LONGMAN
Pronunciation
Dictionary

LONGMAN
Pronunciation
Dictionary

J C Wells

PEARSON
Longman

Pearson Education Limited
Edinburgh Gate
Harlow
Essex CM20 2JE
England
and Associated Companies throughout the World

Visit our website: http://www.longman.com/dictionaries

First edition 1990
Second edition 2000
Third edition 2008
Third impression 2009

ISBN 9781405881173 (cased edition + CD)
ISBN 9781405881180 (paperback edition + CD)

British Library Cataloguing-in-Publication Data
A catalogue record for this book is available from the British Library.

Designed by Richard Jervis
Illustrations by Tony Wilkins

Set in Times and Frutiger by Letterpart, UK
Printed in China
GCC/03

John Wells is Emeritus Professor of Phonetics at UCL in the University of London. He was born in
Lancashire in 1939. Both at school and as an undergraduate at Cambridge he specialized in Classics,
but switched to phonetics as a postgraduate at UCL, where he became a member of the academic
staff (faculty) in 1962. He was elected a Fellow of the British Academy in 1996. Throughout his
career he taught English phonetics, both to native speakers and to EFL learners, as well as general
phonetics and phonology and the phonetics of various other languages.

Among the books he has written are the three-volume *Accents of English* and *English Intonation: an
Introduction*. His first published work was an Esperanto dictionary.

Visit his website at **www.phon.ucl.ac.uk/home/wells**

CONTENTS

Key to phonetic symbols for English   *inside front cover*

Index to notes on pronunciation and phonetics   vii

Acknowledgements   ix

Foreword to the third edition   xiii

A quick guide to the dictionary   xiv

1 Introduction   xvii
1.1 Variants   xvii
1.2 Inflected and derived forms   xvii
1.3 Proper names   xvii
1.4 Compounds and phrases   xvii
1.5 Spelling   xviii
1.6 Homophones   xviii
1.7 Opinion polls   xviii

2 Types of pronunciation recorded   xix
2.1 British pronunciation – RP   xix
2.2 Other varieties of British English   xix
2.3 American pronunciation – General American   xx

3 The English phonemic system and its notation   xxiii
3.1 Vowels and diphthongs   xxiii
3.2 Consonants   xxv
3.3 Stress   xxvi
3.4 Transcription systems   xxvi
3.5 Syllabification   xxvii
3.6 Phonological processes in speech   xxviii

4 Foreign languages   xxix
4.1 Names   xxix
4.2 Transcriptions   xxix

5 Symbols   xxxi
5.1 Phonetic symbols   xxxi
5.2 Key to phonetic symbols for English   xxxiv
5.3 Other symbols   xxxv

6 Abbreviations   xxxvi

The Dictionary A-Z   **1-921**

Typographical conventions, stress marks, other symbols   922

Spelling-to-sound guidelines (grapheme-to-phoneme rules) for each letter of the alphabet are distributed throughout LPD, each at the head of the entries beginning with that letter. (See also DOUBLE CONSONANT LETTERS; SHORT VOWEL, LONG VOWEL.)

CONTENTS

Key to phonetic symbols for English . . . . inside front cover
How to use . . . on pronunciation and phonetics vii
Acknowledgements ix
Foreword to the fourth ed . . . on xiii
A quick guide to the dictionary xv

1 Introduction xvii
1.1 Varieties xvii
1.2 Inflected and derived forms xxi
1.3 Proper names xxi
1.4 Compounds and phrases xxii
1.5 Spelling xxii
1.6 Homophones xxiii
1.7 Optional sounds viii

2 Types of pronunciation recommended xix
2.1 British pronunciation: RP xix
2.2 Observations of British English xxv
2.3 American pronunciation – General American . . xx

3 The English phonemic system and its notation . . xxix
3.1 Vowels and diphthongs xxiii
3.2 Consonants xxxv
3.3 Stress xxxv
3.4 Transcription systems xxxvi
3.5 Syllabification xxxvii
3.6 Phonological processes in speech xxxviii

4 Foreign language xxix
4.1 Names xxix
4.2 Transcriptions xxx

5 Symbols xxxi
5.1 Phonetic symbols xxxvi
5.2 Key to phonetic symbols for English . . . xxxvii
5.3 Other symbols xxxviii

6 Abbreviations xxxvi

The Dictionary A–Z 1–921

Appendix: alphabetic list of names, other symbols . . xxii

Ideally, to some guidelines, if a phoneme-to-phoneme rule found, letters of the alphabet are distributed throughout RP, such as the end of the process beginning with hard k etc. So also not the vowel, letters or that vowel is so vowel . . .

Index to notes on pronunciation and phonetics

Type in blue indicates a Language Panel
on that topic.

abbreviatory conventions	149
accent	783
affricates	**15**, 46, 467
allophone	**609**
approximant	46
alveolar	45
alveolo-palatal	45
articulation	**45**
aspiration	**49**
assimilation	**51**
Australian English	**59**
bilabial	45
breaking	**103**
citation form	**149**
clicks	**153**
clipping	**155**
coalescence	52
coarticulation	51, **159**
combining forms	**165**
compensatory lengthening	270
complementary distribution	609
compounds	**171**
compression	149, **173**
connected speech	149
contracted forms *see A-Z entries for* -'s, -n't, -'d, -'ll, -'ve, *also* don't, I'm, they're *etc.*	
crescendo diphthong	173, 233
dark l	xix, 465
dental	45
devoiced	881
dictionary pronunciation	149
diphthongs	**233**
diminuendo diphthong	233
double consonant letters	**245**
double consonant sounds	**247**
duration	739
early stress	171
elide	269
elision	**269**
e-mail and the web	**271**

Estuary English	xix
falling diphthong	233
fortis	881
free variation	609
fricative	46
geminate	247
glottal	45
glottal stop	**345**
glottalling	345
hard attack	**367**
hiatus	345
hyphenation	801
insertion	567, 663
intrusive r	663
labial-palatal	45
labial-velar	45
labiodental	45
late stress	171
lateral	465
length-mark	739
lenis	881
linking r	663
liquids	46, **465**
long vowel	**739**
manner of articulation	46
median	465
monophthong	233
nasal	46
neutral vowel	539
neutralization	**539**
non-rhotic	663
obstruent	46
opposition	539
optional sounds	149, **567**
palatal	45
palato-alveolar	45
past tense *see A-Z entry for* -ed	
pharyngal	46
phoneme and allophone	**609**
phrasal verbs	**611**
phrases	**171**

pitch-prominence 783
place of articulation 45
plosive 46
plosive releases **621**
plurals, possessives *see A-Z entry*
for -s, -es
post-alveolar 45
pre-fortis clipping 155
pre-l breaking 103
pre-r breaking 103
primary stress 783
progressive assimilation 51
regional accents xix
regressive assimilation 51
retroflex 45
rhotic 663
rhythmic beat 783
rhythmic clipping 155
rising diphthong 233
r-liaison **663**
secondary stress 783
semivowel 46
short vowel, long vowel **739**
sibilant *see A-Z entry for* -s, -es

smoothing 173
sonorant 46
spelling pronunciation **763**
stranded, stranding 891
stress **783**
stress-imposing 165
stress-neutral 165
stress shift **784**
strong form 891
strong vowel 52, 892
suffix 165
syllabic consonants 51, **799**
syllabification xxvi, 149, 801
syllables **801**
t-voicing **805**
unaspirated 49
uvular 46
velar 45
voiced and voiceless **881**
voicing 805, 881
weak forms **891**
weak vowels 52, **892**
the web **271**
yod coalescence 52

Acknowledgements

I am fortunate in the many people who have been ready to help me as I planned and prepared this dictionary. My colleagues in Phonetics and Linguistics at University College London, including several now retired, have patiently tolerated my obsessive questioning: among them I would mention especially the late Prof. A.C. Gimson, with whom I held many discussions on the problems of compiling and maintaining a pronouncing dictionary and on the changing nature of RP (Received Pronunciation).

For detailed advice on American English, I am grateful to Linda Shockey; for checking the Russian transcriptions, to John Baldwin and Sue Barry; for the Arabic, to Janaan Dawood; for the Hindi, to Neil and Saras Smith; and the Japanese, to Kazuhiko Matsuno and Noriko Hattori. Thanks, too, to Graham Pointon of the BBC Pronunciation Unit. Jill House and Dinah Jackson made various helpful suggestions in the course of proof-reading. Any remaining errors are naturally my own responsibility.

I am, of course, greatly indebted to successive editions of Daniel Jones's *English Pronouncing Dictionary* (Dent, 12th edn, 1963; 13th edn revised by A.C. Gimson, 1967; 14th edn, 1977; reprinted with revisions and supplement by S.M. Ramsaran 1988). EPD has set the standard against which other dictionaries must inevitably be judged. Other pronouncing dictionaries I have frequently consulted include *BBC Pronouncing Dictionary of British Names*, 2nd edn by G.E. Pointon (Oxford University Press, 1983); *NBC Handbook of Pronunciation*, 4th edn by Eugene Ehrlich and Raymond Hand, Jr. (Harper and Row, 1984); and *A Pronouncing Dictionary of American English* by J.S. Kenyon and T.A. Knott (Merriam, 1953). For American pronunciation I have also regularly explored *Webster's Ninth New Collegiate Dictionary* (Merriam-Webster, 1983), the *American Heritage Dictionary* (Houghton Mifflin, 1981), and *The Random House Dictionary*, 2nd edn (Random House, 1987). For Australian pronunciation I have used *The Macquarie Dictionary* (Macquarie Library, 1981), and for Indian words *Common Indian Words in English* by R.E. Hawkins (Delhi: Oxford University Press, 1984). I have taken certain medical terms from *Butterworths Medical Dictionary* (2nd edn Butterworth & Co, 1978). Not only for German, but also for information about proper names from a variety of foreign languages, *Duden Aussprachewörterbuch* by Max Mangold (2nd edn, Bibliographisches Institut Mannheim, 1974) has proved invaluable. For French I have drawn particularly on *Dictionnaire de la prononciation* by Alain Lerond (Larousse, 1980); for Italian on *Dizionario d'ortografia e di pronunzia* by Migliorini, Tagliavini & Fiorelli (ERI–Edizioni RAI, 1969). For the entries on affixes and the spelling-to-sound boxes I have taken advantage of ideas contained in *The Groundwork of English Stress* by Roger Kingdon (Longman, 1958), *English Word-Stress* by Erik Fudge (Allen & Unwin, 1984), *Rules of Pronunciation for the English Language* by Axel Wijk (Oxford University Press, 1966), and a number of works by Lionel Guierre, including *Drills in English Stress-Patterns* (4th edn Paris: Armand Colin–Longman, 1984).

Nearly three hundred native speakers of British English took the time and trouble to answer a detailed questionnaire about preferences in the pronunciation of particular words (see 1.7 below, Opinion polls). Thanks to all of them: their chief reward is to have their views recorded in the polling figures presented in this book.

My particular thanks go to Susan Maingay and Stephen Crowdy of Longman Dictionaries, who have been consistently supportive and cooperative, everything a publisher should be; and to Clare Fletcher, who made numerous suggestions for clearer or more felicitous wording and presentation.

John Wells

Note to the second edition

My thanks for helpful suggestions go to the many reviewers and friendly critics of the first edition of the *Longman Pronunciation Dictionary* (LPD), and in particular to Jack Windsor Lewis.

Since the first appearance of LPD there have been new editions of many of the works of reference listed above. I have made particular use of the invaluable Duden *Aussprachewörterbuch* (3rd edn, 1990) and – for Australian names – of *The Macquarie Dictionary* (2nd edn, Macquarie University NSW, 1991).

A much fuller treatment of English spelling-to-sound rules is now available in *A Survey of English Spelling* by Edward Carney (Routledge, 1994).

I have been stimulated by the radical revisions made in the 15th edition of the Daniel Jones *English Pronouncing Dictionary*, now edited by Peter Roach and James Hartman (Cambridge University Press, 1997).

For advice on Chinese names I am indebted to Siew-Yue Killingley and John Maidment, for Cantonese to Cheung Kwan-Hin, for Arabic to Bruce Ingham, and for further information on Japanese to Mitsuhiro Nakamura.

I am grateful to Rebecca Dauer for checking the 5000 new entries from the point of view of American English. Particular thanks also to my graduate student Yuko Shitara for allowing me to include the findings of her 1993 AmE pronunciation preference survey.

Thanks are due to the volunteers who participated in the 1998 pronunciation preference poll – not 275 this time, but over 1900 – to Jonathan Wadman for turning questionnaire responses into computer files, and to my colleague Andy Faulkner for help with processing the data.

Longman have continued to be supportive in every way. Thanks particularly to Adam Gadsby, Emma Campbell, Emma Williams, Dinah Jackson and Sheila Dallas; and to Della Summers who commissioned both the first edition of this dictionary and this current revision.

John Wells
London, March 1999

Note to the third edition

Renewed thanks to Jack Windsor Lewis for helpful comments. Thanks also to Tommaso Francesco Borri for a large number of suggestions concerning pronunciations in Italian and other foreign languages; to Cheung Kwan-hin for help with the transcription of Chinese (Mandarin) and Cantonese words; to Kayoko Yanagisawa for help with new Japanese entries; to Ho-young Lee and Joe-Eun Kim for Korean; for other languages to the BBC Pronunciation Unit and to other colleagues and correspondents too many to name; and to Dinah Jackson for help with proof reading.

Bert Vaux kindly allowed me to use the results of his 2002 polling figures for AmE. Thanks also to all who took part in the new 2007 BrE poll, and to Longman for organizing it.

As my publishers, Pearson Education have given every support. Thanks particularly to Michael Mayor, Editorial Director of the Dictionaries Section, and to my editors, Paola Rocchetti (who also organized the recording sessions) and Nicky Thompson. Allan Ørsnes converted everything to XML/Unicode, and Denise McKeough helped me in the early stages of using the XML editor. Susan Maingay wrote the exercises for the CD-ROM.

John Wells
London, October 2007

Foreword to the third edition

In this edition over 3000 new headwords have been added. They include:

- terms relating to the internet: **Bebo**, **blogging**, **chatroom**, **digicam**, **eBay**, **Google**, **iPod**, **phish**, **podcast**, **unsubscribe**, **Wi-Fi**, **Wikipedia**
- other words that have come into use, or into wider use, since the previous edition: **Asbo**, **Asperger's**, **Botox**, **burqa**, **chav**, **fashionista**, **hijab**, **latte**, **qi**
- proper names previously missing: **al-Qaeda**, **Benfica**, **Beyoncé**, **Condoleezza**, **Federer**, **Lidl**, **Merkel**, **Rowling**, **Sentamu**, **Titchmarsh**
- and many other assorted categories.

This edition is the first to have an accompanying CD-ROM: the Longman Pronunciation Coach. On it you will find hundreds of interactive practice exercises, with help and feedback from me, in addition to the complete text of the *Longman Pronunciation Dictionary* with all words and phrases spoken aloud in both British and American English. Learners whose own language is a tone language are reminded that although the headwords are all spoken here with a falling nuclear tone, stress in English words may, depending on intonation, alternatively involve a rising or falling-rising tone or, if not nuclear, a level high or low tone.

Entries for words containing **be-**, **de-**, **e-**, **pre-**, **re-** and **se-** (also **rede-**, **unre-** etc.) have been simplified. When unstressed, these prefixes are now shown with i. This reflects the fact that, like words ending in i, such as **happy**, they may be pronounced indifferently with ɪ or iː. (These prefixes also have variants with ə, shown explicitly.)

Following research into contemporary RP by Bente Hannisdal, I have removed the § sign from forms with tʃuː and dʒuː deriving from traditional tjuː and djuː.

In view of the declining use in AmE of hw in words with the spelling **wh-**, I have changed the relevant recommendation for those learning AmE and made the corresponding change in the alphabetic entries.

As in previous editions, tone numbers in transcriptions of tone languages are put at the *beginning* of the relevant syllable (contrary to practice in some other circles). This preserves the analogy with stress marks in non-tone languages.

It is sometimes difficult to decide on stress-marking for compound adjectives such as **God-given**, **hard-drinking**, **long-term**. In general I have shown them as having end-stress, with a stress-shift mark. But since they usually precede a noun, itself likely to be stressed, in practice they undergo stress shift much more often than not. There is also a problem in deciding whether to show words such as **one-size-fits-all**, **MRSA** with four stresses or (as they are usually pronounced) just with two; and likewise whether to show three or two stresses in words such as **nondenominational**.

John Wells
London, October 2007

A quick guide to the dictionary

British and American pronunciations

Where only one pronunciation is given this means that the word has a similar pronunciation in both British and American English.

The symbol ‖ is used to introduce American English (AmE) pronunciations when these are different from British English (BrE) forms. Sometimes, when the AmE pronunciation is different in only one part of a word, the dictionary shows only this part.

bad bæd

pronunciation used in both
BrE and AmE

batter ˈbæt ə ‖ ˈbæt̬ ᵊr
　　　　BrE　　AmE

bender ˈbend ə ‖ -ᵊr ~s z

↑ the AmE pronunciation
is ˈbend ᵊr

Main pronunciations and alternatives

All main pronunciations (recommended as models for learners of English) are shown in bold type. If there are alternative pronunciations, these are shown in ordinary black type.

Where only one pronunciation is given for the main pronunciation and for the alternative, this means that both have a similar pronunciation in BrE and AmE.

Sometimes when an alternative pronunciation is different only in one part of a word, the *Longman Pronunciation Dictionary* (LPD) shows only this part.

Pronunciations which are widespread among educated speakers of BrE but which are not, however, considered to belong to RP (Received Pronunciation) are marked with the symbol §.

LPD also includes pronunciations which are generally considered to be incorrect.

main BrE ↓　　　　main AmE ↓
baroque bə ˈrɒk bæ-, -ˈrəʊk ‖ -ˈroʊk -ˈrɑːk
　　alternative BrE ↑　　alternative AmE ↑

bankrupt ˈbæŋk rʌpt -rəpt
pronunciation and alternative both
used in BrE and AmE

ballroom ˈbɔːl ruːm -rʊm ‖ ˈbɑːl-
alternative used only in AmE ↑

bases *pl of* **basis** ˈbeɪs iːz
an alternative pronunciation is ˈbeɪs əz

bath *n* bɑːθ §bæθ ‖ bæθ **baths** bɑːðz §bɑːθs,
the RP form is bɑːθ; in England
bæθ is a localized northern form,
though it is standard in AmE

grievous ˈgriːv əs △ ˈgriːv i̯ əs ~**ly** li ~**ness**
　　　nəs nɪs　　　　　↑
be careful not to use this pronunciation

Pronunciations of foreign words

For words belonging to foreign languages, which are in use in English, LPD shows both their anglicized pronunciations and their pronunciations in the language of origin.

pronunciation in BrE and AmE

Benz benz —*Ger* [bɛnts]

original German pronunciation

Inflected and derived forms

Entries include information about the pronunciation of the different forms of headword (plurals, past tense forms, etc.). Sometimes the different forms are shown in full.

Sometimes just the endings are shown.

Sometimes an ending is added not to the complete word but to just part of it. The symbol | is used to show exactly which part is concerned.

> **blub** blʌb **blubbed** blʌbd **blubbing** ˈblʌb ɪŋ **blubs** blʌbz
>
> **building** ˈbɪld ɪŋ ~s z
> ˈ**building block**; ˈ**building so,ciety**
>
> the plural form **buildings** is pronounced ˈbɪld ɪŋz
>
> **beef|y** ˈbiːf |i ~**ier** i‿ə ‖ i‿ᵊr ~**iest** i‿ɪst i‿əst
> beef + ier = ⬆   beef + iest = ⬆
> ˈbiːfi‿ə   ˈbiːfi‿ɪst

Stress marks

Words of more than one syllable are marked for stress. LPD recognizes two types of stress. (See the panel on 'Stress', p.783.)

When alternative pronunciations are different only in the way in which they are stressed, the full pronunciation is not repeated but small blocks (• •) are used to represent the syllables of the word.

> secondary stress   primary stress
>
> **interchangeability** ˌɪnt ə ˌtʃeɪndʒ ə ˈbɪl ət i
> -ɪt i ‖ ˌɪnt̮ ᵊr ˌtʃeɪndʒ ə ˈbɪl ət̮ i
>
> **backslid|e** ˈbæk slaɪd ˌ·ˈ· ~**er/s** ə/z ‖ ᵊr/z ~**ing** ɪŋ
> an alternative stress pattern is ˌbæk ˈslaɪd

Stress shift

Some words have different stress patterns according to whether they are being used alone or directly before a noun. (See the panel on 'Stress shift', p.784.) The symbol ◄ is used to show words which can behave in this way.

> **academic** ˌæk ə ˈdem ɪk ◄ ~**al/s** ᵊl/z ~**ally** ᵊl‿i
> ~**s** s

Stress in compounds

The pronunciation of compound words can often be derived from their component parts. Stress patterns, however, are not always easy to predict and so important compounds and their patterns are listed after the main entry.

> **bee** biː **bees, bee's** biːz
> ˌbee's ˈknees; ˈbee sting
>
> compounds showing stress pattern

Continued ▶

Special notes

The dictionary makes use of some special symbols to help you to arrive at the right pronunciation.

! This symbol is a warning that the pronunciation is quite different from what the spelling might lead you to expect!

bury 'ber i *(! = berry)* **buried** 'ber id **buries** 'ber iz **burying** 'ber i ˌɪŋ

* This symbol is a warning that the British and American pronunciations are different in an important and unpredictable way.

baton 'bæt ɒn -ᵊn ‖ bə 'tɑːn *(*)—See also phrases with this word* ~s z

= This symbol draws attention to another word which has exactly the same pronunciation as the word looked up.

blew bluː *(= blue)*

→ This symbol shows that an alternative pronunciation is the result of a general rule which affects not just this word but a whole range of words and phrases in the language.

bridegroom 'braɪd gruːm →'braɪg-, -grʊm ~s z

(See the panel on 'Assimilation', p.51.)

For more detailed information see 'Index to notes on pronunciation and phonetics', p.vii, and 'Symbols', p.xxxi.

1 Introduction

This is a specialist dictionary of **pronunciation**. It offers the user three kinds of information about English pronunciation that are not available in a general dictionary: information on **variants**, on **inflected** and **derived** forms, and on **proper names**. It covers both British and American English.

1.1 Variants Many English words have a number of different possible pronunciations. Some of the users of LPD will be teachers and learners of EFL/ESL (English as a foreign or second language), and will look for advice on how to pronounce a given word. For them one **main pronunciation**, printed in bold, is given at each entry. This is the form recommended for EFL purposes. (See the CITATION FORM panel for how to unpack the abbreviatory conventions.) If the British English (BrE) and American English (AmE) recommended forms are different from one another, then both are given in bold. Other users of LPD, especially those who are native speakers of English, will be interested not only to see what form is recommended but also what **variants** are recognized. Where pronunciations other than the main one are in common educated use, they too are included, but as **secondary pronunciations**, printed in ordinary black type. Some pronunciations are controversial, and so as evidence for the selection of a main pronunciation, between 200 and 300 entries include a report of one or more **opinion polls** of pronunciation preferences (see 1.7 below).

The wide coverage of variants makes LPD suitable for use not only in speech production but also in speech recognition: not only for human speakers of English but also for computer applications.

1.2 Inflected and derived forms As well as the uninflected forms of words, LPD systematically includes the plurals of nouns (and possessives if they are pronounced differently from plurals), the third person singular present tense (*s*-forms), present participles (*ing*-forms), past tenses and past participles (*ed*-forms) of verbs, the comparatives and superlatives of adjectives, and derivatives such as those in *-ly*, *-able*, *-er*, *-less*, *-ness*, *-ship*. Where the base form has only one syllable, pronunciations for inflected forms are given in full; otherwise they are usually cut back.

1.3 Proper names LPD includes all the more commonly encountered proper names – **personal** names (first names, Christian names), **family** names (surnames, last names), names of **mythical** and **literary** characters, **place** names, and **commercial** names (particularly names of products). British names are covered as thoroughly as possible within the space available, while American, Irish and Australian ones have not been neglected. Many names from other languages are also included, in most cases with their pronunciation in the language of origin as well as in an anglicized form.

1.4 Compounds and phrases As well as all the above, LPD also includes a good selection of **compounds and phrases**, showing their stress patterns. Some of these illustrate the effect of the highly productive principle of STRESS SHIFT which affects many longer English words. The effects of affixes on word stress are discussed in the special entries devoted to affixes and word endings.

1.5 Spelling **English spelling** is notorious for its shortcomings. Knowing the orthography of a word does not enable one to predict its pronunciation with any confidence. Nevertheless, certain general principles do govern the relationship between spelling and sound (grapheme and phoneme), even though they may be subject to exceptions and uncertainties. Although many handbooks of English pronunciation ignore them entirely, on the implicit grounds that these rules are so chaotic that it is better to learn the pronunciation of each new word separately, it nevertheless seemed helpful for LPD to offer the user something rather than nothing. Accordingly, guidelines designed to be useful particularly to the EFL learner are given at each letter of the alphabet.

1.6 Homophones Learners and native speakers alike can reinforce their grasp of the distinction between sound and spelling by noting **homophones** (= words distinct in spelling but pronounced identically). LPD points them out in notes such as

   bear (= *bare*)   **write** (= *right*)

1.7 Opinion polls For many words of uncertain pronunciation, LPD reports the preferences expressed in five opinion polls:
- a postal opinion poll carried out by the author in 1988 among a panel of 275 native speakers of BrE from throughout Britain;
- a postal opinion poll carried out by Yuko Shitara in 1993 among a panel of 400 native speakers of AmE from throughout the United States;
- an opinion poll carried out by the author in 1998 among a panel of 1932 native speakers of BrE from throughout Britain, some of whom answered by postal questionnaire but others by e-mail or interactively online.
- an on-line dialect survey conducted by Prof. Bert Vaux, then of Harvard University, among a panel of self-selected respondents from the United States in 1999-2002; most questions received about 11,000 answers. Details of the respondents' ages are not available.
- an online poll of BrE conducted by Pearson Education and myself in April-June 2007.

Polling figures in the text are no longer identified by year. Further details of the polls, and of which words were in which poll, can be found on my UCL website. **www.phon.ucl.ac.uk/home/wells**

2 Types of pronunciation recorded

2.1 British pronunciation The model of British English pronunciation recorded in LPD is a modernized version of the type known as **Received Pronunciation**, or **RP**.

In England and Wales, RP is widely regarded as a model for correct pronunciation, particularly for educated formal speech. It is what was traditionally used by BBC news readers – hence the alternative name **BBC pronunciation**, although now that the BBC admits regional accents among its announcers this name has become less appropriate. It is the usual standard in teaching English as a foreign language, in all countries where the model is BrE rather than AmE.

RP itself inevitably changes as the years pass. There is also a measure of diversity within it. Furthermore, the democratization undergone by English society during the second half of the twentieth century means that it is nowadays necessary to define RP in a rather broader way than was once customary. LPD includes a number of pronunciations that diverge from traditional, 'classical' RP. The 'RP' transcriptions shown in LPD in fact cover very much more than a narrowly defined RP.

2.2 Other varieties of British English British Received Pronunciation (RP) is not **localized** (= not associated with any particular city or region). It is to be heard in all parts of the country from those with the appropriate social or educational background. On the other hand, most people do have some degree of local colouring in their speech.

To a large extent, this is manifested in details of phonetic realization (use of particular allophones, for example a glottal rather than an alveolar plosive for t in certain positions – see PHONEME AND ALLOPHONE and GLOTTAL STOP) rather than in any substantial deviation from the RP system (= the inventory of vowel and consonant phonemes). Hence it is automatically covered by the transcription used in LPD.

Pronunciations widespread in England among educated speakers, but which are nevertheless judged to fall outside RP, are marked with the special sign §. Since LPD aims to portray the current state of the English language, we think it important not to ignore them, as other dictionaries do.

one	wʌn §wɒn	The general form is wʌn; wɒn is a localized northern form.
last	lɑːst §læst	The RP form is lɑːst. In England læst is a localized northern form (though it is standard in AmE).

Many other BrE 'educated non-RP' forms are not mentioned explicitly.

Speech with local features of the southeast of England is often referred to as **Estuary English**. This involves, in particular,

- frequent use of ʔ for syllable-final t (see GLOTTAL STOP).
- vocalization of l, i.e. the use of a vowel or semivowel of the o type in place of a dark l, thus **milk** mɪok, **table** ˈteɪb o.
- use of tʃ and dʒ in place of tj and dj, thus **tune** tʃuːn, **reduce** rɪ ˈdʒuːs (= yod coalescence, see ASSIMILATION).

Other widespread but local pronunciation characteristics from various parts of the British Isles include the following:

- ŋg for ŋ at the end of a stem: for example, **sing** sɪŋ is also regionally sɪŋg, and **singer** ˈsɪŋ ə is also regionally ˈsɪŋ gə.
- ɔə for ɔː in certain words: for example, **four** fɔː (also regionally, and formerly in RP, fɔə).
- use of vowel qualities closer to iː, uː than to ɪə, ʊə in words such as **periodic**, **purity**.
- ʌ and ə not distinguished in quality, both being like RP ə.
- r corresponding to spelling r before a consonant sound or at the end of a word: for example, **cart** kɑːt, regionally also kɑːrt (as in AmE).
- many other forms characteristic of Scottish or Irish pronunciation.

These and other pronunciation features associated with regional accents may often be inferred from LPD transcriptions. For example, broad local accents of the north of England have ʊ wherever LPD writes ʌ – for example **love** lʌv, regionally also lʊv. In London and increasingly elsewhere, some people replace θ and ð with f and v respectively, at least in casual speech.

For a few words, LPD includes a pronunciation variant that is not considered correct. These variants are included because of the fact that they are in widespread use. They are marked with the special sign ⚠.

grievous ˈgriːv əs ⚠ ˈgriːv i̯əs

Australian pronunciation is phonemically similar to RP, though with certain important differences. See AUSTRALIAN ENGLISH. For detailed descriptions of many varieties of native English pronunciation throughout the world, see the author's *Accents of English* (three volumes and cassette, Cambridge University Press, 1982).

2.3 American pronunciation The AmE pronunciations shown in LPD are those appropriate to the variety (accent) known as **General American**. This is what is spoken by the majority of Americans, namely those who do not have a noticeable eastern or southern accent. It is the appropriate model for EFL learners who wish to speak AmE rather than BrE.

American pronunciation is shown in LPD entries after the mark ‖. If an entry contains no ‖, then the American pronunciation is the same as the British. If the pronunciation after ‖ is *not* in colour, then the main AmE pronunciation is the same as in BrE.

docile	ˈdəʊs aɪ°l ‖ ˈdɑːs°l	The AmE pronunciation is ˈdɑːs°l.
crown	kraʊn	The AmE pronunciation is kraʊn, the same as in BrE.
tomato	tə ˈmɑːt əʊ ‖ -meɪt̬ oʊ	The AmE pronunciation is tə ˈmeɪt̬ oʊ.
ability	ə ˈbɪl ət i ‖ -ət̬ i	The AmE pronunciation is ə ˈbɪl ət̬ i.
tritium	ˈtrɪt i̯əm ‖ ˈtrɪt̬- ˈtrɪʃ-	The AmE pronunciation is usually ˈtrɪt̬ i̯əm, less commonly ˈtrɪʃ i̯əm
thorax	ˈθɔːr æks ‖ ˈθoʊr-	The AmE pronunciation is usually ˈθɔːr æks, as in BrE. Less commonly it is ˈθoʊr æks.

The mark (*), sparingly used, draws attention to cases where the BrE (RP) and AmE pronunciations differ in unpredictable or unexpected ways.

GenAm is not as tightly codified for EFL purposes as RP. Accordingly, some of the conventions followed in LPD need to be discussed.

There is considerable variability in GenAm vowels in the open back area. LPD follows tradition in continuing to distinguish the vowel of **lot** lɑːt from that of **thought** θɔːt. (Note, though, that books by American scholars generally do not use length marks.) However, fewer and fewer Americans distinguish these two vowel sounds from one another; so a secondary AmE pronunciation with ɑː is given for all words having ɔː (except before r).

LPD distinguishes between the vowels ʌ and ə, although in AmE they can generally be regarded as allophones of the same phoneme, and for some speakers are more or less identical phonetically too. Thus where LPD writes **above** ə ˈbʌv some speakers pronounce ə ˈbəv. Similarly LPD distinguishes between ɜː and ᵊr, as in **further** ˈfɜːð ᵊr, although many speakers have a similar syllabic [r] in both syllables. All these qualities arguably represent the same phoneme ə, with or without a following r.

Where RP has ɜː followed by a vowel sound, most Americans use ɜ:, and that is what is shown in LPD entries: **courage** ˈkʌr ɪdʒ ‖ ˈkɜː-. It should be noted, however, that there are other Americans who use ʌr, as in RP.

AmE pronunciations not explicitly shown in LPD include the use of ɪ rather than e before a nasal, as when **ten** is pronounced tɪn. Although this is typically a 'southern' variant, it can also be heard elsewhere, for example in California. Another southwestern pronunciation not shown is the use of iː rather than ɪ before the velar nasal, as when **thing** is pronounced θiːŋ.

For most Americans ə and ɪ are not distinct as weak vowels (so that **rabbit** rhymes with **abbot**). For AmE LPD follows the rule of showing ɪ before palato-alveolar and velar consonants (ʃ, tʃ, dʒ, k, g, ŋ), but ə elsewhere. Where no separate indication is given for AmE, but both ɪ and ə variants are shown for an entry, it may be assumed that AmE prefers ɪ or ə according to this rule. The actual quality used by Americans for ə varies considerably, being typically more ɪ-like when followed by a consonant but more ʌ-like when at the end of a word.

3 The English phonemic system and its notation

3.1 Vowels and diphthongs
The English vowels and diphthongs are conveniently considered in five groups (A, B, C, D, E below). There are certain differences between RP and GenAm, both in realization (vowel quality) and in the system (vowel inventory).

The **short** vowels are:

A

ɪ	kit, bid
e	dress, bed
æ	trap, bad
ɒ	(RP) lot, odd
ʌ	strut, bud
ʊ	foot, good

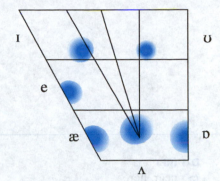

The **long vowels** and **diphthongs** are:

B

iː	fleece, see
eɪ	face, day
aɪ	price, high
ɔɪ	choice, boy

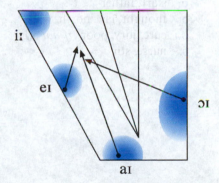

C-1 (RP)

uː	goose, two
əʊ	goat, show
aʊ	mouth, now
ɒʊ	*near-RP variant in* cold *(see 3.6)*

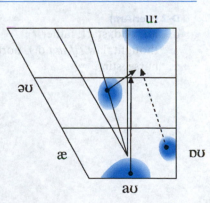

C-2 (GenAm)

u: goose, two
oʊ   goat, show
aʊ   mouth, now

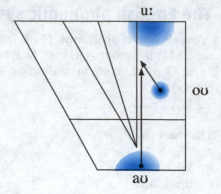

D-1 (RP)

ɪə   near, here
eə   square, fair
ɑ: start, father
ɔ: thought, law, north, war
ʊə   cure, jury, poor *(if not ɔ:)*
ɜ: nurse, stir

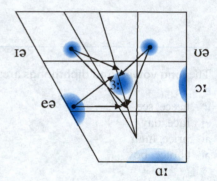

D-2 (GenAm)

ɑ: lot, odd, start, father
ɔ: thought, law *(if not ɑ:)*, north, war
ɜ: nurse, stir

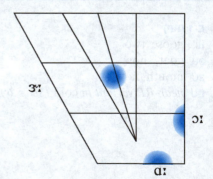

The **weak** vowels are:

E

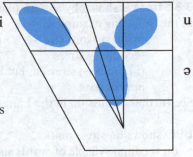

i (happ)y, (rad)i(ation), (glor)i(ous)
ə a(bout), (comm)a, (comm)o(n)
u (infl)u(ence), (sit)u(ation), (biv)ou(ac)

– although the weak vowel system also includes

ɪ i(ntend), (rabb)i(t) *(if not ə)*
ʊ (stim)u(lus), (ed)u(cate) *(if not ə or u)*
and the syllabic consonants (see below).
See WEAK VOWELS.

3.2 Consonants The English consonants are p, b, t, d, k, g, tʃ, dʒ, f, v, θ, ð, s, z, ʃ, ʒ, h, r, l, j, w, m, n, ŋ. For their classification by voicing, place, and manner, see the articles on VOICED AND VOICELESS and ARTICULATION.

The symbols p, b, t, d, k, f, v, h, r, l, w, m, n stand for the English consonant sounds usually so spelled. Keywords for the remaining consonant sounds are as follows:

tʃ	church	dʒ	judge
θ	thin, author, path	ð	this, other, smooth
s	cease, sister	z	zone, roses
ʃ	ship, ocean	ʒ	vision
j	yet	ŋ	sing, long, thanks
g	go, give, gag		

The GenAm transcriptions also make use of the symbol t̬, representing the often voiced alveolar tap used for t in certain positions, as in **atom, better**: see T-VOICING.

In words and names from foreign languages some speakers also use x (Scots *ch*, voiceless velar fricative) and ɬ (Welsh *ll*, voiceless alveolar lateral fricative), which can thus to some extent be considered marginal members of the English consonant system.

As explained at OPTIONAL SOUNDS, symbols written ^raised^ denote sounds that are sometimes optionally inserted. Likely syllabic consonants are shown in this way, since a syllabic consonant always has an optional variant involving ə and a non-syllabic consonant:

ᵊl (midd)le, (tot)al
ᵊn (sudd)en(ly), (serv)an(t)
ᵊr *AmE* (fath)er, (stand)ar(d).

Symbols written in *italics* denote sounds sometimes omitted. See OPTIONAL SOUNDS.

hɪndʒ hinge

3.3 Stress is shown by a mark placed at the beginning of the syllable in question, as in the following examples:

ˈ	primary word stress	reˈMEMber
ˌ	secondary stress	ˌACaˈDEMic; ˈBUTter ˌFINgers
⁝	(in prefixes) stressed, but level undefined: primary or secondary as appropriate.	

See further discussion in the Language Panel on STRESS.

LPD shows no stress mark
- on the final syllable of words such as **celebrate** ˈsel ə breɪt
- on the monosyllabic second element of an early-stressed compound or phrase, for example **selling price** ˈsel ɪŋ praɪs
- on entries that are words of one syllable, for example **time** taɪm.

Stress is always relative; LPD marks it only in branching structures.

3.4 Transcription systems There are various systems of transcription in use for English, including several which conform to the principles of the International Phonetic Alphabet (IPA). The differences between them are in many cases trivial. The system used in LPD conforms to the current de facto standard.

The user's attention is drawn to the abbreviatory conventions explained in the panel on CITATION FORM. Other dictionaries use other abbreviatory conventions and may differ, for example, in how (if at all) syllable divisions are shown. Early editions of Jones's *English Pronouncing Dictionary* (before 1977) used a typographically simpler, 'broad' transcription system for RP. In some parts of the world this system still persists. It involves
- i, ɔ, u for the short vowels LPD writes as ɪ, ɒ, ʊ;
- ei, ou, ai, au, ɔi, iə, ɛə, uə for the diphthongs LPD writes as eɪ, əʊ, aɪ, aʊ, ɔɪ, ɪə, eə, ʊə;
- ə: for the long vowel LPD writes as ɜː.

The current, 17th edition of EPD (CUP, 2006) writes
- ɚ corresponding to LPD's ᵊr.

For AmE, authors in the IPA tradition often use the Kenyon and Knott system, which involves
- no length marks
- ɛ for the vowel which LPD writes as e
- e, o for the normally diphthongal vowels LPD writes as eɪ, oʊ
- ɚ corresponding to LPD's ᵊr.

A different AmE tradition, that of Trager and Smith, involves
- š, ž, č, ǰ for the IPA ʃ, ʒ, tʃ, dʒ
- the representation of long vowels and diphthongs as sequences such as iy, ow, oh (= LPD iː, oʊ, ɔː)
- acute and grave marks over vowels (é, è) to show stress, corresponding to the IPA marks ˈ, ˌ before the syllable.

3.5 Syllabification Syllable divisions are shown in LPD by spacing. This makes the transcriptions of long words easier to read and makes certain details of pronunciation more explicit.

The rhythm of a word or phrase is determined by the number and nature of the syllables it contains. Thus syllables 'carry' stress and intonation. (This is obviously particularly important for poetry and singing.) The division of a word into syllables is its **syllabification**.

The question of syllabification in English is controversial: different phoneticians hold very different views about it. The syllabification principles adopted in LPD are those which most helpfully predict the **distribution of allophones** (see PHONEME AND ALLOPHONE).

LPD assumes that there is a syllable boundary wherever there is a boundary between the elements of a compound: thus **playtime** is 'pleɪ taɪm. It is also assumed that every word consists of whole syllables, and that a consonant cannot belong to two syllables at once. Thus **city** must be either 'sɪt i or 'sɪ ti – the t cannot be in both syllables. (In fact it must be the first, 'sɪt i, because the t is pronounced in a way typical of final t: not aspirated like initial plosives, but on the contrary potentially subject to T-VOICING and glottalling, see GLOTTAL STOP.)

It is generally agreed that phonetic syllable divisions must as far as possible avoid creating consonant clusters which are not found at the edges of words. This is the **phonotactic** constraint. Thus **windy** might be 'wɪn di or 'wɪnd i, but it could not be 'wɪ ndi (because English words cannot begin with nd). LPD takes the view that the syllabification of this word actually parallels its morphology: **wind+y**, 'wɪnd i. For the same reason, **language** must be 'læŋ gwɪdʒ, not 'læŋg wɪdʒ or 'læ ŋgwɪdʒ.

The principle that LPD adopts is that **consonants are syllabified with whichever of the two adjacent vowels is more strongly stressed**. If they are both unstressed, it goes with the leftward one. A **weak** vowel counts as 'less stressed' than an unstressed strong one.

In general, this principle is subject to the phonotactic constraint. However, there are some cases where correct prediction of allophones requires us to override it.

(i) Certain unstressed syllables end in a strong short vowel, even though words cannot. In **nostalgia** the t is unaspirated (as in **stack** stæk, not as in **tack** tæk), so the syllabification is (BrE) nɒ 'stældʒ ə.

(ii) r can end a syllable, even though in BrE it cannot end a word pronounced in isolation. The r in **starry** 'stɑːr i is like the r in **star is**, and different from the more forceful r in **star runner**. Likewise, ʒ can end a syllable: **vision** 'vɪʒ ᵊn.

(iii) Within a morpheme, tr and dr are not split. If **petrol** were 'pet rəl, as the phonotactic constraint leads us to expect (since English words do not end in tr), its t would likely be glottal and its r voiced (as in **rat-race** 'ræt reɪs). In fact, the tr in this word is pronounced as a voiceless affricate; so LPD syllabifies it 'petr əl.

For further discussion, please see the author's article 'Syllabification and allophony' in Ramsaran, S. (ed.), 1990, *Studies in the pronunciation of English*, London: Edward Arnold.

3.6 Phonological processes in speech The mark → precedes secondary pronunciations that can be regarded as derived by automatic rule from the main pronunciation. Examples of processes covered by such a rule include ASSIMILATION and the use of the special allophone ɒʊ before l in some varieties of (near-)RP:

> **include** ɪn ˈkluːd →ɪŋ ˈkluːd
> **cold** kəʊld → kɒʊld

For some speakers, a form shown with → may correspond to the way a word is stored in the mental lexicon, whereas for others the same form may be derived by phonological rule.

The mark → is not applied to phrases exemplifying STRESS SHIFT, since stress shift is shown by the symbol ◄.

In general, LPD shows results only of processes operating within the word, independently of the phonetic context afforded by surrounding words. Hence, for example, it does not show the optional variant of **ribbon** derived by perseverative ASSIMILATION (ˈrɪb m), since this form is restricted to cases where the following word does not begin with a vowel. But the corresponding variant of **vacant** (ˈveɪk ŋt) is included, since its occurrence is context-free.

4 Foreign languages

4.1 Names from foreign languages can either be pronounced in a way that imitates the foreign language or be integrated into the English sound system. Although this applies mainly to personal and geographical names, to some extent it applies to ordinary words too. Accordingly, for many such words LPD shows their pronunciation in the language of origin as well as their anglicized pronunciation. There are two reasons for this: the obvious one of giving the user information about the foreign-language pronunciation, and the less obvious one that those speakers of English who have some knowledge of the foreign language may well pronounce such words or names in a way that imitates the phonetics of the foreign language, or occupies some half-way stage between the foreign-language pronunciation and the anglicization.

Educated speakers of BrE usually know some French. So do Canadians. They will therefore try to pronounce French names in a French way. They may well use nasalized vowels (or attempts at them) and other characteristics of French pronunciation when they pronounce words they perceive as French. The sounds represented as õ, æ̃, ɜ̃ː (as in **bon, vingt-et-un**) may for this reason be regarded as marginal members of the RP vowel system. On the whole, though, it is only those whose knowledge of French goes beyond the average who succeed in differentiating the real-French vowels ɔ̃ and ɑ̃ (as in **bon** and **banc** respectively), or y and u (as in **rue** and **roue**) or in producing œ̃ rather than ɜ̃.

Educated speakers of AmE usually know some Spanish, and may incorporate some characteristics of Spanish phonetics when pronouncing Spanish words or names. Apart from Hispanics, though, most Americans would not distinguish between ɾ (**puro**) and r (**burro**) in the way native speakers of Spanish do.

People living in Wales, whether or not they speak Welsh, can often pronounce the ɬ appropriate for many Welsh names; so can some other speakers of BrE, but usually not of AmE.

Ignorance may lead to surprising results. The German city of **München** (*Ger* ˈmʏn çən) has an English name **Munich** ˈmjuːn ɪk. But British people sometimes think that this is its German name, and attempt to pronounce it as German, producing the quite inappropriate ˈmjuːn ɪx.

Seeing the Pinyin spelling **Beijing** for the city whose traditional English name is **Peking** (Chinese ³pei ¹tɕiŋ), English speakers suppose that the letter **j** should have the same value as in French, ʒ, and say ˌbeɪ ˈʒɪŋ – whereas ˌbeɪ ˈdʒɪŋ would be much closer to the Chinese.

4.2 Transcriptions of foreign languages call for a number of phonetic symbols not included in the list of those used for English. More subtly, they call for certain differences of interpretation in some of the symbols that are also used for English. Thus the symbol t is used not only for the typically alveolar and often aspirated sound of English, but also for the typically dental and unaspirated sound of French. IPA symbols must be always allowed a certain leeway in their interpretation if the transcription is not to be intolerably burdened with diacritic details.

In transcriptions of German, Danish, Swedish, Norwegian, Icelandic, Welsh, Irish, Scottish Gaelic, and Japanese, voiceless plosives may be assumed to be aspirated, at least when at the beginning of a stressed syllable, much as in English. Voiced obstruents in these languages, as in English, may be susceptible to devoicing. In all other foreign languages both plosives and affricates should be assumed to be unaspirated unless explicitly marked as aspirated. Thus both syllables in the Chinese pronunciation of **Beijing** [³pei ¹tɕiŋ] start with voiceless unaspirated consonants, which sound similar to the devoiced b, dʒ of English. In certain cases, including notably Hindi, Chinese, and Korean, aspiration is distinctive in both plosives and affricates.

In general, the transcription LPD uses for foreign languages is a phonemic one for the language in question, sometimes modified in the direction of greater phonetic explicitness. Thus the French vowel of **vin** is shown as æ̃, rather than the more customary ɛ̃, because of the phonetic similarity to the vowel quality of English æ. In Spanish, LPD distinguishes between the plosive and the fricative/approximant allophones of b, d, g, since they sound so different to the English ear. Because LPD uses r for the English consonant as in **red**, it transcribes ɾ or rr in languages that typically have a tongue-tip tapped or rolled r-sound, and ʁ for those that typically have a uvular r-sound.

No stress-marks are used in the transcription of French and Hindi, since these languages have no lexical stress. Nevertheless, there may often appear to be stress on the final syllable of French words and on long vowels in Hindi words.

Japanese pitch-accent is shown in accordance with IPA principles, although this differs from notation that is customary among Japanese scholars. Namely, the accent, if there is one in the word, is shown by the mark ['] **before** the accented mora; this is the mora after which the pitch is typically lower. The pitch upstep that occurs automatically on the second mora of words not bearing an accent on the first two moras is shown as [ˌ]. This mark is not used before a moraic obstruent.

In transcriptions of Swedish and other languages with two types of word-stress, the mark " denotes tone 2. In Chinese (Putonghua), the tones are as follows:

1	high level	[¹ma]	mā *mother*
2	rising	[²ma]	má *hemp*
3	low fall-rise	[³ma]	mǎ *horse*
4	falling	[⁴ma]	mà *to scold*

In Cantonese, they are:

1	high level/ high fall	[¹fan]	*to separate*
2	high rise	[²fan]	*powder*
3	mid level	[³fan]	*to sleep*
4	low fall	[⁴fan]	*tomb*
5	low rise	[⁵fan]	*to work hard*
6	lowish level	[⁶fan]	*participation*

In Burmese, they are:

1	low	[¹kʰà]	*shake*
2	high	[²kʰá]	*be bitter*
3	creaky	[³kʰa̰]	*fee*
4	checked	[⁴kʰaʔ]	*draw off*

5 Symbols

5.1 Phonetic symbols This list includes both the symbols used for English and other symbols of the International Phonetic Alphabet that appear in LPD. These general-phonetic symbols are used for transcribing words in foreign languages and occasionally also for allophonic transcription of English. Their meaning is in most cases somewhat flexible: for example, the symbol e stands for a range of similar but not identical vowel qualities in Danish, German, French, Spanish, Japanese, and English.

For the meaning of the terms used in the definitions, see note at ARTICULATION. 'Chinese' means the Pinyin romanization.

a	open front unrounded vowel; also for open vowel between front and back; French/German/Italian/Spanish *a*; first element of English diphthongs in *price, high* (aɪ), and *mouth, how* (aʊ)
ɑ	open back unrounded vowel; English *father* (ɑː)
ɑ̃	nasalized open back unrounded vowel, French *an*
æ	raised open front unrounded vowel; English *trap, bad*
æ̃	nasalized raised open front unrounded vowel, French *in*
ɐ	open variety of [ə], German *-er*
ɐ̯	non-syllabic ɐ, German *r* in *Uhr*
b	voiced bilabial plosive, English *b*
β	voiced bilabial fricative, Spanish *b/v* between vowels
ɓ	voiced bilabial implosive (glottalic ingressive plosive), Zulu *b*
c	voiceless palatal plosive, like [kj]
ç	voiceless palatal fricative, German *ich*
d	voiced alveolar (sometimes: dental) plosive, English *d*
dʒ	voiced palato-alveolar affricate, English *j*
dr	voiced post-alveolar affricate, English *dr*
dz	voiced alveolo-palatal affricate, Japanese *j*
ð	voiced dental fricative, in English *father*
d̪	voiced dental plosive (where dentality is distinctive)
ɖ	voiced retroflex plosive
ðˤ	pharyngealized ('emphatic') [ð]
e	close-mid front unrounded vowel, French *é*; also for vowel between close-mid and open-mid, English *dress*; first element of English diphthongs in *face* (eɪ) and (RP) *square* (eə)
ɛ	open-mid front unrounded vowel, French *è*
ə	mid central unrounded vowel; English vowel at beginning of *about* and at end of *comma*; first element of RP diphthong in *goat, blow* (əʊ); second element of RP diphthongs in *near, square, cure*
ɚ	rhotacized [ə], in GenAm *better* (= syllabic [r])
ɜ	mid central unrounded vowel, RP *nurse, stir* (ɜː)
ɝ	rhotacized [ɜ], GenAm *nurse, stir* (ɝː)
f	voiceless labiodental fricative, English *f*
g	voiced velar plosive, English 'hard' *g*
ɣ	voiced velar fricative (= voiced [x])
h	voiceless glottal fricative, English *h*

ħ	voiceless pharyngeal fricative
ʰ	aspiration
ɦ	breathy-voiced glottal fricative, Afrikaans *h*
ʱ	breathy-voiced aspiration
i	close front unrounded vowel, French *i*; English *fleece, key* (iː); English neutralization of iː-ɪ, *happy*
i̯	non-syllabic i, German *i* in *Studie*
ɪ	lax (lowered-centralized) [i], English *kit*; second element of English diphthongs in *face, price, choice*
ɨ	close central unrounded vowel, Polish *y*, Russian ы, north Welsh *u*
i̥	voiceless [i]
j	voiced palatal approximant (semivowel), English *y* in *yet*
ɟ	voiced palatal plosive, like [gj]
ʲ	palatalized, [i]-coloured (e.g. tʲ = palatalized t)
k	voiceless velar plosive, English *k*
l	voiced alveolar lateral, English *l*
ɫ	velarized voiced alveolar lateral, English 'dark' l
ɬ	voiceless alveolar lateral fricative, Welsh *ll*
ʎ	voiced palatal lateral, Italian *gl*
m	voiced bilabial nasal, English *m*
m̥	voiceless bilabial nasal
n	voiced alveolar (sometimes: dental) nasal, English *n*
n̪	voiced dental nasal (where dentality is distinctive)
ŋ	voiced velar nasal, English *ng*
ɲ	voiced palatal nasal, Spanish *ñ*
ɳ	voiced retroflex nasal
N	voiced uvular nasal; Japanese *-n*, alternatively pronounced as a nasalized close back vowel; in Burmese either nasalization of the preceding vowel or a nasal consonant homorganic with the following consonant
o	close-mid back rounded vowel, French *o*; also for back rounded vowel between close-mid and open-mid, Spanish *o*; first element of AmE diphthong in *goat, blow* (oʊ)
ɔ	open-mid back rounded vowel; English *north, thought*; first element of English diphthong in *choice*; French o in *pomme*
ɔ̃	nasalized open-mid back rounded vowel, French *on*
ɒ	open back rounded vowel; RP *lot*; first element of BrE diphthong variant in *cold* (ɒʊ)
ø	close-mid front rounded vowel, in French *deux*, German *schön*
œ	open-mid front rounded vowel, in French *neuf*, German *plötzlich*
œ̃	nasalized open-mid front rounded vowel, French *un*
p	voiceless bilabial plosive, English *p*
ɸ	voiceless bilabial fricative, Japanese *f*
q	voiceless uvular plosive, Arabic *q*
r	voiced post-alveolar approximant, English *red* (this differs from the usual IPA value, which is a trill, LPD's rr)
r̝	voiced alveolar fricative trill, Czech *ř*
ɾ	voiced alveolar tap, Spanish single *r*

rr	voiced alveolar trill, Spanish initial *r* or double *rr*
ɽ	voiced retroflex flap
ʁ	voiced uvular fricative/approximant, French *r*
s	voiceless alveolar fricative, English *s*
ʃ	voiceless palato-alveolar fricative, English *sh*
ɕ	voiceless alveolo-palatal fricative, Japanese *sh*, Chinese *x*
ʂ	voiceless retroflex fricative, Chinese *sh*
sˤ	pharyngealized ('emphatic') [s]
t	voiceless alveolar (sometimes: dental) plosive, English *t*
ɾ	alveolar tap, usually voiced, AmE *t* in *city*
tʃ	voiceless palato-alveolar affricate, English *ch*
tr	voiceless post-alveolar affricate, English *tr*
tɕ	voiceless alveolopalatal affricate, Japanese *ch*, Chinese *q*
t̪	voiceless dental plosive (where dentality is distinctive)
θ	voiceless dental fricative, English *th*
ʈ	voiceless retroflex plosive
tˤ	pharyngealized ('emphatic') [t]
u	close back rounded vowel, French *ou*; English *goose* (uː); English neutralization of uː-ʊ, *thank you*
ʊ	lax (lowered-centralized) [u], English *foot*; second element in English diphthongs in *mouth, goat*
ʉ	close central rounded vowel, Swedish *u*
ɯ	close back unrounded vowel, Japanese *u*
ɯ̥	voiceless [ɯ]
ɰ	voiced velar approximant (semivowel), Japanese *w*
v	voiced labiodental fricative, English *v*
ʋ	voiced labiodental approximant, Dutch *w*
ʌ	open-mid back unrounded vowel; also for open-mid unrounded vowel between back and front, English *strut, love*
w	voiced labial-velar approximant (semivowel), English *w*
ʍ	voiceless labial-velar fricative/approximant, Scottish *wh*
x	voiceless velar fricative, German *ach*, Spanish *jota*
χ	voiceless uvular fricative, Welsh *ch*
y	close front rounded vowel, in French *lune*, German *über*
ʏ	lax (lowered-centralized) [y], in German *hübsch*
ɥ	voiced labial-palatal approximant (semivowel), in French *huit*
z	voiced alveolar fricative, English *z*
ʒ	voiced palato-alveolar fricative, in English *measure*
ʑ	voiced alveopalatal fricative, second element of Japanese *j*
ʔ	glottal plosive, glottal stop
ʕ	voiced pharyngeal fricative/approximant, Arabic *'ayn*
ǀ	voiceless dental click, Zulu *c*
ǁ	voiceless lateral click, Zulu *x*
ˈ	primary word stress (re ˈMEMber)
ˌ	secondary stress (ˌACa ˈDEMic)
ˈ ˌ	stress (= ˈ or ˌ as appropriate)
ː	length

5.2 Key to phonetic symbols for English

RP Gen Am   **Consonants**

- • •   p   **p**en, co**p**y, ha**pp**en
- • •   b   **b**ack, **b**u**bb**le, jo**b**
- • •   t   **t**ea, **t**igh**t**, bu**tt**on
-    •   ţ   ci**t**y, be**tt**er
- • •   d   **d**ay, la**dd**er, o**dd**
- • •   k   **c**up, **k**i**ck**, s**ch**ool
- • •   g   **g**et, **g**i**gg**le, **gh**ost
- • •   tʃ   **ch**ur**ch**, ma**tch**, na**t**ure
- • •   dʒ   **j**u**dg**e, a**g**e, sol**d**ier
- • •   f   **f**at, co**ff**ee, rou**gh**
- • •   v   **v**iew, hea**v**y, mo**v**e
- • •   θ   **th**ing, au**th**or, pa**th**
- • •   ð   **th**is, o**th**er, smoo**th**
- • •   s   **s**oon, **c**ea**s**e, **s**i**s**ter
- • •   z   **z**ero, **z**one, ro**s**es, bu**zz**
- • •   ʃ   **sh**ip, **s**ure, sta**t**ion
- • •   ʒ   plea**s**ure, vi**s**ion
- • •   h   **h**ot, **wh**ole, be**h**ind
- • •   m   **m**ore, ha**mm**er, su**m**
- • •   n   **n**ice, **kn**ow, fu**nn**y, su**n**
- • •   ŋ   ri**ng**, lo**ng**, tha**n**ks, su**ng**
- • •   l   **l**ight, va**ll**ey, fee**l**
- • •   r   **r**ight, so**rr**y, a**rr**ange
- • •   j   **y**et, **u**se, be**au**ty
- • •   w   **w**et, **o**ne, **wh**en, q**u**een

In foreign words only:

- • •   x   lo**ch**, **ch**utzpah
-    •   ɫ   **Ll**anelli, H**l**uhluwe

RP Gen Am   **Vowels**

- • •   ɪ   k**i**t, b**i**d, h**y**mn
- • •   e   dr**e**ss, b**e**d
- • •   æ   tr**a**p, b**a**d
-    •   ɒ   l**o**t, **o**dd, w**a**sh
- • •   ʌ   str**u**t, b**u**d, l**o**ve
- • •   ʊ   f**oo**t, g**oo**d, p**u**t
- • •   iː   fl**ee**ce, s**ea**, m**a**chine
- • •   eɪ   f**a**ce, d**a**y, st**ea**k
- • •   aɪ   pr**i**ce, h**igh**, tr**y**
- • •   ɔɪ   ch**oi**ce, b**oy**
- • •   uː   g**oo**se, tw**o**, bl**ue**
- •   əʊ   g**oa**t, sh**ow**, n**o**
-    •   oʊ   g**oa**t, sh**ow**, n**o**
- •   ɒʊ   *variant in* c**o**ld
- • •   aʊ   m**ou**th, n**ow**
- •   ɪə   n**ea**r, h**e**re, s**e**rious
- •   eə   sq**ua**re, f**ai**r, v**a**rious
- •   ɑː   st**a**rt, f**a**ther
-    •   ɑː   l**o**t, **o**dd
- • •   ɔː   th**ough**t, l**aw**, n**or**th, w**ar**
- •   ʊə   c**u**re, p**oo**r, j**u**ry
- •   ɜː   n**ur**se, st**ir**
-    •   ɝː   n**ur**se, st**ir**, c**our**age
- • •   i   happ**y**, rad**i**ation, glor**i**ous
- • •   ə   **a**bout, comm**a**, comm**o**n
-    •   f**a**ther, standard
- • •   u   infl**u**ence, sit**u**ation, thank y**ou**
- • •   ɪ   **i**ntend, bas**i**c
- •   ʊ   stim**u**lus, comm**u**nist

In foreign words only:

- •   ɔ̃   gr**an**d prix, ch**an**son
-    •   ɑ̃ː   gr**an**d prix, ch**an**son
- • •   æ̃   vi**n**gt-et-un
- •   ɜ̃ː   vingt-et-**un**

5.3 Other symbols

‖	GenAm pronunciation follows (see p.xx)
§	BrE non-RP (see p.xix)
⚠	pronunciation considered incorrect (see p.xx)
◄	stress shift possible (see p.784)
→	variant derived by rule (see p.xxviii)
‿	possible compression (see p.173)
(!)	pronunciation unexpected for this spelling
(*)	RP and GenAm differ in an unpredictable and striking way
=	is pronounced the same as
≠	is pronounced differently from
+	(in prefix) attracts consonant from next syllable
~	recapitulates headword up to |, otherwise all of headword
|	end of part to be recapitulated
-	recapitulates as many syllables from the main or preceding pronunciation as it contains, minus the number of syllables preceding/following this mark (count syllables by counting spaces plus ‿ and • symbols

6 Abbreviations

adj	adjective	*Lancs*	Lancashire
adv	adverb	*Leics*	Leicestershire
AK	Alaska	*LI*	Long Island
AL	Alabama	*LPD*	*Longman Pronunciation*
AmE	American English		*Dictionary*
AmSp	American Spanish	*MA*	Massachusetts
AR	Arkansas	*MD*	Maryland
AZ	Arizona	*ME*	Maine
BBC	British Broadcasting	*med*	medical(ly)
	Corporation	*MI*	Michigan
Berks	Berkshire	*MN*	Minnesota
BrE	British English	*MO*	Missouri
BrazPort	Brazilian Portuguese	*ModGk*	Modern Greek
Bucks	Buckinghamshire	*MT*	Montana
CA	California	*mus*	musically, in music
Chi	Chinese	*n*	noun
Co.	County	*N*	North
comb.	combining	*naut*	nautical
conj	conjunction	*NB*	Nebraska; nota bene,
CT	Connecticut		note well
DE	Delaware	*NC*	North Carolina
E	East	*Nfk*	Norfolk
EFL	English as a foreign	*NH*	New Hampshire
	language	*NJ*	New Jersey
e.g.	for example	*NM*	New Mexico
esp.	especially	*Norw*	Norwegian
etc.	et cetera (and the rest)	*Notts*	Nottinghamshire
Fr	French	*NSW*	New South Wales
GA	Georgia; General	*N. Terr*	Northern Territories
	American	*NY*	New York
GenAm	General American	*NYC*	New York City
Glam	Glamorgan	*NYks*	North Yorkshire
Gloucs	Gloucestershire	*NZ*	New Zealand
H&W	Hereford & Worcester	*OH*	Ohio
Hung	Hungarian	*OR*	Oregon
IA	Iowa	*PA*	Pennsylvania
IL	Illinois	*part*	participle
IN	Indiana	*pl*	plural
interj	interjection	*Port*	Portuguese
IPA	International Phonetic	*pp*	past participle
	Alphabet	*PR*	Puerto Rico
It	Italian	*prep*	preposition
Jp	Japanese	*pres*	present
KS	Kansas	*ptcp*	participle

RI	Rhode Island	*Sx*	Sussex
RP	Received Pronunciation	*S Yks*	South Yorkshire
Russ	Russian	*tdmk*	trademark, trade name, proprietary name*
S	South		
SC	South Carolina	*TX*	Texas
ScG	Scottish Gaelic	*UK*	United Kingdom
S-Cr	Serbo-Croat	*US*	United States
SD	South Dakota	*v*	verb
sing.	singular	*VA*	Virginia
Skt	Sanskrit	*VT*	Vermont
Sp	Spanish	*W*	West
Staffs	Staffordshire	*Warks*	Warwickshire
StdEng	Standard English	*W Yks*	West Yorkshire
Swed	Swedish		

* Dictionary entries that we believe to constitute trademarks have been designated *tdmk*. However, neither the presence nor the absence of this designation should be regarded as affecting the legal status of any trademark.

A a

a Spelling-to-sound

1 Where the spelling is **a**, the pronunciation differs according to whether the vowel is short or long, followed or not by **r**, and strong or weak.

2 The 'strong' pronunciation is regularly
æ as in **cat** kæt ('short A') or
eɪ as in **face** feɪs ('long A').

3 Where **a** is followed by **r**, the 'strong' pronunciation is
ɑː as in **start** stɑːt ‖ stɑːrt or
eə ‖ e as in **square** skweə ‖ skwer
or, indeed, there may be the regular 'short' pronunciation
æ as in **carol** ˈkær əl (although in this position many speakers of GenAm use e, thus ˈker əl).

4 Less frequently, the 'strong' pronunciation is
ɑː as in **father** ˈfɑːð ə ‖ ˈfɑːð ᵊr
ɑː ‖ æ as in **bath** bɑːθ ‖ bæθ
ɒ ‖ ɑː as in **watch** wɒtʃ ‖ wɑːtʃ (especially after the sound w)
ɔː ‖ ɔː as in **talk** tɔːk ‖ tɔːk (especially before the letter **l**) or
ɔː ‖ ɔː as in **warm** wɔːm ‖ wɔːrm.

5 The 'weak' pronunciation is
ə as in **about** ə ˈbaʊt or
ɪ as in **village** ˈvɪl ɪdʒ.

6 Because of COMPRESSION, **a** is usually silent in the ending **-ally** as in **basically** ˈbeɪs ɪk li.

7 Note that where the spelling is **a** the pronunciation is not ʌ (except in a few words from foreign languages).

8 **a** also forms part of the digraphs **ai**, **au**, **aw**, **ay**.

ai, ay Spelling-to-sound

1 Where the spelling is one of the digraphs **ai**, **ay**, the pronunciation is regularly
eɪ as in **rain** reɪn, **day** deɪ or before **r**
eə ‖ e as in **fair** feə ‖ fer.

A

2 Occasionally with these digraphs the pronunciation is 'weak':

ə as in **curtain** ˈkɜːt ᵊn ‖ ˈkɜːt ᵊn (for a few speakers ɪ, thus ˈkɜːt ɪn) or

i as in **Murray** ˈmʌr i ‖ ˈmɜː i, when at the end of a word. (For **Monday** etc., see note at **-day**.)

3 Note also the exceptional words **says**, **said**, **again**, **against**, usually pronounced with e.

au, aw Spelling-to-sound

1 Where the spelling is one of the digraphs **au** and **aw**, the pronunciation is regularly

ɔː as in **author** ˈɔːθ ə ‖ ˈɔːθ ᵊr, **law** lɔː.

2 In a few words, the pronunciation is

ɑː ‖ æ as in **laugh** lɑːf ‖ læf

or, in loanwords from foreign languages,

əʊ ‖ oʊ as in **gauche** ɡəʊʃ ‖ ɡoʊʃ or aʊ as in **sauerkraut** ˈsaʊ-

or, in BrE only,

ɒ as in **sausage** ˈsɒs ɪdʒ.

A, a *name of letter* eɪ **A's, As, a's** eɪz
—*Communications code name:* Alfa
ˌAˈ1◂, ˌA-ˈ1; ˌA1(ˈM); ˌA,30ˈ3 —*These patterns apply to all British road numbers.*
ˌAˈ4◂; ˌA4 ˈpaper

a *indef article, before a consonant sound, strong form* eɪ, *weak form* ə —*See also* **an**

a *Latin prep* eɪ ɑː —*See also phrases with this word*

a, à *French prep* æ ɑː —*See also phrases with this word*

a- *comb. form* ¦eɪ, eɪ, ¦æ, æ, ə —*When it has a negative meaning, this prefix is usually* eɪ (ˌatheˈistic), *though in some words there are alternative pronunciations with* æ *or* ə (ˌaˈmoral, aˈmoral), *and sometimes* ə *is the only form* (aˈmorphous). *With other meanings, the pronunciation is regularly* ə (aˈway, aˈspire), *unless stressed because of a suffix, in which case it is* ¦æ (ˌaspiˈration).

Aachen ˈɑːk ən —*Ger* [ˈʔɑː xən]

aah ɑː **aah'd, aahed** ɑːd **aahing, aah'ing** ˈɑːʳ ɪŋ ‖ ˈɑː ɪŋ **aahs, aah's** ɑːz

Aalborg ˈɔːl bɔːɡ ˈɑːl- ‖ -bɔːrɡ —*Danish* Ålborg [ˈʌl bɒːʔ]

Aaliyah *singer* ɑː ˈliː ə

Aalto ˈɑːlt əʊ ‖ -oʊ —*Finnish* [ˈɑːl to]

aardvark ˈɑːd vɑːk ‖ ˈɑːrd vɑːrk **~s** s

aard|wolf ˈɑːd |wʊlf ‖ ˈɑːrd- **~wolves** wʊlvz

aargh ɑːx ɑː, ɑːɡ, ɑːɣ ‖ ɑːrɡ ɜː: —*and various non-speech exclamations involving a mid or open vowel and perhaps a velar component*

Aarhus ˈɔː huːs ˈɑː-, -hʊs ‖ ˈɔːr- ˈɑːr- —*Danish* Århus [ˈɔː huːs]

Aaron (i) ˈeər ən ‖ ˈer ən, (ii) ˈær ən ‖ ˈer- —*In BrE traditionally (i), and still usually so for the biblical character; but the personal name may nowadays be either (i) or (ii)*

Aaronic ₍ᵢ₎eə ˈrɒn ɪk ◂ ‖ æ ˈrɑːn ɪk e-

ab æb —*See also phrases with this word* **abs** æbz

AB ˌeɪ ˈbiː **~s, ~'s** z

ab- (¦)æb, əb —*As a true prefix meaning 'away', ab- is usually* æb, *though with unstressed and reduced-vowel variants* (abˈduct). *It is always* ¦æb *when it means 'cgs unit'* (ˈabvolt, ˌabˈcoulomb). *With a vaguer meaning, it is mostly* əb (abˈstain) *unless stressed* (ˈabdicate, ˈabstract).

aback ə ˈbæk

Abaco ˈæb ə kəʊ ‖ -koʊ

abacus ˈæb ək əs **~es** ɪz əz

Abadan ˌæb ə ˈdɑːn -ˈdæn

Abaddon ə ˈbæd ᵊn

abaft ə ˈbɑːft §-ˈbæft ‖ ə ˈbæft

abalone ˌæb ə ˈləʊn i ‖ -ˈloʊn- **~s** z

abandon ə ˈbænd ən **~ed** d **~ing** ɪŋ **~s** z

abandonment ə ˈbænd ən mənt →-əm-

abase ə ˈbeɪs **abased** ə ˈbeɪst **abases** ə ˈbeɪs ɪz -əz **abasing** ə ˈbeɪs ɪŋ

abasement ə ˈbeɪs mənt

abash ə ˈbæʃ **abashed** ə ˈbæʃt **abashes** ə ˈbæʃ ɪz -əz **abashing** ə ˈbæʃ ɪŋ

abashment ə ˈbæʃ mənt

A

abate ə ˈbeɪt **abated** ə ˈbeɪt ɪd -əd **abates**
  ə ˈbeɪts **abating** ə ˈbeɪt ɪŋ
abatement ə ˈbeɪt mənt ~**s** s
abatis, abattis ˈæb ət ɪs §-əs; æb ə ˈtiː, ˈˑˑˑ
  ‖ -əʈ əs -ə tiː: ~**es** *pl after* s *forms* ɪz əz; *for*
  those who pronounce -ˈtiː, *the pl is written as*
  the sing. but pronounced with added z
abattoir ˈæb ə twɑː ‖ -twɑːr -twɔːr ~**s** z
Abba ˈæb ə
abbac|y ˈæb əs |i ~**ies** iz
Abbado ə ˈbɑːd əʊ ‖ -oʊ —*It* [ab ˈba: do]
Abbas *(i)* ˈæb əs, *(ii)* ə ˈbɑːs
Abbasid ə ˈbæs ɪd ˈæb əs-, §-əd ~**s** z
abbatial ə ˈbeɪʃ ᵊl
abbe, abbé, A~ ˈæb eɪ ‖ æ ˈbeɪ ˈæb eɪ —*Fr*
  [a be] ~**s** z
Abberton ˈæb ət ən ‖ -ˈrt ᵊn
abbess ˈæb es -ɪs, §-əs; æ ˈbes ‖ -əs ~**es** ɪz əz
Abbeville ˈæb vɪl ˈæb ɪ vɪl, -ə- ‖ æb ˈviːᵊl
  ˈæb ɪ vɪl —*Fr* [ab vil]
Abbevillian ˌæb ˈvɪl i ən ◂ ˌæb ɪ ˈvɪl-, §ˌæb ə-
abbey, Abbey ˈæb i ~**s** z
Abbie ˈæb i
abbot, Abbot ˈæb ət ~**s** s
Abbotsbury ˈæb əts bər i ‖ -ˌber i
abbotship ˈæb ət ʃɪp ~**s** s
Abbott ˈæb ət
abbrevi|ate ə ˈbriːv i |eɪt ~**ated** eɪt ɪd -əd
  ‖ eɪʈ əd ~**ates** eɪts ~**ating** eɪt ɪŋ ‖ eɪʈ ɪŋ
abbreviation ə ˌbriːv i ˈeɪʃ ᵊn ~**s** z
abbreviator ə ˈbriːv i eɪt ə ‖ -eɪʈ ᵊr ~**s** z
abbreviatory ə ˈbriːv i ət ər i
  ə ˌbriːv i ˈeɪt ər i ◂ ‖ -i̯ə tɔːr i -tour i
Abbs æbz
Abby ˈæb i
ABC ˌeɪ biː ˈsiː **ABCs** ˌeɪ biː ˈsiːz
abdabs ˈæb dæbz
Abdela æb ˈdel ə
abdi|cate ˈæbd ɪ |keɪt -ə- ~**cated** keɪt ɪd -əd
  ‖ keɪʈ əd ~**cates** keɪts ~**cating** keɪt ɪŋ
  ‖ keɪʈ ɪŋ
abdication ˌæbd ɪ ˈkeɪʃ ᵊn -ə- ~**s** z
abdomen ˈæbd əm ən -ɪn, -ə men; æb ˈdəʊm-
  ~**s** z
abdominal æb ˈdɒm ɪn ᵊl əb-, -ən ᵊl ‖ -ˈdɑːm-
  ~**ly** i ~**s** z
abduct ₍ᵢ₎æb ˈdʌkt əb- ~**ed** ɪd əd ~**ing** ɪŋ ~**s** s
abduction ₍ᵢ₎æb ˈdʌk ʃᵊn əb- ~**s** z
abductor ₍ᵢ₎æb ˈdʌkt ə əb- ‖ -ᵊr ~**s** z
Abdul ˈæbd ʊl -ᵊl
Abdulla, Abdullah æb ˈdʌl ə əb-, -ˈdʊl-
  —*Arabic* [ʕab ˈdʊɫ ɫah]
Abe *short for* Abraham eɪb
Abe *Jp name* ˈɑːb eɪ
à Becket ə ˈbek ɪt §-ət
abed ə ˈbed
Abednego ˌæb ed ˈniːg əʊ ə ˈbed nɪ gəʊ, -nə-
  ‖ ə ˈbed nɪ goʊ
Abel ˈeɪb ᵊl
Abelard ˈæb ə lɑːd -ɪ- ‖ -lɑːrd —*Fr* [a be laːʁ]
abele ə ˈbiːᵊl ˈeɪb ᵊl
Abelian ə ˈbiːl i ən
abelmosk ˈeɪb ᵊl mɒsk ‖ -mɑːsk

Aber ˈæb ə ‖ -ᵊr
Aberaeron, Aberayron ˌæb ər ˈaɪᵊr ən ‖ -ər-
  —*Welsh* [a ber ˈəi ron]
Aberavon ˌæb ər ˈæv ᵊn ‖ -ər- —*Welsh*
  Aberafan [a ber ˈa van]
Abercon|way ˌæb ə ˈkɒn |weɪ ‖ -ᵊr ˈkɑːn-
  ~**wy** wi
Abercorn ˈæb ə kɔːn ‖ -ᵊr kɔːrn
Abercrombie, Abercromby *(i)*
  ˈæb ə ˌkrʌm bi ,ˑˈˑˑ ‖ ˈæb ᵊr-, *(ii)* -ˌkrɒm bi
  ,ˑˈˑˑ ‖ -ˌkrɑːm-
Aberdare ˌæb ə ˈdeə ‖ -ᵊr ˈdeᵊr -ˈdæᵊr
Aberdaron ˌæb ə ˈdær ən ‖ -ᵊr- -ˈder-
Aberdeen *place in Scotland* ˌæb ə ˈdiːn ‖ -ᵊr-
  —*but places in the US are* ˈˑˑˑ ~**shire** ʃə -ʃɪə,
  §-ʃɑɪ̯ə ‖ ʃɪr -ʃᵊr
Aberdonian ˌæb ə ˈdəʊn i ən ◂ ‖ -ᵊr ˈdoʊn- ~**s**
  z
Aberdour ˌæb ə ˈdaʊ ə ‖ -ᵊr ˈdaʊ ᵊr
Aberdovey ˌæb ə ˈdʌv i ‖ -ᵊr-
Aberfan ˌæb ə ˈvæn ‖ -ᵊr- —*also,*
  inappropriately, -ˈfæn —*Welsh* [a ber ˈvan]
Aberfeldy ˌæb ə ˈfeld i ‖ -ᵊr-
Aberffraw ə ˈbeə fraʊ ‖ -ˈber-
Aberfoyle ˌæb ə ˈfɔɪᵊl ‖ -ᵊr-
Abergavenny ˌæb ə gə ˈven i ‖ ˌæb ᵊr- —*as a*
  family name also ˌæb ə ˈgen i ‖ -ᵊr-
Abergele ˌæb ə ˈgel i -eɪ ‖ -ᵊr- —*Welsh*
  [a ber ˈge le]
Abermule ˌæb ə ˈmjuːl ‖ -ᵊr-
Abernethy, a~ ˌæb ə ˈneθ i -ˈniːθ- ‖ -ᵊr- ˈˑˑˑˑ
Aberporth ˌæb ə ˈpɔːθ ‖ -ᵊr ˈpɔːrθ
aberranc|e æ ˈber ᵊnts ə-, ˌæb ər- ~**es** ɪz əz ~**y**
  i
aberrant æ ˈber ənt ə-, ˌæb ər- ~**ly** li
aberration ˌæb ə ˈreɪʃ ᵊn ~**s** z
Abersoch ˌæb ə ˈsəʊk -ˈsɒk ‖ -ᵊr ˈsoʊk
  —*Welsh* [a ber ˈsoːχ]
Abersychan ˌæb ə ˈsɪk ən -ˈsʌk- ‖ -ᵊr- —*Welsh*
  [a ber ˈsə χan]
Abertawe ˌæb ə ˈtaʊ i -eɪ —*Welsh*
  [a ber ˈta we]
Abertillery ˌæb ə tɪ ˈleər i -təˈˑ- ‖ -ᵊr tə ˈler i
Aberystwyth ˌæb ə ˈrɪst wɪθ —*Welsh*
  [a ber ˈə sduɪθ]
abet ə ˈbet **abets** ə ˈbets **abetted** ə ˈbet ɪd -əd
  ‖ ə ˈbeʈ əd **abetting** ə ˈbet ɪŋ ‖ ə ˈbeʈ ɪŋ
abetment ə ˈbet mənt
abetter, abettor ə ˈbet ə ‖ ə ˈbeʈ ᵊr ~**s** z
abey|ance ə ˈbeɪ |ənts ~**ant** ənt
Ab Fab ˌæb ˈfæb
abhor əb ˈhɔː æb-, ə ˈbɔː ‖ æb ˈhɔːr əb-
  abhorred əb ˈhɔːd æb-, ə ˈbɔːd ‖ æb ˈhɔːrd
  əb- **abhorring** əb ˈhɔːr ɪŋ æb-, ə ˈbɔːr- ‖ æb-
  əb- **abhors** əb ˈhɔːz æb-, ə ˈbɔːz ‖ æb ˈhɔːrz
  əb-
abhorrence əb ˈhɒr ənts æb-, ə ˈbɒr-
  ‖ æb ˈhɔːr ənts əb-, -ˈhɑːr-
abhorrent əb ˈhɒr ənt æb-, ə ˈbɒr-
  ‖ æb ˈhɔːr ənt əb-, -ˈhɑːr- ~**ly** li
abide ə ˈbaɪd **abided** ə ˈbaɪd ɪd -əd **abides**
  ə ˈbaɪdz **abiding/ly** ə ˈbaɪd ɪŋ /li **abode**
  ə ˈbəʊd ‖ ə ˈboʊd

A

Abidjan ˌæb i ˈdʒɑːn -ˈdʒæn —*Fr* [a bid ʒɑ̃]
Abigail, a~ ˈæb ɪ geɪᵊl §-ə-
Abilene *places in TX, KS* ˈæb ə liːn -ɪ-
abilit|y ə ˈbɪl ət |i -ɪt- ‖ -əţ |i **~ies** iz
-ability ə ˈbɪl ət i -ɪt- ‖ -əţ i —*A word with this suffix has a secondary stress in the same place as the primary stress in the corresponding word with -able* (ˌcookaˈbility, ˌpreferaˈbility).
Abingdon ˈæb ɪŋ dən
Abinger ˈæb ɪndʒ ə ‖ -ᵊr
ab initio ˌæb ɪ ˈnɪʃ i əʊ ˌ-ə-, -ˈnɪs- ‖ -oʊ
abiotic ˌeɪ baɪ ˈɒt ɪk ◂ ‖ -ˈɑːţ ɪk
abject ˈæb dʒekt **~ly** li ·ˈ··
abjection æb ˈdʒek ʃⁿn
abjuration ˌæb dʒuᵊ ˈreɪʃ ⁿn -dʒɔː-, -dʒə- ‖ -dʒə-
abjure əb ˈdʒʊə æb-, -ˈdʒɔː ‖ æb ˈdʒʊᵊr **~d** d **~s** z **abjuring** əb ˈdʒʊər ɪŋ æb-, -ˈdʒɔːr- ‖ æb ˈdʒʊr ɪŋ
Abkhazi|a æb ˈkɑːz i |ə -ˈkeɪz- **~an/s** ən/z
ab|late ₍ˌ₎æb |ˈleɪt **~lated** ˈleɪt ɪd -əd ‖ ˈleɪţ əd **~lates** ˈleɪts **~lating** ˈleɪt ɪŋ ‖ ˈleɪţ ɪŋ
ablation ₍ˌ₎æb ˈleɪʃ ⁿn
ablatival ˌæb lə ˈtaɪv ᵊl ◂
ablative *'ablating'* ₍ˌ₎æb ˈleɪt ɪv ‖ -leɪţ ɪv
ablative *case* ˈæb lət ɪv ‖ -ləţ- **~s** z
  ˌablative ˈabsolute
ablaut ˈæb laʊt —*Ger* [ˈʔap laʊt]
ablaze ə ˈbleɪz
able ˈeɪb ᵊl **abler** ˈeɪb lə ‖ -lᵊr **ablest** ˈeɪb lɪst -ləst
-able əb ᵊl —*In general, this suffix is stress-neutral* (inˈterpretable, deˈsirable, comˈmunicable). *There are, however, some important exceptions* (ˈadmirable, ˈpreferable, ˈreputable), *and speakers disagree for some words* (applicable, comparable, formidable, hospitable, irrevocable, lamentable, transferable) — *see individual entries.*
able-bodied ˌeɪb ᵊl ˈbɒd id ◂ ‖ -ˈbɑːd-
ablution ə ˈbluːʃ ⁿn æ- **~s** z
ably ˈeɪb li
-ably əb li —*The stress is always as in the corresponding -able form.*
abne|gate ˈæb nɪ |geɪt -nə-, -ne- **~gated** geɪt ɪd -əd ‖ geɪţ əd **~gates** geɪts **~gating** geɪt ɪŋ ‖ geɪţ ɪŋ
abnegation ˌæb nɪ ˈgeɪʃ ⁿn -nə-, -ne-
Abner ˈæb nə ‖ -nᵊr
Abney ˈæb ni
abnormal ₍ˌ₎æb ˈnɔːm ᵊl əb- ‖ -ˈnɔːrm- **~ly** i
abnormalit|y ˌæb nɔː ˈmæl ət |i ˌ-nə-, -ɪt i ‖ -nɔːr ˈmæl əţ |i **~ies** iz
Abo, abo *'aboriginal'* ˈæb əʊ ‖ -oʊ **~s** z
ABO *blood type classification* ˌeɪ biː ˈəʊ ‖ -ˈoʊ
aboard ə ˈbɔːd ‖ ə ˈbɔːrd -ˈboʊrd
abode ə ˈbəʊd ‖ ə ˈboʊd **~s** z
abolish ə ˈbɒl ɪʃ ‖ ə ˈbɑːl- **~ed** t **~es** ɪz əz **~ing** ɪŋ
abolition ˌæb ə ˈlɪʃ ⁿn **~ism** ˌɪz əm **~ist/s** ˌɪst/s əst/s
abomas|um ˌæb əʊ ˈmeɪs |əm ‖ -oʊ- **~a** ə
A-bomb ˈeɪ bɒm ‖ -bɑːm **~s** z

abominab|le ə ˈbɒm ɪn əb |ᵊl -ən ˌəb- ‖ ə ˈbɑːm- **~ly** li
  aˌbominable ˈsnowman, ·ˈ····ˌ··
abomi|nate ə ˈbɒm ɪ |neɪt -ə- ‖ ə ˈbɑːm- **~nated** neɪt ɪd -əd ‖ neɪţ əd **~nates** neɪts **~nating** neɪt ɪŋ ‖ neɪţ ɪŋ
abomination ə ˌbɒm ɪ ˈneɪʃ ⁿn -ə- ‖ ə ˌbɑːm- **~s** z
aboriginal, A~ ˌæb ə ˈrɪdʒ ⁿn əl ◂ -ɪn- ᵊl **~ly** i
aboriginalit|y, A~ ˌæb ə ˌrɪdʒ ə ˈnæl ət |i -ɪˈ--, -ɪt |i -əţ |i **~ies** iz
aborigine, A~ ˌæb ə ˈrɪdʒ ən i -in -m i **~s** z
aborning ə ˈbɔːn ɪŋ ‖ ə ˈbɔːrn ɪŋ
abort ə ˈbɔːt ‖ ə ˈbɔːrt **aborted** ə ˈbɔːt ɪd -əd ‖ ə ˈbɔːrţ əd **aborting** ə ˈbɔːt ɪŋ ‖ ə ˈbɔːrţ ɪŋ **aborts** ə ˈbɔːts ‖ ə ˈbɔːrts
abortifacient ə ˌbɔːt ɪ ˈfeɪʃ ⁿnt §-ə-, -ˈfeɪʃ i ənt ‖ ə ˌbɔːrţ ə- **~s** s
abortion ə ˈbɔːʃ ⁿn ‖ ə ˈbɔːrʃ- **~s** z
abortionist ə ˈbɔːʃ ⁿn ˌɪst §ˌəst ‖ ə ˈbɔːrʃ- **~s** s
abortive ə ˈbɔːt ɪv ‖ ə ˈbɔːrţ ɪv **~ly** li
Aboukir ˌæb u ˈkɪə ‖ -kɪr —*Arabic* [ʔa buː ˈqiːr, -ˈʔiːr]
abound ə ˈbaʊnd **abounded** ə ˈbaʊnd ɪd -əd **abounding/ly** ə ˈbaʊnd ɪŋ /li **abounds** ə ˈbaʊndz
about ə ˈbaʊt
about-fac|e ə ˌbaʊt ˈfeɪs ·ˈ·· **~ed** t **~es** ɪz əz **~ing** ɪŋ
about-turn ə ˌbaʊt ˈtɜːn ‖ -ˈtɜːn **~ed** d **~ing** ɪŋ **~s** z
above ə ˈbʌv
aboveboard ə ˌbʌv ˈbɔːd ◂ ·ˈ·· ‖ ə ˈbʌv bɔːrd -boʊrd
above-mentioned ə ˌbʌv ˈmenʃ ᵊnd ◂
  the aˌbove-ˌmentioned ˈfacts
Aboyne ə ˈbɔɪn
abracadabra ˌæb rə kə ˈdæb rə
abrad|e ə ˈbreɪd **~ed** ɪd əd **~es** z **~ing** ɪŋ
Abraham ˈeɪb rə hæm -həm **~s** z
Abram *place in Greater Manchester* ˈæb rəm ˈɑːb-, -ræm
Abramovich ˌæb rə ˈməʊv ɪtʃ ‖ -ˈmoʊv- —*popularly also* ə ˈbræm ə vɪtʃ —*Russian* [ə brɐ ˈmo vʲitʃ]
Abrams ˈeɪb rəmz
Abramson ˈeɪb rəm sən
abrasion ə ˈbreɪʒ ⁿn **~s** z
abrasive ə ˈbreɪs ɪv -ˈbreɪz- **~ly** li **~ness** nəs nɪs **~s** z
abraxas, A~ ə ˈbræks əs
abreact ˌæb ri ˈækt **~ed** ɪd əd **~ing** ɪŋ **~s** s
abreaction ˌæb ri ˈæk ʃⁿn **~s** z
abreast ə ˈbrest
abridg|e ə ˈbrɪdʒ **~ed** d **~es** ɪz əz **~ing** ɪŋ
Abridge ˈeɪ brɪdʒ
abridgement, abridgment ə ˈbrɪdʒ mənt **~s** s
abroad ə ˈbrɔːd ‖ -ˈbrɑːd *(!)*
abro|gate ˈæb rə |geɪt **~gated** geɪt ɪd -əd ‖ geɪţ əd **~gates** geɪts **~gating** geɪt ɪŋ ‖ geɪţ ɪŋ
abrogation ˌæb rə ˈgeɪʃ ⁿn

abrupt ə 'brʌpt **~ly** li **~ness** nəs nɪs
Abruzzi ə 'brʊts i —*It* [a 'brut tsi]
ABS ˌeɪ biː 'es
Absalom 'æb səl əm
abscess 'æb ses -sɪs, §-səs **~ed** t **~es** ɪz əz
absciss|a æb 'sɪs |ə əb- **~ae** iː **~as** əz
abscission æb 'sɪʃ ᵊn -'sɪʒ-
abscond əb 'skɒnd æb- ‖ -'skɑːnd **~ed** ɪd əd
    ~er/s ə/z ‖ ᵊr/z **~ing** ɪŋ **~s** z
Abse 'æbz i
abseil 'æb seɪᵊl 'æp-, -saɪᵊl **~ed** d **~ing** ɪŋ **~s** z
absenc|e 'æb sən¹s **~es** ɪz əz
absent *adj* 'æb sənt **~ly** li
ab|sent *v* æb |'sent əb- **~sented** 'sent ɪd -əd
    ‖ 'senţ əd **~senting** 'sent ɪŋ ‖ 'senţ ɪŋ **~sents**
    'sents
absentee ˌæb sən 'tiː ◄ **~s** z
absenteeism ˌæb sən 'tiː ˌɪz əm
absentia æb 'sent i̯ə əb-, -'sen¹ʃ-
absently 'æb sənt li
absent-minded ˌæb sənt 'maɪnd ɪd ◄ -əd **~ly**
    li **~ness** nəs nɪs
    ˌabsentˌminded proˈfessor
absinth, absinthe 'æb sɪn¹θ -sæ̃θ
absit omen ˌæb sɪt 'əʊm en ‖ -sɪţ 'oʊm-
absolute 'æb sə luːt -ljuːt, ˌ‧‧'‧◄ **~ness** nəs nɪs
absolutely 'æb sə luːt li -ljuːt li, ˌ‧‧'‧‧◄
    —*There are also casual rapid-speech forms*
    'æbs i, 'æbs li
absolution ˌæb sə 'luːʃ ᵊn -'ljuːʃ- **~s** z
absolutism 'æb sə luːt ˌɪz əm -sə ljuːt-, ˌ‧‧'‧–
    ‖ -luːţ ˌɪz əm
absolutist ˌæb sə 'luːt ɪst -'ljuːt-, §-əst; '‧‧‧‧
    ‖ -'luːţ- **~s** s
absolutive ˌæb sə 'luːt ɪv ◄ -'ljuːt- ‖ -'luːţ- **~s** z
absolv|e əb 'zɒlv §æb-, §-'zɑʊlv ‖ -'zɑːlv
    -'sɑːlv, -'zɔːlv, -'sɔːlv **~ed** d **~es** z **~ing** ɪŋ

absorbedly əb 'zɔːb ɪd li æb-, -'sɔːb-, -əd-;
    -'zɔːbd li, -'sɔːbd li ‖ -'zɔːrb- -'sɔːrb-
absorbency əb 'zɔːb ən¹s i æb-, -'sɔːb-
    ‖ -'zɔːrb- -'sɔːrb-
absorbent əb 'zɔːb ənt æb-, -'sɔːb- ‖ -'zɔːrb-
    -'sɔːrb-
absorber əb 'zɔːb ə æb-, -'sɔːb- ‖ -'zɔːrb ᵊr
    -'sɔːrb- **~s** z
absorption əb 'zɔːp ʃᵊn æb-, -'sɔːp- ‖ -'zɔːrp-
    -'sɔːrp-
absorptive əb 'zɔːpt ɪv æb-, -'sɔːpt- ‖ -'zɔːrpt-
    -'sɔːrpt-
absorptivity ˌæb zɔːp 'tɪv ət i ˌsɔːp-, -ɪt i
    ‖ -zɔːrp 'tɪv əţ i ˌsɔːrp-
abstain əb 'steɪn æb- **~ed** d **~er/s** ə/z ‖ ᵊr/z
    ~ing ɪŋ **~s** z
abstemious əb 'stiːm i̯əs æb- **~ly** li **~ness**
    nəs nɪs
abstention əb 'sten¹ʃ ᵊn æb- **~s** z
abstinence 'æb stɪn ən¹s
abstinent 'æb stɪn ənt **~ly** li
abstract *n* 'æb strækt **~s** s
abstract *v* '*summarize*' 'æb strækt **~ed** ɪd əd
    ~er/s ə/z ‖ ᵊr/z **~ing** ɪŋ **~s** s
abstract *adj* 'æb strækt ‖ ˌ(ˌ)'‧
abstract *v* '*remove*' ₍ˌ₎æb 'strækt əb-, '‧‧ **~ed/ly**
    ɪd /li əd /li **~ing** ɪŋ **~s** s
abstraction ₍ˌ₎æb 'stræk ʃᵊn əb- **~ism** ˌɪz əm
    ~ist/s ˌɪst/s § ˌəst/s **~s** z
abstractive ₍ˌ₎æb 'strækt ɪv əb-
abstract|ly 'æb strækt| li ₍ˌ₎'‧‧ **~ness** nəs
    nɪs
abstruse ₍ˌ₎æb 'struːs əb- **~ly** li **~ness** nəs nɪs
abstrusity ₍ˌ₎æb 'struːs ət i -ɪt- ‖ -əţ i

ABSURD

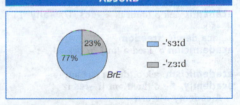

absurd, A~ əb 'sɜːd §æb-, -'zɜːd ‖ -'sɝːd -zɝːd
    ~ism ˌɪz əm **~ist/s** ɪst/s §əst/s **~ly** li
    — *Preference poll, BrE:* -'sɜːd 77%, -'zɜːd
    23%.
absurdit|y əb 'sɜːd ət |i §æb-, -'zɜːd-, -ɪt-
    ‖ -'sɝːd əţ |i -'zɝːd- **~ies** iz
ABTA 'æb tə
Abu Dhabi ˌæb u 'dɑːb i ˌɑːb-, -'dæb- ‖ ˌɑːb-
    —*Arabic* [ʔa buː 'ðˤa bi]
Abu Ghraib ˌæb u 'greɪb ‖ ˌɑːb- —*Arabic*
    [ʔa buː ɣʊ 'reɪb]
Abuja ə 'buːdʒ ə ɑː-
abulia ə 'buːl i̯ə eɪ-, -'bjuːl-
abundance ə 'bʌnd ən¹s
abundant ə 'bʌnd ənt **~ly** li
Abu Nidal ˌæb uː niː 'dɑːl ˌɑːb-, -'dæl ‖ ˌɑːb-
    æb- —*Arabic* [ʔa buː ni 'dˤaːl]
abuse *v* ə 'bjuːz **abused** ə 'bjuːzd **abuses**
    ə 'bjuːz ɪz -əz **abusing** ə 'bjuːz ɪŋ

ABSORB

—'zɔːrb ▢ —'sɔːrb ▢ —'zɔːb ▢ —'sɔːb

75% / 25% *AmE*   83% / 17% *BrE*

━●━ AmE -z- by age   ━●━ BrE -z- by age

Percentage (y-axis: 0, 40, 60, 80, 100)

Older ◄——— Speakers ———► Younger

absorb əb 'zɔːb æb-, -'sɔːb ‖ -'zɔːrb -'sɔːrb **~ed**
    d **~ing/ly** ɪŋ /li **~s** z — *Preference polls,*
    AmE: -'zɔːrb 75%, -'sɔːrb 25%; *BrE,* -'zɔːb
    83%, -'sɔːb 17%.

A

abuse *n* ə 'bjuːs abuses ə 'bjuːs ɪz -əz *(NB verb ≠ noun)*

abuser ə 'bjuːz ə ‖ -ᵊr ~s z

Abu Simbel ˌæb uː 'sɪm bᵊl ˌɑːb-, -bel ‖ ˌɑːb- ˌæb-

abusive ə 'bjuːs ɪv -'bjuːz- ~ly li ~ness nəs nɪs

abut ə 'bʌt abuts ə 'bʌts abutted ə 'bʌt ɪd -əd ‖ ə 'bʌt̬ əd abutting ə 'bʌt ɪŋ ‖ ə 'bʌt̬ ɪŋ

abutilon ə 'bjuːt ɪl ən §-əl-, -ɪ lɒn, -ə lɒn, -ᵊl ɒn ‖ ə 'bjuːt̬ ᵊl ɑːn -ən ~s z

abutment ə 'bʌt mənt ~s s

abutt... —*see* abut

abuttal ə 'bʌt ᵊl ‖ ə 'bʌt̬ ᵊl ~s z

abuzz ə 'bʌz

Abydos ə 'baɪd ɒs -əs ‖ -ɑːs -ɔːs

abysm ə 'bɪz əm

abysmal ə 'bɪz mᵊl ə- ~ly i

abyss ə 'bɪs æ-, 'æb ɪs ~es ɪz əz

abyssal ə 'bɪs ᵊl æ-

Abyssini|a ˌæb ɪ 'sɪn iˌ|ə ˌæb ə- ~an/s ən/z

-ac *This suffix and word-ending is mostly* æk *('cardiac, 'maniac); but note* ˌele'giac *usually with* ək.

a/c —*see* account

ac- *This prefix is a variant of* ad-. *Its pronunciation varies according to context. (1) When followed in spelling by* ce, ci, *it is usually* ək (ac'celerate), *but* ˌæk *if stressed because of a suffix* (ˌacci'dental) *and in a few two-syllable nouns* ('access). *(2) Otherwise, it is* ə, *but* ˌæ *if stressed because of a suffix* (ac'claim; ˌaccla'mation).

AC ˌeɪ 'siː

acacia ə 'keɪʃ ə -'keɪs iˌə ~s z

academe, A~ 'æk ə diːm ˌ‧‧

academia ˌæk ə 'diːm iˌə

academic ˌæk ə 'dem ɪk ◂ ~al/s ᵊl/z ~ally ᵊlˌi ~s s
　ˌacaˌdemic 'freedom

academician ə ˌkæd ə 'mɪʃ ᵊn ˌæk əd-, -ɪ'‧-, -e'‧- ~s z

academicism ˌæk ə 'dem ɪ ˌsɪz əm -ə ‧--

academ|y, A~ ə 'kæd əm |i ~ies iz
　Aˌcademy a'ward

Acadi|a ə 'keɪd iˌ|ə ~an/s ən/z

acai, açaí ə'saɪ —*BrazPort* [asa'i]

acanth|us ə 'kæn'θ |əs ~i aɪ ~uses əs ɪz -əz

a cappella ˌæk ə 'pel ə ˌɑːk-, -æ- ‖ ˌɑː kə- —*It* [ak kap 'pel la]

Acapulco ˌæk ə 'pʊlk əʊ ˌɑːk ə 'puːlk oʊ -'pʊlk- —*Sp* [a ka 'pul ko]

acarid 'æk ər ɪd §-əd ~s z

ACAS 'eɪk æs

acatalectic ˌeɪ ˌkæt ə 'lekt ɪk ◂ ‧,--, æ,--, ə,--

acced|e ək 'siːd æk-, ɪk- ~ed ɪd əd ~es z ~ing ɪŋ

accelerando æk ˌsel ə 'rænd əʊ ək-, ɪk-; ə ˌtʃel- ‖ -'rɑːnd oʊ ɑː ˌtʃel- —*It* [at tʃe le 'ran do]

accelerant ək 'sel ər ənt æk-, ɪk- ~s s

accele|rate ək 'sel ə |reɪt æk-, ɪk- ~rated reɪt ɪd -əd ‖ reɪt̬ əd ~rates reɪts ~rating reɪt ɪŋ ‖ reɪt̬ ɪŋ

acceleration ək ˌsel ə 'reɪʃ ᵊn æk-, ɪk- ~s z

accelerator ək 'sel ə reɪt ə æk-, ɪk- ‖ -reɪt̬ ᵊr ~s z

accelerometer ək ˌsel ə 'rɒm ɪt ə æk-, ɪk-, -ət ə ‖ -'rɑːm ət̬ ᵊr ~s z

accent *n* 'æks ᵊnt 'æk sent ‖ 'æk sent ~s s

ac|cent *v* æk '|sent ək-, ɪk-, 'æk |sent; 'æk |sᵊnt ‖ 'æk |sent ‧·· ~cented sent ɪd sᵊnt-, -əd ‖ sent̬ əd ~centing sent ɪŋ sᵊnt- ‖ sent̬ ɪŋ ~cents sents sᵊnts ‖ sents

accentor æk 'sent ə ək-, ɪk- ‖ -'sent̬ ᵊr ~s z

accentual ək 'sentʃ uˌəl æk-, ɪk-, -'sent ju- ~ly i

accentu|ate ək 'sentʃ u |eɪt æk-, ɪk-, -'sent ju- ~ated eɪt ɪd -əd ‖ eɪt̬ əd ~ates eɪts ~ating eɪt ɪŋ ‖ eɪt̬ ɪŋ

accentuation ək ˌsentʃ u 'eɪʃ ᵊn æk-, ɪk-, -ˌsent ju-

accept ək 'sept æk-, ɪk- ~ed ɪd əd ~ing ɪŋ ~s s

acceptability ək ˌsept ə 'bɪl ət i æk-, ɪk-, -ɪt i ‖ -ət̬ i

acceptab|le ək 'sept əb |ᵊl æk-, ɪk- ~ly li

acceptanc|e ək 'sept ᵊn's æk-, ɪk- ~es ɪz əz

acceptation ˌæks ep 'teɪʃ ᵊn

acceptor ək 'sept ə æk-, ɪk- ‖ -ᵊr ~s z

access *v, n* 'æk ses —*as a v, occasionally also* ‧·· ~ed t ~es ɪz əz ~ing ɪŋ
　'access time

accessibility ək ˌses ə 'bɪl ət i æk-, ɪk-, -,ɪ-, -ɪt i ‖ -ət̬ i

accessib|le ək 'ses əb |ᵊl æk-, ɪk-, -ɪb- ~leness ᵊl nəs -nɪs ~ly li

accession ək 'seʃ ᵊn æk-, ɪk- ~ed d ~ing ˌɪŋ ~s z

accessoris|e, accessoriz|e ək 'ses ə raɪz æk-, ɪk- ~ed d ~es ɪz əz ~ing ɪŋ

accessor|y ək 'ses ər ˌi æk-, ɪk-, △-- ~ies iz

acciaccatura ə ˌtʃæk ə 'tʊər ə △-ˌkæt̬ʃ- ‖ ɑː ˌtʃɑːk ə 'tʊr ə —*It* [at tʃak ka 'tuː ra]

accidence 'æks ɪd ᵊn's -əd- ‖ -ə den's

accident 'æks ɪd ənt -əd- ‖ -ə dent ~s s

accidental ˌæks ɪ 'dent ᵊl ◂ -ə- ‖ -'dent̬ ᵊl ◂ ~ly i ~s z
　ˌacciˌdental 'death

accident-prone 'æks ɪd ənt prəʊn '‧əd- ‖ -proʊn -ə dent-

accidie 'æks ɪd i -əd-

accipiter æk 'sɪp ɪt ə -ət- ‖ -ət̬ ᵊr ~s z

acclaim ə 'kleɪm acclaimed ə 'kleɪmd acclaiming ə 'kleɪm ɪŋ acclaims ə 'kleɪmz

acclaimer ə 'kleɪm ə ‖ -ᵊr ~s z

acclamation ˌæk lə 'meɪʃ ᵊn ~s z

acclamatory ə 'klæm ət ər i ‖ -ə tɔːr i -toʊr i

accli|mate 'æk lɪ |meɪt -lə-; ə 'klaɪ|m eɪt, -ət ~mated meɪt ɪd -əd ‖ meɪt̬ əd ~mates meɪts ~mating meɪt ɪŋ ‖ meɪt̬ ɪŋ

acclimation ˌæk lɪ 'meɪʃ ᵊn -lə-, -laɪ-

acclimatis... —*see* acclimatiz...

acclimatization ə ˌklaɪm ət aɪ 'zeɪʃ ᵊn -ɪ'‧- ‖ -ət̬ ə-

acclimatiz|e ə 'klaɪm ə taɪz ~ed d ~es ɪz əz ~ing ɪŋ

acclivit|y ə 'klɪv ət |i æ-, -ɪt- ‖ -ət̬ |i ~ies iz

accolade 'æk ə leɪd -lɑːd, ˌ·ˈ· ~s z
accommo|date ə 'kɒm ə |deɪt ‖ ə 'kɑːm-
~**dated** deɪt ɪd -əd ‖ deɪt̬ əd ~**dates** deɪts
~**dating/ly** deɪt ɪŋ /li ‖ deɪt̬ ɪŋ /li
accommodation ə ˌkɒm ə 'deɪʃ ᵊn ‖ ə ˌkɑːm-
(*not* ˌæk ɒm-) ~**s** z
accompaniment ə 'kʌmp ən̯i mənt ~**s** s
accompanist ə 'kʌmp ən̯ɪst §ˌəst ~**s** s
accompan|y ə 'kʌmp ən̯|i ~**ied** id ~**ies** iz
~**ying** i ɪŋ
accomplic|e ə 'kʌmp lɪs ə 'kɒmp-, -ləs
‖ ə 'kɑːmp ləs ə 'kʌmp- ~**es** ɪz əz

ACCOMPLISH

8%
92%
□ -'kʌmp-
■ -'kɒmp-
BrE

accomplish ə 'kʌmp lɪʃ ə 'kɒmp- ‖ ə 'kɑːmp-
ə 'kʌmp- — *Preference poll, BrE:* -'kʌmp-
92%, -'kɒmp- *8%. In AmE, however,* -'kɑːmp-
clearly predominates. ~**ed** t ~**er/s** ə/z ‖ ᵊr/z
~**es** ɪz əz ~**ing** ɪŋ ~**ment/s** mənt/s
accord ə 'kɔːd ‖ ə 'kɔːrd ~**ed** ɪd əd ~**ing** ɪŋ ~**s**
z
accordance ə 'kɔːd ᵊn̯s ‖ ə 'kɔːrd ᵊn̯s
accordant ə 'kɔːd ᵊnt ‖ ə 'kɔːrd ᵊnt ~**ly** li
according ə 'kɔːd ɪŋ ‖ ə 'kɔːrd ɪŋ ~**ly** li
accordion ə 'kɔːd i_ən ‖ ə 'kɔːrd- ~**ist/s** ɪst/s
§əst/s ~**s** z
accost ə 'kɒst ‖ ə 'kɔːst ə 'kɑːst ~**ed** ɪd əd ~**ing**
ɪŋ ~**s** s
accouchement ə 'kuːʃ mɒ̃ -mɑ̃ː ‖ -mɑːnt
ˌæk uːʃ 'mɑ̃ː
accoucheur ˌæk uː 'ʃɜː ‖ -'ʃɜː ~**s** z
account ə 'kaʊnt **accounted** ə 'kaʊnt ɪd -əd
‖ ə 'kaʊnt̬ əd **accounting** ə 'kaʊnt ɪŋ
‖ ə 'kaʊnt̬ ɪŋ
accountability ə ˌkaʊnt ə 'bɪl ət i -ɪt i
‖ ə ˌkaʊnt̬ ə 'bɪl ət̬ i
accountable ə 'kaʊnt əb ᵊl ‖ ə 'kaʊnt̬- ~**ness**
nəs nɪs
accountancy ə 'kaʊnt ən̯s i ‖ -ᵊn̯s i
accountant ə 'kaʊnt ənt ‖ -ᵊnt ~**s** s
accoutered, accoutred ə 'kuːt əd
‖ ə 'kuːt̬ ᵊrd
accouterment, accoutrement
ə 'kuːtr ə mənt ə 'kuːt- ‖ ə 'kuːt̬ ᵊr- ə 'kuːtr ə-
~**s** s
Accra ə 'krɑː æ-
accred|it ə 'kred |ɪt §-ət ‖ -|ət ~**ited** ɪt ɪd §ət-,
-əd ‖ ət̬ əd ~**iting** ɪt ɪŋ §ət- ‖ ət̬ ɪŋ ~**its** ɪts
§əts ‖ əts
accreditation ə ˌkred ɪ 'teɪʃ ᵊn -ə-
ac|crete ə |'kriːt æ- ~**creted** 'kriːt ɪd -əd
‖ 'kriːt̬ əd ~**cretes** 'kriːts ~**creting** 'kriːt ɪŋ
‖ 'kriːt̬ ɪŋ
accretion ə 'kriːʃ ᵊn æ- ~**s** z
Accrington 'æk rɪŋ tən

accrual ə 'kruː əl §ə 'kruːl ~**s** z
accrue ə 'kruː **accrued** ə 'kruːd **accrues**
ə 'kruːz **accruing** ə 'kruː ɪŋ
accultu|rate ə 'kʌltʃ ə |reɪt æ- ~**rated** reɪt ɪd
-əd ‖ reɪt̬ əd ~**rates** reɪts ~**rating** reɪt ɪŋ
‖ reɪt̬ ɪŋ
acculturation ə ˌkʌltʃ ə 'reɪʃ ᵊn æ-
accumulable ə 'kjuːm jəl əb ᵊl -'jʊl-
accumu|late ə 'kjuːm jə |leɪt -juː-, △-ə- ~**lated**
leɪt ɪd -əd ‖ leɪt̬ əd ~**lates** leɪts ~**lating**
leɪt ɪŋ ‖ leɪt̬ ɪŋ
accumulation ə ˌkjuːm jə 'leɪʃ ᵊn -juː'-, △-ə'-
~**s** z
accumulative ə 'kjuːm jəl ət ɪv -'·jʊl-, △-'·əl-;
-'·jə leɪt ɪv, -'·juː-, △- ·ə- ‖ -jə leɪt̬ ɪv -jəl ət̬-
~**ly** li ~**ness** nəs nɪs
accumulator ə 'kjuːm jə leɪt ə -'·juː-, △-'·ə-
‖ -leɪt̬ ᵊr ~**s** z
accurac|y 'æk jər əs |i '·jʊr-, -ɪs i ~**ies** iz
accurate 'æk jər ət -jʊr-, -ɪt ~**ly** li ~**ness** nəs
nɪs
Accurist *tdmk* 'æk jʊr ɪst -jər-, §-əst
accursed ə 'kɜːs ɪd ə 'kɜːst ‖ ə 'kɜːst ə 'kɜːs əd
~**ly** li ~**ness** nəs nɪs
accurst ə 'kɜːst ‖ ə 'kɜːst
accusal ə 'kjuːz ᵊl ~**s** z
accusation ˌæk ju 'zeɪʃ ᵊn ‖ -jə- ~**s** z
accusatival ə ˌkjuːz ə 'taɪv ᵊl ◂
accusative ə 'kjuːz ət ɪv ‖ -ət̬- ~**ly** li ~**s** z
accusatorial ə ˌkjuːz ə 'tɔːr i_əl ◂ ‖ -'tour-
accusatory ə 'kjuːz ə ˌtər i ˌæk ju 'zeɪt ər i
‖ -tɔːr i -tour i
accus|e ə 'kjuːz ~**ed** d ~**es** ɪz əz ~**ing/ly** ɪŋ /li
accuser ə 'kjuːz ə ‖ -ᵊr ~**s** z
accustom ə 'kʌst əm ~**ed** d ~**ing** ɪŋ ~**s** z
AC/DC, ac-dc ˌeɪ siː 'diː siː ◂
ace eɪs **aced** eɪst **aces** 'eɪs ɪz -əz **acing** 'eɪs ɪŋ
-acea 'eɪs i_ə 'eɪʃ ə — **Crustacea** krʌ 'steɪs i_ə
-'steɪʃ ə
-aceae 'eɪs i i: 'eɪʃ- — **Rosaceae** rəʊ 'zeɪs i i:
-'zeɪʃ- ‖ rou-
Aceh 'ætʃ eɪ 'ɑːtʃ- ‖ 'ɑːtʃ eɪ —*Indonesian*
[ʔa 'tɕeh]
Aceldama ə 'keld əm ə ə 'seld-; ˌæk el 'dɑːm ə
‖ ə 'seld-
-aceous 'eɪʃ əs — **rosaceous** rəʊ 'zeɪʃ əs
‖ rou-
acephalous ˌeɪ 'sef əl əs ə-
acequia ə 'seɪk i_ə ɑː- ~**s** z
Acer *tdmk* 'eɪs ə ‖ -ᵊr
acerbic ə 'sɜːb ɪk æ- ‖ -'sɜːb ɪk ~**ally** ᵊl_i
acerbit|y ə 'sɜːb ət |i æ-, -ɪt- ‖ -'sɜːb ət̬ |i ~**ies**
iz
acetabul|um ˌæs ɪ 'tæb jʊl |əm ˌ·ə-, -jəl əm
‖ -jəl |əm ~**a** ə
acetaldehyde ˌæs ɪ 'tæld ɪ haɪd ˌ·ə-, -'·ə-
-əf ən; ˌæs ɪt- ‖ ə ˌsiːt̬- ˌæs ət̬-
acetaminophen ə ˌsiːt ə 'mɪn ə fen -ˌset-,
-əf ən; ˌæs ɪt- ‖ ə ˌsiːt̬- ˌæs ət̬-
acetanilide ˌæs ɪ 'tæn ə laɪd ˌ·ə-, -'·ɪ-, -ᵊl aɪd
-ᵊl aɪd -əd
acetate 'æs ə teɪt -ɪ- ~**s** s
acetic ə 'siːt ɪk ə 'set- ‖ ə 'siːt̬ ɪk
a ˌcetic 'acid

acetification ə ˌset ɪf ɪ 'keɪʃ ᵊn -ˌsiːt-, -ˌ-əf-, §-ə'-- ‖ ə ˌset- ə ˌsiːt̬-

aceti|fy ə 'set ɪ |faɪ ə 'siːt-, -ə- ‖ -'set̬- -'siːt̬- **~fied** faɪd **~fier/s** faɪ ə/z ‖ faɪ ᵊr/z **~fies** faɪz **~fying** faɪ ɪŋ

acetone 'æs ə təʊn -ɪ- ‖ -toʊn

acetyl 'æs ɪ taɪᵊl -ə-; -ɪt ɪl, -ət-, -ᵊl; ə 'siːt aɪᵊl, -ɪl, -ᵊl ‖ 'æs ət̬ ᵊl ə 'siːt̬ ᵊl, 'æs ə tiːᵊl

acetylcholine ˌæs ɪ taɪᵊl 'kəʊl iːn ˌ-ə-; ˌæs ɪt ɪl-, ˌæs ət-, -ᵊl'--; ə ˌsiːt aɪᵊl-, -ˌ-ɪl-, -ˌ-ᵊl-; -ɪn ‖ ə ˌsiːt̬ ᵊl 'koʊl- ə ˌset̬-; ˌæs ət̬-, ˌæs ə tiːᵊl-

acetylene ə 'set ə liːn -ɪ-; -ᵊl iːn; -əl ɪn, §-ən ‖ ə 'set̬ ᵊl iːn -ən

acetylsalicylic ˌæs ɪ taɪᵊl ˌsæl ə 'sɪl ɪk ◄ ˌ-ə-, ˌæs ɪt ɪl-, ˌæs ət-, -ᵊl,--; ə ˌsiːt aɪᵊl-, -ˌ-ɪl-, -ˌ-ᵊl-, -ɪ'-- ‖ ə ˌsiːt̬ ᵊl- ˌæs ət̬-

ach ɑːx æx —*Ger* [ʔax]

Achae|a ə 'kiː ‖ə **~an/s** ən/z

Achaemenid ə 'kiːm ən ɪd -'kem-, -ɪn-, §-əd **~s** z

Achai|a ə 'kaɪ ‖ə **~an/s** ən/z

Achates ə 'keɪt iːz -'kɑːt- ‖ ə 'keɪt̬ iːz

ache eɪk (!) **ached** eɪkt **aches** eɪks **aching/ly** 'eɪk ɪŋ /li

Achebe ə 'tʃeɪb i -eɪ

Achelous ˌæk ə 'ləʊ əs -ɪ- ‖ -'loʊ-

achene ə 'kiːn eɪ- **~s** z

Acheron 'æk ər ən -ə rɒn ‖ -ə rɑːn

Acheson 'ætʃ ɪs ən -əs-

Acheulian ə 'ʃuːl i ən -'tʃuːl-

achievable ə 'tʃiːv əb ᵊl

achieve ə 'tʃiːv **achieved** ə 'tʃiːvd **achieves** ə 'tʃiːvz **achieving** ə 'tʃiːv ɪŋ

achievement ə 'tʃiːv mənt **~s** s
 a'**chievement test**

achiever ə 'tʃiːv ə ‖ -ᵊr **~s** z

Achill 'æk ɪl -ᵊl

achillea ˌæk ɪ 'liː ə -ə- **~s** z

Achilles, ~' ə 'kɪl iːz
 A ˌchilles' **'heel**; A ˌchilles' **'tendon**

Achitophel ə 'kɪt ə fel ‖ ə 'kɪt̬-

ach-laut 'æx laʊt 'æk- ‖ 'ɑːx- —*Ger* Achlaut ['ʔax laʊt] **~s** s

Achnasheen ˌæk nə 'ʃiːn ˌæx-

achondroplasia ˌeɪ ˌkɒndr əʊ 'pleɪz i ə ə ˌkɒndr- ‖ ˌeɪ ˌkɑːndr ə 'pleɪʒ i ə -'pleɪʒ ə

achondroplastic ˌeɪ ˌkɒndr əʊ 'plæst ɪk ə ˌkɒndr-, -'plɑːst- ‖ ˌeɪ ˌkɑːndr ə-

achoo ə 'tʃuː

achromatic ˌæk rəʊ 'mæt ɪk ◄ ˌeɪ krəʊ- ‖ ˌæk rə 'mæt̬ ɪk ◄ **~ally** ᵊl i

achromatism ə 'krəʊm ə ˌtɪz əm ₍ᵢ₎æ-, ₍ᵢ₎eɪ- ‖ ₍ᵢ₎eɪ 'kroʊm-

achtung ˌæx 'tʊŋ ˌɑːx-, '· · ‖ ˌɑːx- —*Ger* A~ ['ʔax tʊŋ]

achy 'eɪk i

ach-y-fi ˌæx ə 'viː ˌʌx-, ˌæk-, ˌʌk- —*Welsh* [aːχ ə 'viː]

acicul|a ə 'sɪk jʊl |ə -jəl- ‖ -jəl |ə **~ae** iː **~ar** ə ‖ ᵊr

acid 'æs ɪd §-əd **~ly** li **~ness** nəs nɪs **~s** z
 ˌacid 'rain; ˌacid 'rock; ˌacid 'test

acidhead 'æs ɪd hed §-əd- **~s** z

acidic ə 'sɪd ɪk æ-

acidification ə ˌsɪd ɪf ɪ 'keɪʃ ᵊn -ˌ-əf-, §-ə'--

acidi|fy ə 'sɪd ɪ |faɪ æ-, -ə- **~fied** faɪd **~fier/s** faɪ ə/z ‖ faɪ ᵊr/z **~fies** faɪz **~fying** faɪ ɪŋ

acidity ə 'sɪd ət i æ-, -ɪt- ‖ -ət̬ i

acidophilus ˌæs ɪ 'dɒf ɪl əs ˌ-ə-, -əl əs ‖ -'dɑːf-

acidu|late ə 'sɪd ju |leɪt æ-, -jə-; -'sɪdʒ u-, -ə- ‖ ə 'sɪdʒ ə- **~lated** leɪt ɪd -əd ‖ leɪt̬ əd **~lates** leɪts **~lating** leɪt ɪŋ ‖ leɪt̬ ɪŋ

acidulous ə 'sɪd jʊl əs æ-, -'sɪdʒ ʊl- ‖ ə 'sɪdʒ əl əs

acing 'eɪs ɪŋ

ac|inus 'æs |ɪn əs -ən- **~ini** ɪ naɪ ə-

Acis 'eɪs ɪs §-əs

ack-ack 'æk æk ˌ·'·

ackee 'æk i -iː **~s** z

Ackerley 'æk əl i ‖ -ᵊr li

Ackerman 'æk ə mən ‖ -ᵊr-

Ackland 'æk lənd

acknowledg|e ək 'nɒl ɪdʒ æk-, ɪk- ‖ -'nɑːl- **~ed** d **~es** ɪz əz **~ing** ɪŋ

acknowledgement, acknowledgment ək 'nɒl ɪdʒ mənt æk-, ɪk- ‖ -'nɑːl- **~s** s

Ackroyd 'æk rɔɪd

Acland 'æk lənd

Acle 'eɪk ᵊl

acme 'æk mi **~s** z

acne 'æk ni **~d** d

Acol, acol (i) 'æk ᵊl, (ii) 'eɪk ɒl ‖ -ɑːl —*The place in Kent is* 'eɪk ɒl

acolyte 'æk ə laɪt -ᵊl aɪt **~s** s

Acomb 'eɪk əm

Aconcagua ˌæk ən 'kæg wə →-əŋ-, -ɒn- ‖ -'kɑːg- ˌɑːk- —*Sp* [a koŋ 'ka ɣwa]

aconite 'æk ə naɪt **~s** s

acorn 'eɪk ɔːn ‖ 'eɪk ɔːrn (!) **~s** z

acotyledon ˌeɪ ˌkɒt ɪ 'liːd ᵊn ə ˌkɒt-, æ-, -ə'--, -ᵊl 'iːd- ‖ ˌeɪ ˌkɑːt̬ ᵊl 'iːd ᵊn **~s** z

A'Court 'eɪ kɔːt ‖ 'eɪ kɔːrt -koʊrt

acoustic ə 'kuːst ɪk -'kʊst- —*formerly also* -'kaʊst- **~s** s

acoustical ə 'kuːst ɪk ᵊl **~ly** i

acoustician ˌæk u 'stɪʃ ᵊn **~s** z

acquaint ə 'kweɪnt **acquainted** ə 'kweɪnt ɪd -əd ‖ ə 'kweɪnt̬ əd **acquainting** ə 'kweɪnt ɪŋ ‖ ə 'kweɪnt̬ ɪŋ **acquaints** ə 'kweɪnts

acquaintanc|e ə 'kweɪnt ən̬ts ‖ -ᵊn̬ts **~es** ɪz əz

acquaintanceship ə 'kweɪnt ən ʃɪp -ən̬ts-, →-ən̬tʃ- ‖ ᵊn̬ts- **~s** s

acquiesc|e ˌæk wi 'es **~ed** t **~es** ɪz əz **~ing** ɪŋ

acquiescence ˌæk wi 'es ᵊn̬ts

acquiescent ˌæk wi 'es ᵊnt ◄ **~ly** li

acquire ə 'kwaɪ ə ‖ ə 'kwaɪ ᵊr **~d** d **~ment/s** mənt/s **~s** z **acquiring** ə 'kwaɪ ᵊr ɪŋ ‖ ə 'kwaɪ ᵊr ɪŋ

acquisition ˌæk wɪ 'zɪʃ ᵊn -wə- **~s** z

acquisitive ə 'kwɪz ət ɪv æ-, -ɪt- ‖ -ət̬ ɪv **~ly** li **~ness** nəs nɪs

acquit ə 'kwɪt **acquits** ə 'kwɪts **acquitted** ə 'kwɪt ɪd -əd ‖ ə 'kwɪt̬ əd **acquitting** ə 'kwɪt ɪŋ ‖ ə 'kwɪt̬ ɪŋ

acquittal ə 'kwɪt ᵊl ‖ ə 'kwɪt̬ ᵊl **~s** z

A

acre, Acre 'eɪk ə ‖ 'eɪk ᵊr ~**d** d ~**s** z
  ,Acre 'Lane
Acre *place in Israel* 'eɪk ə 'ɑːk- ‖ -ᵊr
acreag|e 'eɪk ər ɪdʒ ~**es** ɪz əz
acrid 'æk rɪd §-rəd ~**ly** li ~**ness** nəs nɪs
acridity æ 'krɪd ət i ə-, -ɪt- ‖ -əţ i
acriflavine ˌæk rɪ 'fleɪv iːn -rə-, -ɪn, §-ᵊn
Acrilan *tdmk* 'æk rɪ læn -rə-, -lən
acrimonious ˌæk rɪ 'məʊn i əs ◂ ˌ·rə-
  ‖ -'moʊn- ~**ly** li ~**ness** nəs nɪs
acrimony 'æk rɪm ən i '·rəm- ‖ -ə moʊn i
acro- *comb. form*
  with stress-neutral suffix ¦æk rəʊ ‖ ¦æk rə
  -roʊ — **acrophobia** ˌæk rəʊ 'fəʊb i ə
  ‖ -rə 'foʊb-
  with stress-imposing suffix ə 'krɒ +
  ‖ ə 'krɑː + — **acropetal** ə 'krɒp ɪt ᵊl §-ət-
  ‖ ə 'krɑːp əţ ᵊl
acrobat 'æk rə bæt ~**s** s
acrobatic ˌæk rə 'bæt ɪk ◂ ‖ -'bæţ ɪk ~**ally** ᵊl_i
  ~**s** s
acrolect 'æk rəʊ lekt ‖ -roʊ- -rə- ~**s** s
acrolectal ˌæk rəʊ 'lekt ᵊl ‖ -roʊ- -rə-
acromegalic ˌæk rəʊ mə 'gæl ɪk ◂ -mɪ'-
  ‖ ˌæk roʊ-
acromegaly ˌæk rəʊ 'meg əl i ‖ ˌæk roʊ-
acronym 'æk rə nɪm ~**s** z
acrophob|ia ˌæk rəʊ 'fəʊb |i ə ‖ -rə 'foʊb- ~**ic**
  ɪk ◂
acropolis ə 'krɒp əl ɪs §-əs ‖ -'krɑːp-
across ə 'krɒs ‖ ə 'krɔːs -'krɑːs
across-the-board ə ˌkrɒs ðə 'bɔːd ◂
  ‖ ə ˌkrɔːs ðə 'bɔːrd ◂ ə ˌkrɑːs-, -'boʊrd
  an a,cross-the-,board 'increase
acrostic ə 'krɒst ɪk ‖ ə 'krɔːst ɪk -'krɑːst- ~**ally**
  ᵊl_i ~**s** s
acrylic ə 'krɪl ɪk æ- ~**s** s
act ækt **acted** 'ækt ɪd -əd **acting** 'ækt ɪŋ **acts,**
  Acts ækts
  ,act of 'God
Actaeon æk 'tiː ən
ACTH ˌeɪ siː tiː 'eɪtʃ ækθ
actinic æk 'tɪn ɪk
actinide 'ækt ɪ naɪd §-ə- ~**s** z
actinism 'ækt ɪ ˌnɪz əm §-ə-
actinium æk 'tɪn i əm
actinometer ˌækt ɪ 'nɒm ɪt ə §ˌ·ə-, -ət- ə
  ‖ -'nɑːm əţ ᵊr ~**s** z
action 'æk ʃᵊn ~**ed** d ~**ing** ɪŋ ~**s** z
  'action man; ,action 'replay; 'action
  ,stations, ˌ··'··
actionab|le 'æk ʃᵊn̩ əb |ᵊl ~**ly** li
action-packed 'æk ʃᵊn pækt →-ʃᵊm-
Actium 'ækt i əm
acti|vate 'ækt ɪ |veɪt -ə- ~**vated** veɪt ɪd -əd
  ‖ veɪţ əd ~**vates** veɪts ~**vating** veɪt ɪŋ
  ‖ veɪţ ɪŋ
activation ˌækt ɪ 'veɪʃ ᵊn -ə- ~**s** z
activator 'ækt ɪ veɪt ə ‖ -veɪţ ᵊr ~**s** z
active 'ækt ɪv ~**ly** li ~**ness** nəs nɪs ~**s** z
Activex, ActiveX *tdmk* 'ækt ɪ veks -ə-
activism 'ækt ɪv ˌɪz əm §-əv-
activist 'ækt ɪv ɪst §-əv-, §-əst ~**s** s

activit|y æk 'tɪv ət |i -ɪt- ‖ -əţ |i ~**ies** iz
Acton 'ækt ən
actor 'ækt ə ‖ -ᵊr —*There is also a mannered
  pronunciation* -ɔː ‖ -ɔːr ~**s** z
actress 'æk trəs -trɪs, -tres ~**es** ɪz əz
actressy 'æk trəs i -trɪs-
actual 'æk tʃu_əl 'æk tʃᵊl, 'æk ʃu_əl, 'æk ʃᵊl,
  'ækt ju_əl
actualis... —*see* **actualiz...**
actualité ˌækt ju 'æl ɪ teɪ ˌæk tʃu-, -ə-
  ‖ ˌɑːk tʃu ɑːl ə 'teɪ ˌæk- —*Fr* [ak ty al i te]
actualit|y ˌæk tʃu 'æl ət |i ˌ·tju-, ˌˌʃu-, -ɪt i
  ‖ -əţ |i ~**ies** iz
actualization ˌæk tʃu_əl aɪ 'zeɪʃ ᵊn ˌ·tju ˌˌʃu ˌ
  -ɪ'-- ‖ -ə'--
actualiz|e 'æk tʃu_ə laɪz 'ækt ju-, 'æk ʃu ~**ed**
  d ~**es** ɪz əz ~**ing** ɪŋ
actually 'æk tʃu_əl i 'æk tʃᵊl i, 'æk ʃu_əl i,
  'æk ʃᵊl_i, 'ækt ju_əl i —*There is also a very
  casual form* 'æk ʃi
actuarial ˌæk tʃu 'eər i_əl ◂ ˌæk ju-, ˌæk ʃu-
  ‖ -'er- ~**ly** i
actuar|y 'æk tʃu_ər |i 'ækt ju, 'æk ʃu ‖ -er |i
  ~**ies** iz
actu|ate 'æk tʃu |eɪt 'ækt ju-, 'æk ʃu- ~**ated**
  eɪt ɪd -əd ‖ eɪţ əd ~**ates** eɪts ~**ating** eɪt ɪŋ
  ‖ eɪţ ɪŋ
actuation ˌæk tʃu 'eɪʃ ᵊn ˌækt ju-, ˌæk ʃu-
actuator 'æk tʃu eɪt ə 'ækt ju-, 'æk ʃu- ‖ -eɪţ ᵊr
acuity ə 'kjuː ət i -ɪt- ‖ -əţ i
acumen 'æk jʊm ən -jəm-; -ju men, -jə-;
  ə 'kjuːm en, -ən ‖ ə 'kjuːm ən 'æk jəm-
acuminate ə 'kjuːm ɪn ət -ən-, -ɪt; -ɪ neɪt, -ə-
acupuncture 'æk ju ˌpʌŋk tʃə -jə-, §-ə-,
  △-wə-, -ʃə ‖ -jə ˌpʌŋk tʃᵊr
acupuncturist 'æk ju ˌpʌŋk tʃər ɪst '·jə-, §'·ə-,
  △'·wə-, ˌ·'·-, -ʃər ɪst, §-əst ‖ 'æk jə- ~**s** s
acute ə 'kjuːt ~**ly** li ~**ness** nəs nɪs
  a,cute 'accent
-acy əs i —*Words with this suffix are stressed in
  the same way as the corresponding form with
  -ate, if there is one* (le'gitimacy). *Otherwise,
  the stem keeps its usual stress, though
  sometimes with a vowel change* (su'preme —
  su'premacy). *See also* -cracy.
acyclic ⑴eɪ 'saɪk lɪk -'sɪk-
acyclovir eɪ 'saɪk ləʊ vɪə ‖ -oʊ vɪr
AD ˌeɪ 'diː
ad æd (= *add*) **ads** ædz —*See also phrases with
  this word
ad- əd, (¦)æd —*This prefix is strong* ¦æd *when
  stressed,* (1) *because of a suffix* (ˌadap'tation),
  and (2) *in some two-syllable nouns* ('adverb).
  *Otherwise, in RP and GenAm, it is usually
  unstressed and weak* (a'dapt), *although some
  speakers use a strong vowel if the following
  stem begins with a consonant* (ad'mit). *Before
  a stem with initial* d *or* dʒ *the prefix regularly
  loses its* d (ad'diction). *Note the irregularly
  stressed word* 'adjective.
-ad æd, əd — **octad** 'ɒkt æd -əd ‖ 'ɑːkt-
Ada 'eɪd ə
adag|e 'æd ɪdʒ ~**es** ɪz əz

A

adagio ə 'dɑ:dʒ i‿əʊ -'dɑ:ʒ-, -'dɑ:dʒ əʊ
    ‖ ə 'dɑ:dʒ oʊ -'dɑ:dʒ i‿oʊ ~s z
Adair ə 'deə ‖ ə 'deᵊr -'dæᵊr
Adam 'æd əm ~'s z —but for the French
    composer, æ 'dɒ̃ ‖ ɑː 'dɑːm —Fr [a dɑ̃]
    ,Adam's 'apple ‖ '·· ,··
adamancy 'æd əm ən's i
adamant 'æd əm ənt ~ly li
adamantine ,æd ə 'mænt aın ◄ ‖ -iːn -aın, -ᵊn
Adamawa ,æd ə 'mɑː wə
Adamic ə 'dæm ɪk æ-
Adams 'æd əmz
Adamsez 'æd əmz ɪz -əz; -əm sez
Adamson 'æd əm sən
adapt ə 'dæpt adapted ə 'dæpt ɪd -əd
    adapting ə 'dæpt ɪŋ adapts ə 'dæpts
adaptability ə ,dæpt ə 'bɪl ət i -ɪt i ‖ -ət̬ i
adaptab|le ə 'dæpt əb |ᵊl -ly li
adaptation ,æd æp 'teɪʃ ᵊn -əp- ~s z
adapter ə 'dæpt ə ‖ -ᵊr ~s z
adaptive ə 'dæpt ɪv ~ly li ~ness nəs nɪs
adaptor ə 'dæpt ə ‖ -ᵊr ~s z
Adare ə 'deə ‖ ə 'deᵊr -'dæᵊr
ADC ,eɪ diː 'siː ~s, ~'s z
Adcock 'æd kɒk →'æg- ‖ -kɑːk
add æd added 'æd ɪd -əd adding 'æd ɪŋ adds
    ædz
ADD 'attention deficit disorder' ,eɪ diː 'diː
Addams 'æd əmz
addax 'æd æks
addend|um ə 'dend |əm ~a ə
adder 'æd ə ‖ 'æd ᵊr ~s z
addict n 'æd ɪkt addicts 'æd ɪkts
addict v ə 'dɪkt addicted ə 'dɪkt ɪd -əd
    addicting ə 'dɪkt ɪŋ addicts ə 'dɪkts
addiction ə 'dɪk ʃᵊn ~s z
addictive ə 'dɪkt ɪv ~ly li ~ness nəs nɪs
Addie 'æd i
Addington 'æd ɪŋ tən
Addis 'æd ɪs §-əs
    ,Addis 'Ababa 'æb əb ə
Addiscombe 'æd ɪs kəm §-əs-
Addison 'æd ɪs ən §-əs- ~'s z
    'Addison's di,sease
addition ə 'dɪʃ ᵊn ~s z
additional ə 'dɪʃ ᵊn‿ᵊl ~ly i
additive 'æd ət ɪv -ɪt- ‖ -ət̬ ɪv ~s z
addle 'æd ᵊl addled 'æd ᵊld addles 'æd ᵊlz
    addling 'æd ᵊl ɪŋ
Addlebrough 'æd ᵊl bər ə ‖ -,bɜː oʊ
Addlestone 'æd ᵊl stəun ‖ -stoʊn
add-on 'æd ɒn ‖ -ɑːn -ɔːn ~s z
address v ə 'dres æ- ~ed t ~es ɪz əz ~ing ɪŋ

ADDRESS

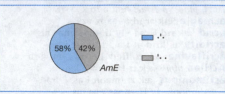

— Preference poll, AmE: '·· 58%, '·· 42%.

AmE

address n ə 'dres ‖ 'ædr es ~es ɪz əz
    — Preference poll, AmE: '·· 58%, '·· 42%.
addressable ə 'dres əb ᵊl
addressee ,ædr es 'iː ə ,dres 'iː ~s z
Addressograph tdmk ə 'dres əʊ grɑːf -græf
    ‖ -ə græf
adduc|e ə 'djuːs æ-, →-'dʒuːs ‖ ə 'duːs -'djuːs
    ~ed t ~es ɪz əz ~ing ɪŋ
adduct ə 'dʌkt æ- ~ed ɪd əd ~ing ɪŋ ~s s
adduction ə 'dʌk ʃᵊn
adductor ə 'dʌkt ə ‖ -ᵊr ~s z
Addy 'æd i
-ade 'eɪd —This suffix is usually stressed
    (,lemo'nade, ,harlequi'nade). When -ade is not
    a true suffix it may be stressed or unstressed,
    taking one of the forms eɪd, 'eɪd, ɑːd, 'ɑːd,
    depending on the particular word
    ('marmelade; ,prome'nade, '···) —see
    individual entries.
Adel 'æd ᵊl
Adela 'æd ɪl ə -əl-; ə 'deɪl ə
Adelaide 'æd ə leɪd -ɪ-, →-ᵊl eɪd
Adele, Adèle ə 'del
Adelie, Adélie ə 'deɪl i -'diːl-, 'æd ɪl i, -əl i
Adelina ,æd ə 'liːn ə -ɪ-; -ᵊl 'iːn-
Adeline 'æd ə laɪn -ɪ-, -liːn; -ᵊl aɪn, -iːn
Adelphi ə 'delf i
Aden 'eɪd ᵊn —Arabic ['ʔa dan]
Adenauer 'æd ə naʊ‿ə 'ɑːd-, →-ᵊn aʊ‿ə
    ‖ -naʊ‿ᵊr —Ger ['ʔaː də nɑʊ ɐ]
Adeney 'eɪd ᵊn‿i
adenine 'æd ə niːn -naɪn, -nɪn ‖ -ᵊn iːn
adenoid 'æd ɪ nɔɪd -ə-, →-ᵊn ɔɪd ‖ -ᵊn ɔɪd ~s z
adenoidal ,æd ɪ 'nɔɪd ᵊl ◄ -ə-, →-ᵊn 'ɔɪd-,
    ‖ ,æd ᵊn 'ɔɪd ᵊl ◄ ~ly i
adenom|a ,æd ɪ 'nəʊm |ə -ə-, →-ᵊn 'əʊm-
    ‖ ,æd ᵊn 'oʊm |ə ~as əz ~ata ət ə ‖ ət̬ ə
adenopathy ,æd ɪ 'nɒp əθ i ,·ə-, →-ᵊn 'ɒp-
    ‖ ,æd ᵊn 'ɑːp-
adenosine ə 'den əʊ siːn æ-; ,æd ɪ 'nəʊs iːn,
    -ə- ‖ -ə siːn -əs ən
adept n 'æd ept ə 'dept, æ 'dept ~s s
adept adj ə 'dept æ-, 'æd ept ~ly li ~ness nəs
    nɪs
adequacy 'æd ɪk wəs i '·ək-, -wɪs i
adequate 'æd ɪk wət -ək-, -wɪt ~ly li ~ness
    nəs nɪs
adessive æ 'des ɪv ə- ~s z
adeste fideles æd ,est i fɪ 'deɪl eɪz əd-, -eɪs
à deux æ 'dɜː ɑː- ‖ -'dʌ —Fr [a dø]
Adger 'ædʒ ə ‖ -ᵊr
adhere əd 'hɪə ₍ᵢ₎æd- ‖ -'hɪᵊr ~d d ~s z
    adhering əd 'hɪər ɪŋ ₍ᵢ₎æd- ‖ -'hɪr ɪŋ

A

adherence əd ˈhɪər ənˈs ⁽ᵢ⁾æd-, -ˈher- ‖ -ˈhɪr-
adherent əd ˈhɪər ənt ⁽ᵢ⁾æd-, -ˈher- ‖ -ˈhɪr- **~ly**
   li **~s** s
adhesion əd ˈhiːʒ ᵊn ⁽ᵢ⁾æd-
adhesive əd ˈhiːs ɪv ⁽ᵢ⁾æd-, -ˈhiːz- **~ly** li **~ness**
   nəs nɪs **~s** z
ad hoc ⁽ᵢ⁾æd ˈhɒk ◂ -ˈhəʊk ‖ -ˈhɑːk ˌɑːd-, -ˈhoʊk
adhoc-ery, adhockery ˌæd ˈhɒk ər i -ˈhəʊk-
   ‖ -ˈhɑːk- ˌɑːd-, -ˈhoʊk-
ad hominem ⁽ᵢ⁾æd ˈhɒm ɪ nem -ə- ‖ -ˈhɑːm-
   ˌɑːd-, -ən əm
adiabatic ˌæd i̯ə ˈbæt ɪk ◂ ˌeɪ ˌdaɪ ə- ‖ -ˈbæt̬ ɪk
   ~ally ᵊl i̯ i
Adidas *tdmk* ˈæd ɪ dæs -ə-, ə ˈdiːd æs, -əz
   ‖ ˈɑːd ə- -ə ˈdiːd əz, -əs
Adie ˈeɪd i
Adiemus ˌæd i ˈeɪm əs
adieu ə ˈdjuː æ-, →-ˈdʒuː:, -ˈdjɜː ‖ -ˈduː -ˈdjuː
   —*Fr* [a djø] **~s** z **~x** z —*or as sing.*
Adi Granth ˌɑːd i ˈɡrʌnt
ad infinitum ˌæd ˌɪn fɪ ˈnaɪt əm ·ˌ-·, -fə'-
   ‖ -ˈnaɪt̬ əm ˌɑːd-
adios ˌæd i ˈɒs ‖ -ˈoʊs ˌɑːd- —*Sp* [a ˈðjos]
adipocere ˈæd ɪ pəʊ sɪə -ə-, -pə-, ˌ···ˈ·
   ‖ -ə poʊ sɪr
adipose ˈæd ɪ pəʊs -ə-, -pəʊz ‖ -poʊs **~ness**
   nəs nɪs
adiposity ˌæd ɪ ˈpɒs ət i ˌ-ə-, -ɪt i ‖ -ˈpaːs ət̬ i
Adirondack ˌæd ə ˈrɒnd æk -ɪ- ‖ -ˈraːnd- **~s** s
adit ˈæd ɪt §-ət **~s** s
adjacency ə ˈdʒeɪs ᵊnˈs i
adjacent ə ˈdʒeɪs ᵊnt **~ly** li
adjectival ˌædʒ ɪk ˈtaɪv ᵊl ◂ -ek-, -ək- **~ly** i **~s**
   z
adjective ˈædʒ ɪkt ɪv -ekt-, -əkt- ‖ △-ət̬- **~s** z
adjoin ə ˈdʒɔɪn æ- **~ed** d **~ing** ɪŋ **~s** z
adjourn ə ˈdʒɜːn ‖ ə ˈdʒɜːɪn **~ed** d **~ing** ɪŋ **~s**
   z
adjournment ə ˈdʒɜːn mənt →-ˈdʒɜːm-
   ‖ -ˈdʒɜːɪn- **~s** s
adjudge ə ˈdʒʌdʒ æ- **~ed** d **~es** ɪz əz **~ing** ɪŋ
adjudi|cate ə ˈdʒuːd ɪ |keɪt -ə- **~cated** keɪt ɪd
   -əd ‖ keɪt̬ əd **~cates** keɪts **~cating** keɪt ɪŋ
   ‖ keɪt̬ ɪŋ
adjudication ə ˌdʒuːd ɪ ˈkeɪʃ ᵊn -ə'- **~s** z
adjudicator ə ˈdʒuːd ɪ keɪt ə -ˈ-ə- ‖ -keɪt̬ ᵊr **~s**
   z
adjunct ˈædʒ ʌŋkt **~s** s
adjunction ə ˈdʒʌŋk ʃᵊn æ-, ˌæd-
adjunctive ə ˈdʒʌŋkt ɪv æ-, ˌæd-
adjuration ˌædʒ ʊᵊ ˈreɪʒ ᵊn -ə- **~s** z
adjure ə ˈdʒʊə -ˈdʒɔː ‖ ə ˈdʒʊᵊr **~d** d **~s** z
   adjuring ə ˈdʒʊər ɪŋ -ˈdʒɔːr- ‖ ə ˈdʒʊᵊr ɪŋ
adjust ə ˈdʒʌst **~ed** ɪd əd **~ing** ɪŋ **~s** s
adjustab|le ə ˈdʒʌst əb ᵊl **~ly** li
adjuster ə ˈdʒʌst ə ‖ -ᵊr **~s** z
adjustment ə ˈdʒʌst mənt **~s** s
adjutancy ˈædʒ ʊt ənˈs i
adjutant ˈædʒ ʊt ənt -ət- **~s** s
Adkins ˈæd kɪnz →ˈæg-
Adlai ˈæd leɪ -laɪ
adland ˈæd lænd
Adlard ˈæd lɑːd -ləd ‖ -lɑːrd

Adler *(i)* ˈæd lə ‖ -lᵊr, *(ii)* ˈɑːd- —*Ger*
   [ˈʔaːd lɐ]
Adlerian æd ˈlɪər i̯ən ‖ -ˈler- **~s** z
Adlestrop ˈæd ᵊl strɒp ‖ -straːp
ad lib ˌæd ˈlɪb
ad-lib ˌæd ˈlɪb ◂ **~bed** d **~bing** ɪŋ **~s** z
ad|man ˈæd |mæn -mən **~men** men mən
admass ˈæd mæs
admeasure æd ˈmeʒ ə əd- ‖ -ᵊr -ˈmeɪʒ- **~s** z
admen ˈæd men -mən
Admetus æd ˈmiːt əs ‖ -ˈmiːt̬-
admin ˈæd mɪn ˌ·ˈ·
administer əd ˈmɪn ɪst ə æd-, →əb-, -əst- ‖ -ᵊr
   ~ed d **administering** əd ˈmɪn ɪst ər ɪŋ -ˈ·əst-;
   →-ˈ·ɪs trɪŋ, →-ˈ·əs trɪŋ **~s** z
admini|strate əd ˈmɪn ɪ |streɪt æd-, →əb-, -ə-
   ~strated streɪt ɪd -əd ‖ streɪt̬ əd **~strates**
   streɪts **~strating** streɪt ɪŋ ‖ streɪt̬ ɪŋ
administration əd ˌmɪn ɪ ˈstreɪʃ ᵊn æd-, →əb-,
   -ə- **~s** z
administrative əd ˈmɪn ɪs trət ɪv æd-, →əb-,
   -ˈ·əs-; -ˈ·ɪ streɪt-, -ˈ·ə- ‖ -ə streɪt̬ ɪv -əs trət̬ ɪv
   ~ly li
administrator əd ˈmɪn ɪ streɪt ə æd-, →əb-,
   -ˈ·ə- ‖ -streɪt̬ ᵊr **~s** z
admirable ˈæd mər əb ᵊl →ˈæb- **~ness** nəs nɪs
admirably ˈæd mər əb li →ˈæb-
admiral ˈæd mᵊr əl →ˈæb- **~s** z
admiral|ty ˈæd mᵊr əl |ti →ˈæb- **~ties** tiz
   Admiralty ˈArch
admiration ˌæd mə ˈreɪʃ ᵊn →ˌæb-, -mɪ-
admire əd ˈmaɪ ə §æd-, →əb- ‖ əd ˈmaɪ ᵊr **~d** d
   ~s z **admiring/ly** əd ˈmaɪ ər ɪŋ /li §æd-
   ‖ əd ˈmaɪ ᵊr ɪŋ /li
admirer əd ˈmaɪ ər ə §æd-, →əb-
   ‖ əd ˈmaɪ ᵊr ər **~s** z
admissibility əd ˌmɪs ə ˈbɪl ət i æd-, →əb-,
   -ˌ·ɪ-, -ɪt i ‖ -ət̬ i
admissib|le əd ˈmɪs əb ᵊl æd-, →əb-, -ɪb- **~ly**
   li
admission əd ˈmɪʃ ᵊn æd-, →əb- **~s** z
ad|mit əd ˈmɪt æd-, →əb- **~mits** ˈmɪts
   ~mitted ˈmɪt ɪd -əd ‖ ˈmɪt̬ əd **~mitting**
   ˈmɪt ɪŋ ‖ ˈmɪt̬ ɪŋ
admittance əd ˈmɪt ᵊnˈs æd-, →əb-
admitted əd ˈmɪt ɪd æd-, →əb-, -əd ‖ -ˈmɪt̬ əd
   ~ly li
admixture əd ˈmɪks tʃə æd-, →əb- ‖ -tʃᵊr **~s** z
admonish əd ˈmɒn ɪʃ æd-, →əb- ‖ -ˈmaːn- **~ed**
   t **~es** ɪz əz **~ing** ɪŋ **~ment/s** mənt/s
admonition ˌæd mə ˈnɪʃ ᵊn →ˌæb- **~s** z
admonitory əd ˈmɒn ɪt ᵊr i æd-, →əb-, -ˈ·ə-
   ‖ -ˈmaːn ə tɔːr i -tour i
ad nauseam ˌæd ˈnɔːz i æm -ˈnɔːs-, -əm
   ‖ -ˈnaːz-
adnominal ⁽ˌ⁾æd ˈnɒm ɪn ᵊl -ən-, -ᵊn̩ əl
   ‖ -ˈnaːm- **~s** z
ado ə ˈduː
adobe ə ˈdəʊb i ‖ ə ˈdoʊb i
adolescence ˌæd ə ˈles ᵊnˈs -ᵊl ˈes-
adolescent ˌæd ə ˈles ᵊnt ◂ -ᵊl ˈes- **~s** s
Adolf ˈæd ɒlf ‖ ˈeɪd ɑːlf ˈæd-
Adolfo ə ˈdɒlf əʊ ‖ ə ˈdaːlf oʊ

A

Adolph 'æd ɒlf ‖ 'eɪd ɑːlf 'æd-
Adolphus ə 'dɒlf əs ‖ ə 'dɑːlf əs
Adonai ˌæd əʊ 'naɪ '·· ·, -ɒ-, ˌ· 'neɪ aɪ;
    ə 'dəʊn i ˌaɪ ‖ ˌɑːd ə 'naɪ -'nɔɪ
Adonis ə 'dəʊn ɪs -'dɒn-, -əs ‖ -'doʊn- -'dɑːn-
adopt ə 'dɒpt ‖ ə 'dɑːpt **~ed** ɪd əd **~er/s** ə/z
    ‖ ᵊr/z **~ing** ɪŋ **~s** s
adoptee ə ˌdɒp 'tiː ‖ ə ˌdɑːp 'tiː **~s** z
adoption ə 'dɒp ʃᵊn ‖ ə 'dɑːp- **~s** z
adoptive ə 'dɒpt ɪv ‖ ə 'dɑːpt- **~ly** li
adorab|le ə 'dɔːr əb |ᵊl ‖ -'doʊr- **~leness**
    ᵊl nəs -nɪs **~ly** li
adoration ˌæd ə 'reɪʃ ᵊn -ɔː-
adore ə 'dɔː ‖ ə 'dɔːr -'doʊr **adored** ə 'dɔːd
    ‖ ə 'dɔːrd -'doʊrd **adores** ə 'dɔːz ‖ ə 'dɔːrz
    -'doʊrz **adoring/ly** ə 'dɔːr ɪŋ /li ‖ -'doʊr-
adorer ə 'dɔːr ə ‖ -ᵊr -'doʊr- **~s** z
adorn ə 'dɔːn ‖ ə 'dɔːrn **~ed** d **~ing** ɪŋ **~s** z
adornment ə 'dɔːn mənt →-'dɔːm- ‖ -'dɔːrn-
    ~s s
adrenal ə 'driːn ᵊl
adrenalin, A~ *tdmk*, **adrenaline** ə 'dren əl ɪn
    -'driːn-, §-ən
adrenocorticotrophic
    ə ˌdriːn əʊ ˌkɔːt ɪk əʊ 'trɒf ɪk ◂
    ‖ -oʊ ˌkɔːrt̬ ɪk oʊ 'troʊf ɪk ◂ -'trɑːf-
Adrian 'eɪdr i ən
Adriana ˌeɪdr i 'ɑːn ə
Adriatic ˌeɪdr i 'æt ɪk ◂ ‖ -'æt̬-
    ˌAdriˌatic 'Sea
Adrienne 'eɪdr i ən ˌ··'en
adrift ə 'drɪft
adroit ə 'drɔɪt **~ly** li **~ness** nəs nɪs
adsorb ₍ᵢ₎æd 'sɔːb əd-, -'zɔːb ‖ -'sɔːrb -'zɔːrb
    ~ed d **~ing** ɪŋ **~s** z
adsorption ₍ᵢ₎æd 'sɔːp ʃᵊn əd-, -'zɔːp- ‖ -'sɔːrp-
    -'zɔːrp-
adstrate 'æd streɪt
adsum 'æd sʊm -sʌm
aduki ə 'duːk i
adu|late 'æd ju |leɪt ‖ˌædʒ u-, 'ædʒ ə- ‖ 'ædʒ ə-
    'æd jə-, 'æd ə- **~lated** leɪt ɪd -əd ‖ leɪt̬ əd
    ~lates leɪts **~lating** leɪt ɪŋ ‖ leɪt̬ ɪŋ
adulation ˌæd ju 'leɪʃ ᵊn ˌædʒ u-, ˌædʒ ə-
    ‖ˌædʒ ə- ˌæd jə-, ˌæd ə-
adulator 'æd ju leɪt ə 'ædʒ u-, 'ædʒ ə-
    ‖ 'ædʒ ə leɪt̬ ᵊr 'æd jə-, 'æd ə- **~s** z
adulatory ˌæd ju 'leɪt ər i ‖ˌædʒ u-, ˌædʒ ə-,
    '····; 'ædʒ ʊl ət̬ ˌər i ‖ 'ædʒ əl ə tɔːr i
    'æd jəl-, 'æd ᵊl-, -toʊr i
Adullam ə 'dʌl əm
Adullamite ə 'dʌl ə maɪt **~s** s
adult *adj, n* 'æd ʌlt ə 'dʌlt ‖ ə 'dʌlt 'æd ʌlt **~s**
    s — *Preference polls (noun), AmE:* '· 88%, '··
    12%; BrE: '·· 84%, '·· 16%.
adulterant ə 'dʌlt ər ənt **~s** s
adulte|rate ə 'dʌlt ə |reɪt **~rated** reɪt ɪd -əd
    ‖ reɪt̬ əd **~rates** reɪts **~rating** reɪt ɪŋ ‖ reɪt̬ ɪŋ
adulteration ə ˌdʌlt ə 'reɪʃ ᵊn **~s** z
adulterator ə 'dʌlt ə reɪt ə ‖ -reɪt̬ ᵊr **~s** z
adulterer ə 'dʌlt ər ə ‖ -ᵊr ər **~s** z
adulteress ə 'dʌlt ər es -ɪs, -əs ‖ -əs **~es** ɪz əz
adulterous ə 'dʌlt ər əs **~ly** li

■ '·· ■ ·'·
84% 16% *BrE*
88% 12% *AmE*

adulter|y ə 'dʌlt ər |i **~ies** iz
adulthood 'æd ʌlt hʊd ə 'dʌlt- ‖ ə 'dʌlt-
    'æd ʌlt-
adum|brate 'æd ʌm |breɪt -əm-; ə 'dʌm-
    ~brated breɪt ɪd -əd ‖ breɪt̬ əd **~brates**
    breɪts **~brating** breɪt ɪŋ ‖ breɪt̬ ɪŋ
adumbration ˌæd ʌm 'breɪʃ ᵊn -əm-
Adur 'eɪd ə ‖ -ᵊr
ad valorem ˌæd və 'lɔːr em -væ-, -əm ‖ -əm
    -'loʊr-
advanc|e əd 'vɑːnts §₍ᵢ₎æd-, §-'vænts ‖ -'vænts
    ~ed t **~ement/s** mənt/s **~es** ɪz əz **~ing** ɪŋ
advantag|e əd 'vɑːnt ɪdʒ §æd-, §-'vænt-
    ‖ -'vænt̬- —*When explicitly opposed to*
    disadvantage, *sometimes contrastively stressed*
    '··· *In public tennis scoring often*
    æd 'vɑːnt eɪdʒ ‖ -'vænt- **~ed** d **~es** ɪz əz
advantageous ˌæd vən 'teɪdʒ əs ◂ -væn-,
    -vɑːn- **~ly** li **~ness** nəs nɪs
advent, Advent 'æd vent -vᵊnt
Advent|ism 'æd vənt |ˌɪz əm -vent-;
    əd 'vent,··, æd- ‖ 'æd vent̬|- əd 'vent|,··, æd-
    ~ist/s ɪst/s §-əst/s
adventitious ˌæd vən 'tɪʃ əs ◂ -ven- **~ly** li
    ~ness nəs nɪs
adventive əd 'vent ɪv æd- ‖ -'vent̬- **~ly** li
adventure əd 'ventʃ ə §æd- ‖ -ᵊr **~d** d **~s** z
    adventuring əd 'ventʃ ər ɪŋ §æd-
adventurer əd 'ventʃ ᵊr ə §æd- ‖ ər **~s** z
adventuress əd 'ventʃ ər əs §æd-, -ɪs, -ə res
    ~es ɪz əz
adventur|ism əd 'ventʃ ər ˌɪz əm §æd- **~ist/s**
    ɪst/s §əst/s
adventurous əd 'ventʃ ər əs §æd- **~ly** li **~ness**
    nəs nɪs
adverb 'æd vɜːb ‖ -vɜːb **~s** z
adverbial əd 'vɜːb i əl æd- ‖ -'vɜːb- **~ly** i **~s** z
adversarial ˌæd vɜː 'seər i əl ◂ ˌ·və-
    ‖ -vᵊr 'ser- ˌ·və- **~ly** i
adversar|y 'æd vəs ər |i -er i; §əd 'vɜːs ər |i,
    §æd- ‖ 'æd vᵊr ser |i '·və- **~ies** iz
adversative əd 'vɜːs ət ɪv æd- ‖ -'vɜːs ət̬- **~ly**
    li **~s** z
adverse 'æd vɜːs əd 'vɜːs, ˌæd- ‖ æd 'vɜːs '··
    ~ly li **~ness** nəs nɪs
adversit|y əd 'vɜːs ət |i æd-, -ɪt-
    ‖ æd 'vɜːs ət̬ |i **~ies** iz
ad|vert *v* əd |'vɜːt æd- ‖ æd |'vɜːt **~verted**
    'vɜːt ɪd -əd ‖ 'vɜːt̬ əd **~verting** 'vɜːt ɪŋ
    ‖ 'vɜːt̬ ɪŋ **~verts** 'vɜːts ‖ 'vɜːts
advert *n* 'æd vɜːt -'vɜːt **~s** s
advertis|e 'æd və taɪz ‖ -vᵊr- **~ed** d **~er/s** ə/z
    ‖ ᵊr/z **~es** ɪz əz **~ing** ɪŋ

A

advertisement əd ˈvɜːt ɪs mənt -ɪz-, -əs-, -əz-;
§ˈæd və taɪz mənt, §ˌ‧ˈ‧‧ ‖ ˌæd vᵊr ˈtaɪz mənt
əd ˈvɜːtʃ əs-, -əz- *(*)* **~s** s

advertorial ˌæd və ˈtɔːr iˌəl -vɜː- ‖ -vᵊr- -ˈtoʊr-
~s z

advice əd ˈvaɪs §æd-

Advil *tdmk* ˈæd vɪl -vᵊl

advisability əd ˌvaɪz ə ˈbɪl ət i §æd- ‖ -əţ i

advisab|le əd ˈvaɪz əb |ᵊl §æd- **~ly** li

advis|e əd ˈvaɪz §æd- **~ed** d **~es** ɪz əz **~ing** ɪŋ

advisedly əd ˈvaɪz ɪd li §æd-, -əd-

adviser, advisor əd ˈvaɪz ə §æd- ‖ -ᵊr **~s** z

advisor|y əd ˈvaɪz ᵊr ˌi §æd- **~ies** iz

advocaat ˈæd vəʊ kɑː- -kɑːt ‖ -voʊ-

advocacy ˈæd vək əs i

advo|cate *v* ˈæd və |keɪt **~cated** keɪt ɪd -əd
‖ keɪţ əd **~cates** keɪts **~cating** keɪt ɪŋ
‖ keɪţ ɪŋ

advocate *n* ˈæd vək ət -ɪt; -və keɪt **~s** s

advokaat ˈæd vəʊ kɑː- -kɑːt ‖ -voʊ-

advowson əd ˈvaʊz ᵊn æd- **~s** z

Adwick-le-Street ˌæd wɪk li ˈstriːt

adz, adze ædz **adzed** ædzd **adzes** ˈædz ɪz -əz
adzing ˈædz ɪŋ

adzuki æd ˈzuːk i —*Jp* [a ˌdzɯ ˈki]
adˈzuki bean

aedes, Aedes, Aëdes eɪ ˈiːd iːz

aedile ˈiːd aɪᵊl ‖ -ᵊl **~s** z **~ship/s** ʃɪp/s

Aegean ɪ ˈdʒiːˌən iː-
    Aeˌgean ˈSea

Aegina i ˈdʒaɪn ə -ˈgiːn- —*ModGk* [ˈe ji na]

aegis ˈiːdʒ ɪs §-əs

Aegisthus i ˈdʒɪs θəs

aegrotat ˈaɪg rəʊ tæt ˈiːg-; i ˈgrəʊt æt ‖ -roʊ-
~s s

Aelfric, Ælfric ˈælf rɪtʃ -rɪk

-aemia *comb. form* ˈiːm iˌə — **septicaemia**
ˌsept ɪ ˈsiːm iˌə ˌ-ə-

Aeneas i ˈniːˌəs -ˈneɪ-, -æs

Aeneid ˈiːn iˌd i ˈniː ɪd

Aeolian i ˈəʊl iˌən eɪ- ‖ i ˈoʊl- **~s** z

Aeolic i ˈɒl ɪk -ˈəʊl- ‖ i ˈɑːl-

Aeolus ˈiːˌəl əs i ˈəʊl-

aeon ˈiːˌən ˈiː ɒn ‖ -ɑːn **~s** z

aepyornis ˌiːp i ˈɔːn ɪs §-əs ‖ -ˈɔːrn-

aer|ate ˈeər |eɪt △ˈeər i |eɪt ‖ ˈer- ˈær- **~ated**
eɪt ɪd -əd ‖ eɪţ əd **~ates** eɪts **~ating** eɪt ɪŋ
‖ eɪţ ɪŋ

aeration ₍ᵢ₎eə ˈreɪʃ ᵊn ‖ ₍ᵢ₎e- ₍ᵢ₎æ-

aerator ˈeər eɪt ə △ˈeər iˌ‧‧ ‖ ˈer eɪţ ᵊr ˈær- **~s**
z

aerial ˈeər iˌəl ‖ ˈer- ˈær-; eɪ ˈɪr- —*in RP*
formerly also eɪ ˈɪər iˌəl **~s** z

aerialist ˈeər iˌəl ɪst §-əst ‖ ˈer- ˈær- **~s** s

aerie ˈɪər i ˈeər-, ˈaɪᵊr- ‖ ˈer i ˈær-, ˈɪr-; ˈeɪ ri **~s**
z

Aer Lingus *tdmk* ˌeə ˈlɪŋ gəs ‖ ˌer- ˌær-

aero, Aero ˈeər əʊ ‖ ˈer oʊ ˈær- **~s** z

aero- *comb. form*
    with stress-neutral suffix |eər əʊ ‖ |er oʊ |ær-,
    -ə — **aerobiosis** ˌeər əʊ baɪ ˈəʊs ɪs §-əs
    ‖ ˌer oʊ baɪ ˈoʊs əs ˌær-
    with stress-imposing suffix ₍ᵢ₎eə ˈrɒ +

‖ ₍ᵢ₎e ˈrɑː + ₍ᵢ₎æ- — **aerography**
₍ᵢ₎eə ˈrɒg rəf i ‖ ₍ᵢ₎e ˈrɑːg- ₍ᵢ₎æ-

aerobatic ˌeər əʊ ˈbæt ɪk ◄ ‖ ˌer ə ˈbæţ ɪk ◄
ˌær- **~ally** ᵊl_i **~s** s

aerobic ₍ᵢ₎eə ˈrəʊb ɪk ‖ ₍ᵢ₎e ˈroʊb ɪk ₍ᵢ₎æ- **~ally**
ᵊl_i **~s** s

aerodrome ˈeər ə drəʊm ‖ ˈer ə droʊm ˈær-
~s z

aerodynamic ˌeər əʊ daɪ ˈnæm ɪk ◄ -dɪ-‧-
‖ ˌer oʊ- ˌær- **~ally** ᵊl_i **~s** s

aerodyne ˈeər əʊ daɪn ‖ ˈer ə- ˈær- **~s** z

Aeroflot *tdmk* ˈeər əʊ flɒt ‖ ˈer ə floʊt ˈær-,
-flɑːt —*Russ* [ʌ ɪ rʌ ˈflɔt]

aerofoil ˈeər əʊ fɔɪᵊl ‖ ˈer oʊ- ˈær- **~s** z

aerogram, aerogramme ˈeər əʊ græm
‖ ˈer ə- ˈær- **~s** z

aerolite ˈeər əʊ laɪt ‖ ˈer ə- ˈær- **~s** s

aerolith ˈeər əʊ lɪθ ‖ ˈer ə- ˈær- **~s** s

aeronaut ˈeər əʊ nɔːt ‖ ˈer ə- ˈær-, -nɑːt **~s** s

aeronautic ˌeər əʊ ˈnɔːt ɪk ◄ ‖ ˌer ə ˈnɔːţ ɪk ◄
ˌær-, -ˈnɑːţ- **~al** ᵊl **~ally** ᵊl_i **~s** s

Aeronwy aɪᵊ ˈrɒn wi ‖ -ˈrɑːn- —*Welsh*
[əi ˈron uɨ, -wi]

aeroplane ˈeər ə pleɪn ‖ ˈer- ˈær- **~s** z

aerosol ˈeər əʊ sɒl ‖ ˈer ə sɑːl ˈær-, -sɔːl **~s** z

aerospace ˈeər əʊ speɪs ‖ ˈer oʊ- ˈær-

aerostatic ˌeər əʊ ˈstæt ɪk ◄
‖ ˌer oʊ ˈstæţ ɪk ◄ ˌær- **~ally** ᵊl_i **~s** s

aertex, A~ *tdmk* ˈeə teks ‖ ˈer- ˈær-

aer|y *ˈnest, high place'* ˈɪər |i ˈeər-, ˈaɪᵊr-
‖ ˈer |i ˈær-, ˈɪr-; ˈeɪ r|i **~ies** iz

aery *ˈethereal'* ˈeər i ‖ ˈer i ˈær-; ˈeɪ ər i

Aeschines ˈiːsk ɪ niːz -ə- ‖ ˈesk- ˈiːsk-

Aeschylus ˈiːsk əl əs -ɪl- ‖ ˈesk- ˈiːsk-

Aesculapi|an ˌiːsk ju ˈleɪp iˌən ˌjə- ‖ ˌesk jə-
ˌ‧ə- **~us** əs

Aesop ˈiːs ɒp ‖ -ɑːp -əp

Aesopian iː ˈsəʊp iˌən -ˈsɒp- ‖ -ˈsoʊp- -ˈsɑːp-

aesthete ˈiːs θiːt ‖ ˈes- *(*)* **~s** s

aesthetic iːs ˈθet ɪk ɪs-, eɪs- ‖ es ˈθeţ ɪk ɪs-
~ally ᵊl_i **~s** s

aestheticism iːs ˈθet ɪ ˌsɪz əm -ə- ‖ es ˈθeţ ə-
ɪs-

aestival iː ˈstaɪv ᵊl ‖ ˈest əv ᵊl

aesti|vate ˈiːst ɪ |veɪt ˈest-, -ə- ‖ ˈest- **~vated**
veɪt ɪd -əd ‖ veɪţ əd **~vates** veɪts **~vating**
veɪt ɪŋ ‖ veɪţ ɪŋ

aestivation ˌiːst ɪ ˈveɪʃ ᵊn ˌest-, -ə- ‖ ˌest- **~s** z

Æthelbert ˈeθ ᵊl bɜːt ‖ -bɜːt

Æthelred ˈeθ ᵊl red

aether, Aether ˈiːθ ə ‖ -ᵊr *(= ether)*

Aetherius iː ˈθɪər iˌəs ɪ- ‖ ɪ ˈθɪr-

aetiological ˌiːt iˌə ˈlɒdʒ ɪk ᵊl ◄
‖ ˌiːţ iˌə ˈlɑːdʒ- **~ly** ˌi

aetiolog|y ˌiːt i ˈɒl ədʒ |i ‖ ˌiːţ i ˈɑːl- **~ies** iz

Aetna ˈet nə

Aetoli|a iː ˈtəʊl iˌə ‖ -ˈtoʊl- **~an/s** ən/z

af- ə, æ —*This variant of* ad- *is usually* ə
(afˈfirm); *but if stressed because of a suffix it
is* ˈæ (ˌaffirˈmation).

afar ə ˈfɑː ‖ ə ˈfɑːr

Afar *African people* ˈæf ɑː æ ˈfɑː, ə- ‖ ˈɑːf ɑːr **~s**
z

A

AFASIC eɪ 'feɪz ɪk
affability ˌæf ə 'bɪl ət i -ɪt i ‖ -ət̬ i
affab|le 'æf əb |əl **~ly** li
affair ə 'feə ‖ ə 'feər ə 'fæər **~s** z
affaire ə 'feə ‖ ə 'feər ə 'fæər —*Fr* [a fɛːʁ] **~s** z
affect *v* ə 'fekt —*Also, to highlight the contrast with* effect, *sometimes* (ˌ)æ- **~ed** ɪd əd **~ing** ɪŋ **~s** s
affect *n* 'æf ekt ə 'fekt **~s** s
affectation ˌæf ek 'teɪʃ ᵊn -ɪk- **~s** z
affected ə 'fekt ɪd -əd **~ly** li **~ness** nəs nɪs
affection ə 'fek ʃᵊn **~s** z
affectionate ə 'fek ʃᵊn ət ˌɪt **~ly** li **~ness** nəs nɪs
affective æ 'fekt ɪv
affenpinscher 'æf ᵊn ˌpɪntʃ ə ‖ -ᵊr **~s** z
afferent 'æf ər ənt
affianc|e ə 'faɪ ənts æ- **~ed** t **~es** ɪz əz **~ing** ɪŋ
affidavit ˌæf ɪ 'deɪv ɪt -ə-, §-ət **~s** s
affiliate *n, adj* ə 'fɪl i ət ˌɪt, -eɪt **~s** s
affili|ate *v* ə 'fɪl i |eɪt **~ated** eɪt ɪd -əd ‖ eɪt̬ əd **~ates** eɪts **~ating** eɪt ɪŋ ‖ eɪt̬ ɪŋ
affiliation ə ˌfɪl i 'eɪʃ ᵊn **~s** z
    af,fili'ation ˌorder
affinit|y ə 'fɪn ət |i -ɪt- ‖ -ət̬ |i **~ies** iz
affirm ə 'fɜːm ‖ ə 'fɝːm **~ed** d **~ing** ɪŋ **~s** z
affirmation ˌæf ə 'meɪʃ ᵊn ‖ -ᵊr- **~s** z
affirmative ə 'fɜːm ət ɪv ‖ ə 'fɝːm ət̬ ɪv **~ly** li
affix *v* ə 'fɪks æ- **~ed** t **~es** ɪz əz **~ing** ɪŋ
affix *n* 'æf ɪks **~es** ɪz əz
affixation ˌæf ɪk 'seɪʃ ᵊn
afflatus ə 'fleɪt əs æ- ‖ -'fleɪt̬-
Affleck 'æf lek
afflict ə 'flɪkt **~ed** ɪd əd **~ing** ɪŋ **~s** s
affliction ə 'flɪk ʃᵊn **~s** z
afflictive ə 'flɪkt ɪv **~ly** li
affluence 'æf lu ənts
affluent 'æf lu ənt **~ly** li
afflux 'æf lʌks **~es** ɪz əz
afford ə 'fɔːd ‖ ə 'fɔːrd -'fourd **~ed** ɪd əd **~ing** ɪŋ **~s** z
affordability ə ˌfɔːd ə 'bɪl ət i -ɪt- ‖ ə ˌfɔːrd ə 'bɪl ət̬ i -ˌfourd-
affordab|le ə 'fɔːd əb| ᵊl ‖ -'fɔːrd- -'fourd- **~ly** li
afforest ə 'fɒr ɪst æ-, -əst ‖ -'fɔːr əst -'fɑːr- **~ed** ɪd əd **~ing** ɪŋ **~s** s
afforestation ə ˌfɒr ɪ 'steɪʃ ᵊn æ-, -ə- ‖ -ˌfɔːr ə- -ˌfɑːr-; ˌæ,·ˑ·ˑ
affray ə 'freɪ **~s** z
Affric 'æf rɪk
affricate *n* 'æf rɪk ət -rək-, -ɪt; -rɪ keɪt, -rə- **~s** s
affri|cate *v* 'æf rɪ |keɪt -rə- **~cated** keɪt ɪd -əd ‖ keɪt̬ əd **~cates** keɪts **~cating** keɪt ɪŋ ‖ keɪt̬ ɪŋ
affrication ˌæf rɪ 'keɪʃ ᵊn -rə-
affricative æ 'frɪk ət ɪv ə-; 'æf rɪ keɪt-, '·rə- ‖ -ət̬- **~ly** li
affright ə 'fraɪt
affront *n, v* ə 'frʌnt **affronted** ə 'frʌnt ɪd -əd ‖ ə 'frʌnt̬ əd **affronting** ə 'frʌnt ɪŋ ‖ ə 'frʌnt̬ ɪŋ **affronts** ə 'frʌnts

Afghan, a~ 'æf gæn -gɑːn, -gən **~s** z
afghani æf 'gɑːn i -'gæn- **~s** z
Afghanistan æf 'gæn ɪ stɑːn -ə-, -stæn, ·, · ·ˑ·, ˌ· · ·ˑ· ‖ -ə stæn
aficionado ə ˌfɪʃ i ə 'nɑːd əʊ ə ˌfɪs-, ə ˌfɪʃ ə'-- ‖ -'nɑːd oʊ —*Sp* [a fi θjo 'na ðo, -sjo'--] **~s** z
afield ə 'fiːᵊld
afire ə 'faɪ ə ‖ ə 'faɪ ᵊr
aflame ə 'fleɪm
aflatoxin ˌæf lə 'tɒks ɪn §-ən ‖ -'tɑːks ən **~s** z
AFL-CIO ˌeɪ ef 'el ˌsiː aɪ 'əʊ ‖ -'oʊ
afloat ə 'fləʊt ‖ ə 'floʊt
aflutter ə 'flʌt ə ‖ ə 'flʌt̬ ᵊr
Afon 'æv ᵊn -ɒn ‖ -ɑːn —*Welsh* ['a von]
afoot ə 'fʊt
afore ə 'fɔː ‖ ə 'fɔːr -'four
aforementioned ə ˌfɔː 'menʃ ᵊnd ◂·ˑ·· ‖ ə ˌfɔːr- -ˌfour-
aforesaid ə 'fɔː sed ‖ ə 'fɔːr- -'four-
aforethought ə 'fɔː θɔːt ‖ ə 'fɔːr- -'four-, -θɑːt
aforetime ə 'fɔː taɪm ‖ ə 'fɔːr- -'four-
a fortiori ˌeɪ ˌfɔːt i 'ɔːr aɪ ˌɑː-, -i ‖ ˌeɪ ˌfɔːrʃ i 'ɔːr i -ˌfɔːrt̬-, -'our-, -aɪ
afoul ə 'faʊl
afraid ə 'freɪd
A-frame 'eɪ freɪm **~s** z
afresh ə 'freʃ
Africa 'æf rɪk ə
African 'æf rɪk ən **~s** z
African-American ˌæf rɪk ən ə 'mer ɪk ən ◂ **~s** z
Africanis... —*see* **Africaniz...**
Africanist 'æf rɪk ən ɪst §-əst **~s** s
Africanization ˌæf rɪk ən aɪ 'zeɪʃ ᵊn -rək-, -ɪ'-- ‖ -ə'-- **~s** z
Africaniz|e 'æf rɪk ə naɪz '·rək- **~ed** d **~es** ɪz əz **~ing** ɪŋ
Afrikaans ˌæf rɪ 'kɑːnts ◂ -rə-, -'kɑːnz ‖ ˌɑːf-
Afrikaner ˌæf rɪ 'kɑːn ə ◂ -rə- ‖ -ᵊr ˌɑːf- **~dom** dəm **~s** z
Afro, afro 'æf rəʊ ‖ -roʊ **~s** z
Afro- *comb. form* ¦æf rəʊ ‖ -roʊ — **Afro-Cuban** ˌæf rəʊ 'kjuːb ən ◂ ‖ -roʊ-
Afro-American ˌæf rəʊ ə 'mer ɪk ən ◂ ‖ ˌæf roʊ- **~s** z
Afro-Asiatic ˌæf rəʊ ˌeɪʃ i 'æt ɪk ◂ -ˌeɪz-, -ˌeɪʒ-, -ˌeɪs- ‖ -roʊ ˌeɪʒ i 'æt̬ ɪk ◂
Afro-Caribbean ˌæf rəʊ ˌkær ə 'biː ən ◂ -ˌ·ɪ-; -kə 'rɪb i ən ‖ -ˌker-; -kə 'rɪb i ən **~s** z
Afrocentric ˌæf rəʊ 'sentr ɪk ◂ ‖ -roʊ-
afrormosia ˌæf rɔː 'məʊz i ə ‖ ˌæf rɔːr 'moʊz ə
aft ɑːft §æft ‖ æft
after 'ɑːft ə §'æft- ‖ 'æft ᵊr **~s** z
after- ¦ɑːft ə §¦æft ə ‖ ¦æft ᵊr —*Compounds with this prefix are almost always early-stressed* ('after,burner). *There is one important exception:* ,after'noon.
afterbirth 'ɑːft ə bɜːθ §'æft- ‖ 'æft ᵊr bɝːθ **~s** s
afterburner 'ɑːft ə ˌbɜːn ə §'æft- ‖ 'æft ᵊr ˌbɝːn ᵊr **~s** z
aftercare 'ɑːft ə keə §'æft- ‖ 'æft ᵊr ker -kær

Affricates

1   An **affricate** is a complex consonant sound consisting of a plosive that is immediately followed by a fricative (see ARTICULATION) made at the same place of articulation. It can therefore also be described as a plosive that has a slow release.

2   English has two affricate phonemes: tʃ as in **church** tʃɜːtʃ ‖ tʃɜːtʃ and dʒ as in **judge** dʒʌdʒ. Their place of articulation is palato-alveolar. In addition to this pair, the clusters tr and dr are pronounced as affricates in RP and GenAm as in **try** traɪ and **dream** driːm. Their place of articulation is post-alveolar.

3   Affricates always belong together in the same syllable: **achieve** ə ˈtʃiːv, **address** ə ˈdres, **natural** ˈnætʃ rəl.

4   Other affricate-like sequences of consonants are found in words such as **obvious** ˈɒb vi‿əs ‖ ˈɑːb vi‿əs, **eighth** eɪtθ, **cats** kæts, **rides** raɪdz; but we do not usually list bv, tθ, ts, dz among the English affricates. Notice also that the t followed by ʃ in **nutshell** ˈnʌt ʃel is not an affricate.

---

aftereffect ˈɑːft ər ɪ ˌfekt §ˈæft-, ˈ·ˌ·ər-, -ə-ˌ· ‖ ˈæft ər- **~s** s

afterglow ˈɑːft ə gləʊ §ˈæft- ‖ ˈæft ᵊr gloʊ

after-hours ˌɑːft ər'aʊ‿əz ◄ §ˌæft- ‖ ˌæft ᵊr ˈaʊ‿ᵊrz

afterlife ˈɑːft ə laɪf §ˈæft- ‖ ˈæft ᵊr-

aftermath ˈɑːft ə mæθ §ˈæft-, -mɑːθ ‖ ˈæft ᵊr-

afternoon ˌɑːft ə ˈnuːn ◄ §ˌæft-, §-ˈnʊn, -ᵊn ˈuːn ‖ ˌæft ᵊr- **~s** z
   ˌafternoon ˈtea

after-sales ˌɑːft ə ˈseɪᵊlz ◄ §ˌæft- ‖ ˌæft ᵊr-

after-school ˌɑːft ə ˈskuːl ◄ §ˌæft- ‖ ˌæft ᵊr-

aftershave ˈɑːft ə ʃeɪv §ˈæft-, ˌ·ˈ· ‖ ˈæft ᵊr- **~s** z
   ˈaftershave ˌlotion, ˌ·ˈ· ˌ··

aftershock ˈɑːft ə ʃɒk §ˈæft- ‖ ˈæft ᵊr ʃɑːk **~s** s

aftertaste ˈɑːft ə teɪst §ˈæft- ‖ ˈæft ᵊr- **~s** s

afterthought ˈɑːft ə θɔːt §ˈæft- ‖ ˈæft ᵊr- -θɑːt **~s** s

afterward ˈɑːft ə wəd §ˈæft- ‖ ˈæft ᵊr wᵊrd **~s** z

afterword ˈɑːft ə wɜːd §ˈæft- ‖ ˈæft ᵊr wɜːd **~s** z

Afton ˈæft ən

ag- ə, æ —*This variant of* ad- *is usually* ə (agˈgression), *but* ˌæ *if stressed because of a suffix* (ˈaggravate).

Aga, aga ˈɑːg ə
   ˌAga ˈKhan

Agadir ˌæg ə ˈdɪə ‖ ˌɑːg ə ˈdɪᵊr ˌæg-

Agag ˈeɪg æg

again ə ˈgen ə ˈgeɪn — *Preference polls, BrE:* -ˈgen *80%,* -ˈgeɪn *20%. Many BrE speakers use both pronunciations. AmE:* -ˈgen *97%,* -ˈgeɪn *3%.*

against ə ˈgenᵗst ə ˈgeɪnᵗst

agama ˈæg əm ə ə ˈgɑːm ə **~s** z

Agamemnon ˌæg ə ˈmem nən -nɒn ‖ -nɑːn

agapanthus ˌæg ə ˈpænᵗθ əs **~es** ɪz əz

agape *n* ˈlove, love feast' ˈæg əp i -eɪ; ə ˈgɑːp i ‖ ɑː ˈgɑːp eɪ ˈɑːg ə peɪ

agape *adv, adj* ˈwide open' ə ˈgeɪp

agar ˈeɪg ə -ɑː ‖ ˈɑːg ᵊr ˈeɪg-, -ɑːr

Agar *family name (i)* ˈeɪg ə ‖ -ᵊr, *(ii)* -ɑː ‖ -ɑːr

agar-agar ˌeɪg ər ˈeɪg ə ‖ ˌɑːg ər ˈɑːg ᵊr

agaric ˈæg ər ɪk ə ˈgær- **~s** s

Agassi, Agassiz ˈæg əs i

agate ˈæg ət -ɪt

Agate *family name (i)* ˈæg ət, *(ii)* ˈeɪg ət

Agatha ˈæg əθ ə

agave ə ˈgeɪv i ə ˈgɑːv i, ˈæg eɪv ‖ ə ˈgɑːv i **~s** z

-age ɪdʒ, (ǃ)ɑːʒ —*In most words* -age *is pronounced* ɪdʒ (perˈcentage), *although some recent French borrowings are pronounced with*

A

ɑːʒ, *stressed in AmE and sometimes in BrE*
(ˌentouˈrage). *Some words have two or more
competing variants* (garage), *and there are
exceptions* (outrage).

age eɪdʒ **aged** *past, pp* eɪdʒd **ageing, aging**
ˈeɪdʒ ɪŋ **ages** ˈeɪdʒ ɪz -əz
ˌage of conˈsent

aged *'having a specified age'; past and pp of*
age eɪdʒd

aged *'very old'* ˈeɪdʒ ɪd -əd; §eɪdʒd

Agee ˈeɪdʒ iː

ageing ˈeɪdʒ ɪŋ

ageism ˈeɪdʒ ˌɪz əm

ageist ˈeɪdʒ ɪst §-əst ~s s

ageless ˈeɪdʒ ləs -lɪs ~ly li ~ness nəs nɪs

age-long ˌeɪdʒ ˈlɒŋ ◂ ‖ ˈeɪdʒ lɔːŋ -lɑːŋ

agenc|y ˈeɪdʒ ənˇs |i ~ies iz

agenda ə ˈdʒend ə ~s z

agene ˈeɪdʒ iːn

agent ˈeɪdʒ ənt ~s s —*See also phrases with
this word*

agentive ˈeɪdʒ ənt ɪv

agent provocateur ˌæʒ õ prə ˌvɒk ə ˈtɜː
ˌeɪdʒ ənt- ‖ ˌɑːʒ ãː prou ˌvɑːk ə ˈtɜː -ˈtʊˀr
—*Fr* [a ʒã pʀɔ vɔ ka tœːʀ] **agents
provocateurs** *same pronunciation, or* -z

age-old ˌeɪdʒ ˈəʊld ◂ →ˈɒʊld ◂ ‖ -ˈoʊld ◂

-ageous ˈeɪdʒ əs —*This suffix may impose
rhythmic stress on the preceding stem*
(ˌadvanˈtageous).

ageratum ˌædʒ ə ˈreɪt əm ‖ -ˈreɪt̬- ~s z

Agfa *tdmk* ˈæg fə

Agg æg

Aggett ˈæg ɪt -ət

Aggie ˈæg i

aggiornamento ə ˌdʒɔːn ə ˈment əʊ ˌæ-
‖ ə ˌdʒɔːrn ə ˈment ou —*It*
[ad dʒor na ˈmen to]

agglome|rate *v* ə ˈglɒm ə |reɪt ‖ ə ˈglɑːm-
~**rated** reɪt ɪd -əd ‖ reɪt̬ əd ~**rates** reɪts
~**rating** reɪt ɪŋ ‖ reɪt̬ ɪŋ

agglomerate *adj, n* ə ˈglɒm ər ət -ɪt, -ə reɪt
‖ ə ˈglɑːm- ~s s

agglomeration ə ˌglɒm ə ˈreɪʃ ᵊn ‖ ə ˌglɑːm-
~s z

agglutinate *adj, n* ə ˈgluːt ɪn ət -ən-, -ɪt;
-ɪ neɪt, -ə- ‖ -ᵊn- ~s s

aggluti|nate *v* ə ˈgluːt ɪ |neɪt -ə- ‖ -ᵊ|n eɪt
~**nated** neɪt ɪd -əd ‖ neɪt̬ əd ~**nates** neɪts
~**nating** neɪt ɪŋ ‖ neɪt̬ ɪŋ

agglutination ə ˌgluːt ɪ ˈneɪʃ ᵊn -ə- ‖ -ᵊn ˈeɪʃ-

agglutinative ə ˈgluːt ɪn ət ɪv -ˈ-ən-; -ɪ neɪt-,
-ə neɪt-, -ᵊn eɪt- ‖ -ᵊn eɪt̬ ɪv -ᵊn ət ɪv ~ly li

aggrandis... —*see* **aggrandiz...**

aggrandiz|e ə ˈgrænd aɪz ˈæg rən daɪz ~**ed** d
~**es** ɪz əz ~**ing** ɪŋ

aggrandizement ə ˈgrænd ɪz mənt -əz-, -aɪz-

aggra|vate ˈæg rə |veɪt ~**vated** veɪt ɪd -əd
‖ veɪt̬ əd ~**vates** veɪts ~**vating/ly** veɪt ɪŋ /li
‖ veɪt̬ ɪŋ /li

aggravation ˌæg rə ˈveɪʃ ᵊn ~s z

aggregate *adj, n* ˈæg rɪg ət -rəg-, -ɪt; -rɪ geɪt,
-rə- ~s s

aggre|gate *v* ˈæg rɪ |geɪt -rə- ~**gated** geɪt ɪd
-əd ‖ geɪt̬ əd ~**gates** geɪts ~**gating** geɪt ɪŋ
‖ geɪt̬ ɪŋ

aggregation ˌæg rɪ ˈgeɪʃ ᵊn -rə- ~s z

aggression ə ˈgreʃ ᵊn

aggressive ə ˈgres ɪv ~ly li ~ness nəs nɪs

aggressor ə ˈgres ə ‖ -ᵊr ~s z

aggrieved ə ˈgriːvd

aggro ˈæg rəʊ ‖ -roʊ

Agha- *comb. form in Irish place names* ˈæx ə
— **Aghacully** ˌæx ə ˈkʌl i

aghast ə ˈgɑːst §-ˈgæst ‖ ə ˈgæst

agile ˈædʒ aɪᵊl ‖ -ᵊl -aɪᵊl ~ly li ~ness nəs nɪs

agility ə ˈdʒɪl ət i -ɪt i ‖ -ət̬ i

agin ə ˈgɪn

Agincourt ˈædʒ ɪn kɔː ˈæʒ-, §-ən-, -kɔːt ‖ -kɔːrt
-kourt

agio ˈædʒ i ˌəʊ ‖ -oʊ ~s z

agiotage ˈædʒ ət ɪdʒ ˈædʒ i ət ɪdʒ, ə tɑːʒ
‖ ˈædʒ i ət̬ ɪdʒ ˌædʒ ə ˈtɑːʒ

agist *v* ə ˈdʒɪst ~**ed** ɪd əd ~**ing** ɪŋ ~**ment/s**
mənt/s ~s s

agi|tate ˈædʒ ɪ |teɪt -ə- ~**tated/ly** teɪt ɪd /li
-əd /li ‖ teɪt̬ əd /li ~**tates** teɪts ~**tating**
teɪt ɪŋ ‖ teɪt̬ ɪŋ

agitation ˌædʒ ɪ ˈteɪʃ ᵊn -ə- ~s z

agitato ˌædʒ ɪ ˈtɑːt əʊ -ə- ‖ -oʊ

agitator ˈædʒ ɪ teɪt ə ˌ-ə- ‖ -teɪt̬ ᵊr ~s z

agitprop ˈædʒ ɪt prɒp §-ət-, ˌ·ˈ· ‖ -prɑːp

Aglaia ə ˈglaɪ ə -ˈgleɪ ə

agleam ə ˈgliːm

aglet ˈæg lət -lɪt ~s s

agley ə ˈgleɪ -ˈglaɪ, -ˈgliː

aglimmer ə ˈglɪm ə ‖ -ᵊr

aglitter ə ˈglɪt ə ‖ ə ˈglɪt̬ ᵊr

aglow ə ˈgləʊ ‖ ə ˈgloʊ

AGM ˌeɪ dʒiː ˈem ~s, ~'s z

agma ˈæg mə ˈæŋ- ~s s

agnail ˈæg neɪᵊl ~s z

agnate ˈæg neɪt ~s s

Agnes ˈæg nɪs -nəs

Agnew ˈæg njuː ‖ -nuː

Agni ˈæg ni ˈʌg- —*Hindi* [əg ɳi]

agnomen æg ˈnəʊm en ‖ -ˈnoʊm ən

agnosia æg ˈnəʊz i ˌə ‖ -ˈnoʊz ə -ˈnoʊʃ-

agnostic ₍ᵢ₎æg ˈnɒst ɪk əg- ‖ -ˈnɑːst- ~**ally** ᵊl i
~s s

agnosticism ₍ᵢ₎æg ˈnɒst ɪ ˌsɪz əm əg-, -ə-
‖ -ˈnɑːst-

Agnus Dei ˌæg nəs ˈdeɪ iː, ˌɑːg-, -nʊs-, ˌɑːn jʊs-,
-ˈdiː aɪ

ago ə ˈgəʊ ‖ ə ˈgoʊ

agog ə ˈgɒg ‖ ə ˈgɑːg

-agogic ə ˈgɒdʒ ɪk -ˈgəʊdʒ- ‖ -ˈgɑːdʒ- -ˈgoʊdʒ-
— **hypnagogic** ˌhɪp nə ˈgɒdʒ ɪk ◂ -ˈgəʊdʒ-
‖ -ˈgɑːdʒ- -ˈgoʊdʒ-

a-go-go, à gogo ə ˈgəʊ gəʊ ‖ ɑː ˈgoʊ goʊ
—*Fr* [a go go]

-agogue *stress-imposing* ə gɒg ‖ ə gɑːg
— **galactogogue** gə ˈlækt ə gɒg ‖ -gɑːg

-agogy ə gɒdʒ i -gɒg-, -gəʊg- ‖ ə gɑːdʒ i
-gɑːg-, -goʊg- — **pedagogy** ˈped ə gɒdʒ i
-gɒg i ‖ -gɑːdʒ i -gɑːg i

agoni... —*see* **agony**
agonis... —*see* **agonize**
agonist 'æg ən ɪst §-əst **~s** s
Agonistes ˌæg əʊ 'nɪst iːz ‖ -ə-
agoniz|e 'æg ə naɪz **~ed** d **~es** ɪz əz **~ing/ly**
  ɪŋ /li
agon|y 'æg ən |i **~ies** iz
  'agony ˌaunt; ''agony ˌcolumn
agora, Agora 'æg ər ə **~s** z
agoraphobia ˌæg ər ə 'fəʊb i ə ‖ -'foʊb-
agoraphobic ˌæg ər ə 'fəʊb ɪk ◄ ‖ -'foʊb- **~s** s
agouti ə 'guːt i ‖ ə 'guːt̬ i **-es, ~s** z
Agra 'ɑːg rə 'æg-
agranulocytosis ə ˌgræn jʊl əʊ saɪ 'təʊs ɪs
  ˌeɪ,ᵻ-, -jəl ˑˑ'-, §-əs
  ‖ ˌeɪ ˌgræn jə loʊ saɪ 'toʊs əs
agrapha 'æg rəf ə
agraphia ₍ᵢ₎eɪ 'græf i ə æ-
agrarian ə 'greər i ən æ- ‖ ə 'grer- ə 'grær-
  ~ism ˌɪz əm **~s** z
agree ə 'griː **agreed** ə 'griːd **agrees** ə 'griːz
  agreeing ə 'griː ɪŋ
agreeab|le ə 'griːˌəb |əl **~leness** əl nəs -nɪs
  ~ly li
agreement ə 'griː mənt **~s** s
agribusiness 'æg ri ˌbɪz nəs -nɪs
Agricola ə 'grɪk əl ə ɑ-
agricultural ˌæg rɪ 'kʌltʃ ᵊr əl ◄ ˌ-rə- **~ly** i
agriculturalist ˌæg rɪ 'kʌltʃ ᵊr əl ɪst ˌ-rə-, §-əst
  ~s s
agriculture 'æg rɪ ˌkʌltʃ ə -rə-, ˌ·ˑ·◄ ‖ -ᵊr
agriculturist ˌæg rɪ 'kʌltʃ ər ɪst ˌ-rə-, §-əst **~s**
  s
Agrigento ˌæg rɪ 'dʒent əʊ -rə- ‖ -oʊ —*It*
  [a gri 'dʒen to]
agrimony 'æg rɪm ən i 'ˑrəm- ‖ -ə moʊn i
Agrippa ə 'grɪp ə
Agrippina ˌæg rɪ 'piːn ə -rə-
agro- *comb. form*
  with stress-neutral suffix |æg rəʊ ‖ -roʊ —
    agrobiology ˌæg rəʊ baɪ 'ɒl ədʒ i
  ‖ -roʊ baɪ 'ɑːl-
  with stress-imposing suffix ə 'grɒ æ- ‖ -'grɑː +
    — **agrology** ə 'grɒl ədʒ i æ- ‖ -'grɑːl-
agronomic ˌæg rəʊ 'nɒm ɪk ◄ ‖ -rə 'nɑːm-
  ~al/ly ᵊl / i **~s** s
agronomist ə 'grɒn əm ɪst §-əst ‖ ə 'grɑːn- **~s**
  s
agronomy ə 'grɒn əm i ‖ ə 'grɑːn-
aground ə 'graʊnd
aguardiente ˌæg wɑːd i 'ent i
  ‖ ˌɑːg wɑːrd i 'ent̬ i -'ent eɪ —*Sp*
  [a ɣwar 'ðjen te]
ague 'eɪg juː **~s** z
Aguecheek 'eɪg juː tʃiːk
Aguilera ˌæg ɪ 'leər ə -ji- ‖ ˌɑːg ə 'ler ə —*Sp*
  [a ɣi 'le ɾa]
aguish 'eɪg juː ɪʃ **~ly** li **~ness** nəs nɪs
Agulhas ə 'gʌl əs
Agutter *(i)* 'æg ət ə ‖ -ət̬ ᵊr, *(ii)* ə 'gʌt ə
  ‖ ə 'gʌt̬ ᵊr
ah ɑː
aha ɑː 'hɑː ə-

Ahab 'eɪ hæb
Ahasuerus ˌeɪ hæz ju 'ɪər əs ə ˌhæz-, -'eər-
  ‖ -'ɪr-
ahead ə 'hed
ahem [ʔm ʔmː] *said with tense voice; also*
  [m 'mm]; *also spelling pronunciation* ə 'hem
Ahenobarbus ə ˌhiːn əʊ 'bɑːb əs -ˌhen-
  ‖ -oʊ 'bɑːrb-
Ahern, Aherne *(i)* ə 'hɜːn ‖ ə 'hɜːn,
  (ii) 'eɪ hɜːn ‖ -hɜːn
ahimsa ə 'hɪm sɑː
ahistorical ˌeɪ hɪ 'stɒr ɪk ᵊl ‖ -'stɔːr- -'stɑːr-
  ~ly i
Ahithophel ə 'hɪθ ə fel
Ahmadabad 'ɑːm əd ə bæd 'ˑɪd-, -bɑːd
Ahmadinejad ˌɑː mə 'diːn ə dʒæd -dʒɑːd
  —*Persian (Farsi)* [æh mæ di ne 'ʒɒd]
Ahmed 'ɑːm ed
Ahmedabad 'ɑːm əd ə bæd 'ˑɪd-, 'ˑed-, -bɑːd
ahoy ə 'hɔɪ
Ahura Mazda ə ˌhʊər ə 'mæz də ‖ ə ˌhʊr- ɑ-,
  -'mɑːz-
ai *'three-toed sloth'* 'aɪ i 'ɑː i, aɪ **ais** 'aɪ iz 'ɑː iz,
  aɪz
AI ˌeɪ 'aɪ
aid eɪd **aided** 'eɪd ɪd -əd **aiding** 'eɪd ɪŋ **aids**
  eɪdz
AID ˌeɪ aɪ 'diː
Aida, Aïda aɪ 'iːd ə ɑː- —*It* [a 'i: da]
Aidan 'eɪd ᵊn
aide eɪd (= *aid*) **aides** eɪdz
aide|-de-camp ˌeɪd| də 'kɑːmp -'kɒ̃, -'kɑ̃-
  ‖ -'kæmp —*Fr* [ɛd də kɑ̃] **aides~** ˌeɪd- ˌeɪdz-
  —*Fr* [ɛd də kɑ̃]
aide-memoire, aide-mémoire
  ˌeɪd mem 'wɑː ˌ·ˑ·· ‖ -'wɑːr —*Fr*
  [ɛd me mwaːʁ]
AIDS, Aids eɪdz
  'AIDS ˌpatient
aigrette 'eɪg ret eɪ 'gret **~s** s
aiguille 'eɪg wiːl -wɪl ‖ ˌeɪ 'gwiːᵊl —*Fr* [e gɥij]
  ~s z *or as sing.*
aiguillette ˌeɪg wɪ 'let -wə- **~s** s
Aiken 'eɪk ən
aikido aɪ 'kiːd əʊ 'aɪk ɪ dəʊ ‖ aɪ 'kiːd oʊ
  ˌaɪk ɪ 'doʊ —*Jp* [a,i 'ki doo]
ail eɪᵊl (= *ale*) **ailed** eɪᵊld **ailing** 'eɪᵊl ɪŋ **ails**
  eɪᵊlz
ailanthus eɪ 'lænᵗθ əs **~es** ɪz əz
Ailbhe 'ælv ə
Aileen *(i)* 'eɪl iːn ‖ eɪ 'liːn, *(ii)* 'aɪl iːn ‖ aɪ 'liːn
aileron 'eɪl ə rɒn ‖ -rɑːn **~s** z
ailment 'eɪᵊl mənt **~s** s
Ailsa 'eɪᵊls ə 'eɪᵊlz ə
  ˌAilsa 'Craig
ailuro- *comb. form* aɪ ¦lʊər əʊ eɪ-, -¦ljʊər-;
  ¦eɪl jʊᵊr əʊ ‖ aɪ ¦lʊr ə — **ailurophobia**
  aɪ ˌlʊər əʊ 'fəʊb i ə eɪ-, -ˌljʊər-; ˌeɪl jʊᵊr-
  ‖ aɪ ˌlʊr ə 'foʊb-
aim eɪm **aimed** eɪmd **aiming** 'eɪm ɪŋ **aims**
  eɪmz
Aimee, Aimée 'eɪm eɪ -i ‖ e 'meɪ eɪ- —*Fr*
  [ɛ me]

A

aimless 'eɪm ləs -lɪs **~ly** li **~ness** nəs nɪs
ain eɪn
Ainscough, Ainscow 'eɪnz kəʊ ‖ -koʊ
Ainsdale 'eɪnz deɪ³l
Ainsley, Ainslie 'eɪnz li
Ainsworth 'eɪnz wɜːθ -wəθ ‖ -wɚθ
ain't eɪnt
Aintree 'eɪn triː 'eɪntr i
Ainu 'aɪn uː **~s** z
aioli, aïoli aɪ 'əʊl i eɪ- ‖ -'oʊl i —*It* [a 'jo li]
air eə ‖ e³r æ³r **aired** eəd ‖ e³rd æ³rd **airing**
   'eər ɪŋ ‖ 'er ɪŋ 'ær- **airs** eəz ‖ e³rz æ³rz
   'air ˌchamber; ˌair chief 'marshal◄; ˌair
   'commodore◄; 'air ˌfreight; ˌair 'marshal◄;
   'air ˌraid; 'air ˌrifle; 'air ˌterminal; ˌair
   ˌtraffic con'trol, ˌ· '·· ·ˌ·, '· ˌ· · ·ˌ·; ˌair
   vice-'marshal◄
airbag 'eə bæg ‖ -er- 'ær- **~s** z
airbas|e 'eə beɪs ‖ 'er- 'ær- **~es** ɪz əz
airbed 'eə bed ‖ 'er- 'ær- **~s** z
airbladder 'eə ˌblæd ə ‖ 'er ˌblæd ³r 'ær- **~s** z
airborne 'eə bɔːn ‖ 'er bɔːrn 'ær-, -boʊrn
airbrake 'eə breɪk ‖ 'er- 'ær- **~s** s
airbrick 'eə brɪk ‖ 'er- 'ær- **~s** s
airbrush 'eə brʌʃ ‖ 'er- 'ær- **~ed** t **~es** ɪz əz
   ~ing ɪŋ
airburst 'eə bɜːst ‖ 'er bɜːst 'ær- **~s** s
airbus, A~ *tdmk* 'eə bʌs ‖ 'er- 'ær- **~es** ɪz əz
air-condition 'eə kən ˌdɪʃ ³n ˌ· '·· · ‖ 'er- 'ær-
   ~ed d **~ing** ˌɪŋ **~s** z
air-cool 'eə kuːl ‖ 'er- 'ær- **~ed** d **~ing** ɪŋ **~s** z
aircraft 'eə krɑːft §-kræft ‖ 'er kræft 'ær-
   'aircraft ˌcarrier
aircraft|man 'eə krɑːft |mən §-kræft-
   ‖ 'er kræft- 'ær- **~men** mən **~woman**
   ˌwʊm ən **~women** ˌwɪm ɪn §-ən
aircrafts|man 'eə krɑːfts |mən §-kræfts-
   ‖ 'er kræfts- 'ær- **~men** mən **~woman**
   ˌwʊm ən **~women** ˌwɪm ɪn §-ən
aircrew 'eə kruː ‖ 'er- 'ær- **~s** z
aircushion 'eə ˌkʊʃ ³n ‖ 'er- 'ær- **~s** z
Airdrie 'eədr i ‖ 'erdr i
air-drie... —*see* air-dry
Airdrieonian ˌeədr i 'əʊn i ən ◄
   ‖ ˌerdr i 'oʊn- **~s** z
airdrop 'eə drɒp ‖ 'er drɑːp 'ær- **~ped** t **~ping**
   ɪŋ **~s** s
air-|dry 'eə |draɪ ‖ 'er- 'ær- **~dries** draɪz
   ~dried draɪd **~drying** draɪ ɪŋ
Aire eə ‖ e³r æ³r
Airedale 'eə deɪ³l ‖ 'er- 'ær- **~s** z
airer 'eər ə ‖ 'er ³r 'ær- **~s** z
Airey 'eər i ‖ 'er i 'ær i
airfare 'eə feə ‖ 'er fer 'ær fær **~s** z
airfield 'eə fiː³ld ‖ 'er- 'ær- **~s** z
airflow 'eə fləʊ ‖ 'er floʊ 'ær- **~s** z
airfoil 'eə fɔɪl ‖ 'er- 'ær- **~s** z
airforc|e 'eə fɔːs ‖ 'er fɔːrs 'ær-, -foʊrs **~es** ɪz
   əz
airframe 'eə freɪm ‖ 'er- 'ær- **~s** z
airgun 'eə gʌn ‖ 'er- 'ær- **~s** z
airhead 'eə hed ‖ 'er- 'ær- **~s** z
airhole 'eə həʊl →-hɒʊl ‖ 'er hoʊl 'ær- **~s** z

airhostess 'eə ˌhəʊst es -ɪs, -əs ‖ 'er ˌhoʊst əs
   'ær- **~es** ɪz əz
airi... —*see* airy
airily 'eər əl i -ɪ li ‖ 'er- 'ær-
airiness 'eər i nəs -nɪs ‖ 'er- 'ær-
airing 'eər ɪŋ ‖ 'er ɪŋ 'ær- **~s** z
   'airing ˌcupboard
air-intake 'eər ˌɪn teɪk ‖ 'er- 'ær- **~s** s
airlane 'eə leɪn ‖ 'er- 'ær- **~s** z
airless 'eə ləs -lɪs ‖ 'er- 'ær- **~ness** nəs nɪs
airletter 'eə ˌlet ə ‖ 'er ˌleţ ³r 'ær- **~s** z
airlift 'eə lɪft ‖ 'er- 'ær- **~ed** ɪd əd **~ing** ɪŋ **~s** s
airline 'eə laɪn ‖ 'er- 'ær- **~s** z
airliner 'eə ˌlaɪn ə ‖ 'er ˌlaɪn ³r 'ær- **~s** z
airlock 'eə lɒk ‖ 'er lɑːk 'ær- **~s** s
airmail 'eə mer³l ‖ 'er- 'ær- **~ed** d **~ing** ɪŋ **~s** z
air|man 'eə |mən -mæn ‖ 'er- 'ær- **~men** mən
   men
airmobile ˌeə 'məʊb aɪ³l ◄ ˌ· '· · ‖ 'er ˌmoʊb ³l
   'ær-, -iː³l, -aɪ³l; -moʊ ˌbiː³l
airplane 'eə pleɪn ‖ 'er- 'ær- **~s** z
airplay 'eə pleɪ ‖ 'er- 'ær-
airpocket 'eə ˌpɒk ɪt §-ət ‖ 'er ˌpɑːk ət 'ær- **~s**
   s
airport 'eə pɔːt ‖ 'er pɔːrt 'ær-, -poʊrt **~s** s
airscrew 'eə skruː ‖ 'er- 'ær- **~s** z
air-sea ˌeə 'siː ◄ ‖ ˌer- ˌær-
   ˌair-sea 'rescue
airshaft 'eə ʃɑːft §-ʃæft ‖ 'er ʃæft 'ær- **~s** s
airship 'eə ʃɪp ‖ 'er- 'ær- **~s** s
airsick 'eə sɪk ‖ 'er- 'ær- **~ness** nəs nɪs
airside 'eə saɪd ‖ 'er- 'ær-
airspace 'eə speɪs ‖ 'er- 'ær-
airspeed 'eə spiːd ‖ 'er- 'ær- **~s** z
airstream 'eə striːm ‖ 'er- 'ær- **~s** z
   'airstream ˌmechanism
airstrike 'eə straɪk ‖ 'er- 'ær- **~s** s
airstrip 'eə strɪp ‖ 'er- 'ær- **~s** s
airtight 'eə taɪt ‖ 'er- 'ær-
airtime 'eə taɪm ‖ 'er- 'ær-
air-to-air ˌeə tu 'eə ◄ -tə- ‖ ˌer tə 'er ◄
   ˌær tə 'ær, -tu-
airwaves 'eə weɪvz ‖ 'er- 'ær-
airway 'eə weɪ ‖ 'er- 'ær- **~s** z
air|woman 'eə |ˌwʊm ən ‖ 'er- 'ær- **~women**
   ˌwɪm ɪn §-ən
airworth|y 'eə ˌwɜːð |i ‖ 'er ˌwɜːð |i 'ær-
   ~iness i nəs i nɪs
air|y, Air|y 'eər |i ‖ 'er |i 'ær i **~ier** i ə ‖ i ³r
   ~iest i ɪst i əst
airy-fairy ˌeər i 'feər i ◄ ‖ ˌer i 'fer i ◄
   ˌær i 'fær i
Aisha (i) aɪ 'iːʃ ə ɑː-, eɪ-, (ii) 'eɪʃ ə 'aɪʃ ə
aisle aɪ³l (= *isle*) **aisles** aɪ³lz
Aisling 'æʃ lɪŋ
Aisne eɪn —*Fr* [ɛn]
ait eɪt (= *eight*) **aits** eɪts
aitch eɪtʃ **aitches** 'eɪtʃ ɪz -əz
aitch-bone 'eɪtʃ bəʊn ‖ -boʊn **~s** z
Aitchison 'eɪtʃ ɪs ən -əs-
Aithne 'eɪθ nə -ni
Aitken, Aitkin (i) 'eɪt kɪn, (ii) 'eɪk ɪn
Aiwa 'aɪ wə —*Jp* [a͈i wa]

Aix eɪks eks —*Fr* [ɛks]
Aix-en-Provence ˌeɪks ɒn prə ˈvɒnˢs ˌeks-,
→ˌ‑ɒm- ‖ ˈ‑ɑːn proʊ ˈvãːs —*Fr*
[ɛk sã pʁɔ vãːs]
Aix-la-Chapelle ˌeɪks lɑː ʃæ ˈpel ˌeks-, ˌ‑læ-,
ˌ‑lə- ‖ -ʃɑː ˈpel —*Fr* [ɛks la ʃa pɛl]
Aix-les-Bains ˌeɪks leɪ ˈbǽ ˌeks-, -ˈbæn —*Fr*
[ɛks le bǽ]
Ajaccio æ ˈdʒæs i əʊ -ˈʒæks- ‖ ɑː ˈjɑːtʃ oʊ -i oʊ
—*Fr* [a ʒak sjo]
ajar ə ˈdʒɑː ‖ ə ˈdʒɑːr
Ajax *(i)* ˈeɪdʒ æks, *(ii)* ˈaɪ æks —*The Greek
hero is (i), as is the scouring powder (tdmk);
the Dutch football team is (ii)*
Ajman ædʒ ˈmɑːn —*Arabic* [ʕa ˈdʒmɑːn]
aka —*see* **also known as**; *sometimes said
aloud as* ˈæk ə *or* ˌeɪ keɪ ˈeɪ
Akabusi ˌæk ə ˈbuːs i
Akai *tdmk* ˈæk aɪ ‖ ə ˈkaɪ
Akan ə ˈkæn ‖ ˈɑːk ɑːn —*Akan* [a kã]
Akbar ˈæk bɑː ‖ -bɑːr
Akela ɑː ˈkeɪl ə
Akerman *(i)* ˈæk ə mən ‖ -ᵊr-, *(ii)* ˈeɪk-
Akhenaten, Akhenaton ˌæk ə ˈnɑːt ᵊn
Akihito ˌæk i ˈhiːt əʊ ‖ ˌɑːk i ˈhiːt oʊ —*Jp*
[a ˈki çi̥ to]
akimbo ə ˈkɪm bəʊ ‖ -boʊ
akin ə ˈkɪn
Akins ˈeɪk ɪnz §-ənz
Akita, akita ə ˈkiːt ə ‖ ə ˈkiːţ ə —*Jp* [ˈa ki̥ ta]
~s z
Akkad ˈæk æd ‖ ˈɑːk ɑːd
Akkadian ə ˈkeɪd i̯ ən æ-, -ˈkæd-
Akron ˈæk rɒn -rən ‖ -rən
Akrotiri ˌæk rəʊ ˈtɪər i ‖ ˌɑːk roʊ ˈtɪr i
Al æl
al æl —*It, Arabic* [al] —*See also phrases with
this word*
al- ə, æ —*This variant of ad- is usually* ə
(alˈlot), *but* æ *if stressed because of a suffix*
(ˌalloˈcation).
-al ᵊl, əl —*When forming an adjective, this
suffix imposes stress one or two syllables back*
(ˌuniˈversal, ˈpersonal). *When forming a noun,
it is stress-neutral* (ˌdisapˈproval).
a la, à la ˌæl ɑː -ə, ˌɑː lɑː ‖ ˌɑː lɑː ˌɑːl ə, ˌæl ə
—*Fr* [a la]
ˌa la ˈcarte, ˌà la ˈcarte kɑːt ‖ kɑːrt —*Fr*
[kaʁt]; ˌa la ˈgrecque, ˌà la ˈgrecque grek
—*Fr* [gʁɛk]; ˌa la ˈmode, ˌà la ˈmode məʊd
‖ moʊd —*Fr* [mɔd]
al|a ˈeɪl |ə ~ae iː
Alabam|a ˌæl ə ˈbæm |ə ◄ -ˈbɑːm- ~an/s ən/z
~ian/s i̯ ən/z
alabaster ˈæl ə bɑːst ə -bæst ə, ˌ‑·ˈ‑·‑ ‖ -bæst ᵊr
alack ə ˈlæk
alackaday ə ˌlæk ə ˈdeɪ ·ˈ‑‑
alacrity ə ˈlæk rət i -rɪt- ‖ -rəţ i
Aladdin ə ˈlæd ɪn §-ᵊn
Alagiah ˌæl ə ˈgaɪ ə
Alaister ˈæl ɪst ə -əst- ‖ -ᵊr
alameda, A~ ˌæl ə ˈmiːd ə -ˈmeɪd- —*Sp*
[a la ˈme ða] ~s z

Alamein ˈæl ə meɪn ˌ‑·ˈ‑·
Alamo ˈæl ə məʊ ‖ -moʊ
Alamogordo ˌæl əm ə ˈgɔːd əʊ ‖ -ˈgɔːrd oʊ
Alan ˈæl ən
Alana ə ˈlæn ə -ˈlɑːn-
Alanbrooke ˈæl ən brʊk →‑əm-
Aland, Åland ˈɔː lənd ˈɑː- —*Swed* [ˈoː land]
alanine ˈæl ə niːn -naɪn
Al-Anon ˌæl ə ˈnɒn ‖ -ˈnɑːn
alar ˈeɪl ə -ɑː ‖ -ᵊr
Alaric ˈæl ər ɪk
alarm ə ˈlɑːm ‖ ə ˈlɑːrm ~ed d ~ing/ly ɪŋ /li
~s z
aˈlarm clock
alarm|ism ə ˈlɑːm |ˌɪz əm ‖ ə ˈlɑːrm- ~ist/s
ɪst/s §əst/s
alarum ə ˈlær əm -ˈlɑːr-, -ˈleər- ‖ -ˈler- ~s z
alas ə ˈlæs -ˈlɑːs
Alasdair ˈæl əst ə -ə steə ‖ -ᵊr
Alask|a, a~ ə ˈlæsk |ə ~an/s ən/z
Alastair ˈæl əst ə -ə steə ‖ -ᵊr
alate ˈeɪl eɪt ~s s
alb ælb **albs** ælbz
Alba, alba ˈælb ə
Albacete ˌælb ə ˈθeɪt i -eɪ —*Spanish*
[al βa ˈθe te]
albacore ˈælb ə kɔː ‖ -kɔːr -koʊr ~s z
Alban ˈɔːlb ən ˈɒlb- ‖ ˈɑːlb-
Albani|a æl ˈbeɪn i̯ |ə ɔːl- ~an/s ən/z
Albany ˈɔːlb ən i ˈɒlb-, §ˈælb- ‖ ˈɑːlb-
Albarn ˈɔːl bɑːn ‖ -bɑːrn ˈɑːl-
albatross ˈælb ə trɒs ‖ -trɑːs -trɔːs ~es ɪz əz
albedo æl ˈbiːd əʊ ‖ -oʊ ~s z
Albee *(i)* ˈɔːlb iː ‖ ˈɔːlb i ˈɑːlb-, *(ii)* ˈælb iː
albeit ₍ₐ₎ɔːl ˈbiː ɪt §₍ₐ₎æl-, ət ‖ ₍ₐ₎ɑːl-, ₍ₐ₎æl-
Albemarle ˈælb ə mɑːl ‖ -mɑːrl
ˌAlbemarle ˈSound
Albéniz æl ˈbeɪn ɪθ ‖ ɑːl ˈbeɪn iːs —*Sp*
[al ˈβe niθ]
Alberich ˈælb ə rɪk -rɪx —*Ger* [ˈal bə ʁɪç]
Albert, a~ ˈælb ət ‖ -ᵊrt —*but as a French
name,* æl ˈbeə ‖ ɑːl ˈbeᵊr —*Fr* [al bɛːʁ] ~s,
~ˈs s
Alberta æl ˈbɜːt ə ‖ -ˈbɜ̃ːţ ə
Albertina ˌælb ə ˈtiːn ə ‖ -ᵊr-
Albertine ˈælb ə tiːn ˌ‑·ˈ‑· ‖ -ᵊr-
albescence æl ˈbes ᵊnts
albescent æl ˈbes ᵊnt
Albigenses ˌælb ɪ ˈdʒenˢs iːz -ə-, -ˈgenˢs-
Albigensian ˌælb ɪ ˈdʒenˢs i̯ ən ◄ ˌ‑ə-, -ˈgenˢs-
‖ -ˈdʒenˢʃ ən ◄ ~s z
albinism ˈælb ɪ ˌnɪz əm -ə-
albino æl ˈbiːn əʊ ‖ -ˈbaɪn oʊ (*) ~s z
Albinoni ˌælb ɪ ˈnəʊn i §-ə- ‖ -ˈnoʊn i —*It*
[al bi ˈnoː ni]
Albion ˈælb i̯ ən
albite ˈælb aɪt
Alborg ˈɔːl bɔːg ˈɑːl- ‖ -bɔːrg —*Danish* Ålborg
[ˈʌl bɔːʔ]
Albright ˈɔːl braɪt ˈɒl- ‖ ˈɑːl-
Albrow ˈɔːl braʊ ‖ ˈɑːl-
Albufeira ˌælb u ˈfeər ə ‖ -ˈfer- —*Port*
[ɐl βu ˈfɐi ɾɐ]

album 'ælb əm ~s z
albumen 'ælb jum ɪn -jəm-, -ən; -ju men, -jə-
∥ æl 'bju:m ən
albumin 'ælb jum ɪn -jəm-, -ən ∥ æl 'bju:m ən
albuminous æl 'bju:m ɪn əs -ən-
albuminuria æl ˌbju:m ɪ 'njʊər i̯ ə -ˌ-ə-
∥ -'nʊr- -'njʊr-
Albuquerque 'ælb ə kɜːk i ˌ·ˈ·· ∥ -kɜːk i
Albury 'ɔːl bər̯ i 'ɒl-, 'ɔː- ∥ 'ɔːl ˌber i 'ɑːl-
Alcaeus æl 'siː̯ əs
Alcaic, a~ æl 'keɪ ɪk ~s s
alcalde æl 'kæld i ∥ -'kɑːld-, -eɪ ~s z
Alcan tdmk 'æl kæn
Alcatraz 'ælk ə træz ˌ·ˈ·
Alcazar, a~ ˌælk ə 'zɑː æl 'kæz ə ∥ 'ælk ə zɑːr
æl 'kæz ʳr, -'kɑːz- —Sp Alcázar [al 'ka θaɾ]
~s z
Alceste æl 'sest
Alcester 'ɔːlst ə ∥ -ʳr 'ɑːlst-
Alcestis æl 'sest ɪs §-əs
alchemist 'ælk əm ɪst -ɪm-, §-əst ~s s
alchemy 'ælk əm i -ɪm-
alcheringa ˌæltʃ ə 'rɪŋ gə
Alcibiades ˌæls ɪ 'baɪ̯ ə diːz ˌ·ə-
Alcinous æl 'sɪn əʊ əs ∥ -oʊ-
Alcmene ælk 'miːn i
Alcoa tdmk æl 'kəʊ ə ∥ -'koʊ-
Alcock (i) 'æl kɒk ∥ -kɑːk, (ii) 'ɔːl- 'ɒl- ∥ 'ɑːl-
alcohol 'ælk ə hɒl ∥ -hɔːl -hɑːl ~s z
alcohol-free ˌælk ə hɒl 'friː ◄ ∥ -ə hɔːl-
-ə hɑːl-
alcoholic ˌælk ə 'hɒl ɪk ◄ ∥ -'hɑːl- -'hɔːl- ~s s
alcoholism 'ælk ə hɒl ˌɪz əm -həl,··
∥ -hɑːl ˌɪz əm -hɔːl,··
Alconbury 'ɔːlk ən bər̯ i 'ɔːk-, 'ɒlk-, →'·əm-
∥ 'ɔːlk ən ˌber i 'ɑːlk-
alcopop 'ælk əʊ pɒp ∥ -oʊ pɑːp ~s s
Alcott (i) 'ɔːlk ət 'ɒlk-, -ɒt ∥ 'ɔːlk ɑːt 'ɑːlk-,
(ii) 'ælk-
alcove 'ælk əʊv ∥ -oʊv ~s z
Alcuin 'ælk wɪn §-wən
Alcyone æl 'saɪ̯ ən i -'siː̯
Alda 'ɔːld ə
Aldabra ˌₐæl 'dæbr ə
Aldebaran æl 'deb ʳr ən -ə ræn
Aldeburgh 'ɔːld bər̯ ə 'ɒld- ∥ 'ɔːld ˌbɜː oʊ
'ɑːld-
aldehyde 'æld ɪ haɪd -ə- ~s z
Alden 'ɔːld ən 'ɒld- ∥ 'ɑːld-
Aldenham 'ɔːld ən̯əm 'ɒld- ∥ 'ɑːld-
al dente ˌₐæl 'dent i -eɪ ∥ ˌₐɑːl- —It
[al 'dɛn te]
alder, Alder 'ɔːld ə 'ɒld- ∥ 'ɔːld ʳr 'ɑːld- ~s z
Aldergrove 'ɔːld ə grəʊv 'ɒld- ∥ 'ɔːld ʳr groʊv
'ɑːld-
Alderley 'ɔːld ə li 'ɒld-, -ʳl i ∥ -ʳr- 'ɑːld-
alder|man 'ɔːld ə |mən 'ɒld- ∥ -ʳr- 'ɑːld- ~men
mən
aldermanic ˌɔːld ə 'mæn ɪk ◄ ˌɒld- ∥ -ʳr- ˌɑːld-
Aldermaston 'ɔːld ə ˌmɑːst ən 'ɒld-, §-ˌmæst-
∥ -ʳr ˌmæst- 'ɑːld-
Alderney 'ɔːld ən i 'ɒld- ∥ -ʳrn i 'ɑːld-

Aldersgate 'ɔːld əz geɪt 'ɒld-, -gɪt, -gət ∥ -ʳrz-
'ɑːld-
Aldershot 'ɔːld ə ʃɒt 'ɒld- ∥ 'ɔːld ʳr ʃɑːt 'ɑːld-
Alderson 'ɔːld əs ən 'ɒld- ∥ -ʳrs- 'ɑːld-
Alderton 'ɔːld ət ən 'ɒld- ∥ 'ɔːld ʳrt ʳn 'ɑːld-
Aldgate 'ɔːld gɪt 'ɒld-, -geɪt, -gət ∥ 'ɔːld geɪt
'ɑːld-
Aldhelm 'ɔːld helm 'ɒld- ∥ 'ɑːld-
Aldi tdmk 'æld i
Aldine 'ɔːld aɪn 'ɒld-, -iːn ∥ 'ɑːld-
Aldington 'ɔːld ɪŋ tən 'ɒld- ∥ 'ɑːld-
Aldis, Aldiss 'ɔːld ɪs 'ɒld-, §-əs ∥ 'ɑːld-
aldol 'æld ɒl ∥ -ɑːl -ɔːl, -oʊl
aldosterone æl 'dɒst ə rəʊn
ˌæld əʊ 'stɪər əʊn ∥ -'dɑːst ə roʊn
ˌæld oʊ stə 'roʊn
Aldous 'ɔːld əs 'ɒld- ∥ 'ɑːld-
Aldrich 'ɔːld rɪtʃ 'ɒld-, -rɪdʒ ∥ 'ɑːld-
Aldridge 'ɔːld rɪdʒ 'ɒld- ∥ 'ɑːld-
Aldrin, a~ 'ɔːldr ɪn 'ɒldr-, §-ən ∥ 'ɑːldr-
Aldus 'ɔːld əs 'ɒld-, 'æld- ∥ 'ɑːld-
Aldwych 'ɔːld wɪtʃ 'ɒld- ∥ 'ɑːld-
ale erʳl **ales** erʳlz
aleatoric ˌæl i̯ ə 'tɒr ɪk ◄ ˌeɪl- ∥ -'tɔːr- -'tɑːr-
~ally ʳl̯ i
aleatory ˌæl i 'eɪt ʳr i 'eɪl i̯ ˌət̯ ʳr i
∥ 'eɪl i̯ ə tɔːr i -toʊr i
Alec, Aleck, a~ 'æl ɪk -ek
Alecto ə 'lekt əʊ æ- ∥ -oʊ
Aled 'æl ed -ɪd —Welsh ['a led]
ale|house 'erʳl |haʊs ~houses haʊz ɪz -əz
aleikum ə 'leɪk ʊm æ- —Arabic [ʔæ 'læɪk um]
Alemannic ˌæl ə 'mæn ɪk ◄ -ɪ-
alembic ə 'lem bɪk ~s s
Alencon, Alençon 'æl ən sɒ̃ ∥ ˌæl ɑːn 'soʊn
—Fr [a lɑ̃ sɔ̃]
aleph 'æl ef 'ɑːl-, -ɪf, §-əf ∥ 'ɑːl əf -ef ~s s
Aleppo ə 'lep əʊ ∥ -oʊ
alert ə 'lɜːt ∥ ə 'lɝːt **alerted** ə 'lɜːt ɪd -əd
∥ ə 'lɝːt̯ əd **alerting** ə 'lɜːt ɪŋ ∥ ə 'lɝːt̯ ɪŋ
alerts ə 'lɜːts ∥ ə 'lɝːts
alert|ly ə 'lɜːt| li ∥ ə 'lɝːt| li ~ness nəs nɪs
Aleut 'æl i uːt ˌ·ˈ·; æ 'luːt, ə-, -'ljuːt ∥ ə 'luːt ~s
s
Aleutian ə 'luːʃ ʳn -'ljuːʃ-, -'i̯ən ~s z
A-level 'eɪ ˌlev ʳl ~s z
ale|wife 'erʳl |waɪf ~wives waɪvz
Alex 'æl ɪks -eks
Alexander ˌæl ɪg 'zɑːnd ə -eg-, -ɪk-, -'zænd-
∥ -'zænd ʳr —There is also a Scottish form
'elʃ ɪnd ə ∥ -ʳr
alexanders ˌæl ɪg 'zɑːnd əz -eg-, -ɪk-, -'zænd-
∥ -'zænd ʳrz
Alexandra ˌæl ɪg 'zɑːndr ə -eg-, -ɪk-, -'zændr-
∥ -'zændr ə
Alexandretta ˌæl ɪg zɑːn 'dret ə ˌ·eg-, ˌ·ɪk-,
-zæn'·- ∥ -zæn 'dreṭ ə
Alexandria ˌæl ɪg 'zɑːnd i̯ ə ˌ·eg-, ˌ·ɪk-,
-'zændr- ∥ -'zændr-
Alexandrian, a~ ˌæl ɪg 'zɑːndr i̯ ən ◄ ˌ·eg-,
ˌ·ɪk-, -'zændr- ∥ -'zændr- ~s z
alexandrine ˌæl ɪg 'zændr aɪn -eg-, -ɪk-,
-'zɑːndr-, -iːn, -ɪn ~s z

A

alexia ˌeɪ 'leks i ə ə'--
Alexis ə 'leks ɪs §-əs
Alf ælf
alfa, Alfa 'ælf ə ~s z
Alfa-Laval ˌælf ə lə 'væl ‖ -'vɑːl
alfalfa æl 'fælf ə
Alfa-Romeo *tdmk* ˌælf ə rəʊ 'meɪ əʊ
   -'rəʊm i əʊ ‖ -roʊ 'meɪ oʊ ~s z
Al-Fayed æl 'faɪ ed
Alfie 'ælf i
Alfonso æl 'fɒnz əʊ -'fɒnˤs- ‖ -'fɑːnˤs oʊ —*Sp*
   [al 'fon so]
Alford *(i)* 'ɔːl fəd 'ɒl- ‖ -'ɔːl fˤrd 'ɑːl-, *(ii)* 'æl-
Alfred 'ælf rɪd -rəd
Alfreda æl 'friːd ə
alfresco æl 'fresk əʊ ‖ -oʊ
Alfreton 'ɔːlf rɪt ən 'ɒlf-, 'ælf-, -rət-
   ‖ 'ɔːlf rət ˤn 'ɑːlf-, 'ælf-
alga 'ælg ə **algae** 'ældʒ iː 'ælg-, -aɪ
Algarve æl 'gɑːv ' · · ‖ ɑːl 'gɑːrv ə —*Port*
   [ał 'garv]
algebra 'ældʒ ɪb rə -əb- ~s z
algebraic ˌældʒ ɪ 'breɪ ɪk ◄ -ə- ~al ˤl ~ally ˤl i
algebraist ˌældʒ ɪ 'breɪ ɪst -ə-, §-əst ~s s
Algeciras ˌældʒ ɪ 'sɪər əs -ə-, -e-, -'sɪr- ‖ -'sɪr-
   —*Sp* [al xe 'θi ras]
Algeo 'ældʒ i əʊ ‖ -oʊ
Alger 'ældʒ ə ‖ -ˤr
Algeri|a æl 'dʒɪər i ˌ|ə ‖ -'dʒɪr- **~an/z** ən/z
Algernon 'ældʒ ən ən ‖ -ˤrn-
Algie 'ældʒ i
Algiers ₍ˌ₎æl 'dʒɪəz ' · · ‖ -'dʒɪˤrz
alginate 'ældʒ ɪ neɪt -ə- ~s s
Algipan *tdmk* 'ældʒ ɪ pæn -ə-
Algoa æl 'gəʊ ə ‖ -'goʊ-
Algol, ALGOL 'ælg ɒl ‖ -ɑːl -ɔːl
algolagnia ˌælg əʊ 'læg ni ə ‖ ˌælg oʊ-
Algonkian æl 'gɒŋk i ən -wi ən ‖ -'gɑːŋk- ~s z
Algonquian æl 'gɒŋk wi ən -i ən ‖ -'gɑːŋk- ~s
   z
Algonquin æl 'gɒŋk wɪn -ɪn, §-wən, §-ən
   ‖ -'gɑːŋk- ~s z
algorithm 'ælg ə ˌrɪð əm ~s z
algorithmic ˌælg ə 'rɪð mɪk ◄ ~ally ˤl i
Algy 'ældʒ i
alhaji æl 'hædʒ i -'hɑːdʒ- —*Arabic*
   [ʔal 'hɑːd dʒi]
Alhambra æl 'hæm brə əl-; ə 'læm- —*Sp*
   [a 'lam bra]
Ali 'æl i 'ɑːl- ‖ 'ɑːl i —*but the former boxer*
   Muhammad Ali *pronounces* ɑː 'liː —*Arabic*
   ['ʕa li]
   ˌAli 'Baba 'bɑːb ɑː
alias 'eɪl i əs -æs ~es ɪz əz ~ing ɪŋ
alibi 'æl ə baɪ -ɪ- ~ed d ~ing ɪŋ ~s z
Alicante ˌæl ɪ 'kænt i -ə-, -eɪ ‖ -'kænt̬ i
   ˌɑːl ə 'kɑːnt̬- —*Sp* [a li 'kan te]
Alice 'æl ɪs §-əs ~'s ɪz əz
   ˌAlice 'Springs
Alicia ə 'lɪʃ ə ə 'lɪs i ə, -'lɪʃ i ə
Alick 'æl ɪk
alidade 'æl ɪ deɪd -ə- ~s z
alien 'eɪl i ən ~s z

alienable 'eɪl i ən əb ˤl
alie|nate 'eɪl i ə |neɪt **~nated** neɪt ɪd -əd
   ‖ neɪt̬ əd **~nates** neɪts **~nating** neɪt ɪŋ
   ‖ neɪt̬ ɪŋ
alienation ˌeɪl i ə 'neɪʃ ˤn ~s z
alienist 'eɪl i ən ɪst §-əst ~s s
alight ə 'laɪt **alighted** ə 'laɪt ɪd -əd ‖ ə 'laɪt̬ əd
   alighting ə 'laɪt ɪŋ ‖ ə 'laɪt̬ ɪŋ **alights**
   ə 'laɪts **alit** ə 'lɪt
align ə 'laɪn **aligned** ə 'laɪnd **aligning**
   ə 'laɪn ɪŋ **aligns** ə 'laɪnz
alignment ə 'laɪn mənt ~s s
alike ə 'laɪk
alimentary ˌæl ɪ 'ment ˤr i ◄ ˌ-ə-
alimentation ˌæl ɪ men 'teɪʃ ˤn ˌ-ə-, -mən-'--
alimon|y 'æl ɪ mən |i '-ə- ‖ -moʊn |i **~ies** iz
aliphatic ˌæl ɪ 'fæt ɪk ◄ -ə- ‖ -'fæt̬-
aliquot 'æl ɪ kwɒt -ə- ‖ -kwɑːt -kwət
Alisha ə 'lɪʃ ə
Alison, a~ 'æl ɪs ən -əs-
A-list 'eɪ lɪst
Alistair 'æl ɪst ə -əst-; -ɪ steə, -ə- ‖ -ə ster
   -əst ˤr
alit ə 'lɪt
Alitalia *tdmk* ˌæl ɪ 'tæl i ə -'tɑːl- ‖ ˌɑːl ɪ 'tɑːl-
   —*It* [a li 'ta: lja]
alive ə 'laɪv
aliyah ə 'liː ə -jə —*Hebrew* [(ʕ)a 'lij jah]
alizarin ə 'lɪz ər ɪn §-ən
al-Jazeera ˌæl dʒə 'zɪər ə ‖ ˌɑːl dʒə 'zɪr ə
   —*Arabic* [al dʒa 'zi: ra:]
alkali 'ælk ə laɪ ~s z
alkaline 'ælk ə laɪn
alkalinity ˌælk ə 'lɪn ət i -ɪt i ‖ -ət̬ i
alkaloid 'ælk ə lɔɪd ~s z
alkane 'ælk eɪn ~s z
alkanet 'ælk ə net ~s s
Alka-Seltzer *tdmk* ˌælk ə 'selts ə ' · · ·
   ‖ 'ælk ə ˌselts ˤr ~s z
alkene 'ælk iːn ~s z
alkyd 'ælk ɪd §-əd
alkyl 'ælk ɪl -aɪˤl, §-ˤl ‖ -ˤl ~s z
alkyne 'ælk aɪn ~s z
all ɔːl ‖ ɑːl
   ˌall 'clear; ˌAll 'Saints; ˌAll 'Saints' Day;
   ˌAll 'Souls'; ˌall the 'same
all- ǀɔːl ǀ ǀɑːl — all-important
   ˌɔːl ɪm 'pɔːt ˤnt ◄ ‖ -'pɔːrt ˤnt ◄ ˌɑːl-
alla 'æl ə 'ɑːl-, -ɑː ‖ 'ɑːl ə 'æl ə —*It* ['al la]
   ˌalla 'breve 'breɪv i -'brev-, -eɪ; 'brev —*It*
   ['bre: ve]
Allah 'æl ə ə 'lɑː:, æ 'lɑː:, ə- —*Arabic* [ał 'ɫɑːh]
Allahabad ˌæl ə hə 'bɑːd -'bæd —*Hindi/Urdu*
   [ɪ la: ha: ba:ɖ]
allamanda ˌæl ə 'mænd ə ~s z
all-American ˌɔːl ə 'mer ɪk ən ◄ ‖ ˌɑːl-
   ˌall-Aˌmerican 'athlete
Allan 'æl ən
Allan-a-Dale ˌæl ən ə 'deɪˤl
Allandale 'æl ən deɪˤl
allanto|in ə 'lænt əʊ| ɪn ˌæl ən 'təʊ|-, §-ən
   ‖ -oʊ|- **~is** ɪs §əs
Allardice 'æl ə daɪs ‖ -ˤr-

all-around ˌɔːl ə ˈraʊnd ◄ ‖ ˌɑː-
Allason ˈæl əs ən
allative ˈæl ət ɪv ‖ -ət̬- ~s z
Allaun ə ˈlɔːn ‖ -ˈlɑːn
allay ə ˈleɪ ~ed d ~ing ɪŋ ~s z
Allbeury ɔːl ˈbjʊər i ‖ ɔːl ˈbjʊr i ɑːl-
All-Black ˈɔːl blæk ‖ ˈɑːl- ~s s
All-Bran tdmk ˈɔːl bræn ‖ ˈɑːl-
all-day ˌɔːl ˈdeɪ ◄ ‖ ˌɑːl-
  ˌall-day ˈmeeting
Allder ˈɔːld ə ˈɒld- ‖ ˈɔːld ³r ˈɑːld- ~'s z
allegation ˌæl ə ˈɡeɪʃ ³n -ɪ- ~s z
alleg|e ə ˈledʒ ₍ᵢ₎æ- ~ed d ~es ɪz əz ~ing ɪŋ
allegedly ə ˈledʒ ɪd li -əd-
Alleghany, Allegheny ˌæl ɪ ˈɡeɪn i -ə-, -ˈɡen-
allegianc|e ə ˈliːdʒ ən's ~es ɪz əz
allegorical ˌæl ə ˈɡɒr ɪk ³l ◄ ˌ-ɪ- ‖ -ˈɡɔːr- -ˈɡɑːr-
  ~ly i
allegor|y ˈæl əɡ ər ˌi ‖ ˈ-ɪɡ- ‖ -ə ɡɔːr ˌi -ɡoʊr i
  ~ies iz ~ist/s ɪst/s §əst/s
allegretto ˌæl ə ˈɡret əʊ -ɪ- ‖ -ˈɡret̬ oʊ ~s z
Allegri ə ˈleɪɡ riː -ˈleɡ-, -ri
allegro ə ˈleɡ rəʊ -ˈleɪɡ- ‖ -roʊ ~s z
allele ə ˈliː³l -s z
all-electric ˌɔːl ə ˈlek trɪk ◄ -ɪ- ‖ ˌɑːl-
allelic ə ˈliːl ɪk
allelomorph ə ˈliːl əʊ mɔːf ‖ -ə mɔːrf ~s s
alleluia ˌæl ə ˈluː jə ◄ -ɪ-, -eɪ- —In hymns also
  occasionally æ ˌleɪ luː ˈjɑː (where final stress is
  called for) ~s z
allemande ˈæl ə mænd -ɪ-, -mɑːnd ‖ -mæn,
  -mɑːnd, ˌ· ·ˈ· —Fr [al mɑ̃ːd] ~s z
all-embracing ˌɔːl ɪm ˈbreɪs ɪŋ ◄ -əm-, -em-
  ‖ ˌɑːl-
Allen ˈæl ən -ɪn
Allenby ˈæl ən bi →-əm-
Allendale ˈæl ən deɪ³l -ɪn-
Allende aɪ ˈend i -ˈjend-, -eɪ ‖ ɑː ˈjend- ˌɑːl-
  —Sp [a ˈʎen de, -ˈjen-]
Allentown ˈæl ən taʊn
allergen ˈæl ə dʒen -ɜː-, -ədʒ ən ‖ -³r- ~s z
allergenic ˌæl ə ˈdʒen ɪk ◄ -ɜː- ‖ -³r-
allergic ə ˈlɜːdʒ ɪk ‖ ə ˈlɜːdʒ ɪk
allerg|y ˈæl ədʒ ˌi ‖ -³rdʒ ˌi ~ies iz ~ist/s
  ɪst/s §əst/s
Allerton ˈæl ət ən ‖ -³rt ³n —but some places of
  this name in Yks are ˈɒl-
allevi|ate ə ˈliːv i ˌeɪt ~ated eɪt ɪd -əd ‖ eɪt̬ əd
  ~ates eɪts ~ating eɪt ɪŋ ‖ eɪt̬ ɪŋ
alleviation ə ˌliːv i ˈeɪʃ ³n
alley ˈæl i ~s z
Alleyn ˈæl ɪn -ən
Alleyne (i) æ ˈleɪn, (ii) -ˈliːn, (iii) ˈæl ən -ɪn
alleyway ˈæl i weɪ ~s z
Allhallows ₍ᵢ₎ɔːl ˈhæl əʊz ‖ -oʊz ₍ᵢ₎ɑːl-
allheal ˈɔːl hiː³l ‖ ˈɑːl-
allianc|e ə ˈlaɪ ən's ~es ɪz əz
Allie ˈæl i
allied adj ˈæl aɪd ə ˈlaɪd
allies n ˈæl aɪz ə ˈlaɪz, v ə ˈlaɪz ˈæl aɪz
alligator ˈæl ɪ ɡeɪt ə ˌ-ə- ‖ -ɡeɪt̬ ³r ~s z
all-important ˌɔːl ɪm ˈpɔːt ³nt ◄ ‖ -ˈpɔːrt- ˌɑːl-

all-in ˌɔːl ˈɪn ◄ ‖ ˌɑː-
  ˌall-in ˈwrestling
all-inclusive ˌɔːl ɪn ˈklus ɪv ◄ →-ɪŋ-, §-ˈkluːz-
  ‖ ˌɑːl-
All-India ˌɔːl ˈɪnd i ə ◄ ‖ ˌɑːl-
  ˌAll- ˌIndia ˈRadio
Allingham ˈæl ɪŋ əm
all-in-one ˌɔːl ɪn ˈwʌn ◄ -ən-, §-ˈwɒn ‖ ˌɑːl-
Allinson ˈæl ɪn sən §-ən-
Allison ˈæl ɪs ən -əs-
allite|rate ə ˈlɪt ə ˌreɪt ‖ ə ˈlɪt̬ ə- ~rated
  reɪt ɪd -əd ‖ reɪt̬ əd ~rates reɪts ~rating
  reɪt ɪŋ ‖ reɪt̬ ɪŋ
alliteration ə ˌlɪt ə ˈreɪʃ ³n ‖ ə ˌlɪt̬- ~s z
alliterative ə ˈlɪt ³r ət ɪv -ə reɪt ɪv
  ‖ ə ˈlɪt̬ ³r ət̬ ɪv -ə reɪt̬ ɪv ~ly li ~ness nəs nɪs
allium ˈæl i əm
all-night ˌɔːl ˈnaɪt ◄ ‖ ˌɑːl-
  ˌall-night ˈparty
all-nighter ˌɔːl ˈnaɪt ə ◄ ‖ ˌɔːl ˈnaɪt̬ ³r ˌɑːl- ~s z
allo- comb. form
  with stress-neutral suffix ¦æl əʊ ‖ ¦æl ə -oʊ
  — allotrope ˈæl əʊ trəʊp ‖ -ə troʊp
  with stress-imposing suffix ə ˈlɒ+ æ ˈlɒ+
  ‖ -ˈlɑː+ — allotropy ə ˈlɒtr əp i æ-
  ‖ ə ˈlɑːtr-
'allo non-standard interjection ə ˈləʊ æ- ‖ -ˈloʊ
Alloa ˈæl əʊ ə ‖ -oʊ ə
allo|cate ˈæl ə ˌkeɪt ~cated keɪt ɪd -əd
  ‖ keɪt̬ əd ~cates keɪts ~cating keɪt ɪŋ
  ‖ keɪt̬ ɪŋ
allocation ˌæl ə ˈkeɪʃ ³n ~s z
allochthonous æ ˈlɒk θən əs ə- ‖ -ˈlɑːk- ~ly li
allocution ˌæl ə ˈkjuːʃ ³n ~s z
allograph ˈæl əʊ ɡrɑːf -ɡræf ‖ -ə ɡræf ~s s
allographic ˌæl əʊ ˈɡræf ɪk ◄ ‖ -ə- ~ally ³l i
allomorph ˈæl əʊ mɔːf ‖ -ə mɔːrf ~s s
allomorphic ˌæl əʊ ˈmɔːf ɪk ◄ ‖ -ə ˈmɔːrf-
  ~ally ³l i
allomorph|ism ˈæl əʊ mɔːf ˌɪz əm ‖ -ə mɔːrf-
  ~y i
allopathic ˌæl ə ˈpæθ ɪk ◄ ~ally ³l i
allopathy ə ˈlɒp əθ i æ- ‖ ə ˈlɑːp-
allophone ˈæl ə fəʊn ‖ -foʊn ~s z
allophonic ˌæl ə ˈfɒn ɪk ◄ ‖ -ˈfɑːn- ~ally ³l i
allophony æ ˈlɒf ən i ə-; ˈæl ə fəʊn i
  ‖ ə ˈlɑːf ən i ˈæl ə foʊn i
all-or-nothing ˌɔːl ɔː ˈnʌθ ɪŋ ◄ ‖ ˌɔːl ³r- ˌɑːl-,
  -ɔːr-
allot ə ˈlɒt ‖ ə ˈlɑːt allots ə ˈlɒts ‖ ə ˈlɑːts
  allotted ə ˈlɒt ɪd -əd ‖ ə ˈlɑːt̬ əd allotting
  ə ˈlɒt ɪŋ ‖ ə ˈlɑːt̬ ɪŋ
allotment ə ˈlɒt mənt ‖ ə ˈlɑːt- ~s s
allotone ˈæl əʊ təʊn ‖ -ə toʊn ~s z
allotrope ˈæl ə trəʊp ‖ -troʊp ~s s
Allott ˈæl ət
allott... —see allot
all-out ˌɔːl ˈaʊt ◄ ‖ ˌɑːl-
  ˌall-out ˈeffort
all-over ˈɔːl ˌəʊv ə ‖ -ˌoʊv ³r ˈɑːl-
allow ə ˈlaʊ allowed ə ˈlaʊd (= aloud)
  allowing ə ˈlaʊ ɪŋ allows ə ˈlaʊz
allowable ə ˈlaʊ əb ³l

allowanc|e ə 'laʊ‿ən's **~es** ɪz əz
Alloway 'æl ə weɪ
allowedly ə 'laʊ ɪd li -əd-
alloy *n* 'æl ɔɪ ə 'lɔɪ **~s** z
alloy *v* ə 'lɔɪ 'æl ɔɪ **~ed** d **~ing** ɪŋ **~s** z
all-party ˌɔːl 'pɑːt i ◄ ‖ -'pɑːɾt i ◄ ˌɑːl-
all-points ˌɔːl 'pɔɪnts ◄ ‖ ˌɑːl-
all-powerful ˌɔːl 'paʊ‿ə fᵊl ◄ -fʊl ‖ -'paʊ‿ᵊr- ˌɑːl-
all-purpose ˌɔːl 'pɜːp əs ◄ ‖ -'pɜːp- ˌɑːl-
all-round ˌɔːl 'raʊnd ◄ ‖ ˌɑːl-
   all-round 'athlete
all-rounder ˌɔːl 'raʊnd ə ‖ -ᵊr ˌɑːl- **~s** z
all-seater ˌɔːl 'siːt ə ◄ ‖ -'siːɾ ᵊr ˌɑːl-
Allsop, Allsopp 'ɔːl sɒp 'ɒl- ‖ 'ɔːl sɑːp 'ɑːl-
allsort 'ɔːl sɔːt ‖ 'ɔːl sɔːrt 'ɑːl- **~s** s
allspice 'ɔːl spaɪs ‖ 'ɑːl-
all-star *adj* ˌɔːl 'stɑː ◄ '· · ‖ -'stɑːr ˌɑːl-
   all-star 'cast
all-star *n* 'ɔːl stɑː ‖ -stɑːr 'ɑːl- **~s** z
Allston 'ɔːlst ən 'ɒlst- ‖ 'ɑːlst-
all-terrain ˌɔːl tə 'reɪn ◄ -te-, -tɪ- ‖ ˌɑːl-
all-time ˌɔːl 'taɪm ◄ ‖ ˌɑːl-
   all-time 'greats
allud|e ə 'luːd ə 'lʲuːd **~ed** ɪd əd **~es** z **~ing** ɪŋ
allure ə 'lʊə -'lʲʊə, -'ljɔː ‖ ə 'lʊᵊr **~d** d **~ment/s** mənt/s **~s** z **alluring/ly** ə 'lʊər ɪŋ /li -'lʲʊər-, -'lʲɔːr- ‖ ə 'lʊr ɪŋ /li
allusion ə 'luːʒ ᵊn -'lʲuːʒ- **~s** z
allusive ə 'luːs ɪv -'lʲuːs- ‖ -'luːz- **~ly** li **~ness** nəs nɪs
alluvi|al ə 'luːv i‿|əl -'lʲuːv- **~a** ə **~on** ən **~um** əm
all-weather ˌɔːl 'weð ə ◄ ‖ - ᵊr ◄ ˌɑːl-
   all-ˌweather 'garments
Allworthy 'ɔːl ˌwɜːð i ‖ 'ɔːl ˌwɜːð i 'ɑːl-
Ally *personal name* 'æl i

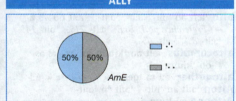

ally *v* ə 'laɪ 'æl aɪ **allied** ə 'laɪd 'æl aɪd —*but in* allied forces *usually* 'æl aɪd **allies** ə 'laɪz 'æl aɪz **allying** ə 'laɪ ɪŋ 'æl aɪ- — *Preference poll, AmE:* ·'· 50%, '· · 50%.
ally *n* 'æl aɪ ə 'laɪ **allies** 'æl aɪz ə 'laɪz
-ally əl i —*but* -ically *is usually reduced by* COMPRESSION *to* ɪk li
allyl 'æl aɪᵊl -ɪl, §-əl ‖ -əl
Alma 'ælm ə —*See also phrases with this word*
Alma Ata ˌæl ˌmɑː ə 'tɑː
almagest, A~ 'ælm ə dʒest
alma mater ˌælm ə 'mɑːt ə -'meɪt- ‖ -'mɑːt̬ ᵊr
almanac, almanack 'ɔːlm ə næk 'ɒlm-, 'ælm- ‖ 'ɑːlm-, 'ælm- **~s** s
almandine 'ælm ən diːn 'ɑːm-, 'ɑːlm-, -dɪn, -daɪn; ˌ·'· **~s** z

Alma-Tadema ˌælm ə 'tæd ɪm ə §-əm ə
Almaty æl 'mɑːt i -ə —*Russ* [al 'ma ti]
Almeida æl 'miːd ə
Almeria ˌælm ə 'riː ə —*Sp* Almería [al me 'ri a]
almight|y ˌͺ)ɔːl 'maɪt |i ‖ ɔːl 'maɪt̬ |i ˌɑːl- **~ily** ɪ li əl i ‖ ᵊl i
Almodóvar ˌælm ə 'dəʊv ɑː -ɒ- ‖ -'doʊv ɑːr —*Sp* [al mo 'ðo βar]

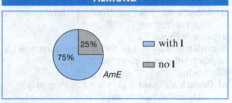

almond, A~ 'ɑːm ənd §'ɑːlm-, §'ælm-, §'ɒlm- ‖ 'ɑːlm- 'ælm-, 'ɑːm-, 'æm- **~s** z — *Preference poll, AmE:* with l 75%, no l 25%.
almond-eyed ˌɑːm ənd 'aɪd ◄ §ˌɑːlm-, ˌælm-, ˌɒlm- ‖ 'ɑːlm- 'ælm-, 'ɑːm-, 'æm-
Almondsbury 'ɑːm əndz bər i §'ɑːlm-, §'ælm-, §'ɒlm- ‖ -ˌber i —*in Avon locally also* 'eɪmz bər i
almoner 'ɑːm ən ə 'ælm-, §'ɒlm- ‖ 'ælm ən ᵊr 'ɑːm- **~s** z
almon|ry 'ɑːm ən| ri **~ries** riz
almost 'ɔːl məʊst 'ɒl-, ˌ·'· ◄ ‖ 'ɔːl moʊst 'ɑːl-
alms ɑːmz §ɑːlmz, §ɒlmz ‖ ɔːlmz
alms-|house 'ɑːmz |haʊs §'ɑːlmz-, §'ɒlmz- ‖ 'ɔːlmz- **~houses** haʊz ɪz -əz
Alne *(i)* ɔːn ‖ ɑːn, *(ii)* ɔːln ‖ ɑːln, *(iii)* æln
Alnmouth æln maʊθ →'ælm-, 'eɪᵊl-
Alnwick 'æn ɪk
aloe 'æl əʊ ‖ -oʊ **~s** z
aloft ə 'lɒft ‖ ə 'lɑːft -'lɔːft
aloha ə 'ləʊ hə -hɑː ‖ ə 'loʊ hɑː ɑː-
alone ə 'ləʊn ‖ ə 'loʊn
along ə 'lɒŋ ‖ ə 'lɔːŋ -'lɑːŋ
alongside ə ˌlɒŋ 'saɪd ◄ ·'· · ‖ ə 'lɔːŋ saɪd -'lɑːŋ-, ·ˌ·
Alonso ə 'lɒnz əʊ -'lɒnˢ- ‖ ə 'lɑːnz oʊ -'lɑːnˢ- —*Sp* [a 'lon so]
Alonzo ə 'lɒnz əʊ ‖ ə 'lɑːnz oʊ —*Sp* [a 'lon θo, -so]
aloof ə 'luːf **~ness** nəs nɪs
alopecia ˌæl ə 'piːʃ ə -'piːʃ i‿ə
aloud ə 'laʊd
Aloysius ˌæl əʊ 'ɪʃ əs -'ɪs i‿əs ‖ ˌæl ə 'wɪʃ əs
alp ælp **alps, Alps** ælps
alpaca æl 'pæk ə **~s** z
Alpen *tdmk* 'ælp ən
alpenglow 'ælp ən gləʊ →-əŋ- ‖ -gloʊ
alpenhorn 'ælp ən hɔːn ‖ -hɔːrn **~s** z
alpenstock 'ælp ən stɒk ‖ -stɑːk **~s** s
Alperton 'ælp ət ən ‖ -ᵊrt ᵊn
Alph ælf
alpha, Alpha 'ælf ə **~s** z
   ˌAlpha Cen'tauri sen 'tɔːr i ken-, -'taʊᵊr-;
   'alpha ˌparticle; 'alpha ˌrhythm

A

alphabet 'ælf ə bet -bɪt, §-bət **~s** s
alphabetic ˌælf ə 'bet ɪk ◄ ‖ -'bet̬- **~al** ᵊl **~ally**
ᵊl_i
alphabetis... —*see* alphabetiz...
alphabetization ˌælf ə bet aɪ 'zeɪʃ ᵊn ˌ·-bɪt-,
-ɪ'-- ‖ -bet̬ ə 'zeɪʃ-
alphabetiz|e 'ælf ə bet aɪz -bə taɪz, -bɪ taɪz
‖ -bə taɪz **~ed** d **~es** ɪz əz **~ing** ɪŋ
alphanumeric ˌælf ə nju 'mer ɪk ◄ §-nu'--
‖ -nu 'mer- -nju'-- **~al** ᵊl
Alphege 'ælf ɪdʒ
Alphonso æl 'fɒnz əʊ -'fɒn's- ‖ -'fɑːn's oʊ
—*Sp* [al 'fon so]
alpine 'ælp aɪn **~s** z
alpin|ism 'ælp ɪn |ˌɪz əm -ən- **~ist/s** ɪst/s əst/s
Alport 'ɔːl pɔːt ‖ -pɔːrt 'ɑːl-, -poʊrt
Alps ælps
al-Qaeda æl 'kaɪd ə əl-, -'keɪd ə, -'kɑː ɪd ə
—*Arabic* [al 'qɑː ʕɪ da]
al-Qaradawi əl ˌkær ə 'dɑː wi æl- ‖ ɑːl-, -'ker-
—*Arabic* [al qa ra 'dˤɑː wi]
already ɔːl 'red i ɒl-, ˌ·- ‖ ɑːl-
Alresford 'ɔːlz fəd ‖ -fᵊrd ɑːlz- —*but places of
this name are locally also* 'ɑːlz-, 'ɑːls-, 'eɪᵊls-
alright ˌɔːl 'raɪt ◄ ‖ ɔːl- ˌɑːl-
Alsace æl 'sæs -'zæs; 'ælz æs —*Fr* [al zas]
Alsager (i) ɔːl 'seɪdʒ ə ‖ -ᵊr ɑːl-, (ii) 'ɔːls ədʒ ə
-ɪdʒ- ‖ -ᵊr 'ɑːls-
Alsatian æl 'seɪʃ ᵊn ˌ·-, -'·i ən **~s** z
alsike 'æls ɪk -aɪk
also 'ɔːls əʊ 'ɒls- ‖ 'ɔːls oʊ 'ɑːls-
Alsop 'ɔːl sɒp 'ɒl- ‖ 'ɔːl sɑːp 'ɑːl-
also-ran 'ɔːls əʊ ræn 'ɒls-, ˌ·'· ‖ -oʊ- 'ɑːls-
Alstom 'ælst ɒm ‖ -ɑːm
Alston 'ɔːlst ən 'ɒlst- ‖ 'ɑːlst-
alt *musical term* ælt ‖ ɑːlt
Alt *name of river; key on computer keyboard* ɔːlt
ɒlt ‖ ɑːlt
Altai ₍ᵢ₎ɑːl 'taɪ
Altaic æl 'teɪ ɪk
Altair 'ælt eə æl 'teə ‖ æl 'teᵊr -'tæᵊr, -'taɪᵊr,
'· ·; -'tɑː ᵊr
Altamira ˌælt ə 'mɪər ə ‖ ˌɑːlt ə 'mɪr ə —*Sp*
[al ta 'mi ɾa]
altar 'ɔːlt ə 'ɒlt- ‖ 'ɔːlt ᵊr 'ɑːlt- (= *alter*) **~s** z
'altar boy
Altarnun ˌɔːlt ə 'nʌn ˌɒlt- ‖ -ᵊr- ˌɑːlt-
altarpiec|e 'ɔːlt ə piːs 'ɒlt- ‖ -ᵊr- 'ɑːlt- **~es** ɪz
əz
Altavista *tdmk* ˌælt ə 'vɪst ə
altazimuth ælt 'æz ɪm əθ §-əm-
Altdorfer 'ælt dɔːf ə ‖ -dɔːrf ᵊr 'ɑːlt- —*Ger*
['ʔalt dɔʁf ɐ]
alter *v* 'ɔːlt ə 'ɒlt- ‖ 'ɔːlt ᵊr 'ɑːlt- **~ed** d
altering 'ɔːlt ᵊr ɪŋ 'ɒlt ‖ 'ɑːlt **~s** z —*See also
phrases with this word*
alteration ˌɔːlt ə 'reɪʃ ᵊn 'ɒlt- ‖ ˌɑːlt- **~s** z
altercation ˌɔːlt ə 'keɪʃ ᵊn ˌɒlt- ‖ -ᵊr- ˌɑːlt- **~s** z
alter ego ˌælt ər 'iːg əʊ ˌɔːlt-, ɒlt-, -'eg-
‖ ˌɑːlt ᵊr 'iːg oʊ ɔːlt- **~s** z
alternant ɔːl 'tɜːn ənt ɒl- ‖ ɔːl 'tɜːn ᵊrn ənt ɑːlt-
~s s

alternate *adj, n* ɔːl 'tɜːn ət ɒl-, -ɪt ‖ 'ɔːlt ᵊrn ət
'ɑːlt- (*) **~ly** li **~s** s
alter|nate *v* 'ɔːlt ə |neɪt 'ɒlt- ‖ -ᵊr- 'ɑːlt-
~nated neɪt ɪd -əd ‖ neɪt̬ əd **~nates** neɪts
~nating neɪt ɪŋ ‖ neɪt̬ ɪŋ
ˌalternating 'current
alternation ˌɔːlt ə 'neɪʃ ᵊn ˌɒlt- ‖ -ᵊr- ˌɑːlt- **~s**
z
alternative ɔːl 'tɜːn ət ɪv ɒl- ‖ ɔːl 'tɜːn ət̬ ɪv
ɑːl-, æl- **~ly** li **~s** z
alternator 'ɔːlt ə neɪt ə 'ɒlt- ‖ 'ɔːlt ᵊr neɪt̬ ᵊr
'ɑːlt-, 'ælt- **~s** z
althaea, althea *'hollyhock'* æl 'θiːr ə **~s** z
Althea *personal name* 'ælᵊθ i ə
Althorp (i) 'ɔːl θɔːp ‖ -θɔːrp 'ɑːl-, (ii) 'æl-
—*but the place in Northants is locally also*
'ɔːltr əp, *as is Viscount A~*
although ɔːl 'ðəʊ ɒl-, ˌ·-, §-'θəʊ ‖ ɔːl 'ðoʊ ɑːl-
Althusser ˌælt u 'seə ‖ ˌɑːlt u: 'seᵊr —*Fr*
[al ty sɛːʁ]
altimeter 'ælt ɪ ˌmiːt ə 'ɔːlt-, 'ɒlt-, -ə-;
æl 'tɪm ɪt ə, -ət- ‖ æl 'tɪm ət̬ ᵊr 'ælt ə ˌmiːt̬ ᵊr
~s z
Altiplano ˌælt ɪ 'plɑːn əʊ ‖ -oʊ ˌɑːlt- —*Sp*
[al ti 'pla no]
altissimo æl 'tɪs ɪ məʊ -ə- ‖ -moʊ ɑːl-
altitude 'ælt ɪ tjuːd 'ɔːlt-, 'ɒlt-, -ə-, →-tʃuːd
‖ -tuːd -tjuːd **~s** z
Altman 'ɔːlt mən ‖ 'ɑːlt-

ALTO

7% — 8%
71% 14%
BrE

☐ 'ælt-
☐ 'ɒlt-
☐ 'ɔːlt-
☐ 'ɑːlt-

alto 'ælt əʊ 'ɒlt-, 'ɔːlt-, 'ɑːlt- ‖ 'ælt oʊ **~s** z
— *Preference poll, BrE:* 'ælt- 71%, 'ɒlt- 14%,
'ɔːlt- 8%, 'ɑːlt- 7%.
altocumulus ˌælt əʊ 'kjuːm jʊl əs -jəl əs
‖ -oʊ 'kjuːm jəl-
altogether ˌɔːlt ə 'geð ə ◄ '· · · · ‖ -ᵊr ◄ ˌɑːl-
Alton 'ɔːlt ən 'ɒlt- ‖ 'ɔːlt ᵊn 'ɑːlt-
Altoona æl 'tuːn ə
alto-relievo ˌælt əʊ rɪ 'liː vəʊ -rə'--
‖ -oʊ rɪ 'liːv oʊ ˌɑːlt-
altostratus ˌælt əʊ 'streɪt əs -'strɑːt-
‖ -oʊ 'streɪt̬ əs -'stræt̬-
altricial æl 'trɪʃ ᵊl
Altrincham 'ɔːltr ɪŋ əm 'ɒltr- ‖ 'ɑːltr-
altruism 'æltr u ˌɪz əm
altruist 'æltr u ɪst §-əst **~s** s
altruistic ˌæltr u 'ɪst ɪk ◄ **~ally** ᵊl_i
alum 'æl əm
alumina ə 'luːm ɪn ə -'ljuːm-
aluminium ˌæl ə 'mɪn i̯əm ◄ ˌ·u-, ˌˌju-, ˌˌjə-
aluminous ə 'luːm ɪn əs -'ljuːm-, -ən-
aluminum ə 'luːm ɪn əm -'ljuːm-, -ən-
alum|na ə 'lʌm |nə **~nae** niː **~ni** naɪ **~nus** nəs
Alun 'æl ɪn —*Welsh* ['a lin, -lin]

Alva 'ælv ə

Alvar 'ælv ɑː -ə ‖ -ɑːr -ᵊr

Alvarez *(i)* æl 'vɑːr ez, *(ii)* 'ælv ə rez —*Sp* Álvarez ['al βa reθ]

alveolar ˌælv i 'əʊl ə ◂ æl 'viːl ə, 'ælv i əl ə ‖ æl 'viː əl ᵊr ~s z

alveolaris... —*see* **alveolariz...**

alveolarity ˌælv i ə 'lær ət i æl ˌviː ə-, -ɪt i ‖ æl ˌviː ə 'lær əɟ i -'ler-

alveolarization ˌælv i ˌəʊl ᵊr aɪ 'zeɪʃ ᵊn æl ˌviː əl-, ˌælv i əl-, -ɪ'-- ‖ æl ˌviː əl ᵊr ə-

alveoriz|e ˌælv i 'əʊl ə raɪz æl 'viːəl-, 'ælv i əl- ‖ æl 'viː əl ə raɪz **~ed** d **~es** ɪz əz **~ing** ɪŋ

alveole 'ælv i əʊl →-ɒʊl **|-oʊl ~s** z

alveol|us ˌælv i 'əʊl |əs æl 'viːᵊl |əs, 'ælv i əl |əs ‖ æl 'viː əl- **~i** aɪ iː

Alvey 'ælv i

Alvin 'ælv ɪn §-ən

Alvis 'ælv ɪs §-əs

always 'ɔːl weɪz §'ɒl-, -wɪz, -wəz ‖ 'ɑːl-

Alwyn *(i)* 'ɔːl wɪn ‖ 'ɑːl-, *(ii)* 'æl-

Alyn 'æl ɪn -ən

Alyson 'æl ɪs ən -əs-

alyssum 'æl ɪs əm -əs- ‖ ə 'lɪs əm

Alzheimer 'ælts haɪm ə -'ælz- ‖ 'ɑːlts haɪm ᵊr —*Ger* ['ʔalts haɪm ɐ] **~'s** z

   'Alzheimer's di‚sease

am *from* be, *strong form* æm, *weak form* əm —*see* I'm, 'm

AM, am, a.m. *'amplitude modulation'; 'ante meridiem'* ˌeɪ 'em ◂

AMA ˌeɪ em 'eɪ

Amadeus ˌæm ə 'deɪ əs ‖ ˌɑːm ə 'deɪ ʊs -əs

amadou 'æm ə duː

amah 'ɑːm ə 'æm-, -ɑː- **~s** z

Amahl 'æm ɑːl ‖ ə 'mɑːl

Amalekite ə 'mæl ə kaɪt ‖ 'æm ə lek aɪt, ·'·'·· **~s** s

Amalfi ə 'mælf i ‖ ə 'mɑːlf i —*It* [a 'mal fi]

amalgam ə 'mælg əm **~s** z

amalga|mate ə 'mælg ə |meɪt **~mated** meɪt ɪd -əd ‖ meɪt əd **~mates** meɪts **~mating** meɪt ɪŋ ‖ meɪt ɪŋ

amalgamation ə ˌmælg ə 'meɪʃ ᵊn **~s** z

Amalthea ˌæm ᵊl 'θiː ə

Amanda ə 'mænd ə

amanita ˌæm ə 'naɪt ə -'niːt- ‖ -'naɪɟ ə -'niːɟ ə **~s** z

Amanpour ˌæm ən 'pʊə ‖ -pʊᵊr

amanuens|is ə ˌmæn ju 'enᵗs |ɪs §-əs **~es** iːz

amaranth 'æm ə rænᵗθ **~s** s

amaranthine ˌæm ə 'rænᵗθ aɪn ◂ -ᵊn ◂ -aɪn

amarett|o ˌæm ə 'ret| əʊ ‖ -'reɟ| oʊ **~i** iː

Amarillo ˌæm ə 'rɪl əʊ ‖ -oʊ

amaryllis, A~ ˌæm ə 'rɪl ɪs §-əs **~es** ɪz əz

amass ə 'mæs **amassed** ə 'mæst **amasses** ə 'mæs ɪz -əz **amassing** ə 'mæs ɪŋ

amassment ə 'mæs mənt

amateur 'æm ət ə 'æm ə tʃʊə, -tʃə, -tjʊə; ˌæm ə 'tɜː ◂ ‖ 'æm ə tʃʊr -əɟ ᵊr, -ə tjur **~s** z

amateurish 'æm ət ər ɪʃ -ətʃ ər-, -ə tʊər-; ˌæm ə 'tjʊər ɪʃ ◂, -'tɜːr- ‖ ˌæm ə 'tʊr ◂ -'tʃʊr-, -'tɜː-, -'tjʊər- **~ly** li **~ness** nəs nɪs

amateurism 'æm ət ər ˌɪz əm '-ətʃ-, -ə tɜːr-, -ə tʊər-, -ə tjʊər- ‖ 'æm ə tʃʊr- -əɟ ᵊr-, -ə tjʊr-

Amati ə 'mɑːt i æ- —*It* [a 'ma: ti]

amatol 'æm ə tɒl ‖ -tɑːl -tɔːl, -toʊl

amatory 'æm ət ᵊr i ‖ -ə tɔːr i -toʊr i

amaurosis ˌæm ɔː 'rəʊs ɪs §-əs ‖ -'roʊs əs -ɑː-

amaze ə 'meɪz **amazed** ə 'meɪzd **amazes** ə 'meɪz ɪz -əz **amazing** ə 'meɪz ɪŋ

amazed|ly ə 'meɪz ɪd| li -'-əd- **~ness** nəs nɪs

amazement ə 'meɪz mənt

amazing ə 'meɪz ɪŋ **~ly** li

amazon, Amazon 'æm əz ən ‖ -ə zɑːn -əz ən **~s** z

Amazonia ˌæm ə 'zəʊn i ə ‖ -'zoʊn-

amazonian, A~ ˌæm ə 'zəʊn i ən ◂ ‖ -'zoʊn- **~s** z

Amazulu ˌæm ə 'zuːl uː

ambassador æm 'bæs əd ə -ɪd- ‖ -ᵊr **~s** z

ambassadorial æm ˌbæs ə 'dɔːr i əl ◂ ˌ·-, -ɪ'-- ‖ -'dour-

ambassadorship æm 'bæs əd ə ʃɪp -'-ɪd- ‖ -ᵊr ʃɪp **~s** s

ambassadress æm 'bæs ə dres -ədr ɪs, -əs; ˌ·ə 'dres ‖ -ədr əs **~es** ɪz əz

amber, Amber 'æm bə ‖ -bᵊr

ambergris 'æm bə griːs -griː, -grɪs ‖ -grɪs -griːs

ambi- *comb. form* ¦æm bi-

Ambi *tdmk* 'æm bi

ambiance 'æm bi‚ənᵗs 'ɒm-, -ɒnᵗs, -ɒ̃s ‖ ˌɑːm bi 'ɑːnᵗs —*Fr* [ɑ̃ bjɑ̃:s]

ambidexterity ˌæm bi dek 'ster ət i -ɪt i ‖ -əɟ i

ambidextrous ˌæm bi 'deks trəs ◂ **~ly** li

ambience 'æm bi‚ənᵗs 'ɒm-, -ɒnᵗs, -ɒ̃s ‖ ˌɑːm bi 'ɑːnᵗs —*Fr* ambiance [ɑ̃ bjɑ̃:s]

ambient 'æm bi‚ənt

ambiguit|y ˌæm bi 'gjuː ət |i ˌ·bə-, -ɪt i ‖ əɟ |i **~ies** iz

ambiguous æm 'bɪg ju‚əs **~ly** li **~ness** nəs nɪs

ambisyllabic ˌæm bi sɪ 'læb ɪk ◂ -sə-

ambisyllabicity ˌæm bi ˌsɪl ə 'bɪs ət i -ɪt i ‖ -əɟ i

ambit 'æm bɪt -bət **~s** s

ambition æm 'bɪʃ ᵊn **~s** z

ambitious æm 'bɪʃ əs **~ly** li **~ness** nəs nɪs

ambivalence æm 'bɪv əl ənᵗs ˌæm bi 'veɪl ənᵗs

ambivalent æm 'bɪv əl ənt ˌæm bi 'veɪl ənt ◂ **~ly** li

amble 'æm bᵊl **ambled** 'æm bᵊld **ambles** 'æm bᵊlz **ambling** 'æm bᵊl ɪŋ

Ambler 'æm blə ‖ 'æm blᵊr

Ambleside 'æm bᵊl saɪd

amblyopia ˌæm bli 'əʊp i ə ‖ -'oʊp-

ambo, Ambo 'æm bəʊ ‖ -boʊ

Amboina, a~ æm 'bɔɪn ə

Amboinese ˌæm bɔɪ 'niːz ◂ ‖ -'niːs ◂

amboyna æm 'bɔɪn ə

Ambridge 'æm brɪdʒ

Ambrose 'æm brəʊz -brəʊs ‖ -broʊz

A

ambrosi|a æm ˈbrəʊz i̯ |ə ˑˈbrəʊʒ |ə ‖ æm ˈbrəʊʒ |ə **~al** əl **~an** ən

ambsace ˈeɪmz eɪs ˈæmz-

ambulac|rum ˌæm bju ˈleɪk |rəm -ˈlæk- ‖ -bjə- **~ra** rə

ambulanc|e ˈæm bjəl ənˈs -bjʊl-, §-bəl- **~es** ɪz əz

ambulance|man ˈæm bjəl ənˈs |mæn ˑ-bjʊl-, §ˑ-bəl- **~men** men **~woman** ˌwʊm ən **~women** ˌwɪm ɪn §-ən

ambulant ˈæm bjəl ənt -bjʊl-

ambu|late ˈæm bju |leɪt -bjə- ‖ -bjə- **~lated** leɪt ɪd -əd ‖ leɪţ əd **~lates** leɪts **~lating** leɪt ɪŋ ‖ leɪţ ɪŋ

ambulation ˌæm bju ˈleɪʃ ᵊn -bjə- ‖ -bjə- **~s** z

ambulator|y ˌæm bju ˈleɪt ər |i ◄ ˑ-bjə-, ˑˑ-lət̬ ər i ‖ ˈæm bjəl ə tɔːr |i -toʊr i **~ies** iz

ambuscad|e ˌæm bə ˈskeɪd ‖ ˈæm bə skeɪd **~ed** ɪd əd **~es** z **~ing** ɪŋ

ambush ˈæm bʊʃ **~ed** t **~es** ɪz əz **~ing** ɪŋ

ambystoma æm ˈbɪst əm ə **~s** z

Amdahl tdmk ˈæm dɑːl

ameb|a ə ˈmiːb |ə **~ae** iː **~as** əz

amebiasis ˌæm iː ˈbar̯ əs ɪs §-əs

amebic ə ˈmiːb ɪk

ameboid ə ˈmiːb ɔɪd

AMEC ˈæm ek

Ameche ə ˈmiːtʃ i

Amelia ə ˈmiːl i̯ ə

amelio|rate ə ˈmiːl i̯ə |reɪt **~rated** reɪt ɪd -əd ‖ reɪţ əd **~rates** reɪts **~rating** reɪt ɪŋ ‖ reɪţ ɪŋ

amelioration ə ˌmiːl i̯ə ˈreɪʒ ᵊn **~s** z

ameliorative ə ˈmiːl i̯ə reɪt ɪv -rət ɪv ‖ -reɪţ ɪv

ameliorator ə ˈmiːl i̯ə reɪt ə ‖ -reɪţ ᵊr **~s** z

amen ˌɑː ˈmen ◄ ˌeɪ- —Although ˌeɪ- is the usual form among Protestants in Britain, ˌeɪ- is preferred by Roman Catholics and also in non-religious contexts, as in ˌAmen ˈCorner. In AmE, ˌeɪ- predominates in speech, but ˌɑː- is preferred in singing. **~s** z

amenability ə ˌmiːn ə ˈbɪl ət i -ˌmen-, -ɪt i ‖ -əţ i

amenab|le ə ˈmiːn əb |ᵊl -ˈmen- **~ly** li

amend ə ˈmend **amended** ə ˈmend ɪd -əd **amending** ə ˈmend ɪŋ **amends** ə ˈmendz

amendment ə ˈmend mənt →-ˈmem- **~s** s

Amenhotep ˌɑːm ən ˈhəʊt ep ‖ -ˈhoʊt-

amenit|y ə ˈmiːn ət |i -ˈmen-, -ɪt- ‖ -əţ |i **~ies** iz

amenorrhea, amenorrhoea ₍ˌ₎eɪ ˌmen ə ˈriː̯ ə ˌæ- ‖ ˌɑː-

ament ˈmentally deficient person' ˈeɪ ment -mənt; æ ˈment **~s** s

ament ˈcatkin' ˈæm ənt ˈeɪm- **~s** s

amentia ₍ˌ₎eɪ ˈmenᵗʃ ə ₍ˌ₎æ-, -ˈmenᵗʃ i̯ə

America ə ˈmer ɪk ə -ək- —also sometimes △-ˈmər-; so also in derivatives **~s**, **~ˈs** z

American ə ˈmer ɪk ən -ək- **~s** z A͵merican ˈEnglish; A͵merican Exˈpress tdmk; A͵merican ˈIndian

Americana ə ˌmer ɪ ˈkɑːn ə -ˌə- ‖ -ˈkæn-

americanis... —see **americaniz...**

Americanism ə ˈmer ɪk ən ˌɪz əm -ˈək- **~s** z

americanization ə ˌmer ɪk ən aɪ ˈzeɪʃ ᵊn -ˌək-, -ɪˑ- ‖ -ə ˈzeɪʃ-

americaniz|e ə ˈmer ɪk ə naɪz -ˈək- **~ed** d **~es** ɪz əz **~ing** ɪŋ

americium ˌæm ə ˈrɪs i̯ əm -ˈrɪʃ-

Amerind ˈæm ə rɪnd **~s** z

Amerindian ˌæm ə ˈrɪnd i̯ ən ◄ **~s** z

Amersham ˈæm əʃ əm ‖ -ᵊrʃ-

Amery ˈeɪm ər i

Ames eɪmz

Amesbury ˈeɪmz bər̯ i ‖ -ˌber i

Ameslan ˈæm ə slæn ˈæm slæn

amethyst ˈæm əθ ɪst -ɪθ-, §-əst **~s** s

amethystine ˌæm ə ˈθɪst aɪn ◄ -ɪ- ‖ -ən -aɪn

Amex tdmk ˈæm eks

Amharic æm ˈhær ɪk əm- ‖ ɑːm ˈhɑːr-

Amherst (i) ˈæm əst ‖ -ᵊrst, (ii) -hɜːst -hɜːrst — (i) is the traditional form in both BrE and AmE, and hence appropriate for Baron A~, the 18th-century general, and for the place in MA.

Amhrán na bhFiann ˌær ɔːn næ ˈviːn —Irish [ˌəu r̯ˠaːn̯ˠ n̯ˠə ˈvʲiːn̯ˠ]

amiability ˌeɪm i̯ ə ˈbɪl ət i -ɪt i ‖ -əţ i

amiab|le ˈeɪm i̯ əb |ᵊl **~leness** ᵊl nəs nɪs **~ly** li

amicability ˌæm ɪk ə ˈbɪl ət i ˌ-ək-, -ɪt i ‖ -əţ i

amicab|le ˈæm ɪk əb |ᵊl ˑ-ək-; ə ˈmɪk- **~leness** ᵊl nəs nɪs **~ly** li

amic|e ˈæm ɪs §-əs **~es** ɪz əz

Amice ˈeɪm ɪs §-əs

amicus, A~ ə ˈmaɪk əs æ-, -ˈmiːk-, -ʊs; ˌæm ɪk- —The trade union is ˈ···

a͵micus ˈcuriae ˈkjʊər i iː -aɪ ‖ ˈkjʊr- ˈkʊr-

amid ə ˈmɪd

amide ˈæm aɪd ˈeɪm- ‖ -əd **~s** z

Amidol tdmk ˈæm ɪ dɒl §-ə- ‖ -dɑːl -dɔːl, -doʊl

amidships ə ˈmɪd ʃɪps

amidst ə ˈmɪdst -ˈmɪtst

Amiens ˈæm i̯ n̩ -æ̃, -ənz —formerly, and as an English-language name, and for the Dublin street, ˈeɪm i̯ ənz; in Shakespeare ˈæm i̯ ənz —Fr [a mjæ̃]

Amies ˈeɪm iz

Amiga tdmk ə ˈmiːg ə

amigo ə ˈmiːg əʊ æ- ‖ -oʊ ɑː- —Sp [a ˈmi ɣo]

Amin ₍ˌ₎ɑː ˈmiːn ₍ˌ₎æ-

amine ə ˈmiːn -ɪn, §-ən; ə ˈmiːn ‖ ə ˈmiːn ˈæm iːn, -ən **~s** z

amino ə ˈmiːn əʊ -ˈmaɪn-; ˈæm ɪn əʊ, -ən- ‖ -oʊ a͵mino ˈacid

amir ə ˈmɪə ‖ ə ˈmɪˑr **~s** z

Amis ˈeɪm ɪs §-əs

Amish ˈɑːm ɪʃ ˈæm-

amiss ə ˈmɪs

Amistad ˈæm ɪ stæd -ə- ‖ ˈɑːm ə stɑːd

amit|y ˈæm ət |i -ɪt i ‖ -əţ |i **~ies** iz

Amlwch ˈæm lʊk -lux —Welsh [ˈam lʊχ]

Amman place in Jordan ə ˈmɑːn æ-, -ˈmæn, ‖ ˈɑːm ɑːn —Arabic [ʕam ˈmaːn]

Amman river in Wales ˈæm ən

ammeter ˈæm iːt ə -ɪt-, -ˌmiːt- ‖ -iːţ ᵊr **~s** z

ammo ˈæm əʊ ‖ -oʊ

Ammon ˈæm ən

ammonia ə ˈməʊn i ə ‖ ə ˈmoʊn-
ammoniac ə ˈməʊn i æk ‖ ə ˈmoʊn-
ammoniated ə ˈməʊn i eɪt ɪd -əd
　‖ ə ˈmoʊn i eɪṭ əd
ammonite, A~ ˈæm ə naɪt ~s s
ammonium ə ˈməʊn i əm ‖ ə ˈmoʊn-
ammunition ˌæm ju ˈnɪʃ ᵊn -jə- ‖ -jə-
amnesia æm ˈniːz i ə -ˈniːʒ ə ‖ -ˈniːʒ ə
amnesiac æm ˈniːz i æk ‖ -ˈniːʒ- ~s s
amnesic æm ˈniːz ɪk -ˈniːs- ~s s
amnest|y, A~ ˈæm nəst |i -nɪst- ~ies iz
　ˌAmnesty ˌInterˈnational
amniocentesis ˌæm ni ˌəʊ sen ˈtiːs ɪs §-əs
　‖ ˌæm ni oʊ-
amnion ˈæm ni ən -ɒn ‖ -ɑːn ən ~s z
amniote ˈæm ni əʊt ‖ -oʊt ~s s
amniotic ˌæm ni ˈɒt ɪk ◄ ‖ -ˈɑːṭ ɪk
Amoco *tdmk* ˈæm ə kəʊ ‖ -koʊ
amoeb|a ə ˈmiːb |ə ~ae iː ~as əz
amoebiasis ˌæm iː ˈbaɪ əs ɪs §-əs
amoebic ə ˈmiːb ɪk
amoeboid ə ˈmiːb ɔɪd
amok ə ˈmɒk ə ˈmʌk, ˈɑːm əʊ ‖ ə ˈmʌk -ˈmɑːk
among ə ˈmʌŋ §-ˈmɒŋ
amongst ə ˈmʌŋkst §-ˈmɒŋkst
amontillado ˌæm ɒnt ɪ ˈlɑːd əʊ əˌmɒnt-, -əˈ--
　‖ ə ˌmɑːnt ə ˈlɑːd oʊ —*Sp* [a mon ti ˈʎa ðo,
　-ˈja-] ~s z
amoral ˌeɪ ˈmɒr əl ◄ ˌæ- ‖ -ˈmɔːr- -ˈmɑːr- ~ly i
amorality ˌeɪ mɒ ˈræl ət i ˌæ-, -ˌmɔ-, -ɪt i
　‖ ˌeɪ mə ˈræl əṭ i -ˌmɔː-
amorett|o, A~ ˌæm ə ˈret |əʊ ‖ -ˈreṭ |oʊ ˌɑːm-
　~i iː
Amorite ˈæm ə raɪt ~s s
amoroso ˌæm ə ˈrəʊs əʊ ‖ ˌɑːm ə ˈroʊs oʊ
amorous ˈæm ər_əs ~ly li ~ness nəs nɪs
amorphous ə ˈmɔːf əs ‖ ə ˈmɔːrf- ~ly li ~ness
　nəs nɪs
amortis... —*see* **amortiz...**
amortizable ə ˈmɔːt aɪz əb ᵊl ‖ ˈæm ᵊr taɪz-
　ə ˈmɔːr-
amortization ə ˌmɔːt aɪ ˈzeɪʃ ᵊn -ɪ-
　‖ ˌæm ᵊrṭ ə- ə ˌmɔːrṭ ə-
amortiz|e ə ˈmɔːt aɪz ‖ ˈæm ᵊr taɪz ə ˈmɔːr-
　~ed d ~ement/s mənt/s ~es ɪz əz ~ing ɪŋ
Amory ˈeɪm ər i
Amos ˈeɪm ɒs ‖ -əs
amount amounted ə ˈmaʊnt amounted ə ˈmaʊnt ɪd -əd
　‖ ə ˈmaʊnṭəd **amounting** ə ˈmaʊnt ɪŋ
　‖ ə ˈmaʊnṭ ɪŋ **amounts** ə ˈmaʊnts
amour ə ˈmʊə, ˌæ- ‖ ə ˈmʊᵊr ɑː- ~s z
amour-propre ˌæm ʊə ˈprɒp rə
　‖ ˌɑːm ʊr ˈproʊp rə ˌæm- —*Fr*
　[a muʁ pʁɔpʁ]
amoxicillin ə ˌmɒks ɪ ˈsɪl ɪn æ- ‖ -ˌmɑːks-
Amoy ə ˈmɔɪ ɑː-, æ- —*Chinese* Xiàmén
　[⁴ɕja ²mən]
amp æmp **amps** æmps
ampelopsis ˌæmp ɪ ˈlɒps ɪs -ə-, §-əs ‖ -ˈlɑːps-
amperag|e ˈæmp ər_ɪdʒ -ɪər- ‖ -ɪr- ~es ɪz əz
ampere, ampère, A~ ˈæmp eə ‖ -ɪr -er —*Fr*
　[ɑ̃ pɛːʁ] ~s z
ampersand ˈæmp ə sænd ‖ -ᵊr- ~s z

Ampex *tdmk* ˈæmp eks
amphetamine æm ˈfet ə miːn -mɪn, §-mən
　‖ -ˈfeṭ- ~s z
amphi- *comb. form*
　with stress-neutral suffix ˌæmᵖf i —
　　amphipathic ˌæmᵖf i ˈpæθ ɪk ◄
　with stress-imposing suffix æm ˈfɪ+ —
　　amphitropous æm ˈfɪtr əp əs
amphibian ⑴æm ˈfɪb i_ən ~s z
amphibious ⑴æm ˈfɪb i_əs ~ly li ~ness nəs
　nɪs
amphibole *mineral* ˈæmᵖf ɪ bəʊl §-ə-, →-bɒʊl
　‖ -boʊl ~s z
amphibolite æm ˈfɪb ə laɪt ~s s
amphibolog|y ˌæmᵖf i ˈbɒl ədʒ| i ‖ -ˈbɑːl-
　~ies iz
amphibrach ˈæmᵖf i bræk ~s s
amphictyonic, A~ æm ˌfɪkt i ˈɒn ɪk ◄ ‖ -ˈɑːn-
amphimacer æm ˈfɪm əs ə ‖ -ᵊr ~s z
amphisbaena ˌæmᵖf ɪs ˈbiːn ə §-əs- ~s z

57% ˈæmp-
43% ˈæmᵖf-
AmE

amphitheater, amphitheatre ˈæmᵖf i ˌθɪət ə
　§ˈ· ·θi ˌet ə ‖ ˈæmp ə ˌθiː əṭ ᵊr ˈæmᵖf- ~s z
　— *Preference poll, AmE:* ˈæmp- 57%, ˈæmᵖf-
　43%.
Amphitrite ˌæmᵖf i ˈtraɪt i ˈ· ·ˌ· · ‖ -ə ˈtraɪṭ i
Amphitryon æm ˈfɪtr i_ən
amph|ora ˈæmᵖf |ər ə ~orae ə riː ~oras ᵊr əz
ampicillin ˌæmp ɪ ˈsɪl ɪn -ə-, §-ən
ample ˈæmp ᵊl **ampler** ˈæm plə ‖ -plᵊr
　amplest ˈæm plɪst -pləst
Ampleforth ˈæmp ᵊl fɔːθ ‖ -fɔːrθ -foʊrθ
Amplex *tdmk* ˈæmp leks
amplexicaul æm ˈpleks ɪ kɔːl §-ə- ‖ -kɑːl
amplification ˌæmp lɪf ɪ ˈkeɪʃ ᵊn ˌ·ləf-, §-ə-
　~s z
ampli|fy ˈæmp lɪ |faɪ -lə- ~fied faɪd ~fier/s
　faɪ_ə/z ‖ faɪ_ᵊr/z ~fies faɪz ~fying faɪ ɪŋ
amplitude ˈæmp lɪ tjuːd -lə-, →-tʃuːd ‖ -tuːd
　-tjuːd ~s z
amply ˈæmp li
Ampney *(i)* ˈæmp ni, *(ii)* ˈæm ni
ampoule ˈæmp uːl -juːl ~s z
Ampthill ˈæmᵖt hɪl -ɪl
ampule ˈæmp juːl ~s z
ampull|a æm ˈpʊl |ə -ˈpʌl- ~ae iː ~as əz
ampu|tate ˈæmp ju |teɪt §-jə- ‖ -jə- ~tated
　teɪt ɪd -əd ‖ teɪṭ əd ~tates teɪts ~tating
　teɪt ɪŋ ‖ teɪṭ ɪŋ
amputation ˌæmp ju ˈteɪʃ ᵊn §-jə- ‖ -jə- ~s z
amputee ˌæmp ju ˈtiː §-jə- ‖ -jə- ~s z
Amritsar æm ˈrɪts ə əm-, -ɑː ‖ -ᵊr —*Hindi*
　[əm rɪṭ sər]
Amstel ˈæm stəl —*Dutch* [ˈɑm stəl]

Amsterdam 'æmᵖst ə dæm ˌ·ˑ·◄ ‖ -ᵊr- —*Dutch*
[ˌɑm stər 'dɑm]
Amstrad *tdmk* 'æm stræd **~s, ~'s** z
Amtrak *tdmk* 'æm træk
amuck ə 'mʌk
Amu Darya ˌɑːm uː 'dɑːr i ə ə ˌmuː-
amulet 'æm jʊl ət §-jəl-, -ɪt, -ju let ‖ -jəl- **~s** s
Amundsen 'ɑːm ənd sən 'æm-, -ʊnd- —*Norw*
['ɑː mun sən]
Amur ə 'mʊə 'æm ʊə ‖ ɑː 'mʊᵊr —*Russ*
[ʌ 'mur]
amuse ə 'mjuːz **amused** ə 'mjuːzd **amuses**
ə 'mjuːz ɪz -əz **amusing** ə 'mjuːz ɪŋ
amusement ə 'mjuːz mənt **~s** s
   a'musement ar,cade; a'musement park
amusing ə 'mjuːz ɪŋ **~ly** li **~ness** nəs nɪs
Amway *tdmk* 'æm weɪ
Amy 'eɪm i
Amyas 'eɪm i ˌəs
amyg|dala ə 'mɪg |dəl ə **~dalae** də liː
   ~daloid də lɔɪd
amygdaloid ə 'mɪgd ə lɔɪd
amyl 'æm ᵊl 'eɪm-, -aɪᵊl, -ɪl
   ˌamyl 'nitrite
amylase 'æm ɪ leɪz -ə-
amytal, A~ *tdmk* 'æm ɪ tæl -ə- ‖ -tɑːl -tɔːl
an *strong form* æn, *weak form* ən —*see also* **a**
an- (¦) æn, ən —*When it is a variant of* ad-,
   this prefix is usually ə (an'nul), *but* æ *if*
   stressed because of a suffix ('annotate). *As a*
   negative prefix, it is usually æn (ˌan'oxia),
   undergoing reduction to ən *only in a few*
   better-known words (a'nonymous).
A.N.Other ˌeɪ ˌen 'ʌð ə ‖ -ᵊr
ana 'ɑːn ə
ana- *comb. form*
   before stress-neutral suffix ¦æn ə
   — **Anabaptist** ˌæn ə 'bæpt ɪst §-əst
   before stress-imposing suffix ə 'næ+
   — **anadromous** ə 'nædr əm əs
Anabaptist ˌæn ə 'bæpt ɪst ◄ §-əst **~s** s
anabasis ə 'næb əs ɪs §-əs
anabatic ˌæn ə 'bæt ɪk ◄ ‖ -'bæt̬-
anabolic ˌæn ə 'bɒl ɪk ◄ ‖ -'bɑːl-
   ˌana,bolic 'steroid
anachronism ə 'næk rə ˌnɪz əm **~s** z
anachronistic ə ˌnæk rə 'nɪst ɪk ◄ **~ally** ᵊl i
Anacin *tdmk* 'æn ə sɪn
anacolutth|on ˌæn ək ə 'luːθ |ᵊn -'ljuːθ-, -|ɒn
   ‖ -|ɑːn **~a** ə **~ons** ᵊnz ɒnz ‖ ɑːnz
anaconda, A~ ˌæn ə 'kɒnd ə ‖ -'kɑːnd ə **~s** z
Anacreon ə 'næk ri ən -ɒn ‖ -ɑːn
anacrus|is ˌæn ə 'kruːs |ɪs §-əs **~es** iːz
anacrustic ˌæn ə 'krʌst ɪk ◄
Anadin *tdmk* 'æn ə dɪn
anaemia ə 'niːm i ə
anaemic ə 'niːm ɪk **~ally** ᵊl i
anaerobic ˌæn ə 'reɪb ɪk ◄ -eə- ‖ -'roʊb- -e-
   ~ally ᵊl i **~s** s
anaesthesia ˌæn əs 'θiːz i ə ˌ·iːs-, ˌ·ɪs-, -'θiːʒ ə
   ‖ -'θiːʒ ə
anaesthesiologist ˌæn əs ˌθiːz i 'ɒl ədʒ ɪst
   §-əst ‖ -'ɑːl- **~s** s

anaesthesiology ˌæn əs ˌθiːz i 'ɒl ədʒ i
   ‖ -'ɑːl-
anaesthetic ˌæn əs 'θet ɪk ◄ -iːs-, -ɪs- ‖ -'θet̬-
   ~s s
anaesthetis... —*see* **anaesthetiz...**
anaesthetist ə 'niːs θət ɪst æ-, -θɪt-, §-əst
   ‖ ə 'nes θət̬ əst *(*)* **~s** s
anaesthetization ə ˌniːs θət aɪ 'zeɪʃ ᵊn -ɪ'--
   ‖ ə ˌnes θət̬ ə-
anaesthetiz|e ə 'niːs θə taɪz -θɪ- ‖ ə 'nes- *(*)*
   ~ed d **~es** ɪz əz **~ing** ɪŋ
anaglyph 'æn ə glɪf **~s** s
anaglypta, A~ *tdmk* ˌæn ə 'glɪpt ə
anagram 'æn ə græm **~med** d **~ming** ɪŋ **~s** z
anagrammatic ˌæn ə grə 'mæt ɪk ◄ ‖ -'mæt̬-
   ~ally ᵊl i
Anaheim 'æn ə haɪm
Anais, Anaïs ˌæn aɪ 'iːs ◄ ə 'nɑɪ̯ əs
anal 'eɪn ᵊl **~ly** i
analect 'æn ə lekt -ᵊl ekt **~s** s
analecta ˌæn ə 'lekt ə
analemma ˌæn ə 'lem ə
analemmatic ˌæn ə le 'mæt ɪk ◄ ‖ -'mæt̬-
analeptic ˌæn ə 'lept ɪk ◄
analgesia ˌæn ᵊl 'dʒiːz i ə ˌ·æl-, -'dʒiːs-
   ‖ -'dʒiːʒ ə
analgesic ˌæn ᵊl 'dʒiːz ɪk ◄ -æl-, -'dʒiːs- **~s** s
analog 'æn ə lɒg -ᵊl ɒg ‖ 'æn ᵊl ɔːg -ɑːg **~s** z
analogical ˌæn ə 'lɒdʒ ɪk ᵊl ◄ -ᵊl 'ɒdʒ-
   ‖ -ᵊl 'ɑːdʒ- **~ly** i
analogis|e, analogiz|e ə 'næl ə dʒaɪz **~ed** d
   ~es ɪz əz **~ing** ɪŋ
analogous ə 'næl əg əs -ədʒ- **~ly** li
analogue 'æn ə lɒg -ᵊl ɒg ‖ 'æn ᵊl ɔːg -ɑːg **~s**
   z
analog|y ə 'næl ədʒ |i **~ies** iz
analphabetic ˌæn ælf ə 'bet ɪk ◄ ˌ·,-- ‖ -'bet̬-
anal-retentive ˌeɪn ᵊl rɪ 'tent ɪv -rə'--, §-riː'·
   ‖ -'tent̬-
analysable 'æn ə laɪz əb ᵊl →'æn ᵊl aɪz-;
   ˌ·ˑ·ˑ·
analysand ə 'næl ɪ sænd -ə- **~s** z
analys|e 'æn ə laɪz -ᵊl aɪz **~ed** d **~er/s** ə/z
   ‖ ᵊr/z **~es** v ɪz əz **~ing** ɪŋ
analysis ə 'næl əs ɪs -ɪs ɪs, §-əs **analyses** n
   ə 'næl ə siːz -ɪ-
analyst 'æn ᵊl ɪst §-əst **~s** s
analytic ˌæn ə 'lɪt ɪk ◄ -ᵊl 'ɪt- ‖ -ᵊl 'ɪt̬ ɪk ◄ **~al**
   ᵊl **~ally** ᵊl i
analyzable 'æn ə laɪz əb ᵊl →'æn ᵊl aɪz-;
   ˌ·ˑ·ˑ·
analyz|e 'æn ə laɪz -ᵊl aɪz **~ed** d **~er/s** ə/z
   ‖ ᵊr/z **~es** ɪz əz **~ing** ɪŋ
anamnesis ˌæn æm 'niːs ɪs §-əs
Anancy ə 'nænᵗs i
Ananda ə 'nænd ə -'nʌnd-
Ananias ˌæn ə 'naɪ̯ əs
anapaest, anapest 'æn ə piːst -pest ‖ -pest **~s**
   s
anapaestic, anapestic ˌæn ə 'piːst ɪk ◄ -'pest-
   ‖ -'pest-
anaphor 'æn ə fɔː -əf ə ‖ -fɔːr **~s** z
anaphora ə 'næf ər ə

A

anaphoric ˌæn ə ˈfɒr ɪk ◂ ‖ -ˈfɔːr- -ˈfɑːr- **~ally**
  əl i

anaphylactic ˌæn ə fɪ ˈlækt ɪk -ə fə- **~ally** əl i

anaphylaxis ˌæn ə fɪ ˈlæks ɪs -ə fə-, §-əs

anaptyctic ˌæn əp ˈtɪkt ɪk ◂ -æp-

anaptyxis ˌæn əp ˈtɪks ɪs -æp-, §-əs

anarch ˈæn ɑːk ‖ -ɑːrk **~s** s

anarchic æ ˈnɑːk ɪk ə- ‖ -ˈnɑːrk- **~al** əl **~ally**
  əl i

anarchism ˈæn ə ˌkɪz əm -ɑː- ‖ -ər- -ɑːr-

anarchist ˈæn ək ɪst -ɑːk-, §-əst ‖ -ərk- -ɑːrk- **~s**
s

anarchistic ˌæn ə ˈkɪst ɪk ◂ -ɑː- ‖ -ər- -ɑːr-

anarchy ˈæn ək i -ɑːk- ‖ -ərk i -ɑːrk-

anarthria æn ˈɑːθ ri ə ‖ -ˈɑːrθ-

anarthric æn ˈɑːθ rɪk ‖ -ˈɑːrθ-

Anastasia ˌæn ə ˈsteɪz i ə -ˈstɑːz- ‖ -ˈsteɪʒ ə
  -ˈstɑːʒ ə

anastigmat æn ˈæst ɪg mæt ən-; ˌæn ə ˈstɪg- **~s**
s

anastigmatic ˌæn ə stɪg ˈmæt ɪk ◂ æn ˌæst ɪg-,
  ən- ‖ -ˈmæt̬-

anastomos|e ə ˈnæst ə məʊz æ- -ˈmoʊz
  -moʊs **~ed** d **~es** ɪz əz **~ing** ɪŋ

anastomos|is ə ˌnæst ə ˈməʊs ǀɪs æ-, ˌæn əst-,
  §-əs ‖ -ˈmoʊs- **~es** iːz

anastrozole ə ˈnæs trə zəʊl →-zɒʊl ‖ -zoʊl

anathema ə ˈnæθ əm ə -ɪm- **~s** z

anathematis|e, anathematiz|e
  ə ˈnæθ əm ə taɪz -ˈɪm- **~ed** d **~es** ɪz əz **~ing**
  ɪŋ

Anatole ˈæn ə təʊl →-tɒʊl ‖ -toʊl —Fr
  [a na tɔl]

Anatoli|a ˌæn ə ˈtəʊl i ǀə ‖ -ˈtoʊl- **~an/s** ən/z

anatomical ˌæn ə ˈtɒm ɪk əl ◂ ‖ -ˈtɑːm- **~ly** i

anatomis|e ə ˈnæt ə maɪz ‖ ə ˈnæt̬- **~ed** d **~es**
  ɪz əz **~ing** ɪŋ

anatomist ə ˈnæt əm ɪst §-əst ‖ ə ˈnæt̬- **~s** s

anatomiz|e ə ˈnæt ə maɪz ‖ ə ˈnæt̬- **~ed** d **~es**
  ɪz əz **~ing** ɪŋ

anatom|y ə ˈnæt əm ǀi ‖ ə ˈnæt̬- **~ies** iz

Anaxagoras ˌæn æk ˈsæg ər əs -ə ræs

Anaximander æ ˌnæks ɪ ˈmænd ə ə-; ˌæn æks-
‖ -ər

ANC ˌeɪ en ˈsiː

-ance ənts —Words with this suffix are stressed
like words in -ant. Examples: conˈtrive,
conˈtrivance; reˈluctant, reˈluctance. Exception:
reˈconnaissance.

ancestor ˈænts est ə -ɪst-, -əst- ‖ -ər **~s** z

ancestral æn ˈses trəl **~ly** i

ancestress ˈænts es tres -ɪs-, -əs-, -trəs, -trɪs
‖ -trəs- **~es** ɪz əz

ances|try ˈænts es ǀtri -ɪs-, -əs- **~tries** triz

Anchises æn ˈkaɪs iːz →æŋ-

anchor ˈæŋk ə ‖ ˈæŋk ər **~ed** d **anchoring**
  ˈæŋk ər ɪŋ **~s** z

anchorag|e, A~ ˈæŋk ər ɪdʒ **~es** ɪz əz

anchoress ˈæŋk ər ɪs -əs, -ə res **~es** ɪz əz

anchorite ˈæŋk ə raɪt **~s** s

anchor|man ˈæŋk ə ǀmæn ‖ -ər- **~men** men
~person ˌpɜːs ən ‖ ˌpɜːs ən **~woman**
  ˌwʊm ən **~women** ˌwɪm ɪn §-ən

anchov|y ˈæntʃ əv ǀi æn ˈtʃəʊv ǀi
‖ ˈæn tʃoʊv ǀi ·ˈ· · **~ies** iz

ancien regime, ancien régime
  ˌɒnˈs i æn reɪ ˈʒiː m i ˌɑːnˈs-, ˌ· ·ɒn-; ɑːn ˌsjæn·ˈ·
‖ ˌɑːnˈs jæn ·ˈ· —Fr [ɑ̃ sjæ ʁe ʒim]

ancient ˈeɪntʃ ənt **~ness** nəs nɪs
  ˌAncient ˈGreek; ˌancient ˈmonument

ancillar|y æn ˈsɪl ər ǀi △-ˈsɪl i ˌər ǀi
‖ ˈænts ə ler ǀi (*) **~ies** iz

Ancoats ˈæŋ kəʊts ‖ -koʊts

Ancona æŋ ˈkəʊn ə ‖ -ˈkoʊn ə —It
  [aŋ ˈko: na]

Ancram ˈæŋk rəm

Ancren Riwle ˌæŋk ren ˈriː ʊl i ˌ·rɪn-, ˌ·rən-,
  -ə

-ancy ənts i —Words with this suffix are
stressed like words in -ant. Example: ˈhesitant,
ˈhesitancy

and strong form ænd, weak forms ənd, ən
  —The presence or absence of d in the weak
form is not sensitive to phonetic context: the
choice depends on the fact that the weak form
ənd is slightly more formal than ən. From ən,
regular processes of SYLLABIC
CONSONANT formation and
ASSIMILATION produce the phonetic
variants m, n, ŋ (all syllabic, though they can
lose their syllabicity by COMPRESSION
before a weak vowel) and əm, əŋ.
  and ˈso on

Andalusi|a ˌænd ə ˈluːs i ǀə -ˈluːz-, -lu ˈsiː ǀə
‖ -ˈluːʒ ǀə —Sp Andalucia [an da lu ˈθi a]
  ~an/s ən/z ‖ ən/z

Andaman ˈænd əm ən -ə mæn **~s** z

Andamanese ˌænd əm ə ˈniːz ◂ ‖ -ˈniːs ◂

andante æn ˈdænt i -eɪ ‖ ɑːn ˈdɑːnt eɪ
  æn ˈdænt̬ i —It [an ˈdan te]

andantino ˌænd æn ˈtiːn əʊ
‖ ˌɑːnd ɑːn ˈtiːn oʊ —It [an dan ˈti: no]

Andean æn ˈdiː ǀən ˈænd i ǀən **~s** z

Andersen, Anderson ˈænd əs ən ‖ -ərs-

Andersonstown ˈænd əs ənz taʊn ‖ ˈ·ərs-

Andes ˈænd iːz

andesite ˈænd ɪ zaɪt -ə-, -saɪt

Andhra Pradesh ˌændr ə prɑː ˈdeʃ ˌɑːndr-,
  -ˈdeɪʃ —Hindi [aːɳd̪ʱr prə d̪eɪʃ]

andiron ˈænd ˌaɪ ən ‖ -ˌaɪ ərn **~s** z

and/or ˌænd ˈɔː ◂ ‖ -ˈɔːr
  ˌapples ˌand/or ˈpears

Andorr|a æn ˈdɔːr ǀə -ˈdɒr- ‖ -ˈdɑːr ə
  —Catalan [ən ˈdɔr rə] **~an/s** ən/z

andouille ɒn ˈdwiː —Fr [ɑ̃ duj]

Andover ˈænd əʊv ə ‖ -oʊv ər

Andre, André ˈɒndr eɪ ˈændr-, ˈɑːndr- ‖ ˈɑːndr-
  —Fr [ɑ̃ dʁe]

Andrea ˈændr i ə —but as an Italian name,
æn ˈdreɪ ə —It [an ˈdrɛː a]
  Anˌdrea del ˈSarto del ˈsɑːt əʊ ‖ -ˈsɑːrt oʊ
  —It [del ˈsar to]

Andreas ˈændr i əs, -æs —but the place in the
Isle of Man is ˈændr əs; as a Spanish name,
æn ˈdreɪ əs —Sp [an ˈdɾe as]

A

Andrei 'ɒndr eɪ 'ɑːndr-, 'ɑːndr- ‖ 'ɑːndr-
— *Russ* [ʌn 'drʲej]
Andrew 'ændr uː
Andrewes, Andrews 'ændr uːz
Andrex *tdmk* 'ændr eks
Andria 'ændr i ə
andro- *comb. form*
    with stress-neutral suffix ˌændr əʊ ‖ -ə
    — **androcentric** ˌændr əʊ 'sentr ɪk ◄ ‖ -ə-
    with stress-imposing suffix æn 'drɒ +
    ‖ -'drɑː + — **androgyny** æn 'drɒdʒ ən i -ɪn-
    ‖ -'drɑːdʒ-
Androcles 'ændr ə kliːz
androgen 'ændr ədʒ ən -ə dʒen **~s** z
androgynous æn 'drɒdʒ ən əs -ɪn- ‖ -'drɑːdʒ-
androgyny æn 'drɒdʒ ən i -ɪn- ‖ -'drɑːdʒ-
android 'ændr ɔɪd **~s** z
Andromache æn 'drɒm ək i ‖ -'drɑːm-
Andromeda æn 'drɒm ɪd ə -əd- ‖ -'drɑːm-
Andronicus *(i)* æn 'drɒn ɪk əs ‖ -'drɑːn-; *(ii)*
    ˌændr ə 'naɪk əs —*in Shakespeare's* Titus A~,
    (i)
Andropov æn 'drɒp ɒf 'ændr ə pɒf
    ‖ ɑːn 'droʊp ɔːf -'drɑːp-, -ɑːf —*Russ*
    [ʌn 'drɔ pəf]
Andros 'ændr ɒs ‖ -əs -ɑːs
-androus 'ændr əs — **polyandrous**
    ˌpɒl i 'ændr əs ◄ ‖ ˌpɑːl-
-andry 'ændr i — **polyandry** ˌpɒl i 'ændr i
    ‖ ˌpɑːl-
Andy 'ænd i
-ane eɪn — **pentane** 'pent eɪn
anecdotage 'æn ɪk dəʊt ɪdʒ '-ek-, '-ək-
    ‖ -doʊt ɪdʒ
anecdotal ˌæn ɪk 'dəʊt ᵊl ◄ -ek-, -ək- ‖ -'doʊt-
anecdote 'æn ɪk dəʊt -ek-, -ək- ‖ -doʊt **~s** s
anecdotist 'æn ɪk dəʊt ɪst -ek-, -ək-, §-əst
    ‖ -doʊt əst **~s** s
anechoic ˌæn ɪ 'kəʊ ɪk ◄ -e-, -ə- ‖ -'koʊ-
Aneirin ə 'naɪᵊr ɪn -ən —*Welsh* [a 'nəi rin]
anemia ə 'niːm i ə
anemic ə 'niːm ɪk **~ally** ᵊl_i
anemometer ˌæn ɪ 'mɒm ɪt ə ˌ-ə-, -ət ə
    ‖ -'mɑːm ət ᵊr **~s** z
anemone ə 'nem ən i △ə 'nen əm i **~s** z
anencephalic ˌæn en ke 'fæl ɪk ◄ →,-eŋ-,
    ˌ-en sɪ-, ˌ-en sə-
anencephaly ˌæn en 'kef əl i →,-eŋ-, -en 'sef-
anent ə 'nent
aneroid 'æn ə rɔɪd
anesthesia ˌæn əs 'θiːz i_ə ˌ-iːs-, ˌ-ɪs-, -'θiːʒ ə
    ‖ -'θiːʒ ə
anesthesiologist ˌæn əs ˌθiːz i 'ɒl ədʒ ɪst
    §-əst ‖ -'ɑːl- **~s** s
anesthesiology ˌæn əs ˌθiːz i 'ɒl ədʒ i ‖ -'ɑːl-
anesthetic ˌæn əs 'θet ɪk ◄ -iːs-, -ɪs- ‖ -'θet̬- **~s**
    s
anesthetist ə 'niːs θət ɪst æ-, -θɪt-, §-əst
    ‖ ə 'nes θət̬ əst **~s** s
anesthetization ə ˌniːs θət aɪ 'zeɪʃ ᵊn -ɪˈ--
    ‖ ə ˌnes θət̬ ə-
anesthetiz|e ə 'niːs θə taɪz -θɪ- ‖ ə 'nes- (*)
    ~ed d **~es** ɪz əz **~ing** ɪŋ

aneurin *'thiamine'* ə 'njʊər ɪn §-'nʊər-;
    'æn jʊr-, -ən ‖ 'æn jər ən
Aneurin ə 'naɪᵊr ɪn -ən —*Welsh* [a 'nəi rin,
    -'nəi-]
aneurism, aneurysm 'æn jə ˌrɪz əm -jʊᵊ- **~s** z
aneurismal, aneurysmal ˌæn jə 'rɪz məl ◄
    -jʊᵊ-
anew ə 'njuː ‖ ə 'nuː -'njuː
Anfield 'æn fiːᵊld
anfractuosit|y ˌæn frækt ju 'ɒs ət |i
    -fræk tʃu-, ˌ-,-, -ɪt i ‖ æn ˌfræk tʃu 'ɑːs ət̬ |i
    ~ies iz
anfractuous ₍ᵢ₎æn 'frækt ju_əs -'fræk tʃu̯
    ‖ -'fræk tʃu̯ əs
angary 'æŋ gər i
angel, Angel 'eɪndʒ ᵊl —*but as a Spanish*
    name, 'ɑːn hel —*Sp* Ángel ['aŋ xel] **~s** z
Angela 'ændʒ əl ə -ɪl-
Angeleno ˌændʒ ə 'liːn əʊ -oʊ —*Sp*
    Angeleño [aŋ xe 'le ɲo] **~s** z
angelfish 'eɪndʒ ᵊl fɪʃ
angelic æn 'dʒel ɪk **~ally** ᵊl_i
angelica, A~ æn 'dʒel ɪk ə
Angelico æn 'dʒel ɪ kəʊ ‖ -koʊ ɑːn-, -'dʒeɪl-
    —*It* [an 'dʒɛː li ko]
Angelina ˌændʒ ə 'liːn ə -e-, -ɪ-
Angell 'eɪndʒ ᵊl
Angelo 'ændʒ ə ləʊ -ɪ- ‖ -loʊ
Angelou 'ændʒ ə luː
angelus, A~ 'ændʒ əl əs -ɪl- **~es** ɪz əz
anger 'æŋ gə ‖ 'æŋ gᵊr **angered** 'æŋ gəd
    ‖ -gᵊrd **angering** 'æŋ gər ˌɪŋ **angers** 'æŋ gəz
    ‖ -gᵊrz
Angers *place in France* ˌɑːn 'ʒeɪ ˌɒ̃- —*Fr*
    [ɑ̃ ʒe]
Angevin 'ændʒ əv ɪn -ɪv-, §-ən
Angharad æŋ 'hær əd æn- ‖ -'her- —*Welsh*
    [aŋ 'ha rad]
angi- *comb. form before vowel* ˌændʒ i
    — **angioma** ˌændʒ i 'əʊm ə ‖ -'oʊm-
Angie 'ændʒ i
angina æn 'dʒaɪn ə
    anˌgina 'pectoris 'pekt ər ɪs §-əs
angio- *comb. form*
    with stress-neutral suffix ˌændʒ i̯əʊ ‖ ə
    — **angiogram** 'ændʒ i̯əʊ græm ‖ ə græm
    with stress-imposing suffix ˌændʒ i 'ɒ +
    ‖ -'ɑː + — **angiography** ˌændʒ i 'ɒg rəf i
    ‖ -'ɑːg-
angioplasty 'ændʒ i̯əʊ ˌplæst i ‖ -i̯ə-
angiosperm 'ændʒ i̯əʊ spɜːm ‖ -ə spɜːm **~s** z
Angkor 'æŋ kɔː ‖ -kɔːr
    ˌAngkor 'Wat
angle, Angle 'æŋ gᵊl **angled** 'æŋ gᵊld
    angles, Angles 'æŋ gᵊlz **angling** 'æŋ glɪŋ
    'æŋ gᵊl_ɪŋ
    'angle ˌbracket
Anglepoise *tdmk* 'æŋ gᵊl pɔɪz
angler 'æŋ glə ‖ -glᵊr **~s** z
Anglesey 'æŋ gᵊls i -iː
anglesite 'æŋ gᵊl saɪt
Angli|a 'æŋ gli_ə **~an/s** ən/z
Anglican 'æŋ glɪk ən **~ism** ˌɪz əm **~s** z

A

anglice, A~ 'æŋ glɪs i -gləs-
anglicis... —*see* **angliciz...**
anglicism, A~ 'æŋ glɪ ˌsɪz əm -glə-
anglicization, A~ ˌæŋ glɪs aɪ 'zeɪʃ ᵊn ˌ·gləs-,
   -ɪ'·- ‖ -ə 'zeɪʒ- **~s** z
angliciz|e, A~ 'æŋ glɪ saɪz -glə- **~ed** d **~es** ɪz
   əz **~ing** ɪŋ
angling 'æŋ glɪŋ
Anglo 'æŋ gləʊ ‖ -gloʊ **~s** z
Anglo- ¦æŋ gləʊ ‖ -gloʊ — **Anglo-Spanish**
   ˌæŋ gləʊ 'spæn ɪʃ ◄ ‖ -gloʊ-
Anglo-American ˌæŋ gləʊ ə 'mer ɪk ən ◄
   -ək ən ‖ ˌ·gloʊ- **~s** z
Anglo-Catholic ˌæŋ gləʊ 'kæθ lɪk ◄
   -'kæθ əl ɪk, -'kɑːθ- ‖ -gloʊ- **~s** s
Anglo-Catholicism
   ˌæŋ gləʊ kə 'θɒl ə ˌsɪz əm -ɪˌ·-
   ‖ -gloʊ kə 'θɑːl-
Anglo-French ˌæŋ gləʊ 'frentʃ ◄ ‖ -gloʊ-
Anglo-Indian ˌæŋ gləʊ 'ɪnd i ə n ◄ ‖ ˌ·gloʊ- **~s**
   z
Anglo-Irish ˌæŋ gləʊ 'aɪᵊr ɪʃ ◄ ‖ -gloʊ-
   the ˌAnglo-ˌIrish A'greement
Anglo-Norman ˌæŋ gləʊ 'nɔːm ən ◄
   ‖ -gloʊ 'nɔːrm-
anglophile 'æŋ gləʊ faɪᵊl ‖ -glə- **~s** z
anglophilia ˌæŋ gləʊ 'fɪl i ə ‖ ˌ·glə-
anglophobe 'æŋ gləʊ fəʊb ‖ -glə foʊb **~s** z
anglophobia ˌæŋ gləʊ 'fəʊb i ə ‖ -glə 'foʊb-
Anglophone, a~ 'æŋ glə fəʊn ‖ -foʊn
Anglo-Saxon ˌæŋ gləʊ 'sæks ᵊn ◄ ‖ -gloʊ- **~s**
   z
Angmering 'æŋ mər ɪŋ
Angol|a æŋ 'gəʊl |ə ‖ -'goʊl |ə **~an/s** ən/z
angora, A~ æŋ 'gɔːr ə ‖ -'goʊr-
angostura, A~ ˌæŋ gə 'stjʊər ə ◄ -gɒ-, -'stʊər-,
   -'stjɔːr- ‖ -'stʊr ə ◄ —*Sp* [aŋ gos 'tu ra]
   ˌAngoˌstura 'bitters
Angouleme, Angoulême ˌɒŋ gu 'lem ‖ ˌɑːŋ-
   —*Fr* [ã gu lɛm]
angry 'æŋ gri **angrier** 'æŋ gri ə ‖ ᵊr **angriest**
   'æŋ griˌɪst əst **angrily** 'æŋ grəl i -grɪ li
angst æŋᵏst ‖ ɑːŋᵏst —*Ger* [ʔaŋst]
angstrom, A~ 'æŋᵏs trəm -trʌm —*Swedish*
   Ångström ['ɔŋ strœm] **~s** z
   'angstrom ˌunit
Anguill|a æŋ 'gwɪl |ə -'gwiː l- **~an/s** ən/z
anguish 'æŋ gwɪʃ **~ed** t **~es** ɪz əz **~ing** ɪŋ
angular 'æŋ gjʊl ə -gjəl- ‖ -gjəl ᵊr **~ly** li **~ness**
   nəs nɪs
angularit|y ˌæŋ gju 'lær ət |i ˌ·gjə-, -ɪt i
   ‖ -gjə 'lær ət̬ |i -'ler- **~ies** iz
Angus 'æŋ gəs
anharmonic ˌæn hɑː 'mɒn ɪk ◄ ‖ -hɑːr 'mɑːn-
anhinga æn 'hɪŋ gə **~s** z
Anhui ˌæn 'hweɪ ‖ ˌɑːn- —*Chinese* Ānhuī
   ['an ¹xwei]
anhydride ₍ᵢ₎æn 'haɪdr aɪd **~s** z
anhydrite ₍ᵢ₎æn 'haɪdr aɪt **~s** z
anhydrous ₍ᵢ₎æn 'haɪdr əs
ani *bird* 'ɑːn i **anis** 'ɑːn iz
aniconic ˌæn aɪ 'kɒn ɪk ◄ ‖ -'kɑːn-
anil 'æn ɪl -ᵊl

Anil ə 'niːᵊl
aniline 'æn əl ɪn -ɪl-, -iːn, §-ən
anilingus ˌeɪn i 'lɪŋ gəs
anima 'æn ɪm ə §-əm-
animadversion ˌæn ɪm æd 'vɜːʃ ᵊn §ˌ·əm-,
   -əd'·-, -'vɜːʒ- ‖ -'vɜːʒ- -'vɜːʃ- **~s** z
animad|vert ˌæn ɪm æd |'vɜːt §ˌ·əm-, -əd'·
   ‖ -|'vɜːt **~verted** 'vɜːt ɪd -əd ‖ 'vɜːt̬ əd
   ~verting 'vɜːt ɪŋ ‖ 'vɜːt̬ ɪŋ **~verts** 'vɜːts
   ‖ 'vɜːts
animal 'æn ɪm ᵊl -əm- **~s** z
   ˌanimal 'husbandry
animalcule ˌæn ɪ 'mæl kjuːl -ə- **~s** z
animalia ˌæn ɪ 'meɪl i ə ˌ·ə-
animalism 'æn ɪm ᵊl ˌɪz əm
animalistic ˌæn ɪm ə 'lɪst ɪk ◄ -ᵊl 'ɪst-
animality ˌæn ɪ 'mæl ət i ˌ·ə-, -ɪt i ‖ -ət̬ i
animate *adj* 'æn ɪm ət -əm-, -ɪt; -ɪ meɪt, -ə-
   ~ness nəs nɪs
ani|mate *v* 'æn ɪ |meɪt -ə- **~mated/ly**
   meɪt ɪd /li -əd ‖ meɪt̬ əd /li **~mates** meɪts
   ~mating meɪt ɪŋ ‖ meɪt̬ ɪŋ
animation ˌæn ɪ 'meɪʃ ᵊn -ə- **~s** z
animator 'æn ɪ meɪt ə '·ə- ‖ -meɪt̬ ᵊr **~s** z
animatronic ˌæn ɪm ə 'trɒn ɪk ◄ ˌ·əm-
   ‖ -'trɑːn- **~s** s
anime, animé 'æn ɪ meɪ -ə- **~s** z
animism 'æn ɪ ˌmɪz əm -ə-
animist 'æn ɪm ɪst -əm-, §-əst **~s** s
animosit|y ˌæn ɪ 'mɒs ət |i ˌ·ə-, -ɪt i
   ‖ -'mɑːs ət̬ |i **~ies** iz
animus 'æn ɪm əs -əm-
anion 'æn ˌaɪ ən **~s** z
anionic ˌæn aɪ 'ɒn ɪk ◄ ‖ -'ɑːn-
anis 'æn iː -iːs; æ 'niːs ‖ ɑː 'niːs -'niː —*Fr* [a ni,
   -nis], *Sp* anís [a 'nis]
anise 'æn ɪs §-əs
aniseed 'æn ɪ siːd -ə-
anisette ˌæn ɪ 'zet §-ə-, -'set **~s** s
anisogamy ˌæn aɪ 'sɒg əm i ‖ -'sɑːg-
anisomorphic æn ˌaɪs əʊ 'mɔːf ɪk ◄ ˌ·ˌ·-
   ‖ -ə 'mɔːrf- **~ally** ᵊl i
anisotropic æn ˌaɪs əʊ 'trɒp ɪk ◄ ˌ·ˌ·-, -'trəʊp-
   ‖ -ə 'traɪp- -ə 'troʊp-
Aniston 'æn ɪst ən §-əst-
Anita ə 'niːt ə ‖ ə 'niːt̬ ə
Anjou ˌɑːn 'ʒuː- ˌ·ᵊ- ‖ 'ɑːndʒ uː —*Fr* [ã ʒu]
Ankara 'æŋk ər ə ‖ 'ɑːŋk- —*Turkish*
   ['aŋ ka ra]
ankh æŋk ɑːŋk **ankhs** æŋks ɑːŋks
ankle 'æŋk ᵊl **~s** z
   'ankle ˌsock
anklebone 'æŋk ᵊl bəʊn ‖ -boʊn **~s** z
anklet 'æŋk lət -lɪt **~s** s
ankylos|e 'æŋk ɪ ləʊz -ə-, -ləʊs ‖ -loʊs -loʊz
   ~ed d ‖ t **~es** ɪz əz **~ing** ɪŋ
ankylosis ˌæŋk ɪ 'ləʊs ɪs -ə-, §-əs ‖ -'loʊs-
Anlaby 'æn ləb i
Ann æn
   ₍ᵢ₎**Ann 'Arbor**
Anna, anna 'æn ə **~'s, ~s** z
Annabel 'æn ə bel
Annabella ˌæn ə 'bel ə

Annalisa ˌæn ə ˈliːz ə -ˈliːs-

annalist ˈæn əl ɪst §-əst *(= analyst)* **~s** s

annals ˈæn ᵊlz

Annam ₍ᵢₐₚₚₐₑ₎æ ˈnæm ˈæn æm

Annamarie, Anna-Marie ˌæn ə mə ˈriː

Annamese ˌæn ə ˈmiːz ◂ -ˈmiːs ◂

Annan ˈæn ən —*but the former Secretary-General of the UN is* -æn, ə ˈnɑːn, ə ˈnæn

Annapolis ə ˈnæp əl ɪs §-əs

Annapurna ˌæn ə ˈpɜːn ə -ˈpʊən- ‖ -ˈpʊrn ə -ˈpɜːn-

annatto, A~ ə ˈnæt əʊ ‖ ə ˈnɑːţ oʊ

Anne æn

anneal ə ˈniːᵊl **annealed** ə ˈniːᵊld **annealing** ə ˈniːᵊl ɪŋ **anneals** ə ˈniːᵊlz

Anneka ˈæn ɪk ə -ək-

annelid ˈæn ə lɪd §-əl əd **~s** z

Annemarie, Anne-Marie ˌæn mə ˈriː →ˌæm-

Annesley *(i)* ˈænz li, *(ii)* ˈæn ɪz li -əz-

Annet, Annett ˈæn ɪt -ət

Annette ə ˈnet æ-

annex *v* ə ˈneks æ- **~ed** t **~es** ɪz əz **~ing** ɪŋ

annex *n* ˈæn eks **~es** ɪz əz

annexation ˌæn ek ˈseɪʃ ᵊn -ɪk- **~s** z

annex|e ˈæn eks **~es** ɪz əz

annexure ˈæn ek ʃʊə ‖ -ʃʊr **~s** z

Annie ˈæn i

Annigoni ˌæn i ˈɡəʊn i ‖ -ˈɡoʊn i —*It* [an ni ˈɡoː ni]

annihi|late ə ˈnaɪ ə |leɪt ɪ- **~lated** leɪt ɪd -əd ‖ leɪţ əd **~lates** leɪts **~lating** leɪt ɪŋ ‖ leɪţ ɪŋ

annihilation ə ˌnaɪ ə ˈleɪʃ ᵊn ɪ-

Annika ˈæn ɪk ə

Annis ˈæn ɪs §-əs

Anniston ˈæn ɪst ən §-əst-

anniversar|y ˌæn ɪ ˈvɜːs ər |i ◂ ˌ-ə-, →-ˈvɜːʃ ri ‖ -ˈvɜːs- **~ies** iz

Anno Domini ˌæn əʊ ˈdɒm ɪ naɪ -ə-, -niː ‖ ˌæn oʊ ˈdɑːm ə niː -ˈdoʊm-, -naɪ

anno|tate ˈæn əʊ |teɪt ‖ -ə- **~tated** teɪt ɪd -əd ‖ teɪţ əd **~tates** teɪts **~tating** teɪt ɪŋ ‖ teɪţ ɪŋ

annotation ˌæn əʊ ˈteɪʃ ᵊn ‖ -ə- **~s** z

annotative ˈæn əʊ teɪt ɪv ‖ -ə teɪţ-

annotator ˈæn əʊ teɪt ə ‖ -ə teɪţ ᵊr **~s** z

announc|e ə ˈnaʊn⸲s **~ed** t **~es** ɪz əz **~ing** ɪŋ

announcement ə ˈnaʊn⸲s mənt **~s** s

announcer ə ˈnaʊn⸲s ə ‖ -ᵊr **~s** z

annoy ə ˈnɔɪ **annoyed** ə ˈnɔɪd **annoying/ly** ə ˈnɔɪ ɪŋ /li **annoys** ə ˈnɔɪz

annoyanc|e ə ˈnɔɪ ən⸲s **~es** ɪz əz

annual ˈæn ju əl **~ly** i **~s** z

annualis|e, annualiz|e ˈæn ju ə laɪz ˈ⸲ju ⸱ **~ed** d **~es** ɪz əz **~ing** ɪŋ

annuitant ə ˈnjuː ɪt ənt ət- ‖ ə ˈnuː ət ᵊnt -ˈnjuː- **~s** s

annuit|y ə ˈnjuː ət |i ɪt- ‖ ə ˈnuː əţ |i -ˈnjuː- **~ies** iz

annul ə ˈnʌl **~led** d **~ling** ɪŋ **~s** z

annular ˈæn jʊl ə -jəl- ‖ -jəl ᵊr

annu|late ˈæn ju |leɪt -jə- ‖ -jə- **~lated** leɪt ɪd -əd ‖ leɪţ əd

annuli ˈæn ju laɪ ‖ -jə-

annull... —*see* **annul**

annulment ə ˈnʌl mənt **~s** s

annulus ˈæn jʊl əs -jəl- ‖ -jəl- **annuli** ˈæn ju laɪ ‖ -jə-

annum ˈæn əm

annunci|ate ə ˈnʌn⸲s i |eɪt ə ˈnʌnʃ- **~ated** eɪt ɪd -əd ‖ eɪţ əd **~ates** eɪts **~ating** eɪt ɪŋ ‖ eɪţ ɪŋ

annunciation, A~ ə ˌnʌn⸲s i ˈeɪʃ ᵊn ə ˌnʌnʃ- **~s** z

annunciative ə ˈnʌn⸲s i ət ɪv ə ˈnʌnʃ-, -eɪt ɪv; -ˈnʌnʃ ət ɪv ‖ -eɪţ ɪv

annunciator ə ˈnʌn⸲s i eɪt ə ə ˈnʌnʃ- ‖ -eɪţ ᵊr **~s** z

annunciatory ə ˈnʌn⸲s i ət ˌər i ə ˈnʌnʃ-, ⸱⸱⸱ˈeɪt ər i; ə ˈnʌnʃ ət ˌər i ‖ -ə tɔːr i -toʊr i

annus ˈæn əs -ʊs ‖ ˈɑːn- ˌannus miˈrabilis mɪ ˈrɑːb əl ɪs mə-, -ˈræb-, -ɪl-, §-əs

Anny ˈæn i

anoa ə ˈnəʊ ə ‖ ə ˈnoʊ ə **anoas** ə ˈnəʊ əz ‖ -ˈnoʊ-

anode ˈæn əʊd ‖ -oʊd **~s** z

anodic æ ˈnɒd ɪk ‖ ə ˈnɑːd ɪk

anodis|e, anodiz|e ˈæn əʊ daɪz ‖ -ə- **~ed** d **~es** ɪz əz **~ing** ɪŋ

anodyne ˈæn əʊ daɪn ‖ -ə- **~s** z

anoint ə ˈnɔɪnt **anointed** ə ˈnɔɪnt ɪd -əd ‖ ə ˈnɔɪnţ əd **anointing** ə ˈnɔɪnt ɪŋ ‖ ə ˈnɔɪnţ ɪŋ **anoints** ə ˈnɔɪnts

anointment ə ˈnɔɪnt mənt **~s** s

anole ə ˈnəʊl i ‖ -ˈnoʊl- **~s** z

anomalistic ə ˌnɒm ə ˈlɪst ɪk ◂ ‖ ə ˌnɑːm- **~ally** ᵊl_i

anomalous ə ˈnɒm əl əs ‖ ə ˈnɑːm- **~ly** li **~ness** nəs nɪs

anomal|y ə ˈnɒm əl |i ‖ ə ˈnɑːm- **~ies** iz

anomic ə ˈnɒm ɪk æ-, -ˈnəʊm- ‖ -ˈnɑːm- -ˈnoʊm-

anomie, anomy ˈæn əʊm i ‖ -əm i

anon ə ˈnɒn ‖ ə ˈnɑːn

Anona ə ˈnəʊn ə ‖ ə ˈnoʊn ə

anonymity ˌæn ə ˈnɪm ət i ˌæn ɒ-, -ɪt i ‖ -əţ i

anonymous ə ˈnɒn ɪ məs -ə- ‖ ə ˈnɑːn- **~ly** li

anopheles, A~ ə ˈnɒf ə liːz -ɪ- ‖ ə ˈnɑːf-

anorak ˈæn ə ræk **~s** s

anorectic ˌæn ə ˈrekt ɪk ◂ **~s** s

anorexia ˌæn ə ˈreks i ə ◂ ˌæn ɒ- **~s** z ˌanoˌrexia nerˈvosa nɜː ˈvəʊs ə -ˈvəʊz- ‖ nᵊr ˈvoʊs ə -ˈvoʊz-

anorexic ˌæn ə ˈreks ɪk ◂ **~s** s

anosmia æn ˈɒz mi ə -ˈɒs- ‖ -ˈɑːz- -ˈɑːs-

another ə ˈnʌð ə ‖ -ᵊr —*There is also an occasional emphatic form* ˌeɪ- **~'s** z

Anouilh ˈæn u iː ˈɒn-, ⸱⸱⸱; æ ˈnuːɪ i ‖ ɑ ˈnuː jə æ-, -i; ⸱⸱ˈiː —*Fr* [a nuj]

ANOVA ˌæn əʊ ˈvɑː ˈ⸱⸱⸱ ‖ -oʊ-

anoxia ₍ᵢₐₙₙₒₓₖₛ₎æn ˈɒks i ə ‖ -ˈɑːks-

ansaphone *tdmk* ˈɑːn⸲s ə fəʊn §ˈæn⸲s- ‖ ˈæn⸲s ə foʊn **~s** z

Ansbacher ˈænz bæk ə ‖ -ᵊr

Anschluss, a~ ˈæn ʃlʊs ‖ ˈɑːn- —*Ger* Anschluß [ˈʔan ʃlʊs]

Anscombe 'æn⁀s kəm

Ansell 'æn⁀s ᵊl

Anselm 'æn⁀s elm

anserine 'æn⁀s ə raɪn -riːn, -rɪn

Ansermet 'ɒn⁀s ə meɪ 'ɑːn⁀s-, -'ð̃-
∥ ˌɑːn⁀s ᵊr 'meɪ —Fr [ɑ̃ sɛʁ mɛ]

Ansett 'æn set

Anshun ˌæn 'ʃʊn ∥ ˌɑːn 'ʃuːn —Chinese
Ānshùn [¹an ⁴şwən]

ANSI 'æn⁀s i

Anson 'æn⁀s ᵊn

Anstey 'æn⁀st i

Anstruther 'æn⁀s trʌð ə ∥ -ᵊr —The place in
Fife is locally also 'eɪn⁀st ə ∥ -ᵊr

Ansty 'æn⁀st i

answer 'ɑːn⁀s ə §'æn⁀s ə ∥ 'æn⁀s ᵊr (!) ~ed d
answering 'ɑːn⁀s ᵊr ɪŋ §'æn⁀s- ∥ 'æn⁀s- ~s z
'answering ma‚chine; 'answering ‚service

answerability ˌɑːn⁀s ᵊr ə 'bɪl ət i §ˌæn⁀s-, -ɪt i
∥ ˌæn⁀s ᵊr ə 'bɪl ət̬ i

answerab|le 'ɑːn⁀s ᵊr əb |ᵊl §'æn⁀s- ∥ 'æn⁀s-
~ly li

answerphone 'ɑːn⁀s ə fəʊn §'æn⁀s-
∥ 'æn⁀s ᵊr foʊn ~s z

ant, Ant ænt **ants** ænts

ant- comb. form before vowel ǀænt, ænt
— **antacid** ₍ᵢ₎ænt 'æs ɪd §-əd , **antonym**
'ænt ən ɪm §-əm

-ant ənt —When attached to an independent
stem, this suffix is usually stress-neutral
(ac'count — ac'countant; in'habit —
in'habitant). Otherwise, it imposes stress: on
the antepenultimate syllable if the penultimate
is weak ('arrogant, 'applicant, sig'nificant), but
on the penultimate itself if it is strong
(flam'boyant, re'luctant). There are several
exceptions: note ex'ecutant, 'ignorant,
'Protestant.

Antabuse tdmk 'ænt ə bjuːs -bjuːz ∥ 'ænt̬-

antacid ₍ᵢ₎ænt 'æs ɪd §-əd ~s z

Antaeus æn 'tiː əs -'teɪ-

antagonis... —see **antagoniz...**

antagonism æn 'tæg ə ˌnɪz əm ~s z

antagonist æn 'tæg ən ɪst §-əst ~s s

antagonistic æn ˌtæg ə 'nɪst ɪk ◂ ˌænt æg-
~ally ᵊl_i

antagoniz|e æn 'tæg ə naɪz ~ed d ~es ɪz əz
~ing ɪŋ

Antalya æn 'tæl jə ∥ ɑːn 'tɑːl jə —Turkish
[ɑn 'tɑl jɑ]

Antananarivo ˌænt ə ˌnæn ə 'riːv əʊ ∥ -oʊ

antarctic, A~ ₍ᵢ₎ænt 'ɑːkt ɪk △-'ɑːt-
∥ ₍ᵢ₎ænt̬ 'ɑːrkt- -'ɑːrt̬-
Ant‚arctic 'Circle, ‚·‚--

Antarctica ₍ᵢ₎ænt 'ɑːkt ɪk ə △-'ɑːt- ∥ -'ɑːrkt-
-'ɑːrt̬-

Antares æn 'teər iːz ∥ -'ter- -'tær-

ant-bear 'ænt beə ∥ -ber -bær ~s z

ante 'ænt i ∥ 'ænt̬ i ~d, ~ed d ~ing ˌɪŋ ~s z
‚ante me'ridiem mə 'rɪd i‚əm -em

ante- comb. form
with stress-neutral suffix ǀænt i ∥ ǀænt̬ i
(= anti-) — **antebellum** ˌænt i 'bel əm ◂
∥ ˌænt̬ i-

anteater 'ænt ˌiːt ə ∥ 'ænt̬ ˌiːt̬ ᵊr ~s z

antecedence ˌænt ɪ 'siːd ᵊn⁀s -ə- ∥ ˌænt̬ ə-

antecedent ˌænt ɪ 'siːd ᵊnt ◂ -ə- ∥ ˌænt̬ ə- ~s s

antechamber 'ænt i ˌtʃeɪm bə
∥ 'ænt̬ i ˌtʃeɪm bᵊr ~s z

ante|date ˌænt i 'ǀdeɪt ◂ '··· ∥ 'ænt̬ i ǀdeɪt
~dated deɪt ɪd -əd ∥ deɪt̬ əd ~dates deɪts
~dating deɪt ɪŋ ∥ deɪt̬ ɪŋ

antediluvian ˌænt i dɪ 'luːv i‚ən ◂ -də'--,
-daɪ'--, -'ljuːv- ∥ ˌænt̬ i- ~s z

antelope 'ænt ɪ ləʊp -ə- ∥ 'ænt̬ ə loʊp ~s s

antenatal ˌænt i 'neɪt ᵊl ◂ ∥ ˌænt̬ i 'neɪt̬ ᵊl ◂ ~s
z

antenn|a æn 'ten |ə ~ae iː ~as əz

antepenult ˌænt i pɪ 'nʌlt -pə'-, -pe'-
∥ ˌænt̬ i 'piːn ʌlt -pɪ 'nʌlt ~s s

antepenultimate ˌænt i pɪ 'nʌlt ɪm ət ◂
-pə'--, -pe'--, -əm ət, -ɪt ∥ ˌænt̬ i- ~ly li ~s s

anterior æn 'tɪər i ə ∥ -'tɪr i‚ᵊr ~ly li

anteriority æn ˌtɪər i 'ɒr ət i -ɪt i
∥ æn ˌtɪr i 'ɔːr ət̬ i

anteroom 'ænt i ruːm -rʊm ∥ 'ænt̬ i- ~s z

Anthea 'æn⁀θ i‚ə

anthelion ænt 'hiːl i‚ən æn 'θiːl- ~s z

anthelminthic ˌæn⁀θ el 'mɪn⁀θ ɪk ◂ ˌænt hel-
~s s

anthelmintic ˌæn⁀θ el 'mɪnt ɪk ◂ ˌænt hel-
∥ -'mɪnt̬- ~s s

anthem 'æn⁀θ əm ~s z

anthemic æn 'θem ɪk -'θiːm-

anther 'æn⁀θ ə ∥ -ᵊr ~s z

anthill 'ænt hɪl ~s z

anthologis... —see **anthologiz...**

anthologist æn 'θɒl ədʒ ɪst §-əst ∥ -'θɑːl- ~s s

anthologiz|e æn 'θɒl ə dʒaɪz ∥ -'θɑːl- ~ed d
~es ɪz əz ~ing ɪŋ

antholog|y æn 'θɒl ədʒ |i ∥ -'θɑːl- ~ies iz

Anthony (i) 'ænt ən i, (ii) 'æn⁀θ- —in BrE (i)
predominates, in AmE (ii).

anthracite 'æn⁀θ rə saɪt

anthracnose æn 'θræk nəʊs -nəʊz ∥ -noʊs

anthrax 'æn⁀θ ræks

anthropic æn 'θrɒp ɪk ∥ -'θrɑːp-

anthropo- comb. form
with stress-neutral suffix ǀæn⁀θ rəʊp əʊ
∥ ǀæn⁀θ rəp ə — **anthropophobia**
ˌæn⁀θ rəʊp əʊ 'fəʊb i‚ə ∥ ˌæn⁀θ rəp ə 'foʊb-
with stress-imposing suffix ˌæn⁀θ rəʊ 'pɒ +
∥ ˌæn⁀θ rə 'pɑː + — **anthroposcopy**
ˌæn⁀θ rəʊ 'pɒsk əp i ∥ -rə 'pɑːsk-

anthropocentric ˌæn⁀θ rəʊp əʊ 'sentr ɪk ◂
∥ -rəp ə- ~ally ᵊl_i

anthropoid 'æn⁀θ rəʊ pɔɪd ∥ -rə- ~s z

anthropological ˌæn⁀θ rəʊp ə 'lɒdʒ ɪk ᵊl ◂
∥ -rəp ə 'lɑːdʒ- ~ly _i

anthropologist ˌæn⁀θ rə 'pɒl ədʒ ɪst §-əst
∥ -'pɑːl- ~s s

anthropology ˌæn⁀θ rə 'pɒl ədʒ i ∥ -'pɑːl-

anthropometry ˌænˈθ rəʊ 'pɒm ətr i -ɪtr i
‖ -rə 'pɑːm-

anthropomorphic ˌænˈθ rəʊp əʊ 'mɔːf ɪk ◂
‖ -rəp ə 'mɔːrf- **~ally** ᵊl i

anthropomorphism
ˌænˈθ rəʊp əʊ 'mɔːf ˌɪz əm ‖ -rəp ə 'mɔːrf-

anthropophagi ˌænˈθ rəʊ 'pɒf ə dʒaɪ -gaɪ
‖ -rə 'pɑːf-

anthropophàgous ˌænˈθ rəʊ 'pɒf əg əs
‖ -rə 'pɑːf-

anthropophagy ˌænˈθ rəʊ 'pɒf ədʒ i
‖ -rə 'pɑːf-

anthroposophy ˌænˈθ rəʊ 'pɒs əf i
‖ -rə 'pɑːs-

anthurium æn 'θjʊər i̯əm -'θʊər- ‖ -'θʊr-
-'θjʊr-

anti 'ænt i ‖ 'ænt̬ i 'ænt aɪ **~s** z

anti- *comb. form*
with stress-neutral suffix ¦ænt i ‖ ¦ænt̬ i
¦ænt aɪ — **antibacterial**
ˌænt i bæk 'tɪər i̯əl ◂ ‖ ˌænt̬i bak 'tɪr-
ˌænt aɪ-
with stress-imposing suffix æn 'tɪ +
— **antiphony** æn 'tɪf ən i

antiabortion ˌænt i ə 'bɔːʃ ᵊn
‖ ˌænt̬ i ə 'bɔːrʃ ᵊn ˌænt aɪ- **~ist/s** ɪst/s §əst/s

antiaircraft, anti-aircraft ˌænt i 'eə krɑːft ◂
§-kræft ‖ ˌænt̬ i 'er kræft ˌænt aɪ-, -'ær-

antialias ˌænt i 'eɪl i̯əs ‖ ˌænt̬ i- ˌænt aɪ- **~ed**
t **~es** ɪz əz **~ing** ɪŋ

antiballistic ˌænt i bə 'lɪst ɪk ◂ ‖ ˌænt̬ i-
ˌænt aɪ-
    ˌantibal ˌlistic 'missile

Antibes ɒn 'tiːb ɑːn-, æn- ‖ ɑːn- —*Fr* [ɑ̃ tib]

antibiotic ˌænt i baɪ 'ɒt ɪk ◂
‖ ˌænt̬ i baɪ 'ɑːt ɪk ◂ ˌænt aɪ- **~ally** ᵊl i **~s** s

antibod|y ˌænt i ˌbɒd |i ‖ 'ænt̬ i ˌbɑːd |i
'ænt aɪ- **~ies** iz

antic 'ænt ɪk ‖ 'ænt̬ ɪk **~s** s

anticholinergic ˌænt i ˌkəʊl ɪ 'nɜːdʒ ɪk -ˌkɒl-,
-ə'-- ‖ ˌænt̬ i ˌkoʊl ə 'nɜːdʒ ɪk ˌænt aɪ-

Antichrist, a~ 'ænt i kraɪst ‖ 'ænt̬ i- 'ænt aɪ-

antici|pate æn 'tɪs i |peɪt ◂ -ə- **~pated** peɪt ɪd
-əd ‖ peɪt̬ əd **~pates** peɪts **~pating** peɪt ɪŋ
‖ peɪt̬ ɪŋ

anticipation æn ˌtɪs ɪ 'peɪʃ ᵊn ˌ·-, -ə'-- **~s** z

anticipatory æn 'tɪs ɪp ət ᵊr i -'--əp-;
ˌ·ˌ·ɪ 'peɪt ər i, ˌ· ˈ--, -ə'-- ‖ æn 'tɪs əp ə tɔːr i
-toʊr i

anticlerical ˌænt i 'kler ɪk ᵊl ◂ ‖ ˌænt̬ i-
ˌænt aɪ- **~ism** ˌɪz əm

anticlimactic ˌænt i klaɪ 'mækt ɪk ◂ -klɪ'--,
-klə'-- ‖ ˌænt̬ i- ˌænt aɪ- **~ally** ᵊl i

anticlimax ˌænt i 'klaɪm æks ‖ ˌænt̬ i- ˌænt aɪ-
~es ɪz əz

anticline 'ænt i klaɪn ‖ 'ænt̬ i- 'ænt aɪ- **~s** z

anticlockwise ˌænt i 'klɒk waɪz ◂
‖ ˌænt̬ i 'klɑːk- ˌænt aɪ-

anticoagulant ˌænt i kəʊ 'æg jʊl ənt ◂
-jəl ənt ‖ ˌænt̬ i koʊ 'æg jəl ənt ˌænt aɪ- **~s** s

anticonvulsant ˌænt i kən 'vʌls ənt ◂ §-kɒn'--
‖ ˌænt̬ i- ˌænt aɪ- **~s** s

Anticosti ˌænt ɪ 'kɒst i -ə- ‖ ˌænt̬ ə 'kɑːst i
-'kɔːst-

anticyclone ˌænt i 'saɪk ləʊn
‖ ˌænt̬ i 'saɪk loʊn ˌænt aɪ- **~s** z

anticyclonic ˌænt i saɪ 'klɒn ɪk ◂
‖ ˌænt̬ i saɪ 'klɑːn ɪk ◂ ˌænt aɪ-

antidepressant ˌænt i dɪ 'pres ᵊnt ◂ -də'--,
§-diː'-- ‖ ˌænt̬ i- ˌænt aɪ- **~s** z

antidote 'ænt i dəʊt ‖ 'ænt̬ i doʊt **~s** s

Antietam æn 'tiːt əm ‖ -'tiːt̬-

antiformant 'ænt i ˌfɔːm ənt ‖ 'ænt̬ i ˌfɔːrm-
'ænt aɪ- **~s** s

antifouling ˌænt i 'faʊl ɪŋ ‖ ˌænt̬ i- ˌænt aɪ-

antifreeze 'ænt i friːz ˌ· '· ‖ 'ænt̬ i-

anti-fungal ˌænt i 'fʌŋ gᵊl ◂ ‖ ˌænt̬ i- ˌænt aɪ-

anti-g ˌænt i 'dʒiː ‖ ˌænt̬ i- ˌænt aɪ-

antigen 'ænt ɪdʒ ən -ədʒ-, -i dʒen ‖ 'ænt̬- **~s** z

Antigone æn 'tɪg ən i

Antigonus æn 'tɪg ən əs

Antigu|a æn 'tiːg |ə —*there is also an
occasional spelling pronunciation* -w|ə **~an/s**
ən/z

antihero 'ænt i ˌhɪər əʊ ‖ 'ænt̬ i ˌhɪr oʊ
ˌænt aɪ-, -ˌhiː roʊ **~es** z

antihistamine ˌænt i 'hɪst ə miːn -mɪn, -mən
‖ ˌænt̬ i- ˌænt̬ ə-

anti-inflammatory ˌænt i ɪn 'flæm ət ᵊr i̯ ◂
‖ ˌænt̬ i ɪn 'flæm ə tɔːr i ◂ ˌænt aɪ-, -toʊr i

antiknock ˌænt i 'nɒk ‖ ˌænt̬ i 'nɑːk ˌænt aɪ-

Antillean æn 'tɪl i̯ən **~s** z

Antilles æn 'tɪl iːz

anti-lock ˌænt i 'lɒk ◂ ‖ ˌænt̬ i 'lɑːk ◂ ˌænt aɪ-

antilog 'ænt i lɒg ‖ 'ænt̬ i lɔːg 'ænt aɪ-, -lɑːg
~s z

antilogarithm ˌænt i 'lɒg ə rɪð əm -rɪθ-
‖ ˌænt̬ i 'lɔːg- ˌænt aɪ-, -'lɑːg- **~s** z

antimacassar ˌænt i mə 'kæs ə
‖ ˌænt̬ i mə 'kæs ᵊr ˌænt aɪ- **~s** z

antimagnetic ˌænt i mæg 'net ɪk ◂ -məg'--
‖ ˌænt̬ i mæg 'net̬ ɪk ◂ ˌænt aɪ-

antimalarial ˌænt i mə 'leər i̯əl ◂
‖ ˌænt̬ i mə 'ler- ˌænt aɪ- **~s** z

antimatter 'ænt i ˌmæt ə ‖ 'ænt̬ i ˌmæt̬ ᵊr
'ænt aɪ-

antimissile ˌænt i 'mɪs aɪᵊl ◂ ‖ ˌænt̬ i 'mɪs ᵊl ◂
ˌænt aɪ- **~s** z

antimony 'ænt ɪ mən i '·ə- ‖ 'ænt̬ ə moʊn i

anting 'ænt ɪŋ ‖ 'ænt̬ ɪŋ

antinomian ˌænt i 'nəʊm i̯ən ◂
‖ ˌænt̬ i 'noʊm- ˌænt aɪ- **~ism** ˌɪz əm

antinomy æn 'tɪn əm i

Antinous æn 'tɪn əʊ əs ‖ -oʊ-

antinovel 'ænt i ˌnɒv ᵊl ‖ 'ænt̬ i ˌnɑːv ᵊl
'ænt aɪ-

antinuclear ˌænt i 'njuːk li̯ə ◂ §-'nuːk-,
△-jəl ə ‖ ˌænt̬ i 'nuːk li̯ᵊr ˌænt aɪ-, -'njuːk-,
△-jəl ᵊr

Antioch 'ænt i ɒk ‖ 'ænt̬ i ɑːk

Antiochus æn 'taɪ̯ək əs

antioxidant ˌænt i 'ɒks ɪd ənt -əd ənt
‖ ˌænt̬ i 'ɑːks- ˌænt aɪ- **~s** s

antiparticle 'ænt i ˌpɑːt ɪk ᵊl ‖ 'ænt̬ i ˌpɑːrt-
'ænt aɪ- **~s** z

Antipas 'ænt i pæs ‖ 'ænt̮ i-
antipasto 'ænt i ˌpæst əʊ -ˌpɑːst-, ˌ·'·· ‖ ˌænt̮ i 'pɑːst oʊ -'pæst-
Antipater æn 'tɪp ət ə ‖ -ət̮ ᵊr
antipathetic ˌænt i pə 'θet ɪk ◂ æn ˌtɪp ə- ‖ ˌænt̮ i pə 'θet̮ ɪk ◂ ~**ally** ᵊl̮i
antipath|y æn 'tɪp əθ |i ~**ies** iz
antipersonnel ˌænt i ˌpɜːs ə 'nel ‖ ˌænt̮ i ˌpɜːs- ˌænt aɪ- ˌanti,person'nel mine
antiperspirant ˌænt i 'pɜːsp ᵊr ənt -ɪr ᵊnt ‖ ˌænt̮ i 'pɜːsp- ˌænt aɪ- ~**s** s
antiphon 'ænt ɪf ən §-əf-; -ɪ fɒn, -ə- ‖ 'ænt̮ ə fɑːn -əf ən ~**s** z
antiphonal æn 'tɪf ᵊn əl ~**ly** i
antiphrasis æn 'tɪf rəs ɪs §-əs
antipodal æn 'tɪp əd ᵊl
antipodean, A~ ˌ₍ᵢ₎æn ˌtɪp ə 'diː ən ~**s** z
antipodes, A~ æn 'tɪp ə diːz
antipyretic ˌænt i paɪᵊ 'ret ɪk ◂ ‖ ˌænt i paɪ 'ret̮ ɪk ◂ ˌænt aɪ- ~**s** s
antiquarian ˌænt ɪ 'kweər i ən ◂ ˌ·ə- ‖ ˌænt̮ ə 'kwer- ~**ism** ˌɪz əm ~**s** z
antiquar|y 'ænt ɪk wər |i '·ək- ‖ 'ænt̮ ə kwer |i ~**ies** iz
antiquated 'ænt ɪ kweɪt ɪd '·ə-, -əd ‖ 'ænt̮ ə kweɪt̮ əd ~**ness** nəs nɪs
antique ₍ᵢ₎æn 'tiːk —*formerly also* 'ænt ɪk ~**ly** li ~**ness** nəs nɪs
antiquit|y æn 'tɪk wət |i -wɪt- ‖ -wət̮ |i ~**ies** iz
anti-rac|ism ˌænt i 'reɪs ˌɪz əm ‖ ˌænt̮ i-, ˌænt aɪ- ~**ist/s** ɪst/s əst/s
antirrhinum ˌænt ɪ 'raɪn əm -ə- ‖ ˌænt̮ ə- ~**s** z
antiscorbutic ˌænt i skɔː 'bjuːt ɪk ◂ ‖ ˌænt̮ i skɔːr 'bjuːt̮ ɪk ◂ ˌænt aɪ- ~**s** s
anti-Semite ˌænt i 'siːm aɪt -'sem- ‖ ˌænt̮ i 'sem- ˌænt aɪ- ~**s** s
anti-Semitic ˌænt i sə 'mɪt ɪk ◂ -'sɪ'·- ‖ ˌænt̮ i sə 'mɪt̮ ɪk ◂ ˌænt aɪ-
anti-Semitism ˌænt i 'sem ə ˌtɪz əm -'·ɪ- ‖ ˌænt̮ i-, ˌænt aɪ-
antisepsis ˌænt i 'seps ɪs ◂ -ə-, §-əs ‖ ˌænt̮ ə-
antiseptic ˌænt i 'sept ɪk ◂ -ə- ‖ ˌænt̮ ə- ~**ally** ᵊl̮i ~**s** s
antisocial ˌænt i 'səʊʃ ᵊl ◂ ‖ ˌænt̮ i 'soʊʃ ᵊl ◂ ˌænt aɪ- ~**ly** i
anti-spam ˌænt i 'spæm ‖ ˌænt̮ i-, ˌænt aɪ-
antispasmodic ˌænt i spæz 'mɒd ɪk ◂ ‖ ˌænt̮ i spæz 'mɑːd- ˌænt aɪ-
antistatic ˌænt i 'stæt ɪk ◂ ‖ ˌænt̮ i 'stæt̮ ɪk ◂ ˌænt aɪ-
Antisthenes æn 'tɪs θə niːz -ɪ-
antistrophe æn 'tɪs trəf i
antitank ˌænt i 'tæŋk ‖ ˌænt̮ i- ˌænt aɪ-
antith|esis æn 'tɪθ |əs ɪs -ɪs-, §-əs ~**eses** ə siːz -ɪ-
antithetic ˌænt i 'θet ɪk ◂ -ə- ‖ ˌænt̮i 'θet̮ ɪk ◂ ~**al** ᵊl ~**ally** ᵊl̮i
antitoxin ˌænt i 'tɒks ɪn §-ᵊn ‖ ˌænt̮ i 'tɑːks ᵊn ˌænt aɪ- ~**s** z
antitrust ˌænt i 'trʌst ‖ ˌænt̮ i-, ˌænt aɪ-
antitussive ˌænt i 'tʌs ɪv ‖ ˌænt̮ i- ˌænt aɪ- ~**s** z

antivir|al ˌænt i 'vaɪᵊr |əl ‖ ˌænt̮ i- ˌænt aɪ- ~**us** əs
antivivisection|ism ˌænt i ˌvɪv ɪ 'sek ʃᵊn| ˌɪz əm §-,-ə- ‖ ˌænt̮ i- ˌænt aɪ- ~**ist/s** ɪst/s əst/s
antler 'ænt lə ‖ -lᵊr ~**ed** d ~**s** z
antlike 'ænt laɪk
antlion 'ænt ˌlaɪ ən ~**s** z
Antofagasta ˌænt əf ə 'gæst ə —*Sp* [an to fa 'ɣas ta]
Antoine ɒn 'twaːn ɑːn-, -'twæn, '·· ‖ ɑːn 'twaːn —*Fr* [ɑ̃ twan]
Antoinette ˌænt wə 'net ˌaːnt-, -waː- —*Fr* [ɑ̃ twa nɛt]
Anton 'ænt ɒn ‖ -ɑːn
Antonia æn 'təʊn i ə ‖ -'toʊn-
Antonian æn 'təʊn i ən ‖ -'toʊn- ~**s** z
Antonine 'ænt ə naɪn ‖ 'ænt̮-
Antoninus ˌænt ə 'naɪn əs ◂ ‖ ˌænt̮- ˌAnto,ninus 'Pius
Antonio æn 'təʊn i əʊ ‖ -'toʊn i oʊ
Antonioni ˌænt əʊn i 'əʊn i æn ˌtəʊn- ‖ ˌɑːnt oʊn 'joʊn i —*It* [an to 'njoː ni]
Antonius æn 'təʊn i əs ‖ -'toʊn-
antonomasia ˌænt ə nəʊ 'meɪz i ə æn ˌtɒn əʊ-, -'meɪʒ- ‖ ˌænt̮ ᵊn oʊ 'meɪʒ i ə -'meɪʒ ə
Antonov æn 'tɒn ɒf ‖ -'tɔːn ɔːf -'tɑːn ɑːf, -'toʊn- —*Russ* [ʌn 'to nəf]
Antony 'ænt ən i ‖ -ᵊn i
antonym 'ænt ə nɪm ‖ -ᵊn ɪm ~**s** z
antonym|ous æn 'tɒn əm |əs -ɪm- ‖ -'tɑːn- ~**y** i
Antrim 'æntr ɪm -əm
Antrobus 'æntr əb əs
antr|um 'æntr| əm ~**a** ə
antsy 'ænts i
Antwerp 'ænt wɜːp ‖ -wɜːp —*Dutch* Antwerpen ['ant vɛrp ən]
Anubis ə 'njuːb ɪs §-əs ‖ ə 'nuːb- ə 'njuːb-
anuresis ˌæn juᵊ 'riːs ɪs §-əs
anuria ₍ᵢ₎æn 'jʊər i ə æn juᵊ 'riː ə ‖ -'jʊr-
anus 'eɪn əs ~**es** ɪz əz
anvil 'æn vɪl -vᵊl ~**s** z
Anwar 'æn waː ‖ 'ɑːn waːr
Anwen 'æn wen
Anwyl 'æn wɪl -wəl
anxiet|y æŋ 'zaɪ ət |i §æŋg-, -ɪt- ‖ -ət̮ |i ~**ies** iz
anxious 'æŋkʃ əs ~**ly** li ~**ness** nəs nɪs
any *strong form* 'en i (!); *occasional weak form* ən i → ᵊn i —*In Irish English,* any *and its compounds are often* 'æn i
Anyang æn 'jæŋ ‖ ˌɑːn 'jaːŋ —*Chinese* Ānyáng [¹an ²jaŋ]
anybody 'en i ˌbɒd i 'en ə-, -ˌbəd i ‖ -ˌbɑːd i —*also weak form* ən-
anyhow 'en i haʊ -ə-
anymore ˌen i 'mɔː ‖ -'mɔːr -'moʊr
anyone 'en i wʌn -ə-, §-wɒn, -wən —*also weak form* ən-
anyplace 'en i pleɪs -ə- —*also weak form* ən-
anyroad 'en i rəʊd -ə- ‖ -roʊd

A

anything 'en i θɪŋ -ə-; △-θɪŋk —*also weak form* ən-
anytime 'en i taɪm
anyway 'en i weɪ -ə-, **~s** z
anywhere 'en i weə -ə-, -hweə ‖ wer -hwer, -wær, -hwær, -wᵊr, -hwᵊr —*also occasional weak form* ən-
Anzac 'ænz æk
Anzio 'ænz i əʊ ‖ -oʊ 'ɑːnz- —*It* ['an tsio]
ANZUS 'ænz əs -ʊs
AOB ˌeɪ əʊ 'biː ‖ -oʊ-
A-OK, A-Okay ˌeɪ əʊ 'keɪ ‖ -oʊ-
AOL *tdmk* ˌeɪ əʊ 'el ‖ -oʊ-
aorist 'eər ɪst 'eɪ ər ɪst, -əst ‖ 'eɪ ər əst **~s** s
aoristic ₍ᵢ₎eə 'rɪst ɪk ◄ ˌeɪ ə'-- ‖ ˌeɪ ə 'rɪst- **~ally** ᵊl i
aort|a eɪ 'ɔːt |ə ‖ -'ɔːrt̬ |ə **~al** ᵊl **~as** əz **~ic** ɪk
Aotearoa ˌɑː əʊ tiːˌə 'rəʊ ə ‖ ˌɑː oʊ tiː ə 'roʊ ə
aoudad 'aʊd æd 'ɑː u dæd **~s** z
ap- ə, æ —*This variant of* ad- *is usually* ə (ap'pear), *but* æ *if stressed because of a suffix* (ˌappa'rition).
Ap *in Welsh names* æp
apace ə 'peɪs
Apache ə 'pætʃ i **~s** z —*for the obsolete sense 'ruffian', the pronunciation was* ə 'pæʃ —*Fr* [a paʃ]
Apalachicola ˌæp ə lætʃ ɪ 'kəʊl ə ◄ -ə'-- ‖ -'koʊl-
apanage 'æp ən ɪdʒ
apart ə 'pɑːt ‖ ə 'pɑːrt
apartheid ə 'pɑːt heɪt -haɪt, -eɪt, -aɪt, -aɪd ‖ ə 'pɑːrt eɪt -aɪt —*Afrikaans* [a 'part heɪt]
apartment ə 'pɑːt mənt ‖ ə 'pɑːrt- **~s** s
   a'partment ˌbuilding; a'partment house
apathetic ˌæp ə 'θet ɪk ◄ ‖ -'θet̬- **~ally** ᵊl i
apathy 'æp əθ i
apatite 'æp ə taɪt
ape eɪp **aped** eɪpt **apes** eɪps **aping** 'eɪp ɪŋ
apelike 'eɪp laɪk
ape|man 'eɪp| mæn **~men** men
Apennines 'æp ə naɪnz -ɪ-, -e-
aperçu ˌæp ɜː 'sjuː -ə-, -'suː ‖ -ᵊr 'suː ˌɑːp- —*Fr* [a pɛʁ sy] **~s** z —*or as singular*
aperient ə 'pɪər iˌənt ‖ ə 'pɪr- **~s** s
aperiodic ˌeɪ ˌpɪər i 'ɒd ɪk ‖ -ˌpɪr i 'ɑːd- **~ally** ᵊl i
aperiodicity ˌeɪ ˌpɪər iˌə 'dɪs ət i -ˌᵢi ɒ-, -ɪt i ‖ -ˌpɪr iˌə 'dɪs ət̬ i
aperitif, apéritif ə ˌper ə 'tiːf æ-, -ˌ-, ·ˑ· -tɪf ‖ ɑː- —*Fr* [a pe ʁi tif] **~s** s
aperture 'æp ə tʃə -tjʊə, -tʃʊə ‖ -ᵊr tʃʊr -tʃᵊr, -tjʊr **~s** z
apeshit 'eɪp ʃɪt
apex, Apex, APEX 'eɪp eks **~es** ɪz əz
apfelstrudel 'æp fəl ˌstruːd ᵊl -ˌʃtruːd-, ·ˑ·· —*Ger* ['apf ᵊl ˌʃtʁuːd ᵊl] **~s** z
aphaeresis æ 'fɪər əs ɪs ə-, -ɪs ɪs, §-əs ‖ ə 'fer-
aphasia ə 'feɪz iˌə eɪ-, æ-, -'feɪʒ ə, -'feɪʒ iˌə ‖ ə 'feɪʒ ə
aphasic ə 'feɪz ɪk eɪ-, æ-
aphelion æ 'fiːl iˌən æp 'hiːl-

apheresis æ 'fɪər əs ɪs ə-, -ɪs ɪs, §-əs ‖ ə 'fer-
aphesis 'æf əs ɪs -ɪs ɪs, §-əs
aphetic ə 'fet ɪk æ- ‖ -'fet̬- **~ally** ᵊl i
aphid 'eɪf ɪd 'æf-, §-əd **~s** z
aph|is 'eɪf |ɪs 'æf-, §-əs **~ides** i diːz §ə-
aphonia ₍ₑᵢ₎ 'fəʊn iˌə ‖ -'foʊn-
aphorism 'æf ə ˌrɪz əm **~s** z
aphorist 'æf ər ɪst §-əst **~s** s
aphoristic ˌæf ə 'rɪst ɪk ◄ **~ally** ᵊl i
Aphra 'æf rə
aphrodisiac ˌæf rə 'dɪz i æk ‖ -'diːz- **~s** s
Aphrodite ˌæf rə 'daɪt i ‖ -'daɪt̬ i
aphtha 'æfθ ə
aphthous 'æfθ əs
Apia ɑː 'piː ə ə-, -ɑː
apian 'eɪp iˌən
apiar|y 'eɪp iˌər |i ‖ -er |i **~ies** iz **~ist/s** ɪst/s §əst/s
apical 'æp ɪk ᵊl 'eɪp-
apices 'eɪp ɪ siːz 'æp-, -ə-
apiculture 'eɪp iˌˌkʌltʃ ə §-ə- ‖ -ᵊr
apiece ə 'piːs
aping 'eɪp ɪŋ
Apis *sacred bull* 'æp ɪs 'ɑːp-, 'eɪp-, §-əs
apish 'eɪp ɪʃ **~ly** li **~ness** nəs nɪs
aplastic ₍ₑᵢ₎ 'plæst ɪk -'plɑːst-
aplenty ə 'plent i ‖ ə 'plent̬ i
aplomb ə 'plɒm æ- ‖ -'plɑːm -'plʌm
apnea, apnoea æp 'niː ə 'æp niˌə
apo- *comb. form*
   with stress-neutral suffix ¦æp əʊ ‖ ¦æp ə
      — **apogamic** ˌæp əʊ 'gæm ɪk ◄ ‖ -ə-
   with stress-imposing suffix ə 'pɒ + æ 'pɒ + ‖ ə 'pɑː + — **apogamous** ə 'pɒg əm əs æ- ‖ -'pɑːg-
apocalyps|e, A~ ə 'pɒk ə lɪps ‖ ə 'pɑːk- **~es** ɪz əz
apocalyptic ə ˌpɒk ə 'lɪpt ɪk ◄ ‖ ə ˌpɑːk- **~ally** ᵊl i
apocope ə 'pɒk əp i ‖ ə 'pɑːk- (!)
apocrypha, A~ ə 'pɒk rəf ə -rɪf ə ‖ ə 'pɑːk-
apocryphal ə 'pɒk rəf ᵊl -rɪf ᵊl ‖ ə 'pɑːk- **~ly** i
apodosis ə 'pɒd əs ɪs §-əs ‖ ə 'pɑːd-
apogee 'æp əʊ dʒiː ‖ -ə-
apolitical ˌeɪ pə 'lɪt ɪk ᵊl ◄ ‖ -'lɪt̬- **~ly** ˌi
Apollinaire ə ˌpɒl ɪ 'neə -ə- ‖ ə ˌpɑːl ə 'neᵊr -'næᵊr —*Fr* [a pɔ li nɛːʁ]
Apollinaris ə ˌpɒl ɪ 'neər ɪs -ə-, -'nɑːr-, §-əs ‖ ə ˌpɑːl ə 'ner əs
Apollo, a~ ə 'pɒl əʊ ‖ ə 'pɑːl oʊ
Apollodorus ə ˌpɒl ə 'dɔːr əs ‖ ə ˌpɑːl- -'doʊr-
Apollonian ˌæp ə 'ləʊn iˌən ‖ -'loʊn-
Apollonius ˌæp ə 'ləʊn iˌəs ‖ -'loʊn-
Apollyon ə 'pɒl iˌən ‖ ə 'pɑːl jən
apologetic ə ˌpɒl ə 'dʒet ɪk ◄ ‖ ə ˌpɑːl ə 'dʒet̬ ɪk ◄ **~ally** ᵊl i **~s** s
apologia ˌæp ə 'ləʊdʒ iˌə -'ləʊdʒ ə ‖ -'loʊdʒ-
apologies ə 'pɒl ədʒ iz ‖ -'pɑːl-
apologis... —*see* **apologiz...**
apologist ə 'pɒl ədʒ ɪst §-əst ‖ ə 'pɑːl- **~s** s
apologiz|e ə 'pɒl ə dʒaɪz ‖ ə 'pɑːl- **~ed** d **~es** ɪz əz **~ing** ɪŋ
apologue 'æp əʊ lɒg ‖ -ə lɔːg -lɑːg **~s** z

apolog|y ə 'pɒl ədʒ |i ‖ ə 'pɑːl- ~ies iz
apophthegm 'æp ə θem ~s z
apoph|ysis ə 'pɒf |əs ɪs -ɪs ɪs, §-əs ‖ ə 'pɑːf-
  ~yses ə siːz ɪ-
apoplectic ˌæp ə 'plekt ɪk ◂ ~ally ᵊl_i
apoplexy 'æp ə pleks i
apoptosis ˌæp əp 'təʊs ɪs ˌeɪ pɒp-, §-əs
  ‖ -'toʊs- ˌeɪ pɑːp-
aport ə 'pɔːt ‖ ə 'pɔːrt -'poʊrt
aposiopesis ˌæp əʊ ˌsaɪ ə 'piːs ɪs §-əs ‖ ˌæp ə-
apostas|y ə 'pɒst əs |i ‖ ə 'pɑːst- ~ies iz
apostate ə 'pɒst eɪt -ət, -ɪt ‖ ə 'pɑːst- (!) ~s s
apostatis|e, apostatiz|e ə 'pɒst ə taɪz
  ‖ ə 'pɑːst- ~ed d ~es ɪz əz ~ing ɪŋ
a posteriori ˌeɪ pɒ ˌster i 'ɔːr aɪ ˌɑː-, -ˌstɪər-, -i
  ‖ ˌɑː poʊ ˌstɪr i 'ɔːr i ˌeɪ-, -ˌpɑː-, -'oʊr i
apostle ə 'pɒs ᵊl ‖ ə 'pɑːs ᵊl ~s, ~s' z ~ship
  ʃɪp
  Aˌpostles' 'Creed
apostolate ə 'pɒst ə leɪt ‖ ə 'pɑːst-
apostolic ˌæp ə 'stɒl ɪk ◂ -ɒ- ‖ -'stɑːl- ~ally
  ᵊl_i
  ˌapoˌstolic suc'cession
apostrophe ə 'pɒs trəf i ‖ ə 'pɑːs- ~s z
apostrophis|e, apostrophiz|e ə 'pɒs trə faɪz
  ‖ ə 'pɑːs- ~ed d ~es ɪz əz ~ing ɪŋ
apothecar|y ə 'pɒθ ək ər_|i -'ɪk-
  ‖ ə 'pɑːθ ə ker |i ~ies, ~ies' iz
apothegm 'æp ə θem ~s z
apotheosis ə ˌpɒθ i 'əʊs ɪs ◂ ˌæp əθ-, §-əs
  ‖ ə ˌpɑːθ i 'oʊs əs ˌæp əθ-
apotheosis|e, apotheosiz|e ə ˌpɒθ i 'əʊs aɪz
  ˌæp əθ- ‖ ə ˌpɑːθ i 'oʊs aɪz ˌæp əθ- ~ed d ~es
  ɪz əz ~ing ɪŋ
app æp apps æps
appal ə 'pɔːl ‖ -'pɑːl ~led d ~ling/ly ɪŋ /li ~s z
Appalach|ia ˌæp ə 'leɪtʃ |i_ə -'leɪtʃ |ə; -'leɪʃ-
  ~ian/s i_ən/z ən/z
appall ə 'pɔːl ‖ -'pɑːl ~ed d ~ing/ly ɪŋ /li ~s z
Appaloosa, a~ ˌæp ə 'luːs ə ~s z
appanag|e 'æp ən ɪdʒ ~es ɪz əz
apparat ˌæp ə 'rɑːt ‖ ˌɑːp- 'æp ə ræt
apparatchik ˌæp ə 'ræt tʃɪk -rɑːt-, -'rætʃ ɪk,
  -'rɑːtʃ ɪk ‖ ˌɑːp ə 'rɑːt- -'rɑːtʃ ɪk ~s s
apparatus sing., pl ˌæp ə 'reɪt əs -'rɑːt-, -'ræt-
  ‖ -'ræt̬ əs -'reɪt̬- ~es ɪz əz
apparel n, v ə 'pær əl ‖ -'per- ~ed, ~led d
  ~ing, ~ling ɪŋ ~s z
apparent ə 'pær ənt -'peər- ‖ -'per- ~ly li
  ~ness nəs nɪs
apparition ˌæp ə 'rɪʃ ᵊn ~s z
appassionata ə ˌpæs i_ə 'nɑːt ə ‖ -'nɑːt̬ ə
  -ˌpɑːs-
appeal ə 'piːᵊl appealed ə 'piːᵊld
  appealing/ly ə 'piːᵊl ɪŋ li appeals ə 'piːᵊlz
appear ə 'pɪə ‖ ə 'pɪᵊr appeared ə 'pɪəd
  ‖ ə 'pɪᵊrd appearing ə 'pɪər ɪŋ ‖ ə 'pɪr ɪŋ
  appears ə 'pɪəz ‖ ə 'pɪᵊrz
appearanc|e ə 'pɪər ənts ‖ ə 'pɪr- ~es ɪz əz
appeas|e ə 'piːz ~ed d ~ement mənt ~er/s
  ə/z ‖ ᵊr/z ~es ɪz əz ~ing ɪŋ
appellant ə 'pel ənt ~s s
appellate ə 'pel ət -ɪt, -eɪt

appellation ˌæp ə 'leɪʃ ᵊn -ɪ-, -e- ~s z
appellation contrôlée
  ˌæp ə ˌlæs i ɒ̃ kɒn 'trəʊl eɪ
  ‖ -ˌlɑːs i oʊn ˌkɑːn troʊ 'leɪ —Fr
  [a pe la sjɔ̃ kɔ̃ tʁɒ le]
appellative ə 'pel ət ɪv æ- ‖ -ət̬ ɪv ~ly li
appellee ˌæp el 'iː -ə 'liː ~s z
append ə 'pend ~ed ɪd əd ~ing ɪŋ ~s z
appendag|e ə 'pend ɪdʒ ~es ɪz əz
appendectom|y ˌæp ən 'dekt əm |i →ˌæp m-;
  ˌæp en- ~ies iz
appendicectom|y ə ˌpend ɪ 'sekt əm |i -ˌ-ə-
  ~ies iz
appendices ə 'pend ɪ siːz -ə-
appendicitis ə ˌpend ə 'saɪt ɪs -ˌɪ-, §-əs
  ‖ -'saɪt̬ əs
append|ix ə 'pend |ɪks ~ices ɪ siːz ə- ~ixes
  ɪks ɪz -əz
apperceiv|e ˌæp ə 'siːv ‖ -ᵊr- ~ed d ~es z ~ing
  ɪŋ
apperception ˌæp ə 'sep ʃᵊn ‖ -ᵊr- ~s z
apperceptive ˌæp ə 'sept ɪv ◂ ‖ -ᵊr-
Apperley 'æp əl i ‖ -ᵊr li
appertain ˌæp ə 'teɪn ‖ -ᵊr- ~ed d ~ing ɪŋ ~s
  z
appestat 'æp ɪ stæt -ə- ~s s
appetenc|e 'æp ɪt ənˑts -ət- ~y i
appetent 'æp ɪt ənt -ət-
appetis|e 'æp ɪ taɪz -ə- ~er/s ə/z ‖ ᵊr/z ~ing/ly
  ɪŋ /li
appetite 'æp ɪ taɪt -ə- ~s s
appetiz|e 'æp ɪ taɪz -ə- ~er/s ə/z ‖ ᵊr/z ~ing/ly
  ɪŋ /li
Appian 'æp i_ən
  ˌAppian 'Way
applaud ə 'plɔːd ‖ -'plɑːd ~ed ɪd əd ~ing ɪŋ ~s
  z
applause ə 'plɔːz ‖ -'plɑːz
apple 'æp ᵊl ~s z
  'apple ˌblossom; ˌapple 'green◂; ˌapple
  'pie; ˌapple 'sauce ‖ '·· ·; 'apple tree
Appleby 'æp ᵊl bi
applecart 'æp ᵊl kɑːt ‖ -kɑːrt ~s s
apple-cheeked ˌæp ᵊl 'tʃiːkt ◂
Appledore 'æp ᵊl dɔː ‖ -dɔːr
Applegarth 'æp ᵊl gɑːθ ‖ -gɑːrθ
applejack 'æp ᵊl dʒæk
apple-pie ˌæp ᵊl 'paɪ ◂
  ˌapple-pie 'order
Appleseed 'æp ᵊl siːd
applet 'æp lət -lɪt ~s s
Appleton 'æp ᵊl tən
Appleyard 'æp ᵊl jɑːd ‖ -jɑːrd
applianc|e ə 'plaɪ_ənts ~es ɪz əz
applicability ə ˌplɪk ə 'bɪl ət i ˌæp lɪk-, -ɪt i
  ‖ -ət̬ i

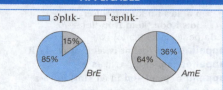

APPLICABLE

■ ə'plɪk- ■ 'æplɪk-

BrE: 85% / 15%
AmE: 64% / 36%

applicab|le ə 'plɪk əb |ᵊl 'æp lɪk əb |ᵊl **~ly** li
— Preference polls, BrE: ə'plɪk- 85%, 'æplɪk-
15%; AmE: 'æplɪk- 64%, ə'plɪk- 36%.
applicant 'æp lɪk ənt -lək- **~s** s
application ˌæp lɪ 'keɪʃ ᵊn -lə- **~s** z
applicator 'æp lɪ keɪt ə '·lə- ‖ -keɪṭ ᵊr **~s** z
applie... —see **apply**
appliqué ə 'pliːk eɪ æ- ‖ ˌæp lə 'keɪ **~d** d **~ing**
ɪŋ **~s** z
apply ə 'plaɪ **applied** ə 'plaɪd **applies** ə 'plaɪz
applying ə 'plaɪ ɪŋ
appoggiatura ə ˌpɒdʒ ə 'tʊər ə -ˌ·i̯ə'--, -'tjʊər-
‖ ə ˌpɑːdʒ ə 'tʊr ə **~s** z
appoint ə 'pɔɪnt **appointed** ə 'pɔɪnt ɪd -əd
‖ ə 'pɔɪnṭ əd **appointing** ə 'pɔɪnt ɪŋ
‖ ə 'pɔɪnṭ ɪŋ **appoints** ə 'pɔɪnts
appointee ə ˌpɔɪn 'tiː ˌæp ɔɪn- **~s** z
appointive ə 'pɔɪnt ɪv ‖ ə 'pɔɪnṭ ɪv
appointment ə 'pɔɪnt mənt **~s** s
Appomattox ˌæp ə 'mæt əks ‖ -'mæṭ-
apport ə 'pɔːt ‖ ə 'pɔːrt -'poʊrt
apportion ə 'pɔːʃ ᵊn ‖ ə 'pɔːrʃ ᵊn -'poʊrʃ- **~ed**
d **~ing** ɪŋ **~ment/s** mənt/s **~s** z
appos|e æ 'pəʊz ə- ‖ -'poʊz **~ed** d **~es** ɪz əz
~ing ɪŋ
apposite 'æp əz ɪt -ət; -ə zaɪt **~ly** li **~ness** nəs
nɪs
apposition ˌæp ə 'zɪʃ ᵊn
appositional ˌæp ə 'zɪʃ ᵊn əl ◂ **~ly** i
appositive ə 'pɒz ət ɪv æ-, -ɪt- ‖ -'pɑːz əṭ- **~ly**
li
appraisal ə 'preɪz ᵊl **~s** z
apprais|e ə 'preɪz **~ed** d **~er/s** ə/z ‖ ᵊr/z **~es**
ɪz əz **~ing** ɪŋ
appraisement ə 'preɪz mənt **~s** s
appreciab|le ə 'priːʃ əb |ᵊl -'·i̯əb-, ə 'priːs i̯
‖ ə 'prɪʃ- **~ly** li
appreci|ate ə 'priːʃ i |eɪt ə 'priːs- ‖ ə 'prɪʃ-
~ated eɪt ɪd -əd ‖ eɪṭ əd **~ates** eɪts **~ating**
eɪt ɪŋ ‖ eɪṭ ɪŋ
appreciation ə ˌpriːʃ i 'eɪʃ ᵊn -ˌpriːs- ‖ ə ˌprɪʃ-
appreciative ə 'priːʃ i̯ ət ɪv -'priːs-, -eɪt-;
-'priːʃ ət ɪv ◂ ‖ ə 'priːʃ əṭ ɪv ə 'prɪʃ-; -'·i eɪṭ- **~ly**
li **~ness** nəs nɪs
appreciatory ə 'priːʃ i̯ ət ᵊr i -'priːs-,
·, ·'eɪt ər i ◂ ‖ ə 'priːʃ ə tɔːr i -'prɪʃ-, -toʊr i
apprehend ˌæp rɪ 'hend ◂ -rə- **~ed** ɪd əd **~ing**
ɪŋ **~s** z
apprehensibility ˌæp rɪ ˌhen⟨s⟩ ə 'bɪl ət i ˌrə-,
-, -ə-, -ɪt i ‖ -əṭ i
apprehensib|le ˌæp rɪ 'hen⟨s⟩ əb |ᵊl ˌrə-, -ɪb ᵊl
~ly li
apprehension ˌæp rɪ 'hen⟨s⟩ ᵊn -rə- **~s** z

apprehensive ˌæp rɪ 'hen⟨s⟩ ɪv -rə- **~ly** li
~ness nəs nɪs
apprentic|e ə 'prent ɪs -əs ‖ ə 'prenṭ- **~ed** t
~es ɪz əz **~ing** ɪŋ
apprenticeship ə 'prent ɪs ʃɪp →-ɪʃ-, -ɪ ·, §-əs ·
‖ ə 'prenṭ əs- →-əʃ-, -ə · **~s** s
appris|e, appriz|e ə 'praɪz **~ed** d **~es** ɪz əz
~ing ɪŋ
appro 'æp rəʊ ‖ -roʊ
approach v, n ə 'prəʊtʃ ‖ ə 'proʊtʃ **~ed** t **~es**
ɪz əz **~ing** ɪŋ
approachability ə ˌprəʊtʃ ə 'bɪl ət i -ɪt i
‖ ə ˌproʊtʃ ə 'bɪl əṭ i
approachab|le ə 'prəʊtʃ əb |ᵊl ‖ ə 'proʊtʃ- **~ly**
li
appro|bate 'æp rəʊ |beɪt ‖ -rə- **~bated** beɪt ɪd
-əd ‖ beɪṭ əd **~bates** beɪts **~bating** beɪt ɪŋ
‖ beɪṭ ɪŋ
approbation ˌæp rəʊ 'beɪʃ ᵊn ‖ -rə-
approbative 'æp rəʊ beɪt ɪv ‖ -rə beɪṭ ɪv
approbatory ˌæp rəʊ 'beɪt ər i ◂
‖ ə 'proʊb ə tɔːr i 'æp rəb-, -toʊr i
appropriacy ə 'prəʊp ri̯ əs i ‖ ə 'proʊp-
appropri|ate v ə 'prəʊp ri |eɪt ‖ ə 'proʊp-
~ated eɪt ɪd -əd ‖ eɪṭ əd **~ates** eɪts **~ating**
eɪt ɪŋ ‖ eɪṭ ɪŋ
appropriate adj ə 'prəʊp ri̯ ət ɪt ‖ ə 'proʊp-
~ly li **~ness** nəs nɪs
appropriation ə ˌprəʊp ri 'eɪʃ ᵊn ‖ ə ˌproʊp-
~s z
approval ə 'pruːv ᵊl **~s** z
approv|e ə 'pruːv **~ed** d **~es** z **~ing/ly** ɪŋ /li
approx. ə 'prɒks ‖ ə 'prɑːks
approximant ə 'prɒks ɪm ənt -əm-
‖ ə 'prɑːks- **~s** s
approxi|mate v ə 'prɒks ɪ |meɪt -ə- ‖ -'prɑːks-
~mated meɪt ɪd -əd ‖ meɪṭ əd **~mates** meɪts
~mating meɪt ɪŋ ‖ meɪṭ ɪŋ
approximate adj ə 'prɒks ɪm ət -əm-, -ɪt
‖ ə 'prɑːks- **~ly** li
approximation ə ˌprɒks ɪ 'meɪʃ ᵊn -ə-
‖ -ˌprɑːks- **~s** z
approximative ə 'prɒks ɪm ət ɪv -'·əm-;
§-ɪ meɪt ɪv, §-ə ·· ‖ ə 'prɑːks ə meɪṭ ɪv **~ly** li
Apps æps
appurtenanc|e ə 'pɜːt ɪn ən⟨t⟩s -ən-
‖ ə 'pɜːt ᵊn ən⟨t⟩s **~es** ɪz əz
appurtenant ə 'pɜːt ɪn ənt -ən-
‖ ə 'pɜːt ᵊn ənt
APR ˌeɪ piː 'ɑː ‖ -'ɑːr
Aprahamian ˌæp rə 'heɪm i̯ ən
apraxia ⟨ɪ⟩eɪ 'præks i̯ə ə-, æ-
apres, après 'æp reɪ ‖ ˌɑː 'preɪ ◂, ˌæ- —Fr
[a pʁɛ]
apres-ski, après-ski ˌæp reɪ 'skiː ◂ ‖ ˌɑːp-
ˌæp-
apricot 'eɪp rɪ kɒt -rə- ‖ -kɑːt 'æp- **~s** s
April 'eɪp rᵊl -rɪl
   ˌApril 'fool, ˌApril 'Fools' Day
a priori ˌeɪ praɪ 'ɔːr aɪ ˌɑː-, -pri-, -i
‖ ˌɑː pri 'ɔːr i ˌeɪ-, ˌæp ri-, -'oʊr-
aprioristic ˌeɪ ˌpraɪ ə 'rɪst ɪk ˌɑː-, -, ˌpriː, -ɔː'--
~ally ᵊl i

A

apriority ˌeɪ praɪ 'ɒr ət i -ɪt- i ‖ ˌɑː pri 'ɔːr ət̬ i
  ˌeɪ-, ˌæp ri-
apron 'eɪp rən ‖ -ᵊrn ~**ed** d ~**ing** ɪŋ ~**s** z
  '**apron strings**
apropos ˌæp rə 'pəʊ ◂'· · · -'poʊ
apse æps **apses** 'æps ɪz -əz
apsidal 'æps ɪd ᵊl §-əd-; æp 'saɪd ᵊl
Apsley 'æps li
apt æpt **apter** 'æpt ə ‖ -ᵊr **aptest** 'æpt ɪst §-əst
Apted 'æpt ɪd -əd
apterous 'æpt ər əs
apteryx 'æpt ə rɪks
aptitude 'æpt ɪ tjuːd -ə-, →§-tʃuːd ‖ -tuːd -tjuːd
  ~**s** z
  '**aptitude test**
apt|ly 'æpt |li ~**ness** nəs nɪs
Apuleius ˌæp ju 'liː əs -'leɪ- ‖ -jə-
Apulia ə 'pjuːl i ə —*It* Puglia ['puʎ ʎa]
Apus 'eɪp əs
Aqaba, 'Aqaba 'æk əb ə ‖ 'ɑːk ə bɑː 'æk-,
  -əb ə —*Arabic* ['ʕa qa bah]
aq|ua 'æk |wə ‖ 'ɑːk- 'æk- ~**uae** wiː waɪ, weɪ
  —*see also phrases with this word*
  ˌaqua 'fortis
aquacade 'æk wə keɪd ‖ 'ɑːk- 'æk- ~**s** z
aquaculture 'æk wə ˌkʌltʃ ə
  ‖ 'ɑːk wə ˌkʌltʃ ᵊr 'æk-
aqualung, Aqua-Lung *tdmk* 'æk wə lʌŋ
  ‖ 'ɑːk- 'æk- ~**s** z
aquamarine ˌæk wə mə 'riːn ◂ ‖ ˌɑːk- ˌæk- ~**s**
  z
aquanaut 'æk wə nɔːt ‖ 'ɑːk- 'æk-, -nɑːt ~**s** s
aquaplan|e 'æk wə pleɪn ‖ 'ɑːk- 'æk- ~**ed** d
  ~**es** z ~**ing** ɪŋ
aqua regia ˌæk wə 'riːdʒ i ə -'riːdʒ ə ‖ ˌɑːk-
  ˌæk-
aquarelle ˌæk wə 'rel ‖ ˌɑːk- ˌæk- ~**s** z
aquarellist ˌæk wə 'rel ɪst §-əst ‖ ˌɑːk- ˌæk- ~**s**
  s
aquaria ə 'kweər i ə ‖ ə 'kwer- ə 'kwær-
Aquarian ə 'kweər i ən ‖ ə 'kwer- ə 'kwær- ~**s**
  z
aquarist 'æk wər ɪst §-əst ‖ ə 'kwer- ə 'kwær-
  (*) ~**s** s
aquari|um ə 'kweər i |əm ‖ ə 'kwer- ə 'kwær-
  ~**a** ə ~**ums** əmz
Aquarius ə 'kweər i əs ‖ ə 'kwer- ə 'kwær-
aquarobics ˌæk wə 'rəʊb ɪks ‖ -'roʊb-
Aquascutum *tdmk* ˌæk wə 'skjuːt əm
  ‖ -'skjuːt̬-
aquatic ə 'kwæt ɪk -'kwɒt- ‖ ə 'kwɑːt̬ ɪk
  -'kwæt̬- ~**ally** ᵊl i ~**s** s
aquatint 'æk wə tɪnt ‖ 'ɑːk- 'æk- ~**s** s
aquavit 'æk wə vɪt -viːt ‖ 'ɑːk wə viːt ~**s** s
aqua vitae ˌæk wə 'vaɪt iː -'viːt aɪ
  ‖ ˌɑːk wə 'vaɪt̬ i ˌæk-
aqueduct 'æk wɪ dʌkt -wə- ~**s** s
aqueous 'eɪk wi əs 'æk-
aquifer 'æk wɪf ə -wəf- ‖ -ᵊr ~**s** z
Aquila 'æk wɪl ə -wəl-; ə 'kwɪl ə
aquilegia ˌæk wɪ 'liːdʒ i ə ˌ-wə-, -'liːdʒ ə ~**s** z
aquiline 'æk wɪ laɪn -wə- ‖ -wəl ən
Aquinas ə 'kwaɪn əs æ-, -æs

Aquino ə 'kiːn əʊ ‖ -oʊ —*Sp* [a 'ki no]
Aquitaine ˌæk wɪ 'teɪn -wə-, '· · · —*Fr*
  [a ki tɛn]
Aquitania ˌæk wɪ 'teɪn i ə ˌ-wə-
aquiver ə 'kwɪv ə ‖ -ᵊr
-ar ə, ɑː ‖ ᵊr, ɑːr —*In most words this ending is
  pronounced weak,* ə ‖ ᵊr *('cedar, 'stellar). In a
  few rarer or newer words it is pronounced
  strong,* ɑː ‖ ɑːr, *either as an alternative or as
  the only form* ('lumbar, 'radar).
ar- ə, æ —*This variant of ad- is usually* ə
  (ar'range), *but* æ *if stressed because of a suffix*
  ('arrogant).
Arab 'ær əb ~**s** z
Arabella ˌær ə 'bel ə ‖ ˌer-
arabesque ˌær ə 'besk ◂ ‖ ˌer- ~**s** s
Arabia ə 'reɪb i ə
Arabian ə 'reɪb i ən ~**s** z
  A ˌrabian 'Nights
Arabic 'ær əb ɪk ‖ 'er-
  ˌArabic 'numeral
arabica ə 'ræb ɪk ə ~**s** z
arabinose ə 'ræb ɪ nəʊz §-ə-, -nəʊs ‖ -**nous**
  -noʊz
arabis 'ær əb ɪs §-əs ‖ 'er-
Arabist 'ær əb ɪst §-əst ‖ 'er- ~**s** s
arable 'ær əb ᵊl ‖ 'er-
Araby 'ær əb i ‖ 'er-
arachnid ə 'ræk nɪd §-nəd ~**s** z
arachnoid ə 'ræk nɔɪd ~**s** z
arachnophobia ə ˌræk nəʊ 'fəʊb i ə
  ‖ -nə 'foʊb-
Arafat 'ær ə fæt ‖ 'er-, -fɑːt —*Arabic*
  [ʕa ra 'fat]
Arafura ˌær ə 'fʊər ə -'fjʊər- ‖ ˌɑːr ə 'fʊr ə
Aragon 'ær əg ən ‖ -ə gɑːn -əg ən —*Sp*
  Aragón [a ra 'ɣon] *but as a Fr family name,*
  [-ə gɔ̃ ‖ -ə gɔːn], *Fr* [a ʁa gɔ̃]
aragonite ə 'ræg ə naɪt 'ær əg-
arak 'ær ək -æk ‖ 'er-; ə 'ræk
Aral 'ær əl 'ɑːr-, 'eər- ‖ 'er-
Araldite *tdmk* 'ær əl daɪt ‖ 'er-
aralia ə 'reɪl i ə ~**s** z
Aramaic ˌær ə 'meɪ ɪk ◂ ‖ ˌer-
Araminta ˌær ə 'mɪnt ə ‖ -'mɪnt̬ ə ˌer-
Aran 'ær ən ‖ 'er-
Aranda 'ær ənd ə ə 'rʌnt ə
Arapaho 'ær əp ə həʊ ‖ -hoʊ
Ararat 'ær ə ræt ‖ 'er-
Araucania ˌær ɔː 'keɪn i ə ‖ ˌer-, ˌɑː-; ə ˌrɔː-,
  ə ˌrɑː-
araucaria ˌær ɔː 'keər i ə ‖ -'ker-, ˌer-, ˌɑː-,
  -'kær- ~**s** z
Arawak 'ær ə wæk ‖ -wɑːk 'er- ~**an** ən ~**s** s
arbalest, arbalist 'ɑːb əl ɪst -əst ‖ 'ɑːrb- ~**s** s
Arbela ɑː 'biːl ə ‖ ɑːr-
arbiter, A~ 'ɑːb ɪt ə -ət- ‖ 'ɑːrb ət̬ ᵊr ~**s** z
arbitrage 'ɑːb ɪ trɑːʒ -ə-, -trɪdʒ, ˌ· · 'trɑːʒ
  ‖ 'ɑːrb-
arbitrageur ˌɑːb ɪ trɑː 'ʒɜː ˌ·ə-, -trə'·, -'ʒʊə
  ‖ ˌɑːrb ə trɑː 'ʒɜː ~**s** z
arbitral 'ɑːb ɪtr əl -ətr- ‖ 'ɑːrb-
arbitrament ɑː 'bɪtr ə mənt ‖ ɑːr- ~**s** s

arbitrarily

40

arbitrarily 'ɑːb ɪtr ər əl i '·ətr-, -ɪ li; △'· ·ə li;
ˌɑːb ə 'treər·ˌ·, -'trer-, §-'trær-
‖ ˌɑːr bə 'trer əl i
arbitrar|y 'ɑːb ɪtr ər| i '·ətr-; △'· ·|i
‖ 'ɑːrb ə trer| i **~iness** i nəs i nɪs
arbi|trate 'ɑːb ɪ |treɪt -ə- ‖ 'ɑːrb- **~trated**
treɪt ɪd -əd ‖ treɪt̬ əd **~trates** treɪts **~trating**
treɪt ɪŋ ‖ treɪt̬ ɪŋ
arbitration ˌɑːb ɪ 'treɪʃ ᵊn -ə- ‖ ˌɑːrb- **~s** z
arbitrator 'ɑːb ɪ treɪt ə '·ə- ‖ 'ɑːrb ə treɪt̬ ᵊr **~s**
z
Arblaster 'ɑːb lɑːst ə §-læst- ‖ 'ɑːrb læst ᵊr
arbor *'tree'* 'ɑːb ə -ɔː ‖ 'ɑːrb ᵊr **~s** z
ˌarbor 'vitae 'vaɪt iː 'viːt aɪ ‖ 'vaɪt̬ i
arbor *'arbour'; 'shaft'* 'ɑːb ə ‖ 'ɑːrb ᵊr **~s** z
Arbor 'ɑːb ə ‖ 'ɑːrb ᵊr
'Arbor Day
arboraceous ˌɑːb ə 'reɪʃ əs ◂ -ɔː- ‖ ˌɑːrb-
arbore|al ɑː 'bɔːr i |əl ‖ ɑːr- -'boʊr- **~ally** ᵊl i
~ous əs
arboresc|ence ˌɑːb ə 'res |ᵊnᵗs ◂ ‖ ˌɑːrb- **~ent**
ᵊnt
arboret|um ˌɑːb ə 'riːt |əm ‖ ˌɑːrb ə 'riːt̬ |əm
~a ə
Arborfield 'ɑːb ə fiːᵊld ‖ 'ɑːrb ᵊr-
arboriculture 'ɑːb ər i ˌkʌltʃ ə ·ˌ·ˌ·ˌ·; ɑː 'bɒr-,
·ˌ·ˌ·ˌ· ‖ 'ɑːrb ər i ˌkʌltʃ ᵊr ɑːr 'bɔːr-, -'boʊr-
arborist 'ɑːb ər ɪst §-əst ‖ 'ɑːrb- **~s** s
Arborite *tdmk* 'ɑːb ə raɪt ‖ 'ɑːrb-
arbour 'ɑːb ə ‖ 'ɑːrb ᵊr **~s** z
arbovirus 'ɑːb əʊ ˌvaɪᵊr əs ‖ 'ɑːrb oʊ- **~es** ɪz
əz
Arbroath ɑː 'brəʊθ ‖ ɑːr 'broʊθ
Arbuckle 'ɑː ˌbʌk ᵊl ˌ·'·· ‖ 'ɑːr-
Arbuthnot ɑː 'bʌθ nət ə-, -nɒt ‖ ɑːr-
arbutus ɑː 'bjuːt əs ‖ ɑːr 'bjuːt̬ əs **~es** ɪz əz
arc ɑːk ‖ ɑːrk (= *ark*) **arced, arcked** ɑːkt
‖ ɑːrkt **arcing, arcking** 'ɑːk ɪŋ ‖ 'ɑːrk ɪŋ **arcs**
ɑːks ‖ ɑːrks —*See also phrases with this word*
arcad|e ₍ᵢ₎ɑː 'keɪd ‖ ɑːr- **~ed** ɪd əd **~es** z
Arcadi|a ɑː 'keɪd i ˌ|ə ‖ ɑːr- **~an/s** ən/z
Arcady 'ɑːk əd i ‖ 'ɑːrk-
arcana ɑː 'keɪn ə -'kɑːn- ‖ ɑːr-
arcane ₍ᵢ₎ɑː 'keɪn ‖ ɑːr-
arcan|um ɑː 'keɪn |əm -'kɑːn- ‖ ɑːr- **~a** ə
Arc de Triomphe ˌɑːk də 'triː ɒmᵖf -əʊmᵖf
‖ ˌɑːrk də tri 'ɑːmᵖf -'ɔːmᵖf —*Fr*
[aʁk də tʁi ɔ̃ːf]
arced ɑːkt ‖ ɑːrkt
arch, Arch ɑːtʃ ‖ ɑːrtʃ **arched** ɑːtʃt ‖ ɑːrtʃt
arches 'ɑːtʃ ɪz -əz ‖ 'ɑːrtʃ- **arching** 'ɑːtʃ ɪŋ
‖ 'ɑːrtʃ-
arch- |ɑːtʃ ‖ |ɑːrtʃ — **arch-rival** ɑːtʃ 'raɪv ᵊl
‖ ˌɑːrtʃ- —*Note however the exception*
archangel |ɑːk- ‖ |ɑːrk-, *and compare* archi-
-arch ɑːk ‖ ɑːrk — **ecclesiarch** ɪ 'kliːz i ɑːk
‖ -ɑːrk —*but in* monarch *usually* ək *in RP.*
Archaean ɑː 'kiː ən ‖ ɑːr-
archaeo- *comb. form*
with stress-neutral suffix |ɑːk i əʊ ‖ |ɑːrk i oʊ
— **archaeoastronomy**
ˌɑːk i əʊ ə 'strɒn əm i ‖ ˌɑːrk i oʊ ə 'strɑːn-
with stress-imposing suffix ˌɑːk i 'ɒ +

archaeopteryx ˌɑːk i 'ɒpt ə rɪks ‖ ˌɑːrk i 'ɑːpt-
archaeological ˌɑːk i ə 'lɒdʒ ɪk ᵊl ◂
‖ ˌɑːrk i ə 'lɑːdʒ- **~ly** i
archaeologist ˌɑːk i 'ɒl ədʒ ɪst §-əst
‖ ˌɑːrk i 'ɑːl- **~s** s
archaeology ˌɑːk i 'ɒl ədʒ i ‖ ˌɑːrk i 'ɑːl-
archaeopteryx ˌɑːk i 'ɒpt ə rɪks
‖ ˌɑːrk i 'ɑːpt-
Archaeozoic, a~ ˌɑːk i ə 'zəʊ ɪk ◂
‖ ˌɑːrk i ə 'zoʊ ɪk ◂
archaic ₍ᵢ₎ɑː 'keɪ ɪk ‖ ɑːr- **~ally** ᵊl i
archais... —*see* **archaiz...**
archaism 'ɑːk eɪ ˌɪz əm ‖ 'ɑːrk i- '·eɪ- **~s** z
archaiz|e 'ɑːk eɪ aɪz -i- ‖ 'ɑːrk i- -eɪ- **~ed** d **~es**
ɪz əz **~ing** ɪŋ
archangel, A~ 'ɑːk ˌeɪndʒ əl ˌ·'·· ‖ 'ɑːrk- **~s** z
archbishop ₍ᵢ₎ɑːtʃ 'bɪʃ əp ‖ ₍ᵢ₎ɑːrtʃ- **~s** s
archbishopric ₍ᵢ₎ɑːtʃ 'bɪʃ əp rɪk ‖ ₍ᵢ₎ɑːrtʃ- **~s** s
Archbold 'ɑːtʃ bəʊld →-bɒʊld ‖ 'ɑːrtʃ boʊld
archdeacon, A~ ₍ᵢ₎ɑːtʃ 'diːk ən ‖ ₍ᵢ₎ɑːrtʃ- **~s** z
archdeacon|ry ₍ᵢ₎ɑːtʃ 'diːk ən |ri ‖ ₍ᵢ₎ɑːrtʃ-
~ries riz
archdi|ocese ˌɑːtʃ 'daɪ |əs ɪs §-əs; ə siːz, -siːs
‖ ˌɑːrtʃ 'daɪ |əs əs **~oceses** ə siːz əs ɪs ɪz, -əs-,
-əz; ə siːz ɪz, -siːs-, -əz ‖ ə səs əz, -iːz
archducal ˌɑːtʃ 'djuːk ᵊl ◂ →§-'dʒuːk-
‖ ˌɑːrtʃ 'duːk ᵊl -'djuːk-
archduchess ˌɑːtʃ 'dʌtʃ ɪs -əs ‖ ˌɑːrtʃ- **~es** ɪz əz
archduch|y ˌɑːtʃ 'dʌtʃ |i ‖ ˌɑːrtʃ- **~ies** iz
archduke ˌɑːtʃ 'djuːk ◂ →§-'dʒuːk
‖ ˌɑːrtʃ 'duːk ◂ -'djuːk **~s** s
Archean ɑː 'kiː ən ‖ ɑːr-
arched ɑːtʃt ‖ ɑːrtʃt
Archelaus ˌɑːk ɪ 'leɪ əs -ə- ‖ ˌɑːrk-
archenem|y ˌɑːtʃ 'en əm |i -ɪm- ‖ ˌɑːrtʃ- **~ies**
iz
archeo- *comb. form*
with stress-neutral suffix |ɑːk i əʊ ‖ |ɑːrk i oʊ
— **archaeoastronomy**
ˌɑːk i əʊ ə 'strɒn əm i ‖ ˌɑːrk i oʊ ə 'strɑːn-
with stress-imposing suffix ˌɑːk i 'ɒ +
‖ ˌɑːrk i 'ɑː + — **archaeopteryx**
ˌɑːk i 'ɒpt ə rɪks ‖ ˌɑːrk i 'ɑːpt-
archeological ˌɑːk i ə 'lɒdʒ ɪk ᵊl ◂
‖ ˌɑːrk i ə 'lɑːdʒ- **~ly** i
archeologist ˌɑːk i 'ɒl ədʒ ɪst §-əst
‖ ˌɑːrk i 'ɑːl- **~s** s
archeology ˌɑːk i 'ɒl ədʒ i ‖ ˌɑːrk i 'ɑːl-
archeopteryx ˌɑːk i 'ɒpt ə rɪks ‖ ˌɑːrk i 'ɑːpt-
Archeozoic, a~ ˌɑːk i ə 'zəʊ ɪk ◂
‖ ˌɑːrk i ə 'zoʊ ɪk ◂
archer, A~ 'ɑːtʃ ə ‖ 'ɑːrtʃ ᵊr **~s** z
archery 'ɑːtʃ ər i ‖ 'ɑːrtʃ-
arches, A~ 'ɑːtʃ ɪz -əz ‖ 'ɑːrtʃ-
archetypal ˌɑːk i 'taɪp ᵊl ◂ ·ˌ·ˌ·· ‖ ˌɑːrk- **~ly** i
archetype 'ɑːk i taɪp ‖ 'ɑːrk- **~s** s
archetypical ˌɑːk ɪ 'tɪp ɪk ᵊl ◂ ˌ·ə- ‖ ˌɑːrk- **~ly**
i
archi- |ɑːk i -ɪ ‖ |ɑːrk i -ə — **archicarp**
'ɑːk i kɑːp ‖ 'ɑːrk i kɑːrp
Archibald 'ɑːtʃ ɪ bɔːld -ə- ‖ 'ɑːrtʃ ə- -bɑːld

A

-archic *comb. form* 'ɑːk ɪk ‖ 'ɑːrk-
— **heptarchic** hep 'tɑːk ɪk ‖ -'tɑːrk-
Archie 'ɑːtʃ i ‖ 'ɑːrtʃ i
archimandrite ˌɑːk i 'mændr aɪt ◂ ‖ ˌɑːrk ə-
  ~s s
Archimedean ˌɑːk ɪ 'miːd i ‿ən -'meɪd-;
  -mi- 'diːˌən ‖ ˌɑːrk-
Archimedes ˌɑːk ɪ 'miːd iːz ◂ -ə-, -'meɪd-
  ‖ ˌɑːrk-
arching 'ɑːtʃ ɪŋ ‖ 'ɑːrtʃ-
archipelago ˌɑːk ɪ 'pel ə ɡəʊ ˌ-ə-, -ɪ ɡəʊ
  ‖ ˌɑːrk ə 'pel ə ɡoʊ **~es, ~s** z
archiphoneme 'ɑːk i ˌfəʊn iːm ˌ·'··
  ‖ 'ɑːrk i ˌfoʊn- **~s** z
archiphonemic ˌɑːk i fəʊ 'niːm ɪk ◂
  ‖ ˌɑːrk i foʊ- **~ally** ᵊl i
architect 'ɑːk ɪ tekt -ə- ‖ 'ɑːrk- **~s** s
architectonic ˌɑːk ɪ tek 'tɒn ɪk ◂ ˌ·ə-,
  ‖ ˌɑːrk ə tek 'tɑːn- **~ally** ᵊl i **~s** s
architectural ˌɑːk ɪ 'tek tʃᵊr ᵊl ◂ ˌ·ə- ‖ ˌɑːrk-
  ~ly i
architecture 'ɑːk ɪ tek tʃə ˌ·ə-
  ‖ 'ɑːrk ə tek tʃᵊr
architrave 'ɑːk ɪ treɪv -ə- ‖ 'ɑːrk- **~s** z
archival ɑː 'kaɪv ᵊl ‖ ɑːr-
archiv|e 'ɑːk aɪv ‖ 'ɑːrk- **~ed** d **~es** z **~ing** ɪŋ
archivist 'ɑːk ɪv ɪst -əv-, §-əst ‖ 'ɑːrk- -aɪv- **~s** s
archly 'ɑːtʃ li ‖ 'ɑːrtʃ li
archon 'ɑːk ən -ɒn ‖ 'ɑːrk ɑːn **~s** z **~ship** ʃɪp
archway 'ɑːtʃ weɪ ‖ 'ɑːrtʃ- **~s** z
-archy ɑːk i ‖ ɑːrk i — **heptarchy** 'hept ɑːk i
  ‖ -ɑːrk i —*but in* 'anarchy, 'monarchy *usually*
  ək i ‖ ᵊrk i
arcing, arck... —*see* **arc**
arco, Arco *tdmk* 'ɑːk əʊ ‖ 'ɑːrk oʊ
arcsin, arcsine 'ɑːk saɪn ˌ·'· ‖ 'ɑːrk-
arctan 'ɑːk tæn ˌ·'· ‖ 'ɑːrk-
arctic, A~ 'ɑːkt ɪk △ 'ɑːt- ‖ 'ɑːrkt- 'ɑːrṭ- **~ally**
  ᵊl i
  ˌArctic 'Circle
Arcturus ɑːk 'tjʊər əs ‖ ɑːrk 'tʊr-
arc-weld ˌɑːk 'weld ‖ ˌɑːrk- **~ed** ɪd əd **~ing** ɪŋ
  ~s z
ard ɑːd ‖ ɑːrd **ards** ɑːdz ‖ ɑːrdz
-ard əd, ɑːd ‖ ᵊrd, ɑːrd —*In well-known words*
  this ending is əd *or* ᵊrd ('standard, 'custard,*
  'wizard, 'Edward). In less familiar words ɑːd
  ‖ ɑːrd *is an alternative or sometimes the only*
  pronunciation, often through the influence of
  the spelling ('bollard, 'mansard). The suffix
  -ward(s) *is usually* wəd(z) ‖ wᵊrd(z), *but* -yard
  is jɑːd ‖ jɑːrd *except usually in* 'vineyard.
Ardagh 'ɑːd ə -ɑː ‖ 'ɑːrd ə
Ardeche, Ardèche ɑː 'deʃ ‖ ɑːr- —*Fr* [aʁ dɛʃ]
Ardee ɑː 'diː ‖ ɑːr-
Arden 'ɑːd ᵊn ‖ 'ɑːrd-
ardency 'ɑːd ᵊnˈs i ‖ 'ɑːrd-
Ardennes ɑː 'den -'denz ‖ ɑːr- —*Fr* [aʁ dɛn]
ardent 'ɑːd ᵊnt ‖ 'ɑːrd- **~ly** li
ard fhéis ˌɑːd 'eɪʃ ˌɔːd- ‖ ˌɑːrd- —*Irish*
  [ɒrḍ 'eːʃ]
Arding 'ɑːd ɪŋ ‖ 'ɑːrd-
Ardingly 'ɑːd ɪŋ laɪ ˌ·'· ‖ 'ɑːrd-

Ardizzone ˌɑːd ɪ 'zəʊn i -ə- ‖ ˌɑːrd ə 'zoʊn i
Ardmore ɑːd 'mɔː →ɑːb- ‖ ɑːrd 'mɔːr -'moʊr
Ardnamurchan ˌɑːd nə 'mɜːk ən -'mɜːx-
  ‖ ˌɑːrd nə 'mɜːk ən
ardor, ardour 'ɑːd ə ‖ 'ɑːrd ᵊr
Ardoyne ɑː 'dɔɪn ‖ ɑːr-
Ardrishaig ɑː 'drɪʃ ɪɡ -eɪɡ ‖ ɑːr-
Ardrossan ɑː 'drɒs ᵊn ‖ ɑːr 'drɑːs ᵊn -'drɔːs-
Ards ɑːdz ‖ ɑːrdz
arduous 'ɑːd juˌəs 'ɑːdʒ uˌ ‖ 'ɑːrdʒ uˌəs **~ly** li
  ~ness nəs nɪs
Ardwick 'ɑːd wɪk ‖ 'ɑːrd-
are *v from* be, *strong form* ɑː ‖ ɑːr, *weak form* ə
  ‖ ᵊr
are *n* '100 m²' eə ɑː ‖ eᵊr æᵊr, ɑːr
area 'eər iˌə ‖ 'er- 'ær- **~s** z
  'area code
areca ə 'riːk ə 'ær ɪk ə **~s** z
arena ə 'riːn ə **~s** z
Arendt 'ɑːr ənt —*German* ['ɑːʁ ənt]
Arenig ə 'ren ɪɡ —*Welsh* [a 're nig]
aren't ɑːnt ‖ ɑːrnt
are|ola ə 'riːˌ|əl ə æ- **~olae** ə liː **~olas** əl əz
areometer ˌeər i 'ɒm ɪt ə ˌær-, -ət ə
  ‖ ˌer i 'ɑːm ət ᵊr ˌær- **~s** z
Areopagite ˌær i 'ɒp ə ɡaɪt -dʒaɪt ‖ ˌær i 'ɑːp-
  ˌer- **~s** s
Areopagitic ˌær i ɒp ə 'dʒɪt ɪk -'ɡɪt-
  ‖ ˌær i ɑːp ə 'dʒɪt̬ ɪk ˌer- **~a** ə
Areopagus ˌær i 'ɒp əɡ əs ‖ -'ɑːp- ˌer-
Ares 'eər iːz ‖ 'er- 'ær-
arete, arête ə 'reɪt æ-, -'ret —*Fr* [a ʁɛt] **~s** s
Aretha ə 'riːθ ə
Arethusa ˌær ɪ 'θjuːz ə -ə-, -e-, -'θuːz-
  ‖ -'θuːz ə ˌer-
Arfon 'ɑːv ᵊn -ɒn ‖ 'ɑːrv- -ɑːn —*Welsh*
  ['ar von]
argali 'ɑːɡ əl i ‖ 'ɑːrɡ- **~s** z
Argand, a~ 'ɑːɡ ænd -ənd ‖ ɑːr 'ɡɑːn ◂ -'ɡæn
  —*Fr* [aʁ ɡɑ̃]
argent, A~ 'ɑːdʒ ənt ‖ 'ɑːrdʒ-
Argentina ˌɑːdʒ ən 'tiːn ə ‖ ˌɑːrdʒ-
Argentine *inhabitant* 'ɑːdʒ ən tiːn -taɪn
  ‖ 'ɑːrdʒ- **~s** z
Argentine *country* 'ɑːdʒ ən taɪn -tiːn ‖ 'ɑːrdʒ-
Argentinian ˌɑːdʒ ən 'tɪn i ən ◂ ‖ ˌɑːrdʒ- **~s** z
Argie 'ɑːdʒ i ‖ 'ɑːrdʒ i **~s** z
argillaceous ˌɑːdʒ ɪ 'leɪʃ əs ◂ -ə- ‖ ˌɑːrdʒ-
arginine 'ɑːdʒ ɪ niːn -ə-, -naɪn ‖ 'ɑːrdʒ-
Argive 'ɑːɡ aɪv 'ɑːdʒ- ‖ 'ɑːrdʒ- 'ɑːrɡ- **~s** z
Argo 'ɑːɡ əʊ ‖ 'ɑːrɡ oʊ
argol 'ɑːɡ ɒl -ᵊl ‖ 'ɑːrɡ ɑːl -ɔːl, -ᵊl
Argolis 'ɑːɡ ə lɪs ‖ 'ɑːrɡ-
argon 'ɑːɡ ɒn -ən ‖ 'ɑːrɡ ɑːn
Argonaut 'ɑːɡ ə nɔːt ‖ 'ɑːrɡ- -nɑːt **~s** s
Argos 'ɑːɡ ɒs ‖ 'ɑːrɡ ɑːs -əs
argos|y 'ɑːɡ əs |i ‖ 'ɑːrɡ- **~ies** iz
argot 'ɑːɡ əʊ -ət, -ɒt ‖ 'ɑːrɡ oʊ -ət
arguab|le 'ɑːɡ juˌəb |ᵊl ‖ 'ɑːrɡ- **~ly** li
argu|e 'ɑːɡ juː ‖ 'ɑːrɡ- **~ed** d **~es** z **~ing** ɪŋ
argument 'ɑːɡ ju mənt -jə- ‖ 'ɑːrɡ jə- **~s** s
argumentation ˌɑːɡ ju men 'teɪʃ ᵊn ˌ·jə-,
  -mən'·- ‖ ˌɑːrɡ jə mən- -men'·-

argumentative ˌɑːg ju 'ment ət ɪv ◄ ˌjə-
‖ ˌɑːrg jə 'menʧ əʧ ɪv ◄ **~ly** li **~ness** nəs nɪs
argus, Argus 'ɑːg əs ‖ 'ɑːrg-
argy-bargy ˌɑːdʒ i 'bɑːdʒ i ‖ ˌɑːrdʒ i 'bɑːrdʒ i
Argyle, a~, Argyll ₍ᵢ₎ɑː 'gaɪᵊl ‖ ₍ᵢ₎ɑːr- ' · · —*For
the name of the type of sock and sock pattern,
AmE prefers the stressing* ' · ·
Argyrol *tdmk* 'ɑːdʒ ə rɒl -ɪ- ‖ 'ɑːrdʒ ə roʊl
-rɑːl, -rɔːl
Arhus 'ɔː huːs 'ɑː-, -hʊs ‖ 'ɑːr- 'ɔːr- —*Danish*
Århus ['ɔː huːʔ s]
aria 'ɑːr i ə **~s** z
Ariadne ˌær i 'æd ni ‖ ˌer-, -'ɑːd-
Arial 'eər i̯əl ‖ 'er- 'ær-
Arian 'eər i̯ən ‖ 'er- 'ær- **~s** z
-arian *comb. form* 'eər i̯ən ‖ 'er- 'ær- —
libertarian ˌlɪb ə 'teər i̯ən ‖ -ᵊr 'ter- -'tær-
Ariane ˌær i 'æn ‖ ˌɑːr i 'ɑːn —*Fr* [a ʁjan]
Arianna ˌær i 'æn ə ‖ ˌer-
arid 'ær ɪd §-əd ‖ 'er- **~ly** li **~ness** nəs nɪs
aridit|y ə 'rɪd ət |i æ-, -ɪt i ‖ -əʈ |i **~ies** iz
Ariel, ariel 'eər i̯əl ‖ 'er- 'ær-
Arien 'eər i̯ən ‖ 'er- 'ær-
Aries 'eər iːz 'eər i iːz ‖ 'er iːz 'ær-, ᵊ i iːz
arietta ˌær i 'et ə ‖ ˌɑːr i 'eʈ ə ˌær-, ˌer- —*It*
[a ɾi 'et ta] **~s** z
aright ə 'raɪt
aril 'ær əl -ɪl ‖ 'er- **~s** z
-arily ᵊr̩əl i ər̩ɪ li; 'er- · , §'ær- · · ‖ 'er əl i
—*Compare* -ary. *The traditional RP form is
now increasingly replaced by* 'er-, *giving a
mismatch between adjective and adverb; see*
(necessarily, primarily, voluntarily)
Arimathaea, Arimathea ˌær ɪm ə 'θiː̩ə ˌəm-
‖ ˌer-
arioso ˌɑːr i 'əʊz əʊ ˌær-, -'əʊs- ‖ -'oʊs oʊ
-'oʊz- **~s** z
Ariosto ˌær i 'ɒst əʊ ‖ ˌɑːr i 'ɑːst oʊ -'ɔːst-,
-'oʊst- —*It* [a 'rjɔs to, a ɾi 'ɔs to]
arise ə 'raɪz **arisen** ə 'rɪz ᵊn *(!)* **arises**
ə 'raɪz ɪz -əz **arising** ə 'raɪz ɪŋ **arose** ə 'rəʊz
‖ ə 'roʊz
Aristaeus ˌær i 'stiː̩əs -ə- ‖ ˌer-
Aristarchus ˌær ɪ 'stɑːk əs -ə- ‖ -'stɑːrk- ˌer-
Aristide ˌær ɪ 'stiːd ‖ ˌer-, -ə- —*Fr* [a ʁis tid]
Aristides ˌær ɪ 'staɪd iːz -ə- ‖ ˌer-
Aristippus ˌær ɪ 'stɪp əs -ə- ‖ ˌer-
aristo ə 'rɪst əʊ ‖ -oʊ **~s** z
Aristoc *tdmk* 'ær ɪ stɒk -ə- ‖ -stɑːk 'er-
aristocrac|y ˌær ɪ 'stɒk rəs |i ˌ·ə- ‖ -'stɑːk- ˌer-
~ies iz
aristocrat 'ær ɪst ə kræt '·əst-, ə 'rɪst- ‖ ə 'rɪst-
~s s
aristocratic ˌær ɪst ə 'kræt ɪk ◄ ˌ·əst-, ə ˌrɪst-
‖ ə ˌrɪst ə 'kræʈ ɪk ◄ **~ally** ᵊl̩i
Aristophanes ˌær ɪ 'stɒf ə niːz ˌ·ə- ‖ -'stɑːf-
ˌer-
Aristophanic ˌær ɪst ə 'fæn ɪk ◄ ˌ·əst-, -ɒ'--
‖ ˌer-
Aristotelian ˌær ɪst ə 'tiːl i̯ən ◄ ˌ·əst-, -ɒ'--,
-'tel- ‖ ˌer- **~s** z
ˌAristoˌtelian 'logic
Aristotle 'ær ɪ stɒt ᵊl '·ə- ‖ -stɑːʈ ᵊl 'er-

arithmetic *n* ə 'rɪθ mə tɪk
arithmetic *adj* ˌær ɪθ 'met ɪk ◄ -əθ-
‖ -'meʈ ɪk ◄ ˌer- **~al** ᵊl **~ally** ᵊl̩i
ˌarithˌmetic pro'gression
arithmetician ə ˌrɪθ mə 'tɪʃ ᵊn ˌær ɪθ-, ˌær əθ-
~s z
-arium *comb. form* 'eər i̯əm ‖ 'er- 'ær-
— **planetarium** ˌplæn ə 'teər i̯əm ˌ·ɪ-
‖ -'ter- -'tær-
Arizon|a ˌær ɪ 'zəʊn |ə ◄ -ə- ‖ -'zoʊn |ə ˌer-
~an/s ən/z **~ian/s** i̯ən/z
Arjuna 'ɑːdʒ ʊn ə ‖ 'ɑːrdʒ- —*Hindi* [ər dʒʊn]
ark, Ark ɑːk ‖ ɑːrk **arks** ɑːks ‖ ɑːrks
Arkansan ɑː 'kænz ᵊn ‖ ɑːr- **~s** z
Arkansas 'ɑːk ən sɔː ‖ 'ɑːrk- -sɑː —*but the* A~
River *is also* ɑː 'kænz əs ‖ ɑːr-
Arkell *(i)* 'ɑːk ᵊl ‖ 'ɑːrk-, *(ii)* ɑː 'kel ‖ ɑːr-
Arkhangelsk ˌɑːk æŋ 'gelsk ɑː 'kæŋ gelsk
‖ ɑːr 'kɑːn gelsk —*Russ* [ʌr ˈxan gᵊilᵊsk]
Arkle 'ɑːk ᵊl ‖ 'ɑːrk-
Arklow 'ɑːk ləʊ ‖ 'ɑːrk loʊ
Arkwright 'ɑːk raɪt ‖ 'ɑːrk-
Arlen 'ɑːl ən ‖ 'ɑːrl-
Arlene 'ɑːl iːn ‖ ɑːr 'liːn
Arles ɑːlz ɑːl ‖ ɑːrl —*Fr* [aʁl]
Arlette ₍ᵢ₎ɑː 'let ‖ ɑːr-
Arlington 'ɑːl ɪŋ tən ‖ 'ɑːrl-
Arlott 'ɑːl ət ‖ 'ɑːrl-
arm ɑːm ‖ ɑːrm **armed** ɑːmd ‖ ɑːrmd **arming**
'ɑːm ɪŋ ‖ 'ɑːrm ɪŋ **arms** ɑːmz ‖ ɑːrmz
armada ɑː 'mɑːd ə ‖ ɑːr- —*formerly* -'meɪd- **~s**
z
Armadale 'ɑːm ə derᵊl ‖ 'ɑːrm-
armadillo ˌɑːm ə 'dɪl əʊ ‖ ˌɑːrm ə 'dɪl oʊ **~s** z
Armageddon ˌɑːm ə 'ged ᵊn ‖ ˌɑːrm-
Armagh ˌɑː 'mɑː ◄ ‖ ˌɑːr-
Armagnac, a~ 'ɑːm ən jæk ‖ ˌɑːrm ən 'jæk
-'jɑːk —*Fr* [aʁ ma njak]
Armalite, ArmaLite *tdmk* 'ɑːm ə laɪt ‖ 'ɑːrm-
~s s
armament 'ɑːm ə mənt ‖ 'ɑːrm- **~s** s
armamentarium ˌɑːm ə men 'teər i̯əm
-mən'-- ‖ ˌɑːrm ə men 'ter-
Armand 'ɑːm ənd ‖ ɑːr 'mɑːn —*Fr* [aʁ mɑ̃]
Armani ɑː 'mɑːn i ‖ ɑːr- —*It* [aɾ 'ma: ni]
Armathwaite 'ɑːm ə θweɪt ‖ 'ɑːrm-
Armatrading ˌɑːm ə 'treɪd ɪŋ ‖ 'ɑːrm-
armature 'ɑːm əʧ ə -ə ʧʊə, -ə ʧʊə
‖ 'ɑːrm ə ʧʊr -tʊr, -əʧ ᵊr **~s** z
armband 'ɑːm bænd ‖ 'ɑːrm- **~s** z
armchair 'ɑːm ʧeə ˌ·'· ‖ 'ɑːrm ʧer -ʧær **~s** z
armed ɑːmd ‖ ɑːrmd
ˌarmed 'forces
Armeni|a ɑː 'miːn i̯ə ‖ ɑːr- **~an/s** ən/z
Armentieres, Armentières 'ɑːm ən tɪəz ˌ·'·
‖ ˌɑːrm ən 'tjeᵊr —*Fr* [aʁ mɑ̃ tjɛːʁ]
armeria ɑː 'mɪər i̯ə ‖ ɑːr 'mɪr-
Armfield 'ɑːm fiːᵊld ‖ 'ɑːrm-
armful 'ɑːm fʊl ‖ 'ɑːrm- **~s** z
armhole 'ɑːm həʊl →-hɒʊl ‖ 'ɑːrm hoʊl **~s** z
Armidale 'ɑːm ɪ derᵊl -ə- ‖ 'ɑːrm-
armie... —*see* **army**

armiger, A~ 'ɑːm ɪdʒ ə §-ədʒ- ‖ 'ɑːrm ɪdʒ ᵊr
~s z
armigerous ɑː 'mɪdʒ ər əs ‖ ɑː-
armillary ɑː 'mɪl ər i 'ɑːm ɪl- ‖ 'ɑːrm ə ler i
ɑːr 'mɪl ər i
Arminian ɑː 'mɪn iˌən ‖ ɑːr- **~ism** ˌɪz əm **~s** z
Arminius ɑː 'mɪn iˌəs ‖ ɑːr-
Armistead 'ɑːm ɪ sted -stɪd ‖ 'ɑːrm-
armistic|e 'ɑːm ɪst ɪs -əst-, §-əs; §ɑː 'mɪst ɪs
‖ 'ɑːrm- **~es** ɪz əz
   'Armistice Day
Armitage 'ɑːm ɪt ɪdʒ -ət- ‖ 'ɑːrm ət̬-
armlet 'ɑːm lət -lɪt ‖ 'ɑːrm- **~s** s
Armley 'ɑːm li ‖ 'ɑːrm-
armload 'ɑːm ləʊd ‖ 'ɑːrm loʊd **~s** z
armlock 'ɑːm lɒk ‖ 'ɑːrm lɑːk **~s** s
armoire ɑː 'mwɑː ‖ ɑːr 'mwɑːr **~s** z
armor, A~ 'ɑːm ə ‖ 'ɑːrm ᵊr **~ed** d **armoring**
'ɑːm ər ɪŋ ‖ 'ɑːrm- **~s** z
   ˌarmored 'car; ˌarmor 'plate ‖ '· ·
armorer 'ɑːm ər ə ‖ 'ɑːrm ər ᵊr **~s** z
armorial ɑː 'mɔːr iˌəl ‖ ɑːr- -'moʊr- **~s** z
Armoric|a ɑː 'mɒr ɪk |ə ‖ ɑːr 'mɔːr- -'mɑːr-
~an/s ən/z
armor|y 'ɑːm ər |i ‖ 'ɑːrm- **~ies** iz
armour, A~ 'ɑːm ə ‖ 'ɑːrm ᵊr **~ed** d
armouring 'ɑːm ər ɪŋ ‖ 'ɑːrm- **~s** z
   ˌarmoured 'car; ˌarmour 'plate ‖ '· ·
armourer 'ɑːm ər ə ‖ 'ɑːrm ər ᵊr **~s** z
armour|y 'ɑːm ər |i ‖ 'ɑːrm- **~ies** iz
armpit 'ɑːm pɪt ‖ 'ɑːrm- **~s** s
armrest 'ɑːm rest ‖ 'ɑːrm- **~s** s
arms ɑːmz ‖ ɑːrmz
   'arms race
Armstrong 'ɑːm strɒŋ ‖ 'ɑːrm strɔːŋ -strɑːŋ
arm|y 'ɑːm |i ‖ 'ɑːrm |i **~ies** iz
   ˌarmy 'officer
Arndale 'ɑːn deɪᵊl ‖ 'ɑːrn-
Arne ɑːn ‖ ɑːrn
Arnhem 'ɑːn əm ‖ 'ɑːrn- —*Dutch* ['ɑrn hɛm,
-əm]
   'Arnhem Land
arnica 'ɑːn ɪk ə ‖ 'ɑːrn-
Arnie 'ɑːn i ‖ 'ɑːrn i
Arno 'ɑːn əʊ ‖ 'ɑːrn oʊ —*It* ['ɑr no]
Arnold 'ɑːn ᵊld ‖ 'ɑːrn-
Arnot, Arnott 'ɑːn ət -ɒt ‖ 'ɑːrn- -ɑːt
A-road 'eɪ rəʊd ‖ -roʊd **~s** z
aroint ə 'rɔɪnt
aroma ə 'rəʊm ə ‖ ə 'roʊm ə **~s** z
aromatherap|y ə ˌrəʊm ə 'θer əp |i ·'· ·ˌ· · ·
‖ -ˌroʊm- **~ist/s** ɪst/s §əst/s
aromatic ˌær ə 'mæt ɪk ◄ -əʊ- ‖ -'mæt̬- ˌer-
~ally ᵊl i
aromaticity ˌær ə mə 'tɪs ət i -mæ'·-,
ə ˌrəʊm ə-, -ɪt i ‖ -ət̬ i ˌer-; ə ˌroʊm ə-
aromatis|e, aromatiz|e ə 'rəʊm ə taɪz
‖ ə 'roʊm- **~ed** d **~es** ɪz əz **~ing** ɪŋ
Aronowitz ə 'rɒn ə wɪts ‖ ə 'rɑːn-
arose ə 'rəʊz ‖ ə 'roʊz
around ə 'raʊnd
around-the-clock ə ˌraʊnd ðə 'klɒk ◄
‖ -'klɑːk ◄

arousal ə 'raʊz ᵊl **~s** z
arous|e ə 'raʊz **~ed** d **~es** ɪz əz **~ing** ɪŋ
Arp ɑːp ‖ ɑːrp
arpeggio ɑː 'pedʒ i əʊ -'pedʒ əʊ
‖ ɑːr 'pedʒ i oʊ -'pedʒ oʊ **~ed** d **~s** z
arquebus 'ɑːk wɪb əs -wəb- ‖ 'ɑːrk- **~es** ɪz əz
arrack 'ær ək -æk ‖ 'er-; ə 'ræk
arraign ə 'reɪn **~ed** d **~ing** ɪŋ **~ment/s** mənt/s
~s z
Arran 'ær ən ‖ 'er-
arrange ə 'reɪndʒ **arranged** ə 'reɪndʒd
arranges ə 'reɪndʒ ɪz -əz **arranging**
ə 'reɪndʒ ɪŋ
arrangement ə 'reɪndʒ mənt **~s** s
arranger ə 'reɪndʒ ə ‖ -ᵊr **~s** z
arrant 'ær ənt ‖ 'er- **~ly** li
arras 'ær əs ‖ 'er- **~es** ɪz əz
Arras 'ær əs ‖ 'er- —*Fr* [a ʁaːs]
Arrau ə 'raʊ —*Sp* [a 'rraʊ]
array ə 'reɪ **arrayed** ə 'reɪd **arraying** ə 'reɪ ɪŋ
arrays ə 'reɪz
arrear ə 'rɪə ‖ ə 'rɪᵊr **~s** z
arrearag|e ə 'rɪər ɪdʒ ‖ ə 'rɪr- **~es** ɪz əz
Arrecife ˌær ə 'siːf eɪ -ɪ-, -e- ‖ ˌɑːr- —*Sp*
[a rre 'θi fe, -'si-]
arrest *v, n* ə 'rest **~ed** ɪd əd **~ing/ly** ɪŋ /li **~s** s
arrestable ə 'rest əb ᵊl
arrester, arrestor ə 'rest ə ‖ -ᵊr **~s** z
arrhythmia ə 'rɪð mi ə eɪ-
Arrian 'ær iˌən ‖ 'er-
arriere-pensee, arrière-pensée
ˌær i eə 'pɒnˈs eɪ -pɒn 'seɪ ‖ -ˌer paːn 'seɪ ˌer-
—*Fr* [a ʁjɛʁ pɑ̃ se]
arris 'ær ɪs §-əs ‖ 'er- **~es** ɪz əz
Arriva *tdmk* ə 'riːv ə
arrival ə 'raɪv ᵊl **~s** z
   ar'rival time
arrive ə 'raɪv **arrived** ə 'raɪvd **arrives** ə 'raɪvz
arriving ə 'raɪv ɪŋ
arrivederci ˌriːv ə 'dɜːtʃ i -'deətʃ- ‖ -'dertʃ i
—*It* [ar ri ve 'der tʃi]
arriving ə 'raɪv ɪŋ
arriviste, ~s ˌær iː 'viːst -'vɪst; ə 'riːv ɪst ‖ ˌer-
—*Fr* [a ʁi vist]
Arrochar 'ær ək ə -əx- ‖ -ᵊr 'er-
arrogance 'ær əg ənˈts ‖ 'er-
arrogant 'ær əg ənt ‖ 'er- **~ly** li
arro|gate 'ær ə |geɪt ‖ 'er- **~gated** geɪt ɪd -əd
‖ geɪt̬ əd **~gates** geɪts **~gating** geɪt ɪŋ
‖ geɪt̬ ɪŋ
arrogation ˌær ə 'geɪʃ ᵊn ‖ ˌer- **~s** z
arrondissement ˌær ɒn 'diːs mɒ̃
‖ ˌæ ˌrɑːnd iːs 'maːn ə- —*Fr* [a ʁɔ̃ dis mɑ̃]
arrow 'ær əʊ ‖ -oʊ 'er- **~ed** d **~ing** ɪŋ **~s** z
arrowhead 'ær əʊ hed ‖ -oʊ- 'er- **~s** z
arrowroot 'ær əʊ ruːt ‖ -oʊ- 'er-
Arrowsmith 'ær əʊ smɪθ ‖ -oʊ- 'er-
arrowwood 'ær əʊ wʊd ‖ -oʊ- 'er-
arroyo ə 'rɔɪ əʊ ‖ -oʊ —*Sp* [a 'rro jo] **~s** z
ars ɑːz ‖ ɑːrs
   ˌars po'etica pəʊ 'et ɪk ə ‖ poʊ 'et̬-

A

arse ɑːs ‖ æs ɑːrs **arsed** ɑːst ‖ æst ɑːrst **arses**
'ɑːs ɪz -əz ‖ 'æs- 'ɑːrs- **arsing** 'ɑːs ɪŋ ‖ 'æs-
'ɑːrs-

arsehole 'ɑːs həʊl →-hɒʊl ‖ 'æs hoʊl 'ɑːrs- **~d**
d **~s** z

arse-lick|er 'ɑːs ˌlɪk ə ‖ 'æs ˌlɪk ᵊr **~ers** əz
‖ ᵊrz **~ing** ɪŋ

arsenal, A~ 'ɑːs ᵊn ᵊl ‖ 'ɑːrs- **~s, ~'s** z

arsenate 'ɑːs ə neɪt -ɪ-; -ən ət, -ɪn-, -ɪt ‖ 'ɑːrs-
~s s

arsenic *adj* ɑː 'sen ɪk ‖ ɑːr- **~al/s** ᵊl/z

arsenic *n* 'ɑːs ᵊn ˌɪk ‖ 'ɑːrs-

arsenide 'ɑːs ə naɪd -ɪ- ‖ 'ɑːrs- **~s** z

arsine 'ɑːs iːn ‖ 'ɑːrs- ɑːr 'siːn

arsis 'ɑːs ɪs §-əs ‖ 'ɑːrs-

arson 'ɑːs ᵊn ‖ 'ɑːrs-

arsonist 'ɑːs ᵊn ɪst §-əst ‖ 'ɑːrs- **~s** s

art *n* ɑːt ‖ ɑːrt —*but in certain French phrases
also* ɑː ‖ ɑːr **arts** ɑːts ‖ ɑːrts —*See also
phrases with this word*
  'art form; **,arts and 'crafts**; **'Arts ,Faculty**

art *v, from* be, *usual form* ɑːt ‖ ɑːrt, *occasional
weak form* ət ‖ ᵊrt

Art *name* ɑːt ‖ ɑːrt

Artaxerxes ˌɑːt ə 'zɜːks iːz -əg-, -ək-, '··,··
‖ ˌɑːrt̬ ə 'zɜːks iːz

art deco, Art Deco ˌɑːt 'dek əʊ ˌɑː-, -'deɪk-
‖ ˌɑːrt̬ deɪ 'koʊ ˌɑːr-, -'deɪk oʊ —*Fr* Art Déco
[aʁ de ko]

artefact 'ɑːt ɪ fækt -ə- ‖ 'ɑːrt̬- **~s** s

Artemis 'ɑːt ɪm ɪs -əm-, §-əs ‖ 'ɑːrt̬-

artemisia ˌɑːt ɪ 'mɪz i̯ə ˌ·ə-, -'miːz-
‖ ˌɑːrt̬ ə 'mɪʒ ə -'mɪʒ i̯ə, -'mɪz- **~s** z

Artemus 'ɑːt ɪm əs -əm- ‖ 'ɑːrt̬-

arterial ɑː 'tɪər i̯əl ‖ ɑːr 'tɪr- **~ly** i

arteries 'ɑːt ər iz ‖ 'ɑːrt̬-

arteriole ɑː 'tɪər i əʊl →-ɒʊl ‖ ɑːr 'tɪr i oʊl **~s**
z

arteriosclerosis ɑː ˌtɪər i əʊ sklə 'rəʊs ɪs
-sklɪə'--, -sklɪ'--, §-əs
‖ ɑːr ˌtɪr i oʊ sklə 'roʊs əs

Arterton 'ɑːt ət ən ‖ 'ɑːrt̬ ᵊrt ᵊn

arter|y 'ɑːt ər |i ‖ 'ɑːrt̬- **~ies** iz

artesian ɑː 'tiːz i̯ən -'tiːʒ-; -'tiːʒ ᵊn
‖ ɑːr 'tiːʒ ᵊn
  ar,tesian 'well

Artex *tdmk* 'ɑːt eks ‖ 'ɑːrt-

artful 'ɑːt fᵊl -fʊl ‖ 'ɑːrt- **~ly** ˌi
  ,Artful 'Dodger

Arthington *(i)* 'ɑːð ɪŋ tən ‖ 'ɑːrð-, *(ii)* 'ɑːθ-
‖ 'ɑːrθ-

arthr- *comb. form before vowel*
  with stressed suffix ɑː θr+ ‖ ɑːr θr+
  — **arthralgia** ɑː 'θrældʒ i̯ə ‖ ɑːr-
  with unstressed suffix |ɑːθ r+ ‖ |ɑːrθ r+
  — **arthrous** 'ɑːθ rəs ‖ 'ɑːrθ-

arthritic ɑː 'θrɪt ɪk ‖ ɑːr 'θrɪt̬ ɪk **~ally** ᵊl_i

arthritis ɑː 'θraɪt ɪs △ ˌɑːθ ə 'raɪt-, §-əs
‖ ɑːr 'θraɪt̬ əs

arthro- *comb. form*
  with stress-neutral suffix |ɑːθ rəʊ ‖ |ɑːrθ rə
  — **arthrospore** 'ɑːθ rəʊ spɔː ‖ 'ɑːrθ rə spɔːr
-spoʊr

with stress-imposing suffix ɑː 'θrɒ+
‖ ɑːr 'θrɑː:+ — **arthropodous** ɑː 'θrɒp əd əs
‖ ɑːr 'θrɑːp-

arthropod 'ɑːθ rə pɒd ‖ 'ɑːrθ rə pɑːd **~s** z

Arthur 'ɑːθ ə ‖ 'ɑːrθ ᵊr

Arthurian ɑː 'θjʊər i̯ən -'θʊər- ‖ ɑːr 'θʊr-

arti... —*see* **arty**

artic *'articulated vehicle'* ɑː 'tɪk 'ɑːt ɪk ‖ ɑːr- **~s**
s

artichoke 'ɑːt ɪ tʃəʊk -ə- ‖ 'ɑːrt̬ ə tʃoʊk **~s** s

article 'ɑːt ɪk ᵊl ‖ 'ɑːrt̬- **~d** d **~s** z

articulacy ɑː 'tɪk jʊl əs i -'·jəl-
‖ ɑːr 'tɪk jəl əs i

articulate *adj* ɑː 'tɪk jʊl ət -jəl-, -ɪt
‖ ɑːr 'tɪk jəl ət **~ly** li **~ness** nəs nɪs

articu|late *v* ɑː 'tɪk ju |leɪt -jə- ‖ ɑːr 'tɪk jə-
~lated leɪt ɪd -əd ‖ leɪt̬ əd **~lates** leɪts
~lating leɪt ɪŋ ‖ leɪt̬ ɪŋ

articulation ɑː ˌtɪk ju 'leɪʃ ᵊn -jə- ‖ ɑːr ˌtɪk jə-
~s z

articulative ɑː 'tɪk jʊl ət ɪv -ju leɪt ɪv
‖ ɑːr 'tɪk jəl ət̬ ɪv -jə leɪt̬-

articulator ɑː 'tɪk ju leɪt ə -'·jə-
‖ ɑːr 'tɪk jə leɪt̬ ᵊr

articulator|y ɑː 'tɪk jʊl ət ᵊr |i -'·jəl-;
ɑː ˌtɪk ju 'leɪt ᵊr |i, -ˌjə-, ·'····
‖ ɑːr 'tɪk jəl ə tɔːr |i -toʊr **~ily** əl i ɪ li

Artie 'ɑːt i ‖ 'ɑːrt̬ i

artifact 'ɑːt ɪ fækt -ə- ‖ 'ɑːrt̬- **~s** s

artific|e 'ɑːt ɪf ɪs -əf-, §-əs ‖ 'ɑːrt̬- **~es** ɪz əz

artificer ɑː 'tɪf ɪs ə -əs- ‖ ɑːr 'tɪf əs ᵊr **~s** z

artificial ˌɑːt ɪ 'fɪʃ ᵊl ◄ -ə- ‖ ˌɑːrt̬- **~ly** i
  ,arti,ficial in'telligence; ,arti,ficial
  'kidney; ,arti,ficial ,respi'ration

artificiality ˌɑːt ɪ ˌfɪʃ i 'æl ət i ˌ·ə-, -ɪt i
‖ ˌɑːrt̬ ə ˌfɪʃ i 'æl ət̬ i

artillery ɑː 'tɪl ər i ‖ ɑːr-

artillery|man ɑː 'tɪl ər i |mən -mæn ‖ ɑːr-
~men mən men

artisan ˌɑːt ɪ 'zæn -ə-, '··· ‖ 'ɑːrt̬ əz ən -əs- (*)
~s z

artisanal ɑː 'tɪz ᵊn ᵊl ˌɑːt ɪ 'zæn ᵊl ◄ ‖ 'ɑːrt̬ əz-

artisanate ˌɑːt ɪ 'zæn eɪt -ə- ‖ 'ɑːrt̬ əz ə neɪt
'·əs-

artist 'ɑːt ɪst §-əst ‖ 'ɑːrt̬ əst **~s** s

artiste ɑː 'tiːst ‖ ɑːr- —*Fr* [aʁ tist] **~s** s

artistic ɑː 'tɪst ɪk ‖ ɑːr- **~ally** ᵊl_i

artistry 'ɑːt ɪst ri §-əst- ‖ 'ɑːrt̬-

artless 'ɑːt ləs -lɪs ‖ 'ɑːrt- **~ly** li **~ness** nəs nɪs

art nouveau, Art Nouveau ˌɑːt nu: 'vəʊ ˌɑː-
‖ ˌɑːrt nu: 'voʊ ˌɑːr- —*Fr* [aʁ nu vo]

Artois ɑː 'twɑː ‖ ɑːr- —*Fr* [aʁ twa]

artsy 'ɑːts i ‖ 'ɑːrts i

artsy-craftsy ˌɑːts i 'krɑːfts i ◄ §-'kræfts-
‖ ˌɑːrts i 'kræfts i ◄

artsy-fartsy ˌɑːts i 'fɑːts i ◄
‖ ˌɑːrts i 'fɑːrts i ◄

Arturo ɑː 'tʊər əʊ ‖ ɑːr 'tʊr oʊ —*It*
[ar 'tu: ɾo]

artwork 'ɑːt wɜːk ‖ 'ɑːrt wɜːk

art|y 'ɑːt |i ‖ 'ɑːrt̬ |i **~ier** i̯ə ‖ i̯ᵊr **~iest** i̯ɪst
i̯əst **~ily** ɪ li əl i **~iness** i nəs i nɪs

Articulation

1   **Articulation** is the production of speech sounds by using the speech organs to modify the air stream set in motion by the lungs. (Regularly in some languages, and very occasionally in English, the air may be set in motion in a way not involving the lungs. This applies, for example, in CLICKS.) Consonants are classified according to their **place** and **manner** of articulation.

2   English consonant sounds have the following **places of articulation**:

p, b, m	are **bilabials**	articulated by the lower lip against the upper lip
f, v	are **labiodentals**	articulated by the lower lip against the upper teeth
θ, ð	are **dentals**	articulated by the tongue tip against the upper teeth
t, d, n, l, s, z	are **alveolars**	articulated by the tongue tip or blade against the alveolar ridge
r, tr, dr	are **post-alveolars**	articulated by raising the tongue tip towards the rear of the alveolar ridge
ʃ, ʒ, tʃ, dʒ	are **palato-alveolars**	articulated by the retracted blade of the tongue against the alveolar ridge and hard palate (usually accompanied by some lip-rounding)
j	is a **palatal**	articulated by raising the front of the body of the tongue towards the hard palate
k, g, ŋ	are **velars**	articulated by the back of the tongue against the soft palate
w	is a **labial-velar**	articulated by raising the back of the tongue towards the soft palate and rounding the lips
ʔ	is a **glottal**	(see GLOTTAL STOP)

3   Note that in some other languages there are also:

- **alveolo-palatals**   articulated by the front of the body of the tongue against the hard palate, together with raising the blade of the tongue towards the alveolar ridge (e.g. the Japanese *sh* ç)
- **labial-palatals**   articulated like palatals but with rounding of the lips (e.g. the French ɥ in *juin* ʒɥæ̃)
- **retroflexes**   articulated by curling the tongue tip back against the alveolar ridge or hard palate (e.g. the Hindi ʈ ʈ)

Articulation ▶

Articulation continued

- **uvulars**   articulated by the extreme back of the tongue against the uvula (e.g. the French *r* ʁ)

- **pharyngals**   articulated by squeezing the pharynx (e.g. the Arabic ʕ)

4   English consonants have the following typical **manners of articulation**:

p, t, k, b, d, g	are **plosives**	articulated with a complete obstruction of the mouth passage, entirely blocking the air-flow for a moment
f, v, θ, ð, s, z, ʃ, ʒ	are **fricatives**	articulated by narrowing the mouth passage so as to make the air-flow turbulent, while allowing it to pass through continuously
tʃ, dʒ (and also usually tr, dr)	are **affricates**	articulated with first a complete obstruction and then a narrowing of the mouth passage (see AFFRICATES)
m, n, ŋ	are **nasals**	articulated by completely obstructing the mouth passage but allowing the air to pass out through the nose
r, l	are **liquids**	articulated by diverting or modifying the air-flow through the mouth
j, w	are **semivowels**	articulatorily like vowels, but functioning as consonants because they are not syllabic

Plosives, fricatives, and affricates are all **obstruents**; nasals, liquids, and semivowels are **sonorants**. Liquids and semivowels are usually **approximants** (= the air escapes freely through the mouth with no turbulence).

---

arty-crafty ˌɑːt i ˈkrɑːft i ◄ §-ˈkræft-
‖ ˌɑːrṭ i ˈkræft i ◄
arty-farty ˌɑːt i ˈfɑːt i ◄ ‖ ˌɑːrṭ i ˈfɑːrṭ i ◄
Arub|a ə ˈruːb |ə —*Dutch* [ɑ ˈry: baː] **~an/s**
    ən/z
arugula ə ˈruːg əl ə -jʊl-, -jəl-
arum ˈeər əm ‖ ˈer- ˈær-
Arun ˈær ən ‖ ˈer-
Arunachal ˌær u ˈnɑːtʃ ᵊl ‖ ˌer- —*Hindi*
    [ə rʊ ṇɑ: tʃəl]
Arundel *(i)* ˈær ənd ᵊl ‖ ˈer-, *(ii)* ə ˈrʌnd ᵊl
    —*The place in Sussex is (i), that in MD (ii).*
arvo ˈɑːv əʊ ‖ -oʊ **~s** z
Arwel ˈɑː wel ‖ ˈɑːr- —*Welsh* [ˈar wel]
Arwyn ˈɑː wɪn ‖ ˈɑːr- —*Welsh* [ˈar wɪn, -wɪn]
-ary əri, eri —*In words of three syllables this*
    suffix is usually weak, ər i (ˈbinary, ˈglossary).
    In longer words it is usually weak in BrE, ər i
    (frequently reduced to ri*); but strong in AmE,*
    er i: *thus* ˈarbitrary ˈɑːb ɪtr ər i

‖ ˈɑːrb ə trer i, ˈcustomary
ˈkʌst əm ər i ‖ ˈkʌst ə mer i. *The stress may*
fall either one or two syllables further back
(exˈemplary, ˌanniˈversary; ˈmercenary,
ˌinterˈplanetary). *A few words differ in stress*
as between BrE and AmE (coˈrollary
‖ ˈcorollary).

Aryan ˈeər i ˌən ˈɑːr- ‖ ˈer- ˈær-, ˈɑːr- **~s** z
aryl ˈær ɪl -əl ‖ ˈer-
arytenoid ˌær ɪ ˈtiːn ɔɪd ◄ -ə- ‖ ə ˈrɪt ᵊn ɔɪd
    ˌær ə ˈtiːn ɔɪd, ˌer- *(*)* **~s** z
    ˌary,tenoid ˈcartilage ‖ ·ˌ· ·—
as *strong form* æz, *weak form* əz
as- *This variant of* ad- *is usually* ə, *but* æ *if*
    stressed because of a suffix (asˈsign;
    ˌassigˈnation).
Asa *(i)* ˈeɪs ə, *(ii)* ˈeɪz ə, *(iii)* ˈɑːs ə
asafetida, asafoetida ˌæs ə ˈfet ɪd ə -ˈfiːt-,
    §-əd- ‖ -ˈfeṭ əd ə

asap *'as soon as possible'* ˌeɪ es eɪ 'piː
—*sometimes spoken as* 'eɪs æp, 'æs-
Asaph 'æs əf
asarabacca ˌæs ər ə 'bæk ə
asbestos æs 'best əs æz-, -ɒs
asbestosis ˌæs be 'stəʊs ɪs ˌæz-, §-əs ‖ -'stoʊs-
Asbo 'æz bəʊ ‖ -boʊ ~s z
Asbury 'æz bər i ‖ 'æz ˌber i -bər i
    ˌAsbury 'Park
Ascalon 'æsk ə lɒn -əl ən ‖ -lɑːn
ascarid 'æsk ə rɪd ~s z
ascend ə 'send —*also, when in contrast with*
    descend, ˌæ- ~ed ɪd əd ~ing ɪŋ ~s z
ascendanc|e ə 'send ənˑs ~y i
ascendant ə 'send ənt
ascendenc|e ə 'send ənˑs ~y i
ascendent ə 'send ənt
ascender ə 'send ə ‖ -ᵊr ~s z
ascension, A~ ə 'senʧ ᵊn
    As'cension Day
Ascensiontide ə 'senʧ ᵊn taɪd
ascent ə 'sent —*also, when in contrast with*
    descent, ˌæ- (= *assent*) ~s s
ascertain ˌæs ə 'teɪn ‖ -ᵊr- ~ed d ~ing ɪŋ ~s z
ascertainable ˌæs ə 'teɪn əb ᵊl ◂ ‖ -ᵊr-
ascertainment ˌæs ə 'teɪn mənt →-'teɪm-
    ‖ -ᵊr-
ascetic ə 'set ɪk æ- ‖ -'seţ ɪk ~ally ᵊl̬_i ~s s
asceticism ə 'set ɪ ˌsɪz əm æ-, -ə,-- ‖ -'seţ-
Asch æʃ
Ascham 'æsk əm
Ascherson 'æʃ əs ən ‖ -ᵊrs-
asci 'æsk aɪ 'æs-, -iː
ascidian ə 'sɪd i ən ~s z
ASCII 'æsk i
ASClization ˌæsk i aɪ 'zeɪʃ ᵊn -i ɪ- ‖ -i ə- ~s z
Asclepius ə 'skliːp i əs æ-
Ascomycetes, a~ ˌæsk əʊ maɪ 'siːt iːz
    ‖ -oʊ maɪ 'siːţ iːz
Ascona æ 'skəʊn ə ‖ -'skoʊn- —*It* [as 'ko: na]
ascorbic ə 'skɔːb ɪk æ- ‖ -'skɔːrb-
Ascot, ascot 'æsk ət §-ɒt ‖ -aːt ~'s, ~s s
ascribable ə 'skraɪb əb ᵊl
ascrib|e ə 'skraɪb ~ed d ~es z ~ing ɪŋ
ascription ə 'skrɪp ʃᵊn æ- ~s z
ascus 'æsk əs **asci** 'æsk aɪ 'æs-, -iː
Asda *tdmk* 'æz də
asdic 'æz dɪk ~s s
-ase eɪz ɛɪs — **oxidase** 'ɒks ɪ deɪz -ə-, -deɪs
    ‖ 'ɑːks-
ASEAN 'æz i ən 'æs-
asepsis ₍ᵢ₎eɪ 'seps ɪs ə-, æ-
aseptic ₍ᵢ₎eɪ 'sept ɪk ə-, æ-
asexual ₍ᵢ₎eɪ 'sek ʃu əl æ-, -'seks ju əl, -'sek ʃᵊl
    ~ly i
Asfordby 'æs fəd bi 'æz-, →-fəb- ‖ -fᵊrd-
Asgarby 'æz gə bi ‖ -gᵊr-
Asgard 'æs gaːd 'æz- ‖ -gaːrd
ash, Ash æʃ **ashes** 'æʃ ɪz -əz
    ˌAsh 'Wednesday
ashamed ə 'ʃeɪmd
Ashanti ə 'ʃænt i ‖ -'ʃaːnt-
Ashbee 'æʃ bi -biː

ashbin 'æʃ bɪn ~s z
Ashbourne 'æʃ bɔːn ‖ -bɔːrn -boʊrn
Ashburton æʃ 'bɜːt ᵊn 'æʃ ˌbɜːt-, -bət-
    ‖ 'æʃ ˌbɜːt ᵊn
Ashby 'æʃ bi
Ashby-de-la-Zouch ˌæʃ bi də lə 'zuːʃ ˌ·ˑ,de·ˑ,
    -laːˑ
ashcan 'æʃ kæn ~s z
Ashcombe 'æʃ kəm
Ashcroft 'æʃ krɒft ‖ -krɔːft -krɑːft
Ashdod 'æʃ dɒd ‖ -daːd
Ashdown 'æʃ daʊn
Ashe æʃ
ashen 'æʃ ᵊn
Asher 'æʃ ə ‖ -ᵊr
ashes, Ashes 'æʃ ɪz -əz
Asheville 'æʃ vɪl
Ashfield 'æʃ fiːᵊld
Ashford 'æʃ fəd ‖ -fᵊrd
Ashgabat ˌæʃ kə 'bæt -xə- ‖ ˌaːʃ kə 'baːt
    —*Turkmen* Aşgabat [aʃ χa 'bat]
ashi... —*see* **ashy**
Ashington 'æʃ ɪŋ tən
Ashkenaz|i, ~y ˌæʃ kə 'naːz |i -kɪ- ‖ ˌaːʃ- ~im
    ɪm §-əm
Ashkhabad 'æʃ kə bæd -baːd; ˌ·ˑ, ˌaːʃ-
    ‖ ˌaːʃ kə 'baːd ˑ·· —*Russ* [əʃ xʌ 'bat]
ashlar 'æʃ lə ‖ -lᵊr ~s z
Ashleigh, Ashley, Ashlie 'æʃ li
Ashman 'æʃ mən
Ashmole 'æʃ məʊl →-mɒʊl ‖ -moʊl
Ashmolean æʃ 'məʊl i ən ‖ -'moʊl-
Ashmore 'æʃ mɔː ‖ -mɔːr -moʊr
ashore ə 'ʃɔː ‖ ə 'ʃɔːr -'ʃoʊr
ashplant 'æʃ plaːnt §-plænt ‖ -plænt ~s s
ashram 'æʃ rəm 'aːʃ-, -ræm ~s z
Ashton 'æʃt ən
Ashton-in-Makerfield
    ˌæʃt ən ɪn 'meɪk ə fiːᵊld →-ɪm'-- ‖ -ᵊr fiːᵊld
Ashton-under-Lyne ˌæʃt ən ˌʌnd ə 'laɪn
    ˌ·ˑ··· ‖ -ˌʌnd ᵊr-
Ashtoreth 'æʃt ə reθ
ashtray 'æʃ treɪ ~s z
Ashurst 'æʃ hɜːst -ɜːst ‖ -hɜːst
Ashwell 'æʃ wel -wᵊl
Ashworth 'æʃ wɜːθ ‖ -wɜːθ
ash|y 'æʃ |i ~ier i ə ‖ i ᵊr ~iest i ɪst i əst
Asia 'eɪʒ ə 'eɪʃ ə — *Preference polls, AmE:*
    'eɪʒ ə 91%, 'eɪʃ ə 9%; *BrE:* 'eɪʒ ə 64%, 'eɪʃ ə
    36%; *those born before 1942,* 'eɪʒ ə 32%, 'eɪʃ ə
    68%. See chart on p. 48.
    ˌAsia 'Minor
Asiago ˌæz i 'aːg əʊ ‖ ˌaːs i 'aːg oʊ ˌaːz-, ˌaːʃ-,
    ˌaːʒ- —*It* [a 'zja: go]
Asian 'eɪʒ ᵊn 'eɪʃ- ~s z *See preference polls at*
    Asia
Asiana *tdmk* ˌæs i 'aːn ə
Asian-American ˌeɪʒ ᵊn ə 'mer ɪk ən ◂ ˌeɪʃ-
Asiatic ˌeɪʒ i 'æt ɪk ◂ ˌeɪz-, ˌeɪʃ-, ˌeɪs- ‖ -'æţ ɪk ◂
    ~s s
Asics *tdmk* 'æz ɪks 'æs-
aside ə 'saɪd ~s z
Asimov 'æs ɪ mɒv 'æz-, -ə- ‖ 'æz ə maːf -mɔːf

ASIA

■ 'eɪʒə   ■ 'eɪʃə

AmE 91% 9%

BrE 64% 36%

● BrE 'eɪʒə by age

Older ← Speakers → Younger

asinine 'æs ɪ naɪn -ə- **~ly** li
asininity ˌæs ɪ 'nɪn ət i ˌ-ə-, -ɪt i ‖ -əţ i
ask ɑːsk §æsk, △ɑːks ‖ æsk **asked** 'ɑːskt §æskt, △ɑːkst ‖ æskt **asking** 'ɑːsk ɪŋ §'æsk-, △'ɑːks- ‖ 'æsk ɪŋ **asks** ɑːsks §æsks, △'ɑːks ɪz ‖ æsks
'asking price
askance ə 'skæn⸴s -'skɑːn⸴s ‖ ə 'skæn⸴s
askari æ 'skɑːr i ə- **~s** z
Aske æsk
Askelon 'æsk əl ən -ɪl-, -ə lɒn, -ɪ- ‖ -ə lɑːn
askew *adv* ə 'skjuː
Askew *family name* 'æsk juː
Askey 'æsk i
Askham 'æsk əm
Askrigg 'æsk rɪg
aslant ə 'slɑːnt §-'slænt ‖ ə 'slænt
asleep ə 'sliːp
ASLEF 'æz lef
A/S level ˌeɪ 'es ˌlev əl **~s** z
ASLIB 'æz lɪb
Asmara æs 'mɑːr ə æz- ‖ -'mær-, -'mer-
Asmodeus æs 'məʊd i ˌəs ˌæs məʊ 'diːˌəs ‖ ˌæz mə 'diːˌəs
asocial ˌeɪ 'səʊʃ əl ‖ -'soʊʃ-
Asoka ə 'səʊk ə -'ʃəʊk- ‖ ə 'soʊk ə —*Hindi* [ə ʃoːk]
asp æsp **asps** æsps
asparagus ə 'spær əg əs -'sper-
aspartame 'æsp ə teɪm ə 'spɑːt eɪm ‖ -ər-
aspartic ə 'spɑːt ɪk ‖ ə 'spɑːrţ-
Aspasia æ 'speɪz iˌə ə-, -'speɪʒ- ‖ æ 'speɪʒ ə
Aspatria ə 'speɪtr iˌə æ-
aspect 'æsp ekt **~s** s
'aspect ˌratio
aspectual æ 'spek tʃuˌəl ə-, -tjuˌ **~ly** i
Aspel, Aspell 'æsp əl
aspen, Aspen 'æsp ən **~s** z
Asperger's 'æsp ɜːg əz ‖ -ɜːg ᵊrz

Asperges, a~ æ 'spɜːdʒ iːz ə- ‖ -'spɜːdʒ-
asperit|y æ 'sper ət i ‖ˌə-, -ɪt- ‖ -əţ ‖i **~ies** iz
aspersion ə 'spɜːʃ ᵊn æ-, §-'spɜːʒ- ‖ -'spɜːʒ- -'spɜːʃ- **~s** z
asphalt 'æs fælt 'æʃ-, -fɔːlt, △-felt ‖ -fɔːlt -fɑːlt **~ed** ɪd əd **~ing** ɪŋ **~s** s
asphodel 'æs fə del 'æʃ- **~s** z
asphyxia æs 'fɪks iˌə əs-
asphyxiant æs 'fɪks iˌənt əs-
asphyxi|ate æs 'fɪks i ˌeɪt əs- **~ated** eɪt ɪd -əd ‖ eɪţ əd **~ates** eɪts **~ating** eɪt ɪŋ ‖ eɪţ ɪŋ
asphyxiation æs ˌfɪks i 'eɪʃ ᵊn əs- **~s** z
aspic 'æsp ɪk
aspidistra ˌæsp ɪ 'dɪs trə -ə- **~s** z
Aspinall 'æsp ɪn ᵊl -ən-; -ɪ nɔːl, -ə-
aspirant 'æsp ər ənt -ɪr-; ə 'spaɪᵊr- **~s** s
aspirate *n* 'æsp ər ət -ɪr-, ɪt **~s** s
aspi|rate *v* 'æsp ə ˌreɪt -ɪ- **~rated** reɪt ɪd -əd ‖ reɪţ əd **~rates** reɪts **~rating** reɪt ɪŋ ‖ reɪţ ɪŋ
aspiration ˌæsp ə 'reɪʃ ᵊn -ɪ- **~al** ᵊl **~s** z
aspirator 'æsp ə reɪt ə -ɪ- ‖ -reɪţ ᵊr **~s** z
aspire ə 'spaɪˌə ə 'spaɪˌᵊr **~d** d **~s** z **aspiring** ə 'spaɪˌər ɪŋ ‖ ə 'spaɪˌᵊr ɪŋ
aspirin 'æsp rɪn -rən; 'æsp ər ən, -ɪn **~s** z
aspiring ə 'spaɪˌər ɪŋ ‖ ə 'spaɪˌᵊr ɪŋ **~ly** li
asplenium æ 'spliːn iˌəm ə- **~s** z
Aspley 'æsp li
Asprey 'æsp ri
Aspro *tdmk* 'æsp rəʊ ‖ -roʊ **~s** z
Asquith 'æsk wɪθ
ass æs —*As a term of abuse, in BrE also* ɑːs (*which may however be taken as a pronunciation rather of* arse) **asses** 'æs ɪz -əz
Assad 'æs æd ‖ 'ɑːs ɑːd —*Arabic* ['as ad]
assagai 'æs ə gaɪ **~s** z
assai æ 'saɪ —*It* [as 'sai]
assail ə 'seɪᵊl **~ed** d **~ing** ɪŋ **~s** z
assailant ə 'seɪl ənt **~s** s
Assam æ 'sæm 'æs æm
Assamese ˌæs ə 'miːz ◂ -æ- ‖ -'miːs
assassin ə 'sæs ɪn -ᵊn **~s** z
assassi|nate ə 'sæs ɪ ˌneɪt -ə- **~nated** neɪt ɪd -əd ‖ neɪţ əd **~nates** neɪts **~nating** neɪt ɪŋ ‖ neɪţ ɪŋ
assassination ə ˌsæs ɪ 'neɪʃ ᵊn -ə- **~s** z
assault ə 'sɔːlt -'sɒlt ‖ -'sɑːlt **~ed** ɪd əd **~ing** ɪŋ **~s** s
as'sault ˌcourse
assay *n* ə 'seɪ æ-; 'æs eɪ ‖ 'æs eɪ æ 'seɪ **~s** z
assay *v* ə 'seɪ æ- **~ed** d **~er/s** ə/z ‖ ᵊr/z **~ing** ɪŋ **~s** z
assegai 'æs ɪ gaɪ -ə- **~s** z
assemblag|e ə 'sem blɪdʒ —*but with reference to wine blending,* ˌæs ɒm 'blɑːʒ ‖ ˌɑːs ɑːm- —*Fr* [a sã bla:ʒ] **~es** ɪz əz
assembl|e ə 'sem bᵊl **~ed** d **~er/s** ᵊ/z ‖ ᵊr/z **~es** z **~ing** ɪŋ
assem|bly ə 'sem |bli **~blies** bliz
as'sembly ˌlanguage; as'sembly line

Aspiration

An **aspirated** consonant is one that is accompanied by a brief h-sound.

In certain environments the English plosives p, t, k are aspirated. That is to say, there is a delay between the release of the primary closure of the articulators and the beginning of voicing for the sound that follows. In the word **pan** pæn, for example, the voicing for æ does not begin immediately after the lips separate for the end of the p. There is a moment's delay, during which the air escapes freely through the mouth, impeded neither by the lips nor by the vocal folds. This constitutes the aspiration of the p. It is one of the ways we recognize the plosive as being a p rather than a b.

We can distinguish three possibilities for the aspiration of English p, t, k, depending on their position.

1 They are **aspirated**
when they occur at the **beginning of a syllable** in which the vowel is strong
as in
pin pɪn (like pʰɪn)
tail teɪᵊl
come kʌm
appeal ə ˈpiːᵊl
retain ri ˈteɪn
maritime ˈmær ɪ taɪm.

If one of l, r, w, j comes between the plosive and the vowel, then aspiration takes the form of making this consonant voiceless as in
play pleɪ (here the l is voiceless)
approve ə ˈpruːv (the r is voiceless)
twin twɪn (the w is voiceless)
accuse ə ˈkjuːz (the j is voiceless).

2 They are **unaspirated**
- when preceded by s at the beginning of a syllable as in **spin** spɪn (the ɪ starts immediately upon the release of the p), **stack** stæk, **school** skuːl, **screen** skriːn (the r may be voiced)
- when followed by any FRICATIVE as in **lapse** læps, **depth** depθ, **sets** sets, **fix** fɪks
- if immediately followed by another plosive as with the k in **doctor** ˈdɒktə ‖ ˈdɑːkt ᵊr. The release stage of the first plosive is then usually inaudible ('masked').

3 Otherwise, they are **unaspirated** or just **slightly aspirated**. For example:
ripe raɪp, **shut** ʃʌt, **lake** leɪk
happy ˈhæp i, **writer** ˈraɪt ə (BrE), **lucky** ˈlʌk i
wasp wɒsp ‖ wɑːsp, **resting** ˈrest ɪŋ, **Oscar** ˈɒsk ə ‖ ˈɑːsk ᵊr, **lifted** ˈlɪft ɪd
today tə ˈdeɪ (note that the t, although at the beginning of a syllable, is followed by a WEAK vowel).

A

assembly|man ə 'sem bli |mən **~men** mən men **~woman** ˌwʊm ən **~women** ˌwɪm ɪn §-ən

assent *n, v* ə 'sent *(= ascent)* **assented** ə 'sent ɪd -əd ‖ ə 'senṯ əd **assenting** ə 'sent ɪŋ ‖ ə 'senṯ ɪŋ **assents** ə 'sents

Asser 'æs ə ‖ -ᵊr

assert ə 'sɜːt ‖ ə 'sɜːt **asserted** ə 'sɜːt ɪd -əd ‖ ə 'sɜːṯ əd **asserting** ə 'sɜːt ɪŋ ‖ ə 'sɜːṯ ɪŋ **asserts** ə 'sɜːts ‖ ə 'sɜːts

assertion ə 'sɜːʃ ᵊn ‖ ə 'sɜːʃ ᵊn **~s** z

assertive ə 'sɜːt ɪv ‖ ə 'sɜːṯ ɪv **~ly** li **~ness** nəs nɪs

assess ə 'ses **~ed** t **~es** ɪz əz **~ing** ɪŋ

assessment ə 'ses mənt **~s** s

assessor ə 'ses ə ‖ -ᵊr **~s** z

asset 'æs et -ɪt **~s** s

asset-strip|per 'æs et ˌstrɪp| ə -ɪt- ‖ -ᵊr **~pers** əz ‖ ᵊrz **~ping** ɪŋ

asseve|rate ə 'sev ə |reɪt æ- **~rated** reɪt ɪd -əd ‖ reɪṯ əd **~rates** reɪts **~rating** reɪt ɪŋ ‖ reɪṯ ɪŋ

asseveration ə ˌsev ə 'reɪʃ ᵊn æ- **~s** z

assez 'æs eɪ ‖ ɑː 'seɪ —*Fr* [a se]

asshole 'ɑːs həʊl 'æs-, →-hɒʊl ‖ 'æs hoʊl **~s** z

assibi|late ə 'sɪb ə |leɪt æ-, -ɪ- **~lated** leɪt ɪd -əd ‖ leɪṯ əd **~lates** leɪts **~lating** leɪt ɪŋ ‖ leɪṯ ɪŋ

assibilation ə ˌsɪb ə 'leɪʃ ᵊn æ-, -ɪ- **~s** z

assiduit|y ˌæs ɪ 'djuː ət |i ˌ·ə-, →-'dʒuːˌ, ɪt i ‖ -'duː əṯ |i -'djuː- **~ies** iz

assiduous ə 'sɪd ju̯ əs §-'sɪdʒ u̯ ‖ ə 'sɪdʒ u̯ əs **~ly** li **~ness** nəs nɪs

assign ə 'saɪn **~ed** d **~ing** ɪŋ **~s** z

assignab|le ə 'saɪn əb |ᵊl **~ly** li

assig|nat 'æs ɪg |næt ˌæs iː 'nja: **~nats** næts 'nja:z —*Fr* [a si nja]

assignation ˌæs ɪg 'neɪʃ ᵊn **~s** z

assignee ˌæs aɪ 'niː -ɪ-, §-ə- ‖ ə ˌsaɪ 'niː ˌæs ə 'niː **~s** z

assignment ə 'saɪn mənt →-'saɪm- **~s** s

assimilable ə 'sɪm əl əb ᵊl -'ɪl-

assimi|late ə 'sɪm ə |leɪt -ɪ- **~lated** leɪt ɪd -əd ‖ leɪṯ əd **~lates** leɪts **~lating** leɪt ɪŋ ‖ leɪṯ ɪŋ

assimilation ə ˌsɪm ə 'leɪʃ ᵊn -ɪ- **~s** z

assimilative ə 'sɪm əl ət ɪv -ə leɪt ɪv ‖ -ə leɪṯ ɪv -əl əṯ- **~ly** li

assimilatory ə 'sɪm əl ət ᵊr i -'ɪl-; ·ˌ·ə 'leɪt ər i, -ˌ·ɪ- ‖ ə 'tɔːr i -toʊr i

Assiniboin, Assiniboine ə 'sɪn ɪ bɔɪn -ə- **~s** z

Assisi ə 'siːs i æ-, -'siːz- ‖ -'sɪs- —*It* [as 'si: zi]

assist ə 'sɪst **~ed** ɪd əd **~ing** ɪŋ **~s** s

assistance ə 'sɪst ᵊnts

assistant ə 'sɪst ənt **~s** s Asˌsistant Pro'fessor; Asˌsistant 'Secretary

assiz|e ə 'saɪz **~es** ɪz əz

associ|ate *v* ə 'səʊs i̯ |eɪt -'səʊʃ- ‖ ə 'soʊs- ə 'soʊs- **~ated** eɪt ɪd -əd ‖ eɪṯ əd **~ates** eɪts **~ating** eɪt ɪŋ ‖ eɪṯ ɪŋ — *Preference poll, BrE:* -'səʊs- *69%,* -'səʊʃ- *31%.*

ASSOCIATE (verb)

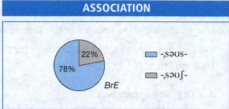

31% ▪ -'səʊs-
69% ▪ -'səʊʃ-
BrE

associate *n, adj* ə 'səʊs i̯ ət -'səʊʃ-, -ɪt, -eɪt ‖ ə 'soʊs- ə 'soʊs- **~s** s

ASSOCIATION

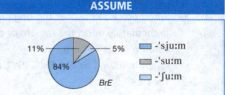

22% ▪ -səʊs-
78% ▪ -səʊʃ-
BrE

association ə ˌsəʊs i 'eɪʃ ᵊn ◄ -ˌsəʊʃ- ‖ ə ˌsoʊs- ə ˌsoʊʃ- **~s** z — *Preference poll, BrE:* -ˌsəʊs- *78%,* -ˌsəʊʃ- *22%.* Asˌsociˌation 'football

associative ə 'səʊs i̯ ət ɪv -'səʊʃ-, -eɪt ɪv ‖ ə 'soʊʃ i eɪṯ ɪv -'soʊs-, əṯ ɪv **~ly** li

associativity ə ˌsəʊs i̯ ə 'tɪv ət i -ˌsəʊʃ-, -ɪt i ‖ ə ˌsoʊʃ i̯ ə 'tɪv əṯ i -ˌsoʊs-

assonanc|e 'æs ən ənᵗs **~es** ɪz əz

assonant 'æs ən ənt **~s** s

assort ə 'sɔːt ‖ ə 'sɔːrt **assorted** ə 'sɔːt ɪd -əd ‖ ə 'sɔːrṯ əd **assorting** ə 'sɔːt ɪŋ ‖ ə 'sɔːrṯ ɪŋ **assorts** ə 'sɔːts ‖ ə 'sɔːrts

assortment ə 'sɔːt mənt ‖ ə 'sɔːrt- **~s** s

Assouan, Assuan ˌæs 'wɑːn ◄ ˌɑːs-, -'wæn, '· · —*Arabic* [ʔa 'sˤwaːn]

assuag|e ə 'sweɪdʒ **~ed** d **~er/s** ə/z ‖ ᵊr/z **~es** ɪz əz **~ement** mənt **~ing** ɪŋ

assuasive ə 'sweɪs ɪv -'sweɪz-

ASSUME

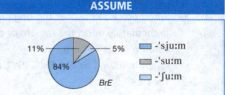

11% ▪ -'sjuːm
5% ▪ -'suːm
84% ▪ -'ʃuːm
BrE

assum|e ə 'sjuːm -'suːm, §-'ʃuːm ‖ ə 'suːm — *Preference poll, BrE:* -'sjuːm *84%,* -'suːm *11%,* -'ʃuːm *5%.* **~ed** d **~es** z **~ing/ly** ɪŋ /li

assumption, A~ ə 'sʌmp ʃᵊn **~s** z

assumptive ə 'sʌmpt ɪv

assuranc|e ə 'ʃɔːr ənᵗs -'ʃʊər- ‖ ə 'ʃʊr- -'ʃɜː- **~es** ɪz əz

assur|e ə 'ʃɔː -'ʃʊə ‖ ə 'ʃʊᵊr -'ʃɜː **~ed** d **~es** z **assuring** ə 'ʃɔːr ɪŋ -'ʃʊər- ‖ ə 'ʃʊr ɪŋ -'ʃɜː-

assuredly ə 'ʃɔːr ɪd li -'ʃʊər-, -əd- ‖ ə 'ʃʊr- -'ʃɜː-

assurer ə 'ʃɔːr ə ə 'ʃʊər ə ‖ ə 'ʃʊr ᵊr -'ɜː- **~s** z

A

Assimilation

1   **Assimilation** is a type of COARTICULATION. It is the alteration of a speech sound to make it more similar to its neighbours. In English it mainly affects PLACE OF ARTICULATION.

2   The alveolar consonants t, d, n, when they occur at the end of a word or syllable, can optionally assimilate to the place of articulation of the next syllable ('regressive' assimilation).

Thus n can become m before p, b, m as in the examples

ten men ˌten 'men → ˌtem 'men

downbeat 'daʊn biːt → 'daʊm biːt.

Similarly, n can become ŋ before k, g as in

fine grade ˌfaɪn 'greɪd → ˌfaɪŋ 'greɪd

incredible ɪn 'kred əb ᵊl → ɪŋ 'kred əb ᵊl.

In the same way d can change to b and g respectively as in

red paint ˌred 'peɪnt → ˌreb 'peɪnt

admit əd 'mɪt → əb 'mɪt

bad guys 'bæd gaɪz → 'bæg gaɪz.

It is also possible for t to change to p and k, though a more frequent possibility is for t, when followed by another consonant, to be realized as a GLOTTAL STOP.

eight boys ˌeɪt 'bɔɪz → ˌeɪp 'bɔɪz

or, more usually, → ˌeɪʔ 'bɔɪz.

3   In the same way s and z can change to ʃ and ʒ respectively, but only before ʃ or j at the beginning of the next syllable. In **you**, **your** the j may then disappear.

this shape ˌðɪs 'ʃeɪp → ˌðɪʃ 'ʃeɪp

these shoes ˌðiːz 'ʃuːz → ˌðiːʒ 'ʃuːz

this unit ˌðɪs 'juːn ɪt → ˌðɪʃ 'juːn ɪt

unless you... ən 'les ju → ən 'leʃ (j)u

as you see ˌæz ju 'siː → ˌæʒ (j)u 'siː

4   Assimilation can also sometimes operate in the other direction: that is, a consonant can assimilate to the place of articulation of the consonant at the end of the preceding syllable ('progressive' assimilation). In English this applies only to SYLLABIC n, changing it to syllabic m or ŋ as appropriate.

ribbon ('rɪb ən →) 'rɪb n̩ → 'rɪb m̩

bacon ('beɪk ən →) 'beɪk n̩ → 'beɪk ŋ̍

up and down (ˌʌp ən 'daʊn →) ˌʌp n̩ 'daʊn → ˌʌp m̩ 'daʊn

Assimilation ▶

A

Assimilation continued

This assimilation can operate only if the words are said without a phonetic ə between the plosive and the nasal. Furthermore, it cannot apply if the sound after the nasal is a vowel.

happens (ˈhæp ənz →) ˈhæp nz → ˈhæp mz

happened (ˈhæp ənd →) ˈhæp nd → ˈhæp md

happening (ˈhæp ən ɪŋ →) ˈhæp n ɪŋ (cannot assimilate further).

5 **Yod coalescence** (or 'coalescent' assimilation) is the process which changes t or d plus j into tʃ or dʒ respectively. Across word boundaries it mainly affects phrases involving **you** or **your**.

let you out ˌlet ju ˈaʊt → ˌletʃ u ˈaʊt

would you try ˌwʊd ju ˈtraɪ → ˌwʊdʒ u ˈtraɪ

get your bags ˌget jɔː ˈbægz → ˌgetʃ ɔː ˈbægz ‖ ˌget jɚr ˈbægz → ˌgetʃ ɚr ˈbægz

6 Within a word, the status of yod coalescence depends on whether the following vowel is STRONG or WEAK.

- Where the vowel is strong, i.e. uː or ʊə, yod coalescence can frequently be heard in BrE, although not in careful RP. (In AmE there is usually no j, so the possibility does not arise.)

  tune tjuːn → tʃuːn

  endure ɪn ˈdjʊə → ɪn ˈdʒʊə

- Where the vowel is weak, i.e. u or ə, assimilation is often variable in BrE, but obligatory in AmE.

  factual ˈfækt ju əl → ˈfæk tʃu əl

  educate ˈed ju keɪt → ˈedʒ u keɪt

7 Historically, a process of yod coalescence is the origin of the tʃ used by all speakers in words such as **nature**, and of the dʒ in words such as **soldier**. Similarly, yod coalescence involving fricatives (sj → ʃ, zj → ʒ) explains the ʃ in words such as **pressure, delicious, patient, Russian**, and the ʒ in words such as **measure**. For example, **delicious** came to English from Latin via the French **délicieux** de li sjø, but in English the sj coalesced into ʃ several centuries ago.

8 Some speakers of BrE assimilate s to ʃ before tr and tʃ, thus **strong** strɒŋ → ʃtrɒŋ, **student** ˈstjuːd ənt → ˈstʃuːd- → ˈʃtʃuːd-. This is not shown in this dictionary.

Assyri|a ə ˈsɪr i ˌ|ə ~**an/s** ən/z
Assyriologist, a~ ə ˌsɪr i ˈɒl ədʒ ɪst §-əst
‖ -ˈɑːl- ~**s** s
Assyriology ə ˌsɪr i ˈɒl ədʒ i ‖ -ˈɑːl-
Asta ˈæst ə
astable ˌ(ˌ)eɪ ˈsteɪb əl

Astaire ə ˈsteə ‖ ə ˈsteɚr -ˈstæɚr
Astarte æ ˈstɑːt i ə- ‖ -ˈstɑːrt-
astatine ˈæst ə tiːn -tɪn
Astbury ˈæst bər i ‖ -ˌber i
aster ˈæst ə ‖ -ɚr ~**s** z

A

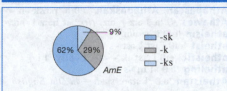

ASTERISK

-sk
-k
-ks

62% 29% 9%

AmE

asterisk *n, v* 'æst ə rɪsk △-rɪks ‖ △-rɪk
— *Preference poll, AmE:* -sk *62%,* -k *29%,*
-ks *9%.* **~ed** t **~ing** ɪŋ **~s** s
asterism 'æst ə ˌrɪz əm **~s** z
Asterix 'æst ə rɪks
astern ə 'stɜːn ‖ ə 'stɝːn
asteroid 'æst ə rɔɪd **~s** z
asthenia æs 'θiːn i ə
asthenic æs 'θen ɪk **~al** ᵊl
asthma 'æs mə 'æsθ- ‖ 'æz- *(*)*
asthmatic æs 'mæt ɪk æsθ- ‖ æz 'mæt̬ ɪk **~ally**
ᵊl i **~s** s
Asti 'æst i -iː ‖ 'ɑːst i —*It* ['as ti]
  ˌAsti spu'mante spu 'mænt i ‖ spu 'mɑːnt i
—*It* [spu 'man te]
astigmatic ˌæst ɪg 'mæt ɪk ◄ ‖ -'mæt̬- **~ally**
ᵊl i
astigmatism ə 'stɪg mə ˌtɪz əm æ- **~s** z
astilbe ə 'stɪlb i **~s** z
astir ə 'stɜː ‖ ə 'stɝː
Astle *(i)* 'æst ᵊl, *(ii)* 'æs ᵊl
Astley 'æst li
Aston 'æst ən
  ˌAston 'Martin *tdmk*; ˌAston 'Villa
astonish ə 'stɒn ɪʃ ‖ ə 'stɑːn ɪʃ **~ed** t **~es** ɪz əz
~ing/ly ɪŋ /li
astonishment ə 'stɒn ɪʃ mənt ‖ -'stɑːn-
Astor 'æst ə ‖ -ᵊr
Astoria ə 'stɔːr i ə æ-
astound ə 'staʊnd **~ed** ɪd əd **~ing/ly** ɪŋ /li **~s**
z
astra, Astra 'æs trə
astragal 'æs trəg ᵊl -trɪg- **~s** z
astrag|alus ə 'stræg |əl əs **~ali** ə laɪ
astrakhan, A~ ˌæs trə 'kæn ◄ -'kɑːn —*Russ*
['as trə xənʲ]
astral 'æs trəl **~ly** i
astray ə 'streɪ
Astrid 'æs trɪd
astride ə 'straɪd
astringency ə 'strɪndʒ ənˢts i
astringent ə 'strɪndʒ ənt **~ly** li **~s** s
astro- *comb. form*
  with stress-neutral suffix ˌæs trəʊ ‖ -trə
  — **astrosphere** 'æs trəʊ sfɪə ‖ -trə sfɪr
  with stress-imposing suffix ə 'strɒ+ æ 'strɒ+
  ‖ ə 'strɑː+ — **astrophorous** ə 'strɒf ər əs æ-
  ‖ -'strɑːf-
astrodome, A~ 'æs trəʊ dəʊm ‖ -trə doʊm
astrolabe 'æs trəʊ leɪb ‖ -trə- **~s** z
astrologer ə 'strɒl ədʒ ə æ- ‖ ə 'strɑːl ədʒ ᵊr
~s z

astrological ˌæs trə 'lɒdʒ ɪk ᵊl ◄ ‖ -'lɑːdʒ- **~ly**
i
astrology ə 'strɒl ədʒ i æ- ‖ -'strɑːl-
astronaut 'æs trə nɔːt ‖ -nɑːt **~s** s
astronautical ˌæs trə 'nɔːt ɪk ᵊl ◄ ‖ -'nɔːt̬-
-'nɑːt̬- **~ly** i
astronautics ˌæs trə 'nɔːt ɪks ‖ -'nɔːt̬- -'nɑːt̬-
astronomer ə 'strɒn əm ə ‖ ə 'strɑːn əm ᵊr **~s**
z
astronomic ˌæs trə 'nɒm ɪk ◄ ‖ -'nɑːm- **~al** ᵊl
~ally ᵊl i
astronomy ə 'strɒn əm i ‖ -'strɑːn-
astrophys|ical ˌæs trəʊ 'fɪz |ɪk ᵊl ◄ ‖ ˌæs trə-
ˌtrəʊ- **-icist/s** ɪs ɪst/s -əs-, §-əst/s **-ics** ɪks
astroturf, AstroTurf *tdmk* 'æs trəʊ tɜːf
‖ -trəʊ tɝːf **-ed** t
Asturias æ 'stʊər i æs ə-, -'stjʊər-, -əs ‖ -'stʊr-
—*Sp* [as 'tur jas]
astute ə 'stjuːt æ-, →-'stʃuːt ‖ ə 'stuːt ə 'stjuːt
~ly li **~ness** nəs nɪs
Astyanax æ 'staɪ ə næks ə-
Asunción æ ˌsʊnˢts i 'ɒn -'əʊn, ·'···
‖ ɑː ˌsuːnˢts i 'oʊn ··— *AmSp* [a sun 'sjon]
asunder ə 'sʌnd ə ‖ -ᵊr
Aswad 'æz wɒd ‖ -wɑːd
Aswan ˌæs 'wɑːn ◄ ˌɑː:-, -'wæn, '·· —*Arabic*
[ʔa 'sˤwaːn]
asyl|um ə 'saɪl |əm **~a** ə **~ums** əmz
asymmetric ˌeɪ sɪ 'metr ɪk ◄ ˌeɪ sə-; ˌæs ɪ-,
ˌæs ə- **~al** ᵊl **~ally** ᵊl i
asymmetry ₍₎æ 'sɪm ətr i ˌeɪ-, -ɪtr- ‖ ˌeɪ-
asymptote 'æs ɪmp təʊt -əmp- ‖ -toʊt **~s** s
asymptotic ˌæs ɪmp 'tɒt ɪk ◄ -əmp-
‖ -'tɑːt̬ ɪk ◄ **~ally** ᵊl i
asynchronous ₍₎eɪ 'sɪŋk rən əs -'sɪn krən- **~ly**
li
asyndetic ˌæs ɪn 'det ɪk ◄ §-ᵊn-; ˌeɪ sɪn-
‖ -'det̬ ɪk ◄
asyndeton æ 'sɪnd ɪt ən ə-, §-ət-; -ɪ tɒn, -ə-
‖ ə 'sɪnd ə tɑːn ˌeɪ-
at *strong form* æt, *weak form* ət —*The phrase* at
all *'in any degree, ever' is usually syllabified*
irregularly as ə 'tɔːl *in BrE and sometimes as*
ə 'tɔːl, ə 'tɑːl *in AmE.*
at- *This variant of* ad- *is usually* ə (at'tach), *but*
|æ *if stressed because of a suffix*
(ˌattri'bution).
AT&T *tdmk* ˌeɪ ˌtiː ən 'tiː
atabrin, atabrine, A~ *tdmk* 'æt əb rɪn §-rən,
-ə briːn ‖ 'æt̬-
Atacama ˌæt ə 'kɑːm ə ◄ ‖ ˌɑːt ɑː- —*Sp*
[a ta 'ka ma]
Atack 'eɪt æk
Atahualpa ˌæt ə 'wɑːlp ə -'wælp- ‖ ˌæt̬-
Atalanta ˌæt ə 'lænt ə ‖ ˌæt̬ ə 'lænt̬ ə
Atari *tdmk* ə 'tɑːr i æ-
Ataturk, Atatürk 'æt ə tɜːk ‖ 'æt̬ ə tɝːk
—*Turkish* [ɑ tɑ 'tyrk]
atavism 'æt ə ˌvɪz əm ‖ 'æt̬-
atavistic ˌæt ə 'vɪst ɪk ◄ ‖ ˌæt̬- **~ally** ᵊl i
ataxia ə 'tæks i ə ₍₎eɪ-, æ-
ataxic ə 'tæks ɪk **~s** s
ataxy ə 'tæks i

Atchison 'ætʃ ɪs ən -əs-
atchoo ə 'tʃuː
Atco *tdmk* 'æt kəʊ ‖ -koʊ
Ate *Greek goddess* 'ɑːt i 'eɪt-, -iː ‖ 'eɪt i

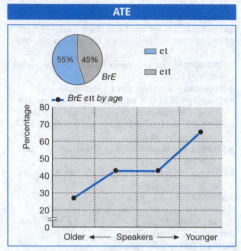

ATE

et
eɪt

BrE

BrE eɪt by age

Percentage

Older ← Speakers → Younger

ate *past of* **eat** et eɪt ‖ eɪt △et — *Preference poll, BrE:* et 55%, eɪt 45%. *In AmE, however,* et *is considered non-standard.*

-ate eɪt, ət ɪt, ¦eɪt —*This suffix is regularly strong,* eɪt, *in verbs, but often weakened to* ət, ɪt *in nouns and adjectives. Its influence on stress depends on the length of the word.* (1) *In two-syllable verbs stress usually falls on the suffix in BrE* (vi'brate, cre'ate), *but on the stem in AmE* ('vibrate, 'create). (2) *In longer verbs, the stress generally falls on the antepenultimate* ('demonstrate, dis'criminate, as'sociate). *There are a few exceptions and cases where speakers disagree* ('sequestrate *or* se'questrate). (3) *In nouns and adjectives the suffix is unstressed* ('private, 'climate), *and in longer words the primary stress generally falls two syllables back from the suffix* ('delegate, 'vertebrate, ap'propriate; *important exceptions are* in'nate, or'nate, se'date). *The suffix vowel is generally weak in familiar words* ('climate, 'private), *though in some words speakers vary* ('candidate, 'magistrate). *In more technical words a strong vowel is retained* ('sulphate, 'caudate). (4) *Note the distinction between verb and noun/adj in cases such as* 'separate, as'sociate, 'moderate, 'delegate.

A-team 'eɪ tiːm
atebrin *tdmk* 'æt əb rɪn §-rən, -ə briːn ‖ 'æt̬-
atelier ə 'tel i ̪eɪ æ-; 'æt ᵊl jeɪ ‖ ̩æt ᵊl 'jeɪ —*Fr* [a tə lje] **~s** z
a tempo ⑴ɑː 'temp əʊ ‖ -oʊ
atenolol ə 'ten ə lɒl ə- ‖ -lɑːl -lɔːl
Athabasc|a, Athabask|a ̩æθ ə 'bæsk |ə **~an** ən
Athanasian ̩æθ ə 'neɪʃ ᵊn ◄ -'neɪʒ-; -'neɪʃ i̯ən, -'neɪs-, -'neɪz- ‖ -'neɪʒ-
the ̩Atha̩nasian 'creed

Athanasius ̩æθ ə 'neɪʃ əs ◄ -'neɪʒ-; -'neɪʃ i̯əs, -'neɪs-, -'neɪz- ‖ -'neɪʒ-
Athapascan, Athapaskan ̩æθ ə 'pæsk ən ◄
Athawes *(i)* 'æθ ɔːz ‖ -ɑːz, *(ii)* 'æt hɔːz ‖ -hɑːz
atheism 'eɪθ i ˌɪz əm
atheist 'eɪθ i ɪst §-əst **~s** s
atheistic ̩eɪθ i 'ɪst ɪk ◄ **~al** ᵊl **~ally** ᵊl ̯i
atheling 'æθ əl ɪŋ **~s** z
Athelstan 'æθ ᵊl stən -stæn —*in Old English was* 'æð ᵊl stɑːn
athematic ̩æθ iː 'mæt ɪk ◄ -ɪ-, -ə-; ̩eɪ θiː-, -θɪ-, -θə- ‖ -'mæt̬-
Athena ə 'θiːn ə
Athenaeum ̩æθ ə 'niː əm -ə-
Athene ə 'θiːn i -iː
Athenian ə 'θiːn i̯ən **~s** z
Athenry ̩æθ ᵊn 'raɪ -ɪn-
Athens 'æθ ɪnz -ᵊnz
atherom|a ̩æθ ə 'rəʊm |ə ‖ -'roʊm |ə **~as** əz **~ata** ət ə ‖ ət̬ ə
atheroscle|rosis ̩æθ ə rəʊ sklə |'rəʊs ɪs -sklɪ'--, -sklɪ'--, §-əs ‖ -roʊ sklə |'roʊs əs **~rotic** 'rɒt ɪk ◄ ‖ 'rɑːt̬ ɪk ◄
Atherstone 'æθ ə stəʊn ‖ -ᵊr stoʊn
Atherton *(i)* 'æθ ət ən ‖ -ᵊrt ᵊn, *(ii)* 'æð- —*the place near Manchester is (ii).*
athetoid 'æθ ə tɔɪd -ɪ-
athetosis ̩æθ ə 'təʊs ɪs -ɪ-, §-əs ‖ -'toʊs-
Athey 'æθ i
athirst ə 'θɜːst ‖ ə 'θɝːst
athlete 'æθ liːt △'æθ ə liːt **~s, ~'s** s
̩athlete's 'foot
athletic æθ 'let ɪk əθ-; △̩æθ ə 'let- ‖ -'let̬- **~ally** ᵊl ̯i
athleticism æθ 'let ɪ ̩sɪz əm əθ-, -'-ə-; △̩æθ ə 'let- ‖ -'let̬-
Athlone ⑴æθ 'ləʊn ‖ -'loʊn
Athol *place in MA* 'æθ ɒl ‖ -ɑːl -ɔːl, -ᵊl
Atholl *place in Scotland* 'æθ ᵊl
at-home ət 'həʊm æt-; ə 'təʊm ‖ -'hoʊm **~s** z
Athos 'æθ ɒs -eɪθ- ‖ -ɑːs —*ModGk* ['a θɔs]
athwart ə 'θwɔːt ‖ ə 'θwɔːrt
Athy ə 'θaɪ
-ation 'eɪʃ ᵊn —*This suffix bears the primary word stress. In words of four or more syllables, a further rhythmic (secondary) stress falls two syllables further back* (̩conso'lation, con̩side'ration, ne̩goti'ation, as̩soci'ation). *Words in* -isation/-ization, *however, have the secondary stress earlier if possible, namely in the same place as the primary stress of the corresponding* -ise/-ize *word* (̩organi'zation, ̩atomi'zation, ̩dramati'zation, ̩actuali'zation).

atishoo ə 'tɪʃ uː
Ativan *tdmk* 'æt ɪ væn §-ə- ‖ 'æt̬ ə-
-ative ət ɪv, eɪt ɪv ‖ ət̬ ɪv, eɪt̬ ɪv *In words of three syllables, the first receives the stress, and the suffix vowel is weak* ('fricative, 'vocative, 'laxative, 'narrative; *exception* cre'ative). *In longer words, the stress usually falls on the same syllable as in the underlying stem:* ac'cusative, con'sultative, pre'servative; 'operative, 'qualitative, ag'glutinative,

ˌarguˈmentative; adˈministrative. *There is
sometimes a vowel change* (deˈrive —
deˈrivative), *and there are several exceptional
cases* (comˈbine —ˈcombinative, ˈalternate —
alˈternative, inˈterrogate —ˌinterˈrogative,
ˈdemonstrate — deˈmonstrative). *Where the
primary stress is on the last syllable of the
stem, the suffix has a reduced vowel*
(ˌinterˈrogative); *but otherwise in these longer
words* (ˈcumulative, ˈlegislative) *the choice
between weak-vowelled* ət ɪv ‖ əţ ɪv *and
strong-vowelled* eɪt ɪv ‖ eɪţ ɪv *depends partly
on social or regional factors, with BrE RP
tending to prefer* ət ɪv, *AmE* eɪţ ɪv: *see
individual entries.*

Atka ˈæt kə ‖ ˈɑːt-

Atkins ˈæt kɪnz

Atkinson ˈæt kɪnˈs ən

Atlanta ət ˈlænt ə æt- ‖ æt ˈlænţ ə ət-

Atlantean ˌæt læn ˈtiːˌən ◄ æt ˈlænt iˌən, ət-

atlantes ət ˈlænt iːz æt-

Atlantic, a~ ət ˈlænt ɪk §ˌ(ˌ)æt- ‖ -ˈlænţ-
    Atˌlantic ˈCity; Atˌlantic ˈOcean

Atlantis ət ˈlænt ɪs ˌ(ˌ)æt-, §-əs ‖ -ˈlænţ-

atlas, Atlas ˈæt ləs **~es** ɪz əz

Atletico æt ˈlet ɪ kəʊ ‖ ɑːt ˈlet ɪ koʊ —*Sp*
    Atlético [at ˈle ti ko]

ATM ˌeɪ tiː ˈem **~s** z

atman ˈɑːt mən

atmosphere ˈæt məs fɪə ‖ -fɪr **~s** z

atmospheric ˌæt məs ˈfer ɪk ◄ ‖ -ˈfɪr- **~al** ᵊl
    ~ally ᵊlˌi **~s** s
    ˌatmosˌpheric ˈpressure

atoll ˈæt ɒl ə ˈtɒl ‖ ˈæt ɔːl -ɑːl **~s** z

atom ˈæt əm ‖ ˈæţ əm **~s** z
    ˈatom bomb

atomic ə ˈtɒm ɪk ‖ ə ˈtɑːm- **~ally** ᵊlˌi
    aˌtomic ˈbomb; aˌtomic ˈenergy

atomis... —*see* **atomiz...**

atomism ˈæt ə ˌmɪz əm ‖ ˈæţ-

atomistic ˌæt ə ˈmɪst ɪk ◄ ‖ ˌæţ- **~ally** ᵊlˌi

atomiz|e ˈæt ə maɪz ‖ ˈæţ ə- **~ed** d **~er/s** ə/z
    ‖ ᵊr/z **~es** ɪz əz **~ing** ɪŋ

atonal ˌ(ˌ)eɪ ˈtəʊn ᵊl æ-, ə- ‖ -ˈtoʊn- **~ism** ˌɪz əm
    ~ly i

atonality ˌeɪ təʊ ˈnæl ət i ˌæ-, ˌtə-, -ɪt i
    ‖ -toʊ ˈnæl əţ i

aton|e ə ˈtəʊn ‖ ə ˈtoʊn **~ed** d **~es** z **~ing** ɪŋ

atonement ə ˈtəʊn mənt ‖ ə ˈtoʊn- **~s** s

atoneness ˌ(ˌ)æt ˈwʌn nəs -nɪs

atonic ˌ(ˌ)eɪ ˈtɒn ɪk ˌ(ˌ)æ-, ə- ‖ -ˈtɑːn-

atoning ə ˈtəʊn ɪŋ ‖ ə ˈtoʊn ɪŋ

atony ˈæt ən i ‖ ˈæt ᵊn i

atop ə ˈtɒp ‖ ə ˈtɑːp

atopic ˌeɪ ˈtɒp ɪk ◄ ‖ -ˈtɑːp- -ˈtoʊp- **~ally** ᵊlˌi

atopy ˈæt əp i ‖ ˈæţ-

-ator eɪt ə ‖ eɪţ ᵊr —*Stress falls on the same
syllable(s) as for the corresponding verb in* -ate
— **radiator** ˈreɪd i eɪt ə ‖ -eɪţ ᵊr

Atora *tdmk* ə ˈtɔːr ə

atorvastatin ə ˌtɔːv ə ˈstæt ɪn -ᵊn, ·ˈ··ˌ··
    ‖ -ˌtɔːrv-

-atory *The BrE and AmE pronunciations of
this suffix differ. In BrE the vowel of the
penultimate syllable is always weak: the suffix
is either* ət ᵊr i *or* eɪt ᵊr i *and, if the latter,
may be stressed. Different speakers often
pronounce differently. Thus* arˈticulatory *may
have* -jʊl ət ᵊr i *or* -ju leɪt ᵊr i, *or
alternatively may be stressed* arˌticuˈlatory ◄.
In AmE the suffix always has a strong vowel,
ə tɔːr i ə tour i, *stress remaining as for the
corresponding verb in* -ate: arˈticulatory,
ˈmandatory.

ATP ˌeɪ tiː ˈpiː

atrabilious ˌætr ə ˈbɪl iˌəs ◄ **~ness** nəs nɪs

atresia ə ˈtriːz iˌə æ-, -ˈtriːʒ-, -ˈtriːʒ ə
    ‖ ə ˈtriːʒ ə

Atreus ˈeɪtr iˌəs -uːs; ˈeɪtr uːs

at-risk ˌ(ˌ)æt ˈrɪsk ət-

atri|um ˈeɪtr iˌəm ˈætr- **~a** ə **~al** əl

atrocious ə ˈtrəʊʃ əs ‖ ə ˈtroʊʃ əs **~ly** li **~ness**
    nəs nɪs

atrocit|y ə ˈtrɒs ət ˌi -ɪt i ‖ ə ˈtrɑːs əţ ˌi **~ies**
    iz

atrophic æ ˈtrɒf ɪk ˌ(ˌ)eɪ-, ə- ‖ -ˈtrɑːf-

atr|ophy *n, v* ˈætr ˌəf i △-ə faɪ **~ophied** əf id
    △ə faɪd **~ophies** əf iz △ə faɪz **~ophying**
    əf iˌɪŋ △ə faɪ ɪŋ

atropine ˈætr ə piːn -əp ɪn, §-əp ən

Atropos ˈætr ə pɒs -əp əs ‖ -pɑːs

attaboy ˈæt ə bɔɪ ‖ ˈæţ-

attach ə ˈtætʃ **attached** ə ˈtætʃt **attaches**
    ə ˈtætʃ ɪz əz **attaching** ə ˈtætʃ ɪŋ

attaché ə ˈtæʃ eɪ -i ‖ ˌæţ ə ˈʃeɪ ˌæt æ- (*) **~s** s
    atˈtaché case ! ˌattaˈché case

attachment ə ˈtætʃ mənt **~s** s

attack ə ˈtæk **attacked** ə ˈtækt **attacking**
    ə ˈtæk ɪŋ **attacks** ə ˈtæks

attacker ə ˈtæk ə ‖ -ᵊr **~s** z

attain ə ˈteɪn **~ed** d **~ing** ɪŋ **~s** z

attainability ə ˌteɪn ə ˈbɪl ət i -ɪt i ‖ -əţ i

attainable ə ˈteɪn əb ᵊl

attainder ə ˈteɪnd ə ‖ -ᵊr

attainment ə ˈteɪn mənt →-ˈteɪm- **~s** s

attar ˈæt ə -ɑː ‖ ˈæţ ᵊr ˈæt ɑːr **~s** z

attempt ə ˈtempt **~ed** ɪd əd **~ing** ɪŋ **~s** s

Attenborough ˈæt ᵊn bər ə →ˈ·əm-, §-ˌbʌr ə
    ‖ -ˌbɜː oʊ

attend ə ˈtend **~ed** ɪd əd **~ing** ɪŋ **~s** z

attendanc|e ə ˈtend ᵊnˈs **~es** ɪz əz

attendant ə ˈtend ənt **~s** s

attendee ə ˌten ˈdiː ˌæt en- **~s** z

attention ə ˈtenʃ ᵊn **~s** z

attentive ə ˈtent ɪv ‖ ə ˈtenţ ɪv **~ly** li **~ness**
    nəs nɪs

attenuate *adj* ə ˈten juˌət ɪt, -eɪt

attenu|ate *v* ə ˈten ju eɪt **~ated** eɪt ɪd -əd
    ‖ eɪţ əd **~ates** eɪts **~ating** eɪt ɪŋ ‖ eɪţ ɪŋ

attenuation ə ˌten ju ˈeɪʃ ᵊn **~s** z

attenuator ə ˈten ju eɪt ə ‖ -eɪţ ᵊr **~s** z

Attercliffe ˈæt ə klɪf ‖ ˈæţ ᵊr-

attest ə ˈtest **~ed** ɪd əd **~ing** ɪŋ **~s** s

attestation ˌæt e ˈsteɪʃ ᵊn -ə- **~s** z

attestor ə ˈtest ə ‖ -ᵊr **~s** z

attic, Attic 'æt ɪk ‖ 'æt̬- ~s s
Attica 'æt ɪk ə ‖ 'æt̬-
Atticism 'æt ɪ ˌsɪz əm §-ə- ‖ 'æt̬-
Attila ə 'tɪl ə 'æt ɪl-
attire ə 'taɪ‿ə ‖ ə 'taɪ‿ᵊr ~d d ~s z **attiring**
    ə 'taɪ‿ər ɪŋ ‖ ə 'taɪ‿ᵊr ɪŋ

ATTITUDE

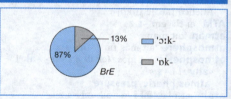

88% 12%
■ -tuːd
■ -tjuːd
AmE

attitude 'æt ɪ tjuːd -ə-, →-tʃuːd ‖ 'æt̬ ə tuːd
    -tjuːd ~s z — *Preference poll, AmE:* -tuːd *88%,*
    -tjuːd *12%.*
attitudinal ˌæt ɪ 'tjuːd ɪn ᵊl ◂ -ˌə-, →-'tʃuːd-,
    -ᵊn ᵊl ‖ ˌæt̬ ə 'tuːd ᵊn ᵊl ◂ -'tjuːd- **~ly** i
attitudinis|e, attitudiniz|e ˌæt ɪ 'tjuːd ɪ naɪz
    ˌ-ə-, →-'tʃuːd-, -ə naɪz, -ᵊn aɪz
    ‖ ˌæt̬ ə 'tuːd ᵊn aɪz -'tjuːd- **~ed** d **~es** ɪz əz
    ~ing ɪŋ
Attleborough 'æt ᵊl bər ə ‖ 'æt̬ ᵊl ˌbɜː ou
Attlee 'æt li
atto- ˌæt əu ‖ ˌæt̬ ou — **attogram**
    'æt əu græm ‖ 'æt̬ ou-
attorney ə 'tɜːn i ‖ ə 'tɜːn i (!) **~ship/s** ʃɪp/s
    ~s z
    at,torney 'general
attract ə 'trækt **~ed** ɪd əd **~ing** ɪŋ **~s** s
attractant ə 'trækt ənt **~s** s
attraction ə 'træk ʃᵊn **~s** z
attractive ə 'trækt ɪv **~ly** li **~ness** nəs nɪs
attractor ə 'trækt ə ‖ -ᵊr **~s** z
attributab|le ə 'trɪb jut əb ‖ᵊl -'ˌjət-, -'ˌjuːt-
    ‖ -'trɪb jət̬- **~ly** li
attribute *v* ə 'trɪb juːt §'ætr ɪ bjuːt, §-ə-
    ‖ ə 'trɪb jət -juːt **attributed** ə 'trɪb jut ɪd
    'ætr ɪ bjuːt-, '-ə-, -əd ‖ ə 'trɪb jət̬ əd -juːt̬ əd
    attributes *v* ə 'trɪb juːts §'ætr ɪ bjuːts, §-ə-
    ‖ ə 'trɪb jəts -juːts **attributing** ə 'trɪb jut ɪŋ
    'ætr ɪ bjuːt-, '-ə- ‖ ə 'trɪb jət̬ ɪŋ -juːt̬ ɪŋ
attribute *n* 'ætr ɪ bjuːt -ə- **~s** s
attribution ˌætr ɪ 'bjuːʃ ᵊn -ə- **~s** z
attributive ə 'trɪb jut ɪv -jət ɪv, -juːt ɪv;
    §'ætr ɪ bjuːt ɪv, §'-ə- ‖ -jət̬ ɪv **~ly** li **~ness** nəs
    nɪs
attrition ə 'trɪʃ ᵊn æ-
Attu 'æt uː
Attucks 'æt əks ‖ 'æt̬-
attun|e ə 'tjuːn æ-, →-'tʃuːn ‖ ə 'tuːn ə 'tjuːn
    ~ed d **~es** z **~ing** ɪŋ
Attw... —*see* **Atw...**
ATV ˌeɪ tiː 'viː **~s** z
Atwater 'æt ˌwɔːt ə ‖ -ˌwɔːt̬ ᵊr -ˌwɑːt̬ ᵊr
Atwell 'æt wel
atwitter ə 'twɪt ə ‖ ə 'twɪt̬ ᵊr
Atwood 'æt wud
atypical ˌeɪ 'tɪp ɪk ᵊl **~ly** i

au əu ‖ ou —*Fr* [o] —*See also phrases with this
    word*
aubade əu 'bɑːd ‖ ou- —*Fr* [o bad] **~s** z
auberge, ~s əu 'beəʒ ‖ ˌou 'beᵊrʒ —*Fr*
    [o bɛʁʒ]
aubergine 'əub ə ʒiːn -dʒiːn ‖ 'oub ᵊr- **~s** z
Auberon 'ɔːb ᵊr ən 'əub-, -ə rɒn, '·rɒn ‖ 'ɑːb-,
    -ə rɑːn —*The writer* A~ Waugh *pronounced*
    'ɔːb-
Aubrey 'ɔːb ri ‖ 'ɑːb-
aubrietia ɔː 'briːʃ ə -'briːʃ i ə ‖ ɑː-, ou- **~s** z
auburn, A~ 'ɔːb ən 'ɔː bɜːn ‖ 'ɔːb ᵊrn 'ɑːb-
Aubusson 'əub ju sɒn ‖ ˌoub ə 'sɑːn -'soun
    —*Fr* [o by sɔ̃]
Auchinleck 'ɔːk ɪn lek 'ɒx-, -ən-, ˌ · '· ‖ 'ɑːk-
Auchterarder ˌɒxt ər 'ɑːd ə ˌɒxt-
    ‖ ˌɔːkt ər 'ɑːrd ᵊr ˌɑːkt-
Auchtermuchty ˌɔːxt ə 'mʌkt i ˌɒkt-;
    ˌɒxt ə 'mʌxt i ‖ -ᵊr- ˌɑːkt-
Auckland 'ɔːk lənd ‖ 'ɑːk-
au contraire ˌəu kɒn 'treə ‖ ˌou kɑːn 'treᵊr
    -'træᵊr —*Fr* [o kɔ̃ tʁɛːʁ]
au courant əu 'kur ɒ̃ ‖ ˌou ku 'rɑːn —*Fr*
    [o ku ʁɑ̃]

AUCTION

87% 13%
■ 'ɔːk-
■ 'ɒk-
BrE

auction 'ɔːk ʃᵊn 'ɒk- ‖ 'ɑːk- — *Preference poll,
    BrE:* 'ɔːk- *87%,* 'ɒk- *13%.* **~ed** d **~ing** ɪŋ **~s** z
auctioneer ˌɔːk ʃə 'nɪə ◂ ˌɒk- ‖ -'nɪᵊr ˌɑːk- **~s** z
auctorial ɔːk 'tɔːr i əl ‖ ɑːk-, -'tour-
audacious ɔː 'deɪʃ əs ‖ ɑː- **~ly** li **~ness** nəs nɪs
audacit|y ˌ₍ᵢ₎ɔː 'dæs ət |i -ɪt i ‖ -ət̬ |i ˌ₍ᵢ₎ɑː- **~ies**
    iz
Auden 'ɔːd ᵊn ‖ 'ɑːd-
Audenshaw 'ɔːd ᵊn ʃɔː ‖ 'ɑːd ᵊn ʃɑː
Audi *tdmk* 'aud i 'ɔːd- ‖ 'ɔːd-, 'ɑːd-
audibility ˌɔːd ə 'bɪl ət i ˌ·ɪ-, -ɪt i ‖ -ət̬ i ˌɑːd-
audib|le 'ɔːd əb ‖ᵊl -ɪb- ‖ 'ɑːd- **~ly** li
Audie 'ɔːd i ‖ 'ɑːd-
audienc|e 'ɔːd i ənᵗs ‖ 'ɑːd- **~es** ɪz əz
audile 'ɔːd aɪᵊl -ɪl ‖ 'ɑːd-
audio 'ɔːd i əu ‖ -ou 'ɑːd- **~s** z
    ˌaudio cas'sette
audiolingual ˌɔːd i əu 'lɪŋ gwəl ◂ -'lɪŋ gjuˌəl
    ‖ ˌou- ˌɑːd- **~ly** i
audiological ˌɔːd i ə 'lɒdʒ ɪk ᵊl ◂ ‖ -'lɑːdʒ-
    ˌɑːd- **~ly** i
audiologist ˌɔː di 'ɒl ədʒ ɪst §-əst ‖ -'ɑːl- ˌɑːd-
    ~s s
audiology ˌɔːd i 'ɒl ədʒ i ‖ -'ɑːl- ˌɑːd-
audiometer ˌɔːd i 'ɒm ɪt ə -ət- ə ‖ -'ɑːm ət̬ ᵊr
    ˌɑːd- **~s** z
audiometry ˌɔːd i 'ɒm ətr i -ɪtr i ‖ -'ɑːm- ˌɑːd-
audiophile 'ɔːd i əu faɪl ‖ ˌou- 'ɑːd- **~s** z
audiotape 'ɔːd i əu teɪp ‖ ˌou- 'ɑːd- **~s** s

audiotyp|ing 'ɔːd i ˌəʊ ˌtaɪp |ɪŋ ‖ ˌ_oʊ- 'ɑːd-
~**ist/s** ɪst/s əst/s
audiovisual ˌɔːd i ˌəʊ 'vɪʒ u ᵊl ◂ -'vɪz ju ˌəl,
-'vɪʒ ᵊl ‖ ˌ_oʊ- ˌɑːd-, -'vɪʒ ᵊl ~**ly** i
  ˌaudio ˌvisual 'aids
aud|it 'ɔːd |ɪt §-ət ‖ 'ɔːd |ət 'ɑːd- ~**ited** ɪt ɪd
§ət-, -əd ‖ ət əd ~**iting** ɪt ɪŋ §ət- ‖ ət ɪŋ ~**its**
ɪts §əts ‖ əts
audition ɔː 'dɪʃ ᵊn ‖ ɑː- ~**ed** d ~**ing** ɪŋ ~**s** z
auditor 'ɔːd ɪt ə -ət- ‖ -ət ᵊr 'ɑːd- ~**s** z
auditori|um ˌɔːd ɪ 'tɔːr i ˌəm ‖ˌ-ə- ‖ ˌɑːd-,
-'toʊr- ~**a** ə ~**ums** əmz
auditor|y 'ɔːd ɪt ər |i ˌ-ət ˌ| ‖ 'ɔːd ə tɔːr |i 'ɑːd-,
-toʊr i ~**ily** əl i ɪ li
Audlab *tdmk* 'ɔːd læb ‖ 'ɑːd-
Audlem 'ɔːd ləm ‖ 'ɑːd-
Audley 'ɔːd li ‖ 'ɑːd-
Audrey 'ɔːdr i ‖ 'ɑːd-
Audubon 'ɔːd ə bɒn -əb ən ‖ -bɑːn 'ɑːd-,
-əb ən
AUEW ˌeɪ ju: ˌi: 'dʌb ᵊl ju
auf *German prepn* aʊf —*Ger* [auf] —*See also
phrases with this word*
au fait ˌ_əʊ 'feɪ ‖ ˌ_oʊ- —*Fr* [o fɛ]
au fond ˌ_əʊ 'fɒ̃ ‖ ˌ_oʊ 'foʊn -'fɔ̃: —*Fr* [o fɔ̃]
auf Wiedersehen ˌ_aʊf 'viːd ə zeɪn -'wiːd-,
-'‧‧,zeɪ ən ‖ -ᵊr- —*Ger* [auf 'viː dɐ ˌzeː ən]
Augean ɔː 'dʒiː ˌən ‖ ɑː-
auger, Auger 'ɔːg ə ‖ -ᵊr 'ɑːg- ~**s** z
aught ɔːt ‖ ɑːt (= *ought*)
Aughton 'ɔːt ᵊn ‖ 'ɑːt- —*but there is one village
of this name, near Lancaster, which is* 'æft ən
augite 'ɔːdʒ aɪt ‖ 'ɑːdʒ-
aug|ment ɔːg |'ment ˌ_oʊg- ‖ ˌ_ɑːg- ~**mented**
'ment ɪd -əd ‖ 'menţ əd ~**menting** 'ment ɪŋ
‖ 'menţ ɪŋ ~**ments** 'ments
augment *n* 'ɔːg ment -mənt ‖ 'ɑːg- ~**s** s
augmentation ˌɔːg men 'teɪʃ ᵊn -mən- ‖ ˌɑːg-
~**s** z
augmentative ɔːg 'ment ət ɪv ‖ -'menţ əţ ɪv
ɑːg- ~**s** z
Augrabies ə 'grɑːb iːz
au gratin əʊ 'græt æn ‖ oʊ 'grɑːt ᵊn —*Fr*
[o gʁa tæ̃]
Augsburg 'aʊgz bɜːg 'aʊks-, -bʊəg ‖ -bɝːg
'aːgz-, -bʊrg —*Ger* ['auks bʊʁk]
augur *n, v* 'ɔːg ə -jə ‖ -ᵊr 'ɑːg- ~**ed** d **auguring**
'ɔːg ər ɪŋ -jər- ‖ 'ɑːg- ~**s** z
augur|y 'ɔːg jʊr |i -jər-, -ər- ‖ -jər |i 'ɑːg-, -ər-
~**ies** iz
august *adj* ˌ_ɔː 'gʌst ‖ ˌ_ɑː-; '‧‧ ~**ly** li ~**ness**
nəs nɪs
August *n, name of month* 'ɔːg əst ‖ 'ɑːg-
August *personal name*, **august** *n 'clown'*
'aʊg ʊst ~**s** s
Augusta ɔː 'gʌst ə ə- ‖ ɑː-
Augustan ɔː 'gʌst ən ə- ‖ ɑː- ~**s** z
Augustine ɔː 'gʌst ɪn ə-, §-ən ‖ 'ɔːg ə stiːn
'ɑːg- (*)
Augustinian ˌɔːg ə 'stɪn i ən ◂ ˌ‧ʌ- ‖ ˌɑːg- ~**s** z
Augustus ɔː 'gʌst əs ə- ‖ ɑː-
au jus əʊ 'ʒuː- -'ʒuːs ‖ oʊ- —*Fr* [o ʒy]
auk ɔːk ‖ ɑːk **auks** ɔːks ‖ ɑːks

auklet 'ɔːk lət -lɪt ‖ 'ɑːk- ~**s** s
aul|a 'ɔːl |ə -aʊl- ‖ 'ɑːl- ~**ae** iː
au lait əʊ 'leɪ ‖ oʊ- —*Fr* [o lɛ]
auld, Auld ɔːld ‖ ɑːld
  ˌauld ˌlang 'syne zaɪn saɪn; ˌAuld 'Reekie
  'riːk i
Aulis 'ɔːl ɪs -aʊl-, §-əs ‖ 'ɑːl-
Aum ɔːm ‖ ɑːm
au naturel əʊ ˌnæt ju 'rel -ˌnætʃ ə-, -ˌnæt jə-,
ˌ‧ˌ‧- ‖ oʊ ˌnɑːtʃ ə 'rel —*Fr* [o na ty ʁɛl]
Aung San Suu Kyi aʊŋ ˌsæn su: 'tʃiː ‖ -ˌsɑːn-

---

aunt ɑːnt §ænt ‖ ænt ɑːnt **aunts** ɑːnts §ænts
‖ ænts ɑːnts — *Preference poll, AmE:* ænt
70%, ɑːnt *30%.*
  ˌAunt 'Sally
aunt|ie, aunt|y, Auntly 'ɑːnt |i §'ænt-
‖ 'ænţ |i 'ɑːnt- ~**ies** iz
au pair ˌ_əʊ 'peə ‖ ˌ_oʊ 'peᵊr -'pæᵊr —*Fr*
[o pɛːʁ] ~**s** z
au poivre əʊ 'pwɑːv -'‧rə ‖ oʊ- —*Fr*
[o pwaːvʁ]
aur|a 'ɔːr |ə ‖ ~**ae** iː
aural 'ɔːr əl —*Sometimes* 'aʊᵊr əl, *to avoid
confusion with oral* ~**ly** i
Aurangzeb 'ɔːr əŋ zeb
aureate 'ɔːr i eɪt ət, ɪt ~**ly** li ~**ness** nəs nɪs
Aurelian ɔː 'riːl i ˌən
Aurelius ɔː 'riːl i ˌəs
aureola ɔː 'riː əl ə ˌɔːr i 'əʊl ə, ˌɒr-
‖ ˌɔːr i 'oʊl ə ~**s** z
aureole 'ɔːr i əʊl ‖ -oʊl ~**s** z
aureomycin, A~ *tdmk* ˌɔːr i əʊ 'maɪs ɪn §-ᵊn
‖ -oʊ-‧-
au revoir ˌ_əʊ rə 'vwɑː -rɪ-, §-riː-
‖ ˌoʊ rə 'vwɑːr —*Fr* [o ʁə vwaːʁ]
auricle 'ɔːr ɪk ᵊl 'ɒr- ~**s** z
auricul|a ɔː 'rɪk jʊl |ə ɒ-, -jəl- ‖ -jəl |ə ~**ar** ə
‖ ᵊr ~**as** əz
Auriel 'ɔːr i ˌəl
auriferous ɔː 'rɪf ər əs
Auriga ɔː 'raɪg ə ‖ ɑː-
Aurignacian ˌɔːr ɪg 'neɪʃ ᵊn ◂ -iːn 'jeɪʃ-
aurochs 'ɔːr ɒks 'aʊᵊr- ‖ -ɑːks ~**es** ɪz əz
auror|a, A~ ɔː 'rɔːr |ə ɒ- ~**ae** iː ~**as** əz
  auˌrora auˈstralis ɒ 'streɪl ɪs ɔː-, ə-, -'strɑːl-,
  §-əs ‖ ɔː 'streɪl əs ɑː-; auˌrora ˌboreˈalis
Auschwitz 'aʊʃ wɪts -vɪts —*Ger* ['auʃ vɪts]
auscultation ˌɔːsk ᵊl 'teɪʃ ᵊn ˌɒsk-, -ʌl- ‖ ˌɑːsk-
auslese, A~ 'aʊs leɪz ə —*Ger* ['aus leː zə]
auspices 'ɔːsp ɪs ɪz 'ɒsp-, -əs-, -əz, -iːz ‖ 'ɑːsp-
auspicious ɔː 'spɪʃ əs ɒ- ‖ ɑː- ~**ly** li ~**ness** nəs
nɪs
Aussie 'ɒz i ‖ 'ɔːs i 'ɑːs-, 'ɔːz-, 'ɑːz- ~**s** z

A

Aust ɔːst ‖ ɑːst
Austell 'ɒst ᵊl 'ɔːst- ‖ 'ɑːst- — St A~'s *in Cornwall is locally also* -'ɔːs ᵊlz
Austen 'ɒst ɪn 'ɔːst-, §-ən ‖ 'ɔːst- 'ɑːst-
Auster 'ɔːst ə ‖ -ᵊr 'ɑːst-
austere ɔː 'stɪə ɒ- ‖ ɔː 'stɪᵊr ɑː-, -'steᵊr **~ly** li
austerit|y ɔː 'ster ət |i ɒ-, -ɪt i ‖ ɔː 'ster ət |i ɑː-, -'stɪr- **~ies** iz
Austerlitz 'ɔːst ə lɪts 'aʊst- ‖ -ᵊr- 'ɑːst-
Austick 'ɔːst ɪk ‖ 'ɑːst-
Austin 'ɒst ɪn 'ɔːst-, §-ən ‖ 'ɔːst ən 'ɑːst-
austral 'ɔːs trəl 'ɒs- ‖ 'ɑːs-
Austra|lasia ˌɒs trə |'leɪʒ ə ◂ ˌɔːs-, -'leɪʃ-, -|'leɪz i ə ‖ ˌɔːs- ˌɑːs- **~lasian/s** 'leɪʒ ᵊn/z 'leɪʃ-, 'leɪz i ᵊn/z
Australi|a ɒ 'streɪl i ˌ|ə ɔː-, ə- ‖ ɔː- ɑː-, ə- **~an** ən **~ans** ənz —*locally* ə-
Australoid 'ɒs trə lɔɪd 'ɔːs- ‖ 'ɔːs- 'ɑːs- **~s** z
australopithecine ˌɒs trəl əʊ 'pɪθ ə saɪn ˌɔːs-, -ɪ-, -siːn ‖ ɔː ˌstreɪl oʊ- ɑː- **~s** z
australopithecus ˌɒs trəl əʊ 'pɪθ ɪk əs -ək əs ‖ ɔː ˌstreɪl oʊ '·- ɑː-
Austri|a 'ɒs tri ˌ|ə 'ɔːs- ‖ 'ɔːs- 'ɑːs- **~an/s** ən/z
Austro- *comb. form* |ɒs trəʊ |ɔːs trəʊ ‖ |ɔːs troʊ — **Austro-Hungarian** ˌɒs trəʊ hʌŋ 'geər i ˌən ◂ ˌɔːs- ‖ ˌɔːs troʊ hʌŋ 'ger- ˌɑːs-, -'gær-
Austronesi|a ˌɒs trəʊ 'niːz i ˌ|ə ◂ ˌɔːs-, -'niːʒ ˌ|ə, -'niːs i ˌ|ə, -'niːʃ ˌ|ə ‖ ˌɔːs troʊ 'niːʒ ˌ|ə ˌɑːs-, -'niːʃ- **~an/s** ən/z
Austyn 'ɒst ɪn 'ɔːst-, §-ən ‖ 'ɔːst- ɑːst-
AUT ˌeɪ juː 'tiː
autarchic ɔː 'tɑːk ɪk ‖ -'tɑːrk- ɑː- **~al** ᵊl
autarchy 'ɔːt ɑːk i ‖ -ɑːrk i 'ɑːt-
autarkic ɔː 'tɑːk ɪk ‖ -'tɑːrk- ɑː- **~al** ᵊl
autarky 'ɔːt ɑːk i ‖ -ɑːrk i 'ɑːt-
auteur ɔː 'tɜː ₍ₒ₎əʊ- ‖ oʊ 'tɜː —*Fr* [o tœːʁ]
authentic ɔː 'θent ɪk ‖ -'θenṱ ɪk ɑː- **~ally** ᵊl_i
authenti|cate ɔː 'θent ɪ |keɪt §-ə- ‖ -'θenṱ- ɑː- **~cated** keɪt ɪd -əd ‖ keɪṱ əd **~cates** keɪts **~cating** keɪt ɪŋ ‖ keɪṱ ɪŋ **~cator/s** keɪt ə/z ‖ keɪṱ ᵊr/z
authentication ɔː ˌθent ɪ 'keɪʃ ᵊn §-ə- ‖ -ˌθenṱ- ɑː- **~s** z
authenticity ˌɔːθ en 'tɪs ət i ˌ·ᵊn-, -ɪt i ‖ -əṱ i ˌɑːθ-, -ᵊn-
author 'ɔːθ ə ‖ 'ɔːθ ᵊr 'ɑːθ- **~ed** d **authoring** 'ɔːθ ᵊr_ɪŋ ‖ 'ɑːθ- **~s** z
authoress 'ɔːθ ə res -ər ɪs, -ər əs, ˌɔːθ ə 'res ‖ 'ɔːθ ᵊr əs 'ɑːθ- **~es** ɪz əz
authorial ɔː 'θɔːr i ˌəl ‖ ɑː- **~ly** i
authoris... —*see* **authoriz...**
authoritarian ɔː ˌθɒr ɪ 'teər i ˌən ◂ -ə'·- ‖ -ˌθɔːr ə 'ter- ɑː-, ə- **~ism** ˌɪz əm **~s** z
authoritative ɔː 'θɒr ɪt ət ɪv -'·ət-; -ɪ teɪt ɪv, -ə·· ‖ ə 'θɔːr ə teɪṱ ɪv ɔː-, ɑː- **~ly** li **~ness** nəs nɪs
authorit|y ɔː 'θɒr ət |i ə-, -ɪt i ‖ ə 'θɔːr əṱ |i ɔː-, ɑː- **~ies** iz
authorization ˌɔːθ ᵊr_aɪ 'zeɪʃ ᵊn -ᵊr ɪ- ‖ ə- ˌɑːθ- **~s** z

authoriz|e 'ɔːθ ə raɪz ‖ 'ɑːθ- **~ed** d **~es** ɪz əz **~ing** ɪŋ ˌAuthorized 'Version
authorship 'ɔːθ ə ʃɪp ‖ -ᵊr- 'ɑːθ-
autism 'ɔːt ˌɪz əm ‖ 'ɑːt-
autistic ɔː 'tɪst ɪk ‖ ɑː- **~ally** ᵊl_i
auto 'ɔːt əʊ ‖ 'ɔːt oʊ 'ɑːt- **~s** z
auto- *comb. form* with stress-neutral suffix |ɔːt əʊ ‖ |ɔːt oʊ |ɑːt- — **autoimmune** ˌɔːt əʊ ɪ 'mjuːn ‖ ˌɔːt oʊ- ˌɑːt- with stress-imposing suffix ɔː 'tɒ + ‖ ɔː 'tɑː + ɑː- — **autolysis** ɔː 'tɒl əs ɪs -ɪs-, §-əs ‖ ɔː 'tɑːl- ɑː-
autobahn 'ɔːt əʊ bɑːn 'aʊt- ‖ 'ɔːt oʊ- 'ɑːt- —*Ger* ['au to baːn] **~s** z
autobiographer ˌɔːt əʊ baɪ 'ɒg rəf ə ‖ ˌɔːt ə baɪ 'ɑːg rəf ᵊr ˌɑːt- **~s** z
autobiographic ˌɔːt əʊ ˌbaɪ_ə 'græf ɪk ◂ -ˌbaɪ əʊ- ‖ ˌɔːt ə ˌbaɪ ə- ˌɑːt- **~al** ᵊl **~ally** ᵊl_i
autobiograph|y ˌɔːt əʊ baɪ 'ɒg rəf |i ‖ ˌɔːt ə baɪ 'ɑːg- ˌɑːt- **~ies** iz
autocar, A~ 'ɔːt əʊ kɑː ‖ 'ɔːt oʊ kɑːr 'ɑːt- **~s** z
autochang|e 'ɔːt əʊ tʃeɪndʒ ‖ 'ɔːt oʊ- 'ɑːt- **~es** ɪz əz
autochanger 'ɔːt əʊ ˌtʃeɪndʒ ə ‖ 'ɔːt oʊ ˌtʃeɪndʒ ᵊr 'ɑːt- **~s** z
autochthon ɔː 'tɒk θᵊn -θɒn ‖ -'tɑːk- ɑː-, -θɑːn **~s** z
autochthonous ɔː 'tɒk θən əs ‖ -'tɑːk- ɑː- **~ly** li
autoclav|e 'ɔːt əʊ kleɪv ‖ 'ɔːt oʊ- 'ɑːt- **~ed** d **~es** z **~ing** ɪŋ
autocorrelation ˌɔːt əʊ ˌkɒr ə 'leɪʃ ᵊn -ɪ'·- ‖ ˌɔːt oʊ ˌkɔːr- ˌɑːt-, -ˌkɑːr-
autocrac|y ɔː 'tɒk rəs |i ‖ -'tɑːk- ɑː- **~ies** iz
autocrat 'ɔːt ə kræt ‖ 'ɔːt ə- 'ɑːt- **~s** s
autocratic ˌɔːt ə 'kræt ɪk ◂ ‖ ˌɔːt ə 'kræṱ ɪk ˌɑːt- **~al** ᵊl **~ally** ᵊl_i
autocross 'ɔːt əʊ krɒs ‖ 'ɔːt oʊ krɔːs 'ɑːt-, -krɑːs
autocue, A~ *tdmk* 'ɔːt əʊ kjuː ‖ 'ɔːt oʊ- 'ɑːt- **~s** z
autocycle 'ɔːt əʊ ˌsaɪk ᵊl ‖ 'ɔːt oʊ- 'ɑːt- **~s** z
auto-da-fé ˌɔːt əʊ dɑː 'feɪ ˌaʊt-, -dɑː'· ‖ ˌɔːt oʊ- ˌɑːt- —*Port* [au tu da 'fe]
autodestruct ˌɔːt əʊ di 'strʌkt -də'· ‖ ˌɔːt oʊ- ˌɑːt- **~ed** ɪd əd **~ing** ɪŋ **~s** s
autodidact 'ɔːt əʊ dɪ ˌdækt -ˌdaɪd ækt, ˌ··'· ‖ 'ɔːt oʊ 'daɪd ækt ˌɑːt-, -də 'dækt **~s** s
autodidactic ˌɔːt əʊ dɪ 'dækt ɪk ◂ -daɪ'-- ‖ ˌɔːt oʊ daɪ- ˌɑːt-, ˌ·-də- **~ally** ᵊl_i
autoerotic ˌɔːt əʊ ɪ 'rɒt ɪk ◂ -ə'-- ‖ ˌɔːt oʊ ɪ 'rɑːṱ ɪk ◂ ˌɑːt-
autoeroticism ˌɔːt əʊ ɪ 'rɒt ɪ ˌsɪz əm -ə'--, -ə,-- ‖ ˌɔːt oʊ ɪ 'rɑːṱ ə- ˌɑːt-
autoerotism ˌɔːt əʊ 'er ə ˌtɪz əm ‖ ˌɔːt oʊ- ˌɑːt-
autogiro ˌɔːt əʊ 'dʒaɪᵊr əʊ ‖ ˌɔːt oʊ 'dʒaɪᵊr oʊ ˌɑːt- **~s** z
autograph 'ɔːt ə grɑːf -græf ‖ 'ɔːt ə græf 'ɑːt- **~ed** t **~ing** ɪŋ **~s** s

A

Australian English

The pronunciation of English in Australia is generally similar to BrE rather than AmE. Some of the points of difference are as follows:

- If there is a choice between ɪ and ə as a weak vowel, Australian English prefers ə.

  valid ˈvæl əd (rhymes with **salad** ˈsæl əd)

  boxes ˈbɒks əz (sounds just like **boxers**).

- Australian English uses fewer GLOTTAL STOPs than BrE. When t is between vowels it is often voiced as in AmE; and, as in AmE, it may be elided after n (see T-VOICING).

  better ˈbeṭ ə

  entertain ˌenṭ ə ˈteɪn.

- The vowels ɪ, e and æ tend to be closer than in BrE RP; ɑː tends to be fronter; ɪə and eə are monophthongal (like ɪː, eː); and the diphthongs eɪ and əʊ tend to be wider (almost like aɪ and aʊ), while aɪ and aʊ sound more like ɑɪ, æʊ.

---

autogyro ˌɔːt əʊ ˈdʒaɪʳr əʊ ‖ ˌɔːt̬ oʊ ˈdʒaɪʳr oʊ ˌɑːt̬- **~s** z

autoharp, A~ *tdmk* ˈɔːt əʊ hɑːp ‖ ˈɔːt̬ oʊ hɑːrp ˈɑːt̬- **~s** s

autoimmun|e ˌɔːt əʊ ɪ ˈmjuːn ◂ ‖ ˌɔːt̬ oʊ- ˌɑːt̬- **~ity** ət i ɪt i ‖ əṭ i

autoload ˌɔːt əʊ ˈləʊd ˈ · · · ‖ ˌɔːt̬ oʊ ˈloʊd ˌɑːt̬- **~ed** ɪd əd **~ing** ɪŋ ◂ **~s** z

autologous ɔː ˈtɒl əg əs ‖ -ˈtɑːl- ɑː- **~ly** li

Autolycus ɔː ˈtɒl ɪk əs ‖ -ˈtɑːl- ɑː-

automaker ˈɔːt əʊ ˌmeɪk ə ‖ ˈɔːt̬ oʊ ˌmeɪk ᵊr **~s** z

automat, A~ *tdmk* ˈɔːt ə mæt ‖ ˈɔːt̬- ˈɑːt̬- **~s** s

automata ɔː ˈtɒm ət ə ‖ ɔː ˈtɑːm əṭ ə ɑː-

auto|mate ˈɔːt ə |meɪt ‖ ˈɔːt̬- ˈɑːt̬- **~mated** meɪt ɪd -əd ‖ ˈmeɪt̬ əd **~mates** meɪts **~mating** meɪt ɪŋ ‖ ˈmeɪt̬ ɪŋ

automatic ˌɔːt ə ˈmæt ɪk ◂ ‖ ˌɔːt̬ ə ˈmæt̬ ɪk ◂ ˌɑːt̬- **~ally** ᵊl̬ i

  autoˌ**matic ˈpilot**

automation ˌɔːt ə ˈmeɪʃ ᵊn ‖ ˌɔːt̬- ˌɑːt̬-

automatism ɔː ˈtɒm ə ˌtɪz əm ‖ ɔː ˈtɑːm- ɑː-

autom|aton ɔː ˈtɒm |ət ən ‖ ɔː ˈtɑːm |ət ᵊn ɑː-, -|ə taɪn **~ata** ət ə ‖ əṭ ə **~atons** ət ənz ‖ ət ᵊnz

automobile ˈɔːt ə məʊ ˌbiːᵊl ˌ · · · · ‖ ˈɔːt̬ ə moʊ ˌbiːᵊl ˈɑːt̬-; ˌ · · · ·; ˌ · · · · · **~s** z

automotive ˌɔːt əʊ ˈməʊt ɪv ◂ ‖ ˌɔːt̬ ə ˈmoʊt̬ ɪv ◂ ˌɑːt̬-

autonomic ˌɔːt ə ˈnɒm ɪk ◂ ‖ ˌɔːt̬ ə ˈnɑːm ɪk ◂ ˌɑː- **~ally** ᵊl̬ i

  ˌ**autonomic ˈnervous ˌsystem**

autonomous ɔː ˈtɒn əm əs ‖ ɔː ˈtɑːn- ɑː- **~ly** li

autonom|y ɔː ˈtɒn əm |i ‖ ɔː ˈtɑːn- ɑː- **~ies** iz

autopilot ˈɔːt əʊ ˌpaɪl ət ‖ ˈɔːt̬ oʊ- ˈɑːt̬- **~s** s

autopista ˌaʊt əʊ ˈpiːst ə ‖ -oʊ- —*Sp* [au to ˈpis ta]

autops|y ˈɔːt ɒps |i -əps-; ɔː ˈtɒps |i ‖ ˈɔːt̬ ɑːps |i -ˈɑːt-; ɔːt̬ əps i, ˈɑːt̬- **~ies** iz

autoreverse ˌɔːt əʊ ri ˈvɜːs -rəˈ · ‖ ˌɔːt̬ oʊ ri ˈvɜ˞ːs ˌɑːt̬-

autoroute ˈɔːt əʊ ruːt ‖ ˈɔːt̬ oʊ- ˈɑːt̬- —*Fr* [o to ʁut] **~s** s

autosegmental ˌɔːt əʊ seg ˈment ᵊl ◂ -səgˈ · -, -sɪgˈ · - ‖ ˌɔːt̬ oʊ seg ˈment̬ ᵊl ◂ ˌɑːt̬- **~ly** i

autostrada ˈɔːt əʊ ˌstrɑːd ə ˈaʊt- ‖ ˈaʊt oʊ- ˈɔːt̬-, ˈɑːt̬- —*It* [au to ˈstraː da] **~s** z

autosuggestion ˌɔːt əʊ sə ˈdʒes tʃən -ˈdʒeʃ- ‖ ˌɔːt̬ oʊ səg ˈdʒes tʃən ˌɑːt̬-

Autrey ˈɔːtr i ‖ ˈɑːtr-

autumn, A~ ˈɔːt əm ‖ ˈɔːt̬ əm ˈɑːt̬- **~s** z

autumnal ɔː ˈtʌm nəl ‖ ɑː- **~ly** i

Auty ˈɔːt i ‖ ˈɔːt̬ i ˈɑːt̬ i

Auvergne əʊ ˈveən -ˈvɜːn ‖ oʊ ˈveᵊrn -ˈvɜ˞ːn —*Fr* [o vɛʁnj, ɔ-]

au vin əʊ ˈvæ̃ -ˈvæn ‖ oʊ- —*Fr* [o væ̃]

AUX ɔːks ‖ ɑːks

  ˈ**AUX node**

Auxerre əʊ ˈseə ‖ oʊ ˈseᵊr —*Fr* [o sɛːʁ]

auxiliar|y ɔːg ˈzɪl i ər |i ɔːk-, ɔːk ˈsɪl-, △-ˈ · ər |i ‖ ɑːg-, -ˈzɪl ər |i **~ies** iz

auxin ˈɔːks ɪn §-ən ‖ ˈɑːks- **~s** z

Ava *(i)* ˈɑːv ə, *(ii)* ˈeɪv ə

avail ə ˈveᵊl **~ed** d **~ing** ɪŋ **~s** z

availabilit|y ə ˌveɪl ə ˈbɪl ət |i -ɪt i ‖ -ət̬ |i **~ies** iz

availab|le ə ˈveɪl əb |ᵊl **~ly** li

avalanch|e ˈæv ə lɑːntʃ §-læntʃ ‖ -læntʃ **~es** ɪz əz

Avalon ˈæv ə lɒn ‖ -lɑːn

avant-garde ˌæv ɒŋ ˈgɑːd ◂ -ᵊnt-, -ɒ̃- ‖ ˌɑːv ɑːn ˈgɑːrd ◂ ˌæv-; ə ˈvɑːnt gɑːrd —*Fr* [a vɑ̃ gaʁd]

Avar ˈæv ɑː ˈeɪv- ‖ -ɑːr

avarice ˈæv ər ɪs §-əs

A

avaricious ˌæv ə ˈrɪʃ əs ◂ ~ly li ~ness nəs nɪs
avast ə ˈvɑːst §-ˈvæst ‖ ə ˈvæst
Avastin tdmk eɪ ˈvæst ɪn
avatar ˈæv ə tɑː ˌ·ˈ· ‖ -tɑːr ~s z
avaunt ə ˈvɔːnt ‖ -ˈvɑːnt
ave, Ave 'hail'; 'prayer' ˈɑːv eɪ -i
   ˌAve Maˈria; ˌAve Maˌria ˈLane
Ave. —see Avenue; sometimes spoken as æv
Avebury ˈeɪv bər i ‖ -ˌber i —locally also
   ˈeɪb ər i
avenge ə ˈvendʒ avenged ə ˈvendʒd avenges
   ə ˈvendʒ ɪz -əz avenging/ly ə ˈvendʒ ɪŋ /li
avenger ə ˈvendʒ ə ‖ -ᵊr ~s z
avens ˈeɪv ᵊnz ˈæv-, -ɪnz ‖ ˈæv-
Aventine ˈæv ᵊn taɪn
aventurine ə ˈventʃ ə riːn -ər ɪn, -ər ən
avenue ˈæv ə njuː -ɪ- ‖ -nuː -njuː ~s z
aver ə ˈvɜː ‖ ə ˈvɜː averred ə ˈvɜːd ‖ ə ˈvɜːd
   averring ə ˈvɜːr ɪŋ ‖ ə ˈvɜː ɪŋ avers ə ˈvɜːz
   ‖ ə ˈvɜːz
averag|e ˈæv ər ɪdʒ ~ed d ~es ɪz əz ~ing ɪŋ
Averil, Averill ˈæv ər ɪl ᵊr ᵊl
Avernus ə ˈvɜːn əs ‖ ə ˈvɜːn əs
averr... —see aver
Averroes, Averroës ə ˈver əʊ iːz ˌæv ə ˈrəʊ-
   ‖ -oʊ-
averse ə ˈvɜːs ‖ ə ˈvɜːs ~ly li ~ness nəs nɪs
aversion ə ˈvɜːʃ ᵊn §-ˈvɜːʒ- ‖ ə ˈvɜːʒ ᵊn -ˈvɜːʃ-
   ~s z
   aˈversion ˌtherapy
aversive ə ˈvɜːs ɪv §-ˈvɜːz- ‖ ə ˈvɜːs ɪv -ˈvɜːz-
avert ə ˈvɜːt ‖ ə ˈvɜːt averted ə ˈvɜːt ɪd -əd
   ‖ ə ˈvɜːt̬ əd averting ə ˈvɜːt ɪŋ ‖ ə ˈvɜːt̬ ɪŋ
   averts ə ˈvɜːts ‖ ə ˈvɜːts
Avery ˈeɪv ər i
Aves, aves ˈeɪv iːz
Avesta ə ˈvest ə
Avestan ə ˈvest ən
avgolemono ˌæv gəʊ ˈlem ə nəʊ
   ‖ ˌɑːv goʊ ˈlem ə noʊ —Gk
   [av ɣɔ ˈle mɔ nɔ]
Avia tdmk ˈeɪv i ə
avian ˈeɪv i ən
aviar|y ˈeɪv i ər |i |i ‖ -er |i ~ies iz
aviation ˌeɪv i ˈeɪʃ ᵊn
aviator ˈeɪv i eɪt ə ‖ -eɪt̬ ᵊr ~s z
Avicenna ˌæv ɪ ˈsen ə §-ə-
avid ˈæv ɪd §-əd ~ly li
avidity ə ˈvɪd ət i æ-, -ɪt- ‖ -ət̬ i
Aviemore ˌæv i ˈmɔː -ˈmɔːr -ˈmoʊr
avifauna ˈeɪv ɪ ˌfɔːn ə ˈæv-, §-ə- ‖ -ˌfɑːn-
Avignon ˈæv iːn jõ ‖ ˌæv iːn ˈjoʊn -ˈjɑːn, -ˈjɔːn
   —Fr [a vi njɔ̃]
Avila ˈæv ɪl ə -əl- ‖ ˈɑːv- —Sp [ˈa βi la]
avionic ˌeɪv i ˈɒn ɪk ◂ -ˈɑːn- ~s s
avirulent ˌeɪ ˈvɪr ʊl ənt ◂ ə'--, jʊl-, -jəl-, -əl-
   ‖ -əl- -jəl-
Avis ˈeɪv ɪs §-əs
Avoca ə ˈvəʊk ə ‖ ə ˈvoʊk ə
avocado ˌæv ə ˈkɑːd əʊ ◂ ‖ -oʊ ˌɑːv- ~s z
   ˌavoˌcado ˈpear
avocation ˌæv əʊ ˈkeɪʃ ᵊn ‖ -ə- ~al ᵊl ~s z
avocet ˈæv ə set ~s s

Avogadro ˌæv əʊ ˈgɑːdr əʊ -ˈgædr-
   ‖ -ə ˈgɑːdr oʊ ˌɑːv-, -ˈgædr- —It
   [a vo ˈgaː dro] ~'s z
   ˌAvoˌgadro('s) ˈnumber
avoid ə ˈvɔɪd avoided ə ˈvɔɪd ɪd -əd avoiding
   ə ˈvɔɪd ɪŋ avoids ə ˈvɔɪdz
avoidab|le ə ˈvɔɪd əb| ᵊl ~ly li
avoidance ə ˈvɔɪd ᵊnˢs
avoirdupois ˌæv wɑː dju ˈpwɑː ◂ -ˈ·ˌ·,
   ˌæv ə də ˈpɔɪd ◂ ‖ ˌæv ᵊr də ˈpɔɪz ˈ···ˌ·
Avon (i) ˈeɪv ᵊn -ɒn ‖ -ɑːn, (ii) ˈæv ᵊn, (iii) ɑːn
   —In most senses, (i), though the brand of
   cosmetics is usually -ɒn ‖ -ɑːn; the river in
   England is (ii), while the river and loch in
   Grampian are (iii).
Avonmouth ˈeɪv ᵊn maʊθ
Avory ˈeɪv ər i
avow ə ˈvaʊ avowed ə ˈvaʊd avowing
   ə ˈvaʊ ɪŋ avows ə ˈvaʊz
avowal ə ˈvaʊ əl ə ˈvaʊl ~s z
avowedly ə ˈvaʊ ɪd li -əd-
Avril ˈæv rəl -rɪl
avuncular ə ˈvʌŋk jʊl ə -jəl- ‖ -jəl ᵊr
aw ɔː ‖ ɑː
AWACS, Awacs ˈeɪ wæks
await ə ˈweɪt awaited ə ˈweɪt ɪd -əd
   ‖ ə ˈweɪt̬ əd awaiting ə ˈweɪt ɪŋ ‖ ə ˈweɪt̬ ɪŋ
   awaits ə ˈweɪts
awake ə ˈweɪk awaked ə ˈweɪkt awakes
   ə ˈweɪks awaking ə ˈweɪk ɪŋ awoke
   ə ˈwəʊk ‖ ə ˈwoʊk awoken ə ˈwəʊk ən
   ‖ ə ˈwoʊk ən
awaken ə ˈweɪk ən ~ed d ~ing/s ɪŋ/z ~s z
award ə ˈwɔːd ‖ ə ˈwɔːrd ~ed ɪd əd ~er/s ə/z
   ‖ ᵊr/z ~ing ɪŋ ~s z
awardable ə ˈwɔːd əb ᵊl ‖ ə ˈwɔːrd-
aware ə ˈweə ‖ ə ˈweᵊr
awareness ə ˈweə nəs -nɪs ‖ -ˈwer-
awash ə ˈwɒʃ ‖ ə ˈwɔːʃ -ˈwɑːʃ
away ə ˈweɪ
Awbery ˈɔː bər i ‖ ˈɔː ˌber i ˈɑː-
awe, Awe ɔː ‖ ɑː awed ɔːd ‖ ɑːd
aweigh ə ˈweɪ (= away)
awe-inspiring ˈɔːr ɪn ˌspaɪ ᵊr ɪŋ
   ‖ ˈɔː ɪn ˌspaɪ ᵊr ɪŋ ˈɑː- ~ly li
awesome ˈɔː səm ‖ ˈɑː- ~ly li ~ness nəs nɪs
awestricken ˈɔː ˌstrɪk ən ‖ ˈɑː-
awestruck ˈɔː strʌk ‖ ˈɑː-
awful ˈɔːf ᵊl -ʊl ‖ ˈɑːf- —but in the literal
   meaning 'awe-inspiring', ˈɔː fʊl ‖ ˈɔː-, ˈɑː-
   ~ness nəs nɪs
awfully ˈɔːf li ˈɔːf əl i, -ʊl i ‖ ˈɑːf-
awhile ə ˈwarᵊl -ˈhwarᵊl ‖ ə ˈhwarᵊl
awkward ˈɔːk wəd ‖ -wᵊrd ˈɑːk- ~ly li ~ness
   nəs nɪs
awl ɔːl ‖ ɑːl (= all) awls ɔːlz ‖ ɑːlz
awn ɔːn ‖ ɑːn awns ɔːnz ‖ ɑːnz
awning ˈɔːn ɪŋ ‖ ˈɑːn- ~s z
awoke ə ˈwəʊk ‖ ə ˈwoʊk
awoken ə ˈwəʊk ən ‖ ə ˈwoʊk ən
AWOL ˈeɪ wɒl ‖ -wɑːl -wɔːl —or as letters
   ˌeɪ ˌdʌb ᵊl ju ˌəʊ ˈel -ˌoʊ·

A

awry ə 'raɪ —*jocularly, or by confusion, also* 'ɔːr i

ax, axe æks **axes** 'æks ɪz -əz

axel, Axel 'æks ᵊl (= *axle*) ~**s** z

axe|man 'æks |mən -mæn **~men** mən men

axes *pl of* **axis** 'æks iːz

axes *from* **ax, axe** 'æks ɪz -əz

Axholme 'æks həʊm ‖ -hoʊm

axial 'æks i̯əl **~ly** i

axil 'æks ɪl -ᵊl ~**s** z

axill|a æk 'sɪl |ə **~ae** iː

axiom 'æks i̯əm ~**s** z

axiomatic ˌæks i̯ə 'mæt ɪk ◂ ‖ -'mæt̬- **~al** ᵊl **~ally** ᵊl̬ i

axis 'æks ɪs §-əs **axes** 'æks iːz

axle 'æks ᵊl ~**s** z

ax|man 'æks |mən -mæn **~men** mən men

Axminster 'æks ˌmɪnᵗst ə ‖ -ᵊr ~**s** z

axolotl ˌæks ə 'lɒt ᵊl '·· · ‖ 'æks ə lɑːt̬ ᵊl ~**s** z

axon 'æks ɒn ‖ -ɑːn ~**s** z

axonometric ˌæks ᵊn əʊ 'metr ɪk ◂ ‖ -ᵊn oʊ- **~ally** ᵊl̬ i

ay *'always'* eɪ aɪ

ay *'yes'* aɪ (= *I, eye*)

ayah 'aɪ ə ~**s** z

ayatollah ˌaɪ̯ə 'tɒl ə ‖ -'toʊl ə ˌɑː jə- ~**s** z

Ayckbourn 'eɪk bɔːn ‖ -bɔːrn -boʊrn

Aycliffe 'eɪ klɪf

aye *'always'* eɪ aɪ

aye *'yes'* aɪ (= *I, eye*) **ayes** aɪz

aye-aye *n* 'aɪ aɪ ~**s** z

Ayenbite of Inwyt ˌeɪ ən baɪt əv 'ɪn wɪt ‖ ˌ· ·baɪt̬-

Ayer eə ‖ eᵊr æᵊr

Ayers eəz ‖ eᵊrz æᵊrz
     ˌAyers 'Rock

Ayesha aɪ 'iːʃ ə ɑː-; 'aɪʃ ə

Ayia Napa ˌaɪ̯ə 'næp ə —*ModGk* [ˌa ja 'na pa]

Aylesbury 'eɪᵊlz bər i̯ ‖ -ˌber i

Aylesford 'eɪᵊlz fəd 'eɪᵊls- ‖ -fᵊrd

Aylesham *place in Kent* 'eɪᵊl ʃəm

Ayling 'eɪl ɪŋ

Aylmer 'eɪᵊl mə ‖ -mᵊr

Aylsham *place in Nfk* 'eɪᵊl ʃəm —*locally also* -səm; 'ɑːl ʃəm

Aylward 'eɪᵊl wəd -bɔːd ‖ -wᵊrd -wɔːrd

Aymara ˌaɪm ə 'rɑː ◂ '· · ·; aɪ 'mɑːr ə —*Sp* Aymará [ai ma ˈɾa] ~**s** z

Aynho 'eɪn həʊ ‖ -hoʊ

Ayot 'eɪ ət

Ayr eə ‖ eᵊr æᵊr

Ayrshire 'eə ʃə -ʃɪə, §'eə ˌʃaɪ̯ə ‖ 'er ʃᵊr 'ær-, -ʃɪr, -ˌʃaɪ̯ᵊr

Ayrton 'eət ᵊn ‖ 'ert ᵊn 'ært-

Aysgarth 'eɪz gɑːθ ‖ -gɑːrθ

Ayto 'eɪt əʊ ‖ -oʊ

Ayton, Aytoun 'eɪt ᵊn

ayurved|a, A~ ˌɑɪ̯ə 'veɪd ə -ʊə-, ˌɑː jʊə-, -'viːd- ‖ ˌɑː jʊr- **~ic** ɪk ◂

A-Z ˌeɪ tə 'zed ‖ ˌeɪt̬ ə 'ziː

azalea ə 'zeɪl i̯ə ~**s** z

Azani|a ə 'zeɪn i̯|ə **~an/s** ən/z

Azariah ˌæz ə 'raɪ̯ə

azathioprine ˌæz ə 'θaɪ əʊ priːn ‖ -ə priːn

Azerbaijan ˌæz ə baɪ 'dʒɑːn -'ʒɑːn ‖ ˌɑːz ᵊr- —*Russ* [ʌ zʲɪr bʌj 'dʒan]

Azerbaijani ˌæz ə baɪ 'dʒɑːn i ◂ -'ʒɑːn- ‖ ˌɑːz ᵊr- ~**s** z

Azeri æ 'zeər i ə- ‖ ɑː 'zer i ˌæ- ~**s** z

azide 'eɪz aɪd ~**s** z

azimuth 'æz ɪm əθ -əm- ~**s** s

azimuthal ˌæz ɪ 'mʌθ ᵊl ◂ -ə-, -'mjuːθ- **~ly** i

Aziz ə 'ziːz -'zɪz

Aznavour 'æz nə vʊə -vɔː ‖ ˌɑːz nə 'vʊᵊr -'vɔːr —*Fr* [az na vuːʁ]

azo 'eɪz əʊ 'æz- ‖ -oʊ

azo- *comb. form* ǀeɪz əʊ ǀæz əʊ ‖ -oʊ —
     azobenzene ˌeɪz əʊ 'benz iːn ˌæz- ‖ -oʊ-

azoic ₍ᵢ₎eɪ 'zəʊ ɪk -'zoʊ-

Azores ə 'zɔːz ‖ 'eɪz ɔːrz -oʊrz (*)

Azov 'eɪz ɒv 'ɑːz-, 'æz- ‖ -ɑːv -ɔːv —*Russ* [ʌ 'zɔf]

AZT *tdmk* ˌeɪ zed 'tiː ‖ -ziː-

Aztec 'æz tek ~**s** s

Aztecan 'æz tek ən ·'··

azure 'æʒ ə 'eɪʒ-, -ʊə, -jʊə; 'æz jʊə, 'eɪz-; ə 'zjʊə ‖ 'æʒ ᵊr

azygous 'æz ɪg əs ₍ᵢ₎eɪ 'zaɪg əs, ə-

Bb

b Spelling-to-sound

1 Where the spelling is **b**, the pronunciation is regularly b as in **baby** 'beɪb i.

2 Where the spelling is double **bb** the pronunciation is again b as in **shabby** 'ʃæb i.

3 **b** is silent in two groups of words:
- before **t** in **debt** det, **doubt** daʊt, **subtle** 'sʌt ᵊl ‖ 'sʌt̬ ᵊl
- after **m** at the end of a word or stem as in **climb** klaɪm, **lamb** læm, **thumb** θʌm, **bomber** 'bɒm ə ‖ 'bɑːm ᵊr.

B, b biː: **Bs, B's, b's** biːz —*Communications code name:* Bravo
ˌB and 'B, ˌb and 'b
BA ˌbiː 'eɪ
baa bɑː ‖ bæ bɑː: **baaed** bɑːd ‖ bæd bɑːd
  baaing 'bɑːʳ ɪŋ ‖ 'bæ ɪŋ 'bɑː ɪŋ **baas** bɑːz ‖ bæz bɑːz
Baader-Meinhof ˌbɑːd ə 'maɪn hɒf ‖ -ᵊr 'maɪn hoʊf —*Ger* [ˌbaː dɐ 'maɪn hɔf, -hoːf]
Baal 'beɪ əl beɪᵊl, bɑːl
baa-lamb 'bɑː læm ‖ 'bæ- ~s z
Baalbek, Ba'albek 'bɑːl bek —*Arabic* [ba 'ʕal bak]
baas *from* **baa** bɑːz ‖ bæz bɑːz
baas *'master'* bɑːs
Ba'ath bɑːθ —*Arabic* [baʕθ]
Bab *religious leader* bɑːb
baba 'bɑːb ɑː -ə ~s z
  ˌbaba ga'nush gə 'nuʃ
babaco bə 'bɑːk əʊ ‖ -oʊ ~s z
Babar 'bɑːb ɑː ‖ bɑː 'bɑːr
Babbage 'bæb ɪdʒ
Babbitt, b~ 'bæb ɪt §-ət
Babbittry 'bæb ɪtr i §-ətr-
babbl|e 'bæb ᵊl **~ed** d **~er/s** ᵊ/z ‖ ᵊr/z **~es** z **~ing** ɪŋ
Babcock 'bæb kɒk ‖ -kɑːk
babe beɪb **babes** beɪbz
Babel, babel 'beɪb ᵊl ‖ 'bæb-
babi... —*see* **baby**
Babington 'bæb ɪŋ tən
Babinski bə 'bɪn ski
babiroussa, babirussa ˌbæb ɪ 'ruːs ə ˌbɑːb-, -ə- ~s z
Babi Yar ˌbɑːb i 'jɑː ‖ -'jɑːr —*Russ* [ˌba bʲi 'jar]
baboon bə 'buːn ‖ bæ- ~s z

Babs bæbz
babu, Babu 'bɑːb u: —*Hindi* [ba: bu:]
babushka bə 'buːʃ kə bæ-, -'bʊʃ- —*Russ* ['ba buʃ kə]
baby, Baby 'beɪb i **babied** 'beɪb id **babies** 'beɪb iz **babying** 'beɪb i ɪŋ
  ˌbaby 'blue◄; 'baby ˌboomer; ˌbaby 'boy; 'baby ˌbuggy; 'baby ˌcarriage; ˌbaby 'girl; ˌbaby 'grand; 'baby talk; 'baby tooth
baby-bouncer, B~ *tdmk* 'beɪb i ˌbaʊnᵗs ə ‖ -ᵊr ~s z
Babycham *tdmk* 'beɪb i ʃæm
baby-faced 'beɪb i feɪst
Babygro *tdmk* 'beɪb i grəʊ ‖ -groʊ ~s z
babyhood 'beɪb i hʊd
babyish 'beɪb i ɪʃ **~ly** li **~ness** nəs nɪs
Babylon 'bæb ɪl ən -əl-; -ɪ lɒn, -ə- ‖ -ə lɑːn -əl ən
Babyloni|a ˌbæb ɪ 'ləʊn i ˌə -ˌə-, -ˌə- ‖ -'loʊn- **~an/s** ən/z
baby-mind|er 'beɪb i ˌmaɪnd |ə ‖ -|ᵊr **~ers** əz ‖ ᵊrz **~ing** ɪŋ
Babyshambles 'beɪb i ˌʃæm bᵊlz
baby-|sit 'beɪb i |sɪt **~sitter/s** sɪt ə/z ‖ sɪt̬ ᵊr/z **~sitting** sɪt ɪŋ ‖ sɪt̬ ɪŋ
baby-walker 'beɪb i ˌwɔːk ə ‖ -ᵊr ~s z
BAC ˌbiː eɪ 'siː
Bacall bə 'kɔːl ‖ -'kɑːl
Bacardi *tdmk* bə 'kɑːd i ‖ -'kɑːrd- —*Sp* Bacardí [ba kaɾ 'ði] ~s z
baccalaureate ˌbæk ə 'lɔːr i ət ɪt ‖ -'lɑːr- ~s z
baccara, baccarat 'bæk ə rɑː ˌ·ˌ·' ‖ 'bɑːk- ˌbæk- —*Fr* [ba ka ʁa]
baccate 'bæk eɪt
Bacchae 'bæk iː -aɪ
bacchanal ˌbæk ə 'næl '·ˌ·; 'bæk ən ᵊl ‖ ˌbɑːk- ~s z
bacchanalia, B~ ˌbæk ə 'neɪl i ə

B

bacchanalian ˌbæk ə ˈneɪl i ən ◄
bacchant ˈbæk ənt →-ŋt ‖ bə ˈkænt -ˈkɑːnt;
    ˈbæk ənt ~s s
bacchante bə ˈkænt i bə ˈkænt ‖ -ˈkænt̬ i
    -ˈkɑːnt-; bə ˈkɑːnt **bacchantes** bə ˈkænt iz
    bə ˈkænts ‖ bə ˈkænt̬ iz -ˈkɑːnt̬-; bə ˈkɑːnts
Bacchic, b~ ˈbæk ɪk
Bacchus ˈbæk əs
bacciferous bæk ˈsɪf ər əs
baccy ˈbæk i
Bach, bach bɑːk bɑːx —*Ger* [bax]; *Welsh*
    [bɑːχ]
Bacharach ˈbæk ə ræk
bachelor, B~ ˈbætʃ əl ə -ɪl ə ‖ -ᵊl ər ~**hood**
    hʊd ~**ship** ʃɪp ~**s** z
    ˈbachelor girl; ˌBachelor of ˈArts;
    ˈbachelor's deˌgree
bacillar bə ˈsɪl ə ˈbæs ɪl ə, -əl- ‖ -ᵊr
bacillary bə ˈsɪl ər i ˈbæs ɪl-, ˈ-əl- ‖ ˈbæs ə ler i
    bə ˈsɪl ər i
bacilliform bə ˈsɪl ɪ fɔːm bæ-, -ə- ‖ -fɔːrm
bacill|us bə ˈsɪl |əs ~**i** aɪ iː
bacitracin ˌbæs ɪ ˈtreɪs ɪn -ə-, §-ᵊn
back bæk **backed** bækt **backing** ˈbæk ɪŋ
    backs bæks
    ˈback ˌcountry; ˌback ˈdoor◄; ˈback
    forˌmation; ˌback ˈgarden; ˌback ˈnumber;
    ˌback ˈpassage; ˌback ˈseat; ˌback ˈstreet;
    ˈback talk; ˌback ˈup; ˌback ˈyard
backache ˈbæk eɪk ~**s** s
backbench ˌbæk ˈbentʃ ◄ ˈ·· ~**es** ɪz əz
backbencher ˌbæk ˈbentʃ ə ◄ ˈ··· ‖ -ᵊr ~**s** z
backbit|er ˈbæk baɪt |ə ‖ -baɪt̬ ᵊr ~**ers** əz ‖ ᵊrz
    ~**ing** ɪŋ
backblocks ˈbæk blɒks ‖ -blɑːks
backboard ˈbæk bɔːd ‖ -bɔːrd -boʊrd ~**s** z
backbone ˈbæk bəʊn ‖ -boʊn ~**d** d ~**s** z
backbreak|er ˈbæk ˌbreɪk |ə ‖ -|ᵊr ~**ers** əz
    ‖ ᵊrz ~**ing** ɪŋ
backchat ˈbæk tʃæt
backcloth ˈbæk klɒθ ‖ -klɔːθ -klɑːθ
backcomb ˈbæk kəʊm ‖ -koʊm ~**ed** d ~**ing** ɪŋ
    ~**s** z
back|date ˌbæk ˈ|deɪt ◄ ˈ·· ‖ ˈbæk |deɪt
    ~**dated** deɪt ɪd əd ‖ deɪt̬ əd ~**dates** deɪts
    ~**dating** deɪt ɪŋ ‖ deɪt̬ ɪŋ
backdrop ˈbæk drɒp ‖ -drɑːp ~**s** s
backer, B~ ˈbæk ə ‖ -ᵊr ~**s** z
backfield ˈbæk fiːᵊld
backfill ˈbæk fɪl ~**ed** d ~**ing** ɪŋ ~**s** z
backfire *n* ˈbæk ˌfaɪ ə ‖ -ˌfaɪ ᵊr ~**s** z
backfire *v* ˌbæk ˈfaɪ ə ◄ ˈ·ˌ·· ‖ ˈbæk ˌfaɪ ᵊr ~**d** d
    ~**s** z **backfiring** ˌbæk ˈfaɪ ər ɪŋ ˈ·ˌ--
    ‖ ˈbæk ˌfaɪ ᵊr ɪŋ
backflip ˈbæk flɪp ~**s** s
back-formation ˈbæk fɔː ˌmeɪʃ ᵊn ‖ -fɔːr- ~**s** z
backgammon ˈbæk ˌgæm ən ·ˈ··
background ˈbæk graʊnd ~**ed** ɪd əd ~**ing** ɪŋ
    ~**s** z
backhand ˈbæk hænd ~**ed** *v* ɪd əd ~**ing** ɪŋ ~**s**
    z
backhanded *adj* ˌbæk ˈhænd ɪd ◄ -əd
    ‖ ˈbæk hænd əd ~**ly** li ~**ness** nəs nɪs

backhander ˈbæk hænd ə ˌ·ˈ·· ‖ -ᵊr ~**s** z
backhoe ˈbæk həʊ ‖ -hoʊ ~**s** z
Backhouse, b~ ˈbæk haʊs -əs
backing ˈbæk ɪŋ
    ˈbacking store
backlash ˈbæk læʃ
backless ˈbæk ləs -lɪs
backlighting ˌbæk ˈlaɪt ɪŋ ˈ·ˌ·· ‖ ˈbæk ˌlaɪt̬ ɪŋ
    ˌ·ˈ··
backlist ˈbæk lɪst ~**s** s
backlit ˌbæk ˈlɪt ◄ ˈ··
backlog ˈbæk lɒg ‖ -lɔːg -lɑːg ~**s** z
backlot ˈbæk lɒt ‖ -lɑːt ~**s** s
backmost ˈbæk məʊst ‖ -moʊst
backpack ˈbæk pæk ~**ed** t ~**er/s** ə/z ‖ -ᵊr/z
    ~**ing** ɪŋ ~**s** s
backpedal, back-pedal ˌbæk ˈped ᵊl ◄ ˈ·ˌ··
    ‖ ˈbæk ˌped ᵊl ~**ed, ~led** d ~**ing, ~ling** ɪŋ ~**s**
    z
backra ˈbʌk rə ˈbæk- ‖ ˈbæk- ˈbʊk-
backrest ˈbæk rest ~**s** s
backroom ˈbæk ruːm -rʊm ~**s** z
    ˈbackroom boys
Backs bæks
backscratcher ˈbæk ˌskrætʃ ə ‖ -ᵊr ~**s** z
back-seat ˌbæk ˈsiːt ◄
    ˌback-seat ˈdriver
backsheesh ˌbæk ˈʃiːʃ ˈ··
backside ˈbæk saɪd ˌ·ˈ· ~**s** z
backsight ˈbæk saɪt ~**s** s
backslapping ˈbæk ˌslæp ɪŋ ~**s** z
backslash ˈbæk slæʃ ~**es** ɪz əz
backslid|e ˈbæk slaɪd ˌ·ˈ· ~**er/s** ə/z ‖ ᵊr/z ~**ing**
    ɪŋ
backspac|e *n* ˈbæk speɪs ~**es** ɪz əz
backspac|e *v* ˌbæk ˈspeɪs ◄ ˈ·· ~**ed** t ~**es** ɪz əz
    ~**ing** ɪŋ
backspin ˈbæk spɪn
backstage ˌbæk ˈsteɪdʒ ◄
    ˌbackstage ˈworkers
backstair ˌbæk ˈsteə ◄ ‖ ˈbæk ster ~**s** z
    ˌbackstairs ˈinfluence
backstay ˈbæk steɪ ~**s** z
backstitch ˈbæk stɪtʃ ~**ed** t ~**es** ɪz əz ~**ing** ɪŋ
backstop ˈbæk stɒp ‖ -stɑːp ~**s** s
backstreet ˈbæk striːt
backstroke ˈbæk strəʊk ‖ -stroʊk ~**s** s
backswing ˈbæk swɪŋ ~**s** z
back-to-back ˌbæk tə ˈbæk ◄
    ˌback-to-back ˈhousing
backtrack ˈbæk træk ˌ·ˈ· ~**ed** t ~**ing** ɪŋ ~**s** s
backup ˈbæk ʌp ~**s** s
Backus ˈbæk əs
backward ˈbæk wəd ‖ -wᵊrd ~**ly** li ~**ness** nəs
    nɪs
backwardation ˌbæk wə ˈdeɪʃ ᵊn ‖ -wᵊr-
backward-looking ˌbæk wəd ˈlʊk ɪŋ ◄ §-ˈluːk-
    ‖ -wᵊrd-
backwards ˈbæk wədz ‖ -wᵊrdz
backwash ˈbæk wɒʃ ‖ -wɔːʃ -wɑːʃ ~**es** ɪz əz
backwater ˈbæk ˌwɔːt ə ‖ -ˌwɔːt̬ ᵊr -ˌwɑːt̬ ᵊr ~**s**
    z
backwoods ˈbæk wʊdz

B

backwoods|man 'bæk wʊdz |mən ˌ'·'·- ~men mən men

backyard ˌbæk 'jɑːd ◄ ‖ -'jɑːrd ◄ ~s z

Bacofoil tdmk 'beɪk əʊ fɔɪʳl ‖ -oʊ-

bacon, Bacon 'beɪk ən ~s z ˌbacon 'sandwich

Baconian beɪ 'kəʊn iˌən bə- ‖ -'koʊn- ~s z

bacteria bæk 'tɪər iˌə ‖ -'tɪr-

bacterial bæk 'tɪər iˌəl ‖ -'tɪr- ~ly i

bactericidal bæk ˌtɪər ɪ 'saɪd ᵊl ◄ -ə- ‖ -ˌtɪr ə- ~ly i

bactericide bæk 'tɪər ɪ saɪd -ə- ‖ -'tɪr ə- ~s z

bacteriological bæk ˌtɪər iˌə 'lɒdʒ ɪk ᵊl ◄ ‖ -ˌtɪr iˌə 'lɑːdʒ- ~ly ˌi

bacteriologist bæk ˌtɪər i 'ɒl ədʒ ɪst §-əst ‖ -ˌtɪr i 'ɑːl- ~s s

bacteriology bæk ˌtɪər i 'ɒl ədʒ i ‖ -ˌtɪr i 'ɑːl-

bacteriophage bæk 'tɪər iˌəʊ feɪdʒ ‖ -'tɪr iˌə- ~s z

bacterium bæk 'tɪər iˌəm ‖ -'tɪr-

Bactria 'bæk tri ə

Bactrian 'bæk tri ən ~s z

Bacup 'beɪk əp -ʌp

bad bæd ˌbad 'blood; ˌbad 'debt; ˌbad 'faith; ˌbad 'feeling; ˌbad 'form; ˌbad 'news

Bad in German place names bæd bɑːd ‖ bɑːd —Ger [baːt] —See also phrases with this word

Badajoz ˌbæd ə 'hɒz -həʊz, '···‖ ˌbɑːd ə 'hoʊs —Sp [ba ða 'xoθ]

badass 'bæd æs ~es ɪz əz

Badawi bə 'dɑː wi

Badcock 'bæd kɒk →'bæg- ‖ -kɑːk

Baddeley 'bæd ᵊlˌi

Baddesley (i) 'bæd ɪz li -əz-, (ii) 'bædz li

baddie, baddy 'bæd i baddies 'bæd iz

Baddiel bə 'diːᵊl

baddish 'bæd ɪʃ

bade bæd beɪd

Badedas tdmk 'bɑːd ə dæs -ɪ-; bə 'deɪd æs, -əs

Badel bə 'del

Baden British or American name 'beɪd ᵊn

Baden places in German-speaking countries 'bɑːd ᵊn —Ger ['baː dᵊn]

Baden-Baden ˌbɑːd ᵊn 'bɑːd ᵊn —Ger [ˌba: dᵊn 'ba: dᵊn]

Baden-Powell ˌbeɪd ᵊn 'pəʊ əl -'paʊˌəl, -el, -ɪl, -'paʊl ‖ -'poʊ əl

Bader 'bɑːd ə ‖ -ᵊr

badge bædʒ badges 'bædʒ ɪz -əz

badger 'bædʒ ə ‖ -ᵊr ~ed d badgering 'bædʒ ᵊrˌɪŋ ~s z

Bad Godesberg ˌbæd 'gəʊd əz bɜːg -beəg; -'gəʊdz· ‖ ˌbɑːt 'goʊd əz bɜːg -berg —Ger [ˌbaːt 'go: dəs bɛʁk]

badinage 'bæd ɪ nɑːʒ -ə-, -nɑːdʒ, ˌ··'· —Fr [ba di naːʒ]

badlands 'bæd lændz

badly 'bæd li

badly-behaved ˌbæd li bi 'heɪvd ◄ -li bə-

badly-off ˌbæd li 'ɒf ◄ -'ɔːf ‖ -'ɔːf -'ɑːf

badminton, B~ 'bæd mɪn tən →'bæb-, △-mɪŋ-

bad-|mouth 'bæd |maʊθ →'bæb-, -maʊð ~mouthed maʊθt maʊðd ~mouthing maʊθ ɪŋ maʊð ɪŋ ~mouths v maʊθs maʊðz

badness 'bæd nəs -nɪs

Badoit tdmk 'bæd wɑː ‖ bɑː 'dwɑː —Fr [ba dwa]

bad-tempered ˌbæd 'temp əd ◄ ‖ -ᵊrd '···~ly li

Baedeker 'beɪd ɪk ə -ək-, -ek- ‖ -ᵊr ~s z —Ger ['bɛː də kɐ]

Baer beə ‖ beᵊr

Baerlein 'beə laɪn ‖ 'ber-

Baez 'baɪ ez ·'· —but the singer Joan Baez prefers baɪz

Baffin 'bæf ɪn §-ᵊn

baffl|e 'bæf ᵊl ~ed d ~es z ~ing ˌɪŋ

bafflement 'bæf ᵊl mənt

BAFTA 'bæft ə

bag bæg bagged bægd bagging 'bæg ɪŋ bags bægz 'bag ˌlady

Baganda bə 'gænd ə -'gɑːnd-

bagasse bə 'gæs bæ-, -'gɑːs

bagatelle ˌbæg ə 'tel ~s z

Bagdad ˌbæg 'dæd '·· ‖ 'bæg dæd —Arabic [baɣ 'daːd]

Bagehot (i) 'bædʒ ət, (ii) 'bæg ət —The economist Walter B~ was (i).

bagel 'beɪg ᵊl ~s z

bagful 'bæg fʊl ~s z bagsful 'bægz fʊl

bagg... —see bag

baggag|e 'bæg ɪdʒ ~es ɪz əz 'baggage car; 'baggage room; 'baggage tag

Baggally 'bæg əl i

Baggie tdmk 'bæg i ~s z

Baggins 'bæg ɪnz §-ənz

bagg|y 'bæg |i ~ier iˌə ‖ iˌᵊr ~iest iˌɪst iˌəst ~ily ɪ li əl i ~iness i nəs -nɪs

Baghdad ˌbæg 'dæd '·· ‖ 'bæg dæd —Arabic [baɣ 'daːd]

Bagley 'bæg li

bag|man 'bæg |mən ~men mən men

Bagnall, Bagnell 'bæg nᵊl

bagnio 'bæn jəʊ 'bɑːn- ‖ 'bɑːn joʊ ~s z

Bagnold 'bæg nəʊld →-nɒʊld ‖ -noʊld

bagpip|e 'bæg paɪp ~er/s ə/z ‖ ᵊr/z ~es s ~ing ɪŋ

bagsful 'bægz fʊl

Bagshaw 'bæg ʃɔː ‖ -ʃɑː

Bagshot 'bæg ʃɒt ‖ -ʃɑːt

baguette bæ 'get bə- ~s s —Fr [ba gɛt]

Baguley 'bæg əlˌi -jʊl-

bagwash 'bæg wɒʃ ‖ -wɔːʃ -wɑːʃ ~s ɪz əz

bah bɑː ‖ bæ (= baa)

bahadur bə 'hɑːd ə -ʊə ‖ -ᵊr -ʊr ~s z

Bahai, Baha'i, Bahá'í bə 'haɪ bɑː:-, -'hɑː i, -'haɪ i ~s z —Persian [ba hɑː ʔiː]

Baha|ism bə 'haɪ |ˌɪz əm bɑː:-, -'hɑː:- ~ist/s ɪst/s əst/s

Bahama bə 'hɑːm ə ~s z

Bahamian bə 'heɪm iˌən -'hɑːm- ~s z

Bahasa bə 'hɑːs ə bɑː:-

B

Baha'ullah, Bahá'-u'lláh ˌbɑː hɑː 'ʊl ə
   bə ˌhɑː ʊ 'lɑː
Bahia bə 'hiː ə bɑː 'iː ə —*Port* [bɐ 'i ɐ]
Bahrain, Bahrein ˌbɑː 'reɪn ˌbɑːx-;
   ˌbɑː hə 'reɪn —*Arabic* [baħ 'reːn] **~i/s** i/z
baht bɑːt **bahts** bɑːts
bahuvrihi bɑː huː 'vriː hi
Baikal baɪ 'kæl -'kɑːl, '·· —*Russ* [bʌj 'kał]
Baikonur ˌbaɪk ə 'nʊə ‖ -'nʊər —*Russ*
   [bəj kʌ 'nur]
bail berˀl **bailed** berˀld **bailing** 'berˀl ɪŋ **bails**
   berˀlz
bailable 'berˀl əb ˀl
Baildon 'berˀl ən
Baile Atha Cliath, Baile Átha Cliath
   ˌblɑː 'klɪə ˌblɔː- ‖ -'kliː ə ˌblɔː- —*Irish*
   [błɑː 'kliə]
bailee ˌbeɪ 'liː ˌberˀl 'i: **~s** z
bailey, B~ 'beɪl i **~s, ~'s** z
   ˌBailey 'bridge, '···
bailie 'beɪl i **~s** z
bailiff 'beɪl ɪf §-əf **~s** s
bailiwick 'beɪl i wɪk §-ə- **~s** s
Baillie 'beɪl i
Baillieu 'beɪl ju:
Bailly 'beɪl i
bailment 'berˀl mənt
bailor ˌber 'lɔː 'berˀl ə, ˌberˀl 'ɔː ‖ -'lɔːr **~s** z
bailout 'berˀl aʊt **~s** s
bails|man 'berˀlz |mən **~men** mən men
Baily 'beɪl i **~'s** z
Bain beɪn
Bainbridge 'beɪn brɪdʒ →'beɪm-
Baines beɪnz
bain-marie ˌbæn mə 'ri: →ˌbæm-, -mə- **~s** z
   —*Fr* [bæ̃ ma ʁi]
Bairam baɪ 'rɑːm -'ræm; 'baɪˀr əm **~s** z
Baird beəd ‖ beˀrd
bairn beən ‖ beˀrn **bairns** beənz ‖ beˀrnz
Bairnsfather 'beənz ˌfɑːð ə ‖ 'bernz ˌfɑːð ˀr
Bairstow 'beə stəʊ ‖ 'ber stoʊ
bait beɪt **baited** 'beɪt ɪd -əd ‖ 'beɪt̬ əd **baiting**
   'beɪt ɪŋ ‖ 'beɪt̬ ɪŋ **baits** beɪts
baize beɪz (= *bays*)
Baja 'bɑː hɑː —*Sp* ['ba xa]
   ˌBaja ˌCali'fornia
Bajan 'beɪdʒ ən **~s** z
bajra 'bɑːdʒ rə
bake beɪk **baked** beɪkt **bakes** beɪks **baking**
   'beɪk ɪŋ
   ˌbaked 'beans
bake|house 'beɪk| haʊs **~houses** haʊz ɪz -əz
bakelite, B~ *tdmk* 'beɪk ə laɪt 'beɪk laɪt
baker, Baker 'beɪk ə ‖ -ˀr **~s** z
   ˌbaker's 'dozen; 'Baker Street
bakeries 'beɪk ər iz
Bakerloo ˌbeɪk ə 'lu: ‖ -ˀr-
   ˌBaker'loo line
Bakersfield 'beɪk əz fi:ˀld ‖ -ˀrz-
baker|y 'beɪk ər |i **~ies** iz
Bakewell 'beɪk wel -wəl
   ˌBakewell 'tart

baking 'beɪk ɪŋ
   'baking ˌpowder
baklava 'bɑːk lə vɑː 'bæk-; ˌ··'· **~s** z
baksheesh ˌbæk 'ʃi:ʃ ··
Bakst bækst ‖ bɑːkst —*Russ* [bakst]
Baku ₍ˌ₎bɑː 'ku: bæ-
Bakunin bə 'ku:n ɪn bɑː-, §-ən —*Russ*
   [bʌ 'ku nʲɪn]
Bala 'bæl ə 'bɑːl ə
Balaam 'beɪl əm -æm
balaclava, B~ ˌbæl ə 'klɑːv ə ◂ —*Russ*
   [bə łʌ 'kła və] **~s** z
balalaika ˌbæl ə 'laɪk ə —*Russ* [bə łʌ 'łaj kə]
   ~s z
balanc|e 'bæl ənˀs **~ed** t **~es** ɪz əz **~ing** ɪŋ
   ˌbalanced 'diet; ˌbalance of 'power;
   'balance ˌsheet; 'balance ˌwheel;
   'balancing ˌact
Balanchine 'bæl ən tʃiːn -ʃiːn
balas 'bæl əs 'beɪl-
balata 'bæl ət ə bə 'lɑːt ə ‖ bə 'lɑːt̬ ə **~s** z
Balaton 'bæl ə tɒn 'bɒl- ‖ 'bɑːl ə tɑːn 'bæl-,
   -toʊn —*Hung* ['bɒ lɒ ton]
Balboa, b~ bæl 'bəʊ ə ‖ -'boʊ- **~s** z —*Sp*
   [bal 'βo a]
Balbriggan, b~ bæl 'brɪg ən
Balbus 'bælb əs
Balchin 'bɔːltʃ ɪn 'bɒltʃ-, §-ən ‖ 'bɑːltʃ-
Balcomb, Balcombe 'bɔːlk əm 'bɒlk- ‖ 'bɑːlk-
Balcon 'bɔːlk ən 'bɒlk- ‖ 'bɑːlk-
balcon|y 'bælk ən |i **~ies** iz
bald bɔːld ‖ bɑːld (= *bawled*) **balder** 'bɔːld ə
   §'bɒld- ‖ 'bɔːld ˀr 'bɑːld- **baldest** 'bɔːld ɪst
   §'bɒld-, əst ‖ 'bɑːld-
   'bald ˌeagle
baldachin, baldaquin 'bɔːld ək ɪn §'bɒld-,
   §-ən ‖ 'bɑːld-
Balder *name* 'bɔːld ə 'bɒld- ‖ 'bɔːld ˀr 'bɑːld-
balderdash 'bɔːld ə dæʃ §'bɒld- ‖ -ˀr- 'bɑːld-
bald-faced ˌbɔːld 'feɪst ◂ §ˌbɒld- ‖ ˌbɑːld-
baldhead 'bɔːld hed ‖ 'bɑːld- **~s** z
baldheaded ˌbɔːld 'hed ɪd ◂ §ˌbɒld-, -əd
   ‖ ˌbɑːld-
baldie 'bɔːld i §'bɒld i ‖ 'bɑːld i **~s** z
baldish 'bɔːld ɪʃ §'bɒld- ‖ 'bɑːld-
bald|ly 'bɔːld |li §'bɒld- ‖ 'bɑːld- **~ness** nəs nɪs
Baldock 'bɔːld ɒk 'bɒld- ‖ -ɑːk 'bɑːld-
baldric 'bɔːldr ɪk §'bɒldr- ‖ 'bɑːldr-
Baldry 'bɔːldr i 'bɒldr i ‖ 'bɑːldr i
Baldwin 'bɔːld wɪn §'bɒld-, §-wən ‖ 'bɑːld-
bald|y 'bɔːld |i ‖ 'bɑːld |i **~ies** iz
bale berˀl (= *bail*) **baled** berˀld **bales** berˀlz
   baling 'berˀl ɪŋ
Bale, Bâle *place in Switzerland* bɑːl —*Fr* [bɑːl]
Bale *family name* berˀl
Balearic ˌbæl i 'ær ɪk ◂ bə 'lɪər ɪk ‖ -'er- **~s** s
baleen bə 'liːn bæ-, beɪ-
baleful 'berˀl fˀl -fʊl **~ly** i **~ness** nəs nɪs
Balenciaga bə ˌlen⁀s i 'ɑːg ə bæ- —*Sp*
   [ba len 'θja ɣa]
baler 'berˀl ə ‖ -ˀr **~s** z
Balfe bælf

B

Balfour *(i)* 'bælf ə ‖ -ᵊr, *(ii)* 'bæl fɔː ‖ -fɔːr
-four
   the ˌBalfour ˌdeclaˈration
Balham 'bæl əm
Bali 'bɑːl i
Balinese ˌbɑːl ɪ 'niːz ◄ -ə- ‖ -'niːs
Baliol 'beɪl i‿əl
balk bɔːk bɒːlk ‖ bɑːk **balked** bɔːkt bɔːlkt
   ‖ bɑːkt **balking** 'bɔːk ɪŋ 'bɔːlk- ‖ 'bɑːk- **balks**
   bɔːks bɔːlks ‖ bɑːks
Balkan 'bɔːlk ən 'bɒlk- ‖ 'bɑːlk- ~s z
Balkanis..., b~ —*see* **Balkaniz...**
Balkanization, b~ ˌbɔːlk ən aɪ 'zeɪʃ ᵊn ˌbɒlk-,
   -ɪ'- ‖ -ə '- ˌbɑːlk-
Balkaniz|e, b~ 'bɔːlk ə naɪz 'bɒlk- ‖ 'bɑːlk-
   ~ed d ~es ɪz əz ~ing ɪŋ
balk|y 'bɔːk |i ‖ 'bɑːk- ~ier i‿ə ‖ i‿ᵊr ~iest i‿ɪst
   i‿əst
ball, Ball bɔːl ‖ bɑːl **balled** bɔːld ‖ bɑːld
   (= bald) **balling** 'bɔːl ɪŋ ‖ 'bɑːl- **balls** bɔːlz
   ‖ bɑːlz
   'ball boy; 'ball games; 'ball park
Ballachulish ˌbæl ə 'huːl ɪʃ
ballad 'bæl əd ~s z
ballade bæ 'lɑːd bə- ~s z —*Fr* [ba lad]
balladeer ˌbæl ə 'dɪə ‖ -'dɪᵊr ~s z
Ballance 'bæl ənˢs
ball-and-socket ˌbɔːl ən 'sɒk ɪt -ənd-, §-ət
   ‖ -'sɑːk ət ˌbɑːl-
Ballantine 'bæl ən taɪn
Ballantrae ˌbæl ən 'treɪ
Ballantyne 'bæl ən taɪn
Ballarat 'bæl ə ræt ˌ·'·
Ballard 'bæl ɑːd -əd ‖ -ɑːrd -ᵊrd
ballast 'bæl əst ~ed ɪd əd ~ing ɪŋ ~s s
Ballater 'bæl ət ə ‖ -əţ ᵊr
ballbearing ˌbɔːl 'beər ɪŋ ‖ -'ber- ˌbɑːl-, -'bær-
   ~s z
ballcock 'bɔːl kɒk ‖ -kɑːk 'bɑːl- ~s s
ballerina ˌbæl ə 'riːn ə ~s z
Ballesteros ˌbæl ɪ 'stɪər ɒs -ə-, -e-, -'steər-,
   -'ster- ‖ ˌbaɪ ə 'ster oʊs ˌbæl- —*Sp*
   [ba ʎe 'ste ros, ba je-]
ballet 'bæl eɪ ‖ bæ 'leɪ 'bæl eɪ ~s z
   'ballet ˌdancer ‖ ·'· ˌ··
balletic bæ 'let ɪk bə- ‖ -'leţ-
balletomane 'bæl ɪt əʊ meɪn '·et-, '·et-;
   bə 'let ·, bæ- ‖ bə 'leţ ə meɪn
balletomania ˌbæl ɪt əʊ 'meɪn i ə '·et-, '·et-
   ‖ bə ˌleţ ə 'meɪn i ə (*)
Balliol 'beɪl i‿əl
ballist|a bə 'lɪst |ə ~ae iː ~as əz
ballistic bə 'lɪst ɪk ~ally ᵊl‿i ~s s
Balloch 'bæl ək -əx —*but the place in Highland*
   region is bæ 'lɒx
ballock 'bɒl ək ‖ 'bɔːl- 'bɑːl- ~s s
balloon bə 'luːn ~ed d ~ing ɪŋ ~s z
balloonist bə 'luːn ɪst §-əst ~s s
ballot 'bæl ət **balloted** 'bæl ət ɪd -əd
   ‖ 'bæl əţ əd **balloting** 'bæl ət ɪŋ ‖ 'bæl əţ ɪŋ
   ballots 'bæl əts
   'ballot box; 'ballot ˌpaper
ballpark 'bɔːl pɑːk ‖ -pɑːrk 'bɑːl- ~s s

ball-peen, ball-pein 'bɔːl piːn ‖ 'bɑːl- ~s z
ballplayer 'bɔːl ˌpleɪ ə ‖ -ᵊr 'bɑːl- ~s z
ballpoint 'bɔːl pɔɪnt ‖ 'bɑːl- ~s s
ballroom 'bɔːl ruːm -rʊm ‖ 'bɑːl- ~s z
   ˌballroom 'dancing
balls, Balls bɔːlz ‖ bɑːlz **ballsed** bɔːlzd
   ‖ bɑːlzd **ballses** 'bɔːlz ɪz -əz ‖ 'bɑːlz- **ballsing**
   'bɔːlz ɪŋ ‖ 'bɑːlz- —*These are parts of the*
   slang verb to balls up
balls-up *n* 'bɔːlz ʌp ‖ 'bɑːlz- ~s s
balls|y 'bɔːlz |i ‖ 'bɑːlz- ~ier i‿ə ‖ i‿ᵊr ~iest
   i‿ɪst i‿əst ~iness i nəs i nɪs
bally, Bally 'bæl i —*but the tdmk for shoes is*
   properly Fr [ba ji]
Ballycastle ˌbæl i 'kɑːs ᵊl §-'kæs- ‖ -'kæs-
ballyhoo ˌbæl i 'huː ‖ 'bæl i huː ~ed d ~ing
   ɪŋ ~s z
Ballymacarrett ˌbæl i mə 'kær ət -ɪt ‖ -'ker-
Ballymena ˌbæl i 'miːn ə
Ballymoney ˌbæl i 'mʌn i
balm bɑːm §bɑːlm, §bɒlm **balms** bɑːmz
   §bɑːlmz, §bɒlmz
Balmain *(i)* ˌbæl 'meɪn; *(ii)* ˌbæl mæ -mæn
   ‖ -meɪn ·'· —*Fr* [bal mæ̃] —*as an English or*
   Scottish name, and for the place in Australia,
   (i); as a French name, (ii)
Balmoral, b~ bæl 'mɒr əl ˌ·'- ‖ -'mɔːr- -'mɑːr-
balm|y 'bɑːm |i §'bɑːlm-, §'bɒlm- ~ier i‿ə ‖ i‿ᵊr
   ~iest i‿ɪst i‿əst ~ily ɪ li əl i ~iness i nəs -nɪs
balneal 'bæln i‿əl
balneology ˌbæln i 'ɒl ədʒ i ‖ -'ɑːl-
Balniel bæl 'niːᵊl
Balogh 'bæl ɒg ‖ -ɑːg
baloney bə 'ləʊn i ‖ -'loʊn-
Baloo bə 'luː 'bɑːl uː
BALPA 'bælp ə
Balquhidder bæl 'wɪd ə -'hwɪd-, -'kwɪd-
   ‖ -'hwɪd ᵊr
balsa 'bɔːls ə 'bɒls- ‖ 'bɑːls- ~s z
Balsall 'bɔːls ᵊl 'bɒls- ‖ -ɔːl 'bɑːls ɑːl
balsam 'bɔːls əm 'bɒls- ‖ 'bɑːls- ~s z
balsamic bɔːl 'sæm ɪk bɒl- ‖ bɑːl-
Balt bɔːlt bɒlt ‖ bɑːlt **Balts** bɔːlts bɒlts ‖ bɑːlts
Balthazar bæl 'θæz ə 'bælθ ə zɑː, ˌ·'·
   ‖ bæl 'θeɪz ᵊr —*in Shakespeare* ˌbælθ ə 'zɑː,
   '··· ‖ -'zɑːr
balti 'bɔːlt i 'bɒlt-, 'bælt- ‖ 'bɑːlt i 'bɔːlt-
Baltic 'bɔːlt ɪk ‖ 'bɑːlt-
   ˌBaltic 'Sea
Baltimore 'bɔːlt ɪ mɔː 'bɒlt-, -ə- ‖ -ə mɔːr
   'bɑːlt-, -moʊr; -əm ᵊr
Balto-Slavic ˌbɔːlt əʊ 'slɑːv ɪk ◄ ˌbɒlt-
   ‖ -oʊ 'slæv- ˌbɑːlt-, -'slɑːv-
Balto-Slavonic ˌbɔːlt əʊ slə 'vɒn ɪk ◄ ˌbɒlt-
   ‖ -oʊ slə 'vɑːn- ˌbɑːlt-
Baluchi bə 'luːtʃ i ~s z
Baluchistan bə ˌluːtʃ ɪ 'stɑːn -ə-, -'stæn, ·'···
   ‖ -ə 'stæn
baluster 'bæl əst ə ‖ -ᵊr ~s z
balustrade ˌbæl ə 'streɪd ‖ 'bæl ə streɪd ~s z
Balzac 'bælz æk △'bɔːlz-, △'bɒlz-; bæl 'zæk
   ‖ 'bɔːlz- 'bɑːlz-, -ɑːk —*Fr* [bal zak]
Bamako ˌbæm ə 'kəʊ '··· ‖ -'koʊ ˌbɑːm-

Bamber 'bæm bə ‖ -bᵊr
Bamberg 'bæm bɜːg ‖ -bɜːg 'baːm-, -berg
　—*Ger* ['bam bɛʁk]
Bambi 'bæm bi
bambin|o bæm 'biːn |əʊ ‖ -|oʊ baːm- ~**i** i ~**os**
　əʊz ‖ oʊz —*It* [bam 'biː no]
bamboo ˌbæm 'buː ◄ ~**s** z
　ˌbamboo 'furniture
bamboozl|e ₍ᵢ₎bæm 'buːz ᵊl ~**ed** d ~**es** z ~**ing**
　ɪŋ
Bamburgh 'bæm bər ə
Bamford 'bæm fəd ‖ -fᵊrd
Bamforth 'bæm fɔːθ ‖ -fɔːrθ -foʊrθ
Bamian ₍ᵢ₎baːm 'jaːn
ban bæn **banned** bænd (= *band*) **banning**
　'bæn ɪŋ **bans** bænz
banal bə 'naːl bæ-, -'næl, §'beɪn ᵊl ~**ly** li
banalit|y bə 'næl ət |i bæ-, beɪ-, -ɪt i ‖ -əṭ |i
　~**ies** iz
banana bə 'naːn ə ‖ -'næn- ~**s** z
　ba'nana oil; ba'nana skin; baˌnana 'split
Bananarama bə ˌnaːn ə 'raːm ə
　‖ bə ˌnæn ə 'ræm ə
Banaras bə 'naːr əs
banausic bə 'nɔːz ɪk -'nɔːs- ‖ -'nɔːs- -'naːs-,
　-'nɔːz-, -'naːz-
Banbridge bæn 'brɪdʒ →bæm-, '· ·
Banbury 'bæn bər i →'bæm- ‖ -ˌber i
　ˌBanbury 'Cross
Banchory 'bæŋk ər i 'bæŋx-
banco 'bæŋk əʊ ‖ -oʊ ~**s** z
Bancroft 'bæn krɒft →'bæŋ- ‖ -krɔːft -kraːft
band bænd **banded** 'bænd ɪd -əd **banding**
　'bænd ɪŋ **bands** bændz
　'band saw
Banda 'bænd ə ‖ 'baːnd-
bandag|e 'bænd ɪdʒ ~**ed** d ~**es** ɪz əz ~**ing** ɪŋ
Band-Aid *tdmk*, **band-aid** 'bænd eɪd ~**s** z
bandana, bandanna ₍ᵢ₎bæn 'dæn ə ~**s** z
Bandaranaike ˌbænd ᵊr ə 'naɪ ɪk ə -'naɪk ə
　‖ ˌbaːnd-
Bandar Seri Begawan
　ˌbænd ə ˌser i bə 'gaː wən ˌaː-, -be'--, -bɪ'--,
　-'gaʊ ən ‖ ˌbaːnd ᵊr-
bandbox 'bænd bɒks →'bæm- ‖ -baːks ~**es** ɪz
　əz
bandeau 'bænd əʊ ‖ bæn 'doʊ ~**s**, ~**x** z —*Fr*
　[bã do]
banderol, banderole 'bænd ə rəʊl →-rɒʊl
　‖ -roʊl ~**s** z
bandersnatch 'bænd ə snætʃ ‖ -ᵊr-
bandicoot 'bænd i kuːt ~**s** s
bandie... —*see* **bandy**
bandit 'bænd ɪt §-ət ~**s** s
banditry 'bænd ɪtr i -ətr-
banditti bæn 'dɪt i ‖ -'dɪṭ-
bandleader 'bænd ˌliːd ə ‖ -ᵊr ~**s** z
bandmaster 'bænd ˌmaːst ə §-ˌmæst ə
　‖ -ˌmæst ᵊr ~**s** z
bandoleer, bandolier ˌbænd ə 'lɪə ‖ -'lɪᵊr ~**s**
　z
bandore bæn 'dɔː 'bænd ɔː ‖ 'bænd ɔːr -oʊr ~**s**
　z

band-pass 'bænd paːs §-pæs ‖ -pæs ~**es** ɪz əz
bandsaw 'bænd sɔː ~**s** z
bands|man 'bændz |mən ~**men** mən men
bandstand 'bænd stænd ~**s** z
Bandung 'bæn dʊŋ ˌ·'· ‖ 'baːn-
bandwagon 'bænd ˌwæg ən ~**s** z
bandwidth 'bænd wɪdθ -wɪtθ ~**s** s
band|y 'bænd |i ~**ied** id ~**ies** iz ~**ying** i ɪŋ
bandy-legged ˌbænd i 'legd ◄ -'leg ɪd, -'leg əd
bane beɪn **banes** beɪnz
baneful 'beɪn fᵊl -fʊl ~**ly** i
Banff bæn⸣f →bæmᵖf
Banfield 'bæn fiːᵊld
bang bæŋ **banged** bæŋd **banging** 'bæŋ ɪŋ
　bangs bæŋz
Bangalore ˌbæŋ gə 'lɔː ‖ -'lɔːr -'loʊr, '· · ·
banger 'bæŋ ə ‖ -ᵊr ~**s** z
Bangkok, b~ ˌbæŋ 'kɒk '· · ‖ 'bæŋ kaːk ~'**s**, ~**s**
　s
Bangladesh ˌbæŋ glə 'deʃ ◄ -'deɪʃ ‖ ˌbaːŋ-
Bangladeshi ˌbæŋ glə 'deʃ i ◄ -'deɪʃ- ‖ ˌbaːŋ-
　~**s** z
bangle 'bæŋ gᵊl ~**s** z
bang-on ˌbæŋ 'ɒn ‖ -'ɔːn -'aːn
Bangor (*i*) 'bæŋ gə △'bæŋ ə ‖ -gᵊr, (*ii*) -gɔː
　‖ -gɔːr —*Welsh* ['baŋ gɔr] —*The places in the
　UK are usually* (i), *but the place in ME* (ii).
Bangui ˌbɒŋ 'giː ˌbaːŋ- ‖ ˌbaːŋ- —*Fr* [bã gi]
bang-up ˌbæŋ 'ʌp ◄
Banham 'bæn əm
banian 'bæn i ən 'bæn jæn ~**s** z
banish 'bæn ɪʃ ~**ed** t ~**es** ɪz əz ~**ing** ɪŋ ~**ment**
　mənt
banister 'bæn ɪst ə -əst ə ‖ -ᵊr ~**s** z
Banja Luka ˌbæn jə 'luːk ə ˌbaːn- ‖ ˌbaːn-
　—*Serbian* ['baː ɲa: '·'luː ka]
banjax 'bæn dʒæks ~**ed** t
banjo 'bæn dʒəʊ ˌ·'· ‖ -dʒoʊ ~**es**, ~**s** z
banjoist 'bæn dʒəʊ ɪst ˌ·'·, §-əst ‖ -dʒoʊ- ~**s** s
Banjul bæn 'dʒuːl ‖ 'baːn dʒuːl
bank bæŋk **banked** bæŋkt **banking** 'bæŋk ɪŋ
　banks bæŋks
　'bank acˌcount; 'bank ˌbalance; 'bank
　draft; ˌbank 'holiday; 'bank loan; 'bank
　ˌmanager; 'bank rate; 'bank ˌstatement
bankable 'bæŋk əb ᵊl
bankbill 'bæŋk bɪl ~**s** z
bankbook 'bæŋk bʊk ~**s** s
banker 'bæŋk ə ‖ -ᵊr ~**s** z
　'banker's card; ˌbanker's 'order
Bankes bæŋks
Bankhead 'bæŋk hed
Ban Ki-Moon ˌbæn ˌkiː 'muːn →ˌbæŋ- ‖ ˌbaːn-
　—*Korean* [ban ˈɡi mun]
banknote 'bæŋk nəʊt -wɪtθ ‖ -noʊt ~**s** s
bankroll 'bæŋk rəʊl →-rɒʊl ‖ -roʊl ~**ed** d ~**ing**
　ɪŋ ~**s** z
bankrupt 'bæŋk rʌpt -rəpt ~**ed** ɪd əd ~**ing** ɪŋ
　~**s** s
bankrupt|cy 'bæŋk rʌpt |si -rəpt- ~**cies** siz
Banks bæŋks **Banks's** 'bæŋks ɪz -əz
banksia 'bæŋks i ə ~**s** z
Banksy 'bæŋks i

B

Ban-Lon *tdmk* 'bæn lɒn ‖ -laːn
Bann bæn
bann... —*see* **ban**
banner, B~ 'bæn ə ‖ -ᵊr ~s z
　,banner 'headline
Bannerman 'bæn ə mən ‖ -ᵊr-
Banning 'bæn ɪŋ
Bannister 'bæn ɪst ə §-əst- ‖ -ᵊr
bannock 'bæn ək ~s s
Bannockburn 'bæn ək bɜːn ‖ -bɝːn
banns bænz *(= bans)*
banq|uet 'bæŋk |wɪt §-wət ‖ -|wət -wet
　~ueted wɪt ɪd wət əd ‖ wət əd wet əd
　~ueter/s wɪt ə/z wət- ‖ wət ᵊr/z wet̮-
　~ueting wɪt ɪŋ wət- ‖ wət̮ ɪŋ wet̮- **~uets** wɪts
　wəts ‖ wət̮s wets
banquette ₍₎bæŋ 'ket ~s s
Banquo 'bæŋk wəʊ ‖ -woʊ ~'s z
banshee, banshie 'bæn ʃiː ·ˈ· ~s z
Banstead 'bæn⸝st ɪd §-əd, 'bæn sted
bantam, B~ 'bænt əm ‖ 'bæn̮t̮- ~s z
bantamweight 'bænt əm weɪt ‖ 'bæn̮t̮- ~s s
banter 'bænt ə ‖ 'bæn̮t̮ ᵊr **~ed** d **bantering/ly**
　'bænt ər ɪŋ /li ‖ 'bæn̮t̮ ər ɪŋ /li **~s** z
banterer 'bænt ər ə ‖ 'bæn̮t̮ ər ᵊr **~s** z
Banting, b~ 'bænt ɪŋ ‖ 'bæn̮t̮ ɪŋ
Bantoid 'bænt ɔɪd 'baːnt-
Bantry 'bæntr i
　,Bantry 'Bay
Bantu ⸝bæn 'tuː ◂ ⸝baːn-, '·· ~s z
　,Bantu 'languages
bantustan, B~ ⸝bæn tu: 'staːn ⸝baːn-, -'stæn,
　'··· ~s z
banyan 'bæn jən -i⸝ən, -jæn ~s z
　'banyan tree
banzai ₍₎bæn 'zaɪ ◂ ₍₎baːn-, '·· ‖ ₍₎baːn- ~s z
　—*Jp* [ba⸝n 'dzai]
baobab 'beɪ əʊ bæb 'baʊ bæb ‖ -ə- ~s z
　'baobab tree
BAOR ⸝biː eɪ əʊ 'aː ‖ -oʊ 'aːr ~'s z
bap bæp **baps** bæps
baptis... —*see* **baptiz...**
baptism 'bæpt ⸝ɪz əm ~s z
baptismal ₍₎bæp 'tɪz məl ~ly i
Baptist 'bæpt ɪst §-əst ~s s
baptister|y 'bæpt ɪst ər⸝|i §'⸝-əst- ~ies iz
baptis|try 'bæpt ɪs |tri §-əs- ~tries triz

BAPTIZE		

92% ← 8%

'··

·ˈ·

AmE

baptiz|e bæp 'taɪz ⸝bæp- ‖ 'bæpt aɪz bæp 'taɪz
　~ed d **~er/s** ə/z ‖ ᵊr/z **~es** ɪz əz **~ing** ɪŋ
　— *Preference poll, AmE:* '·· 92%, ·ˈ· 8%.
Baquba, Baqubah baː'kuːb ə —*Arabic*
　[baʕ 'quː bah]

bar, Bar baː ‖ baːr **barred** baːd ‖ baːrd
　(= bard) **barring** 'baːr ɪŋ **bars** baːz ‖ baːrz
　,bar 'billiards; 'bar chart; 'bar graph;
　,bar 'none; ,bar 'sinister
Barabbas bə 'ræb əs
Barack 'bær æk -ək ‖ bə 'raːk -'ræk
barathea ⸝bær ə 'θiː⸝ə ‖ ⸝ber-
barb baːb ‖ baːrb **barbed** baːbd ‖ baːrbd
　barbing 'baːb ɪŋ ‖ 'baːrb ɪŋ **barbs** baːbz
　‖ baːrbz
　,barbed 'wire
Barbadian baː 'beɪd i⸝ən -'beɪdʒ ən ‖ baːr- ~s
　z
Barbados baː 'beɪd ɒs -əʊz, -əs, -əʊs
　‖ baːr 'beɪd oʊs ~'s ɪz əz
Barbara 'baːb rə 'baːb ər ə ‖ 'baːrb- ~'s z
barbarian baː 'beər i⸝ən ‖ baːr 'ber i⸝ən -'bær-
　~s z
barbaric baː 'bær ɪk ‖ baːr- -'ber- ~ally ᵊl⸝i
barbaris... —*see* **barbariz...**
barbarism 'baːb ə ⸝rɪz əm ‖ 'baːrb- ~s z
barbarit|y baː 'bær ət |i -ɪt- ‖ baːr 'bær ət̮ |i
　-'ber- ~ies iz
barbariz|e 'baːb ə raɪz ‖ 'baːrb- ~ed d ~es ɪz
　əz ~ing ɪŋ
Barbarossa ⸝baːb ə 'rɒs ə ‖ ⸝baːrb ə 'rɔːs ə
　-'raːs-
barbarous 'baːb ər⸝əs ‖ 'baːrb- ~ly li ~ness
　nəs nɪs
Barbary 'baːb ər⸝i ‖ 'baːrb-
　,Barbary 'ape
barbate 'baːb eɪt ‖ 'baːrb-
barbecu|e 'baːb ɪ kjuː -ə- ‖ 'baːrb- ~ed d ~es
　z ~ing ɪŋ
barbel 'baːb ᵊl ‖ 'baːrb- ~s z
barbell 'baː bel ‖ 'baːr- ~s z
barbequ|e 'baːb i kjuː -ə- ‖ 'baːrb- ~ed d ~es
　z ~ing ɪŋ
barber, B~ 'baːb ə ‖ 'baːrb ᵊr ~ed d
　barbering 'baːb ər ɪŋ ‖ 'baːrb ər ɪŋ ~s z
barberr|y 'baːb ər⸝|i ‖ 'baːr ⸝ber |i ~ies iz
barbershop 'baːb ə ʃɒp ‖ 'baːrb ᵊr ʃaːp ~s s
barbet 'baːb ɪt §-ət ‖ 'baːrb ət ~s s
barbette baː 'bet ‖ baːr- ~s s
barbican, B~ 'baːb ɪk ən -ək- ‖ 'baːrb- ~s z
Barbie, b~ 'baːb i ‖ 'baːrb i
　'Barbie doll
Barbirolli ⸝baːb ɪ 'rɒl i -ə- ‖ ⸝baːrb ə 'raːl i
　-'rɔːl-
barbital 'baːb ɪt ᵊl -ət- ‖ 'baːrb ə taːl -tɔːl
barbitone 'baːb ɪ təʊn -ə- ‖ 'baːrb ə toʊn
barbiturate baː 'bɪtʃ ʊr ət -'bɪtʃ ᵊr ⸝ət,
　-'bɪt jʊr-, -ɪt, -jə reɪt, -juᵊ- ‖ baːr 'bɪtʃ ᵊr ət
　-u⸝ət; ⸝baːrb ə 'tjʊr ət, -eɪt ~s s
Barbizon 'baːb ɪ zɒn §-ə- ‖ ⸝baːrb ə 'zoʊn
　-'zaːn —*Fr* [baʁ bi zɔ̃]
Barbour 'baːb ə ‖ 'baːrb ᵊr
bar-b-que 'baːb i kjuː -ə- ‖ 'baːrb- ~s z
Barbra 'baːb rə ‖ 'baːrb-
Barbuda baː 'bjuːd ə ‖ baːr- -'buːd-
barbule 'baːb juːl ‖ 'baːrb juːᵊl
barbwire ⸝baːb 'waɪ⸝ə ◂ ‖ ⸝baːrb 'waɪ⸝ᵊr ◂ '··
Barça 'baːs ə ‖ 'baːrs ə —*Catalan* ['bar sɐ]

barcarole, barcarolle ˌbɑːk ə ˈrəʊl →-ˈrɒʊl,
'··· ‖ ˈbɑːrk ə roʊl ~s z
Barcelona ˌbɑːs ɪ ˈləʊn ə ◂ -ə-
‖ ˌbɑːrs ə ˈloʊn ə ◂ —Sp [bar θe ˈlo na],
Catalan [bər sə ˈlo nə]
Barchester ˈbɑː tʃɪst ə -tʃəst-, ˌtʃest ə
‖ ˈbɑːr ˌtʃest ər -tʃəst-
Barclay ˈbɑːk li -leɪ ‖ ˈbɑːrk- ~'s z
Barclaycard tdmk ˈbɑːk li kɑːd -leɪ-
‖ ˈbɑːrk li kɑːrd -leɪ- ~s z
barcod|e ˈbɑː kəʊd ‖ ˈbɑːr koʊd ~ed ɪd əd ~es
z ~ing ɪŋ
Barcoo ˌbɑː ˈkuː ◂ ‖ ˌbɑːr-
    ˌBarcoo ˈdog
bard bɑːd ‖ bɑːrd **barded** ˈbɑːd ɪd -əd
‖ ˈbɑːrd əd **barding** ˈbɑːd ɪŋ ‖ ˈbɑːrd ɪŋ
    bards bɑːdz ‖ bɑːrdz
Bardell (i) bɑː ˈdel ‖ bɑːr-, (ii) ˈbɑːd əl -el
‖ ˈbɑːrd-
bardic ˈbɑːd ɪk ‖ ˈbɑːrd ɪk
bardolater bɑː ˈdɒl ət ə ‖ bɑːr ˈdɑːl əţ ər ~s z
bardolatry bɑː ˈdɒl ətr i ‖ bɑːr ˈdɑːl-
Bardolph ˈbɑːd ɒlf ‖ ˈbɑːrd ɑːlf
Bardon ˈbɑːd ən ‖ ˈbɑːrd ən
Bardot bɑː ˈdəʊ ‖ bɑːr ˈdoʊ —Fr [baʁ do]
Bardsey ˈbɑːd si ‖ ˈbɑːrd-
Bardsley ˈbɑːdz li ‖ ˈbɑːrdz-
bard|y ˈbɑːd| i ‖ ˈbɑːrd| i ~ies iz
bare beə ‖ beər bæər (= bear) **bared** beəd
‖ beərd bæərd **barer** ˈbeər ə ‖ ˈber ər ˈbær-
    bares beəz ‖ beərz bæərz **barest** ˈbeər ɪst
    -əst ‖ ˈber əst ˈbær- **baring** ˈbeər ɪŋ ‖ ˈber ɪŋ
    ˈbær-
bare-arsed, bare-assed ˈbeər ɑːst ‖ ˈber æst
ˈbær-
bareback ˈbeə bæk ‖ ˈber- ˈbær-
barebacked ˌbeə ˈbækt ◂ ‖ ˈber bækt ˈbær-
Barebones ˈbeə bəʊnz ‖ ˈber boʊnz ˈbær-
barefaced ˌbeə ˈfeɪst ◂ ‖ ˌber- ˌbær-
barefacedly ˌbeə ˈfeɪst li ◂ -ˈfeɪs ɪd-, -əd-; '· ··
‖ ˌber- ˌbær-
bare|foot ˈbeə |fʊt ˌ·ˈ· ‖ ˈber- ˈbær- ~footed
fʊt ɪd -əd ‖ fʊţ əd
bare-handed ˌbeə ˈhænd ɪd ◂ -əd ◂ ‖ ˌber-
ˌbær-
bareheaded ˌbeə ˈhed ɪd ◂ -əd ‖ ˌber- ˌbær-
barelegged ˌbeə ˈlegd ◂ -ˈleg ɪd, -əd ‖ ˌber-
ˌbær-
barely ˈbeə li ‖ ˈber li ˈbær-
Barenboim ˈbær ən bɔɪm ˈbeər-, →-əm- ‖ ˈber-
ˈbær-
bareness ˈbeə nəs -nɪs ‖ ˈber- ˈbær-
Barents ˈbær ənts ‖ ˈber- ˈbær-, ˈbɑːr-
barf bɑːf ‖ bɑːrf **barfed** bɑːft ‖ bɑːrft **barfing**
ˈbɑːf ɪŋ ‖ ˈbɑːrf ɪŋ **barfs** bɑːfs ‖ bɑːrfs
bar|fly ˈbɑː |flaɪ ‖ ˈbɑːr- ~flies flaɪz
Barford ˈbɑː fəd ‖ ˈbɑːr fərd
bargain ˈbɑːg ɪn -ən ‖ ˈbɑːrg- ~ed d ~er/s ə/z
‖ ər/z ~ing ɪŋ ~s z
    'bargaining ˌcounter
barge bɑːdʒ ‖ bɑːrdʒ **barged** bɑːdʒd
‖ bɑːrdʒd **barges** ˈbɑːdʒ ɪz -əz ‖ ˈbɑːrdʒ əz
    barging ˈbɑːdʒ ɪŋ ‖ ˈbɑːrdʒ ɪŋ

bargeboard ˈbɑːdʒ bɔːd ‖ ˈbɑːrdʒ bɔːrd
-boʊrd ~s z
bargee (ˌ)bɑː ˈdʒiː ‖ (ˌ)bɑːr- ~s z
barge|man ˈbɑːdʒ |mən -mæn ‖ ˈbɑːrdʒ-
~men mən men
bargepole ˈbɑːdʒ pəʊl →-pɒʊl ‖ ˈbɑːrdʒ poʊl
~s z
barging ˈbɑːdʒ ɪŋ ‖ ˈbɑːrdʒ ɪŋ
Bargoed ˈbɑː gɔɪd ‖ ˈbɑːr-
Barham (i) ˈbɑːr əm, (ii) ˈbær əm ‖ ˈber-
Barhaugh ˈbɑː hʌf ‖ ˈbɑːr-
barhop ˈbɑː hɒp ‖ ˈbɑːr hɑːp ~ped t ~ping ɪŋ
~s s
Bari ˈbɑːr i —It [ˈbaː ri]
baric ˈbeər ɪk ˈbær- ‖ ˈber ɪk
baring ˈbeər ɪŋ ‖ ˈber ɪŋ ˈbær-
Baring (i) ˈbeər ɪŋ ‖ ˈber-, (ii) ˈbær ɪŋ ‖ ˈber-
Baring-Gould ˌbeər ɪŋ ˈguːld ‖ ˌber- ˌbær-
barista bɑː ˈriːst ə bə-, -ˈrɪst-, -ɑː- ~s z
baritone ˈbær ɪ təʊn -ə- ‖ ˈbær ə toʊn ˈber- ~s
z
barium ˈbeər i əm ‖ ˈber- ˈbær-
    ˌbarium ˈmeal
bark bɑːk ‖ bɑːrk **barked** bɑːkt ‖ bɑːrkt
    barking ˈbɑːk ɪŋ ‖ ˈbɑːrk ɪŋ **barks** bɑːks
‖ bɑːrks
barkeep ˈbɑː kiːp ‖ ˈbɑːr- ~ing ɪŋ ~s s
barkeeper ˈbɑː ˌkiːp ə ‖ ˈbɑːr ˌkiːp ər ~s z
barker, B~ ˈbɑːk ə ‖ ˈbɑːrk ər ~s z
Barking ˈbɑːk ɪŋ ‖ ˈbɑːrk ɪŋ ~'s z
Barkley, Barkly ˈbɑːk li ‖ ˈbɑːrk-
Barkston ˈbɑːkst ən ‖ ˈbɑːrkst-
Barlaston ˈbɑːl əst ən ‖ ˈbɑːrl-
barley ˈbɑːl i ‖ ˈbɑːrl i
    ˈbarley ˌsugar, ˈbarley ˌwater, ˌbarley
    ˈwine
barleycorn, B~ ˈbɑːl i kɔːn ‖ ˈbɑːrl i kɔːrn
Barlinnie bɑː ˈlɪn i ‖ bɑːr-
Barlow, Barlowe ˈbɑːl əʊ ‖ ˈbɑːrl oʊ
barm bɑːm ‖ bɑːrm
    ˈbarm cake
barmaid ˈbɑː meɪd ‖ ˈbɑːr-
bar|man ˈbɑː |mən -mæn ‖ ˈbɑːr- ~men mən
men
barmecidal, B~ ˌbɑːm ɪ ˈsaɪd əl ◂ -ə- ‖ ˌbɑːrm-
Barmecide ˈbɑːm ɪ saɪd -ə- ‖ ˈbɑːrm-
barmi... —see barmy
bar mitz|vah, bar miz|vah (ˌ)bɑː ˈmɪts |və
‖ (ˌ)bɑːr- ~vahed vəd ~vahing vər ɪŋ ‖ və ɪŋ
~vahs vəz
Barmouth ˈbɑː məθ ‖ ˈbɑːr-
barm|y ˈbɑːm |i ‖ ˈbɑːrm |i ~ier i ə ‖ i ər ~iest
i ɪst i əst ~iness i nəs -nɪs
barn bɑːn ‖ bɑːrn **barns** bɑːnz ‖ bɑːrnz
    ˈbarn dance; ˌbarn ˈdoor; ˈbarn owl
Barnabas ˈbɑːn əb əs -ə bæs ‖ ˈbɑːrn-
Barnaby ˈbɑːn əb i ‖ ˈbɑːrn-
barnacle ˈbɑːn ək əl -ɪk- ‖ ˈbɑːrn- ~d d ~s z
    ˈbarnacle goose
Barnard (i) ˈbɑːn əd ‖ ˈbɑːrn ərd, (ii) -ɑːd
‖ -ɑːrd, (iii) bə ˈnɑːd ‖ bər ˈnɑːrd
Barnardo bə ˈnɑːd əʊ bɑː- ‖ bər ˈnɑːrd oʊ ~'s
z

Barnehurst ˈbɑːn hɜːst ‖ ˈbɑːrn hɜ˞ːst
Barnes bɑːnz ‖ bɑːrnz
Barnet ˈbɑːn ɪt §-ət ‖ ˈbɑːrn-
Barnett *(i)* ˈbɑːn ɪt §-ət ‖ ˈbɑːrn ət, *(ii)* bɑː ˈnet ‖ bɑːr-
barney, B~ ˈbɑːn i ‖ ˈbɑːrn i **~ed** d **~ing** ɪŋ **~s** z
Barnoldswick bɑː ˈnəʊldz wɪk →-ˈnɒʊldz- ‖ bɑːr ˈnoʊldz- —*locally also* ˈbɑːl ɪk
Barnsley ˈbɑːnz li ‖ ˈbɑːrnz-
Barnstable ˈbɑːnᵗst əb ᵊl ‖ ˈbɑːrnᵗst-
Barnstaple ˈbɑːnᵗst əp ᵊl ‖ ˈbɑːrnᵗst-
barnstorm ˈbɑːn stɔːm ‖ ˈbɑːrn stɔːrm **~ed** d **~er/s** ə/z ‖ ᵊr/z **~ing** ɪŋ **~s** z
Barnum ˈbɑːn əm ‖ ˈbɑːrn-
barnyard ˈbɑːn jɑːd ‖ ˈbɑːrn jɑːrd **~s** z
baro- *comb. form*
with stress-neutral suffix ¦bær ə ‖ ¦ber- — **barogram** ˈbær ə græm ‖ ˈber-
with stress-imposing suffix bə ˈrɒ+ ‖ bə ˈrɑː+ — **barometry** bə ˈrɒm ətr i -ɪtr- ‖ bə ˈrɑːm-
Baroda bə ˈrəʊd ə ‖ -ˈroʊd-
barograph ˈbær ə grɑːf -græf ‖ -græf ˈber- **~s** s
barographic ˌbær ə ˈgræf ɪk ◂ ‖ ˌber- **~al** ᵊl **~ally** ᵊl‿i
barometer bə ˈrɒm ɪt ə -ət- ‖ -ˈrɑːm əţ ᵊr
barometric ˌbær ə ˈmetr ɪk ◂ ‖ ˌber- **~al** ᵊl **~ally** ᵊl‿i
baron ˈbær ən ‖ ˈber- *(= barren)* **~s** z
Baron *(i)* ˈbær ən ‖ ˈber-, *(ii)* ˈbeər ən ‖ ˈber-
baronag|e ˈbær ən ɪdʒ ‖ ˈber- **~es** ɪz əz
baroness ˈbær ə nes ˌ· ·ˈ◂; ˈbær ən ɪs, -əs ‖ ˈber- **~es** ɪz əz
baronet ˈbær ən ɪt -ət; -ə net, ˌbær ə ˈnet ‖ ˈber- **~s** s
baronetag|e ˈbær ən ɪt ɪdʒ -ət ɪdʒ; -ə net-, ˌbær ə ˈnet- ‖ -əţ ɪdʒ ˈber- **~es** ɪz əz
baronet|cy ˈbær ən ɪt |si -ət si; -ə net- ‖ ˈber- **~cies** siz
baronial bə ˈrəʊn i‿əl ‖ -ˈroʊn- **~ly** i
baron|y ˈbær ən |i ‖ ˈber- **~ies** iz
baroque bə ˈrɒk bæ-, -ˈrəʊk ‖ -ˈroʊk -ˈrɑːk
Barossa bə ˈrɒs ə ‖ -ˈrɑːs- -ˈrɔːs-
Barotse bə ˈrɒts i ‖ -ˈrɑːts- **~land** lænd
barouch|e bə ˈruːʃ bæ- **~es** ɪz əz
barque bɑːk ‖ bɑːrk *(= bark)* **barques** bɑːks ‖ bɑːrks
barquentine ˈbɑːk ən tiːn →-ŋ- ‖ ˈbɑːrk-
Barr bɑː ‖ bɑːr
Barra ˈbær ə ‖ ˈber-
barrack ˈbær ək ‖ ˈber- **~s** s
Barraclough ˈbær ə klʌf ‖ˈber-
barracoon ˌbær ə ˈkuːn ‖ ˌber- **~s** z
barracouta ˌbær ə ˈkuːt ə ‖ -ˈkuːţ ə ˌber- **~s** z
barracuda ˌbær ə ˈkjuːd ə -ˈkuːd- ‖ -ˈkuːd ə ˌber- **~s** z
barrag|e *'dam'* ˈbær ɑːʒ -ɑːdʒ ‖ ˈbɑːr ɪdʒ *(*)* **~es** ɪz əz
barrag|e *'artillery fire'* ˈbær ɑːʒ -ɑːdʒ ‖ bə ˈrɑːʒ -ˈrɑːdʒ **~es** ɪz əz
ˈbarrage balˌloon ‖ ·ˈ· ·ˌ·
barramunda ˌbær ə ˈmʌnd ə ‖ ˌber- **~s** z
barramundi ˌbær ə ˈmʌnd i ‖ ˌber- **~s** z
Barranquilla ˌbær ən ˈkiːl jə ‖ ˌbɑːr ən ˈkiː jə ˌbær-, ˌber- —*AmSp* [ba ɾraŋ ˈki ja]
Barrat, Barratt ˈbær ət ‖ ˈber-
barratry ˈbær ətr i ‖ ˈber-
barre bɑː ‖ bɑːr —*Fr* [baːʁ] **~s** z
barré ˈbær eɪ ‖ bɑː ˈreɪ —*Fr* [ba ʁe]
barred bɑːd ‖ bɑːrd
barrel ˈbær əl ‖ ˈber- **~ed, ~led** d **~ing, ~ling** ɪŋ **~s** z
ˈbarrel ˌorgan
barrel-chested ˌbær əl ˈtʃest ɪd ◂ -əd, ˈ· ·ˌ· · ‖ ˌber-
barrelhouse ˈbær əl haʊs ‖ ˈber-
Barrell ˈbær əl ‖ ˈber-
barren ˈbær ən ‖ ˈber- **~ly** li **~ness** nəs nɪs
Barrett ˈbær ət -ɪt ‖ ˈber-
barrette bə ˈret bɑː- **~s** s
Barri ˈbær i ‖ ˈber-
barricad|e ˌbær ɪ ˈkeɪd -ə-, ˈ· · · ‖ ˈbær ə keɪd ˈber-, ˌ· ·ˈ· **~ed** ɪd əd **~es** z **~ing** ɪŋ
Barrie ˈbær i ‖ ˈber-
barrier ˈbær i‿ə ‖ ᵊr ˈber- **~s** z
ˈbarrier cream; **ˌbarrier ˈreef**, ˈ· · · ·
barring ˈbɑːr ɪŋ
Barrington ˈbær ɪŋ tən ‖ ˈber-
barrio ˈbær i‿əʊ ‖ ˈbɑːr i oʊ ˈbær-, ˈber- —*Sp* [ˈba rrjo] **~s** z —*Sp* [s]
barrister ˈbær ɪst ə -əst- ‖ -ᵊr ˈber- **~s** z
Barron ˈbær ən ‖ ˈber-
barroom ˈbɑː ruːm -rʊm ‖ ˈbɑːr- **~s** z
barrow, B~ ˈbær əʊ ‖ -oʊ ˈber- **~s** z
ˈbarrow boy
Barrow-in-Furness ˌbær əʊ ɪn ˈfɜːn ɪs §-ənˈ·-, -əs ‖ ˌbær oʊ ən ˈfɜ˞ːn əs ˌber-
Barry ˈbær i ‖ ˈber-
Barrymore ˈbær i mɔː ‖ -mɔːr ˈber-, -moʊr
Barsac, b~ ˈbɑːs æk ‖ bɑːr ˈsæk —*Fr* [baʁ sak]
Barset ˈbɑːs ɪt -ət, -et ‖ ˈbɑːrs- **~shire** ʃə ʃɪə ‖ ʃᵊr ʃɪr
Barsham ˈbɑːʃ əm ‖ ˈbɑːrʃ-
Barstow ˈbɑːst əʊ ‖ ˈbɑːr stoʊ
Bart, bart, BART bɑːt ‖ bɑːrt —*see also* **baronet**
bartender ˈbɑː ˌtend ə ‖ ˈbɑːr ˌtend ᵊr **~s** z
barter ˈbɑːt ə ‖ ˈbɑːrţ ᵊr **~ed** d **bartering** ˈbɑːt ər ɪŋ ‖ ˈbɑːrţ ər ɪŋ **~s** z
Barth bɑːt ‖ bɑːrt —*Ger* [baʁt, baːɐt]
Barthes bɑːt ‖ bɑːrt —*Fr* [baʁt]
Bartholdi bɑː ˈtɒld i -ˈθɒld- ‖ bɑːr ˈθɑːld i -ˈtɑːld-, -ˈθɔːld-, -ˈtɔːld- —*Fr* [baʁ tɔl di]
Bartholin ˈbɑːθ əl ɪn ˈbɑːt-, §-ən ‖ ˈbɑːrθ- ˈbɑːrţ-
Bartholomew bɑː ˈθɒl ə mjuː bə- ‖ bɑːr ˈθɑːl- bᵊr-
Bartle ˈbɑːt ᵊl ‖ ˈbɑːrţ ᵊl
Bartlett ˈbɑːt lət -lɪt ‖ ˈbɑːrt-
Bartok, Bartók ˈbɑːt ɒk ‖ ˈbɑːrt ɑːk -ɔːk —*Hungarian* [ˈbɒr toːk]
Bartoli ˈbɑːt əl i ‖ ˈbɑːrt- —*It* [ˈbar to li]

Bartolommeo bɑː ˌtɒl ə ˈmeɪ əʊ ˌ··ˈ··
‖ ˌbɑːr ˌtɑːl ə ˈmeɪ oʊ -ˌtɔːl- —*It*
[bar to lom ˈmɛː o]
Barton ˈbɑːt ᵊn ‖ ˈbɑːrt ᵊn
Barts, Bart's bɑːts ‖ bɑːrts
bartsia bɑːts i ə ‖ ˈbɑːrts- ~s z
Baruch *name in the Bible (Apocrypha)* ˈbɑːr ʊk
ˈbeər-, -ək ‖ bə ˈruːk ˈbɑːr uːk, ˈber-, -ək
Baruch *family name* bə ˈruːk
Barugh bɑːf ‖ bɑːrf
Barwick ˈbær ɪk ˈbɑː wɪk ‖ ˈbɑːr wɪk
baryon ˈbær i ɒn ‖ -ɑːn ˈber- ~s z
Baryshnikov bə ˈrɪʃ nɪ kɒf -nə- ‖ -kɑːf -kɔːf
—*Russ* [bʌ ˈrɪʃ nʲɪ kəf]
barysphere ˈbær ɪ sfɪə -ə- ‖ -sfɪr ˈber-
baryta bə ˈraɪt ə ‖ -ˈraɪt̬-
barytes bə ˈraɪt iːz ‖ -ˈraɪt̬ iz
barytone ˈbær ɪ təʊn -ə- ‖ -toʊn ˈber- ~s z
basal ˈbeɪs ᵊl §ˈbeɪz-
  ˌbasal ˈganglia; ˌbasal meˈtaboˌlism
basalt ˈbæs ɔːlt -ᵊlt; bə ˈsɔːlt, -ˈsɒlt ‖ bə ˈsɔːlt
  -ˈsɑːlt; ˈbeɪs ɔːlt, -ɑːlt ~s s
basaltic bə ˈsɔːlt ɪk -ˈsɒlt- ‖ -ˈsɑːlt-
Basan ˈbeɪs æn
bascule ˈbæsk juːl ~s z
base beɪs **based** beɪst **bases** ˈbeɪs ɪz -əz
  basing ˈbeɪs ɪŋ
  ˌbase ˈmetal; ˈbase rate
baseball ˈbeɪs bɔːl ‖ -bɑːl ~s z
  ˈbaseball bat; ˈbaseball cap
baseboard ˈbeɪs bɔːd ‖ -bɔːrd -boʊrd ~s z
base-born ˈbeɪs bɔːn ˌ·ˈ· ‖ ˌbeɪs ˈbɔːrn ◂
Basel ˈbɑːz ᵊl —*Ger* [ˈbɑː zᵊl]
baseless ˈbeɪs ləs -lɪs ~ly li ~ness nəs nɪs
baseline ˈbeɪs laɪn ~s z
base|man ˈbeɪs mən ~men mən
basement ˈbeɪs mənt ~s s
basenji bə ˈsendʒ i ~s z
baseplate ˈbeɪs pleɪt ~s s
baser ˈbeɪs ə ‖ -ᵊr
bases *pl of* **basis** ˈbeɪs iːz
bases *pl of* **base** ˈbeɪs ɪz -əz
basest ˈbeɪs ɪst -əst
Basford *(i)* ˈbeɪs fəd ‖ -fᵊrd, *(ii)* ˈbæs- —*The*
  place in Notts is (i); those in Cheshire and
  Staffs are (ii)
bash bæʃ **bashed** bæʃt **bashes** ˈbæʃ ɪz -əz
  bashing/s ˈbæʃ ɪŋ/z
Bashan ˈbeɪʃ æn
-basher ˌbæʃ ə ‖ -ᵊr ~s z — **gay-basher/s**
  ˈgeɪ ˌbæʃə/z ‖ ᵊr/z
bashful ˈbæʃ fᵊl -fʊl ~ly ˌi ~ness nəs nɪs
-bashing ˌbæʃ ɪŋ — **square-bashing**
  ˈskweə ˌbæʃ ɪŋ ‖ ˈskwer-
Bashir bə ˈʃɪə ‖ -ˈʃɪᵊr
Bashkir ₍ˌ₎bæʃ ˈkɪə ‖ bɑːʃ ˈkɪᵊr ~s z
Bashkiria ₍ˌ₎bæʃ ˈkɪər i ə -ˈkɪr- ‖ bɑːʃ ˈkɪr-
basho ˈbæʃ əʊ ‖ bɑː ˈʃoʊ ~s z —*Jp* [ba ˌɕo]
basic, BASIC ˈbeɪs ɪk ~s s
  ˌBasic ˈEnglish
basically ˈbeɪs ɪk li -ɪk ᵊl_i
basidiomycete bə ˌsɪd i ˌəʊ maɪ ˈsiːt
  ·ˌ···ˈmaɪs iːt ‖ -oʊ ˈmaɪs iːt ·ˌ···maɪ ˈsiːt

basidi|um bə ˈsɪd i‖əm bæ- **~a** ə **~al** əl
Basie ˈbeɪs i
basil, Basil ˈbæz ᵊl -ɪl ‖ ˈbeɪz ᵊl ˈbeɪs-, ˈbæs-
basilar ˈbæz ɪl ə ˈbæs-, -əl- ‖ -ᵊr
Basildon ˈbæz ᵊl dən
basilect ˈbæz ɪ lekt ˈbeɪs-, -ə- **~s s**
basilectal ˌbæz ɪ ˈlekt ᵊl ◂ ˌbeɪs-, -ə- **~ly** i
basilica bə ˈzɪl ɪk ə -ˈsɪl- ‖ -ˈsɪl- **~s z**
basilisk ˈbæz ə lɪsk ˈbæs-, -ɪ- **~s s**
basin ˈbeɪs ᵊn **~s z**
basinet ˈbæs ɪ net -ə-, -nɪt, ˌ··ˈnet
basinful ˈbeɪs ᵊn fʊl **~s z**
basing *pres part of* **base** ˈbeɪs ɪŋ
Basing *name* ˈbeɪz ɪŋ
Basinger ˈbeɪs ɪndʒ ə ˈbæs-, -əndʒ- ‖ -ᵊr
Basingstoke ˈbeɪz ɪŋ stəʊk ‖ -stoʊk
-basis *stress-imposing* bəs ɪs §-əs — **anabasis**
  ə ˈnæb əs ɪs §-əs
basis ˈbeɪs ɪs §-əs **bases** ˈbeɪs iːz
bask bɑːsk §bæsk ‖ bæsk **basked** bɑːskt §bæskt
  ‖ bæskt **basking** ˈbɑːsk ɪŋ §ˈbæsk- ‖ ˈbæsk ɪŋ
  basks bɑːsks §bæsks ‖ bæsks
Baskerville ˈbæsk ə vɪl ‖ -ᵊr- **~s z**
basket ˈbɑːsk ɪt §ˈbæsk-, -ət ‖ ˈbæsk ət **~s s**
  ˈbasket case
basketball ˈbɑːsk ɪt bɔːl §ˈbæsk-, -ət-
  ‖ ˈbæsk ət bɔːl -bɑːl
basketful ˈbɑːsk ɪt fʊl §ˈbæsk-, -ət- ‖ ˈbæsk-
basketry ˈbɑːsk ɪtr i §ˈbæsk-, -ətr- ‖ ˈbæsk-
basketwork ˈbɑːsk ɪt wɜːk §ˈbæsk-, §-ət-
  ‖ ˈbæsk ət wɜːrk
Baskin ˈbæsk ɪn §-ən
Baskin-Robbins *tdmk* ˌbæsk ɪn ˈrɒb ɪnz §-ən-,
  §-ənz ‖ -ˈrɑːb-
Basle bɑːl —*Ger* Basel [ˈbɑː zᵊl]
Baslow ˈbæz ləʊ ‖ -loʊ
basmati, B~ bæz ˈmɑːt i bæs-, bəz-, bəs-
  ‖ bɑːz ˈmɑːt̬ i —*Hindi* [bɑː smə ʈiː]
Basnett ˈbæz nɪt -nət, -net
basophil ˈbeɪs əʊ fɪl ˈbeɪz- ‖ -ə-
basophilic ˌbeɪs əʊ ˈfɪl ɪk ◂ ˌbeɪz- ‖ -ə-
Basotho bə ˈsuːt uː -ˈsəʊt əʊ ‖ -ˈsoʊt oʊ
Basque, basque bæsk bɑːsk **Basques,**
  basques bæsks bɑːsks
Basra, Basrah ˈbæz rə ˈbɑːz- ‖ ˈbɑːs rə ˈbæs-,
  ˈbɑːz-, ˈbæz- —*Arabic* [ˈbasˤ rɑ]
bas-relief ˌbɑː ri ˈliːf ◂ ˌbæs-, -rə- **~s s**
bass *in music* (= *base*) **basses** ˈbeɪs ɪz -əz
  ˌbass ˈclef; ˌbass ˈfiddle; ˌbass guiˈtar
bass *'fish', 'bast'* bæs **basses** ˈbæs ɪz -əz
Bass *family name; place name element; beer*
  tdmk bæs **Basses, Bass's** ˈbæs ɪz -əz
  ˌBass ˈRock
Bassanio bə ˈsɑːn i əʊ bæ- ‖ -oʊ
Bassenthwaite ˈbæs ᵊn θweɪt
basset, B~ ˈbæs ɪt -ət **~s s**
  ˈbasset horn; ˈbasset hound
Basseterre ˌbæs ˈteə ‖ -ˈteᵊr
Bassetlaw ˌbæs ɪt ˈlɔː -ət- ‖ -ˈlɑː
Bassett ˈbæs ɪt -ət
Bassey ˈbæs i
bassinet, bassinette ˌbæs ɪ ˈnet -ə- **~s s**
Bassingbourn ˈbæs ɪŋ bɔːn ‖ -bɔːrn -boʊrn

B

bassist 'beɪs ɪst §-əst ~s s
basso 'bæs əʊ 'bɑːs- ‖ -oʊ —*It* ['bas so] ~s z
  ˌbasso pro'fundo prəʊ 'fʌnd əʊ -'fund- ‖ -proʊ 'fʌnd oʊ —*as if It* [pro 'fun do]
bassoon bə 'suːn bæ- ~ist/s ɪst/s §əst/s ~s s
basswood 'bæs wʊd
bast bæst
Bastable 'bæst əb ᵊl
bastard 'bɑːst əd 'bæst- ‖ 'bæst ᵊrd ~s z
bastardis... —*see* bastardiz...
bastardization ˌbɑːst əd aɪ 'zeɪʃ ᵊn ˌbæst-, -ɪ'-- ‖ ˌbæst ᵊrd ə-
bastardiz|e 'bɑːst ə daɪz 'bæst- ‖ 'bæst ᵊr- ~ed d ~es ɪz əz ~ing ɪŋ
bastard|y 'bɑːst əd |i 'bæst- ‖ 'bæst ᵊrd |i ~ies iz
baste beɪst (= *based*) basted 'beɪst ɪd -əd
  bastes beɪsts basting 'beɪst ɪŋ
Bastedo bə 'stiːd əʊ ‖ -oʊ
Basten 'bæst ən -ɪn
Bastille, b~ ₍ᵢ₎bæ 'stiːᵊl —*Fr* [bas tij]
Bastin 'bæst ɪn §-ən
bastinado ˌbæst ɪ 'neɪd əʊ -ə-, -'nɑːd- ‖ -oʊ
bastion 'bæst i ən ‖ 'bæs tʃən ~s z
Basuto bə 'suːt əʊ ‖ -'suːt̬ oʊ
Basutoland bə 'suːt əʊ lænd ‖ -'suːt̬ oʊ-
bat bæt bats bæts batted 'bæt ɪd -əd ‖ 'bæt̬ əd batting 'bæt ɪŋ ‖ 'bæt̬ ɪŋ
Bata *tdmk* 'bɑːt ə ‖ 'bɑːt̬ ə
Batavia bə 'teɪv i ə
batboy 'bæt bɔɪ ~s z
batch bætʃ batches 'bætʃ ɪz -əz
  ˌbatch 'processing
Batchelor 'bætʃ əl ə -ɪl- ‖ -ᵊl ᵊr
bate, Bate beɪt bated 'beɪt ɪd -əd ‖ 'beɪt̬ əd
  bates beɪts bating 'beɪt ɪŋ ‖ 'beɪt̬ ɪŋ
  ˌbated 'breath
bateleur ˌbæt ə 'lɜː →-ᵊl 'ɜː; '· · · ‖ ˌbæt̬ ᵊl 'ɜː '· · · ~s z
Bately 'beɪt li
Bateman 'beɪt mən
Bates beɪts
Batesian 'beɪts i ən
Bateson 'beɪt sən
Batey 'beɪt i ‖ 'beɪt̬ i

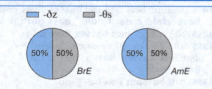

BATHS

- -ðz
- -θs

50% 50%   50% 50%

BrE   AmE

bath *n* bɑːθ §bæθ ‖ bæθ baths bɑːðz §bɑːθs, §bæθs, §bæðz ‖ bæðz bæθs — *Preference polls, BrE: -ðz 50%, -θs 50%; AmE, -ðz 50%, -θs 50%. Surprisingly, exactly half of each panel preferred the -θs form, traditionally considered non-standard. Some people differentiate between 'acts of bathing', with -θs, and 'bathtubs, bathhouses', with -ðz.* bath's bɑːθs

§bæθs ‖ bæθs
  'bath mat; 'bath night; 'bath salts
bath *v* bɑːθ §bæθ ‖ bæθ bathed bɑːθt §bæθt ‖ bæθt bathing 'bɑːθ ɪŋ §'bæθ- ‖ 'bæθ ɪŋ
  baths bɑːθs §bæθs ‖ bæθs —*This verb is not current in AmE.*
Bath *place name* bɑːθ §bæθ ‖ bæθ
  ˌBath 'bun; ˌBath 'chair, '· ·
bathe beɪð bathed beɪðd bathes beɪðz
  bathing 'beɪð ɪŋ
bathed *past & pp of* bath bɑːθt §bæθt ‖ bæθt
bathed *past & pp of* bathe beɪðd
bather 'beɪð ə ‖ -ᵊr ~s z
bathetic bə 'θet ɪk bæ- ‖ -'θet̬ ɪk
bath|house 'bɑːθ| haʊs §'bæθ|- ‖ 'bæθ|-
  ~houses haʊz ɪz -əz
bathing *from* bathe 'beɪð ɪŋ
  'bathing ˌbeauty; 'bathing ˌcostume; 'bathing maˌchine; 'bathing suit
bathing *from* bath 'bɑːθ ɪŋ §'bæθ- ‖ 'bæθ ɪŋ
Batho (i) 'bæθ əʊ ‖ -oʊ, (ii) 'beɪθ-
bathos 'beɪθ ɒs ‖ -ɑːs -ɔːs, -oʊs
bathrobe 'bɑːθ rəʊb §'bæθ- ‖ 'bæθ roʊb ~s z
bathroom 'bɑːθ ruːm §'bæθ-, -rʊm ‖ 'bæθ- ~s z
Bathsheba bæθ 'ʃiːb ə 'bæθ ʃɪb ə
bathtub 'bɑːθ tʌb §'bæθ- ‖ 'bæθ- ~s z
Bathurst 'bæθ ɜːst 'bɑːθ-, -əst, -hɜːst ‖ -ɜːst
bathy- *comb. form*
  with stress-neutral suffix ˌbæθ ɪ
  — bathymetric ˌbæθ ɪ 'metr ɪk ◂
  with stress-imposing suffix bə 'θɪ+ bæ-
  — bathymetry bə 'θɪm ətr i bæ-, -ɪtr i
bathyal 'bæθ i əl
bathypelagic ˌbæθ i pə 'lædʒ ɪk ◂
bathyscaphe 'bæθ i skeɪf §-ə- ~s s
bathysphere 'bæθ i sfɪə -ə- ‖ -sfɪr ~s z
batik bə 'tiːk bæ-; 'bæt ɪk, 'bɑːt ɪk ~s s
bating 'beɪt ɪŋ ‖ 'beɪt̬ ɪŋ
Batista bə 'tiːst ə bæ-, bɑː- —*Sp* [ba 'tis ta]
batiste bæ 'tiːst bə- ~s s
Batley 'bæt li
batman *'army servant'* 'bæt mən batmen 'bæt mən -men
Batman *cartoon character* 'bæt mæn
bat mitzvah ˌbɑːt 'mɪts və
baton 'bæt ɒn -ᵊn ‖ bə 'tɑːn (*) —*See also phrases with this word* ~s z
Baton Rouge ˌbæt ᵊn 'ruːʒ
bats bæts
Batsford 'bæts fəd ‖ -fᵊrd
bats|man 'bæts| mən ~men mən
Batson 'bæts ən
batt, Batt bæt
batt... —*see* bat
battalion bə 'tæl jən -'tæl i ən ~s z
battels 'bæt ᵊlz ‖ 'bæt̬-
batten, B~ 'bæt ᵊn ~ed d ~ing ɪŋ ~s z
Battenberg 'bæt ᵊn bɜːg ‖ -bɜːg —*Ger* ['bat ᵊn bɛʁk]
  ˌBattenberg 'cake

batter 'bæt ə ‖ 'bæt ᵊr **~ed** d **battering/s**
'bæt ər ɪŋ/z ‖ 'bæt ər ɪŋ/z **~s** z
'**battering ˌram**
batteries —*see* **battery**
Battersby 'bæt əz bi ‖ 'bæt ᵊrz-
Battersea 'bæt əs i -ə si: ‖ 'bæt ᵊr si:
batter|y 'bætr |i 'bæt ər ˌ|i ‖ 'bæt ər |i
→'bætr |i **~ies** iz
batti... —*see* **batty**
batting 'bæt ɪŋ ‖ 'bæt ɪŋ
'**batting ˌaverage**
battl|e, B~ 'bæt ᵊl ‖ 'bæt ᵊl **~ed** d **~es** z **~ing**
ɪŋ
'**battle ˌcruiser**; '**battle cry**; '**battle**
fa ˌtigue; ˌ**battle 'royal**
battleax, battleax|e 'bæt ᵊl æks ‖ 'bæt- **~es**
ɪz əz
battledore 'bæt ᵊl dɔː ‖ 'bæt ᵊl dɔːr -door **~s** z
battledress 'bæt ᵊl dres ‖ 'bæt-
battlefield, B~ 'bæt ᵊl fiːᵊld ‖ 'bæt- **~s** z
battlefront 'bæt ᵊl frʌnt ‖ 'bæt- **~s** s
battleground 'bæt ᵊl graʊnd ‖ 'bæt- **~s** z
battlement 'bæt ᵊl mənt ‖ 'bæt- **~ed** ɪd əd **~s**
s
battleship 'bæt ᵊl ʃɪp ‖ 'bæt- **~s** s
ˌ**battleship 'grey**
battue bæ 'tuː -'tjuː —*Fr* [ba ty]
batt|y 'bæt |i ‖ 'bæt |i **~ier** i ə ‖ i ᵊr **~iest** i ɪst
i ˌəst **~iness** i nəs -nɪs
Batty, Battye 'bæt i ‖ 'bæt i
batwing 'bæt wɪŋ **~s** z
bauble 'bɔːb ᵊl ‖ 'baːb- **~s** z
Baucis 'bɔːs ɪs §-əs ‖ 'baːs-
baud bɔːd bəʊd ‖ baːd
Baudelaire 'bəʊd ə leə -ᵊl eə, ˌ··'·
‖ ˌboʊd ᵊl 'eᵊr —*Fr* [bod lɛːʁ]
Bauer 'baʊ ə ‖ 'baʊ ᵊr —*Ger* ['bau ɐ]
Baugh bɔː ‖ baː
Baughan (i) bɔːn ‖ baːn, (ii) 'bɒf ᵊn ‖ 'baːf-
'bɔːf-
Bauhaus 'baʊ haʊs —*Ger* ['bau haus]
bauhinia bəʊ 'hɪn i ə bɔː- ‖ bɔː- baː-
Baulch bɒlʃ ‖ baːlʃ bɔːlʃ
baulk bɔːk bɔːlk ‖ baːk **baulked** bɔːkt bɔːlkt
‖ baːkt **baulking** 'bɔːk ɪŋ 'bɔːlk- ‖ 'baːk-
baulks bɔːks bɔːlks ‖ baːks
Baum baʊm —*as an American family name,
also* baːm, bɔːm
Baumé 'bəʊm eɪ ‖ boʊ 'meɪ —*Fr* [bo me]
bauxite 'bɔːks aɪt ‖ 'baːks-
Bavari|a bə 'veər i ˌ|ə ‖ -'ver- -'vær- **~an/s**
ən/z
bavarois|e ˌbæv ə 'waːz -aː- ‖ -aːr- **~es** ɪz əz
—*Fr* [ba va ʁwaːz]
Baverstock 'bæv ə stɒk ‖ -ᵊr staːk
Baw Baw 'bɔː bɔː ‖ 'baː baː
bawbee ˌbɔː 'biː 'bɔːb i ‖ 'bɔːb i 'baːb-;
ˌbɔː 'biː;, ˌbaː- **~s** z
bawd bɔːd ‖ baːd **bawds** bɔːdz ‖ baːdz
Bawden 'bɔːd ᵊn ‖ 'baːd-
bawd|y 'bɔːd |i ‖ 'baːd- **~ier** i ə ‖ i ᵊr **~iest**
i ɪst i ˌəst **~ily** ɪ li əl i **~iness** i nəs i nɪs

bawdyhouse 'bɔːd i haʊs ‖ 'baːd-
bawl bɔːl ‖ baːl (= *ball*) **bawled** bɔːld ‖ baːld
bawling 'bɔːl ɪŋ ‖ 'baːl- **bawls** bɔːlz ‖ baːlz
Bawtree, Bawtry 'bɔːtr i ‖ 'baːtr-
Bax bæks
Baxendale 'bæks ᵊn derᵊl
Baxter 'bækst ə ‖ -ᵊr
bay beɪ **bays** beɪz (= *baize*)
'**bay leaf**; ˌ**bay 'rum**; '**Bay Stater**; '**Bay
Street**; '**bay tree**; ˌ**bay 'window**
bayadere ˌbaɪ ə 'dɪə -'deə ‖ 'baɪ ə dɪr
Bayard, b~ 'beɪ aːd -əd ‖ -ᵊrd -aːrd
bayberry 'beɪ ˌber i
Bayer *tdmk* 'beɪ ə ‖ -ᵊr
Bayes beɪz
Bayesian 'beɪz i ˌən ‖ 'beɪʒ ᵊn
Bayeux ˌ₍₎baɪ 'ɜː ˌ₍₎beɪ-, -'jɜː ‖ 'beɪ u 'baɪ- —*Fr*
[ba jø]
Bayh baɪ
Bayley 'beɪl i
Baylis, Bayliss 'beɪl ɪs §-əs
Bayne beɪn
Baynes beɪnz
bay|onet 'beɪ |ən ɪt -ət; -ə net, ˌ··'· ‖ -|ən ət
-ə net, ˌ··'net **~oneted, ~onetted** ən ɪt ɪd
-ət-, -əd; ə net-, ˌ··'· ‖ ən ət əd ə net-, ˌ··'·
~oneting, ~onetting ən ɪt ɪŋ -ət ɪŋ; ə net-,
ˌ··'· ‖ ən ət ɪŋ ə net-, ˌ··'· **~onets** ən ɪts
-əts; ə nets, ˌ··'· ‖ ən əts ə nets, ˌ·· 'nets
Bayonne *place in France* baɪ 'ɒn ‖ -'ɔːn -'oʊn,
-'aːn —*Fr* [ba jɔn]
Bayonne *place in NJ* beɪ 'əʊn ‖ -'oʊn
bayou 'baɪ uː -juː ‖ -oʊ -uː **~s** z
Bayreuth ˌbaɪᵊ 'rɔɪt 'baɪᵊr ɔɪt —*Ger* [baɪ ʁɔyt]
Bayswater 'beɪz ˌwɔːt ə ‖ -ˌwɔːt ᵊr -ˌwaːt-
Baywatch 'beɪ wɒtʃ ‖ -waːtʃ
Baz bæz
bazaar, bazar bə 'zaː ‖ -'zaːr **~s** z
Bazalgette 'bæz ᵊl dʒet
Bazell bə 'zel
bazooka bə 'zuːk ə **~s** z
B-ball 'biː bɔːl ‖ -baːl
BBC ˌbiː biː 'siː ◂ ˌbiːb i-
ˌBBC-'2; ˌBBC ˌWorld 'Service, ˌ···'·, ··
BB gun 'biːb i gʌn **~s** z
BBQ, bbq 'baːb ɪ kjuː -ə- ‖ 'baːrb-
bdellium 'del i ˌəm bə 'del-
be *strong form* biː, *weak form* bi —*For* am, are,
aren't, art, been, being, is, isn't, was, wasn't,
wast, were, weren't, *see separate entries*
be- bi bə *This prefix is always unstressed:*
be'neath, be'friend.
Bea biː
beach biːtʃ **beached** biːtʃt **beaches** 'biːtʃ ɪz
-əz **beaching** 'biːtʃ ɪŋ
'**beach ball**; '**beach ˌbuggy**
beachchair 'biːtʃ tʃeə ‖ -tʃer **~s** z
beachcomber 'biːtʃ ˌkəʊm ə ‖ -ˌkoʊm ᵊr **~s** z
beachfront 'biːtʃ frʌnt
beachhead 'biːtʃ hed **~s** z
Beach-la-Mar, beach-la-mar ˌbiːtʃ lə 'maː
‖ -'maːr
beachwear 'biːtʃ weə ‖ -wer

B

Beachy 'biːtʃ i
　ˌBeachy 'Head
beacon, B~ 'biːk ən ~s z
Beaconsfield *(i)* 'bek ənz fiːᵊld *(ii)* 'biːk-
　—*The place in Bucks is (i); Disraeli's title and
　the places in Tasmania and Canada are (ii)*
bead biːd **beaded** 'biːd ɪd -əd **beading/s**
　'biːd ɪŋ/z **beads** biːdz
beadi... —*see* **beady**
beadle, B~ 'biːd ᵊl ~s z
beadwork 'biːd wɜːk ‖ -wɝːk
bead|y 'biːd |i ~ier iˌə ‖ iˌᵊr ~iest iˌɪst iˌəst
　~ily ɪ li əl i ~iness i nəs -nɪs
beady-eyed ˌbiːd i 'aɪd ◂
beagle 'biːg ᵊl ~s z **beagling** 'biːg ᵊlˌɪŋ
beak biːk **beaked** biːkt **beaks** biːks
Beaken 'biːk ən
beaker 'biːk ə ‖ -ᵊr ~s z
　'Beaker Folk
beakerful 'biːk ə fʊl ‖ -ᵊr-
beaklike 'biːk laɪk
Beal, Beale biːᵊl
be-all and end-all ˌbiː ɔːl ən 'end ɔːl -ənd'-‑
　‖ -ɑːl ən 'end ɑːl
beam biːm **beamed** biːmd **beaming** 'biːm ɪŋ
　beams biːmz
beam-ends ˌbiːm 'endz
Beamer 'biːm ə ‖ -ᵊr ~s z
Beaminster 'bem ɪnˈst ə ‖ -ᵊr —*There is also a
　spelling pronunciation* 'biːm-
Beamish 'biːm ɪʃ
bean, Bean biːn **beans** biːnz
　'bean curd
beanbag 'biːn bæg →'biːm- ~s z
beanfeast 'biːn fiːst ~s s
beanie 'biːn i ~s z
　'beanie ˌbaby
beano, Beano 'biːn əʊ ‖ -oʊ ~s z
beanpole 'biːn pəʊl →'biːm-, →-pɒʊl ‖ -poʊl
　~s z
beanshoot 'biːn ʃuːt ~s s
beansprout 'biːn spraʊt ~s s
beanstalk 'biːn stɔːk ‖ -stɑːk ~s s
bear *n, v* beə ‖ beᵊr bæᵊr (= *bare*) **bearing**
　'beər ɪŋ ‖ 'ber ɪŋ 'bær- **bears** beəz ‖ beᵊrz
　bæᵊrz **bore** bɔː ‖ bɔːr boʊr **borne** bɔːn
　‖ bɔːrn boʊrn
　'bear ˌgarden; 'bear hug; 'bear ˌmarket;
　ˌbear 'up
bearab|le 'beər əb |ᵊl ‖ 'ber- 'bær- ~ly li
bear-baiting 'beə ˌbeɪt ɪŋ ‖ 'ber ˌbeɪt ɪŋ 'bær-
beard, Beard bɪəd ‖ bɪᵊrd **bearded** 'bɪəd ɪd
　-əd ‖ 'bɪrd əd **bearding** 'bɪəd ɪŋ ‖ 'bɪrd ɪŋ
　beards bɪədz ‖ bɪᵊrdz
beardless 'bɪəd ləs -lɪs ‖ 'bɪrd ləs ~ness nəs
　nɪs
Beardsall, Beardsell 'bɪəd sᵊl ‖ 'bɪrd-
Beardsley 'bɪədz li ‖ 'bɪrdz-
Beare bɪə ‖ bɪr —*but* ˌBeare 'Green *in Surrey is*
　beə
bearer 'beər ə ‖ 'ber ᵊr ~s z
bearhug 'beə hʌg ‖ 'ber- ~s z
bearing 'beər ɪŋ ‖ 'ber ɪŋ 'bær- ~s z

bearish 'beər ɪʃ ‖ 'ber ɪʃ 'bær- ~ly li ~ness
　nəs nɪs
bearnaise, béarnaise, B~ ˌbeɪ ə 'neɪz ◂ -ɑː-,
　-'nez ‖ 'beɪ ᵊr neɪz -ɑːr- —*Fr* [be aʁ nɛːz]
Bearsden ⑴beəz 'den ‖ ⑴berz-
bearskin 'beə skɪn ‖ 'ber- ~s z
Bearsted *(i)* 'bɜː sted ‖ 'bɝː-, *(ii)* 'beə- ‖ 'ber-
Beasant 'bez ᵊnt
beast biːst **beasts** biːsts
　ˌbeast of 'burden
beastie 'biːst i ~s z
beast|ly 'biːst |li ~liness li nəs -nɪs
beat biːt **beaten** 'biːt ᵊn **beating** 'biːt ɪŋ
　‖ 'biːt̬ ɪŋ **beats** biːts
beatbox 'biːt bɒks ‖ -bɑːks ~er/s ə/z ‖ ᵊr/z
　~ing ɪŋ
beater 'biːt ə ‖ 'biːt̬ ᵊr ~s z
beatific ˌbiːˌə 'tɪf ɪk ◂ ~ally ᵊl i
beatification bi ˌæt ɪ fɪ 'keɪʃ ᵊn -ˌə-, §-fə'-‑
　‖ -ˌæt̬-
beati|fy bi 'æt ɪ |faɪ -ə- ‖ -'æt̬- ~fied faɪd
　~fies faɪz ~fying faɪ ɪŋ
beating 'biːt ɪŋ ‖ 'biːt̬ ɪŋ ~s z
beatitude, B~ bi 'æt ɪ tjuːd -ə-, →-tʃuːd
　‖ -'æt̬ ə tuːd -tjuːd ~s z
Beatle 'biːt ᵊl ‖ 'biːt̬ ᵊl (= *beetle*) ~s z
beatnik 'biːt nɪk ~s s
Beaton 'biːt ᵊn
Beatrice 'bɪətr ɪs -əs ‖ 'biː ətr əs —*also, in
　imitated Italian,* ˌbeɪ ə 'triːtʃ eɪ, -ɑː-, -i
　—*Italian* [be a 'triː tʃe]
Beatrix 'bɪətr ɪks ‖ 'biː ə trɪks
Beattie 'biːt i ‖ 'biːt̬ i
Beattock 'biːt ək ‖ 'biːt̬ ək
Beatty *(i)* 'biːt i ‖ 'biːt̬ i, *(ii)* 'beɪt i ‖ 'beɪt̬ i
　—*The film actor Warren B~ is (ii)*
beat-up 'biːt ʌp ‖ 'biːt̬-
beau bəʊ ‖ boʊ —*Fr* [bo] **beaus, beaux** bəʊz
　bəʊ ‖ boʊz —*See also phrases with this word*
Beaucaire ˌbəʊ 'keə ‖ ˌboʊ 'keᵊr
Beauchamp 'biːtʃ əm
Beauclerk 'bəʊ kleə ·ˈ· ‖ 'boʊ klɜːk
beaucoup 'bəʊ kuː ˌ·ˈ· ◂ ‖ 'boʊ- —*Fr* [bo ku]
Beaufort *(i)* 'bəʊ fət -fɔːt ‖ 'boʊ fᵊrt, *(ii)* 'bjuː-
　—*The British dukedom, the personal and
　family name, the places in NC and Australia,
　the Arctic sea, and the wind scale are (i); the
　place in SC is (ii).*
　'Beaufort scale; ˌBeaufort 'Sea
beau geste ˌbəʊ 'ʒest ‖ ˌboʊ- —*Fr* [bo ʒɛst]
Beaujolais 'bəʊʒ ə leɪ -ɒ- ‖ ˌboʊʒ ə 'leɪ —*Fr*
　[bo ʒɔ lɛ]
　ˌBeaujolais nou'veau nu 'vəʊ ‖ -'voʊ —*Fr*
　[nu vo]
Beaulieu 'bjuːl i *(!)*
Beauly 'bjuːl i
Beaumaris bəʊ 'mær ɪs bjuː:-, §-əs ‖ boʊ-
　-'mer-
beau monde ˌbəʊ 'mɒnd ‖ ˌboʊ 'mɔːnd
　-'mɑːnd —*Fr* [bo mɔ̃ːd]
Beaumont 'bəʊ mənt -mɒnt ‖ 'boʊ mɑːnt ˌ·ˈ·
　—*but the place in Cumbria is* 'biː-
Beaune bəʊn ‖ boʊn —*Fr* [boːn]

beaut bjuːt **beauts** bjuːts
beauteous ˈbjuːt i ˌəs ‖ ˈbjuːt̬- **~ly** li
beautician bjuː ˈtɪʃ ᵊn **~s** z
beauties ˈbjuːt iz ‖ ˈbjuːt̬ iz
beautifi... —*see* **beautify**
beautification ˌbjuːt ɪf ɪ ˈkeɪʃ ᵊn ˌ-əf-, §-ə'-- ‖ ˌbjuːt̬-
beautiful ˈbjuːt əf ᵊl -ɪf-; -ɪ fʊl, -ə- ‖ ˈbjuːt̬-
beautifully ˈbjuːt əf li -ɪf-; -ɪ fʊl i, -ə fʊl i ‖ ˈbjuːt̬-
beauti|fy ˈbjuːt ɪ |faɪ -ə- ‖ ˈbjuːt̬- **~fied** faɪd **~fies** faɪz **~fying** faɪ ɪŋ
beauty ˈbjuːt i ‖ ˈbjuːt̬ i **beauties** ˈbjuːt iz ‖ ˈbjuːt̬ iz
   ˈbeauty ˌcontest; ˈbeauty ˌparlour; ˈbeauty queen; ˈbeauty ˌsalon ‖ -ˌ·; ˈbeauty sleep; ˈbeauty spot
Beauvais ₍ˌ₎bəʊ ˈveɪ ‖ ₍ˌ₎boʊ- —*Fr* [bo vɛ]
Beauvoir ˈbəʊv wɑː ‖ ˈboʊv ˈwɑːr —*Fr* [bo vwaːʁ]
beaux bəʊz bəʊ ‖ boʊz
beaux-arts ₍ˌ₎bəʊ ˈzɑː ‖ ₍ˌ₎boʊ ˈzɑːr —*Fr* [bo zaːʁ]
Beavan ˈbev ᵊn
beaver, B~ ˈbiːv ə ‖ -ᵊr **~ed** d **beavering** ˈbiːv ᵊr ɪŋ **~s** z
Beaverbrook ˈbiːv ə brʊk ‖ -ᵊr-
Beavis ˈbiːv ɪs §-əs
Beazley ˈbiːz li
Bebb beb
Bebbington, Bebington ˈbeb ɪŋ tən
Bebo ˈbiː bəʊ ‖ -boʊ
bebop ˈbiː bɒp ‖ -bɑːp
bebopper ˈbiː bɒp ə ‖ -bɑːp ᵊr **~s** z
becalm bɪ ˈkɑːm bə-, -ˈkɑːlm, §-ˈkɒlm **~ed** d **~ing** ɪŋ **~s** z
became bɪ ˈkeɪm bə-

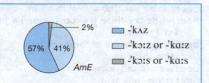

BECAUSE

2%
57% 41%
■ -ˈkʌz
■ -ˈkɔːz or -ˈkɑːz
■ -ˈkɔːs or -ˈkɑːs
AmE

because bɪ ˈkɒz bə-, -ˈkəz, -ˈkəz, §-ˈkɔːz, §-ˈkɒs, §-ˈkɔːs ‖ -ˈkʌz -ˈkɔːz, -ˈkɑːz, -ˈkəz, -kəz —*Many speakers use* bɪ kəz *(or* bə kəz*) as the weak form,* bɪ ˈkɒz ‖ -ˈkɔːz *(etc.) as the strong form. Some, though, also use an irregular strong form* bɪ ˈkəz, bə ˈkəz. *There are also casual variants* kɒz, kəz *(etc.) —see* **cos.**
— *Preference poll, AmE:* -ˈkʌz 57%, -ˈkɔːz or -ˈkɑːz 41%, -ˈkɔːs or -ˈkɑːs 2%.
Beccles ˈbek ᵊlz
bechamel, béchamel ˌbeɪʃ ə ˈmel ◂ —*Fr* [be ʃa mɛl]
beche-de-mer, bêche-de-mer ˌbeʃ də ˈmeə ˌbeɪʃ- ‖ -ˈmeᵊr —*This is not a true French expression.*
Becher's ˈbiːtʃ əz ‖ -ᵊrz

Bechet ˈbeʃ eɪ
Bechstein ˈbek staɪn
Bechtel ˈbekt el
Bechuana ˌbetʃ u ˈɑːn ə △ˌbek ju- **~land** lænd
beck, Beck bek **becks** beks
Beckenbauer ˈbek ᵊn baʊ ə ‖ -baʊ ᵊr —*Ger* [ˈbɛk ᵊn bau ɐ]
Beckenham ˈbek ᵊn ᵊm
Becker ˈbek ə ‖ -ᵊr —*Ger* [ˈbɛk ɐ]
Becket, Beckett ˈbek ɪt §-ət
Beckford ˈbek fəd ‖ -fᵊrd
Beckham ˈbek əm
Beckinsale ˈbek ɪn seɪᵊl §-ən-
Beckmann ˈbek mən —*Ger* [ˈbɛk man]
beckon ˈbek ən **~ed** d **~ing/ly** ɪŋ /li **~s** z
Beckton ˈbekt ən
Beckwith ˈbek wɪθ
Becky ˈbek i
becloud bɪ ˈklaʊd bə- **~ed** ɪd əd **~ing** ɪŋ **~s** z
be|come bɪ |ˈkʌm bə- **~came** ˈkeɪm **~comes** ˈkʌmz **~coming** ˈkʌm ɪŋ
becoming bɪ ˈkʌm ɪŋ bə- **~ly** li
Becontree ˈbek ən triː ‖ ˈbiːk-
Becquerel, b~ ˈbek ᵊr ᵊl ˌbek ə ˈrel —*Fr* [bɛ kʁɛl] **~s** z
Becton ˈbekt ən
bed bed **bedded** ˈbed ɪd -əd **bedding** ˈbed ɪŋ **beds** bedz
   ˌbed and ˈbreakfast; ˈbed ˌlinen
BEd ˌbiː ˈed
bedad bɪ ˈdæd bə-
Bedale *place in NYks* ˈbiːd ᵊl ˈbiː deɪᵊl
Bedales ˈbiː deɪᵊlz
bedaub bɪ ˈdɔːb bə- ‖ -ˈdɑːb **~ed** d **~ing** ɪŋ **~s** z
bedazzl|e bɪ ˈdæz ᵊl bə- **~ed** d **~es** z **~ing** ɪŋ
bedblock|er ˈbed ˌblɒk ə ‖ -ˌblɑːk ᵊr **~ers** əz ‖ ᵊrz **~ing** ɪŋ
bedbug ˈbed bʌg →ˈbeb- **~s** z
bedchamber ˈbed ˌtʃeɪm bə ‖ -bᵊr **~s** z
bedclothes ˈbed kləʊðz -kləʊz ‖ -kloʊðz -kloʊz
bedd... —*see* **bed**
beddable ˈbed əb ᵊl
Beddau ˈbeð aɪ —*Welsh* [ˈbe ðai, -ðe]
bedder ˈbed ə ‖ -ᵊr **~s** z
Beddgelert beð ˈgel ət bed-, beɪð- ‖ -ᵊrt —*Welsh* [ˌbeːð ˈge lert]
bedding, B~ ˈbed ɪŋ
   ˈbedding plant
Beddoes, Beddowes, Beddows ˈbed əʊz ‖ -oʊz
beddy-bye ˈbed i baɪ **~s** z
Bede biːd
bedeck bɪ ˈdek bə- **~ed** t **~ing** ɪŋ **~s** s
bedel, bedell ˈbiːd ᵊl **~s** z
Bedevere ˈbed ə vɪə -ɪ- ‖ -vɪr
bedevil bɪ ˈdev ᵊl bə- **~ed, ~led** d **~ing, ~ling** ɪŋ **~ment** mənt **~s** z
bedew bɪ ˈdjuː bə-, →-ˈdʒuː ‖ -ˈduː -ˈdjuː **~ed** d **~ing** ɪŋ **~s** z
bedfellow ˈbed ˌfel əʊ ‖ -oʊ **~s** z
Bedford ˈbed fəd ‖ -fᵊrd

B

Bedfordshire 'bed fəd ʃə -ʃɪə ‖ -fᵊrd ʃᵊr -ʃɪr
bedhead 'bed hed ~s z
bedim bɪ 'dɪm bə- ~med d ~ming ɪŋ ~s z
Bedivere 'bed ə vɪə -ɪ- ‖ -vɪr
bedizen bɪ 'daɪz ᵊn bə-, -'dɪz- ~ed d ~ing ɪŋ ~s z
bedjacket 'bed ˌdʒæk ɪt §-ət ~s s
bedlam 'bed ləm
bedlinen 'bed ˌlɪn ɪn §-ən
Bedlington 'bed lɪŋ tən
bedmaker 'bed ˌmeɪk ə →'beb- ‖ -ᵊr ~s z
bedouin, B~ 'bed u ɪn -æ, -ən ~s z
bedpan 'bed pæn →'beb- ~s z
bedpost 'bed pəʊst →'beb- ‖ -poʊst ~s s
bedraggl|e bɪ 'dræg ᵊl bə- ~ed d ~es z ~ing ɪŋ
bedridden 'bed ˌrɪd ᵊn
bedrock 'bed rɒk ‖ -rɑːk
bedroll 'bed rəʊl →-rɒʊl ‖ -roʊl ~s z

BEDROOM

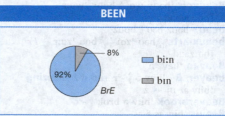

BrE

bedroom 'bedr uːm 'bedr ʊm, 'bed ruːm, -rʊm
— Preference poll, BrE: -uː- 63%, -ʊ- 37%. ~s z
ˌbedroom 'slippers
Bedruthan bɪ 'drʌð ᵊn bə-
Beds bedz —see also **Bedfordshire**
bedside 'bed saɪd
ˌbedside 'manner
bedsit, bed-sit ˌbed 'sɪt ' · · ~s s
bedsitter, bed-sitter ˌbed 'sɪt ə ‖ -'sɪt ᵊr ~s z
bed-sitting room ˌbed 'sɪt ɪŋ ruːm -rʊm
‖ -'sɪt- ~s z
bedsock 'bed sɒk ‖ -sɑːk ~s s
bedsore 'bed sɔː ‖ -sɔːr -soʊr ~s z
bedspread 'bed spred ~s z
bedspring 'bed sprɪŋ ~s z
bedstead 'bed sted ~s z
bedstraw 'bed strɔː ‖ -strɑː ~s z
bedtime 'bed taɪm ~s z
ˌbedtime 'story
Bedwell 'bed wəl -wel
Bedwellty bed 'welt i -'weɫt- —Welsh
[bed 'weɫ ti]
bed-wett|er 'bed ˌwet| ə ‖ -ˌweţ| ᵊr ~ers əz
‖ ᵊrz ~ing ɪŋ
bee biː ~s **bees, bee's** biːz
ˌbee's 'knees; 'bee sting
Beeb biːb
beech, Beech biːtʃ (= beach) **beeches** 'biːtʃ ɪz -əz
Beecham 'biːtʃ əm
Beecher 'biːtʃ ə ‖ -ᵊr
Beeching 'biːtʃ ɪŋ
beechnut 'biːtʃ nʌt ~s s

beechwood 'biːtʃ wʊd
bee-eater 'biː ˌiːt ə ‖ -ˌiːţ ᵊr ~s z
beef biːf **beefed** biːft **beefing** 'biːf ɪŋ **beefs** biːfs **beeves** biːvz
ˌbeef 'tea
beefburger 'biːf ˌbɜːg ə ‖ -ˌbɜːg ᵊr ~s z
beefcake 'biːf keɪk
beefeater 'biːf ˌiːt ə ‖ -ˌiːţ ᵊr ~s z
beefi... —see **beefy**
beefsteak 'biːf steɪk ~s s
beefwood 'biːf wʊd
beef|y 'biːf |i ~ier i ə ‖ i ᵊr ~iest i ɪst i əst
Bee Gee 'biː dʒiː ~s z
beehive 'biː haɪv ~s z
beekeep|er 'biː ˌkiːp ə ‖ -ᵊr ~ers əz ‖ ᵊrz ~ing ɪŋ
beeline 'biː laɪn
Beelzebub bɪ 'elz ɪ bʌb -ə-

BEEN

8% ▮ biːn
92% ▮ bɪn

BrE

been biːn bɪn ‖ bɪn —Some BrE speakers have biːn as strong form, bɪn as weak form.
— Preference poll, BrE (for strong form): biːn 92%, bɪn 8%.
beep biːp **beeped** biːpt **beeping** 'biːp ɪŋ **beeps** biːps
beeper 'biːp ə ‖ -ᵊr ~s z
beer, Beer bɪə ‖ bɪᵊr ~ed bɪəd ‖ bɪᵊrd **beers** bɪəz ‖ bɪᵊrz
Beerbohm 'bɪə bəʊm ‖ 'bɪr boʊm
beeri... —see **beery**
Beersheba bɪə 'ʃiːb ə 'bɪəʃ ɪb ə ‖ bɪr-
beer|y, Beery 'bɪər |i ‖ 'bɪr |i ~ier i ə ‖ i ᵊr ~iest i ɪst i əst
beestings 'colostrum' 'biːst ɪŋz
Beeston 'biːst ən
beeswax 'biːz wæks
beeswing 'biːz wɪŋ
beet biːt (= beat) **beets** biːts
Beethoven 'beɪt həʊv ᵊn -əʊv- ‖ 'beɪt oʊv ᵊn —Ger ['beːt hoː fᵊn] ~'s z
beetl|e 'biːt ᵊl ‖ 'biːţ ᵊl ~ed d ~es z ~ing ɪŋ
Beeton 'biːt ᵊn
beetroot 'biːtr uːt 'biːt ruːt ~s s
beeves biːvz
beezer 'biːz ə ‖ -ᵊr
befall bɪ 'fɔːl bə- ‖ -'fɑːl ~en ən ~ing ɪŋ ~s z
befell bɪ 'fel bə-
be|fit bɪ |'fɪt bə- ~fits 'fɪts ~fitted 'fɪt ɪd -əd ‖ 'fɪţ əd ~fitting/ly 'fɪt ɪŋ /li ‖ 'fɪţ ɪŋ /li
befog bɪ 'fɒg bə- ‖ -'fɔːg -'fɑːg ~ged d ~ging ɪŋ ~s z
before bɪ 'fɔː bə- ‖ -'fɔːr -'foʊr
beforehand bɪ 'fɔː hænd bə- ‖ -'fɔːr- -'foʊr-
befoul bɪ 'faʊl bə- ~ed d ~ing ɪŋ ~s z

befriend bi 'frend bə- ~**ed** ɪd əd ~**ing** ɪŋ ~**s** z

befuddl|e bi 'fʌd ᵊl bə- ~**ed** d ~**ement** mənt ~**es** z ~**ing** ɪŋ

beg beg **begged** begd **begging** 'beg ɪŋ **begs** begz

begad bi 'gæd bə-

began bi 'gæn bə-

be|get bi |'get bə- ~**gat/s** gæt/s ~**gets** 'gets ~**getting** 'get ɪŋ ‖ 'geṭ ɪŋ ~**got** 'gɒt ‖ 'gɑːt ~**gotten** 'gɒt ᵊn ‖ 'gɑːt ᵊn

begetter bi 'get ə bə- ‖ -'geṭ ᵊr ~**s** z

beggar 'beg ə ‖ -ᵊr ~**ed** d **beggaring** 'beg ər ɪŋ ~**s** z

beggar|ly 'beg ə |li -ᵊl i ‖ -ᵊr- ~**liness** li nəs -nɪs

beggar-my-neighb|our, ~or ‚beg ə mi 'neɪb ə -maɪ'- ‖ ‚beg ᵊr maɪ 'neɪb ᵊr

beggary 'beg ər i

be|gin bi |'gɪn bə- ~**gan** 'gæn ~**ginning** 'gɪn ɪŋ ~**gins** 'gɪnz ~**gun** 'gʌn

Begin *Israeli name* 'beɪg ɪn 'beg-

beginner bi 'gɪn ə bə- ‖ -ᵊr ~**s** z be‚ginner's 'luck

beginning bi 'gɪn ɪŋ bə- ~**s** z

begone bi 'gɒn bə-, §-'gɑːn, §-'gɔːn ‖ -'gɔːn -'gɑːn

begonia bi 'gəʊn i ə bə- ‖ -'goʊn jə ~**s** z

begorra bi 'gɒr ə bə- ‖ -'gɔːr- -'gɑːr-

begot bi 'gɒt bə- ‖ -'gɑːt ~**ten** ᵊn

begrim|e bi 'graɪm bə- ~**ed** d ~**es** z ~**ing** ɪŋ

begrudg|e bi 'grʌdʒ bə- ~**ed** d ~**es** ɪz əz ~**ing/ly** ɪŋ /li

beguil|e bi 'gaɪᵊl bə- ~**ed** d ~**es** z ~**ing/ly** ɪŋ /li

beguine *'dance', 'music'* bi 'giːn bə- ~**s** z

Beguine *'member of sisterhood'* 'beg iːn 'beɪg-; bi 'giːn, bə-, ‚beɪ- ~**s** z

begum, Begum 'beɪg əm 'biːg- ~**s** z

begun bi 'gʌn bə-

behalf bi 'hɑːf bə- ‖ -'hæf

Behan 'biː ən

behav|e bi 'heɪv bə- ~**ed** d ~**es** z ~**ing** ɪŋ

behavior, behaviour bi 'heɪv jə bə- ‖ -jᵊr ~**s** z be'havio(u)r ‚pattern; be'havio(u)r ‚therapy

behavior|al, behaviour~ bɪ 'heɪv jər əl ~**ism** ‚ɪz əm ~**ist/s** ɪst/s §əst/s ~**ly** i

behavio|ristic, behaviou~ bi ‚heɪv jə 'rɪst ɪk ◄ bə-

behead bi 'hed bə- ~**ed** ɪd əd ~**ing** ɪŋ ~**s** z

beheld bi 'held bə-

behemoth, B~ bi 'hiːm ɒθ bə-, -əθ ‖ -ɑːθ -əθ

behest bi 'hest bə-

behind bi 'haɪnd bə- ~**s** z

behindhand bi 'haɪnd hænd bə-

Behn ben

behold bi 'həʊld bə-, →-'hɒʊld ‖ -'hoʊld ~**ing** ɪŋ ~**s** z

beholden bɪ 'həʊld ən bə-, §biː-, →-'hɒʊld- ‖ -'hoʊld-

beholder bi 'həʊld ə bə-, →'hɒʊld- ‖ -'hoʊld ᵊr ~**s** z

behoov|e bi 'huːv bə- ~**ed** d ~**es** z ~**ing** ɪŋ

behov|e bi 'həʊv bə- ‖ -'hoʊv ~**ed** d ~**es** z ~**ing** ɪŋ

Behrens 'beər ənz ‖ 'ber- —*Ger* ['beːʁ əns]

Beiderbecke 'baɪd ə bek ‖ -ᵊr-

beige beɪʒ beɪdʒ

Beighton *(i)* 'beɪt ᵊn, *(ii)* 'baɪt ᵊn

beignet 'beɪn jeɪ ‚·'· —*Fr* [bɛ njɛ] ~**s** z

Beijing ‚beɪ 'dʒɪŋ -'ʒɪŋ —*Note: there is no justification in Chinese for the* -'ʒɪŋ *pronunciation frequently heard in English.* —*Chi* Běijīng [³peɪ ¹tɕɪŋ]

being 'biː ɪŋ ~**s** z

Beinn *in ScGaelic names* ben

Beira 'baɪᵊr ə ‖ 'beɪ rə —*Port* ['bɐi ɾɐ]

Beirut ‚beɪ 'ruːt ◄ ‚beə- —*Arabic* [bej 'ruːt]

Beit baɪt

Beith biːθ —*but the place in Strathclyde is* biːð

bejeweled, bejewelled bi 'dʒuː‚ əld bə-, -'dʒuːld

Bekaa, Beqaa be 'kɑː —*Arabic* [bɛ 'qɑːʕ]

Bekonscot 'bek ənz kɒt ‖ -kɑːt

bel, Bel bel *(= bell)* —*It* [bɛl] **bels** belz ‚bel 'canto 'kænt əʊ ‖ 'kɑːnt oʊ —*It* ['kan to]; ‚Bel Pa'ese paɪ 'eɪz i paː- —*It* [pa 'e: ze]

belabor, belabour bi 'leɪb ə bə- ‖ -ᵊr ~**ed** d **belaboring, belabouring** bɪ 'leɪb ər ɪŋ ~**s** z

Belafonte ‚bel ə 'fɒnt i ‖ -'fɑːnṭ i -eɪ

Belarius bi 'leər i əs bə-, -'lɑːr- ‖ -'ler- -'lær-

Belarus ‚bel ə 'ruːs —*Belorussian* [‚bʲe ła 'rus], *Russian* [‚bʲe łə 'rus] ~**ian/s** i ᵊn/z

belated bi 'leɪt ɪd bə-, -əd ‖ -'leɪṭ- ~**ly** li ~**ness** nəs nɪs

Belau bə 'laʊ bi-, be-; 'bel aʊ

belay bi 'leɪ bə- ~**ed** d ~**ing** ɪŋ ~**s** z be'laying pin

belch, Belch beltʃ **belched** beltʃt **belching** 'beltʃ ɪŋ **belches** 'beltʃ ɪz -əz

Belcher 'beltʃ ə 'belʃ- ‖ -ᵊr

beldam, beldame 'beld əm 'bel dæm, -dɑːm

beleagu|er bi 'liːg |ə bə- ‖ -|ᵊr ~**ered** əd ‖ ᵊrd ~**ering** ər ɪŋ ~**ers** əz ‖ ᵊrz

Belem be 'lem bə- —*Port* [bə 'lẽi, be 'lẽi]

belemnite 'bel əm naɪt ~**s** z

Belfast ‚bel 'fɑːst ◄ '· ·, §-'fæst ‖ 'bel fæst ‚·'·

belf|ry 'belf |ri ~**ries** riz

Belgae 'belg aɪ 'beldʒ iː

Belgian 'beldʒ ən ~**s** z

Belgic 'beldʒ ɪk

Belgium 'beldʒ əm

Belgrade ‚bel 'greɪd ‖ '· ·

Belgrano bel 'grɑːn əʊ ‖ -oʊ —*Sp* [bel 'ɣra no]

Belgrave 'bel greɪv ‚Belgrave 'Square

Belgravia bel 'greɪv i ə

Belial 'biːl i əl

be|lie bi |'laɪ bə- ~**lied** 'laɪd ~**lies** 'laɪz ~**lying** 'laɪ ɪŋ

B

belief bi 'liːf bə- ~s s
believab|le bi 'liːv əb |ᵊl bə- ~ly li
believ|e bi 'liːv bə- ~er/s ə/z ‖ ᵊr/z ~ed d ~es
z ~ing ıŋ
Belinda bə 'lınd ə bi-
Belisarius ˌbel ı 'saːr i̯ əs ˌ-ə-, -'seər- ‖ -'ser-
Belisha bə 'liːʃ ə bi-
Beˌlisha 'beacon
belittl|e bi 'lıt ᵊl bə- ‖ -'lıt̬- ~ed d ~es z ~ing
ıŋ
Belize bi 'liːz bə-, be-
Belizean bı 'liːz i̯ ən bə-, be-, -'lız- ~s z
bell, Bell bel belled beld belling 'bel ıŋ
bells belz
'bell jar; ˌBell 'Rock; 'bell tent
Bella 'bel ə
ˌBella 'Coola 'kuːl ə
belladonna ˌbel ə 'dɒn ə ‖ -'daːn-
Bellamy 'bel əm i
bellbird, B~ 'bel bɜːd ‖ -bɜːd ~s z
bell-bottom 'bel ˌbɒt əm ‖ -ˌbaːt̬ əm ~s z
bellboy 'bel bɔı ~s z
belle, Belle bel (= bell) belles belz
ˌbelle é'poque eı 'pɒk ‖ -'pɔːk -'paːk —Fr
[bɛ le pɔk]; ˌBelle 'Fourche river in US fuːʃ
Belleek bə 'liːk bı-
Bellenden Ker ˌbel ənd ən 'kɜː ‖ -'kɜː
Bellerophon bə 'ler əf ən bı-
belles-lettres ˌbel 'letr ə —Fr [bɛl lɛtχ]
Belleville 'bel vıl
Bellevue ˌbel 'vjuː ‖ 'bel vjuː
Bellew 'bel juː
bellflower, B~ 'bel ˌflaʊ ə ‖ -ˌflaʊ ᵊr ~s z
bellhop 'bel hɒp ‖ -haːp ~s s
bellicose 'bel ı kəʊs -ə-, -kəʊz ‖ -koʊs ~ly li
~ness nəs nıs
bellicosity ˌbel ı 'kɒs ət i ˌ-ə-, -ıt i ‖ -'kaːs ət̬ i
bellie... —see belly
belligerenc|e bə 'lıdʒ ᵊr ᵊn⁀s bı- ~y i
belligerent bə 'lıdʒ ᵊr ᵊnt bı-
Belling 'bel ıŋ
Bellingham (i) 'bel ıŋ əm -həm, (ii) -ındʒ əm,
(iii) -ıŋ hæm —The place in Greater London
is (i), that in Northumberland (ii), and that in
Washington State (iii). The family name may
be any of the three.
Bellingshausen 'bel ıŋz ˌhaʊz ᵊn
Bellini be 'liːn i bə- —It [bel 'liː ni]
bell|man 'bel |mən ~men mən men
Bellmawr ⁽ˌ⁾bel 'mɔː ‖ ⁽ˌ⁾bel 'maːr -'cmɔːr
Belloc 'bel ɒk -ək ‖ -aːk
Bellona be 'ləʊn ə ‖ -'loʊn-
bellow, B~ 'bel əʊ ‖ -oʊ ~ed d ~ing ıŋ ~s z
Bellows 'bel əʊz ‖ -oʊz
bellpull 'bel pʊl ~s z
bellring|er 'bel ˌrıŋ ə ‖ -ᵊr ~ers əz ‖ ᵊrz ~ing
ıŋ
bellwether 'bel ˌweð ə ˌ·'·· ‖ -ᵊr ~s z
bell|y 'bel |i ~ied id ~ies iz ~ying i̯ ıŋ
'belly ˌbutton; 'belly flop; 'belly laugh
bellyach|e 'bel i eık ~ed t ~es s ~ing ıŋ
belly-danc|e 'bel i daːn⁀s §-dæn⁀s ‖ -dæn⁀s
~er/s ə/z ‖ ᵊr/z ~ing ıŋ

bellyful 'bel i fʊl
belly-landing 'bel i ˌlænd ıŋ ~s z
Belmondo bel 'mɒnd əʊ ‖ -'maːnd oʊ —Fr
[bɛl mɔ̃ do]
Belmont 'bel mɒnt -mənt ‖ -maːnt
Belmopan ˌbelm əʊ 'pæn ‖ -oʊ-
Belmore 'bel mɔː ‖ -mɔːr -moʊr
Beloff 'bel ɒf ‖ -aːf
Belo Horizonte ˌbel əʊ ˌhɒr ı 'zɒnt i ˌbeıl-,
-ə'··-, -eı ‖ -oʊ ˌhɔːr ə 'zaːnt i —Port
[ˌbɛ lo ɾi 'zon ti]
belong bi 'lɒŋ bə- ‖ -'lɔːŋ -'laːŋ ~ed d ~ing/s
ıŋ/z ~s z
Belorussia ˌbel əʊ 'rʌʃ ə bi ˌel-, -'ruːs i̯ ə
Belorussian ˌbel əʊ 'rʌʃ ᵊn bi ˌel-, -'ruːs i̯ ən ~s
z
beloved bi 'lʌv ıd bə-, -əd, -'lʌvd —but
predicatively always -'lʌvd
below bi 'ləʊ bə- ‖ -'loʊ
Belper 'belp ə ‖ -ᵊr
Belsen 'bels ᵊn —Ger ['bɛl zᵊn]
Belshazzar bel 'ʃæz ə ‖ -ᵊr
Belsize 'bel saız
ˌBelsize 'Park
Belstead 'bel stıd -sted, §-stəd
belt belt belted 'belt ıd -əd belting 'belt ıŋ
belts belts
'belt drive
Beltane 'belt eın -ən
beltway 'belt weı ~s z
beluga bə 'luːg ə bi-, be- ~s z
Belushi bə 'luːʃ i
belvedere, B~ 'belv ə dıə -ı-, ˌ·ˑ· ‖ -dır ~s z
Belvoir place in Leics; family name 'biːv ə ‖ -ᵊr
(!)
bem|a 'biːm |ə ~as əz ~ata ət ə ‖ ət̬ ə
Bemba 'bem bə ~s z
Bembo 'bem bəʊ ‖ -boʊ
Bembridge 'bem brıdʒ
bemoan bi 'məʊn bə- ‖ -'moʊn ~ed d ~ing ıŋ
~s z
bemus|e bi 'mjuːz bə- ~ed d ~edly ıd li əd li
~ement mənt ~es ız əz ~ing ıŋ
Ben, ben ben bens benz —See also phrases
with this word
benadryl, B~ tdmk 'ben ə drıl ~s z
Benares bı 'naːr ız bə-, be-, -əz
Benaud 'ben əʊ ‖ -oʊ
Benbecula ben 'bek jʊl ə →bem-
Benbow 'ben bəʊ →'bem- ‖ -boʊ
Bence ben⁀s
bench bentʃ benched bentʃt benches
'bentʃ ız -əz benching 'bentʃ ıŋ
bencher 'bentʃ ə ‖ -ᵊr ~s z
Benchley 'bentʃ li
benchmark 'bentʃ maːk ‖ -maːrk ~ed t ~ing
ıŋ ~s s
benchwarmer 'ben⁀tʃ ˌwɔːm ə ‖ -ˌwɔːrm ᵊr ~s
z
bend bend bended 'bend ıd -əd bending
'bend ıŋ bends bendz bent bent
ˌbend 'over; ˌbend 'sinister
bendable 'bend əb ᵊl

bender 'bend ə ‖ -ᵊr ~s z
Bendigo 'bend ɪ gəʊ -ə- ‖ -goʊ
Bendix 'bend ɪks
bend|y 'bend |i ~ier i ə ‖ i ᵊr ~iest i ɪst i əst
~iness i nəs -nɪs
beneath bi 'ni:θ bə-
Benecol _tdmk_ 'ben ɪ kɒl -ə- ‖ -kɑ:l
Benedicite, b~ ˌben ɪ 'daɪs ət i ˌ·ə-, -'di:tʃ-,
-ɪt i; -ɪ teɪ, -ə teɪ ‖ -ət i ~s z
Benedick, b~ 'ben ɪ dɪk -ə-
Benedict 'ben ɪ dɪkt -ə- —_The former
pronunciation_ 'ben ɪt _is nowadays spelt
correspondingly as_ Bene't _or_ Benet.
benedictine, B~ _'liqueur'_ ˌben ɪ 'dɪkt i:n ◄ -ə-
‖ -dɪk 'ti:n ~s z
Benedictine _'monk'_ ˌben ɪ 'dɪkt ɪn ◄ -ə-, -i:n,
-aɪn ~s z
benediction ˌben ɪ 'dɪkʃ ᵊn -ə- ~s z
Benedictus ˌben ɪ 'dɪkt əs -ə-, -ʊs
benefaction ˌben ɪ 'fæk ʃᵊn -ə- ~s z
benefactive ˌben ɪ 'fækt ɪv -ə-, '···· ~s z
benefactor 'ben ɪ fækt ə '·ə- ‖ -ᵊr ~s z
benefactress 'ben ɪ fæk trəs '·ə-, -trəs, ˌ·'··
~es ɪz əz
benefice 'ben ɪf ɪs -əf-, §-əs ~ed t ~s ɪz əz
beneficence bə 'nef ɪs ᵊn̩ts bɪ-, -əs-
beneficent bə 'nef ɪs ᵊnt bɪ-, -əs- ~ly li
beneficial ˌben ɪ 'fɪʃ ᵊl ◄ -ə- ~ly ˌi ~ness nəs
nɪs
beneficiar|y ˌben ɪ 'fɪʃ ər ˌi ˌ·ə-, -'fɪʃ i ər ˌi
‖ -'fɪʃ i er ˌi -'·ər ˌi ~ies iz
bene|fit 'ben ɪ |fɪt -ə-, §-fət ~fited, ~fitted
fɪt ɪd §fət-, -əd ‖ fɪt̬ əd ~fiting, ~fitting fɪt ɪŋ
§fət- ‖ fɪt̬ ɪŋ ~fits fɪts §fəts
Benelux 'ben ɪ lʌks -ə-
the 'Benelux ˌcountries
Benenden 'ben ənd ən —_formerly also_
ˌben ən 'den
Benet, Bene't 'ben ɪt §-ət
Benét _American family name_ bə 'neɪ be-
Benetton _tdmk_ 'ben ɪt ən -ət-; -ɪ tɒn, -ə-
‖ -ə tɑːn
benevolence bə 'nev əl ᵊn̩ts bɪ-
benevolent bə 'nev əl ᵊnt bɪ- ~ly li
Benfica ben 'fi:k ə —_Port_ [bẽ 'fi kɐ]
Benfleet 'ben fli:t
BEng ˌbi: 'endʒ
Bengal ˌben 'gɔ:l ◄ →ˌbeŋ-, -'gɑ:l
Bengali ben 'gɔ:l i →beŋ-, -'gɑ:l-, ˌ·'·· ◄ ~s z
Benghazi ben 'gɑ:z i →beŋ- —_Arabic_
[ˌba ni 'ɣa: zi]
Benguela ben 'gwel ə →beŋ-, -'gweɪl-, -'gel-,
-'geɪl- —_Port_ [beŋ 'gwe lɐ]
Ben Gurion, Ben-Gurion ben 'gʊər i ən
→beŋ- ‖ -'gʊr- ˌben gʊr 'jɑːn, -'jɔːn
Ben Hur, Ben-Hur ˌben 'hɜː ‖ -'hɜːr
Benidorm 'ben ɪ dɔːm -ə- ‖ -dɔːrm
benighted bi 'naɪt ɪd bə-, -əd ‖ -'naɪt̬- ~ly li
~ness nəs nɪs
benign bə 'naɪn bɪ- ~ly li
benignanc|y bə 'nɪg nən̩ts |i bɪ- ~ies ɪz
benignant bə 'nɪg nənt bɪ- ~ly li

benignit|y bə 'nɪg nət |i bi-, -nɪt i ‖ -nət̬ |i
~ies iz
Benin be 'ni:n bɪ-, bə-, -'nɪn
Beninese ˌben ɪ 'ni:z ◄ be ˌni:-, bɪ-, bə-, -ˌnɪ-
benison 'ben ɪz ən -ɪs-, -əz-, -əs- ~s z
Benita be 'ni:t ə bi-, bə- ‖ -'ni:t̬-
Benito be 'ni:t əʊ bi-, bə- ‖ -'ni:t̬ oʊ
Benjamin, b~ 'bendʒ əm ɪn ən
Ben Macdhui ˌben mək 'du: i
Benn ben
benne 'ben i
Bennelong 'ben ə lɒŋ -ɪ- ‖ -lɔːŋ -lɑːŋ
Bennet, Bennett 'ben ɪt §-ət
Ben Nevis ˌben 'nev ɪs §-əs
Bennie, b~ 'ben i ~s z
Bennington 'ben ɪŋ tən
Benn|y, benn|y 'ben |i ~ies, ~y's iz
Benoni bə 'nəʊn i bɪ-, be- ‖ -'noʊn-
Ben Rhydding ˌben 'rɪd ɪŋ
Benson 'ben̩ts ᵊn
bent bent **bents** bents
Bentall 'bent ᵊl -ɔːl ‖ -ɔːl -ɑːl ~'s z
Bentham 'ben̩θ əm 'bent-
Benthamism 'ben̩θ ə ˌmɪz əm 'bent-
Benthamite 'ben̩θ ə maɪt 'bent-
benthic 'ben̩θ ɪk
benthos 'ben̩θ ɒs ‖ 'ben θɑːs
Bentinck 'bent ɪŋk
Bentine ben 'ti:n '··
Bentley 'bent li ~s z
Benton 'bent ən ‖ -ᵊn
bentonite 'bent ə naɪt ‖ -ᵊn aɪt
ben trovato ˌben trəʊ 'vɑːt əʊ
‖ -troʊ 'vɑːt̬ oʊ —_It_ [ˌben tro 'vaː to]
Bentsen 'bents ən
bentwood 'bent wʊd
Benue 'ben u eɪ ‖ 'beɪn weɪ
Benue-Congo ˌben u eɪ 'kɒŋ gəʊ
‖ ˌbeɪn weɪ 'kɑːŋ goʊ
benumb bi 'nʌm bə- ~ed d ~ing ɪŋ ~s z
Benylin _tdmk_ 'ben ə lɪn -i-, -ᵊl ɪn
Benyon 'ben jən
Benz benz —_Ger_ [bɛnts]
benzedrine, B~ _tdmk_ 'benz ə dri:n -ɪ-, -drɪn ~s
z
benzene 'benz i:n ben 'zi:n
ˌbenzene 'ring
benzidine 'benz ɪ di:n -ə-, -dɪn
benzine 'benz i:n ben 'zi:n
benzo- _comb. form
with stress-neutral suffix_ ¦benz əʊ ‖ -oʊ
— **benzosulfate, benzosulphate**
ˌbenz əʊ 'sʌlf eɪt ‖ -oʊ-
benzocaine 'benz əʊ keɪn ‖ -ə-
benzodiazepine ˌbenz əʊ daɪ 'æz ə pi:n -'eɪz-
‖ ˌbenz oʊ-
benzoic ben 'zəʊ ɪk ‖ -'zoʊ-
benzoin 'benz əʊ ɪn ben 'zəʊ-, §-ən; 'benz ɔɪn
‖ -oʊ- —_Some people claim to distinguish_
'benz əʊ ɪn _etc._ 'phenyl benzoyl carbinol' _from_
'benz ɔɪn _'gum benjamin'_
benzol 'benz ɒl ‖ -oʊl -ɑːl, -ɔːl
benzole 'benz əʊl →-ɒʊl ‖ -oʊl

B

benzoyl 'benz əʊ ɪl §-əl ‖ -oʊ-
benzpyrene ˌbenz 'paɪᵊr iːn
benzyl 'benz ɪl -ᵊl ‖ -iːᵊl -ᵊl
Beowulf 'beɪ əʊ wʊlf ‖ -ə-

BEQUEATH

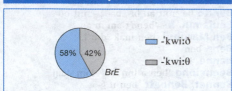

58% 42%   ▬ -'kwiːð
              ▬ -'kwiːθ
        BrE

be|queath bi ‖'kwiːð bə-, -'kwiːθ — *Preference poll, BrE:* -'kwiːð *58%,* -'kwiːθ *42%.*
  ~queathed 'kwiːðd 'kwiːθt ~queathes 'kwiːðz 'kwiːθs ~queathing 'kwiːð ɪŋ 'kwiːθ ɪŋ
bequest bi 'kwest bə- ~s s
Bequia *Caribbean island* 'bek wi -weɪ (!)
be|rate bi ‖'reɪt bə- ~rated 'reɪt ɪd -əd ‖ 'reɪt̬ əd ~rates 'reɪts ~rating 'reɪt ɪŋ ‖ 'reɪt̬ ɪŋ
Berber 'bɜːb ə ‖ 'bɜːb ᵊr ~s z
Berbera 'bɜːb ər ə ‖ 'bɜːb-
berberis 'bɜːb ər ɪs §-əs ‖ 'bɜːb- ~es ɪz əz
Berbice bɜː 'biːs 'bɜːb ɪs ‖ bɜː-
berceuse beə 'sɜːz ‖ ber 'sʊz -'sɜːz —*Fr* [bɛʁ søːz]
Berchtesgaden 'beəkt əz gɑːd ᵊn 'beəxt- ‖ 'berkt- —*Ger* [bɛʁç təs 'gɑːd ᵊn]
Bere bɪə ‖ bɪᵊr
bereav|e bi 'riːv bə- ~ed d ~ement/s mənt/s ~es z ~ing ɪŋ
bereft bi 'reft bə-
Berengaria ˌber əŋ 'geər i ə ˌ-ɪŋ-, ˌ-eŋ- ‖ -'ger-
Berenger 'ber ɪndʒ ə -əndʒ ə ‖ -ᵊr
Berenice ˌber ɪ 'naɪs i -ə-, -'naɪk-, -iː; -'niːtʃ eɪ, -i; -'niːs
Berenson 'ber ənˡs ən
Beresford 'ber ɪs fəd -əs-, -ɪz-, -əz- ‖ -fᵊrd
beret 'ber eɪ -i; bə 'reɪ ‖ bə 'reɪ —*Formerly also* 'ber ɪt. ~s z
berg, Berg bɜːg ‖ bɜːg —*Ger* [bɛʁk] bergs bɜːgz ‖ bɜːgz
Bergamo 'bɜːg ə məʊ ‖ 'bɜːg ə moʊ —*It* ['bɛr ga mo]
bergamot 'bɜːg ə mɒt ‖ 'bɜːg ə mɑːt ~s s 'bergamot oil
Bergen 'bɜːg ən 'beəg- ‖ 'bɜːg- —*Norw* ['bær gən, 'bæʁ-]
Berger (i) 'bɜːdʒ ə ‖ 'bɜːdʒ ᵊr, (ii) 'bɜːg ə ‖ 'bɜːg ᵊr —*as a British name,* (i); *as an American name,* (ii)
Bergerac 'bɜːʒ ə ræk ‖ ˌberʒ ə 'ræk -'rɑːk
Bergman 'bɜːg mən ‖ 'bɜːg-
bergschrund 'bɜːg ʃrʊnd ‖ 'bɜːg- ~s z —*Ger* B~ ['bɛʁk ʃʁʊnt]
Bergson 'bɜːg sᵊn ‖ 'bɜːg- —*Fr* [bɛʁk sɔn]
Bergsonian bɜːg 'səʊn i ən ‖ bɜːg 'soʊn- berg- ~s z
beribboned bi 'rɪb ənd bə-

beriberi ˌber i 'ber i ˈ·ˌ·ˌ·
Bering 'beər ɪŋ 'ber- ‖ 'bɪr ɪŋ 'ber- —*Danish* ['beː ʁeŋ]
  ˌBering 'Sea, ˌBering 'Strait
Berisford 'ber ɪs fəd -əs-, -ɪz-, -əz- ‖ -fᵊrd
berk bɜːk ‖ bɜːk berks bɜːks ‖ bɜːks
Berkeley (i) 'bɑːk li ‖ 'bɑːrk-, (ii) 'bɜːk li ‖ 'bɜːk- —*British and Irish places and names are* (i), *American places and names are* (ii).
berkelium bɜː 'kiːl i əm bə-, 'bɜːk li ˌəm ‖ 'bɜːk li ˌəm
Berkhamsted 'bɜːk əm sted 'bɑːk-, -əmᵖst ɪd, -əd ‖ 'bɜːk-
Berkley *place in Michigan* 'bɜːk li ‖ 'bɜːk-
Berkoff 'bɜːk ɒf ‖ 'bɜːk ɑːf
Berkowitz 'bɜːk ə wɪts ‖ 'bɜːk-
Berks *name of county* bɑːks §bɜːks ‖ bɜːks bɑːrks —*see also* **Berkshire**
Berkshire (i) 'bɑːk ʃə -ʃɪə ‖ 'bɑːrk ʃᵊr -ʃɪr, (ii) 'bɜːk- ‖ 'bɜːk- —*The English county is* (i), *though with a non-standard variant* (ii). *The hills in MA are* (ii). ~s z
Berlei *tdmk* 'bɜːl i -aɪ ‖ 'bɜːl-
Berlin ˌ(ˌ)bɜː 'lɪn ‖ ˌ(ˌ)bɜː- —*Ger* [bɛʁ 'liːn] —*but the town in New Hampshire is* 'bɜːl ən
Berliner ˌ(ˌ)bɜː 'lɪn ə ‖ bᵊr 'lɪn ᵊr ~s z
Berlioz 'beəl i əʊz 'bɜːl- ‖ 'berl i oʊz —*Fr* [bɛʁ ljoːz]
Berlitz 'bɜːl ɪts §-əts ‖ 'bɜːl ɪts bɜː 'lɪts
Berlusconi ˌbɜːl ə 'skəʊn i ˌbeəl-, -u- ‖ ˌbɜːl ə 'skoʊn i —*It* [ber lu 'sko: ni]
berm, berme bɜːm ‖ bɜːm bermes, berms bɜːmz ‖ bɜːmz
Bermondsey 'bɜːm əndz i ‖ 'bɜːm-
Bermuda bə 'mjuːd ə ‖ bᵊr- ~s z
  Ber,muda 'shorts; Ber,muda 'Triangle
Bermudan bə 'mjuːd ᵊn ‖ bᵊr- ~s z
Bern bɜːn beən ‖ bɜːn bern —*Ger* [bɛʁn]
Bernadette ˌbɜːn ə 'det ‖ ˌbɜːn-
Bernadotte ˌbɜːn ə 'dɒt ˈ·ˌ·ˌ· ‖ 'bɜːn ə dɑːt
Bernal (i) bə 'næl ‖ bᵊr-, (ii) 'bɜːn ᵊl ‖ 'bɜːn-
Bernanke bə 'næŋk i ‖ bᵊr-
Bernard (i) 'bɜːn əd ‖ 'bɜːn ᵊrd, (ii) bə 'nɑːd ‖ bᵊr 'nɑːrd —*As a British name usually* (i), *as an American name usually* (ii).
Bernardette ˌbɜːn ə 'det ‖ ˌbɜːn ᵊr- -ə-
Bernardine 'bɜːn ə dɪn -diːn ‖ 'bɜːn ᵊr-
Berne bɜːn beən ‖ bɜːn bern —*Fr* [bɛʁn]
Berners 'bɜːn əz ‖ 'bɜːn ᵊrz
Berners-Lee ˌbɜːn əz 'liː ‖ ˌbɜːn ᵊrz 'li
Bernese ˌbɜː 'niːz ◄ ‖ ˌbɜː- -'niːs
Bernhardt 'bɜːn hɑːt ‖ 'bɜːn hɑːrt —*Fr* [bɛʁ naːʁ]
Bernice (i) 'bɜːn ɪs -əs ‖ 'bɜːn-, (ii) bə 'niːs bɜː- ‖ bᵊr-, (iii) bɜː 'naɪs i ‖ bᵊr- —*In AmE usually* (ii).
Bernini bɜː 'niːn i bə- ‖ bᵊr- —*It* [ber 'ni: ni]
Bernoulli bɜː 'nuːl i bə- ‖ bᵊr- —*Fr* [bɛʁ nu ji], *Ger* [bɛʁ 'nʊl i]
  Ber'nouilli ef,fect
Bernstein (i) 'bɜːn staɪn ‖ 'bɜːn-, (ii) -stiːn
Be-Ro *tdmk* 'biː rəʊ ‖ -roʊ
Berol *tdmk* 'biː rɒl -rəʊl ‖ -rɑːl -rɔːl, -roʊl

Berridge 'ber ɪdʒ
Berriew 'ber i uː
berr‖y 'ber ‖i **~ied** id **~ies** iz **~ying** i ɪŋ
Berry 'ber i
Berryman 'ber i mən
berserk bə 'zɜːk bɜː-, -'sɜːk; 'bɜːs ɜːk, 'bɜːz-
‖ bᵊr 'sɝːk -'zɝːk **~er/s** ə/z ‖ ᵊr/z
Bert bɜːt ‖ bɝːt
Bertelsmann *tdmk* 'bɜːt ᵊlz mæn -mən ‖ 'bɝːt̮-
—*Ger* ['bɛʁ tᵊls man]
berth bɜːθ ‖ bɝːθ (= *birth*) **berthed** bɜːθt
‖ bɝːθt **berthing** 'bɜːθ ɪŋ ‖ 'bɝːθ ɪŋ **berths**
bɜːθs bɜːðz ‖ bɝːθs
Bertha 'bɜːθ ə ‖ 'bɝːθ ə
Bertie 'bɜːt i ‖ 'bɝːt̮ i —*but as a family name
in BrE*, 'baːt i
Bertolucci ˌbɜːt ə 'lʊtʃ i -'luːtʃ- ‖ ˌbɝːt̮ ə 'luːtʃ i
—*It* [ber to 'lut tʃi]
Bertram 'bɜːtr əm ‖ 'bɝːtr-
Bertrand 'bɜːtr ənd ‖ 'bɝːtr-
Berwick 'ber ɪk
Berwick-on-Tweed ˌber ɪk ɒn 'twiːd ‖ -aːn·
-ɔːn'-
Berwickshire 'ber ɪk ʃə -ʃɪə; '· ·ˌʃaɪ ə ‖ -ʃɪr -ʃᵊr;
'· ·ˌʃaɪˌᵊr
Berwyn 'beə wɪn 'bɜː- ‖ 'bɝː-
beryl, Beryl 'ber əl -ɪl **~s** z
beryllium bə 'rɪl i əm be-
Berzelius bə 'ziːl i əs -'zeɪl- ‖ bᵊr- —*Swed*
[bær 'seː li ʊs]
Besançon bə 'zɒs n̆ ə ‖ -'zaːn soʊn -'zænˈs ᵊn
—*Fr* [bə zã sɔ̃]
Besant *(i)* 'bes ᵊnt 'bez-, *(ii)* bɪ 'zænt bə-
beseech bɪ 'siːtʃ bə- **~ed** t **~es** ɪz əz **~ing/ly**
ɪŋ /li **besought** bɪ 'sɔːt bə- ‖ -'saːt
beseem bɪ 'siːm bə- **~ed** d **~ing** ɪŋ **~s** z
be‖set bɪ ‖'set bə- **~sets** 'sets **~setting** 'set ɪŋ
‖ 'set̮ ɪŋ
beside bɪ 'saɪd bə- **~s** z
besieg‖e bɪ 'siːdʒ bə-, -'siːʒ **~ed** d **~ement**
mənt **~er/s** ə/z ‖ ᵊr/z **~es** ɪz əz **~ing** ɪŋ
be‖smear bɪ ‖'smɪə bə- ‖ -‖'smɪᵊr **~smeared**
smɪəd ‖ 'smɪᵊrd **~smearing** 'smɪər ɪŋ
‖ 'smɪr ɪŋ **~smears** 'smɪəz ‖ 'smɪᵊrz
besmirch bɪ 'smɜːtʃ bə- ‖ -'smɝːtʃ **~ed** t **~ment**
mənt **~es** ɪz əz **~ing** ɪŋ
besom 'biːz əm **~ed** d **~ing** ɪŋ **~s** z
besotted bɪ 'sɒt ɪd bə-, -'zɒt-, -əd ‖ -'saːt̮ əd
besought bɪ 'sɔːt bə- ‖ -'saːt
bespangl‖e bɪ 'spæŋ gᵊl bə- **~ed** d **~es** z **~ing**
ɪŋ
bespatt‖er bɪ 'spæt ‖ə bə- ‖ -'spæt̮ ‖ᵊr **~ered**
əd ‖ ᵊrd **~ering** ˌər ɪŋ ‖ ər ɪŋ **~ers** əz ‖ ᵊrz
be‖speak bɪ ‖'spiːk bə- **~speaking** 'spiːk ɪŋ
~speaks 'spiːks **~spoke** 'spəʊk ‖ 'spoʊk
~spoken 'spəʊk ᵊn ‖ 'spoʊk ᵊn
bespectacled bɪ 'spekt ək ᵊld bə-, -ɪk-
bespok‖e bɪ 'spəʊk bə- ‖ -'spoʊk **~en** ən
besprinkl‖e bɪ 'sprɪŋk ᵊl bə- **~ed** d **~es** z **~ing**
ɪŋ
Bess bes **Bess's** 'bes ɪz -əz
Bessarabi‖a ˌbes ə 'reɪb iˌə **~an/s** ən/z ◂
Bessborough 'bez bᵊrˌə ‖ -ˌbɝː oʊ

Bessbrook 'bes brʊk
Bessel, Bessell 'bes ᵊl
'Bessel ˌfunction
Bessemer 'bes ɪm ə -əm- ‖ -ᵊr
ˌBessemer conˈverter
Besses o' th' Barn ˌbes ɪz əð 'baːn ˌ·əz-
‖ -'baːrn
Bessey, Bessie, Bessy 'bes i
best, Best best **bested** 'best ɪd -əd **besting**
'best ɪŋ **bests** bests
ˌbest 'man
bestial 'best iˌəl ‖ 'bes tʃəl →'beʃ-, 'biːs- **~ly** i
(*)
bestialit‖y ˌbest i 'æl ət ‖i -ɪt i
‖ ˌbes tʃi 'æl ət̮ ‖i →ˌbeʃ-, ˌbiːs- (*) **~ies** iz
bestiar‖y 'best iˌər ‖i ‖ 'bes tʃi er ‖i →'beʃ-,
'biːs- (*) **~ies** iz
be‖stir bɪ ‖'stɜː bə- -‖'stɝː **~stirred** 'stɜːd
‖ 'stɝːd **~stirring** 'stɜːr ɪŋ ‖ 'stɝː ɪŋ **~stirs**
'stɜːz ‖ 'stɝːz
bestow bɪ 'stəʊ bə- ‖ -'stoʊ **~ed** d **~ing** ɪŋ **~s**
z
bestowal bɪ 'stəʊ əl bə- ‖ -'stoʊ-
bestrew bɪ 'struː bə-
bestrewn bɪ 'struːn bə-
be‖stride bɪ ‖'straɪd bə- **~strides** 'straɪdz
~stridden 'strɪd ᵊn **~strode** 'strəʊd
‖ 'stroʊd
bestseller, best-seller ˌbest 'sel ə ◂ ‖ -ᵊr
~dom dəm **~s** z
bestselling, best-selling ˌbest 'sel ɪŋ ◂
Beswick 'bez ɪk
bet, Bet bet **betted** 'bet ɪd -əd ‖ 'bet̮- **betting**
'bet ɪŋ ‖ 'bet̮- **bets** bets
beta, Beta 'biːt ə ‖ 'beɪt̮ ə (*) **~s** z
'beta ˌparticle; 'beta ˌrhythm
beta-blocker 'biːt ə ˌblɒk ə ‖ 'beɪt̮ ə ˌblaːk ᵊr
~s z
betaine 'biːt ə iːn -ɪn; bɪ 'teɪ-, bə- ‖ 'biːt̮-
be‖take bɪ ‖'teɪk bə- **~taken** 'teɪk ən **~takes**
'teɪks **~taking** 'teɪk ɪŋ **~took** 'tʊk
Betamax *tdmk* 'biːt ə mæks ‖ 'beɪt̮-
betatron 'biːt ə trɒn ‖ 'beɪt̮ ə traːn **~s** z
betcha 'betʃ ə
betel 'biːt ᵊl ‖ 'biːt̮ ᵊl (= *beetle*)
'betel nut
Betelgeuse 'biːt ᵊl dʒɜːz -ʒɜːz, -dʒuːz, ˌ·'·
‖ 'biːt̮ ᵊl dʒuːs 'bet̮-, -dʒuːz
bete noire, bête noire ˌbeɪt 'nwaː ˌbet-
‖ ˌbet nə 'waːr ˌbeɪt- —*Fr* [bɛt nwaːʁ] **betes
noires, bêtes noires** ˌbeɪt 'nwaːz ˌbet-,
'nwaː ‖ ˌbet nə 'waːrz ˌbeɪt-, -'nwaːr —*Fr*
[bɛt nwaːʁ]
beth *Hebrew letter* bet beθ ‖ beɪt beɪθ, beɪs
Beth *personal name* beθ
Beth-Ann, Bethanne, Beth-Anne ˌbeθ 'æn
Bethany 'beθ ən i
Bethel, bethel 'beθ ᵊl **~'s, ~s** z
Bethell *(i)* 'beθ ᵊl, *(ii)* be 'θel
Bethesda be 'θezd ə bɪ-, bə-
be‖think bɪ ‖'θɪŋk bə- **~thinking** 'θɪŋk ɪŋ
~thinks 'θɪŋks **~thought** 'θɔːt ‖ 'θaːt
Bethlehem 'beθ lɪ hem -lə-, -liˌəm

Bethnal 'beθ nᵊl
  ,Bethnal 'Green
bethought bɪ 'θɔːt bə- ‖ -'θɑːt
Bethune, Béthune be 'θjuːn bi-, bə-, -'tjuːn,
-'tuːn ‖ -'θuːn —Fr [be tyn] —As a family
name, also 'biːt ᵊn
betid|e bɪ 'taɪd bə- ~**ed** ɪd əd ~**es** z ~**ing** ɪŋ
betimes bɪ 'taɪmz bə-
betise, bêtise be 'tiːz ₍ᵢ₎beɪ- —Fr [bɛ tiːz] ~**s**
same pronunciation
Betjeman 'betʃ ə mən -ɪ-
betoken bɪ 'təʊk ən bə- ‖ -'toʊk- ~**ed** d ~**er/s**
ə/z ‖ ᵊr/z ~**ing** ᵢŋ ~**s** z
beton|y 'bet ən |i ‖ -ᵊn i ~**ies** iz
betook bɪ 'tʊk bə-
betray bɪ 'treɪ bə- ~**ed** d ~**er/s** ə/z ‖ ᵊr/z ~**ing**
ɪŋ ~**s** z
betrayal bɪ 'treɪ əl bə- ~**s** z
betrayment bɪ 'treɪ mənt bə- ~**s** s
be|troth bɪ |'trəʊθ bə-, -'trəʊθ ‖ -|'trəʊð -'trɑːθ
~**trothed** 'trəʊðd 'trəʊθt ‖ -'trəʊðd -'trɑːθt
~**trothing** 'trəʊð ɪŋ 'trəʊθ- ‖ -'trəʊð ɪŋ
-'trɑːθ- ~**troths** 'trəʊðz 'trəʊθs ‖ -'trɑːðz
-'trɑːθs
betrothal bɪ 'trəʊð ᵊl bə-, -'trəʊθ- ‖ -'trɑːð-
-'trɑːθ- ~**s** z
Betsy 'bets i
bett... —see **bet**
Bettany 'bet ən i ‖ -ᵊn i
Bette 'bet i bet
Bettelheim 'bet ᵊl haɪm ‖ 'beţ-
better 'bet ə ‖ 'beţ ᵊr ~**ed** d **bettering**
  'bet ər ɪŋ ‖ 'beţ ər ɪŋ ~**s** z
betterment 'bet ə mənt ‖ 'beţ ᵊr-
better-off ,bet ər 'ɒf -'ɔːf ‖ ,beţ ər 'ɔːf -'ɑːf
Betterton 'bet ət ən ‖ 'beţ ᵊrt ᵊn
Betteshanger 'bets ,hæŋ ə ‖ -ᵊr
Bettina be 'tiːn ə bə, bɪ-
betting 'bet ɪŋ ‖ 'beţ ɪŋ
  'betting shop
Betton 'bet ᵊn
bettor 'bet ə ‖ 'beţ ᵊr ~**s** z
Bettws 'bet əs -ʊs ‖ 'beţ- —Welsh ['bet us]
Bettws... —see **Betws...**
Betty 'bet i ‖ 'beţ i ~**'s** z
between bɪ 'twiːn bə-
betweentimes bɪ 'twiːn taɪmz bə-
betwixt bɪ 'twɪkst bə-
Betws-y-Coed ,bet əs i 'kɔɪd ,-ʊs-, -'kəʊ ɪd, -ed
‖ ,beţ- —Welsh [,bet us ə 'koːɪd]
Betws-yn-Rhos ,bet əs ɪn 'rəʊs ,-ʊs-, -ən'-
‖ ,beţ əs ən 'roʊs — Welsh [,bet us ən 'hroːs]
Beulah 'bjuːl ə
Bevan 'bev ᵊn
bevatron 'bev ə trɒn ‖ -trɑːn ~**s** z
bevel 'bev ᵊl ~**ed**, ~**led** d ~**ing**, ~**ling** ɪŋ ~**s** z
  'bevel gear
beverag|e 'bev ər ɪdʒ ~**es** ɪz əz
Beveridge 'bev ər ɪdʒ
Beverley, Beverly 'bev əl i ‖ -ᵊr li
  ,Beverly 'Hills
Bevin 'bev ɪn §-ᵊn
Bevis (i) 'bev ɪs §-əs, (ii) 'biːv-

bevv|y 'bev |i ~**ied** id ~**ies** iz
bev|y 'bev |i (= bevvy) ~**ies** iz
bewail bɪ 'weɪᵊl bə- ~**ed** d ~**ing** ɪŋ ~**s** z
beware bɪ 'weə bə- ‖ -'weᵊr -'wæᵊr
Bewdley 'bjuːd li
Bewes bjuːz
bewhiskered bɪ 'wɪsk əd bə-, -'hwɪsk- ‖ -ᵊrd
Bewick, Bewicke 'bjuː ɪk
bewigged bɪ 'wɪgd bə-
bewild|er bɪ 'wɪld |ə bə- ‖ -|ᵊr **~ered** əd ‖ ᵊrd
  ~ering/ly ᵊr ɪŋ /li **~erment** ə mənt
  ‖ ᵊr mənt **~ers** əz ‖ ᵊrz
bewitch bɪ 'wɪtʃ bə- ~**ed** t ~**er/s** ə/z ‖ ᵊr/z ~**es**
  ɪz əz ~**ing/ly** ɪŋ /li ~**ment/s** mənt/s
Bewley 'bjuːl i
Bexar county in TX beə ‖ beᵊr
Bexhill ,beks 'hɪl ◄
  ,Bexhill-on-'Sea
Bexley 'beks li
Bexleyheath ,beks li 'hiːθ
bey, Bey beɪ (= bay) **beys, Beys** beɪz
Beyfus 'beɪf əs 'baɪf-
Beynon 'baɪn ən 'beɪn-
Beyoncé bɪ 'jɒn's eɪ ‖ -'jɑːn's-
beyond bɪ 'jɒnd bə- bi 'ɒnd ‖ bi 'ɑːnd
bezant, B~ 'bez ᵊnt ~**s** s
bezel 'bez ᵊl ~**s** z
Beziers, Béziers 'bez i eɪ —Fr [be zje]
bezique bɪ 'ziːk bə- ~**s** s
bezoar 'biːz ɔː ‖ -ɔːr -oʊr ~**s** z
Bhagavad-Gita ,bʌg əv əd 'giːt ə ,bæg-,
  -ə væd- ‖ ,bɑːg ə ,vɑːd-
bhagwan, B~ 'bæg wɑːn bʌ 'gwɑːn —Hindi
  [bʱəg ʋaːn]
bhaji, bhajee 'bɑːdʒ i ~**s** z —Hindi
  [bʱaː dʒi]
bhang bæŋ —Hindi [bʱaːŋ]
bhangra 'bæŋ grə 'bɑːŋ- —Hindi [bʱaːŋgr]
bharal 'bʌr əl ‖ 'bɜː əl ~**s** z —Hindi [bʱərəl]
bhikku 'bɪk uː
bhindi 'bɪnd i —Hindi [bʱɪn ɖi]
Bhojpuri bəʊdʒ 'pʊər i ‖ boʊdʒ 'pʊr i
  —Hindi [bʱoːdʒ pʊ riː]
Bhopal ₍ᵢ₎bəʊ 'pɑːl ‖ ₍ᵢ₎boʊ- —Hindi
  [bʱoː paːl]
Bhreathnach 'vræn ɒk ‖ -ɑːk
Bhumibol 'buːm i bɒn -bɒl ‖ -boʊn -boʊl
  —Thai [pʰuː mi pʰon]
bhuna 'buːn ə
Bhutan ,bu: 'tɑːn -'tæn
Bhutanese ,buːt ə 'niːz ◄ ‖ -'niːs
Bhutto 'buːt əʊ 'bʊt- ‖ 'buːţ oʊ
bi baɪ
bi- comb. form ₍ᵢ₎baɪ — **biaxial** ₍ᵢ₎baɪ 'æks i əl
Biaf|ra bɪ 'æf |rə baɪ- ~**ran/s** rən/z
Bialystok bɪ 'æl ɪ stɒk -'-ə-; ,biː ə 'lɪst ɒk
  ‖ bi 'ɑːl ə stɑːk —Polish Białystok
  [bja 'wɨ stɔk]
Bianca bi 'æŋk ə
biannual ,baɪ 'æn ju əl ~**ly** i ~**s** z
Biarritz ,biə 'rɪts '·· ‖ ,biː ə 'rɪts '···—Fr
  [bja ʀits]

bias, Bias 'baɪ‿əs **~ed, ~sed** t **~es, ~ses** ɪz əz
  ~ing, ~sing ɪŋ
  ˌbias 'binding
biathlete baɪ 'æθ liːt **~s** z
biathlon baɪ 'æθ lən -lɒn ‖ -lɑːn **~s** z
bib bɪb **bibbed** bɪbd **bibbing** 'bɪb ɪŋ **bibs** bɪbz
Bibb bɪb
bibb... —*see* **bib**
Bibby 'bɪb i ~'s z
bibelot 'bɪb ləʊ ‖ 'biːb ə loʊ **~s** z —*or as sing.*
bible, Bible 'baɪb ᵊl **~s** z
  'Bible belt; 'Bible ˌstudy
biblical, B~ 'bɪb lɪk ᵊl **~ly** ˌi
biblio- *comb. form*
  with stress-neutral suffix ˌbɪb li əʊ ‖ -ə
  — **bibliomania** ˌbɪb li əʊ 'meɪn i‿ə ‖ -ə'--
  with stress-imposing suffix ˌbɪb li 'ɒ+ ‖ -'ɑː+
  — **bibliolatry** ˌbɪb li 'ɒl ətr i ‖ -'ɑːl-
bibliographer ˌbɪb li 'ɒg rəf ə ‖ -'ɑːg rəf ᵊr **~s**
  z
bibliographic ˌbɪb li‿ə 'græf ɪk ◂ **~al** ᵊl **~ally**
  ᵊl i
bibliograph|y ˌbɪb li 'ɒg rəf |i ‖ -'ɑːg- **~ies** iz
bibliophile 'bɪb li‿ə faɪ ᵊl **~s** z
bibulous 'bɪb jʊl əs -jəl- ‖ -jəl- **~ly** li **~ness**
  nəs nɪs
Bic, BiC *tdmk* bɪk **Bics, BiCs** bɪks
bicameral ˌ(ˌ)baɪ 'kæm ᵊr‿əl
bicameralism ˌ(ˌ)baɪ 'kæm ᵊr‿ə ˌlɪz əm
bicarb 'baɪ kɑːb ˌˑˑ ‖ -kɑːrb
bicarbonate ˌ(ˌ)baɪ 'kɑːb ən‿ət -ɪt, -eɪt
  ‖ -'kɑːrb-
  biˌcarbonate of 'soda
bice baɪs
  ˌbice 'green
bicentenar|y ˌbaɪ sen 'tiːn ər‿|i -'ten-;
  ˌ(ˌ)baɪ 'sent ɪn ər‿|i, -'sent ən- ‖ -'ten-
  ˌ(ˌ)'sent ᵊn er |i **~ies** iz
bicentennial ˌbaɪ sen 'ten i‿əl **~s** z
biceps 'baɪ seps **~es** ɪz əz
Bicester 'bɪst ə ‖ -ᵊr (!)
Biche-la-mar ˌbiːtʃ lə 'mɑː biːʃ-, -læ- ‖ -'mɑːr
bichon frise ˌbiːʃ ᵊn 'friːz -ɒn- —*Fr* bichon
  frisé [bi ʃɔ̃ fʁi ze] **~s** ɪz əz
bichromate ˌ(ˌ)baɪ 'krəʊm eɪt -ət, -ɪt ‖ -'kroʊm-
bicker 'bɪk ə ‖ -ᵊr **~ed** d **~ing** 'bɪk ər ɪŋ **~s** s
Bickerstaff, Bickerstaffe 'bɪk ə stɑːf §-stæf
  ‖ -ᵊr stæf
Bickersteth 'bɪk ə steθ -stɪθ ‖ -ᵊr-
Bickerton 'bɪk ət ən ‖ -ᵊrt ᵊn
Bickford 'bɪk fəd ‖ -fᵊrd
bickie 'bɪk i **~s** z
Bickley 'bɪk li
Bicknell 'bɪk nᵊl
bicoastal ˌ(ˌ)baɪ 'kəʊst ᵊl ‖ -'koʊst-
bicolor, bicolour 'baɪ ˌkʌl ə ‖ -ᵊr
biconcave ˌ(ˌ)baɪ 'kɒŋ keɪv -'kɒn-,
  ˌbaɪ kɒn 'keɪv ˌ(ˌ)baɪ 'kɑːn-
biconcavity ˌbaɪ kɒn 'kæv ət i -ɪt i
  ‖ ˌbaɪ kɑːn 'kæv ət̬ i
biconvex ˌ(ˌ)baɪ 'kɒn veks ˌbaɪ kɒn 'veks
  ‖ ˌ(ˌ)baɪ 'kɑːn-

biconvexity ˌbaɪ kɒn 'veks ət i -ɪt i
  ‖ ˌbaɪ kɑːn 'veks ət̬ i
bicuspid ˌbaɪ 'kʌsp ɪd §-əd **~s** z
bicuspidate ˌbaɪ 'kʌsp ɪ deɪt §-ə-
bicycl|e 'baɪs ɪk ᵊl -ək- **~ed** d **~es** z **~ing** ˌɪŋ
  'bicycle clip; 'bicycle pump
bicyclist 'baɪs ɪk lɪst -ək-, §-ləst **~s** s
bid bɪd **bade** beɪd **bidden** 'bɪd ᵊn
  bidding 'bɪd ɪŋ **bids** bɪdz
  'bid price
biddable 'bɪd əb ᵊl
Biddell (i) 'bɪd ᵊl, (ii) bɪ 'del
bidden 'bɪd ᵊn
bidder, B~ 'bɪd ə ‖ -ᵊr **~s** z
Biddie 'bɪd i
bidding 'bɪd ɪŋ
Biddle 'bɪd ᵊl
Biddulph 'bɪd ʌlf
Biddy, bidd|y 'bɪd |i **~ies** iz
bide, Bide baɪd **bided** 'baɪd ɪd -əd **biding**
  'baɪd ɪŋ **bides** baɪdz **bode** bəʊd ‖ boʊd
Bideford 'bɪd ɪ fəd -ə- ‖ -fᵊrd (!)
Biden 'baɪd ᵊn
bidet 'biːd eɪ ‖ bɪ 'deɪ —*Fr* [bi dɛ] (*) **~s** z
bidialectal ˌbaɪ ˌdaɪ‿ə 'lekt ᵊl
bidialectalism ˌbaɪ ˌdaɪ‿ə 'lekt ə ˌlɪz əm
  -ᵊl ˌɪz-
bidirectional ˌbaɪ daɪᵊ 'rek ʃᵊn əl ◂ ˌdə-, ˌdɪ-
  ~ly i
Bidwell 'bɪd wel
Bieber 'biːb ə ‖ -ᵊr
Biedermeier 'biːd ə ˌmaɪ‿ə ‖ -ᵊr ˌmaɪˌᵊr —*Ger*
  ['biː dɐ ˌmai ɐ]
Bielefeld 'biːl ə feld -felt —*Ger* ['biː lə fɛlt]
biennale ˌbi: e 'nɑːl eɪ **~s** z
biennial baɪ 'en i‿əl **~ly** i
bien-pensant ˌbjæ̃ 'pɒ̃s ɒ̃ ‖ -pɑ̃: 'sɑ̃: —*Fr*
  [bjæ̃ pɑ̃ sɑ̃]
bier bɪə ‖ bɪᵊr (= *beer*) **biers** bɪəz ‖ bɪᵊrz
Bierce bɪəs ‖ bɪᵊrs
bierkeller 'bɪə ˌkel ə ‖ 'bɪr ˌkel ᵊr —*Ger* B~
  ['biːɐ ˌkɛl ɐ]
biff bɪf **biffed** bɪft **biffing** 'bɪf ɪŋ **biffs** bɪfs
Biffen 'bɪf ɪn §-ᵊn
Biffo 'bɪf əʊ ‖ -oʊ
bifid 'baɪ fɪd **~ly** li
bifocal ˌbaɪ 'fəʊk ᵊl ◂ ‖ -'foʊk- **~s** z
bifoliate ˌbaɪ 'fəʊl i eɪt -i‿ət, ɪt ‖ -'foʊl-
bifurcate *adj* ˌbaɪ 'fɜːk eɪt -ət, -ɪt; 'baɪ fə keɪt,
  -kət, -kɪt ‖ -'fɜːk- **~ly** li
bifur|cate *v* 'baɪ fə |keɪt -fɜː- ‖ -fᵊr- **~cated**
  keɪt ɪd əd ‖ keɪt̬ əd **~cates** keɪts **~cating**
  keɪt ɪŋ ‖ keɪt̬ ɪŋ
bifurcation ˌbaɪ fə 'keɪʃ ᵊn -fɜː- ‖ -fᵊr- **~s** z
big bɪg **bigger** 'bɪg ə ‖ -ᵊr **biggest** 'bɪg ɪst -əst
  ˌBig 'Apple; ˌbig 'bang ˌtheory; ˌBig 'Ben;
  ˌBig 'Brother; ˌbig 'business; ˌbig 'deal;
  ˌbig 'game; ˌbig 'stick; ˌBig 'Sur sɜː ‖ sɜˑ;
  'big time, ˌˑ'ˑ; ˌbig 'top; ˌbig 'wheel
bigami... —*see* **bigamy**
bigamist 'bɪg əm ɪst §-əst **~s** s
bigamous 'bɪg əm əs **~ly** li
bigam|y 'bɪg əm |i **~ies** iz

B

Bigbury 'bɪg bər‿i ‖ -ˌber i
Bigelow 'bɪg ə ləʊ -ɪ- ‖ -loʊ
Bigfoot 'bɪg fʊt
bigg... —see big
Biggar 'bɪg ə ‖ -ᵊr
biggie 'bɪg i ~s z
Biggin 'bɪg ɪn §-ən
biggish 'bɪg ɪʃ
Biggles 'bɪg ᵊlz
Biggleswade 'bɪg ᵊlz weɪd
Biggs bɪgz
bigg|y 'bɪg| i ~ies iz
bighead 'bɪg hed ~s z
bigheaded ˌbɪg 'hed ɪd ◂ -əd ~ly li ~ness nəs
   nɪs
big-hearted ˌbɪg 'hɑːt ɪd ◂ -əd ‖ -'hɑːrt̬- ~ly li
   ~ness nəs nɪs
bighorn 'bɪg hɔːn ‖ -hɔːrn ~s z
bight baɪt (= bite, byte) bighted 'baɪt ɪd -əd
   ‖ 'baɪt̬- bighting 'baɪt ɪŋ ‖ 'baɪt̬- bights
   baɪts
bigmouth 'bɪg maʊθ ~s s
bigmouthed ˌbɪg 'maʊðd ◂ -'maʊθt, '··
Bignell 'bɪg nᵊl
bigness 'bɪg nəs -nɪs
bignonia bɪg 'nəʊn i‿ə ‖ -'noʊn- ~s z
bigot 'bɪg ət ~s s
bigoted 'bɪg ət ɪd -əd ‖ -ət̬ əd ~ly li ~ness nəs
   nɪs
bigotr|y 'bɪg ətr |i ~ies iz
big-time 'bɪg taɪm
bigwig 'bɪg wɪg ~s z
Bihar bɪ 'hɑː ‖ -'hɑːr —Hindi [bɪ hɑːr]
Bihari bɪ 'hɑːr i ~s z
bijou 'biːʒ uː biː 'ʒuː ~s, ~x z
bijouterie bi 'ʒuːt ər i ‖ -'ʒuːt̬- —Fr
   [bi ʒu tʁi]
bike baɪk biked baɪkt bikes baɪks biking
   'baɪk ɪŋ
biker, Biker 'baɪk ə ‖ -ᵊr ~s z
bikeshed 'baɪk ʃed ~s z
bikini, B~ bɪ 'kiːn i bə- ~s z
Biko 'biːk əʊ ‖ -oʊ
bilabial ₍ˌ₎baɪ 'leɪb i‿əl ~ly i ~s z
bilateral ₍ˌ₎baɪ 'læt̬ ᵊr əl ‖ -'læt̬ ər əl
   →-'lætr əl ~ly i ~ness nəs nɪs
Bilbao bɪl 'baʊ -'bɑː əʊ ‖ -'bɑː oʊ —Sp
   [bil 'βa o]
bilberr|y 'bɪl bər‿|i ‖ -ˌber |i ~ies iz
bilbo, Bilbo 'bɪlb əʊ ‖ -oʊ ~es, ~s z
Bildungsroman 'bɪld ʊŋz rəʊ ˌmɑːn ‖ -roʊ‿·
   —Ger ['bɪl dʊŋs ʁo ˌmaːn]
bile baɪᵊl
   'bile duct
bilge bɪldʒ bilged bɪldʒd bilges 'bɪldʒ ɪz -əz
   bilging 'bɪldʒ ɪŋ
bilgy 'bɪldʒ i
bilharzia bɪl 'hɑːz i‿ə -'hɑːts- ‖ -'hɑːrz-
biliary 'bɪl i‿ər i ‖ -er i
bilingual ₍ˌ₎baɪ 'lɪŋ gwəl -'lɪŋ gju‿əl ~ism
   ˌɪz əm ~ly i ~s z
bilious 'bɪl i‿əs ~ly li ~ness nəs nɪs
bilirubin ˌbɪl i 'ruːb ɪn ˌbaɪl-, §-ən

-bility 'bɪl ət i -ɪt- ‖ -ət̬-
bilk bɪlk bilked bɪlkt bilker/s 'bɪlk ə/z ‖ -ᵊr/z
   bilking 'bɪlk ɪŋ bilks bɪlks
Bilko 'bɪlk əʊ ‖ -oʊ
bill, Bill bɪl billed bɪld billing 'bɪl ɪŋ bills
   bɪlz
   ˌbill of 'fare; ˌbill of 'rights; ˌbill of 'sale
billable 'bɪl əb ᵊl
billabong 'bɪl ə bɒŋ ‖ -bɔːŋ -bɑːŋ ~s z
billboard 'bɪl bɔːd ‖ -bɔːrd -boʊrd ~s z
Billerica ˌbɪl 'rɪk ə ˌbel ə '··
Billericay ˌbɪl ə 'rɪk i
bill|et 'bɪl |ɪt -ət ‖ -|ət ~eted ɪt ɪd ət-, -əd
   ‖ ət̬ əd ~eting ɪt ɪŋ ət- ‖ ət̬ ɪŋ ~ets ɪts əts
billet-doux ˌbɪl eɪ 'duː -i- —Fr [bi ʒɛ du]
   billets-doux ˌbɪl eɪ 'duːz -i-, -'duː- —Fr
   [bi ʒɛ du]
billeter 'bɪl ɪt ə -ət- ‖ -ət̬ ᵊr ~s z
Billett 'bɪl ɪt §-ət
billettee ˌbɪl ɪ 'tiː -ə- ~s z
billfold 'bɪl fəʊld →-fɒʊld ‖ -foʊld ~s z
billhook 'bɪl hʊk §-huːk ~s s
billiard 'bɪl i‿əd ‖ 'bɪl jᵊrd ~s z
   'billiard ball; 'billiard ˌtable
Billie 'bɪl i
Billie-Jean ˌbɪl i 'dʒiːn ◂
billies —see billy
Billinge 'bɪl ɪndʒ
Billingham 'bɪl ɪŋ əm -həm
Billings 'bɪl ɪŋz
Billingsgate 'bɪl ɪŋz geɪt
Billingshurst 'bɪl ɪŋz hɜːst ‖ -hɜːst
Billingsley 'bɪl ɪŋz li
billion 'bɪl jən 'bɪl i‿ən ~s z
billionaire ˌbɪl jə 'neə ◂ ‖ -'neᵊr ◂ ~s z
billionth 'bɪl jənθ 'bɪl i‿ənθ ~s s
billow 'bɪl əʊ ‖ -oʊ ~ed d ~ing ɪŋ ~s z
billowy 'bɪl əʊ i ‖ -oʊ-
billposter 'bɪl ˌpəʊst ə ‖ -ˌpoʊst ᵊr ~s z
billposting 'bɪl ˌpəʊst ɪŋ ‖ -ˌpoʊst-
billsticker 'bɪl ˌstɪk ə ‖ -ᵊr ~s z
Billy, billy 'bɪl i Billy's, billies 'bɪl iz
   'billy goat
billy-can 'bɪl i kæn ~s z
billycock 'bɪl i kɒk -kɑːk ~s s
billy-o, billy-oh 'bɪl i əʊ ‖ -oʊ
Biloxi bɪ 'lʌks i bə-, -'lɒks- ‖ -'lɑːks- —In MS,
   locally -'lʌks-
Bilston 'bɪlst ən
Biltmore 'bɪlt mɔː ‖ -mɔːr -moʊr
biltong 'bɪl tɒŋ ‖ -tɔːŋ -tɑːŋ
Bim bɪm
bimbo 'bɪm bəʊ ‖ -boʊ ~s z
bimetallic ˌbaɪ me 'tæl ɪk ◂ -mə-, -mɪ-
   ˌbimeˌtallic 'strip
bimetallism ˌbaɪ 'met ᵊl ˌɪz əm -əl ˌɪz- ‖ -'met̬-
bimillenni|al ˌbaɪ mɪ 'len i |əl ˌ·mə- ~um əm
Bimini, b~ 'bɪm ən i -ɪn- ~s z
bimodal ₍ˌ₎baɪ 'məʊd ᵊl ‖ -'moʊd-
bimodality ˌbaɪ məʊ 'dæl ət i -ɪt- i
   ‖ -moʊ 'dæl ət̬ i
bimonth|ly ˌbaɪ 'mʌnθ |li ~lies liz
bin bɪn bins bɪnz

B

Bina (i) 'baɪn ə, (ii) 'biːn ə
binar|y 'baɪn ər |i ~ies iz
binaural ⑴baɪ 'nɔːr əl bɪ-
Binchy 'bɪntʃ i
bind baɪnd **binding** 'baɪnd ɪŋ **binds** baɪndz
  bound baʊnd
binder, B~ 'baɪnd ə ‖ -ᵊr ~s z
binder|y 'baɪnd ˏər |i ~ies iz
bindi 'bɪn di —Hindi [bɪɳ ɖiː] ~s z
binding 'baɪnd ɪŋ ~ly li ~ness nəs nɪs ~s z
bindweed 'baɪnd wiːd
bine baɪn **bines** baɪnz
Binet 'biːn eɪ ‖ bɪ 'neɪ —Fr [bi nɛ]
Binet-Simon ˌbiːn eɪ 'saɪm ən
  ‖ bɪ ˌneɪ siː 'moʊn
bing, Bing bɪŋ **bings, Bing's** bɪŋz
binge, Binge bɪndʒ **binged** bɪndʒd **bingeing,**
  binging 'bɪndʒ ɪŋ **binges** 'bɪndʒ ɪz -əz
Bingen 'bɪŋ ən —Ger ['bɪŋ ən]
Bingham 'bɪŋ əm
Binghamton 'bɪŋ əm tən
Bingley 'bɪŋ li
bingo, Bingo 'bɪŋ gəʊ ‖ -goʊ
  'bingo hall
Binks bɪŋks
bin Laden ˌbɪn 'lɑːd ᵊn —Arabic [bɪn 'laː dɪn]
bin-liner 'bɪn ˌlaɪn ə ‖ -ᵊr ~s z
bin|man 'bɪn |mæn →'bɪm-, -mən ~men men
  -mən
binnacle 'bɪn ək ᵊl -ɪk- ~s z
Binney, Binnie 'bɪn i
Binns bɪnz
Binoche bɪ 'nɒʃ bə- ‖ -'noʊʃ —Fr [bi nɔʃ]
binocular n bɪ 'nɒk jʊl ə bə-, baɪ-, -jəl-
  ‖ -'nɑːk jəl ᵊr ~s z
binocular adj baɪ 'nɒk jʊl ə bɪ-, bə-
  ‖ -'nɑːk jəl ᵊr -ly li
  bi,nocular 'vision
binocularity baɪ ˌnɒk jʊ 'lær ət i bɪ-, bə-,
  -ˌjə-, -ɪt i ‖ -ˌnɑːk jə 'lær ət i -'ler-
binomial ⑴baɪ 'nəʊm i əl ‖ -'noʊm- ~ly i ~s z
  bi'nomial ˌtheorem
bint bɪnt **bints** bɪnts
binturong 'bɪnt jʊ rɒŋ -jə- ‖ bɪn 'tʊr ɔːŋ -ɑːŋ
  ~s z
Binyon 'bɪn jən
bio, Bio 'baɪ əʊ ‖ -oʊ
bio- comb. form
  with stress-neutral suffix ˌbaɪ əʊ ‖ -oʊ —In
  some well-known words, the weakening of the
  second diphthong to ə has become thoroughly
  established, with the consequence in RP that
  SMOOTHING from ˌbaɪ ə to ˌbaə is also
  heard. But in some other cases, where the
  separateness of the prefix is strongly felt, əʊ
  ‖ oʊ remains strong. —**biolytic**
  ˌbaɪ əʊ 'lɪt ɪk ◄ ‖ ˌbaɪ oʊ 'lɪt̬ ɪk ◄
  with stress-imposing suffix baɪ 'ɒ+ ‖ -'ɑː+
  —**biolysis** baɪ 'ɒl əs ɪs -ɪs-, §-əs ‖ -'ɑːl-
biochemical ˌbaɪ əʊ 'kem ɪk ᵊl ◄ ‖ ˌ‑oʊ- ~ly ˌi
  ~s z
biochemist ˌbaɪ əʊ 'kem ɪst §-əst ‖ -oʊ- ~s s
biochemistry ˌbaɪ əʊ 'kem ɪs tri -əs tri ‖ ˌ‑oʊ-

biodata 'baɪ əʊ ˌdeɪt ə -ˌdɑːt- ‖ -oʊ ˌdæt̬ ə
biodegradability ˌbaɪ əʊdi ˌgreɪd ə 'bɪl ət i
  -də-,‑-, -ɪt i ‖ ˌbaɪ oʊ di ˌgreɪd ə 'bɪl ət̬ i
biodegradab|le ˌbaɪ əʊ di 'greɪd əb |ᵊl ◄
  -də'- ‖ ˌ‑oʊ- ~ly li
biodegradation ˌbaɪ əʊ ˌdeg rə 'deɪʒ ᵊn
  ‖ ˌ‑oʊ-
biodegrad|e ˌbaɪ əʊdi 'greɪd -də'- ‖ ˌbaɪ oʊ-
  ~ed ɪd əd ~es z ~ing ɪŋ
biodiversity ˌbaɪ əʊ daɪ 'vɜːs ət i -dɪ'-, -ɪt i
  ‖ ˌbaɪ oʊ də 'vɜːs ət̬ i -daɪ'-
bioengineering ˌbaɪ əʊ ˌendʒ ɪ 'nɪər ɪŋ -‑,ə-
  ‖ -oʊ ˌendʒ ə 'nɪr-
biofeedback ˌbaɪ əʊ 'fiːd bæk →‑'fiːb- ‖ -oʊ-
biogas 'baɪ əʊ gæs ‖ -oʊ-
biographer baɪ 'ɒg rəf ə ‖ -'ɑːg rəf ᵊr ~s z
biographic ˌbaɪ ə 'græf ɪk ◄ ~al ᵊl ~ally ᵊl i
biograph|y baɪ 'ɒg rəf |i ‖ -'ɑːg- ~ies iz
biohazard 'baɪ əʊ ˌhæz əd ‖ -oʊ ˌhæz ᵊrd ~s z
Bioko bi 'əʊk əʊ ‖ -'oʊk oʊ
biological ˌbaɪ ə 'lɒdʒ ɪk ᵊl ◄ ‖ -'lɑːdʒ- ~ly li
  ˌbio,logical 'clock
biologist baɪ 'ɒl ədʒ ɪst §-əst ‖ -'ɑːl- ~s s
biology baɪ 'ɒl ədʒ i ‖ -'ɑːl-
biomass 'baɪ əʊ mæs ‖ -oʊ-
biome 'baɪ əʊm ‖ -oʊm ~s z
biometric ˌbaɪ əʊ 'metr ɪk ◄ ‖ -oʊ- ~al ᵊl ~s s
Bion 'baɪ ˌən -ɒn ‖ 'baɪ ɑːn
bionic ⑴baɪ 'ɒn ɪk ‖ -'ɑːn- ~s s
biopharmaceutic ˌbaɪ əʊ ˌfɑːm ə 'suːt ɪk ◄
  -'sjuːt- ‖ ˌbaɪ oʊ ˌfɑːrm ə 'suːt̬ ɪk ◄ ~als ᵊl/z
biophysical ˌbaɪ əʊ 'fɪz ɪk ᵊl ‖ ˌ‑oʊ- ~ly ˌi
biophysicist ˌbaɪ əʊ 'fɪz ɪs ɪst -əs ɪst, §-əst
  ‖ ˌ‑oʊ- ~s s
biophysics ˌbaɪ əʊ 'fɪz ɪks ‖ -oʊ-
biopic 'baɪ əʊ pɪk ‖ -oʊ- ~s s
bioprogram 'baɪ əʊ ˌprəʊ græm ˌ·‑·'·
  ‖ -oʊ ˌproʊ- ~s z
biops|y 'baɪ ɒps |i ·'·‑· ‖ -ɑːps- ~ies iz
biorhythm 'baɪ əʊ ˌrɪð əm ‖ -oʊ- ~s z
biorhythmic ˌbaɪ əʊ 'rɪð mɪk ◄ ‖ -oʊ-
BIOS 'baɪ ɒs ‖ -ɑːs
bioscope 'baɪ ə skəʊp ‖ -skoʊp ~s s
biosphere 'baɪ əʊ sfɪə ‖ -ə sfɪr ~s z
Bio-Strath tdmk 'baɪ əʊ stræθ ‖ -oʊ-
biota baɪ 'əʊt ə ‖ -'oʊt̬-
biotech 'baɪ əʊ tek ‖ -oʊ-
biotechnology ˌbaɪ əʊ tek 'nɒl ədʒ i
  ‖ -oʊ tek 'nɑːl-
biotic baɪ 'ɒt ɪk ‖ -'ɑːt̬-
bipartisan ˌbaɪ ˌpɑːt ɪ 'zæn -ə-; ⑴·'·‑·‑·, -ɪz ən,
  -əz- ‖ ⑴baɪ 'pɑːrt̬ əz ən -əs- ~ship ʃɪp
bipartite ⑴baɪ 'pɑːt aɪt '·‑·‑· ‖ -'pɑːrt- ~ly li
bipartition ˌbaɪ pɑː 'tɪʃ ᵊn -pə- ‖ -pɑːr-
biped 'baɪ ped ~s z
bipedal ˌbaɪ 'piːd ᵊl ◄ -'ped- ~ly i
biplane 'baɪ pleɪn ~s z
bipod 'baɪ pɒd ‖ -pɑːd ~s z
bipolar ˌbaɪ 'pəʊl ə ◄ ‖ -'poʊl ᵊr ◄
bipolarity ˌbaɪ pəʊ 'lær ət i -ɪt i
  ‖ -poʊ 'lær ət̬ i -'ler-
biquadratic ˌbaɪ kwɒ 'dræt ɪk ◄
  ‖ -kwɑː 'dræt̬-

biracial ˌbaɪ 'reɪʃ ᵊl ◂
birch, Birch bɜːtʃ ‖ bɜ˞ːtʃ **birches, Birch's**
 'bɜːtʃ ɪz -əz ‖ 'bɜ˞ːtʃ-
Birchall (i) 'bɜːtʃ ɔːl ‖ 'bɜ˞ːtʃ- -ɑːl, (ii) -ᵊl
Bircher 'bɜːtʃ ə ‖ 'bɜ˞ːtʃ ᵊr
Birchington 'bɜːtʃ ɪŋ tən ‖ 'bɜ˞ːtʃ-
bird, Bird bɜːd ‖ bɜ˞ːd **birding** 'bɜːd ɪŋ
 ‖ 'bɜ˞ːd ɪŋ **birds** bɜːdz ‖ bɜ˞ːdz
 'bird ˌfancier; 'bird flu; ˌbird of 'passage;
 ˌbird of 'prey; 'bird ˌtable
birdbath 'bɜːd bɑːθ →'bɜːb-, §-bæθ
 ‖ 'bɜ˞ːd bæθ
bird-brained 'bɜːd breɪnd →'bɜːb- ‖ 'bɜ˞ːd-
birdcag|e 'bɜːd keɪdʒ →'bɜːg- ‖ 'bɜ˞ːd- **~es** ɪz
 əz
birder 'bɜːd ə ‖ 'bɜ˞ːd ᵊr **~s** z
birdie, B~ 'bɜːd i ‖ 'bɜ˞ːd i **~s** z
birdlike 'bɜːd laɪk ‖ 'bɜ˞ːd-
birdlim|e 'bɜːd laɪm ‖ 'bɜ˞ːd- **~ed** d **~ing** ɪŋ **~s**
 z
bird|man 'bɜːd |mæn →'bɜːb-, -mən ‖ 'bɜ˞ːd-
 ~men men -mən
Birdsall (i) 'bɜːd sɔːl ‖ 'bɜ˞ːd- -sɑːl, (ii) -sᵊl
birdseed 'bɜːd siːd ‖ 'bɜ˞ːd-
bird's-eye, Birdseye 'bɜːdz aɪ ‖ 'bɜ˞ːdz-
bird's-foot 'bɜːdz fʊt ‖ 'bɜ˞ːdz- **~s** s
birdshot 'bɜːd ʃɒt ‖ 'bɜ˞ːd-
bird's-nest 'bɜːdz nest ‖ 'bɜ˞ːdz- **~s** s
birdsong 'bɜːd sɒŋ ‖ 'bɜ˞ːd sɔːŋ -sɑːŋ **~s** z
bird-watch|er 'bɜːd ˌwɒtʃ |ə ‖ 'bɜ˞ːd ˌwɑːtʃ |ᵊr
 -ˌwɔːtʃ- **~ers** əz ‖ ᵊrz **~ing** ɪŋ
birefring|ence ˌbaɪ ri 'frɪndʒ |ənᵗs -rə- **~ent**
 ənt
bireme 'baɪ riːm **~s** z
biretta bə 'ret ə bɪ- ‖ -'reṭ- **~s** z
Birgit 'bɪəg ɪt 'bɜːg-, §-ət ‖ 'bɪrg-
Birgitta bɪə 'gɪt ə bɪr 'gɪt ə —Swedish
 [bɪr ''gɪt a]
biriani ˌbɪr i 'ɑːn i **~s** z
Birkbeck 'bɜːk bek ‖ 'bɜ˞ːk- —but as a family
 name sometimes 'bɜː bek ‖ 'bɜ˞ː-
Birkenhead ˌbɜːk ən 'hed '·· ‖ ˌbɜ˞ːk-
Birkenshaw 'bɜːk ən ʃɔː ‖ 'bɜ˞ːk- -ʃɑː
Birkenstock 'bɜːk ən stɒk ‖ 'bɜ˞ːk ən stɑːk **~s**
 s
Birkett 'bɜːk ɪt §-ət ‖ 'bɜ˞ːk-
birl bɜːl ‖ bɜ˞ːl **birled** bɜːld ‖ bɜ˞ːld **birling**
 'bɜːl ɪŋ ‖ 'bɜ˞ːl- **birls** bɜːlz ‖ bɜ˞ːlz
Birley 'bɜːl i ‖ 'bɜ˞ːl i
Birling 'bɜːl ɪŋ ‖ 'bɜ˞ːl ɪŋ
Birmingham (i) 'bɜːm ɪŋ əm -həm ‖ 'bɜ˞ːm-,
 (ii) -hæm —The place in England is (i), but
 places in the US are (ii).
Birnam 'bɜːn əm ‖ 'bɜ˞ːn-
Birney, Birnie 'bɜːn i ‖ 'bɜ˞ːn i
biro, Biro tdmk 'baɪᵊr əʊ ‖ -oʊ —Hungarian
 Biró ['bi roː] **~s** z
Birobidzhan ˌbɪr əʊ bɪ 'dʒɑːn ‖ ˌ·oʊ- —Russ
 [bʲɪ rə bʲɪ 'dʒan]
birr bɜː ‖ bɜ˞ː **birred** bɜːd ‖ bɜ˞ːd **birring**
 'bɜːr ɪŋ ‖ 'bɜ˞ː- **birrs** bɜːz ‖ bɜ˞ːz
Birrane bɪ 'reɪn bə-
Birrell 'bɪr əl

Birt bɜːt ‖ bɜ˞ːt
birth bɜːθ ‖ bɜ˞ːθ **birthed** bɜːθt ‖ bɜ˞ːθt
 birthing 'bɜːθ ɪŋ ‖ 'bɜ˞ːθ- **births** bɜːθs
 ‖ bɜ˞ːθs
 'birth cerˌtificate; 'birth conˌtrol
birthday 'bɜːθ deɪ -di ‖ 'bɜ˞ːθ- —See note at
 -day **~s** z
 'birthday cake; 'birthday card; ˌBirthday
 'honours; 'birthday ˌparty; 'birthday
 ˌpresent; 'birthday suit
birthmark 'bɜːθ mɑːk ‖ 'bɜ˞ːθ mɑːrk **~s** s
birthplace 'bɜːθ pleɪs ‖ 'bɜ˞ːθ- **~s** ɪz əz
birthrate 'bɜːθ reɪt ‖ 'bɜ˞ːθ- **~s** s
birthright 'bɜːθ raɪt ‖ 'bɜ˞ːθ- **~s** s
birthroot 'bɜːθ ruːt ‖ 'bɜ˞ːθ-
birthstone 'bɜːθ stəʊn ‖ 'bɜ˞ːθ stoʊn **~s** z
birthwort 'bɜːθ wɜːt §-wɔːt ‖ 'bɜ˞ːθ wɜ˞ːt -wɔːrt
 ~s s
Birtles 'bɜːt ᵊlz ‖ 'bɜ˞ːṭ-
Birtwhistle, Birtwistle 'bɜːt ˌwɪs ᵊl -ˌhwɪs-
 ‖ 'bɜ˞ːt ˌhwɪs-
biryani ˌbɪr i 'ɑːn i **~s** z
bis bɪs
Biscay 'bɪsk eɪ -i
Biscayne ˌbɪs 'keɪn ◂
 ˌBiscayne 'Boulevard
biscotti bɪ 'skɒt i ‖ -'skɑːṭ- —It [bi 'skɔt ti]
biscuit 'bɪsk ɪt §-ət **~s** s
bisect ˌ(ˌ)baɪ 'sekt '·· ‖ '···· **~ed** ɪd əd **~ing** ɪŋ **~s**
 s
bisection ˌ(ˌ)baɪ 'sek ʃᵊn '·,·· ‖ '·,··· **~al** ᵊl **~ally**
 ᵊl i
bisector ˌ(ˌ)baɪ 'sekt ə ‖ 'baɪ ˌsekt ᵊr **~s** z
bisexual ˌbaɪ 'sek ʃu əl ◂ -'seks ju əl, -'sekʃ ᵊl
 ~ly -i **~s** z
bisexuality ˌbaɪ ˌsek ʃu 'æl ət i -ˌseks ju-, -ɪt i
 ‖ -əṭ i
bish bɪʃ **bishes** 'bɪʃ ɪz -əz
Bishkek ˌbɪʃ 'kek
bishop, B~ 'bɪʃ əp **~s** s
 ˌBishop's 'Stortford
bishophood 'bɪʃ əp hʊd
bishopric 'bɪʃ əp rɪk **~s** s
Bishopsgate 'bɪʃ əps geɪt
Bishopston 'bɪʃ əps tən
Bislama 'bɪʃ lə mɑː
Bisley 'bɪz li
Bismag tdmk 'bɪz mæg
Bismarck 'bɪz mɑːk ‖ -mɑːrk —Ger
 ['bɪs maʁk]
bismuth 'bɪz məθ
bismuthic bɪz 'mjuː θ ɪk -'mʌθ-; 'bɪz məθ-
BiSoDol tdmk 'baɪ səʊ dɒl ‖ -soʊ dɑːl -dɔːl
bison 'baɪs ᵊn ‖ 'baɪz- **~s** z
Bispham 'bɪsp əm —but as a family name
 sometimes 'bɪs fəm
bisque bɪsk —Fr [bisk] **bisques** bɪsks
Bissau bɪ 'saʊ 'bɪs aʊ —Port [bi 'sau]
Bissell 'bɪs ᵊl
Bisset, Bissett (i) 'bɪs ɪt §-ət, (ii) 'bɪz-
bissextile bɪ 'sekst arᵊl ‖ -ᵊl
bistable ˌbaɪ 'steɪb ᵊl
bister 'bɪst ə ‖ -ᵊr **~ed** d

B

Bisto *tdmk* 'bɪst əʊ ‖ -oʊ
bistort 'bɪst ɔːt ‖ -ɔːrt **~s** s
bistour|y 'bɪst ər |i **~ies** iz
bistre 'bɪst ə ‖ -ᵊr **~d** d
bistro 'biːs trəʊ 'bɪs- ‖ -troʊ —*Fr (usually*
   bistrot) [bis tʁo] **~s** z
bit bɪt **bits** bɪts
   'bit part
bitch bɪtʃ **bitched** bɪtʃt **bitches** 'bɪtʃ ɪz -əz
   bitching 'bɪtʃ ɪŋ
bitchin 'bɪtʃ ɪn -ən
bitch|y 'bɪtʃ |i **~ier** i‿ə ‖ i‿ᵊr **~iest** i‿ɪst i‿əst
   ~ily ɪ li əl i **~iness** i nəs i nɪs
bite baɪt **bit** bɪt **bites** baɪts **biting** 'baɪt ɪŋ
   ‖ 'baɪt̬ ɪŋ **bitten** 'bɪt ᵊn
biter 'baɪt ə ‖ 'baɪt̬ ᵊr **~s** z
bite-size 'baɪt saɪz **~d** d
Bithell *(i)* 'bɪθ ᵊl, *(ii)* bɪ 'θel
Bithynia baɪ 'θɪn i‿ə bɪ-
biting 'baɪt ɪŋ ‖ 'baɪt̬ ɪŋ **~ly** li
bitmap 'bɪt mæp **~ped** t **~ping** ɪŋ **~s** s
bitsy 'bɪts i
bitt bɪt (= *bit*) **bitts** bɪts
bitten 'bɪt ᵊn
bitt|er 'bɪt |ə ‖ 'bɪt̬ |ᵊr **~erer** ər ə ‖ ᵊr ər
   ~erest ər ɪst -əst **~ers** əz ‖ ᵊrz
   ˌbitter 'end; ˌbitter 'lemon
bittercress 'bɪt ə kres ‖ 'bɪt̬ ᵊr-
bitterly 'bɪt ə li -ᵊl i ‖ 'bɪt̬ ᵊr li
bittern 'bɪt ᵊn -ɜːn ‖ 'bɪt̬ ᵊrn **~s** z
bitterness 'bɪt ə nəs -nɪs; -ᵊn əs, -ɪs ‖ 'bɪt̬ ᵊr-
bitternut 'bɪt ə nʌt ‖ 'bɪt̬ ᵊr- **~s** s
bittersweet 'bɪt ə swiːt ˌ·'· ‖ 'bɪt̬ ᵊr-
bitt|y 'bɪt |i ‖ 'bɪt̬ |i **~iness** i nəs i nɪs
bitumen 'bɪtʃ ʊm ɪn -əm-, -ən; -u men, -ə-;
   'bɪt jʊm ɪn ‖ bə 'tuːm ən bɪ-, baɪ-, -'tjuːm- *(*)*
bituminiz|e bɪ 'tjuːm ɪ naɪz bə-, →-'tʃuːm-, -ə-;
   'bɪtʃ ʊm ɪ-, '·əm-, '·ə- ‖ bə 'tuːm- bɪ-, baɪ-,
   -'tjuːm- **~ed** d **~es** ɪz əz **~ing** ɪŋ
bituminous bɪ 'tjuːm ɪn əs bə-, →-'tʃuːm-,
   -ən əs ‖ -'tuːm- -'tjuːm-
biunique ˌbaɪ ju 'niːk ◄ **~ly** li **~ness** nəs nɪs
bivalenc|e ⁽ˌ⁾baɪ 'veɪl ənˢs ◄ 'bɪv əl ənˢs **~y** i
bivalent ⁽ˌ⁾baɪ 'veɪl ənt ◄ 'bɪv əl ənt
bivalve 'baɪ vælv **~s** z
bivariate ˌbaɪ 'veər i‿ət ◄ ‿ɪt ‖ -'ver- -'vær-
bivouac 'bɪv u‿æk **~ked** t **~king** ɪŋ **~s** s
bivv|y 'bɪv |i **~ies** iz
biweek|ly ⁽ˌ⁾baɪ 'wiːk |li **~lies** liz
biz bɪz
bizarre bɪ 'zɑː bə- ‖ -'zɑːr **~ly** li **~ness** nəs nɪs
Bizet 'biːz eɪ bɪ 'zeɪ —*Fr* [bi zɛ] **~'s** z
Bjelke-Petersen ˌbjelk i 'piːt əs ən ‖ -'piːt̬ ᵊr-
Björk bjɔːk bjɜːk, bi 'ɔːk ‖ bjɜːrk bjɜːk
   —*Icelandic* [bjœ̠k]
Bjorn, Björn bi 'ɔːn bjɜːn ‖ bi 'ɔːrn bjɜːn
   —*Swedish* [bjœːn]
blab blæb **blabbed** blæbd **blabbing** 'blæb ɪŋ
   blabs blæbz
blabb|er 'blæb |ə ‖ -|ᵊr **~ered** əd ‖ ᵊrd **~ering**
   ər ɪŋ **~ers** əz ‖ ᵊrz
blabber|mouth 'blæb ə |maʊθ ‖ -ᵊr- **~mouths**
   maʊðz maʊθs

blabby 'blæb i
Blaby 'bleɪb i
black, Black blæk **blacked** blækt **blacker**
   'blæk ə ‖ -ᵊr **blackest** 'blæk ɪst -əst **blacking**
   'blæk ɪŋ **blacks, Blacks** blæks
   ˌblack and 'blue◄; ˌblack and 'white◄;
   'Black ˌCountry; ˌBlack 'Death; ˌblack
   'eye; ˌBlack 'Forest; ˌblack 'hole; ˌblack
   'ice; ˌblack 'magic; ˌBlack Ma'ria; ˌblack
   'market; ˌblack ˌmarke'teer; ˌBlack 'Mass;
   'black ˌpeople; ˌblack 'power; ˌblack
   'pudding; ˌBlack 'Sea; 'black spot
Blackadder 'blæk ˌæd ə ˌ·'·ˌ·; 'blæk əd ə ‖ -ᵊr
Blackall 'blæk ɔːl ‖ -ɑːl
blackamoor 'blæk ə mɔː -mʊə ‖ -mʊr **~s** z
black-and-white ˌblæk ən 'waɪt ◄ -ənd-,
   →-ŋ-, -'hwaɪt
blackball 'blæk bɔːl ‖ -bɑːl **~ed** d **~ing** ɪŋ **~s** z
blackberr|y, BlackBerr|y *tdmk* 'blæk bər |i
   ‖ -ˌber |i **~ied** id **~ies** iz **~ying** i ɪŋ
blackbird 'blæk bɜːd ‖ -bɜːd **~s** z
blackboard 'blæk bɔːd ‖ -bɔːrd -boʊrd **~s** z
   ˌblackboard 'jungle
Blackburn 'blæk bɜːn -bən ‖ -bɜːn —*locally*
   also 'blæg-
blackcap 'blæk kæp **~s** s
blackcock 'blæk kɒk ‖ -kɑːk
blackcurrant ˌblæk 'kʌr ənt ◄ ·'·ˌ·, '·ˌ··
   ‖ 'blæk ˌkɜː ənt **~s** s
blacken 'blæk ən **~ed** d **~ing** ˌɪŋ **~s** z
Blacket, Blackett 'blæk ɪt §-ət
black-eyed ˌblæk 'aɪd ◄
   ˌblack-eyed 'Susan
blackface 'blæk feɪs
black|fly 'blæk |flaɪ **~flies** flaɪz
Blackfoot 'blæk fʊt
Blackford 'blæk fəd ‖ -fᵊrd
Blackfriars ˌblæk 'fraɪ‿əz ◄ '·ˌ·· ‖ -'fraɪ‿ᵊrz
   ˌBlack ˌfriars 'Bridge
blackguard 'blæg ɑːd -əd ‖ -ɑːrd -ᵊrd **~ly** li **~s**
   z
blackhead 'blæk hed **~s** z
Blackheath ˌblæk 'hiːθ ◄
Blackie *(i)* 'blæk i, *(ii)* 'bleɪk i
blacking 'blæk ɪŋ **~s** z
blackish 'blæk ɪʃ **~ly** li
blackjack 'blæk dʒæk **~ed** t **~ing** ɪŋ **~s** s
blacklead 'blæk led ˌ·'· **~ed** ɪd əd **~ing** ɪŋ **~s** z
blackleg 'blæk leg **~ged** d **~ging** ɪŋ **~s** z
Blackley 'blæk li —*but the place in Manchester*
   is 'bleɪk-
blacklist 'blæk lɪst **~ed** ɪd əd **~ing** ɪŋ **~s** s
Blacklock 'blæk lɒk ‖ -lɑːk
blackly 'blæk li
blackmail 'blæk meɪᵊl **~ed** d **~er** ə ‖ -ᵊr **~ers**
   əz ‖ ᵊrz **~ing** ɪŋ **~s** z
Blackman 'blæk mən
Blackmore 'blæk mɔː ‖ -mɔːr -moʊr
blackness 'blæk nəs -nɪs
blackout 'blæk aʊt **~s** s
Blackpool 'blæk puːl
Blackshirt 'blæk ʃɜːt ‖ -ʃɜːt **~s** s
blacksmith 'blæk smɪθ **~ing** ɪŋ **~s** s

Blackstone 'blæk stəʊn -stən ‖ -stoʊn -stən
blackthorn 'blæk θɔːn ‖ -θɔːrn ~s z
black-tie ˌblæk 'taɪ ◂
blacktop 'blæk tɒp ‖ -tɑːp
Blacktown 'blæk taʊn
Blackwall 'blæk wɔːl ‖ -wɑːl
   ˌBlackwall 'Tunnel
blackwater, B~ 'blæk ˌwɔːt ə ‖ -ˌwɔːt̬ ᵊr
   -ˌwɑːt̬-
Blackwell 'blæk wᵊl -wel
Blackwood, b~ 'blæk wʊd —but the place in
   Gwent is ˌ·'·
bladder 'blæd ə ‖ -ᵊr ~ed d ~s z
bladderwort 'blæd ə wɜːt -wɔːt ‖ -ᵊr wɜːt
   -wɔːrt ~s s
bladderwrack 'blæd ə ræk ‖ -ᵊr-
blade bleɪd bladed 'bleɪd ɪd -əd blades bleɪdz
blader 'bleɪd ə ‖ -ᵊr ~s z
Bladon 'bleɪd ᵊn
blaeberry 'bleɪ bər_i ‖ -ˌber i
Blaenau 'blaɪn aɪ △-aʊ; 'bleɪn i —Welsh
   ['bləi nai, 'bləi-, -na, -ne]
   ˌBlaenau 'Gwent
blag blæg blagged blægd blagging 'blæg ɪŋ
   blags blægz
Blagden, Blagdon 'blæg dən
blagger 'blæg ə ‖ -ᵊr ~s z
blah blɑː blahs blɑːz
Blahnik 'blɑːn ɪk
blain, Blain, Blaine bleɪn blains, Blaine's
   bleɪnz
Blair bleə ‖ bleᵊr
Blairgowrie ˌbleə 'gaʊᵊr i ‖ ˌbler-
Blairism 'bleər ˌɪz əm ‖ 'bler-
Blairite 'bleər aɪt ‖ 'bler- ~s s
Blaise bleɪz
Blake bleɪk Blake's bleɪks
Blakemore 'bleɪk mɔː ‖ -mɔːr -moʊr
Blakeney 'bleɪk ni
Blakenham 'bleɪk ən_əm
blame bleɪm blamed bleɪmd blames bleɪmz
   blaming 'bleɪm ɪŋ
blameless 'bleɪm ləs -lɪs ~ly li ~ness nəs nɪs
blameworth|y 'bleɪm ˌwɜːð |i ‖ -ˌwɜːð |i
   ~iness i nəs i nɪs
Blanc blɒ̃ ‖ blɑː: —Fr [blɑ̃]
blanch, B~ blɑːntʃ §blæntʃ ‖ blæntʃ blanched
   blɑːntʃt §blæntʃt ‖ blæntʃt blanches
   'blɑːntʃ ɪz §'blæntʃ-, -əz ‖ 'blæntʃ əz
   blanching 'blɑːntʃ ɪŋ §'blæntʃ- ‖ 'blæntʃ ɪŋ
Blanchard 'blæntʃ əd -ɑːd ‖ -ᵊrd -ɑːrd
Blanche blɑːntʃ ‖ blæntʃ
Blanchett 'blɑːntʃ ət 'blæntʃ-, -ɪt ‖ 'blæntʃ-
Blanchflower 'blɑːntʃ ˌflaʊ_ə §'blæntʃ-
   ‖ 'blæntʃ ˌflaʊ_ᵊr
blancmang|e blə 'mɒndʒ ‖ -'mɑːndʒ (!) ~es
   ɪz əz
blanco, B~ tdmk 'blæŋk əʊ ‖ -oʊ ~ed d ~s z
   ~ing ɪŋ
bland, Bland blænd blander 'blænd ə ‖ -ᵊr
   blandest 'blænd ɪst -əst
Blandford 'blænd fəd ‖ -fᵊrd

blandish 'blænd ɪʃ ~ed t ~es ɪz əz ~ing ɪŋ
   ~ment/s mənt/s
bland|ly 'blænd |li ~ness nəs nɪs
blank blæŋk blanked blæŋkt blanking
   'blæŋk ɪŋ blanks blæŋks
   ˌblank 'cartridge; ˌblank 'cheque or
   'check; ˌblank 'verse
blank|et 'blæŋk |ɪt §-ət ‖ -|ət ~eted ɪt ɪd §ət-,
   əd ‖ ət̬ əd ~eting ɪt ɪŋ ‖ ət̬ ɪŋ ~ets ɪts §əts
   ‖ əts
blankety-blank ˌblæŋk ət i 'blæŋk ◂ ‖ -ət̬ i-
blank|ly 'blæŋk| li ~ness nəs nɪs
blanquette (ˌ)blɒŋ 'ket (ˌ)blæŋ- ‖ (ˌ)blɑː-ŋ-
   —Fr [blɑ̃ kɛt]
blan,quette de 'veau vəʊ ‖ voʊ —Fr [vo]
Blantyre 'blæn ˌtaɪ_ə ˌblæn 'taɪ_ə ‖ ˌblæn 'taɪᵊr
blare bleə ‖ bleᵊr blared bleəd ‖ bleᵊrd blares
   bleəz ‖ bleᵊrz blaring 'bleər ɪŋ ‖ 'bler ɪŋ
blarney, B~ 'blɑːn i ‖ 'blɑːrn i ~ed d ~s z
   ~ing ɪŋ
blase, blasé 'blɑːz eɪ ‖ ˌblɑː 'zeɪ —Fr [blɑ ze]
blasphem|e (ˌ)blæs 'fiːm (ˌ)blɑːs- ‖ '·· ~ed d
   ~er ə ‖ ᵊr ~ers əz ‖ ᵊrz ~es z ~ing ɪŋ
blasphemi... —see blasphemy
blasphemous 'blæs fəm əs 'blɑːs-, -fɪm- ~ly li
blasphem|y 'blæs fəm |i 'blɑːs-, -fɪm- ~ies iz
blast blɑːst §blæst ‖ blæst blasted 'blɑːst ɪd
   §'blæst-, -əd ‖ 'blæst əd blasting 'blɑːst ɪŋ
   §'blæst- ‖ 'blæst ɪŋ blasts blɑːsts §blæsts
   ‖ blæsts
   'blast ˌfurnace
blasto- comb. form
   with stress-neutral suffix ǀblæst əʊ ‖ -ə
   — blastopore 'blæst əʊ pɔː ‖ -ə pɔːr -poʊr
   with stress-imposing suffix blæ 'stɒ+
   ‖ -'stɑː+ — blastolysis blæ 'stɒl əs ɪs -ɪs-,
   §-əs ‖ -'stɑːl-
blast-off 'blɑːst ɒf §'blæst-, -ɔːf ‖ 'blæst ɔːf -ɑːf
blastula 'blæst jʊl ə →'blæs tʃʊl ə
   ‖ 'blæs tʃəl ə
blastulation ˌblæst ju 'leɪʃ ᵊn →ˌblæs tʃə-
   ‖ ˌblæs tʃə-
blat blæt blats blæts blatted 'blæt ɪd -əd
   ‖ 'blæt̬- blatting 'blæt ɪŋ ‖ 'blæt̬-
blatancy 'bleɪt ᵊn's i
blatant 'bleɪt ᵊnt ~ly li
Blatchford 'blætʃ fəd ‖ -fᵊrd
blath|er 'blæð |ə ‖ -|ᵊr ~ered əd ‖ ᵊrd ~ering
   ᵊr_ɪŋ ~ers əz ‖ ᵊrz
Blavatsky blə 'væt ski ‖ -'vɑːt-
Blawith (i) blɑːð, (ii) 'bleɪ wɪθ —The places in
   Cumbria are (i).
Blaydes bleɪdz
Blaydon 'bleɪd ᵊn
blaze bleɪz blazed bleɪzd blazes 'bleɪz ɪz -əz
   blazing/ly 'bleɪz ɪŋ /li
blazer 'bleɪz ə ‖ -ᵊr ~s z
blazon 'bleɪz ᵊn ~ed d ~ing ˌɪŋ ~ment/s
   mənt/s ~s z
blazon|ry 'bleɪz ᵊn |ri ~ries riz
Blea bliː
bleach bliːtʃ bleached bliːtʃt bleaches
   'bliːtʃ ɪz -əz bleaching 'bliːtʃ ɪŋ

bleacher 'bliːtʃ ə ‖ -ᵊr ~s z

bleak bliːk **bleaker** 'bliːk ə ‖ -ᵊr **bleakest**
'bliːk ɪst -əst

bleak|ly 'bliːk |li ~ness nəs nɪs

blear blɪə ‖ blɪᵊr **bleared** blɪəd ‖ blɪᵊrd
blearing 'blɪər ɪŋ ‖ 'blɪr ɪŋ **blears** blɪəz
‖ blɪᵊrz

blear|y 'blɪər |i ‖ 'blɪr |i **~ier** i‿ə ‖ i‿ᵊr **~iest**
i‿ɪst i‿əst **~ily** əl i ɪ li **~iness** i nəs i nɪs

bleary-eyed ˌblɪər i 'aɪd ◂ ‖ ˌblɪr-

Bleasdale 'bliːz deɪᵊl

bleat bliːt **bleated** 'bliːt ɪd -əd ‖ 'bliːt̬ əd
bleats bliːts **bleating** 'bliːt ɪŋ ‖ 'bliːt̬ ɪŋ

bleb bleb **blebs** blebz

bled, Bled bled

Bleddyn 'bleð ɪn

Bledisloe 'bled ɪs ləʊ -əs-, -ɪz- ‖ -loʊ

bleed bliːd **bled** bled **bleeding** 'bliːd ɪŋ
bleeds bliːdz

bleeder 'bliːd ə ‖ -ᵊr ~s z

bleep bliːp **bleeped** bliːpt **bleeping** 'bliːp ɪŋ
bleeps bliːps

bleeper 'bliːp ə ‖ -ᵊr ~s z

blemish 'blem ɪʃ **~ed** t **~es** ɪz əz **~ing** ɪŋ

Blencathra blen 'kæθ rə

blench blentʃ **blenched** blentʃt **blenches**
'blentʃ ɪz -əz **blenching** 'blentʃ ɪŋ

blend blend **blended** 'blend ɪd -əd **blending**
'blend ɪŋ **blends** blendz

blende blend (= blend)

blender 'blend ə ‖ -ᵊr ~s z

Blenheim 'blen ɪm -əm

Blenkinsop 'bleŋk ɪn sɒp -ən- ‖ -sɑːp

Blennerhassett ˌblen ə 'hæs ɪt §-ət, '·· · · ‖ -ᵊr-

blenn|y 'blen |i **~ies** iz

blent blent

blepharitis ˌblef ə 'raɪt ɪs §-əs ‖ -'raɪt̬ əs

blepharo- comb. form
with stress-neutral suffix ⎪blef ə rəʊ ‖ -ər ə
— **blepharoplasty** 'blef ə rəʊ ˌplæst i
‖ -'blef ər ə-
with stress-imposing suffix ˌblef ə 'rɒ +
‖ -'rɑː + — **blepharotomy** ˌblef ə 'rɒt əm i
‖ -'rɑːt̬-

Bleriot, Blériot 'bler i əʊ ‖ ˌbler i 'oʊ '·· ·
—Fr [ble ʁjo]

Bles bles

blesbok 'bles bɒk -bʌk ‖ -bɑːk ~s s

blesbuck 'bles bʌk ~s s

bless bles **blesses** 'bles ɪz -əz **blessing**
'bles ɪŋ **blest** blest

blessed past & pp of **bless** blest

blessed adj, B~ 'bles ɪd -əd **~ly** li **~ness** nəs
nɪs

blessing 'bles ɪŋ **~s** z

Blessington 'bles ɪŋ tən

blest blest

blet blet

Bletchingley 'bletʃ ɪŋ li

Bletchley 'bletʃ li

bleth|er 'bleð |ə ‖ -|ᵊr **~ered** əd ‖ ᵊrd **~ering**
ər ɪŋ **~ers** əz ‖ ᵊrz

Blethyn 'bleθ ɪn -ᵊn

blew bluː (= blue)

Blewett 'bluː ɪt §ˌ ət

blewits 'bluː ɪts §ˌ əts

Blewitt 'bluː ɪt §ˌ ət

Blige blaɪdʒ

Bligh blaɪ

blight blaɪt **blighted** 'blaɪt ɪd -əd ‖ 'blaɪt̬ əd
blighting 'blaɪt ɪŋ ‖ 'blaɪt̬ ɪŋ **blights** blaɪts

blighter 'blaɪt ə ‖ 'blaɪt̬ ᵊr ~s z

Blighty 'blaɪt i ‖ 'blaɪt̬ i

blimey 'blaɪm i

blimp, Blimp blɪmp **blimps** blɪmps

blimpish 'blɪmp ɪʃ

blind blaɪnd **blinded** 'blaɪnd ɪd -əd **blinder**
'blaɪnd ə ‖ -ᵊr **blindest** 'blaɪnd ɪst -əst
blinding/ly 'blaɪnd ɪŋ /li **blinds** blaɪndz
ˌblind 'alley; ˌblind 'date; ˌblind 'drunk;
ˌblind man's 'buff; 'blind spot

blinder 'blaɪnd ə ‖ -ᵊr ~s z

blindfold 'blaɪnd fəʊld →-fɒʊld ‖ -foʊld **~ed**
ɪd əd **~ing** ɪŋ **~s** z

Blindley 'blaɪnd li

blindly 'blaɪnd li

blindness 'blaɪnd nəs -nɪs

blindworm 'blaɪnd wɜːm ‖ -wɜːm **~s** z

bling blɪŋ
ˌbling'bling

blini 'blɪn i 'bliːn- **~s** z

blink blɪŋk **blinked** blɪŋkt **blinking** 'blɪŋk ɪŋ
blinks blɪŋks

blinker 'blɪŋk ə ‖ -ᵊr **~ed** d **~s** z

blinks blɪŋks

blintz blɪnts **blintzes** 'blɪnts ɪz -əz

blintze 'blɪnts ə ~s z

blip blɪp **blipped** blɪpt **blipping** 'blɪp ɪŋ **blips**
blɪps

bliss, Bliss blɪs

Blissett 'blɪs ɪt §-ət

blissful 'blɪs fᵊl -fʊl **~ly** ˌi **~ness** nəs nɪs

B-list 'biː lɪst

blist|er 'blɪst |ə ‖ -|ᵊr **~ered** əd ‖ ᵊrd **~ering/ly**
ər ɪŋ /li **~ers** əz ‖ -ᵊrz
'blister pack

BLit ˌbiː 'lɪt

blithe blaɪð ‖ blaɪθ

blithe|ly 'blaɪð |li ‖ 'blaɪθ- **~ness** nəs nɪs

blithering 'blɪð ər ɪŋ

blithesome 'blaɪð səm §'blaɪθ- **~ly** li **~ness**
nəs nɪs

Blithfield 'blɪθ fiːᵊld —locally also 'blɪf iːᵊld

BLitt ˌbiː 'lɪt

blitz blɪts **blitzed** blɪtst **blitzes** 'blɪts ɪz -əz
blitzing 'blɪts ɪŋ

Blitzer 'blɪts ə ‖ -ᵊr

blitzkrieg 'blɪts kriːg —Ger B~ ['blɪts kʁiːk]
~s z

Blix blɪks —Norw [bliks]

Blixen 'blɪks ᵊn

blizzard 'blɪz əd ‖ -ᵊrd ~s z

bloat bləʊt ‖ bloʊt **bloated** 'bləʊt ɪd -əd
‖ 'bloʊt̬ əd **bloating** 'bləʊt ɪŋ ‖ 'bloʊt̬ ɪŋ
bloats bləʊts ‖ bloʊts

bloater 'bləʊt ə ‖ 'bloʊt̬ ᵊr ~s z

B

blob blɒb ‖ blɑːb **blobs** blɒbz ‖ blɑːbz
bloc blɒk ‖ blɑːk (= *block*) **blocs** blɒks
‖ blɑːks
Bloch blɒk blɒx ‖ blɑːk
block blɒk ‖ blɑːk **blocked** blɒkt ‖ blɑːkt
blocking 'blɒk ɪŋ ‖ 'blɑːk ɪŋ **blocks** blɒks
‖ blɑːks
ˌblock and 'tackle; ˌblock 'letters; ˌblock
re'lease; ˌblock 'vote
blockad|e blɒ 'keɪd ‖ blɑː- **~ed** ɪd əd **~er** ə
‖ ᵊr **~ers** əz ‖ ᵊrz **~es** z **~ing** ɪŋ
blockag|e 'blɒk ɪdʒ ‖ 'blɑːk- **~es** ɪz əz
blockboard 'blɒk bɔːd ‖ 'blɑːk bɔːrd -boʊrd
blockbuster 'blɒk ˌbʌst ə ‖ 'blɑːk ˌbʌst ᵊr **~s**
z
blockhead 'blɒk hed ‖ 'blɑːk- **~s** z
block|house 'blɒk |haʊs ‖ 'blɑːk- **~houses**
haʊz ɪz -əz
Blodwen 'blɒd wɪn -wen ‖ 'blɑːd- —*Welsh*
['blod wen]
Bloemfontein 'bluːm fən ˌteɪn -fɒn- ‖ -faːn-
Blofeld 'bləʊ feld ‖ 'bloʊ-
blog blɒg ‖ blɔːg blɑːg **blogged** blɒgd
‖ blɔːgd blɑːgd **blogging** 'blɒg ɪŋ ‖ 'blɔːg ɪŋ
'blɑːg ɪŋ **blogs** blɒgz ‖ blɔːgz blɑːgz
blogger 'blɒg ə ‖ 'blɑːg ᵊr **~s** z
blogosphere 'blɒg əʊ sfɪə ‖ 'blɑːg ə sfɪr
bloke bləʊk ‖ bloʊk **blokes** bləʊks ‖ bloʊks
blokeish, blokish 'bləʊk ɪʃ ‖ 'bloʊk- **~ness**
nəs nɪs
Blom blɒm ‖ blɑːm
Blomefield 'bluːm fiːᵊld
Blomfield 'blɒm fiːᵊld 'blʌm-, 'blʊm-, 'bluːm-
‖ 'blɑːm-
blond, blonde blɒnd ‖ blɑːnd **blondes,
blonds** blɒndz ‖ blɑːndz
Blondel ˌblɒn 'del ‖ ˌblɑːn- —*Fr* [blɔ̃ dɛl]
blondie, B~ 'blɒnd i ‖ 'blɑːnd i
Blondin 'blɒnd ɪn ‖ blɑːn 'dæn —*Fr* [blɔ̃ dæ̃]
blondish 'blɒnd ɪʃ ‖ 'blɑːnd-
blood, Blood blʌd **blooded** 'blʌd ɪd -əd
blooding 'blʌd ɪŋ **bloods** blʌdz
'blood bank; ˌblood 'brother; 'blood
count; 'blood ˌdonor; 'blood group;
'blood lust; 'blood ˌmoney; 'blood
ˌplasma; 'blood ˌpoisoning; 'blood
ˌpressure; ˌblood 'red◂; 'blood reˌlation,
ˌ· ·ˈ··; 'blood sports; 'blood transˌfusion;
'blood type; 'blood ˌvessel
blood-and-thunder ˌblʌd ᵊn 'θʌnd ə ‖ -ᵊr
blood|bath 'blʌd| baːθ →'blʌb-, §-bæθ ‖ -bæθ
~baths baːðz §baːθs, §bæθs, §bæðz ‖ bæðz
bæθs
-blooded 'blʌd ɪd ◂ -əd — **hot-blooded**
ˌhɒt 'blʌd ɪd ◂ -əd ‖ ˌhaːt-
bloodhound 'blʌd haʊnd **~s** z
bloodi... —*see* **bloody**
bloodless 'blʌd ləs -lɪs **~ly** li **~ness** nəs nɪs
bloodletting 'blʌd ˌlet ɪŋ ‖ -ˌleṭ-
bloodline 'blʌd laɪn
bloodmobile 'blʌd mə ˌbiːᵊl **~s** z
bloodshed 'blʌd ʃed
bloodshot 'blʌd ʃɒt ‖ -ʃaːt

bloodstain 'blʌd steɪn **~ed** d **~s** z
bloodstock 'blʌd stɒk ‖ -staːk
bloodstream 'blʌd striːm
bloodsucker 'blʌd ˌsʌk ə ‖ -ᵊr **~s** z
bloodsucking 'blʌd ˌsʌk ɪŋ
bloodthirst|y 'blʌd ˌθɜːst |i ‖ -ˌθɜːst |i **~ily**
ɪ li əl i **~iness** i nəs i nɪs
blood|y 'blʌd |i **~ied** id **~ier** i ə ‖ i ᵊr **~ies** iz
~iest i ɪst i əst **~ily** ɪ li əl i **~iness** i nəs i nɪs
ˌBloody 'Mary
bloody-minded ˌblʌd i 'maɪnd ɪd ◂ -əd **~ly** li
~ness nəs nɪs
bloom, Bloom bluːm **bloomed** bluːmd
blooming 'bluːm ɪŋ **blooms** bluːmz
Bloomberg 'bluːm bɜːg ‖ -bɜːɡ
bloomer, B~ 'bluːm ə ‖ -ᵊr **~s** z
Bloomfield 'bluːm fiːᵊld
blooming *euphemistic intensifier* 'bluːm ɪŋ
'blʊm-, -ɪn, -ən **~ly** li **~ness** nəs nɪs —*The
forms with final* n, *although non-standard, are
sometimes used in RP for jocular effect*
Bloomingdale 'bluːm ɪŋ derᵊl **~'s** z
Bloomington 'bluːm ɪŋ tən
Bloomsbury 'bluːmz bər i ‖ -ˌber i
'Bloomsbury Group
bloop bluːp **blooped** bluːpt **blooping**
'bluːp ɪŋ **bloops** bluːps
blooper 'bluːp ə ‖ -ᵊr **~s** z
Bloor, Blore blɔː ‖ blɔːr bloʊr
Blorenge 'blɒr ɪndʒ ‖ 'blɔːr-
blossom, B~ 'blɒs əm ‖ 'blaːs- **~ed** d **~ing** ɪŋ
~s z
blot blɒt ‖ blaːt **blots** blɒts ‖ blaːts **blotted**
'blɒt ɪd -əd ‖ 'blaːṭ əd **blotting** 'blɒt ɪŋ
‖ 'blaːṭ ɪŋ
'blotting ˌpaper
blotch blɒtʃ ‖ blaːtʃ **blotched** blɒtʃt ‖ blaːtʃt
blotch|y 'blɒtʃ |i ‖ 'blaːtʃ |i **~ier** i ə ‖ i ᵊr
~iest i ɪst i əst **~ily** ɪ li əl i **~iness** i nəs i nɪs
blott... —*see* **blot**
blotter 'blɒt ə ‖ 'blaːṭ ᵊr **~s** z
blotto 'blɒt əʊ ‖ 'blaːṭ oʊ
Blount (i) blʌnt, (ii) blaʊnt
blouse blaʊz ‖ blaʊs (*) —*in RP formerly also*
bluːz **blouses** 'blaʊz ɪz -əz ‖ 'blaʊs-
blouson 'bluːz ɒn ‖ 'blaʊs aːn 'bluːs-, 'blaʊz-,
'bluːz-, -oʊn —*Fr* [blu zɔ̃] **~s** z
blovi|ate 'bləʊv i |eɪt ‖ 'bloʊv i |eɪt **~ated**
eɪt ɪd -əd ‖ eɪt̬ əd **~ates** eɪts **~ating** eɪt ɪŋ
‖ eɪt̬ ɪŋ
bloviation ˌbləʊv i 'eɪʃ ᵊn ‖ ˌbloʊv-
blow bləʊ ‖ bloʊ **blew** bluː **blowed** bləʊd
‖ bloʊd **blowing** 'bləʊ ɪŋ ‖ 'bloʊ ɪŋ **blown**
bləʊn §'bləʊ ən ‖ bloʊn **blows** bləʊz ‖ bloʊz
blowback 'bləʊ bæk ‖ 'bloʊ- **~s** s
blow-by-blow ˌbləʊ baɪ 'bləʊ ◂
‖ ˌbloʊ baɪ 'bloʊ ◂
ˌblow-by-ˌblow ac'count
blow-drier 'bləʊ draɪ ə ˌ·ˈ·· ‖ 'bloʊ draɪ ᵊr
blow-dry 'bləʊ draɪ ˌ·ˈ· ‖ 'bloʊ-
blower 'bləʊ ə ‖ 'bloʊ ᵊr **~s** z
blowfish 'bləʊ fɪʃ ‖ 'bloʊ- **~es** ɪz əz
blow|fly 'bləʊ |flaɪ ‖ 'bloʊ- **~flies** flaɪz

B

blowgun 'bləʊ gʌn ‖ 'bloʊ- ~s z
blowhard 'bləʊ hɑːd ‖ 'bloʊ hɑːrd ~s z
blowhole 'bləʊ həʊl →-hɒʊl ‖ 'bloʊ hoʊl ~s z
blowlamp 'bləʊ læmp ‖ 'bloʊ- ~s s
blown bləʊn §'bləʊ ən ‖ bloʊn
blowout 'bləʊ aʊt ‖ 'bloʊ- ~s s
blowpipe 'bləʊ paɪp ‖ 'bloʊ- ~s s
blows|y 'blaʊz |i ~ier i ə ‖ i ᵊr ~iest i ɪst i əst
~ily ɪ li əl i
blowtorch 'bləʊ tɔːtʃ ‖ 'bloʊ tɔːrtʃ ~es ɪz əz
blow-up 'bləʊ ʌp ‖ 'bloʊ- ~s s
blow|y 'bləʊ |i ‖ 'bloʊ |i ~ier i ə ‖ i ᵊr ~iest
i ɪst əst
blowz|y 'blaʊz |i ~ier i ə ‖ i ᵊr ~iest i ɪst i əst
~ily ɪ li əl i
Bloxham 'blɒks əm ‖ 'blɑːks-
BLT, blt ˌbiː el 'tiː
blub blʌb **blubbed** blʌbd **blubbing** 'blʌb ɪŋ
blubs blʌbz
blubb|er 'blʌb |ə ‖ -|ᵊr ~ered əd ‖ ᵊrd ~ering
ər ɪŋ ~ers əz ‖ ᵊrz
Blucher, Blücher, b~ 'bluːk ə 'bluːtʃ- ‖ -ᵊr
—Ger ['blyː çɐ]
bludge blʌdʒ **bludged** blʌdʒd **bludges**
'blʌdʒ ɪz -əz **bludging** 'blʌdʒ ɪŋ
bludgeon 'blʌdʒ ən ~ed d ~ing ɪŋ ~s z
bludger 'blʌdʒ ə ‖ -ᵊr ~s z
blue, Blue bluː **blued** bluːd **blueing, bluing**
'bluː ɪŋ **bluer** 'bluː ə ‖ ᵊr **blues** bluːz **bluest**
'bluː ɪst əst
ˌblue 'blood; ˌblue 'moon; ˌblue 'peter
bluebag 'bluː bæg
bluebeard, B~ 'bluː bɪəd ‖ -bɪrd
bluebell, B~ 'bluː bel ~s z
blueberr|y 'bluː bər |i -ˌber i ‖ -ˌber |i ~ies iz
ˌblueberry 'pie
bluebird 'bluː bɜːd ‖ -bɝːd ~s z
blue-black ˌbluː 'blæk ◀
ˌblue-black 'ink
blue-blooded ˌbluː 'blʌd ɪd ◀ -əd
bluebook 'bluː bʊk §-buːk ~s s
bluebottle 'bluː ˌbɒt ᵊl ‖ -ˌbɑːt̬- ~s z
bluecoat 'bluː kəʊt ‖ -koʊt ~s s
Bluecol tdmk 'bluː kɒl ‖ -kɑːl
blue-collar ˌbluː 'kɒl ə ◀ ‖ -'kɑːl ᵊr
blue-eyed ˌbluː 'aɪd ◀
ˌblue-eyed 'boy
Bluefields 'bluː fiːᵊldz
bluefish 'bluː fɪʃ
bluegrass 'bluː grɑːs §-græs ‖ -græs
blue-green ˌbluː 'griːn ◀
ˌblue-green 'algae
blueish 'bluː ɪʃ ~ness nəs nɪs
bluejacket 'bluː ˌdʒæk ɪt §-ət ~s s
bluejay 'bluː dʒeɪ ~s z
blueness 'bluː nəs -nɪs
bluenose 'bluː nəʊz ‖ -noʊz
blue-pencil ˌbluː 'penˑs ᵊl -ɪl ~ed, ~led d
~ing, ~ling ɪŋ ~s z
blue|print 'bluː |prɪnt ~printed prɪnt ɪd -əd
‖ prɪnt̬ əd ~printing prɪnt ɪŋ ‖ prɪnt̬ ɪŋ
~prints prɪnts
blue-ribbon ˌbluː 'rɪb ən ◀

blues bluːz
blue-sky ˌbluː 'skaɪ ◀
bluestocking 'bluː ˌstɒk ɪŋ ‖ -ˌstɑːk- ~s z
bluesy 'bluːz i
bluet 'bluː ɪt §-ət
bluethroat 'bluː θrəʊt ‖ -θroʊt ~s s
bluetit 'bluː tɪt ~s s
Bluetooth 'bluː tuːθ §-tʊθ
Bluett 'bluː ɪt §ˌət
bluey 'bluː i ~s z
bluff blʌf **bluffed** blʌft **bluffer** 'blʌf ə ‖ -ᵊr
bluffest 'blʌf ɪst -əst **bluffing** 'blʌf ɪŋ
bluffs blʌfs
bluffer 'blʌf ə ‖ -ᵊr ~s z
bluff|ly 'blʌf |li ~ness nəs nɪs
Bluford 'bluː fəd ‖ -fᵊrd
bluing 'bluː ɪŋ
bluish 'bluː ɪʃ ~ness nəs nɪs
Blum bluːm
Blume bluːm
Blundell 'blʌnd ᵊl
Blundellsands ˌblʌnd ᵊl 'sændz
Blunden 'blʌnd ən
blund|er 'blʌnd |ə ‖ -|ᵊr ~ered əd ‖ ᵊrd
~ering/ly ᵊr ɪŋ /li ~ers əz ‖ ᵊrz
blunderbuss 'blʌnd ə bʌs ‖ -ᵊr- ~s ɪz əz
blunderer 'blʌnd ᵊr ə ‖ ᵊr ər ~s z
blunge blʌndʒ **blunged** blʌndʒd **blunges**
'blʌndʒ ɪz -əz **blunging** 'blʌndʒ ɪŋ
Blunkett 'blʌŋk ɪt -ət
blunt, Blunt blʌnt **blunted** 'blʌnt ɪd əd
‖ 'blʌnt̬ əd **blunter** 'blʌnt ə ‖ 'blʌnt̬ ᵊr
bluntest 'blʌnt ɪst əst ‖ 'blʌnt̬ əst **blunting**
'blʌnt ɪŋ ‖ 'blʌnt̬ ɪŋ **blunts** blʌnts
blunt|ly 'blʌnt |li ~ness nəs nɪs
blur, Blur blɜː ‖ blɝː **blurred** blɜːd ‖ blɝːd
blurring 'blɜːr ɪŋ ‖ 'blɝː ɪŋ **blurs** blɜːz
‖ blɝːz
blurb blɜːb ‖ blɝːb **blurbs** blɜːbz ‖ blɝːbz
blurr... —see blur
blurry 'blɜːr i ‖ 'blɝː i
blurt blɜːt ‖ blɝːt **blurted** 'blɜːt ɪd -əd
‖ 'blɝːt̬ əd **blurting** 'blɜːt ɪŋ ‖ 'blɝːt̬ ɪŋ
blurts blɜːts ‖ blɝːts
blush blʌʃ **blushed** blʌʃt **blushes** 'blʌʃ ɪz -əz
blushing/ly 'blʌʃ ɪŋ /li
blusher 'blʌʃ ə ‖ -ᵊr ~s z
blust|er 'blʌst |ə ‖ -|ᵊr ~ered əd ‖ ᵊrd
~ering/ly ər ɪŋ /li ~ers əz ‖ ᵊrz
blusterous 'blʌst ᵊr əs ~ly li
blustery 'blʌst ər i
Blu-Tack tdmk 'bluː tæk
Bly blaɪ
Blyth (i) blaɪð, (ii) blaɪθ, (iii) blaɪ —The place
in Northumberland is (i).
Blythe blaɪð
Blyton 'blaɪt ᵊn
B-movie 'biː ˌmuːv i
BMus ˌbiː 'mʌz
BMW tdmk ˌbiː em 'dʌb ᵊl juː ~s, ~'s z
BMX ˌbiː em 'eks
B'nai B'rith bə ˌneɪ bə 'riːθ ·ˌ·'brɪθ
BNOC 'biː nɒk ‖ -nɑːk

bo, Bo bəʊ ‖ boʊ
BO ˌbiː ˈəʊ ‖ -ˈoʊ
boa ˈbəʊ ə ‖ ˈboʊ ə —*in RP formerly also* bɔː
  boas ˈbəʊ əz ‖ ˈboʊ əz
Boadicea ˌbəʊ əd ɪ ˈsiːˌə -əˈ- ‖ ˌboʊ-
Boakes, Boaks bəʊks ‖ boʊks
Boanerges ˌbəʊ ə ˈnɜːdʒ iːz ‖ ˌboʊ ə ˈnɜːdʒ-
boar bɔː ‖ bɔːr boʊr (= *bore*) **boars** bɔːz ‖ bɔːrz
  bɔʊrz
board bɔːd ‖ bɔːrd boʊrd **boarded** ˈbɔːd ɪd -əd
  ‖ ˈbɔːrd əd ˈboʊrd- **boarding** ˈbɔːd ɪŋ
  ‖ ˈbɔːrd ɪŋ ˈboʊrd- **boards** bɔːdz ‖ bɔːrdz
  boʊrdz
  ˈboarding card; **ˈboarding school**
boarder ˈbɔːd ə ‖ ˈbɔːrd ᵊr ˈboʊrd- **~s** z
boarding|house ˈbɔːd ɪŋ |haʊs ‖ ˈbɔːrd-
  ˈboʊrd- **~houses** haʊz ɪz -əz
Boardman ˈbɔːd mən →ˈbɔːb- ‖ ˈbɔːrd- boʊrd-
boardroom ˈbɔːd ruːm -rʊm ‖ ˈbɔːrd- ˈboʊrd-
  ~s z
boardwalk ˈbɔːd wɔːk ‖ ˈbɔːrd- ˈboʊrd-, -wɑːk
  ~s s
Boas ˈbəʊ æz -æs, -əz, -əs ‖ ˈboʊ-
boast bəʊst ‖ boʊst **boasted** ˈbəʊst ɪd -əd
  ‖ ˈboʊst- **boasting/ly** ˈbəʊst ɪŋ /li ‖ ˈboʊst-
  boasts bəʊsts ‖ boʊsts
boaster ˈbəʊst ə ‖ ˈboʊst ᵊr **~s** z
boastful ˈbəʊst fᵊl -fʊl ‖ ˈboʊst- **~ly** i **~ness**
  nəs nɪs
boat bəʊt ‖ boʊt **boated** ˈbəʊt ɪd -əd
  ‖ ˈboʊt̬ əd **boating** ˈbəʊt ɪŋ ‖ ˈboʊt̬ ɪŋ **boats**
  bəʊts ‖ boʊts
  ˈboat ˌpeople; **ˈboat race**; **ˈboat train**
boatel ⁽ˌ⁾bəʊ ˈtel ‖ ⁽ˌ⁾boʊ- **~s** z
Boateng ˈbwaːt eŋ —*but popularly usually*
  ˈbəʊt- ‖ ˈboʊt-
boater ˈbəʊt ə ‖ ˈboʊt̬ ᵊr **~s** z
boathook ˈbəʊt hʊk §-huːk ‖ ˈboʊt- **~s** s
boat|house ˈbəʊt |haʊs ‖ ˈboʊt- **~houses**
  haʊz ɪz -əz
boatload ˈbəʊt ləʊd ‖ ˈboʊt loʊd **~s** z
boat|man ˈbəʊt |mən ‖ ˈboʊt- **~men** mən men
boatshed ˈbəʊt ʃed ‖ ˈboʊt- **~s** z
boatswain ˈbəʊs ᵊn ‖ ˈboʊs ᵊn —*There is also
  a spelling pronunciation* ˈbəʊt sweɪn ‖ ˈboʊt-
  ~s z
boatyard ˈbəʊt jaːd ‖ ˈboʊt jaːrd **~s** z
Boaz ˈbəʊ æz ‖ ˈboʊ-
bob, Bob bɒb ‖ baːb **bobbed** bɒbd ‖ baːbd
  bobbing ˈbɒb ɪŋ ‖ ˈbaːb ɪŋ **bobs, Bob's**
  bɒbz ‖ baːbz
bobbi... —*see* **bobby**
Bobbie ˈbɒb i ‖ ˈbaːb i
bobbin ˈbɒb ɪn §-ən ‖ ˈbaːb ən **~s** z
Bobbitt ˈbɒb ɪt §-ət ‖ ˈbaːb ət
bobble ˈbɒb ᵊl ‖ ˈbaːb ᵊl **~s** z
bobbly ˈbɒb ᵊl_i ‖ ˈbaːb-
bobby, Bobby ˈbɒb i ‖ ˈbaːb i **bobbies**,
  Bobby's ˈbɒb iz ‖ ˈbaːb-
  ˈbobby pin; **ˈbobby socks**
bobby-soxer ˈbɒb i ˌsɒks ə ‖ ˈbaːb i ˌsaːks ᵊr
bobcat ˈbɒb kæt ‖ ˈbaːb- **~s** s
bobolink ˈbɒb ə lɪŋk ‖ ˈbaːb- **~s** s

bobsled ˈbɒb sled ‖ ˈbaːb- **~der/s** ə/z ‖ ᵊr/z
  ~ding ɪŋ **~s** z
bobsleigh ˈbɒb sleɪ ‖ ˈbaːb- **~s** z
bobstay ˈbɒb steɪ ‖ ˈbaːb- **~s** z
bobtail ˈbɒb teɪᵊl ‖ ˈbaːb- **~ed** d **~ing** ɪŋ **~s** z
bobwhite ˌbɒb ˈwaɪt -ˈhwaɪt ‖ ˌbaːb ˈhwaɪt **~s**
  s
Boca Raton ˌbəʊk ə rə ˈtəʊn
  ‖ ˌboʊk ə rə ˈtoʊn
Boccaccio bɒ ˈkaːtʃ i əʊ bə-, -ˈkætʃ-
  ‖ boʊ ˈkaːtʃ i oʊ —*It* [bok ˈkat tʃo]
Boccherini ˌbɒk ə ˈriːn i ‖ ˌbaːk- ˌboʊk- —*It*
  [bok ke ˈri: ni]
Bocelli bɒ ˈtʃel i ‖ boʊ- —*It* [bo ˈtʃɛl li]
Boche, boche bɒʃ ‖ baːʃ boʊʃ
Bochum ˈbəʊk əm ‖ ˈboʊk- —*Ger* [ˈboːx ʊm]
bock, Bock bɒk ‖ baːk **bocks** bɒks ‖ baːks
  ˌbock ˈbeer
bod bɒd ‖ baːd **bods** bɒdz ‖ baːdz
bodacious bəʊ ˈdeɪʃ əs ‖ boʊ- **~ly** li
Boddington ˈbɒd ɪŋ tən ‖ ˈbaːd-
bode bəʊd ‖ boʊd **boded** ˈbəʊd ɪd -əd
  ‖ ˈboʊd əd **bodes** bəʊdz ‖ boʊdz **boding**
  ˈbəʊd ɪŋ ‖ ˈboʊd ɪŋ
bodega bəʊ ˈdiːg ə -ˈdeɪg- ‖ boʊ ˈdeɪg ə —*Sp*
  [bo ˈðe ɣa] **~s** z
Bo ˌdega ˈBay
bodge bɒdʒ ‖ baːdʒ **bodged** bɒdʒd ‖ baːdʒd
  bodges ˈbɒdʒ ɪz -əz ‖ ˈbaːdʒ əz **bodging**
  ˈbɒdʒ ɪŋ ‖ ˈbaːdʒ ɪŋ
bodger ˈbɒdʒ ə ‖ ˈbaːdʒ ᵊr **~s** z
bodgie ˈbɒdʒ i ‖ ˈbaːdʒ i **~s** z
Bodhisattva ˌbɒd ɪ ˈsæt və ˌbəʊd-, §-ə-, -ˈsʌt-,
  -ˈsaːt-, -wə ‖ ˌboʊd ə ˈsʌt və
bodhrán ˈbɔːr aːn baʊ ˈraːn
Bodiam (i) ˈbəʊd i_əm ‖ ˈboʊd-, (ii) ˈbɒd-
  ‖ ˈbaːd-
bodic|e ˈbɒd ɪs -əs ‖ ˈbaːd- **~es** ɪz əz
bodice-ripper ˈbɒd ɪs ˌrɪp ə -əs-
  ‖ ˈbaːd əs ˌrɪp ᵊr **~s** z
Bodie ˈbəʊd i ‖ ˈboʊd i
bodie... —*see* **body**
-bodied ˈbɒd id ◄ ‖ -ˈbaːd id ◄ — **full-bodied**
  ˌfʊl ˈbɒd id ◄ ‖ -ˈbaːd-
bodily ˈbɒd ɪ li -ᵊl i ‖ ˈbaːd ᵊl i
bodkin, B~ ˈbɒd kɪn ‖ ˈbaːd- **~s** z
Bodleian bɒd ˈliː_ən ˈbɒd li_ən ‖ baːd-
Bodley ˈbɒd li ‖ ˈbaːd-
Bodmer ˈbɒd mə ‖ ˈbaːd mᵊr
Bodmin ˈbɒd mɪn →ˈbɒb-, §-mən ‖ ˈbaːd-
Bodnant ˈbɒd nænt ‖ ˈbaːd-
Bodoni bə ˈdəʊn i ‖ -ˈdoʊn- —*It* [bo ˈdo: ni]
Bodrum ˈbɒdr əm -ʊm ‖ ˈboʊdr əm
body, Body ˈbɒd i ‖ ˈbaːd i **bodies** ˈbɒd iz
  ‖ ˈbaːd iz
  ˈbody blow; **ˈbody ˌbuilding**; **ˈbody
  count**; **ˈbody ˌdouble**; **ˈbody ˌlanguage**;
  ˈbody ˌpopping; **ˈbody ˌsnatcher**; **ˈbody
  ˌstocking**; **ˈbody ˌwarmer**
bodycheck ˈbɒd i tʃek ‖ ˈbaːd- **~s** s
bodyguard ˈbɒd i gaːd ‖ ˈbaːd i gaːrd **~s** z
bodyline ˈbɒd i laɪn ‖ ˈbaːd- **~s** z
bodywork ˈbɒd i wɜːk ‖ ˈbaːd i wɜːrk

B

Boehm (i) bəʊm 'bəʊ əm ‖ boʊm, (ii) biːm, (iii) bɜːm ‖ bɝːm (iv) beɪm —Ger [bøːm]
boehmite 'bɜːm aɪt ‖ 'beɪm- 'boʊm- (*)
Boeing tdmk 'bəʊ ɪŋ ‖ 'boʊ ɪŋ
Boeotia bi 'əʊʃ ə -i‿ə ‖ -'oʊʃ ə
Boeotian bi 'əʊʃ ᵊn -i‿ən ‖ -'oʊʃ ᵊn ~s z
Boer bɔː 'bəʊ ə, bʊə ‖ bɔːr boʊr, bʊᵊr **Boers** bɔːz 'bəʊ əz, bʊəz ‖ bɔːrz boʊrz, bʊᵊrz
Boethius bəʊ 'iːθ i‿əs ‖ boʊ-
boeuf bɜːf ‖ bʊf bʌf, boʊf —Fr [bœf]
  ,boeuf ,bourgui'gnon ,bʊəg iːn 'jɒn ,bɔːg-, -ɪn-, -ən- ‖ ,bʊrg iːn 'jaːn -'jɔːn, -'joʊn —Fr [buʁ gi njɔ̃]
boff bɒf ‖ baːf **boffed** bɒft ‖ baːft **boffing** 'bɒf ɪŋ ‖ 'baːf ɪŋ **boffs** bɒfs ‖ baːfs
boffin 'bɒf ɪn §-ᵊn ‖ 'baːf- ~s z
boffo 'bɒf əʊ ‖ 'baːf oʊ
Bofors 'bəʊf əz ‖ 'boʊ fɔːrz -fɔːrs —Swed [buː 'fɔʂ]
bog bɒg ‖ baːg bɔːg **bogged** bɒgd ‖ baːgd bɔːgd **bogging** 'bɒg ɪŋ ‖ 'baːg ɪŋ 'bɔːg- **bogs** bɒgz ‖ baːgz bɔːgz
Bogalusa place in LA ,bɒg ə 'luːs ə ‖ ,boʊg-
Bogarde 'bəʊg aːd ‖ 'boʊg aːrd
Bogart 'bəʊg aːt ‖ 'boʊg aːrt
bogbean 'bɒg biːn ‖ 'baːg- 'bɔːg-
Bogdanov bɒg 'daːn əv ‖ baːg-
bogey, Bogey 'bəʊg i ‖ 'boʊg i ~s z
bogey|man 'bəʊg i |mæn ‖ 'boʊg- ~men men
boggie... —see **boggy**
bogginess 'bɒg i nəs -nɪs ‖ 'baːg- 'bɔːg-
Boggis 'bɒg ɪs §-əs ‖ 'baːg-
boggl|e 'bɒg ᵊl ‖ 'baːg ᵊl ~ed d ~es z ~ing ɪŋ
boggl|y 'bɒg |i ‖ 'baːg |i 'bɔːg- ~ier i‿ə ‖ i‿ᵊr ~iest i‿ɪst i‿əst
bogie 'bəʊg i ‖ 'boʊg i (= bogey) ~s z
Bognor 'bɒg nə ‖ 'baːg nᵊr
BOGOF, bogof 'bɒg ɒf ‖ 'baːg ɔːf -aːf
Bogota, Bogotá ,bɒg ə 'taː ,bəʊg- ‖ ,boʊg ə 'taː: '··· —Sp [bo ɣo 'ta] —but the place in NJ is bə 'goʊt ə
bog-standard ,bɒg 'stænd əd ◂ ‖ ,baːg 'stænd ᵊrd ◂ ,bɔːg-
bogus 'bəʊg əs ‖ 'boʊg-
bogy 'bəʊg i ‖ 'boʊg i (= bogey)
bohea bəʊ 'hiː ‖ boʊ-
Boheme, Bohème, b~ bəʊ 'em -'eɪm ‖ boʊ-
Bohemia bəʊ 'hiːm i‿ə ‖ boʊ-
bohemian, B~ bəʊ 'hiːm i‿ən ‖ boʊ- ~s z
Böhm bɜːm ‖ boʊm —Ger [bøːm]
boho 'bəʊ həʊ ‖ 'boʊ hoʊ
Bohr bɔː ‖ bɔːr boʊr —Danish [boːʁ]
bohrium 'bɔːr i‿əm ‖ 'boʊr-
Bohun (i) buːn, (ii) 'bəʊ ən ‖ 'boʊ-
bohunk 'bəʊ hʌŋk ‖ 'boʊ- ~s s
boil bɔɪᵊl **boiled** bɔɪᵊld **boiling** 'bɔɪl ɪŋ **boils** bɔɪᵊlz
Boileau 'bɔɪl əʊ bwæ 'ləʊ ‖ bwaː 'loʊ —Fr [bwa lo]
boiler 'bɔɪl ə ‖ -ᵊr ~s z
  'boiler suit
boilermak|er 'bɔɪl ə ,meɪk |ə ‖ -ᵊr ,meɪk |ᵊr ~ers əz ‖ ᵊrz ~ing ɪŋ

boilerplate 'bɔɪl ə pleɪt ‖ -ᵊr- ~s s
boiling 'bɔɪᵊl ɪŋ
  'boiling point; ,boiling 'water
boil-in-the-bag ,bɔɪᵊl ɪn ðə 'bæg ◂
boing bɔɪŋ
boink bɔɪŋk
Bois bɔɪz —but in French place names bwaː
Boise place in ID 'bɔɪz i 'bɔɪs i
boisterous 'bɔɪst ər əs →'bɔɪs trəs ~ly li ~ness nəs nɪs
bok choy ,bɒk 'tʃɔɪ ‖ ,baːk-
Bokhara bɒ 'kaːr ə bəʊ- ‖ boʊ- —Russ [bu 'xa rə]
Bokmål 'bʊk mɔːl 'buːk- ‖ -maːl —Norw ['buːk mɔːl]
bola 'bəʊl ə 'boʊl ə —Sp ['bo la] ~s z
Bolam 'bəʊl əm ‖ 'boʊl-
Bolan 'bəʊl ən ‖ 'boʊl-
bolas 'bəʊl əs ‖ 'boʊl- —Sp ['bo las]
bold, Bold bəʊld →bɒʊld ‖ boʊld **bolder** 'bəʊld ə →'bɒʊld ə ‖ 'boʊld ᵊr **boldest** 'bəʊld ɪst →'bɒʊld-, -əst ‖ 'boʊld-
boldface 'bəʊld feɪs →'bɒʊld-, ,·'· ‖ 'boʊld- ~d t
bold|ly 'bəʊld |li →'bɒʊld- ‖ 'boʊld- ~ness nəs nɪs
Boldre 'bəʊld ə →'bɒʊld- ‖ 'boʊld ᵊr
bole bəʊl →bɒʊl ‖ boʊl (= bowl) **boles** bəʊlz ‖ boʊlz
Boleat, Boléat 'bəʊl i‿ət -i aː ‖ 'boʊl-
bolero 'garment' 'bɒl ə rəʊ bə 'leər əʊ ‖ bə 'ler oʊ ~s z
bolero 'dance' bə 'leər əʊ ‖ -'ler oʊ ~s z
bo|letus bəʊ |'liːt əs ‖ boʊ |'liːt̬ əs ~leti 'liːt aɪ -iː ~letuses 'liːt əs ɪz -əz ‖ 'liːt̬-
Boleyn (i) bə 'lɪn ‖ boʊ-, (ii) 'bʊl ɪn, (iii) bʊ 'liːn
Bolger 'bɒldʒ ə 'bɒlʒ- ‖ 'boʊldʒ ᵊr 'baːldʒ-
bolide 'bəʊl aɪd -ɪd, §-əd ‖ 'boʊl- ~s z
Bolingbroke 'bɒl ɪŋ brʊk 'bʊl- ‖ 'baːl-
Bolinger 'bɒl ɪndʒ ə -əndʒ- ‖ 'baːl əndʒ ᵊr
Bolitho bə 'laɪθ əʊ ‖ -oʊ
Bolivar, b~ 'bɒl ɪ vaː: -ə-; bɒ 'liːv aː ‖ 'baːl əv ᵊr bə 'liːv aːr —Sp Bolívar [bo 'li βaɾ]
Bolivia bə 'lɪv i‿ə
Bolivian bə 'lɪv i‿ən ~s z
boliviano bə ,lɪv i 'aːn əʊ bɒ- ‖ -oʊ ~s z
boll bəʊl →bɒʊl. bɒl ‖ boʊl (= bowl) **bolls** bəʊlz →bɒʊlz. bɒlz ‖ boʊlz
  ,boll 'weevil
bollard 'bɒl aːd -əd ‖ 'baːl ᵊrd ~s z
Bollin 'bɒl ɪn §-ən ‖ 'baːl-
Bollinger 'bɒl ɪndʒ ə -əndʒ- ‖ 'baːl əndʒ ᵊr
bollix 'bɒl ɪks ~ed t ~es ɪz əz ~ing ɪŋ
bollock 'bɒl ək ‖ 'baːl- ~ed t ~ing/s ɪŋ/z ~s s
bollocks-up 'bɒl əks ʌp ‖ 'baːl-
Bollywood 'bɒl i wʊd ‖ 'baːl-
bologna 'sausage' bə 'ləʊn i ‖ bə 'loʊn i
Bologna bə 'ləʊn jə -'lɒn- ‖ -'loʊn- —It [bo 'loɲ ɲa]

B

bolognaise, bolognese ˌbɒl ə 'neɪz ◄ △-əg-,
-'nez ‖ ˌboʊl ən 'jeɪz ◄
　ˌbolognaise 'sauce
boloney bə 'ləʊn i ‖ bə 'loʊn i
bolo tie 'bəʊl əʊ taɪ ‖ 'boʊl oʊ taɪ ~s z
Bolshevik 'bɒlʃ ə vɪk -ɪ- ‖ 'boʊlʃ- ~s s
Bolshevism 'bɒlʃ ə ˌvɪz əm -ɪ- ‖ 'boʊlʃ-
Bolshevist 'bɒlʃ əv ɪst -ɪv-, §-əst ‖ 'boʊlʃ- ~s s
Bolshevistic ˌbɒlʃ ə 'vɪst ɪk ◄ -ɪ- ‖ ˌboʊlʃ-
bolshi|e 'bɒlʃ i ‖ 'boʊlʃ i ~es z ~ness nəs nɪs
Bolshoi, Bolshoy ˌbɒl 'ʃɔɪ ◄ ‖ ˌboʊl- —*Russ*
　[bʌlʲ 'ʃɔj]
　ˌBolshoi 'Ballet ‖ ˌˌ· '··
bolshy 'bɒlʃ i ‖ 'boʊlʃ i
Bolsover 'bɒls ˌəʊv ə 'bəʊlz- ‖ 'boʊls ˌoʊv ᵊr
　—*The place in Derbyshire is locally* 'bəʊlz-,
　→'bɒʊlz-
bolst|er, B~ 'bəʊlst |ə →'bɒʊlst-; §'bɒlst-
　‖ 'boʊlst |ᵊr **~ered** əd ‖ ᵊrd **~ering** ᵊr ɪŋ **~ers**
　əz ‖ ᵊrz
bolt, Bolt bəʊlt →bɒʊlt, §bɒlt ‖ boʊlt **bolted**
　'bəʊlt ɪd →'bɒʊlt-, §'bɒlt-, -əd ‖ 'boʊlt əd
　bolting 'bəʊlt ɪŋ →'bɒʊlt-, §'bɒlt- ‖ 'boʊlt ɪŋ
　bolts, Bolt's bəʊlts →bɒʊlts, §bɒlts ‖ boʊlts
bolter 'bəʊlt ə →'bɒʊlt-, §'bɒlt- ‖ 'boʊlt ᵊr ~s z
bolthole 'bəʊlt həʊl →'bɒʊlt hɒʊl, §'bɒlt-
　‖ 'boʊlt hoʊl ~s z
Bolton 'bəʊlt ən →'bɒʊlt- ‖ 'boʊlt- ~s z
Bolton-le-Sands ˌbəʊlt ən li 'sændz →ˌbɒʊlt-,
　-lə'· ‖ ˌboʊlt-
Boltzmann 'bɒlts mən 'bəʊlts- ‖ 'boʊlts-
　—*Ger* ['bɔlts man]
bolus 'bəʊl əs ‖ 'boʊl- ~es ɪz əz
bomb bɒm ‖ bɑːm **bombed** bɒmd ‖ bɑːmd
　bombing 'bɒm ɪŋ ‖ 'bɑːm ɪŋ **bombs** bɒmz
　‖ bɑːmz
　'bomb diˌsposal
bombard *v* bɒm 'bɑːd ‖ bɑːm 'bɑːrd **~ed** ɪd əd
　~ing ɪŋ **~s** z
bombardier ˌbɒm bə 'dɪə ◄ ‖ ˌbɑːm bᵊr 'dɪᵊr
　-bə- ~s z
bombardment bɒm 'bɑːd mənt →-'bɑːb-
　‖ bɑːm 'bɑːrd- ~s s
bombasine ˌbɒm bə 'ziːn ˌ· '·· ‖ ˌbɑːm bə 'ziːn
bombast 'bɒm bæst ‖ 'bɑːm-
bombastic bɒm 'bæst ɪk ‖ bɑːm- **~ally** ᵊl_i
Bombay ˌbɒm 'beɪ ◄ ‖ ˌbɑːm-
　ˌBombay 'duck
bombazine ˌbɒm bə 'ziːn ˌ· '·· ‖ ˌbɑːm bə 'ziːn
bombe bɒm bɒmb ‖ bɑːm —*Fr* [bɔ̃ːb] **bombes**
　bɒmz bɒmbz ‖ bɑːmz
bomber 'bɒm ə ‖ 'bɑːm ᵊr ~s z
bomblet 'bɒm lət -lɪt ‖ 'bɑːm- ~s s
bombproof 'bɒm pruːf §-prʊf ‖ 'bɑːm- **~ed** t
bombshell 'bɒm ʃel ‖ 'bɑːm- ~s z
bombsight 'bɒm saɪt ‖ 'bɑːm- ~s s
bombsite 'bɒm saɪt ‖ 'bɑːm- ~s s
Bompas 'bʌmp əs
bon bɒn bɔ̃ ‖ bɑːn —*Fr* [bɔ̃] —*See also phrases
　with this word*
bona 'bəʊn ə ‖ 'boʊn ə
　ˌbona 'fide 'faɪd i 'fiːd eɪ; ˌbona 'fides
　'faɪd iːz 'fiːd eɪz, -eɪs

Bonaire bɒn 'eə ‖ bə 'neᵊr
Bonallack bə 'næl ək
bonanza bə 'nænz ə ~s z
Bonaparte 'bəʊn ə pɑːt ‖ 'boʊn ə pɑːrt —*Fr*
　[bɔ na paʁt]
Bonapartism 'bəʊn ə pɑːt ˌɪz əm
　‖ 'boʊn ə pɑːrt̬-
Bonapartist 'bəʊn ə pɑːt ɪst §-əst
　‖ 'boʊn ə pɑːrt̬ əst ~s s
bon appetit ˌbɒn æp e 'tiː -ɪ 'tiː
　‖ ˌboʊn æp eɪ 'tiː ˌbɑːn, -ɑːp ə- —*Fr*
　[bɔ na pe ti]
Bonar *(i)* 'bəʊn ə ‖ 'boʊn ᵊr, *(ii)* 'bɒn ə
　‖ 'bɑːn ᵊr
Bonaventure ˌbɒn ə ˌventʃ ə ˌ·'·'··
　‖ ˌbɑːn ə ˌventʃ ᵊr ·'·'··
bonbon 'bɒn bɒn →'bɒm- ‖ 'bɑːn bɑːn ~s z
bonce bɒnᵗs ‖ bɑːnᵗs **bonces** 'bɒnᵗs ɪz -əz
　‖ 'bɑːnᵗs-
bond, Bond bɒnd ‖ bɑːnd **bonded** 'bɒnd ɪd
　-əd ‖ 'bɑːnd əd **bonding** 'bɒnd ɪŋ
　‖ 'bɑːnd ɪŋ **bonds, Bond's** bɒndz ‖ bɑːndz
bondage 'bɒnd ɪdʒ ‖ 'bɑːnd-
Bondfield 'bɒnd fiːᵊld ‖ 'bɑːnd-
bondholder 'bɒnd ˌhəʊld ə →-ˌhɒʊld-
　‖ 'bɑːnd ˌhoʊld ᵊr ~s z
Bondi *place in Australia* 'bɒnd aɪ ‖ 'bɑːnd-
bondservant 'bɒnd ˌsɜːv ᵊnt
　‖ 'bɑːnd ˌsɜːv ᵊnt ~s s
bonds|man 'bɒndz mən ‖ 'bɑːndz- **~men** mən
　men
bone, Bone bəʊn ‖ boʊn **boned** bəʊnd
　‖ boʊnd **boning** 'bəʊn ɪŋ ‖ 'boʊn ɪŋ **bones**
　bəʊnz ‖ boʊnz
　ˌbone 'china; 'bone ˌmarrow; 'bone meal
bone-dry ˌbəʊn 'draɪ ◄ ‖ ˌboʊn-
bonehead 'bəʊn hed ‖ 'boʊn- ~s z
bone-idle ˌbəʊn 'aɪd ᵊl ◄ ‖ ˌboʊn-
bone-lazy ˌbəʊn 'leɪz i ◄ ‖ ˌboʊn-
boneless 'bəʊn ləs -lɪs ‖ 'boʊn-
bonemeal 'bəʊn miːᵊl →'bəʊm- ‖ 'boʊn-
boner 'bəʊn ə ‖ 'boʊn ᵊr ~s z
bone-setter 'bəʊn ˌset ə ‖ 'boʊn ˌset̬ ᵊr ~s z
bone-shaker 'bəʊn ˌʃeɪk ə ‖ 'boʊn ˌʃeɪk ᵊr ~s
　z
Bo'ness ˌbəʊ 'nes ‖ ˌboʊ-
bonfire 'bɒn ˌfaɪ ə ‖ 'bɑːn ˌfaɪ ᵊr ~s z
bong bɒŋ ‖ bɑːŋ bɔːŋ **bonged** bɒŋd ‖ bɑːŋd
　bɔːŋd **bonging** 'bɒŋ ɪŋ ‖ 'bɑːŋ ɪŋ 'bɔːŋ-
　bongs bɒŋz ‖ bɑːŋz bɔːŋz
bongo 'bɒŋ gəʊ ‖ 'bɑːŋ goʊ 'bɔːŋ- ~s z
Bonham 'bɒn əm ‖ 'bɑːn-
Bonham Carter ˌbɒn əm 'kɑːt ə
　‖ ˌbɑːn əm 'kɑːrt̬ ᵊr
Bonhoeffer 'bɒn ˌhɜːf ə ‖ 'bɑːn ˌhoʊf ᵊr —*Ger*
　['boːn hœf ɐ, 'bɔn-]
bonhomie 'bɒn əm i -ɒm-, -iː ‖ ˌbɑːn ə 'miː
　'···
boni... —*see* **bony**
Boniface 'bɒn ɪ feɪs -ə- ‖ 'bɑːn-
Bonington 'bɒn ɪŋ tən ‖ 'bɑːn-
Bonio *tdmk* 'bəʊn i əʊ ‖ 'boʊn i oʊ ~s z
Bonita bə 'niːt ə ‖ -'niːt̬-

B

bonito bə ˈniːt əʊ ‖ -ˈniːt̬ oʊ -ə **~s** z
Bon Jovi ˌbɒn ˈdʒəʊv i ‖ ˌbaːn ˈdʒoʊv i
bonk bɒŋk ‖ baːŋk **bonked** bɒŋkt ‖ baːŋkt
　bonking ˈbɒŋk ɪŋ ‖ ˈbaːŋk ɪŋ **bonks** bɒŋks
　‖ baːŋks
bonkbuster ˈbɒŋk ˌbʌst ə ‖ ˈbaːŋk ˌbʌst ᵊr **~s**
　z
bonkers ˈbɒŋk əz ‖ ˈbaːŋk ᵊrz
bon mot ˌbɒ̃ ˈməʊ ˌbɒn- ‖ ˌbaːn ˈmoʊ ˌbɔːn-
　—Fr [bɔ̃ mo] **~s** z
Bonn bɒn ‖ baːn —Ger [bɔn]
bonne bɒn ‖ baːn bɔːn, bʌn —Fr [bɔn]
　ˌbonne ˈbouche buːʃ —Fr [buʃ]; ˌbonne
　ˈfemme fæm —Fr [fam]
bonnet ˈbɒn ɪt §-ət ‖ ˈbaːn- **~s** s
Bonneville ˈbɒn ə vɪl ‖ ˈbaːn-
Bonnie ˈbɒn i ‖ ˈbaːn i
　ˌBonnie ˌPrince ˈCharlie
bonn|y, Bonny ˈbɒn |i ‖ ˈbaːn |i **~ier** i ə ‖ i ᵊr
　~iest i ɪst i ᵊst **~ily** ɪ li əl i **~iness** i nəs i nɪs
Bono (i) ˈbəʊn əʊ ‖ ˈboʊn oʊ (ii) ˈbɒn əʊ
　‖ ˈbaːn oʊ —The American singer is (i), the
　Irish singer (ii).
bonobo bə ˈnəʊb əʊ ˈbɒn ə bəʊ ‖ bə ˈnoʊb oʊ
　~s z
bonsai ˈbɒn saɪ ˈbəʊn- ‖ ˌbaːn ˈsaɪ ˌboʊn-, ˈ· ·
　—Jp [bo̞ˌn sai] **~s** z
Bonser, Bonsor ˈbɒnˢs ə ‖ ˈbaːnˢs ᵊr
bonus ˈbəʊn əs ‖ ˈboʊn- **-es** ɪz əz
bon vivant ˌbɒ̃ ˈviːv ɒ̃ -viː ˈvɒ̃
　‖ ˌbaːn viː ˈvaːnt —Fr [bɔ̃ vi vɑ̃]
bon viveur ˌbɒ̃ viː ˈvɜː ‖ ˌbaːn viː ˈvɜː —not a
　true French expression **~s** z
bon voyage ˌbɒ̃ vwaɪ ˈɑːʒ ˌˈ· · ‖ ˌbaːn- ˌbɔːn-
　—Fr [bɔ̃ vwa jaːʒ]
bon|y ˈbəʊn |i ‖ ˈboʊn |i **~ier** i ə ‖ i ᵊr **~iest**
　i ɪst i ᵊst **~ily** ɪ li əl i **~iness** i nəs i nɪs
Bonython bə ˈnaɪθ ᵊn
bonze bɒnz ‖ baːnz **bonzes** ˈbɒnz ɪz -əz
　‖ ˈbaːnz əz
bonzer ˈbɒnz ə ‖ ˈbaːnz ᵊr
Bonzo ˈbɒnz əʊ ‖ ˈbaːnz oʊ
boo buː **booed** buːd **booing** ˈbuː ɪŋ **boos** buːz
boob buːb **boobed** buːbd **boobing** ˈbuːb ɪŋ
　boobs buːbz
boo-boo ˈbuː buː **~s** z
booby ˈbuːb i **boobies** ˈbuːb iz
　ˈbooby hatch; ˈbooby prize; ˈbooby trap
booby-trap ˈbuːb i træp **~ped** t **~ping** ɪŋ **~s** s
boodl|e, B~ ˈbuːd ᵊl **~ed** d **~es** z **~e's** z **~ing**
　ɪŋ
boogaloo ˈbuːg ə luː
booger ˈbʊg ə ˈbuːg- ‖ -ᵊr **~s** z
boogie ˈbuːg i ˈbʊg i ‖ ˈbʊg i ˈbuːg i **~d** d **~ing**
　ɪŋ z
boogie-woogie ˌbuːg i ˈwuːg i ˌbʊg i ˈwʊg i
　‖ ˌbʊg i ˈwʊg i ˌbuːg i ˈwuːg i
boohoo ˌbuː ˈhuː **~ed** d **~ing** ɪŋ **~s** z
boojum ˈbuːdʒ əm
book bʊk §buːk **booked** bʊkt §buːkt **booking**
　ˈbʊk ɪŋ §ˈbuːk- **books** bʊks §buːks
　ˈbook club; ˈbook shelf; ˈbook ˌtoken
bookable ˈbʊk əb ᵊl §ˈbuːk-

bookbinder ˈbʊk ˌbaɪnd ə §ˈbuːk- ‖ -ᵊr **~s** z
bookbinder|y ˈbʊk ˌbaɪnd ᵊr |i §ˈbuːk- **~ies** iz
bookbinding ˈbʊk ˌbaɪnd ɪŋ §ˈbuːk-
bookcas|e ˈbʊk keɪs §ˈbuːk- **~es** ɪz əz
bookend ˈbʊk end §ˈbuːk-, ˌˈ· **~s** z
Booker, b~ ˈbʊk ə §ˈbuːk- ‖ -ᵊr
Bookham ˈbʊk əm
bookie ˈbʊk i §ˈbuːk- **~s** z
bookish ˈbʊk ɪʃ §ˈbuːk- **~ly** li **~ness** nəs nɪs
bookkeep|er ˈbʊk ˌkiːp |ə §ˈbuːk- ‖ -|ᵊr **~ers**
　əz ‖ ᵊrz **~ing** ɪŋ
booklet ˈbʊk lət §ˈbuːk-, -lɪt **~s** s
booklover ˈbʊk ˌlʌv ə §ˈbuːk- ‖ -ᵊr **~s** z
bookmaker ˈbʊk ˌmeɪk ə §ˈbuːk- ‖ -ᵊr **~s** z
book|man ˈbʊk| mən §ˈbuːk|-, -mæn **~men**
　mən men
bookmark ˈbʊk maːk §ˈbuːk- ‖ -maːrk **~s** s
bookmobile ˈbʊk məʊ ˌbiːl §ˈbuːk- **~s** z
bookplate ˈbʊk pleɪt §ˈbuːk- **~s** s
bookseller ˈbʊk ˌsel ə §ˈbuːk- ‖ -ᵊr **~s** z
book|shelf ˈbʊk |ʃelf §ˈbuːk- **~shelves** ʃelvz
bookshop ˈbʊk ʃɒp §ˈbuːk- ‖ -ʃaːp **~s** s
bookstall ˈbʊk stɔːl §ˈbuːk- ‖ -staːl **~s** z
bookstore ˈbʊk stɔː §ˈbuːk- ‖ -stɔːr -stoʊr **~s** z
bookwork ˈbʊk wɜːk §ˈbuːk- ‖ -wɜːk
bookworm ˈbʊk wɜːm §ˈbuːk- ‖ -wɜːm **~s** z
Boole buːl
Boolean, b~ ˈbuːl i ən **~s** z
boom buːm **boomed** buːmd **booming**
　ˈbuːm ɪŋ **booms** buːmz
　ˈboom town
boomer, B~ ˈbuːm ə ‖ -ᵊr **~s** z
boomerang ˈbuːm ə ræŋ **~ed** d **~ing** ɪŋ **~s** z
boomlet ˈbuːm lət -lɪt **~s** s
boomslang ˈbuːm slæŋ **~s** z
boon, Boon buːn **boons** buːnz
　ˌboon comˈpanion
boondocks ˈbuːn dɒks ‖ -daːks
boondoggl|e ˈbuːn ˌdɒg ᵊl ‖ -ˌdaːg- -ˌdɔːg-
　~ed d **~es** z **~ing** ᵊɪŋ
Boone buːn
boong bʊŋ **boongs** bʊŋz
boonies ˈbuːn iz
boor bʊə bɔː ‖ bʊᵊr bɔːr **boors** bʊəz bɔːz
　‖ bʊᵊrz bɔːrz
boorish ˈbʊər ɪʃ ˈbɔːr- ‖ ˈbʊr- ˈbɔːr- **~ly** li
　~ness nəs nɪs
Boosey ˈbuːz i
boost buːst **boosted** ˈbuːst ɪd -əd **boosting**
　ˈbuːst ɪŋ **boosts** buːsts
booster ˈbuːst ə ‖ -ᵊr **~s** z
boot, Boot buːt **booted** ˈbuːt ɪd -əd ‖ ˈbuːt̬ əd
　booting ˈbuːt ɪŋ ‖ ˈbuːt̬ ɪŋ **boots, Boots**
　buːts
　ˈboot camp
bootable ˈbuːt əb ᵊl ‖ ˈbuːt̬-
bootblack ˈbuːt blæk **~s** s
bootee ˈbuːt iː ˌ(ˌ)buː ˈtiː ‖ ˌ(ˌ)buː ˈtiː ˈbuːt̬ i **~s** z
Bootes, Boötes bəʊ ˈəʊt iːz ‖ boʊ ˈoʊt iːz

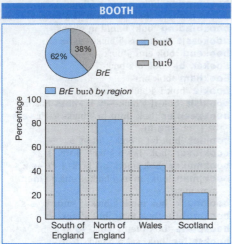

BOOTH

62% 38%

■ buːð
■ buːθ

BrE

■ BrE buːð by region

Percentage

100
80
60
40
20
0

South of England | North of England | Wales | Scotland

booth, Booth buːð buːθ ‖ buːθ **booths, Booth's** buːðz buːθs ‖ buːθs — *Preference poll, BrE:* buːð 62%, buːθ 38%
Bootham 'buːð əm
Boothby 'buːð bi
Boothe buːð buːθ ‖ buːθ
Boothia 'buːθ i ə
Boothroyd 'buːθ rɔɪd 'buːð-
bootie 'buːt i ‖ 'buːţ i **~s** z
bootjack 'buːt dʒæk **~s** s
bootlac|e 'buːt leɪs **~es** ɪz əz
Bootle 'buːt ᵊl ‖ 'buːţ ᵊl
bootleg 'buːt leg **~ged** d **~ging** ɪŋ **~s** z
bootlegger 'buːt leg ə ‖ -ᵊr **~s** z
bootless 'buːt ləs -lɪs
Boots *tdmk* buːts
bootstrap 'buːt stræp **~ped** t **~ping** ɪŋ **~s** s
boot|y 'buːt |i ‖ 'buːţ |i **~ies** iz
bootylicious ˌbuːt i 'lɪʃ əs ◄ -ə- ‖ ˌbuːţ-
booze buːz **boozed** buːzd **boozes** 'buːz ɪz -əz **boozing** 'buːz ɪŋ
boozer 'buːz ə ‖ -ᵊr **~s** z
booze-up 'buːz ʌp **~s** z
booz|y 'buːz|i **~ier** i ə ‖ i ᵊr **~iest** i ɪst ‿əst **~ily** ɪ li əl i **~iness** i nəs -nɪs
bop bɒp ‖ bɑːp **bopped** bɒpt ‖ bɑːpt **bopping** 'bɒp ɪŋ ‖ 'bɑːp ɪŋ **bops** bɒps ‖ bɑːps
bo-peep, B~ ₍ˌ₎bəʊ 'piːp ‖ ₍ˌ₎boʊ-
Bophuthatswana ˌbɒp uːt ət 'swɑːn ə ˌˑuː tæt'‑-; bɒ ˌpuːt ət'‑-, bəʊ- ‖ ˌboʊ ˌpuːţ ət- -ˌpuːt ɑːt-
bopp... —*see* **bop**
bopper 'bɒp ə ‖ 'bɑːp ᵊr **~s** z
boracic bə 'ræs ɪk bɒ-
borage 'bɒr ɪdʒ 'bʌr- ‖ 'bɔːr- 'bɑːr-
Borat 'bɔːr æt -ɑːt
borate 'bɔːr eɪt -ət, -ɪt ‖ 'boʊr- **~s** s
borax 'bɔːr æks ‖ 'boʊr-
borborygmus ˌbɔːb ə 'rɪg məs ‖ ˌbɔːrb-
Bordeaux ₍ˌ₎bɔː 'dəʊ ◄ ‖ ₍ˌ₎bɔːr 'doʊ —*Fr* [bɔʁ do]
Bor'deaux ˌmixture

Bordelaise, b~ ˌbɔːd ə 'leɪz -ᵊl 'eɪz ‖ ˌbɔːrd- —*Fr* [bɔʁ də lɛːz]
bordello bɔː 'del əʊ ‖ bɔːr 'del oʊ **~s** z
Borden 'bɔːd ᵊn ‖ 'bɔːrd ᵊn
border, B~ 'bɔːd ə ‖ 'bɔːrd ᵊr **~ed** d **bordering** 'bɔːd ᵊr ɪŋ ‖ 'bɔːrd ᵊr ɪŋ **~s** z **'border ˌterrier**
borderer 'bɔːd ᵊr ə ‖ 'bɔːrd ᵊr ᵊr **~s** z
borderland 'bɔːd ə lænd -ᵊl ænd ‖ 'bɔːrd ᵊr- **~s** z
borderline 'bɔːd ə laɪn -ᵊl aɪn ‖ 'bɔːrd ᵊr- **~s** z
bore bɔː ‖ bɔːr boʊr **bored** bɔːd ‖ bɔːrd boʊrd **bores** bɔːz ‖ bɔːrz boʊrz **boring** 'bɔːr ɪŋ ‖ 'boʊr-
boreal 'bɔːr i əl ‖ 'boʊr-
borealis ˌbɔːr i 'eɪl ɪs -'ɑːl-, §-əs ‖ -'æl əs ˌboʊr-
Boreas 'bɒr i æs 'bɔːr-, əs ‖ 'bɔːr- 'boʊr-
boredom 'bɔː dəm ‖ 'bɔːr- 'boʊr-
Boreham 'bɔːr əm ‖ 'boʊr-
Borehamwood ˌbɔːr əm 'wʊd ‖ ˌboʊr-
borehole 'bɔː həʊl →-hɒʊl ‖ 'bɔːr hoʊl 'boʊr- **~s** z
borer 'bɔːr ə ‖ -ᵊr 'boʊr- **~s** z
Borg bɔːg ‖ bɔːrg —*Swedish* [bɔrj]
Borges 'bɔːx es 'bɔːg-, -ez ‖ 'bɔːr hes —*Sp* ['boɾ xes]
Borgia 'bɔːdʒ i ə 'bɔːʒ-; '-ə ‖ 'bɔːrdʒ- 'bɔːrʒ- —*It* ['bɔr dʒa]
boric 'bɔːr ɪk 'bɒr- ‖ 'boʊr-
Boris 'bɒr ɪs §-əs ‖ 'bɔːr- —*Russ* [bʌ 'rʲis]
Bork bɔːk ‖ bɔːrk
Borland 'bɔː lənd ‖ 'bɔːr-
Borlotti, b~ bɔː 'lɒt i ‖ bɔːr 'lɑːţ i —*It* [bor 'lɔt ti]
Bormann 'bɔː mæn -mən ‖ 'bɔːr- —*Ger* ['boːɐ man]
-born 'bɔːn ◄ ‖ 'bɔːrn ◄ — **free-born** ˌfriː 'bɔːn ◄ ‖ -'bɔːrn ◄
born bɔːn ‖ bɔːrn
born-again ˌbɔːn ə 'gen ◄ -'geɪn ‖ ˌbɔːrn- ˌborn-aˌgain 'Christian
borne bɔːn ‖ bɔːrn boʊrn
Borneo 'bɔːn i əʊ ‖ 'bɔːrn i oʊ
Bornholm 'bɔːn həʊm -hɒlm ‖ 'bɔːrn hoʊm —*Danish* [bɔʁn 'hɒlʔm]
Borodin 'bɒr ə dɪn ‖ 'bɔːr ə diːn 'bɑːr- —*Russ* [bə rʌ 'dʲin]
Borodino ˌbɒr ə 'diːn əʊ ‖ ˌbɔːr ə 'diːn oʊ ˌbɑːr- —*Russ* [bə rə dʲɪ 'no]
boron 'bɔːr ɒn ‖ -ɑːn 'boʊr-
borough 'bʌr ə ‖ 'bɝː oʊ (*) **~s** z
borrow, B~ 'bɒr əʊ ‖ 'bɔːr oʊ 'bɑːr- **~ed** d **~ing** ɪŋ **~s** z
Borrowdale 'bɒr əʊ derᵊl ‖ 'bɔːr oʊ- 'bɑːr-
borrower 'bɒr əʊ ə ‖ 'bɔːr oʊ ᵊr 'bɑːr- **~s** z
borsch bɔːʃ ‖ bɔːrʃ
borscht, borshch bɔːʃt bɔːʃtʃ ‖ bɔːrʃt —*Russ* [borɕtɕ]
Borsley 'bɔːz li ‖ 'bɔːrz-
borstal, B~ 'bɔːst ᵊl ‖ 'bɔːrst- **~s** z
bort bɔːt ‖ bɔːrt
Borth bɔːθ ‖ bɔːrθ

Borthwick 'bɔːθ wɪk ‖ 'bɔːrθ-
Borussia bəʊ 'ruːs i‿ə ‖ boʊ- —*Ger*
   [bo 'ʀʊs i‿a]
borzoi 'bɔːz ɔɪ ‚bɔː 'zɔɪ ‖ 'bɔːrz- ~**s** z
Bosanquet 'bəʊz ᵊn ket →-ᵊŋ-, -kɪt ‖ 'boʊz-
boscage 'bɒsk ɪdʒ ‖ 'bɑːsk-
Boscastle 'bɒs ‚kɑːs ᵊl -‚kæs- ‖ 'bɑːs ‚kæs-
Boscawen *(i)* bɒ 'skəʊ ən bə-, -'skɔː-
  ‖ bɑː 'skoʊ ən, *(ii)* 'bɒsk wɪn -§wən, -waɪn,
  -ə wən ‖ 'bɑːsk- —*The British family name is
  usually (i); the place in NH is (ii).*
Bosch bɒʃ ‖ bɑːʃ bɔːʃ —*Dutch* [bɔs]; *Ger* [bɔʃ]
Boscobel 'bɒsk ə bel ‖ 'bɑːsk-
Bose *(i)* bəʊz ‖ boʊz, *(ii)* bəʊs ‖ boʊs
bosh bɒʃ ‖ bɑːʃ
Bosham 'bɒz əm ‖ 'bɑːz- —*There is also a
  spelling pronunciation* 'bɒʃ- ‖ 'bɑːʃ-
Bosie 'bəʊz i ‖ 'boʊz i
boskiness 'bɒsk i nəs -nɪs ‖ 'bɑːsk-
bosky 'bɒsk i ‖ 'bɑːsk i
Bosley 'bɒz li ‖ 'bɑːz-
bos'n, bo's'n 'bəʊs ᵊn ‖ 'boʊs-
Bosnia 'bɒz ni‿ə ‖ 'bɑːz-
Bosnian 'bɒz ni‿ən ‖ 'bɑːz- ~**s** z
bosom 'bʊz əm §'buːz- ~**s** z
bosomy 'bʊz əm i 'buːz-
boson 'bəʊs ɒn 'bəʊz- ‖ 'boʊs ɑːn 'boʊz-
Bosphorus 'bɒsp ər‿əs 'bɒs fər ‖ 'bɑːsp-
  'bɑːs fər
Bosporus 'bɒsp ər‿əs ‖ 'bɑːsp-
boss bɒs ‖ bɔːs bɑːs **bossed** bɒst ‖ bɔːst bɑːst
  bosses 'bɒs ɪz -əz ‖ 'bɔːs əz 'bɑːs- **bossing**
  'bɒs ɪŋ ‖ 'bɔːs ɪŋ 'bɑːs-
  ‚boss 'shot
bossa nova ‚bɒs ə 'nəʊv ə ‖ ‚bɑːs ə 'noʊv ə
boss-eyed 'bɒs aɪd ‚·'·◄ ‖ 'bɑːs- 'bɔːs-
bossi... —*see* **bossy**
Bossom 'bɒs əm ‖ 'bɑːs-
boss|y 'bɒs |i ‖ 'bɔːs |i 'bɑːs- ~**ier** i‿ə ‖ i‿ᵊr
  ~**iest** i‿ɪst i‿əst ~**ily** ɪ li əl i ~**iness** i nəs i nɪs
bossy-boots 'bɒs i buːts ‖ 'bɔːs- 'bɑːs-
Bostik *tdmk* 'bɒst ɪk ‖ 'bɑːst-
Bostock 'bɒst ɒk ‖ 'bɔːst ɑːk 'bɑːst-
Boston, b~ 'bɒst ən ‖ 'bɔːst- 'bɑːst-
  ‚Boston 'Tea ‚Party
bosun 'bəʊs ᵊn ‖ 'boʊs- ~**s** z
Boswell 'bɒz wᵊl -wel ‖ 'bɑːz-
Bosworth 'bɒz wəθ -wɜːθ ‖ 'bɑːz wᵊrθ -wɜːθ
  ‚Bosworth 'Field
bot bɒt ‖ bɑːt **bots** bɒts ‖ bɑːts **botted** 'bɒt ɪd
  -əd ‖ 'bɑːt̬- **botting** 'bɒt ɪŋ ‖ 'bɑːt̬ ɪŋ
botanic bə 'tæn ɪk bɒ- ~**al** ᵊl ~**ally** ᵊl i
botanis... —*see* **botaniz...**
botanist 'bɒt ən ɪst §-əst ‖ 'bɑːt ᵊn ‚əst ~**s** s
botaniz|e 'bɒt ə naɪz -ᵊn aɪz ‖ 'bɑːt ᵊn aɪz ~**ed**
  d ~**er/s** ə/z ‖ ᵊr/z ~**es** ɪz əz ~**ing** ɪŋ
botany 'bɒt ən i ‖ 'bɑːt ᵊn i
  ‚Botany 'Bay
botch bɒtʃ ‖ bɑːtʃ **botched** bɒtʃt ‖ bɑːtʃt
  botches 'bɒtʃ ɪz -əz ‖ 'bɑːtʃ əz **botching**
  'bɒtʃ ɪŋ ‖ 'bɑːtʃ ɪŋ
botcher 'bɒtʃ ə ‖ 'bɑːtʃ ᵊr ~**s** z
botch-up 'bɒtʃ ʌp ‖ 'bɑːtʃ- ~**s** s

botch|y 'bɒtʃ |i ‖ 'bɑːtʃ |i ~**ier** i‿ə ‖ i‿ᵊr ~**iest**
  i‿ɪst i‿əst ~**ily** ɪ li əl i
botel ‚(ˌ)bəʊ 'tel ‖ ‚(ˌ)boʊ- ~**s** z
bot|fly 'bɒt |flaɪ ‖ 'bɑːt- ~**flies** flaɪz
both bəʊθ ‖ boʊθ
Botha 'bəʊt ə 'bʊət- ‖ 'boʊt ə —*Afrikaans*
  ['bʊə ta]
Botham *(i)* 'bəʊθ əm ‖ 'boʊθ-, *(ii)* 'bɒθ əm
  ‖ 'bɑːθ- —*The cricketer Ian B~ is (i).*
bother 'bɒð ə ‖ 'bɑːð ᵊr ~**ed** d **bothering**
  'bɒð ᵊr ɪŋ ‖ 'bɑːð ᵊr ɪŋ ~**s** z
botheration ‚bɒð ə 'reɪʃ ᵊn ‖ ‚bɑːð-
bothersome 'bɒð ə səm ‖ 'bɑːð ᵊr-
bothi... —*see* **bothy**
Bothnia 'bɒθ ni‿ə ‖ 'bɑːθ-
Bothwell 'bɒθ wəl 'bɒð-, -wel ‖ 'bɑːθ- 'bɑːð-
both|y 'bɒθ |i ‖ 'bɑːθ |i ~**ies** iz
Botley 'bɒt li ‖ 'bɑːt-
Botolph 'bɒt ɒlf ‖ 'bɑːt ɑːlf
Botox *tdmk* 'bəʊ tɒks ‖ 'boʊ tɑːks
botryoid 'bɒtr ɪ ɔɪd ‖ 'bɑːtr-
botryoidal ‚bɒtr i 'ɔɪd ᵊl ◄ ‖ ‚bɑːtr-
botrytis bɒ 'traɪt ɪs bə-, §-əs ‖ boʊ 'traɪt̬ əs
Botswan|a bɒt 'swɑːn |ə ‖ bɑːt- —*Tswana*
  [bʊ 'tswa: na] ~**an/s** ən/z
Bott, bott bɒt ‖ bɑːt
bott... —*see* **bot**
Botticelli ‚bɒt ɪ 'tʃel i §-ə- ‖ ‚bɑːt̬ ə- —*It*
  [bot ti 'tʃel li]
bottl|e 'bɒt ᵊl ‖ 'bɑːt̬ ᵊl ~**ed** d ~**es** z ~**ing** ɪŋ
  'bottle bank; ‚bottle 'green◄; 'bottle
  ‚party
bottlebrush 'bɒt ᵊl brʌʃ ‖ 'bɑːt̬- ~**es** ɪz əz
bottled-up ‚bɒt ᵊld 'ʌp ◄ ‖ ‚bɑːt̬-
bottle-|feed 'bɒt ᵊl |fiːd ‖ 'bɑːt̬- ~**fed** fed
  ~**feeding** fiːd ɪŋ ~**feeds** fiːdz
bottleful 'bɒt ᵊl fʊl ‖ 'bɑːt̬- ~**s** z
bottleneck 'bɒt ᵊl nek ‖ 'bɑːt̬- ~**s** s
bottlenose 'bɒt ᵊl nəʊz ‖ 'bɑːt̬ ᵊl noʊz ~**d** d
bottler 'bɒt ᵊl ə ‖ 'bɑːt̬ ᵊl ᵊr ~**s** z
bottle-washer 'bɒt ᵊl ‚wɒʃ ə
  ‖ 'bɑːt̬ ᵊl ‚wɑːʃ ᵊr -‚wɔːʃ- ~**s** z
bottom, B~ 'bɒt əm ‖ 'bɑːt̬- ~**ed** d ~**ing** ɪŋ ~**s**
  z
  ‚bottom 'drawer; ‚bottom 'line
Bottome bə 'təʊm ‖ -'toʊm
bottomless 'bɒt əm ləs -lɪs ‖ 'bɑːt̬-
Bottomley 'bɒt əm li ‖ 'bɑːt̬-
bottommost 'bɒt əm məʊst ‖ 'bɑːt̬ əm moʊst
bottomry 'bɒt əm ri ‖ 'bɑːt̬-
bottom-up ‚bɒt əm 'ʌp ◄ ‖ ‚bɑːt̬-
botulin 'bɒt jʊl ɪn 'bɒtʃ əl-, §-ᵊn ‖ 'bɑːtʃ əl ᵊn
botulinus ‚bɒt ju 'laɪn əs ‚bɒtʃ u-, ‚bɒtʃ ə-,
  -'liːn- ‖ ‚bɑːtʃ ə-
botulism 'bɒt ju ‚lɪz əm 'bɒtʃ u-, ‚'bɒtʃ ə-
  ‖ 'bɑːtʃ ə-
bouchee, bouchée 'buːʃ eɪ buː 'ʃeɪ ‖ buː 'ʃeɪ
  —*Fr* [bu ʃe] ~**s** z
Boucher *(i)* 'baʊtʃ ə -ᵊr, *(ii)* 'buːʃ eɪ buː 'ʃeɪ
Boucicault 'buːs i kəʊ -kɔːlt -kɑːlt, -koʊ
boucle, bouclé, bouclee, bouclée 'buːk leɪ
  ‖ buː 'kleɪ
Boudicca 'buːd ɪk ə bəʊ 'dɪk ə ‖ buː 'dɪk ə

Boudin 'buːd æ̃ ‖ buː 'dæn —*Fr* [bu dæ̃]
boudoir 'buːd wɑː -wɔː ‖ 'buːd wɑːr 'bʊd- ~**s** z
bouffant 'buːf ɒ̃ -ɒŋ, -ɒnt ‖ buː 'fɑːnt 'buːf ɑːnt
bougainvillaea, bougainvillea
   ˌbuːg ən 'vɪl iˌə ˌbəʊg- ‖ ˌboʊg-, ˌbʊg-, →ˌ·ŋ-
   ~**s** z
Bougainville 'buːg ən vɪl →-ŋ- —*in
   Australian English*, 'bɒʊg- —*Fr* [bu gæ vil]
bough *'branch'* baʊ (= *bow 'bend'*) **boughed**
   baʊd **boughs** baʊz
Bough *name(i)* bɒf ‖ bɔːf bɑːf, *(ii)* baʊ
bought bɔːt ‖ bɑːt
Boughton *(i)* 'baʊt ᵊn, *(ii)* 'bɔːt ᵊn ‖ 'bɑːt-
bougie 'buːʒ iː 'buːdʒ-, buː 'ʒiː —*Fr* [bu ʒi] ~**s**
   z
bouillabaisse ˌbuː jə 'bes -'beɪs, '···· —*Fr*
   [bu ja bɛs]
bouillon 'buː jɒn 'bwiː-, -jɒ̃ ‖ 'bʊl jɑːn —*Fr*
   [bu jɔ̃]
   'bouillon cube
Boulby 'bəʊl bi →'bɒʊl- ‖ 'boʊl-
boulder, B~ 'bəʊld ə →'bɒʊld- ‖ 'boʊld ᵊr
   (= *bolder*) ~**s** z
   'boulder clay
boule *'council in ancient Athens'* 'buːl eɪ 'baʊl-,
   -iː
boule *'gem'* buːl **boules** *'gems'* buːlz
boules *game* buːl —*Fr* [bul]
boulevard 'buːl ə vɑːd 'buːl vɑːd, -vɑː
   ‖ 'bʊl ə vɑːrd (*) ~**s** z
boulevardier ₍ᵢ₎buːl 'vɑːd i eɪ ˌbuːl ə'--
   ‖ ˌbʊl ə vɑːr 'diᵊr ˌbuːl-, -'djeɪ ~**s** z
Boulez 'buːl ez -eɪ ‖ buː 'lez —*Fr* [bu lɛːz]
Boulogne bu 'lɔɪn bə- ‖ -'loʊn -'lɔɪn —*Fr*
   [bu lɔnj]
Boult bəʊlt →bɒʊlt ‖ boʊlt
Boulter 'bəʊlt ə →'bɒʊlt- ‖ 'boʊlt ᵊr
Boulting 'bəʊlt ɪŋ →'bɒʊlt- ‖ 'boʊlt ɪŋ
Boulton 'bəʊlt ən →'bɒʊlt- ‖ 'boʊlt ᵊn
bounce baʊnᵗs **bounced** baʊnᵗst **bounces**
   'baʊnᵗs ɪz -əz **bouncing** 'baʊnᵗs ɪŋ
bouncer 'baʊnᵗs ə ‖ -ᵊr ~**s** z
bounc|y 'baʊnᵗs |i ~**ier** iˌə ‖ iˌᵊr ~**iest** iˌɪst
   iˌəst ~**ily** ɪ li əl i ~**iness** i nəs i nɪs
-bound baʊnd — **southbound** ˌsaʊθ baʊnd
bound, Bound baʊnd **bounded** 'baʊnd ɪd -əd
   bounding 'baʊnd ɪŋ **bounds** baʊndz
   ˌbound 'form
boundar|y 'baʊndˌᵊr |i ~**ies** iz
   'boundary ˌlayer
bounden 'baʊnd ən
bounder 'baʊnd ə ‖ -ᵊr ~**s** z
boundless 'baʊnd ləs -lɪs ~**ly** li ~**ness** nəs nɪs
bounteous 'baʊnt iˌəs ‖ 'baʊnṭ- ~**ly** li ~**ness**
   nəs nɪs
bounti... —*see* **bounty**
bountiful 'baʊnt ɪf ᵊl -əf-; -ɪ fʊl, -ə- ‖ 'baʊnṭ-
   ~**ly** ˌi ~**ness** nəs nɪs
bount|y, B~ 'baʊnt |i ‖ 'baʊnṭ |i ~**ies** iz
   'bounty ˌhunter

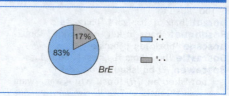

83%
17%
∴
∵
BrE

bouquet bu 'keɪ bəʊ-, 'buːk eɪ ‖ boʊ-
   — *Preference poll, BrE:* ∴ *83%,* ∵ *17%. Some
   people say* bu- *for the aroma,* bəʊ- ‖ boʊ- *for
   the flowers.* ~**s** z
bouˌquet garˈni gɑː 'niː ‖ gɑːr-, ˌ· --
bourbon *drink* 'bɜːb ən 'bʊəb- ‖ 'bɜːb- ~**s** z
Bourbon *dynasty* 'bʊəb ən 'bɔːb-, -ɒn
   ‖ 'bʊrb ən 'bɔːrb-, 'boʊrb- —*Fr* [buʁ bɔ̃] ~**s** z
   —*in French pronounced as the sing.*
bourdon, B~ 'bʊəd ᵊn 'bɔːd- ‖ 'bʊrd- ~**s** z
bourgeois, B~ 'bʊəʒ wɑː 'bɔːʒ-, ˌ·'· ‖ 'bʊrʒ-, ˌ·'·
   —*Fr* [buʁ ʒwa] —*In the noun the plural
   (spelt identically with the sing.) is pronounced
   either with* z *or, as in French, identically with
   the sing.* —*But the type size is* bɜː 'dʒɔɪs ‖ bɜː-
bourgeoisie ˌbʊəʒ wɑː 'ziː ˌbɔːʒ- ‖ ˌbʊrʒ- —*Fr*
   [buʁ ʒwa zi]
Bourke bɜːk ‖ bɜːk
bourn, Bourn, bourne bɔːn bʊən ‖ bɔːrn
   bʊᵊrn, boʊrn **bourns, bournes** bɔːnz bʊənz
   ‖ bɔːrnz bʊᵊrnz, boʊrnz
Bourne *(i)* bɔːn ‖ bɔːrn boʊrn, *(ii)* bʊən
   ‖ bʊᵊrn, *(iii)* bɜːn ‖ bɜːn
Bournemouth 'bɔːn məθ →'bɔːm- ‖ 'bɔːrn-
   'bʊrn-, 'boʊrn-
Bournville 'bɔːn vɪl ‖ 'bɔːrn- 'bʊrn-, 'boʊrn-
Bournvita *tdmk* ˌbɔːn 'viːt ə ‖ ˌbɔːrn 'viːṭ ə
   ˌbʊrn-, ˌboʊrn-
bourree, bourrée 'bʊr eɪ 'bʊər- ‖ bʊ 'reɪ —*Fr*
   [bu ʁe] ~**s** z
bourse, B~ bʊəs bɔːs ‖ bʊᵊrs **bourses** 'bʊəs ɪz
   'bɔːs-, -əz ‖ 'bʊrs əz
Boursin *tdmk* 'bʊəs æ̃ 'bɔːs-; bʊə 'sæ̃, bɔː-
   ‖ bʊr 'sæn —*Fr* [buʁ sæ̃]
Bourton 'bɔːt ᵊn ‖ 'bɔːrt ᵊn 'boʊrt-
boustrophedon ˌbuːs trə 'fiːd ᵊn ˌbaʊs-, -ɒn
   ‖ -ɑːn
bout baʊt **bouts** baʊts
boutique buː 'tiːk ~**s** s
boutonniere bu ˌtɒn i 'eə ˌbʊt ɒn 'jeə, ˌbuːt-
   ‖ ˌbuːt ᵊn 'iᵊr (*) ~**s** z
Boutros 'buːtr ɒs ‖ -oʊs
   ˌBoutros 'Ghali 'gɑːl i
Bouverie 'buːv ᵊr i
bouzouki bu 'zuːk i bə- —*Gk* [bu 'zu ci] ~**s** z
Bovary 'bəʊv ᵊr i ‖ 'boʊv- —*Fr* [bo va ʁi]
Bovey *family name (i)* 'bəʊv i ‖ 'boʊv i
   (ii) 'buːv- *(iii)* 'bʌv-
Bovey Tracey ˌbʌv i 'treɪs i
bovine 'bəʊv aɪn ‖ 'boʊv- -iːn ~**s** z
Bovingdon 'bɒv ɪŋ dən 'bʌv- ‖ 'bɑːv-
Bovington 'bɒv ɪŋ tən ‖ 'bɑːv-
Bovis 'bəʊv ɪs §-əs ‖ 'boʊv-

B

Bovril *tdmk* 'bɒv rəl -rɪl ‖ 'bɑːv-
bovver 'bɒv ə ‖ 'bɑːv ᵊr ~ed d
   'bovver boots; 'bovver boy
bow *v* '*play a stringed instrument*'; '*curve*' bəʊ
   ‖ boʊ **bowed** bəʊd ‖ boʊd **bowing** 'bəʊ ɪŋ
   ‖ 'boʊ ɪŋ **bows** bəʊz ‖ boʊz
bow *n* ('*act of bending*'; *of boat or ship*) baʊ
   bows baʊz
bow *v* '*bend the head/body forward*' baʊ
   bowed baʊd **bowing** 'baʊ ɪŋ **bows** baʊz
bow *n* (*for arrows*, '*knot*', *for violin*) bəʊ ‖ boʊ
   bows bəʊz ‖ boʊz
   ,bow 'legs
Bow *place name* bəʊ ‖ boʊ
Bowater 'bəʊ ˌwɔːt ə ‖ 'boʊ ˌwɔːt̬ ᵊr -ˌwɑːt̬-
Bowden (i) 'bəʊd ᵊn ‖ 'boʊd ᵊn, (ii) 'baʊd ᵊn
Bowdler 'baʊd lə ‖ -lᵊr
bowdleris... —*see* **bowdleriz...**
bowdlerism 'baʊd lər ˌɪz əm ‖ 'boʊd-
bowdlerization ˌbaʊd lər aɪ 'zeɪʃ ᵊn -ɪ'--
   ‖ -ə 'zeɪʃ- ˌboʊd-
bowdleriz|e 'baʊd lə raɪz ‖ 'boʊd- ~ed d ~er/s
   ə/z ‖ ᵊr/z ~es ɪz əz ~ing ɪŋ
Bowdoin, Bowdon 'bəʊd ᵊn ‖ 'boʊd-
Bowe bəʊ ‖ boʊ
bowel 'baʊ əl baʊl ‖ 'baʊ əl ~s z
   'bowel ˌmovement
Bowen 'bəʊ ɪn §-ən ‖ 'boʊ-
bower, Bower 'baʊ ə ‖ 'baʊ ᵊr ~ed d
   bowering 'baʊ ᵊr ɪŋ ‖ 'baʊ ᵊr ɪŋ ~s z
bowerbird 'baʊ ə bɜːd ‖ 'baʊ ᵊr bɜ:d ~s z
Bowers 'baʊ əz ‖ 'baʊ ᵊrz
Bowery, b~ 'baʊ ər i ‖ 'baʊ ᵊr i
Bowes bəʊz ‖ boʊz
Bowie *name(i)* 'baʊ i, (ii) 'bəʊ i ‖ 'boʊ i, (iii)
   'buː i —*The musician David B~ is (ii). In*
   'bowie knife, (ii) or (iii)
Bowker 'baʊk ə ‖ -ᵊr
bowl bəʊl →bɒʊl ‖ boʊl **bowled** bəʊld
   →bɒʊld ‖ boʊld **bowling** 'bəʊl ɪŋ →'bɒʊl-
   ‖ 'boʊl ɪŋ **bowls** bəʊlz →bɒʊlz ‖ boʊlz
Bowland 'bəʊ lənd ‖ 'boʊ-
Bowlby 'bəʊl bi →'bɒʊl- ‖ 'boʊl-
bow-legged ˌbəʊ 'leg ɪd ◄ -əd, '·ˌ·; ˌbəʊ 'legd,
   '· · ‖ 'boʊ ˌleg əd 'boʊ legd
bowler, B~ 'bəʊl ə →'bɒʊl- ‖ 'boʊl ᵊr ~s z
Bowles bəʊlz →bɒʊlz ‖ boʊlz
bowlful 'bəʊl fʊl →'bɒʊl- ‖ 'boʊl-
bowline 'bəʊl ɪn §-ən, §'bəʊ laɪn ‖ 'boʊl-
   'boʊ laɪn ~s z
bowling, B~ 'bəʊl ɪŋ →'bɒʊl- ‖ 'boʊl ɪŋ
   'bowling ˌalley; 'bowling ˌaverage;
   'bowling green
bow|man '*archer*', **B~** 'bəʊ |mən ‖ 'boʊ- ~men
   mən men
bow|man '*oarsman*' baʊ |mən ~men mən
   men
Bown baʊn
Bowness bəʊ 'nes ‖ boʊ-
Bowra 'baʊᵊr ə
Bowring 'baʊᵊr ɪŋ
bowsaw 'bəʊ sɔː ‖ 'boʊ- -sɑː ~s z
bowser, B~ 'baʊz ə ‖ -ᵊr ~s z

bowshot 'bəʊ ʃɒt ‖ 'boʊ ʃɑːt
bowsprit 'bəʊ sprɪt ‖ 'boʊ- ~s s
bowstring 'bəʊ strɪŋ ‖ 'boʊ- ~s z
bow tie ˌbəʊ 'taɪ ‖ ˌboʊ-
bow window ˌbəʊ 'wɪnd əʊ ‖ ˌboʊ 'wɪnd oʊ
bowwow *interj* ˌbaʊ 'waʊ
bowwow *n* 'baʊ waʊ ~s z
bowyang 'bəʊ jæŋ ‖ 'boʊ- ~s z
bowyer, B~ 'bəʊ jə ‖ 'boʊ jᵊr
box, Box bɒks ‖ bɑːks **boxed** bɒkst ‖ bɑːkst
   boxes 'bɒks ɪz -əz ‖ 'bɑːks əz **boxing**
   'bɒks ɪŋ ‖ 'bɑːks ɪŋ
   ˌBox and 'Cox; 'box ˌcamera; ˌbox end
   'wrench; 'box ˌjunction; 'box ˌnumber
boxcar 'bɒks kɑː ‖ 'bɑːks kɑːr ~s z
boxer, Boxer 'bɒks ə ‖ 'bɑːks ᵊr ~s z
boxercise 'bɒks ə saɪz ‖ 'bɑːks ᵊr-
boxful 'bɒks fʊl ‖ 'bɑːks- ~s z
boxing 'bɒks ɪŋ ‖ 'bɑːks-
   'Boxing Day; 'boxing gloves; 'boxing
   ring
box-offic|e 'bɒks ˌɒf ɪs §-əs ‖ 'bɑːks ˌɑːf əs
   -ˌɔːf- ~es ɪz əz
boxroom 'bɒks ruːm -rʊm ‖ 'bɑːks- ~s z
boxwood 'bɒks wʊd ‖ 'bɑːks-
boxy 'bɒks i ‖ 'bɑːks i
-boy bɔɪ — **schoolboy** 'skuːl bɔɪ
boy, Boy bɔɪ **boys** bɔɪz
   ˌboy 'scout ‖ '· ·
boyar 'bɔɪ ə -ɑː; 'bəʊ jɑː, ·'· ‖ boʊ 'jɑːr 'bɔɪ ᵊr
   ~s z
Boyce bɔɪs
boy|cott, B~ 'bɔɪ |kɒt -kət ‖ -|kɑːt ~cotted
   kɒt ɪd kət-, -əd ‖ kɑːt̬ əd ~cotting kɒt ɪŋ kət-
   ‖ kɑːt̬ ɪŋ ~cotts kɒts kəts ‖ kɑːts
Boyd bɔɪd
boyfriend 'bɔɪ frend ~s z
boyhood 'bɔɪ hʊd
boyish 'bɔɪ ɪʃ ~ly li ~ness nəs nɪs
Boyle bɔɪᵊl
Boyne bɔɪn
boyo 'bɔɪ əʊ ‖ -oʊ ~s z
boysenberr|y 'bɔɪz ᵊn bər ˌi →'·ᵊm-, -ˌber ˌi
   ‖ -ˌber ˌi ~ies iz
Boyson 'bɔɪs ᵊn
Boyzone 'bɔɪ zəʊn ‖ -zoʊn
Boz bɒz ‖ bɑːz —*Dickens apparently*
   pronounced bəʊz
bozo 'bəʊz əʊ ‖ 'boʊz oʊ ~s z
BP ˌbiː 'piː
BPhil ˌbiː 'fɪl
BR ˌbiː 'ɑː ‖ -'ɑːr
bra brɑː **bras** brɑːz
Brabant brə 'bænt —*Dutch* ['brɑː bant]; *Fr*
   [bʁa bɑ̃]
Brabantio brə 'bænt i əʊ -'bæntʃ- ‖ oʊ
Brabazon 'bræb əz ᵊn -ə zɒn ‖ -ə zɑːn
Brabham 'bræb əm
Brabin 'breɪb ɪn §-ən
Brabourne 'breɪ bɔːn -bən ‖ -bɔːrn -boʊrn
brace breɪs **braced** breɪst **braces** 'breɪs ɪz -əz
   bracing 'breɪs ɪŋ
   ˌbrace and 'bit

Bracegirdle 'breɪs ˌgɜːd ᵊl ‖ -ˌgɜːd-
bracelet 'breɪs lət -lɪt **~s** s
bracer 'breɪs ə ‖ -ᵊr **~s** z
bracero, B~ brə 'seər əʊ brɑː- ‖ brɑː 'ser oʊ
—*AmSp* [brɑ 'se ɾo] **~s** z
brachial 'breɪk i̯əl 'bræk-
brachiate *adj* 'breɪk i eɪt ət, ɪt
brachi|ate *v* 'breɪk i |eɪt **~ated** eɪt ɪd -əd
‖ eɪt̬ əd **~ates** eɪts **~ating** eɪt ɪŋ ‖ eɪt̬ ɪŋ
brachiation ˌbreɪk i 'eɪʃ ᵊn
brachiopod 'breɪk i̯ə pɒd 'bræk- ‖ -pɑːd **~s** z
brachiosaur|us ˌbreɪk i̯ə 'sɔːr |əs ˌbræk- **~i** aɪ
~uses əs ɪz əs əz
brachy- *comb. form*
with stress-neutral suffix ˈbræk i
— **brachyglossal** ˌbræk i 'glɒs ᵊl ◄ ‖ -'glɑːs-
with stress-imposing suffix bræ 'kɪ +
— **brachylogy** bræ 'kɪl ədʒ i
brachycephalic ˌbræk i sə 'fæl ɪk ◄ -sɪ'--
bracken 'bræk ən
Brackenbury 'bræk ən bər̯i →'·əm- ‖ -ˌber i
brack|et 'bræk |ɪt §-ət ‖ -|ət **~eted** ɪt ɪd §ət-,
-əd ‖ ət̬ əd **~eting** ɪt ɪŋ §ət- ‖ ət̬ ɪŋ **~ets** ɪts
§əts ‖ əts
brackish 'bræk ɪʃ **~ness** nəs nɪs
Brackley 'bræk li
Brackman 'bræk mən
Bracknell 'bræk nᵊl
bract brækt **bracts** brækts
bracteole 'brækt i əʊl →→-ɒʊl ‖ -oʊl **~s** z
brad, Brad bræd **brads** brædz
bradawl 'bræd ɔːl ‖ -ɑːl **~s** z
Bradbourne 'bræd bɔːn →'bræb- ‖ -bɔːrn
-boʊrn
Bradbrook 'bræd brʊk →'bræb-
Bradbury 'bræd bər̯i →'bræb- ‖ -ˌber i
Braddock 'bræd ək
Braddon 'bræd ᵊn
Braden 'breɪd ᵊn
Bradenton 'breɪd ᵊn tən
Bradfield 'bræd fiːᵊld
Bradford 'bræd fəd ‖ -fᵊrd —*in WYks locally
also* 'bræt-
Bradlaugh 'bræd lɔː ‖ -lɑː
Bradley *(i)* 'bræd li, *(ii)* 'breɪd li
Bradman 'bræd mən →'bræb-
Bradshaw 'bræd ʃɔː ‖ -ʃɑː
Bradwell 'bræd wəl -wel
brady- *comb. form* ˈbræd i -ə — **bradycardia**
ˌbræd i 'kɑːd i̯ə ˌ·ə- ‖ -'kɑːrd-
Brady 'breɪd i
bradykinin ˌbræd ɪ 'kaɪn ɪn ˌbreɪd-, §-ən
brae breɪ (= *bray*) **braes** breɪz
Braeburn 'breɪ bɜːn ‖ -bɜːn
Braemar ˌbreɪ 'mɑː ◄ ‖ -'mɑːr ◄
Braeuisge breɪ 'wɪsk i
brag bræg **bragged** brægd **bragging/ly**
'bræg ɪŋ /li **brags** brægz
Braganza brə 'gænz ə *Port* Bragança
[brɐ 'ɣɐ̃ sɐ]
Bragg bræg
bragg... —*see* **brag**

braggadocio ˌbræg ə 'dəʊtʃ i̯əʊ -'dəʊʃ-
‖ -'doʊʃ i̯oʊ -'doʊs- **~s** z
braggart 'bræg ət -ɑːt ‖ -ᵊrt **~s** s
Brahe 'brɑː hə -ə, -hi —*Danish* ['bʁɑː ə]
Brahma 'brɑːm ə —*but as the name of a breed
of fowl or cattle, also* 'breɪm ə
Brahman 'brɑːm ən
Brahmani, Brahmanee brɑː 'mɑːn i **~s** z
Brahmanic brɑː 'mæn ɪk
Brahmaputra ˌbrɑːm ə 'puːtr ə —*Hindi*
[brəhm pʊtr]
brahmin, B~ 'brɑːm ɪn §-ən **~s** z
Brahminism 'brɑːm ɪn ˌɪz əm §-ən-
Brahms brɑːmz —*Ger* [bʁɑːms]
Brahui brɑː 'huː i
braid, Braid breɪd **braided** 'breɪd ɪd -əd
braiding 'breɪd ɪŋ **braids** breɪdz
braider 'breɪd ə ‖ -ᵊr **~s** z
brail breɪᵊl **brailed** breɪᵊld **brailing** 'breɪᵊl ɪŋ
brails breɪᵊlz
braille, B~ breɪᵊl —*Fr* [bʁaj]
brailler 'breɪᵊl ə ‖ -ᵊr **~s** z
brain, Brain breɪn **brained** breɪnd **braining**
'breɪn ɪŋ **brains** breɪnz
'**brain ˌdamage**; '**brain drain**; '**brain(s)
trust**
brainbox 'breɪn bɒks ‖ -bɑːks **~es** ɪz əz
brain|child 'breɪn |tʃaɪᵊld **~children** tʃɪldr ən
Braine breɪn
brainfart 'breɪn fɑːt ‖ -fɑːrt **~s** s
braini... —*see* **brainy**
brainiac, B~ 'breɪn i æk **~s** s
brainless 'breɪn ləs -lɪs **~ly** li **~ness** nəs nɪs
brainpan 'breɪn pæn →'breɪm- **~s** z
brainpower 'breɪn ˌpaʊ ə ‖ -ˌpaʊ ᵊr
brainstem 'breɪn stem **~s** z
brainstorm 'breɪn stɔːm ‖ -stɔːrm **~ed** d **~ing**
ɪŋ **~s** z
brainteaser 'breɪn ˌtiːz ə ‖ -ᵊr **~s** z
Braintree 'breɪn triː 'breɪntr i
brainwash 'breɪn wɒʃ ‖ -wɔːʃ -wɑːʃ **~ed** t **~es**
ɪz əz **~ing/s** ɪŋ/z
brainwave 'breɪn weɪv **~s** z
brain|y 'breɪn |i **~ier** i̯ə ‖ i̯ᵊr **~iest** i̯ɪst i̯əst
~ily ɪ li əl i **~iness** i nəs i nɪs
braise breɪz (= *brays*) **braised** breɪzd **braises**
'breɪz ɪz -əz **braising** 'breɪz ɪŋ
Braithwaite 'breɪθ weɪt
brake, Brake breɪk (= *break*) **braked** breɪkt
brakes breɪks **braking** 'breɪk ɪŋ
'**brake ˌfluid**; '**brake shoe**
brake|man 'breɪk |mən **~men** mən men
braless 'brɑː ləs -lɪs
Bram bræm
Bramah *(i)* 'brɑːm ə, *(ii)* 'bræm ə
Bramall 'bræm ɔːl ‖ -ɑːl
Brambell 'bræm bᵊl
bramble, B~ 'bræm bᵊl **~s** z
brambling 'bræm blɪŋ **~s** z
Bramhope 'bræm həʊp ‖ -hoʊp
Bramley 'bræm li **~s** z
Brammer 'bræm ə ‖ -ᵊr
Brampton 'bræmpt ən

B

Bramwell 'bræm wəl -wel
bran bræn
  'bran tub
Branagh 'bræn ə
-**branch** bræŋk — **lamellibranch**
  lə 'mel ɪ bræŋk §-ə-
branch brɑːntʃ §bræntʃ ‖ bræntʃ **branched**
  brɑːntʃt §bræntʃt ‖ bræntʃt **branches**
  'brɑːntʃ ɪz §'bræntʃ-, -əz ‖ 'bræntʃ əz
  branching 'brɑːntʃ ɪŋ §'bræntʃ- ‖ 'bræntʃ ɪŋ
branchi|a 'bræŋk i ˌ|ə **~ae** iː **~al** əl
brand, Brand brænd **branded** 'brænd ɪd -əd
  branding 'brænd ɪŋ **brands, Brand's**
  brændz
  'brand name
Brandeis 'brænd aɪs
Brandenburg 'brænd ən bɜːg →-əm- ‖ -bɜːg
  —Ger ['bʁan dⁿ buʁk] **~s** z
  ˌBrandenburg Con'certo; ˌBrandenburg
  'Gate
Brander 'brænd ə ‖ -ᵊr
Brandi 'brænd i
brandi... —see **brandy**
brandish 'brænd ɪʃ **~ed** t **~er/s** ə/z ‖ ᵊr/z **~es**
  ɪz əz **~ing** ɪŋ
brandling 'brænd lɪŋ **~s** z
brand-new ˌbrænd 'njuː ◄ ‖ -'nuː ◄ -'njuː ◄
  ˌbrand-new 'clothes
Brando 'brænd əʊ ‖ -oʊ
Brandon 'brænd ən
Brandreth 'brændr ɪθ -əθ, -eθ
Brandt brænt —Ger [bʁant]
brand|y, B~ 'brænd ˌ|i **~ied** id **~ies** iz **~ying**
  i ɪŋ
Brangwyn 'bræŋ gwɪn
Braniff 'bræn ɪf §-əf
Branigan, Brannigan 'bræn ɪg ən §-əg-
branks bræŋks
Branksome 'bræŋk səm
Branson 'bræn⸜s ᵊn
Branston 'bræn⸜st ən
brant, Brant brænt **brants** brænts
Branwell 'bræn wəl -wel
Braque brɑːk bræk —Fr [bʁak]
Brasenose 'breɪz nəʊz ‖ -noʊz
brash bræʃ **brasher** 'bræʃ ə ‖ -ᵊr **brashest**
  'bræʃ ɪst -əst
Brasher family name 'breɪʃ ə ‖ -ᵊr
brash|ly 'bræʃ ˌ|li **~ness** nəs nɪs
Brasilia brə 'zɪl i ˌə —Port Brasília [bʁʌ 'zi lja]
brass, Brass brɑːs §bræs ‖ bræs **brassed**
  brɑːst §bræst ‖ bræst **brasses** 'brɑːs ɪz
  §'bræs-, -əz ‖ 'bræs əz
  ˌbrass 'band; ˌbrassed 'off; ˌbrass 'hat;
  ˌbrass 'knuckles; ˌbrass 'tacks
brassard 'bræs ɑːd ‖ -ɑːrd brə 'sɑːrd **~s** z
brassbound, B~ 'brɑːs baʊnd §'bræs- ‖ 'bræs-
brasserie 'bræs ər i ˌbræs ə 'riː ‖ ˌbræs ə 'riː
  ~s z
brassi- —see **brassy**
brassica 'bræs ɪk ə **~s** z
brassie 'brɑːs i 'bræs- ‖ 'bræs i **~s** z

brassiere 'bræz i ˌə 'bræs-, -i eə ‖ brə 'zɪᵊr (*)
  ~s z
Brassington 'bræs ɪŋ tən
brass-monkey ˌbrɑːs 'mʌŋk i ◄ §ˌbræs-
  ‖ ˌbræs-
  ˌbrass-'monkey ˌweather
Brasso tdmk 'brɑːs əʊ §'bræs- ‖ 'bræs oʊ
brass|y 'brɑːs ˌ|i §'bræs- ‖ 'bræs ˌ|i **~ier** i ə
  ‖ i ᵊr **~iest** i ɪst i əst **~ily** ɪ li əl i **~iness** i nəs
  i nɪs
Brasted 'breɪst ed -ɪd, -əd
brat bræt **brats** bræts
Bratby 'bræt bi
Bratislava ˌbræt ɪ 'slɑːv ə -ə-, '·· ·· ‖ ˌbrɑːt̮-
  ˌbræt̮- —Slovak ['bra t̮i sla va]
bratpack 'bræt pæk
brattish 'bræt ɪʃ ‖ 'bræt̮-
Brattleboro 'bræt ᵊl bər ə ‖ 'bræt̮ ᵊl ˌbɜː oʊ
Bratton 'bræt ᵊn
bratty 'bræt i ‖ 'bræt̮ i
bratwurst 'bræt wɜːst 'brɑːt- ‖ 'brɑːt wɜːst
  —Ger B~ ['bʁaːt vʊʁst]
Bratz tdmk bræts
Braun (i) brɔːn ‖ brɑːn, (ii) braʊn —As a tdmk,
  (i)
Braunton 'brɔːnt ən ‖ 'brɔːnt ᵊn 'brɑːnt-
bravado brə 'vɑːd əʊ ‖ -oʊ **~es, ~s** z
brave breɪv **braved** breɪvd **braver** 'breɪv ə
  ‖ -ᵊr **braves** breɪvz **bravest** 'breɪv ɪst -əst
  braving 'breɪv ɪŋ
brave|ly 'breɪv ˌ|li **~ness** nəs nɪs
braver|y 'breɪv ər ˌ|i **~ies** iz
Bravington 'bræv ɪŋ tən
bravo name for letter B, b 'brɑːv əʊ ‖ -oʊ
bravo n 'assassin' 'brɑːv əʊ ‖ -oʊ **~es, ~s** z
bravo interj; n 'shout of approval' ₍ᵢ₎ˌbrɑː 'vəʊ
  'brɑːv əʊ ‖ 'brɑːv oʊ brɑː 'voʊ **~s** z
Bravo 'brɑːv əʊ ‖ -oʊ
bravura brə 'vjʊər ə -'vʊər- ‖ -'vjʊr- -'vʊr-
braw brɔː ‖ brɑː
Brawdy 'brɔːd i ‖ 'brɑːd-
brawl brɔːl ‖ brɑːl **brawled** brɔːld ‖ brɑːld
  brawling/ly 'brɔːl ɪŋ /li ‖ 'brɑːl- **brawls**
  brɔːlz ‖ brɑːlz
brawler 'brɔːl ə ‖ -ᵊr 'brɑːl- **~s** z
brawn brɔːn ‖ brɑːn
brawn|y 'brɔːn ˌ|i ‖ 'brɑːn- **~ier** i ə ‖ i ᵊr **~iest**
  i ɪst i əst **~ily** ɪ li əl i **~iness** i nəs i nɪs
Braxton 'brækst ən
bray, Bray breɪ **brayed** breɪd (= braid)
  braying 'breɪ ɪŋ **brays** breɪz
braze breɪz (= braise, brays) **brazed** breɪzd
  brazes 'breɪz ɪz -əz **brazing** 'breɪz ɪŋ
brazen 'breɪz ᵊn **~ed** d **~ing** ˌɪŋ **~ly** li **~ness**
  nəs nɪs **~s** z
brazer 'breɪz ə ‖ -ᵊr **~s** z
brazier, B~ 'breɪz i ə 'breɪʒ ə, 'breɪʒ i ə
  ‖ 'breɪʒ ᵊr **~s** z
Brazil country, b~ 'nut', 'wood', 'dye' brə 'zɪl
  Bra'zil nut
Brazil family name(i) 'bræz ᵊl -ɪl, (ii) brə 'zɪl
Brazilian brə 'zɪl i ən **~s** z

B

Brazzaville ˈbræz ə vɪl ˈbrɑːz- —*Fr*
[bʁa za vil]
Brčko ˈbɜːtʃ kəʊ ‖ ˈbɜːtʃ koʊ —*S-Cr* [ˈbr̩tʃ kɔː]
breach, B~ briːtʃ (= *breech*) **breached** briːtʃt
breaches ˈbriːtʃ ɪz -əz **breaching** ˈbriːtʃ ɪŋ
bread bred (= *bred*) **breaded** ˈbred ɪd -əd
breading ˈbred ɪŋ **breads** bredz
ˈbread bin; ˈbread box; ˌbread ˈpudding;
ˌbread ˈsauce
Breadalbane brə ˈdɔːlb ɪn brɪ-, -ˈdælb-, -ən
‖ -ˈdɑːlb-
bread-and-butter ˌbred ᵊn ˈbʌt ə ◂ →-əm-,
→ˌbreb m- ‖ -ˈbʌt ᵊr ◂
ˌbread-andˈbutter ˌissues
breadbasket ˈbred ˌbɑːsk ɪt →ˈbreb-, §-ˌbæsk-,
§-ət ‖ -ˌbæsk ət ~**s** s
breadboard ˈbred bɔːd →ˈbreb- ‖ -bɔːrd
-boʊrd ~**s** z
breadcrumb ˈbred krʌm →ˈbreg- ~**s** z
breadfruit ˈbred fruːt ~**s** s
bread|knife ˈbred| naɪf ~**knives** naɪvz
breadline ˈbred laɪn ~**s** z
breadnut ˈbred nʌt ~**s** s
breadth bredθ bretθ, §breθ **breadths** bredθs
bretθs, §breθs
breadth|ways ˈbredθ |weɪz ˈbretθ-, §ˈbreθ-
~**wise** waɪz
breadwinner ˈbred ˌwɪn ə ‖ -ᵊr ~**s** z
break breɪk (= *brake*) **breaking** ˈbreɪk ɪŋ
breaks breɪks **broke** brəʊk ‖ broʊk **broken**
ˈbrəʊk ən ‖ ˈbroʊk ən
breakable ˈbreɪk əb ᵊl ~**s** z
breakag|e ˈbreɪk ɪdʒ ~**es** ɪz əz
breakaway ˈbreɪk ə ˌweɪ ~**s** z
breakbeat ˈbreɪk biːt
breakdanc|e ˈbreɪk dɑːnᵗs §-dænᵗs ‖ -dænᵗs
~**ed** t ~**er/s** ə/z ‖ ᵊr/z ~**es** ɪz əz ~**ing** ɪŋ
breakdown ˈbreɪk daʊn ~**s** z
breaker ˈbreɪk ə ‖ -ᵊr ~**s** z
break-even, breakeven ˌbreɪk ˈiːv ᵊn ˈ·ˌ··
breakfast ˈbrek fəst §ˈbreɪk- ~**ed** ɪd əd ~**er/s**
ə/z ‖ ᵊr/z ~**ing** ɪŋ ~**s** s
breakfront ˈbreɪk frʌnt
break-in ˈbreɪk ɪn ~**s** z
breaking ˈbreɪk ɪŋ
ˌbreaking and ˈentering; ˈbreaking point
breakneck ˈbreɪk nek
breakout ˈbreɪk aʊt ~**s** s
breakpoint ˈbreɪk pɔɪnt ~**s** s
Breakspear ˈbreɪk spɪə ‖ -spɪr
breakthrough ˈbreɪk θruː ~**s** z
breakup ˈbreɪk ʌp ~**s** s
breakwater ˈbreɪk ˌwɔːt ə ‖ -ˌwɔːt̬ ᵊr -ˌwɑːt̬- ~**s**
z
bream, Bream briːm
Brean briːn
Brearley ˈbrɪə li ‖ ˈbrɪr-
breast brest **breasted** ˈbrest ɪd -əd **breasting**
ˈbrest ɪŋ **breasts** brests
breastbone ˈbrest bəʊn ‖ -boʊn ~**s** z
breast-|feed ˈbrest |fiːd ~**fed** fed ~**feeding**
fiːd ɪŋ ~**feeds** fiːdz
breastplate ˈbrest pleɪt ~**s** s

breaststroke ˈbrest strəʊk ‖ -stroʊk
breastwork ˈbrest wɜːk ‖ -wɜːk ~**s** s
breath breθ **breaths** breθs (!)
ˈbreath test
breathable ˈbriːð əb ᵊl
breathalys|e, breathalyz|e ˈbreθ ə laɪz
→-ᵊl aɪz ~**ed** d ~**er/s** *tdmk* ə/z ‖ -ᵊr/z ~**es** ɪz
əz ~**ing** ɪŋ
breathe briːð **breathed** briːðd (!) **breathes**
briːðz (!) **breathing** ˈbriːð ɪŋ
breathed *past and pp of* **breathe** briːðd
breathed *adj* '*having breath; voiceless*' breθt
briːðd
breather ˈbriːð ə ‖ -ᵊr ~**s** z
breathi... —*see* **breathy**
breathing ˈbriːð ɪŋ
ˈbreathing space
breathless ˈbreθ ləs lɪs ~**ly** li ~**ness** nəs nɪs
breathtaking ˈbreθ ˌteɪk ɪŋ ~**ly** li
breath|y ˈbreθ |i ~**ier** i ə ‖ i ᵊr ~**iest** i ɪst i əst
~**ily** ɪ li əl i ~**iness** i nəs i nɪs
breathy-voiced ˌbreθ i ˈvɔɪst ◂
Brebner ˈbreb nə ‖ -nᵊr
breccia ˈbretʃ i ə ˈbretʃ ə
brecciated ˈbretʃ i eɪt ɪd -əd ‖ -eɪt̬-
Brechin ˈbriːk ɪn ˈbriːx-, §-ən
Brecht brext brekt —*Ger* [bʁɛçt]
Brechtian ˈbrext i ən ˈbrekt- ‖ ˈbrekt- ~**s** s
Breckenridge ˈbrek ən rɪdʒ →-ŋ-
Breckland ˈbrek lənd -lænd
Brecknock ˈbrek nɒk -nək ‖ -nɑːk -nək
Brecon ˈbrek ən
bred bred (= *bread*)
Breda briːd ə ˈbreɪd ə, breɪ ˈdɑː —*Dutch*
[bʁe ˈdaː, bʁa-]
Bredon ˈbriːd ᵊn
breech briːtʃ **breeches** *pl of* **breech** ˈbriːtʃ ɪz
-əz
ˈbreeches buoy
breeches '*trousers*' ˈbrɪtʃ ɪz ˈbriːtʃ-, -əz
breeching ˈbrɪtʃ ɪŋ ˈbriːtʃ-
breech-load|er ˈbriːtʃ ˌləʊd |ə ˌ·ˈ·· ‖ -ˌloʊd |ᵊr
~**ers** əz ‖ ᵊrz ~**ing** ɪŋ
breed briːd **bred** bred **breeding** ˈbriːd ɪŋ
breeds briːdz
breeder ˈbriːd ə ‖ -ᵊr ~**s** z
breeding-ground ˈbriːd ɪŋ graʊnd ~**s** z
breeks briːks
Breen briːn
breeze, B~ briːz **breezed** briːzd **breezes**
ˈbriːz ɪz -əz **breezing** ˈbriːz ɪŋ
breezeblock ˈbriːz blɒk ‖ -blɑːk ~**s** s
breezeway ˈbriːz weɪ ~**s** z
breez|y ˈbriːz |i ~**ier** i ə ‖ i ᵊr ~**iest** i ɪst i əst
~**ily** ɪ li əl i ~**iness** i nəs i nɪs
Breitling ˈbraɪt lɪŋ
Brekkies *tdmk* ˈbrek iz
Bremen ˈbreɪm ən ˈbrem- —*Ger* [ˈbʁeː mən]
—*but the places in the US are* ˈbriːm ən
Bremerhaven ˈbreɪm ə hɑːv ᵊn ˈbrem- ‖ ˈ·ᵊr-
—*Ger* [breːm ɐ ˈhaːf ᵊn]
Bremner ˈbrem nə ‖ -nᵊr

B

Breaking

When a vowel is followed in the same syllable by r or l, a glide sound ə may develop before the liquid. The vowel then becomes a diphthong, and is said to undergo **breaking**.

Two types of breaking are particularly frequent in English, and are shown explicitly in this dictionary:

- **feel** fiːᵊl Besides the traditional pronunciation fiːl, the form fiːəl (or fiəl) is often to be heard, especially in BrE. This happens when l follows iː, eɪ, aɪ, ɔɪ, and is termed **pre-l breaking**. (Some speakers of GenAm have pre-l breaking after uː, oʊ, aʊ, thus **rule** ruːᵊl. This is *not* shown in this dictionary.)

- **fear** fɪə ‖ fɪᵊr In AmE, the usual pronunciation involves the phoneme ɪ. (Unlike BrE, AmE has no phoneme ɪə.) However, this word may actually sound more like fiər or fiᵊr, especially if said slowly. This is due to **pre-r breaking**, which arises in GenAm when r follows ɪ, e, æ.

Both kinds of breaking are particularly common in the last syllable of a stressed word (including words of one syllable).

Bren bren
  'Bren gun
Brend brend
Brenda 'brend ə
Brendan 'brend ən
Brennan 'bren ən
Brenner 'bren ə ‖ -ᵊr —*Ger* ['bʁɛn ɐ]
  ,Brenner 'Pass
Brent, brent brent
Brentford 'brent fəd ‖ -fᵊrd
Brenton 'brent ən
Brentwood 'brent wʊd
bre'r, br'er breə brɜː ‖ brɜː brer
Brereton *(i)* 'brɪət ᵊn ‖ 'brɪrt ᵊn, *(ii)* 'breət ᵊn ‖ 'brert ᵊn
bresaola bre 'saʊl ə —*It* [bre 'sa o la]
Brescia 'breʃ i ə 'breʃ ə —*It* ['breʃ ʃa]
Brest brest —*Fr* [bʁɛst]
Brest-Litovsk ,brest lɪ 'tɒfsk -'tɒvsk ‖ -'tɔːfsk -'tɑːfsk, -'toʊfsk —*Russ* [,brʲest lʲɪ 'tofsk]
brethren 'breð rən -rɪn
Breton 'bret ɒn -ᵊn, -ɒ̃ ‖ -ᵊn —*Fr* [bʁə tɔ̃] ~s z
Brett bret
Bretton 'bret ᵊn
Breughel 'brɔɪg ᵊl 'brɜːg- ‖ 'bruːg- —*Dutch* ['brøː xəl] ~s, ~'s z
breve briːv ‖ brev **breves** briːvz ‖ brevz
brevet 'brev ɪt §-ət ~s s
breviar|y 'brev i ə|r i 'briːv-, -ᵊr |i ‖ -i er |i ~ies iz
brevier brə 'vɪə brɪ- ‖ -'vɪᵊr
brevity 'brev ət i -ɪt- ‖ -ət̬-
brew bruː **brewed** bruːd (= *brood*) **brewing** 'bruː ɪŋ **brews** bruːz (= *bruise*)

brewer, B~ 'bruː ə ‖ ᵊr ~s, ~'s z
brewer|y 'bruː ər |i ~ies iz
brewski 'bruː ski ~s z
Brewster 'bruːst ə ‖ -ᵊr
brew-up 'bruː ʌp
Brezhnev 'breʒ nef —*Russ* ['brʲeʒ nʲɪf]
Brian 'braɪ ən —*occasionally also* 'briː ən
  ,Brian Bo'ru bə 'ruː
briar 'braɪ ə ‖ 'braɪ ᵊr ~s z
briarroot 'braɪ ə ruːt ‖ 'braɪ ᵊr- -rʊt
bribable 'braɪb əb ᵊl
bribe braɪb **bribed** braɪbd **bribes** braɪbz
  bribing 'braɪb ɪŋ
briber 'braɪb ə ‖ -ᵊr ~s z
briber|y 'braɪb ər |i ~ies iz
bric-a-brac, bric-à-brac 'brɪk ə bræk
Brice braɪs
bricht brɪxt —*The StdEng equivalent of this Scots dialect word is* **bright** braɪt
brick brɪk **bricked** brɪkt **bricking** 'brɪk ɪŋ
  bricks brɪks
brickbat 'brɪk bæt ~s s
brickfield 'brɪk fiːᵊld ~s z
brickie 'brɪk i ~s z
bricklay|er 'brɪk ,leɪ |ə ‖ -|ᵊr ~ers əz ‖ ᵊrz
  ~ing ɪŋ
brick-red ,brɪk 'red ◄
brickwork 'brɪk wɜːk ‖ -wɜːk ~s s
brickyard 'brɪk jɑːd ‖ -jɑːrd ~s z
bridal 'braɪd ᵊl (= *bridle*)
bride, Bride braɪd **brides** braɪdz
  'bride price
bridegroom 'braɪd gruːm →'braɪg-, -grʊm ~s z

Brideshead 'braɪdz hed
bridesmaid 'braɪdz meɪd ~s z
bride-to-be ˌbraɪd tə 'bi: -tu- brides-to-be
　ˌbraɪdz tə 'bi: -tu-
Bridewell, b~ 'braɪd wəl -wel
bridge, Bridge brɪdʒ bridged brɪdʒd bridges
　'brɪdʒ ɪz -əz bridging 'brɪdʒ ɪŋ
　'bridge ˌplayer
bridgeable 'brɪdʒ əb əl
bridgehead 'brɪdʒ hed ~s z
Bridgeman 'brɪdʒ mən
Bridgend ˌbrɪdʒ 'end ˈ· · —The town in Mid
　Glam is locally brɪ 'dʒend
Bridgeport 'brɪdʒ pɔːt ‖ -pɔːrt -pourt
Bridger 'brɪdʒ ə ‖ -ər
Bridges 'brɪdʒ ɪz -əz
Bridget 'brɪdʒ ɪt -ət
Bridgetown 'brɪdʒ taʊn —but in Barbados
　locally §-tʌn
Bridgewater 'brɪdʒ ˌwɔːt ə ‖ -ˌwɔːt̬ ər -ˌwɑːt̬-
bridgework 'brɪdʒ wɜːk ‖ -wɜːk ~s s
bridging 'brɪdʒ ɪŋ
　'bridging loan
Bridgman 'brɪdʒ mən
Bridgnorth 'brɪdʒ nɔːθ ‖ -nɔːrθ
Bridgwater 'brɪdʒ ˌwɔːt ə ‖ -ˌwɔːt̬ ər -ˌwɑːt̬-
Bridie, b~ 'braɪd i ~s, ~'s z
bridl|e, B~ 'braɪd əl ~ed d ~es z ~ing ɪŋ
　'bridle path
bridleway 'braɪd əl weɪ ~s z
Bridlington 'brɪd lɪŋ tən
bridoon brɪ 'duːn ~s z
Bridport 'brɪd pɔːt →'brɪb- ‖ -pɔːrt -pourt
Brie, brie bri: —Fr [bʁi]
brief bri:f briefed bri:ft briefer 'bri:f ə ‖ -ər
　briefest 'bri:f ɪst -əst briefing 'bri:f ɪŋ
　briefs bri:fs
briefcas|e 'bri:f keɪs ~es ɪz əz
brief|ly 'bri:f |li ~ness nəs nɪs
brier 'braɪ ə ‖ 'braɪ ər ~s z
Brierley, Brierly (i) 'braɪ ə li ‖ 'braɪ ər-,
　(ii) 'brɪə li ‖ 'brɪr-
Briers 'braɪ əz ‖ 'braɪ ərz
brig brɪg brigs brɪgz
brigade brɪ 'geɪd brə- ~s z
brigadier ˌbrɪg ə 'dɪə ◂ ‖ -'dɪər ◂ ~s z
brigadier-general ˌbrɪg ə ˌdɪə 'dʒen ər əl
　‖ -ˌdɪr- ~s z
Brigadoon ˌbrɪg ə 'duːn
brigalow 'brɪg ə ləʊ ‖ -loʊ
brigand 'brɪg ənd ~s z
brigandage 'brɪg ənd ɪdʒ
brigantine 'brɪg ən tiːn -taɪn ~s z
Brigg brɪg
Briggs brɪgz
Brigham 'brɪg əm
Brighouse 'brɪg haʊs
bright, Bright braɪt brighter 'braɪt ə
　‖ 'braɪt̬ ər brightest 'braɪt ɪst -əst ‖ 'braɪt̬ əst
　brights braɪts
　ˌbright 'lights; 'Bright's diˌsease; ˌbright
　'spark
brighten 'braɪt ən ~ed d ~ing ɪŋ ~s z

bright-eyed ˌbraɪt 'aɪd ◂ ‖ ˌbraɪt̬-
Brightlingsea 'braɪt lɪŋ si:
bright|ly 'braɪt |li ~ness nəs nɪs
Brighton 'braɪt ən (= brighten)
brightwork 'braɪt wɜːk ‖ -wɜːk
Brigid 'brɪdʒ ɪd §-əd
Briginshaw 'brɪg ɪn ʃɔː ‖ -ʃɑː
Brigitte brɪ 'ʒiːt 'brɪʒ ɪt —Fr [bʁi ʒit]
brill, Brill brɪl brills brɪlz
brillianc|e 'brɪl jənˈs 'brɪl i ənˈs ~y i
brilliant 'brɪl jənt 'brɪl i ənt ~ly li ~ness nəs
　nɪs
brilliantine 'brɪl jən tiːn ˌ·ˈ· ~d d
Brillo tdmk 'brɪl əʊ ‖ -oʊ
　'Brillo pad
brim brɪm brimmed brɪmd brimming
　'brɪm ɪŋ brims brɪmz
Brimble 'brɪm bəl
brimful, brimfull ˌbrɪm 'fʊl ◂ ˈ· ·
-brimmed 'brɪmd — wide-brimmed
　ˌwaɪd 'brɪmd ◂
brimstone 'brɪm stəʊn -stən ‖ -stoʊn
Brindisi 'brɪnd ɪz i -əz- —It ['brin di zi]
brindle 'brɪnd əl ~d d
Brindley 'brɪnd li
brine braɪn brined braɪnd brines braɪnz
　brining 'braɪn ɪŋ
Brinell brɪ 'nel brə-
　Bri'nell ˌnumber
bring brɪŋ bringing 'brɪŋ ɪŋ brings brɪŋz
　brought brɔːt ⚠bɒːt ‖ brɑːt
　ˌbring-and-'buy sale
bringer 'brɪŋ ə ‖ -ər ~s z
brini... —see briny
brinjal 'brɪndʒ əl -ɔːl
brink, Brink brɪŋk brinks brɪŋks
brinkmanship 'brɪŋk mən ʃɪp
brinksmanship 'brɪŋks mən ʃɪp
Brinks-Mat tdmk ˌbrɪŋks 'mæt
Brinley 'brɪn li
Brinton 'brɪnt ən ‖ -ən
brin|y 'braɪn |i ~ier i ə ‖ i ər ~iest i ɪst i əst
　~iness i nəs i nɪs
Bri-Nylon tdmk ˌbraɪ 'naɪl ɒn ‖ -ɑːn
brio, Brio 'bri: əʊ ‖ -oʊ
brioch|e bri 'ɒʃ -'əʊʃ, ˈ· · ‖ -'oʊʃ —Fr [bʁi ɔʃ]
　~es ɪz əz
briolette ˌbri: əʊ 'let ‖ -ə- ~s s
briony, B~ 'braɪ ən i
briquet, briquette brɪ 'ket ~s s
Brisbane 'brɪz bən -beɪn
Brisco, Briscoe 'brɪsk əʊ ‖ -oʊ
Briseis braɪ 'siː ɪs §-əs
brisk brɪsk brisker 'brɪsk ə ‖ -ər briskest
　'brɪsk ɪst -əst
brisket 'brɪsk ɪt §-ət
brisk|ly 'brɪsk |li ~ness nɪs nəs
brisling 'brɪz lɪŋ 'brɪs- ~s z
bristl|e 'brɪs əl ~ed d ~es z ~ing ɪŋ
bristlecone 'brɪs əl kəʊn ‖ -koʊn
bristletail 'brɪs əl teɪl ~s z
bristl|y 'brɪs əl i ~iness i nəs -nɪs

B

Bristol 'brɪst ᵊl
 ,Bristol 'Channel; 'Bristol ,fashion
Bristolian brɪs 'təʊl i ᵊn ǁ -'toʊl- ~s z
Bristow, Bristowe 'brɪst əʊ ǁ -oʊ
Brit, brit brɪt **Brits, brits** brɪts
Britain 'brɪt ᵊn ~'s z
Britannia brɪ 'tæn jə brə-
Britannic brɪ 'tæn ɪk brə-
Britax tdmk 'brɪt æks
britches 'brɪtʃ ɪz -əz
Briticism 'brɪt ɪ ,sɪz əm -ə- ǁ 'brɪt̮- ~s z
British 'brɪt ɪʃ ǁ 'brɪt̮ ɪʃ
 ,British 'English; ,British 'Isles; ,British
 'Summer Time
Britisher 'brɪt ɪʃ ə ǁ 'brɪt̮ ɪʃ ᵊr ~s z
Britishness 'brɪt ɪʃ nəs -nɪs ǁ 'brɪt̮-
Britoil tdmk 'brɪt ɔɪᵊl
Briton 'brɪt ᵊn (= Britain) ~s z
Britpop 'brɪt pɒp ǁ -pɑːp
Britt brɪt
Brittain, Brittan 'brɪt ᵊn
Brittany 'brɪt ən i ǁ -ᵊn-
Britten 'brɪt ᵊn
brittl|e 'brɪt ᵊl ǁ 'brɪt̮ ᵊl ~er ə ǁ ᵊr ~eness nəs
 nɪs ~est ɪst əst
brittle-star 'brɪt ᵊl stɑː ǁ 'brɪt̮ ᵊl stɑːr ~s z
Britvic tdmk 'brɪt vɪk
Brix brɪks
Brixham 'brɪks əm
Brixton 'brɪkst ən
Brize Norton ,braɪz 'nɔːt ᵊn ǁ -'nɔːrt-
Brno 'bɜːn əʊ brə 'nəʊ ǁ 'bɜːn oʊ —Czech
 ['br̩ no]
bro brəʊ ǁ broʊ
Bro., bro. —see **Brother**
broach brəʊtʃ ǁ broʊtʃ **broached** brəʊtʃt
 ǁ broʊtʃt **broaches** 'brəʊtʃ ɪz -əz ǁ 'broʊtʃ əz
 broaching 'brəʊtʃ ɪŋ ǁ 'broʊtʃ ɪŋ
Broackes brəʊks ǁ broʊks
broad, Broad brɔːd ǁ brɑːd (!) **broader**
 'brɔːd ə ǁ -ᵊr 'brɑːd- **broadest** 'brɔːd ɪst -əst
 ǁ 'brɑːd- **broads, Broads** brɔːdz ǁ brɑːdz
 ,broad 'beans; 'broad jump
B-road 'biː rəʊd ǁ -roʊd
broadband 'brɔːd bænd →'brɔːb- ǁ 'brɑːd-
broad-based ,brɔːd 'beɪst ◄ ǁ ,brɑːd-
Broadbent 'brɔːd bent →'brɔːb- ǁ 'brɑːd-
Broadbridge 'brɔːd brɪdʒ →'brɔːb- ǁ 'brɑːd-
broadbrush 'brɔːd brʌʃ ǁ 'brɑːd-
broadcast 'brɔːd kɑːst →'brɔːg-, §-kæst ǁ -kæst
 'brɑːd- ~er/s ə/z ǁ ᵊr/z ~ing ɪŋ ~s s
broadcloth 'brɔːd klɒθ →'brɔːg-, -klɔːθ ǁ -klɔːθ
 'brɑːd-, -klɑːθ
broaden 'brɔːd ᵊn ǁ 'brɑːd- ~ed d ~ing ˌɪŋ ~s
 z
Broadhead 'brɔːd hed ǁ 'brɑːd-
Broadhurst 'brɔːd hɜːst ǁ -hɜ˞ːst 'brɑːd-
broad-leaved ,brɔːd 'liːvd ◄ ǁ ,brɑːd-
broadloom 'brɔːd luːm ǁ 'brɑːd-
broadly 'brɔːd li ǁ 'brɑːd-
broadminded ,brɔːd 'maɪnd ɪd ◄ →,brɔːb-, -əd
 ǁ ,brɑːd- ~ly li ~ness nəs nɪs

Broadmoor 'brɔːd mɔː →'brɔːb-, -mʊə ǁ -mʊr
 'brɑːd-, -mɔːr
broadness 'brɔːd nəs -nɪs ǁ 'brɑːd-
Broadribb 'brɔːd rɪb ǁ 'brɑːd-
broadsheet 'brɔːd ʃiːt ǁ 'brɑːd- ~s s
broadside 'brɔːd saɪd ǁ 'brɑːd- ~s z
broad-spectrum ,brɔːd 'spek trəm ◄ ǁ ,brɑːd-
Broadstairs 'brɔːd steəz ǁ -sterz 'brɑːd-
broadsword 'brɔːd sɔːd ǁ -sɔːrd 'brɑːd-, -soʊrd
 ~s z
Broadwater 'brɔːd ,wɔːt ə ǁ -,wɔːt̮ ᵊr 'brɑːd-,
 -,wɑːt̮-
broadway, B~ 'brɔːd weɪ ǁ 'brɑːd- ~s z
broadwise 'brɔːd waɪz ǁ 'brɑːd-
Broadwood 'brɔːd wʊd ǁ 'brɑːd-
Brobat tdmk 'brəʊb æt ǁ 'broʊb-
Brobdingnag 'brɒbd ɪŋ næg ǁ 'brɑːbd-
Brobdingnagian ,brɒbd ɪŋ 'næg i ᵊn ◄
 ǁ ,brɑːbd-
Broca 'brəʊk ə ǁ 'broʊk ə —Fr [bʁɔ ka] ~'s z
brocad|e brə 'keɪd brəʊ- ǁ broʊ- ~ed ɪd əd ~es
 z ~ing ɪŋ
brocatel, brocatelle ,brɒk ə 'tel ǁ ,brɑːk-
broccoli 'brɒk ᵊl i §-ə laɪ ǁ 'brɑːk-
broch brɒk brɒx ǁ brɑːx **brochs** brɒks brɒxs
 ǁ brɑːxs

brochure 'brəʊʃ ə -ʊə, -jʊə; brɒ 'ʃʊə, brə-
 ǁ broʊ 'ʃʊᵊr — Preference poll, BrE: '·· 90%,
 ·'· 10%. ~s z
brock, Brock brɒk ǁ brɑːk **brocks, Brock's**
 brɒks ǁ brɑːks
Brocken 'brɒk ən ǁ 'brɑːk- —Ger ['bʁɔk ᵊn]
 ,Brocken 'spectre
Brockenhurst 'brɒk ən hɜːst ǁ 'brɑːk ən hɜ˞ːst
brocket 'brɒk ɪt §-ət ǁ 'brɑːk ət ~s s
Brocklebank 'brɒk ᵊl bæŋk ǁ 'brɑːk-
Brockley 'brɒk li ǁ 'brɑːk-
Brockway 'brɒk weɪ ǁ 'brɑːk-
Brockwell 'brɒk wᵊl -wel ǁ 'brɑːk-
Broderick 'brɒd ᵊr ɪk ǁ 'brɑːd
broderie anglaise ,brəʊd ər i 'ɒŋ gleɪz
 ,brɒd-, -'ɑːŋ-, -glez, ·,··(ᵢ)·
 ǁ ,broʊd ə ,riː ɑːŋ 'gleɪz —Fr
 [bʁɔd ʁi ɑ̃ glɛːz]
Brodick 'brɒd ɪk ǁ 'brɑːd-
Brodie, b~ 'brəʊd i ǁ 'broʊd i
Brodsky 'brɒd ski ǁ 'brɑːd- —Russ ['brɔt skʲɪj]
Broederbond 'bruːd ə bɒnd 'brʊd-, -bɒnt,
 -bɔːnt ǁ -ᵊr bɑːnt -bɔːnt —Afrikaans
 ['bru dər bɔnt]
Brogan, b~ 'brəʊg ən ǁ 'broʊg-
brogue brəʊg ǁ broʊg **brogues** brəʊgz
 ǁ broʊgz

B

broil brɔɪᵊl **broiled** brɔɪᵊld **broiling** ˈbrɔɪᵊl ɪŋ **broils** brɔɪᵊlz
broiler ˈbrɔɪᵊl ə ‖ -ᵊr **~s** z
Brokaw ˈbrəʊk ɔː ‖ ˈbroʊk ɔː -ɑː
broke brəʊk ‖ broʊk
Broke brʊk
broken ˈbrəʊk ən ‖ ˈbroʊk-
ˌBroken ˈHill
broken-down ˌbrəʊk ən ˈdaʊn ◂ ‖ ˌbroʊk-
broken-hearted ˌbrəʊk ən ˈhɑːt ɪd ◂ -əd ‖ ˌbroʊk ən ˈhɑːrt̬ əd ◂
ˌbroken-ˌhearted ˈlover
brokenly ˈbrəʊk ən li ‖ ˈbroʊk-
brok|er ˈbrəʊk |ə ‖ ˈbroʊk |ᵊr **~ering** ər ɪŋ **~ers** əz ‖ ᵊrz
brokerage ˈbrəʊk ər ɪdʒ ‖ ˈbroʊk-
Brolac *tdmk* ˈbrəʊ læk ‖ ˈbroʊ-
broll|y ˈbrɒl |i ‖ ˈbrɑːl |i **~ies** iz
bromate ˈbrəʊm eɪt ‖ ˈbroʊm-
brome brəʊm ‖ broʊm
Brome *(i)* brəʊm ‖ broʊm, *(ii)* bruːm
bromegrass ˈbrəʊm grɑːs §-græs ‖ ˈbroʊm græs
bromeliad brəʊ ˈmiːl i æd ‖ broʊ- **~s** z
Bromfield ˈbrɒm fiːᵊld ‖ ˈbrɑːm-
bromic ˈbrəʊm ɪk ‖ ˈbroʊm-
bromide ˈbrəʊm aɪd ‖ ˈbroʊm- **~s** z
bromidic brəʊ ˈmɪd ɪk ‖ broʊ-
bromine ˈbrəʊm iːn -ɪn, -aɪn ‖ ˈbroʊm-
Bromley *(i)* ˈbrɒm li ‖ ˈbrɑːm li, *(ii)* ˈbrʌm li —*The places in London are (i), but were formerly also (ii). The family name may be either.*
bromocriptine, bromocryptine ˌbrəʊm əʊ ˈkrɪpt iːn ‖ ˌbroʊm oʊ-
bromoform ˈbrəʊm əʊ fɔːm ‖ ˈbroʊm ə fɔːrm
Brompton ˈbrɒmpt ən ˈbrʌmpt- ‖ ˈbrɑːmpt ən
Bromsgrove ˈbrɒmz grəʊv ‖ ˈbrɑːmz groʊv
Bromwich ˈbrɒm ɪtʃ ˈbrʌm-, -ɪdʒ ‖ ˈbrɑːm-
Bromyard ˈbrɒm jɑːd -jəd ‖ ˈbrɑːm jɑːrd
bronc brɒŋk ‖ brɑːŋk **~s** s
bronchi ˈbrɒŋk aɪ -iː ‖ ˈbrɑːŋk-
bronchia ˈbrɒŋk i ə ‖ ˈbrɑːŋk-
bronchial ˈbrɒŋk i əl ‖ ˈbrɑːŋk-
bronchiole ˈbrɒŋk i əʊl →-ɒʊl ‖ ˈbrɑːŋk i oʊl **~s** z
bronchitic brɒŋ ˈkɪt ɪk brɒn- ‖ brɑːŋ ˈkɪt̬ ɪk brɑːn-
bronchitis ₍ₗ₎brɒŋ ˈkaɪt ɪs ₍ₗ₎brɒn-, §-əs ‖ brɑːŋ ˈkaɪt̬ əs brɑːn-
broncho- *comb. form* *with stress-neutral suffix* ¦brɒŋk əʊ ‖ ¦brɑːŋk ə -oʊ — **bronchogram** ˈbrɒŋk əʊ græm ‖ ˈbrɑːŋk ə- *with stress-imposing suffix* brɒŋ ˈkɒ+ brɒn- ‖ brɑːŋ ˈkɑː+ brɑːn- — **bronchography** brɒŋ ˈkɒg rəf i ‖ brɑːŋ ˈkɑːg-
bronchodilator ˌbrɒŋk əʊ daɪ ˈleɪt ə -dɪˈ--, -dəˈ-- ‖ ˌbrɑːŋk oʊ daɪ ˈleɪt̬ ᵊr -ˈdaɪl eɪt̬ ᵊr **~s** z
bronch|us ˈbrɒŋk |əs ‖ ˈbrɑːŋk- **~i** aɪ iː
bronco ˈbrɒŋk əʊ ‖ ˈbrɑːŋk oʊ **~s** z
Bronski ˈbrɒn ski ‖ ˈbrɑːn-
Bronson ˈbrɒnᵗs ᵊn ‖ ˈbrɑːnᵗs ᵊn
Bronstein ˈbrɒn stiːn ‖ ˈbrɑːn-
Bronte, Brontë ˈbrɒnt i -eɪ ‖ ˈbrɑːnt i -eɪ **~s, ~'s** z
brontosaur ˈbrɒnt ə sɔː ‖ ˈbrɑːnt̬ ə sɔːr
brontosaur|us ˌbrɒnt ə ˈsɔːr |əs ◂ ‖ ˌbrɑːnt̬- **~i** aɪ **~uses** əs ɪz əs əz
Bronwen ˈbrɒn wen -wən, -wɪn ‖ ˈbrɑːn-
Bronx brɒŋks ‖ brɑːŋks
ˌBronx ˈcheer
bronze brɒnz ‖ brɑːnz **bronzed** brɒnzd ‖ brɑːnzd **bronzes** ˈbrɒnz ɪz -əz ‖ ˈbrɑːnz əz **bronzing** ˈbrɒnz ɪŋ ‖ ˈbrɑːnz ɪŋ
ˈBronze Age; **ˌbronze ˈmedal**
bronzer ˈbrɒnz ə ‖ ˈbrɑːnz ᵊr **~s** z
bronzy ˈbrɒnz i ‖ ˈbrɑːnz i
brooch brəʊtʃ ‖ broʊtʃ bruːtʃ *(!)* **brooches** ˈbrəʊtʃ ɪz -əz ‖ ˈbroʊtʃ əz ˈbruːtʃ-
brood bruːd **brooded** ˈbruːd ɪd -əd **brooding/ly** ˈbruːd ɪŋ /li **broods** bruːdz
brooder ˈbruːd ə ‖ -ᵊr **~s** z
brood|y ˈbruːd |i **~ier** i ə ‖ i ᵊr **~iest** i ɪst i əst **~ily** ɪ li əl i **~iness** i nəs i nɪs
brook brʊk §bruːk **brooked** brʊkt §bruːkt **brooking** ˈbrʊk ɪŋ §ˈbruːk- **brooks** brʊks §bruːks
Brook, Brooke brʊk §bruːk
Brookeborough ˈbrʊk bər ə
Brookes brʊks §bruːks
Brookfield ˈbrʊk fiːᵊld §ˈbruːk-
Brooking ˈbrʊk ɪŋ §ˈbruːk- **~s** z
Brook|land ˈbrʊk |lənd §ˈbruːk- **~lands** ləndz
brooklime ˈbrʊk laɪm §ˈbruːk- **~s** z
Brookline ˈbrʊk laɪn
Brooklyn ˈbrʊk lɪn -lən
ˌBrooklyn ˈBridge
Brookner ˈbrʊk nə ‖ -nᵊr
Brooks brʊks §bruːks
Brookside ˌbrʊk ˈsaɪd §ˌbruːk-
brookweed ˈbrʊk wiːd
Brookwood ˈbrʊk wʊd

BROOM

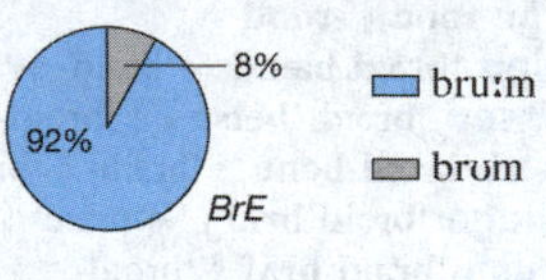

broom bruːm brʊm — *Preference poll, BrE:* bruːm *92%,* brʊm *8%.* **brooms** bruːmz brʊmz
Broom, Broome bruːm brʊm
Broomfield ˈbrʊm fiːᵊld ˈbruːm-
broomrape ˈbruːm reɪp brʊm- **~s** s
broomstick ˈbruːm stɪk ˈbrʊm- **~s** s
Brophy ˈbrəʊf i ‖ ˈbroʊf i
Bros brɒs brɒz ‖ brɔːs brɑːs —*or see* **Brothers**
brose brəʊz ‖ broʊz
Brosnahan *(i)* ˈbrɒz nə hən ‖ ˈbrɑːz-, *(ii)* ˈbrɒs- ‖ ˈbrɑːs-
Brosnan ˈbrɒz nən ‖ ˈbrɑːz-

broth brɒθ brɔ:θ ‖ brɔ:θ brɑ:θ **broths** brɒθs
  brɔ:θs, brɔ:ðz ‖ brɔ:θs brɑ:θs

brotha *non-standard variant of* brother 'brʌð ə
  ~s z

brothel 'brɒθ ᵊl ‖ 'brɑ:θ- 'brɔ:θ-, 'brɑ:ð-,
  'brɔ:ð- ~s z

brother, B~ 'brʌð ə ‖ -ᵊr ~s z
  ˌBrother 'Jonathan

brotherhood 'brʌð ə hʊd ‖ -ᵊr- ~s z

broth|er-in-law 'brʌð |ər ɪn ˌlɔ: 'ɪ-'-ə-, ən ˌlɔ:
  ‖ -ˌlɑ: **~ers-in-law** əz ɪn ˌlɔ: §-ənˌ· ‖ ᵊrz ən-
  -ˌlɑ:

brother|ly 'brʌð ə |li ‖ -ᵊr- **~liness** li nəs li nɪs

brothers-in-law 'brʌð əz ɪn ˌlɔ: §-ənˌ·
  ‖ -ᵊrz ən- -ˌlɑ:

Brotherton 'brʌð ət ən ‖ -ᵊrt ᵊn

Brough brʌf —*but the place in Highland,*
  Scotland, is brɒx ‖ brɔ:x, brɑ:x

brougham 'bru:ˌəm bru:m **~s** z

Brougham *(i)* brʊm, *(ii)* bru:m, *(iii)* brɔ:m
  ‖ brɑ:m, *(iv)* 'bru:ˌəm, *(v)* 'brəʊ əm ‖ 'brou-

brought brɔ:t △bɔ:t ‖ brɑ:t

Broughton *(i)* 'brɔ:t ᵊn ‖ 'brɑ:t-, *(ii)* 'braʊt ᵊn,
  (iii) 'brʌft ən —*Most places with this name*
  are (i), but the place in Northants is (ii) and
  places in Wales are (iii).

brouhaha 'bru: hɑ: hɑ: ·'·· ~s z

brow braʊ **brows** braʊz (= browse)

brow|beat 'braʊ |bi:t **~beaten** bi:t ᵊn
  ~beating bi:t ɪŋ ‖ bi:t̬ ɪŋ **~beats** bi:ts

brown, Brown braʊn **browned** braʊnd
  browner 'braʊn ə ‖ -ᵊr **brownest** 'braʊn ɪst
  -əst **browning** 'braʊn ɪŋ **browns** braʊnz
  ˌbrown 'Betty; ˌbrown 'rat; ˌbrown 'rice;
  ˌbrown 'sugar

brown-bag ˌbraʊn 'bæg **~ging** ɪŋ

Browne braʊn

browned-off ˌbraʊnd 'ɒf ◄ -'ɔ:f ◄ ‖ -'ɔ:f ◄ -'ɑ:f

brownfield 'braʊn fi:ᵊld

Brownhills 'braʊn hɪlz

Brownian 'braʊn iˌən

brownie, B~ 'braʊn i ~s z
  'Brownie Guide; 'brownie point

Browning, b~ 'braʊn ɪŋ

brownish 'braʊn ɪʃ

Brownjohn 'braʊn dʒɒn ‖ -dʒɑ:n

Brownlee, Brownlie 'braʊn li -li:

Brownlow 'braʊn ləʊ ‖ -loʊ

brownness 'braʊn nəs -nɪs

brown-nos|e ˌbraʊn 'nəʊz '·· ‖ -'noʊz **~ed** d
  ~es ɪz əz **~ing** ɪŋ

brownout 'braʊn aʊt ~s s

Brownrigg 'braʊn rɪg

brownshirt, B~ 'braʊn ʃɜ:t ‖ -ʃɜ:t ~s s

brownstone 'braʊn stəʊn ‖ -stoʊn ~s z

browse braʊz **browsed** braʊzd **browses**
  'braʊz ɪz -əz **browsing** 'braʊz ɪŋ

browser 'braʊz ə ‖ -ᵊr ~s z

Broxbourne 'brɒks bɔ:n ‖ 'brɑ:ks bɔ:rn -boʊrn

Broxtowe 'brɒkst əʊ ‖ 'brɑ:kst oʊ

brr bə hə hə ‖ bɜ: —*or non-speech sounds, often*
  including the voiced bilabial trill [ʙ]

Brubeck 'bru: bek

Bruce bru:s

brucellosis ˌbru:s ɪ 'ləʊs ɪs -ə-, §-əs ‖ -'loʊs-

Bruch brʊk —*Ger* [bʁʊx]

Bruckner 'brʊk nə ‖ -nᵊr —*Ger* ['bʁʊk nɐ]
  —*but as an American name,* 'brʌk-

Bruegel, Brueghel 'brɔɪg ᵊl 'brɜ:g-, 'brɜ:x-
  ‖ 'bru:g- —*Dutch* ['brø: xəl]

Bruford 'bru: fəd ‖ -fᵊrd

Bruges bru:ʒ bru:dʒ —*Fr* [bʁy:ʒ], *Flemish*
  Brugge ['bryɣə]

Bruin, bruin 'bru: ɪn §ˌən ~s, ~'s z

bruise bru:z **bruised** bru:zd **bruises** 'bru:z ɪz
  -əz **bruising/ly** 'bru:z ɪŋ /li

bruiser 'bru:z ə ‖ -ᵊr ~s z

bruit bru:t (= *brute*) **bruited** 'bru:t ɪd -əd
  ‖ 'bru:t̬ əd **bruiting** 'bru:t ɪŋ ‖ 'bru:t̬ ɪŋ
  bruits bru:ts

Brum brʌm

brumal 'bru:m ᵊl

brum|by, B~ 'brʌm| bi ~**bies** biz

Brummagem, b~ 'brʌm ədʒ əm

Brummell 'brʌm ᵊl

Brumm|ie, Brumm|y, b~ 'brʌm |i ~**ies** iz

brunch brʌntʃ **brunches** 'brʌntʃ ɪz -əz

Brundisium brʌn 'dɪz iˌəm brʊn- ‖ -'dɪʒ-

Brunei 'bru:n aɪ bru 'naɪ

Bruneian bru 'naɪ ən ~s z

Brunel bru 'nel

brunet, brunette bru 'net ~s s

Brünnhilde brʊn 'hɪld ə '··· —*Ger*
  [bʁʏn 'hɪl də]

Bruno 'bru:n əʊ ‖ -oʊ

Brunson 'brʌnˀs ᵊn

Brunswick 'brʌnz wɪk

brunt, Brunt brʌnt

Brunton 'brʌnt ən ‖ -ᵊn

bruschetta bru 'sket ə -'ʃet ə —*It*
  [bru 'sket ta]

brush brʌʃ **brushed** brʌʃt **brushes** 'brʌʃ ɪz -əz
  brushing 'brʌʃ ɪŋ

brushi... —*see* **brushy**

brush-off 'brʌʃ ɒf -ɔ:f ‖ -ɔ:f -ɑ:f

brush-up 'brʌʃ ʌp

brushwood 'brʌʃ wʊd

brushwork 'brʌʃ wɜ:k ‖ -wɜ:k

brush|y 'brʌʃ |i ~**ier** iˌə ‖ iˌᵊr ~**iest** i ɪst i əst
  ~**iness** i nəs i nɪs

brusque brʊsk bru:sk, brʌsk ‖ brʌsk

brusque|ly 'brʊsk |li 'bru:sk-, 'brʌsk- ‖ 'brʌsk-
  ~**ness** nəs nɪs

Brussels, b~ 'brʌs ᵊlz —*Fr* Bruxelles [bʁy sɛl],
  Dutch Brussel ['brʏs əl]
  ˌbrussels 'sprouts

brut bru:t —*Fr* [bʁyt]

Brut *tdmk* bru:t

brutal 'bru:t ᵊl ‖ 'bru:t̬ ᵊl ~**ly** i

brutalis... —*see* **brutaliz...**

brutalism 'bru:t ᵊl ˌɪz əm -ə ˌlɪz- ‖ 'bru:t̬-

brutalist 'bru:t ᵊl ɪst §-əst ‖ 'bru:t̬- ~**s** s

brutalit|y bru 'tæl ət |i -ɪt- ‖ -ət̬ |i ~**ies** iz

brutalization ˌbru:t ᵊl aɪ 'zeɪʃ ᵊn -ɪ'··-
  ‖ ˌbru:t̬ ᵊl ə-

B

brutaliz|e 'bruːt ə laɪz -ᵊl aɪz ‖ 'bruːt̬ ᵊl aɪz
~ed d ~es ɪz əz ~ing ɪŋ
brute bruːt **brutes** bruːts
brutish 'bruːt ɪʃ ‖ 'bruːt̬- ~ly li ~ness nəs nɪs
Bruton 'bruːt ᵊn
Brutus 'bruːt əs ‖ 'bruːt̬-
bruxism 'brʊks ɪz əm 'brʌks-
Bryan 'braɪ ˌən
Bryant 'braɪ ˌənt
Bryce braɪs
Bryden, Brydon 'braɪd ᵊn
Brylcreem tdmk 'brɪl kriːm ~ed d
Brymon tdmk 'braɪm ən -ɒn ‖ -aːn
Bryn brɪn
Brynley 'brɪn li
Bryn Mawr place in the US ˌbrɪn 'mɔː → ˌbrɪm-
‖ -'mɑːr
Brynmawr place in Gwent brɪn 'maʊ ə →brɪm-
‖ -'maʊ ᵊr —Welsh [brɪn 'maur, brɪn-]
Brynmor 'brɪn mɔː →'brɪm- ‖ -mɔːr
Brynner 'brɪn ə ‖ -ᵊr
bryon|y, B~ 'braɪ ən |i ~ies iz
bryophyte 'braɪ əʊ faɪt ‖ -ə- ~s s
bryozoan ˌbraɪ əʊ 'zəʊ ən ‖ -ə 'zoʊ- ~s z
Bryson 'braɪs ᵊn
Brythonic brɪ 'θɒn ɪk brə- ‖ -'θaːn-
Brzezinski brə 'zɪnˈsk i -'ʒɪn-
BSc, B.Sc. ˌbiː es 'siː
BSE ˌbiː es 'iː
B-side 'biː saɪd ~s z
BSkyB tdmk ˌbiː skaɪ 'biː
BST ˌbiː es 'tiː
BTEC ˌbiː 'tek '· ·
btw, BTW ₍ˌ₎baɪ ðə 'weɪ
bub bʌb **bubs** bʌbz
bubal 'bjuːb ᵊl ~s z
bubbl|e 'bʌb ᵊl ~ed d ~er/s ˌə/z ‖ ˌᵊr/z ~es z
~ing ˌɪŋ
ˌbubble and 'squeak; 'bubble bath;
'bubble ˌchamber; 'bubble gum; 'bubble
sort; 'bubble wrap
bubbl|y 'bʌb ᵊl|ˌi ~ier ˌi ə ‖ ˌi ᵊr ~iest ˌi ɪst
i əst
Buber 'buːb ə ‖ -ᵊr —Ger ['buː bɐ]
bubo 'bjuːb əʊ 'buːb- ‖ -oʊ ~s z
bubonic bju 'bɒn ɪk bu- ‖ -'baːn-
buˌbonic 'plague
buccal 'bʌk ᵊl (= buckle)
buccaneer ˌbʌk ə 'nɪə ‖ -'nɪᵊr ~neered 'nɪəd
‖ 'nɪᵊrd ~neering 'nɪər ɪŋ ‖ 'nɪr ɪŋ ~neers
'nɪəz ‖ 'nɪrz
buccinator 'bʌks ɪ neɪt ə '·ə- ‖ -neɪt̬ ᵊr ~s z
Buccleuch bə 'kluː (!)
Bucephalus bju 'sef əl əs
Buchan 'bʌk ən 'bʌx-
Buchanan bju 'kæn ən bə- —In Scotland
usually bə-
Bucharest ˌbuːk ə 'rest ˌbjuːk-, ˌbʊk-, ˌbuːx-,
'· · · ‖ 'buːk ə rest —Romanian Bucureşti
[bu ku reʃ ti]
Buchenwald 'buːk ən væld ‖ -waːld -wɔːld
—Ger ['buː xᵊn valt]
Buchman (i) 'bʌk mən, (ii) 'bʊk-

Buchmanism 'bʌk mən ˌɪz əm 'bʊk-
buck, Buck bʌk **bucked** bʌkt **bucking** 'bʌk ɪŋ
bucks bʌks
buckaroo ˌbʌk ə 'ruː '· · · ~s z
buckbean 'bʌk biːn ~s z
buckboard 'bʌk bɔːd ‖ -bɔːrd -boʊrd ~s z
Buckden 'bʌk dən
bucker 'bʌk ə ‖ -ᵊr ~s z
buck|et 'bʌk |ɪt §-ət ‖ -|ət ~eted ɪt ɪd §ət-, -əd
‖ ət̬ əd ~eting ɪt ɪŋ §ət- ‖ ət̬ ɪŋ ~ets ɪts §əts
‖ əts
'bucket seat; 'bucket shop
bucketful 'bʌk ɪt fʊl §-ət- ~s z
buckeye 'bʌk aɪ ~s z
Buckfastleigh ˌbʌk faːst 'liː §-fæst- ‖ -fæst-
Buckhurst 'bʌk hɜːst -ɜːst ‖ -hɜːst
Buckie 'bʌk i
Buckingham 'bʌk ɪŋ əm △-ən ˌəm, §-həm
~shire ʃə ʃɪə ‖ ʃᵊr ʃɪr
ˌBuckingham 'Palace
buckish 'bʌk ɪʃ ~ly li ~ness nəs nɪs
Buckland 'bʌk lənd
buckl|e 'bʌk ᵊl ~ed d ~es z ~ing ˌɪŋ
buckler, B~ 'bʌk lə ‖ -lᵊr ~s z
Buckley 'bʌk li
buckling 'bʌk lɪŋ ~s z
Buckmaster 'bʌk ˌmaːst ə §-ˌmæst- ‖ -ˌmæst ᵊr
Buckminster 'bʌk ˌmɪnˈst ə ‖ -ᵊr
Bucknall, Bucknell 'bʌk nᵊl
buckram 'bʌk rəm
Bucks, Bucks. bʌks
bucksaw 'bʌk sɔː ‖ -saː ~s z
buckshee ˌbʌk 'ʃiː ◂ '· · ‖ 'bʌk ʃiː
buckshot 'bʌk ʃɒt ‖ -ʃaːt
buckskin 'bʌk skɪn
buckteeth ˌbʌk 'tiːθ
buckthorn 'bʌk θɔːn ‖ -θɔːrn ~s z
Buckton 'bʌkt ən
buck|tooth ˌbʌk |'tuːθ §-'tʊθ ~teeth 'tiːθ
buckwheat 'bʌk wiːt -hwiːt ‖ -ʍiːt
buckyball 'bʌk i bɔːl ‖ -baːl ~s z
bucolic bju 'kɒl ɪk ‖ -'kaːl- ~ally ᵊl_i
Buczacki bu 'tʃæt ski bju-
bud, Bud bʌd **budded** 'bʌd ɪd -əd **budding**
'bʌd ɪŋ **buds** bʌdz
Budapest ˌbjuːd ə 'pest ◂ ˌbuːd-, ˌbʊd-, '· · ·
‖ 'buːd ə pest —Hung ['bu dɒ peʃt]
Budd bʌd
budd... —see bud
Buddha, b~ 'bʊd ə ‖ 'buːd ə —Hindi [buḍḍʰ]
~s z
Buddhism 'bʊd ɪz əm ‖ 'buːd-
Buddhist 'bʊd ɪst §-əst ‖ 'buːd-
Buddhistic bu 'dɪst ɪk
buddi... —see buddy
Buddig 'bɪð ɪg —Welsh ['bɪ ðig, 'bi-]
buddleia 'bʌd li ə bʌd 'liː ə ~s z
budd|y 'bʌd |i ~ied id ~ies iz ~ying i ˌɪŋ
buddy-buddy ˌbʌd i 'bʌd i '· · ˌ· ·
Bude bjuːd
budge, Budge bʌdʒ **budged** bʌdʒd **budges**
'bʌdʒ ɪz -əz **budging** 'bʌdʒ ɪŋ
budgerigar 'bʌdʒ ər ˌi gɑː ‖ -gɑːr ~s z

B

budg|et, B~ 'bʌdʒ |ɪt §-ət ‖ -|ət **~eted** ɪt ɪd
§ət-, -əd ‖ əʧ əd **~eting** ɪt ɪŋ §ət- ‖ əʧ ɪŋ **~ets**
ɪts §əts ‖ əts
  '**budget ac,count**; '**Budget Day**
budgetary 'bʌdʒ ɪt ər i '-ət ‖ -ə ter i
budgie, B~ 'bʌdʒ i **~s** z
Budleigh 'bʌd li
Budweiser *tdmk* 'bʌd waɪz ə ‖ -ᵊr
Buenos Aires ˌbweɪn ɒs 'aɪᵊr iz ˌbwen-, -əs-,
-əz-, -'eər-, -iːz, ˌ· -'eəz ‖ ˌbweɪn əs- —*Spanish*
[ˌbwe nos 'ai res], *locally also* [-noh 'ai re]
Buerk bɜːk ‖ bɜ·k
buff bʌf **buffed** bʌft **buffing** 'bʌf ɪŋ **buffs**
bʌfs
buffalo, B~ 'bʌf ə ləʊ -ᵊl əʊ ‖ -loʊ **~es, ~s** z
  '**buffalo grass**
buffer 'bʌf ə ‖ -ᵊr **~ed** d **buffering** 'bʌf ər ɪŋ
~s z
  '**buffer state**; '**buffer stock**; '**buffer zone**
buff|et *v, n 'blow'* 'bʌf |ɪt §-ət ‖ -|ət **~eted**
ɪt ɪd ət-, -əd ‖ əʧ əd **~eting/s** ɪt ɪŋ/z ət-
‖ əʧ ɪŋ/z **~ets** ɪts §əts ‖ əts
buffet *n 'meal, sideboard, counter'* 'bʊf eɪ 'bʌf-,
-i ‖ bə 'feɪ bu- (*)
  '**buffet car** ‖ ·ˌ· ·
bufflehead 'bʌf ᵊl hed **~ed** ɪd əd **~s** z
buffo 'bʊf əʊ ‖ 'buːf oʊ —*It* ['buf fo]
buffoon bə 'fuːn bʌ- **~s** z
buffooner|y bə 'fuːn ər |i bʌ- **~ies** iz
Buffs bʌfs
bug bʌg **bugged** bʌgd **bugging** 'bʌg ɪŋ **bugs**
bʌgz
  ˌ**Bugs 'Bunny**
Bug *river* buːg —*Russ, Polish* [buk]
bugaboo 'bʌg ə buː
Buganda bu 'gænd ə
Bugatti bju 'gæt i bu- ‖ -'gɑːʧ-
bugbear 'bʌg beə ‖ -ber **~s** z
bug-eyed ˌbʌg 'aɪd ◄ '·· ‖ '··
  ˌ**bug-eyed 'monster**
bugg... —*see* **bug**
bugger 'bʌg ə ‖ -ᵊr **~ed** d **buggering**
'bʌg ər ɪŋ **~s** z
bugger-all, bugger all ˌbʌg ər 'ɔːl ◄ ‖ -ər-
-'ɑːl
buggery 'bʌg ər i
buggi... —*see* **buggy**
Buggins 'bʌg ɪnz §-ənz **~'s** ɪz -əz
  '**Buggins'(s) turn**
bugg|y 'bʌg |i **~ier** i,ə ‖ i,ᵊr **~ies** iz **~iest** i,ɪst
i,əst **~iness** i nəs i nɪs
bug|house 'bʌg |haʊs **~houses** haʊz ɪz -əz
bugl|e, Bugle 'bjuːg ᵊl **~ed** d **~es** z **~ing** ɪŋ
bugler 'bjuːg lə ‖ -lᵊr **~s** z
bugloss 'bjuː glɒs ‖ -glɑːs -glɔːs **~es** ɪz əz
Bugner (*i*) 'bʌg nə ‖ -nᵊr, (*ii*) 'bʊg-
bugrake 'bʌg reɪk **~s** s
buhl buːl
Buick *tdmk* 'bjuː ɪk **~s** s
build bɪld **building** 'bɪld ɪŋ **builds** bɪldz **built**
bɪlt
builder 'bɪld ə ‖ -ᵊr **~s** z

building 'bɪld ɪŋ **~s** z
  '**building block**; '**building so,ciety**
buildup 'bɪld ʌp **~s** s
built bɪlt
Builth bɪlθ
  ˌ**Builth 'Wells**
built-in ˌbɪlt 'ɪn ◄
  ˌ**built-in 'cupboards**
built-up ˌbɪlt 'ʌp ◄
  ˌ**built-up 'area**
Buist (*i*) bjuːst, (*ii*) 'bjuː,ɪst
Buitoni *tdmk* bju 'təʊn i ‖ -'toʊn-
Bujumbura ˌbuːdʒ əm 'bʊər ə -ʊm- ‖ -'bʊr-
Bukhara bu 'kɑːr ə -'xɑːr- —*Russ* [bu 'xa rə]
Bukta *tdmk* 'bʌkt ə
Bulawayo ˌbʊl ə 'weɪ əʊ ˌbuːl- ‖ -oʊ —*Ndebele*
[ɓu la 'wa: jɔ]
bulb bʌlb **bulbs** bʌlbz
bulbar 'bʌlb ə ‖ -ᵊr -ɑːr
bulbil 'bʌlb ɪl §-ᵊl **~s** z
bulbous 'bʌlb əs **~ly** li
bulbul 'bʊl bʊl **~s** z
Bulgar, b~ 'bʌlg ɑː 'bʊlg-, -ə ‖ -ɑːr -ᵊr **~s** z
Bulgari *tdmk* 'bʊlg ər i —*It* ['bul ga ri]
Bulgari|a bʌl 'geər i |ə bʊl- ‖ -'ger- -'gær-
~an/s ən/z
bulge bʌldʒ **bulged** bʌldʒd **bulges** 'bʌldʒ ɪz
-əz **bulging** 'bʌldʒ ɪŋ
bulgur 'bʌlg ə ‖ -ᵊr
bulg|y 'bʌldʒ |i **~ier** i,ə ‖ i,ᵊr **~iest** i,ɪst i,əst
~iness i nəs i nɪs
bulim|ia bu 'lɪm |i,ə bju-, bə-, -'liːm|- **~ic** ɪk
bulk bʌlk **bulked** bʌlkt **bulking** 'bʌlk ɪŋ
bulks bʌlks
bulkhead 'bʌlk hed **~s** z
bulk|y 'bʌlk |i **~ier** i,ə ‖ i,ᵊr **~iest** i,ɪst i,əst
~ily i li əl i **~iness** i nəs i nɪs
bull, Bull bʊl **bulls** bʊlz
  '**bull ,terrier**
bull|a 'bʊl |ə 'bʌl- **~ae** iː
bullac|e 'bʊl ɪs -əs **~es** ɪz əz
Bullard (*i*) 'bʊl ɑːd ‖ -ɑːrd, (*ii*) -əd ‖ -ᵊrd
bulldog 'bʊl dɒg ‖ -dɔːg -dɑːg **~s** z
  '**bulldog clip**
bulldoz|e 'bʊl dəʊz ‖ -doʊz **~ed** d **~es** ɪz əz
~ing ɪŋ
bulldozer 'bʊl ˌdəʊz ə ‖ -ˌdoʊz ᵊr **~s** z
Bullen 'bʊl ən -ɪn
Buller 'bʊl ə ‖ -ᵊr
bullet 'bʊl ɪt -ət **~s** s
bullet-headed ˌbʊl ɪt 'hed ɪd ◄ -ət-, -əd
bulletin 'bʊl ət ɪn -ɪt-, §-ən ‖ -ᵊn **~s** z
  '**bulletin board**
bulletproof 'bʊl ɪt pruːf §-ət-, §-pruf
bullfight 'bʊl faɪt **~s** s
bullfight|er 'bʊl ˌfaɪt |ə ‖ -ˌfaɪt |ᵊr **~ers** əz
‖ ᵊrz **~ing** ɪŋ
bullfinch 'bʊl fɪntʃ **~es** ɪz əz
bullfrog 'bʊl frɒg ‖ -frɑːg -frɔːg **~s** z
bullhead 'bʊl hed **~s** z
bullheaded ˌbʊl 'hed ɪd ◄ -əd **~ly** li **~ness** nəs
nɪs
bullhorn 'bʊl hɔːn ‖ -hɔːrn **~s** z

bulli... —*see* **bully**
bullion ˈbʊl i‿ən
bullish ˈbʊl ɪʃ ~**ly** li ~**ness** nəs nɪs
bullnecked ˌbʊl ˈnekt ◂
bullnose ˈbʊl nəʊz ‖ -noʊz ~**d** d
bullock, B~ ˈbʊl ək ‖ -ɑːk ~**s** s
Bullokar ˈbʊl ə kɑː -ək ə ‖ -ə kɑːr -ək ᵊr
Bullough ˈbʊl əʊ ‖ -oʊ
bullpen ˈbʊl pen ~**s** z
bullring ˈbʊl rɪŋ ~**s** z
bullroarer ˈbʊl ˌrɔːr ə ‖ -ᵊr -ˌroʊr- ~**s** z
bull's-eye ˈbʊlz aɪ ~**s** z
bull|shit ˈbʊl |ʃɪt ~**shitter/s** ʃɪt ə/z ‖ ʃɪt̬ ᵊr/z
   ~**shitting** ʃɪt ɪŋ ‖ ʃɪt̬ ɪŋ ~**shits** ʃɪts
bullwhip ˈbʊl wɪp -hwɪp ‖ -*h*wɪp ~**ped** t ~**ping**
   ɪŋ ~**s** s
bull|y ˈbʊl |i ~**ied** id ~**ies** iz ~**ying** i‿ɪŋ
   ˌbully ˈbeef, ˈ· ·
bullyboy ˈbʊl i bɔɪ ~**s** z
bully-off ˌbʊl i ˈɒf -ɔːf ‖ -ɔːf -ɑːf
bullyrag ˈbʊl i ræg ~**ged** d ~**ging** ɪŋ ~**s** z
Bulmer ˈbʊlm ə ‖ -ᵊr
Bulow, Bülow ˈbjuːl əʊ ‖ -oʊ —*Ger* [ˈbyː lo]
bulrush ˈbʊl rʌʃ ~**es** ɪz əz
Bulstrode (*i*) ˈbʊl strəʊd ‖ -stroʊd, (*ii*) ˈbʌl-
Bultitude ˈbʌlt ɪ tjuːd -ə-, →-tʃuːd ‖ -tuːd -tjuːd
bulwark ˈbʊl wək ˈbʌl-, -wɜːk ‖ -wᵊrk ~**s** s
Bulwer ˈbʊl wə ‖ -wᵊr
bum bʌm **bummed** bʌmd **bumming** ˈbʌm ɪŋ
   bums bʌmz
   ˌbum's ˈrush
bumbag ˈbʌm bæg ~**s** z
bumbl|e ˈbʌm bᵊl ~**ed** d ~**es** z ~**ing/ly** ɪŋ /li
bumblebee ˈbʌm bᵊl biː ~**s** z
bumbledom ˈbʌm bᵊl dəm
bumble-puppy ˈbʌm bᵊl ˌpʌp i
bumbler ˈbʌm blə ‖ ᵊr ~**s** z
bumboat ˈbʌm bəʊt ‖ -boʊt ~**s** s
bumf bʌmᵖf
bumfuzzled bʌm ˈfʌz ᵊld
Bumiputra ˌbuːm ɪ ˈpuːtr ə
bummalo ˈbʌm ə ləʊ ‖ -loʊ
bummaree ˌbʌm ə ˈriː ˈ· · · ~**s** z
bummer ˈbʌm ə ‖ -ᵊr ~**s** z
bump bʌmp **bumped** bʌmpt **bumping**
   ˈbʌmp ɪŋ **bumps** bʌmps
   ˌbump ˈstart
bumper ˈbʌmp ə ‖ -ᵊr ~**s** z
bumper-to-bumper ˌbʌmp ə tə ˈbʌmp ə ◂
   ‖ -ᵊr tə ˈbʌmp ᵊr ◂
bumph bʌmᵖf
bumpi... —*see* **bumpy**
bumpkin ˈbʌmp kɪn ~**s** z
bumptious ˈbʌmp ʃəs ~**ly** li ~**ness** nəs nɪs
Bumpus ˈbʌmp əs
bump|y ˈbʌmp |i ~**ier** i ə ‖ i‿ᵊr ~**iest** i‿ɪst i‿əst
   ~**ily** ɪ li əl i ~**iness** i nəs i nɪs
bun bʌn **buns** bʌnz
Buna *tdmk* ˈbuːn ə ˈbjuːn-
Bunbury ˈbʌn bər‿i →ˈbʌm- ~**ed** d ~**ing** ɪŋ
   ~**ish** ɪʃ ~**ist/s** ɪst/s §əst/s
bunch, Bunch bʌntʃ **bunched** bʌntʃt **bunches**
   ˈbʌntʃ ɪz -əz **bunching** ˈbʌntʃ ɪŋ

Bunche bʌntʃ
bunco ˈbʌŋk əʊ ‖ -oʊ ~**ed** d ~**ing** ɪŋ ~**s** z
Buncombe ˈbʌŋk əm
bund, Bund bʌnd **bunds** bʌndz
Bundes|bank ˈbʊnd əz |bæŋk ˈbʌnd- —*Ger*
   [ˈbʊn dəs |baŋk] ~**rat** rɑːt —*Ger* [ʁaːt] ~**tag**
   tɑːg —*Ger* [taːk] ~**wehr** veə ‖ -ver —*Ger*
   [veːɐ]
bundl|e ˈbʌnd ᵊl ~**ed** d ~**es** z ~**ing** ɪŋ
Bundy ˈbʌnd i
bunfight ˈbʌn faɪt ~**s** s
bung bʌŋ **bunged** bʌŋd **bunging** ˈbʌŋ ɪŋ
   bungs bʌŋz
bungalow ˈbʌŋ gə ləʊ ‖ -loʊ ~**s** z
Bungay ˈbʌŋ gi
bungee ˈbʌndʒ i -iː
   ˈbungee ˌjumping
bunghole ˈbʌŋ həʊl →-hɒʊl ‖ -hoʊl ~**s** z
bungl|e ˈbʌŋ gᵊl ~**ed** d ~**er/s** ə/z ‖ ᵊr/z ~**es** z
   ~**ing/ly** ɪŋ /li
bunion ˈbʌn jən ~**s** z
bunk bʌŋk **bunked** bʌŋkt **bunking** ˈbʌŋk ɪŋ
   bunks bʌŋks
bunker, B~ ˈbʌŋk ə ‖ -ᵊr ~**ed** d **bunkering**
   ˈbʌŋk ər‿ɪŋ ~**s** z
bunk|house ˈbʌŋk |haʊs ~**houses** haʊz ɪz -əz
bunko ˈbʌŋk əʊ ‖ -oʊ ~**ed** d ~**ing** ɪŋ ~**s** z
bunkum ˈbʌŋk əm
bunk-up ˈbʌŋk ʌp
bunn|y, Bunny ˈbʌn |i ~**ies** iz
   ˈbunny ˌgirl
bunraku bʊn ˈrɑːk uː ‖ bʌn- —*Jp*
   [ˈbʊn ɾa kɯ]
bunsen, B~ ˈbʌnˢ ᵊn —*Ger* [ˈbʊn zᵊn] ~**s** z
   ˌBunsen ˈburner ‖ ˈ· · , ·
bunt bʌnt **bunted** ˈbʌnt ɪd -əd ‖ ˈbʌnt̬ əd
   bunting ˈbʌnt ɪŋ ‖ ˈbʌnt̬ ɪŋ **bunts** bʌnts
Bunter ˈbʌnt ə ‖ ˈbʌnt̬ ᵊr
bunting, B~ ˈbʌnt ɪŋ ‖ ˈbʌnt̬ ɪŋ ~**s** z
Bunty ˈbʌnt i
Buñuel ˈbuːn ju el ˌ· ˈ·· ‖ ˌbuːn ˈwel —*Sp*
   [bu ˈɲwel]
bunya ˈbʌn jə ~**s** z
Bunyan ˈbʌn jən
Bunyanesque ˌbʌn jə ˈnesk ◂
bunyip ˈbʌn jɪp ~**s** s
buoy bɔɪ ‖ ˈbuːɪ bɔɪ (*in BrE* = **boy**) **buoyed**
   bɔɪd ‖ ˈbuːɪd bɔɪd **buoying** ˈbɔɪ ɪŋ ‖ ˈbuːɪ ɪŋ
   ˈbɔɪ ɪŋ **buoys** bɔɪz ‖ ˈbuːɪz bɔɪz
buoyancy ˈbɔɪ ənˢ i ‖ ˈbuː jənˢ i
buoyant ˈbɔɪ ənt ‖ ˈbuː jənt ~**ly** li
BUPA ˈbuːp ə ˈbjuːp-
bur bɜː ‖ bɝː **burs** bɜːz ‖ bɝːz
Burbage ˈbɜːb ɪdʒ ‖ ˈbɝːb-
Burbank ˈbɜː bæŋk ‖ ˈbɝː-
Burberr|y ˈbɜː bər‿|i ‖ ˈbɝː- -ˌber |i ~**ies** iz
burbl|e ˈbɜːb ᵊl ‖ ˈbɝːb- ~**ed** d ~**es** z ~**ing** ɪŋ
burbot ˈbɜːb ət ‖ ˈbɝːb- ~**s** s
burbs bɜːbz ‖ bɝːbz
Burbury ˈbɜː bər‿i ‖ ˈbɝː- -ˌber i
Burch bɜːtʃ ‖ bɝːtʃ
Burchell ˈbɜːtʃ əl ‖ ˈbɝːtʃ-
Burcher ˈbɜːtʃ ə ‖ ˈbɝːtʃ ᵊr

B

Burchill 'bɜːtʃ əl -ɪl ‖ 'bɜːtʃ-
Burco *tdmk* 'bɜːk əʊ ‖ 'bɜːk oʊ
burden, B~ 'bɜːd ᵊn ‖ 'bɜːd ᵊn **~ed** d **~ing** ɪŋ
  ~s z
burdensome 'bɜːd ᵊn səm ‖ 'bɜːd- **~ly** li
  ~ness nəs nɪs
Burdett (i) 'bɜːd et ‖ 'bɜːd-, (ii) ˌbɜː 'det bə-
  ‖ bᵊr 'det
burdock 'bɜː dɒk ‖ 'bɜː dɑːk **~s** s
Burdon 'bɜːd ᵊn ‖ 'bɜːd-
bure *'Fijian cottage'* 'bʊr eɪ 'bjʊər- **~s** z
Bure bjʊə ‖ bjʊᵊr
bureau 'bjʊər əʊ 'bjɔːr-; bjʊ 'rəʊ ‖ 'bjʊr oʊ
  —Fr [by ʁo] **~s, ~x** z —or as sing.
  ˌbureau de 'change ʃɒndʒ ʃɒ̃ʒ, ʃɑːndʒ
  ‖ ʃɑːndʒ —Fr [ʃãːʒ]
bureaucrac|y bjʊᵊ 'rɒk rəs |i bjɔː-, bjə-
  ‖ -'rɑːk- **~ies** iz
bureaucrat 'bjʊər ə kræt 'bjɔːr- ‖ 'bjʊr- **~s** s
bureaucratic ˌbjʊər ə 'kræt ɪk ◂ ˌbjɔːr-
  ‖ ˌbjʊr ə 'kræt̬ ɪk ◂ **~ally** ᵊl i
bureaux 'bjʊər əʊz 'bjɔːr-, -əʊ; bjʊᵊ 'rəʊz,
  -'rəʊ ‖ 'bjʊr oʊz
buret, burette bjʊᵊ 'ret **~s** s
Burford 'bɜː fəd ‖ 'bɜː fᵊrd
burg, Burg bɜːg ‖ bɜːg **burgs** bɜːgz ‖ bɜːgz
Burge bɜːdʒ ‖ bɜːdʒ
burgee 'bɜːdʒ iː ‖ 'bɜːdʒ iː **~s** z
burgeon 'bɜːdʒ ᵊn ‖ 'bɜːdʒ- **~ed** d **~ing** ɪŋ **~s**
  z
burger, B~ 'bɜːg ə ‖ 'bɜːg ᵊr **~s** z
  'Burger ˌKing, ; ˌ‧◂ '‧
burgess, B~ 'bɜːdʒ ɪs -əs, -es ‖ 'bɜːdʒ- **~es** ɪz
  əz
burgh 'bʌr ə ‖ 'bɜː oʊ (= borough) **~s** z
Burgh (i) 'bʌr ə ‖ 'bɜː oʊ, (ii) bɜːg ‖ bɜːg,
  (iii) bɜː ‖ bɜː
Burgh-by-Sands *place in Cumbria*
  ˌbrʌf baɪ 'sændz
Burghclere 'bɜː kleə ‖ 'bɜː kler
burgher 'bɜːg ə ‖ 'bɜːg ᵊr **~s** z
Burghfield 'bɜː fiːᵊld ‖ 'bɜː-
Burghley 'bɜːl i ‖ 'bɜːl i
burglar 'bɜːg lə ‖ 'bɜːg lᵊr **~s** z
  'burglar aˌlarm
burglari... —see **burglary**
burglaris|e, burglariz|e 'bɜːg lə raɪz ‖ 'bɜːg-
  ~ed d **~es** ɪz əz **~ing** ɪŋ
burglar|y 'bɜːg lər |i △-ᵊl r|i ‖ 'bɜːg- **~ies** iz
burgl|e 'bɜːg ᵊl ‖ 'bɜːg ᵊl **~ed** d **~es** z **~ing** ɪŋ
burgomaster 'bɜːg əʊ ˌmɑːst ə § -ˌmæst-
  ‖ 'bɜːg ə ˌmæst ᵊr **~s** z
burgoo 'bɜːg uː ‖ 'bɜːg- bᵊr 'guː
Burgos 'bʊəg ɒs ‖ 'bʊr goʊs -gɑːs —Sp
  ['bur ɣos]
Burgoyne 'bɜːg ɔɪn bɜː 'gɔɪn ‖ bᵊr 'gɔɪn
Burgundian bɜː 'gʌnd i ən bə- ‖ bᵊr- **~s** z
Burgund|y, b~ 'bɜːg ᵊnd |i →-ŋd- ‖ 'bɜːg-
  ~ies iz
Burhop 'bʌr əp ‖ 'bɜː-
buri... —see **bury**
burial 'ber i əl (!) **~s** z

Buriat ˌbʊr i 'ɑːt ◂ ˌbʊər-, -'æt; ˌbʊə 'jɑːt
  ‖ ˌbʊr 'jɑːt ◂ **~s** s
Buridan 'bjʊər ɪd ən -əd- ‖ 'bjʊr-
burin 'bjʊər ɪn -ən ‖ 'bjʊr- 'bɜː- **~s** z
burk bɜːk ‖ bɜːk **~s** s
burka 'bɜːk ə ‖ 'bɜːk ə **~s** z
Burke, burke bɜːk ‖ bɜːk **burked** bɜːkt ‖ bɜːkt
  burking 'bɜːk ɪŋ ‖ 'bɜːk ɪŋ **burkes** bɜːks
  ‖ bɜːks
Burkina Faso bɜː ˌkiːn ə 'fæs əʊ
  ‖ bᵊr ˌkiːn ə 'fɑːs oʊ bʊr-
Burkitt 'bɜːk ɪt §-ət ‖ 'bɜːk- **~'s** s
burl, Burl bɜːl ‖ bɜːl **burled** bɜːld ‖ bɜːld
  burling 'bɜːl ɪŋ ‖ 'bɜːl ɪŋ **burls** bɜːlz ‖ bɜːlz
burlap 'bɜː læp ‖ 'bɜː-
Burleigh 'bɜːl i ‖ 'bɜːl i
burlesqu|e bɜː 'lesk ‖ bɜː- **~ed** t **~ely** li **~es** s
  ~ing ɪŋ
Burley 'bɜːl i ‖ 'bɜːl i
burli... —see **burly**
Burlington 'bɜːl ɪŋ tən ‖ 'bɜːl-
burl|y, Burly 'bɜːl |i ‖ 'bɜːl |i **~ier** i ə ‖ i ᵊr
  ~iest i ɪst i əst **~ily** ɪ li əl i **~iness** i nəs i nɪs
Burma 'bɜːm ə ‖ 'bɜːm ə
Burmah 'bɜːm ə ‖ 'bɜːm ə
Burman 'bɜːm ən ‖ 'bɜːm ən **~s** z
Burmese ˌbɜː 'miːz ◂ -'miːs ‖ ˌbɜː- -'miːs
burn, Burn bɜːn ‖ bɜːn **burned** bɜːnd ‖ bɜːnd
  burning 'bɜːn ɪŋ ‖ 'bɜːn ɪŋ **burns** bɜːnz
  ‖ bɜːnz **burnt** bɜːnt ‖ bɜːnt
Burnaby 'bɜːn əb i ‖ 'bɜːn-
Burnage 'bɜːn ɪdʒ ‖ 'bɜːn-
Burnaston 'bɜːn əst ən ‖ 'bɜːn-
Burne bɜːn ‖ bɜːn
burned-out ˌbɜːnd 'aʊt ◂ ˌbɜːnd-
Burne-Jones ˌbɜːn 'dʒəʊnz ‖ ˌbɜːn 'dʒoʊnz
Burnell bɜː 'nel ‖ bᵊr-
burner 'bɜːn ə ‖ 'bɜːn ᵊr **~s** z
burnet 'bɜːn ɪt §-ət ‖ bᵊr 'net 'bɜːn ət **~s** z
Burnet, Burnett (i) bə 'net bɜː- ‖ bᵊr-,
  (ii) 'bɜːn ɪt §-ət ‖ 'bɜːn-
Burney 'bɜːn i ‖ 'bɜːn i
Burnham 'bɜːn əm ‖ 'bɜːn-
Burnham-on-Crouch ˌbɜːn əm ɒn 'kraʊtʃ
  ‖ ˌbɜːn əm ɑːn- ˌ-ɔːn-
burning 'bɜːn ɪŋ ‖ 'bɜːn ɪŋ **~ly** li **~s** z
  ˌburning 'bush
burnish 'bɜːn ɪʃ ‖ 'bɜːn ɪʃ **~ed** t **~er/s** ə/z
  ‖ ᵊr/z **~es** ɪz əz **~ing** ɪŋ
Burnley 'bɜːn li ‖ 'bɜːn-
burnoos|e, burnous, burnous|e bɜː 'nuːs
  -'nuːz ‖ bᵊr- **~es** ɪz əz
burnout 'bɜːn aʊt ‖ 'bɜːn- **~s** s
Burns bɜːnz ‖ bɜːnz —In Scottish
  pronunciation, bʌrnz
  'Burns night
Burnside 'bɜːn saɪd ‖ 'bɜːn- **b~s** z
burnt bɜːnt ‖ bɜːnt
  ˌburnt 'offering
Burntisland bɜːnt 'aɪl ənd ‖ 'bɜːnt̬-
burnt-out ˌbɜːnt 'aʊt ◂ ‖ ˌbɜːnt̬-
  ˌburnt-out 'case
Burntwood 'bɜːnt wʊd ‖ 'bɜːnt-

burn-up ˈbɜːn ʌp ‖ ˈbɜːn-
buroo bə ˈruː bruː **~s** z
burp bɜːp ‖ bɜːp **burped** bɜːpt ‖ bɜːpt **burping**
ˈbɜːp ɪŋ ‖ ˈbɜːp- **burps** bɜːps ‖ bɜːps
Burpham ˈbɜːf əm ‖ ˈbɜːf-
burqa ˈbɜːk ə ‖ ˈbɜːk ə —*Arabic* [ˈbur qˤah] **~s**
z
burr, Burr bɜː ‖ bɜː **burred** bɜːd ‖ bɜːd
(= *bird*) **burring** ˈbɜːr ɪŋ ‖ ˈbɜː ɪŋ **burrs** bɜːz
‖ bɜːz
burrawang ˈbʌr ə wæŋ **~s** z
Burrell ˈbʌr əl ‖ ˈbɜː-
Burren ˈbʌr ən ‖ ˈbɜː-
burrito bə ˈriːt əʊ bʊ- ‖ bə ˈriːt̬ oʊ —*Sp*
[bu ˈrri to] **~s** z —*Sp* [-s]
burro ˈbʊr əʊ ‖ ˈbɜː oʊ ˈbʊr- —*Sp* [ˈbu rro] **~s**
z
Burrough ˈbʌr əʊ ‖ ˈbɜː oʊ -ə
Burroughes, Burroughs ˈbʌr əʊz ‖ ˈbɜː oʊz
burrow, B~ ˈbʌr əʊ ‖ ˈbɜː oʊ **~ed** d **~ing** ɪŋ **~s**
z
Burrows ˈbʌr əʊz ‖ ˈbɜː oʊz
burry *adj* 'prickly' ˈbɜːr i ‖ ˈbɜː i
burry *n* 'aboriginal' ˈbʊr i
Burry *family name* ˈbʌr i ‖ ˈbɜː i
burs|a ˈbɜːs |ə ‖ ˈbɜːs |ə **~ae** iː **~al** əl **~as** əz
bursar ˈbɜːs ə ‖ ˈbɜːs ər -ɑːr **~s** z
bursarial bɜː ˈseər i̯ əl ‖ bər ˈser-
bursarship ˈbɜːs ə ʃɪp ‖ ˈbɜːs ər- **~s** s
bursar|y ˈbɜːs ər |i ‖ ˈbɜːs- **~ies** iz
Burscough ˈbɜːsk əʊ ‖ ˈbɜːsk oʊ
burse bɜːs ‖ bɜːs **burses** ˈbɜːs ɪz -əz ‖ ˈbɜːs əz
bursitis bɜː ˈsaɪt ɪs §-əs ‖ bər ˈsaɪt̬-
Burslem ˈbɜːz ləm ‖ ˈbɜːz-
burst bɜːst ‖ bɜːst **bursting** ˈbɜːst ɪŋ
‖ ˈbɜːst ɪŋ **bursts** bɜːsts ‖ bɜːsts
Burstall ˈbɜːst ɔːl ‖ ˈbɜːst- -ɑːl
Burt bɜːt ‖ bɜːt
burthen ˈbɜːð ³n ‖ ˈbɜːð- **~ed** d **~ing** ɪŋ **~s** z
Burton, b~ ˈbɜːt ³n ‖ ˈbɜːt- **~s, ~'s** z
Burtonwood ˌbɜːt ³n ˈwʊd ‖ ˌbɜːt-
Burundi bʊ ˈrʊnd i bə- **~an/s** ən/z
Burwash *place in Sussex* ˈbɜː wɒʃ ‖ ˈbɜː wɑːʃ
—*locally also* ˈbʌr əʃ
Burwell ˈbɜː wel -wəl ‖ ˈbɜː-
bury ˈber i (! = *berry*) **buried** ˈber id **buries**
ˈber iz **burying** ˈber i̯ ɪŋ
Bury ˈber i —*As a family name, also*
ˈbjʊər i ‖ ˈbjʊr i
ˌBury St ˈEdmunds
Buryat ˌbʊr i ˈɑːt ◂ ˌbʊər-, -ˈæt; ˌbʊə ˈjɑːt
‖ ˌbʊr ˈjɑːt ◂ **~s** s
bus bʌs **bused, bussed** bʌst (= *bust*) **buses,**
busses ˈbʌs ɪz -əz **busing, bussing** ˈbʌs ɪŋ
ˈbus bar; **ˈbus boy**; **ˈbus ˌshelter**; **ˈbus**
ˌstation; **ˈbus stop**
Busan ˌbuː ˈsæn ‖ -ˈsɑːn —*Korean* [b̥u san]
busbar ˈbʌs bɑː ‖ -bɑːr **~s** z
bus|by, Busby ˈbʌz |bi **~bies** biz
Busch bʊʃ
Buse bjuːz

bush, Bush bʊʃ **bushed** bʊʃt **bushes, Bush's**
ˈbʊʃ ɪz -əz **bushing** ˈbʊʃ ɪŋ
ˌbush ˈtelegraph
bushbab|y ˈbʊʃ ˌbeɪb |i **~ies** iz
bushbuck ˈbʊʃ bʌk
bushcraft ˈbʊʃ krɑːft §-kræft ‖ -kræft
bushel ˈbʊʃ ³l **~s** z
Bushell (i) ˈbʊʃ ³l (ii) bʊ ˈʃel
Bushey ˈbʊʃ i
bushfire ˈbʊʃ ˌfaɪ‿ə ‖ -ˌfaɪ‿ər **~s** z
bushhammer ˈbʊʃ ˌhæm ə ‖ -³r **~s** z
bushi... —*see* **bushy**
Bushido bu ˈʃiːd əʊ ˌbʊʃ i ˈdəʊ ‖ ˈbuːʃ i doʊ
ˈbʊʃ- —*Jp* [bɯ ˈɕi doo]
Bushire bu ˈʃaɪ‿ə bju-, -ˈʃɪə ‖ bu ˈʃɪˀr
bush|man, B~ ˈbʊʃ |mən **~men** mən men
Bushmills ˈbʊʃ mɪlz
Bushnell ˈbʊʃ n³l
bushranger ˈbʊʃ ˌreɪndʒ ə ‖ -³r **~s** z
bushveld, B~ ˈbʊʃ felt -velt
bushwhack ˈbʊʃ wæk -hwæk **~ed** t **~er/s** ə/z
‖ ³r/z **~ing** ɪŋ **~s** s
bush|y ˈbʊʃ |i **~ier** i̯ ə ‖ i̯ ³r **~iest** i̯ ɪst i̯ əst
~ily ɪ li əl i **~iness** i nəs i nɪs
bushy-tailed ˌbʊʃ i ˈteɪ³ld ◂
busi... —*see* **busy**
busily ˈbɪz ɪ li -əl i
business ˈbɪz nəs -nɪs **~es** ɪz əz
ˈbusiness card; **ˈbusiness class**; **ˈbusiness**
end; **ˈbusiness hours, ˌ · · ˈ·**; **ˈbusiness suit**
businesslike ˈbɪz nəs laɪk -nɪs-
business|man ˈbɪz nəs |mæn -nɪs-, -mən **~men**
men mən **~woman** ˌwʊm ən **~women**
ˌwɪm ɪn §-ən
busing ˈbʌs ɪŋ
busk, Busk bʌsk **busked** bʌskt **busking**
ˈbʌsk ɪŋ **busks** bʌsks
busker ˈbʌsk ə ‖ -³r **~s** z
buskin ˈbʌsk ɪn §-ən **~ed** d **~s** z
busload ˈbʌs ləʊd ‖ -loʊd **~s** z
bus|man ˈbʌs |mən -mæn **~men** mən men
ˌbusman's ˈholiday
buss, Buss bʌs **bussed** bʌst **busses** ˈbʌs ɪz -əz
bussing ˈbʌs ɪŋ
buss... —*see* **bus**
Bussell ˈbʌs ³l
bust bʌst **busted** ˈbʌst ɪd -əd **busting** ˈbʌst ɪŋ
busts bʌsts
bustard ˈbʌst əd ‖ -³rd **~s** z
-buster ˌbʌst ə ‖ -³r — **pricebuster**
ˈpraɪs ˌbʌst ə ‖ -³r
buster, B~ ˈbʌst ə ‖ -³r **~s** z
bustier ˈbʌst i eɪ ˈbust-, -i̯ ə ‖ ˌbuːst i ˈeɪ ˌbʌst-
~s z
bustl|e ˈbʌs ³l **~ed** d **~es** z **~ing/ly** ɪŋ /li
bust-up ˈbʌst ʌp **~s** s
bust|y ˈbʌst |i **~ier** i̯ ə ‖ i̯ ³r **~iest** i̯ ɪst i̯ əst
~iness i nəs i nɪs
bus|y ˈbɪz |i **~ier** i̯ ə ‖ i̯ ³r **~iest** i̯ ɪst i̯ əst **~ily**
ɪ li əl i **~yness** i nəs i nɪs
ˌbusy ˈLizzie
busybod|y ˈbɪz i ˌbɒd |i ‖ -ˌbɑːd |i **~ies** iz
busywork ˈbɪz i wɜːk ‖ -wɜːk

B

but *strong form* bʌt, *weak form* bət
butadiene ˌbjuːt ə ˈdaɪ iːn -ˈ- ‖ ˌbjuːt̬-
butane ˈbjuːt eɪn bjuː ˈteɪn
butanoic ˌbjuːt ə ˈnəʊ ɪk ◄ -ⁿn ˈəʊ-
‖ ˌbjuːt̬ ⁿn ˈoʊ ɪk ◄
butanol ˈbjuːt ə nɒl -ⁿn ɒl ‖ -ⁿn oʊl -aːl, -ɔːl
butanone ˈbjuːt ə nəʊn -ⁿn əʊn ‖ -ⁿn oʊn
butch, Butch bʊtʃ
butch|er, B~ ˈbʊtʃ |ə ‖ -|ᵊr ~ered əd ‖ ᵊrd
   ~ering ər ɪŋ ~ers əz ‖ ᵊrz
butcherbird ˈbʊtʃ ə bɜːd ‖ -ᵊr bɜːd ~s z
butcher|y ˈbʊtʃ ər |i ~ies iz
Bute bjuːt
butene ˈbjuːt iːn
Buthelezi ˌbuːt ə ˈleɪz i ‖ ˌbuːt̬- —*Zulu*
   [bu te ˈle: zi]
butler, B~ ˈbʌt lə ‖ -|ᵊr ~s z
Butlin ˈbʌt lɪn -lən ~'s z
Butskellite ˈbʌts kə laɪt -kɪ- ~s s
butt, Butt bʌt **butted** ˈbʌt ɪd -əd ‖ ˈbʌt̬ əd
   butting ˈbʌt ɪŋ ‖ ˈbʌt̬ ɪŋ **butts** bʌts
butte, Butte bjuːt
butter ˈbʌt ə ‖ ˈbʌt̬ ᵊr ~ed d **buttering**
   ˈbʌt ᵊr ɪŋ ‖ ˈbʌt̬ ər ɪŋ ~s z
   ˈbutter bean; ˌbutter ˈicing; ˈbutter
   ˌmountain
butterball ˈbʌt ə bɔːl ‖ ˈbʌt̬ ᵊr- -baːl ~s z
butterbur ˈbʌt ə bɜː ‖ ˈbʌt̬ ᵊr bɜː ~s z
buttercream ˈbʌt ə kriːm ‖ ˈbʌt̬ ᵊr-
buttercup ˈbʌt ə kʌp ‖ ˈbʌt̬ ᵊr- ~s s
butterfat ˈbʌt ə fæt ‖ ˈbʌt̬ ᵊr- ~s s
Butterfield ˈbʌt ə fiːᵊld ‖ ˈbʌt̬ ᵊr-
butterfingers ˈbʌt ə ˌfɪŋ gəz
   ‖ ˈbʌt̬ ᵊr ˌfɪŋ gᵊrz
butter|fly ˈbʌt ə |flaɪ ‖ ˈbʌt̬ ᵊr- ~flies flaɪz
   ˈbutterfly bush; ˈbutterfly stroke;
   ˈbutterfly valve
butteri... —*see* **buttery**
Butterkist *tdmk* ˈbʌt ə kɪst ‖ ˈbʌt̬ ᵊr-
Buttermere ˈbʌt ə mɪə ‖ ˈbʌt̬ ᵊr mɪr
buttermilk ˈbʌt ə mɪlk ‖ ˈbʌt̬ ᵊr-
butternut ˈbʌt ə nʌt ‖ ˈbʌt̬ ᵊr- ~s s
Butters ˈbʌt əz ‖ ˈbʌt̬ ᵊrz
butterscotch ˈbʌt ə skɒtʃ ‖ ˈbʌt̬ ᵊr skaːtʃ
Butterwick ˈbʌt ə wɪk -ᵊr ɪk ‖ ˈbʌt̬ ᵊr wɪk
butterwort ˈbʌt ə wɜːt §-wɔːt ‖ ˈbʌt̬ ᵊr wɜːt
   -wɔːrt ~s s
Butterworth ˈbʌt ə wəθ -wɜːθ ‖ ˈbʌt̬ ᵊr wᵊrθ
   ~'s s
butter|y ˈbʌt ər |i ‖ ˈbʌt̬- ~ies iz
Butthead ˈbʌt hed
butthole ˈbʌt həʊl →-hɒʊl ‖ -hoʊl ~s s
butti... —*see* **butty**
buttinski bʌ ˈtɪn ski ‖ bə ˈdɪn ski ~s z
buttock ˈbʌt ək ‖ ˈbʌt̬- ~s s
button, B~ ˈbʌt ⁿn ~ed d ~ing ˌɪŋ ~s z
button-down ˌbʌt ⁿn ˈdaʊn ◄
   ˌbutton-down ˈcollar
buttonhol|e ˈbʌt ⁿn həʊl →-hɒʊl ‖ -hoʊl ~ed
   d ~es z ~ing ɪŋ
buttonhook ˈbʌt ⁿn hʊk §-huːk ~s s
buttress ˈbʌtr əs -ɪs ~ed t ~es ɪz əz ~ing ɪŋ
butt|y ˈbʌt |i ‖ ˈbʌt̬ |i ~ies iz

butyl ˈbjuːt aɪᵊl -ɪl, §-ᵊl ‖ ˈbjuːt̬ ᵊl
butyric bjuː ˈtɪr ɪk
buxom ˈbʌks əm ~ly li ~ness nəs nɪs
Buxted ˈbʌkst ɪd -əd, -ed
Buxtehude ˌbʊkst ə ˈhuːd ə ˈ·····—*Ger*
   [bʊks tə ˈhuː də], *Danish* [bʊks də ˈhuː ðə]
Buxton ˈbʌkst ən
buy baɪ *(= by)* **bought** bɔːt ‖ baːt **buying**
   ˈbaɪ ɪŋ **buys** baɪz
buyback ˈbaɪ bæk ~s s
buyer ˈbaɪ ə ‖ ˈbaɪ ᵊr ~s z
   ˌbuyer's ˈmarket, ˈ····
buyout ˈbaɪ aʊt ~s s
Buys Ballot ˌbaɪs bə ˈlɒt ˌbɔɪs-, ˌbaɪz-, -ˈbæl ət
   ‖ -ˈlaːt —*Dutch* [ˌbœys ba ˈlɔt]
Buzby ˈbʌz bi
Buzfuz ˈbʌz fʌz
buzz bʌz **buzzed** bʌzd **buzzes** ˈbʌz ɪz -əz
   buzzing ˈbʌz ɪŋ
buzzard, B~ ˈbʌz əd ‖ -ᵊrd ~s z
buzzcut ˈbʌz kʌt ~s s
buzzer ˈbʌz ə ‖ -ᵊr ~s z
buzzword ˈbʌz wɜːd ‖ -wɜːd ~s z
BVD *tdmk* ˌbiː viː ˈdiː ~'s z
bwana ˈbwɑːn ə ~s z
Bwlch bʊlk bʊlx —*Welsh* [bʊlχ]
by baɪ —*This word normally has no weak form.*
   However there is an occasional weak form **bi,**
   bə, *which is stylistically marked and in RP*
   restricted to set phrases. The EFL learner
   should always use the pronunciation **baɪ.**
Byars ˈbaɪ əz ‖ ˈbaɪ ᵊrz
Byatt ˈbaɪ ət
by-blow ˈbaɪ bləʊ ‖ -bloʊ ~s z
Bydgoszcz ˈbɪd gɒʃ ‖ -gɔːʃ -goʊʃ —*Polish*
   [ˈbɨd gɔʃtʃ]
bye, Bye baɪ *(= by, buy)* **byes** baɪz
bye- *comb. form* ¦baɪ — **bye-election**
   ˈbaɪ ɪ ˌlek ʃⁿn -ə-
bye-bye *interj* ₍ₒ₎baɪ ˈbaɪ
bye-byes *n* ˈbaɪ baɪz
byelaw ˈbaɪ lɔː ‖ -laː ~s z
by-election ˈbaɪ ɪ ˌlek ʃⁿn -ə- ~s z
Byeloruss|ia bi ˌel əʊ ˈrʌʃ |ə ¦bel əʊˈ--,
   -ˈruːs |i ə ‖ -oʊ ˈrʌʃ |ə —*Also, inappropriately,*
   ˌbaɪ ə ləʊ- ~ian/s ⁿn/z i ən/z
Byers ˈbaɪ əz ‖ ˈbaɪ ᵊrz
Byfield ˈbaɪ fiːᵊld
Byfleet ˈbaɪ fliːt
bygone ˈbaɪ gɒn §-gaːn ‖ -gɔːn -gaːn ~s z
Bygraves ˈbaɪ greɪvz
Byker ˈbaɪk ə ‖ -ᵊr
bylaw ˈbaɪ lɔː ‖ -laː ~s z
byline ˈbaɪ laɪn ~s s
Byng bɪŋ
BYO ˌbiː waɪ ˈəʊ ‖ -ˈoʊ
BYOB ˌbiː waɪ əʊ ˈbiː ‖ -oʊ ˈbiː
bypass ˈbaɪ paːs §-pæs ‖ -pæs ~ed t ~es ɪz əz
   ~ing ɪŋ
   ˈbypass ˌsurgery
by|path ˈbaɪ |paːθ §-pæθ ‖ -|pæθ ~paths
   paːðz paːθs, §pæθs, §pæðz ‖ -pæðz -pæθs
byplay ˈbaɪ pleɪ

byproduct 'baɪ ˌprɒd ʌkt ‖ -ˌprɑːd əkt **~s** s
Byrd bɜːd ‖ bɝːd
byre 'baɪ‿ə ‖ 'baɪ‿ᵊr **byres** 'baɪ‿əz ‖ 'baɪ‿ᵊrz
Byrne bɜːn ‖ bɝːn
byroad 'baɪ rəʊd ‖ -roʊd **~s** z
Byrom 'baɪ‿ᵊr əm
Byron 'baɪ‿ᵊr ən **~'s** z
Byronic baɪ‿ᵊ 'rɒn ɪk ‖ -'rɑːn- **~ally** ᵊl̩ i
Bysshe bɪʃ
byssinosis ˌbɪs ɪ 'nəʊs ɪs -ə-, §-əs ‖ -'noʊs-
byss|us 'bɪs| əs **~i** aɪ **~uses** əs ɪz -əz
bystander 'baɪ ˌstænd ə ‖ -ᵊr **~s** z

byte baɪt (= *bite*) **bytes** baɪts
Byward 'baɪ wəd ‖ -wᵊrd
byway 'baɪ weɪ **~s** z
byword 'baɪ wɜːd ‖ -wɝːd **~s** z
by-your-leave ˌbaɪ jɔː 'liːv -jʊə-, -jə- ‖ -jᵊr-
Byzantian bɪ 'zænt i ən bə-, baɪ-, -'zænʃ ᵊn **~s** z
Byzantine, b~ bɪ 'zænt aɪn bə-, baɪ-, -iːn; 'bɪz ᵊn taɪn, -tiːn ‖ 'bɪz ᵊn tiːn -taɪn **~s** z
Byzantium bɪ 'zænt i əm bə-, baɪ-, -'zænʃ- ‖ -'zænʃ- -'zænʈ-

Cc

c Spelling-to-sound

1 Where the spelling is **c**, the pronunciation is regularly

k as in **cut** kʌt ('hard C') or

s as in **nice** naɪs ('soft C').

Less frequently, it is

ʃ as in **ocean** ˈəʊʃ ᵊn ‖ ˈoʊʃ ᵊn.

c may also form part of the digraphs **ch** and **ck**.

2 The pronunciation is regularly k when **c**

- is at the end of a word, as in **basic** ˈbeɪs ɪk or

- is followed by one of **a, o, u**, as in **camp** kæmp, **copy** ˈkɒp i ‖ ˈkɑːp i, **curl** kɜːl ‖ kɝːl or

- is followed by a consonant letter as in **cry** kraɪ.

3 The pronunciation is regularly s when **c**

- is followed by one of **e, i, y**, as in **central** ˈsentr əl, **city** ˈsɪt i, **cycle** ˈsaɪk ᵊl, **face** feɪs.

Note also **Caesar** ˈsiːz ə ‖ -ᵊr.

4 Where **c** at the end of a stressed syllable is followed by **e** or **i** plus a vowel within a word, the pronunciation is regularly ʃ as in **precious** ˈpreʃ əs, **special** ˈspeʃ ᵊl, **musician** mju ˈzɪʃ ᵊn. In these cases the **e** or **i** is silent, as usually applies when the following vowel is weak; but when the vowel after the **e** or **i** is strong, the pronunciation is i as in **speciality** ˌspeʃ i ˈæl ət i ‖ -ət̬ i. Sometimes, there is an alternative possibility with s as in **appreciate, associate, oceanic**; and where there is another ʃ in the same word as in **association, pronunciation**, many speakers prefer s.

5 Correspondingly, where the spelling is double **cc**, the pronunciation is k in most positions as in **account** ə ˈkaʊnt, but ks when followed by one of **e, i, y** as in **accept** ək ˈsept.

6 Correspondingly, too, where the spelling is **sc** the pronunciation is

sk in most positions as in **describe** dɪ ˈskraɪb, but

s when followed by one of **e, i, y** as in **scent** sent, **disciple** dɪ ˈsaɪp ᵊl

ʃ when at the end of a stressed syllable and followed by **i** plus a vowel within a word as in **luscious** ˈlʌʃ əs.

sc may also form part of the trigraph **sch** (see **ch** 4).

7 **c** is silent in one or two exceptional words, including **muscle** ˈmʌs ᵊl, **indict** ɪn ˈdaɪt, **Connecticut** kə ˈnet ɪk ət ‖ -ˈnet-.

ch Spelling-to-sound

1 Where the spelling is the digraph **ch**, the pronunciation is regularly

tʃ as in **chip** tʃɪp or

ʃ as in **machine** mə ˈʃiːn or

k as in **chemistry** ˈkem ɪs tri.

ch may also form part of the trigraph **sch** (see 4).

2 Where the spelling is the trigraph **tch**, the pronunciation is regularly tʃ as in **fetch** fetʃ.

3 Otherwise, there is no reliable rule for choosing between the three possibilities for **ch**. In general,

tʃ is the pronunciation in long-established words as in **cheese** tʃiːz, **chain** tʃeɪn, **coach** kəʊtʃ ‖ koʊtʃ

ʃ is the pronunciation in recent loanwords from French as in **champagne** ʃæm ˈpeɪn, **parachute** ˈpær ə ʃuːt

nʃ is also a less usual option in place of ntʃ at the end of a syllable, as in **lunch** lʌntʃ or lʌnʃ

k is the pronunciation in words of Greek origin, as in **chaos** ˈkeɪ-, **monarch** -ək ‖ -ᵊrk. Where **ch** is followed by a consonant letter, the pronunciation is always k as in **Christmas** ˈkrɪs məs, **technical** ˈtek nɪk ᵊl.

4 After **s**, the pronunciation is usually k as in **school** skuːl. Occasionally **sch** is a trigraph, and the pronunciation is ʃ; this applies in words borrowed from German, certain proper names, and the traditional BrE pronunciation of **schedule** ˈʃed-.

5 Occasionally, the pronunciation is

dʒ as in the usual version of **sandwich** ˈsæn wɪdʒ and some other British place-names ending in **-ich** or

x, in certain words from foreign languages, as in **loch** (with k as an anglicizing alternative).

6 **ch** is silent in one or two exceptional words, including **yacht** jɒt ‖ jɑːt.

7 The sound tʃ is also sometimes written **t** as in **question**, **natural**, and **c** as in **cello**.

ck Spelling-to-sound

Where the spelling is the digraph **ck**, the pronunciation is always k as in **back** bæk, **acknowledge** ək ˈnɒl ɪdʒ ‖ ək ˈnɑːl ɪdʒ.

C, c siː **C's, Cs, c's** siːz —*Communications code
name:* Charlie
  ,C of 'E
C++ ,siː plʌs 'plʌs
C3PO ,siː 'θriː piː əʊ ‖ -oʊ
CAA ,siː eɪ 'eɪ
Caan kɑːn
cab kæb **cabs** kæbz
  'cab rank
cabal kə 'bæl ‖ -'bɑːl **~s** z
cabala kə 'bɑːl ə kæ- **~s** z
cabalism 'kæb ə ,lɪz əm
cabalistic ,kæb ə 'lɪst ɪk ◂
Caballé kə 'baɪ eɪ kæ- ‖ ,kæb ɑː 'jeɪ -ɑːl —*Sp*
  [ka 'βa ʎe, -je]
caballero ,kæb ə 'leər əʊ ‖ -'jer oʊ ,kæb ᵊl-
  —*Sp* [ka βa 'ʎe ɾo, -'je-]
cabana kə 'bɑːn ə ‖ kə 'bæn ə -'bɑːn-, -jə —*Sp*
  cabaña [ka 'βa ɲa]
cabaret 'kæb ə reɪ ,···· **~s** z
cabbage 'kæb ɪdʒ **~s** ɪz əz
  ,cabbage 'white
cabbala kə 'bɑːl ə kæ- **~s** z
cabbalism 'kæb ə ,lɪz əm
cabbalistic ,kæb ə 'lɪst ɪk ◂
cabbie, cabby 'kæb i **cabbies** 'kæb iz
cabdriver 'kæb ,draɪv ə ‖ -ᵊr **~s** z
caber 'keɪb ə ‖ -ᵊr 'kɑːb- **~s** z
cabernet sauvignon, C~ S~
  ,kæb ə neɪ ,səʊv iːn 'jɒn -'jɒ̃, -'···
  ‖ ,kæb ᵊr ,neɪ ,soʊv iːn 'joʊn —*Fr*
  [ka bɛʁ nɛ so vi njɔ̃]
Cabildo, c~ kə 'bɪld əʊ ‖ kə 'biːld oʊ —*Sp*
  [ka 'βil do] **~s** z
cabin 'kæb ɪn §-ən **~s** z
  'cabin boy; 'cabin class; 'cabin crew;
  'cabin ,cruiser; 'cabin ,fever
Cabinda kə 'bɪnd ə -'biːnd- —*Port* [kɐ 'βin dɐ]
cabinet 'kæb ɪn ət -ən ,ət, -ɪt **~s** s
cabinet-mak|er 'kæb ɪn ət ,meɪk ə -ən ,ət-,
  -ɪn ɪt- ‖ -ᵊr **~ers** əz ‖ ᵊrz **~ing** ɪŋ
cabl|e 'keɪb ᵊl **~ed** d **~es** z **~ing** ɪŋ
  'cable car; ,cable 'tele,vision, ,··· ,··'·,
  '·· ,····
cablecast 'keɪb ᵊl kɑːst §-kæst ‖ -kæst **~s** s
cablegram 'keɪb ᵊl græm **~s** z
cable-knit 'keɪb ᵊl nɪt
cableway 'keɪb ᵊl weɪ **~s** z
cab|man 'kæb mən **~men** mən men
cabochon 'kæb ə ʃɒn ‖ -ʃɑːn —*Fr* [ka bɔ ʃɔ̃]
caboodle kə 'buːd ᵊl
caboos|e kə 'buːs **~es** ɪz əz
Caborn 'keɪ bɔːn ‖ -bɔːrn
Cabot 'kæb ət **~s** s
cabotage 'kæb ə tɑːʒ -ət ɪdʒ
Cabrillo kə 'brɪl əʊ ‖ -'briː joʊ —*AmSp*
  [ka 'βɾi jo]
Cabrini kə 'briːn i
cabriole 'kæb ri əʊl →-ɒʊl, ,··'· ‖ -oʊl
cabriolet 'kæb ri ə leɪ -ri əʊ-, ,··'·
  ‖ ,kæb ri ə 'leɪ **~s** z
cabstand 'kæb stænd **~s** z
ca'canny ,kɔː 'kæn i ‖ ,kɑː-

cacao kə 'kaʊ -'kɑː əʊ, -'keɪ əʊ ‖ -oʊ
Caccia, c~ 'kætʃ ə '·i̯ ə ‖ 'kɑːtʃ-
cacciatore ,kætʃ ə 'tɔːr i ,kɑːtʃ-, -eɪ ‖ ,kɑːtʃ-
  -'toʊr- —*It* [kat tʃa 'tɔː re]
cachaca, cachaça kə 'ʃæs ə ‖ -'ʃɑːs- —*BrPort*
  [ka 'ʃa sa]
cachalot 'kæʃ ə lɒt ‖ -loʊ -lɑːt
cache kæʃ *(= cash)* **cached** kæʃt **caches**
  'kæʃ ɪz -əz **caching** 'kæʃ ɪŋ
cachectic kæ 'kekt ɪk kə-
cachepot 'kæʃ pəʊ -pɒt, ,·'· ‖ 'kæʃ paɪt -poʊ
cache-sexe ,kæʃ 'seks
cachet 'kæʃ eɪ kæ 'ʃeɪ ‖ kæ 'ʃeɪ **~s** z
cachexia kæ 'keks i̯ ə kə-
cachexy kæ 'keks i kə-
cachin|nate 'kæk ɪ |neɪt -ə- **~nated** neɪt ɪd
  -əd ‖ neɪt̮ əd **~nates** neɪts **~nating** neɪt ɪŋ
  ‖ neɪt̮ ɪŋ
cachinnation ,kæk ɪ 'neɪʃ ᵊn -ə- **~s** z
cachou kə 'ʃuː kæ-; 'kæʃ uː **~s** z
cacique kæ 'siːk kə- ‖ kə- **~s** s
cack-handed ,kæk 'hænd əd ◂ -əd **~ly** li
cackl|e 'kæk ᵊl **~ed** d **~er/s** ,ə/z ‖ ,ᵊr/z **~es** z
  ~ing ,ɪŋ
caco- *comb. form*
  with stress-neutral suffix ¦kæk əʊ ‖ -ə
  — **cacographic** ,kæk əʊ 'græf ɪk ◂ ‖ -ə-
  with stress-imposing suffix kæ 'kɒ+ kə-
  ‖ kæ 'kɑː+ — **cacography** kæ 'kɒg rəf i kə-
  ‖ -'kɑːg-
cacoethes ,kæk əʊ 'iːθ iːz ‖ -oʊ-
cacophoni... —*see* **cacophony**
cacophonous kə 'kɒf ən əs kæ- ‖ kæ 'kɑːf- **~ly**
  li
cacophon|y kə 'kɒf ən |i kæ- ‖ kæ 'kɑːf- **~ies**
  iz
cact|us 'kækt |əs **~i** aɪ iː **~uses** əs ɪz əs əz
cacuminal kæ 'kjuːm ɪn ᵊl kə-, -ən- **~s** z
cad, CAD kæd **cads** kædz
cadastral kə 'dæs trᵊl
cadaver kə 'dæv ə -'dɑːv-, -'deɪv- ‖ -ᵊr **~s** z
cadaveric kə 'dæv ər ɪk
cadaverous kə 'dæv ər əs **~ly** li **~ness** nəs nɪs
Cadbury 'kæd bər i →'kæb- ‖ -,ber i **~'s** z
Cadby 'kæd bi →'kæb-
CAD-CAM, CAD/CAM 'kæd kæm →'kæg-
caddie 'kæd i **~s** z
caddis 'kæd ɪs §-əs
  'caddis fly
caddish 'kæd ɪʃ **~ly** li **~ness** nəs nɪs
cadd|y 'kæd |i **~ies** iz
cade, Cade keɪd
Cadeby 'keɪd bi →'keɪb-
Cadell *(i)* kə 'del, *(ii)* 'kæd ᵊl
cadenc|e 'keɪd ᵊnts **~ed** t **~es** ɪz əz
cadency 'keɪd ᵊnts i
cadent 'keɪd ᵊnt
cadenza kə 'denz ə **~s** z
Cader Idris ,kæd ər 'ɪdr ɪs ‖ ,kɑːd ᵊr- —*Welsh*
  [,ka der 'i drɪs]
cadet kə 'det **~s** s
  ca'det corps
cadetship kə 'det ʃɪp **~s** s

cadge kædʒ **cadged** kædʒd **cadges** 'kædʒ ɪz
-əz **cadging** 'kædʒ ɪŋ
cadger 'kædʒ ə ‖ -ᵊr ~s z
cadi 'kɑːd i 'keɪd i ~s z
Cadillac *tdmk* 'kæd ɪ læk -ə-, -ᵊl æk ~s s
Cadiz *place in Spain* kə 'dɪz —*Sp* Cádiz
['ka ðiθ]
Cadmean kæd 'miː ən
cadmic 'kæd mɪk →'kæb-
cadmium 'kæd mi əm →'kæb-
Cadmus 'kæd məs →'kæb-
Cadogan kə 'dʌg ən
cadre 'kɑːd ə 'keɪd-, -rə ‖ 'kædr i 'kɑːdr-, -eɪ *(*)*
~s z
caduce|us kə 'djuːs i ǀ_əs →-'dʒuːs- ‖ -'duːs-
-'duːʃ ǀəs, -'djuːʃ- ~i aɪ
caducous kə 'djuːk əs →-'dʒuːk- ‖ -'duːk-
-'djuːk-
Cadwallader kæd 'wɒl əd ə ‖ -'wɑːl əd ᵊr
caec|um 'siːk ǀəm ~a ə ~al ᵊl
Caedmon 'kæd mən →'kæb-
Caen kɒ̃ kɑːn ‖ kɑːn —*Fr* [kɑ̃]
Caerau 'kaɪᵊr aɪ —*Welsh* ['kəi rai, -rai, -re]
Caerleon kɑː 'liː ən ˌkɑɪ ə- ‖ kɑːr-
Caernarfon, Caernarvon kə 'nɑːv ᵊn
‖ kɑːr 'nɑːrv- —*Welsh* [kəir 'nar von] ~shire
ʃə ʃɪə ‖ ʃᵊr ʃɪr
Caerphilly kə 'fɪl i keə-, kɑː- ‖ kɑːr- —*Welsh*
[kəir 'fil i, kar-]
Caersws ˌkaɪ ə 'suːs ˌkaɪ ᵊr- —*Welsh*
[kəir 'suːs]
Caesar 'siːz ə ‖ -ᵊr —*Classical Latin* ['kai sar]
~s, ~'s z
Caesarea ˌsiːz ə 'riː ə
caesarean, caesarian sɪ 'zeər i ən sə-, siː-
‖ -'zer- -'zær-
cae ˌsarean 'section
caesium 'siːz i əm ‖ 'siːs-
caesur|a sɪ 'zjʊər ǀə sə-, siː-, -'zjɔːr-, -'ʒʊər-
‖ -'zʊr- ~ae iː aɪ ~as əz
cafe, café 'kæf eɪ -i; kæ 'feɪ ‖ kæ 'feɪ kə- —*Fr*
[ka fe] —*Sometimes also (but in RP only
facetiously)* kæf, keɪf ~s z
ˌcafé au 'lait əʊ 'leɪ ‖ -oʊ- —*Fr* [o lɛ]
cafeteria ˌkæf ə 'tɪər i ə -ɪ- ‖ -'tɪr- ~s z
cafetière ˌkæf ti 'eə ˌ-ə ti'- ‖ ˌkæf ə 'tɪᵊr —*Fr*
[kaf tjɛːʁ] ~s z —*or as sing.*
caff kæf **caffs** kæfs
caffè 'kæf eɪ kæ 'feɪ ‖ kæ 'feɪ ~ latte 'læt eɪ
'lɑːt- ‖ 'lɑːt- ~ macchiato ˌmæk i 'ɑːt əʊ
‖ ˌmɑːk i 'ɑːt oʊ —*It* [kaf 'fe, kaf ˌfel 'lat te,
kaf ˌfem ma 'kja: to]
caffeinated 'kæf ɪ neɪt ɪd '-ə-, -əd ‖ -neɪt̬-
caffeine 'kæf iːn ‖ kæ 'fiːn *(*)*
Cafferty 'kæf ət i ‖ -ᵊrt̬ i
Caffin, Caffyn 'kæf ɪn §-ᵊn
Caffrey 'kæf ri
CAFOD, Cafod 'kæf ɒd ‖ -ɑːd
caftan 'kæft æn -ɑːn ‖ 'kæft ən kæf 'tæn ~s z
cage, Cage keɪdʒ **caged** keɪdʒd **cages**
'keɪdʒ ɪz -əz **caging** 'keɪdʒ ɪŋ
'cage bird

cag|ey 'keɪdʒ ǀi ~ier i ə ‖ i ᵊr ~iest i ɪst i ˌəst
~ily ɪ li -əl i ~iness i nəs -nɪs
Cagliari ˌkæl i 'ɑːr i 'kæl jər i —*It* ['kaʎ ʎa ri]
Cagliostro ˌkæl i 'ɒs trəʊ ‖ kæl 'jɑːs troʊ
kɑːl-, -'jɔːs- —*It* [kaʎ 'ʎɔs tro]
Cagney 'kæg ni
cagoule kə 'guːl kæ- ~s z
cag|ly 'keɪdʒ ǀi ~ier i ə ‖ i ᵊr ~iest i ɪst i ˌəst
~ily ɪ li -əl i ~iness i nəs -nɪs
Cahill (i) 'kɑː hɪl, (ii) 'keɪ hɪl
cahoots kə 'huːts
Caiaphas 'kaɪ ə fæs
Caicos 'keɪk əs -ɒs
caiman 'keɪm ən keɪ 'mæn, kaɪ- ~s z
Cain, Caine keɪn (= *cane*) —*but* Cain *as a
Welsh female name is* kaɪn
caipirinha ˌkaɪp ɪ 'rɪn jə -'riːn- —*BrPort*
[kai pi 'ri ɲɐ]
caique, caïque kaɪ 'iːk kɑː- ~s s
Caird keəd ‖ keᵊrd
Cairene 'kaɪᵊr iːn
cairn keən ‖ keᵊrn **cairned** keənd ‖ keᵊrnd
cairns keənz ‖ keᵊrnz
ˌcairn 'terrier
Cairncross 'keən krɒs →'keəŋ-, -krɔːs, ˌ·'·
‖ 'kern krɔːs -krɑːs
Cairngorm, c~ ˌkeən 'gɔːm →ˌkeəŋ-, '· ·
‖ 'kern gɔːrm
Cairns keənz ‖ keᵊrnz —*but in Australia the
town in Queensland is usually* kænz
Cairo *in Egypt* 'kaɪᵊr əʊ ‖ -oʊ —*but places in
the US are* 'ker oʊ, 'keɪ roʊ. —*Arabic* El
Qahira [el 'qɑː hi rɑ, il qɑ 'hi rɑ]
caisson 'keɪs ᵊn -ɒn; kə 'suːn ‖ 'keɪs ɑːn -ᵊn ~s
z
Caister, Caistor 'keɪst ə ‖ -ᵊr
Caithness 'keɪθ nes -nɪs, -nəs, ˌ·'nes
caitiff 'keɪt ɪf §-əf ‖ 'keɪt̬ əf ~s s
Caitlin 'keɪt lɪn 'kæt liːn
Caius 'kaɪ əs ‖ 'keɪ əs —*but as a family name
and for the Cambridge college,* kiːz
cajol|e kə 'dʒəʊl →-'dʒɒʊl ‖ -'dʒoʊl ~ed d ~es
z ~ing/ly ɪŋ /li
cajoler|y kə 'dʒəʊl ər ǀi ‖ -'dʒoʊl- ~ies iz
Cajun 'keɪdʒ ən ~s z
cajuput 'kædʒ ə pʊt -pət ~s s
cake keɪk **caked** keɪkt **cakes** keɪks **caking**
'keɪk ɪŋ
cakewalk 'keɪk wɔːk ‖ -wɑːk ~s s
CAL kæl ˌsiː eɪ 'el
Calabar ˌkæl ə 'bɑː ◄ '· · · ‖ -'bɑːr ◄
ˌCalabar 'bean
calabash 'kæl ə bæʃ ~es ɪz əz
calaboos|e ˌkæl ə 'buːs ˌ·'·· ~es ɪz əz
calabrese ˌkæl ə 'briːs -briːz, -breɪz; ˌ·'·, -'· i
Calabri|a kə 'læb ri ǀə -'lɑːb- ‖ -'leɪb- -'lɑːb-
—*It* [ka 'lɑː bria] ~an/s ən/z
caladium kə 'leɪd i əm ~s z
Calais 'kæl eɪ -i ‖ kæ 'leɪ —*Fr* [ka lɛ]
calaloo, calalu 'kæl ə luː
calamari ˌkæl ə 'mɑːr i ‖ ˌkɑːl- —*It*
[ka la 'ma: ri]
calami 'kæl ə maɪ

calamine 'kæl ə maɪn
  'calamine ˌlotion, ˌ · · · ' · ·
calamint 'kæl ə mɪnt
calamitous kə 'læm ɪt əs -ət- ‖ -əţ əs **~ly** li
  ~ness nəs nɪs
calamit|y kə 'læm ət |i -ɪt- ‖ -əţ |i **~ies** iz
  Caˌlamity 'Jane
cal|amus 'kæl |əm əs **~ami** ə maɪ
calathea ˌkæl ə 'θi: ə
calcane|us kæl 'keɪn i|əs **~a** ə **~al** əl **~i** aɪ
  ~um əm
calcareous kæl 'keər i əs ‖ -'ker- -'kær-
calceolaria ˌkæls i ə 'leər i ə ‖ -'ler- **~s** z
calciferol kæl 'sɪf ə rɒl ‖ -roʊl -ɑːl, -ɔːl
calciferous kæl 'sɪf ər əs
calcifi... —see **calcify**
calcification ˌkæls ɪf ɪ 'keɪʃ ᵊn ˌ·əf-, §-ə'-
calcifug|e 'kæls ɪ fjuːdʒ §-ə- **~es** ɪz əz
calci|fy 'kæls ɪ |faɪ -ə- **~fied** faɪd **~fies** faɪz
  ~fying faɪ ɪŋ
calcination ˌkæls ɪ 'neɪʃ ᵊn -ə-
calcin|e 'kæls aɪn -ɪn **~ed** d **~es** z **~ing** ɪŋ
calcite 'kæls aɪt **~s** s
calcitic kæl 'sɪt ɪk ‖ -'sɪţ-
calcium 'kæls i əm
  ˌcalcium 'carbonate
Calcot, Calcott (i) 'kælk ət -ɒt,
  (ii) 'kɒlk- 'kɒlk- ‖ 'kɑːlk-
calculability ˌkælk jʊl ə 'bɪl ət i ˌ·jəl-, -ɪt i
  ‖ -jəl ə 'bɪl əţ i
calculable 'kælk jʊl əb ᵊl '·jəl- ‖ 'kælk jəl-
calcu|late 'kælk ju |leɪt -jə- ‖ -jə- **~lated/ly**
  leɪt ɪd /li -əd /li ‖ leɪţ əd /li **~lates** leɪts
  ~lating/ly leɪt ɪŋ /li ‖ leɪţ ɪŋ /li
calculation ˌkælk ju 'leɪʃ ᵊn -jə- ‖ -jə- **~s** z
calculative 'kælk jʊl ət ɪv '·jəl-, -ju leɪt-
  ‖ -jə leɪţ-
calculator 'kælk ju leɪt ə '·jə- ‖ -jə leɪţ ᵊr **~s** z
calc|ulus 'kælk |jʊl əs -jəl- ‖ -jəl əs **~uli** ju laɪ
  jə- ‖ jə laɪ
Calcutta ₍ˌ₎kæl 'kʌt ə ‖ -'kʌţ- Bengali Kolkata
  ['kol ka ţa]
Caldecote 'kɔːld ɪk ət 'kɒld-, -ək-
  ‖ 'kɔːld ə koʊt 'kɑːld-
Caldecott 'kɔːld ɪ kɒt 'kɒld-, -ə-, -kət
  ‖ 'kɔːld ə kɑːt 'kɑːld-
Calder 'kɔːld ə 'kɒld- ‖ 'kɔːld ᵊr 'kɑːld-
caldera kæl 'deər ə 'kɔːld ər ə ‖ kæl 'der ə **~s**
  z
Calderdale 'kɔːld ə der ᵊl 'kɒld- ‖ -ᵊr- 'kɑːld-
caldron 'kɔːldr ən 'kɒldr- ‖ 'kɑːldr- **~s** z
Caldwell 'kɔːld wel 'kɒld- ‖ 'kɑːld-
Caldy 'kɔːld i 'kɒld- ‖ 'kɑːld-
Cale ker ᵊl
Caleb 'keɪl eb ‖ -əb
Caledon 'kæl ɪd ən -əd-
Caledoni|a ˌkæl ɪ 'dəʊn i |ə ˌ·ə- ‖ -'doʊn-
  ~an/s ən/z
calefacient ˌkæl ɪ 'feɪʃ i ənt -'feɪʃ ᵊnt
calefaction ˌkæl ɪ 'fæk ʃᵊn -ə-
calefactory ˌkæl ɪ 'fæk tər i
calendar 'kæl ənd ə -ɪnd- ‖ -ᵊr **~s** z
  ˌcalendar 'month

calend|er 'kæl ənd |ə -ɪnd- ‖ -|ᵊr (= calendar)
  ~ered əd ‖ ᵊrd **~ering** ər ɪŋ **~ers** əz ‖ ᵊrz
calendrical kə 'lendr ɪk ᵊl kæ-
calends 'kæl endz 'keɪl-, -ɪndz, -əndz
calendula kæ 'lend jʊl ə kə-, -jəl-
  ‖ -'lendʒ əl ə **~s** z
calf kɑːf ‖ kæf **calves** kɑːvz ‖ kævz
  'calf love
calf-length 'kɑːf leŋᵏθ §'kæf-, §-lenᵗθ ‖ 'kæf-
calfskin 'kɑːf skɪn ‖ 'kæf-
Calgary 'kælg ər i
Calhoun (i) kæl 'huːn, (ii) kə 'huːn
Caliban 'kæl ə bæn -ɪ-
caliber 'kæl əb ə -ɪb-; kə 'liːb ə, -'laɪb- ‖ -ᵊr
cali|brate 'kæl ə |breɪt -ɪ- **~brated** breɪt ɪd -əd
  ‖ breɪţ əd **~brates** breɪts **~brating** breɪt ɪŋ
  ‖ breɪţ ɪŋ
calibration ˌkæl ə 'breɪʃ ᵊn -ɪ- **~s** z
calibrator 'kæl ə breɪt ə '·ɪ- ‖ -breɪţ ᵊr **~s** z
calibre 'kæl əb ə -ɪb-; kə 'liːb ə, -'laɪb- ‖ -ᵊr
calico 'kæl ɪ kəʊ -ə- ‖ -koʊ **~es, ~s** z
Calicut 'kæl ɪk ət -ɪ kʌt
California ˌkæl ə 'fɔːn i ə ˌ·ɪ- ‖ -'fɔːrn jə
Californian ˌkæl ə 'fɔːn i ən ˌ·ɪ-
  ‖ -'fɔːrn jən ◂ **~s** z
  ˌCaliˌfornian 'Desert
californium ˌkæl ə 'fɔːn i əm ˌ·ɪ- ‖ -'fɔːrn-
Caligula kə 'lɪg jʊl ə -jəl-
caliper 'kæl ɪp ə -əp- ‖ -ᵊr **~ed** d **~s** z
caliph 'keɪl ɪf 'kæl-, -əf; kæ 'liːf **~s** s
caliphate 'kæl ɪ feɪt 'keɪl-, -ə- **~s** s
calisthenic ˌkæl ɪs 'θen ɪk ◂ -əs- **~s** s
Calistoga ˌkæl ɪ 'stəʊg ə -ə- ‖ -'stoʊg ə
calk kɔːk ‖ kɑːk **calked** kɔːkt ‖ kɑːkt **calking**
  'kɔːk ɪŋ ‖ 'kɑːk- **calks** kɔːks ‖ kɑːks
Calke kɔːk ‖ kɑːk
call, CALL kɔːl ‖ kɑːl **called** kɔːld ‖ kɑːld
  calling 'kɔːl ɪŋ ‖ 'kɑːl- **calls** kɔːlz ‖ kɑːlz
  'call box; 'call girl; 'call sign
calla 'kæl ə **~s** z
Callaghan 'kæl ə hən -hæn
Callander 'kæl ənd ə ‖ -ᵊr
Callanetics tdmk ˌkæl ə 'net ɪks ‖ -neţ-
Callard 'kæl ɑːd ‖ -ɑːrd
Callas 'kæl əs -æs
Callaway 'kæl ə weɪ
callback 'kɔːl bæk ‖ 'kɑːl-
callboy 'kɔːl bɔɪ ‖ 'kɑːl- **~s** z
caller 'one that calls' 'kɔːl ə ‖ 'kɔːl ᵊr 'kɑːl- **~s**
  z
calligrapher kə 'lɪg rəf ə kæ- ‖ -ᵊr **~s** z
calligraphic ˌkæl ɪ 'græf ɪk ◂ -ə- **~ally** ᵊl i
calligraphist kə 'lɪg rəf ɪst kæ-, §-əst **~s** s
calligraphy kə 'lɪg rəf i kæ-
Callil kə 'lɪl
Callimachus kə 'lɪm ək əs
call-in 'kɔːl ɪn ‖ 'kɑːl-
calling 'kɔːl ɪŋ ‖ 'kɑːl- **~s** z
  'calling card
Calliope, c~ kə 'laɪ əp i kæ- **~s** z
calliper 'kæl ɪp ə -əp- ‖ -ᵊr **~ed** d **~s** z
callipygian ˌkæl ɪ 'pɪdʒ i ən ◂ ˌ·ə-
callipygous ˌkæl ɪ 'paɪg əs ◂ -ə-

callisthenic ˌkæl ɪs ˈθen ɪk ◀ -əs- **~s** s
Callisto kə ˈlɪst əʊ kæ- ‖ -oʊ
callosit|y kə ˈlɒs ət |i kæ-, -ɪt- ‖ -ˈlɑːs əţ |i
　~ies iz
callous ˈkæl əs **~ed** t **~ly** li **~ness** nəs nɪs
callout ˈkɔːl aʊt ‖ ˈkɑːl- **~s** s
callow, C~ ˈkæl əʊ ‖ -oʊ **~ness** nəs nɪs
Calloway ˈkæl ə weɪ
calltime ˈkɔːl taɪm ‖ ˈkɑːl-
Callum ˈkæl əm
call-up ˈkɔːl ʌp ‖ ˈkɑːl- **~s** s
callus ˈkæl əs (= callous) **~es** ɪz əz
calm kɑːm kɑːlm, §kɒlm **calmer** ˈkɑːm ə
　ˈkɑːlm-, §ˈkɒlm- ‖ -ᵊr **calmest** ˈkɑːm ɪst
　ˈkɑːlm-, §ˈkɒlm-, -əst
Calman ˈkæl mən
calmative ˈkælm ət ɪv ˈkɑːm- ‖ -əţ- **~s** z
calm|ly ˈkɑːm |li ˈkɑːlm-, §ˈkɒlm- **~ness** nəs
　nɪs
Calne kɑːn §kɑːln, §kɒln
calomel ˈkæl ə mel -əm ᵊl
calor, Calor tdmk ˈkæl ə ‖ -ᵊr
　ˈCalor gas
caloric kə ˈlɒr ɪk kæ-; ˈkæl ər- ‖ -ˈlɔːr- -ˈlɑːr-
calorie, C~ ˈkæl ər i **~s** z
　ˈcalorie ˌcounting
calorific ˌkæl ə ˈrɪf ɪk ◀
calorimeter ˌkæl ə ˈrɪm ɪt ə -ət ə ‖ -əţ ᵊr **~s** z
calotte kə ˈlɒt ‖ -ˈlɑːt **~s** s
Calpurnia kæl ˈpɜːn i ə ‖ -ˈpɜːn-
calque kælk **calqued** kælkt **calques** kælks
　calquing ˈkælk ɪŋ
Calthorpe (i) ˈkæl θɔːp ‖ -θɔːrp, (ii) ˈkɔːl- ˈkɒl-
　‖ ˈkɑːl-
Calton ˈkɔːlt ən ‖ ˈkɑːlt- —but in Strathclyde
　locally ˈkɑːlt-
caltrap, caltrop ˈkæltr əp ˈkɔːltr- **~s** s
Calum ˈkæl əm
calumet ˈkæl ju met -jə-, ˌ·ˈ· **~s** s
calumni|ate kə ˈlʌm ni |eɪt **~ated** eɪt ɪd -əd
　‖ eɪţ əd **~ates** eɪts **~ating** eɪt ɪŋ ‖ eɪţ ɪŋ
calumniation kə ˌlʌm ni ˈeɪʃ ᵊn **~s** z
calumnious kə ˈlʌm ni əs **~ly** li
calum|ny ˈkæl əm |ni **~nies** niz
Calvados, c~ ˈkælv ə dɒs ‖ ˌkælv ə ˈdoʊs
　ˌkɑːlv- —Fr [kal va doːs]
Calvar|y, c~ ˈkælv ər |i **~ies** iz
calve kɑːv ‖ kæv (in RP = carve) **calved** kɑːvd
　‖ kævd **calves** kɑːvz ‖ kævz **calving** ˈkɑːv ɪŋ
　‖ ˈkæv-
Calverley ˈkɑːv ə li ˈkælv- ‖ -ᵊr-
Calvert (i) ˈkælv ət ‖ -ᵊrt, (ii) ˈkɔːlv- ‖ ˈkɑːlv-
Calverton (i) ˈkælv ət ən ‖ -ᵊrt ᵊn, (ii) ˈkɑːlv-
calves from **calf, calve** kɑːvz ‖ kævz
Calvin ˈkælv ɪn §-ən
Calvinism ˈkælv ə ˌnɪz əm -ɪ-
Calvinist, c~ ˈkælv ən ɪst §-ᵊn-, §-əst **~s** s
Calvinistic ˌkælv ə ˈnɪst ɪk ◀ -ɪ- **~al** ᵊl
Calvocoressi ˌkælv ə kə ˈres i
calx kælks **calxes** ˈkælks ɪz -əz
calyces ˈkeɪl ɪ siːz ˈkæl-, -ə-
Calydon ˈkæl ɪd ən -əd-
calypso, C~ kə ˈlɪps əʊ ‖ -oʊ **~s** z

calypsonian ˌkæl ɪp ˈsəʊn i ən ‖ -ˈsoʊn- **~s** z
calyx ˈkeɪl ɪks ˈkæl- **~es** ɪz əz
calzone kæl ˈzəʊn i -eɪ ‖ -ˈzoʊn- -ˈzoʊn i;
　ˌkælt ˈsoʊn i **~s** z —It [kal ˈtsoː ne]
cam, Cam kæm **cammed** kæmd **camming**
　ˈkæm ɪŋ **cams** kæmz
camaraderie ˌkæm ə ˈrɑːd ər i -ˈræd-, -ə riː
　‖ ˌkɑːm-
Camargue kæ ˈmɑːg kə- ‖ -ˈmɑːrg —Fr
　[ka maʁg]
camarilla ˌkæm ə ˈrɪl ə -jə ‖ -ˈriː jə —Sp
　[ka ma ˈri ʎa, -ja] **~s** z
Camay tdmk kæ ˈmeɪ ˈkæm eɪ
cam|ber, C~ ˈkæm |bə ‖ -|bᵊr **~bered** bəd
　‖ bᵊrd **~bering** bər ɪŋ **~bers** bəz ‖ bᵊrz
Camberley ˈkæm bə li -bᵊl i ‖ -bᵊr-
Camberwell ˈkæm bə wᵊl -wel ‖ -bᵊr-
　ˌCamberwell ˈbeauty
cambium ˈkæm bi əm
Cambodi|a kæm ˈbəʊd i |ə ‖ -ˈboʊd- **~an/s**
　ən/z
Camborne ˈkæm bɔːn ‖ -bɔːrn -boʊrn
Cambray ˈkɒm breɪ ˈkɒ̃- ‖ kɑːm ˈbreɪ —Fr
　[kɑ̃ bʁɛ]
Cambri|a ˈkæm bri |ə ˈkeɪm- **~an/s** ən/z
cambric ˈkeɪm brɪk **~s** s
Cambridge ˈkeɪm brɪdʒ **~shire** ʃə -ʃɪə ‖ ʃᵊr ʃɪr
Cambuslang ˌkæm bəs ˈlæŋ
Cambyses kæm ˈbaɪs iːz
camcorder ˈkæm ˌkɔːd ə ˌ·ˈ·· ‖ -ˌkɔːrd ᵊr **~s** z
Camden ˈkæm dən
　ˌCamden ˈTown
came keɪm
camel ˈkæm ᵊl **~s** z
Camelford ˈkæm ᵊl fəd ‖ -fᵊrd
camelhair ˈkæm ᵊl heə ‖ -her
Camelia kə ˈmiːl i ə
camellia kə ˈmiːl i ə -ˈmel- **~s** z
Camelot ˈkæm ə lɒt -ɪ- ‖ -lɑːt
Camembert ˈkæm əm beə -bɜːt ‖ -ber -bɜːt
　—Fr [ka mɑ̃ bɛːʁ] **~s** z
cameo ˈkæm i əʊ ‖ -oʊ **~s** z
camera ˈkæm ər ə **~s** z
cameral ˈkæm ər əl
camera|man ˈkæm rə |mæn -mən **~men** men
　mən
camera obscura ˌkæm ər ə ᵊr əb ˈskjʊər ə -ɒb-·
　‖ -ə əb ˈskjʊr ə
camera-ready ˌkæm rə ˈred i ◀
　ˌcamera-ˌready ˈcopy
camera-shy ˈkæm rə ʃaɪ -ər ə-
camera|woman ˈkæm rə ˌwʊm ən **~women**
　ˌwɪm ɪn -ən
Cameron ˈkæm ᵊr ən
Cameronian ˌkæm ə ˈrəʊn i ən ‖ -ˈroʊn- **~s** z
Cameroon ˌkæm ə ˈruːn ˈ··· **~s** z
Cameroonian ˌkæm ə ˈruːn i ən **~s** z
camiknicker ˈkæm i ˌnɪk ə ˌ·ˈ·· ‖ -ᵊr **~s** z
camiknicks ˈkæm i nɪks
Camilla kə ˈmɪl ə
Camille kə ˈmɪl -ˈmiːᵊl
camisole ˈkæm ɪ səʊl -ə-, ə→-soʊl ‖ -soʊl **~s** z
camlet ˈkæm lət -lɪt

Camoens, Camoëns 'kæm əʊ enz -en's ‖ -oʊ-
  —*Port* Camões [kɐ 'mõiʃ]
camomile 'kæm ə maɪ^əl ~**s** z
  ˌcamomile 'tea
camouflag|e 'kæm ə flɑːʒ -u-, -flɑːdʒ ~**ed** d
  ~**es** ɪz əz ~**ing** ɪŋ
Camoys *(i)* 'kæm ɔɪz, *(ii)* kə 'mɔɪz
camp, Camp kæmp **camped** kæmpt **camping**
  'kæmp ɪŋ **camps** kæmps
  ˌcamp 'bed; ˌCamp 'David; ˌcamp
  'follower, ' ˌ · · ·
campaign ₍ˌ₎kæm 'peɪn ~**ed** d ~**er/s** ə/z ‖ ^ər/z
  ~**ing** ɪŋ ~**s** z
Campanella ˌkæmp ə 'nel ə
campanile ˌkæmp ə 'niːl i -eɪ; -'niːl^əl ‖ ˌkɑːmp-
  ~**s** z
campanologist ˌkæmp ə 'nɒl ədʒ ɪst §-əst
  ‖ -'nɑːl- ~**s** s
campanology ˌkæmp ə 'nɒl ədʒ i ‖ -'nɑːl-
campanula kæm 'pæn jul ə kəm-, -jəl- ~**s** z
Campari kæm 'pɑːr i ‖ kɑːm- —*It*
  [kam 'pa: ɾi]
Campbell 'kæm b^əl ~**s, 's** z
Campbeltown 'kæm b^əl taʊn
Campden 'kæm dən 'kæmp-
camper 'kæmp ə ‖ -^ər ~**s** z
campfire 'kæmp ˌfaɪ ə ‖ -ˌfaɪ ^ər ~**s** z
campground 'kæmp graʊnd ~**s** z
camphor 'kæm^pf ə ‖ -^ər
campho|rate 'kæm^pf ə |reɪt ~**rated** reɪt ɪd -əd
  ‖ reɪt̬ əd
camping 'kæmp ɪŋ
campion, C~ 'kæmp i ən ~**s** z
Campling 'kæmp lɪŋ
camp-out 'kæmp aʊt ~**s** s
Campsie 'kæmps i
campsite 'kæmp saɪt ~**s** s
campstool 'kæmp stuːl ~**s** z
campus 'kæmp əs ~**es** ɪz əz
camp|y 'kæmp i ~**ier** i ə ‖ i ^ər ~**iest** i ɪst ˌəst
campylobacter ˌkæmp ɪl əʊ 'bækt ə ˌ-əl-,
  kæm ˌpɪl-, ' · · · , · · ‖ -oʊ 'bækt ^ər
CAMRA 'kæm rə
Camrose 'kæm rəʊz ‖ -roʊz
camshaft 'kæm ʃɑːft §-ʃæft ‖ -ʃæft ~**s** s
Camus kæ 'muː kə-, kɑː- —*Fr* [ka my]
can *n, v 'tin'* kæn **canned** kænd **canning**
  'kæn ɪŋ **cans** kænz
can *v 'be able' strong form* kæn, *weak form* kən
Cana 'keɪn ə
Canaan 'keɪn ən 'keɪn i ən
Canaanite 'keɪn ə naɪt -i ə- ~**s** s
Canada 'kæn əd ə §-ɪd- ~**'s** z
Canadian kə 'neɪd i ən ~**s** z
canal kə 'næl ~**s** z
  ca'nal boat
Canaletto ˌkæn ə 'let əʊ →-^əl 'et- ‖ -^əl 'eʈ oʊ
  —*It* [ka na 'let to] ~**s, ~'s** z
canalis... —see* **canaliz...**
canalization ˌkæn əl aɪ 'zeɪʃ ^ən -ɪ'--
  ‖ -^əl ə 'zeɪʃ-
canaliz|e 'kæn ə laɪz -^əl aɪz ‖ -^əl aɪz ~**ed** d ~**es**
  ɪz əz ~**ing** ɪŋ

canape, canapé 'kæn ə peɪ -əp -i ~**s** z
canard 'kæn ɑːd kæ 'nɑːd, kə- ‖ kə 'nɑːrd —*Fr*
  [ka naːʁ] ~**s** z
canar|y, C~ kə 'neər |i ‖ -'ner |i ~**ies** iz
canasta kə 'næst ə
Canavan 'kæn əv ən
Canaveral kə 'næv ^ər_əl
Canberra 'kæn bər_ə →'kæm- ‖ -bər ə
cancan 'kæn kæn →'kæŋ-
cancel 'kæn's ^əl ~**ed, ~led** d ~**ing, ~ling** ɪŋ
  ~**s** z
cancela... —see* **cancella...**
cancellable 'kæn's ^əl_əb ^əl
canc|ellate 'kæn's| ^əl ət -ɪt; ' · ə leɪt ~**ellated**
  ə leɪt ɪd -əd; →^əl eɪt- ‖ ^əl eɪt̬ əd
cancellation ˌkæn's ə 'leɪʃ ^ən -ɪ-; -^əl 'eɪʃ- ~**s** z
cancellous 'kæn's l əs
cancer, C~ 'kæn's ə ‖ -^ər ~**s** z
Cancerian ₍ˌ₎kæn 'sɪər i ən -'seər- ‖ -'sɪr- ~**s** z
cancerous 'kæn's ər_əs ~**ly** li
cancroid 'kæŋk rɔɪd ~**s** z
Cancun, Cancún kæn 'kuːn ‖ kɑː- —*Sp*
  Cancún [kaŋ 'kun]
Candace 'kænd ɪs -əs; kæn 'deɪs i
candela kæn 'diːl ə -'del-, -'deɪl- ~**s** z
candelab|ra ˌkænd ə 'lɑːb |rə -ɪ-, -'læb- ~**ras**
  rəz ~**rum/s** rəm/z
Canderel *tdmk* 'kænd ə rel ˌ · ·'·
Candi 'kænd i
candi... —see* **candy**
Candia 'kænd i_ə
Candice 'kænd ɪs -əs
candid 'kænd ɪd §-əd ~**ly** li ~**ness** nəs nɪs
Candida, c~ 'kænd ɪd ə §-əd-
candidac|y 'kænd ɪd əs |i -'əd- ‖ 'kæn- ~**ies** iz
candidate 'kænd ɪ deɪt -ə-; -ɪd ət, -əd-, -ɪt
  ‖ 'kæn- ~**s** s
candidature 'kænd ɪd ət̬ ʃ ə '-əd-, -ɪtʃ-; -ɪ deɪtʃ-,
  -ə deɪtʃ- ‖ 'kænd əd ə tʃʊr 'kæn-, -ətʃ ^ər ~**s** z
Candide ₍ˌ₎kɒn 'diːd kɒ̃- ‖ ₍ˌ₎kɑːn- —*Fr*
  [kɑ̃ did]
candidiasis ˌkænd ɪ 'daɪ_əs ɪs ˌ-ə-, §-əs
candle 'kænd ^əl ~**s** z
candleholder 'kænd ^əl ˌhəʊld ə →-ˌhɒʊld ə
  ‖ -ˌhoʊld ^ər ~**s** z
candle|light 'kænd ^əl| laɪt ~**lit** lɪt
Candlemas 'kænd ^əl mæs -məs
candlepower 'kænd ^əl ˌpaʊ_ə ‖ -ˌpaʊ_^ər
Candler 'kænd lə ‖ -l^ər
candlestick 'kænd ^əl stɪk ~**s** s
candlewick 'kænd ^əl wɪk
Candlin 'kænd lɪn -lən
can-do ˌkæn 'duː ◄
candor, candour 'kænd ə ‖ -^ər
cand|y, Candy 'kænd |i ~**ied** id ~**ies** iz ~**ying**
  i ɪŋ
  'candy stripe; 'candy ˌstriper
candyfloss 'kænd i flɒs ‖ -flɔːs -flɑːs
candy-striped 'kænd i straɪpt
candytuft 'kænd i tʌft
cane, Cane keɪn **caned** keɪnd **canes** keɪnz
  caning 'keɪn ɪŋ
canebrake 'keɪn breɪk →'keɪm-

C

Canes Venatici ˌkeɪn iːz vɪ 'næt ɪ saɪ ˌkɑːn-, ˌ-eɪz-, -vəˈ--, veˈ--, -ə ˋ, -kiː
Canewdon kə 'njuːd ᵊn
Canfield, c~ 'kæn fiːᵊld
Canicula kə 'nɪk jʊl ə -jəl-
canicular kə 'nɪk jʊl ə -jəl- ‖ -jəl ᵊr
canine 'keɪn aɪn 'kæn- ~s z
caning 'keɪn ɪŋ ~s z
Canis 'keɪn ɪs 'kæn-, §-əs
canister 'kæn ɪst ə -əst- ‖ -ᵊr ~s z
cank|er 'kæŋk |ə ‖ -|ᵊr ~ered əd ‖ ᵊrd ~ering
    ər ɪŋ ~ers əz ‖ ᵊrz
cankerous 'kæŋk ər əs
Cann kæn
cann... —see can
canna 'kæn ə ~s z
cannabis 'kæn əb ɪs §-əs
Cannae 'kæn iː
cannel 'kæn ᵊl
cannelloni, canneloni ˌkæn ə 'ləʊn i -ɪ-;
    -ᵊl 'əʊn- ‖ -ᵊl 'oʊn i —It [kan nel 'loː ni]
canner, C~ 'kæn ə ‖ -ᵊr
canner|y 'kæn ər |i ~ies iz
Cannes kæn kænz —Fr [kan]
canni... —see canny
cannibal 'kæn ɪb ᵊl -əb- ~s z
cannibalis... —see cannibaliz...
cannibalism 'kæn ɪb ə ˌlɪz əm '-əb-, -ᵊl ˌɪz-
cannibalistic ˌkæn ɪb ə 'lɪst ɪk ◂ ˌ-əb-, -ᵊl ˈɪst-
cannibalization ˌkæn ɪb ᵊl aɪ 'zeɪʃ ᵊn ˌ-əb-,
    -ɪˈ-- ‖ -ə 'zeɪʃ-
cannibaliz|e 'kæn ɪb ə laɪz '-əb-, -ᵊl aɪz ~ed d
    ~es ɪz əz ~ing ɪŋ
cannikin 'kæn ɪk ɪn -ək-, §-ən ~s z
Canning 'kæn ɪŋ
Cannizzaro ˌkæn ɪ 'zɑːr əʊ -ə-, -ˈzeər- ‖ -oʊ
    —It [kan nit 'tsa: ro]
Cannock 'kæn ək
cannon, C~ 'kæn ən ~ed d ~ing ɪŋ ~s z
    'cannon ˌfodder
cannonad|e ˌkæn ə 'neɪd ~ed ɪd əd ~es z
    ~ing ɪŋ
cannonball 'kæn ən bɔːl →-əm- ‖ -bɑːl ~s z
cannot 'kæn ɒt -ət; §kæ 'nɒt, kə- ‖ 'kæn ɑːt
    kə 'nɑːt, kæ- —see also can't
cann|ula 'kæn |jʊl ə -jəl- ‖ -|jəl ə ~ulae ju liː
    jə-, -laɪ ‖ jə- ~ulas jʊl əz jəl- ‖ jəl əz
cann|y 'kæn |i ~ier i ə ‖ i ᵊr ~iest i ɪst i əst
    ~ily ɪ li əl i ~iness i nəs i nɪs
canoe kə 'nuː ~d d ~ing ɪŋ ~s z
canoeist kə 'nuː ɪst § əst ~s s
canola kə 'nəʊl ə ‖ -'noʊl-
canon, Canon 'kæn ən (= cannon) ~s z
    ˌcanon 'law
cañon 'kæn jən —AmSp cañón [ka 'ɲon] ~s z
Canonbury 'kæn ən bər i →'-əm- ‖ -ˌber i
canoness ˌkæn ə 'nes 'kæn ən ɪs, §-əs, -ə nes
    ‖ 'kæn ən əs ~es ɪz əz
canonical kə 'nɒn ɪk ᵊl ‖ -'nɑːn- ~ly ˌi ~s z
canonicity ˌkæn ə 'nɪs ət i ˌ-ɒ-, -ɪt i ‖ -ət i
canonis... —see canoniz...
canonization ˌkæn ən aɪ 'zeɪʃ ᵊn -ɪˈ--
    ‖ -ə 'zeɪʃ- ~s z

canoniz|e 'kæn ə naɪz ~ed d ~es ɪz əz ~ing ɪŋ
canon|ry 'kæn ən |ri ~ries riz
canoodl|e kə 'nuːd ᵊl ~ed d ~es z ~ing ɪŋ
can-opener 'kæn ˌəʊp ən ə ‖ -ˌoʊp ᵊn ᵊr ~s z
canopi... —see canopy
Canopic kə 'nəʊp ɪk kæ-, -'nɒp- ‖ -'noʊp-
    -'nɑːp-
Canopus kə 'nəʊp əs kæ- ‖ -'noʊp-
canop|y 'kæn əp |i ~ied id ~ies iz
Canossa kə 'nɒs ə kæ- ‖ -'nɑːs- —It
    [ka 'nos sa]
canst strong form kænst, weak form kənst
cant, Cant kænt canted 'kænt ɪd -əd
    ‖ 'kænt̬ əd canting/ly 'kænt ɪŋ /li ‖ 'kænt̬-
    cants kænts
can't kɑːnt ‖ kænt △keɪnt —Before a
    consonant (less frequently before a vowel) also
    kɑːn ‖ kæn. Unlike can, this word has no
    weak form.
Cantab 'kænt æb
cantabile kæn 'tɑːb ɪ leɪ -ə leɪ; -əl i, -ɪl i
Cantabrian kæn 'teɪb ri ən ~s z
Cantabrigian ˌkænt ə 'brɪdʒ i ən ◂ ~s z
cantaloup, cantaloupe 'kænt ə luːp
    ‖ 'kænt̬ ə loʊp (*) ~s s
cantankerous kæn 'tæŋk ər əs kən- ~ly li
    ~ness nəs nɪs
cantata kæn 'tɑːt ə kən- ‖ kən 'tɑːt̬ ə ~s z
canteen ₍₎kæn 'tiːn ~s z
canter, C~ 'kænt ə ‖ 'kænt̬ ᵊr ~ed d cantering
    'kænt ᵊr ɪŋ ‖ 'kænt̬ ər ɪŋ ~s z
Canterbury, c~ 'kænt ə bər i -ˌber i
    ‖ 'kænt̬ ᵊr ˌber i
cantharides kæn 'θær ɪ diːz -ə- ‖ -'θer-
canth|us 'kænᵗθ |əs ~i aɪ
canticle 'kænt ɪk ᵊl §-ək- ‖ 'kænt̬ ək ᵊl ~s z
cantilena ˌkænt ɪ 'leɪn ə -ə-, -'liːn- ‖ ˌkænt̬- ~s
    z
cantilev|er 'kænt ɪ liːv |ə '-ə-; -ᵊl iːv-
    ‖ 'kænt̬ ᵊl iːv |ᵊr -ev ᵊr ~ered əd ‖ ᵊrd ~ering
    ər ɪŋ ~ers əz ‖ ᵊrz
canto 'kænt əʊ ‖ -oʊ ~s z
canton in heraldry; on flag 'kænt ən ~ed d
    ~ing ɪŋ ~s z
canton v 'quarter (soldiers)' kæn 'tuːn kən-
    ‖ -'tɑːn -'toʊn ~ed d ~ing ɪŋ ~s z
canton 'political division, esp. Swiss' 'kænt ɒn
    ₍ˌ₎kæn 'tɒn ‖ 'kænt ɑːn -ᵊn; kæn 'tɑːn ~s z
Canton places in the UK, US; family name
    'kænt ən
Canton place in China ˌkæn 'tɒn ◂ ‖ -'tɑːn ◂
    —Chi Guǎngzhōu [³kwaŋ ¹tsou]
Cantona ˌkænt ə 'nɑː —Fr [kã tɔ na]
cantonal 'kænt ən ᵊl kæn 'təʊn ᵊl, -'tɒn-
    ‖ 'kænt ᵊn əl kæn 'tɑːn ᵊl
Cantonese ˌkænt ə 'niːz ◂ ‖ -ᵊn 'iːz ◂ -'iːs
cantonment kæn 'tuːn mənt kən-, →-'tuːm-
    ‖ -'tɑːn- -'toʊn- ~s z
cantor, C~ 'kænt ɔː -ə ‖ -ᵊr
cantorial kæn 'tɔːr i əl ‖ -'toʊr-
cantoris kæn 'tɔːr ɪs §-əs ‖ -'toʊr-
Cantuar 'kænt ju ɑː ‖ -ɑːr
Canuck kə 'nʌk ~s s

can|ula 'kæn |jʊl ə -jəl- ‖ -|jəl ə ~ulae ju li:
jə-, -laɪ ‖ jə- ~ulas jʊl əz jəl- ‖ jəl əz

Canute kə 'njuːt -'nuːt ‖ -'nuːt -'njuːt

canvas 'kæn vəs ~es ɪz əz

canvasback 'kæn vəs bæk ~s s

canvass 'kæn vəs ~ed t ~er/s ə/z ‖ ᵊr/z ~es ɪz
əz ~ing ɪŋ

Canvey 'kæn vi

canyon 'kæn jən ~ing ɪŋ ~s z

Canyon de 'Chelly place in AZ də 'ʃeɪ

cap kæp capped kæpt capping 'kæp ɪŋ caps
kæps

CAP ˌsiː eɪ 'piː

capabilit|y ˌkeɪp ə 'bɪl ət |i -ɪt i ‖ -əţ |i ~ies iz

capable 'keɪp əb ᵊl ~ness nəs nɪs

capably 'keɪp əb li

capacious kə 'peɪʃ əs ~ly li ~ness nəs nɪs

capacitanc|e kə 'pæs ɪt ənts -ət- ~es ɪz əz

capacitor kə 'pæs ɪt ə -ət- ‖ -əţ ᵊr ~s z

capacit|y kə 'pæs ət |i -ɪt- ‖ -əţ |i ~ies iz

cap-a-pie ˌkæp ə 'piː -'peɪ

caparison kə 'pær ɪs ən -əs- ‖ -'per- ~ed d
~ing ɪŋ ~s z

cape, Cape keɪp capes keɪps —See also
phrases with this word
ˌCape Ca'naveral; ˌCape 'Horn; ˌCape of
'Good 'Hope; ˌCape 'Province; 'Cape Town

Cape Girardeau place in MO
ˌkeɪp dʒə 'rɑːd əʊ ‖ -'rɑːrd oʊ

Čapek 'tʃæp ek ‖ 'tʃɑːp- —Czech ['tʃa pek]

Capel 'keɪp ᵊl —but in Welsh place names
'kæp- —Welsh ['kap el]
ˌCapel 'Curig 'kɪr ɪg -'kjʊər- —Welsh
['ki rig, 'ke-]

capelin 'keɪp ᵊl ɪn §ˌən

Capell 'keɪp ᵊl

Capella kə 'pel ə

capellini ˌkæp ə 'liːn i -e- —It [ka pel 'li: ni]

Capenhurst 'keɪp ən hɜːst ‖ -hɝːst

cap|er 'keɪp| ə ‖ -ᵊr ~ered əd ‖ ᵊrd ~ering
ər ɪŋ ~ers əz ‖ ᵊrz

capercaillie, capercailzie ˌkæp ə 'keɪl i -ji
‖ -ᵊr- ~s z

Capernaum kə 'pɜːn i əm -eɪ-; ·'·əm ‖ -'pɝːn-

Capetian kə 'piːʃ ᵊn ~s z

Cape Verd|e ˌkeɪp 'vɜːd -'veəd ‖ -'vɝːd ~ean/s
i ˌən/z

capful 'kæp fʊl ~s z

capillarit|y ˌkæp ɪ 'lær ət |i ˌ·ə-, -ɪt i ‖ -əţ |i
-'ler- ~ies iz

capillar|y kə 'pɪl ər |i ‖ 'kæp ə ler |i (*) ~ies
iz

Capistrano ˌkæp ɪ 'strɑːn əʊ §-ə- ‖ -oʊ

Capita 'kæp ɪt ə -ət- ‖ -əţ ə

capital 'kæp ɪt ᵊl -ət- ‖ -əţ- ~s z
ˌcapital 'gain; ˌcapital 'punishment

capital-intensive ˌkæp ɪt ᵊl ɪn 'ten¹s ɪv ◂ ˌ·ət-,
§-ən'·- ‖ ˌkæp əţ- ~ly li

capitalis... —see capitaliz...

capitalism 'kæp ɪt ə ˌlɪz əm '·ət-, -ᵊl ˌɪz-;
kæ 'pɪt-, kə- ‖ -əţ ᵊl ˌɪz-

capitalist 'kæp ɪt ᵊl ɪst '·ət-, kæ 'pɪt-, kə 'pɪt-,
§-əst ‖ 'kæp əţ ᵊl əst ~s s

capitalistic ˌkæp ɪt ə 'lɪst ɪk ◂ ˌ·ət-, -ᵊl 'ɪst-
‖ -əţ ᵊl 'ɪst- ~ally ᵊl_i

capitalization ˌkæp ɪt ᵊl aɪ 'zeɪʃ ᵊn ˌ·ət-, -ɪ'·-;
kæ 'pɪt-, kə- ‖ -ə 'zeɪʃ- ~s z

capitaliz|e 'kæp ɪt ə laɪz '·ət-, -ᵊl aɪz; kæ 'pɪt-,
kə- ‖ -əţ ᵊl aɪz ~ed d ~es ɪz əz ~ing ɪŋ

capitation ˌkæp ɪ 'teɪʃ ᵊn -ə-

capitol, C~ 'kæp ɪt ᵊl -ət-; -ɪ tɒl, -ə- ‖ -əţ ᵊl
-ə tɑːl (usually = capital) ~s z

Capitoline kə 'pɪt əʊ laɪn 'kæp ɪt-, '·ət-, -ᵊl aɪn
‖ 'kæp əţ ᵊl aɪn

capitul|a kə 'pɪt jʊl |ə -jəl- ‖ -'pɪtʃ əl |ə ~ar ə
‖ ᵊr

capitu|late kə 'pɪt ju |leɪt -jə-; -'pɪtʃ u-, -ə-
‖ -'pɪtʃ ə- ~lated leɪt ɪd əd ‖ leɪţ əd ~lates
leɪts ~lating leɪt ɪŋ ‖ leɪţ ɪŋ

capitulation kə ˌpɪt ju 'leɪʃ ᵊn -jə-; -ˌpɪtʃ u-, -ə-
‖ -ˌpɪtʃ ə- ~s z

capitul|um kə 'pɪt jʊl |əm -jəl- ‖ -'pɪtʃ əl- ~a ə

Caplan 'kæp lən

caplet, C~ tdmk 'kæp lət -lɪt

capo 'Mafia leader' 'kɑːp əʊ 'kæp- ‖ -oʊ ~s z

capo for guitar 'kæp əʊ 'keɪp- ‖ 'keɪp oʊ ~s z

Capodimonte, Capo-di-Monte
ˌkæp əʊ di 'mɒnt eɪ ˌkɑːp-, -i
‖ ˌkɑːp oʊ di 'mɑːnt eɪ —It
[ka po di 'mon te]

capoeira ˌkæp əʊ 'eər ə -u- ‖ ˌkɑːp oʊ 'er ə
—BrPort [ka po 'ej ɾa, ka 'pwej ɾa]

capon, Capon 'keɪp ən -ɒn ‖ -ɑːn -ən ~s z

Capone kə 'pəʊn ‖ -'poʊn

capote kə 'pəʊt ‖ -'poʊt —Fr [ka pɔt] ~s s

Capote kə 'pəʊt i ‖ -'poʊţ i

Capp kæp

capp... —see cap

Cappa, Cappagh 'kæp ə

Cappadoci|a ˌkæp ə 'dəʊs i |ə -'dəʊʃ-,
-'dəʊʃ |ə ‖ -'doʊʃ- ~an/s ən/z

cappelletti ˌkæp ə 'let i ‖ -'leţ i —It
[kap pel 'let ti]

capper, C~ 'kæp ə ‖ -ᵊr

cappuccino ˌkæp u 'tʃiːn əʊ -ə-
‖ ˌkɑːp ə 'tʃiːn oʊ -jə- ~s z

Capra 'kæp rə

Capri kə 'priː kæ-; 'kæp riː —It ['ka: pri]

Capriati ˌkæp ri 'ɑːt i

capric 'kæp rɪk

capriccio kə 'priːtʃ i əʊ -'prɪtʃ- ‖ ˌ·oʊ ~s z

capriccioso kə ˌpriːtʃ i 'əʊs əʊ -ˌprɪtʃ-, -'əʊz-
‖ -'oʊs oʊ

capric|e kə 'priːs ~es ɪz əz

capricious kə 'prɪʃ əs ‖ -'priːʃ- ~ly li ~ness
nəs nɪs

Capricorn 'kæp rɪ kɔːn -rə- ‖ -kɔːrn ~s z

Capricorn|ian ˌkæp rɪ 'kɔːn i |ən ◂ ˌ·rə-
‖ -'kɔːrn|- ~ians i ˌənz ~us əs

caprine 'kæp raɪn

capriol|e 'kæp ri əʊl →-ʊl ‖ -oʊl ~ed d ~es z
~ing ɪŋ

Caprivi kə 'priːv i kæ-

caproic kə 'prəʊ ɪk kæ- ‖ -'proʊ-

capsicum 'kæps ɪk əm -ək- ~s z

capsid 'kæps ɪd §-əd ~s z

C

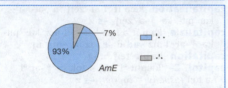

CAPSIZE

AmE — 93%, 7%

capsiz|e (ˌ)kæp ˈsaɪz ‖ ˈkæps aɪz — *Preference poll, AmE:* ˈ· · 93%, ·ˈ· 7%. **~ed** d **~es** ɪz əz **~ing** ɪŋ
capstan ˈkæpst ən ‖ -æn **~s** z
   ˈcapstan lathe
capstone ˈkæp stəʊn ‖ -stoʊn **~s** z
capsular ˈkæps jʊl ə -jəl- ‖ -ᵊl ər
capsule ˈkæps juːl -ᵊl ‖ -ᵊl -uːl **~s** z
captain ˈkæpt ɪn -ən ‖ -ən —*also, particularly nautical or as a vocative,* ˈkæp ən; *with this pronunciation also spelt* cap'n **~ed** d **~ing** ɪŋ **~s** z
captain|cy ˈkæpt ən |si -ɪn- **~cies** siz
captainship ˈkæpt ɪn ʃɪp -ən-
caption ˈkæp ʃᵊn **~ed** d **~ing** ɪŋ **~s** z
captious ˈkæp ʃəs **~ly** li **~ness** nəs nɪs
capti|vate ˈkæpt ɪ |veɪt -ə- **~vated** veɪt ɪd -əd ‖ veɪt̬ əd **~vates** veɪts **~vating** veɪt ɪŋ ‖ veɪt̬ ɪŋ
captivation ˌkæpt ɪ ˈveɪʃ ᵊn -ə-
captivator ˈkæpt ɪ veɪt ə ˈ·ə- ‖ -veɪt̬ ᵊr **~s** z
captive ˈkæpt ɪv **~s** z
captivit|y kæp ˈtɪv ət |i -ɪt- ‖ -ət̬ |i **~ies** iz
captor ˈkæpt ə ‖ -ᵊr -ɔːr **~s** z
cap|ture ˈkæp |tʃə -ʃə ‖ -|tʃᵊr -ʃᵊr **~tured** tʃəd ʃəd ‖ tʃᵊrd ʃᵊrd **~tures** tʃəz ʃəz ‖ tʃᵊrz ʃᵊrz **~turing** tʃər ɪŋ ʃər-
Capua ˈkæp ju ə —*It* [ˈkaː pu a]
capuch|e kə ˈpuːʃ -ˈpuːtʃ **~es** ɪz əz
capuchin ˈkæp jʊtʃ ɪn -jʊʃ-, §-ən; kə ˈpuːtʃ-, -ˈpuːʃ- ‖ ˈkæp jəʃ ᵊn kə ˈpjuːtʃ ən **~s** z
Capulet ˈkæp ju let -lət, -lɪt ‖ -jəl ət **~s** s
capybara ˌkæp i ˈbɑːr ə ‖ -ˈbær-, -ˈber- **~s** z
car kɑː ‖ kɑːr cars kɑːz ‖ kɑːrz
   ˌcar ˈboot sale; ˈcar park; ˈcar pool; ˈcar wash
Cara ˈkɑːr ə ‖ ˈkær-, ˈker-
carabiner ˌkær ə ˈbiːn ə ‖ -ᵊr ˌker- **~s** z
carabinieri ˌkær ə bɪn i ˈeər i ‖ ˌkær əb ən ˈjer i ˌker- —*It* [ˌka ra bi ˈnjeː ri]
caracal ˈkær ə kæl ‖ ˈker- **~s** z
Caracalla ˌkær ə ˈkæl ə ‖ ˌker-
caracara ˌkær ə ˈkɑːr ə ˌkɑːr- ‖ ˌker-, -kə ˈrɑː **~s** z
Caracas kə ˈræk əs -ˈrɑːk- ‖ -ˈrɑːk- —*Sp* [ka ˈra kas]
caracol|e ˈkær ə kəʊl →-kɒl ‖ -koʊl ˈker- **~ed** d **~es** z **~ing** ɪŋ
Caractacus kə ˈrækt ək əs
caracul ˈkær ə kʌl -ək ᵊl ‖ ˈker-
Caradoc kə ˈræd ɒk -ək ‖ -ɑːk

Caradog kə ˈræd ɒg ‖ -ɑːg -ɔːg —*Welsh* [ka ˈra dog]
Caradon ˈkær əd ən ‖ ˈker-
carafe kə ˈræf -ˈrɑːf **~s** s
carambola ˌkær əm ˈbəʊl ə ‖ -ˈboʊl ə ˌker- **~s** z

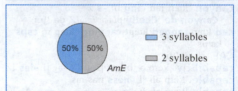

CARAMEL

AmE — 50% 50% — 3 syllables / 2 syllables

caramel ˈkær ə mel -əm ᵊl ‖ -əm ᵊl ker-, -ə mel; ˈkɑːrm ᵊl — *Preference poll, AmE: three syllables 50%, two syllables 50%.* **~s** z
caramelis|e, carameliz|e ˈkær əm ə laɪz →-ᵊl aɪz; -ə mel aɪz ‖ ˈker-; ˈkɑːrm ə laɪz **~ed** d **~es** ɪz əz **~ing** ɪŋ
Caran d'Ache tdmk ˌkær ən ˈdæʃ ‖ ˌkɑːr ən ˈdɑːʃ ˌkær-, ˌker-
carapac|e ˈkær ə peɪs ‖ ˈker- **~es** ɪz əz
carat ˈkær ət ‖ ˈker- (= *carrot*) **~s** s
Caravaggio ˌkær ə ˈvædʒ i əʊ ˌkɑːr-, -ˈvɑːdʒ-, -ˈvædʒ- ‖ ˌkær ə ˈvɑːdʒ oʊ ˌker- —*It* [ka ra ˈvad dʒo]
caravan ˈkær ə væn ˌ·ˈ· ‖ ˈker- **~er/s, ~ner/s** ə/z ‖ ᵊr/z **~ing, ~ning** ɪŋ **~s** z
caravansary ˌkær ə ˈvæn sər i ‖ ˌker-
caravanserai ˌkær ə ˈvæn sə raɪ -reɪ, -sər i ‖ ˌker- **~s** z
caravel ˈkær ə vel ˌ·ˈ·; ˈkær əv ᵊl ‖ ˈker- **~s** z
caraway ˈkær ə weɪ ‖ ˈker-
carb kɑːb ‖ kɑːrb carbs kɑːbz ‖ kɑːrbz
carbamate ˈkɑːb ə meɪt ‖ ˈkɑːrb-
carbazole ˈkɑːb ə zəʊl →-zɒʊl ‖ ˈkɑːrb ə zoʊl
carbide ˈkɑːb aɪd ‖ ˈkɑːrb- **~s** z
carbine ˈkɑːb aɪn ‖ ˈkɑːrb iːn -aɪn **~s** z
carbineer ˌkɑːb ɪ ˈnɪə -ə- ‖ ˌkɑːrb ə ˈnɪᵊr **~s** z
Carbis ˈkɑːb ɪs §-əs ‖ ˈkɑːrb-
carbo ˈkɑːb əʊ ‖ ˈkɑːrb oʊ **~s** z
carbohydrate ˌkɑːb əʊ ˈhaɪdr eɪt ‖ ˌkɑːrb oʊ- -ə- **~s** s
carbolic kɑː ˈbɒl ɪk ‖ kɑːr ˈbɑːl ɪk
carbon ˈkɑːb ən ‖ ˈkɑːrb- **~s** z
   ˌcarbon ˈcopy; ˌcarbon ˈdating; ˌcarbon diˈoxide; ˈcarbon eˌmission; ˈcarbon ˌfootprint; ˈcarbon ˌpaper; ˈcarbon sink; ˈcarbon tax
carbonade ˌkɑːb ə ˈneɪd -ˈnɑːd, ˈ··· ‖ ˌkɑːrb- **~s** z
carbonado ˌkɑːb ə ˈneɪd əʊ -ˈnɑːd- ‖ ˌkɑːrb ə ˈneɪd oʊ **~es, ~s** z
carbonara ˌkɑːb ə ˈnɑːr ə ‖ ˌkɑːrb-
carbonate n ˈkɑːb ə neɪt -ən ət, -ɪt ‖ ˈkɑːrb- **~s** s
carbo|nate v ˈkɑːb ə |neɪt ‖ ˈkɑːrb- **~nated** neɪt ɪd -əd ‖ neɪt̬ əd **~nates** neɪts **~nating** neɪt ɪŋ ‖ neɪt̬ ɪŋ
carbonation ˌkɑːb ə ˈneɪʃ ᵊn ‖ ˌkɑːrb-

carbonic kɑː ˈbɒn ɪk ‖ kɑːr ˈbɑːn ɪk
carboniferous, C~ ˌkɑːb ə ˈnɪf ər_əs ◄
‖ ˌkɑːrb-
carbonis... —see **carboniz...**
carbonization ˌkɑːb ən aɪ ˈzeɪʃ ᵊn -ɪ'--
‖ ˌkɑːrb ən ə- ~s z
carboniz|e ˈkɑːb ə naɪz ‖ ˈkɑːrb- ~ed d ~es ɪz
əz ~ing ɪŋ
carbon-neutral ˌkɑːb ən ˈnjuːtrə l ◄ §-ˈnuːtr-
‖ ˌkɑːrb ən ˈnuːtr ə l ◄ -ˈnjuːtr-
carbonyl ˈkɑːb ə naɪᵊl -nɪl, -ən ᵊl ‖ ˈkɑːrb ə nɪl
-niːᵊl, ‧‧'‧
carborundum, C~ tdmk ˌkɑːb ə ˈrʌnd əm
‖ ˌkɑːrb-
Carbost ˈkɑːb ɒst ‖ ˈkɑːrb ɔːst -ɑːst
carboxyl kɑː ˈbɒks ɪl -aɪᵊl, §-ᵊl ‖ kɑːr ˈbɑːks ᵊl
carboy ˈkɑːb ɔɪ ‖ ˈkɑːrb- ~s z
carbuncle ˈkɑːb ʌŋk ᵊl ‖ ˈkɑːrb- ~s z
carburant ˈkɑːb jʊr ənt -jər-, -ər- ‖ ˈkɑːrb ər-
-jər- ~s s
carburation ˌkɑːb juᵊ ˈreɪʃ ᵊn -jə-, -ə-
‖ ˌkɑːrb ə- -jə-
carburetor, carburetter, carburettor
ˌkɑːb ə ˈret ə -juᵊ-, ˈ‧‧‧‧ ‖ ˈkɑːrb ə reɪt ᵊr (*)
~s z
carcajou ˈkɑːk ə dʒuː -ʒuː ‖ ˈkɑːrk- ~s z
carcas|e, carcass ˈkɑːk əs ‖ ˈkɑːrk- ~es ɪz əz
Carcassonne ˌkɑːk ə ˈsɒn ‖ ˌkɑːrk ə ˈsɑːn
-ˈsɔːn —Fr [kaʁ ka sɔn]
Carchemish ˈkɑːk ə mɪʃ -ɪ-; kɑː ˈkiːm ɪʃ
‖ ˈkɑːrk- kɑːr ˈkiːm ɪʃ
carcinogen kɑː ˈsɪn ədʒ ən ˈkɑːs ɪn-, -ə dʒen
‖ kɑːr- ˈkɑːrs ən ə dʒen ~s z
carcinogenic ˌkɑːs ɪn ə ˈdʒen ɪk ◄ ˌ-ən-;
kɑː ˌsɪn- ‖ ˌkɑːrs ᵊn oʊ- kɑːr ˌsɪn-, -ə'--
‖ ˌkɑːrs ᵊn ˈoʊm ə ~s z
carcinoma ˌkɑːs ɪ ˈnəʊm ə -ə-, -ᵊn ˈəʊm-
‖ ˌkɑːrs ᵊn ˈoʊm ə ~s z
card kɑːd ‖ kɑːrd **carded** ˈkɑːd ɪd -əd ‖ ˈkɑːrd-
carding ˈkɑːd ɪŋ ‖ ˈkɑːrd- **cards** kɑːdz
‖ kɑːrdz
ˌcard ˈindex, ‧ ‧‧
cardamom, cardamum ˈkɑːd əm əm
‖ ˈkɑːrd- -ə mɑːm
cardan, C~ ˈkɑːd ᵊn -æn ‖ ˈkɑːrd-
cardboard ˈkɑːd bɔːd →ˈkɑːb- ‖ ˈkɑːrd bɔːrd
-boʊrd
card-carrying ˈkɑːd ˌkær i ɪŋ →ˈkɑːg- ‖ ˈkɑːrd-
-ˌker-
Cardew ˈkɑː djuː ‖ ˈkɑːr duː
cardi- comb. form ¦kɑːd i ‖ ¦kɑːrd i —
cardialgia ˌkɑːd i ˈældʒ i_ə -ˈældʒ ə ‖ ˌkɑːrd-
cardiac ˈkɑːd i æk ‖ ˈkɑːrd-
cardie ˈkɑːd i ‖ ˈkɑːrd i ~s z
Cardiff ˈkɑːd ɪf §-əf ‖ ˈkɑːrd əf
cardigan, C~ ˈkɑːd ɪg ən ‖ ˈkɑːrd- ~s z
Cardin ˈkɑːd æ̃ -æn ‖ kɑːr ˈdæn —Fr [kaʁ dæ̃]
cardinal ˈkɑːd ɪn ᵊl -ᵊn_əl ‖ ˈkɑːrd- ~s z
ˌcardinal ˈpoint; ˌcardinal ˈvowel
cardinality ˌkɑːd ɪ ˈnæl ət i ˌ-ə-, -ᵊn ˈæl-, -ɪt i
‖ ˌkɑːrd ᵊn ˈæl ət̬ i
cardio- comb. form with stress-neutral suffix
¦kɑːd i_əʊ ‖ ¦kɑːrd i_oʊ_ə —
cardiomyopathy ˌkɑːrd i_əʊ maɪ ˈɒp əθ i

‖ ˌkɑːrd i_oʊ maɪ ˈɑːp-
with stress-imposing suffix ˌkɑːd i ˈɒ+
‖ ˌkɑːrd i ˈɑː+ — **cardiography**
ˌkɑːd i ˈɒg rəf i ‖ ˌkɑːrd i ˈɑːg-
cardiogram ˈkɑːd i_əʊ græm ‖ ˈkɑːrd i_ə- ~s z
cardiograph ˈkɑːd i_əʊ grɑːf -græf ‖ ˈkɑːrd i_ə græf ~s s
cardioid ˈkɑːd i ɔɪd ‖ ˈkɑːrd- ~s z
cardiological ˌkɑːd i ə ˈlɒdʒ ɪk ᵊl ◄
‖ ˌkɑːrd i ə ˈlɑːdʒ- ~ly i
cardiologist ˌkɑːd i ˈɒl ədʒ ɪst §-əst
‖ ˌkɑːrd i ˈɑːl- ~s s
cardiology ˌkɑːd i ˈɒl ədʒ i ‖ ˌkɑːrd i ˈɑːl-
cardiopulmonary ˌkɑːd i_əʊ ˈpʌlm ən ər i ◄
-ˈpʊlm- ‖ ˌkɑːrd i_ə ˈpʌlm ə ner i ◄
cardiovascular ˌkɑːd i_əʊ ˈvæsk jʊl ə ◄ -jəl ə
‖ ˌkɑːrd i oʊ ˈvæsk jəl ᵊr
cardoon ₍ₗ₎kɑː ˈduːn ‖ ₍ₗ₎kɑːr- ~s z
cardpunch ˈkɑːd pʌntʃ →ˈkɑːb- ‖ ˈkɑːrd- ~es
ɪz əz
cardsharp ˈkɑːd ʃɑːp ‖ ˈkɑːrd ʃɑːrp ~ing ɪŋ ~s
s
cardsharper ˈkɑːd ˌʃɑːp ə ‖ ˈkɑːrd ˌʃɑːrp ᵊr ~s
z
Cardus ˈkɑːd əs ‖ ˈkɑːrd-
card|y ˈkɑːd| i ‖ ˈkɑːrd| i ~ies iz
care keə ‖ keᵊr kæᵊr **cared** keəd ‖ keᵊrd kæᵊrd
cares keəz ‖ keᵊrz kæᵊrz **caring** ˈkeər ɪŋ
‖ ˈker ɪŋ ˈkær-
careen kə ˈriːn ~ed d ~ing ɪŋ ~s z
career kə ˈrɪə ‖ -ˈrɪᵊr **careered** kə ˈrɪəd
‖ -ˈrɪᵊrd **careering** kə ˈrɪər ɪŋ ‖ -ˈrɪr ɪŋ
careers kə ˈrɪəz ‖ -ˈrɪᵊrz
careerism kə ˈrɪər ˌɪz əm ‖ -ˈrɪr-
careerist kə ˈrɪər ɪst §-əst ‖ -ˈrɪr- ~s s
carefree ˈkeə friː ‧'‧ ‖ ˈker- ˈkær-
careful ˈkeəf ᵊl -ʊl ‖ ˈkerf- ˈkærf- ~ly i ~ness
nəs nɪs
caregiver ˈkeə ˌgɪv ə ‖ ˈker ˌgɪv ᵊr ˈkær- ~s z
careless ˈkeə ləs -lɪs ‖ ˈker- ˈkær- ~ly li ~ness
nəs nɪs —See poll figures at -less
carer ˈkeər ə ‖ ˈker ᵊr ˈkær- ~s z
caress kə ˈres ~ed t ~es ɪz əz ~ing ɪŋ
caret ˈkær ɪt -ət, -et ‖ ˈker- ~s s
caretaker ˈkeə ˌteɪk ə ‖ ˈker ˌteɪk ᵊr ˈkær- ~s z
ˈcaretaker ˌgovernment
Carew place in Dyfed ˈkeər uː -i ‖ ˈker-
Carew family name (i) kə ˈruː, (ii) ˈkeər i
‖ ˈker i
careworn ˈkeə wɔːn ‖ ˈker wɔːrn -woʊrn
Carey ˈkeər i ‖ ˈker i
carfare ˈkɑː feə ‖ ˈkɑːr fer
Carfax ˈkɑː fæks ‖ ˈkɑːr-
Cargill (i) ˈkɑː gɪl ‖ ˈkɑːr-, (ii) kɑː ˈgɪl ‖ kɑːr-
cargo ˈkɑːg əʊ ‖ ˈkɑːrg oʊ ~es, ~s z
Carholme ˈkɑː həʊm ‖ ˈkɑːr hoʊm
carhop ˈkɑː hɒp ‖ ˈkɑːr hɑːp ~s s
Caria ˈkeər i_ə ‖ ˈker- ˈkær-
Carib ˈkær ɪb §-əb ‖ ˈker- ~s z

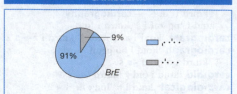

CARIBBEAN

9%

91%

BrE

Caribbean ˌkær ə 'biː ən ◂ -ɪ-; kə 'rɪb i‿ən ‖ ˌker- — *Preference poll, BrE:* ˌ‧ˑ‧‧ 91%, ‧ˑ‧‧ 9%.

　ˌCarib ˌbean 'Sea, ˑˌ‧‧‧ˑ.

caribou 'kær ə buː -ɪ- ‖ 'ker- ~s z

caricatur|e 'kær ɪk ə tʃʊə '‧ək-, -tjʊə, -tʃɔː, -tjɔː; ˌ‧‧ˑˑ ‖ -tʃʊr 'ker-, -tʊr, -tjʊr; -ətʃ ᵊr ~ed d ~es z **caricaturing** 'kær ɪk ə tʃʊər ɪŋ '‧ək-, -tjʊər ɪŋ, -tʃɔːr ɪŋ, -tjɔːr ɪŋ; ˌ‧‧ˑˑ ‖ -tʃʊr ɪŋ 'ker-, -tʊr ɪŋ, -tjʊr ɪŋ; -ətʃ ər ɪŋ

caricaturist 'kær ɪk ə tʃʊər ɪst '‧ək-, -tjʊər ‧, -tʃɔːr ‧, -tjɔːr ‧, §-əst; ˌ‧‧ˑˑ ‖ -tʃʊr əst 'ker-, -tʊr-, -tjʊr ‧, -tʃᵊr ‧ ~s s

CARICOM 'kær ɪ kɒm -ə- ‖ -kɑːm 'ker-

caries 'keər iz -iːz; 'keər i iːz ‖ 'ker- 'kær-

carillon kə 'rɪl jən -ɒn; 'kær ɪl-, -əl- ‖ 'kær ə lɑːn 'ker- ~s z

carin|a, C~ kə 'riːn |ə -'raɪn- ~ae iː aɪ ~as əz

caring 'keər ɪŋ ‖ 'ker ɪŋ 'kær- ~ly li

Carinthi|a kə 'rɪntᵊθ i |ə ~an/s ən/z

carioca, C~ ˌkær i 'əʊk ə ǁ -'oʊk ə ˌker- ~s z

carious 'keər i əs ‖ 'ker- 'kær-

Carisbrooke 'kær ɪz brʊk -ɪs-, -əz-, -əs- ‖ 'ker-

carjack 'kɑː dʒæk ‖ 'kɑːr- ~ed t ~er/s ə/z ᵊr/z ~ing ɪŋ ~s s

Carl kɑːl ‖ kɑːrl

Carla 'kɑːl ə ‖ 'kɑːrl ə

Carleen, Carlene 'kɑːl iːn ‖ 'kɑːrl-

Carleton 'kɑːlt ən ‖ 'kɑːrlt-

carline, C~ 'kɑːl aɪn -ɪn, §-ən ‖ 'kɑːrl ən ~s z

Carling 'kɑːl ɪŋ ‖ 'kɑːrl ɪŋ

Carlingford 'kɑːl ɪŋ fəd ‖ 'kɑːrl ɪŋ fᵊrd

Carlisle (i) ˌkɑː 'laɪᵊl ‖ ˌkɑːr- kᵊr-, (ii) 'kɑː laɪᵊl ‖ 'kɑːr- — *In BrE usually* (i), *although the place in Cumbria is locally* (ii); *in AmE usually* (ii).

Carlist 'kɑːl ɪst §-əst ‖ 'kɑːrl- ~s s

Carlo 'kɑːl əʊ ‖ 'kɑːrl oʊ ~'s z

carload 'kɑː ləʊd ‖ 'kɑːr loʊd ~s z

Carlos 'kɑːl ɒs ‖ 'kɑːrl oʊs -əs — *Sp* ['kar los]

Carlotta kɑː 'lɒt ə ‖ kɑːr 'lɑːt̬ ə

Carlovingian ˌkɑːl əʊ 'vɪndʒ i‿ən ◂ -'vɪndʒ ən ‖ ˌkɑːrl ə- ~s z

Carlow 'kɑːl əʊ ‖ 'kɑːrl oʊ

Carlsbad 'kɑːlz bæd ‖ 'kɑːrlz-

Carlsberg 'kɑːlz bɜːg ‖ 'kɑːrlz bɜːg ~s, 's z

Carlson 'kɑːls ən ‖ 'kɑːrls-

Carlton 'kɑːlt ən ‖ 'kɑːrlt-

Carly 'kɑːl i ‖ 'kɑːrl i

Carlyle ˌkɑː 'laɪᵊl ‖ ˌkɑːr- ‧ˑ

Carman 'kɑːm ən ‖ 'kɑːrm-

Carmarthen kə 'mɑːð ᵊn ‖ kɑːr 'mɑːrð-

Carmel (i) 'kɑːm el -ᵊl ‖ 'kɑːrm-, (ii) ˌ‧ˌkɑː 'mel ‖ ˌ‧ˌkɑːr- — *The mountain is usually* (i); *the place in California is* (ii).

Carmelite 'kɑːm ə laɪt -ɪ-; -el aɪt ‖ 'kɑːrm- ~s s

Carmelle ˌ‧ˌkɑː 'mel ‖ ˌ‧ˌkɑːr-

Carmen 'kɑːm en ‖ 'kɑːrm ən — *Sp* ['kar men]

Carmichael kɑː 'maɪk ᵊl -'mɪx-, ˑˌ‧‧ ‖ 'kɑːr ˌmaɪk ᵊl

Carmina Burana ˌkɑːm ɪn ə bə 'rɑːn ə §ˌ-ən-, ˌkɑː ˌmiːn ə-, -bu 'rɑːn- ‖ ˌkɑːrm ən- kɑːr ˌmiːn-

carminative 'kɑːm ɪn ət ɪv '‧ən- ‖ kɑːr 'mɪn ət̬ ɪv 'kɑːrm ə neɪt̬- ~s z

carmine 'kɑːm aɪn -ɪn, §-ən ‖ 'kɑːrm- ~s z

Carmody 'kɑːm əd i ‖ 'kɑːrm-

Carnaby 'kɑːn əb i ‖ 'kɑːrn-

Carnac 'kɑːn æk ‖ kɑːr 'næk — *Fr* [kaʁ nak]

carnage 'kɑːn ɪdʒ ‖ 'kɑːrn-

Carnaghan 'kɑːn əg ən ‖ 'kɑːrn- -ə hæn

carnal 'kɑːn ᵊl ‖ 'kɑːrn ᵊl ~ly i

carnality kɑː 'næl ət i -ɪt- ‖ kɑːr 'næl ət̬ i

carnallite 'kɑːn ə laɪt -ᵊl aɪt ‖ 'kɑːrn ᵊl aɪt

Carnap 'kɑːn æp ‖ 'kɑːrn-

Carnarvon kə 'nɑːv ᵊn ‖ kᵊr 'nɑːrv-

carnassial kɑː 'næʃ i əl ‖ kɑːr-

Carnatic kɑː 'næt ɪk ‖ kɑːr 'næt̬ ɪk

carnation kɑː 'neɪʃ ᵊn ‖ kɑːr- ~s z

carnauba kɑː 'nɔːb ə -'naʊb- ‖ kɑːr- -'nɑːb-

Carnegie (i) kɑː 'neg i ‖ kɑːr-, (ii) -'neɪg-, (iii) -'niːg-, (iv) 'kɑːn əg i ‖ 'kɑːrn- — *Andrew C~ was* (ii); *but C~ Hall is usually* (iv).

carnelian kɑː 'niːl i‿ən kə- ‖ kɑːr- ~s z

carnet 'kɑːn eɪ ‖ kɑːr 'neɪ — *Fr* [kaʁ nɛ] ~s z

Carney 'kɑːn i ‖ 'kɑːrn i

Carnforth 'kɑːn fɔːθ -fəθ ‖ 'kɑːrn fɔːrθ -foʊrθ

carnie 'kɑːn i ‖ 'kɑːrn i ~s z

carnival 'kɑːn ɪv ᵊl -əv- ‖ 'kɑːrn- ~s z

carnivore 'kɑːn ɪ vɔː -ə- ‖ 'kɑːrn ə vɔːr -voʊr ~s z

carnivorous kɑː 'nɪv ᵊr əs ‖ kɑːr- ~ly li ~ness nəs nɪs

Carnochan 'kɑːn ək ən -əx- ‖ 'kɑːrn-

Carnot 'kɑːn əʊ ‖ kɑːr 'noʊ — *Fr* [kaʁ no]

Carnoustie kɑː 'nuːst i ‖ kɑːr-

carn|y 'kɑːn |i ‖ 'kɑːrn i ~ies iz

carob 'kær əb ‖ 'ker- ~s z

carol, Carol 'kær əl ‖ 'ker- ~ed, ~led d ~ing, ~ling ɪŋ ~s z

Carola 'kær əl ə ‖ 'ker-

Carole 'kær əl ‖ 'ker-

Carolina ˌkær ə 'laɪn ə ◂ ‖ ˌker- ~s, ~'s z

Caroline (i) 'kær ə laɪn ‖ 'ker-, (ii) -əl ɪn §-ən

Carolingian ˌkær ə 'lɪndʒ i‿ən ◂ ‖ ˌker- ~s z

Carolinian ˌkær ə 'lɪn i‿ən ◂ ‖ ˌker- ~s z

Carolyn 'kær əl ɪn §-ən ‖ 'ker-

carom 'kær əm ‖ 'ker- ~ed d ~ing ɪŋ ~s z

caron 'kær ən ‖ 'ker- ~s z

Caron (i) 'kær ən ‖ 'ker-, (ii) kə 'rɒn ‖ -'rɑːn -'rɔːn

carotene 'kær ə tiːn ‖ 'ker-

carotid kə 'rɒt ɪd §-əd ‖ -'rɑːt̬- ~s z

carousal kə 'raʊz ᵊl ~s z

carous|e kə 'raʊz ~ed d ~es ɪz əz ~ing ɪŋ

carousel ˌkær ə 'sel -u-, -'zel ‖ ˌker-, ˑ‧‧‧ ~s z

C

carp kɑːp ‖ kɑːrp **carped** kɑːpt ‖ kɑːrpt
  carping ˈkɑːp ɪŋ ‖ ˈkɑːrp- **carps** kɑːps
  ‖ kɑːrps
carpaccio kɑː ˈpætʃ i əʊ -ˈpɑːtʃ-; ·ˈ·əʊ
  ‖ kɑːr ˈpɑːtʃ oʊ —*It* [kar ˈpat tʃo]
carpal ˈkɑːp əl ‖ ˈkɑːrp- **~s** z
Carpathian kɑː ˈpeɪθ i ən ‖ kɑːr- **~s** z
carpe diem ˌkɑːp i ˈdiː em ‖ ˌkɑːrp-
carpel ˈkɑːp əl -el ‖ ˈkɑːrp- **~s** z
Carpentaria ˌkɑːp ən ˈteər i ə →ˌm-, ˌen-
  ‖ ˌkɑːrp ən ˈter-
carpenter, C~ ˈkɑːp ənt ə -ɪnt-, →ˌmt-
  ‖ ˈkɑːrp ənt ʲr →ˌmt- **~ed** d **carpentering**
  ˈkɑːp ənt ər ɪŋ -ɪnt-, →ˌmt ‖ ˈkɑːrp ənt ʲr ɪŋ
  →ˈ·əntr ɪŋ, →-mtr- **~s** z
carpentry ˈkɑːp əntr i -ɪntr i, →-m tri ‖ ˈkɑːrp-
carp|et ˈkɑːp |ɪt §-ət ‖ ˈkɑːrp |ət **~eted** ɪt ɪd
  §ət-, -əd ‖ ət əd **~eting** ɪt ɪŋ §ət- ‖ ət ɪŋ **~ets**
  ɪts §əts ‖ əts
  ˈcarpet ˌbeetle; ˈcarpet ˌbombing; ˈcarpet
  ˌslippers
carpetbag ˈkɑːp ɪt bæg §-ət- ‖ ˈkɑːrp- **~ger/s**
  ə/z ‖ ʲr/z **~ging** ɪŋ **~s** z
carpet-bomb ˈkɑːp ɪt bɒm §-ət-
  ‖ ˈkɑːrp ət bɑːm **~ed** d **~ing** ɪŋ **~s** z
carpet-sweeper ˈkɑːp ɪt ˌswiːp ə §-ət-
  ‖ ˈkɑːrp ət ˌswiːp ʲr **~s** z
carphone ˈkɑː fəʊn ‖ ˈkɑːr foʊn **~s** z
carpi ˈkɑːp aɪ ‖ ˈkɑːrp-
carping ˈkɑːp ɪŋ ‖ ˈkɑːrp ɪŋ **~ly** li
carpo- *comb. form with stress-neutral suffix*
  ¦kɑːp əʊ ‖ ¦kɑːrp ə
  — **carpophore** ˈkɑːp əʊ fɔː ‖ ˈkɑːrp ə fɔːr
  with stress-imposing suffix kɑ ˈpɒ +
  ‖ kɑːr ˈpɑː +
  — **carpophagous** kɑː ˈpɒf əg əs ‖ kɑːr ˈpɑːf-
carpool ˈkɑː puːl ‖ ˈkɑːr puːl **~ing** ɪŋ **~s** z
carport ˈkɑː pɔːt ‖ ˈkɑːr pɔːrt -poʊrt **~s** s
-carpous ˈkɑːp əs ‖ ˈkɑːrp- — **polycarpous**
  ˌpɒl i ˈkɑːp əs ◄ ‖ ˌpɑːl i ˈkɑːrp-
carp|us ˈkɑːp |əs ‖ ˈkɑːrp- **~i** aɪ iː
carr, Carr kɑː ‖ kɑːr **~s** z
carrageen, carragheen ˌkær ə giːn ˌ·ˈ·
  ‖ ˈker-
Carrantuohill, Carrauntoohill
  ˌkær ən ˈtuː əl ‖ ˌker-
Carrara kə ˈrɑːr ə —*It* [kar ˈra ra]
Carrbridge ˌkɑː ˈbrɪdʒ ‖ ˌkɑːr-
carrel ˈkær əl ‖ ˈker- (= *carol*) **~s** z
Carrhae ˈkær iː ‖ ˈker-
carri... —*see* **carry**
Carriacou ˌkær i ə ˈkuː ˈ·· ·· ‖ ˌker-
carriag|e ˈkær ɪdʒ ‖ ˈker- **~es** ɪz əz
carriageway ˈkær ɪdʒ weɪ ‖ ˈker- **~s** z
Carrick, c~ ˈkær ɪk ‖ ˈker-
Carrickfergus ˌkær ɪk ˈfɜːg əs ‖ -ˈfɜːg əs ˌker-
Carrie ˈkær i ‖ ˈker-
carrier ˈkær i ə ‖ ˈkær iʲr ˈker- **~s** z
  ˈcarrier bag, ˌ·· ˈ·; ˌcarrier ˈpigeon, ˈ··· ˌ·;
  ˈcarrier wave
Carrington ˈkær ɪŋ tən ‖ ˈker-
carrion ˈkær i ən ‖ ˈker-
  ˌcarrion ˈcrow, ˈ· · · ·

Carrol, Carroll ˈkær əl ‖ ˈker-
Carron ˈkær ən ‖ ˈker-
carrot ˈkær ət ‖ ˈker-
carrot-and-stick ˌkær ət ʲn ˈstɪk -ət ʲnd-
  ‖ ˌker-
carroty ˈkær ət i -ət i ˈker-
carrousel ˌkær ə ˈsel -u-, -ˈzel ‖ ˌker-, ˈ· · · **~s** z
Carruthers kə ˈrʌð əz ‖ -ʲrz
carry, Carry ˈkær i ‖ ˈker- **carried** ˈkær id
  ‖ ˈker- **carries** ˈkær iz ˈker- **carrying**
  ˈkær i ɪŋ ‖ ˈker-
carryall ˈkær i ɔːl ‖ ˈker-, -ɑːl **~s** z
carrycot ˈkær i kɒt ‖ -kɑːt ˈker- **~s** s
carrying ˈkær i ɪŋ ‖ ˈker-
  ˈcarrying case; ˈcarrying charge
carryings-on ˌkær i ɪŋz ˈɒn ‖ -ˈɑːn ˌker-, -ˈɔːn
carry-on ˈkær i ɒn ˌ· ·ˈ· ◄ ‖ -ɑːn ˈker-, -ɔːn **~s** z
carryout ˈkær i aʊt ‖ ˈker- **~s** s
carry-over ˈkær i ˌəʊv ə ‖ -ˌoʊv ʲr ˈker- **~s** z
Carse kɑːs ‖ kɑːrs
Carshalton kɑː ˈʃɔːlt ən kə- ‖ kɑːr- -ˈʃɑːlt-
  —*formerly also* keɪs ˈhɔːt ʲn
carsick ˈkɑː sɪk ‖ ˈkɑːr-
Carson ˈkɑːs ʲn ‖ ˈkɑːrs ʲn
  ˌCarson ˈCity
Carstairs ˌkɑː ˈsteəz ·· ‖ ˈkɑːr sterz
cart kɑːt ‖ kɑːrt **carted** ˈkɑːt ɪd -əd ‖ ˈkɑːrt əd
  carting ˈkɑːt ɪŋ ‖ ˈkɑːrt ɪŋ **carts** kɑːts
  ‖ kɑːrts
  ˈcart track
Carta ˈkɑːt ə ‖ ˈkɑːrt ə
cartage ˈkɑːt ɪdʒ ‖ ˈkɑːrt-
Cartagena ˌkɑːt ə ˈdʒiːn ə ‖ ˌkɑːrt ə ˈheɪn ə
  -ˈgeɪn- —*Sp* [kar ta ˈxe na]
carte blanche ˌkɑːt ˈblɑːnʃ -ˈblɒ̃ʃ ‖ ˌkɑːrt-
  —*Fr* [kaʁ tə blɑ̃ːʃ]
cartel kɑː ˈtel ‖ kɑːr- **~s** z
carter, C~ ˈkɑːt ə ‖ ˈkɑːrt ʲr **~s** z
Carteret ˈkɑːt ə ret -rɪt, -rət ‖ ˈkɑːrt-, ˌ· ·ˈret
Cartesian (ˌ)kɑː ˈtiːz i ən -ˈtiːʒ ʲn
  ‖ kɑːr ˈtiːʒ ʲn **~s** z
Carthage ˈkɑːθ ɪdʒ ‖ ˈkɑːrθ-
Carthaginian ˌkɑːθ ə ˈdʒɪn i ən ◄ ‖ ˌkɑːrθ- **~s**
  z
Carthew ˈkɑːθ juː ‖ ˈkɑːrθ uː
carthors|e ˈkɑːt hɔːs ‖ ˈkɑːrt hɔːrs **~es** ɪz əz
Carthusian kɑː ˈθjuːz i ən -ˈθuːz-
  ‖ kɑːr ˈθuːʒ ʲn -ˈθjuːʒ- **~s** z
Cartier ˈkɑːt i eɪ ‖ ˈkɑːrt- —*but as a French or*
  French Canadian name, ˌ· ·ˈ· —*Fr* [kaʁ tje]
  ~'s z
cartilage ˈkɑːt əl ɪdʒ -ɪl- ‖ ˈkɑːrt- **~es** ɪz əz
cartilaginous ˌkɑːt ə ˈlædʒ ɪn əs ◄ ˌ·ɪ-,
  -ʲl ˈædʒ-, -ən əs ‖ ˌkɑːrt ʲl ˈædʒ ən əs
Cartland ˈkɑːt lənd ‖ ˈkɑːrt-
cartload ˈkɑːt ləʊd ‖ ˈkɑːrt loʊd **~s** z
Cartmel ˈkɑːt məl -mel ‖ ˈkɑːrt-
cartographer kɑː ˈtɒg rəf ə ‖ kɑːr ˈtɑːg rəf ʲr
  ~s z
cartographic ˌkɑːt ə ˈgræf ɪk ◄ ‖ ˌkɑːrt- **~al** ʲl
  ~ally ʲl i
cartography kɑː ˈtɒg rəf i ‖ kɑːr ˈtɑːg-
cartomancy ˈkɑːt əʊ ˌmæn‖s i ‖ ˈkɑːrt ə-

C

carton, C~ 'kɑːt ᵊn ‖ 'kɑːrt ᵊn ~s z
cartoon kɑ: 'tuːn ‖ kɑːr- ~s z
cartoonish kɑ: 'tuːn ɪʃ ‖ kɑːr-
cartoonist kɑ: 'tuːn ɪst §-əst ‖ kɑːr- ~s s
cartophilist kɑ: 'tɒf əl ɪst -ɪl-, §-əst
 ‖ kɑːr 'tɑːf- ~s s
cartophily kɑ: 'tɒf əl i -ɪl- ‖ kɑːr 'tɑːf-
cartouch|e kɑ: 'tuːʃ ‖ kɑːr- ~es ɪz əz
cartridg|e 'kɑːtr ɪdʒ ‖ 'kɑːrtr- §'kætr- ~es ɪz
 əz
 'cartridge belt; 'cartridge ˌpaper
cartwheel 'kɑːt wiːᵊl -hwiːᵊl ‖ 'kɑːrt- ~ed d
 ~ing ɪŋ ~s z
Cartwright, c~ 'kɑːt raɪt ‖ 'kɑːrt-
caruncle kə 'rʌŋk ᵊl kæ-; 'kær əŋk- ~s z
Caruso kə 'ruːs əʊ -'ruːz- ‖ -oʊ —It
 [ka 'ru: zo]
Caruthers kə 'rʌð əz ‖ -ᵊrz
carve kɑːv ‖ kɑːrv carved kɑːvd ‖ kɑːrvd
 carves kɑːvz ‖ kɑːrvz carving 'kɑːv ɪŋ
 ‖ 'kɑːrv ɪŋ
carvel 'kɑːv ᵊl -el ‖ 'kɑːrv- ~s z
carvel-built 'kɑːv ᵊl bɪlt -el- ‖ 'kɑːrv-
carver, C~ 'kɑːv ə ‖ 'kɑːrv ᵊr ~s z
carver|y 'kɑːv ər |i ‖ 'kɑːrv- ~ies iz
carve-up 'kɑːv ʌp ‖ 'kɑːrv-
carving 'kɑːv ɪŋ ‖ 'kɑːrv ɪŋ ~s z
 'carving knife
Carwardine 'kɑː wə diːn ‖ 'kɑːr wᵊr-
Cary family name 'keər i ‖ 'ker i 'kær-
Cary personal name 'kær i 'keər- ‖ 'ker-
caryatid ˌkær i 'æt ɪd §-əd; 'kær i ə tɪd
 ‖ -'æt əd ˌker-; 'kær i ə tɪd, 'ker- ~s z
Caryl 'kær əl -ɪl ‖ 'ker-
Carys 'kær ɪs -əs ‖ 'ker-
Carysfort 'kær ɪs fɔːt -əs- ‖ -fɔːrt 'ker-, -foʊrt
carzey 'kɑːz i ‖ — ~s z
Casablanca ˌkæs ə 'blæŋk ə ˌkæz-
 ‖ ˌkɑːs ə 'blɑːŋk ə —Fr [ka za blɑ̃ ka]
Casals kə 'sælz ‖ -'sɑːlz kɑ:- —Sp [ka 'sals],
 Catalan [kə 'zals]
Casanova ˌkæs ə 'nəʊv ə ˌkæz-
 ‖ ˌkæz ə 'noʊv ə ˌkæs- —It [ka sa 'nɔ: va]
Casaubon kə 'sɔːb ən 'kæz ə bɒn ‖ -'sɑːb-;
 'kæz ə bɑːn —Fr [ka zo bɔ̃]
casbah 'kæz bɑː -bə ‖ 'kɑːz-
cascad|e, C~ ₍ᵢ₎kæ 'skeɪd ~ed ɪd əd ~es z ~ing
 ɪŋ
cascara kæ 'skɑːr ə ‖ -'skær- -'sker-
cascarilla ˌkæsk ə 'rɪl ə ‖ -'ri: jə, -'rɪl jə
case, Case keɪs cased keɪst cases 'keɪs ɪz -əz
 casing keɪs ɪŋ
 'case ˌending; ˌcase 'history; 'case ˌstudy
casebook 'keɪs bʊk §-buːk ~s s
casebound 'keɪs baʊnd
case-harden 'keɪs ˌhɑːd ᵊn ‖ -ˌhɑːrd- ~ed d
 ~ing ˌɪŋ ~s z
casein 'keɪs i ɪn 'keɪs iːn ‖ keɪ 'siːn
caseload 'keɪs ləʊd ‖ -loʊd ~s z
casemate 'keɪs meɪt ~s s
casement, C~ 'keɪs mənt ~ed ɪd əd ~s s
 ˌcasement 'window
casework 'keɪs wɜːk ‖ -wɜːk

caseworker 'keɪs ˌwɜːk ə ‖ -ˌwɜːk ᵊr ~s z
Casey 'keɪs i
cash, Cash kæʃ cashed kæʃt cashes 'kæʃ ɪz
 -əz cashing 'kæʃ ɪŋ
 'cash card; 'cash crop; ˌcash 'discount;
 'cash diˌspenser; 'cash flow; 'cash
 maˌchine; 'cash ˌregister
cashable 'kæʃ əb ᵊl
cash-and-carry ˌkæʃ ᵊn 'kær i →-ᵊn- ‖ -'ker-
cashback 'kæʃ bæk
cashbook 'kæʃ bʊk ~s s
cashew 'kæʃ u: kæ 'ʃu:, kə- ~s z
ca|shier kæ |'ʃɪə kə- ‖ -'|ʃᵊr ~shiered 'ʃɪəd
 ‖ 'ʃɪᵊrd ~shiering 'ʃɪər ɪŋ ‖ 'ʃɪr ɪŋ ~shiers
 'ʃɪəz ‖ 'ʃɪᵊrz
Cashin 'kæʃ ɪn §-ᵊn
cash-in-hand ˌkæʃ ɪn 'hænd §-ᵊn-
cashless 'kæʃ ləs -lɪs
Cashman 'kæʃ mən
cashmere 'kæʃ mɪə ˌ·'· ‖ 'kæʒ mɪr 'kæʃ- ~s z
cashpoint 'kæʃ pɔɪnt ~s s
cash-rich ˌkæʃ 'rɪtʃ ◂
cash-starved ˌkæʃ 'stɑːvd ◂ ‖ -'stɑːrvd ◂
cash-strapped ˌkæʃ 'stræpt ◂
casing 'keɪs ɪŋ ~s z
casino kə 'siːn əʊ ‖ -oʊ ~s z
Casio tdmk 'kæs i əʊ ‖ oʊ
cask kɑːsk §kæsk ‖ kæsks casks kɑːsks §kæsks
 ‖ kæsks
casket 'kɑːsk ɪt §'kæsk-, §-ət ‖ 'kæsk ət ~s s
Caslon 'kæz lɒn -lən ‖ -lɑːn -lən
Caspar 'kæsp ə -ɑ: ‖ -ᵊr -ɑːr
Caspian 'kæsp i ən
casque kæsk kɑːsk casques kæsks kɑːsks
Cass kæs
Cassandra kə 'sændr ə -'sɑːndr- ~s, ~'s z
cassareep 'kæs ə riːp
cassata kə 'sɑːt ə kæ- ‖ -'sɑːt̬ ə —It
 [kas 'sa: ta]
cassava kə 'sɑːv ə
Cassel, Cassell 'kæs ᵊl —but as a French
 name, kæ 'sel —Fr [ka sɛl]
casserol|e 'kæs ə rəʊl →-rɒʊl ‖ -roʊl 'kæz-
 ~ed d ~es z ~ing ɪŋ
cassette kə 'set kæ- ~s s
 cas'sette reˌcorder
cassia 'kæs i ə ‖ 'kæʃ ə (*)
Cassidy 'kæs əd i -ɪd-
Cassie 'kæs i
Cassillis 'kæs ᵊlz
Cassio 'kæs i əʊ ‖ oʊ
Cassiopeia ˌkæs i əʊ 'piː ə -'peɪ ə ‖ ˌkæs i oʊ-
cassis kæ 'siːs kɑː-; 'kæs iːs —Fr [ka sis]
cassiterite kə 'sɪt ə raɪt ‖ -'sɪt̬-
Cassius 'kæs i əs ‖ 'kæʃ əs -i əs (*)
Cassivelaunus ˌkæs ɪv ə 'lɔːn əs ˌ·əv-, -ɪ'··,
 -'laʊn- ‖ -'lɑːn-
cassock 'kæs ək ~s s
Casson 'kæs ᵊn
cassoulet ˌkæs u 'leɪ -ə-, '··· ‖ -ə- —Fr
 [ka su lɛ] ~s z
cassowar|y 'kæs ə weər |i -wər i ‖ -wer |i
 ~ies iz

cast kɑːst §kæst ‖ kæst **casting** ˈkɑːst ɪŋ
§ˈkæst- ‖ ˈkæst ɪŋ **casts** kɑːsts §kæsts ‖ kæsts

Castali|a kæ ˈsteɪl i‿|ə **~an** ən

castanet ˌkæst ə ˈnet **~s** s

castaway ˈkɑːst ə ˌweɪ §ˈkæst- ‖ ˈkæst- **~s** z

caste kɑːst §kæst ‖ kæst *(= cast)* **castes** kɑːsts
§kæsts ‖ kæsts

Castel Gandolfo ˌkæst el gæn ˈdɒlf əʊ
‖ -ˈdɑːlf oʊ — *It* [kas tel gan ˈdɔl fo]

castellated ˈkæst ə leɪt ɪd ˈˌ·ɪ-, -ᵊl eɪt-, -əd
‖ -leɪt̬ əd

caster ˈkɑːst ə §ˈkæst- ‖ ˈkæst ᵊr **~s** z
    ˈcaster ˌsugar, ˌ··ˈ··

Casterbridge ˈkɑːst ə brɪdʒ §ˈkæst- ‖ ˈkæst ᵊr-

casti|gate ˈkæst ɪ |geɪt -ə- **~gated** geɪt ɪd -əd
‖ geɪt̬- **~gates** geɪts **~gating** geɪt ɪŋ ‖ geɪt̬ ɪŋ

castigation ˌkæst ɪ ˈgeɪʃ ᵊn -ə- **~s** z

castigator ˈkæst ɪ geɪt ə ˈˌ·ə- ‖ -geɪt̬ ᵊr **~s** z

Castile kæ ˈstiːᵊl —*but the place in NY is*
    -ˈstaɪᵊl

Castilian kæ ˈstɪl i‿ən **~s** z

casting ˈkɑːst ɪŋ §ˈkæst- ‖ ˈkæst ɪŋ **~s** z
    ˌcasting ˈvote

cast-iron ˌkɑːst ˈaɪ‿ən ◂ §ˌkæst-
‖ ˌkæst ˈaɪ‿ᵊrn ◂

castl|e, C~ ˈkɑːs ᵊl §ˈkæs- ‖ ˈkæs ᵊl **~ed** d **~es**
z **~ing** ɪŋ

Castlebar ˌkɑːs ᵊl ˈbɑː §ˌkæs- ‖ ˌkæs ᵊl ˈbɑːr

Castleford ˈkɑːs ᵊl fəd §ˈkæs- ‖ ˈkæs ᵊl fᵊrd

Castlemaine ˈkɑːs ᵊl meɪn §ˈkæs- ‖ ˈkæs-

Castlenau ˈkɑːs ᵊl nɔː §ˈkæs-, -nəʊ ‖ ˈkæs- -nɑː

Castlerea, Castlereagh ˈkɑːs ᵊl reɪ §ˈkæs-,
ˌ··ˈ· ‖ ˈkæs-

Castleton ˈkɑːs ᵊl tən §ˈkæs- ‖ ˈkæs-

Castlewellan ˌkɑːs ᵊl ˈwel ən §ˌkæs- ‖ ˌkæs-

castoff, cast-off ˈkɑːst ɒf §ˈkæst-, -ɔːf
‖ ˈkæst ɔːf -ɑːf **~s** s

castor, C~ ˈkɑːst ə §ˈkæst- ‖ ˈkæst ᵊr *(= caster)*
~s z
    ˌcastor ˈoil; ˈcastor ˌsugar, ˌ··ˈ··

castrate kæ ˈstreɪt ‖ ˈkæs treɪt *(*)* **castrated**
kæ ˈstreɪt ɪd -əd ‖ ˈkæs treɪt̬ əd **castrates**
kæ ˈstreɪts ‖ ˈkæs treɪts **castrating**
kæ ˈstreɪt ɪŋ ‖ ˈkæs treɪt̬ ɪŋ

castration kæ ˈstreɪʃ ᵊn **~s** z

castrat|o kæ ˈstrɑːt |əʊ kə- ‖ -|oʊ **~i** iː

Castries kæ ˈstriːz -ˈstriːs

Castro ˈkæs trəʊ ‖ -troʊ —*Sp* [ˈkas tro]

Castrol *tdmk* ˈkæs trɒl ‖ -troʊl -trɑːl, -trɔːl

CASUAL

BrE
- 77% ˈkæʒ-
- 23% ˈkæz-

---

casual ˈkæʒ u‿əl -ju‿, ˈkæz juː; ˈkæʒ ᵊl
— *Preference poll, BrE:* ˈkæʒ- 77%, ˈkæz-
23%. **~ly** i **~ness** nəs nɪs **~s** z

---

casualization, casualisation
ˌkæʒ u‿əl aɪ ˈzeɪʃ ᵊn ˌ·ju‿, ˌkæz juː;
ˌkæʒ ᵊl aɪ-, -ɪ-·· ‖ -ə-··

casualiz|e, casualis|e ˈkæʒ u‿ə laɪz -ju‿,
ˈkæz juː; ˈkæʒ ə laɪz **~ed** d **~ing** ɪŋ **~es** ɪz əz

casual|ty ˈkæʒ u‿əl |ti ·ju‿, ˈkæz juː;
ˈkæʒ ᵊl |ti **~ties** tiz
    ˈcasualty ward

casuarina ˌkæz ju‿ə ˈriːn ə ˌkæʒ juː, ˌkæʒ u‿,
ˌkæʒ ə ˈriːn ə; -ˈraɪn- ‖ ˌkæʒ u‿ **~s** z

casuist ˈkæz ju‿ɪst ˈkæʒ juː, ˈkæʒ u‿, §-əst
‖ ˈkæʒ u‿əst **~s** s

casuistic ˌkæz ju ˈɪst ɪk ◂ ˌkæʒ juː-, ˌkæʒ u-
‖ ˌkæʒ u- **~ally** ᵊl i

casuis|try ˈkæz ju‿ɪs |tri ˈkæʒ juː, ˈkæʒ u‿, §-əs·
‖ ˈkæʒ u‿ **~tries** triz

casus belli ˌkɑːs ʊs ˈbel iː -əs-; ˌkeɪs əs ˈbel aɪ

cat kæt **cats** kæts
    ˈcat ˌburglar; ˈcat ˌcracker; ˈcat ˌdoor; ˈcat
    flap; ˌcat's ˈcradle; ˌcat's ˈwhisker

CAT kæt
    ˈCAT scan, ˈCAT ˌscanner

cata- *comb. form with stress-neutral suffix*
    ¦kæt ə ‖ ¦kæt̬ ə
    — **cataclastic** ¦kæt ə ˈklæst ɪk ◂ ‖ ¦kæt̬- *with*
    stress-imposing suffix kə ˈtæ+
    — **catadromous** kə ˈtædr əm əs

catabolic ˌkæt ə ˈbɒl ɪk ◂ ‖ ˌkæt̬ ə ˈbɑːl- **~ally**
    ᵊl i

catabolism kə ˈtæb ə ˌlɪz əm

catachresis ˌkæt ə ˈkriːs ɪs §-əs ‖ ˌkæt̬-

catachrestic ˌkæt ə ˈkrest ɪk ◂ ‖ ˌkæt̬-

cataclysm ˈkæt ə ˌklɪz əm ‖ ˈkæt̬- **~s** z

cataclysmal ˌkæt ə ˈklɪz mᵊl ‖ ˌkæt̬- **~ly** i

cataclysmic ˌkæt ə ˈklɪz mɪk ◂ ‖ ˌkæt̬- **~ally**
    ᵊl i

catacomb ˈkæt ə kuːm -kəʊm ‖ ˈkæt̬ ə koʊm
    ~s z

catafalque ˈkæt ə fælk ‖ ˈkæt̬ ə fɔːk -fɑːk,
    -fɔːlk, -fælk **~s** s

Catalan ˈkæt ə læn -ᵊl ən, ᵊl æn; ˌkæt ə ˈlæn
    ‖ ˈkæt̬ ᵊl ən -æn, ˌkɑːt ə ˈlɑːn **~s** z

catalectic ˌkæt ə ˈlekt ɪk ◂ -ᵊl ˈekt-
    ‖ ˌkæt̬ ᵊl ˈekt ɪk ◂

catalepsy ˈkæt ə leps i -ᵊl eps- ‖ ˈkæt̬ ᵊl eps i

cataleptic ˌkæt ə ˈlept ɪk ◂ -ᵊl ˈept-
    ‖ ˌkæt̬ ᵊl ˈept ɪk ◂

Catalina ˌkæt ə ˈliːn ə -ᵊl ˈiːn- ‖ ˌkæt̬ ᵊl ˈiːn ə

catalog, catalogu|e ˈkæt ə lɒg -ᵊl ɒg
    ‖ ˈkæt̬ ᵊl ɔːg -ɑːg **~ed** d **~ing** ɪŋ **catalogs,**
    catalogues ˈkæt ə lɒgz -ᵊl ɒgz ‖ ˈkæt̬ ᵊl ɔːgz
    -ɑːgz

Catalonia ˌkæt ə ˈləʊn i‿ə -ᵊl ˈəʊn-
    ‖ ˌkæt̬ ᵊl ˈoʊn-

catalpa kə ˈtælp ə ‖ -ˈtɑːlp-, -ˈtɔːlp- **~s** z

catalysis kə ˈtæl əs ɪs §-əs

catalyst ˈkæt ᵊl ɪst §-əst ‖ ˈkæt̬- **~s** s

catalytic ˌkæt ə ˈlɪt ɪk ◂ -ᵊl ˈɪt- ‖ ˌkæt̬ ᵊl ˈɪt̬ ɪk ◂
    ~ally ᵊl i

catamaran ˌkæt əm ə ˈræn ˈ···· ‖ ˌkæt̬- **~s** z

catamite ˈkæt ə maɪt ‖ ˈkæt̬- **~s** s

catamount ˈkæt ə maʊnt ‖ ˈkæt̬- **~s** s

catamountain ˌkæt ə 'maʊnt ɪn -ən
‖ ˌkæt̮ ə 'maʊnt ᵊn **~s** z
cat-and-dog ˌkæt ᵊn 'dɒg ◄ ‖ -'dɔːg -'dɑːg
cat-and-mouse ˌkæt ᵊn 'maʊs ◄
cataphora kə 'tæf ər ə
cataphoresis ˌkæt ə fə 'riːs ɪs -fɒˈ--, §-əs
‖ ˌkæt̮-
cataphoretic ˌkæt ə fə 'ret ɪk ◄ -fɒˈ--
‖ ˌkæt̮ ə fə 'ret̮ ɪk ◄ **~ally** ᵊl̩ i
cataphoric ˌkæt ə 'fɒr ɪk ◄ ‖ ˌkæt̮ ə 'fɔːr ɪk ◄
-'fɑːr- **~ally** ᵊl̩ i
cataplasm 'kæt ə ˌplæz əm ‖ 'kæt̮- **~s** z
cataplexy 'kæt ə pleks i ‖ 'kæt̮-
catapult 'kæt ə pʌlt §-pʊlt ‖ 'kæt̮- **~ed** ɪd -əd
~ing ɪŋ **~s** s
cataract 'kæt ə rækt ‖ 'kæt̮- **~s** s
catarrh kə 'tɑː ‖ -'tɑːr
catarrhal kə 'tɑːr əl
catarrhine 'kæt ə raɪn ‖ 'kæt̮- **~s** z
catastasis kə 'tæst əs ɪs §-əs
catastrophe kə 'tæs trəf i **~s** z
catastrophic ˌkæt ə 'strɒf ɪk ◄ ‖ ˌkæt̮ ə 'strɑːf-
~ally ᵊl̩ i
ˌcata,strophic 'failure
catastrophism kə 'tæs trə ˌfɪz əm
catatonia ˌkæt ə 'təʊn i ə ‖ ˌkæt̮ ə 'toʊn-
catatonic ˌkæt ə 'tɒn ɪk ◄ ‖ ˌkæt̮ ə 'tɑːn- **~ally**
ᵊl̩ i
Catawba, c~ kə 'tɔːb ə ‖ -'tɑːb-
catbird 'kæt bɜːd ‖ -bɜːd **~s** z
catcall 'kæt kɔːl ‖ -kɑːl **~s** z
catch kætʃ △ketʃ **catches** 'kætʃ ɪz △'ketʃ-, -əz
catching 'kætʃ ɪŋ △'ketʃ- **caught** kɔːt ‖ kɑːt
'catch crop
catch-22 ˌkætʃ ˌtwent i 'tuː △ˌketʃ-, △-ˌtwen-
‖ -ˌtwent̮-
catch-all 'kætʃ ɔːl △'ketʃ- ‖ -ɑːl
catch-as-catch-can ˌkætʃ əz ˌkætʃ 'kæn
△ˌketʃ əz ˌketʃ-
catcher 'kætʃ ə △'ketʃ- ‖ -ᵊr **~s** z
catch|fly 'kætʃ |flaɪ △'ketʃ- **~flies** flaɪz
catchi... —see **catchy**
catchment 'kætʃ mənt △'ketʃ-
'catchment ˌarea
catchpenny 'kætʃ ˌpen i △'ketʃ-
catchphras|e 'kætʃ freɪz △'ketʃ- **~es** ɪz əz
Catchpole, c~ 'kætʃ pəʊl →-pɒʊl ‖ -poʊl **~s** z
catchweight 'kætʃ weɪt △'ketʃ- **~s** s
catchword 'kætʃ wɜːd △'ketʃ- ‖ -wɜːd **~s** z
catch|y 'kætʃ |i △'ketʃ- **~ier** i ə ‖ i ᵊr **~iest**
i ɪst i ᵊst
cate keɪt **cates** keɪts
catechesis ˌkæt ɪ 'kiːs ɪs -ə-, §-əs ‖ ˌkæt̮-
catechis... —see **catechiz...**
catechism 'kæt ə ˌkɪz əm -ɪ- ‖ 'kæt̮- **~s** z
catechist 'kæt ək ɪst -ɪk-, §-əst ‖ 'kæt̮- **~s** s
catechiz|e 'kæt ə kaɪz -ɪ- ‖ 'kæt̮- **~ed** d **~er/s**
ə/z ‖ ᵊr/z **~es** ɪz əz **~ing** ɪŋ
catechu 'kæt ə tʃuː -ɪ-, -ʃu- ‖ 'kæt̮-
catechumen ˌkæt ə 'kjuːm en -ɪ-, -ɪn, -ən
‖ ˌkæt̮- **~s** z
categori... —see **category**

categorial ˌkæt ə 'gɔːr i əl ◄ ˌ-ɪ- ‖ ˌkæt̮- -'goʊr-
~ly i
categoric ˌkæt ə 'gɒr ɪk ◄ -ɪ-
‖ ˌkæt̮ ə 'gɔːr ɪk ◄ -'gɑːr-
categorical ˌkæt ə 'gɒr ɪk ᵊl ◄ ˌ-ɪ-
‖ ˌkæt̮ ə 'gɔːr ɪk ᵊl ◄ -'gɑːr- **~ly** i
ˌcate,gorical de'nial
categoris... —see **categoriz...**
categorization ˌkæt ɪg ər ˌaɪ 'zeɪʃ ᵊn ɪˈ--
‖ ˌkæt̮ ɪg ər ə-
categoriz|e 'kæt ɪg ə raɪz ˈ-əg- ‖ 'kæt̮- **~ed** d
~es ɪz əz **~ing** ɪŋ
categor|y 'kæt əg ər ˌi ˈ-ɪg- ‖ 'kæt̮ ə gɔːr ˌi
-goʊr- **(*) ~ies** iz
catenar|y kə 'tiːn ər ˌi ‖ 'kæt ᵊn er ˌi **(*) ~ies**
iz
cate|nate v 'kæt ɪ |neɪt -ə-; -ᵊn eɪt
‖ 'kæt ᵊn eɪt **~nated** neɪt ɪd -əd ‖ neɪt̮ əd
~nates neɪts **~nating** neɪt ɪŋ ‖ neɪt̮ ɪŋ
catenation ˌkæt ɪ 'neɪʃ ᵊn -ə-; -ᵊn 'eɪʃ-
‖ ˌkæt ᵊn 'eɪʃ ᵊn **~s** z
cater, Cater 'keɪt ə ‖ 'keɪt̮ ᵊr **~ed** d **catering**
'keɪt ᵊr ɪŋ ‖ 'keɪt̮ ᵊr ɪŋ **~s** z
cater-cornered ˌkæt ə 'kɔːn əd ◄
‖ ˌkæt̮ ə 'kɔːrn ᵊrd ◄ -i-, -ᵊr-, '·· , · ·
caterer 'keɪt ᵊr ə ‖ 'keɪt̮ ᵊr ᵊr **~s** z
Caterham 'keɪt ᵊr əm ‖ 'keɪt̮ ᵊr hæm
Caterina ˌkæt ə 'riːn ə ‖ ˌkæt̮-
caterpillar 'kæt ə pɪl ə ‖ 'kæt̮ ᵊr pɪl ᵊr **~s** z
caterwaul 'kæt ə wɔːl ‖ 'kæt̮ ᵊr wɔːl -wɑːl **~ed**
d **~ing** ɪŋ **~s** z
Catesby 'keɪts bi
catfight 'kæt faɪt **~s** s
catfish 'kæt fɪʃ **~es** ɪz əz
catfood 'kæt fuːd
Catford 'kæt fəd ‖ -fᵊrd
catgut 'kæt gʌt
Cath kæθ **Cath's** kæθs —but St Catherine's
College, Cambridge, is colloquially known as
kæts
Cathar 'kæθ ə -ɑː ‖ -ɑːr **~s** z
Catharine 'kæθ ᵊr ˌɪn ən
Catharism 'kæθ ə ˌrɪz əm
Catharist 'kæθ ər ɪst §-əst **~s** s
cathars|is kə 'θɑːs |ɪs kæ-, §-əs ‖ -'θɑːrs- **~es**
iːz
cathartic kə 'θɑːt ɪk kæ- ‖ -'θɑːrt̮- **~s** s
Cathay 'China' ₍ᵢ₎kæ 'θeɪ kə-
ˌCathay Pa'cific tdmk, · , · · ·˙·
Cathays place in SGlam kə 'teɪz
Cathcart 'kæθ kɑːt ˌ·˙· ‖ -kɑːrt —The place in
Strathclyde is ˌ·˙·
cathedra kə 'θiːdr ə -'θedr-, -'tedr-
cathedral kə 'θiːdr əl **~s** z
Cather 'kæð ə ‖ -ᵊr
Catherine, c~ 'kæθ ᵊr ˌɪn ən **~'s** z
'catherine wheel
Catherwood 'kæθ ə wʊd 'kæð- ‖ -ᵊr-
catheter 'kæθ ɪt ə -ət- ‖ 'kæθ ət̮ ᵊr 'kæθt ᵊr **~s**
z
catheteris... —see **catheteriz...**
catheterization ˌkæθ ɪt ˌər aɪ 'zeɪʃ ᵊn ˌət ˌ, -ɪˈ--
‖ ˌkæθ ət̮ ᵊr ə- ˌkæθt ᵊr əˈ--

catheteriz|e 'kæθ ɪt ə raɪz '·ət- ‖ 'kæθ ət-
  'kæθ ə raɪz **~ed d ~es** ɪz əz **~ing** ɪŋ
cathexis kæ 'θeks ɪs kə-, §-əs
Cathleen 'kæθ liːn ˌ·'·
cathode 'kæθ əʊd ‖ -oʊd **~s** z
  ˌcathode 'ray
cathode-ray tube ˌkæθ əʊd 'reɪ tjuːb →-tʃuːb
  ‖ -oʊd 'reɪ tuːb -tjuːb
cathodic kæ 'θɒd ɪk kə-, -'θəʊd- ‖ -'θɑːd-
catholic, C~ 'kæθ lɪk 'kæθ əl ɪk, §'kæːθ- **~s** s
Catholicism, c~ kə 'θɒl ə ˌsɪz əm -ɪ- ‖ -'θɑːl-
catholicity, C~ ˌkæθ ə 'lɪs ət i -ɪt i ‖ -ət i
cat|house 'kæt |haʊs **~houses** haʊz ɪz -əz
Cathrine 'kæθ rɪn -rən
Cathy 'kæθ i
Catiline 'kæt ə laɪn -ɪ-, -əl aɪn ‖ 'kæt əl aɪn
cation 'kæt ˌaɪ ən ‖ 'kæt- **~s** z
catkin 'kæt kɪn §-kən **~s** z
Catling, c~ 'kæt lɪŋ
catmint 'kæt mɪnt **~s** s
catnap 'kæt næp **~s** s
catnip 'kæt nɪp **~s** s
Cato 'keɪt əʊ ‖ 'keɪt oʊ **~'s** z
Caton 'keɪt ᵊn
cat-o'-nine tails ˌkæt ə 'naɪn teᵊlz ‖ ˌkæt-
Catrina kə 'triːn ə
Catrine 'kætr iːn
Catriona kə 'triːˌən ə kæ-; -'triːn ə;
  ˌkætr i 'əʊn ə ‖ -'oʊn-
CAT scan 'kæt skæn ‖ -ᵊr **~er/s** ə/z ‖ ᵊr/z **~s** z
cat's-ear 'kæts ɪə ‖ -ɪr **~s** z
cat's-eye, Catseye *tdmk* 'kæts aɪ **~s** z
Catskill 'kæts kɪl **~s** z
cat's-paw 'kæts pɔː ‖ -pɑː **~s** z
catsuit 'kæt suːt -sjuːt **~s** s
catsup 'kæts əp 'ketʃ-, 'kætʃ- —*see also*
  ketchup **~s** s
cattail 'kæt teᵊl **~s** z
Catterick 'kæt ᵊr ɪk ‖ 'kæt ər ɪk
catter|y 'kæt ər |i ‖ 'kæt- **~ies** iz
cattish 'kæt ɪʃ ‖ 'kæt ɪʃ **~ly** li **~ness** nəs nɪs
cattle 'kæt ᵊl ‖ 'kæt ᵊl
  'cattle cake; 'cattle grid; 'cattle truck
cattle|man 'kæt ᵊl mən -mæn ‖ 'kæt- **~men**
  mən men
cattleya 'kæt li ə **~s** z
Catto 'kæt əʊ ‖ 'kæt oʊ
Cotton 'kæt ᵊn
catt|y 'kæt |i ‖ 'kæt |i **~ier** i ə ‖ i ᵊr **~iest** i ɪst
  i əst **~ily** ɪ li ᵊl i ‖ ᵊl i **~iness** i nəs -nɪs
catty-corner 'kæt i ˌkɔːn ə ‖ 'kæt i ˌkɔːrn ᵊr
Catullus kə 'tʌl əs
catwalk 'kæt wɔːk ‖ -wɑːk **~s** s
Caucasian kɔː 'keɪz iˌən -'keɪʒ-, -'keɪʒ ᵊn
  ‖ kɔː- 'keɪʒ ᵊn kɑː-, -'kæʒ- **~s** z
Caucasoid 'kɔːk ə sɔɪd -zɔɪd ‖ 'kɑːk-
Caucasus 'kɔːk əs əs ‖ 'kɑːk-
caucus 'kɔːk əs ‖ 'kɑːk- **~es** ɪz əz
caudal 'kɔːd ᵊl ‖ 'kɑːd- **~ly** i
caudate 'kɔːd eɪt ‖ 'kɑːd-
caudillo kɔː 'diːl jəʊ kaʊ-, -'dɪl əʊ
  ‖ kaʊ 'diː joʊ -'dɪl· —*Sp* [kau 'ði ʎo, -jo] **~s**
  z

Caudine 'kɔːd aɪn ‖ 'kɑːd-
caudle, C~ 'kɔːd ᵊl ‖ 'kɑːd- **~s** z
caught kɔːt ‖ kɑːt
caul kɔːl ‖ kɑːl (= *call*) **~s** z
cauldron 'kɔːldr ən 'kɒldr- ‖ 'kɑːldr- **~s** z
Caulfield 'kɔːl fiːᵊld 'kɔː- ‖ 'kɑːl-, 'kɔː-
cauliflower 'kɒl i ˌflaʊ ə ‖ 'kɑːl i ˌflaʊ ᵊr
  'kɔːl- **~s** z
  ˌcauliˌflower 'cheese; ˌcauliˌflower 'ear
caulk kɔːk ‖ kɑːk **caulked** kɔːkt ‖ kɑːkt
  caulking 'kɔːk ɪŋ ‖ 'kɑːk- **caulks** kɔːks
  ‖ kɑːks
Caunce *(i)* kɔːnts ‖ kɑːnts; *(ii)* kɒnts ‖ kɑːnts
causal 'kɔːz ᵊl ‖ 'kɑːz- **~ly** i
causalit|y kɔː 'zæl ət |i -ɪt- ‖ -ət |i kɑː- **~ies** iz
causation kɔː 'zeɪʃ ᵊn ‖ kɑː- **~s** z
causative 'kɔːz ət ɪv ‖ -ət- 'kɑːz- **~ly** li **~s** z
cause kɔːz ‖ kɑːz **caused** kɔːzd ‖ kɑːzd **causes**
  'kɔːz ɪz -əz ‖ 'kɑːz- **causing** 'kɔːz ɪŋ ‖ 'kɑːz-
  —*See also phrases with this word*
cause celebre, cause célèbre ˌkəʊz sə 'leb
  ˌkɔːz-, -se-, -sɪ-, ˌ·'·rə ‖ ˌkɔːz sə 'leb rə ˌkɑːz-,
  ˌkoʊz- —*Fr* [koz se lɛbʁ]
causerie 'kəʊz ər i ‖ ˌkoʊz ə 'riː —*Fr* [koz ʁi]
  ~s z
causeway 'kɔːz weɪ ‖ 'kɑːz- **~s** z
caustic 'kɔːst ɪk 'kɒst- ‖ 'kɑːst- **~ally** ᵊl i **~s** s
causticity kɔː 'stɪs ət i kɒ-, -ɪt- ‖ -ət i kɑː-
Caute kəʊt ‖ koʊt
cauteri... —*see* **cautery**
cauteris... —*see* **cauteriz...**
cauterization ˌkɔːt ər aɪ 'zeɪʃ ᵊn -ɪ'·-
  ‖ ˌkɔːt ər ə- ˌkɑːt- **~s** z
cauteriz|e 'kɔːt ə raɪz ‖ 'kɔːt- 'kɑːt- **~ed d ~es**
  ɪz əz **~ing** ɪŋ
cauter|y 'kɔːt ər |i ‖ 'kɔːt- 'kɑːt- **~ies** iz
Cauthen 'kɔːθ ᵊn ‖ 'kɑːθ-
caution 'kɔːʃ ᵊn ‖ 'kɑːʃ- **~ed d ~ing** ɪŋ **~s** z
cautionary 'kɔːʃ ᵊn ər i -ᵊn ər i ‖ 'kɔːʃ ə ner i
  'kɑːʃ-
cautious 'kɔːʃ əs ‖ 'kɑːʃ- **~ly** li **~ness** nəs nɪs
cava 'kɑːv ə —*Sp* ['ka βa]
Cavafy kə 'væf i ‖ -'vɑːf i —*Greek* Kaváfis
  [ka 'va fis]
cavalcade ˌkæv ᵊl 'keɪd ◂ '···**~s** z
cavalier ˌkæv ə 'lɪə ◂ ‖ -'lɪᵊr **~ly** li **~s** z
cavalla kə 'væl ə **~s** z
Cavalleria Rusticana
  ˌkæv əl ə 'riːˌə ˌrʊst ɪ 'kɑːn ə kə ˌvæl-, -ˌrʌst-
  —*It* [ka val le 'riː a ʁus ti 'kaː na]
cavall|y kə 'væl |i **~ies** iz
caval|ry 'kæv ᵊl |ri **~ries** riz
cavalry|man 'kæv ᵊl ri |mən -mæn **~men** mən
  men
Cavan 'kæv ᵊn
Cavanagh *(i)* 'kæv ən ə, *(ii)* kə 'væn ə
cavatina ˌkæv ə 'tiːn ə ‖ ˌkɑːv-
cave *n 'watch'* 'keɪv i
cave *n, v 'hollow'* keɪv **caved** keɪvd **caves**
  keɪvz **caving** 'keɪv ɪŋ
  'cave ˌpainting
cave *interj* ˌkeɪ 'viː 'keɪv i
Cave *name* keɪv

caveat ˈkæv i æt ˈkeɪv-, -ət ‖ ˈkɑːv i ɑːt ˈkæv-, -æt **~s** s
ˌcaveat ˈemptor ˈempt ɔː -ə ‖ -ɔːr -ᵊr
cave-in ˈkeɪv ɪn **~s** z
Cavell (i) ˈkæv ᵊl; (ii) kə ˈvel —Nurse Edith C~ was (i).
cave|man ˈkeɪv |mæn **~men** men
Cavendish, c~ ˈkæv ᵊnd ɪʃ
caver ˈkeɪv ə ‖ -ᵊr **~s** z
cavern ˈkæv ᵊn ‖ -ᵊrn **~ed** d **~ing** ɪŋ **~s** z
cavernous ˈkæv ən əs ‖ -ᵊrn- **~ly** li
Caversham ˈkæv əʃ əm ‖ -ᵊrʃ-
cavi... —see **cavy**

CAVIAR

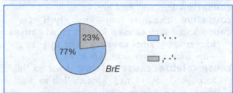

caviar, caviare ˈkæv i ɑː ˌ·ˈ· ‖ -ɑːr ˈkɑːv- **~s** z
— Preference poll, BrE: ˈ··· 77%, ˌ·ˈ· 23%.
cavil ˈkæv ᵊl -ɪl **~ed, ~led** d **~ing, ~ling** ɪŋ **~s** z
cavitation ˌkæv ɪ ˈteɪʃ ᵊn -ə- **~s** z
cavit|y ˈkæv ət |i -ɪt- ‖ -əţ |i **~ies** iz
ca|vort kə |ˈvɔːt ‖ -|ˈvɔːrt **~vorted** ˈvɔːt ɪd -əd ‖ ˈvɔːrţ əd **~vorting** ˈvɔːt ɪŋ ‖ ˈvɔːrţ ɪŋ **~vorts** ˈvɔːts ‖ ˈvɔːrts
Cavour kə ˈvʊə -ˈvɔː ‖ -ˈvʊᵊr —It [ka ˈvuːr]
cavy ˈkeɪv i **cavies** ˈkeɪv iz
caw kɔː ‖ kɑː **cawed** kɔːd ‖ kɑːd **cawing** ˈkɔːˑ ɪŋ ‖ ˈkɔː- ɪŋ ˈkɑː- **caws** kɔːz ‖ kɑːz (= cause)
Cawdor ˈkɔːd ə -ɔː ‖ -ᵊr ˈkɑːd-, -ɔːr
Cawdrey ˈkɔːdr i ‖ ˈkɑːdr-
Cawley ˈkɔːl i ‖ ˈkɑːl-
Cawnpore ˌkɔːn ˈpɔː ‖ ˈkɔːn pɔːr ˈkɑːn-
Cawood ˈkeɪ wʊd
Caxton ˈkækst ən
cay kiː keɪ **cays** kiːz keɪz
cayenne, C~ ₍ᵢ₎keɪ ˈen ₍ᵢ₎kaɪ- —Fr [ka jɛn]
Cayley ˈkeɪl i
cayman, C~ ˈkeɪm ən **~s** z
ˈCayman ˌIslands ‖ ˌ·ˈ··
Caymanian keɪ ˈmæn i ən **~s** z
Cayuga ki ˈuːg ə keɪ-, kaɪ- **~s** z
Cazenove ˈkæz ə nəʊv -ɪ- ‖ -noʊv —but the road in north London is usually ˈkeɪz nəʊv
CB ˌsiː ˈbiː **~er/s** ə/z ‖ ᵊr/z
CBE ˌsiː biː ˈiː
CBeebies ˌsiː ˈbiːb iz
CBS ˌsiː biː ˈes ◄
CD ˌsiː ˈdiː **~s** z
ˌCˈD ˌplayer
C. diff. ˌsiː ˈdɪf
CD-R ˌsiː diː ˈɑː ‖ -ˈɑːr **~s** z
CD-ROM ˌsiː diː ˈrɒm ‖ -ˈrɑːm **~s** z
CD-RW ˌsiː diː ɑː ˈdʌb ᵊl juː ‖ -ˈɑːrˈ- -jə; -ˈdʌb jə **~s** z

céad míle fáilte ˌkeɪd ˌmiːl ə ˈfɔːltʃ ə ‖ -ˈfɑːltʃ- —Irish [ˌkʲeːd̪ ˌmʲiːlʲə ˈfɑːlʲ tʲə]
ceanothus ˌsiːˑ ə ˈnəʊθ əs ‖ -ˈnoʊθ- **~es** ɪz əz
cease siːs **ceased** siːst **ceases** ˈsiːs ɪz -əz **ceasing** ˈsiːs ɪŋ
cease-fire ˈsiːs ˌfaɪ ə ˌ·ˈ·· ‖ -ˌfaɪ ᵊr **~s** z
ceaseless ˈsiːs ləs -lɪs **~ly** li
Ceausescu tʃaʊ ˈʃesk uː -ˈtʃesk-, -juː —Romanian Ceauşescu [tʃau ˈʃes ku]
cecal ˈsiːk ᵊl
Cecil (i) ˈses ᵊl -ɪl, (ii) ˈsiːs-, (iii) ˈsɪs- —In BrE usually (i), though the English landed family is (iii). In AmE usually (ii).
Cecile siː ˈiːᵊl -ɪl; se ˈsiːᵊl ‖ se ˈsiːᵊl
Cecilia sə ˈsiːl i ə sɪ-, -ˈsɪl- ‖ -ˈsiːl jə -ˈsɪl-
Cecily (i) ˈsɪs əl i -ɪl-, (ii) ˈses-
cecum ˈsiːk əm **ceca** ˈsiːk ə
cedar ˈsiːd ə ‖ -ᵊr (= seeder) **~s** z
ˌCedar ˈRapids
cedarwood ˈsiːd ə wʊd ‖ -ᵊr- **~s** z
cede siːd (= seed) **ceded** ˈsiːd ɪd -əd **cedes** siːdz **ceding** ˈsiːd ɪŋ
cedi ˈsiːd i (= seedy) **~s** z
cedilla sə ˈdɪl ə sɪ- **~s** z
Cedric (i) ˈsedr ɪk, (ii) ˈsiːdr ɪk —Usually (i) in BrE, (ii) in AmE
Ceefax ˈsiːˑ fæks
Cefn ˈkev ᵊn
ceili, ceilidh ˈkeɪl i **~s** z
ceiling ˈsiːl ɪŋ (usually = sealing) **~s** z
Ceinwen ˈkaɪn wen —Welsh [ˈkəin wen]
celadon ˈsel əd ən -ə dɒn ‖ -ə dɑːn
ˈceladon ware
celandine ˈsel ən daɪn -diːn **~s** z
Celanese tdmk ˌsel ə ˈniːz
-cele siːᵊl — hydrocele ˈhaɪdr ə siːᵊl
celeb sə ˈleb sɪ- **~s** z
Celebes sə ˈliːb iz se-, sɪ-, -ˈleɪb-; ˈsel ɪ biːz, -ə-
celebrant ˈsel əb rənt -ɪb- **~s** s
cele|brate ˈsel ə |breɪt -ɪ- **~brated** breɪt ɪd -əd ‖ breɪţ əd **~brates** breɪts **~brating** breɪt ɪŋ ‖ breɪţ ɪŋ
celebration ˌsel ə ˈbreɪʃ ᵊn -ɪ- **~s** z
celebrator ˈsel ə breɪt ə ˈ·ɪ- ‖ -breɪţ ᵊr **~s** z
celebratory ˌsel ə ˈbreɪt ər i ◄ ˌ·ɪ-, ˈ·····, ˈ·ˑbrət ᵊr i ‖ ˈsel əb rə tɔːr i sə ˈleb-, -toʊr i
celebrit|y sə ˈleb rət |i sɪ-, -rɪt- ‖ -rəţ |i **~ies** iz
celeriac sə ˈler i æk sɪ-
celerity sə ˈler ət i sɪ-, -ɪt- ‖ -əţ i
celery ˈsel ər i
celesta sə ˈlest ə sɪ- **~s** z
Celeste, c~ sə ˈlest sɪ- **~'s, ~s** s
celestial sə ˈlest i əl sɪ- ‖ -ˈles tʃəl →-ˈleʃ- **~ly** li
celestite ˈsel ə staɪt -ɪ-; sə ˈlest aɪt, sɪ-
Celia ˈsiːl i ə
celiac ˈsiːl i æk
celibacy ˈsel əb əs i ˈ·ɪb-
celibate ˈsel əb ət -ɪb-, -ɪt **~s** s
Celine, Céline se ˈliːn sə-, sɪ-, seɪ-
cell sel (= sell) **celled** seld **cells** selz
cell|ar ˈsel |ə ‖ -|ᵊr (= seller) **~ared** əd ‖ ᵊrd **~aring** ər ɪŋ **~ars** əz ‖ ᵊrz
cellarage ˈsel ər ɪdʒ

C

cellarer 'sel ər ə ‖ -ᵊr ər ~s z
cellaret, cellarette ˌsel ə 'ret ~s s
cellar|man 'sel ə mən -mæn ‖ -ᵊr- ~men mən
   men
Cellini tʃe 'liːn i tʃɪ-, tʃə- —*It* [tʃel 'liː ni]
cellist 'tʃel ɪst §-əst ~s s
cellmate 'sel meɪt ~s s
Cellnet *tdmk* 'sel net
cello 'tʃel əʊ ‖ -oʊ ~s z
cellophane, C~ *tdmk* 'sel ə feɪn
cellphone 'sel fəʊn ‖ -foʊn ~s z
cellular 'sel jʊl ə -jəl- ‖ -jəl ᵊr
cellularity ˌsel ju 'lær ət i ˌjə-, -ɪt i
   ‖ -jə 'lær ət̬ i -'ler-
cellule 'sel juːl ~s z
cellulite 'sel ju laɪt -jə-, ˌ‧ ‧'liːt ‖ -jə-
celluloid, C~ *tdmk* 'sel ju lɔɪd -jə- ‖ -jə- -ə-
cellulose 'sel ju ləʊs -jə-, -ləʊz ‖ -jə loʊs
Celsius 'sels i̯əs ‖ 'selʃ əs
celt *'stone implement'* selt **celts** selts
Celt (i) kelt, (ii) selt **Celts** (i) kelts, (ii) selts
   —*In England and Wales usually (i), in
   Scotland (ii)*
Celtic (i) 'kelt ɪk, (ii) 'selt ɪk —*The sea is (i),
   the football, baseball and basketball teams are
   (ii). The languages are usually (i).*
Cemaes Bay ˌkem aɪs 'beɪ
cembalo 'tʃem bə ləʊ ‖ -loʊ ~s z
cement *n, v* sə 'ment sɪ- **cemented**
   sə 'ment ɪd sɪ-, -əd ‖ -'ment̬ əd **cementing**
   sə 'ment ɪŋ sɪ- ‖ -'ment̬ ɪŋ **cements**
   sə 'ments sɪ-
   ce'ment ˌmixer
cementation ˌsiːm en 'teɪʃ ᵊn -ən-
cementite sə 'ment aɪt sɪ-
cementum sə 'ment əm sɪ- ‖ -'ment̬-
cemeter|y 'sem ətr ‖i -ɪtr-; '‧ət̬ ᵊr ‖i, '‧ɪt̬
   ‖ 'sem ə ter ‖i ~ies iz
Cemmaes ˌkem aɪs
Cenci 'tʃentʃ i —*It* ['tʃen tʃi]
CEng ˌsiː 'endʒ
Cenis sə 'niː se- —*Fr* [sə ni]
cenobite 'siːn əʊ baɪt 'sen- ‖ -ə- ~s s
cenotaph, C~ 'sen ə tɑːf -tæf ‖ -tæf ~s s
Cenozoic ˌsiːn əʊ 'zəʊ ɪk ◂ ‖ -ə 'zoʊ- ˌsen-
cense senˢs (= *sense*) **censed** senˢst **censes**
   'senˢs ɪz -əz **censing** 'senˢs ɪŋ
censer 'senˢs ə ‖ -ᵊr (= *censor, sensor*) ~s z
cens|or 'senˢs |ə ‖ -|ᵊr ~ored əd ‖ ᵊrd ~oring
   ər ɪŋ ~ors əz ‖ ᵊrz
censorial sen 'sɔːr i̯əl ‖ -'soʊr-
censorious sen 'sɔːr i̯əs ‖ -'soʊr- ~ly li ~ness
   nəs nɪs
censorship 'senˢs ə ʃɪp ‖ -ᵊr-
censurab|le 'senˢʃ ər əb |ᵊl ~ly li
censure 'senˢʃ ə 'senˢs jʊə ‖ 'senˢʃ ᵊr **censured**
   'senˢʃ əd 'senˢs jʊəd ‖ 'senˢʃ ᵊrd **censures**
   'senˢʃ əz 'senˢs jʊəz ‖ 'senˢʃ ᵊrz **censuring**
   'senˢʃ ər ɪŋ 'senˢs jʊər ɪŋ
census 'senˢs əs ~es ɪz əz
cent sent (= *sent*) **cents** sents
cental 'sent ᵊl ~s z
centaur 'sent ɔː ‖ -ɔːr ~s z

Centaur|us sen 'tɔːr |əs ~i aɪ iː
centaury 'sent ɔːr i
centavo sen 'tɑːv əʊ ‖ -oʊ —*Sp* [sen 'ta βo]
   ~s z
centenarian ˌsent ɪ 'neər i̯ən ˌ‧ə-
   ‖ ˌsent ᵊn 'er- ~s z
centenar|y ₍₁₎sen 'tiːn ər ‖i sᵊn-, -'ten- ‖ -'ten-
   'sent ᵊn er ‖i ~ies iz
centennial sen 'ten i̯əl sᵊn- ~ly i ~s z
center 'sent ə ‖ 'sent̬ ᵊr ~ed d **centering**
   'sent ər ɪŋ →'sentr ɪŋ ‖ 'sent̬ ər ɪŋ ~s z
centerboard 'sent ə bɔːd ‖ 'sent̬ ᵊr bɔːrd
   -boʊrd ~s z
centerfold 'sent ə fəʊld →-foʊld
   ‖ 'sent̬ ᵊr foʊld ~s z
centerpiec|e 'sent ə piːs ‖ 'sent̬ ᵊr- ~es ɪz əz
centesimal sen 'tes əm ᵊl -ɪm- ~ly i
centi- ˌsent i -ə ‖ ˌsent̬ ə ˌsaɪnt̬ ə
centigrade 'sent ɪ greɪd -ə- ‖ 'sent̬ ə- ~s z
centigram, centigramme 'sent ɪ græm -ə-
   ‖ 'sent̬ ə- ˌsaɪnt̬- ~s z
centiliter, centilitre 'sent ɪ ˌliːt ə -ə-
   ‖ 'sent̬ ə ˌliːt̬ ᵊr 'saɪnt̬- ~s z
centime 'sɒnt iːm 'saɪnt- ‖ 'saɪnt- 'sent- —*Fr*
   [sɑ̃ tim] ~s z
centimeter, centimetre 'sent ɪ ˌmiːt ə -ə-
   ‖ 'sent̬ ə ˌmiːt̬ ᵊr 'saɪnt̬- ~s z
centimo 'sent ɪ məʊ -ə- ‖ -moʊ ~s z —*Sp*
   céntimo ['θen ti mo, 'sen-]
centipede 'sent ɪ piːd -ə- ‖ 'sent̬ ə- ~s z
centner 'sent nə ‖ -nᵊr —*Ger* Zentner
   ['tsɛnt nɐ] ~s z
cento 'sent əʊ ‖ -oʊ ~s z
central, C~ 'sentr əl
   ˌCentral 'Africa; ˌCentral ˌAfrican
   Re'public; ˌcentral 'heating; ˌcentral
   'nervous ˌsystem; ˌcentral 'processing
   ˌunit; ˌcentral ˌreser'vation; 'Central
   Time
centralis... —*see* **centraliz...**
centralism 'sentr ə ˌlɪz əm
centralist 'sentr əl ɪst -əst
centralistic ˌsentr ə 'lɪst ɪk ◂
centralit|y sen 'træl ət i -ɪt- ‖ -ət̬ i ~ies iz
centralization ˌsentr əl aɪ 'zeɪʃ ᵊn -ɪ'‧- ‖ -əl ə-
centraliz|e 'sentr ə laɪz ~ed d ~er/s ə/z ‖ ᵊr/z
   ~es ɪz əz ~ing ɪŋ
centrally 'sentr əl i
centre 'sent ə ‖ 'sent̬ ᵊr ~d d **centring**
   'sent ər ɪŋ ‖ 'sent̬ ər ɪŋ ~s z
   'centre bit; ˌcentre 'forward
centreboard 'sent ə bɔːd ‖ 'sent̬ ᵊr bɔːrd
   -boʊrd ~s z
centrefold 'sent ə fəʊld →-foʊld
   ‖ 'sent̬ ᵊr foʊld ~s z
centrepiec|e 'sent ə piːs ‖ 'sent̬ ᵊr- ~es ɪz əz
-centric 'sentr ɪk — **heliocentric**
   ˌhiːl i̯əʊ 'sentr ɪk ◂ ‖ -oʊ 'sentr-
Centrica *tdmk* 'sentr ɪk ə
centrifugal ˌsentr ɪ 'fjuːg ᵊl ◂ -ə-;
   sen 'trɪf jʊg ᵊl, -jəg- ‖ sen 'trɪf jəg ᵊl -əg- ~ly
   i
centrifugation ˌsentr ɪ fju 'geɪʃ ᵊn ˌ‧ə- ‖ -fjə'‧--

centrifug|e 'sentr ɪ fjuːdʒ -ə-, -fjuːʒ **~ed** d **~es**
ɪz əz **~ing** ɪŋ
centripetal sen 'trɪp ɪt ³l -ət-; ˌsentr ɪ 'piːt ³l,
-ə- ‖ -ət̬ ³l **~ly** i
centrist 'sentr ɪst §-əst **~s** s
centro- *comb. form*
with stress-neutral suffix |sentr əʊ ‖ -ə
— **centrosome** 'sentr əʊ səʊm ‖ -ə soʊm
centroid 'sentr ɔɪd **~s** z
centromere 'sentr əʊ mɪə ‖ -ə mɪr **~s** z
centum 'kent əm
centupl|e 'sent jʊp ³l -jəp-; →'sentʃ ʊp-, -əp-;
sen 'tjuːp- ‖ sen 'tuːp ³l -'tjuːp-, -'tʌp- **~ed** d
~es z **~ing** ɪŋ
centurion sen 'tjʊər i̯ ən -'tʃʊər-, -'tjɔːr-, -'tʃɔːr-
‖ -'tʊr- -'tjʊr- **~s** z
century 'sentʃ ər i
CEO ˌsiː iː 'əʊ ‖ -'oʊ **~s** z
ceorl tʃeəl ‖ 'tʃer ɔːrl
cep, cèpe sep **ceps, cèpes** seps
cephalic sə 'fæl ɪk sɪ-, ke-, kɪ- —*In words
containing* (-)cephal-, *the medical profession in
Britain generally prefers* k. *The alternative
pronunciation with* s *is nevertheless
widespread, and preferred in AmE.*
Cephalonia ˌkef ə 'ləʊn i̯ ə ˌsef- ‖ -'loʊn-
—*ModGk* Kefallinía [cε fa li 'ni a]
cephalopod 'sef əl ə pɒd ‖ -paːd **~s** z
cephalosporin ˌsef əl əʊ 'spɔːr ɪn ˌkef-, §-ən
‖ -ə 'spɔːr ən -'spoʊr-
cephalothorax ˌsef əl əʊ 'θɔːr æks ‖ -əl ə-
-'θoʊr-
-cephalous 'sef əl əs 'kef- — **autocephalous**
ˌɔːt əʊ 'sef əl əs ◄ ‖ ˌɔːt̬ ə- ˌɑːt-
-cephaly 'kef əl i 'sef- — **microcephaly**
ˌmaɪk rəʊ 'kef əl i -'sef- ‖ ˌ-oʊ-
Cephas 'siːf æs
Cepheid, c~ 'siːf i ɪd 'sef-, §-əd
Cepheus 'siːf juːs 'siːf i̯ əs
cepstral 'keps trəl
cepstrum 'keps trəm **~s** z
ceramic sə 'ræm ɪk sɪ-, kə-, kɪ-, ke- **~s** s
cerastes sə 'ræst iːz sɪ-, se-
Cerberus 'sɜːb ər_əs ‖ 'sɜːb-
cercaria sɜː 'keər i̯ ə sə- ‖ s³r 'ker-
cere sɪə ‖ sɪ³r (= *sere*) **cered** sɪəd ‖ sɪ³rd
cereal 'sɪər i̯ əl ‖ 'sɪr- (= *serial*) **~s** z
cerebell|um ˌser ə 'bel |əm -ɪ- **~a** ə **~ar a** ‖ ³r
Cerebos *tdmk* 'ser ə bɒs -ɪ- ‖ -baːs -boʊs
cerebra sə 'riːb rə sɪ-; 'ser əb rə, -ɪb-
cerebral 'ser əb rəl -ɪ-; sə 'riːb rəl, sɪ- **~ly** i
cere|brate 'ser ə |breɪt -ɪ- **~brated** breɪt ɪd
-əd ‖ breɪt̬ əd **~brates** breɪts **~brating**
breɪt ɪŋ ‖ breɪt̬ ɪŋ
cerebration ˌser ə 'breɪʃ ³n -ɪ- **~s** z
cerebrospinal ˌser əb rəʊ 'spaɪn ³l ◄ ˌ-ɪb-;
sə 'riːb- ‖ -əb roʊ-
cerebrovascular ˌser əb rəʊ 'væsk jʊl ə ◄
ˌ-ɪb-, -jəl ə; sə ˌriːb- ‖ -roʊ 'væsk jəl ³r ◄
cerebrum sə 'riːb rəm sɪ-; 'ser əb-, -ɪb-
Ceredig kə 'red ɪg —*Welsh* [ke 're dig]
Ceredigion ˌker ə 'dɪg i ɒn ‖ -aːn —*Welsh*
[ke re 'dig jon]

cerement 'sɪə mənt 'ser ə mənt ‖ 'sɪr- **~s** s
ceremonial ˌser ə 'məʊn i̯ əl ◄ ˌ-ɪ- ‖ -'moʊn-
~ism ˌɪz əm **~ist/s** ɪst/s ə̯st/s **~ly** i
ceremonious ˌser ə 'məʊn i̯ əs ◄ ˌ-ɪ- ‖ -'moʊn-
~ly li **~ness** nəs nɪs
ceremon|y 'ser əm ən |i ˌ-ɪm- ‖ -ə moʊn |i
~ies iz
Ceres 'sɪər iːz ‖ 'sɪr-
Cerf sɜːf ‖ sɜːf
Ceri 'ker i
cerise sə 'riːz sɪ-, -'riːs
cerium 'sɪər i̯ əm ‖ 'sɪr-
CERN sɜːn ‖ sɜːn
Cerne Abbas ˌsɜːn 'æb əs ‖ ˌsɜːn-
Cerrig-y-Drudion ˌker ɪg ə 'drɪd jɒn ‖ -jaːn
-jɔːn
cert sɜːt ‖ sɜːt **certs** sɜːts ‖ sɜːts
certain 'sɜːt ³n -ɪn ‖ 'sɜːt-
certainly 'sɜːt ³n li -ɪn- ‖ 'sɜːt-
certain|ty 'sɜːt ³n |ti -ɪn- ‖ 'sɜːt- **~ties** tiz
CertEd ˌsɜːt 'ed ‖ ˌsɜːt-
certes 'sɜːt ɪz -əz, -iːz; sɜːts ‖ 'sɜːt̬ iːz sɜːts
certifiab|le 'sɜːt ɪ faɪ_əb |³l ˌ-ə-, ˌ·'··· ‖ 'sɜːt̬-
~ly li
certifi|cate *v* sə 'tɪf ɪ |keɪt -ə- ‖ s³r- **~cated**
keɪt ɪd -əd ‖ keɪt̬ əd **~cates** keɪts **~cating**
keɪt ɪŋ ‖ keɪt̬ ɪŋ
certificate *n* sə 'tɪf ɪk ət -ək-, -ɪt ‖ s³r- **~s** s
certification ˌsɜːt ɪf ɪ 'keɪʒ ³n ˌ-əf-, -ə'·- ‖ ˌsɜːt̬-
—*Occasionally also* sə ˌtɪf- ‖ s³r-, *but only in
the sense 'certificating', not in the sense
'certifying'*
certi|fy 'sɜːt ɪ |faɪ -ə- ‖ 'sɜːt̬- **~fied** faɪd **~fies**
faɪz **~fying** faɪ ɪŋ
certiorari ˌsɜːt i̯ ə 'reər aɪ ˌsɜːt-, -i ɔː-, -'raːr i
‖ ˌsɜːʃ i̯ ə 'rer i ˌ·ə'··
certitude 'sɜːt ɪ tjuːd -ə-, →-tʃuːd ‖ 'sɜːt̬ ə tuːd
-tjuːd **~s** z
cerulean sə 'ruːl i̯ ən sɪ-
Cerullo sə 'rʊl əʊ se-, -'ruːl- ‖ -oʊ
cerumen sə 'ruːm en sɪ-, -ən
Cervantes sɜː 'vænt iːz -ɪz ‖ s³r- —*Sp*
[θer 'βan tes]
cervelat ˌsɜːv ə 'laːt -'laː, -'læt, '···
‖ 'sɜːv ə laːt -laː, -læt
cervical sə 'vaɪk ³l sɜː-; 'sɜːv ɪk ³l ‖ 'sɜːv ɪk ³l
cervices sə 'vaɪs iːz sɜː-; 'sɜːv ɪ siːz, -ə- ‖ s³r-
'sɜːv ə siːz
cervine 'sɜːv aɪn ‖ 'sɜːv-
cervix 'sɜːv ɪks ‖ 'sɜːv- **~es** ɪz əz
Cesar, César 'seɪz ɑː ‖ seɪ 'zaːr —*Fr* [se zaːʁ]
cesarean, cesarian sɪ 'zeər i̯ ən sə-, siː-
‖ -'zer- -'zær-
Cesarewitch sɪ 'zær ə wɪtʃ sə-, -ɪ- ‖ -'zer-
cesium 'siːz i̯ əm ‖ 'siːs-
cess ses
cessation se 'seɪʃ ³n sɪ-, sə-
cession 'seʃ ³n (= *session*) **~s** z
Cessna *tdmk* 'ses nə **~s, ~'s** z
cesspit 'ses pɪt **~s** s
cesspool 'ses puːl **~s** z
cesta 'sest ə **~s** z
c'est la vie ˌseɪ lɑː 'viː -lə- —*Fr* [sɛ la vi]

cestode 'sest əʊd ‖ -oʊd **~s** z
cestus 'sest əs **~es** ɪz əz
cesur|a sɪ 'zjʊər |ə sə-, siː-, -'zjɔːr-, -'ʒʊər-
‖ -'zʊr- **~ae** iː aɪ **~as** əz
cetacean sɪ 'teɪʃ ᵊn sə-, -'teɪʃ i̯ ən, -'teɪs i̯ ən **~s** z
cetane 'siːt eɪn
   'cetane ˌnumber
ceteris paribus ˌket ə riːs 'pær ɪb əs ˌkeɪt-, ˌset-, -ər ɪs-, -'pɑːr-, -əb-, -ʊs ‖ ˌkeɪt̬ ər əs- -'per-
Ceti 'siːt aɪ
cetological ˌsiːt ə 'lɒdʒ ɪk ᵊl ◂ ‖ ˌsiːt ə 'lɑːdʒ-
cetolog|ist siː 'tɒl ədʒ |ɪst sɪ-, §-əst ‖ -'tɑːl- **~ists** ɪsts §əsts **~y** i
cetrimide 'setr ɪ maɪd -ə-
Cetshwayo ketʃ 'waɪ əʊ ‖ -oʊ —*Zulu* [|ɛ 'tʃwa: jɔ]
Cetus 'siːt əs ‖ 'siːt̬-
cetyl 'siːt ɪl -ᵊl ‖ 'siːt̬ ᵊl
Ceuta 'sjuːt ə 'suːt- ‖ 'seɪ uːt̬ ə —*Sp* ['θeu ta, 'seu-]
Cevennes, Cévennes sɪ 'ven seɪ-, sə- —*Fr* [se vɛn]
ceviche sɪ 'viːtʃ eɪ sə-, seɪ-, -i; seɪ 'viːʃ —*AmSp* [se 'βi tʃe]
Ceylon sɪ 'lɒn sə- ‖ -'lɑːn
Ceylonese ˌsel ə 'niːz ◂ ˌsiːl- ‖ -'niːs
Cezanne, Cézanne sɪ 'zæn seɪ-, sə- ‖ seɪ 'zɑːn —*Fr* [se zan]
cf —*see* **compare**
Chablis, c~ 'ʃæb liː 'ʃɑːb-, -li ‖ ʃæ 'bliː ʃɑː-, ʃə- —*Fr* [ʃa bli]
Chabrier 'ʃæb ri eɪ 'ʃɑːb-; ʃɑː 'briː- ‖ ˌʃɑːb ri 'eɪ —*Fr* [ʃa bʁi je]
Chabrol ʃæ 'brɒl ʃə- ‖ ʃɑː 'brɔʊl —*Fr* [ʃa bʁɔl]
cha-cha 'tʃɑː tʃɑː **~ed** d **cha-chaing** 'tʃɑː tʃɑːʳ ɪŋ ‖ -tʃɑː ɪŋ **~s** z
cha-cha-cha ˌtʃɑː tʃɑː 'tʃɑː
chacma 'tʃæk mə ‖ 'tʃɑːk- **~s** z
chaconne ʃə 'kɒn ʃæ- ‖ ʃɑː 'kɑːn -kɔːn —*Fr* [ʃa kɔn] **~s** z
chacun à son goût ˌʃæk ɜːn ˌɑː sɒŋ 'guː -,æ- ‖ ˌʃɑː ˌkuːn ɑː saːn- -sɔːn'· —*Fr* [ʃa kœ̃ a sɔ̃ gu]
Chad, chad tʃæd
Chadband 'tʃæd bænd →'tʃæb-
Chadburn 'tʃæd bɜːn 'tʃæb- ‖ -bɝːn
Chadderton 'tʃæd ət ən ‖ -ᵊrt ᵊn
Chadian 'tʃæd i̯ ən **~s** z
Chadic 'tʃæd ɪk
chador 'tʃɑːd ɔː 'tʃʌd-, -ə ‖ -ɔːr
Chadwick 'tʃæd wɪk
chaebol 'tʃeɪ bɒl ‖ -bɔːl -bɑːl, -boʊl —*Kor* [tʃɛ bol]
Chaeronea ˌkaɪᵊr ə 'niː̯ ə ˌkɪər-, ˌker-
chaeto- *comb. form*
   with stress-neutral suffix |kiːt əʊ ‖ kiːt̬ ə
   — **chaetopod** 'kiːt əʊ pɒd ‖ 'kiːt̬ ə pɑːd
   with stress-imposing suffix kiː 'tɒ + ‖ -'tɑː +
   — **chaetophorous** kiː 'tɒf ər əs ‖ -'tɑːf-
chafe tʃeɪf **chafed** tʃeɪft **chafes** tʃeɪfs **chafing** 'tʃeɪf ɪŋ

chafer 'tʃeɪf ə ‖ -ᵊr **~s** z
chaff tʃɑːf tʃæf ‖ tʃæf **chaffed** tʃɑːft tʃæft ‖ tʃæft **chaffing** 'tʃɑːf ɪŋ 'tʃæf- ‖ 'tʃæf- **chaffs** tʃɑːfs tʃæfs ‖ tʃæfs
chaffer 'tʃæf ə ‖ -ᵊr **~ed** d **chaffering** 'tʃæf ᵊr ɪŋ **~s** z
Chaffey 'tʃæf i
chaffinch 'tʃæf ɪntʃ **~es** ɪz əz
chafing 'tʃeɪf ɪŋ
   'chafing dish
Chagall ʃæ 'gæl ʃə-, -'gɑːl —*Fr* [ʃa gal] **~s, ~'s** z
Chagas 'ʃɑːg əs —*Port* ['ʃa ɣɐʃ] —*The possessive form* **~'** *has the same pronunciation, or sometimes an extra* ɪz əz
   'Chagas' diˌsease
Chagford 'tʃæg fəd ‖ -fᵊrd
Chagos 'ʃɑːg ɒs 'ʃæg-, 'tʃɑːg-, 'tʃæg-, -əʊs ‖ 'ʃɑːg oʊs -əs
chagrin 'ʃæg rɪn -rən ‖ ʃə 'grɪn (*) **~ed** d
Chagrin 'ʃæg ræ ‖ ʃɑː 'græn —*Fr* [ʃa gʁæ̃]
Chaim haɪm xaɪm —*Hebrew* ['xa jim, xa 'jiːm]
chain, Chain tʃeɪn **chained** tʃeɪnd **chaining** 'tʃeɪn ɪŋ **chains** tʃeɪnz
   'chain gang; 'chain ˌletter; ˌchain link 'fencing; ˌchain re'action; 'chain stitch; 'chain store
chain-link 'tʃeɪn lɪŋk
   ˌchain-link 'fence
chainsaw 'tʃeɪn sɔː ‖ -sɑː **~s** z
chain-smok|e 'tʃeɪn sməʊk ‖ -smoʊk **~ed** t **~er/s** ə/z ‖ ᵊr/z **~es** s **~ing** ɪŋ
chair tʃeə ‖ tʃeᵊr **chaired** tʃeəd ‖ tʃeᵊrd **chairing** 'tʃeər ɪŋ ‖ 'tʃer ɪŋ **chairs** tʃeəz ‖ tʃeᵊrz
   'chair lift
chairbound 'tʃeə baʊnd ‖ 'tʃer-
chair|man 'tʃeə |mən ‖ 'tʃer- **~men** mən men **~manship/s** ʃɪp/s **~person/s** ˌpɜːs ᵊn/z ‖ ˌpɝːs ᵊn/z **~woman** ˌwʊm ən **~women** ˌwɪm ɪn §-ən
chaise ʃeɪz ‖ tʃeɪs **chaises** 'ʃeɪz ɪz -əz; ʃeɪz ‖ 'tʃeɪs əz
   ˌchaise 'longue lɒŋ ‖ lɔːŋ laːŋ —*Fr* [ʃez lɔ̃ːg] —*The plural,* **~(s) longues,** *is pronounced identically to the singular, or sometimes with added* **z***. Particularly in AmE,* longue *is sometimes changed by popular etymology to* lounge.
chakra 'tʃʌk rə 'tʃæk-, 'tʃɑːk-
chalaz|a kə 'leɪz |ə **~ae** iː **~as** əz
Chalcedon 'kæls ɪd ən -əd-; -ɪ dɒn, -ə- ‖ -ə dɑːn
chalcedon|y kæl 'sed ən |i ‖ 'kæls ə doʊn |i **~ies** iz
Chalcidice kæl 'sɪd əs i -ɪs-
Chalcis 'kæls ɪs §-əs
chalcopyrite ˌkælk əʊ 'paɪʳr aɪt ‖ -ə-
Chalde|a kæl 'diː |ə kɔːl- ‖ kɔːl-, kɑːl- **~an/s** ən/z
Chaldee kæl 'diː kɔːl-, '·· ‖ kɔːl-, kɑːl- **~s** z
Chaldon 'tʃɔːld ən 'tʃɒld- ‖ 'tʃɑːld-
chaldron 'tʃɔːldr ən ‖ 'tʃɑːldr- **~s** z

chalet 'ʃæl eɪ -i ‖ ʃæ 'leɪ *(*)* ~**s** z
Chalfont 'tʃæl fɒnt 'tʃælf ᵊnt ‖ -fɑːnt —*locally
also* 'tʃɑːf ᵊnt
chalic|e 'tʃæl ɪs -əs ~**es** ɪz əz
chalk, Chalk tʃɔːk ‖ tʃɑːk **chalked** tʃɔːkt
‖ tʃɑːkt **chalking** 'tʃɔːk ɪŋ ‖ 'tʃɑːk- **chalks**
tʃɔːks ‖ tʃɑːks
chalkboard 'tʃɔːk bɔːd ‖ -bɔːrd 'tʃɑːk-, -boʊrd
~**s** z
Chalker 'tʃɔːk ə ‖ -ᵊr 'tʃɑːk-
chalkface 'tʃɔːk feɪs ‖ 'tʃɑːk-
chalkstripe 'tʃɔːk straɪp ‖ 'tʃɑːk- ~**s** s
chalk|y 'tʃɔːk |i ‖ 'tʃɑːk- ~**ier** i ə ‖ i ᵊr ~**iest**
i ɪst i əst ~**iness** i nəs i nɪs
challah 'hɑːl ə xɑː 'lɑː- ~**s** z **challoth** xɑː 'lɒt
‖ -'loʊt
challeng|e 'tʃæl ɪndʒ -əndʒ ~**ed** d ~**es** ɪz əz
~**ing/ly** ɪŋ /li
challenger, C~ 'tʃæl ɪndʒ ə -əndʒ- ‖ -ᵊr ~**s** z
Challenor 'tʃæl ən ə -ɪn- ‖ -ᵊr
Challes, Challis 'tʃæl ɪs -əs
Challock 'tʃɒl ək ‖ 'tʃɑːl-
Challoner 'tʃæl ən ə ‖ -ᵊr
Chalmers *(i)* 'tʃɑːm əz 'tʃɑːlm- ‖ -ᵊrz,
(ii) 'tʃælm-
chalybeate kə 'lɪb i ət ɪt, -eɪt ‖ -'liːb-
Cham *ethnonym* tʃæm **Chams** tʃæmz
chamber 'tʃeɪm bə ‖ -bᵊr ~**ed** d ~**s** z
'**chamber ,music**; '**chamber ,orchestra**;
'**chamber pot**
chamberlain 'tʃeɪm bə lɪn -lən ‖ -bᵊr- ~**s** z
Chamberlain, Chamberlaine,
Chamberlayne *(i)* 'tʃeɪm bə lɪn -lən ‖ -bᵊr-,
(ii) -leɪn
chambermaid 'tʃeɪm bə meɪd ‖ -bᵊr- ~**s** z
Chambers 'tʃeɪm bəz ‖ -bᵊrz
Chambourcy *tdmk* ʃæm 'boʊs i
‖ ,ʃɑːm boʊr 'siː —*Fr* [ʃã buʁ si]
chambray 'ʃæm breɪ -bri
chambré 'ʃɒm breɪ ‖ ʃɑːm 'breɪ —*Fr* [ʃã bʁe]
chameleon kə 'miːl i ən ~**s** z
chameleonic kə ,miːl i 'ɒn ɪk ◀ ‖ -'ɑːn-
chameleon-like kə 'miːl i ən laɪk
chamfer 'tʃæmᵖf ə 'ʃæmᵖf- ‖ -ᵊr 'tʃæmp- ~**ed** d
chamfering 'tʃæmᵖf ər ɪŋ 'ʃæmᵖf- ‖ 'tʃæmp-
~**s** z
chamm|y 'ʃæm |i ~**ies** iz
chamois *(i)* 'ʃæm wɑː ‖ ʃæm 'wɑː, *(ii)* 'ʃæm i
—*(ii) is used mainly in reference to chamois
leather, and is then alternatively spelt*
chammy, shammy. *The plural may have* z, *or
may — particularly in reference to the goats
— be pronounced identically with the singular.*
chamomile 'kæm ə maɪᵊl -miːᵊl
Chamonix 'ʃæm ə ni: -ɒ- ‖ ,ʃæm ə 'ni: —*Fr*
[ʃa mɔ ni]
champ tʃæmp **champed** tʃæmpt **champing**
'tʃæmp ɪŋ **champs** tʃæmps
champagne, C~ ,ʃæm 'peɪn ◀ —*Fr* [ʃã panj]
,**champagne 'cocktail**
Champaign ʃæm 'peɪn
champak 'tʃʌmp ək 'tʃæmp æk
Champernowne 'tʃæmp ə naʊn ‖ -ᵊr-

champers 'ʃæmp əz ‖ -ᵊrz
champerty 'tʃæmp ət i -ɜːt- ‖ -ᵊrt̬ i
champignon 'ʃæmp iːn jõ ,·'·; ʃæm 'pɪn jən
‖ ʃæm 'pɪn jən tʃæm- —*Fr* [ʃã pi njõ] ~**s** z
—*or as singular*
champion, C~ 'tʃæmp jən -i ən ~**ed** d ~**ing** ɪŋ
~**s** z
championship 'tʃæmp jən ʃɪp -i ən- ~**s** s
Champlain ⑴ʃæm 'pleɪn —*Fr* [ʃã plɛ̃]
Champneys 'tʃæmp niz
Champs Elysees, Champs Elysées
,ʃɒnz ə 'liːz eɪ ,ʃɒmz-, ,ʃõz-, -ɪ-, -eɪ-
‖ ,ʃɑːnz ,eɪl i 'zeɪ —*Fr* [ʃã ze li ze]
Chan tʃæn —*Cantonese* [⁴tsʰen]

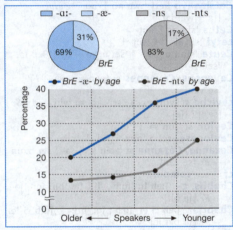

CHANCE

chance tʃɑːnᵗs §tʃænᵗs ‖ tʃænᵗs — *Preference
polls, BrE (not restricted to RP):* -ɑː- 69%, -æ-
31%; -ns 83%, -nts 17%. **chanced** tʃɑːnᵗst
§tʃænᵗst ‖ tʃænᵗst **chances** 'tʃɑːnᵗs ɪz
§'tʃænᵗs-, -əz ‖ 'tʃænᵗs əz **chancing**
'tʃɑːnᵗs ɪŋ §'tʃænᵗs- ‖ 'tʃænᵗs ɪŋ
chancel 'tʃɑːnᵗs ᵊl §'tʃænᵗs- ‖ 'tʃænᵗs ᵊl ~**s** z
chanceller|y 'tʃɑːnᵗs ᵊl ər |i §'tʃænᵗs-, '·ᵊl ər |i
‖ 'tʃænᵗs- ~**ies** iz
chancellor, C~ 'tʃɑːnᵗs əl ə §'tʃænᵗs-
‖ 'tʃænᵗs ᵊl ər ~**s** z
chancer 'tʃɑːnᵗs ə §'tʃænᵗs ə ‖ 'tʃænᵗs ᵊr ~**s** z
chancer|y 'tʃɑːnᵗs ər |i §'tʃænᵗs- ‖ 'tʃænᵗs- ~**ies**
iz
chanciness 'tʃɑːnᵗs i nəs §'tʃænᵗs-, -nɪs
‖ 'tʃænᵗs-
chancre 'ʃæŋk ə ‖ -ᵊr ~**s** z
chancroid 'ʃæŋk rɔɪd ~**s** z
Chanctonbury 'tʃæŋkt ən bər i →·'·əm-, -,ber i
‖ -,ber i
chanc|y 'tʃɑːnᵗs |i §'tʃænᵗs i ‖ 'tʃænᵗs |i ~**ier**
i ə ‖ i ᵊr ~**iest** i ɪst i əst
chandelier ,ʃænd ə 'lɪə ,ʃɒnd-, -ᵊl 'ɪə ‖ -ᵊl 'ɪᵊr
~**s** z
chandelle ʃæn 'del ʃɑːn- ~**s** z
Chandigarh ,tʃʌnd i 'gɜː ,tʃænd-, -'gɑː, '·ˌ·gə
‖ -'gɜː -'gɑːr

chandler, C~ 'tʃɑːnd lə §'tʃænd- ‖ 'tʃænd lᵊr ~s
z

chandler|y 'tʃɑːnd lər |i §'tʃænd-, §-ᵊl r|i
‖ 'tʃænd- ~ies iz

Chandos *(i)* 'ʃænd ɒs ‖ -oʊs, *(ii)* 'tʃænd-

Chanel ʃə 'nel ʃæ- —*Fr* [ʃa nɛl]

Chang tʃæŋ ‖ dʒɑːŋ —*Chi* Zhāng [¹tʂaŋ]

Changchun ˌtʃæŋ 'tʃʊn ‖ ˌtʃɑːŋ- —*Chi*
Chángchūn [²tʂʰaŋ ¹tʂʰwən]

change tʃeɪndʒ **changed** tʃeɪndʒd **changes**
'tʃeɪndʒ ɪz -əz **changing** 'tʃeɪndʒ ɪŋ
'**change ˌringing**

changeability ˌtʃeɪndʒ ə 'bɪl ət i -ɪt i ‖ -ət̬ i

changeab|le 'tʃeɪndʒ əb |ᵊl ~**leness** ᵊl nəs -nɪs
~**ly** li

changeless 'tʃeɪndʒ ləs -lɪs ~**ly** li ~**ness** nəs
nɪs

changeling 'tʃeɪndʒ lɪŋ ~s z

changeover *n* 'tʃeɪndʒ ˌəʊv ə ‖ -ˌoʊv ᵊr ~s z

changer 'tʃeɪndʒ ə ‖ -ᵊr ~s z

changeround 'tʃeɪndʒ raʊnd ~s z

Changi *place in Singapore* 'tʃæŋ i

changing 'tʃeɪndʒ ɪŋ
'**changing room**

channel, C~ 'tʃæn ᵊl ~**ed**, ~**led** d ~**ing**, ~**ling**
ɪŋ ~s z
'**channel ˌhopping**; '**Channel ˌIslands**,
ˌ·'··; '**channel ˌsurfing**

Channing 'tʃæn ɪŋ

Channon *(i)* 'tʃæn ən, *(ii)* 'ʃæn ən

chanson 'ʃɒ̃ sɒ̃ 'ʃɒn-, -sɒn ‖ ʃɑːn 'sɔːn -'soʊn,
-'sɑːn; 'ʃænˢs ən —*Fr* [ʃɑ̃ sɔ̃] ~s z —*or as*
singular

chant, Chant tʃɑːnt §tʃænt ‖ tʃænt **chanted**
'tʃɑːnt ɪd §'tʃænt- ‖ 'tʃænt̬ əd **chanting**
'tʃɑːnt ɪŋ §'tʃænt- ‖ 'tʃænt̬ ɪŋ

Chantal ˌʃɑːn 'tæl ˌʃɒn-, ˌʃæn-, -'tɑːl ‖ ʃɑːn 'tɑːl
—*Fr* [ʃɑ̃ tal]

Chantelle ˌʃɑːn 'tel ˌʃɒn-, ˌʃæn- —*Fr* [ʃɑ̃ tɛl]

chanter, C~ 'tʃɑːnt ə §'tʃænt- ‖ 'tʃænt̬ ᵊr ~s z

chanterelle ˌʃɒnt ə 'rel ˌʃænt-, ˌtʃænt- ‖ ˌʃænt̬-
ˌʃɑːnt̬- ~s z

chanteus|e ˌʃɒn 'tɜːz ˌʃɑːn- ‖ ʃɑːn 'tuːz ʃæn- *(*)*
—*Fr* [ʃɑ̃ tøːz] ~**es** ɪz əz —*or as singular*

chantey 'ʃænt i ‖ 'ʃænt̬ i ~s z

chanti... —*see* **chanty**

Chanticleer, c~ 'ʃɑːnt ə klɪə 'ʃɒnt-, 'tʃɑːnt-,
'tʃænt-, -ɪ-, ˌ·'· ‖ 'tʃænt̬ ə klɪr ~s, ~'s z

Chantilly ʃæn 'tɪl i ʃɒn- ‖ ˌʃɑːnt i 'ji: —*Fr*
[ʃɑ̃ ti ji]

chantr|y, C~ 'tʃɑːntr |i §'tʃæntr- ‖ 'tʃæntr |i
~**ies** iz
'**chantry ˌchapel**

chant|y 'ʃænt |i 'tʃænt-, 'tʃɑːnt- ‖ 'ʃænt̬ |i ~**ies**
iz

Chanukah 'hɑːn ək ə 'hɒn-, 'kɑːn-, -ʊk-, -ɑː
—*Hebrew* [xa nu 'ka]

Chao tʃaʊ
ˌ**Chao ˌYuen 'Ren** ˌju: en 'ren —*Chi* Zhào
Yuánrèn [⁴tʂɐu ²ɥɛn ⁴ʐən]

chaology keɪ 'ɒl ədʒ i ‖ -'ɑːl-

chaos 'keɪ ɒs ‖ -ɑːs

chaotic keɪ 'ɒt ɪk ‖ -'ɑːt̬- ~**ally** ᵊl i

chap tʃæp **chapped** tʃæpt **chapping** 'tʃæp ɪŋ
chaps tʃæps

chaparral ˌʃæp ə 'ræl ˌtʃæp-, -'rɑːl

chapati, chapatti tʃə 'pɑːt i -'pæt- ‖ -'pɑːt̬ i
—*Hindi* [tʃə pa: ʈi] ~s z

chapbook 'tʃæp bʊk §-buːk ~s s

chapel, C~ 'tʃæp ᵊl ~s z

Chapel-en-le-Frith ˌtʃæp ᵊl ˌen lə 'frɪθ
-ᵊl ən lə-

chapelgo|er 'tʃæp ᵊl ˌɡəʊ |ə ‖ -ˌɡoʊ |ᵊr ~**ers**
əz ‖ ᵊrz ~**ing** ɪŋ

Chapeltown 'tʃæp ᵊl taʊn

chaperon, chaperon|e 'ʃæp ə rəʊn ‖ -roʊn
~**ed** d ~**es**, ~s z ~**ing** ɪŋ

chapfallen 'tʃæp ˌfɔːl ən ‖ -ˌfɑːl-

chaplain 'tʃæp lɪn -lən ~s z

chaplain|cy 'tʃæp lən |si -lɪn- ~**cies** siz

chaplet 'tʃæp lət -lɪt ~s s

Chaplin 'tʃæp lɪn -lən

Chaplinesque ˌtʃæp lɪ 'nesk ◂ -lə-

Chapman 'tʃæp mən

chapp... —*see* **chap**

chappal 'tʃʌp ᵊl ~s z

Chappaquiddick ˌtʃæp ə 'kwɪd ɪk

Chappell 'tʃæp ᵊl

chapp|ie, chapp|y, Chappie *tdmk* 'tʃæp |i
~**ies** iz

chaps tʃæps

chapstick 'tʃæp stɪk ~s s

chaptalis... —*see* **chaptaliz...**

chaptalization ˌtʃæpt əl aɪ 'zeɪʃ ᵊn ˌʃæpt-, -ɪ'--
‖ -əl ə-

chaptaliz|e 'tʃæpt ə laɪz 'ʃæpt- ~**ed** d ~**es** ɪz
əz ~**ing** ɪŋ

chapter 'tʃæpt ə ‖ -ᵊr ~s z
ˌ**chapter and 'verse**; '**chapter house**

char tʃɑː ‖ tʃɑːr **charred** tʃɑːd ‖ tʃɑːrd
charring 'tʃɑːr ɪŋ **chars** tʃɑːz ‖ tʃɑːrz

charabanc 'ʃær ə bæŋ -bɒŋ ‖ 'ʃer- ~s z

character 'kær əkt ə -ɪkt- ‖ -ᵊr 'ker- ~s z
'**character sketch**

characteris... —*see* **characteriz...**

characteristic ˌkær əkt ə 'rɪst ɪk ◂ -ˌɪkt- ‖ ˌker-
~**ally** ᵊl i ~s s

characterization ˌkær əkt ər ˌaɪ 'zeɪʃ ᵊn -ˌɪkt-,
ɪ'-- ‖ -ɪkt ər ə- ˌker-

characteriz|e 'kær əkt ə raɪz '-ɪkt- ‖ 'ker- ~**ed**
d ~**es** ɪz əz ~**ing** ɪŋ

characterless 'kær əkt ə ləs '-ɪkt-, -lɪs ‖ -ᵊr ləs
'ker- ~**ly** li

charade ʃə 'rɑːd -'reɪd ‖ -'reɪd ~s z —*The*
-'reɪd *form, previously only AmE, is now*
occasionally also heard in BrE

charbroil 'tʃɑː brɔɪᵊl ‖ 'tʃɑːr- ~**ed** d ~**ing** ɪŋ ~s
z

charcoal 'tʃɑː kəʊl →-kɒʊl ‖ 'tʃɑːr koʊl ~**ed** d
~**ing** ɪŋ ~s z

charcoal-burner 'tʃɑː kəʊl ˌbɜːn ə →-kɒʊl-
‖ 'tʃɑːr koʊl ˌbɜːn ᵊr ~s z

Charcot 'ʃɑːk əʊ ‖ ʃɑːr 'koʊ —*Fr* [ʃaʁ ko]

charcuterie ʃɑː 'kuːt ər i -'kjuːt-
‖ ʃɑːr ˌkuːt̬ ə 'riː -'··· —*Fr* [ʃaʁ ky tʁi]

chard, Chard tʃɑːd ‖ tʃɑːrd

Chardonnay, c~ 'ʃɑːd ə neɪ →-ˀn eɪ
‖ ˌʃɑːrd ᵊn 'eɪ **~s** z —*Fr* Chardonnet
[ʃaʁ dɔ nɛ]
charge tʃɑːdʒ ‖ tʃɑːrdʒ **charged** tʃɑːdʒd
‖ tʃɑːrdʒd **charges** 'tʃɑːdʒ ɪz -əz ‖ 'tʃɑːrdʒ əz
charging 'tʃɑːdʒ ɪŋ ‖ 'tʃɑːrdʒ ɪŋ
'**charge ac,count**; '**charge card**; '**charge
hand**; '**charge nurse**; '**charge sheet**
chargeable 'tʃɑːdʒ əb ᵊl ‖ 'tʃɑːrdʒ-
chargeback 'tʃɑːdʒ bæk ‖ 'tʃɑːrdʒ- **~s** s
chargé d'affaires ˌʃɑːʒ eɪ dæ 'feə -də·
‖ ʃɑːr ˌʒeɪ də 'feˀr -dæ· —*Fr* [ʃaʁ ʒe da fɛːʁ]
—*The plural,* **chargés d'affaires***, is
pronounced identically with the singular, as in
French; or, alternatively, as* ˌeɪz- · ˌʒeɪz-
charger 'tʃɑːdʒ ə ‖ 'tʃɑːrdʒ ᵊr **~s** z
chargrill 'tʃɑː grɪl ‖ 'tʃɑːr- **~ed** d **~ing** ɪŋ **~s** z
Chari 'tʃɑːr i
chari... —*see* **chary**
Charing 'tʃær ɪŋ 'tʃeər- ‖ 'tʃer-
ˌCharing 'Cross
chari|ot 'tʃær i ˌ|ət ‖ 'tʃer- **~oted** ət ɪd -əd
‖ ət əd **~oting** ət ɪŋ ‖ ət ɪŋ **~ots** əts
charioteer ˌtʃær i ə 'tɪə ‖ -'tɪᵊr ˌtʃer- **~s** z
charisma kə 'rɪz mə **charismata** kə 'rɪz mət ə
ˌkær ɪz 'mɑːt ə, -əz- ‖ kə 'rɪz mət ə
charismatic ˌkær ɪz 'mæt ɪk ◄ -əz- ‖ -'mæt̬-
ˌker- **~ally** ᵊl i
charitab|le 'tʃær ɪt əb ᵊl '·ət- ‖ 'tʃær ət- 'tʃer-
~leness ᵊl nəs -nɪs **~ly** li
charit|y, C~ 'tʃær ət |i -ɪt- ‖ -ət |i 'tʃer- **~ies** iz
charivari ˌʃɑːr ɪ 'vɑːr i ˌʃær-, -ə- ‖ ʃə ˌrɪv ə 'riː
ˌʃɪv ə 'riː *(*)*
charivaria ˌʃɑːr ɪ 'vɑːr i ə ˌʃær-, -ə- ‖ ʃə ˌrɪv ə 'riː
charka 'tʃɜːk ɑː 'tʃɑːk-, -ə ‖ 'tʃɜːk- **~s** z
charlad|y 'tʃɑː ˌleɪd |i ‖ 'tʃɑːr- **~ies** iz
charlatan 'ʃɑːl ət ən -ə tæn ‖ 'ʃɑːrl ət ᵊn **~ism**
ˌɪz əm **~ry** ri **~s** z
Charlbury 'tʃɑːl bər i ‖ 'tʃɑːrl ˌber i
Charlecote 'tʃɑːl kəʊt ‖ 'tʃɑːrl koʊt
Charleen (i) 'tʃɑːl iːn ₍ˌ₎tʃɑː 'liːn ‖ 'tʃɑːrl-,
(ii) 'ʃɑːl iːn ₍ˌ₎ʃɑː 'liːn ‖ 'ʃɑːrl iːn ˌʃɑːr 'liːn
Charlemagne 'ʃɑːl ə meɪn -maɪn, ·'·· ‖ 'ʃɑːrl-
—*Fr* [ʃaʁ lə manj]
Charlene (i) 'tʃɑːl iːn ₍ˌ₎tʃɑː 'liːn ‖ 'tʃɑːrl-,
(ii) 'ʃɑːl iːn ₍ˌ₎ʃɑː 'liːn ‖ 'ʃɑːrl iːn ˌʃɑːr 'liːn
Charles tʃɑːlz ‖ tʃɑːrlz —*but as a French name,*
ʃɑːl ‖ ʃɑːrl —, *Fr* [ʃaʁl] **Charles', Charles's**
'tʃɑːlz ɪz əz; tʃɑːlz ‖ 'tʃɑːrlz əz tʃɑːrlz
Charleston, c~ 'tʃɑːlst ən 'tʃɑːlz tən
‖ 'tʃɑːrlst ən **~s** z
Charlestown 'tʃɑːlz taʊn ‖ 'tʃɑːrlz-
Charley, Charlie, c~ 'tʃɑːl i ‖ 'tʃɑːrl i
'**charley horse**
Charlie, c~ 'tʃɑːl i ‖ 'tʃɑːrl i **~s**, **~'s** z
charlock 'tʃɑː lɒk ‖ 'tʃɑːr lɑːk
charlotte, C~ 'ʃɑːl ət ‖ 'ʃɑːrl- **~s**, **~'s** s
ˌCharlotte A'malie ə 'mɑːl i ə ‖ ə 'mɑːl jə;
ˌcharlotte 'russe ruːs
Charlottenburg ʃɑː 'lɒt ᵊn bɜːg
‖ ʃɑːr 'lɑːt ᵊn bɜːg —*Ger* [ʃaʁ 'lɔt ᵊn bʊʁk]
Charlottesville 'ʃɑːl əts vɪl ‖ 'ʃɑːrl- -vᵊl
Charlottetown 'ʃɑːl ət taʊn ‖ 'ʃɑːrl-

Charlton 'tʃɑːlt ən ‖ 'tʃɑːrlt-
charm tʃɑːm ‖ tʃɑːrm **charmed** tʃɑːmd
‖ tʃɑːrmd **charming** 'tʃɑːm ɪŋ ‖ 'tʃɑːrm ɪŋ
charms tʃɑːmz ‖ tʃɑːrmz
Charmaine ₍ˌ₎ʃɑː 'meɪn ‖ ʃɑːr-
charmer 'tʃɑːm ə ‖ 'tʃɑːrm ᵊr **~s** z
Charmian (i) 'tʃɑːm i ən ‖ 'tʃɑːrm-, (ii) 'ʃɑːm-
‖ 'ʃɑːrm-, (iii) 'kɑːm- ‖ 'kɑːrm-
charming 'tʃɑːm ɪŋ ‖ 'tʃɑːrm ɪŋ **~ly** li
charnel 'tʃɑːn ᵊl ‖ 'tʃɑːrn ᵊl
'**charnel house**
Charnock 'tʃɑːn ɒk -ək ‖ 'tʃɑːrn ɑːk
Charnwood 'tʃɑːn wʊd ‖ 'tʃɑːrn-
Charolais, Charollais 'ʃær ə leɪ ‖ ˌʃær ə 'leɪ
ˌʃer-, ˌʃɑːr- —*As a pl n, also with final* z
Charon 'keər ən -ɒn ‖ 'ker- 'kær-
charpoy 'tʃɑːp ɔɪ ‖ 'tʃɑːrp- **~s** z
Charrington 'tʃær ɪŋ tən ‖ 'tʃer-
chart, Chart tʃɑːt ‖ tʃɑːrt **charted** 'tʃɑːt ɪd -əd
‖ 'tʃɑːrt̬ əd **charting** 'tʃɑːt ɪŋ ‖ 'tʃɑːrt̬ ɪŋ
charter 'tʃɑːt ə ‖ 'tʃɑːrt̬ ᵊr **~ed** d **chartering**
'tʃɑːt ᵊr ɪŋ ‖ 'tʃɑːrt̬ ᵊr ɪŋ **~s** z
ˌchartered ac'countant; 'charter flight;
ˌcharter 'member
charterer 'tʃɑːt ᵊr ə ‖ 'tʃɑːrt̬ ᵊr ᵊr **~s** z
Charterhouse 'tʃɑːt ə haʊs ‖ 'tʃɑːrt̬ ᵊr-
Charteris (i) 'tʃɑːt ər ɪs -əs ‖ 'tʃɑːrt̬-,
(ii) 'tʃɑːt əz ‖ 'tʃɑːrt̬ ᵊrz
Chartham 'tʃɑːt əm ‖ 'tʃɑːrt̬-
Chartism 'tʃɑːt ˌɪz əm ‖ 'tʃɑːrt̬-
Chartist 'tʃɑːt ɪst §-əst ‖ 'tʃɑːrt̬- **~s** s
Chartres *place in France* 'ʃɑːtr ə ʃɑːtr, ʃɑːt
‖ 'ʃɑːrtr ə —*Fr* [ʃaʁtχ]
chartreuse, C~ *tdmk* ʃɑː 'trɜːz ‖ ʃɑːr 'truːz
-'truːs *(*)* —*Fr* [ʃaʁ tʁøːz]
Chartwell 'tʃɑːt wel -wᵊl ‖ 'tʃɑːrt-
char|woman 'tʃɑː ˌ|ˌwʊm ən ‖ 'tʃɑːr- **~women**
ˌwɪm ɪn §-ən
char|y 'tʃeər |i ‖ 'tʃer |i 'tʃær- **~ier** i ə ‖ i ᵊr
~iest i ɪst i əst **~ily** əl i ɪl i **~iness** i nəs i nɪs
Charybdis kə 'rɪbd ɪs §-əs
Chas. tʃæz tʃæs —*or see* Charles
chase, Chase tʃeɪs **chased** tʃeɪst (= *chaste*)
chases 'tʃeɪs ɪz -əz **chasing** 'tʃeɪs ɪŋ
chaser 'tʃeɪs ə ‖ -ᵊr **~s** z
chasm 'kæz əm *(!)* **~s** z
chassé 'ʃæs eɪ ‖ ʃæ 'seɪ **~d** d **~ing** ɪŋ **~s** z
chasseur ₍ˌ₎ʃæ 'sɜː ‖ -'sɜː —*Fr* [ʃa sœːʁ]
chassis *sing.* 'ʃæs i ‖ 'tʃæs-, △-əs **chassis**
pl 'ʃæs iz -i ‖ tʃæs-
chaste tʃeɪst (= *chased*) **chaster** 'tʃeɪst ə ‖ -ᵊr
chastest 'tʃeɪst ɪst -əst
chastely 'tʃeɪst li
chasten 'tʃeɪs ᵊn **~ed** d **~ing** ˌɪŋ **~s** z
chasteness 'tʃeɪst nəs -nɪs
chastis|e ₍ˌ₎tʃæ 'staɪz ‖ 'tʃæst aɪz **~ed** d **~es** ɪz
əz **~ing** ɪŋ
chastisement ₍ˌ₎tʃæ 'staɪz mənt 'tʃæst ɪz mənt,
-əz- ‖ 'tʃæst aɪz- **~s** s
chastiser ₍ˌ₎tʃæ 'staɪz ə ‖ -ᵊr **~s** z
chastity, C~ 'tʃæst ət i -ɪt- ‖ -ət̬ i
'**chastity belt**
chasuble 'tʃæz jʊb ᵊl -jəb- ‖ -jəb- -əb- **~s** z

chat tʃæt **chats** tʃæts **chatted** 'tʃæt ɪd -əd
‖ 'tʃæt̬ əd **chatting** 'tʃæt ɪŋ ‖ 'tʃæt̬ ɪŋ
'**chat show**
Chataway 'tʃæt ə weɪ ‖ 'tʃæt̬-
chateau, château 'ʃæt əʊ ‖ ʃæ 'toʊ —*Fr*
[ʃa to] **~s** z
Chateaubriand, c~ ˌʃæt əʊ bri 'ɒn ◂ -'ɒ̃,
-'ɒnd; -'briː; ʃæ 'təʊb ri· ‖ ʃæ ˌtoʊ bri 'ɑːn ◂
—*Fr* [ʃa to bri jɑ̃]
Châteauneuf-du-Pape ˌʃæt əʊ nɜːf dju 'pæp
-du'·, -'pɑːp ‖ ʃæ ˌtoʊ nʌf du 'pɑːp —*Fr*
[ʃa to nœv dy pap]
chateaux, châteaux 'ʃæt əʊz -əʊ ‖ ʃæ 'toʊz
-'toʊ —*Fr* [ʃa to]
chatelain, châtelain 'ʃæt ə leɪn -ᵊl eɪn
‖ 'ʃæt̬ ᵊl eɪn —*Fr* [ʃat læ̃] **~s** z
chatelaine, châtelaine 'ʃæt ə leɪn -ᵊl eɪn
‖ 'ʃæt̬ ᵊl eɪn —*Fr* [ʃat lɛn] **~s** z
Chater 'tʃeɪt ə ‖ 'tʃeɪt̬ ᵊr
Chatham 'tʃæt əm ‖ 'tʃæt̬-
chatline 'tʃæt laɪn **~s** z
chatroom 'tʃæt ruːm -rʊm **~s** z
Chatsworth 'tʃæts wəθ -wɜːθ ‖ -wᵊrθ
chatt... —*see* **chat**
Chattahoochee ˌtʃæt ə 'huːtʃ i ◂ ‖ ˌtʃæt̬-
ˌChatta‚hoochee 'River
Chattanooga ˌtʃæt ᵊn 'uːg ə ˌtʃæt ə 'nuːg ə
‖ ˌChatta‚nooga 'choo-choo
chattel 'tʃæt ᵊl ‖ 'tʃæt̬- **~s** z
chatter 'tʃæt ə ‖ 'tʃæt̬ ᵊr **~ed** d **chattering**
'tʃæt ᵊr ɪŋ ‖ 'tʃæt̬ ər ɪŋ **~s** z
chatterbox 'tʃæt ə bɒks ‖ 'tʃæt̬ ᵊr bɑːks **~es** ɪz
əz
chatterer 'tʃæt ər ə ‖ 'tʃæt̬ ər ᵊr **~s** z
Chatteris 'tʃæt ər ɪs §-əs ‖ 'tʃæt̬-
Chatterjee, Chatterji 'tʃæt ə dʒiː ‖ 'tʃæt̬ ᵊr-
Chatterley 'tʃæt ə li -ᵊl i ‖ 'tʃæt̬ ᵊr- ~'s z
Chatterton 'tʃæt ət ᵊn ‖ 'tʃæt̬ ᵊrt ᵊn
chattie... —*see* **chatty**
Chatto 'tʃæt əʊ ‖ 'tʃæt̬ oʊ
chatt|y 'tʃæt |i ‖ 'tʃæt̬ |i **~ier** i ə ‖ i ᵊr **~iest**
i ɪst i əst **~ily** ɪ li əl i **~iness** i nəs i nɪs
chat-up 'tʃæt ʌp ‖ 'tʃæt̬-
'**chat-up line**
Chatwin 'tʃæt wɪn
Chaucer 'tʃɔːs ə ‖ -ᵊr 'tʃɑːs-
Chaucerian tʃɔː 'sɪər i ən ‖ -'sɪr- tʃɑː- **~s** z
chaudfroid 'ʃəʊ fwɑː -frwɑː ‖ 'ʃoʊ- —*Fr*
[ʃo fʁwa]
Chaudhuri, Chaudhury 'tʃaʊd ᵊr i
chauffeur 'ʃəʊf ə ʃəʊ 'fɜː, ʃə- ‖ ʃoʊ 'fɜː **~ed** d
chauffeuring 'ʃəʊf ᵊr ɪŋ ‖ ʃoʊ 'fɜː ɪŋ **~s** z
chaulmoog|ra tʃɔːl 'muːg rə tʃəʊl- ‖ tʃɑːl- **~ric**
rɪk
Chauncey, Chauncy 'tʃɔːn⁀s i ‖ 'tʃɑːn⁀s-
chausses ʃəʊs ‖ ʃoʊs
chautauqua, C~ ʃə 'tɔːk wə ‖ -'tɑːk- **~s** z
chauvinism 'ʃəʊv ə ˌnɪz əm -ɪ- ‖ 'ʃoʊv-
chauvinist 'ʃəʊv ən ɪst -ɪn-, əst ‖ 'ʃoʊv- **~s** s
chauvinistic ˌʃəʊv ə 'nɪst ɪk ◂ -ɪ- ‖ ˌʃoʊv- **~ally**
ᵊl i
chav tʃæv **chavs** tʃævz
Chavasse ʃə 'væs

Chavez 'tʃæv es ‖ 'tʃɑːv ez 'ʃɑːv-, -es —*Sp*
Chávez ['tʃa βeθ, -βes]
Chavon, Chavonne ʃə 'vɒn ‖ -'vɑːn
chaw tʃɔː ‖ tʃɑː **chaws** tʃɔːz ‖ tʃɑːz
Chawton 'tʃɔːt ᵊn ‖ 'tʃɑːt-
Chay tʃeɪ
Chayefsky tʃaɪ 'ef ski
chayote tʃaɪ 'əʊt i ‖ -'oʊt- **~s** z
Chaz tʃæz
Che tʃeɪ
Cheadle 'tʃiːd ᵊl
Cheam tʃiːm
cheap tʃiːp **cheaper** 'tʃiːp ə ‖ -ᵊr **cheapest**
'tʃiːp ɪst -əst
cheapen 'tʃiːp ən **~ed** d **~ing** ɪŋ **~s** z
cheapie 'tʃiːp i **~s** z
cheap-jack 'tʃiːp dʒæk **~s** s
cheap|ly 'tʃiːp |li **~ness** nəs nɪs
cheapo 'tʃiːp əʊ ‖ -oʊ
Cheapside 'tʃiːp saɪd ˌ·'·
cheapskate 'tʃiːp skeɪt **~s** s
cheat tʃiːt **cheated** 'tʃiːt ɪd -əd ‖ 'tʃiːt̬ əd
cheating/ly 'tʃiːt ɪŋ /li ‖ 'tʃiːt̬ ɪŋ /li **cheats**
tʃiːts
cheater 'tʃiːt ə ‖ 'tʃiːt̬ ᵊr **~s** z
Cheatham 'tʃiːt əm ‖ 'tʃiːt̬-
Chechen 'tʃetʃ en -ən; tʃɪ 'tʃen, tʃe-
Chechenia tʃɪ 'tʃen jə tʃe-
Chechnya tʃetʃ 'njɑː 'tʃetʃ ni ə
check tʃek **checked** tʃekt **checking** 'tʃek ɪŋ
checks tʃeks
'**checking ac‚count**
checkbook 'tʃek bʊk §-buːk **~s** s
checkbox 'tʃek bɒks ‖ -bɑːks **~es** ɪz əz
checker, C~ 'tʃek ə ‖ -ᵊr **~ed** d **checkering**
'tʃek ᵊr ɪŋ **~s** z
checkerboard 'tʃek ə bɔːd ‖ -ᵊr bɔːrd -boʊrd
~s z
check-in 'tʃek ɪn **~s** z
Checkland 'tʃek lənd
Checkley 'tʃek li
checklist 'tʃek lɪst **~s** s
check|mate 'tʃek |meɪt ˌ·'· **~mated** meɪt ɪd
-əd ‖ meɪt̬ əd **~mates** meɪts **~mating** meɪt ɪŋ
‖ meɪt̬ ɪŋ
checkout 'tʃek aʊt **~s** s
checkpoint 'tʃek pɔɪnt **~s** s
checkrail 'tʃek reɪᵊl **~s** z
checkrein 'tʃek reɪn **~s** z
checkroom 'tʃek ruːm -rʊm **~s** z
checksum 'tʃek sʌm **~s** z
checkup 'tʃek ʌp **~s** s
Cheddar, c~ 'tʃed ə ‖ -ᵊr
ˌCheddar 'cheese
Chedzoy 'tʃedz ɔɪ
cheek, Cheek tʃiːk **cheeked** tʃiːkt **cheeking**
'tʃiːk ɪŋ **cheeks** tʃiːks
cheekbone 'tʃiːk bəʊn ‖ -boʊn **~s** z
-cheeked 'tʃiːkt — **rosy-cheeked**
ˌrəʊz i 'tʃiːkt ◂ ‖ ˌroʊz-
cheek|y 'tʃiːk |i **~ier** i ə ‖ i ᵊr **~iest** i ɪst i əst
~ily ɪ li əl i **~iness** i nəs i nɪs

cheep tʃiːp (= *cheap*) **cheeped** tʃiːpt **cheeping** ˈtʃiːp ɪŋ **cheeps** tʃiːps

cheer tʃɪə ‖ tʃɪˀr **cheered** tʃɪəd ‖ tʃɪˀrd **cheering** ˈtʃɪər ɪŋ ‖ ˈtʃɪr ɪŋ **cheers** tʃɪəz ‖ tʃɪˀrz

cheerful ˈtʃɪəf ˀl -ʊl ‖ ˈtʃɪrf- **~ly** ᵢ **~ness** nəs nɪs

cheeri... —*see* **cheery**

cheerio, C~ ˌtʃɪər i ˈəʊ ◄ ‖ ˌtʃɪr i ˈoʊ ˈ··· **~s** z

cheerlead|er ˈtʃɪə ˌliːd ə ‖ ˈtʃɪr ˌliːd ˀr **~ers** əz ‖ ˀrz **~ing** ɪŋ

cheerless ˈtʃɪə ləs -lɪs ‖ ˈtʃɪr- **~ly** li **~ness** nəs nɪs

cheers tʃɪəz ‖ tʃɪˀrz

cheer|y ˈtʃɪər |i ‖ ˈtʃɪr |i **~ier** i̯ə ‖ i̯ˀr **~iest** i̯ɪst i̯əst **~ily** əl i ɪl i **~iness** i nəs i nɪs

cheese tʃiːz **cheesed** tʃiːzd **cheeses** ˈtʃiːz ɪz -əz

ˌcheesed ˈoff; ˌcheese ˈstraw

cheeseboard ˈtʃiːz bɔːd ‖ -bɔːrd -boʊrd **~s** z

cheeseburger ˈtʃiːz ˌbɜːg ə ‖ -ˌbɜːg ˀr **~s** z

cheesecake ˈtʃiːz keɪk **~s** s

cheesecloth ˈtʃiːz klɒθ -klɔːθ ‖ -klɔːθ -klɑːθ

Cheeseman ˈtʃiːz mən

cheesemonger ˈtʃiːz ˌmʌŋ gə ‖ -gˀr **~s** z

cheeseparing ˈtʃiːz ˌpeər ɪŋ ‖ -ˌper- -ˌpær-

Cheesewright ˈtʃiːz raɪt

Cheesman ˈtʃiːz mən

cheesy ˈtʃiːz i

cheetah ˈtʃiːt ə ‖ ˈtʃiːt̬ ə **~s** z

Cheetham ˈtʃiːt əm ‖ ˈtʃiːt̬-

Cheetos *tdmk* ˈtʃiːt əʊz ‖ ˈtʃiːt̬ oʊz

Cheever ˈtʃiːv ə ‖ -ˀr

Cheez Whiz *tdmk* ˌtʃiːz ˈwɪz

chef ʃef **chefs** ʃefs —*but in French phrases both sing. and pl are* ʃeɪ —*See also phrases with this word*

chef d'oeuvre, chefs d'oeuvre ˌʃeɪ ˈdɜːv rə -ˈdɜːv ‖ ˌʃeɪ ˈdʌv —*Fr* [ʃɛ dœːvʁ]

Chegwin ˈtʃeg wɪn

Cheke tʃiːk

Chekhov ˈtʃek ɒf -ɒv ‖ -ɔːf -ɑːf —*Russ* [ˈtʃɛ xəf]

Chekhovian tʃe ˈkəʊv i̯ən -ˈkɒv- ‖ -ˈkoʊv-

Chek Lap Kok ˌtʃek læp ˈkɒk ‖ -lɑːp ˈkoʊk —*Cantonese* [³tsʰeːk ⁶laːp ³kɔːk]

chel|a *'claw'* ˈkiːl| ə **~ae** iː

chela *'disciple'* ˈtʃeɪl ə —*Hindi* [tʃeː laː] **~s** z

chelate *v* kiː ˈleɪt kɪ-, kə-, tʃiː-; ˈkiːl eɪt, ˈtʃiːl- ‖ ˈkiːl eɪt **chelated** kiː ˈleɪt ɪd kɪ-, kə-, tʃiː-, -əd; ˈkiːl eɪt-, ˈtʃiːl- ‖ ˈkiːl eɪt̬ əd

chelate *n, adj* ˈkiːl eɪt ˈtʃiːl- **~s** s

chelation kiː ˈleɪʃ ˀn kɪ-, kə-, tʃiː-

Chelmer ˈtʃelm ə ‖ -ˀr

Chelmsford ˈtʃelmz fəd ˈtʃelmᵖs- ‖ -fˀrd —*locally also* ˈtʃemz-, ˈtʃɒmz-

Chelsea ˈtʃels i
ˌChelsea ˈbun

Cheltenham ˈtʃelt ˀn̩ əm
ˌCheltenham ˈSpa

chemical ˈkem ɪk ˀl **~ly** ᵢ **~s** z
ˌchemical ˌengiˈneering

chemin de fer ʃə ˌmæn də ˈfeə ‖ -ˈfeˀr —*Fr* [ʃə mæt fɛːʁ, ʃmæt fɛːʁ]

chemis|e ʃə ˈmiːz **~es** ɪz əz

chemist ˈkem ɪst §-əst **~s, ~'s** s

chemis|try ˈkem ɪs |tri -əs- **~tries** triz

Chemnitz ˈkem nɪts —*Ger* [ˈkɛm nɪts]

chemo- *comb. form*
with stress-neutral suffix ˌkiːm əʊ ˌkem əʊ ‖ -oʊ — **chemosynthesis** ˌkiːm əʊ ˈsɪnˀθ əs ɪs ˌkem-, -ɪs ɪs, §-əs ‖ ˌ·oʊ-
with stress-imposing suffix kiː ˈmɒ+ ke ˈmɒ+ ‖ -ˈmɑː+ — **chemolysis** kiː ˈmɒl əs ɪs ke-, -ɪs ɪs, §-əs ‖ -ˈmɑːl-

chemotherapy ˌkiːm əʊ ˈθer əp i ˌkem- ‖ ˌ·oʊ-

Chenevix *(i)* ˈtʃen ə vɪks, *(ii)* ˈʃen-

Cheney *(i)* ˈtʃeɪn i, *(ii)* ˈtʃiːn i —*The American politician Dick C~ is* (i)

Chengdu ˌtʃeŋ ˈduː ˌtʃʌŋ- —*Chi* Chéngdū [²tʂʰən ¹tu]

Chenies *(i)* ˈtʃeɪn iz, *(ii)* ˈtʃiːn iz —*The place in Bucks may be either* (i) *or* (ii).

chenille ʃə ˈniːˀl

Chennai ˈtʃen aɪ tʃe ˈnaɪ

cheongsam ˌtʃɒŋ ˈsæm tʃi ˌɒŋ- ‖ ˈtʃɔːŋ sɑːm ˈtʃɑːŋ- **~s** z

Cheops ˈkiː ɒps ‖ -ɑːps

Chepstow ˈtʃep stəʊ ‖ -stoʊ

cheque (= *check*) **cheques** tʃeks
ˈcheque card

chequebook ˈtʃek bʊk §-buːk **~s** s

chequer ˈtʃek ə ‖ -ˀr (= *checker*) **~ed** d **chequering** ˈtʃek ᵊr ɪŋ **~s** z

Chequers ˈtʃek əz ‖ -ˀrz

Cher ʃeə ‖ ʃeˀr

Cherbourg ˈʃeə bʊəg ˈʃɜː-, -bɔːg, -bɜːg ‖ ˈʃer bʊrg —*Fr* [ʃɛʁ buːʁ]

cherchez la femme ˌʃeəʃ eɪ læ ˈfæm -lɑː· ‖ ˌʃer ˌʃeɪ- —*Fr* [ʃɛʁ ʃe la fam]

Cheremis, Cheremiss ˈtʃer ə mɪs -miːs, ˌ·ˈ·

Cherenkov tʃə ˈreŋk ɒf tʃɪ-, -ɒv ‖ -ɑːf —*Russ* [tʃɪ ˈrʲen kəf]

Cherie, Chérie ʃə ˈriː ʃe-

Cherilyn *(i)* ˈtʃer əl ɪn -ɪl-, -ən, *(ii)* ˈʃer-

cherimoya ˌtʃer ɪ ˈmɔɪ ə -ə-

cherish ˈtʃer ɪʃ **~ed** t **~es** ɪz əz **~ing** ɪŋ

Cheriton ˈtʃer ɪt ən -ət- ‖ -ˀn

Chernobyl tʃɜː ˈnəʊb ˀl tʃə-, -ˈnɒb-, -ɪl; ˈtʃɜːn əb- ‖ tʃˀr ˈnoʊb- —*Russ* [tʃɪr ˈno bilʲ]

Chernomyrdin ˌtʃɜːn ə ˈmɪəd ɪn -ˈmɜːd-, -ˀn ‖ ˌtʃɪrn ə ˈmɪrd- ˌtʃɜːn- —*Russ* [tʃɪr nʌ ˈmɪr dʲɪn]

chernozem ˈtʃɜːn əʊ zem ˌ··ˈzjɒm ‖ ˌtʃɜːn ə ˈzem -ˈʒɑːm, -ˈʒɔːm —*Russ* [tʃɪr nʌ ˈzʲɔm]

Cherokee ˈtʃer ə kiː ˌ··ˈ· **~s** z

cheroot ʃə ˈruːt **~s** s

cherr|y, C~ ˈtʃer |i **~ies** iz

cherry-pick ˈtʃer i pɪk **~ed** t **~ing** ɪŋ **~s** s

Chersonese, c~ ˈkɜːs ə niːs -niːz, ˌ··ˈ· ‖ ˈkɜːs-

chert tʃɜːt ‖ tʃɜːt **cherts** tʃɜːts ‖ tʃɜːts

Chertsey ˈtʃɜːts i ‖ ˈtʃɜːts i

cherub ˈtʃer əb **~s** z

cherubic tʃə ˈruːb ɪk tʃe- **~ally** ˀl_i

C

cherubim 'tʃer ə bɪm 'ker-, -u-
Cherubini ˌker u 'biːn i -ə-, -iː —*It*
   [ke ru 'biː ni]
chervil 'tʃɜːv əl -ɪl ‖ 'tʃɜːv-
Cherwell 'tʃɑː wəl -wel ‖ 'tʃɑːr-
Cheryl *(i)* 'tʃer əl -ɪl, *(ii)* 'ʃer-
Chesapeake 'tʃes ə piːk
   ˌChesapeake 'Bay
Chesebrough 'tʃiːz brə ‖ -broʊ
Chesham 'tʃeʃ əm —*formerly* 'tʃes-
Cheshire 'tʃeʃ ə -ɪə ‖ -ᵊr
   ˌCheshire 'cat, ˌCheshire 'cheese
Cheshunt 'tʃes ᵊnt 'tʃez- —*There is also a
   spelling pronunciation* 'tʃeʃ-
Chesil 'tʃez əl
   ˌChesil 'Beach
Chesney *(i)* 'tʃez ni, *(ii)* 'tʃes ni
chess tʃes
chessboard 'tʃes bɔːd ‖ -bɔːrd -boʊrd ~s z
chess|man 'tʃes |mæn -mən ~**men** men mən
chest tʃest **chested** 'tʃest ɪd -əd **chests** tʃests
   ˌchest of 'drawers
-chested 'tʃest ɪd -əd
Chester 'tʃest ə ‖ -ᵊr
Chesterfield, C~ 'tʃest ə fiːᵊld ‖ -ᵊr- ~s z
Chester-le-Street 'tʃest ə li striːt -ᵊl i-;
   'tʃes li striːt ‖ ˌ·ᵊr-
Chesterton 'tʃest ət ən ‖ -ᵊrt ᵊn
chestnut, C~ 'tʃes nʌt 'tʃest- ~s s
   'chestnut tree
chest|y 'tʃest |i ~**ier** i ə ‖ i ᵊr ~**iest** i ɪst i əst
   ~**iness** i nəs i nɪs
Chet tʃet
Chetham *(i)* 'tʃiːt əm ‖ 'tʃiːt̬-, *(ii)* 'tʃet- ‖ 'tʃet̬-
Chetnik 'tʃet nɪk ~s s
Chetwode 'tʃet wʊd
Chetwyn 'tʃet wɪn
Chetwynd 'tʃet wɪnd
Cheung tʃʌŋ —*Cantonese* ['tsœːŋ]
cheval glass ʃə 'væl glɑːs §-glæs ‖ -glæs
chevalier *n* ˌʃev ə 'lɪə ‖ -'lɪᵊr ~s z
Chevalier *name* ʃə 'væl i eɪ ʃɪ-
Chevening 'tʃiːv nɪŋ
Chevette *tdmk* ʃə 'vet ʃe- ~s s
Chevington 'tʃev ɪŋ tən
Cheviot 'tʃiːv i ət 'tʃev- ‖ 'ʃev- —*locally* 'tʃiːv-
   ~s s
Chevon, Chevonne ʃə 'vɒn ʃɪ- ‖ -'vɑːn
chèvre 'ʃev rə ˌʃeəv- —*Fr* [ʃɛːvʁ]
Chevrolet *tdmk* 'ʃev rə leɪ ˌ·'· ‖ ˌʃev rə 'leɪ ~s
   z
chevron 'ʃev rən -rɒn ~s z
chevv|y, chev|y *v* 'tʃev |i ~**ied** id ~**ies** iz
   ~**ying** i ɪŋ
Chevvy, Chevy *n 'Chevrolet'* 'ʃev i
chew tʃuː **chewed** tʃuːd **chewing** 'tʃuː ɪŋ
   chews tʃuːz
   'chewing gum
Chewton 'tʃuːt ᵊn
chew|y 'tʃuː |i ~**iness** i nəs -nɪs
Chex *tdmk* tʃeks
Cheyenne ˌʃaɪ 'æn ◂ -'en ~s z
Cheyne *(i)* 'tʃeɪn i, *(ii)* tʃeɪn, *(iii)* tʃiːn

Cheyne-Stokes ˌtʃeɪn 'stəʊks ‖ -'stoʊks
chez ʃeɪ —*Fr* [ʃe]
  ₍₁₎**chez 'nous** nu: —*Fr* [nu]
chi *Greek letter* kaɪ **chis** kaɪz
Chiang Kaishek ˌtʃæŋ kaɪ 'ʃek tʃi ˌæŋ-
  ‖ tʃi ˌɑːŋ- —*Chi* Jiǎng Jièshí [³tɕjaŋ ⁴tɕje ²ʂɨ¹]
Chiang Mai tʃi ˌæŋ 'maɪ ‖ -ˌɑːŋ-
Chianti, c~ ki 'ænt i ‖ -'ɑːnt̬ i —*It* ['kjan ti]
  ~**shire** ʃə ʃɪə, ˌʃaɪ ə ‖ ʃᵊr ʃɪr, ˌʃaɪ ᵊr
Chiapas tʃi 'æp əs ‖ -'ɑːp- —*Sp* ['tʃja pas]
chiaroscuro ki ˌɑːr ə 'skʊər əʊ -'skjʊər-
  ‖ -'skʊr oʊ -'skjʊr- —*It* [kja ros 'kuː ro] ~s z
chias|ma kaɪ 'æz |mə ~**mas** məz ~**mata** mət ə
  ‖ mət̬ ə
chiasmus kaɪ 'æz məs
Chibcha 'tʃɪb tʃə
Chibchan 'tʃɪb tʃən
chibouk tʃɪ 'buːk tʃə- ~s s
chic ʃiːk ʃɪk
Chicago ʃɪ 'kɑːg əʊ ʃə- ‖ -oʊ —*locally also*
  -'kɔːg-
Chicana, c~ tʃɪ 'kɑːn ə ʃɪ-, tʃə-, ʃə- ‖ -'kæn-
  —*Sp* [tʃi 'ka na] ~s z
chican|e ʃɪ 'keɪn ʃə- ~**ed** d ~**es** z ~**ing** ɪŋ
chicaner|y ʃɪ 'keɪn ᵊr |i ʃə- ~**ies** iz
Chicano, c~ tʃɪ 'kɑːn əʊ ʃɪ-, tʃə-, ʃə- ‖ -oʊ
  -'kæn- —*Sp* [tʃi 'ka no] ~s z
Chichele 'tʃɪtʃ əl i -ɪl-
Chichén Itzá tʃɪ ˌtʃen ɪt 'sɑː -iːt- —*AmSp*
  [tʃi ˌtʃe nit 'sa]
Chichester 'tʃɪtʃ ɪst ə -əst- ‖ -ᵊr —*but the place
  in upstate NY is* 'tʃaɪ ˌtʃest ᵊr
Chichewa tʃɪ 'tʃeɪ wə
chi-chi 'ʃiː ʃiː 'tʃiː tʃiː
chick, Chick tʃɪk **chicks** tʃɪks
chickabidd|y 'tʃɪk ə bɪd |i ~**ies** iz
chickadee 'tʃɪk ə diː ˌ·'· ~s z
chickaree 'tʃɪk ə riː ~s z
Chickasaw 'tʃɪk ə sɔː ‖ -sɑː ~s z
chicken 'tʃɪk ɪn -ən ~**ed** d ~**ing** ɪŋ ~s z
  'chicken pox, 'chicken ˌwire
chickenfeed 'tʃɪk ɪn fiːd -ən-
chicken-fried 'tʃɪk ɪn fraɪd -ən-
chickenhearted ˌtʃɪk ɪn 'hɑːt ɪd ◂ -ən-, -əd
  ‖ -'hɑːrt̬ əd ◂
chickenlivered ˌtʃɪk ɪn 'lɪv əd ◂ -ən- ‖ -ᵊrd ◂
  '·ˌ·ˌ·
chickenshit 'tʃɪk ɪn ʃɪt -ən-
chickpea 'tʃɪk piː ~s z
chickweed 'tʃɪk wiːd
chicle 'tʃɪk əl
chicory 'tʃɪk ᵊr i
chid... —*see* **chide**
Chiddingly *place in Sussex* ˌtʃɪd ɪŋ 'laɪ
chide tʃaɪd **chid** tʃɪd **chidden** 'tʃɪd ᵊn **chided**
  'tʃaɪd ɪd -əd **chides** tʃaɪdz
chief tʃiːf **chiefly** 'tʃiːf li **chiefs** tʃiːfs
  ˌchief 'constable; ˌChief E'xecutive; ˌchief
  in'spector; ˌChief 'Justice◂; ˌchief of
  'staff; ˌchief ˌsuperin'tendent◂
chieftain 'tʃiːf tən -ɪn ~s z
chieftain|cy 'tʃiːf tən |si -ɪn- ~**cies** siz
chiffchaff 'tʃɪf tʃæf ~s s

C

chiffon 'ʃɪf ɒn ʃɪ 'fɒn ‖ ʃɪ 'fɑːn ~s z
chiffonier, chiffonnier ˌʃɪf ə 'nɪə ‖ -'nɪ°r ~s z
chigger 'tʃɪg ə 'dʒɪg- ‖ -°r ~s z
chignon 'ʃiːn jɒn -jɔ̃ ‖ -jɑːn —Fr [ʃi njɔ̃] ~s z
chigoe 'tʃɪg əʊ ‖ -oʊ 'tʃiːg- ~s z
Chigwell 'tʃɪg wəl -wel
chihuahua, C~ tʃɪ 'wɑː wə tʃə-, ʃɪ-, ʃə-, -wɑːː -'waʊ ə —Sp [tʃi 'wa wa] ~s z
chikungunya ˌtʃɪk ʊŋ 'gun jə
chilblain 'tʃɪl bleɪn ~ed d ~s z
child, Child tʃaɪ°ld **children** 'tʃɪldr ən 'tʃʊldr- ‖ 'tʃɪld °rn **children's** 'tʃɪldr ənz 'tʃʊldr- ‖ 'tʃɪld °rnz **child's** tʃaɪ°ldz
    'child a‚buse; 'child care; 'child's play; ‚child 'prodigy
childbearing 'tʃaɪ°ld ‚beər ɪŋ ‖ -‚ber- -‚bær-
childbed 'tʃaɪ°ld bed
childbirth 'tʃaɪ°ld bɜːθ ‖ -bɜːθ
Childe, c~ 'tʃaɪ°ld
childermas, C~ 'tʃɪld ə mæs ‖ -°r-
Childers 'tʃɪld əz ‖ -°rz
childhood 'tʃaɪ°ld hʊd
childish 'tʃaɪ°ld ɪʃ ~ly li ~ness nəs nɪs
childless 'tʃaɪld ləs -lɪs ~ness nəs nɪs
childlike 'tʃaɪ°ld laɪk
childmind|er 'tʃaɪld ‚maɪnd| ə ‖ -°r ~ers əz ‖ -°rz ~ing ɪŋ
childproof 'tʃaɪ°ld pruːf §-prʊf
children 'tʃɪldr ən 'tʃʊldr- ‖ 'tʃɪld °rn ~'s z
    'children's home
Childs tʃaɪ°ldz
Childwall 'tʃɪl wɔːl 'tʃɪld- ‖ -wɑːl
Chile, chile 'tʃɪl i ‖ -eɪ —Sp ['tʃi le]
    ‚chile con 'carne kɒn 'kɑːn i →kɒŋ-, kən-, -eɪ ‖ kɑːn 'kɑːrn i kən-
Chilean 'tʃɪl i ‚ən ‖ tʃɪ 'liː ən, -'leɪ- ~s z
chili 'tʃɪl i (= chilly) ~es z
    'chili dog
chiliad 'kɪl i æd 'kaɪl-, -əd ~s z
chiliasm 'kɪl i ‚æz əm
chiliast 'kɪl i æst ~s s
chiliastic ˌkɪl i 'æst ɪk ◄
Chilkoot 'tʃɪl kuːt
chill tʃɪl **chilled** tʃɪld **chilling** 'tʃɪl ɪŋ **chills** tʃɪlz
chiller 'tʃɪl ə ‖ -°r ~s z
chilli 'tʃɪl i (= chilly) ~es z
    ‚chilli con 'carne kɒn 'kɑːn i →kɒŋ-, kən-, -eɪ ‖ kɑːn 'kɑːrn i kən-; 'chilli ‚powder
chilling 'tʃɪl ɪŋ ~ly li
chillness 'tʃɪl nəs -nɪs
Chillon ʃɪ 'lɒn ʃə-; 'ʃɪl ən, -ɒn ‖ ʃə 'lɑːn —Fr [ʃi jɔ̃]
chillum 'tʃɪl əm
chill|y 'tʃɪl |i ~ier i ‚ə ‖ i ‚°r ~iest i ‚ɪst i ‚əst ~ily ɪ li əl i ~iness i nəs i nɪs
Chilpruf tdmk 'tʃɪl pruːf §-prʊf
Chiltern 'tʃɪlt ən ‖ -°rn ~s z
    ‚Chiltern 'Hills; ‚Chiltern 'Hundreds
Chilton 'tʃɪlt ən ‖ -°n
Chilver 'tʃɪlv ə ‖ -°r ~s z
chimaera kaɪ 'mɪər ə kɪ-, kə-, ʃɪ-, ʃə-, -'meər-; 'kɪm ər ə, 'ʃɪm- ‖ -'mɪr ə ~s z

Chimborazo ˌtʃɪm bə 'rɑːz əʊ ˌʃɪm- ‖ -oʊ —AmSp [tʃim bo 'ra so]
chime tʃaɪm **chimed** tʃaɪmd **chimes** tʃaɪmz **chiming** 'tʃaɪm ɪŋ
chimer 'tʃaɪm ə ‖ -°r ~s z
chimera kaɪ 'mɪər ə kɪ-, kə-, ʃɪ-, ʃə-, -'meər-; 'kɪm ər ə, 'ʃɪm- ‖ -'mɪr ə ~s z
chimeric kaɪ 'mer ɪk kɪ-, kə-, ʃɪ- ~al °l ~ally °l i
chimichanga ˌtʃɪm i 'tʃæŋ gə ‖ -'tʃɑːŋ- —Sp [tʃi mi 'tʃaŋ ga] ~s z
chimichurri ˌtʃɪm i 'tʃʊr i -'tʃʌr i
chimney 'tʃɪm ni ~s z
chimneybreast 'tʃɪm ni brest ~s s
chimneypiec|e 'tʃɪm ni piːs ~es ɪz əz
chimneypot 'tʃɪm ni pɒt ‖ -pɑːt ~s s
chimneystack 'tʃɪm ni stæk ~s s
chimneysweep 'tʃɪm ni swiːp ~s s
chimneysweeper 'tʃɪm ni ‚swiːp ə ‖ -°r ~s z
chimp tʃɪmp **chimps** tʃɪmps
chimpanzee ˌtʃɪm pæn 'ziː ◄ -ən- ‖ ˌʃɪmp-; tʃɪm 'pænz i ~s z
chin tʃɪn **chinned** tʃɪnd **chinning** 'tʃɪn ɪŋ **chins** tʃɪnz
China, china 'tʃaɪn ə
China|man, c~ 'tʃaɪn ə |mən ~men mən men
Chinatown 'tʃaɪn ə taʊn
chinaware 'tʃaɪn ə weə ‖ -wer
chinch tʃɪntʃ **chinches** 'tʃɪntʃ ɪz -əz
    'chinch bug
chincherinchee ˌtʃɪntʃ ə 'rɪntʃ i -rɪn 'tʃiː, -rən 'tʃi- ~s z
chinchilla tʃɪn 'tʃɪl ə ~s z
chin-chin ˌtʃɪn 'tʃɪn
Chincoteague 'ʃɪŋk ə tiːg 'tʃɪŋk-
Chindit 'tʃɪnd ɪt §-ət ~s s
chine tʃaɪn **chines** tʃaɪnz
Chinese ˌtʃaɪ 'niːz ◄ ‖ -'niːs ◄
    ‚Chinese 'chequers; ‚Chinese 'gooseberry; ‚Chinese 'restaurant
Chingford 'tʃɪŋ fəd ‖ -f°rd
chink tʃɪŋk **chinked** tʃɪŋkt **chinking** 'tʃɪŋk ɪŋ **chinks** tʃɪŋks
chinless 'tʃɪn ləs -lɪs
    ‚chinless 'wonder
Chinnor 'tʃɪn ə ‖ -°r
chino 'tʃiːn əʊ 'ʃiːn- ‖ -oʊ ~s z
chinoiserie ʃɪn 'wɑːz ər i (ᵢ)ʃiːn-, -ˌwɑːz ə 'riː- —Fr [ʃi nwaz ʁi]
chinook, C~ (ᵢ)tʃɪ 'nuːk ʃɪ-, §tʃə-, -'nʊk ‖ ʃə 'nʊk ʃɪ- ~s s
chinquapin 'tʃɪŋk ə pɪn -ɪ- ~s z
chinstrap 'tʃɪn stræp ~s s
chintz tʃɪnts **chintzes** 'tʃɪnts ɪz -əz
chintz|y 'tʃɪnts |i ~ier i ‚ə ‖ i ‚°r ~iest i ‚ɪst i ‚əst
chin-up, chinup 'tʃɪn ʌp ~s s
chinwag 'tʃɪn wæg ~s z
chinwagging 'tʃɪn ‚wæg ɪŋ
chionodoxa kaɪ ‚ɒn ə 'dɒks ə -‚əʊn-, ˌkaɪ ən- ‖ kaɪ ‚oʊn ə 'dɑːks ə ~s z
Chios 'kaɪ ɒs 'kiː- ‖ -ɑːs

C

chip tʃɪp **chipped** tʃɪpt **chipping** 'tʃɪp ɪŋ **chips**
tʃɪps
'chip ˌbasket; 'chip shot
chipboard 'tʃɪp bɔːd ‖ -bɔːrd -boʊrd
chipmunk 'tʃɪp mʌŋk ~s s
chipolata ˌtʃɪp ə 'lɑːt ə ‖ -'lɑːt ə ~s z
chipotle tʃɪ 'pɒt leɪ tʃə-, -li ‖ tʃə 'poʊt- -'pɑːt-
—Sp [tʃi 'pot le] ~s z
chipp... —see **chip**
Chippendale 'tʃɪp ən deɪ°l →-m- ~s z
Chippenham 'tʃɪp ən ˌəm
chipper 'tʃɪp ə ‖ -°r
Chippewa 'tʃɪp ɪ wɑː -ə-, -wə
chippi... —see **chip; chippy**
chipping, C~ 'tʃɪp ɪŋ ~s z
ˌChipping 'Sodbury 'sɒd bər i →'sɒb-
‖ 'sɑːd ˌber i -bər ˌi
chipp|y 'tʃɪp |i ~ies iz
Chirac 'ʃɪr æk ‖ ʃɪ 'rɑːk —Fr [ʃi ʁak]
chiral 'kaɪ°r əl
chirality kaɪ° 'ræl ət i -ɪt- ‖ -ət̬ i
Chirk tʃɜːk ‖ tʃɜːk
chiromancy 'kaɪ°r əʊ ˌmæn°s i ‖ -ə-
Chiron 'kaɪ°r ən -ɒn ‖ -ɑːn
chiropodist kɪ 'rɒp əd ɪst kə-, ʃɪ-, ʃə-, §-əst
‖ kə 'rɑːp- —formerly also kaɪ°- ~s s
chiropody kɪ 'rɒp əd i kə-, ʃɪ-, ʃə- ‖ kə 'rɑːp-
—formerly also kaɪ°-
chiropractic ˌkaɪ°r əʊ 'prækt ɪk ◄ '···ˌ·
‖ 'kaɪ°r ə ˌprækt ɪk
chiropractor 'kaɪ°r əʊ ˌprækt ə ‖ -ə ˌprækt °r
~s z
chirp tʃɜːp ‖ tʃɜːp **chirped** tʃɜːpt ‖ tʃɜːpt
chirping 'tʃɜːp ɪŋ ‖ 'tʃɜːp ɪŋ **chirps** tʃɜːps
‖ tʃɜːps
chirper 'tʃɜːp ə ‖ 'tʃɜːp °r ~s z
chirp|y 'tʃɜːp |i ‖ 'tʃɜːp |i **-ier** i ə ‖ i ˌ°r **-iest**
i ˌɪst i ˌəst **-ily** ɪ li əl i **-iness** i nəs i nɪs
chirr tʃɜː ‖ tʃɜː **chirred** tʃɜːd ‖ tʃɜːd **chirring**
'tʃɜːr ɪŋ ‖ 'tʃɜː ɪŋ **chirrs** tʃɜːz ‖ tʃɜːz
chirrup 'tʃɪr əp ‖ 'tʃɜː- **-ed** t **-ing** ɪŋ ~s s
chisel 'tʃɪz °l ~ed, ~led d ~ing, ~ling ˌɪŋ ~s z
chiseler, chiseller 'tʃɪz °l ə ‖ °r ~s z
Chisholm 'tʃɪz əm
Chisinau ˌkɪʃ ɪ 'naʊ —Moldovan Chişinău
[ki ʃi 'nəu]
Chislehurst 'tʃɪz °l hɜːst ‖ -hɜːst
chi-square ˌkaɪ skweə ‖ -skwer ~d d
'chi-square test
Chiswick 'tʃɪz ɪk §-ək
chit tʃɪt **chits** tʃɪts
chitchat 'tʃɪt tʃæt
chitin 'kaɪt ɪn -°n ‖ -°n
chitinous 'kaɪt ɪn əs -ən- ‖ -°n-
chitlings 'tʃɪt lɪŋz
chitlins 'tʃɪt lɪnz -lənz
chiton 'kaɪt °n -ɒn ‖ -ɑːn ~s z
Chittagong 'tʃɪt ə gɒŋ ‖ 'tʃɪt̬ ə gɔːŋ -gɑːŋ
Chittenden 'tʃɪt °nd ən
chitterling 'tʃɪt ə lɪŋ →-°l ɪŋ ‖ 'tʃɪt̬ °r lɪŋ
'tʃɪt lən ~s z
Chitty, c~ 'tʃɪt i ‖ 'tʃɪt̬ i
chiv tʃɪv ʃɪv **chivs** tʃɪvz ʃɪvz

chivalric 'ʃɪv °l rɪk ʃə 'væl-
chivalrous 'ʃɪv °l rəs **-ly** li ~ness nəs nɪs
chival|ry 'ʃɪv °l |ri ~ries riz
Chivas (i) 'ʃɪv æs, (ii) 'ʃiːvəs
chive tʃaɪv **chives** tʃaɪvz
Chivers 'tʃɪv əz ‖ -°rz
chivv|y, chiv|y 'tʃɪv |i ~ied id ~ies iz ~ying
i ˌɪŋ
chiz, chizz tʃɪz
chlamydi|a klə 'mɪd i |ə ~ae i: ~al ˌəl
Chloe, Chloë 'kləʊ i ‖ 'kloʊ i
chloracne ˌklɔːr 'æk ni ‖ ˌkloʊr-
chloral 'klɔːr əl ‖ 'kloʊr-
chlorambucil klɔːr 'æm bju sɪl ‖ -bjə- kloʊr-
chloramine 'klɔːr ə miːn ˌklɔːr 'æm iːn
‖ 'kloʊr-
chloramphenicol ˌklɔːr æm 'fen ɪ kɒl ˌ·əm-,
§-ə kɒl ‖ -koʊl ˌkloʊr-, -kɑːl, -kɔːl
chlorate 'klɔːr eɪt ‖ 'kloʊr- ~s s
chlordane 'klɔːd eɪn ‖ 'klɔːrd- 'kloʊrd-
chloric 'klɔːr ɪk 'klɒr- ‖ 'kloʊr-
chloride 'klɔːr aɪd ‖ 'kloʊr- ~s z
chlori|nate 'klɔːr ɪ |neɪt 'klɒr-, -ə- ‖ 'kloʊr-
~nated neɪt ɪd -əd ‖ neɪt̬ əd ~nates neɪts
~nating neɪt ɪŋ ‖ neɪt̬ ɪŋ
chlorination ˌklɔːr ɪ 'neɪʃ °n ˌklɒr-, -ə-
‖ ˌkloʊr-
chlorine 'klɔːr iːn -ɪn, §-ən ‖ 'kloʊr-
chlorite 'klɔːr aɪt ‖ 'kloʊr-
chloro- comb. form
with stress-neutral suffix ˌklɔːr əʊ ˌklɒr-
‖ ˌklɔːr ə ˌkloʊr- — **chlorobenzene**
ˌklɔːr əʊ 'benz iːn ˌklɒr- ‖ ˌklɔːr ə- ˌkloʊr-
chlorodyne 'klɔːr ə daɪn 'klɒr- ‖ 'kloʊr-
chlorofluorocarbon
ˌklɔːr əʊ ˌfluər əʊ 'kɑːbən -ˌflɔːr əʊ-;
-ˌfluː ə rəʊ- ‖ ˌklɔːr ə ˌflʊr oʊ 'kɑːrb ən
ˌkloʊr- ~s z
chloroform 'klɒr ə fɔːm 'klɔːr- ‖ 'klɔːr ə fɔːrm
'kloʊr- ~ed d ~ing ɪŋ ~s z
chlorophyl, chlorophyll 'klɒr ə fɪl 'klɔːr-
‖ 'klɔːr- 'kloʊr-
chloroplast 'klɔːr əʊ plɑːst -plæst
‖ 'klɔːr ə plæst 'kloʊr- ~s s
chloroquine, C~ 'klɔːr ə kwɪn 'klɒr-, -kwiːn
‖ 'klɔːr ə kwiːn 'kloʊr-
chlorosis klɔː 'rəʊs ɪs §-əs ‖ klə 'roʊs-
chlorpromazine ˌklɔː 'prəʊm ə ziːn -'prɒm-
‖ ˌklɔːr 'prɑːm ə ziːn ˌkloʊr-
Choat, Choate tʃəʊt ‖ tʃoʊt
Chobham 'tʃɒb əm ‖ 'tʃɑːb-
choc tʃɒk ‖ tʃɑːk (= chock) **chocs** tʃɒks ‖ tʃɑːks
chocaholic ˌtʃɒk ə 'hɒl ɪk ◄
‖ ˌtʃɑːk ə 'hɑːl ɪk ◄ ˌtʃɔːk-, -'hɔːl- ~s s
choc-bar 'tʃɒk bɑː ‖ 'tʃɑːk bɑːr ~s z
chocc|y 'tʃɒk |i ‖ 'tʃɑːk |i ~ies iz
chocho 'tʃəʊ tʃəʊ ‖ 'tʃoʊ tʃoʊ ~s z
choc-ice 'tʃɒk aɪs ‖ 'tʃɑːk- ~es ɪz əz
chock tʃɒk ‖ tʃɑːk **chocked** tʃɒkt ‖ tʃɑːkt
chocking 'tʃɒk ɪŋ ‖ 'tʃɑːk ɪŋ **chocks** tʃɒks
‖ tʃɑːks
chock-a-block ˌtʃɒk ə 'blɒk ◄ ‖ 'tʃɑːk ə blɑːk ◄
chock-full ˌtʃɒk 'fʊl ◄ ‖ ˌtʃɑːk- ˌtʃʌk-

C

chocoholic ˌtʃɒk ə 'hɒl ɪk ◂
‖ ˌtʃɑːk ə 'hɑːl ɪk ◂ ˌtʃɔːk-, -'hɔːl- **~s** s
chocolate 'tʃɒk lət -lɪt; 'tʃɒk əl ət, -ɪt ‖ 'tʃɔːk-
'tʃɑːk- **~s** s
ˌchocolate 'biscuit; 'chocolate cake, ˌ· · '·;
ˌchocolate 'pudding
chocolate-box 'tʃɒk lət bɒks -lɪt-
‖ 'tʃɔːk lət bɑːks 'tʃɑːk-
chocolatey 'tʃɒk lət i ‖ 'tʃɑːk lət i
Choctaw, c~ 'tʃɒkt ɔː ‖ 'tʃɑːkt ɔː -ɑː- **~s** z
CHOGM 'tʃɒg əm ‖ 'tʃɑːg-
choice tʃɔɪs **choicer** 'tʃɔɪs ə ‖ -ᵊr **choices**
'tʃɔɪs ɪz -əz **choicest** 'tʃɔɪs ɪst əst **choicely**
'tʃɔɪs li **choiceness** 'tʃɔɪs nəs -nɪs
choir 'kwaɪ ə ‖ 'kwaɪ ᵊr (! = quire) **choirs**
'kwaɪ əz ‖ 'kwaɪ ᵊrz
'choir school
choirboy 'kwaɪ ə bɔɪ ‖ 'kwaɪ ᵊr- **~s** z
choirmaster 'kwaɪ ə ˌmɑːst ə §-ˌmæst-
‖ 'kwaɪ ᵊr ˌmæst ᵊr **~s** z
choke tʃəʊk ‖ tʃoʊk **choked** tʃəʊkt ‖ tʃoʊkt
choking 'tʃəʊk ɪŋ ‖ 'tʃoʊk ɪŋ **chokes** tʃəʊks
‖ tʃoʊks
chokeberr|y 'tʃəʊk ˌber| i ‖ 'tʃoʊk- **~ies** iz
chokecherr|y 'tʃəʊk ˌtʃer| i ‖ 'tʃoʊk- **~ies** iz
choker 'tʃəʊk ə ‖ 'tʃoʊk ᵊr **~s** z
chokey, choky 'tʃəʊk i ‖ 'tʃoʊk i
cholecystectom|y ˌkɒl ɪ sɪst 'ekt əm |i ˌ·ə-
‖ ˌkoʊl ə- **~ies** iz
choler 'kɒl ə ‖ 'kɑːl ᵊr 'koʊl- (usually = collar)
cholera 'kɒl ər ə ‖ 'kɑːl-
choleraic ˌkɒl ə 'reɪ ɪk ◂ ‖ ˌkɑːl-
choleric 'kɒl ər ɪk kɒ 'ler- ‖ 'kɑːl- kə 'ler- **~ally**
ᵊl i
cholesterol kə 'lest ə rɒl kɒ-, -ᵊr ˌɒl ‖ -roʊl
-rɑːl, -rɔːl
choline 'kəʊl iːn ‖ 'koʊl-
cholinergic ˌkəʊl ɪ 'nɜːdʒ ɪk ◂ ˌkɒl-, -ə-
‖ ˌkoʊl ə 'nɜːdʒ ɪk ◂
cholinesterase ˌkəʊl ɪ 'nest ə reɪz ˌkɒl-, ˌ·ə-,
-reɪs ‖ ˌkoʊl-
cholla 'tʃɒl ə **~s** z
Cholmeley 'tʃʌm li
Cholmondeley 'tʃʌm li
Chomolungma ˌtʃəʊm əʊ 'lʊŋ mə
‖ ˌtʃoʊm oʊ-
chomp tʃɒmp ‖ tʃɑːmp **chomped** tʃɒmpt
‖ tʃɑːmpt **chomping** 'tʃɒmp ɪŋ ‖ 'tʃɑːmp ɪŋ
chomps tʃɒmps ‖ tʃɑːmps
Chomsky 'tʃɒmᵖsk i ‖ 'tʃɑːmᵖsk i
Chomskyan 'tʃɒmᵖsk i ˌən ‖ 'tʃɑːmᵖsk- **~s** z
chondroma kɒn 'drəʊm ə ‖ kɑːn 'droʊm ə **~s**
z
Chongqing ˌtʃʊŋ 'tʃɪŋ —Chi Chóngqìng
[²tʂʰʊŋ ⁴tɕʰiŋ]
Choo tʃuː
choo-choo 'tʃuː tʃuː **~s** z
chook tʃʊk **chooks** tʃʊks
choose tʃuːz (= chews) **chooses** 'tʃuːz ɪz -əz
choosing 'tʃuːz ɪŋ **chose** tʃəʊz ‖ tʃoʊz
chosen 'tʃəʊz ᵊn ‖ 'tʃoʊz ᵊn
chooser 'tʃuːz ə ‖ -ᵊr **~s** z

choos|y, choos|ey 'tʃuːz |i **~ier** i ə ‖ i ᵊr
~iest i ɪst i əst **~iness** i nəs i nɪs
chop tʃɒp ‖ tʃɑːp **chopped** tʃɒpt ‖ tʃɑːpt
chopping 'tʃɒp ɪŋ ‖ 'tʃɑːp ɪŋ **chops** tʃɒps
‖ tʃɑːps
ˌchop 'suey 'suː i
chop-chop ˌtʃɒp 'tʃɒp ‖ 'tʃɑːp tʃɑːp ˌ·'·
chopfallen 'tʃɒp ˌfɔːl ən ‖ 'tʃɑːp- ˌ-ˌfɑːl-
chop|house 'tʃɒp |haʊs ‖ 'tʃɑːp- **~houses**
haʊz ɪz -əz
Chopin 'ʃɒp æ 'ʃəʊp- ‖ 'ʃoʊp æn —Fr [ʃɔ pæ̃]
chopp... —see **chop**
chopper 'tʃɒp ə ‖ 'tʃɑːp ᵊr **~s** z
chopp|y 'tʃɒp |i ‖ 'tʃɑːp |i **~ier** i ə ‖ i ᵊr **~iest**
i ɪst i əst **~ily** i li əl i **~iness** i nəs -nɪs
chopstick 'tʃɒp stɪk ‖ 'tʃɑːp- **~s** s
choral 'kɔːr əl ‖ 'koʊr- **~ly** i
chorale kɒ 'rɑːl kɔː-, kə- ‖ kə 'ræl -'rɑːl **~s** z
-chord kɔːd ‖ kɔːrd — **octachord** 'ɒkt ə kɔːd
‖ 'ɑːkt ə kɔːrd
chord kɔːd ‖ kɔːrd (= cord) **chords** kɔːdz
‖ kɔːrdz
chordal 'kɔːd ᵊl ‖ 'kɔːrd-
chordate 'kɔːd eɪt -ɪt, -ət ‖ 'kɔːrd- **~s** s
chore tʃɔː ‖ tʃɔːr tʃoʊr **chores** tʃɔːz ‖ tʃɔːrz
tʃoʊrz
chorea kɔː 'rɪə kɒ-, kə- ‖ kə 'riː ə
choreograph 'kɒr i ə grɑːf 'kɔːr-, -græf
‖ 'kɔːr i ə græf 'koʊr- **~ed** t **~ing** ɪŋ **~s** s
choreographer ˌkɒr i 'ɒg rəf ə ˌkɔːr-
‖ ˌkɔːr i 'ɑːg rəf ᵊr ˌkoʊr- **~s** z
choreographic ˌkɒr i ə 'græf ɪk ◂ ˌkɔːr-
‖ ˌkɔːr- ˌkoʊr- **~ally** ᵊl i
choreography ˌkɒr i 'ɒg rəf i ˌkɔːr-
‖ ˌkɔːr i 'ɑːg- ˌkoʊr-
choriamb 'kɒr i æmb 'kɔːr-, -æm ‖ 'kɔːr- 'koʊr-
~s z
choriambic ˌkɒr i 'æm bɪk ◂ ˌkɔːr- ‖ ˌkɔːr-
ˌkoʊr-
choriambus ˌkɒr i 'æm bəs ˌkɔːr- ‖ ˌkɔːr-
ˌkoʊr-
choric 'kɒr ɪk ‖ 'kɔːr ɪk 'kɑːr-, 'koʊr-
chorine 'kɔːr iːn ‖ 'koʊr- **~s** z
chorion 'kɔːr i ˌən -ɒn ‖ -i ɑːn 'koʊr-
chorionic ˌkɔːr i 'ɒn ɪk ◂ ‖ -'ɑːn- ˌkoʊr-
chorister 'kɒr ɪst ə -əst- ‖ 'kɔːr əst ᵊr 'kɑːr-,
'koʊr- **~s** z
chorizo tʃə 'riːz əʊ tʃɒ-, -'rɪts- ‖ -oʊ -'riːs- —Sp
[tʃo 'ri θo, -so] **~s** z
Chorley 'tʃɔːl i ‖ 'tʃɔːrl i
Chorleywood ˌtʃɔːl i 'wʊd ‖ ˌtʃɔːrl-
Chorlton 'tʃɔːlt ən ‖ 'tʃɔːrlt ᵊn
Chorlton-cum-Hardy ˌtʃɔːlt ən kʌm 'hɑːd i
→ˌ·əŋ- ‖ ˌtʃɔːrlt ᵊn kʌm 'hɑːrd i
choroid 'kɔːr ɔɪd 'koʊr-
chortl|e 'tʃɔːt ᵊl ‖ 'tʃɔːrt ᵊl **~ed** d **~es** z **~ing**
ɪŋ
chorus 'kɔːr əs ‖ 'koʊr- **~ed** t **~es** ɪz əz **~ing** ɪŋ
'chorus girl
chose tʃəʊz ‖ tʃoʊz
chosen 'tʃəʊz ᵊn ‖ 'tʃoʊz ᵊn
chota 'tʃəʊt ə ‖ 'tʃoʊt̬ ə

Chou En-lai ˌtʃəʊ en ˈlaɪ -ən- ‖ ˌtʃoʊ- —*Chi Zhōu Ēnlái* [¹tʂou ¹ən ²lai]
chough tʃʌf **choughs** tʃʌfs
choux ʃuː *(= shoe)*
chow tʃaʊ **chows** tʃaʊz
 ˈchow chow; ˌchow ˈmein meɪn
Chow tʃaʊ —*Cantonese* [¹tsɐw]
chow-chow ˈtʃaʊ tʃaʊ ~s z
chowder ˈtʃaʊd ə ‖ -ᵊr ~s z
chowderhead ˈtʃaʊd ə hed ‖ -ᵊr- ~s z
chrestomath|y kre ˈstɒm əθ |i ‖ -ˈstɑːm- ~ies iz
Chrimbo ˈkrɪm bəʊ ‖ -boʊ
Chris krɪs **Chris's** ˈkrɪs ɪz -əz
chrism ˈkrɪz əm
chrisom ˈkrɪz əm ~s z
Chrissie, Chrissy ˈkrɪs i
Christ kraɪst **Christ's** kraɪsts
Christabel ˈkrɪst ə bel
Christadelphian ˌkrɪst ə ˈdelf i̯ən ◂ ~s z
Christchurch ˈkraɪst tʃɜːtʃ ‖ -tʃɜːtʃ
christen ˈkrɪs ᵊn ~ed d ~ing ɪŋ ~s z
Christendom ˈkrɪs ᵊn dəm
christening ˈkrɪs ᵊn ɪŋ ~s z
 ˈchristening robe
Christi ˈkrɪst i
Christian ˈkrɪs tʃən →ˈkrɪʃ-; ˈkrɪst i̯ən ~s z
 ˈChristian name; ˌChristian ˈScience
Christiana ˌkrɪst i ˈɑːn ə ˌkrɪs tʃi- ‖ -ˈæn ə
christiania, C~ ˌkrɪst i ˈɑːn i̯ə ~s z
Christianis... —*see* **Christianiz...**
Christianit|y ˌkrɪst i ˈæn ət |i ˌkrɪs tʃi-, →ˌkrɪʃ tʃi-, -ɪt i ‖ ˌkrɪs tʃi ˈæn ət |i ~ies iz
Christianization ˌkrɪs tʃən aɪ ˈzeɪʃ ᵊn →ˌkrɪʃ-, -ɪ'--; ˌkrɪst i̯ən aɪ ˈzeɪʃ- ‖ -ə ˈzeɪʃ-
Christianiz|e ˈkrɪs tʃə naɪz →ˈkrɪʃ-; ˈkrɪst i̯ə naɪz ~ed d ~er/s ə/z ‖ ᵊr/z ~es ɪz əz ~ing ɪŋ
Christianly ˈkrɪs tʃən li →ˈkrɪʃ-; ˈkrɪst i̯ən li
Christie, c~ ˈkrɪst i ~s, ~'s z
Christina krɪ ˈstiːn ə
Christine ˈkrɪst iːn
Christlike ˈkraɪst laɪk ~ness nəs nɪs
Christmas ˈkrɪs məs §ˈkrɪz- —*in very careful speech sometimes* ˈkrɪst- ~es ɪz əz
 ˈChristmas box; ˈChristmas cake; ˈChristmas card; ˌChristmas ˈcracker; ˌChristmas ˈDay; ˌChristmas ˈEve; ˈChristmas ˌIsland ‖ ˌ· ·ˈ·; ˈChristmas ˌpresent; ˌChristmas ˈpudding; ˌChristmas ˈstocking; ˈChristmas tree
Christmassy ˈkrɪs məs i
Christmastide ˈkrɪs məs taɪd ˈkrɪst-
Christmastime ˈkrɪs məs taɪm ˈkrɪst-
Christobel ˈkrɪst ə bel
Christophe krɪ ˈstɒf ‖ kriː ˈstɑːf -ˈstɔːf —*Fr* [kʁi stɔf]
christophene ˈkrɪst ə fiːn ~s z
Christopher ˈkrɪst əf ə ‖ -ᵊr
Christopherson krɪ ˈstɒf əs ən ‖ -ˈstɑːf ᵊrs-
Christy, c~ ˈkrɪst i
chroma ˈkrəʊm ə ‖ ˈkroʊm ə
chromate ˈkrəʊm eɪt ‖ ˈkroʊm- ~s s

chromatic krə ˈmæt ɪk krəʊ- ‖ kroʊ ˈmæt̬ ɪk
 ~ally ᵊl̬ i ~ness nəs nɪs
chromaticity ˌkrəʊm ə ˈtɪs ət i -ɪt i ‖ ˌkroʊm ə ˈtɪs ət̬ i
chromatid ˈkrəʊm ət ɪd §-əd ‖ -ət̬ əd -ə tɪd ~s z
chromatin ˈkrəʊm ət ɪn §-ən ‖ ˈkroʊm- ~s z
chromatogram ˈkrəʊm ət ə græm krəʊ ˈmæt- ‖ kroʊ ˈmæt̬ ə græm krə- ~s z
chromatographic ˌkrəʊm ət ə ˈgræf ɪk ◂ ‖ kroʊ ˌmæt̬ ə- krə-
chromatography ˌkrəʊm ə ˈtɒg rəf i ‖ ˌkroʊm ə ˈtɑːg-
chrome krəʊm ‖ kroʊm **chromed** krəʊmd ‖ kroʊmd **chromes** krəʊmz ‖ kroʊmz
 chroming ˈkrəʊm ɪŋ ‖ ˈkroʊm ɪŋ
 ˌchrome ˈyellow
chrominance ˈkrəʊm ɪn ənᵗs §-ən- ‖ ˈkroʊm-
chromite ˈkrəʊm aɪt ‖ ˈkroʊm-
chromium ˈkrəʊm i̯əm ‖ ˈkroʊm-
chromo ˈkrəʊm əʊ ‖ ˈkroʊm oʊ ~s z
chromolithograph ˌkrəʊm əʊ ˈlɪθ ə grɑːf -græf ‖ ˌkroʊm ə ˈlɪθ ə græf ~s s
chromolithographic ˌkrəʊm əʊ ˌlɪθ ə ˈgræf ɪk ‖ ˌkroʊm ə-
chromolithography ˌkrəʊm əʊ lɪ ˈθɒg rəf i ‖ ˌkroʊm ə lɪ ˈθɑːg-
chromophob|ia ˌkrəʊm əʊ ˈfəʊb |i̯ə ‖ ˌkroʊm ə ˈfoʊb |i̯ə ~ic ɪk
chromosomal ˌkrəʊm ə ˈsəʊm ᵊl ◂ ‖ ˌkroʊm ə ˈzoʊm ᵊl ◂ -ˈsoʊm- ~ly i

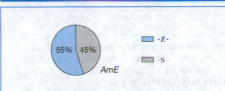

CHROMOSOME

55% 45%

AmE

-z-

-s

chromosome ˈkrəʊm ə səʊm ‖ ˈkroʊm ə zoʊm -soʊm — *Preference poll, AmE:* -zoʊm 55%, -soʊm 45%. ~s z
chromosphere ˈkrəʊm ə sfɪə ‖ ˈkroʊm ə sfɪr
chronax|ie, chronax|y ˈkrəʊn æks |i krɒn ˈæks i ‖ ˈkroʊn- ˈkrɑːn- ~ies iz
chroneme ˈkrəʊn iːm ‖ ˈkroʊn- ~s z
chronemic krəʊ ˈniːm ɪk ‖ kroʊ-
chronic ˈkrɒn ɪk ‖ ˈkrɑːn ɪk ~ally ᵊl̬ i
chronicl|e, C~ ˈkrɒn ɪk ᵊl ‖ ˈkrɑːn- ~ed d ~es z ~ing ɪŋ
chronicler ˈkrɒn ɪk lə ‖ ˈkrɑːn ɪk lᵊr ~s z
chrono- *comb. form*
 with stress-neutral suffix ¦krɒn ə ¦krəʊn əʊ ‖ ¦krɑːn ə ¦kroʊn ə — **chronoscopic** ˌkrɒn ə ˈskɒp ɪk ◂ ˌkrəʊn- ‖ ˌkrɑːn ə ˈskɑːp ɪk ◂ ˌkroʊn-
 with stress-imposing suffix krə ˈnɒ+ ‖ krə ˈnɑː+ — **chronoscopy** krə ˈnɒsk əp i ‖ -ˈnɑːsk-
chronograph ˈkrɒn ə grɑːf ˈkrəʊn-, -græf ‖ ˈkrɑːn ə græf ˈkroʊn- ~s s

chronological ˌkrɒn ə ˈlɒdʒ ɪk ᵊl ◂ ˌkrəʊn-,
-ᵊl ˈɒdʒ- ‖ ˌkrɑːn ᵊl ˈɑːdʒ ɪk ᵊl ◂ ˌkroʊn- **~ly**
ˌi

chronolog|y krə ˈnɒl ədʒ |i krɒ-, krəʊ-
‖ -ˈnɑːl- **~ies** iz

chronometer krə ˈnɒm ɪt ə krɒ-, krəʊ-, -ət-
‖ -ˈnɑːm ət̬ ᵊr **~s** z

chronometric ˌkrɒn ə ˈmetr ɪk ◂ ˌkrəʊn-
‖ ˌkrɑːn-, ˌkroʊn- **~al** ᵊl **~ally** ᵊl̬i

chronometry krə ˈnɒm ətr i krɒ-, krəʊ-, -ɪtr-
‖ -ˈnɑːm-

chrysalid ˈkrɪs əl ɪd §-əd **~s** z

chrysalides krɪ ˈsæl ɪ diːz krə-, -ə-

chrysalis ˈkrɪs əl ɪs §-əs **~es** ɪz əz

chrysanth krə ˈsæn̆θ krɪ-, -ˈzæn̆θ **~s** s

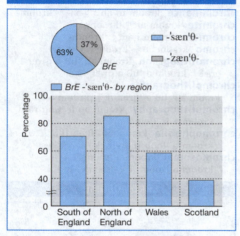

CHRYSANTHEMUM

chrysanthemum krə ˈsæn̆θ ɪm əm krɪ-,
-ˈzæn̆θ-, -əm̩ əm — *Preference poll, BrE:*
-ˈsæn̆θ- *63%,* -ˈzæn̆θ- *37%.* **~s** z

Chryseis kraɪ ˈsiː ɪs §ˌəs

chryselephantine ˌkrɪs ˌel ɪ ˈfænt aɪn -ə-

Chrysler *tdmk* ˈkraɪz lə ‖ ˈkraɪs lᵊr **~s** z

chrysolite ˈkrɪs ə laɪt

chrysoprase ˈkrɪs ə preɪz

Chrysostom ˈkrɪs əst əm

chrysotile ˈkrɪs ə taɪᵊl -tɪl, §-tᵊl

chthonian ˈθəʊn i ən ˈkθəʊn- ‖ ˈθoʊn-

chthonic ˈθɒn ɪk ˈkθɒn- ‖ ˈθɑːn-

chub tʃʌb **chubs** tʃʌbz

Chubb tʃʌb

chubb|y ˈtʃʌb |i **~ier** i ə ‖ i ᵊr **~iest** i ɪst i ˌəst
~iness i nəs i nɪs

chuck, Chuck tʃʌk **chucked** tʃʌkt **chucking**
ˈtʃʌk ɪŋ **chucks** tʃʌks

chucker-out ˌtʃʌk ər ˈaʊt ‖ -ᵊr- **chuckers-out**
ˌtʃʌk əz ˈaʊt ‖ -ᵊrz-

chuckl|e ˈtʃʌk ᵊl **~ed** d **~es** z **~ing** ˌɪŋ

chucklehead ˈtʃʌk ᵊl hed **~s** z

chuckwalla ˈtʃʌk wɒl ə ‖ -wɑːl ə **~s** z

chuff tʃʌf **chuffed** tʃʌft **chuffing** ˈtʃʌf ɪŋ
chuffs tʃʌfs

chug tʃʌg **chugged** tʃʌgd **chugging** ˈtʃʌg ɪŋ
chugs tʃʌgz

chugalug ˈtʃʌg ə lʌg **~ged** d **~ging** ɪŋ **~s** z

Chukchee, Chukchi ˈtʃʊk tʃiː ˈtʃʌk- **~s** z

chukka, chukker ˈtʃʌk ə ‖ -ᵊr **~s** z

Chula Vista ˌtʃuːl ə ˈvɪst ə

chum tʃʌm **chummed** tʃʌmd **chumming**
ˈtʃʌm ɪŋ **chums** tʃʌmz

Chumash ˈtʃuːm æʃ

Chumbawamba ˌtʃʌm bə ˈwɑːm bə -ˈwʌm-

chumm|y ˈtʃʌm |i **~ier** i ə ‖ i ᵊr **~iest** i ɪst i ˌəst
~ily ɪ li əl i **~iness** i nəs i nɪs

chump tʃʌmp **chumps** tʃʌmps

chunder ˈtʃʌnd ə ‖ -ᵊr **~ed** d **chundering**
ˈtʃʌnd ᵊr ɪŋ **~s** z

Chungking ˌtʃʊŋ ˈkɪŋ ˌtʃʌŋ- —*Chi* Chóngqìng
[²tʂʰʊŋ ⁴tɕʰiŋ]

chunk tʃʌŋk **chunked** tʃʌŋkt **chunking**
ˈtʃʌŋk ɪŋ **chunks** tʃʌŋks

chunk|y ˈtʃʌŋk |i **~ier** i ə ‖ i ᵊr **~iest** i ɪst i ˌəst
~iness i nəs i nɪs

chunnel, C~ ˈtʃʌn ᵊl

chunter ˈtʃʌnt ə ‖ ˈtʃʌnt̬ ᵊr **~ed** d **chuntering**
ˈtʃʌnt ᵊr ɪŋ ‖ ˈtʃʌnt̬ ər ɪŋ **~s** z

church, Church tʃɜːtʃ ‖ tʃɝːtʃ **churched** tʃɜːtʃt
‖ tʃɝːtʃt **churches** ˈtʃɜːtʃ ɪz -əz ‖ ˈtʃɝːtʃ əz
churching ˈtʃɜːtʃ ɪŋ ‖ ˈtʃɝːtʃ ɪŋ **church's, C~**
ˈtʃɜːtʃ ɪz -əz ‖ ˈtʃɝːtʃ əz
ˌChurch ˈArmy; ˌChurch Comˈmissioners;
ˌChurch ˈmilitant; ˌChurch Slaˈvonic

Churchdown ˈtʃɜːtʃ daʊn ‖ ˈtʃɝːtʃ-

churchgo|er ˈtʃɜːtʃ ˌgəʊ |ə ‖ ˈtʃɝːtʃ ˌgoʊ |ᵊr
~ers əz ‖ ᵊrz **~ing** ɪŋ

Churchill ˈtʃɜːtʃ ɪl ‖ ˈtʃɝːtʃ-

Churchillian tʃɜː ˈtʃɪl i ən ‖ tʃɝː-

church|man, C~ ˈtʃɜːtʃ |mən ‖ ˈtʃɝːtʃ- **~men**
mən men

churchwarden ˌtʃɜːtʃ ˈwɔːd ᵊn ◂
‖ ˈtʃɝːtʃ ˌwɔːrd ᵊn **~s** z

church|woman ˈtʃɜːtʃ ˌwʊm ən ‖ ˈtʃɝːtʃ-
~women ˌwɪm ɪn -ən

church|y ˈtʃɜːtʃ| i ‖ ˈtʃɝːtʃ| i **~iness** i nəs -nɪs

churchyard ˈtʃɜːtʃ jɑːd ‖ ˈtʃɝːtʃ jɑːrd **~s** z

churl tʃɜːl ‖ tʃɝːl **churls** tʃɜːlz ‖ tʃɝːlz

churlish ˈtʃɜːl ɪʃ ‖ ˈtʃɝːl- **~ly** li **~ness** nəs nɪs

churn tʃɜːn ‖ tʃɝːn **churned** tʃɜːnd ‖ tʃɝːnd
churning ˈtʃɜːn ɪŋ ‖ ˈtʃɝːn ɪŋ **churns** tʃɜːnz
‖ tʃɝːnz

chute ʃuːt (= *shoot*) **chutes** ʃuːts

Chuter ˈtʃuːt ə ‖ ˈtʃuːt̬ ᵊr

chutney ˈtʃʌt ni

chutzpah ˈhʊts pə ˈxʊts-, -pɑː

Chuvash ˈtʃuːv æʃ tʃu ˈvɑːʃ **~es** ɪz əz

Chuzzlewit ˈtʃʌz ᵊl wɪt

chyle kaɪᵊl

chyme kaɪm

chymotrypsin ˌkaɪm əʊ ˈtrɪps ɪn §-ᵊn ‖ -oʊ-

chypre ˈʃiːp rə —*Fr* [ʃipχ]

CIA ˌsiː aɪ ˈeɪ

ciabatta tʃə ˈbæt ə ˌtʃiː ə-, -ˈbɑːt- ‖ -ˈbæt̬ ə —*It*
[tʃa ˈbat ta]

Ciampino tʃæm ˈpiːn əʊ ‖ tʃɑːm ˈpiːn oʊ —*It*
[tʃam ˈpi: no]

ciao tʃaʊ

Ciaran ˈkɪər ən ‖ ˈkɪr-

Ciba *tdmk* 'siːb ə —*Ger* [ˈtsiː ba]
Ciba-Geigy *tdmk* ˌsiːb ə 'gaɪg i
Cibber 'sɪb ə ‖ -ᵊr
cibori|um sɪ 'bɔːr i ˌləm sə- ‖ -'bour- **~a** ə
cicada sɪ 'kɑːd ə sə- ‖ -'keɪd ə saɪ-, -'kɑːd- **~s** z
cicala sɪ 'kɑːl ə sə- **~s** z
cicatric|e 'sɪk ətr ɪs §-əs **~es** ɪz əz
cicatris... —*see* **cicatriz...**
cicatrix 'sɪk ə trɪks sə 'keɪtr ɪks, sɪ- **cicatrices**
   ˌsɪk ə 'traɪs iːz
cicatrization ˌsɪk ətr aɪ 'zeɪʃ ᵊn -ətr ɪ- ‖ -ətr ə-
cicatriz|e 'sɪk ə traɪz **~ed** d **~es** ɪz əz **~ing** ɪŋ
cicely, C~ 'sɪs əl i -ɪl-
Cicero, C~ 'sɪs ə rəʊ ‖ -roʊ
ciceron|e ˌtʃɪtʃ ə 'rəʊn |i ˌsɪs- ‖ -'roʊn |i **~i** iː
Ciceronian ˌsɪs ə 'rəʊn i ˌən ◀ ‖ -'roʊn- **~s** z
cichlid 'sɪk lɪd §-ləd **~s** z
cicisbe|o ˌtʃɪtʃ ɪz 'beɪ |əʊ ‖ -|oʊ —*It*
   [tʃi tʃiz 'bɛː o] **~i** iː
Cid sɪd
CID ˌsiː aɪ 'diː
-cidal 'saɪd ᵊl — **genocidal** ˌdʒen ə 'saɪd ᵊl ◀
-cide saɪd — **insecticide** ɪn ˌsekt ɪ saɪd -ə-
cider 'saɪd ə ‖ -ᵊr **~s** z
Cif *tdmk* sɪf
cig sɪg **cigs** sɪgz
cigar sɪ 'gɑː sə- ‖ -'gɑːr **~s** z

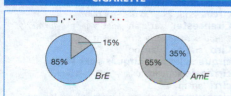

CIGARETTE

15%
85%
BrE

35%
65%
AmE

cigaret, cigarette ˌsɪg ə 'ret ˈ··· ‖ ˈ··· ˌ·ˈ· **~s**
   s —*Preference polls, BrE:* ˌ·ˈ· 85%, ˈ··· 15%;
   AmE: ˈ··· 65%, ˌ·ˈ· 35%.
   ˌciga'rette ˌholder, ˈ···—; ˌciga'rette
   ˌlighter, ˈ···—
cigarillo ˌsɪg ə 'rɪl əʊ ‖ -oʊ -'riː joʊ **~s** z
cigg|ie, cigg|y 'sɪg |i **~ies** iz
ciguatera ˌsɪg wə 'teər ə ˌsiːg-, -'tɪər- ‖ -'ter-
   —*AmSp* [si ɣwa 'te ɾa]
cilantro sɪ 'læntr əʊ sə- ‖ -'lɑːntr oʊ -'læntr-
   —*AmSp* [si 'lan tro]
Cilcennin kɪl 'ken ɪn §-ən
Cilento sɪ 'lent əʊ sə- ‖ -oʊ
cilia 'sɪl i ə 'siːl-
ciliary 'sɪl i ˌər i ‖ -i er i
ciliat|e 'sɪl i eɪt -i̯ət, -i̯ɪt **~ed** ɪd əd **~es** s
Cilic|ia saɪ 'lɪs |i ə sɪ-, sə-, -'lɪʃ- ‖ sə 'lɪʃ |ə
   ~ian/s i ən/z ‖ ᵊn/z
cili|um 'sɪl i ˌəm **~a** ə
cill sɪl (= *sill*) **cills** sɪlz
Cilla 'sɪl ə
Cillit Bang *tdmk* ˌsɪl ɪt 'bæŋ §-ət-
Cimabue ˌtʃɪm ə 'buː eɪ ˌtʃiːm-, -i —*It*
   [tʃi ma 'buː e]
cimetidine saɪ 'met ɪ diːn sɪ-, sə-, -ə- ‖ -'met ə-

Cimmerian sɪ 'mɪər i ˌən sə-, -'mer- ‖ -'mɪr- **~s**
   z
C-in-C ˌsiː ɪn 'siː §-ən- **~s** z
cinch sɪntʃ **cinched** sɪntʃt **cinches** 'sɪntʃ ɪz -əz
   cinching 'sɪntʃ ɪŋ
cinchona sɪŋ 'kəʊn ə ‖ -'koʊn- **~s** z
Cincinnati ˌsɪn's ə 'næt i ◀ -ɪ- ‖ -'næt i
Cincinnatus ˌsɪn's ə 'nɑːt əs ◀ -ɪ-, -'neɪt-
   ‖ -'næt-
cincture 'sɪŋk tʃə ‖ -tʃᵊr **~s** z
cinder 'sɪnd ə ‖ -ᵊr **~s** z
Cinderella ˌsɪnd ə 'rel ə ◀ §sɪn 'drel ə
Cindy 'sɪnd i
cine 'sɪn i
cine- ˌsɪn i — **cinephotography**
   ˌsɪn i fəʊ 'tɒg rəf i ‖ -fə 'tɑːg-
cineaste, cinéaste 'sɪn i æst -eɪ-, ˌ·ˈ· **~s** s
cinecamera 'sɪn i ˌkæm ᵊr ə ˌ·ˈ··· **~s** z
cinefilm 'sɪn i fɪlm **~s** z
cinema 'sɪn əm ə -ɪm-; -ɪ mɑː, -ə- **~s** z
cinemago|er 'sɪn əm ə ˌgəʊ| ə ˈ·ɪm-
   ‖ -ˌgoʊ| ᵊr **~ers** əz ‖ ᵊrz **~ing** ɪŋ
cinemascope, CinemaScope *tdmk*
   'sɪn əm ə skəʊp ˈ·ɪm- ‖ -skoʊp
cinematic ˌsɪn ə 'mæt ɪk ◀ -ə- ‖ -'mæt- **~ally**
   ᵊl i
cinematograph ˌsɪn ə 'mæt ə grɑːf ˌ·ɪ-, -græf
   ‖ -'mæt ə græf **~s** s
cinematography ˌsɪn əm ə 'tɒg rəf i ˌ·ɪm-
   ‖ -'tɑːg-
cinema verite, cinéma vérité
   ˌsɪn əm ə 'ver ɪ teɪ ˌ·ɪm-, -ɪ mɑː-, -ə mɑː-,
   -ə teɪ ‖ -ˌver ə 'teɪ —*Fr* [si ne ma ve ʁi te]
cine-projector 'sɪn i prə ˌdʒekt ə ‖ -ᵊr **~s** z
cineradiographic ˌsɪn i ˌreɪd i ˌə 'græf ɪk
   ~ally ᵊl i
cineradiography ˌsɪn i ˌreɪd i 'ɒg rəf i
   ‖ -'ɑːg-
Cinerama *tdmk* ˌsɪn ə 'rɑːm ə -ɪ-
cineraria ˌsɪn ə 'reər i̯ə ‖ -'rer- **~s** z
Cinna 'sɪn ə
cinnabar 'sɪn ə bɑː ‖ -bɑːr
cinnamon 'sɪn əm ən
cinque, C~ sɪŋk (= *sink*)
   ˌCinque 'Ports, ˈ··
cinquecento ˌtʃɪŋk wɪ 'tʃent əʊ §-wə- ‖ -oʊ
   —*It* [tʃiŋ kwe 'tʃen to]
cinquefoil 'sɪŋk fɔɪ ᵊl 'sæŋk- **~s** z
Cinzano *tdmk* tʃɪn 'zɑːn əʊ sɪn-; tʃɪnt 'sɑːn-,
   sɪnt- ‖ -oʊ **~s** z
cipher 'saɪf ə ‖ -ᵊr **~ed** d **ciphering** 'saɪf ᵊr ɪŋ
   ~s z
Cipriani ˌsɪp ri 'ɑːn i
circa 'sɜːk ə ‖ 'sɜːk ə
circadian sɜː 'keɪd i ˌən ‖ sᵊr-
Circassian sə 'kæs i ˌən sɜː- ‖ sᵊr 'kæʃ ᵊn -i ˌən
   ~s z
Circe 'sɜːs i ‖ 'sɜːs i
circl|e 'sɜːk ᵊl ‖ 'sɜːk ᵊl **~ed** d **~es** z **~ing** ˌɪŋ
circlet 'sɜːk lət -lɪt ‖ 'sɜːk- **~s** s
circlip 'sɜːk lɪp ‖ 'sɜːk- **~s** s
circs sɜːks ‖ sɜːks

circu|it 'sɜːk |ɪt §-ət ‖ 'sɝːk |ət **~ited** ɪt ɪd §ət-, -əd ‖ əṱ əd **~iting** ɪt ɪŋ §ət- ‖ əṱ ɪŋ **~its** ɪts §əts ‖ əts
   'circuit ˌbreaker; 'circuit ˌdiagram; 'circuit judge

circuitous sɜː 'kjuː ɪt əs sə-, ət- ‖ sɚ 'kjuː əṱ əs **~ly** li **~ness** nəs nɪs

circuitry 'sɜːk ətr i -ɪtr- ‖ 'sɝːk-

circuity sɜː 'kjuː ət i sə-, ɪt i ‖ sɚ 'kjuː əṱ i

circular 'sɜːk jʊl ə -jəl- ‖ 'sɝːk jəl ᵊr **~s** z
   ˌcircular 'saw

circularis... —*see* **circulariz...**

circularit|y ˌsɜːk ju 'lær ət |i ˌjə-, -ɪt i ‖ ˌsɝːk jə 'lær əṱ |i -'ler- **~ies** iz

circularization ˌsɜːk jʊl ər aɪ 'zeɪʃ ᵊn ˌjəl-, -ɪ'-- ‖ ˌsɝːk jəl ər ə-

circulariz|e 'sɜːk jʊl ə raɪz '-jəl- ‖ 'sɝːk jəl- **~ed** d **~es** ɪz əz **~ing** ɪŋ

circu|late 'sɜːk ju |leɪt -jə- ‖ 'sɝːk jə- **~lated** leɪt ɪd -əd ‖ leɪṱ əd **~lates** leɪts **~lating** leɪt ɪŋ ‖ leɪṱ ɪŋ

circulation ˌsɜːk ju 'leɪʃ ᵊn -jə- ‖ ˌsɝːk jə- **~s** z

circulator 'sɜːk ju leɪt ə '-jə- ‖ 'sɝːk jə leɪt ᵊr **~s** z

circulatory ˌsɜːk ju 'leɪt ər i ˌjə-; 'sɜːk jʊl ət ᵊr i, '-jəl- ‖ 'sɝːk jəl ə tɔːr i -tour i

circum- *comb. form* ˌsɜːk əm ‖ ˌsɝːk əm
  — **circumlunar** ˌsɜːk əm 'luːn ə ◄ -'ljuːn- ‖ ˌsɝːk əm 'luːn ᵊr ◄

circumcentre, circumcenter 'sɜːk əm ˌsent ə ‖ 'sɝːk əm ˌsen ṱ ᵊr **~s** z

circumcis|e 'sɜːk əm saɪz ‖ 'sɝːk- **~ed** d **~er/s** ə/z ‖ ᵊr/z **~es** ɪz əz **~ing** ɪŋ

circumcision ˌsɜːk əm 'sɪʒ ᵊn ‖ ˌsɝːk- **~s** z

circumferenc|e sə 'kʌmᵖf ᵊr ᵊn ᵗs ‖ sɚ- sə- **~es** ɪz əz

circumferential sə ˌkʌmᵖf ə 'renᵗʃ ᵊl ◄ ‖ sɚ- sə-

circumflex 'sɜːk əm fleks ‖ 'sɝːk- **~ed** t **~es** ɪz əz **~ing** ɪŋ

circumlocution ˌsɜːk əm lə 'kjuːʃ ᵊn ‖ ˌsɝːk əm loʊ- **~s** z

circumlocutory ˌsɜːk əm 'lɒk jʊt ər i -'jət, -lə 'kjuːt ər i ‖ ˌsɝːk əm 'lɑːk jə tɔːr i -tour i

circumnavi|gate ˌsɜːk əm 'næv ɪ |geɪt -'ə- ‖ ˌsɝːk- **~gated** geɪt ɪd -əd ‖ geɪṱ əd **~gates** geɪts **~gating** geɪt ɪŋ ‖ geɪṱ ɪŋ

circumnavigation ˌsɜːk əm ˌnæv ɪ 'geɪʃ ᵊn -ˌ-ə- ‖ ˌsɝːk- **~s** z

circumscrib|e 'sɜːk əm skraɪb ˌ-ˈ- ‖ 'sɝːk- **~ed** d **~es** z **~ing** ɪŋ

circumscription ˌsɜːk əm 'skrɪp ʃᵊn ‖ ˌsɝːk- **~s** z

circumspect 'sɜːk əm spekt ‖ 'sɝːk- **~ly** li **~ness** nəs nɪs

circumspection ˌsɜːk əm 'spek ʃᵊn ‖ ˌsɝːk-

circumstanc|e 'sɜːk əm stænᵗs -stɑːnᵗs, -stənᵗs ‖ 'sɝːk əm stænᵗs **~ed** t **~es** ɪz əz
  — *Preference poll, BrE:* -stænᵗs 65%, -stɑːnᵗs 24%, -stənᵗs 11%.

circumstantial ˌsɜːk əm 'stænᵗʃ ᵊl ◄ -'stɑːnᵗʃ- ‖ ˌsɝːk- **~ly** i

CIRCUMSTANCE

Pie chart (BrE): -stænᵗs 65%, -stɑːnᵗs 24%, -stənᵗs 11%

Line graph: BrE by age -æ- / -ɑː- / -ə-; Percentage (y-axis 0–80); x-axis: Older ← Speakers → Younger

circumvallation ˌsɜːk əm və 'leɪʃ ᵊn -væ'-- ‖ ˌsɝːk- **~s** z

circum|vent ˌsɜːk əm |'vent '··· ‖ ˌsɝːk- **~vented** 'vent ɪd -əd ‖ 'venṱ əd **~venting** 'vent ɪŋ ‖ 'venṱ ɪŋ **~vents** 'vents

circumvention ˌsɜːk əm 'venᵗʃ ᵊn ‖ ˌsɝːk- **~s** z

circumventive ˌsɜːk əm 'vent ɪv ◄ ‖ ˌsɝːk əm 'venṱ ɪv ◄

circus 'sɜːk əs ‖ 'sɝːk- **~es** ɪz əz

Cirencester 'saɪᵊr ᵊn ˌsest ə ‖ -ᵊr —*formerly, and occasionally still,* 'sɪs ɪt ə ‖ -əṱ ᵊr

Ciro 'sɪər əʊ ‖ 'sɪr oʊ

cirque sɜːk ‖ sɝːk **cirques** sɜːks ‖ sɝːks

cirrhosis sə 'rəʊs ɪs sɪ-, §-əs ‖ -'roʊs-

cirri 'sɪr aɪ

cirrocumulus ˌsɪr əʊ 'kjuːm jʊl əs -jəl əs ‖ ˌsɪr oʊ 'kjuːm jəl əs

cirrostratus ˌsɪr əʊ 'strɑːt əs -'streɪt- ‖ ˌsɪr oʊ 'streɪṱ əs -'stræṱ-

cirr|us 'sɪr |əs **~i** aɪ

cis- *comb. form* ˌsɪs — **cis-butadiene** ˌsɪs ˌbjuːt ə 'daɪ iːn ‖ -ˌbjuːṱ-

Cisalpine ⑴sɪs 'ælp aɪn

cisco 'sɪsk əʊ ‖ -oʊ **~es, ~s** z

Ciskei ˌsɪs 'kaɪ '··

cisplatin ⑴sɪs 'plæt ɪn -ᵊn

Cissie 'sɪs i

cissoid 'sɪs ɔɪd **~s** z

cissus 'sɪs əs

ciss|y, Cissy 'sɪs |i **~ies** iz

Cistercian sɪ 'stɜːʃ ᵊn sə- ‖ -'stɝːʃ- **~s** z

cistern 'sɪst ən ‖ -ᵊrn **~s** z

cis-trans ˌsɪs 'trænz ◄ -'trɑːnz

cistron 'sɪs trɒn -trɒn ‖ -trɑːn **~s** z

cistus 'sɪst əs

citadel 'sɪt əd ᵊl -ə del ‖ 'sɪṱ- **~s** z

citation saɪ 'teɪʃ ᵊn sɪ- **~s** z
   ci'tation form

cite saɪt (= *sight, site*) **cited** 'saɪt ɪd -əd ‖ 'saɪṱ əd **cites** saɪts **citing** 'saɪt ɪŋ ‖ 'saɪṱ ɪŋ

cithara 'sɪθ ər ə **~s** z

cither 'sɪθ ə ‖ -ᵊr **~s** z

Citation form, dictionary entry and connected speech

1 The *Longman Pronunciation Dictionary* (LPD), like other dictionaries, makes use of various **abbreviatory conventions**. This enables LPD to show a number of possible pronunciations with a single transcription of a word. However, it means that if you want to convert a passage in ordinary spelling into phonetic transcription you must 'unpack' these conventions.

2 For example, some phonetic symbols in LPD are printed in *italic* or raised and in smaller type, to denote OPTIONAL SOUNDS. If you are writing a transcription, you should choose either to include the sound or to omit it. The simplest rule is to convert italic symbols into roman (= plain), and to omit raised symbols.

Dictionary entry	**glimpse**	glɪmps
You can write		glɪmps
Dictionary entry	**fail**	feɪᵊl
You can write		feɪl

3 LPD uses spaces to show SYLLABIFICATION. You will probably want to omit these spaces in your transcription.

| Dictionary entry | **running** | ˈrʌn ɪŋ |
| You can write | | ˈrʌnɪŋ |

4 The LPD mark ‿, too, shows a syllable boundary, though it is a boundary that may be removed by COMPRESSION. You can ignore this mark.

Dictionary entry	**hideous**	ˈhɪd i‿əs
You can write		ˈhɪdiəs
Dictionary entry	**listening**	ˈlɪs ᵊn‿ɪŋ
You can write		ˈlɪsnɪŋ

5 Carrying out the procedure described above will give you a possible **citation** form (= dictionary pronunciation) for a word. This is the way the word might typically be pronounced if spoken in isolation. However, when a word occurs in a phrase or sentence, its pronunciation may sometimes be different from this.

Some of the special phonetic characteristics of **connected speech** are discussed in the articles on ASSIMILATION, COMPOUNDS AND PHRASES, DOUBLE CONSONANTS, ELISION, R-LIAISON, STRESS SHIFT, T-VOICING, and WEAK FORMS.

Citibank *tdmk* ˈsɪt i bæŋk ‖ ˈsɪt̬-
Citicorp *tdmk* ˈsɪt i kɔːp ‖ ˈsɪt̬ i kɔːrp
citified ˈsɪt i faɪd ‖ ˈsɪt̬-
Citigroup ˈsɪt i gruːp ‖ ˈsɪt̬-
citizen ˈsɪt ɪz ən -əz- ‖ ˈsɪt̬ əz ən -əs- **~s** z
— *Preference poll, AmE: -əz- 64%, -əs- 36%. See chart on p. 150.*
 ˌCitizens Adˈvice ˌBureau
citizenry ˈsɪt ɪz ən ri ˈ-əz- ‖ ˈsɪt̬-

citizenship ˈsɪt ɪz ən ʃɪp ˈ-əz- ‖ ˈsɪt̬- **~s** s
citral ˈsɪtr əl -æl
citrate ˈsɪtr eɪt ˈsaɪtr-, -ət, -ɪt **~s** s
citric ˈsɪtr ɪk
 ˌcitric ˈacid
citrine ˈsɪtr iːn -iːn, §-ən
Citrine sɪ ˈtriːn sə-
Citroen, Citroën *tdmk* ˈsɪtr əʊ ən ˈsɪtr ən ‖ ˌsɪtr oʊ ˈen —*Fr* [si tʁɔ ɛn] **~s** z

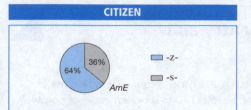

CITIZEN

64% / 36%
■ -z-
■ -s-
AmE

citron 'sɪtr ən ~s z
citronella ˌsɪtr ə 'nel ə
citrous 'sɪtr əs (= *citrus*)
citrus 'sɪtr əs ~es ɪz əz
cittern 'sɪt ɜːn -ᵊn ‖ 'sɪṭ ᵊrn ~s z
cit|y 'sɪt |i ‖ 'sɪṭ |i ~ies iz
  'city ˌeditor; ˌcity 'fathers; ˌcity 'hall
city-dweller 'sɪt i ˌdwel ə ‖ 'sɪṭ i ˌdwel ᵊr ~s z
cityscape 'sɪt i skeɪp ‖ 'sɪṭ- ~s s
city-state ˌsɪt i 'steɪt ‖ ˌsɪṭ- '· · ·~s s
citywide ˌsɪt i 'waɪd ◄ ‖ ˌsɪṭ-
Ciudad θju 'dɑːd ˌθiːˌu 'dɑːd ‖ sju 'dɑːd
  ˌsiˌu 'dɑːd —*Sp* [θju 'ðað, sju-]
civet 'sɪv ɪt §-ət ~s s
civic 'sɪv ɪk ~s s
civies 'sɪv iz
civil 'sɪv ᵊl -ɪl
  ˌcivil de'fence; ˌcivil ˌengi'neering; ˌcivil
  'liberties; 'civil list; ˌcivil 'partner(ship);
  ˌcivil 'rights; ˌcivil 'servant; ˌcivil 'war
civilian sə 'vɪl iˌən sɪ- ~s z
civilis... —*see* **civiliz...**
civilit|y sə 'vɪl ət |i sɪ-, -ɪt- ‖ -əṭ |i ~ies iz
civilization ˌsɪv ᵊl aɪ 'zeɪʃ ᵊn ˌ·ɪl-, -ɪ'·- ‖ -ᵊl ə-
  ~s z
civiliz|e 'sɪv ə laɪz -ɪ-; -ᵊl aɪz ~ed d ~er/s ə/z
  ‖ ᵊr/z ~es ɪz əz ~ing ɪŋ
civilly 'sɪv ᵊl i -ɪl-
civv|y 'sɪv |i ~ies iz
  'civvy street
CJD ˌsiː dʒeɪ 'diː
clachan, C~ 'klæx ən 'klæk-, 'klɑːx-
clack klæk **clacked** klækt **clacking** 'klæk ɪŋ
  clacks klæks
Clackmannan klæk 'mæn ən ~shire ʃə ʃɪə,
  ˌʃaɪˌə ‖ ʃᵊr ʃɪr, ˌʃaɪˌᵊr
Clacton 'klækt ən
clad klæd **cladding/s** 'klæd ɪŋ/z **clads** klædz
clade kleɪd **clades** kleɪdz
cladist 'kleɪd ɪst -əst ~s s
cladistics klə 'dɪst ɪks klæ-
Clady 'klæd i
clafouti, clafoutis klæ 'fuːt i ‖ ˌklɑːf uː 'tiː
  —*Fr* [kla fu ti]
clag klæg **clagged** klægd **clagging** 'klæg ɪŋ
  clags klægz
claggy 'klæg i
Claiborne 'kleɪ bɔːn ‖ -bɔːrn
claim kleɪm **claimed** kleɪmd **claiming**
  'kleɪm ɪŋ **claims** kleɪmz
claimable 'kleɪm əb ᵊl
claimant 'kleɪm ənt ~s s
claimer 'kleɪm ə ‖ -ᵊr ~s z

Clair kleə ‖ kleᵊr klæᵊr
clairaudi|ence ˌ‚kleər 'ɔːd iˌ‚ənᵗs ‖ ˌ‚kler-
  ˌ‚klær-, -'ɑːd- ~ent/s ənt/s
Claire kleə ‖ kleᵊr klæᵊr
Clairol *tdmk* 'kleər ɒl ‖ 'kler ɔːl 'klær-, -ɑːl
clairvoyance ˌ‚kleə 'vɔɪ ənᵗs ‖ ˌ‚kler- ˌ‚klær-
clairvoyant ˌ‚kleə 'vɔɪ ənt ‖ ˌ‚kler- ˌ‚klær-
  ~ly li ~s s
clam klæm **clammed** klæmd **clamming**
  'klæm ɪŋ **clams** klæmz
  ˌclam 'chowder
clamant 'kleɪm ənt 'klæm-
clambake 'klæm beɪk ~s s
clamber 'klæm bə ‖ -bᵊr ~ed d **clambering**
  'klæm bər ɪŋ ~s z
clamm|y 'klæm |i ~ier iˌə ‖ iˌᵊr ~iest iˌɪst iˌəst
  ~ily ɪ li əl i ~iness i nəs i nɪs
clamor 'klæm ə ‖ -ᵊr ~ed d **clamoring**
  'klæm ər ɪŋ ~s z
clamorous 'klæm ər_əs ~ly li ~ness nəs nɪs
clamour 'klæm ə ‖ -ᵊr ~ed d **clamouring**
  'klæm ər ɪŋ ~s z
clamp, Clamp klæmp **clamped** klæmpt
  clamping 'klæmp ɪŋ **clamps** klæmps
clampdown 'klæmp daʊn ~s z
clamshell 'klæm ʃel ~s z
clan klæn **clans** klænz
Clancarty klæn 'kɑːt i →klæŋ- ‖ -'kɑːrṭ i
Clancey, Clancy 'klænᵗs i

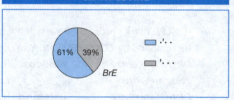

CLANDESTINE

61% / 39%
■ ·'· ·
■ '· · ·
BrE

clandestine klæn 'dest ɪn -aɪn, §-ən;
  'klænd e staɪn, -ɪ-, -ə-, -stɪn —*Preference poll*
  BrE: ·'· · 61%, '· · · 39%. ~ly li ~ness nəs nɪs
clang klæŋ **clanged** klæŋd **clanging** 'klæŋ ɪŋ
  clangs klæŋz
clanger 'klæŋ ə ‖ -ᵊr ~s z
clangor 'klæŋ gə -ə ‖ -ᵊr -gᵊr
clangorous 'klæŋ gər əs -ər- ~ly li
clangour 'klæŋ gə -ə ‖ -ᵊr -gᵊr
clank klæŋk **clanked** klæŋkt **clanking**
  'klæŋk ɪŋ **clanks** klæŋks
Clanmaurice, Clanmorris ˌ‚klæn 'mɒr ɪs
  →ˌ‚klæm-, §-əs ‖ -'mɔːr- -'mɑːr-
clannish 'klæn ɪʃ ~ly li ~ness nəs nɪs
Clanricarde *(i)* ˌ‚klæn 'rɪk əd ‖ -ᵊrd, *(ii)*
  ˌklæn rɪ 'kɑːd ◄ ‖ -'kɑːrd ◄
clanship 'klæn ʃɪp
clans|man 'klænz |mən ~men mən men
  ~woman ˌwʊm ən ~women ˌwɪm ɪn §-ən
clap klæp **clapped** klæpt **clapping** 'klæp ɪŋ
  claps klæps
clapboard 'klæp bɔːd 'klæb əd ‖ 'klæb ᵊrd
  'klæp bɔːrd, -boʊrd

Clapham 'klæp əm
 ,Clapham 'Junction
clapp... —*see* **clap**
clapped-out ,klæpt 'aʊt ◂
clapper 'klæp ə ‖ -ᵊr **~s** z
clapperboard 'klæp ə bɔːd ‖ -ᵊr bɔːrd -boʊrd
 ~s z
Clapton 'klæpt ən
claptrap 'klæp træp
claque klæk (= *clack*) **claques** klæks
Clara 'kleər ə ‖ 'kler ə 'klær- —*As a foreign
name, also* 'klɑːr ə
clarabella, C~ ,klær ə 'bel ə ‖ ,kler-
Clare kleə ‖ kleᵊr klæᵊr
Claremont 'kleə mɒnt -mənt ‖ 'kler mɑːnt
 'klær-
Clarence 'klær ənᵗs ‖ 'kler-
Clarenceux 'klær ən suː -sjuː: ‖ 'kler-
Clarendon, c~ 'klær ənd ən ‖ 'kler-
claret 'klær ət -ɪt ‖ 'kler- **~s** s
Clarges 'klɑːdʒ ɪz -əz ‖ 'klɑːrdʒ əz
Clarice 'klær ɪs §-əs ‖ 'kler-
Claridg|e 'klær ɪdʒ ‖ 'kler- **~e's** ɪz əz
clarification ,klær ɪf ɪ 'keɪʃ ᵊn -ᵊf-, §-ə'--
 ‖ ,kler- **~s** z
clarificatory ,klær əf ɪ 'keɪt ər i ◂ ,ɪf-, §-ə'--;
 'klær əf ɪ kət ᵊr i, -ᵊf-, §'· -ə-
 ‖ 'klær əf ɪk ə tɔːr i 'kler-, klə 'rɪf-, -toʊr i *(*)*
clari|fy 'klær ə |faɪ -ɪ- ‖ 'kler- **~fied** faɪd
 ~fier/s faɪ ə/z ‖ faɪ ᵊr/z **~fies** faɪz **~fying**
 faɪ ɪŋ
Clarinda klə 'rɪnd ə klæ-
clarinet ,klær ə 'net -ɪ- ‖ ,kler- **~s** s
clarinetist, clarinettist ,klær ə 'net ɪst -ɪ-,
 §-əst ‖ -'net- ,kler- **~s** s
clarion 'klær i ən ‖ 'kler- **~s** z
Clarissa klə 'rɪs ə
clarity 'klær ət i -ɪt- ‖ -əṭ i 'kler-
Clark, Clarke klɑːk ‖ klɑːrk
clarkia 'klɑːk i ə ‖ 'klɑːrk- **~s** z
Clarkson 'klɑːks ᵊn ‖ 'klɑːrks ᵊn
Claro 'kleər əʊ ‖ 'kler oʊ
Clarrie 'klær i ‖ 'kler-
clart klɑːt ‖ klɑːrt **clarts** klɑːts ‖ klɑːrts
clarty 'klɑːt i ‖ 'klɑːrṭ i
clar|y, Clary 'kleər |i ‖ 'kler |i 'klær- **~ies** iz
-clase kleɪz kleɪs — **orthoclase** 'ɔːθ əʊ kleɪz
 -kleɪs ‖ 'ɔːrθ ə-
clash klæʃ **clashed** klæʃt **clashes** 'klæʃ ɪz -əz
 clashing 'klæʃ ɪŋ
clasp klɑːsp §klæsp ‖ klæsp **clasped** klɑːspt
 §klæspt ‖ klæspt **clasping** 'klɑːsp ɪŋ §'klæsp-
 ‖ 'klæsp ɪŋ **clasps** klɑːsps §klæsps ‖ klæsps
 'clasp knife
class klɑːs §klæs ‖ klæs **classed** klɑːst §klæst
 ‖ klæst **classes** 'klɑːs ɪz §'klæs-, -əz ‖ 'klæs-
 classing 'klɑːs ɪŋ §'klæs- ‖ 'klæs ɪŋ
 ,class 'action; 'class ,system; ,class
 'struggle, ˈ· ˌ··; ,class 'war, ˈ· ·
class-conscious ,klɑːs 'kɒnᵗʃ əs ◂ §,klæs-
 ‖ 'klæs ,kɑːnᵗʃ əs **~ness** nəs nɪs
classi... —*see* **classy**

classic 'klæs ɪk **~s** s
classical 'klæs ɪk ᵊl **~ly** i **~ism** ,ɪz əm
 ,Classical 'Latin
classicism 'klæs ɪ ,sɪz əm -ə-
classicist 'klæs ɪs ɪst -əs-, §-əst **~s** s
classifiable 'klæs ɪ faɪ ˌəb ᵊl '·ə-, ,··'· ··
classification ,klæs ɪf ɪ 'keɪʃ ᵊn ,-əf-, -ə'-- **~s** z
classificatory ,klæs ɪf ɪ 'keɪt ər i ◂ ,-əf-, §-ə'--;
 '· ·ɪk ət ˌər i ‖ 'klæs əf ɪk ə tɔːr i klə 'sɪf-,
 klæ 'sɪf-, -toʊr i *(*)*
classifier 'klæs ɪ faɪ ə §'·ə- ‖ -faɪ ᵊr **~s** z
classi|fy 'klæs ɪ |faɪ -ə- **~fied/s** faɪd/z **~fies**
 faɪz **~fying** faɪ ɪŋ
classism 'klɑːs ,ɪz əm §'klæs- ‖ 'klæs-
classless 'klɑːs ləs §'klæs-, -lɪs ‖ 'klæs- **~ness**
 nəs nɪs
classmate 'klɑːs meɪt §'klæs- ‖ 'klæs- **~s** s
classroom 'klɑːs ruːm §'klæs-, →'klɑːʃ-,
 →§'klæʃ-, -rʊm ‖ 'klæs- →'klæʃ- **~s** z
classwork 'klɑːs wɜːk §'klæs- ‖ 'klæs wɜːk
class|y 'klɑːs |i §'klæs- ‖ 'klæs |i **~ier** i ə ‖ i ᵊr
 ~iest i ɪst i əst
clast klæst **clasts** klæsts
clastic 'klæst ɪk
clathrate 'klæθ reɪt **~s** s
clatter 'klæt ə ‖ 'klæt ᵊr **~ed** d **clattering**
 'klæt ᵊr ɪŋ ‖ 'klæt ᵊr ɪŋ **~s** z
Claud klɔːd ‖ klɑːd
Claude *(i)* kləʊd ‖ kloʊd, *(ii)* klɔːd ‖ klɑːd —*Fr*
 [klo:d]
Claudette ⁽ˌ⁾klɔː 'det ‖ ⁽ˌ⁾klɑː-
Claudia 'klɔːd i ə ‖ 'klɑːd-
Claudian 'klɔːd i ən ‖ 'klɑːd-
claudication ,klɔːd ɪ 'keɪʃ ᵊn -ə- ‖ ,klɑːd-
Claudius 'klɔːd i əs ‖ 'klɑːd-
Claughton 'klɔːt ᵊn ‖ 'klɑːt- —*but places with
this spelling in Lancashire are* 'klæft ən *(near
Lancaster) and* 'klaɪt ᵊn *(near Preston)*
clausal 'klɔːz ᵊl ‖ 'klɑːz-
clause klɔːz ‖ klɑːz (= *claws*) **clauses** 'klɔːz ɪz
 -əz ‖ 'klɑːz-
Clausewitz 'klaʊz ə vɪts 'klaʊs- —*Ger*
 ['klaʊ zə vɪts]
claustrophobia ,klɔːs trə 'fəʊb i ə ,klɒs-
 ‖ -'foʊb- ,klɑːs-
claustrophobic ,klɔːs trə 'fəʊb ɪk ◂ ,klɒs-
 ‖ -'foʊb- ,klɑːs- **~ally** ᵊl i **~s** s
clave kleɪv klɑːv **claves** kleɪvz klɑːvz
Claverhouse 'kleɪv ə haʊs ‖ -ᵊr-
Clavering *(i)* 'kleɪv ᵊr ɪŋ, *(ii)* 'klæv-
Claverton 'klæv ət ən ‖ -ᵊrt ᵊn
clavichord 'klæv ɪ kɔːd -ə- ‖ -kɔːrd **~s** z
clavicle 'klæv ɪk ᵊl **~s** z
clavier klə 'vɪə 'klæv i ə ‖ -'vɪᵊr **~s** z
claviform 'klæv ɪ fɔːm §-ə- ‖ -fɔːrm
Clavius 'kleɪv i əs
claw klɔː ‖ klɑː **clawed** klɔːd ‖ klɑːd **clawing**
 'klɔːˑ ɪŋ ‖ 'klɔː- ɪŋ 'klɑː- **claws** klɔːz ‖ klɑːz
 'claw ,hammer
clawback 'klɔː bæk ‖ 'klɑː- **~s** s
Claxton 'klækst ən
clay, Clay kleɪ **clays** kleɪz
 ,clay 'pigeon, ,clay 'pigeon ,shooting

C

Claydon 'kleɪd ᵊn
clayey 'kleɪ i
claymore 'kleɪ mɔː ‖ -mɔːr -moʊr **~s** z
claypan 'kleɪ pæn **~s** z
Clayton 'kleɪt ᵊn
claytonia kleɪ 'təʊn i ə ‖ -'toʊn- **~s** z
clean kliːn **cleaned** kliːnd **cleaning** 'kliːn ɪŋ
   cleans kliːnz
clean-cut ˌkliːn 'kʌt ◂ →ˌkliːŋ-
cleaner 'kliːn ə ‖ -ᵊr **~s, ~'s** z
cleanli... —see **cleanly**
clean-limbed ˌkliːn 'lɪmd ◂
   ˌclean-limbed 'heroes
cleanliness 'klen li nəs -nɪs
clean-living ˌkliːn 'lɪv ɪŋ ◂
cleanly adv 'kliːn li
clean|ly adj 'klen |li §'kliːn- **-lier** li ə ‖ li ᵊr
   ~liest li ɪst li əst
cleanness 'kliːn nəs -nɪs
cleanse klenz **cleansed** klenzd **cleansing**
   'klenz ɪŋ **cleanses** 'klenz ɪz -əz
cleanser 'klenz ə ‖ -ᵊr **~s** z
clean-shaven ˌkliːn 'ʃeɪv ᵊn ◂
Cleanthes kli 'ænᵗθ iːz
cleanup 'kliːn ʌp **~s** s
clear klɪə ‖ klɪᵊr **cleared** klɪəd ‖ klɪᵊrd **clearer**
   'klɪər ə ‖ 'klɪr ᵊr **clearest** 'klɪər ɪst -əst
   ‖ 'klɪr əst **clearing** 'klɪər ɪŋ ‖ 'klɪr ɪŋ
clearanc|e 'klɪər ᵊnᵗs ‖ 'klɪr- **~es** ɪz əz
   'clearance ˌsale
Clearasil tdmk 'klɪər ə sɪl ‖ 'klɪr-
clearcole 'klɪə kəʊl →-kɒʊl ‖ 'klɪr koʊl
clear-cut ˌklɪə 'kʌt ◂ ‖ ˌklɪr-
   ˌclear-cut de'cision
clearer 'klɪər ə ‖ 'klɪr ᵊr **~s** z
clear-headed ˌklɪə 'hed ɪd ◂ -əd ‖ ˌklɪr- **~ly** li
   ~ness nəs nɪs
   ˌclear-ˌheaded 'attitude
clearing 'klɪər ɪŋ ‖ 'klɪr ɪŋ **~s** z
   'clearing ˌbank
clearing|house 'klɪər ɪŋ |haʊs ‖ 'klɪr-
   ~houses haʊz ɪz -əz
clear|ly 'klɪə |li ‖ 'klɪr |li **~ness** nəs nɪs
clearout 'klɪər aʊt ‖ 'klɪr- **~s** s
clear-sighted ˌklɪə 'saɪt ɪd ◂ -əd
   ‖ ˌklɪr 'saɪt̬ əd ◂ **~ly** li **~ness** nəs nɪs
clear-up 'klɪər ʌp ‖ 'klɪr- **~s** s
clearway 'klɪə weɪ ‖ 'klɪr- **~s** z
cleat kliːt **cleated** 'kliːt ɪd -əd ‖ 'kliːt̬ əd
   cleats kliːts
Cleator 'kliːt ə ‖ 'kliːt̬ ᵊr
cleavag|e 'kliːv ɪdʒ **~es** ɪz əz
cleave, C~ kliːv **cleaved** kliːvd **cleaves** kliːvz
   cleaving 'kliːv ɪŋ **cleft** kleft **clove** kləʊv
   ‖ kloʊv **cloven** 'kləʊv ᵊn ‖ 'kloʊv ᵊn
cleaver, C~ 'kliːv ə ‖ -ᵊr **~s** z
Cleckheaton ₍ᵢ₎klek 'hiːt ᵊn
Cleddau 'kleð aɪ —Welsh ['kle ðai, -ðe]
Cledwyn 'kled wɪn
Clee kliː
cleek kliːk **cleeks** kliːks
Cleese kliːz

Cleethorpes 'kliː θɔːps ‖ -θɔːrps
clef klef **clefs** klefs
cleft kleft **clefts** klefts
   ˌcleft 'palate; ˌcleft 'stick
cleg kleg **clegs** klegz
Clegg kleg
Cleisthenes 'klaɪsθ ə niːz -ɪ-
cleistogamy klaɪ 'stɒg əm i ‖ -'staːg-
Cleland (i) 'klel ənd, (ii) 'kliːl ənd
Clem, clem klem
clematis 'klem ət ɪs §-əs; klə 'meɪt-, klɪ-
   ‖ 'klem ət̬ əs klɪ 'mæt-, -'meɪt-, -'maːt̬- **~es** ɪz
   əz
Clemence 'klem ənᵗs
Clemenceau 'klem ən səʊ ‖ ˌklem ən 'soʊ
   —Fr [kle mɑ̃ so]
clemenc|y, C~ 'klem ənᵗs |i **~ies** iz
Clemens 'klem ənz
clement, C~ 'klem ənt **~ly** li
Clementina ˌklem ən 'tiːn ə
clementine, C~ 'klem ən taɪn -tiːn- **~s** z
clenbuterol klen 'bjuːt ə rɒl ‖ -'bjuːt̬ ə rɔːl
   -raːl
clench klentʃ **clenched** klentʃt **clenches**
   'klentʃ ɪz -əz **clenching** 'klentʃ ɪŋ
Cleo 'kliː əʊ ‖ -oʊ
Cleobury places in Shropshire 'klɪb ər i 'kleb-,
   'klɪəb-
Cleobury family name (i) 'kləʊ bər ‿i
   ‖ 'kloʊ ˌber i, (ii) 'kliː-
Cleon 'kliː ən -ɒn ‖ -aːn
Cleopatra, c~ ˌkliː ə 'pætr ə -'pɑːtr- **~'s** z
clepsydr|a 'kleps ɪdr |ə -ədr-; klep 'sɪdr |ə **~ae**
   iː **~as** əz
clerestor|y 'klɪə ˌstɔːr |i 'klɪəst ər ˌ|i ‖ 'klɪr-
   -ˌstoʊr- **~ies** iz
clerg|y 'klɜːdʒ |i ‖ 'klɜːdʒ |i **~ies** iz
clergy|man 'klɜːdʒ i |mən ‖ 'klɜːdʒ- **~men**
   mən **~woman** ˌwʊm ən **~women** ˌwɪm ɪn
   §-ən
cleric 'kler ɪk **~s** s
clerical 'kler ɪk ᵊl **~ly** ‿i
clericalism 'kler ɪk ə ˌlɪz əm -ᵊl ˌɪz-
clerihew, C~ 'kler i hjuː -ə- **~s** z
clerisy 'kler əs i -ɪs-
clerk, Clerk klɑːk ‖ klɜːk (*) **clerked** klɑːkt
   ‖ klɜːkt **clerking** 'klɑːk ɪŋ ‖ 'klɜːk ɪŋ **clerks**
   klɑːks ‖ klɜːks
Clerkenwell 'klɑːk ən wel -wəl ‖ 'klɜːk-
   'klɑːrk-
Clermont 'kleə mɒnt 'klɜː-, -mənt
   ‖ 'kler mɑːnt 'klɜː-
Clery 'klɪər i ‖ 'klɪr i
Clevedon 'kliːv dən
Cleveland 'kliːv lənd
Cleveleys 'kliːv liz
clever 'klev ə ‖ -ᵊr **cleverer** 'klev ᵊr ə ‖ -ᵊr ər
   cleverest 'klev ᵊr ɪst -əst **~ly** li **~ness** nəs
   nɪs
   ˌclever 'dick, ˌ·‿·'·
clever-clever ˌklev ə 'klev ə ◂ ‖ -ᵊr 'klev ᵊr
Cleverdon 'klev əd ᵊn ‖ -ᵊrd-

C

Clicks

A **click** is a speech sound made with an air stream set in motion within the mouth rather than by the lungs.

In English, isolated clicks are sometimes used as meaningful noises, but they are not part of the phoneme system and do not form part of the pronunciation of words.

An alveolar click | can be used as a sign of disapproval (see the entry **tut-tut**). If accompanied by a breathy-voiced ŋ, it is a kind of sneer. A lateral click ‖ can be used to encourage horses.

Cleves kliːvz —*Fr* Clèves [klɛːv], *Ger* Kleve ['kleː və]

clevis 'klev ɪs §-əs **~es** ɪz əz

clew kluː (= *clue*) **clewed** kluːd **clewing** 'kluː ɪŋ **clews** kluːz

Clewer 'kluː_ə ‖ _³r

Clewes, Clews kluːz

Cley (i) kleɪ, (ii) klaɪ

Clibborn 'klɪb ən ‖ -³rn

Cliburn 'klaɪ bɜːn ‖ -bɜ˞n

cliche, cliché 'kliːʃ eɪ ‖ kliː 'ʃeɪ (*) **~d, ~'d** d **~s** z

click klɪk **clicked** klɪkt **clicking** 'klɪk ɪŋ **clicks** klɪks
   'click ˌbeetle; 'click ˌlanguage

clickable 'klɪk əb ³l

clicker 'klɪk ə ‖ -³r **~s** z

clickety-|clack ˌklɪk ət i ‖ 'klæk ‖ ˌklɪk əţ- **~click** 'klɪk

click-fit 'klɪk fɪt

clickstream 'klɪk striːm **~s** z

click-through 'klɪk θruː **~s** z

client 'klaɪ_ənt **~s** s

clientele ˌkliː ɒn 'tel -ð-, -ɑːn-, ˌkliː_ən- ‖ ˌklaɪ ən- **~s** z

Clifden 'klɪft ən

cliff klɪf **cliffs** klɪfs
   'cliff ˌdweller

Cliff, Cliffe klɪf

cliffhang|er 'klɪf ˌhæŋ ə ‖ -³r **~ers** əz ‖ ³rz **~ing** ɪŋ

Clifford 'klɪf əd ‖ -³rd

Clift klɪft

Clifton 'klɪft ən

Cliftonville 'klɪft ən vɪl

climacteric klaɪ 'mækt ər ɪk ˌklaɪ mæk 'ter ɪk **~s** s

climactic klaɪ 'mækt ɪk **~ally** ³l_i

climate 'klaɪm ət -ɪt **~s** s
   'climate ˌchange

climatic klaɪ 'mæt ɪk ‖ -'mæţ- **~ally** ³l_i

climatologic ˌklaɪm ət ə 'lɒdʒ ɪk ◂ ‖ -əţ ə 'laːdʒ- **~al** ³l **~ally** ³l_i

climatolog|ist ˌklaɪm ə 'tɒl ədʒ| ɪst §-əst ‖ -'taːl- **~ists** ɪsts §əsts **~y** i

climax 'klaɪm æks **climaxed** 'klaɪm ækst **climaxes** 'klaɪm æks ɪz -əz **climaxing** 'klaɪm æks ɪŋ

climb klaɪm (= *clime*) **climbed** klaɪmd **climbing** 'klaɪm ɪŋ **climbs** klaɪmz

climbable 'klaɪm əb ³l

climb-down 'klaɪm daʊn **~s** z

climber 'klaɪm ə ‖ -³r **~s** z

climbing 'klaɪm ɪŋ
   'climbing frame; 'climbing ˌirons

clime klaɪm **climes** klaɪmz

clinch, Clinch klɪntʃ **clinched** klɪntʃt **clinches** 'klɪntʃ ɪz -əz **clinching** 'klɪntʃ ɪŋ

clincher 'klɪntʃ ə ‖ -³r **~s** z

cline, Cline klaɪn **clines** klaɪnz

cling klɪŋ **clinging** 'klɪŋ ɪŋ **clings** klɪŋz **clung** klʌŋ

clingfilm 'klɪŋ fɪlm

clingstone 'klɪŋ stəʊn ‖ -stoʊn

cling|y 'klɪŋ |i **~ier** i_ə ‖ i_³r **~iest** i_ɪst i_əst **~iness** i nəs -nɪs

clinic 'klɪn ɪk **~s** s

clinical 'klɪn ɪk ³l **~ly** i

clinician klɪ 'nɪʃ ³n klə- **~s** z

clink klɪŋk **clinked** klɪŋkt **clinking** 'klɪŋk ɪŋ **clinks** klɪŋks

clinker 'klɪŋk ə ‖ -³r **~ed** d **clinkering** 'klɪŋk_ər ɪŋ **~s** z

clinker-built ˌklɪŋk ə 'bɪlt ◂ ‖ -³r-

clinkety-clank ˌklɪŋk ət i 'klæŋk ‖ -əţ i-

clinometer klaɪ 'nɒm ɪt ə klɪ-, -ət- ‖ -'naːm əţ ³r **~s** z

clint, Clint klɪnt **clints** klɪnts

Clinton 'klɪnt ən ‖ -³n

Clio (i) 'klaɪ əʊ ‖ -oʊ, (ii) 'kliː- —*The muse is usually (i), the model of car (ii).*

cliometric ˌklaɪ əʊ 'metr ɪk ◂ ‖ -ə- **~s** s

clip klɪp **clipped** klɪpt **clipping** 'klɪp ɪŋ **clips** klɪps
   'clip joint

clipboard 'klɪp bɔːd ‖ -bɔːrd -boʊrd **~s** z

clip-clop 'klɪp klɒp ˌ·'· ‖ klɑːp **~ped** t **~ping** ɪŋ **~s** s

clip-on 'klɪp ɒn ‖ -ɑːn -ɔːn

clipper 'klɪp ə ‖ -³r **~s** z

clippie 'klɪp i **~s** z

C

clipping ˈklɪp ɪŋ ~s z
Clipsham ˈklɪp ʃəm
Clipstone ˈklɪp stəʊn ‖ -stoʊn
clique kliːk §klɪk cliques kliːks §klɪks
cliquey ˈkliːk i §ˈklɪk i
cliquish ˈkliːk ɪʃ §klɪk ɪʃ ~ly li ~ness nəs nɪs
cliquy ˈkliːk i §ˈklɪk i
Clissold ˈklɪs əʊld →-ɒʊld, -ᵊld ‖ -oʊld
Clitheroe ˈklɪð ə rəʊ ‖ -roʊ
clitic ˈklɪt ɪk ‖ ˈklɪt̬ ɪk ~s s
cliticis... —see cliticiz...
cliticization ˌklɪt ɪs aɪ ˈzeɪʃ ᵊn ˌ-əs-, -ɪˈ--
‖ ˌklɪt̬ əs ə-
cliticiz|e ˈklɪt ɪ saɪz -ə- ‖ ˈklɪt̬- ~ed d ~es ɪz əz
~ing ɪŋ
clitoral ˈklɪt ər əl ˈklaɪt- ‖ ˈklɪt̬-
clitoridectom|y ˌklɪt ər ɪ ˈdekt əm |i -əˈ--
‖ ˌklɪt̬- ~ies iz
clitoris ˈklɪt ər ɪs ˈklaɪt-, §-əs ‖ ˈklɪt̬-
Clive klaɪv
Cliveden ˈklɪvd ən
clivia ˈklaɪv i ˌə ~s z
cloac|a kləʊ ˈeɪk |ə ‖ kloʊ- ~ae iː
cloak kləʊk ‖ kloʊk cloaked kləʊkt ‖ kloʊkt
cloaking ˈkləʊk ɪŋ ‖ ˈkloʊk ɪŋ cloaks kləʊks
‖ kloʊks
cloak-and-dagger ˌkləʊk ən ˈdæg ə →-ŋ-
‖ ˌkloʊk ən ˈdæg ᵊr
cloakroom ˈkləʊk ruːm -rʊm ‖ ˈkloʊk-
clobber ˈklɒb ə ‖ ˈklɑːb ᵊr ~ed d clobbering
ˈklɒb ər ɪŋ ‖ ˈklɑːb- ~s z
cloche klɒʃ kləʊʃ ‖ kloʊʃ cloches ˈklɒʃ ɪz
ˈkləʊʃ-, -əz ‖ ˈkloʊʃ əz
clock klɒk ‖ klɑːk clocked klɒkt ‖ klɑːkt
clocking ˈklɒk ɪŋ ‖ ˈklɑːk ɪŋ clocks klɒks
‖ klɑːks
ˌclock ˈradio; ˈclock ˌtower
clock-watch|er ˈklɒk ˌwɒtʃ |ə
‖ ˈklɑːk ˌwɑːtʃ |ᵊr ~ers əz ‖ ᵊrz ~ing ɪŋ
clockwise ˈklɒk waɪz ‖ ˈklɑːk-
clockwork ˈklɒk wɜːk ‖ ˈklɑːk wɜːk
clod klɒd ‖ klɑːd clods klɒdz ‖ klɑːdz
Clodagh ˈkləʊd ə ‖ ˈkloʊd ə
cloddish ˈklɒd ɪʃ ‖ ˈklɑːd ɪʃ ~ness nəs nɪs
clodhopper ˈklɒd ˌhɒp ə ‖ ˈklɑːd ˌhɑːp ᵊr ~s z
clog klɒg ‖ klɑːg klɔːg clogged klɒgd ‖ klɑːgd
klɔːgd clogging ˈklɒg ɪŋ ‖ ˈklɑːg ɪŋ ˈklɔːg-
clogs klɒgz ‖ klɑːgz klɔːgz
ˈclog dance
cloggy ˈklɒg i ‖ ˈklɑːg i ˈklɔːg-
Clogher ˈklɒx ə ˈklɒ hə; klɔː ‖ klɔːr
cloisonné klwaː ˈzɒn eɪ klwʌ- ‖ ˌklɔɪz ə ˈneɪ
cloister ˈklɔɪst ə ‖ -ᵊr ~ed d cloistering
ˈklɔɪst ər ɪŋ ~s z
cloistral ˈklɔɪs trəl
clomp klɒmp ‖ klɑːmp clomped klɒmpt
‖ klɑːmpt clomping ˈklɒmp ɪŋ ‖ ˈklɑːmp ɪŋ
clomps klɒmps ‖ klɑːmps
clonal ˈkləʊn ᵊl ‖ ˈkloʊn ᵊl ~ly i
clone kləʊn ‖ kloʊn cloned kləʊnd ‖ kloʊnd
clones kləʊnz ‖ kloʊnz cloning ˈkləʊn ɪŋ
‖ ˈkloʊn ɪŋ
Clones place in Ireland ˈkləʊn ɪs -əs ‖ ˈkloʊn-

clonic ˈklɒn ɪk ‖ ˈklɑːn ɪk
clonk klɒŋk ‖ klɑːŋk klɔːŋk clonked klɒŋkt
‖ klɑːŋkt klɔːŋkt clonking ˈklɒŋk ɪŋ
‖ ˈklɑːŋk ɪŋ ˈklɔːŋk- clonks klɒŋks ‖ klɑːŋks
klɔːŋks
Clonmel, Clonmell ˌklɒn ˈmel →ˌklɒm-, '· ·
‖ ˌklɑːn-
clonus ˈkləʊn əs ‖ ˈkloʊn əs ~es ɪz əz
Clooney ˈkluːn i
clop klɒp ‖ klɑːp clopped klɒpt ‖ klɑːpt
clopping ˈklɒp ɪŋ ‖ ˈklɑːp ɪŋ clops klɒps
‖ klɑːps
Clophill ˈklɒp hɪl ‖ ˈklɑːp-
clopp... —see clop
Clorox tdmk ˈklɔːr ɒks ‖ -ɑːks ˈkloʊr-
close adj, adv kləʊs ‖ kloʊs closer ˈkləʊs ə
‖ ˈkloʊs ᵊr closest ˈkləʊs ɪst -əst ‖ ˈkloʊs əst
ˌclose ˈcall; ˌclose ˈquarters; ˌclose
ˈshave; ˌclose ˈthing
close n 'end' kləʊz ‖ kloʊz closes ˈkləʊz ɪz -əz
‖ ˈkloʊz əz
close v kləʊz ‖ kloʊz closed kləʊzd ‖ kloʊzd
closes ˈkləʊz ɪz -əz ‖ ˈkloʊz əz closing
ˈkləʊz ɪŋ ‖ ˈkloʊz ɪŋ
ˌclosed ˈbook; ˌclosed ˌcircuit ˈteleˌvision;
ˌclosed ˈshop
close n 'courtyard' kləʊs ‖ kloʊs closes
ˈkləʊs ɪz -əz ‖ ˈkloʊs əz
Close family name kləʊs ‖ kloʊs
close-cropped ˌkləʊs ˈkrɒpt ◄
‖ ˌkloʊs ˈkrɑːpt ◄
close-cut ˌkləʊs ˈkʌt ◄ ‖ ˌkloʊs-
closed-door ˌkləʊzd ˈdɔː ◄ ‖ ˌkloʊzd ˈdɔːr ◄
-ˈdoʊr
closedown ˈkləʊz daʊn ‖ ˈkloʊz-
closefisted ˌkləʊs ˈfɪst ɪd ◄ -əd ‖ ˌkloʊs-
close-fitting ˌkləʊs ˈfɪt ɪŋ ◄ ‖ ˌkloʊs ˈfɪt̬ ɪŋ ◄
close-grained ˌkləʊs ˈgreɪnd ◄ ‖ ˌkloʊs-
close-hauled ˌkləʊs ˈhɔːld ◄ ‖ ˌkloʊs- -ˈhɑːld
close-knit ˌkləʊs ˈnɪt ◄ ‖ ˌkloʊs-
close-lipped ˌkləʊs ˈlɪpt ◄ ‖ ˌkloʊs-
closely ˈkləʊs li ‖ ˈkloʊs-
closely-knit ˌkləʊs li ˈnɪt ◄ ‖ ˌkloʊs-
ˌclosely-knit ˈgroup
close-mouthed ˌkləʊs ˈmaʊðd ◄ -ˈmaʊθt ◄
‖ ˌkloʊs-
closeness ˈkləʊs nəs -nɪs ‖ ˈkloʊs-
closeout ˈkləʊz aʊt ‖ ˈkloʊz-
closer n ˈkləʊz ə ‖ ˈkloʊz ᵊr ~s z
closer comparative adj ˈkləʊs ə ‖ ˈkloʊs ᵊr
close-run ˌkləʊs ˈrʌn ◄ ‖ ˌkloʊs-
close season ˈkləʊs ˌsiːz ᵊn '· ·· ‖ ˈkloʊzd-
close-set ˌkləʊs ˈset ◄ ‖ ˌkloʊs-
ˌclose-set ˈeyes
clos|et ˈklɒz |ɪt §-ət ‖ ˈklɑːz |ət ~eted ɪt ɪd
§ət-, -əd ‖ ət̬ əd ~eting ɪt ɪŋ §ət- ‖ ət̬ ɪŋ ~ets
ɪts §-əts ‖ əts
close-up ˈkləʊs ʌp ‖ ˈkloʊs- ~s s
closing ˈkləʊz ɪŋ ‖ ˈkloʊz ɪŋ
ˈclosing date; ˈclosing price; ˈclosing
time
clostridi|um klɒ ˈstrɪd i ˌ|əm ‖ klɑː- ~a ə

Clipping

1 A **clipped** vowel is one that is pronounced more quickly than an unclipped vowel. For example, **rice** raɪs has a quick aɪ (and a slow s) when compared with **rise** raɪz (slow aɪ, quicker z).

In English, a vowel (or vowel plus nasal, or vowel plus LIQUID) is clipped when it is followed by one of the consonants p, t, ʈ, k, tʃ, f, θ, s, ʃ within the same syllable (when 'syllable' is determined as in this dictionary). These are the FORTIS consonants, and we call this phenomenon **pre-fortis clipping**. It is particularly noticeable with long vowels and diphthongs when they are stressed.

The vowels have pre-fortis clipping in the words

feet fiːt (compare **feed** fiːd)

loose luːs (compare **lose** luːz)

rate reɪt (compare **raid** reɪd).

So do the vowels in the stressed syllables in the words

seeking ˈsiːk ɪŋ (compare **intriguing** ɪn ˈtriːg ɪŋ)

paper ˈpeɪp ə ‖ ˈpeɪp ᵊr (compare **labo(u)r** ˈleɪb ə ‖ -ᵊr)

total ˈtəʊt ᵊl ‖ ˈtoʊʈ ᵊl (compare **modal** ˈməʊd ᵊl ‖ ˈmoʊd ᵊl).

The eɪ in **plating** ˈpleɪt ɪŋ has pre-fortis clipping, but the eɪ in **play-time** does not, since here the t is in a different syllable.

2 Clipping does not involve any change of vowel quality ('timbre'). Clipped iː in **teach** tiːtʃ does not sound like ɪ in **rich** rɪtʃ.

3 Both the e and the n of **tent** tent are affected by pre-fortis clipping: compare **tend** tend with no clipping. Both the ɪ and the l of **milk** mɪlk are clipped. In **fierce**, clipping affects the ɪə of BrE fɪəs and the ɪᵊr of AmE fɪᵊrs: compare **fears** fɪəz ‖ fɪᵊrz, where there is no clipping.

4 Another, less noticeable, kind of clipping in English depends on the presence within a word of one or more unstressed syllables after the stressed syllable. The iː in **leader** ˈliːd ə ‖ ˈliːd ᵊr is somewhat clipped in comparison with the iː in **lead** liːd, because in **leader** an unstressed syllable follows. The iː in **leadership** ˈliːd ə ʃɪp ‖ ˈliːd ᵊr ʃɪp is rather more clipped, because two unstressed syllables follow. This kind of clipping is called **rhythmic clipping**.

5 In **teacher** ˈtiːtʃ ə ‖ ˈtiːtʃ ᵊr the iː is affected both by pre-fortis clipping (because of the tʃ) and by rhythmic clipping (because of the **-er**). As a result, it is phonetically quite short. (We still call it a long vowel, because it is still an allophone of the phoneme iː.)

6 The contrary process to clipping may be called **stretching**. This tends to affect the vowel of the last syllable a speaker makes before taking a breath or stopping talking.

C

closure 'kləʊʒ ə ‖ 'kloʊʒ ᵊr ~d d closuring
  'kləʊʒ ər ɪŋ ‖ 'kloʊʒ- ~s z
clot klɒt ‖ klɑːt clots klɒts ‖ klɑːts clotted
  'klɒt ɪd -əd ‖ 'klɑːt̬ əd clotting 'klɒt ɪŋ
  ‖ 'klɑːt̬ ɪŋ
  ˌclotted 'cream
cloth klɒθ klɔːθ ‖ klɔːθ klɑːθ cloths klɒθs
  klɒðz, klɔːðz, klɔːθs ‖ klɔːðz klɔːθs, klɑːðz,
  klɑːθs
clothbound 'klɒθ baʊnd 'klɔː-θ- ‖ 'klɔːθ-
  'klɑː-θ-
clothe v kləʊð ‖ kloʊð clothed kləʊðd
  ‖ kloʊðd clothes kləʊðz ‖ kloʊðz clothing
  'kləʊð ɪŋ ‖ 'kloʊð ɪŋ
cloth-eared ˌklɒθ 'ɪəd ◂ ˌklɔː-θ- ‖ ˌklɔːθ 'ɪᵊrd ◂
  ˌklɑː-θ-
clothes n kləʊðz kləʊz ‖ kloʊz kloʊðz
  'clothes ˌhanger; 'clothes moth; 'clothes
  peg
clothesbasket 'kləʊðz ˌbɑːsk ɪt 'kləʊz-,
  §-, bæsk-, §-ət ‖ 'kloʊz ˌbæsk ət 'kloʊðz- ~s s
clotheshors|e 'kləʊðz hɔːs 'kləʊz-
  ‖ 'kloʊz hɔːrs 'kloʊðz- ~es ɪz əz
clothesline 'kləʊðz laɪn 'kləʊz- ‖ 'kloʊz-
  'kloʊðz- ~s z
clothespin 'kləʊðz pɪn 'kləʊz- ‖ 'kloʊz-
  'kloʊðz- ~s z
clothier, C~ 'kləʊð i‿ə ‖ 'kloʊð i‿ᵊr ~s z
clothing 'kləʊð ɪŋ ‖ 'kloʊð ɪŋ
Clotho 'kləʊθ əʊ ‖ 'kloʊθ oʊ
clott... —see clot
cloture 'kləʊtʃ ə ‖ 'kloʊtʃ ᵊr ~s z
cloud klaʊd clouded 'klaʊd ɪd -əd clouding
  'klaʊd ɪŋ clouds klaʊdz
  'cloud ˌchamber; ˌcloud 'nine
cloudbank 'klaʊd bæŋk →'klaʊb- ~s s
cloudberr|y 'klaʊd bər ˌi →'klaʊb-, -ˌber ˌi
  ‖ -ˌber ˌi ~ies iz
cloudburst 'klaʊd bɜːst →'klaʊb- ‖ -bɜːst ~s s
cloud-capped ˌklaʊd 'kæpt ◂ →ˌklaʊg-, '· ·
  ˌcloud-capped 'mountains
cloud-cuckoo-land ˌklaʊd 'kʊk uː lænd
  →ˌklaʊg- ‖ -'kuːk-
Cloudesley 'klaʊdz li
cloudi... —see cloudy
cloudless 'klaʊd ləs -lɪs ~ly li
cloudscape 'klaʊd skeɪp ~s s
cloud|y 'klaʊd ˌi ~ier i‿ə ‖ i‿ᵊr ~iest i‿ɪst i‿əst
  ~ily ɪ li əl i ~iness i nəs i nɪs
clough, Clough klʌf —but the place in Co.
  Down is klɒx
Clouseau 'kluːz əʊ ‖ kluː 'zoʊ —Fr [klu zo]
clout, Clout klaʊt clouted 'klaʊt ɪd -əd
  ‖ 'klaʊt̬ əd clouting 'klaʊt ɪŋ ‖ 'klaʊt̬ ɪŋ
  clouts klaʊts
Clouzot 'kluːz əʊ ‖ kluː 'zoʊ —Fr [klu zo]
clove kləʊv ‖ kloʊv cloves kləʊvz ‖ kloʊvz
  ˌclove 'hitch, '· ·
Clovelly klə 'vel i
cloven 'kləʊv ᵊn ‖ 'kloʊv ᵊn
cloven-footed ˌkləʊv ᵊn 'fʊt ɪd ◂ -əd
  ‖ ˌkloʊv ᵊn 'fʊt̬ əd ◂

cloven-hoofed ˌkləʊv ᵊn 'huːft ◂ -'hʊft
  ‖ ˌkloʊv ᵊn 'hʊft ◂ -'huːft, -'hʊvd, -'huːvd
clover 'kləʊv ə ‖ 'kloʊv ᵊr ~s z
clover|leaf 'kləʊv ə ˌliːf ‖ 'kloʊv ᵊr- ~leafs
  liːfs ~leaves liːvz
Clovis 'kləʊv ɪs §-əs ‖ 'kloʊv-
Clowes (i) klaʊz, (ii) kluːz
clown klaʊn clowned klaʊnd clowning
  'klaʊn ɪŋ clowns klaʊnz
clownery 'klaʊn ər i
clownish 'klaʊn ɪʃ ~ly li ~ness nəs nɪs
cloy klɔɪ cloyed klɔɪd cloying/ly 'klɔɪ ɪŋ /li
  cloys klɔɪz
cloze kləʊz ‖ kloʊz
club klʌb clubbed klʌbd clubbing 'klʌb ɪŋ
  clubs klʌbz
  ˌClub 'Med; ˌclub 'sandwich; ˌclub 'soda
clubb... —see club
clubbable 'klʌb əb ᵊl
clubber 'klʌb ə ‖ -ᵊr ~s z
clubby 'klʌb i
club|foot ˌklʌb |'fʊt '· · ~feet 'fiːt ~footed
  'fʊt ɪd ◂ -əd ‖ 'fʊt̬ əd
club|house 'klʌb |haʊs ~houses haʊz ɪz -əz
clubland 'klʌb lænd -lənd
club|man 'klʌb |mən -mæn ~men mən men
clubmate 'klʌb meɪt ~s s
clubs klʌbz
cluck klʌk clucked klʌkt clucking 'klʌk ɪŋ
  clucks klʌks
clue kluː clued kluːd clueing, cluing 'kluː ˌɪŋ
  clues kluːz
clued-in ˌkluːd 'ɪn ◂
Cluedo tdmk 'kluːd əʊ ‖ -oʊ
clued-up ˌkluːd 'ʌp ◂
clueless 'kluː ləs -lɪs ~ly li ~ness nəs nɪs
Cluj kluːʒ —Romanian [kluʒ]
Clumber, c~ 'klʌm bə ‖ -bᵊr
clump klʌmp clumped klʌmpt clumping
  'klʌmp ɪŋ clumps klʌmps
clumpy 'klʌmp i
clums|y 'klʌmz ˌi ~ier i‿ə ‖ i‿ᵊr ~iest i‿ɪst i‿əst
  ~ily ɪ li əl i ~iness i nəs i nɪs
Clun klʌn
Clunes kluːnz
clung klʌŋ
Clunie 'kluːn i
Clunies 'kluːn iz
clunk klʌŋk clunked klʌŋkt clunking
  'klʌŋk ɪŋ clunks klʌŋks
clunk-click ˌklʌŋk 'klɪk
clunker 'klʌŋk ə ‖ -ᵊr ~s z
Cluny 'kluːn i —Fr [kly ni]
clupeid 'kluːp i ɪd §-əd ~s z
clupeoid 'kluːp i ɔɪd
cluster 'klʌst ə ‖ -ᵊr ~ed d clustering
  'klʌst ər ɪŋ ~s z
  'cluster bomb; 'cluster pine
clutch klʌtʃ clutched klʌtʃt clutches 'klʌtʃ ɪz
  -əz clutching 'klʌtʃ ɪŋ
  'clutch bag
clutter 'klʌt ə ‖ 'klʌt̬ ᵊr ~ed d cluttering
  'klʌt ər ɪŋ ‖ 'klʌt̬ ər ɪŋ ~s z

Clutterbuck ˈklʌt ə bʌk ‖ ˈklʌʧ ᵊr-
Clutton ˈklʌt ᵊn
Clwyd ˈkluː ɪd —*Welsh* [kluɪd, klʊid]
Clwydian klu ˈɪd i ən
Clydach ˈklɪd əx ˈklʌd-, -ək
Clyde klaɪd
Clydebank ˈklaɪd bæŋk →ˈklaɪb-
Clydella *tdmk* klaɪ ˈdel ə
Clydesdale ˈklaɪdz deɪᵊl
Clydeside ˈklaɪd saɪd
Clyne klaɪn
Clyro ˈklaɪᵊr əʊ ‖ -oʊ
Clyst klɪst
clyster ˈklɪst ə ‖ -ᵊr ~s z
Clytemnestra ˌklaɪt əm ˈniːs trə ˌklɪt-, -ɪm-, -em-, -ˈnes- ‖ ˌklaɪʧ-
cm —*see* **centimeter/s**
c'mon kəm ˈɒn ‖ -ˈɑːn -ˈɔːn
CND ˌsiː en ˈdiː
cnidarian naɪ ˈdeər i ən knaɪ- ‖ -ˈder- -ˈdær-
Cnidus ˈnaɪd əs ˈknaɪd-
CNN ˌsiː en ˈen
C-note ˈsiː nəʊt ‖ -noʊt ~s s
Cnut kə ˈnjuːt
c/o ˌsiː ˈəʊ ◂ ‖ -ˈoʊ —*or see* **care of, carried over**
co *WWW and e-mail* kəʊ ‖ koʊ
co- ˌkəʊ ‖ ˌkoʊ —*New compounds in* co- *vary between early and late stress, with a preference for late* (ˌco-arˈranger) *except when the second element has only one syllable* (ˈco-heir). *In established words, note however* ˈco͵pilot, ˈcosine.
Co. kəʊ ‖ koʊ —*or see* Company, County
CO ˌsiː ˈəʊ ◂ ‖ -ˈoʊ
coach kəʊʧ ‖ koʊʧ **coached** kəʊʧt ‖ koʊʧt **coaches** ˈkəʊʧ ɪz -əz ‖ ˈkoʊʧ əz **coaching** ˈkəʊʧ ɪŋ ‖ ˈkoʊʧ ɪŋ
'coach ͵station
coachbuilder ˈkəʊʧ ͵bɪld ə ‖ ˈkoʊʧ ͵bɪld ᵊr ~s z
Coachella kəʊ ˈtʃel ə ‖ koʊ- kə-
coach|man ˈkəʊʧ |mən ‖ ˈkoʊʧ- ~men mən men
coachwork ˈkəʊʧ wɜːk ‖ ˈkoʊʧ wɜːk
Coad, Coade kəʊd ‖ koʊd
coadjutor kəʊ ˈædʒ ʊt ə -ət- ‖ koʊ ˈædʒ əʈ ᵊr ˌkoʊ ə ˈdʒuːʈ ᵊr ~s z
coagulant kəʊ ˈæg jʊl ənt -jəl- ‖ koʊ ˈæg jəl- ~s s
coagu|late kəʊ ˈæg ju |leɪt -jə- ‖ koʊ ˈæg jə- ~lated leɪt ɪd -əd ‖ leɪʈ əd ~lates leɪts ~lating leɪt ɪŋ ‖ leɪʈ ɪŋ
coagulation kəʊ ˌæg ju ˈleɪʃ ᵊn -jə- ‖ koʊ ˌæg jə-
Coahuila ˌkəʊ ə ˈwiːl ə ‖ ˌkoʊ- —*AmSp* [ko a ˈwi la]
coal kəʊl →kɒʊl ‖ koʊl **coaled** kəʊld →kɒʊld ‖ koʊld (= *cold*) **coaling** ˈkəʊl ɪŋ →ˈkɒʊl- ‖ ˈkoʊl ɪŋ **coals** kəʊlz →kɒʊlz ‖ koʊlz
'coal gas; 'coal tar; 'coal tit
coal-black ˌkəʊl ˈblæk ◂ →ˌkɒʊl- ‖ ˌkoʊl-

Coalbrookdale ˌkəʊl brʊk ˈdeɪᵊl →ˌkɒʊl-, §-bruːk- ‖ ˌkoʊl-
coalbunker ˈkəʊl ͵bʌŋk ə →ˈkɒʊl- ‖ ˈkoʊl ͵bʌŋk ᵊr ~s z
coalesc|e ˌkəʊ ə ˈles ‖ ˌkoʊ- ~ed t ~es ɪz əz ~ing ɪŋ
coalescenc|e ˌkəʊ ə ˈles ᵊnᵗs ‖ ˌkoʊ- ~es ɪz əz
coalescent ˌkəʊ ə ˈles ᵊnt ◂ ‖ ˌkoʊ-
coalfac|e ˈkəʊl feɪs →ˈkɒʊl- ‖ ˈkoʊl- ~es ɪz əz
coalfield ˈkəʊl fiːᵊld →ˈkɒʊl- ‖ ˈkoʊl- ~s z
coal-fired ˌkəʊl ˈfaɪ‿əd ◂ →ˌkɒʊl- ‖ ˌkoʊl ˈfaɪ‿ᵊrd ◂
coalfish ˈkəʊl fɪʃ →ˈkɒʊl- ‖ ˈkoʊl-
coalhole ˈkəʊl həʊl →ˈkɒʊl- ‖ ˈkoʊl hoʊl ~s z
coal|house ˈkəʊl |haʊs →ˈkɒʊl- ‖ ˈkoʊl- ~houses haʊz ɪz -əz
Coalisland kəʊl ˈaɪl ənd ‖ koʊl-
Coalite *tdmk* ˈkəʊl aɪt ‖ ˈkoʊl-
coalition ˌkəʊ ə ˈlɪʃ ᵊn ‖ ˌkoʊ- ~s z
coal|man ˈkəʊl mən →ˈkɒʊl-, -mæn ‖ ˈkoʊl- ~men mən men
coalmine ˈkəʊl maɪn →ˈkɒʊl- ‖ ˈkoʊl- ~s z
coalminer ˈkəʊl ͵maɪn ə →ˈkɒʊl- ‖ ˈkoʊl ͵maɪn ᵊr ~s z
coalpit ˈkəʊl pɪt →ˈkɒʊl- ‖ ˈkoʊl- ~s s
Coalport ˈkəʊl pɔːt →ˈkɒʊl- ‖ ˈkoʊl pɔːrt -poʊrt
Coalsack ˈkəʊl sæk →ˈkɒʊl- ‖ ˈkoʊl-
coalscuttle ˈkəʊl ͵skʌt ᵊl →ˈkɒʊl- ‖ ˈkoʊl ͵skʌʈ ᵊl ~s z
Coalville ˈkəʊl vɪl →ˈkɒʊl-, -vᵊl ‖ ˈkoʊl-
coaming ˈkəʊm ɪŋ ‖ ˈkoʊm ɪŋ ~s z
coarse kɔːs ‖ kɔːrs koʊrs (= *course*) **coarser** ˈkɔːs ə ‖ ˈkɔːrs ᵊr ˈkoʊrs- **coarsest** ˈkɔːs ɪst -əst ‖ ˈkɔːrs əst ˈkoʊrs-
coarse-grained ˌkɔːs ˈɡreɪnd ◂ ‖ ˌkɔːrs- ˌkoʊrs-
coarsely ˈkɔːs li ‖ ˈkɔːrs- ˈkoʊrs-
coarsen ˈkɔːs ᵊn ‖ ˈkɔːrs ᵊn ˈkoʊrs- ~ed d ~ing ɪŋ ~s z
coarseness ˈkɔːs nəs -nɪs ‖ ˈkɔːrs- ˈkoʊrs-
coarticu|late ˌkəʊ ɑː ˈtɪk ju |leɪt -jə- ‖ ˌkoʊ ɑːr ˈtɪk jə- ~lated leɪt ɪd -əd ‖ leɪʈ əd ~lates leɪts ~lating leɪt ɪŋ ‖ leɪʈ ɪŋ
coarticulation ˌkəʊ ɑː ͵tɪk ju ˈleɪʃ ᵊn -jə- ‖ ˌkoʊ ɑːr ͵tɪk jə- ~s z
coarticulatory ˌkəʊ ɑː ˈtɪk jʊl ət‿ᵊr i -ˈjəl-; -,tɪk ju ˈleɪt ᵊr i, -,·jə-, ,·ˑ·◂·· ‖ ˌkoʊ ɑːr ˈtɪk jəl ə tɔːr i -toʊr i
coast kəʊst ‖ koʊst **coasted** ˈkəʊst ɪd -əd ‖ ˈkoʊst əd **coasting** ˈkəʊst ɪŋ ‖ ˈkoʊst ɪŋ **coasts** kəʊsts ‖ koʊsts
coastal ˈkəʊst ᵊl ‖ ˈkoʊst-
coaster ˈkəʊst ə ‖ ˈkoʊst ᵊr ~s z
coastguard ˈkəʊst ɡɑːd ‖ ˈkoʊst ɡɑːrd ~s z
coastguards|man ˈkəʊst ɡɑːdz |mən ‖ ˈkoʊst ɡɑːrdz- ~men mən men
coastline ˈkəʊst laɪn ‖ ˈkoʊst-
coastward ˈkəʊst wəd ‖ ˈkoʊst wᵊrd ~s z
coastwise ˈkəʊst waɪz ‖ ˈkoʊst-

C

C

coat kəʊt ‖ koʊt **coated** ˈkəʊt ɪd -əd
‖ ˈkoʊt̬ əd **coating** ˈkəʊt ɪŋ ‖ ˈkoʊt̬ ɪŋ **coats**
kəʊts ‖ koʊts
ˈcoat ˌhanger
Coatbridge ˈkəʊt brɪdʒ ˌ·ˈ· ‖ ˈkoʊt- —locally
ˌ·ˈ·
coatee ˈkəʊt iː ˌkəʊ ˈtiː ‖ ˌkoʊ ˈtiː **~s** z
Coates, Coats kəʊts ‖ koʊts
coati kəʊ ˈɑːt i ‖ koʊ ˈɑːt̬ i **~s** z
coati-mundi kəʊ ˌɑːt i ˈmʌnd i -ˈmʊnd-
‖ koʊ ˌɑːt̬-
coating ˈkəʊt ɪŋ ‖ ˈkoʊt̬ ɪŋ **~s** z
coatroom ˈkəʊt ruːm -rʊm ‖ ˈkoʊt- **~s** z
coatstand ˈkəʊt stænd ‖ ˈkoʊt- **~s** z
coat-tail ˈkəʊt teɪᵊl ‖ ˈkoʊt- **~s** z
coauthor ˌkəʊ ˈɔːθ ə ˈ·ˌ·· ‖ ˌkoʊ ˈɔːθ ᵊr -ˈɑːθ-
~ed d **coauthoring** ˌkəʊ ˈɔːθ ər ɪŋ ‖ ˌkoʊ-
-ˈɑːθ- **~s** z
coax v kəʊks ‖ koʊks (= cokes) **coaxed** kəʊkst
‖ koʊkst **coaxes** ˈkəʊks ɪz -əz ‖ ˈkoʊks əz
coaxing/ly ˈkəʊks ɪŋ /li ‖ ˈkoʊks-
coax n 'cable' ˈkəʊ æks ‖ ˈkoʊ- **~es** ɪz əz
coaxial ˌ₍ᵢ₎kəʊ ˈæks i əl ‖ ˌ₍ᵢ₎koʊ- **~ly** i
cob kɒb ‖ kɑːb **cobs** kɒbz ‖ kɑːbz
Cobain kəʊ ˈbeɪn ‖ koʊ- ˈ··
cobalt ˈkəʊb ɔːlt -ɒlt ‖ ˈkoʊb- -ɑːlt
Cobb kɒb ‖ kɑːb
cobber ˈkɒb ə ‖ ˈkɑːb ᵊr **~s** z
Cobbett ˈkɒb ɪt §-ət ‖ ˈkɑːb-
cobbl|e ˈkɒb ᵊl ‖ ˈkɑːb- **~ed** d **~es** z **~ing** ɪŋ
Cobbleigh ˈkɒb li ‖ ˈkɑːb li
cobbler ˈkɒb lə ‖ ˈkɑːb lᵊr **~s** z
cobblestone ˈkɒb ᵊl stəʊn ‖ ˈkɑːb ᵊl stoʊn **~s**
z
Cobbold ˈkɒb əʊld →-ɒʊld ‖ ˈkɑːb oʊld
Cobden ˈkɒb dən ‖ ˈkɑːb-
cobelligerent ˌkəʊ bə ˈlɪdʒ ᵊr_ənt ◂ -bɪ-
‖ ˌkoʊ- **~s** s
Cobh, Cóbh kəʊv ‖ koʊv —Irish [koːv]
Cobham ˈkɒb əm ‖ ˈkɑːb-
coble ˈkəʊb ᵊl ˈkɒb- ‖ ˈkoʊb- **~s** z
Cobleigh, Cobley ˈkɒb li ‖ ˈkɑːb-
Coblenz kəʊ ˈblenˢs ‖ koʊ- —Ger Koblenz
[ˈkoː blɛnts]
cobnut ˈkɒb nʌt ‖ ˈkɑːb- **~s** s
COBOL, Cobol ˈkəʊb ɒl ‖ ˈkoʊb ɔːl -ɑːl
cobra ˈkəʊb rə ˈkɒb- ‖ ˈkoʊb- **~s** z
coburg, C~ ˈkəʊ bɜːg ‖ ˈkoʊ bɜːg —Ger
[ˈkoː bʊʁk]
cobweb ˈkɒb web ‖ ˈkɑːb- **~bed** d **~s** z
coca ˈkəʊk ə ‖ ˈkoʊk ə
Coca-Cola tdmk ˌkəʊk ə ˈkəʊl ə
‖ ˌkoʊk ə ˈkoʊl ə
cocaine ₍ᵢ₎kəʊ ˈkeɪn kə- ‖ ₍ᵢ₎koʊ- ·ˈ·
coccal ˈkɒk ᵊl ‖ ˈkɑːk ᵊl
cocci ˈkɒks aɪ ˈkɒk- ‖ ˈkɑːks-
coccidiosis kɒk ˌsɪd i ˈəʊs ɪs ˌkɒks ɪd-, §-əs
‖ kɑːk ˌsɪd i ˈoʊs əs ˌkɑːks ɪd-
coccus ˈkɒk əs ‖ ˈkɑːk-
coccyx ˈkɒks ɪks ‖ ˈkɑːks- **coccyges**
kɒk ˈsaɪdʒ iːz ‖ kɑːk-
Coch in Welsh names kəʊx kəʊk ‖ koʊk
—Welsh [koːχ]

co|chair ˌkəʊ |ˈtʃeə ·· ‖ ˌkoʊ |ˈtʃeᵊr —Some
speakers stress the v ˌ·ˈ· but the n ˈ·ˌ·. **~chaired**
ˈtʃeəd ‖ ˈtʃeᵊrd **~chairing** ˈtʃeər ɪŋ ‖ ˈtʃer ɪŋ
~chairs ˈtʃeəz ‖ ˈtʃeᵊrz
Cochin ˈkəʊtʃ ɪn ˈkɒtʃ-, §-ən ‖ ˈkoʊtʃ-
cochineal ˌkɒtʃ ɪ ˈniːᵊl -ə-, ·ˈ·· ‖ ˌkɑːtʃ- ˌkoʊtʃ-
Cochise kəʊ ˈtʃiːs -ˈtʃiːz ‖ koʊ-
cochle|a ˈkɒk li ˌə ‖ ˈkoʊk- ˈkɑːk- **~ae** iː **~ar** ə
‖ ᵊr
Cochran, Cochrane ˈkɒk rən ˈkɒx- ‖ ˈkɑːk-
cock kɒk ‖ kɑːk **cocked** kɒkt ‖ kɑːkt **cocking**
ˈkɒk ɪŋ ‖ ˈkɑːk ɪŋ **cocks** kɒks ‖ kɑːks (= cox)
ˌcocked ˈhat
cockad|e kɒ ˈkeɪd ‖ kɑ- **~ed** ɪd əd **~es** z
cock-a-doodle-doo ˌkɒk ə ˌduːd ᵊl ˈduː
‖ ˌkɑːk-
cock-a-hoop ˌkɒk ə ˈhuːp ‖ ˌkɑːk-
Cockaigne kɒ ˈkeɪn kə- ‖ kɑː-
cock-a-leekie ˌkɒk ə ˈliːk i ‖ ˌkɑːk-
cockalorum ˌkɒk ə ˈlɔːr əm ‖ ˌkɑːk- -ˈloʊr- **~s**
z
cockamamie, cockamamy ˌkɒk ə ˈmeɪm i ◂
‖ ˌkɑːk-
cock-and-bull ˌkɒk ən ˈbʊl →-ŋ-, →-əm-
‖ ˌkɑːk-
cockateel, cockatiel ˌkɒk ə ˈtiːᵊl ‖ ˌkɑːk- **~s** z
cockatoo ˌkɒk ə ˈtuː ·ˈ·· ‖ ˈkɑːk ə tuː **~s** z
cockatric|e ˈkɒk ə traɪs -trɪs, -trəs ‖ ˈkɑːk- **~es**
ɪz əz
Cockayne kɒ ˈkeɪn kə- ‖ kɑː-
Cockburn ˈkəʊb ən -ɜːn ‖ ˈkoʊ bɜːn (!)
cockchafer ˈkɒk ˌtʃeɪf ə ‖ ˈkɑːk ˌtʃeɪf ᵊr **~s** z
Cockcroft (i) ˈkɒk krɒft -rɒft ‖ ˈkɑːk krɔːft
-rɔːft, -krɑːft, -rɑːft; (ii) ˈkəʊ krɒft
‖ ˈkoʊ krɔːft -krɑːft
cockcrow ˈkɒk krəʊ ‖ ˈkɑːk kroʊ
cocker, C~ ˈkɒk ə ‖ ˈkɑːk ᵊr **~s** z
ˌcocker ˈspaniel
cockerel ˈkɒk ᵊr_əl ‖ ˈkɑːk- **~s** z
Cockermouth ˈkɒk ə maʊθ -məθ ‖ ˈkɑːk ᵊr-
cockeyed ˌkɒk ˈaɪd ◂ ·ˈ· ‖ ˌkɑːk-
Cockfield ˈkəʊ fiːᵊld ‖ ˈkoʊ- (!)
cockfight ˈkɒk faɪt ‖ ˈkɑːk- **~s** s
cockfighting ˈkɒk ˌfaɪt ɪŋ ‖ ˈkɑːk ˌfaɪt̬ ɪŋ
Cockfosters ˈkɒk fɒst əz ˌ·ˈ·· ‖ ˈkɑːk fɔːst ᵊrz
-fɑːst-, ˌ·ˈ··
cockhorse ˌkɒk ˈhɔːs ◂ ‖ ˌkɑːk ˈhɔːrs ◂
cockieleekie ˌkɒk ə ˈliːk i -i- ‖ ˌkɑːk-
cockle ˈkɒk ᵊl ‖ ˈkɑːk ᵊl **~s** z
cockleshell ˈkɒk ᵊl ʃel ‖ ˈkɑːk ᵊl- **~s** z
cockney, C~ ˈkɒk ni ‖ ˈkɑːk- **~ism/s** ˌɪz əm/z
~s z
cock-of-the-rock ˌkɒk əv ðə ˈrɒk
‖ ˌkɑːk əv ðə ˈrɑːk
cockpit ˈkɒk pɪt ‖ ˈkɑːk- **~s** s
cockroach ˈkɒk rəʊtʃ ‖ ˈkɑːk roʊtʃ **~es** ɪz əz
Cockroft (i) ˈkɒk rɒft ‖ ˈkɑːk rɔːft -rɑːft,
(ii) ˈkəʊ krɒft ‖ ˈkoʊ krɔːft -krɑːft
Cocks kɒks ‖ kɑːks
cockscomb ˈkɒks kəʊm ‖ ˈkɑːks koʊm **~s** z
cocksfoot ˈkɒks fʊt ‖ ˈkɑːks- **~s** s
cock|shy ˈkɒk |ʃaɪ ‖ ˈkɑːk- **~shies** ʃaɪz
cockspur ˈkɒk spɜː ‖ ˈkɑːk spɜː **~s** z

Coarticulation

1 Speech sounds tend to be influenced by the speech sounds that surround them. **Coarticulation** is the retention of a phonetic feature that was present in a preceding sound, or the anticipation of a feature that will be needed for a following sound. Most ALLOPHONIC variation — though not all — is coarticulatory.

2 For example, a vowel or LIQUID that is adjacent to a nasal tends to be somewhat nasalized. This **coarticulation of nasality** applies to the vowels in **money** 'mʌn i and to the l in **elm** elm

3 The English lenis ('voiced') obstruents tend to lose their voicing when adjacent to a voiceless consonant or to a pause. For example, this applies to the consonants in **good** gʊd when said in isolation, or in a phrase such as **the first good thing**. This is **coarticulation of voicing** (see VOICED AND VOICELESS).

4 Many consonants vary somewhat, depending on which vowel comes after them. Thus the ʃ in **sheep** ʃiːp is more iː-like, the ʃ in **short** ʃɔːt ‖ ʃɔːrt is more ɔː-like. This is **coarticulation of place of articulation**. Other examples are the d in **dream** driːm (post-alveolar because of the r) and the b in **obvious** 'ɒb vi‿əs ‖ 'ɑːb vi‿əs (sometimes labiodental because of the v).

5 For cases where coarticulation is variable, and may result in what sounds like a different phoneme, see ASSIMILATION.

---

cocksucker 'kɒk ˌsʌk ə ‖ 'kɑːk ˌsʌk ᵊr ~s z
cocksure ˌkɒk 'ʃɔː ◄ -'ʃʊə ‖ ˌkɑːk 'ʃʊᵊr ◄ -'ʃɜː ~ly li ~ness nəs nɪs
cocktail 'kɒk teɪᵊl ‖ 'kɑːk- ~s z
'cocktail ˌlounge; 'cocktail ˌparty; 'cocktail ˌstick
cock-up 'kɒk ʌp ‖ 'kɑːk- ~s s
cock|y 'kɒk |i ‖ 'kɑːk |i ~ier i‿ə ‖ i‿ᵊr ~iest i‿ɪst i‿əst ~ily ɪ li əl i ~iness i nəs i nɪs
cocky-leeky ˌkɒk i 'liːk i -ə- ‖ ˌkɑːk-
coco, Coco 'kəʊk əʊ ‖ 'koʊk oʊ ˌcoco de 'mer meə ‖ meᵊr
cocoa 'kəʊk əʊ ‖ 'koʊk oʊ ~s z
coconut 'kəʊk ə nʌt ‖ 'koʊk- ~s s ˌcoconut 'matting; 'coconut ˌshy
cocoon kə 'kuːn ~ed d ~ing ɪŋ ~s z
Cocos 'kəʊk əs -ɒs ‖ 'koʊk əs -oʊs
cocotte kə 'kɒt kɒ-, kəʊ- ‖ koʊ 'kɑːt kɑː-, -'kɔːt —Fr [kɔ kɔt] ~s s
cocoyam 'kəʊk əʊ jæm ‖ 'koʊk oʊ- ~s z
Cocteau 'kɒkt əʊ ‖ kɑːk 'toʊ kɔːk- —Fr [kɔk to]
cod kɒd ‖ kɑːd **codded** 'kɒd ɪd -əd ‖ 'kɑːd əd **codding** 'kɒd ɪŋ ‖ 'kɑːd ɪŋ **cods** kɒdz ‖ kɑːdz
COD 'cash on delivery' ˌsiː əʊ 'diː ‖ -oʊ-
coda 'kəʊd ə ‖ 'koʊd ə ~s z
coddl|e 'kɒd ᵊl ‖ 'kɑːd- ~ed d ~es z ~ing ɪŋ

code kəʊd ‖ koʊd **coded** 'kəʊd ɪd -əd ‖ 'koʊd əd **codes** kəʊdz ‖ koʊdz **coding/s** 'kəʊd ɪŋ/z ‖ 'koʊd ɪŋ/z
codec 'kəʊd ek ‖ 'koʊd- ~s s
codeine 'kəʊd iːn ‖ 'koʊd-
co-dependenc|e ˌkəʊ di 'pend ənˈs ˌdə- ‖ ˌkoʊ- ~y i
co-dependent ˌkəʊ di 'pend ənt ◄ -də- ‖ ˌkoʊ- ~s s
coder 'kəʊd ə ‖ 'koʊd ᵊr ~s z
code-|share 'kəʊd |ʃeə ‖ 'koʊd |ʃer -ʃær ~sharing ˌʃeər ɪŋ ‖ ˌʃer ɪŋ
codeword 'kəʊd wɜːd ‖ 'koʊd wɜːd ~s z
codex 'kəʊd eks ‖ 'koʊd- ~es ɪz əz **codices** 'kəʊd ɪ siːz 'kɒd-, -ə- ‖ 'koʊd ə- 'kɑːd-
codfish 'kɒd fɪʃ ‖ 'kɑːd-
codger 'kɒdʒ ə ‖ 'kɑːdʒ ᵊr ~s z
codice... —see **codex**
codicil 'kəʊd ɪ sɪl 'kɒd-, -ə- ‖ 'kɑːd ə sɪl -əs ᵊl ~s z
codification ˌkəʊd ɪf ɪ 'keɪʃ ᵊn ˌəf-, §-ə'-- ‖ ˌkɑːd- koʊd- ~s z
codi|fy 'kəʊd ɪ |faɪ -ə- ‖ 'kɑːd- 'koʊd- ~fied faɪd ~fier/s faɪ‿ə/z ‖ faɪ‿ᵊr/z ~fies faɪz ~fying faɪ ɪŋ
coding 'kəʊd ɪŋ ‖ 'koʊd- ~s z
codlin 'kɒd lɪn §-lən ‖ 'kɑːd- ~s z
codling 'kɒd lɪŋ ‖ 'kɑːd- ~s z

cod-liver oil ˌkɒd lɪv ər ˈɔɪᵊl ◂
‖ ˈkɑːd lɪv ᵊr ˌɔɪᵊl
codomain ˌkəʊ də ˈmeɪn -dəʊ-, ˈˌˌˌˌ
‖ ˌkoʊ doʊ- **~s** z
codon ˈkəʊd ɒn ‖ ˈkoʊd ɑːn **~s** z
codpiec|e ˈkɒd piːs →ˈkɒb- ‖ ˈkɑːd- **~es** ɪz əz
Codrington ˈkɒdr ɪŋ tən ‖ ˈkɑːdr-
codriver ˈkəʊ ˌdraɪv ə ˌˈˌˌ ‖ ˈkoʊ ˌdraɪv ᵊr **~s** z
codswallop ˈkɒdz ˌwɒl əp ‖ ˈkɑːdz ˌwɑːl-
Cody ˈkəʊd i ‖ ˈkoʊd i
Coe kəʊ ‖ koʊ
coed ˈkəʊ ed ˌˈˌ ‖ ˈkoʊ- **~s** z
Coed in Welsh place names kɔɪd —Welsh [kɔid, koːd, koïd]
coeducation ˌkəʊ ˌed ju ˈkeɪʃ ᵊn -ˌedʒ u-
‖ ˌkoʊ ˌedʒ ə-
coeducational ˌkəʊ ˌed ju ˈkeɪʃ ᵊn ᵊl ◂
-ˌedʒ u- ‖ ˌkoʊ ˌedʒ ə- **~ly** i
coefficient ˌkəʊ ɪ ˈfɪʃ ᵊnt ◂ -ə- ‖ ˌkoʊ- **~s** s
ˌcoefˌficient of ˈfriction
coelacanth ˈsiːl ə kænᵗθ **~s** s
coelenterate si ˈlent ə reɪt sə-, -ɚ ət, -ɚ ɪt
‖ -ˈlenț- **~s** s
Coelho ˈkwel ju ku ˈel-, -jəʊ ‖ -joʊ —BrPort
[ko ˈe ʎu]
coeliac ˈsiːl i æk
ˈcoeliac diˌsease
coelom ˈsiːl əm **~s** z
coelomate ˈsiːl ə meɪt **~s** s
coelomic si ˈlɒm ɪk -ˈləʊm- ‖ -ˈlɑːm- -ˈloʊm-
Coen ˈkəʊ ɪn -ən ‖ ˈkoʊ ən
coenobite ˈsiːn əʊ baɪt ‖ -ə- **~s** s
coenzyme ₍ˌ₎kəʊ ˈenz aɪm ‖ ₍ˌ₎koʊ- **~s** z
coequal ₍ˌ₎kəʊ ˈiːk wəl ‖ ₍ˌ₎koʊ- **~ly** i **~s** z
coerc|e kəʊ ˈɜːs ‖ koʊ ˈɝːs **~ed** t **~er/s** ə/z
ᵊr/z **~es** ɪz əz **~ing** ɪŋ
coercible kəʊ ˈɜːs əb ᵊl -ɪb ᵊl ‖ koʊ ˈɝːs-
coercion kəʊ ˈɜːʃ ᵊn ‖ koʊ ˈɝːʃ ᵊn -ˈɝːʒ-
coercive kəʊ ˈɜːs ɪv ‖ koʊ ˈɝːs- **~ly** li **~ness**
nəs nɪs
coercivity ˌkəʊ ɜː ˈsɪv ət i -ɪt i
‖ ˌkoʊ ɝː ˈsɪv əț i
coeternal ˌkəʊ i ˈtɜːn ᵊl ◂ -iː- ‖ ˌkoʊ i ˈtɝːn ᵊl ◂
~ly i
Coetzee ₍ˌ₎kuːt ˈsiːˌə -ˈsiː- —Afrikaans [ku ˈtsɪə]
Coeur d'Alene ˌkɔː də ˈleɪn -dᵊl ˈeɪn
‖ ˌkɔːrd ᵊl ˈeɪn
Coeur de Lion ˌkɜː də ˈliː ð̃ ˌkɜːd ᵊl ˈiː-, -ɒn,
ˌən ‖ ˌkɜː də ˈlaɪ ən ˌkɜːd ᵊl ˈaɪ ən —Fr
[kœʁ də ljɔ̃]
coeval kəʊ ˈiːv ᵊl ‖ koʊ- **~ly** i **~s** z
coevolution ˌkəʊ iːv ə ˈluːʃ ᵊn -ev ə-, -ˈljuːʃ-
‖ ˌkoʊ ev-
coexist ˌkəʊ ɪg ˈzɪst -ɪk-, -əg-, -ək-, -eg-, -ek-
‖ ˌkoʊ- **~ed** ɪd əd **~ing** ɪŋ **~s** s
coexist|ence ˌkəʊ ɪg ˈzɪst ᵊnᵗs -ɪk-, -əg-, -ək-,
-eg-, -ek- ‖ ˌkoʊ- **~ent/ly** ᵊnt /li
coextensive ˌkəʊ ɪk ˈstenᵗs ɪv -ek-, -ək- ‖ ˌkoʊ-
~ly li **~ness** nəs nɪs
cofactor ˈkəʊ ˌfækt ə ‖ ˈkoʊ ˌfækt ᵊr **~s** z
CofE ˌsiː ˌəv ˈiː

6% ▮ ˈkɔːf-
57% 37% ▮ ˈkɑːf-
▮ no distinction
AmE

coffee ˈkɒf i ‖ ˈkɔːf i ˈkɑːf- **~s** z — Preference
poll, AmE: ˈkɔːf- 57%, ˈkɑːf- 6%; no
distinction made between ɔː and ɑː, 37%.
ˈcoffee bar; ˈcoffee break; ˈcoffee cup;
ˈcoffee klatch klætʃ ‖ klɑːtʃ, klʌtʃ; ˈcoffee
house; ˈcoffee ˌmorning; ˈcoffee shop;
ˈcoffee ˌtable
coffeemaker ˈkɒf i ˌmeɪk ə ‖ ˈkɔːf i ˌmeɪk ᵊr
ˈkɑːf- **~s** z
Coffeemate tdmk ˈkɒf i meɪt ‖ ˈkɔːf- ˈkɑːf-
coffeepot ˈkɒf i pɒt ‖ ˈkɔːf i pɑːt ˈkɑːf- **~s** s
coffee-table book ˈkɒf i teɪb ᵊl ˌbʊk §-ˌbuːk
‖ ˈkɔːf- ˈkɑːf-
coffer ˈkɒf ə ‖ ˈkɔːf ᵊr ˈkɑːf- **~s** z
cofferdam ˈkɒf ə dæm ‖ ˈkɔːf ᵊr- ˈkɑːf- **~s** z
Coffey ˈkɒf i ‖ ˈkɔːf i ˈkɑːf-
coffin, C~ ˈkɒf ɪn §-ᵊn ‖ ˈkɔːf ᵊn ˈkɑːf- **~s** z
coffle ˈkɒf ᵊl ‖ ˈkɔːf- ˈkɑːf- **~s** z
cog kɒg ‖ kɑːg **cogs** kɒgz ‖ kɑːgz
Cogan ˈkəʊg ən ‖ ˈkoʊg ən
cogency ˈkəʊdʒ ᵊnᵗs i ‖ ˈkoʊdʒ-
cogent ˈkəʊdʒ ᵊnt ‖ ˈkoʊdʒ- **~ly** li
Coggan ˈkɒg ən ‖ ˈkɑːg-
Coggeshall (i) ˈkɒg ɪʃ ᵊl ˈkɒks ᵊl ‖ ˈkɑːg-,
(ii) ˈkɒgz ɔːl ‖ ˈkɑːgz- -ɑːl —The place in
Essex is (i), the family name (ii)
Coghill ˈkɒg hɪl -ɪl ‖ ˈkɑːg-
Coghlan (i) ˈkəʊl ən ‖ ˈkoʊl-, (ii) ˈkɒx lən
ˈkɒg- ‖ ˈkɔːk- ˈkɑːk-
cogi|tate ˈkɒdʒ ɪ |teɪt -ə- ‖ ˈkɑːdʒ- **~tated**
teɪt ɪd -əd ‖ teɪt̬ əd **~tates** teɪts **~tating**
teɪt ɪŋ ‖ teɪt̬ ɪŋ
cogitation ˌkɒdʒ ɪ ˈteɪʃ ᵊn -ə- ‖ ˌkɑːdʒ-
cogitative ˈkɒdʒ ɪt ət ɪv ˈ-ət-; -ɪ teɪt-, -ə teɪt-
‖ ˈkɑːdʒ ə teɪt̬ ɪv **~ly** li **~ness** nəs nɪs
cogito ergo sum ˌkɒg ɪt əʊ ˌɜːg əʊ ˈsʊm
§-ˌət-, -ˈsʌm ‖ ˌkoʊg ə toʊ ˌɝːg oʊ ˈsʊm -ˌerg-
cognac, C~ ˈkɒn jæk ‖ ˈkoʊn- —Fr [kɔ njak]
~s s
cognate ˈkɒg neɪt ₍ˌ₎ˈˌ ‖ ˈkɑːg- **~ly** li **~s** s
cognis... —see **cogniz...**
cognition kɒg ˈnɪʃ ᵊn ‖ kɑːg-
cognitive ˈkɒg nət ɪv -nɪt- ‖ ˈkɑːg nət̬ ɪv **~ly** li
cogniz|ance ˈkɒg nɪz |ᵊnᵗs -nəz-; kɒg ˈnaɪz-;
ˈkɒn ɪz-, -əz- ‖ ˈkɑːg- **~ant** ənt
cognomen ₍ˌ₎kɒg ˈnəʊm en -ən
‖ ₍ˌ₎kɑːg ˈnoʊm ən ˈkɑːg nəm-
cognoscent|e ˌkɒg nə ˈʃent| i -nəʊ-, -ˈsent-
-iː; ˌkɒn jəʊ- ‖ ˌkɑːn jə ˈʃenț| i -ə- **~i** i iː
cogwheel ˈkɒg wiːᵊl -hwiːᵊl ‖ ˈkɑːg- **~s** z
cohab|it ₍ˌ₎kəʊ ˈhæb |ɪt §-ət ‖ ₍ˌ₎koʊ ˈhæb |ət
~ited ɪt əd §ət-, -əd ‖ ət̬ əd **~iting** ɪt ɪŋ §ət-
‖ ət̬ ɪŋ **~its** ɪts §əts ‖ əts

C

cohabitation ˌ(ˌ)kəʊ ˌhæb ɪ 'teɪʃ ⁿn
-ə- ‖ ˌ(ˌ)koʊ-
cohabitee ˌ(ˌ)kəʊ ˌhæb ɪ 'tiː -ə'- ‖ ˌ(ˌ)koʊ- ~s z
Cohen 'kəʊ ɪn §-ən ‖ 'koʊ ən
coher|e kəʊ 'hɪə ‖ koʊ 'hɪ³r ~ed d ~es z
  cohering kəʊ 'hɪər ɪŋ ‖ koʊ 'hɪr ɪŋ
coherenc|e kəʊ 'hɪər ənˢts ‖ koʊ 'hɪr- ~y i
coherent kəʊ 'hɪər ənt ‖ koʊ 'hɪr- ~ly li
cohesion kəʊ 'hiːʒ ⁿn ‖ koʊ-
cohesive kəʊ 'hiːs ɪv -'hiːz- ‖ koʊ- ~ly li ~ness
  nəs nɪs
coho 'kəʊ həʊ ‖ 'koʊ hoʊ
coho|bate 'kəʊ həʊ |beɪt ‖ 'koʊ hoʊ- ~bated
  beɪt ɪd -əd ‖ beɪt̬ əd ~bates beɪts ~bating
  beɪt ɪŋ ‖ beɪt̬ ɪŋ
cohobation ˌkəʊ həʊ 'beɪʃⁿn ‖ ˌkoʊ hoʊ-
Cohoes kə 'həʊz ‖ -'hoʊz
cohort 'kəʊ hɔːt ‖ 'koʊ hɔːrt ~s s
cohosh 'kəʊ hɒʃ ‖ 'koʊ haːʃ ~es ɪz əz
COHSE 'kəʊz i ‖ 'koʊz i
coif 'headdress' kɔɪf **coifs** kɔɪfs
coif 'coiffure' kwaːf kwæf **coiffed** kwaːft kwæft
  coiffing 'kwaːf ɪŋ 'kwæf- **coifs** kwaːfs kwæfs
coiffeur kwaː 'fɜː kwɒ-, kwæ-, kwʌ- ‖ -'fɜː
  —Fr [kwa fœːʁ] ~s z
coiffure kwaː 'fjʊə kwɒ-, kwæ-, kwʌ- ‖ -'fjʊ³r
  —Fr [kwa fyːʁ] ~d d ~s z
coign kɔɪn (= coin)
coil kɔɪ³l **coiled** kɔɪ³ld **coiling** 'kɔɪl ɪŋ **coils**
  kɔɪ³lz
  'coil spring
Coimbra 'kwɪm brə 'kwiːm- —Port
  ['kwim brɐ]
coin kɔɪn 'kɔɪ ɪn **coined** kɔɪnd 'kɔɪ ɪnd **coining**
  'kɔɪn ɪŋ 'kɔɪ ɪn ɪŋ **coins** kɔɪnz 'kɔɪ ɪnz
coinag|e 'kɔɪn ɪdʒ ~es ɪz əz
coincid|e ˌkəʊ ɪn 'saɪd -ən- ‖ ˌkoʊ- ~ed ɪd əd
  ~es z ~ing ɪŋ
coincidenc|e kəʊ 'ɪnˢts ɪd ənˢts -əd- ‖ koʊ-
  -ə denˢts ~es ɪz əz
coincident kəʊ 'ɪnˢts ɪd ənt -əd- ‖ koʊ- -ə dent
coincidental kəʊ ˌɪnˢts ɪ 'dent ³l ◂ ˌ· ·⁝, -ə'--
  ‖ koʊ ˌɪnˢts ə 'dent̬ ³l ˌ· ·-- ~ly i
coin-op 'kɔɪn ɒp ‖ -aːp ~s s
coinsurance ˌkəʊ ɪn 'ʃʊər ənˢts -ˌən-, -'ʃɔːr-
  ‖ ˌkoʊ ɪn 'ʃʊr- -'ʃɜː-, ˌkoʊ 'ɪn ʃʊr-
Cointreau tdmk 'kwɒntr əʊ 'kwaːntr-,
  'kwæntr- ‖ kwaːn 'troʊ —Fr [kwæ̃ tʁo] ~s z
coir 'kɔɪ ə ‖ 'kɔɪ³r
coit, Coit kɔɪt
coital 'kəʊ ɪt ³l §-ət-; 'kɔɪt ³l ‖ 'koʊ ət̬ ³l
coition kəʊ 'ɪʃ ⁿn ‖ koʊ-
coitus 'kəʊ ɪt əs §-ət-; 'kɔɪt əs ‖ 'koʊ ət̬ əs
  'kɔɪt əs
  ˌcoitus ˌinter'ruptus ˌɪnt ə 'rʌpt əs ‖ ˌɪnt̬-;
  ˌcoitus ˌreser'vatus ˌrez ə 'vaːt əs ‖ -ɜː-,
  -'veɪt- -³r 'veɪt̬ əs
cojones kə 'həʊn iz -eɪz ‖ -'hoʊn- -eɪs —Sp
  [ko 'xo nes]
coke kəʊk ‖ koʊk **coked** kəʊkt ‖ koʊkt **cokes**
  kəʊks ‖ koʊks **coking** 'kəʊk ɪŋ ‖ 'koʊk ɪŋ
Coke tdmk kəʊk ‖ koʊk **Cokes** kəʊks ‖ koʊks

Coke family name (i) kʊk §kuːk, (ii) kəʊk
  ‖ koʊk
Coker 'kəʊk ə ‖ 'koʊk ³r
col, Col kɒl ‖ kaːl **cols** kɒlz ‖ kaːlz
col- ǀkɒ, kə ‖ ǀkaː, kə —This prefix, found only
  before l, is pronounced stressed ǀkɒ ‖ ǀkaː: (1) if
  the following syllable is unstressed
  (ˌcolloˈcation), (2) in a few two-syllable nouns
  ('colleague; but colˈlapse with kə-); and (3)
  occasionally, in context, when contrastively
  stressed (to select and 'collect). Otherwise it is
  usually weak kə (colˈlision).
cola 'kəʊl ə ‖ 'koʊl ə ~s z
colander 'kʌl ənd ə 'kɒl-, -ɪnd- ‖ -³r 'kaːl- ~s z
Colby (i) 'kəʊl bi →'kɒʊl- ‖ 'koʊl-, (ii) 'kɒl-
  ‖ 'kaːl-
colcannon kɒl 'kæn ən ‖ kaːl-
Colchester 'kəʊltʃ ɪst ə →'kɒʊltʃ-, §'kɒltʃ-,
  -əst- ‖ 'koʊl ˌtʃest ³r
colchicum 'kɒltʃ ɪk əm 'kɒlk- ‖ 'kaːltʃ- ~s z
Colchis 'kɒlk ɪs §-əs ‖ 'kaːlk-
cold kəʊld →kɒʊld ‖ koʊld **colder** 'kəʊld ə
  →'kɒʊld- ‖ 'koʊld ³r **coldest** 'kəʊld ɪst
  →'kɒʊld, -əst ‖ 'koʊld- **colds** kəʊldz →kɒʊldz
  ‖ koʊldz
  ˌcold 'chisel; ˌcold 'comfort; 'cold cream;
  'cold cuts, ˌ· '·; ˌcold 'feet; ˌcold 'fish;
  'cold frame; ˌcold 'front, '· ·; ˌcold 'snap;
  'cold sore; ˌcold 'steel; ˌcold 'storage;
  ˌcold 'sweat; ˌcold 'turkey; ˌcold 'war◂
cold-blooded ˌkəʊld 'blʌd ɪd ◂ →ˌkɒʊld-, -əd
  ‖ ˌkoʊld- ~ly li ~ness nəs nɪs
cold-drawn ˌkəʊld 'drɔːn ◂ →ˌkɒʊld- ‖ ˌkoʊld-
  -'draːn
Coldfield 'kəʊld fiː³ld →'kɒʊld- ‖ 'koʊld-
cold-hearted ˌkəʊld 'haːt ɪd ◂ →ˌkɒʊld-, -əd
  ‖ ˌkoʊld 'haːrt̬ əd ◂ ~ly li ~ness nəs nɪs
coldish 'kəʊld ɪʃ →'kɒʊld- ‖ 'koʊld ɪʃ
Colditz 'kəʊld ɪts →'kɒʊld-, 'kɒld-, §-əts
  ‖ 'koʊld- 'kaːld- —Ger ['kɔl dɪts]
cold|ly 'kəʊld |li →'kɒʊld- ‖ 'koʊld- ~ness
  nəs nɪs
Coldplay 'kəʊld pleɪ →'kɒʊld- ‖ 'koʊld-
cold-shoulder ˌkəʊld 'ʃəʊld ə →ˌkɒʊld 'ʃɒʊld-
  ‖ ˌkoʊld 'ʃoʊld ³r ~ed d
Coldstream 'kəʊld striːm →'kɒʊld- ‖ 'koʊld-
cole, Cole kəʊl →kɒʊl ‖ koʊl (= coal)
Colebrook 'kəʊl brʊk →'kɒʊl- ‖ 'koʊl-
Coleclough (i) 'kəʊl klʌf →'kɒʊl- ‖ 'koʊl-,
  (ii) -klaʊ
colectom|y kəʊ 'lekt əm |i ‖ koʊ- ~ies iz
Coleford 'kəʊl fəd →'kɒʊl- ‖ 'koʊl f³rd
Coleherne 'kəʊl hɜːn →'kɒʊl- ‖ 'koʊl hɜːn ˌ·'·
Coleman 'kəʊl mən →'kɒʊl- ‖ 'koʊl-
Colenso kə 'lenz əʊ ‖ -oʊ
coleoptera ˌkɒl i 'ɒpt ər ə ‖ ˌkaːl i 'aːpt-
coleopterous ˌkɒl i 'ɒpt ər əs ◂ ‖ ˌkaːl i 'aːpt-
Coleraine ˌ(ˌ)kəʊl 'reɪn →ˌ(ˌ)kɒʊl- ‖ ˌ(ˌ)koʊl-
Coleridge 'kəʊl ər ɪdʒ ‖ 'koʊl- ~'s ɪz əz
Colerne (i) kə 'lɜːn ‖ -'lɜːn; (ii) 'kɒl ən
  ‖ 'kaːl ³rn, (iii) 'kʌl ən ‖ -³rn
coleslaw 'kəʊl slɔː →'kɒʊl- ‖ 'koʊl- -slaː ~s z
Colet 'kɒl ɪt -ət ‖ 'kaːl-

C

Colette kɒ 'let kə-, ˌkɒ- ‖ koʊ- —*Fr* [kɔ lɛt]
coleus 'kəʊl i ˌəs ‖ 'koʊl-
coley 'kəʊl i ‖ 'koʊl i ~s z
Colgate *tdmk* 'kəʊl geɪt →'kɒʊl-, 'kɒl-, -gət,
  -gɪt ‖ 'koʊl- 'kɑːl-
colibri, C~ *tdmk* 'kɒl ɪb ri -əb- ‖ 'kɑːl-
colic 'kɒl ɪk ‖ 'kɑːl- ~s s
colicky 'kɒl ɪk i ‖ 'kɑːl-
coliform 'kəʊl i fɔːm 'kɒl- ‖ 'koʊl ə fɔːrm
  'kɑːl-
Colima kə 'liːm ə —*Sp* [ko 'li ma]
Colin (i) 'kɒl ɪn -ən ‖ 'kɑːl-, (ii) 'kəʊ lɪn
  ‖ 'koʊ- —*as a British name*, (i).
Colindale 'kɒl ɪn deɪ°l -ən- ‖ 'kɑːl-
Coliseum ˌkɒl ə 'siːˌəm -ɪ- ‖ ˌkɑːl-
colitis kəʊ 'laɪt ɪs kɒ-, §-əs ‖ koʊ 'laɪt̬ əs kə-
Coll kɒl ‖ kɑːl
collabo|rate kə 'læb ə |reɪt **~rated** reɪt ɪd -əd
  ‖ reɪt̬ əd **~rates** reɪts **~rating** reɪt ɪŋ ‖ reɪt̬ ɪŋ
collaboration kə ˌlæb ə 'reɪʃ ᵊn **~ist/s** ɪst/s
  §əst/s **~s** z
collaborative kə 'læb ər ət ɪv -ə reɪt-
  ‖ -ə reɪt̬ ɪv -ərˌət̬- **~ly** li
collaborator kə 'læb ə reɪt ə ‖ -reɪt̬ ᵊr **~s** z
collag|e kɒ 'lɑːʒ kə-; 'kɒl ɑːʒ ‖ kə- kɑ:-, kɔ:-,
  koʊ- —*Fr* [kɔ laːʒ] **~es** ɪz əz
collagen 'kɒl ədʒ ən -ɪn ‖ 'kɑːl-
collaps|e kə 'læps **~ed** t **~es** ɪz əz **~ing** ɪŋ
collapsibility kə ˌlæps ə 'bɪl ət i -ˌɪ-, -ɪt i
  ‖ -ət̬ i
collapsible kə 'læps əb ᵊl -ɪb-
collar 'kɒl ə ‖ 'kɑːl ᵊr **~ed** d **collaring**
  'kɒl ər ɪŋ ‖ 'kɑːl- **~s** z
  'collar stud
collarbone 'kɒl ə bəʊn ‖ 'kɑːl ᵊr boʊn **~s** z
collard 'kɒl əd ‖ 'kɑːl ᵊrd **~s** z
collarette ˌkɒl ə 'ret ‖ ˌkɑːl- **~s** s
collarless 'kɒl ə ləs -lɪs ‖ 'kɑːl ᵊr-
col|late kə |'leɪt kɒ-, kəʊ- ‖ kɑː-, koʊ-, 'kɑːl eɪt
  ~lated 'leɪt ɪd -əd ‖ 'leɪt̬ əd **~lates** 'leɪts
  ~lating 'leɪt ɪŋ ‖ 'leɪt̬ ɪŋ
collateral kə 'læt ᵊr əl kɒ- ‖ -'læt̬ ər əl
  →-'lætr əl **~ly** i
collateraliz|e, collateralis|e kə 'læt ᵊr ə laɪz
  ‖ kə 'læt̬ ər ə laɪz **~ed** d **~es** ɪz əz **~ing** ɪŋ
collation kə 'leɪʃ ᵊn kɒ-, kəʊ- ‖ kɑ:-, koʊ- **~s** z
collator kə 'leɪt ə kɒ-, kəʊ-; 'kɒl eɪt ə, 'kəʊl-
  ‖ kə 'leɪt̬ ᵊr kɑ:-, koʊ-, 'kɑːl eɪt̬ ᵊr **~s** z
colleague 'kɒl iːg ‖ 'kɑːl- -ɪg **~s** z
collect *n 'prayer'* 'kɒl ekt -ɪkt ‖ 'kɑːl- **~s** s
collect *v, adj, adv* kə 'lekt **~ed** ɪd əd **~ing** ɪŋ
  ~s s
collectable kə 'lekt əb ᵊl -ɪb- **~s** z
collectanea ˌkɒl ek 'teɪn iˌə ‖ ˌkɑːl-
collected kə 'lekt ɪd -əd **~ly** li **~ness** nəs nɪs
collectible kə 'lekt əb ᵊl -ɪb- **~s** z
collection kə 'lek ʃᵊn **~s** z
collective kə 'lekt ɪv **~ly** li **~ness** nəs nɪs **~s** z
  colˌlective 'farm
collectivis... —*see* **collectiviz...**
collectivism kə 'lekt ɪ ˌvɪz əm -ə-
collectivist kə 'lekt ɪv ɪst -əv ɪst, §-əst **~s** s
collectivistic kə ˌlekt ɪ 'vɪst ɪk ◂ -ə-

collectivit|y ˌkɒl ek 'tɪv ət |i kə ˌlek-, -ɪt i
  ‖ kə ˌlek 'tɪv ət̬ |i ˌkɑːl ek- **~ies** iz
collectivization kə ˌlekt ɪv aɪ 'zeɪʃ ᵊn -ˌəv-,
  -ɪ'-- ‖ -ɪv ə- **~s** z
collectiviz|e kə 'lekt ɪ vaɪz -ə- **~ed** d **~es** ɪz əz
  ~ing ɪŋ
collector kə 'lekt ə ‖ -ᵊr **~s** z
  col'lector's ˌitem
colleen, C~ kɒ 'liːn 'kɒl iːn ‖ kɑ: 'liːn 'kɑːl iːn
  ~s z
colleg|e 'kɒl ɪdʒ ‖ 'kɑːl- **~es** ɪz əz
collegial kə 'liːdʒ iˌəl -'liːg-
collegiality kə ˌliːdʒ i 'æl ət i -ɪt i ‖ -ət̬ i
collegian kə 'liːdʒ iˌən -'liːdʒ ən **~s** z
collegiate kə 'liːdʒ iˌət kɒ-, ɪt; -'liːdʒ ət, -ɪt
collegium kə 'liːdʒ iˌəm -'leg-; -'liːdʒ əm **~s** z
collenchyma kə 'leŋk ɪm ə kɒ-, §-əm-
Colles 'kɒl ɪs -əs ‖ 'kɑːl- **Colles'** *same, or with*
  added ɪz əz
  ˌColles' 'fracture
collet, Collet, Collett 'kɒl ɪt -ət ‖ 'kɑːl- **~s** s
Colley 'kɒl i ‖ 'kɑːl i
collid|e kə 'laɪd **~ed** ɪd əd **~es** z **~ing** ɪŋ
collie 'kɒl i ‖ 'kɑːl i **~s** z
collier, C~ 'kɒl iˌə ‖ 'kɑːl jᵊr **~s** z
collier|y 'kɒl jər |i ‖ 'kɑːl- **~ies** iz
colli|gate 'kɒl ɪ |geɪt -ə- ‖ 'kɑːl- **~gated**
  geɪt ɪd -əd ‖ geɪt̬ əd **~gates** geɪts **~gating**
  geɪt ɪŋ ‖ geɪt̬ ɪŋ
colligation ˌkɒl ɪ 'geɪʃ ᵊn -ə- ‖ ˌkɑːl- **~s** z
colligative kə 'lɪg ət ɪv ‖ 'kɑːl ə geɪt̬ ɪv
colli|mate 'kɒl ɪ |meɪt -ə- ‖ 'kɑːl- **~mated**
  meɪt ɪd -əd ‖ meɪt̬ əd **~mates** meɪts **~mating**
  meɪt ɪŋ ‖ meɪt̬ ɪŋ
collimation ˌkɒl ɪ 'meɪʃ ᵊn -ə- ‖ ˌkɑːl- **~s** z
collimator 'kɒl ɪ meɪt ə '-ə- ‖ 'kɑːl ə meɪt̬ ᵊr
  ~s z
Collin 'kɒl ɪn -ən ‖ 'kɑːl-
collinear kɒ 'lɪn iˌə kə-, kəʊ- ‖ kə 'lɪn iˌᵊr kɑ:-
Collinge 'kɒl ɪndʒ -əndʒ ‖ 'kɑːl-
Collingham 'kɒl ɪŋ əm ‖ 'kɑːl-
Collingwood 'kɒl ɪŋ wʊd ‖ 'kɑːl-
Collins, c~ 'kɒl ɪnz -ənz ‖ 'kɑːl-
Collinson 'kɒl ɪnᵗs ən -ənᵗs- ‖ 'kɑːl-
Collis 'kɒl ɪs -əs ‖ 'kɑːl-
collision kə 'lɪʒ ᵊn **~s** z
  col'lision course
collocate *n* 'kɒl ək ət -ɪt; -ə keɪt ‖ 'kɑːl- **~s** s
collo|cate *v* 'kɒl ə |keɪt -əʊ- ‖ 'kɑːl- **~cated**
  keɪt ɪd -əd ‖ keɪt̬ əd **~cates** keɪts **~cating**
  keɪt ɪŋ ‖ keɪt̬ ɪŋ
collocation ˌkɒl ə 'keɪʃ ᵊn -əʊ- ‖ ˌkɑːl- **~s** z
collocutor kə 'lɒk jʊt ə -jət-; 'kɒl ə kjuːt ə
  ‖ -'lɑːk jət̬ ᵊr **~s** z
collodi|on kə 'ləʊd iˌ|ən ‖ -'loʊd- **~um** əm
colloid 'kɒl ɔɪd ‖ 'kɑːl- **~s** z
colloidal kə 'lɔɪd ᵊl kɒ-
collop 'kɒl əp ‖ 'kɑːl- **~s** s
colloquia kə 'ləʊk wiˌə ‖ -'loʊk-
colloquial kə 'ləʊk wiˌəl ‖ -'loʊk- **~ly** i
colloquialism kə 'ləʊk wiˌə ˌlɪz əm ‖ -'loʊk-
  ~s z
colloquium kə 'ləʊk wiˌəm ‖ -'loʊk- **~s** z

colloq|uy 'kɒl ək| wi ‖ 'kɑːl- **~uies** wiz
collotype 'kɒl əʊ taɪp ‖ 'kɑːl ə- **~s** s
Colls kɒlz ‖ kɑːlz
collud|e kə 'luːd kʊ-, -'ljuːd **~ed** ɪd əd **~es** z
~ing ɪŋ
collusion kə 'luːʒ ᵊn kʊ-, -'ljuːʒ- **~s** z
collusive kə 'luːs ɪv kʊ-, -'ljuːs-, -'luːz-, -'ljuːz-
~ly li **~ness** nəs nɪs
colluvi|um kə 'luːv i ˌ|əm kʊ-, -'ljuːv- **~a** ə
~ums əmz
colly, Colly 'kɒl i ‖ 'kɑːl i
collyri|um kə 'lɪr i ˌ|əm **~a** ə
collywobbles 'kɒl i ˌwɒb ᵊlz
‖ 'kɑːl i ˌwɑːb ᵊlz
Colman (i) 'kəʊl mən →'kɒʊl- ‖ 'koʊl-,
(ii) 'kɒl- ‖ 'kɑːl-
Colnaghi kɒl 'nɑːg i ‖ kɑːl-
Colnbrook 'kəʊln brʊk →'kɒʊln-, 'kəʊn-
‖ 'koʊln-
Colne kəʊn kəʊln ‖ koʊn
Colney 'kəʊn i 'kəʊln i ‖ 'koʊn i
colobus 'kɒl əb əs ‖ 'kɑːl- **~es** ɪz əz
colocynth 'kɒl ə sɪntθ ‖ 'kɑːl- **~s** s
cologne, C~ kə 'ləʊn ‖ -'loʊn **~s, C~'s** z
Colombi|a kə 'lɒm bi ˌ|ə -'lʌm- ‖ -'lʌm- -'loʊm-
~an/s ən/z
Colombo kə 'lʌm bəʊ -'lɒm- ‖ -boʊ
Co'lombo Plan
colon *'colonial farmer'* kɒ 'lɒn kə- ‖ kə 'loʊn
koʊ- —*Fr* [kɔ lɔ̃] **~s** z
colon *'punctuation mark'; 'part of intestine'*
'kəʊl ən -ɒn ‖ 'koʊl ən **~s** z
Colon, Colón *place in Panama*, **colon, colón**
currency unit kɒ 'lɒn kə- ‖ kə 'loʊn koʊ-
—*Sp* [ko 'lon]
colonel, C~ 'kɜːn ᵊl ‖ 'kɜːn ᵊl (= *kernel*) **~s** z
ˌColonel 'Blimp
colonel|cy 'kɜːn ᵊl |si ‖ 'kɜːn- **~cies** siz
coloni... —*see* **colony**
colonial kə 'ləʊn i ˌəl ‖ -'loʊn- **~ly** i **~s** z
colonialism kə 'ləʊn i ˌə ˌlɪz əm ‖ -'loʊn-
colonialist kə 'ləʊn i ˌəl ɪst §-əst ‖ -'loʊn- **~s** s
colonic kəʊ 'lɒn ɪk kə- ‖ koʊ 'lɑːn-
colonis... —*see* **coloniz...**
colonist 'kɒl ən ɪst §-əst ‖ 'kɑːl- **~s** s
colonization ˌkɒl ən aɪ 'zeɪʃ ᵊn -ən ɪ-
‖ ˌkɑːl ən ə- **~s** z
coloniz|e 'kɒl ə naɪz ‖ 'kɑːl- **~ed** d **~es** ɪz əz
~ing ɪŋ
colonizer 'kɒl ə naɪz ə ‖ 'kɑːl ə naɪz ᵊr **~s** z
colonnad|e ˌkɒl ə 'neɪd '·· ‖ ˌkɑːl- **~ed** ɪd əd
~es z
colonoscope kə 'lɒn ə skəʊp ‖ -'lɑːn ə skoʊp
~s s
Colonsay 'kɒl ənz eɪ -ən seɪ ‖ 'kɑːl-
Colonus kə 'ləʊn əs -'lɒn- ‖ -'loʊn-
colon|y 'kɒl ən |i ‖ 'kɑːl- **~ies** iz
colophon 'kɒl ə fɒn -əf ᵊn ‖ 'kɑːl ə fɑːn -əf ən
~s z
colophony kɒ 'lɒf ᵊn i kə- ‖ kə 'lɑːf-

color 'kʌl ə ‖ -ᵊr **colored** 'kʌl əd ‖ -ᵊrd
coloring 'kʌl ər ɪŋ **colors** 'kʌl əz ‖ -ᵊrz
'color bar, 'color line; 'color scheme;
ˌcolor 'supplement
Colorado, c~ ˌkɒl ə 'rɑːd əʊ ◂
‖ ˌkɑːl ə 'ræd oʊ ◂ -'rɑːd-
ˌColoˌrado 'beetle; ˌColoˌrado 'Springs
colorant 'kʌl ər ənt **~s** s
coloration ˌkʌl ə 'reɪʃ ᵊn **~s** z
coloratura ˌkɒl ər ə 'tʊər ə -'tjʊər-
‖ ˌkʌl ər ə 'tʊr ə -'tjʊr- **~s** z
color-blind 'kʌl ə blaɪnd ‖ -ᵊr- **~ness** nəs nɪs
color-cod|e ˌkʌl ə 'kəʊd '··· ‖ ˌkʌl ᵊr 'koʊd
~ed ɪd əd **~ing** ɪŋ **~es** z
color-cod|e ˌkʌl ə 'kəʊd '··· ‖ ˌkʌl ᵊr ˌkoʊd
·'· **~ed** ɪd ◂ əd **~ing** ɪŋ **~es** z
color-coordinated ˌkʌl ə kəʊ 'ɔːd ɪ neɪt ɪd ◂
-'ə-, -'· ᵊn eɪt-, -əd
‖ ˌkʌl ᵊr koʊ 'ɔːrd n eɪt əd ◂
color-coordination ˌkʌl ə kəʊ ˌɔːd ɪ 'neɪʃ ᵊn
-ə'··, -ᵊn 'eɪʃ- ‖ ˌkʌl ᵊr koʊ ˌɔːrd ᵊn 'eɪʃ ᵊn
colored 'kʌl əd ‖ -ᵊrd **~s** z
colorfast 'kʌl ə fɑːst §-fæst ‖ -ᵊr fæst **~ness**
nəs nɪs
colorful 'kʌl ə fᵊl -fʊl ‖ -ᵊr- **~ly** i
colorimeter ˌkʌl ə 'rɪm ɪt ə -ət ‖ -əṭ ᵊr **~s** z
colorimetry ˌkʌl ə 'rɪm ətr i -ɪtr i
coloring 'kʌl ər ɪŋ
'coloring ˌmatter
colorist 'kʌl ər ɪst §-əst **~s** s
colorization ˌkʌl ə raɪ 'zeɪʃ ᵊn
coloriz|e 'kʌl ə raɪz **~ed** d **~es** ɪz əz **~ing** ɪŋ
colorless 'kʌl ə ləs -lɪs ‖ -ᵊr- **~ly** li **~ness** nəs
nɪs
Coloroll *tdmk* 'kʌl ə rəʊl →-rɒʊl ‖ -roʊl
colorwash 'kʌl ə wɒʃ ‖ -ᵊr wɔːʃ -wɑːʃ **~ed** t
~es ɪz əz **~ing** ɪŋ
colorway 'kʌl ə weɪ ‖ -ᵊr- **~s** z
Colossae kə 'lɒs iː -aɪ ‖ -'lɑːs-
colossal kə 'lɒs ᵊl ‖ -'lɑːs- **~ly** i
Colosseum, c~ ˌkɒl ə 'siː əm ‖ ˌkɑːl-
colossi kə 'lɒs aɪ ‖ -'lɑːs-
Colossian kə 'lɒʃ ᵊn kə 'lɒs i ˌən, -'lɒʃ- ‖ -'lɑːʃ-
~s z
coloss|us kə 'lɒs |əs ‖ -'lɑːs- **~i** aɪ **~uses** əs ɪz
-əz
colostom|y kə 'lɒst əm |i ‖ -'lɑːst- **~ies** iz
co'lostomy bag
colostrum kə 'lɒs trəm ‖ -'lɑːs-
colour 'kʌl ə ‖ -ᵊr **coloured** 'kʌl əd ‖ -ᵊrd
colouring 'kʌl ər ɪŋ **colours** 'kʌl əz ‖ -ᵊrz
'colour bar, 'color line; 'colour scheme;
ˌcolour 'supplement
colourant 'kʌl ər ənt **~s** s
colour-blind 'kʌl ə blaɪnd ‖ -ᵊr- **~ness** nəs nɪs
colour-coordinated ˌkʌl ə kəʊ 'ɔːd ɪ neɪt ɪd ◂
-'ə-, -'·ᵊn eɪt-, -əd
‖ ˌkʌl ᵊr koʊ 'ɔːrd ᵊn eɪt əd ◂
colour-coordination ˌkʌl ə kəʊ ˌɔːd ɪ 'neɪʃ ᵊn
-ə'··, -ᵊn 'eɪʃ- ‖ ˌkʌl ᵊr koʊ ˌɔːrd ᵊn 'eɪʃ ᵊn
coloured 'kʌl əd ‖ -ᵊrd **~s** z
colourfast 'kʌl ə fɑːst §-fæst ‖ -ᵊr fæst **~ness**
nəs nɪs

colourful 'kʌl ə fᵊl -fʊl ‖ -ᵊr- **~ly** ˌi
colouring 'kʌl ər ɪŋ
  'colouring ˌmatter
colourist 'kʌl ər ɪst §-əst **~s** s
colourization, colourisation
  ˌkʌl ə raɪ 'zeɪʃ ᵊn
colouriz|e, colouris|e 'kʌl ə raɪz **~ed** d **~es**
  ɪz əz **~ing** ɪŋ
colourless 'kʌl ə ləs -lɪs ‖ -ᵊr- **~ly** li **~ness** nəs
  nɪs
colourwash 'kʌl ə wɒʃ ‖ -ᵊr wɔːʃ -waːʃ **~ed** t
  ~es ɪz əz **~ing** ɪŋ
colourway 'kʌl ə weɪ ‖ -ᵊr- **~s** z
-colous stress-imposing kəl əs — **sanguicolous**
  sæŋ 'gwɪk əl əs
colpitis kɒl 'paɪt ɪs §-əs ‖ kaːl 'paɪt̬ əs
colpo- comb. form
  with stress-neutral suffix ˌkɒlp əʊ ‖ ˌkaːlp oʊ
  — **colpomycosis** ˌkɒlp əʊ maɪ 'kəʊs ɪs §-əs
  ‖ ˌkaːlp oʊ maɪ 'koʊs əs
  with stress-imposing suffix kɒl 'pɒ +
  ‖ kaːl 'paː + — **colporrhaphy** kɒl 'pɒr əf i
  ‖ kaːl 'paːr-
colporteur ˌkɒl pɔː 'tɜː ˌkəʊl-; kɒl ˌpɔːt ə,
  'kəʊl-, ˌ·'·· ‖ ˌkaːl pɔːr 'tɜː -poʊr-;
  'kaːl ˌpɔːrt̬ ᵊr, -ˌpoʊrt̬- —Fr [kɔl pɔʁ tœːʁ] **~s**
  z
colposcope 'kɒlp ə skəʊp ‖ 'kaːlp ə skoʊp **~s**
  s
Colquhoun kə 'huːn
Colson 'kəʊls ᵊn →'kɒʊls- ‖ 'koʊls-
Colston 'kəʊlst ən →'kɒʊlst- ‖ 'koʊlst-
colt, Colt kəʊlt →kɒʊlt ‖ koʊlt **colts, Colts**
  kəʊlts →kɒʊlts ‖ koʊlts
coltan 'kɒl tæn ‖ 'kaːl-
colter 'kəʊlt ə §'kuː- ‖ 'koʊlt ᵊr **~s** z
coltish 'kəʊlt ɪʃ ‖ 'koʊlt- **~ly** li **~ness** nəs nɪs
Coltrane kɒl 'treɪn ‖ koʊl-
coltsfoot 'kəʊlts fʊt →'kɒʊlts- ‖ 'koʊlts- **~s** s
colubrine 'kɒl ju braɪn -brɪn, -brən ‖ 'kaːl ə-
  -jə-
Colum, Columb 'kɒl əm ‖ 'kaːl-
Columba kə 'lʌm bə **~'s** z
columbari|um ˌkɒl əm 'beər i ˌ|əm
  ‖ ˌkaːl əm 'ber i ˌ|əm -'bær- **~a** ə
Columbia kə 'lʌm bi ə
Columbian kə 'lʌm bi ən **~s** z
columbine, C~ 'kɒl əm baɪn ‖ 'kaːl- **~s** z
columbite kə 'lʌm baɪt 'kɒl əm- ‖ 'kaːl əm-
columbium kə 'lʌm bi əm
Columbo kə 'lʌm bəʊ ‖ -boʊ
Columbus kə 'lʌm bəs
column 'kɒl əm ‖ 'kaːl əm **~ed** d **~s** z
columnar kə 'lʌm nə ‖ -nᵊr
columnist 'kɒl əm nɪst -ɪst, §-nəst, §-əst
  ‖ 'kaːl- **~s** s
colure kə 'lʊə -'ljʊə; 'kəʊ- ‖ -'lʊᵊr **~s** z
Colville 'kɒl vɪl ‖ 'koʊl-
Colvin 'kɒlv ɪn §-ən ‖ 'koʊlv ən
Colwich 'kɒl wɪtʃ ‖ 'kaːl- —formerly -ɪtʃ
Colwyn 'kɒl wɪn -wən ‖ 'kaːl-
  ˌColwyn 'Bay
Colyer 'kɒl jə ‖ 'kaːl jᵊr

Colyton 'kɒl ɪt ən -ət- ‖ 'kaːl ət ᵊn
colza 'kɒlz ə ‖ 'kaːlz ə 'koʊlz-
com WWW and e-mail kɒm ‖ kaːm
com- This prefix is pronounced stressed kɒm
  ‖ kaːm (1) if the following syllable is
  unstressed (ˌcombiˈnation); (2) in many
  disyllabic nouns ('combine; but comˈmand);
  and (3) occasionally, in context, when
  contrastively stressed (ˌdepartments and
  'compartments). Otherwise it is usually weak
  kəm in RP and GenAm, though strong in
  some regional British speech (com'puter).
  Before a stem beginning m, one m is lost
  ('commerce, com'mit).
coma 'kəʊm ə ‖ 'koʊm ə **~s** z
Comanche kə 'mæntʃ i **~s** z
comatose 'kəʊm ə təʊs -təʊz ‖ 'koʊm ə toʊs
  ~ly li
comb kəʊm ‖ koʊm **combed** kəʊmd ‖ koʊmd
  combing 'kəʊm ɪŋ ‖ 'koʊm ɪŋ **combs**
  kəʊmz ‖ koʊmz
com|bat v 'kɒm ˌ|bæt 'kʌm-, -bæt; kəm 'ˌ|bæt,
  ₍ˌ₎kɒm- ‖ kəm 'ˌ|bæt 'kaːm bæt **~bated,**
  ~batted bæt ɪd -əd ‖ 'bæt̬ əd **~bating,**
  ~batting bæt ɪŋ ‖ 'bæt̬ ɪŋ **~bats** bæts
  ‖ 'bæts
combat n, adj 'kɒm bæt 'kʌm-, -bət ‖ 'kaːm-
  'combat faˌtigue
combatant 'kɒm bət ənt 'kʌm-; kəm 'bæt ᵊnt,
  ₍ˌ₎kɒm- ‖ kəm 'bæt ᵊnt **~s** s
combative 'kɒm bət ɪv 'kʌm-; kəm 'bæt ɪv,
  ₍ˌ₎kɒm- ‖ kəm 'bæt̬ ɪv **~ly** li **~ness** nəs nɪs
Combe, combe kuːm —as a family name, also
  kəʊm ‖ koʊm
comber fish 'kɒm bə ‖ 'kaːm bᵊr **~s** z
comber 'thing that combs' 'kəʊm ə ‖ 'koʊm ᵊr
  ~s z
combination ˌkɒm bɪ 'neɪʃ ᵊn -bə- ‖ ˌkaːm- **~s**
  z
  ˌcombiˈnation lock
combinative 'kɒm bɪ nət ɪv ˌ·bə-, -neɪt ɪv
  ‖ 'kaːm bə neɪt̬ ɪv kəm 'baɪn ət̬-
combinatorial ˌkɒm bɪn ə 'tɔːr i ˌəl ◂ ˌ·bən-
  ‖ ˌkaːm- kəm ˌbaɪn-, -'toʊr-
combine n 'kɒm baɪn ‖ 'kaːm- **~s** z
  ˌcombine 'harvester
combin|e v 'join, unite' kəm 'baɪn §₍ˌ₎kɒm-
  ~ed d **~er/s** ə/z ‖ ᵊr/z **~es** z **~ing** ɪŋ
  com'bining form
combin|e v 'harvest' 'kɒm baɪn ‖ 'kaːm- **~ed** d
  ~es z **~ing** ɪŋ
combing 'kəʊm ɪŋ ‖ 'koʊm ɪŋ **~s** z
combo 'kɒm bəʊ ‖ 'kaːm boʊ **~s** z
comb-out 'kəʊm aʊt ‖ 'koʊm- **~s** s
combover 'kəʊm ˌəʊv ə ‖ 'koʊm ˌoʊv ᵊr
combust kəm 'bʌst §₍ˌ₎kɒm- **~ed** ɪd əd **~ing** ɪŋ
  ~s s
combustibility kəm ˌbʌst ə 'bɪl ət i §kɒm-,
  §ˌkɒm bʌst-, -ɪ'··, -ɪt i ‖ -ət̬ i
combustib|le kəm 'bʌst əb |ᵊl §₍ˌ₎kɒm-, -ɪb-
  ~ly li
combustion kəm 'bʌs tʃən §₍ˌ₎kɒm-
  com'bustion ˌchamber

Combining forms

1 Many literary and scientific words are composed of **combining forms** derived from Greek or Latin. Typically, they consist of a first element and a second element. For example, **microscopic** consists of **micro-** plus **-scopic**. The *Longman Pronunciation Dictionary* has entries for these separate elements, which makes it possible to work out the pronunciation of many rare or new words not listed in this dictionary.

2 One problem is that of deciding the stress pattern of such a word. Most combining form **suffixes** (= second elements) are **stress-neutral** (= they preserve the location of stresses in the first element; the suffix may well be stressed itself). Others are **stress-imposing** (= they cause the main stress to fall on a particular syllable of the first element).

For example, **-graphic** ˈɡræf ɪk is stress-neutral, but **-graphy** is stress-imposing (as in **epigraphy** e ˈpɪɡ rəf i).

3 A first element usually has two different pronunciations, one used with stress-neutral suffixes, the other with stress-imposing suffixes. For the pronunciation of the whole word, the pronunciation for the suffix must be combined with the appropriate pronunciation for the first element.

4 The mark ¦ in the pronunciation of a first element means a stress. This will be a secondary stress (ˌ) if the suffix includes a main stress; if not, it will be a main stress (ˈ). In general, suffixes of two or more syllables are stressed, but those of one syllable are not.

5 For example, take the first element **cata-**.

- With a stress-neutral suffix, it is pronounced ¦kæt ə. Combining this with **-graphic** ˈɡræf ɪk we get **catagraphic** ˌkæt ə ˈɡræf ɪk. Combining it with **-phyte** faɪt we get **cataphyte** ˈkæt ə faɪt.

- With a stress-imposing suffix, it is pronounced kə ˈtæ⁺. (The sign ⁺ is a reminder that this syllable is incomplete and must attract at least one consonant from the suffix.) Combining **cata-** with **-logy** lədʒ i (stress-imposing) we get **catalogy** kə ˈtæl ədʒ i.

(The words **catagraphic**, **cataphyte**, **catalogy** do not exist. But if they did, we know that this is how they would be pronounced.)

---

combustive kəm ˈbʌst ɪv §ˌkɒm-

come kʌm —*There is also an occasional weak form* kəm. *See* c'mon **came** keɪm **comes** kʌmz **coming** ˈkʌm ɪŋ

come-all-ye kʌm ˈɔːl ji kə ˈmɔːl-, -jə ‖ -ˈɑːl-

come-at-able ˌkʌm ˈæt əb əl ‖ -ˈæt-

comeback ˈkʌm bæk ~s s

Comecon ˈkɒm i kɒn ‖ ˈkɑːm i kɑːn

comedi... —*see* comedy

comedian kə ˈmiːd i ‿ən ~s z

comedic kə ˈmiːd ɪk ~ally əl i

comedienne kə ˌmiːd i ˈen ~s z

comedo ˈkɒm ɪ dəʊ -ə-; kə ˈmiːd əʊ ‖ ˈkɑːm ə doʊ ~s z **comedones** ˌkɒm ɪ ˈdəʊn iːz -ə- ‖ ˌkɑːm ə ˈdoʊn iːz

comedown ˈkʌm daʊn ~s z

comed|y ˈkɒm əd |i -ɪd- ‖ ˈkɑːm- ~ies iz

come-hither ˌkʌm ˈhɪð ə ‖ -ᵊr -ˈhɪθ-

come|ly ˈkʌm |li ~lier li‿ə ‖ li‿ᵊr ~liest li‿ɪst li‿əst ~liness li nəs li nɪs

Comenius kə 'meɪn i̯əs kɒ-, -'miːn-
come-on 'kʌm ɒn ‖ -aːn -ɔːn ~s z
-comer ˌkʌm ə ‖ -ᵊr — **late-comer**
'leɪt ˌkʌm ə ‖ -ᵊr ~s z
comer 'kʌm ə ‖ -ᵊr ~s z
Comer *family name* 'kəʊm ə ‖ 'koʊm ᵊr
comestible kə 'mest əb ᵊl -ɪb- ~s z
comet 'kɒm ɪt §-ət ‖ 'kaːm- ~s s
comeuppanc|e ˌkʌm 'ʌp ənˀs →-mᵖs ~es ɪz əz
comfit 'kʌmᵖf ɪt 'kɒmᵖf-, §-ət ‖ 'kaːmᵖf- ~s s
comf|ort, C~ 'kʌmᵖf |ət | -|-ᵊrt ~orted ət ɪd
-əd ‖ -ᵊrt̬ əd ~orting ət ɪŋ ‖ ᵊrt̬ ɪŋ ~orts əts
‖ ᵊrts
'**comfort** ˌstation
comfortab|le 'kʌmᵖft əb |ᵊl 'kʌmᵖf ət əb |ᵊl
‖ -ᵊrb-, 'kʌmᵖf ət̬ əb |ᵊl, '-ᵊrt̬- ~ly li ~ness nəs
nɪs
ˌcomfortably 'off
comforter 'kʌmᵖf ət ə ‖ -ᵊrt̬ ᵊr -ət̬- ~s z
comfortless 'kʌmᵖf ət ləs -lɪs ‖ -ᵊrt-
comfrey 'kʌmᵖf ri ~s z
comf|y 'kʌmᵖf |i ~ier i̯ə ‖ i̯ᵊr ~iest i̯ɪst i̯əst
comic 'kɒm ɪk ‖ 'kaːm- ~s s
ˌcomic 'opera; 'comic strip
comical 'kɒm ɪk ᵊl ‖ 'kaːm- ~ly ˌi ~ness nəs
nɪs
Cominform 'kɒm ɪn ˌfɔːm -ən-
‖ 'kaːm ən ˌfɔːrm
coming 'kʌm ɪŋ ~s z
coming-out ˌkʌm ɪŋ 'aʊt
Comintern 'kɒm ɪn ˌtɜːn -ən- ‖ 'kaːm ən ˌtɜːrn
Comiskey kə 'mɪsk i
comit|y 'kɒm ət |i -ɪt- ‖ 'kaːm ət̬ |i 'koʊm-
~ies iz
comma 'kɒm ə ‖ 'kaːm ə ~s z
command kə 'maːnd §-'mænd ‖ -'mænd ~ed
ɪd əd ~ing ɪŋ ~s z
com'mand ˌmodule; com'mand
per'formance
commandant 'kɒm ən dænt -daːnt, ˌ· ·'·
‖ 'kaːm- ~s s
comman|deer ˌkɒm ən |'dɪə -aːn-, §-æn-
‖ ˌkaːm ən |'dɪᵊr ~deered 'dɪəd ‖ 'dɪᵊrd
~deering 'dɪər ɪŋ ‖ 'dɪr ɪŋ ~deers 'dɪəz
‖ 'dɪᵊrz
commander kə 'maːnd ə §-'mænd-
‖ -'mænd ᵊr ~s z
com,mander in 'chief
commanding kə 'maːnd ɪŋ §-'mænd-
‖ -'mænd- ~ly li
com,manding 'officer
commandment kə 'maːnd mənt →-'maːm-,
§-'mænd- ‖ -'mænd- ~s s
commando kə 'maːnd əʊ §-'mænd-
‖ -'mænd oʊ ~s z
comme ci comme ça kɒm ˌsiː kɒm 'saː
‖ kaːm ˌsiː kaːm- —*Fr* [kɔm si kɔm sa]
Comme des Garçons *tdmk* ˌkɒm deɪ 'gaːs ɒ̃
-gaː 'sɒ̃ ‖ ˌkaːm deɪ gaːr 'soʊn —*Fr*
[kɔm de gaʁ sɔ̃]
commedia dell'arte kɒ ˌmeɪd i̯ə del 'aːt eɪ
kə-, -ˌmed- ‖ kə ˌmeɪd i̯ə del 'aːrt̬ i -ˌmed-
—*It* [kom 'mɛː dja del 'lar te]

comme il faut ˌkɒm iːᵊl 'fəʊ ‖ ˌkʌm iːᵊl 'foʊ
ˌkaːm-, ˌkɔːm- —*Fr* [kɔ mil fo]
commemo|rate kə 'mem ə |reɪt ~rated
reɪt ɪd -əd ‖ reɪt̬ əd ~rates reɪts ~rating
reɪt ɪŋ ‖ reɪt̬ ɪŋ ~rator/s reɪt ə/z ‖ reɪt̬ ᵊr/z
commemoration kə ˌmem ə 'reɪʃ ᵊn ~s z
commemorative kə 'mem ᵊr_ət ɪv -ə reɪt-
‖ ət̬ ɪv -ə reɪt̬- ~s z
commenc|e kə 'menˀs ~ed t ~es ɪz əz ~ing ɪŋ
commencement kə 'menˀs mənt ~s s
commend kə 'mend ~ed ɪd əd ~ing ɪŋ ~s z
commendab|le kə 'mend əb |ᵊl ~ly li
commendation ˌkɒm en 'deɪʃ ᵊn -ən-
‖ ˌkaːm ən- -en- ~s z
commendatory kə 'mend ə ˌtər i
ˌkɒm en 'deɪt ər i, ˌ·ən- ‖ -ə tɔːr i -tour i
commensal kə 'menˀs ᵊl ~ism ˌɪz əm ~ly i ~s
z
commensurability kə ˌmenˀʃ ᵊr ə 'bɪl ət i
-ˌmenˀs-, -jər ə-, -ɪt i ‖ kə ˌmenˀs ᵊr ə 'bɪl ət̬ i
commensurab|le kə 'menˀʃ ᵊr əb |ᵊl -'menˀs-,
-jər əb- ‖ -'menˀs- ~ly li
commensurate kə 'menˀʃ ᵊr ət -'menˀs-, -jər-,
-ɪt ‖ -'menˀs- ~ly li
comment *n* 'kɒm ent ‖ 'kaːm- ~s s
comm|ent *v* 'kɒm |ent §kɒ 'm|ent, kə-
‖ 'kaːm- ~ented ent ɪd -əd ‖ ent̬ əd ~enting
ent ɪŋ ‖ ent̬ ɪŋ ~ents ents
commentar|y 'kɒm ənt_ᵊr |i ‖ 'kaːm ən ter |i
~ies iz
commen|tate 'kɒm ən |teɪt -en- ‖ 'kaːm-
~tated teɪt ɪd -əd ‖ teɪt̬ əd ~tates teɪts
~tating teɪt ɪŋ ‖ teɪt̬ ɪŋ
commentator 'kɒm ən teɪt ə '·en-
‖ 'kaːm ən teɪt̬ ᵊr ~s z
Commer *tdmk* 'kɒm ə ‖ 'kaːm ᵊr ~s z
commerce 'kɒm ɜːs ‖ 'kaːm ᵊrs kə 'mɜːs
commercial kə 'mɜːʃ ᵊl ‖ -'mɜːʃ- ~ly i ~s z
com,mercial 'traveller
commercialis... —*see* **commercializ...**
commercialism kə 'mɜːʃ ə ˌlɪz əm -ᵊl ˌɪz-
‖ -'mɜːʃ-
commerciality kə ˌmɜːʃ i 'æl ət i -ɪt i
‖ kə ˌmɜːʃ i 'æl ət̬ i
commercialization kə ˌmɜːʃ ᵊl aɪ 'zeɪʃ ᵊn -ᵊl ɪ-
‖ -ˌmɜːʃ ᵊl ə-
commercializ|e kə 'mɜːʃ ə laɪz -ᵊl aɪz ‖ -'mɜːʃ-
~ed d ~es ɪz əz ~ing ɪŋ
commie 'kɒm i ‖ 'kaːm i ~s z
commination ˌkɒm ɪ 'neɪʃ ᵊn -ə- ‖ ˌkaːm-
commingl|e kɒ 'mɪŋ gᵊl kə- ‖ kə- kaː- ~ed d
~es z ~ing ˌɪŋ
commi|nute 'kɒm ɪ |njuːt §-ə- ‖ 'kaːm ə |nuːt
-njuːt ~nuted njuːt ɪd -əd ‖ nuːt̬ əd njuːt̬-
~nutes njuːts ‖ nuːts njuːts ~nuting njuːt ɪŋ
‖ nuːt̬ ɪŋ njuːt̬-
comminution ˌkɒm ɪ 'njuːʃ ᵊn §-ə-
‖ ˌkaːm ə 'nuːʃ- -'njuːʃ-
commis 'kɒm i -ɪs ‖ ˌkaː 'miː ◂ kə-
'commis chef, ˌcommis 'chef
commise|rate kə 'mɪz ə |reɪt ~rated reɪt ɪd
-əd ‖ reɪt̬ əd ~rates reɪts ~rating reɪt ɪŋ
‖ reɪt̬ ɪŋ

commiseration kə ˌmɪz ə 'reɪʃ ᵊn ~s z
commiserative kə 'mɪz ər̩ ət ɪv -ə reɪt ɪv
  ‖ -ə reɪt ɪv ~**ly** li
commissar ˌkɒm ɪ 'sɑː -ə-, '· · · ‖ 'kɑːm ə sɑːr
  ~**s** z
commissariat ˌkɒm ɪ 'seər i ət ˌ-ə-, -'sær-,
  -'sɑːr-, -æt ‖ ˌkɑːm ə 'ser- ~**s** s
commissar|y 'kɒm ɪs ər |i '·əs-
  ‖ 'kɑːm ə ser |i ~**ies** iz
commission kə 'mɪʃ ᵊn ~**ed** d ~**ing** ɪŋ ~**s** z
  com'mission ˌagent
commissionaire kə ˌmɪʃ ə 'neə -ᵊn- ‖ -'neᵊr
  ~**s** z
commissional kə 'mɪʃ ᵊn əl
commissionary kə 'mɪʃ ᵊn ər i ‖ -ə ner i
commissioner kə 'mɪʃ ᵊn ə ‖ ər ~**s** z
commissure 'kɒm ɪ sjʊə -ə-, -ʃʊə ‖ 'kɑːm ə ʃʊr
  ~**s** z
commit kə 'mɪt **commits** kə 'mɪts **committed**
  kə 'mɪt ɪd -əd ‖ -'mɪt̬ əd **committing**
  kə 'mɪt ɪŋ ‖ -'mɪt̬ ɪŋ
commitment kə 'mɪt mənt ~**s** s
committable kə 'mɪt əb ᵊl ‖ -'mɪt̬-
committal kə 'mɪt ᵊl ‖ -'mɪt̬- ~**s** z
committee kə 'mɪt i ‖ -'mɪt̬ i —*but*
  ˌkɒm ɪ 'tiː ‖ ˌkɑːm- *in the obsolete sense*
  'person to whom someone or something is
  committed' ~**s** z
  com'mittee stage
committee|man kə 'mɪt i |mən mæn ‖ -'mɪt̬-
  ~**men** mən men ~**woman** ˌwʊm ən ~**women**
  ˌwɪm ɪn §-ən
commode kə 'məʊd ‖ -'moʊd ~**s** z
commodification kə ˌmɒd ɪf ɪ 'keɪʃ ᵊn -ˌ·əf-,
  §-ə'·- ‖ -ˌmɑːd-
commodi|fy kə 'mɒd ɪ| faɪ -ə- ‖ -'mɑːd- ~**fied**
  faɪd ~**fies** faɪz ~**fying** faɪ ɪŋ
commodious kə 'məʊd i ̯əs ‖ -'moʊd- ~**ly** li
  ~**ness** nəs nɪs
commodit|y kə 'mɒd ət |i -ɪt- ‖ -'mɑːd ət̬ |i
  ~**ies** iz
commodore 'kɒm ə dɔː ‖ 'kɑːm ə dɔːr -doʊr
  ~**s** z
Commodus 'kɒm əd əs kə 'məʊd- ‖ 'kɑːm-
common 'kɒm ən ‖ 'kɑːm- ~**er** ə ‖ ᵊr ~**est** ɪst
  əst ~**ly** li ~**ness** nəs nɪs ~**s, C~s** z
  ˌcommon de'nominator; ˌCommon
  'Market; ˌcommon 'noun; 'common room;
  ˌcommon 'sense
commonage 'kɒm ən ɪdʒ ‖ 'kɑːm-
commonalit|y ˌkɒm ə 'næl ət |i -ɪt i
  ‖ ˌkɑːm ə 'næl ət̬ |i ~**ies** iz
commonal|ty 'kɒm ən ᵊl |ti ‖ 'kɑːm- ~**ties** tiz
commoner 'kɒm ən ə ‖ 'kɑːm ən ᵊr ~**s** z
common-law ˌkɒm ən 'lɔː ◀ ‖ ˌkɑːm- -'lɑː
  ˌcommon-law 'marriage
common-or-garden ˌkɒm ən ɔː 'gɑːd ᵊn ◀
  -ə'·- ‖ ˌkɑːm ən ᵊr 'gɑːrd ᵊn ◀
commonplac|e 'kɒm ən pleɪs →-əm- ‖ 'kɑːm-
  ~**es** ɪz əz
commonsense ˌkɒm ən 'sen̪s ◀ ‖ ˌkɑːm-
  ˌcommonsense de'cision

commonsensical ˌkɒm ən 'sen̪s ɪk ᵊl ◀
  ‖ ˌkɑːm- ~**ly** ˌi
commonsensicality
  ˌkɒm ən ˌsen̪s ɪ 'kæl ət i -ˌ·ə-, -ɪt i
  ‖ ˌkɑːm ən ˌsen̪s ɪ 'kæl ət̬ i
commonweal 'kɒm ən wiːᵊl ‖ 'kɑːm-
commonwealth, C~ 'kɒm ən welθ ‖ 'kɑːm-
commotion kə 'məʊʃ ᵊn ‖ -'moʊʃ- ~**s** z
commotional kə 'məʊʃ ᵊn əl ‖ -'moʊʃ-
comms kɒmz ‖ kɑːmz

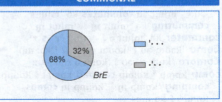

BrE

communal 'kɒm jʊn ᵊl -jən-; kə 'mjuːn ᵊl
  ‖ kə 'mjuːn ᵊl 'kɑːm jən- — *Preference poll,*
  BrE: '· · · 68%, ·'· · 32%. ~**ly** i
communality ˌkɒm ju 'næl ət i -ɪt i
  ‖ ˌkɑːm ju 'næl ət̬ i
communard, C~ 'kɒm ju nɑːd -nɑː
  ‖ 'kɑːm ju nɑːrd -nɑːr ~**s** z
commun|e *v* kə 'mjuːn 'kɒm juːn ~**ed** d ~**es** z
  ~**ing** ɪŋ
commune, C~ *n* 'kɒm juːn ‖ 'kɑːm- kə 'mjuːn
  ~**s** z
communicability kə ˌmjuːn ɪk ə 'bɪl ət i -ɪt i
  ‖ -ət̬ i
communicable kə 'mjuːn ɪk əb ᵊl ~**ness** nəs
  nɪs
communicant kə 'mjuːn ɪk ənt ~**s** s
communi|cate kə 'mjuːn ɪ |keɪt -ə- ~**cated**
  keɪt ɪd -əd ‖ keɪt̬ əd ~**cates** keɪts ~**cating**
  keɪt ɪŋ ‖ keɪt̬ ɪŋ
communication kə ˌmjuːn ɪ 'keɪʃ ᵊn -ə- ~**s** z
  com ˌmuni'cation cord; com ˌmuni'cations
  ˌsatellite
communicative kə 'mjuːn ɪk ət ɪv -'·ək-;
  -ɪ keɪt-, -ə keɪt- ‖ -ə keɪt̬ ɪv -ɪk ət̬- ~**ly** li ~**ness**
  nəs nɪs
  com ˌmunicative 'competence
communicator kə 'mjuːn ɪ keɪt ə ‖ -keɪt̬ ᵊr
communion, C~ kə 'mjuːn i ̯ən ~**s** z
  com'munion rail
communique, communiqué kə 'mjuːn ɪ keɪ
  -ə- ~**s** z
communism, C~ 'kɒm ju ˌnɪz əm -jə-
  ‖ 'kɑːm jə-
communist, C~ 'kɒm jʊn ɪst -jən-, -juːn-, §-əst
  ‖ 'kɑːm jən əst ~**s** s
communitarian kə ˌmjuːn ɪ 'teər i ̯ən ◀ -ə'·-
  ‖ -'ter- ~**s** z
communit|y kə 'mjuːn ət |i -ɪt- ‖ -ət̬ |i ~**ies** iz
  com'munity ˌcentre; com'munity chest,
  ·ˌ· · · '·; com ˌmunity 'medicine; com ˌmunity
  'singing
commutability kə ˌmjuːt ə 'bɪl ət i -ɪt i
  ‖ kə ˌmjuːt̬ ə 'bɪl ət̬ i

commutable kə ˈmjuːt əb ᵊl ‖ -ˈmjuːt̬-

commu|tate ˈkɒm ju |teɪt ‖ ˈkɑːm jə- **~tated** teɪt ɪd -əd ‖ teɪt̬ əd **~tates** teɪts **~tating** teɪt ɪŋ ‖ teɪt̬ ɪŋ

commutation ˌkɒm ju ˈteɪʃ ᵊn ‖ ˌkɑːm jə- **~s** z

ˌcommuˈtation ˌticket

commutative kə ˈmjuːt ət ɪv ˈkɒm ju teɪt ɪv ‖ ˈkɑːm jə teɪt̬ ɪv kə ˈmjuːt̬ ət̬ ɪv **~ly** li

commutator ˈkɒm ju teɪt ə ‖ ˈkɑːm jə teɪt̬ ᵊr **~s** z

commute kə ˈmjuːt **commuted** kə ˈmjuːt ɪd -əd ‖ -ˈmjuːt̬ əd **commutes** kə ˈmjuːts **commuting** kə ˈmjuːt ɪŋ ‖ -ˈmjuːt̬ ɪŋ

commuter kə ˈmjuːt ə ‖ -ˈmjuːt̬ ᵊr **~s** z

Como ˈkəʊm əʊ ‖ ˈkoʊm oʊ —*It* [ˈkɔː mo]

Comoro ˈkɒm ə rəʊ ‖ ˈkɑːm ə roʊ **~s** z

comp kɒmp ‖ kɑːmp **comped** kɒmpt ‖ kɑːmpt **comping** ˈkɒmp ɪŋ ‖ ˈkɑːm ɪŋ **comps** kɒmps ‖ kɑːmps

compact *v* ˈpress together' kəm ˈpækt ₍ˌ₎kɒm- ‖ ₍ˌ₎kɑːm- **~ed** ɪd əd **~ing** ɪŋ **~s** s

compact *v* ˈmake an agreement' ˈkɒm pækt ‖ ˈkɑːm- **~ed** ɪd əd **~ing** ɪŋ **~s** s

compact *adj* kəm ˈpækt ₍ˌ₎kɒm- ‖ ₍ˌ₎kɑːm- —*In stress-shifting environments usually* ˌkɒm pækt ‖ ˌkɑːm-, *as if underlyingly* ˌkɒm ˈpækt ◄ ‖ ˌkɑːm- *(even for speakers who otherwise say* kəm ˈpækt) **~ly** li **~ness** nəs nɪs ˌcompact ˈdisc/ˈdisk

compact *n* ˈkɒm pækt ‖ ˈkɑːm-

CompactFlash *tdmk* ˌkɒm pækt ˈflæʃ ‖ ˌkɑːm-

compaction kəm ˈpæk ʃᵊn §₍ˌ₎kɒm-

compactor kəm ˈpækt ə §₍ˌ₎kɒm- ‖ -ᵊr **~s** z

compadre kəm ˈpɑːdr eɪ **~s** z

companion kəm ˈpæn jən §₍ˌ₎kɒm-, -ˈpæn i ən **~able** əb ᵊl **~ably** əb li **~ate** ət ɪt **~s** z **~ship** ʃɪp **~way/s** weɪ/z

compan|y ˈkʌmp ən‿|i **~ies** iz ˌcompany ˈsecretary

Compaq *tdmk* ˈkɒm pæk ‖ ˈkɑːm-

comparability ˌkɒmp ᵊr‿ə ˈbɪl ət i -ɪt i; kəm ˌpær ə-, §kɒm-, -ˌpeər- ‖ ˌkɑːm ᵊr‿ə ˈbɪl ət̬ i kəm ˌper ə-, -ˌpær-

comparab|le ˈkɒmp ᵊr‿əb ᵊl kəm ˈpær əb ᵊl, §₍ˌ₎kɒm-, -ˈpeər- ‖ ˈkɑːm- kəm ˈper-, -ˈpær- **~ly** li

comparative kəm ˈpær ət ɪv §₍ˌ₎kɒm- ‖ -ət̬- -ˈper- **~ly** li

comparator kəm ˈpær ət ə §₍ˌ₎kɒm- ‖ -ət̬ ᵊr -ˈper- **~s** z

com|pare kəm |ˈpeə §₍ˌ₎kɒm- ‖ -|ˈpeᵊr -ˈpæᵊr **~pared** ˈpeəd ‖ ˈpeᵊrd ˈpæᵊrd **~pares** ˈpeəz ‖ ˈpeᵊrz ˈpæᵊrz **~paring** ˈpeər ɪŋ ‖ ˈper ɪŋ ˈpær-

comparison kəm ˈpær ɪs ən §₍ˌ₎kɒm-, -əs-, §-ɪz-, §-əz- ‖ -ˈper- **~s** z

comparison-|shop kəm ˈpær ɪs ən |ʃɒp §₍ˌ₎§kɒm-, -ˈ-əs-, §- -ɪz-, §- -əz- ‖ -|ʃɑːp -ˈper- **~shopping** ʃɒp ɪŋ ‖ ʃɑːp ɪŋ

compartment *n* kəm ˈpɑːt mənt §₍ˌ₎kɒm- ‖ -ˈpɑːrt- **~s** s

compartmentalization ˌkɒm pɑːt ˌment ᵊl aɪ ˈzeɪʃ ᵊn -ᵊl ɪ- ‖ kəm ˌpɑːrt ˌment̬ ᵊl ə- ˌkɑːm pɑːrt-

compartmentaliz|e ˌkɒm pɑːt ˈment ᵊl aɪz -ə laɪz ‖ kəm ˌpɑːrt ˈment̬ ᵊl aɪz ˌkɑːm pɑːrt- **~ed** d **~es** ɪz əz **~ing** ɪŋ

compass ˈkʌmp əs §ˈkɒmp- ‖ ˈkɑːmp- **~ed** t **~es** ɪz əz **~ing** ɪŋ ˈcompass point

compassion kəm ˈpæʃ ᵊn §₍ˌ₎kɒm-

compassionate kəm ˈpæʃ ᵊn‿ət §₍ˌ₎kɒm-, ɪt **~ly** li **~ness** nəs nɪs

compatibility kəm ˌpæt ə ˈbɪl ət i §kɒm-, §ˌkɒm pæt-, -ɪˈ--, -ɪt i ‖ -ˌpæt̬ ə ˈbɪl ət̬ i

compatib|le kəm ˈpæt əb ‖ ᵊl §₍ˌ₎kɒm-, -ɪb- ‖ -ˈpæt̬- **~ly** li

compatriot kəm ˈpætr i ət ₍ˌ₎kɒm- ‖ -ˈpeɪtr- ₍ˌ₎kɑːm-, -ɑːt *(*)* **~s** s

compeer ˈkɒm pɪə ˈ- ‖ kəm ˈpɪᵊr ₍ˌ₎kɑːm-, ˈkɑːm pɪr **~s** z

compel kəm ˈpel §₍ˌ₎kɒm- **~led** d **~ling/ly** ɪŋ /li **~s** z

compellab|le kəm ˈpel əb ‖ ᵊl §₍ˌ₎kɒm- **~ly** li

compendious kəm ˈpend i‿əs §₍ˌ₎kɒm- **~ly** li **~ness** nəs nɪs

compendium kəm ˈpend i‿əm §₍ˌ₎kɒm- **~s** z

compensable kəm ˈpen⸴s əb ᵊl

compen|sate ˈkɒmp ən |seɪt -en- ‖ ˈkɑːmp- **~sated** seɪt ɪd -əd ‖ seɪt̬ əd **~sates** seɪts **~sating** seɪt ɪŋ ‖ seɪt̬ ɪŋ

compensation ˌkɒmp ən ˈseɪʃ ᵊn -en- ‖ ˌkɑːmp- **~s** z

compensatory ˌkɒmp ən ˈseɪt̬ ᵊr i ◄ ˌ-en-, ˈ- - - -; kəm ˈpen⸴s ət ᵊr i, §₍ˌ₎kɒm- ‖ kəm ˈpen⸴s ə tɔːr i -tour i

compere, compère ˈkɒm peə ‖ ˈkɑːm per **~d** d **~s** z **compering, compèring** ˈkɒm peᵊr ɪŋ ‖ ˈkɑːm per ɪŋ

com|pete kəm |ˈpiːt §₍ˌ₎kɒm- **~peted** ˈpiːt ɪd -əd ‖ ˈpiːt̬ əd **~petes** ˈpiːts **~peting** ˈpiːt ɪŋ ‖ ˈpiːt̬ ɪŋ

competenc|e ˈkɒmp ɪt ᵊn⸴s -ət- ‖ ˈkɑːmp ət ᵊn⸴s **~y** i

competent ˈkɒmp ɪt ənt -ət- ‖ ˈkɑːmp ət ᵊnt **~ly** li

competition ˌkɒmp ə ˈtɪʃ ᵊn -ɪ- ‖ ˌkɑːmp- **~s** z

competitive kəm ˈpet ət ɪv §₍ˌ₎kɒm-, -ɪt- ‖ -ˈpet̬ ət̬- **~ly** li **~ness** nəs nɪs

competitor kəm ˈpet ɪt ə §₍ˌ₎kɒm-, -ət- ‖ -ˈpet̬ ət̬ ᵊr **~s** z

compilation ˌkɒmp ɪ ˈleɪʃ ᵊn -ə-, -aɪ- ‖ ˌkɑːmp- **~s** z

compil|e kəm ˈpaᵊl §₍ˌ₎kɒm- **~ed** d **~es** z **~ing** ɪŋ

compiler kəm ˈpaɪl ə ₍ˌ₎kɒm- ‖ -ᵊr **~s** z

complacenc|e kəm ˈpleɪs ᵊn⸴s §₍ˌ₎kɒm- **~y** i

complacent kəm ˈpleɪs ᵊnt §₍ˌ₎kɒm- **~ly** li

complain kəm ˈpleɪn §₍ˌ₎kɒm- **~ed** d **~er/s** ə/z ‖ ᵊr/z **~ing/ly** ɪŋ /li **~s** z

complainant kəm ˈpleɪn ənt §₍ˌ₎kɒm- **~s** s

complaint kəm ˈpleɪnt §₍ˌ₎kɒm- **~s** s

C

complaisance kəm ˈpleɪz ᵊnᵗs §₍ˌ₎kɒm-
∥ -ˈpleɪs- -ˈpleɪz-; ˌkɑːm pleɪ ˈzænᵗs, -plə-,
-ˈzɑːnᵗs, ˈ··· *(*)*
complaisant kəm ˈpleɪz ᵊnt §₍ˌ₎kɒm- ∥ -ˈpleɪs-
-ˈpleɪz-; ˌkɑːm pleɪ ˈzænt, -plə-, -ˈzɑːnt, ˈ··· *(*)*
~ly li
Complan *tdmk* ˈkɒm plæn ∥ ˈkɑːm-
compleat kəm ˈpliːt ₍ˌ₎kɒm-
complected kəm ˈplekt ɪd §₍ˌ₎kɒm-, -əd
comple|ment *v* ˈkɒmp lɪ |ment -lə-, ˌ·ˈ·
∥ ˈkɑːmp lə- *(= compliment) —see note at*
-ment ~mented ment ɪd -əd ∥ menţ əd
~menting ment ɪŋ ∥ menţ ɪŋ **~ments** ments
complement *n* ˈkɒmp lɪ mənt -lə- ∥ ˈkɑːmp lə-
(= compliment) **~s** s
complemental ˌkɒmp lɪ ˈment ᵊl ◄ -lə-
∥ ˌkɑːmp lə ˈmenţ ᵊl ◄
complementarity ˌkɒmp lɪ men ˈtær ət i ˌ·lə-,
-mən·-, -ɪt i ∥ ˌkɑːmp lə men ˈtær əţ i
-mən·-, -ˈter-
complementary ˌkɒmp lɪ ˈment ᵊr i ◄ ˌ·lə-
∥ ˌkɑːmp lə ˈmenţ ᵊr i ◄ →-ˈmentr i *(=*
complimentary)
ˌcomple ˌmentary ˈcolours
complementation ˌkɒmp lɪ men ˈteɪʃ ᵊn ˌ·lə-,
-mən·- ∥ ˌkɑːmp lə-
complementiser, complementizer
ˈkɒmp lɪ ment aɪz ə ˈ·lə-, -mən taɪz ə
∥ ˈkɑːmp lə ment aɪz ᵊr -mən taɪz ᵊr **~s** z
com|plete kəm |ˈpliːt §₍ˌ₎kɒm- **~pleted**
ˈpliːt ɪd -əd ∥ ˈpliːţ əd **~pletes** ˈpliːts
~pleting ˈpliːt ɪŋ ∥ ˈpliːţ ɪŋ
complete|ly kəm ˈpliːt li §₍ˌ₎kɒm- **~ness** nəs
nɪs
completion kəm ˈpliːʃ ᵊn §₍ˌ₎kɒm- **~s** z
completive kəm ˈpliːt ɪv ₍§₎kɒm- ∥ -ˈpliːţ-

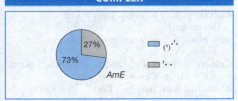

27%
73%
□ ₍ˌ₎·ˈ·
□ ˈ··
AmE

complex *adj* ˈkɒm pleks kəm ˈpleks, ˌkɒm-
∥ ˌkɑːm ˈpleks ◄ kəm-, ˈkɑːm pleks
— *Preference poll, AmE:* ₍ˌ₎·ˈ· *73%,* ˈ·· *27%.*
~ly li
ˌcomplex ˈnumber; **ˌcomplex ˈsentence**
complex *n* ˈkɒm pleks ∥ ˈkɑːm- **~es** ɪz əz
complexion kəm ˈplekʃ ᵊn §₍ˌ₎kɒm- **~ed** d **~s**
z
complexit|y kəm ˈpleks ət |i §₍ˌ₎kɒm-, -ɪt-
∥ -əţ |i **~ies** iz
complianc|e kəm ˈplaɪ‿ənᵗs §₍ˌ₎kɒm- **~es** ɪz əz
~y i
compliant kəm ˈplaɪ‿ənt §₍ˌ₎kɒm- **~ly** li
compli|cate ˈkɒmp lɪ |keɪt -lə- ∥ ˈkɑːmp lə-
~cated keɪt ɪd -əd ∥ keɪţ əd **~cates** keɪts
~cating keɪt ɪŋ ∥ keɪţ ɪŋ

complicated ˈkɒmp lɪ keɪt ɪd -əd
∥ ˈkɑːmp lə keɪţ əd **~ly** li **~ness** nəs nɪs
complication ˌkɒmp lɪ ˈkeɪʃ ᵊn -lə-
∥ ˌkɑːmp lə- **~s** z
complicit kəm ˈplɪs ɪt §kɒm-, -ət
complicity kəm ˈplɪs ət i §₍ˌ₎kɒm-, -ɪt- ∥ -əţ i
complie... —*see* **comply**
compliment *n* ˈkɒmp lɪ mənt -lə- ∥ ˈkɑːmp lə-
~s s
compli|ment *v* ˈkɒmp lɪ |ment -lə-, ˌ·ˈ·
∥ ˈkɑːmp lə- —*see note at* **-ment ~mented**
ment ɪd -əd ∥ menţ əd **~menting** ment ɪŋ
∥ menţ ɪŋ **~ments** ments
complimentar|y ˌkɒmp lɪ ˈment ᵊr |i ◄ ˌ·lə-
∥ ˌkɑːmp lə ˈmenţ ᵊr |i ◄ →-ˈmentr |i **~ies** iz
~ily əl i ɪ li **~iness** i nəs i nɪs
complin ˈkɒmp lɪn -lən ∥ ˈkɑːmp-
compline ˈkɒmp lɪn -lən, -laɪn ∥ ˈkɑːmp-
com|ply kəm |ˈplaɪ §₍ˌ₎kɒm- **~plied** ˈplaɪd
~plies ˈplaɪz **~plying** ˈplaɪ ɪŋ
compo ˈkɒmp əʊ ∥ ˈkɑːmp oʊ
component kəm ˈpəʊn ənt §₍ˌ₎kɒm- ∥ -ˈpoʊn-
~s s
com ˌponent ˈparts
componential ˌkɒmp əʊ ˈnenᵗʃ ᵊl ◄
∥ ˌkɑːmp ə-
com|port *v* kəm |ˈpɔːt §₍ˌ₎kɒm- ∥ -|ˈpɔːrt
-ˈpoʊrt **~ported** ˈpɔːt ɪd -əd ∥ ˈpɔːrţ əd ˈpoʊrţ-
~porting ˈpɔːt ɪŋ ∥ ˈpɔːrţ ɪŋ ˈpoʊrţ- **~ports**
ˈpɔːts ∥ ˈpɔːrts ˈpoʊrts
comportment kəm ˈpɔːt mənt §₍ˌ₎kɒm-
∥ -ˈpɔːrt- -ˈpoʊrt-
compos|e kəm ˈpəʊz §₍ˌ₎kɒm- ∥ -ˈpoʊz **~ed** d
~es ɪz əz **~ing** ɪŋ
composedly kəm ˈpəʊz ɪd li §₍ˌ₎kɒm-, -əd·
∥ -ˈpoʊz-
composer kəm ˈpəʊz ə §₍ˌ₎kɒm- ∥ -ˈpoʊz ᵊr **~s**
z
Compositae kəm ˈpɒz ɪ taɪ §₍ˌ₎kɒm-, -ə-, -tiː
∥ -ˈpɑːz-
composite *adj* ˈkɒmp əz ɪt -əs-, §-ət; -ə zaɪt,
-saɪt ∥ kəm ˈpɑːz ət kɑːm- **~s** s
composite *v* ˈkɒmp ə zaɪt -saɪt, ˌ·ˈ·;
kəm ˈpɒz ɪt ∥ kəm ˈpɑːz ət kɑːm- **composited**
ˈkɒmp ə zaɪt ɪd -saɪt ɪd, -əd, ˌ·ˈ·· ·;
kəm ˈpɒz ɪt- ∥ kəm ˈpɑːz əţ əd kɑːm-
composites ˈkɒmp ə zaɪts -saɪts, ˌ·ˈ·;
kəm ˈpɒz ɪts ∥ kəm ˈpɑːz əts kɑːm-
compositing ˈkɒmp ə zaɪt ɪŋ -saɪt ɪŋ, ˌ·ˈ·· ·;
kəm ˈpɒz ɪt ɪŋ ∥ kəm ˈpɑːz əţ ɪŋ kɑːm-
composition ˌkɒmp ə ˈzɪʃ ᵊn ∥ ˌkɑːmp- **~s** z
compositional ˌkɒmp ə ˈzɪʃ ᵊn əl ◄ ∥ ˌkɑːmp-
compositor kəm ˈpɒz ɪt ə §₍ˌ₎kɒm-, -ət-
∥ -ˈpɑːz əţ ᵊr **~s** z
compos mentis ˌkɒmp əs ˈment ɪs ˌkɒm pɒs-,
§-əs ∥ ˌkɑːmp əs ˈmenţ əs ˌkoʊm poʊs-
compost ˈkɒmp ɒst ∥ ˈkɑːm poʊst *(*)* **~ed** ɪd
əd **~ing** ɪŋ **~s** s
composure kəm ˈpəʊʒ ə §₍ˌ₎kɒm- ∥ -ˈpoʊʒ ᵊr
compote ˈkɒm pəʊt -pɒt ∥ ˈkɑːm poʊt **~s** s
compound *v* kəm ˈpaʊnd ₍ˌ₎kɒm-, ˈ·· **~ed** ɪd
əd **~ing** ɪŋ **~s** z
compound *n* ˈkɒm paʊnd ∥ ˈkɑːm- **~s** z

C

compound *adj* ˈkɒm paʊnd ‖ ˈkɑːm-
kəm ˈpaʊnd, ˌkɑːm ˈpaʊnd ◂
  ˌcompound ˈfracture; ˌcompound
ˈinterest; ˌcompound ˈtense
comprehend ˌkɒmp rɪ ˈhend -rə- ‖ ˌkɑːm- ~ed
ɪd əd ~ing ɪŋ ~s z
comprehensibility ˌkɒmp rɪ ˌhenˢ ə ˈbɪl ət i
ˌ-rə-, -ˌ-ɪ-, -ɪt i ‖ ˌkɑːmp rɪ ˌhenˢ ə ˈbɪl əṱ i
comprehensib|le ˌkɒmp rɪ ˈhenˢ əb ‖ᵊl ˌ-rə-,
-ɪb ᵊl ‖ ˌkɑːmp- ~ly li
comprehension ˌkɒmp rɪ ˈhenʃ ᵊn -rə-
‖ ˌkɑːmp-
comprehensive ˌkɒmp rɪ ˈhenˢ ɪv ◂ -rə-
‖ ˌkɑːmp- ~ly li ~s z
comprehensivis... —*see* **comprehensiviz...**
comprehensivization
  ˌkɒmp rɪ ˌhenˢ ɪv aɪ ˈzeɪʃ ᵊn ˌ-rə-, -ɪˈ--
‖ ˌkɑːmp rɪ ˌhenˢ ɪv ə-
comprehensiviz|e ˌkɒmp rɪ ˈhenˢ ɪ vaɪz ˌ-rə-
‖ ˌkɑːmp- ~ed d ~es ɪz əz ~ing ɪŋ
compress *n* ˈkɒm pres ‖ ˈkɑːm- ~es ɪz əz
compress *v* kəm ˈpres §₍ᵢ₎kɒm- ~ed t ~es ɪz əz
~ing ɪŋ
  com,pressed ˈair
compressibility kəm ˌpres ə ˈbɪl ət i §kɒm-,
§ˌkɒm pres-, -ˌ-ɪ-, -ɪt i ‖ -əṱ i
compressible kəm ˈpres əb ᵊl §₍ᵢ₎kɒm-
compression kəm ˈpreʃ ᵊn §₍ᵢ₎kɒm- ~s z
compressor kəm ˈpres ə §₍ᵢ₎kɒm- ‖ -ᵊr ~s z
compris|e kəm ˈpraɪz §₍ᵢ₎kɒm- ~ed d ~es ɪz əz
~ing ɪŋ
compromis|e ˈkɒmp rə maɪz ‖ ˈkɑːmp- ~ed d
~es ɪz əz ~ing ɪŋ
comptometer, C~ *tdmk* ˌkɒmp ˈtɒm ɪt ə -ət-
‖ ˌkɑːmp ˈtɑːm əṱ ᵊr ~s z
Compton *(i)* ˈkɒmpt ən ‖ ˈkɑːmpt ən,
(ii) ˈkʌmpt ən
comptroller kən ˈtrəʊl ə kəmp-, ₍ᵢ₎kɒmp-,
§₍ᵢ₎kɒn- ‖ -ˈtroʊl ᵊr kɑːmp-, ˈ··· ~s z
compulsion kəm ˈpʌlʃ ᵊn §₍ᵢ₎kɒm- ~s z
compulsive kəm ˈpʌls ɪv §₍ᵢ₎kɒm- ~ly li ~ness
nəs nɪs
compulsor|y kəm ˈpʌls ᵊr |i ~ily əl i ɪ li
~iness i nəs i nɪs
compunction kəm ˈpʌŋk ʃᵊn §₍ᵢ₎kɒm-
computability kəm ˌpjuːt ə ˈbɪl ət i §kɒm-,
§ˌkɒm pjuːt-, ˌkɒm pjʊt-, -ɪt i
‖ -ˌpjuːt ə ˈbɪl əṱ i
computable kəm ˈpjuːt əb ᵊl ˈkɒm pjʊt-
‖ -ˈpjuːṱ-
computation ˌkɒm pju ˈteɪʃ ᵊn ‖ ˌkɑːm- ~s z
computational ˌkɒm pju ˈteɪʃ ᵊn ᵊl ◂ ‖ ˌkɑːm-
~ly i
com|pute kəm ‖ˈpjuːt §₍ᵢ₎kɒm- ~puted
ˈpjuːt ɪd -əd ‖ ˈpjuːṱ əd ~putes ˈpjuːts
~puting ˈpjuːt ɪŋ ‖ ˈpjuːṱ ɪŋ
computer kəm ˈpjuːt ə §₍ᵢ₎kɒm- ‖ -ˈpjuːṱ ᵊr ~s
z
  comˈputer ˌlanguage
computer-aided kəm ˌpjuːt ᵊrˈeɪd ɪd ◂
§₍ᵢ₎kɒm-, -əd ‖ -ˌpjuːṱ ᵊr-
computer-assisted kəm ˌpjuːt ərə ˈsɪst ɪd ◂
§₍ᵢ₎kɒm-, -əd ‖ -ˌpjuːṱ ᵊr-

computerate kəm ˈpjuːt ər ət §₍ᵢ₎kɒm-, -ɪt
‖ -ˈpjuːṱ-
computer-based kəm ˌpjuːt ə ˈbeɪst ◂
§₍ᵢ₎kɒm- ‖ -ˌpjuːṱ ᵊr-
computeris... —*see* **computeriz...**
computerization kəm ˌpjuːt ə raɪ ˈzeɪʃ ᵊn
§₍ᵢ₎kɒm-, -ər ɪ- ‖ -ˌpjuːṱ ər ə-
computeriz|e kəm ˈpjuːt ə raɪz §₍ᵢ₎kɒm-
‖ -ˈpjuːṱ- ~ed d ~es ɪz əz ~ing ɪŋ
comrade ˈkɒm reɪd ˈkʌm-, -rɪd, -rəd
‖ ˈkɑːm ræd -rəd (*) ~ly li ~s z ~ship ʃɪp
Comrie ˈkɒm ri ‖ ˈkɑːm-
coms kɒmz ‖ kɑːmz
comsat, C~ *tdmk* ˈkɒm sæt ‖ ˈkɑːm- ~s s
Comstock ˈkɒm stɒk ˈkʌm- ‖ ˈkɑːm stɑːk
comstockery ˈkɒm stɒk ər i ˈkʌm-, ˌ·ˈ--
‖ ˈkɑːm stɑːk-
Comte kɒnt kɔːnt ‖ koʊnt —*Fr* [kɔ̃ːt]
Comus ˈkəʊm əs ‖ ˈkoʊm-
Comyn ˈkʌm ɪn §-ən
Comyns ˈkʌm ɪnz §-ənz
con, Con kɒn ‖ kɑːn —*but as an Italian prep,
in AmE also* kɔːn, koʊn **conned** kɒnd ‖ kɑːnd
conning ˈkɒn ɪŋ ‖ ˈkɑːn ɪŋ **cons** kɒnz
‖ kɑːnz —*see also phrases with this word.*
con- *This prefix is pronounced stressed* kɒn
‖ kɑːn *(1) if the following syllable is
unstressed* (ˌconfronˈtation), *(2) in many
two-syllable noun* (ˈcontract, *but* conˈtrol); *and
(3) in context, when contrastively stressed*
(ˌuniˌformity and ˈconˌformity). *Otherwise it is
usually weak* kən *in RP and GenAm, though
strong in some regional British speech*
(conˈsider). *Before a stem beginning* n, *one* n
is lost (conˈnect, ˌconnoˈtation).
Cona *tdmk* ˈkəʊn ə ‖ ˈkoʊn ə
conacre ˈkɒn ˌeɪk ə kən ˈeɪk ə ‖ ˈkɑːn ˌeɪk ᵊr
~s z
Conakry ˌkɒn ə ˈkriː ‖ ˈkɑːn ə kriː —*Fr*
[kɔ na kʁi]
con amore ˌkɒn ə ˈmɔːr eɪ -i ‖ ˌkɑːn-, kɔːn,
ˌkoʊn-, -ˈmoʊr-
Conan *(i)* ˈkəʊn ən ‖ ˈkoʊn-, *(ii)* ˈkɒn- ‖ ˈkɑːn-
—*For Sir A. Conan Doyle,* (i)
conation kəʊ ˈneɪʃ ᵊn ‖ koʊ-
Concannon kɒn ˈkæn ən ‖ kɑːn-
concate|nate kən ˈkæt ə |neɪt →kəŋ-, ₍ᵢ₎kɒn-,
→₍ᵢ₎kɒŋ-, -ɪ-, -ᵊ|n eɪt ‖ kɑːn ˈkæt ᵊ|n eɪt
~nated neɪt ɪd -əd ‖ neɪṱ əd ~nates neɪts
~nating neɪt ɪŋ ‖ neɪṱ ɪŋ
concatenation kən ˌkæt ə ˈneɪʃ ᵊn →kəŋ-,
kɒn-, ˌkɒn kæt-, -ɪ--, -ᵊn ˈeɪʃ-
‖ kɑːn ˌkæt ᵊn ˈeɪʃ ᵊn ˌ·ˈ-- ~s z
concatenative kən ˈkæt ən əṱ ɪv →kəŋ-,
ˌkɒn-, →₍ᵢ₎kɒŋ-, -ˈ·ɪn-, -ə neɪt-, -ɪ neɪt-
‖ ₍ᵢ₎kɑːn ˈkæt ᵊn eɪṱ ɪv
concave ₍ᵢ₎kɒn ˈkeɪv ◂ →₍ᵢ₎kɒŋ-, kən-, →kəŋ-,
ˈ·· ‖ ₍ᵢ₎kɑːn- ~ly li ~ness nəs nɪs
concavit|y ₍ᵢ₎kɒn ˈkæv ət |i →₍ᵢ₎kɒŋ-, kən-,
→kəŋ-, -ɪt- ‖ ₍ᵢ₎kɑːn ˈkæv əṱ |i ~ies iz
concavo-concave kɒn ˌkeɪv əʊ kɒn ˈkeɪv ◂
kən-, -kən·- ‖ kɑːn ˌkeɪv oʊ kɑːn ˈkeɪv

Compounds and phrases

1 A two-element **compound** is typically pronounced with **early stress**: that is to say, its first element has more stress than its second.

'bedtime 'bed taɪm

'block‚buster 'blɒk ‚bʌst ə ‖ 'blɑːk ‚bʌst ᵊr

Although many compounds are written as single words, others are written as two words.

'Christmas card
'visitors' book
'music ‚lessons
'beauty ‚contest

2 On the other hand, a **phrase** is typically pronounced with **late stress**: that is to say, the second of two words has more stress than the first.

‚next 'time
‚printed 'cards
‚several 'books
‚weekly 'lessons

3 These stress patterns, and all others, can be changed if the speaker wants to emphasize a particular contrast (to focus on a particular element).

I ‚don't want ‚music 'lessons – just some ‚time to 'practise!
It ‚wasn't a ‚beauty 'contest – ‚more a ‚beauty com'mercial.

The stress patterns shown in this dictionary are those that apply if *no* special emphasis (no contrastive focus) is required.

4 Some expressions, grammatically compounds, are nevertheless pronounced with late stress (= as if they were phrases). Among them are compounds in which the first element names the **material or ingredient** of which a thing is made.

a ‚rubber 'duck
‚paper 'plates
‚cheese 'sandwiches
a ‚pork 'pie
a ‚gold 'ring

However, expressions involving **cake**, **juice** and **water** take early stress.

'almond cake
'orange juice
'barley ‚water

5 Names of roads and streets all take late stress except those involving **street** itself, which take early stress.

‚Melrose 'Road
‚Lavender 'Crescent
‚Oxford 'Square
‚King's 'Avenue but 'Gower Street

C

concavo-convex ˌkɒn ˌkeɪv əʊ kɒn ˈveks ◂
kən-, -ˈkən'· ‖ ˌkɑːn ˌkeɪv oʊ kɑːn ˈveks
conceal kən ˈsiːᵊl §₍ᵢ₎kɒn- **~ed** d **~ing** ɪŋ
~ment mənt **~s** z
conced|e kən ˈsiːd §₍ᵢ₎kɒn- **~ed** ɪd əd **~es** z
~ing ɪŋ
conceit kən ˈsiːt §₍ᵢ₎kɒn- **~s** s
conceited kən ˈsiːt ɪd §₍ᵢ₎kɒn-, -əd ‖ -ˈsiːt̬ əd
~ly li **~ness** nəs nɪs
conceivab|le kən ˈsiːv əb |ᵊl §₍ᵢ₎kɒn- **~ly** li
conceiv|e kən ˈsiːv §₍ᵢ₎kɒn- **~ed** d **~er/s** ə/z
‖ ᵊr/z **~es** z **~ing** ɪŋ
concele|brate ˌkɒn ˈsel ə |breɪt kən-, -ɪ-
‖ ˌkɑːn- **~brated** breɪt ɪd -əd ‖ breɪt̬ əd
~brates breɪts **~brating** breɪt ɪŋ ‖ breɪt̬ ɪŋ
concelebration ˌkɒn ˌsel ə ˈbreɪʃ ᵊn kən ˌsel-,
-ɪ'·· ‖ ˌkɑːn- **~s** z
concen|trate ˈkɒn⁺s ᵊn |treɪt -en- ‖ ˈkɑːn⁺s-
~trated treɪt ɪd -əd ‖ treɪt̬ əd **~trates** treɪts
~trating treɪt ɪŋ ‖ treɪt̬ ɪŋ
concentration ˌkɒn⁺s ᵊn ˈtreɪʃ ᵊn -en-
‖ ˌkɑːn⁺s- **~s** z
    ˌconcenˈtration camp
concentrator ˈkɒn⁺s ᵊn treɪt ə |·en-
‖ ˈkɑːn⁺s ᵊn treɪt̬ ᵊr **~s** z
concentric kən ˈsentr ɪk ₍ᵢ₎kɒn- ‖ ₍ᵢ₎kɑːn- **~ally**
ᵊl_i
concept ˈkɒn sept ‖ ˈkɑːn- **~s** s
conception kən ˈsep ʃᵊn §₍ᵢ₎kɒn- **~s** z
conceptual kən ˈsep tʃu_əl §₍ᵢ₎kɒn-, -ʃu_əl;
-ˈsept ju_ ‖ kɑːn-, -ˈsep tʃəl
conceptualis... —*see* **conceptualiz...**
conceptualization kən ˌsep tʃu_əl aɪ ˈzeɪʃ ᵊn
§kɒn-, -ˌʃu_əl-, -ˌsept ju_, -ɪ'·· ‖ -ə ˈzeɪʃ- kɑːn-,
-ˌsep tʃəl ə ˈzeɪʃ- **~s** z
conceptualiz|e kən ˈsep tʃu_ə laɪz §₍ᵢ₎kɒn-,
-ˈsept ju_; -ˈsep tʃu laɪz, -ˈsep tʃə laɪz ‖ kɑːn-,
-ˈsep ʃu_ **~ed** d **~es** ɪz əz **~ing** ɪŋ
conceptually kən ˈsep tʃu_əl i §₍ᵢ₎kɒn-,
-ʃu_əl i; -ˈsept ju_ ‖ kɑːn-, -ˈsep tʃəl i
concern kən ˈsɜːn §₍ᵢ₎kɒn- ‖ -ˈsɜːn **~ed** d **~ing**
ɪŋ **~s** z
concerned|ly kən ˈsɜːn ɪd |li §₍ᵢ₎kɒn-, -əd-;
-ˈsɜːnd |li ‖ -ˈsɜːn əd- **~ness** nəs nɪs
con|cert *v* kən |ˈsɜːt §₍ᵢ₎kɒn- ‖ -|ˈsɜːt **~certed**
ˈsɜːt ɪd -əd ‖ ˈsɜːt̬ əd **~certing** ˈsɜːt ɪŋ
‖ ˈsɜːt̬ ɪŋ **~certs** ˈsɜːts ‖ ˈsɜːts
concert *n* '*agreement*' ˈkɒn⁺s ət ˈkɒn sɜːt
‖ ˈkɑːn⁺s ᵊrt ˈkɑːn sɜːt
concert *n* '*musical performance*' ˈkɒn⁺s ət
‖ ˈkɑːn⁺s ᵊrt **~s** s
    ˌconcert ˈgrand
concertante ˌkɒntʃ ə ˈtænt eɪ -i
‖ ˌkoʊn tʃᵊr ˈtɑːnt eɪ
concerted kən ˈsɜːt ɪd §₍ᵢ₎kɒn-, -əd ‖ -ˈsɜːt̬ əd
~ly li
Concertgebouw ₍ᵢ₎kɒn ˈsɜːt gə baʊ kən-,
-gɪ baʊ ‖ kɑːn ˈsɜːt- —*Dutch*
[kɔn ˈsɛrt χə ˌbʌu]
concertgo|er ˈkɒn⁺s ət ˌgəʊ |ə
‖ ˈkɑːn⁺s ᵊrt ˌgoʊ |ᵊr **~ers** əz ‖ ᵊrz **~ing** ɪŋ
concerti kən ˈtʃeət i: §₍ᵢ₎kɒn-, -ˈtʃɜːt- ‖ -ˈtʃert i:
    conˌcerti ˈgrossi ˈgrɒs i: ‖ ˈgroʊs i:

concertina ˌkɒn⁺s ə ˈtiːn ə ‖ ˌkɑːn⁺s ᵊr- **~ed** d
concertinaing ˌkɒn⁺s ə ˈtiːn ᵊr ɪŋ
‖ ˌkɑːn⁺s ᵊr ˈtiːn ə ɪŋ **~s** z
concertin|o ˌkɒntʃ ə ˈtiːn |əʊ
‖ ˌkɑːntʃ ᵊr ˈtiːn |oʊ **~i** i: **~os** əʊz ‖ oʊz
concertmaster ˈkɒn⁺s ət ˌmɑːst ə §-mæst-
‖ ˈkɑːn⁺s ᵊrt ˌmæst ᵊr **~s** z
concert|o kən ˈtʃeət |əʊ §₍ᵢ₎kɒn-, -ˈtʃɜːt-
‖ -ˈtʃert̬ |oʊ **~i** i: **~os** əʊz ‖ oʊz
    conˌcerto ˈgrosso ˈgrɒs əʊ ‖ ˈgroʊs oʊ
concession kən ˈseʃ ᵊn §₍ᵢ₎kɒn- **~s** z
concessionaire kən ˌseʃ ə ˈneə §₍ᵢ₎kɒn-
‖ -ˈneᵊr **~s** z
concessionary kən ˈseʃ ᵊn ᵊr i -ᵊn_ᵊr i
‖ -ə ner i
concessive kən ˈses ɪv §₍ᵢ₎kɒn-
conch kɒŋk kɒntʃ ‖ kɑːŋk kɑːntʃ, kɔːŋk
    conches ˈkɒntʃ ɪz -əz ‖ ˈkɑːntʃ ɪz **conchs**
    kɒŋks ‖ kɑːŋks kɔːŋks
conch|a ˈkɒŋk |ə ‖ ˈkɑːŋk |ə **~ae** iː
conchie ˈkɒntʃ i ‖ ˈkɑːntʃ i **~s** z
Conchobar ˈkɒn u_ə ˈkɒŋk əʊ ə ‖ ˈkɑːn u_ᵊr
ˈkɑːŋk oʊ ᵊr
conchoid ˈkɒŋk ɔɪd ‖ ˈkɑːŋk- **~s** z
conchoidal kɒŋ ˈkɔɪd ᵊl ‖ kɑːŋ-
conchological ˌkɒŋk ə ˈlɒdʒ ɪk ᵊl ◂
‖ ˌkɑːŋk ə ˈlɑːdʒ- **~ly** i
conchologist ₍ᵢ₎kɒŋ ˈkɒl ədʒ ɪst ₍ᵢ₎kɒn-, §-əst
‖ ₍ᵢ₎kɑːŋ ˈkɑːl- **~s** s
conchology ₍ᵢ₎kɒŋ ˈkɒl ədʒ i ₍ᵢ₎kɒn-
‖ ₍ᵢ₎kɑːŋ ˈkɑːl-
concierg|e ˈkɒn si eəʒ 'kō-, ˌ·'·· ‖ koʊn ˈsjeᵊrʒ
—*Fr* [kɔ̃ sjɛʁʒ] **~es** ɪz əz
conciliar kən ˈsɪl i_ə §₍ᵢ₎kɒn- ‖ _ᵊr
concili|ate kən ˈsɪl i |eɪt §₍ᵢ₎kɒn- **~ated** eɪt ɪd
-əd ‖ eɪt̬ əd **~ates** eɪts **~ating** eɪt ɪŋ ‖ eɪt̬ ɪŋ
conciliation kən ˌsɪl i ˈeɪʃ ᵊn §₍ᵢ₎kɒn- **~s** z
conciliator kən ˈsɪl i eɪt ə ‖ -eɪt̬ ᵊr **~s** z
conciliatory kən ˈsɪl i_ət_ər i §₍ᵢ₎kɒn-,
-i eɪt ər i; kən ˌsɪl i ˈeɪt ər i ‖ -i_ə tɔːr i -tour i
concise kən ˈsaɪs §₍ᵢ₎kɒn- **~ly** li **~ness** nəs nɪs
concision kən ˈsɪʒ ᵊn §₍ᵢ₎kɒn-
conclave ˈkɒŋ kleɪv ˈkɒn- ‖ ˈkɑːn- **~s** z
conclud|e kən ˈkluːd →kəŋ-, §₍ᵢ₎kɒn- **~ed** ɪd
əd **~es** z **~ing** ɪŋ
conclusion kən ˈkluːʒ ᵊn →kəŋ-, §₍ᵢ₎kɒn- **~s** z
conclusive kən ˈkluːs ɪv →kəŋ-, §₍ᵢ₎kɒn-,
§-ˈkluːz- **~ly** li **~ness** nəs nɪs
conclusory kən ˈkluːs ər i →kəŋ-, §₍ᵢ₎kɒn-,
-ˈkluːz-
concoct kən ˈkɒkt →kəŋ-, §₍ᵢ₎kɒn- ‖ -ˈkɑːkt
~ed ɪd əd **~ing** ɪŋ **~s** s
concoction kən ˈkɒk ʃᵊn →kəŋ-, §₍ᵢ₎kɒn-
‖ -ˈkɑːk- **~s** z
concomitanc|e kən ˈkɒm ɪt ᵊn's →kəŋ-,
§₍ᵢ₎kɒn-, -ət- ‖ -ˈkɑːm ət ᵊn's **~y** i
concomitant kən ˈkɒm ɪt ənt →kəŋ-, §₍ᵢ₎kɒn-,
-ət- ‖ -ˈkɑːm ət ᵊnt **~ly** li **~s** s
concord ˈkɒŋ kɔːd ˈkɒn- ‖ ˈkɑːn kɔːrd →ˈkɑːŋ-
~s z
Concord *(i)* ˈkɒŋ kɔːd ˈkɒn- ‖ ˈkɑːn kɔːrd
→ˈkɑːŋ-, *(ii)* ˈkɒŋk əd ˈkɒn kɔːd, ˈkɒŋ-

Compression

1 Sometimes a sequence of sounds has two possible pronunciations: either as two separate syllables, or **compressed** into a single syllable. Possible compressions are shown in this dictionary by the symbol ‿ between the syllables affected.

lenient ˈliːn i‿ənt — Two pronunciations are possible: a slower one ˈliːn i ənt, and a faster one ˈliːn jənt.

maddening ˈmæd ᵊn‿ɪŋ — Two pronunciations are possible: a slower one with three syllables, ˈmæd n ɪŋ or ˈmæd ən ɪŋ and a faster one with two syllables, ˈmæd nɪŋ.

diagram ˈdaɪ‿ə græm — Two pronunciations are possible: a slower one ˈdaɪ ə græm, and a faster one ˈdaə græm.

2 Generally the uncompressed version is more usual
• in rarer words
• in slow or deliberate speech
• the first time a word is used in a given discourse.

The compressed version is more usual
• in frequently used words
• in fast or casual speech
• if the word has already been used in the discourse.

3 When a syllable is compressed, one of the following phonetic changes takes place. (They are also exemplified in 1 above.)
• A weak vowel i or u is changed into the corresponding semivowel, j or w, producing in combination with the following vowel a crescendo DIPHTHONG.
influence ˈɪn flu‿ən's (= ˈɪn.flu.ən's or ˈɪn.flwən's)
• A syllabic consonant is changed into a plain non-syllabic consonant. (See SYLLABIC CONSONANTS for this dictionary's use of superscript schwa (ᵊ) to indicate a potential syllabic consonant.)
doubling ˈdʌb ᵊl‿ɪŋ (= ˈdʌb.l.ɪŋ or ˈdʌb.lɪŋ)
• A long vowel or diphthong changes: iː becomes ɪ, uː becomes ʊ, and a diphthong loses its second element, so that aɪ and aʊ become a. In this dictionary this possibility is shown by printing the length-mark or the second element in italics (i*ː*, a*ɪ*, a*ʊ*). These changes, known as **smoothing**, are often to be heard in BrE RP, but not in GenAm.
agreeable ə ˈgriː‿əb ᵊl (= ə.ˈgriː.əb.l or ə.ˈgrɪəb.l)
ruinous ˈruː‿ɪn əs (= ˈruː.ɪn.əs or ˈrʊɪn.əs)
scientist ˈsaɪ‿ənt ɪst (= ˈsaɪ.ənt.ɪst or ˈsaənt.ɪst)
nowadays ˈnaʊ‿ə deɪz (= ˈnaʊ.ə.deɪz or ˈnaə.deɪz)

4 In the case of two potential syllabic consonants, it is always the one **before** the mark ‿ that can lose its syllabicity through compression.
national ˈnæʃ ᵊn əl (= ˈnæʃ.n.əl or ˈnæʃ.nəl)
liberal ˈlɪb ᵊr əl (= ˈlɪb.r.əl or ˈlɪb.rəl)

Compression ▶

C

Compression continued

5 Sometimes a pronunciation that was originally the result of compression has become the only possibility. For example, the comparative of **simple** ˈsɪmp ᵊl might be expected to be **simpler** ˈsɪmp ᵊl ə ‖ -ər (three syllables). In fact it is always ˈsɪmp lə ‖ -lᵊr (two syllables). There are also words where speakers differ: most people always pronounce **factory** ˈfæk tri with two syllables, but a few may sometimes say it with three, ˈfækt ər i.

Many historical compressions are shown as such in the spelling: **angry**, **disastrous**, **remembrance**. In such words an uncompressed pronunciation (e.g. ri ˈmem bər ənˈs) is not considered standard.

‖ ˈkɑːŋk ᵊrd —*The place in NC is (i), that in MA (ii). Authorities disagree about the places in CA and NH.*

concordanc|e kən ˈkɔːd ᵊnˈs →kən-, §₍ᵢ₎kɒn- ‖ -ˈkɔːrd- kɑːn- **~ed** t **~es** ɪz əz **~ing** ɪŋ

concordant kən ˈkɔːd ᵊnt →kən-, §₍ᵢ₎kɒn- ‖ -ˈkɔːrd ᵊnt **~ly** li

concordat kɒn ˈkɔːd æt →kɒn-, kən-, →kən- ‖ kən ˈkɔːrd æt **~s** s

Concorde *aircraft* ˈkɒŋ kɔːd ˈkɒn- ‖ ˈkɑːn kɔːrd →ˈkɑːŋ-, ·ˈ· **~s** z

concours ˈkɒŋ kʊə ‖ koʊn ˈkʊᵊr —*Fr* [kɔ̃ kuːʁ]

ˌconcours/conˌcours dˈeleˈgance, c~ dˈéléˈgance ˌdel eɪ ˈgɒnˈs ‖ ˌdeɪ leɪ ˈgɑːnˈs —*Fr* [de lə gɑ̃ːs]

concours|e ˈkɒŋ kɔːs ˈkɒn- ‖ ˈkɑːn kɔːrs →ˈkɑːŋ-, -koʊrs **~es** ɪz əz

concrete *n; adj 'made of ~'* ˈkɒŋ kriːt ˈkɒn- ‖ ˈkɑːn- ₍ᵢ₎·ˈ·

ˌconcrete ˈjungle; ˈconcrete ˌmixer

concrete *adj 'not abstract'* ˈkɒŋ kriːt ˈkɒn- ‖ ₍ᵢ₎kɑːn ˈkriːt ˈ· ·, kən ˈkriːt **~ly** li **~ness** nəs nɪs

con|crete *v 'cover with ~'* ˈkɒŋ ǀkriːt ˈkɒn- ‖ ˈkɑːn- ₍ᵢ₎·ˈ· **~creted** kriːt ɪd -əd ‖ ˈkriːt̬ əd **~cretes** kriːts **~creting** kriːt ɪŋ ‖ ˈkriːt̬ ɪŋ

con|crete *v 'solidify'* kən ǀˈkriːt →kən-, ₍ᵢ₎kɒn- ‖ ˈkɑːn ǀkriːt ₍ᵢ₎·ˈ· **~creted** ˈkriːt ɪd -əd ‖ ˈkriːt̬ əd **~cretes** ˈkriːts ‖ kriːts **~creting** ˈkriːt ɪŋ ‖ ˈkriːt̬ ɪŋ

concretion kən ˈkriːʃ ᵊn →kən-, ₍ᵢ₎kɒn- ‖ kɑːn- kən- **~s** z

concretis... —*see* **concretiz...**

concretization ˌkɒŋ kriːt aɪ ˈzeɪʃ ᵊn ‖ ˌkɑːn ˌkriːt̬ ə-, ·ˌ· --

concretiz|e ˈkɒŋ kriːt aɪz ‖ ˈkɑːn ˈkriːt aɪz ˈ· -- **~ed** d **~es** ɪz əz **~ing** ɪŋ

concubinage kɒn ˈkjuːb ɪn ɪdʒ →kɒŋ-, kən-, →kən-, -ən- ‖ kɑːn-

concubine ˈkɒŋ kju baɪn ˈkɒn-, -kjə- ‖ ˈkɑːn- **~s** z

concupiscence kən ˈkjuːp ɪs ᵊnˈs →kən-, kɒn-, →kɒŋ-, §-əs-; ˌkɒŋ kju ˈpɪs- ‖ kɑːn-

concupiscent kən ˈkjuːp ɪs ənt →kən-, kɒn-, →kɒŋ-, §-əs-; ˌkɒŋ kju ˈpɪs- ‖ kɑːn-

con|cur kən ǀˈkɜː →kən-, §₍ᵢ₎kɒn- ‖ -ǀˈkɜː kɑːn- **~curred** ˈkɜːd ‖ ˈkɜːd **~curring** ˈkɜːr ɪŋ ‖ ˈkɜː ɪŋ **~curs** ˈkɜːz ‖ ˈkɜːz

concurrence kən ˈkʌr ənˈs →kən-, §₍ᵢ₎kɒn- ‖ -ˈkɜː- kɑːn-

concurrent kən ˈkʌr ənt →kən-, §₍ᵢ₎kɒn- ‖ -ˈkɜː- kɑːn- **~ly** li

concuss kən ˈkʌs →kən-, §₍ᵢ₎kɒn- **~ed** t **~es** ɪz əz **~ing** ɪŋ

concussion kən ˈkʌʃ ᵊn →kən-, §₍ᵢ₎kɒn-

concussive kən ˈkʌs ɪv →kən-, §₍ᵢ₎kɒn-

Conde, Condé ˈkɒnd eɪ ‖ ˈkɑːnd-

ˌCondé ˈNast nɑːst næst ‖ næst

condemn kən ˈdem §₍ᵢ₎kɒn- **~ed** d **~ing** ɪŋ **~s** z

conˈdemned cell, ·ˌ· ˈ·

condemnable kən ˈdem nəb ᵊl

condemnation ˌkɒn dem ˈneɪʃ ᵊn -dəm- ‖ ˌkɑːn- **~s** z

condemnatory kən ˈdem nət̬ ər i §₍ᵢ₎kɒn-; ˌkɒn dem ˈneɪt ər i ◄, ·ˈdəm- ‖ kən ˈdem nə tɔːr i -toʊr i

condensate ˈkɒn denˈs eɪt ˈkɒnd ən seɪt; kən ˈdenˈs eɪt ‖ ˈkɑːn- **~s** s

condensation ˌkɒn den ˈseɪʃ ᵊn -dən- ‖ ˌkɑːn- **~s** z

condens|e kən ˈdenˈs §₍ᵢ₎kɒn- **~ed** t **~es** ɪz əz **~ing** ɪŋ

conˌdensed ˈmilk

condenser kən ˈdenˈs ə §₍ᵢ₎kɒn- ‖ -ᵊr **~s** z

condescend ˌkɒn dɪ ˈsend -də- ‖ ˌkɑːn- **~ed** ɪd əd **~ing/ly** ɪŋ /li **~s** z

condescension ˌkɒn dɪ ˈsenʧ ᵊn -də- ‖ ˌkɑːn-

condign kən ˈdaɪn ˈkɒn daɪn ‖ ˈkɑːn daɪn kən daɪn **~ly** li

condiment ˈkɒnd ɪ mənt -ə- ‖ ˈkɑːnd- **~s** s

condition kən ˈdɪʃ ᵊn §₍ᵢ₎kɒn- **~ed** d **~ing** ɪŋ **~s** z

conˌditioned ˈreflex

conditional kən ˈdɪʃ ᵊnˌᵊl §₍ᵢ₎kɒn- **~ly** i

conditionality kən ˌdɪʃ ə ˈnæl ət i §kɒn-, §ˌkɒn ˌdɪʃ-, -ɪt i ‖ -ət̬ i

conditioner kən ˈdɪʃ ᵊnˌə §₍ᵢ₎kɒn- ‖ -ᵊr **~s** z

condo 'kɒnd əʊ ‖ 'kɑːnd oʊ ~**s** z
condol|e kən 'dəʊl §₍ᵢ₎kɒn-, →-'dɒʊl ‖ -'doʊl
  ~**ed** d ~**es** z ~**ing** ɪŋ
Condoleezza ˌkɒnd ə 'liːz ə ‖ ˌkɑːnd-
condolenc|e kən 'dəʊl ən̩ts §₍ᵢ₎kɒn- ‖ -'doʊl-
  ~**es** ɪz əz
condom 'kɒnd əm 'kɒn dɒm ‖ 'kʌnd əm
  'kɑːnd- ~**s** z
condominium ˌkɒnd ə 'mɪn i əm ‖ ˌkɑːnd- ~**s**
  z
Condon 'kɒnd ən -ɒn ‖ 'kɑːnd ən
condonation ˌkɒnd ə 'neɪʃ ᵊn ˌkɒn dəʊ-
  ‖ ˌkɑːnd- ˌkɑːn doʊ-
condon|e kən 'dəʊn §₍ᵢ₎kɒn- ‖ -'doʊn ~**ed** d
  ~**es** z ~**ing** ɪŋ
condor 'kɒnd ɔː -ə ‖ 'kɑːnd ᵊr -ɔːr ~**s** z
condottier|e ˌkɒn ˌdɒt i 'eər ˌeɪ kən ˌdɒt-
  ‖ ˌkɑːn də 'tjer ‖i ˌkɑːn ˌdɑːţ i 'er ‖i —*It*
  [kon dot 'tjɛː re] ~**i** iː
Condover 'kʌnd əʊv ə ‖ -oʊv ᵊr
conduc|e kən 'djuːs §₍ᵢ₎kɒn-, →§-'dʒuːs
  ‖ -'duːs -'djuːs ~**ed** t ~**es** ɪz əz ~**ing** ɪŋ
conducive kən 'djuːs ɪv §₍ᵢ₎kɒn-, →§-'dʒuːs-
  ‖ -'duːs- -'djuːs- ~**ness** nəs nɪs
conduct *n* 'kɒn dʌkt -dəkt ‖ 'kɑːn- ~**s** s
conduct *v* kən 'dʌkt §₍ᵢ₎kɒn- ~**ed** ɪd əd ~**ing** ɪŋ
  ~**s** s
conductance kən 'dʌkt ən̩ts §₍ᵢ₎kɒn-
conduction kən 'dʌk ʃᵊn §₍ᵢ₎kɒn-
conductive kən 'dʌkt ɪv §₍ᵢ₎kɒn- ~**ly** li
conductivity ˌkɒn dʌk 'tɪv ət i ˌ-dək-, -ɪt i
  ‖ ˌkɑːn dʌk 'tɪv əţ i kən ˌdʌk 'tɪv-
conductor kən 'dʌkt ə §₍ᵢ₎kɒn- ‖ -ᵊr ~**s** z
  ~**ship/s** ʃɪp/s
  con'**ductor rail**
conductress kən 'dʌk trəs §₍ᵢ₎kɒn-, -trɪs, -tres
  ~**es** ɪz əz
conduit 'kɒn djuˌɪt 'kʌn-, -duˌɪt, →§-dʒuˌɪt,
  §ˌət; 'kɒnd ɪt, 'kʌnd-, §-ət ‖ 'kɑːn duˌət -djuˌ
  ~**s** s
Condy 'kɒnd i ‖ 'kɑːnd i
condyle 'kɒn daɪᵊl -dɪl, §-dᵊl ‖ 'kɑːn- ~**s** z
condylom|a ˌkɒnd ɪ 'ləʊm ‖ə -ə-
  ‖ ˌkɑːnd ə 'loʊm ‖ə ~**ata** ət ə ‖ əţ ə ~**as** əz
cone kəʊn ‖ koʊn **coned** kəʊnd ‖ koʊnd
  coning 'kəʊn ɪŋ ‖ 'koʊn ɪŋ **cones** kəʊnz
  ‖ koʊnz
conehead 'kəʊn hed ‖ 'koʊn- ~**s** z
Conestoga ˌkɒn ɪ 'stəʊg ə -ə-
  ‖ ˌkɑːn ə 'stoʊg ə
coney, Coney 'kəʊn i ‖ 'koʊn i ~**s** z
  ˌConey 'Island
confab *v* kən 'fæb 'kɒn fæb ‖ 'kɑːn fæb ~**bed** d
  ~**bing** ɪŋ ~**s** z
confab *n* 'kɒn fæb kən 'fæb ‖ 'kɑːn- ~**s** z
confabu|late kən 'fæb ju ‖leɪt ₍ᵢ₎kɒn- ‖ -jə-
  ~**lated** leɪt ɪd -əd ‖ leɪţ əd ~**lates** leɪts
  ~**lating** leɪt ɪŋ ‖ leɪţ ɪŋ
confabulation kən ˌfæb ju 'leɪʃ ᵊn ₍ᵢ₎kɒn-
  ‖ -jə- ~**s** z
confect *v* kən 'fekt §₍ᵢ₎kɒn- ~**ed** ɪd əd ~**ing** ɪŋ
  ~**s** s
confection kən 'fek ʃᵊn §₍ᵢ₎kɒn- ~**s** z

confectioner kən 'fek ʃᵊn ə §₍ᵢ₎kɒn- ‖ ᵊr ~**s** z
confectioner|y kən 'fek ʃᵊn ᵊr ‖i §₍ᵢ₎kɒn-,
  -ʃᵊn ər ˌi ‖ -ʃə ner ‖i ~**ies** iz
confederac|y, C~ kən 'fed ᵊr əs ‖i §₍ᵢ₎kɒn-
  ~**ies** iz
confede|rate *v* kən 'fed ə ‖reɪt §₍ᵢ₎kɒn-
  ~**rated** reɪt ɪd -əd ‖ reɪţ əd ~**rates** reɪts
  ~**rating** reɪt ɪŋ ‖ reɪţ ɪŋ
confederate *adj, n* kən 'fed ᵊr ət §₍ᵢ₎kɒn-, -ɪt
  ~**s** s
confederation, C~ kən ˌfed ə 'reɪʃ ᵊn §kɒn-,
  §ˌkɒn,·· ~**s** z
con|fer kən ‖'fɜː §₍ᵢ₎kɒn- ‖ -‖'fɝ: ~**ferred** 'fɜːd
  ‖ 'fɝ:d ~**ferring** 'fɜːr ɪŋ ‖ 'fɜ: ɪŋ ~**fers** 'fɜːz
  ‖ 'fɝːz
conferee ˌkɒn fə 'riː -fɜ:- ‖ ˌkɑːn- ~**s** z
conferenc|e 'kɒn fᵊr ən̩ts ‖ 'kɑːn- ~**es** ɪz əz
conferral kən 'fɜːr əl §₍ᵢ₎kɒn- ‖ -'fɝ:- ~**s** z
conferv|a kən 'fɜːv ‖ə ₍ᵢ₎kɒn- ‖ -fɝ:v ‖ə ~**ae** iː
  ~**as** əz
confess kən 'fes §₍ᵢ₎kɒn- ~**ed** t ~**es** ɪz əz ~**ing**
  ɪŋ
confession kən 'feʃ ᵊn §₍ᵢ₎kɒn- ~**s** z
confessional kən 'feʃ ᵊn əl §₍ᵢ₎kɒn- ~**s** z
confessor kən 'fes ə ₍ᵢ₎kɒn-, -ɔː ‖ -ᵊr 'kɑːn fes-,
  -ɔːr ~**s** z
confetti kən 'fet i kɒn- ‖ -'feţ i
confidant, confidante 'kɒn fɪ dænt -fə-, ˌ·'·,
  ˌ·'·ˌdɑːnt, '·ˌdənt ‖ 'kɑːn- -dɑːnt ~**s** s
confid|e kən 'faɪd §₍ᵢ₎kɒn- ~**ed** ɪd əd ~**er/s** ə/z
  ‖ ᵊr/z ~**es** z ~**ing** ɪŋ
confidence 'kɒn fɪd ən̩ts -fəd- ‖ 'kɑːn- ~**es** ɪz
  əz
  '**confidence ˌlimit**; '**confidence trick**
confidence-building 'kɒn fɪd ən̩ts ˌbɪld ɪŋ
  ‖ 'kɑːn-
confident 'kɒn fɪd ənt -fəd- ‖ 'kɑːn- ~**ly** li
confidential ˌkɒn fɪ 'den'ʃ ᵊl ◂ -fə- ‖ ˌkɑːn-
  ~**ly** i
confidentiality ˌkɒn fɪ ˌden'ʃ i 'æl ət i ˌ·fə-
  ‖ ˌkɑːn fə ˌden'ʃ i 'æl əţ i
confiding kən 'faɪd ɪŋ §₍ᵢ₎kɒn- ~**ly** li
configuration kən ˌfɪg jə 'reɪʃ ᵊn ˌkɒn ˌfɪg-,
  -juᵊ-, -ə- ‖ ˌkɑːn ˌfɪg- ~**al/ly** əl /i ~**s** z
configure kən 'fɪg ə §₍ᵢ₎kɒn- ‖ -jᵊr *(*)* ~**ed** d
  ~**es** z **configuring** kən 'fɪg ər ɪŋ ₍ᵢ₎kɒn-
  ‖ -jər ɪŋ
confin|e *v* kən 'faɪn §₍ᵢ₎kɒn- ~**ed** d ~**es** z ~**ing**
  ɪŋ
confine *n* 'kɒn faɪn ‖ 'kɑːn- ~**s** z
confinement kən 'faɪn mənt §₍ᵢ₎kɒn-,
  →-'faɪm- ~**s** s
confirm kən 'fɜːm §₍ᵢ₎kɒn- ‖ -'fɝ:m ~**ed** d ~**ing**
  ɪŋ ~**s** z
confirmation ˌkɒn fə 'meɪʃ ᵊn ‖ ˌkɑːn fᵊr- ~**s**
  z
confirmatory kən 'fɜːm ət ᵊr i
  ˌkɒn fə 'meɪt ər i ◂, '·····‖ -'fɝ:m ə tɔːr i
  -toʊr i
con|firmed kən ‖'fɜːmd §₍ᵢ₎kɒn- ‖ -‖'fɝ:md
  ~**firmedly** 'fɜːm ɪd li -əd- ‖ 'fɝ:m əd li

C

confi|scate *v* 'kɒn fɪ |skeɪt -fə- ‖ 'kɑːn-
~**scated** skeɪt ɪd -əd ‖ skeɪʈ əd ~**scates**
skeɪts ~**scating** skeɪt ɪŋ ‖ skeɪʈ ɪŋ
confiscation ˌkɒn fɪ 'skeɪʃ ᵊn -fə- ‖ ˌkɑːn- ~**s** z
confiscatory kən 'fɪsk ət ᵊr i kɒn-;
ˌkɒn fɪ 'skeɪt ər i, -ˌfə-, '· · · · · ‖ -ə tɔːr i
-tour i
confit 'kɒn fiː ‖ ˌkɔːn 'fiː ˌkɑːn- —*Fr* [kɔ̃ fi]
Confiteor kɒn 'fɪt i ɔː kən- ‖ kən 'fɪʈ i ɔːr
-'fiːʈ-, -iˌᵊr
conflagration ˌkɒn flə 'ɡreɪʃ ᵊn ‖ ˌkɑːn- ~**s** z
con|flate kən |'fleɪt ₍ᵢ₎kɒn- ~**flated** 'fleɪt ɪd
-əd ‖ 'fleɪʈ əd ~**flates** 'fleɪts ~**flating** 'fleɪt ɪŋ
‖ 'fleɪʈ ɪŋ
conflation kən 'fleɪʃ ᵊn ₍ᵢ₎kɒn- ~**s** z
conflict *n* 'kɒn flɪkt ‖ 'kɑːn- ~**s** s
conflict *v* kən 'flɪkt §₍ᵢ₎kɒn-; 'kɒn flɪkt
‖ 'kɑːn flɪkt ~**ed** ɪd əd ~**ing/ly** ɪŋ /li ~**s** s
confluenc|e 'kɒn flu ᵊnᵗs ‖ 'kɑːn- ~**es** ɪz əz
confluent 'kɒn flu ᵊnt ‖ 'kɑːn- ~**s** s
conform kən 'fɔːm §₍ᵢ₎kɒn- ‖ -'fɔːrm ~**ed** d
~**ing** ɪŋ ~**s** z
conformab|le kən 'fɔːm əb |ᵊl §₍ᵢ₎kɒn-
‖ -'fɔːrm- ~**leness** ᵊl nəs -nɪs ~**ly** li
conformal kən 'fɔːm ᵊl ₍ᵢ₎kɒn- ‖ -'fɔːrm-
₍ᵢ₎kɑːn- ~**ly** i
conformance kən 'fɔːm ᵊnᵗs §₍ᵢ₎kɒn- ‖ -'fɔːrm-
conformation ˌkɒn fɔː 'meɪʃ ᵊn -fə-
‖ ˌkɑːn fɔːr- -fᵊr-
conformer kən 'fɔːm ə §₍ᵢ₎kɒn- ‖ -'fɔːrm ᵊr ~**s**
z
conformist kən 'fɔːm ɪst §₍ᵢ₎kɒn-, §-əst
‖ -'fɔːrm- ~**s** s
conformit|y kən 'fɔːm ət |i §₍ᵢ₎kɒn-, -ɪt-
‖ -'fɔːrm əʈ |i ~**ies** iz
confound kən 'faʊnd ₍ᵢ₎kɒn- ₍ᵢ₎kɑːn- ~**ed** ɪd
əd ~**ing** ɪŋ ~**s** z
confounded kən 'faʊnd ɪd ₍ᵢ₎kɒn-, -əd
‖ ₍ᵢ₎kɑːn- ~**ly** li ~**ness** nəs nɪs
confraternity ˌkɒn frə 'tɜːn ət i -ɪt i
‖ ˌkɑːn frə 'tɜːn əʈ i
confrere, confrère 'kɒn freə ‖ 'kɑːn frer
'koʊn-, ·'· —*Fr* [kɔ̃ fʁɛːʁ] ~**s** z
con|front kən |'frʌnt §₍ᵢ₎kɒn- ~**fronted**
'frʌnt ɪd -əd ‖ 'frʌnʈ əd ~**fronting** 'frʌnt ɪŋ
‖ 'frʌnʈ ɪŋ ~**fronts** 'frʌnts
confrontation ˌkɒn frʌn 'teɪʃ ᵊn -frən-
‖ ˌkɑːn-
confrontational ˌkɒn frʌn 'teɪʃ ᵊn ᵊl ◂ ˌ·frən-
‖ ˌkɑːn- ~**ly** i
confrontationist ˌkɒn frʌn 'teɪʃ ᵊn ɪst ˌ·frən-,
§ˌəst ‖ ˌkɑːn- ~**s** s
Confucian kən 'fjuːʃ ᵊn ₍ᵢ₎kɒn-, -'fjuːʃ iˌən
~**ism** ˌɪz əm
Confucius kən 'fjuːʃ əs ₍ᵢ₎kɒn-, -'fjuːʃ iˌəs
—*Chi* Kǒng Fūzǐ [³kʰʊŋ ¹fu ³tsuɪ]
confus|e kən 'fjuːz §₍ᵢ₎kɒn- ~**ed** d ~**es** ɪz əz
~**ing/ly** ɪŋ /li
confused|ly kən 'fjuːz ɪd |li §₍ᵢ₎kɒn-, -əd-;
-'fjuːzd |li ~**ness** nəs nɪs
confusion kən 'fjuːʒ ᵊn §₍ᵢ₎kɒn- ~**s** z
confutation ˌkɒn fju 'teɪʃ ᵊn ‖ ˌkɑːn- ~**s** z

con|fute kən |'fjuːt §₍ᵢ₎kɒn- ~**futed** 'fjuːt ɪd
-əd ‖ 'fjuːʈ əd ~**futes** 'fjuːts ~**futing** 'fjuːt ɪŋ
‖ 'fjuːʈ ɪŋ
conga 'kɒŋ ɡə ‖ 'kɑːŋ ɡə ~**ed** d **congaing**
'kɒŋ ɡəʳ ɪŋ ‖ 'kɑːŋ ɡə ɪŋ ~**s** z
congé 'kɒn ʒeɪ 'kɔ̃- ‖ koʊn 'ʒeɪ kɑːn-, kɔːn-;
'kɑːn ʒeɪ —*Fr* [kɔ̃ ʒe] ~**s** z
congeal kən 'dʒiːᵊl §₍ᵢ₎kɒn- ~**ed** d ~**ing** ɪŋ ~**s**
z
congelation ˌkɒn dʒɪ 'leɪʃ ᵊn -dʒə- ‖ ˌkɑːn-
congener kən 'dʒiːn ə kɒn-; 'kɒnd*ʒ* ɪn ə, -ən-
‖ 'kɑːnd*ʒ* ən ᵊr kən 'dʒiːn ᵊr ~**s** z
congenial kən 'dʒiːn i əl §₍ᵢ₎kɒn- ~**ly** i
congeniality kən ˌdʒiːn i 'æl ət i §ˌkɒn dʒiːn-,
-ɪt i ‖ -əʈ i
congenital kən 'dʒen ɪt ᵊl §₍ᵢ₎kɒn-, §-ət- ‖ -əʈ-
~**ly** ˌi
conger 'kɒŋ ɡə ‖ 'kɑːŋ ɡᵊr ~**s** z
ˌconger 'eel
congeries kɒn 'dʒɪər iːz kən-, -'dʒer-, -ɪz,
-'dʒer i iːz ‖ 'kɑːnd*ʒ* ə riːz
congest kən 'dʒest §₍ᵢ₎kɒn- ~**ed** ɪd əd ~**ing** ɪŋ
~**s** s
congestion kən 'dʒes tʃən §₍ᵢ₎kɒn-, →-'dʒeʃ-
Congleton 'kɒŋ ɡᵊl tən ‖ 'kɑːŋ-
conglomerate *adj, n* kən 'ɡlɒm ᵊrˌət →kəŋ-,
§₍ᵢ₎kɒn-, ɪt, -ə reɪt ‖ -'ɡlɑːm- ~**s** s
conglomeration kən ˌɡlɒm ə 'reɪʃ ᵊn →kəŋ-,
§kɒn-, §ˌkɒn ˌɡlɒm- ‖ -ˌɡlɑːm- ˌkɑːn ˌɡlɑːm- ~**s**
z
Congo 'kɒŋ ɡəʊ ‖ 'kɑːŋ ɡoʊ
Congolese ˌkɒŋ ɡə 'liːz ◂ ‖ ˌkɑːŋ- -'liːs
congrats kən 'ɡræts →kəŋ-, §₍ᵢ₎kɒn-
congratters kən 'ɡræt əz →kəŋ-, §₍ᵢ₎kɒn-
‖ -'ɡræʈ ᵊrz

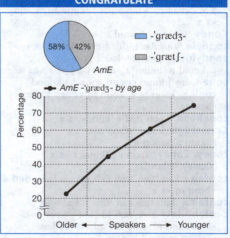

CONGRATULATE

58% -'ɡrædʒ-
42% -'ɡrætʃ-
AmE

AmE -'ɡrædʒ- *by age*

congratu|late kən 'ɡrætʃ u |leɪt →kəŋ-,
§₍ᵢ₎kɒn-, -ə-; -'ɡræt ju- ‖ -'ɡrædʒ ə |leɪt
-'ɡrætʃ- — *Preference poll, AmE:* -'ɡrædʒ-
58%, -'ɡrætʃ- *42%.* ~**lated** leɪt ɪd -əd ‖ leɪʈ əd
~**lates** leɪts ~**lating** leɪt ɪŋ ‖ leɪʈ ɪŋ

congratulation kən ˌgrætʃ u 'leɪʃ ᵊn →kəŋ-, §kɒn-, §ˌkɒn ˌgrætʃ-, -ə-; -ˌgræt ju- ‖ kən ˌgrætʃ ə- -ˌgrædʒ- **~s** z

congratulatory kən ˌgrætʃ u 'leɪt ər i ◂ →kəŋ-, §kɒn-, §ˌkɒn ˌgrætʃ-, -ə'--; -ˌgræt ju-; kən 'grætʃ əl ət ˌər i, -'-ᵊl- ‖ kən 'grætʃ əl ə tɔːr i -'grædʒ-, -toʊr i (*)

congregant 'kɒŋ grɪg ənt -grəg- ‖ 'kɑːŋ- **~s** s

congre|gate v 'kɒŋ grɪ |geɪt -grə- ‖ 'kɑːŋ- **~gated** geɪt ɪd -əd ‖ geɪt̬ əd **~gates** geɪts **~gating** geɪt ɪŋ ‖ geɪt̬ ɪŋ

congregation ˌkɒŋ grɪ 'geɪʃ ᵊn -grə- ‖ ˌkɑːŋ- **~s** z

congregational, C~ ˌkɒŋ grɪ 'geɪʃ ᵊn ᵊl ◂ ˌ-grə- ‖ ˌkɑːŋ-

Congregationalism ˌkɒŋ grɪ 'geɪʃ ᵊn ə ˌlɪz əm ˌ-grə-, əl ˌɪz- ‖ ˌkɑːŋ-

Congregationalist ˌkɒŋ grɪ 'geɪʃ ᵊn ᵊl ɪst ˌ-grə-, §-əst ‖ ˌkɑːŋ- **~s** s

Congresbury 'kʌnz bər i 'kuːmz- ‖ 'kɑːŋz ber i

congress 'kɒŋ gres ‖ 'kɑːŋ grəs -rəs **~es** ɪz əz

congressional kən 'greʃ ᵊn ᵊl →kəŋ-, (ˌ)kɒn-, →(ˌ)kɒŋ- ‖ (ˌ)kɑːn-

congress|man 'kɒŋ gres |mən -grɪs-, -grəs- ‖ 'kɑːŋ grəs- **~men** mən men **~woman** ˌwʊm ən **~women** ˌwɪm ɪn §-ən

Congreve 'kɒŋ griːv ‖ 'kɑːn- →'kɑːŋ-

congruenc|e 'kɒŋ gru ənᵗs ‖ 'kɑːŋ- kən 'gruː̯ **~es** ɪz əz **~y** i

congruent 'kɒŋ gru ənt ‖ 'kɑːŋ- kən 'gruː̯ **~ly** li

congruential ˌkɒŋ gru 'enᵗʃ ᵊl ◂ ‖ ˌkɑːŋ-

congruit|y kən 'gruː̯ ət |i →(ˌ)kɒŋ-, →(ˌ)kɒn-, ɪt- ‖ ət̬ |i (ˌ)kɑːn- **~ies** iz

congruous 'kɒŋ gru əs ‖ 'kɑːŋ- **~ly** li **~ness** nəs nɪs

conic 'kɒn ɪk ‖ 'kɑːn ɪk **~s** s
  ˌconic 'section

conical 'kɒn ɪk ᵊl ‖ 'kɑːn-

conidi|um kəʊ 'nɪd i |əm ‖ kə- **~a** ə **~al** əl

conie... —see **cony**

conifer 'kɒn ɪf ə 'kəʊn-, -əf- ‖ 'kɑːn əf ᵊr **~s** z

coniferous kəʊ 'nɪf ər əs kɒ- ‖ koʊ- kə-

coning 'kəʊn ɪŋ ‖ 'koʊn ɪŋ

Coningham 'kʌn ɪŋ əm ‖ -hæm

Coningsby 'kɒn ɪŋz bi 'kʌn- ‖ 'kʌn-

Conisborough, Conisbrough 'kɒn ɪs bər̩ ə ˈ-əs- ‖ 'kɑːn əs ˌbɜː oʊ

Coniston 'kɒn ɪst ən §-əst- ‖ 'kɑːn-

conium 'kəʊn i əm ‖ 'koʊn-

conjectural kən 'dʒek tʃᵊr̩ əl §(ˌ)kɒn-, -ʃᵊr̩ əl **~ly** i

conjecture kən 'dʒek tʃə §(ˌ)kɒn-, -ʃə ‖ -tʃᵊr **~d** d **~s** z **conjecturing** kən 'dʒek tʃər ɪŋ §(ˌ)kɒn-, -ʃər-

conjoin kən 'dʒɔɪn (ˌ)kɒn- ‖ (ˌ)kɑːn- **~ed** d **~ing** ɪŋ **~s** z

conjoint kən 'dʒɔɪnt (ˌ)kɒn-, '·· ‖ (ˌ)kɑːn- **~ly** li

conjugal 'kɒndʒ ʊg ᵊl -əg- ‖ 'kɑːndʒ əg ᵊl kən 'dʒuːg- **~ly** i

conjugality ˌkɒndʒ u 'gæl ət i -ɪt i ‖ ˌkɑːndʒ ə 'gæl ət̬ i ˌ-u-

conjugate adj, n 'kɒndʒ ʊg ət -əg-, -ɪt; -u geɪt ‖ 'kɑːndʒ əg ət -ə geɪt **~ly** li **~s** s

conju|gate v 'kɒndʒ u |geɪt -ə- ‖ 'kɑːndʒ ə- **~gated** geɪt ɪd -əd ‖ geɪt̬ əd **~gates** geɪts **~gating** geɪt ɪŋ ‖ geɪt̬ ɪŋ

conjugation ˌkɒndʒ u 'geɪʃ ᵊn -ə- ‖ ˌkɑːndʒ ə- **~al/ly** ᵊl /i **~s** z

conjunct 'kɒn dʒʌŋkt kən 'dʒʌŋkt, (ˌ)kɒn- ‖ 'kɑːn- **~ly** li **~s** s

conjunction kən 'dʒʌŋk ʃᵊn §(ˌ)kɒn- **~al/ly** ᵊl /i **~s** z

conjunctiv|a ˌkɒn dʒʌŋk 'taɪv |ə ‖ ˌkɑːn- kən ˌdʒʌŋk 'taɪv |ə **~ae** iː **~al** ᵊl **~as** z

conjunctive kən 'dʒʌŋkt ɪv (ˌ)kɒn-

conjunctivitis kən ˌdʒʌŋkt ɪ 'vaɪt ɪs §kɒn-, §ˌkɒn dʒʌŋkt ɪ '·-, -ə'--, §-əs ‖ -'vaɪt̬ əs

conjuncture kən 'dʒʌŋk tʃə §(ˌ)kɒn- ‖ -tʃᵊr **~s** z

conjuration ˌkɒn dʒu 'reɪʃ ᵊn ˌkʌndʒ ə- ‖ ˌkɑːndʒ ə-

conjure 'do magic; evoke' 'kʌndʒ ə ‖ 'kɑːndʒ ᵊr **~d** d **~s** z **conjuring** 'kʌndʒ ər ɪŋ ‖ 'kɑːndʒ-

conjure 'ask solemnly' kən 'dʒʊə (ˌ)kɒn-, -'dʒɔː ‖ -'dʒʊᵊr **~d** d **~s** z **conjures** kən 'dʒʊəz (ˌ)kɒn-, -'dʒɔːz ‖ -'dʒʊᵊrz

conjurer, conjuror 'kʌndʒ ᵊr ə ‖ 'kɑːndʒ ᵊr ər 'kʌndʒ- **~s** z

conk kɒŋk ‖ kɑːŋk kɔːŋk **conked** kɒŋkt ‖ kɑːŋkt kɔːŋkt **conking** 'kɒŋk ɪŋ ‖ 'kɑːŋk ɪŋ 'kɔːŋk- **conks** kɒŋks ‖ kɑːŋks kɔːŋks

conked-out ˌkɒŋkt 'aʊt ◂ ‖ ˌkɑːŋkt- ˌkɔːŋkt-

conker 'kɒŋk ə ‖ 'kɑːŋk ᵊr **~s** z

Conleth 'kɒn ləθ ‖ 'kɑːn-

con|man 'kɒn |mæn ‖ 'kɑːn- **~men** men

con moto (ˌ)kɒn 'məʊt əʊ ‖ (ˌ)kɑːn 'moʊt̬ oʊ (ˌ)koʊn-

Connacht 'kɒn ɔːt -ət ‖ 'kɑːn ɔːt -ɑːt

Connah 'kɒn ə ‖ 'kɑːn ə

connate 'kɒn eɪt kɒ 'neɪt ‖ 'kɑːn- kɑ 'neɪt **~ly** li

Connaught 'kɒn ɔːt ‖ 'kɑːn ɔːt -ɑːt

connect kə 'nekt **~ed** ɪd əd **~ing** ɪŋ **~s** s
  conˌnected 'speech; conˌnecting rod

connected|ly kə 'nekt ɪd /li -əd- **~ness** nəs nɪs

Connecticut kə 'net ɪk ət §-ək- ‖ -'net̬- (!)

connection kə 'nek ʃᵊn **~al** ᵊl **~ism** ˌɪz əm **~ist/s** ɪst/s §əst/s ‖ əst/s **~s** z

connective kə 'nekt ɪv **~ly** li

connectivity ˌkɒn ek 'tɪv ət i kə ˌnek '·-, -ɪt i ‖ ˌkɑːn ek 'tɪv ət̬ i

connector kə 'nekt ə ‖ -ᵊr **~s** z

conned kɒnd ‖ kɑːnd

Connell (i) 'kɒn ᵊl ‖ 'kɑːn ᵊl; (ii) kə 'nel

Connemara ˌkɒn ɪ 'mɑːr ə -ə- ‖ ˌkɑːn-

Connery 'kɒn ər i ‖ 'kɑːn-

Connex tdmk 'kɒn eks kə 'neks ‖ 'kɑːn-

connexion kə 'nek ʃᵊn **~al** ᵊl **~s** z

Connibere 'kɒn ɪ bɪə -ə- ‖ 'kɑːn ə bɪr

Connie 'kɒn i ‖ 'kɑːn i

conning 'kɒn ɪŋ ‖ 'kɑːn ɪŋ
  'conning ˌtower
conniption kə 'nɪp ʃⁿn
connivance kə 'naɪv ⁿts
conniv|e kə 'naɪv **~ed** d **~er/s** ə/z ‖ ⁿr/z **~es** z
  ~ing ɪŋ
connoisseur ˌkɒn ə 'sɜː -ɪ- ‖ ˌkɑːn ə 'sɜː -'suʳr
  ~s z **~ship** ʃɪp
Connolly 'kɒn əl i ‖ 'kɑːn-
Connor 'kɒn ə ‖ 'kɑːn ⁿr
Connors 'kɒn əz ‖ 'kɑːn ⁿrz
connotation ˌkɒn ə 'teɪʃ ⁿn -əʊ-, △-ju-
  ‖ ˌkɑːn- **~s** z
connotative 'kɒn ə teɪt ɪv '-əʊ-, △'-ju-;
  kə 'nəʊt ət ɪv, kɒ- ‖ 'kɑːn ə teɪt ɪv
  kə 'nəʊt̬ ət̬ ɪv **~ly** li
con|note kə |'nəʊt kɒ- | -|'nəʊt kɑː- **~noted**
  'nəʊt ɪd -əd ‖ 'nəʊt̬ əd **~notes** 'nəʊts
  ‖ 'nəʊts **~noting** 'nəʊt ɪŋ ‖ 'nəʊt̬ ɪŋ
connubial kə 'njuːb i əl kɒ- ‖ -'nuːb- -'njuːb-
  ~ly i
connubiality kə ˌnjuːb i 'æl ət i kɒ-
  ‖ -ˌnuːb i 'æl ət̬ i -ˌnjuːb-
conoid 'kəʊn ɔɪd ‖ 'koʊn- **~s** z
Conor 'kɒn ə ‖ 'kɑːn ⁿr
conquer 'kɒŋk ə ‖ 'kɑːŋk ⁿr (= conker) **~ed** d
  conquering 'kɒŋk ər ɪŋ ‖ 'kɑːŋk- **~s** z
conqueror 'kɒŋk ər ə ‖ 'kɑːŋk ⁿr ‿ər **~s** z
conquest, C~ 'kɒŋ kwest ‖ 'kɑːn kwest
  →'kɑːŋ-, -kwəst **~s** s
conquistador kɒn 'kwɪst ə dɔː →kɒŋ-, ˌ• • •ˈ•,
  •ˌ• •ˈ• ‖ kɑːn 'kiːst ə dɔːr kən-, kɔːŋ-, -'kwɪst-
  —Sp [koŋ kis ta 'ðoɾ] **conquistadores**
  kɒn ˌkwɪst ə 'dɔːr eɪz →kɒŋ-, ˌ• • •ˈ• • ‖ kɑːn-
  kən-, kɔːŋ-, -ˌkiːst-, -'doʊr-, -eɪs —Sp
  [koŋ kis ta 'ðo res]
Conrad 'kɒn ræd ‖ 'kɑːn-
Conrail, ConRail tdmk 'kɒn reɪ³l ˌ•ˈ• ‖ 'kɑːn-
Conran 'kɒn rən -ræn ‖ 'kɑːn-
Conroy 'kɒn rɔɪ ‖ 'kɑːn-
consanguineous ˌkɒn sæŋ 'gwɪn i əs ◂
  ‖ ˌkɑːn- -ˌsæn- **~ly** li
consanguinity ˌkɒn sæŋ 'gwɪn ət i -ɪt i
  ‖ ˌkɑːn sæŋ 'gwɪn ət̬ i -ˌsæn-
conscienc|e 'kɒnʧ ⁿnts ‖ 'kɑːnʧ ⁿnts **~es** ɪz əz
  'conscience clause; 'conscience ˌmoney
conscienceless 'kɒnʧ ⁿnts ləs -lɪs ‖ 'kɑːnʧ-
conscience-stricken 'kɒnʧ ⁿnts ˌstrɪk ən
  ‖ 'kɑːnʧ-
conscientious ˌkɒnʧ i 'enʧ əs ◂ ˌkɒnts-
  ‖ ˌkɑːnʧ- **~ly** li **~ness** nəs nɪs
  ˌconsciˌentious ob'jector
conscionable 'kɒnʧ ⁿn_əb ³l ‖ 'kɑːnʧ-
conscious 'kɒnʧ əs ‖ 'kɑːnʧ əs **~ly** li
consciousness 'kɒnʧ əs nəs -nɪs ‖ 'kɑːnʧ-
  'consciousness ˌraising
conscript n 'kɒn skrɪpt ‖ 'kɑːn- **~s** s
conscript v kən 'skrɪpt §₍₁₎kɒn- **~ed** ɪd əd **~ing**
  ɪŋ **~s** s
conscription kən 'skrɪp ʃⁿn §₍₁₎kɒn-
conse|crate 'kɒnts ɪ |kreɪt -ə- ‖ 'kɑːnts ə-
  ~crated kreɪt ɪd -əd ‖ kreɪt̬ əd **~crates** kreɪts
  ~crating kreɪt ɪŋ ‖ kreɪt̬ ɪŋ

consecration ˌkɒnts ɪ 'kreɪʃ ⁿn -ə- ‖ ˌkɑːnts ə-
consecrator 'kɒnts ɪ kreɪt ə '-ə-
  ‖ 'kɑːnts ə kreɪt̬ ⁿr **~s** z
consecutive kən 'sek jʊt ɪv §₍₁₎kɒn-, -jət-,
  §-ət- ‖ -jət̬ ɪv -ət̬- **~ly** li **~ness** nəs nɪs
consensual kən 'senʧ ju əl ₍₁₎kɒn-, -'senʧ u əl
  ‖ -'senʧ u əl -'senʧ əl **~ly** i
consensus kən 'senʧ əs §₍₁₎kɒn-
con|sent v, n kən |'sent §₍₁₎kɒn- **~sented**
  'sent ɪd -əd ‖ 'sent̬ əd **~senting** 'sent ɪŋ
  ‖ 'sent̬ ɪŋ **~sents** 'sents
consequenc|e 'kɒnts ɪk wənts -ək-; §-ɪ kwents,
  §-ə- ‖ 'kɑːnts ə kwents -ɪk wənts **~es** ɪz əz
consequent 'kɒnts ɪk wənt -ək-; §-ɪ kwent, §-ə-
  ‖ 'kɑːnts ə kwent -ɪk wənt **~ly** li
consequential ˌkɒnts ɪ 'kwenʧ ³l ◂ -ə-
  ‖ ˌkɑːnts- **~ly** i
conservanc|y kən 'sɜːv ⁿts |i §₍₁₎kɒn- ‖ -'sɜːv-
  ~ies iz
conservation ˌkɒnts ə 'veɪʃ ⁿn ‖ ˌkɑːnts ⁿr- **~al**
  ³l ◂
conservationism ˌkɒnts ə 'veɪʃ ə ˌnɪz əm
  -ⁿn ˌɪz- ‖ ˌkɑːnts ⁿr-
conservationist ˌkɒnts ə 'veɪʃ ⁿn_ɪst əst
  ‖ ˌkɑːnts ⁿr- **~s** s
conservatism kən 'sɜːv ə ˌtɪz əm §₍₁₎kɒn-
  ‖ -'sɜːv-
conservative, C~ kən 'sɜːv ət ɪv §₍₁₎kɒn-
  ‖ -'sɜːv ət̬ ɪv **~ly** li **~s** z
  Con'servative ˌParty
conservatoire kən 'sɜːv ə twɑː ₍₁₎kɒn-
  ‖ -'sɜːv ə twɑːr •ˌ• •ˈ• **~s** z
conservator kən 'sɜːv ət ə §₍₁₎kɒn-;
  'kɒnts ə veɪt ə ‖ -'sɜːv ət̬ ⁿr ə tɔːr;
  'kɑːnts ⁿr veɪt̬ ⁿr **~s** z
conservator|y kən 'sɜːv ətr |i -'sɜːv ət ər |i
  ‖ kən 'sɜːv ə tɔːr |i -tour i **~ies** iz
conserv|e v kən 'sɜːv §₍₁₎kɒn- ‖ -'sɜːv **~ed** d
  ~es z **~ing** ɪŋ
conserve n 'kɒn sɜːv kən 'sɜːv ‖ 'kɑːn sɜːv **~s**
  z
Consett 'kɒnts ɪt -ət, -et ‖ 'kɑːnts-
consider kən 'sɪd ə §₍₁₎kɒn- ‖ -ⁿr **~ed** d
  considering kən 'sɪd ər ɪŋ ‖ -ⁿr **~s** z
considerab|le kən 'sɪd ər əb |³l §₍₁₎kɒn- **~ly** li
considerate kən 'sɪd ər ət §₍₁₎kɒn-, -ɪt **~ly** li
  ~ness nəs nɪs
consideration kən ˌsɪd ə 'reɪʃ ⁿn §₍₁₎kɒn- **~s** z
Considine 'kɒnts ɪ daɪn -ə- ‖ 'kɑːnts-
consigliere ˌkɒn sɪl i 'eər eɪ -i
  ‖ ˌkɑːn sɪl i 'er eɪ —It [kon siʎ 'ʎɛː re]
consign kən 'saɪn §₍₁₎kɒn- **~ed** d **~ing** ɪŋ **~s** z
consignee ˌkɒnts aɪ 'niː -ɪ-, -ə- ‖ ˌkɑːnts- **~s** z
consignment kən 'saɪn mənt §₍₁₎kɒn-,
  →-'saɪm- **~s** s
consignor kən 'saɪn ə §₍₁₎kɒn-, ˌkɒnts aɪ 'nɔː,
  kən ˌsaɪ 'nɔː ‖ -ⁿr ˌkɑːnts aɪ 'nɔːr, -ə-;
  kən ˌsaɪ 'nɔːr **~s** z
consist kən 'sɪst §₍₁₎kɒn- **~ed** ɪd əd **~ing** ɪŋ **~s**
  s
consistence kən 'sɪst ⁿnts §₍₁₎kɒn-
consistenc|y kən 'sɪst ⁿnts |i §₍₁₎kɒn- **~ies** iz
consistent kən 'sɪst ⁿnt **~ly** li

C

consistorial ˌkɒn sɪ 'stɔːr i ˌəl ‖ ˌkaːn- -'stoʊr-
consistor|y kən 'sɪst ər ˌi **~ies** iz
consolation ˌkɒn's ə 'leɪʃ ᵊn ‖ ˌkaːn's- **~s** z
  ˌconso'lation prize
consolatory kən 'sɒl ət ᵊr i §₍ₜ₎kɒn-, -'səʊl-
  ‖ -'soʊl ə tɔːr i -'saːl-, -toʊr i
consol|e v kən 'səʊl §₍ₜ₎kɒn-, →-'sɒʊl ‖ -'soʊl
  ~ed d **~es** z **~ing/ly** ɪŋ /li
console n 'kɒn səʊl →-sɒʊl ‖ 'kaːn soʊl **~s** z
consoli|date kən 'sɒl ɪ |deɪt §₍ₜ₎kɒn-, -ə-
  ‖ -'saːl- **~dated** deɪt ɪd -əd ‖ deɪt̬ əd **~dates**
  deɪts **~dating** deɪt ɪŋ ‖ deɪt̬ ɪŋ
consolidation kən ˌsɒl ɪ 'deɪʃ ᵊn §kɒn-,
  §ˌkɒn ˌsɒl-, -əˈ-- ‖ -ˌsaːl-
consolidator kən 'sɒl ɪ deɪt ə §₍ₜ₎kɒn-, -'·ə-
  ‖ -'saːl ə deɪt̬ ᵊr
consols kən 'sɒlz 'kɒn's ɒlz, -ᵊlz ‖ -'saːlz
consomme, consommé kɒn 'sɒm eɪ kən-,
  'kɒn's ə meɪ, -ɒ- ‖ ˌkaːn's ə 'meɪ *(*)* —Fr
  [kɔ̃ sɔ me] **~s** z
consonance 'kɒn's ən ᵊn's ‖ 'kaːn's-
consonant 'kɒn's ən ənt ‖ 'kaːn's- **~s** s
consonantal ˌkɒn's ə 'nænt ᵊl ◂
  ‖ ˌkaːn's ə 'nænt̬ ᵊl ◂ **~ly** i
con|sort v kən |'sɔːt ₍ₜ₎kɒn- ‖ -|'sɔːrt ₍ₜ₎kaːn-,
  '·· **~sorted** 'sɔːt ɪd -əd ‖ 'sɔːrt̬ əd **~sorting**
  'sɔːt ɪŋ ‖ 'sɔːrt̬ ɪŋ **~sorts** 'sɔːts 'sɔːrts
consort n 'kɒn sɔːt ‖ 'kaːn sɔːrt **~s** s
consorti|um kən 'sɔːt i ˌ|əm §₍ₜ₎kɒn-, -'sɔːʃ-,
  -'sɔːʃ |əm ‖ -'sɔːrt i ˌ|əm -'sɔːrʃ-; -'sɔːrʃ |əm **~a**
  ə **~ums** əmz
conspecific ˌkɒn spə 'sɪf ɪk ◂ -spɪ- ‖ ˌkaːn-
conspectus kən 'spekt əs §₍ₜ₎kɒn- **~es** ɪz əz
conspicuous kən 'spɪk ju ˌəs §₍ₜ₎kɒn- **~ly** li
  ~ness nəs nɪs
conspirac|y kən 'spɪr əs ˌ|i §₍ₜ₎kɒn- **~ies** iz
conspirator kən 'spɪr ət ə §₍ₜ₎kɒn- ‖ -ət̬ ᵊr **~s** z
conspiratorial kən ˌspɪr ə 'tɔːr i ˌəl ◂ ₍ₜ₎kɒn-
  ‖ -'toʊr- **~ly** i
conspire kən 'spaɪ ə §₍ₜ₎kɒn- ‖ -'spaɪ ᵊr **~d** d
  ~s z **conspiring** kən 'spaɪər ɪŋ §₍ₜ₎kɒn-
  ‖ -'spaɪ ᵊr ɪŋ
constable, C~ 'kʌn's təb ᵊl 'kɒn'st- ‖ 'kaːn'st-
  'kʌn'st- **~s** z —The painter John C~ was
  'kʌn'st-
constabular|y kən 'stæb jʊl ər ˌ|i §₍ₜ₎kɒn-,
  -'·jəl- ‖ -jə ler ˌ|i **~ies** iz
Constance 'kɒn'st ən's ‖ 'kaːn'st-
constancy 'kɒn'st ən's i ‖ 'kaːn'st-
constant, C~ 'kɒn'st ənt ‖ 'kaːn'st- **~ly** li
Constanta, Constantsa kən 'stæn's ə kɒn-
  ‖ -'staːn's ə —Romanian Constanța
  [kon 'stan tsa]
Constantine 'kɒn'st ən taɪn -tiːn ‖ 'kaːn'st-
Constantinople ˌkɒn ˌstænt ɪ 'nəʊp ᵊl -ə-
  ‖ ˌkaːn ˌstænt ᵊn 'oʊp ᵊl
constatation ˌkɒn'st ə 'teɪʃ ᵊn ‖ ˌkaːn'st- **~s** z
constellation ˌkɒn'st ə 'leɪʃ ᵊn -ɪ- ‖ ˌkaːn'st-
  ~s z
consternation ˌkɒn'st ə 'neɪʃ ᵊn ‖ ˌkaːn'st ᵊr-
consti|pate 'kɒn'st ɪ |peɪt -ə- ‖ 'kaːn'st-
  ~pated peɪt ɪd -əd ‖ peɪt̬ əd **~pates** peɪts
  ~pating peɪt ɪŋ ‖ peɪt̬ ɪŋ

constipation ˌkɒn'st ɪ 'peɪʃ ᵊn -ə- ‖ ˌkaːn'st-
constituenc|y kən 'stɪt ju ən's ˌ|i §₍ₜ₎kɒn-,
  -'stɪtʃ u ˌ ‖ -'stɪtʃ u ˌ **~ies** iz
constituent kən 'stɪt ju ənt §₍ₜ₎kɒn-, -'stɪtʃ u
  ‖ -'stɪtʃ u ˌ **~s** s
  con ˌstituent as'sembly
consti|tute 'kɒn'st ɪ |tjuːt -ə-, →§-tʃuːt
  ‖ 'kaːn'st ə |tuːt -tjuːt **~tuted** tjuːt ɪd -əd
  →§tʃuːt-, -əd ‖ tuːt̬ əd tjuːt- **~tutes** tjuːts
  →§tʃuːts ‖ tuːts tjuːts **~tuting** tjuːt ɪŋ →§tʃuːt-
  ‖ tuːt̬ ɪŋ tjuːt̬ ɪŋ
constitution ˌkɒn'st ɪ 'tjuːʃ ᵊn -ə-, →§-'tʃuːʃ-
  ‖ ˌkaːn'st ə 'tuːʃ ᵊn -'tjuːʃ- **~s** z
constitutional ˌkɒn'st ɪ 'tjuːʃ ᵊn ˌəl ◂ ˌ·ə-,
  →§-'tʃuːʃ- ‖ ˌkaːn'st ə 'tuːʃ- -'tjuːʃ- **~ly** i
constitutionalism ˌkɒn'st ɪ 'tjuːʃ ᵊn ˌə ˌlɪz əm
  ˌ·ə-, →§-'tʃuːʃ-, ˌəl ˌɪz- ‖ ˌkaːn'st ə 'tuːʃ- -'tjuːʃ-
constitutionalist ˌkɒn'st ɪ 'tjuːʃ ᵊn ˌəl ɪst ˌ·ə-,
  →§-'tʃuːʃ- ‖ ˌkaːn'st ə 'tuːʃ- -'tjuːʃ-, §-əst **~s** s
constitutionality ˌkɒn'st ɪ ˌtjuːʃ ə 'næl ət i
  ˌ·ə-, →§-ˌtʃuːʃ-, -ɪt i
  ‖ ˌkaːn'st ə ˌtuːʃ ə 'næl ət̬ i -ˌtjuːʃ-
constitutive kən 'stɪt jʊt ɪv §₍ₜ₎kɒn-, -'stɪtʃ ət-;
  'kɒn'st ɪ tjuːt ɪv, ˌ·ə-, -tʃuːt ɪv
  ‖ 'kaːn'st ə tuːt̬ ɪv -tjuːt̬ ɪv; kən 'stɪtʃ ət̬- **~ly** li
constrain kən 'streɪn §₍ₜ₎kɒn- **~ed** d **~ing** ɪŋ
  ~s z
constraint kən 'streɪnt §₍ₜ₎kɒn- **~s** s
constrict kən 'strɪkt §₍ₜ₎kɒn- **~ed** ɪd əd **~ing**
  ɪŋ **~s** s
constriction kən 'strɪk ʃᵊn §₍ₜ₎kɒn- **~s** z
constrictive kən 'strɪkt ɪv §₍ₜ₎kɒn- **~ly** li
constrictor kən 'strɪkt ə §₍ₜ₎kɒn- ‖ -ᵊr **~s** z
construct n 'kɒn strʌkt ‖ 'kaːn- **~s** s
construct v kən 'strʌkt §₍ₜ₎kɒn- **~ed** ɪd əd
  ~ing ɪŋ **~s** s
construction kən 'strʌk ʃᵊn §₍ₜ₎kɒn- **~s** z
constructional kən 'strʌk ʃᵊn ˌəl §₍ₜ₎kɒn- **~ly** i
constructionist kən 'strʌk ʃᵊn ˌɪst §₍ₜ₎kɒn-,
  §ˌəst **~s** s
constructive kən 'strʌkt ɪv §₍ₜ₎kɒn- **~ly** li
  ~ness nəs nɪs
constructiv|ism kən 'strʌkt ɪv ˌɪz əm §₍ₜ₎kɒn-
  ~ist/s ɪst/s §əst/s
constructor kən 'strʌkt ə §₍ₜ₎kɒn- ‖ -ᵊr **~s** z
construe kən 'struː §₍ₜ₎kɒn- **~d** d **~s** z
  construing kən 'struː ɪŋ §₍ₜ₎kɒn-
consubstantial ˌkɒn səb 'stæn'ʃ ᵊl ◂ §-sʌb-,
  -'staːn'ʃ- ‖ ˌkaːn-
consubstantiation ˌkɒn səb ˌstæn'ʃ i ˌeɪʃ ᵊn
  §ˌ·sʌb-, -ˌstæn's-, -ˌstaːn'ʃ-, -ˌstaːn's- ‖ ˌkaːn-
consuetude 'kɒn's wɪ tjuːd -wə-, →-tʃuːd
  ‖ 'kaːn's wɪ tuːd kən 'suː; ə-, -tjuːd
consul 'kɒn's ᵊl ‖ 'kaːn's ᵊl **~s** z
  ˌconsul 'general
consular 'kɒn's jʊl ə -jəl- ‖ 'kaːn's ᵊl ᵊr *(*)*
consulate 'kɒn's jʊl ət -jəl-, -ɪt ‖ 'kaːn's ᵊl ət
  ~s s
consulship 'kɒn's ᵊl ʃɪp ‖ 'kaːn's- **~s** s
consult v kən 'sʌlt §₍ₜ₎kɒn- **~ed** ɪd əd **~ing** ɪŋ
  ~s s
  con'sulting room
consult n kən 'sʌlt §₍ₜ₎kɒn-; 'kɒn sʌlt **~s** s

consultanc|y kən 'sʌlt ənᵗs |i §₍ᵢ₎kɒn- **~ies** iz
consultant kən 'sʌlt ənt §₍ᵢ₎kɒn- **~s** s
consultation ˌkɒnᵗs ᵊl 'teɪʃ ᵊn -ʌl- ‖ ˌkɑːnᵗs- **~s** z
consultative kən 'sʌlt ət ɪv §₍ᵢ₎kɒn- ‖ -əʈ ɪv 'kɑːnᵗs ᵊl teɪʈ ɪv
consultatory kən 'sʌlt ət ᵊr i §₍ᵢ₎kɒn- ‖ -ə tɔːr i -toʊr i
consumable kən 'sjuːm əb ᵊl §₍ᵢ₎kɒn-, -'suːm-, §-'ʃuːm- ‖ -'suːm- **~s** z
consum|e kən 'sjuːm §₍ᵢ₎kɒn-, -'suːm, §-'ʃuːm ‖ -'suːm **~ed** d **~es** z **~ing** ɪŋ
consumer kən 'sjuːm ə §₍ᵢ₎kɒn-, -'suːm-, §-'ʃuːm- ‖ -'suːm ᵊr **~s** z
con͵sumer 'durable; con'sumer goods
consumerism kən 'sjuːm ə ˌrɪz əm §₍ᵢ₎kɒn-, -'suːm-, §-'ʃuːm-, -ᵊr ˌɪz- ‖ -'suːm-
consuming kən 'sjuːm ɪŋ §₍ᵢ₎kɒn-, -'suːm-, §-'ʃuːm- ‖ -'suːm-
consummate adj kən 'sʌm ət §₍ᵢ₎kɒn-, -ɪt; 'kɒnᵗs əm-, -jʊm-, -juːm- ‖ 'kɑːnᵗs əm- **~ly** li
consum|mate v 'kɒnᵗs ə |meɪt -ju- ‖ 'kɑːnᵗs- **~mated** meɪt ɪd -əd ‖ meɪʈ əd **~mates** meɪts **~mating** meɪt ɪŋ ‖ meɪʈ ɪŋ
consummation ˌkɒnᵗs ə 'meɪʃ ᵊn -ju- ‖ ˌkɑːnᵗs- **~s** z
consumption kən 'sʌmp ʃᵊn §₍ᵢ₎kɒn-
consumptive kən 'sʌmpt ɪv §₍ᵢ₎kɒn- **~ly** li **~s** z
Contac tdmk 'kɒn tæk ‖ 'kɑːn-
contact v 'kɒn tækt kən 'tækt, ₍ᵢ₎kɒn- ‖ 'kɑːn- **~ed** ɪd əd **~ing** ɪŋ **~s** s
contact n 'kɒn tækt ‖ 'kɑːn- **~s** s
'contact lens, ˌ·'·
contagion kən 'teɪdʒ ən §₍ᵢ₎kɒn-, -'teɪdʒ i ən **~s** z
contagious kən 'teɪdʒ əs §₍ᵢ₎kɒn-, -'teɪdʒ i əs **~ly** li **~ness** nəs nɪs
contain kən 'teɪn §₍ᵢ₎kɒn- **~ed** d **~ing** ɪŋ **~s** z
container kən 'teɪn ə §₍ᵢ₎kɒn- ‖ -ᵊr **~s** z
containeris... —see **containeriz...**
containerization kən ˌteɪn ər aɪ 'zeɪʃ ᵊn §kɒn-, ˌkɒn ˌteɪn-, -ər ɪ- ‖ -ər ə-
containeriz|e kən 'teɪn ə raɪz §₍ᵢ₎kɒn- **~ed** d **~es** ɪz əz **~ing** ɪŋ
containment kən 'teɪn mənt §₍ᵢ₎kɒn-, →-'teɪm-
contaminant kən 'tæm ɪn ənt §₍ᵢ₎kɒn-, -ən- **~s** s
contami|nate kən 'tæm ɪ |neɪt §₍ᵢ₎kɒn-, -ə- **~nated** neɪt ɪd -əd ‖ neɪʈ əd **~nates** neɪts **~nating** neɪt ɪŋ ‖ neɪʈ ɪŋ
contamination kən ˌtæm ɪ 'neɪʃ ᵊn §₍ᵢ₎kɒn-, -ə-
contango kən 'tæŋ gəʊ kɒn- ‖ -goʊ **~s** z
conte 'story' kɒnt ‖ koʊnt —Fr [kɔ̃ːt] **~s** s
conté 'crayon' 'kɒnt eɪ -i ‖ 'kɑːnt- —Fr [kɔ̃ te] **~s** z
Conteh 'kɒnt eɪ ‖ 'kɑːnt-
contemn kən 'tem §₍ᵢ₎kɒn- **~ed** d **~ing** ɪŋ **~s** z

contem|plate 'kɒnt əm |pleɪt 'kɒn tem- ‖ 'kɑːnʈ əm- 'kɑːn tem- **~plated** pleɪt ɪd -əd ‖ pleɪʈ əd **~plates** pleɪts **~plating** pleɪt ɪŋ ‖ pleɪʈ ɪŋ
contemplation ˌkɒnt əm 'pleɪʃ ᵊn ˌkɒn tem- ‖ ˌkɑːnʈ əm- ˌkɑːn tem-
contemplative kən 'temp lət ɪv §₍ᵢ₎kɒn-; 'kɒnt əm pleɪt ɪv, kɒn tem-, -plət ɪv ‖ -ləʈ- 'kɑːnʈ əm pleɪʈ ɪv, 'kɑːn tem- —Some speakers may distinguish between ·'· · · (with reference to monks and nuns) and '· · · · 'pensive'. **~ly** li **~ness** nəs nɪs **~s** z
contemporaneity kən ˌtemp ər ə 'niː ət i kɒn-, ˌkɒn ˌtemp-, -'neɪ-, ɪt i ‖ -əʈ i
contemporaneous kən ˌtemp ə 'reɪn i əs kɒn-, ˌkɒn ˌtemp- **~ly** li **~ness** nəs nɪs
contemporar|y kən 'temp ᵊr ər |i §₍ᵢ₎kɒn- ‖ -ə rer |i —casually also -'temp r|i **~ies** iz
contempt kən 'tempt §₍ᵢ₎kɒn- **~s** s
contemptibility kən ˌtempt ə 'bɪl ət i §₍ᵢ₎kɒn-, -ɪt i ‖ -əʈ i
contemptib|le kən 'tempt əb |ᵊl §₍ᵢ₎kɒn- **~leness** ᵊl nəs -nɪs **~ly** li
contemptuous kən 'tempt ju əs §₍ᵢ₎kɒn-, -'temp tʃu ‖ -'temp tʃu əs -ʃu əs **~ly** li **~ness** nəs nɪs
contend kən 'tend §₍ᵢ₎kɒn- **~ed** ɪd əd **~er/s** ə/z ‖ -ᵊr/z **~ing** ɪŋ **~s** z
con|tent adj, v, n 'contentment' kən |'tent §₍ᵢ₎kɒn- **~tented** 'tent ɪd -əd ‖ 'tenʈ əd **~tenting** 'tent ɪŋ ‖ 'tenʈ ɪŋ **~tents** 'tents
content n 'matter contained' 'kɒn tent ‖ 'kɑːn- **~s** s
contented kən 'tent ɪd §₍ᵢ₎kɒn-, -əd ‖ -'tenʈ əd **~ly** li **~ness** nəs nɪs
contention kən 'tenᵗʃ ᵊn §₍ᵢ₎kɒn- **~s** z
contentious kən 'tenᵗʃ əs §₍ᵢ₎kɒn- **~ly** li **~ness** nəs nɪs
contentment kən 'tent mənt §₍ᵢ₎kɒn-
conterminous kɒn 'tɜːm ɪn əs kən-, -ən- ‖ -'tɜːm- ₍ᵢ₎kɑːn- **~ly** li
contessa 'kɒn 'tes ə ‖ kɑːn- —It [kon 'tes sa]
contest n 'kɒn test ‖ 'kɑːn- **~s** s
contest v kən 'test §₍ᵢ₎kɒn-; 'kɒn test ‖ 'kɑːn test **~ed** ɪd əd **~ing** ɪŋ **~s** s
contestant kən 'test ənt §₍ᵢ₎kɒn- **~s** s
contestation ˌkɒnt e 'steɪʃ ᵊn ‖ ˌkɑːnt-
context 'kɒn tekst ‖ 'kɑːn- **~s** s
context-free ˌkɒn tekst 'friː ◄ ‖ ˌkɑːn-
context-sensitive ˌkɒn tekst 'senᵗs ət ɪv ◄ -ɪt ɪv ‖ ˌkɑːn tekst 'senᵗs əʈ ɪv ◄
contextual kən 'tekst ju əl §₍ᵢ₎kɒn-, -'teks tʃu ‖ kɑːn 'teks tʃu əl kən-, -'teks tʃəl **~ly** i
contextualis... —see **contextualiz...**
contextualization kən ˌtekst ju əl aɪ 'zeɪʃ ᵊn §₍ᵢ₎kɒn-, -ˌteks tʃu, -ɪ'- ‖ kɑːn ˌteks tʃu əl ə 'zeɪʃ ᵊn kən-, -ˌteks tʃəl ə 'zeɪʃ-
contextualiz|e kən 'tekst ju ə laɪz §₍ᵢ₎kɒn-, -'teks tʃu ‖ kɑːn 'teks tʃu ə laɪz kən-, -'teks tʃə laɪz **~ed** d **~es** ɪz əz **~ing** ɪŋ
Contiboard tdmk 'kɒnt i bɔːd ‖ 'kɑːnʈ i bɔːrd -boʊrd

contiguit|y ˌkɒnt ɪ ˈgjuːˌət |i ˌ-ə-, -ɪt i
‖ ˌkaːnt̬ ə ˈgjuː əˌt |i ~**ies** iz
contiguous kən ˈtɪg ju‿əs §₍₁₎kɒn- ~**ly** li ~**ness**
nəs nɪs
Contin ˈkɒnt ɪn §-ən ‖ ˈkaːnt-
continence ˈkɒnt ɪn ənˢs -ən- ‖ ˈkaːnt ᵊn-
continent ˈkɒnt ɪn ənt -ən- ‖ ˈkaːnt ᵊn ənt ~**ly**
li ~**s** s
continental ˌkɒnt ɪ ˈnent ᵊl ◀ -ə-
‖ ˌkaːnt ᵊn ˈent̬ ᵊl ◀ ~**ly** i
   ˌconti,nental ˈbreakfast; ˌconti,nental
   ˈshelf
contingenc|y kən ˈtɪndʒ ənˢs |i §₍₁₎kɒn- ~**ies**
iz
contingent kən ˈtɪndʒ ənt §₍₁₎kɒn- ~**ly** li ~**s** s
continua kən ˈtɪn ju‿ə §₍₁₎kɒn-
continual kən ˈtɪn ju‿əl §₍₁₎kɒn- ~**ly** i
continuance kən ˈtɪn ju‿ənˢs §₍₁₎kɒn-
continuant kən ˈtɪn ju‿ənt §₍₁₎kɒn- ~**s** s
continuation kən ˌtɪn ju ˈeɪʃ ᵊn §₍₁₎kɒn- ~**s** z
continuative kən ˈtɪn ju‿ət ɪv -eɪt ɪv ‖ -eɪt̬ ɪv
~**ly** li
continu|e kən ˈtɪn juː §₍₁₎kɒn-, -ju ‖ -ju ~**ed** d
~**es** z ~**ing** ɪŋ
continuit|y ˌkɒnt ɪ ˈnjuːˌət |i ˌ-ə-, -ɪt i
‖ ˌkaːnt ᵊn ˈuː əˌt |i -ˈjuː- ~**ies** iz
continuo kən ˈtɪn ju əʊ ₍₁₎kɒn-, -u- ‖ -oʊ ~**s** z
continuous kən ˈtɪn ju‿əs §₍₁₎kɒn- ~**ly** li ~**ness**
nəs nɪs
continu|um kən ˈtɪn juˌəm §₍₁₎kɒn- ~**a** ə
contoid ˈkɒnt ɔɪd ‖ ˈkaːnt- ~**s** z
contoidal kɒn ˈtɔɪd ᵊl ‖ kaːn-
con|tort kən |ˈtɔːt §₍₁₎kɒn- ◀ -|ˈtɔːrt ~**torted**
   ˈtɔːt ɪd -əd ‖ ˈtɔːrt̬ əd ~**torting** ˈtɔːt ɪŋ
   ‖ ˈtɔːrt̬ ɪŋ ~**torts** ˈtɔːts ‖ ˈtɔːrts
contorted kən ˈtɔːt ɪd §₍₁₎kɒn-, -əd ‖ ˈtɔːrt̬ əd
~**ly** li ~**ness** nəs nɪs
contortion kən ˈtɔːʃ ᵊn §₍₁₎kɒn- ‖ -ˈtɔːrʃ ᵊn ~**s**
z
contortionist kən ˈtɔːʃ ᵊnˌɪst ₍₁₎kɒn-, §ˌəst
‖ -ˈtɔːrʃ- ~**s** s
contour ˈkɒn tʊə -ɔː ‖ ˈkaːn tʊr ~**ed** d
   contouring ˈkɒn tʊər ɪŋ ‖ ˈkaːn tʊr ɪŋ ~**s** z
   ˈcontour line
contra, C~ ˈkɒntr ə -aː ‖ ˈkaːntr ə ~**s** z
contra- *comb. form* ¦kɒntr ə ‖ ¦kaːntr ə —
   contraposition ˌkɒntr ə pə ˈzɪʃ ᵊn ‖ ˌkaːntr-
contraband ˈkɒntr ə bænd ‖ ˈkaːntr- ~**ist/s**
ɪst/s §əst/s ‖ əst/s
contrabass ˌkɒntr ə ˈbeɪs ˈ · · ‖ ˈkaːntr ə beɪs
~**ist/s** ɪst/s §əst/s ‖ əst/s
contraception ˌkɒntr ə ˈsep ʃᵊn ‖ ˌkaːntr-
contraceptive ˌkɒntr ə ˈsept ɪv ◀ ‖ ˌkaːntr- ~**s**
z
contract *v* kən ˈtrækt §₍₁₎kɒn- —*but in the*
   meaning 'agree under contract, make a
   contract' sometimes ˈkɒn trækt ‖ ˈkaːn- ~**ed**
   ɪd əd ~**ing** ɪŋ ~**s** s
contract *n* ˈkɒn trækt ‖ ˈkaːn- ~**s** s
contractible kən ˈtrækt əb ᵊl §₍₁₎kɒn-
contractile kən ˈtrækt aɪᵊl §₍₁₎kɒn- ‖ -ᵊl -aɪᵊl
contractility ˌkɒn træk ˈtɪl ət i -ɪt i
‖ ˌkaːn træk ˈtɪl ət̬ i

contraction kən ˈtræk ʃᵊn §₍₁₎kɒn- ~**s** z
contractor kən ˈtrækt ə §₍₁₎kɒn-; ˈkɒn trækt ə
‖ ˈkaːn trækt ᵊr ~**s** z
contractual kən ˈtræk tʃu‿əl §₍₁₎kɒn-,
   -ˈtrækt ju‿ ‖ kaːn-, -ˈtræk tʃəl ~**ly** i
contracture kən ˈtræk tʃə §₍₁₎kɒn-, -tjʊə, -ʃə
‖ -tʃᵊr ~**s** z
contradict ˌkɒntr ə ˈdɪkt ‖ ˌkaːntr- ~**ed** ɪd əd
~**ing** ɪŋ ~**s** s
contradiction ˌkɒntr ə ˈdɪk ʃᵊn ‖ ˌkaːntr- ~**s** z
contradictor|y ˌkɒntr ə ˈdɪkt ərˌ|i ◀ ‖ ˌkaːntr-
~**ies** iz ~**ily** əl i ɪ li ~**iness** i nəs i nɪs
contradistinction ˌkɒntr ə dɪ ˈstɪŋk ʃᵊn -ə də-
‖ ˌkaːntr-
contradistinctive ˌkɒntr ə dɪ ˈstɪŋkt ɪv ◀
-ə də- ‖ ˌkaːntr- ~**ly** li
contrafactual ˌkɒntr ə ˈfæk tʃu‿əl ◀ -ʃu‿əl;
   -ˈfækt ju‿ ‖ ˌkaːntr- ~**ly** i ~**s** z
contraflow ˈkɒntr ə fləʊ ˌ · ˈ· ‖ ˈkaːntr ə floʊ
~**s** z
contrail ˈkɒn treɪᵊl ‖ ˈkaːn- ~**s** z
contraindi|cate ˌkɒntr ə ˈɪnd ɪ |keɪt →ˌ·ᵊr-
‖ ˌkaːntr- ~**cated** keɪt ɪd -əd ‖ keɪt̬ əd ~**cates**
   keɪts ~**cating** keɪt ɪŋ ‖ keɪt̬ ɪŋ
contraindication ˌkɒntr ə ˌɪnd ɪ ˈkeɪʃ ᵊn
→ˌ·ᵊr-, -ˌ·ə- ‖ ˌkaːntr- ~**s** z
contralateral ˌkɒntr ə ˈlætˌᵊr əl ◀
‖ ˌkaːntr ə ˈlæt̬ ər əl →-ˈlætr əl
contralto kən ˈtraːlt əʊ §₍₁₎kɒn-, -ˈtrælt-
‖ -ˈtrælt oʊ ~**s** z
contraption kən ˈtræp ʃᵊn §₍₁₎kɒn- ~**s** z
contrapuntal ˌkɒntr ə ˈpʌnt ᵊl ◀
‖ ˌkaːntr ə ˈpʌnt̬ ᵊl ◀ ~**ly** i
contrari... —*see* **contrary**
contrariet|y ˌkɒntr ə ˈraɪ ət |i -ɪt i
‖ ˌkaːntr ə ˈraɪ ət̬ |i ~**ies** iz
contrarily kən ˈtreər əl i -ɪ li; ˈkɒntr ər-
‖ ˈkaːn trer əl i ˌ·ˈ·-
contrariwise kən ˈtreər i waɪz §₍₁₎kɒn-;
   ˈkɒntr ər- ‖ ˈkaːn trer- kən ˈtrer-
contrar|y *adj 'perverse, obstinate'* kən ˈtreər |i
   §₍₁₎kɒn- ‖ -ˈtrer |i ˈkaːn trer |i ~**iness** i nəs
i nɪs
contrar|y *n; adj 'different, opposed'*
   ˈkɒntr ər |i ‖ ˈkaːn trer |i ~**ies** iz ~**iness**
i nəs i nɪs
contrast *v* kən ˈtraːst §₍₁₎kɒn-, §-ˈtræst;
   ˈkɒn traːst, §-ˈtræst ‖ -ˈtræst ˈkaːn træst —*The*
   -ˈtræst *form was apparently used in RP until*
   at least the 1940s. ~**ed** ɪd əd ~**ing** ɪŋ ~**s** s
contrast *n* ˈkɒn traːst §-træst ‖ ˈkaːn træst ~**s**
s
contrastive kən ˈtraːst ɪv §₍₁₎kɒn-, §-ˈtræst-
‖ -ˈtræst- ~**ly** li ~**ness** nəs nɪs
contrasty ˈkɒn traːst i §-ˈtræst- ‖ ˈkaːn træst i
contraven|e ˌkɒntr ə ˈviːn ‖ ˌkaːntr- ~**ed** d
~**es** z ~**ing** ɪŋ
contravention ˌkɒntr ə ˈvenˢʃ ᵊn ‖ ˌkaːntr- ~**s**
z
contretemps ˈkɒntr ə tɒ̃ -tɒŋ, -tɒm
‖ ˈkaːntr ə tãː —*Fr* [kɔ̃ trə tãː] —*The plural*
   (spelled identically) is pronounced with -z *or,*
   as in French, like the singular.

CONTRIBUTE

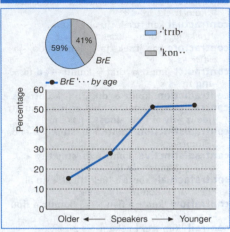

■ ·'trɪb·
■ 'kɒn··

BrE

— ●— BrE '··· by age

CONTROVERSY

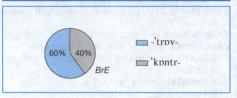

■ -'trɒv-
■ 'kɒntr-

BrE

widespread. Preference poll, BrE: -'trɒv- 60%,
'kɒntr- 40%. In AmE 'kɑːntr- is the only
possibility.

contribute kən 'trɪb juːt §₍₁₎kɒn-;
'kɒntr ɪ bjuːt, -ə- ‖ kən 'trɪb jət -juːt
— *Preference poll, BrE: ·'·· 59%, '··· 41%;
born before 1942, ·'·· 84% '··· 16%.*
   contributed kən 'trɪb jʊt ɪd §₍₁₎kɒn-;
'kɒntr ɪ bjuːt ɪd, '·ə- ‖ -'trɪb jət əd -əʈ-, -juːʈ-
   contributes kən 'trɪb juːts §₍₁₎kɒn-;
'kɒntr ɪ bjuːts, -ə- ‖ -'trɪb jəts -juːts
   contributing kən 'trɪb jʊt ɪŋ -jət-, §-juːt-;
'kɒntr ɪ bjuːt ɪŋ, '·ə- ‖ -'trɪb jəʈ ɪŋ -əʈ-, -juːʈ-
contribution ˌkɒntr ɪ 'bjuːʃ ᵊn -ə- ‖ ˌkɑːntr- ~s
z
contributive kən 'trɪb jʊt ɪv §₍₁₎kɒn-, -jət-,
§-juːt-; 'kɒntr ɪ bjuːt-, '·ə- ‖ -jəʈ ɪv -əʈ- ~ly li
 ~ness nəs nɪs
contributor kən 'trɪb jʊt ə §₍₁₎kɒn-, -jət-,
§-juːt-; 'kɒntr ɪ bjuːt ə, '·ə- ‖ -jəʈ ᵊr -əʈ- ~s z
contributor|y kən 'trɪb jʊ tər |i §₍₁₎kɒn-, -'·jə-,
§-'ju:; ˌkɒntr ɪ 'bjuːt ər |i, ·ə- ‖ -jə tɔːr |i
-tʊər i ~ies iz
contrite 'kɒn traɪt kən 'traɪt ‖ kən 'traɪt
'kɑːn traɪt ~ly li ~ness nəs nɪs
contrition kən 'trɪʃ ᵊn §₍₁₎kɒn-
contrivanc|e kən 'traɪv ᵊn⸝s §₍₁₎kɒn- ~es ɪz əz
contriv|e kən 'traɪv §₍₁₎kɒn- ~ed d ~es z ~ing
ɪŋ
control kən 'trəʊl §₍₁₎kɒn-, →-'trɒʊl ‖ -'troʊl
 ~led d ~ling ɪŋ ~s z
  con'trol freak; con'trol group; con'trol
  room; con'trol ˌtower
controllable kən 'trəʊl əb ᵊl §₍₁₎kɒn-,
→-'trɒʊl- ‖ -'troʊl-
controller kən 'trəʊl ə §₍₁₎kɒn-, →-'trɒʊl-
‖ -'troʊl ᵊr ~s z
controversial ˌkɒntr ə 'vɜːʃ ᵊl ◄ -'vɜːs i əl
‖ ˌkɑːntr ə 'vɜːʃ ᵊl -'vɜːs i̯əl ~ist/s ɪst/s §əst/s
‖ əst/s ~ly li
controvers|y 'kɒntr ə vɜːs |i -vəs i;
kən 'trɒv əs |i, §₍₁₎kɒn- ‖ 'kɑːntr ə vɜːs |i
 ~ies iz —*Among RP speakers the* 'kɒntr- *form
perhaps still predominates; but in BrE in
general the* -'trɒv- *form is now clearly more*

contro|vert ˌkɒntr ə |'vɜːt ◄ '··
‖ 'kɑːntr ə |vɜːt ˌ·'·· ~verted 'vɜːt ɪd -əd
‖ vɜːʈ əd ~verting 'vɜːt ɪŋ ‖ vɜːʈ ɪŋ ~verts
'vɜːts ‖ vɜːts
contumacious ˌkɒn tju 'meɪʃ əs ◄ ‖ ˌkɑːn tə-
-tjə, -tʃə- ~ly li ~ness nəs nɪs
contumac|y 'kɒnt jʊm əs |i '·jəm-
‖ kən 'tuːm əs |i -'tjuːm- ~ies iz
contumelious ˌkɒn tju 'miːl i̯əs ◄ ‖ ˌkɑːn tə-
ˌ·tjə-, ˌ·tʃə- ~ly li
contumely 'kɒn tjuːm li -tjʊm ɪl i, -əl i;
kən 'tjuːm əl ˌi, -ɪl i ‖ kɑːn 'tuːm əl i kən-,
-'tjuːm-; 'kɑːn tə miːl i, '·tjə-, '·tʃə-
contus|e kən 'tjuːz §₍₁₎kɒn-, →§-'tʃuːz ‖ -'tuːz
-'tjuːz ~ed d ~es ɪz əz ~ing ɪŋ
contusion kən 'tjuːʒ ᵊn §₍₁₎kɒn-, →§-'tʃuːʒ-
‖ -'tuːʒ- -'tjuːʒ- ~s z
conundrum kə 'nʌndr əm ~s z
conurbation ˌkɒn ɜː 'beɪʃ ᵊn -ə- ‖ ˌkɑːn ᵊr- ~s
z
conure 'kɒn jʊə ‖ 'kɑːn jʊr ~s z
Convair *tdmk* 'kɒn veə ‖ 'kɑːn ver
convalesc|e ˌkɒn və 'les ‖ ˌkɑːn- ~ed t ~es
əz ~ing ɪŋ
convalescence ˌkɒn və 'les ᵊn⸝s ‖ ˌkɑːn-
convalescent ˌkɒn və 'les ᵊnt ◄ ‖ ˌkɑːn- ~s s
convect kən 'vekt §₍₁₎kɒn- ~ed ɪd əd ~ing ɪŋ
 ~s s
convection kən 'vek ʃᵊn §₍₁₎kɒn-
convective kən 'vekt ɪv §₍₁₎kɒn- ~ly li
convector kən 'vekt ə §₍₁₎kɒn- ‖ -ᵊr ~s z
conven|e kən 'viːn §₍₁₎kɒn- ~ed d ~er/s ə/z
‖ ᵊr/z ~es z ~ing ɪŋ
convenienc|e kən 'viːn i̯ən⸝s §₍₁₎kɒn- ~es ɪz
əz
  con'venience food
convenient kən 'viːn i̯ənt §₍₁₎kɒn- ~ly li
convenor kən 'viːn ə §₍₁₎kɒn- ‖ -ᵊr ~s z
convent 'kɒn vənt ‖ 'kɑːn- -vent ~s s
conventicle kən 'vent ɪk ᵊl §₍₁₎kɒn- ‖ -'venʈ-
 ~s z
convention kən 'ven⸝ʃᵊn §₍₁₎kɒn- ~s z
conventional kən 'ven⸝ʃ ᵊn⸝ᵊl §₍₁₎kɒn- ~ism
ɪz əm ~ly i
conventionalis... —*see* **conventionaliz...**
conventionality kən ˌven⸝ʃ ə 'næl ət i
§₍₁₎kɒn-, -ɪt i ‖ -əʈ i
conventionalized kən 'ven⸝ʃ ᵊn⸝ə laɪzd
§₍₁₎kɒn-

conventio|neer kən ˌvenʃ ə 'nɪə §kɒn-
‖ -'nɪ³r **~ed** d **conventioneering**
kən ˌvenʃ ə 'nɪə³ ɪŋ §₍ᵢ₎kɒn- ‖ -'nɪr ɪŋ **~s** z
converb 'kɒn vɜːb ‖ 'kɑːn vɜːb **~s** z
converg|e kən 'vɜːdʒ ₍ᵢ₎kɒn- ‖ -'vɜːdʒ —*but in*
contrast to diverge, 'kɒn vɜːdʒ ‖ 'kɑːn vɜːdʒ
~ed d **~es** ɪz əz **~ing** ɪŋ
convergenc|e kən 'vɜːdʒ ən‡s §₍ᵢ₎kɒn-
‖ -'vɜːdʒ- —*but in contrast to* divergence,
'kɒn vɜːdʒ- ‖ 'kɑːn vɜːdʒ- **~es** ɪz əz **~ies** iz
~y i
convergent kən 'vɜːdʒ ənt §₍ᵢ₎kɒn- ‖ -'vɜːdʒ-
—*but in contrast to* divergent, 'kɒn vɜːdʒ-
‖ 'kɑːn vɜːdʒ- **~ly** li
conversab|le kən 'vɜːs əb |ᵊl ‖ -'vɜːs- **~leness**
ᵊl nəs -nɪs **~ly** li
conversant kən 'vɜːs ᵊnt §₍ᵢ₎kɒn- ‖ -'vɜːs-
'kɑːn v³rs- **~ly** li
conversation ˌkɒn və 'seɪʃ ᵊn ‖ ˌkɑːn v³r- **~s** z
ˌconver'sation piece
conversational ˌkɒn və 'seɪʃ ᵊn̯ əl ◄
‖ ˌkɑːn v³r- **~ly** i
conversationalist ˌkɒn və 'seɪʃ ᵊn̯ əl ɪst §-əst
‖ ˌkɑːn v³r- **~s** s
conversazion|e ˌkɒn və sæts i 'əʊn |i
‖ ˌkɑːn v³r saːts i 'oʊn |i ˌkoʊn- —*It*
[kɒn ver sat 'tsjoː ne] **~es** ɪz **~i** iː
converse n 'kɒn vɜːs ‖ 'kɑːn vɜːs
convers|e v kən 'vɜːs §₍ᵢ₎kɒn- ‖ -'vɜːs **~ed** t
~es ɪz əz **~ing** ɪŋ
converse adj 'kɒn vɜːs kən 'vɜːs ‖ kən 'vɜːs
'kɑːn vɜːs **~ly** li
conversion kən 'vɜːʃ ᵊn §₍ᵢ₎kɒn-, §-'vɜːʒ-
‖ -'vɜːʒ- -'vɜːʃ- **~s** z
con'version ˌfactor
con|vert v kən |'vɜːt §₍ᵢ₎kɒn- ‖ -|'vɜːt **~verted**
'vɜːt ɪd -əd ‖ 'vɜːt̬ əd **~verts** 'vɜːts ‖ 'vɜːts
~verting 'vɜːt ɪŋ ‖ 'vɜːt̬ ɪŋ
convert n 'kɒn vɜːt ‖ 'kɑːn vɜːt **~s** s
converter kən 'vɜːt ə §₍ᵢ₎kɒn- ‖ -'vɜːt̬ ³r **~s** z
convertibility kən ˌvɜːt ə 'bɪl ət i §kɒn-,
§ˌkɒn ˌvɜːt-, -ɪ'--, -ɪt i ‖ -ˌvɜːt̬ ə 'bɪl ət̬ i
convertible kən 'vɜːt əb ᵊl §₍ᵢ₎kɒn-, -ɪb-
‖ -'vɜːt̬-
convertor kən 'vɜːt ə §₍ᵢ₎kɒn- ‖ -'vɜːt̬ ³r **~s** z
convex ˌkɒn 'veks ◄ kən- ‖ ˌkɑːn kən-;
'kɑːn veks **~ly** li
convexit|y kən 'veks ət |i ˌkɒn-, -ɪt- ‖ -ət̬ |i
ˌkɑːn- **~ies** iz
convexo-concave kən ˌveks əʊ kɒn 'keɪv ◄
kɒn-, ˌkɒn,--, →-kɒŋ'-, -kən'- ‖ -oʊ kɑːn-
convexo-convex kən ˌveks əʊ kɒn 'veks ◄
kɒn-, ˌkɒn,--, -kən'- ‖ -oʊ kɑːn-
convey kən 'veɪ §₍ᵢ₎kɒn- **~ed** d **~ing** ɪŋ **~s** z
conveyanc|e kən 'veɪ ən‡s §₍ᵢ₎kɒn- **~ed** t **~er/s**
ə/z ‖ ³r/z **~es** ɪz əz **~ing** ɪŋ
conveyer, conveyor kən 'veɪ ə §₍ᵢ₎kɒn- ‖ -³r
~s z
con'veyor belt
convict v kən 'vɪkt §₍ᵢ₎kɒn- **~ed** ɪd əd **~ing** ɪŋ
~s s
convict n 'kɒn vɪkt ‖ 'kɑːn- **~s** s
conviction kən 'vɪk ʃᵊn §₍ᵢ₎kɒn- **~s** z

convinc|e kən 'vɪn‡s §₍ᵢ₎kɒn- **~ed** t **~es** ɪz əz
~ing/ly ɪŋ /li
convivial kən 'vɪv i ᵊl §₍ᵢ₎kɒn- **~ly** i
conviviality kən ˌvɪv i 'æl ət i §₍ᵢ₎kɒn-, -ɪt i
‖ -ət̬ i
convocation, C~ ˌkɒn və 'keɪʃ ᵊn ‖ ˌkɑːn- **~s**
z
convok|e kən 'vəʊk §₍ᵢ₎kɒn- ‖ -'voʊk **~ed** t
~es s **~ing** ɪŋ
convoluted 'kɒn və ˌluːt ɪd -ˌljuːt-, -əd, ˌ· ·'· ·◄
‖ 'kɑːn və ˌluːt̬ əd **~ly** li
convolution ˌkɒn və 'luːʃ ᵊn -'ljuːʃ- ‖ ˌkɑːn- **~s**
z
convolv|e kən 'vɒlv §-'vəʊlv ‖ -'vɑːlv **~ed** d
~es z **~ing** ɪŋ
convolv|ulus kən 'vɒlv |jʊl əs §₍ᵢ₎kɒn-, -jəl-
‖ -'vɑːlv |jəl- -'vɔːlv-, -'vɑːv-, -'vɔːv- **~uli**
ju laɪ jə-, |jə laɪ **~uluses** jʊl əs ɪz jəl-, -əz
‖ jəl əs əz
convoy v 'kɒn vɔɪ ‖ 'kɑːn- kən 'vɔɪ **~ed** d **~ing**
ɪŋ **~s** z
convoy n 'kɒn vɔɪ ‖ 'kɑːn- **~s** z
convulsant kən 'vʌls ᵊnt §₍ᵢ₎kɒn- **~s** s
convuls|e kən 'vʌls §₍ᵢ₎kɒn- **~ed** t **~es** ɪz əz
~ing ɪŋ
convulsion kən 'vʌlʃ ᵊn §₍ᵢ₎kɒn- **~s** z
convulsive kən 'vʌls ɪv §₍ᵢ₎kɒn- **~ly** li **~ness**
nəs nɪs
Conway 'kɒn weɪ ‖ 'kɑːn-
Conwy 'kɒn wi ‖ 'kɑːn- —*Welsh* ['kɒn uɪ]
con|y 'kəʊn |i ‖ 'koʊn |i —*formerly* 'kʌn i **~ies**
iz
Conybeare (i) 'kɒn i bɪə ‖ 'kɑːn i bɪr,
(ii) 'kʌn-
coo ku: **cooed** ku:d **cooing** 'ku: ɪŋ **coos** ku:z
Coober Pedy ˌku:b ə 'pi:d i ‖ -³r-
Cooch ku:tʃ
cooee, cooey 'ku: iː ˌˌ'·; 'ku: i **~s** z
Coogan 'ku:g ən
cook, Cook kʊk §ku:k **cooked** kʊkt §ku:kt
cooking 'kʊk ɪŋ §'ku:k- **cooks** kʊks §ku:ks
'cook book
cook-chill ˌkʊk 'tʃɪl ◄ §ˌku:k- **~ed** d **~ing** ɪŋ **~s**
z
Cooke kʊk §ku:k
Cookeen tdmk ₍ᵢ₎kʊ 'ki:n
cooker 'kʊk ə §'ku:k- ‖ -³r **~s** z
cookery 'kʊk ᵊr i §'ku:k-
'cookery book
cook|house 'kʊk |haʊs §'ku:k- **~houses**
haʊz ɪz -əz
cookie 'kʊk i **~s** z
cooking 'kʊk ɪŋ §'ku:k-
'cooking ˌapple
cookout 'kʊk aʊt §'ku:k- **~s** s
Cookson 'kʊks ᵊn
Cooktown 'kʊk taʊn
cookware 'kʊk weə §'ku:k- ‖ -wer -wær **~s** z
cook|y 'kʊk |i **~ies** iz
cool ku:l **cooled** ku:ld **cooler** 'ku:l ə ‖ -³r
coolest 'ku:l ɪst -əst **cooling** 'ku:l ɪŋ **cools**
ku:lz
'cooling ˌtower

C

coolabah 'ku:l ə bɑː ~s z

coolamon 'ku:l ə mɒn ‖ -mɑːn

Coolangatta ˌku:l əŋ 'gæt ə -ən- ‖ -'gæt̬ ə

coolant 'ku:l ənt ~s s

coolbag 'ku:l bæg ~s z

coolbox 'ku:l bɒks ‖ -bɑːks ~es ɪz əz

cooler 'ku:l ə ‖ -ʲr ~s z

Cooley 'ku:l i

Coolgardie ku:l 'gɑːd i ‖ -'gɑːrd i

cool-headed ˌku:l 'hed ɪd ◄ -əd

coolibah, coolibar 'ku:l ə bɑː -ɪ- ~s z

Coolidge 'ku:l ɪdʒ

coolie 'ku:l i ~s z

Coolin 'ku:l ɪn §-ən

cooling-off ˌku:l ɪŋ 'ɒf -'ɔːf ‖ -'ɔːf -'ɑːf
  ˌcooling-'off ˌperiod

coolly 'ku:l li -i

coolness 'ku:l nəs -nɪs

Cooloola kə 'lu:l ə

coolth ku:lθ

coomb, coombe, C~ ku:m **coombs** ku:mz

Coombes, Coombs, Coomes ku:mz

coon ku:n **coons** ku:nz

Coonawarra ˌku:n ə 'wɒr ə ‖ -'wɑːr ə -'wɔːr ə

cooncan 'ku:n kæn →'ku:ŋ-

Cooney 'ku:n i

coonskin 'ku:n skɪn ~s z

coontie 'ku:nt i ~s z

coop ku:p ‖ kʊp **cooped** ku:pt ‖ kʊpt **cooping**
  'ku:p ɪŋ ‖ 'kʊp- **coops** ku:ps ‖ kʊps

Co-op, co-op 'kəʊ ɒp ‖ 'koʊ ɑːp ~s s

Coope ku:p

cooper, C~ 'ku:p ə ‖ -ʲr 'kʊp- ~ed d
  coopering 'ku:p ər ɪŋ ‖ 'kʊp- ~s z

cooperage 'ku:p ər ɪdʒ 'kʊp-

coope|rate, co-ope|rate kəʊ 'ɒp ə |reɪt
  ‖ koʊ 'ɑːp- ~**rated** reɪt ɪd -əd ‖ reɪt̬ əd ~**rates**
  reɪts ~**rating** reɪt ɪŋ ‖ reɪt̬ ɪŋ

cooperation, co-operation
  kəʊ ˌɒp ə 'reɪʃ ᵊn ˌkəʊ ˌɒp- ‖ koʊ ˌɑːp-
  ˌkoʊ ˌɑːp-

cooperative, co-operative, C~
  kəʊ 'ɒp ər_ət ɪv ‖ koʊ 'ɑːp ər_ət̬ ɪv -ə reɪt̬- ~**ly**
  li ~**ness** nəs nɪs

coopt, co-opt kəʊ 'ɒpt ‖ koʊ 'ɑːpt ~**ed** ɪd əd
  ~**ing** ɪŋ ~s s

cooptation, co-optation ˌkəʊ ɒp 'teɪʃ ᵊn
  ‖ ˌkoʊ ɑːp- ~s z

cooption, co-option kəʊ 'ɒp ʃᵊn ‖ koʊ 'ɑːp-
  ~s z

coordin|ate, co-ordin|ate v kəʊ 'ɔːd ɪ n|eɪt
  -ə-, -ᵊn |eɪt ‖ koʊ 'ɔːrd ᵊn |eɪt ~**ated** eɪt ɪd
  -əd ‖ eɪt̬ əd ~**ates** eɪts ~**ating** eɪt ɪŋ ‖ eɪt̬ ɪŋ

coordinate, co-ordinate adj, n kəʊ 'ɔːd ɪn ət
  -ᵊn_ət, -ɪt ‖ koʊ 'ɔːrd ᵊn_ət -eɪt ~**ly** li ~**ness**
  nəs nɪs ~s s

coordination, co-ordination
  kəʊ ˌɔːd ɪ 'neɪʃ ᵊn ˌkəʊ -ɔːd-, -ə-, -ᵊn 'eɪʃ-
  ‖ koʊ ˌɔːrd ᵊn 'eɪʃ ᵊn ˌkoʊ ˌɔːrd-

coordinator, co-ordinator kəʊ 'ɔːd ɪ neɪt ə
  -'-ə-, -ᵊn eɪt- ‖ koʊ 'ɔːrd ᵊn eɪt̬ ᵊr ~s z

Coors tdmk kɔːz kʊəz ‖ kʊᵊrz

coot ku:t **coots** ku:ts

Coot, Coote ku:t

Cootamundra ˌku:t ə 'mʌndr ə ◄ ‖ ˌku:t̬-
  ˌCoota,mundra 'wattle

cootie 'ku:t i ‖ 'ku:t̬ i ~s z

co-own ˌkəʊ 'əʊn ‖ ˌkoʊ 'oʊn ~**ed** d ~**er/s** ə/z
  ‖ -ʲr/z ~**ership** ə ʃɪp ‖ -ʲr ʃɪp ~**ing** ɪŋ ~s z

cop kɒp ‖ kɑːp **copped** kɒpt ‖ kɑːpt **copping**
  'kɒp ɪŋ ‖ 'kɑːp ɪŋ **cops** kɒps ‖ kɑːps

Copacabana ˌkəʊp ə kə 'bæn ə ‖ ˌkoʊp- —Sp
  [ko pa ka 'βa na], BrazPort
  [kɔ pa ka 'bɐ na]

copacetic ˌkəʊp ə 'si:t ɪk ◄ ‖ ˌkoʊp ə 'set̬ ɪk ◄
  -'si:t̬-

copaiba kəʊ 'paɪb ə kɒ- ‖ koʊ-

copal 'kəʊp ᵊl -æl ‖ 'koʊp-

copartner ˌkəʊ 'pɑːt nə ‖ ˌkoʊ 'pɑːrt nᵊr ~s z
  ~**ship/s** ʃɪp/s

-cope stress-imposing kəp i — apocope
  ə 'pɒk əp i ‖ -'pɑːk-

cope, Cope kəʊp ‖ koʊp **coped** kəʊpt ‖ koʊpt
  copes kəʊps ‖ koʊps **coping** 'kəʊp ɪŋ
  ‖ 'koʊp ɪŋ

copeck 'kəʊp ek ‖ 'koʊp- ~s s

Copeland 'kəʊp lənd ‖ 'koʊp-

Copenhagen ˌkəʊp ən 'heɪg ən ◄ -'hɑːg-, ˌ·'··
  ‖ 'koʊp ən ˌheɪg ən ˌ·'··, -'hɑːg ən —Danish
  København [køb ən 'hau̯ˀn]

coper 'kəʊp ə ‖ 'koʊp ᵊr ~s z

Copernic|an kəʊ 'pɜːn ɪk |ən ‖ koʊ 'pɝːn- kə-
  ~**us** əs

Copestake 'kəʊp steɪk ‖ 'koʊp-

copestone 'kəʊp stəʊn ‖ 'koʊp stoʊn ~s z

copi... —see **copy**

copier 'kɒp i ə ‖ 'kɑːp i ᵊr ~s z

copilot 'kəʊ ˌpaɪl ət ˌ·'·· ‖ 'koʊ- ~s s

coping 'kəʊp ɪŋ ‖ 'koʊp ɪŋ

copingstone 'kəʊp ɪŋ stəʊn ‖ 'koʊp ɪŋ stoʊn
  ~s z

copious 'kəʊp i_əs ‖ 'koʊp- ~**ly** li ~**ness** nəs
  nɪs

copita kəʊ 'pi:t ə kɒ- ‖ koʊ 'pi:t̬ ə —Sp
  [ko 'pi ta] ~s z —Sp [s]

Copland (i) 'kəʊp lənd ‖ 'koʊp-, (ii) 'kɒp-
  ‖ 'kɑːp- —The composer, Aaron C~, is (i)

Copley 'kɒp li ‖ 'kɑːp-

copolymer ₍₎kəʊ 'pɒl ɪm ə -əm-
  ‖ ₍₎koʊ 'pɑːl əm ᵊr ~s z

cop-out, copout 'kɒp aʊt ‖ 'kɑːp- ~s s

copp... —see **cop**

copper 'kɒp ə ‖ 'kɑːp ᵊr ~ed d ~s z
  ˌcopper 'beech; 'Copper Belt; ˌcopper
  'sulphate

copperas 'kɒp ər əs ‖ 'kɑːp-

copper-bottomed ˌkɒp ə 'bɒt əmd ◄
  ‖ ˌkɑːp ᵊr 'bɑːt̬ əmd ◄

Copperfield 'kɒp ə fiːld ‖ 'kɑːp ᵊr-

copperhead 'kɒp ə hed ‖ 'kɑːp ᵊr- ~s z

coppermine, C~ 'kɒp ə maɪn ‖ 'kɑːp ᵊr- ~s z

copperplate 'kɒp ə pleɪt ˌ·'· ‖ 'kɑːp ᵊr-

coppersmith, C~ 'kɒp ə smɪθ ‖ 'kɑːp ᵊr- ~s s

coppery 'kɒp ər i ‖ 'kɑːp-

coppic|e 'kɒp ɪs §-əs ‖ 'kɑːp əs ~**ed** t ~**es** ɪz əz
  ~**ing** ɪŋ

Coppola 'kɒp əl ə ‖ 'koʊp- 'kɑːp-
Coppull 'kɒp ᵊl ‖ 'kɑːp-
copra 'kɒp rə ‖ 'koʊp- 'kɑːp-
copro- *comb. form*
  with stress-neutral suffix ˌkɒp rəʊ ‖ ˌkɑːp rə-
  — **coprophilia** ˌkɒp rəʊ 'fɪl i ə ‖ ˌkɑːp rə-
  with stress-imposing suffix kɒ 'prɒ +
  ‖ kɑː 'prɑː + — **coprophagous**
  kɒ 'prɒf əg əs ‖ kɑː 'prɑːf-
coprocessor, co-processor ˌkəʊ 'prəʊs es ə
  '·, · · · ‖ ˌkoʊ 'prɑːs es ᵊr -'proʊs- **~s** z
coproduc|e ˌkəʊ prə 'djuːs §-'duːs, →§-'dʒuːs
  ‖ ˌkoʊ prə 'duːs -'djuːs **~ed** t **~es** ɪz əz **~ing**
  ɪŋ
coproduction ˌkəʊ prə 'dʌk ʃᵊn ‖ ˌkoʊ-
copse kɒps ‖ kɑːps (= *cops*) **copses** 'kɒps ɪz
  -əz ‖ 'kɑːps əz
Copt kɒpt ‖ kɑːpt **Copts** kɒpts ‖ kɑːpts
copter, 'copter 'kɒpt ə ‖ 'kɑːpt ᵊr **~s** z
Copthall 'kɒpt ɔːl -hɔːl ‖ 'kɑːpt ɔːl -hɔːl, -ɑːl,
  -hɑːl
Coptic 'kɒpt ɪk ‖ 'kɑːpt-
cop|ula 'kɒp |jʊl ə -jəl- ‖ 'kɑːp |jəl ə **~ulae**
  ju liː -jə-, -leɪ ‖ jə liː **~ulas** jʊl əz jəl- ‖ jəl əz
copu|late 'kɒp ju |leɪt -jə- ‖ 'kɑːp jə- **~lated**
  leɪt ɪd -əd ‖ leɪt̬ əd **~lates** leɪts **~lating**
  leɪt ɪŋ ‖ leɪt̬ ɪŋ
copulation ˌkɒp ju 'leɪʃ ᵊn -jə- ‖ ˌkɑːp jə- **~s** z
copulative 'kɒp jʊl ət ɪv 'jəl-; -ju leɪt-, -jə leɪt-
  ‖ 'kɑːp jəl ət̬ ɪv -jə leɪt̬- **~ly** li
cop|y 'kɒp |i ‖ 'kɑːp |i **~ied** id **~ies** iz **~ying**
  i ɪŋ
  'copy ˌtaster; 'copy ˌtypist
copybook 'kɒp i bʊk §-buːk ‖ 'kɑːp- **~s** s
copyboy 'kɒp i bɔɪ ‖ 'kɑːp- **~s** z
copycat 'kɒp i kæt ‖ 'kɑːp- **~s** s
copydesk 'kɒp i desk ‖ 'kɑːp- **~s** s
Copydex *tdmk* 'kɒp i deks ‖ 'kɑːp-
copy-ed|it 'kɒp i ˌed |ɪt §-ət ‖ 'kɑːp i ˌed |ət
  ~ited ɪt ɪd §ət-, -əd ‖ ət̬ əd **~iting** ɪt ɪŋ §ət-
  ‖ ət̬ ɪŋ **~its** ɪts §əts ‖ əts
copygirl 'kɒp i gɜːl ‖ 'kɑːp i gɝːl **~s** z
copyhold 'kɒp i həʊld →-hɒʊld
  ‖ 'kɑːp i hoʊld **~s** z
copyholder 'kɒp i ˌhəʊld ə →-ˌhɒʊld-
  ‖ 'kɑːp i ˌhoʊld ᵊr **~s** z
copyist 'kɒp i ɪst §-əst ‖ 'kɑːp- **~s** s
copyreader 'kɒp i ˌriːd ə ‖ 'kɑːp i ˌriːd ᵊr **~s** z
copy|right 'kɒp i |raɪt ‖ 'kɑːp- **~righted**
  raɪt ɪd -əd ‖ raɪt̬ əd **~righting** raɪt ɪŋ
  ‖ raɪt̬ ɪŋ **~rights** raɪts
copywrit|er 'kɒp i ˌraɪt |ə ‖ 'kɑːp i ˌraɪt̬ |ᵊr
  ~ers əz ‖ ᵊrz **~ing** ɪŋ
coq au vin ˌkɒk əʊ 'væn -'væ̃ ‖ ˌkoʊk oʊ-
  ˌkɑːk- —*Fr* [kɔ ko væ̃]
co|quet kɒ |'ket kəʊ- ‖ koʊ |'ket **~quets** 'kets
  ~quetted 'ket ɪd -əd ‖ 'ket̬ əd **~quetting**
  'ket ɪŋ ‖ 'ket̬ ɪŋ
Coquet 'kəʊk ɪt §-ət ‖ 'koʊk-
coquetr|y 'kɒk ɪtr |i 'kəʊk-, -ətr- ‖ 'koʊk-
  koʊ 'ketr |i **~ies** iz
coquette kɒ 'ket kəʊ- ‖ koʊ- **~s** s

coquettish kɒ 'ket ɪʃ kəʊ- ‖ koʊ 'ket̬ ɪʃ **~ly** li
  ~ness nəs nɪs
coquille kɒ 'kiː ‖ koʊ 'kiːᵊl —*Fr* [kɔ kij]
  co,quilles ˌSt 'Jacques ˌsæn 'ʒæk -ˌsæ-
  ‖ ˌsɑːn 'ʒɑːk —*Fr* [sæ ʒak]
coquina kəʊ 'kiːn ə ‖ koʊ-
cor kɔː ‖ kɔːr —*See also phrases with this word*
  ˌcor 'blimey
Cora 'kɔːr ə ‖ 'koʊr-
coracle 'kɒr ək ᵊl ‖ 'kɔːr- 'kɑːr- **~s** z
coral, Coral 'kɒr əl ‖ 'kɔːr- 'kɑːr- **~s** z
  ˌCoral 'Sea; 'coral snake
coralline 'kɒr ə laɪn ‖ 'kɔːr- 'kɑːr- **~s** z
coralroot 'kɒr əl ruːt ‖ 'kɔːr- 'kɑːr- **~s** s
Coram 'kɔːr əm
cor anglais ˌkɔːr 'ɒŋ gleɪ -'ɑːŋ-
  ‖ ˌkɔːr ɑːŋ 'gleɪ ˌkoʊr-, -ːŋ- **cors anglais**
  ˌkɔːz- ‖ ˌkɔːrz- ˌkoʊrz-
corban 'kɔː bæn 'kɔːb ən ‖ 'kɔːr-
corbel 'kɔːb ᵊl ‖ 'kɔːrb- **~ed, ~led** d **~ing,**
  ~ling ɪŋ **~s** z
Corbet, Corbett 'kɔːb ɪt §-ət ‖ 'kɔːrb-
Corbin 'kɔːb ɪn §-ən ‖ 'kɔːrb-
Corbishley 'kɔːb ɪʃ li ‖ 'kɔːrb-
Corbridge 'kɔː brɪdʒ ‖ 'kɔːr-
Corbusier kɔː 'buːz i eɪ -'bjuːz- ‖ ˌkɔːrb uːz 'jeɪ
  -uːs- —*Fr* [kɔʁ by zje]
Corby 'kɔːb i ‖ 'kɔːrb i
Corbyn 'kɔːb ɪn §-ən ‖ 'kɔːrb ən
Corcoran 'kɔːk ᵊr ən ‖ 'kɔːrk-
Corcyra kɔː 'saɪᵊr ə ‖ kɔːr- —*ModGk* Kérkira
  ['cɛr ci ɾa]
cord kɔːd ‖ kɔːrd **corded** 'kɔːd ɪd -əd ‖ 'kɔːrd-
  cording 'kɔːd ɪŋ ‖ 'kɔːrd- **cords** kɔːdz
  ‖ kɔːrdz
cordage 'kɔːd ɪdʒ ‖ 'kɔːrd-
cordate 'kɔːd eɪt ‖ 'kɔːrd- **~ly** li
Cordelia kɔː 'diːl i ə ‖ kɔːr-
cordelier, C~ ˌkɔːd ə 'lɪə -ɪ- ‖ ˌkɔːrd ə 'lɪʳr **~s**
  z
Cordell ˌkɔː 'del ‖ ˌkɔːr-
cordial 'kɔːd i əl ‖ 'kɔːrdʒ əl (*) **~ly** i **~s** z
cordiality ˌkɔːd i 'æl ət i -ɪt i
  ‖ ˌkɔːrdʒ i 'æl ət̬ i kɔːr 'dʒæl ət̬ i (*)
cordillera ˌkɔːd ɪl 'jeər ə -ᵊl- ‖ ˌkɔːrd ᵊl 'jer ə
  kɔːr 'dɪl ər ə —*Sp* [kor ði 'ʎe ɾa, -'je-]
cordite 'kɔːd aɪt ‖ 'kɔːrd-
cordless 'kɔːd ləs -lɪs ‖ 'kɔːrd-
cordoba, córdoba, C~ 'kɔːd əb ə ‖ 'kɔːrd-
  —*Sp* Córdoba ['kor ðo βa]
cordon 'kɔːd ᵊn ‖ 'kɔːrd ᵊn **~s** z —*but in*
  French words -õ, -ɒn, -ɒŋ ‖ kɔːr 'dõː, -'dɑːn,
  -'dɔːn —*See also phrases with this word*
cordon bleu ˌkɔːd n̆ 'blɜː ◄ -ɒn-, -ɒm-, -ɒŋ-
  ‖ kɔːr ˌdõː 'blʊ —*Fr* [kɔʁ dõ blø]
cordon sanitaire ˌkɔːd n̆ ˌsæn ɪ 'teə ˌ·ɒn-, -ə'·
  ‖ kɔːr ˌdõː ˌsɑːn i 'teᵊr —*Fr*
  [kɔʁ dõ sa ni tɛːʁ]
Cordova 'kɔːd əv ə ‖ 'kɔːrd- —*Sp* Córdoba
  ['kor ðo βa]
cordovan 'kɔːd əv ᵊn ‖ 'kɔːrd-
corduroy 'kɔːd ə rɔɪ -jʊ-, -jə-; ˌkɔːdʒ ə-, -ʊ-;
  ˌ· ·ˋ·, 'kɔːdr ɔɪ ‖ 'kɔːrd- **~ed** d **~s** z

cordwain 'kɔːd weɪn ‖ 'kɔːrd- **~er/s** ə/z ‖ ᵊr/z
core kɔː ‖ kɔːr koʊr **cored** kɔːd ‖ kɔːrd koʊrd
  cores kɔːz ‖ kɔːrz koʊrz **coring** 'kɔːr ɪŋ
  ‖ 'koʊr-
  'core time
coreferential ˌkəʊ ˌref ə 'ren'ʃ ᵊl ◄ ‖ ˌkoʊ- **~ly**
i
Corel tdmk kə 'rel kɒ-; 'kɒr əl ‖ 'kɔːr əl, 'kɑːr-
core|late 'kɒr ə |leɪt -ɪ-; 'kəʊ ri-, -rə-, ˌ·'·
  ‖ 'koʊ ri- **~lated** leɪt ɪd -əd ‖ leɪt̬ əd **~lates**
  leɪts **~lating** leɪt ɪŋ ‖ leɪt̬ ɪŋ
Coreldraw, CorelDraw! tdmk kə ˌrel 'drɔː
  ˌkɒr əl '· ‖ -'drɑː
coreligionist, co-religionist
  ˌkəʊ rɪ 'lɪdʒ ᵊn ɪst ˌ·rə-, §ˌ·riː-, §ˌ_əst ‖ ˌkoʊ- **~s**
s
Corelli kə 'rel i kɒ- ‖ koʊ- —It [ko 'rɛl li]
Coren 'kɒr ən ‖ 'kɔːr-
coreopsis ˌkɒr i 'ɒps ɪs §-əs ‖ ˌkɔːr i 'ɑːps-
  ˌkoʊr-
corer 'kɔːr ə ‖ -ᵊr 'koʊr- **~s** z
corespondent, co-respondent
  ˌkəʊ rɪ 'spɒnd ənt -rə-, §-riː-
  ‖ ˌkoʊ rɪ 'spɑːnd- **~s** s
Corey 'kɔːr i ‖ 'koʊr-
corf kɔːf ‖ kɔːrf **corves** kɔːvz ‖ kɔːrvz
Corfam tdmk 'kɔː fæm ‖ 'kɔːr-
Corfe kɔːf ‖ kɔːrf
Corfu ˌkɔː 'fuː -'fjuː ‖ 'kɔːr fuː -fjuː, ˌ·'·
  —ModGk Kérkira ['cɛr ci ɾ a]
  ˌCorfu 'Channel
corgi, Corgi 'kɔːg i ‖ 'kɔːrg i **~s** z
coriander ˌkɒr i 'ænd ə '···· ‖ 'kɔːr i ænd ᵊr
  'koʊr-, ˌ·'·-
Corin 'kɒr ɪn -ən ‖ 'kɔːr-
Corinne kə 'rɪn
Corinth place in Greece 'kɒr ɪn'θ -ᵊn'θ ‖ 'kɔːr-
  'kɑːr- —but places in the US are kə 'rɪn'θ
Corinthian kə 'rɪn'θ i ᵊn **~s** z
Coriolanus ˌkɒr i ˌəʊ 'leɪn əs kə ˌraɪ ə-, -'lɑːn-
  ‖ ˌkɔːr i ə-, ˌkɑːr-
Coriolis ˌkɒr i 'əʊl ɪs §-əs ‖ ˌkɔːr i 'oʊl əs
  ˌkoʊr-, -ə 'liːs —Fr [kɔʁ jɔ lis]
cork, Cork kɔːk ‖ kɔːrk **corked** kɔːkt ‖ kɔːrkt
  corking 'kɔːk ɪŋ ‖ 'kɔːrk ɪŋ **corks** kɔːks
  ‖ kɔːrks
corkage 'kɔːk ɪdʒ ‖ 'kɔːrk-
corkboard 'kɔːk bɔːd ‖ 'kɔːrk bɔːrd -boʊrd
corker 'kɔːk ə ‖ 'kɔːrk ᵊr **~s** z
corkscrew 'kɔːk skruː ‖ 'kɔːrk- **~ed** d **~ing** ɪŋ
  ~s z
corkwood 'kɔːk wʊd ‖ 'kɔːrk-
cork|y 'kɔːk |i ‖ 'kɔːrk |i **~ier** i ə ‖ i ᵊr **~iest**
  i ɪst i əst **~iness** i nəs i nɪs
Corlett 'kɔːl ɪt -ət ‖ 'kɔːrl-
Corley 'kɔːl i ‖ 'kɔːrl i
corm kɔːm ‖ kɔːrm **corms** kɔːmz ‖ kɔːrmz
Cormac, Cormack 'kɔːm æk -ək ‖ 'kɔːrm-
cormel 'kɔːm ᵊl ‖ 'kɔːrm ᵊl kɔːr 'mel **~s** z
cormorant 'kɔːm ᵊr_ənt ‖ 'kɔːrm- -ə rænt **~s** s
corn kɔːn ‖ kɔːrn **corned** kɔːnd ‖ 'kɔːrnd
  corning 'kɔːn ɪŋ ‖ 'kɔːrn ɪŋ **corns** kɔːnz
  ‖ kɔːrnz

'corn bread; ˌcorned 'beef◄; ˌcorned beef
  'sandwich; 'corn exˌchange; 'Corn Laws
cornball 'kɔːn bɔːl →'kɔːm- ‖ 'kɔːrn- -baːl **~s** z
corncob 'kɔːn kɒb →'kɔːŋ- ‖ 'kɔːrn kaːb **~s** z
corncockle 'kɔːn ˌkɒk ᵊl →'kɔːŋ-
  ‖ 'kɔːrn ˌkaːk ᵊl **~s** z
corncrake 'kɔːn kreɪk →'kɔːŋ- ‖ 'kɔːrn- **~s** s
corne|a 'kɔːn i ǀə kɔː 'niː ǀə ‖ 'kɔːrn i ǀə **~ae** iː
  ~al əl **~as** əz
Corneille kɔː 'neɪ -'neɪ'l ‖ kɔːr- —Fr [kɔʁ nɛj]
cornel 'kɔːn ᵊl ‖ 'kɔːrn ᵊl -el **~s** z
Cornelia kɔː 'niːl i ə ‖ kɔːr-
cornelian kɔː 'niːl i ən ‖ kɔːr- **~s** z
Cornelius kɔː 'niːl i əs ‖ kɔːr-
Cornell ˌkɔː 'nel ˌkɔːr-
corner, C~ 'kɔːn ə ‖ 'kɔːrn ᵊr 'kɔːn- **~ed** d
  cornering 'kɔːn ər ɪŋ ‖ 'kɔːrn ər ɪŋ 'kɔːn- **~s**
z
  ˌcorner 'shop, '···
-cornered 'kɔːn əd ‖ 'kɔːrn ᵊrd 'kɔːn- —
  three-cornered ˌθriː 'kɔːn əd ◄ ‖ -'kɔːrn ᵊrd
  -'kɔːn-
cornerstone 'kɔːn ə stəʊn ‖ 'kɔːrn ᵊr stoʊn
  'kɔːn- **~s** z
cornet 'kɔːn ɪt §-ət ‖ kɔːr 'net (*) **~s** s
cornetto, C~ tdmk ₍ₒ₎kɔː 'net əʊ
  ‖ ₍ₒ₎kɔːr 'net̬ oʊ **~s** z
corn-fed 'kɔːn fed ‖ 'kɔːrn-
cornfield 'kɔːn fiːᵊld ‖ 'kɔːrn- **~s** z
cornflakes 'kɔːn fleɪks ‖ 'kɔːrn-
cornflour 'kɔːn ˌflaʊ_ə ‖ 'kɔːrn ˌflaʊ_ᵊr
cornflower 'kɔːn ˌflaʊ ə ‖ 'kɔːrn ˌflaʊ_ᵊr **~s** z
Cornford 'kɔːn fəd ‖ 'kɔːrn fᵊrd
Cornhill ˌkɔːn 'hɪl '·· ‖ 'kɔːrn hɪl
cornic|e 'kɔːn ɪs §-əs ‖ 'kɔːrn əs -ɪs **~es** ɪz əz
cornich|e, C~ ₍ₒ₎kɔː 'niːʃ 'kɔːn iːʃ, -ɪʃ ‖ ₍ₒ₎kɔːr-
  ~es ɪz əz
corn|ily 'kɔːn |ɪ li əl i ‖ 'kɔːrn- **~iness** i nəs
i nɪs
Corning 'kɔːn ɪŋ ‖ 'kɔːrn ɪŋ
Cornish 'kɔːn ɪʃ ‖ 'kɔːrn-
  ˌCornish 'pasty
Cornish|man 'kɔːn ɪʃ |mən ‖ 'kɔːrn- **~men**
mən men **~woman** ˌwʊm ən **~women**
ˌwɪm ɪn §-ən
cornmeal 'kɔːn miːᵊl →'kɔːm- ‖ 'kɔːrn-
corn pone 'kɔːn pəʊn ‖ 'kɔːrn poʊn
cornrow 'kɔːn rəʊ ‖ 'kɔːrn roʊ **~s** z
cornstarch 'kɔːn staːtʃ ‖ 'kɔːrn staːrtʃ
cornucopia ˌkɔːn ju 'kəʊp i ə
  ‖ ˌkɔːrn ə 'koʊp- ˌ·jə- **~s** z
Cornwall 'kɔːn wɔːl -wəl ‖ 'kɔːrn waːl -wɔːl
Cornwallis ₍ₒ₎kɔːn 'wɒl ɪs §-əs ‖ kɔːrn 'waːl-
corn|y 'kɔːn |i ‖ 'kɔːrn |i **~ier** i ə ‖ i'ᵊr **~iest**
i ɪst i əst
corolla, C~ kə 'rɒl ə ‖ -'roʊl ə -'raːl ə
corollar|y kə 'rɒl ər |i ‖ 'kɔːr ə ler |i 'kaːr- (*)
  ~ies iz
Coromandel ˌkɒr əʊ 'mænd ᵊl ‖ ˌkɔːr ə-, ˌkaːr-
coron|a, C~ kə 'rəʊn ǀə ‖ -'roʊn ǀə **~ae** iː **~s** z
coronach 'kɒr ən ək -əx ‖ 'kɔːr- 'kaːr- **~s** s
Coronado ˌkɒr ə 'naːd əʊ ‖ ˌkɔːr ə 'naːd oʊ
  ˌkaːr-

coronal 'kɒr ən ᵊl kə 'rəʊn ᵊl ‖ 'kɔːr- 'kɑːr-;
kə 'roʊn- **~s** z

coronar|y 'kɒr ən ər‿|i ‖ 'kɔːr ə ner |i 'kɑːr-
~ies iz

coronation ˌkɒr ə 'neɪʃ ᵊn ◄ ‖ ˌkɔːr- ˌkɑːr- **~s** z

coroner 'kɒr ən ə ‖ 'kɔːr ᵊn ər 'kɑːr- **~s** z

coronet 'kɒr ən ɪt -et; -ə net, ˌ· 'net
‖ ˌkɔːr ə 'net ˌkɑːr- **~s** s

Corot 'kɒr əʊ ‖ kɑː 'roʊ kɔ:-, kə- —*Fr* [kɔ ʁo]

Corp. kɔːp ‖ kɔːrp —*or see* **Corporal**

corpora 'kɔːp ər‿ə -ə rɑː ‖ 'kɔːrp-
ˌcorpora cal'losa kə 'ləʊs ə ‖ -'loʊs-;
ˌcorpora 'lutea 'luːt i ə ‖ 'luːt̬-; ˌcorpora
stri'ata straɪ 'eɪt ə ‖ -'eɪt̬-

corporal 'kɔːp ᵊr‿əl ‖ 'kɔːrp- **~s** z

corporate 'kɔːp ər‿ət ɪt ‖ 'kɔːrp- **~ly** li

corporation ˌkɔːp ə 'reɪʃ ᵊn ◄ ‖ ˌkɔːrp- **~s** z
ˌcorpo'ration tax

corporatism 'kɔːp ər‿ə ˌtɪzəm ˌ-ɪ- ‖ 'kɔːrp-

corporeal kɔː 'pɔːr i‿əl ‖ kɔːr- -'poʊr- **~ly** i

corps *sing.* kɔː ‖ kɔːr koʊr (= *core*) **corps** *pl*
kɔːz ‖ kɔːrz koʊrz
ˌcorps de 'ballet ‖ ˌ · ᐧ ᐧ ᐧ.

corpse kɔːps ‖ kɔːrps **corpsed** kɔːpst ‖ kɔːrpst
corpsing 'kɔːps ɪŋ ‖ 'kɔːrps ɪŋ **corpses**
'kɔːps ɪz -əz ‖ 'kɔːrps əz

corps|man 'kɔːz |mən -mæn ‖ 'kɔːrz- 'koʊrz-
~men mən

corpulenc|e 'kɔːp jʊl ənᵗs -jəl- ‖ 'kɔːrp jəl- **~y**
i

corpulent 'kɔːp jʊl ənt -jəl- ‖ 'kɔːrp jəl- **~ly** li

corpus, Corpus 'kɔːp əs ‖ 'kɔːrp- **~es** ɪz əz
ˌcorpus cal'losum kə 'ləʊs əm ‖ -'loʊs-;
ˌCorpus 'Christi 'krɪst i; ˌcorpus de'licti
di 'lɪkt aɪ də-, -iː; ˌcorpus 'luteum 'luːt i‿əm
‖ 'luːt̬-; ˌcorpus stri'atum straɪ 'eɪt əm
‖ -'eɪt̬-

corpus-based 'kɔːp əs beɪst ˌ· ᐧ'◄ ‖ 'kɔːrp-

corpuscle 'kɔːp ʌs ᵊl kɔː 'pʌs ᵊl ‖ 'kɔːrp- **~s** z

corpuscular kɔː 'pʌsk jʊl ə -jəl-
‖ kɔːr 'pʌsk jəl ᵊr

Corr kɔː ‖ kɔːr **Corrs** kɔːz ‖ kɔːrz

corral kə 'rɑːl kɒ- ‖ -'ræl (*may = chorale*) **~led**
d **~ling** ɪŋ **~s** z

correct kə 'rekt **~ed** ɪd əd **~ing** ɪŋ **~ly** li **~ness**
nəs nɪs **~s** s

correction kə 'rek ʃᵊn **~s** z

correctional kə 'rek ʃᵊn ᵊl

correctitude kə 'rekt ɪ tjuːd §-ə-, →§-tʃuːd
‖ -tuːd -tjuːd

corrective kə 'rekt ɪv **~ly** li **~s** z

corrector kə 'rekt ə ‖ -ᵊr **~s** z

Correggio kɒ 'redʒ i‿əʊ kə-, -'redʒ əʊ
‖ kə 'redʒ i‿oʊ -'redʒ oʊ —*It* [kor 'red dʒo]
~s, ~'s z

corre|late *v* 'kɒr ə |leɪt -ɪ- ‖ 'kɔːr- 'kɑːr-
~lated leɪt ɪd -əd ‖ leɪt̬ əd **~lates** leɪts
~lating leɪt ɪŋ ‖ leɪt̬ ɪŋ

correlate *n* 'kɒr ə leɪt -ɪ-; -əl ət, -ɪt ‖ 'kɔːr-
'kɑːr- **~s** s

correlation ˌkɒr ə 'leɪʃ ᵊn -ɪ- ‖ ˌkɔːr- ˌkɑːr- **~s**
z
ˌcorre'lation coef,ficient

correlative kə 'rel ət ɪv kɒ- ‖ -ət̬ ɪv **~ly** li
~ness nəs nɪs **~s** z

correspond ˌkɒr ə 'spɒnd -ɪ- ‖ ˌkɔːr ə 'spɑːnd
ˌkɑːr- **~ed** ɪd əd **~ing/ly** ɪŋ /li **~s** z

correspondenc|e ˌkɒr ə 'spɒnd ənᵗs -ɪ-
‖ ˌkɔːr ə 'spɑːnd- ˌkɑːr- **~es** ɪz əz
ˌcorre'spondence course

correspondent ˌkɒr ə 'spɒnd ənt -ɪ-
‖ ˌkɔːr ə 'spɑːnd- ˌkɑːr- **~ly** li **~s** s

corrida kɒ 'riːd ə kə- ‖ kɔː 'riːð ə —*Sp*
[ko 'rri ða] **~s** z

corridor 'kɒr ɪ dɔː -ə-; -ɪd ə, -əd- ‖ 'kɔːr əd ᵊr
'kɑːr-, -ə dɔːr **~s** z

corrie, C~ 'kɒr i ‖ 'kɔːr i 'kɑːr i **~s** z

Corriedale 'kɒr i deɪᵊl ‖ 'kɔːr- 'kɑːr- **~s** z

Corrigan 'kɒr ɪg ən -əg- ‖ 'kɔːr- 'kɑːr-

corrigend|um ˌkɒr ɪ 'dʒend |əm -ə-, -'gend-
‖ ˌkɔːr- ˌkɑːr- **~a** ə

Corris 'kɒr ɪs §-əs ‖ 'kɔːr- 'kɑːr-

corrobo|rate kə 'rɒb ə |reɪt ‖ -'rɑːb- **~rated**
reɪt ɪd -əd ‖ reɪt̬ əd **~rates** reɪts **~rating**
reɪt ɪŋ ‖ reɪt̬ ɪŋ

corroboration kə ˌrɒb ə 'reɪʃ ᵊn ‖ -ˌrɑːb- **~s** z

corroborative kə 'rɒb ər‿ət ɪv -ə reɪt-
‖ -'rɑːb ə reɪt̬ ɪv -ər‿ət̬ ɪv **~ly** li

corroborator kə 'rɒb ə reɪt ə ‖ -'rɑːb ə reɪt̬ ᵊr
~s z

corroboree kə 'rɒb ər i -ə riː ‖ -'rɑːb- **~s** z

corrod|e kə 'rəʊd ‖ -'roʊd **~ed** ɪd əd **~es** z
~ing ɪŋ

corrodible kə 'rəʊd əb ᵊl -ɪb- ‖ -'roʊd-

corrosion kə 'rəʊʒ ᵊn ‖ -'roʊʒ-

corrosive kə 'rəʊs ɪv -'rəʊz- ‖ -'roʊs- -'roʊz-
~ly li **~ness** nəs nɪs

corru|gate 'kɒr ə |geɪt -u-, -ju- ‖ 'kɔːr- 'kɑːr-
~gated geɪt ɪd -əd ‖ geɪt̬ əd **~gates** geɪts
~gating geɪt ɪŋ ‖ geɪt̬ ɪŋ

corrugation ˌkɒr ə 'geɪʃ ᵊn -u-, -ju- ‖ ˌkɔːr-
ˌkɑːr- **~s** z

corrupt kə 'rʌpt **~ed** ɪd əd **~ing** ɪŋ **~s** s

corruptibility kə ˌrʌpt ə 'bɪl ət i -ˌ·ɪ-, -ɪt i
‖ -ət̬ i

corruptib|le kə 'rʌpt əb |ᵊl -ɪb- **~ly** li

corruption kə 'rʌp ʃᵊn **~s** z

corruptive kə 'rʌpt ɪv **~ly** li

corrupt|ly kə 'rʌpt |li **~ness** nəs nɪs

corruptor kə 'rʌpt ə ‖ -ᵊr **~s** z

Corsa *tdmk* 'kɔːs ə ‖ 'kɔːrs ə

corsag|e ⁽₁⁾kɔː 'sɑːʒ ᐧ· ‖ ⁽₁⁾kɔːr- -'sɑːdʒ, ᐧ·· **~es**
ɪz əz

corsair 'kɔːs eə ⁽₁⁾kɔː 'seə ‖ 'kɔːrs er
⁽₁⁾kɔːr 'seᵊr **~s** z

corse kɔːs ‖ kɔːrs **corses** 'kɔːs ɪz -əz ‖ 'kɔːrs-

corselet 'kɔːs lət -lɪt ‖ 'kɔːrs- —*but for the
undergarment, properly* Corselette *tdmk,*
ˌkɔːs ə 'let ‖ ˌkɔːrs- **~s** s

cors|et 'kɔːs |ɪt §-ət ‖ 'kɔːrs |ət **~eted** ɪt ɪd
§ət-, -əd ‖ ət̬ əd **~eting** ɪt ɪŋ §ət- ‖ ət̬ ɪŋ **~ets**
ɪts §əts ‖ əts

corsetry 'kɔːs ɪtr i §-ətr- ‖ 'kɔːrs-

Corsica 'kɔːs ɪk ə ‖ 'kɔːrs-

Corsican 'kɔːs ɪk ən ‖ 'kɔːrs- **~s** z

Corstorphine kə 'stɔːf ɪn §-ᵊn ‖ kᵊr 'stɔːrf-

corteg|e, cortèg|e ˌkɔː ˈteɪʒ -ˈteʒ, ' · ·
‖ ˌkɔːr ˈteʒ —Fr [kɔʁ tɛːʒ] **~es** ɪz əz
Cortes *'parliament'* ˈkɔːt ez -ɪz, -es ‖ ˈkɔːrt-
Cortes, Cortés ˈkɔːt ez kɔː ˈtez ‖ kɔːr ˈtez
—Sp Cortés [kor ˈtes]
cortex ˈkɔːt eks ‖ ˈkɔːrt- **~es** ɪz əz **cortices**
ˈkɔːt ɪ siːz -ə- ‖ ˈkɔːrt̬-
Cortez ˈkɔːt ez kɔː ˈtez ‖ kɔːr ˈtez —Sp Cortés
[kor ˈtes]
Corti ˈkɔːt i ‖ ˈkɔːrt̬ i —It [ˈkor ti]
cortical ˈkɔːt ɪk ᵊl ‖ ˈkɔːrt̬-
cortices ˈkɔːt ɪ siːz -ə- ‖ ˈkɔːrt̬-
corticosteroid ˌkɔːt ɪk əʊ ˈstɪər ɔɪd
‖ ˌkɔːrt̬ ɪ koʊ ˈstɪr ɔɪd **~s** z
corticosterone ˌkɔːt ɪk əʊ ˈstɪər əʊn
-ɪ ˈkɒst ə rəʊn ‖ ˌkɔːrt̬ ɪ koʊ ˈstɪr oʊn
-ˈkaːst ə roʊn
Cortina kɔː ˈtiːn ə ‖ kɔːr- **~s** z
cortisone, C~ ˈkɔːt ɪ zəʊn -ə-, -səʊn
‖ ˈkɔːrt̬ ə zoʊn -soʊn
Cortland ˈkɔːt lənd ‖ ˈkɔːrt-
Corton ˈkɔːt ᵊn ‖ ˈkɔːrt ᵊn
corundum kə ˈrʌnd əm
Corunna kə ˈrʌn ə kɒ- —Sp La Coruña
[la ko ˈru ɲa], —Galician A Coruñha
[a ko ˈru ɲa]
coru|scate ˈkɒr ə |skeɪt ‖ ˈkɔːr- ˈkaːr- **~scated**
skeɪt ɪd -əd ‖ skeɪt̬ əd **~scates** skeɪts
~scating skeɪt ɪŋ ‖ skeɪt̬ ɪŋ
coruscation ˌkɒr ə ˈskeɪʃ ᵊn ‖ ˌkɔːr- ˌkaːr- **~s** z
corvee, corvée ˈkɔːv eɪ ‖ ˌkɔːr ˈveɪ ' · · —Fr
[kɔʁ ve] **~s** z
corvette ˌkɔː ˈvet ‖ ˌkɔːr- **~s** s
corvine ˈkɔːv aɪn ‖ ˈkɔːrv-
Corvo ˈkɔːv əʊ ‖ ˈkɔːrv oʊ
Corvus ˈkɔːv əs ‖ ˈkɔːrv-
Corwen ˈkɔː wən ‖ ˈkɔːr- —Welsh [ˈkor wen]
Cory ˈkɔːr i
corybant, C~ ˈkɒr ɪ bænt -ə- ‖ ˈkɔːr- **~s** s
corybantes, C~ ˌkɒr ɪ ˈbænt iːz -ə- ‖ ˌkɔːr-
Corydon ˈkɒr ɪd ən -əd, -ɒn ‖ ˈkɔːr-
corymb ˈkɒr ɪmb -ɪm, §-əm ‖ ˈkɔːr- ˈkaːr- **~s** z
coryphae|us ˌkɒr ɪ ˈfiː ˌ|əs -ə- ‖ ˌkɔːr- ˌkaːr- **~i**
aɪ iː
Coryton (i) ˈkɒr ɪt ən -ət- ‖ ˈkɔːr ət ᵊn, (ii)
ˈkɔːr- —in Devon, (i); in Essex, (ii)
coryza kə ˈraɪz ə
cos *'lettuce'* kɒs kɒz ‖ kaːs koʊs
cos *'cosine'* kɒz kɒs ‖ kaːs koʊs
cos *'because'* kəz kəs, occasional strong form
kɒz kɒs ‖ kaːz kɔːz
Cos island in Greece kɒs ‖ kaːs koʊs
Cosa Nostra ˌkəʊz ə ˈnɒs trə ‖ ˌkoʊs ə ˈnoʊs-
Cosby ˈkɒz bi ‖ ˈkaːz bi
cosec ˈkəʊ sek ‖ ˈkoʊ-
cosecant ˌkəʊ ˈsiːk ənt ‖ ˌkoʊ- -ænt **~s** s
cosech ˈkəʊ seʃ ‖ ˈkoʊ- —or as cosec h
coset ˈkəʊ set ‖ ˈkoʊ- **~s** s
Cosford ˈkɒs fəd ‖ ˈkaːs fᵊrd
Cosgrave ˈkɒz greɪv ‖ ˈkaːz-
cosh *'bludgeon'* kɒʃ ‖ kaːʃ **coshed** kɒʃt ‖ kaːʃt
coshes ˈkɒʃ ɪz -əz ‖ ˈkaːʃ əz **coshing** ˈkɒʃ ɪŋ
‖ ˈkaːʃ ɪŋ

cosh *'hyperbolic cosine'* kɒʃ ‖ kaːʃ —or as cos h
Cosham ˈkɒs əm ˈkɒʃ- ‖ ˈkaːs əm ˈkaːʃ-
Cosi Fan Tutte, Cosi Fan Tutte
ˌkəʊs i ˌfæn ˈtʊt i ˌkəʊz-, kəʊ ˌsiː-
‖ koʊ ˌsiː faːn ˈtuːt eɪ -ˈtʊt- —It
[ko ˌsif fan ˈtut te]
co-sign ˈkəʊ saɪn ‖ ˈkoʊ- **~ed** d **~er/s** ə/z
‖ ᵊr/z **~ing** ɪŋ **~s** z
cosignator|y ˌkəʊ ˈsɪg nət ər |i
‖ ˌkoʊ ˈsɪg nə tɔːr |i -tour i **~ies** iz
cosine ˈkəʊ saɪn ‖ ˈkoʊ- **~s** z
CoSIRA kəʊ ˈsaɪᵊr ə ‖ koʊ-
cosmetic kɒz ˈmet ɪk ‖ kaːz ˈmet̬ ɪk **~ally** ᵊl i
~s s
cos,metic 'surgery
cosmetician ˌkɒz mə ˈtɪʃ ᵊn -mɪ- ‖ ˌkaːz- **~s** z
cosmetolog|ist ˌkɒz mə ˈtɒl ədʒ ɪst -me-,
§-əst ‖ ˌkaːz mə ˈtaːl- **~ists** ɪsts §əsts **~y** i
cosmic ˈkɒz mɪk ‖ ˈkaːz- **~ally** ᵊl i
,cosmic 'ray
cosmo- comb. form
with stress-neutral suffix ˌkɒz məʊ ‖ ˌkaːz mə
-moʊ — **cosmographic** ˌkɒz məʊ ˈgræf ɪk ◂
‖ ˌkaːz mə-
with stress-imposing suffix kɒz ˈmɒ +
‖ kaːz ˈmaː + — **cosmographer**
kɒz ˈmɒg rəf ə ‖ kaːz ˈmaːg rəf ᵊr
Cosmo ˈkɒz məʊ ‖ ˈkaːz moʊ
cosmogon|y kɒz ˈmɒg ən |i ‖ kaːz ˈmaːg-
~ies iz
cosmography kɒz ˈmɒg rəf i ‖ kaːz ˈmaːg-
cosmological ˌkɒz məʊ ˈlɒdʒ ɪk ᵊl
‖ ˌkaːz mə ˈlaːdʒ- **~ly** i
cosmolog|y kɒz ˈmɒl ədʒ |i ‖ kaːz ˈmaːl- **~ies**
iz
cosmonaut ˈkɒz mə nɔːt ‖ ˈkaːz- -naːt **~s** s
cosmopolitan ˌkɒz mə ˈpɒl ɪt ən ◂
‖ ˌkaːz mə ˈpaːl ət ᵊn ◂ **~ism** ˌɪz əm **~s** z
cosmos ˈkɒz mɒs ‖ ˈkaːz məs -moʊs, -maːs
Cossack ˈkɒs æk ‖ ˈkaːs- -ək **~s** s
coss|et ˈkɒs |ɪt §-ət ‖ ˈkaːs |ət **~eted** ɪt ɪd §ət-,
-əd ‖ ət̬ əd **~eting** ɪt ɪŋ §ət- ‖ ət ɪŋ **~ets** ɪts
§əts ‖ əts
cossie ˈkɒz i ‖ ˈkaːz i **~s** z
cossie ˈkɒz i ‖ ˈkaːz i **~s** z
cost kɒst kɔːst ‖ kɔːst kaːst **costed** ˈkɒst ɪd
ˈkɔːst-, -əd ‖ ˈkɔːst əd ˈkaːst- **costing/s**
ˈkɒst ɪŋ/z ˈkɔːst- ‖ ˈkɔːst ɪŋ/z ˈkaːst- **costs**
kɒsts kɔːsts ‖ kɔːsts kaːsts
**,cost of 'living, ,cost of 'living ,index;
,cost 'price**
costa, Costa ˈkɒst ə ‖ ˈkoʊst ə ˈkaːst ə, ˈkɔːst ə
—See also phrases with this word —Sp
[ˈkos ta] **~s** z
,Costa 'Brava ˈbraːv ə —Sp [-ˈβra βa]
,Costa del 'Sol del ˈsɒl ‖ -ˈsoʊl —Sp
[-ðel ˈsol]
Costain (i) ˈkɒst eɪn ‖ ˈkaːst-, (ii) kɒ ˈsteɪn
‖ kaː-
costal ˈkɒst ᵊl ‖ ˈkaːst ᵊl
co-star ˈkəʊ staː ‖ ˈkoʊ staːr **~red** d
co-starring ˈkəʊ staːr ɪŋ ‖ ˈkoʊ- **~s** z
costard ˈkʌst əd ˈkɒst- ‖ ˈkaːst ᵊrd **~s** z

Costard 'kɒst əd -ɑːd ‖ 'kɑːst ᵊrd
Costa Ric|a ˌkɒst ə 'riːk |ə ‖ ˌkoʊst- ˌkɔːst-,
ˌkɑːst- —*Sp* [ˌkos ta 'rri ka] **~an/s** ən/z
cost-benefit ˌkɒst 'ben ɪf ɪt -əf-, §-ət ‖ ˌkɔːst-
ˌkɑːst-
cost-effective ˌkɒst ɪ 'fekt ɪv ◀ ˌkɔːst-, -ə-,
'· ·, · · ‖ ˌkɔːst- ˌkɑːst- **~ly** li **~ness** nəs nɪs
Costello (i) kɒ 'stel əʊ kə- ‖ kɑː 'stel oʊ, (ii)
'kɒst əl əʊ -ɪl- ‖ 'kɑːst ə loʊ —*In Ireland*
usually (ii), *elsewhere* (i)
costermonger 'kɒst ə ˌmʌŋ gə
‖ 'kɑːst ᵊr ˌmʌŋ gᵊr -ˌmɑːŋ- **~s** z
Costessey *place in Norfolk* 'kɒs i ‖ 'kɑːs i (!)
costive 'kɒst ɪv ‖ 'kɑːst- 'kɔːst- **~ly** li **~ness**
nəs nɪs
cost|ly 'kɒst |li 'kɔːst- ‖ 'kɔːst |li 'kɑːst- **~lier**
li ə ‖ li ᵊr **~liest** li ˌɪst li ˌəst **~liness** li nəs
li nɪs
costmary 'kɒst ˌmeər i ‖ 'kɔːst ˌmer i 'kɑːst-
Costner 'kɒst nə ‖ 'kɑːst nᵊr
cost-plus ˌkɒst 'plʌs ◀ ˌkɔːst- ‖ ˌkɔːst- ˌkɑːst-
cost-push ˌkɒst 'pʊʃ ˌkɔːst- ‖ ˌkɔːst- ˌkɑːst-

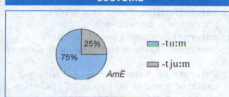

25%

75%

■ -tuːm

■ -tjuːm

AmE

costume *n, adj* 'kɒs tjuːm →-tʃuːm, →'kɒʃ-
‖ 'kɑːs tuːm -tjuːm **~d** d **~s** z — *Preference*
poll, AmE: -tuːm 75%, -tjuːm 25%.
'costume ˌjewellery
costumier kɒ 'stjuːm i ə →§-'stʃuːm-, -i eɪ
‖ kɑː 'stuːm i eɪ -'stjuːm-, -ᵊr **~s** z
cos|y 'kəʊz |i ‖ 'koʊz |i **~ier** i ə ‖ i ᵊr **~ies** iz
~iest i ˌɪst i ˌəst **~ily** ɪ li ə l i **~iness** i nəs i nɪs
cot kɒt ‖ kɑːt **cots** kɒts ‖ kɑːts
'cot death
cotan 'kəʊ tæn ‖ 'koʊ-
cotangent ˌkəʊ 'tændʒ ənt '· ·, · · ‖ ˌkoʊ- **~s** s
cotanh 'kəʊ θæn -tænʃ ‖ 'koʊ- —*or as* cotan h
cote kəʊt ‖ koʊt (= *coat*) —*formerly also* kɒt
‖ kɑːt **cotes** kəʊts ‖ koʊts
Cote d'Azur, Côte d'Azur ˌkəʊt də 'zjʊə -dæ-
‖ ˌkoʊt də 'zʊᵊr —*Fr* [kot da zyʁ]
Cote d'Ivoire, Côte d'Ivoire ˌkəʊt diː 'vwɑː
‖ ˌkoʊt diː 'vwɑːr —*Fr* [kot di vwaʁ]
coterie 'kəʊt ᵊr i ˌkəʊt ə 'riː ‖ 'koʊt ᵊr i
ˌkoʊt ə 'riː **~s** z
coterminous ₍ˌ₎kəʊ 'tɜːm ɪn əs -ən-
‖ ₍ˌ₎koʊ 'tɜːm- **~ly** li
coth kɒθ ‖ kɑːθ -*or as* cot h
Cothi 'kɒθ i ‖ 'kɑːθ i 'kɔːθ-
cothurn|us kəʊ 'θɜːn |əs kɒ- ‖ koʊ 'θɜːn |əs
~i aɪ
cotillion kə 'tɪl i ˌən kəʊ-, kɒ- ‖ koʊ- **~s** z
cotinga kəʊ 'tɪŋ gə ‖ koʊ-
Coton 'kəʊt ᵊn ‖ 'koʊt ᵊn

cotoneaster kə ˌtəʊn i 'æst ə
‖ -'toʊn i ˌæst ᵊr —*There is also a spelling*
pronunciation, considered incorrect,
ˌkɒt ᵊn 'iːst ə ‖ 'kɑːt ᵊn ˌiːst ᵊr **~s** z
Cotopaxi ˌkɒt ə 'pæks i ˌkəʊt-, -əʊ- ‖ ˌkoʊt ə-
-'pɑːks i —*Sp* [ko to 'pak si]
Cotswold 'kɒts wəʊld →-wɒʊld, -wəld
‖ 'kɑːts woʊld **~s** z
cotta 'kɒt ə ‖ 'kɑːt ə **~s** z
cottag|e 'kɒt ɪdʒ ‖ 'kɑːt ɪdʒ **~ed** d **~es** ɪz əz
~ing ɪŋ
ˌcottage 'cheese ‖ '· · ·; ˌcottage 'hospital;
ˌcottage 'industry; ˌcottage 'loaf;
ˌcottage 'pie
cottager 'kɒt ɪdʒ ə ‖ 'kɑːt ɪdʒ ᵊr **~s** z
cottar 'kɒt ə ‖ 'kɑːt ᵊr **~s** z
Cottenham 'kɒt ən ˌəm ‖ 'kɑːt ᵊn ˌəm
cotter, C~ 'kɒt ə ‖ 'kɑːt ᵊr **~s** z
Cotterell 'kɒtr əl ‖ 'kɑːtr-
Cottesloe 'kɒts ləʊ 'kɒt əz ləʊ ‖ 'kɑːts loʊ
'kɑːt əz loʊ
Cottesmore 'kɒts mɔː ‖ 'kɑːts mɔːr -moʊr
Cottle 'kɒt ᵊl ‖ 'kɑːt ᵊl
cotton, C~ 'kɒt ᵊn ‖ 'kɑːt ᵊn **~s** z
ˌcotton 'candy; 'cotton gin; 'cotton
grass; ˌcotton 'waste; ˌcotton 'wool◀
cotton-picking 'kɒt ᵊn ˌpɪk ɪŋ ‖ 'kɑːt-
cottonseed 'kɒt ᵊn siːd ‖ 'kɑːt-
cottontail 'kɒt ᵊn teᵊl ‖ 'kɑːt- **~s** z
cottonwood 'kɒt ᵊn wʊd ‖ 'kɑːt- **~s** z
cottony 'kɒt ᵊn i ‖ 'kɑːt-
cotyledon ˌkɒt ɪ 'liːd ᵊn -ə-; -ᵊl 'iːd-
‖ ˌkɑːt ᵊl 'iːd ᵊn **~ous** əs **~s** z
coucal 'kuːk ᵊl 'kʊk-, -æl, -ɑːl **~s** z
couch kaʊtʃ —*but in*
'couch grass *also* kuːtʃ **couched** kaʊtʃt
couches 'kaʊtʃ ɪz -əz **couching** 'kaʊtʃ ɪŋ
Couch kuːtʃ
couchant 'kaʊtʃ ənt 'kuːʃ ᵊnt
couchette ₍ˌ₎kuː 'ʃet **~s** s
Coué 'kuː eɪ ‖ ku 'eɪ —*Fr* [kwe, ku e]
cougar 'kuːg ə -ɑː ‖ -ᵊr **~s** z
cough kɒf kɔːf ‖ kɔːf kɑːf **coughed** kɒft kɔːft
‖ kɔːft kɑːft **coughing** 'kɒf ɪŋ 'kɔːf- ‖ 'kɔːf ɪŋ
'kɑːf- **coughs** kɒfs kɔːfs ‖ kɔːfs kɑːfs
'cough drop; 'cough ˌmixture
Coughlan (i) 'kɒf lən 'kɒx-, 'kɒk- ‖ 'kɔːf-
'kɑːf-, 'koʊk-, (ii) 'kɒg lən ‖ 'kɔːg- 'kɑːg-,
(iii) 'kəʊl ən ‖ 'koʊl ən
Coughton (i) 'kəʊt ᵊn ‖ 'koʊt-, (ii) 'kaʊt ᵊn
could *strong form* kʊd, *occasional weak form*
kəd
couldn't 'kʊd ᵊnt —*There is also a form*
'kʊd ᵊn, *in standard speech used mainly before*
a consonant. This word has no weak form.
couldst kʊdst
coulee 'kuːl i -eɪ **~s** z
coulis *sing.* 'kuːl i ‖ ku 'liː **coulis** *pl* 'kuːl iz -i
‖ ku 'liːz -'liː —*Fr* [ku li]
coulomb, C~ 'kuːl ɒm ‖ -ɑːm -oʊm —*Fr*
[ku lɔ̃] **~s** z
Coulsdon 'kuːlz dən 'kəʊlz-

Coulson (i) 'kəʊls ᵊn →'kɒʊls- ‖ 'koʊls ᵊn, (ii) 'kuːls ᵊn
Coulston 'kuːlst ən
coulter 'kəʊlt ə →'kɒʊlt-, 'kuːt- ‖ 'koʊlt ᵊr ~s z
Coulthard (i) 'kuːlt ɑːd ‖ -ɑːrd, (ii) 'kəʊlθ- →'kɒʊlθ- ‖ 'koʊlθ-
Coulton 'kəʊlt ən →'kɒʊlt- ‖ 'koʊlt ᵊn
coumarin 'kuːm ər ɪn §-ən
council 'kaʊn⟨t⟩s ᵊl -ɪl (usually = counsel) ~s z ¦Council 'Bluffs; 'council house; 'council tax
councillor, councilor 'kaʊn⟨t⟩s ᵊl̩ə -ɪl- ‖ ər ~s z
council|man 'kaʊn⟨t⟩s ᵊl |mən -ɪl-, -mæn ~men mən men ~woman ˌwʊm ən ~women ˌwɪm ɪn -ən
counsel 'kaʊn⟨t⟩s ᵊl ~ed, ~led d ~ing, ~ling ɪŋ ~s z
counsellor, counselor 'kaʊn⟨t⟩s ᵊl̩ə ‖ ər ~s z ~ship ʃɪp
count kaʊnt **counted** 'kaʊnt ɪd -əd ‖ 'kaʊnt̬ əd **counting** 'kaʊnt ɪŋ ‖ 'kaʊnt̬ ɪŋ **counts** kaʊnts 'count noun
countab|le 'kaʊnt əb |ᵊl ‖ 'kaʊnt̬- ~ly li
countdown 'kaʊnt daʊn ~s z
countenanc|e 'kaʊnt ən ən⟨t⟩s -ɪn- ‖ -ᵊn̩ən⟨t⟩s ~ed t ~es ɪz əz ~ing ɪŋ
counter 'kaʊnt ə ‖ 'kaʊnt̬ ᵊr ~ed d **countering** 'kaʊnt ər ɪŋ ‖ 'kaʊnt̬ ər ɪŋ ~s z
counter- prefix ¦kaʊnt ə ‖ ¦kaʊnt̬ ᵊr —In context, this prefix often bears a contrastive nuclear accent (not shown in the entries below).
counteract ˌkaʊnt ər 'ækt -ə 'rækt ‖ ˌkaʊnt̬ ər- ~ed ɪd əd ~ing ɪŋ ~s s
counteraction ˌkaʊnt ər 'æk ʃᵊn -ə 'ræk-, '···· ‖ ˌkaʊnt̬ ər- ~s z
counterattack v, n 'kaʊnt ər ə ˌtæk ˌ···'· ‖ 'kaʊnt̬ ər- ~ed t ~ing ɪŋ ~s s
counterattraction ˌkaʊnt ər ə 'træk ʃᵊn '···,·· ‖ ˌkaʊnt̬ ər- ~s z
counterbalanc|e v 'kaʊnt ə 'bæl ən⟨t⟩s ‖ ˌkaʊnt̬ ᵊr-, ~ed t ~es ɪz əz ~ing ɪŋ
counterbalanc|e n 'kaʊnt ə ˌbæl ən⟨t⟩s ‖ 'kaʊnt̬ ᵊr- ~es ɪz əz
counterbid 'kaʊnt ə bɪd ‖ 'kaʊnt̬ ᵊr- ~ding ɪŋ ~s z
counterblast 'kaʊnt ə blɑːst §-blæst ‖ 'kaʊnt̬ ᵊr blæst ~s s
countercharg|e v, n 'kaʊnt ə tʃɑːdʒ ‖ 'kaʊnt̬ ᵊr tʃɑːrdʒ ~ed d ~es ɪz əz ~ing ɪŋ
counterclaim v, n 'kaʊnt ə kleɪm ‖ 'kaʊnt̬ ᵊr- ~ed d ~ing ɪŋ ~s z
counterclockwise ˌkaʊnt ə 'klɒk waɪz ‖ ˌkaʊnt̬ ᵊr 'klɑːk-
counterculture 'kaʊnt ə ˌkʌltʃ ə ‖ 'kaʊn t̬ ᵊr ˌkʌltʃ ᵊr
counterespionage ˌkaʊnt ər 'esp i ə nɑːʒ -nɑːdʒ, -nɪdʒ ‖ ˌkaʊnt̬ ər-
counterexample 'kaʊnt ər ɪg ˌzɑːmp ᵊl -eg,-, -ɪk,-, §-ˌzæmp- ‖ 'kaʊn t̬ ᵊr ɪg ˌzæmpᵊl ~s z

counterfactual ˌkaʊnt ə 'fæk tʃu əl -'fæk tju əl ‖ ˌkaʊnt̬ ᵊr- -ʃu əl, -'fæk tʃə l ~ly i ~s z
counter|feit 'kaʊnt ə |fɪt -fiːt ‖ 'kaʊnt̬ ᵊr- ~feited fɪt ɪd fiːt-, -əd ‖ fɪt̬ əd ~feiting fɪt ɪŋ fiːt- ‖ fɪt̬ ɪŋ ~feits fɪts fiːts
counterfoil 'kaʊnt ə fɔɪᵊl ‖ 'kaʊnt̬ ᵊr- ~s z
counterinflationary ˌkaʊnt ər ɪn 'fleɪʃ ᵊn ər i ◂ -ᵊn ᵊr- ‖ ˌkaʊnt̬ ᵊr ɪn 'fleɪʃ ə ner i ◂
counterinsurgency ˌkaʊnt ər ɪn 'sɜːdʒ ən⟨t⟩s i ‖ ˌkaʊnt̬ ər ɪn 'sɜːdʒ-
counterintelligence ˌkaʊnt ər ɪn 'tel ɪdʒ ən⟨t⟩s -ədʒ ən⟨t⟩s, '···· ‖ ˌkaʊnt̬ ər-
counterintuitive ˌkaʊnt ər ɪn 'tjuː ət ɪv ◂ →§-'tʃuː- ‖ ˌkaʊnt̬ ər ɪn 'tuː ət̬ ɪv -'tjuː- ~ly li
counterirritant ˌkaʊnt ər 'ɪr ɪt ənt §-ət ənt ‖ ˌkaʊnt̬ ər 'ɪr ət ᵊnt ~s s
countermand ˌkaʊnt ə 'mɑːnd §-'mænd, '··· ‖ 'kaʊnt̬ ᵊr mænd ˌ·'· ~ed ɪd əd ~ing ɪŋ ~s z
countermarch 'kaʊnt ə mɑːtʃ ‖ 'kaʊnt̬ ᵊr mɑːrtʃ ~ed t ~es ɪz əz ~ing ɪŋ
countermeasure 'kaʊnt ə ˌmeʒ ə ‖ 'kaʊnt̬ ᵊr ˌmeʒ ᵊr -ˌmeɪʒ- ~s z
counteroffensive ˌkaʊnt ər ə 'fen⟨t⟩s ɪv '···,·· ‖ 'kaʊnt̬ ər ə ˌfen⟨t⟩s ɪv ~s z
counterpane 'kaʊnt ə peɪn ‖ 'kaʊnt̬ ᵊr- ~s z
counterpart 'kaʊnt ə pɑːt ‖ 'kaʊnt̬ ᵊr pɑːrt ~s s
counter|point 'kaʊnt ə |pɔɪnt ‖ 'kaʊnt̬ ᵊr- ~pointed pɔɪnt ɪd -əd ‖ pɔɪnt̬ əd ~pointing pɔɪnt ɪŋ ‖ pɔɪnt̬ ɪŋ ~points pɔɪnts
counterpois|e 'kaʊnt ə pɔɪz ‖ 'kaʊnt̬ ᵊr- ~ed d ~es ɪz əz ~ing ɪŋ
counterpresuppositional ˌkaʊnt ə ˌpriː sʌp ə 'zɪʃ ᵊn əl ‖ ˌkaʊnt̬ ᵊr- s z
counterproductive ˌkaʊnt ə prə 'dʌkt ɪv ◂ ‖ ˌkaʊnt̬ ᵊr- ~ly li ~ness nəs nɪs
counterproposal 'kaʊnt ə prə ˌpəʊz ᵊl ‖ 'kaʊnt̬ ᵊr prə ˌpoʊz ᵊl ~s z
Counter-Reformation ˌkaʊnt ə ˌref ə 'meɪʃ ᵊn ‖ ˌkaʊnt̬ ᵊr ˌref ᵊr-
counterrevolution ˌkaʊnt ə ˌrev ə 'luːʃ ᵊn -'ljuːʃ-, '····,·· ‖ ˌkaʊnt̬ ᵊr- ~s z
counterrevolutionar|y ˌkaʊnt ə ˌrev ə 'luːʃ ᵊn_ər |i -'ljuːʃ-, -ᵊn ər_|i, '····,·· ‖ ˌkaʊnt̬ ᵊr rev ə 'luːʃ ə ner |i ~ies iz
countersank 'kaʊnt ə sæŋk ˌ·'· ‖ 'kaʊnt̬ ᵊr-
countershaft 'kaʊnt ə ʃɑːft §-ʃæft ‖ 'kaʊnt̬ ᵊr ʃæft ~s s
countersign n 'kaʊnt ə saɪn ‖ 'kaʊnt̬ ᵊr- ~s z
countersign v 'kaʊnt ə saɪn ˌ·'· ‖ 'kaʊnt̬ ᵊr- ~ed d ~ing ɪŋ ~s z
counter|sink 'kaʊnt ə sɪŋk ˌ·'· ‖ 'kaʊnt̬ ᵊr- ~sank sæŋk ~sinking sɪŋk ɪŋ ~sunk sʌŋk
countertenor 'kaʊnt ə 'ten ə '··,·· ‖ 'kaʊnt̬ ᵊr ˌten ᵊr ~s z
counterterror|ist ˌkaʊnt ə 'ter ər |ɪst -|əst ‖ ˌkaʊnt̬ ᵊr- ~ism ˌɪz əm
countervail ˌkaʊnt ə 'verᵊl '··· ˌkaʊnt̬ ᵊr- ~ed d ~ing ɪŋ ~s z
counterweight 'kaʊnt ə weɪt ‖ 'kaʊnt̬ ᵊr- ~s s

countess 'kaʊnt ɪs -es, -əs, ˌkaʊn 'tes
∥ 'kaʊnt̬ əs **~es** ɪz əz
counti... —*see* **county**
counting|house 'kaʊnt ɪŋ |haʊs ∥ 'kaʊnt̬ ɪŋ-
~houses haʊz ɪz -əz
countless 'kaʊnt ləs -lɪs
countrified 'kʌntr i faɪd
countr|y 'kʌntr |i **~ies** iz
  ˌcountry and 'western; ˌcountry
  'bumpkin; 'country club; ˌcountry
  'cousin; ˌcountry 'dance ∥ '· · ·; ˌcountry
  'house; ˌcountry 'seat
country|man 'kʌntr i |mən **~men** mən
countryside 'kʌntr i saɪd
countrywide ˌkʌntr i 'waɪd ◂ '· · ·
country|woman 'kʌntr i |ˌwʊm ən **~women**
  ˌwɪm ɪn §-ən
count|y 'kaʊnt |i ∥ 'kaʊnt̬ |i **~ies** iz
  ˌcounty 'council; ˌcounty 'court; ˌcounty
  'town
coup ku: (!) **coups** ku:z —*See also phrases with*
  this word
coup de grace, coup de grâce
  ˌku: də 'grɑːs —*Fr* [kud grɑs]
coup d'état ˌku: deɪ 'tɑː —*Fr* [ku de ta]
coup de théâtre ˌku: də teɪ 'ɑːtr ə —*Fr*
  [kud te ɑːtχ]
coupe '*dish*' ku:p **~s** s
coupe, coupé '*vehicle*' 'ku:p eɪ ∥ ku: 'peɪ ku:p
  coupes, coupés 'ku:p eɪz ∥ ku: 'peɪz ku:ps
Couper 'ku:p ə ∥ -ᵊr
Couperin 'ku:p ə ræn -ræ̃ —*Fr* [ku pʁæ̃]
Coupland (i) 'ku:p lənd, (ii) 'kəʊp-
coupl|e 'kʌp ᵊl **~ed** d **~es** z **~ing** ɪŋ
coupler 'kʌp lə ∥ -lᵊr **~s** z
couplet 'kʌp lət -lɪt **~s** s
coupling *n* 'kʌp lɪŋ **~s** z
coupling *pres part of* **couple** 'kʌp ᵊl ɪŋ

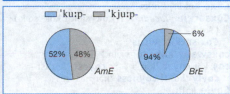

COUPON

□ 'ku:p- □ 'kju:p-

—6%

52% 48%
AmE

94%
BrE

coupon 'ku:p ɒn ⚠ 'kju:p- ∥ -ɑːn **~s** z
  — *Preference polls, AmE:* 'ku:p- *52%,* 'kju:p-
  48%; BrE: 'ku:p- *94%,* 'kju:p- *6%.*
coups ku:z —*In French phrases usually* ku:, *as*
  singular —*Fr* [ku] —*See* **coup**
courage, C~ 'kʌr ɪdʒ ∥ 'kɝː ɪdʒ
courageous kə 'reɪdʒ əs **~ly** li **~ness** nəs nɪs
Courbet 'kʊə beɪ 'kɔː- ∥ kʊr 'beɪ —*Fr* [kuʁ bɛ]
courgette �ₒkɔː 'ʒet ⚠kʊə- ∥ kʊr- **~s** s
courier 'kʊr i ə 'kʊər-, 'kʌr- ∥ 'kɝː i ᵊr 'kʊr- **~s**
  z
Courland 'kʊə lənd -lænd ∥ 'kʊr-
Courrèges ku 'reʒ -'reɪʒ —*Fr* [ku ʁɛːʒ]

course kɔːs ∥ kɔːrs koʊrs (= *coarse*) **coursed**
  kɔːst ∥ kɔːrst koʊrst **courses** 'kɔːs ɪz -əz
  ∥ 'kɔːrs əz 'koʊrs- **coursing** 'kɔːs ɪŋ
  ∥ 'kɔːrs ɪŋ 'koʊrs-
coursebook 'kɔːs bʊk §-buːk ∥ 'kɔːrs- **~s** s
courser 'kɔːs ə ∥ 'kɔːrs ᵊr 'koʊrs- **~s** z
coursework 'kɔːs wɜːk ∥ 'kɔːrs wɝːk 'koʊrs-
court, Court kɔːt ∥ kɔːrt koʊrt **courted**
  'kɔːt ɪd -əd ∥ 'kɔːrt̬ əd 'koʊrt̬- **courting**
  'kɔːt ɪŋ ∥ 'kɔːrt̬ ɪŋ 'koʊrt̬- **courts** kɔːts
  ∥ kɔːrts koʊrts
  'court card; ˌcourt 'circular; 'court shoe
Courtauld 'kɔːt əʊld →-ɒʊld, -əʊ ∥ 'kɔːrt oʊld
  'koʊrt-
court-bouillon ˌkɔːt 'buː jɒn ˌkʊət-, ˌkʊə-
  ∥ ˌkɔːr 'buːl jɑːn —*Fr* [kuʁ bu jɔ̃]
Courtelle *tdmk* ⚠kɔː 'tel ∥ ⚠kɔːr- ⚠koʊr-
Courtenay 'kɔːt ni ∥ 'kɔːrt̬- 'koʊrt̬-
courteous 'kɜːt i əs 'kɔːt- ∥ 'kɝːt̬- **~ly** li **~ness**
  nəs nɪs
courtesan ˌkɔːt ɪ 'zæn -ə-, '· · · ∥ 'kɔːrt̬ əz ən
  'koʊrt̬-, -ə zæn **~s** z
courtes|y 'kɜːt əs |i 'kɔːt-, -ɪs- ∥ 'kɝːt̬- **~ies** iz
  'courtesy car; 'courtesy light; 'courtesy
  ˌtitle
court|house 'kɔːt |haʊs ∥ 'kɔːrt̬- 'koʊrt̬-
  ~houses haʊz ɪz -əz
courtier 'kɔːt i ə 'kɔːt jə ∥ 'kɔːrt̬ i ᵊr 'koʊrt̬-;
  'kɔːrtʃ ᵊr, 'koʊrtʃ- **~s** z
court|ly 'kɔːt |li ∥ 'kɔːrt̬- 'koʊrt̬- **~liness** li nəs
  li nɪs
court-martial ˌkɔːt 'mɑːʃ ᵊl ◂ ∥ 'kɔːrt ˌmɑːrʃ ᵊl
  'koʊrt-, ˌ·'·· **courts-martial** ˌkɔːts 'mɑːʃ ᵊl
  ∥ 'kɔːrts ˌmɑːrʃ ᵊl 'koʊrts-, ˌ·'··
Courtneidge 'kɔːt nɪdʒ ∥ 'kɔːrt̬- 'koʊrt̬-
Courtney 'kɔːt ni ∥ 'kɔːrt̬- 'koʊrt̬-
courtroom 'kɔːt ruːm -rʊm ∥ 'kɔːrt̬- 'koʊrt̬- **~s**
  z
courtship 'kɔːt ʃɪp ∥ 'kɔːrt̬- 'koʊrt̬-
courts-martial —*see* **court-martial**
courtyard 'kɔːt jɑːd ∥ 'kɔːrt jɑːrd 'koʊrt- **~s** z
Courvoisier *tdmk* ⚠kʊə 'vwæz i eɪ -'vwɑːz-
  ∥ ˌkɔːrv wɑːs i 'eɪ —*Fr* [kuʁ vwa zje] **~s** z
couscous 'kuːs kuːs
cousin 'kʌz ᵊn **~s** z
Cousins 'kʌz ᵊnz
Cousteau 'kuːst əʊ ∥ ku 'stoʊ —*Fr* [ku sto]
couth kuːθ
Coutts kuːts
couture ku 'tjʊə -'tʊə, →§-'tʃʊə ∥ -'tʊr -'tjʊr
  —*Fr* [ku ty:ʁ]
couturier ku 'tjʊər i eɪ -'tʊər-, →§-'tʃʊər-, -i ə
  ∥ -'tʊr- -i ᵊr **~s** z
couvade ⚠kuː 'vɑːd
covalenc|y ˌkəʊ 'veɪl ᵊnᵗs |i '·ˌ··· ∥ ˌkoʊ- **~ies**
  iz
covalent ˌkəʊ 'veɪl ᵊnt ◂ ∥ ˌkoʊ- **~ly** li
  ˌcoˌvalent 'bond
covariance ˌkəʊ 'veər i ᵊnᵗs '·ˌ··· ∥ ˌkoʊ 'ver-
  -'vær-
cove, Cove kəʊv ∥ koʊv **coves** kəʊvz ∥ koʊvz
coven 'kʌv ᵊn **~s** z
covenant *n* 'kʌv ᵊn ənt **~s** s

C

C

coven|ant *v* 'kʌv ən ˌ|ənt ‖ -ə n|ænt **~anted**
ənt ɪd -əd ‖ əɲ əd æɲ əd **~anting** ənt ɪŋ
‖ əɲ ɪŋ æɲ ɪŋ **~ants** ənts ‖ ænts

covenanter, covenantor, C~ 'kʌv ən ˌ|ənt ə
ˌkʌv ə 'nænt ə, ˌkʌv ə næn 'tɔː
‖ 'kʌv ə næɲ ᵊr ˌ·'·ˌ·, ˌkʌv ə næn 'tɔːr **~s** z

Covent 'kɒv ᵊnt 'kʌv- ‖ 'kʌv- 'kɑːv-
ˌCovent 'Garden◄

Coventry 'kɒv ᵊntr i 'kʌv- ‖ 'kʌv- 'kɑːv-

cover 'kʌv ə ‖ -ᵊr **covered** 'kʌv əd ‖ -ᵊrd
covering 'kʌv ər ɪŋ **covers** 'kʌv əz ‖ -ᵊrz
'cover charge; ˌcovered 'wagon; 'cover
girl; 'cover ˌletter; 'cover note; ˌcover
'point

Coverack *(i)* 'kʌv ə ræk -ər ək, *(ii)* 'kɒv-
‖ 'kɑːv-

coverage 'kʌv ər ɪdʒ

coverall 'kʌv ər ɔːl ‖ -ər ɔːl -ɑːl **~s** z

Coverdale 'kʌv ə deɪᵊl ‖ -ᵊr-

covering 'kʌv ər ɪŋ **~s** z
ˌcovering 'letter

cover|let 'kʌv ə |lət -lɪt ‖ -ᵊr- -lɪd **~lets** ləts lɪts
‖ lɪdz

Coverley 'kʌv ə li ‖ -ᵊr-

covermount 'kʌv ə maʊnt ‖ -rᵊ- **~s** s

covert *n* 'kʌv ət -ə ‖ -ᵊrt 'koʊ vɜːt **~s** s

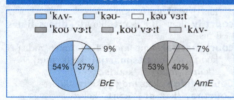

COVERT

☐ 'kʌv-   ☐ 'kəʊ-   ☐ ˌkəʊ 'vɜːt
☐ 'koʊ vɜːt   ☐ ˌkoʊ'vɜːt   ☐ 'kʌv-

BrE: 9% pie chart 54% 37%
AmE: 7% pie chart 53% 40%

BrE   AmE

covert *adj* 'kʌv ət 'kəʊ vɜːt, ˌkəʊ 'vɜːt ◄
‖ 'koʊ vɜːt ˌ·'·; 'kʌv ᵊrt — *Preference polls,*
BrE: 'kʌv- 54%, 'kəʊ- 37%, ˌkəʊ 'vɜːt 9%;
AmE: 'koʊ vɜːt 53%, ˌkoʊ 'vɜːt 40%, 'kʌv-
7%. **~ly** li **~ness** nəs nɪs

cover-up 'kʌv ər ʌp ‖ -ər ʌp **~s** s

cov|et 'kʌv |ɪt -ət ‖ -|ət **~eted** ɪt ɪd §ət-, -əd
‖ əɲ əd **~eting** ɪt ɪŋ §ət- ‖ əɲ ɪŋ **~ets** ɪts §əts
‖ əts

covetable 'kʌv ɪt əb ᵊl '·ət- ‖ '·əɲ-

covetous 'kʌv ɪt əs -ət- ‖ -əɲ əs **~ly** li **~ness**
nəs nɪs

covey 'kʌv i **~s** z

coving 'kəʊv ɪŋ ‖ 'koʊv ɪŋ

cow, Cow kaʊ **cows** kaʊz
ˌcow 'parsley

cowabunga ˌkaʊ ə 'bʌŋ gə

cowage 'kaʊ ɪdʒ

Cowan 'kaʊ ən

coward, C~ 'kaʊ əd ‖ 'kaʊ ᵊrd **~s** z

cowardice 'kaʊ əd ɪs §-əs ‖ 'kaʊ ᵊrd-

coward|ly 'kaʊ əd |li ‖ 'kaʊ ᵊrd- **~liness**
li nəs li nɪs

cowbell 'kaʊ bel **~s** z

cowberr|y 'kaʊ bər ˌ|i -ˌber |i ‖ -ˌber |i **~ies** iz

cowbird 'kaʊ bɜːd ‖ -bɜːd **~s** z

cowboy 'kaʊ bɔɪ **~s** z

Cowbridge 'kaʊ brɪdʒ

cowcatcher 'kaʊ ˌkætʃ ə ‖ -ᵊr §-ˌketʃ- **~s** z

Cowdenbeath ˌkaʊd ᵊn 'biːθ

Cowdray, Cowdrey 'kaʊdr i -eɪ

cowed kaʊd

Cowell *(i)* 'kaʊ əl kaʊl ‖ 'kaʊ ˌəl, *(ii)* 'kəʊ əl
‖ 'koʊ əl

Cowen *(i)* 'kaʊ ən -ɪn, *(ii)* 'kəʊ- ‖ 'koʊ-

cower 'kaʊ ə ‖ 'kaʊ ᵊr **cowered** 'kaʊ əd
‖ 'kaʊ ᵊrd **cowering** 'kaʊ ər ɪŋ ‖ 'kaʊ ᵊr ɪŋ
cowers 'kaʊ əz ‖ 'kaʊ ᵊrz

Cowes kaʊz

Cowgill 'kaʊ gɪl

cowgirl 'kaʊ gɜːl ‖ -gɜːl **~s** z

cowhand 'kaʊ hænd **~s** z

cowheel 'kaʊ hiːᵊl

cowherd 'kaʊ hɜːd ‖ -hɜːd **~s** z

cowhide 'kaʊ haɪd **~s** z

Cowie 'kaʊ i

cowl kaʊl **cowled** kaʊld **cowling** 'kaʊl ɪŋ
cowls kaʊlz

Cowley 'kaʊl i

cowlick 'kaʊ lɪk **~s** s

cowling, C~ 'kaʊl ɪŋ **~s** z

cow|man 'kaʊ |mən -mæn **~men** mən men

co-worker ˌkəʊ 'wɜːk ə ˌ·'·ˌ· ‖ 'koʊ ˌwɜːk ᵊr **~s**
z

cowpat 'kaʊ pæt **~s** s

Cowper *(i)* 'kuːp ə ‖ -ᵊr, *(ii)* 'kaʊp-

cowpoke 'kaʊ pəʊk ‖ -poʊk **~s** s

cowpox 'kaʊ pɒks ‖ -pɑːks

cowrie, cowry 'kaʊᵊr i **cowries** 'kaʊᵊr iz

cowshed 'kaʊ ʃed **~s** z

cowslip 'kaʊ slɪp **~s** s

cowtown 'kaʊ taʊn **~s** z

cox, Cox kɒks ‖ kɑːks *(= cocks)* **coxed** kɒkst
‖ kɑːkst **coxes, Cox's** 'kɒks ɪz -əz ‖ 'kɑːks əz
coxing 'kɒks ɪŋ ‖ 'kɑːks ɪŋ **Cox's** 'kɒks ɪz
-əz ‖ 'kɑːks əz

coxalgia kɒk 'sældʒ ə -'sældʒ i ə ‖ kɑːk-

coxcomb 'kɒks kəʊm ‖ 'kɑːks koʊm **~s** z

Coxe kɒks ‖ kɑːks

Coxsackie *place in NY* kɒk 'sæk i kʊk 'sɑːk i
‖ kɑːk-
Cox'sackie ˌvirus

coxswain 'kɒks ᵊn -weɪn ‖ 'kɑːks- **~s** z

coy kɔɪ **coyer** 'kɔɪ ə ‖ -ᵊr **coyest** 'kɔɪ ɪst -əst
coyly 'kɔɪ li **coyness** 'kɔɪ nəs -nɪs

Coyle kɔɪᵊl

coyote 'kɔɪ 'əʊt i kaɪ-; 'kɔɪ əʊt, 'kaɪ- ‖ kaɪ 'oʊṯ i
'kaɪ oʊt **coyotes** kɔɪ 'əʊt iz kaɪ-; 'kɔɪ əʊts,
'kaɪ- ‖ kaɪ 'oʊṯ iz 'kaɪ oʊts

coypu 'kɔɪp uː -juː; kɔɪ 'puː **~s** z

coz kʌz

cozen 'kʌz ᵊn **~ed** d **~ing** ɪŋ **~s** z

Cozens 'kʌz ᵊnz

Cozumel ˌkɒz u 'mel ˌkɒs- ‖ ˌkoʊs- —*AmSp*
[ko su 'mel]

coz|y 'kəʊz |i ‖ 'koʊz |i **~ier** i ə ‖ i ᵊr **~iest**
i ɪst i ə st **~ily** ɪ li əl i **~iness** i nəs i nɪs

CPA ˌsiː piː 'eɪ **~s** z

CP'er ˌsiː 'piː ə ‖ -ᵊr **~s** z

CP/M ˌsiː piː 'em

CPU ˌsiː piː 'juː ~s z

crab, Crab kræb crabbing 'kræb ɪŋ crabs
kræbz
'crab ˌapple; 'crab louse; ˌCrab 'Nebula;
ˌcrab 'paste

Crabb, Crabbe kræb

crabbed 'kræb ɪd -əd; kræbd ~ly li ~ness nəs
nɪs

crabb|y 'kræb |i ~ier i̯ə ǁ i̯ᵊr ~iest i̯ɪst i̯əst

crabgrass 'kræb grɑːs §-græs ǁ -græs

crabtree, C~ 'kræb triː ~s z

crabways 'kræb weɪz

crabwise 'kræb waɪz

crack kræk cracked krækt cracking 'kræk ɪŋ
cracks kræks

crackbrained 'kræk breɪnd

crackdown 'kræk daʊn ~s z

cracker 'kræk ə ǁ -ᵊr ~s z

cracker-barrel 'kræk ə ˌbær əl ǁ -ᵊr- -ˌber-

crackerjack 'kræk ə dʒæk ǁ -ᵊr-

crackhead 'kræk hed ~s z

Crackington 'kræk ɪŋ tən

crackjaw 'kræk dʒɔː ǁ -dʒɑː

crackl|e 'kræk ᵊl ~ed d ~es z ~ing ɪŋ

crackleware 'kræk ᵊl weə ǁ -wer -wær

crackling n 'crisp pork skin' 'kræk lɪŋ -lən

crackling part, verbal n 'kræk ᵊl ɪŋ

crackly 'kræk ᵊl i

cracknel 'kræk nᵊl ~s z

Cracknell 'kræk nᵊl

crackpot 'kræk pɒt ǁ -pɑːt ~s s

cracks|man 'kræks |mən ~men mən men

crackup 'kræk ʌp ~s s

Cracow 'kræk aʊ -əʊ, -ɒf ǁ 'krɑːk aʊ —Polish
Kraków ['kra kuf]

-cracy stress-imposing krəs i — plutocracy
pluː 'tɒk rəs i ǁ -'tɑːk-

Craddock 'kræd ək

cradl|e 'kreɪd ᵊl ~ed d ~es z ~ing ɪŋ

cradle-rob 'kreɪd ᵊl rɒb ǁ -rɑːb ~bing ɪŋ

cradle-snatch|er 'kreɪd ᵊl ˌsnætʃ |ə ǁ -|ᵊr ~ers
əz ǁ ᵊrz ~ing ɪŋ

Cradley (i) 'kreɪd li, (ii) 'kræd-

craft krɑːft §kræft ǁ kræft crafted 'krɑːft ɪd
§'kræft-, -əd ǁ 'kræft əd crafting 'krɑːft ɪŋ
§'kræft- ǁ 'kræft ɪŋ crafts krɑːfts §kræfts
ǁ kræfts
'craft ˌunion

-craft krɑːft §kræft ǁ kræft — woodcraft
'wʊd krɑːft §-kræft ǁ -kræft

crafts|man 'krɑːfts |mən §'kræfts- ǁ 'kræfts-
~men mən men

craftsmanship 'krɑːfts mən ʃɪp §'kræfts-
ǁ 'kræfts-

crafts|woman 'krɑːfts ˌwʊm ən §'kræfts-
ǁ 'kræfts- ~women ˌwɪm ɪn -ən

craft|y 'krɑːft |i §'kræft- ǁ 'kræft |i ~ier i̯ə
ǁ i̯ᵊr ~iest i̯ɪst i̯əst ~ily ɪ li əl i ~iness i nəs
i nɪs

crag kræg crags krægz

Cragg kræg

Craggs krægz

cragg|y 'kræg |i ~ier i̯ə ǁ i̯ᵊr ~iest i̯ɪst i̯əst
~ily ɪ li əl i ~iness i nəs i nɪs

craic Irish spelling of 'crack' kræk

Craig kreɪg

Craigavon ˌkreɪg 'æv ᵊn

Craigie 'kreɪg i

Craignure ₍ˌ₎kreɪg 'njʊə ǁ -'nʊᵊr -'njʊᵊr

crake kreɪk crakes kreɪks

cram, Cram kræm crammed kræmd
cramming 'kræm ɪŋ crams kræmz

crambo 'kræm bəʊ ǁ -boʊ

cram-full ˌkræm 'fʊl ◂

crammer 'kræm ə ǁ -ᵊr ~s z

Cramond 'kræm ənd 'krɑːm-

cramp kræmp cramped kræmpt cramping
'kræmp ɪŋ cramps kræmps

crampon 'kræmp ɒn -ən ǁ -ɑːn ~s z

cran, Cran kræn crans krænz

cranage 'kreɪn ɪdʒ

cranberr|y 'kræn bər ˌ|i →'kræm- ǁ -ˌber |i
~ies iz

Cranborne, Cranbourn, Cranbourne
'kræn bɔːn →'kræm- ǁ -bɔːrn -bourn

Cranbrook 'kræn brʊk →'kræm-

crane, Crane kreɪn craned kreɪnd craning
'kreɪn ɪŋ cranes kreɪnz
'crane fly

cranesbill 'kreɪnz bɪl ~s z

Cranfield 'kræn fiːᵊld

Cranford 'kræn fəd ǁ -fᵊrd

crania 'kreɪn i̯ə

cranial 'kreɪn i̯əl

cranio- comb. form
with stress-neutral suffix ¦kreɪn i̯əʊ ǁ oʊ
— craniometric ˌkreɪn i̯əʊ 'metr ɪk ◂ ǁ -oʊ'--
with stress-imposing suffix ˌkreɪn i 'ɒ+
ǁ -'ɑː+ — craniotomy ˌkreɪn i 'ɒt əm i
ǁ -'ɑːt̬-

crani|um 'kreɪn i̯ˌ|əm ~a ə

crank, Crank kræŋk cranked kræŋkt
cranking 'kræŋk ɪŋ cranks kræŋks

crankcas|e 'kræŋk keɪs ~es ɪz əz

cranki... —see cranky

Cranko 'kræŋk əʊ ǁ -oʊ

crankpin 'kræŋk pɪn ~s z

crankshaft 'kræŋk ʃɑːft §-ʃæft ǁ -ʃæft ~s s

Crankshaw 'kræŋk ʃɔː ǁ -ʃɑː

crank|y 'kræŋk |i ~ier i̯ə ǁ i̯ᵊr ~iest i̯ɪst i̯əst
~ily ɪ li əl i ~iness i nəs i nɪs

Cranleigh, Cranley 'kræn li

Cranmer 'kræn mə →'kræm- ǁ -mᵊr

crannog 'kræn əg ~s z

crann|y 'kræn |i ~ied id ~ies iz

Cranston 'kræn'st ən

Cranwell 'kræn wəl -wel

crap kræp crapped kræpt crapping 'kræp ɪŋ
craps kræps

crape kreɪp

crapper 'kræp ə ǁ -ᵊr ~s z

crappie, crappy 'kræp i crappies 'kræp iz

crapp|y 'kræp| i ~ier i̯ə ǁ i̯ᵊr ~iest i̯ɪst i̯əst
~ily ɪ li əl i ~iness i nəs i nɪs

craps kræps

crapshoot ˈkræp ʃuːt **~s** s
crapshooter ˈkræp ˌʃuːt ə ‖ -ˌʃuːt̬ ᵊr **~s** z
crapulence ˈkræp jʊl ənᵗs -jəl- ‖ -jəl-
crapulent ˈkræp jʊl ənt -jəl- ‖ -jəl- **~ly** li
crapulous ˈkræp jʊl əs -jəl- ‖ -jəl- **~ness** nəs nɪs
craquelure ˈkræk ə lʊə -ljʊə ‖ -lʊr
crases ˈkreɪs iːz
crash kræʃ **crashed** kræʃt **crashes** ˈkræʃ ɪz -əz
  crashing ˈkræʃ ɪŋ
  ˈcrash ˌbarrier; ˈcrash ˌhelmet
Crashaw ˈkræʃ ɔː ‖ -ɑː
crash-div|e ˈkræʃ daɪv ˌ‧‧ **~ed** d **~es** z **~ing** ɪŋ
  crashdove ˈkræʃ dəʊv ‖ -doʊv
crash-land ˈkræʃ lænd ˌ‧‧ **~ed** ɪd əd **~s** z
  ~ing/s ɪŋ/z
crasis ˈkreɪs ɪs §-əs **crases** ˈkreɪs iːz
crass kræs **crasser** ˈkræs ə ‖ -ᵊr **crassest**
  ˈkræs ɪst -əst
crass|ly ˈkræs |li **~ness** nəs nɪs
Crassus ˈkræs əs
-crat kræt — **plutocrat** ˈpluːt əʊ kræt
  ‖ ˈpluːt̬ ə-
Cratchit ˈkrætʃ ɪt §-ət
crate kreɪt **crated** ˈkreɪt ɪd -əd ‖ ˈkreɪt̬ əd
  crates kreɪts **crating** ˈkreɪt ɪŋ ‖ ˈkreɪt̬ ɪŋ
crater ˈkreɪt ə ‖ ˈkreɪt̬ ᵊr **~ed** d **cratering**
  ˈkreɪt ər ɪŋ ‖ ˈkreɪt̬ ər ɪŋ **~s** z
Crathes ˈkræθ ɪz -əz
Crathorn, Crathorne ˈkreɪ θɔːn ‖ -θɔːrn
Crathy ˈkræθ i
-cratic ˈkræt ɪk ‖ ˈkræt̬ ɪk — **plutocratic**
  ˌpluːt əʊ ˈkræt ɪk ◄ ‖ ˌpluːt̬ ə ˈkræt̬ ɪk ◄
cra|vat krə| ˈvæt **~vats** ˈvæts **~vatted** ˈvæt ɪd
  -əd ‖ ˈvæt̬ əd
crave kreɪv **craved** kreɪvd **craves** kreɪvz
  craving ˈkreɪv ɪŋ
craven, Craven ˈkreɪv ᵊn **~ly** li **~ness** nəs nɪs
craving ˈkreɪv ɪŋ **~s** z
craw krɔː ‖ krɑː **craws** krɔːz ‖ krɑːz
crawdad ˈkrɔː dæd ‖ ˈkrɑː- **~s** z
crawfish ˈkrɔː fɪʃ ‖ ˈkrɑː-
Crawford ˈkrɔː fəd ‖ -fᵊrd ˈkrɑː-
crawl krɔːl ‖ krɑːl **crawled** krɔːld ‖ krɑːld
  crawling ˈkrɔːl ɪŋ ‖ ˈkrɑːl- **crawls** krɔːlz
  ‖ krɑːlz
crawler ˈkrɔːl ə ‖ -ᵊr ˈkrɑːl- **~s** z
Crawley ˈkrɔːl i ‖ ˈkrɑːl-
crawl|y ˈkrɔːl |i ‖ ˈkrɑːl- **~ier** i ə ‖ i ᵊr **~iest**
  i ɪst i əst
Crawshaw ˈkrɔː ʃɔː ‖ ˈkrɑː ʃɑː
Crawshay ˈkrɔː ʃeɪ ‖ ˈkrɑː-
Cray kreɪ
crayfish ˈkreɪ fɪʃ
Crayford ˈkreɪ fəd ‖ -fᵊrd
Crayola *tdmk* kreɪ ˈəʊl ə ‖ -ˈoʊl-
crayon ˈkreɪ ɒn -ən ‖ -ɑːn -ən; kræn **~ed** d
  ~ing ɪŋ **~s** z
craze kreɪz **crazed** kreɪzd **crazes** ˈkreɪz ɪz -əz
  crazing ˈkreɪz ɪŋ
craz|y ˈkreɪz |i **~ier** i ə ‖ i ᵊr **~iest** i ɪst i əst
  ~ily ɪ li əl i **~iness** i nəs i nɪs
  ˌCrazy ˈHorse, ˌcrazy ˈpaving

CRE ˌsiː ɑːr ˈiː ‖ -ɑːr-
Creagh kreɪ
creak kriːk **creaked** kriːkt **creaking** ˈkriːk ɪŋ
  creaks kriːks
creak|y ˈkriːk |i **~ier** i ə ‖ i ᵊr **~iest** i ɪst i əst
  ~ily ɪ li əl i **~iness** i nəs i nɪs

CREAM CHEESE

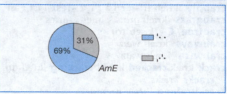

AmE

cream kriːm **creamed** kriːmd **creaming**
  ˈkriːm ɪŋ **creams** kriːmz
  ˌcream ˈcheese, ˈcream cheese
  — *Preference poll, AmE:* ˈ‧ ‧ 69%, ˌ‧ ‧ 31%;
  ˌcream ˈcracker; ˌcream ˈpuff; ˌcream
  ˈsauce; ˌcream ˈsoda; ˌcream ˈtea
cream-coloured, cream-colored
  ˈkriːm ˌkʌl əd ‖ -ᵊrd
creamer ˈkriːm ə ‖ -ᵊr **~s** z
creamer|y ˈkriːm ər |i **~ies** iz
cream|y ˈkriːm |i **~ier** i ə ‖ i ᵊr **~iest** i ɪst i əst
  ~ily ɪ li əl i **~iness** i nəs i nɪs
crease kriːs **creased** kriːst **creases** ˈkriːs ɪz -əz
  creasing ˈkriːs ɪŋ
crease-resistant ˈkriːs rɪ ˌzɪst ənt -rə-, ˌ‧‧ˈ‧‧◄
Creasey, Creasy ˈkriːs i

CREATE

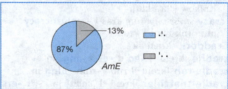

AmE

cre|ate kri |ˈeɪt ˌkriː:-, ˈ‧ ‧ — *Preference poll,*
  AmE: ‧ˈ‧ 87%, ˈ‧ ‧ 13%. **~ated** ˈeɪt ɪd -əd
  ‖ ˈeɪt̬ əd **~ates** ˈeɪts **~ating** ˈeɪt ɪŋ ‖ ˈeɪt̬ ɪŋ
creatine ˈkriː ə tiːn -tɪn, §-ət ᵊn
creatinine kri ˈæt ə niːn -ɪ-; ᵊn iːn; ᵊn ɪn,
  -ɪn ɪn, §-ᵊn ən ‖ -ᵊn iːn -ən
creation kri ˈeɪʃ ᵊn ˌkriː:- **~s** z
creationism kri ˈeɪʃ ᵊn ˌɪz əm ˌkriː:-
creationist kri ˈeɪʃ ᵊn ɪst ˌkriː:-, §ˌəst **~s** s
creative kri ˈeɪt ɪv ˌkriː:- ‖ -ˈeɪt̬ ɪv **~ly** li **~ness**
  nəs nɪs
creativity ˌkriː eɪ ˈtɪv ət i ˌkriː:ə-, -ɪt i ‖ -ət̬ i
creator kri ˈeɪt ə ˌkriː:-; ˈkriː eɪt ə ‖ -ˈeɪt̬ ᵊr **~s** z
creature ˈkriːtʃ ə ‖ -ᵊr **~s** z
  ˌcreature ˈcomforts ‖ ˈ‧‧ ˌ‧‧
creche, crèche kreʃ kreɪʃ —*Fr* [kʀɛʃ] **creches,**
  crèches ˈkreʃ ɪz ˈkreɪʃ-, -əz
Crecy, Crécy ˈkres i ‖ kreɪ ˈsiː —*Fr* [kʀe si]
cred kred
Creda *tdmk* ˈkriːd ə
credal ˈkriːd ᵊl

credenc|e 'kriːd ᵊnᵗs **~es** ɪz əz

credential krə 'denᵗʃ ᵊl krɪ- **~ed, ~led** d **~s** z

credenza krə 'denz ə krɪ- **~s** z

credibility ˌkred ə 'bɪl ət i ˌ·ɪ-, -ɪt i ‖ -əţ i
ˌcrediˈbility gap

credib|le 'kred əb |ᵊl -ɪb- **~ly** li

cred|it 'kred |ɪt §-ət ‖ -|əţ **~ited** ɪt ɪd §ət-, -əd ‖ əţ əd **~iting** ɪt ɪŋ §ət- ‖ əţ ɪŋ **~its** ɪts §əts ‖ əts
'credit acˌcount; **'credit card**; **'credit ˌlimit**; **'credit note**; **'credit squeeze**

creditab|le 'kred ɪt əb |ᵊl §'·ət- ‖ 'kred əţ- **~ly** li

Crediton 'kred ɪt ən §-ət- ‖ -əţ ᵊn

creditor 'kred ɪt ə §-ət- ‖ -əţ ᵊr **~s** z

creditworth|y 'kred ɪt ˌwɜːð |i §-ət- ‖ -ˌwɜːð |i **~iness** i nəs i nɪs

credo, Credo 'kreɪd əʊ 'kriːd- ‖ -oʊ **~s** z

credulity krə 'djuːl ət i krɪ-, kre-, →§-'dʒuːl-, -ɪt- ‖ -'duːl əţ i -'djuːl-

credulous 'kred jʊl əs -jəl- ‖ 'kredʒ əl əs **~ly** li **~ness** nəs nɪs

Cree kriː **Crees** kriːz

creed, Creed kriːd **creeds** kriːdz

CREEK

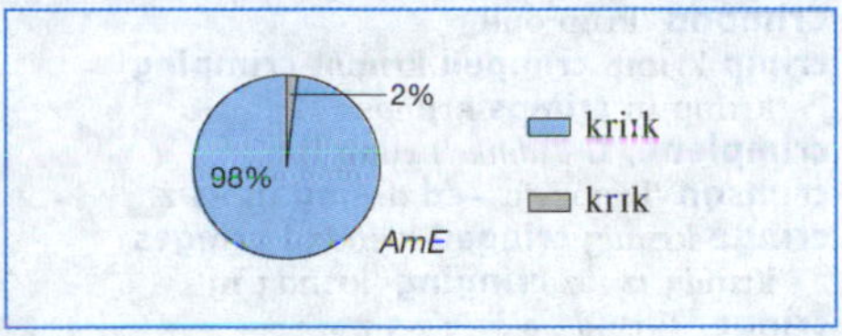

creek kriːk ‖ krɪk — *Preference poll, AmE:* kriːk *98%,* krɪk *2%.* **creeks** kriːks ‖ krɪks

Creek kriːk *(= creak)* **Creeks** kriːks

creel kriːᵊl **creels** kriːᵊlz

Creeley 'kriːl i

creep kriːp **creeping** 'kriːp ɪŋ **creeps** kriːps **crept** krept

creeper 'kriːp ə ‖ -ᵊr **~s** z

creep|y 'kriːp |i **~ier** i‿ə ‖ i‿ᵊr **~iest** i‿ɪst i‿əst **~ily** ɪ li əl i **~iness** i nəs i nɪs

creepy-crawl|y ˌkriːp i 'krɔːl |i '· ·ˌ· · ‖ -'krɑːl- **~ies** iz

Creevey 'kriːv i

Creighton *(i)* 'kraɪt ᵊn, *(ii)* 'kreɪt-

Creigiau 'kraɪg ə —*Welsh* ['krəig jai, -je]

cremains krə 'meɪnz kri-

cremate krə 'meɪt kri- ‖ 'kriːm eɪt **cremated** krə 'meɪt ɪd kri-, -əd ‖ 'kriːm eɪţ əd **cremates** krə 'meɪts kri- ‖ 'kriːm eɪts **cremating** krə 'meɪt ɪŋ kri- ‖ 'kriːm eɪţ ɪŋ

cremation krə 'meɪʃ ᵊn kri- ‖ kri- **~s** z

cremator|ium ˌkrem ə 'tɔːr i‿əm ‖ ˌkriːm- ˌkrem-, -'toʊr- **~a** ə

crematory 'krem ət‿ər |i ‖ 'kriːm ə tɔːr |i 'krem-, -toʊr- **~ies** iz

creme, crème krem kreɪm, kriːm —*Fr* [kʁɛm] **cremes, crèmes** kremz kreɪmz, kriːmz —*Fr* [kʁɛm] —*See also phrases with this word*

Creme kriːm

creme brulee, crème brûlée ˌkrem bruː 'leɪ ˌkreɪm-, ˌ· '· · —*Fr* [kʁɛm bʁy le]

creme caramel, crème caramel ˌkrem ˌkær ə 'mel ˌkreɪm- ‖ -ˌker-; ˌ·'· · ·

creme de la creme, crème de la crème ˌkrem də lɑː 'krem ˌkreɪm-, -'kreɪm —*Fr* [kʁɛm də la kʁɛm]

creme de menthe, crème de menthe ˌkrem də 'mɒnᵗθ ˌkreɪm-, -'mɑːnt ‖ -'mɑːnt —*Fr* [kʁɛm də mɑ̃ːt]

creme fraiche, crème fraîche ˌkrem 'freʃ ˌkreɪm-, -'freɪʃ —*Fr* [kʁɛm fʁɛʃ]

Cremona krɪ 'məʊn ə krə- ‖ -'moʊn ə —*It* [kre 'moː na]

Cremora *tdmk* krɪ 'mɔːr ə krə-

crenate 'kriːn eɪt

crenel|ate, crenell|ate 'kren ə l|eɪt -ᵊl |eɪt ‖ -ᵊl |eɪt **~ated** eɪt ɪd -əd ‖ eɪţ əd **~ates** eɪts ‖ eɪts **~ating** eɪt ɪŋ ‖ eɪţ ɪŋ

crenelation, crenellation ˌkren ə 'leɪʃ ᵊn -ᵊl 'eɪʃ- ‖ ˌkren ᵊl 'eɪʃ ᵊn **~s** z

creole, Creole 'kriː əʊl 'kreɪ-, →-ɒʊl ‖ -oʊl **~s** z

creolis... —*see* **creoliz...**

creolization ˌkriː‿əl aɪ 'zeɪʃ ᵊn ˌkreɪ-, '·əʊl-, -ɪ'-- ‖ -əl ə-

creoliz|e 'kriː‿ə laɪz 'kreɪ-, -əʊ- **~ed** d **~es** ɪz əz **~ing** ɪŋ

Creon 'kriː‿ən -ɒn ‖ -ɑːn

creosol 'kriː‿ə sɒl ‖ -soʊl -sɑːl, -sɔːl

creo|sote 'kriː‿ə |səʊt ‖ -|soʊt **~soted** səʊt ɪd -əd ‖ soʊţ əd **~sotes** səʊts ‖ soʊts **~soting** səʊt ɪŋ ‖ soʊţ ɪŋ
'creosote bush

crepe, crêpe kreɪp krep —*Fr* [kʁɛp] **crepes, crêpes** kreɪps kreps
ˌcrepe de 'Chine ʃiːn —*Fr* [də ʃin]; **ˌcrepe 'paper** ‖ '· ˌ· ·; **ˌcrepe su'zette, ˌcrepes su'zettes** su 'zet —*Fr* [sy zɛt]

crepi|tate 'krep ɪ |teɪt §-ə- **~tated** teɪt ɪd -əd ‖ teɪţ əd **~tates** teɪts **~tating** teɪt ɪŋ ‖ teɪţ ɪŋ

crepitation ˌkrep ɪ 'teɪʃ ᵊn §-ə- **~s** z

crept krept

crepuscular krɪ 'pʌsk jʊl ə krə-, kre-, -jəl- ‖ -jəl ᵊr

crescend|o krə 'ʃend |əʊ krɪ- ‖ -|oʊ **~i** iː **~os** əʊz ‖ oʊz

crescent 'krez ᵊnt 'kres- ‖ 'kres- — *Preference poll, BrE:* 'krez- *55%,* 'kres- *45%. See chart on p. 196.* **~s** s

cresol 'kriːs ɒl ‖ -ɑːl -ɔːl, -oʊl

cress kres

cresset 'kres ɪt §-ət **~s** s

Cressida 'kres ɪd ə -əd-

Cresswell 'kres wel 'krez-, -wəl

crest krest **crested** 'krest ɪd -əd **cresting** 'krest ɪŋ **crests** krests

Cresta 'krest ə

crestfallen 'krest ˌfɔːl ən ‖ -ˌfɑːl-

Creswell 'kres wel 'krez-, -wəl

cretaceous, C~ krɪ 'teɪʃ əs krə-, kre-, -'teɪʃ i‿əs

Cretan 'kriːt ᵊn **~s** z

Crete kriːt

CRESCENT

'krez-
'kres-

BrE

BrE 'krez- by age

Percentage

100
80
60
40
0

Older ← Speakers → Younger

cretic 'kri:t ɪk ‖ 'kri:t̬ ɪk **~s** s
cretin 'kret ɪn -ᵊn ‖ 'kri:t ᵊn *(*)* **~ism** ˌɪz əm **~s** z
cretinous 'kret ɪn əs -ən- ‖ 'kri:t ᵊn əs *(*)*
cretonne kre 'tɒn krə-, krɪ-; 'kret ɒn ‖ 'kri:t ɑːn krɪ 'tɑːn
Creutzfeldt-Jakob ˌkrɔɪts felt 'jæk ɒb ‖ -'jɑːk oʊb
   ˌCreutzfeldt-'Jakob diˌsease
crevass|e krə 'væs krɪ- **~es** ɪz əz
crevic|e 'krev ɪs §-əs **~ed** t **~es** ɪz əz
crew kru: **crewed** kru:d *(= crude)* **crewing**
   'kru: ɪŋ **crews** kru:z
   'crew cut; ˌcrew 'neck, '· ·
Crewe kru:
crewel 'kru: əl ɪl
Crewkerne 'kru: kɜːn ‖ -kɝːn
crew|man 'kru: |mən -mæn **~men** mən men
crewmember 'kru: ˌmem bə ‖ -bᵊr **~s** z
cri kri: **cris** kri: kri:z
   ˌcri de 'coeur də 'kɜː ‖ də 'kɝː —*Fr*
   [kʁid kœːʁ]
Crianlarich ˌkri:ˌ ən 'lær ɪx -ɪk ‖ -'ler-
crib krɪb **cribbed** krɪbd **cribbing** 'krɪb ɪŋ
   cribs krɪbz
   'crib death
Cribb krɪb
cribb... —*see* **crib**
cribbage 'krɪb ɪdʒ
cribber 'krɪb ə ‖ -ᵊr **~s** z
Cribbins 'krɪb ɪnz §-ənz
Criccieth 'krɪk iˌ əθ -eθ —*Welsh* ['krik jeθ]
Crich kraɪtʃ
Crichel 'krɪtʃ ᵊl
Crichton 'kraɪt ᵊn
crick, Crick krɪk **cricked** krɪkt **cricking**
   'krɪk ɪŋ **cricks, Crick's** krɪks
crick|et 'krɪk |ɪt §-ət ‖ -|ət **~eter/s** ɪt ə/z §ət-
   ‖ ət ᵊr/z **~eting** ɪt ɪŋ ət- ‖ ət̬ ɪŋ
Crickhowell ₍ₗ₎krɪk 'haʊ ̬əl -'haʊl; krɪ 'kaʊ ̬əl,
   -'kaʊl
cricoid 'kraɪk ɔɪd **~s** z

cried kraɪd
Crieff kri:f
crier, Crier 'kraɪˌ ə ‖ 'kraɪˌ ᵊr **~s** z
cries kraɪz
crikey 'kraɪk i
crime kraɪm —*but in French expressions* kri:m
   crimes kraɪmz —*See also phrases with this
   word*
Crimea kraɪ 'mɪə -'mi:ˌ ə ‖ -'mi:ˌ ə
Crimean kraɪ 'mɪən -'mi:ˌ ən ‖ -'mi:ˌ ən **~s** z
crime passionnel ˌkri:m ˌpæs iˌ ə 'nel
   -ˌpæʃ ə 'nel —*Fr* [kʁim pa sjɔ nɛl]
criminal 'krɪm ɪn ᵊl -ən- **~ly** i **~s** z
criminalis... —*see* **criminaliz...**
criminalit|y ˌkrɪm ɪ 'næl ət |i ˌ·ə-, -ɪt i ‖ -ət̬ |i
   ~ies iz
criminalization ˌkrɪm ɪn ᵊl aɪ 'zeɪʃ ᵊn -ᵊn ˌəl-,
   -ɪ'·· ‖ -ə 'zeɪʃ-
criminaliz|e 'krɪm ɪn ᵊl aɪz -ᵊn ˌəl- **~ed** d **~es**
   ɪz əz **~ing** ɪŋ
crimini 'kri:m ɪ ni: 'krɪm-, -ə-
criminological ˌkrɪm ɪn ə 'lɒdʒ ɪk ᵊl ◂ ˌ·ən-
   ‖ -'lɑːdʒ- **~ly** i
criminologist ˌkrɪm ɪ 'nɒl ədʒ ɪst ˌ·ə-, §-əst
   ‖ -'nɑːl- **~s** s
criminology ˌkrɪm ɪ 'nɒl ədʒ i ˌ·ə- ‖ -'nɑːl-
Crimond 'krɪm ənd
crimp krɪmp **crimped** krɪmpt **crimping**
   'krɪmp ɪŋ **crimps** krɪmps
crimplene, C~ *tdmk* 'krɪmp li:n
crimson 'krɪmz ᵊn **~ed** d **~ing** ɪŋ **~s** z
cringe krɪndʒ **cringed** krɪndʒd **cringes**
   'krɪndʒ ɪz -əz **cringing** 'krɪndʒ ɪŋ
cringer 'krɪndʒ ə ‖ -ᵊr **~s** z
cringle 'krɪŋ gᵊl **~s** z
crinkl|e 'krɪŋk ᵊl **~ed** d **~es** z **~ing** ɪŋ
crinkle-cut 'krɪŋk ᵊl kʌt
crinkly 'krɪŋk li
crinoid 'kraɪn ɔɪd 'krɪn- **~s** z
crinoline 'krɪn əl ɪn §-ən **~s** z
cripes kraɪps
Crippen 'krɪp ɪn -ən
crippl|e 'krɪp ᵊl **~ed** d **~es** z **~ing** ˌɪŋ
Cripplegate 'krɪp ᵊl geɪt
Cripps krɪps
Crisco *tdmk* 'krɪsk əʊ ‖ -oʊ
crisis 'kraɪs ɪs §-əs **crises** 'kraɪs i:z
crisp, Crisp krɪsp **crisped** krɪspt **crisping**
   'krɪsp ɪŋ **crisps** krɪsps
crispbread 'krɪsp bred **~s** z
Crispian 'krɪsp iˌ ən
Crispin 'krɪsp ɪn §-ən
crisply 'krɪsp li
crispness 'krɪsp nəs -nɪs
crisp|y 'krɪsp |i **~ier** iˌ ə ‖ iˌ ᵊr **~iest** iˌ ɪst iˌ əst
   ~ily ɪ li əl i **~iness** i nəs i nɪs
crisscross 'krɪs krɒs -krɔːs ‖ -krɔːs -krɑːs **~ed** t
   ~es ɪz əz **~ing** ɪŋ
Cristobal, Cristóbal krɪ 'stəʊb ᵊl ‖ -'stoʊb-
   —*Sp* [kris 'to βal]
Critchley 'krɪtʃ li
criteri|on kraɪ 'tɪər iˌ |ən ‖ -'tɪr- **~a** ə **~al** əl
critic 'krɪt ɪk ‖ 'krɪt̬ ɪk **~s** s

C

critical 'krɪt ɪk ᵊl ‖ 'krɪt̬- **~ly** ̬i
  ,critical 'mass
criticality ,krɪt ɪ 'kæl ət i ,-ə-, -ɪt i
  ‖ ,krɪt̬ ə 'kæl ət̬ i
criticis|e, criticiz|e 'krɪt ɪ saɪz -ə- ‖ 'krɪt̬ ə-
  ~ed d **~es** ɪz əz **~ing** ɪŋ
criticism 'krɪt ɪ ,sɪz əm -ə- ‖ 'krɪt̬ ə- **~s** z
critique krɪ 'tiːk krə- **~s** s
Crittall 'krɪt ɔːl ‖ -ɑːl
critter 'krɪt ə ‖ 'krɪt̬ ᵊr **~s** z
CRO ,siː ɑːr 'əʊ ‖ -ɑːr 'oʊ
croak krəʊk ‖ kroʊk **croaked** krəʊkt ‖ kroʊkt
  croaking/s 'krəʊk ɪŋ/z ‖ 'kroʊk ɪŋ/z **croaks**
  krəʊks ‖ kroʊks
croak|y 'krəʊk |i ‖ 'kroʊk |i **~ily** ɪ li əl i
  ~iness i nəs i nɪs
Croat 'krəʊ æt -ət ‖ 'kroʊ- **~s** s
Croatia krəʊ 'eɪʃ ə ‖ kroʊ-
Croatian krəʊ 'eɪʃ ᵊn ‖ kroʊ- **~s** z
crochet 'krəʊʃ eɪ -i, §-ə ‖ kroʊ 'ʃeɪ **~ed** d **~ing**
  ɪŋ **~s** z
crocidolite krəʊ 'sɪd ə laɪt ‖ kroʊ-
crock krɒk ‖ krɑːk **crocked** krɒkt ‖ krɑːkt
  crocks krɒks ‖ krɑːks
Crocker 'krɒk ə ‖ 'krɑːk ᵊr
crockery 'krɒk ər i ‖ 'krɑːk-
crocket 'krɒk ɪt §-ət ‖ 'krɑːk- **~s** s
Crockett 'krɒk ɪt §-ət ‖ 'krɑːk-
Crockford 'krɒk fəd ‖ 'krɑːk fᵊrd
crocodile 'krɒk ə daɪᵊl ‖ 'krɑːk- **~s** z
  'crocodile clip; 'crocodile tears, ⸱⸱⸱⸱'.
crocodilian ,krɒk ə 'dɪl i_ən ‖ ,krɑːk- **~s** z
Crocs krɒks ‖ krɑːks *tdmk*
crocus 'krəʊk əs ‖ 'kroʊk əs **~es** ɪz əz
Croes- *in Welsh place names* krɔɪs — **Croeserw**
  krɔɪs 'er uː
Croesus 'kriːs əs
croft, Croft krɒft krɔːft ‖ 'krɔːft krɑːft **crofting**
  'krɒft ɪŋ 'krɔːft- ‖ 'krɔːft ɪŋ 'krɑːft- **crofts**
  krɒfts krɔːfts ‖ krɔːfts krɑːfts
crofter 'krɒft ə 'krɔːft- ‖ 'krɔːft ᵊr 'krɑːft- **~s** z
Crofton 'krɒft ən 'krɔːft- ‖ 'krɔːft- 'krɑːft-
Crohn krəʊn ‖ kroʊn
  'Crohn's di,sease
croiss|ant 'kwæs |ɒ̃ 'krwæs-, 'krwʌs-, 'kwɑːs-
  ‖ kwɑː: 's|ɑ̃: krə-, krwɑː:-, -'s|ɑːnt —*Fr*
  [kʁwa sɑ̃] **~ants** ɒ̃z ‖ ɑːz ɑːnts
Croix krwɑː kwɑː —*but in the name of the*
  island St Croix, krɔɪ —*Fr* [kʁwa]
  ,Croix de 'Guerre də 'geə ‖ -'geᵊr —*Fr*
  [kʁwad gɛːʁ]
Croker 'krəʊk ə ‖ 'kroʊk ᵊr
Cro-Magnon ₍ᵢ₎krəʊ 'mæn jɒn -jən; -'mæg nən,
  -nɒn ‖ ₍ᵢ₎kroʊ 'mæg nən -nɑːn —*Fr*
  [kʁɔ ma njɔ̃]
Cromartie, Cromarty 'krɒm ət i
  ‖ 'krɑːm ᵊrt̬ i
Crombie *(i)* 'krɒm bi ‖ 'krɑːm-, *(ii)* 'krʌm-
Crome krəʊm ‖ kroʊm
Cromer 'krəʊm ə ‖ 'kroʊm ᵊr
Cromford 'krɒm fəd ‖ 'krɑːm fᵊrd
cromlech 'krɒm lek ‖ 'krɑːm- **~s** s

Crompton *(i)* 'krɒmpt ən ‖ 'krɑːmpt-,
  (ii) 'krʌmpt-
Cromwell 'krɒm wəl -wel ‖ 'krɑːm- —*formerly*
  'krʌm-, -ᵊl
Cromwellian ₍ᵢ₎krɒm 'wel i_ən ‖ ₍ᵢ₎krɑːm-
crone krəʊn ‖ kroʊn **crones** krəʊnz ‖ kroʊnz
Cronin 'krəʊn ɪn §-ən ‖ 'kroʊn-
cronk krɒŋk ‖ krɑːŋk
Cronkite 'krɒŋk aɪt ‖ 'krɑːn kaɪt 'krɑːŋk aɪt
cron|y 'krəʊn |i ‖ 'kroʊn |i **~ies** iz **~yism**
  i ,ɪz əm
crook, Crook krʊk §kruːk **crooks** krʊks
  §kruːks
crookback, C~ 'krʊk bæk §'kruːk- **~ed** t **~s** s
Crooke krʊk §kruːk
crooked 'krʊk ɪd §'kruːk-, -əd **~er** ə ‖ ᵊr **~est**
  ɪst əst **~ly** li **~ness** nəs nɪs
Crookes krʊks §kruːks
Croom, Croome kruːm
croon kruːn **crooned** kruːnd **crooning**
  'kruːn ɪŋ **croons** kruːnz
crooner 'kruːn ə ‖ -ᵊr **~s** z
crop krɒp ‖ krɑːp **cropped** krɒpt ‖ krɑːpt
  cropping 'krɒp ɪŋ ‖ 'krɑːp ɪŋ **crops** krɒps
  ‖ krɑːps
  'crop ,spraying
crop-dusting 'krɒp ,dʌst ɪŋ ‖ 'krɑːp-
cropper 'krɒp ə ‖ 'krɑːp ᵊr **~s** z
croquet 'krəʊk i -eɪ ‖ kroʊ 'keɪ
croquette krɒ 'ket krəʊ- ‖ kroʊ 'ket **~s** s
crore krɔː ‖ krɔːr kroʊr **crores** krɔːz ‖ krɔːrz
  kroʊrz
Crosbie, Crosby 'krɒz bi 'krɒs- ‖ 'krɔːz bi
  'krɑːz-
crosier, C~ 'krəʊz i_ə 'krəʊʒ ə ‖ 'kroʊʒ ᵊr **~s** z
Crosland 'krɒs lənd ‖ 'krɔːs- 'krɑːs-
cross, Cross krɒs krɔːs ‖ krɔːs krɑːs **crossed**
  krɒst krɔːst ‖ krɔːst krɑːst **crosses** 'krɒs ɪz
  'krɔːs-, -əz ‖ 'krɔːs əz 'krɑːs- **crossing**
  'krɒs ɪŋ 'krɔːs- ‖ 'krɔːs ɪŋ 'krɑːs-
  ,crossed 'line
cross- ˌkrɒs ˌkrɔːs ‖ ˌkrɔːs ˌkrɑːs
  — **cross-cultural** ˌkrɒs 'kʌltʃ ᵊr_əl ◂ ˌkrɔːs-
  ‖ ˌkrɔːs- ˌkrɑːs-
crossbar 'krɒs bɑː 'krɔːs- ‖ 'krɔːs bɑːr 'krɑːs-
  ~s z
crossbeam 'krɒs biːm 'krɔːs- ‖ 'krɔːs- 'krɑːs- **~s**
  z
crossbench 'krɒs bentʃ 'krɔːs-, ˌ·'· ‖ 'krɔːs-
  'krɑːs- **~er/s** ə/z ‖ ᵊr/z **~es** ɪz əz
crossbill 'krɒs bɪl 'krɔːs- ‖ 'krɔːs- 'krɑːs- **~s** z
crossbones 'krɒs bəʊnz 'krɔːs- ‖ 'krɔːs boʊnz
  'krɑːs-
cross-border ˌkrɒs 'bɔːd ə ◂ ˌkrɔːs-
  ‖ ˌkrɔːs 'bɔːrd ᵊr ˌkrɑːs-
crossbow 'krɒs bəʊ 'krɔːs- ‖ 'krɔːs boʊ 'krɑːs-
  ~s z
crossbred 'krɒs bred 'krɔːs- ‖ 'krɔːs- 'krɑːs-
crossbreed 'krɒs briːd 'krɔːs- ‖ 'krɔːs- 'krɑːs-
  ~s z
cross-channel ˌkrɒs 'tʃæn ᵊl ◂ ˌkrɔːs- ‖ ˌkrɔːs-
  ˌkrɑːs-

C

crosscheck v ˌkrɒs 'tʃek ˌkrɔːs-, '·· ‖ ˌkrɔːs- ˌkrɑːs- **~ed** t **~ing** ɪŋ **~s** s
crosscheck n 'krɒs tʃek 'krɔːs-, ˌ·'· ‖ 'krɔːs- 'krɑːs- **~s** s
cross-country ˌkrɒs 'kʌntr i ◂ ˌkrɔːs- ‖ ˌkrɔːs- ˌkrɑːs-
   ˌcross-ˌcountry 'running
crosscourt 'krɒs kɔːt 'krɔːs- ‖ 'krɔːs kɔːrt 'krɑːs-, -koʊrt
cross-cultural ˌkrɒs 'kʌltʃ ᵊr_əl ◂ ˌkrɔːs- ‖ ˌkrɔːs- ˌkrɑːs-
crosscurrent 'krɒs ˌkʌr ənt 'krɔːs- ‖ 'krɔːs ˌkɝː ənt 'krɑːs- **~s** s
crosscut n 'krɒs kʌt 'krɔːs- ‖ 'krɔːs- 'krɑːs- **~s** s
cross|cut v, adj 'krɒs |kʌt 'krɔːs-, ˌ·'· ‖ 'krɔːs- 'krɑːs- **~cuts** kʌts **~cutting** kʌt ɪŋ ‖ kʌt̬ ɪŋ
cross-dress|er ˌkrɒs 'dres |ə ˌkrɔːs- ‖ ˌkrɔːs 'dres |ᵊr ˌkrɑːs- **~ers** əz ‖ ᵊrz **~ing** ɪŋ
crosse krɒs ‖ krɔːs krɑːs
cross-examination ˌkrɒs ɪg ˌzæm ə 'neɪ ᵊn ˌkrɔːs-, -ˌɪk-, -ˌəg-, -ˌək-, -ˌeg-, -ˌek-, -ɪ'·- ‖ ˌkrɔːs- ˌkrɑːs- **~s** s
cross-examin|e ˌkrɒs ɪg 'zæm ɪn ˌkrɔːs-, -ɪk-, -əg-, -ək-, -eg-, -ek-, §-ən ‖ ˌkrɔːs- ˌkrɑːs- **~ed** d **~es** z **~ing** ɪŋ
cross-eyed ˌkrɒs 'aɪd ◂ ˌkrɔːs-, '·· ‖ 'krɔːs aɪd 'krɑːs-, ˌ·'·
cross-fertilis... —see **cross-fertiliz...**
cross-fertilization ˌkrɒs ˌfɜːt ᵊl aɪ 'zeɪʃ ᵊn ˌkrɔːs-, -ɪl aɪ-, -ɪ'·-, -ə'- ‖ ˌkrɔːs ˌfɜːt̬ ᵊl ə- ˌkrɑːs-
cross-fertiliz|e ˌkrɒs 'fɜːt ə laɪz ˌkrɔːs-, -ɪ-, -ᵊl aɪz ‖ ˌkrɔːs 'fɜːt̬ ᵊl aɪz ˌkrɑːs- **~ed** d **~es** ɪz əz **~ing** ɪŋ
crossfire 'krɒs ˌfaɪ ə 'krɔːs- ‖ 'krɔːs ˌfaɪ ᵊr 'krɑːs-
cross-grained ˌkrɒs 'greɪnd ◂ ˌkrɔːs- ‖ ˌkrɔːs- ˌkrɑːs-
cross-hatching 'krɒs ˌhætʃ ɪŋ 'krɔːs- ‖ 'krɔːs- 'krɑːs-
cross-index ˌkrɒs 'ɪnd eks ˌkrɔːs- ‖ ˌkrɔːs- ˌkrɑːs- **~ed** t **~es** ɪz əz **~ing** ɪŋ
crossing 'krɒs ɪŋ 'krɔːs- ‖ 'krɔːs ɪŋ 'krɑːs- **~s** z
crossjack 'krɒs dʒæk 'krɔːs- ‖ 'krɔːs- 'krɑːs- —nautically also 'krɔːdʒ ɪk, 'krɒdʒ-, -ək ‖ 'krɑːdʒ-, 'krɔːdʒ-
cross-legged ˌkrɒs 'legd ◂ ˌkrɔːs-, '·; -'leg ɪd, -əd ‖ 'krɔːs legd 'krɑːs-, ˌ·'·
Crossley 'krɒs li 'krɔːs- ‖ 'krɔːs- 'krɑːs-
Crossmaglen ˌkrɒs mə 'glen ˌkrɔːs- ‖ ˌkrɑːs-
Crossman 'krɒs mən 'krɔːs- ‖ 'krɔːs- 'krɑːs-
crossmatch ˌkrɒs 'mætʃ ˌkrɔːs-, '·· ‖ ˌkrɔːs- ˌkrɑːs- **~ed** t **~es** ɪz əz **~ing** ɪŋ
crossover 'krɒs ˌəuv ə 'krɔːs- ‖ 'krɔːs ˌoʊv ᵊr 'krɑːs- **~s** z
crosspatch 'krɒs pætʃ 'krɔːs- ‖ 'krɔːs- 'krɑːs- **~es** ɪz əz
crosspiec|e 'krɒs piːs 'krɔːs- ‖ 'krɔːs- 'krɑːs- **~es** ɪz əz
cross|ply 'krɒs |plaɪ 'krɔːs- ‖ 'krɔːs- 'krɑːs- **~plies** plaɪz

cross-polli|nate ˌkrɒs 'pɒl ə |neɪt ˌkrɔːs-, -ɪ- ‖ ˌkrɔːs 'pɑːl- ˌkrɑːs- **~nated** neɪt ɪd -əd ‖ neɪt̬ əd **~nates** neɪts **~nating** neɪt ɪŋ ‖ neɪt̬ ɪŋ
cross-pollination ˌkrɒs ˌpɒl ə 'neɪʃ ᵊn ˌkrɔːs-, -ɪ- ‖ ˌkrɔːs ˌpɑːl- ˌkrɑːs-
cross-purposes ˌkrɒs 'pɜːp əs ɪz ˌkrɔːs-, -əz ‖ ˌkrɔːs 'pɝːp-, ˌkrɑːs-, '·,···
cross-question ˌkrɒs 'kwes tʃən ˌkrɔːs-, →-'kweʃ- ‖ ˌkrɔːs- ˌkrɑːs- **~ed** d **~ing** ɪŋ **~s** z
cross-re|fer ˌkrɒs rɪ |'fɜː ˌkrɔːs-, -rə-, §-riː- ‖ ˌkrɔːs rɪ |'fɜːɪ ˌkrɑːs- **~ferred** 'fɜːd ‖ 'fɝːd **~ferring** 'fɜːr ɪŋ ‖ 'fɝː ɪŋ **~fers** 'fɜːz ‖ 'fɝːz
cross-referenc|e ˌkrɒs 'ref ᵊr_ᵊn's ˌkrɔːs- ‖ ˌkrɔːs-, '·,··· **~ed** t **~es** ɪz əz **~ing** ɪŋ
crossroad 'krɒs rəʊd 'krɔːs- ‖ 'krɔːs roʊd 'krɑːs- **~s** z
cross-section 'krɒs ˌsek ʃᵊn 'krɔːs-, ˌ·'·· ‖ 'krɔːs- 'krɑːs- **~ed** d **~s** z
cross-sectional ˌkrɒs 'sek ʃᵊn_əl ◂ ˌkrɔːs- ‖ ˌkrɔːs- ˌkrɑːs-
cross-selling ˌkrɒs 'sel ɪŋ ˌkrɔːs- ‖ ˌkrɔːs- ˌkrɑːs-
cross-stitch 'krɒs stɪtʃ 'krɔːs- ‖ 'krɔːs- 'krɑːs-
crosstalk 'krɒs tɔːk 'krɔːs- ‖ 'krɔːs tɔːk 'krɑːs tɑːk
crosstown ˌkrɒs 'taʊn ◂ ˌkrɔːs- ‖ ˌkrɔːs- ˌkrɑːs-
cross-train ˌkrɒs 'treɪn ˌkrɔːs- ‖ ˌkrɔːs- ˌkrɑːs- **~ed** d **~er/s** ə/z ‖ ᵊr/z **~ing** ɪŋ **~s** z
crosstree 'krɒs triː 'krɔːs- ‖ 'krɔːs- 'krɑːs- **~s** z
crosswalk 'krɒs wɔːk 'krɔːs- ‖ 'krɔːs wɔːk 'krɑːs wɑːk **~s** s
crossways 'krɒs weɪz 'krɔːs- ‖ 'krɔːs- 'krɑːs-
crosswind 'krɒs wɪnd 'krɔːs- ‖ 'krɔːs- 'krɑːs- **~s** z
crosswise 'krɒs waɪz 'krɔːs- ‖ 'krɔːs- 'krɑːs-
crossword 'krɒs wɜːd 'krɔːs- ‖ 'krɔːs wɝːd 'krɑːs- **~s** z
   'crossword ˌpuzzle
crosswort 'krɒs wɜːt 'krɔːs-, -wɔːt ‖ 'krɔːs wɝːt 'krɑːs-, -wɔːrt
Crosthwaite 'krɒs θweɪt 'krɔːs- ‖ 'krɔːs- 'krɑːs-
crostini krɒ 'stiːn i ‖ krɑː- —It [kro 'stiː ni]
crotch krɒtʃ ‖ krɑːtʃ **crotched** krɒtʃt ‖ krɑːtʃt **crotches** 'krɒtʃ ɪz -əz ‖ 'krɑːtʃ əz
crotchet 'krɒtʃ ɪt -ət ‖ 'krɑːtʃ ət **~s** s
crotchet|y 'krɒtʃ ət |i |ɪ -ɪt- ‖ 'krɑːtʃ ət̬ |i |i **~iness** i nəs i nɪs
croton, Croton 'krəʊt ᵊn ‖ 'kroʊt- **~s** z
crouch, Crouch kraʊtʃ —but the place in Kent is kruːtʃ **crouched** kraʊtʃt **crouches** 'kraʊtʃ ɪz -əz **crouching** 'kraʊtʃ ɪŋ
Crouchback 'kraʊtʃ bæk
croup kruːp
croupier 'kruːp i ə -i eɪ ‖ ᵊr **~s** z
croupy 'kruːp i
crouton 'kruːt ɒn -õ ‖ -ɑːn kruː 'tɑːn —Fr [kʁu tɔ̃] **~s** z
crow, Crow krəʊ ‖ kroʊ **crew** kruː **crowed** krəʊd ‖ kroʊd **crowing** 'krəʊ ɪŋ ‖ 'kroʊ ɪŋ **crows** krəʊz ‖ kroʊz
crowbar 'krəʊ bɑː ‖ 'kroʊ bɑːr **~s** z

Crowborough 'krəʊ bər ə ‖ 'kroʊ ˌbɜː oʊ
crowd kraʊd **crowded** 'kraʊd ɪd -əd
  crowding 'kraʊd ɪŋ **crowds** kraʊdz
  ˌcrowded 'out
crowdedness 'kraʊd ɪd nəs -əd-, -nɪs
crowd-pleas|er 'kraʊd ˌpliːz ə ‖ -ᵊr **~ers** əz
  ‖ ᵊrz **~ing** ɪŋ
Crowe krəʊ ‖ kroʊ
crowfoot 'krəʊ fʊt ‖ 'kroʊ- **~s** s
Crowhurst 'krəʊ hɜːst ‖ 'kroʊ hɜːst
Crowley (i) 'krəʊ li ‖ 'kroʊ li; (ii) 'kraʊ-
crown kraʊn **crowned** kraʊnd **crowning**
  'kraʊn ɪŋ **crowns** kraʊnz
  ˌcrown 'colony; ˌcrown 'court; ˌCrown
  'Derby; ˌcrowned 'head; ˌcrown 'jewels;
  ˌcrown 'prince◂, ˌCrown Prince 'George
Crowndale 'kraʊn deɪᵊl
Crowne kraʊn
crown-of-thorns ˌkraʊn əv 'θɔːnz ‖ -'θɔːrnz
crow's-|foot 'krəʊz| fʊt ‖ 'kroʊz- **~feet** fiːt
crow's-nest 'krəʊz nest ‖ 'kroʊz- **~s** s
Crowther 'kraʊð ə ‖ -ᵊr
Crowthorne 'krəʊ θɔːn ‖ 'kroʊ θɔːrn
Croxford 'krɒks fəd ‖ 'krɑːks fᵊrd
Croyde krɔɪd
Croydon 'krɔɪd ᵊn
crozier, C~ 'krəʊz iˌə 'krəʊʒ ə ‖ 'kroʊʒ ᵊr **~s** z
cru kruː —Fr [kʁy]
cruces 'kruːs iːz
crucial 'kruːʃ ᵊl 'kruːʃ iˌəl **~ly** i
cruciality ˌkruːʃ i 'æl ət i -ɪt i ‖ -əţ i
crucian 'kruːʃ ᵊn
cruciate 'kruːʃ i eɪt 'kruːs-, ˌ_ət, ˌɪt
crucible 'kruːs əb ᵊl -ɪb- **~s** z
crucifer 'kruːs ɪf ə -əf- ‖ -əf ᵊr **~s** z
Cruciferae kruː 'sɪf ə riː
cruciferous kruː 'sɪf ər əs
crucifix 'kruːs ə fɪks -ɪ- **~es** ɪz əz
crucifixion ˌkruːs ə 'fɪk ʃᵊn -ɪ- **~s** z
cruciform 'kruːs ɪ fɔːm -ə- ‖ -fɔːrm
cruci|fy 'kruːs ɪ |faɪ -ə- **~fied** faɪd **~fier/s**
  faɪ ə/z ‖ faɪ ᵊr/z **~fies** faɪz **~fying** faɪ ɪŋ
cruck krʌk **crucks** krʌks
crud krʌd
Cruddas 'krʌd əs
cruddy 'krʌd i
crude kruːd **cruder** 'kruːd ə ‖ -ᵊr **crudest**
  'kruːd ɪst -əst
crudely 'kruːd li
Cruden 'kruːd ᵊn **~'s** z
crudeness 'kruːd nəs -nɪs
crudites, crudités 'kruːd ɪ teɪ -ə-
  ‖ ˌkruːd ɪ 'teɪ —Fr [kʁy di te]
crudit|y 'kruːd ət i |i -ɪt- ‖ -əţ |i **~ies** iz
cruel 'kruː əl kruːl **crueler, crueller** 'kruː əl ə
  'kruːl ə ‖ -ᵊr **cruelest, cruellest** 'kruː əl ɪst
  -əst; 'kruːl ɪst, -əst
Cruella de Vil kru ˌel ə də 'vɪl
cruelly 'kruː əl i -li; 'kruːl i, -li
cruel|ty 'kruː əl |ti |ti 'kruːl |ti **~ties** tiz
cruelty-free ˌkruː əl ti 'friː ◂ ˌkruːl ti 'friː ◂
cruet 'kruː ɪt §ˌət **~s** s
Cruft krʌft **Crufts, Cruft's** krʌfts

Cruickshank, Cruikshank 'krʊk ʃæŋk
  §'kruːk-
cruise, C~ kruːz (= crews) **cruised** kruːzd
  cruises 'kruːz ɪz -əz **cruising** 'kruːz ɪŋ
  ˌcruise 'missile ‖ '· ·ˌ·
cruiser 'kruːz ə ‖ -ᵊr **~s** z
cruiserweight 'kruːz ə weɪt ‖ -ᵊr- **~s** s
cruising 'kruːz ɪŋ
  'cruising speed
cruller 'krʌl ə ‖ -ᵊr **~s** z
crumb krʌm **crumbed** krʌmd **crumbing**
  'krʌm ɪŋ **crumbs** krʌmz
crumbl|e 'krʌm bᵊl **~ed** d **~es** z **~ing** ɪŋ
crum|bly 'krʌm |bli **-blier** bli ə ‖ bli ᵊr
  ~bliest bli ɪst bli əst
crumb|y 'krʌm |i **~ier** i ə ‖ i ᵊr **~iest** i ɪst i əst
crumhorn 'krʌm hɔːn ‖ -hɔːrn
Crumlin 'krʌm lɪn -lən
Crummock 'krʌm ək
crumm|y 'krʌm |i **~ier** i ə ‖ i ᵊr **~iest** i ɪst i əst
crump, Crump krʌmp **crumped** krʌmpt
  crumping 'krʌmp ɪŋ **crumps, Crump's**
  krʌmps
crumpet 'krʌmp ɪt §ˌət **~s** s
crumpl|e 'krʌmp ᵊl **~ed** d **~es** z **~ing** ɪŋ
crunch krʌntʃ **crunched** krʌntʃt **crunches**
  'krʌntʃ ɪz -əz **crunching** 'krʌntʃ ɪŋ
Crunchie tdmk 'krʌntʃ i **~s** z
crunch|y 'krʌntʃ |i **~iness** i nəs i nɪs
crupper 'krʌp ə ‖ -ᵊr
crusad|e kruː 'seɪd **~ed** ɪd əd **~es** z **~ing** ɪŋ
crusader kruː 'seɪd ə ‖ -ᵊr **~s** z
cruse, Cruse kruːz ‖ kruːs (usually = cruise)
  cruses 'kruːz ɪz -əz ‖ 'kruːs-
crush krʌʃ **crushed** krʌʃt **crushes** 'krʌʃ ɪz -əz
  crushing/ly 'krʌʃ ɪŋ /li
  'crush ˌbarrier
crushable 'krʌʃ əb ᵊl
Crusoe 'kruːs əʊ 'kruːz- ‖ -oʊ
crust krʌst **crusted** 'krʌst ɪd -əd **crusting**
  'krʌst ɪŋ **crusts** krʌsts
crustacean krʌ 'steɪʃ ᵊn -'steɪʃ ᵊn **~s** z
crustal 'krʌst ᵊl
crust|y 'krʌst |i **~ier** i ə ‖ i ᵊr **~iest** i ɪst i əst
  ~ily ɪ li əl i **~iness** i nəs i nɪs
crutch, Crutch krʌtʃ **crutched** krʌtʃt
  crutches 'krʌtʃ ɪz -əz **crutching** 'krʌtʃ ɪŋ
Cruttenden 'krʌt ᵊnd ən
Cruttwell, Crutwell 'krʌt wəl
crux krʌks krʊks **cruces** 'kruːs iːz **cruxes**
  'krʌks ɪz -əz
Cruyff kraɪf —Dutch [kʁœyf]
Cruyff krɔɪf kraɪf —Dutch [krœyf]
Cruz kruːz —Sp [kruθ], AmSp [krus], Port
  [kruʃ], BrazPort [krus]
cruzeiro kru 'zeər əʊ ‖ -'zer oʊ —Port
  [kru 'zei ru] **~s** z
crwth kruːθ
cry kraɪ **cried** kraɪd **cries** kraɪz **crying** 'kraɪ ɪŋ
crybab|y 'kraɪ ˌbeɪb |i **~ies** iz
Cryer 'kraɪ ə ‖ 'kraɪ ᵊr
cryo- comb. form
  with stress-neutral suffix |kraɪ əʊ -ə ‖ -ə -oʊ

C

— **cryoscopic** ˌkraɪ əʊ ˈskɒp ɪk ◄
‖ -ə ˈskɑːp ɪk ◄
with stress-imposing suffix kraɪ ˈɒ + ‖ -ˈɑː +
— **cryoscopy** kraɪ ˈɒsk əp i ‖ -ˈɑːsk-
cryogenic ˌkraɪ əʊ ˈdʒen ɪk ◄ ‖ -ə- **~s** s
cryonic kraɪ ˈɒn ɪk ‖ -ˈɑːn- **~s** s
cryostat ˈkraɪˌə stæt **~s** s
cryotron ˈkraɪˌə trɒn ‖ -trɑːn **~s** z
crypt krɪpt **crypts** krɪpts
crypt- *comb. form before vowel* ¦krɪpt —
cryptanalysis ˌkrɪpt ə ˈnæl əs ɪs -ɪs ɪs, §-əs
cryptic ˈkrɪpt ɪk **~ally** ᵊl i
crypto ˈkrɪpt əʊ ‖ -oʊ **~s** z
crypto- *comb. form before consonant*
with stress-neutral suffix ¦krɪpt əʊ ‖ -oʊ —
crypto-Fascist ˌkrɪpt əʊ ˈfæʃ ɪst §-əst ‖ -oʊ-
with stress-imposing suffix krɪp ˈtɒ + ‖ -ˈtɑː +
— **cryptogamous** krɪp ˈtɒg əm əs ‖ -ˈtɑːg-
cryptogam ˈkrɪpt ə gæm **~s** z
cryptogram ˈkrɪpt ə græm **~s** z
cryptographer krɪp ˈtɒg rəf ə ‖ -ˈtɑːg rəf ᵊr
~s z
cryptographic ˌkrɪpt ə ˈgræf ɪk ◄ **~ally** ᵊl i
cryptography krɪp ˈtɒg rəf i ‖ -ˈtɑːg-
cryptorchidism krɪp ˈtɔːk ɪ ˌdɪz əm -ˈə-
‖ -ˈtɔːrk-
crystal, C~ ˈkrɪst ᵊl **~s** z
ˌcrystal ˈball; ˌcrystal ˈclear◄; ˈcrystal
ˌgazing; ˌCrystal ˈPalace; ˈcrystal set
crystaliz... —*see* **crystalliz...**
crystalline ˈkrɪst ə laɪn -liːn; -ᵊl aɪn, -iːn
‖ -ᵊl ən -ə laɪn, -ə liːn
crystallis... —*see* **crystalliz...**
crystallization ˌkrɪst ᵊl aɪ ˈzeɪʃ ᵊn -ᵊl ɪ-, -ᵊl ə-
‖ -ᵊl ə-
crystalliz|e ˈkrɪst ə laɪz -ᵊl aɪz **~ed** d **~es** ɪz əz
~ing ɪŋ
crystallographer ˌkrɪst ə ˈlɒg rəf ə -ᵊl ˈɒg-
‖ -ᵊl ˈɑːg rəf ᵊr **~s** z
crystallographic ˌkrɪst ᵊl ə ˈgræf ɪk ◄ **~al** ᵊl
~ally ᵊl i
crystallography ˌkrɪst ə ˈlɒg rəf i -ᵊl ˈɒg-
‖ -ᵊl ˈɑːg-
csardas, csárdás ˈtʃɑːd æʃ -ɑːʃ; ˈzɑːd əs
‖ ˈtʃɑːrd ɑːʃ —*Hung* [ˈtʃɑːr dɑːʃ]
CSE ˌsiː es ˈiː **~s, ˈs** z
C-section ˈsiː ˌsek ʃᵊn
CS gas ˌsiː es ˈgæs
ctenoid ˈtiːn ɔɪd ˈten-
CT scan ˌsiː ˈtiː skæn ˈkæt skæn **~s** z
cub kʌb **cubbing** ˈkʌb ɪŋ **cubs** kʌbz
ˈCub Scout
Cuba ˈkjuːb ə —*Sp* [ˈku βa]
Cuban ˈkjuːb ən **~s** z
cubbyhole ˈkʌb i həʊl →-hɒʊl ‖ -hoʊl **~s** z
cube kjuːb **cubed** kjuːbd **cubes** kjuːbz **cubing**
ˈkjuːb ɪŋ
ˌcube ˈroot ‖ ˈ· ·
cubeb ˈkjuːb eb **~s** z
cubic ˈkjuːb ɪk
cubical ˈkjuːb ɪk ᵊl (= *cubicle*) **~ly** i
cubicle ˈkjuːb ɪk ᵊl **~s** z
cubism ˈkjuːb ˌɪz əm

cubist ˈkjuːb ɪst §-əst **~s** s
cubit ˈkjuːb ɪt §-ət **~s** s
Cubitt ˈkjuːb ɪt §-ət
Cublington ˈkʌb lɪŋ tən
cuboid ˈkjuːb ɔɪd **~s** z
Cuckfield ˈkʊk fiːᵊld
cucking-stool ˈkʌk ɪŋ stuːl **~s** z
Cuckmere ˈkʊk mɪə ‖ -mɪr
Cuckney ˈkʌk ni
cuckold ˈkʌk əʊld →-ɒʊld, -ᵊld ‖ -oʊld -ᵊld
~ed ɪd əd **~er/s** ə/z ‖ -ᵊr/z **~ing** ɪŋ **~s** z
cuckoldry ˈkʌk ᵊld ri -əʊld- ‖ -oʊld-
cuckoo ˈkʊk uː ‖ ˈkuːk- ˈkʊk- **~s** z
ˈcuckoo clock
cuckoopint ˈkʊk uː paɪnt -pɪnt ‖ ˈkuːk- ˈkʊk-
~s s
cuckoo-spit ˈkʊk uː spɪt ‖ ˈkuːk- ˈkʊk-
cucumber ˈkjuːk ʌm bə ‖ -bᵊr **~s** z
cucurbit kju ˈkɜːb ɪt §-ət ‖ -ˈkɜːb- **~s** s
cud kʌd
cudbear ˈkʌd beə →ˈkʌb- ‖ -ber
Cuddesdon ˈkʌdz dən
cuddl|e ˈkʌd ᵊl **~ed** d **~es** z **~ing** ɪŋ
cuddlesome ˈkʌd ᵊl səm
cuddly ˈkʌd ᵊl i
Cuddy, cudd|y ˈkʌd |i **~ies** iz
cudgel ˈkʌdʒ əl **~ed, ~led** d **~ing, ~ling** ɪŋ **~s**
z
Cudlipp ˈkʌd lɪp
cudweed ˈkʌd wiːd
Cudworth ˈkʌd wəθ -wɜːθ ‖ -wᵊrθ —*locally
also* -əθ
cue kjuː **cued** kjuːd **cueing, cuing** ˈkjuːˌ ɪŋ
cues kjuːz
ˈcue ball
cuff, Cuff kʌf **cuffed** kʌft **cuffing** ˈkʌf ɪŋ
cuffs kʌfs
Cuffley ˈkʌf li
cufflink ˈkʌf lɪŋk **~s** s
cui bono ˌkuː i ˈbəʊn əʊ ˌkwiː ˈ·-, -ˈbɒn-
‖ ˌkwiː ˈboʊn oʊ
Cuillin ˈkuːl ɪn -ən
cuirass kwɪ ˈræs kwə-, kjuᵊ- **~ed** t **~es** ɪz əz
cuirassier ˌkwɪr ə ˈsɪə kjʊər- ‖ -ˈsɪᵊr **~s** z
Cuisenaire, c~ ˌkwiːz ə ˈneə ‖ -ˈneᵊr —*Fr*
[kɥiz nɛːʁ]
Cuisinart, c~ ˈkwiːz ɪn ɑːt ˈkwɪz- ‖ -ɑːrt **~s** s
cuisine kwɪ ˈziːn kwə-, △kju- —*Fr* [kɥi zin]
ˌcui,sine minˈceur mæn ˈsɜː ‖ -ˈsɜːr —*Fr*
[mæ̃ sœːʁ]
cuisse kwɪs **cuisses** ˈkwɪs ɪz -əz
Culbertson ˈkʌlb ət sən ‖ -ᵊrt-
Culcheth ˈkʌltʃ əθ -ɪθ
cul-de-sac ˈkʌl də sæk ˈkʊl-, ˌ· ·ˈ· —*Fr*
[kyd sak, kyt-] **~s** s
Culham ˈkʌl əm
culinary ˈkʌl ɪn ər i ˈkjuːl-, ˈ-ən- ‖ -ə ner i
Culkin ˈkʌlk ɪn §-ən
cull kʌl **culled** kʌld **culling** ˈkʌl ɪŋ **culls** kʌlz
Cullen ˈkʌl ən -ɪn
cullender ˈkʌl ənd ə -ɪnd- ‖ -ᵊr **~s** z
culler, C~ ˈkʌl ə ‖ -ᵊr **~s** z
cullet ˈkʌl ɪt -ət

Cullinan 'kʌl ɪn ən -ən-
Culloden kə 'lɒd ᵊn kʌ-, -'ləʊd- ‖ -'lɑːd- -'loʊd-
   Cul,loden 'Moor
Cullompton kə 'lʌmpt ən 'kʌl əmpt-
culm, Culm kʌlm
culmi|nate 'kʌlm ɪ |neɪt -ə- **~nated** neɪt ɪd
   -əd ‖ neɪt̬ əd **~nates** neɪts **~nating** neɪt ɪŋ
   ‖ neɪt̬ ɪŋ
culmination ,kʌlm ɪ 'neɪʃ ᵊn -ə- **~s** z
culminative 'kʌlm ɪn ət ɪv '-ən-; -ɪ neɪt ɪv, -ə · ·
   ‖ -ə neɪt̬ ɪv **~ly** li
culotte kju 'lɒt ku- ‖ 'kuːl ɑːt 'kjuːl-; ku 'lɑːt,
   kju- —Fr [ky lɔt] **~s** s
culpa 'kʊlp ə -ɑː
culpability ,kʌlp ə 'bɪl ət i -ɪt i ‖ -ət̬ i
culpab|le 'kʌlp əb |ᵊl **~ly** li
Culpeper, Culpepper 'kʌl ,pep ə ‖ -ᵊr
culprit 'kʌlp rɪt -rət **~s** s
Culross (i) 'kʌl rɒs ,·'·; 'kuː-, -rəs ‖ -rɔːs -rɑːs;
   (ii) 'kuː- —In Scotland, (ii); otherwise usually
   (i)
culs-de-sac 'kʌl də sæk 'kʊl-, ,·'· —Fr
   [kyd sak, kyt-]
Culshaw 'kʌl ʃɔː ‖ -ʃɑː
cult kʌlt **cults** kʌlts
Culter 'kuːt ə ‖ 'kuːt̬ ᵊr (!)
cultic 'kʌlt ɪk
cultism 'kʌlt ,ɪz əm
cultist 'kʌlt ɪst §-əst **~s** s
cultivable 'kʌlt ɪv əb ᵊl '·əv-
cultivar 'kʌlt ɪ vɑː -ə- ‖ -vɑːr **~s** z
culti|vate 'kʌlt ɪ |veɪt -ə- **~vated** veɪt ɪd -əd
   ‖ veɪt̬ əd **~vates** veɪts **~vating** veɪt ɪŋ
   ‖ veɪt̬ ɪŋ
cultivation ,kʌlt ɪ 'veɪʃ ᵊn -ə- **~s** z
cultivator 'kʌlt ɪ veɪt ə '·ə- ‖ -veɪt̬ ᵊr **~s** z
cultural 'kʌltʃ ᵊr_əl **~ly** i
culture 'kʌltʃ ə ‖ -ᵊr **~d** d **~s** z **culturing**
   'kʌltʃ ər_ɪŋ
   'culture ,medium; 'culture shock
Culver 'kʌlv ə ‖ -ᵊr
culvert 'kʌlv ət ‖ -ᵊrt **~s** s
Culzean kə 'leɪn
cum 'come' kʌm
cum, -cum- Latin prep kʌm kʊm —may be
   stressed or unstressed —See also phrases with
   this word
Cumae 'kjuːm iː
cumber 'kʌm bə ‖ -bᵊr **~ed** d **cumbering**
   'kʌm bər_ɪŋ **~s** z
Cumberland 'kʌm bə lənd ‖ -bᵊr-
Cumberledge 'kʌm bə ledʒ -lɪdʒ ‖ -bᵊr-
Cumbernauld ,kʌm bə 'nɔːld '· · · ‖ -bᵊr-
   -'nɑːld
cumbersome 'kʌm bə səm ‖ -bᵊr- **~ly** li **~ness**
   nəs nɪs
Cumbrae 'kʌm breɪ
Cumbria 'kʌm bri_ə
Cumbrian 'kʌm bri_ən **~s** z
cumbrous 'kʌm brəs
cum grano salis kʌm ,greɪn əʊ 'seɪl ɪs kʊm-,
   -,grɑːn-, -'sɑːl-, -'sæl-, §-əs
   ‖ kʊm ,grɑːn oʊ 'sɑːl əs

cumin 'kʌm ɪn 'kuːm-, 'kjuːm-, §-ən
cum laude ⑴kʌm 'laʊd eɪ ⑴kʊm-, 'lɔːd-, -i
   ‖ kʊm 'laʊd i -ə
cummerbund 'kʌm ə bʌnd ‖ -ᵊr- **~s** z
cummin, C~ 'kʌm ɪn §-ən
Cummings, cummings 'kʌm ɪŋz
Cumnock 'kʌm nək
Cumnor 'kʌm nə ‖ -nᵊr
cumquat 'kʌm kwɒt ‖ -kwɑːt **~s** s
cumshaw 'kʌm ʃɔː ‖ -ʃɑː **~s** z
cumulative 'kjuːm jʊl ət ɪv '-jəl-; -ju leɪt-,
   -jə leɪt- ‖ -jəl ət̬ ɪv -jə leɪt̬ ɪv **~ly** li **~ness** nəs
   nɪs
cumulonimbus ,kjuːm jʊl əʊ 'nɪm bəs ,·jəl-
   ‖ -jə loʊ-
cumulostratus ,kjuːm jʊl əʊ 'streɪt əs ,·jəl-,
   -'strɑːt- ‖ -jə loʊ 'streɪt̬ əs -'stræt̬-
cumulus 'kjuːm jʊl əs -jəl- ‖ -jəl əs
Cunard ⑴kjuː 'nɑːd ‖ -'nɑːrd ,kuː- **~er/s** ə/z
   ‖ -ᵊr/z
cunctation ⑴kʌŋk 'teɪʃ ᵊn
cunctator ⑴kʌŋk 'teɪt ə ‖ -'teɪt̬ ᵊr **~s** z
Cundy 'kʌnd i
cuneal 'kjuːn i_əl
cuneate 'kjuːn i eɪt ət, ɪt
cuneiform 'kjuːn ɪ fɔːm 'kjuːn i_ɪ fɔːm, -i_ə-;
   kju 'neɪ ɪ fɔːm, -'niː-, -ə fɔːm ‖ -fɔːrm
Cuningham, Cuninghame 'kʌn ɪŋ əm
   ‖ -hæm
Cunliffe 'kʌn lɪf
cunnilinctus ,kʌn ɪ 'lɪŋkt əs -ə-
cunnilingus ,kʌn ɪ 'lɪŋ gəs -ə-
cunning 'kʌn ɪŋ **~ly** li **~ness** nəs nɪs
Cunningham 'kʌn ɪŋ əm ‖ -hæm
Cunobelin, Cunobeline kju 'nɒb əl ɪn §-ən
   ‖ -'noʊb-
Cunobelinus ,kjuːn əʊ bə 'laɪn əs -bɪ'--, -'liːn-
   ‖ ,kjuːn oʊ-
cunt kʌnt **cunts** kʌnts
Cunynghame 'kʌn ɪŋ əm ‖ -hæm
Cuomo 'kwəʊm əʊ ‖ 'kwoʊm oʊ
cup kʌp **cupped** kʌpt **cupping** 'kʌp ɪŋ **cups**
   kʌps
   'cup ,final, ,·'· ·
Cupar 'kuːp ə ‖ -ᵊr
cupbearer 'kʌp ,beər ə ‖ -,ber ᵊr **~s** z
cupboard 'kʌb əd ‖ -ᵊrd **~s** z
   'cupboard love
cupcake 'kʌp keɪk **~s** s
Cupertino ,kuːp ə 'tiːn əʊ ‖ -ᵊr 'tiːn oʊ
cupful 'kʌp fʊl **~s** z
cupid, Cupid 'kjuːp ɪd §-əd **~s, ~'s** z
cupidity kju 'pɪd ət i -ɪt- ‖ -ət̬ i
Cupit, Cupitt 'kjuːp ɪt §-ət
cupola 'kjuːp əl ə -ə **~s** z
cuppa 'kʌp ə
cupreous 'kjuːp ri_əs
cupric 'kjuːp rɪk
Cuprinol tdmk 'kjuːp rɪ nɒl -rə- ‖ -nɑːl -nɔːl,
   -noʊl
cupronickel ,kjuːp rəʊ 'nɪk ᵊl ,kuːp- ‖ -roʊ-
cuprous 'kjuːp rəs
cup-tie 'kʌp taɪ **~s** z

cupule 'kju:p ju:l ~s z
cur kɜː ‖ kɜ·ː **curs** kɜːz ‖ kɜ·ːz
curable 'kjʊər əb ᵊl 'kjɔːr- ‖ 'kjʊr-
curacao, curaçao, C~ 'kjʊər ə səʊ 'kjɔːr-, ˌ·ˈ· ‖ 'kjʊr ə soʊ 'kʊr-, -saʊ, ˌ·ˈ·
curac|y 'kjʊər əs |i 'kjɔːr- ‖ 'kjʊr- **~ies** iz
curare, curari kjuᵊ 'rɑːr i
curassow 'kjʊər ə səʊ 'kjɔːr- ‖ 'kjʊr ə soʊ ~s z
cur|ate v kjuᵊ 'r|eɪt ‖ 'kjʊr |eɪt **~ated** eɪt ɪd -əd ‖ eɪt̬ əd **~ates** eɪts **~ating** eɪt ɪŋ ‖ eɪt̬ ɪŋ
curate n 'kjʊər ət 'kjɔːr-, -ɪt ‖ 'kjʊr- -eɪt **~s** s
　'curate's 'egg
curative 'kjʊər ət ɪv 'kjɔːr- ‖ 'kjʊr ət̬ ɪv **~ly** li **~ness** nəs nɪs
curator kjuᵊ 'reɪt ə 'kjʊr eɪt̬ ᵊr -ət̬-; kju 'reɪt̬ ᵊr **~s** z
curb kɜːb ‖ kɜ·ːb **curbed** kɜːbd ‖ kɜ·ːbd **curbing** 'kɜːb ɪŋ ‖ 'kɜ·ːb ɪŋ **curbs** kɜːbz ‖ kɜ·ːbz
curbstone 'kɜːb stəʊn ‖ 'kɜ·ːb stoʊn ~s z
curd kɜːd ‖ kɜ·ːd **curds** kɜːdz ‖ kɜ·ːdz
　'curd 'cheese, '· ·
curdl|e 'kɜːd ᵊl ‖ 'kɜ·ːd ᵊl **~ed** d **~es** z **~ing** _ɪŋ
cure kjʊə kjɔː ‖ kjʊᵊr **cured** kjʊəd kjɔːd ‖ kjʊᵊrd **cures** kjʊəz kjɔːz ‖ kjʊᵊrz **curing** 'kjʊər ɪŋ 'kjɔːr- ‖ 'kjʊr ɪŋ
curé 'kjʊər eɪ 'kjɔːr- ‖ kju 'reɪ 'kjʊr eɪ —Fr [ky ʁe] **~s** z
cure-all 'kjʊər ɔːl 'kjɔːr- ‖ 'kjʊr ɔːl -ɑːl **~s** z
curettage kjuᵊ 'ret ɪdʒ ˌkjʊər ɪ 'tɑːʒ, -ə- ‖ ˌkjʊr ə 'tɑːʒ
curette kjuᵊ 'ret **~s** s
curfew 'kɜːf ju: ‖ 'kɜ·ːf- **~s** z
cur|ia 'kjʊər |i̯ə 'kjɔːr-, 'kʊər- ‖ 'kjʊr- **~iae** i i: i aɪ
Curie, curie 'kjʊər i -i: ‖ 'kjʊr i kju 'ri: —Fr [ky ʁi] **~s** z
curing —see **cure**
curio 'kjʊər i əʊ 'kjɔːr- ‖ 'kjʊr i oʊ
curiosa ˌkjʊər i 'əʊs ə ‖ ˌkjʊr i 'oʊs ə -'oʊz-
curiosity ˌkjʊər i 'ɒs ət i ˌkjɔːr-, -ɪt i ‖ ˌkjʊr i 'ɑːs ət̬ i
curious 'kjʊər i̯əs 'kjɔːr- ‖ 'kjʊr- **~er** ə ‖ ᵊr **~ly** li **~ness** nəs nɪs
curium 'kjʊər i̯əm 'kjɔːr- ‖ 'kjʊr-
cur|l kɜːl ‖ kɜ·ːᵊl **curled** kɜːld ‖ kɜ·ːᵊld **curling** 'kɜːl ɪŋ ‖ 'kɜ·ːl ɪŋ **curls** kɜːlz ‖ kɜ·ːᵊlz
curler 'kɜːl ə ‖ 'kɜ·ːl ᵊr **~s** z
curlew 'kɜːl ju: -u: ‖ 'kɜ·ːl- **~s** z
curlicue 'kɜːl i kju: ‖ 'kɜ·ːl- **~s** z
curling 'kɜːl ɪŋ ‖ 'kɜ·ːl ɪŋ
curl|y 'kɜːl |i ‖ 'kɜ·ːl |i **~ier** i̯ə ‖ i̯ᵊr **~ies** iz **~iest** i̯ɪst i̯əst **~iness** i nəs i nɪs
curlycue 'kɜːl i kju: ‖ 'kɜ·ːl- **~s** z
curmudgeon kɜː 'mʌdʒ ən kə- ‖ kᵊr- **~ly** li **~s** z
Curr kɜː ‖ kɜ·ː
curragh, C~ 'kʌr ə -əx ‖ 'kɜ·ː ə **~s** z
Curran 'kʌr ən ‖ 'kɜ·ː-
currant 'kʌr ənt ‖ 'kɜ·ː- (= current) **~s** s
　ˌcurrant 'bun
currawong 'kʌr ə wɒŋ ‖ 'kɜ·ː ə wɑːŋ **~s** z
currenc|y 'kʌr ən̩ts |i ‖ 'kɜ·ː- **~ies** iz

current 'kʌr ənt ‖ 'kɜ·ː- **~ly** li **~ness** nəs nɪs **~s** s
　ˌcurrent af'fairs
curricul|um kə 'rɪk jʊl |əm -jəl- ‖ -jəl- **~a** ə **~ar** ə ‖ ᵊr
　curˌriculum 'vitae 'vi:t aɪ -eɪ; 'vaɪt i: ‖ 'vaɪt̬ i 'wi:t aɪ
Currie 'kʌr i ‖ 'kɜ·ː i
currier 'kʌr i̯ə ‖ 'kɜ·ː i̯ᵊr **~s** z
currish 'kɜːr ɪʃ ‖ 'kɜ·ː-
curr|y, Curry 'kʌr |i ‖ 'kɜ·ː |i **~ied** id **~ies** iz **~ying** i_ɪŋ
　'curry ˌpowder
curse kɜːs ‖ kɜ·ːs **cursed** kɜːst ‖ kɜ·ːst **curses** 'kɜːs ɪz -əz ‖ 'kɜ·ːs əz **cursing** 'kɜːs ɪŋ ‖ 'kɜ·ːs ɪŋ **curst** kɜːst ‖ kɜ·ːst
cursed adj 'kɜːs ɪd -əd; kɜːst ‖ 'kɜ·ːs əd kɜ·ːst **~ly** li **~ness** nəs nɪs
cursed past, pp kɜːst ‖ kɜ·ːst
cursive 'kɜːs ɪv ‖ 'kɜ·ːs ɪv **~ly** li **~s** z
cursor 'kɜːs ə ‖ 'kɜ·ːs ᵊr **~s** z
cursorial kɜː 'sɔːr i̯əl ‖ kᵊr- -'soʊr-
cursor|y 'kɜːs ᵊr ˌi ‖ 'kɜ·ːs- **~ily** əl i ɪ li **~iness** i nəs i nɪs
curst kɜːst ‖ kɜ·ːst
curt, Curt kɜːt ‖ kɜ·ːt
curtail kɜː 'teɪᵊl kə- ‖ kᵊr- **~ed** d **~ing** ɪŋ **~ment** mənt **~s** z
curtain 'kɜːt ᵊn ‖ 'kɜ·ːt- **~ed** d **~ing** _ɪŋ **~s** z
　'curtain call
curtain-raiser 'kɜːt ᵊn ˌreɪz ə ‖ 'kɜ·ːt ᵊn ˌreɪz ᵊr **~s** z
curtain-up ˌkɜːt ᵊn 'ʌp ‖ ˌkɜ·ːt-
curtilage 'kɜːt əl ɪdʒ -ɪl- ‖ 'kɜ·ːt̬ ᵊl-
Curtin 'kɜːt ɪn §-ᵊn ‖ 'kɜ·ːt ᵊn
Curtis, Curtiss 'kɜːt ɪs §-əs ‖ 'kɜ·ːt̬-
Curtius 'kɜːt i̯əs ‖ 'kɜ·ːt̬- —but as a German name sometimes 'kɜːts- ‖ 'kɜ·ːts- —Ger ['kʊʁ tsi ʊs]
curtly 'kɜːt li ‖ 'kɜ·ːt-
curtness 'kɜːt nəs -nɪs ‖ 'kɜ·ːt-
curts|ey, curts|y 'kɜːts |i ‖ 'kɜ·ːts |i **~eyed, ~ied** id **~eying, ~ying** i_ɪŋ **~eys, ~ies** iz
curvaceous, curvacious kɜː 'veɪʃ əs ‖ kᵊr- **~ly** li **~ness** nəs nɪs
curvature 'kɜːv ətʃ ə -ə tjʊə ‖ 'kɜ·ːv ə tʃʊr -tʃᵊr, -tʊr, -tjʊr
curve kɜːv ‖ kɜ·ːv **curved** kɜːvd ‖ kɜ·ːvd **curves** kɜːvz ‖ kɜ·ːvz **curving** 'kɜːv ɪŋ ‖ 'kɜ·ːv-
curvet kɜː 'vet ‖ kᵊr- 'kɜ·ːv ət **curveted, curvetted** kɜː 'vet ɪd -əd ‖ kᵊr 'vet̬ əd 'kɜ·ːv ət̬ əd **curveting, curvetting** kɜː 'vet ɪŋ ‖ kᵊr 'vet̬ ɪŋ 'kɜ·ːv ət̬ ɪŋ **curvets** kɜː 'vets ‖ kᵊr- 'kɜ·ːv əts
curvilinear ˌkɜːv ɪ 'lɪn i̯ə ◂ ˌ·ə- ‖ ˌkɜ·ːv ə 'lɪn i̯ᵊr ◂ **~ly** li
curvy 'kɜːv i ‖ 'kɜ·ːv i
Curwen 'kɜː wɪn -wən ‖ 'kɜ·ː-
Curzon 'kɜːz ᵊn ‖ 'kɜ·ːz-
Cusack (i) 'kju:s æk, (ii) 'kju:z-
cuscus 'kʌs kʌs 'kʌsk əs **~es** ɪz əz
Cush kʌʃ kʊʃ
Cushing 'kʊʃ ɪŋ

cushion 'kʊʃ ᵊn ~**ed** d ~**ing** ɪŋ ~**s** z
Cushite 'kʌʃ aɪt 'kʊʃ- ~**s** s
Cushitic kʌ 'ʃɪt ɪk kʊ- ‖ -'ʃɪt̬-
cush|y 'kʊʃ |i ~**ier** i ə ‖ i ᵊr ~**iest** i ɪst i ‿əst
cusp kʌsp **cusped** kʌspt **cusps** kʌsps
cuspid 'kʌsp ɪd §-əd
cuspidor 'kʌsp ɪ dɔː §-ə- ‖ -dɔːr -doʊr ~**s** z
cuss kʌs **cussed** kʌst **cusses** 'kʌs ɪz -əz
    cussing 'kʌs ɪŋ
cussed *past, pp* kʌst
cussed *adj* 'kʌs ɪd -əd ~**ly** li ~**ness** nəs nɪs
Cusson 'kʌs ᵊn
custard 'kʌst əd ‖ -ᵊrd ~**s** z
    ˌcustard 'apple; ˌcustard 'pie; 'custard
    ˌpowder
Custer 'kʌst ə ‖ -ᵊr ~'**s** z
custodial kʌ 'stəʊd i ə l kə- ‖ -'stoʊd-
custodian kʌ 'stəʊd i ‿ən kə- ‖ -'stoʊd- ~**ship**
    ʃɪp
custod|y 'kʌst əd |i ~**ies** iz
custom 'kʌst əm ~**s** z
    'custom(s) house
customable 'kʌst əm əb ᵊl
customarily 'kʌst əm ᵊr_əl i ɪ li, ˌkʌst ə 'mer-
    ‖ ˌkʌst ə 'mer əl i
customary 'kʌst əm ər‿i ‖ -ə mer i
custom-built ˌkʌst əm 'bɪlt ◄ ' · ·
customer 'kʌst əm ə ‖ -ᵊr ~**s** z
customis|e, customiz|e 'kʌst ə maɪz ~**able**
    əb ᵊl ~**ed** d ~**es** ɪz əz ~**ing** ɪŋ
custom-made ˌkʌst əm 'meɪd ◄ ' · ·
cut kʌt **cuts** kʌts **cutting** 'kʌt ɪŋ ‖ 'kʌt̬ ɪŋ
    ˌcut 'glass ◄, ˌcut glass 'bowls
cut-and-cover ˌkʌt ᵊn 'kʌv ə ◄ ‖ -ᵊr
cut-and-dried ˌkʌt ᵊn 'draɪd ◄
cut-and-dry ˌkʌt ᵊn 'draɪ
cutaneous kju 'teɪn i ‿əs ~**ly** li
cutaway 'kʌt ə ˌweɪ ‖ 'kʌt̬- ~**s** z
cutback 'kʌt bæk ~**s** s
cutch, Cutch kʌtʃ
cute kjuːt **cuter** 'kjuːt ə ‖ 'kjuːt̬ ᵊr **cutest**
    'kjuːt ɪst -əst ‖ 'kjuːt̬ əst
cute|ly 'kjuːt |li ‖ **-ness** nəs nɪs
cutesy 'kjuːts i
Cutex *tdmk* 'kjuːt eks
cutey 'kjuːt i ‖ 'kjuːt̬ i ~**s** z
Cutforth 'kʌt fɔːθ ‖ -fɔːrθ -foʊrθ
Cuthbert 'kʌθ bət ‖ -bᵊrt
Cuthbertson 'kʌθ bət sən ‖ -bᵊrt-
cuticle 'kjuːt ɪk ᵊl ‖ 'kjuːt̬- ~**s** z
Cuticura *tdmk* ˌkjuːt ɪ 'kjʊər ə -ə-, -'kjɔːr-
    ‖ ˌkjuːt̬ ə 'kjʊr ə
cutie 'kjuːt i ‖ 'kjuːt̬ i ~**s** z
cutis 'kjuːt ɪs §-əs ‖ 'kjuːt̬-
cutlas, cutlass 'kʌt ləs ~**es** ɪz əz
cutler, C~ 'kʌt lə ‖ -lᵊr ~**s** z
cutlery 'kʌt lər i -ler i
cutlet 'kʌt lət -lɪt ~**s** s
cutoff 'kʌt ɒf -ɔːf ‖ 'kʌt̬ ɔːf -ɑːf ~**s** s
cutout 'kʌt aʊt ‖ 'kʌt̬- ~**s** s
cut-price ˌkʌt 'praɪs ◄
cutpurse 'kʌt pɜːs ‖ -pɝːs ~**es** ɪz əz
cut-rate ˌkʌt 'reɪt ◄

cutter, C~ 'kʌt ə ‖ 'kʌt̬ ᵊr ~**s** z
cutthroat 'kʌt θrəʊt ‖ -θroʊt ~**s** s
cutting 'kʌt ɪŋ ‖ 'kʌt̬ ɪŋ ~**ly** li ~**s** z
    ˌcutting 'edge
cuttle 'kʌt ᵊl ‖ 'kʌt̬ ᵊl
cuttlebone 'kʌt ᵊl bəʊn ‖ 'kʌt̬ ᵊl boʊn
cuttlefish 'kʌt ᵊl fɪʃ ‖ 'kʌt̬- ~**es** ɪz əz
Cutty Sark ˌkʌt i 'saːk ‖ 'kʌt̬ i saːrk
cutup 'kʌt ʌp ‖ 'kʌt̬- ~**s** s
cutwater 'kʌt ˌwɔːt ə ‖ -ˌwɔːt̬ ᵊr -ˌwaːt̬ ᵊr ~**s** z
cutworm 'kʌt wɜːm ‖ -wɝːm ~**s** z
Cuvier 'kjuːv i eɪ ‖ ˌ · '· — *Fr* [ky vje]
Cuxhaven 'kʊks ˌhaːv ᵊn — *Ger* [kʊks 'haːf ᵊn]
Cuyahoga ˌkaɪ ə 'həʊg ə ◄ -'hɒg- ‖ -'hoʊg ə ◄
    -'hɔːg-, -'haːg-; kə'· -
    ˌCuya ˌhoga 'River
Cuyp kaɪp kɔɪp — *Dutch* [kœyp]
cuz '*because*' kəz
Cuzco 'kʊsk əʊ ‖ 'kuːsk oʊ — *AmSp* ['kus ko]
CV ˌsiː 'viː ~**s**, ~'**s** z
CVA ˌsiː viː 'eɪ ~**s**, ~'**s** z
cwm, Cwm kʊm kuːm — *Welsh* [kʊm] **cwms**
    kʊmz kuːmz
    ₍ᵢ₎Cwm 'Rhondda
Cwmbran, Cwmbrân kʊm 'braːn kuːm-
Cwmyoy kʊm 'jɔɪ
cwt —*see* **hundredweight**
-cy si — **bankruptcy** 'bæŋk rʌpts i -rəpts-
Cy saɪ
cyan 'saɪ ən -æn
cyanamid saɪ 'æn əm ɪd §-əd; 'saɪ ˌən-
cyanamide saɪ 'æn ə maɪd -əm ɪd, §-əm əd;
    'saɪ ˌən- ‖ -əm əd
cyanate 'saɪ ə neɪt ~**s** s
cyanic saɪ 'æn ɪk
cyanide 'saɪ ə naɪd ~**s** z
cyano 'saɪ ə nəʊ saɪ 'æn əʊ ‖ 'saɪ ə noʊ
cyanogen saɪ 'æn ədʒ ən -ɪn, -en
cyanosis ˌsaɪ ə 'nəʊs ɪs §-əs ‖ -'noʊs-
Cybele 'sɪb əl i -ɪl-
cybercafe, cybercafé 'saɪb ə ˌkæf eɪ -i
    ‖ -ᵊr kæ ˌfeɪ ˌ · ·'· ~**s** z
cybercrime 'saɪb ə kraɪm ‖ -ᵊr-
cyberfraud 'saɪb ə frɔːd ‖ -ᵊr- -frɑːd
cybernetic ˌsaɪb ə 'net ɪk ◄ ‖ -ᵊr 'net̬- ~**ally**
    ᵊl_i ~**s** s
cyber|punk 'saɪb ə |pʌŋk ‖ -ᵊr- ~**punks** pʌŋks
cyberspace 'saɪb ə speɪs ‖ -ᵊr-
cyber-squatt|er 'saɪb ə ˌskwɒt |ə
    ‖ -ᵊr ˌskwaːt̬ |ᵊr ~**ers** əz ‖ ᵊrz ~**ing** ɪŋ
cyborg 'saɪb ɔːg ‖ -ɔːrg ~**s** z
cycad 'saɪk æd -əd ~**s** z
Cyclades 'sɪk lə diːz
cyclamate 'saɪk lə meɪt 'sɪk- ~**s** s
cyclamen 'sɪk ləm ən 'saɪk-, -lə men ~**s** z
cycle 'saɪk ᵊl — *In the senses 'bicycle', 'ride a*
    bicycle' only, there is also an AmE
    pronunciation 'sɪk- **cycled** 'saɪk ᵊld **cycles**
    'saɪk ᵊlz **cycling** 'saɪk ᵊl_ɪŋ
    'cycle track
cycleway 'saɪk ᵊl weɪ ~**s** z
cyclic 'saɪk lɪk 'sɪk-

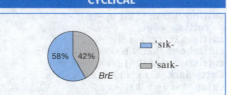

CYCLICAL

58% 42%

■ 'sɪk-
■ 'saɪk-

BrE

cyclical 'sɪk lɪk ᵊl 'saɪk- — *Preference poll, BrE:* 'sɪk- *58%*, 'saɪk- *42%*. **~ly** ˌi
cycling 'saɪk lɪŋ
cyclist 'saɪk lɪst §-ləst **~s** s
cyclo- *comb. form*
    with stress-neutral suffix ¦saɪk ləʊ ¦sɪk ləʊ
    ‖ -loʊ — **cyclohexane** ˌsaɪk ləʊ 'heks eɪn
    ˌsɪk- ‖ -loʊ-
    with stress-imposing suffix saɪ 'klɒ +
    ‖ -'klɑː+ — **cyclometer** saɪ 'klɒm ɪt ə -ət-
    ‖ -'klɑːm əṱ ᵊr
cyclo-cross 'saɪk ləʊ krɒs -krɔːs ‖ -loʊ krɔːs
    -krɑːs
cycloid 'saɪk lɔɪd **~s** z
cyclometer saɪ 'klɒm ɪt ə -ət- ‖ -'klɑːm əṱ ᵊr
    ~s z
cyclone 'saɪk ləʊn ‖ -loʊn **~s** z
cyclonic saɪ 'klɒn ɪk ‖ -'klɑːn- **~al** ᵊl
cyclopaedia ˌsaɪk ləʊ 'piːd i ə ‖ ˌ-lə- **~s** z
cyclopaedic ˌsaɪk ləʊ 'piːd ɪk ◄ ‖ -lə- **~ally** ᵊl_i
Cyclopean, c~ ˌsaɪk ləʊ 'piː ən ◄
    saɪ 'kləʊp i ən ‖ -lə-
cyclopedia ˌsaɪk ləʊ 'piːd i ə ‖ ˌ-lə- **~s** z
cyclopedic ˌsaɪk ləʊ 'piːd ɪk ◄ ‖ -lə- **~ally** ᵊl_i
cyclopes, C~ saɪ 'kləʊp iːz ‖ -'kloʊp-
cyclops, C~ 'saɪk lɒps ‖ -lɑːps
cyclorama ˌsaɪk ləʊ 'rɑːm ə ‖ -lə 'ræm ə
    -'rɑːm- **~s** z
cyclosporin ˌsaɪk ləʊ 'spɔːr ɪn §-ən ‖ -loʊ-
    -'spoʊr-
cyclostyl|e 'saɪk ləʊ staɪᵊl ‖ -lə- **~ed** d **~es** z
    ~ing ɪŋ
cyclothym|ia ˌsaɪk ləʊ 'θaɪm ¦i ə ˌsɪk- ‖ ˌ-lə-
    ~ic ɪk ◄
cyclotron 'saɪk ləʊ trɒn ‖ -lə trɑːn **~s** z
cyder 'saɪd ə ‖ -ᵊr **~s** z
Cydrax *tdmk* 'saɪdr æks
Cyfeiliog kə 'vaɪl i ɒg ‖ -ɑːg -ɔːg — *Welsh*
    [kə 'vəɪl jog]
cygnet 'sɪg nət -nɪt *(= signet)* **~s** s
Cygnus 'sɪg nəs
cylinder 'sɪl ɪnd ə -ənd- ‖ -ᵊr **~s** z
cylindrical sə 'lɪndr ɪk ᵊl sɪ-, -ək- **~ly** ˌi
cyma 'saɪm ə
cymbal 'sɪm bᵊl *(= symbol)* **~s** z
cymbalist 'sɪm bᵊl ɪst §-əst
cymbalo 'sɪm bə ləʊ ‖ -loʊ **~s** z
Cymbeline 'sɪm bə liːn -bɪ-
cymbidium sɪm 'bɪd i əm **~s** z
cyme saɪm **cymes** saɪmz
Cymric 'kɪm rɪk 'kʌm-
Cymru, Cymry 'kʌm ri △'kʊm-, 'kɪm- —*Other*
    pronunciations may be heard from those not

familiar with Welsh —Welsh ['kəm ri, -rɨ] *(in
Welsh these two words are homophones)*
ˌ**Cymru am 'byth** æm 'bɪθ —*Welsh*
    [am 'bɪθ, -'bɨθ]
Cynan 'kʌn ən —*Welsh* ['kə nan]
Cynara 'sɪn ər ə sɪ 'nɑːr ə
Cyncoed kɪn 'kɔɪd →kɪŋ-
Cynewulf 'kɪn ɪ wʊlf -ə-
cynghanedd kən 'hæn eð kʌŋ-, -'hɑːn-
    —*Welsh* [kəŋ 'ha neð]
cynic, Cynic 'sɪn ɪk **~s** s
cynical 'sɪn ɪk ᵊl **~ly** ˌi **~ness** nəs nɪs
cynicism 'sɪn ɪ ˌsɪz əm -ə-
Cynon 'kʌn ən —*Welsh* ['kə nɒn]
cynosure 'saɪn ə sjʊə 'sɪn-, -zjʊə, -ʃʊə, -ʒʊə
    ‖ -ʃʊr **~s** z
Cynthia 'sɪnᵗθ i ə
cypher 'saɪf ə ‖ -ᵊr **~s** z
cy pres, cy près ˌsiː 'preɪ ˌsaɪ-
cy pres, cy près ˌsiː 'preɪ ˌsaɪ-
cypress 'saɪp rəs -rɪs **~es** ɪz əz
Cyprian 'sɪp ri ən
Cypriot 'sɪp ri ət **~s** s
Cypriote 'sɪp ri əʊt ‖ -oʊt **~s** s
cypripedium ˌsɪp rɪ 'piːd i əm ˌ-rə- **~s** z
Cyprus 'saɪp rəs
Cyrano de Bergerac
    ˌsɪr ə nəʊ də 'bɜːʒ ə ræk -'beəʒ-
    ‖ -noʊ də 'bɜːʒ- -rɑːk —*Fr*
    [si ʁa nod bɛʁ ʒə ʁak]
Cyrenaic ˌsaɪᵊr ə 'neɪ ɪk ◄ ˌsɪr-, -ɪ- ‖ ˌsɪr-
Cyrenaica ˌsaɪᵊr ə 'neɪ ɪk ə ˌsɪr-, -ɪ-, -'naɪ-
    ‖ ˌsɪr-
Cyrene saɪᵊ 'riːn i
Cyrenian saɪᵊ 'riːn i ən i_ən **~s** z
Cyriac 'sɪr i æk
Cyriax 'sɪr i æks
Cyril 'sɪr əl -ɪl
Cyrillic sə 'rɪl ɪk sɪ-, kɪ-
Cyrus 'saɪᵊr əs
-cyst sɪst — **otocyst** 'əʊt əʊ sɪst ‖ 'oʊṱ oʊ-
cyst sɪst **cysts** sɪsts
cystectom|y sɪ 'stekt əm ¦i **~ies** iz
cysteine 'sɪst i iːn -ɪn; 'sɪst eɪn ‖ -ə-
cystic 'sɪst ɪk
cystine 'sɪst iːn -ɪn
cystitis sɪ 'staɪt ɪs §-əs ‖ -'staɪṱ-
cysto- *comb. form*
    with stress-neutral suffix ¦sɪst ə
    — **cystoscope** 'sɪst ə skəʊp ‖ -skoʊp
    with stress-imposing suffix sɪ 'stɒ + sə-
    ‖ -'stɑː+ — **cystoscopy** sɪ 'stɒsk əp i
    ‖ -'stɑːsk-
-cyte saɪt — **leucocyte** 'luːk ə saɪt 'ljuː-k-
Cythera sɪ 'θɪər ə sə- ‖ -'θɪr ə
Cytherea ˌsɪθ ə 'riː_ə
cyto- *comb. form*
    with stress-neutral suffix ¦saɪt əʊ ‖ ¦saɪṱ ə -oʊ
    — **cytolytic** ˌsaɪt əʊ 'lɪt ɪk ◄ ‖ ˌsaɪṱ ə 'lɪṱ-
    with stress-imposing suffix saɪ 'tɒ + ‖ -'tɑː+
    — **cytolysis** saɪ 'tɒl əs ɪs -ɪs-, §-əs ‖ -'tɑːl-
cytogenetic ˌsaɪt əʊ dʒə 'net ɪk ◄ -dʒɪ'--
    ‖ ˌsaɪṱ oʊ dʒə 'neṱ- **~s** s **~ally** ᵊl_i **~s** s

cytological ˌsaɪt ə 'lɒdʒ ɪk ᵊl ◄
  ‖ ˌsaɪţ ə 'lɑːdʒ- **~ly** ˌi
cytologist saɪ 'tɒl ədʒ ɪst §-əst ‖ -'tɑːl- **~s** s
cytology saɪ 'tɒl ədʒ i ‖ -'tɑːl-
cytomegalovirus ˌsaɪt əʊ 'meg ə ləʊ ˌvaɪᵊr əs
  -ᵊl əʊ- ‖ ˌsaɪţ ə 'meg ə loʊ-
cytoplasm 'saɪt əʊ ˌplæz əm ‖ 'saɪţ ə-
cytoplasmic ˌsaɪt əʊ 'plæz mɪk ◄ ‖ ˌsaɪţ ə-
cytosine 'saɪt əʊ siːn ‖ 'saɪţ ə-
cytotoxic ˌsaɪt əʊ 'tɒks ɪk ◄ ‖ ˌsaɪţ ə 'tɑːks-
cytotoxin ˌsaɪt əʊ 'tɒks ɪn §-ᵊn
  ‖ ˌsaɪţ ə 'tɑːks ᵊn **~s** z

czar zɑː tsɑː ‖ zɑːr tsɑːr **czars** zɑːz tsɑːz ‖ zɑːrz
  tsɑːrz
czardas 'tʃɑːd æʃ -ɑːʃ; 'zɑːd əs ‖ 'tʃɑːrd ɑːʃ
  —Hung csárdás ['tʃɑːr dɑːʃ]
czardom 'zɑː dəm 'tsɑː- ‖ 'zɑːr- 'tsɑːr-
czarina zɑː 'riːn ə tsɑː- **~s** z
czarism 'zɑːr ˌɪz əm 'tʃɑːr-
Czech tʃek *(= check)* **Czechs** tʃeks
Czechoslovak ˌtʃek əʊ 'sləʊv æk ◄
  ‖ -oʊ 'sloʊv- -ə-, -ɑːk **~s** s
Czechoslovaki|a ˌtʃek əʊ sləʊ 'væk iˌ|ə
  -'vɑːk- ‖ -ə sloʊ 'vɑːk- -'væk- **~an/s** ən/z

Dd

d Spelling-to-sound

1 Where the spelling is **d**, the pronunciation is regularly d as in **dead** ded.

2 Where the spelling is double **dd**, the pronunciation is again d as in **middle** ˈmɪd ᵊl.

3 Less frequently, the pronunciation is dʒ as in **gradual** ˈgrædʒ u ˌəl, **procedure** prə ˈsiːdʒ ə ‖ -ᵊr. This pronunciation comes about through yod coalescence (see ASSIMILATION), and applies where the spelling is **du**, most typically where **u** counts as a weak vowel. Some BrE speakers also do this where **u** counts as a strong vowel, and likewise where the spelling is **eu**, **ew** as in **dew**, **due** djuː or dʒuː.

4 The verb ending **-ed** has three regular pronunciations (see alphabetic entry at **-ed**). Note that after a voiceless consonant the pronunciation is regularly t as in **clapped** klæpt.

5 **d** is usually silent in **sandwich** and **Wednesday**.

D, d diː **D's, d's, Ds** diːz —*Communications code name:* Delta
-d —*see* **-ed**
-'d d —*This contracted form of* had *and* would *is used only after words (usually pronouns) ending in a vowel sound:* he'd hiːd, I'd aɪd, she'd ʃiːd, they'd ðeɪd, we'd wiːd, you'd juːd, who'd huːd, Joe'd dʒəʊd ‖ dʒoʊd. *After a word ending in a consonant the spelling* 'd *implies merely a weak form,* əd*:* it'd ɪt əd ‖ ɪţ əd. *The occasional contracted form of* did *(esp. AmE) is pronounced in the same way.*
d' d —*This contracted form of* do *is found principally in* d'you djuː, →dʒuː, dʒə
da *in Italian phrases* daː də —*It* [da] —*See also phrases with this word*
DA ˌdiː ˈeɪ
dab dæb **dabbed** dæbd **dabbing** ˈdæb ɪŋ **dabs** dæbz
　ˌdab ˈhand
dabbl|e ˈdæb ᵊl **~ed** d **~er/s** ˌə/z ‖ ᵊr/z **~es** z **~ing** ˌɪŋ
dabchick ˈdæb tʃɪk **~s** s
D'Abernon ˈdæb ən ən ‖ ˈdaːb- ‖ -ᵊrn-
dabster ˈdæb stə ‖ -stᵊr **~s** z
da capo daː ˈkaːp əʊ də- ‖ -oʊ —*It* [dak ˈkaː po]
Dacca ˈdæk ə —*see* Dhaka
dace deɪs **daces** ˈdeɪs ɪz -əz
dacha ˈdætʃ ə ‖ ˈdaːtʃ ə —*Russ* [ˈda tʃə] **~s** z

Dachau ˈdæk aʊ ˈdæx- ‖ ˈdaːk- —*Ger* [ˈdax aʊ]
dachshund ˈdæks ᵊnd ˈdæʃ-, -hʊnd, -hʊnt ‖ ˈdaːks hʊnt —*Ger* [ˈdaks hʊnt] **~s** z
Dacia ˈdeɪs i ə ˈdeɪʃ ə, ˈdeɪʃ i ə
Dacian ˈdeɪs i ən ˈdeɪʃ ᵊn, ˈdeɪʃ i ən **~s** z
dacoit də ˈkɔɪt **~s** s
Dacre ˈdeɪk ə ‖ -ᵊr
dacron, D~ *tdmk* ˈdæk rɒn ˈdeɪk- ‖ ˈdeɪk raːn ˈdæk-
dactyl ˈdækt ɪl -ᵊl **~s** z
dactylic dæk ˈtɪl ɪk **~ally** ᵊl_i
dactylogram dæk ˈtɪl ə græm **~s** z
dactylographic ˌdæk ˌtɪl ə ˈgræf ɪk ◂
dactylography ˌdækt ɪ ˈlɒg rəf i ˌ ə- ‖ -ˈlaːg-
-dactylous ˈdækt ɪl əs -əl- — **polydactylous** ˌpɒl i ˈdækt ɪl əs ◂ -əl əs ‖ ˌpaːl-
dad, Dad dæd **dads, Dad's** dædz
dada, Dada ˈdaːd aː
dadaism, D~ ˈdaːd aːʳ ˌɪz əm ‖ -aː-
dadaist, D~ ˈdaːd aːʳ ɪst §-əst ‖ -aː- **~s** s
dadaistic, D~ ˌdaːd aːʳ ˈɪst ɪk ◂ ‖ -aː-
daddy, Daddy ˈdæd i **daddies, Daddy's** ˈdæd iz
ˌdaddy ˈlonglegs ˈlɒŋ legz ‖ ˈlɔːŋ- ˈlaːŋ-
Dade deɪd
dado ˈdeɪd əʊ ‖ -oʊ **~s** z
Daedalus ˈdiːd əl əs ‖ ˈded- (*)
daemon ˈdiːm ən ˈdaɪm-, ˈdeɪm- **~s** z

D

daemonic dɪ 'mɒn ɪk də-, di:- ‖ -'mɑ:n- **~ally**
əl i

Daewoo 'deɪ u: ‖ ˌdaɪ 'wu: —*Korean* [dɛ u]

DAF, Daf *tdmk* dæf

daff, Daff dæf **daffs** dæfs

daffodil 'dæf ə dɪl **~s** z

daff|y, Daffy 'dæf |i **~ier** i ə ‖ i ᵊr **~iest** i ɪst
i əst

daft dɑ:ft §dæft ‖ dæft **dafter** 'dɑ:ft ə §'dæft-
‖ 'dæft ᵊr **daftest** 'dɑ:ft ɪst §'dæft-, -əst
‖ 'dæft-

daft|ly 'dɑ:ft |li §'dæft- ‖ 'dæft- **~ness** nəs nɪs

Dafydd 'dæv ɪð 'dɑ:v- —*Also sometimes* 'dæf-,
-ɪd *by those not familiar with Welsh.* —*Welsh*
['da vɪð, -vɪð]

  Dafydd ap 'Gwilym æp 'gwɪl ɪm ɑ:p-

dag dæg **dags** dægz

da Gama də 'gɑ:m ə ‖ -'gæm- —*Port*
[dɐ 'ɣɐ mɐ]

Dagenham 'dæg ən əm

Dagestan ˌdɑ:g ɪ 'stɑ:n -ə-

Dagg dæg

dagga 'dæx ə 'dæg-, 'dʌx-, 'dɑ:g-

dagger 'dæg ə ‖ -ᵊr **~s** z

Daggett 'dæg ɪt §-ət

dagg|y 'dæg |i **~ier** i ə ‖ i ᵊr **~iest** i ɪst i əst

Daglish 'dæg lɪʃ

daglock 'dæg lɒk ‖ -lɑ:k **~s** s

Dagmar 'dæg mɑ: ‖ -mɑ:r

dago 'deɪg əʊ ‖ -oʊ **~es, ~s** z

Dagon 'deɪg ɒn -ən ‖ -ɑ:n

daguerreotype, daguerrotype
də 'ger əʊ taɪp ‖ -ə- **~s** s

Dagwood 'dæg wʊd

Dahl dɑ:l

dahlia, D~ 'deɪl i ə ‖ 'dæl jə 'dɑ:l- (*) **~s** z

Dahmer 'dɑ:m ə ‖ -ᵊr

Dahomey də 'həʊm i ‖ -'hoʊm i

Dahrendorf 'dær ən dɔ:f 'dɑ:r- ‖ -dɔ:rf —*Ger*
['da: ʁən dɔʁf]

Dai daɪ

Daiches *(i)* 'deɪʃ ɪz -əz, -ɪs, -əs, *(ii)* 'deɪtʃ-,
(iii) 'daɪx- ‖ 'daɪk-

Daihatsu *tdmk* daɪ 'hæts u: ‖ -'hɑːts- —*Jp*
[da ˌi ha tsɯ]

daikon 'daɪk ɒn ‖ -ɑ:n —*Jp* [da ˌi kon]

Dail, Dáil dɔɪᵊl dɔ:l, daɪᵊl —*Irish* [dɑːlʲ]

  Dail 'Eireann, ˌDáil 'Éireann 'eər ən
‖ 'eɪ rən 'er- —*Irish* ['e: rʲən]

dail|y 'deɪl |i **~ies** iz

  ˌdaily 'bread

Daimler 'deɪm lə ‖ -lᵊr —*Ger* ['daim lɐ] **~s** z

daimon 'daɪm ɒn -ən ‖ -oʊn

daimyo 'daɪm jəʊ ‖ -joʊ —*Jp* [da ˌi 'mjoo]

daint|y, D~ 'deɪnt |i ‖ 'deɪnt̬ |i **~ier** i ə ‖ i ᵊr
~ies iz **~iest** i ɪst i əst **~ily** ɪ li əl i **~iness**
i nəs i nɪs

daiquiri, D~ 'daɪk ər i 'dæk-, -ɪr- **~s** z

dair|y 'deər |i ‖ 'der |i 'dær- **~ies** iz

  'dairy ˌcattle; 'dairy ˌfarmer

Dairylea *tdmk* ˌdeər i 'li: ◄ ' · · · ‖ ˌder-

dairymaid 'deər i meɪd ‖ 'der- 'dær- **~s** z

dairy|man 'deər i |mən -mæn ‖ 'der- 'dær-
~men mən men

dais 'deɪ ɪs §-əs; deɪs ‖ 'daɪ- **daises** 'deɪ ɪs ɪz
§-əs-, -əz; 'deɪs ɪz, -əz ‖ 'daɪ-

daisy, Daisy 'deɪz i **daisies, Daisy's** 'deɪz iz

  'daisy chain; 'daisy wheel

Daiwa 'daɪ wa: —*Jp* [da ˌi ɰa]

dak dɑːk dɔːk, dæk —*Hindi* [ɖɑːk]

Dakar 'dæk ɑ: -ə ‖ də 'kɑːr —*Fr* [da kaːʁ]

Dakin 'deɪk ɪn §-ən

Dakota də 'kəʊt ə ‖ -'koʊt̬ ə **~s** z

Dakotan də 'kəʊt ᵊn ‖ -'koʊt̬- **~s** z

DAKS *tdmk* dæks

dal *in Italian phrases* dæl dɑ:l ‖ dɑ:l —*It* [dal]

dal *'pulse'* dɑːl

Dalai Lama ˌdæl aɪ 'lɑːm ə ˌdɑːl- ‖ ˌdɑːl-, -i-

Dalaman 'dæl ə mæn ˌ · ' · —*Turkish*
[da la 'man]

dalasi də 'lɑːs i

Dalbeattie dæl 'bi:t i dəl- ‖ -'bi:t̬ i —*locally*
dəl-

Dalberg 'dæl bɜːg ‖ -bɜːg

Dalby *(i)* 'dɔ:l bi 'dɒl- ‖ 'dɑːl-, *(ii)* 'dæl bi

dale, Dale deɪᵊl **dales, Dales** deɪᵊlz

dalek 'dɑːl ek **~s** s

dales|man 'deɪᵊlz |mən -mæn **~men** mən men
~woman ˌwʊm ən **~women** ˌwɪm ɪn §-ən

Daley 'deɪl i

Dalgarno dæl 'gɑːn əʊ ‖ -'gɑːrn oʊ

Dalgetty, Dalgety ₍ₗ₎dæl 'get i dəl- ‖ -'get̬ i

Dalgleish, Dalglish dæl 'gliːʃ dəl-

Dalhousie *(i)* dæl 'haʊz i, *(ii)* -'huːz i —*(i) is
appropriate for the current Earl of D~. The
19th-century governor of Canada is often
referred to as (ii).*

Dali 'dɑːl i —*Sp* Dalí [da 'li], *Catalan* [də 'li]

Dalian ˌdɑː li 'æn —*Chi* Dàlián [⁴da ²ljɛn]

Dalit, dalit 'dʌl ɪt **~s** s

Dalkeith dæl 'kiːθ

Dalkey 'dɔːk i 'dɔːlk- ‖ 'dɔːlk i 'dɑːlk i

Dallaglio də 'læl i əʊ ‖ -'lɑːl i oʊ

Dallapiccola ˌdæl ə 'pɪk əl ə —*It*
[dal la 'pik ko la]

Dallas 'dæl əs

Dallasite 'dæl ə saɪt **~s** s

Dalles dælz

dalliance 'dæl i ənᵗs **~es** ɪz əz

Dalloway 'dæl ə weɪ

dall|y 'dæl |i **~ied** id **~ies** iz

Dalmatia dæl 'meɪʃ ə -'meɪʃ i ə

dalmatian, D~ dæl 'meɪʃ ᵊn -'meɪʃ i ᵊn **~s** z

dalmatic dæl 'mæt ɪk ‖ -'mæt̬- **~s** s

Dalmeny dæl 'men i dəl-

Dalry dəl 'raɪ dæl-

Dalrymple dæl 'rɪmp ᵊl, ' · · ·, dəl 'rɪmp-

dal segno ₍ₗ₎dæl 'sen jəʊ ₍ₗ₎dɑːl-
‖ ₍ₗ₎dɑːl 'seɪn joʊ —*It* [dal 'seɲ ɲo]

Dalston 'dɔːlst ən 'dɒlst- ‖ 'dɑːlst-

Dalton, d~ 'dɔːlt ən 'dɒlt- ‖ 'dɑːlt- **~ism** ˌɪz əm

Daltrey, Daltry 'dɔːltr i 'dɒltr- ‖ 'dɑːltr-

Dalwhinnie dæl 'wɪn i dəl-, -'hwɪn- —*locally*
dəl 'hwɪn i

Daly 'deɪl i

Dalyell *(i)* di 'el daɪ-, *(ii)* 'dæl jəl
Dalzell *(i)* di 'el, *(ii)* 'dæl zel
Dalziel *(i)* di 'el, *(ii)* 'dæl ziːʔl
dam dæm **dammed** dæmd **damming** 'dæm ɪŋ
  dams dæmz
damag|e 'dæm ɪdʒ **~ed** d **~es** ɪz əz **~ing/ly**
  ɪŋ /li
Daman 'deɪm ən
Damara də 'mɑːr ə **~s** z
Damaraland də 'mɑːr ə lænd
Damart *tdmk* 'dæm ɑːt 'deɪm- ‖ -ɑːrt
damascene, D~ 'dæm ə siːn ˌ·'· **~d** d **~s** z
Damascus də 'mæsk əs -'mɑːsk- —*Arabic*
  Dimashq [di 'maʃq]
damask 'dæm əsk **~ed** t **~s** s
D'Amato də 'mɑːt əʊ ‖ -oʊ
dame, Dame deɪm **dames** deɪmz
Damen 'deɪm ən
Damian, Damien, Damion 'deɪm i ən —*As a*
  French name, Damien *is* [da mjæ̃]
damm... —*see* **dam**
dammar 'dæm ə ‖ -ʔr
dammit 'dæm ɪt §-ət
damn dæm *(= dam)* **damned** dæmd **damning**
  'dæm ɪŋ -nɪŋ **damns** dæmz
damnab|le 'dæm nəb |ʔl **~ly** li
damnation ˌ(ˌ)dæm 'neɪʃ ʔn
damnedest 'dæmd ɪst -əst
damn-fool ˌdæm fuːl
Damoclean ˌdæm ə 'kliː ən ◂
Damocles 'dæm ə kliːz
Damon 'deɪm ən
damosel, damozel ˌdæm ə 'zel **~s** z
damp dæmp **damped** dæmpt **damper**
  'dæmp ə ‖ -ʔr **dampest** 'dæmp ɪst -əst
  damping 'dæmp ɪŋ **damps** dæmps
  'damp course; ˌdamp 'squib
dampen 'dæmp ən **~ed** d **~ing** ɪŋ **~s** z
damper, D~ 'dæmp ə ‖ -ʔr **~s** z
Dampier 'dæmp i ə 'dæmp ɪə ‖ ˌʔr
dampish 'dæmp ɪʃ
damp|ly 'dæmp |li **~ness** nəs nɪs
damp-proof 'dæmp pruːf §-prʊf
damsel 'dæmz ʔl 'dæmᵖs ʔl **~s** z
damsel|fly 'dæmz ʔl |flaɪ **~flies** flaɪz
damson 'dæmz ən **~s** z
dan dæn —*Jp* ['daɴ]
Dan dæn
Dana *(i)* 'dɑːn ə, *(ii)* 'deɪn ə, *(iii)* 'dæn ə
  —*Generally (i) in BrE, (ii) in AmE.*
Danae, Danaë 'dæn i iː -eɪ-
Danaides, Danaïdes də 'neɪ ɪ diːz dæ-, -ə-
Dan-Air *tdmk* ˌdæn 'eə ‖ -'eʔr -'æʔr
Da Nang ˌdɑː 'næŋ ‖ də 'nɑːŋ ˌ(ˌ)dɑː-, -'næŋ
Danaus, Danaüs 'dæn i əs -eɪ-
Danbury 'dæn bər i →'dæm- ‖ -ˌber i
Danby 'dæn bi →'dæm-
dance, Dance dɑːnts §dænts ‖ dænts **danced**
  dɑːntst §dæntst ‖ dæntst **dances** 'dɑːnts ɪz
  §'dænts-, -əz ‖ 'dænts- **dancing/ly**
  'dɑːnts ɪŋ /li §'dænts- ‖ 'dænts ɪŋ /li
dancer, D~ 'dɑːnts ə §'dænts- ‖ 'dænts ʔr **~s** z
Dancy 'dænts i

dandelion 'dænd i laɪ ən '·ə-, -ʔl aɪ ‖ -ʔl aɪ ən
  ~s z
Dandenong 'dænd ə nɒŋ ‖ -nɑːŋ
dander 'dænd ə ‖ -ʔr
dandi... —*see* **dandy**
Dandie 'dænd i
  ˌDandie 'Dinmont 'dɪn mənt →-'dɪm-, -mɒnt
dandi|fy 'dænd ɪ |faɪ §-ə- **~fied** faɪd **~fier/s**
  faɪ ə/z ‖ faɪ ʔr/z **~fies** faɪz **~fying** faɪ ɪŋ
Dandini dæn 'diːn i
dandl|e 'dænd ʔl **~ed** d **~es** z **~ing** ɪŋ
Dando 'dænd əʊ ‖ -oʊ
dandruff 'dændr əf -ʌf
dand|y, Dandy 'dænd |i **~ies** iz
Dane deɪn **Danes** deɪnz
Danegeld 'deɪn geld →'deɪŋ-
Danelagh, Danelaw 'deɪn lɔː ‖ -lɑː
dang dæŋ
danger 'deɪndʒ ə ‖ -ʔr **~s** z
  'danger ˌmoney
Dangerfield 'deɪndʒ ə fiːʔld ‖ -ʔr-
dangerous 'deɪndʒ ər əs **~ly** li
dangl|e 'dæŋ gʔl **~ed** d **~er/s** ˌə/z ‖ ˌʔr/z **~es**
  z **~ing** ɪŋ
dangly 'dæŋ gli
Daniel, Daniell 'dæn jəl
Daniella ˌdæn i 'el ə dæn 'jel ə
Danielle ˌdæn i 'el dæn 'jel
Daniels 'dæn jəlz
danio, Danio 'deɪn i əʊ ‖ -oʊ
Danish, d~ 'deɪn ɪʃ
  ˌDanish 'blue; ˌDanish 'pastry
dank dæŋk **danker** 'dæŋk ə ‖ -ʔr **dankest**
  'dæŋk ɪst -əst **dankly** 'dæŋk li **dankness**
  'dæŋk nəs -nɪs
Dankworth 'dæŋk wɜːθ -wəθ ‖ -wʔrθ
Dannie 'dæn i
Dannimac *tdmk* 'dæn i mæk
d'Annunzio dæ 'nʊnts i əʊ ‖ dɑː 'nʊnts i oʊ
  —*It* [dan 'nun tsjo]
Danny 'dæn i
Dano-Norwegian ˌdeɪn əʊ nɔː 'wiːdʒ ən ◂
  ‖ -oʊ nɔːr-
danse dɒnˢ dɑːnˢ ‖ dɑːnˢ —*Fr* [dɑ̃ːs]
danseur ˌ(ˌ)dɒn 'sɜː ˌ(ˌ)dɑːn- ‖ ˌ(ˌ)dɑːn 'sʊʔr -'sɜː
  —*Fr* [dɑ̃ sœːʁ] **~s** z
danseuse ˌ(ˌ)dɒn 'sɜːz ˌ(ˌ)dɑːn- ‖ ˌ(ˌ)dɑːn 'suːz
  -'sʊz —*Fr* [dɑ̃ søːz] **~s** *same pronunciation*
Dante 'dænt i 'dɑːnt-, -eɪ ‖ 'dɑːnt eɪ —*It*
  ['dan te]
Dantean 'dænt i ən 'dɑːnt-; dæn 'tiː ən, dɑːn-
  ~s z
Dantesque ˌ(ˌ)dæn 'tesk ˌ(ˌ)dɑːn-
Danton 'dænt ɒn -ən; dɒ̃ 'tɒ̃ ‖ -ʔn ˌdɑːn 'toʊn
  —*Fr* [dɑ̃ tɔ̃]
Danube 'dæn juːb
Danubian dæ 'njuːb i ən də- ‖ -'nuːb- -'njuːb-
Danvers 'dæn vəz ‖ -vʔrz
Danville 'dæn vɪl -vəl
Danzig 'dænts ɪg -ɪk —*Ger* ['dan tsɪç], *Polish*
  Gdańsk [gdajsk]
Danziger 'dænts ɪg ə ‖ -ʔr
dap dæp **daps** dæps

daphne, D~ 'dæf ni
daphnia 'dæf ni̯ə
Daphnis 'dæf nɪs §-nəs
dapper 'dæp ə ‖ -ᵊr **~ly** li **~ness** nəs nɪs
dappl|e 'dæp ᵊl **~ed** d **~es** z **~ing** ˌɪŋ
dapple-gray, dapple-grey ˌdæp ᵊl 'greɪ ◄
dapsone 'dæps əʊn ‖ -oʊn
Dar dɑː ‖ dɑːr —*See also phrases with this word*
DAR ˌdiː eɪ 'ɑː ‖ -'ɑːr
Dara 'dɑːr ə
Darbishire 'dɑːb i ʃə -ʃɪə ‖ 'dɑːrb i ʃᵊr -ʃɪr
d'Arblay 'dɑːb leɪ ‖ 'dɑːrb-
Darby 'dɑːb i ‖ 'dɑːrb i
  ˌDarby and 'Joan club
d'Arc dɑːk ‖ dɑːrk
Darcus 'dɑːk əs ‖ 'dɑːrk-
Darcy, D'Arcy 'dɑːs i ‖ 'dɑːrs i
Dardanelles ˌdɑːd ə 'nelz -ᵊn 'elz
  ‖ ˌdɑːrd ᵊn 'elz
Dardanus 'dɑːd ən əs ‖ 'dɑːrd-
Dardic 'dɑːd ɪk ‖ 'dɑːrd-
dare, Dare deə ‖ deᵊr dæᵊr **dared** deəd
  ‖ deᵊrd dæᵊrd **dares** deəz ‖ deᵊrz dæᵊrz
  daring 'deər ɪŋ ‖ 'der ɪŋ ' d&r-
daredevil 'deə ˌdev ᵊl ‖ 'der- 'dær- **~ry** ri **~s** z
daren't deənt §'deər ᵊnt ‖ 'der ᵊnt 'dærˌ
Darent 'dær ənt ‖ 'der-
Darenth 'dær ənᵗθ ‖ 'der-
daresay ˌdeə 'seɪ ◄ 'des eɪ ‖ ˌder- ˌdær- —*The*
  'des eɪ *form is not used at the end of a*
  sentence.
Daresbury 'dɑːz bər̯i ‖ 'dɑːrz- -ˌber i
Dar es Salaam, Dar-es-Salaam
  ˌdɑːr es sə 'lɑːm ˌɪs-, ˌez-, ˌɪz-
Darfur ₍ˌ₎dɑː 'fʊə ‖ ₍ˌ₎dɑːr 'fʊᵊr
darg dɑːg ‖ dɑːrg **dargs** dɑːgz ‖ dɑːrgz
daric 'dær ɪk ‖ 'der- **~s** s
Darien 'deər i ən 'dær- ‖ ˌder i 'en ˌdær-, ˌdɑːr-
  —*Sp* Darién [da 'rjen]
Darin 'dær ən -ɪn ‖ 'der-
daring 'deər ɪŋ ‖ 'der- 'dær- **~ly** li **~ness** nəs
  nɪs
dariole 'dær i əʊl →-ɒl ‖ -oʊl 'der-, 'dɑːr- **~s**
  z
Darius (i) də 'raɪ‿əs, (ii) 'deər i‿əs 'dær-
  ‖ 'der-, (iii) 'dɑːr- —(i) *is appropriate for the*
  ancient Persian king
Darjeeling dɑː 'dʒiːl ɪŋ ‖ dɑːr-
dark dɑːk ‖ dɑːrk **darker** 'dɑːk ə ‖ 'dɑːrk ᵊr
  darkest 'dɑːk ɪst -əst ‖ 'dɑːrk-
  'Dark ˌAges, ˌ· '·‿·; ˌdark 'glasses; ˌdark
  'horse
darken 'dɑːk ən ‖ 'dɑːrk- **~ed** d **~ing** ˌɪŋ **~s** z
darkey 'dɑːk i ‖ 'dɑːrk i **~s** z
darkie 'dɑːk i ‖ 'dɑːrk i **~s** z
darkish 'dɑːk ɪʃ ‖ 'dɑːrk-
darkling 'dɑːk lɪŋ ‖ 'dɑːrk-
dark|ly 'dɑːk |li ‖ 'dɑːrk- **~ness** nəs nɪs
darkroom 'dɑːk ruːm -rʊm ‖ 'dɑːrk- **~s** z
dark|y 'dɑːk |i ‖ 'dɑːrk |i **~ies** iz
Darlaston 'dɑːl əst ən ‖ 'dɑːrl-
Darleen, Darlene 'dɑːl iːn ‖ ˌdɑːr 'liːn
Darley 'dɑːl i ‖ 'dɑːrl i

darling, D~ 'dɑːl ɪŋ ‖ 'dɑːrl- **~s** z
Darlington 'dɑːl ɪŋ tən ‖ 'dɑːrl-
Darmstadt 'dɑːm stæt ‖ 'dɑːrm- —*Ger*
  ['daʁm ʃtat]
darmstadtium ˌdɑːm 'stæt i‿əm -'ʃtæt-
  ‖ ˌdɑːrm 'stæt̬ i‿əm
darn dɑːn ‖ dɑːrn **darned** dɑːnd ‖ dɑːrnd
  darning 'dɑːn ɪŋ ‖ 'dɑːrn- **darns** dɑːnz
  ‖ dɑːrnz
  'darning ˌneedle
darnel 'dɑːn ᵊl ‖ 'dɑːrn- **~s** z
darner 'dɑːn ə ‖ 'dɑːrn ᵊr **~s** z
Darnley 'dɑːn li ‖ 'dɑːrn-
Darrel, Darrell 'dær əl ‖ 'der-
Darren, Darron 'dær ən ‖ 'der-
Darrow 'dær əʊ ‖ -oʊ 'der-
Darryl 'dær əl -ɪl ‖ 'der-
dart, Dart dɑːt ‖ dɑːrt **darted** 'dɑːt ɪd -əd
  ‖ 'dɑːrt̬ əd **darting** 'dɑːt ɪŋ ‖ 'dɑːrt̬ ɪŋ **darts**
  dɑːts ‖ dɑːrts
D'Artagnan, Dartagnan dɑː 'tæn jɒn -jən
  ‖ ˌdɑːrt ᵊn 'jɑːn —*Fr* [daʁ ta njɑ̃]
dartboard 'dɑːt bɔːd ‖ 'dɑːrt bɔːrd -boʊrd **~s** z
darter 'dɑːt ə ‖ 'dɑːrt̬ ᵊr **~s** z
Dartford 'dɑːt fəd ‖ 'dɑːrt fᵊrd
Darth Vader ˌdɑːθ 'veɪd ə ‖ ˌdɑːrθ 'veɪd ᵊr
Dartmoor 'dɑːt mɔː -mʊə ‖ 'dɑːrt mʊr -mʊᵊr
Dartmouth 'dɑːt məθ ‖ 'dɑːrt-
dartre 'dɑːt ə ‖ 'dɑːrt̬ ᵊr (= *darter*)
Darwen 'dɑː wɪn §-wən ‖ 'dɑːr- —*locally also*
  'dær ən
Darwin 'dɑː wɪn §-wən ‖ 'dɑːr-
Darwinian dɑː 'wɪn i‿ən ‖ dɑːr- **~s** z
Darwinism 'dɑː wɪn ˌɪz əm -wən- ‖ 'dɑːr-
Daryll 'dær əl -ɪl ‖ 'der-
Daschle 'dæʃ ᵊl
dash, Dash dæʃ **dashed** dæʃt **dashes** 'dæʃ ɪz
  -əz **dashing** 'dæʃ ɪŋ
dashboard 'dæʃ bɔːd ‖ -bɔːrd -boʊrd **~s** z
dasheen dæ 'ʃiːn 'dæʃ iːn
dashiki də 'ʃiːk i dɑː-, dæ- **~s** z
dashing 'dæʃ ɪŋ **~ly** li **~ness** nəs nɪs
dashpot 'dæʃ pɒt ‖ -pɑːt **~s** s
Dashwood 'dæʃ wʊd
dassie 'dæs i 'dʌs i **~s** z
dastardly 'dæst əd li ‖ 'dɑːst- ‖ -ᵊrd-
dasyure 'dæs i jʊə 'dæz- ‖ -jʊr **~s** z
DAT dæt ˌdiː eɪ 'tiː

DATA					
■ 'deɪt ə	■ 'dɑːt ə	▢ 'dæt ə			
■ 'deɪt ə	■ 'dæt ə	▢ 'dɑːt̬ ə			

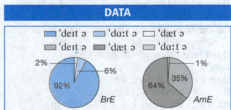

data 'deɪt ə 'dɑːt ə, §'dæt ə ‖ 'deɪt̬ ə 'dæt̬ ə,
  'dɑːt̬ ə — *Preference polls, BrE:* 'deɪt ə 92%,

'dɑːt ə 6%, 'dæt ə 2%; *AmE:* 'deɪʧ ə 64%,
'dæʧ ə 35%, 'dɑːʧ ə 1%.
'**data bus**; '**data ˌcapture**; ˌ**data**
'**processing**
databank 'deɪt ə bæŋk 'dɑːt- ‖ 'deɪʧ- 'dæʧ-,
'dɑːʧ- **~s** s
database 'deɪt ə beɪs 'dɑːt- ‖ 'deɪʧ- 'dæʧ-, 'dɑːʧ-
~es ɪz əz
datafile 'deɪt ə faɪ³l 'dɑːt- ‖ 'deɪʧ- 'dæʧ-, 'dɑːʧ-
~s z
Datapost *tdmk* 'deɪt ə pəʊst 'dɑːt-
‖ 'deɪʧ ə poʊst 'dæʧ-, 'dɑːʧ-
Datchet 'dæʧ ɪt §-ət
date deɪt **dated** 'deɪt ɪd -əd ‖ 'deɪʧ əd **dates**
deɪts **dating** 'deɪt ɪŋ ‖ 'deɪʧ ɪŋ
'**date palm**; '**dating ˌagency**
datebook 'deɪt bʊk §-buːk **~s** s
dateline 'deɪt laɪn **~d** d **~s** z
date-mark 'deɪt mɑːk ‖ -mɑːrk **~ed** t **~ing** ɪŋ
~s s
date-stamp 'deɪt stæmp **~ed** t **~ing** ɪŋ **~s** s
datival də 'taɪv ³l deɪ- **~ly** i **~s** z
dative 'deɪt ɪv ‖ 'deɪʧ- **~s** z
Datsun *tdmk* 'dæts ³n ‖ 'dɑːts- —*Jp*
[dat 'to san] **~s** z
datum 'deɪt əm 'dɑːt- ‖ 'deɪʧ- 'dæʧ-, 'dɑːʧ-
datura də 'tjʊər ə ‖ -'tʊr- -'tjʊr- **~s** z
daub dɔːb ‖ dɑːb **daubed** dɔːbd ‖ dɑːbd **daubs**
dɔːbz ‖ dɑːbz **daubing** 'dɔːb ɪŋ ‖ 'dɑːb-
daube dəʊb ‖ doʊb —*Fr* [doːb] **~s** z
Daubeney, Daubney 'dɔːb ni ‖ 'dɑːb-
Daudet 'dəʊd eɪ ‖ doʊ 'deɪ —*Fr* [do dɛ]
daughter 'dɔːt ə ‖ 'dɔːt ³r 'dɑːʧ- **~ly** li **~s** z
daughter-in-law 'dɔːt ər ɪn ˌlɔː →'dɔːtr·,·,
-ən,· ‖ 'dɔːʧ ər ³n ˌlɔː 'dɑːʧ ər ³n ˌlɑː **~s** z
daughters-in-law 'dɔːt əz ɪn ˌlɔː -³n,·
‖ 'dɔːʧ ³rz ³n ˌlɔː 'dɑːʧ ³rz ³n ˌlɑː
daunt, Daunt dɔːnt ‖ dɑːnt **daunted** 'dɔːnt ɪd
-əd ‖ 'dɔːnʧ əd 'dɑːnʧ- **daunting/ly**
'dɔːnt ɪŋ /li ‖ 'dɔːnʧ ɪŋ /li 'dɑːnʧ- **daunts**
dɔːnts ‖ dɑːnts
dauntless 'dɔːnt ləs -lɪs ‖ 'dɑːnt- **~ly** li **~ness**
nəs nɪs
dauphin, D~ 'dɔːf ɪn 'dəʊf-, §-³n, -æ̃
‖ doʊ 'fæn 'doʊf ³n —*Fr* [do fæ̃] **~s** z
dauphine, D~ 'dɔːf iːn 'dəʊf- ‖ doʊ 'fiːn —*Fr*
[do fin] **~s** z
Dave deɪv
davenport, D~ 'dæv ³n pɔːt →-³m- ‖ -pɔːrt
-poʊrt **~s** s
Daventry 'dæv ³ntr i —*formerly also* 'deɪntr i
Davey 'deɪv i
David 'deɪv ɪd §-əd —*but as a non-English*
name also dæ 'viːd
Davidson 'deɪv ɪd sən §-əd-
Davie 'deɪv i
Davies 'deɪv ɪs §-əs, -iːz
Davina də 'viːn ə
da Vinci də 'vɪnʧ i —*It* [dav 'vin tʃi]
Davis 'deɪv ɪs §-əs
Davison 'deɪv ɪs ³n §-əs-
davit 'dæv ɪt 'deɪv-, §-ət **~s** s

Davos dæ 'vəʊs 'dæv ɒs, 'dɑːv-, -əs ‖ dɑː 'voʊs
—*Ger* [da 'voːs]
Davro 'dæv rəʊ ‖ -roʊ
Davy 'deɪv i
ˌ**Davy ˌJones's 'locker**; '**Davy lamp**
Davyhulme 'deɪv i hjuːm
daw, Daw dɔː ‖ dɑː **daws, Daw's** dɔːz ‖ dɑːz
dawdl|e 'dɔːd ³l ‖ 'dɑːd- **~ed** d **~er/s** ə/z
‖ ³r/z **~es** z **~ing/ly** ɪŋ /li
Dawe dɔː ‖ dɑː
Dawes dɔːz ‖ dɑːz
Dawkins 'dɔːk ɪnz §-ənz ‖ 'dɑːk-
Dawlish 'dɔːl ɪʃ ‖ 'dɑːl-
dawn, Dawn dɔːn ‖ dɑːn **dawned** dɔːnd
‖ dɑːnd **dawning** 'dɔːn ɪŋ ‖ 'dɑːn- **dawns**
dɔːnz ‖ dɑːnz
ˌ**dawn 'chorus**; ˌ**dawn 'redwood**
Dawnay 'dɔːn i ‖ 'dɑːn-
Dawson 'dɔːs ³n ‖ 'dɑːs-
Dax dæks
day, Day deɪ **days** deɪz
'**day bed**; ˌ**Day 'Lewis**; '**day ˌnursery**; ˌ**day**
of 'reckoning; ˌ**day re'lease course**; ˌ**day**
re'turn; '**day school**
-day deɪ, di —*Although RP and GenAm are*
both traditionally considered to prefer **di**, *most*
speakers in practice use both pronunciations
for this suffix, often in a strong form—weak
form relationship. The **deɪ** *form is generally*
preferred in exposed positions, for example at
the end of a sentence: I'll do it on Monday
'mʌn deɪ; *the* **di** *form is preferred in close-knit*
expressions such as Monday morning.
ˌmʌnd i 'mɔːn ɪŋ ‖ -'mɔːrn-.
Dayak 'daɪ æk **~s** s
Dayan daɪ 'æn -'ɑːn ‖ dɑː 'jɑːn
daybook 'deɪ bʊk §-buːk **~s** s
dayboy 'deɪ bɔɪ **~s** z
daybreak 'deɪ breɪk
day-care 'deɪ keə ‖ -ker -kær
daydream 'deɪ driːm **~er/s** ə/z ‖ ³r/z **~ing** ɪŋ
~s z
daygirl 'deɪ gɜːl ‖ -gɜːl **~s** z
dayglo, Day-Glo *tdmk* 'deɪ gləʊ ‖ -gloʊ
Day-Lewis ˌdeɪ 'luː ɪs §-əs
daylight 'deɪ laɪt **~s** s
ˌ**daylight 'robbery**; ˌ**daylight 'saving**
(time)
daylong ˌdeɪ 'lɒŋ ◂ ‖ -'lɔːŋ ◂ -'lɑːŋ ◂
dayroom 'deɪ ruːm -rʊm **~s** z
dayspring 'deɪ sprɪŋ
daystar 'deɪ stɑː ‖ -stɑːr
daytime 'deɪ taɪm
day-to-day ˌdeɪ tə 'deɪ ◂ ‖ ˌdeɪʧ ə-
ˌ**day-to-ˌday 'running**
Dayton 'deɪt ³n
Daytona deɪ 'təʊn ə ‖ -'toʊn ə
Day.tona 'Beach
Daz *tdmk* dæz
daze deɪz **dazed** deɪzd **dazes** 'deɪz ɪz -əz
dazing 'deɪz ɪŋ
dazzl|e 'dæz ³l **~ed** d **~er/s** ə/z ‖ ³r/z **~es** z
~ing/ly ɪŋ /li

D

D

DC ˌdiː ˈsiː
DC10 ˌdiː siː ˈten **~s, ~'s** z
D-day ˈdiː deɪ
DDT ˌdiː diː ˈtiː
de *in French phrases* də di —*Fr* [də]
de *in Latin phrases* deɪ diː
De, de *in English family names* də
de- ˌdiː, di, də —*Attached to free forms, meaning 'do the opposite of' or 'remove', this prefix is usually pronounced strong,* ⑴diː (ˌde'nasalized). *With these meanings it is freely productive, and most words made this way are not included in the dictionary. Otherwise the prefix is usually weak,* **di** (de'cide, de'pend), *with variant* də; *but strong* ˌde+ *before an unstressed syllable* ('deference, ˌdere'liction).
deacon, D~ ˈdiːk ən **~s** z
deaconess ˌdiːk ə ˈnes '···; ˈdiːk ənˌɪs, əs
   ‖ ˈdiːk ən əs **~es** ɪz əz
deacti|vate di ˈækt ɪ |veɪt ˌdiː-, -ə- **~vated**
   veɪt ɪd -əd ‖ veɪt̬ əd **~vates** veɪts **~vating**
   veɪt ɪŋ ‖ veɪt̬ ɪŋ
deactivation di ˌækt ɪ ˈveɪʃ ᵊn ˌdiː,-, -ə-
dead ded **deader** ˈded ə ‖ -ᵊr **deadest** ˈded ɪst
   -əst
   ˌdead ˈcentre; ˌdead ˈduck; ˌdead ˈend;
   ˌdead ˈheat; ˌdead ˈletter; ˌdead ˈloss;
   ˈdead march; ˈdead ˌnettle; ˌdead
   ˈreckoning; ˌdead ˈringer; ˌDead ˈSea◄;
   ˌDead Sea ˈScrolls; ˌdead ˈweight
dead-and-alive ˌded ᵊnˌə ˈlaɪv ◄ -ᵊnd ə-
dead beat *adj* ˌded ˈbiːt ◄ → ˌdeb-
deadbeat *n* ˈded biːt →ˈdeb- **~s** s
deadbolt ˈded bəʊlt →ˈdeb-, →-bɒʊlt ‖ -boʊlt
   ~s s
deaden ˈded ᵊn **~ed** d **~ing** ɪŋ **~s** z
dead-end ˌded ˈend ◄
deadeye ˈded aɪ
deadhead *v* ˌded ˈhed '·· ‖ '·· **~ed** ɪd əd **~ing**
   ɪŋ **~s** z
Deadhead *n* ˈded hed **~s** z
deadli... —*see* **deadly**
deadlight ˈded laɪt **~s** s
deadline ˈded laɪn **~s** z
deadliness ˈded li nəs -nɪs
deadlock ˈded lɒk ‖ -lɑːk **~ed** t **~s** s
dead|ly ˈded |li **~lier** li ə ‖ li ᵊr **~liest** li ɪst
   li əst
   ˌdeadly ˈnightshade; ˌdeadly ˈsin
deadman ˈded mæn →ˈdeb-
   ˌdeadman's ˈfingers
deadness ˈded nəs -nɪs
deadpan ˈded pæn →ˈdeb-
deadweight ˈded weɪt
deadwood ˈded wʊd ˌ·ˈ·
deaf def **deafer** ˈdef ə ‖ -ᵊr **deafest** ˈdef ɪst
   -əst
deaf-aid ˈdef eɪd **~s** z
deaf-and-dumb ˌdef ᵊn ˈdʌm ◄
deafen ˈdef ᵊn **~ed** d **~ing** ˌɪŋ **~s** z
deafly ˈdef li
deaf-mute ˌdef ˈmjuːt ◄ **~s** s

deafness ˈdef nəs -nɪs
Deakin ˈdiːk ɪn §-ən
deal, Deal diːᵊl **dealing/s** ˈdiːᵊl ɪŋ/z **deals**
   diːᵊlz **dealt** delt (!)
dealer ˈdiːᵊl ə ‖ -ᵊr **~s** z **~ship/s** ʃɪp/s
dealt delt
dean, Dean diːn **deans, Dean's** diːnz
Deana (i) di ˈæn ə, (ii) ˈdiːn ə
Deane (i) diːn, (ii) di ˈæn
deaner|y ˈdiːn ər |i **~ies** iz
deanship ˈdiːn ʃɪp **~s** s
dear, Dear dɪə ‖ dɪᵊr **dearer** ˈdɪər ə ‖ ˈdɪr ᵊr
   dearest ˈdɪər ɪst -əst ‖ ˈdɪr- **dears** dɪəz
   ‖ dɪᵊrz
Dearborn ˈdɪə bɔːn -bən ‖ ˈdɪr bɔːrn -bᵊrn
Deare dɪə ‖ dɪᵊr
dearie ˈdɪər i ‖ ˈdɪr i **~s** z
Dearing ˈdɪər ɪŋ ‖ ˈdɪr ɪŋ
dearly ˈdɪə li ‖ ˈdɪr li
Dearne dɜːn ‖ dɜːrn
dearness ˈdɪə nəs -nɪs ‖ ˈdɪr-
dearth dɜːθ ‖ dɜːθ **dearths** dɜːθs ‖ dɜːθs
deary ˈdɪər i ‖ ˈdɪr i
death deθ **deaths** deθs
   ˈdeath camp; ˈdeath cell; ˈdeath
   cerˌtificate; ˈdeath ˌduties; ˈdeath knell;
   ˈdeath mask; ˈdeath ˌpenalty; ˈdeath
   rate; ˈdeath ˌrattle; ˌdeath ˈrow; ˈdeath
   squad; ˈdeath tax; ˈdeath toll; ˈdeath
   trap; ˌDeath ˈValley; ˈdeath ˌwarrant;
   ˈdeath wish
DeAth, De'ath di ˈæθ deɪ-, -ˈɑːθ; deɪθ, deθ,
   diːθ
deathbed ˈdeθ bed **~s** z
deathblow ˈdeθ bləʊ ‖ -bloʊ **~s** z
death-dealing ˈdeθ ˌdiːᵊl ɪŋ
death-defying ˈdeθ di ˌfaɪ ɪŋ -də-
deathless ˈdeθ ləs -lɪs **~ly** li **~ness** nəs nɪs
deathlike ˈdeθ laɪk
death|ly ˈdeθ |li **~liness** li nəs -nɪs
death's-head ˈdeθs hed **~s** z
deathwatch ˈdeθ wɒtʃ ‖ -wɑːtʃ **~es** ɪz əz
   ˌdeathwatch ˈbeetle
Deauville ˈdəʊ vɪl -viːᵊl ‖ ˈdoʊ- —*Fr* [do vil]
Deayton ˈdiːt ᵊn
deb deb **debs** debz
debacle, débâcle deɪ ˈbɑːk ᵊl dɪ-, də-; -ˈbækl;
   ˈdeɪb ɑːk ᵊl; ⚠ˈdeb ək ᵊl —*Fr* [de bɑːkl] **~s** z
   —*or as sing.*
debag ˌdi ˈbæg **~ged** d **~ging** ɪŋ **~s** z
de|bar di |ˈbɑː də-, ˌdiː- ‖ -|ˈbɑːr **~barred**
   ˈbɑːd ‖ ˈbɑːrd **~barring** ˈbɑːr ɪŋ **~bars** ˈbɑːz
   ‖ ˈbɑːrz
debark *'strip the bark from (wood)', 'disable
   vocal cords of (dog)'* ˌdi ˈbɑːk ‖ -ˈbɑːrk **~ed** t
   ~ing ɪŋ **~s** s
debark *'disembark'* di ˈbɑːk ˌdiː-, də- ‖ -ˈbɑːrk
   ~ed t **~ing** ɪŋ **~s** s
debarkation ˌdiː bɑː ˈkeɪʃ ᵊn ‖ -bɑːr- **~s** z
debarment di ˈbɑː mənt də-, ˌdiː- ‖ -ˈbɑːr-
debarr... —*see* **debar**
debas|e di ˈbeɪs də- **~ed** t **~ement/s** mənt/s
   ~er/s ə/z ‖ ᵊr/z **~es** ɪz əz **~ing** ɪŋ

debatab|le di 'beɪt əb |ᵊl də- ‖ -'beɪt̬- **~ly** li
de|bate di |'beɪt də- **~bated** 'beɪt ɪd -əd
‖ 'beɪt̬ əd **~bater/s** 'beɪt ə/z ‖ 'beɪt̬ ᵊr/z
~bates 'beɪts **~bating** 'beɪt ɪŋ ‖ 'beɪt̬ ɪŋ
debauch di 'bɔːtʃ də- ‖ -'bɑːtʃ **~ed** t **~es** ɪz əz
~ing ɪŋ
debauchee ˌdeb ɔː 'tʃiː -'ʃiː; dɪ ˌbɔː-, də- ‖ -ɑː-
~s z
debaucher|y di 'bɔːtʃ ər_|i də- ‖ -'bɑːtʃ- **~ies** iz
Debbie, Debby 'deb i
De Beauvoir də 'bəʊ vwɑː ‖ -ˌbəʊ 'vwɑːr
—*Fr* [də bo vwaːʁ]
De Beer də 'bɪə ‖ -'bɪᵊr
Deben 'diːb ən
Debenham 'deb ən_əm
debenture di 'bentʃ ə də- ‖ -ᵊr **~s** z
debili|tate di 'bɪl ɪ |teɪt də-, -ə- **~tated** teɪt ɪd
-əd ‖ teɪt̬ əd **~tates** teɪts **~tating** teɪt ɪŋ
‖ teɪt̬ ɪŋ
debilitation di ˌbɪl ɪ 'teɪʃ ᵊn də-, -ə-
debilit|y di 'bɪl ət i də-, -ɪt- ‖ -ət̬ |i **~ies** iz
deb|it 'deb |ɪt §-ət ‖ -|ət **~ited** ɪt ɪd §ət-, -əd
‖ ət̬ əd **~iting** ɪt ɪŋ §ət- ‖ ət̬ ɪŋ **~its** ɪts §əts
‖ əts
debonair, debonaire ˌdeb ə 'neə ◄ ‖ -'neᵊr
-'næᵊr **~ly** li **~ness** nəs nɪs
debon|e ˌdiː 'bəʊn ‖ -'boʊn **~ed** d **~es** z **~ing**
ɪŋ
de Bono də 'bəʊn əʊ ‖ -'boʊn oʊ
Deborah 'deb ər_ə
debouch di 'baʊtʃ də-, ˌdiː-, -'buːʃ **~ed** t **~es**
ɪz əz **~ing** ɪŋ
Debra 'deb rə
Debrett də 'bret dɪ- **~'s** s
debrid|e di 'briːd də-, deɪ- **~ed** ɪd əd **~es** z
~ing ɪŋ
debridement, débridement dɪ 'briːd mənt
də-, ₍ₗ₎diː-, deɪ-, ˌˌ'mɑ̃ —*Fr* [de bʁid mɑ̃]
debrief ˌdiː 'briːf **~ed** t **~ing** ɪŋ **~s** s

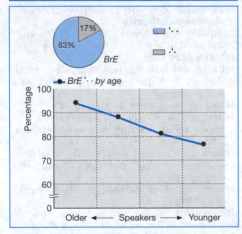

debris, débris 'deb ri: 'deɪb-; də 'briː
‖ də 'briː: 'deɪb ri: — *Preference poll, BrE:* 'ˌˌ
83%, ˌˌ *17%.*

De Broglie də 'brəʊg li ‖ də 'brɔɪ —*Fr*
[də bʁɔj]
Debs debz
debt det *(!)* **debts** dets
debt-laden 'det ˌleɪd ᵊn
debtor 'det ə ‖ 'det̬ ᵊr **~s** z
debt-ridden 'det ˌrɪd ᵊn
debug ˌdiː 'bʌg **~ged** d **~ging** ɪŋ **~s** z
de|bunk ˌdiː: |'bʌŋk **~bunked** 'bʌŋkt
~bunker/s 'bʌŋk ə/z ‖ 'bʌŋk ᵊr/z **~bunking**
'bʌŋk ɪŋ **~bunks** 'bʌŋks
De Burgh də 'bɜːg ‖ -'bɜːg
Debussy də 'buːs i -'bjuːs-, -'bʊs-; 'deɪb juːs i
‖ ˌdeɪb ju 'siː —*Fr* [də by si]

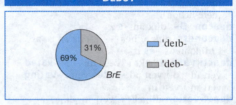

'deɪb-
'deb-
BrE

debut, début 'deɪb juː -uː; 'deb juː ‖ deɪ 'bjuː
— *Preference poll, BrE:* 'deɪb- *69%,* 'deb-
31%. —*Fr* [de by] **~s** z
debutant, débutant 'deb ju tɒ̃ 'deɪb- —*Fr*
[de by tɑ̃]
debutante, débutante 'deb ju tɑːnt 'deɪb-,
-tænt, -tɒnt —*Fr* [de by tɑ̃ːt] **~s** s
DEC *tdmk* dek
Dec —*see* **December**
deca- *comb. form*
with stress-neutral suffix |dek ə — **decagram**
'dek ə græm
with stress-imposing suffix dɪ 'kæ+ də- —
Decapolis dɪ 'kæp əl ɪs də-, §-əs

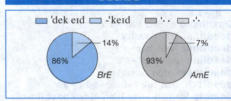

'dek eɪd -'keɪd ˌˌ ˌˌ
14%   7%
86%   93%
BrE   *AmE*

decade 'dek eɪd di 'keɪd, de-; 'dek əd
— *Preference polls, BrE:* 'dek eɪd *86%,* -'keɪd
14%; AmE: 'ˌˌ *93%,* ˌˌ *7%. The form* 'dek əd
is associated mainly with the religious sense,
'part of the rosary, set of ten Hail Marys'. **~s**
z
decadence 'dek əd ᵊn⁺s
decadent 'dek əd ənt **~ly** li **~s** s
decaf, decaff 'diː kæf **~s** s
decaffei|nate ˌdiː 'kæf ɪ |neɪt dɪ-, -ə- **~nated**
neɪt ɪd -əd ‖ neɪt̬ əd **~nates** neɪts **~nating**
neɪt ɪŋ ‖ neɪt̬ ɪŋ
decagon 'dek əg ən -ə gɒn ‖ -ə gɑːn **~s** z
decahedr|on ˌdek ə 'hiːdr |ən -'hedr-; 'ˌˌ,ˌˌ **~a**
ə **~ons** ənz

D

decal dɪ 'kæl 'diː kæl ‖ 'diː kæl dɪ 'kæl ~s z
decalcomania dɪ ˌkælk ə 'meɪn i̯ə
Decalogue 'dek ə lɒg ‖ -lɔːg -lɑːg
Decameron dɪ 'kæm ᵊr̩ən də-, de-
decamp dɪ 'kæmp ˌdiː- ~ed t ~ing ɪŋ ~s s
decanal dɪ 'keɪn ᵊl də-; 'dek ən ᵊl ~ly i
decane 'dek eɪn
decani dɪ 'keɪn aɪ
de|cant dɪ |'kænt ˌdiː-, də- ~canted 'kænt ɪd -əd ‖ 'kænt̬ əd ~canting 'kænt ɪŋ ‖ 'kænt̬ ɪŋ ~cants 'kænts
decanter dɪ 'kænt ə də-, ˌdiː- ‖ -'kænt̬ ᵊr ~s z
decapi|tate dɪ 'kæp ɪ |teɪt də-, ˌdiː-, -ə- ~tated teɪt ɪd -əd ‖ teɪt̬ əd ~tates teɪts ~tating teɪt ɪŋ ‖ teɪt̬ ɪŋ
decapitation dɪ ˌkæp ɪ 'teɪʃ ᵊn ˌdiː ˌkæp-, -ə- ~s z
decapod 'dek ə pɒd ‖ -pɑːd ~s z
decarbonis... —see decarboniz...
decarbonization ˌdiː ˌkɑːb ən aɪ 'zeɪʃ ᵊn ·ˌ·-, -ɪ'·- ‖ diː ˌkɑːrb ən ə- ~s z
decarboniz|e ⑴diː 'kɑːb ə naɪz ‖ -'kɑːrb- ~ed d ~es ɪz əz ~ing ɪŋ
decasyllabic ˌdek ə sɪ 'læb ɪk ◂ -sə'·-
decasyllable 'dek ə ˌsɪl əb ᵊl ˌ·'···· ~s z
decathlete dɪ 'kæθ liːt de-, də- ~s s
decathlon dɪ 'kæθ lɒn de-, də-, -lən ‖ -lɑːn -lən ~s z
Decatur dɪ 'keɪt ə də- ‖ -'keɪt̬ ᵊr
decay dɪ 'keɪ də- ~ed d ~ing ɪŋ ~s z
Decca tdmk 'dek ə
Deccan 'dek ən —Hindi [ɖək kʰɪŋ, ɖe: kəŋ]
deceas|e dɪ 'siːs də- ~ed t ~es ɪz əz ~ing ɪŋ
decedent dɪ 'siːd ᵊnt də- ~s s
deceit dɪ 'siːt də- ~s s
deceitful dɪ 'siːt fᵊl də-, -fʊl ~ly i ~ness nəs nɪs
deceiv|e dɪ 'siːv də- ~ed d ~er/s ə/z ‖ ᵊr/z ~es z ~ing ɪŋ
decele|rate ˌdiː 'sel ə |reɪt ~rated reɪt ɪd -əd ‖ reɪt̬ əd ~rates reɪts ~rating reɪt ɪŋ ‖ reɪt̬ ɪŋ
deceleration ˌdiː ˌsel ə 'reɪʃ ᵊn ·ˌ·- ~s z
December dɪ 'sem bə də-, §-'zem- ‖ -bᵊr
Decembrist dɪ 'sem brɪst də-, §-brəst ~s s
decenc|y 'diːs ᵊn's |i ~ies iz
decennial dɪ 'sen i̯əl də-, de- ~ly i
decent 'diːs ᵊnt ~ly li ~ness nəs nɪs
decentralis... —see decentraliz...
decentralization ˌdiː ˌsentr əl aɪ 'zeɪʃ ᵊn ·ˌ·-, -ɪ'·- ‖ -əl ə- ~s z
decentraliz|e ⑴diː 'sentr ə laɪz ~ed d ~es ɪz əz ~ing ɪŋ
deception dɪ 'sep ʃᵊn də- ~s z
deceptive dɪ 'sept ɪv də- ~ly li ~ness nəs nɪs
deci- ¦des i ‖ ¦des ə — decimetre 'des i ˌmiːt ə ‖ -ə ˌmiːt̬ ᵊr
decibel 'des ɪ bel -ə-; -ɪb ᵊl, -əb- ~s z
decid|e dɪ 'saɪd də- ~ed ɪd əd ~er/s ə/z ‖ ᵊr/z ~es z ~ing ɪŋ
decided|ly dɪ 'saɪd ɪd |li də-, -əd- ~ness nəs nɪs
deciduous dɪ 'sɪd ju̯əs də- ‖ dɪ 'sɪdʒ u̯əs ~ly li ~ness nəs nɪs

decile 'des aɪᵊl -ɪl ~s z
Decima 'des ɪm ə -əm-
decimal 'des əm ᵊl -ɪm- ~ly i ~s z
ˌdecimal 'point; 'decimal ˌsystem
decimalis... —see decimaliz...
decimalization ˌdes əm ᵊl aɪ 'zeɪʃ ᵊn ˌ·ɪm-, -ɪ'·- ‖ -ə 'zeɪʃ-
decimaliz|e 'des əm ə laɪz '·ɪm-, -ᵊl aɪz ~ed d ~es ɪz əz ~ing ɪŋ
deci|mate 'des ɪ |meɪt -ə- ~mated meɪt ɪd -əd ‖ meɪt̬ əd ~mates meɪts ~mating meɪt ɪŋ ‖ meɪt̬ ɪŋ
decimation ˌdes ɪ 'meɪʃ ᵊn -ə- ~s z
Decimus 'des ɪm əs -əm-
decipher dɪ 'saɪf ə də-, ˌdiː- ‖ -ᵊr ~ed d deciphering dɪ 'saɪf ᵊr ɪŋ də-, ˌdiː- ~s z
decipherable dɪ 'saɪf ᵊr əb ᵊl də-, ˌdiː-
decipherer dɪ 'saɪf ᵊr ə də-, ˌdiː- ‖ -ᵊr ᵊr ~s z
decipherment dɪ 'saɪf ə mənt də-, ˌdiː- ‖ -ᵊr- ~s s
decision dɪ 'sɪʒ ᵊn də-, -'zɪʃ-, -'zɪʒ-, -'sɪʃ- ~s z
decision-mak|er dɪ 'sɪʒ ᵊn ˌmeɪk |ə də-, -'zɪʃ-, -'zɪʒ-, -'sɪʃ- ‖ -|ᵊr ~ers əz ‖ ᵊrz ~ing ɪŋ
decisive dɪ 'saɪs ɪv də-, -'saɪz- ~ly li ~ness nəs nɪs
deck dek decked dekt decking 'dek ɪŋ decks deks
deckchair 'dek tʃeə ˌ·'· ‖ -tʃer -tʃær ~s z
-decker 'dek ə ‖ -ᵊr — single-decker ˌsɪŋ gᵊl 'dek ə ◂ ‖ -ᵊr
Decker 'dek ə ‖ -ᵊr
deckhand 'dek hænd ~s z
deckhouse 'dek haʊs
deckle 'dek ᵊl ~s z
ˌdeckle 'edge
deckle-edged ˌdek ᵊl 'edʒd ◂
declaim dɪ 'kleɪm də- ~ed d ~ing ɪŋ ~s z
declamation ˌdek lə 'meɪʃ ᵊn ~s z
declamator|y dɪ 'klæm ət ᵊr |i də- ‖ -ə tɔːr |i -tour i ~ily əl i ɪ li
Declan 'dek lən
declarable dɪ 'kleər əb ᵊl də- ‖ -'kler- -'klær-
declaration ˌdek lə 'reɪʃ ᵊn ~s z
declarative dɪ 'klær ət ɪv də-, -'kleər- ‖ -ət̬ ɪv -'kler- ~ly li
declaratory dɪ 'klær ət ᵊr i də-, -'kleər- ‖ -ə tɔːr i -'kler-, -tour i
declare dɪ 'kleə də- ‖ dɪ 'kleᵊr -'klæᵊr ~d d ~s z declaring dɪ 'kleər ɪŋ də- ‖ dɪ 'kler ɪŋ -'klær-
declaredly dɪ 'kleər ɪd li də-, -əd- ‖ -'kler- -'klær-
declasse, déclassé, declassee, déclassée ˌdeɪ 'klæs eɪ -'klɑːs-, ˌ·'·· ‖ ˌdeɪ klæ 'seɪ -klɑː- —Fr [de kla se]
declassifiable ⑴diː 'klæs ɪ faɪˌəb ᵊl -'·ə-, ˌ·ˌ·'···
declassification ⑴diː ˌklæs ɪf ɪ 'keɪʃ ᵊn ·ˌ·-, -əf ɪ'·-, §-ə'·◂
declassi|fy ⑴diː 'klæs ɪ |faɪ -ə- ~fied faɪd ~fies faɪz ~fying faɪ ɪŋ
declension dɪ 'klenʧ ᵊn də- ~al ᵊl ~s z
declinable dɪ 'klaɪn əb ᵊl də-
declination ˌdek lɪ 'neɪʃ ᵊn -lə- ~al ᵊl ~s z

D

decline *n* di ˈklaɪn də- ˈdiː klaɪn ~s z

declin|e *v* di ˈklaɪn də- ~ed d ~er/s ə/z ‖ ᵊr/z
~es z ~ing ɪŋ

declivit|y di ˈklɪv ət |i də-, -ɪt- ‖ -əṭ |i ~ies iz

declutch ˌdiː ˈklʌtʃ di-, də- ~ed t ~es ɪz əz
~ing ɪŋ

decoct di ˈkɒkt də- ‖ -ˈkɑːkt ~ed ɪd əd ~ing ɪŋ
~s s

decoction di ˈkɒk ʃᵊn də- ‖ -ˈkɑːk- ~s z

decod|e ⁽ˌ⁾diː ˈkəʊd ‖ -ˈkoʊd ~ed ɪd əd ~er/s
ə/z ‖ ᵊr/z ~es z ~ing ɪŋ

decok|e *v* ˌdiː ˈkəʊk dɪ-, də- ‖ -ˈkoʊk ~ed t ~es
s ~ing ɪŋ

decoke *n* ˈdiː kəʊk ˌ·ˈ· ‖ -koʊk ~s s

decolletage, décolletage ˌdeɪ kɒl ˈtɑːʒ
deɪ ˈkɒl ɪ tɑːʒ, -ə- ‖ -ˈkɑːl- ˌ·ˈ·ˈ, ˌdek əl əˈ·
—*Fr* [de kɔl taːʒ]

decollete, décolleté deɪ ˈkɒl teɪ -ˈkɒl ɪ teɪ,
-ə teɪ ‖ ˌdeɪ kɑːl ˈteɪ ˌ·ˈ·ˈ· —*Fr* [de kɔl te]

decolonis... —*see* decoloniz...

decolonization ˌdiː ˌkɒl ən aɪ ˈzeɪʃ ᵊn ·ˌˈ·, -ɪˈ·-
‖ ˌdiː ˌkɑːl ən əˈ·- ~s z

decoloniz|e ⁽ˌ⁾diː ˈkɒl ə naɪz ‖ -ˈkɑːl- ~ed d
~es ɪz əz ~ing ɪŋ

decommission ˌdiː kə ˈmɪʃ ᵊn ~ed d ~ing ˌɪŋ
~s z

decomposable ˌdiː kəm ˈpəʊz əb ᵊl ‖ -ˈpoʊz-

decompos|e ˌdiː kəm ˈpəʊz §-kɒm- ‖ -ˈpoʊz
~ed d ~er/s ə/z ‖ ᵊr/z ~es ɪz əz ~ing ɪŋ

decomposition ˌdiː ˌkɒmp ə ˈzɪʃ ᵊn ‖ -ˌkɑːmp-

decompress ˌdiː kəm ˈpres §-kɒm- ~ed t ~es
ɪz əz ~ing ɪŋ

decompression ˌdiː kəm ˈpreʃ ᵊn §-kɒm- ~s z
ˌdecomˈpression ˌchamber

decongestant ˌdiː kən ˈdʒest ənt §-kɒn- ~s s

deconse|crate ˌdiː ˈkɒnˀs ɪ |kreɪt -ə-
‖ -ˈkɑːnˀs- ~crated kreɪt ɪd -əd ‖ kreɪṭ əd
~crates kreɪts ~crating kreɪt ɪŋ ‖ kreɪṭ ɪŋ

deconsecration ˌdiː ˌkɒnˀs ɪ ˈkreɪʃ ᵊn ·ˌ·-
‖ -ˌkɑːnˀs- ~s z

deconstruct ˌdiː kən ˈstrʌkt §-kɒn- ~ed ɪd əd
~ing ɪŋ ~s s

deconstruction ˌdiː kən ˈstrʌk ʃᵊn §-kɒn-
~ism ˌɪz əm ~ist/s ɪst/s §əst/s ‖ əst/s ~s z

decontami|nate ˌdiː kən ˈtæm ɪ |neɪt §ˌ-kɒn-,
-ə neɪt ~nated neɪt ɪd -əd ‖ neɪṭ əd ~nates
neɪts ~nating neɪt ɪŋ ‖ neɪṭ ɪŋ

decontamination ˌdiː kən ˌtæm ɪ ˈneɪʃ ᵊn
§ˌ-kɒn-, -əˈ·- ~s z

decontrol ˌdiː kən ˈtrəʊl §-kɒn-, →-ˈtrɒʊl
‖ -ˈtroʊl ~led d ~ling ɪŋ ~s z

decor, décor ˈdeɪk ɔː ˈdek- ‖ deɪ ˈkɔːr ˈdeɪk ɔːr
~s z

deco|rate ˈdek ə |reɪt ~rated reɪt ɪd -əd
‖ reɪṭ əd ~rates reɪts ~rating reɪt ɪŋ ‖ reɪṭ ɪŋ

decoration ˌdek ə ˈreɪʃ ᵊn ~s z

decorative ˈdek ᵊr ˌət ɪv ‖ əṭ ɪv -ə reɪṭ- ~ly li
~ness nəs nɪs

decorator ˈdek ə reɪt ə ‖ -reɪṭ ᵊr ~s z

decorous ˈdek ᵊr əs —*formerly* dɪ ˈkɔːr əs ~ly
li ~ness nəs nɪs

decorti|cate ˌdiː ˈkɔːt ɪ |keɪt §-ə- ‖ -ˈkɔːrṭ-
~cated keɪt ɪd -əd ‖ keɪṭ əd ~cates keɪts
~cating keɪt ɪŋ ‖ keɪṭ ɪŋ

decortication ˌdiː ˌkɔːt ɪ ˈkeɪʃ ᵊn §-ə-
‖ ˌdiː ˌkɔːrṭ əˈ·- ~s z

decorum dɪ ˈkɔːr əm də- ‖ -ˈkoʊr-

decoupage, découpage ˌdeɪ ku ˈpɑːʒ —*Fr*
[de ku paːʒ]

decoupl|e ⁽ˌ⁾diː ˈkʌp ᵊl ~ed d ~es z ~ing ˌɪŋ

De Courcey, De Courcy (*i*) də ˈkɔːs i
‖ -ˈkɔːrs i -ˈkoʊrs-, (*ii*) -ˈkʊəs i ‖ -ˈkʊrs i,
(*iii*) -ˈkɜːs i ‖ -ˈkɜːs i

decoy *v* di ˈkɔɪ də- ~ed d ~ing ɪŋ ~s z

decoy *n* ˈdiː kɔɪ dɪ ˈkɔɪ, də-, §diː- ~s z

decreas|e *v* ˌdiː ˈkriːs ◂ di-, də-, ˈ··ˈ ~ed t ~es
ɪz əz ~ing/ly ɪŋ /li

decreas|e *n* ˈdiː kriːs di ˈkriːs, də-, ˌdiː- ~es ɪz
əz

decree di ˈkriː də- ~d d ~ing ɪŋ ~s z
deˌcree ˈnisi

decrement *n* ˈdek rɪ mənt -rə- ~s s

decre|ment *v* ˈdek rɪ |ment -rə- —*See note at*
-ment ~mented ment ɪd -əd ‖ menṭ əd
~menting ment ɪŋ ‖ menṭ ɪŋ ~ments ments

decreolis... —*see* decreoliz...

decreolization ˌdiː ˌkriː əl aɪ ˈzeɪʃ ᵊn -ˌkreɪ-,
-ˌəʊl-, -ɪˈ·- ‖ -ə ˈzeɪʃ-

decreoliz|e ˌdiː ˈkriː ə laɪz -ˈkreɪ-, -əʊ- ~ed d
~es ɪz əz ~ing ɪŋ

decrepit di ˈkrep ɪt də-, §-ət ~ly li

decrepi|tate di ˈkrep ɪ |teɪt də-, -ə- ~tated
teɪt ɪd -əd ‖ teɪṭ əd ~tates teɪts ~tating
teɪt ɪŋ ‖ teɪṭ ɪŋ

decrepitude di ˈkrep ɪ tjuːd də-, -ə-, →-tʃuːd
‖ -tuːd -tjuːd

decrescendo ˌdiː krə ˈʃend əʊ ˌdeɪ-, -krɪ- ‖ -oʊ
~s z

De Crespigny (*i*) də ˈkrep ɪn i -ən-, (*ii*)
-ˈkresp-

decretal di ˈkriːt ᵊl də- ‖ -ˈkriːṭ ᵊl ~s z

decri... —*see* decry

decriminalis... —*see* decriminaliz...

decriminalization ˌdiː ˌkrɪm ɪn ᵊl aɪ ˈzeɪʃ ᵊn
-ˌᵊn ᵊl-, ·ˌ·-, -ɪˈ·- ‖ -ə ˈzeɪʃ-

decriminaliz|e ⁽ˌ⁾diː ˈkrɪm ɪn ə laɪz -ᵊn ə-,
-əl aɪz ~ed d ~es ɪz əz ~ing ɪŋ

de|cry di |ˈkraɪ də- ~cried ˈkraɪd ~cries ˈkraɪz
~crying ˈkraɪ ɪŋ

decrypt ⁽ˌ⁾diː ˈkrɪpt ~ed ɪd əd ~ing ɪŋ ~s s

decryption ⁽ˌ⁾diː ˈkrɪp ʃᵊn ~s z

decubitus di ˈkjuːb ɪt əs də-, -ət- ‖ -əṭ-

decumbent di ˈkʌm bənt də-

decurion de ˈkjʊər i ən di- ‖ -ˈkjʊr- ~s z

decurrent di ˈkʌr ənt də- ‖ -ˈkɜː- ~ly li

decussate *adj* di ˈkʌs eɪt ˌdiː-, -ət, -ɪt ~ly li

decuss|ate *v* di ˈkʌs |eɪt ˌdiː-; ˈdek əs- ~ated
eɪt ɪd -əd ‖ eɪṭ əd ~ates eɪts ~ating eɪt ɪŋ
‖ eɪṭ ɪŋ

Dedalus ˈdiːd əl əs ‖ ˈded-

Deddington ˈded ɪŋ tən

Dedham ˈded əm

D

dedi|cate 'ded ɪ |keɪt §-ə- **~cated/ly** keɪt ɪd /li
-əd /li ‖ keɪṭ əd /li **~cates** keɪts **~cating**
keɪt ɪŋ ‖ keɪṭ ɪŋ
dedicatee ˌded ɪk ə 'tiː ˌ·ək- **~s** z
dedication ˌded ɪ 'keɪʃ ³n §-ə- **~s** z
dedicator 'ded ɪ keɪt ə §'·-ə- ‖ -keɪṭ ³r **~s** z
dedicatory 'ded ɪk ət ³r i -ɪ keɪt ər i ‖ -ə tɔːr i
-toʊr i
deduc|e di 'dju:s də-, →§-'dʒu:s ‖ -'du:s -'dju:s
~ed t **~es** ɪz əz **~ing** ɪŋ
deducible di 'dju:s əb ³l də-, →§-'dʒu:s-, -ɪb-
‖ -'du:s- -'dju:s-
deduct di 'dʌkt də- **~ed** ɪd əd **~ing** ɪŋ **~s** s
deductible di 'dʌkt əb ³l də-, -ɪb- **~s** z
deduction di 'dʌk ʃ³n də- **~s** z
deductive di 'dʌkt ɪv də- **~ly** li
Dee di:
deed di:d **deeded** 'di:d ɪd -əd **deeding** 'di:d ɪŋ **deeds** di:dz
   'deed poll
Deedes di:dz
deejay 'di: dʒeɪ ˌ·'· **~s** z
Deekes, Deeks di:ks
Deeko *tdmk* 'di:k əʊ ‖ -oʊ
Deeley 'di:l i
deem di:m **deemed** di:md **deeming** 'di:m ɪŋ **deems** di:mz
Deemer 'di:m ə ‖ -³r
Deeming 'di:m ɪŋ
de-emphasis|e, de-emphasiz|e
   ˌdi: 'emᵖf ə saɪz **~ed** d **~es** ɪz əz **~ing** ɪŋ
deemster 'di:m stə ‖ -st³r **~s** z
deep di:p **deeper** 'di:p ə ‖ -³r **deepest**
   'di:p ɪst -əst **deeps** di:ps
   ˌdeep 'end; ˌDeep 'South; ˌdeep 'space;
   ˌdeep 'water
deep-dyed ˌdi:p 'daɪd ◄
deepen 'di:p ən **~ed** d **~ing** ˌɪŋ **~s** z
deep-freez|e *n*, **Deepfreeze** *tdmk* ˌdi:p 'fri:z
   ‖ 'di:p fri:z **~es** ɪz əz
deep-freez|e *v* ˌdi:p 'fri:z **~er/s** ə/z ‖ ³r/z **~es**
   ɪz əz **~ing** ɪŋ
deep-frozen ˌdi:p 'frəʊz ³n ◄ ‖ -'froʊz-
deep-|fry ˌdi:p |'fraɪ ˌ·'· **~fried** 'fraɪd **~fries**
   'fraɪz **~frying** 'fraɪ ɪŋ
Deeping 'di:p ɪŋ
deep-laid ˌdi:p 'leɪd ◄
deep|ly 'di:p |li **~ness** nəs nɪs
deep-pocketed ˌdi:p 'pɒk ɪt ɪd ◄ -ət-, -əd
   ‖ -'pɑːk əṭ əd ◄
deep-rooted ˌdi:p 'ru:t ɪd ◄ -əd ‖ -'ru:ṭ- **~ness**
   nəs nɪs
deep-sea ˌdi:p 'si: ◄
deep-seated ˌdi:p 'si:t ɪd ◄ -əd ‖ -'si:ṭ-
deep-set ˌdi:p 'set ◄
deer dɪə ‖ dɪ³r (= *dear*)
Deer, Deere dɪə ‖ dɪ³r
deerhound 'dɪə haʊnd ‖ 'dɪr- **~s** z
deerskin 'dɪə skɪn ‖ 'dɪr- **~s** z
deerstalker 'dɪə ˌstɔːk ə ‖ 'dɪr ˌstɔːk ³r -ˌstɑːk-
   ~s z

de-esca|late ₍₁₎di: 'esk ə |leɪt **~lated** leɪt ɪd
-əd ‖ leɪṭ əd **~lates** leɪts **~lating** leɪt ɪŋ
‖ leɪṭ ɪŋ
de-escalation ˌdi: ˌesk ə 'leɪʃ ³n ·ˌ·- **~s** z
Deeside 'di: saɪd
defac|e di 'feɪs də- **~ed** t **~es** ɪz əz **~ing** ɪŋ
defacement di 'feɪs mənt də- **~s** s
de facto ₍₁₎deɪ 'fækt əʊ di- ‖ -oʊ
defalc|ate 'di: fælk |eɪt -fɔːlk- ‖ di 'fælk-
-'fɔːlk-; 'def ³l k|eɪt **~ated** eɪt ɪd -əd ‖ eɪṭ əd
~ates eɪts **~ating** eɪt ɪŋ ‖ eɪṭ ɪŋ
defalcation ˌdi:f æl 'keɪʃ ³n -ɔːl- ‖ ˌdef ³l- **~s** z
defamation ˌdef ə 'meɪʃ ³n ˌdi:f- **~s** z
defamator|y di 'fæm ə ˌtər i də- ‖ -ə tɔːr |i
-toʊr i **~ily** əl i ɪ li
defam|e di 'feɪm də- **~ed** d **~es** z **~ing** ɪŋ
default *v* di 'fɔːlt də-, -'fɒlt ‖ -'fɑːlt **~ed** ɪd əd
~er/s ə/z ‖ ³r/z **~ing** ɪŋ **~s** s
default *n* di 'fɔːlt də-, -'fɒlt; 'di:· ‖ -'fɑːlt **~s** s
defeasance di 'fi:z ³n's də-
defeasible di 'fi:z əb ³l də-, -ɪb-
de|feat *v, n* di |'fi:t də- **~feated** 'fi:t ɪd -əd
‖ 'fi:ṭ əd **~feating** 'fi:t ɪŋ ‖ 'fi:ṭ ɪŋ **~feats**
'fi:ts
defeatism di 'fi:t ˌɪz əm də- ‖ -'fi:ṭ-
defeatist di 'fi:t ɪst də-, §-əst ‖ -'fi:ṭ- **~s** s
defe|cate 'def ə |keɪt 'di:f-, -ɪ- **~cated** keɪt ɪd
-əd ‖ keɪṭ əd **~cates** keɪts **~cating** keɪt ɪŋ
‖ keɪṭ ɪŋ
defecation ˌdef ə 'keɪʃ ³n ˌdi:f-, -ɪ- **~s** z

DEFECT

14%
86%
'··
·'·
BrE

defect *n* 'di: fekt di 'fekt, də- — *Preference*
poll, BrE: '·· 86%, ·'· 14%. **~s** s
defect *v* di 'fekt də- **~ed** ɪd əd **~ing** ɪŋ **~s** s
defection di 'fek ʃ³n də- **~s** z
defective di 'fekt ɪv də- **~ly** li **~ness** nəs nɪs
defector di 'fekt ə də- ‖ -³r **~s** z
defenc|e di 'fen's də- **~es** ɪz əz
defenceless di 'fen's ləs də-, -lɪs **~ly** li **~ness**
nəs nɪs
defence|man di 'fen's| mən də- **~men** mən
defend di 'fend də- **~ed** ɪd əd **~ing** ɪŋ **~s** z
defendant di 'fend ənt də- ‖ -ænt **~s** s
defender di 'fend ə də- ‖ -³r **~s** z
defene|strate ₍₁₎di: 'fen ɪ |streɪt -ə- **~strated**
streɪt ɪd -əd ‖ streɪṭ əd **~strates** streɪts
~strating streɪt ɪŋ ‖ streɪṭ ɪŋ
defenestration ˌdi: ˌfen ɪ 'streɪʃ ³n -ə'·- **~s** z
defens|e di 'fen's də- ‖ 'di:· **~es** ɪz əz
defenseless di 'fen's ləs də-, -lɪs **~ly** li **~ness**
nəs nɪs
defense|man di 'fen's| mən də- **~men** mən
defensibility di ˌfen's ə 'bɪl ət i də-, -ˌ·ɪ-, -ɪt i
‖ -əṭ i

defensib|le di 'fen⟨s⟩ əb |ᵊl də-, -ıb- **~ly** li
defensive di 'fen⟨s⟩ ıv də- **~ly** li **~ness** nəs nıs
de|fer di |'fɜː də- ‖ -|'fɝː **~ferred** 'fɜːd ‖ 'fɝːd
    ~ferring 'fɜːr ıŋ ‖ 'fɝː ıŋ **~fers** 'fɜːz ‖ 'fɝːz
deference 'def ᵊr_ᵊn⟨t⟩s
deferent 'def ᵊr_ᵊnt
deferential ˌdef ə 'ren⟨t⟩ʃ ᵊl ◀ **~ly** i
deferment di 'fɜː mənt də- ‖ -'fɝː- **~s** s
deferral di 'fɜːr əl də- ‖ -'fɝː- **~s** z
deferrer di 'fɜːr ə də- ‖ -'fɝː ᵊr **~s** z
deffo 'def əʊ ‖ -oʊ
defiance di 'faɪ_ᵊn⟨t⟩s də-
defiant di 'faɪ_ᵊnt də- **~ly** li
defibril|late ₍ᵢ₎di: 'fɪb rı |leıt -'faıb-, -rə-
    ~lated leıt ıd -əd ‖ leıt̬ əd **~lates** leıts
    ~lating leıt ıŋ ‖ leıt̬ ıŋ
defibrillation di: ˌfɪb rı 'leıʃ ᵊn -ˌfaıb-, ˌ·ˌ·-,
    -rə'--
defibrillator ₍ᵢ₎di: 'fɪb rı leıt ə -'faıb-, -'·rə-
    ‖ -leıt̬ ᵊr **~s** z
deficienc|y di 'fıʃ ᵊn⟨t⟩s |i də- **~ies** iz
    de'ficiency di,sease
deficient di 'fıʃ ᵊnt də- **~ly** li
deficit 'def əs ıt -ıs-, -ət; dı 'fıs-, də-, §di:-
    —*formerly also* 'di:f- **~s** s
de fide di 'faıd i ˌdi:-; ˌdeı 'fi:d eı
defie... —*see* **defy**
defilad|e ˌdef ı 'leıd -ə-, '··· **~ed** ıd əd **~es** z
    ~ing ıŋ
defile *n* di 'faıᵊl də- 'di: faıᵊl **~s** z
defil|e *v* di 'faıᵊl də- **~ed** d **~es** z **~ing** ıŋ
defilement di 'faıᵊl mənt də- **~s** s
definab|le di 'faın əb |ᵊl də- **~ly** li
defin|e di 'faın də- **~ed** d **~er/s** ə/z ‖ -ᵊr/z **~es**
    z **~ing** ıŋ
definite 'def ᵊn_ət -ın-, -ıt **~ly** li **~ness** nəs nıs
    ˌdefinite 'article
definition ˌdef ə 'nıʃ ᵊn -ı- **~al** ᵊl
definitive di 'fın ət ıv də-, -ıt- ‖ -ət̬ ıv **~ly** li
    ~ness nəs nıs
de|flate ˌdi: |'fleıt dı-, də- **~flated** 'fleıt ıd -əd
    ‖ 'fleıt̬ əd **~flates** 'fleıts **~flating** 'fleıt ıŋ
    ‖ 'fleıt̬ ıŋ
deflation ˌdi: 'fleıʃ ᵊn dı-, də- **~s** z
deflationary ˌdi: 'fleıʃ ᵊn ᵊr_i dı-, də-, -ᵊn_ᵊr i
    ‖ -ə ner i
deflator di 'fleıt ə də- ‖ -'fleıt̬ ᵊr **~s** z
deflect di 'flekt də- **~ed** ıd əd **~ing** ıŋ **~s** s
deflection di 'flek ʃᵊn də- **~s** z
defloration ˌdi: flɔ: 'reıʃ ᵊn ˌdef lɔ:- ‖ ˌdef lə-
    ˌdi:f- **~s** z
deflower ˌdi: 'flaʊ ə dı-, də- ‖ -'flaʊ ᵊr **~ed** d
    deflowering ˌdi: 'flaʊ ᵊr ıŋ dı-, də-
    ‖ -'flaʊ ᵊr ıŋ **~s** z
Defoe di 'fəʊ də- ‖ -'foʊ
defog ˌdi: 'fɒg -'fɑːg -'fɔːg **~ged** d **~ger/s**
    ə/z ‖ -ᵊr/z **~ging** ıŋ **~s** z
defoliant di 'fəʊl i ənt ˌdi:-, də- ‖ -'foʊl- **~s** s
defoli|ate di 'fəʊl i |eıt ˌdi:-, də- ‖ -'foʊl-
    ~ated eıt ıd -əd ‖ eıt̬ əd **~ates** eıts **~ating**
    eıt ıŋ ‖ eıt̬ ıŋ
defoliation di ˌfəʊl i 'eıʃ ᵊn də-, ˌdi: ˌfəʊl-
    ‖ -ˌfoʊl- **~s** z

deforest ˌdi: 'fɒr ıst dı-, də-, -əst ‖ -'fɔːr- -'fɑːr-
    ~ed ıd əd **~ing** ıŋ **~s** s
deforestation di: ˌfɒr ı 'steıʃ ᵊn dı-, də-,
    ˌdi: -ˌfɒr-, -ə- ‖ -ˌfɔːr- -ˌfɑːr- **~s** z
deform di 'fɔːm də-, ˌdi:- ‖ -'fɔːrm **~ed** d **~ing**
    ıŋ **~s** z
deformation ˌdi: fɔ: 'meıʃ ᵊn ˌdef ə- ‖ ˌdi: fɔːr-
    ˌdef ᵊr- **~s** z
deformit|y di 'fɔːm ət |i də-, -ıt- ‖ -'fɔːrm ət̬ |i
    ~ies iz
DEFRA 'def rə
defrag *n* 'di: fræg
defrag *v* ˌdi: 'fræg **~ged** d **~ging** ıŋ **~s** z
defrag|ment ˌdi: fræg 'ment **~mented**
    'ment ıd -əd ‖ 'ment̬- **~menting** 'ment ıŋ
    ‖ 'ment̬ ıŋ **~ments** 'ments
defraud di 'frɔːd də-, ˌdi:- ‖ -'frɑːd **~ed** ıd əd
    ~er/s ə/z ‖ ᵊr/z **~ing** ıŋ **~s** z
defraudation ˌdi: frɔ: 'deıʃ ᵊn ‖ -frɑː- **~s** z
defray di 'freı də- **~ed** d **~ing** ıŋ **~s** z
defrayal di 'freı əl də- **~s** z
De Freitas də 'freıt əs ‖ -'freıt̬-
defrock ˌdi: 'frɒk ‖ -'frɑːk **~ed** t **~ing** ıŋ **~s** s
defrost ˌdi: 'frɒst dı-, də-, -'frɔːst ‖ -'frɔːst
    -'frɑːst **~ed** ıd əd **~ing** ıŋ **~s** s
deft deft **defter** 'deft ə ‖ -ᵊr **deftest** 'deft ıst
    -əst **deftly** 'deft li **deftness** 'deft nəs -nıs
defunct di 'fʌŋkt də-; 'di: fʌŋkt **~ness** nəs nıs
defus|e ˌdi: 'fju:z də-, dı- —*Some people
    disapprove of the pronunciation* di-, *since it
    can lead to confusion with* diffuse (v). **~ed** d
    ~es ız əz **~ing** ıŋ
de|fy di |'faı də- **~fied** 'faıd **~fier/s** 'faı_ə/z
    ‖ 'faı ᵊr/z **~fies** 'faız **~fying** 'faı ıŋ
degage, dégagé ˌdeı gɑ: 'ʒeı -gæ-;
    ₍ᵢ₎deı 'gɑːʒ eı
Deganwy dı 'gæn wi də- —*Welsh* [de 'ga nui,
    -nui-]
Degas 'deıg ɑ: ‖ də 'gɑː —*Fr* [də 'ga]
De Gaulle də 'gəʊl di-, →-'gɒʊl, -'gɔːl ‖ -'gɔːl
    -'goʊl —*Fr* [də gol]
degauss ˌdi: 'gaʊs -'gɔːs **~ed** t **~es** ız əz **~ing**
    ıŋ
degemi|nate ˌdi: 'dʒem ı |neıt -ə- **~nated**
    neıt ıd -əd ‖ neıt̬ əd **~nates** neıts **~nating**
    neıt ıŋ ‖ neıt̬ ıŋ
degemination ˌdi: ˌdʒem ı 'neıʃ ᵊn -ə- **~s** z
degenerac|y di 'dʒen ᵊr_əs |i də- **~ies** iz
degenerate *adj, n* di 'dʒen ᵊr_ət də-, -ıt **~ly** li
    ~ness nəs nıs **~s** s
degene|rate *v* di 'dʒen ə |reıt də- **~rated**
    reıt ıd -əd ‖ reıt̬ əd **~rates** reıts **~rating**
    reıt ıŋ ‖ reıt̬ ıŋ
degeneration di ˌdʒen ə 'reıʃ ᵊn də- **~s** z
degenerative di 'dʒen ᵊr_ət ıv də-, -ə reıt ıv
    ‖ ət̬ ıv -ə reıt̬ ıv **~ly** li
DeGeneres də 'dʒen ᵊr əs di-
deglutition ˌdi: glu 'tıʃ ᵊn
degradability di ˌgreıd ə 'bıl ət i də-, -ıt i
    ‖ -ət̬ i
degradable di 'greıd əb |ᵊl də-
degradation ˌdeg rə 'deıʃ ᵊn **~s** z

D

degrad|e di 'greɪd də- **~ed** ɪd əd **~es** z **~ing/ly**
ɪŋ /li

de|grease ˌdi: |'gri:s -'gri:z **~greased** 'gri:st
'gri:zd **~greases** 'gri:s ɪz 'gri:z-, -əz
~greasing 'gri:s ɪŋ ' gri:z-

degree di 'gri: də- **~s** z

De Havilland di 'hæv ɪl ənd də-, -ᵊl-

dehisc|e di 'hɪs də- **~ed** t **~es** ɪz əz **~ing** ɪŋ

dehiscence di 'hɪs ᵊn's də-

dehiscent di 'hɪs ᵊnt də-

dehorn ˌdi: 'hɔ:n ‖ -'hɔ:rn **~ed** d **~ing** ɪŋ **~s** z

Dehra Dun ˌdeər ə 'du:n ‖ ˌder-

dehumanis... —*see* **dehumaniz...**

dehumanization ⁽ˌ⁾di: ˌhju:m ən aɪ 'zeɪʃ ᵊn
-ən ɪ- ‖ -ən ə- -ˌju:m-

dehumaniz|e ⁽ˌ⁾di: 'hju:m ə naɪz ‖ -'ju:m- **~ed**
d **~es** ɪz əz **~ing** ɪŋ

dehumidi|fy ˌdi: hju 'mɪd ɪ |faɪ §-'ə- ‖ ˌju-
~fied faɪd **~fier/s** faɪ ə/z ‖ faɪ ᵊr/z **~fies** faɪz
~fying faɪ ɪŋ

dehydr|ate ⁽ˌ⁾di: 'haɪdr |eɪt ◄ -haɪ 'dr|eɪt; '···
~ated eɪt ɪd -əd ‖ eɪţ əd **~ates** eɪts **~ating**
eɪt ɪŋ ‖ eɪţ ɪŋ

dehydration ˌdi: haɪ 'dreɪʃ ᵊn **~s** z

dehydrogenase ˌdi: haɪ 'drɒdʒ ə neɪz
ˌdi: 'haɪdr ədʒ-, -neɪs ‖ -'drɑ:dʒ-

Deianira ˌdeɪ ə 'naɪᵊr ə ˌdi:

deic|e, de-ic|e ˌdi: 'aɪs **~ed** t **~es** ɪz əz **~ing**
ɪŋ

deicide 'deɪ ɪ saɪd 'di:ˌ, -ə- **~s** z

deictic 'daɪkt ɪk 'deɪkt- —*Also sometimes, by*
misanalysis, di 'ɪkt ɪk, deɪ- **~ally** ᵊl i **~s** s

deification ˌdeɪ ɪf ɪ 'keɪʃ ᵊn ˌdiˌ, ˌ-əf-, §-ə'-- **~s**
z

dei|fy 'deɪ ɪ |faɪ 'di:ˌ, -ə- **~fied** faɪd **~fier/s**
faɪ ə/z ‖ faɪ ᵊr/z **~fies** faɪz **~fying** faɪ ɪŋ

Deighton *(i)* 'deɪt ᵊn, *(ii)* 'daɪt ᵊn, *(iii)* 'di:t ᵊn

deign deɪn *(= Dane)* **deigned** deɪnd **deigning**
'deɪn ɪŋ **deigns** deɪnz

Dei gratia ˌdeɪ i: 'graːt iˌə ˌdi: aɪ 'greɪʃ-

Deimos 'deɪm ɒs 'daɪm- ‖ -ɑːs

deindustriali|sation, ~zation
ˌdi: ɪn ˌdʌs tri əl aɪ 'zeɪʃ ᵊn -ɪ'-- ‖ -ə'--

deinonychus daɪ 'nɒn ɪk əs ‖ -'nɑːn- **~es** ɪz əz

Deirdre 'dɪədr i ‖ 'dɪrdr i —*but in Ireland* -ə
—*Ir* ['dʲerʲ dʲrʲe]

deism 'deɪ ˌɪz əm 'di:- ‖ 'di:- 'deɪ-

deist 'deɪ ɪst 'di:-, §-əst ‖ 'di:- 'deɪ- **~s** s

DEITY

pie chart: 'deɪ- 80%, 'di:- 20% (BrE)

deit|y 'deɪ ət |i 'di:-, -ɪt- ‖ 'di: əţ |i 'deɪ- —
Preference poll, BrE: 'deɪ- *80%,* 'di:- *20%.* **~ies**
iz

deixis 'daɪks ɪs 'deɪks-, §-əs —*Also sometimes,*
by misanalysis, di 'ɪks ɪs, deɪ-, §-əs.

deja vu, déjà vu ˌdeɪʒ ɑ: 'vu: -'vju: —*Fr*
[de ʒa vy]

dejected di 'dʒekt ɪd də-, -əd **~ly** li **~ness** nəs
nɪs

dejection di 'dʒek ʃᵊn də- **~s** z

De Jong, De Jongh də 'jɒŋ ‖ -'jɔːŋ -'jɑːŋ,
-'dʒɔːŋ, -'dʒɑːŋ

de jure ⁽ˌ⁾deɪ 'dʒʊər i di-, -'jʊər-, -eɪ
‖ ⁽ˌ⁾di: 'dʒʊr i ⁽ˌ⁾deɪ 'jʊr eɪ

de Keyser də 'kaɪz ə ‖ -ᵊr

Dekker 'dek ə ‖ -ᵊr

dekko 'dek əʊ ‖ -oʊ **~s** z

de Klerk də 'kleək ‖ -'kleᵊrk —*Afrikaans*
[də 'klɛrk]

De Kooning də 'ku:n ɪŋ

del, Del del

Delacour 'del ə kʊə -kɔː ‖ -kʊr

Delacourt 'del ə kɔːt ‖ -kɔːrt -koʊrt

Delacroix 'del ə krwɑː ˌ·'·· —*Fr* [də la krwa]

Delafield 'del ə fi:ᵊld

Delagoa ˌdel ə 'gəʊ ə ◄ ‖ -'goʊ ə
ˌDelaˌgoa 'Bay

Delahaye 'del ə heɪ

de la Mare ˌdel ə 'meə də lɑː-; 'del ə meə
‖ -'meᵊr -'mæᵊr

Delamere 'del ə mɪə ˌ·'·· ‖ -mɪr

Delancey də 'læn's i

Delaney də 'leɪn i dɪ-

Delano *(i)* 'del ə nəʊ ‖ -noʊ, *(ii)* də 'leɪn əʊ
‖ -oʊ -*Franklin D~ Roosevelt was (i); the place*
in CA is (ii).

De-La-Noy 'del ə nɔɪ

Delany də 'leɪn i dɪ-

de la Renta ˌdel ə 'rent ə dəl-

Delargy də 'lɑːg i ‖ -'lɑːrg i

De La Rue, de la Rue ˌdel ə 'ru: dəl ə-;
'del ə ru:

delation di 'leɪʃ ᵊn də- **~s** z

Delaware 'del ə weə ‖ -wer -wær

De La Warr 'del ə weə ‖ -wer -wær

delay di 'leɪ də- **~ed** d **~er/s** ə/z ‖ -ᵊr/z **~ing**
ɪŋ **~s** z

delayed-action di ˌleɪd 'æk ʃᵊn ◄ də-

Delbert 'delb ət ‖ -ᵊrt

Delbridge 'del brɪdʒ

del credere ˌdel 'kreɪd ər i -'kred- **~s** z

Delderfield 'deld ə fi:ᵊld ‖ -ᵊr-

dele 'di:l i: -i **~d** d **~ing** ɪŋ **~s** z

delectab|le di 'lekt əb |ᵊl də- **~ly** li

delectation ˌdi: lek 'teɪʃ ᵊn

delegac|y 'del ɪg əs |i ˌ·əg- **~ies** iz

delegate *n* 'del ɪg ət -əg-, -ɪt; -ɪ geɪt, -ə- **~s** s

dele|gate *v* 'del ɪ |geɪt -ə- **~gated** geɪt ɪd -əd
‖ geɪţ əd **~gates** geɪts **~gating** geɪt ɪŋ
‖ geɪţ ɪŋ

delegation ˌdel ɪ 'geɪʃ ᵊn -ə- **~s** z

de|lete di |'li:t də- **~leted** 'li:t ɪd -əd ‖ 'li:ţ əd
~letes 'li:ts **~leting** 'li:t ɪŋ ‖ 'li:ţ ɪŋ

deleterious ˌdel ɪ 'tɪər iˌəs ◄ ˌdi:l-, ˌ-ə- ‖ -'tɪr-
~ly li **~ness** nəs nɪs

deletion di 'li:ʃ ᵊn də- **~s** z

delf delf

Delfont 'del fɒnt ‖ -fɑːnt

D

delft, Delft delft
delftware 'delft weə ‖ -wer -wær
Delgado del 'gɑːd əʊ ‖ -oʊ
Delhi 'del i
deli 'del i ~s z
Delia 'diːl i̯ə
Delian 'diːl i̯ən ~s z
deliberate *adj* di 'lɪb ər̩ət də-, ɪt ~ly li ~ness
    nəs nɪs
delibe|rate *v* di 'lɪb ə |reɪt də- ~rated reɪt ɪd
    -əd ‖ reɪt̬ əd ~rates reɪts ~rating reɪt ɪŋ
    ‖ reɪt̬ ɪŋ
deliberation di ˌlɪb ə 'reɪʃ ᵊn də- ~s z
deliberative di 'lɪb ər̩ət ɪv də- ‖ -ə reɪt̬ ɪv
    -ər̩ət̬- ~ly li ~ness nəs nɪs
Delibes də 'liːb dɪ- —*Fr* [də lib]
delicac|y 'del ɪk əs |i '·ək- ~ies iz
delicate 'del ɪk ət -ək-, -ɪt ~ly li ~ness nəs nɪs
    ~s s
delicatessen ˌdel ɪk ə 'tes ᵊn ˌ·ək- ~s z
delicious di 'lɪʃ əs də- ~ly li ~ness nəs nɪs
de|light *n, v* di |'laɪt də- ~lighted 'laɪt ɪd -əd
    ‖ 'laɪt̬ əd ~lighting 'laɪt ɪŋ ‖ 'laɪt̬ ɪŋ ~lights
    'laɪts
delighted di 'laɪt ɪd də-, -əd ‖ -'laɪt̬ əd ~ly li
    ~ness nəs nɪs
delightful di 'laɪt fᵊl də-, -fʊl ~ly ̩i ~ness nəs
    nɪs
Delilah di 'laɪl ə də-
delim|it ₍ᵢ₎diː 'lɪm |ɪt dɪ-, də-, §-ət ‖ -|ət ~ited
    ɪt ɪd §ət-, -əd ‖ ət̬ əd ~iting ɪt ɪŋ §ət- ‖ ət̬ ɪŋ
    ~its ɪts §əts ‖ əts
delimi|tate di 'lɪm ɪ |teɪt də- ~tated teɪt ɪd
    -əd ‖ teɪt̬ əd ~tates teɪts ~tating teɪt ɪŋ
    ‖ teɪt̬ ɪŋ
delimitation di ˌlɪm ɪ 'teɪʃ ᵊn də- ~s z
delimitative di 'lɪm ɪt ət ɪv də-, §-'·ət-;
    -ɪ teɪt ɪv, -ə · · ‖ -ə teɪt̬ ɪv
deline|ate di 'lɪn i |eɪt də- ~ated eɪt ɪd -əd
    ‖ eɪt̬ əd ~ates eɪts ~ating eɪt ɪŋ ‖ eɪt̬ ɪŋ
delineation di ˌlɪn i 'eɪʃ ᵊn də- ~s z
delineator di 'lɪn i eɪt ə də- ‖ -eɪt̬ ᵊr ~s z
delinquenc|y di 'lɪŋk wən̩t̬s |i də- ~ies iz
delinquent di 'lɪŋk wənt də- ~ly li ~s s
deliquesc|e ˌdel ɪ 'kwes -ə- ~ed t ~es ɪz əz
    ~ing ɪŋ
deliquescence ˌdel ɪ 'kwes ᵊn̩t̬s -ə-
deliquescent ˌdel ɪ 'kwes ᵊnt ◄ -ə-
delirious di 'lɪr i̯ əs də-, -'lɪər- — *Preference*
    poll, BrE: -'lɪr- 46%, -'lɪər- 54% *(those born*
    since 1973: 80%). ~ly li ~ness nəs nɪs
deliri|um di 'lɪr i̯ |əm də-, -'lɪər- ~a ə ~ums
    əmz
de ˌlirium 'tremens 'triːm enz 'trem-, -ənz
De Lisle, De L'Isle də 'laɪᵊl
delist ˌdiː 'lɪst ~ed ɪd əd ~ing ɪŋ ~s s
Delius 'diːl i̯əs
deliver di 'lɪv ə də- ‖ -ᵊr ~ed d delivering
    dɪ 'lɪv ər ɪŋ ~s z
deliverability di ˌlɪv ər̩ə 'bɪl ət i də-, -ɪt i
    ‖ -ət̬ i
deliverable di 'lɪv ər̩əb ᵊl də- ~s z
deliverance di 'lɪv ᵊr̩ən̩t̬s də-

DELIRIOUS

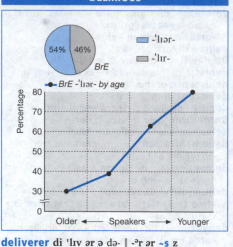

deliverer di 'lɪv ər̩ə də- ‖ -ᵊr̩ᵊr ~s z
deliver|y di 'lɪv ər̩|i də- ~ies iz
delivery|man di 'lɪv ər̩ i |mæn də-, -mən
    ~men men mən
dell, Dell del dells, Dell's delz
Della 'del ə
Deller 'del ə ‖ -ᵊr
Dellums 'del əmz
Delmar, Del Mar del 'mɑː '·· ‖ 'del mɑːr ·'·
Delmarva del 'mɑːv ə ‖ -'mɑːrv ə
Delmonico del 'mɒn ɪ kəʊ ‖ -'mɑːn ɪ koʊ
Del Monte *tdmk* del 'mɒnt eɪ -i ‖ -'mɑːnt-
Deloitte də 'lɔɪt
Delorean də 'lɔːr i̯ən
Delores də 'lɔːr ɪz di-, -əz ‖ -ɪs
Delors də 'lɔː ‖ -'lɔːr —*Fr* [də lɔːʁ]
Delos 'diːl ɒs ‖ -ɑːs
de|louse ˌdiː |'laʊs -'laʊz ~loused 'laʊst
    'laʊzd ~louses 'laʊs ɪz 'laʊz-, -əz ~lousing
    'laʊs ɪŋ 'laʊz-
Delph delf
Delphi 'delf aɪ -i —*Mod Gk* [ðel 'fi]
Delphian 'delf i̯ən
Delphic 'delf ɪk
Delphine del 'fiːn
delphinium del 'fɪn i̯əm ~s z
Delphinus del 'faɪn əs
Delroy 'del rɔɪ
Delsey *tdmk* 'dels i
delta, Delta 'delt ə ~s z
deltaic del 'teɪ ɪk
delta-winged ˌdelt ə 'wɪŋd ◄
deltic 'delt ɪk
deltiology ˌdelt i 'ɒl ədʒ i ‖ -'ɑːl-
deltoid 'delt ɔɪd ~s z
delud|e di 'luːd də-, -'ljuːd ~ed ɪd əd ~es z
    ~ing ɪŋ
delug|e *n, v* 'del juːdʒ -juːʒ ~ed d ~es ɪz əz
    ~ing ɪŋ
delusion di 'luːʒ ᵊn də-, -'ljuːʒ- ~al ᵊl ~s z
delusive di 'luːs ɪv də-, -'ljuːs-, §-'luːz-, §-'ljuːz-
    ~ly li ~ness nəs nɪs

delusory di ˈluːs ər i də-, -ˈljuːs-, -ˈluːz-, -ˈljuːz-
deluxe, de luxe də ˈlʌks di-, -ˈlʊks, -ˈluːks
　—*Fr* [də lyks]
delve delv **delved** delvd **delver/s** ˈdelv ə/z
　‖ -ᵊr/z **delves** delvz **delving** ˈdelv ɪŋ
Delwyn ˈdel wɪn
Delyn ˈdel ɪn
Delyth ˈdel ɪθ
Dem dem —*or as* Democrat, Democratic
demagnetis... —*see* **demagnetiz...**
demagnetization ˌdiː ˌmæg nət aɪ ˈzeɪʃ ᵊn
　·ˌ-, -nɪt ·ˈ-, -ɪˈ- ‖ -nət ə-
demagnetiz|e ₍ˌ₎diː ˈmæg nə taɪz -nɪ- **~ed** d
　~es ɪz əz **~ing** ɪŋ
demagog ˈdem ə gɒg ‖ -gɑːg **~s** z
demagogic ˌdem ə ˈgɒg ɪk ◀ -ˈgɒdʒ- ‖ -ˈgɑːg-
　-ˈgɑːdʒ-, -ˈgoʊdʒ- **~ally** ᵊl_i
demagogue ˈdem ə gɒg ‖ -gɑːg **~s** z
demagoguer|y ˈdem ə gɒg ər |i ˌ·ˈ·-
　‖ -gɑːg ər |i **~ies** iz
demagogy ˈdem ə gɒg i -gɒdʒ- ‖ -gɑːg i
　-gɑːdʒ-, -goʊdʒ-
deman ˌdiː ˈmæn **~ned** d **~ning** ɪŋ **~s** z
demand *n, v* di ˈmɑːnd də-, §-ˈmænd ‖ -ˈmænd
　~ed ɪd əd **~ing/ly** ɪŋ /li **~s** z
de Manio də ˈmæn i əʊ ‖ -oʊ
demarc|ate ˈdiː mɑːk |eɪt ‖ di ˈmɑːrk |eɪt
　ˈdiː mɑːrk eɪt **~ated** eɪt ɪd -əd ‖ eɪṱ əd **~ates**
　eɪts **~ating** eɪt ɪŋ ‖ eɪṱ ɪŋ
demarcation ˌdiː mɑː ˈkeɪʃ ᵊn ‖ -mɑːr-
　ˌdemarˈcation diˌspute, -ˌ·ˈ·
demarcative di ˈmɑːk ət ɪv ˌdiː-
　‖ -ˈmɑːrk əṱ ɪv
demarcator ˈdiː mɑːk eɪt ə ‖ di ˈmɑːrk eɪṱ ᵊr
　ˈdiː mɑːrk eɪṱ ᵊr **~s** z
demarch|e, démarch|e ˈdeɪ mɑːʃ ˌ·ˈ·
　‖ deɪ ˈmɑːrʃ dɪ- **~es** ɪz əz —*or as sing.* —*Fr*
　[de maʁʃ]
dematerialis... —*see* **dematerializ...**
dematerialization ˌdiː mə ˌtɪər i̯əl aɪ ˈzeɪʃ ᵊn
　-ɪˈ- ‖ -ˌtɪr i̯əl ə- **~s** z
dematerializ|e ˌdiː mə ˈtɪər i̯ə laɪz ‖ -ˈtɪr-
　~ed d **~es** ɪz əz **~ing** ɪŋ
deme diːm **demes** diːmz
demean di ˈmiːn də- **~ed** d **~ing** ɪŋ **~s** z
demeanor, demeanour di ˈmiːn ə də- ‖ -ᵊr **~s**
　z
de|ment *v, n* di |ˈment də- **~mented** ˈment ɪd
　-əd ‖ ˈmenṱ əd **~menting** ˈment ɪŋ
　‖ ˈmenṱ ɪŋ **~ments** ˈments
demented di ˈment ɪd də-, ₍ˌ₎diː-, -əd
　‖ -ˈmenṱ əd **~ly** li **~ness** nəs nɪs
dementia di ˈmenʃ ə də-, ₍ˌ₎diː-, -ˈmenʃ i̯ə,
　-ˈment i̯ə **~s** z
　deˌmentia ˈpraecox
demerara, D~ ˌdem ə ˈreər ə ◀ -ˈrɑːr- ‖ -ˈrer ə
　-ˈrɑːr ə
　ˌdemeˌrara ˈsugar
demerg|e ˌdiː ˈmɜːdʒ ‖ -ˈmɜːdʒ **~ed** d **~es** ɪz əz
　~ing ɪŋ
demerger ˌdiː ˈmɜːdʒ ə dɪ ·ˈ· ‖ -ˈmɜːdʒ ᵊr **~s** z
demerit ₍ˌ₎diː ˈmer ɪt §-ət **~s** s —*but, with
　contrastive stress*, (ˌmerits and) ˈdeˌmerits

Demerol *tdmk* ˈdem ə rɒl ‖ -roʊl -rɑːl, -rɔːl
demersal di ˈmɜːs ᵊl də- ‖ -ˈmɜːs-
demesne di ˈmeɪn də-, -ˈmiːn **~s** z
Demeter di ˈmiːt ə də- ‖ -ˈmiːṱ ᵊr
Demetrius di ˈmiːtr i̯əs də-
demi- ¦dem i
demie... —*see* **demy**
demigod ˈdem i gɒd ‖ -gɑːd **~s** z
demigoddess ˈdem i ˌgɒd es -ɪs, -əs
　‖ -ˌgɑːd əs **~es** ɪz əz
demijohn ˈdem i dʒɒn ‖ -dʒɑːn **~s** z
demilitaris... —*see* **demilitariz...**
demilitarization ˌdiː ˌmɪl ɪt ər aɪ ˈzeɪʃ ᵊn ·ˌ-,
　-ət ər aɪ-, -ɪˈ- ‖ -əṱ ᵊr ə- **~s** z
demilitariz|e ₍ˌ₎diː ˈmɪl ɪt ə raɪz -ˈət- **~ed** d
　~es ɪz əz **~ing** ɪŋ
de Mille də ˈmɪl
demilune ˈdem i luːn -ljuːn **~s** z
demimondaine ˌdem i mɒn ˈdeɪn -ˈmɒnd eɪn
　‖ -mɑːn ˈdeɪn -ˈmɑːnd eɪn —*Fr*
　[də mi mɔ̃ dɛn]
demimonde ˌdem i ˈmɒnd ·ˈ··
　‖ ˈdem i mɑːnd —*Fr* [də mi mɔ̃d]
demin|e ˌdiː ˈmaɪn **~ed** d **~es** z **~ing** ɪŋ
de minimis ₍ˌ₎deɪ ˈmɪn ɪ miːs -ə-
demis|e di ˈmaɪz də-, -ˈmiːz **~ed** d **~es** ɪz əz
　~ing ɪŋ
demisemiquaver ˌdem i sem i ˌkweɪv ə ˌ·ˈ··-
　‖ -ᵊr **~s** z
demist ˌdiː ˈmɪst **~ed** ɪd əd **~ing** ɪŋ **~s** s
demister ˌdiː ˈmɪst ə ‖ -ᵊr **~s** z
demitasse ˈdem i tæs -tɑːs, ˌ·ˈ· —*Fr*
　[də mi tas]
demiurge ˈdem i ɜːdʒ ˈdiːm- ‖ -ɜːdʒ
demo ˈdem əʊ ‖ -oʊ **~s** z
demo- *comb. form*
　with stress-neutral suffix ¦dem ə ¦diːm ə
　— **demographic** ˌdem ə ˈgræf ɪk ◀ ˌdiːm-
　with stress-imposing suffix dɪ ˈmɒ+ də-, diː-
　‖ -ˈmɑː+ — **demography** dɪ ˈmɒg rəf i də-,
　diː- ‖ -ˈmɑːg-
demob ₍ˌ₎diː ˈmɒb ‖ -ˈmɑːb **~bed** d **~bing** ɪŋ
　~s z
demobilis... —*see* **demobiliz...**
demobilization di ˌməʊb əl aɪ ˈzeɪʃ ᵊn ₍ˌ₎diː-,
　-ɪl aɪ-, -ɪˈ- ‖ -ˌmoʊb əl ə- **~s** z
demobiliz|e di ˈməʊb ə laɪz ₍ˌ₎diː-, -ɪ-, -ᵊl aɪz
　‖ -ˈmoʊb- **~ed** d **~es** ɪz əz **~ing** ɪŋ
democrac|y di ˈmɒk rəs |i də- ‖ -ˈmɑːk- **~ies**
　iz
democrat ˈdem ə kræt **~s** s
democratic ˌdem ə ˈkræt ɪk ◀ ‖ -ˈkræṱ ɪk ◀
　~ally ᵊl_i
democratis... —*see* **democratiz...**
democratization di ˌmɒk rət aɪ ˈzeɪʃ ᵊn də-,
　-ɪˈ- ‖ -ˌmɑːk rəṱ ə-
democratiz|e di ˈmɒk rə taɪz də- ‖ -ˈmɑːk-
　~ed d **~es** ɪz əz **~ing** ɪŋ
Democritus di ˈmɒk rɪt əs də-, -rət-
　‖ -ˈmɑːk rəṱ əs
demode, démodé ₍ˌ₎deɪ ˈməʊd eɪ
　‖ ˌdeɪ moʊ ˈdeɪ —*Fr* [de mɔ de]

D

demodu|late ˌdiː ˈmɒd ju |leɪt dɪ-, -ˈmɒdʒ u-
‖ -ˈmɑːdʒ ə- ~lated leɪt ɪd -əd ‖ leɪt ̬əd
~lates leɪts ~lating leɪt ɪŋ ‖ leɪt ̬ɪŋ
demodulation ˌdiː ˌmɒd ju ˈleɪʃ ᵊn -ˌmɒdʒ u-;
dɪ ˌmɒd- ‖ -ˌmɑːdʒ ə- dɪ ˌmɑːdʒ ə- ~s z
demodulator ˌdiː ˈmɒd ju leɪt ə dɪ-, -ˈmɒdʒ u-
‖ -ˈmɑːdʒ ə leɪt ̬ᵊr ~s z
demographer dɪ ˈmɒg rəf ə də-
‖ -ˈmɑːg rəf ᵊr ~s z
demographic ˌdem ə ˈgræf ɪk ◂ ˌdiːm- ~ally
ᵊl̬ i
demography dɪ ˈmɒg rəf i də- ‖ -ˈmɑːg-
demoiselle ˌdem wɑː ˈzel -wə- —Fr
[də mwa zɛl] ~s z —or as sing.
demolish dɪ ˈmɒl ɪʃ də- ‖ -ˈmɑːl- ~ed t ~es ɪz
əz ~ing ɪŋ
demolition ˌdem ə ˈlɪʃ ᵊn ˌdiːm- ~s z
demolitionist ˌdem ə ˈlɪʃ ᵊn ˌɪst ˌdiːm-, §ˌəst ~s
s
demon ˈdiːm ən ~s z
demonetis|e, demonetiz|e ₍ˌ₎diː ˈmʌn ɪ taɪz
-ˈmɒn-, -ə- ‖ -ˈmɑːn- -ˈmʌn- ~ed d ~es ɪz əz
~ing ɪŋ
demoniac dɪ ˈməʊn i æk də- ‖ -ˈmoʊn- ~s s
demoniacal ˌdiːm əʊ ˈnaɪ ək ᵊl ◂ ‖ ˌ-ə- ~ly ̬i
demonic dɪ ˈmɒn ɪk də- ‖ -ˈmɑːn- ~ally ᵊl̬ i
demonis... —see demoniz...
demonization ˌdiːm ən aɪ ˈzeɪʃ ᵊn -ɪˈ-- ‖ -əˈ-·
demoniz|e ˈdiːm ən aɪz ~ed d ~es ɪz əz ~ing
ɪŋ
demonology ˌdiːm ə ˈnɒl ədʒ i ‖ -ˈnɑːl-
demonstrability dɪ ˌmɒnˢ trə ˈbɪl ət i də-,
-ɪt i; ˈdem ənˢ- ‖ dɪ ˌmɑːnˢ trə ˈbɪl ət̬ i

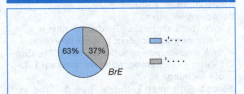

DEMONSTRABLE

63% 37%

BrE

◾ ·ˈ···
◾ ˈ····

demonstrab|le dɪ ˈmɒnˢ trəb |ᵊl də-;
ˈdem ənˢ- ‖ dɪ ˈmɑːnˢ- — Preference poll,
BrE: ·ˈ··· 63%, ˈ···· 37%. ~ly li
demon|strate ˈdem ən |streɪt ~strated
streɪt ɪd -əd ‖ streɪt̬ əd ~strates streɪts
~strating streɪt ɪŋ ‖ streɪt̬ ɪŋ
demonstration ˌdem ən ˈstreɪʃ ᵊn ~s z
demonstrative dɪ ˈmɒnˢ trət ɪv də-
‖ -ˈmɑːnˢ trət̬ ɪv ~ly li ~ness nəs nɪs
demonstrator ˈdem ən streɪt ə ‖ -streɪt̬ ᵊr ~s
z
de Montfort də ˈmɒnt fət -fɔːt ‖ dɪ ˈmɑːnt fᵊrt
demoralis... —see demoraliz...
demoralization dɪ ˌmɒr əl aɪ ˈzeɪʃ ᵊn ˌdiː,--,
-ɪˈ-- ‖ dɪ ˌmɔːr əl ə-, -ˌmɑːr-
demoraliz|e dɪ ˈmɒr ə laɪz ₍ˌ₎diː- ‖ -ˈmɔːr-
-ˈmɑːr- ~ed d ~es ɪz əz ~ing ɪŋ
Demos ˈdiːm ɒs ‖ -ɑːs
demosaic ˌdiː məʊ ˈzeɪ ɪk ‖ -moʊ- ~ed, ~ked t
~ing, ~king ɪŋ ~s s

Demosthenes dɪ ˈmɒsθ ə niːz də-, -ɪ-
‖ -ˈmɑːsθ-
de|mote ˌdiː |ˈməʊt dɪ-, də- ‖ -|ˈmoʊt ~moted
ˈməʊt ɪd -əd ‖ ˈmoʊt̬ əd ~motes ˈməʊts
‖ ˈmoʊts ~moting ˈməʊt ɪŋ ‖ ˈmoʊt̬ ɪŋ
demotic dɪ ˈmɒt ɪk də- ‖ -ˈmɑːt̬ ɪk
demotion ˌdiː ˈməʊ ʃᵊn dɪ-, də- ‖ -ˈmoʊ ʃᵊn ~s
z
demoti|vate ˌdiː ˈməʊt ɪ |veɪt -ə- ‖ -ˈmoʊt̬ ə-
~vated veɪt ɪd -əd ‖ veɪt̬ əd ~vates veɪts
~vating veɪt ɪŋ ‖ veɪt̬ ɪŋ
demotivation ˌdiː ˌməʊt ɪ ˈveɪʃ ᵊn -ə-
‖ diː ˌmoʊt̬ ə-
Dempsey ˈdemps i
Dempster, d~ ˈdempst ə ‖ -ᵊr
demulcent dɪ ˈmʌls ᵊnt də- ~s s
de|mur v, n dɪ |ˈmɜː də- ‖ -|ˈmɜː ~murred
ˈmɜːd ‖ ˈmɜːd ~murring ˈmɜːr ɪŋ ‖ ˈmɜː ɪŋ
~murs ˈmɜːz ‖ ˈmɜːz
de|mure dɪ |ˈmjʊə də- ‖ -|ˈmjʊᵊr ~murer
ˈmjʊər ə ‖ ˈmjʊr ᵊr ~murest ˈmjʊər ɪst -əst
‖ ˈmjʊr əst ~murely ˈmjʊə li ‖ ˈmjʊr li
~mureness ˈmjʊə nəs nɪs ‖ ˈmjʊr-
demurr... —see demur
demurrage dɪ ˈmʌr ɪdʒ də- ‖ -ˈmɜː-
demurral dɪ ˈmʌr əl də- ‖ -ˈmɜː- ~s z
demurrer 'objector' dɪ ˈmɜːr ə də- ‖ -ˈmɜː ᵊr
demurrer 'objection' dɪ ˈmʌr ə də- ‖ -ˈmɜː ᵊr
demutualization, demutualisation
ˌdiː ˌmjuːtʃ u əl aɪ ˈzeɪʃ ᵊn -ɪˈ-· ‖ -əˈ-· ·
demutualiz|e, demutualis|e
ˌdiː ˈmjuːtʃ u ə laɪz ~ed d ~es ɪz əz ~ing ɪŋ
de|my dɪ |ˈmaɪ də- ~mies ˈmaɪz
demystification ˌdiː ˌmɪst ɪf ɪ ˈkeɪʃ ᵊn ·,·-,
-əf ɪ-, §-əˈ-· ‖ ˌdiː ˌmɪst-
demysti|fy ₍ˌ₎diː ˈmɪst ɪ |faɪ -ə- ~fied faɪd
~fier/s faɪ ə/z ‖ faɪ ᵊr/z ~fies faɪz ~fying
faɪ ɪŋ
demythologis... —see demythologiz...
demythologization
ˌdiː mɪ ˌθɒl ədʒ aɪ ˈzeɪʃ ᵊn ˌ·mə-, -ɪˈ-·
‖ -ˌθɑːl ədʒ ə-
demythologiz|e ˌdiː mɪ ˈθɒl ə dʒaɪz ˌ·mə-
‖ -ˈθɑːl- ~ed d ~es ɪz əz ~ing ɪŋ
den, Den den dens, Den's denz
Dena ˈdiːn ə
Denaby ˈden əb i
Denali də ˈnɑːl i dɪ-
denari|us dɪ ˈneər i|əs də-, -ˈnɑːr- ‖ -ˈner-
-ˈnær- ~i aɪ iː
denary ˈdiːn ᵊr i ˈden-
denationalis... —see denationaliz...
denationalization ˌdiː ˌnæʃ ᵊn ᵊl aɪ ˈzeɪʃ ᵊn
·,·-, -ɪˈ-· ‖ ˌdiː ˌnæʃ ᵊn ᵊl ə- ~s z
denationaliz|e ₍ˌ₎diː ˈnæʃ ᵊn ə laɪz ᵊl aɪz ~ed
d ~es ɪz əz ~ing ɪŋ
denaturalization, denaturalisation
ˌdiː ˌnætʃ ᵊr ə laɪ ˈzeɪʃ ᵊn -ᵊr ᵊl aɪ-, -ᵊr ᵊl ɪ-
‖ -ᵊr ᵊl ə-
denaturaliz|e, denaturalis|e
ˌdiː ˈnætʃ ᵊr ə laɪz ˌᵊl aɪz ~ed d ~es ɪz əz
~ing ɪŋ

denature ˌdiː 'neɪtʃ ə ‖ -ᵊr ~**d** d ~**s** z
  denaturing ˌdiː 'neɪtʃ ər ɪŋ
denaturiz|e ˌdiː 'neɪtʃ ə raɪz ~**ed** d ~**es** ɪz əz
  ~**ing** ɪŋ
Denbigh, Denby 'den bi →'dem-
Dench dentʃ
dendrite 'dendr aɪt ~**s** s
dendritic ˌden 'drɪt ɪk ‖ -'drɪt̮ ɪk ~**ally** ᵊl_i
dendrochronology ˌdendr əʊ krə 'nɒl ədʒ i
  ˌ‧‧krɒ- ‖ -oʊ krə 'nɑːl-
dendrogram 'dendr ə græm ~**s** z
dendroid 'dendr ɔɪd
dendrology den 'drɒl ədʒ i ‖ -'drɑːl-
dene, Dene *British name* diːn **denes** diːnz
  'dene hole
Dene, Déné *Canadian indigenous people* 'den i
  -eɪ
Deneb 'den eb
Denebola di 'neb əl ə də-, de-
dengue 'deŋ gi -geɪ
Deng Xiaoping ˌdʌŋ ʃaʊ 'pɪŋ ˌdeŋ- —*Chi*
  Dēng Xiǎopíng [¹təŋ ³ɕjɛu ²pʰiŋ]
Den Haag den 'hɑːg dən- —*Dutch* [dɛn 'haːx]
Denham, Denholm, Denholme 'den əm
  —*but Denholme, W.Yks., is usually*
  -hɒlm ‖ -hoʊlm
deniable di 'naɪ_əb ᵊl
denial di 'naɪ_əl də-, §di:- ~**s** z
denie... —*see* **deny**
denier *measure of fineness* 'den i_ə -eɪ
  ‖ 'den jᵊr
denier *coin* 'den i_ə -eɪ; də 'nɪə ‖ də 'nɪᵊr —*Fr*
  [də nje] ~**s** z
denier *'one that denies'* di 'naɪ_ə də- ‖ -'naɪ_ᵊr
  ~**s** z
deni|grate 'den ɪ |greɪt -ə-; 'diː naɪ |greɪt
  ~**grated** greɪt ɪd -əd ‖ greɪt̮ əd ~**grates**
  greɪts ~**grating** greɪt ɪŋ ‖ greɪt̮ ɪŋ
denigration ˌden ɪ 'greɪʃ ᵊn -ə-; ˌdiː naɪ- ~**s** z
denigratory ˌden ɪ 'greɪt ər i ◂ ˌ‧ə-; '‧‧‧‧‧
  ‖ 'den ɪg rə tɔːr i -toʊr i (*)
denim 'den ɪm -əm ~**ed** d ~**s** z
De Niro də 'nɪər əʊ ‖ -'nɪr oʊ
Denis 'den ɪs §-əs ~**'s** ɪz əz
Denise də 'niːz de-, di-, -'niːs
Denison 'den ɪs ən -əs-
denitrification ˌdiː ˌnaɪtr ɪf ɪ 'keɪʃ ᵊn -ˌəf-,
  -əˈ‧‧
denitri|fy ˌdiː 'naɪtr ɪ |faɪ -ə- ~**fied** faɪd ~**fies**
  faɪz ~**fying** faɪ ɪŋ
denizen 'den ɪz ən -əz- ~**s** z
Denmark 'den mɑːk →'dem- ‖ -mɑːrk
Denne den
Dennie 'den i
Denning 'den ɪŋ
Dennis 'den ɪs §-əs
Dennison 'den ɪs ən §-əs-
Denny 'den i
denominable di 'nɒm ɪn əb ᵊl də-, -'‧ən-
  ‖ -'nɑːm-
denominate *adj* di 'nɒm ɪn ət də-, -ən-, -ɪt;
  -ɪ neɪt, -ə- ‖ -'nɑːm-

denomi|nate *v* di 'nɒm ɪ |neɪt də-, -ə-
  ‖ -'nɑːm- ~**nated** neɪt ɪd -əd ‖ neɪt̮ əd ~**nates**
  neɪts ~**nating** neɪt ɪŋ ‖ neɪt̮ ɪŋ
denomination di ˌnɒm ɪ 'neɪʃ ᵊn də-, -ə-
  ‖ -ˌnɑːm- ~**s** z
denominational di ˌnɒm ɪ 'neɪʃ ᵊn_əl ◂ də-,
  -ˌ‧ə- ‖ -ˌnɑːm- ~**ism** ˌɪz əm ~**ly** i
denominative di 'nɒm ɪn ət ɪv ˌdiː-, -ən_ət-
  ‖ -'nɑːm ən_ət̮ ɪv ~**s** z
denominator di 'nɒm ɪ neɪt ə də-, -'‧ə-
  ‖ -'nɑːm ə neɪt̮ ᵊr ~**s** z
denotation ˌdiː nəʊ 'teɪʃ ᵊn ‖ -noʊ- ~**s** z
denotative di 'nəʊt ət ɪv ˌdiː-, də-;
  'diː nəʊ teɪt ɪv ‖ 'diː noʊ teɪt̮ ɪv di 'noʊt̮ ət̮ ɪv
  ~**ly** li
de|note di |'nəʊt də- ‖ -|'noʊt ~**noted**
  'nəʊt ɪd -əd ‖ 'noʊt̮ əd ~**notes** 'nəʊts
  ‖ 'noʊts ~**noting** 'nəʊt ɪŋ ‖ 'noʊt̮ ɪŋ
denouement, dénouement deɪ 'nuː mɒ̃ dɪ-,
  də- ˌdeɪ nuː 'mɑ̃: —*Fr* [de nu mɑ̃] ~**s** z
  —*or as sing.*
denounc|e di 'naʊnts də- ~**ed** t ~**er/s** ə/z
  ‖ -ᵊr/z ~**es** ɪz əz ~**ing** ɪŋ
de novo ˌdeɪ 'nəʊv əʊ diː-, dɪ-, də
  ‖ -'noʊv oʊ
Denpasar den 'pæs ɑː →dem-, -'pɑːs- ‖ -ɑːr
dense dents **denser** 'dents ə ‖ -ᵊr **densest**
  'dents ɪst -əst **densely** 'dents li **denseness**
  'dents nəs -nɪs
Denselow 'denz ə ləʊ ‖ -loʊ
densit|y 'dents ət i |-ɪt- ‖ -ət̮ i ~**ies** iz
dent, Dent dent **dented** 'dent ɪd -əd
  ‖ 'dent̮ əd **denting** 'dent ɪŋ ‖ 'dent̮ ɪŋ **dents**
  dents
dental 'dent ᵊl ‖ 'dent̮ ᵊl ~**ly** i ~**s** z
  ˌdental 'floss; ˌdental 'surgeon, '‧‧ ˌ‧‧
dentate 'dent eɪt ~**ly** li
denticle 'dent ɪk ᵊl ‖ 'dent̮- ~**s** z
denticulate den 'tɪk jʊl ət -jəl-, -ɪt; -ju leɪt, -jə-
  ‖ -jəl ət ~**ly** li
dentiform 'dent ɪ fɔːm §-ə- ‖ 'dent̮ ə fɔːrm
dentifric|e 'dent ɪ frɪs -ə-, §-frəs ‖ 'dent̮ə- ~**es**
  ɪz əz
dentil 'dent ɪl -ᵊl ‖ 'dent̮ ᵊl ~**s** z
dentilabial ˌdent i 'leɪb i_əl ◂ ‖ ˌdent̮- ~**s** z
dentilingual ˌdent i 'lɪŋ gwəl ◂ -'lɪŋ gju_əl
  ‖ ˌdent̮- ~**s** z
dentin 'dent ɪn §-ən
dentine 'dent iːn ˌden 'tiːn
dentist 'dent ɪst §-əst ‖ 'dent̮ əst ~**s** s
dentistry 'dent ɪst ri -əst- ‖ 'dent̮-
dentition den 'tɪʃ ᵊn
Denton 'dent ən ‖ -ᵊn
D'Entrecasteaux ˌdɒntr ə kæ 'stəʊ ◂
  ˌ‧‧'kæst əʊ ‖ ˌdɑːntr ə kæ 'stoʊ ◂ ˌ‧‧'kæst oʊ
  —*Fr* [dɑ̃ tʁə ka sto]
denture 'dentʃ ə ‖ -ᵊr ~**s** z
denudation ˌdiː nju 'deɪʃ ᵊn §-nu-; ˌden ju-
  ‖ -nu- -nju- ~**s** z
denud|e di 'njuːd də-, §-'nuːd ‖ -'nuːd -'njuːd
  ~**ed** ɪd əd ~**es** z ~**ing** ɪŋ
denumerability di ˌnjuːm ər ə 'bɪl ət i də-,
  §-ˌnuːm- ‖ -ˌnuːm ər ə 'bɪl ət̮ i -ˌnjuːm-

D

denumerab|le di ˈnjuːm ər_əb |ᵊl də-, §-ˈnuːm-
∥ -ˈnuːm- -ˈnjuːm- **~ly** li
denunciation di ˌnʌntˢ i ˈeɪʃ ᵊn də- **~s** z
denunciatory di ˈnʌntˢ i ˌət_ər i də-, -ˈnʌntˢ-
∥ -ə tɔːr i -toʊr-
Denver ˈden və ∥ -vᵊr
de|ny di |ˈnaɪ də- **~nied** ˈnaɪd **~nies** ˈnaɪz
~nying ˈnaɪ ɪŋ
Denys ˈden ɪs §-əs
Denzil ˈdenz ᵊl -ɪl
Deo ˈdeɪ əʊ ˈdiː- ∥ -oʊ —See also phrases with
this word
deoch an doris, deoch an doruis
ˌdɒx ən ˈdɒr ɪs ˌdjɒx-, -ˈdɒr ɪs ∥ —
deodand ˈdiː əʊ dænd ∥ -ə- **~s** z
deodar ˈdiː əʊ dɑː ∥ -ə dɑːr **~s** z
deodorant di ˈəʊd_ər ənt ∥ -ˈoʊd_ **~s** s
deodoris|e, deodoriz|e di ˈəʊd ə raɪz -ər aɪz
∥ -ˈoʊd- **~ed** d **~er/s** ə/z ∥ -ᵊr/z **~es** ɪz əz
~ing ɪŋ
deo gratias ˌdeɪ əʊ ˈɡrɑːt i_əs ˌdiː-, -æs, -ɑːs
∥ ˌ-oʊ-
deontic di ˈɒnt ɪk ∥ -ˈɑːnt̬-
deontological di ˌɒnt ə ˈlɒdʒ ɪk ᵊl ◂ ˌdiː-
∥ -ˌɑːnt̬ ə ˈlɑːdʒ- **~ly** _i
deontology ˌdiː ɒn ˈtɒl ədʒ i ∥ -ɑːn ˈtɑːl-
deo volente ˌdeɪ əʊ və ˈlent i ˌdiː-, - vɒ'--, -eɪ
∥ ˌ-oʊ-
deoxy- ¦diː ¦ɒks i di ¦ɒks i ∥ di ¦ɑːks i —
deoxycorticosterone
ˌdiː ˌɒks i ˌkɔːt ɪ kəʊ ˈstɪər əʊn di ˌɒks-,
-ˈkɒst ə rəʊn ∥ di ˌɑːks i ˌkɔːrt̬ ɪ ˈkɑːst ə roʊn
-ˈkoʊst-
deoxyge|nate ˌdiː ˈɒks ɪdʒ ə |neɪt di-,
§-ˈ-ədʒ-; ˌdiː ɒk ˈsɪdʒ- ∥ -ˈɑːks- **~nated** neɪt ɪd
-əd ∥ neɪt̬ əd **~nates** neɪts **~nating** neɪt ɪŋ
∥ neɪt̬ ɪŋ
deoxyribonucleic
ˌdiː ɒks i ˌraɪb əʊ nju ˈkliː ɪk ◂ di ˌɒks-,
-ˈkleɪ- ∥ di ˌɑːks i ˌraɪb oʊ nu- -nˈjuː'--, -ˈkleɪ-
ˌdeoxyˌribonuˌcleic ˈacid
dep —see **depart, departure**
Depardieu ˈdep ɑː djɜː, ˌ· ˈ· ∥ -ɑːr ˈdjʌ —Fr
[də paʁ djø]
de|part di |ˈpɑːt də- ∥ -|ˈpɑːrt **~parted** ˈpɑːt ɪd
-əd ∥ ˈpɑːrt̬ əd **~parts** ˈpɑːts ∥ ˈpɑːrts
~parting ˈpɑːt ɪŋ ∥ ˈpɑːrt̬ ɪŋ
department di ˈpɑːt mənt də- ∥ -ˈpɑːrt- **~s** s
deˈpartment store
departmental ˌdiː pɑːt ˈment ᵊl ◂ di ˌpɑːt-, də-
∥ ˌdiː pɑːrt ˈment̬ ᵊl di ˌpɑːrt- **~ly** i
departmentaliz|e, departmentalis|e
ˌdiː pɑːt ˈment ə laɪz di ˌpɑːt-, də ˌpɑːt-,
-ᵊl aɪz ∥ ˌdiː pɑːrt ˈment̬ ᵊl aɪz **~ed** d **~es** ɪz
əz **~ing** ɪŋ
departure di ˈpɑːtʃ ə də- ∥ -ˈpɑːrtʃ ᵊr **~s** z
deˈparture lounge; deˈparture time
Depeche Mode di ˌpeʃ ˈməʊd də- ∥ -ˈmoʊd
depend di ˈpend də- **~ed** ɪd əd **~ing** ɪŋ **~s** z
dependability di ˌpend ə ˈbɪl ət i də-, -ɪt i
∥ -ət̬ i
dependab|le di ˈpend əb |ᵊl də- **~ly** li
dependanc... —see **dependenc...**

dependant di ˈpend ənt də- **~s** s
dependence di ˈpend əntˢ də- **~es** ɪz əz
dependenc|y di ˈpend əntˢ |i də- **~ies** iz
dependent di ˈpend ənt də- **~s** s
depict di ˈpɪkt də- **~ed** ɪd əd **~ing** ɪŋ **~s** s
depiction di ˈpɪk ʃᵊn də- **~s** z
depi|late ˈdep ɪ |leɪt -ə- **~lated** leɪt ɪd -əd
∥ leɪt̬ əd **~lates** leɪts **~lating** leɪt ɪŋ ∥ leɪt̬ ɪŋ
depilation ˌdep ɪ ˈleɪʃ ᵊn -ə-
depilator|y di ˈpɪl ət_ər |i də- ∥ -ə tɔːr |i
-toʊr i **~ies** iz
deplan|e ˌdiː ˈpleɪn **~ed** d **~es** z **~ing** ɪŋ
de|plete di |ˈpliːt də- **~pleted** ˈpliːt ɪd -əd
∥ ˈpliːt̬ əd **~pletes** ˈpliːts **~pleting** ˈpliːt ɪŋ
∥ ˈpliːt̬ ɪŋ
depletion di ˈpliːʃ ᵊn də- **~s** z
deplorab|le di ˈplɔːr əb |ᵊl də- ∥ -ˈploʊr- **~ly** li
deplore di ˈplɔː də- ∥ -ˈplɔːr -ˈploʊr **~d** d **~s** z
deploring di ˈplɔːr ɪŋ də- ∥ -ˈploʊr-
deploy di ˈplɔɪ də- **~ed** d **~ing** ɪŋ **~ment** mənt
~s z
de-policing, depolicing ˌdiː pə ˈliːs ɪŋ
depoliticization, depoliticisation
ˌdiː pə ˌlɪt ɪ saɪ ˈzeɪʃ ᵊn -ˌ-ə-, -sɪˈ- · · ∥ -ˌlɪt̬ əs ə-
depoliticiz|e, depoliticis|e ˌdiː pə ˈlɪt ɪ saɪz
-ə- ∥ -ˈlɪt̬ ə- **~ed** d **~es** ɪz əz **~ing** ɪŋ
deponent di ˈpəʊn ənt də- ∥ -ˈpoʊn- **~s** s
Depo-Provera tdmk ˌdep əʊ prəʊ ˈvɪər ə
∥ -oʊ proʊ ˈver ə
depopu|late ˌ_di ˈpɒp ju |leɪt -jə- ∥ -ˈpɑːp jə-
~lated leɪt ɪd -əd ∥ leɪt̬ əd **~lates** leɪts
~lating leɪt ɪŋ ∥ leɪt̬ ɪŋ
depopulation ˌdiː ˌpɒp ju ˈleɪʃ ᵊn ˌ·ˌ-, -jə'--
∥ ˌdiː ˌpɑːp jə-
de|port di |ˈpɔːt də- ∥ -|ˈpɔːrt -ˈpoʊrt **~ported**
ˈpɔːt ɪd -əd ∥ ˈpɔːrt̬ əd ˈpoʊrt̬- **~porting**
ˈpɔːt ɪŋ ∥ ˈpɔːrt̬ ɪŋ ˈpoʊrt̬- **~ports** ˈpɔːts
∥ ˈpɔːrts ˈpoʊrts
deportation ˌdiː pɔː ˈteɪʃ ᵊn ∥ -pɔːr- -pᵊr-,
-poʊr- **~s** z
deportee ˌdiː pɔː ˈtiː ∥ -pɔːr- -poʊr- **~s** z
deportment di ˈpɔːt mənt də- ∥ -ˈpɔːrt-
-ˈpoʊrt-
depos|e di ˈpəʊz də- ∥ -ˈpoʊz **~ed** d **~es** ɪz əz
~ing ɪŋ
depos|it di ˈpɒz |ɪt də-, §-ət ∥ -ˈpɑːz |ət **~ited**
ɪt ɪd §ət-, -əd ∥ ət̬ əd **~iting** ɪt ɪŋ §ət- ∥ ət̬ ɪŋ
~its ɪts §əts ∥ əts
deˈposit acˌcount
depositar|y di ˈpɒz ɪt_ər |i də-, -ˈ-ət_
∥ -ˈpɑːz ə ter |i **~ies** iz
deposition ˌdep ə ˈzɪʃ ᵊn ˌdiː pə- **~s** z
depositor di ˈpɒz ɪt ə də-, -ət- ∥ -ˈpɑːz ət̬ ᵊr **~s**
z
depositor|y di ˈpɒz ɪt_ər |i də-, -ˈ-ət_
∥ -ˈpɑːz ə tɔːr |i -toʊr i **~ies** iz
depot ˈdep əʊ ∥ ˈdiːp oʊ ˈdep- — Preference
poll, AmE: ˈdiːp- 95%, ˈdep- 5%. **~s** z
Depp dep
depravation ˌdep rə ˈveɪʃ ᵊn
deprav|e di ˈpreɪv də- **~ed** d **~es** z **~ing** ɪŋ
depravit|y di ˈpræv ət |i də-, -ɪt- ∥ -ət̬ |i **~ies**
iz

DEPOT

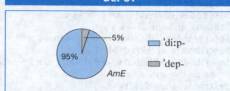

- 5% ■ 'di:p-
- 95% ■ 'dep-
- *AmE*

depre|cate 'dep rə |keɪt -rɪ- **~cated** keɪt ɪd -əd
‖ keɪt̬ əd **~cates** keɪts **~cating/ly** keɪt ɪŋ /li
‖ keɪt̬ ɪŋ /li

deprecation ˌdep rə 'keɪʃ ᵊn -rɪ-

deprecatory 'dep rə keɪt ər i '·rɪ-, ·ˑ·ˑ·;
-kət̬ ər i ‖ -kə tɔːr i -tour i

depreci|ate di 'priːʃ i |eɪt də-, -'priːs- **~ated**
eɪt ɪd -əd ‖ eɪt̬ əd **~ates** eɪts **~ating** eɪt ɪŋ
‖ eɪt̬ ɪŋ

depreciation di ˌpriːʃ i 'eɪʃ ᵊn də-, -ˌpriːs-

depreciatory di 'priːʃ i ət ər i də-, -'priːs-,
-'priːʃ ət̬ ər i ‖ ə tɔːr i -tour i

depre|date 'dep rə |deɪt -rɪ- **~dated** deɪt ɪd
-əd ‖ deɪt̬ əd **~dates** deɪts **~dating** deɪt ɪŋ
‖ deɪt̬ ɪŋ

depredation ˌdep rə 'deɪʃ ᵊn -rɪ- **~s** z

depredatory di 'pred ət ər i də-;
ˌdep rə 'deɪt ər i, ·ˌrɪ-, '····· ‖ -ə tɔːr i -tour i

depress di 'pres də- **~ed** t **~es** ɪz əz **~ing/ly**
ɪŋ /li

depressant di 'pres ᵊnt də- **~s** s

depression di 'preʃ ᵊn də- **~s** z

depressive di 'pres ɪv də- **~ly** li **~ness** nəs nɪs
~s z

depressor di 'pres ə də- ‖ -ᵊr **~s** z

depressuris... —*see* **depressuriz...**

depressurization ˌdiː ˌpreʃ ər aɪ 'zeɪʒ ᵊn ·ˌ·-,
dɪˌ-, -ɪ'- ‖ dɪ ˌpreʃ ər ə- **~s** z

depressuriz|e ₍ˌ₎diː 'preʃ ə raɪz dɪ- **~ed** d **~es**
ɪz əz **~ing** ɪŋ

DEPRIVATION

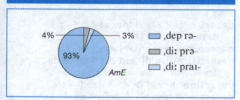

- 4% — 3% ■ ˌdep rə-
- 93% ■ ˌdiː prə-
- *AmE* ■ ˌdiː praɪ-

deprivation ˌdep rɪ 'veɪʃ ᵊn -rə-; ˌdiː prə-, prɪ-,
-praɪ- — *Preference poll, AmE:* ˌdep rə- *93%,*
ˌdiː prə- *4%,* ˌdiː praɪ- *3%.* **~s** z

depriv|e di 'praɪv də- **~ed** d **~es** z **~ing** ɪŋ

de profundis ˌdeɪ prə 'fʊnd iːs ˌdiː-, -prɒ-,
-'fʌnd-, -ɪs ‖ -proʊ-

deprogram ˌdiː 'prəʊ græm §-grəm ‖ -'proʊ-
~med d **~ming** ɪŋ **~s** z

depside 'deps aɪd -ɪd, §-əd **~s** z

dept —*see* **department**

Deptford 'det fəd 'dept- ‖ -fᵊrd

depth depθ **depths** depθs
'depth charge

deputation ˌdep ju 'teɪʃ ᵊn -jə- ‖ -jə- **~s** z

de|pute di |'pjuːt də- **~puted** 'pjuːt ɪd -əd
‖ 'pjuːt̬ əd **~putes** 'pjuːts **~puting** 'pjuːt ɪŋ
‖ 'pjuːt̬ ɪŋ

deputi... —*see* **deputy**

deputis|e, deputiz|e 'dep ju taɪz -jə- ‖ -jə-
~ed d **~es** ɪz əz **~ing** ɪŋ

deput|y 'dep jʊt |i -jət- ‖ -jət̬ |i **~ies** iz

De Quincey də 'kwɪn(t)s i

derail ₍ˌ₎di: 'reᵊl di- **~ed** d **~ing** ɪŋ **~s** z

derailleur di 'reɪl jə də-, ˌdiː-, -ə ‖ -ᵊr **~s** z

derailment ₍ˌ₎di: 'reᵊl mənt dɪ- **~s** s

derang|e di 'reɪndʒ də- **~ed** d **~es** ɪz əz **~ing**
ɪŋ

derangement di 'reɪndʒ mənt də-

de|rate ˌdiː- |'reɪt **~rated** 'reɪt ɪd -əd ‖ 'reɪt̬ əd
~rates 'reɪts **~rating** 'reɪt ɪŋ ‖ 'reɪt̬ ɪŋ

derb|y 'daːb |i §'dɜːb- ‖ 'dɝːb |i *(*)* **~ies** iz

Derby *(i)* 'daːb i ‖ 'daːrb i, *(ii)* 'dɜːb i ‖ 'dɝːb i
—*For the place in England, usually (i); for
places in the US, (ii).*

Derbyshire 'daːb i ʃə §'dɜːb-, -ʃɪə ‖ 'daːrb i ʃᵊr
'dɝːb-, -ʃɪr

deregu|late ˌdiː 'reg ju |leɪt di-, -jə- ‖ -jə-
~lated leɪt ɪd -əd ‖ leɪt̬ əd **~lates** leɪts
~lating leɪt ɪŋ ‖ leɪt̬ ɪŋ

deregulation ˌdiː ˌreg ju 'leɪʃ ᵊn -jə-
‖ diː ˌreg jə- ·ˌ·-

Dereham 'dɪər əm ‖ 'dɪr-

Derek 'der ɪk

derelict 'der ə lɪkt -ɪ- **~s** s

dereliction ˌder ə 'lɪk ʃᵊn -ɪ- **~s** z

derequisition ˌdiː ˌrek wɪ 'zɪʃ ᵊn -wə- **~ed** d
~ing ɪŋ **~s** z

derestrict ˌdiː ri 'strɪkt -rə- **~ed** ɪd əd **~ing** ɪŋ
~s s

derestriction ˌdiː ri 'strɪk ʃᵊn -rə- **~s** z

De Reszke də 'resk i

Derg dɜːg ‖ dɝːg

derid|e di 'raɪd də- **~ed** ɪd əd **~es** z **~ing** ɪŋ

de rigueur ₍ˌ₎də rɪ 'gɜː ₍ˌ₎deɪ-, ₍ˌ₎diː-, -riː-
‖ -'gɝː —*Fr* [də ʁi gœːʁ]

derision di 'rɪʒ ᵊn də-

derisive di 'raɪs ɪv də-, -'raɪz-, -'rɪz- **~ly** li
~ness nəs nɪs

deris|ory dɪ 'raɪs |ər i də-, §di:-, -'raɪz- **~orily**
ᵊr əl i ᵊr ɪ li

derivable di 'raɪv əb ᵊl də-

derivation ˌder ɪ 'veɪʃ ᵊn -ə- **~al** ᵊl **~s** z

derivative di 'rɪv ət ɪv də- ‖ -ət̬ ɪv **~ly** li **~s** z

deriv|e di 'raɪv də- **~ed** d **~es** z **~ing** ɪŋ

d'Erlanger 'deᵊl ɒ̃ʒ eɪ ‖ 'derl ɑːn ˈʒeɪ

-derm dɜːm ‖ dɝːm — **periderm** 'per i dɜːm
‖ -dɝːm

derm dɜːm ‖ dɝːm

dermabrasion ˌdɜːm ə 'breɪʒ ᵊn ‖ ˌdɝːm-

-dermal 'dɜːm ᵊl ‖ 'dɝːm ᵊl — **peridermal**
ˌper i 'dɜːm ᵊl ◄ ‖ -'dɝːm-

dermal 'dɜːm ᵊl ‖ 'dɝːm-

dermatitis ˌdɜːm ə 'taɪt ɪs §-əs
‖ ˌdɝːm ə 'taɪt̬ əs

dermatologist ˌdɜːm ə 'tɒl ədʒ ɪst §-əst
‖ ˌdɝːm ə 'taːl- **~s** s

dermatology ˌdɜːm ə ˈtɒl ədʒ i
‖ ˌdɝːm ə ˈtɑːl-
dermis ˈdɜːm ɪs §-əs ‖ ˈdɝːm-
Dermod ˈdɜːm əd ‖ ˈdɝːm-
Dermot, Dermott ˈdɜːm ət ‖ ˈdɝːm-
dernier cri ˌdɜːn i eɪ ˈkriː ‖ ˌdɝːn- —*Fr*
[dɛʁ nje kʁi]
dero|gate ˈder ə |ɡeɪt ˈdiː rəʊ ˌ|ɡeɪt **~gated**
ɡeɪt ɪd -əd ‖ ɡeɪt̬ əd **~gates** ɡeɪts **~gating**
ɡeɪt ɪŋ ‖ ɡeɪt̬ ɪŋ
derogation ˌder ə ˈɡeɪʃ ᵊn ˌdiː rəʊ- **~s** z
derogator|y di ˈrɒg ət ᵊr |i də-
‖ -ˈrɑːg ə tɔːr |i -tour i **~ily** əl i ɪl i **~iness**
i nəs i nɪs
Deronda də ˈrɒnd ə di- ‖ -ˈrɑːnd ə
derrick, D~ ˈder ɪk **~s** s
Derrida də ˈriːd ə de-; ˈder ɪd ə, -əd-
‖ ˌder i ˈdɑː ˈ··· —*Fr* [dɛ ʁi da]
Derrie ˈder i
derriere, derrière ˈder i eə ˌ·ˈ· ‖ ˌder i ˈeᵊr
—*Fr* [dɛʁ jɛːʁ] **~s** z —*or as sing.*
derring-do ˌder ɪŋ ˈduː ˌdeər-, ˌdɜːr-
derringer, D~ ˈder ɪndʒ ə -əndʒ- ‖ -ᵊr **~s** z
derris ˈder ɪs §-əs
Derry, derry ˈder i
Dershowitz ˈdɜːʃ ə wɪts ‖ ˈdɝːʃ-
derv dɜːv ‖ dɝːv
dervish ˈdɜːv ɪʃ ‖ ˈdɝːv- **~es** ɪz əz
Dervla ˈdɜːv lə ‖ ˈdɝːv-
Derwent ˈdɜː wənt -went ‖ ˈdɝː- —*but Baron*
D~ is ˈdɑː-
Derwentwater ˈdɜː wənt ˌwɔːt ə -went-
‖ ˈdɝː wənt ˌwɔːt̬ ᵊr -ˌwɑːt̬ ᵊr
Deryck ˈder ɪk
Deryn ˈder ɪn §-ən
Des dez ‖ des —*See also phrases with this word*
DES ˌdiː iː ˈes
Desai de ˈsaɪ ˈdeɪs aɪ
De Sales də ˈsɑːlz
desali|nate ˌ(ˌ)diː ˈsæl ɪ |neɪt -ə- **~nated**
neɪt ɪd -əd ‖ neɪt̬ əd **~nates** neɪts **~nating**
neɪt ɪŋ ‖ neɪt̬ ɪŋ
desalination ˌdiː ˌsæl ɪ ˈneɪʃ ᵊn -ə-
‖ diː ˌsæl ə-
desalinis... —*see* **desaliniz...**
desalinization ˌdiː ˌsæl ɪn aɪ ˈzeɪʃ ᵊn diː ˌsæl-,
-ən aɪ-, -ɪˈ·· ‖ -ən ə-
desaliniz|e ˌ(ˌ)diː ˈsæl ɪ naɪz -ə- **~ed** d **~es** ɪz əz
~ing ɪŋ
De Salis *(i)* də ˈsæl ɪs §-əs, *(ii)* -ˈseɪl-, *(iii)*
də ˈsɑːlz
desalt ˌdiː ˈsɒlt -ˈsɔːlt ‖ -ˈsɔːlt -ˈsɑːlt **~ed** ɪd əd
~ing ɪŋ **~s** s
De Saumarez, De Sausmarez də ˈsɒm ər ɪz
-ə rez ‖ -ˈsɑːm-
Desborough ˈdez bər ə ‖ -ˌbɝː oʊ
descal|e ˌdiː ˈskeɪᵊl **~ed** d **~es** z **~ing** ɪŋ
de|scant *v* di ‖ˈskænt də-, de- **~scanted**
ˈskænt ɪd -əd ‖ ˈskænt̬ əd **~scanting**
ˈskænt ɪŋ ‖ ˈskænt̬ ɪŋ **~scants** ˈskænts
descant *n* ˈdesk ænt **~s** s
Descartes ˈdeɪ kɑːt ·ˈ· ‖ deɪ ˈkɑːrt —*Fr*
[de kaʁt]

descend di ˈsend də- **~ed** ɪd əd **~ing** ɪŋ **~s** z
descendant di ˈsend ənt də- **~s** s
descender di ˈsend ə də- ‖ -ᵊr **~s** z
descent di ˈsent də- **~s** s
descrambler ˌ(ˌ)diː ˈskræm blə ‖ -blᵊr **~s** z
describable di ˈskraɪb əb ᵊl də-
describ|e di ˈskraɪb də- **~ed** d **~er/s** ə/z ‖ ᵊr/z
~es z **~ing** ɪŋ
descrie... —*see* **descry**
description di ˈskrɪp ʃᵊn də- **~s** z
descriptive di ˈskrɪpt ɪv də- **~ly** li **~ness** nəs
nɪs
descriptiv|ism di ˈskrɪpt ɪv ˌ|ɪz əm də- **~ist/s**
ɪst/s §-əst/s
descriptor di ˈskrɪpt ə də- ‖ -ᵊr **~s** z
de|scry di ‖ˈskraɪ də- **~scried** ˈskraɪd **~scries**
ˈskraɪz **~scrying** ˈskraɪ ɪŋ
Desdemona ˌdez dɪ ˈməʊn ə -də- ‖ -ˈmoʊn-
dese|crate ˈdes ɪ |kreɪt -ə- **~crated** kreɪt ɪd
-əd ‖ kreɪt̬ əd **~crates** kreɪts **~crating**
kreɪt ɪŋ ‖ kreɪt̬ ɪŋ
desecration ˌdes ɪ ˈkreɪʃ ᵊn -ə- **~s** z
deseed ˌdiː ˈsiːd **~ed** ɪd əd **~ing** ɪŋ **~s** z
desegre|gate ˌ(ˌ)diː ˈseg rɪ |ɡeɪt -rə- **~gated**
ɡeɪt ɪd -əd ‖ ɡeɪt̬ əd **~gates** ɡeɪts **~gating**
ɡeɪt ɪŋ ‖ ɡeɪt̬ ɪŋ
desegregation ˌdiː ˌseg rɪ ˈɡeɪʃ ᵊn -rə-
‖ diː ˌseg-
deselect ˌdiː sə ˈlekt -sɪ- **~ed** ɪd əd **~ing** ɪŋ **~s**
s
deselection ˌdiː sə ˈlek ʃᵊn -sɪ- **~s** z
de Selincourt də ˈsel ɪn kɔːt →-ɪŋ- ‖ -kɔːrt
-koʊrt
desensitis... —*see* **desensitiz...**
desensitization ˌdiː ˌsen⁺s ət aɪ ˈzeɪʃ ᵊn -ɪt aɪ-,
-ɪˈ·· ‖ diː ˌsen⁺s ət̬ ə- **~s** z
desensitiz|e ˌ(ˌ)diː ˈsen⁺s ə taɪz -ɪ- **~ed** d **~es** ɪz
əz **~ing** ɪŋ
de|sert *v* di ‖ˈzɜːt də- ‖ -‖ˈzɝːt **~serted** ˈzɜːt ɪd
-əd ‖ ˈzɝːt̬ əd **~serting** ˈzɜːt ɪŋ ‖ ˈzɝːt̬ ɪŋ
~serts ˈzɜːts ‖ ˈzɝːts
desert *n* '*what is deserved*' di ˈzɜːt də- ‖ -ˈzɝːt
~s s
desert *n* '*arid place*' ˈdez ət ‖ -ᵊrt **~s** s
ˌdesert ˈrat
deserter di ˈzɜːt ə də- ‖ -ˈzɝːt̬ ᵊr **~s** z
desertification di ˌzɜːt ɪf ɪ ˈkeɪʃ ᵊn də-,
ˌdez ət-, -əfˈ··, §-əˈ- ‖ -ˌzɝːt̬ əf-
desertion di ˈzɜːʃ ᵊn də- ‖ -ˈzɝːʃ- **~s** z
deserv|e di ˈzɜːv də- ‖ -ˈzɝːv **~ed** d **~es** z **~ing**
ɪŋ
deserved|ly di ˈzɜːv ɪd |li də-, -əd- ‖ -ˈzɝːv-
~ness nəs nɪs
desexualization, desexualisation
ˌ(ˌ)diː ˌsek ʃu əl aɪ ˈzeɪʃ ᵊn -ˌseks juˌ, -ɪˈ··
‖ -əˈ··
desexualiz|e, desexualis|e
ˌ(ˌ)diː ˈsek ʃu ə laɪz -ˈseks juˌ **~ed** d **~es** ɪz əz
~ing ɪŋ
deshabille ˌdez ə ˈbiːᵊl ˌdeɪz-, ˌdes-, -æ-
déshabillé ˌdez ə ˈbiː eɪ ˌdeɪz-, ˌdes-, -æ-;
-ˈbiːᵊl —*Fr* [de za bi je]
desiccant ˈdes ɪk ənt -ək- **~s** s

D

desic|cate 'des ɪ |keɪt -ə- **~cated** keɪt ɪd -əd
‖ keɪt̬ əd **~cates** keɪts **~cating** keɪt ɪŋ
‖ keɪt̬ ɪŋ
desiccation ˌdes ɪ 'keɪʃ ᵊn -ə- **~s** z
desiccator 'des ɪ keɪt ə '·ə- ‖ -keɪt̬ ᵊr **~s** z
desiderata di ˌzɪd ə 'rɑːt ə də-, -ˌsɪd-, -'reɪt-
‖ -'rɑːt̬ ə -'reɪt̬-
desiderative di 'zɪd ᵊr ət ɪv də- ‖ -ə reɪt̬ ɪv
ᵊr ət̬ ɪv **~s** z
desiderat|um di ˌzɪd ə 'rɑːt |əm də-, -ˌsɪd-,
-'reɪt- ‖ -'rɑːt̬- -'reɪt̬- **~a** ə
design di 'zaɪn də- **~ed** d **~ing/ly** ɪŋ /li **~s** z
designate *adj* 'dez ɪg nət -nɪt, -neɪt
desig|nate *v* 'dez ɪg |neɪt **~nated** neɪt ɪd -əd
‖ neɪt̬ əd **~nates** neɪts **~nating** neɪt ɪŋ
‖ neɪt̬ ɪŋ
designation ˌdez ɪg 'neɪʃ ᵊn **~s** z
designator 'dez ɪg neɪt ə ‖ -neɪt̬ ᵊr **~s** z
designedly di 'zaɪn ɪd li də-, -əd-
designer di 'zaɪn ə də- ‖ -ᵊr **~s** z
de͵signer 'jeans
desinenc|e 'dez ɪn ənˢs 'des-, -ən- **~es** ɪz əz
desinential ˌdez ɪ 'nenˢʃ ᵊl ◂ ˌdes-, -ə-
desirability di ˌzaɪ ᵊr ə 'bɪl ət i də-, -ɪt i
‖ -ˌzaɪ ᵊr ə 'bɪl ət̬ i
desirab|le di 'zaɪ ᵊr əb |ᵊl də- ‖ -'zaɪ ᵊr-
~leness ᵊl nəs -nɪs **~les** ᵊlz **~ly** li
desire di 'zaɪ ə də- ‖ -'zaɪ ᵊr **~d** d **~s** z
de͵siring di 'zaɪ ᵊr ɪŋ də-, §di:- ‖ -'zaɪ ᵊr ɪŋ
Desiree, Désirée deɪ 'zɪər eɪ de-, dɪ-
‖ ˌdez ə 'reɪ
desirous di 'zaɪ ᵊr əs də- ‖ -'zaɪ ᵊr- **~ly** li
~ness nəs nɪs
desist di 'zɪst də-, -'sɪst **~ed** ɪd əd **~ing** ɪŋ **~s** s
desk desk **desks** desks
deskill ˌdiː 'skɪl **~ed** d **~ing** ɪŋ **~s** z
desktop 'desk tɒp ˌ·'· ‖ -tɑːp **~s** s
deskwork 'desk wɜːk ‖ -wɜːk
desman 'des mən 'dez- **~s** z
desmid 'dez mɪd §-məd **~s** z
desmoid 'dez mɔɪd 'des- **~s** z
Des Moines də 'mɔɪn di-
Desmond 'dez mənd
desolate *adj* 'des əl ət 'dez-, -ɪt **~ly** li
deso|late *v* 'des ə |leɪt 'dez- **~lated** leɪt ɪd -əd
‖ leɪt̬ əd **~lates** leɪts **~lating** leɪt ɪŋ ‖ leɪt̬ ɪŋ
desolation ˌdes ə 'leɪʃ ᵊn ˌdez-
De Soto də 'səʊt əʊ ‖ -'soʊt̬ oʊ —*Sp*
[de 'so to]
Desoutter di 'suːt ə də- ‖ -'suːt̬ ᵊr
De Souza də 'suːz ə
desoxy- ˌdez ˌɒks i ‖ -ˌɑːks- —
desoxymorphine ˌdez ˌɒks i 'mɔːf iːn
‖ dez ˌɑːks i 'mɔːrf-
despair dɪ 'speə də- ‖ -'speᵊr -'spæᵊr **~ed** d
despairing/ly dɪ 'speər ɪŋ /li də- ‖ -'sper-
-'spær- **~s** z
Despard 'desp ɑːd ‖ -ɑːrd
despatch *n* di 'spætʃ də-; 'dɪs pætʃ **~es** ɪz əz
despatch *v* di 'spætʃ də- **~ed** t **~es** ɪz əz **~ing**
ɪŋ
Despenser dɪ 'spenˢs ə də- ‖ -ᵊr

desperado ˌdesp ə 'rɑːd əʊ ‖ -oʊ -'reɪd- **~es,**
~s z
desperate 'desp ᵊr ət ɪt **~ly** li **~ness** nəs nɪs
desperation ˌdesp ə 'reɪʃ ᵊn
despicability di ˌspɪk ə 'bɪl ət i də-, ˌdesp ɪk-,
-ɪt i ‖ -ət̬ i
despicab|le di 'spɪk əb |ᵊl də- 'desp ɪk-
~leness ᵊl nəs -nɪs **~ly** li
despis|e di 'spaɪz də- **~ed** d **~es** ɪz əz **~ing** ɪŋ
despite di 'spaɪt də-
Des Plaines *place in IL* des 'pleɪnz
despoil di 'spɔɪᵊl də- **~ed** d **~ing** ɪŋ **~s** z
despoliation di ˌspəʊl i 'eɪʃ ᵊn də- ‖ -ˌspoʊl-
despond di 'spɒnd də- 'desp ɒnd ‖ -'spɑːnd
~ed ɪd əd **~ing** ɪŋ **~s** z
despondenc|e di 'spɒnd ənˢs də- ‖ -'spɑːnd-
~ies iz **~y** i
despondent di 'spɒnd ənt də- ‖ -'spɑːnd- **~ly**
li
despot 'desp ɒt -ət ‖ -ɑːt -ət **~s** s
despotic di 'spɒt ɪk də-, de- ‖ -'spɑːt̬ ɪk **~ally**
ᵊl i
despotism 'desp ə ˌtɪz əm
des res ˌdez 'rez
dessert di 'zɜːt də- ‖ -'zɜːt **~s** s
des'sert wine
dessertspoon di 'zɜːt spuːn də- ‖ -'zɜːt- **~s** z
dessert|spoonful di 'zɜːt |spuːn fʊl də-
‖ -'zɜːt- ·ˌ·'·· **~spoonful spuːnz fʊl
destabilis... —*see* **destabiliz...**
destabilization ˌdiː ˌsteɪb ᵊl aɪ 'zeɪʃ ᵊn
dɪ ˌsteɪb-, -ɪl'··-, -ɪ'·- ‖ diː ˌsteɪb ᵊl ə- **~s** z
destabiliz|e ˌdiː 'steɪb ə laɪz dɪ-, -ɪ-, -ᵊl aɪz
~ed d **~es** ɪz əz **~ing** ɪŋ
deStalinis... —*see* **deStaliniz...**
deStalinization ˌdiː ˌstɑːl ɪn aɪ 'zeɪʃ ᵊn -ˌstæl-,
-ˌ·ən-, -ɪ'·- ‖ diː ˌstɑːl ən ə- -ˌstæl-
deStaliniz|e ˌdiː 'stɑːl ɪ naɪz -'stæl-, -ə- **~ed** d
~es ɪz əz **~ing** ɪŋ
De Stijl də 'staɪᵊl —*Dutch* [də 'steɪl]
destination ˌdest ɪ 'neɪʃ ᵊn -ə- **~s** z
destine 'dest ɪn -ən **~d** d **~s** z
destin|y 'dest ən |i -ɪn- **~ies** iz
destitute 'dest ɪ tjuːt -ə-, →-tʃuːt ‖ -tuːt -tjuːt
destitution ˌdest ɪ 'tjuːʃ ᵊn -ə-, →-'tʃuːʃ-
‖ -'tuːʃ ᵊn -'tjuːʃ-
destroy di 'strɔɪ də- **~ed** d **~ing** ɪŋ **~s** z
destroyer di 'strɔɪ ə də- ‖ -ᵊr **~s** z
destruct di 'strʌkt də- **~ed** ɪd əd **~ing** ɪŋ **~s** s
destructib|le di 'strʌkt əb |ᵊl də-, -ɪb- **~leness**
ᵊl nəs -nɪs **~ly** li
destruction di 'strʌk ʃᵊn də- **~s** z
destructive di 'strʌkt ɪv də- **~ly** li **~ness** nəs
nɪs
destructor di 'strʌkt ə də- ‖ -ᵊr **~s** z
Destry 'des tri
desuetude 'des wɪ tjuːd →-tʃuːd; di 'sjuː ɪ-,
də-, -'suː, ə- ‖ -tuːd -tjuːd; di 'suː ə-
desultor|y 'des ᵊlt ᵊr |i 'dez- ‖ -ᵊl tɔːr |i -toʊr i
~ily əl i i li **~iness** i nəs i nɪs
detach di 'tætʃ də- **~ed** t **~es** ɪz əz **~ing** ɪŋ
detachable di 'tætʃ əb ᵊl də-
detachedly di 'tætʃ ɪd li də-, -əd-; -'tætʃt li

detachment di 'tætʃ mənt də- **~s** s

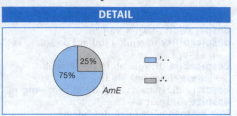

DETAIL

AmE

detail *n, v* 'diː teɪəl ; di 'teɪəl, də- **~ed** d **~ing** ɪŋ **~s** z — *Preference poll, AmE:* 'ˑ ˑ 75%, ˑ⋮ˑ 25%.

detain di 'teɪn də- **~ed** d **~ing** ɪŋ **~s** z
detainee ˌdiː teɪ 'niː; di ˌteɪ-, də-; ˌdɪt eɪ- **~s** z
detangl|e ˌdiː 'tæŋ gəl **~ed** d **~s** z **~ing** ɪŋ
detect di 'tekt də- **~ed** ɪd əd **~ing** ɪŋ **~s** s
detectab|le, detectib|le di 'tekt əb |əl də-, -ɪb- **~ly** li
detection di 'tek ʃən də-
detective di 'tekt ɪv də- **~s** z
detector di 'tekt ə də- ‖ -ər **~s** z
   de'tector van
detent di 'tent də- **~s** s
detente, détente 'deɪ tɒnt -tɑːnt; deɪ 'tɒnt, -'tɑːnt ‖ deɪ 'tɑːnt —*Fr* [de tɑ̃ːt]
detention di 'tenʧ ən də- **~s** z
   de'tention ˌcentre
deter di 'tɜː də- ‖ -'tɜː **~red** d **deterring** di 'tɜːr ɪŋ də- ‖ -'tɜː ɪŋ **~s** z
Deterding 'det əd ɪŋ ‖ 'deʈ ərd ɪŋ
detergent di 'tɜːdʒ ənt də- ‖ -'tɜːdʒ- **~s** s
deterior|ate di 'tɪər i ə r|eɪt də-, △-'tɪər ə r|eɪt, △-'tɪər i |eɪt ‖ -'tɪr- **~ated** eɪt ɪd -əd ‖ eɪʈ əd **~ates** eɪts **~ating** eɪt ɪŋ ‖ eɪʈ ɪŋ
deterioration di ˌtɪər i ə 'reɪʃ ən də-, △-ˌtɪər ə 'reɪʃ ən, △-ˌtɪər i 'eɪʃ ən ‖ -ˌtɪr- **~s** z
determinable di 'tɜːm ɪn əb əl də-, -ən ˌəb- ‖ -'tɜːm-
determinant di 'tɜːm ɪn ənt də-, -ən- ‖ -'tɜːm- **~s** s
determinate di 'tɜːm ɪn ət də-, -ən-, -ɪt ‖ -'tɜːm- **~ly** li **~ness** nəs nɪs
determination di ˌtɜːm ɪ 'neɪʃ ən də-, -ə- ‖ -ˌtɜːm- **~s** z
determinative di 'tɜːm ɪn ət ɪv də-, -ən ˌət- ‖ -'tɜːm ə neɪʈ ɪv -ən ˌəʈ- **~ness** nəs nɪs **~s** z
determin|e di 'tɜːm ɪn də-, -ən ‖ -'tɜːm- **~ed/ly** d /li **~ing** ɪŋ
determiner di 'tɜːm ɪn ə də-, -ən- ‖ -'tɜːm ən ər **~s** z
determinism dɪ 'tɜːm ɪ ˌnɪz əm də-, §diː-, -ə- ‖ -'tɜːm-
deterministic di ˌtɜːm ɪ 'nɪst ɪk ◂ də-, -ə- ‖ -ˌtɜːm- **~ally** əl i
deterrence di 'ter ənts də-, §-'tɜːr- ‖ -'tɜː- -'ter-
deterrent di 'ter ənt də-, §-'tɜːr- ‖ -'tɜː- -'ter- **~s** s

detest di 'test də- **~ed** ɪd əd **~ing** ɪŋ **~s** s
detestab|le di 'test əb |əl də- **~leness** əl nəs -nɪs **~ly** li

detestation ˌdiː te 'steɪʃ ən
dethron|e di 'θrəʊn də-, ˌdiː- ‖ -'θroʊn **~ed** d **~ement** mənt **~es** z **~ing** ɪŋ
Detmold 'det məʊld →-mɒʊld ‖ -moʊld —*Ger* ['det mɔlt]
deton|ate 'det ə n|eɪt -ᵊn |eɪt ‖ 'det ᵊn |eɪt 'deʈ ə n|eɪt **~ated** eɪt ɪd -əd ‖ eɪʈ əd **~ates** eɪts **~ating** eɪt ɪŋ ‖ eɪʈ ɪŋ
detonation ˌdet ə 'neɪʃ ən -ᵊn 'eɪʃ- ‖ ˌdet ᵊn 'eɪʃ ᵊn ˌdeʈ ə 'neɪʃ- **~s** z
detonator 'det ə neɪt ə -ᵊn eɪt- ‖ 'det ᵊn eɪʈ ᵊr 'deʈ ə neɪʈ ᵊr **~s** z
detour 'diː tʊə 'deɪ-, -tɔː; ˌdeɪ 'tʊə, di-, də-, -'tɔː ‖ -tʊr di 'tʊᵊr **~ed** d **~s** z
detox di 'tɒks di-; 'diː tɒks ‖ -'tɑːks
detoxi|cate ˌdiː 'tɒks ɪ 'keɪʃ di-, -ə- ‖ -'tɑːks- **~cated** keɪt ɪd -əd ‖ keɪʈ əd **~cates** keɪts **~cating** keɪt ɪŋ ‖ keɪʈ ɪŋ
detoxication ˌdiː ˌtɒks ɪ 'keɪʃ ən di ˌtɒks-, -ə- ‖ di ˌtɑːks-
detoxi|fy ˌdiː 'tɒks ɪ faɪ di-, -ə- ‖ -'tɑːks- **~fied** faɪd **~fies** faɪz **~fying** faɪ ɪŋ
detract di 'trækt də- , ˌdiː- **~ed** ɪd əd **~ing** ɪŋ **~s** s
detraction di 'træk ʃən də-, ˌdiː- **~s** z
detractor di 'trækt ə də-, ˌdiː- ‖ -ər **~s** z
detrain ˌdiː 'treɪn **~ed** d **~ing** ɪŋ **~s** z
detribalis... —*see* **detribaliz...**
detribalization ˌdiː ˌtraɪb əl aɪ 'zeɪʃ ən dɪ ˌtraɪb-, -əl ɪ- ‖ -əl ə-
detribaliz|e ˌdiː 'traɪb ə laɪz dɪ-, -əl aɪz **~ed** d **~es** ɪz əz **~ing** ɪŋ
detriment 'detr ɪ mənt -ə-
detrimental ˌdetr ɪ 'ment əl ◂ -ə- ‖ -'menʈ əl ◂ **~ly** i
detritus di 'traɪt əs də- ‖ -'traɪʈ əs
Detroit di 'trɔɪt də-
de trop də 'trəʊ ‖ -'troʊ —*Fr* [də tʁo]
Dettol 'det ɒl -ᵊl ‖ -ɑːl
Dettori də 'tɔːr i di-, de-
detumesc|ence ˌdiː tju 'mes |ᵊn⌐s →-tʃu- ‖ -tu- -tju- **~ent** ᵊnt
Deucalion dju 'keɪl i ən →dʒu- ‖ du- dju-
deuce djuːs →dʒuːs ‖ duːs djuːs **deuces** 'djuːs ɪz →'dʒuːs-, -əz ‖ 'duːs- 'djuːs-
deuced djuːst →dʒuːst; 'djuːs ɪd, →'dʒuːs-, -əd
deucedly 'djuːs ɪd li →'dʒuːs-, -əd- ‖ 'duːs- 'djuːs-
deus, Deus 'deɪ ʊs 'diː əs
   ˌdeus ex 'machina 'mæk ɪn ə 'mɑːk-, §-ən-; -mə 'ʃiːn ə ‖ -'mɑːk ɪ nɑː -'mæk-, -ən ə
deuterium dju 'tɪər i əm →dʒu- ‖ du 'tɪr- dju-
deutero- ˌdjuːt ə rəʊ →ˌdʒuːt- ‖ ˌduːʈ ə roʊ —
   Deutero-Isaiah ˌdjuːt ə rəʊ aɪ 'zaɪ ə →ˌdʒuːt- ‖ ˌduːʈ ə roʊ aɪ 'zeɪ ə
deuteron ˌdjuːt ə rɒn →ˌdʒuːt- ‖ ˌduːʈ ə rɑːn 'djuːʈ- **~s** z
Deuteronomy ˌdjuːt ə 'rɒn əm i →ˌdʒuːt-; 'djuːt ər ə nɒm i, →'dʒuːt- ‖ ˌduːʈ ə 'rɑːn- ˌdjuːʈ-
Deutsch dɔɪtʃ

Deutsche Mark ,dɔɪtʃ ə 'mɑːk ‖ -'mɑːrk
—*Ger* [,dɔy tʃə 'maʁk]
Deutschland 'dɔɪtʃ lənd -lænd —*Ger*
['dɔytʃ lant]
deutschmark, D~ 'dɔɪtʃ mɑːk ‖ -mɑːrk
deutzia 'djuːts i̯ə →'dʒuːts-; 'dɔɪts- ‖ 'duːts-
'djuːts- ~**s** z
deva 'deɪv ə 'diːv- —*Hindi* [ɖeːʋ]
De Valera də və 'leər ə ,dev ə-, -'lɪər- ‖ -'ler ə
-'lɪr-
de Valois də 'væl wɑː
devaluation ,diː ,væl ju 'eɪʃ ᵊn dɪ ,væl-
‖ diː ,væl- ~**s** z
devalue ,diː 'væl juː dɪ- ~**d** d ~**s** z **devaluing**
,diː 'væl juː ɪŋ dɪ-
Devanagari ,deɪv ə 'nɑːg ᵊr i̯ ,dev-
Devaney di 'veɪn i də-
deva|state 'dev ə |steɪt ~**stated** steɪt ɪd -əd
‖ steɪt̬ əd ~**states** steɪts ~**stating/ly**
steɪt ɪŋ /li ‖ steɪt̬ ɪŋ /li
devastation ,dev ə 'steɪʃ ᵊn
develop di 'vel əp də- ~**ed** t ~**er/s** ə/z ‖ ᵊr/z
~**ing** ɪŋ ~**s** s
de'veloping ,country, ·,·· · '··
development di 'vel əp mənt də- ~**s** s
de'velopment ,area
developmental di ,vel əp 'ment ᵊl ◄ də-
‖ -'ment̬ ᵊl ◄ ~**ly** i
deverbal ,diː 'vɜːb ᵊl ◄ ‖ -'vɜːb- ~**s** z
deverbative ,diː 'vɜːb ət ɪv di- ‖ -'vɜːb ət̬ ɪv
~**s** z
De Vere də 'vɪə di- ‖ -'vɪᵊr
Devereux *(i)* 'dev ə ruːks, *(ii)* -rɜː -ər ə ‖ -ər ə,
(iii) -reks, *(iv)* -ruː, *(v)* -rəʊ ‖ -roʊ
devianc|e 'diːv i̯ənˢ ~**y** i
deviant 'diːv i̯ənt ~**ly** li ~**s** s
deviate n 'diːv i̯ət -ɪt ~**s** s
devi|ate v 'diːv i̯ eɪt ~**ated** eɪt ɪd -əd ‖ eɪt̬ əd
~**ates** eɪts ~**ating** eɪt ɪŋ ‖ eɪt̬ ɪŋ
deviation ,diːv i 'eɪʃ ᵊn ~**ism** ,ɪz əm ~**ist/s**
ɪst/s §-əst/s ~**s** z
deviator 'diːv i eɪt ə ‖ -eɪt̬ ᵊr ~**s** z
devic|e di 'vaɪs də- ~**es** ɪz əz
devil 'dev ᵊl -ɪl ~**ed, ~led** d ~**ing, ~ling** ɪŋ ~**s**
z
,devil's 'advocate; 'devil's food cake,
,··'· ·; ,devils-on-'horseback
devilish 'dev ᵊl ɪʃ ~**ly** li ~**ness** nəs nɪs
de Villiers də 'vɪl jəz ‖ -jᵊrz
devil-may-care ,dev ᵊl meɪ 'keə ◄ ‖ -'keᵊr
-'kæᵊr
devilment 'dev ᵊl mənt
devil|ry 'dev ᵊl |ri ~**ries** riz
Devine *(i)* di 'viːn də-, *(ii)* -'vaɪn
devious 'diːv i̯əs ~**ly** li ~**ness** nəs nɪs
devis|e di 'vaɪz də- ~**ed** d ~**er/s** ə/z ‖ ᵊr/z ~**es**
ɪz əz ~**ing** ɪŋ
devitalis... —*see* **devitaliz...**
devitalization ,diː ,vaɪt ᵊl aɪ 'zeɪʃ ᵊn -ᵊl ɪ-
‖ diː ,vaɪt̬ ᵊl ə-
devitaliz|e ⑴diː 'vaɪt ə laɪz -ᵊl aɪz
‖ -'vaɪt̬ ᵊl aɪz ~**ed** d ~**es** ɪz əz ~**ing** ɪŋ
DeVito də 'viːt əʊ ‖ də 'viːt̬ oʊ

Devizes di 'vaɪz ɪz də-, -əz
Devlin 'dev lɪn -lən
devoic|e ⑴di: 'vɔɪs ~**ed** t ~**es** ɪz əz ~**ing** ɪŋ
devoid di 'vɔɪd də-
devolution ,diːv ə 'luːʃ ᵊn ,dev-, -'ljuːʃ- ‖ ,dev-
~**ist/s** ɪst/s ~**s** z
devolv|e di 'vɒlv də-, §-'vəʊlv ‖ -'vɑːlv ~**ed** d
~**es** z ~**ing** ɪŋ ~**ement** mənt
Devon 'dev ᵊn —*but the river in Notts. is* 'diːv-
Devonian de 'vəʊn i̯ən də-, dɪ- ‖ -'voʊn- ~**s** z
Devonish 'dev ᵊn ɪʃ
Devonport 'dev ᵊn pɔːt →-ᵊm- ‖ -pɔːrt -poʊrt
Devonshire 'dev ᵊn ʃə -ʃɪə ‖ -ʃᵊr -ʃɪr
de|vote di |'vəʊt də- ‖ -|'voʊt ~**voted** 'vəʊt ɪd
-əd ‖ 'voʊt̬ əd ~**votes** 'vəʊts ‖ 'voʊts
~**voting** 'vəʊt ɪŋ ‖ 'voʊt̬ ɪŋ
devoted|ly di 'vəʊt ɪd |li də-, -əd- ‖ -'voʊt̬ əd-
~**ness** nəs nɪs
devotee ,dev əʊ 'tiː ‖ -ə 'tiː -'teɪ ~**s** z
devotion di 'vəʊʃ ᵊn də- ‖ -'voʊʃ- ~**s** z
devotional di 'vəʊʃ ᵊn ᵊl də--'voʊʃ- ~**ly** i
devour di 'vaʊ̯ə də- ‖ 'vaʊ̯ᵊr ~**ed** d
devouring di 'vaʊ̯ ᵊr ɪŋ də- ‖ -'vaʊ̯ᵊr ɪŋ ~**s** z
devout di 'vaʊt də- ~**ly** li ~**ness** nəs nɪs
De Vries *(i)* də 'vriːs, *(ii)* -'vriːz
dew djuː →dʒuː ‖ duː djuː **dewed** djuːd
→dʒuːd ‖ duːd djuːd **dewing** 'djuː ɪŋ →'dʒuː-
‖ 'duː ɪŋ 'djuː- **dews** djuːz →dʒuːz ‖ duːz
djuːz
'dew point
Dewar, dewar 'djuː̯ə →'dʒuː̯ə ‖ 'duː ᵊr
'djuː ᵊr ~**s** z
dewberr|y 'djuː bər |i →'dʒuː- ‖ 'duː ,ber |i
'djuː- ~**ies** iz
dewclaw 'djuː klɔː →'dʒuː- ‖ 'duː- 'djuː-, -klɑ-
~**s** z
dewdrop 'djuː drɒp →'dʒuː- ‖ 'duː drɑːp 'djuː-
~**s** s
Dewey 'djuː i →'dʒuː i ‖ 'duː i 'djuː i
,Dewey 'decimal ,system
dewfall 'djuː fɔːl →'dʒuː- ‖ 'duː- 'djuː-, -fɑːl
Dewhurst 'djuː hɜːst →'dʒuː- ‖ 'duː hɜːst 'djuː-
Dewi 'de wi —*this Welsh name is occasionally
anglicized as* 'djuː i
dewi... —*see* **dewy**
de Wint də 'wɪnt
dewlap 'djuː læp →'dʒuː- ‖ 'duː- 'djuː- ~**s** s
dewpond 'djuː pɒnd →'dʒuː- ‖ 'duː pɑːnd
'djuː- ~**s** z
Dewsbury 'djuːz bər i →'dʒuːz- ‖ 'duːz ,ber i
'djuːz-
dew-worm 'djuː wɜːm →'dʒuː- ‖ 'duː wɜːm
'djuː- ~**s** z
dew|y 'djuː |i →'dʒuː i ‖ 'duː |i 'djuː i ~**ier** i̯ə
‖ i̯ᵊr ~**iest** i̯ɪst i̯əst ~**ily** ɪ li əl i ~**iness** i nəs
i nɪs
dewy-eyed ,djuː i 'aɪd ◄ →,dʒuː- ‖ ,duː- ,djuː-
Dexedrine *tdmk* 'deks ɪ driːn -ə-
Dexter, d~ 'dekst ə ‖ -ᵊr
dexterity dek 'ster ət i -ɪt- ‖ -ət̬ i
dexterous 'deks tᵊr̯əs ~**ly** li ~**ness** nəs nɪs
dextral 'deks trəl ~**ly** i
dextrality dek 'stræl ət i -ɪt- ‖ -ət̬ i

dextrin 'deks trɪn
dextro- ¦deks trəʊ ‖ -troʊ
dextrorotatory ˌdeks trəʊ rəʊ 'teɪt ər i ◂
-'rəʊt ət ər i ‖ -troʊ 'roʊt̬ ə tɔːr i ◂ -tour i (*)
dextrorse 'deks trɔːs ₍₁₎dek 'strɔːs ‖ -trɔːrs ~ly
li
dextrose 'deks trəʊz -trəʊs ‖ -troʊs -troʊz
dextrous 'deks trəs ~ly li ~ness nəs nɪs
dey deɪ (= *day*) **deys** deɪz
De Zoete də 'zuːt
DFID 'dɪf ɪd
Dhahran ˌdɑː 'ræn -'rɑːn ‖ -'rɑːn —*Arabic*
[ðˤɑh 'rɑːn]
Dhaka 'dæk ə
dhal dɑːl —*Hindi* [d̪ɑːl]
dhansak dʌn 'sɑːk —*Hindi* [d̪ən sɑːk]
dharma 'dɑːm ə ‖ 'dɑːrm ə —*Hindi* [d̪ʰərm]
Dharug, Dharuk, Dharruk dɑː 'ruːg 'dɑr ʊk
Dhekelia di 'keɪl i ə də-
dhobi 'dəʊb i ‖ 'doʊb i —*Hindi* ['d̪ʰoː bi] ~s z
'dhobi('s) itch
dhole dəʊl →dɒʊl ‖ doʊl (= *dole*) **dholes**
dəʊlz →dɒʊlz ‖ doʊlz
dhoti 'dəʊt i ‖ 'doʊt̬ i —*Hindi* ['d̪ʰoː t̪i] ~s z
dhow daʊ **dhows** daʊz
dhurrie 'dʌr i ‖ 'dɝː i ~s z
di- ¦daɪ — **dimorphemic** ˌdaɪ mɔː 'fiːm ɪk ◂
‖ -mɔːr-
Di daɪ **Di's** daɪz
dia- *comb. form*
with stress-neutral suffix ¦daɪ ə — **diatropic**
ˌdaɪ ə 'trɒp ɪk ◂ ‖ -'trɑːp-
with stress-imposing suffix daɪ 'æ+
— **diatropism** daɪ 'ætr ə ˌpɪz əm
diabesity ˌdaɪ ə 'biːs ət i -ɪt i ‖ -ət̬ i
diabetes ˌdaɪ ə 'biːt iːz ◂ -ɪs, §-əs ‖ -'biːt̬ əs -iːz
ˌdiaˌbetes in'sipidus ɪn 'sɪp ɪd əs §-əd əs;
ˌdiaˌbetes mel'litus mə 'laɪt əs mɪ-, me-
‖ -'laɪt̬- 'mel ət̬ əs
diabetic ˌdaɪ ə 'bet ɪk ◂ ‖ -'bet̬- ~s s
diablerie di 'ɑːb lər i —*Fr* [dja blə ʁi]
diabolic ˌdaɪ ə 'bɒl ɪk ◂ ‖ -'bɑːl- ~al ᵊl ~ally
ᵊl_i
diabolism daɪ 'æb ə ˌlɪz əm
diabolo daɪ 'æb ə ləʊ di- ‖ -loʊ ~s z
diachronic ˌdaɪ ə 'krɒn ɪk ◂ ‖ -'krɑːn- ~ally
ᵊl_i
diachrony daɪ 'æk rən i
diacidic ˌdaɪ ə 'sɪd ɪk ◂
diaconal daɪ 'æk ən ᵊl di-
diaconate daɪ 'æk ə neɪt di-, -ən ət, -ən ɪt
diacritic ˌdaɪ ə 'krɪt ɪk ‖ -'krɪt̬- ~al ᵊl ~ally ᵊl_i
~s s
diadem 'daɪ ə dem -əd əm ~ed d ~s z
Diadochi daɪ 'æd ə kaɪ
diaer|esis daɪ 'ɪər |əs ɪs -'er-, -ɪs ɪs, §-əs ‖ -'er-
~eses ə siːz ɪ-
Diageo *tdmk* di 'ædʒ i əʊ ‖ -oʊ
Diaghilev di 'æg ə lef -ɪ-

DIAGNOSE

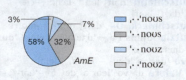

3% 7%
58% 32%
AmE
| ˌ·ˈnəʊs |
| ·ˈˈnəʊs |
| ·ˈnəʊz |
| ˌ·ˈnəʊz |

diagnos|e 'daɪ_əg nəʊz -nəʊs, ˌ·ˈˈ ‖ ˌ·· 'nəʊs
-'nəʊz, 'ˈˈˈ — *Preference poll. AmE:* ˌ·ˈnəʊs
58%, 'ˈ ·nəʊs *32%,* 'ˈ ·nəʊz *7%,* ˌ·ˈnəʊz *3%.*
~ed d ‖ t ~es v ɪz əz ~ing ɪŋ
diagnos|is ˌdaɪ_əg 'nəʊs |ɪs -'nəʊz-, §-əs
‖ -'nəʊs- ~es n iːz
diagnostic ˌdaɪ_əg 'nɒst ɪk ◂ ‖ -'nɑːst- ~ally
ᵊl_i ~s s
diagnostician ˌdaɪ_əg nɒ 'stɪʃ ᵊn ‖ -nɑː-ˈ·· ~s z
diagonal daɪ 'æg ᵊn_əl ~ly i ~s z
diagram 'daɪ_ə græm ~ed d ~ing ɪŋ ~med d
~ming ɪŋ ~s z
diagrammatic ˌdaɪ_ə grə 'mæt ɪk ◂ ‖ -'mæt̬-
~al ᵊl ~ally ᵊl_i
dial 'daɪ_əl daɪᵊl **dialed, dialled** 'daɪ_əld daɪᵊld
dialing, dialling 'daɪ_əl ɪŋ 'daɪᵊl ɪŋ **dials**
'daɪ_əlz daɪᵊlz
'dialling code; 'dialling tone; 'dial tone
dialect 'daɪ_ə lekt ~s s
dialectal ˌdaɪ_ə 'lekt ᵊl ◂ ~ly i
dialectic ˌdaɪ_ə 'lekt ɪk ◂ ~al ᵊl ~ally ᵊl_i ~s s
dialectician ˌdaɪ_ə lek 'tɪʃ ᵊn ~s z
dialectological ˌdaɪ_ə lekt ə 'lɒdʒ ɪk ᵊl
‖ -'lɑːdʒ- ~ly_i
dialectologist ˌdaɪ_ə lek 'tɒl ədʒ ɪst §-əst
‖ -'tɑːl- ~s s
dialectology ˌdaɪ_ə lek 'tɒl ədʒ i ‖ -'tɑːl-
dialog, dialogue 'daɪ_ə lɒg ‖ -lɔːg -lɑːg ~s z
dialup 'daɪ_əl ʌp 'daɪᵊl ʌp
dialys|e 'daɪ_ə laɪz ~ed d ~es ɪz əz ~ing ɪŋ
dialyses *from v* 'daɪ_ə laɪz ɪz -əz
dialyses *n pl* daɪ 'æl ə siːz -ɪ-
dial|ysis daɪ 'æl |əs ɪs -ɪs-, §-əs ~yses ə siːz -ɪ-
diamagnetic ˌdaɪ_ə mæg 'net ɪk ◂ -məg'--
‖ -'net̬-
diamante, diamanté ˌdiː ə 'mɒnt eɪ ˌdaɪ_,
-'mænt-, -i ‖ -mɑːn 'teɪ
diameter daɪ 'æm ɪt ə -ət- ‖ -ət̬ ᵊr ~s z
diametral daɪ 'æm ɪtr əl -ətr-
diametric ˌdaɪ_ə 'metr ɪk ◂ ~al ᵊl ~ally ᵊl_i
ˌdiaˌmetrically op'posed
diamond, D~ 'daɪ_əm ənd §'daɪm ənd
‖ 'daɪm ənd ~ed ɪd əd ~s z
ˌdiamond 'jubilee; ˌdiamond 'wedding
(anniˌversary)
diamondback 'daɪ_əm əndbæk §'daɪm··
‖ 'daɪm·· ~s s
Dian ₍₁₎daɪ 'æn di-
Diana daɪ 'æn ə
Diane ₍₁₎daɪ 'æn di-
dianetics *tdmk* ˌdaɪ_ə 'net ɪks ‖ -'net̬-
dianoetic ˌdaɪ_ə nəʊ 'et ɪk ◂ ‖ -noʊ 'et̬-
dianthus daɪ 'ænᵗθ əs ~es ɪz əz

D

diapason ˌdaɪ ə ˈpeɪz ᵊn -ˈpeɪs- **~s** z
diaper ˈdaɪ əp ə §ˈdaɪp ə ‖ ˈdaɪp ᵊr **~ed** d
   diapering ˈdaɪ əp ər ɪŋ §ˈdaɪp ər ɪŋ
   ‖ ˈdaɪp ᵊr ɪŋ **~s** z
diaphanous daɪ ˈæf ən əs **~ly** li **~ness** nəs nɪs
diaphone ˈdaɪ ə fəʊn ‖ -foʊn **~s** z
diaphoneme ˈdaɪ ə ˌfəʊn iːm ˌ· ·ˈ· · ‖ -ˌfoʊn- **~s**
   z
diaphonemic ˌdaɪ ə fəʊ ˈniːm ɪk ‖ -fə'-- **~ally**
   ᵊl i
diaphonic ˌdaɪ ə ˈfɒn ɪk ◄ ‖ -ˈfɑːn- **~ally** ᵊl i
diaphoresis ˌdaɪ ə fə ˈriːs ɪs -fɒˈ-, -fɔːˈ-, §-əs
diaphoretic ˌdaɪ ə fə ˈret ɪk ◄ -fɒˈ-, -fɔːˈ--
   ‖ -ˈreţ ɪk ◄ **~s** s
diaphragm ˈdaɪ ə fræm **~s** z
diaphragmatic ˌdaɪ ə fræg ˈmæt ɪk ◄ ‖ -ˈmæţ-
   ~ally ᵊl i
diaph|ysis daɪ ˈæf |əs ɪs -ɪs ɪs, §-əs **~yses** ə siːz
   ɪ-
diarch|y ˈdaɪ ɑːk |i ‖ -ɑːrk |i **~ies** iz
diaries ˈdaɪ ər iz
diarist ˈdaɪ ər ɪst §-əst; △ˈdaɪ ər i ɪst **~s** s
diarrhea, diarrhoea ˌdaɪ ə ˈrɪə §-ˈriː ə ‖ -ˈriː ə
diar|y ˈdaɪ ər |i **~ies** iz
Dias ˈdiː əs —Port [ˈdi ɐʃ]
diaspora, D~ daɪ ˈæsp ər ə ˌdaɪ ə ˈspɔːr ə **~s** z
diaspore ˈdaɪ ə spɔː ‖ -spɔːr -spoʊr
diastase ˈdaɪ ə steɪz -steɪs
diastole daɪ ˈæst əl i
diastolic ˌdaɪ ə ˈstɒl ɪk ◄ ‖ -ˈstɑːl-
diathermy ˈdaɪ ə ˌθɜːm i ‖ -ˌθɜːm i
diath|esis daɪ ˈæθ |əs ɪs -ɪs ɪs, §-əs **~eses**
   ə siːz ɪ-
diatom ˈdaɪ ə tɒm ət əm ‖ -tɑːm **~s** z
diatomaceous ˌdaɪ ət ə ˈmeɪʃ əs ‖ -əţ ə-
diatomic ˌdaɪ ə ˈtɒm ɪk ◄ ‖ -ˈtɑːm-
diatomite daɪ ˈæt ə maɪt ‖ -ˈæţ-
diatonic ˌdaɪ ə ˈtɒn ɪk ◄ ‖ -ˈtɑːn- **~ally** ᵊl i
   ˌdia ˌtonic ˈscale
diatribe ˈdaɪ ə traɪb **~s** z
Diaz ˈdiː æs -æθ ‖ -ɑːs —Sp Díaz [ˈdi aθ],
   AmSp [-as]; Port Diaz [ˈdi ɐʃ]
diazepam daɪ ˈeɪz ə pæm -ˈæz-, -ɪ- ‖ -ˈæz-
diazo ˌdaɪ ˈeɪz əʊ -ˈæz- ‖ -ˈæz oʊ
diazonium ˌdaɪ ə ˈzəʊn i əm ‖ -ˈzoʊn-
dib dɪb **dibbed** dɪbd **dibbing** ˈdɪb ɪŋ **dibs**
   dɪbz
dibber ˈdɪb ə ‖ -ᵊr **~s** z
dibbl|e, D~ ˈdɪb ᵊl **~ed** d **~er/s** ə/z ‖ -ᵊr/z **~es**
   z **~ing** ɪŋ
Dibden ˈdɪb dən
dibs dɪbz
DiCaprio di ˈkæp ri əʊ ‖ -oʊ
dicast ˈdɪk æst **~s** s
Diccon ˈdɪk ən
dice daɪs **diced** daɪst **dices** ˈdaɪs ɪz -əz **dicing**
   ˈdaɪs ɪŋ
dicentra ˌdaɪ ˈsentr ə **~s** z
dic|ey ˈdaɪs |i **~ier** i ə ‖ i ᵊr **~iest** i ɪst i əst
dichlorvos daɪ ˈklɔː vɒs ‖ -ˈklɔːr voʊs -ˈkloʊr-
dichotic ˌdaɪ ˈkɒt ɪk dɪ- ‖ -ˈkɑːţ ɪk
dichotom|y daɪ ˈkɒt əm |i dɪ- ‖ -ˈkɑːţ- **~ies** iz
Dick, dick dɪk **Dick's, dicks** dɪks

Dicken ˈdɪk ɪn §-ən
Dickens, d~ ˈdɪk ɪnz §-ənz **D~'** ɪz əz —or as
   nominative
Dickensian dɪ ˈkenz i ən də- **~s** z
dicker, D~ ˈdɪk ə ‖ -ᵊr **~ed** d **dickering**
   ˈdɪk ər ɪŋ **~s** z
Dickerson ˈdɪk əs ən ‖ -ᵊrs-
dickey, dickie, D~ ˈdɪk i **~s** z
dickhead ˈdɪk hed **~s** z
Dickie ˈdɪk i
Dickins ˈdɪk ɪnz §-ənz
Dickinson ˈdɪk ɪn sən §-ən-
Dickon ˈdɪk ən
Dickson ˈdɪks ᵊn
dick|y, Dicky ˈdɪk |i **~ies, ~y's** iz
dickybird ˈdɪk i bɜːd ‖ -bɜːd **~s** z
dicotyledon ˌdaɪ ˌkɒt ɪ ˈliːd ᵊn -ə-, -ᵊl ˈiːd-
   ‖ -ˌkɑːţ ᵊl ˈiːd ᵊn -ˌ·- **~s** z
dicoumarol ˌᵢ daɪ ˈkuːm ə rɒl ‖ -roʊl -rɑːl, -rɔːl
dicta ˈdɪkt ə
dictaphone, D~ tdmk ˈdɪkt ə fəʊn ‖ -foʊn **~s**
   z
dictate n ˈdɪkt eɪt **~s** s
dict|ate v ˌᵢ dɪk ˈt|eɪt ‖ ˈdɪkt |eɪt dɪk ˈt|eɪt
   ~ated eɪt ɪd -əd ‖ eɪţ əd **~ates** eɪts **~ating**
   eɪt ɪŋ ‖ eɪţ ɪŋ
dictation dɪk ˈteɪʃ ᵊn **~s** z
dictator dɪk ˈteɪt ə ‖ ˈdɪkt eɪţ ᵊr dɪk ˈteɪţ ᵊr **~s**
   z
dictatorial ˌdɪkt ə ˈtɔːr i əl ◄ ‖ -ˈtoʊr- **~ly** i
   ~ness nəs nɪs
dictatorship dɪk ˈteɪt ə ʃɪp ‖ ˈdɪkt eɪţ ᵊr ʃɪp
   dɪk ˈteɪţ ᵊr- **~s** s
diction ˈdɪkʃ ᵊn
dictionar|y ˈdɪk ʃən ᵊr |i ˈdɪk ʃᵊn ər |i,
   §-ʃə ner |i ‖ ˈdɪk ʃə ner |i **~ies** iz
dict|um ˈdɪkt |əm **~a** ə **~ums** əmz
did dɪd occasional weak forms §dəd, d —see **'d**
didactic daɪ ˈdækt ɪk dɪ-, də- **~ally** ᵊl i **~s** s
didacticism daɪ ˈdækt ɪ ˌsɪz əm dɪ-, də-, -ə-
Didcot ˈdɪd kət →ˈdɪg-, -kɒt ‖ -kɑːt
diddl|e ˈdɪd ᵊl **~ed** d **~es** z **~ing** ɪŋ
diddly ˈdɪd ᵊl i
diddlysquat ˌdɪd ᵊl i ˈskwɒt ˈ· · · · ‖ -ˈskwɑːt
diddums ˈdɪd əmz
diddy, Diddy ˈdɪd i
Diderot ˈdiːd ə rəʊ ‖ ˌdiːd ə ˈroʊ —Fr
   [di dʁo]
didgeridoo ˌdɪdʒ ər i ˈduː **~s** z
didicoy, didikoi ˈdɪd ɪ kɔɪ -ə- **~s** z
Didier ˈdɪd i eɪ —Fr [di dje]
didn't ˈdɪd ᵊnt △ˈdɪt- —non-final also ˈdɪd ᵊn
Dido, dido ˈdaɪd əʊ ‖ -oʊ
didst dɪdst dɪtst
did|y ˈdaɪd |i **~ies** iz
didymous, Didymus ˈdɪd ɪm əs -əm-
die daɪ **died** daɪd **dieing** ˈdaɪ ɪŋ **dies** daɪz
   dying ˈdaɪ ɪŋ
dieback ˈdaɪ bæk
die-cast ˈdaɪ kɑːst §-kæst ‖ -kæst **~ing** ɪŋ **~s** s
dieffenbachia ˌdiːf ᵊn ˈbæk i ə →ˌ·ᵊm-
   ‖ -ˈbɑːk- **~s** z
Diego di ˈeɪg əʊ ‖ -oʊ —Sp [ˈdje ɣo]

diehard 'daɪ hɑːd ‖ -hɑːrd ~s z
dieldrin 'diːᵊldr ɪn -ən
dielectric ˌdaɪ ɪ 'lek trɪk ◄ -ə- ~**ally** ᵊl i ~s s
diene, -diene 'daɪ iːn
Dieppe di 'ep ˌdiː- —Fr [djɛp]
dier|esis daɪ 'ɪər |əs ɪs -'er-, -ɪs ɪs, §-əs ‖ -'er-
   ~**eses** ə siːz ɪ-
dies from **die** daɪz
dies Latin, 'day' 'diː eɪz 'daɪ iːz ‖ -eɪs —See
   also phrases with this word
diesel, D~ 'diːz ᵊl ‖ 'diːs- ~s z
   'diesel ˌengine; 'diesel ˌfuel; 'diesel oil
diesel-electric ˌdiːz ᵊl ɪ 'lek trɪk ◄ -əˈ-- ‖ ˌdiːs-
   ~s s
dieselisation, dieselization
   ˌdiːz ᵊl aɪ 'zeɪʃ ᵊn -ᵊl ɪ- ‖ -ᵊl ə- ˌdiːs-
Dies Irae ˌdiː eɪz 'ɪər aɪ -ez-, -es-, -eɪ
   ‖ -eɪs 'ɪr eɪ
di|esis 'daɪ |əs ɪs ɪs ɪs, §-əs ~**eses** ə siːz ɪ-
dies non ˌdaɪ iːz 'nɒn ˌdiː eɪz-, -'nəʊn ‖ -'nɑːn
   ˌdiː eɪs-, -'noʊn
di|et 'daɪ |ət ~**eted** ət ɪd -əd ‖ ət əd ~**eting**
   ət ɪŋ ‖ ət ɪŋ ~**ets** əts
dietar|y 'daɪ ət ᵊr |i ‖ 'daɪ ə ter |i ~**ies** iz
dieter 'one that diets' 'daɪ ət ə ‖ 'daɪ ət ᵊr ~s z
Dieter name 'diːt ə ‖ 'diːt ᵊr —Ger ['diː tɐ]
dietetic ˌdaɪ ə 'tet ɪk ◄ ɪ- ‖ -'tet̬- ~**ally** ᵊl i ~s s
diethylstil|bestrol, ~boestrol
   ˌdaɪ ˌeθ ᵊl stɪl 'biːs trɒl -ˌiːθ-, -ˌɪl-, -'bes-,
   -trəl ‖ ˌdaɪ ˌeθ ᵊl stɪl 'bes troʊl -trɑːl, -trɔːl
dietician, dietitian ˌdaɪ ə 'tɪʃ ᵊn ~s z
Dietrich 'diːtr ɪk 'dɪətr-, -ɪx, -ɪʃ —Ger
   ['diː tʁɪç]
Dieu et mon droit ˌdjɜːʳ eɪ mɒn 'drwɑː
   ‖ ˌdjuː eɪ mɔːn 'dwɑː: -ən 'dwɑː -əʳ 'dwɑː —Fr [djø e mɔ̃ dʁwa]
differ 'dɪf ə ‖ -ᵊr ~**ed** d **differing** 'dɪf ər ɪŋ ~s
   z
differenc|e 'dɪf rənts 'dɪf ᵊr ənts ‖ 'dɪf ər ᵊnts
   ~**ed** t ~**es** ɪz əz ~**ing** ɪŋ
different 'dɪf rənt 'dɪf ᵊr ənt ‖ 'dɪf ər ᵊnt ~**ly** li
   ~**ness** nəs nɪs
different|ia ˌdɪf ə 'renʧ| i ə ~**iae** i iː i aɪ, i eɪ
differential ˌdɪf ə 'renʧ ᵊl ◄ ~**ly** i ~s z
   ˌdiffe ˌrential 'calculus; ˌdiffe ˌrential
   e'quation; ˌdiffe ˌrential 'gear
differenti|ate ˌdɪf ə 'renʧ i |eɪt ~**ated** eɪt ɪd
   -əd ‖ eɪt̬ əd ~**ates** eɪts ~**ating** eɪt ɪŋ ‖ eɪt̬ ɪŋ
differentiation ˌdɪf ə ˌrenʧ i 'eɪʃ ᵊn ~s z
difficile 'dɪf ɪ sɪl -ə-; ˌdɪf ɪ 'siːᵊl —The name of
   the bacterium Clostridium d~ is Latin, not
   French —Latin [dif 'fi ki le]
difficult 'dɪf ɪk ᵊlt -ək-; §-ɪ kʌlt, -ə- ~**ly** li
difficult|y 'dɪf ɪk ᵊlt |i ‖ '-ək-; §-ɪ kʌlt-, §-ə kʌlt-
   ~**ies** iz
diffidence 'dɪf ɪd ənts -əd-
diffident 'dɪf ɪd ənt -əd- ~**ly** li
diffract dɪ 'frækt də- ~**ed** ɪd əd ~**ing** ɪŋ ~s s
diffraction dɪ 'fræk ʃᵊn də- ~s z
diffus|e v dɪ 'fjuːz də- ~**ed** d ~**es** ɪz əz ~**ing** ɪŋ
diffuse adj dɪ 'fjuːs də-, daɪ- ~**ly** li ~**ness** nəs
   nɪs
diffuser n dɪ 'fjuːz ə də- ‖ -ᵊr ~s z
diffusion dɪ 'fjuːʒ ᵊn də- ~s z

diffusive dɪ 'fjuːs ɪv də-, §-'fjuːz- ~**ly** li ~**ness**
   nəs nɪs
diffusivity ˌdɪf ju 'sɪv ət i dɪ ˌfjuː-, də ˌfjuː-,
   -ɪt i ‖ -ət̬ i
dig dɪg **digging** 'dɪg ɪŋ **digs** dɪgz **dug** dʌg
digamma 'daɪ ˌgæm ə (ˌ)·'· · ~s z
Digbeth 'dɪg bəθ
Digby 'dɪg bi
digerati ˌdɪdʒ ə 'rɑːt i ‖ -'rɑːt̬ i
digest v daɪ 'dʒest dɪ-, də- ~**ed** ɪd əd ~**ing** ɪŋ
   ~s s
digest n 'daɪ dʒest ~s s
digestant daɪ 'dʒest ᵊnt dɪ-, də- ~s s
digestibility daɪ ˌdʒest ə 'bɪl ət i dɪ-, də-, -ˌ·ɪ-,
   -ɪt i ‖ -ət̬ i
digestib|le daɪ 'dʒest əb |ᵊl dɪ-, də-, -ɪb- ~**ly** li
digestif dɪ 'ʒest iːf ˌdiːʒ es 'tiːf —Fr
   [di ʒes tif] ~s s
digestion daɪ 'dʒes tʃən dɪ-, də-, →-'dʒeʃ- ~s z
digestive daɪ 'dʒest ɪv dɪ-, də- ~**ly** li ~s z
digger, D~ 'dɪg ə ‖ -ᵊr ~s z
digging 'dɪg ɪŋ ~s z
Diggle 'dɪg ᵊl
dight daɪt
digibox, D~ tdmk 'dɪdʒ i bɒks ‖ -bɑːks ~**es** ɪz
   əz
digicam 'dɪdʒ i kæm ~s z
digipack, Digipak tdmk 'dɪdʒ i pæk ~s s
digit 'dɪdʒ ɪt §-ət ~s s
digital 'dɪdʒ ɪt ᵊl -ət- ‖ -ət̬ ᵊl ~**ly** i ~s z
digitalin ˌdɪdʒ ɪ 'teɪl ɪn -ə-, §-ən ‖ -'tæl-
digitalis ˌdɪdʒ ɪ 'teɪl ɪs -ə-, §-əs ‖ -'tæl- (*)
digitis... —see **digitiz...**
digitization ˌdɪdʒ ɪt aɪ 'zeɪʃ ᵊn ˌ·ət-, -ɪ'·-
   ‖ -ət ə-
digitiz|e 'dɪdʒ ɪ taɪz -ə- ~**ed** d ~**er/s** ə/z ‖ ᵊr/z
   ~**es** ɪz əz ~**ing** ɪŋ
diglossia (ˌ)daɪ 'glɒs i ə ‖ -'glɑːs- -'glɔːs-
diglossic (ˌ)daɪ 'glɒs ɪk ‖ -'glɑːs-
diglot 'daɪ glɒt ‖ -glɑːt ~s s
digni|fy 'dɪg nɪ |faɪ -nə- ~**fied/ly** faɪd /li ~**fies**
   faɪz ~**fying** faɪ ɪŋ
dignitar|y 'dɪg nət ᵊr |i ‖ '·nɪt̬ ‖ -nə ter |i ~**ies**
   iz
dignity 'dɪg nət |i -nɪt- ‖ -nət̬ |i ~**ies** iz
digoxin dɪ 'dʒɒks ɪn -ᵊn ‖ -'dʒɑːks-
digraph 'daɪ grɑːf -græf ‖ -græf ~s s
digress daɪ 'gres ~**ed** t ~**es** ɪz əz ~**ing** ɪŋ
digression daɪ 'greʃ ᵊn -s z
digressive daɪ 'gres ɪv ~**ly** li ~**ness** nəs nɪs
dihedral (ˌ)daɪ 'hiːdr əl ~s z
Dijkstra 'daɪks trə —Dutch ['dɛik strɑ]
Dijon 'diːʒ ɒ̃ -ɒn ‖ diː 'ʒɑːn -'ʒɔːn, -'ʒoʊn —Fr
   [di ʒɔ̃]
dik-dik 'dɪk dɪk ~s s
dike daɪk **diked** daɪkt **dikes** daɪks **diking**
   'daɪk ɪŋ
diktat 'dɪkt æt -ɑːt ‖ dɪk 'tɑːt ~s s
dilapi|date dɪ 'læp ɪ |deɪt də-, -ə- ~**dated**
   deɪt ɪd -əd ‖ deɪt̬ əd ~**dates** deɪts ~**dating**
   deɪt ɪŋ ‖ deɪt̬ ɪŋ
dilapidation dɪ ˌlæp ɪ 'deɪʃ ᵊn də-, -ə- ~s z
dilatation ˌdaɪl eɪ 'teɪʃ ᵊn ˌdɪl-, -ə- ~s z

di|late daɪ '|leɪt dɪ-, də- ‖ 'daɪ |leɪt **~lated**
leɪt ɪd -əd ‖ leɪt̬ əd **~lates** leɪts **~lating**
leɪt ɪŋ ‖ leɪt̬ ɪŋ

dilation daɪ 'leɪʃ ᵊn dɪ-, də- **~s** z

dilator daɪ 'leɪt ə dɪ-, də- ‖ -'leɪt̬ ᵊr 'daɪ leɪt̬ ᵊr
~s z

dilator|y 'dɪl ət̬ ᵊr |i ‖ -ə tɔːr |i -tour i **~ily** əl i
ɪ li **~iness** i nəs i nɪs

Dilbert 'dɪl bət -bɜːt ‖ -bᵊrt

dildo, dildoe 'dɪld əʊ ‖ -oʊ **~s** z

dildonics dɪl 'dɒn ɪks ‖ -'dɑːn-

dilemma dɪ 'lem ə daɪ-, də- **~s** z

dilet|tante ˌdɪl ə |'tænt i -ɪ- ‖ -|'tɑːnt '···
~tantes 'tænt iz ‖ 'tɑːnts **~tanti** 'tænt iː
‖ -'tɑːnt̬ i

dilettantism ˌdɪl ə 'tænt ˌɪz əm -ɪ- ‖ -'tɑːnt-
'····

Dilhorne 'dɪl ən -ɔːn ‖ -ᵊrn -hɔːrn

Dili, Díli 'diːl i

diligenc|e 'dɪl ɪdʒ ən{s -ədʒ- **~es** ɪz əz

diligent 'dɪl ɪdʒ ənt -ədʒ- **~ly** li

Dilke dɪlk

dill, Dill dɪl
 ˌdill 'pickle

Diller 'dɪl ə ‖ -ᵊr

dilli... —*see* **dilly**

Dillinger 'dɪl ɪndʒ ə ‖ -ᵊr

Dillon 'dɪl ən

Dillwyn 'dɪl wɪn -ɪn

dill|y, Dilly 'dɪl |i **~ies** iz
 ˈdilly bag

dilly-dall|y 'dɪl i ˌdæl |i ˌ·'·· **~ied** id **~ies** iz
~ying i ɪŋ

diluent 'dɪl ju ənt **~s** s

di|lute *v, adj* ⁽ˌ⁾daɪ |'luːt dɪ-, də-, -'ljuːt **~luted**
'luːt ɪd 'ljuːt-, -əd ‖ 'luːt̬ əd **~lutes** 'luːts '
ljuːts **~luting** 'lut ɪŋ 'ljuːt- ‖ 'luːt̬ ɪŋ

dilution ⁽ˌ⁾daɪ 'luːʃ ᵊn dɪ-, də-, -'ljuːʃ- **~s** z

diluvi|al daɪ 'luːv i ˌ|əl dɪ-, də-, -'ljuːv- **~an** ən
~um əm

Dilworth 'dɪl wɜːθ -wəθ ‖ -wᵊrθ

Dilwyn 'dɪl wɪn

Dilys 'dɪl ɪs §-əs

dim dɪm **dimmed** dɪmd **dimmer** 'dɪm ə ‖ -ᵊr
dimmest 'dɪm ɪst §-əst **dimming** 'dɪm ɪŋ
dims dɪmz —*See also phrases with this word*

DiMaggio dɪ 'mædʒ i əʊ ‖ -oʊ ·'·oʊ

Dimbleby 'dɪm bᵊl bi

dime daɪm **dimes** daɪmz

dimension daɪ 'men⌐ʃ ᵊn dɪ-, də- ‖ də- **~ed** d
~ing ɪŋ **~s** z

dimensional daɪ 'men⌐ʃ ᵊn ᵊl dɪ-, də- ‖ də- **~ly**
i

dimensionality daɪ ˌmen⌐ʃ ə 'næl ət i dɪ-, də-,
-ɪt i ‖ də ˌmen⌐ʃ ə 'næl ət̬ i

Diment 'daɪm ənt

dimer 'daɪm ə 'daɪ mɜː ‖ -ᵊr **~s** z

dimercaprol ˌdaɪ mɜː 'kæp rɒl -mə-
‖ -mᵊr 'kæp roʊl -rɑːl, -rɔːl

dimerism 'dɪm ər ˌɪz əm

dimerous 'dɪm ər əs

dimeter 'dɪm ɪt ə -ət- ‖ -ət̬ ᵊr **~s** z

diminish dɪ 'mɪn ɪʃ də- **~ed** t **~es** ɪz əz **~ing** ɪŋ
~ment mənt
 diˌminished reˌsponsi'bility; diˌminishing
 re'turns

diminuendo dɪ ˌmɪn ju 'end əʊ də- ‖ -oʊ **~es,
~s** z

diminution ˌdɪm ɪ 'njuːʃ ᵊn -ə-, △-ju- ‖ -'nuːʃ-
-'njuːʃ- **~s** z

diminutive dɪ 'mɪn jut ɪv də-, -jət- ‖ -jət̬ ɪv **~ly**
li **~ness** nəs nɪs **~s** z

dimit|y, D~ 'dɪm ət |i -ɪt- ‖ -ət̬ |i **~ies** iz

dimly 'dɪm li

dimmer 'dɪm ə ‖ -ᵊr **~s** z
 'dimmer switch

dimmish 'dɪm ɪʃ

Dimmock 'dɪm ək

dimness 'dɪm nəs -nɪs

dimorph|ism ⁽ˌ⁾daɪ 'mɔːf |ˌɪz əm ‖ -'mɔːrf-
~ous əs

dimout 'dɪm aʊt **~s** s

dimpl|e 'dɪmp ᵊl **~ed** d **~es** z **~ing** ɪŋ

Dimplex *tdmk* 'dɪmp leks

dimply 'dɪmp li

dim sum ˌdɪm 'sʌm -'sum —*Cantonese*
[²dim ¹sɐm]

dimwit 'dɪm wɪt **~s** s

dim-witted ˌdɪm 'wɪt ɪd ◄ -əd ‖ -'wɪt̬ əd ◄ **~ly**
li **~ness** nəs nɪs

din, DIN dɪn **dinned** dɪnd **dinning** 'dɪn ɪŋ
dins dɪnz

Dina *(i)* 'diːn ə, *(ii)* 'daɪn-

Dinah 'daɪn ə

dinar 'diːn ɑː ‖ dɪ 'nɑːr 'diːn ɑːr **~s** z

Dinaric dɪ 'nær ɪk də-, daɪ- ‖ -'ner-
 Diˌnaric 'Alps

Dinas 'diːn æs

din-din 'dɪn dɪn **~s** z

dine daɪn **dined** daɪnd **dines** daɪnz **dining**
'daɪn ɪŋ

Dineen dɪ 'niːn də-

Dinefwr dɪ 'nev ʊə ‖ -ʊr

diner 'daɪn ə ‖ -ᵊr **~s** z

dinero di 'neər əʊ ‖ -'ner oʊ

Dinesen 'dɪn ɪs ən 'diːn-, -əs-, -ɪn

dinette ⁽ˌ⁾daɪ 'net **~s** s

ding dɪŋ **dinged** dɪŋd **dinging** 'dɪŋ ɪŋ **dings**
dɪŋz —*See also phrases with this word*

Dingaan 'dɪŋ gɑːn

dingaling ˌdɪŋ ə 'lɪŋ '··· **~s** z

Ding an sich ˌdɪŋ æn 'sɪk -'sɪx ‖ -ɑːn 'zɪk
—*Ger* [ˌdɪŋ an 'zɪç]

dingbat 'dɪŋ bæt **~s** s

dingdong 'dɪŋ dɒŋ ˌ·'·◄ ‖ -dɔːŋ -dɑːŋ **~s** z

dinge dɪndʒ **dinges** 'dɪndʒ ɪz -əz

dinger 'dɪŋ ə ‖ -ᵊr **~s** z

dingh|y 'dɪŋ |i -g|i **~ies** iz

dingi... —*see* **dingy**

dingle, D~ 'dɪŋ gᵊl **~s** z

Dingley 'dɪŋ li

dingo 'dɪŋ gəʊ ‖ -goʊ **~es** z

dingus 'dɪŋ əs -gəs **~es** ɪz əz

Dingwall 'dɪŋ wɔːl -wəl ‖ -wɑːl

ding|y 'dɪndʒ |i ~ier i ə ‖ i ᵊr ~iest i ɪst i əst
~ily ɪ li əl i ~iness i nəs i nɪs

dining 'daɪn ɪŋ
'dining car; 'dining room; 'dining ˌtable

dink dɪŋk **dinks** dɪŋks

Dinka 'dɪŋk ə ~s z

dinki... —see **dinky**

Dinkins 'dɪŋk ɪnz §-ənz ‖ 'dɪn kɪnz

dinkum 'dɪŋk əm

dink|y 'dɪŋk |i ~ier i ə ‖ i ᵊr ~ies iz ~iest i ɪst
i əst

dinner 'dɪn ə ‖ -ᵊr ~s z
'dinner bell; 'dinner ˌjacket; 'dinner
ˌparty; 'dinner plate; 'dinner ˌservice;
'dinner set; 'dinner ˌtable

dinnertime 'dɪn ə taɪm ‖ -ᵊr- ~s z

dinoflagellate ˌdaɪn əʊ 'flædʒ ə leɪt -'ˌɪ-;
-əl ət, -ɪt ‖ ˌ-oʊ- ~s s

Dinorwic dɪ 'nɔː wɪk də- ‖ -'nɔːr-

dinosaur 'daɪn ə sɔː ‖ -sɔːr ~s z

dinosaurian ˌdaɪn ə 'sɔːr i ən ◂ ~s z

dinothere 'daɪn əʊ θɪə ‖ -ə θɪr ~s z

Dinsdale 'dɪnz deɪᵊl

dint dɪnt

Dinwiddie, Dinwiddy (i) dɪn 'wɪd i,
(ii) 'dɪn wɪd i

Dio 'daɪ əʊ ‖ -oʊ

diocesan daɪ 'ɒs ɪs ən -əs-, -ɪz-, -əz- ‖ -'ɑːs- ~s
z

di|ocese 'daɪ |əs ɪs §-əs; ə siːz, -siːs ~oceses
ə siːz əs ɪs ɪz, -əz; ə siːz ɪz, ə siːs ɪz, -əz

Diocletian ˌdaɪ ə 'kliːʃ ᵊn -'kliːʃ i ən

diode 'daɪ əʊd ‖ -oʊd ~s z

Diodorus ˌdaɪ ə 'dɔːr əs ‖ -'doʊr-
ˌDioˌdorus 'Siculus 'sɪk jʊl əs ‖ -jəl əs

dioecious daɪ 'iːʃ əs ~ly li

Diogenes daɪ 'ɒdʒ ə niːz -ɪ- ‖ -'ɑːdʒ-

Diomede 'daɪ ə miːd

Diomedes ˌdaɪ ə 'miːd iːz

Dion modern name di 'ɒn 'diː ən -ɒn ‖ di 'oʊn
—Fr [djɔ̃]

Dion classical name 'daɪ ən

Dione daɪ 'əʊn i ‖ -'oʊn i

Dionne ˌdiː 'ɒn di- ‖ -'ɑːn

Dionysia ˌdaɪ ə 'nɪz i ə -'nɪs- ‖ -'nɪʃ-

Dionysiac ˌdaɪ ə 'nɪz i æk ◂ -'nɪs- ‖ -'nɪʃ-

Dionysian ˌdaɪ ə 'nɪz i ən ◂ -'nɪs-, -'naɪs-
‖ -'nɪʃ ᵊn -'naɪs i ən ~s z

Dionysius ˌdaɪ ə 'nɪz i əs -'nɪs- ‖ -'nɪʃ- (*)

Dionysus ˌdaɪ ə 'naɪs əs -'niːs-

Diophantine ˌdaɪ əʊ 'fænt aɪn ◂ -ə- -ᵊn

Diophantus ˌdaɪ əʊ 'fænt əs ‖ -ə 'fænt̬ əs

diopside daɪ 'ɒps aɪd ‖ -'ɑːps-

dioptase daɪ 'ɒpt eɪz -eɪs ‖ -'ɑːpt-

diopter, dioptre daɪ 'ɒpt ə ‖ -'ɑːpt ᵊr ~s z

Dior 'diː ɔː ˑˈˑ ‖ di 'ɔːr —Fr [djɔːʁ]

diorama ˌdaɪ ə 'rɑːm ə ‖ -'ræm ə -'rɑːm ə

dioramic ˌdaɪ ə 'ræm ɪk ◂

diorite 'daɪ ə raɪt

Dioscuri daɪ 'ɒsk jʊr i -aɪ; ˌdaɪ ə 'skjʊər-, -ɒ-
‖ ˌdaɪ ə 'skjʊr aɪ

diotic daɪ 'əʊt ɪk -'ɒt- ‖ -'oʊt̬ ɪk -'ɑːt̬- ~ally ᵊl i

dioxide ˌ(ˌ)daɪ 'ɒks aɪd ‖ -'ɑːks- ~s z

dioxin daɪ 'ɒks ɪn §-ᵊn ‖ -'ɑːks-

dip, DIP dɪp **dipped** dɪpt **dipping** 'dɪp ɪŋ **dips**
dɪps
'DIP switch

diphenylamine ˌdaɪ ˌfiːn arᵊl 'æm iːn -ˌfen-,
-ᵊl-, -ɪn, -ən, -ə 'miːn ‖ daɪ ˌfen ᵊl ə 'miːn
-'æm ən

diphone 'daɪ fəʊn ‖ -foʊn ~s z

diphtheria dɪf 'θɪər i ə dɪp- ‖ -'θɪr-

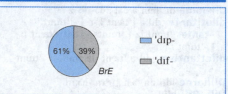

61% 39%

☐ 'dɪp-

☐ 'dɪf-

BrE

diphthong 'dɪf θɒŋ 'dɪp- ‖ -θɔːŋ -θɑːŋ —
Preference poll, BrE: 'dɪf- 39%, 'dɪp- 61%.
Phoneticians, however, prefer 'dɪf-. *Native
speakers of English do not say* -tɒŋ ‖ -tɔːŋ.
~ed d ~ing ɪŋ ~s z

diphthongal ˌ(ˌ)dɪf 'θɒŋ gᵊl ˌ(ˌ)dɪp- ‖ -'θɔːŋ-
-'θɑːŋ- ~ly i

diphthongis... —see **diphthongiz...**

diphthongization ˌdɪf θɒŋ gaɪ 'zeɪʃ ᵊn ˌdɪp-,
-aɪ'--, -gɪ'--, -ɪ'-- ‖ -θɔːŋ ə- -θɑːŋ ə-, -gə'-- ~s z

diphthongiz|e 'dɪf θɒŋ gaɪz 'dɪp-, -aɪz
‖ -θɔːŋ aɪz -θɑːŋ-, -gaɪz ~ed d ~es ɪz əz ~ing
ɪŋ

diplo- comb. form
with stress-neutral suffix ˌdɪp ləʊ ‖ -lə
— **diplocardiac** ˌdɪp ləʊ 'kɑːd i æk ◂
‖ -lə 'kɑːrd-

Diplock 'dɪp lɒk ‖ -lɑːk

diplodocus dɪ 'plɒd ək əs daɪ-;
ˌdɪp ləʊ 'dəʊk əs ‖ -'plɑːd- ~es ɪz əz

diploid 'dɪp lɔɪd ~s z

diploma dɪ 'pləʊm ə də- ‖ -'ploʊm ə ~s z

diplomac|y dɪ 'pləʊm əs |i də- ‖ -'ploʊm- ~ies
iz

diplomat 'dɪp lə mæt ~s s

diplomate 'dɪp lə meɪt ~s s

diplomatic ˌdɪp lə 'mæt ɪk ◂ ‖ -'mæt̬ ɪk ◂
~ally ᵊl i
ˌdiplo·matic 'bag; ˌdiplo'matic corps;
ˌdiplo·matic im'munity

diplomatist dɪ 'pləʊm ət ɪst də-, §-əst ‖ -ət̬- ~s
s

diplophonia ˌdɪp ləʊ 'fəʊn i ə ‖ -lə 'foʊn-

diplosis dɪ 'pləʊs ɪs §də-, §-əs ‖ -'ploʊs-

dipole 'daɪ pəʊl →-pɒʊl ‖ -poʊl ~s z

dipp.. —see **dip**

dipper, D~ 'dɪp ə ‖ -ᵊr ~s z

dipp|y 'dɪp |i ~ier i ə ‖ i ᵊr ~iest i ɪst i əst

dipshit 'dɪp ʃɪt

dipsomania ˌdɪps əʊ 'meɪn i ə ‖ ˌ-ə-

dipsomaniac ˌdɪps əʊ 'meɪn i æk ‖ ˌ-ə- ~s s

dipstick 'dɪp stɪk ~s s

dipswitch 'dɪp swɪtʃ ~es ɪz əz

Dipsy 'dɪps i

D

Diphthongs

1 A **diphthong** is a complex vowel: a sequence of two vowel qualities within a single syllable. Compare **monophthong**, a vowel whose quality remains constant (as is the case with most vowels).

2 Several English vowel phonemes are diphthongal. The aɪ of **time** taɪm, for example, involves a movement of the tongue from a starting-point a towards an endpoint ɪ.

3 Ordinary diphthongs are **diminuendo** (or **falling**), in that the prominence decreases as we pass from the first element to the second. The a part of aɪ is more prominent than the ɪ part. Compare sequences such as the je in **yes** jes, which is a kind of **crescendo** (**rising**) diphthong (see also COMPRESSION).

4 In English, the distinction between diphthong and monophthong is not always clear-cut. For example, some speakers pronounce eə as a monophthong, ɛː. In some positions iː and uː may be somewhat diphthongal, ɪi, ʊu.

D

---

dipter|al 'dɪpt ər əl **~an** ən **~ous** əs
diptych 'dɪp tɪk **~s** s
Dirac dɪ 'ræk də-; 'dɪr æk
dire 'daɪ‿ə ‖ 'daɪ‿ᵊr **direr** 'daɪ‿ər ə ‖ 'daɪ‿ᵊr ər
  direst 'daɪ‿ər ɪst -əst ‖ 'daɪ‿ᵊr əst

DIRECT

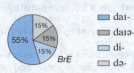
```
        22%
   78%
        AmE
```
🟦 də-
🟦 daɪ-

direct *v, adj, adv* ₍ᵢ₎**daɪᵊ 'rekt** də-, dɪ- ‖ də- daɪ-
  ~ed ɪd əd **~ing** ɪŋ **~s** s —*In the case of* direct, *the stress-shifted form* ˌdaɪᵊ rekt *is frequent in BrE in phrases such as* ˌdirect 'debit; *but the weak-vowelled variant is also heard,* də 'rekt, dɪ-, *with no stress shift, thus* dɪˌrect 'debit.
  — *Preference poll, AmE:* də- 78%, daɪ- 22%.
  ˌdirect 'debit, ·ˌ--; ˌdirect 'method, ·ˌ--;
  ˌdirect 'object, ·ˌ--; ˌdirect 'speech, ·ˌ--;
  ˌdirect 'tax, ·ˌ-
direction daɪᵊ 'rek ʃᵊn də-, dɪ- ‖ də- daɪ- **~s** z
  — *Preference poll, BrE:* daɪ- 55%, daɪə- 15%,
  dɪ- 15%, də- 15%
directional daɪᵊ 'rek ʃᵊn‿əl də-, dɪ- ‖ də- daɪ-
  ~ly i
directionality daɪᵊ ˌrek ʃə 'næl ət i də-, dɪ-,
  -ɪt i; ˌdaɪᵊ·'-- ‖ də ˌrek ʃə 'næl ət̬ i daɪ-
directionless daɪᵊ'rek ʃᵊn ləs də-, dɪ-, -lɪs ‖ də-
  daɪ- **~ly** li
directive daɪᵊ 'rekt ɪv də-, dɪ- ‖ də- daɪ- **~s** z
direct|ly daɪᵊ'rekt |li də-, dɪ- ‖ də- daɪ- —*In the senses 'immediately, as soon as' there is*

also a casual form 'drek li, *becoming old-fashioned* **~ness** nəs nɪs
Directoire, d~ ˌdɪr ek 'twɑː ˌdɪər-, ˌdiː rek-;
  də 'rekt wɑː, dɪ-, daɪᵊ- ‖ ˌdiː rek 'twɑɪr —*Fr*
  [di ʁɛk twaːʁ]
director daɪᵊ 'rekt ə də-, dɪ- ‖ də 'rekt ᵊr daɪ-
  ~s z
directorate daɪᵊ 'rekt ər‿ət də-, dɪ-, ‿ɪt ‖ də-
  daɪ- **~s** s
directorial ˌdaɪᵊr ek 'tɔːr i‿əl ◂ də ˌrek-, dɪ-
  ‖ -'toʊr-
directorship daɪᵊ 'rekt ə ʃɪp də-, dɪ-
  ‖ də 'rekt ᵊr- daɪ- **~s** s
director|y daɪᵊ 'rekt ər |i də-, dɪ- ‖ də- daɪ-
  ~ies iz
directrix daɪᵊ 'rek trɪks də-, dɪ-
direct-to-consumer
  daɪᵊˌrekt tə kən 'sjuːm ə ◂ də-, dɪ-, §-kɒn'--,
  -'suːm-, §-'ʃuːm- ‖ də ˌrekt tə kən 'suːmᵊr ◂
  daɪ-
direful 'daɪ‿ə fᵊl -fʊl ‖ 'daɪ‿ᵊr- **~ly** i **~ness** nəs
  nɪs
dire|ly 'daɪ‿ə |li ‖ 'daɪ‿ᵊr |li **~ness** nəs nɪs
dirge dɜːdʒ ‖ dɜːdʒ **dirges** 'dɜːdʒ ɪz -əz
  ‖ 'dɜːdʒ-
dirham 'dɪər æm 'dɪr-, -əm ‖ də 'ræm **~s** z

DIRECTION

```
        15%
   55%   15%
        15%
        BrE
```
🟦 daɪ-
⬜ daɪə-
🟦 di-
⬜ də-

D

dirigible 'dır ıdʒ əb ᵊl '‧ədʒ-, -ıb ᵊl; də 'rıdʒ-, dı- ~s z

dirigisme 'dır ı ˌʒız əm -ə- —*Fr* [di ʁi ʒism]

dirigiste ˌdır ı 'ʒiːst ◂ -ə-, 'dır ıʒ ıst, -əst —*Fr* [di ʁi ʒist] ~s s —*or as sing.*

diriment 'dır ım ənt -əm-

dirk, Dirk dɜːk ‖ dɜːk **dirks, Dirk's** dɜːks ‖ dɜːks

dirndl 'dɜːnd ᵊl ‖ 'dɜːnd- ~s z

dirt dɜːt ‖ dɜːt
   ˌdirt 'cheap; 'dirt ˌfarmer; ˌdirt 'road, '‧ ‧; 'dirt track

dirtbag 'dɜːt bæg ‖ 'dɜːt- ~s z

dirt-disher 'dɜːt ˌdıʃ ə ‖ 'dɜːt ˌdıʃ ᵊr ~s z

dirt|y 'dɜːt |i ‖ 'dɜːt |i ~ied id ~ier i ə ‖ i ᵊr ~ies iz ~iest i ıst i əst ~ily ı li əl i ~iness i nəs i nıs ~ying i ıŋ
   ˌdirty old 'man; ˌdirty 'trick; ˌdirty 'word; 'dirty work

Dis dıs

dis dıs **dissed** dıst **disses** 'dıs ız -əz **dissing** 'dıs ıŋ

dis- (¦) dıs —*Stressed when followed by an unstressed syllable, and often even when not:* ˌdisaf'firm, (ˌ)dis'relish.

disabilit|y ˌdıs ə 'bıl ət |i -ıt i ‖ -əţ |i ~ies iz

disabl|e dıs 'eıb ᵊl §dız- ~ed d ~ement mənt ~es z ~ing ıŋ

disabus|e ˌdıs ə 'bjuːz ~ed d ~es ız əz ~ing ıŋ

disadvantag|e ˌdıs əd 'vɑːnt ıdʒ §-æd-, §-'vænt- ‖ -'vænţ- ~ed d ~es ız əz ~ing ıŋ

disadvantageous ˌdıs ˌæd vən 'teıdʒ əs ‧,‧-, -væn'‧-, -vɑːn'‧- ~ly li ~ness nəs nıs

disaffected ˌdıs ə 'fekt ıd -əd ~ly li

disaffection ˌdıs ə 'fek ʃᵊn

disaffili|ate ˌdıs ə 'fıl i |eıt ~ated eıt ıd -əd ‖ eıţ əd ~ates eıts ~ating eıt ıŋ ‖ eıţ ıŋ

disaffiliation ˌdıs ə ˌfıl i 'eıʃ ᵊn ~s z

disafforest ˌdıs ə 'fɒr ıst -əst ‖ -'fɔːr- -'fɑːr- ~ed ıd əd ~ing ıŋ ~s s

disafforestation ˌdıs ə ˌfɒr ı 'steıʃ ᵊn -ə'‧- ‖ -ˌfɔːr- -ˌfɑːr- ~s z

disagree ˌdıs ə 'griː —*Often with contrastive stress:* Do you agree or 'dıs ə ˌgriː ? ~d d ~ing ıŋ ~s z

disagreeab|le ˌdıs ə 'griː əb |ᵊl ◂ ~ly li

disagreement ˌdıs ə 'griː mənt ~s s

disallow ˌdıs ə 'laʊ ~ed d ~ing ıŋ ~s z

disambigu|ate ˌdıs æm 'bıg ju |eıt ~ated eıt ıd -əd ‖ eıţ əd ~ates eıts ~ating eıt ıŋ ‖ eıţ ıŋ

disambiguation ˌdıs æm ˌbıg ju 'eıʃ ᵊn ~s z

disappear ˌdıs ə 'pıə ‖ -'pıᵊr ~ed d
   disappearing ˌdıs ə 'pıər ıŋ ‖ -'pır ıŋ ~s z

disappearanc|e ˌdıs ə 'pıər ənᵗs ‖ -'pır- ~es ız əz

disap|point ˌdıs ə |'pɔınt ~pointed/ly 'pɔınt ıd /li -əd /li ‖ 'pɔınţ əd /li ~pointing/ly 'pɔınt ıŋ /li ‖ 'pɔınţ ıŋ /li ~points 'pɔınts

disappointment ˌdıs ə 'pɔınt mənt ~s s

disapprobation ˌdıs ˌæp rəʊ 'beıʃ ᵊn ‖ -ə-

disapproval ˌdıs ə 'pruːv ᵊl ~s z

disapprov|e ˌdıs ə 'pruːv ~ed d ~es z ~ing/ly ıŋ /li

disarm dıs 'ɑːm dız- ‖ -'ɑːrm ~ed d ~ing/ly ıŋ /li ~s z

disarmament dıs 'ɑːm ə mənt dız- ‖ -'ɑːrm- ~s s

disarrang|e ˌdıs ə 'reındʒ ~ed d ~ement mənt ~es ız əz ~ing ıŋ

disarray ˌdıs ə 'reı ~ed d ~ing ıŋ ~s z

disassembl|e ˌdıs ə 'sem bᵊl ~ed d ~er/s ə/z ‖ ᵊr/z ~es ız əz ~ing ıŋ

disassoci|ate ˌdıs ə 'səʊʃ i |eıt -'səʊs- ‖ -'soʊʃ- -'soʊs- ~ated eıt ıd -əd ‖ eıţ əd ~ates eıts ~ating eıt ıŋ ‖ eıţ ıŋ

disaster dı 'zɑːst ə də-, §-'zæst- ‖ -'zæst ᵊr ~s z
   di'saster ˌarea

disastrous dı 'zɑːs trəs də-, §-'zæs-, △-'zæst ər əs ‖ -'zæs- ~ly li ~ness nəs nıs

disavow ˌdıs ə 'vaʊ ~ed d ~ing ıŋ ~s z

disavowal ˌdıs ə 'vaʊ əl -'vaʊl ~s z

disband dıs 'bænd ~ed ıd əd ~ing ıŋ ~s z

disbandment dıs 'bænd mənt ~s s

dis|bar dıs |'bɑː ‖ -|'bɑːr ~barred 'bɑːd ‖ 'bɑːrd ~barring 'bɑːr ıŋ ~bars 'bɑːz ‖ 'bɑːrz

disbarment dıs 'bɑː mənt ‖ -'bɑːr- ~s s

disbelief ˌdıs bı 'liːf -bə-

disbeliev|e ˌdıs bı 'liːv -bə- ~ed d ~er/s ə/z ‖ ᵊr/z ~es z ~ing/ly ıŋ /li

disbud (ˌ)dıs 'bʌd ~ded ıd əd ~ding ıŋ ~s z

disburden dıs 'bɜːd ᵊn ‖ -'bɜːd- ~ed d ~ing ıŋ ~s z

disburs|e dıs 'bɜːs ‖ -'bɜːs ~ed t ~es ız əz ~ing ıŋ

disbursement dıs 'bɜːs mənt ‖ -'bɜːs- ~s s

disc dısk **discs** dısks
   'disc ˌbrakes; 'disc ˌharrow; 'disc ˌjockey

discalced dıs 'kælst

discard *v* dıs 'kɑːd ‧- ‖ -'kɑːrd ~ed ıd əd ~ing ıŋ ~s z

discard *n* 'dıs kɑːd ‖ -kɑːrd ~s z

discern dı 'sɜːn də-, -'zɜːn ‖ 'sɜːn -'zɜːn ~ed d ~ing/ly ıŋ /li ~s z

discernib|le dı 'sɜːn əb |ᵊl də-, -'zɜːn-, -ıb- ‖ -'sɜːn- -'zɜːn- ~ly li

discernment dı 'sɜːn mənt də-, -'zɜːn- ‖ -'sɜːn- -'zɜːn-

discharg|e *n* 'dıs tʃɑːdʒ ‧'‧ ‖ -tʃɑːrdʒ ~es ız əz

discharg|e *v* dıs 'tʃɑːdʒ ‧-, '‧ ‧ ‖ -'tʃɑːrdʒ ~ed d ~es ız əz ~ing ıŋ

disci 'dısk aı 'dıs-

disciple dı 'saıp ᵊl də- ~s z ~ship ʃıp

disciplinarian ˌdıs ə plı 'neər i ən ˌ‧ı-, -plə'‧- ‖ -'ner- ~s z

disciplinary 'dıs ə plın ər i '‧ı-, '‧ ‧plən-, ˌ‧ ‧'plın ər i ‖ -plə ner i

disciplin|e *n, v* 'dıs əp lın -ıp-, -lən; §dı 'sıp-, də- ~ed d ~es z ~ing ıŋ

disclaim dıs 'kleım ~ed d ~ing ıŋ ~s z

disclaimer dıs 'kleım ə ‖ -ᵊr ~s z

disclos|e dıs 'kləʊz ‖ -'kloʊz ~ed d ~es ız əz ~ing ıŋ

disclosure dıs 'kləʊʒ ə ‖ -'kloʊʒ ᵊr ~s z

disco ˈdɪsk əʊ ‖ -oʊ ~s z
discob|olus dɪ ˈskɒb |əl əs ‖ -ˈskɑːb- ~oli ə laɪ əl aɪ
discograph|y dɪ ˈskɒɡ rəf |i ‖ -ˈskɑːɡ- ~ies iz
discolor (ˌ)dɪs ˈkʌl ə ‖ -ᵊr ~ed d **discoloring** dɪs ˈkʌl ər ɪŋ ~s z
discoloration dɪs ˌkʌl ə ˈreɪʃ ᵊn ˌˌˌˌ- ~s z
discolour (ˌ)dɪs ˈkʌl ə ‖ -ᵊr ~ed d **discolouring** dɪs ˈkʌl ər ɪŋ ~s z
discombobu|late ˌdɪsk əm ˈbɒb ju |leɪt -jə- ‖ -ˈbɑːb jə- ~lated leɪt ɪd -əd ‖ leɪt̬ əd ~lates leɪts ~lating leɪt ɪŋ ‖ leɪt̬ ɪŋ
discomf|it dɪs ˈkʌmᵖf |ɪt -ət ‖ -|ət ~ited ɪt ɪd §ət-, -əd ‖ ət̬ əd ~iting ɪt ɪŋ §ət- ‖ ət̬ ɪŋ ~its ɪts §əts ‖ əts
discomfiture dɪs ˈkʌmᵖf ɪtʃ ə -ətʃ- ‖ -ᵊr ~s z
discomfort dɪs ˈkʌmᵖf ət ‖ -ᵊrt
discommod|e ˌdɪs kə ˈməʊd ‖ -ˈmoʊd ~ed ɪd əd -es z ~ing ɪŋ
discompos|e ˌdɪs kəm ˈpəʊz §-kɒm- ‖ -ˈpoʊz ~ed d ~es z ~ing/ly ɪŋ /li
discomposure ˌdɪs kəm ˈpəʊʒ ə §-kɒm- ‖ -ˈpoʊʒ ᵊr
discon|cert ˌdɪs kən |ˈsɜːt §-kɒn- ‖ -|ˈsɜːt ~certed ˈsɜːt ɪd -əd ‖ ˈsɜːt̬ əd ~certing/ly ˈsɜːt ɪŋ /li ‖ ˈsɜːt̬ ɪŋ /li ~certs ˈsɜːts ‖ ˈsɜːts
disconfirm ˌdɪs kən ˈfɜːm §-kɒn- ‖ -ˈfɜːm ~ed d ~ing ɪŋ ~s z
disconformit|y ˌdɪs kən ˈfɔːm ət |i §ˌ·kɒn-, -ɪt i ‖ -ˈfɔːrm ət̬ |i ~ies iz
disconnect v ˌdɪs kə ˈnekt ~ed/ly ɪd /li əd /li ~ing ɪŋ ~s s
disconnect n ˌdɪs kə ˈnekt ˈ·ˌ·
disconnection, disconnexion ˌdɪs kə ˈnek ʃᵊn ~s z
disconsolate dɪs ˈkɒnˢ əl ət -ɪt ‖ -ˈkɑːnˢ- ~ly li ~ness nəs nɪs
discon|tent ˌdɪs kən |ˈtent §-kɒn- ~tented ˈtent ɪd -əd ‖ ˈtent̬ əd ~tenting ˈtent ɪŋ ‖ ˈtent̬ ɪŋ ~tents ˈtents
discontented ˌdɪs kən ˈtent ɪd -əd ‖ -ˈtent̬ əd ~ly li ~ness nəs nɪs
discontinuance ˌdɪs kən ˈtɪn ju ᵊnˢ §ˌ·kɒn-
discontinuation ˌdɪs kən ˌtɪn ju ˈeɪʃ ᵊn §ˌ·kɒn-
discontinu|e ˌdɪs kən ˈtɪn juː §-kɒn-, -ju ~ed d ~es z ~ing ɪŋ
discontinuit|y ˌdɪs ˌkɒnt ɪ ˈnjuː ət |i -əˈ·ˌ·, ɪt i ‖ ˌdɪs ˌkɑːnt ᵊn ˈuː ət̬ |i -ˈjuː- ~ies iz
discontinuous ˌdɪs kən ˈtɪn ju əs ◄ §ˌ·kɒn- ~ly li ~ness nəs nɪs
discord n ˈdɪs kɔːd ‖ -kɔːrd ~s z
discordanc|e dɪs ˈkɔːd ᵊnˢ ‖ -ˈkɔːrd ᵊnˢ ~es ɪz əz
discordant dɪs ˈkɔːd ᵊnt ‖ -ˈkɔːrd ᵊnt ~ly li
discotheque ˈdɪsk ə tek ˌ·ˈˌ· ~s s
dis|count v ˈdɪs |kaʊnt ·ˈ· — *Preference poll, AmE:* ˈ·· 82%, ·ˈ· 18%. **~counted** kaʊnt ɪd -əd ‖ kaʊnt̬ əd **~counting** kaʊnt ɪŋ ‖ kaʊnt̬ ɪŋ **~counts** kaʊnts

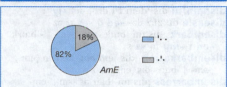

DISCOUNT (verb)
18%
82%
AmE
■ ˈ··
■ ·ˈ·

discount n ˈdɪs kaʊnt ~s s
ˈdiscount house; ˈdiscount store
discountenanc|e dɪs ˈkaʊnt ɪn ənˢ -ən- ‖ -ˈkaʊnt ᵊn- ~ed t ~es ɪz əz ~ing ɪŋ
discounter ˈdɪs kaʊnt ə ‖ -kaʊnt̬ ᵊr ~s z
discourag|e dɪs ˈkʌr ɪdʒ ‖ -ˈkɜː- ~ed d ~es ɪz əz ~ing/ly ɪŋ /li
discouragement dɪs ˈkʌr ɪdʒ mənt ‖ -ˈkɜː- ~s s
discours|e v dɪs ˈkɔːs ‖ -ˈkɔːrs -ˈkoʊrs ~ed t ~es ɪz əz ~ing ɪŋ
discours|e n ˈdɪs kɔːs ·ˈ· ‖ -kɔːrs -koʊrs ~es ɪz əz
discourteous dɪs ˈkɜːt i əs ‖ -ˈkɜːt̬- ~ly li ~ness nəs nɪs
discourtes|y dɪs ˈkɜːt əs |i -ɪ- ‖ -ˈkɜːt̬- ~ies iz
discover dɪ ˈskʌv ə də- ‖ -ᵊr ~ed d **discovering** dɪ ˈskʌv ər ɪŋ ~s z
discoverable dɪ ˈskʌv ᵊr əb ᵊl
discoverer dɪ ˈskʌv ᵊr ə də- ‖ -ᵊr ᵊr ~s z
discover|y dɪ ˈskʌv ᵊr |i də- ~ies iz
discred|it v, n (ˌ)dɪs ˈkred |ɪt §-ət ‖ -|ət ~ited ɪt ɪd §ət-, -əd ‖ ət̬ əd ~iting ɪt ɪŋ §ət- ‖ ət̬ ɪŋ ~its ɪts §əts ‖ əts
discreditab|le (ˌ)dɪs ˈkred ɪt əb |ᵊl §-ət əb- ‖ -ət̬ əb- ~ly li
discreet dɪ ˈskriːt də- ~ly li ~ness nəs nɪs
discrepanc|y dɪs ˈkrep ᵊnˢ |i ~ies iz
discrepant dɪs ˈkrep ᵊnt ~ly li
discrete dɪ ˈskriːt ˌdɪs ˈkriːt ◄ *(usually =* discreet*)* ~ly li ~ness nəs nɪs
discretion dɪ ˈskreʃ ᵊn
discretionar|y dɪ ˈskreʃ ᵊn ᵊr ˌ|i ᵊn ᵊr |i ‖ -ə ner |i -ily əl ɪ i li
discriminant dɪ ˈskrɪm ɪn ənt də-, -ən ᵊnt ~s s
discrimi|nate dɪ ˈskrɪm ɪ |neɪt də-, -ə- ~nated neɪt ɪd -əd ‖ neɪt̬ əd ~nates neɪts ~nating neɪt ɪŋ ‖ neɪt̬ ɪŋ
discrimination dɪ ˌskrɪm ɪ ˈneɪʃ ᵊn də-, -ə- ~s z
discriminative dɪ ˈskrɪm ɪn ət ɪv də-, -ən ət-; -ɪ neɪt ɪv, -ə- ·· ‖ -ə neɪt̬ ɪv -ən ət̬ ɪv ~ly li
discriminator dɪ ˈskrɪm ɪ neɪt ə də-, -ˈ·ə- ‖ -neɪt̬ ᵊr ~s z
discriminator|y dɪ ˈskrɪm ɪn ət ᵊr |i də-, -ˈ·ən-; ˌskrɪm ɪ ˈneɪt ər |i, -ˌ·ə- ‖ -ə tɔːr |i -tour i ~ily əl ɪ i li
discursive dɪs ˈkɜːs ɪv ‖ -ˈkɜːs- ~ly li ~ness nəs nɪs
discus ˈdɪsk əs **disci** ˈdɪsk aɪ ˈdɪs aɪ ~es ɪz əz
discuss dɪ ˈskʌs də- ~ed t ~es ɪz əz ~ing ɪŋ
discussable dɪ ˈskʌs əb ᵊl
discussant dɪ ˈskʌs ᵊnt də- ~s s

D

D

discussion dɪ 'skʌʃ ᵊn də- ~s z
disdain *n, v* dɪs 'deɪn dɪz- ~ed d ~ing ɪŋ ~s z
disdainful dɪs 'deɪn fᵊl dɪz-, -fʊl ~ly ˌi
diseas|e dɪ 'ziːz də- ~ed d ~es ɪz əz
disembark ˌdɪs ɪm 'bɑːk -əm-, -em- ‖ -'bɑːrk ~ed t ~ing ɪŋ ~s s
disembarkation ˌdɪs ˌem bɑː 'keɪʃ ᵊn ˌɪm-, ˌəm- ‖ -bɑːr- dɪs ˌem- ~s z
disembarrass ˌdɪs ɪm 'bær əs -əm-, -em- ‖ -'ber- ~ed t ~es ɪz əz ~ing ɪŋ ~ment mənt
disembod|y ˌdɪs ɪm 'bɒd |i -əm-, -em- ‖ -'bɑːd |i ~ied ɪd ~ies iz ~iment i mənt ~ying i ɪŋ
disembogu|e ˌdɪs ɪm 'bəʊg -əm-, -em- ‖ -'boʊg ~ed d ~es z ~ing ɪŋ
disembowel ˌdɪs ɪm 'baʊ əl ᵊm-, -em-, ˌ· ·'baʊl ‖ -'baʊ əl ~ed, ~led d ~ing, ~ling ɪŋ ~ment mənt ~s z
disembroil ˌdɪs ɪm 'brɔɪᵊl -əm-, -em- ~ed d ~ing ɪŋ ~s z
disen|chant ˌdɪs ɪn |'tʃɑːnt -ən, -en-, §-|'tʃænt ‖ -|'tʃænt ~chanted 'tʃɑːnt ɪd §'tʃænt-, -əd ‖ 'tʃænt̬ əd ~chanting 'tʃɑːnt ɪŋ §'tʃænt- ‖ 'tʃænt̬ ɪŋ ~chants 'tʃɑːnts §'tʃænts ‖ 'tʃænts
disencum|ber ˌdɪs ɪn 'kʌm |bə →-ɪŋ-, -ən-, -en- ‖ -|bᵊr ~bered bəd ‖ bᵊrd ~bering bər ɪŋ ~bers bəz ‖ bᵊrz
disendow ˌdɪs ɪn 'daʊ -ən-, -en- ~ed d ~ing ɪŋ ~ment mənt ~s z
disenfranchis|e ˌdɪs ɪn 'fræntʃ aɪz -ən-, -en- ~ed d ~ement mənt ~es ɪz əz ~ing ɪŋ
disengag|e ˌdɪs ɪn 'geɪdʒ -ən-, -en- ~ed d ~ement mənt ~es ɪz əz ~ing ɪŋ
disentangl|e ˌdɪs ɪn 'tæŋ gᵊl -ən-, -en- ~ed d ~ement mənt ~es z ~ing ɪŋ
disequilibrium ˌdɪs ˌiːk wɪ 'lɪb ri əm -ˌek-, -wə'·- ‖ dɪs ˌek-
disestablish ˌdɪs ɪ 'stæb lɪʃ -ə-, -e- ~ed t ~es ɪz əz ~ing ɪŋ ~ment mənt
disestablishmentarian ˌdɪs ɪ ˌstæb lɪʃ mən 'teər i ən ˌ·ə-, ˌ·e- ‖ -'ter- ~s z
disfav|or, disfav|our ⑴dɪs 'feɪv |ə ‖ -|ᵊr ~ored, ~oured əd ‖ ᵊrd ~oring, ~ouring ər ɪŋ ~ors, ~ours əz ‖ ᵊrz
disfig|ure dɪs 'fɪg |ə ‖ -|jᵊr *(*)* ~ured əd ‖ jᵊrd ~ures əz ‖ jᵊrz ~uring ər ɪŋ ‖ jər ɪŋ
disfigurement dɪs 'fɪg ə mənt ‖ -jᵊr- ~s z
disforest ⑴dɪs 'fɒr ɪst -əst ‖ -'fɔːr- -'fɑːr- ~ed ɪd əd ~ing ɪŋ ~s s
disforestation ˌdɪs ˌfɒr ɪ 'steɪʃ ᵊn ·ˌ·-, -ə- ‖ dɪs ˌfɔːr- -ˌfɑːr-
disfranchis|e dɪs 'fræntʃ aɪz ~ed d ~es ɪz əz ~ing ɪŋ
disfranchisement dɪs 'fræntʃ ɪz mənt -əz-, -aɪz- ~s s
disfrock ˌdɪs 'frɒk ‖ -'frɑːk ~ed t ~ing ɪŋ ~s s
disgorg|e dɪs 'gɔːdʒ ‖ -'gɔːrdʒ ~ed d ~es ɪz əz ~ing ɪŋ
disgrac|e *v, n* dɪs 'greɪs dɪz-, dəs- ~ed t ~es ɪz əz ~ing ɪŋ
disgraceful dɪs 'greɪs fᵊl dɪz-, dəs-, -fʊl ~ly ˌi
disgruntled dɪs 'grʌnt ᵊld ‖ -'grʌnt̬-

disgruntlement dɪs 'grʌnt ᵊl mənt ‖ -'grʌnt̬-
disguis|e *v, n* dɪs 'gaɪz dɪz-, dəs- ~ed d ~er/s ə/z ‖ ᵊr/z ~es ɪz əz ~ing ɪŋ
disgust *n, v* dɪs 'gʌst dɪz-, dəs- ~ed/ly ɪd /li əd /li ~ing/ly ɪŋ /li ~s s
dish dɪʃ **dished** dɪʃt **dishes** 'dɪʃ ɪz -əz **dishing** 'dɪʃ ɪŋ
    'dish ˌtowel
dishabille ˌdɪs ə 'biːᵊl -æ-
disharmonious ˌdɪs hɑː 'məʊn i əs ‖ -hɑːr 'moʊn- ~ly li
disharmon|y ⑴dɪs 'hɑːm ən |i ‖ -'hɑːrm- ~ies iz
dish|cloth 'dɪʃ |klɒθ -klɔːθ ‖ -|klɑːθ -klɔːθ ~cloths klɒθs klɒðz, klɔːðz, klɔːθs ‖ klɔːðz klɑːθs, klɑːðz, klɑːθs
dishdasha 'dɪʃ dæʃ ə ‖ -dɑːʃ- ~s z
dishearten dɪs 'hɑːt ᵊn ‖ -'hɑːrt- ~ed d ~ing/ly ˌɪŋ /li ~ment mənt ~s z
disher 'dɪʃ ə ‖ -ᵊr ~s z
dishevel dɪ 'ʃev ᵊl ~ed, ~led d ~ing, ~ling ɪŋ ~ment mənt ~s z
Dishforth 'dɪʃ fəθ -fɔːθ ‖ -fᵊrθ -fɔːrθ —*The place in N Yks is locally* -fəθ
dishful 'dɪʃ fʊl ~s z
dishi... —*see* **dishy**
dishonest ⑴dɪs 'ɒn ɪst dɪz-, -əst ‖ -'ɑːn- ~ly li
dishonest|y ⑴dɪs 'ɒn əst |i dɪz-, -ɪst- ‖ -'ɑːn- ~ies iz
dishon|or, dishon|our *n, v* dɪs 'ɒn |ə dɪz- ‖ -'ɑːn |ᵊr ~ored, ~oured əd ‖ ᵊrd ~oring, ~ouring ər ɪŋ ~ors, ~ours əz ‖ ᵊrz
dishonorab|le, dishonourab|le dɪs 'ɒn ər əb |ᵊl dɪz- ‖ -'ɑːn- ~ly li
dishpan 'dɪʃ pæn ~s z
dishrag 'dɪʃ ræg ~s z
dishware 'dɪʃ weə ‖ -wer -wær
dishwash|er 'dɪʃ ˌwɒʃ |ə ‖ -ˌwɔːʃ ᵊr -ˌwɑːʃ |ᵊr ~ers əz ‖ ᵊrz ~ing ɪŋ
dishwater 'dɪʃ ˌwɔːt ə ‖ -ˌwɔːt̬ ᵊr -ˌwɑːt̬ ᵊr
dish|y 'dɪʃ |i ~ier i ə ‖ i ᵊr ~iest i ɪst i əst
disillusion ˌdɪs ɪ 'luːʒ ᵊn -ə-, -'ljuːʒ- ~ed d ~ing ɪŋ ~ment/s mənt/s ~s z
disincentive ˌdɪs ɪn 'sent ɪv ‖ -'sent̬ ɪv ~s z
disinclination ˌdɪs ˌɪn klɪ 'neɪʃ ᵊn →-ˌɪŋ-, ˌ·ən-, -klə'·- ~s z
disinclin|e ˌdɪs ɪn 'klaɪn →-ɪŋ-, -ən- ~ed d ~es z ~ing ɪŋ
disinfect ˌdɪs ɪn 'fekt -ən- ~ed ɪd əd ~ing ɪŋ ~s s
disinfectant ˌdɪs ɪn 'fekt ənt -ən- ~s s
disinfection ˌdɪs ɪn 'fek ʃᵊn -ən- ~s z
disinfest ˌdɪs ɪn 'fest -ən- ~ed ɪd əd ~ing ɪŋ ~s s
disinfestation ˌdɪs ˌɪn fe 'steɪʃ ᵊn ˌ·ən- ~s z
disinflationary ˌdɪs ɪn 'fleɪʃ ᵊn ər i ˌ·ən-, -'fleɪʃ ᵊn ri ‖ -ə ner i
disinformation ˌdɪs ˌɪn fə 'meɪʃ ᵊn ˌ· ·-, ˌ·ən- ‖ -fᵊr'·-
disingenuous ˌdɪs ɪn 'dʒen ju əs ◄ ˌ·ən- ~ly li ~ness nəs nɪs

disinher|it ˌdɪs ɪn ˈher |ɪt -ən-, -ət ‖ -|ət **~ited**
ɪt ɪd ət-, -əd ‖ ət̬ əd **~iting** ɪt ɪŋ -ət- ‖ ət̬ ɪŋ
~its ɪts əts ‖ əts

disinheritance ˌdɪs ɪn ˈher ɪt ən‿s ˌ-ən-
‖ -ət ᵊn‿s

disinte|grate dɪs ˈɪnt ɪ |greɪt -ə- ‖ -ˈɪnt̬ ə-
~grated greɪt ɪd -əd ‖ greɪt̬ əd **~grates**
greɪts **~grating** greɪt ɪŋ ‖ greɪt̬ ɪŋ

disintegration dɪs ˌɪnt ɪ ˈgreɪʃ ᵊn ˌ‿ˌ-, ˌənt-,
-ə'-- ‖ -ˌɪnt̬ ə- **~s** z

disin|ter ˌdɪs ɪn |ˈtɜː- ‖ -|ˈtɜː **~terred** ˈtɜːd
‖ ˈtɜːd **~terring** ˈtɜːr ɪŋ ‖ ˈtɜː ɪŋ **~ters** ˈtɜːz
‖ ˈtɜːz

disinterest ˌ‿dɪs ˈɪntr əst -ɪst, -est; -ˈɪnt ə rest
‖ -ˈɪnt̬ ər əst, -ə rest

disinterested ˌ‿dɪs ˈɪntr əst ɪd -ɪst-, -est-, -əd;
-ˈɪnt ə rest ɪd, -əd ‖ -ˈɪnt̬ ər əst əd, -ə rest əd
~ly li **~ness** nəs nɪs

disintermediation ˌ‿dɪs ˌɪnt ə miːd i ˈeɪʃ ᵊn
‖ -ˌɪn t̬ ᵊr-

disinterment ˌdɪs ɪn ˈtɜː mənt -ən- ‖ -ˈtɜː- **~s**
s

disinvest ˌdɪs ɪn ˈvest -ən- **~ed** ɪd əd **~ing** ɪŋ
~ment/s mənt/s **~s** s

disjoin ˌ‿dɪs ˈdʒɔɪn **~ed** d **~ing** ɪŋ **~s** z

disjoint dɪs ˈdʒɔɪnt **~ly** li

disjointed dɪs ˈdʒɔɪnt ɪd -əd ‖ -ˈdʒɔɪnt̬ əd **~ly**
li **~ness** nəs nɪs

disjunct dɪs ˈdʒʌŋkt ˋ‿‧ **~ly** li **~s** s

disjunction ˌ‿dɪs ˈdʒʌŋk ʃᵊn **~s** z

disjunctive ˌ‿dɪs ˈdʒʌŋkt ɪv **~ly** li **~s** s

disjuncture ˌ‿dɪs ˈdʒʌŋk tʃə -ʃə ‖ -tʃᵊr **~s** z

disk dɪsk **disks** dɪsks
   ˈdisk drive

diskette dɪ ˈsket ˌdɪsk ˈet **~s** s

Disley ˈdɪz li

dislik|e v, n ˌ‿dɪs ˈlaɪk —but with contrastive
stress, ˌlikes and ˈdislikes **~ed** t **~es** s **~ing** ɪŋ

dislo|cate ˈdɪs lə |keɪt -ləʊ- ‖ dɪs ˈloʊ|k eɪt
~cated keɪt ɪd -əd ‖ keɪt̬ əd **~cates** keɪts
~cating keɪt ɪŋ ‖ keɪt̬ ɪŋ

dislocation ˌdɪs lə ˈkeɪʃ ᵊn -ləʊ- ‖ -loʊ- **~s** z

dislodg|e dɪs ˈlɒdʒ ‖ -ˈlɑːdʒ **~ed** d **~es** ɪz əz
~ing ɪŋ

dislodgement, dislodgment dɪs ˈlɒdʒ mənt
‖ -ˈlɑːdʒ- **~s** s

disloyal ˌ‿dɪs ˈlɔɪ əl **~ly** i

disloyal|ty ˌ‿dɪs ˈlɔɪ əl |ti **~ties** tiz

dismal ˈdɪz məl **~ly** i **~ness** nəs nɪs

dismantl|e dɪs ˈmænt ᵊl **~ed** d **~ement/s**
mənt/s **~es** z **~ing** ɪŋ

dismast ˌdɪs ˈmɑːst §-ˈmæst ‖ -ˈmæst **~ed** ɪd əd
~ing ɪŋ **~s** s

dismay v, n dɪs ˈmeɪ dɪz- **~ed** d **~ing** ɪŋ **~s** z

dismember ˌ‿dɪs ˈmem bə ‖ -bᵊr **~ed** d
  dismembering ˌ‿dɪs ˈmem bər ɪŋ **~s** z

dismemberer ˌ‿dɪs ˈmem bər ə ‖ -bᵊr ər **~s** z

dismemberment dɪs ˈmem bə mənt ‖ -bᵊr- **~s**
s

dismiss dɪs ˈmɪs §ˌ‿dɪz- **~ed** t **~es** ɪz əz **~ing**
ɪŋ

dismissal dɪs ˈmɪs ᵊl §dɪz- **~s** z

dismissive dɪs ˈmɪs ɪv §dɪz- **~ly** li **~ness** nəs
nɪs

dis|mount ˌ‿dɪs |ˈmaʊnt **~mounted**
ˈmaʊnt ɪd -əd ‖ ˈmaʊnt̬ əd **~mounting**
ˈmaʊnt ɪŋ ‖ ˈmaʊnt̬ ɪŋ **~mounts** ˈmaʊnts

Disney ˈdɪz ni
  ˌDisney ˈWorld tdmk, ˈ‧‧‧

Disneyland tdmk ˈdɪz ni lænd

disobedience ˌdɪs ə ˈbiːd i ən‿s ˌ-əʊ-

disobedient ˌdɪs ə ˈbiːd i ənt ◂ ˌ-əʊ- **~ly** li

disobey ˌdɪs ə ˈbeɪ -əʊ- **~ed** d **~ing** ɪŋ **~s** z

disoblig|e ˌdɪs ə ˈblaɪdʒ §-əʊ- **~ed** d **~es** ɪz əz
~ing/ly ɪŋ /li

disord|er dɪs ˈɔːd |ə dɪz- ‖ -ˈɔːrd |ᵊr **~ered** əd
‖ ᵊrd **~ering** ər ɪŋ **~ers** əz ‖ ᵊrz

disorder|ly dɪs ˈɔːd ə |li dɪz-, -ə|l i ‖ -ˈɔːrd ᵊr-
~liness li nəs -nɪs
  disˌorderly ˈconduct; disˌorderly ˈhouse

disorganis... —see **disorganiz...**

disorganization dɪs ˌɔːg ən aɪ ˈzeɪʃ ᵊn dɪz-,
ˌ‧ˌ-, -ɪˈ-- ‖ -ˌɔːrg ən ə-

disorganiz|e dɪs ˈɔːg ə naɪz dɪz-, ˌ-- ‖ -ˈɔːrg-
~ed d **~es** ɪz əz **~ing** ɪŋ

disori|ent ˌ‿dɪs ˈɔːr i |ent ənt ‖ -ˈoʊr- **~ented**
ent ɪd ənt-, -əd ‖ ent̬ əd **~enting** ent ɪŋ ənt-
‖ ent̬ ɪŋ **~ents** ents ənts

disorien|tate ˌ‿dɪs ˈɔːr i ən |teɪt -ˈɒr-, -i en-
‖ -ˈoʊr- **~tated** teɪt ɪd -əd ‖ teɪt̬ əd **~tates**
teɪts **~tating** teɪt ɪŋ ‖ teɪt̬ ɪŋ

disorientation dɪs ˌɔːr i ən ˈteɪʃ ᵊn -ˌɒr-, ˌ‧ˌ-,
-i en- ‖ -ˌoʊr-

disown dɪs ˈəʊn ˌ- ‖ -ˈoʊn **~ed** d **~ing** ɪŋ **~s** z

disparag|e dɪ ˈspær ɪdʒ də- ‖ -ˈsper- **~ed** d
~ement/s mənt/s **~es** ɪz əz **~ing/ly** ɪŋ /li

disparate ˈdɪsp ər ət -ɪt; -ə reɪt ‖ dɪs ˈpær-,
-ˈper- **~ly** li **~ness** nəs nɪs

disparit|y ˌ‿dɪs ˈpær ət |i -ɪt- ‖ -ət̬ |i -ˈper-
~ies iz

dispassionate dɪs ˈpæʃ ᵊn ət ɪt **~ly** li **~ness**
nəs nɪs

dispatch v dɪ ˈspætʃ də- **~ed** t **~er/s** ə/z ‖ ᵊr/z
~es ɪz əz **~ing** ɪŋ

dispatch n dɪ ˈspætʃ də-; ˈdɪs pætʃ **~es** ɪz əz
  diˈspatch box; diˈspatch ˌrider

dispel dɪ ˈspel **~led** d **~ling** ɪŋ **~s** z

dispensable dɪ ˈspen‿s əb ᵊl **~ness** nəs nɪs

dispensar|y dɪ ˈspen‿s ər |i **~ies** iz

dispensation ˌdɪsp ən ˈseɪʃ ᵊn -en- **~s** z

dispens|e dɪ ˈspen‿s **~ed** t **~er/s** ə/z ‖ ᵊr/z **~es**
ɪz əz **~ing** ɪŋ

dispersal dɪ ˈspɜːs ᵊl də- ‖ -ˈspɜːs- **~s** z

dispersant dɪ ˈspɜːs ᵊnt də- ‖ -ˈspɜːs- **~s** s

dispers|e dɪ ˈspɜːs də- ‖ -ˈspɜːs **~ed** t **~es** ɪz əz
~ing ɪŋ

dispersion, D~ dɪ ˈspɜːʃ ᵊn də-, §-ˈspɜːʒ-
‖ -ˈspɜːʒ- -ˈspɜːʃ- **~s** z

dispersive dɪ ˈspɜːs ɪv də- ‖ -ˈspɜːs- -ˈspɜːz-

dispir|it dɪ ˈspɪr |ɪt -ət ‖ -|ət **~ited/ly** ɪt ɪd /li
ət-, -əd /li ‖ ət̬ əd /li **~iting** ɪt ɪŋ ət- ‖ ət̬ ɪŋ
~its ɪts əts ‖ əts

displac|e ˌ‿dɪs ˈpleɪs **~ed** t **~es** ɪz əz **~ing** ɪŋ
  ˌdisplaced ˈperson, ˌ‧ˌ--

displacement ˌ‿dɪs ˈpleɪs mənt **~s** s

display dɪ 'spleɪ **~ed** d **~ing** ɪŋ **~s** z

displeas|e ₍ᵢ₎dɪs 'pliːz **~ed** d **~es** ɪz əz **~ing/ly**
ɪŋ /li

displeasure ₍ᵢ₎dɪs 'pleʒ ə ‖ -ᵊr

di|sport dɪ |'spɔːt ‖ -|'spɔːrt -'spoʊrt **~sported**
'spɔːt ɪd -əd ‖ 'spɔːrt̬ əd 'spoʊrt̬- **~sporting**
'spɔːt ɪŋ ‖ 'spɔːrt̬ ɪŋ 'spoʊrt̬- **~sports** 'spɔːts
‖ 'spɔːrts 'spoʊrts

disposability dɪ ˌspəʊz ə 'bɪl ət i də-, -ɪt i
‖ -ˌspoʊz ə 'bɪl ət̬ i

disposable dɪ 'spəʊz əb ᵊl də- ‖ -'spoʊz-

disposal dɪ 'spəʊz ᵊl də- ‖ -'spoʊz- **~s** z

dispos|e dɪ 'spəʊz də- ‖ -'spoʊz **~ed** d **~es** ɪz
əz **~ing** ɪŋ

disposition ˌdɪsp ə 'zɪʃ ᵊn **~s** z

dispossess ˌdɪs pə 'zes **~ed** t **~es** ɪz əz **~ing**
ɪŋ

dispossession ˌdɪs pə 'zeʃ ᵊn **~s** z

Disprin tdmk 'dɪsp rɪn -rən **~s** z

disproof ₍ᵢ₎dɪs 'pruːf §-'prʊf **~s** s

disproportion ˌdɪs prə 'pɔːʃ ᵊn ‖ -'pɔːrʃ ᵊn
-'poʊrʃ- **~al/ly** ᵊl /i **~ed** d **~ing** ɪŋ **~s** z

disproportionate ˌdɪs prə 'pɔːʃ ᵊn ət ◄ ɪt
‖ -'pɔːrʃ- -'poʊrʃ- **~ly** li **~ness** nəs nɪs

disprov|e ₍ᵢ₎dɪs 'pruːv **~ed** d **~es** z **~ing** ɪŋ

disputab|le dɪ 'spjuːt əb ᵊl də-; 'dɪs pjʊt-
‖ dɪ 'spjuːt̬ əb ᵊl 'dɪs pjət̬- **~ly** li

disputant dɪ 'spjuːt ᵊnt də-; 'dɪs pjʊt ənt
‖ 'dɪs pjət ᵊnt **~s** s

disputation ˌdɪs pju 'teɪʃ ᵊn ‖ -pjə- **~s** z

disputatious ˌdɪs pju 'teɪʃ əs ◄ ‖ -pjə- **~ly** li
~ness nəs nɪs

di|spute v dɪ |'spjuːt də- **~sputed** 'spjuːt ɪd
-əd ‖ 'spjuːt̬ əd **~sputes** 'spjuːts **~sputing**
'spjuːt ɪŋ ‖ 'spjuːt̬ ɪŋ

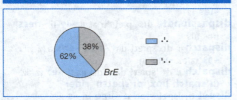

DISPUTE (noun)

62% / 38% □ .ˈ. □ ˈ.. *BrE*

dispute n dɪ 'spjuːt də-; 'dɪs pjuːt — *Preference
poll, BrE:* .ˈ. *62%,* ˈ.. *38%.* **~s** s

disqualification dɪs ˌkwɒl ɪf ɪ 'keɪʃ ᵊn ˌ·ˌ·-,
-əf ɪ-, §-ə'·- ‖ -ˌkwɑːl- **~s** z

disquali|fy dɪs 'kwɒl ɪ |faɪ ˌdɪs-, -ə- ‖ -'kwɑːl-
~fied faɪd **~fies** faɪz **~fying** faɪ ɪŋ

disqui|et dɪs 'kwaɪˌ|ət **~eted** ət ɪd -əd ‖ ət̬ əd
~eting ət ɪŋ ‖ ət̬ ɪŋ **~ets** əts

disquietude dɪs 'kwaɪˌə tjuːd -ɪ-, →-tʃuːd
‖ -tuːd -tjuːd

disquisition ˌdɪs kwɪ 'zɪʃ ᵊn -kwə- **~al** ᵊl **~s** z

Disraeli dɪz 'reɪl i dɪs-

disregard v, n ˌdɪs rɪ 'gɑːd -rə- ‖ -'gɑːrd **~ed**
ɪd əd **~ing** ɪŋ **~s** z

disrelish ₍ᵢ₎dɪs 'rel ɪʃ **~ed** t **~es** ɪz əz **~ing** ɪŋ

disremem|ber ˌdɪs rɪ 'mem |bə -rə- ‖ -|bᵊr
~bered bəd ‖ bᵊrd **~bering** bər ɪŋ **~bers** bəz
‖ bᵊrz

disrepair ˌdɪs rɪ 'peə -rə- ‖ -'peᵊr -'pæᵊr

disreputab|le dɪs 'rep jʊt əb |ᵊl -jət əb-
‖ -jət̬ əb- **~leness** ᵊl nəs -nɪs **~ly** li

disrepute ˌdɪs rɪ 'pjuːt -rə-

disrespect ˌdɪs rɪ 'spekt -rə- **~ed** ɪd əd **~ing** ɪŋ
~s s

disrespectful ˌdɪs rɪ 'spekt fᵊl ◄ -rə-, -fʊl **~ly** ˌi
~ness nəs nɪs

disrob|e ₍ᵢ₎dɪs 'rəʊb ‖ -'roʊb **~ed** d **~es** z **~ing**
ɪŋ

disrupt dɪs 'rʌpt **~ed** ɪd əd **~er/s** ə/z ‖ ᵊr/z
~ing ɪŋ **~s** s

disruption dɪs 'rʌp ʃᵊn **~s** z

disruptive dɪs 'rʌpt ɪv **~ly** li **~ness** nəs nɪs

disruptor dɪs 'rʌpt ə ‖ -ᵊr **~s** z

Diss dɪs

diss dɪs **dissed** dɪst **disses** 'dɪs ɪz -əz **dissing**
'dɪs ɪŋ

dissatisfaction ˌdɪs ˌsæt ɪs 'fæk ʃᵊn ˌdɪs æt-,
dɪ ˌsæt-, -əs'·- ‖ ˌdɪs ˌsæt̬ əs- ˌdɪs æt̬-, dɪ ˌsæt̬-
~s z

dissatis|fy ˌdɪs 'sæt ɪs |faɪ ₍ᵢ₎dɪ-, -əs- ‖ -'sæt̬-
~fied/ly faɪd /li **~fies** faɪz **~fying** faɪ ɪŋ

DISSECT

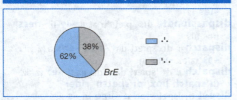

11% / 89% □ daɪ- □ dɪ- *BrE*

BrE daɪ- *by age*

Percentage — Older ◄— Speakers —► Younger

dissect daɪ 'sekt dɪ-, də- ‖ dɪ-; 'daɪ sekt
— *Preference poll, BrE:* daɪ- *89% (born since
1981, 95%),* dɪ- *11%.* **~ed** ɪd əd **~ing** ɪŋ **~s** s

dissection dɪ 'sek ʃᵊn də-, daɪ- **~s** z

dissemblance dɪ 'sem blən‹s də-

dissembl|e dɪ 'sem bᵊl də- **~ed** d **~er/s** ˌə/z
‖ ᵊr/z **~es** z **~ing** ˌɪŋ

dissemi|nate dɪ 'sem ɪ |neɪt də-, -ə- **~nated**
neɪt ɪd -əd ‖ neɪt̬ əd **~nates** neɪts **~nating**
neɪt ɪŋ ‖ neɪt̬ ɪŋ

dissemination dɪ ˌsem ɪ 'neɪʃ ᵊn də-, -ə-

disseminator dɪ 'sem ɪ neɪt ə də-, -'·ə-
‖ -neɪt̬ ᵊr **~s** z

dissension dɪ 'sen‹ʃ ᵊn də- **~s** z

dis|sent v, n dɪ |'sent də- *(usually = descent)*
~sented 'sent ɪd -əd ‖ 'sent̬ əd **~senting/ly**
'sent ɪŋ /li ‖ 'sent̬ ɪŋ /li **~sents** 'sents

dissenter, D~ dɪ 'sent ə də- ‖ -'sent̬ ᵊr **~s** z

dissentient dɪ 'sen‹ʃ i ənt də-, -'sen‹ʃ ᵊnt **~s** s

dissertation ˌdɪs ə ˈteɪʃ ᵊn -ɜː- ‖ -ᵊr- **~s** z
disservic|e dɪ ˈsɜːv ɪs, ₍ˌ₎dɪs-, §-əs ‖ -ˈsɜːv- **~es** ɪz əz
dissev|er dɪ ˈsev |ə ‖ -|ᵊr **~ered** əd ‖ ᵊrd **~ering** ər ɪŋ **~ers** əz ‖ ᵊrz
dissidence ˈdɪs ɪd ᵊnˢs -əd-
dissident ˈdɪs ɪd ᵊnt -əd- **~s** s
dissimilar ₍ˌ₎dɪ ˈsɪm ɪl ə ₍ˌ₎dɪs-, -əl- ‖ -ᵊr **~ly** li
dissimilarit|y ˌdɪs ɪm ɪ ˈlær ət |i ˌ-əm-, dɪ ˌsɪm-, ˌdɪs ˌsɪm-, -ə-ˈ--, -ɪt i ‖ -əʈ |i -ˈler- **~ies** iz
dissimi|late ₍ˌ₎dɪ ˈsɪm ɪ |leɪt -ə- **~lated** leɪt ɪd -əd ‖ leɪʈ əd **~lates** leɪts **~lating** leɪt ɪŋ ‖ leɪʈ ɪŋ
dissimilation ˌdɪs ɪm ɪ ˈleɪʃ ᵊn dɪ ˌsɪm-, ˌdɪs ˌsɪm-, -ə-ˈ-- ‖ dɪ ˌsɪm- **~s** z
dissimilitude ˌdɪs ɪ ˈmɪl ɪ tjuːd ˌ-ə-, ˌ-sɪ-, ˌ-sə-, -ə ·, →-tʃuːd ‖ -tuːd -tjuːd **~s** z
dissimu|late dɪ ˈsɪm ju |leɪt də-, -jə- ‖ -jə- **~lated** leɪt ɪd -əd ‖ leɪʈ əd **~lates** leɪts **~lating** leɪt ɪŋ ‖ leɪʈ ɪŋ
dissimulation dɪ ˌsɪm ju ˈleɪʃ ᵊn də-, -jə- ‖ -jə- **~s** z
dissi|pate ˈdɪs ɪ |peɪt -ə- **~pated** peɪt ɪd -əd ‖ peɪʈ əd **~pates** peɪts **~pating** peɪt ɪŋ ‖ peɪʈ ɪŋ
dissipation ˌdɪs ɪ ˈpeɪʃ ᵊn -ə- **~s** z
dissoci|ate dɪ ˈsəʊs i |eɪt -ˈsəʊʃ- ‖ -ˈsoʊʃ- -ˈsoʊs- **~ated** eɪt ɪd -əd ‖ eɪʈ əd **~ates** eɪts **~ating** eɪt ɪŋ ‖ eɪʈ ɪŋ
dissociation dɪ ˌsəʊs i ˈeɪʃ ᵊn -ˌsəʊs- ‖ -ˌsoʊʃ-, -ˌsoʊs- **~s** z
dissolubility dɪ ˌsɒl ju ˈbɪl ət i -ˌjə-, -ɪt i ‖ dɪ ˌsɑːl jə ˈbɪl əʈ i
dissoluble dɪ ˈsɒl jʊb ᵊl -jəb- ‖ dɪ ˈsɑːl jəb ᵊl **~ness** nəs nɪs
dissolute ˈdɪs ə luːt -ljuːt **~ly** li **~ness** nəs nɪs
dissolution ˌdɪs ə ˈluːʃ ᵊn -ljuːʃ- **~s** z
dissolv|e dɪ ˈzɒlv də-, §-ˈzəʊlv ‖ -ˈzɑːlv **~ed** d **~es** z **~ing** ɪŋ
dissonanc|e ˈdɪs ᵊn ᵊnˢs **~es** ɪz əz
dissonant ˈdɪs ᵊn ᵊnt **~ly** li
dissuad|e dɪ ˈsweɪd **~ed** ɪd əd **~es** z **~ing** ɪŋ
dissuasion dɪ ˈsweɪʒ ᵊn **~s** z
dissuasive dɪ ˈsweɪs ɪv -ˈsweɪz- **~ly** li **~ness** nəs nɪs
dissy... —see **disy...**
distaff ˈdɪst ɑːf §-æf ‖ -æf **~s** s
distal ˈdɪst ᵊl **~ly** i
distanc|e ˈdɪst ᵊnˢs **~ed** t **~es** ɪz əz **~ing** ɪŋ
distant ˈdɪst ᵊnt **~ly** li
distaste ₍ˌ₎dɪs ˈteɪst **~s** s
distasteful ₍ˌ₎dɪs ˈteɪst fᵊl -fʊl **~ly** i **~ness** nəs nɪs
distemp|er dɪ ˈstemp |ə də- ‖ -|ᵊr **~ered** əd ‖ ᵊrd **~ering** ər ɪŋ **~ers** əz ‖ ᵊrz
distend dɪ ˈstend də- **~ed** ɪd əd **~ing** ɪŋ **~s** z
distension, distention dɪ ˈstenˢʃ ᵊn də-
distich ˈdɪst ɪk **~s** s
di|stil, di|still dɪ |ˈstɪl də- **~stilled** ˈstɪld **~stilling** ˈstɪl ɪŋ **~stills, ~stils** ˈstɪlz
distillate ˈdɪst ɪl ət -əl-, -ɪt; -ɪ leɪt, -ə- **~s** s

distillation ˌdɪst ɪ ˈleɪʃ ᵊn -ə-, -ᵊl ˈeɪʃ- **~s** z
ˌdistilˈlation ˌcolumn
distiller dɪ ˈstɪl ə də- ‖ -ᵊr **~s** z
distiller|y dɪ ˈstɪl ər |i də- **~ies** iz
distinct dɪ ˈstɪŋkt də- **~ly** li **~ness** nəs nɪs
distinction dɪ ˈstɪŋk ʃᵊn də- **~s** z
distinctive dɪ ˈstɪŋkt ɪv də- **~ly** li **~ness** nəs nɪs
distingué dɪ ˈstæŋ geɪ də- ‖ ˌdiːst æŋ ˈgeɪ ˌdɪst- —Fr [dis tæ ge]
distinguish dɪ ˈstɪŋ gwɪʃ də-, -wɪʃ **~ed** t **~es** ɪz əz **~ing** ɪŋ
distinguishab|le dɪ ˈstɪŋ gwɪʃ əb |ᵊl də-, -ˈ·wɪʃ- **~ly** li
di|stort dɪ |ˈstɔːt də- ‖ -|ˈstɔːrt **~storted** ˈstɔːt ɪd -əd ‖ ˈstɔːrʈ əd **~storting** ˈstɔːt ɪŋ ‖ ˈstɔːrʈ ɪŋ **~storts** ˈstɔːts ‖ ˈstɔːrts
distortion dɪ ˈstɔːʃ ᵊn də- ‖ -ˈstɔːrʃ ᵊn **~s** z
distract dɪ ˈstrækt də- **~ed/ly** ɪd /li əd /li **~ing/ly** ɪŋ /li **~s** s
distraction dɪ ˈstræk ʃᵊn də- **~s** z
distractor dɪ ˈstrækt ə də- ‖ -ᵊr **~s** z
distrain dɪ ˈstreɪn də- **~ed** d **~ing** ɪŋ **~s** z
distraint dɪ ˈstreɪnt də-
distrait ˈdɪs treɪ dɪ ˈstreɪ, də- ‖ dɪ ˈstreɪ —Fr [dis tʁɛ]
distraught dɪ ˈstrɔːt də- ‖ -ˈstrɑːt **~ly** li
distress dɪ ˈstres də- **~ed** t **~es** ɪz əz **~ing/ly** ɪŋ /li
distressful dɪ ˈstres fᵊl də-, -fʊl **~ly** i **~ness** nəs nɪs

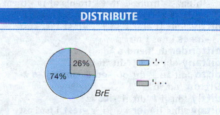

BrE

distribute dɪ ˈstrɪb juːt də-; ˈdɪs trɪ bjuːt, -trə- ‖ -jət —The stressing ˈ···, although disliked by many, is widely used in BrE. — Preference poll, BrE: ·ˈ·· 74%, ˈ··· 26%. **distributed** dɪ ˈstrɪb jʊt ɪd də-, -jət-, -əd; ˈdɪs trɪ bjuːt ɪd, -ˈtrə-, -əd ‖ -jəʈ əd **distributes** dɪ ˈstrɪb juːts də-; ˈdɪs trɪ bjuːts, -trə- ‖ -jəts **distributing** dɪ ˈstrɪb jʊt ɪŋ də-, -jət-; ˈdɪs trɪ bjuːt ɪŋ, -ˈtrə- ‖ -jəʈ ɪŋ
distribution ˌdɪs trɪ ˈbjuːʃ ᵊn -trə- **~s** z
distributional ˌdɪs trɪ ˈbjuːʃ ᵊn ᵊl **~ly** i
distributive dɪ ˈstrɪb jʊt ɪv də-, -jə-; §ˈdɪs trɪ bjuːt ɪv, -ˈtrə- ‖ -jəʈ ɪv **~ly** li **~ness** nəs nɪs
distributor dɪ ˈstrɪb jʊt ə də-, -jət ə; §ˈdɪs trɪ bjuːt ə, -ˈtrə- ‖ -jəʈ ᵊr **~ship/s** ʃɪp/s **~s** z
district ˈdɪs trɪkt **~s** s
ˌdistrict atˈtorney; ˌdistrict ˈnurse; ˌDistrict of Coˈlumbia
distrust ₍ˌ₎dɪs ˈtrʌst **~ed** ɪd əd **~ing** ɪŋ **~s** s

distrustful 240

distrustful ˌdɪs 'trʌst fᵊl -fʊl **~ly** i **~ness** nəs nɪs

disturb dɪ 'stɜːb də- ‖ -'stɝːb **~ed** d **~ing/ly** ɪŋ /li **~s** z

disturbanc|e dɪ 'stɜːb ənts də-, →-mᵖs ‖ -'stɝːb- **~es** ɪz əz

disunion ˌdɪs 'juːn i‿ən →§ˌdɪʃ-

disu|nite ˌdɪs ju |'naɪt →§ˌdɪʃ- **~nited** 'naɪt ɪd -əd ‖ 'naɪt̬ əd **~nites** 'naɪts **~niting** 'naɪt ɪŋ ‖ 'naɪt̬ ɪŋ

disunit|y ˌdɪs 'juːn ət |i →§ˌdɪʃ-, -ɪt- ‖ -ət̬ |i **~ies** iz

disuse n ˌdɪs 'juːs →§ˌdɪʃ-

disused ˌdɪs 'juːzd ◄ dɪs-, →§ˌdɪʃ- ˌdisused 'railway

disyllabic ˌdaɪ sɪ 'læb ɪk ◄ -sə-; ˌdɪs ɪ-, -ə- **~ally** ᵊl̩ i

disyllable ˌdaɪ 'sɪl əb ᵊl ˌdɪ-, '·ˌ··· **~s** z

dit dɪt **dits** dɪts

ditch dɪtʃ **ditched** dɪtʃt **ditches** 'dɪtʃ ɪz -əz **ditching** 'dɪtʃ ɪŋ

ditcher 'dɪtʃ ə ‖ -ᵊr **~s** z

Ditchling 'dɪtʃ lɪŋ

ditchwater 'dɪtʃ ˌwɔːt ə ‖ -ˌwɔːt̬ ᵊr -ˌwɑːt̬ ᵊr

dith|er 'dɪð |ə ‖ -|ᵊr **~ered** əd ‖ ᵊrd **~ering** ər ɪŋ **~ers** əz ‖ ᵊrz

ditherer 'dɪð ər ə ‖ -ᵊr ər **~s** z

dithery 'dɪð ər i

dithyramb 'dɪθ ɪ ræm -ə-, -ræmb **~s** z

dithyrambic ˌdɪθ ɪ 'ræm bɪk ◄ -ə-

ditransitive ˌdaɪ 'trænᵗs ət ɪv -'trɑːnᵗs-, -'trænz-, -'trɑːnz-, -ɪt- ‖ -'trænᵗs ət̬ ɪv -'trænz- **~ly** li **~s** z

dits|y 'dɪts |i **~ier** i‿ə ‖ i‿ᵊr **~iest** i‿ɪst i‿əst **~iness** i nəs i nɪs

dittander dɪ 'tænd ə §də- ‖ -ᵊr

dittany 'dɪt ən i ‖ 'dɪt ᵊn i

ditto 'dɪt əʊ ‖ 'dɪt̬ oʊ **~ed** d **~ing** ɪŋ **~s** z

Ditton 'dɪt ᵊn

ditt|y 'dɪt |i ‖ 'dɪt̬ |i **~ies** iz

ditz|y 'dɪts |i **~ier** i‿ə ‖ i‿ᵊr **~iest** i‿ɪst i‿əst **~iness** i nəs i nɪs

diuresis ˌdaɪ juᵊ 'riːs ɪs §-əs ‖ -jə-

diuretic ˌdaɪ juᵊ 'ret ɪk ◄ -jə 'ret̬ ɪk **~s** s

diurnal daɪ 'ɜːn ᵊl ‖ -'ɝːn ᵊl **~ly** i

diva 'diːv ə **~s** z

diva|gate 'daɪv ə |geɪt 'daɪ veɪ-, 'dɪv ə- **~gated** geɪt ɪd -əd ‖ geɪt̬ əd **~gates** geɪts **~gating** geɪt ɪŋ ‖ geɪt̬ ɪŋ

divagation ˌdaɪv ə 'geɪʃ ᵊn ˌdaɪ veɪ-, ˌdɪv ə- **~s** z

divalent ˌdaɪ 'veɪl ənt '·ˌ··

Divali dɪ 'vɑːl i

divan dɪ 'væn də-, ˌdaɪ-, 'daɪv æn **~s** z

dive daɪv **dived** daɪvd **dives** daɪvz **diving** 'daɪv ɪŋ **dove** dəʊv ‖ doʊv

dive-bomb 'daɪv bɒm ‖ -bɑːm **~ed** d **~er/s** ə/z ‖ ᵊr/z **~ing** ɪŋ **~s** z

diver, Diver 'daɪv ə ‖ -ᵊr **~s** z

diverg|e daɪ 'vɜːdʒ dɪ-, də- ‖ də 'vɝːdʒ daɪ- **~ed** d **~es** ɪz əz **~ing** ɪŋ

divergenc|e daɪ 'vɜːdʒ ənᵗs dɪ-, də- ‖ də 'vɝːdʒ- daɪ- **~es** ɪz əz

divergent ˌdaɪ 'vɜːdʒ ənt dɪ-, də- ‖ də 'vɝːdʒ- daɪ- —but with contrastive stress, against convergent, 'daɪ,·· **~ly** li

divers 'daɪv əz -ɜːz; ˌdaɪ 'vɜːs, '· · ‖ -ᵊrz

diverse daɪ 'vɜːs ˌdaɪ-, '· · ‖ də 'vɝːs daɪ-, 'daɪ vɜːs **~ly** li **~ness** nəs nɪs

diversification daɪ ˌvɜːs ɪf ɪ 'keɪʃ ᵊn dɪ-, də-, -ˌ·əf-, §-ə'·- ‖ də ˌvɝːs- daɪ- **~s** z

diversi|fy daɪ 'vɜːs ɪ |faɪ -ə- ‖ də 'vɝːs- daɪ- **~fied** faɪd **~fies** faɪz **~fying** faɪ ɪŋ

diversion daɪ 'vɜːʃ ᵊn dɪ-, də-, §-'vɜːʒ- ‖ də 'vɝːʒ ᵊn daɪ-, -'vɝːʃ- **~ist/s** ɪst/s §əst/s **~s** z

diversionary daɪ 'vɜːʃ ᵊn ər i dɪ-, də-, §-'vɜːʒ-, -ᵊn ˌər- ‖ də 'vɝːʒ ə ner i daɪ-

diversit|y daɪ 'vɜːs ət |i dɪ-, də-, -ɪt- ‖ də 'vɝːs ət̬ |i daɪ- **~ies** iz

di|vert daɪ |'vɜːt dɪ-, də- ‖ də |'vɝːt daɪ- **~verted** 'vɜːt ɪd -əd ‖ 'vɝːt̬ əd **~verting** 'vɜːt ɪŋ ‖ 'vɝːt̬ ɪŋ **~verts** 'vɜːts ‖ 'vɝːts

diverticulitis ˌdaɪv ə ˌtɪk ju 'laɪt ɪs ˌ·ɜː-, §-əs ‖ ˌdaɪv ᵊr ˌtɪk jə 'laɪt̬ əs

diverticul|um ˌdaɪv ə 'tɪk jʊl |əm ˌ·ɜː-, -jəl əm ‖ ˌdaɪv ᵊr 'tɪk jəl |əm **~a** ə

divertiment|o dɪ ˌvɜːt ɪ 'ment |əʊ -ˌveət-, -ə- ‖ dɪ ˌvɝːt̬ ə 'ment |oʊ **~i** iː

divertissement ˌdiː veə 'tiːs mõ dɪ 'vɜːt ɪs mənt, -əs-, -mõ ‖ dɪ 'vɝːt̬ əs mənt —Fr [di vɛʁ tis mɑ̃]

Dives name 'daɪv iːz

divest daɪ 'vest dɪ-, də- **~ed** ɪd əd **~ing** ɪŋ **~s** s

divestiture daɪ 'vest ɪtʃ ə dɪ-, də- ‖ -ᵊr -ə tʃʊr **~s** z

divestment daɪ 'vest mənt dɪ-, də- **~s** s

divid|e dɪ 'vaɪd də- **~ed** ɪd əd **~es** z **~ing** ɪŋ

dividend 'dɪv ɪ dend -ə-; -ɪd ənd, -əd- **~s** z

divider dɪ 'vaɪd ə də- ‖ -ᵊr **~s** z

divi-divi ˌdɪv i 'dɪv i ˌdiːv i 'diːv i **~s** z

divination ˌdɪv ɪ 'neɪʃ ᵊn -ə- **~s** z

divin|e adj, n, v, D~ dɪ 'vaɪn də- **~ed** d **~ely** li **~eness** nəs nɪs **~er/s** ə/z ‖ ᵊr/z **~est** ɪst əst **~ing** ɪŋ di,vine 'right; Di,vine 'Service; di'vining rod

diving 'daɪv ɪŋ 'diving bell; 'diving suit

divingboard 'daɪv ɪŋ bɔːd ‖ -bɔːrd -boʊrd **~s** z

divinit|y, D~ dɪ 'vɪn ət |i də-, -ɪt- ‖ -ət̬ |i **~ies** iz

Divis 'dɪv ɪs §-əs

divisibility dɪ ˌvɪz ə 'bɪl ət i də-, -ˌ·ɪ-, -ɪt i ‖ -ət̬ i

divisib|le dɪ 'vɪz əb |ᵊl də-, -ɪb- **~ly** li

division dɪ 'vɪʒ ᵊn də- **~al** ᵊl **~s** z di'vision ˌlobby

divisive dɪ 'vaɪs ɪv də-, §-'vaɪz-, §-'vɪz-, §-'vɪs- **~ly** li **~ness** nəs nɪs

divisor dɪ 'vaɪz ə də- ‖ -ᵊr (= deviser) **~s** z

divorc|e n, v dɪ 'vɔːs də- ‖ -'vɔːrs -'voʊrs **~ed** t **~es** ɪz əz **~ing** ɪŋ

D

divorcé, divorcee, divorcée dɪ ˌvɔː ˈsiː də-,
-ˈseɪ; ˌdɪv ɔː-, ˌdiːv ɔː-, -ˈseɪ; dɪ ˈvɔːs iː, də-, -eɪ
‖ də ˌvɔːr ˈseɪ -ˌvoʊr-, -ˈsiː; -ˈvɔːrs iː, -ˈvoʊrs-,
-eɪ ~s z

divot ˈdɪv ət ~s s

divulg|e daɪ ˈvʌldʒ dɪ-, də- ‖ də- daɪ- ~**ed** d
~**es** ɪz əz ~**ing** ɪŋ

divulgenc|e daɪ ˈvʌldʒ ənˀs dɪ-, də- ‖ də- daɪ-
~**es** ɪz əz

divv|y ˈdɪv |i ~**ied** id ~**ies** iz ~**ying** i ɪŋ

Diwali dɪ ˈwɑːl i

Dix dɪks

Dixey, Dixie, d~ ˈdɪks i
  ˈDixie Cup *tdmk*

Dixiecrat ˈdɪks i kræt ~**s** s

Dixieland, d~ ˈdɪks i lænd

Dixon ˈdɪks ən

DIY, diy ˌdiː aɪ ˈwaɪ ~**ing** ɪŋ
  ˌDIˈY shop

dizygotic ˌdaɪ zaɪ ˈɡɒt ɪk ◀ -ˈɡɑːt-

dizz|y ˈdɪz |i ~**ied** id ~**ier** i̯ə ‖ i̯ˀr ~**ies** iz
~**iest** i ɪst i̯əst ~**ily** ɪ li əl i ~**iness** i nəs i nɪs
~**ying/ly** i̯ ɪŋ /li

DJ, D.J. ˌdiː ˈdʒeɪ ‖ ˈ· · **DJs, D.J.s** ˌdiː ˈdʒeɪz
‖ ˈ· ·

Djakarta dʒə ˈkɑːt ə ‖ -ˈkɑːrt̬ ə

djellaba, djellabah ˈdʒel əb ə dʒə ˈlɑːb ə ~**s**
z

Djibouti dʒɪ ˈbuːt i dʒə- ‖ -ˈbuːt̬ i ~**an/s** ən/z

djinn dʒɪn **djinns** dʒɪnz

DLit, DLitt ˌdiː ˈlɪt ~**s**, ~ˈ**s** s

DNA ˌdiː en ˈeɪ

Dneper, Dnieper ˈniːp ə ˈdniːp- ‖ -ˀr —*Russ*
[dⁿˈɛpr]

Dnepropetrovsk ˌnep rəʊ pe ˈtrɒfsk -pɪˈ·, -pəˈ·
‖ -roʊ pə ˈtrɔːfsk -ˈtrɑːvsk —*Russ*
[dⁿnⁱ prə pⁱˈ trɔfsk]

Dniester ˈniːst ə ˈdniːst- ‖ -ˀr —*Russ* [dⁿnⁱɛstr]

D-notic|e ˈdiː ˌnəʊt ɪs §-əs ‖ -ˌnoʊt̬- ~**es** ɪz əz

do *n, other senses* duː **dos, do's** duːz

do *n 'musical note'* dəʊ ‖ doʊ **dos** dəʊz ‖ doʊz

do *v, strong form* duː; *weak forms* dʊ, də, d **did**
dɪd **didn't** ˈdɪd ənt **does** dʌz *(see)* **doesn't**
ˈdʌz ənt **doing** ˈduː ɪŋ **done** dʌn **don't**
dəʊnt ‖ doʊnt

DOA ˌdiː əʊ ˈeɪ ‖ -oʊ-

doable ˈduː əb əl

Doane dəʊn ‖ doʊn

dobbin, D~ ˈdɒb ɪn §-ən ‖ ˈdɑːb- ~**s**, ~ˈ**s** z

Dobbs dɒbz ‖ dɑːbz

Dobell *(i)* dəʊ ˈbel ‖ doʊ-, *(ii)* ˈdəʊb əl
‖ ˈdoʊb-

Doberman, d~ ˈdəʊb ə mən ‖ ˈdoʊb ˀr mən
~**s** z
  ˌDoberman ˈpinscher ˈpɪntʃ ə ‖ ˀr

Dobie ˈdəʊb i ‖ ˈdoʊb i

Dobson ˈdɒb sən ‖ ˈdɑːb-

doc, Doc dɒk ‖ dɑːk **docs, Doc's** dɒks ‖ dɑːks

docent ˈdəʊs ənt dəʊ ˈsent ‖ ˈdoʊs- ~**s** s

Docetism dəʊ ˈsiːt ˌɪz əm ˈdəʊs ɪ ˌtɪz əm, -ə-
‖ doʊ ˈsiːt̬-

Docherty ˈdɒx ət i ˈdɒk- ‖ ˈdɑːk ˀrt̬ i

docile ˈdəʊs aɪˀl ‖ ˈdɑːs ˀl *(*)* ~**ly** li

docility dəʊ ˈsɪl ət i də-, -ɪt- ‖ dɑː ˈsɪl ət̬ i doʊ-

dock dɒk ‖ dɑːk **docked** dɒkt ‖ dɑːkt **docking**
ˈdɒk ɪŋ ‖ ˈdɑːk ɪŋ **docks** dɒks ‖ dɑːks

docker, D~ ˈdɒk ə ‖ ˈdɑːk ˀr ~**s** z

dock|et ˈdɒk |ɪt §-ət ‖ ˈdɑːk |ət ~**eted** ɪt ɪd
§ət-, -əd ‖ ət̬ əd ~**eting** ɪt ɪŋ §ət- ‖ ət̬ ɪŋ ~**ets**
ɪts §əts ‖ əts

dockland, D~ ˈdɒk lənd -lænd ‖ ˈdɑːk- ~**s** z

dockside ˈdɒk saɪd ‖ ˈdɑːk-

dockworker ˈdɒk ˌwɜːk ə ‖ ˈdɑːk ˌwɜːk ˀr ~**s**
z

dockyard ˈdɒk jɑːd ‖ ˈdɑːk jɑːrd ~**s** z

doctor, D~ ˈdɒkt ə ‖ ˈdɑːkt ˀr ~**ed** d
  doctoring ˈdɒkt ər ɪŋ ‖ ˈdɑːkt- ~**s** z

doctoral ˈdɒkt ər əl →ˈdɒk trəl; dɒk ˈtɔːr əl
‖ ˈdɑːkt-

doctorate ˈdɒkt ər ət -ɪt; →ˈdɒk trət, -trɪt
‖ ˈdɑːkt- ~**s** s

Doctorow ˈdɒkt ə rəʊ ‖ ˈdɑːkt ə roʊ

doctrinaire ˌdɒk trɪ ˈneə ◀ -trə-
‖ ˌdɑːk trə ˈneˀr -ˈnæˀr ~**s** z

doctrinal dɒk ˈtraɪn əl ˈdɒk trɪn əl, -trən-
‖ ˈdɑːk trən əl ~**ly** i

doctrinarian ˌdɒk trɪ ˈneər i ən ◀ ˌtrə-
‖ ˌdɑːk trə ˈner- ~**s** z

doctrine ˈdɒk trɪn -trən ‖ ˈdɑːk- ~**s** z

docudrama ˈdɒk ju ˌdrɑːm ə ‖ ˈdɑːk jə-
-ˌdræm ə ~**s** z

docu|ment *v* ˈdɒk ju |ment ‖ ˈdɑːk jə- —*See
note at* -ment ~**mented** ment ɪd -əd
‖ ment̬ əd ~**menting** ment ɪŋ ‖ ment̬ ɪŋ
~**ments** ments

document *n* ˈdɒk ju mənt -jə- ‖ ˈdɑːk jə- ~**s** s

documentar|y ˌdɒk ju ˈment ˌər |i
‖ ˌdɑːk jə ˈment̬ ˀr |i →-ˈmentr |i ~**ies** iz
~**ist/s** ɪst/s §əst/s

documentation ˌdɒk ju men ˈteɪʃ ˀn -mən-ˈ·-
‖ ˌdɑːk jə-

docusoap ˈdɒk ju səʊp -jə- ‖ ˈdɑːk jə soʊp ~**s**
s

Docwra ˈdɒk rə ‖ ˈdɑːk-

Dod, Dodd dɒd ‖ dɑːd

dodd|er ˈdɒd |ə ‖ ˈdɑːd |ˀr ~**ered** əd ‖ ˀrd
~**ering/ly** ər ɪŋ /li ~**ers** əz ‖ ˀrz

doddery ˈdɒd ər i ‖ ˈdɑːd-

Doddington ˈdɒd ɪŋ tən ‖ ˈdɑːd-

doddle ˈdɒd əl ‖ ˈdɑːd- ~**s** z

dodeca- *comb. form*
  with stress-neutral suffix ˌdəʊ ˌdek ə
  ‖ doʊ ˌdek ə — **dodecasyllable**
  ˌdəʊ ˌdek ə ˈsɪl əb əl ‖ doʊ ˌdek-
  with stress-imposing suffix ˌdəʊd ɪ ˈkæ+ -e-,
  -ə- ‖ ˌdoʊd- — **dodecagonal**
  ˌdəʊd ɪ ˈkæɡ ən əl ◀ -ˌe-, -ˌə-‖ ˌdoʊd-

dodecagon ˌdəʊ ˈdek əɡ ən -ə ɡɒn ‖ doʊ- ~**s** z

dodecahedr|on ˌdəʊ ˌdek ə ˈhiːdr |ən -ˈhedr-
‖ doʊ ˌdek- ~**a** ə ~**ons** ənz

Dodecanese ˌdəʊd ɪk ə ˈniːz ˌek-, §-ˈniːs
‖ doʊ ˌdek ə niːz -niːs, -ˌ-ˈ-ˈ

dodecaphonic ˌdəʊd ek ə ˈfɒn ɪk ◀ -ɪk-, -ˌek-
‖ doʊ ˌdek ə ˈfɑːn ɪk ◀

D

dodge, Dodge dɒdʒ ‖ da:dʒ **dodged** dɒdʒd
‖ da:dʒd **dodges** 'dɒdʒ ɪz -əz ‖ 'da:dʒ-
dodging 'dɒdʒ ɪŋ ‖ 'da:dʒ ɪŋ
dodgem, D~ *tdmk* 'dɒdʒ əm ‖ 'da:dʒ- **~s** z
'**dodgem cars**
dodger 'dɒdʒ ə ‖ 'da:dʒ ʰr **~s** z
Dodgson (i) 'dɒdʒ sʰn ‖ 'da:dʒ-, (ii) 'dɒd sʰn
‖ 'da:d- —*Lewis Carroll (Charles D~)*
reportedly was (ii)
dodg|y 'dɒdʒ |i ‖ 'da:dʒ |i **~ier** i ə ‖ i ʰr **~iest**
i ɪst i əst
Dodi 'dəʊd i ‖ 'doʊd i
dodo 'dəʊd əʊ ‖ 'doʊd oʊ **~es, ~s** z
Dodoma *place in Tanzania* 'dəʊd əm ə -ə mɑː
‖ 'doʊd-
Dodona *place in Greece* dəʊ 'dəʊn ə
‖ də 'doʊn ə
Dodson 'dɒd sʰn ‖ 'da:d-
doe, Doe dəʊ ‖ doʊ **does** dəʊz ‖ doʊz
-doer ˌduː ə ‖ 'duː ʰr — **wrong-doer**
'rɒŋ ˌduː ə ‖ ˌrɔːŋ 'duː ʰr ˌra:ŋ-
doer 'duː ə ‖ 'duː ʰr **~s** z
does *from* **do**, *strong form* dʌz, *weak forms* dəz,
dz
does *n*, *'female animals'* dəʊz ‖ doʊz
doeskin 'dəʊ skɪn ‖ 'doʊ- **~s** z
doesn't 'dʌz ʰnt —*also, when non-final,*
'dʌz ʰn
doeth 'duː ɪθ ˌ əθ
doff dɒf ‖ dɔːf da:f **doffed** dɒft ‖ dɔːft da:ft
doffing 'dɒf ɪŋ ‖ 'dɔːf ɪŋ 'da:f- **doffs** dɒfs
‖ dɔːfs da:fs
dog dɒg ‖ dɔːg da:g **dogged** dɒgd ‖ dɔːgd
da:gd **dogging** 'dɒg ɪŋ ‖ 'dɔːg ɪŋ 'da:g- **dogs**
dɒgz ‖ dɔːgz da:gz
'**dog ˌbiscuit**; '**dog ˌcollar**; '**dog days**;
ˌ**dog in the 'manger**; '**dog ˌpaddle**; '**dog
rose**; ˌ**dog's 'breakfast**; '**dog tag**
Dogberry 'dɒg ˌber i -bər i ‖ 'dɔːg- 'da:g-
dogcart 'dɒg ka:t ‖ 'dɔːg ka:rt 'da:g- **~s** s
dogcatcher 'dɒg ˌkætʃ ə §-ˌketʃ-
‖ 'dɔːg ˌkætʃ ʰr 'da:g- **~s** z
doge dəʊdʒ dəʊʒ ‖ doʊdʒ **doges** 'dəʊdʒ ɪz
'dəʊʒ-, -əz ‖ 'doʊdʒ-
dog-eared 'dɒg ɪəd ˌ·'· ‖ 'dɔːg ɪrd 'da:g-
dog-eat-dog ˌdɒg i:t 'dɒg ‖ ˌdɔːg i:t 'dɔːg
ˌda:g i:t 'da:g
dog-end ˌdɒg 'end '·· ‖ 'dɔːg- ˌda:g- **~s** z
dogfight 'dɒg faɪt ‖ 'dɔːg- 'da:g- **~s** s
dogfish 'dɒg fɪʃ ‖ 'dɔːg- 'da:g- **~es** ɪz əz
dogfood 'dɒg fu:d ‖ 'dɔːg- 'da:g- **~s** z
dogged *adj* 'dɒg ɪd -əd ‖ 'dɔːg- 'da:g- **~ly** li
~ness nəs nɪs
dogged *past & pp of* **dog** dɒgd ‖ dɔːgd da:gd
dogger, D~ 'dɒg ə ‖ 'dɔːg ʰr 'da:g ʰr **~s** z
doggerel 'dɒg ʰr əl ‖ 'dɔːg- 'da:g-
doggie 'dɒg i ‖ 'dɔːg i 'da:g i **~s** z
doggish 'dɒg ɪʃ ‖ 'dɔːg- 'da:g- **~ly** li
doggo 'dɒg əʊ ‖ 'dɔːg oʊ 'da:g-
doggone 'dɒg ɒn ‖ ˌda:g 'ga:n ◂ ˌdɔːg-, -'gɔːn
~d d

dogg|y 'dɒg |i ‖ 'dɔːg |i 'da:g- **~ier** i ə ‖ i ʰr
~iest i ɪst i əst
'**doggy bag**; '**doggy ˌpaddle**
doggy-style 'dɒg i staɪʰl ‖ 'dɔːg- 'da:g-
dog|house 'dɒg |haʊs ‖ 'dɔːg- 'da:g- **~houses**
haʊz ɪz -əz
dogie 'dəʊg i ‖ 'doʊg i **~s** z
dogleg 'dɒg leg ‖ 'dɔːg- 'da:g- **~s** z
doglegged ˌdɒg 'leg ɪd ◂ -əd; -'legd ‖ ˌdɔːg-
ˌda:g-
dogma 'dɒg mə ‖ 'dɔːg- 'da:g- **~s** z
dogmatic dɒg 'mæt ɪk ‖ dɔːg 'mæt̬ ɪk da:g-
~ally ʰl i
dogmatism 'dɒg mə ˌtɪz əm ‖ 'dɔːg- 'da:g-
dogmatist 'dɒg mət ɪst §-əst ‖ 'dɔːg mət̬ əst
'da:g- **~s** s
dogmatiz|e, dogmatis|e 'dɒg mə taɪz
‖ 'dɔːg- 'da:g- **~ed** d **~es** ɪz əz **~ing** ɪŋ
Dogon 'dəʊg ɒn ‖ 'doʊg a:n
do-good|er ˌdu: 'gʊd |ə ‖ ˌdu: gʊd |ʰr **~ers** əz
‖ ʰrz **~ing** ɪŋ
dogsbod|y 'dɒgz ˌbɒd |i ‖ 'dɔːgz ˌba:d |i
'da:gz- **~ies** iz
dogsled 'dɒg sled ‖ 'dɔːg- 'da:g- **~s** z
dog's-tail 'dɒgz teɪʰl ‖ 'dɔːgz- 'da:gz- **~s** z
dog-tired ˌdɒg 'taɪ əd ◂ ‖ ˌdɔːg 'taɪ ʰrd ◂
ˌda:g-
dogtooth 'dɒg tu:θ §-tʊθ ‖ 'dɔːg- 'da:g-
dogtrot 'dɒg trɒt ‖ 'dɔːg tra:t 'da:g-
dogwatch 'dɒg wɒtʃ ‖ 'dɔːg wa:tʃ 'da:g-,
-wɔːtʃ **~es** ɪz əz
dogwood 'dɒg wʊd ‖ 'dɔːg- 'da:g- **~s** z
doh *musical note* dəʊ ‖ doʊ (= *doe*) **dohs** dəʊz
‖ doʊz
doh, d'oh *interjection* dɜː dəʊ ‖ dʌ doʊ
Doha 'dəʊ ha: 'dəʊ ə ‖ 'doʊ-
Doherty (i) 'dɒ hət i 'dɒx ət i ‖ 'da: hʰrt̬ i,
(ii) 'dəʊ hət i -ət i ‖ 'doʊ ʰrt̬ i
Dohnányi dɒk 'na:n ji dɒx-, -ji: ‖ 'doʊn a:n ji
—*Hung* ['doh na: ɲi]
Doig (i) dɔɪg, (ii) 'dəʊ ɪg ‖ 'doʊ-
doil|y 'dɔɪl |i **~ies** iz
Doi moi ˌdɔɪ 'mɔɪ
doing 'du: ɪŋ **~s** z
doit dɔɪt **doits** dɔɪts
do-it-yourself ˌdu: ɪt jə 'self ◂ →ˌtʃ ə-, -jɔː'·,
-jʊə'·; §,-ət-, §-ətʃ ə- ‖ ˌdu: ət jʰr- **~er/s** ə/z
‖ ʰr/z
dojo 'dəʊ dʒəʊ ‖ 'doʊ dʒoʊ —*Jp* ['doo dʑoo]
Doktorow 'dɒkt ər əʊ ‖ 'da:kt ər oʊ
Dolan 'dəʊl ən ‖ 'doʊl-
Dolby 'dɒl bi ‖ 'doʊl- 'dɔːl-, 'da:l-
dolce 'dɒltʃ i -eɪ ‖ 'doʊltʃ eɪ —*It* ['dol tʃe]
ˌ**dolce ˌfar ni'ente** ˌfa: ni 'ent i -eɪ ‖ ˌfa:r-
—*It* [far 'njen te]; ˌ**dolce 'vita** 'vi:t ə
‖ 'vi:t̬ ə —*It* ['vi: ta]
Dolcis *tdmk* 'dɒls ɪs 'dɒltʃ-, §-əs ‖ 'da:ls-
doldrums 'dɒldr əmz 'dəʊldr- ‖ 'doʊldr-
'da:ldr-, 'dɔːldr-
dole dəʊl →dɒʊl ‖ doʊl **doled** dəʊld →dɒʊld
‖ doʊld **doles** dəʊlz →dɒʊlz ‖ doʊlz **doling**
'dəʊl ɪŋ →'dɒʊl- ‖ 'doʊl ɪŋ

doleful 'dəʊl fᵊl →'dɒʊl-, -fʊl ‖ 'doʊl- **~ly** i
~ness nəs nɪs
dolerite 'dɒl ə raɪt ‖ 'dɑːl-
Dolgellau, Dolgelley dɒl 'geθ li -laɪ ‖ dɑːl-
— *Welsh* [dol 'ge ɬaɪ, -ɬa, -ɬe]
doli... —*see* **dole**
dolichocephalic ˌdɒl ɪ kəʊ sɪ 'fæl ɪk ◂ -sə'--,
-ke'--, -kɪ'-- ‖ ˌdɑːl ɪ koʊ-
dolichosaur|us ˌdɒl ɪ kəʊ 'sɔːr |əs
‖ ˌdɑːl ɪ koʊ- **~i** aɪ
Dolin 'dɒl ɪn §-ən ‖ 'doʊl-
dolina dɒ 'liːn ə dəʊ- ‖ doʊ- **~s** z
doline dɒ 'liːn dəʊ- ‖ doʊ- **~s** z
Dolittle 'duː ˌlɪt ᵊl ‖ -ˌlɪt̬-
doll, Doll dɒl ‖ dɑːl dɔːl **dolled** dɒld ‖ dɑːld
dɔːld **dolling** 'dɒl ɪŋ ‖ 'dɑːl ɪŋ 'dɔːl- **dolls,**
doll's dɒlz ‖ dɑːlz dɔːlz
'**doll's house**
dollar, D~ 'dɒl ə ‖ 'dɑːl ᵊr **~s** z
ˌdollar 'bill; 'dollar sign
dollarization, dollarisation
ˌdɒl ər aɪ 'zeɪʃᵊn -ɪ- ‖ ˌdɑːl ər ə-
doll|house 'dɒl |haʊs ‖ 'dɑːl- 'dɔːl- **~houses**
haʊz ɪz -əz
dollie, D~ 'dɒl i ‖ 'dɑːl i 'dɔːl i **~s** z
Dollond 'dɒl ənd ‖ 'dɑːl- 'dɔːl-
dollop 'dɒl əp ‖ 'dɑːl- **~s** s
doll|y, Dolly 'dɒl |i ‖ 'dɑːl |i 'dɔːl- **~ies, ~y's**
iz
'dolly bird; 'dolly ˌmixture
dolma 'dɒlm ə -ɑː ‖ 'dɑːlm- 'dɔːlm- —*Turkish*
[doɬ 'ma] **~s** z **dolmades** dɒl 'mɑːð ez
-'mɑːd iːz ‖ dɑːl- dɔːl- —*ModGk* [dol 'ma ðes]
dolman 'dɒlm ən ‖ 'doʊlm- **~s** z
dolmen 'dɒl men -mən ‖ 'doʊlm ən **~s** z
Dolmetsch 'dɒl metʃ ‖ 'dɑːl- 'dɔːl-
Dolmio *tdmk* dɒl 'miː əʊ ‖ dɑːl 'miː oʊ
dolomite, D~ 'dɒl ə maɪt ‖ 'doʊl- 'dɑːl- **~s** s
dolor 'dɒl ə ‖ 'doʊl ᵊr 'dɑːl- **~s** z
Dolores də 'lɔːr es dɒ-, -ɪs, -əs, -ez, -ɪz, -əz ‖ -əs
-'loʊr- —*Sp* [do 'lo ɾes]
doloroso ˌdɒl ə 'rəʊs əʊ -'rəʊz-
‖ ˌdoʊl ə 'roʊs oʊ —*It* [do lo 'ro: so]
dolorous 'dɒl ər əs ‖ 'doʊl- 'dɑːl- **~ly** li **~ness**
nəs nɪs
dolour 'dɒl ə ‖ 'doʊl ᵊr 'dɑːl- **~s** z
dolphin, D~ 'dɒlf ɪn §-ᵊn ‖ 'dɑːlf- 'dɔːlf- **~s** z
dolphinarium ˌdɒlf ɪ 'neər i_əm ˌ-ə-
‖ ˌdɑːlf ə 'ner- ˌdɔːlf- **~s** z
dolphin-safe ˌdɒlf ɪn 'seɪf ◂ §-ᵊn- ‖ ˌdɑːlf-
ˌdɔːlf-
Dolphus 'dɒlf əs ‖ 'dɑːlf-
dolt dəʊlt →dɒʊlt ‖ doʊlt **dolts** dəʊlts →dɒʊlts
‖ doʊlts
doltish 'dəʊlt ɪʃ →'dɒʊlt- ‖ 'doʊlt- **~ly** li **~ness**
nəs nɪs
dom, Dom dɒm ‖ dɑːm
-dom dəm — **martyrdom** 'mɑːt ə dəm
‖ 'mɑːrt̬ ᵊr dəm
domain dəʊ 'meɪn ‖ doʊ- də- **~s** z
Dombey 'dɒm bi ‖ 'dɑːm-
dome dəʊm ‖ doʊm **domed** dəʊmd ‖ doʊmd
domes dəʊmz ‖ doʊmz

Domecq dəʊ 'mek ‖ doʊ-
Domesday 'duːmz deɪ (= *Doomsday*)
'Domesday Book
domestic də 'mest ɪk **~ally** ᵊl_i **~s** s
do,mestic 'science; do,mestic 'service
domesti|cate də 'mest ɪ |keɪt **~cated** keɪt ɪd
-əd ‖ keɪt̬ əd **~cates** keɪts **~cating** keɪt ɪŋ
‖ keɪt̬ ɪŋ
domestication də ˌmest ɪ 'keɪʃ ᵊn
domesticity ˌdəʊm e 'stɪs ət i ˌdɒm-, ˌ-ə-, -ɪt i
‖ ˌdoʊm e 'stɪs ət̬ i ˌdɑːm-, ˌ-ə-; də ˌme-
Domestos *tdmk* də 'mest ɒs dəʊ- ‖ -oʊs
domicil|e 'dɒm ɪ saɪᵊl 'dəʊm-, -ə-, əs ɪl, §-əs ᵊl
‖ 'dɑːm- 'doʊm-, -əs ᵊl **~ed** d **~es** z **~ing** ɪŋ
domiciliary ˌdɒm ɪ 'sɪl i_ər i ˌ-ə-, -'sɪl ər i
‖ ˌdɑːm ə 'sɪl i er i ˌdoʊm-
dominance 'dɒm ɪn ən²s -ən- ‖ 'dɑːm-
dominant 'dɒm ɪn ənt -ən- ‖ 'dɑːm- △-ət **~s** s
domi|nate 'dɒm ɪ |neɪt -ə- ‖ 'dɑːm- **~nated**
neɪt ɪd -əd ‖ neɪt̬ əd **~nates** neɪts **~nating**
neɪt ɪŋ ‖ neɪt̬ ɪŋ
domination ˌdɒm ɪ 'neɪʃ ᵊn -ə- ‖ ˌdɑːm- **~s** z
dominatr|ix ˌdɒm ɪ 'neɪtr| ɪks -ə- ‖ ˌdɑːm-
~ices ɪ siːz ə- **~ixes** ɪks ɪz -əz
domineer ˌdɒm ɪ 'nɪə -ə- ‖ ˌdɑːm ə 'nɪᵊr **~ed** d
domineering/ly ˌdɒm ɪ 'nɪər ɪŋ /li ˌ-ə-
‖ ˌdɑːm ə 'nɪr ɪŋ /li **~s** z
Domingo də 'mɪŋ gəʊ dəʊ-, dɒ- ‖ -goʊ —*Sp*
[do 'mɪŋ go]
Dominic 'dɒm ɪ nɪk -ə- ‖ 'dɑːm-
Dominica *in the Leeward Islands*
ˌdɒm ɪ 'niːk ə -ə- ‖ ˌdɑːm- —*but often called*
də 'mɪn ɪk ə *by those not familiar with the*
name
dominical də 'mɪn ɪk ᵊl dɒ-, dəʊ-
Dominican *'of the D~ Republic'; religious*
də 'mɪn ɪk ən **~s** z
Do,minican Re'public
Dominican *'of Dominica'* ˌdɒm ɪ 'niːk ən ˌ-ə-
‖ ˌdɑːm- —*see note at* Dominica **~s** z
Dominick 'dɒm ɪ nɪk -ə- ‖ 'dɑːm-
dominie 'dɒm ɪn i -ən- ‖ 'dɑːm- **~s** z
dominion də 'mɪn jən -'mɪn i ən **~s** z
Dominique ˌdɒm ɪ 'niːk -ə-, '· · · ‖ ˌdɑːm- —*Fr*
[dɔ mi nik]
domino, D~ 'dɒm ɪ nəʊ -ə- ‖ 'dɑːm ə noʊ **~es,**
~s z
'domino ef,fect; 'domino ˌtheory
Dominus 'dɒm ɪn ʊs -ən-, -əs ‖ 'doʊm ɪ nuːs
'dɑːm-, -ə-
ˌdominus vo'biscum vəʊ 'bɪsk ʊm -əm
‖ voʊ-
Domitian də 'mɪʃ ᵊn dəʊ-, dɒ-, -'mɪʃ i_ən
Domremy, Domrémy dɒm 'reɪm i
‖ ˌdoʊm reɪ 'miː —*Fr* [dɔ̃ ʁe mi]
don, Don dɒn ‖ dɑːn —*See also phrases with*
this word **donned** dɒnd ‖ dɑːnd **donning**
'dɒn ɪŋ ‖ 'dɑːn ɪŋ **dons** dɒnz ‖ dɑːnz
Donaghadee ˌdɒn ə hə 'diː ˌ-ək- ‖ ˌdɑːn-
Donahue 'dɒn ə hjuː 'dʌn-, -huː ‖ 'dɑːn-
Donal 'dəʊn ᵊl ‖ 'doʊn ᵊl
Donald 'dɒn ᵊld ‖ 'dɑːn ᵊld
Donaldson 'dɒn ᵊld sən ‖ 'dɑːn-

D

Donat 'dəʊn æt ‖ 'doʊn-

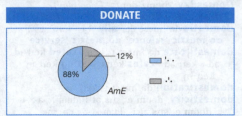

DONATE

88% / 12% '·· / ·'·

AmE

donate dəʊ 'neɪt ‖ 'doʊn eɪt doʊ 'neɪt
— *Preference poll, AmE:* '·· 88%, ·'· 12%.
donated dəʊ 'neɪt ɪd -əd ‖ 'doʊn eɪt̮ əd
doʊ 'neɪt̮- **donates** dəʊ 'neɪts ‖ 'doʊn eɪts
doʊ 'neɪts **donating** dəʊ 'neɪt ɪŋ
‖ 'doʊn eɪt̮ ɪŋ doʊ 'neɪt-
Donatello ˌdɒn ə 'tel əʊ ‖ ˌdɑːn ə 'tel oʊ
ˌdoʊn- —*It* [do na 'tɛl lo] **~s, ~'s** z
donation dəʊ 'neɪʃ ᵊn ‖ doʊ- **~s** z
Donatist 'dəʊn ət ɪst 'dɒn-, §-əst
‖ 'doʊn ət̮ əst 'dɑːn- **~s** z
donative 'dəʊn ət ɪv 'dɒn- ‖ 'doʊn ət̮ ɪv 'dɑːn-
~s z
donator dəʊ 'neɪt ə ‖ 'doʊn eɪt̮ ᵊr doʊ 'neɪt̮- **~s**
z
Don Carlos ˌdɒn 'kɑːl ɒs →ˌdɒŋ-
‖ ˌdɑːn 'kɑːrl oʊs -əs —*It, Sp* [doŋ 'kaɾ los]
Doncaster 'dɒŋk əst ə 'dɒŋ ˌkɑːst ə, -ˌkæst-
‖ 'dɑːŋ ˌkæst ᵊr 'dɑːn-, -kəst-
done dʌn (= *dun*)
donee ˌdəʊ 'niː ‖ doʊ- **~s** z
Donegal ˌdɒn ɪ 'ɡɔːl ◄ ‖ˌdʌn-, -ə-, '··· ‖ ˌdɑːn-
-'ɡɑːl, '···
Donegan 'dɒn ɪɡ ən -əɡ- ‖ 'dɑːn-
Donelly 'dɒn əl i ‖ 'dɑːn-
Doner, Döner 'dɒn ə ‖ 'doʊn ᵊr —*Turkish*
[dø 'neɾ]
ˌdoner ke'bab
dong dɒŋ ‖ dɑːŋ dɔːŋ **donged** dɒŋd ‖ dɑːŋd
dɔːŋd **donging** 'dɒŋ ɪŋ ‖ 'dɑːŋ ɪŋ 'dɔːŋ-
dongs dɒŋz ‖ dɑːŋz dɔːŋz
donga 'dɒŋ ɡə ‖ 'dɑːŋ- 'dɔːŋ- **~s** z
Don Giovanni ˌdɒn dʒəʊ 'vɑːn i -'væn i
‖ ˌdɑːn dʒi̯ə 'vɑːn i —*It* [dɔn dʒo 'van ni]
dongle 'dɒŋ ɡᵊl ‖ 'dɑːŋ- **~s** z
Donington 'dɒn ɪŋ tən 'dʌn- ‖ 'dɑːn-
Donizetti ˌdɒn ɪ 'zet i -ə-, -ɪd- ‖ ˌdɑːn ə 'zet̮ i
—*It* [do nid 'dzet ti]
donjon 'dɒndʒ ən 'dʌndʒ- ‖ 'dɑːndʒ- **~s** z
Don Juan (i) ˌdɒn 'dʒuː ən ‖ ˌdɑːn-, (ii) -'wɑːn
-'hwɑːn —*Sp* [doŋ 'xwan] —*in English
literature, including Byron, and usually when
used metaphorically, BrE prefers (i); in
imitated Spanish, and generally in AmE, (ii)
is preferred.*
donkey 'dɒŋk i ‖ 'dɑːŋk i 'dʌŋk-, 'dɔːŋk- **~s** z
'donkey ˌengine; 'donkey ˌjacket;
'donkey's ˌyears
donkeywork 'dɒŋk i wɜːk ‖ 'dɑːŋk i wɜːk
'dʌŋk-, 'dɔːŋk-
Donkin 'dɒŋk ɪn ‖ 'dɑːŋk-

Donleavy, Donlevy (i) dɒn 'liːv i ‖ dɑːn-,
(ii) -'lev i
Donmar 'dɒn mɑː →'dɒm- ‖ 'dɑːn mɑːr
donn... —*see* **don**
Donna, donna 'dɒn ə ‖ 'dɑːn ə —*It* ['dɔn na]
Donne (i) dʌn, (ii) dɒn ‖ dɑːn —*The poet John
Donne was probably* (i).
Donnegan 'dɒn ɪɡ ən -əɡ- ‖ 'dɑːn-
Donnell 'dɒn ᵊl ‖ 'dɑːn-
Donnelly 'dɒn əl i ‖ 'dɑːn-
Donner, d~ 'dɒn ə ‖ 'dɑːn ᵊr
Donnie 'dɒn i ‖ 'dɑːn i
donnish 'dɒn ɪʃ ‖ 'dɑːn- **~ly** li **~ness** nəs nɪs
Donny 'dɒn i ‖ 'dɑːn i
Donnybrook, d~ 'dɒn i brʊk §-bruːk ‖ 'dɑːn-
~s s
Donoghue, Donohue 'dɒn ə hjuː 'dʌn-, -huː
‖ 'dɑːn-
donor 'dəʊn ə ‖ 'doʊn ᵊr —*but in contrast
with* **donee** *also* -ɔː, ˌdəʊ 'nɔː ‖ -ɔːr,
ˌdoʊ 'nɔːr **~s** z
do-nothing 'duː ˌnʌθ ɪŋ **~s** z
Donovan (i) 'dɒn əv ən ‖ 'dɑːn-, (ii) 'dʌn-
Don Pasquale ˌdɒn pæ 'skwɑːl eɪ →ˌdɒm-,
-pə-, -i ‖ ˌdɑːn- —*It* [dɔm pas 'kwa: le]
Don Quixote ˌdɒn 'kwɪks ət →ˌdɒŋ-,
ˌkɪ 'həʊt i ‖ ˌdɑːn- ˌki: 'hoʊt eɪ —*Sp*
[doŋ ki 'xo te]
don't dəʊnt ‖ doʊnt —*also, non-finally, esp.
before a consonant sound,* dəʊn ‖ doʊn. *This
word has no weak form except occasionally* də
in don't mind, don't know *(see* **dunno***).* **don'ts**
dəʊnts ‖ doʊnts
ˌdon't ˈknows
do|nut 'dəʊ |nʌt ‖ 'doʊ- **~nuts** nʌts **~nutted**
nʌt ɪd -əd ‖ nʌt̮ əd **~nutting** nʌt ɪŋ ‖ nʌt̮ ɪŋ
doobie 'duːb i **~s** z
doodad 'duː dæd **~s** z
doodah 'duː dɑː **~s** z
doodl|e 'duːd ᵊl **~ed** d **~es** z **~ing** ɪŋ
doodlebug 'duːd ᵊl bʌɡ **~s** z
doo-doo 'duː duː
doofus 'duːf əs **~es** ɪz əz
doohickey 'duː ˌhɪk i **~s** z
doolally ˌduː 'læl i
Doolan 'duːl ən
Dooley 'duːl i
Doolittle 'duː ˌlɪt ᵊl ‖ -ˌlɪt̮ ᵊl
doom duːm **doomed** duːmd **dooming**
'duːm ɪŋ **dooms** duːmz
doom-laden 'duːm ˌleɪd ᵊn
doomsayer 'duːm ˌseɪ ə ‖ -ᵊr **~s** z
Doomsday, d~ 'duːmz deɪ
doomster 'duːm stə ‖ -stᵊr **~s** z
doomwatch 'duːm wɒtʃ ‖ -wɑːtʃ -wɔːtʃ **~er/s**
ə/z ‖ ᵊr/z **~es** ɪz əz
Doon, Doone duːn
Doonesbury 'duːnz bər_i ‖ -ˌber i
door dɔː ‖ dɔːr doʊr **doors** dɔːz ‖ dɔːrz doʊrz
doorbell 'dɔː bel ‖ 'dɔːr- 'doʊr- **~s** z
doorcas|e 'dɔː keɪs ‖ 'dɔːr- 'doʊr- **~es** ɪz əz
do-or-die ˌduː ɔː 'daɪ ◄ ‖ -ᵊr- -ɔːr-
doorframe 'dɔː freɪm ‖ 'dɔːr- 'doʊr- **~s** z

D

Double consonant letters

1 Double **consonant** letters in English spelling normally correspond to a single sound in pronunciation. So **happy** is pronounced ˈhæp i (not ˈhæp pi), **rabbit** rhymes perfectly with **habit**, **Ellen** rhymes perfectly with **Helen**.

For double **vowel** letters, see **ee** (under **e**), **oo** (under **o**).

2 An exception arises in a few words with **cc** before **i** or **e**, for example **succeed** sək ˈsiːd. See also the article on **s**, **ss**.

3 The other important exception is where the two letters in question belong to two different parts of a compound word, or one to a stem and one to an affix. Then the two letters usually correspond to two phonemes (see DOUBLE CONSONANT SOUNDS). Examples: **nighttime** ˈnaɪt taɪm, **unnamed** ˌʌn ˈneɪmd, **meanness** ˈmiːn nəs.

Adverbs in **-ly**, however, usually drop one l sound when attached to a stem ending in l: **fully** ˈfʊl i.

doorjamb ˈdɔː dʒæm ‖ ˈdɔːr- ˈdoʊr- ~**s** z
doorkeeper ˈdɔː ˌkiːp ə ‖ ˈdɔːr ˌkiːp ʰr ˈdoʊr-
   ~**s** z
doorknob ˈdɔː nɒb ‖ ˈdɔːr naːb ˈdoʊr- ~**s** z
doorknocker ˈdɔː ˌnɒk ə ‖ ˈdɔːr ˌnaːk ʰr
   ˈdoʊr- ~**s** z
door|man ˈdɔː |mæn -mən ‖ ˈdɔːr- ˈdoʊr-
   ~**men** mən men
doormat ˈdɔː mæt ‖ ˈdɔːr- ˈdoʊr- ~**s** s
doornail ˈdɔː neɪ³l ‖ ˈdɔːr- ˈdoʊr- ~**s** z
doorplate ˈdɔː pleɪt ‖ ˈdɔːr- ˈdoʊr- ~**s** s
doorpost ˈdɔː pəʊst ‖ ˈdɔːr poʊst ˈdoʊr- ~**s** s
doorscraper ˈdɔː ˌskreɪp ə ‖ ˈdɔːr ˌskreɪp ʰr
   ˈdoʊr- ~**s** z
doorstep ˈdɔː step ‖ ˈdɔːr- ˈdoʊr- ~**ped** t
   ~**ping** ɪŋ ~**s** s
doorstop ˈdɔː stɒp ‖ ˈdɔːr staːp ˈdoʊr- ~**per/s**
   ə/z ‖ ʰr/z ~**s** z
door-to-door ˌdɔː tə ˈdɔː ◄ ‖ ˌdɔːr tə ˈdɔːr ◄
   ˌdoʊr tə ˈdoʊr
doorway ˈdɔː weɪ ‖ ˈdɔːr- ˈdoʊr- ~**s** z
dooryard ˈdɔː jaːd ‖ ˈdɔːr jaːrd ˈdoʊr- ~**s** z
dooz|ie, dooz|y ˈduːz i ~**ies** iz
dopa ˈdəʊp ə ‖ ˈdoʊp ə -aː
dopamine ˈdəʊp ə miːn -mɪn ‖ ˈdoʊp-
dopant ˈdəʊp ənt ‖ ˈdoʊp- ~**s** s
dope dəʊp ‖ doʊp **doped** dəʊpt ‖ doʊpt
   dopes dəʊps ‖ doʊps **doping** ˈdəʊp ɪŋ
   ‖ ˈdoʊp ɪŋ
   ˈdope fiend; ˈdope ˌpeddler; ˈdope sheet
dopehead ˈdəʊp hed ‖ ˈdoʊp- ~**s** z
dop|ey ˈdəʊp |i ‖ ˈdoʊp |i ~**ier** i ə ‖ i ʰr ~**iest**
   i ɪst i əst
doppelganger, doppelgänger
   ˈdɒp ³l ˌgæŋ ə -ˌgeŋ- ‖ ˈdaːp ³l ˌgæŋ ʰr —*Ger*
   [ˈdɔp ³l ˌgeŋ ɐ] ~**s** z

Doppler ˈdɒp lə ‖ ˈdaːp lʰr
   ˈDoppler efˌfect
dopy —*see* **dopey**
Dora ˈdɔːr ə ‖ ˈdoʊr-
Dorabella ˌdɔːr ə ˈbel ə ‖ ˌdoʊr-
dorado də ˈraːd əʊ dɒ- ‖ -oʊ ~**s** z
Doran ˈdɔːr ən ‖ ˈdoʊr-
Dorcas ˈdɔːk əs ‖ ˈdɔːrk-
Dorchester ˈdɔːtʃ ɪst ə §-est- ‖ ˈdɔːr tʃest ʰr
   ˈdɔːtʃ əst ʰr
Dordogne ⁽ˌ⁾dɔː ˈdɔɪn ‖ dɔːr ˈdoʊn —*Fr*
   [dɔʁ dɔnj]
Dore dɔː ‖ dɔːr doʊr
Doré ˈdɔːr eɪ ‖ dɔː ˈreɪ —*Fr* [dɔ ʁe]
Doreen ˈdɔːr iːn dɔː ˈriːn, dɒ-, də- ‖ ˌdɔː ˈriːn
Doria ˈdɔːr i ə ‖ ˈdoʊr-
Dorian ˈdɔːr i ən ‖ ˈdoʊr-
Doric ˈdɒr ɪk ‖ ˈdɔːr- ˈdaːr-
dorie... —*see* **dory**
Dorinda də ˈrɪnd ə dɔː-, dɒ-
Doris *in Greece* ˈdɔːr ɪs ˈdɒr-, -əs ‖ ˈdaːr-, ˈdoʊr-
Doris *personal name* ˈdɒr ɪs -əs ‖ ˈdɔːr- ˈdaːr-,
   ˈdoʊr-
Doritos *tdmk* də ˈriːt əʊz ‖ -ˈriːt͡ oʊz
dork dɔːk ‖ dɔːrk **dorks** dɔːks ‖ dɔːrks
Dorking ˈdɔːk ɪŋ ‖ ˈdɔːrk-
dorky ˈdɔːk i ‖ ˈdɔːrk i
Dorling ˈdɔː lɪŋ ‖ ˈdɔːr-
dorm dɔːm ‖ dɔːrm **dorms** dɔːmz ‖ dɔːrmz
Dorman ˈdɔːm ən ‖ ˈdɔːrm-
dormanc|y ˈdɔːm ənt͡s |i ‖ ˈdɔːrm- ~**ies** iz
dormant ˈdɔːm ənt ‖ ˈdɔːrm-
dormer, D~ ˈdɔːm ə ‖ ˈdɔːrm ʰr ~**s** z
dormie ˈdɔːm i ‖ ˈdɔːrm i
dormition dɔː ˈmɪʃ ³n ‖ dɔːr-

dormitor|y 'dɔːm ətr |i -ɪtr-; '·ət,ər |i, '·ɪt,
‖ 'dɔːrm ə tɔːr |i **~ies** iz
'dormitory ,suburb

Dormobile *tdmk* 'dɔːm əʊ biːᵊl ‖ 'dɔːrm ə- **~s**
z

dor|mouse 'dɔː |maʊs ‖ 'dɔːr- **~mice** maɪs

dormy 'dɔːm i ‖ 'dɔːrm i

Dornoch 'dɔːn ɒk -ɒx, -ək, -əx ‖ 'dɔːrn ɑːk
—*locally* -əx

Dorothea ,dɒr ə 'θɪə -'θiː: ə ‖ ,dɔːr ə 'θiː: ə
,dɑːr-

Dorothy 'dɒr əθ i ‖ 'dɔːr- 'dɑːr- —*formerly* -ət-

Dorow, Dorrow 'dɒr əʊ ‖ 'dɔːr oʊ 'dɑːr-

dorp dɔːp ‖ dɔːrp **dorps** dɔːps ‖ dɔːrps

Dorr dɔː ‖ dɔːr

Dorrington 'dɒr ɪŋ tən ‖ 'dɔːr- 'dɑːr-

Dorrit 'dɒr ɪt §-ət ‖ 'dɔːr- 'dɑːr-

Dors dɔːz ‖ dɔːrz

dorsal 'dɔːs ᵊl ‖ 'dɔːrs- **~ly** i

Dorset 'dɔːs ɪt -ət ‖ 'dɔːrs-

Dorsey 'dɔːs i ‖ 'dɔːrs i

dorsum 'dɔːs əm ‖ 'dɔːrs-

Dortmund 'dɔːt mənd -mʊnd ‖ 'dɔːrt- —*Ger*
['dɔɐt mʊnt]

dor|y, Dory 'dɔːr |i ‖ 'doʊr- **~ies** iz

do's duːz

DOS dɒs ‖ dɑːs dɔːs

dosag|e 'dəʊs ɪdʒ §'dəʊz- ‖ 'doʊs- **~es** ɪz əz

dose dəʊs §dəʊz ‖ doʊs **dosed** dəʊst §dəʊzd
‖ doʊst **doses** 'dəʊs ɪz §'dəʊz-, -əz ‖ 'doʊs əz
dosing 'dəʊs ɪŋ §'dəʊz- ‖ 'doʊs ɪŋ

dosh dɒʃ ‖ dɑːʃ

do-si-do ,dəʊs i 'dəʊ ,dəʊ saɪ 'dəʊ
‖ ,doʊ siː 'doʊ **~s** z

dosimeter dəʊ 'sɪm ɪt ə -ət- ‖ doʊ 'sɪm ət ᵊr
~s z

dosimetry dəʊ 'sɪm ətr i -ɪtr- ‖ doʊ-

Dos Passos ₍ₒ₎dɒs 'pæs ɒs ‖ doʊs 'pæs oʊs
dəs-, -əs

doss dɒs ‖ dɑːs **dossed** dɒst ‖ dɑːst **dosses**
'dɒs ɪz -əz ‖ 'dɑːs əz **dossing** 'dɒs ɪŋ
‖ 'dɑːs ɪŋ

dosser 'dɒs ə ‖ 'dɑːs ᵊr **~s** z

doss|house 'dɒs |haʊs ‖ 'dɑːs- **-houses**
haʊz ɪz -əz

dossier 'dɒs i eɪ -i,ə ‖ 'dɔːs i eɪ 'dɑːs-, -i,ᵊr
—*Fr* [do sje] **~s** z

dost *from do* dʌst, *weak form* dəst

Dostoevski, Dostoevsky, Dostoyevski,
Dostoyevsky ,dɒst ɔɪ 'ef ski ‖ ,dɑːst ə 'jef-
,dʌst- —*Russ* [də stʌ 'jef skʲɪj]

dot, Dot dɒt ‖ dɑːt **dots** dɒts ‖ dɑːts **dotted**
'dɒt ɪd -əd ‖ 'dɑːt̬ əd **dotting** 'dɒt ɪŋ
‖ 'dɑːt̬ ɪŋ
,dotted 'line

dotage 'dəʊt ɪdʒ ‖ 'doʊt̬-

dotard 'dəʊt əd -ɑːd ‖ 'doʊt̬ ᵊrd **~s** z

dot-com ,dɒt 'kɒm ‖ ,dɑːt 'kɑːm **~s** z

dote dəʊt ‖ doʊt **doted** 'dəʊt ɪd -əd ‖ 'doʊt̬ əd
dotes dəʊts ‖ doʊts **doting** 'dəʊt ɪŋ
‖ 'doʊt̬ ɪŋ

doth *from do* dʌθ, *weak form* dəθ

Dotheboys 'duː ðə ,bɔɪz

doting 'dəʊt ɪŋ ‖ 'doʊt̬ ɪŋ **~ly** li

dot-matrix ,dɒt 'meɪtr ɪks '·,·· ‖ ,dɑːt-

Dotrice də 'triːs dɒ-

dott... —*see* **dot**

dotterel 'dɒtr əl ‖ 'dɑːtr- **~s** z

Dottie 'dɒt i ‖ 'dɑːt̬ i

dottle 'dɒt ᵊl ‖ 'dɑːt̬ ᵊl

dott|y 'dɒt |i ‖ 'dɑːt̬ |i **~ier** i,ə ‖ i,ᵊr **~iest** i,ɪst
i,əst **~ily** ɪ li əl i **~iness** i nəs i nɪs

Douai 'daʊ i 'duː,, -eɪ ‖ duː 'eɪ —*but the place*
in France is 'duː eɪ ‖ ·'· —*Fr* [dwe, du e]

Douala du 'ɑːl ə —*Fr* [dwa la]

doubl|e 'dʌb ᵊl **~ed** d **~es** z **~ing** ,ɪŋ **~y** ,i
,double 'agent, ,double 'bar; ,double
'bass; ,double 'bed; ,double 'bind;
,double 'bluff—*but* ,bluff and 'double
bluff; ,double 'chin; ,double 'cream;
,double 'date; ,double 'fault; ,double
'feature; ,double 'figures; ,Double
'Gloucester; 'doubles ,match; ,double
'take, '·· ·; ,double 'time

double-barreled, double-barrelled
,dʌb ᵊl 'bær əld ◀ ‖ -'ber-

double-bedded ,dʌb ᵊl 'bed ɪd ◀ -əd

double-blind ,dʌb ᵊl 'blaɪnd ◀

double-book ,dʌb ᵊl 'bʊk §-'buːk **~ed** t **~ing**
ɪŋ **~s** s

double-breasted ,dʌb ᵊl 'brest ɪd ◀ -əd

double-check ,dʌb ᵊl 'tʃek '···**~ed** t **~ing** ɪŋ
~s s

double-click ,dʌb ᵊl 'klɪk **~ed** t **~ing** ɪŋ **~s** s

double-clutch 'dʌb ᵊl klʌtʃ **~ed** t **~es** ɪz əz
~ing ɪŋ

double-cross ,dʌb ᵊl 'krɒs -'krɔːs ‖ -'krɔːs
-'krɑːs **~ed** t **~er/s** ə/z ‖ ᵊr/z **~es** ɪz əz **~ing**
ɪŋ

Doubleday 'dʌb ᵊl deɪ

double-deal|er ,dʌb ᵊl 'diː ᵊl |ə ‖ -|ᵊr **~ers** əz
‖ ᵊrz **~ing** ɪŋ

double-decker ,dʌb ᵊl 'dek ə ◀ ‖ -ᵊr **~s** z

double-declutch ,dʌb ᵊl di: 'klʌtʃ -dɪ'·, -də'·
~ed t **~es** ɪz əz **~ing** ɪŋ

double-digit ,dʌb ᵊl 'dɪdʒ ɪt ◀ §-ət

double-dip ,dʌb ᵊl 'dɪp **~ped** t **~ping** ɪŋ **~s** s

double-dotted ,dʌb ᵊl 'dɒt ɪd ◀ -əd
‖ -'dɑːt̬ əd ◀

double-dutch ,dʌb ᵊl 'dʌtʃ

double-dyed ,dʌb ᵊl 'daɪd ◀

double-edged ,dʌb ᵊl 'edʒd ◀
,double-edged 'compliment

double entendre ,duːb ᵊl ɒn 'tɒnd rə ,dʌb-
‖ ,ɑːn 'tɑːnd rə —*as if Fr* [du blɑ̃ tɑ̃:dʁ]

double-entry ,dʌb ᵊl 'entr i ◀

double-figure ,dʌb ᵊl 'fɪg ə ◀ ‖ -jᵊr

double-glaz|e ,dʌb ᵊl 'gleɪz **~ed** d **~es** ɪz əz
~ing ɪŋ

double-header ,dʌb ᵊl 'hed ə ‖ -ᵊr

double-jointed ,dʌb ᵊl 'dʒɔɪnt ɪd ◀ -əd
‖ -'dʒɔɪnt̬ əd ◀

double-park ,dʌb ᵊl 'pɑːk ‖ -'pɑːrk **~ed** t **~ing**
ɪŋ **~s** s

double-quick ,dʌb ᵊl 'kwɪk ◀
,double-quick 'time

Double consonant sounds

1 Double consonant sounds ('geminates') are found in English only across grammatical boundaries: where two words occur next to one another in connected speech, or in the two parts of a compound word, or a stem and an affix. They always straddle a syllable boundary, too. Examples are **a nice sight** ə ˌnaɪs ˈsaɪt, **midday** ˌmɪd ˈdeɪ, **soulless** ˈsəʊl ləs ‖ ˈsoʊl ləs.

2 Although cases like these consist of two identical phonemes in succession, they are not usually pronounced as two distinct complete sounds. The details depend on their manner of ARTICULATION.

- **Fricatives, nasals, liquids**: a geminate is pronounced like a single sound, except that it lasts longer. In **this set** ˌðɪs ˈset the two s's come together to make a long s: between the two vowels, straddling the syllable boundary. In **ten names** ˌten ˈneɪmz we get a long n:.

- **Plosives**: a geminate is pronounced like a single sound, with just one sequence of approach—hold—release (see PLOSIVES); but in a geminate the hold is longer. In **big game** ˌbɪg ˈɡeɪm there is a single phonetic ɡ: between the two vowels, straddling the syllable boundary. Exceptionally, because of the possibility of a GLOTTAL STOP, a geminated t may consist phonetically of ʔt: **that time** ˌðæt ˈtaɪm; but a single long alveolar tː is also possible.

- **Affricates** are the only case where two successive complete consonant sounds are pronounced independently, one after the other. In **rich choice** ˌrɪtʃ ˈtʃɔɪs the fricative part of the first tʃ can be separately heard before the beginning of the second tʃ. In **orange juice** there are two separate dʒs.

doubler 'dʌb ᵊl ə ‖ ᵊr ~s z
double-sided ˌdʌb ᵊl ˈsaɪd ɪd ◂ -əd
double-spac|e ˌdʌb ᵊl ˈspeɪs ~ed t ~es ɪz əz
  ~ing ɪŋ
doublespeak 'dʌb ᵊl spiːk
double-stop ˌdʌb ᵊl ˈstɒp ‖ -ˈstɑːp ~ped t
  ~ping ɪŋ ~s s
doublet 'dʌb lət -lɪt ~s s
double-talk 'dʌb ᵊl tɔːk ‖ -tɑːk ~ed t ~er/s ə/z
  ‖ ᵊr/z ~ing ɪŋ ~s s
doublethink 'dʌb ᵊl θɪŋk
doubleton 'dʌb ᵊl tən ~s z
double-tongu|e ˌdʌb ᵊl ˈtʌŋ §-ˈtɒŋ ~ing ɪŋ
double-wide 'dʌb ᵊl waɪd ~s z
doubling 'dʌb ᵊlˌɪŋ ~s z
doubloon dʌ ˈbluːn ~s z
doubly 'dʌb li
doubt daʊt **doubted** 'daʊt ɪd -əd ‖ 'daʊţ əd
  doubting 'daʊt ɪŋ ‖ 'daʊţ ɪŋ **doubts** daʊts
  ˌdoubting ˈThomas
doubter 'daʊt ə ‖ 'daʊţ ᵊr ~s z
doubtful 'daʊt fᵊl -fʊl ~ly i
doubtless 'daʊt ləs -lɪs ~ly li
douceur duː ˈsɜː ‖ -ˈsɝː —Fr [du sœːʁ] ~s z

douche duːʃ **douched** duːʃt **douches** 'duːʃ ɪz
  -əz **douching** 'duːʃ ɪŋ
Doug dʌg
Dougal, Dougall 'duːg ᵊl
Dougan 'duːg ən
dough dəʊ ‖ doʊ (= doe) **doughs** dəʊz ‖ doʊz
doughboy 'dəʊ bɔɪ ‖ 'doʊ- ~s z
Dougherty (i) 'dɒx ət i 'dɒk- ‖ 'dɑːk ᵊrţ i,
  (ii) 'dəʊ- ‖ 'doʊ- 'dɔːrţ i, (iii) 'dɑː-
dough|nut 'dəʊ |nʌt ‖ 'doʊ- ~nuts nʌts
  ~nutted nʌt ɪd -əd ‖ nʌţ əd ~nutting nʌt ɪŋ
  ‖ nʌţ ɪŋ
dought|y, D~ 'daʊt |i ‖ 'daʊţ |i ~ier i ə ‖ i ᵊr
  ~iest i ɪst i əst ~ily ɪ li əl i ~iness i nəs i nɪs
dough|y 'dəʊ |i ‖ 'doʊ |i ~ier i ə ‖ i ᵊr ~iest
  i ɪst i əst ~iness i nəs i nɪs
Dougie 'dʌg i
Douglas, Douglass 'dʌg ləs
Douglas-Home ˌdʌg ləs ˈhjuːm
Doukhobor 'duːk ə bɔː ‖ -bɔːr ~s z
doula 'duːlə ~s z
Doulton 'dəʊlt ən →'dɒʊlt- ‖ 'doʊlt ᵊn
Doune duːn
Dounreay 'duːn reɪ ˌ·ˈ·
dour dʊə 'daʊ_ə ‖ dʊᵊr daʊ_ᵊr

dourine 'dʊər iːn ‖ dʊ 'riːn
dour|ly 'dʊə |li 'daʊ ə |li ‖ 'dʊᵊr- 'daʊ ᵊr-
~**ness** nəs nɪs
Douro 'dʊər əʊ ‖ 'dʊr oʊ —*Port* ['do ɾu]
douse daʊs **doused** daʊst **douses** 'daʊs ɪz -əz
dousing 'daʊs ɪŋ
Douwe Egberts *tdmk* ˌdaʊ 'eg bəts -bɜːts
‖ -bᵊrts
dove *n* dʌv **doves** dʌvz
dove *v from* **dive** dəʊv ‖ doʊv
dovecot 'dʌv kɒt ‖ -kɑːt ~**s** s
dovecote 'dʌv kəʊt -kɒt ‖ -koʊt ~**s** s
Dovedale 'dʌv deɪᵊl
dovekey, dovekie 'dʌv ki ~**s** z
Dover 'dəʊv ə ‖ 'doʊv ᵊr
ˌDover 'sole
Dovercourt 'dəʊv ə kɔːt ‖ 'doʊv ᵊr kɔːrt
-koʊrt
Doveridge 'dʌv ər ɪdʒ
dovetail *n, v* 'dʌv teɪᵊl ~**ed** d ~**ing** ɪŋ ~**s** z
Dovey 'dʌv i —*Welsh* Dyfi ['də vi]
dovish 'dʌv ɪʃ
Dow daʊ
dowager 'daʊ ədʒ ə ɪdʒ- ‖ -ᵊr ~**s** z
Dowd daʊd
Dowdeswell 'daʊdz wəl -wel
Dowding 'daʊd ɪŋ
dowd|y 'daʊd |i ~**ier** i ə ‖ i ᵊr ~**ies** iz ~**iest**
i ɪst i əst ~**ily** ɪ li əl i ~**iness** i nəs i nɪs
dowel 'daʊ əl daʊl ‖ 'daʊ əl **doweled,**
dowelled 'daʊ əld daʊld ‖ 'daʊ əld
doweling, dowelling 'daʊ əl ɪŋ 'daʊl ɪŋ
‖ 'daʊ əl ɪŋ **dowels** 'daʊəlz daʊlz ‖ 'daʊ əlz
Dowell 'daʊ əl daʊl ‖ 'daʊ əl
dower, Dower 'daʊ ə ‖ 'daʊ ᵊr ~**s** z
dowitcher 'daʊ ɪtʃ ə ‖ -ᵊr ~**s** z
Dow-Jones ˌdaʊ 'dʒəʊnz ◂ ‖ -'dʒoʊnz ◂
ˌDow-Jones 'average
Dowlais 'daʊ laɪs -ləs
Dowland 'daʊ lənd
down, Down daʊn **downed** daʊnd **downing**
'daʊn ɪŋ **downs, Down's** daʊnz
ˌdown 'payment; 'Down's ˌsyndrome
down- ˌdaʊn
down-and-out ˌdaʊn ən 'aʊt ◂ -ənd- ~**s** s
down-and-outer ˌdaʊn ən 'aʊt ə ‖ -'aʊt ᵊr ~**s**
z
down-at-heel ˌdaʊn ət 'hiːᵊl ◂
downbeat 'daʊn biːt →'daʊm- ~**s** s
downcast 'daʊn kɑːst →'daʊŋ-, §-kæst ‖ -kæst
downdraft, downdraught 'daʊn drɑːft
§-dræft ‖ -dræft ~**s** s
downdrift 'daʊn drɪft
Downe daʊn
downer 'daʊn ə ‖ -ᵊr ~**s** z
Downes daʊnz
Downey 'daʊn i
downfall 'daʊn fɔːl ‖ -fɑːl ~**s** z
downgrad|e *v* ˌdaʊn 'greɪd →ˌdaʊn-; '·· ~**ed**
ɪd əd ~**es** z ~**ing** ɪŋ
downgrade *n* 'daʊn greɪd →'daʊŋ- ~**s** z
Downham 'daʊn əm

downhearted ˌdaʊn 'hɑːt ɪd ◂ -əd
‖ -'hɑːrt əd ◂ ~**ly** li ~**ness** nəs nɪs
downhill ˌdaʊn 'hɪl ◂ -**er/s** ə/z ‖ -ᵊr/z
down-home ˌdaʊn 'həʊm ◂ ‖ -'hoʊm ◂
downi... —*see* **downy**
Downie 'daʊn i
Downing 'daʊn ɪŋ
'Downing Street
downland, D~ 'daʊn lænd -lənd ~**s** z
downlighter 'daʊn ˌlaɪt ə ‖ -'laɪt ᵊr ~**s** z
download ˌdaʊn 'ləʊd '·· ‖ 'daʊn loʊd ~**ed** ɪd
əd ~**ing** ɪŋ ~**s** z
downloadable ˌdaʊn 'ləʊd əb ᵊl ◂ '····
‖ 'daʊn loʊd əb ᵊl
downmarket ˌdaʊn 'mɑːk ɪt ◂ →ˌdaʊm-, §-ət
‖ -'mɑːrk-
Downpatrick ₍ₜ₎daʊn 'pætr ɪk →₍ₜ₎daʊm-
downpipe 'daʊn paɪp →'daʊm- ~**s** s
downplay ˌdaʊn 'pleɪ ~**ed** d ~**ing** ɪŋ ~**s** z
downpour 'daʊn pɔː →'daʊm- ‖ -pɔːr -poʊr ~**s**
z
downrange ˌdaʊn 'reɪndʒ ◂
downright 'daʊn raɪt
downriver ˌdaʊn 'rɪv ə ◂ ‖ -ᵊr ◂
Downs daʊnz
downscale ˌdaʊn 'skeᵊl ◂
downshift 'daʊn ʃɪft ˌ·'· ~**ed** ɪd əd ~**ing** ɪŋ ~**s**
s
Downside, d~ 'daʊn saɪd
downsiz|e 'daʊn saɪz ˌ·'· ~**ed** d ~**es** ɪz əz ~**ing**
ɪŋ
downspout 'daʊn spaʊt ~**s** s
downstage ˌdaʊn 'steɪdʒ ◂
downstairs ˌdaʊn 'steəz ◂ ‖ -'steᵊrz ◂
-'stæᵊrz◂
downstate *n* 'daʊn steɪt
downstate *adj, adv* ˌdaʊn 'steɪt ◂
downstream ˌdaʊn 'striːm ◂
downstroke 'daʊn strəʊk ‖ -stroʊk ~**s** s
downswing 'daʊn swɪŋ ~**s** z
downtime 'daʊn taɪm
down-to-earth ˌdaʊn tu 'ɜːθ ◂ ‖ -'ɜːθ ◂
downtown ˌdaʊn 'taʊn ◂
downtrend 'daʊn trend ~**s** z
downtrodden 'daʊn ˌtrɒd ᵊn ˌ·'·· ‖ -ˌtrɑːd-
downturn 'daʊn tɜːn ‖ -tɜːn ~**s** z
downward 'daʊn wəd ‖ -wᵊrd ~**ly** li ~**ly** li ~**s**
z
downwash 'daʊn wɒʃ ‖ -wɔːʃ -wɑːʃ
downwind ˌdaʊn 'wɪnd ◂
down|y 'daʊn |i ~**ier** i ə ‖ i ᵊr ~**iest** i ɪst i əst
dowr|y 'daʊᵊr |i ~**ies** iz
dowse *'drench', 'extinguish'* daʊs **dowsed**
daʊst **dowses** 'daʊs ɪz -əz **dowsing** 'daʊs ɪŋ
dowse *'seek underground water or minerals'*
daʊz **dowsed** daʊzd **dowses** 'daʊz ɪz əz
dowsing 'daʊz ɪŋ
Dowse *name* daʊs
dowser 'daʊz ə ‖ -ᵊr ~**s** z
Dowsing 'daʊz ɪŋ
dowsing rod 'daʊz ɪŋ rɒd ‖ -rɑːd
Dowson 'daʊs ᵊn
doxastic dɒk 'sæst ɪk ‖ dɑːk-

doxolog|y dɒk 'sɒl ədʒ |i ‖ dɑːk 'sɑːl- **~ies** iz
dox|y 'dɒks |i ‖ 'dɑːks |i **~ies** iz
doyen 'dɔɪ ən -en —*Fr* [dwa jæ] **~s** z
doyenne ˌ(ˌ)dɔɪ 'en —*Fr* [dwa jɛn] **~s** z
Doyle dɔɪᵊl
doyley, D'Oyley, doyly, D'Oyly 'dɔɪl i **~s** z
doze dəʊz ‖ doʊz (= *doughs*) **dozed** dəʊzd
　‖ doʊzd **dozes** 'dəʊz ɪz -əz ‖ 'doʊz əz **dozing**
　'dəʊz ɪŋ ‖ 'doʊz ɪŋ
dozen 'dʌz ᵊn **~s** z
dozer 'dəʊz ə ‖ 'doʊz ᵊr **~s** z
doz|y 'dəʊz |i ‖ 'doʊz |i **~ier** i ə ‖ i ᵊr **~iest**
　i ɪst i əst **~ily** ɪ li əl i **~iness** i nəs i nɪs
DPhil ˌdiː 'fɪl
Dr '*debtor*' 'det ə ‖ 'deṭ ᵊr
Dr '*doctor*' 'dɒkt ə ‖ 'dɑːkt ᵊr
drab dræb **drabber** 'dræb ə ‖ -ᵊr **drabbest**
　'dræb ɪst -əst **drabs** dræbz
Drabble 'dræb ᵊl
drably 'dræb li
drabness 'dræb nəs -nɪs
dracaena drə 'siːn ə **~s** z
drachm dræm (= *dram*) **drachms** dræmz
drach|ma 'dræk |mə **~mae** miː meɪ **~mas** məz
Draco 'dreɪk əʊ ‖ -oʊ
draconian drə 'kəʊn i ən dreɪ- ‖ -'koʊn-
draconic drə 'kɒn ɪk dreɪ- ‖ -'kɑːn ɪk **~ally** ᵊl_i
Dracula 'dræk jʊl ə -jəl- ‖ -jəl ə
draff dræf
draft drɑːft §dræft ‖ dræft **drafted** 'drɑːft ɪd
　§'dræft-, -əd ‖ 'dræft əd **drafting** 'drɑːft ɪŋ
　§'dræft- ‖ 'dræft ɪŋ **drafts** drɑːfts §dræfts
　‖ dræfts
　'draft ˌdodger
draftee ˌ(ˌ)drɑːf 'tiː §ˌ(ˌ)dræf- ‖ ˌ(ˌ)dræf- **~s** z
drafter 'drɑːft ə §'dræft ə ‖ 'dræft ᵊr **~s** z
drafts|man 'drɑːfts |mən §'dræfts- ‖ 'dræfts-
　~manship mən ʃɪp **~men** mən men
draft|y 'drɑːft |i §'dræft- ‖ 'dræft |i **~ier** i ə
　‖ i ᵊr **~iest** i ɪst i əst **~iness** i nəs i nɪs
drag dræg **dragged** drægd **dragging** 'dræg ɪŋ
　drags drægz
　'drag ˌartist; 'drag race
Drage dreɪdʒ
dragee, dragée dræ 'ʒeɪ **~s** z
draggled 'dræg ᵊld
dragg|y 'dræg |i **~ier** i ə ‖ i ᵊr **~iest** i ɪst i əst
dragline 'dræg laɪn **~s** z
dragnet 'dræg net **~s** z
drago|man 'dræg ə |mən -mæn **~mans** mənz
　mænz **~men** mən men
dragon 'dræg ən **~s** z
dragonet 'dræg ən ɪt -ət, -ə net **~s** s
dragon|fly 'dræg ən |flaɪ →-ŋ- **~flies** flaɪz
dragonnad|e ˌdræg ə 'neɪd **~ed** ɪd əd **~es** z
　~ing ɪŋ
dragoon drə 'guːn **~ed** d **~ing** ɪŋ **~s** z
dragster 'dræg stə ‖ -stᵊr **~s** z
drail dreɪᵊl **drails** dreɪᵊlz
drain dreɪn **drained** dreɪnd **draining**
　'dreɪn ɪŋ **drains** dreɪnz
　'draining board
drainage 'dreɪn ɪdʒ

drainer 'dreɪn ə ‖ -ᵊr **~s** z
drainpipe 'dreɪn paɪp →'dreɪm- **~s** s
drake, Drake dreɪk **drakes, Drake's** dreɪks
Drakelow 'dreɪk ləʊ ‖ -loʊ —*locally also* '-ə ·
Drakensberg 'drɑːk ənˈs bɜːg 'dræk-, -ənz-
　‖ -bɜːg
Dralon *tdmk* 'dreɪl ɒn ‖ -ɑːn
dram dræm **drams** dræmz

DRAMA

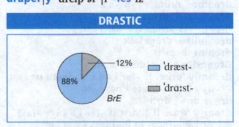

1%　　　　　　　11%

88%

　■ 'drɑːm-
　■ 'dræm-
　■ 'dreɪm-

AmE

drama 'drɑːm ə ‖ 'dræm ə — *Preference poll,*
　AmE: 'drɑːm- *88%,* 'dræm- *11%,* 'dreɪm- *1%.*
　~s z
drama-doc ˌdrɑːm ə 'dɒk ‖ -'dɑːk ˌdræm- **~s** s
Dramamine *tdmk* 'dræm ə miːn -mɪn **~s** z
dramatic drə 'mæt ɪk ‖ -'mæṭ- **~ally** ᵊl_i **~s** s
dramatis... —*see* **dramatiz...**
dramatis personae ˌdræm ət ɪs pɜː 'səʊn aɪ
　ˌdrɑːm-, drə 'mæt-, -iː ‖ -əṭ əs pᵊr 'soʊn iː -aɪ
dramatist 'dræm ət ɪst 'drɑːm-, §-əst ‖ -əṭ əst
　~s s
dramatization ˌdræm ət aɪ 'zeɪʃ ᵊn ˌdrɑːm-,
　-ət ɪ- ‖ -əṭ ə- **~s** z
dramatiz|e 'dræm ə taɪz 'drɑːm- **~ed** d **~es** ɪz
　əz **~ing** ɪŋ
dramaturg|e 'dræm ə tɜːdʒ 'drɑːm- ‖ -tɜːdʒ
　~es ɪz əz
dramaturgic ˌdræm ə 'tɜːdʒ ɪk ◄ ˌdrɑːm-
　‖ -'tɜːdʒ- **~al** ᵊl
dramaturgy 'dræm ə tɜːdʒ i 'drɑːm- ‖ -tɜːdʒ i
Drambuie dræm 'bjuː_i -'buː_i **~s** z
dramed|y 'drɑːm əd |i ‖ 'dræm- **~ies** iz
drank dræŋk
drape dreɪp **draped** dreɪpt **drapes** dreɪps
　draping 'dreɪp ɪŋ
draper, D~ 'dreɪp ə ‖ -ᵊr **~s** z
draper|y 'dreɪp ər |i **~ies** iz

DRASTIC

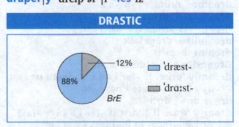

　　　　　　　12%

88%

　■ 'dræst-
　■ 'drɑːst-

BrE

drastic 'dræst ɪk 'drɑːst- — *Preference poll,*
　BrE: 'dræst- *88% (southerners 92%),* 'drɑːst-
　12% (southerners 8%). In AmE always
　'dræst-. **~ally** ᵊl_i
drat dræt **dratted** 'dræt ɪd -əd ‖ 'dræṭ əd
draught drɑːft §dræft ‖ dræft **~s** s
　'draught exˌcluder

draughtboard 'drɑːft bɔːd §'dræft-
‖ 'dræft bɔːrd -bourd ~s z
draughts|man 'drɑːfts |mən §'dræfts-
‖ 'dræfts- ~**manship** mən ʃɪp ~**men** mən
men
draught|y 'drɑːft |i §'dræft- ‖ 'dræft |i ~**ier** i ə
‖ i ͵ᵊr ~**iest** i ɪst i ͵əst ~**iness** i nəs i nɪs
Drava 'drɑːv ə
Dravidian drə 'vɪd i ͚ən ~s z
draw drɔː ‖ drɑː **drawing** 'drɔːͬ ɪŋ ‖ 'drɔː ɪŋ
'drɑː- **drawn** drɔːn ‖ drɑːn **draws** drɔːz
‖ drɑːz
drawback 'drɔː bæk ‖ 'drɑː- ~s s
drawbar 'drɔː bɑː ‖ -bɑːr 'drɑː- ~s z
drawbridg|e 'drɔː brɪdʒ ‖ 'drɑː- ~**es** ɪz əz
drawdown 'drɔː daʊn ‖ 'drɑː- ~s z
drawee ͵drɔːͬ 'iː ‖ drɔː 'iː drɑː- ~s z
drawer *'sliding container'* drɔː ‖ drɔːr ~s z
drawer *'one that draws'* 'drɔːͬ ə ‖ 'drɔː ͵ᵊr
'drɑː ͵ᵊr ~s z
drawers *'undergarment'* drɔːz ‖ drɔːrz
drawing 'drɔːͬ ɪŋ ‖ 'drɔː ɪŋ 'drɑː- ~s z
'**drawing board**; '**drawing pin**; '**drawing
room** *also* 'drɔɪŋ
drawl drɔːl ‖ drɑːl **drawled** drɔːld ‖ drɑːld
drawling 'drɔːl ɪŋ ‖ 'drɑːl- **drawls** drɔːlz
‖ drɑːlz
drawn drɔːn ‖ drɑːn
drawsheet 'drɔː ʃiːt ‖ 'drɑː- ~s s
drawstring 'drɔː strɪŋ ‖ 'drɑː- ~s z
Drax dræks
dray, Dray dreɪ **drays** dreɪz
Draycott *(i)* 'dreɪk ət, *(ii)* ͵'dreɪ kɒt ‖ -kɑːt
Drayton 'dreɪt ᵊn
dread dred **dreaded** 'dred ɪd -əd **dreading**
'dred ɪŋ **dreads** dredz
dreadful 'dred fᵊl -ful ~**ly** i ~**ness** nəs nɪs
dreadlock 'dred lɒk ‖ -lɑːk ~**ed** t ~s s
dreadnaught, dreadnought, D~ 'dred nɔːt
‖ -nɑːt ~s s
dream driːm **dreamed** dremᵖt driːmd ‖ driːmd
dreaming 'driːm ɪŋ **dreams** driːmz **dreamt**
dremᵖt
'**dream world**
dreamboat 'driːm bəʊt ‖ -boʊt ~s s
dreamer 'driːm ə ‖ -ᵊr ~s z
dreamland 'driːm lænd
dreamless 'driːm ləs -lɪs ~**ly** li
dreamlike 'driːm laɪk
dreamt dremᵖt
Dreamtime, d~ 'driːm taɪm
dream|y 'driːm |i ~**ier** i ə ‖ i ͵ᵊr ~**iest** i ɪst i ͵əst
~**ily** ɪ li əl i ~**iness** i nəs i nɪs
drear drɪə ‖ drɪᵊr
drear|y 'drɪər |i ‖ 'drɪr |i ~**ier** i ə ‖ i ͵ᵊr ~**iest**
i ɪst i ͵əst ~**ily** əl i ɪ li ~**iness** i nəs i nɪs
dreck drek
dredge dredʒ **dredged** dredʒd **dredges**
'dredʒ ɪz -əz **dredging** 'dredʒ ɪŋ
dredger 'dredʒ ə ‖ -ᵊr ~s z
dree driː **dreed** driːd **dreeing** 'driː ɪŋ **drees**
driːz
Dreena 'driːn ə

Dreft *tdmk* dreft
dreg dreg **dregs** dregz
dreidel 'dreɪd ᵊl ~s z
Dreiser *(i)* 'draɪs ə ‖ -ᵊr, *(ii)* 'draɪz ə ‖ -ᵊr
drench drentʃ **drenched** drentʃt **drenches**
'drentʃ ɪz -əz **drenching** 'drentʃ ɪŋ
Drene *tdmk* driːn
Dresden 'drezd ən —*Ger* ['dʁeːs dᵊn]
dress dres **dressed** drest **dresses** 'dres ɪz -əz
dressing 'dres ɪŋ
͵**dress 'circle**, '· ·͵·; ͵**dress re'hearsal**;
'**dress shield**; ͵**dress 'suit** ‖ '· ·
dressage 'dres ɑːʒ -ɑːdʒ, -ɪdʒ, dre 'sɑːʒ
‖ drə 'sɑːʒ dre-
dresser 'dres ə ‖ -ᵊr ~s z
dressing 'dres ɪŋ ~s z
'**dressing room**; '**dressing ͵table**
dressing-down ͵dres ɪŋ 'daʊn
dressing-gown 'dres ɪŋ gaʊn ~s z
dressing-up ͵dres ɪŋ 'ʌp
dressmaker 'dres ͵meɪk ə ‖ -ᵊr ~s z
dressmaking 'dres ͵meɪk ɪŋ
dress-up 'dres ʌp
dress|y 'dres |i ~**ier** i ə ‖ i ͵ᵊr ~**iest** i ɪst i ͵əst
~**ily** ɪ li əl i ~**iness** i nəs i nɪs
drew, Drew druː
Drexel 'dreks ᵊl
drey dreɪ **dreys** dreɪz
Dreyfus, Dreyfuss 'dreɪf əs 'draɪf-, -ʊs —*Fr*
[dʁɛ fys]
Drian 'driː͵ ən
dribbl|e 'drɪb ᵊl ~**ed** d ~**er/s** ͚ə/z ‖ ͚ᵊr/z ~**es** z
~**ing** ͚ɪŋ
Driberg 'draɪ bɜːg ‖ -bɜːg
driblet 'drɪb lət -lɪt ~s s
dribs and drabs ͵drɪbz ən 'dræbz
dried draɪd
dried-up ͵draɪd 'ʌp ◂
drier 'draɪ͵ ə ‖ 'draɪ ͵ᵊr ~s z
dries draɪz
driest 'draɪ ɪst 'draɪ ͵əst
Driffield 'drɪf iːᵊld
drift drɪft **drifted** 'drɪft ɪd -əd **drifting**
'drɪft ɪŋ **drifts** drɪfts
'**drift ice**
driftage 'drɪft ɪdʒ
drifter 'drɪft ə ‖ -ᵊr ~s z
driftnet 'drɪft net ~s s
driftwood 'drɪft wʊd
Drighlington 'drɪg lɪŋ tən 'drɪl ɪŋ-
drill drɪl **drilled** drɪlds **drilling** 'drɪl ɪŋ **drills**
drɪlz
drillstock 'drɪl stɒk ‖ -stɑːk ~s s
drily 'draɪ li
drink drɪŋk **drank** dræŋk **drinking** 'drɪŋk ɪŋ
drinks drɪŋks **drunk** drʌŋk
'**drinking ͵fountain**; '**drinking ͵water**
drinkable 'drɪŋk əb ᵊl ~s z
drink-driv|er ͵drɪŋk 'draɪv| ə ‖ -ᵊr ~**ers** əz
‖ ᵊrz ~**ing** ɪŋ
drinker 'drɪŋk ə ‖ -ᵊr ~s z
drinking-up ͵drɪŋk ɪŋ 'ʌp
͵**drinking-'up time**

Drinkwater 'drɪŋk ˌwɔːt ə ‖ -ˌwɔːʈ ʰr -ˌwɑːʈ-
drip drɪp **dripped** drɪpt **dripping** 'drɪp ɪŋ
  drips drɪps
  '**drip feed**; '**drip pan**
drip-|dry v 'drɪp |draɪ ˌ·'·◂ **~dried** draɪd
  ~dries draɪz **~drying** draɪ ɪŋ
drip-dry adj ˌdrɪp 'draɪ ◂
  ˌdrip-dry 'shirts
drip-|feed 'drɪp| fiːd ˌ·'·◂ **~fed** fed **~feeding**
  fiːd ɪŋ **~feeds** fiːdz
drip-mat 'drɪp mæt **~s** s
dripping 'drɪp ɪŋ **~s** z
dripp|y 'drɪp |i **~ier** i ə ‖ i ʰr **~iest** i ɪst i əst
Driscoll 'drɪsk ʰl
drive draɪv **driven** 'drɪv ʰn **drives** draɪvz
  driving 'draɪv ɪŋ **drove** drəʊv ‖ droʊv
  '**drive shaft**; '**driving ˌlicence**; '**driving**
  seat; '**driving test**
driveaway 'draɪv ə ˌweɪ
drive-by 'draɪv baɪ
drive-in 'draɪv ɪn **~s** z
drivel 'drɪv ʰl **~ed, ~led** d **~ing, ~ling** ɪŋ **~s** z
driveler, driveller 'drɪv ʰl ə ‖ ər **~s** z
driven 'drɪv ʰn
driver, D~ 'draɪv ə ‖ -ʰr **~s** z
  '**driver ant**; '**driver's ˌlicense**; '**driver's**
  seat
drive-through, drive-thru 'draɪv θruː **~s** z
drivetime 'draɪv taɪm
driveway 'draɪv weɪ **~s** z
Driza-bone tdmk 'draɪz ə bəʊn ‖ -boʊn
drizzl|e 'drɪz ʰl **~ed** d **~es** z **~ing** ˌɪŋ
drizzly 'drɪz ʰl i
Drogheda 'drɒɪ ɪd ə 'drɒh-, -əd-
drogue drəʊg ‖ droʊg **drogues** drəʊgz
  ‖ droʊgz
droid drɔɪd **droids** drɔɪdz
droit de seigneur ˌdrwɑː də seɪn 'jɜː -sen'·,
  -siːn'· ‖ -'jɜː: —Fr [dʁwad sɛ njœːʁ]
Droitwich 'drɔɪt wɪtʃ
droll drəʊl →drɒʊl ‖ droʊl **drolls** drəʊlz
  →drɒʊlz ‖ droʊlz
droller|y 'drəʊl ər |i →'drɒʊl- ‖ 'droʊl- **~ies** iz
drollness 'drəʊl nəs →'drɒʊl-, -nɪs ‖ 'droʊl-
drolly 'drəʊl li →'drɒʊl- ‖ 'droʊl-
-drome drəʊm ‖ droʊm — **palindrome**
  'pæl ɪn drəʊm -ən- ‖ -droʊm
dromedar|y 'drɒm əd ər |i ‖ 'drʌm-, '·ɪd ;
  -ə der i, -ɪ · · ‖ 'drɑːm ə der |i 'drʌm- **~ies** iz
Dromio 'drəʊm i əʊ 'drɒm- ‖ 'droʊm i oʊ
Dromore drə 'mɔː ‖ -'mɔːr -'moʊr
-dromous stress-imposing drəm əs —
  catadromous kə 'tæd rəm əs əs
drone drəʊn ‖ droʊn **droned** drəʊnd
  ‖ droʊnd **drones** drəʊnz ‖ droʊnz **droning**
  'drəʊn ɪŋ ‖ 'droʊn ɪŋ
Dronfield 'drɒn fiːʰld ‖ 'drɑːn-
drongo 'drɒŋ gəʊ ‖ 'drɑːŋ goʊ **~es, ~s** z
Drood druːd
drool druːl **drooled** druːld **drooling** 'druːl ɪŋ
  drools druːlz
droop druːp **drooped** druːpt **drooping/ly**
  'druːp ɪŋ /li **droops** druːps

droop|y 'druːp |i **~ier** i ə ‖ i ʰr **~iest** i ɪst i əst
  ~ily ɪ li əl i **~iness** i nəs -nɪs
drop drɒp ‖ drɑːp **dropped** drɒpt ‖ drɑːpt
  dropping 'drɒp ɪŋ ‖ 'drɑːp ɪŋ **drops** drɒps
  ‖ drɑːps
  '**drop scone**; '**drop shot**
drop-dead ˌdrɒp 'ded ◂ ‖ ˌdrɑːp-
drop-down 'drɒp daʊn ‖ 'drɑːp- **~s** z
drophead 'drɒp hed ‖ 'drɑːp- **~s** z
drop-in 'drɒp ɪn ˌ·'· ‖ 'drɑːp-
dropkick 'drɒp kɪk ‖ 'drɑːp- **~ed** t **~ing** ɪŋ **~s**
  s
drop-leaf 'drɒp liːf ‖ 'drɑːp-
droplet 'drɒp lət -lɪt ‖ 'drɑːp- **~s** s
drop-off 'drɒp ɒf -ɔːf ‖ 'drɑːp ɔːf -ɑːf **~s** s
dropout 'drɒp aʊt ‖ 'drɑːp- **~s** s
dropper 'drɒp ə ‖ 'drɑːp ʰr **~s** z
dropping 'drɒp ɪŋ ‖ 'drɑːp- **~s** z
dropsical 'drɒps ɪk ʰl ‖ 'drɑːps- **~ly** i
dropsy 'drɒps i ‖ 'drɑːps i
dropwort 'drɒp wɜːt §-wɔːt ‖ 'drɑːp wɜːt
  -wɔːrt **~s** s
drosh|ky 'drɒʃ |ki ‖ 'drɑːʃ- **~kies** kiz
drosophila drɒ 'sɒf ɪl ə drə-, -əl-
  ‖ drə 'sɑːf əl ə drə- **~s** z
dross drɒs ‖ drɑːs drɔːs
drought draʊt ‖ ⚠drauθ **droughts** draʊts
  ‖ ⚠drauθs —*The pronunciation with θ*
  properly belongs with a now archaic doublet
  spelled drouth.
drove drəʊv ‖ droʊv **droves** drəʊvz ‖ droʊvz
drover 'drəʊv ə ‖ 'droʊv ʰr **~s** z
drown draʊn **drowned** 'draʊnd **drowning**
  'draʊn ɪŋ **drowns** draʊnz
drowse draʊz **drowsed** draʊzd **drowses**
  'draʊz ɪz -əz **drowsing** 'draʊz ɪŋ
drows|y 'draʊz |i **~ier** i ə ‖ i ʰr **~iest** i ɪst i əst
  ~ily ɪ li əl i **~iness** i nəs i nɪs
Droylsden 'drɔɪʰlz dən
drub drʌb **drubbed** drʌbd **drubbing** 'drʌb ɪŋ
  drubs drʌbz
Druce druːs
drudge, Drudge drʌdʒ **drudged** drʌdʒd
  drudges 'drʌdʒ ɪz -əz **drudging/ly**
  'drʌdʒ ɪŋ /li
drudger|y 'drʌdʒ ər |i **~ies** iz
drug drʌg **drugged** drʌgd **drugging** 'drʌg ɪŋ
  drugs drʌgz
  '**drug ˌaddict**
drugged-out ˌdrʌgd 'aʊt ◂
drugget 'drʌg ɪt §-ət **~s** s
druggie 'drʌg i **~s** z
druggist 'drʌg ɪst §-əst **~s** s
drugg|y 'drʌg |i **~ies** iz
drugstore 'drʌg stɔː ‖ -stɔːr -stoʊr **~s** z
Druid, druid 'druː ɪd **~s** z
druidic dru 'ɪd ɪk **~al** ʰl
drum drʌm **drummed** drʌmd **drumming**
  'drʌm ɪŋ **drums** drʌmz
  ˌdrum 'major ‖ '· ˌ· ·; ˌdrum ˌmajo'rette
  ‖ '· · ·ˌ·
Drumalbyn drʌm 'ælb ɪn §-ən
drumbeat 'drʌm biːt **~s** s

D

Drumcondra drʌm 'kɒndr ə ‖ -'kɑːndr ə
drumfire 'drʌm ˌfaɪ ə ‖ -ˌfaɪ ˌʳr
drumhead 'drʌm hed ~s z
drumlin 'drʌm lɪn -lən ~s z
drumm... —*see* **drum**
drummer 'drʌm ə ‖ -ʳr ~s z
Drummond 'drʌm ənd
Drumnadrochit ˌdrʌm nə 'drɒx ɪt -'drɒk-, §-ət
‖ -'drɑːk-
Drumochter drə 'mɒxt ə -'mɒkt- ‖ -'mɑːkt ʳr
drum-roll 'drʌm rəʊl →-rɒʊl ‖ -roʊl ~s z
drumstick 'drʌm stɪk ~s s
drunk drʌŋk **drunks** drʌŋks
drunkard 'drʌŋk əd ‖ -ʳrd ~s z
drunken 'drʌŋk ən ~ly li ~ness nəs nɪs
drunkometer drʌŋ 'kɒm ɪt ə -ət-
‖ -'kɑːm ət ʳr 'drʌŋk ə ˌmiːt ʳr ~s z
drupe druːp (= *droop*) **drupes** druːps
drupel 'druːp ³l ~s z
Drury 'drʊər i ‖ 'drʊr i
Druse, druse druːz **Druses, druses** 'druːz ɪz
-əz
Drusilla dru 'sɪl ə
druther 'drʌð ə ‖ -ʳr ~s z
Druze druːz **Druzes** 'druːz ɪz -əz
dry draɪ **dried** draɪd **drier, dryer** 'draɪ ə
‖ 'draɪ ʳr **dries** draɪz **driest, dryest** 'draɪ ɪst
'draɪ ˌəst **drying** 'draɪ ɪŋ
'dry ˌbattery, ˌ· '· ·; ˌdry 'cleaner's; 'dry
dock, ˌ· '·; 'dry goods; ˌdry 'ice; ˌdry 'land;
ˌdry 'rot; ˌdry 'run
dryad 'draɪ æd 'draɪ ˌəd **dryades** 'draɪ ə diːz
dryads 'draɪ ædz 'draɪ ˌədz
Dryburgh 'draɪ bər ə ‖ 'draɪ bɜːg
dry-clean ˌdraɪ 'kliːn ◄ ~ed d ~ing ɪŋ ~s z
Dryden 'draɪd ³n
dryer 'draɪ ə ‖ 'draɪ ʳr **dryest** 'draɪ ɪst 'draɪ ˌəst
dry-eyed ˌdraɪ 'aɪd ◄
dryish 'draɪ ɪʃ
dryly 'draɪ li
dryness 'draɪ nəs -nɪs
drypoint 'draɪ pɔɪnt ~s s
dry-roasted ˌdraɪ 'rəʊst ɪd ◄ -əd ◄ ‖ -'roʊst-
Drysdale 'draɪz deɪ³l
dry-shod ˌdraɪ 'ʃɒd ◄ 'draɪ ʃɑːd
dry-stone 'draɪ stəʊn ˌ·'· ‖ -stoʊn
drywall 'draɪ wɔːl ‖ -wɑːl
DTI ˌdiː tiː 'aɪ
DTs, d t's, DT's ˌdiː 'tiːz
Du *in names* (i) dju →dʒu, (ii) du —*See also*
phrases with this word—*This prefix is*
unstressed.
dual 'djuː ˌəl →'dʒuː ˌ, §'duː ˌ; djuːl, →dʒuːl;
§duːl ‖ 'duː əl 'djuː- ~s z
ˌdual 'carriageway
Duala du 'ɑːl ə
dual-band ˌdjuː əl 'bænd ◄ →ˌdʒuː ˌ, §ˌduː ˌ;
ˌdjuːl'·, →ˌdʒuːl'·, §ˌduːl'· ‖ ˌduː əl- ˌdjuː əl-
dualism 'djuː ˌəl ˌɪz əm →'dʒuː ˌ, §'duː ˌ ‖ 'duː-
'djuː- ~s z
dualist 'djuː ˌəl ɪst →'dʒuː ˌ, §'duː ˌ §-əst ‖ 'duː-
'djuː- ~s s

dualistic ˌdjuː ə 'lɪst ɪk ◄ →ˌdʒuː ˌ, §ˌduə ˌ
‖ ˌduː- ˌdjuː- ~ally ³l i
dualit|y dju 'æl ət |i →dʒu-, §du-, -ɪt i
‖ du 'æl ət |i djuː- ~ies iz
dual-purpose ˌdjuː ˌəl 'pɜːp əs ◄ →ˌdʒuː ˌ,
§ˌduː ˌ; ˌdjuːl'· ·, →ˌdʒuːl'· ·, §ˌduːl'· ·
‖ ˌduː əl 'pɜːp əs ◄ ˌdjuː-
Duane ⑴duː 'eɪn dweɪn
dub dʌb **dubbed** dʌbd **dubbing** 'dʌb ɪŋ **dubs**
dʌbz
Dubai ˌdu: 'baɪ ˌdjuː-, →ˌdʒuː-, du-, dju-,
→dʒu-; →'baɪ i —*Arabic* [du 'bajj]
Dubarry dju 'bær i du- ‖ du- dju-, -'ber i
dubbin 'dʌb ɪn §-ən ~ed d ~s z
Dubček 'dʊb tʃek ‖ 'duːb- —*Slovak*
['dup tʃek]
dubiet|y dju 'baɪ ət |i →dʒu-, -ɪt-
‖ du 'baɪ ət |i djuː- ~ies iz
dubious 'djuːb i əs →'dʒuːb- ‖ 'duːb- 'djuːb-
~ly li ~ness nəs nɪs
Dublin 'dʌb lɪn §-lən
ˌDublin 'Bay, ˌDublin Bay 'prawn
Dubliner 'dʌb lɪn ə §-lən- ‖ -ʳr ~s z
dubnium 'dʌb ni əm 'duːb-, 'dʊb-
Dubois, Du Bois *American family name*
du 'bɔɪs də-, -'bɔɪz
Dubois *French or Dutch family name* du 'bwɑː
dju- —*Fr* [dy bwa]
Dubonnet *tdmk*, **d~** du 'bɒn eɪ dju-, →dʒu-
‖ ˌduːb ə 'neɪ —*Fr* [dy bɔ nɛ] ~s z
Dubrovnik du 'brɒv nɪk dju- ‖ -'brɑːv-
—*Croatian* [''du brov niːk]
Dubuque də 'bjuːk
ducal 'djuːk ³l →'dʒuːk- ‖ 'duːk ³l 'djuːk- ~ly i
Du Cane dju 'keɪn du- ‖ du- dju-
Du Cann dju 'kæn du- ‖ du- dju-
ducat 'dʌk ət ~s s
duce 'duːtʃ eɪ —*It* ['dut tʃe]
Duchamp 'dju: ʃɒ̃ 'duː-, -ʃɒm ‖ du 'ʃɑː -'ʃɑːm
—*Fr* [dy ʃɑ̃]
Duchenne du 'ʃen dju-
Duchesne dju 'ʃeɪn du-
duchess 'dʌtʃ ɪs -əs, -es, ˌdʌtʃ 'es ~es ɪz əz
duchesse dju 'ʃes du- —*Fr* [dy ʃɛs]
duch|y 'dʌtʃ |i ~ies iz
Ducie 'djuːs i →'dʒuːs- ‖ 'duːs i 'djuːs-
duck, Duck dʌk **ducked** dʌkt (= *duct*)
ducking 'dʌk ɪŋ **ducks** dʌks
'ducking stool; ˌducks and 'drakes
duckbill 'dʌk bɪl ~ed d ~s z
ˌduckbilled 'platypus
duckboard 'dʌk bɔːd ‖ -bɔːrd -boʊrd ~s z
duck-egg 'dʌk eg ~s z
Duckett 'dʌk ɪt §-ət
Duckham 'dʌk əm ~'s z
duckie 'dʌk i ~s z
duckling 'dʌk lɪŋ ~s z
duckweed 'dʌk wiːd
Duckworth 'dʌk wəθ -wɜːθ ‖ -wʳθ
duck|y 'dʌk |i ~ier i ə ‖ i ʳr ~ies iz ~iest i ɪst
i ˌəst
duct dʌkt **ducted** 'dʌkt ɪd -əd **ducting**
'dʌkt ɪŋ **ducts** dʌkts

ductile 'dʌkt aɪ³l ‖ -³l
ductility dʌk 'tɪl ət i -ɪt- ‖ -əţ i
ductless 'dʌkt ləs -lɪs
dud dʌd **duds** dʌdz
Dudden, Duddon 'dʌd ³n
dude duːd djuːd **dudes** duːdz djuːdz
  'dude ranch
dudgeon 'dʌdʒ ən
Dudley 'dʌd li

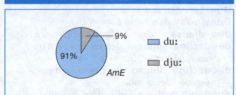

DUE

9% ☐ duː
91% ☐ djuː
AmE

due djuː →dʒuː ‖ duː djuː — *Preference poll,*
  AmE: duː *91%,* djuː *9%.* **dues** djuːz →dʒuːz
  ‖ duːz djuːz
duel 'djuː‿əl →'dʒuː‿; djuːl, →dʒuːl ‖ 'duː‿əl
  'duː- *(= dual)* **~ed, ~led** d **~er/s, ~ler/s** ə/z
  ‖ ³r/z **~ing, ~ling ~s** z
duelist, duellist 'djuː‿əl ɪst →'dʒuː‿, §-əst;
  'djuːl-, →'dʒuːl- ‖ 'duː‿əl əst 'duː- **~s** s
duenna dju 'en ə duː- ‖ duː- djuː- **~s** z
Duerden 'djʊəd ³n ‖ 'dʊrd ³n 'djʊrd-
duet dju 'et →dʒuː- ‖ duː- djuː- **~s** s
duettist dju 'et ɪst →dʒuː-, §-əst ‖ du 'eţ ɪst
  djuː- **~s** s
duff, Duff dʌf **duffed** dʌft **duffing** 'dʌf ɪŋ
  duffs dʌfs
duffel, D~ *tdmk* 'dʌf ³l
duffer 'dʌf ə ‖ -³r **~s** z
Dufferin 'dʌf ər ɪn -³r‿ən
Duffey, Duffie 'dʌf i
Duffield 'dʌf iː³ld
duffle 'dʌf ³l
  'duffle bag; 'duffle coat
Duffy 'dʌf i
Dufton 'dʌft ən
Dufy 'duːf i ‖ du 'fiː — *Fr* [dy fi]
dug dʌg **dugz** dʌgz
Dugald 'duːg ³ld
Dugan 'duːg ən
Dugdale 'dʌg deɪ³l
Duggan 'dʌg ən
Duggleby 'dʌg ³l bi
dugong 'duː gɒŋ 'djuː- ‖ -gɑːŋ -gɔːŋ **~s** z
dugout 'dʌg aʊt **~s** s
Duguid 'djuːɡ ɪd 'duːg-
duh dɜː ‖ də dʌ
duiker 'daɪk ə ‖ -³r **~s** z
Duisburg 'djuːz bɜːg 'djuːs- ‖ 'duːs bɜːg 'duːz-
  — *Ger* ['dyːs bʊʁk]
Duisenberg 'daɪz ³n bɜːg 'dɔɪz- ‖ 'duːz ³n bɜːg
  — *Dutch* ['dœy s³n bɛrx]
Dukakis du 'kɑːk ɪs djuː-, də-, §-əs
Dukas 'djuːk ɑː 'duːk- ‖ du 'kɑː djuː- — *Fr*
  [dy ka]

duke, Duke djuːk →dʒuːk ‖ duːk djuːk **dukes,**
  Duke's djuːks →dʒuːks ‖ duːks djuːks
dukedom 'djuːk dəm →'dʒuːk- ‖ 'duːk- 'djuːk-
  ~s z
Dukeries 'djuːk ər iz →dʒuːk- ‖ 'duːk- 'djuːk-
Dukhobor 'duːk ə bɔː -əʊ- ‖ -bɔːr **~s** z
Dukinfield 'dʌk ɪn fiː³ld -ən-
Dulais 'dɪl aɪs -əs
dulcet 'dʌls ɪt -ət
dulciana ˌdʌls i 'ɑːn ə ‖ -'æn ə -'ɑːn ə
Dulcie 'dʌls i
dulcimer 'dʌls ɪm ə -əm- ‖ -³r **~s** z
Dulcinea ˌdʌls ɪ 'niː‿ə -ə-, -'neɪ ə
Dulcy 'dʌls i
dulia du 'laɪ ə djuː-; 'djuːl i‿ə, 'duːl-
dull dʌl **dulled** dʌld **duller** 'dʌl ə ‖ -³r **dullest**
  'dʌl ɪst -əst **dulling** 'dʌl ɪŋ **dulls** dʌlz
dullard 'dʌl əd ‖ -³rd **~s** z
Dulles 'dʌl ɪs -əs
dullish 'dʌl ɪʃ
dullness 'dʌl nəs -nɪs
dullsville 'dʌlz vɪl §-v³l **~s** z
dull-witted ˌdʌl 'wɪt ɪd ◄ -əd ‖ -'wɪţ əd ◄
  ~ness nəs nɪs
dully 'dʌl li 'dʌl i
dulness 'dʌl nəs -nɪs
dulse dʌls
Duluth də 'luːθ du-, djuː-
Dulux *tdmk* 'djuː lʌks →'dʒuː- ‖ 'duː- 'djuː-
Dulverton 'dʌlv ət ən ‖ -³rt ³n
Dulwich 'dʌl ɪdʒ -ɪtʃ
duly 'djuː li →'dʒuː- ‖ 'duː li djuː-
Duma, duma 'duːm ə
Dumaresq, d~ dju 'mer ɪk →dʒuː- ‖ duː- djuː-
  ~s s
Dumas 'djuːm ɑː 'duːm-; du 'mɑː ‖ du 'mɑː
  —*Fr* [dy ma]
Du Maurier du 'mɒr i eɪ djuː- ‖ də 'mɔːr-
dumb dʌm **dumbed** dʌmd **dumber** 'dʌm ə
  ‖ -³r **dumbest** 'dʌm ɪst -əst **dumbing**
  'dʌm ɪŋ **dumbs** dʌmz
  'dumb show
Dumbarton ˌ(ˌ)dʌm 'bɑːt ³n dəm- ‖ -'bɑːrt ³n
  ˌDumbarton 'Oaks; ˌDumbarton 'Bridge *in*
  CA
dumbbell 'dʌm bel **~s** z
dumbfound ˌ(ˌ)dʌm 'faʊnd '·· **~ed** ɪd əd **~ing**
  ɪŋ **~s** z
Dumbledore 'dʌm b³l dɔː ‖ -dɔːr
dumb|ly 'dʌm |li **~ness** nəs nɪs
Dumbo 'dʌm bəʊ ‖ -boʊ
dumbstruck 'dʌm strʌk
dumbwaiter ˌdʌm 'weɪt ə ‖ -'weɪţ ³r **~s** z
dumdum, dum-dum 'dʌm dʌm
dumfound ˌ(ˌ)dʌm 'faʊnd '·· **~ed** ɪd əd **~ing** ɪŋ
  ~s z
Dumfries ˌ(ˌ)dʌm 'friːs dəm-, -'friːz
Dummer 'dʌm ə ‖ -³r
dumm|y 'dʌm |i **~ies** iz
dump dʌmp **dumped** dʌmpt **dumping**
  'dʌmp ɪŋ **dumps** dʌmps
  'dump truck
dumper 'dʌmp ə ‖ -³r **~s** z

dumpi... —*see* **dumpy**
dumpling 'dʌmp lɪŋ ~s z
dumpster, D~ *tdmk* 'dʌmpst ə ‖ -ᵊr ~s z
dump|y 'dʌmp |i ~ier i‿ə ‖ i‿ᵊr ~iest i‿ɪst i‿əst
~ily ɪ li əl i ~iness i nəs i nɪs
dun, Dun dʌn **dunned** dʌnd **dunner** 'dʌn ə
‖ -ᵊr **dunnest** 'dʌn ɪst -əst **dunning** 'dʌn ɪŋ
duns dʌnz —*See also phrases with this word*
Dunaway 'dʌn ə weɪ
Dunbar dʌn 'bɑː →dʌm- ‖ -'bɑːr '··
Dunblane dʌn 'bleɪn →dʌm-
Duncan 'dʌŋk ən
Duncannon dʌn 'kæn ən →dʌŋ-
dunce dʌn's **dunces, dunce's** 'dʌn's ɪz -əz
'dunce's cap
Dunciad 'dʌn's i æd
Dundalk *in Ireland* ₍ᵢ₎dʌn 'dɔːk -'dɔːlk ‖ -'dɑːk
—*but the place in MD is* '··
Dundas dʌn 'dæs 'dʌnd əs
Dundee ₍ᵢ₎dʌn 'diː
₍ᵢ₎Dun'dee cake; ,Dundee U'nited, ·,--
dunderhead 'dʌnd ə hed ‖ -ᵊr- ~ed əd ~s z
Dundonald dʌn 'dɒn ᵊld ‖ -'dɑːn-
Dundonian dʌn 'dəʊn i‿ən ‖ -'doʊn- ~s z
Dundrear|y, d~ dʌn 'drɪər |i ‖ -'drɪr |i ~ies iz
dune djuːn →dʒuːn ‖ duːn djuːn **dunes** djuːnz
→dʒuːnz ‖ duːnz djuːnz
'dune ,buggy
Dunedin dʌn 'iːd ɪn -ᵊn —*in NZ* -ᵊn
Dunfermline dʌn 'fɜːm lɪn -lən ‖ -'fɝːm-
dung dʌŋ **dunged** dʌŋd **dunging** 'dʌŋ ɪŋ
dungs dʌŋz
'dung ,beetle
Dungannon dʌn 'gæn ən →dʌŋ-
dungaree ,dʌŋ gə 'riː '··· ~s z
Dungeness ,dʌnd'ʒ ə 'nes ◄
,Dungeness 'B; ,Dungeness 'crab
dungeon 'dʌndʒ ən ~s z
dunghill 'dʌŋ hɪl ~s z
Dunhill 'dʌn hɪl ~s, ~'s z
dunk dʌŋk **dunked** dʌŋkt **dunking** 'dʌŋk ɪŋ
dunks dʌŋks
Dunkeld dʌn 'keld →dʌŋ-
Dunkery 'dʌŋk ər i
,Dunkery 'Beacon
Dunkirk ₍ᵢ₎dʌn 'kɜːk →₍ᵢ₎dʌŋ- ‖ 'dʌn kɜːk —*Fr*
Dunkerque [dœ̃ kɛʁk]
Dunkley 'dʌŋk li
Dunkling 'dʌŋk lɪŋ
Dun Laoghaire, Dún Laoghaire, Dún
Laoire ₍ᵢ₎dʌn 'lɪər i ₍ᵢ₎duːn-, -'leər-, -ə ‖ -'ler-
—*Irish* [dun 'l̪ˠeː rʲe]
dunlin 'dʌn lɪn -lən ~s z
Dunlop 'dʌn lɒp ‖ -lɑːp —*but as placename*
and family name, in BrE usually ·'·
Dunmail ,dʌn 'meᵊl →,dʌm-
,Dunmail 'Raise
Dunmow 'dʌn məʊ →'dʌm- ‖ -moʊ
Dunn, Dunne dʌn
dunn... —*see* **dun**
dunnage 'dʌn ɪdʒ
Dunnet, Dunnett 'dʌn ɪt §-ət
,Dunnet 'Head

dunno '*don't know*' də 'nəʊ ₍ᵢ₎dʌ- ‖ -'noʊ
dunnock 'dʌn ək ~s s
dunn|y 'dʌn |i ~ies iz
Dunoon dʌn 'uːn də 'nuːn
Duns dʌnz
,Duns 'Scotus 'skəʊt əs -'skɒt- ‖ 'skoʊt̬-
Dunsany dʌn 'seɪn i -'sæn-
Dunsinane dʌn 'sɪn ən —*but in Shakespeare's*
'*Macbeth*' ,dʌn'ts ɪ 'neɪn, -ə-, '···
Dunstable 'dʌn'st əb ᵊl
Dunstan 'dʌn'st ən
Dunster 'dʌn'st ə ‖ -ᵊr
Dunwoody dʌn 'wʊd i
duo 'djuː əʊ →'dʒuː- ‖ 'duː oʊ 'djuː- ~s z
duodecimal ,djuː əʊ 'des ɪm ᵊl ◄ →,dʒuː-,
-'·əm- ‖ ,duː oʊ- ,djuː- ~ly i ~s z
duodecimo ,djuː əʊ 'des ɪ məʊ →,dʒuː-, -'·ə-
‖ ,duː oʊ 'des ə moʊ
duoden|um ,djuː əʊ 'diːn |əm →,dʒuː-
‖ ,duː ə- ,djuː-: ~a ə ~al ᵊl ◄ ~ums əmz
,duo,denal 'ulcer
duologue 'djuː‿ə lɒg →'dʒuː‿‿ ‖ 'duː ə lɔːg
'djuː-, -lɑːg ~s z
duopol|y djuː 'ɒp əl |i →dʒuː- ‖ duː 'ɑːp- djuː-
~ies iz
dupe djuːp →dʒuːp ‖ duːp djuːp **duped** djuːpt
→dʒuːpt ‖ duːpt djuːpt **dupes** djuːps →dʒuːps
‖ duːps djuːps **duping** 'djuːp ɪŋ →'dʒuːp-
‖ 'duːp ɪŋ djuːp-
duple 'djuːp ᵊl →'dʒuːp- ‖ 'duːp ᵊl 'djuːp-
duplex 'djuːp leks →'dʒuːp- ‖ 'duː p- 'djuːp-
~es ɪz əz
duplicate *adj, n* 'djuːp lɪk ət →'dʒuː p-, -lək-,
-ɪt ‖ 'duː p- 'djuːp- ~s s
dupli|cate *v* 'djuːp lɪ |keɪt →'dʒuː p-, -lə-
‖ 'duː p- 'djuːp- ~cated keɪt ɪd -əd ‖ keɪt̬ əd
~cates keɪts ~cating keɪt ɪŋ ‖ keɪt̬ ɪŋ
duplication ,djuːp lɪ 'keɪʃ ᵊn →,dʒuː p-, -lə-
‖ ,duːp- ,djuːp- ~s z
duplicator 'djuːp lɪ keɪt ə →'dʒuː p-, '·lə-
‖ 'duːp lɪ keɪt̬ ᵊr 'djuːp- ~s z
duplicitous djuː 'plɪs ɪt əs →dʒuː-, -ət-
‖ duː 'plɪs ət̬ əs djuː- ~ly li
duplicity djuː 'plɪs ət i →dʒuː-, -ɪt-
‖ duː 'plɪs ət̬ i djuː-
Dupont *(i)* djuː 'pɒnt →dʒuː- ‖ duː 'pɑːnt djuː-,
(ii) 'djuː pɒnt →'dʒuː- ‖ 'duː pɑːnt 'djuː-
—*Fr* [dy põ]
Dupré, Duprée, Duprez duː 'preɪ djuː- —*but*
as an English name, also -'priː
Dupuytren duː 'pwiːtr ən djuː-; 'djuːp i trõ, ·'··
—*Fr* [dy pɥi tʁæ̃]
Duquesne duː 'keɪn djuː- —*Fr* [dy kɛn]
durability ,djʊər ə 'bɪl ət i ,djɔː-, →,dʒʊər-,
-ɪt i ‖ ,dʊr ə 'bɪl ət̬ i ,djʊr-
durab|le 'djʊər əb |ᵊl 'djɔːr-, →'dʒʊər- ‖ 'dʊr-
'djʊr- ~leness ᵊl nəs -nɪs ~les ᵊlz ~ly li
Duracell *tdmk* 'djʊər ə sel →'dʒʊər- ‖ 'dʊr-
'djʊr-
Durack 'djʊər æk ‖ 'dʊr- 'djʊr-
Duraglit *tdmk* 'djʊər ə glɪt →'dʒʊər- ‖ 'dʊr-
'djʊr-

duralumin, D~ *tdmk* djuᵊ 'ræl jυ mɪn →dʒuᵊ-,
-jə-, §-mən ‖ du 'ræl jəm ən dju-
dura mater ˌdjυər ə 'meɪt ə →ˌdʒυər-
‖ ˌdυr ə 'mɑːt ᵊr ˌdjυr-, '·· , ··
Duran djuᵊ 'ræn duᵊ-, →dʒuᵊ-
durance 'djυər ənˤs 'djɔːr-, →'dʒυər- ‖ 'dυr-
'djυr-
Durango dju 'ræŋ gəυ →dʒu-, də-
‖ du 'ræŋ goυ dju-, də-
duration djuᵊ 'reɪʃ ᵊn djɔː-, →dʒuᵊ- ‖ du- dju-
~s z
durative 'djυər ət ɪv 'djɔːr-, →'dʒυər-
‖ 'dυr ət ɪv 'djυr-
Durban 'dɜːb ən ‖ 'dɝːb-
durbar 'dɜːb ɑː ˌdɜː 'bɑː ‖ 'dɝːb ɑːr ~s z
Durbin 'dɜːb ɪn §-ən ‖ 'dɝːb-
Durbridge 'dɜː brɪdʒ ‖ 'dɝː-
Durer, Dürer 'djυər ə ‖ 'dυr ᵊr —*Ger* ['dy: ʁɐ]
duress djuᵊ 'res →dʒuᵊ-, 'djυər es ‖ dυ 'res
durex, Durex *tdmk* 'djυər eks 'djɔːr-, →dʒυər-
‖ 'dυr- 'djυr- ~es ɪz əz
Durham 'dʌr əm ‖ 'dɝː-
durian 'dυər i ən 'djυr-, -i ɑːn ‖ 'dυr- ~s z
Durie 'djυər i ‖ 'dυr i 'djυər-

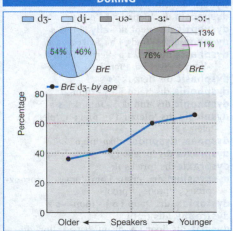

DURING

□ dʒ-　□ dj-　▨ -υə-　■ -ɜː-　□ -ɔː-

54% | 46%
BrE

76% | -13% | -11%
BrE

●─ *BrE* dʒ- by age

Percentage
80
60
40
20
0
Older ◄── Speakers ──► Younger

during 'dʒυər ɪŋ 'djυər-, 'dʒɜːr-, -'djɜːr-, 'dʒɔːr-,
'djɔːr- ‖ 'dɝː ɪŋ 'dυr-, 'djυr- — *Preference poll,*
BrE: 'dʒ- *54% (born since 1981, 67%)* 'dj-
46%; -υə- *76%,* -ɜː- *13%,* -ɔː- *10%.*
Durkheim 'dɜːk haɪm ‖ 'dɝːk- —*Fr* [dyʁ kɛm]
durmast 'dɜː mɑːst §-mæst ‖ 'dɝː mæst ~s s
Durness 'dɜːn əs -ɪs ‖ 'dɝːn-
Durrant (i) 'dʌr ənt ‖ 'dɝː-, (ii) də 'rænt
Durrell 'dʌr əl ‖ 'dɝːr-
Durrenmatt, Dürrenmatt 'djυər ən mæt
'dυər- ‖ 'dυr ən mɑːt —*Ger* ['dʏʁ ən mat]
durr|ie, durr|y 'dʌr |i ‖ 'dɝː |i ~ies ɪz
durst dɜːst ‖ dɝːst **durstn't** 'dɜːs ᵊnt ‖ 'dɝːs-
durum 'djυər əm →'dʒυər- ‖ 'dυr- 'djυr-, 'dɜː-
Dushanbe ˌdu: ʃæn 'beɪ →-ʃæm- ‖ ˌʃɑːn- -ʃæn-,
→-ʃɑːm-, →-ʃæm-
dusk dʌsk **dusked** dʌskt **dusking** 'dʌsk ɪŋ
dusks dʌsks

dusk|y 'dʌsk |i ~ier i ə ‖ i ᵊr ~iest i ɪst i ˌəst
~ily ɪ li əl i ~iness i nəs i nɪs
Dusseldorf, Düsseldorf 'dυs ᵊl dɔːf
‖ 'duːs ᵊl dɔːrf 'dυs- —*Ger* ['dʏs ᵊl dɔʁf]
dust dʌst **dusted** 'dʌst ɪd -əd **dusting** 'dʌst ɪŋ
dusts dʌsts
'dust ˌcover; 'dust ˌdevil; 'dusting
ˌpowder; 'dust ˌjacket; 'dust storm
dustbin 'dʌst bɪn ~s z
dustbowl 'dʌst bəυl -→bυl ‖ -boυl ~s z
dustcart 'dʌst kɑːt ‖ -kɑːrt ~s s
dustcoat 'dʌst kəυt ‖ -koυt ~s s
duster 'dʌst ə ‖ -ᵊr ~s z
dusti... —*see* **dusty**
Dustin 'dʌst ɪn §-ən
dust|man 'dʌst |mən ~men mən men
dustpan 'dʌst pæn ~s z
dustsheet 'dʌst ʃiːt →'dʌʃ- ~s s
dustup 'dʌst ʌp ~s s
dust|y, Dusty 'dʌst |i ~ier i ə ‖ i ᵊr ~iest i ɪst
i ˌəst ~ily ɪ li əl i ~iness i nəs i nɪs
Dutch, dutch dʌtʃ
ˌDutch 'auction; ˌDutch 'courage; ˌDutch
'elm diˌsease; ˌDutch 'oven; ˌDutch 'treat;
ˌDutch 'uncle
Dutch|man 'dʌtʃ |mən ~men mən men
~woman ˌwυm ən ~women ˌwɪm ɪn §-ən
duteous 'djuːt i əs →'dʒuːt- ‖ 'duːʈ i əs 'djuːʈ-
~ly li ~ness nəs nɪs
Duthie 'dʌθ i
duti... —*see* **duty**
dutiable 'djuːt i əb ᵊl →'dʒuːt- ‖ 'duːʈ- 'djuːʈ-
dutiful 'djuːt ɪ fᵊl →'dʒuːt-, -ə-, -fυl ‖ 'duːʈ-
'djuːʈ- ~ly ˌi ~ness nəs nɪs
Du Toit dju 'twɑː du- ‖ du- dju-
Dutton 'dʌt ᵊn
dut|y 'djuːt |i →'dʒuːt i ‖ 'duːʈ |i 'djuːʈ i ~ies
ɪz
duty-free ˌdjuːt i 'friː ◄ →ˌdʒuːt- ‖ ˌduːʈ- ˌdjuːʈ-
ˌduty-'free shop, ˌduty-free 'whisky
duum|vir dju 'ʌm |və du-, -'υm- ‖ du 'ʌm |vᵊr
~virate vər ət vɪr-, -ɪt; -və reɪt, vɪ- ~viri və riː
vɪ-, -raɪ
Duvalier du 'væl i eɪ dju- ‖ ˌduː vɑːl 'jeɪ ·'··
—*Fr* [dy va lje]
duvet 'duːv eɪ 'djuːv- ‖ du 'veɪ ~s z
dux dʌks
Duxford 'dʌks fəd ‖ -fᵊrd
duyker 'daɪk ə ‖ -ᵊr ~s z
DVD ˌdi: vi: 'di: ~s z
Dvorak, Dvořák 'dvɔːʒ æk 'vɔːʒ-, -ɑːk
‖ 'dvɔːʒ ɑːk —*Czech* ['dvɔ ˌraːk] —*but as an*
American family name, and for the keyboard
design, also 'dvɔːr æk
dwale dweɪᵊl
dwarf dwɔːf ‖ dwɔːrf **dwarfed** dwɔːft
‖ dwɔːrft **dwarfing** 'dwɔːf ɪŋ ‖ 'dwɔːrf ɪŋ
dwarfs dwɔːfs ‖ dwɔːrfs **dwarves** dwɔːvz
‖ dwɔːrvz
dwarfish 'dwɔːf ɪʃ ‖ 'dwɔːrf-
dwarfism 'dwɔːf ˌɪz əm ‖ 'dwɔːrf-
dwarves dwɔːvz ‖ dwɔːrvz
Dwayne dweɪn

dweeb dwiːb **dweebs** dwiːbz

dwell dwel **dwelled** dweld dwelt **dwelling**
  ˈdwel ɪŋ **dwells** dwelz **dwelt** dwelt

dweller ˈdwel ə ‖ -ᵊr ~s z

dwelling ˈdwel ɪŋ ~s z
  ˈdwelling house

dwelt dwelt

Dwight dwaɪt

dwindl|e ˈdwɪnd ᵊl ~ed d ~es z ~ing ɪŋ

Dworkin ˈdwɔːk ɪn §-ən ‖ ˈdwɔːrk-

Dwyer ˈdwaɪ ə ‖ -ᵊr

Dwynwen ˈduː ɪn wen

dyad ˈdaɪ æd ~s z

dyadic daɪ ˈæd ɪk ~s s

Dyak ˈdaɪ æk -ək ~s s

dyarch|y ˈdaɪ ɑːk |i ‖ -ɑːrk |i ~ies iz

dybbuk ˈdɪb ək di: ˈbuːk ~ed t ~s s

Dyce daɪs

Dyck daɪk

dye daɪ (= die) **dyed** daɪd **dyes** daɪz **dyeing**
  ˈdaɪ ɪŋ

dyed-in-the-wool ˌdaɪd ɪn ðə ˈwʊl ◂ ˌ-ᵊn-

dyer, Dyer ˈdaɪ ə ‖ ˈdaɪ ᵊr ~s z

dyestuff ˈdaɪ stʌf ~s s

dyeworks ˈdaɪ wɜːks ‖ -wɜːks

Dyfed ˈdʌv ɪd -ed, -əd —Welsh [ˈdə ved]
  —Also, by those not familiar with the name,
  ˈdɪf-

Dyffryn ˈdʌf rɪn -rən —Welsh [ˈdəf rin, -rin]

Dyfrig ˈdʌv rɪg —Welsh [ˈdəv rig]

dying ˈdaɪ ɪŋ

Dyirbal ˈdʒɪəb ɑːl ‖ ˈdʒɪrb-

dyke daɪk (= dike) **dyked** daɪkt **dykes** daɪks
  dyking ˈdaɪk ɪŋ

Dykes daɪks

Dylan ˈdɪl ən ˈdʌl- —Welsh [ˈdə lan]

Dymchurch ˈdɪm tʃɜːtʃ ‖ -tʃɜːtʃ

dymo, Dymo tdmk ˈdaɪm əʊ ‖ -oʊ ~ˈd, ~ed d
  ~s z ~ing ɪŋ

Dymock, Dymoke ˈdɪm ək

Dympna ˈdɪmp nə

dynamic daɪ ˈnæm ɪk dɪ-, də- ~ally ᵊl i ~s s

dynamism ˈdaɪn ə ˌmɪz əm ~s z

dyna|mite ˈdaɪn ə |maɪt ~mited maɪt ɪd -əd
  ‖ maɪt̬ əd ~mites maɪts ~miting maɪt ɪŋ
  ‖ maɪt̬ ɪŋ

dynamo ˈdaɪn ə məʊ ‖ -moʊ ~s z

dynamometer ˌdaɪn ə ˈmɒm ɪt ə -ət ə
  ‖ -ˈmɑːm ət̬ ᵊr ~s z

dynast ˈdɪn əst ˈdaɪn-, -æst ‖ ˈdaɪn æst -əst ~s
  s

dynastic dɪ ˈnæst ɪk də-, daɪ- ‖ daɪ- ~ally ᵊl i

dynast|y ˈdɪn əst |i ‖ ˈdaɪn- (*) ~ies iz

dyne daɪn (= dine) **dynes** daɪnz

Dynevor ˈdɪn ɪv ə -əv- ‖ -ᵊr —but in Wales
  often dɪ ˈnev ə. Welsh Dinefwr [di ˈne vur]

d'you djuː, dju, djə →dʒuː, →dʒu, →dʒə

dys- ˌ(ˌ)dɪs — **dysfunction** ˌ(ˌ)dɪs ˈfʌŋk ʃᵊn

Dysart ˈdaɪz ət ˈdaɪs-, -ɑːt ‖ -ɑːrt

dysarthria dɪs ˈɑːθ ri ə ‖ -ˈɑːrθ-

dyscalculia ˌdɪs kæl ˈkjuːl i ə

dysentery ˈdɪs ᵊntr i ˈdɪs ᵊnt ər i, §-ᵊn ter i
  ‖ ˈdɪs ᵊn ter i

dysfunction ˌ(ˌ)dɪs ˈfʌŋk ʃᵊn ~al ᵊl ~s z

dyslalia dɪs ˈleɪl i ə -ˈlæl- ~s z

dyslectic ˌ(ˌ)dɪs ˈlekt ɪk ~s s

dyslexia ˌ(ˌ)dɪs ˈleks i ə

dyslexic ˌ(ˌ)dɪs ˈleks ɪk ~s s

dysmenorrhea, dysmenorrhoea
  ˌdɪs ˌmen ə ˈrɪə ‖ -ˈriː ə

Dyson ˈdaɪs ᵊn

dyspepsia dɪs ˈpeps i ə -ˈpep ʃə

dyspeptic dɪs ˈpept ɪk ~ally ᵊl i ~s s

dysphagia dɪs ˈfeɪdʒ i ə -ˈfeɪdʒ ə

dysphasia dɪs ˈfeɪz i ə -ˈfeɪʒ-, -ˈfeɪʒ i ə
  ‖ -ˈfeɪʒ ə -ˈfeɪʒ i ə, -ˈfeɪz i ə

dysphasic dɪs ˈfeɪz ɪk ~s s

dysphonia dɪs ˈfəʊn i ə ‖ -ˈfoʊn-

dysphonic dɪs ˈfɒn ɪk ‖ -ˈfɑːn ɪk ~s s

dysplasia dɪs ˈpleɪz i ə -ˈpleɪʒ ə -ˈpleɪʒ i ə,
  -ˈpleɪz i ə

dyspnea, dyspnoea dɪsp ˈniː ə

dyspraxia dɪs ˈpræks i ə

dyspraxic dɪs ˈpræks ɪk

dysprosium dɪs ˈprəʊz i əm -ˈprəʊs- ‖ -ˈproʊz-
  -ˈprouʒ-, -ˈprous-, -ˈprouʃ-

dystopia ˌ(ˌ)dɪs ˈtəʊp i ə ‖ -ˈtoʊp- ~s z

dystrophy ˈdɪs trəf i

dysuria dɪs ˈjʊər i ə ˌdɪs juˈ ˈriː ə ‖ -ˈjʊr- dɪʃ-

dziggetai ˈdʒɪg ə taɪ ˈdzɪg-, ˈzɪg-, -ɪ-, ˌˈˈ ~s z

Ee

e Spelling-to-sound

1. Where the spelling is **e**, the pronunciation differs according to whether the vowel is short or long, followed or not by **r**, and strong or weak.

2. The 'strong' pronunciation is regularly
   e as in **dress** dres ('short E') or
   iː as in **cathedral** kə ˈθiːdr əl ('long E').

3. Where **e** is followed by **r**, the 'strong' pronunciation is
   ɜː ‖ ɝː as in **serve** sɜːv ‖ sɝːv or
   ɪə ‖ ɪ as in **severe** sə ˈvɪə ‖ sə ˈvɪr
   or, indeed, there may be the regular 'short' pronunciation
   e as in **very** ˈver i.

4. The 'weak' pronunciation is
   ɪ as in **wasted** ˈweɪst ɪd or
   i as in **review** ri ˈvjuː
   (although some speakers use ə instead, thus ˈweɪst əd, rə ˈvjuː) or
   ə as in **agent** ˈeɪdʒ ənt (especially where the spelling is **el, ence, ent, er**).

5. Less frequently, the 'strong' pronunciation is
   ɪ in the exceptional words **pretty** ˈprɪt i ‖ ˈprɪt̮ i, **England, English** ˈɪŋ-
   eə ‖ e in **where** weə ‖ wer, **there** ðeə ‖ ðer (strong forms), and a few others
   eɪ, in foreign borrowings such as **suede** sweɪd, and often also in words ending in
   -eity, -eic as in **deity** ˈdeɪ- (also ˈdiː-), **nucleic** -ˈkleɪ-
   and, in BrE only, ɑː in **clerk** klɑːk, **Derby** ˈdɑːb i, and a few others.

6. **e** is frequently silent. At the end of a word, for example, it is silent if it follows a consonant letter as in **make** meɪk, **life** laɪf, **these** ðiːz, **nice** naɪs, **orange** -ndʒ, **face** feɪs, **huge** hjuːdʒ, **collapse** kə ˈlæps, **twelve** twelv. In this position it may have the function of indicating that the vowel before the consonant is long (**make, life, these**); or that **c** or **g** is 'soft' (**notice, orange**); or both of these (**face, huge**); or neither (**collapse, twelve**).

7. In a few cases at the end of a word after a consonant, the pronunciation is i as in **apostrophe** ə ˈpɒs trəf i ‖ ə ˈpɑːs trəf i.

8. **e** also forms part of the digraphs **ea, ee, ei, eu, ew, ey**.

ea Spelling-to-sound

1   Where the spelling is the digraph **ea**, there are several different pronunciations. The most usual are

i: as in **tea** tiː, and

e as in **bread** bred.

Less frequent are

eɪ, notably in **great** greɪt, **steak** steɪk, **break** breɪk

ɪə ‖ iːə, notably in **idea** aɪ ˈdɪə ‖ aɪ ˈdiː ə, **theatre** ˈθɪət ə ‖ ˈθiː əţ ər.

2   Where **ea** is followed by **r**, the pronunciation is regularly

ɪə ‖ ɪ as in **near** nɪə ‖ nɪr.

Less frequently it is

ɜː ‖ ɜ: as in **early** ˈɜːl i ‖ ˈɜːl i and several others

ɑː notably in **heart** hɑːt ‖ hɑːrt, **hearth**

eə ‖ e notably in **bear** beə ‖ ber, **pear** peə ‖ per, **swear** sweə ‖ swer, **wear** weə ‖ wer, and one meaning of **tear**.

3   **ea** is not a digraph in words such as **creation**, **react**, **area**.

ee Spelling-to-sound

1   Where the spelling is the digraph **ee**, the pronunciation is regularly

i: as in **tree** triː

or, before **r**,

ɪə ‖ ɪ as in **beer** bɪə ‖ bɪr.

2   Exceptionally, the pronunciation is ɪ in AmE **been** bɪn (sometimes also in BrE) and sometimes in **Greenwich** (although here many speakers use e).

3   At the end of a few words the pronunciation is weak i as in **coffee** ˈkɒfi ‖ ˈkɔːfi.

ei, ey Spelling-to-sound

1   Where the spelling is one of the digraphs **ei**, **ey**, the pronunciation is most frequently

eɪ as in **veil** veɪl, **convey** kən ˈveɪ.

2   Less frequently, it is

i: as in **receive** ri ˈsiːv, **key** kiː,

and in a few words

aɪ as in **height** haɪt, **eye** aɪ or

e as in **heifer** ˈhef ə ‖ ˈhef ər, **Reynolds** ˈren əldz.

E

3 Where the spelling is **ei** before **r**, the pronunciation is either

eə ‖ e as in **their** ðeə ‖ ðer or

ɪə ‖ ɪ as in **weird** wɪəd ‖ wɪrd.

4 The exceptional **either**, **neither** may have aɪ or iː, with BrE preferring the former and AmE the latter.

5 **ei** is not a digraph in words such as **atheism**, **deity**.

eu, ew Spelling-to-sound

1 Where the spelling is one of the digraphs **eu**, **ew**, the pronunciation is regularly

juː as in **feudal** ˈfjuːd ᵊl, **few** fjuː or

uː as in **rheumatism** ˈruːm ə tɪz əm, **crew** kruː.

(For the dropping of j, see **u** 3.)

2 Exceptionally, it is also

əʊ ‖ oʊ as in **sew** səʊ ‖ soʊ

ɜː ‖ uː in French words as in **masseuse** mæ ˈsɜːz ‖ mə ˈsuːs or

ɔɪ in German-derived words as in **Freudian** ˈfrɔɪd i ən.

Note also **lieutenant**, BrE lef ˈten ənt.

3 Where the spelling is **eu** before **r**, the pronunciation is regularly

juə ‖ ju as in **Europe** ˈjuər əp ‖ ˈjur əp,

or when weak

ju as in **neurology** nju ˈrɒl ədʒ i ‖ -ˈrɑːl-.

E, e *name of letter* iː **Es, E's, e's** iːz
—*Communications code name:* Echo
'E ˌnumber
e *Latin prepn* eɪ iː —*See also phrases with this word*
each iːtʃ
  ₍ᵢ₎**each 'other**; **ˌeach 'way◄**
Eadie ˈiːd i
Eads iːdz
Eady ˈiːd i
eager ˈiːg ə ‖ -ᵊr **~ly** li **~ness** nəs nɪs
  ˌeager 'beaver
eagle, Eagle ˈiːg ᵊl **~s** z
eagle-eyed ˌiːg ᵊl ˈaɪd ◄
eaglet ˈiːg lət -lɪt **~s** s
eagre ˈeɪg ə ˈiːg- ‖ -ᵊr **~s** z
Eakins ˈeɪk ɪnz §-ənz
Eakring ˈiːk rɪŋ
Ealing ˈiːl ɪŋ
Eames *(i)* iːmz, *(ii)* eɪmz

Eamon, Eamonn ˈeɪm ən
-ean ˈiː‿ən, i ən —*In some words this suffix is stressed (ˌEuro'pean), but in others stress-imposing (Shake'spearean). Both possibilities are heard in Caribbean.*
ear ɪə ‖ ɪʳr **eared** ɪəd ‖ ɪʳrd **earing** ˈɪər ɪŋ ‖ ˈɪr ɪŋ **ears** ɪəz ‖ ɪʳrz
  'ear ˌtrumpet
earache ˈɪər eɪk ‖ ˈɪr-
Eardley ˈɜːd li ‖ ˈɜːd-
eardrop ˈɪə drɒp ‖ ˈɪr drɑːp **~s** s
eardrum ˈɪə drʌm ‖ ˈɪr- **~s** z
eared ɪəd ‖ ɪʳrd
-eared ˈɪəd ‖ ˈɪʳrd
earflap ˈɪə flæp ‖ ˈɪr- **~s** s
earful ˈɪə fʊl ‖ ˈɪr-
Earhart ˈeə hɑːt ‖ ˈer hɑːrt
earhole ˈɪə həʊl →-hɒʊl ‖ ˈɪr hoʊl **~s** z
earl, Earl ɜːl ‖ ɜːl **earls, Earl's** ɜːlz ‖ ɜːlz
  ˌEarl's 'Court; **ˌEarl 'Grey**

earldom 'ɜːl dəm ‖ 'ɜːl- ~s z
Earle ɜːl ‖ ɜːl
earless 'ɪə ləs -lɪs ‖ 'ɪr-
Earley 'ɜːl i ‖ 'ɜːl i
earli... —*see* **early**
earlobe 'ɪə ləʊb ‖ 'ɪr ləʊb ~s z
earl|y 'ɜːl |i ‖ 'ɜːl |i **~ier** i ə ‖ i ʲr **~iest** i ɪst
i‿əst **~iness** i nəs i nɪs **~ies** iz
‚early 'bird, ‚·· '·; ‚early 'closing day;
‚Early 'English; ‚early 'warning ‚system
earmark 'ɪə mɑːk ‖ 'ɪr mɑːrk **~ed** t **~ing** ɪŋ **~s**
s
earmuff 'ɪə mʌf ‖ 'ɪr- **~s** s
earn, Earn ɜːn ‖ ɜːn (= *urn*) **earned** ɜːnd ɜːnt
‖ ɜːnd **earning/s** 'ɜːn ɪŋ/z ‖ 'ɜːn ɪŋ/z **earns**
ɜːnz ‖ ɜːnz
earner 'ɜːn ə ‖ 'ɜːn ʲr **~s** z
earnest 'ɜːn ɪst -əst ‖ 'ɜːn- **~ly** li **~ness** nəs nɪs
~s s
earnings-related ‚ɜːn ɪŋz ri 'leɪt ɪd ◀ -rə '··
‖ ‚ɜːn ɪŋz ri 'leɪt əd ◀
Earnshaw 'ɜːn ʃɔː ‖ 'ɜːn- -ʃɑː
Earp ɜːp ‖ ɜːp
earphone 'ɪə fəʊn ‖ 'ɪr foʊn **~s** z
earpiec|e 'ɪə piːs ‖ 'ɪr- **~es** ɪz əz
earplug 'ɪə plʌg ‖ 'ɪr- **~s** z
earring 'ɪə rɪŋ 'ɪər ɪŋ ‖ 'ɪr ɪŋ -rɪŋ **~s** z
earshot 'ɪə ʃɒt ‖ 'ɪr ʃɑːt
ear-splitting 'ɪə ‚splɪt ɪŋ ‖ 'ɪr ‚splɪt ɪŋ **-ly** li
earth ɜːθ ‖ ɜːθ **earthed** ɜːθt ‖ ɜːθt **earthing**
'ɜːθ ɪŋ ‖ 'ɜːθ ɪŋ **earths** *v* ɜːθs ‖ ɜːθs **earths** *n*
pl ɜːθs ɜːðz ‖ ɜːθs **earth's** ɜːθs ‖ ɜːθs
'earth ‚closet; 'earth ‚satellite; 'earth
‚science
Eartha 'ɜːθ ə ‖ 'ɜːθ ə
earthborn 'ɜːθ bɔːn ‖ 'ɜːθ bɔːrn
earthbound 'ɜːθ baʊnd ‖ 'ɜːθ-
earthen 'ɜːθ ʲn 'ɜːð- ‖ 'ɜːθ-
earthenware 'ɜːθ ʲn weə 'ɜːð- ‖ 'ɜːθ ʲn wer
-wær
earthi... —*see* **earthy**
earthling 'ɜːθ lɪŋ ‖ 'ɜːθ- **~s** z
earthly 'ɜːθ li ‖ 'ɜːθ-
earth|man 'ɜːθ |mæn ‖ 'ɜːθ- **~men** men
earthnut 'ɜːθ nʌt ‖ 'ɜːθ- **~s** s
earthquake 'ɜːθ kweɪk ‖ 'ɜːθ- **~s** s
earthshaking 'ɜːθ ‚ʃeɪk ɪŋ ‖ 'ɜːθ-
earthshattering 'ɜːθ ‚ʃæt ʲr ɪŋ
‖ 'ɜːθ ‚ʃæt̬ ʲr ɪŋ **-ly** li
earthstar 'ɜːθ stɑː ‖ 'ɜːθ stɑːr **~s** z
earthward 'ɜːθ wəd ‖ 'ɜːθ wʲrd **~s** z
earthwork 'ɜːθ wɜːk ‖ 'ɜːθ wɜːk **~s** s
earthworm 'ɜːθ wɜːm ‖ 'ɜːθ wɜːm **~s** z
earth|y 'ɜːθ |i ‖ 'ɜːθ |i **~ier** i ə ‖ i ʲr **~iest** i ɪst
i‿əst **~iness** i nəs i nɪs
earwax 'ɪə wæks ‖ 'ɪr-
earwig 'ɪə wɪg ‖ 'ɪr- **~s** z
earworm 'ɪə wɜːm ‖ 'ɪr wɜːm **~s** z
Easdale 'iːz deɪʲl
ease iːz **eased** iːzd **eases** 'iːz ɪz -əz **easing**
'iːz ɪŋ
easeful 'iːz fʲl -fʊl **~ly** i **~ness** nəs nɪs
easel 'iːz ʲl **~s** z

easement 'iːz mənt **~s** s
easi... —*see* **easy**
easily 'iːz ɪ li -əl i
Easington 'iːz ɪŋ tən
Eason 'iːs ʲn
east, East iːst
‚East 'Anglia; ‚East 'End; ‚East 'Indies;
‚East 'London
eastbound 'iːst baʊnd
Eastbourne 'iːst bɔːn ‖ -bɔːrn -boʊrn
Eastcheap 'iːst tʃiːp
East Ender, Eastender ‚iːst 'end ə ‖ -ʲr **~s** z
Easter 'iːst ə ‖ -ʲr **~s** z
‚Easter 'Day; 'Easter egg; 'Easter ‚Island
‖ ‚·· '·‚·; ‚Easter 'Sunday
Easterbrook 'iːst ə brʊk §-bruːk ‖ -ʲr-
easterly 'iːst əl i ‖ -ʲr li **easterlies** 'iːst əl iz
‖ -ʲr liz
eastern 'iːst ən ‖ -ʲrn
Easterner, e~ 'iːst ən ə ‖ -ʲrn ʲr -ən ʲr **~s** z
easternmost 'iːst ən məʊst →-əm-
‖ -ʲrn moʊst
Eastertide 'iːst ə taɪd ‖ -ʲr- **~s** z
easting 'iːst ɪŋ **~s** z
Eastleigh ‚iːst 'liː ◀ '··
Eastman 'iːst mən
east-northeast ‚iːst nɔːθ 'iːst ‖ -nɔːrθ- —*also*
naut -nɔːr- ‖ -nɔːr-
Easton 'iːst ən
east-southeast ‚iːst saʊθ 'iːst —*also naut*
-saʊ-
eastward 'iːst wəd ‖ -wʲrd **~ly** li **~s** z
East-West ‚iːst 'west ◀
Eastwood 'iːst wʊd
eas|y 'iːz |i ‖ -ʲr **~iest** i ɪst i‿əst **~ily**
ɪ li əl i **~iness** i nəs i nɪs
‚easy 'chair, '·· ·; 'easy street; ‚easy
'terms; ‚easy 'virtue
easygoing ‚iːz i 'gəʊ ɪŋ ◀ ‖ -'goʊ ɪŋ ◀
easyJet *tdmk* 'iːz i dʒet
easy-peasy ‚iːz i 'piːz i ◀
eat iːt **ate** et eɪt ‖ eɪt ⚠et **eaten** 'iːt ʲn **eating**
'iːt ɪŋ ‖ 'iːt̬ ɪŋ **eats** iːts
'eating ‚apple; 'eating dis‚order
eatable 'iːt əb ʲl ‖ 'iːt̬- **~s** z
eaten 'iːt ʲn
eater 'iːt ə ‖ 'iːt̬ ʲr **~s** z
eater|y 'iːt ər |i ‖ 'iːt̬- **~ies** iz
eating-|house 'iːt ɪŋ |haʊs ‖ 'iːt̬- **~houses**
haʊz ɪz -əz
eating-plac|e 'iːt ɪŋ pleɪs ‖ 'iːt̬- **~es** ɪz əz
Eaton 'iːt ʲn
‚Eaton 'Socon 'səʊk ən ‖ 'soʊk-
eau əʊ ‖ oʊ —*Fr* [o]
‚eau de co'logne də kə 'ləʊn di- ‖ -'loʊn
—*Fr* [od kɔ lɔnj]; ‚eau de 'nil də 'niːʲl —*Fr*
[od nil]; ‚eau de toi'lette —*Fr* [ot twa lɛt];
‚eau de 'vie də 'viː —*Fr* [od vi]
eaves, Eaves iːvz
eavesdrop 'iːvz drɒp ‖ -drɑːp **~ped** t **~per/s**
ə/z ‖ ʲr/z **~ping** ɪŋ **~s** s
e-banking 'iː ‚bæŋk ɪŋ
eBay 'iː beɪ

ebb eb **ebbed** ebd **ebbing** 'eb ɪŋ **ebbs** ebz
  ˌebb 'tide, ' · ·
Ebbsfleet 'ebz fliːt
Ebbw 'eb u -ə
  ˌEbbw 'Vale
EBCDIC 'eb si dɪk
Ebenezer ˌeb ə 'niːz ə ◂ -ɪ- ‖ -ᵊr ' · · · ·
Eblis 'eb lɪs §-ləs
Ebola i 'bəʊl ə ‖ i 'boʊl ə
ebon 'eb ən
Ebonics i 'bɒn ɪks ‖ -'bɑːn-
ebonite 'eb ə naɪt
ebon|y, Ebony 'eb ən |i ~**ies** iz
e-book 'iː bʊk ~**s** s
Ebor 'iːb ɔː ‖ -ɔːr
Eboracum i 'bɒr ək əm ˌiːb ɔː 'rɑːk- ‖ i 'bɔːr-
  i 'bɑːr-
Ebro 'iːb rəʊ 'eb- ‖ -roʊ 'eɪb- —*Sp* ['e βro]
ebullience i 'bʌl i ‿ən‿s ə-, -'bʊl-
ebullient i 'bʌl i ‿ənt ə-, -'bʊl- ~**ly** li
ebullition ˌeb ə 'lɪʃ ᵊn -ʊ-
Ebury 'iːb ər‿i
EC ˌiː 'siː
ecarte, écarté eɪ 'kɑːt eɪ ‖ ˌeɪ kɑːr 'teɪ —*Fr*
  [e kaʁ te]
Ecbatana ek 'bæt ən ə ˌek bə 'tɑːn ə
  ‖ ek 'bæt ᵊn ə
Ecce Homo ˌek eɪ 'həʊm əʊ ˌeks-, ˌetʃ-, -i-,
  -'hɒm- ‖ -'hoʊm oʊ
eccentric ɪk 'sentr ɪk ek-, ək- ~**ally** ᵊl‿i ~**s** s
eccentricit|y ˌeks en 'trɪs ət |i ˌ·ᵊn-, -ɪt i
  ‖ -ət̬ |i ~**ies** iz
Ecclefechan ˌek ᵊl 'fek ən -'fex-
Eccles 'ek ᵊlz
  'Eccles cake
ecclesia ɪ 'kliːz i‿ə
Ecclesiastes ɪ ˌkliːz i 'æst iːz ə-
ecclesiastic ɪ ˌkliːz i 'æst ɪk ◂ ə- ~**al** ᵊl ~**ally**
  ᵊl‿i ~**s** s
ecclesiasticism ɪ ˌkliːz i 'æst ɪ ˌsɪz əm ə-, -'·ə-
Ecclesiasticus ɪ ˌkliːz i 'æst ɪk əs ə-
ecclesio- *comb. form*
  with stress-neutral suffix ɪ ¦kliːz i‿ə ə-
  — **ecclesiological** ɪ ˌkliːz i‿ə 'lɒdʒ ɪk ᵊl ◂ ə-
  ‖ -'lɑːdʒ-
  with stress-imposing suffix ɪ ˌkliːz i 'ɒ+ ə-
  ‖ ɪ ˌkliːz i 'ɑː+ — **ecclesiology**
  ɪ ˌkliːz i 'ɒl ədʒ i ə- ‖ -'ɑːl-
Eccleston 'ek ᵊlst ən
eccrine 'ek rɪn -riːn, -rən, -raɪn
ecdysiast ek 'dɪz i æst ~**s** s
ECG ˌiː siː 'dʒiː ~**s**, ~'**s** z
echelon 'eʃ ə lɒn 'eɪʃ- ‖ -lɑːn ~**ed** d ~**ing** ɪŋ ~**s**
  z
echeveria, E~ ˌetʃ ɪ 'vɪər i‿ə ˌ·ə-
  ‖ ˌetʃ əv ə 'riː ə ˌetʃ- ~**s** z
echid|na ɪ 'kɪd |nə ə-, e- ~**nae** niː ~**nas** nəz
echinacea ˌek ɪ 'neɪʃ ə -ə-, ˌ · ·'eɪs i‿ə
echinoderm i 'kaɪn əʊ dɜːm ə-, -'kɪn-
  ‖ -ə dɜːm ~**s** z
echin|us i 'kaɪn |əs ə-, e-; 'ek ɪn-, -ən- ~**i** aɪ
echo, Echo 'ek əʊ ‖ -oʊ ~**ed** d ~**er/s** ə/z ‖ ᵊr/z
  ~**es** z ~**ing** ɪŋ

echocardiogram ˌek əʊ 'kɑːd i‿əʊ græm
  ‖ -oʊ 'kɑːrd i‿ə- ~**s** z
echoey 'ek əʊ i ‖ -oʊ i
echoic e 'kəʊ ɪk i-, ə- ‖ -'koʊ- ~**ally** ᵊl‿i
echolalia ˌek əʊ 'leɪl i‿ə ‖ ˌ·oʊ-
echolocation ˌek əʊ ləʊ 'keɪʃ ᵊn ‖ -oʊ loʊ-
echt ext ekt —*Ger* [ʔɛçt]
Eckersley 'ek əz li ‖ -ᵊrz-
Eckhart 'ek hɑːt ‖ -hɑːrt —*Ger* ['ʔɛk haʁt]
eclair, éclair i 'kleə eɪ-, 'eɪk leə ‖ eɪ 'kleᵊr i-,
  -'klæᵊr —*Fr* [e klɛːʁ] ~**s** z
eclampsia ɪ 'klæmps i‿ə e-, ə-
eclat, éclat eɪ 'klɑː 'eɪk lɑː —*Fr* [e kla]
eclectic ɪ 'klekt ɪk e-, ə- ~**ally** ᵊl‿i ~**s** s
eclecticism ɪ 'klekt ɪ ˌsɪz əm e-, ə-, -ə-
eclips|e ɪ 'klɪps ə-, iː- ~**ed** t ~**es** ɪz əz ~**ing** ɪŋ
eclipsis ɪ 'klɪps ɪs ə-, iː-, §-əs
ecliptic ɪ 'klɪpt ɪk ə-, iː- ~**s** s
eclogue 'ek lɒg ‖ -lɔːg -lɑːg ~**s** z
Eco 'ek əʊ ‖ -oʊ —*It* ['ɛː ko]
eco- *comb. form* ¦iːk əʊ ¦ek əʊ ‖ ¦iːk oʊ ¦ek-, -ə
  — **ecocide** 'iːk əʊ saɪd 'ek- ‖ -ə-
eco-friendly ¦iːk əʊ 'frendli ◂ ˌek- ‖ -oʊ-
E. coli ˌiː 'kəʊl aɪ ‖ -'koʊl-
ecological ˌiːk ə 'lɒdʒ ɪk ᵊl ◂ ˌek- ‖ -'lɑːdʒ- ~**ly**
  i
ecologist ɪ 'kɒl ədʒ ɪst e-, ə-, iː- ‖ -'kɑːl- ~**s** s
ecology i 'kɒl ədʒ i e-, ə- ‖ -'kɑːl-
econometric i ˌkɒn ə 'metr ɪk ◂ ə- ‖ -ˌkɑːn-
  ~**al** ᵊl ~**s** s
econometrician i ˌkɒn ə me 'trɪʃ ᵊn ə-, iː-,
  -mə'·- ‖ -ˌkɑːn ə mə- ~**s** z

ECONOMIC

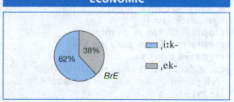

62% | 38%

▨ ˌiːk-

▨ ˌek-

BrE

economic ˌiːk ə 'nɒm ɪk ◂ ˌek- ‖ -'nɑːm-
  — *Preference poll, BrE:* ˌiːk- 62%, ˌek- 38%.
  ~**al** ᵊl ~**ally** ᵊl‿i ~**s** s
economie... —*see* **economy**
economise —*see* **economize**
economist i 'kɒn əm ɪst ə-, §iː-, §-əst ‖ -'kɑːn-
  ~**s** s
economiz|e i 'kɒn ə maɪz ə-, §iː- ‖ -'kɑːn- ~**ed**
  d ~**er/s** ə/z ‖ ᵊr/z ~**es** ɪz əz ~**ing** ɪŋ
econom|y i 'kɒn əm |i ə-, §iː- ‖ -'kɑːn- ~**ies** iz
  e'conomy class
ecorche, écorché ˌeɪk ɔː 'ʃeɪ ‖ -ɔːr-
Ecorse *place in MI* 'iː kɔːs ɪ 'kɔːs ‖ 'iː kɔːrs
  ɪ 'kɔːrs
ecosphere 'iːk əʊ sfɪə 'ek- ‖ -oʊ sfɪr
ecosystem 'iːk əʊ ˌsɪst əm 'ek-, -ɪm ‖ -oʊ- ~**s** z
  — *Preference poll, BrE:* 'iːk- 88%, 'ek- 12%.
  See chart on p.262.
ecraseur, écraseur ˌeɪk rɑː 'zɜː ‖ -'zɝː —*Fr*
  [e kʁɑ zœːʁ] ~**s** z
ecru, écru 'eɪk ruː 'ek-

E

ECOSYSTEM

88% — 12%
■ 'iːk-
■ 'ek-
BrE

● BrE 'iːk- by age

Percentage (y-axis: 0, 60, 80, 100)

Older ◄— Speakers —► Younger

ecstas|y 'ekst əs |i **~ies** iz
ecstatic ɪk 'stæt ɪk ek-, ək- ‖ -'stæt̬ ɪk **~ally** ᵊl_i
~s s
ECT ˌiː siː 'tiː
ecto- comb. form
  with stress-neutral suffix ¦ekt əʊ ‖ ¦ekt oʊ -ə
  — **ectogenic** ˌekt əʊ 'dʒen ɪk ◄ ‖ -oʊ- -ə-
  with stress-imposing suffix ek 'tɒ+ ‖ ek 'tɑː+
  — **ectogenous** ek 'tɒdʒ ən əs -ɪn- ‖ -'tɑːdʒ-
ectoderm 'ekt əʊ dɜːm ‖ -ə dɜːm **~s** z
ectomorph 'ekt əʊ mɔːf ‖ -ə mɔːrf **~s** s
ectomorphic ˌekt əʊ 'mɔːf ɪk ◄ ‖ -ə 'mɔːrf-
-ectomy 'ekt əm i — **gastrectomy**
  gæ 'strekt əm i
ectopic ₍ᵢ₎ek 'tɒp ɪk ‖ -'tɑːp-
ectoplasm 'ekt əʊ ˌplæz əm ‖ -ə-
ectype 'ek taɪp **~s** s
ecu, e.c.u., ECU 'European currency unit'
  'ek juː 'eɪk-, 'iːk-; ˌiː siː 'juː ‖ eɪ 'kuː —Fr
  [e ky] **~s, ~'s** z
ecu, écu old coin, 'shield' 'eɪk juː eɪ 'kjuː
  ‖ eɪ 'kjuː —Fr [e ky] **~s** z
Ecuador 'ek wə dɔː ‖ -dɔːr —Sp [e kwa 'ðoɾ]
Ecuadoran ˌek wə 'dɔːr ən ◄ **~s** z
Ecuadorean, Ecuadorian ˌek wə 'dɔːr i_ən ◄
  ~s z
ecumenical ˌiːk ju 'men ɪk ᵊl ◄ ˌek- ‖ ˌek jə-
  ~ly i
ecumenicism ˌiːk ju 'men ɪ ˌsɪz əm -'·ə-
  ‖ ˌek jə-
ecumenism ɪ 'kjuːm ə ˌnɪz əm iː-, 'ek jum-
eczema 'eks ɪm ə -əm ˌə; 'ek zɪm ə ‖ ɪg 'ziːm ə
  'egz əm ə, 'eks-
eczematous ek 'sem ət əs ɪk-, -'siːm-; -'zem-,
  -'ziːm-, ɪg- ‖ ɪg 'zem ət̬ əs -'ziːm-
Ed ed
-ed, -d t, d, ɪd əd —This unstressed ending has
  three regular pronunciations: 1. After **t** or **d** it
  is pronounced ɪd or, less commonly in BrE but
  regularly in AmE, əd, as hated 'heɪt ɪd
  ‖ 'heɪt̬ əd, needed 'niːd ɪd ‖ -əd. (In singing,

exceptionally, a strong-vowelled variant **ed** is
usual, as 'niːd ed.)
2. After the other VOICED consonants or a
vowel sound, it is pronounced **d**, as called
kɔːld, seemed siːmd, vowed vaʊd, tied taɪd,
feared fɪəd ‖ fɪᵊrd.
3. After the other VOICELESS consonants (**p,
k, tʃ, f, θ, s, ʃ**), it is pronounced **t**, as gripped
grɪpt, patched pætʃt, knifed naɪft.
Certain adjectives have ɪd, əd against these
rules, as wicked 'wɪk ɪd, -əd. The same
applies also to most words in -edly, -edness as
markedly 'mɑːk ɪd li, -əd- ‖ 'mɑːrk əd li. This
'syllabic' pronunciation of the ending formerly
applied to all -ed formations, and is still heard
when people recite older literature, where it
may be required for scansion purposes: thus
(only in imitated old pronunciation) seemed
'siːm ɪd.
Edale 'iː deɪᵊl
Edam 'iːd æm -əm —Dutch [eː 'dɑm]
edaphic i 'dæf ɪk ə- **~ally** ᵊl_i
Edda 'ed ə **~s** z
Eddery 'ed ər i
Eddic 'ed ɪk
Eddie 'ed i
eddie... —see **eddy**
Eddington 'ed ɪŋ tən
eddo 'ed əʊ ‖ -oʊ **~es** z
edd|y, Eddy 'ed |i **~ied** id **~ies** iz **~ying** i_ɪŋ
Eddystone 'ed ɪst ən -əst-; -i stəʊn ‖ -i stoʊn
Ede family name iːd
edelweiss 'eɪd ᵊl vaɪs ⚠'aɪd-, -waɪs —Ger
  Edelweiß ['ʔeː dᵊl vais]
edema i 'diːm ə ə- **~s** z
edematous i 'diːm ət əs ə- ‖ -ət̬ əs
Eden 'iːd ᵊn
Edenbridge 'iːd ᵊn brɪdʒ
Edenfield 'iːd ᵊn fiːᵊld
edentate i 'dent eɪt **~s** s
Edessa i 'des ə
Edexcel ˌed ek 'sel
Edgar 'ed gə →'eg- ‖ -gᵊr
Edgbaston 'edʒ bəst ən -bæst-
edge, Edge edʒ **edged** edʒd **edges** 'edʒ ɪz
  -əz **edging** 'edʒ ɪŋ
Edgecomb, Edgecombe 'edʒ kəm
-edged 'edʒd — **blunt-edged** ˌblʌnt 'edʒd ◄
Edgehill ˌedʒ 'hɪl —but as a family name, '· ·
Edgerton 'edʒ ət ən ‖ -ᵊrt ᵊn
edgeways 'edʒ weɪz
edgewise 'edʒ waɪz
Edgeworth 'edʒ wɜːθ -wəθ ‖ -wɜːθ
edging 'edʒ ɪŋ **~s** z
Edgware 'edʒ weə ‖ -wer
edg|y 'edʒ |i **~ier** i_ə ‖ i_ᵊr **~iest** i_ɪst i_əst **~ily**
  ɪ li əl i **~iness** i nəs i nɪs
edh eð **edhs** eðz
Ediacaran ˌiːd i 'æk ər ən ◄ -i_ə 'kɑːr-
  ‖ -i_ə 'kær-
edibility ˌed ə 'bɪl ət i ˌ·ɪ-, -ɪt i ‖ -ət̬ i
edible 'ed əb ᵊl -ɪb-
edict 'iːd ɪkt **~s** s

Edie 'iːd i

edification ˌed ɪf ɪ 'keɪʃ ᵊn ˌ-əf-, §-ə'--

edific|e 'ed ɪf ɪs -əf-, §-əs **~es** ɪz əz

edi|fy 'ed ɪ |faɪ -ə- **~fied** faɪd **~fier/s** faɪ‿ə/z ‖ faɪ‿ᵊr/z **~fies** faɪz **~fying** faɪ ɪŋ

Edina (i) e 'diːn ə ɪ-, (ii) i 'daɪn ə —*The place in MI is* (ii)

Edinburgh 'ed ɪn bər‿ə →'-ɪm-, '-ᵊn-, §-ˌbʌr ə ‖ -ˌbɜː ə -oʊ —*but the place in TX is locally* 'ed ᵊn bɜːg

Edington 'ed ɪŋ tən

Edison 'ed ɪs ən -əs-

edit 'ed ɪt §-ət **edited** 'ed ɪt ɪd §-ət-, -əd ‖ -ət-
   editing 'ed ɪt ɪŋ §-ət- ‖ -ət- **edits** 'ed ɪts §-əts

Edith 'iːd ɪθ -əθ **~'s** s

edition i 'dɪʃ ᵊn ə- **~s** z

editor 'ed ɪt ə §-ət- ‖ -ət ᵊr **~s** z

editorial ˌed ɪ 'tɔːr i‿əl ◂ ˌ-ə- ‖ -'toʊr- **~ly** i **~s** z

editorialis... —*see* **editorializ...**

editorialization ˌed ɪ ˌtɔːr i‿əl aɪ 'zeɪʃ ᵊn ˌˌ-ə-, -ɪ'-- ‖ -ə 'zeɪʃ- -ˌtoʊr- **~s** z

editorializ|e ˌed ɪ 'tɔːr i‿ə laɪz ˌ-ə- ‖ -'toʊr- **~ed** d **~er/s** ə/z ‖ ᵊr/z **~es** ɪz əz **~ing** ɪŋ

editorship 'ed ɪt ə ʃɪp ‖ -ət ᵊr- **~s** s

-edly ɪd li əd li — **designedly** di 'zaɪn ɪd li də-, -əd-

Edmead, Edmeade 'ed miːd →'eb-

Edmond 'ed mənd →'eb-

Edmonds 'ed məndz →'eb-

Edmondson 'ed mənd sən →'eb-

Edmonton 'ed mən tən →'eb-

Edmund 'ed mənd →'eb- **~s** z

Edmundson 'ed mənd sən →'eb-

Edna 'ed nə

Ednyfed ed 'nʌv ɪd -ed, §-əd —*Welsh* [ed 'nə ved]

Edo 'ed əʊ ‖ -oʊ —*Jp* [e ˌdo]

Edom 'iːd əm

Edomite 'iːd ə maɪt **~s** s

Edrich 'edr ɪtʃ

Edridge 'edr ɪdʒ

Edsel 'ed sᵊl

educability ˌed jʊk ə 'bɪl ət i ˌedʒ ʊk-, ˌedʒ ək-, -ɪt i ‖ ˌedʒ ək ə 'bɪl ət i

educable 'ed jʊk əb ᵊl 'edʒ ʊk-, 'edʒ ək- ‖ 'edʒ ək-

edu|cate 'ed ju |keɪt 'edʒ u-, 'edʒ ə- ‖ 'edʒ ə- **~cated** keɪt ɪd -əd ‖ keɪt̬ əd **~cates** keɪts **~cating** keɪt ɪŋ ‖ keɪt̬ ɪŋ

education ˌed ju 'keɪʃ ᵊn ˌedʒ u-, ˌedʒ ə- ‖ ˌedʒ ə- **~s** z

educational ˌed ju 'keɪʃ ᵊn əl ◂ ˌedʒ u-, ˌedʒ ə- ‖ ˌedʒ ə- **~ly** i

educationalist ˌed ju 'keɪʃ ᵊn əl ɪst ˌedʒ u-, ˌedʒ ə-, §-əst ‖ ˌedʒ ə- **~s** s

educative 'ed jʊk ət ɪv 'edʒ ʊk-, 'edʒ ək-; 'ed ju keɪt ɪv, 'edʒ u-, 'edʒ ə- ‖ 'edʒ ə keɪt̬ ɪv

educator 'ed ju keɪt ə 'edʒ u-, 'edʒ ə- ‖ 'edʒ ə keɪt̬ ᵊr **~s** z

educ|e i 'djuːs ə-, →-'dʒuːs ‖ -'duːs -'djuːs **~ed** t **~es** ɪz əz **~ing** ɪŋ

eduction ɪ 'dʌk ʃᵊn ə-, iː- **~s** z

edutainment ˌed ju 'teɪn mənt ˌedʒ u-, ˌedʒ ə-, →-'teɪm- ‖ ˌedʒ ə-

Edward 'ed wəd ‖ -wᵊrd

Edwardes 'ed wədz ‖ -wᵊrdz

Edwardian ed 'wɔːd i‿ən -'wɑːd- ‖ -'wɔːrd- -'wɑːrd-

Edwards 'ed wədz ‖ -wᵊrdz

Edwin 'ed wɪn §-wən

Edwina ed 'wiːn ə

Edwinstowe 'ed wɪn stəʊ §-wən- ‖ -stoʊ

-ee iː, eɪ, i —*Where this is a genuine suffix, it is usually stressed, as* ˌpay'ee, ˌabsen'tee. *In words spelt* -ee *where it is not a genuine suffix, it may be stressed* (ˌrefe'ree); *or unstressed but strong* ('pedigree **-griː**); *or weak* (committee kə 'mɪt i ‖ -'mɪt̬ i). *If alternatively spelt* -ée, *it is pronounced* eɪ (*see next entry*).

-ee, -ée eɪ —*Often unstressed in BrE, but usually stressed in AmE, as* matinee '· · · ‖ ˌ· '·ˌ·, fiancee ·' · · ‖ ˌ· ˌ·'·

EEC ˌiː iː 'siː

EEG ˌiː iː 'dʒiː **~s** z

eek iːk

eel iːᵊl **eels** iːᵊlz

eelgrass 'iːᵊl grɑːs §-græs ‖ -græs

eelpout 'iːᵊl paʊt **~s** s

eelworm 'iːᵊl wɜːm ‖ -wɜːm **~s** z

-een 'iːn — **velveteen** ˌvelv ə 'tiːn -ə-

e'en iːn

eeny meeny miny mo ˌiːn i ˌmiːn i ˌmaɪn i 'məʊ ‖ -'moʊ

-eer 'ɪə ‖ 'ɪ³r — *This suffix is stressed:* **mountaineer** ˌmaʊnt ɪ 'nɪə -ə- ‖ -ᵊn 'ɪ³r

e'er eə ‖ e³r æ³r (= air)

eer|ie 'ɪər |i ‖ 'ɪr |i **-ier** i‿ə ‖ i‿³r **~iest** i‿ɪst i‿əst **~ily** əl i ɪ li **~iness** i nəs i nɪs

Eeyore 'iː ɔː ‖ -ɔːr

eff ef **effed** eft **effing** 'ef ɪŋ **effs** efs

effable 'ef əb ᵊl

effac|e i 'feɪs e-, ə- **~ed** t **~es** ɪz əz **~ing** ɪŋ

effaceable i 'feɪs əb ᵊl e-, ə-

effacement i 'feɪs mənt e-, ə-

effect ə'fekt i- **~ed** ɪd əd **~ing** ɪŋ **~s** s

effective ə 'fekt ɪv i- **~ly** li **~ness** nəs nɪs

effectual i 'fek tʃu‿əl ə-, -tju‿əl **~ly** i

effectu|ate i 'fek tʃu |eɪt ə-, -tju- **~ated** eɪt ɪd -əd ‖ eɪt̬ əd **~ates** eɪts **~ating** eɪt ɪŋ ‖ eɪt̬ ɪŋ

effectuation i ˌfek tʃu 'eɪʃ ᵊn ə-, -tju-

effeminacy i 'fem ɪn əs i ə-, e-, -'-ən-

effeminate i 'fem ɪn ət ə-, e-, -'-ən-, -ɪt **~ly** li **~s** s

effendi, E~ e 'fend i i-, ə- **~s** z

efferent 'ef ər ənt 'iːf-, -er-

effervesc|e ˌef ə 'ves ‖ -³r- **~ed** t **~es** ɪz əz **~ing** ɪŋ

effervescence ˌef ə 'ves ᵊnts ‖ -³r-

effervescent ˌef ə 'ves ᵊnt ◂ ‖ -³r- **~ly** li

effete i 'fiːt e-, ə- **~ly** li **~ness** nəs nɪs

efficacious ˌef ɪ 'keɪʃ əs ◂ ə- **~ly** li **~ness** nəs nɪs

efficacity ˌef ɪ 'kæs ət i ˌ-ə-, -ɪt i ‖ -ət̬ i

efficacy 'ef ɪk əs i '-ək-

efficienc|y ə ˈfɪʃ ənˈs |i i- **~ies** iz
  efˈficiency bar
efficient ə ˈfɪʃ ənt i- **~ly** li
Effie ˈef i
effig|y ˈef ɪdʒ |i -ədʒ- **~ies** iz
Effingham *(i)* ˈef ɪŋ əm §-həm, *(ii)* -hæm
  —*The place in England is (i), those in the US (ii)*
effleurage ˈef lɜː rɑːʒ -ə-, ˌ· ·ˈ· ‖ ˌef lə ˈrɑːʒ
  —*Fr* [ɛ flœ ʁɑːʒ]
effloresc|e ˌef lə ˈres -lɔː- **~ed** t **~es** ɪz əz **~ing** ɪŋ
efflorescenc|e ˌef lə ˈres ənˈs -lɔː- **~es** ɪz əz
efflorescent ˌef lə ˈres ənt ◂ -lɔː-
effluence ˈef lu ənˈs
effluent ˈef lu ənt **~s** s
effluvi|um ɪ ˈfluːv i ˌ|əm e-, ə- **~a** ə **~al** əl **~ums** əmz
efflux ˈef lʌks **~es** ɪz əz
effort ˈef ət ‖ -ərt -ɔːrt **~s** s
effortless ˈef ət ləs -lɪs ‖ -ərt- **~ly** li **~ness** nəs nɪs
effronter|y ɪ ˈfrʌnt ər |i e-, ə- ‖ -ˈfrʌnt̬- **~ies** iz
effulgence i ˈfʌldʒ ənˈs e-, ə-, -ˈfʊldʒ-
effulgent i ˈfʌldʒ ənt e-, ə-, -ˈfʊldʒ- **~ly** li
effusion i ˈfjuːʒ ən e-, ə- **~s** z
effusive ɪ ˈfjuːs ɪv e-, ə-, §-ˈfjuːz- **~ly** li **~ness** nəs nɪs
Efik ˈef ɪk **~s** s
e-fit ˈiː fɪt **~s** s
EFL ˌiː ef ˈel
eft eft **efts** efts
EFTA ˈeft ə
e.g. ˌi: ˈdʒiː: *or as* for example
egad i ˈgæd
egalitarian i ˌgæl ɪ ˈteər i ən ə-, -əˈ·-; ˌiːg æl- ‖ -ˈter- **~ism** ˌɪz əm **~s** z
Egan ˈiːg ən
Egbert ˈeg bɜːt -bət ‖ -bɜːt
Egeria i ˈdʒɪər i ə ‖ -ˈdʒɪr-
Egerton ˈedʒ ət ən ‖ -ərt ən
egest i ˈdʒest **~ed** ɪd əd **~ing** ɪŋ **~s** s
Egeus ɪ ˈdʒiː əs iː-; ˈiːdʒ uːs, -juːs
egg eg **egged** egd **egging** ˈeg ɪŋ **eggs** egz
  ˌegg and ˈspoon race; ˌegg ˈroll ‖ ˈ· ·; ˈegg ˌtimer; ˈegg white
eggar, Eggar ˈeg ə ‖ -ər **~s** z
eggbeater ˈeg ˌbiːt ə ‖ -ˌbiːt̬ ər **~s** z
egg-bound ˈeg baʊnd
eggcorn ˈeg kɔːn ‖ -kɔːrn **~s** z
eggcup ˈeg kʌp **~s** s
egghead ˈeg hed **~s** z
Egginton ˈeg ɪn tən
Eggleton ˈeg əl tən
eggnog ˌeg ˈnɒg ˈ· · ‖ ˈeg nɑːg **~s** z
eggplant ˈeg plɑːnt §-plænt ‖ -plænt **~s** s
eggshell ˈeg ʃel **~s** z
eggwhisk ˈeg wɪsk -hwɪsk **~s** s
Egham ˈeg əm
egis ˈiːdʒ ɪs §-əs
eglantine ˈeg lən taɪn -tiːn **~s** z
Eglon ˈeg lɒn ‖ -lɑːn
Eglwys ˈeg lu ɪs ˈeg lɔɪs —*Welsh* [ˈe glujs]

Egmont ˈeg mɒnt -mənt ‖ -mɑːnt
ego ˈiːg əʊ ˈeg- ‖ -oʊ **~s** z
  ˈego trip
egocentric ˌiːg əʊ ˈsentr ɪk ◂ ˌeg- ‖ -oʊ- **~ally** əlˌi
egocentricity ˌiːg əʊ sen ˈtrɪs ət i ˌeg-, -sənˈ·-, -ɪt i ‖ -oʊ sen ˈtrɪs ət̬ i
egocentrism ˌiːg əʊ ˈsentr ˌɪz əm ˌeg- ‖ -oʊ-
egoism ˈiːg əʊ ˌɪz əm ˈeg- ‖ -oʊ-
egoist ˈiːg əʊ ɪst ˈeg-, §-əst ‖ -oʊ- **~s** s
egoistic ˌiːg əʊ ˈɪst ɪk ◂ ˌeg- ‖ -oʊ- **~ally** əlˌi
egomania ˌiːg əʊ ˈmeɪn i ə ˌeg- ‖ ˌ·oʊ-
egomaniac ˌiːg əʊ ˈmeɪn i æk ˌeg- ‖ ˌ·oʊ- **~s** s
egomaniacal ˌiːg əʊ mə ˈnaɪ ək əl ◂ ˌeg-, -ɪk əl ‖ ˌ·oʊ-
Egon ˈiːg ɒn ˈeg-, -ən ‖ ˈeɪg ɑːn
egotism ˈeg əʊ ˌtɪz əm ˈiːg- ‖ ˈiːg ə-
egotist ˈeg əʊt ɪst ˈiːg-, §-əst ‖ ˈiːg ət̬ əst **~s** s

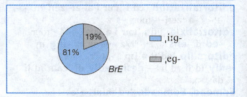

BrE

egotistic ˌeg əʊ ˈtɪst ɪk ◂ ˌiːg- ‖ ˌiːg ə-
  — *Preference poll, BrE:* ˌiːg- *81%,* ˌeg- *19%.*
  ~al əl **~ally** əlˌi
egregious ɪ ˈgriːdʒ əs ə-, -ˈgriːdʒ i əs **~ly** li **~ness** nəs nɪs
Egremont ˈeg rə mənt -rɪ-, -mɒnt ‖ -mɑːnt
egress ˈiː gres
egressive i ˈgres ɪv —*in contrast to* ingressive, *also* ˌiː-
egret ˈiːg rət -rɪt, -ret ‖ ˈeg-; iː ˈgret, ɪ- **~s** s
Egypt ˈiːdʒ ɪpt §-əpt
Egyptian i ˈdʒɪp ʃən ə- **~s** z
Egyptological ˌiːdʒ ɪpt ə ˈlɒdʒ ɪk əl ◂ §ˌ·əpt-; i ˌdʒɪpt- ‖ -ˈlɑːdʒ-
Egyptologist ˌiːdʒ ɪp ˈtɒl ədʒ ɪst §ˌ·əp-, §-əst ‖ -ˈtɑːl- **~s** s
Egyptology ˌiːdʒ ɪp ˈtɒl ədʒ i §ˌ·əp- ‖ -ˈtɑːl- eh eɪ
Ehrlich ˈeə lɪk -lɪx ‖ ˈer- —*Ger* [ˈʔeːɐ lɪç] —*but as an American family name,* ˈɜː- ‖ ˈɜːr-
Eichmann ˈaɪk mən ˈaɪx- —*Ger* [ˈʔaɪç man]
Eid iːd
Eid-al-... —*see* Eid-ul-...
eider ˈaɪd ə ‖ -ər **~s** z
eiderdown ˈaɪd ə daʊn ‖ -ər- **~s** z
eidetic aɪ ˈdet ɪk ‖ -ˈdet̬ ɪk **~ally** əlˌi
Eid-ul-Adha ˌiːd ʌl ˈæd ə -ˈʌd ə —*Arabic* [ˈʕiːd al ˈʔadˤ ˈħaː]
Eid-ul-Fitr ˌiːd ʌl ˈfɪt ə ‖ -fɪt̬ ər —*Arabic* [ˈʕiːd al ˈfɪtˤr]
Eifel, Eiffel ˈaɪf əl —*Ger* [ˈʔaɪ fəl], *Fr* [ɛ fɛl]
  ˌEiffel ˈTower
Eifion ˈaɪv i ɒn ‖ -ɑːn —*Welsh* [ˈəiv jon]
eigenfunction ˈaɪg ən ˌfʌŋk ʃən →-ŋ- **~s** z
eigenvalue ˈaɪg ən ˌvæl juː →-ŋ- **~s** z

Eiger 'aɪg ə ‖ -ʰr —*Ger* ['ʔai gɐ]
Eigg eg
eight eɪt **eights** eɪts
eighteen ˌeɪ 'tiːn ◂ §ˌeɪt-, §ˌeɪt 'iːn
  ˌeighteen 'months
eighteenth ˌeɪ 'tiːnᵗθ ◂ §ˌeɪt-, §ˌeɪt 'iːnᵗθ ~s s
  ˌeighteenth 'century
eighteen-wheeler ˌeɪ tiːn 'wiːᵊl ə §ˌeɪt-,
  'hwiːl- ‖ -ʰr ~s z
eightfold 'eɪt fəʊld →ᵊ-fɒʊld ‖ -foʊld
eighth eɪtθ ‖ eɪθ **eighths** eɪtθs ‖ eɪθs
  'eighth note
eighti... —*see* **eighty**
eightieth 'eɪt i‿əθ §-ti-, ɪθ ‖ 'eɪʈ i‿əθ ~s s
eightsome 'eɪt səm ~s z
  ˌeightsome 'reel
eight|y 'eɪt |i §'eɪt t|i ‖ 'eɪʈ |i ~ies iz
  ˌeighty-'four◂
Eilat eɪ 'lɑːt
Eilean 'el ən
  ˌEilean 'Donan 'dɒn ən ‖ -'doʊn-
Eileen 'aɪl iːn ‖ ˌaɪ 'liːn ˌeɪ-
Eilidh 'eɪl i
Eiloart 'aɪl əʊ ɑːt ‖ -oʊ ɑːrt
Eindhoven 'aɪnd həʊv ᵊn 'aɪnt- ‖ -hoʊv-
  —*Dutch* ['ɛint hoː vən]
einkorn 'aɪn kɔːn →'aɪŋ- ‖ -kɔːrn
Einstein 'aɪn staɪn —*Ger* ['ʔain ʃtain]
einsteinium aɪn 'staɪn i‿əm
Eire, Éire 'eər ə ‖ 'er ə 'ær-; 'eɪ rə —*Irish*
  ['eː rʲə]
eirenicon aɪᵊ 'riːn ɪ kɒn -'ren- ‖ -kɑːn
Eirian 'aɪʳr i‿ən —*Welsh* ['əir jan]
Eirlys 'aɪ‿ə lɪs -ləs ‖ ᵊr- —*Welsh* ['əir lɪs, -lɪs]
Eisenhower 'aɪz ᵊn ˌhaʊ‿ə ‖ -ˌhaʊˌʰr
Eisenstein 'aɪz ᵊn staɪn -ʃtaɪn —*Russ*
  ['ɛj zʲɪn ʃtijn]
eisteddfod aɪ 'sted fəd ɪ-, ə-, -'steð vɒd ‖ -vɑːd
  —*Welsh* [əi 'sdeð vod] ~s z

EITHER

☐ 'aɪð-   ☐ 'iːð-
       13%   16%
87%   84%
  BrE   AmE

●━ BrE iː- by age   ●━ AmE aɪ- by age
●━ AmE iː- by age

Older ◂━ Speakers ━▸ Younger

either 'aɪð ə 'iːð- ‖ 'iːð ʰr 'aɪð- — *Preference
polls, BrE:* 'aɪð- *87%,* 'iːð- *13%; AmE:* 'iːð-
84%, 'aɪð- *16%.*

E

either-or ˌaɪð ər 'ɔː ˌiːð- ‖ ˌiːð ər 'ɔːr ˌaɪð-
Eithne 'eθ ni —*Irish* ['e hə nə]
ejaculate *n* i 'dʒæk jʊl ət ə-, -jəl-, -ɪt; -ju leɪt,
  -jə- ‖ -jəl- ~s s
ejacu|late *v* i 'dʒæk ju |leɪt ə-, -jə- ‖ -jə-
  ~lated leɪt ɪd -əd ‖ leɪʈ əd ~lates leɪts
  ~lating leɪt ɪŋ ‖ leɪʈ ɪŋ
ejaculatio i ˌdʒæk ju 'leɪʃ i əʊ ‖ -jə 'leɪʃ i oʊ
ejaculation i ˌdʒæk ju 'leɪʃ ᵊn ə-, -jə- ‖ -jə- ~s
  z
eject i 'dʒekt ə- ~ed ɪd əd ~ing ɪŋ ~s s
ejecta i 'dʒekt ə ə-
ejection i 'dʒek ʃᵊn ə- ~s z
  e'jection seat
ejective i 'dʒekt ɪv ə- ~ly li ~s z
ejectment i 'dʒekt mənt ə- ~s s
ejector i 'dʒekt ə ə- ‖ -ʰr ~s z
  e'jector seat
Ekco *tdmk* 'ek əʊ ‖ -oʊ
eke iːk **eked** iːkt **ekes** iːks **eking** 'iːk ɪŋ
EKG ˌiː keɪ 'dʒiː ~s z
ekistics i 'kɪst ɪks ə-
Ektachrome *tdmk* 'ekt ə krəʊm ‖ -kroʊm
el el —*See also phrases with this word*
elabo|rate *v* i 'læb ə |reɪt ə- ~rated reɪt ɪd -əd
  ‖ reɪʈ əd ~rates reɪts ~rating reɪt ɪŋ ‖ reɪʈ ɪŋ
elaborate *adj* i 'læb ᵊr‿ət ə-, ɪt ~ly li ~ness
  nəs nɪs
elaboration i ˌlæb ə 'reɪʃ ᵊn ə- ~s z
Elaine ɪ 'leɪn e-, ə-
El Al *tdmk* ˌel 'æl
El Alamein ₍ᵢ₎el 'æl ə meɪn ·ˌ- ·'·
Elam 'iːl əm
Elamite 'iːl ə maɪt ~s s
elan, élan eɪ 'lɒ̃ i-, -'lɑːn, -'læn; 'eɪl ɒn
  ‖ eɪ 'lɑːn —*Fr* [e lɑ̃]
  é,lan vi'tal viː 'tæl -'tɑːl —*Fr* [vi tal]
Elan *valley in Wales* 'iːl ən
Elan *tdmk for car* i' læn eɪ-
eland 'iːl ənd ~s z
elapid 'el ə pɪd §-əp əd ~s z
elaps|e i 'læps ə- ~ed t ~es ɪz əz ~ing ɪŋ
elastic i 'læst ɪk ə-, -'lɑːst- ~ally ᵊl‿i ~s s
  e,lastic 'band
elasti|cate i 'læst ɪ |keɪt ə-, -'lɑːst- ~cated
  keɪt ɪd -əd ‖ keɪʈ əd ~cates keɪts ~cating
  keɪt ɪŋ ‖ keɪʈ ɪŋ
elasticity ˌiːl ət 'stɪs ət i ˌel-, ˌˌɑː-, -ɪt i; i ˌlæ-,
  ə-, -ˌlɑː- ‖ -əʈ i
Elastoplast *tdmk* i 'læst əʊ plɑːst ə-, -'lɑːst-,
  -plæst ‖ -ə plæst
e|late i |'leɪt ə- ~lated 'leɪt ɪd -əd ‖ 'leɪʈ əd
  ~lates 'leɪts ~lating 'leɪt ɪŋ ‖ 'leɪʈ ɪŋ
elated i 'leɪt ɪd ə-, -əd ‖ -'leɪʈ əd ~ly li ~ness
  nəs nɪs
elation i 'leɪʃ ᵊn ə-
elative 'iːl ət ɪv i'leɪt- ‖ -əʈ- ~s z
Elba 'elb ə —*It* ['el ba, 'el-]
ElBaradei əl 'bær ə daɪ el-, -deɪ
Elbe elb —*Ger* ['ʔɛl bə]
Elbert 'elb ət ‖ -ᵊrt
elbow 'el bəʊ ‖ -boʊ ~ed d ~ing ɪŋ ~s z
  'elbow grease

elbowroom 'el bəʊ ruːm -rʊm ‖ -boʊ-
Elbrus el 'bruːs -'brʊs, '· · —*Russ* [ɛlʲ 'brus]
El Cajon ˌel kə 'həʊn ‖ -'hoʊn —*Sp* El Cajón
   [el ka 'xon]
elder, Elder 'eld ə ‖ -ᵊr ~s z
   ˌelder 'brother; ˌelder 'statesman
elderberr|y 'eld ə ˌber |i -bərˌ|i ‖ -ᵊr ˌber |i
   ~ies iz
   ˌelderberry 'wine
eldercare 'eld ə keə ‖ -ᵊr ker -kær
elderflower 'eld ə ˌflaʊ ə ‖ -ᵊr ˌflaʊ ᵊr ~s z
elderl|y 'eld əl |i ‖ -ᵊr l|i ~iness i nəs i nɪs
eldership 'eld ə ʃɪp ‖ -ᵊr- ~s s
eldest 'eld ɪst -əst
Eldon 'eld ən
El Dorado ˌel də 'raːd əʊ ‖ -oʊ -'reɪd-
Eldred 'eldr ɪd -ed, -əd
eldrich 'eldr ɪtʃ 'el rɪtʃ
Eldridge 'eldr ɪdʒ
Elea 'iːl i ə
Eleanor 'el ən ə -ɪn- ‖ -ᵊr -ə nɔːr
Eleanora ˌel i ə 'nɔːr ə
Eleatic ˌel i 'æt ɪk ◀ ˌiːl- ‖ -'æt-
Eleazar ˌel i 'eɪz ə ‖ -ᵊr
elecampane ˌel ɪ kæm 'peɪn ˌ·ə-
elect *adj, n, v* i 'lekt ə- ~ed ɪd əd ~ing ɪŋ ~s s
election i 'lek ʃᵊn ə- ~s z
electio|neer i ˌlek ʃə |'nɪə ə- ‖ -|'nɪᵊr ~neered
   'nɪəd ‖ 'nɪᵊrd ~neering 'nɪər ɪŋ ‖ 'nɪr ɪŋ
   ~neers 'nɪəz ‖ 'nɪᵊrz
elective i 'lekt ɪv ə- ~ly li ~s z
elector i 'lekt ə ə- ‖ -ᵊr ~s z

ELECTORAL

83% -'lekt-
17% -'tɔːr-
BrE

---

electoral i 'lekt ər əl ə-, →-'lek trəl;
   -ˌlek 'tɔːr əl ◀ —*Preference poll, BrE:* -'lekt-
   83%, -'tɔːr- *17%.* ~ly i
   eˌlectoral 'college
electorate i 'lekt ər_ət ə-, ɪt ~s s
Electra i 'lek trə ə-
   E'lectra ˌcomplex
electret 'lek trət ə-, -trɪt, -tret ~s s
electric i 'lek trɪk ə- ~s s
   eˌlectric 'blanket; eˌlectric 'chair; eˌlectric
   'eel; eˌlectric 'eye; eˌlectric gui'tar;
   eˌlectric 'shock, eˌlectric 'shock ˌtherapy
electrical i 'lek trɪk ᵊl ə- ~ly ˌi
   eˌlectrical ˌengi'neering
electrician i ˌlek 'trɪʃ ᵊn ə-, ˌel ek-, ˌel ɪk-,
   ˌɪl ek-, ˌiːl ek-, -'trɪʒ- ~s z

---

electricity i ˌlek 'trɪs ət i ə-, ˌel ek-, ˌel ɪk-,
   ˌɪl ek-, ˌiːl ek-, -'trɪz-, -ɪt i ‖ -ət̬ i
electrification i ˌlek trɪf ɪ 'keɪʃ ᵊn ə-, -ˌ·trəf-,
   §-ə'·- ~s z
electri|fy i 'lek trɪ |faɪ ə-, -trə- ~fied faɪd
   ~fier/s faɪ_ə/z ‖ faɪ_ᵊr/z ~fies faɪz ~fying
   faɪ ɪŋ
electro- *comb. form*
   with stress-neutral suffix i ˌlek trəʊ ə-
   ‖ i ˌlek troʊ -trə — electrographic
   i ˌlek trəʊ 'græf ɪk ◀ ə- ‖ -troʊ- -trə-
   with stress-imposing suffix i ˌlek 'trɒ+ ə-,
   ˌel ek-, ˌel ɪk-, ˌɪl ek-, ˌiːl ek- ‖ i ˌlek 'traː+
   — electrography i ˌlek 'trɒg rəf i ə-, ˌel ek-,
   ˌel ɪk-, ˌɪl ek-, ˌiːl ek- ‖ -'traːg-
electrocardiogram
   i ˌlek trəʊ 'kaːd i_əʊ græm ə-
   ‖ -troʊ 'kaːrd i_ə- ~s z
electrocardiograph
   i ˌlek trəʊ 'kaːd i_əʊ graːf ə-, -græf
   ‖ -troʊ 'kaːrd i_ə græf ~s s
electrocardiography
   ɪ ˌlek trəʊ ˌkaːd i 'ɒg rəf i ə-
   ‖ -troʊ ˌkaːrd i 'aːg-
electroconvulsive i ˌlek trəʊ kən 'vʌls ɪv ə-
   ‖ -ˌtroʊ-
   eˌlectroconˌvulsive 'therapy
electro|cute i'lek trə |kjuːt ə- ~cuted kjuːt ɪd
   -əd ‖ kjuːt̬ əd ~cutes kjuːts ~cuting kjuːt ɪŋ
   ‖ kjuːt̬ ɪŋ
electrocution i ˌlek trə 'kjuːʃ ᵊn ə- ~s z
electrode i 'lek trəʊd ə- ‖ -troʊd ~s z
electrodynamic i ˌlek trəʊ daɪ 'næm ɪk ◀ ə-,
   dɪ'·- ‖ -ˌtroʊ- ~ally ᵊl i ~s s
electroencephalogram
   i ˌlek trəʊ ɪn 'sef əl_ə græm ə-, -en'·-, -'kef-,
   -əʊ- ‖ -ˌtroʊ- ~s z
electroencephalograph
   i ˌlek trəʊ ɪn 'sef əl_ə graːf ə-, -en'·-, -'kef-,
   -əʊ-, -græf ‖ -troʊ ɪn 'sef əl_ə græf ~s s
electrolier i ˌlek trəʊ 'lɪə ə- ‖ -trə 'lɪᵊr ~s z
Electrolux *tdmk* i 'lek trəʊ lʌks ə- ‖ -troʊ-
electrolysis i ˌlek 'trɒl əs ɪs ə-, ˌel ek-, ˌel ɪk-,
   ˌɪl ek-, ˌiːl ek-, -ɪs ɪs, §-əs ‖ -'traːl-
electrolyte i 'lek trəʊ laɪt ‖ -trə- ~s s
electrolytic i ˌlek trəʊ 'lɪt ɪk ◀ -trə ‖ -'lɪt̬-
electromagnet i ˌlek trəʊ 'mæg nɪt ə-, -nət
   ‖ -troʊ- ~s s
electromagnetic i ˌlek trəʊ mæg 'net ɪk ◀ ə-,
   -məg'·- ‖ -troʊ mæg 'net̬- ~ally ᵊl i
   eˌlectromagˌnetic 'spectrum
electromagnetism
   i ˌlek trəʊ 'mæg nə ˌtɪz əm ə-, -'·nɪ- ‖ -ˌtroʊ-
electromotive i ˌlek trəʊ 'məʊt ɪv ◀ ə-
   ‖ -troʊ 'moʊt̬ ɪv -trə-
   eˌlectroˌmotive 'force
electromyogram i ˌlek trəʊ 'maɪ_ə græm ə-
   ‖ -ˌtroʊ-
electromyography i ˌlek trəʊ maɪ 'ɒg rəf i ə-
   ‖ -troʊ maɪ 'aːg-
electron i 'lek trɒn ə- ‖ -traːn ~s z
   eˌlectron 'microscope ‖ -·'· · ·, ·· ·

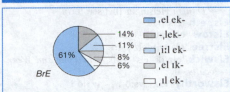

ELECTRONIC

,el ek- 61%
-,lek- 14%
,i:l ek- 11%
,el ɪk- 8%
,ɪl ek- 6%

BrE

electronic ˌel ek ˈtrɒn ɪk ◄ i ˌlek-, ə-; ˌel ɪk-, ˌɪl ek-, ˌi:l ek- ‖ i ˌlek ˈtrɑːn ɪk ◄ **~a ə ~ally**
ᵊl i **~s s** — *Preference poll, BrE:* ˌel ek- *61%,*
-ˌlek- *14%,* ˌi:l ek- *11%,* ˌel ɪk- *8%,* ˌɪl ek- *6%*
electropalatogram
i ˌlek trəʊ ˈpæl ət ə græm ə-, -ˈə təʊ-
‖ -troʊ ˈpæl əʈ ə-
electropalatography
i ˌlek trəʊ ˌpæl ə ˈtɒg rəf i ə-
‖ -troʊ ˌpæl ə ˈtɑːg-
electro|plate i ˈlek trəʊ |pleɪt ə-, ·ˌ·ˈ· ‖ -trə-
~plated pleɪt ɪd -əd ‖ pleɪʈ əd **~plates** pleɪts
~plating pleɪt ɪŋ ‖ pleɪʈ ɪŋ
electroscope i ˈlek trəʊ skəʊp ə- ‖ -trə skoʊp
~s s
electroshock i ˈlek trəʊ ʃɒk ə- ‖ -troʊ ʃɑːk
-trə-
electrostatic i ˌlek trəʊ ˈstæt ɪk ◄ ə-
‖ -trə ˈstæʈ ɪk ◄ **~ally** ᵊl i **~s s**
electrotyp|e i ˈlek trəʊ taɪp ə- ‖ -trə- **~ed** t
~es s **~ing** ɪŋ
electrum i ˈlek trəm ə-
electuar|y i ˈlekt ju̯ ̯ər |i ə- ‖ i ˈlek tʃu er |i
~ies iz
eleemosynary ˌel i i: ˈmɒz ɪn ər̯i ˌel i: ˈmɒz-,
ˌ·ɪ-, -ˈmɒs-, -ˈməʊz-, -ˈᵊn-
‖ ˌel ə ˈmɑːs ə ner i ˌ·ɪ-, -ˈmɑːz-, -ˈmoʊs-
elegance ˈel ɪg ən̩ts -əg-
elegant ˈel ɪg ənt -əg- **~ly** li
elegiac ˌel ɪ ˈdʒaɪ̯ ̯ək ◄ -ə-, -æk **~s s**
ˌeleˌgiac ˈcouplet
elegis|e, elegiz|e ˈel ə dʒaɪz -ɪ- **~ed** d **~es** ɪz
əz **~ing** ɪŋ
elegist ˈel ədʒ ɪst -ɪdʒ-, §-əst **~s s**
eleg|y ˈel ədʒ |i -ɪdʒ- **~ies** iz
element ˈel ɪ mənt -ə- **~s s**
elemental ˌel ɪ ˈment ᵊl ◄ -ə- ‖ -ˈmenʈ ᵊl ◄ **~ly**
i
elementar|y ˌel ɪ ˈment ̯ər |i ◄ ˌ·ə-
‖ -ˈmenʈ ̯ər |i ◄ →-ˈmentr |i **~ily** ᵊl i ɪ li
~iness i nəs i nɪs
ˌeleˌmentary ˈparticle; ˌeleˈmentary
school
elenchus ɪ ˈleŋk əs ə-
Eleonora ˌel i ̯ə ˈnɔːr ə ɪ ˌleɪ ə-
elephant ˈel ɪf ənt -əf- **~s s**
elephantiasis ˌel ɪf ən ˈtaɪ̯ ̯əs ɪs -əf ən-,
-ɪ fæn-, -ə fæn-, §-əs
elephantine ˌel ɪ ˈfænt aɪn ◄ -ə- ‖ -i:n ◄ -aɪn;
ˈel əf ən ti:n, -taɪn
Eleusinian ˌel ju ˈsɪn i̯ ̯ən ◄ ˌ·u- **~s z**
Eleusis ɪ ˈlju:s ɪs e-, ə-, -ˈlu:s-, §-əs ‖ -ˈlu:s-
Eleuthera ɪ ˈlu:θ ər̯ə ̯ə-, e-, -ˈlju:θ-

ele|vate ˈel ɪ |veɪt -ə- **~vated** veɪt ɪd -əd
‖ veɪʈ əd **~vates** veɪts **~vating** veɪt ɪŋ
‖ veɪʈ ɪŋ
elevation ˌel ɪ ˈveɪʃ ᵊn -ə- **~s z**
elevator ˈel ɪ veɪt ə ˈ·ə- ‖ -veɪʈ ᵊr **~s z**
ˈelevator ˌoperator
eleven i ˈlev ᵊn ə- **~s z**
eleven-plus i ˌlev ᵊn ˈplʌs ə-, →-ˈᵊm-
elevenses i ˈlev ᵊnz ɪz ə-, -əz
eleventh i ˈlev ᵊnᵗθ ə- **~s s**
eˌleventh ˈhour
elf, Elf elf **elf's** elfs **elves** elvz
Elfed ˈelv ed
elfin ˈelf ɪn §-ən
elfish ˈelf ɪʃ **~ly** li **~ness** nəs nɪs
Elfreda, Elfrida el ˈfri:d ə
Elgar ˈelg ɑː -ə ‖ -ɑːr -ᵊr
Elgin *(i)* ˈelg ɪn §-ən, *(ii)* ˈeldʒ ɪn -ən —*For the
marbles, the place in Scotland, and as a
British name, (i); for place in IL, and as an
American name, (ii).*
El Greco el ˈgrek əʊ ‖ -oʊ
Eli ˈi:l aɪ
Elia ˈi:l i̯ə
Elias ɪ ˈlaɪ̯ ̯əs ə-, -æs
elic|it i ˈlɪs |ɪt ə-, §-|ət ‖ -|ət *(usually = illicit)*
~ited ɪt ɪd §ət-, -əd ‖ əʈ əd **~iting** ɪt ɪŋ §ət-
‖ əʈ ɪŋ **~its** ɪts §əts ‖ əts
elicitation i ˌlɪs ɪ ˈteɪʃ ᵊn ə-, i:-, -ə- **~s z**
elid|e i ˈlaɪd ə-, i:- **~ed** ɪd əd **~es** z **~ing** ɪŋ
eligibility ˌel ɪdʒ ə ˈbɪl ət i ˌ·ədʒ-, -ɪˈ··, -ɪt i
‖ -əʈ i
eligib|le ˈel ɪdʒ əb |ᵊl ˈ·ədʒ-, -ɪb- **~ly** li
Elihu ɪ ˈlaɪ hju: e-, ə- ‖ ˈel ə hju:
Elijah ɪ ˈlaɪdʒ ə ə-
Elim ˈi:l ɪm §-əm
elimi|nate i ˈlɪm ɪ |neɪt ə- -ə- **~nated** neɪt ɪd
-əd ‖ neɪʈ əd **~nates** neɪts **~nating** neɪt ɪŋ
‖ neɪʈ ɪŋ
elimination i ˌlɪm ɪ ˈneɪʃ ᵊn ə-, -ə- **~s z**
eliminator i ˈlɪm ɪ neɪt ə ə-, -ˈ·ə- ‖ -ˈneɪʈ ᵊr **~s**
z
Elin ˈel ɪn -ən
Elinor ˈel ən ə -ɪn- ‖ -ən ᵊr -ə nɔːr
Eliot, Eliott ˈel i̯ ̯ət
Elis ˈi:l ɪs §-əs
Elisa i ˈli:s ə e-, -ˈli:z-, -ˈlɪz-
Elisabeth i ˈlɪz əb əθ ə-
Elise i ˈli:z ə-, e-
Elisha i ˈlaɪʃ ə ə-
elision i ˈlɪʒ ᵊn ə-, §i:- **~s z**
elite, élite i ˈli:t ₍ᵢ₎eɪ-, ə- **~s s**
elitism, élitism i ˈli:t ˌɪz əm eɪ-, -ɪ- ‖ -ˈli:ʈ-
elitist, élitist i ˈli:t ɪst ə-, §-əst ‖ -ˈli:ʈ- **~s s**
elixir i ˈlɪks ə e-, ə-, -ɪə; ˈel ɪk sɪə ‖ -ᵊr **~s z**
Eliza i ˈlaɪz ə-
Elizabeth i ˈlɪz əb əθ ə- **~s, ~'s s**
Elizabethan i ˌlɪz ə ˈbi:θ ᵊn ◄ ə- **~s z**
elk, Elk elk **elks** elks
Elkan *(i)* ˈelk ən, *(ii)* -ɑːn
elkhound ˈelk haʊnd **~s z**
Elkie ˈelk i
Elkins ˈelk ɪnz

ell el **ells** elz

Ella 'el ə

Elland 'el ənd

Ellen 'el ən -ɪn

Ellery 'el ər i

Ellesmere 'elz mɪə ‖ -mɪr
  Ellesmere 'Port

Ellice 'el ɪs §-əs

Ellie 'el i

Ellington 'el ɪŋ tən

Elliot, Elliott 'el i ət

ellips|e i 'lɪps ə-, e- **~es** ɪz əz

ellipses pl of **ellipse** i 'lɪps ɪz ə-, e-, -əz

ellipses pl of **ellipsis** i 'lɪps iːz ə-, e-

ellips|is i 'lɪps |ɪs ə-, e-, §-əs **~es** iːz

ellipsoid i 'lɪps ɔɪd ə-, e- **~s** z

ellipsoidal ˌel ɪp 'sɔɪd ᵊl ◂ i ˌlɪp-, ə-, e-

ellipt i 'lɪpt ə-, e- **~ed** ɪd əd **~ing** ɪŋ **~s** s

elliptic i 'lɪpt ɪk ə-, e- **~al** ᵊl **~ally** ᵊl̩ i

Ellis 'el ɪs §-əs

Ellison 'el ɪs ən -əs-

Ellsworth 'elz wɜːθ -wəθ ‖ -wɜːθ

elm elm **elms** elmz

Elmer 'elm ə ‖ -ᵊr

Elmes elmz

Elmet 'elm et -ɪt, §-ət

Elmhurst 'elm hɜːst ‖ -hɜːst

Elmira el 'maɪᵊr ə

Elmo 'elm əʊ ‖ -oʊ

El Monte el 'mɒnt i ‖ -'mɑːnt̬ i —Sp
  [el 'mon te]

Elmwood 'elm wʊd

El Niño el 'niːn jəʊ ‖ -joʊ —Sp [el 'ni ɲo]

elocution ˌel ə 'kjuːʃ ᵊn

elocutionary ˌel ə 'kjuːʃ ᵊn ər i ◂ -'·ᵊn̩r i
  ‖ -ə ner i

elocutionist ˌel ə 'kjuːʃ ᵊn ɪst §ˌəst **~s** s

Elohim e 'ləʊ hɪm ɪ-, ə-; ˌel əʊ 'hiːm ‖ -'loʊ-
  ˌel oʊ 'hiːm

Eloise ˌel əʊ 'iːz ‖ -oʊ- '··

elon|gate 'iː lɒŋ |geɪt ‖ i 'lɔːŋ |geɪt -'lɑːŋ- (*)
  ~gated geɪt ɪd -əd ‖ geɪt̬ əd **~gates** geɪts
  ~gating geɪt ɪŋ ‖ geɪt̬ ɪŋ

elongation ˌiː lɒŋ 'geɪʃ ᵊn ‖ i ˌlɔːŋ 'geɪʃ ᵊn
  -ˌlɑːŋ-; ˌiː lɔːŋ-, -lɑːŋ- **~s** z

elop|e i 'ləʊp ə- ‖ -'loʊp **~ed** t **~ement/s**
  mənt/s **~es** s **~ing** ɪŋ

eloquence 'el ək wənts

eloquent 'el ək wənt **~ly** li **~ness** nəs nɪs

El Paso el 'pæs əʊ ‖ -oʊ —Sp [el 'pa so]

Elphick 'elf ɪk

Elphinstone 'elf ɪn stən §-ən-, -stəʊn ‖ -stoʊn

El Portal place in FL ˌel pɔː 'tæl ‖ -pɔːr-

Elroy 'el rɔɪ

Elsa 'els ə —but as a German name, also 'elz-
  —Ger ['ʔɛl za]

El Salvador ⑴el 'sælv ə dɔː ‖ -dɔːr —Sp
  [el sal βa 'ðor]

Elsan tdmk 'el sæn

Elsbeth 'els bəθ

else, Else els

elsewhere ˌels 'weə -'hweə, '·· ‖ 'els ʰwer
  -ʰwær

Elsie 'els i

Elsinore 'els ɪ nɔː -ə-, ˌ·'·ˑ ‖ ˌels ə 'nɔːr -'noʊr
  —Danish Helsingør [hɛl seŋ 'øːʔʁ]

Elspeth 'els pəθ

Elstow 'el stəʊ ‖ -stoʊ

Elstree 'els triː 'elz-, -tri

Elswick 'elz ɪk 'els-, -wɪk —In Tyne and Wear,
  locally -ɪk

Elsworthy 'elz ˌwɜːð i ‖ -ˌwɜːð i

ELT ˌi: el 'ti:

Eltham (i) 'elt əm, (ii) 'elθ əm —The place in
  London is (i); those in Australia and NZ, (ii)

Elton 'elt ən

eluci|date i 'luːs ɪ |deɪt ə-, -'ljuːs-, -ə- **~dated**
  deɪt ɪd -əd ‖ deɪt̬ əd **~dates** deɪts **~dating**
  deɪt ɪŋ ‖ deɪt̬ ɪŋ

elucidation i ˌluːs ɪ 'deɪʃ ᵊn ə-, -ˌljuːs-, -ə- **~s** z

elucidatory i 'luːs ɪ deɪt ər i ə-, -ˌ·'··ˑ
  ‖ -əd ə tɔːr i -toʊr i

elud|e i 'luːd ə-, -'ljuːd **~ed** ɪd əd **~es** z **~ing**
  ɪŋ

Eluned e 'lɪn ed -'liːn-

elusion i 'luːʒ ᵊn ə-, -'ljuːʒ-

elusive i 'luːs ɪv ə-, -'ljuːs- **~ly** li **~ness** nəs nɪs

elusory i 'luːs ər i ə-, -'ljuːs-

elute i 'luːt ə-, -'ljuːt **eluted** i 'luːt ɪd ə-,
  -'ljuːt-, -əd ‖ -'luːt̬- **~s** s **eluting** i 'luːt ɪŋ ə-,
  -'ljuːt- ‖ -'luːt̬-

Elva 'elv ə

elver 'elv ə ‖ -ᵊr **~s** z

elves elvz

Elvin 'elv ɪn §-ən

Elvira (i) el 'vɪər ə ‖ -'vɪr ə, (ii) -'vaɪᵊr ə

Elvis 'elv ɪs §-əs

elvish 'elv ɪʃ

Elwes 'el wɪz -wəz

Elwyn 'el wɪn

Ely American personal name 'iːl aɪ

Ely place name 'iːl i

Elyot 'el i ət

Elysee, Elysée eɪ 'liːz eɪ i-, ə- ‖ ˌeɪl iː 'zeɪ
  —Fr [e li ze]

Elysian, e~ i 'lɪz i ən ə- ‖ i 'lɪʒ ᵊn -'liːʒ-

Elysium i 'lɪz i əm ə- ‖ i 'lɪʒ- -'liːʒ-, -'lɪz-

elytron 'el ɪ trɒn -ə-; -ɪtr ən, -ətr- ‖ -ə trɑːn

Elzevier, Elzevir 'elz ə vɪə 'els- ‖ -vɪr —Dutch
  ['ɛl zə viːr]

em em

em- ɪm, (¦)em —This prefix is stressed ¦em if
  the following syllable is unstressed
  (ˌembro'cation). Otherwise it is unstressed
  (em'balm). When it is unstressed, a
  weak-vowel form ɪm is preferred in RP,
  although some speakers, particularly regional
  ones, use a strong-vowel form em.

'em pronoun əm —This variant of them has no
  strong form.

emaci|ate i 'meɪʃ i |eɪt ə-, -'meɪs- **~ated** eɪt ɪd
  -əd ‖ eɪt̬ əd **~ates** eɪts **~ating** eɪt ɪŋ ‖ eɪt̬ ɪŋ

emaciation i ˌmeɪʃ i 'eɪʃ ᵊn ə-, -ˌmeɪs-

email, e-mail 'iː meɪᵊl **~ed** d **~ing** ɪŋ **~s** z

Elision

1   **Elision** is the eliding (= omission, deletion) of a sound that would otherwise be present. It is particularly characteristic of rapid or casual speech. It is not random, but follows certain rules, which differ from one language to another.

2   Some types of possible elision can occur within words in isolation. They are shown in this dictionary by the use of *italic* symbols (or occasionally by raised symbols or by transcribing a second pronunciation). In English they include

- the elision of the middle part of ntʃ and ndʒ. For example, **lunch** lʌntʃ is pronounced lʌntʃ or, alternatively, lʌnʃ; **strange** streɪndʒ is streɪndʒ or streɪnʒ.

- the elision of the middle part of mps, mpt, nts, ŋks, ŋkt. For example, **jumped** dʒʌmpt is pronounced dʒʌmpt or, alternatively, dʒʌmt; **lynx** lɪŋks is lɪŋks or lɪŋs.

3   Other types of possible elision apply in compound words and in connected speech. They are shown in this dictionary for compounds, but naturally cannot be shown for connected speech. They include the elision of t and d at the end of a word, before a consonant at the beginning of the next word. Then

- t may be elided in ft, st, and less commonly in pt, kt, tʃt, θt, ʃt
- d may be elided in ld, nd, and less commonly in bd, gd, dʒd, vd, ðd, zd, md, ŋd.

next   nekst   In isolation, or before a vowel sound, this word is pronounced nekst. But in a phrase such as **next thing**, **next question** it is often pronounced neks, with elision of the t.

stand   stænd   In isolation, or before a vowel sound, this word is pronounced stænd. But in a phrase such as **stand clear**, **stand firm** it is often pronounced stæn, with elision of the d.

4   The contracted negative **n't** ᵊnt is a special case. Its t may be elided in connected speech, no matter what kind of sound follows. Thus when **didn't** ˈdɪd ᵊnt is followed by another word or phrase, it is sometimes pronounced ˈdɪd ᵊn.

5   The consonant h is often elided in unstressed syllables, and especially in weak forms of function words. Thus **him** is hɪm in isolation, or if stressed, but often ɪm when unstressed in a phrase such as **tell him**.

6   The vowel ə is subject to elision as follows.

- often (though not always) when it is followed by a nasal or liquid and then a WEAK vowel. There are two stages: first, the ə combines with the nasal or liquid, making the latter syllabic (see SYLLABIC CONSONANTS); then, the nasal or liquid may become non-syllabic (see COMPRESSION), in which case all trace of the ə has disappeared.

Elision continued

camera ˈkæm ər‿ə The full form is ˈkæm.ər.ə. If ə is elided, in the first instance it makes the r syllabic: ˈkæm.r̩.ə. This is usually compressed to give ˈkæm.rə. All three possibilities occur.

- sometimes, in casual speech, in the first syllable of a word in which the second syllable is stressed and begins with a liquid. The first syllable then undergoes compression. Thus **terrific** tə ˈrɪf ɪk sometimes becomes ˈtrɪf ɪk, or **collide** kə ˈlaɪd becomes klaɪd. Since they are not found except in casual speech, these forms are not shown in this dictionary. The same applies to cases of apparent elision of ə in some speakers' occasional pronunciation of words such as **incident** ˈɪnˈs əd ənt, **capacity** kə ˈpæs ət i, where there seems to be a compensatory lengthening of the preceding consonant, giving the effect of ˈɪnˈs dənt, kə ˈpæsː ti.

7 A pronunciation that originated through elision may become the only possibility for some speakers. Some people have ˈkæm rə as the only pronunciation for **camera**, or pliːs as the only form for **police**. For many people it would feel very artificial to pronounce a t in **postman** ˈpəʊs mən ‖ ˈpoʊs mən.

---

ema|nate ˈem ə |neɪt **~nated** neɪt ɪd -əd
‖ neɪt̬ əd **~nates** neɪts **~nating** neɪt ɪŋ
‖ neɪt̬ ɪŋ
emanation ˌem ə ˈneɪʃ ᵊn **~s** z
emanative ˈem ə neɪt ɪv -nət ɪv ‖ -neɪt̬ ɪv
emanatory ˈem ə neɪt ər i ˌ·ˈ·ˈ·ˌ;
ˈem ən ət ər i ‖ -ən ə tɔːr i -toʊr i
emanci|pate i ˈmænˈs ɪ |peɪt ə-, -ə- **~pated**
peɪt ɪd -əd ‖ peɪt̬ əd **~pates** peɪts **~pating**
peɪt ɪŋ ‖ peɪt̬ ɪŋ
emancipation i ˌmænˈs ɪ ˈpeɪʃ ᵊn ə-, -ə- **~s** z
emancipator i ˈmænˈs ɪ peɪt ə ə-, -ˈ·ə-
‖ -peɪt̬ ᵊr **~s** z
Emanuel i ˈmæn ju‿əl ə- —*but in singing
usually* -el
emascu|late v i ˈmæsk ju |leɪt ə- ‖ -jə- **~lated**
leɪt ɪd -əd ‖ leɪt̬ əd **~lates** leɪts **~lating**
leɪt ɪŋ ‖ leɪt̬ ɪŋ
emasculate *adj* i ˈmæsk jʊl ət ə-, -ɪt, -ju leɪt
‖ -jəl-
emasculation i ˌmæsk ju ˈleɪʃ ᵊn ə- ‖ -jə- **~s** z
embalm ɪm ˈbɑːm em-, §-ˈbɑːlm **~ed** d **~er/s**
ə/z ‖ ᵊr/z **~ing** ɪŋ **~s** z
embalmment ɪm ˈbɑːm mənt em-, §-ˈbɑːlm- **~s**
s
embankment ɪm ˈbæŋk mənt em- **~s** s
embarcadero, E~ em ˌbɑːk ə ˈdeər əʊ ɪm-,
əm- ‖ -ˌbɑːrk ə ˈder oʊ **~s** z
embargo ɪm ˈbɑːg əʊ em- ‖ -ˈbɑːrg oʊ **~ed** d
~es z **~ing** ɪŋ
embark ɪm ˈbɑːk em- ‖ -ˈbɑːrk **~ed** t **~ing** ɪŋ
~s s
embarkation ˌem bɑː ˈkeɪʃ ᵊn ‖ -bɑːr- **~s** z
embarras de richesses ɒm ˌbær ɑː də riː ˈʃes
‖ ˌɑːm bɑː ˌrɑː- —*Fr* [ɑ̃ ba ʁa dʁi ʃɛs]

embarrass ɪm ˈbær əs em- ‖ -ˈber- **~ed** t **~es** ɪz
əz **~ing/ly** ɪŋ /li **~ment/s** mənt/s
embass|y ˈem bəs |i **~ies** iz
embattl|e ɪm ˈbæt ᵊl em- ‖ -ˈbæt̬ ᵊl **~ed** d **~es**
z **~ing** ɪŋ
embed ɪm ˈbed em- **~ded** ɪd əd **~ding** ɪŋ **~s** z
embellish ɪm ˈbel ɪʃ em- **~ed** t **~es** ɪz əz **~ing**
ɪŋ **~ment/s** mənt/s
ember, Ember ˈem bə ‖ -bᵊr **~s** z
 ˈEmber day
embezzl|e ɪm ˈbez ᵊl em- **~ed** d **~es** z **~ing** ɪŋ
embezzlement ɪm ˈbez ᵊl mənt em- **~s** s
embezzler ɪm ˈbez ᵊl ə em- ‖ ᵊr **~s** z
embitter ɪm ˈbɪt ə em- ‖ -ˈbɪt̬ ᵊr **~ed** d
 embittering ɪm ˈbɪt ər ɪŋ em- ‖ -ˈbɪt̬ ər- **~s** z
embitterment ɪm ˈbɪt ə mənt em- ‖ -ˈbɪt̬ ᵊr-
emblazon ɪm ˈbleɪz ᵊn em- **~ed** d **~ing** ɪŋ
 ~ment mənt **~s** z
emblem ˈem bləm -blɪm **~s** z
emblematic ˌem blə ˈmæt ɪk ◄ -blɪ- ‖ -ˈmæt̬-
 ~ally ᵊl i
emblement ˈem blə mənt -bᵊl- **~s** s
embodiment ɪm ˈbɒd i mənt em- ‖ -ˈbɑːd- **~s**
s
embod|y ɪm ˈbɒd |i em- ‖ -ˈbɑːd |i **~ied** id
 ~ies iz **~ying** i‿ɪŋ
embolden ɪm ˈbəʊld ən em-, →-ˈbʊʊld-
‖ -ˈboʊld- **~ed** d **~ing** ɪŋ **~s** z
emboli ˈem bə laɪ
embolic em ˈbɒl ɪk ‖ -ˈbɑːl-
embolism ˈem bə ˌlɪz əm **~s** z
em|bolus ˈem |bəl əs **~boli** bə laɪ
embonpoint ˌɒm bɒn ˈpwæ̃ ˌɒ̃-, →-bɒm-, -bɒ̃-,
-ˈpwɒ̃ ‖ ˌɑːm boʊn ˈpwæn —*Fr* [ɑ̃ bɔ̃ pwæ̃]
embosomed ɪm ˈbʊz əmd em-, §-ˈbuːz-

E-mail and the web

In an e-mail address the character @ is read as **at**. The punctuation mark **<.>** is read as dot, both in e-mail addresses and in URLs (= website addresses). The punctuation mark **</>** is usually read as **slash** or **forward slash**, and **<#>** as **hash** (BrE) or **pound sign** (AmE).

So **<j.wells@ucl.ac.uk>** is read as **J dot Wells at U C L dot A C dot U K.** **<www.pearsonlongman.com/elt-world>** is read as **W W W dot PearsonLongman dot com slash E L T hyphen world.**

E

---

emboss ɪm ˈbɒs em- ‖ -ˈbɑːs -ˈbɔːs **~ed** t **~es** ɪz əz **~ing** ɪŋ
embouchure ˌɒm bu ˈʃʊə '··· ‖ ˌɑːm bu ˈʃʊər ˈɑːm bə ʃʊr —*Fr* [ɑ̃ bu ʃyːʁ] **~s** z
embourgeoisement ˌɒm bu ˈwɑːz mɒ̃ ‖ em ˈbʊrʒ wɑːz mɑːnt ɑːm-, -mənt —*Fr* [ɑ̃ buʁ ʒwaz mɑ̃]
embowered ɪm ˈbaʊ ̯əd em- ‖ -ˈbaʊ ̯ərd
embrac|e ɪm ˈbreɪs em- **~ed** t **~er/s** ə/z ‖ ər/z **~es** ɪz əz **~ing** ɪŋ
embrasure ɪm ˈbreɪʒ ə em- ‖ -ər **~s** z
embrocation ˌem brə ˈkeɪʃ ən **~s** z
embroider ɪm ˈbrɔɪd ə em- ‖ -ər **~ed** d
  embroidering ɪm ˈbrɔɪd ər ɪŋ **~s** z
embroider|y ɪm ˈbrɔɪd ər_i em- **~ies** ɪz
embroil ɪm ˈbrɔɪəl em- **~ed** d **~ing** ɪŋ **~s** z
embryo ˈem bri əʊ ‖ -oʊ **~s** z
embryo- *comb. form*
  with stress-neutral suffix ˈem bri əʊ ‖ -ə
  — **embryotome** ˈem bri əʊ təʊm ‖ -ə toʊm
  with stress-imposing suffix ˌem bri ˈɒ+
  ‖ -ˈɑː+ — **embryotomy** ˌem bri ˈɒt əm i
  ‖ -ˈɑːt̬-
embryolog|ist ˌem bri ˈɒl ədʒ| ɪst §-əst ‖ -ˈɑːl- **~ists** ɪsts §əsts **~y** i
embryonic ˌem bri ˈɒn ɪk ◄ ‖ -ˈɑːn- **~ally** ᵊl_i
Emburey, Embury ˈem bər i -bjʊr-
embus ɪm ˈbʌs em- **~ed, ~sed** t **~es, ~ses** ɪz əz **~ing, ~sing** ɪŋ
emcee ˌem ˈsiː **~d** d **~ing** ɪŋ **~s** z
-eme iːm — **grapheme** ˈgræf iːm —*Although strong-vowelled, this suffix is unstressed.*
Emeline ˈem ə liːn -ɪ-
emend i ˈmend ə- **~ed** ɪd əd **~ing** ɪŋ **~s** z
emendation ˌiːm en ˈdeɪʃ ən ˌem-, -ən- **~s** z
Emeney, Emeny ˈem ən i
emerald ˈem ᵊr_əld **~s** z
emerg|e i ˈmɜːdʒ ə- ‖ -ˈmɜːdʒ **~ed** d **~es** ɪz əz **~ing** ɪŋ
emergenc|e i ˈmɜːdʒ ən⁀s ə- ‖ -ˈmɜːdʒ- **~es** ɪz əz
emergenc|y i ˈmɜːdʒ ən⁀s |i ə- ‖ -ˈmɜːdʒ- **~ies** iz
emergent i ˈmɜːdʒ ənt ə- ‖ -ˈmɜːdʒ-
emerit|us i ˈmer ɪt| əs ə-, -ət|- ‖ -ət̬| əs **~a** ə
Emerson ˈem əs ən ‖ -ᵊrs-

emery, Emery ˈem ər_i
  ˈemery ˌpaper
emetic i ˈmet ɪk ə- ‖ -ˈmet̬ ɪk **~ally** ᵊl_i **~s** s
emetine ˈem ɪ tiːn -ə-, -tɪn, -taɪn
EMF, emf ˌiː em ˈef
EMG ˌiː em ˈdʒiː
EMI *tdmk* ˌiː em ˈaɪ
emic ˈiːm ɪk **~ally** ᵊl_i
emigrant ˈem ɪg rənt -əg- **~s** s
emi|grate ˈem ɪ |greɪt -ə- **~grated** greɪt ɪd -əd ‖ greɪt̬ əd **~grates** greɪts **~grating** greɪt ɪŋ ‖ greɪt̬ ɪŋ
emigration ˌem ɪ ˈgreɪʃ ən -ə-
emigre, émigré, émigré ˈem ɪ greɪ -ə- **~s** z
Emil e ˈmiːᵊl eɪ- —*Ger* [ˈʔeː miːl]
Emile, Émile e ˈmiːᵊl eɪ- —*Fr* [e ˈmil]
Emily ˈem əl i -ɪl-
Emin ˈem ɪn
Eminem ˈem ə nem -ɪ-
eminenc|e, E~ ˈem ɪn ən⁀s -ən-, **~es** ɪz əz —*but as a French word see next entry*
eminence grise, éminence grise, éminences grises ˌem i nɒ̃s ˈgriːz ‖ ˌeɪm i nɑːs- —*Fr* [e mi nɑ̃s griːz]
eminent ˈem ɪn ənt -ən- **~ly** li
emir e ˈmɪə ɪ-, ə-, eɪ-; ˈem ɪə ‖ -ˈmɪᵊr **~s** z
emirate ˈem ər ət -ɪər-, -ɪt, -eɪt; e ˈmɪər-, i- ‖ ɪ ˈmɪr- **~s** s
emissar|y ˈem ɪs ər_|i ‖ -ə ser |i **~ies** iz
emission i ˈmɪʃ ən ə- **~s** z
emissive i ˈmɪs ɪv ə-
emissivity ˌiːm ɪ ˈsɪv ət i ˌem-, ˌ·ə-, -ɪt i ‖ -ət̬ i
e|mit i |ˈmɪt ə- **~mits** ˈmɪts **~mitted** ˈmɪt ɪd -əd ‖ ˈmɪt̬ əd **~mitting** ˈmɪt ɪŋ ‖ ˈmɪt̬ ɪŋ
Emley ˈem li
Emlyn ˈem lɪn §-lən
Emma ˈem ə
Emmanuel i ˈmæn ju_əl ə-
Emmaus i ˈmeɪ əs e-, ə-
Emmeline ˈem ə liːn -ɪ-
emmenagogue i ˈmen ə gɒg ə-, e-, -ˈmiːn- ‖ -gɑːg **~s** z
Emmental, Emmenthal ˈem ən tɑːl **~er/s** ə/z ‖ -ᵊr/z
emmer ˈem ə ‖ -ᵊr
Emmerdale ˈem ə deɪᵊl ‖ -ᵊr-

Emmerson 'em əs ən ‖ -ᵊrs-
emmet, Emmet, Emmett 'em ɪt §-ət ~s s
emmetropia ˌem ɪ 'trəʊp i ə ˌ·ə- ‖ -'troʊp-
emmetropic ˌem ɪ 'trɒp ɪk ◄ -ə- ‖ -'trɑːp-
Emmie, Emmy 'em i ~s z
emo 'iːm əʊ ‖ -oʊ
emollient i 'mɒl i ənt ə- ‖ -'mɑːl- ~s s
emolument i 'mɒl ju mənt ə- ‖ -'mɑːl jə-
e-money 'iː ˌmʌn i
Emory 'em ər i
e|mote i |'məʊt ə-, iː- ‖ -|'moʊt **~moted** 'məʊt ɪd -əd ‖ 'moʊt̬ əd **~motes** 'məʊts ‖ 'moʊts **~moting** 'məʊt ɪŋ ‖ 'moʊt̬ ɪŋ
emoticon i 'məʊt ɪ kɒn ə-, -'mɒt-, -ɪk ən, -ˌaɪk ɒn ‖ -'moʊt̬ ɪ kɑːn **~s** z
emotion i 'məʊʃ ᵊn ə- ‖ -'moʊʃ- **~s** z
emotional i 'məʊʃ ᵊn ᵊl ə- ‖ -'moʊʃ- **~ism** ˌɪz əm **~ly** i
emotionless i 'məʊʃ ᵊn ləs ə- ‖ -'moʊʃ- **~ly** li
emotive i 'məʊt ɪv ə- ‖ -'moʊt̬ ɪv **~ly** li **~ness** nəs nɪs
empanada ˌemp ə 'nɑːd ə **~s** z —*Sp* [em pa 'na ða]
empanel ɪm 'pæn ᵊl em- **~ed, ~led** d **~ing, ~ling** ɪŋ **~s** z
empathetic ˌemp ə 'θet ɪk ◄ ‖ -'θet̬- **~ally** ᵊl_i
empathis|e, empathiz|e 'emp ə θaɪz **~ed** d **~es** ɪz əz **~ing** ɪŋ
empathy 'emp əθ i
Empedocles em 'ped ə kliːz ɪm-
emperor 'emp ər_ə ‖ -ᵊr_ər **~s** z **~ship** ʃɪp
emph|asis 'emᵖf |əs ɪs §-əs **~ases** ə siːz
emphasis|e, emphasiz|e 'emᵖf ə saɪz **~ed** d **~es** ɪz əz **~ing** ɪŋ
emphatic ɪm 'fæt ɪk em- ‖ -'fæt̬ ɪk **~ally** ᵊl_i **~s** s
emphysema ˌemᵖf ɪ 'siːm ə -ə-, -aɪ-, -'ziːm-; ⚠ -'ziːm i ə
emphysematous ˌemᵖf ɪ 'sem ət əs ◄ -ə-, -'siːm- ‖ -ət̬ əs
empire, E~ 'emp aɪ_ə ‖ 'emp aɪᵊr **~s** z **Empire 'State ˌBuilding**
empire-build|er 'emp aɪ_ə ˌbɪld| ə ‖ 'emp aɪᵊr ˌbɪld| ᵊr **~ers** əz ‖ ᵊrz **~ing** ɪŋ
empiric ɪm 'pɪr ɪk em- **~s** s
empirical ɪm 'pɪr ɪk ᵊl em- **~ly** ˌi
empiricism ɪm 'pɪr ɪ ˌsɪz əm em-, -'·ə-
emplacement ɪm 'pleɪs mənt em- **~s** s
emplan|e ɪm 'pleɪn em- **~ed** d **~es** z **~ing** ɪŋ
employ ɪm 'plɔɪ em-, əm- **~ed** d **~ing** ɪŋ **~s** z
employable ɪm 'plɔɪ əb ᵊl em-, əm-
employee ɪm 'plɔɪ iː em-, əm-; ˌem plɔɪ 'iː, ˌɪm- ‖ ˌ··ˈ· **~s** z
employer ɪm 'plɔɪ ə em-, əm- ‖ -ᵊr **~s** z
employment ɪm 'plɔɪ mənt em-, əm- **~s** s **em'ployment ˌagency**
empori|um em 'pɔːr i ˌəm ɪm- ‖ -'poʊr- **~a** ə **~ums** əmz
empower ɪm 'paʊ ə em- ‖ -'paʊ_ᵊr **~ed** d **empowering** ɪm 'paʊ ər ɪŋ em- ‖ -'paʊ_ᵊr ɪŋ **~ment** mənt **~s** z
empress 'emp rəs -rɪs **~es** ɪz əz
Empson 'emᵖs ᵊn

empt|y 'emᵖt |i **~ied** id **~ier** i_ə ‖ i_ᵊr **~ies** iz **~iest** i_ɪst i_əst **~ily** ɪ li əl i **~iness** i nəs i nɪs **~ying** i_ɪŋ
empty-handed ˌemᵖt i 'hænd ɪd ◄ -əd
empty-headed ˌemᵖt i 'hed ɪd ◄ -əd **~ness** nəs nɪs
empurpled ɪm 'pɜːp ᵊld em- ‖ -'pɜːp-
empyema ˌemp aɪ 'iːm ə
empyre|al ˌemp ɪ 'riː ˌəl ◄ -aɪᵊ-, -ə-, **~an** ən
Emrys 'em rɪs —*Welsh* ['em ris, -ris]
Ems emz —*Ger* [ʔems]
EMS ˌiː em 'es
Emsworth 'emz wəθ -wɜːθ ‖ -wɜːθ
emu 'iːm juː **~s** z
EMU ˌiː em 'juː 'iːm juː
emu|late 'em ju |leɪt -jə- ‖ -jə- **~lated** leɪt ɪd -əd ‖ leɪt̬ əd **~lates** leɪts **~lating** leɪt ɪŋ ‖ leɪt̬ ɪŋ
emulation ˌem ju 'leɪʃ ᵊn -jə- ‖ -jə- **~s** z
emulator 'em ju leɪt ə '·jə- ‖ -jə leɪt̬ ᵊr **~s** z
emulous 'em jʊl əs -jəl- ‖ -jəl- **~ly** li **~ness** nəs nɪs
emulsification i ˌmʌls ɪf ɪ 'keɪʃ ᵊn ə-, -ˌəf-, §-ə'·.
emulsi|fy i 'mʌls ɪ |faɪ ə-, -ə- **~fied** faɪd **~fier/s** faɪ ə/z ‖ faɪ ᵊr/z **~fies** faɪz **~fying** faɪ ɪŋ
emulsion i 'mʌl ʃᵊn ə- **~ed** d **~ing** ɪŋ **~s** z **e'mulsion ˌpaint**
Emyr 'em ɪə ‖ -ɪr —*Welsh* ['em ir, -ir]
en *printer's measure* en ens enz
en *in French phrases* ɒ̃ ɒn, ɑːn ‖ ɑ̃: ɑːn —*Fr* [ɑ̃] —See also phrases with this word
en- ɪn ən, (ˌ)en —*This prefix is stressed* ˌen *if the following syllable is unstressed* (ˌenhar'monic). *Otherwise the prefix is unstressed, and the weak-vowel form* ɪn *is preferred in RP* (en'large), *although some speakers, in Britain particularly regional ones, use* en *or* ən.
-en ᵊn, ən, ən — **wooden** 'wʊd ᵊn **blacken** 'blæk ən **woollen** 'wʊl ən
Ena 'iːn ə
enabl|e ɪn 'eɪb ᵊl en-, ən- **~ed** d **~ement** mənt **~er/s** _ə/z ‖ _ᵊr/z **~es** z **~ing** ˌɪŋ
enact ɪn 'ækt en-, ən- **~ed** ɪd əd **~ing** ɪŋ **~ment/s** mənt/s **~s** s
enamel i 'næm ᵊl ə- **~ed, ~led** d **~er/s, ~ler/s** ə/z ‖ ᵊr/z **~ing, ~ling** ɪŋ **~ist/s, ~list/s** ɪst/s §-əst/s **~s** z
enamelware i 'næm ᵊl weə ə- ‖ -wer
enamor, enamour ɪn 'æm ə en-, ən- ‖ -ᵊr **~ed** d
enantio- *comb. form with stress-neutral suffix* en ˌænt i_əʊ ɪn- ‖ ɪn ˌænt̬i_ə — **enantiomorph** en 'ænt i əʊ mɔːf ɪn- ‖ ɪn 'ænt̬i ə mɔːrf *with stress-imposing suffix* en ˌænt i 'ɒ+ ɪn- ‖ ɪn ˌænt̬ i 'ɑː+ — **enantiopathy** en ˌænt i 'ɒp əθ i ɪn- ‖ ɪn ˌænt̬ i 'ɑːp-
enarthrosis ˌen ɑː 'θrəʊs ɪs §-əs ‖ -ɑːr 'θroʊs-
en bloc ɒ̃ 'blɒk ˌɒn-, →ˌɒm-, ˌɑːn-, →ˌɑːm- ‖ ˌɑ̃: 'blɑːk ˌɑːn- —*Fr* [ɑ̃ blɔk]

en brochette ˌɒ̃ brɒ ˈʃet ˌɒn-, →ˌ, ˌɒm-
‖ ˌɑ̃: broʊ- —*Fr* [ɑ̃ bʁɔ ʃɛt]
en brosse ˌɒ̃ ˈbrɒs ˌɒn-, →ˌ, ˌɒm- ‖ ˌɑːn ˈbrɔːs
-ˈbrɑːs —*Fr* [ɑ̃ bʁɔs]

encaenia, E~ en ˈsiːn i ə

encamp ɪn ˈkæmp en-, →ɪŋ-, →eŋ- **~ed** t **~ing**
ɪŋ **~ment/s** mənt/s **~s** s

encapsu|late ɪn ˈkæps ju ˌleɪt en-, ən-, →ɪŋ-,
→eŋ-, →əŋ-, §-ə-, §-ˈkæp ʃə- ‖ -ə- **~lated**
leɪt ɪd -əd ‖ ˌleɪţ əd **~lates** leɪts **~lating**
leɪt ɪŋ ‖ ˌleɪţ ɪŋ

encapsulation ɪn ˌkæps ju ˈleɪʃ ᵊn en-, ən-,
→ɪŋ-, →eŋ-, →əŋ-, §-ə-, §-ˌkæp ʃə- ‖ -ə- **~s** z

Encarta *tdmk* ɪn ˈkɑːt ə en-, →ɪŋ-, →eŋ-
‖ -ˈkɑːrţ ə

encas|e ɪn ˈkeɪs en-, →ɪŋ-, →eŋ- **~ed** t **~ement**
mənt **~es** ɪz əz **~ing** ɪŋ

encash ɪn ˈkæʃ en-, →ɪŋ-, →eŋ- **~able** əb ᵊl
~ed t **~es** ɪz əz **~ing** ɪŋ **~ment/s** mənt/s

encaustic ɪn ˈkɔːst ɪk en-, →ɪŋ-, →eŋ-, -ˈkɒst-
‖ -ˈkɔːst- -ˈkɑːst- **~s** s

-ence ən̩s —*The two possible stress-effects of
this suffix are illustrated in* ˌcorreˈspondence
and maˈlevolence. *In a few words it triggers a
vowel change and shift of stress in the stem, as*
prevail prɪ ˈveɪᵊl → prevalence ˈprev ᵊl ən̩s,
confide kən ˈfaɪd → confidence ˈkɒn fɪd ᵊn̩s.
There is fluctuation in precedence, subsidence.

enceinte ˌ(ˌ)ɒn ˈsænt ˌ(ˌ)ɒ̃- ‖ ˌ(ˌ)ɑ̃:- —*Fr* [ɑ̃ sæːt]

Enceladus en ˈsel əd əs

encephalic ˌen kɪ ˈfæl ɪk ◀ →ˌeŋ-, -kə-, -ke-;
ˌen sɪ-, -sə-, -se- ‖ -sə-

encepha|litic en ˌkef ə ˈlɪt ɪk ◀ →eŋ-,
en ˌsef-, ɪn-, ˌen kef-, ˌen sef-
‖ ɪn ˌsef ə ˈlɪţ ɪk ◀ **~litis** ˈlaɪt ɪs §-əs
‖ ˈlaɪţ əs

encephalo- *comb. form*
with stress-neutral suffix en ˌkef əl əʊ →eŋ-,
ɪn-, →ɪŋ-, en ˌsef-, ɪn ˌsef- ‖ ɪn ˌsef əl ə
— **encephalogram** en ˈkef əl əʊ græm
→eŋ-, ɪn-, →ɪŋ-, en ˈsef-, ɪn ˈsef-
‖ ɪn ˈsef əl ə græm
with stress-imposing suffix en ˌkef ə ˈlɒ+
→eŋ-, en ˌsef-, ˌ ˌ ˈ ˌ, ɪn ˌ ˈ ‖ ɪn ˌsef ə ˈlɑː+
— **encephalopathy** en ˌkef ə ˈlɒp əθ i
→eŋ-, en ˌsef-, ˌ ˌ ˈ ˌ, ɪn ˌ ˈ ‖ ɪn ˌsef ə ˈlɑːp-

encephalomyelitis
en ˌkef ə ləʊ ˌmaɪ ə ˈlaɪt ɪs →eŋ-, en ˌsef-,
ˌ ˌ ˈ ˌ, ɪn ˌ ˈ ‖ ɪn ˌsef ə loʊ ˌmaɪ ə ˈlaɪţ əs

enchain ɪn ˈtʃeɪn en-, ən- **~ed** d **~ing** ɪŋ
~ment mənt **~s** z

en|chant ɪn ‖ˈtʃɑːnt en-, ən-, §-ˈtʃænt ‖ -ˈtʃænt
~chanted ˈtʃɑːnt ɪd §ˈtʃænt-, -əd ‖ ˈtʃænţ əd
~chanting ˈtʃɑːnt ɪŋ §ˈtʃænt- ‖ ˈtʃænţ ɪŋ

enchanter ɪn ˈtʃɑːnt ə en-, ən-, §-ˈtʃænt-
‖ -ˈtʃænţ ᵊr **~s** z

enchanting ɪn ˈtʃɑːnt ɪŋ en-, ən-, §ˈtʃænt-
‖ -ˈtʃænţ ɪŋ **~ly** li

enchantment ɪn ˈtʃɑːnt mənt §-ˈtʃænt-
‖ -ˈtʃænt- **~s** s

enchantress ɪn ˈtʃɑːntr əs en-, ən-, §-ˈtʃæntr-,
-ɪs, -es ‖ -ˈtʃæntr- **~es** ɪz əz

enchilada ˌen tʃɪ ˈlɑːd ə -tʃə- **~s** z

Encinitas ˌen̩s ɪ ˈniːt əs -ə- ‖ -ˈniːţ-

enciph|er ɪn ˈsaɪf |ə en-, ən- ‖ -|ᵊr **~ered** əd
‖ ᵊrd **~ering** ər ɪŋ **~ers** əz ‖ ᵊrz

encircl|e ɪn ˈsɜːk ᵊl en-, ən- ‖ -ˈsɜːk- **~ed** d
~ement/s mənt/s **~es** z **~ing** ɪŋ

enclasp ɪn ˈklɑːsp en-, ən-, →ɪŋ-, →eŋ-, →əŋ-,
§-ˈklæsp ‖ -ˈklæsp **~ed** t **~ing** ɪŋ **~s** s

enclave ˈen kleɪv →ˈeŋ-, ˈɒŋ-, ˈˌ ˈ ‖ ˈɑːn- **~s** z

enclitic ɪn ˈklɪt ɪk en-, →ɪŋ-, →eŋ- ‖ -ˈklɪţ ɪk **~s**
s

enclos|e ɪn ˈkləʊz en-, ən-, →ɪŋ-, →eŋ-, →əŋ-
‖ -ˈkloʊz **~ed** d **~es** ɪz əz **~ing** ɪŋ

enclosure ɪn ˈkləʊʒ ə en-, ən-, →ɪŋ-, →eŋ-,
→əŋ- ‖ -ˈkloʊʒ ᵊr **~s** z

encod|e ɪn ˈkəʊd ˌ(ˌ)en-, →ɪŋ-, →ˌ(ˌ)eŋ- ‖ -ˈkoʊd
~ed ɪd əd **~er/s** ə/z ‖ ᵊr/z **~es** z **~ing** ɪŋ

encomiast ɪn ˈkəʊm i æst en-, ən-, →ɪŋ-,
→eŋ-, →əŋ-, -əst ‖ -ˈkoʊm- **~s** s

encomienda ɪn ˌkəʊm i ˈend ə en-, ən-
‖ -ˌkoʊm- —*Sp* [eŋ ko ˈmjen da]

encomi|um ɪn ˈkəʊm i ̩əm en-, ən-, →ɪŋ-,
→eŋ-, →əŋ- ‖ -ˈkoʊm- **~a** ə **~ums** əmz

encompass ɪn ˈkʌmp əs en-, →ɪŋ-, →eŋ-,
→əŋ- ‖ -ˈkɑːmp- **~ed** t **~es** ɪz əz **~ing** ɪŋ
~ment mənt

encore ˈɒŋ kɔː ˈˌ ˈ ‖ ˈɑːn kɔːr -kour

encounter ɪn ˈkaʊnt ə en-, ən-, →ɪŋ-, →eŋ-,
→əŋ- ‖ -ˈkaʊnţ ᵊr **~ed** d **encountering**
ɪn ˈkaʊnt_ər ɪŋ en-, ən-, →ɪŋ-, →eŋ-, →əŋ-
‖ -ˈkaʊnţ ər ɪŋ →ˈkaʊntr ɪŋ **~s** z

en'counter group

encourag|e ɪn ˈkʌr ɪdʒ en-, ən-, →ɪŋ-, →eŋ-,
→əŋ- ‖ -ˈkɝː- **~ed** d **~ement/s** mənt/s **~es** ɪz
əz **~ing/ly** ɪŋ /li

encroach ɪn ˈkrəʊtʃ en-, ən-, →ɪŋ-, →eŋ-, →əŋ-
‖ -ˈkroʊtʃ **~ed** t **~es** ɪz əz **~ing** ɪŋ **~ment/s**
mənt/s

en croute, en croûte ˌɒn ˈkruːt →ˌ, ˌɒŋ- ‖ ˌɑːn-
—*Fr* [ɑ̃ kʁut]

encrust ɪn ˈkrʌst en-, ən-, →ɪŋ-, →eŋ-, →əŋ-
~ed ɪd əd **~ing** ɪŋ **~s** s

encrustation ˌɪn krʌs ˈteɪʃ ᵊn ˌen-, →ˌ, ˌ→ɪŋ-,
→eŋ-, ˌ ˌ,-- **~s** z

encrypt ɪn ˈkrɪpt en-, ən-, →ɪŋ-, →eŋ-, →əŋ-
~ed ɪd əd **~ing** ɪŋ **~s** s

encryption ɪn ˈkrɪp ʃᵊn en-, ən-, →ɪŋ-, →eŋ-,
→əŋ- **~s** z

encum|ber ɪn ˈkʌm |bə en-, ən-, →ɪŋ-, →eŋ-,
→əŋ- ‖ -|bᵊr **~bered** bəd ‖ bᵊrd **~bering**
bər ɪŋ **~bers** bəz ‖ bᵊrz

encumbranc|e ɪn ˈkʌm brən̩s en-, ən-, →ɪŋ-,
→eŋ-, →əŋ- **~s** z

-ency ən̩s i —*Stress always as in the
corresponding* -ent *word:* sufˈficiency, ˈurgency,
ˈexcellency.

encyclical ɪn ˈsɪk lɪk ᵊl en-, ən- **~s** z

encyclopaed... —*see* **encycloped...**

encyclopedia ɪn ˌsaɪk lə ˈpiːd i ̩ə en-, ən- **~s** z

encyclopedic ɪn ˌsaɪk lə ˈpiːd ɪk ◀ en-, ən-
~ally ᵊl ̩i

encyclopedist ɪn ˌsaɪk lə ˈpiːd ɪst en-, ən-,
§-əst **~s** s

encyst en ˈsɪst **~ed** ɪd əd **~ing** ɪŋ **~s** s

E

end end **ended** 'end ɪd -əd **ending** 'end ɪŋ
ends endz
'end ˌmatter; **'end ˌproduct**, ˌ· '· ·; **'end ˌuser**, ˌ· '· ·
endang|er ɪn 'deɪndʒ |ə en-, ən- ‖ -|ᵊr **~ered** əd ‖ ᵊrd **~ering** ər‿ɪŋ **~erment** ə mənt ‖ ᵊr mənt **~ers** əz ‖ ᵊrz
endear ɪn 'dɪə en-, ən- ‖ -'dɪᵊr **~ed** d
endearing/ly ɪn 'dɪər ɪŋ /li en-, ən- ‖ -'dɪr ɪŋ /li **~ment/s** mənt/s **~s** z
endeavor, endeavour ɪn 'dev ə en-, ən- ‖ -ᵊr **~ed** d **endeavoring, endeavouring** ɪn 'dev ər‿ɪŋ en-, ən- **~s** z
Endell 'end ᵊl
endemic en 'dem ɪk ɪn- **~al** ᵊl **~ally** ᵊl‿i
Enderby 'end ə bi ‖ -ᵊr-
'Enderby Land
Enders 'end əz ‖ -ᵊrz
endgame 'end geɪm →'eŋ- **~s** z
Endicott 'end ɪ kɒt -ə-; -ɪk ət, -ək- ‖ -kɑːt
ending 'end ɪŋ **~s** z
endive 'end ɪv -aɪv ‖ 'end aɪv 'ɑːnd iːv **~s** z
endless 'end ləs -lɪs **~ly** li **~ness** nəs nɪs
endo- *comb. form*
with stress-neutral suffix ¦end əʊ ‖¦end ə — **endocranial** ˌend əʊ 'kreɪn i‿əl ◂ ‖ ˌ-ə-
with stress-imposing suffix en 'dɒ+ ‖ en 'dɑː+ — **endogenous** en 'dɒdʒ ən əs -ɪn- ‖ -'dɑːdʒ-
endocarditis ˌend əʊ kɑː 'daɪt ɪs §-əs ‖ -oʊ kɑːr 'daɪţ əs
endocarp 'end əʊ kɑːp ‖ -ə kɑːrp **~s** s
endocentric ˌend əʊ 'sentr ɪk ◂ ‖ -oʊ- **~ally** ᵊl‿i
endocrine 'end əʊ kraɪn -krɪn, -kriːn, §-krən ‖ -ə- **~s** z
endocrinology ˌend əʊ krɪ 'nɒl ədʒ i -kraɪ'-- ‖ -oʊ krɪ 'nɑːl-
endogam|ous en 'dɒg əm |əs ‖ -'dɑːg- **~y** i
endogenous en 'dɒdʒ ən əs ɪn-, -ɪn- ‖ -'dɑːdʒ- **~ly** li
endometriosis ˌend əʊ ˌmiːtr i 'əʊs ɪs §-əs ‖ -oʊ ˌmiːtr i 'oʊs əs
endometri|um ˌend əʊ 'miːtr i‿|əm ‖ ˌ-oʊ- **~a** ə **~al** əl
endomorph 'end əʊ mɔːf ‖ -ə mɔːrf **~s** s
endomorph|ic ˌend əʊ 'mɔːf |ɪk◂ ‖ -ə 'mɔːrf- **~ism** ˌɪz əm
endoplasm 'end əʊ ˌplæz əm ‖ -ə-
endoplasmic ˌend əʊ 'plæz mɪk ◂ ‖ -oʊ-
Endor 'end ɔː ‖ -ɔːr
endorphin en 'dɔːf ɪn §-ən ‖ -'dɔːrf- **~s** z
endorsable ɪn 'dɔːs əb ᵊl en-, ən- ‖ -'dɔːrs-
endors|e ɪn 'dɔːs en-, ən- ‖ -'dɔːrs **~ed** t **~ement/s** mənt/s **~er/s** ə/z ‖ ᵊr/z **~es** ɪz əz **~ing** ɪŋ
endorsee ˌen dɔː 'siː ‖ -dɔːr- **~s** z
endoscope 'end ə skəʊp ‖ -skoʊp **~s** s
endoscopic ˌend ə 'skɒp ɪk ◂ ‖ -'skɑːp- **~ally** ᵊl‿i
endoscop|y en 'dɒsk əp |i ‖ -'dɑːsk- **~ies** iz
endosmosis ˌend ɒz 'məʊs ɪs -ɒs-, §-əs ‖ -ɑːz 'moʊs- -ɑːs-
endosperm 'end əʊ spɜːm ‖ -oʊ spɜːm
endotherm 'end əʊ θɜːm ‖ -oʊ θɜːm **~s** z
endothermic ˌend əʊ 'θɜːm ɪk ◂ ‖ -ə 'θɜːm- **~ally** ᵊl‿i
endow ɪn 'daʊ en-, ən- **~ed** d **~ing** ɪŋ **~ment/s** mənt/s **~s** z
en'dowment ˌmortgage; **en'dowment ˌpolicy**
endpaper 'end ˌpeɪp ə →'em- ‖ -ᵊr **~s** z
endplay 'end pleɪ →'em- **~ed** d **~ing** ɪŋ **~s** z
Endsleigh 'endz li -liː
end-stopped 'end stɒpt ˌ·'· ‖ -stɑːpt
endu|e ɪn 'djuː en-, ən-, →-'dʒuː ‖ -'duː -'djuː **~ed** d **~es** z **~ing** ɪŋ
endurable ɪn 'djʊər əb ᵊl en-, ən-, →-'dʒʊər-, -'djɔːr- ‖ -'dʊr- -djʊr-, -'dɜːr-
endurance ɪn 'djʊər ənᵗs en-, ən-, -'djɔːr-, →-'dʒʊər- ‖ -'dʊr- -'djʊr-, -'dɜːr-
endure ɪn 'djʊə en-, ən-, -'djɔː, →-'dʒʊə ‖ -'dʊᵊr -'djʊᵊr, -'dɜː **~d** d **~s** z **enduring/ly** ɪn 'djʊər ɪŋ /li en-, ən-, -'djɔːr-, →-'dʒʊər- ‖ -'dʊr ɪŋ /li -'djʊr-, -'dɜː-
endways 'end weɪz
endwise 'end waɪz
Endymion en 'dɪm i‿ən ɪn-
-ene iːn — **toluene** 'tɒl ju iːn ‖ 'toʊl- —*Although strong-vowelled, this suffix is unstressed.*
Eneas i 'niː‿əs -'neɪ-, -æs
Eneid 'iːn i‿ɪd ɪ 'niː-, §-əd
enema 'en əm ə -ɪm- **~s** z
enem|y 'en əm |i -ɪm- **~ies** iz
ˌenemy 'alien
Energen *tdmk* 'en ədʒ ən ‖ -ᵊrdʒ-
energetic ˌen ə 'dʒet ɪk ◂ ‖ -ᵊr 'dʒeţ ɪk ◂ **~ally** ᵊl‿i **~s** s
Energis *tdmk* 'en ədʒ ɪs §-əs ‖ -ᵊrdʒ-
energis|e, energiz|e 'en ə dʒaɪz ‖ -ᵊr- **~ed** d **~es** ɪz əz **~ing** ɪŋ
energ|y 'en ədʒ |i ‖ -ᵊrdʒ |i **~ies** iz
ener|vate 'en ə |veɪt -ɜː- ‖ -ᵊr- **~vated** veɪt ɪd -əd ‖ veɪţ əd **~vates** veɪts **~vating** veɪt ɪŋ ‖ veɪţ ɪŋ
enervation ˌen ə 'veɪʃ ᵊn -ɜː- ‖ -ᵊr-
en famille ˌɒ̃ fæ 'miː ˌɒn-, ˌɑːn- ‖ ˌɑːn fə- —*Fr* [ɑ̃ fa mij]
enfant terrible ˌɒ̃f ɒ̃ tə 'riːb lə ˌɒn fɒn-, ˌɑːn fɑːn-, -te'-- ‖ ɑːn ˌfɑːn- —*Fr* [ɑ̃ fɑ̃ tɛ ʁibl]
enfants terribles *as singular*
enfeebl|e ɪn 'fiːb ᵊl en-, ən- **~ed** d **~ement/s** mənt/s **~es** z **~ing** ‿ɪŋ
enfeoff ɪn 'fiːf en-, ən-, -'fef **~ed** t **~ing** ɪŋ **~s** s
en fete, en fête ₍ᵢ₎ɒ̃ 'feɪt ₍ᵢ₎ɒn-, -'fet ‖ ₍ᵢ₎ɑ̃ː —*Fr* [ɑ̃ fɛt]
Enfield 'en fiːᵊld
enfilad|e *v* ˌen fɪ 'leɪd -fə-, '· · · ‖ 'en fə leɪd -lɑːd **~ed** ɪd əd **~es** z **~ing** ɪŋ
enfilade *n* 'en fɪ leɪd -fə-, ˌ· '· ‖ -lɑːd **~s** z
enfold ɪn 'fəʊld en-, ən-, →-'fɒʊld ‖ -'foʊld **~ed** ɪd əd **~ing** ɪŋ **~s** z
enforc|e ɪn 'fɔːs en-, ən- ‖ -'fɔːrs -'foʊrs **~ed** t **~es** ɪz əz **~ing** ɪŋ

E

enforceab|le ɪn 'fɔːs əb |ᵊl en-, ən- ‖ -'fɔːrs-
-'foʊrs- **~ly** li

enforcement ɪn 'fɔːs mənt en-, ən- ‖ -'fɔːrs-
-'foʊrs-

enforcer ɪn 'fɔːs ə en-, ən- ‖ -'fɔːrs ᵊr -'foʊrs-
~s z

enfranchis|e ɪn 'fræntʃ aɪz en-, ən- **~ed** d **~es**
ɪz əz **~ing** ɪŋ

enfranchisement ɪn 'fræntʃ ɪz mənt en-, ən-,
-əz- ‖ -aɪz-, -əz- **~s** s

Engadine 'eŋ gə diːn ˌ·ˑˑ

engag|e ɪn 'geɪdʒ en-, ən-, →ɪŋ-, →eŋ-, →əŋ-
~ed d **~es** ɪz əz **~ing/ly** ɪŋ /li

engagé ˌɒŋ gæ 'ʒeɪ -gɑː- ‖ ˌɑːŋ gɑː- —*Fr*
[ɑ̃ ga ʒe]

engagement ɪn 'geɪdʒ mənt en-, ən-, →ɪŋ-,
→eŋ-, →əŋ- **~s** s
en'gagement book; en'gagement ring

en garde ˌ(ˌ)ɒ̃ 'gɑːd ˌ(ˌ)ɒn-, →ˌ(ˌ)ɒŋ-
‖ ˌ(ˌ)ɑːn 'gɑːrd —*Fr* [ɑ̃ gaʀd]

Engelbert 'eŋ gᵊl bɜːt ‖ -bɜːt —*Ger*
['ʔeŋ ᵊl bɛʀt]

Engels 'eŋ gᵊlz —*Ger* ['ʔeŋ ᵊls]

engender ɪn 'dʒend ə en-, ən- ‖ -ᵊr **~ed** d
engendering ɪn 'dʒend ᵊr ɪŋ **~s** z

engine 'endʒ ɪn §ɪndʒ-, -ən **~s** z
'engine ˌdriver

-engined 'endʒ ɪnd §'ɪndʒ-, -ənd
— twin-engined ˌtwɪn 'endʒ ɪnd ◄ §-'ɪndʒ-,
-ənd

engi|neer ˌendʒ ɪ |'nɪə §ˌɪndʒ-, -ə- ‖ -|'nɪᵊr
~neered 'nɪəd ‖ 'nɪᵊrd **~neering** 'nɪər ɪŋ
‖ 'nɪr ɪŋ **~neers** 'nɪəz ‖ 'nɪᵊrz

England 'ɪŋ glənd -lənd **~'s** z

Englefield 'eŋ gᵊl fiːᵊld

Englewood 'eŋ gᵊl wʊd

English 'ɪŋ glɪʃ -lɪʃ **~man** mən **~men** mən men
~ness nəs nɪs **~woman** ˌwʊm ən **~women**
ˌwɪm ɪn §-ən
ˌEnglish 'Channel; ˌEnglish 'literature

Eng Lit ˌɪŋ 'lɪt

Eng. lit. ˌɪŋ 'lɪt ˌeŋ-

engorg|e ɪn 'gɔːdʒ en-, ən-, →ɪŋ-, →eŋ-, →əŋ-
‖ -'gɔːrdʒ **~ed** d **~ement** mənt **~es** ɪz əz **~ing**
ɪŋ

engraft ɪn 'grɑːft en-, ən-, →ɪŋ-, →eŋ-, →əŋ-,
§-'græft ‖ -'græft **~ed** ɪd əd **~ing** ɪŋ **~s** s

engram 'en græm →'eŋ- **~s** z

engrav|e ɪn 'greɪv en-, ən-, →ɪŋ-, →eŋ-, →əŋ-
~ed d **~er/s** ə/z ‖ ᵊr/z **~es** z **~ing/s** ɪŋ/z

engross ɪn 'grəʊs en-, ən-, →ɪŋ-, →eŋ-, →əŋ-,
§-'grɒs ‖ -'groʊs **~ed** t **~es** ɪz əz **~ing** ɪŋ

engulf ɪn 'gʌlf en-, ən-, →ɪŋ-, →eŋ-, →əŋ- **~ed**
t **~ing** ɪŋ **~s** s

enhanc|e ɪn 'hɑːnᵗs en-, ən-, -'hænᵗs ‖ -'hænᵗs
~ed t **~ement/s** mənt/s **~er/s** ə/z ‖ ᵊr/z **~es**
ɪz əz **~ing** ɪŋ

enharmonic ˌen hɑː 'mɒn ɪk ◄ ‖ -hɑːr 'mɑːn-
~ally ᵊl_i

Enid 'iːn ɪd §-əd —*but in Wales sometimes* 'en-

enigma i 'nɪg mə e-, ə- **~s** z

enigmatic ˌen ɪg 'mæt ɪk ◄ ‖ -'mæt̮ ɪk ◄ **~ally**
ᵊl_i

enjambment ɪn 'dʒæm mənt en-, ən-,
-'dʒæmb- —*Fr* enjambement [ɑ̃ ʒɑ̃b mɑ̃] **~s** s

enjoin ɪn 'dʒɔɪn en-, ən- **~ed** d **~ing** ɪŋ **~s** z

enjoy ɪn 'dʒɔɪ en-, ən- **~ed** d **~ing** ɪŋ **~s** z

enjoyab|le ɪn 'dʒɔɪ əb |ᵊl en-, ən- **~ly** li

enjoyment ɪn 'dʒɔɪ mənt en-, ən- **~s** s

enlarg|e ɪn 'lɑːdʒ en-, ən- ‖ -'lɑːrdʒ **~ed** d
~ement/s mənt/s **~er/s** ə/z ‖ ᵊr/z **~es** ɪz əz
~ing ɪŋ

enlighten ɪn 'laɪt ᵊn en-, ən- **~ed** d **~ing** ˌɪŋ **~s**
z

enlightenment, E~ ɪn 'laɪt ᵊn mənt en-, ən-

enlist ɪn 'lɪst en-, ən- **~ed** ɪd əd **~ing** ɪŋ **~s** s
en'listed man

enlistment ɪn 'lɪst mənt en-, ən- **~s** s

enliven ɪn 'laɪv ᵊn en-, ən- **~ed** d **~ing** ˌɪŋ **~s** z

en masse ˌ(ˌ)ɒ̃ 'mæs ˌ(ˌ)ɒn-, →ˌ(ˌ)ɒm- ‖ ˌ(ˌ)ɑːn-
-'mɑːs —*Fr* [ɑ̃ mas]

enmesh ɪn 'meʃ en-, ən-, →ɪm-, →em-, →əm-
~ed t **~es** ɪz əz **~ing** ɪŋ

enmit|y 'en mət |i →'em-, -mɪt-; △'em nət i
‖ 'en mət̮ |i **~ies** ɪz

Ennals 'en ᵊlz

enneahedr|on ˌen i ə 'hiːdr |ən -'hedr- **~a** ə

Ennerdale 'en ə deɪᵊl ‖ -ᵊr-

Ennis 'en ɪs §-əs

Enniskillen ˌen ɪs 'kɪl ən ◄ -əs-, -ɪn

Ennius 'en i əs

ennobl|e ɪ 'nəʊb ᵊl e-, ə-, ɪn-, en-, ən- ‖ -'noʊb-
~ed d **~ement** mənt **~es** z **~ing** ɪŋ

ennui 'ɒn wiː ˑˑ ‖ ˌɑːn 'wiː —*Fr* [ɑ̃ nɥi]

Eno 'iːn əʊ ‖ -oʊ **~'s** z

Enoch 'iːn ɒk ‖ -ək -ɑːk

Enola Gay ɪ ˌnəʊl ə 'geɪ ‖ -ˌnoʊl-

enology i 'nɒl ədʒ i ‖ -'nɑːl-

Enone i 'nəʊn i ‖ -'noʊn i

enophile 'iːn əʊ faɪᵊl ‖ 'iːn ə- **~s** z

enormit|y i 'nɔːm ət |i i ə-, -ɪt- ‖ i 'nɔːrm ət̮ |i
~ies ɪz

enormous i 'nɔːm əs ə- ‖ i 'nɔːrm- **~ly** li
~ness nəs nɪs

Enos 'iːn ɒs ‖ -ɑːs

enosis 'en əʊs ɪs §-əs ‖ ɪ 'noʊs-

enough ə 'nʌf i 'nʌf —*After* t, d *(and
sometimes other obstruents) the* ə *and* n *may
combine to give a syllabic consonant, thus
good enough* ˌgʊd n 'ʌf.

enounc|e ɪ 'naʊnᵗs **~ed** t **~es** ɪz əz **~ing** ɪŋ

enow i 'naʊ ə-

en papillote ˌɒ̃ ˌpæp i 'ɒt ɒn-, →ɒm-
‖ ˌɑːn ˌpaːp i 'oʊt —*Fr* [ɑ̃ pa pi jɔt]

en passant ˌɒn 'pæs ɒn →ˌ-, ɒm-, ˌɒ̃-, -ɒnt,
-ɒ̃; -pæ 'sɒnt, -'sɑːnt ‖ ˌɑːn pɑː 'sɑːn -pə- —*Fr*
[ɑ̃ pa sɑ̃]

enplan|e ɪn 'pleɪn en-, →ɪm-, →em- **~ed** d **~es**
z **~ing** ɪŋ

enquire ɪn 'kwaɪ_ə en-, ən-, →ɪŋ-, →eŋ-, →əŋ-
‖ -'kwaɪ_ᵊr **~d** d **~s** z enquiring/ly
ɪn 'kwaɪ_ər ɪŋ /li en-, ən-, →ɪŋ-, →eŋ-, →əŋ-
‖ -'kwaɪ_ᵊr ɪŋ /li

enquirer ɪn 'kwaɪ_ər ə en-, ən-, →ɪŋ-, →eŋ-,
→eŋ- ‖ -'kwaɪ_ᵊr ᵊr **~s** z

enquir|y ɪn 'kwaɪ‿ər |i en-, ən-, →ɪŋ-, →eŋ-, →əŋ- ‖ ɪn 'kwaɪ‿ər |i ' · · ·; 'ɪŋk wər |i **~ies** iz

enrag|e ɪn 'reɪdʒ en-, ən- **~ed** d **~es** ɪz əz **~ing** ɪŋ

enrapture ɪn 'ræp tʃə en-, ən- ‖ -tʃ⁰r **~d** d **~s** z **enrapturing** ɪn 'ræp tʃər ɪŋ en-, ən-

enrich ɪn 'rɪtʃ en-, ən- **~ed** t **~er/s** ə/z ‖ ⁰r/z **~es** ɪz əz **~ing** ɪŋ **~ment/s** mənt/s

Enrico en 'riːk əʊ ‖ -oʊ —*It* [en 'riː ko]

Enright 'en raɪt

enrob|e ɪn 'rəʊb en-, ən- ‖ -'roʊb **~ed** d **~es** z **~ing** ɪŋ

enrol, enroll ɪn 'rəʊl en-, ən-, →-'rɒʊl ‖ -'roʊl **~ed** d **~ing** ɪŋ **~ment/s** mənt/s **~s** z

Enron 'en rɒn ‖ -rɑːn

en route ˌɒn 'ruːt ˌŏ- ‖ ˌɑːn- —*Fr* [ã ʁut]

ENSA 'enˢ ə

ensanguined ɪn 'sæŋ gwɪnd en-, ən-

Enschede 'enˢ kə deɪ —*Dutch* ['en sxə de]

ensconc|e ɪn 'skɒnˢ en-, ən- ‖ -'skɑːnˢ **~ed** t **~es** ɪz əz **~ing** ɪŋ

ensemble ɒn 'sɒm b⁰l ŏ-, -'sŏ- ‖ ɑːn 'sɑːm- —*Fr* [ã sã:bl] **~s** z

enshrin|e ɪn 'ʃraɪn en-, ən- **~ed** d **~ement** mənt **~es** z **~ing** ɪŋ

enshroud ɪn 'ʃraʊd en-, ən- **~ed** ɪd əd **~ing** ɪŋ **~s** z

ensign 'en saɪn —*but in the sense 'flag', naut, usually* 'enˢ ⁰n **~s** z

ensilag|e 'enˢ əl ɪdʒ -ɪl-; ɪn 'saɪl-, en-, ənˢ **~ed** d **~es** ɪz əz **~ing** ɪŋ

ensil|e en 'saɪ⁰l 'enˢ aɪ⁰l, -⁰l **~ed** d **~es** z **~ing** ɪŋ

enslav|e ɪn 'sleɪv en-, ən- **~ed** d **~ement/s** mənt/s **~er/s** ə/z ‖ ⁰r/z **~es** z **~ing** ɪŋ

ensnare ɪn 'sneə en-, ən- ‖ -'sne⁰r -'snæ⁰r **~d** d **~ment/s** mənt/s **~s** z **ensnaring** ɪn 'sneər ɪŋ en-, ən- ‖ -'sner ɪŋ -'snær-

Ensor 'enˢ ɔː -ə ‖ -ɔːr -⁰r

enstatite 'enˢt ə taɪt

ensu|e ɪn 'sjuː en-, ən-, -'suː ‖ -'suː **~ed** d **~es** z **~ing** ɪŋ

en suite ˌŏ 'swiːt ˌɒn-, ˌɑːn- ‖ ˌɑːn- —*Fr* [ã sɥit]

ensure ɪn 'ʃɔː en-, ən-, -'ʃʊə, -'sjʊə ‖ -'ʃʊ⁰r -'ʃɜː **~d** d **~s** z **ensuring** ɪn 'ʃɔːr ɪŋ en-, ən-, -'ʃʊər-, -'sjʊər- ‖ -'ʃʊr ɪŋ -'ʃɜː-

ENT ˌiː en 'tiː
ˌEN'T ˌspecialist

-ent ənt —*This suffix has the same stress-effects as -ence, thus* ad'jacent, in'telligent, 'eminent; *note* ap'parent. *It triggers a vowel change and change of stress in the stem of some words, as* excel ɪk 'sel → excellent 'eks əl ənt, provide prə 'vaɪd → provident 'prɒv ɪd ənt ‖ 'prɑːv-. *Note change of vowel but not of stress in* ap'pear → ap'parent.

entablature en 'tæb lətʃ ə ɪn-, -lɪtʃ-; -lɪ tʃʊə, lə- ‖ -lə tʃʊr -tʊr; -lətʃ ⁰r **~s** z

entail ɪn 'ter⁰l en-, ən- **~ed** d **~ing** ɪŋ **~ment/s** mənt/s **~s** z

entameb|a, entamoeb|a ˌent ə 'miːb |ə ‖ ˌenṯ- **~ae** iː **~as** əz

entangl|e ɪn 'tæŋ g⁰l en-, ən- **~ed** d **~ement/s** mənt/s **~es** z **~ing** ɪŋ

entasis 'ent əs ɪs §-əs ‖ 'enṯ-

Entebbe en 'teb i ɪn-, ən-

entelech|y en 'tel ək |i ɪn-, ən- **~ies** iz

entendre —*see* **double entendre**

Entenmann 'ent ən mæn →-əm- ‖ 'enṯ-

entente ₍ˌ₎ɒn 'tɒnt ₍ˌ₎ŏ- ‖ ₍ˌ₎ɑːn 'tɑːnt —*Fr* [ã tã:t]
ˌentente ˌcordi'ale, ·ˌ-- ˌkɔːd i 'ɑːl ‖ ˌkɔːrd- —*Fr* [kɔʁ djal]

enter 'ent ə ‖ 'enṯ ⁰r **entered** 'ent əd ‖ 'enṯ ⁰rd **entering** 'ent ər ɪŋ ‖ 'enṯ ər ɪŋ →'entr ɪŋ **enters** 'ent əz ‖ 'enṯ ⁰rz

enteric en 'ter ɪk

enteritis ˌent ə 'raɪt ɪs §-əs ‖ ˌenṯ ə 'raɪṯ əs

entero- *comb. form with stress-neutral suffix* ¦ent ər əʊ ‖ ¦enṯ ə roʊ- — **enterobacterium** ˌent ər əʊ bæk 'tɪər i‿əm ‖ ˌenṯ ə roʊ bæk 'tɪr- *with stress-imposing suffix* ˌent ə 'rɒ+ ‖ ˌenṯ ə 'rɑː+ — **enterostomy** ˌent ə 'rɒst əm i ‖ ˌenṯ ə 'rɑːst-

enterpris|e 'ent ə praɪz ‖ 'enṯ ⁰r- **~es** ɪz əz **~ing/ly** ɪŋ /li

entertain ˌent ə 'teɪn ‖ ˌenṯ ⁰r- **~ed** d **~er/s** ə/z ‖ ⁰r/z **~ing/ly** ɪŋ /li **~s** z

entertainment ˌent ə 'teɪn mənt →-'teɪm- ‖ ˌenṯ ⁰r- **~s** s

enthalpy 'en θælp i -θ⁰lp-; en 'θælp i, ɪn-, ən-

enthral, enthral|l ɪn 'θrɔːl en-, ən- ‖ -'θrɑːl **~led** d **~ling** ɪŋ **~ment** mənt **~s** z

enthron|e ɪn 'θrəʊn en-, ən- ‖ -'θroʊn **~ed** d **~es** z **~ement** mənt **~ing** ɪŋ

enthus|e ɪn 'θjuːz en-, ən-, -'θuːz ‖ -'θuːz **~ed** d **~es** ɪz əz **~ing** ɪŋ

enthusiasm ɪn 'θjuːz i ˌæz əm en-, ən-, -'θuːz-, §-əz- ‖ -'θuːz- **~s** z

enthusiast ɪn 'θjuːz i æst en-, ən-, -'θuːz-, §-əst ‖ -'θuːz- **~s** s

enthusiastic ɪn ˌθjuːz i 'æst ɪk ◂ en-, ən-, -ˌθuːz- ‖ -ˌθuːz- **~ally** ⁰l i

entia 'ent i‿ə 'enˢ-

entic|e ɪn 'taɪs en-, ən- **~ed** t **~ement/s** mənt/s **~er/s** ə/z ‖ ⁰r/z **~es** ɪz əz **~ing/ly** ɪŋ/ li

entire ɪn 'taɪ‿ə en-, ən-, §ˌen-, §ˌɪn- ‖ -'taɪ‿⁰r **~ly** li **~ness** nəs nɪs

entiret|y ɪn 'taɪ‿ər ət |i en-, ən-, -ɪt i, -'taɪ‿ət |i ‖ -'taɪ‿⁰rṯ |i -'taɪ‿⁰r əṯ |i **~ies** iz

entiti... —*see* **entity**

entitl|e ɪn 'taɪt ⁰l en-, ən- ‖ -'taɪṯ ⁰l **~ed** d **~ement/s** mənt/s **~es** z **~ing** ɪŋ

entit|y 'ent ət |i -ɪt- ‖ 'enṯ əṯ |i **~ies** iz

entomb ɪn 'tuːm en-, ən- **~ed** d **~ing** ɪŋ **~ment** mənt **~s** z

entomological ˌent əm ə 'lɒdʒ ɪk ⁰l ◂ ‖ ˌenṯ əm ə 'lɑːdʒ- **~ly** i

entomologist ˌent ə 'mɒl ədʒ ɪst §-əst ‖ ˌenṯ ə 'mɑːl- **~s** s

entomology ˌent ə 'mɒl ədʒ i ‖ ˌenṯ ə 'mɑːl-

entourag|e ˌɒn tuˀ rɑːʒ ŏ-, ·ˌ·'· ‖ ˌɑːn tu 'rɑːʒ —*Fr* [ã tu ʁaːʒ] **~es** ɪz əz

entracte, entr'acte 'ɒntr ækt 'õtr-, ˌ·'·
‖ ˌɑːntr- —*Fr* [ã tʁakt] **~s** s
entrails 'entr erᵊlz ‖ 'entr ᵊlz
entrain ɪn 'treɪn en-, ən- **~ed** d **~ing** ɪŋ **~ment**
mənt **~s** z
entrammel ɪn 'træm ᵊl en-, ən- **~ed, ~led** d
~ing, ~ling ɪŋ **~s** z
entranc|e *n 'way in'* 'entr ənts **~es** ɪz əz
entranc|e *v 'charm'* ɪn 'trɑːnts en-, ən-,
§-'trænts ‖ -'trænts **~ed** t **~ement/s** mənt/s
~es ɪz əz **~ing/ly** ɪŋ /li
entrant 'entr ənt **~s** s
entrap ɪn 'træp en-, ən- **~ment/s** mənt/s **~ped**
t **~ping** ɪŋ **~s** s
en|treat ɪn 'triːt en-, ən- **~treated** 'triːt ɪd -əd
‖ 'triːt̬ əd **~treating/ly** 'triːt ɪŋ /li
‖ 'triːt̬ ɪŋ /li **~treats** 'triːts
entreatment ɪn 'triːt mənt en-, ən- **~s** s
entreat|y ɪn 'triːt |i en-, ən- ‖ -'triːt̬ |i **~ies** iz
entrechat 'ɒntr ə ʃɑː 'õtr-, 'ɑːntr-, ˌ·ˌ·'·
‖ ˌɑːntr ə 'ʃɑː —*Fr* [ã tʁə ʃa] **~s** z
entrecote, entrecôte 'ɒntr ə kəʊt ˌ·ˌ·'·
‖ 'ɑːntr ə koʊt ˌ·ˌ·'· —*Fr* [ã tʁə kot] **~s** s
Entre-Deux-Mers ˌɒntr ə ˈdɜː 'meə
‖ ˌɑːntr ə ˈduː 'meᵊr —*Fr* [ã tʁə dø mɛːʁ]
entree, entrée 'ɒntr eɪ 'õtr- ‖ 'ɑːntr- —*Fr*
[ã tʁe] **~s** z
entremets *sing.* 'ɒntr ə meɪ 'õtr-, 'ɑːntr-, ˌ·ˌ·'·
‖ 'ɑːntr- —*Fr* [ã tʁə mɛ] **~** *pl* z
entrench ɪn 'trentʃ en-, ən- **~ed** t **~es** ɪz əz
~ing ɪŋ **~ment/s** mənt/s
entre nous ˌɒntr ə 'nuː 'õtr-, ˌɑːntr- ‖ ˌɑːntr-
—*Fr* [ã tʁə nu]
entrepot, entrepôt 'ɒntr ə pəʊ 'õtr-
‖ 'ɑːntr ə poʊ —*Fr* [ã tʁə po] **~s** z
entrepreneur ˌɒntr ə prə 'nɜː ˌõtr-, -pre'-,
-'njʊə ‖ ˌɑːntr ə prə 'nɜː: -pə'-, -'nuᵊr —*Fr*
[ã tʁə pʁə nœːʁ] **~s** z **~ship** ʃɪp
entrepreneurial ˌɒntr ə prə 'nɜːr i əl ◂ ˌõtr-,
-pre'-, -'njʊər- ‖ ˌɑːntr ə prə 'nɜː:- -'nʊr- **~ly** i
entresol 'ɒntr ə sɒl 'õtr- ‖ 'ɑːntr ə sɑːl —*Fr*
[ã tʁə sɔl] **~s** z
entries 'entr iz
entropic en 'trɒp ɪk ‖ -'trɑːp- **~ally** ᵊl i
entropy 'entr əp i
entrust ɪn 'trʌst en-, ən- **~ed** ɪd əd **~ing** ɪŋ
~ment mənt **~s** s
entr|y 'entr |i **~ies** iz
 'entry cerˌtificate
entryism 'entr i ˌɪz əm
entryist 'entr i ɪst §-əst **~s** s
entryphone 'entr i fəʊn ‖ -foʊn **~s** z
entryway 'entr i weɪ **~s** z
entwin|e ɪn 'twaɪn en-, ən- **~ed** d **~es** z **~ing**
ɪŋ
Entwistle 'ent wɪs ᵊl
enucleate *adj* i 'njuːk li ət ə-, -ɪt, -eɪt ‖ i 'nuːk-
i 'njuːk-
enucle|ate *v* i 'njuːk li |eɪt ə- ‖ -'nuːk- -'njuːk-
~ated eɪt ɪd -əd ‖ eɪt̬ əd **~ates** eɪts **~ating**
eɪt ɪŋ ‖ eɪt̬ ɪŋ
Enugu e 'nuːg uː ɪ-

enumerable i 'njuːm ər ˌəb ᵊl ə-, §-'nuːm-
‖ i 'nuːm- i 'njuːm- *(usually = innumerable)*
enume|rate ɪ 'njuːm ə |reɪt ə-, §-'nuːm-
‖ ɪ 'nuːm- ɪ 'njuːm- **~rated** reɪt ɪd -əd
‖ reɪt̬ əd **~rates** reɪts **~rating** reɪt ɪŋ ‖ reɪt̬ ɪŋ
enumeration ɪ ˌnjuːm ə 'reɪʃ ᵊn ə-, §-'nuːm-
‖ ɪ ˌnuːm- ɪ ˌnjuːm- **~s** z
enumerator ɪ 'njuːm ə reɪt ə ə-, §-'nuːm-
‖ ɪ 'nuːm ə reɪt̬ ᵊr ɪ 'njuːm- **~s** z
enunci|ate ɪ 'nʌnˀs i |eɪt ə-, -'nʌnˀʃ- **~ated**
eɪt ɪd -əd ‖ eɪt̬ əd **~ates** eɪts **~ating** eɪt ɪŋ
‖ eɪt̬ ɪŋ
enunciation ɪ ˌnʌnˀs i 'eɪʃ ᵊn ə-, -ˌnʌnˀʃ- **~s** z
enunciative ɪ 'nʌnˀs i ət ɪv ə-, -'nʌnˀʃ-, -eɪt-
‖ -i eɪt̬ ɪv **~ly** li
enunciator ɪ 'nʌnˀs i eɪt ə ə-, -'nʌnˀʃ- ‖ -eɪt̬ ᵊr
~s z
enure —*see* **inure**
enuresis ˌen juᵊ 'riːs ɪs §-əs ‖ -jə-
envelop *v* ɪn 'vel əp en-, ən- **~ed** t **~er/s** ə/z
‖ ᵊr/z **~ing** ɪŋ **~s** s

---

envelope *n* 'en və ləʊp 'ɒn- ‖ -loʊp 'ɑːn-
— *Preference poll, BrE:* 'en- 78%, 'ɒn- 22%.
~s s
envelopment ɪn 'vel əp mənt en-, ən-
envenom ɪn 'ven əm en-, ən- **~ed** d **~ing** ɪŋ **~s**
z
enviab|le 'en vi ˌəb |ᵊl **~ly** li
envie... —*see* **envy**
envious 'en vi əs **~ly** li **~ness** nəs nɪs
environ *v* ɪn 'vaɪᵊr ən en-, ən- **~ed** d **~ing** ɪŋ
~s z
environment ɪn 'vaɪᵊr ən mənt en-, ən-,
→-əm-, -ə- **~s** s
environmental ɪn ˌvaɪᵊr ən 'ment ᵊl ◂ en-,
ən-, →-əm-, -ə- ‖ -'ment̬ ᵊl ◂ **~ism** ˌɪz əm
~ist/s ɪst/s §əst/s **~ly** i
environs *n* ɪn 'vaɪᵊr ənz en-, ən-; 'en vɪr-, -vər-
envisag|e ɪn 'vɪz ɪdʒ en-, ən- **~ed** d **~es** ɪz əz
~ing ɪŋ
envision ɪn 'vɪʒ ᵊn en-, ən- **~ed** d **~ing** ɪŋ **~s**
z
envoi, envoy 'en vɔɪ ‖ 'ɑːn- **~s** z
en|vy 'en |vi **~vied** vid **~vies** viz **~vying/ly**
vi ˌɪŋ /li
enwrap ɪn 'ræp en-, ən- **~ped** t **~ping** ɪŋ **~s** s
enwreath|e ɪn 'riːð en-, ən- **~ed** d **~es** z **~ing**
ɪŋ
Enya 'en jə
enzyme 'en zaɪm **~s** z
Eocene 'iː əʊ siːn ‖ -ə-
eohippus ˌiː əʊ 'hɪp əs ‖ -oʊ-
Eoin *(i)* 'əʊ ɪn -ən ‖ 'oʊ ən, *(ii)* jəʊn ‖ joʊn

eolian i ˈəʊl i ̩ən ‖ i ˈoʊl-
Eolic i ˈɒl ɪk -ˈəʊl- ‖ i ˈɑːl ɪk
eolith ˈiː əʊ lɪθ ‖ -ə- ~**s** s
eolithic, e~ ˌiː əʊ ˈlɪθ ɪk ◂ ‖ -ə-
eon ˈiː ̩ən -ɒn ‖ -ɑːn ~**s** z
Eos ˈiː ɒs ‖ -ɑːs
eosin ˈiː əʊs ɪn §-ən ‖ -əs-
eosinophil ˌiː əʊ ˈsɪn əʊ fɪl ‖ ˌiː ə ˈsɪn ə fɪl ~**s** z
Eothen ˈiː əʊ θen i ˈəʊθ en ‖ -ə-
-eous i ̩əs — **piteous** ˈpɪt i ̩əs —*This suffix imposes stress on the preceding syllable:* couˈrageous. *In some words its compressed form* jəs *has coalesced with the final consonant of the stem:* righteous ˈraɪtʃ əs
EP ˌiː ˈpiː ~**s**, ~ˈ**s** z
epact ˈiːp ækt ˈep- ~**s** s
Epaminondas e ˌpæm ɪ ˈnɒnd æs ɪ-, -ə- ‖ -ˈnɑːnd əs
eparch ˈep ɑːk ‖ -ɑːrk ~**s** s
eparch|y ˈep ɑːk |i ‖ -ɑːrk |i ~**ies** iz
epaulet, epaulette ˌep ə ˈlet -ɔː-, ˈ··· ~**s** s
Epcot *tdmk* ˈep kɒt ‖ -kɑːt
epee, épée ˈep eɪ -ˈeɪp-; ˌe ˈpeɪ ‖ eɪ ˈpeɪ ˈep eɪ —*Fr* [e pe] —**ist/s** ɪst/s §əst/s ~**s** z
epenthesis e ˈpen'θ əs ɪs ɪ-, -ə-, §-əs
epenthesis|e, epenthesiz|e e ˈpen'θ ə saɪz ~**ed** d ~**es** ɪz əz ~**ing** ɪŋ
epenthetic ˌep en ˈθet ɪk ◂ -ən-, →·-m- ‖ -ˈθeţ- ~**ally** ᵊl ̩i
epergne ɪ ˈpɜːn e-, -ˈpeən ‖ ɪ ˈpɜːn eɪ- —*not actually a French word* ~**s** z
epexegesis e ˌpeks ɪ ˈdʒiːs ɪs ɪ-, -ə-, -ə-, §-əs
epexegetic e ˌpeks ɪ ˈdʒet ɪk ◂ ɪ-, -ə-, -ə- ‖ -ˈdʒeţ- ~**ally** ᵊl ̩i
epha, ephah ˈiːf ə ‖ ˈef ə ~**s** z
ephebe ˈef iːb ɪ ˈfiːb, e- ~**s** z
ephedrine ˈef ɪ driːn -ə-; -ɪdr ɪn, -ədr-, -ən; ɪ ˈfedr ɪn, -ən ‖ ɪ ˈfedr ən e-
ephemera ɪ ˈfem ər ̩ə e-, ə-, -ˈfiːm- ~**s** z

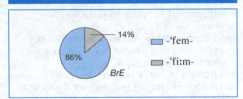

14%
86%
BrE
-ˈfem-
-ˈfiːm-

ephemeral ɪ ˈfem ᵊr ̩əl e-, ə-, -ˈfiːm- ~**ly** i
— *Preference poll, BrE:* -ˈfem- *86%,* -ˈfiːm- *14%*
ephemerality ɪ ˌfem ə ˈræl ət i e-, ə-, -ˌfem- ‖ -əţ i
ephemeris ɪ ˈfem ər ɪs e-, ə-, -ˈfiːm-, §-əs
 ephemerides ˌef ɪ ˈmer ɪ diːz ˌə-, -ˈə-
Ephesian ɪ ˈfiːʒ ᵊn e-, ə-, -ˈfiːʒ i ̩ən ~**s** z
Ephesus ˈef ɪs əs -əs-
Ephialtes ˌef i ˈælt iːz
ephod ˈiːf ɒd ˈef- ‖ -ɑːd ~**s** z
ephor ˈiːf ɔː ˈef-, -ə ‖ -ɔːr -ᵊr ~**s** z
Ephraim ˈiːf reɪ ɪm -ri ̩, -əm; ˈiːf rəm ‖ ˈiːf ri ̩əm

epi- *comb. form*
 with stress-neutral suffix ˌep i ̩ |ep ə
 — **epistatic** ˌep ɪ ˈstæt ɪk ◂ -ə- ‖ -ˈstæţ-
 with stress-imposing suffix ɪ ˈpɪ+ e-
 — **epistasis** ɪ ˈpɪst əs ɪs e-, §-əs
epic ˈep ɪk ~**s** s
epicanth|ic ˌep ɪ ˈkæn'θ |ɪk ◂ §-ə- ~**us** əs
 ˌepi ̩canthic ˈfold
epicene ˈep ɪ siːn §-ə- ~**s** z
epicenter, epicentre ˈep ɪ ̩sent ə §-ə- ‖ -ˌsent ᵊr ~**s** z
epiclesis ˌep ɪ ˈkliːs ɪs §-ə-, -əs
Epictetus ˌep ɪk ˈtiːt əs ‖ -ˈtiːţ-
epicure ˈep ɪ kjʊə §-ə-, -kjɔː ‖ -kjʊr ~**s** z
epicurean, E~ ˌep ɪ kjuˈ ˈriːˌən §-ə- ~**s** z
Epicurus ˌep ɪ ˈkjʊər əs §-ə-, -ˈkjɔːr- ‖ -ˈkjʊr-
epicycle ˈep ɪ ̩saɪk ᵊl §-ə- ~**s** z
epicyclic ˌep ɪ ˈsaɪk lɪk ◂ §-ə-, -ˈsɪk-
 ˌepi ̩cyclic ˈtrain
epicycloid ˌep ɪ ˈsaɪk lɔɪd §-ə- ~**s** z
Epidaurus ˌep ɪ ˈdɔːr əs §-ə- —*ModGk* Epidhavros [ɛ ˈpi ða vrɔs]
epideictic ˌep ɪ ˈdaɪkt ɪk ◂ -ə-
epidemic ˌep ɪ ˈdem ɪk ◂ §-ə- ~**ally** ᵊl ̩i ~**s** s
epidemiological ˌep ɪ ˌdiːm i ̩ə ˈlɒdʒ ɪk ᵊl §ˌ-ə-, -ˌdem- ‖ -ˈlɑːdʒ- ~**ly** ̩i
epidemiologist ˌep ɪ ˌdiːm i ˈɒl ədʒ ɪst §ˌ-ə-, -ˌdem-, §-əst ‖ -ˈɑːl- ~**s** s
epidemiology ˌep ɪ ˌdiːm i ˈɒl ədʒ i §ˌ-ə-, -ˌdem- ‖ -ˈɑːl-
epidermis ˌep ɪ ˈdɜːm ɪs §-ə-, §-əs ‖ -ˈdɜːm-
epidiascope ˌep ɪ ˈdaɪˌə skəʊp §ˌ-ə- ‖ -skoʊp ~**s** s
epi|didymis ˌep ɪ |ˈdɪd əm ɪs §ˌ-ə-, -ɪm ɪs, §-əs ~**didymides** dɪ ˈdɪm ɪ diːz §də-, -ə-; ˈdɪd əm ɪ diːz, -ə-
epidote ˈep ɪ dəʊt §-ə- ‖ -doʊt
epidural ˌep ɪ ˈdjʊər əl ◂ §-ə-, -ˈdjɔːr-, →·-ˈdʒʊər- ‖ -ˈdʊr- -ˈdjʊr- ~**ly** i ~**s** z
epigastrium ˌep ɪ ˈgæs tri ̩əm §ˌ-ə-
epiglottal ˌep ɪ ˈglɒt ᵊl ◂ -ə- ‖ -ˈglɑːţ ᵊl ◂
epiglottis ˌep ɪ ˈglɒt ɪs -ə-, §-əs, -ˈ·ˌ·· ‖ -ˈglɑːţ- ~**es** ɪz əz
epigone ˈep ɪ gəʊn -ə- ‖ -goʊn ~**s** z
Epigoni e ˈpɪg ə naɪ ɪ-, -iː
epigram ˈep ɪ græm -ə- ~**s** z
epigrammatic ˌep ɪ grə ˈmæt ɪk ◂ ˌ-ə- ‖ -ˈmæţ- ~**ally** ᵊl ̩i
epigrammatist ˌep ɪ ˈgræm ət ɪst ˌ-ə-, §-əst ‖ -əţ- ~**s** s
epigraph ˈep ɪ grɑːf -ə-, -græf ‖ -græf ~**s** s
epigrapher e ˈpɪg rəf ə ɪ- ‖ -ᵊr ~**s** z
epigraphic ˌep ɪ ˈgræf ɪk ◂ -ə- ~**al** ᵊl ~**ally** ᵊl ̩i
epigraphy e ˈpɪg rəf i ɪ-
epilepsy ˈep ɪ leps i ˈ-ə-
epileptic ˌep ɪ ˈlept ɪk ◂ -ə- ~**s** s
 ˌepi ̩leptic ˈfit
epilog, epilogue ˈep ɪ lɒg -ə- ‖ -lɔːg -lɑːg ~**s** z
EpiPen *tdmk* ˈep i pen
epiphan|y, E~ ɪ ˈpɪf ən |i ə- ~**ies** iz
epiphenom|enon ˌep ɪ fɪ ˈnɒm |ɪn ən -fə'·-, -ˈ·ən- ‖ -ˈnɑːm |ə nɑːn -ən ən ~**ena** ɪn ə ən- ‖ ən ə -**enal** ɪn ᵊl ən- ‖ ən ᵊl

epiph|ysis e ˈpɪf |əs ɪs ɪ-, §-əs **~yses** ə siːz ɪ-
epiphyte ˈep ɪ faɪt -ə- **~s** s
epiphytic ˌep ɪ ˈfɪt ɪk ◂ -ə- ‖ -ˈfɪt̬-
Epirus ɪ ˈpaɪ°r əs e-, ə-
episcopac|y ɪ ˈpɪsk əp əs |i e-, ə- **~ies** iz
episcopal ɪ ˈpɪsk əp °l e-, ə- **~ly** i
episcopalian, E~ ɪ ˌpɪsk ə ˈpeɪl i ̩ən ◂ e-, ə- **~s** z
episcopate ɪ ˈpɪsk əp ət e-, ə-, -ɪt, -eɪt **~s** s
episcope ˈprojector' ˈep ɪ skəʊp ‖ -skoʊp **~s** s
episiotom|y ɪ ˌpɪz i ˈɒt əm |i e-, ə-, -ˌpiːz-, ˌep ɪz- ‖ -ˈɑːt̬ əm |i **~ies** iz
episode ˈep ɪ səʊd -ə- ‖ -soʊd **~s** z
episodic ˌep ɪ ˈsɒd ɪk ◂ -ə- ‖ -ˈsaːd- **~ally** °l_i
epistemic ˌep ɪ ˈstiːm ɪk ◂ -ə-, -ˈstem-
epistemological ɪ ˌpɪst ɪ mə ˈlɒdʒ ɪk °l ◂ e-, ə-, -ˌ·ə-, -ˌ·iː- ‖ -ˈlɑːdʒ- **~ly** ̩i
epistemology ɪ ˌpɪst ɪ ˈmɒl ədʒ i e-, ə-, -ˌ·ə-, -ˌ·iː- ‖ -ˈmɑːl-
epistle, E~ ɪ ˈpɪs °l ə- **~s** z
epistolary ɪ ˈpɪst əl ər i e-, ə-; ˌep ɪ ˈstɒl ər i ◂, §ˌ·ə- ‖ -ə ler i
epistyle ˈep ɪ staɪ°l -ə- **~s** z
epitaph ˈep ɪ tɑːf -ə-, -tæf ‖ -tæf **~s** s
epitaxial ˌep ɪ ˈtæks i əl ◂ ˌ·ə-
epithalami|um ˌep ɪθ ə ˈleɪm i ̩|əm ˌ·əθ- **~a** ə
epitheli|um ˌep ɪ ˈθiːl i ̩|əm ˌ·ə- **~al** əl
epithet ˈep ɪ θet -ə- **~s** s
epitome ɪ ˈpɪt əm i ə- ‖ ɪ ˈpɪt̬ əm i **~s** z
epitomis|e, epitomiz|e ɪ ˈpɪt ə maɪz ə- ‖ ɪ ˈpɪt̬ ə- **~ed** d **~es** ɪz əz **~ing** ɪŋ
epizootic ˌep ɪ zəʊ ˈɒt ɪk ◂ ‖ -zoʊ ˈɑːt̬ ɪk ◂ **~s** s
e pluribus unum eɪ ˌplʊər ɪb əs ˈuːn əm iː-, -ˌplɔːr-, ˌ·ˌ·-, -əb ·ˈ·-, -ʊs·ˈ·-, -ˈjuːn- -ʊm ‖ -ˌplʊr-
epoch ˈiːp ɒk ‖ ˈep ək -ɑːk (*) **~s** s
epochal ˈep ɒk °l ˈiːp-, -ək-; iː ˈpɒk °l ‖ ˈep ək °l
epoch-making ˈiːp ɒk ˌmeɪk ɪŋ ‖ ˈep ək-
epode ˈep əʊd ‖ -oʊd **~s** z
eponym ˈep ə nɪm **~s** z
eponymous ɪ ˈpɒn ɪm əs ə-, -əm- ‖ ɪ ˈpɑːn- **~ly** li
epos ˈep ɒs ‖ -ɑːs
EPOS ˈiː pɒs ‖ -pɑːs
epox|y ɪ ˈpɒks |i e-, ə- ‖ e ˈpɑːks |i ɪ- **~ies** iz e ˌpoxy ˈresin
epoxide ɪ ˈpɒks aɪd e-, ə- ‖ e ˈpɑːks- ɪ- **~s** z
Epping ˈep ɪŋ ˌEpping ˈForest
EPROM ˈiː prɒm ‖ -prɑːm **~s** z
epsilon ep ˈsaɪl ən ɪp-, -ɒn; ˈeps ɪ lɒn, -ə-, -lən ‖ ˈeps ə lɑːn -əl ən (*) **~s** z
Epsom ˈeps əm ˌEpsom ˈDowns; ˌEpsom ˈsalts ‖ ˈ·· ·
Epson tdmk ˈeps ɒn -ən ‖ -ɑːn
Epstein ˈep staɪn
Epstein-Barr ˌep staɪn ˈbɑː →-staɪm- ‖ -ˈbɑːr
e-publishing ˈiː ˌpʌb lɪʃ ɪŋ
epylli|on e ˈpɪl i ̩|ən ɪ-, -ɒn- **~a** ə
equability ˌek wə ˈbɪl ət i -ɪt i ‖ -ət̬ i
equab|le ˈek wəb |°l **~leness** °l nəs -nɪs **~ly** li

equal ˈiːk wəl **~ed, ~led** d **~ing, ~ling** ɪŋ **~ly** i **~s** z
ˌEqual ˈRights Aˌmendment; ˈequal(s) sign
equalis... —*see* **equaliz...**
equalitarian ɪ ˌkwɒl ɪ ˈteər i ̩ən ◂ iː-, ə-, -ˌ·ə- ‖ ɪ ˌkwɔːl ə ˈter i ̩ən ◂ -ˌkwɑːl-, -ˈtær- **~s** z
equalit|y ɪ ˈkwɒl ət |i ə-, -ɪt- ‖ -ˈkwɑːl ət̬- **~ies** iz
equalization ˌiːk wəl aɪ ˈzeɪʃ °n -ɪˈ·- ‖ -əˈ·- **~s** z
equaliz|e ˈiːk wə laɪz **~ed** d **~er/s** ə/z ‖ °r/z **~es** ɪz əz **~ing** ɪŋ
equally ˈiːk wəl i
equanimity ˌek wə ˈnɪm ət i ˌiːk-, -ɪti -ət̬ i
equanimous ɪ ˈkwæn ɪm əs e-, -ˈkwɒn-, -əm- **~ly** li
equatable i ˈkweɪt əb °l iː-, ə- ‖ -ˈkweɪt̬-
e|quate i |ˈkweɪt ə- **~quated** ˈkweɪt ɪd -əd ‖ ˈkweɪt̬ əd **~quates** ˈkweɪts **~quating** ˈkweɪt ɪŋ ‖ ˈkweɪt̬ ɪŋ

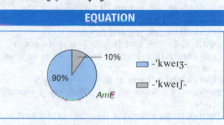

EQUATION

-ˈkweɪʒ-
-ˈkweɪʃ-
90%
10%
AmE

equation i ˈkweɪʒ °n ə-, -ˈkweɪʃ- — *Preference poll, AmE:* -ˈkweɪʒ- *90%,* -ˈkweɪʃ- *10%.* **~s** z
equative i ˈkweɪt ɪv ə- ‖ -ˈkweɪt̬- **~s** z
equator, E~ i ˈkweɪt ə ə- ‖ i ˈkweɪt̬ °r **~s** z
equatorial ˌek wə ˈtɔːr i əl ◂ ˌiːk- ‖ ˌiːk- -ˈtoʊr- **~ly** i ˌEquaˌtorial ˈGuinea
equerr|y ɪ ˈkwer |i ə-; ˈek wər |i ‖ ˈek wər |i —*at court,* ɪ ˈkwer i **~ies** iz
equestrian ɪ ˈkwes tri ̩ən e-, ə- **~ism** ̩ɪz əm **~s** z
equestrienne ɪ ˌkwes tri ˈen e-, ə- **~s** z
equi ˈek wi ˈiːk-
equi- *comb. form*
with stress-neutral suffix |iːk wi |ek-, -wə- — **equiprobable** ˌiːk wi ˈprɒb əb °l ◂ ˌek-, ˌ·wə- ‖ -ˈprɑːb-
equiangular ˌiːk wi ˈæŋ gjʊl ə ˌek-, -gjəl- ‖ -gjəl °r
equidistant ˌiːk wi ˈdɪst ənt ◂ ˌek-, -wə- **~ly** li
equilateral ˌiːk wi ˈlæt °r əl ◂ ˌ·wə- ‖ -ˈlæt̬ ər əl →-ˈlætr əl **~ly** i ˌequiˌlateral ˈtriangle
equilib|rate ˌiːk wi ˈlaɪb |reɪt ˌek-, -wə-, -ˈlɪb-; iː ˈkwɪl ɪ b|reɪt, ɪ-, ə-, -ə- ‖ ɪ ˈkwɪl ə b|reɪt **~rated** reɪt ɪd -əd ‖ reɪt̬ əd **~rates** reɪts **~rating** reɪt ɪŋ ‖ reɪt̬ ɪŋ
equilibration ˌiːk wi laɪ ˈbreɪʃ °n ˌek-, ˌ·wə-, -lɪˈ·-; iː ˌkwɪl ɪ-, ɪ-, -əˈ·- ‖ ɪ ˌkwɪl ə-
equilibrium ˌiːk wi ˈlɪb ri ̩əm ˌek-, ˌ·wə-
equine ˈek waɪn ˈiːk- ‖ ˈiːk- ˈek- **~s** z

equinoctial ,iːk wi 'nɒk ʃʳl ◂ ,ek-, -wə-
‖ -'nɑːk- ~s z
,equi,noctial 'gales

EQUINOX

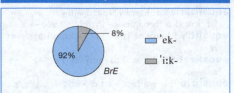

- 92% (BrE) 'iːk-
- 8% 'ek-

equinox 'ek wi nɒks 'iːk-, -wə- ‖ -nɑːks ~es ɪz
əz — Preference poll, BrE: 'ek- 92%, 'iːk- 8%
equip ɪ 'kwɪp ə- ~ped t ~ping ɪŋ ~s s
equipag|e 'ek wɪp ɪdʒ -wəp- ~es ɪz əz
equipment ɪ 'kwɪp mənt ə-
equipoise 'ek wi pɔɪz 'iːk-, -wə- ~d d
equipollent ,iːk wi 'pɒl ənt ◂ ,ek-, -wə-
‖ -'pɑːl-
equitab|le 'ek wɪt əb |ʳl '·wət- ‖ -wəţ əb-
~leness ʳl nəs -nɪs ~ly li
equitation ,ek wɪ 'teɪʃ ʳn -wə-
equit|y, E~ 'ek wət |i -wɪt- ‖ -wəţ |i ~ies iz
equivalenc|e ɪ 'kwɪv əl ənʦ ə- ~es ɪz əz ~ies
iz ~y i
equivalent ɪ 'kwɪv əl ənt ə- ~ly li ~s s
equivocal ɪ 'kwɪv ək ʳl ə-, -ɪk ʳl ~ly i ~ness
nəs nɪs
equivo|cate ɪ 'kwɪv ə |keɪt ə- ~cated keɪt ɪd
-əd ‖ keɪţ əd ~cates keɪts ~cating keɪt ɪŋ
‖ keɪţ ɪŋ
equivocation ɪ ,kwɪv ə 'keɪʃ ʳn ə- ~s z
equus, Equus 'ek wəs
ER ,iː 'ɑː ‖ -'ɑːr
er hesitation noise, BrE ɜː ə —The AmE
equivalent is written uh
-er ə ‖ ʳr dirtier 'dɜːt i ə ‖ 'dɜːţ i ʳr —On rare
occasions this suffix receives contrastive stress,
and is then pronounced 'ɜː ‖ 'ɜːt, thus not
early, but earliER ,ɜːl i 'ɜː ‖ ,ɜːl i 'ɜːt,
interviewEE and interviewER ,ɪnt ə vjuː 'ɜː
‖ ,ɪnţ ʳr vjuː: 'ɜːt
era 'ɪər ə ‖ 'ɪr ə 'er ə, 'iː rə ~s z
ERA ,iː ɑːr 'eɪ ‖ -ɑːr-
eradi|cate ɪ 'ræd ɪ |keɪt ə-, §-ə- ~cated keɪt ɪd
-əd ‖ keɪţ əd ~cates keɪts ~cating keɪt ɪŋ
‖ keɪţ ɪŋ
eradication ɪ ,ræd ɪ 'keɪʃ ʳn ə-, §-ə- ~s z
eradicator ɪ 'ræd ɪ keɪt ə ə-, §-'-ə- ‖ -keɪţ ʳr ~s
z
erase ɪ 'reɪz ə- ‖ ɪ 'reɪs (*) erased ɪ 'reɪzd ə-
‖ ɪ 'reɪst erases ɪ 'reɪz ɪz ə-, -əz ‖ ɪ 'reɪs əz
erasing ɪ 'reɪz ɪŋ ə- ‖ ɪ 'reɪs ɪŋ
eraser ɪ 'reɪz ə ə- ‖ ɪ 'reɪs ʳr ~s z
Erasmian ɪ 'ræz mi ən e-, ə-, ~s z
Erasmus ɪ 'ræz məs e-, ə-
Erastian ɪ 'ræst i ən e-, ə-, ‖ -'ræs tʃən ~ism
,ɪz əm ~s z
erasure ɪ 'reɪʒ ə ə- ‖ ɪ 'reɪʒ ʳr ~s z
Erato 'er ə təʊ ‖ -toʊ
Eratosthenes ,er ə 'tɒsθ ə niːz ‖ -'tɑːsθ-

erbium 'ɜːb i əm ‖ 'ɜːb-
Erdington 'ɜːd ɪŋ tən ‖ 'ɜːd-
ere 'before' eə ‖ eʳr æʳr (= air)
'ere 'here' ɪə ‖ ɪʳr —a nonstandard form of here
Erebus 'er ɪb əs -əb-
Erechtheum ,er ek 'θiː əm -ɪk-, -ək-
‖ ɪ 'rek θi əm
Erechtheus ɪ 'rek θjuːs e-, ə-, -'ˈθi əs
‖ -'rek θi əs
erect adj, v ɪ 'rekt ə- ~ed ɪd əd ~ing ɪŋ ~ly li
~ness nəs nɪs ~s s
erectile ɪ 'rekt aɪʳl ə- ‖ -ʳl -aɪʳl
erection ɪ 'rek ʃʳn ə- ~s z
erector ɪ 'rekt ə ə- ‖ -ʳr ~s z
eremite 'er ə maɪt -ɪ- ~s s
eremitic ,er ə 'mɪt ɪk ◂ -ɪ- ‖ -'mɪţ- ~al ʳl
e-resume, e-résumé 'iː ,rez jʊ meɪ -jə- ‖ -ə-
-·-'meɪ
erethism 'er ə ,θɪz əm -ɪ-
Eretz 'er ets -ɪts, §-əts —Hebrew ['ɛ rets]
Erewhon 'er ɪ wɒn -ə-, -hwɒn ‖ -hwɑːn -hwʌn
Erfurt 'eə fɜːt ‖ 'er- —Ger ['ɛʁ fʊʁt]
erg ɜːg ‖ ɜːg ergs ɜːgz ‖ ɜːgz
ergative 'ɜːg ət ɪv ‖ 'ɜːg əţ ɪv ~ly li ~s z
ergativity ,ɜːg ə 'tɪv ət i -ɪt i ‖ ,ɜːg ə 'tɪv əţ i
ergo 'ɜːg əʊ 'eəg- ‖ 'erg oʊ 'ɜːg-
ergonomic ,ɜːg ə 'nɒm ɪk ◂
‖ ,ɜːg ə 'nɑːm ɪk ◂ ~ally ʳl_i ~s s
ergonomist ɜː 'gɒn əm ɪst §-əst ‖ ɜː 'gɑːn- ~s
s
ergosterol ɜː 'gɒst ə rɒl ‖ ɜː 'gɑːst ə roʊl
-rɔːl, -rɑːl
ergot 'ɜːg ət -ɒt ‖ 'ɜːg- -ɑːt
ergotism 'ɜːg ə ,tɪz əm ‖ 'ɜːg-
Eric 'er ɪk
Erica, erica 'er ɪk ə ~s, ~'s z
ericaceous ,er ɪ 'keɪʃ əs ◂ -ə-
Ericsson tdmk 'er ɪks ən —Swed ["eː rik sɔn]
Eridan|us e 'rɪd ən |əs ɪ-, ə- ~i aɪ
Erie 'ɪər i ‖ 'ɪr i
,Erie Ca'nal
Erik 'er ɪk
Erika 'er ɪk ə
Eriksson 'er ɪks ʳn
Erin 'er ɪn 'ɪər-, 'eər-, §-ən
Eris 'er ɪs §-əs
Eriskay 'er ɪ skeɪ -ə-
eristic e 'rɪst ɪk ɪ-, ə- ~s s
Erith 'ɪər ɪθ §-əθ ‖ 'ɪr-
Eritre|a ,er ɪ 'treɪ |ə -ə-, -'triː |ə ‖ -'triː |ə
~an/s ən/z
erk ɜːk ‖ ɜːk (= irk) erks ɜːks ‖ ɜːks
Erle ɜːl ‖ ɜːl
erlking 'ɜːl kɪŋ ‖ 'ɜːl-
ERM ,iː ɑːr 'em ‖ -ɑːr-
ermine 'ɜːm ɪn §-ən ‖ 'ɜːm- ~d d ~s z
erne, Erne ɜːn ‖ ɜːn (= earn) ernes ɜːnz
‖ ɜːnz
Ernest 'ɜːn ɪst -əst ‖ 'ɜːn-
Ernestina ,ɜːn ɪ 'stiːn ə -ə- ‖ ,ɜːn-
Ernie 'ɜːn i ‖ 'ɜːn i
Ernle 'ɜːn li ‖ 'ɜːn-
Ernst eənˈst ɜːnˈst ‖ ɜːnˈst —Ger [ʔɛʁnst]

erod|e ɪ 'rəʊd ə- ‖ ɪ 'roʊd **~ed** ɪd əd **~es** z
~ing ɪŋ
erogenous ɪ 'rɒdʒ ən əs e-, ə-, -ɪn- ‖ ɪ 'rɑːdʒ-
Eroica ɪ 'rəʊ ɪk ə e-, ə- ‖ ɪ 'roʊ-
Eros 'ɪər ɒs 'er-, -əʊz ‖ 'er ɑːs 'ɪr-
erosion ɪ 'rəʊʒ ᵊn ə- ‖ ɪ 'roʊʒ ᵊn **~s** z
erosive ɪ 'rəʊs ɪv ə- ‖ ɪ 'roʊs- **~ly** li
erotic ɪ 'rɒt ɪk ə- ‖ ɪ 'rɑːt̬ ɪk **~ally** ᵊl_i
erotica ɪ 'rɒt ɪk ə ə- ‖ ɪ 'rɑːt̬ ɪk ə
eroticis... —*see* **eroticiz...**
eroticism ɪ 'rɒt ɪ ˌsɪz əm ə-, -ə- ‖ ɪ 'rɑːt̬ ə-
eroticization ɪ ˌrɒt ɪs aɪ 'zeɪʃ ᵊn ə-, ˌ-əs-, -ɪ'-- ‖ ɪ 'rɑːt̬ əs ə-
eroticiz|e ɪ 'rɒt ɪ saɪz ə-, -ə- ‖ ɪ 'rɑːt̬ ə- **~ed** d
~es ɪz əz **~ing** ɪŋ
erotogenic ɪ ˌrɒt ə 'dʒen ɪk ◂ ə-, -ˌrəʊt- ‖ ɪ ˌroʊt̬ ə- ɪ ˌrɑːt̬ ə- **~ally** ᵊl_i
erotoman|ia ɪ ˌrɒt əʊ 'meɪn |i_ə ə-, -ˌrəʊt- ‖ ɪ ˌroʊt̬ ə- ɪ ˌrɑːt̬ ə- **~iac/s** i æk/s
Erpingham 'ɜːp ɪŋ əm ‖ 'ɜːp ɪŋ hæm
err ɜː §eə ‖ eᵊr ɜː **erred** ɜːd §eəd ‖ eᵊrd ɜːd
erring 'ɜːr ɪŋ §'er-, §'eər- ‖ 'er ɪŋ 'ɜː- **errs** ɜːz §eəz ‖ eᵊrz ɜːz
errancy 'er ᵊn's i
errand 'er ənd **~s** z
errant 'er ənt **~ly** li
errata e 'rɑːt ə ɪ-, ə-, -'reɪt- ‖ e 'rɑːt̬ ə -'reɪt̬-, -'ræt̬-
erratic ɪ 'ræt ɪk e-, ə- ‖ ɪ 'ræt̬ ɪk **~ally** ᵊl_i **~s** s
errat|um e 'rɑːt |əm ɪ-, ə-, -'reɪt- ‖ e 'rɑːt̬ |əm -'reɪt̬-, -'ræt̬- **~a** ə
errhine 'er aɪn -ɪn
erring 'ɜːr ɪŋ §'er-, §'eər- ‖ 'er- 'ɜː- **~ly** li
Errol, Erroll 'er əl
erroneous ɪ 'rəʊn i_əs e-, ə- ‖ ɪ 'roʊn- **~ly** li **~ness** nəs nɪs
error 'er ə ‖ -ᵊr **~s** z
ersatz 'eə zæts 'ɜː-, -sæts, -zɑːts, ˌ·' ‖ 'er zɑːts 'ɜː-, -sɑːts, -sæts, ˌ·' —*Ger* [ʔeɐ 'zats]
Erse ɜːs ‖ ɜːs
Erskine 'ɜːsk ɪn §-ən ‖ 'ɜːsk-
erstwhile 'ɜːst waɪᵊl -hwaɪᵊl ‖ 'ɜːst hwaɪᵊl
erubescence ˌer u 'bes ᵊn's
erubescent ˌer u 'bes ᵊnt ◂ **~ly** li
eructation ˌiː rʌk 'teɪʃ ᵊn ɪ ˌrʌk-; ˌer ʌk-, -ək- **~s** z
erudite 'er u daɪt -ju- ‖ -jə- -ə- **~ly** li **~ness** nəs nɪs
erudition ˌer u 'dɪʃ ᵊn -ju- ‖ -jə- -ə-
erupt ɪ 'rʌpt ə- **~ed** ɪd əd **~ing** ɪŋ **~s** s
eruption ɪ 'rʌp ʃᵊn ə- **~s** z
eruptive ɪ 'rʌpt ɪv ə- **~ly** li
eruv 'er ʊv ‖ eɪ 'ruːv **eruvin** 'er ʊv ɪn ‖ ˌer u 'viːn
Ervine 'ɜːv ɪn §-ən, -aɪn ‖ 'ɜːv-
-ery ər i —*This stress-neutral suffix is used only after a strong-vowelled syllable* (maˈchinery); *after a weak-vowelled syllable the variant* -ry ri *is used instead* ('dentistry).
Erymanthian ˌer ɪ 'mænᵗθ i_ən ◂
erysipelas ˌer ɪ 'sɪp əl əs ˌə-, ˌ-ə-, -ɪl əs
erythema ˌer ɪ 'θiːm ə ə-
erythrocyte ɪ 'rɪθ rəʊ saɪt ə- ‖ -rə- **~s** s

erythromycin ɪ ˌrɪθ rəʊ 'maɪs ɪn ə-, §-ᵊn ‖ -rə-
erythropoietic ɪ ˌrɪθ rəʊ pɔɪ 'et ɪk ◂ ə- ‖ -rə pɔɪ 'et̬-
-es *ending of pl or 3rd person sing.*, **-es'** *possessive pl ending—There are two pronunciations: 1. After a sibilant sound* (**s, z, ʃ, ʒ, tʃ, dʒ**) *the ending is pronounced* ɪz *or, less commonly in BrE but regularly in AmE*, əz, *as* pushes **'pʊʃ** ɪz, -əz, churches' **'tʃɜːtʃ** ɪz, -əz. (*In singing a strong-vowelled variant* ez *is occasionally used.) 2. Where the spelling* y *is changed to* i, *this ending is pronounced* z, *as* cry — cries kraɪz —*See also* **-s**.
Esau 'iːs ɔː ‖ -ɑː
Esbjerg 'es bjɜːg ‖ -bjɜːg —*Danish* ['ɛs bjɛʁʔ]
escalad|e ˌesk ə 'leɪd '···· **~ed** ɪd əd **~es** z **~ing** ɪŋ
esca|late 'esk ə |leɪt **~lated** leɪt ɪd -əd ‖ leɪt̬ əd **~lates** leɪts **~lating** leɪt ɪŋ ‖ leɪt̬ ɪŋ
escalation ˌesk ə 'leɪʃ ᵊn **~s** z
escalator 'esk ə leɪt ə △'·jə- ‖ -leɪt̬ ᵊr **~s** z
escallonia ˌesk ə 'ləʊn i_ə ‖ -'loʊn- **~s** z
escallop, escalope 'esk ə lɒp ◂ ˌ·'·; e 'skæl əp, ɪ-, -ɒp ‖ ɪ 'skɑːl əp *(*)* **~s** s
escapade ˌesk ə 'peɪd '···· ‖ 'esk ə peɪd **~s** z
escap|e ɪ 'skeɪp e-, ə- **~ed** t **~es** s **~ing** ɪŋ
e'scape road; e'scape ve,locity; e'scape wheel
escapee ɪ ˌskeɪ 'piː ˌesk eɪ 'piː **~s** z
escapement ɪ 'skeɪp mənt e-, ə- **~s** s
escapism ɪ 'skeɪp ˌɪz əm e-, ə-
escapist ɪ 'skeɪp ɪst e-, ə-, §-əst **~s** s
escapologist ˌesk ə 'pɒl ədʒ ɪst ˌer-, §-əst ‖ -'pɑːl- **~s** z
escapology ˌesk ə 'pɒl ədʒ i ˌer- ‖ -'pɑːl-
escargot ɪ 'skɑːg əʊ e- ‖ ˌesk ɑːr 'goʊ *(*)* —*Fr* [ɛs kaʁ go] **~s** z
escarole 'esk ə rəʊl →-rɒʊl ‖ -roʊl
escarpment ɪ 'skɑːp mənt e-, ə- ‖ ɪ 'skɑːrp- **~s** s
-esce 'es — opalesce ˌəʊp ə 'les ‖ ˌoʊp-
-escence 'es ᵊn's — phosphorescence ˌfɒs fə 'res ᵊn's ‖ ˌfɑːs-
-escent 'es ᵊnt — frutescent fruː 'tes ᵊnt
eschatological ˌesk ət ə 'lɒdʒ ɪk ᵊl ◂ ˌæt- ‖ -ət̬ ə 'lɑːdʒ- **~ly** _i
eschatology ˌesk ə 'tɒl ədʒ i ‖ -'tɑːl-
es|cheat ɪs |'tʃiːt es-, əs- **~cheated** 'tʃiːt ɪd -əd ‖ 'tʃiːt̬ əd **~cheating** 'tʃiːt ɪŋ ‖ 'tʃiːt̬ ɪŋ **~cheats** 'tʃiːts
Escher 'eʃ ə ‖ -ᵊr —*Dutch* ['ɛʃ ər]
escherichia ˌeʃ ə 'rɪk i_ə
eschew ɪs 'tʃuː es-, əs-; i 'ʃuː, ə-; ɪ 'skjuː, ə- **~ed** d **~ing** ɪŋ **~s** z
eschscholtzia ɪ 'ʃɒlts i_ə e-, ə-, -'skɒlts-; -'skɒlʃ ə, -'skɒlt̬ ə ‖ ɪ 'ʃɑːlts- **~s** z
Escoffier ɪ 'skɒf i eɪ e-, ə- ‖ ˌesk ɑːf 'jeɪ —*Fr* [ɛs kɔ fje]
Escondido ˌesk ən 'diːd əʊ ‖ -oʊ -ɑːn-
Escorial e 'skɔːr i æl -ɑːl, -i_əl, ˌesk ɒr i 'ɑːl ‖ -i_əl -'skoʊr- —*Sp* [es ko 'rjal]
escort n 'esk ɔːt ‖ -ɔːrt **~s** s

e|scort *v* ɪ '|skɔːt e-, ə-; 'e|sk ɔːt ‖ ɪ '|skɔːrt e-
~scorted skɔːt ɪd -əd ‖ skɔːrt̬ əd ~scoring
skɔːt ɪŋ ‖ skɔːrt̬ ɪŋ ~scorts skɔːts ‖ skɔːrts
escritoire ˌesk rə 'twaː -riː-, -rɪ- ‖ -'twaːr ~s z
escrow 'esk rəʊ es 'krəʊ ‖ 'esk roʊ es 'kroʊ
escudo ɪ 'ʃkuːd əʊ e-, ə-, -'skuːd-, -'skjuːd- ‖ -oʊ
—*Port* [ɪʃ 'ku ðu] ~s z
esculent 'esk jʊl ənt ‖ -jəl-
escutcheon ɪ 'skʌtʃ ən e- ~s z
Esda 'es də 'ez-
Esdras 'ez dræs -drəs ‖ -drəs
-ese 'iːz ‖ -'iːs — journalese ˌdʒɜːn ə 'liːz ◄
‖ ˌdʒɜːn- -'liːs Japanese ˌdʒæp ə 'niːz ◄
‖ -'niːs
Esher 'iːʃ ə ‖ -ᵊr
e-signature 'iː ˌsɪg nətʃ ə -nɪtʃ- ‖ -ᵊr ~s z
Esk esk
Eskdale 'esk derᵊl
esker 'esk ə ‖ -ᵊr ~s z
Eskimo 'esk ɪ məʊ -ə- ‖ -moʊ ~s z
ESL ˌiː es 'el
Esling 'ez lɪŋ
Esme, Esmé 'ez mi
Esmeralda ˌez mə 'ræld ə
Esmond 'ez mənd
ESN ˌiː es 'en
ESOL 'iːs ɒl ‖ -aːl
esophageal iː ˌsɒf ə 'dʒiːr əl ◄ ɪ-, ə-, ˌiːs ɒf-
‖ ɪ ˌsaːf-
esophagus iː 'sɒf əg əs ɪ-, ə- ‖ ɪ 'saːf- ~es ɪz
əz
esoteric ˌes əʊ 'ter ɪk ◄ ˌiːs- ‖ ˌes ə- ~ally ᵊl ̩i
ESP ˌiː es 'piː
espadrille ˌesp ə 'drɪl '··· ‖ 'esp ə drɪl ~s z
espalier ɪ 'spæl i eɪ e-, ə-, ə ‖ -'spæl jᵊr -jeɪ ~s
z
esparto e 'spaːt əʊ ɪ- ‖ ɪ 'spaːrt̬ oʊ
especial ɪ 'speʃ ᵊl e-, ə-, △ɪk-, △ək- ~ly i
Esperantist ˌesp ə 'rænt ɪst ◄ -'raːnt-, §-əst
‖ -'raːnt̬- ~s s
Esperanto ˌesp ə 'rænt əʊ -'raːnt- ‖ -'raːnt̬ oʊ
—*Esperanto* [es pe 'ran to]
espial ɪ 'spaɪ əl e-, ə-
espie... —*see* espy
espionage 'esp i̯ə naːʒ -naːdʒ, ˌ···',
'esp i̯ən ɪdʒ
esplanade ˌesp lə 'neɪd -'naːd, '···
‖ 'esp lə naːd -neɪd ~s z
Esposito ˌesp ə 'ziːt əʊ -'siːt- ‖ -'ziːt̬ oʊ -'siːt̬-
—*Sp* [es po 'si to]
espousal ɪ 'spaʊz ᵊl e-, ə- ~s z
espouse ɪ 'spaʊz e-, ə-, §-'spaʊs espoused
ɪ 'spaʊzd e-, ə-, §-'spaʊst espouses
ɪ 'spaʊz ɪz e-, ə-, §-'spaʊs-, -əz espousing
ɪ 'spaʊz ɪŋ e-, ə-, §-'spaʊs-
espresso e 'spres əʊ ‖ -oʊ —*It* [e 'sprɛs so] ~s
z
esprit, E~ e 'spriː ɪ-, ə- —*See also phrases with
this word*
esprit de corps e ˌspriː də 'kɔː ɪ-, ə-; ˌesp riː-
‖ -'kɔːr -'koʊr —*Fr* [ɛs pʁi kɔːʁ]
esprit d'escalier e ˌspriː de 'skæl i eɪ ɪ-, ə-
‖ e ˌspriː ˌdesk aːl 'jeɪ —*Fr* [ɛs pʁi dɛs ka lje]

e|spy ɪ '|spaɪ e-, ə- ~spied 'spaɪd ~spies
'spaɪz ~spying 'spaɪ ɪŋ
Espy 'esp i
Esq. —*see* Esquire
-esque 'esk — Chaplinesque ˌtʃæp lɪn 'esk ◄
-lən-
Esquiline 'esk wɪ laɪn -wə-
Esquimalt ɪ 'skwaɪm ɔːlt e-, ə-, -ɒlt ‖ -aːlt
esquire ɪ 'skwaɪ‿ə e-, ə- ‖ 'esk waɪ‿ᵊr
ɪ 'skwaɪ‿ᵊr, e- ~s z
ESRC ˌiː es aː 'siː ‖ -aːr '·
-ess 'es, es, ɪs əs —*There is great inter-speaker
variability in the treatment of this suffix. See
individual entries.*
essay *v* e 'seɪ 'es eɪ ~ed d ~ing ɪŋ ~s z
essay *n 'attempt'* 'es eɪ e 'seɪ ~s z
essay *n 'piece of writing'* 'es eɪ ~s z
essayist 'es eɪ ɪst §-əst ~s s
esse 'es i
Essen 'es ᵊn —*Ger* ['ʔɛs ᵊn]
essenc|e 'es ᵊn̩s ~es ɪz əz
Essendon 'es ᵊn dən
Essene 'es iːn e -'siːn ‖ ɪ 'siːn e-; 'es iːn ~s z
essential ɪ 'sentʃ ᵊl e-, ə- ~ly i ~ness nəs nɪs
~s z
essentialit|y ɪ ˌsentʃ i 'æl ət |i e-, ə-, -ɪt |i
‖ -ət̬ |i ~ies iz
Essex 'es ɪks -əks
essive 'es ɪv ~s z
Essling 'es lɪŋ
Esso *tdmk* 'es əʊ ‖ -oʊ
Essoldo e 'sɒld əʊ ɪ-, ə- ‖ -'saːld oʊ
-est *superlative ending* ɪst əst — biggest
'bɪg ɪst -əst nicest 'naɪs ɪst -əst
-est *archaic and liturgical second person sing.
ending* ɪst əst sendest 'send ɪst -əst takest
'teɪk ɪst -əst
establish ɪ 'stæb lɪʃ e-, ə- ~ed t ~er/s ə/z
‖ ᵊr/z ~es ɪz əz ~ing ɪŋ
e,stablished 'church
establishment, E~ ɪ 'stæb lɪʃ mənt e-, ə- ~s s
establishmentarian
ɪ ˌstæb lɪʃ mən 'teər i‿ən ◄ e-, ə- ‖ -'ter- ~s z
estaminet e 'stæm ɪ neɪ ɪ-, -ə-
‖ e ˌstaːm iː 'neɪ —*Fr* [ɛs ta mi nɛ] ~s z
estancia ɪ 'stæn̩s i̯ə e- ‖ e 'staːn̩s- —*AmSp*
[es 'tan sja] ~s z
estate ɪ 'steɪt e-, ə- ~s s
e'state ˌagent; e'state car
Estcourt 'est kɔːt ‖ -kɔːrt -koʊrt
Este 'est i —*It* ['ɛs te]
Estee, Estée 'est eɪ -i
esteem ɪ 'stiːm e-, ə- ~ed d ~ing ɪŋ ~s z
Estefan 'est ə fæn -ɪ-
Estella ɪ 'stel ə e-, ə-
Estelle ɪ 'stel e-, ə-
ester 'est ə ‖ -ᵊr ~s z
esteras|e 'est ə reɪz -reɪs ~es ɪz əz
Esterhazy 'est ə haːz i ‖ '·ᵊr- —*Hung*
Eszterházy ['ɛs tɛr ha zi]
Esther 'est ə 'esθ- ‖ -ᵊr
esthete 'iːs θiːt ‖ 'es- (*) ~s s

esthetic iːs 'θet ɪk ɪs- ‖ es 'θet̬ ɪk ~al ᵊl ~ally
ᵊl i ~s s

estheticism iːs 'θet ɪ ˌsɪz əm -ə- ‖ es 'θet̬ ə- ɪs-

Esthwaite 'es θweɪt

estimab|le 'est ɪm əb ǀᵊl '·əm- ~leness ᵊl nəs
-nɪs ~ly li

esti|mate v 'est ɪ ǀmeɪt -ə-, -mət ~mated
meɪt ɪd -əd ‖ meɪt̬ əd ~mates meɪts ~mating
meɪt ɪŋ ‖ meɪt̬ ɪŋ

estimate n 'est ɪm ət -əm-, -ɪt; -ɪ meɪt, -ə- ~s s

estimation ˌest ɪ 'meɪʃ ᵊn -ə- ~s z

estimator 'est ɪ meɪt ə '·ə- ‖ -meɪt̬ ᵊr ~s z

estival i 'staɪv ᵊl ‖ 'est əv ᵊl

esti|vate 'iːst ɪ ǀveɪt 'est-, -ə- ~vated veɪt ɪd
-əd ‖ veɪt̬ əd ~vates veɪts ~vating veɪt ɪŋ
‖ veɪt̬ ɪŋ

estivation ˌiːst ɪ 'veɪʃ ᵊn ˌest-, -ə- ~s z

Estoni|a e 'stəʊn i ǀə ɪ-, ə- ‖ -'stoʊn- ~an/s
ən/z

estop ɪ 'stɒp e-, ə- ‖ e 'stɑːp ~ped t ~ping ɪŋ
~s s

estoppel ɪ 'stɒp ᵊl e-, ə- ‖ e 'stɑːp-

Estoril ˌest ə 'rɪl '···—Port [ɪʃ tu 'ril]

estovers ɪ 'stəʊv əz e-, ə- ‖ e 'stoʊv ᵊrz ɪ-

estrade e 'strɑːd ɪ-, ə- ~s z

estradiol ˌes trə 'daɪ ɒl ˌiːs- ‖ -oʊl -ɔːl, -ɑːl

estragon, E~ 'es trə gɒn ‖ -gɑːn —Fr
[ɛs tʁa gɔ̃]

estrang|e ɪ 'streɪndʒ e-, ə- ~ed d ~es ɪz əz
~ing ɪŋ

estrangement ɪ 'streɪndʒ mənt e-, ə- ~s s

estreat ɪ 'striːt e- ~s s

estrogen 'iːs trədʒ ən 'es- ‖ 'es-

estrous, estrus 'iːs trəs 'es- ‖ 'es-

estuarine 'est ju ə raɪn -rɪn ‖ 'es tʃu

estuar|y 'est jʊr ǀi '·ju ᵊr ǀi; 'es tʃʊr ǀi, 'eʃ-
‖ 'es tʃu er ǀi ~ies iz

esurienc|e ɪ 'sjʊər i ᵊn's ‖ ɪ 'sʊr- ~y i

esurient ɪ 'sjʊər i ᵊnt ‖ ɪ 'sʊr- ~ly li

et et —See also phrases with this word

ET ˌiː 'tiː

eta Greek letter 'iːt ə ‖ 'eɪt̬ ə 'iːt̬ ə (*)

ETA 'estimated time of arrival' ˌiː tiː 'eɪ

ETA Basque organization 'et ə

etagere, étagère ˌeɪt ə 'ʒeə ˌet-, -æ-, -ɑː-
‖ ˌeɪt̬ ə 'ʒeᵊr —Fr [e ta ʒɛːʁ] ~s z

et al, et al. ⒧et 'æl ‖ ⒧et̬ 'ɑːl -'æl, -'ɔːl

Etam tdmk 'iːt æm

etc., etcetera, et cetera ⒧et 'setr ə ɪt-, ət-,
△ ⒧ek-, -'set ər ə ‖ -'set̬ ər ə →-'setr ə

etch etʃ **etched** etʃt **etches** 'etʃ ɪz -əz
etching/s 'etʃ ɪŋ/z

etch-a-sketch 'etʃ ə sketʃ

etcher 'etʃ ə ‖ -ᵊr ~ers əz ‖ ᵊrz

Etchingham ˌetʃ ɪŋ 'hæm

Eteocles 'et iˌə kliːz ɪ 'tiːˌə- ‖ ɪ 'tiː ə-

eternal ɪ 'tɜːn ᵊl iː-, ə- ‖ ɪ 'tɜːn ᵊl ~ly i
e ˌternal 'triangle

eternalis|e, eternaliz|e ɪ 'tɜːn ə laɪz iː-, ə-,
-ᵊl aɪz ‖ ɪ 'tɜːn- ~ed d ~es ɪz əz ~ing ɪŋ

eternit|y ɪ 'tɜːn ət |i ǀi iː-, ə-, -ɪt- ‖ ɪ 'tɜːn ət̬ |i
~ies iz
e'ternity ring

Etesian ɪ 'tiːʒ i ən -'tiːz-; -'tiːʒ ᵊn ‖ ɪ 'tiːʒ ᵊn

eth letter name eð

Eth woman's name eθ

-eth archaic and liturgical third person sing.
ending ɪθ əθ **sendeth** 'send ɪθ -əθ, **taketh**
'teɪk ɪθ -əθ

Ethan 'iːθ ᵊn

ethane 'iːθ eɪn 'eθ- ‖ 'eθ-

ethanoic ˌeθ ə 'nəʊ ɪk ◂ ˌiːθ- ‖ -'noʊ-

ethanol 'eθ ə nɒl 'iːθ- ‖ -noʊl -nɔːl, -nɑːl

Ethel 'eθ ᵊl

Ethelbert 'eθ ᵊl bɜːt ‖ -bɜːt

Ethelberta ˌeθ ᵊl 'bɜːt ə ‖ -'bɜːt̬ ə

Ethelburga ˌeθ ᵊl 'bɜːg ə ‖ -'bɜːg ə

Etheldreda 'eθ ᵊl driːd ə

Ethelred 'eθ ᵊl red

ether 'iːθ ə ‖ -ᵊr

ethereal ɪ 'θɪər i əl iː-, ə- ‖ ɪ 'θɪr- ~ly i ~ness
nəs nɪs

etherealis|e, etherealiz|e ɪ 'θɪər i ə laɪz iː-,
ə- ‖ ɪ 'θɪr- ~ed d ~es ɪz əz ~ing ɪŋ

Etheredge, Etherege, Etheridge 'eθ ər ɪdʒ

Ethernet, e~ tdmk 'iːθ ə net ‖ -ᵊr-

ethic 'eθ ɪk ~s s

ethical 'eθ ɪk ᵊl ~ly i ~ness nəs nɪs

Ethiop 'iːθ i ɒp ‖ -ɑːp ~s s

Ethiope 'iːθ i əʊp ‖ -oʊp ~s s

Ethiopi|a ˌiːθ i 'əʊp i ǀə ‖ -'oʊp- ~an/s ən/z

Ethiopic ˌiːθ i 'ɒp ɪk ◂ -'əʊp- ‖ -'ɑːp- -'oʊp-

ethmoid 'eθ mɔɪd ~s z

ethnarch 'eθ nɑːk ‖ -nɑːrk ~s s

Ethne 'eθ ni

ethnic 'eθ nɪk ~ally ᵊl i ~s s

ethnicity eθ 'nɪs ət i -ɪt- ‖ -ət̬ i

ethno- comb. form
with stress-neutral suffix ǀeθ nəʊ ‖ ǀeθ noʊ
— **ethnobotany** ˌeθ nəʊ 'bɒt ən i
‖ ˌeθ noʊ 'bɑːt ᵊn i
with stress-imposing suffix eθ 'nɒ+
‖ eθ 'nɑː+ — **ethnogeny** eθ 'nɒdʒ ən i
‖ -'nɑːdʒ-

ethnocentric ˌeθ nəʊ 'sentr ɪk ◂ -noʊ-

ethnocentricity ˌeθ nəʊ sen 'trɪs ət i -ɪt i
‖ -noʊ sen 'trɪs ət̬ i

ethnocentrism ˌeθ nəʊ 'sentr ˌɪz əm ‖ -noʊ-

ethnographer eθ 'nɒg rəf ə ‖ -'nɑːg rəf ᵊr ~s
z

ethnographic ˌeθ nə 'græf ɪk ◂ ~al ᵊl ~ally
ᵊl i

ethnography eθ 'nɒg rəf i ‖ -'nɑːg-

ethnological ˌeθ nə 'lɒdʒ ɪk ᵊl ◂ ‖ -'lɑːdʒ- ~ly
i

ethnologist eθ 'nɒl ədʒ ɪst §-əst ‖ -'nɑːl- ~s s

ethnology eθ 'nɒl ədʒ i ‖ -'nɑːl-

ethnomethodolog|ist
ˌeθ nəʊ ˌmeθ ə 'dɒl ədʒ ǀɪst §-əst
‖ -noʊ ˌmeθ ə 'dɑːl- ~ists ɪsts §əsts ~y i

ethnomusicological
ˌeθ nəʊ ˌmjuːz ɪk ə 'lɒdʒ ɪk ᵊl
‖ -noʊ ˌmjuːz ɪk ə 'lɑːdʒ- ~ly i

ethnomusicolog|ist
ˌeθ nəʊ ˌmjuːz ɪ 'kɒl ədʒ ǀɪst -ˌ·ə-, §-əst
‖ -noʊ ˌmjuːz ɪ 'kɑːl- ~ists ɪsts §əsts ~y i

E

ethological ˌeθ ə ˈlɒdʒ ɪk ᵊl ◂ ˌiːθ- ‖ -ˈlɑːdʒ-
~ly i
etholog|ist iː ˈθɒl ədʒ |ɪst ɪ-, §-əst ‖ -ˈθɑːl-
~ists ɪsts §əsts ~y i
ethos ˈiːθ ɒs ‖ -ɑːs ˈeθ-, -oʊs
ethyl ˈeθ ᵊl -ɪl; ˈiːθ aɪᵊl
ˌethyl ˈalcohol
ethylene ˈeθ ə liːn -ɪ-
ˌethylene ˈglycol
etic ˈet ɪk ‖ ˈeţ ɪk ~ally ᵊl i
e-ticket ˈiː ˌtɪk ɪt §-ət ~s s
Etienne ˌet i ˈen —Fr [e tjɛn]
etio|late ˈiːt i ə |leɪt -i əʊ- ‖ ˈiːţ- ~lated leɪt ɪd
-əd ‖ leɪţ əd ~lates leɪts ~lating leɪt ɪŋ
‖ leɪţ ɪŋ
etiolation ˌiːt i ə ˈleɪʃ ᵊn -i əʊ- ‖ ˌiːţ-
etiological ˌiːt i ə ˈlɒdʒ ɪk ᵊl ◂ ‖ ˌiːţ i ə ˈlɑːdʒ-
~ly i
etiolog|y ˌiːt i ˈɒl ədʒ |i ‖ ˌiːţ i ˈɑːl- ~ies iz
etiquette ˈet i ket -ɪk ət, ˌet i ˈket ‖ ˈeţ ɪk ət
-ɪ ket ~s s
Etive ˈet ɪv ‖ ˈeţ-
Etna ˈet nə
Eton ˈiːt ᵊn (= eaten)
ˌEton ˈcollar
Etonian i ˈtəʊn i ən ‖ -ˈtoʊn- ~s z
Etruria ɪ ˈtrʊər i ə ə- ‖ ɪ ˈtrʊr-
Etruscan ɪ ˈtrʌsk ən ə- ~s z
-ette ˈet — lecturette ˌlek tʃə ˈret
Ettie ˈet i ‖ ˈeţ i
Ettrick ˈetr ɪk
Etty ˈet i ‖ ˈeţ i
etude, étude ˈeɪ tjuːd →-tʃuːd, ˈ· ‖ eɪ ˈtuːd
-ˈtjuːd, ˈ· · —Fr [e tyd] ~s z
etui, étui e ˈtwiː ‖ eɪ- —Fr [e tɥi] ~s z
Etwall ˈet wɔːl ‖ -wɑːl
etyma ˈet ɪm ə -əm- ‖ ˈeţ-
etymological ˌet ɪm ə ˈlɒdʒ ɪk ᵊl ◂ -əm-
‖ ˌeţ əm ə ˈlɑːdʒ- ~ly i
etymologis... —see etymologiz...
etymologist ˌet ɪ ˈmɒl ədʒ ɪst -ə-, §-əst
‖ ˌeţ ə ˈmɑːl- ~s s
etymologiz|e ˌet ɪ ˈmɒl ə dʒaɪz ˌə-
‖ ˌeţ ə ˈmɑːl- ~ed d ~es ɪz əz ~ing ɪŋ
etymolog|y ˌet ɪ ˈmɒl ədʒ |i ˌə- ‖ ˌeţ ə ˈmɑːl-
~ies iz
ety|mon ˈet ɪ |mɒn -ə- ‖ ˈeţ ə |mɑːn ~ma mə
E-type ˈiː taɪp
EU ˌiː ˈjuː
eu- ˌjuː, ju — eubacteria ˌjuː bæk ˈtɪər i ə
‖ -ˈtɪr- eupeptic ju ˈpept ɪk
Euan ˈjuː ən
Eubank ˈjuː bæŋk
Euboea ju ˈbɪə -ˈbiː ə ‖ -ˈbiː ə
eucalypt ˈjuːk ə lɪpt ~s s
eucalypt|us ˌjuːk ə ˈlɪpt |əs ~i aɪ ~uses əs ɪz
-əz
eucharist, E~ ˈjuːk ər ɪst §-əst ~s s
eucharistic, E~ ˌjuːk ə ˈrɪst ɪk ◂
euch|re ˈjuːk |ə ‖ -|ᵊr ~red əd ‖ ᵊrd ~res əz
‖ ᵊrz ~ring ər ɪŋ
Euclid ˈjuːk lɪd §-ləd
Euclidean, Euclidian, e~ ju ˈklɪd i ən ~s z

Eucryl tdmk ˈjuːk rɪl -rəl
eudiometer ˌjuːd i ˈɒm ɪt ə -ət ə ‖ -ˈɑːm əţ ᵊr
~s z
Eudora ju ˈdɔːr ə ‖ -ˈdoʊr-
Eudoxus ju ˈdɒks əs ‖ -ˈdɑːks-
Euen ˈjuː ən
Eugene ˈjuː dʒiːn -ʒiːn, ·ˈ·; ju ˈʒeɪn
eugenic ju ˈdʒen ɪk ~ally ᵊl i ~s s
Eugenie, Eugénie ju ˈʒeɪn i -ˈʒiːn-, -ˈdʒiːn-
—Fr [ø ʒe ni]
eukaryote ju ˈkær i əʊt -ɒt, -i ət ‖ -oʊt -ˈker-
~s s
Eulalia ju ˈleɪl i ə
Euler ˈɔɪl ə ˈjuːl- ‖ -ᵊr —Ger [ˈʔɔy lɐ]
eulogies ˈjuːl ədʒ iz
eulogis|e ˈjuːl ə dʒaɪz ~ed d ~es ɪz əz ~ing ɪŋ
eulogist ˈjuːl ədʒ ɪst §-əst ~s s
eulogistic ˌjuːl ə ˈdʒɪst ɪk ◂ ~ally ᵊl i
eulogi|um ju ˈləʊdʒ i |əm ‖ -ˈloʊdʒ- ~a ə
~ums əmz
eulogiz|e ˈjuːl ə dʒaɪz ~ed d ~es ɪz əz ~ing ɪŋ
eulog|y ˈjuːl ədʒ |i ~ies iz
Eumenides ju ˈmen ɪ diːz -ə-
Eunice ˈjuːn ɪs -əs, ju ˈnaɪs i
Eunson ˈjuːn sᵊn
eunuch ˈjuːn ək ~s s
euonymus ju ˈɒn ɪm əs -əm- ‖ -ˈɑːn- ~es ɪz əz
Eupen ˈɜːp ən ˈjuːp-, ˈɔɪp- ‖ ˈɔɪp- —Fr [ø pɛn],
Ger [ˈʔɔy pᵊn]
eupeptic ju ˈpept ɪk
Euphemia ju ˈfiːm i ə
euphemism ˈjuːf ə ˌmɪz əm -ɪ- ~s z
euphemistic ˌjuːf ə ˈmɪst ɪk ◂ -ɪ- ~ally ᵊl i
euphonic ju ˈfɒn ɪk ‖ -ˈfɑːn- ~ally ᵊl i
euphonious ju ˈfəʊn i əs ‖ -ˈfoʊn- ~ly li
~ness nəs nɪs
euphonium ju ˈfəʊn i əm ‖ -ˈfoʊn- ~s z
euphon|y ˈjuːf ən |i ~ies iz
euphorbia ju ˈfɔːb i ə ‖ -ˈfɔːrb- ~s z
euphorbiaceous ju ˌfɔːb i ˈeɪʃ əs ◂ ‖ -ˌfɔːrb-
euphoria ju ˈfɔːr i ə -ˈfɒr- ‖ -ˈfoʊr-
euphoric ju ˈfɒr ɪk ‖ -ˈfɔːr- -ˈfɑːr- ~ally ᵊl i
Euphrates ju ˈfreɪt iːz
Euphrosyne ju ˈfrɒz ɪ ni: -ə- ‖ -ˈfrɑːs- -ˈfrɑːz-
Euphues ˈjuːf ju iːz
euphuism ˈjuːf ju ˌɪz əm ~s z
euphuistic ˌjuːf ju ˈɪst ɪk ◂
euploid ˈjuːp lɔɪd ~s z
Eurailpass ˈjʊər eɪᵊl pɑːs ˈjɔːr-, §-pæs;
juᵊ ˈreɪᵊl- ‖ ˈjʊr eɪᵊl pæs ~es ɪz əz
Eurasia juᵊ ˈreɪʒ ə -ˈreɪʃ-
Eurasian juᵊ ˈreɪʒ ᵊn -ˈreɪʃ- ~s z
Euratom juᵊr ˈæt əm ‖ -ˈæţ-
eureka juᵊ ˈriːk ə
eurhythmic juᵊ ˈrɪð mɪk -ˈrɪθ- ~ally ᵊl i ~s s
Eurig ˈaɪᵊr ɪg —Welsh [ˈəɪ rɪg, ˈəi-]
Euripides juᵊ ˈrɪp ɪ diːz -ə-
euripus, E~ juᵊ ˈraɪp əs
euro ˈjʊər əʊ ˈjɔːr- ‖ ˈjʊr oʊ ~s z
Euro- comb. form
with stress-neutral suffix ˌjʊər əʊ ˌjɔːr- ‖ ˌjʊr ə
-oʊ — Eurocrat ˈjʊər əʊ kræt ˈjɔːr- ‖ ˈjʊr ə-

E

with stress-imposing suffix juə ˈrɒ +
‖ juə ˈrɑː + — **Eurocracy** juə ˈrɒk rəs i
‖ -ˈrɑːk-

Eurocentric ˌjuər əu ˈsentr ɪk ◄ ˌjɔːr- ‖ ˌjur ou-
Eurocheque ˈjuər əu tʃek ˈjɔːr- ‖ ˈjur ou- ~**s** s
Eurocommunism ˈjuər əu ˌkɒm ju nɪz əm
ˈjɔːr-, -,-,jə-; ,·ˑ·,·ˑ ‖ ˈjur ou ˌkɑːm jə-
Eurocommunist ˈjuər əu ˌkɒm jun ɪst ˈjɔːr-,
-,jən-, §-əst; ,·ˑ·- ‖ ˈjur ou ˌkɑːm jən əst ~**s** s
Eurodisney *tdmk* ˈjuər əu ˌdɪz ni ˈjɔːr-
‖ ˈjur ou-
Eurodollar ˈjuər əu ˌdɒl ə ˈjɔːr-, ,·ˑ··
‖ ˈjur ou ˌdɑːl ²r ~**s** z
Eurofighter ˈjuər əu ˌfaɪt ə ˈjɔːr-, ,·ˑ··
‖ ˈjur ou ˌfaɪt ²r ~**s** z
Euroland ˈjuər əu lænd ˈjɔːr- ‖ ˈjur ou-
Europa juə ˈrəup ə ‖ -ˈroup ə
Europe ˈjuər əp ˈjɔːr- ‖ ˈjur əp ˈjɜː-
European ˌjuər ə ˈpiː ən ◄ ˌjɔːr- ‖ ˌjur- ˌjɜː- ~**s**
z
ˌEuroˌpean Comˈmunities; ˌEuroˌpean
ˈParliament; ˌEuroˈpean plan
europium juə ˈrəup i əm ‖ -ˈroup-
Europoort, Europort ˈjuər əu pɔːt ˈjɔːr-
‖ ˈjur ou pɔːrt -pourt —*Dutch* [ˈøː roː poːrt]
Eurosceptic ˌjuər əu ˈskept ɪk ◄ ˌjɔːr-
‖ ˌjur ou- ~**s** s
Eurostar *tdmk* ˈjuər əu stɑː ˈjɔːr- ‖ ˈjur ou stɑːr
~**s** z
Eurotra juə ˈrəutr ə ‖ -ˈroutr ə
Eurotrash ˈjuər əu træʃ ˈjɔːr- ‖ ˈjur ou-
Eurotunnel *tdmk* ˈjuər əu ˌtʌn ²l ˈjɔːr-
‖ ˈjur ou-
Eurovision ˈjuər əu ˌvɪʒ ²n ˈjɔːr- ‖ ˈjur ou-
ˌEuroˌvision ˈSong ˌContest
Eurus ˈjuər əs ˈjɔːr- ‖ ˈjur-
Eurydice juə ˈrɪd ɪs i -əs-, -iː; ˌjuər i ˈdiːtʃ i, -eɪ
‖ ˌjur- —*Also, where appropriate, pronounced
in imitated Italian* Euridice — *It*
[eu ri ˈdiː tʃe]
eurythmic juə ˈrɪð mɪk -ˈrɪθ- ~**ally** ²l̩ i ~**s** s
Eusebio, Eusébio ju ˈseɪb i əu -ˈseb- ‖ -ou
—*Port* [eu ˈze bju]
Eusebius ju ˈsiːb i̯əs
Eustace ˈjuːst əs -ɪs
eustachian, E~ ju ˈsteɪʃ ²n -ˈsteɪʃ i̯ən;
ju ˈsteɪk i̯ən
Euˌstachian ˈtube
Euston ˈjuːst ən
eutectic ju ˈtekt ɪk ~**s** s
Eutelsat *tdmk* ˈjuːt ²l sæt ˈjuː tel- ‖ ˈjuːt̬-
Euterpe ju ˈtɜːp i ‖ -ˈtɜːp i
euthanas|e ˈjuːθ ə neɪz ~**ed** d ~**es** ɪz əz ~**ing**
ɪŋ
euthanasia ˌjuːθ ə ˈneɪz i_ə -ˈneɪz i_ə, -ˈneɪʒ ə
‖ -ˈneɪʒ ə
euthanis|e, euthaniz|e ˈjuːθ ə naɪz ~**ed** d
~**es** ɪz əz ~**ing** ɪŋ
eutrophic ju ˈtrɒf ɪk -ˈtrəuf- ‖ -ˈtrouf-
eutrophication ju ˌtrɒf ɪ ˈkeɪʃ ²n ˌju:-, -ə-
‖ -ˌtrouf-
Euxine ˈjuːks aɪn ‖ -²n
Euxton ˈekst ən

Eva ˈiːv ə —*as a foreign name also* ˈeɪv ə *or* (*esp
AmE*) ˈev ə
evacu|ate iˈvæk ju ˌeɪt ə- ~**ated** eɪt ɪd -əd
‖ eɪt̬ əd ~**ates** eɪts ~**ating** eɪt ɪŋ ‖ eɪt̬ ɪŋ
evacuation i ˌvæk ju ˈeɪʃ ²n ə- ~**s** z
evacuee i ˌvæk ju ˈiː ə- ~**s** z
evad|e i ˈveɪd ə- ~**ed** ɪd əd ~**er/s** ə/z ‖ ²r/z ~**es**
z ~**ing** ɪŋ
Evadne ɪ ˈvæd ni
evalu|ate i ˈvæl ju ˌeɪt ə- ~**ated** eɪt ɪd -əd
‖ eɪt̬ əd ~**ates** eɪts ~**ating** eɪt ɪŋ ‖ eɪt̬ ɪŋ
evaluation i ˌvæl ju ˈeɪʃ ²n ə- ~**s** z
evaluative i ˈvæl ju̯ət ɪv ə-, -ju eɪt- ‖ -ju eɪt̬ ɪv
~**ly** li
Evan ˈev ²n
Evander ɪ ˈvænd ə ə- ‖ -²r
evanescence ˌev ə ˈnes ²nts ˌiːv-
evanescent ˌev ə ˈnes ²nt ◄ ˌiːv- ~**ly** li
evangel i ˈvændʒ əl -el ~**s** z
evangelic ˌiːv æn ˈdʒel ɪk ◄ ‖ ˌev ²n- ~**s** s
evangelical ˌiːv æn ˈdʒel ɪk ²l ◄ ‖ ˌev ²n- ~**ly**
i ~**s** s
Evangeline i ˈvændʒ ə liːn -ɪ-, -laɪn
evangelis... —*see* **evangeliz...**
evangelism ɪ ˈvændʒ ə ˌlɪz əm ə-, -ɪ-
evangelist ɪ ˈvændʒ əl ɪst ə-, -ɪl-, §-əst ~**s** s
evangelistic ɪ ˌvændʒ ə ˈlɪst ɪk ◄ ə-, -ɪ- ~**ally**
²l̩ i
evangelization ɪ ˌvændʒ əl aɪ ˈzeɪʃ ²n ə-, -ˌɪl-,
-ɪˈ- ‖ -əl ə-
evangeliz|e ɪ ˈvændʒ ə laɪz ə-, -ɪ- ~**ed** d ~**es** ɪz
əz ~**ing** ɪŋ
Evans ˈev ²nz
Evanston ˈev ²nst ən
Evansville ˈev ²nz vɪl
evapo|rate i ˈvæp ə ˌreɪt ə- ~**rated** reɪt ɪd -əd
‖ reɪt̬ əd ~**rates** reɪts ~**rating** reɪt ɪŋ ‖ reɪt̬ ɪŋ
eˌvaporated ˈmilk
evaporation i ˌvæp ə ˈreɪʃ ²n ə- ~**s** z
evaporator i ˈvæp ə reɪt ə ə- ‖ -reɪt̬ ²r ~**s** z
evasion i ˈveɪʒ ²n ə- ~**s** z
evasive i ˈveɪs ɪv ə-, §-ˈveɪz- ~**ly** li ~**ness** nəs
nɪs
Evatt ˈev ət
eve, Eve iːv
Evelina ˌev ə ˈliːn ə -ɪ-
Eveline ˈiːv lɪn -lən
Evelyn (*i*) ˈiːv lɪn -lən, (*ii*) ˈev- ˈev ə- —*As a
man's name, and as an English family name,
* (*i*); *as a woman's name, either. In AmE
usually* (*ii*).
even ˈiːv ²n ~**ed** d ~**ing** ˌɪŋ ~**s** z
even-handed ˌiːv ²n ˈhænd ɪd ◄ -əd ~**ly** li
~**ness** nəs nɪs
evening *v* 'making even' ˈiːv ²n ˌɪŋ
evening *n* 'period between afternoon and night'
ˈiːv nɪŋ ~**s** z
ˈevening dress, ,·ˑˈ·; ˌevening ˈprayer;
ˌevening ˈstar
Evenki ɪ ˈveŋk i ə-
Evenlode ˈiːv ²n ləud ‖ -loud
evenly ˈiːv ²n li
evenness ˈiːv ²n nəs -nɪs

evensong 'iːv ᵊn sɒŋ ‖ -sɔːŋ -sɑːŋ
even-steven ˌiːv ᵊn 'stiːvᵊn
e|vent ɪ|'vent ə- ~vented 'vent ɪd -əd
  ‖ 'venṭ əd ~venting 'vent ɪŋ ‖ 'venṭ ɪŋ
  ~vents 'vents
even-tempered ˌiːv ᵊn 'temp əd ◂ ‖ -ᵊrd ~ly li
  ~ness nəs nɪs
eventer ɪ 'vent ə ə- ‖ -ᵊr ~s z
eventful ɪ 'vent fᵊl ə-, -fʊl ~ly i ~ness nəs nɪs
eventide 'iːv ᵊn taɪd
eventual ɪ 'ventʃ u əl ə-, -'ventʃ əl —In formal
  style also -'vent ju əl
eventualit|y ɪ ˌventʃ u 'æl ət |i ə-, -'vent ju-,
  -ɪt i ‖ -əṭ |i ~ies iz
eventually ɪ 'ventʃ u əl i ə-, -'ventʃ əl i —In
  formal style also -'vent ju əl i
eventu|ate ɪ 'ventʃ u |eɪt ə-, -'vent ju- ~ated
  eɪt ɪd -əd ‖ eɪṭ əd ~ates eɪts ~ating eɪt ɪŋ
  ‖ eɪṭ ɪŋ
ever 'ev ə ‖ -ᵊr
Everage 'ev ər ɪdʒ
Everard 'ev ə rɑːd ‖ -rɑːrd
ever-changing ˌev ə 'tʃeɪndʒ ɪŋ ◂ ‖ -ᵊr- ~ly li
Everest 'ev ər ɪst -əst, -ə rest
Everett 'ev ər ɪt -ət, -ə ret
Everglades 'ev ə gleɪdz ‖ -ᵊr-
evergreen 'ev ə griːn ‖ -ᵊr- ~s z
everlasting ˌev ə 'lɑːst ɪŋ ◂ §-'læst- ‖ -ᵊr 'læst-
  ~ly li ~ness nəs nɪs ~s z
  ˌever ˌlasting 'life
Everley, Everly 'ev ə li ‖ -ᵊr-
evermore ˌev ə 'mɔː ◂ ‖ -ᵊr 'mɔːr -'moʊr
everpresent ˌev ə 'prez ᵊnt ◂ ‖ -ᵊr-
EverReady tdmk ˌev ə 'red i ◂ ·ˌ·ˌ· ‖ '·ᵊrˌ··
Evers 'ev əz ‖ -ᵊrz
Evershed 'ev ə ʃed ‖ -ᵊr-
Eversholt 'ev ə ʃɒlt -ʃəʊlt ‖ -ᵊr ʃoʊlt
eversion ɪ'vɜːʃ ᵊn ə-, -'vɜːʒ- ‖ -'vɜːʒ ᵊn -'vɜːʃ-
e|vert ɪ |'vɜːt iː-, ə- ‖ ɪ |'vɜːrt ~verted 'vɜːt ɪd
  -əd ‖ 'vɜːṭ əd ~verting 'vɜːt ɪŋ ‖ 'vɜːṭ ɪŋ
  ~verts 'vɜːts ‖ 'vɜːts
Evert 'ev ət ‖ -ᵊrt
Everton 'ev ət ən ‖ -ᵊrt ᵊn
every 'ev ri —In very formal style occasionally
  also 'ev ər i (and in compounds too)
  ˌevery 'which way
everybody 'ev ri ˌbɒd i ‖ -ˌbɑːd i
everyday ˌev ri 'deɪ ◂
Everyman 'ev ri mæn
everyone 'ev ri wʌn §-wɒn
everyplace 'ev ri pleɪs
everything 'ev ri θɪŋ ⚠-θɪŋk
everywhere 'ev ri weə -hweə ‖ -hwer -hwær
Evesham 'iːv ʃəm 'iːv ɪʃ əm, 'iːs əm
Evett 'ev ɪt -ət
Evian tdmk 'ev i ɒ̃ ‖ ˌeɪv i 'ɑːn —Fr Évian
  [e vjɑ]
evict ɪ 'vɪkt ə- ~ed ɪd əd ~ing ɪŋ ~s s
eviction ɪ 'vɪk ʃᵊn ə- ~s z
evidenc|e n, v 'ev ɪd ᵊnᵗs -əd-; §-ɪ denᵗs, §-ə-
  ~ed t ~es ɪz əz ~ing ɪŋ
evident 'ev ɪd ənt -əd-; §-ɪ dent, §ə- ~ly li
evidential ˌev ɪ 'denᵗʃ ᵊl ◂ -ə- ~ly i

evil 'iːv ᵊl -ɪl ~s z
  ˌevil 'eye; 'Evil One
evildoer 'iːv ᵊl ˌduː ə -ɪl-, ˌ·'·· ‖ -ᵊr ~s z
evilly 'iːv əl i -ɪl i
evil-minded ˌiːv ᵊl 'maɪnd ɪd ◂ -ɪl-, -əd ~ly li
  ~ness nəs nɪs
evilness 'iːv ᵊl nəs -ɪl-, -nɪs
evil-tempered ˌiːv ᵊl 'temp əd ◂ -ɪl- ‖ -ᵊrd ~ly
  li ~ness nəs nɪs
evinc|e ɪ 'vɪnᵗs ə- ~ed t ~es ɪz əz ~ing ɪŋ
evisce|rate ɪ 'vɪs ə |reɪt ə- ~rated reɪt ɪd -əd
  ‖ reɪṭ əd ~rates reɪts ~rating reɪt ɪŋ ‖ reɪṭ ɪŋ
evisceration ɪ ˌvɪs ə 'reɪʃ ᵊn ə- ~s z
Evita e 'viːt ə e-, ə- —Sp [e 'βi ta]
evocation ˌiːv əʊ 'keɪʃ ᵊn ˌev- ‖ ˌiːv oʊ- ˌev ə-
  ~s z
evocative ɪ 'vɒk ət ɪv ə- ‖ -'vɑːk əṭɪv ~ly li
  ~ness nəs nɪs
evok|e ɪ 'vəʊk ə- ‖ -'voʊk ~ed t ~es s ~ing ɪŋ
evolute 'iːv ə luːt 'ev-, -ljuːt ‖ 'ev-

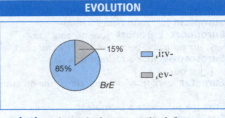

EVOLUTION

BrE

evolution ˌiːv ə 'luːʃ ᵊn ˌev-, -'ljuːʃ- ‖ ˌev- ~s z
  — Preference poll, BrE: ˌiːv- 85%, ˌev- 15%
evolutionar|y ˌiːv ə 'luːʃ ᵊnᵊr |i ◂ ˌev-,
  -'ljuːʃ-, -ᵊn ᵊr |i ‖ ˌev ə 'luːʃ ə ner |i -ily əl i
  ɪ li
evolutive ɪ 'vɒl jʊt ɪv iː-, ə-, -jət- ‖ -'vɑːl jəṭ ɪv
evolv|e ɪ'vɒlv ə-, §-'vəʊlv ‖ -'vɑːlv ~ed d ~es z
  ~ing ɪŋ
Evonne ˌiː 'vɒn ɪ-, ə- ‖ -'vɑːn
Evo-stik tdmk 'iːv əʊ stɪk ‖ -oʊ-
evzone 'ev zəʊn ‖ -zoʊn ~s z
Ewan 'juː ən
Ewart 'juː ət ‖ ᵊrt
Ewbank 'juː bæŋk
ewe juː §jəʊ (= yew, you) ewes juːz
Ewe loch in Scotland juː
Ewe African people and language 'e weɪ 'eɪ-
Ewell 'juː əl juːl
Ewelme 'juː elm
Ewen 'juː ən m
ewer 'juː ə ‖ ᵊr ~s z
Ewhurst 'juː hɜːst ‖ -hɜːst
Ewing 'juː ɪŋ
Ewins 'juː ɪnz
Ewyas 'juː əs
ex eks —See also phrases with this word exes,
  ex's 'eks ɪz -əz
ex- ¦eks, ɪks, əks, eks —or with gz, kz. —This
  prefix is always stressed ¦eks when it has the
  specific meaning 'formerly' (ˌex-'chairman).
  When it has no such specific meaning, it is
  still stressed ¦eks, ¦egz (1) if the following
  syllable is unstressed (ˌexca'vation), and (2) in

some disyllabic nouns and adjectives ('extract).
*Otherwise, in RP, the prefix is usually
unstressed and weak* ɪks, ɪgz (ex'pect). *But
both vowel and consonants are subject to
variation: some speakers use the weak vowel* ə
rather than ɪ, *though others (particularly BrE
regional speakers) have strong* e *and may even
stress it. The forms with* ks *are used before a
following consonant sound, those with* gz
before a vowel sound (exact ɪg 'zækt, exhaust
ɪg 'zɔːst). *(However, some speakers voice only
the second consonant, thus* ɪk 'zækt, ɪk 'zɔːst.)
In words with the spellings exce-, exci- *the
consonants are simplified to* ks (excite
ɪk 'saɪt). *Several words are irregular, as shown
in the entries below.*

exacer|bate ɪg 'zæs ə |beɪt eg-, əg-, ɪk-, ek-,
ək-; ek 'sæs- ‖ -ᵊr- **~bated** beɪt ɪd -əd
‖ beɪt̬ əd **~bates** beɪts **~bating** beɪt ɪŋ
‖ beɪt̬ ɪŋ
exacerbation ɪg ˌzæs ə 'beɪʃ ᵊn eg-, əg-, ɪk-,
ek-, ək-; ek ˌsæs- ‖ -ᵊr-
exact *adj, v* ɪg 'zækt eg-, əg-, ɪk-, ek-, ək- **~ed**
ɪd əd **~ing** ɪŋ **~s** s
exacting ɪg 'zækt ɪŋ eg-, əg-, ɪk-, ek-, ək- **~ly** li
~ness nəs nɪs
exaction ɪg 'zæk ʃᵊn eg-, əg-, ɪk-, ek-, ək- **~s** z
exactitude ɪg 'zækt ɪ tjuːd eg-, əg-, ɪk-, ek-,
ək-, -ə-, →-tʃuːd ‖ **-tuːd** -tjuːd
exactly ɪg 'zækt li eg-, əg-, ɪk-, ek-, ək- —*In
rapid casual speech this word may lose its
initial vowel or even the whole initial syllable.*
exactness ɪg 'zækt nəs eg-, əg-, ɪk-, ek-, ək-,
-nɪs
ex-actor *'former actor'* ˌeks 'ækt ə ‖ -ᵊr **~s** z
exactor *'one that exacts'* ɪg 'zækt ə eg-, əg-,
ɪk-, ek-, ək- ‖ -ᵊr **~s** z
exagge|rate ɪg 'zædʒ ə |reɪt eg-, əg-, ɪk-, ek-,
ək- **~rated/ly** reɪt ɪd /li -əd /li ‖ reɪt̬ əd /li
~rates reɪts **~rating** reɪt ɪŋ ‖ reɪt̬ ɪŋ
exaggeration ɪg ˌzædʒ ə 'reɪʃ ᵊn eg-, əg-, ɪk-,
ek-, ək- **~s** z
exalt ɪg 'zɔːlt eg-, əg-, ɪk-, ek-, ək-, -'zɒlt
‖ -'zɑːlt **~ed** ɪd əd **~ing** ɪŋ **~s** s
exaltation ˌegz ɔːl 'teɪʃ ᵊn ˌeks-, -ɒl- ‖ -ɑːl-
exalted ɪg 'zɔːlt ɪd eg-, əg-, ɪk-, ek-, ək-, -'zɒlt-,
-əd ‖ -'zɑːlt- **~ly** li **~ness** nəs nɪs
exam ɪg 'zæm eg- əg-, ɪk-, ek-, ək-; §'egz æm **~s**
z
   e'xam ˌpaper
examination ɪg ˌzæm ɪ 'neɪʃ ᵊn eg-, əg-, ɪk-,
ek-, ək-, -ə- **~s** z
   e͵xami'nation ˌpaper
examin|e ɪg 'zæm ɪn eg-, əg-, ɪk-, ek-, ək-, §-ən
~ed d **~es** z **~ing** ɪŋ
examinee ɪg ˌzæm ɪ 'niː eg-, əg-, ɪk-, ek-, ək-,
-ə- **~s** z
examiner ɪg 'zæm ɪn ə eg-, əg-, ɪk-, ek-, ək-,
§-ən- ‖ -ᵊr **~s** z
example ɪg 'zɑːmp ᵊl eg-, əg-, ɪk-, ek-, ək-,
§-'zæmp- ‖ -'zæmp- **~s** z
exanthema ˌeks æn 'θiːm ə ‖ ˌegz æn-
exarch 'eks ɑːk ‖ -ɑːrk **~s** s

exarchate 'eks ɑːk eɪt ‖ -ɑːrk- **~s** s

exaspe|rate ɪg 'zæsp ə |reɪt eg-, əg-, ɪk-, ek-,
ək-, -'zɑːsp- — *Preference poll, BrE:* -'zæsp-
54% (English southerners 33%), -'zɑːsp- *46%
(English southerners 67%). In AmE always*
-'zæsp-. **~rated/ly** reɪt ɪd /li -əd /li
‖ reɪt̬ əd /li **~rates** reɪts **~rating/ly**
reɪt ɪŋ /li ‖ reɪt̬ ɪŋ /li
exasperation ɪg ˌzæsp ə 'reɪʃ ᵊn eg-, əg-, ɪk-,
ek-, ək-, -ˌzɑːsp-
Excalibur ek 'skæl ɪb ə -əb- ‖ -ᵊr
ex cathedra ˌeks kə 'θiːdr ə -'θedr-, -'tedr-
exca|vate 'eks kə |veɪt **~vated** veɪt ɪd -əd
‖ veɪt̬ əd **~vates** veɪts **~vating** veɪt ɪŋ
‖ veɪt̬ ɪŋ
excavation ˌeks kə 'veɪʃ ᵊn **~s** z
excavator 'eks kə veɪt ə ‖ -veɪt̬ ᵊr **~s** z
Excedrin *tdmk* ek 'sedr ɪn ɪk-, -ən
exceed ɪk 'siːd ek-, ək- **~ed** ɪd əd **~ing/ly** ɪŋ /li
~s z
excel ɪk 'sel ek-, ək- **~led** d **~ling** ɪŋ **~s** z
excellence 'eks ᵊl ᵊn‿s
Excellenc|y, e~ 'eks ᵊl ᵊn‿s |i **~ies** iz
excellent 'eks ᵊl ᵊnt **~ly** li
excelsior ek 'sels i ɔː ɪk-, -i ə ‖ -i ᵊr -i ɔːr
except *v, prep, conj* ɪk 'sept ek-, ək- **~ed** ɪd əd
~ing ɪŋ **~s** s
exception ɪk 'sep ʃᵊn ek-, ək- **~s** z
exceptionab|le ɪk 'sep ʃᵊn‿əb |ᵊl ek-, ək- **~ly**
li
exceptional ɪk 'sep ʃᵊn‿əl ek-, ək- **~ly** i
excerpt *n* 'eks ɜːpt ek 'sɜːpt, 'egz ɜːpt
‖ 'eks ɜːpt 'egz ɜːpt **~s** s
excerpt *v* ek 'sɜːpt ɪk-, ək-; ɪg 'zɜːpt ‖ ek 'sɜːpt
eg 'zɜːpt, '· · **~ed** ɪd əd **~ing** ɪŋ **~s** s
excess *n* ɪk 'ses ek-, ək-; 'eks es **~es** ɪz əz —*In
stress-shifting environments usually* ˌeks es, *as
if underlyingly* ˌek 'ses ◂: ˌexcess 'baggage
(see excess adj)*
excess *adj* 'eks es ek 'ses, ɪk-, ək-
excessive ɪk 'ses ɪv ek-, ək- **~ly** li
exchang|e *n, v* ɪks 'tʃeɪndʒ eks-, əks- **~ed** d
~es ɪz əz **~ing** ɪŋ
   ex'change rate
exchangeable ɪks 'tʃeɪndʒ əb ᵊl eks-, əks-
exchequer ɪks 'tʃek ə eks-, əks- ‖ -ᵊr **~s** z
excipient ɪk 'sɪp i ənt ek-, ək- **~s** s
excise *n* *'tax'* 'eks aɪz ɪk 'saɪz, ek-, ək-
excis|e *v* *'remove'* ɪk 'saɪz ₍ᵢ₎ek-, ək- **~ed** d **~es**
ɪz əz **~ing** ɪŋ
excision ɪk 'sɪʒ ᵊn ek-, ək- **~s** z
excitability ɪk ˌsaɪt ə 'bɪl ət i ek-, ək-, -ɪt i
‖ -ˌsaɪt̬ ə 'bɪl ət̬ i

E

excitab|le ɪk 'saɪt əb |ᵊl ek-, ək- ‖ -'saɪt̬ əb-
~**leness** ᵊl nəs -nɪs ~**ly** li
excitation ˌeks ɪ 'teɪʃ ᵊn -ə-, -aɪ- ~**s** z
ex|cite ɪk |'saɪt ek-, ək- ~**cited/ly** 'saɪt ɪd /li
əd /li ‖ 'saɪt̬ əd /li ~**cites** 'saɪts ~**citing/ly**
'saɪt ɪŋ /li ‖ 'saɪt̬ ɪŋ /li
excitement ɪk 'saɪt mənt ek-, ək- ~**s** s
exciter, excitor ɪk 'saɪt ə ek-, ək- ‖ -'saɪt̬ ᵊr ~**s**
z
exclaim ɪk 'skleɪm ek-, ək- ~**ed** d ~**er/s** ə/z
‖ ᵊr/z ~**ing** ɪŋ ~**s** z
exclamation ˌeks klə 'meɪʃ ᵊn ~**s** z
ˌexcla'mation mark; ˌexcla'mation point
exclamator|y ɪk 'sklæm ət̚ ər |i ek-, ək-
‖ -ə tɔːr |i -toʊr i ~**ily** əl i ɪ i li
exclave 'eks kleɪv ~**s** z
exclud|e ɪk 'skluːd ek-, ək- ~**ed** ɪd əd ~**er/s** ə/z
‖ ᵊr/z ~**es** z ~**ing** ɪŋ
exclusion ɪk 'skluːʒ ᵊn ek-, ək- ~**s** z
exclusionary ɪk 'skluːʒ ᵊn ər ˌi -ᵊn ˌəri
‖ -ə ner i
exclusive ɪk 'skluːs ɪv ek-, ək-, §-'skluːz- ~**ly** li
~**ness** nəs nɪs
exclusivity ˌeks klu 'sɪv ət i -ɪt i ‖ -ət̬ i
excogi|tate eks 'kɒdʒ ɪ |teɪt ɪks-, -ə- ‖ -'kɑːdʒ-
~**tated** teɪt ɪd -əd ‖ teɪt̬ əd ~**tates** teɪts
~**tating** teɪt ɪŋ ‖ teɪt̬ ɪŋ
excogitation ˌeks ˌkɒdʒ ɪ 'teɪʃ ᵊn ·ˌ-,
ɪks ˌkɒdʒ- ‖ ˌkɑːdʒ- ~**s** z
excommunicate n, adj ˌeks kə 'mjuːn ɪk ət
-ɪt, -ɪ keɪt ~**s** s
excommuni|cate v ˌeks kə 'mjuːn ɪ |keɪt -'ə-
~**cated** keɪt ɪd -əd ‖ keɪt̬ əd ~**cates** keɪts
~**cating** keɪt ɪŋ ‖ keɪt̬ ɪŋ
excommunication ˌeks kə ˌmjuːn ɪ 'keɪʃ ᵊn
-·ˌə- ~**s** z
ex-con ˌeks 'kɒn ‖ -'kɑːn ~**s** z
ex-convict ˌeks 'kɒn vɪkt ‖ -'kɑːn- ~**s** s
excori|ate ɪk 'skɔːr i |eɪt ek-, ək-, -'skɒr-
‖ -'skoʊr- ~**ated** eɪt ɪd -əd ‖ eɪt̬ əd ~**ates** eɪts
~**ating** eɪt ɪŋ ‖ eɪt̬ ɪŋ
excoriation ɪk ˌskɔːr i 'eɪʃ ᵊn ek-, ək-, -ˌskɒr-
‖ -ˌskoʊr- ~**s** z
excrement 'eks krɪ mənt -krə-
excremental ˌeks krɪ 'ment ᵊl ◂ -krə-
‖ -'ment̬ ᵊl ◂
excrescenc|e ɪk 'skres ᵊn's ek-, ək- ~**es** ɪz əz
excrescent ɪk 'skres ᵊnt ek-, ək- ~**ly** li
excreta ɪk 'skriːt ə ek-, ək- ‖ -'skriːt̬ ə
ex|crete ɪk |'skriːt ek-, ək- ~**creted** 'skriːt ɪd
-əd ‖ 'skriːt̬ əd ~**cretes** 'skriːts ~**creting**
'skriːt ɪŋ ‖ 'skriːt̬ ɪŋ
excretion ɪk 'skriːʃ ᵊn ek-, ək-
excretive ɪk 'skriːt ɪv ek-, ək- ‖ -'skriːt̬ ɪv
excretory ɪk 'skriːt ər i ek-, ək-
‖ 'eks krə tɔːr i -toʊr i
excruciating ɪk 'skruːʃ i eɪt ɪŋ ek-, ək- ‖ -eɪt̬ ɪŋ
~**ly** li
exculp|ate 'eks kʌlp |eɪt ɪks 'kʌlp-, eks- ~**ated**
eɪt ɪd -əd ‖ eɪt̬ əd ~**ates** eɪts ~**ating** eɪt ɪŋ
‖ eɪt̬ ɪŋ
exculpation ˌeks kʌl 'peɪʃ ᵊn ~**s** z

excursion ɪk 'skɜːʃ ᵊn ek-, ək-, -'skɜːʒ-
‖ -'skɜːʒ ᵊn ~**s** z
ex'cursion train
excursive ɪk 'skɜːs ɪv ek-, ək-, §-'skɜːz-
‖ -'skɜːs- ~**ly** li ~**ness** nəs nɪs
excursus ek 'skɜːs əs ɪk- ‖ -'skɜːs- ~**es** ɪz əz
excusab|le ɪk 'skjuːz əb |ᵊl ek-, ək- ~**ly** li
excusatory ɪk 'skjuːz ət ˌər i ek-, ək-;
ˌeks kju: 'zeɪt ər i ‖ -'skjuːz ə tɔːr i -toʊr i
excus|e v ɪk 'skjuːz ek-, ək- ~**ed** d ~**er/s** ə/z
‖ ᵊr/z ~**es** ɪz əz ~**ing** ɪŋ
excus|e n ɪk 'skjuːs ek-, ək- (!) ~**es** ɪz əz
excuse-me ɪk 'skjuːz mi ek-, ək-, -mi: ~**s**, ~'**s** z
ex-directory ˌeks də 'rekt ər ˌi ˌ-dɪ-, ˌ-daɪ-
Exe eks
exeat 'eks i æt -eɪ- ~**s** s
exec ɪg 'zek eg-, əg-, ɪk-, ek-, ək- ~**s** s
execrab|le 'eks ɪk rəb |ᵊl '-ək- ~**ly** li
exe|crate 'eks ɪ |kreɪt -ə- ~**crated** kreɪt ɪd -əd
‖ kreɪt̬ əd ~**crates** kreɪts ~**crating** kreɪt ɪŋ
‖ kreɪt̬ ɪŋ
execration ˌeks ɪ 'kreɪʃ ᵊn -ə- ~**s** z
executable 'eks ɪ kjuːt əb ᵊl ‖ -kjuːt̬ əb ᵊl
executant ɪg 'zek jʊt ənt eg-, əg-, ɪk-, ek-, ək-,
-jət-, §-ət- ‖ -jət ᵊnt -ət- ~**s** s
exe|cute 'eks ɪ |kjuːt -ə- ~**cuted** kjuːt ɪd -əd
‖ 'kjuːt̬ əd ~**cutes** kjuːts ~**cuting** kjuːt ɪŋ
‖ kjuːt̬ ɪŋ
execution ˌeks ɪ 'kjuːʃ ᵊn -ə- ~**s** z
executioner ˌeks ɪ 'kjuːʃ ᵊn ə ˌ-ə- ‖ ᵊr ~**s** z
executive ɪg 'zek jʊt ɪv eg-, əg-, ɪk-, ek-, ək-,
-jət-, §-ət- ‖ -jət̬ ɪv -ət̬- ~**s** z
e,xecutive 'officer
executor ɪg 'zek jʊt ə eg-, əg-, ɪk-, ek-, ək-,
-jət-, §-ət- ‖ -jət̬ ᵊr -ət̬ ᵊr —but in the sense
'performer' also 'eks ɪ kjuːt ə ‖ -kjuːt̬ ᵊr ~**s** z
executrix ɪg 'zek ju trɪks eg-, əg-, ɪk-, ek-, ək-
‖ -jə- -ə-
exeges|is ˌeks ɪ 'dʒiːs ‖ɪs -ə-, §-əs ~**es** iːz
exegete 'eks ɪ dʒiːt -ə- ~**s** s
exegetic ˌeks ɪ 'dʒet ɪk ◂ -ə- ‖ -'dʒet̬- ~**al** ᵊl ~**s**
s
exemplar ɪg 'zemp lɑː eg-, əg-, ɪk-, ek-, ək-, -lə
‖ -lɑːr -lᵊr ~**s** z
exemplary ɪg 'zemp lər i eg-, əg-, ɪk-, ek-, ək-
exemplification ɪg ˌzemp lɪf ɪ 'keɪʃ ᵊn eg-,
əg-, ɪk-, ek-, ək-, -ˌləf-, §-ə'- ~**s** z
exempli|fy ɪg 'zemp lɪ |faɪ eg-, əg-, ɪk-, ek-,
ək-, -lə- ~**fied** faɪd ~**fier/s** faɪ ə/z ‖ faɪ ᵊr/z
~**fies** faɪz ~**fying** faɪ ɪŋ
exempli gratia eg ˌzemp li: 'grɑːt i ɑː ɪg-,
əg-; -laɪ 'greɪʃ i ə, -eɪ
exempt adj, v ɪg 'zempt eg-, əg-, ɪk-, ek-, ək-
~**ed** ɪd əd ~**ing** ɪŋ ~**s** s
exemption ɪg 'zempʃᵊn eg-, əg-, ɪk-, ek-, ək-
~**s** z
exequatur ˌeks ɪ 'kweɪt ə -ə- ‖ -'kweɪt̬ ᵊr ~**s** z
exequies 'eks ɪk wiz -ək-
exercis|e n, v 'eks ə saɪz ‖ -ᵊr- ~**ed** d ~**er/s** ə/z
‖ ᵊr/z ~**es** ɪz əz ~**ing** ɪŋ
'exercise bike; 'exercise book
exergue ek 'sɜːg 'eks ɜːg ‖ 'eks ɜːg 'egz- ~**s** z

ex|ert ɪg |ˈzɜːt eg-, əg-, ɪk-, ek-, ək- ‖ -|ˈzɜːt
~**erted** ˈzɜːt ɪd -əd ‖ ˈzɜːtʃ əd ~**erting** ˈzɜːt ɪŋ
‖ ˈzɜːtʃ ɪŋ ~**erts** ˈzɜːts ‖ ˈzɜːts
exertion ɪg ˈzɜːʃ ᵊn eg-, əg-, ɪk-, ek-, ək-
‖ -ˈzɜːʃ ᵊn ~**s** z
Exeter ˈeks ɪt ə -ət- ‖ -əṭ ᵊr
exeunt ˈeks i ʌnt -eɪ-, -ʊnt, -i ənt
ˌexeunt ˈomnes ˈɒm neɪz -niːz ‖ ˈɑːm- ˈɔːm-
exfoli|ate ₍ₗ₎eks ˈfəʊl i |eɪt ‖ -ˈfoʊl- ~**ated**
eɪt ɪd -əd ‖ eɪṭ əd ~**ates** eɪts ~**ating** eɪt ɪŋ
‖ eɪṭ ɪŋ
exfoliation ₍ₗ₎eks ˌfəʊl i ˈeɪʃ ᵊn ‖ -ˌfoʊl-
ex gratia ₍ₗ₎eks ˈgreɪʃ ə -ˈgreɪʃ i ə
exhalation ˌeks hə ˈleɪʃ ᵊn -ə- ~**s** z
exhalatory eks ˈheɪl ət ᵊr i ɪks-, əks-, -ˈhæl-
‖ -ə tɔːr i -toʊr i
exhal|e eks ˈher ᵊl ɪks-, əks-; eg ˈzer ᵊl, ɪg-, əg-
~**ed** d ~**es** z ~**ing** ɪŋ
exhaust v ɪg ˈzɔːst eg-, əg-, ɪk-, ek-, ək- ‖ -ˈzɑːst
~**ed** ɪd əd ~**ing** ɪŋ ~**s** s
exhaust n ɪg ˈzɔːst eg-, əg-, ɪk-, ek-, ək-,
§ˈeg zɔːst ‖ -ˈzɑːst ~**s** s
ex'**haust pipe**
exhaustion ɪg ˈzɔːs tʃən eg-, əg-, ɪk-, ek-, ək-
‖ -ˈzɑːs-
exhaustive ɪg ˈzɔːst ɪv eg-, əg-, ɪk-, ek-, ək-
‖ -ˈzɑːst- ~**ly** li ~**ness** nəs nɪs
exhib|it v ɪg ˈzɪb |ɪt eg-, əg-, ɪk-, ek-, ək-, §-ət
‖ -|ət ~**ited** ɪt ɪd §ət-, -əd ‖ əṭ əd ~**iting** ɪt ɪŋ
§ət- ‖ əṭ ɪŋ ~**its** ɪts §əts ‖ əts
exhibit n ɪg ˈzɪb ɪt eg-, əg-, ɪk-, ek-, ək-, §-ət;
ˈeks ɪb-, -əb- ~**s** s
exhibition ˌeks ɪ ˈbɪʃ ᵊn -ə- ~**s** z
exhibitioner ˌeks ɪ ˈbɪʃ ᵊn‿ə ‿ə- ‖ ᵊr ~**s** z
exhibitionism ˌeks ɪ ˈbɪʃ ᵊn ‿ɪz əm ‿ə-
exhibitionist ˌeks ɪ ˈbɪʃ ᵊn‿ɪst ‿ə-, §‿əst ~**s** s
exhibitionistic ˌeks ɪ ˌbɪʃ ə ˈnɪst ɪk ‿ə- ~**ally**
ᵊl i
exhibitor ɪg ˈzɪb ɪt ə eg-, əg-, §-ət- ‖ -əṭ ᵊr ~**s** z
exhila|rate ɪg ˈzɪl ə |reɪt eg-, əg-, ɪk-, ek-, ək-,
ek ˈsɪl- ~**rated** reɪt ɪd -əd ‖ reɪṭ əd ~**rates**
reɪts ~**rating/ly** reɪt ɪŋ /li ‖ reɪṭ ɪŋ /li
exhilaration ɪg ˌzɪl ə ˈreɪʃ ᵊn eg-, ɪk-, ek-,
ək-, ek ˌsɪl- ~**s** z
ex|hort ɪg |ˈzɔːt eg-, əg-, ɪk-, ek-, ək- ‖ -|ˈzɔːrt
~**horted** ˈzɔːt ɪd -əd ‖ ˈzɔːrṭ əd ~**horting**
ˈzɔːt ɪŋ ‖ ˈzɔːrṭ ɪŋ ~**horts** ˈzɔːts ‖ ˈzɔːrts
exhortation ˌegz ɔː ˈteɪʃ ᵊn ˌeks- ‖ -ɔːr- -ᵊr- ~**s**
z
exhortative ɪg ˈzɔːt ət ɪv eg-, əg-, ɪk-, ek-, ək-
‖ -ˈzɔːrṭ əṭ ɪv
exhortatory ɪg ˈzɔːt ət‿ər i eg-, əg-, ɪk-, ek-,
ək- ‖ -ˈzɔːrṭ ə tɔːr i -toʊr i
exhumation ˌeks hju ˈmeɪʃ ᵊn -ju- ‖ ˌegz ju- ~**s**
z
exhum|e eks ˈhjuːm ɪg ˈzjuːm, eg-, əg-, ɪk-, ek-,
ək-, -ˈzuːm ‖ ɪg ˈzuːm -ˈzjuːm, eks ˈhjuːm ~**ed**
d ~**es** z ~**ing** ɪŋ
ex hypothesi ˌeks haɪ ˈpɒθ ə saɪ -əs i
‖ -ˈpɑːθ-
Exide tdmk ˈeks aɪd
exigenc|e ˈeks ɪdʒ ənᵗs ˈegz-, -ədʒ- ~**es** ɪz əz

exigenc|y ˈeks ɪdʒ ənᵗs |i ˈegz-, ˈ‿ədʒ-;
ɪg ˈzɪdʒ-, eg-, əg-, ɪk-, ek-, ək- ~**ies** iz
exigent ˈeks ɪdʒ ənt ˈegz-, -ədʒ- ~**ly** li
exiguity ˌeks ɪ ˈgjuː‿ət i ɪt i ‖ ˌegz ɪ ˈgjuː əṭ i
exiguous ɪg ˈzɪg ju‿əs eg-, əg-, ɪk-, ek-, ək-;
ek ˈsɪg-, ɪk-, ək- ~**ly** li ~**ness** nəs nɪs
exil|e n, v ˈeks aɪ ᵊl ˈegz- ~**ed** d ~**es** z ~**ing** ɪŋ
exist ɪg ˈzɪst eg-, əg-, ɪk-, ek-, ək- ~**ed** ɪd əd
~**ing** ɪŋ ~**s** s
existence ɪg ˈzɪst ənᵗs eg-, əg-, ɪk-, ek-, ək-
existent ɪg ˈzɪst ənt eg-, əg-, ɪk-, ek-, ək-
existential ˌegz ɪ ˈstenᵗʃ ᵊl ◂ ˌeks-, -ə- ~**ism**
ˌɪz əm ~**ist/s** ɪst/s §əst/s ~**ly** i

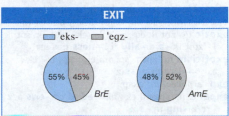

EXIT

□ ˈeks- □ ˈegz-

55% 45% *BrE*
48% 52% *AmE*

ex|it ˈeks |ɪt ˈegz, §-ət ‖ -|ət — *Preference
polls, BrE:* ˈeks- *55%,* ˈegz- *45%; AmE:* ˈeks-
48%, ˈegz- *52%.* ~**ited** ɪt ɪd §ət-, -əd ‖ əṭ əd
~**iting** ɪt ɪŋ §ət- ‖ əṭ ɪŋ ~**its** ɪts §əts ‖ əts
ˈexit poll
Ex-lax tdmk ˈeks læks
ex libris ˌeks ˈliːb rɪs -ˈlaɪb-, -riːs, §-rəs
Exmoor ˈeks mʊə -mɔː ‖ -mʊr
ˌExmoor ˈpony
Exmouth ˈeks məθ -maʊθ
exo- *comb. form*
with stress-neutral suffix |eks əʊ ‖ |eks oʊ
— **exosphere** ˈeks əʊ sfɪə ‖ -oʊ sfɪr
with stress-imposing suffix ek ˈsɒ +
‖ ek ˈsɑː + — **exogenous** ek ˈsɒdʒ ən əs -ɪn-
‖ -ˈsɑːdʒ-
exocentric ˌeks əʊ ˈsentr ɪk ◂ ‖ -oʊ- ~**ally** ᵊl i
Exocet tdmk ˈeks əʊ set ‖ -oʊ- ~**s** s
exocrine ˈeks əʊ kraɪn -krɪn, §-ək rən
‖ -ək rən
exodus, E~ ˈeks əd əs §ˈegz- ~**es** ɪz əz
ex-officio, ex officio ˌeks ə ˈfɪʃ i əʊ ◂ ˌ‿ɒ-,
-ˈfɪs- ‖ -oʊ
exogamous ek ˈsɒg əm əs ‖ -ˈsɑːg- ~**ly** li
exogamy ek ˈsɒg əm i ‖ -ˈsɑːg-
exogenous ek ˈsɒdʒ ən əs ɪk-, -ɪn- ‖ -ˈsɑːdʒ-
~**ly** li
exon ˈeks ɒn ‖ -ɑːn ~**s** z
exone|rate ɪg ˈzɒn ə |reɪt eg-, əg-, ɪk-, ek-, ək-
‖ -ˈzɑːn- ~**rated** reɪt ɪd -əd ‖ reɪṭ əd ~**rates**
reɪts ~**rating** reɪt ɪŋ ‖ reɪṭ ɪŋ
exoneration ɪg ˌzɒn ə ˈreɪʃ ᵊn eg-, əg-, ɪk-,
ek-, ək- ‖ -ˌzɑːn- ~**s** z
exonym ˈeks əʊ nɪm ‖ -ə- ~**s** z
exophora ek ˈsɒf ər ə ‖ -ˈsɑːf-
exophoric ˌeks əʊ ˈfɒr ɪk ◂ ‖ -ə ˈfɔːr- -ˈfɑːr-
exophthalm|ic ˌeks ɒf ˈθælm |ɪk ◂ -əf-, -ɒp-
‖ -ɑːf- -əf-, -ɑːp- ~**os** əs ɒs ‖ ɑːs
ˌexophˌthalmic ˈgoitre

E

exorbitance ɪg 'zɔːb ɪt ən's eg-, əg-, ɪk-, ek-, ək-, -ət- ‖ -'zɔːrb ət ən's

exorbitant ɪg 'zɔːb ɪt ənt eg-, əg-, ɪk-, ek-, ək-, -ət- ‖ -'zɔːrb ət ənt **~ly** li

exorcis... —*see* **exorciz...**

exorcism 'eks ɔː ˌsɪz əm 'egz-, -ə- ‖ -ɔːr- -ʰr- **~s** z

exorcist 'eks ɔːs ɪst 'egz-, -əs-, §-əst ‖ -ɔːrs--ʰrs- **~s** s

exorciz|e 'eks ɔːs aɪz 'egz-, -ə saɪz ‖ -ɔːrs aɪz -ʰr saɪz **~ed** d **~es** ɪz əz **~ing** ɪŋ

exordi|um ek 'sɔːd i ˌəm eg 'zɔːd- ‖ eg 'zɔːrd- **~a** ə **~ums** əmz

exoskeleton 'eks əʊ ˌskel ɪt ʰn -ət- ‖ -'oʊ- **~s** z

exothermic ˌeks əʊ 'θɜːm ɪk ◂ ‖ -oʊ 'θɜːm-

exotic ɪg 'zɒt ɪk eg-, əg-, ɪk-, ek-, ək-; ek 'sɒt ɪk ‖ -'zɑːt̬ ɪk **~a** ə **~ally** ʰl ̩i **~ness** nəs nɪs

exoticism ɪg 'zɒt ɪ ˌsɪz əm eg-, əg-, ɪk-, ek-, ək-, -ə- ‖ -'zɑːt̬ ə- **~s** z

exp *'exponential'* eksp

expand ɪk 'spænd ek-, ək- **~ed** ɪd əd **~er/s** ə/z ‖ ʰr/z **~ing** ɪŋ **~s** z

expans|e ɪk 'spæn's ek-, ək- **~es** ɪz əz

expansibility ɪk ˌspæn's ə 'bɪl ət i -ˌ·ɪ-, -ɪt i ‖ -ət̬ i

expansible ɪk 'spæn's əb ʰl ek-, ək-, -ɪb-

expansion ɪk 'spæn'ʃ ʰn ek-, ək- **~s** z
ex'pansion bolt

expansionary ɪk 'spæn'ʃ ən ˌʰr i ek-, ək- ‖ -ə ner i

expansion|ism ɪk 'spæn'ʃ ʰn| ˌɪz əm ek-, ək- **~ist/s** ɪst/s §əst/s

expansive ɪk 'spæn's ɪv ek-, ək- **~ly** li **~ness** nəs nɪs

ex parte ˌeks 'pɑːt i -eɪ ‖ -'pɑːrt̬ i

expat, ex-pat ˌeks 'pæt ◂ **~s** s

expati|ate ek 'speɪʃ i |eɪt ◂, əks- **~ated** eɪt ɪd -əd ‖ eɪt̬ əd **~ates** eɪts **~ating** eɪt ɪŋ ‖ eɪt̬ ɪŋ

expatri|ate *v* ⁽ᵢ⁾eks 'pætr i |eɪt ɪks-, -'peɪtr- ‖ -'peɪtr- **~ated** eɪt ɪd -əd ‖ eɪt̬ əd **~ates** eɪts **~ating** eɪt ɪŋ ‖ eɪt̬ ɪŋ

expatriate *n, adj* ⁽ᵢ⁾eks 'pætr i ˌət ɪks-, -'peɪtr-, ɪt, -eɪt ‖ -'peɪtr- **~s** s

expatriation eks ˌpætr i 'eɪʃ ʰn ɪks-, -ˌpeɪtr-, ˌeks ˌpeɪtr- ‖ -ˌpeɪtr-

expect ɪk 'spekt ⁽ᵢ⁾ek-, ək- **~ed** ɪd əd **~ing** ɪŋ **~s** s

expectanc|e ɪk 'spekt ən's ek-, ək- **~es** ɪz əz **~ies** iz **~y** i

expectant ɪk 'spekt ənt ek-, ək- **~ly** li

expectation ˌeks pek 'teɪʃ ʰn **~s** z

expectorant ɪk 'spekt ər ənt ek-, ək- **~s** s

expecto|rate ɪk 'spekt ə |reɪt ek-, ək- **~rated** reɪt ɪd -əd ‖ reɪt̬ əd **~rates** reɪts **~rating** reɪt ɪŋ ‖ reɪt̬ ɪŋ

expectoration ɪk ˌspekt ə 'reɪʃ ʰn ek-, ək- **~s** z

Expedia *tdmk* ɪk 'spiːd i ə ek-, ək-

expedienc|e ɪk 'spiːd i ən's ek-, ək- **~es** ɪz əz **~ies** iz **~y** i

expedient ɪk 'spiːd i ənt ek-, ək- **~ly** li

expe|dite 'eks pə |daɪt -pɪ- **~dited** daɪt ɪd -əd ‖ daɪt̬ əd **~diter/s** daɪt ə/z ‖ daɪt̬ ʰr/z **~dites** daɪts **~diting** daɪt ɪŋ ‖ daɪt̬ ɪŋ

expedition ˌeks pə 'dɪʃ ʰn -pɪ- **~s** z

expeditionary ˌeks pə 'dɪʃ ʰn ər ̩i ◂ ˌ·pɪ-, -ʰn ˌər i ‖ -ə ner i

expeditious ˌeks pə 'dɪʃ əs ◂ -pɪ- **~ly** li **~ness** nəs nɪs

expel ɪk 'spel ek-, ək- **~led** d **~ling** ɪŋ **~s** z

expellee ˌeks pe 'liː ɪk ˌspel 'iː, ek-, ək- **~s** z

expend ɪk 'spend ek-, ək- **~ed** ɪd əd **~ing** ɪŋ **~s** z

expendab|le ɪk 'spend əb| ʰl ek-, ək- **~ly** li

expenditure ɪk 'spend ɪtʃ ə ek-, ək- ‖ -ʰr -ə tʃʊr **~s** z

expens|e ɪk 'spen's ek-, ək- **~es** ɪz əz
ex'pense acˌcount

expensive ɪk 'spen's ɪv ek-, ək- **~ly** li **~ness** nəs nɪs

experienc|e *n, v* ɪk 'spɪər i ən's ek-, ək- ‖ -'spɪr- **~ed** t **~es** ɪz əz **~ing** ɪŋ

experiential ɪk ˌspɪər i 'en'ʃ ʰl ◂ ek-, ək-, ˌ·spɪr- **~ly** i

experi|ment *v* ɪk 'sper ɪ |ment ek-, ək-, -ə- ‖ -'spɪr- —*See note at* -ment **~mented** ment ɪd -əd ‖ men̬t əd **~menting** ment ɪŋ ‖ men̬t ɪŋ **~ments** men̬ts

experiment *n* ɪk 'sper ɪ mənt ek-, ək-, -ə- ‖ -'spɪr- **~s** s

experimental ɪk ˌsper ɪ 'ment ʰl ◂ ⁽ᵢ⁾ek-, ək-, -ə- ‖ -'men̬t ʰl ◂ -ˌspɪr- **~ism** ˌɪz əm **~ist/s** ɪst/s §əst/s **~ly** i

experimentation ɪk ˌsper ɪ men 'teɪʃ ʰn ek-, ək-, -ˌ·ə-, -mən'·- ‖ -ˌspɪr- **~s** z

expert 'eks pɜːt ˌek 'spɜːt, ɪk-, ək- ‖ 'eks pɜːt ɪk 'spɜːt **~ly** li **~ness** nəs nɪs **~s** s
ˌexpert 'system

expertis|e, expertiz|e *v* 'eks pə taɪz -pɜːt aɪz ‖ -pʰr- **~ed** d **~es** ɪz əz **~ing** ɪŋ

expertise *n* ˌeks pɜː 'tiːz -pə-, '··· ‖ -pʰr 'tiːz -'tiːs

expiable 'eks pi əb ʰl

expi|ate 'eks pi |eɪt **~ated** eɪt ɪd -əd ‖ eɪt̬ əd **~ates** eɪts **~ating** eɪt ɪŋ ‖ eɪt̬ ɪŋ

expiation ˌeks pi 'eɪʃ ʰn **~s** z

expiatory 'eks pi ˌət ər i -eɪt ər i, ˌeks pi 'eɪt ər i ‖ ə tɔːr i -tour i

expiration ˌeks pə 'reɪʃ ʰn -pɪ-, -paɪ³- **~s** z

expiratory ɪk 'spaɪ³r ət ər i ⁽ᵢ⁾ek-, ək-, -'spɪr- ‖ -ə tɔːr i -tour i

expir|e ɪk 'spaɪ³ ⁽ᵢ⁾ek-, ək- ‖ ɪk 'spaɪ³r **~ed** d **~es** z **~ing** ɪŋ

expir|y ɪk 'spaɪ³r |i ek-, ək- ‖ ɪk 'spaɪ³r |i 'eks pər |i **~ies** iz
ex'piry date

explain ɪk 'spleɪn ek-, ək- **~ed** d **~ing** ɪŋ **~s** z

explainable ɪk 'spleɪn əb ʰl ek-, ək-

explanation ˌeks plə 'neɪʃ ʰn **~s** z

explanator|y ɪk 'splæn ət ər |i ek-, ək- ‖ -ə tɔːr |i -tour i **~ily** əl ɪ i li

expletive ɪk 'spliːt ɪv ek-, ək-; 'eks plət- ‖ 'eks plət̬ ɪv **~s** z

explicable ɪk 'splɪk əb ʰl ek-, ək-; 'eks plɪk-

expli|cate 'eks plı |keıt -plə- **~cated** keıt ıd
-əd ‖ keıt̮ əd **~cates** keıts **~cating** keıt ıŋ
‖ keıt̮ ıŋ

explication ˌeks plı 'keıʃ ᵊn -plə- —*also as a*
French word, Fr [ɛks pli ka sjɔ̃] **~s** z

explicative ek 'splık ət ıv ık-, ək-; 'eks plık-
‖ -ət̮ ıv

explicatory ek 'splık ət̮ ər i ık-, ək-;
ˌeks plı 'keıt ər i ◂ ‖ -ə tɔːr i 'eks plık-,
-ə toʊr i

explicature ek 'splık ətʃ ə ık-, ək-, -ə tjʊə ‖ -ᵊr
~s z

explicit ık 'splıs ıt ek-, ək-, §-ət —*For contrast*
with implicit, *also* ˌeks 'plıs-, '·ˌ·-- **~ly** li **~ness**
nəs nıs

explod|e ık 'spləʊd ek-, ək- ‖ -'sploʊd **~ed** ıd
əd **~er/s** ə/z ‖ ᵊr/z **~es** z **~ing** ıŋ

exploit *n* 'eks plɔıt **~s** s

ex|ploit *v* ık ‖'splɔıt ₍ᵢ₎ek-, ək- **~ploited**
'plɔıt ıd -əd ‖ 'plɔıt̮ əd **~ploiting** 'plɔıt ıŋ
‖ 'plɔıt̮ ıŋ **~ploits** 'plɔıts

exploitable ık 'splɔıt əb ᵊl ₍ᵢ₎ek-, ək-
‖ -'splɔıt̮-

exploitation ˌeks plɔı 'teıʃ ᵊn **~s** z

exploitative ık 'splɔıt ət ıv ₍ᵢ₎ek-, ək-
‖ -'splɔıt̮ ət̮ ıv **~ly** li

exploiter ık 'splɔıt ə ₍ᵢ₎eks-, əks- ‖ -'splɔıt̮ ᵊr
~s z

exploration ˌeks plə 'reıʃ ᵊn -plɔː- **~s** z

explorative ık 'splɒr ət ıv ek-, ək-, -'splɔːr-
‖ -'splɔːr ət̮ ıv -'sploʊr- **~ly** li

exploratory ık 'splɒr ət̮ ər i ek-, ək-, -'splɔːr-
‖ -'splɔːr ə tɔːr i -'sploʊr ə toʊr i

explore ık 'splɔː ek-, ək- ‖ -'splɔːr -'sploʊr **~d** d
~s z **exploring** ık 'splɔːr ıŋ ek-, ək-
‖ -'sploʊr-

explorer ık 'splɔːr ə ek-, ək- ‖ -'splɔːr ᵊr
-'sploʊr- **~s** z

explosion ık 'spləʊʒ ᵊn ek-, ək- ‖ -'sploʊʒ ᵊn
~s z

explosive ık 'spləʊs ıv ek-, ək-, -'spləʊz-
‖ -'sploʊs- **~ly** li **~ness** nəs nıs **~s** z

expo, Expo 'eks pəʊ ‖ -poʊ **~s** z

exponent ık 'spəʊn ənt ek-, ək- ‖ ık 'spoʊn-
'eks poʊn- **~s** s

exponential ˌeks pə 'nentʃ ᵊl ◂ -pəʊ- ‖ -poʊ-
~ly i
ˌexpoˌnential 'growth

exponenti|ate ˌeks pə 'nentʃ i |eıt -ˌpəʊ-
‖ -ˌpoʊ- **~ated** eıt ıd -əd ‖ eıt̮ əd **~ates** eıts
~ating eıt ıŋ ‖ eıt̮ ıŋ

exponentiation ˌeks pə ˌnentʃ i 'eıʃ ᵊn -ˌpəʊ-
‖ -ˌpoʊ- **~s** z

ex|port *v* ık ‖'spɔːt ek-, ək-; ˌeks 'pɔːt, '··
‖ ık 'spɔːrt ek-, -'spoʊrt; 'eks pɔːrt, -poʊrt
~ported 'spɔːt ıd -əd ‖ 'spɔːrt̮ əd -'spoʊrt̮-
~porting 'spɔːt ıŋ ‖ 'spɔːrt̮ ıŋ -'spoʊrt̮-
~ports 'spɔːts ‖ 'spɔːrts -'spoʊrts

export *n* 'eks pɔːt ‖ -pɔːrt -poʊrt **~s** s

exportable ık 'spɔːt əb ᵊl ek-, ək-; ˌeks 'pɔːt-,
'·-- ‖ ık 'spɔːrt̮ əb ᵊl ek-, -'spoʊrt̮-; 'eks pɔːrt̮-,
-poʊrt̮-

exportation ˌeks pɔː 'teıʃ ᵊn ‖ -pɔːr- -poʊr-,
-pᵊr- **~s** z

exporter ık 'spɔːt ə ek-, ək-; 'eks pɔːt ə
‖ -'spɔːrt̮ ᵊr -'spoʊrt̮-; 'eks pɔːrt̮- **~s** z

export-import ˌeks pɔːt 'ım pɔːt ◂
‖ ˌeks pɔːrt̮ 'ım pɔːrt ◂ -poʊrt ◂

expos|e *v* ık 'spəʊz ek-, ək- ‖ -'spoʊz **~ed** d
~es ız əz **~ing** ıŋ

exposé *n* ek 'spəʊz eı ık-, ək-; ˌeks poʊ 'zeı
—*Fr* [ɛk spo ze] **~s** z

exposition ˌeks pə 'zıʃ ᵊn **~s** z

expositor ık 'spɒz ət ə ek-, ək-, -ıt-
‖ -'spɑːz ət̮ ᵊr **~s** z

expository ık 'spɒz ət̮ ər i ek-, ək-, -'·ıt̮
‖ -'spɑːz ə tɔːr i -toʊr i

ex post facto ˌeks ˌpəʊst 'fækt əʊ ·ˌ·--
‖ -ˌpoʊst 'fækt oʊ

expostu|late ık 'spɒs tʃu |leıt ek-, ək-, -tju-
‖ -'spɑːs tʃə- **~lated** leıt ıd -əd ‖ leıt̮ əd
~lates leıts **~lating** leıt ıŋ ‖ leıt̮ ıŋ

expostulation ık ˌspɒs tʃu 'leıʃ ᵊn ek-, ək-,
-tju- ‖ -ˌspɑːs tʃə- **~s** z

exposure ık 'spəʊʒ ə ek-, ək- ‖ -'spoʊʒ ᵊr
—*There is also an occasional very careful form*
-'spəʊz jə ‖ -'spoʊz jᵊr **~s** z
ex'posure ˌmeter

expound ık 'spaʊnd ek-, ək- **~ed** ıd əd **~ing** ıŋ
~s z

express ık 'spres ek-, ək- —*In a stress-shifting*
environment the adj or n is sometimes
ˌeks pres, *as if underlyingly* ˌeks 'pres ◂ꞏ
ˌExpress 'Dairies. *There is usually no*
stress-shifting in the v: to exˌpress 'sympathy
~ed t **~es** ız əz **~ing** ıŋ **~ly** li

expressible ık 'spres əb ᵊl -ıb-

expression ık 'spreʃ ᵊn ek-, ək- **~ism** ˌız əm
~ist/s ıst/s §əst/s **~s** z

expressionistic ık ˌspreʃ ə 'nıst ık ◂ ek-, ək-,
→-ᵊn 'ıst- **~ally** ᵊl i

expressionless ık 'spreʃ ᵊn ləs ek-, ək-, -lıs
~ly li **~ness** nəs nıs

expressive ık 'spres ıv ek-, ək- **~ly** li **~ness**
nəs nıs

expressivity ˌeks pre 'sıv ət i -ıt i ‖ -ət̮ i

expressway ık 'spres weı ek-, ək- **~s** z

expropri|ate ık 'sprəʊp ri |eıt ₍ᵢ₎ek-, ək-
‖ -'sproʊp- **~ated** eıt ıd -əd ‖ eıt̮ əd **~ates**
eıts **~ating** eıt ıŋ ‖ eıt̮ ıŋ

expropriation ık ˌsprəʊp ri 'eıʃ ᵊn ek-, ək-,
ˌeks ˌprəʊp- ‖ -ˌsproʊp- **~s** z

expulsion ık 'spʌlʃ ᵊn ek-, ək- **~s** z

expung|e ık 'spʌndʒ ₍ᵢ₎ek-, ək- **~ed** d **~es** ız
əz **~ing** ıŋ

expur|gate 'eks pə |geıt -pɜː- ‖ -pᵊr- **~gated**
geıt ıd -əd ‖ geıt̮ əd **~gates** geıts **~gating**
geıt ıŋ ‖ geıt̮ ıŋ

expurgation ˌeks pə 'geıʃ ᵊn -pɜː- ‖ -pᵊr- **~s** z

expurgatory ek 'spɜːg ət̮ ər i ‖ -ə tɔːr i -toʊr i

EXQUISITE

69% · 31% BrE
76% · 24% AmE

■ ·'·· ■ '···

-●- BrE stress on second syllable, by age
-●- AmE stress on second syllable, by age

Percentage (100, 80, 60, 40, 20, 0)

Older ◄— Speakers —► Younger

exquisite ɪk 'skwɪz ɪt ek-, ək-, 'eks kwɪz-, -ət
— *Preference polls, BrE:* ·'·· 69%, '··· 31%;
AmE: ·'·· 76%, '··· 24%. **~ly** li **~ness** nəs nɪs
ex-service ˌeks 'sɜːv ɪs ◄ ˌek-, §-əs ‖ -'sɜːv əs
ex-service|man ˌeks 'sɜːv ɪs |mən ˌek-, -əs-
‖ -'sɜːv- **~men** mən men **~woman** ˌwʊm ən
~women ˌwɪm ɪn §-ən
extant ₍ᵢ₎ek 'stænt ɪk-, ək-; 'ekst ənt
Extel *tdmk* 'eks tel
extemporaneous ɪk ˌstemp ə 'reɪn i_əs ◄
₍ᵢ₎ek-, ək- **~ly** li **~ness** nəs nɪs
extempore ɪk 'stemp ər i ₍ᵢ₎ek-, ək-
extemporis... —*see* **extemporiz...**
extemporization ɪk ˌstemp ər aɪ 'zeɪʃ ᵊn ek-,
ək-, -ər ɪ- ‖ -ər ə- **~s** z
extemporiz|e ɪk 'stemp ə raɪz ek-, ək- **~ed** d
~es ɪz əz **~ing** ɪŋ
extend ɪk 'stend ek-, ək- **~ed** ɪd əd **~ing** ɪŋ **~s**
z
   ex‚tended 'family
extender ɪk 'stend ə ek-, ək- ‖ -ᵊr **~s** z
extensibility ɪk ˌstenᵗs ə 'bɪl ət i -ˌɪ-, -ɪt i
‖ -əţ i
extensible ɪk 'stenᵗs əb ᵊl ek-, ək-, -ɪb-
extension ɪk 'stenᵗʃ ᵊn ek-, ək- **~s** z
extensional ɪk 'stenᵗʃ ᵊn_əl ek-, ək-
extensionality ɪk ˌstenᵗʃ ə 'næl ət i ek-, ək-,
-ɪt i ‖ -əţ i
extensive ɪk 'stenᵗs ɪv ek-, ək- **~ly** li **~ness**
nəs nɪs
extensor ɪk 'stenᵗs ə ek-, ək-, -ɔː ‖ -ᵊr **~s** z
extent ɪk 'stent ek-, ək- **~s** s
extenu|ate ɪk 'sten ju |eɪt ek-, ək- **~ated**
eɪt ɪd -əd ‖ eɪţ əd **~ates** eɪts **~ating** eɪt ɪŋ
‖ eɪţ ɪŋ
extenuation ɪk ˌsten ju 'eɪʃ ᵊn ek-, ək- **~s** z
exterior ɪk 'stɪər i_ə ₍ᵢ₎ek-, ək- ‖ -'stɪr i_ᵊr **~ly**
li **~s** z
exterioris... —*see* **exterioriz...**
exteriority ɪk ˌstɪər i 'ɒr ət i ek-, ək-,
ˌekst ɪər-, -ɪt i ‖ -ˌstɪr i 'ɔːr əţ i -'ɑːr-

exteriorization ɪk ˌstɪər i_ər aɪ 'zeɪʃ ᵊn ek-,
ək-, ˌekst ɪər-, -ɪ'- ‖ -ˌstɪr i_ər ə- **~s** z
exterioriz|e ɪk 'stɪər i_ə raɪz ₍ᵢ₎ek-, ək- ‖ -'stɪr-
~ed d **~es** ɪz əz **~ing** ɪŋ
extermi|nate ɪk 'stɜːm ɪ |neɪt ek-, ək-, -ə-
‖ -'stɜːm- **~nated** neɪt ɪd -əd ‖ neɪţ əd
~nates neɪts **~nating** neɪt ɪŋ ‖ neɪţ ɪŋ
extermination ɪk ˌstɜːm ɪ 'neɪʃ ᵊn ek-, ək-, -ə-
‖ -ˌstɜːm- **~s** z
exterminator ɪk 'stɜːm ɪ neɪt ə ek-, ək-, -ˈə-
‖ -'stɜːm ə neɪţ ᵊr **~s** z
extern 'eks tɜːn ‖ -tɜːn **~s** z **~ship/s** ʃɪp/s
external ɪk 'stɜːn ᵊl ₍ᵢ₎ek-, ək- ‖ -'stɜːn ᵊl **~ly** i
~s z
externalis... —*see* **externaliz...**
externalit|y ˌekst ɜː 'næl ət i |i -ɪt i
‖ ˌekst ɜː 'næl əţ i |i **~ies** iz
externalization ɪk ˌstɜːn ᵊl aɪ 'zeɪʃ ᵊn ek-, ək-,
ekst ɜːn-, -ᵊl ɪ- ‖ -ˌstɜːn ᵊl ə- **~s** z
externaliz|e ɪk 'stɜːn ə laɪz ₍ᵢ₎ek-, ək-, -ᵊl aɪz
‖ -'stɜːn- **~ed** d **~es** ɪz əz **~ing** ɪŋ
exterritorial ˌeks ˌter ɪ 'tɔːr i_əl ◄ ‖ -'toʊr- **~ly**
i
extinct ɪk 'stɪŋkt ₍ᵢ₎ek-, ək-
extinction ɪk 'stɪŋk ʃᵊn ₍ᵢ₎ek-, ək- **~s** z
extinguish ɪk 'stɪŋ gwɪʃ ek-, ək-, §-wɪʃ **~ed** t
~er/s ə/z ‖ ᵊr/z **~es** ɪz əz **~ing** ɪŋ
extir|pate 'ekst ɜː |peɪt -ə- ‖ -ᵊr- **~pated**
peɪt ɪd -əd ‖ peɪţ əd **~pates** peɪts **~pating**
peɪt ɪŋ ‖ peɪţ ɪŋ
extirpation ˌekst ɜː 'peɪʃ ᵊn -ə- ‖ -ᵊr- **~s** z
extol, extol|l ɪk 'stəʊl ek-, ək-, →-'stɒʊl, -'stɒl
‖ -'stoʊl **~led** d **~ling** ɪŋ **~s** z
Exton 'ekst ən
ex|tort ɪk |'stɔːt ek-, ək- ‖ -|'stɔːrt **~started**
'stɔːt ɪd -əd ‖ 'stɔːrţ əd **~storting** 'stɔːt ɪŋ
‖ 'stɔːrţ ɪŋ **~storts** 'stɔːts ‖ 'stɔːrts
extortion ɪk 'stɔːʃ ᵊn ek-, ək- ‖ -'stɔːrʃ ᵊn **~s** z
extortionate ɪk 'stɔːʃ ᵊn_ət ek-, ək-, ɪt
‖ -'stɔːrʃ- **~ly** li
extortioner ɪk 'stɔːʃ ᵊn_ə ek-, ək-
‖ -'stɔːrʃ ᵊn_ər **~s** z
extortionist ɪk 'stɔːʃ ᵊn_ɪst ek-, ək-, §_əst
‖ -'stɔːrʃ- **~s** s
extra 'eks trə **~s** z
   ˌextra 'cover
extra- *comb. form*
  with stress-neutral suffix |eks trə —
  extracanonical ˌeks trə kə 'nɒn ɪk ᵊl ◄
  ‖ -'nɑːn-
  with stress-imposing suffix ɪk 'stræ+ ek-, ək-
  — **extrapolate** ɪk 'stræp ə leɪt ek-, ək-
extracellular ˌeks trə 'sel jʊl ə ◄ -jəl·
‖ -jəl ᵊr ◄
extract *n* 'eks trækt **~s** s
extract *v* ɪk 'strækt ek-, ək- —*In AmE, in the
sense 'select and cite excerpts' also* 'eks trækt
~ed ɪd əd **~ing** ɪŋ **~s** s
extraction ɪk 'stræk ʃᵊn ek-, ək- **~s** z
extractive ɪk 'strækt ɪv ek-, ək-
extractor ɪk 'strækt ə ek-, ək- ‖ -ᵊr **~s** z
   ex'tractor fan

extracurricular ˌeks trə kə 'rɪk jʊl ə ◂ -jəl ə
‖ -jəl ᵊr

extraditable 'eks trə daɪt əb ᵊl ˌ·'··
‖ -daɪt̬ əb ᵊl

extra│dite 'eks trə │daɪt **~dited** daɪt ɪd -əd
‖ daɪt̬ əd **~dites** daɪts **~diting** daɪt ɪŋ
‖ daɪt̬ ɪŋ

extradition ˌeks trə 'dɪʃ ᵊn **~s** z

extrados *sing.* ek 'streɪd ɒs ‖ 'eks trə dɑːs **~es**
ɪz əz **extrados** *pl* ek 'streɪd əʊz
‖ 'eks trə dəʊz

extragalactic ˌek strə gə 'lækt ɪk ◂

extrajudicial ˌeks trə dʒu 'dɪʃ ᵊl ◂ **-ly** i

extramarital ˌeks trə 'mær ɪt ᵊl ◂ -ət ᵊl
‖ -ət̬ ᵊl ◂ -'mer- **-ly** i

extrametrical ˌeks trə 'metr ɪk ᵊl ◂

extramural ˌeks trə 'mjʊər əl ◂ -'mjɔːr-
‖ -'mjʊr əl **-ly** i

extraneous ɪk 'streɪn i ‿əs ek-, ək- **~ly** li **~ness**
nəs nɪs

extranet 'eks trə net

extraordinaire ɪk ˌstrɔːd ɪ 'neə ek-, ək-, -ə-,
-ᵊn ˌ'eə ‖ ɪk ˌstrɔːrd ᵊn 'eᵊr —*Fr*
[ɛk stʁa ɔʁ di nɛːʁ]

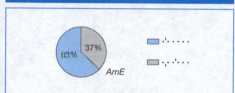

EXTRAORDINARILY

AmE

63% ·'····· 37% ˌ·ˌ·'··

extraordinarily ɪk 'strɔːd ᵊn ᵊr ‿əl i ek-, ək-,
-'·ɪn-, -ᵊn ˌər əl i, §-ˌstrɔːd ᵊn 'er əl i◂, -ɪ li;
ˌeks trə 'ɔːd ᵊn ᵊr ‿əl i◂, -ᵊn ˌər əl i, -ɪ li
‖ ɪk ˌstrɔːrd ᵊn 'er əl i ◂ ·'····· — *Preference
poll, AmE:* ·'····· *63%,* ˌ·ˌ·'·· *37% (figures
perhaps unreliable because of confusion over
possible stress shifting).*

extraordinary ɪk 'strɔːd ᵊn ər ‿i ek-, ək-, -'·ɪn-,
§-er i, -ᵊn ˌər i, ˌeks trə 'ɔːd ᵊn ər ‿i◂, -ᵊn ˌər-
‖ ɪk 'strɔːrd ᵊn er i ˌeks trə 'ɔːrd ᵊn er i◂

extrapo│late ɪk 'stræp ə │leɪt ek-, ək-, △-jə-
~lated leɪt ɪd -əd ‖ leɪt̬ əd **~lates** leɪts
~lating leɪt ɪŋ ‖ leɪt̬ ɪŋ

extrapolation ɪk ˌstræp ə 'leɪʃ ᵊn ek-, ək-,
△-jə- **~s** z

extrapos│e ˌeks trə 'pəʊz ‖ -'poʊz **~ed** d **~es**
ɪz əz **~ing** ɪŋ

extraposition ˌeks trə pə 'zɪʃ ᵊn **~s** z

extrasensory ˌeks trə 'sen̩s ər ‿i ◂
ˌextra ˌsensory per'ception

extra-special ˌeks trə 'speʃ ᵊl ◂ **-ly** ˌi

extraterrestrial ˌeks trə tə 'res tri ˌəl ◂ -tɪ'·-,
-te'·-, △-'res tʃəl

extraterritorial ˌeks trə ˌter ɪ 'tɔːr i ˌəl -ˌ·ə-
‖ -'toʊr- **-ly** i

extraterritoriality
ˌeks trə ˌter ɪ tɔːr i 'æl ət i -ˌ·ə-, -ɪt i ‖ -ət̬ i
-toʊr i'·-

extravaganc│e ɪk 'stræv əg ən̩s ek-, ək- **~es**
ɪz əz

extravagant ɪk 'stræv əg ənt ek-, ək- **-ly** li
~ness nəs nɪs

extravaganza ɪk ˌstræv ə 'gænz ə ₍ˌ₎ek-, ək-
~s z

extrava│sate ek 'stræv ə │seɪt ˌek-, ɪk-, ək-
~sated seɪt ɪd -əd ‖ seɪt̬ əd **~sates** seɪts
~sating seɪt ɪŋ ‖ seɪt̬ ɪŋ

extravasation ek ˌstræv ə 'seɪʃ ᵊn ɪk-, ək-,
ˌeks træv-, -'zeɪʃ- **~s** z

extraversion ˌeks trə 'vɜːʃ ᵊn -'vɜːʒ-
‖ -'vɜːʒ ᵊn

extra│vert 'eks trə │vɜːt ‖ -│vɜːt **~verted**
vɜːt ɪd -əd ‖ vɜːt̬ əd **~verts** 'vɜːts ‖ 'vɜːts

extreme ɪk 'striːm ek-, ək- —*In a
stress-shifting environment occasionally*
ˌeks triːm, *as if underlyingly* ˌek 'striːm ◂·
ˌextreme 'unction **-ly** li **~ness** nəs nɪs **~s** z

extremis ɪk 'striːm ɪs ek-, ək-

extremism ɪk 'striːm ˌɪz əm ek-, ək-

extremist ɪk 'striːm ɪst ek-, ək-, §-əst **~s** s

extremit│y ɪk 'strem ət ‖i ek-, ək-, -ɪt- ‖ -ət̬ ‖i
~ies iz

extricable ɪk 'strɪk əb ᵊl ek-, ək-, 'eks trɪk-

extri│cate 'eks trɪ │keɪt -trə- **~cated** keɪt ɪd -əd
‖ keɪt̬ əd **~cates** keɪts **~cating** keɪt ɪŋ
‖ keɪt̬ ɪŋ

extrication ˌeks trɪ 'keɪʃ ᵊn -trə-

extrinsic ₍ˌ₎eks 'trɪn̩s ɪk ɪks-, -'trɪnz- **-ally** ᵊl ˌi

extroversion ˌeks trə 'vɜːʃ ᵊn -'vɜːʒ-
‖ -'vɜːʒ ᵊn

extro│vert 'eks trəʊ │vɜːt ‖ -ə │vɜːt **~verted**
vɜːt ɪd -əd ‖ vɜːt̬ əd **~verts** 'vɜːts ‖ 'vɜːts

extrud│e ɪk 'struːd ek-, ək- **~ed** ɪd əd **~es** z
~ing ɪŋ

extrusion ɪk 'struːʒ ᵊn ek-, ək- **~s** z

exuberance ɪg 'zjuːb ᵊr ˌən̩s eg-, əg-, ɪk-, ek-,
ək-, -'zuːb- ‖ -'zuːb-

exuberant ɪg 'zjuːb ᵊr ənt eg-, əg-, ɪk-, ek-, ək-,
-'zuːb- ‖ -'zuːb- **-ly** li

exudation ˌeks ju 'deɪʃ ᵊn ˌegz-, -u-, ˌekʃ u-
~s z

exud│e ɪg 'zjuːd eg-, əg-, ɪk-, ek-, ək-, -'zuːd
‖ -'zuːd **~ed** ɪd əd **~es** z **~ing** ɪŋ

exult ɪg 'zʌlt eg-, əg-, ɪk-, ek-, ək- **~ed** ɪd əd
~ing ɪŋ **~s** s

exultant ɪg 'zʌlt ənt eg-, əg-, ɪk-, ek-, ək- **-ly** li

exultation ˌegz ʌl 'teɪʃ ᵊn ˌeks-, -ᵊl- **~s** z

Exuma ek 'suːm ə

exurb 'eks ɜːb 'egz- ‖ -ɜːb **~s** z

exurban ₍ˌ₎eks 'ɜːb ən ₍ˌ₎egz- ‖ ek 'sɜːb ən
eg 'zɜːb-

exurbanite ₍ˌ₎eks 'ɜːb ə naɪt ₍ˌ₎egz- ‖ ek 'sɜːb-
eg 'zɜːb- **~s** s

exurbia ₍ˌ₎eks 'ɜːb i ə ‖ ek 'sɜːb- eg 'zɜːb- **~s** z

exuvi│ae ɪg 'zjuːv i ˌ‖i eg-, əg-, ɪk-, ek-, ək-,
-'zuːv-, -aɪ ‖ -'zuːv- **~al** əl

Exxon *tdmk* 'eks ɒn ‖ -ɑːn

Eyam iːm *(!)*

Eyck aɪk

E

eye, Eye aɪ (= I) **eyed** aɪd **eyeing, eying**
  'aɪ ɪŋ **eyes** aɪz
  'eye ˌcontact; 'eye rhyme; 'eye ˌshadow
eyeball 'aɪ bɔːl ‖ -bɑːl **~ed** d **~ing** ɪŋ **~s** z
eyebath 'aɪ bɑːθ §-bæθ ‖ -bæθ **~s** s
eyebright 'aɪ braɪt **~s** s
eyebrow 'aɪ braʊ **~s** z
  'eyebrow ˌpencil
eye-catching 'aɪ ˌkætʃ ɪŋ △-,ketʃ- **~ly** li
eyecup 'aɪ kʌp **~s** s
-eyed 'aɪd — **brown-eyed** ˌbraʊn 'aɪd ◄
eyeful 'aɪ fʊl **~s** z
eyeglass 'aɪ glɑːs §-glæs ‖ -glæs **~es** ɪz əz
eyelash 'aɪ læʃ **~es** ɪz əz
eyeless 'aɪ ləs -lɪs
eyelet 'aɪ lət -lɪt **~s** s
eyelevel 'aɪ ˌlev ᵊl ˌ·'··
eyelid 'aɪ lɪd **~s** z
eyeliner 'aɪ ˌlaɪn ə ‖ -ᵊr **~s** z
eye-opener 'aɪ ˌəʊp ən ə ‖ -ˌoʊp ᵊn ər **~s** z
eyepatch 'aɪ pætʃ **~es** ɪz əz
eyepiec|e 'aɪ piːs **~es** ɪz əz
eye-popping 'aɪ ˌpɒp ɪŋ ‖ -ˌpɑːp-
eyeshade 'aɪ ʃeɪd **~s** z

eyeshot 'aɪ ʃɒt ‖ -ʃɑːt
eyesight 'aɪ saɪt
eyesore 'aɪ sɔː ‖ -sɔːr -soʊr **~s** z
eyestalk 'aɪ stɔːk -stɑːk **~s** s
eyestrain 'aɪ streɪn
eyeteeth 'aɪ tiːθ
Eyetie 'aɪ taɪ **~s** z
eye|tooth 'aɪ |tuːθ §-tʊθ, ˌ·'· **~teeth** tiːθ
eyewash 'aɪ wɒʃ ‖ -wɑːʃ -wɔːʃ
eyewear 'aɪ weə ‖ -wer -wær
eyewitness 'aɪ ˌwɪt nəs -nɪs, ˌ·'·· **~es** ɪz əz
eying 'aɪ ɪŋ
Eynon 'aɪn ən —*Welsh* ['əi non]
Eynsford 'eɪnz fəd ‖ -fᵊrd
Eynsham 'eɪn ʃəm —*but locally* 'en-
eyot eɪt 'eɪ ət, aɪt **eyots** eɪts 'eɪ əts, aɪts
Eyre, eyre eə ‖ eᵊr æᵊr
eyr|ie, eyr|y 'ɪər |i 'eər-, 'aɪᵊr- ‖ 'er |i 'ɪr-,
  'aɪᵊr- **~ies** iz
Eysenck 'aɪz eŋk
Eyton *(i)* 'iːt ᵊn, *(ii)* 'aɪt ᵊn, *(iii)* 'eɪt ᵊn
Ezekiel ɪ 'ziːk i əl ə-
e-zine 'iː ziːn **~s** z
Ezra 'ez rə

Ff

f Spelling-to-sound

1 Where the spelling is **f**, the pronunciation is regularly f as in **fifty** ˈfɪft i.

2 Where the spelling is double **ff**, the pronunciation is again f as in **stiff** stɪf.

3 Exceptionally, the word **of** is pronounced with v: **a piece of wood** ə ˌpiːs əv ˈwʊd.

4 **f** is silent in the old pronunciation of **halfpenny** ˈheɪp ni.

5 The sound f is also regularly written **ph** as in **photograph**, and occasionally **gh** as in **rough** rʌf.

F, f ef **Fs, fs, F's, f's** efs —*Communications code name:* Foxtrot
fa fɑː
FA ˌef ˈeɪ ◂
   ˌFA ˈCup
fab fæb
Faber ˈfeɪb ə ‖ -ᵊr
Fabergé ˈfæb ə ʒeɪ -dʒeɪ ‖ ˌfæb ᵊr ˈʒeɪ
Fabian ˈfeɪb iˌən ~s z
   ˈFabian Soˌciety
Fabius ˈfeɪb iˌəs
fable ˈfeɪb ᵊl ~d d ~s z
fabliau ˈfæb li əʊ ‖ -oʊ ~x z —*Fr* [fab li jo]
Fablon *tdmk* ˈfæb lɒn -lən ‖ -lɑːn
fabric ˈfæb rɪk ~s s
fabri|cate ˈfæb rɪ |keɪt -rə- **~cated** keɪt ɪd -əd ‖ keɪt əd **~cates** keɪts **~cating** keɪt ɪŋ ‖ keɪt ɪŋ
fabrication ˌfæb rɪ ˈkeɪʃ ᵊn -rə- ~s z
fabricator ˈfæb rɪ keɪt ə ˈ·rə- ‖ -keɪt ᵊr ~s z
fabulist ˈfæb jʊl ɪst -jəl-, §-əst ‖ -jəl- ~s s
fabulous ˈfæb jʊl əs -jəl- ‖ -jəl- **~ly** li **~ness** nəs nɪs
facade, façade fə ˈsɑːd fæ-; ˈfæs ɑːd ~s z
face feɪs **faced** feɪst **faces** ˈfeɪs ɪz -əz **facing/s** ˈfeɪs ɪŋ/z
   ˈface card; ˈface ˌflannel; ˈface pack; ˈface ˌpowder; ˌface ˈvalue, ˈ· ˌ· ·
face-ache ˈfeɪs eɪk ~s s
Facebook ˈfeɪs bʊk §-buːk
face-|cloth ˈfeɪs |klɒθ -klɔːθ ‖ -|klɔːθ -klɑːθ **~cloths** klɒθs klɔːs, klɔːðz ‖ klɔːθs klɔːðz, klɑːθs, klɑːðz
-faced ˈfeɪst feɪst — **stony-faced** ˌstəʊn i ˈfeɪst ◂ ˈ· · · ‖ ˌstoʊn-
faceless ˈfeɪs ləs -lɪs
face-lift ˈfeɪs lɪft ~s s
face-off ˈfeɪs ɒf -ɔːf ‖ -ɔːf -ɑːf ~s s
faceplate ˈfeɪs pleɪt ~s s
facer ˈfeɪs ə ‖ -ᵊr ~s z
face-sav|er ˈfeɪs ˌseɪv |ə ‖ -|ᵊr **~ers** əz ‖ ᵊrz **~ing** ɪŋ
fac|et ˈfæs |ɪt -ət, -et **~eted** ɪt ɪd ət-, et-, -əd ‖ əţ əd **~ets** ɪts əts, ets
facetiae fə ˈsiːʃ iˌiː
facetious fə ˈsiːʃ əs ~**ly** li **~ness** nəs nɪs
face-to-face ˌfeɪs tə ˈfeɪs ◂
facetted ˈfæs ɪt ɪd -ət-, -əd ‖ -əţ-
Fach vɑːk vaːx —*Welsh* [vaːχ]
facia ˈfeɪʃ ə ˈfeɪʃ iˌə ~s z
facial ˈfeɪʃ ᵊl ˈfeɪʃ iˌəl; ˈfeɪs iˌəl **~ly** i ~s z
   ˈfacial nerve
facies ˈfeɪʃ iˌiːz ˈfeɪʃ iːz
facile ˈfæs aɪᵊl ‖ -ᵊl **~ly** li **~ness** nəs nɪs
facili|tate fə ˈsɪl ə |teɪt -ɪ- **~tated** teɪt ɪd -əd ‖ teɪţ əd **~tates** teɪts **~tating** teɪt ɪŋ ‖ teɪţ ɪŋ
facilitation fə ˌsɪl ə ˈteɪʃ ᵊn -ɪ-
facilitative fə ˈsɪl ət ət ɪv -ˈ·ɪt-; -ə teɪt ɪv ‖ -ə teɪţ ɪv
facilitator fə ˈsɪl ə teɪt ə -ˈ·ɪ- ‖ -teɪţ ᵊr ~s z
facilit|y fə ˈsɪl ət |i -ɪt- ‖ -əţ |i **~ies** iz
facing ˈfeɪs ɪŋ ~s z
Facit *tdmk* ˈfeɪs ɪt §-ət
facsimile fæk ˈsɪm əl i -ɪl- **~d** d **~ing** ɪŋ ~s z
fact fækt **facts** fækts
fact-finding ˈfækt ˌfaɪnd ɪŋ
faction ˈfæk ʃᵊn ~s z
factional ˈfæk ʃᵊnˌᵊl **~ism** ˌɪz əm
factious ˈfæk ʃəs **~ly** li **~ness** nəs nɪs
factitious fæk ˈtɪʃ əs **~ly** li **~ness** nəs nɪs
factitive ˈfækt ət ɪv -ɪt- ‖ -əţ ɪv **~ly** li ~s z
factive ˈfækt ɪv ~s z
factoid ˈfækt ɔɪd ~s z

F

factor 'fækt ə ‖ -ᵊr **~ed** d **factoring**
'fækt ər ɪŋ **~s** z
factorage 'fækt ər ɪdʒ
factorial fæk 'tɔːr i_əl ‖ -'tour- **~ly** i **~s** z
factoris... —*see* **factoriz...**
factorization ˌfækt ər aɪ 'zeɪʃ ᵊn -ər ɪ- ‖ -ər ə-
~s z
factoriz|e 'fækt ə raɪz **~ed** d **~es** ɪz əz **~ing** ɪŋ
factory 'fæk tri 'fækt ər i **factories** 'fæk triz
'fækt ər iz
ˌfactory 'farm; 'factory ˌship
factotum fæk 'təʊt əm ‖ -'toʊt əm **~s** z
factual 'fæk tʃu_əl -ʃu_əl; 'fækt ju_əl **~ly** i **~s** z
facula 'fæk jʊl ə -jəl- ‖ -jəl ə
facultative 'fæk ᵊlt ət ɪv -ᵊl teɪt-
‖ 'fæk ᵊl teɪt̬ ɪv **~ly** li
facult|y 'fæk ᵊlt |i **~ies** iz
fad fæd **fads** fædz
Fadden 'fæd ᵊn
faddish 'fæd ɪʃ **~ly** li **~ness** nəs nɪs
faddism 'fæd ˌɪz əm
faddy 'fæd i
fade feɪd **faded** 'feɪd ɪd -əd **fades** feɪdz
fading 'feɪd ɪŋ
fade-in 'feɪd ɪn **~s** z
fadeless 'feɪd ləs -lɪs **~ly** li
fade-out 'feɪd aʊt **~s** s
fadge fædʒ **fadges** 'fædʒ ɪz -əz
fading 'feɪd ɪŋ **~s** z
fado 'fɑːd əʊ ‖ -oʊ **~s** z —*Port* ['fa ðu]
faecal 'fiːk ᵊl
faeces 'fiːs iːz
faerie 'feɪ ər i 'feər i ‖ 'fer i, 'fær i
Faeroe 'feər əʊ ‖ 'fer oʊ 'fær- *(= pharaoh)* **~s** z
Faeroese ˌfeər əʊ 'iːz ◂ ‖ ˌfer oʊ- ˌfær-, -'iːs ◂
faery 'feɪ ər i 'feər i ‖ 'fer i, 'fær i
faff fæf **faffed** fæft **faffing** 'fæf ɪŋ **faffs** fæfs
fag fæg **fagged** fægd **fagging** 'fæg ɪŋ **fags**
fægz
ˌfag 'end ◂, '· ·; ˌfagged 'out
Fagan 'feɪg ən
fagg|ot 'fæg |ət **~oted** ət ɪd -əd ‖ ət̬ əd
~oting ət ɪŋ ‖ ət̬ ɪŋ **~ots** əts
faggotry 'fæg ətr i
faggotty, faggoty 'fæg ət i ‖ -ət̬ i
fag-hag 'fæg hæg **~s** z
Fagin 'feɪg ɪn §-ən
fag|ot 'fæg |ət **~oted** ət ɪd -əd **~oting**
ət ɪŋ ‖ ət̬ ɪŋ **~ots** əts
fah fɑː
Fahd fɑːd
Fahrenheit 'fær ən haɪt 'fɑːr- ‖ 'fer-
Fahy 'fɑː hi -i
faience, faïence faɪ 'ɒ̃s feɪ-, -'ɑːnᵗs, -'ɒnᵗs
‖ feɪ 'ɑːnᵗs faɪ- —*Fr* [fa jɑ̃ːs]
fail feɪᵊl **failed** feɪᵊld **failing** 'feɪᵊl ɪŋ **fails**
feɪᵊlz
failing *n* 'feɪl ɪŋ **~s** z
fail-safe 'feɪᵊl seɪf ˌ·'·
Failsworth 'feɪᵊlz wɜːθ -wəθ ‖ -wᵊrθ
fáilte 'fɔːltʃ ə ‖ 'fɑːltʃ ə —*Irish* ['fɑːlʲ tʲə]
failure 'feɪl jə ‖ -jᵊr **~s** z
fain feɪn

faineant, feinéant 'feɪn i_ənt —*Fr* [fɛ ne ɑ̃]
fainites 'feɪn aɪts
fains feɪnz
faint feɪnt **fainted** 'feɪnt ɪd -əd ‖ 'feɪnt̬ əd
fainter 'feɪnt ə ‖ 'feɪnt̬ ᵊr **faintest** 'feɪnt ɪst
§-əst ‖ 'feɪnt̬ əst **fainting** 'feɪnt ɪŋ ‖ 'feɪnt̬ ɪŋ
faints feɪnts
faint-hearted ˌfeɪnt 'hɑːt ɪd ◂ -əd
‖ -'hɑːrt̬ əd ◂ **~ly** li **~ness** nəs nɪs
faintly 'feɪnt li
faintness 'feɪnt nəs -nɪs
fair feə ‖ feᵊr fæᵊr **fairer** 'feər ə ‖ 'fer ᵊr
'fær ᵊr **fairest** 'feər ɪst §-əst ‖ 'fer əst 'fær-
ˌfair 'copy; ˌfair 'dinkum; ˌfair 'game;
'Fair ˌIsle; ˌfair 'sex, '· ·
Fairbairn, Fairbairne 'feə beən ‖ 'fer bern
'fær bærn
Fairbank 'feə bæŋk ‖ 'fer- 'fær-
Fairbanks 'feə bæŋks ‖ 'fer- 'fær-
Fairbourn, Fairbourne 'feə bɔːn ‖ 'fer bɔːrn
'fær-, -boʊrn
Fairbrother 'feə ˌbrʌð ə ‖ 'fer ˌbrʌð ᵊr 'fær-
Fairchild 'feə tʃaɪᵊld ‖ 'fer- 'fær-
Fairclough *(i)* 'feə klʌf ‖ 'fer- 'fær-, *(ii)* -kləʊ
‖ -kloʊ
Fairfax 'feə fæks ‖ 'fer- 'fær-
Fairfield 'feə fiːᵊld ‖ 'fer- 'fær-
Fairford 'feə fəd ‖ 'fer fᵊrd 'fær-
fairground 'feə graʊnd ‖ 'fer- 'fær- **~s** z
fair-haired ˌfeə 'heəd ◂ ‖ ˌfer 'heᵊrd ◂
Fairhaven 'feə ˌheɪv ᵊn ‖ 'fer- 'fær-
fairi... —*see* **fairy**
fairing 'feər ɪŋ ‖ 'fer ɪŋ 'fær- **~s** z
fairish 'feər ɪʃ ‖ 'fer ɪʃ 'fær-
Fairley, Fairlie 'feə li ‖ 'fer- 'fær-
Fairlight 'feə laɪt ‖ 'fer- 'fær-
fairly 'feə li ‖ 'fer- 'fær-
Fairman 'feə mən ‖ 'fer- 'fær-
fair-minded ˌfeə 'maɪnd ɪd ◂ -əd ‖ ˌfer- ˌfær-
~ness nəs nɪs
Fairmont 'feə mɒnt -mənt ‖ 'fer mɑːnt 'fær-
fairness 'feə nəs -nɪs ‖ 'fer- 'fær-
Fairport 'feə pɔːt ‖ 'fer pɔːrt 'fær-, -poʊrt
fair-to-middling ˌfeə tə 'mɪd ᵊl_ɪŋ ◂ ‖ ˌfer-
ˌfær-
fairway 'feə weɪ ‖ 'fer- 'fær- **~s** z
fair-weather, Fairweather 'feə ˌweð ə
‖ 'fer ˌweð ᵊr 'fær-
fair|y 'feər |i ‖ 'fer |i 'fær- **~ies** iz
'fairy ˌcycle, ˌfairy 'god,mother; 'fairy
ˌlight; ˌfairy 'ring ‖ '· · ·; 'fairy ˌstory
fairyland 'feər i lænd ‖ 'fer- 'fær-
fairy-tale 'feər i teɪᵊl ‖ 'fer- 'fær- **~s** z
Faisal 'faɪs ᵊl
Faisalabad ˌfaɪs əl ə bæd 'faɪz-, -bɑːd
fait accompli ˌfeɪt ə 'kɒmp liː ˌfet-, -'kʌmp-
‖ ˌfeɪt̬ ə kɑːm 'pliː —*Fr* [fɛ ta kɔ̃ pli] **faits**
accomplis ˌfeɪz ə 'kɒmp liː ˌfeɪts-, ˌfeɪt-, ˌfez-,
-'kʌmp-, -liːz ‖ ˌfeɪz ə kɑːm 'pliː —*Fr*
[fɛ za kɔ̃ pli]
faites vos jeux ˌfeɪt vəʊ 'ʒɜː ˌfet- ‖ -voʊ 'ʒuː
—*Fr* [fɛt vo ʒø]

faith, Faith feɪθ **faiths, Faith's** feɪθs
  'faith ˌhealing
faithful 'feɪθ fˀl -fʊl **~ly** ˌi **~ness** nəs nɪs
Faithful, Faithfull 'feɪθ fˀl -fʊl
faithless 'feɪθ ləs -lɪs **~ly** li **~ness** nəs nɪs
fajita fæ 'hiːt ə fə- ‖ -'hiːt ə fɑː- **~s** z —*Sp*
  [fa 'xi ta|s]
fake feɪk **faked** feɪkt **fakes** feɪks **faking**
  'feɪk ɪŋ
Fakenham 'feɪk ən_əm
faker 'feɪk ə ‖ -ᵊr **~s** z
fakie 'feɪk i
fakir 'feɪk ɪə 'fɑːk-, 'fæk-; fə 'kɪə, fæ- ‖ fə 'kɪᵊr
  fɑː-; 'feɪk ᵊr **~s** z
Fal fæl
falafel fə 'lɑːf ᵊl
Falange fə 'lændʒ fæ-; 'fæl ændʒ ‖ 'feɪl ændʒ
  —*Sp* [fa 'laŋ xe]
Falangist fə 'lændʒ ɪst §-əst **~s** s
Falasha fə 'læʃ ə ‖ -'lɑːʃ ə **~s** z
falcate 'fælk eɪt
falchion 'fɔːltʃ ən 'fɔːlʃ- ‖ 'fɑːltʃ- **~s** z
falciform 'fæls ɪ fɔːm -ə- ‖ -fɔːrm

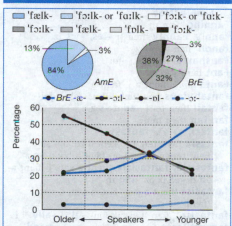

FALCON

falcon, F~ 'fɔːlk ən 'fælk-, 'fɒlk-, 'fɔːk- ‖ 'fælk-
  'fɔːlk-, 'fɑːlk-, 'fɔːk-, 'fɑːk- — *Preference polls,*
  AmE: 'fælk- 84%, 'fɔːlk- *or* 'fɑːlk- 13%, 'fɔːk-
  or 'fɑːk- 3%; *BrE:* 'fɔːlk- 38%, 'fælk- 32%,
  'fɒlk- 27%, 'fɔːk- 3%. **~s** z
Falconbridge 'fɔːlk ən brɪdʒ 'fælk-, 'fɒlk-,
  'fɔːk-, →-əm- ‖ 'fælk- 'fɔːlk-, 'fɑːlk-
Falconcrest ˌfælk ən 'krest ◂ ˌfɔːlk-, ˌfɔːk-,
  ˌfɒlk-, →əŋ- ‖ ˌfælk-, ˌfɑːlk-
falconer, F~ 'fɔːlk ən ə 'fælk-, 'fɒlk-, 'fɔːk-
  ‖ 'fælk ᵊn_ər 'fɔːlk-, 'fɑːlk- **~s** z
falconry 'fɔːlk ən ri 'fælk-, 'fɒlk-, 'fɔːk- ‖ 'fælk-
  'fɔːlk-, 'fɑːlk-
Falder 'fɔːld ə 'fɒld- ‖ 'fɔːld ᵊr 'fɑːld-
falderal ˌfæld ə ræl -ɪ- ‖ 'fɑːld ə rɑːl **~s** z
Faldo 'fæld əʊ ‖ 'fɑːld oʊ
faldstool 'fɔːld stuːl ‖ 'fɑːld- **~s** z
Falernian fə 'lɜːn i_ən ‖ -'lɜːn-
Faliscan fə 'lɪsk ən **~s** z

Falk fɔːlk fɔːk ‖ fɑːlk
Falkender 'fɔːlk ənd ə ‖ -ᵊr 'fɑːlk-
Falkirk 'fɔːl kɜːk 'fɒl-, §'fæl, -kək ‖ -kɜːk 'fɑːl-
Falkland 'fɔːlk lənd 'fɔːk-, 'fɒlk- ‖ 'fɔːk- 'fɑːk-
  ~s z
  'Falkland ˌIslands ‖ ˌ·· '··
Falkner 'fɔːlk nə 'fɔːk-, 'fɒlk-, 'fælk- ‖ 'fɔːk nᵊr
  'fɑːk-
Falkus 'fɔːlk əs ‖ 'fɑːlk-
fall, Fall fɔːl ‖ fɑːl **fallen** 'fɔːl ən ‖ 'fɑːl-
  falling 'fɔːl ɪŋ ‖ 'fɑːl- **falls, Falls** fɔːlz ‖ fɑːlz
  fell fel
  'fall guy; ˌfalling 'star; 'fall line
Falla 'fæl ə 'fɑːl-, -jə ‖ 'fɑː jə —*Sp* ['fa ʌay, -jaj]
fallacious fə 'leɪʃ əs **~ly** li **~ness** nəs nɪs
fallac|y 'fæl əs |i **~ies** iz
fal-lal ₍ₗ₎fæl 'læl ₍ₗ₎fæ- **~s** z
fallback 'fɔːl bæk ‖ 'fɑːl- **~s** s
fallen 'fɔːl ən ‖ 'fɑːl-
Faller 'fæl ə ‖ -ᵊr
fallibility ˌfæl ə 'bɪl ət i ˌ·ɪ-, -ɪt i ‖ -əţ i
fallib|le 'fæl əb |ᵊl -ɪb- **~ly** li
falling-off ˌfɔːl ɪŋ 'ɒf -'ɔːf ‖ -'ɔːf ˌfɑːl ɪŋ 'ɑːf
falling-out ˌfɔːl ɪŋ 'aʊt ˌfɑːl-
fall-off 'fɔːl ɒf -ɔːf ‖ -ɔːf 'fɑːl-, -ɑːf **~s** s
Fallon 'fæl ən
fallopian, F~ fə 'ləʊp i_ən ‖ -'loʊp-
  falˌlopian 'tube
fallout 'fɔːl aʊt ‖ 'fɑːl-
fallow, F~ 'fæl əʊ ‖ -oʊ **~ed** d **~ing** ɪŋ **~s** z
  'fallow deer
Fallowes 'fæl əʊz ‖ -oʊz
Fallowfield 'fæl əʊ fiːᵊld ‖ -oʊ-
Falls fɔːlz ‖ fɑːlz
Falluja fə 'luːdʒ ə —*Arabic* [fa 'lu: dʒah]
Falmer 'fælm ə ‖ -ᵊr
Falmouth 'fæl məθ

FALSE

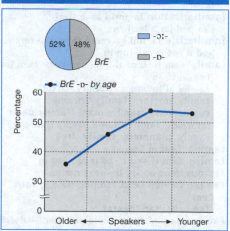

false fɔːls fɒls ‖ fɑːls **falser** 'fɔːls ə 'fɒls ə
  ‖ 'fɔːls ᵊr 'fɑːls ᵊr **falsest** 'fɔːls ɪst 'fɒls-, §-əst
  ‖ 'fɔːls əst 'fɑːls- — *Preference poll, BrE:* -ɔː-
  52%, -ɒ- *48%.*

F

,false a'larm; ,false ar'rest; ,false
'bottom; ,false pre'tenses; ,false 'start;
,false 'teeth
false-hearted ,fɔːls 'hɑːt ɪd ◂ ,fɒls-, -əd
‖ ,fɔːls 'hɑːrt̬ əd ◂ ,fɑːls-, '·,··
falsehood 'fɔːls hʊd 'fɒls- ‖ 'fɑːls- ~s z
falsely 'fɔːls li 'fɒls- ‖ 'fɑːls-
falseness 'fɔːls nəs 'fɒls-, -nɪs ‖ 'fɑːls-
falsetto fɔːl 'set əʊ fɒl- ‖ fɔːl 'set̬ oʊ fɑːl- ~s z
falsies 'fɔːls iz 'fɒls- ‖ 'fɑːls-
falsifiability ,fɔːls ɪ faɪ ə 'bɪl ət i ,fɒls-, -ɪt i
‖ ,fɑːls ə faɪ ə 'bɪl ət̬ i ,fɑːls-
falsifiab|le ,fɔːls ɪ faɪ əb |ᵊl 'fɒls-, '·ə-, ,·'··· ‖
'fɑːls- ~ly li
falsification ,fɔːls ɪf ɪ 'keɪʃ ᵊn ,fɒls-, ,-əf-, §-ə'--
‖ ,fɑːls- ~s z
falsi|fy 'fɔːls ɪ |faɪ 'fɒls-, -ə- ‖ 'fɑːls- ~fied faɪd
~fier/s faɪ ə/z ‖ faɪ ᵊr/z ~fies faɪz ~fying
faɪ ɪŋ
falsit|y 'fɔːls ət |i 'fɒls-, -ɪt- ‖ 'fɔːls ət̬ |i 'fɑːls-
~ies iz
Falstaff 'fɔːlst ɑːf 'fɒlst-, §-æf ‖ -æf 'fɑːlst-
Falstaffian ₍ˌ₎fɔːl 'stɑːf i ən ₍ˌ₎fɒl-, §-'stæf-
‖ -'stæf- ₍ˌ₎fɑːl-
faltboat 'fælt bəʊt 'fɑːlt-, 'fɔːlt-, 'fɒlt-
‖ 'fɔːlt boʊt 'fɑːlt- ~s s
falter 'fɔːlt ə 'fɒlt ə ‖ 'fɔːlt ᵊr 'fɑːlt ᵊr ~ed d
faltering/ly 'fɔːlt ᵊr ɪŋ /li 'fɒlt‿ ‖ 'fɑːlt‿ ~s z
Falun Gong ,fɑː lʊn 'gʊŋ ,fæl-, -'gʊŋ ‖ -'gɔːŋ
-'gɑːŋ —Chi Fǎlún Gōng [³fa ²lwən ¹gʊŋ]
Falwell 'fɔːl wel ‖ 'fɑːl-
Famagusta ,fæm ə 'gʊst ə ◂ ,fɑːm-
‖ ,fɑːm ə 'gʊːst ə
fame feɪm famed feɪmd
familial fə 'mɪl i əl ‖ fə 'mɪl jəl
familiar fə 'mɪl i ə ‖ fə 'mɪl jᵊr ~ly li
familiaris... —see familiariz...
familiarit|y fə ˌmɪl i 'ær ət |i -ɪt i
‖ fə ˌmɪl 'jær ət̬ |i -'jer-; -ˌmɪl i 'ær-, -'er- ~ies
iz
familiarization fə ˌmɪl i ər aɪ 'zeɪʃ ᵊn -ɪ'--
‖ fə ˌmɪl jər ə 'zeɪʃ ᵊn
familiariz|e fə 'mɪl i ə raɪz ‖ fə 'mɪl jə raɪz
~ed d ~es ɪz əz ~ing ɪŋ
family 'fæm li 'fæm əl i, -ɪl- families 'fæm liz
'fæm əl iz, -ɪl-
,family al'lowance; ,family 'circle;
,family 'doctor; ,family 'income
,supplement; 'family man; 'family name
'surname', ,family 'name 'family reputation';
,family 'planning; ,family 'tree
famine 'fæm ɪn §-ən ~s z
famish 'fæm ɪʃ ~ed t ~es ɪz əz ~ing ɪŋ
famous 'feɪm əs ~ly li ~ness nəs nɪs
fan fæn fanned fænd fanning 'fæn ɪŋ fans
fænz
'fan belt; 'fan ,heater
Fan in names of Welsh mountains væn —Welsh
[van]
Fanagalo ,fæn ə gə 'ləʊ '····‖ ,fɑːn ə gə 'loʊ
fan-assisted ,fæn ə 'sɪst ɪd ◂ -əd
fanatic fə 'næt ɪk ‖ -'næt̬ ɪk ~s s
fanatical fə 'næt ɪk ᵊl ‖ -'næt̬ ɪk- ~ly ‿i

fanaticism fə 'næt ɪ ˌsɪz əm -ə- ‖ -'næt̬ ə-
fanciable 'fæn⸍s i əb ᵊl
fancier 'fæn⸍s i ə ‖ ᵊr ~s z
fanciful 'fæn⸍s ɪ fᵊl -ə-, -fʊl ~ly ‿i ~ness nəs
nɪs
fanc|y, Fanc|y 'fæn⸍s |i ~ied id ~ier i ə ‖ i‿ᵊr
~ies iz ~iest i‿ɪst i‿əst ~ily ɪ li əl i ~iness
i nəs i nɪs ~ying i ɪŋ
,fancy 'dress; 'fancy goods; 'fancy man;
'fancy ,woman
fancy-dress ,fæn⸍s i 'dres ◂
fancy-free ,fæn⸍s i 'friː ◂
fancywork 'fæn⸍s i wɜːk ‖ -wɜːk
fandango fæn 'dæŋ gəʊ ‖ -goʊ ~s z
fane, Fane feɪn fanes feɪnz
Faneuil 'fæn jəl -ᵊl; 'fæn ju‿əl
,Faneuil 'Hall
fanfare 'fæn feə ‖ -fer -fær ~s z
fanfaronade ,fæn fær ə 'neɪd -fər‿ə-, -'nɑːd ~s
z
fanfold 'fæn fəʊld →-fɒʊld ‖ -foʊld
fang fæŋ fanged fæŋd fangs fæŋz
Fang African people and language fæŋ fɑːŋ
fanlight 'fæn laɪt ~s s
Fannie 'fæn i
,Fannie 'Mae
Fanning 'fæn ɪŋ
fann|y, Fann|y 'fæn |i ~ies, ~y's iz
fanon 'fæn ən ~s z
Fanshawe 'fæn ʃɔː ‖ -ʃɑː
Fant fænt ‖ fɑːnt
Fanta tdmk 'fænt ə ‖ 'fænt̬ ə
fantabulous fæn 'tæb jʊl əs -jəl- ‖ -jəl-
fantail 'fæn teɪᵊl ~ed d ~s z
fan-tan 'fæn tæn
fantasi... —see fantasy
fantasia fæn 'teɪz i ə ,fænt ə 'ziː ə, -'siː ə
‖ fæn 'teɪʒ ə -ˌteɪʒ i ə; ,fænt̬ ə 'ziː ə ~s z
fantasis|e, fantasiz|e 'fænt ə saɪz ‖ 'fænt̬ ə-
~ed d ~es ɪz əz ~ing ɪŋ
fantasist 'fænt ə sɪst -zɪst, §-səst, §-zəst
‖ 'fænt̬- ~s s
fantastic ₍ˌ₎fæn 'tæst ɪk fən- ~al ᵊl ~ally ᵊl‿i
fantasti|cate fæn 'tæst ɪ| keɪt -ə- ~cated
keɪt ɪd -əd ‖ keɪt̬ əd ~cates keɪts ~cating
keɪt ɪŋ ‖ keɪt̬ ɪŋ
fantas|y 'fænt əs |i -əz- ‖ 'fænt̬- ~ied id ~ies
iz ~ying i ɪŋ
Fante, Fanti 'fænt i ‖ 'fɑːnt i
Fanthorpe 'fæn θɔːp ‖ -θɔːrp
fantoccini ,fænt ə 'tʃiːn i ‖ ,fænt̬- ,fɑːnt̬- —It
[fan tot 'tʃiː ni]
Fantom 'fænt əm ‖ 'fænt̬-
Fanum 'feɪn əm
fanzine 'fæn ziːn ~s z
FAO ,ef eɪ 'əʊ ‖ -'oʊ
FAQ ,ef eɪ 'kjuː FAQs, FAQ's ,ef eɪ 'kjuːz fæks
far fɑː ‖ fɑːr farther 'fɑːð ə ‖ 'fɑːrð ᵊr farthest
'fɑːð ɪst §-əst ‖ 'fɑːrð- further 'fɜːð ə
‖ 'fɜːð ᵊr furthest 'fɜːð ɪst §-əst ‖ 'fɜːð-
,Far 'East; ,Far 'Eastern◂
Fara island in Orkney 'fær ə ‖ 'fer ə
farad 'fær əd -æd ‖ 'fer- ~s z

Faraday 'fær ə deɪ -di ‖ 'fer-
faradic fə 'ræd ɪk
farandole 'fær ən dəʊl →-dɒʊl ‖ -doʊl 'fer-
　　—*Fr* [fa ʁɑ̃ dɔl] **~s** z
farang fæ 'ræŋ fə- **~s** z
faraway ˌfɑː r ə 'weɪ ◄
　　ˌfaraway 'looks
farce fɑːs ‖ fɑːrs **farces** 'fɑːs ɪz -əs ‖ 'fɑːrs-
farceur ˌfɑː 'sɜː ‖ ˌfɑːr 'sɜː —*Fr* [faʁ sœːʁ] **~s** z
farci, farcie ˌfɑː 'siː ‖ ˌfɑːr- —*Fr* [faʁ si]
farcical 'fɑːs ɪk əl -ək- ‖ 'fɑːrs- **~ly** ˌi **~ness** nəs
　　nɪs
farcy 'fɑːs i ‖ 'fɑːrs i
fare feə ‖ feər fæər (= *fair*) **fared** feəd ‖ feərd
　　fæərd **fares** feəz ‖ feərz fæərz **faring** 'feər ɪŋ
　　‖ 'fer ɪŋ 'fær-
Fareham 'feər əm ‖ 'fer- 'fær-
farewell ˌfeə 'wel ◄ ‖ ˌfer- ˌfær-
Farewell *family name* 'feə wel -wəl ‖ 'fer- 'fær-
farfalle fɑː 'fæl eɪ ‖ fɑːr- -'fɑːl- —*It* [far 'fal le]
farfetched ˌfɑː 'fetʃt ◄ ‖ ˌfɑːr-
far-flung ˌfɑː 'flʌŋ ◄ ‖ ˌfɑːr-
Fargo 'fɑːg əʊ ‖ 'fɑːrg oʊ
far-gone ˌfɑː 'gɒn ◄ §-'gɑːn, §-'gɔːn
　　‖ ˌfɑːr 'gɔːn ◄ -'gɑːn
farina fə 'riːn ə -'raɪn ə
farinaceous ˌfær ɪ 'neɪʃ əs ◄ -ə- ‖ ˌfer-
Faringdon 'fær ɪŋ dən ‖ 'fer-
Farjeon 'fɑːdʒ ən ‖ 'fɑːrdʒ-
farl fɑːl ‖ fɑːrl **farls** fɑːlz ‖ fɑːrlz
Farleigh, Farley 'fɑːl i ‖ 'fɑːrl i
farm fɑːm ‖ fɑːrm **farmed** fɑːmd ‖ fɑːrmd
　　farming 'fɑːm ɪŋ ‖ 'fɑːrm ɪŋ **farms** fɑːmz
　　‖ fɑːrmz
farmer, F~ 'fɑːm ə ‖ 'fɑːrm ər **~s** z
farmhand 'fɑːm hænd ‖ 'fɑːrm- **~s** z
farm|house 'fɑːm |haʊs ‖ 'fɑːrm- **~houses**
　　haʊz ɪz -əz
Farmington 'fɑːm ɪŋ tən ‖ 'fɑːrm-
farmland 'fɑːm lænd -lənd ‖ 'fɑːrm-
farmstead 'fɑːm sted ‖ 'fɑːrm- **~s** z
farmyard 'fɑːm jɑːd ‖ 'fɑːrm jɑːrd **~s** z
Farnaby 'fɑːn əb i ‖ 'fɑːrn-
Farnborough 'fɑːn bər ə →'fɑːm-, §-ˌbʌr-
　　‖ 'fɑːrn ˌbɜː oʊ
Farncombe 'fɑːn kəm →'fɑːŋ- ‖ 'fɑːrn-
Farne fɑːn ‖ fɑːrn
　　'Farne ˌIslands
Farnham 'fɑːn əm ‖ 'fɑːrn-
Farnley 'fɑːn li ‖ 'fɑːrn-
Farnworth 'fɑːn wɜːθ ‖ 'fɑːrn wɜːθ
faro 'feər əʊ ‖ 'fer oʊ 'fær- (= *pharaoh*)
Faro *place in Portugal* 'fɑːr əʊ 'feər- ‖ -oʊ
　　—*Port* ['fa ru]
Faroe 'feər əʊ ‖ 'fer oʊ 'fær- (= *pharaoh*) **~s** z
Faroese ˌfeər əʊ 'iːz ◄ ‖ ˌfer oʊ- ˌfær-, -'iːs◄
far-off ˌfɑːr 'ɒf ◄ -'ɔːf ‖ ˌfɑːr 'ɔːf ◄ -'ɑːf
　　ˌfar-off 'lands
farouche fə 'ruːʃ fæ- —*Fr* [fa ʁuʃ]
Farouk fə 'ruːk
far-out ˌfɑːr 'aʊt ◄ ‖ ˌfɑːr-
Farquhar 'fɑːk ə -wə ‖ 'fɑːrk wɜr -ər, -wɑːr

Farquharson 'fɑːk əs ən -wəs- ‖ 'fɑːrk wɜrs ən
　　-ərs-
Farr fɑː ‖ fɑːr
farraginous fə 'rædʒ ɪn əs -'reɪdʒ-, -ən-
farrago fə 'rɑːg əʊ -'reɪg- ‖ -oʊ **~s** z
Farrah 'fær ə ‖ 'fer-
Farrakhan 'fær ə kæn
Farrant 'fær ənt ‖ 'fer-
Farrar 'fær ə ‖ -ər 'fer-
far-reaching ˌfɑː 'riːtʃ ɪŋ ◄ ‖ ˌfɑːr-
　　ˌfar-ˌreaching 'consequences
Farrell 'fær əl ‖ 'fer-
farrier 'fær i ə ‖ ər 'fer- **~s** z
Farringdon 'fær ɪŋ dən ‖ 'fer-
farrow, F~ 'fær əʊ ‖ -oʊ 'fer- **~ed** d **~ing** ɪŋ **~s**
　　z
far-seeing ˌfɑː 'siː ɪŋ ◄ ‖ ˌfɑːr-
Farsi 'fɑːs i ‖ 'siː ‖ 'fɑːrs i
farsighted ˌfɑː 'saɪt ɪd ◄ -əd ‖ ˌfɑːr 'saɪt əd ◄
　　~ly li **~ness** nəs nɪs
fart fɑːt ‖ fɑːrt **farted** 'fɑːt ɪd -əd ‖ 'fɑːrt̬ əd
　　farting 'fɑːt ɪŋ ‖ 'fɑːrt̬ ɪŋ **farts** fɑːts ‖ fɑːrts
farth|er 'fɑːð| ə ‖ 'fɑːrð| ər **~est** ɪst -əst
farthermost 'fɑːð ə məʊst ‖ 'fɑːrð ər moʊst
farthing, F~ 'fɑːð ɪŋ ‖ 'fɑːrð- **~s** z
farthingale 'fɑːð ɪŋ geɪl ‖ 'fɑːrð- **~s** z
fartlek 'fɑːt lek ‖ 'fɑːrt- **~ked** t **~king** ɪŋ **~s** s
　　—*Swedish* ['faʈ lek]
fasces 'fæs iːz
fascia 'feɪʃ ə 'feɪʃ i ə, 'fæʃ- ‖ 'fæʃ i ə 'feɪʃ ə —*In
　　BrE* 'fæʃ- *as a medical term, otherwise
　　generally* 'feɪʃ-; *as a term in classical
　　architecture, also* 'feɪs i ə. *In AmE, generally*
　　'fæʃ i ə, *but* 'feɪʃ ə *in the sense of* 'board above
　　shopfront' **~s** z
fasci|ate 'fæʃ i |eɪt **~ated** eɪt ɪd -əd ‖ eɪt̬ əd
fascicle 'fæs ɪk əl -ək- **~s** z
fascicule 'fæs ɪ kjuːl -ə- **~s** z
fasciitis ˌfæʃ i 'aɪt ɪs §-əs ‖ -'aɪt̬ əs
fasci|nate 'fæs ɪ |neɪt -ə- **~nated** neɪt ɪd -əd
　　‖ neɪt̬ əd **~nates** neɪts **~nating** neɪt ɪŋ
　　‖ neɪt̬ ɪŋ
fascinating 'fæs ɪ neɪt ɪŋ -ə- ‖ -neɪt̬ ɪŋ **~ly** li
fascination ˌfæs ɪ 'neɪʃ ən -ə- **~s** z
fascism 'fæʃ ˌɪz əm
fascist 'fæʃ ɪst §-əst **~s** s
fascistic fæ 'ʃɪst ɪk fə-
fash fæʃ **fashed** fæʃt **fashes** 'fæʃ ɪz -əz
　　fashing 'fæʃ ɪŋ
Fashanu 'fæʃ ə nuː
fashion 'fæʃ ən **~ed** d **~ing** ˌɪŋ **~s** z
　　'fashion ˌplate
-fashion ˌfæʃ ən — Chinese-fashion
　　ˌtʃaɪ 'niːz ˌfæʃ ən
fashionab|le 'fæʃ ən əb |əl **~leness** əl nəs -nɪs
　　~ly li
fashionista ˌfæʃ ə 'niːst ə -'nɪst ə; →-ən 'iːst-,
　　→ən 'ɪst- **-s** z
Fashoda fə 'ʃəʊd ə fæ- ‖ -'ʃoʊd ə
Faslane fæz 'leɪn fəs-
Fassbinder 'fæs bɪnd ə ‖ 'fɑːs bɪnd ər 'fæs-
　　—*Ger* Faßbinder ['fas bɪn dɐ]

F

fast fɑːst §fæst ‖ fæst **fasted** 'fɑːst ɪd §'fæst-,
-əd ‖ 'fæst əd **faster** 'fɑːst ə §'fæst ə
‖ 'fæst ᵊr **fastest** 'fɑːst ɪst §'fæst-, §-əst
‖ 'fæst- **fasting** 'fɑːst ɪŋ §'fæst- ‖ 'fæst ɪŋ
fasts fɑːsts §fæsts ‖ fæsts
'fast ˌday; ˌfast 'food, '· ·; ˌfast 'lane
fastback 'fɑːst bæk §'fæst- ‖ 'fæst- ~s s
fastball 'fɑːst bɔːl ‖ 'fæst- -bɑːl ~er/s ə/z
‖ -ᵊr/z
fasten 'fɑːs ᵊn §'fæs- ‖ 'fæs ᵊn ~ed d ~ing ˌɪŋ
~s z
fastener 'fɑːs nə §'fæs-, '·ᵊn ə ‖ 'fæs ᵊn‿ᵊr ~s z
fastening n 'fɑːs nɪŋ §'fæs-, '·ᵊn ɪŋ ‖ 'fæs ᵊn‿ɪŋ
~s z
fast-forward ˌfɑːst 'fɔː wəd §ˌfæst-
‖ ˌfæst 'fɔːr wᵊrd
fastidious fæ 'stɪd i‿əs fə- ~ly li ~ness nəs nɪs
fastigiate fæ 'stɪdʒ i‿ət -eɪt
fastness 'fɑːst nəs §'fæst-, -nɪs ‖ 'fæst- ~es ɪz
əz
Fastnet 'fɑːst net §'fæst-, -nɪt ‖ 'fæst-
fast-talk ˌfɑːst 'tɔːk §ˌfæst- ‖ ˌfæst- -'tɑːk ~ed t
~er/s ə/z ‖ ᵊr/z ~ing ɪŋ ~s s
fat fæt **fatted** 'fæt ɪd -əd ‖ 'fæt̬ əd **fatter**
'fæt ə ‖ 'fæt̬ ᵊr **fattest** 'fæt ɪst §-əst ‖ 'fæt̬ əst
fatting 'fæt ɪŋ ‖ 'fæt̬ ɪŋ
ˌfat 'cat; ˌfat 'hen
Fatah 'fæt ə 'fʌt ə ‖ 'fɑːt ə —Arabic ['fa taħ]
fatal 'feɪt ᵊl ‖ 'feɪt̬ ᵊl ~ism ˌɪz əm ~ist/s ɪst/s
§-əst/s
fatalistic ˌfeɪt ᵊl 'ɪst ɪk ◄ ‖ ˌfeɪt̬- ~ally ᵊl i
fatality fə 'tæl ət i feɪ-, -ɪt- ‖ feɪ 'tæl ət̬ i fə-
~ies iz
fatally 'feɪt ᵊl i ‖ 'feɪt̬ ᵊl i
fata morgana ˌfɑːt ə mɔː 'gɑːn ə
‖ ˌfɑːt̬ ə mɔːr-
fate, Fate feɪt **fated** 'feɪt ɪd -əd ‖ 'feɪt̬ əd
fates, Fates feɪts
fateful 'feɪt fᵊl -fʊl ~ly i
fat-free ˌfæt 'friː ◄
fathead 'fæt hed ~s z
fatheaded ˌfæt 'hed ɪd ◄ -əd, '· · · ~ness nəs
nɪs
fath|er 'fɑːð |ə ‖ -|ᵊr ~ered əd ‖ ᵊrd ~ering
ər ɪŋ ~ers əz ‖ ᵊrz
ˌFather 'Christmas; 'father ˌfigure;
'Father's Day; ˌFather 'Time
fatherhood 'fɑːð ə hʊd ‖ -ᵊr-
father-in-law 'fɑːð ər ˌɪn ˌlɔː →'·ə-, ᵊr ˌən-
‖ 'fɑːð ᵊr ˌən ˌlɔː -ər‿ᵊn-, -ˌlɑː **fathers-in-law**
'fɑːð əz ɪn ˌlɔː §-ən‿· ‖ -ᵊrz ən ˌlɔː -ˌlɑː
fatherland 'fɑːð ə lænd ‖ -ᵊr- ~s z
fatherly 'fɑːð ə li -ᵊl i ‖ -ᵊr-
fathers-in-law —see **father-in-law**
fathom 'fæð əm ~ed d ~ing ɪŋ ~s z
fathomless 'fæð əm ləs -lɪs
fatigu|e fə 'tiːg ~ed d ~es z ~ing ɪŋ
Fatima 'fæt ɪm ə -əm- ‖ 'fæt̬-
fatling 'fæt lɪŋ ~s z
fat|ly 'fæt |li ~ness nəs nɪs
fatshedera ˌfæts 'hed ər ə ~s z
fatsia 'fæts i‿ə ~s z
fatso, Fatso 'fæts əʊ ‖ -oʊ ~es, ~s z

fat-soluble ˌfæt 'sɒl jʊb ᵊl ◄ -jəb-, '·,·-
‖ 'fæt ˌsɑːl jəb ᵊl
fatstock 'fæt stɒk ‖ -stɑːk
fatt... —see **fat**
fatten 'fæt ᵊn ~ed d ~er/s ə/z ‖ ᵊr/z ~ing ˌɪŋ
~s z
fattish 'fæt ɪʃ ‖ 'fæt̬ ɪʃ ~ness nəs nɪs
fatt|y 'fæt |i ‖ 'fæt̬ |i ~ier i‿ə ‖ i‿ᵊr ~ies iz
~iest i‿ɪst i‿əst ~iness i nəs i nɪs
ˌfatty 'acid
fatuit|y fə 'tjuː ət |i fæ-, →-'tʃuː-, ɪt-
‖ -'tuː ət̬ |i -'tjuː-, -'tʃuː- ~ies iz
fatuous 'fæt ju‿əs ‖ 'fætʃ u‿əs ~ly li
~ness nəs nɪs
fatwa 'fæt wɑː ~s z —Arabic ['fat wɑː]
faucal 'fɔːk ᵊl ‖ 'fɑːk-
fauces 'fɔːs iːz ‖ 'fɑːs-
faucet 'fɔːs ɪt -ət ‖ 'fɑːs- ~s s
Faucett, Faucitt 'fɔːs ɪt -ət ‖ 'fɑːs-
faugh fɔː ‖ fɑː —or non-speech sequences such
as [pɸ, pɸ̩ə]
Faulds (i) fəʊldz →fɒʊldz ‖ foʊldz, (ii) fɔːldz
‖ fɑːldz
Faulkner 'fɔːk nə 'fɒːlk- ‖ -nᵊr 'fɑːk-
Faull fɔːl ‖ fɑːl
fault fɔːlt fɒlt ‖ fɔːlt fɑːlt **faulted** 'fɔːlt ɪd 'fɒlt-,
-əd ‖ 'fɔːlt əd 'fɑːlt- **faulting** 'fɔːlt ɪŋ 'fɒlt-
‖ 'fɔːlt ɪŋ 'fɑːlt- **faults** fɔːlts fɒlts ‖ fɔːlts fɑːlts
'fault line; 'fault plane
faultfind|er 'fɔːlt ˌfaɪnd |ə 'fɒlt-
‖ 'fɔːlt ˌfaɪnd -|ᵊr 'fɑːlt- ~ing ɪŋ
faultless 'fɔːlt ləs 'fɒlt-, -lɪs ‖ 'fɔːlt- 'fɑːlt- ~ly
li ~ness nəs nɪs
fault-tolerant 'fɔːlt ˌtɒl ər ənt 'fɒlt-, -ᵊr‿ənt
‖ -ˌtɑːl-
fault|y 'fɔːlt |i 'fɒlt- ‖ 'fɔːlt |i 'fɑːlt- ~ier i‿ə
‖ i‿ᵊr ~iest i‿ɪst i‿əst ~ily ɪ li əl i ~iness i nəs
i nɪs
faun fɔːn ‖ fɑːn (= fawn) **fauns** fɔːnz ‖ fɑːnz
fauna 'fɔːn ə 'faʊn- ‖ 'fɑːn ə ~s z
Fauntleroy 'fɒnt lə rɔɪ 'fɔːnt- ‖ 'fɔːnt- 'fɑːnt-
'Fauntleroy suit
Faure fɔː ‖ fɔːr —Fr [fɔːʁ]
Fauré 'fɔːr eɪ 'fɒr- ‖ foʊ 'reɪ fɔː- —Fr [fo ʁe]
Faust faʊst —but the place in NY is fɔːst
Faustian 'faʊst i‿ən
Faustus 'faʊst əs 'fɔːst- ‖ 'fɔːst-, 'faːst-
faute de mieux ˌfəʊt də 'mjɜː
‖ ˌfoʊt də 'mjuː —Fr [fot də mjø]
Fauve fəʊv ‖ foʊv —Fr [foːv]
Fauvism 'fəʊv ˌɪz əm ‖ 'foʊv-
Fauvist 'fəʊv ɪst §-əst ‖ 'foʊv- ~s s
faux fəʊ ‖ foʊ —see also phrases with this word
Faux name (i) fɔːks ‖ fɑːks, (ii) fəʊ ‖ foʊ
faux ami ˌfəʊz æ 'mi: ‖ ˌfoʊz- —Fr [fo za mi]
~s z or as sing.
faux-naif, faux-naïf ˌfəʊ naɪ 'iːf ◄ ‖ ˌfoʊ nɑː-
—Fr [fo na if]
faux pas sing. ˌfəʊ 'pɑː '· · ‖ ˌfoʊ- —Fr [fo pɑ]
faux pas pl ˌfəʊ 'pɑːz -'pɑː, '· · ‖ ˌfoʊ- —Fr
[fo pɑ]
fava 'fɑːv ə
'fava bean

fave feɪv
favela fə 'vel ə fæ- **~s** z —*BrPort* [fa 've lɐ, -s]
Favell 'feɪv ᵊl
Faversham 'fæv əʃ əm ‖ -ᵊrʃ-
favonian, F~ fə 'vəʊn i ən feɪ- ‖ -'vəʊn-
favor 'feɪv ə ‖ -ᵊr **~ed** d **favoring/ly**
   'feɪv ər ɪŋ /li **~s** z
favorab|le 'feɪv ər ᵊb |ᵊl **~leness** ᵊl nəs -nɪs
   ~ly li
favorite 'feɪv rət -rɪt; 'feɪv ər ət, -ɪt
   ‖ △'feɪv ᵊrt **~s** s
   ,favorite 'son
favoritism 'feɪv rə ˌtɪz əm -rɪt-; '·ər əˌ··, -ər ɪ-
   ‖ △-ᵊr-
favour 'feɪv ə ‖ -ᵊr **~ed** d **favouring/ly**
   'feɪv ər ɪŋ /li **~s** z
favourab|le 'feɪv ər ᵊb |ᵊl **~leness** ᵊl nəs -nɪs
   ~ly li
favourite 'feɪv rət -rɪt; 'feɪv ər ə, -ɪt
   ‖ △'feɪv ᵊrt **~s** s
   ,favorite 'son
favouritism 'feɪv rə ˌtɪz əm -rɪt-; '·ər əˌ··, -ər ɪ-
   ‖ △-ᵊr-
Fawcett 'fɔːs ɪt -ət ‖ 'faːs-
Fawcus 'fɔːk əs ‖ 'faːk-
Fawkes fɔːks ‖ faːks
Fawley 'fɔːl i ‖ 'faːl i
Fawlty 'fɔːlt i 'fɒlt i ‖ 'fɔːlt i 'faːlt i
fawn fɔːn ‖ faːn **fawned** fɔːnd ‖ faːnd
   fawner/s 'fɔːn ə/z ‖ -ᵊr/z 'faːn- **fawning/ly**
   'fɔːn ɪŋ /li ‖ 'faːn- **fawns** fɔːnz ‖ faːnz
Fawr 'vaʊ ə ‖ 'vaʊˌᵊr —*Welsh* [vaur]
fax, Fax fæks **faxed** fækst **faxes** 'fæks ɪz -əz
   faxing 'fæks ɪŋ
fay, Fay, Faye feɪ
Fayed 'faɪ ed
Fayette ˌfeɪ 'et
Fayetteville 'feɪ et vɪl -ɪt-, -ət- ‖ -ət vᵊl -vɪl
Faygate 'feɪ geɪt
Fazackerley, Fazakerley fə 'zæk ə li ‖ -ᵊr-
faze feɪz (= *phase, Fay's*) **fazed** feɪzd **fazes**
   'feɪz ɪz -əz **fazing** 'feɪz ɪŋ
Fazeley 'feɪz li
FBI ˌef biː 'aɪ -bi-
feal|ty 'fiːᵊl |ti **~ties** tiz
fear fɪə ‖ fɪᵊr **feared** fɪəd ‖ fɪᵊrz **fearer/s**
   'fɪər ə/z ‖ 'fɪr ᵊr/z **fearing** 'fɪər ɪŋ ‖ 'fɪr ɪŋ
   fears fɪəz ‖ fɪᵊrz
fearful 'fɪəf ᵊl 'fɪə fʊl ‖ 'fɪrf ᵊl **~ly** ˌi **~ness** nəs
   nɪs
Feargal, Fearghal 'fɜːg ᵊl ‖ 'fɜːg-
Feargus 'fɜːg əs ‖ 'fɜːg-
fearless 'fɪə ləs -lɪs ‖ 'fɪr- **~ly** li **~ness** nəs nɪs
Fearn, Fearne (i) fɜːn ‖ fɜːn, (ii) feən ‖ fern
fearsome 'fɪəs əm ‖ 'fɪrs- **~ly** li **~ness** nəs nɪs
feasibility ˌfiːz ə 'bɪl ət i ˌ·ɪ-, -ɪt i ‖ -əˌt i
   ,feasi'bility ,study
feasib|le 'fiːz əb |ᵊl -ɪb- **~leness** ᵊl nəs -nɪs **~ly**
   li
feast fiːst **feasted** 'fiːst ɪd -əd **feaster/s**
   'fiːst ə/z ‖ -ᵊr/z **feasting** 'fiːst ɪŋ **feasts**
   fiːsts
   'feast day

feat fiːt (= *feet*) **feats** fiːts
feath|er 'feð |ə ‖ -|ᵊr **~ered** əd ‖ ᵊrd **~ering**
   ər ɪŋ **~ers** əz ‖ ᵊrz
   ,feather 'bed; ,feather 'boa; ,feather
   'duster; 'feather star
featherbed v 'feð ə bed ˌ·ˈ· ‖ -ᵊr- **~ded** ɪd əd
   ~ding ɪŋ **~s** z
featherbrained 'feð ə breɪnd ˌ·ˈ·◂ ‖ -ᵊr-
featheredg|e 'feð ər edʒ ˌ·ˈ· ‖ -ər- **~ed** d **~es**
   ɪz əz
featheriness 'feð ər i nəs -nɪs
featherstitch 'feð ə stɪtʃ ‖ -ᵊr- **~ed** t **~es** ɪz əz
   ~ing ɪŋ
Featherstone (i) 'feð əst ən -ə stəʊn
   ‖ -ᵊr stəʊn, (ii) 'fɜːst ən ‖ 'fɜːst-
Featherstonehaugh (i) 'feð əst ən hɔː
   ‖ 'feð ᵊrst- -haː, (ii) 'fæn ʃɔː ‖ -ʃaː, (iii)
   'fest ən hɔː ‖ -haː, (iv) 'fiːs ᵊn heɪ, (v)
   'fɪəst ən hɔː ‖ 'fɪrst- -haː
featherweight 'feð ə weɪt ‖ -ᵊr- **~s** s
feathery 'feð ər i
feature 'fiːtʃ ə ‖ -ᵊr **~ed** d **~es** z **featuring**
   'fiːtʃ ər ɪŋ
   'feature film
featureless 'fiːtʃ ə ləs -lɪs ‖ -ᵊr-
Feaver 'fiːv ə ‖ -ᵊr
Febreze *tdmk* fə 'briːz
febrifug|e 'feb rɪ fjuːdʒ -rə- **~es** ɪz əz
febrile 'fiːb raɪᵊl 'feb- ‖ 'feb-

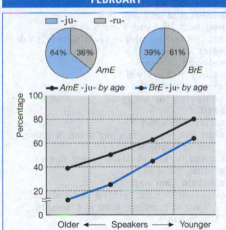

FEBRUARY

February 'feb ru ər i 'feb juˌ-, -er i; 'feb rʊr i,
   -rər-, -jʊr-, -jər- ‖ 'feb ju er i 'feb ru- —*The
   forms with* j, *although sometimes criticized,
   are often heard from educated speakers (esp.
   AmE) and preferred by them. Casually also
   'feb ri. — Preference polls, AmE:* -ju- *64%,
   *-ru- *36%; BrE:* -ru- *61%,* -ju- *39%, with vowel
   in* -ary *weak 57%, strong* -eri *43%.*
fecal 'fiːk ᵊl
feces 'fiːs iːz
fecit 'feɪk ɪt 'fiːs-, §-ət
feck fek **fecking** 'fek ɪŋ
feckless 'fek ləs -lɪs **~ly** li **~ness** nəs nɪs

fecund 'fek ənd 'fiːk-, -ʌnd; fɪ 'kʌnd, fə-

fecun|date 'fek ən |deɪt 'fiːk-, -ʌn- **~dated**
deɪt ɪd -əd ‖ deɪt̬ əd **~dates** deɪts **~dating**
deɪt ɪŋ ‖ deɪt̬ ɪŋ

fecundity fɪ 'kʌnd ət i fə-, fe-, fiː-, -ɪt- ‖ -ət̬ i

fed, Fed fed **feds, Feds** fedz
,fed 'up◄

fedayeen, F~ fə 'dɑː jiːn fe-, fɪ-; ,fed aɪ 'iːn
‖ ,fed ɑː 'jiːn

federal 'fed ər əl **~ism** ,ɪz əm **~ist/s** ɪst/s
§əst/s **~ly** li
,Federal Re'serve

fede|rate v 'fed ə |reɪt **~rated** reɪt ɪd -əd
‖ reɪt̬ əd **~rates** reɪts **~rating** reɪt ɪŋ ‖ reɪt̬ ɪŋ

federation ,fed ə 'reɪʃ ᵊn **~s** z

federative 'fed ər ət ɪv -ə reɪt ɪv
‖ 'fed ə reɪt̬ ɪv ər ət̬ ɪv **~ly** li

Federer 'fed ər ə ‖ -ᵊr —Ger ['feː də ʁɐ]

Fedex, FedEx tdmk 'fed eks **~ed** t **~es** ɪz əz
~ing ɪŋ

fedora, F~ fɪ 'dɔːr ə fə- ‖ -'doʊr- **~s** z

fee fiː **fees** fiːz

feeble 'fiːb ᵊl **~ness** nəs nɪs

feebleminded ,fiːb ᵊl 'maɪnd ɪd ◄ -əd ‖ '· · · ·
~ly li **~ness** nəs nɪs

feebly 'fiːb li

feed fiːd **fed** fed **feeding** 'fiːd ɪŋ **feeds** fiːdz
'feeding ,bottle

feedback 'fiːd bæk →'fiːb-

feedbag 'fiːd bæg →'fiːb- **~s** z

feeder 'fiːd ə ‖ -ᵊr **~s** z

feedlot 'fiːd lɒt ‖ -lɑːt **~s** s

feedstock 'fiːd stɒk ‖ -stɑːk **~s** s

feel fiːᵊl **feeling** 'fiːᵊl ɪŋ **feels** fiːᵊlz **felt** felt

feeler 'fiːl ə ‖ -ᵊr **~s** z

feelgood 'fiːᵊl gʊd

feeling 'fiːᵊl ɪŋ **~ly** li **~s** z

Feeney, Feeny 'fiːn i

fee-paying 'fiː ,peɪ ɪŋ

feet fiːt

Feiffer 'faɪf ə ‖ -ᵊr

feign feɪn (= fane) **feigned** feɪnd **feigning**
'feɪn ɪŋ **feigns** feɪnz

feigned|ly 'feɪn ɪd |li |li -əd- **~ness** nəs nɪs

Feilding 'fiːᵊld ɪŋ

Feinstein 'faɪn staɪn

feint feɪnt (= faint) **feinted** 'feɪnt ɪd -əd
‖ 'feɪnt̬ əd **feinting** 'feɪnt ɪŋ ‖ 'feɪnt̬ ɪŋ
feints feɪnts

Feisal 'faɪs ᵊl

feist|y 'faɪst |i —but the Jamaican word of
similar meaning, sometimes so spelt, is 'feɪst |i
~ier i ə ‖ i ᵊr **~iest** i ɪst i əst **~ily** ɪ li əl i
~iness i nəs i nɪs

felafel fə 'læf ᵊl fɪ-, fe-, -'lɑːf- ‖ -'lɑːf-

feldspar 'feld spɑː ‖ -spɑːr **~s** z

feldspathic feld 'spæθ ɪk '· · ·

Felice fə 'liːs fɪ-

Felicia fə 'lɪs i ə fɪ-, -'lɪʃ- ‖ -'lɪʃ ə -'liːʃ ə

felici|tate fə 'lɪs ɪ |teɪt fɪ-, fe-, -ə- **~tated**
teɪt ɪd -əd ‖ teɪt̬ əd **~tates** teɪts **~tating**
teɪt ɪŋ ‖ teɪt̬ ɪŋ

felicitation fə ,lɪs ɪ 'teɪʃ ᵊn fɪ-, fe-, -ə- **~s** z

felicitous fə 'lɪs ɪt əs fɪ-, fe-, -ət- ‖ -ət̬ əs **~ly** li
~ness nəs nɪs

felicit|y, F~ fə 'lɪs ət |i fɪ-, fe-, -ɪt- ‖ -ət̬ |i **~ies**
iz

Felindre ve 'lɪndr ə və- —Welsh [ve 'lin dre]

feline 'fiːl aɪn **~ly** li **~ness** nəs nɪs **~s** z

Felix 'fiːl ɪks

Felixstowe 'fiːl ɪk stəʊ ‖ -stoʊ

fell, Fell fel **felled** feld **felling** 'fel ɪŋ **fells**
felz

fella 'fel ə **~s** z

fellah 'fel ə -ɑː; fə 'lɑː **fellaheen, fellahin**
,fel ə 'hiːn '· · ·; fə ,lɑː 'hiːn

fel|late fe 'ᵊleɪt fə-, fɪ- ‖ 'fe|l eɪt **~lated** leɪt ɪd
-əd ‖ leɪt̬ əd **~later/s** leɪt ə/z ‖ leɪt̬ ᵊr/z
~lates leɪts **~lating** leɪt ɪŋ ‖ leɪt̬ ɪŋ

fellatio fe 'leɪʃ i əʊ fə-, fɪ-, -'lɑːt- ‖ -oʊ

fellation fe 'leɪʃ ᵊn fə-, fɪ- **~s** z

feller 'fel ə ‖ -ᵊr **~s** z

Felling 'fel ɪŋ

Fellini fe 'liːn i fə-, fɪ- —It [fel 'liː ni]

felloe 'fel əʊ ‖ -oʊ (= fellow) **~s** z

fellow 'fel əʊ ‖ -oʊ **~s** z
,fellow 'creature; ,fellow 'feeling; ,fellow
'men; ,fellow 'traveller

Fellowes, Fellows 'fel əʊz ‖ -oʊz

fellowship 'fel əʊ ʃɪp ‖ -oʊ- **~s** s

felo de se ,fiːl əʊ di 'siː ,fel-, -'seɪ; -deɪ 'seɪ
‖ ,fel oʊ-

felon 'fel ən **~s** z

felonious fə 'ləʊn i ˌəs fe-, fɪ- ‖ -'loʊn- **~ly** li
~ness nəs nɪs

felon|y 'fel ən |i **~ies** iz

Felpham 'felp əm -həm; 'felf-

felspar 'fel spɑː ‖ -spɑːr **~s** z

Felstead, Felsted 'fel stɪd -sted

felt felt **felted** 'felt ɪd -əd **felting** 'felt ɪŋ **felts**
felts

Feltham 'felt əm —as a family name, also
'felθ-

Felton 'felt ən

felt-tip 'felt tɪp ,·'· **~s** s

Feltz felts

felucca fe 'lʌk ə fə-, fɪ- ‖ -'luːk ə -'lʊk ə, -'lʌk ə
~s z

felwort 'fel wɜːt -wɔːt ‖ -wɜːt -wɔːrt

fem. fem

FEMA 'fiːm ə

female 'fiːm eɪᵊl **~ness** nəs nɪs
,female im'personator

Femidom tdmk 'fem ɪ dɒm -ə- ‖ -dɑːm

Feminax tdmk 'fem ɪ næks -ə-

feminine 'fem ən ɪn -ɪn-, §-ən **~ly** li **~ness** nəs
nɪs

femininit|y ,fem ə 'nɪn ət i -ɪ-, -ɪt ‖ -ət̬ |i
~ies iz

feminis... —see **feminiz...**

feminism 'fem ə ,nɪz əm -ɪ-

feminist 'fem ən ɪst -ɪn-, §-əst **~s** s

feminization ,fem ən aɪ 'zeɪʃ ᵊn ,·ɪn-, -ɪ'··
‖ -ən ə-

feminiz|e 'fem ə naɪz -ɪ- **~ed** d **~es** ɪz əz **~ing**
ɪŋ

femme fem —*but as a French word,* fæm —*Fr* [fam] **femmes** femz

femme fatale ˌfæm fə ˈtɑːl ‖ ˌfem fə ˈtæl ˌfæm-, -ˈtɑːl —*Fr* [fam fa tal] **femmes fatales** —*same pronunciation*

femora ˈfem ər ə ‖ ˈfiːm-

femoral ˈfem ᵊr ᵊl ‖ ˈfiːm-

femto- ¦femᵖt əʊ ‖ ¦femᵖt oʊ — **femtogram** ˈfemᵖt əʊ græm ‖ -oʊ-

femur ˈfiːm ə ‖ -ᵊr ~**s** z

fen fen **fens** fenz

Fenby ˈfen bi →ˈfem-

fence fen¦s **fenced** fen¦st **fences** ˈfen¦s ɪz -əz **fencing** ˈfen¦s ɪŋ

fenced-in ˌfen¦st ˈɪn ◂

fence-mending ˈfen¦s ˌmend ɪŋ

fencer ˈfen¦s ə ‖ -ᵊr ~**s** z

fence-sitter ˈfen¦s ˌsɪt ə ‖ -ˌsɪt̬ ᵊr ~**s** z

Fenchurch ˈfen tʃɜːtʃ ‖ -tʃɜːtʃ

fend fend **fended** ˈfend ɪd -əd **fending** ˈfend ɪŋ **fends** fendz

fender, F~ ˈfend ə ‖ -ᵊr ~**s** z

fender-bender ˈfend ə ˌbend ə ‖ -ᵊr ˌbend ᵊr ~**s** z

Fenella fə ˈnel ə fɪ-

fenes|trate fə ˈnes ¦treɪt fɪ-, fe-; ˈfen ɪ s¦treɪt, -ə- ~**trated** treɪt ɪd -əd ‖ treɪt̬ əd ~**trates** treɪts ~**trating** treɪt ɪŋ ‖ treɪt̬ ɪŋ

fenestration ˌfen ɪ ˈstreɪʃ ᵊn -ə- ~**s** z

feng shui ˌfʌŋ ˈʃweɪ ˌfʊŋ-, ˌfeŋ-, ˌˈʃuː i —*Chi* fēng shǔi [¹faŋ ³ʃweɪ]

Fenian ˈfiːn i ᵊn ~**s** z

Fenimore ˈfen ɪ mɔː -ə- ‖ -mɔːr -moʊr

fenland, F~ ˈfen lænd -lænd

Fenn fen

fennec ˈfen ek -ɪk ~**s** s

fennel ˈfen ᵊl

Fennel, Fennell ˈfen ᵊl

Fenner ˈfen ə ‖ -ᵊr ~**'s** z

Fennimore ˈfen ɪ mɔː -ə- ‖ -mɔːr -moʊr

fenny ˈfen i

Fenoulhet ˈfen ə leɪ -ᵊl eɪ

Fenstanton fen ˈstænt ən

fentanyl ˈfent ə nɪl

Fentiman ˈfent ɪ mən -ə-

Fenton ˈfent ən ‖ -ᵊn

fenugreek ˈfen ju griːk -u- ‖ -jə-

Fenway ˈfen weɪ

Fenwick (i) ˈfen ɪk (ii) -wɪk —*The place in Northumberland is* (i)*. The US family name is* (ii)*, the UK one may be either.*

Feodor ˈfiː ə dɔː ‖ -dɔːr —*Russ* [fɪ ˈɔ dər]

feoff fiːf fef **feoffed** fiːft feft **feoffing** ˈfiːf ɪŋ ˈfef- **feoffs** fiːfs fefs

feoffee fe ˈfiː ₍ₒ₎fiː- ~**s** z

feral ˈfer ᵊl ˈfɪər- ‖ ˈfɪr-

ferbam ˈfɜː bæm ˈfɜːb əm ‖ ˈfɜː bæm

fer-de-lanc|e ˌfeə də ˈlɑːn¦s ˌfɜː-, §-ˈlæn¦s ‖ ˌferd ᵊl ˈæn¦s -ˈɑːn¦s ~**es** ɪz əz

Ferdinand ˈfɜːd ɪ nænd -ə-, -ᵊn ænd; -ɪn ənd, -ən ənd ‖ ˈfɜːd ᵊn ænd

Ferens ˈfer ənz

Fergal ˈfɜːg ᵊl ‖ ˈfɜːg ᵊl

Fergie ˈfɜːg i ‖ ˈfɜːg i

Fergus ˈfɜːg əs ‖ ˈfɜːg-

Ferguson, Fergusson ˈfɜːg əs ən ‖ ˈfɜːg-

ferial ˈfɪər i ᵊl ˈfer- ‖ ˈfɪr- ˈfer-

Ferlinghetti ˌfɜːl ɪŋ ˈget i ‖ ˌfɜːl ɪŋ ˈget̬ i

Fermanagh fə ˈmæn ə fɜː- ‖ fᵊr-

Fermat fə ˈmæt fɜː-; ˈfɜːm æt, -ɑː ‖ fer ˈmɑː —*Fr* [fɛʁ ma]

ferment n ˈfɜː ment ‖ ˈfɜː- ~**s** s

fer|ment v fə ¦ment fɜː- ‖ fᵊr- ~**mented** ˈment ɪd -əd ‖ ˈment̬ əd ~**menting** ˈment ɪŋ ‖ ˈment̬ ɪŋ ~**ments** ˈments

fermentation ˌfɜːm en ˈteɪʃ ᵊn -ən-, fə ˌmen- ‖ ˌfɜːm- ~**s** z

Fermi ˈfɜːm i ˈfeəm- ‖ ˈfɜːm i ˈferm i —*It* [ˈfer mi]

fermion ˈfɜːm i ɒn ‖ ˈfɜːm i ɑːn ˈferm- ~**s** z

fermium ˈfɜːm i əm ‖ ˈfɜːm- ˈferm-

Fermor ˈfɜːm ɔː ‖ ˈfɜːm ɔːr

Fermoy fə ˈmɔɪ fɜː-; ˈfɜːm ɔɪ ‖ fᵊr-

fern, Fern fɜːn ‖ fɜːn **ferns** fɜːnz ‖ fɜːnz

Fernandez fə ˈnænd ez fɜː-, -ɪz ‖ fᵊr- fer- —*Sp* Fernández [fer ˈnan deθ]

Fernando fə ˈnænd əʊ ‖ fᵊr ˈnænd oʊ fer-, -ˈnɑːnd- —*Sp* [fer ˈnan do]*, Port* [fər ˈnɐn du]

Fer¦nando 'Po

Ferndale ˈfɜːn deɪ ᵊl ‖ ˈfɜːn-

Ferndown ˈfɜːn daʊn ‖ ˈfɜːn-

ferner|y ˈfɜːn ər |i ‖ ˈfɜːn- ~**ies** iz

Ferneyhough, Fernihough (i) ˈfɜːn i hʌf ‖ ˈfɜːn-, (ii) -həʊ ‖ -hoʊ

Fernley ˈfɜːn li ‖ ˈfɜːn-

ferny ˈfɜːn i ‖ ˈfɜːn i

Fernyhalgh (i) ˈfɜːn i hʌf ‖ ˈfɜːn-, (ii) -hælʃ

Fernyhough (i) ˈfɜːn i hʌf ‖ ˈfɜːn-, (ii) -həʊ ‖ -hoʊ

ferocious fə ˈrəʊʃ əs fɪ- ‖ -ˈroʊʃ- ~**ly** li ~**ness** nəs nɪs

ferocit|y fə ˈrɒs ət |i fɪ-, -ɪt- ‖ -ˈrɑːs ət̬ |i ~**ies** iz

Ferodo *tdmk* fə ˈrəʊd əʊ fɪ- ‖ -ˈroʊd oʊ

-ferous *stress-imposing* fər əs — **ferriferous** fe ˈrɪf ər əs

Ferranti fə ˈrænt i fɪ-, fe- ‖ -ˈrænt̬ i -ˈrɑːnt̬ i

Ferrar (i) ˈfer ə ‖ -ᵊr, (ii) fə ˈrɑː ‖ -ˈrɑːr

Ferrara fə ˈrɑːr ə —*It* [fer ˈra: ra]

Ferrari fə ˈrɑːr i —*It* [fer ˈra: ri]

Ferraro fə ˈrɑːr əʊ ‖ -oʊ

ferrel, F~ ˈfer ᵊl ~**s**, **F~'s** z

Ferrer (i) ˈfer ə ‖ -ᵊr, (ii) fə ˈreə ‖ -ˈreᵊr

Ferrero Rocher *tdmk* fə ˌreər əʊ ˈrɒʃ eɪ -rɒ ˈʃeɪ ‖ fə ˌrer oʊ roʊ ˈʃeɪ

ferr|et ˈfer |ɪt -ət ‖ -|ət ~**eted** ɪt ɪd ət-, -əd ‖ ət əd ~**eting** ɪt ɪŋ ət- ‖ ət̬ ɪŋ ~**ets** ɪts əts ‖ əts

ferri- *comb. form* with *stress-neutral suffix* ¦fer i -aɪ — **ferricyanide** ˌfer i ˈsaɪ ə naɪd ˌaɪ- with *stress-imposing suffix* fe ˈrɪ+ — **ferriferous** fe ˈrɪf ər əs

ferric ˈfer ɪk

ferrie... —*see* **ferry**

Ferrier ˈfer i ə ‖ ᵊr

Ferris, f~ 'fer ɪs §-əs
  'Ferris wheel
ferrite 'fer aɪt
ferro- *comb. form* ˌfer əʊ ‖ -oʊ
— **ferrochromium** ˌfer əʊ 'krəʊm i ˌəm
  ‖ -oʊ 'kroʊm-
ferroconcrete ˌfer əʊ 'kɒŋ kriːt -'kɒn-
  ‖ -oʊ 'kɑːn- ·'·
Ferrograph *tdmk* 'fer əʊ grɑːf -græf ‖ -oʊ græf
ferrous 'fer əs
ferruginous fe 'ruːdʒ ɪn əs fə-, fɪ-, -ən-
ferrule 'fer uːl -əl, -juːl ‖ -əl ~s z
ferr|y, Ferry 'fer |i ~ied id ~ies iz ~ying i ɪŋ
ferryboat 'fer i bəʊt ‖ -boʊt ~s s
ferry|man 'fer i |mən -mæn ~men mən men
fertile 'fɜːt aɪᵊl ‖ 'fɜːt ᵊl (*) ~ly li ~ness nəs
  nɪs
fertilis... —*see* **fertiliz...**
fertility fɜː 'tɪl ət i fə-, -ɪt- ‖ fᵊr 'tɪl ət i
  fer'tility drug; fer'tility ˌsymbol
fertilization ˌfɜːt əl aɪ 'zeɪʃ ᵊn ˌ-ɪl-, -ɪ'-
  ‖ ˌfɜːt̬ ᵊl ə- ~s z
fertiliz|e 'fɜːt ə laɪz -ɪ-, -ᵊl aɪz ‖ 'fɜːt̬ ᵊl aɪz ~ed
  d ~es ɪz əz ~ing ɪŋ
fertilizer 'fɜːt ə laɪz ə '·ɪ-, -ᵊl aɪz-
  ‖ 'fɜːt̬ ᵊl aɪz ᵊr ~s z
ferule 'fer uːl -əl, -juːl ‖ -əl ~s z
fervenc|y 'fɜːv ᵊnts |i ‖ 'fɜːv- ~ies iz
fervent 'fɜːv ᵊnt ‖ 'fɜːv- ~ly li ~ness nəs nɪs
fervid 'fɜːv ɪd §-əd ‖ 'fɜːv- ~ly li ~ness nəs nɪs
fervor, fervour 'fɜːv ə ‖ 'fɜːv ᵊr ~s z
fescue 'fesk juː ~s z
fess, Fess, fesse fes **fesses** 'fes ɪz -əz
fest fest **fests** fests
festal 'fest ᵊl ~ly i
Feste 'fest i
fest|er 'fest |ə ‖ -|ᵊr ~ered əd ‖ ᵊrd ~ering
  ər ɪŋ ~ers əz ‖ ᵊrz
festination ˌfest ɪ 'neɪʃ ᵊn -ə-
Festiniog fe 'stɪn i ɒg ‖ -ɑːg —*Welsh*
  Ffestiniog [fe 'sdin jog]
festival 'fest ɪv ᵊl -əv- ~s z
festive 'fest ɪv ~ly li ~ness nəs nɪs
festivit|y fe 'stɪv ət |i -ɪt- ‖ -ət̬ |i ~ies iz
festoon ₍ₗ₎fe 'stuːn ~ed d ~ing ɪŋ ~s z
festschrift 'fest ʃrɪft →'feʃ- ~s s —*Ger* F~
  ['fɛst ʃʁɪft]
Festus 'fest əs
feta 'fet ə —*ModGk* ['fɛ ta]
fetal 'fiːt ᵊl ‖ 'fiːt̬ ᵊl
fetch fetʃ **fetched** fetʃt **fetches** 'fetʃ ɪz -əz
  fetcher/s 'fetʃ ə/z ‖ -ᵊr/z **fetching/ly**
  'fetʃ ɪŋ /li
fete, fête feɪt ‖ fet (*usually* = *fate*) —*Fr* [fɛt]
  feted, fêted 'feɪt ɪd -əd ‖ 'feɪt̬ əd **fetes,
  fêtes** feɪts **feting, fêting** 'feɪt ɪŋ ‖ 'feɪt̬ ɪŋ
  ˌfête cham'pêtre, ˌfêtes cham'pêtres
  ʃɒm 'peɪtr ə '·peɪtr ‖ ʃɑːm- —*Fr* [ʃɑ̃ pɛtχ]
feticide 'fiːt ɪ saɪd §-ə- ‖ 'fiːt̬- ~s z
fetid 'fet ɪd 'fiːt-, §-əd ‖ 'fet̬ əd ~ly li ~ness
  nəs nɪs
fetish 'fet ɪʃ 'fiːt- ‖ 'fet̬ ɪʃ ~es ɪz əz ~ism ˌɪz əm
  ~ist/s ɪst/s §əst/s

fetishistic ˌfet ɪ 'ʃɪst ɪk ◂ ˌfiːt- ‖ ˌfet̬ ɪ- ~ally
  ᵊl i
fetlock 'fet lɒk ‖ -lɑːk ~s s
fetor 'fiːt ə -ɔː ‖ 'fiːt̬ ᵊr 'fiːt ɔːr ~s z
fetta 'fet ə —*ModGk* feta ['fɛ ta]
fetter 'fet ə ‖ 'fet̬ ᵊr ~ed d **fettering** 'fet ᵊr ɪŋ
  ‖ 'fet̬ ᵊr ɪŋ ~s z
Fettes 'fet ɪs -ɪz, -əs, -əz ‖ 'fet̬ əs
fettl|e 'fet ᵊl ‖ 'fet̬ ᵊl ~ed d ~er/s ə/z ‖ ᵊr/z
  ~es z ~ing ɪŋ
fettuccin|e, ~i ˌfet u 'tʃiːn i ‖ ˌfet̬ ə- —*It* ~e
  [fet tut 'tʃi: ne]
fetus 'fiːt əs ‖ 'fiːt̬ əs ~es ɪz əz
feu fjuː (= *few*) **feued** 'fjuːd **feuing** 'fjuː ɪŋ
  feus fjuːz
feud fjuːd **feuded** 'fjuːd ɪd -əd **feuding**
  'fjuːd ɪŋ **feuds** fjuːdz
feudal 'fjuːd ᵊl ~ly i
  'feudal ˌsystem
feudalism 'fjuːd ᵊl ˌɪz əm
feudalistic ˌfjuːd ᵊl 'ɪst ɪk ◂ -ə 'lɪst- ~ally ᵊl i
feudatory 'fjuːd ə ˌtər i ‖ -ə tɔːr i -toʊr i
fever 'fiːv ə ‖ -ᵊr ~ed d ~s z
  'fever pitch, ·'·
feverfew 'fiːv ə fjuː ‖ -ᵊr-
feverish 'fiːv ᵊr ɪʃ ~ly li ~ness nəs nɪs
Feversham 'fev ə ʃəm ‖ -ᵊr-
few fjuː **fewer** 'fjuː ə ‖ ᵊr **fewest** 'fjuː ɪst §əst
Fewkes fjuːks
fewness 'fjuː nəs -nɪs
Fewston 'fjuːst ən
fey, Fey feɪ
Feydeau 'feɪd əʊ ‖ feɪ 'doʊ —*Fr* [fɛ do]
Feyenoord 'faɪ ə nɔːd ‖ -nɔːrd —*Dutch*
  ['fɛɪ ə noːrt]
Feynman 'faɪn mən
fez, Fez fez **fezes, fezzes** 'fez ɪz -əz
ff..., Ff... *in family names* —*see* **F...**
Ffestiniog fe 'stɪn i ɒg ‖ -ɑːg —*Welsh*
  [fe 'sdin jog]
Ffion 'fiː ɒn ‖ -ɑːn —*Welsh* ['fi ɔn]
Ffolkes fəʊks ‖ foʊks
Ffoulkes (i) fəʊks ‖ foʊks, (ii) fuːks
Ffrangcon 'fræŋk ən
Ffynnongroew, Ffynnongroyw
  ˌfʌn ən 'grɔɪ uː ˌfɪn-, →-əŋ- —*Welsh*
  [ˌfə non 'groi u, -'groɪ-]
-fiable faɪ əb ᵊl '··· —*Although this suffix is
  usually unstressed in RP and GenAm, in some
  other varieties it is stressed, and this variant is
  increasingly heard in RP too:* i'dentifiable *or*
  iˌdenti'fiable
fiance, fiancé, fiancee, fiancée fi 'ɒnts eɪ
  -'ɑːnts-, -'ɒ̃s- ‖ ˌfiː ɑːn 'seɪ fi 'ɑːnts eɪ —*Fr*
  [fjɑ̃ se] — *Preference poll, AmE:* ˌ··'· 53%, ·'··
  47%. ~s z
Fianna Fail, Fianna Fáil ˌfiː ən ə 'fɔɪᵊl -'fɔːl;
  ˌfiːn ə ·' —*Irish* [ˌfiə nə 'faːlʲ]
fiasco fi 'æsk əʊ ‖ -oʊ ~es, ~s z
fiat 'fiː æt 'faɪ-, -ət ‖ -ɑːt
Fiat *tdmk* 'fiː ət -æt ‖ -ɑːt ~s s
fib fɪb **fibbed** fɪbd **fibbing** 'fɪb ɪŋ **fibs** fɪbz
fibber 'fɪb ə ‖ -ᵊr ~s z

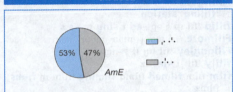

fiber 'faɪb ə ‖ -ᵊr **~s** z
  ˌfiber 'optics
fiberboard 'faɪb ə bɔːd ‖ -ᵊr bɔːrd -bourd
fiberfill 'faɪb ə fɪl ‖ -ᵊr-
Fiberglas *tdmk,* **fiberglass** 'faɪb ə glɑːs §-glæs
  ‖ -ᵊr glæs
Fibonacci ˌfɪb ə 'nɑːtʃ i ˌfiːb- —*It*
  [fi bo 'nat tʃi]
  ˌFibo'nacci ˌnumbers
fibre 'faɪb ə ‖ -ᵊr **~s** z
  ˌfibre 'optics
fibreboard 'faɪb ə bɔːd ‖ -ᵊr bɔːrd -bourd
fibreglass 'faɪb ə glɑːs §-glæs ‖ -ᵊr glæs
fibril 'faɪb rɪl -rəl **~s** z
fibril|late 'fɪb rɪ |leɪt 'faɪb-, -rə- **~lated** leɪt ɪd
  -əd ‖ leɪt̬ əd **~lates** leɪts **~lating** leɪt ɪŋ
  ‖ leɪt̬ ɪŋ
fibrillation ˌfɪb rɪ 'leɪʃ ᵊn ˌfaɪb-, -rə- **~s** z
fibrin 'faɪb rɪn 'fɪb-, §-rən
fibro 'faɪb rəʊ ‖ -roʊ
fibro- *comb. form* |faɪb rəʊ ‖ -roʊ —
  fibrocement ˌfaɪb rəʊ sɪ 'ment -sə' ‖ ˌroʊ-
fibroid 'faɪb rɔɪd **~s** z
fibrom|a faɪ 'brəʊm |ə ‖ -'broʊm |ə **~as** əz
  ~ata ət ə ‖ ət̬ ə
fibrosis faɪ 'brəʊs ɪs §-əs ‖ -'broʊs-
fibrositis ˌfaɪb rə 'saɪt ɪs §-əs ‖ -'saɪt̬ əs
fibrous 'faɪb rəs
fib|ula 'fɪb |jʊl ə ‖ -|jəl ə **~ulae** ju liː jə-
  ‖ jə liː **~ulas** jʊl əz ‖ jəl əz
fiche fiːʃ **fiches** 'fiːʃ ɪz -əz
fichu 'fiːʃ uː 'fɪʃ- **~s** z
fickle 'fɪk ᵊl **~ness** nəs nɪs
fiction 'fɪk ʃᵊn **~s** z
fictional 'fɪk ʃᵊn ᵊl **~ly** i
fictionalis... —*see* **fictionaliz...**
fictionalization ˌfɪk ʃᵊn ᵊl aɪ 'zeɪʃ ᵊn əl ɪ-
  ‖ əl ə- **~s** z
fictionaliz|e ˌfɪk ʃᵊn ə laɪz **~ed** d **~es** ɪz əz
  ~ing ɪŋ
fictitious fɪk 'tɪʃ əs **~ly** li **~ness** nəs nɪs
fictive 'fɪkt ɪv **~ness** nəs nɪs
ficus, Ficus 'faɪk əs 'fiːk-
fid fɪd **fids** fɪdz
fiddl|e 'fɪd ᵊl **~ed** d **~es** z **~ing** ˌɪŋ
fiddleback 'fɪd ᵊl bæk **~s** s
fiddle-de-dee ˌfɪd ᵊl di 'diː
fiddle-faddle 'fɪd ᵊl ˌfæd ᵊl
fiddler, F~ 'fɪd lə 'fɪd ᵊlˌə ‖ 'fɪd lᵊr 'fɪd ᵊlˌᵊr **~s**
  z
  'fiddler crab
fiddlestick 'fɪd ᵊl stɪk **~s** s
fiddlewood 'fɪd ᵊl wʊd

fiddling 'fɪd ᵊl ɪŋ
fiddl|y 'fɪd ᵊlˌ|i **~ier** i ə ‖ i ᵊr **~iest** i ˌəst i əst
Fidel fɪ 'del ⍛fiː-, §fə- —*Sp* [fi 'ðel]
Fidelio fɪ 'deɪl i əʊ fə- ‖ oʊ
Fidelis fɪ 'deɪl ɪs fə-, §-əs
fidelit|y fɪ 'del ət i |i fə-, faɪ-, -ɪt-⍛ ‖ -ət̬ |i **~ies** iz
Fidelma fɪ 'delm ə fə-
fidg|et 'fɪdʒ |ɪt -ət ‖ -|ət **~eted** ɪt ɪd §ət-, -əd
  ‖ ət̬ əd **~eting** ɪt ɪŋ §ət- ‖ ət̬ ɪŋ **~ets** ɪts §əts
  ‖ əts
fidget|y 'fɪdʒ ət i |i -ɪt- ‖ -ət̬ |i **~iness** i nəs
  i nɪs
Fidler *(i)* 'fɪd lə ‖ -lᵊr, *(ii)* 'fiːd-
Fido 'faɪd əʊ ‖ -oʊ
fiducial fɪ 'djuːʃ i əl fə-, faɪ-, -'djuːs-, →-'dʒuːʃ-,
  →-'dʒuːs- ‖ fə 'duːʃ ᵊl -'djuːʃ- **~ly** i
fiduciar|y fɪ 'djuːʃ i ər |i fə-, faɪ-, -'djuːs-,
  →-'dʒuːʃ-, →-'dʒuːs-, -'ər |i ‖ fə 'duːʃ i er |i
  -'djuːʃ-; -'ər |i **~ies** iz
fie faɪ
Fiedler 'fiːd lə ‖ -lᵊr
fief fiːf **fiefs** fiːfs
fiefdom 'fiːf dəm **~s** z
field, Field fiːᵊld **fielded** 'fiːᵊld ɪd -əd
  fielding 'fiːᵊld ɪŋ **fields** fiːᵊldz
  'field day; 'field eˌvent; 'field ˌglasses;
  'field hand; 'field ˌhockey; ˌfield
  'marshal◂, ·ˌ··; 'field ˌmushroom; 'field
  test; 'field ˌtrial; 'field trip
fieldcraft 'fiːᵊld krɑːft §-kræft ‖ -kræft
Fielden 'fiːᵊld ən
fielder, F~ 'fiːᵊld ə ‖ -ᵊr **~s** z
fieldfare 'fiːᵊld feə ‖ -fer -fær **~s** z
Fielding 'fiːᵊld ɪŋ
field|mouse 'fiːᵊld |maʊs **~mice** maɪs
Fields fiːᵊldz
fields|man 'fiːᵊldz |mən **~men** mən men
field-test 'fiːᵊld test **~ed** ɪd əd **~ing** ɪŋ **~s** s
fieldwork 'fiːᵊld wɜːk ‖ -wɜːk **~er/s** ə/z ‖ ᵊr/z
fiend fiːnd **fiends** fiːndz
fiendish 'fiːnd ɪʃ **~ly** li **~ness** nəs nɪs
Fiennes faɪnz
fierce fɪəs ‖ fɪᵊrs **fiercely** 'fɪəs li ‖ 'fɪᵊrs-
  fierceness 'fɪəsnɪs -nəs ‖ 'fɪᵊrs- **fiercer** 'fɪəs ə
  ‖ 'fɪᵊrs ᵊr **fiercest** 'fɪəs ɪst -əst ‖ 'fɪᵊrs-
fier|y 'faɪᵊr |i **~ier** i ə ‖ i ᵊr **~iest** i ˌɪst i əst **~ily**
  əl i ɪ li **~iness** i nəs i nɪs
fiesta, F~ fi 'est ə **~s** z
FIFA 'fiːf ə
fife, Fife faɪf **fifed** faɪft **fifes** faɪfs **fifing**
  'faɪf ɪŋ
fife-rail 'faɪf reɪᵊl
Fifi 'fiː fiː
Fifield 'faɪ fiːᵊld
fifteen ˌfɪf 'tiːn ◂ **~s** z
  ˌfifteen 'days
fifteenth ˌfɪf 'tiːnθ ◂ **~s** s
fifth fɪfθ fɪftθ, fɪθ **fifths** fɪfθs fɪftθs, fɪfs, fɪθs
  ˌFifth A'mendment; ˌfifth 'column
fifth-generation ˌfɪfθ ˌdʒen ə 'reɪʃ ᵊn ◂
  ˌfɪftθ-, ˌfɪθ-
fiftieth 'fɪft i əθ ˌɪθ **~s** s
fift|y 'fɪft |i **~ies** iz

F

fifty-fifty ˌfɪft i ˈfɪft i ◄
ˌfifty-ˌfifty 'chance

fig fɪɡ **figged** fɪɡd **figging** 'fɪɡ ɪŋ **figs** fɪɡz
'fig leaf; 'fig tree

Figaro 'fɪɡ ə rəʊ ‖ -roʊ

Figg fɪɡ

Figgis 'fɪɡ ɪs §-əs

fight faɪt **fighting** 'faɪt ɪŋ ‖ 'faɪt̬ ɪŋ **fights**
faɪts **fought** fɔːt ‖ fɑːt
ˌfighting 'chance

fightback 'faɪt bæk ~s s

fighter 'faɪt ə ‖ 'faɪt̬ ər ~s z

figment 'fɪɡ mənt ~s s

Figueroa ˌfɪɡ ə 'rəʊ ə ‖ -'roʊ ə

figurative 'fɪɡ ər_ət ɪv '·jʊr- ‖ -jər ət̬ ɪv ~ly li
~ness nəs nɪs

fig|ure 'fɪɡ |ə §-|jə ‖ 'fɪɡ |jər -jʊr (*) —The
pronunciation without **j**, standard and usual
in BrE, is in AmE generally condemned.
~**ured** əd §jəd ‖ jərd jʊrd ~**ures** əz §jəz ‖ jərz
jʊrz ~**uring** ər ɪŋ §jər- ‖ jər ɪŋ jʊr ɪŋ
ˌfigured 'bass; ˌfigure of 'eight; ˌfigure
of 'speech; 'figure ˌskating

figurehead 'fɪɡ ə hed ‖ -jər- ~s z

figurine ˌfɪɡ ə riːn -jʊ°-, ˌ·'· ‖ ˌfɪɡ jə 'riːn -ju-
~s z

figwort 'fɪɡ wɜːt §-wɔːt ‖ -wɜːt -wɔːrt ~s s

Fiji 'fiː dʒiː ˌ·'·

Fijian fi 'dʒiː_ən ˌfiː- ‖ 'fiː dʒiː ən fɪ 'dʒiː ən ~s
z

Fila tdmk 'fiː l ɑː -ə

filament 'fɪl ə mənt ~s s

filamentous ˌfɪl ə 'ment əs ◄ ‖ -'ment̬-

filari|a fɪ 'leər i_|ə fə- ‖ -'ler- -'lær- ~**ae** iː

filariasis ˌfɪl ə 'raɪ_əs ɪs §-əs; fɪ ˌleər i 'eɪs-, fə-

filbert 'fɪlb ət ‖ -ərt ~s s

filch fɪltʃ **filched** fɪltʃt **filches** 'fɪltʃ ɪz -əz
filching 'fɪltʃ ɪŋ

file faɪ°l **filed** faɪ°ld **files** faɪ°lz **filing** 'faɪ°l ɪŋ
'file ˌserver

filename 'faɪ°l neɪm ~s z

filet 'fɪl eɪ -ɪt, §-ət ‖ fɪ 'leɪ ~s z
ˌfilet 'mignon 'miːn jɒn -'mɪn- ‖; fiˌlet
mi'gnon mɪn 'jɒn -'jɑːn, -'joʊn —Fr
[fi le mi njɔ̃]

Filey 'faɪl i

filial 'fɪl i_əl ~**ly** i ~**ness** nəs nɪs

filibeg 'fɪl ɪ beɡ -ə- ~s z

filibuster 'fɪl ɪ bʌst ə '·ə- ‖ -°r ~**ed** d
filibustering 'fɪl ɪ bʌst ər_ɪŋ '·ə- ~s z

filigree 'fɪl ɪ griː -ə- ~**d** d ~**ing** ɪŋ ~s z

filing 'faɪ°l ɪŋ ~s z
'filing ˌcabinet; 'filing clerk

Filioque ˌfiːl i 'əʊ kwi ˌfɪl-, ˌfaɪl- ‖ -'oʊ-
the ˌFili'oque clause

Filipin|o ˌfɪl ɪ 'piːn| əʊ ◄ -ə- ‖ -oʊ ◄ ~**a** ə ɑː ~**as**
əz ɑːz ~**os** əʊz ‖ oʊz

fill fɪl **filled** fɪld **filling** 'fɪl ɪŋ **fills** fɪlz

filler 'fɪl ə ‖ -°r ~s z
'filler cap

fill|et 'fɪl| ɪt §-ət ~**eted** ɪt ɪd §ət-, -əd ‖ -ət̬ əd
~**eting** ɪt ɪŋ §ət- ‖ ət̬ ɪŋ ~**ets** ɪts §əts

Filleul 'fɪl i_əl

fill-in 'fɪl ɪn ~s z

filling 'fɪl ɪŋ ~s z
'filling ˌstation

fillip 'fɪl ɪp §-əp ~**ed** t ~**ing** ɪŋ ~s s

Fillmore 'fɪl mɔː ‖ -mɔːr -moʊr

Fillongley 'fɪl ɒŋ li ‖ -ɑːŋ-

fill|y 'fɪl |i ~**ies** iz

film fɪlm **filmed** fɪlmd **filming** 'fɪlm ɪŋ **films**
fɪlmz
'film ˌpremière ‖ 'film preˌmière; 'film
ˌsetting; 'film star; 'film stock

filmgoer 'fɪlm ˌɡəʊ ə ‖ -ˌɡoʊ °r ~s z

filmic 'fɪlm ɪk

film-maker 'fɪlm ˌmeɪk ə ‖ -°r ~s z

filmstrip 'fɪlm strɪp ~s s

film|y 'fɪlm |i ~**ier** i_ə ‖ i_°r ~**iest** i_ɪst i_əst ~**ily**
ɪ li ə li ~**iness** i nəs i nɪs

filo 'fiːl əʊ ~'faɪl- ‖ -oʊ —ModGk ['fi lo]

Filofax tdmk 'faɪl əʊ fæks ‖ -ə- ~**es** ɪz əz

fils monetary unit, coin fɪls

fils 'son' fiːs —Fr [fis]

filter 'fɪlt ə ‖ -°r ~**ed** d **filtering** 'fɪlt_ər ɪŋ ~s z
'filter bed; 'filter ˌpaper; 'filter tip, ˌ·'·

filterable 'fɪlt_ər əb °l

filter-tipped ˌfɪlt ə 'tɪpt ◄ ‖ -°r-

filth fɪlθ

filth|y 'fɪlθ |i ~**ier** i_ə ‖ i_°r ~**iest** i_ɪst i_əst ~**ily**
ɪ li əl i ~**iness** i nəs i nɪs

filtrable 'fɪltr əb °l

filtrate n 'fɪltr eɪt ~s s

filtration fɪl 'treɪʃ °n ~s z

fin fɪn —but as a French word fæ̃, fæn; see also
phrases with this word **finned** fɪnd **fins** fɪnz

Fina tdmk 'fiːn ə -faɪn-

finable 'faɪn əb °l

finagl|e fɪ 'neɪɡ °l fə- ~**ed** d ~**es** z ~**ing** ˌɪŋ

final 'faɪn °l ~**ly** i ~s z

finale fɪ 'nɑːl i fə- ‖ -'næl i -'nɑːl i ~s z

finalis... —see **finaliz...**

finalist 'faɪn °l ɪst §-əst ~s s

finality faɪ 'næl ət i -ɪt- ‖ -ət̬ i

finaliz|e 'faɪn ə laɪz -°l aɪz ~**ed** d ~**es** ɪz əz
~**ing** ɪŋ

finally 'faɪn əl i

FINANCE

financ|e n 'faɪn ænts faɪ 'nænts, fɪ-, fə- —
Preference polls, AmE: '·· 87%, ·'· 13%; BrE:
'·· 81%, ·'· 19%. ~**es** ɪz əz

financ|e v faɪ 'nænts fɪ-, fə- ‖ fə- faɪ-;
'faɪn ænts ~**ed** t ~**es** ɪz əz ~**ing** ɪŋ

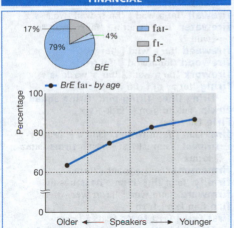

FINANCIAL

fai-
fi-
fə-

BrE

BrE faɪ- *by age*

Percentage

Older ◄— Speakers —► Younger

financial faɪ ˈnænʦ ᵊl fɪ-, fə- ‖ fə- faɪ- —
Preference poll, BrE: faɪ- 79%, fɪ- 17%, fə- 4%.
~ly i
fi₁nancial ˈyear
financier faɪ ˈnænʦ i ₚə fɪ-, fə- ‖ ˌfɪn ən ˈsɪᵊr
ˌfaɪn- *(*)* **~s** z
Finbar ˈfɪn bɑː →ˈfɪm- ‖ -bɑːr
Finborough ˈfɪn bər ₚə →ˈfɪm-, §-ˌbʌr ə
‖ -ˌbɜː oʊ
finch, Finch fɪnʧ **finches** ˈfɪnʧ ɪz -əz
Finchale ˈfɪŋk ᵊl
Finchampstead ˈfɪnʧ əm sted -əmp-, -stɪd
Finchingfield ˈfɪnʧ ɪŋ fiːᵊld
Finchley ˈfɪnʧ li
find faɪnd **finding** ˈfaɪnd ɪŋ **finds** faɪndz
found faʊnd
finder ˈfaɪnd ə ‖ -ᵊr **~s** z
Findern ˈfɪnd ən ‖ -ᵊrn
fin de siècle ˌfæ̃ də ˈsjek lə ˌfæn-, -si ˈeɪk ᵊl
—*Fr* [fæ̃d sjɛkl]
Findhorn ˈfɪnd hɔːn ‖ -hɔːrn
finding ˈfaɪnd ɪŋ **~s** z
Findlater ˈfɪn lət ə ˈfɪnd- ‖ -lət ᵊr
Findlay ˈfɪn li ˈfɪnd-
Findon ˈfɪnd ən
Findus *tdmk* ˈfɪnd əs
fine *ordinary senses* faɪn **fined** faɪnd **finer**
ˈfaɪn ə ‖ -ᵊr **fines** faɪnz **finest** ˈfaɪn ɪst -əst
fining ˈfaɪn ɪŋ
ˌfine ˈart; ˌfine ˈprint
fine *Irish word* ˈfɪn ə —*Irish* [ˈfi nⁱə]
ˌFine ˈGael
fine *French word, ‘liqueur’* fiːn —*Fr* [fin]
fineable ˈfaɪn əb ᵊl
fine-drawn ˌfaɪn ˈdrɔːn ◄ ‖ -ˈdrɑːn ◄
ˌfine-drawn ˈfeatures
finely ˈfaɪn li
finer|y ˈfaɪn ər |i **~ies** iz
fines herbes ˌfiːnz ˈeəb ˌfiːn-, -ˈɜːb ‖ -ˈeᵊrb
—*Fr* [fin zɛʁb]
finespun ˌfaɪn ˈspʌn ◄ ˈ··
finess|e fɪ ˈnes fə- **~ed** t **~es** ɪz əz **~ing** ɪŋ

fine-tooth ˌfaɪn ˈtuːθ ◄ §-ˈtʊθ, ˈ·· **~ed** t
ˌfine-ˈtooth comb, ˌfine-tooth ˈcomb
fine-tun|e ˌfaɪn ˈtjuːn →-ˈʧuːn ‖ -ˈtuːn -ˈtjuːn
~ed d **~es** z **~ing** ɪŋ
Fingal ˈfɪŋ gᵊl
finger ˈfɪŋ gə ‖ -gᵊr **fingered** ˈfɪŋ gəd ‖ -gᵊrd
fingering ˈfɪŋ gər ɪŋ **fingers** ˈfɪŋ gəz ‖ gᵊrz
ˈfinger bowl
fingerboard ˈfɪŋ gə bɔːd ‖ -gᵊr bɔːrd -boʊrd **~s**
z
-fingered ˈfɪŋ gəd ‖ -gᵊrd
fingering ˈfɪŋ gər ɪŋ **~s** z
fingermark ˈfɪŋ gə mɑːk ‖ -gᵊr mɑːrk **~s** s
fingernail ˈfɪŋ gə neɪᵊl ‖ -gᵊr- **~s** z
finger-|paint ˈfɪŋ gə |peɪnt ‖ -gᵊr- **~painting**
ˌpeɪnt ɪŋ ‖ ˌpeɪnt̬ ɪŋ **~paints** peɪnts
fingerplate ˈfɪŋ gə pleɪt ‖ -gᵊr- **~s** s
finger-pointing ˈfɪŋ gə ˌpɔɪnt ɪŋ
‖ -gᵊr ˌpɔɪnt̬ ɪŋ
fingerpost ˈfɪŋ gə pəʊst ‖ -gᵊr poʊst **~s** s
finger|print ˈfɪŋ gə |prɪnt ‖ -gᵊr- **~printed**
prɪnt ɪd -əd ‖ prɪnt̬ əd **~printing** prɪnt ɪŋ
‖ prɪnt̬ ɪŋ **~prints** prɪnts
fingerspelling ˈfɪŋ gə ˌspel ɪŋ ‖ -gᵊr-
fingerstall ˈfɪŋ gə stɔːl ‖ -gᵊr- -stɑːl **~s** z
fingertip ˈfɪŋ gə tɪp ‖ -gᵊr- **~s** s
Fingest ˈfɪndʒ ɪst §-əst
finial ˈfaɪn i ᵊl ˈfɪn- **~s** z
finical ˈfɪn ɪk ᵊl **~ly** i **~ness** nəs nɪs
finicking ˈfɪn ɪk ɪŋ
finickity fɪ ˈnɪk ət i fə-, -ɪt- ‖ -ət̬ i
finicky ˈfɪn ɪk i
fining ˈfaɪn ɪŋ **~s** z
finis ˈfɪn ɪs ˈfiːn-, ˈfaɪn-, §-əs
finish ˈfɪn ɪʃ **finished** ˈfɪn ɪʃt **finishes**
ˈfɪn ɪʃ ɪz -əz **finishing** ˈfɪn ɪʃ ɪŋ
ˈfinishing school; ˌfinishing ˈtouch
finisher ˈfɪn ɪʃ ə ‖ -ᵊr **~s** z
Finisterre ˌfɪn ɪ ˈsteə ◄ -ə- ‖ -ˈsteᵊr
finite ˈfaɪn aɪt **~ly** li **~ness** nəs nɪs
finito fɪ ˈniːt əʊ fə- ‖ -oʊ —*It* [fi ˈniː to]
fink, Fink, Finke fɪŋk **finked** fɪŋkt **finking**
ˈfɪŋk ɪŋ **finks** fɪŋks
Finkelstein ˈfɪŋk ᵊl staɪn
Finland ˈfɪn lənd
Finlandia fɪn ˈlænd i ə
Finlandi|sation, ~zation ˌfɪn lənd aɪ ˈzeɪʃ ᵊn
-ɪ- ‖ -ə ˈzeɪʃ-
Finlay ˈfɪn li -leɪ
Finlayson ˈfɪn lɪs ən
Finn fɪn **Finns** fɪnz
Finnair *tdmk* ˈfɪn eə ˌ·ˈ· ‖ -er -ær
finnan ˈfɪn ən
ˌfinnan ˈhaddie ˈhæd i
Finnegan ˈfɪn ɪg ən -əg- **~s, ~'s** z
ˌFinnegans ˈWake
Finney ˈfɪn i
Finnic ˈfɪn ɪk
Finnish ˈfɪn ɪʃ
Finno-Ugrian ˌfɪn əʊ ˈjuːg ri ən ◄ -ˈuːg- ‖ ˌ·oʊ-
Finno-Ugric ˌfɪn əʊ ˈjuːg rɪk ◄ -ˈuːg- ‖ ˌ·oʊ-
Finnuala fɪəˈnʊələ ‖ ˌfiːᵊˈnuːələ
fino ˈfiːn əʊ ‖ -oʊ **~s** z —*Sp* [ˈfi no]

finocchio, finochio fɪ ˈnɒk i əʊ fə-
‖ -ˈnoʊk i oʊ
Finola fɪ ˈnəʊl ə fə- ‖ -ˈnoʊl ə
Finsberg ˈfɪnz bɜːg ‖ -bɜːg
Finsbury ˈfɪnz bər i §-ˌber i ‖ -ˌber i
  ˌFinsbury ˈPark
Finucane fɪ ˈnuːk ən fə-
Finzi ˈfɪnz i
Fiona fi ˈəʊn ə ‖ fi ˈoʊn ə
Fionnuala fiə ˈnʊəl ə ‖ ˈfiːə ˈnu əl ə
fiord fi ˈɔːd ˈfiːˌɔːd, fjɔːd ‖ fi ˈɔːrd bɪɔːrd ~s z
fipple ˈfɪp ᵊl ~s z
fir fɜː ‖ fɜ˞ː (= fur) **firs** fɜːz ‖ fɜ˞ːz
Firbank ˈfɜː bæŋk ‖ ˈfɜ˞ː-
fire ˈfaɪ ə ‖ ˈfaɪ ᵊr ~d d **firing** ˈfaɪ ər ɪŋ
  ‖ ˈfaɪ ᵊr ɪŋ ~s z
  ˈfire aˌlarm; ˈfire briˌgade; ˈfire
  deˌpartment; ˈfire drill; ˈfire ˌengine;
  ˈfire eˌscape; ˈfire exˌtinguisher; ˈfire
  ˌfighter; ˈfire ˌfighting; ˈfire hose; ˈfire
  ˌhydrant; ˈfire inˌsurance; ˈfire ˌirons;
  ˈfire screen; ˈfire ship; ˈfire ˌstation; ˈfire
  ˌwarden
firearm ˈfaɪ ər ɑːm ‖ ˈfaɪ ᵊr ɑːrm ~s z
fireball ˈfaɪ ə bɔːl ‖ ˈfaɪ ᵊr- -bɑːl ~s z
fireboat ˈfaɪ ə bəʊt ‖ ˈfaɪ ᵊr boʊt ~s s
firebomb ˈfaɪ ə bɒm ‖ ˈfaɪ ᵊr bɑːm ~ed d ~ing
  ɪŋ ~s z
firebox ˈfaɪ ə bɒks ‖ ˈfaɪ ᵊr bɑːks ~es ɪz əz
firebrand ˈfaɪ ə brænd ‖ ˈfaɪ ᵊr- ~s z
firebrat ˈfaɪ ə bræt ‖ ˈfaɪ ᵊr- ~s s
firebreak ˈfaɪ ə breɪk ‖ ˈfaɪ ᵊr- ~s s
firebrick ˈfaɪ ə brɪk ‖ ˈfaɪ ᵊr- ~s s
fireclay ˈfaɪ ə kleɪ ‖ ˈfaɪ ᵊr-
firecracker ˈfaɪ ə ˌkræk ə ‖ ˈfaɪ ᵊr ˌkræk ᵊr ~s
  z
firecrest ˈfaɪ ə krest ‖ ˈfaɪ ᵊr- ~s s
firedamp ˈfaɪ ə dæmp ‖ ˈfaɪ ᵊr-
firedog ˈfaɪ ə dɒg ‖ ˈfaɪ ᵊr dɔːg -dɑːg ~s z
fire-eat|er ˈfaɪ ərˌiːt| ə ‖ ˈfaɪ ᵊr ˌiːt| ᵊr ~ing ɪŋ
  ~s z
firefight ˈfaɪ ə faɪt ‖ ˈfaɪ ᵊr- ~s s
fire|fly ˈfaɪ ə |flaɪ ‖ ˈfaɪ ᵊr- ~flies flaɪz
firefox, F~ tdmk ˈfaɪ ə fɒks ‖ ˈfaɪ ᵊr fɑːks
fireguard ˈfaɪ ə gɑːd ‖ ˈfaɪ ᵊr gɑːrd ~s z
fire|house ˈfaɪ ə |haʊs ‖ ˈfaɪ ᵊr- ~houses
  haʊz ɪz -əz
firelight ˈfaɪ ə laɪt ‖ ˈfaɪ ᵊr-
firelighter ˈfaɪ ə ˌlaɪt ə ‖ ˈfaɪ ᵊr ˌlaɪt ᵊr ~s z
fire|man ˈfaɪ ə |mən ‖ ˈfaɪ ᵊr- ~man's mənz
  ~men mən men
fireplac|e ˈfaɪ ə pleɪs ‖ ˈfaɪ ᵊr- ~es ɪz əz
fireplug ˈfaɪ ə plʌg ‖ ˈfaɪ ᵊr- ~s z
firepower ˈfaɪ ə ˌpaʊ ə ‖ ˈfaɪ ᵊr ˌpaʊ ᵊr
fireproof ˈfaɪ ə pruːf §-prʊf ‖ ˈfaɪ ᵊr-
fire-rais|er ˈfaɪ ə ˌreɪz |ə ‖ ˈfaɪ ᵊr ˌreɪz |ᵊr ~ers
  əz ‖ ᵊrz ~ing ɪŋ
fireside ˈfaɪ ə saɪd ‖ ˈfaɪ ᵊr- ~s z
firestone, F~ ˈfaɪ ə stəʊn ‖ ˈfaɪ ᵊr stoʊn ~s z
firestorm ˈfaɪ ə stɔːm ‖ ˈfaɪ ᵊr stɔːrm ~s z
firethorn ˈfaɪ ə θɔːn ‖ ˈfaɪ ᵊr θɔːrn ~s z
firetrap ˈfaɪ ə træp ‖ ˈfaɪ ᵊr- ~s s

firewalk|er ˈfaɪ ə ˌwɔːk |ə ‖ ˈfaɪ ᵊr ˌwɔːk |ᵊr
  -ˌwɑːk- ~ers əz ‖ ᵊrz ~ing ɪŋ
firewall ˈfaɪ ə wɔːl ‖ ˈfaɪ ᵊr wɔːl -wɑːl ~s z
firewater ˈfaɪ ə ˌwɔːt ə ‖ ˈfaɪ ᵊr ˌwɔːt̬ ᵊr
  -ˌwɑːt̬ ᵊr
fireweed ˈfaɪ ə wiːd ‖ ˈfaɪ ᵊr-
firewood ˈfaɪ ə wʊd ‖ ˈfaɪ ᵊr-
firework ˈfaɪ ə wɜːk ‖ ˈfaɪ ᵊr wɜːk ~s s
firing ˈfaɪ ər ɪŋ ‖ ˈfaɪ ᵊr ɪŋ ~s z
  ˈfiring line; ˈfiring pin; ˈfiring squad
firkin ˈfɜːk ɪn §-ən ‖ ˈfɜ˞ːk- ~s z
Firle fɜːl ‖ fɜ˞ːl
firm fɜːm ‖ fɜ˞ːm **firmer** ˈfɜːm ə ‖ ˈfɜ˞ːm ᵊr
  firmest ˈfɜːm ɪst -əst ‖ ˈfɜ˞ːm- **firms** fɜːmz
  ‖ fɜ˞ːmz
firmament ˈfɜːm ə mənt ‖ ˈfɜ˞ːm-
firm|ly ˈfɜːm |li ‖ ˈfɜ˞ːm- ~ness nəs nɪs
firmware ˈfɜːm weə ‖ ˈfɜ˞ːm wer -wær
firn fɪən fɜːn ‖ fɪ˞rn
first fɜːst ‖ fɜ˞ːst **firsts** fɜːsts ‖ fɜ˞ːsts
  ˌfirst ˈaid; ˌfirst ˈaider/s ˈeɪd ə/z ‖ -ᵊr/z;
  ˌfirst ˈbase; ˌfirst ˈclass◂; ˌfirst ˈcousin;
  ˌfirst-day ˈcover; ˌfirst ˈfloor; ˌfirst ˈlady;
  ˌfirst lieuˈtenant◂; ˌfirst ˈmate; ˌfirst
  name; ˌfirst ˈnight; ˌfirst ofˈfender; ˌfirst
  ˌpast the ˈpost; ˌfirst ˈperson◂; ˌfirst
  reˈfusal; ˌfirst ˈstrike
firstborn ˈfɜːst bɔːn ‖ ˈfɜ˞ːst bɔːrn ~s z
first-class ˌfɜːst ˈklɑːs ◂ §-ˈklæs ‖ ˌfɜ˞ːst ˈklæs ◂
  ˌfirst-class hoˈtel
first-degree ˌfɜːst dɪ ˈgriː ◂ -də- ‖ ˌfɜ˞ːst-
  ˌfirst-deˌgree ˈmurder
first-ever ˌfɜːst ˈev ə ◂ ‖ ˌfɜ˞ːst ˈev ᵊr ◂
firstfruits ˈfɜːst fruːts ‖ ˈfɜ˞ːst-
firsthand ˌfɜːst ˈhænd ◂ ‖ ˌfɜ˞ːst-
firstly ˈfɜːst li ‖ ˈfɜ˞ːst-
first-nighter ˌfɜːst ˈnaɪt ə ‖ ˌfɜ˞ːst ˈnaɪt̬ ᵊr ~s z
first-person ˌfɜːst ˈpɜːs ᵊn ◂ ‖ ˌfɜ˞ːst ˈpɜ˞ːs n ◂
first-rate ˌfɜːst ˈreɪt ◂ ‖ ˌfɜ˞ːst-
first-string ˌfɜːst ˈstrɪŋ ◂ ‖ ˌfɜ˞ːst-
first-time ˌfɜːst ˈtaɪm ◂ ‖ ˌfɜ˞ːst-
  ˌfirst-time ˈbuyer
firth, Firth fɜːθ ‖ fɜ˞ːθ **firths** fɜːθs ‖ fɜ˞ːθs
firtree ˈfɜː triː ‖ ˈfɜ˞ː- ~s z
fiscal ˈfɪsk ᵊl ~ly i
  ˌfiscal ˈyear
Fischer ˈfɪʃ ə ‖ -ᵊr
fish, Fish fɪʃ **fished** fɪʃt **fishing** ˈfɪʃ ɪŋ **fishes**
  ˈfɪʃ ɪz -əz
  ˈfish farm; ˌfish ˈfinger; ˈfishing rod;
  ˈfish knife; ˌfish 'n' ˈchips; ˈfish slice;
  ˈfish stick
Fishbourne ˈfɪʃ bɔːn ‖ -bɔːrn -boʊrn
fishbowl ˈfɪʃ bəʊl →-bɒʊl ‖ -boʊl ~s z
fishcake ˈfɪʃ keɪk ~s s
fisher, F~ ˈfɪʃ ə ‖ -ᵊr ~s z
fisher|man ˈfɪʃ ə |mən ‖ -ᵊr- ~man's mənz
  ~men mən men
fisher|y ˈfɪʃ ər |i ~ies iz
fish-eye ˈfɪʃ aɪ
  ˌfish-eye ˈlens
Fishguard ˈfɪʃ gɑːd ‖ -gɑːrd
fishhook ˈfɪʃ hʊk §-huːk ~s s

fishi... —*see* fish, fishy
Fishley 'fɪʃ li
Fishlock 'fɪʃ lɒk ‖ -lɑːk
fishmonger 'fɪʃ ˌmʌŋ gə ‖ -gˀr -ˌmɑːŋ- **~s** z
fishnet 'fɪʃ net **~s** s
fishplate 'fɪʃ pleɪt **~s** s
fishpond 'fɪʃ pɒnd ‖ -pɑːnd **~s, F~s** z
fishtail 'fɪʃ teɪˀl **~ed** d **~ing** ɪŋ **~s** z
Fishwick 'fɪʃ wɪk
fish|wife 'fɪʃ |waɪf **~wives** waɪvz
fish|y 'fɪʃ |i **~ier** iˌə ‖ iˌˀr **~iest** iˌɪst iˌəst **~ily**
ɪ li əl i **~iness** i nəs i nɪs
Fisk, Fiske fɪsk
Fison 'faɪs ˀn
fissile 'fɪs aɪˀl ‖ -ˀl (*)
fission 'fɪʃ ˀn **~s** z
fissionable 'fɪʃ ˀn_əb ˀl
fissiparous fɪ 'sɪp ər əs fə-
fissure 'fɪʃ ə -ʊə ‖ -ˀr **~d** d **fissuring** 'fɪʃ ər ɪŋ
-ʊər- **~s** z
fist fɪst **fisted** 'fɪst ɪd -əd **fisting** 'fɪst ɪŋ **fists**
fɪsts
-fisted 'fɪst ɪd ◂ -əd
fistful 'fɪst fʊl **~s** z
fisticuffs 'fɪst i kʌfs
fistul|a 'fɪst jʊl |ə ‖ 'fɪs tʃəl |ə →'fɪʃ- **~ae** iː
~ar ə ‖ ˀr **~as** əz **~ous** əs
fit fɪt **fits** fɪts **fitted** 'fɪt ɪd -əd **fitter** 'fɪt ə
‖ 'fɪţ ˀr **fittest** 'fɪt ɪst -əst ‖ 'fɪţ əst **fitting**
'fɪt ɪŋ ‖ 'fɪţ ɪŋ
fitch, Fitch fɪtʃ **fitches** 'fɪtʃ ɪz -əz
fitchew, F~ 'fɪtʃ uː **~s** z
fitful 'fɪt fˀl -fʊl **~ly** i **~ness** nəs nɪs
fitment 'fɪt mənt **~s** s
fitness 'fɪt nəs -nɪs
fitter, F~ 'fɪt ə ‖ 'fɪţ ˀr **~s** z
fitting 'fɪt ɪŋ ‖ 'fɪţ ɪŋ **~ly** li **~ness** nəs nɪs
Fitz fɪts
Fitzgerald, FitzGerald ˌₜfɪts 'dʒer əld
Fitzgibbon ˌₜfɪts 'gɪb ən
Fitzhardinge ˌₜfɪts 'hɑːd ɪŋ ‖ -'hɑːrd-
Fitzherbert ˌₜfɪts 'hɜːb ət ‖ -'hɜːb ˀrt
Fitzjames ˌₜfɪts 'dʒeɪmz
Fitzjohn ˌₜfɪts 'dʒɒn ‖ -'dʒɑːn
Fitzpatrick ˌₜfɪts 'pætr ɪk
Fitzrovia ˌₜfɪts 'rəʊv iˌə ‖ -'roʊv-
Fitzroy ˌₜfɪts 'rɔɪ ˈ ◂
Fitzsimmons ˌₜfɪts 'sɪm ənz
Fitzwalter ˌₜfɪts 'wɔːlt ə ‖ -'wɔːlt ˀr -'wɑːlt ˀr
Fitzwilliam ˌₜfɪts 'wɪl jəm
five faɪv —*but for clarity in communications
code*, fife faɪf **fives** faɪvz
ˌfive-ˌfinger 'exercise; ˌfive o''clock◂,
ˌfive o'ˌclock 'shadow; Five-'Year Plan
five-and-dime ˌfaɪv ˀnd 'daɪm ◂
five-and-ten ˌfaɪv ənd 'ten ◂
five-a-side ˌfaɪv ə 'saɪd ◂
five-barred ˌfaɪv 'bɑːd ◂ ‖ -'bɑːrd ◂
five-eighth ˌfaɪv 'eɪtθ ◂ §-'eɪθ **~s** s
fivefold 'faɪv fəʊld →-fɒʊld ‖ -foʊld
fivepenc|e 'faɪf pən𝗌 'faɪv- **~es** ɪz əz
fivepenn|y 'faɪf pən |i 'faɪv- **~ies** iz
fiver 'faɪv ə ‖ -ˀr **~s** z

five-spot 'faɪv spɒt ‖ -spɑːt **~s** s
five-star ˌfaɪv 'stɑː ◂ ‖ -'stɑːr ◂
ˌfive-star ho'tel
fix fɪks **fixed** fɪkst **fixes** 'fɪks ɪz -əz **fixing/s**
'fɪks ɪŋ/z
fixable 'fɪks əb ˀl
fix|ate fɪk 's|eɪt 'fɪks |eɪt ‖ 'fɪks |eɪt **~ated**
eɪt ɪd -əd ‖ eɪţ əd **~ates** eɪts **~ating** eɪt ɪŋ
‖ eɪţ ɪŋ
fixation fɪk 'seɪʃ ˀn **~s** z
fixative 'fɪks ət ɪv ‖ -əţ ɪv **~s** z
fixedly 'fɪks ɪd li -əd-
fixed-rate ˌfɪkst'reɪt ◂
fixer 'fɪks ə ‖ -ˀr **~s** z
fixit|y 'fɪks ət |i -ɪt- ‖ -əţ |i **~ies** iz
fixture 'fɪks tʃə ‖ -tʃˀr **~s** z
fizgig 'fɪz gɪg **~s** z
fizz fɪz **fizzed** fɪzd **fizzes** 'fɪz ɪz -əz **fizzing**
'fɪz ɪŋ
fizzl|e 'fɪz ˀl **~ed** d **~es** z **~ing** ɪŋ
fizz|y 'fɪz |i **~ier** iˌə ‖ iˌˀr **~iest** iˌɪst iˌəst
~ily ɪ li əl i **~iness** i nəs i nɪs
fjord fi 'ɔːd 'fiː ɔːd, fjɔːd ‖ fi 'ɔːrd fjɔːrd **~s** z
flab flæb
flabbergast 'flæb ə gɑːst §-gæst ‖ -ˀr gæst
~ed ɪd əd **~ing** ɪŋ **~s** s
flabb|y 'flæb |i **~ier** iˌə ‖ iˌˀr **~iest** iˌɪst iˌəst
~ily ɪ li əl i **~iness** i nəs i nɪs
flaccid 'flæks ɪd 'flæs-, §-əd **~ly** li **~ness** nəs
nɪs
flaccidity flæk 'sɪd ət i flæ-, flə-, -ɪt- ‖ -əţ i
Flack, flack flæk
flag flæg **flagged** flægd **flagging** 'flæg ɪŋ
flags flægz
'flag day
flagellant 'flædʒ əl ənt -ɪl-; flə 'dʒel- **~s** s
flagellate *n, adj* 'flædʒ əl ət -ɪl-, -ɪt; -ə leɪt **~s** s
flagel|late *v* 'flædʒ ə |leɪt -ɪ- **~lated** leɪt ɪd
-əd ‖ leɪţ əd **~lates** leɪts **~lating** leɪt ɪŋ
‖ leɪţ ɪŋ
flagellation ˌflædʒ ə 'leɪʃ ˀn -ɪ- **~s** z
flagell|um flə 'dʒel| əm flæ- **~a** ə **~ar** ə ‖ ˀr
~ums əmz
flageolet ˌflædʒ ə 'let -'leɪ **~s** s
Flagg flæg
flagon 'flæg ən **~s** z
flagpole 'flæg pəʊl →-pɒʊl ‖ -poʊl **~s** z
flagrancy 'fleɪg rən𝗌 i
flagrant 'fleɪg rənt **~ly** li
flagrante flə 'grænt i flæ-
fla·grante de'licto dɪ 'lɪkt əʊ də-, deɪ- ‖ -oʊ
flagship 'flæg ʃɪp **~s** s
flagstaff, F~ 'flæg stɑːf §-stæf ‖ -stæf **~s** s
flagstone 'flæg stəʊn ‖ -stoʊn **~s** z
flag-waving 'flæg ˌweɪv ɪŋ
Flaherty 'flɑː hət i 'flæ-, -ət-; 'fleət i ‖ 'flæ ˀrţ i
'flɑːrţ i
flail fleɪˀl **flailed** fleɪˀld **flailing** 'fleɪˀl ɪŋ
flails fleɪˀlz
flair fleə ‖ fleˀr flæˀr **flairs** fleəz ‖ fleˀrz flæˀrz
flak flæk
flake fleɪk **flaked** fleɪkt **flakes** fleɪks **flaking**
'fleɪk ɪŋ

F

flak|y 'fleɪk |i ~**ier** i ə ‖ i ʰr ~**iest** i ɪst i əst
~**ily** ɪ li əl i ~**iness** i nəs i nɪs
flam flæm **flams** flæmz
flambe, flambé 'flɒm beɪ 'flɑːm-, 'flæm-, -bi
‖ flɑːm 'beɪ —*Fr* [flɑ̃ be] ~**ed** d
flambeau 'flæm bəʊ ‖ -boʊ ~**x** z
flambee, flambée 'flɒm beɪ 'flɑːm-, 'flæm-,
-bi ‖ flɑːm 'beɪ —*Fr* [flɑ̃ be] ~**d** d
Flamborough 'flæm bər ə ‖ -ˌbɜː oʊ
ˌFlamborough 'Head
flamboyance flæm 'bɔɪ ənᵗs
flamboyant flæm 'bɔɪ ənt ~**ly** li ~**s** s
flame fleɪm **flamed** fleɪmd **flames** fleɪmz
flaming/ly 'fleɪm ɪŋ /li
flamenco flə 'meŋ kəʊ ‖ -koʊ ~**s** z
flameproof 'fleɪm pruːf §-pruf ~**ed** t ~**ing** ɪŋ
~**s** s
flame-thrower 'fleɪm ˌθrəʊ ə ‖ -ˌθroʊ ʰr ~**s** z
flaming 'fleɪm ɪŋ
flamingo flə 'mɪŋ gəʊ flæ- ‖ -goʊ ~**es**, ~**s** z
Flaminian flə 'mɪn i ən flæ-
flammability ˌflæm ə 'bɪl ət i -ɪt i ‖ -əṭ i
flammable 'flæm əb ᵊl
Flamsteed 'flæm stiːd
flan flæn ‖ flɑːn **flans** flænz ‖ flɑːnz
Flanagan 'flæn əg ən
Flanders 'flɑːnd əz §'flænd- ‖ 'flænd ʰrz
flange flændʒ **flanged** flændʒd **flanges**
'flændʒ ɪz -əz **flanging** 'flændʒ ɪŋ
flank flæŋk **flanked** flæŋkt **flanking**
'flæŋk ɪŋ **flanks** flæŋks
flanker 'flæŋk ə ‖ -ʰr ~**s** z
flannel 'flæn ᵊl ~**ed**, ~**led** d ~**ing**, ~**ling** ɪŋ ~**s**
z
flannelboard 'flæn ᵊl bɔːd ‖ -bɔːrd -bourd ~**s**
z
flannelette ˌflæn ᵊl 'et -ə 'let
flannelgraph 'flæn ᵊl grɑːf -græf ‖ -græf ~**s** s
flannelly 'flæn ᵊl i
flap flæp **flapped** flæpt **flapping** 'flæp ɪŋ
flaps flæps
flapdoodle 'flæp ˌduːd ᵊl
flapjack 'flæp dʒæk ~**s** s
flapper 'flæp ə ‖ -ʰr ~**s** z
flare fleə ‖ fleʰr flæʰr **flared** fleəd ‖ fleʰrd
flæʰrd **flares** fleəz ‖ fleʰrz flæʰrz **flaring**
'fleər ɪŋ ‖ 'fler ɪŋ 'flær-
'flare path
flare-up 'fleər ʌp ‖ 'fler- 'flær- ~**s** s
flash, Flash flæʃ **flashed** flæʃt **flashes**
'flæʃ ɪz -əz **flashing** 'flæʃ ɪŋ
ˌflash 'flood; 'flash point
flashback 'flæʃ bæk ~**s** s
flashbulb 'flæʃ bʌlb ~**s** z
flashcard 'flæʃ kɑːd ‖ -kɑːrd ~**s** z
flashcube 'flæʃ kjuːb ~**s** z
flasher 'flæʃ ə ‖ -ʰr ~**s** z
flashgun 'flæʃ gʌn ~**s** z
flashi... —*see* **flashy**
flashlight 'flæʃ laɪt ~**s** s
Flashman 'flæʃ mən
flashmob 'flæʃ mɒb ‖ -mɑːb ~**s** z
flashover 'flæʃ ˌəʊv ə ‖ -ˌoʊv ʰr ~**s** z

flash|y 'flæʃ |i ~**ier** i ə ‖ i ʰr ~**iest** i ɪst i əst
~**ily** ɪ li əl i ~**iness** i nəs i nɪs
flask, Flask flɑːsk §flæsk ‖ flæsk **flasks** flɑːsks
§flæsks ‖ flæsks
flat flæt **flats** flæts **flatted** 'flæt ɪd -əd
‖ 'flæṭ əd **flatter** 'flæt ə ‖ 'flæṭ ʰr **flattest**
'flæt ɪst -əst ‖ 'flæṭ əst **flatting** 'flæt ɪŋ
‖ 'flæṭ ɪŋ
ˌflat 'feet; ˌflat 'racing; ˌflat 'spin
flatbed 'flæt bed ~**s** z
flatboat 'flæt bəʊt ‖ -boʊt ~**s** s
flat-bottomed ˌflæt 'bɒt əmd ◄ ‖ -'bɑːṭ əmd ◄
flatbread 'flæt bred
Flatbush 'flæt bʊʃ
flatcar 'flæt kɑː ‖ -kɑːr ~**s** z
flat-chested ˌflæt 'tʃest ɪd ◄ -əd
flatfeet —*see* **flatfoot**
flatfish 'flæt fɪʃ ~**es** ɪz əz
flat|foot 'flæt |fʊt ~**feet** fiːt ~**foots** fʊts
flat-footed ˌflæt 'fʊt ɪd ◄ -əd ‖ -'fʊṭ əd ◄ ~**ly**
li ~**ness** nəs nɪs
flathead, F~ 'flæt hed ~**s** z
flatiron 'flæt ˌaɪ ən ‖ 'flæṭ ˌaɪ ʰrn ~**s** z
Flatland 'flæt lænd
flatlet 'flæt lət -lɪt ~**s** s
Flatley 'flæt li
flatlin|e 'flæt laɪn ~**ing** ɪŋ
flatly 'flæt li
flatmate 'flæt meɪt ~**s** s
flatness 'flæt nəs -nɪs
flat-pack 'flæt pæk ~**s** s
flatshare 'flæt ʃeə ‖ -ʃer -ʃær ~**s** z
flatten 'flæt ᵊn ~**ed** d ~**ing** ˌɪŋ ~**s** z
flatter 'flæt ə ‖ 'flæṭ ʰr ~**ed** d **flattering/ly**
'flæt ˌər ɪŋ /li ‖ 'flæṭ- ~**s** z
flatterer 'flæt ər ə ‖ 'flæṭ ər ər ~**s** z
flatter|y 'flæt ər |i ‖ 'flæṭ- ~**ies** iz
flattie 'flæt i ‖ 'flæṭ i ~**s** z
flattish 'flæt ɪʃ ‖ 'flæṭ ɪʃ
flattop 'flæt tɒp ‖ -tɑːp ~**s** s
flatulenc|e 'flæt jʊl ənᵗs 'flætʃ ʊl- ‖ 'flætʃ əl-
~**y** i
flatulent 'flæt jʊl ənt 'flætʃ ʊl- ‖ 'flætʃ əl- ~**ly**
li
flatus 'fleɪt əs ‖ 'fleɪṭ- ~**es** ɪz əz
flatware 'flæt weə ‖ -wer -wær
flatworm 'flæt wɜːm ‖ -wɜːm ~**s** z
Flaubert 'fləʊb eə ‖ floʊ 'beʰr —*Fr* [flo bɛʁ]
flaunt flɔːnt ‖ flɑːnt **flaunted** 'flɔːnt ɪd -əd
‖ 'flɔːnṭ əd 'flɑːnṭ- **flaunting/ly** 'flɔːnt ɪŋ /li
‖ 'flɔːnṭ ɪŋ /li 'flɑːnṭ- **flaunts** flɔːnts ‖ flɑːnts
flaunter 'flɔːnt ə ‖ 'flɔːnṭ ʰr 'flɑːnṭ- ~**s** z
flautist 'flɔːt ɪst §-əst ‖ 'flɔːṭ- 'flɑːṭ-, 'flaʊṭ- ~**s** s
flava 'fleɪv ə
Flavell (*i*) 'fleɪv ᵊl, (*ii*) flə 'vel
Flavia 'fleɪv i ə
Flavian 'fleɪv i ən
flavin 'fleɪv ɪn 'flæv-, §-ᵊn ~**s** z
flavine 'fleɪv iːn 'flæv-, -ɪn
Flavius 'fleɪv i əs
flavone 'fleɪv əʊn ‖ -oʊn
flavonoid 'fleɪv ə nɔɪd 'flæv- ~**s** z
flavonol 'fleɪv ə nɒl 'flæv- ‖ -nɔːl -nɑːl, -noʊl

flavor 'fleɪv ə ‖ -ᵊr **~ed** d **flavoring/s**
  'fleɪv ər ɪŋ/z **~s** z

flavor|ful 'fleɪv ə fʊl -fᵊl ‖ -ᵊr- **~less** ləs lɪs
  ~some səm

flavour 'fleɪv ə ‖ -ᵊr **~ed** d **flavouring/s**
  'fleɪv ər ɪŋ/z **~s** z

flavour|ful 'fleɪv ə fʊl -fᵊl ‖ -ᵊr- **~less** ləs lɪs
  ~some səm

flaw flɔː ‖ flɑː **flawed** flɔːd ‖ flɑːd **flawing**
  'flɔːʳ ɪŋ ‖ 'flɔː ɪŋ 'flɑː- **flaws** flɔːz ‖ flɑːz

flawless 'flɔː ləs -lɪs ‖ 'flɑː- **~ly** li **~ness** nəs
  nɪs

flax flæks

flaxen 'flæks ᵊn

Flaxman 'flæks mən

flay fleɪ **flayed** fleɪd **flaying** 'fleɪ ɪŋ **flays**
  fleɪz

flea fliː (= *flee*) **fleas** fliːz
  'flea ˌmarket

fleabag 'fliː bæg **~s** z

fleabane 'fliː beɪn **~s** z

fleabite 'fliː baɪt **~s** s

flea-bitten 'fliː ˌbɪt ᵊn

fleadh flɑː —*Irish* [flʲa(ɣ)]

fleapit 'fliː pɪt **~s** s

fleawort 'fliː wɜːt §-wɔːt ‖ -wɝːt -wɔːrt **~s** s

fleche, flèche fleɪʃ fleʃ **fleches, flèches**
  'fleɪʃ ɪz 'fleʃ-, -əz

fleck flek **flecked** flekt **flecking** 'flek ɪŋ
  flecks fleks (= *flex*)

Flecker 'flek ə ‖ -ᵊr

flection 'flek ʃᵊn **~s** z

flectional 'flek ʃᵊn ᵊl

flectionless 'flek ʃᵊn ləs -lɪs

fled fled

fledge fledʒ **fledged** fledʒd **fledges** 'fledʒ ɪz
  -əz **fledging** 'fledʒ ɪŋ

fledgeling, fledgling 'fledʒ lɪŋ **~s** z

flee fliː (= *flea*) **fled** fled **fleeing** 'fliː ɪŋ **flees**
  fliːz

fleece fliːs **fleeced** fliːst **fleeces** 'fliːs ɪz -əz
  fleecing 'fliːs ɪŋ

fleec|y 'fliːs |i **~ier** i‿ə ‖ i‿ᵊr **~iest** i‿ɪst i‿əst
  ~ily ɪ li əl i **~iness** i nəs i nɪs

fleet, Fleet fliːt **fleeted** 'fliːt ɪd -əd ‖ 'fliːt̬ əd
  fleeter 'fliːt ə ‖ 'fliːt̬ ʳr **fleetest** 'fliːt ɪst -əst
  ‖ 'fliːt̬- **fleeting** 'fliːt ɪŋ ‖ 'fliːt̬ ɪŋ
  'fleet ˌadmiral; 'Fleet Street

fleeting 'fliːt ɪŋ ‖ 'fliːt̬ ɪŋ **~ly** li **~ness** nəs nɪs

Fleetwood 'fliːt wʊd

Fleming 'flem ɪŋ **~s** z, **~'s** z

Flemington 'flem ɪŋ tən

Flemish 'flem ɪʃ

flense flenᵗs flenz **flensed** flenᵗst flenzd
  flenses 'flenᵗs ɪz 'flenz-, -əz **flensing**
  'flenᵗs ɪŋ 'flenz-

flenser 'flenᵗs ə 'flenz- ‖ -ᵊr **~s** z

flesh fleʃ **fleshed** fleʃt **fleshes** 'fleʃ ɪz -əz
  fleshing 'fleʃ ɪŋ
  'flesh wound

flesh-colored, flesh-coloured 'fleʃ ˌkʌl əd
  ‖ -ᵊrd

fleshi... —*see* **fleshy**

flesh|ly 'fleʃ |li **~lier** li‿ə ‖ li‿ᵊr **~liest** li‿ɪst
  li‿əst **~liness** li nəs li nɪs

fleshpot 'fleʃ pɒt ‖ -pɑːt **~s** s

flesh|y 'fleʃ |i **~ier** i‿ə ‖ i‿ᵊr **~iest** i‿ɪst i‿əst
  ~iness i nəs i nɪs

fletcher, F~ 'fletʃ ə ‖ -ᵊr **~s**, **~'s** z

Fletton, f~ 'flet ᵊn

Fleur flɜː ‖ flɝː —*Fr* [flœːʁ]

fleur-de-lis, fleur-de-lys *sing.* ˌflɜː də 'liː
  -'liːs ‖ ˌflɝː- —*Fr* [flœʁ də lis]

flew, Flew fluː **flews** fluːz

flex fleks **flexed** flekst **flexes** 'fleks ɪz -əz
  flexing 'fleks ɪŋ

flexibility ˌfleks ə 'bɪl ət i ˌ-ɪ-, -ɪt i ‖ -ət̬ i

flexib|le 'fleks əb |ᵊl -ɪb- **~leness** ᵊl nəs -nɪs
  ~ly li

flexion 'flek ʃᵊn

flexional 'flek ʃᵊn ᵊl

flexionless 'flek ʃᵊn ləs -lɪs

flexitime 'fleks i taɪm

Flexner 'fleks nə ‖ -nᵊr

flexor 'fleks ə -ɔː ‖ -ᵊr -ɔːr **~s** z

flextime 'fleks taɪm

flexuous 'fleks ju‿əs ‖ 'flek ʃu‿əs **~ly** li

flexure 'flek ʃə 'fleks jʊə ‖ -ʃᵊr **~s** z

flibbertigibbet ˌflɪb ət i 'dʒɪb ɪt -ət ‖ -ᵊrt̬ i-
  '·ˌ·ˌ·· **~s** s

flick flɪk **flicked** flɪkt **flicking** 'flɪk ɪŋ **flicks**
  flɪks
  'flick knife

flicker 'flɪk ə ‖ -ᵊr **~ed** d **flickering** 'flɪk ər‿ɪŋ
  ~s z

Flickr *tdmk* 'flɪk ə ‖ -ᵊr

flier 'flaɪ‿ə ‖ 'flaɪ‿ᵊr **~s** z

flies flaɪz

flight flaɪt **flighted** 'flaɪt ɪd -əd ‖ 'flaɪt̬ əd
  flighting 'flaɪt ɪŋ ‖ 'flaɪt̬ ɪŋ **flights** flaɪts
  'flight deck; ˌflight lieu'tenant◂; 'flight
  ˌnumber; 'flight path; 'flight reˌcorder;
  'flight ˌsergeant

flighti... —*see* **flighty**

flightless 'flaɪt ləs -lɪs

flight|y 'flaɪt |i ‖ 'flaɪt̬ |i **~ier** i‿ə ‖ i‿ᵊr **~iest**
  i‿ɪst i‿əst **~ily** ɪ li əl i **~iness** i nəs i nɪs

flimflam 'flɪm flæm **~med** d **~ming** ɪŋ **~s** z

flims|y 'flɪmz |i **~ier** i‿ə ‖ i‿ᵊr **~iest** i‿ɪst i‿əst
  ~ily ɪ li əl i **~iness** i nəs i nɪs

flinch flɪntʃ **flinched** flɪntʃt **flinches** 'flɪntʃ ɪz
  -əz **flinching** 'flɪntʃ ɪŋ

Flinders, f~ 'flɪnd əz ‖ -ᵊrz

fling flɪŋ **flinging** 'flɪŋ ɪŋ **flings** flɪŋz **flung**
  flʌŋ

Flinn flɪn

flint, Flint flɪnt **flints** flɪnts

flintlock 'flɪnt lɒk ‖ -lɑːk **~s** s

Flintshire 'flɪnt ʃə -ʃɪə ‖ -ʃᵊr -ʃɪr

flintstone, F~ 'flɪnt stəʊn ‖ -stoʊn **~s** z

flint|y 'flɪnt |i ‖ 'flɪnt̬ |i **~ier** i‿ə ‖ i‿ᵊr **~iest**
  i‿ɪst i‿əst **~ily** ɪ li əl i **~iness** i nəs i nɪs

flip flɪp **flipped** flɪpt **flipping** 'flɪp ɪŋ **flips**
  flɪps
  'flip side

flip-flop 'flɪp flɒp ‖ -flɑːp **~s** s

F

flippancy 'flɪp ən^ts i
flippant 'flɪp ənt **~ly** li
flipper 'flɪp ə ‖ -ªr **~s** z
flirt flɜːt ‖ flɜːt **flirted** 'flɜːt ɪd -əd ‖ 'flɜːt̬ əd
  flirting 'flɜːt ɪŋ ‖ 'flɜːt̬ ɪŋ **flirts** flɜːts ‖ flɜːts
flirtation flɜː 'teɪʃ ªn ‖ flɜː-
flirtatious flɜː 'teɪʃ əs ‖ flɜː- **~ly** li **~ness** nəs
  nɪs
flirty 'flɜːt i ‖ 'flɜːt̬ i
flit flɪt **flits** flɪts **flitted** 'flɪt ɪd -əd ‖ 'flɪt̬ əd
  flitting 'flɪt ɪŋ ‖ 'flɪt̬ ɪŋ
flitch flɪtʃ **flitches** 'flɪtʃ ɪz -əz
flitter 'flɪt ə ‖ 'flɪt̬ ªr **~ed** d **flittering**
  'flɪt̬ ər ɪŋ ‖ 'flɪt̬ ər ɪŋ **~s** z
Flitton 'flɪt ªn
Flitwick 'flɪt ɪk ‖ 'flɪt̬-
flivver 'flɪv ə ‖ -ªr **~s** z
Flixton 'flɪkst ən
Flo fləʊ ‖ floʊ
float fləʊt ‖ floʊt **floated** 'fləʊt ɪd -əd
  ‖ 'floʊt̬ əd **floating** 'fləʊt ɪŋ ‖ 'floʊt̬ ɪŋ
  floats fləʊts ‖ floʊts
  ,floating 'voter
floatation fləʊ 'teɪʃ ªn ‖ floʊ- **~s** z
floating-point ˌfləʊt ɪŋ 'pɔɪnt ◂ ‖ ˌfloʊt̬-
flocculent 'flɒk jʊl ənt ‖ 'flɑːk jəl- **~ly** li
flock flɒk ‖ flɑːk **flocked** flɒkt ‖ flɑːkt
  flocking 'flɒk ɪŋ ‖ 'flɑːk ɪŋ **flocks** flɒks
  ‖ flɑːks
Flockhart 'flɒk hɑːt ‖ 'flɑːk hɑːrt
Flodden 'flɒd ªn ‖ 'flɑːd-
floe fləʊ ‖ floʊ (= flow) **floes** fləʊz ‖ floʊz
Floella fləʊ 'el ə ‖ floʊ-
flog flɒg ‖ flɑːg **flogged** flɒgd ‖ flɑːgd
  flogging/s 'flɒg ɪŋ/z ‖ 'flɑːg ɪŋ/z **flogs**
  flɒgz ‖ flɑːgz
flogger 'flɒg ə ‖ 'flɑːg ªr **~s** z
Flo-Jo 'fləʊ dʒəʊ ‖ 'floʊ dʒoʊ
flong flɒŋ ‖ flɔːŋ flɑːŋ **flongs** flɒŋz ‖ flɔːŋz
  flɑːŋz
flood, Flood flʌd **flooded** 'flʌd ɪd -əd
  flooding 'flʌd ɪŋ **floods** flʌdz
  'flood tide
floodgate 'flʌd geɪt →'flʌg- **~s** s
flood|light 'flʌd |laɪt **~lighted** laɪt ɪd -əd
  ‖ laɪt̬ əd **~lighting** laɪt ɪŋ ‖ laɪt̬ ɪŋ **~lights**
  laɪts **~lit** lɪt
floodwater 'flʌd ˌwɔːt ə ‖ -ˌwɔːt̬ ªr -ˌwɑːt̬ ªr
Flook flʊk fluːk
floor flɔː ‖ flɔːr flour **floored** flɔːd ‖ flɔːrd
  flourd **flooring** 'flɔːr ɪŋ ‖ 'flour- **floors** flɔːz
  ‖ flɔːrz flourz
  'floor cloth; 'floor ˌmanager; 'floor show
floorboard 'flɔː bɔːd ‖ 'flɔːr bɔːrd 'flour bourd
  ~s z
flooring 'flɔːr ɪŋ ‖ 'flour-
floor-length 'flɔː leŋkθ §-lentθ ‖ 'flɔːr- 'flour-
floorspace 'flɔː speɪs ‖ 'flɔːr- 'flour-
floortime 'flɔː taɪm ‖ 'flɔːr- 'flour-
floorwalker 'flɔː ˌwɔːk ə ‖ 'flɔːr ˌwɔːk ªr
  'flour-, -ˌwɑːk ªr
floos|ie, floos|y, floozie, floozly 'fluːz |i
  ~ies iz

flop flɒp ‖ flɑːp **flopped** flɒpt ‖ flɑːpt
  flopping 'flɒp ɪŋ ‖ 'flɑːp ɪŋ **flops** flɒps
  ‖ flɑːps
flop|house 'flɒp |haʊs ‖ 'flɑːp- **~houses**
  haʊz ɪz -əz
flopp|y 'flɒp |i ‖ 'flɑːp |i **~ier** i ə ‖ i ªr **~ies** iz
  ~iest i ɪst i əst **~ily** ɪ li ə l i **~iness** i nəs i nɪs
  ,floppy 'disk
Flopsy, f~ 'flɒps i ‖ 'flɑːps i
flora, Flora 'flɔːr ə ‖ 'flour- **~s** z
floral 'flɔːr əl ‖ 'flour- **~ly** i
floreat 'flɒr i æt 'flɔː-, -ɪt ‖ 'flɔːr- 'flɑːr-
Florence 'flɒr ən^ts ‖ 'flɔːr- 'flɑːr- **~'s** ɪz əz
Florentine, f~ 'flɒr ən taɪn -tiːn; flə 'rent aɪn
  ‖ 'flɔːr ən tiːn 'flɑːr- **~s** z
Flores 'flɔːr ɪz -iːz, -ɪs, §-əs ‖ 'flour-
  ,Flores 'Sea
florescence flɔː 'res ªn^ts flɒ-, flə- ‖ flou-
floret 'flɒr ət 'flɔː-, -ɪt ‖ 'flɔːr- 'flour- **~s** s
Florey 'flɔːr i 'flɒr- ‖ 'flour-
floribunda ˌflɒr ɪ 'bʌnd ə ˌflɔːr-, §-ə- ‖ ˌflɔːr ə-
  ˌflour- **~s** z
floricultural ˌflɔːr ɪ 'kʌltʃ ªr əl ˌflɒr-, -ˌ·ə-
  ‖ ˌflour-
floriculture 'flɔːr ɪ ˌkʌltʃ ə 'flɒr-, -ə- ‖ -ªr
  'flour-
floriculturist ˌflɔːr ɪ 'kʌltʃ ər ɪst 'flɒr-, -ˌ·ə-,
  §-əst ‖ ˌflour- **~s** s
florid 'flɒr ɪd §-əd ‖ 'flɔːr- 'flɑːr- **~ly** li **~ness**
  nəs nɪs
Florida 'flɒr ɪd ə -əd- ‖ 'flɔːr- 'flɑːr-
  ,Florida 'Keys
Floridan 'flɒr ɪd ən -əd- ‖ 'flɔːr- 'flɑːr- **~s** z
Floridian flɒ 'rɪd i ən flə- ‖ flə- **~s** z
floridity flɒ 'rɪd ət i flɔː-, flə-, -ɪt- ‖ flə 'rɪd ət̬ i
  flɔː-
florin 'flɒr ɪn -ən ‖ 'flɔːr- 'flɑːr- **~s** z
Florio 'flɔːr i əʊ ‖ -oʊ 'flour-
florist 'flɒr ɪst 'flɔːr-, §-əst ‖ 'flɔːr- 'flɑːr-,
  'flour- **~s** s
floristry 'flɒr ɪs tri 'flɔːr-, -əs- ‖ 'flɔːr- 'flɑːr-,
  'flour-
Florrie 'flɒr i ‖ 'flɔːr i 'flɑːr i
floruit 'flɒr u ɪt 'flɔːr- ‖ 'flɔːr- 'flɑːr-, 'flour-,
  -ju-
floss, Floss flɒs ‖ flɔːs flɑːs **flossed** flɒst
  ‖ flɔːst flɑːst **flosses** 'flɒs ɪz -əz ‖ 'flɔːs əz
  'flɑːs- **flossing** 'flɒs ɪŋ ‖ 'flɔːs ɪŋ 'flɑːs-
Flossie 'flɒs i ‖ 'flɔːs i 'flɑːs i
floss|y 'flɒs |i ‖ 'flɔːs |i 'flɑːs- **~ier** i ə ‖ i ªr
  ~iest i ɪst i əst **~ily** ɪ li ə l i **~iness** i nəs i nɪs
flotation fləʊ 'teɪʃ ªn ‖ floʊ- **~s** z
flote fləʊt ‖ floʊt
flotilla fləʊ 'tɪl ə ‖ floʊ- **~s** z
flotsam 'flɒts əm ‖ 'flɑːts-
Flotta 'flɒt ə ‖ 'flɑːt̬ ə
flounce flaʊn^ts **flounced** flaʊn^tst **flounces**
  'flaʊn^ts ɪz -əz **flouncing** 'flaʊn^ts ɪŋ
flounder 'flaʊnd ə ‖ -ªr **~ed** d **floundering**
  'flaʊnd ər ɪŋ ‖ -ªr ɪŋ **~s** z
flour 'flaʊ ə ‖ 'flaʊ ªr (= flower) **floured**
  'flaʊ əd ‖ 'flaʊ ªrd **flouring** 'flaʊ ər ɪŋ
  ‖ 'flaʊ ªr ɪŋ **flours** 'flaʊ əz ‖ 'flaʊ ªrz

flourish ˈflʌr ɪʃ ‖ ˈflɝː- **~ed** t **~es** ɪz əz **~ing** ɪŋ
flourmill ˈflaʊ‿ə mɪl ‖ ˈflaʊ‿ʳr- **~s** z
floury ˈflaʊ‿ər i ‖ ˈflaʊ‿ʳr i (= *flowery*)
flout flaʊt **flouted** ˈflaʊt ɪd -əd ‖ ˈflaʊt̬ əd
  flouting ˈflaʊt ɪŋ ‖ ˈflaʊt̬ ɪŋ **flouts** flaʊts
flow fləʊ ‖ floʊ **flowed** fləʊd ‖ floʊd
  flowing/ly ˈfləʊ ɪŋ /li ‖ ˈfloʊ ɪŋ /li **flows**
  fləʊz ‖ floʊz
  ˈflow ˌdiagram
flow|chart ˈfləʊ |tʃɑːt ‖ ˈfloʊ |tʃɑːrt **~charted**
  tʃɑːt ɪd -əd ‖ tʃɑːrt̬ əd **~charting** tʃɑːt ɪŋ
  ‖ tʃɑːrt̬ ɪŋ **~charts** tʃɑːts ‖ tʃɑːrts
flower ˈflaʊ‿ə ‖ ˈflaʊ‿ʳr (= *flour*) **flowered**
  ˈflaʊ‿əd ‖ ˈflaʊ‿ʳrd **flowering/s** ˈflaʊ‿ə ɪŋ/z
  ‖ ˈflaʊ‿ʳr ɪŋ/z **flowers** ˈflaʊ‿əz ‖ ˈflaʊ‿ʳrz
  ˈflower girl; ˌflowering ˈcurrant; ˈflower
  ˌpower
flowerbed ˈflaʊ‿ə bed ‖ ˈflaʊ‿ʳr- **~s** z
flowerless ˈflaʊ‿ə ləs -lɪs ‖ ˈflaʊ‿ʳr-
flowerpot ˈflaʊ‿ə pɒt ‖ ˈflaʊ‿ʳr pɑːt **~s** s
flower|y ˈflaʊ‿ər |i ‖ ˈflaʊ‿ʳr |i **~ier** i‿ə ‖ i‿ʳr
  ~iest i‿ɪst i‿əst **~ily** əl i ɪ li **~iness** i nəs i nɪs
flown fləʊn §ˈfləʊ ən ‖ floʊn
Floyd flɔɪd
flu fluː (= *flew, flue*)
flub flʌb **flubbed** flʌbd **flubbing** ˈflʌb ɪŋ
  flubs flʌbz
Fluck flʌk
fluctu|ate ˈflʌk tʃu |eɪt -tju- **~ated** eɪt ɪd -əd
  ‖ eɪt̬ əd **~ates** eɪts **~ating** eɪt ɪŋ ‖ eɪt̬ ɪŋ
fluctuation ˌflʌk tʃu ˈeɪʃ ən -tju- **~s** z
flue fluː (= *flew*) **flues** fluːz
fluellen, F~ flu ˈel ɪn -ən
fluency ˈfluː ən‿s i
fluent ˈfluː ənt **~ly** li
fluff flʌf **fluffed** flʌft **fluffing** ˈflʌf ɪŋ **fluffs**
  flʌfs
fluff|y ˈflʌf |i **~ier** i‿ə ‖ i‿ʳr **~iest** i‿ɪst i‿əst **~ily**
  ɪ li əl i **~iness** i nəs i nɪs
flugelhorn, flügelhorn ˈfluːg əl hɔːn ‖ -hɔːrn
  ~s z
fluid ˈfluːɪd **~ly** li **~ness** nəs nɪs **~s** z
  ˌfluid ˈounce
fluidis|e, fluidiz|e ˈfluːɪ daɪz **~ed** d **~es** ɪz əz
  ~ing ɪŋ
fluidity flu ˈɪd ət i -ɪt- ‖ -ət̬ i
fluke fluːk **fluked** fluːkt **flukes** fluːks **fluking**
  ˈfluːk ɪŋ
fluk|ey, fluk|y ˈfluːk |i **~ier** i‿ə ‖ i‿ʳr **~iest**
  i‿ɪst i‿əst
flume fluːm **flumed** fluːmd **flumes** fluːmz
  fluming ˈfluːm ɪŋ
flummer|y ˈflʌm ər |i **~ies** iz
flummox ˈflʌm əks **~ed** t **~es** ɪz əz **~ing** ɪŋ
flung flʌŋ
flunk flʌŋk **flunked** flʌŋkt **flunking** ˈflʌŋk ɪŋ
  flunks flʌŋks
flunk|ey, flunk|y ˈflʌŋk |i **~eys, ~ies** iz
Fluon *tdmk* ˈfluː ɒn ‖ -ɑːn
fluor ˈfluː ɔː ə ‖ -ɔːr -ʳr
fluoresc|e flɔː ˈres fluˢ-, flə-; ˌfluː‿ə ˈres ‖ floʊ-;
  ˌfluː‿ə ˈres **~ed** t **~es** ɪz əz **~ing** ɪŋ

fluoresc|ence flɔː ˈres |ən‿s fluˢ-, flə-;
  ˌfluː‿ə ˈres- ‖ floʊ-; ˌfluː‿ə ˈres- **~ent** ənt
fluoric flu ˈɒr ɪk ‖ -ˈɔːr ɪk -ˈɑːr ɪk
fluori|date ˈflɔːr ɪ |deɪt -ə-; ˈfluː‿ər ɪ deɪt,
  -ə deɪt ‖ ˈflʊr- ˈflɔːr-, ˈfloʊr- **~dated** deɪt ɪd
  -əd ‖ deɪt̬ əd **~dates** deɪts **~dating** deɪt ɪŋ
  ‖ deɪt̬ ɪŋ
fluoridation ˌflɔːr ɪ ˈdeɪʃ ᵊn ˌfluː‿ər ɪ ˈdeɪʃ-,
  -ə'-- ‖ ˌflʊr- ˌflɔːr-, ˌfloʊr- **~s** z
fluoride ˈflʊər aɪd ˈflɔːr-; ˈfluː‿ə raɪd ‖ ˈflʊr-
  ˈflɔːr-, ˈfloʊr- **~s** z
fluori|nate ˈflɔːr ɪ |neɪt ˈfluː‿ər ɪ neɪt, -ə neɪt
  ‖ ˈflʊr- ˈflɔːr-, ˈfloʊr- **~nated** neɪt ɪd -əd
  ‖ neɪt̬ əd **~nates** neɪts **~nating** neɪt ɪŋ
  ‖ neɪt̬ ɪŋ
fluorination ˌflɔːr ɪ ˈneɪʃ ᵊn ˌfluː‿ər ɪ ˈneɪʃ-,
  -ə ˈneɪʃ- ‖ ˌflʊr- ˌflɔːr-, ˌfloʊr- **~s** z
fluorine ˈflʊər iːn ˈflɔːr-, ˈfluː‿ə riːn ‖ ˈflʊr-
  ˈflɔːr-, ˈfloʊr-
fluorite ˈflʊər aɪt ˈflɔːr-, ˈfluː‿ə raɪt ‖ ˈflʊr-
  ˈflɔːr-, ˈfloʊr-
fluoro- *comb. form*
  with stress-neutral suffix ˌflʊər əʊ ˌflɔːr-;
  ˌfluː‿ə rəʊ ‖ ˌflʊr oʊ ˌflɔːr-, ˌfloʊr-
  — **fluorocarbon** ˌflʊər əʊ ˈkɑːb ən ˌflɔːr-;
  ˌfluː‿ə rəʊ- ‖ ˌflʊr oʊ ˈkɑːrb ən ˌflɔːr-, ˌfloʊr-
  with stress-imposing suffix flɔː ˌrɒ + fluˢ-, flə-;
  ˌfluː‿ə ˈrɒ + ‖ flu ˌrɑː + flɔː-, floʊ-
  — **fluoroscopy** flɔː ˈrɒsk əp ɪ fluˢ-, flə-;
  ˌfluː‿ə'-- ‖ flu ˈrɑːsk əp ɪ flɔː-, floʊ-
fluorosis flɔː ˈrəʊs ɪs fluˢ-, flə-; ˌfluː‿ə'--, §-əs
  ‖ flu ˈroʊs əs flɔː-, floʊ-
fluorspar ˈflʊə spɑː ˈflɔː-; ˈfluː‿ə spɑː
  ‖ ˈflʊr spɑːr ˈfluː‿ʳr spɑːr, -ɔːr-
fluothane ˈfluː‿ə θeɪn
flurr|y, F~ ˈflʌr |i ‖ ˈflɝː |i **~ied** id **~ies** iz
  ~ying i‿ɪŋ
flush flʌʃ **flushed** flʌʃt **flusher** ˈflʌʃ ə ‖ -ʳr
  flushes ˈflʌʃ ɪz -əz **flushest** ˈflʌʃ ɪst -əst
  flushing/s ˈflʌʃ ɪŋ/z
Flushing ˈflʌʃ ɪŋ
fluster ˈflʌst ə ‖ -ʳr **~ed** d **flustering**
  ˈflʌst ər ɪŋ **~s** z
flute fluːt **fluted** ˈfluːt ɪd -əd ‖ ˈfluːt̬ əd **flutes**
  fluːts **fluting/s** ˈfluːt ɪŋ/z ‖ ˈfluːt̬ ɪŋ/z
flutist ˈfluːt ɪst §-əst ‖ ˈfluːt̬ əst **~s** s
flutter ˈflʌt ə ‖ ˈflʌt̬ ʳr **~ed** d **fluttering**
  ˈflʌt ər ɪŋ ‖ ˈflʌt̬ ər ɪŋ **~s** z
fluvial ˈfluːv i‿əl
flux flʌks **fluxed** flʌkst **fluxes** ˈflʌks ɪz -əz
  fluxing ˈflʌks ɪŋ
fluxion ˈflʌk ʃᵊn **~s** z
fly flaɪ **flew** fluː **flies** flaɪz **flown** fləʊn
  ‖ floʊn **flying** ˈflaɪ ɪŋ
  ˌfly ˈhalf; ˈflying boat; ˌflying ˈbuttress;
  ˌflying ˈcolours; ˌflying ˈdoctor; ˌflying
  ˈfish; ˌflying ˈfox; ˈflying maˌchine;
  ˈflying ˌofficer; ˌflying ˈpicket; ˌflying
  ˈsaucer; ˈflying squad; ˌflying ˈstart
flyaway ˈflaɪ ə ˌweɪ
flyback ˈflaɪ bæk
flyblown ˈflaɪ bləʊn ‖ -bloʊn
flyboy ˈflaɪ bɔɪ **~s** z

flyby 'flaɪ baɪ **~s** z
fly-by-night 'flaɪ baɪ ˌnaɪt §-bɪ-, §-bə-
fly-by-wire ˌflaɪ baɪ 'waɪ‿ə ◂ ‖ -'waɪ‿ʳr ◂
flycatcher 'flaɪ ˌkætʃ ə △-ˌketʃ- ‖ -ʳr **~s** z
fly-drive 'flaɪ draɪv ˌ·'· **~s** z
flyer 'flaɪ‿ə ‖ 'flaɪ‿ʳr **~s** z
fly-fish 'flaɪ fɪʃ **~er/s** ə/z ‖ ʳr/z **~ing** ɪŋ
fly|leaf 'flaɪ |liːf **~leaves** liːvz
Flymo *tdmk* 'flaɪ məʊ ‖ -moʊ **~s** z
Flynn flɪn
Flynt flɪnt
fly-on-the-wall ˌflaɪ ɒn ðə 'wɔːl ◂ ‖ -ɑːn-
-ɔːn-, -'wɑːl ◂
flyover 'flaɪ ˌəʊv ə ‖ -ˌoʊv ʳr **~s** z
flypaper 'flaɪ ˌpeɪp ə ‖ -ʳr **~s** z
flypast 'flaɪ pɑːst §-pæst ‖ -pæst **~s** s
flypost 'flaɪ pəʊst ‖ -poʊst **~ed** ɪd əd **~er/s** ə/z
‖ -ʳr/z **~ing** ɪŋ **~s** s
flyscreen 'flaɪ skriːn **~s** z
flysheet 'flaɪ ʃiːt **~s** s
flyspeck 'flaɪ spek **~ed** t **~s** s
flyswatter 'flaɪ ˌswɒt ə ‖ -ˌswɑːt ʳr **~s** z
Flyte flaɪt
flytrap 'flaɪ træp **~s** s
flyweight 'flaɪ weɪt **~s** s
flywheel 'flaɪ wiːʳl -hwiːʳl **~s** z
flywhisk 'flaɪ wɪsk -hwɪsk **~s** s
FM ˌef 'em ◂
ˌFM 'radio
f-number 'ef ˌnʌm bə ‖ -bʳr **~s** z
Fo fəʊ ‖ foʊ —*It* [fo]
FO ˌef 'əʊ ‖ -'oʊ
foal fəʊl →fɒʊl ‖ foʊl **foaled** fəʊld →fɒʊld
‖ foʊld **foaling** 'fəʊl ɪŋ →'fɒʊl- ‖ 'foʊl ɪŋ
foals fəʊlz →fɒʊlz ‖ foʊlz
foam fəʊm ‖ foʊm **foamed** fəʊmd ‖ foʊmd
foaming/ly 'fəʊm ɪŋ /li ‖ 'foʊm ɪŋ /li
foams fəʊmz ‖ foʊmz
ˌfoam 'rubber◂
foam|y 'fəʊm |i ‖ 'foʊm |i **~ier** i ə ‖ i ʳr **~iest**
i ɪst i əst **~ily** ɪ li əl i **~iness** i nəs i nɪs
fob fɒb ‖ fɑːb **fobbed** fɒbd ‖ fɑːbd **fobbing**
'fɒb ɪŋ ‖ 'fɑːb ɪŋ **fobs** fɒbz ‖ fɑːbz
'fob watch
f.o.b. ˌef əʊ 'biː ‖ -oʊ-
focaccia, foccaccia fəʊ 'kætʃ i‿ə ‖ foʊ 'kɑːtʃ-
—*It* focaccia [fo 'kat tʃa]
focal 'fəʊk ʳl ‖ 'foʊk ʳl **~ly** i
ˌfocal 'length ‖ '·· ·; 'focal point
Foch fɒʃ ‖ fɔːʃ fɑːʃ —*Fr* [fɔʃ]
Fochabers 'fɒk əb əz 'fɒx- ‖ 'fɑːk əb ʳrz
foci 'fəʊs aɪ 'fəʊk-, -iː ‖ 'foʊs- 'foʊk-
fo'c'sle 'fəʊks ʳl ‖ 'foʊks ʳl **~s** z
focus 'fəʊk əs ‖ 'foʊk əs **~ed, ~sed** t **~es,**
~ses ɪz əz **~ing, ~sing** ɪŋ
fodder 'fɒd ə ‖ 'fɑːd ʳr
Foden 'fəʊd ʳn ‖ 'foʊd-
foe fəʊ ‖ foʊ **foes** fəʊz ‖ foʊz
foehn, föhn fɜːn ‖ feɪn —*Ger* [føːn]
foe|man 'fəʊ |mən ‖ 'foʊ- **~men** mən men
foetal 'fiːt ʳl ‖ 'fiːt̬ ʳl
foetid 'fet ɪd 'fiːt-, §-əd ‖ 'fet̬ əd
foetus 'fiːt əs ‖ 'fiːt̬ əs **~es** ɪz əz

fog fɒg ‖ fɑːg fɔːg **fogged** fɒgd ‖ fɑːgd fɔːgd
fogging 'fɒg ɪŋ ‖ 'fɑːg ɪŋ 'fɔːg- **fogs** fɒgz
‖ fɑːgz fɔːgz
'fog lamp, 'fog light
Fogarty 'fəʊg ət i ‖ 'foʊg ʳrt i
fogbank 'fɒg bæŋk ‖ 'fɑːg- 'fɔːg- **~s** s
fogbound 'fɒg baʊnd ‖ 'fɑːg- 'fɔːg-
Fogerty 'fəʊg ət i ‖ 'foʊg ʳrt i
fogey 'fəʊg i ‖ 'foʊg i **~s** z
Fogg fɒg ‖ fɑːg fɔːg
fogg|y 'fɒg |i ‖ 'fɑːg |i 'fɔːg- **~ier** i ə ‖ i ʳr
~iest i ɪst i əst **~ily** ɪ li əl i **~iness** i nəs i nɪs
ˌFoggy 'Bottom
foghorn 'fɒg hɔːn ‖ 'fɑːg hɔːrn 'fɔːg- **~s** z
fog|y 'fəʊg |i ‖ 'foʊg |i **~ies** iz
fohn, föhn fɜːn ‖ feɪn —*Ger* [føːn]
foible 'fɔɪb ʳl **~s** z
foie gras ˌfwɑː 'grɑː —*Fr* [fwa gʁa]
foil fɔɪʳl **foiled** fɔɪʳld **foiling** 'fɔɪʳl ɪŋ **foils**
fɔɪʳlz
foist fɔɪst **foisted** 'fɔɪst ɪd -əd **foisting**
'fɔɪst ɪŋ **foists** fɔɪsts
Fokker 'fɒk ə ‖ 'fɑːk ʳr **~s** z
fold fəʊld →fɒʊld ‖ foʊld **folded** 'fəʊld ɪd
→'fɒʊld-, -əd ‖ 'foʊld əd **folding** 'fəʊld ɪŋ
→'fɒʊld- ‖ 'foʊld ɪŋ **folds** fəʊldz →fɒʊldz
‖ foʊldz
foldaway 'fəʊld ə ˌweɪ →'fɒʊld- ‖ 'foʊld-
folder 'fəʊld ə →'fɒʊld- ‖ 'foʊld ʳr **~s** z
folderol 'fɒld ə rɒl -ɪ- ‖ 'fɑːld ə rɑːl **~s** z
foldout 'fəʊld aʊt →'fɒʊld- ‖ 'foʊld- **~s** s
Foley 'fəʊl i ‖ 'foʊl i
Folger 'fəʊldʒ ə →'fɒʊldʒ- ‖ 'foʊldʒ ʳr
folia 'fəʊl i‿ə ‖ 'foʊl-
foliage 'fəʊl i ɪdʒ ‖ 'foʊl- **~d** d
'foliage plant
foliar 'fəʊl i‿ə ‖ 'foʊl i‿ʳr
foliate *adj* 'fəʊl i‿ət ɪt, eɪt ‖ 'foʊl-
foli|ate *v* 'fəʊl i |eɪt ‖ 'foʊl- **~ated** eɪt ɪd -əd
‖ eɪt̬ əd **~ates** eɪts **~ating** eɪt ɪŋ ‖ eɪt̬ ɪŋ
foliation ˌfəʊl i 'eɪʃ ʳn ‖ ˌfoʊl- **~s** z
folic 'fəʊl ɪk 'fɒl- ‖ 'foʊl- 'fɑːl-
ˌfolic 'acid
folie à deux ˌfɒl i æ 'dɜː -i ɑː- ‖ foʊ ˌliː ə 'dʌ
fɑː- —*Fr* [fɔ li a dø]
folie de grandeur ˌfɒl i də 'grɒnd ɜː
‖ foʊ ˌliː də grɑːn 'dɜː fɑː- —*Fr*
[fɔ li də gʁɑ̃ dœːʁ]
Folies Bergere, Folies Bergère
ˌfɒl i bɜː 'ʒeə -bə'-, -beə'- ‖ foʊ ˌliː ber 'ʒeʳr
—*Fr* [fɔ li bɛʁ ʒɛːʁ]
folio 'fəʊl i‿əʊ ‖ 'foʊl i‿oʊ **~s** z
foli|um 'fəʊl i‿|əm ‖ 'foʊl- **~a** ə
Foljambe 'fʊldʒ əm
folk fəʊk §fəʊlk ‖ foʊk **folks** fəʊks §fəʊlks
‖ foʊks
'folk dance; 'folk ˌdancer; ˌfolk
ˌety'mology; 'folk ˌmedicine; 'folk
ˌsinger; 'folk song
Folkestone 'fəʊkst ən ‖ 'foʊkst-
folkie 'fəʊk i ‖ 'foʊk i **~s** z
folklore 'fəʊk lɔː §'fəʊlk- ‖ 'foʊk lɔːr -loʊr
folkloric ˌfəʊk 'lɔːr ɪk ◂ §'fəʊlk- ‖ ˌfoʊk- -'loʊr-

folklorist 'fəʊk lɔːr ɪst §'fəʊlk-, §-əst ‖ 'foʊk-
-lɔʊr- ~s s

folkloristic ˌfəʊk lɔː 'rɪst ɪk ◄ ‖ ˌfoʊk- -loʊ-

folks|y 'fəʊks |i §'fəʊlks- ‖ 'foʊks |i ~ier i ə
‖ i ˌ°r ~iest i ˌɪst i ˌəst ~iness i nəs i nɪs

folktale 'fəʊk ter°l §'fəʊlk- ‖ 'foʊk- ~s z

folkway 'fəʊk wer §'fəʊlk- ‖ 'foʊk- ~s z

Follett 'fɒl ɪt -ət ‖ 'fɑːl-

Follick 'fɒl ɪk ‖ 'fɑːl-

follicle 'fɒl ɪk °l ‖ 'fɑːl- ~s z

follicular fɒ 'lɪk jʊl ə fə-, -jəl- ‖ fə 'lɪk jəl °r
fɑ:-

follie... —*see* **folly**

follow 'fɒl əʊ ‖ 'fɑːl oʊ ~ed d **following**
ˌfɒl əʊ ɪŋ -u ɪŋ ‖ 'fɑːl oʊ ɪŋ ~s z

follower 'fɒl əʊ ə §-u ə ‖ 'fɑːl oʊ °r ~s z

follow-my-leader ˌfɒl əʊ mə 'liːd ə -mɪˈ-,
-maɪˈ- ‖ ˌfɑːl oʊ maɪ 'liːd °r

follow-on ˌfɒl əʊ 'ɒn ‖ ˌfɑːl oʊ 'ɑːn -'ɔːn ~s z

follow-the-leader ˌfɒl əʊ ðə 'liːd ə
‖ ˌfɑːl oʊ ðə 'liːd °r

follow-through ˌfɒl əʊ 'θruː ‖ ˌfɑːl oʊ- ~s z

follow-up 'fɒl əʊ ʌp ‖ 'fɑːl oʊ- ~s s

foll|y 'fɒl |i ‖ 'fɑːl |i ~ies iz

Folsom (i) 'fəʊl səm →'fɒʊl- ‖ 'foʊl səm,
(ii) 'fɒl- ‖ 'fɑːl- —*The places in CA and NM
are (i); the family name may be either.*

Fomalhaut 'fɒm ə ləʊt 'fəʊm-, -əl hɔːt
‖ 'foʊm °l hɔːt -hɑːt; -ə loʊ

fo|ment fəʊ |'ment ‖ foʊ- ˈ·· ~mented
'ment ɪd -əd ‖ 'menţ əd ~menting 'ment ɪŋ
‖ 'menţ ɪŋ ~ments 'ments

fomentation ˌfəʊm en 'teɪʃ °n -ən- ‖ ˌfoʊm-
~s z

fond fɒnd ‖ fɑːnd **fonder** 'fɒnd ə ‖ 'fɑːnd °r
fondest 'fɒnd ɪst -əst ‖ 'fɑːnd-

Fonda 'fɒnd ə ‖ 'fɑːnd ə

fondant 'fɒnd ənt ‖ 'fɑːnd- ~s s

fondl|e 'fɒnd °l ‖ 'fɑːnd- ~ed d ~es z ~ing ɪŋ

fond|ly 'fɒnd |li ‖ 'fɑːnd- ~ness nəs nɪs

fondu, fondue 'fɒnd juː -uː ‖ fɑːn 'duː -'djuː,
ˈ·· —*Fr* [fɔ̃ dy] ~s z

Fongafale ˌfɒŋ ə 'fɑːl eɪ -gə- ‖ ˌfɑːŋ- ˌfɔːŋ-

font fɒnt ‖ fɑːnt **fonts** fɒnts ‖ fɑːnts

Fontaine 'fɒnt eɪn ‖ fɑːn 'teɪn

Fontainebleau 'fɒnt ɪn bləʊ →-ɪm-, -ən-
‖ 'fɑːnt °n bloʊ △'faʊnt °n bluː —*Fr*
[fɔ̃ tɛn blo]

Fontana *tdmk* fɒn 'tɑːn ə ‖ fɑːn 'tæn ə

fontanel, fontanelle ˌfɒnt ə 'nel
‖ ˌfɑːnt °n 'el ˈ···~s z

Fonteyn (i) ₍ˌ₎fɒn 'teɪn ‖ ₍ˌ₎fɑːn-, (ii) 'fɒnt eɪn
‖ 'fɑːn teɪn —*In AmE usually (i).*

Fonz fɒnz ‖ fɑːnz

Foochow ˌfuː 'tʃaʊ —*Chi* Fúzhōu [²fu ¹tʂou]

food fuːd §fʊd **foods** fuːdz §fʊdz
'food chain; 'food ˌpoisoning; 'food
ˌprocessor; 'food stamp

foodie 'fuːd i ~s z

foodstuff 'fuːd stʌf §'fʊd- ~s s

Fookes fuːks

fool fuːl **fooled** fuːld **fooling** 'fuːl ɪŋ **fools**
fuːlz
'fool's 'errand; ˌfool's 'paradise

fooler|y 'fuːl ər |i ~ies iz

foolhard|y 'fuːl ˌhɑːd |i ‖ -ˌhɑːrd |i ~ier i ə
‖ i ˌ°r ~iest i ˌɪst i ˌəst ~ily ɪ li əl i ~iness i nəs
i nɪs

foolish 'fuːl ɪʃ ~ly li ~ness nəs nɪs

foolproof 'fuːl pruːf §-prʊf

foolscap 'fuːl skæp 'fuːlz kæp ~s s

Foord fɔːd ‖ fɔːrd foʊrd

Foosball 'fuːz bɔːl 'fuːs- ‖ -bɑːl

fooser 'fuːz ə ‖ -°r ~s z

foot, Foot fʊt **feet** fiːt **footed** 'fʊt ɪd -əd
‖ 'fʊţ əd **footing** 'fʊt ɪŋ ‖ 'fʊţ ɪŋ **foots** fʊts
'foot brake; 'foot fault; 'foot ˌsoldier

footag|e 'fʊt ɪdʒ ‖ 'fʊţ ɪdʒ ~es ɪz əz

foot-and-mouth ˌfʊt °n 'maʊθ
ˌfoot-and-'mouth diˌsease

football 'fʊt bɔːl §-b°l ‖ -bɑːl ~er/s ə/z ˌ°r/z
~s z
'football ˌplayer; 'football pools

foot|bath 'fʊt |bɑːθ §-bæθ ‖ -|bæθ (*not* 'fʊd-₎
~baths bɑːðz §bæθs, §bɑːθs, §bæðz ‖ bæðz
bæθs

footboard 'fʊt bɔːd ‖ -bɔːrd -boʊrd (*not* 'fʊd-₎
~s z

footbridg|e 'fʊt brɪdʒ ~es ɪz əz

Footdee *place in Grampian* fʊt 'diː —*locally
also* 'fɪt i

foot-dragging 'fʊt ˌdræg ɪŋ

Foote fʊt

-footed 'fʊt ɪd -əd ‖ 'fʊţ əd — **splay-footed**
ˌspleɪ 'fʊt ɪd ◄ -əd ‖ -'fʊţ əd ◄

-footer 'fʊt ə ‖ 'fʊţ °r — **six-footer**
ˌsɪks 'fʊt ə ‖ -'fʊţ °r

footer *n* 'football', 'line at end of page' 'fʊt ə
‖ 'fʊţ °r ~s z

footfall 'fʊt fɔːl ‖ -fɑːl ~s z

foot-fault *v* 'fʊt fɔːlt -fɒlt ‖ -fɔːlt -fɑːlt ~ed ɪd
əd ~ing ɪŋ ~s s

foothill 'fʊt hɪl ~s z

foothold 'fʊt həʊld →-hɒʊld ‖ -hoʊld ~s z

footie 'fʊt i ‖ 'fʊţ i

footing 'fʊt ɪŋ ‖ 'fʊţ ɪŋ ~s z

footl|e 'fuːt °l ‖ 'fuːţ °l ~ed d ~es z ~ing ˌɪŋ

footlight 'fʊt laɪt ~s s

footling 'fuːt lɪŋ

footloose 'fʊt luːs

foot|man 'fʊt |mən ~men mən

footmark 'fʊt mɑːk ‖ -mɑːrk ~s s

footnote 'fʊt nəʊt ‖ -noʊt ~s s

footpad 'fʊt pæd ~s z

foot|path 'fʊt |pɑːθ §-pæθ ‖ -|pæθ ~paths
pɑːðz §pæθs, §pɑːθs, §pæðz ‖ pæðz pæθs

footplate 'fʊt pleɪt ~man mən mæn ~men
mən men ~s s

footprint 'fʊt prɪnt ~s s

footrac|e 'fʊt reɪs ~es ɪz əz

footrest 'fʊt rest ~s s

footsie 'fʊts i

footslog 'fʊt slɒg ‖ -slɑːg ~ged d ~ger/s ə/z ‖ ˀr/z ~ging ɪŋ ~s z

footsore 'fʊt sɔː ‖ -sɔːr -soʊr ~ness nəs nɪs

footstep 'fʊt step ~s s

footstool 'fʊt stuːl ~s z

footsure 'fʊt ʃɔː -ʃʊə ‖ -ʃʊr -ʃɜː ~ness nəs nɪs

footway 'fʊt weɪ ~s z

footwear 'fʊt weə ‖ -wer -wær

footwork 'fʊt wɜːk ‖ -wɜːk

footy 'fʊt i ‖ 'fʊt̬ i

foo yong, foo yoong, foo young ˌfuː 'jʌŋ -'jɒŋ, -'jʊŋ ‖ -'jʌŋ -'jɒːŋ, -'jɑːŋ, -'jʊŋ

foozl|e 'fuːz ᵊl ~ed d ~er/s ə/z ‖ ˀr/z ~es z ~ing ɪŋ

fop fɒp ‖ fɑːp **fops** fɒps ‖ fɑːps

fopper|y 'fɒp ər |i ‖ 'fɑːp- ~ies iz

foppish 'fɒp ɪʃ ‖ 'fɑːp- ~ly li ~ness nəs nɪs

for strong form fɔː ‖ fɔːr, weak form fə ‖ fˀr
— In both RP and GenAm ELISION gives rise to an occasional prevocalic weak form fr, used before weak vowels: stay for a week ˌsteɪ frə 'wiːk. There is also a very casual or rapid weak form f. In RP some speakers also have an occasional prevocalic strong form fɒr, used (if at all) only in the phrases for her fɒr ə, for him fɒr ɪm, for it fɒr ɪt, for us fɒr əs.

forag|e 'fɒr ɪdʒ ‖ 'fɔːr- 'fɑːr- ~ed d ~er/s ə/z ‖ ˀr/z ~es ɪz əz ~ing ɪŋ

'forage cap

foramen fə 'reɪm en fɒ-, -ən ‖ -ən fɔː- ~s z

foramina fə 'ræm ɪn ə fɒ-, -'reɪm-, §-ən-

foraminifer ˌfɒr ə 'mɪn ɪf ə -əf ə ‖ ˌfɔːr ə 'mɪn əf ˀr -s z

foraminif|era fə ˌræm ɪ 'nɪf |ər ə ˌfɒr əm-, ˌfɔːr əm-, -ə'- ~eral ˀr əl ~erous ər əs

forasmuch fər ˌəz 'mʌtʃ ˌfɔːr əz 'mʌtʃ, ˌfɒr- ‖ ˌfɔːr əz 'mʌtʃ ˈ··

foray v, n 'fɒr eɪ ‖ 'fɔːr eɪ 'fɑːr- ~ed d ~ing ɪŋ ~s z

forbad fə 'bæd fɔː- ‖ fˀr- fɔːr-

forbade fə 'bæd fɔː-, -'beɪd ‖ fˀr- fɔːr-

for|bear v 'hold oneself back' fɔː ‖'beə fə- ‖ fɔːr ‖'beˀr fˀr-, -'bæˀr ~bearing 'beər ɪŋ ‖ 'ber ɪŋ 'bær ɪŋ ~bears 'beəz ‖ 'beˀrz 'bæˀrz ~bore 'bɔː ‖ 'bɔːr -'boʊr ~borne 'bɔːn ‖ 'bɔːrn -'boʊrn

forbear n 'ancestor' 'fɔː beə ‖ 'fɔːr ber 'foʊr-, -bær ~s z

forbearance fɔː 'beər ənⁱs fə- ‖ fɔːr 'ber- fˀr-, -'bær-

Forbes fɔːbz 'fɔːb ɪs, -əs ‖ fɔːrbz —in Scotland usually as two syllables.

for|bid fə |'bɪd fɔː- ‖ fˀr- fɔːr- ~bad 'bæd ~bade 'bæd 'beɪd ~bidden 'bɪd ᵊn ~bidding 'bɪd ɪŋ

for,bidden 'fruit

forbidding fə 'bɪd ɪŋ fɔː- ‖ fˀr- fɔːr- ~ly li ~ness nəs nɪs

forbore fə 'bɔː ‖ fɔːr 'bɔːr -'boʊr

forborne fə 'bɔːn ‖ fɔːr 'bɔːrn -'boʊrn

Forbush 'fɔː bʊʃ ‖ 'fɔːr-

force fɔːs ‖ fɔːrs foʊrs **forced** fɔːst ‖ fɔːrst foʊrst **forces** 'fɔːs ɪz -əz ‖ 'fɔːrs əz 'foʊrs-

forcing 'fɔːs ɪŋ ‖ 'fɔːrs ɪŋ 'foʊrs-

,forced 'march; ,force ma'jeure mæ 'ʒɜː mə- ‖ mɑː- 'ʒɜː mæ-, mə- —Fr [fɔʁs ma ʒœːʁ]

force-|feed ˌfɔːs |'fiːd '·· ‖ ˌfɔːrs-, ˌfoʊrs- ~fed 'fed ~feeding 'fiːd ɪŋ ~feeds 'fiːdz

forceful 'fɔːs fᵊl -fʊl ‖ 'fɔːrs- 'foʊrs- ~ly i ~ness nəs nɪs

forcemeat 'fɔːs miːt ‖ 'fɔːrs- 'foʊrs-

forceps 'fɔːs eps -ɪps, -əps ‖ 'fɔːrs əps -eps

forcib|le 'fɔːs əb ᵊl -ɪb- ‖ 'fɔːrs- 'foʊrs- ~leness ᵊl nəs -nɪs ~ly li

ford, Ford fɔːd ‖ fɔːrd foʊrd **forded** 'fɔːd ɪd -əd ‖ 'fɔːrd əd 'foʊrd- **fording** 'fɔːd ɪŋ ‖ 'fɔːrd ɪŋ 'foʊrd- **fords, Ford's** fɔːdz ‖ fɔːrdz foʊrdz

fordable 'fɔːd əb ᵊl ‖ 'fɔːrd- 'foʊrd-

Forde fɔːd ‖ fɔːrd foʊrd

Fordham 'fɔːd əm ‖ 'fɔːrd- 'foʊrd-

Fordingbridge 'fɔːd ɪŋ brɪdʒ ‖ 'fɔːrd- 'foʊrd-

Fordyce 'fɔːd aɪs fɔː 'daɪs ‖ 'fɔːrd- —in Scotland ·'·

fore fɔː ‖ fɔːr four (= four)

,fore and 'aft

fore- |fɔː ‖ |fɔːr- |foʊr-

forearm n 'limb from elbow to wrist' 'fɔːr ɑːm ‖ 'fɔːr ɑːrm 'foʊr- ~s z

forearm v 'prepare' (ˌ)fɔːr 'ɑːm ‖ (ˌ)fɔːr 'ɑːrm (ˌ)foʊr- ~ed d ~ing ɪŋ ~s z

forebear n 'ancestor' 'fɔː beə ‖ 'fɔːr ber 'foʊr-, -bær ~s z

forebod|e fɔː 'bəʊd fə- ‖ fɔːr 'boʊd foʊr- ~ed ɪd əd ~es z ~ing ɪŋ

foreboding fɔː 'bəʊd ɪŋ fə- ‖ fɔːr 'boʊd ɪŋ foʊr- ~ly li ~s z

forebrain 'fɔː breɪn ‖ 'fɔːr- 'foʊr- ~s z

forecast n 'fɔː kɑːst §-kæst ‖ 'fɔːr kæst 'foʊr- ~s s

forecast v 'fɔː kɑːst §-kæst, (ˌ)·'· ‖ 'fɔːr kæst 'foʊr- ~ed ɪd əd ~er/s ə/z ‖ ˀr/z ~ing ɪŋ ~s s

forecastle 'fəʊks ᵊl ‖ 'foʊks- ~s z

foreclos|e (ˌ)fɔː 'kləʊz ‖ (ˌ)fɔːr 'kloʊz (ˌ)foʊr- ~ed d ~es ɪz əz ~ing ɪŋ

foreclosure (ˌ)fɔː 'kləʊʒ ə ‖ (ˌ)fɔːr 'kloʊʒ ˀr (ˌ)foʊr- ~s z

forecourt 'fɔː kɔːt ‖ 'fɔːr kɔːrt 'four kourt ~s s

foredeck 'fɔː dek ‖ 'fɔːr- 'four- ~s s

foredoomed (ˌ)fɔː 'duːmd ‖ (ˌ)fɔːr- (ˌ)four-

forefather 'fɔː ˌfɑːð ə ‖ 'fɔːr ˌfɑːð ˀr 'four- ~s z

forefeet 'fɔː fiːt ‖ 'fɔːr- 'four-

forefinger 'fɔː ˌfɪŋ gə ‖ 'fɔːr ˌfɪŋ gˀr 'four- ~s z

fore|foot 'fɔː |fʊt ‖ 'fɔːr- 'four- ~feet fiːt

forefront 'fɔː frʌnt ‖ 'fɔːr- 'four-

foregather fɔː 'gæð ə ‖ fɔːr 'gæð ˀr ~ed d **foregathering** fɔː 'gæð ər ɪŋ ‖ fɔːr- ~s z

fore|go (ˌ)fɔː |'gəʊ ‖ (ˌ)fɔːr |'goʊ (ˌ)four- ~goes 'gəʊz ‖ 'goʊz ~going 'gəʊ ɪŋ ‖ 'goʊ ɪŋ ~gone 'gɒn §'gɔːn, §'gɑːn ‖ 'gɔːn 'gɑːn ~went 'went

foregoing *adj 'preceding'* 'fɔː ˌgəʊ ɪŋ ₍ₗ₎'·· ‖ ₍ₗ₎fɔːr 'goʊ ɪŋ ₍ₗ₎foʊr-
foregoing *part 'giving up'* ₍ₗ₎fɔː 'gəʊ ɪŋ ‖ ₍ₗ₎fɔːr 'goʊ ɪŋ
foregone *pp 'given up'* ₍ₗ₎fɔː 'gɒn §-'gɔːn, §-'gɑːn ‖ ₍ₗ₎fɔːr 'gɔːn -'gɑːn
foregone *adj, 'certain'* 'fɔː gɒn §-gɔːn, §-gɑːn ‖ 'fɔːr gɔːn 'foʊr-, -gɑːn
ˌforegone con'clusion
foreground 'fɔː graʊnd ‖ 'fɔːr- 'foʊr- **~ed** ɪd əd **~ing** ɪŋ **~s** z
forehand 'fɔː hænd ‖ 'fɔːr- 'foʊr- **~ed** ɪd əd **~s** z

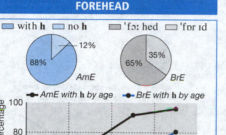

FOREHEAD

with h
no h
'fɔː hed
'fɒr ɪd
12%
88%
AmE
35%
65%
BrE
AmE with h by age
BrE with h by age
Percentage
100
80
60
40
0
Older
Speakers
Younger

forehead 'fɔː hed 'fɒr ɪd -əd, -ed ‖ 'fɔːr hed 'foʊr-, -ed; 'fɔːr əd, 'fɑːr- — *Preference polls, AmE: with* h *88%, no* h *12%; BrE:* 'fɒr ɪd *35%,* 'fɔː hed *65%. Several BrE respondents said they would have voted for* 'fɒr ed, *an option not offered.* **~s** z
foreign 'fɒr ən -ɪn ‖ 'fɔːr ən 'fɑːr- **~ness** nəs nɪs
ˌforeign af'fairs; **ˌForeign 'Legion**; **ˌforeign 'minister**; **'Foreign ˌOffice**; **ˌForeign 'Secretary**
foreigner 'fɒr ən ə -ɪn- ‖ 'fɔːr ən ᵊr 'fɑːr- **~s** z
foreknowledge ₍ₗ₎fɔː 'nɒl ɪdʒ ‖ ₍ₗ₎fɔːr 'nɑːl- ₍ₗ₎foʊr-
foreland, F~ 'fɔː lənd ‖ 'fɔːr- 'foʊr- **~s** z
foreleg 'fɔː leg ‖ 'fɔːr- 'foʊr- **~s** z
forelimb 'fɔː lɪm ‖ 'fɔːr- 'foʊr- **~s** z
forelock 'fɔː lɒk ‖ 'fɔːr lɑːk 'foʊr- **~s** s
fore|man, F~ 'fɔː |mən ‖ 'fɔːr- 'foʊr- **~men** mən men
foremast 'fɔː mɑːst §-mæst, -məst ‖ 'fɔːr mæst 'foʊr-, -məst —*naut* -məst **~s** s
foremost 'fɔː məʊst ‖ 'fɔːr moʊst 'foʊr-
forename 'fɔː neɪm ‖ 'fɔːr- 'foʊr- **~s** z
forenoon 'fɔː nuːn §-nʊn ‖ 'fɔːr- 'foʊr- **~s** z
forensic fə 'rentˢ ɪk fɒ-, -'renz- **~ally** ᵊl‿i **~s** s
foˌrensic 'science
foreordain ˌfɔːr ɔː 'deɪn ‖ ˌfɔːr ɔːr- ˌfoʊr- **~ed** d **~ing** ɪŋ **~ment** mənt **~s** z

forepart 'fɔː pɑːt ‖ 'fɔːr pɑːrt 'foʊr- **~s** s
forepaw 'fɔː pɔː ‖ 'fɔːr- 'foʊr-, -pɑː **~s** z
foreplay 'fɔː pleɪ ‖ 'fɔːr- 'foʊr-
forerunner 'fɔː ˌrʌn ə ‖ 'fɔːr ˌrʌn ᵊr 'foʊr- **~s** z
foresail 'fɔː seɪᵊl -sᵊl ‖ 'fɔːr- 'foʊr- —*naut* -sᵊl **~s** z
fore|see ₍ₗ₎fɔː |'siː fə- ‖ ₍ₗ₎fɔːr- ₍ₗ₎foʊr- **~saw** 'sɔː ‖ 'sɑː **~seeing** 'siː ɪŋ **~seen** 'siːn
foreseeable fɔː 'siː‿əb ᵊl fə- ‖ fɔːr- foʊr-
foreshadow ₍ₗ₎fɔː 'ʃæd əʊ ‖ ₍ₗ₎fɔːr 'ʃæd oʊ ₍ₗ₎foʊr- **~ed** d **~ing** ɪŋ **~s** z
foreshore 'fɔː ʃɔː ‖ 'fɔːr ʃɔːr 'foʊr ʃoʊr **~s** z
foreshorten ₍ₗ₎fɔː 'ʃɔːt ᵊn ‖ ₍ₗ₎fɔːr 'ʃɔːrt ᵊn ₍ₗ₎foʊr- **~ed** d **~ing** ‿ɪŋ **~s** z
foreshow ₍ₗ₎fɔː 'ʃəʊ ‖ ₍ₗ₎fɔːr 'ʃoʊ **~ed** d **~ing** ɪŋ **~n** n **~s** z
foresight 'fɔː saɪt ‖ 'fɔːr- 'foʊr-
foreskin 'fɔː skɪn ‖ 'fɔːr- 'foʊr- **~s** z
forest, F~ 'fɒr ɪst -əst ‖ 'fɔːr əst 'fɑːr- **~s** s
forestall ₍ₗ₎fɔː 'stɔːl ‖ ₍ₗ₎fɔːr- ₍ₗ₎foʊr-, -'stɑːl **~ed** d **~ing** ɪŋ **~s** z
forestation ˌfɒr ə 'steɪʃ ᵊn -ɪ- ‖ ˌfɔːr- ˌfɑːr-
forested 'fɒr ɪst ɪd -əst-, -əd ‖ 'fɔːr- 'fɑːr-
forester, F~ 'fɒr ɪst ə -əst- ‖ 'fɔːr əst ᵊr 'fɑːr- **~s** z
forestry 'fɒr ɪst ri -əst- ‖ 'fɔːr- 'fɑːr-
foretast|e *v* ₍ₗ₎fɔː 'teɪst ‖ ₍ₗ₎fɔːr- ₍ₗ₎foʊr- **~ed** ɪd əd **~es** s **~ing** ɪŋ
foretaste *n* 'fɔː teɪst ‖ 'fɔːr- 'foʊr- **~s** s
fore|tell ₍ₗ₎fɔː |'tel ‖ ₍ₗ₎fɔːr- ₍ₗ₎foʊr- **~telling** 'tel ɪŋ **~tells** 'telz **~told** 'təʊld →'tɒʊld ‖ 'toʊld
forethought 'fɔː θɔːt ‖ 'fɔːr- 'foʊr-, -θɑːt
foretold ₍ₗ₎fɔː 'təʊld →'tɒʊld ‖ ₍ₗ₎fɔːr 'toʊld ₍ₗ₎foʊr-
forever fər 'ev ə ‖ fər 'ev ᵊr
forewarn ₍ₗ₎fɔː 'wɔːn ‖ ₍ₗ₎fɔːr 'wɔːrn ₍ₗ₎foʊr- **~ed** d **~ing** ɪŋ **~s** z
forewent ₍ₗ₎fɔː 'went ‖ ₍ₗ₎fɔːr- ₍ₗ₎foʊr-
fore|woman 'fɔː |ˌwʊm ən ‖ 'fɔːr- 'foʊr- **~women** ˌwɪm ɪn -ən
foreword 'fɔː wɜːd ‖ 'fɔːr wɜːd 'foʊr- **~s** z
forex 'fɒr eks ‖ 'fɔːr- 'fɑːr-
Forfar 'fɔːf ə ‖ 'fɔːrf ᵊr —*also spelling pronunciation* 'fɔː fɑː ‖ 'fɔːr fɑːr
forf|eit *n, v, adj* 'fɔːf |ɪt -ət ‖ 'fɔːrf |ət **~eited** ɪt ɪd §ət-, -əd ‖ əṭ əd **~eiting** ɪt ɪŋ §ət- ‖ əṭ ɪŋ **~eits** ɪts §əts ‖ əts
forfeitable 'fɔːf ɪt əb ᵊl §'·ət- ‖ 'fɔːrf əṭ əb ᵊl
forfeiter 'fɔːf ɪt ə §-ət ə ‖ 'fɔːrf əṭ ᵊr **~s** z
forfeiture 'fɔːf ɪtʃ ə §-ətʃ- ‖ 'fɔːrf ətʃ ᵊr -ə tʃʊr, -tjʊr **~s** z
forfend fɔː 'fend ‖ fɔːr- **~ed** ɪd əd **~ing** ɪŋ **~s** z
forgather fɔː 'gæð ə ‖ fɔːr 'gæð ᵊr **~ed** d
forgathering fɔː 'gæð ər‿ɪŋ ‖ fɔːr- **~s** z
forgave fə 'geɪv ‖ fᵊr-
forge fɔːdʒ ‖ fɔːrdʒ foʊrdʒ **forged** fɔːdʒd ‖ fɔːrdʒd foʊrdʒd **forges** 'fɔːdʒ ɪz -əz ‖ 'fɔːrdʒ əz 'foʊrdʒ- **forging** 'fɔːdʒ ɪŋ ‖ 'fɔːrdʒ ɪŋ 'foʊrdʒ-
forger 'fɔːdʒ ə ‖ 'fɔːrdʒ ᵊr 'foʊrdʒ- **~s** z
forger|y 'fɔːdʒ ər‿|i ‖ 'fɔːrdʒ- 'foʊrdʒ- **~ies** iz

F

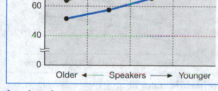

for|get fə |'get ‖ fʳ- —*but in formal style sometimes* fɔː- ‖ fɔːr- **~gets** 'gets **~getting** 'get ɪŋ ‖ 'get ɪŋ **~got** 'gɒt ‖ 'gɑːt **~gotten** 'gɒt ᵊn ‖ 'gɑːt ᵊn

forgetful fə 'get fᵊl -fʊl ‖ fʳ- **~ly** i **~ness** nəs nɪs

forget-me-not fə 'get mi nɒt ‖ fʳ 'get mi nɑːt **~s** s

forgettable fə 'get əb ᵊl ‖ fʳ 'get əb ᵊl

forging 'fɔːdʒ ɪŋ ‖ 'fɔːrdʒ ɪŋ 'foʊrdʒ- **~s** z

forgivab|le fə 'gɪv əb |ᵊl fɔː- ‖ fʳ- fɔːr- **~ly** li

for|give fə |'gɪv ‖ fʳ- —*but in formal style sometimes* fɔː- ‖ fɔːr- **~gave** 'geɪv **~given** 'gɪv ᵊn **~gives** 'gɪvz **~giving** 'gɪv ɪŋ

forgiveness fə 'gɪv nəs fɔː-,-nɪs ‖ fʳ- fɔːr-

forgiving fə 'gɪv ɪŋ fɔː- ‖ fʳ- fɔːr- **~ly** li **~ness** nəs nɪs

for|go ₍ₒ₎fɔː |'gəʊ ‖ ₍ₒ₎fɔːr |'goʊ **~goes** 'gəʊz ‖ 'goʊz **~going** 'gəʊ ɪŋ ‖ 'goʊ ɪŋ **~gone** 'gɒn §'gɔːn, §'gɑːn ‖ 'gɔːn 'gɑːn **~went** 'went

forgot fə 'gɒt ‖ fʳ 'gɑːt **~ten** ᵊn

forint 'fɒr ɪnt §-ənt ‖ 'fɔːr- —*Hungarian* ['fo rint] **~s** s

fork fɔːk ‖ fɔːrk **forked** fɔːkt ‖ fɔːrkt **forking** 'fɔːk ɪŋ ‖ 'fɔːrk ɪŋ **forks** fɔːks ‖ fɔːrks ,forked 'lightning

forkful 'fɔːk fʊl ‖ 'fɔːrk- **~s** z

forklift 'fɔːk lɪft ˌ·ˈ· ‖ 'fɔːrk- ,fork-lift 'truck ‖ ˈ· ·

forlorn fə 'lɔːn ₍ₒ₎fɔː- ‖ fʳ 'lɔːrn ,fɔːr- **~ly** li **~ness** nəs nɪs for,lorn 'hope

form fɔːm ‖ fɔːrm **formed** fɔːmd ‖ fɔːrmd **forming** 'fɔːm ɪŋ ‖ 'fɔːrm ɪŋ **forms** fɔːmz ‖ fɔːrmz

formal 'fɔːm ᵊl ‖ 'fɔːrm ᵊl

formaldehyde fɔː 'mæld ɪ haɪd -ə- ‖ fɔːr- fʳ-

formalin, F~ *tdmk* 'fɔːm ᵊl ɪn §-ən ‖ 'fɔːrm- -ə liːn

formalis... —*see* **formaliz...**

formalism 'fɔːm ə ,lɪz əm -ᵊl ,ɪz- ‖ 'fɔːrm- **~s** z

formalist 'fɔːm ᵊl ɪst §-əst ‖ 'fɔːrm- **~s** s

formalit|y fɔː 'mæl ət |i -ɪt- ‖ fɔːr 'mæl ət |i **~ies** iz

formalization ,fɔːm ᵊl aɪ 'zeɪʃ ᵊn -ɪ'·- ‖ ,fɔːrm ᵊl ə- **~s** z

formaliz|e 'fɔːm ə laɪz -ᵊl aɪz ‖ 'fɔːrm- **~ed** d **~es** ɪz əz **~ing** ɪŋ

formally 'fɔːm ᵊl i ‖ 'fɔːrm-

Forman 'fɔː mən ‖ 'fɔːr- 'foʊr-

formant 'fɔːm ənt ‖ 'fɔːrm- **~s** s 'formant ,structure

form|at *n*, *v* 'fɔːm |æt ‖ 'fɔːrm- **~ats** æts **~atted** æt ɪd -əd ‖ æt əd **~atting** æt ɪŋ ‖ æt ɪŋ

for|mate *v* 'take one's place in a formation' fɔː 'meɪt ‖ 'fɔːr|m eɪt **~mated** meɪt ɪd -əd ‖ meɪt əd **~mates** meɪts **~mating** meɪt ɪŋ ‖ meɪt ɪŋ

formate *n* 'salt or ester of formic acid' 'fɔːm eɪt ‖ 'fɔːrm- **~s** s

formation fɔː 'meɪʃ ᵊn ‖ fɔːr- **~al** ᵊl **~s** z

formative 'fɔːm ət ɪv ‖ 'fɔːrm ət ɪv **~ly** li **~ness** nəs nɪs **~s** z

formatter 'fɔːm æt ə ‖ 'fɔːrm æt ᵊr **~s** z

formbook 'fɔːm bʊk ‖ 'fɔːrm- **~s** s

Formby 'fɔːm bi ‖ 'fɔːrm-

forme fɔːm ‖ fɔːrm (= *form*) **formes** fɔːmz ‖ fɔːrmz

former 'fɔːm ə ‖ 'fɔːrm ᵊr **~s** z

formerly 'fɔːm ə li -ᵊl i ‖ 'fɔːrm ᵊr-

formic 'fɔːm ɪk ‖ 'fɔːrm- ,formic 'acid

Formica *tdmk*, **f~** fɔː 'maɪk ə ‖ fɔːr-

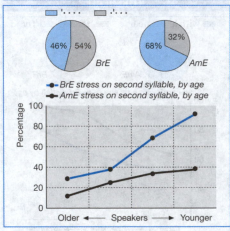

FORMIDABLE

- **BrE stress on second syllable, by age**
- **AmE stress on second syllable, by age**

BrE: 46% / 54% — BrE
AmE: 68% / 32% — AmE

formidab|le 'fɔːm ɪd əb |ᵊl '·əd-; fə 'mɪd-, fɔː- ‖ 'fɔːrm- fʳ 'mɪd-, fɔːr- —*Also in an imitated French form,* ,fɔːm ɪ 'dɑːb ᵊl ‖ ,fɔːrm- —*Fr* [fɔʁ mi dabl] — *Preference polls, BrE:* '· · · · 46%, ·'· · · 54%; *AmE:* '· · · · 68%, ·'· · · 32%. **~ly** li

formless 'fɔːm ləs -lɪs ‖ 'fɔːrm- **~ly** li **~ness** nəs nɪs

Formos|a fɔː 'məʊs ə -'məʊz- ‖ fɔːr 'moʊs ə **~an/s** ᵊn/z

form|ula 'fɔːm |jʊl ə -jəl ə ‖ 'fɔːrm |jᵊl ə **~ulae** ju liː jə-, -laɪ ‖ jə liː **~ulas** jʊl əz jəl əz ‖ jᵊl əz

formulaic ,fɔːm ju 'leɪ ɪk ◀ -jə- ‖ ,fɔːrm jə- **~ally** ᵊl i

formular|y 'fɔːm jʊl ər |i '·jəl- ‖ 'fɔːrm jə ler |i **~ies** iz

formu|late 'fɔːm ju |leɪt -jə- ‖ 'fɔːrm jə- **~lated** leɪt ɪd -əd ‖ leɪt əd **~lates** leɪts **~lating** leɪt ɪŋ ‖ leɪt ɪŋ

formulation ,fɔːm ju 'leɪʃ ᵊn -jə- ‖ ,fɔːrm jə- **~s** z

Fornax 'fɔːn æks ‖ 'fɔːrn-

Forney 'fɔːn i ‖ 'fɔːrn i

forni|cate 'fɔːn ɪ |keɪt -ə- ‖ 'fɔːrn- **~cated** keɪt ɪd -əd ‖ keɪt əd **~cates** keɪts **~cating** keɪt ɪŋ ‖ keɪt ɪŋ

fornication ,fɔːn ɪ 'keɪʃ ᵊn -ə- ‖ ,fɔːrn- **~s** z

fornicator 'fɔːn ɪ keɪt ə '·ə- ‖ 'fɔːrn ə keɪt ᵊr **~s** z

fornix 'fɔːn ɪks ‖ 'fɔːrn- **fornices** 'fɔːn ɪ siːz -ə-
‖ 'fɔːrn-
forrader, forrarder 'fɒr əd ə ‖ 'fɔːr əd ᵊr
'fɑːr-
Forres 'fɒr ɪs -əs ‖ 'fɔːr- 'fɑːr-
Forrest 'fɒr ɪst -əst ‖ 'fɔːr- 'fɑːr-
Forrester 'fɒr ɪst ə -əst- ‖ 'fɔːr əst ᵊr 'fɑːr-
for|sake fə ‖'seɪk fɔː- ‖ ᶠr- fɔːr- **~saken**
'seɪk ən **~sakes** 'seɪks **~saking** 'seɪk ɪŋ
~sook 'sʊk
forsooth fə 'suːθ fɔː- ‖ ᶠr- fɔːr-
Forster 'fɔːst ə 'fɒst- ‖ 'fɔːrst ᵊr
for|swear ₍ᵢ₎fɔː ‖'sweə ‖ ₍ᵢ₎fɔːr ‖'sweᵊr 'swæᵊr
~swearing 'sweər ɪŋ ‖ 'swer ɪŋ 'swær ɪŋ
~swears 'sweəz ‖ 'sweᵊrz 'swæᵊrz **~swore**
'swɔː ‖ 'swɔːr 'swoʊr **~sworn** 'swɔːn
‖ 'swɔːrn 'swoʊrn
Forsyte 'fɔː saɪt ‖ 'fɔːr-
Forsyth (i) fɔː 'saɪθ ‖ 'fɔːr-, (ii) 'fɔː saɪθ ‖ 'fɔːr-
—*The Scottish family name is (i).*
forsythia fɔː 'saɪθ i ə fə-, -'sɪθ- ‖ fɔːr 'sɪθ i ə
fᵊr-, -'saɪθ- **~s** z
fort, Fort fɔːt ‖ fɔːrt foʊrt **forts** fɔːts ‖ fɔːrts
foʊrts
₍ᵢ₎Fort 'Knox; ₍ᵢ₎Fort 'Lauderdale; ₍ᵢ₎Fort
'William
forte *loud,* **Forte** *family name* 'fɔːt eɪ -i
‖ 'fɔːrt eɪ **~s** z
forte *'positive characteristic'* 'fɔːt eɪ -i; fɔːt
‖ fɔːrt foʊrt; 'fɔːrt̬ i, 'fɔːrt eɪ **fortes** 'fɔːt eɪz
-iz; fɔːts ‖ 'fɔːrts foʊrts; 'fɔːrt̬ iz, 'fɔːrt eɪz
Fortean 'fɔːt i ən ‖ 'fɔːrt̬-
fortepiano, forte-piano ‚fɔːt i pi 'æn əʊ
‚eɪ-, -'ɑːn-; ‚· ·'pjæn-, ‚· ·'pjɑːn-
‖ ‚fɔːrt̬ i pi 'ɑːn oʊ ‚fɔːrt eɪ- **~s** z
fortes —*see* **forte, fortis**
Fortescue 'fɔːt ɪ skjuː -ə- ‖ 'fɔːrt̬-
forth, Forth fɔːθ ‖ fɔːrθ foʊrθ
forthcoming ₍ᵢ₎fɔːθ 'kʌm ɪŋ ‖ ₍ᵢ₎fɔːrθ- ₍ᵢ₎foʊrθ-
~ness nəs nɪs
forthright 'fɔːθ raɪt ‚·'· ‖ 'fɔːrθ- 'foʊrθ- **~ly** li
~ness nəs nɪs
forthwith ‚fɔːθ 'wɪθ -'wɪð ‖ ‚fɔːrθ- ‚foʊrθ-
forties, F~ 'fɔːt iz §-tiz ‖ 'fɔːrt̬ iz
fortieth 'fɔːt i əθ ɪθ ‖ 'fɔːrt̬ i əθ **~s** s
fortifiable 'fɔːt ɪ faɪ ‚əb ᵊl '·ə-, ‚· ·'· ·· ‖ 'fɔːrt̬ ə-
fortification ‚fɔːt ɪf ɪ 'keɪʃ ᵊn ‚əf-, §-ə'-‚··
‖ ‚fɔːrt̬ əf- **~s** z
forti|fy 'fɔːt ɪ ‖faɪ -ə- ‖ 'fɔːrt̬ ə- **~fied** faɪd
~fier/s faɪ ə/z ‖ faɪ ᵊr/z **~fies** faɪz **~fying**
faɪ ɪŋ
Fortinbras 'fɔːt ɪn bræs →-ɪm-, §-ᵊn-
‖ 'fɔːrt̬ ᵊn-
fortis 'fɔːt ɪs §-əs ‖ 'fɔːrt̬ əs **fortes** 'fɔːt iːz -eɪz
‖ 'fɔːrt̬-
fortissimo fɔː 'tɪs ɪ məʊ -ə- ‖ fɔːr 'tɪs ə moʊ
~s z
fortitude 'fɔːt ɪ tjuːd -ə-, →-tʃuːd ‖ 'fɔːrt̬ ə tuːd
-tjuːd
fortnight 'fɔːt naɪt ‖ 'fɔːrt- 'foʊrt- **~s** s
fortnight|ly 'fɔːt naɪt |li ‖ 'fɔːrt- 'foʊrt- **~lies**
liz
Fortnum 'fɔːt nəm ‖ 'fɔːrt- **~'s** z

Fortran, FORTRAN 'fɔː træn ‖ 'fɔːr-
fortress 'fɔːtr əs -ɪs ‖ 'fɔːrtr əs **~es** ɪz əz
fortuitous fɔː 'tjuːˌ ɪt əs →-'tʃuːˌ, -ət-,
⚠ ‚fɔːtʃ u 'ɪʃ əs ◂ ‖ fɔːr 'tuː ət̬ əs ᶠr-, -'tjuː-
~ly li **~ness** nəs nɪs
fortunate 'fɔːtʃ ən ‚ət ɪt ‖ 'fɔːrtʃ- **~ly** li
fortune 'fɔːtʃ ən -uːn; 'fɔːt juːn ‖ 'fɔːrtʃ ən **~s** z
'fortune ‚hunter
fortune-tell|er 'fɔːtʃ ən ‚tel |ə -uːn-; 'fɔːt juːn-
‖ 'fɔːrtʃ ən ‚tel |ᵊr **~ers** əz ‖ ᵊrz **~ing** ɪŋ
fort|y, Forty 'fɔːt |i §'fɔːt t|i ‖ 'fɔːrt̬ |i **~ies** iz
‚forty 'winks
forty-five ‚fɔːt i 'faɪv ◂ §-ti- ‖ ‚fɔːrt̬ i- **~s** z
forty-niner ‚fɔːt i 'naɪn ə §-ti-
‖ ‚fɔːrt̬ i 'naɪn ᵊr **~s** z
forum 'fɔːr əm ‖ 'foʊr- **~s** z
forward 'fɔː wəd ‖ 'fɔːr wᵊrd —*but the
adjective and adverb, in BrE nautical use, are*
'fɒr əd **~ed** ɪd əd **~er/s** ə/z ‖ ᵊr/z **~ing** ɪŋ **~s**
z
forward-looking ‚fɔː wəd 'lʊk ɪŋ ◂ '·· ‚· ·
‖ ‚fɔːr wᵊrd-
‚forward-‚looking 'policies
forward|ly 'fɔː wəd |li ‖ 'fɔːr wᵊrd |li **~ness**
nəs nɪs
forwards 'fɔː wədz ‖ 'fɔːr wᵊrdz
forwent ₍ᵢ₎fɔː 'went ‖ ₍ᵢ₎fɔːr-
Fosbury 'fɒz bər i ‖ 'fɑːz ‚ber i
‚Fosbury 'flop
Fosdick 'fɒz dɪk ‖ 'fɑːz-
Fosdyke 'fɒz daɪk ‖ 'fɑːz-
foss, Foss fɒs ‖ fɑːs **fosses** 'fɒs ɪz -əz
‖ 'fɑːs əz
foss|a 'fɒs |ə ‖ 'fɑːs |ə **~ae** iː **~as** əz
fosse, Fosse fɒs ‖ fɑːs **fosses** 'fɒs ɪz -əz
‖ 'fɑːs əz
‚Fosse 'Way
fossick 'fɒs ɪk ‖ 'fɑːs- **~ed** t **~er/s** ə/z ‖ ᵊr/z
~ing ɪŋ **~s** s
fossil 'fɒs ᵊl -ɪl ‖ 'fɑːs ᵊl **~s** z
fossilis... —*see* **fossiliz...**
fossilization ‚fɒs ᵊl aɪ 'zeɪʃ ᵊn ‚·ɪl-, -ɪ'-
‖ ‚fɑːs ᵊl ə- **~s** z
fossiliz|e 'fɒs ᵊl aɪz -ɪ laɪz ‖ 'fɑːs- **~ed** d **~es** ɪz
əz **~ing** ɪŋ
foster, F~ 'fɒst ə ‖ 'fɑːst ᵊr **~ed** d **fostering**
'fɒst ᵊr ɪŋ ‖ 'fɑːst ər ɪŋ **~s** z
foster- 'fɒst ə ‖ 'fɑːst ᵊr — **foster-brother**
'fɒst ə ‚brʌð ə ‖ 'fɑːst ᵊr ‚brʌð ᵊr
fosterage 'fɒst ər ɪdʒ ‖ 'fɑːst-
fosterling 'fɒst ə lɪŋ ‖ 'fɑːst ᵊr- **~s** z
Fothergill 'fɒð ə gɪl ‖ 'fɑːð ᵊr-
Fotheringay, Fotheringhay 'fɒð ər ɪŋ geɪ
‖ 'fɑːð- —*but the Northants village is
nowadays called* -heɪ
Fotheringham 'fɒð ər ɪŋ əm ‖ 'fɑːð ər ɪŋ hæm
Foucault 'fuːk əʊ ₍ᵢ₎fuː 'kəʊ ‖ fuː 'koʊ —*Fr*
[fu ko]
fouetté 'fuːˌ ə teɪ ‚fuː ə 'teɪ —*Fr* [fwɛ te] **~s**
z
fought fɔːt ‖ fɑːt

foul faʊl (= *fowl*) **fouled** faʊld **fouler** 'faʊl ə
‖ -ᵊr **foulest** 'faʊl ɪst -əst **fouling** 'faʊl ɪŋ
foully 'faʊl li -i **fouls** faʊlz
  ,foul 'play
Foula 'fuːl ə
foulard 'fuːl ɑː -ɑːd; fu 'lɑː, -'lɑːd ‖ fu 'lɑːrd ~s
z
Foulds fəʊldz →fɒʊldz ‖ foʊldz
Foulkes (i) fəʊks ‖ foʊks, (ii) faʊks
foul-mouthed ,faʊl 'maʊðd ◄ ‖ -'maʊθt ◄
foulness 'faʊl nəs -nɪs ~es ɪz əz
Foulness ,faʊl 'nes
foul-up 'faʊl ʌp ~s s
found faʊnd **founded** 'faʊnd ɪd -əd **founding**
  'faʊnd ɪŋ **founds** faʊndz
  ,founding 'father
foundation faʊn 'deɪʃ ᵊn ~s z
  foun'dation course; foun'dation
  ,garment; foun'dation stone
foundationer faʊn 'deɪʃ ᵊn ə ‖ ˌər ~s z
founder 'faʊnd ə ‖ -ᵊr ~ed d **foundering**
  'faʊnd ᵊr ɪŋ ~s z
foundling 'faʊnd lɪŋ ~s z
foundr|y 'faʊndr |i **~ies** iz
fount *'set of printing type'* fɒnt faʊnt ‖ fɑːnt
  faʊnt **founts** fɒnts faʊnts ‖ fɑːnts faʊnts
fount *'spring, origin'* faʊnt **founts** faʊnts
fountain 'faʊnt ɪn -ən ‖ 'faʊnt ᵊn ~s z
  'fountain pen; ,Fountains 'Abbey
Fountain, Fountaine 'faʊnt ɪn -ən ‖ 'faʊnt ᵊn
fountainhead 'faʊnt ɪn hed -ən-, ˌ·'·
  ‖ 'faʊnt ᵊn- ~s z
four fɔː ‖ fɔːr four (= *fore*) **fours** fɔːz ‖ fɔːrz
  foʊrz
  'four flush; ,four 'hundred◄
four by four, 4×4 ,fɔː baɪ 'fɔː -bi-
  ‖ 'fɔːr baɪ fɔːr 'four baɪ four ~s z
Fourcin 'fɔːs ɪn §-ᵊn ‖ 'fɔːrs-
foureyes 'fɔːr aɪz ‖ 'fɔːr- 'foʊr-
fourfold 'fɔː fəʊld →-fɒʊld ‖ 'fɔːr foʊld 'foʊr-
four-footed ,fɔː 'fʊt ɪd ◄ -əd ‖ ,fɔːr 'fʊt̬ əd ◄
  ,foʊr-
Fourier 'fʊr i ə 'fʊər-, -eɪ ‖ 'fʊr i eɪ -i ᵊr —*Fr*
  [fu ʁje]
four-in-hand ,fɔːr ɪn 'hænd §-ən- ‖ ,fɔːr ən-
  ,foʊr-
four-|leaf 'fɔː |liːf ‖ 'fɔːr- 'foʊr-
four-leaved ,fɔː 'liːvd ◄ ‖ ,fɔːr- ,foʊr-
  ,four-leaved 'clover
four-legged ,fɔː 'leg ɪd ◄ -əd; -'legd ◄ ‖ ,fɔːr-
  ,foʊr-
four-letter ,fɔː 'let ə ◄ ‖ ,fɔːr 'let̬ ᵊr ◄ ,foʊr-
  ,four-,letter 'word
four-o'clock ,fɔːr ə 'klɒk ◄ ‖ ,fɔːr ə 'klɑːk ◄
  ,foʊr-
four-part ,fɔː 'pɑːt ◄ ‖ ,fɔːr 'pɑːrt ◄ ,foʊr-
fourpence 'fɔːp ᵊn's →-mᵖs; 'fɔː pen's, ˌ·'·
  ‖ 'fɔːrp- foʊrp-
fourpenny 'fɔːp ən i ‖ 'fɔːr ,pen i 'foʊr-
four-poster ,fɔː 'pəʊst ə ◄ ‖ ,fɔːr 'poʊst ᵊr ◄
  ,foʊr- ~s z
  ,four-,poster 'bed

four-pounder ,fɔː 'paʊnd ə ‖ ,fɔːr 'paʊnd ᵊr
  ,four- ~s z
fourscore ,fɔː 'skɔː ◄ '·· ‖ ,fɔːr 'skɔːr ◄
  ,four 'skoʊr
  ,fourscore and 'ten
foursome 'fɔː səm ‖ 'fɔːr- 'foʊr- ~s z
foursquare ,fɔː 'skweə ◄ '·· ‖ ,fɔːr 'skweᵊr
  foʊr-, -'skwæᵊr
four-star 'fɔː stɑː ‖ 'fɔːr stɑːr 'foʊr-
four-stroke 'fɔː strəʊk ‖ 'fɔːr stroʊk 'foʊr-
fourteen ,fɔː 'tiːn ◄ §,fɔːt- ‖ ,fɔːr- ,fɔːrt-, ,foʊr-,
  ,foʊrt- ~s z
fourteenth ,fɔː 'tiːnᵗθ ◄ §,fɔːt- ‖ ,fɔːr- ,fɔːrt-,
  ,foʊr-, ,foʊrt- ~s s
fourth fɔːθ ‖ fɔːrθ foʊrθ (= *forth*) **fourthly**
  'fɔːθ li ‖ 'fɔːrθ li 'foʊrθ- **fourths** fɔːθs
  ‖ fɔːrθs foʊrθs
  ,fourth di'mension; ,fourth e'state;
  ,Fourth of Ju'ly
four-wheel ,fɔː 'wiːᵊl ◄ -'hwiːᵊl ‖ ,fɔːr 'hwiːᵊl ◄
  ,four-
  ,four-wheel 'drive
four-wheeler ,fɔː 'wiːl ə ◄ -'hwiːl-
  ‖ ,fɔːr 'hwiːl ᵊr ,foʊr- ~s z
fove|a 'fəʊv i |ə 'fɒv- ‖ 'foʊv- **~ae** iː
Foveaux fə 'vəʊ ‖ -'voʊ
Fowey fɔɪ
Fowke (i) fəʊk ‖ foʊk, (ii) faʊk
Fowkes (i) fəʊks ‖ foʊks, (ii) faʊks
fowl faʊl **fowls** faʊlz
  'fowl pest
fowler, F~ 'faʊl ə ‖ -ᵊr ~s z
Fowles faʊlz
Fowlmere 'faʊl mɪə ‖ -mɪr
fox, Fox fɒks ‖ fɑːks **foxed** fɒkst ‖ fɑːkst
  foxes 'fɒks ɪz -əz ‖ 'fɑːks əz **foxing** 'fɒks ɪŋ
  ‖ 'fɑːks ɪŋ
  ,fox 'terrier
Foxcroft 'fɒks krɒft ‖ 'fɑːks krɔːft -krɑːft
Foxe fɒks ‖ fɑːks
foxfire 'fɒks ,faɪ ə ‖ 'fɑːks ,faɪ ᵊr
foxglove 'fɒks glʌv ‖ 'fɑːks- ~s z
foxhole 'fɒks həʊl →-hɒʊl ‖ 'fɑːks hoʊl ~s z
foxhound 'fɒks haʊnd ‖ 'fɑːks- ~s z
foxhunt 'fɒks hʌnt ‖ 'fɑːks- ~s s
foxhunt|er, F~ 'fɒks ,hʌnt |ə
  ‖ 'fɑːks ,hʌnt̬ |ᵊr **~ers** əz ‖ ᵊrz **~ing** ɪŋ
foxi... —*see* **foxy**
foxtail 'fɒks teᵊl ‖ 'fɑːks- ~s z
Foxton 'fɒkst ən ‖ 'fɑːkst-
foxtrot 'fɒks trɒt ‖ 'fɑːks trɑːt ~s s
fox|y 'fɒks |i ‖ 'fɑːks |i **~ier** i ə ‖ i ᵊr **~iest**
  i ɪst i əst **~ily** ɪ li əl i **~iness** i nəs i nɪs
Foy fɔɪ
foyer 'fɔɪ eɪ -ə; 'fwaɪ eɪ ‖ 'fɔɪ ᵊr -eɪ; 'fwɑː jeɪ
  —*Fr* [fwa je] ~s z
Foyle fɔɪᵊl **Foyles, Foyle's** fɔɪᵊlz
Fra frɑː —*It* [fra]
frabjous 'fræb dʒəs
fracas *sing.* 'fræk ɑː ‖ 'freɪk əs 'fræk- (*)
  fracas *pl* 'fræk ɑːz ‖ 'feɪk əs 'fræk- **~es** ɪz əz
fractal 'frækt ᵊl ~s z
fraction 'fræk ʃᵊn ~s z

fractional 'fræk ʃⁿ‿əl ~**ly** i
fractio|nate 'fræk ʃə |neɪt ~**nated** neɪt ɪd -əd
‖ neɪt̬ əd ~**nates** neɪts ~**nating** neɪt ɪŋ
‖ neɪt̬ ɪŋ
fractionation ‚fræk ʃə 'neɪʃ ⁿn ~**s** z
fractionator 'fræk ʃə neɪt ə ‖ -neɪt̬ ʳr ~**s** z
fractious 'fræk ʃəs ~**ly** li ~**ness** nəs nɪs
fracture 'fræk tʃə -ʃə ‖ -tʃ ʳr -ʃʳr ~**d** d
fracturing 'fræk tʃər ɪŋ -ʃər‿ ~**s** z
frag fræg **fragged** frægd **fragging** 'fræg ɪŋ
frags frægz
fragile 'frædʒ aɪʳl ‖ -ⁿl (*) ~**ly** li ~**ness** nəs nɪs
fragility frə 'dʒɪl ət i fræ-, -ɪt- ‖ -ət̬ i
fragment n 'fræg mənt ~**s** s
frag|ment v ‿fræg |'ment ~**mented** 'ment ɪd
-əd ‖ 'ment̬ əd ~**menting** 'ment ɪŋ
‖ 'ment̬ ɪŋ ~**ments** 'ments
fragmental fræg 'ment ⁿl ‖ -'ment̬ ⁿl
fragmentary 'fræg mənt‿ər i fræg 'ment-
‖ 'fræg mən ter i
fragmentation ‚fræg mən 'teɪʃ ⁿn -men- ~**s** z
Fragonard 'fræg ə nɑː -ɒ- ‖ ‚frɑːg oʊ 'nɑːr
‚fræg-, -ə- —Fr [fʁa ɡɔ naːʁ]
fragranc|e 'freɪg rənt̬s ~**es** ɪz əz
fragrant 'freɪg rənt ~**ly** li ~**ness** nəs nɪs
fraidy cat 'freɪd i kæt ~**s** s
frail freɪʳl **frailer** 'freɪʳl ə ‖ -ʳr **frailest**
'freɪʳl ɪst -əst **frailly** 'freɪʳl li **frailness**
'freɪl nəs -nɪs
frail|ty 'freɪʳl |ti ~**ties** tiz
Frain freɪn
frame, Frame freɪm **framed** freɪmd **framer/s**
'freɪm ə/z ‖ -ʳr/z **frames** freɪmz **framing**
'freɪm ɪŋ
‚frame of 'mind; ‚frame of 'reference
frame-up 'freɪm ʌp ~**s** s
framework 'freɪm wɜːk ‖ -wɜːk ~**s** s
Framingham (i) 'freɪm ɪŋ əm ‖ -hæm,
(ii) 'fræm-
Framlingham 'fræm lɪŋ əm ‖ -hæm
Framlington 'fræm lɪŋ tən
Frampton 'fræmpt ən
Fran fræn
franc fræŋk (= frank) —Fr [fʁɑ̃] **francs**
fræŋks
France frɑːnts §frænts ‖ frænts **France's**
'frɑːnts ɪz §'frænts-, -əz ‖ 'frænts əz
Frances personal name 'frɑːnts ɪs §'frænts-, -əs
‖ 'frænts-
Francesca fræn 'tʃesk ə -'sesk- ‖ frɑːn- fræn-
franchis|e 'fræntʃ aɪz 'frɑːntʃ- ~**ed** d ~**es** ɪz əz
~**ing** ɪŋ
franchisee ‚fræntʃ aɪ 'ziː ‚frɑːntʃ- ~**s** z
franchisement 'fræntʃ ɪz mənt 'frɑːntʃ-, §-əz-
‖ -aɪz-‿-əz- ~**s** s
franchisor ‚fræntʃ aɪ 'zɔː ‚frɑːntʃ-, -ɪ- ‖ -'zɔːr
-ə- ~**s** z
Francis 'frɑːnts ɪs §'frænts-, -əs ‖ 'frænts-
Franciscan fræn 'sɪsk ən ~**s** z
francium 'frænts i‿əm 'frɑːnts-
Franck composer frɒŋk frɑːŋk ‖ frɑːŋk —Fr
[fʁɑ̃ːk]
Franco 'fræŋk əʊ ‖ -oʊ 'frɑːŋk- —Sp ['fraŋ ko]

Franco- ¦fræŋk əʊ ‖ -oʊ — **Franco-British**
‚fræŋk əʊ 'brɪt ɪʃ ◂ ‖ -oʊ 'brɪt̬ ɪʃ ◂
Francois, François 'frɒnts wɑː 'frɑːnts-,
'frænts-, ‚·'· ‖ frɑːn 'swɑː —Fr [fʁɑ̃ swa]
Francoise, Françoise 'frɒnts wɑːz 'frɑːnts-,
'frænts-, ‚·'· ‖ frɑːn 'swɑːz —Fr [fʁɑ̃ swaːz]
francolin 'fræŋk əʊl ɪn §-ən ‖ -əl‿ən ~**s** z
Franconi|a fræn 'kəʊn i‿|ə ‖ -'koʊn- ~**an/s**
ən/z
Francophile 'fræŋk əʊ faɪʳl ‖ -ə- ~**s** z
francophobe, F~ 'fræŋk əʊ fəʊb ‖ -ə foʊb ~**s**
z
francophone, F~ 'fræŋk əʊ fəʊn ‖ -ə foʊn ~**s**
z
frangible 'frændʒ əb ⁿl -ɪb-
frangipani ‚frændʒ ɪ 'pɑːn i §-ə-, -'pæn-
‖ -'pæn i ~**s** z
Franglais, f~ 'frɒŋ ɡleɪ 'frɑː‿ŋ- ‖ frɑːn 'ɡleɪ
—Fr [fʁɑ̃ ɡlɛ]
frank, Frank fræŋk **franked** fræŋkt **franker**
'fræŋk ə ‖ -ʳr **frankest** 'fræŋk ɪst -əst
franking 'fræŋk ɪŋ **franks** fræŋks
Frankau (i) 'fræŋk əʊ ‖ -oʊ, (ii) -aʊ
frankenfood 'fræŋk ən fuːd ~**s** z
Frankenstein 'fræŋk ən staɪn -ɪn- —Ger
['fʁaŋk ⁿn ʃtaɪn]
Frankfort places in US 'fræŋk fət ‖ -fʳrt
Frankfurt 'fræŋk fɜːt -fət ‖ -fʳrt —Ger
['fʁaŋk fʊʁt]
frankfurter, F~ 'fræŋk fɜːt ə -fət- ‖ -fʳrt̬ ʳr ~**s**
z
Frankie 'fræŋk i
frankincense 'fræŋk ɪn ‚sents -ən-
Frankish 'fræŋk ɪʃ
Frankland 'fræŋk lənd
franklin, F~ 'fræŋk lɪn -lən ~**s, ~'s** z
frankly 'fræŋk li
Franklyn 'fræŋk lɪn -lən
frankness 'fræŋk nəs -nɪs
Frannie 'fræn i
Frant frænt
frantic 'frænt ɪk ‖ 'frænt̬ ɪk ~**ally** ⁿl‿i ~**ness**
nəs nɪs
Franz frænts frɑːnts ‖ frɑːnts —Ger [fʁants]
—but as an American name also frænz
frap fræp **frapped** fræpt **frapping** 'fræp ɪŋ
fraps fræps
frappe, frappé 'fræp eɪ ‖ fræ 'peɪ —Fr
[fʁa pe] ~**s** z
Frascati fræ 'skɑːt i —It [fra 'ska: ti]
Fraser 'freɪz ə ‖ -ʳr
Fraserburgh 'freɪz ə bər‿ə -ə ‚bʌr ə
‖ -ʳr ‚bɜː oʊ
Frasier 'freɪz i‿ə 'freɪʒ ə ‖ 'freɪʒ ʳr
frass fræs
frat fræt **frats** fræts
fratch|y 'frætʃ |i ~**iness** i nəs i nɪs
Frater, f~ 'freɪt ə ‖ 'freɪt̬ ʳr
fraternal frə 'tɜːn ⁿl ‖ -'tɜːn- ~**ism** ‚ɪz əm ~**ly** i
fraternis... —see **fraterniz...**
fraternit|y frə 'tɜːn ət |i ‖ -ɪt- ‖ -'tɜːn ət̬ |i ~**ies**
iz

fraternization ˌfræt ən aɪ ˈzeɪʃ ən -ɪˈ-- ‖ ˌfræg ᵊrn ə-

fraterniz|e ˈfræt ə naɪz -ᵊn aɪz ‖ -ᵊr- **~ed** d **~er/s** ə/z ‖ ᵊr/z **~es** ɪz əz **~ing** ɪŋ

fratricidal ˌfrætr ɪ ˈsaɪd ᵊl ◂ ˌfreɪtr-, -ə- **~ly** i

fratricide ˈfrætr ɪ saɪd ˈfreɪtr-, -ə- **~s** z

Fratton ˈfræt ᵊn

Frau frau — *Ger* [fʁau]
₍ˌ₎**Frau ˈBecker**

fraud frɔːd ‖ frɑːd **frauds** frɔːdz ‖ frɑːdz

fraudster ˈfrɔːd stə ‖ -stᵊr ˈfrɑːd- **~s** z

fraudulence ˈfrɔːd jʊl ənts -jəl-, ˈfrɔːdʒ əl- ‖ ˈfrɔːdʒ əl- ˈfrɑːdʒ-

fraudulent ˈfrɔːd jʊl ənt -jəl-, ˈfrɔːdʒ əl- ‖ ˈfrɔːdʒ əl- ˈfrɑːdʒ- **~ly** li

fraught frɔːt ‖ frɑːt

fraulein, fräulein ˈfrɔɪ laɪn ˈfrau- — *Ger* Fräulein [ˈfʁɔy laɪn] **~s** z

Fraunhofer ˈfraun həʊf ə ‖ -hoʊf ᵊr — *Ger* [ˈfʁaun hoːf ɐ]
ˈFraunhofer lines

fray freɪ **frayed** freɪd **fraying** ˈfreɪ ɪŋ **frays** freɪz

Fray Bentos ˌfreɪ ˈbent ɒs ‖ -oʊs — *Sp* [frai ˈβen tos]

Frayn, Frayne freɪn

Frazer ˈfreɪz ə ‖ -ᵊr

Frazier ˈfreɪz iˌə ‖ ˈfreɪʒ ᵊr -iˌᵊr (*)

frazil ˈfreɪz ɪl ˈfræz-, -ᵊl

frazzl|e ˈfræz ᵊl **~ed** d **~es** z **~ing** ɪŋ

freak friːk **freaked** friːkt **freaking** ˈfriːk ɪŋ **freaks** friːks

freakish ˈfriːk ɪʃ **~ly** li **~ness** nəs nɪs

freak-out ˈfriːk aʊt **~s** s

freak|y ˈfriːk| i **~ier** iˌə ‖ iˌᵊr **~iest** iˌɪst ˌəst **~ily** ɪ li əl i **~iness** i nəs -nɪs

Frean friːn

freckle ˈfrek ᵊl **~d** d **~s** z

Fred fred

Freda ˈfriːd ə

Freddie, Freddy ˈfred i

Frederic ˈfredr ɪk ˈfred ər ɪk

Frederica ˌfred ə ˈriːk ə fre ˈdriːk ə

Frederick ˈfredr ɪk ˈfred ər ɪk

Fredericksburg ˈfred ᵊr ɪks bɜːg ‖ -bɝːg

Fredericton ˈfredr ɪk tən ˈfred ər ɪk tən

Fredonia frɪ ˈdəʊn iˌə frə- ‖ -ˈdoʊn-

free friː **freed** friːd **freeing** ˈfriː ɪŋ **freely** ˈfriː li **freer** ˈfriːˌə ‖ ᵊr **frees** friːz **freest** ˈfriːˌɪst ˌəst

ˌfree ˈagent; ˌfree asˌsociˈation; ˌFree ˈChurch; ˌfree colˌlective ˈbargaining; ˌfree ˈenterprise; ˌfree ˈgift; ˌfree ˈhand; ˌfree ˈhouse; ˌfree ˈkick; ˌFree ˈKirk; ˌfree ˈlove; ˌfree ˈpardon; ˌfree ˈpass; ˌfree ˈport; ˌfree ˈspeech; ˌfree ˈtrade; ˌFree Trade ˈHall; ˌfree ˈverse; ˌfree ˈwill

-free friː — *New formations with this suffix tend to be late-stressed* (ˌlead-ˈfree), *long-established ones early-stressed* (ˈcarefree)

freebas|e ˈfriː beɪs **~ed** t **~es** ɪz əz **~ing** ɪŋ

freebee, freebie ˈfriːb i **~s** z

freeboard ˈfriː bɔːd ‖ -bɔːrd -boʊrd

freebooter ˈfriː ˌbuːt ə ‖ -ˌbuːt̬ ᵊr **~s** z

freeborn ˌfriː ˈbɔːn ◂ ˈ·· ‖ -ˈbɔːrn ◂

freed friːd

freed|man ˈfriːd |mən -mæn **~men** mən men

freedom ˈfriː dəm **~s** z
ˈfreedom ˌfighter

freed|woman ˈfriːd |ˌwʊm ən **~women** ˌwɪm ɪn -ən

free-fall ˌfriː ˈfɔːl ◂ ˈ·· ‖ -ˈfɑːl **~ing** ɪŋ

free-floating ˌfriː ˈfləʊt ɪŋ ◂ ‖ -ˈfloʊt̬ ɪŋ

Freefone *tdmk* ˈfriː fəʊn ‖ -foʊn

free-for-all ˌfriː fər ˌɔːl ˌ·ˈ· ‖ -fər- -ˌɑːl **~s** z

freeform ˈfriː fɔːm ‖ -fɔːrm

freehand ˈfriː hænd

freehanded ˌfriː ˈhænd ɪd ◂ -əd **~ly** li **~ness** nəs nɪs

freehold ˈfriː həʊld →-hɒʊld ‖ -hoʊld **~s** z

freeholder ˈfriː həʊld ə →-hɒʊld- ‖ -hoʊld ᵊr **~s** z

freelanc|e ˈfriː lɑːnts §-lænts ‖ -lænts **~ed** t **~es** ɪz əz **~ing** ɪŋ

free-liver ˌfriː ˈlɪv ə ‖ -ᵊr **~s** z

free-living ˌfriː ˈlɪv ɪŋ ◂

freeload ˌfriː ˈləʊd ˈ·· ‖ -ˈloʊd **~ed** ɪd əd **~er/s** ə/z ‖ ᵊr/z **~ing** ɪŋ **~s** z

Freelove ˈfriː lʌv

freely ˈfriː li

free|man, F~ ˈfriː |mən -mæn **~men** mən men

freemartin ˈfriː ˌmɑːt ɪn §-ᵊn ‖ -ˌmɑːrt ᵊn **~s** z

freemason, F~ ˈfriː ˌmeɪs ᵊn ˌ·ˈ·· **~s** z

freemasonry, F~ ˈfriː ˌmeɪs ᵊn ri ˌ·ˈ···

freemen ˈfriː mən -men

freenet ˈfriː net **~s** s

freephone ˈfriː fəʊn ‖ -foʊn

Freeport ˈfriː pɔːt ‖ -pɔːrt -pourt

freepost, F~ *tdmk* ˈfriː pəʊst ‖ -poʊst

freer ˈfriːˌə ‖ ᵊr **~s** z

Freer frɪə ‖ frɪᵊr

free-range ˌfriː ˈreɪndʒ ◂

free-running *adj* ˌfriː ˈrʌn ɪŋ ◂

freerunning *n* ˈfriː ˌrʌn ɪŋ

freesheet ˈfriː ʃiːt **~s** s

freesia ˈfriːz iˌə ˈfriːʒ ə, ˈfriːʒ iˌə ‖ ˈfriːʒ ə **~s** z

Freeson ˈfriːs ᵊn

free-spoken ˌfriː ˈspəʊk ən ◂ ‖ -ˈspoʊk- **~ness** nəs nɪs

freest ˈfriːˌɪst ˌəst

free-standing ˌfriː ˈstænd ɪŋ ◂

freestone, F~ ˈfriː stəʊn ‖ -stoʊn

freestyle ˈfriː staɪᵊl

freethinker ˌfriː ˈθɪŋk ə ‖ -ᵊr **~s** z

freethinking ˌfriː ˈθɪŋk ɪŋ

free-to-air ˌfriː tu ˈeə ◂ -tə- ‖ -ˈeᵊr ◂ -ˈæᵊr ◂

Freetown ˈfriː taʊn

Freeview *tdmk* ˈfriː vjuː

freeware ˈfriː weə ‖ -wer -wær

freeway ˈfriː weɪ **~s** z

freewheel ˌfriː ˈwiːᵊl -ˈhwiːᵊl, ˈ·· **~ed** d **~ing** ɪŋ **~s** z

freewill ˌfriː ˈwɪl ◂
ˌfreewill ˈofferings

freeze friːz (= *frees*) **freezes** 'friːz ɪz -əz
  freezing 'friːz ɪŋ **froze** frəʊz ‖ froʊz **frozen**
  'frəʊz ᵊn ‖ 'froʊz ᵊn
  ˌfreezing 'cold; 'freezing comˌpartment;
  'freezing point
freeze-|dry ˌfriːz |'draɪ ◂ **~dried** 'draɪd ◂
  ~dries 'draɪz ◂ **~drying** 'draɪ ɪŋ ◂
freeze-frame ˌfriːz 'freɪm '··
freezer 'friːz ə ‖ -ᵊr **~s** z
freeze-up 'friːz ʌp **~s** s
Freiburg 'fraɪ bɜːg -bʊəg ‖ -bɜːg —*Ger*
  ['fʁaɪ bʊʁk]
freight freɪt **freighted** 'freɪt ɪd -əd ‖ 'freɪt̬ əd
  freighting 'freɪt ɪŋ ‖ 'freɪt̬ ɪŋ **freights** freɪts
freightage 'freɪt ɪdʒ ‖ 'freɪt̬-
freighter 'freɪt ə ‖ 'freɪt̬ ᵊr **~s** z
freightliner 'freɪt ˌlaɪn ə ‖ -ᵊr **~s** z
Freixenet *tdmk* 'freʃ ə net ˌ·ˈ· —*Catalan*
  [frə ʃə 'net]
Fremantle 'friː mænt ᵊl ·ˈ·· ‖ -mænt̬ ᵊl
fremitus 'frem ɪt əs §-ət- ‖ -ət̬ əs
Fremont 'friː mɒnt frɪ 'mɒnt ‖ -mɑːnt
French, f~ frentʃ
  ˌFrench 'bean; ˌFrench 'bread; ˌFrench
  Ca'nadian; 'French doors, ˌ· ˈ·; ˌFrench
  'dressing; ˌFrench 'fries; ˌFrench 'horn;
  ˌFrench 'kiss; ˌFrench 'leave; ˌFrench
  'loaf; ˌFrench 'polish; ˌFrench 'toast;
  ˌFrench 'windows
frenchi|fy, F~ 'frentʃ ɪ |faɪ -ə- **~fied** faɪd **~fies**
  faɪz **~fying** faɪ ɪŋ
French|man 'frentʃ |mən **~men** mən **~woman**
  ˌwʊm ən **~women** ˌwɪm ɪn §-ən
frenetic frə 'net ɪk frɪ-, fre- ‖ -'net̬ ɪk **~ally** ᵊl i
frenum 'friːn əm
frenz|y 'frenz |i **~ied/ly** id /li **~ies** iz
freon, Freon *tdmk* 'friː ɒn ‖ -ɑːn
frequenc|y 'friːk wən's |i **~ies** iz
  'frequency ˌcurve
frequent *v* frɪ 'kwent frə-, friː-; §'friːk wənt
  frequented frɪ 'kwent ɪd frə-, friː-, -əd;
  §'friːk wənt- ‖ -'kwent̬ əd **frequenting**
  frɪ 'kwent ɪŋ frə-, friː-; §'friːk wənt-
  ‖ -'kwent̬ ɪŋ **frequents** frɪ 'kwents frə-, friː-;
  §'friːk wənts
frequent *adj* 'friːk wənt **~ly** li **~ness** nəs nɪs
frequentative frɪ 'kwent ət ɪv frə-, friː-
  ‖ -'kwent̬ ət̬ ɪv **~s** z
Frere (i) frɪə ‖ frɪᵊr, (ii) freə ‖ freᵊr
fresco 'fresk əʊ ‖ -oʊ **~ed** d **~es, ~s** z **~ing** ɪŋ
fresh freʃ **freshed** freʃt **fresher** 'freʃ ə ‖ -ᵊr
  freshes 'freʃ ɪz -əz **freshest** 'freʃ ɪst -əst
  freshing 'freʃ ɪŋ
freshen 'freʃ ᵊn **~ed** d **~ing** ˌɪŋ **~s** z
fresher 'freʃ ə ‖ -ᵊr **~s** z
freshet 'freʃ ɪt -ət **~s** s
fresh-faced ˌfreʃ 'feɪst ◂
freshly 'freʃ li
fresh|man 'freʃ |mən **~men** mən
freshness 'freʃ nəs -nɪs
freshwater, F~ 'freʃ ˌwɔːt ə ˌ·ˈ·· ‖ -ˌwɔːt̬ ᵊr
  -ˌwɑːt̬ ᵊr

Fresnel, f~ 'freɪn el 'fren-, -ᵊl, freɪ 'nel
  ‖ freɪ 'nel —*Fr* [fʁɛ nɛl]
Fresno 'frez nəʊ ‖ -noʊ
fret fret **frets** frets **fretted** 'fret ɪd -əd
  ‖ 'fret̬ əd **fretting** 'fret ɪŋ ‖ 'fret̬ ɪŋ
fretboard 'fret bɔːd ‖ -bɔːrd -boʊrd **~s** z
fretful 'fret fᵊl -fʊl **~ly** i **~ness** nəs nɪs
fretsaw 'fret sɔː ‖ -sɑː **~s** z
fretwork 'fret wɜːk ‖ -wɜːk
Freud frɔɪd —*Ger* [fʁɔʏt]
Freudian 'frɔɪd i ən **~s** z
  ˌFreudian 'slip
Freya 'freɪ ə
Freycinet 'freɪs ə neɪ —*Fr* [fʁɛ si nɛ]
friability ˌfraɪ ə 'bɪl ət i -ɪt i ‖ -ət̬ i
friable 'fraɪ əb ᵊl **~ness** nəs nɪs
friar 'fraɪ ə ‖ 'fraɪ ᵊr **~s** z
  ˌFriar 'Tuck
friar|y 'fraɪ ᵊr |i **~ies** iz
fricandeau 'frɪk ən dəʊ ‖ -doʊ ˌ·ˈ· **~x** z —*or*
  as sing.
fricassee *n, v* 'frɪk ə seɪ -siː, ˌ·ˈ· ‖ ˌfrɪk ə 'siː
  ~d d **~ing** ɪŋ **~s** z
frication frɪ 'keɪʃ ᵊn frə-
fricative 'frɪk ət ɪv ‖ -ət̬ ɪv **~s** z
fricking 'frɪk ɪŋ
friction 'frɪk ʃᵊn **~s** z
frictional 'frɪk ʃᵊn ᵊl **~ly** i **~s** z
Friday 'fraɪ deɪ 'fraɪd i —*see note at* -day **~s** z
fridge frɪdʒ **fridges** 'frɪdʒ ɪz -əz
fridge-freezer ˌfrɪdʒ 'friːz ə ‖ -ᵊr **~s** z
fried fraɪd
Friedan 'friːd ᵊn friː 'dæn
Friedman 'friːd mən
Friedrich 'friːdr ɪk —*Ger* ['fʁiːd ʁɪç]
Friel friːᵊl
friend, F~ frend **friends** frendz
friendless 'frend ləs -lɪs **~ness** nəs nɪs
friend|ly, F~ 'frend |li **~lies** liz **~liness** li nəs
  -nɪs
  'friendly soˌciety
friendship 'frend ʃɪp **~s** s
frier 'fraɪ ə ‖ 'fraɪ ᵊr **~s** z
Friern 'fraɪ ən 'friː ən ‖ 'fraɪ ᵊrn
  ˌFriern 'Barnet
fries fraɪz
Fries *American family name* friːz
Friesian 'friːz i ən 'friːz-; 'friːʒ ᵊn, 'friːʒ i ən
  ‖ 'friːʒ ᵊn **~s** z
Friesland 'friːz lənd -lænd —*Dutch* ['fris lɑnt]
frieze friːz (= *frees*) **friezes** 'friːz ɪz -əz
frig *v* 'masturbate; copulate' frɪg **frigged** frɪgd
  frigging 'frɪg ɪŋ **frigs** frɪgz
frig *n* 'refrigerator' frɪdʒ
frigate 'frɪg ət -ɪt **~s** s
Frigg frɪg
Frigga 'frɪg ə
fright fraɪt **frights** fraɪts
frighten 'fraɪt ᵊn **~ed** d **~er/s** ə/z ‖ ᵊr/z
  ~ing/ly ˌɪŋ /li **~s** z
fright|ful 'fraɪt |fᵊl -fʊl **~fully** fli fᵊl i, fʊl i
  ~fulness fᵊl nəs fʊl-, -nɪs
frigid 'frɪdʒ ɪd §-əd **~ly** li **~ness** nəs nɪs

F

Frigidaire _tdmk_ ˌfrɪdʒ ɪ ˈdeə -ə- ‖ -ˈdeəʳ ˈdæəʳ
~s z

frigidity frɪ ˈdʒɪd ət i -ɪt- ‖ -əʈ i

frijole frɪ ˈhəʊl i -eɪ ‖ -ˈhoʊl i —_Sp_ [fri ˈxo le]
~s z

frill frɪl **frilled** frɪld **frilling** ˈfrɪl ɪŋ **frills** frɪlz

frill|y ˈfrɪl |i ~**ier** i ə ‖ i ˚r ~**iest** i ɪst i ̩əst
~**iness** i nəs i nɪs

Frimley ˈfrɪm li

fringe frɪndʒ **fringed** frɪndʒd **fringes**
ˈfrɪndʒ ɪz -əz **fringing** ˈfrɪndʒ ɪŋ
ˈfringe ˌbenefit

Frinton ˈfrɪnt ən ‖ -ᵊn

fripper|y ˈfrɪp ər |i ~**ies** iz

frisbee, F~ _tdmk_ ˈfrɪz bi ~**s** z

Frisby ˈfrɪz bi

Frisch frɪʃ —_Ger_ [fʁɪʃ]

Frisco ˈfrɪsk əʊ ‖ -oʊ

frise, frisé, frisee, frisée ˈfrɪz eɪ ‖ frɪ ˈzeɪ
—_Fr_ [fʁi ze]

Frisian ˈfrɪz i ən ˈfrɪʒ ᵊn, ˈfrɪʒ i ən; ˈfriːz i ən;
ˈfriːʒ ᵊn, ˈfriːʒ i ən ‖ ˈfrɪʒ ᵊn ˈfriːʒ- ~**s** z

frisk frɪsk **frisked** frɪskt **frisker/s** ˈfrɪsk ə/z
‖ -ᵊr/z **frisking** ˈfrɪsk ɪŋ **frisks** frɪsks

frisk|y ˈfrɪsk |i ~**ier** i ə ‖ i ˚r ~**iest** i ɪst i ̩əst
~**ily** ɪ li əl i ~**iness** i nəs i nɪs

frisson ˈfriːs ɒn ˈfrɪs-, -ɒ̃; friː ˈsɒ̃, frɪ-
‖ friː ˈsoʊn —_Fr_ [fʁi sɔ̃] ~**s** z

Frist frɪst

frit frɪt **frits** frɪts **fritted** ˈfrɪt ɪd -əd ‖ ˈfrɪʈ əd
fritting ˈfrɪt ɪŋ ‖ ˈfrɪʈ ɪŋ

Frith frɪθ

fritillar|y frɪ ˈtɪl ər |i frə- ‖ ˈfrɪʈ ᵊl er |i (*)
~**ies** iz

Frito|-Lay _tdmk_ ˈfriːt əʊ| leɪ ‖ ˈfriːʈ oʊ- ~**s** z

frittata frɪ ˈtɑːt ə —_It_ [frit ˈta: ta]

fritter ˈfrɪt ə ‖ ˈfrɪʈ ᵊr ~**ed** d **frittering**
ˈfrɪt ər ɪŋ ‖ ˈfrɪʈ ər ɪŋ ~**s** z

fritto misto ˌfrɪt əʊ ˈmɪst əʊ ˌfriːt-
‖ ˌfriːt oʊ ˈmiːst oʊ —_It_ [ˌfrit to ˈmis to]

Fritz, fritz frɪts

Friuli fri ˈuːl i —_It_ [fri ˈu: li]

Friulian fri ˈuːl i ən ~**s** z

frivolit|y frɪ ˈvɒl ət |i frə-, -ɪt- ‖ -ˈvɑːl əʈ |i
~**ies** iz

frivolous ˈfrɪv əl əs ~**ly** li ~**ness** nəs nɪs

frizz frɪz **frizzed** frɪzd **frizzes** ˈfrɪz ɪz -əz
frizzing ˈfrɪz ɪŋ

frizzl|e ˈfrɪz ᵊl ~**ed** d ~**es** z ~**ing** ̩ɪŋ

frizz|ly ˈfrɪz |li ~**lier** li ə ‖ li ˚r ~**liest** li ɪst
li ̩əst

frizz|y ˈfrɪz |i ~**ier** i ə ‖ i ˚r ~**iest** i ɪst i ̩əst ~**ily**
ɪ li əl i ~**iness** i nəs i nɪs

fro frəʊ ‖ froʊ

Frobisher ˈfrəʊb ɪʃ ə ‖ ˈfroʊb ɪʃ ᵊr
ˌFrobisher ˈBay

frock frɒk ‖ frɑːk **frocks** frɒks ‖ frɑːks
ˌfrock ˈcoat ‖ ˈ· ·

Frodo ˈfrəʊd əʊ ‖ ˈfroʊd oʊ

Frodsham ˈfrɒd ʃəm ‖ ˈfrɑːd-

Froebel, Fröbel ˈfrəʊb ᵊl ˈfrɜːb- ‖ ˈfreɪb- ˈfrɔɪb-
—_Ger_ [ˈfʁøː bᵊl]

frog frɒg ‖ frɑːg frɔːg **frogs** frɒgz ‖ frɑːgz
frɔːgz

frogbit ˈfrɒg bɪt ‖ ˈfrɑːg- ˈfrɔːg- ~**s** s

Froggatt ˈfrɒg ət -ɪt ‖ ˈfrɑːg-

Frogg|ie, frogg|y, F~ ˈfrɒg |i ‖ ˈfrɑːg |i
ˈfrɔːg- ~**ies** iz

frogging ˈfrɒg ɪŋ ‖ ˈfrɑːg- ˈfrɔːg-

froghopper ˈfrɒg ˌhɒp ə ‖ ˈfrɑːg ˌhɑːp ᵊr
ˈfrɔːg- ~**s** z

frog|man ˈfrɒg |mən ‖ ˈfrɑːg- ˈfrɔːg- ~**men**
mən men

frogmarch ˈfrɒg mɑːtʃ ‖ ˈfrɑːg mɑːrtʃ ˈfrɔːg-
~**ed** t ~**es** ɪz əz ~**ing** ɪŋ

Frogmore ˈfrɒg mɔː ‖ ˈfrɑːg mɔːr ˈfrɔːg-, -moʊr

frogspawn ˈfrɒg spɔːn ‖ ˈfrɑːg- ˈfrɔːg-, -spɑːn

frolic ˈfrɒl ɪk ‖ ˈfrɑːl- ~**ked** t ~**ker/s** ə/z ‖ ᵊr/z
~**king** ɪŋ ~**s** s

frolicsome ˈfrɒl ɪk səm ‖ ˈfrɑːl-

from _strong form_ frɒm ‖ frʌm frɑːm, _weak form_
frəm

fromage frais ˌfrɒm ɑːʒ ˈfreɪ ‖ frə ˌmɑːʒ-
—_Fr_ [fʁɔ maʒ fʁɛ]

Frome (i) fruːm, (ii) frəʊm ‖ froʊm —_The_
places and rivers in England and Jamaica are
all (i), although the spelling pronunciation (ii)
can be heard from people not familiar with the
name. Lake F~ in Australia is (ii).

Fromm frɒm ‖ frɑːm froʊm

Fron vrɒn ‖ vrɑːn —_Welsh_ [vrɔn]

Froncysyllte ˌvrɒn kə ˈsʌlt eɪ -ˌvrɒŋ-
‖ ˌvrɑːn- —_Welsh_ [vrɔn kə ˈsəɬ te]

frond frɒnd ‖ frɑːnd **fronded** ˈfrɒnd ɪd -əd
‖ ˈfrɑːnd əd **fronds** frɒndz ‖ frɑːndz

front frʌnt **fronted** ˈfrʌnt ɪd -əd ‖ ˈfrʌnʈ əd
fronter ˈfrʌnt ə ‖ ˈfrʌnʈ ᵊr **frontest**
ˈfrʌnt ɪst -əst ‖ ˈfrʌnʈ əst **fronting** ˈfrʌnt ɪŋ
‖ ˈfrʌnʈ ɪŋ **fronts** frʌnts
ˌfront ˈdoor; ˌfront ˈline; ˈfront man;
ˌfront ˈpage; ˌfront ˈroom

frontag|e ˈfrʌnt ɪdʒ ‖ ˈfrʌnʈ ɪdʒ ~**es** ɪz əz

frontal ˈfrʌnt ᵊl ‖ ˈfrʌnʈ ᵊl ~**ly** i

frontbench ˌfrʌnt ˈbentʃ ◄ ˈ·· ~**er/s** ə/z ‖ ᵊr/z

Frontenac ˈfrɒnt ə næk ‖ ˈfrɑːnt ᵊn æk —_Fr_
[fʁɔ̃t nak]

frontier ˈfrʌnt ɪə ˈfrɒnt-; frʌn ˈtɪə ‖ frʌn ˈtɪᵊr
frɑːn- ~**s** z

frontiers|man ˈfrʌnt ɪəz |mən ˈfrɒnt-;
frʌn ˈtɪəz- ‖ frʌn ˈtɪrz- ~**men** mən ~**woman**
ˌwʊm ən ~**women** ˌwɪm ɪn §-ən

frontispiec|e ˈfrʌnt ɪ spiːs -ə- ‖ ˈfrʌnʈ ə- ~**es**
ɪz əz

front-line ˌfrʌnt ˈlaɪn ◄ ˈ··
ˌfront-line ˈtroops

front-loader ˌfrʌnt ˈləʊd ə ‖ -ˈloʊd ᵊr ~**s** z

front-loading ˌfrʌnt ˈləʊd ɪŋ ◄ ‖ -ˈloʊd ɪŋ ◄

front-of-house ˌfrʌnt əv ˈhaʊs ◄ ‖ ˌfrʌnʈ əv-

front-page ˌfrʌnt ˈpeɪdʒ ◄ ˈ··

front-rank ˌfrʌnt ˈræŋk

front-runn|er ˌfrʌnt ˈrʌn| ə ◄ ˈ·ˌ·· ‖ -ᵊr ~**ers** əz
‖ ᵊrz ~**ing** ɪŋ

front-wheel ˌfrʌnt ˈwiːᵊl ‖ -ˈhwiːᵊl
ˌfront-wheel ˈdrive

frosh frɒʃ ‖ frɑːʃ **froshes** ˈfrɒʃ ɪz -əz ‖ ˈfrɑːʃ-

frost, Frost frɒst frɔːst ‖ frɔːst **frosted**
'frɒst ɪd 'frɔːst-, -əd ‖ 'frɔːst əd 'frɑːst-
frosting 'frɒst ɪŋ 'frɔːst- ‖ 'frɔːst ɪŋ 'frɑːst-
frosts frɒsts frɔːsts ‖ frɔːsts frɑːsts
frostbite 'frɒst baɪt 'frɔːst- ‖ 'frɔːst- 'frɑːst- **~s**
s
frostbitten 'frɒst ˌbɪt ᵊn 'frɔːst- ‖ 'frɔːst-
'frɑːst-
frostbound 'frɒst baʊnd 'frɔːst- ‖ 'frɔːst-
'frɑːst-
frost-free ˌfrɒst'friː ◄ ‖ ˌfrɔːst- ˌfrɑːst-
frostie 'frɒst i 'frɔːst- ‖ 'frɔːst i 'frɑːst- **~s, F~s**
tdmk z
frost|y 'frɒst |i 'frɔːst- ‖ 'frɔːst |i 'frɑːst- **~ier**
i ə ‖ i ᵊr **~iest** i ɪst i əst **~ily** ɪ li əl i **~iness**
i nəs i nɪs
froth v frɒθ frɔːθ ‖ frɔːθ frɑːθ, frɔːð **frothed**
frɒθt frɔːθt ‖ frɔːθt frɑːθt, frɔːðd **frothing**
'frɒθ ɪŋ 'frɔːθ- ‖ 'frɔːθ ɪŋ 'frɑːθ-, 'frɔːð- **froths**
frɒθs frɔːθs ‖ frɔːθs frɑːθs, frɔːðz
froth n frɒθ frɔːθ ‖ frɔːθ frɑːθ **froths** frɒθs
frɔːθs ‖ frɔːθs frɑːθs
froth|y 'frɒθ |i 'frɔːθ- ‖ 'frɔːθ |i 'frɑːθ-, 'frɔːð-
~ier i ə ‖ i ᵊr **~iest** i ɪst i əst **~ily** ɪ li əl i
~iness i nəs i nɪs
frottage 'frɒt ɑːʒ -ɪdʒ; frɒ 'tɑːʒ ‖ frɔː 'tɑːʒ frɑː-
—Fr [frɔ taːʒ]
Froud fraʊd
Froude fruːd
froufrou 'fruː fruː
froward 'frəʊ əd ‖ 'frəʊ ᵊrd **~ly** li **~ness** nəs
nɪs
frown fraʊn **frowned** fraʊnd **frowner/s**
'fraʊn ə/z ‖ -ᵊr/z **frowning/ly** 'fraʊn ɪŋ /li
frowns fraʊnz
frowst fraʊst **frowsted** 'fraʊst ɪd -əd
frowsting 'fraʊst ɪŋ **frowsts** fraʊsts
frowst|y 'fraʊst |i **~ier** i ə ‖ i ᵊr **~iest** i ɪst
i əst **~ily** ɪ li əl i **~iness** i nəs i nɪs
frows|y, frowz|y 'fraʊz |i **~ier** i ə ‖ i ᵊr **~iest**
i ɪst i əst **~iness** i nəs -nɪs
froyo 'frəʊ jəʊ ‖ 'frəʊ joʊ **~s** z
froze frəʊz ‖ froʊz
frozen 'frəʊz ᵊn ‖ 'froʊz ᵊn **~ly** li **~ness** nəs
nɪs
fructification ˌfrʌkt ɪf ɪ 'keɪʃ ᵊn ˌfrʊkt-, ˌəf-,
§-ə'-
fructi|fy 'frʌkt ɪ |faɪ 'frʊkt-, -ə- **~fied** faɪd
~fies faɪz **~fying** faɪ ɪŋ
fructose 'frʌkt əʊz 'frʊkt-, -əʊs ‖ -oʊs
frugal 'fruːg ᵊl **~ly** i **~ness** nəs nɪs
frugality fruː 'gæl ət i -ɪt- ‖ -əţ i
fruit fruːt **fruited** 'fruːt ɪd -əd ‖ 'fruːţ əd
fruiting 'fruːt ɪŋ ‖ 'fruːţ ɪŋ **fruits** fruːts
'**fruit bat**; ˌfruit '**cocktail**; '**fruit fly**; '**fruit**
knife; '**fruit ma**ˌ**chine**; ˌfruit '**salad**
fruitarian fruː 'teər i ən ‖ -'ter- -'tær- **~ism**
ˌɪz əm **~s** z
fruitcake 'fruːt keɪk **~s** s
fruiterer 'fruːt ər ə ‖ 'fruːţ ər ər **~s** z
fruitful 'fruːt fᵊl -fʊl **~ly** i **~ness** nəs nɪs
fruiti... —see **fruity**
fruition fruː 'ɪʃ ᵊn

fruitless 'fruːt ləs -lɪs **~ly** li **~ness** nəs nɪs
fruit|y 'fruːt |i ‖ 'fruːţ |i **~ier** i ə ‖ i ᵊr **~iest**
i ɪst i əst **~iness** i nəs i nɪs
frumenty 'fruːm ənt i
frump frʌmp **frumps** frʌmps
frumpish 'frʌmp ɪʃ **~ly** li **~ness** nəs nɪs
frump|y 'frʌmp |i **~ier** i ə ‖ i ᵊr **~iest** i ɪst i əst
~ily ɪ li əl i **~iness** i nəs i nɪs
frus|trate frʌ 's|treɪt 'frʌs |treɪt ‖ 'frʌs |treɪt
~trated treɪt ɪd -əd ‖ treɪţ əd **~trater/s**
treɪt ə/z ‖ treɪţ ᵊr/z **~trates** treɪts
~trating/ly treɪt ɪŋ /li ‖ treɪţ ɪŋ /li
frustration frʌ 'streɪʃ ᵊn **~s** z
frust|um 'frʌst |əm **~a** ə **~ums** əmz
frutesc|ence fruː 'tes |ᵊn¹s **~ent** ᵊnt
fry fraɪ **fried** fraɪd **fries** fraɪz **frying** 'fraɪ ɪŋ
'**frying pan**
Fry, Frye fraɪ
fryer, frier 'fraɪ ə ‖ 'fraɪ ᵊr **~s** z
Fryston 'fraɪst ən
fry-up 'fraɪ ʌp **~s** s
f-stop 'ef stɒp ‖ -stɑːp **~s** s
ftp ˌef tiː 'piː **~'d** d **~'ing** ɪŋ **~'s** z
FTSE, FT-SE 'fʊts i
fubs|y 'fʌbz| i **~ier** i ə ‖ i ᵊr **~iest** i ɪst əst
Fuchs (i) fʊks, (ii) fuːks, (iii) fjuːks —The
explorer was (i). (iii) is AmE only.
fuchsia 'fjuːʃ ə **~s** z
fuchsin 'fuːks ɪn §-ən
fuchsine 'fuːks iːn -ɪn ‖ 'fʊks ᵊn 'fjuːks- (*)
fuck fʌk **fucked** fʌkt **fucker/s** 'fʌk ə/z ‖ -ᵊr/z
fucking 'fʌk ɪŋ **fucks** fʌks
ˌfuck '**all**, '· ·
fucker 'fʌk ə ‖ -ᵊr **~s** z
fuckhead 'fʌk hed **~s** z
fuck-up 'fʌk ʌp **~s** s
fuckwit 'fʌk wɪt **~s** s
fucous 'fjuːk əs
fucus 'fjuːk əs
fuddl|e 'fʌd ᵊl **~ed** d **~es** z **~ing** ɪŋ
fuddy-dudd|y 'fʌd i ˌdʌd |i **~ies** iz
fudge, Fudge fʌdʒ **fudged** fʌdʒd **fudges**
'fʌdʒ ɪz -əz **fudging** 'fʌdʒ ɪŋ
fudgy 'fʌdʒ i
Fuegian 'fweɪdʒ ᵊn 'fweɪg i ən **~s** z
fuehrer 'fjʊər ə 'fjɔːr- ‖ 'fjʊr ᵊr —Ger Führer
['fyː ʁɐ] **~s** z
fuel 'fjuː əl §fjuːl **~ed, ~led** d **~ing, ~ling** ɪŋ
~s z
'**fuel cell**; '**fuel oil**
fuel-efficient 'fjuː əl ɪ ˌfɪʃ ᵊnt §'fjuːl i-
Fuerteventura ˌfweət i ven 'tjʊər ə ˌeɪ,
→-'tʃʊər-, →-tʃɔːr- ‖ ˌfwert eɪ ven 'tʊr ə —Sp
[fwer te βen 'tu ɾa]
fug fʌg **fugs** fʌgz
fugacious fju 'geɪʃ əs **~ly** li **~ness** nəs nɪs
fugacity fju 'gæs ət i -ɪt- ‖ -əţ i
fugal 'fjuːg ᵊl **~ly** i
fuggles, F~ 'fʌg ᵊlz
fugg|y 'fʌg| i **~ier** i ə ‖ i ᵊr **~iest** i ɪst əst
~iness i nəs -nɪs
fugitive 'fjuːdʒ ət ɪv -ɪt- ‖ -əţ ɪv **~ly** li **~ness**
nəs nɪs **~s** z

fugu ˈfuːg uː —*Jp* [ˈɸɯ ŋɯ, -gɯ]
fugue fjuːg **fugues** fjuːgz
fuhrer, führer ˈfjʊər ə ˈfjɔːr- ‖ ˈfjʊr ᵊr —*Ger*
  Führer [ˈfyː ʁɐ] **~s** z
Fujairah fu ˈdʒaɪᵊr ə
Fuji ˈfuːdʒ i —*Jp* [ˈɸɯ dzi]
Fujian ˌfuːdʒ i ˈɑːn ˈfuːdʒ i ˌən —*Chi* Fújiàn
  [²fu ⁴dzjɛn]
Fujica *tdmk* ˈfuːdʒ ɪk ə
Fujitsu *tdmk* fuː ˈdʒɪts uː —*Jp* [ɸɯ ˈdzi tsɯɯ]
Fukuoka ˌfuːk u ˈəʊk ə ˌfʊk- ‖ -ˈoʊk- —*Jp*
  [ɸɯ ˈkɯ o ka]
-ful (i) suffix to form adjectives, fᵊl fʊl **painful**
  ˈpeɪn fᵊl, -fʊl; (ii) suffix to form nouns
  specifying a quantity, fʊl **spoonful** ˈspuːn fʊl
Fula ˈfuːl ə **~s** z
Fulani fu ˈlɑːn i ˈfuːl ɑːn i
Fulbourn ˈfʊl bɔːn ‖ -bɔːrn -boʊrn
Fulbright ˈfʊl braɪt
Fulbrighter ˈfʊl braɪt ə ‖ -braɪt ᵊr **~s** z
Fulcher ˈfʊltʃ ə ‖ -ᵊr
fulc|rum ˈfʌlk |rəm ˈfʊlk- **~ra** rə
ful|fil, ~fill fʊl| ˈfɪl **~filled** fɪld **~filler/s**
  ˈfɪl ə/z ‖ ˈfɪl ᵊr/z **~filling** ˈfɪl ɪŋ **~fils, ~fills**
  ˈfɪlz
fulfillment, fulfilment fʊl ˈfɪl mənt
Fulford ˈfʊl fəd ‖ -fᵊrd
Fulham ˈfʊl əm
fuliginous fju ˈlɪdʒ ɪn əs §-ən- **~ly** li
full fʊl **fuller** ˈfʊl ə ‖ -ᵊr **fullest** ˈfʊl ɪst -əst
  ˌfull ˈdress; ˌfull ˈhouse; ˌfull ˈmarks; ˌfull
  ˈmoon; ˌfull ˈstop; ˌfull ˈtoss
fullback ˌfʊl ˈbæk '·· ‖ ˈfʊl bæk **~s** s
full-blooded ˌfʊl ˈblʌd ɪd ◂ -əd **~ness** nəs nɪs
full-blown ˌfʊl ˈbləʊn ◂ ‖ -ˈbloʊn ◂
full-bodied ˌfʊl ˈbɒd id ◂ ‖ -ˈbɑːd-
full-color, full-colour ˌfʊl ˈkʌl ə ◂ ‖ -ᵊr ◂
full-court ˌfʊl ˈkɔːt ◂ ‖ -ˈkɔːrt ◂ -koʊrt ◂
  ˌfull-court ˈpress
full-cream ˌfʊl ˈkriːm ◂
  ˌfull-cream ˈmilk
full-dress ˌfʊl ˈdres ◂
fuller, F~ ˈfʊl ə ‖ -ᵊr **~s, ~'s** z
  ˌfuller's ˈearth
Fullerton ˈfʊl ət ən ‖ -ᵊrt ᵊn
full-face ˌfʊl ˈfeɪs ◂
full-fashioned ˌfʊl ˈfæʃ ᵊnd ◂
full-fat ˌfʊl ˈfæt ◂
full-figured ˌfʊl ˈfɪg əd ◂ ‖ -jᵊrd ◂
full-fledged ˌfʊl ˈfledʒd ◂
full-frontal ˌfʊl ˈfrʌnt ᵊl ◂ ‖ -ˈfrʌnt̬ ᵊl ◂
full-grown ˌfʊl ˈgrəʊn ◂ ‖ -ˈgroʊn ◂
full-hearted ˌfʊl ˈhɑːt ɪd ◂ -əd ‖ -ˈhɑːrt̬ əd ◂
full-length ˌfʊl ˈleŋᵏθ ◂ -ˈlenᵗθ
  ˌfull-length ˈportrait
fullness ˈfʊl nəs -nɪs
full-on ˌfʊl ˈɒn ◂ ‖ -ˈɑːn ◂ -ˈɔːn ◂
full-page ˌfʊl ˈpeɪdʒ ◂
full-scale ˌfʊl ˈskeɪᵊl ◂
  ˌfull-scale ˈwar
full-size ˌfʊl ˈsaɪz ◂
full-term ˌfʊl ˈtɜːm ◂ ‖ -ˈtɜːm ◂

full-throated ˌfʊl ˈθrəʊt ɪd ◂ -əd
  ‖ -ˈθroʊt̬ əd ◂
  ˌfull-ˌthroated ˈroar
full-time ˌfʊl ˈtaɪm ◂
  ˌfull-time ˈwork
fully ˈfʊl i
-fully fᵊl i fʊl i **painfully** ˈpeɪn fᵊl i -fʊl i
fully-fashioned ˌfʊl i ˈfæʃ ᵊnd ◂
fully-fledged ˌfʊl i ˈfledʒd ◂
fully-grown ˌfʊl i ˈgrəʊn ◂ ‖ -ˈgroʊn ◂
fulmar ˈfʊlm ə -ɑː ‖ -ᵊr -ɑːr **~s** z
Fulmer ˈfʊlm ə ‖ -ᵊr
fulminant ˈfʊlm ɪn ənt ˈfʌlm-, -ən-
fulmi|nate ˈfʊlm ɪ |neɪt ˈfʌlm-, -ə- **~nated**
  neɪt ɪd -əd ‖ neɪt̬ əd **~nates** neɪts **~nating**
  neɪt ɪŋ ‖ neɪt̬ ɪŋ
fulmination ˌfʊlm ɪ ˈneɪʃ ᵊn ˌfʌlm-, -ə- **~s** z
fulness ˈfʊl nəs -nɪs
fulsome ˈfʊls əm **~ly** li **~ness** nəs nɪs
Fulton ˈfʊlt ən
fulvous ˈfʌlv əs ˈfʊlv-
Fulwell ˈfʊl wel
Fulwood ˈfʊl wʊd
Fu Manchu ˌfuː mæn ˈtʃuː
fumaric fju ˈmær ɪk ‖ -ˈmer-
fumarole ˈfjuːm ə rəʊl →-rɒʊl ‖ -roʊl **~s** z
fumbl|e ˈfʌm bᵊl **~ed** d **~es** z **~ing** ɪŋ
fumbler ˈfʌm blə ‖ -blᵊr **~s** z
fume fjuːm **fumed** fjuːmd **fumes** fjuːmz
  fuming ˈfjuːm ɪŋ
fumigant ˈfjuːm ɪg ənt -əg- **~s** s
fumi|gate ˈfjuːm ɪ |geɪt -ə- **~gated** geɪt ɪd -əd
  ‖ geɪt̬ əd **~gates** geɪts **~gating** geɪt ɪŋ
  ‖ geɪt̬ ɪŋ
fumigation ˌfjuːm ɪ ˈgeɪʃ ᵊn -ə- **~s** z
fumigator ˈfjuːm ɪ geɪt ə '·ə- ‖ -geɪt̬ ᵊr **~s** z
fumitor|y ˈfjuːm ɪt ˌᵊr |i '·ət- ‖ -ə tɔːr |i -toʊr i
  ~ies iz
fun fʌn
  ˈfun fur; ˈfun run
Funafuti ˌfuːn ə ˈfuːt i
funambulist fju ˈnæm bjʊl ɪst -bjəl-, §-əst **~s**
  s
Funchal ˌfʊn ˈtʃɑːl -ˈʃɑːl —*Port* [fũ ˈʃal]
function ˈfʌŋk ʃᵊn **~ed** d **~ing** ɪŋ **~s** z
functional ˈfʌŋk ʃᵊn ᵊl **~ism** ˌɪz əm **~ist/s**
  ɪst/s §əst/s **~ly** i
functionality ˌfʌŋk ʃə ˈnæl ət i -ɪt i ‖ -ət̬ i
functionar|y ˈfʌŋk ʃᵊn ˌər |i -ʃᵊn ˌər ˌ|i
  ‖ -ʃə ner |i **~ies** iz
functor ˈfʌŋkt ə ‖ -ᵊr **~s** z
fund fʌnd **funded** ˈfʌnd ɪd -əd **funding**
  ˈfʌnd ɪŋ **funds** fʌndz
fundament ˈfʌnd ə mənt **~s** s
fundamental ˌfʌnd ə ˈment ᵊl ◂ ‖ -ˈment̬ ᵊl ◂
  ~ism ˌɪz əm **~ist/s** ɪst/s §əst/s **~ly** i **~s** z
fund-rais|er ˈfʌnd ˌreɪz| ə ‖ -ᵊr **~ers** əz ‖ ᵊrz
  ~ing ɪŋ
fund|us ˈfʌnd| əs **~i** aɪ
Fundy ˈfʌnd i
funeral ˈfjuːn ᵊr ᵊl **~s** z
  ˈfuneral diˌrector; ˈfuneral home;
  ˈfuneral ˌparlor

funerary ˈfjuːn ər ər i △ ˈfjuːn ər i ‖ -ə rer i
funereal fju ˈnɪər i əl ‖ -ˈnɪr- **~ly** i
funfair ˈfʌn feə ‖ -fer -fær **~s** z
fungal ˈfʌŋ gəl
fungi ˈfʌŋ giː -gaɪ; ˈfʌndʒ aɪ, -iː
fungible ˈfʌndʒ əb əl -ɪb- **~s** z
fungicidal ˌfʌŋ gɪ ˈsaɪd əl ◄ §-gə-; ˌfʌndʒ ɪ-, §-ə-
fungicide ˈfʌŋ gɪ saɪd §-gə-; ˈfʌndʒ ɪ-, §-ə- **~s** z
fungoid ˈfʌŋ gɔɪd
fungous ˈfʌŋ gəs (= *fungus*)
fungus ˈfʌŋ gəs **fungi** ˈfʌŋ gaɪ -giː -gaɪ; ˈfʌndʒ aɪ, -iː: **funguses** ˈfʌŋ gəs ɪz -əz
funicular fju ˈnɪk jʊl ə fə-, -jəl- ‖ -jəl ər **~s** z **fuˌnicular ˈrailway**
funk fʌŋk **funked** fʌŋkt **funking** ˈfʌŋk ɪŋ **funks** fʌŋks
funk|y ˈfʌŋk |i **~ier** i ə ‖ i ər **~iest** i ɪst i əst **~ily** ɪ li əl i **~iness** i nəs i nɪs
fun-loving ˈfʌn ˌlʌv ɪŋ
funnel ˈfʌn əl **~ed, ~led** d **~ing, ~ling** ɪŋ **~s** z
funn|y ˈfʌn |i **~ier** i ə ‖ i ər **~ies** iz **~iest** i ɪst i əst **~ily** ɪ li əl i **~iness** i nəs i nɪs **ˈfunny bone**; **ˈfunny ˌbusiness**; **ˈfunny farm**; **ˌfunny haˈha** hɑː ˈhɑː ˈˈ; **ˌfunny ˈman** *'strange man'*; **ˈfunny man** *'comedian'*
funny-looking ˈfʌn i ˌlʊk ɪŋ
Funt fʌnt
fur fɜː ‖ fɜ: **furred** fɜːd ‖ fɜːd **furring** ˈfɜːr ɪŋ ‖ ˈfɜː ɪŋ **furs** fɜːz ‖ fɜːz **ˈfur seal**
furan ˈfjʊər æn ˈfjɔːr-; fjuə ˈræn ‖ ˈfjʊr æn fjʊ ˈræn
furbelow ˈfɜːb ə ləʊ -ɪ- ‖ ˈfɜːb ə loʊ **~ed** d **~ing** ɪŋ **~s** z
furbish ˈfɜːb ɪʃ ‖ ˈfɜːb- **~ed** t **~er/s** ə/z ‖ ər/z **~es** ɪz əz **~ing** ɪŋ
Furby *tdmk* ˈfɜːb i ‖ ˈfɜːb i **~s** z
Furies, f~ ˈfjʊər iz ˈfjɔːr- ‖ ˈfjʊr iz
furious ˈfjʊər i əs ˈfjɔːr- ‖ ˈfjʊr- **~ly** li **~ness** nəs nɪs
furl fɜːl ‖ fɜːl **furled** fɜːld ‖ fɜːld **furling** ˈfɜːl ɪŋ ‖ ˈfɜːl ɪŋ **furls** fɜːlz ‖ fɜːlz
furlong ˈfɜːl ɒŋ ‖ ˈfɜːl ɔːŋ -ɑːŋ **~s** z
Furlong, Furlonge ˈfɜːl ɒŋ ‖ ˈfɜːl ɔːŋ -ɑːŋ
furlough ˈfɜːl əʊ ‖ ˈfɜːl oʊ **~ed** d **~ing** ɪŋ **~s** z
furnac|e, F~ ˈfɜːn ɪs -əs ‖ ˈfɜːn- **~es** ɪz əz
Furneaux ˈfɜːn əʊ ‖ ˈfɜː ˈnoʊ
Furnell fɜː ˈnel ‖ fɜː-
Furness ˈfɜːn ɪs -əs; fɜː ˈnes ‖ ˈfɜːn əs
furnish ˈfɜːn ɪʃ ‖ ˈfɜːn- **~ed** t **~er/s** ə/z ‖ ər/z **~es** ɪz əz **~ing/s** ɪŋ/z
furniture ˈfɜːn ɪtʃ ə §-ətʃ- ‖ ˈfɜːn ɪtʃ ər
Furnival, Furnivall ˈfɜːn ɪv əl -əv- ‖ ˈfɜːn-
furor ˈfjʊər ɔː ˈfjɔːr- ‖ ˈfjʊr ər -ɔːr, -oʊr **~s** z
furore fjuə ˈrɔːr i ˈfjʊər ɔː, ˈfjɔːr- ‖ ˈfjʊr ər -ɔːr, -oʊr **~s** z —*This word sounds different from* furor *in BrE, but not in AmE.*
furph|y, F~ ˈfɜːf |i ‖ ˈfɜːf |i **~ies** iz
furred fɜːd ‖ fɜːd
furrier ˈfʌr i ə ‖ ˈfɜː i ər **~s** z
furrier|y ˈfʌr i ər| i ‖ ˈfɜː i er| i **~ies** iz

furring ˈfɜːr ɪŋ ‖ ˈfɜː ɪŋ
furrow ˈfʌr əʊ ‖ ˈfɜː oʊ **~ed** d **~ing** ɪŋ **~s** z
furr|y ˈfɜːr |i §ˈfʌr- ‖ ˈfɜː |i **~ier** i ə ‖ i ər **~iest** i ɪst i əst **~iness** i nəs i nɪs
Furtado fɜː ˈtɑːd əʊ ‖ fⁱr ˈtɑːd oʊ
further ˈfɜːð ə ‖ ˈfɜːð ər **~ed** d **furthering** ˈfɜːð ər ɪŋ ‖ ˈfɜːð ər ɪŋ **~s** z **ˌfurther ˌeduˈcation**
furtherance ˈfɜːð ər ən's ‖ ˈfɜːð-
furtherer ˈfɜːð ər ə ‖ ˈfɜːð ər ər **~s** z
furthermore ˌfɜːð ə ˈmɔː ˈˈˈ ‖ ˈfɜːð ər mɔːr -moʊr
furthermost ˈfɜːð ə məʊst ‖ ˈfɜːð ər moʊst
furthest ˈfɜːð ɪst -əst ‖ ˈfɜːð-
furtive ˈfɜːt ɪv ‖ ˈfɜːt̬ ɪv **~ly** li **~ness** nəs nɪs
Furtwängler ˈfʊət veŋ glə ‖ ˈfʊrt weŋ glⁱr —*Ger* [ˈfʊʁt veŋ lɐ]
furuncle ˈfjʊər ʌŋk əl ˈfjɔːr- ‖ ˈfjʊr- **~s** z
fur|y, Fur|y ˈfjʊər |i ˈfjɔːr- ‖ ˈfjʊr |i **~ies** iz
furze fɜːz ‖ fɜːz (= *furs*)
fusarium fju ˈzeər i əm ‖ -ˈzer- -ˈzær- **fuˈsarium wilt**
fuse *n*, *v* fjuːz **fused** fjuːzd **fuses** ˈfjuːz ɪz -əz **fusing** ˈfjuːz ɪŋ **ˈfuse box**; **ˈfuse wire**
fusee fju ˈziː **~s** z
fusel ˈfjuːz əl **ˈfusel oil**
fuselag|e ˈfjuːz ə lɑːʒ ˈfjuːs-, -ɪ-, -lɪdʒ ‖ ˈfjuːs- ˈfjuːz- **~es** ɪz əz
Fuseli ˈfjuːz əl i fju ˈzel i
fusibility ˌfjuːz ə ˈbɪl ət i ˌˈɪ-, -ɪt i ‖ -ət̬ i
fusible ˈfjuːz əb əl -ɪb- **~ness** nəs nɪs
fusiform ˈfjuːz ɪ fɔːm -ə- ‖ -fɔːrm
fusilier ˌfjuːz ə ˈlɪə -ɪ- ‖ -ˈlⁱr **~s** z
fusillad|e ˌfjuːz ə ˈleɪd -ɪ-, -ˈlɑːd, ˈˈˈ ‖ ˈfjuːs ə leɪd ˈfjuːz-, -lɑːd **~ed** ɪd əd **~es** z **~ing** ɪŋ
fusilli fu ˈzɪl i fju-, -ˈsɪl-, -ˈsiːl- —*It* [fu ˈzil li, -ˈsil-]
fusion ˈfjuːʒ ən **~al** əl **~ism** ˌɪz əm **~ist/s** ɪst/s §əst/s **~s** z **ˈfusion bomb**
fuss fʌs **fussed** fʌst **fusses** ˈfʌs ɪz -əz **fussing** ˈfʌs ɪŋ
fussbudget ˈfʌs ˌbʌdʒ ɪt -ət **~s** s
fussi... —*see* fussy
fusspot ˈfʌs pɒt ‖ -pɑːt **~s** s
fuss|y ˈfʌs |i **~ier** i ə ‖ i ər **~iest** i ɪst i əst **~ily** ɪ li əl i **~iness** i nəs i nɪs
fustanella ˌfʌst ə ˈnel ə **~s** z
fustian ˈfʌst i ən ‖ ˈfʌs tʃən
fustic ˈfʌst ɪk
fust|y ˈfʌst |i **~ier** i ə ‖ i ər **~iest** i ɪst i əst **~ily** ɪ li əl i **~iness** i nəs i nɪs
futharc, futhark ˈfuːθ ɑːk ‖ -ɑːrk
futile ˈfjuːt aɪəl ‖ ˈfjuːt̬ əl ˈfjuːt aɪəl **~ly** li ‖ i li **~ness** nəs nɪs
futilit|y fju ˈtɪl ət i ‖ i -ɪt- ‖ -ət̬ i **~ies** iz
futon ˈfuːt ɒn ˈfjuːt-, ˈfʊt-, -ⁿn; fuː ˈtɒn ‖ -ɑːn —*Jp* [ɸɯ ˌton] **~s** z
futtock ˈfʌt ək ‖ ˈfʌt̬ ək **~s** s
Futura fju ˈtjʊər ə →-ˈtʃʊər ə ‖ -ˈtʊr ə -ˈtjʊr ə

future 'fjuːtʃ ə ‖ -ᵊr ~s z
  ˌfuture 'perfect
future-proof 'fjuːtʃ ə pruːf §-prʊf ‖ -ᵊr- ~ed t
  ~ing ɪŋ ~s s
futur|ism 'fjuːtʃ ər |ˌɪz əm ~ist/s ɪst/s §əst/s
futuristic ˌfjuːtʃ ə 'rɪst ɪk ◂ ~ally ᵊl̩ i
futurit|y fju 'tjʊər ət |i -'tjɔːr-, →-'tʃʊər-,
  →§-'tʃɔːr-, -ɪt- ‖ -'tʊr ət̬ |i ~ies iz
futurologist ˌfjuːtʃ ə 'rɒl ədʒ ɪst §-əst ‖ -'rɑːl-
  ~s s
futurology ˌfjuːtʃ ə 'rɒl ədʒ i ‖ -'rɑːl-
futz fʌts **futzed** fʌtst **futzes** 'fʌts ɪz -əz
  futzing 'fʌts ɪŋ
fuze fjuːz **fuzed** fjuːzd **fuzes** 'fjuːz ɪz -əz
  fuzing 'fjuːz ɪŋ

Fuzhou ˌfuː 'dʒəʊ ‖ -'dʒoʊ —*Chi* Fúzhōu
  [²fu ¹tsou]
fuzz fʌz **fuzzed** fʌzd **fuzzes** 'fʌz ɪz -əz **fuzzing**
  'fʌz ɪŋ
fuzz|y 'fʌz |i ~ier i ə ‖ i ᵊr ~iest i ɪst i əst ~ily
  ɪ li əl i ~iness i nəs i nɪs
fuzzy-wuzz|y ˌfʌz i ˌwʌz |i ~ies iz
f-word 'ef wɜːd ‖ -wɜːd
-fy faɪ —*This suffix imposes antepenultimate*
  stress (so'lidify, per'sonify).
Fybogel *tdmk* 'faɪb əʊ dʒel ‖ -ə-
Fyfe, Fyffe faɪf
Fylde faɪᵊld
Fylingdales 'faɪl ɪŋ derᵊlz
Fyne faɪn

G g

g Spelling-to-sound

1 Where the spelling is **g**, the pronunciation is regularly
g as in **gas** gæs ('hard G').
Less frequently, it is
dʒ as in **gentle** ˈdʒent ᵊl ('soft G').
Occasionally, it is ʒ as usually in **garage** ˈgær ɑːʒ ‖ gə ˈrɑːʒ.
g also forms part of the digraphs **gh, gu**, and **ng** (see under **n**).

2 Hard G is the usual pronunciation. Soft G and ʒ are found in certain words where **g** is followed by **e, i, y** — mostly words of French or Latin origin. Thus on the one hand we have
g in **get** get, **give** gɪv
but on the other
dʒ in **general** ˈdʒen rəl, **ginger** ˈdʒɪndʒ ə.

3 Where the spelling is the digraph **dg** before **e, i, y**, the pronunciation is always dʒ as in **edge** edʒ, **elegy** ˈel ədʒ i.

4 Where the spelling is double **gg**, the pronunciation is again regularly g as in **egg** eg.
Occasionally it is dʒ as in **exaggerate** ɪg ˈzædʒ ə reɪt. Note **suggest** BrE usually sə ˈdʒest but AmE səg ˈdʒest.

5 **g** is silent before **m n** but only at the beginning or end of a word or stem as in **gnat** næt, **sign** saɪn, **phlegm** flem, **foreigner** ˈfɒr ən ə ‖ ˈfɔːr ən ᵊr.

6 The sound g is also occasionally written **gh** as in **ghost** or **gu** as in **guess** ges.

gh Spelling-to-sound

Where the spelling is the occasional digraph **gh** there are several possible pronunciations:
g as in **ghost** gəʊst ‖ goʊst
f as in **rough** rʌf or
silent, after **i** and sometimes other vowel letters as in **high** haɪ, **eight** eɪt, **daughter** ˈdɔːt ə ‖ ˈdɔːt ᵊr.

gu Spelling-to-sound

1 Where the spelling is the digraph **gu**, the pronunciation may be
ɡ as in **guess** ɡes, **vague** veɪɡ or
ɡw as in **language** ˈlæŋ ɡwɪdʒ.

2 Generally speaking, ɡ is found at the beginning of a word, and at the end of a word before silent **e**; ɡw is found in the middle of a word.

3 Most instances of **gu** are not a digraph: **gun** ɡʌn, **regular** ˈreɡ jəl ə ‖ ˈreɡ jəl ᵊr, **argue** ˈɑːɡ juː ‖ ˈɑːrɡ juː.

G

G, g dʒiː **Gs, G's, g's** dʒiːz —*Communications code name:* Golf
Ga ɡɑː
gab ɡæb **gabbed** ɡæbd **gabbing** ˈɡæb ɪŋ **gabs** ɡæbz
Gabalfa ɡə ˈbælv ə -ˈbælf ə —*Welsh* [ɡa ˈbal va]
gabardine —*see* **gaberdine**
Gabbana ɡə ˈbɑːn ə -ˈbæn-
Gabbitas ˈɡæb ɪ tæs §-ə-
gabbl|e ˈɡæb ᵊl **~ed** d **~es** z **~ing** ɪŋ
gabbro ˈɡæb rəʊ ‖ -roʊ **~s** z
gabby, Gabby ˈɡæb i
gaberdine ˌɡæb ə ˈdiːn ◄ ··· ‖ ˈɡæb ᵊr diːn **~s** z
gabfest ˈɡæb fest **~s** s
Gabi *name(i)* ˈɡæb i, *(ii)* ˈɡɑːb i
Gabi *Australian language* ˈɡʌb i
gabion ˈɡeɪb i ən **~s** z
gable, Gable ˈɡeɪb ᵊl **~d** d **~s** z
Gabon ˈɡæb ɒn ɡæ ˈbɒn, ɡə-, -ˈbɔ̃ ‖ ɡə ˈboʊn —*Fr* [ɡa bɔ̃]
Gabonese ˌɡæb ə ˈniːz ◄ -ɒ-
Gabor *(i)* ɡə ˈbɔː ‖ -ˈbɔːr, *(ii)* ˈɡɑːb ɔː ‖ -ɔːr —*Hungarian* Gábor [ˈɡɑː bor]
Gaborone ˌɡæb ə ˈrəʊn i ˌxæb-, -ˈruːn- ‖ ˌɡɑːb ə ˈroʊn i
Gabriel ˈɡeɪb ri əl
Gabriella ˌɡæb ri ˈel ə ˌɡeɪb-
Gabrielle ˌɡæb ri ˈel ˌɡeɪb-, ···
Gaby *(i)* ˈɡæb i, *(ii)* ˈɡɑːb i
gad, Gad ɡæd **gadded** ˈɡæd ɪd -əd **gadding** ˈɡæd ɪŋ **gads** ɡædz
gadabout ˈɡæd ə ˌbaʊt **~s** s
Gadarene ˌɡæd ə ˈriːn ◄ ··· ‖ ˈɡæd ə riːn ˌGadarene ˈswine
Gaddafi ɡə ˈdɑːf i -ˈdæf- —*Arabic* [ɣað ˈðɑː fi]
Gaddesden ˈɡædz dən
gad|fly ˈɡæd |flaɪ **~flies** flaɪz
gadget ˈɡædʒ ɪt -ət **~s** s
gadgetry ˈɡædʒ ɪtr i -ətr i
gadolinium ˌɡæd ə ˈlɪn i_əm -ᵊl ˈɪn-
gadroon ɡə ˈdruːn **~s** z

Gadsby ˈɡædz bi
Gadsden, Gadsdon ˈɡædz dən
gadwall ˈɡæd wɔːl ‖ -wɑːl **~s** z
gadzooks ₍ₗ₎ɡæd ˈzuːks
Gaea ˈdʒiːˌə
Gael ɡeɪᵊl **Gaels** ɡeɪᵊlz
Gaelic ˈɡeɪl ɪk ˈɡæl-, ˈɡɑːl- ˌGaelic ˈfootball
Gaeltacht ˈɡeɪᵊl tæxt -təxt —*Irish* [ˈɡeːl tᵊxt]
Gaenor ˈɡeɪn ə ˈɡaɪn-, -ɔː ‖ -ɔːr —*Welsh* [ˈɡəi nor]
gaff ɡæf **gaffed** ɡæft **gaffing** ˈɡæf ɪŋ **gaffs** ɡæfs
gaffe ɡæf **gaffes** ɡæfs
gaffer ˈɡæf ə ‖ -ᵊr **~s** z
gag ɡæg **gagged** ɡægd **gagging** ˈɡæg ɪŋ **gags** ɡægz
gaga ˈɡɑː ɡɑː
Gagarin ɡə ˈɡɑːr ɪn §-ən —*Russ* [ɡʌ ˈɡa rʲɪn]
Gagauz ˌɡæg ɑː ˈuːz
Gagauzi ˌɡæg ɑː ˈuːz i ◄
gage, Gage ɡeɪdʒ **gages** ˈɡeɪdʒ ɪz -əz
gaggl|e ˈɡæg ᵊl **~ed** d **~es** z **~ing** ɪŋ
Gaia ˈɡaɪ ə ˈɡeɪ ə
Gaidhealtachd ˈɡeɪᵊl tək -tæxt —*ScG* [ˈɡeːɫ təxk]
gaiet|y ˈɡeɪ ət |i -ɪt- ‖ -əţ |i **~ies** iz
gaijin ˌɡaɪ ˈdʒɪn -ˈdʒiːn; ··· —*Jp* [ɡa ˈi dʑiN]
Gail, Gaile ɡeɪᵊl
gaillardia ɡeɪ ˈlɑːd i_ə ɡə- ‖ -ˈlɑːrd- **~s** z
gaily ˈɡeɪ li
gain ɡeɪn **gained** ɡeɪnd **gainer/s** ˈɡeɪn ə/z ‖ -ᵊr/z **gaining** ˈɡeɪn ɪŋ **gains** ɡeɪnz
gainer ˈɡeɪn ə ‖ -ᵊr **~s** z
Gaines ɡeɪnz
Gainesville ˈɡeɪnz vɪl -vᵊl
gainful ˈɡeɪn fᵊl -fʊl **~ly** _i **~ness** nəs nɪs
gain|say ˌɡeɪn |ˈseɪ **~said** ˈsed ˈseɪd **~sayer/s** ˈseɪ ə/z ‖ -ᵊr/z **~saying** ˈseɪ ɪŋ **~says** ˈseɪz ˈsez
Gainsborough ˈɡeɪnz bᵊr_ə ‖ -ˌbɝː oʊ **~s** z
ˈgainst ɡenˈst ɡeɪnˈst

Gairdner *(i)* 'geəd nə ‖ 'gerd nᵊr, *(ii)* 'gɑːd-
  ‖ 'gɑːrd-
Gairloch 'geə lɒx -lɒk ‖ 'ger lɑːk
Gaisford 'geɪs fəd ‖ -fᵊrd
gait geɪt (= *gate*)
gaiter 'geɪt ə ‖ 'geɪt ᵊr ~s z
Gaitskell, Gaitskill 'geɪt skəl -skɪl
Gaius 'gaɪ̯əs
gal gæl **gals** gælz
gala 'gɑːl ə 'geɪl ə ‖ 'geɪl ə 'gæl ə ~s z
galactagogue gə 'lækt ə gɒg ‖ -gɑːg ~s z
galactic gə 'lækt ɪk
Galactica gə 'lækt ɪk ə
galacto- *comb. form*
  with stress-neutral suffix gə ˌlækt əʊ ‖ -ə
  — **galactopoietic** gə ˌlækt əʊ pɔɪ 'et ɪk ◂
  ‖ -ə pɔɪ 'eʈ ɪk ◂
  with stress-imposing suffix ˌgæl ək 'tɒ+ -æk-
  ‖ -'tɑː+ — **galactometer** ˌgæl ək 'tɒm ɪt ə
  ˌæk-, -ət ə ‖ -'tɑːm əʈ ᵊr
galactose gə 'lækt əʊs -əʊz ‖ -oʊs
galah gə 'lɑː ~s z
Galahad 'gæl ə hæd
galantine 'gæl ən tiːn ˌ·'· ~s z
Galapagos, Galápagos gə 'læp əg əs -ə gɒs
  ‖ gə 'lɑːp ə goʊs -əg əs — *Sp* [ga 'la pa ɣos]
Galashiels ˌgæl ə 'ʃiːᵊlz
Galatea ˌgæl ə 'tiː̯ə
Galatia gə 'leɪʃ ə -'leɪʃ i̯ə
Galatian gə 'leɪʃ ᵊn -'leɪʃ i̯ən ~s z
galax|y 'gæl əks |i ~ies iz
Galba 'gælb ə
galbanum 'gælb ən əm
Galbraith gæl 'breɪθ ‖ 'gælb reɪθ
gale, Gale geɪᵊl **gales** geɪᵊlz
gale-force 'geɪᵊl fɔːs ‖ -fɔːrs -foʊrs
Galen 'geɪl ən -ɪn
galena, G~ gə 'liːn ə
Galenic, g~ geɪ 'len ɪk gə-
galere, galère gæ 'leə ‖ -'leᵊr — *Fr* [ga lɛːʁ]
Galicia gə 'lɪs i̯ə -'lɪʃ ə, -'lɪʃ i̯ə ‖ -'lɪʃ ə -'liːʃ-
Galician gə 'lɪs i̯ən -'lɪʃ ᵊn, -'lɪʃ i̯ən ‖ -'lɪʃ ᵊn
  -'liːʃ- ~s z
Galilean ˌgæl ɪ 'liː̯ən ◂ -ə- ~s z
Galilee 'gæl ɪ liː -ə-
Galileo ˌgæl ɪ 'leɪ əʊ -ə-, -'liː- ‖ -oʊ — *It*
  [ga li 'lɛː o]
galingale 'gæl ɪŋ geɪᵊl ~s z
galipot 'gæl ɪ pɒt ‖ -pɑːt
gall, Gall gɔːl ‖ gɑːl **galled** gɔːld ‖ gɑːld
  galling 'gɔːl ɪŋ ‖ 'gɑːl- **galls** gɔːlz ‖ gɑːlz
  'gall ˌbladder; 'gall wasp
Galla 'gæl ə ~s z
Gallacher, Gallaher 'gæl ə hə -əx ə ‖ -ə hᵊr
Gallagher 'gæl ə hə -əx ə, -əg ə ‖ -əg ᵊr
gallant *n, adj 'attentive to women'* gə 'lænt
  'gæl ənt ‖ gə 'lɑːnt ~ly li ~s s
gallant *adj 'brave'* 'gæl ənt ~ly li
gallant|ry 'gæl ənt |ri ~ries riz
Gallaudet ˌgæl ə 'det
galleon 'gæl i̯ən ~s z
galleria ˌgæl ə 'riː̯ə ~s z
galler|y 'gæl ᵊr |i ~ies iz

galley, G~ 'gæl i ~s z
  'galley proof; 'galley slave
Galliano ˌgæl i 'ɑːn əʊ ‖ -oʊ
galliard 'gæl i ɑːd -i̯əd ‖ 'gæl jᵊrd ~s z
Gallic, g~ 'gæl ɪk
gallicism 'gæl ɪ ˌsɪz əm -ə- ~s z
gallimauf|ry ˌgæl ɪ 'mɔːf |ri -ə- ‖ -'mɑːf- ~ries
  riz
gallinaceous ˌgæl ɪ 'neɪʃ əs -ə-
galling 'gɔːl ɪŋ ‖ 'gɑːl- ~ly li
gallinule 'gæl ɪ njuːl -ə- ‖ -nuːl -njuːl ~s z
Gallipoli gə 'lɪp əl i
gallipot 'gæl i pɒt ‖ -pɑːt
gallium 'gæl i̯əm
galli|vant 'gæl ɪ |vænt -ə-, vɑːnt, ˌ··'·
  ‖ -ə |vænt ~vanted vænt ɪd vɑːnt-, -əd
  ‖ vænt̬ əd ~vanting vænt ɪŋ vɑːnt- ‖ vænt̬ ɪŋ
  ~vants vænts
Gallo 'gæl əʊ ‖ -oʊ
Gallo- ˌgæl əʊ ‖ -oʊ — **Gallo-Romance**
  ˌgæl əʊ rəʊ 'mæn‖s ◂ ‖ -oʊ roʊ-
gallon 'gæl ən ~s z
galloon gə 'luːn
gallop 'gæl əp ~ed t ~er/s ə/z ‖ ᵊr/z ~ing ɪŋ
  ~s s
Galloway, g~ 'gæl ə weɪ
gallowglass 'gæl əʊ glɑːs §-glæs ‖ -oʊ glæs
  ~es ɪz əz
gallows 'gæl əʊz ‖ -oʊz
  'gallows ˌhumour
gallstone 'gɔːl stəʊn ‖ -stoʊn 'gɑːl- ~s z
Gallup 'gæl əp
  ˌGallup 'poll, '···‖'···
gallus 'gæl əs ~es ɪz əz
galoot gə 'luːt ~s s
galop 'gæl əp gæ 'lɒp ~s s
galore gə 'lɔː ‖ -'lɔːr -'loʊr
galosh gə 'lɒʃ ‖ -'lɑːʃ ~es ɪz əz
Galsworthy *(i)* 'gɔːlz ˌwɜːð i ‖ -ˌwɝːð i 'gɑːlz-,
  (ii) 'gælz-
Galt gɔːlt gɒlt ‖ gɑːlt
Galtieri ˌgælt i 'eər i ‖ ˌgɑːlt i 'er i — *Sp*
  [gal 'tje ɾi]
Galton 'gɔːlt ən 'gɒlt- ‖ 'gɑːlt-
galtonia gɔːl 'təʊn i ə gɒl- ‖ -toʊn- gɑːl- ~s z
galumph gə 'lʌmᵖf ~ed t ~ing ɪŋ ~s s
galvanic gæl 'væn ɪk ~ally ᵊl i
galvanis... —*see* **galvaniz...**
galvanism 'gælv ə ˌnɪz əm
galvanization ˌgælv ə naɪ 'zeɪʃ ᵊn -ən ɪ-
  ‖ -ən ə-
galvaniz|e 'gælv ə naɪz ~ed d ~er/s ə/z ‖ ᵊr/z
  ~es ɪz əz ~ing ɪŋ
galvano- *comb. form*
  with stress-neutral suffix ˌgælv ən ə
  gæl |væn ə — **galvanoscope**
  'gælv ən ə skəʊp gæl 'væn- ‖ -skoʊp
  with stress-imposing suffix ˌgælv ə 'nɒ+
  ‖ -'nɑː+ — **galvanoscopy**
  ˌgælv ə 'nɒsk əp i ‖ -'nɑːsk-
galvanometer ˌgælv ə 'nɒm ɪt ə -ət ə
  ‖ -'nɑːm əʈ ᵊr ~s z
Galveston, Galvestone 'gælv əst ən -ɪst-

G

Galway 'gɔːl weɪ ‖ 'gɑːl-
gam gæm **gammed** gæmd **gamming** 'gæm ɪŋ
  gams gæmz
Gama, gama 'gɑːm ə
Gamage 'gæm ɪdʒ ~**'s** ɪz əz
Gamaliel gə 'meɪl i‿əl -'mɑːl-
Gambaccini ˌgæm bə 'tʃiːn i
Gambi|a 'gæm bi‿|ə ~**an/s** ən/z
Gambier, g~ 'gæm bi‿ə ‖ ‿ər
gambit 'gæm bɪt §-bət ~**s** s
gambl|e, G~ 'gæm bəl **gambled** 'gæm bəld
  gambler/s 'gæm blə/z ‖ -blər/z **gambles**
  'gæm bəlz **gambling** 'gæm blɪŋ
gamboge gæm 'bəʊdʒ -'bəʊʒ, -'buːʒ ‖ -'bəʊdʒ
gambol 'gæm bəl (= gamble) ~**ed, ~led** d
  ~**ing, ~ling** ɪŋ ~**s** z
gambrel 'gæm brəl ~**s** z
game geɪm **gamer** 'geɪm ə ‖ -ər **games** geɪmz
  gamest 'geɪm ɪst -əst
  '**game plan**; '**games ˌmistress**
gamecock 'geɪm kɒk ‖ -kɑːk ~**s** s
gamekeeper 'geɪm ˌkiːp ə ‖ -ər ~**s** z
gamelan 'gæm ə læn -ɪ-
gamely 'geɪm li
gameplay 'geɪm pleɪ
gamesmanship 'geɪmz mən ʃɪp
gamete 'gæm iːt gə 'miːt ~**s** s
gameto- comb. form
  with stress-neutral suffix gə ¦miːt əʊ
  ¦gæm ɪt ə, -ət- ‖ gə ¦miːt ə ¦gæm ət ə
  — **gametocyte** gə 'miːt əʊ saɪt 'gæm ɪt ə-,
  -ət- ‖ -'miːt̬ ə- 'gæm ət̬ ə-
  with stress-imposing suffix ˌgæm ɪ 'tɒ+ §-ə-
  ‖ -'tɑː+ — **gametogeny** ˌgæm ɪ 'tɒdʒ ən i
  ˌ,ə- ‖ -'tɑːdʒ-
gamey 'geɪm i
gamin 'gæm ɪn §-ən —Fr [ga mæ̃] ~**s** z —or as
  sing.
gamine 'gæm iːn gæ 'miːn —Fr [ga min] ~**s** z
gaming 'geɪm ɪŋ
  '**gaming ˌtable**
Gamlen, Gamlin 'gæm lɪn -lən
gamma 'gæm ə ~**s** z
  ˌgamma 'globulin; ˌgamma ˌradi'ation;
  'gamma ray
Gammell 'gæm əl
gammer 'gæm ə ‖ -ər ~**s** z
gammon, G~ 'gæm ən ~**ed** d ~**ing** ɪŋ ~**s** z
gammy 'gæm i
-gamous stress-imposing gəm əs — **bigamous**
  'bɪg əm əs
gamp, Gamp gæmp **gamps** gæmps
gamut 'gæm ət -ʌt, -ʊt
gam|y 'geɪm |i ~**ier** i‿ə ‖ i‿ər ~**iest** i‿ɪst i‿əst
  ~**iness** i nəs i nɪs
-gamy stress-imposing gəm i — **monogamy**
  mə 'nɒg əm i ‖ -'nɑːg-
gan gæn
Ganda 'gænd ə 'gɑːnd ə
Gandalf 'gænd ælf ‖ -ɑːlf
gander, G~ 'gænd ə ‖ -ər ~**s** z
Gandhi 'gænd i 'gɑːnd i —Hindi [gãː ḍi]
ganef 'gɑːn əf ~**s** s

Ganesh gə 'neɪʃ -'neʃ —Hindi [gə neːʃ]
gang gæŋ **ganged** gæŋd **ganging** 'gæŋ ɪŋ
  gangs gæŋz
gang-bang 'gæŋ bæŋ ~**ed** d ~**ing** ɪŋ ~**s** z
gangbuster 'gæŋ ˌbʌst ə ‖ -ər ~**s** z
ganger 'gæŋ ə ‖ -ər ~**s** z
Ganges 'gændʒ iːz
gangland 'gæŋ lænd -lənd
ganglia 'gæŋ gli ə
gangling 'gæŋ glɪŋ
gangli|on 'gæŋ gli |ən ~**a** ə ~**ons** ənz
gan|gly 'gæŋ |gli ~**glier** gli ə ‖ gli ‿ər ~**gliest**
  gli ɪst əst
gangmaster 'gæŋ ˌmɑːst ə §-ˌmæst- ‖ -mæst ər
  ~**s** z
gangplank 'gæŋ plæŋk ~**s** s
gangren|e 'gæŋ griːn ‖ ˑˑˑ ~**ed** d ~**es** z ~**ing** ɪŋ
gangrenous 'gæŋ grɪn əs -grən-
gangsta 'gæŋkst ə ~**s** z
gangster 'gæŋkst ə ‖ -ər ~**s** z
gangue gæŋ (= gang)
gangway 'gæŋ weɪ ~**s** z
ganister 'gæn ɪst ə -əst- ‖ -ər
ganja 'gændʒ ə 'gɑːndʒ-
gannet 'gæn ɪt -ət ~**s** s
Gannex tdmk 'gæn eks
gansey 'gænz i ~**s** z
Gansu ˌgæn 'suː ‖ ˌgɑːn- —Chi Gānsù
  [¹kan ⁴su]
Gant gænt
gantlet 'gænt lət 'gɔːnt-, -lɪt ‖ 'gɔːnt- 'gɑːnt-,
  'gænt- ~**s** s
gantr|y 'gæntr |i ~**ies** iz
Ganymede 'gæn ɪ miːd -ə-
gaol dʒeɪəl (= jail) **gaoled** dʒeɪəld **gaoling**
  'dʒeɪəl ɪŋ **gaols** dʒeɪəlz
gaolbird 'dʒeɪəl bɜːd ‖ -bɝːd ~**s** z
gaoler 'dʒeɪl ə ‖ -ər ~**s** z
gap gæp **gaps** gæps
gape geɪp **gaped** geɪpt **gaper/s** 'geɪp ə/z
  ‖ -ər/z **gapes** geɪps **gaping/ly** 'geɪp ɪŋ /li
gap-toothed ˌgæp 'tuːθt ◂ -'tuːðd, §-'tʊθt
gar gɑː ‖ gɑːr
garag|e n, v 'gær ɑːʒ -ɑːdʒ, -ɪdʒ; gə 'rɑːʒ,
  -'rɑːdʒ ‖ gə 'rɑːʒ -'rɑːdʒ (*) — Preference
  polls, AmE: -'rɑːʒ 52%, -'rɑːdʒ 48%; BrE:
  'gær ɑːdʒ 56% (dʒ 31%, ʒ 25%), -ɪdʒ 38%,
  gə 'rɑːdʒ 6%. ~**ed** d ~**es** ɪz əz ~**ing** ɪŋ
  'garage sale ‖ ga'rage sale
garam masala ˌgɑːr əm mə 'sɑːl ə ˌgʌr-,
  -mɑː'-- —Hindi-Urdu [gə rəm mə ʃaː lah]
Garamond 'gær ə mɒnd ‖ -mɑːnd
Garand 'gær ənd ‖ 'ger-; gə 'rænd
Garard 'gær ɑːd ‖ -ɑːrd 'ger-
garb gɑːb ‖ gɑːrb **garbed** gɑːbd ‖ gɑːrbd
garbage 'gɑːb ɪdʒ ‖ 'gɑːrb-
  'garbage can; 'garbage col,lector;
  'garbage truck
garbanzo gɑː 'bænz əʊ ‖ gɑːr 'bɑːnz oʊ ~**s** z
garbl|e 'gɑːb əl ‖ 'gɑːrb əl ~**ed** d ~**es** z ~**ing**
  ɪŋ
Garbo, garbo 'gɑːb əʊ ‖ 'gɑːrb oʊ ~**s** z

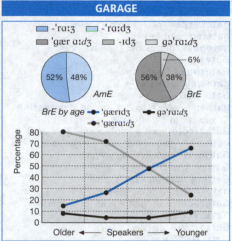

GARAGE

- ▨ -'rɑ:ʒ   ▨ -'rɑ:dʒ
- ■ 'gær ɑ:dʒ   ■ -ɪdʒ   ▨ gə'rɑ:dʒ

AmE: 52% | 48%

BrE: 56% | 38% | 6%

BrE by age —●— 'gærɪdʒ   —●— gə'rɑ:dʒ
—●— 'gærɑ:dʒ

Percentage chart: 80 70 60 50 40 30 20 10 0
Older ← Speakers → Younger

Garcia *English family name (i)* 'gɑːs i̯ə
‖ 'gɑːrs-, *(ii)* 'gɑːʃ- ‖ 'gɑːrʃ-
Garcia *Spanish name* gɑ: 'siː̯ə ‖ gɑːr- —*Sp*
García [gar 'θi a], *AmSp* [-'si-]
garcon, garçon 'gɑːs ɒn -ɔ̃ ‖ gɑːr 'soʊn -'sɔ̃:
—*Fr* [gaʁ sɔ̃]
garda, Garda *Irish policeman* 'gɑːd ə
‖ 'gɑːrd ə —*Irish* ['gar də] **gardai, gardaí,**
G~ ⑴gɑ: 'diː ‖ ⑴gɑːr- —*Irish* ['gar di:]
ˌGarda ˌSíoˈchǎna ˌʃiː̯ə ˈkɔːn ə -ˈxɔːn-
‖ -ˈkɑːn-
Garda *lake in Italy* 'gɑːd ə ‖ 'gɑːrd ə —*It*
['gar da]
garden, G~ 'gɑːd ᵊn ‖ 'gɑːrd ᵊn **~ed** d **~ing**
ɪŋ **~s** z
'garden ˌcentre; ˌgarden 'city; 'garden
ˌparty; ˌgarden 'suburb
gardener 'gɑːd nə ‖ 'gɑːrd nᵊr **~s** z
gardenia gɑ: 'diːn i̯ə ‖ gɑːr 'diːn jə **~s** z
gardening *n* 'gɑːd nɪŋ ‖ 'gɑːrd-
garden-variety 'gɑːd ᵊn və ˌraɪ ət i
‖ 'gɑːrd ᵊn və ˌraɪ ət̬ i
Gardiner 'gɑːd nə ‖ 'gɑːrd nᵊr
Gardyne gɑ: 'daɪn ‖ gɑːr-
Gare du Nord ˌgɑ: dju: 'nɔː ‖ ˌgɑːr du: 'nɔːr
—*Fr* [gaʁ dy nɔːʁ]
Garel 'gær əl ‖ 'ger-
Gareloch 'geə lɒx -lɒk ‖ 'ger lɑːk 'gær-
Gareth 'gær əθ -ɪθ, -eθ ‖ 'ger- —*Welsh*
['ga reθ]
Garfield 'gɑː fiːᵊld ‖ 'gɑːr-
garfish 'gɑː fɪʃ ‖ 'gɑːr-
Garforth 'gɑː fəθ -fɔːθ ‖ 'gɑːr fᵊrθ -fɔːrθ, -foʊrθ
Garfunkel gɑ: 'fʌŋk ᵊl 'gɑːf ʌŋk ᵊl ‖ gɑːr-
garganey 'gɑːg ən i ‖ 'gɑːrg- **~s** z
Gargantua gɑ: 'gænt ju̯ə ‖ gɑːr 'gæntʃ u̯ə
gargantuan gɑ: 'gænt ju̯ən
‖ gɑːr 'gæntʃ u̯ən
gargl|e 'gɑːg ᵊl ‖ 'gɑːrg ᵊl **~ed** d **~es** z **~ing**
ɪŋ
gargoyle 'gɑː gɔɪᵊl ‖ 'gɑːrg- **~s** z

Garibaldi, g~ ˌgær ɪ 'bɔːld i -ə-, -'bɒld- ‖ ˌger-,
-'bɑːld i —*It* [ga ri 'bal di] **~s** z
garish 'geər ɪʃ 'gɑːr- ‖ 'ger- 'gær- **~ly** li **~ness**
nəs nɪs
garland, G~ 'gɑːl ənd ‖ 'gɑːrl- **~s** z
garlic, G~, Garlick, Garlicke 'gɑːl ɪk
‖ 'gɑːrl-
garlicky 'gɑːl ɪk i ‖ 'gɑːrl-
Garman 'gɑːm ən ‖ 'gɑːrm-
garment 'gɑːm ənt ‖ 'gɑːrm- **~ed** ɪd əd **~s** s
Garmin *tdmk* 'gɑː mɪn ‖ 'gɑːr-
Garmisch 'gɑːm ɪʃ ‖ 'gɑːrm- —*Ger* ['gaʁ mɪʃ]
Garmondsway, Garmonsway 'gɑːm ənz weɪ
‖ 'gɑːrm-
garn|er, G~ 'gɑːn |ə ‖ 'gɑːrn |ᵊr **~ered** əd
‖ ᵊrd **~ering** ᵊr ɪŋ **~ers** əz ‖ ᵊrz
garnet, G~, Garnett 'gɑːn ɪt -ət ‖ 'gɑːrn- **~s** s
garnish 'gɑːn ɪʃ ‖ 'gɑːrn- **~ed** t **~er/s** ə/z
‖ ᵊr/z **~es** ɪz əz **~ing** ɪŋ
garnishee ˌgɑːn ɪ 'ʃiː §-ə- ‖ ˌgɑːrn- **~s** z
garott... —*see* **garrot...**
Garrard 'gær ɑːd -əd ‖ -ɑːrd 'ger-, -ᵊrd
Garratt 'gær ət ‖ 'ger-
Garraway 'gær ə weɪ ‖ 'ger-
garret, G~, Garrett 'gær ət -ɪt ‖ 'ger- **~s** s
Garrick 'gær ɪk ‖ 'ger-
garrison, G~ 'gær ɪs ən -əs- ‖ 'ger- **~ed** d **~ing**
ɪŋ **~s** z
gar|rote, gar|rotte gə |'rɒt -|'rɑːt -'roʊt
~roted, ~rotted 'rɒt ɪd -əd ‖ 'rɑːt̬ əd 'roʊt̬-
~rotes, ~rottes 'rɒts ‖ 'rɑːts 'roʊts **~roting,**
~rotting 'rɒt ɪŋ ‖ 'rɑːt̬ ɪŋ 'roʊt̬-
garrulity gə 'ruːl ət i gæ-, -'rjuːl-, -ɪt- ‖ -ət̬ i
garrulous 'gær əl əs -jʊl- ‖ 'ger- **~ly** li **~ness**
nəs nɪs
Garry 'gær i ‖ 'ger-
garrya 'gær i̯ə ‖ 'ger- **~s** z
Garryowen, g~ ˌgær i 'əʊ ɪn -ən
‖ ˌgær i 'oʊ ən ˌger-
Garscadden gɑ: 'skæd ᵊn ‖ gɑːr-
Garside 'gɑː saɪd ‖ 'gɑːr-
Garston 'gɑːst ən ‖ 'gɑːrst-
Gartcosh ⑴gɑːt 'kɒʃ ⑴gɑːrt 'kɑːʃ
garter, G~ 'gɑːt ə ‖ 'gɑːrt̬ ᵊr **~ed** d **gartering**
'gɑːt ᵊr ɪŋ ‖ 'gɑːrt̬ ᵊr ɪŋ **~s** z
'garter snake
garth, Garth gɑːθ ‖ gɑːrθ **garths, Garth's**
gɑːθs ‖ gɑːrθs
Garton 'gɑːt ᵊn ‖ 'gɑːrt ᵊn
Garuda *tdmk* gə 'ruːd ə gæ-
Garvagh 'gɑːv ə ‖ 'gɑːrv ə
Garvaghy gɑ: 'væ hi ‖ gɑːr-
Gary *family name* 'geər i ‖ 'ger i 'gær i
Gary *personal name; place in IN* 'gær i ‖ 'ger-
gas gæs **gases, gasses** 'gæs ɪz -əz **gassed**
gæst **gassing** 'gæs ɪŋ
'gas ˌchamber; ˌgas 'fire; ˌgas ˌfitter; 'gas
mask; 'gas ˌpedal; 'gas ring; 'gas
ˌstation; ˌgas 'turbine ‖ '· ˌ··
gasbag 'gæs bæg **~s** z
Gascoigne, Gascoin, Gascoine, Gascoyne
'gæsk ɔɪn
Gascon 'gæsk ən **~s** z

G

Gascony 'gæsk ən i
gaseous 'gæs i‿əs 'geɪs-, 'geɪz-ǁ 'gæʃ əs **~ness**
  nəs nɪs
gas-fired 'gæs ˌfaɪ‿əd ǁ -ˌfaɪ‿ərd
gas-guzzl|er 'gæs ˌgʌz ᵊl|ə ǁ -ᵊr **~ing** ɪŋ
gash, Gash gæʃ **gashed** gæʃt **gashes** 'gæʃ ɪz
  -əz **gashing** 'gæʃ ɪŋ
gasholder 'gæs ˌhəʊld ə ǁ -ˌhoʊld ᵊr **~s** z
gasifiable 'gæs ɪ faɪ‿əb ᵊl §'·ə-; ˌ··'··
gasification ˌgæs ɪf ɪ 'keɪʃ ᵊn ˌ·əf-, §-ə'·--
gasi|fy 'gæs ɪ |faɪ -ə- **~fied** faɪd **~fier/s** faɪ‿ə/z
  ǁ faɪ‿ᵊr/z **~fies** faɪz **~fying** faɪ ɪŋ
Gaskell 'gæsk ᵊl
gasket 'gæsk ɪt -ət **~s** s
gaskin 'gæsk ɪn §-ən **~s** z
gaslamp 'gæs læmp **~s** s
gaslight 'gæs laɪt **~s** s
gas|man 'gæs |mæn **~men** men
gasohol 'gæs ə hɒl ǁ -hɔːl -hɑːl
gasolene, gasoline 'gæs ə liːn ˌ··'·
gasometer gæ 'sɒm ɪt ə gə-, -ət ə
  ǁ -'sɑːm ət̬ ᵊr **~s** z
gasp gɑːsp §gæsp ǁ gæsp **gasped** gɑːspt
  §gæspt ǁ gæspt **gasping** 'gɑːsp ɪŋ §'gæsp-
  ǁ 'gæsp ɪŋ **gasps** gɑːsps §gæsps ǁ gæsps
Gaspar 'gæsp ə -ɑː ǁ -ᵊr -ɑːr
Gaspé 'gæsp eɪ ǁ gæ 'speɪ —Fr [gas pe]
gass|y 'gæs |i **~ier** i ə ǁ i‿ᵊr **~iest** i ɪst i əst
  ~iness i nəs i nɪs
gasteropod 'gæs tər‿ə pɒd ǁ -pɑːd **~s** z
gastrectom|y gæ 'strekt əm |i **~ies** iz
gastric 'gæs trɪk
gastritis gæ 'straɪt ɪs §-əs ǁ -'straɪt̬ əs
gastro- comb. form
  with stress-neutral suffix |gæs trəʊ ǁ -troʊ
  — **gastroenteric** ˌgæs trəʊ en 'ter ɪk ◂
  ǁ -troʊ-
  with stress-imposing suffix gæ 'strɒ +
  ǁ -'strɑː + — **gastroscopy** gæ 'strɒsk əp i
  ǁ -'strɑːsk-
gastroenteritis ˌgæs trəʊ ˌent ə 'raɪt ɪs §-əs
  ǁ -troʊ ˌent̬ ə 'raɪt̬ əs
gastrointestinal ˌgæs trəʊ ɪn 'test ɪn ᵊl ◂
  -ᵊn əl; -ˌɪnt es 'taɪn- ǁ -troʊ ɪn 'test ᵊn‿əl ◂
  ~ly i
gastronome 'gæs trə nəʊm ǁ -noʊm **~s** z
gastronomic ˌgæs trə 'nɒm ɪk ◂ ǁ -'nɑːm-
  ~ally ᵊl‿i
gastronomy gæ 'strɒn əm i ǁ -'strɑːn-
gastropod 'gæs trə pɒd ǁ -pɑːd **~s** z
gastropub 'gæs trəʊ pʌb ǁ -troʊ- **~s** z
gasworks 'gæs wɜːks ǁ -wɜːks
gat gæt **gats** gæts
Gatcomb, Gatcombe 'gæt kəm
gate, Gate geɪt **gated** 'geɪt ɪd -əd ǁ 'geɪt̬ əd
  gates geɪts **gating** 'geɪt ɪŋ ǁ 'geɪt̬ ɪŋ
  'gate ˌmoney
Gateacre 'gæt ək ə ǁ -ᵊr
gateau, gâteau 'gæt əʊ ǁ gæ 'toʊ —Fr
  [ɡa to] **~s, ~x** z -or as sing.
gatecrash 'geɪt kræʃ **~ed** t **~er/s** ə/z ǁ ᵊr/z
  ~es ɪz əz **~ing** ɪŋ
gatefold 'geɪt fəʊld →-fɒʊld ǁ -foʊld **~s** z

gate|house, G~ 'geɪt |haʊs **~houses** haʊz ɪz
  -əz
gatekeeper 'geɪt ˌkiːp ə ǁ -ᵊr **~s** z
gateleg 'geɪt leg **~s** z
gatepost 'geɪt pəʊst ǁ -poʊst **~s** s
Gates geɪts
Gateshead 'geɪts hed ˌ·'·
gateway 'geɪt weɪ **~s** z
Gath gæθ
gather 'gæð ə §'gɑːð- ǁ -ᵊr **~ed** d **gathering**
  'gæð ᵊr ɪŋ §'gɑːð- **~s** z
Gathercole 'gæð ə kəʊl →-kɒʊl ǁ -ᵊr koʊl
gatherer 'gæð ᵊr‿ə §'gɑːð- ǁ -ᵊr‿ᵊr **~s** z
Gathurst 'gæθ ɜːst -əst ǁ -ᵊrst
Gatley 'gæt li
Gatling 'gæt lɪŋ **~s, ~'s** z
gator 'geɪt ə ǁ 'geɪt̬ ᵊr **~s** z
Gatorade tdmk 'geɪt ə reɪd ˌ·'· ǁ 'geɪt̬-
Gatsby 'gæts bi
Gatso tdmk 'gæts əʊ ǁ -oʊ
Gatt, GATT gæt
Gatting 'gæt ɪŋ ǁ 'gæt̬ ɪŋ
Gatwick 'gæt wɪk
gauche gəʊʃ ǁ goʊʃ
gauche|ly 'gəʊʃ |li ǁ 'goʊʃ- **~ness** nəs nɪs
Gaucher 'gəʊ 'ʃeɪ ǁ goʊ 'ʃeɪ **-'s** z —Fr
  [go ʃe]
  'Goucher's di,sease
gaucherie 'gəʊʃ ᵊr i ˌgəʊʃ ə 'riː ǁ ˌgoʊʃ ə 'riː
  —Fr [goʃ ʁi] **~s** z
gaucho 'gaʊtʃ əʊ ǁ -oʊ **~s** z
gaudeamus ˌgaʊd i 'ɑːm ʊs ˌgɔːd-, -'eɪm-, -əs
  ˌgaude ˌamus 'igitur
Gaudi, Gaudí gaʊ 'diː 'gaʊd i —Catalan
  [ɡəu 'ði], Sp [ɡau 'ði]
gaud|y 'gɔːd |i ǁ 'gɑːd- **~ier** i ə ǁ i‿ᵊr **~iest** i ɪst
  i əst **~ily** ɪ li əl i **~iness** i nəs i nɪs
gauge geɪdʒ **gauged** geɪdʒd **gauges** 'geɪdʒ ɪz
  -əz **gauging** 'geɪdʒ ɪŋ
Gauguin 'gəʊg æ̃ -æn ǁ goʊ 'gæn —Fr
  [go gæ̃] **~s, ~'s** z
Gaul gɔːl ǁ gɑːl **Gauls** gɔːlz ǁ gɑːlz
gauleiter, G~ 'gaʊ ˌlaɪt ə ǁ -laɪt̬ ᵊr —Ger
  ['gau lai tɐ] **~s** z
Gaulish 'gɔːl ɪʃ ǁ 'gɑːl-
Gaullism 'gəʊl ˌɪz əm →'gɒʊl- ǁ 'gɔːl- 'gɑːl-,
  'goʊl-
Gaullist 'gəʊl ɪst →'gɒʊl-, §-əst ǁ 'gɔːl- 'gɑːl-,
  'goʊl- **~s** s
Gauloise, Gauloises tdmk 'gəʊl wɑːz ˌ·'·
  ǁ goʊl 'wɑːz —Fr [go lwɑːz]
gault, Gault gɔːlt gɒlt ǁ gɑːlt
Gaultier 'gəʊt i eɪ 'gɔːlt-, ˌ·'· ǁ 'goʊt- 'goʊlt-
  —Fr [go tje]
Gaumont 'gəʊ mɒnt -mənt ǁ 'goʊ mɑːnt
gaunt, Gaunt gɔːnt ǁ gɑːnt **gaunter** 'gɔːnt ə
  ǁ 'gɔːnt̬ ᵊr 'gɑːnt̬ ᵊr **gauntest** 'gɔːnt ɪst -əst
  ǁ 'gɔːnt̬ əst 'gɑːnt̬-
gauntlet 'gɔːnt lət -lɪt ǁ 'gɑːnt- **~s** s
gaunt|ly 'gɔːnt |li ǁ 'gɑːnt- **~ness** nəs nɪs
Gausden 'gɔːz dən ǁ 'gɑːz-
gauss, Gauss gaʊs
Gaussian 'gaʊs i‿ən

Gautama 'gaʊt əm ə 'gəʊt- ‖ 'goʊt-
Gauteng 'gaʊt eŋ 'xaʊt-
gauze gɔːz ‖ gɑːz **gauzes** 'gɔːz ɪz -əz ‖ 'gɑːz-
gauz|y 'gɔːz |i ‖ 'gɑːz- **~ier** i ə ‖ i ʲr **~iest** i ɪst
   i ˌəst **~ily** ɪ li əl i **~iness** i nəs i nɪs
Gavan 'gæv ³n
gave geɪv
gavel 'gæv ³l **~s** z
gavelkind 'gæv ³l kaɪnd -kɪnd
Gaveston 'gæv ɪst ən -əst-
gavial 'geɪv i əl 'gæv- **~s** z
Gavin 'gæv ɪn -³n
gavotte gə 'vɒt ‖ -'vɑːt **~s** s
Gawain 'gɑː weɪn 'gæ-, -wɪn; gə 'weɪn
gawd gɔːd gɑːd
Gawith (i) 'gaʊ ɪθ, (ii) 'geɪ wɪθ
gawk gɔːk ‖ gɑːk **gawked** gɔːkt ‖ gɑːkt
   gawking 'gɔːk ɪŋ ‖ 'gɑːk- **gawks** gɔːks
   ‖ gɑːks
gawk|y 'gɔːk |i ‖ 'gɑːk- **~ier** i ə ‖ i ʲr **~iest**
   i ɪst i ˌəst **~ily** ɪ li əl i **~iness** i nəs i nɪs
Gawler 'gɔːl ə ‖ -ʲr 'gɑːl-
gawp gɔːp ‖ gɑːp **gawped** gɔːpt ‖ gɑːpt
   gawping 'gɔːp ɪŋ ‖ 'gɑːp- **gawps** gɔːps
   ‖ gɑːps
gay, Gay geɪ **gaily** 'geɪ li **gayer** 'geɪ ə ‖ -ʲr
   gayest 'geɪ ɪst -əst **gays** geɪz
gaydar, G~ 'geɪd ɑː ‖ -ɑːr
Gaydon 'geɪd ³n
Gaye geɪ
Gayle geɪ³l
Gaylord 'geɪ lɔːd ‖ -lɔːrd
Gay-Lussac ˌgeɪ 'luːs æk ‖ -lə 'sæk —Fr
   [gɛ ly sak]
gayness 'geɪ nəs -nɪs
Gaynor 'geɪn ə ‖ -ʲr
Gayton 'geɪt ³n
Gaza 'gɑːz ə ‖ 'gæz-
   ˌGaza 'Strip
gazania gə 'zeɪn i ə **~s** z
Gazdar 'gæz dɑː ‖ -dɑːr
gaze geɪz **gazed** geɪzd **gazes** 'geɪz ɪz -əz
   gazing 'geɪz ɪŋ
gazebo gə 'ziːb əʊ ‖ -'zeɪb oʊ -'ziːb- **~s** z
gazelle gə 'zel **~s** z
gazer 'geɪz ə ‖ -ʲr **~s** z
ga|zette gə |'zet **~zetted** 'zet ɪd -əd ‖ 'zeţ əd
   ~zettes 'zets **~zetting** 'zet ɪŋ ‖ 'zeţ ɪŋ
gazetteer ˌgæz ə 'tɪə -ɪ- ‖ -'tɪʲr **~s** z
gazillion gə 'zɪl i ən ‖ -'zɪl jən **~s** z
gazpacho gæz 'pætʃ əʊ gæs-, gəs-, -'pɑːtʃ-
   ‖ gə 'spɑːtʃ oʊ —Sp [gaθ 'pa tʃo]
gazump gə 'zʌmp **~ed** t **~ing** ɪŋ **~s** s
gazund|er gə 'zʌnd| ə ‖ -ʲr **~ered** əd ‖ ʲrd
   ~ering ər ɪŋ **~ers** əz ‖ ʲrz
Gazza 'gæz ə
GB ˌdʒiː 'biː
GCE ˌdʒiː siː 'iː ◂ **~s** z
GCSE ˌdʒiː siː es 'iː ◂ **~s** z
Gdansk dæn'sk gə'dæn'sk ‖ -'dɑːn'sk —Polish
   Gdańsk [gdajsk]
g'day gə 'deɪ
GDP ˌdʒiː diː 'piː

gean giːn **geans** giːnz
gear gɪə ‖ gɪʲr **geared** gɪəd ‖ gɪʲrd **gearing**
   'gɪər ɪŋ ‖ 'gɪr ɪŋ **gears** gɪəz ‖ gɪʲrz
   'gear ˌlever; 'gear ˌshift; 'gear ˌstick
gearbox 'gɪə bɒks ‖ 'gɪʲr bɑːks **~es** ɪz əz
Geary 'gɪər i ‖ 'gɪr i
Gebhard 'geb hɑːd ‖ -hɑːrd
gecko 'gek əʊ ‖ -oʊ **~es, ~s** z
Geddes 'ged ɪs §-əs ‖ -iːz
geddit 'ged ɪt §-ət ‖ 'geţ ət —This
   non-standard spelling of get it reflects a casual
   pronunciation with ţ (= d).
gee, Gee dʒiː **geed** dʒiːd **geeing** 'dʒiː ɪŋ
   gees dʒiːz
geegaw 'dʒiː gɔː 'giː- ‖ -gɑː **~s** z
gee-gee 'dʒiː dʒiː **~s** z
geek giːk **geeks** giːks
geek|y 'giːk| i **~ier** i ə ‖ i ʲr **~iest** i ɪst ˌəst
Geelong dʒɪ 'lɒŋ dʒə- ‖ -'lɔːŋ -'lɑːŋ
Geen (i) giːn, (ii) dʒiːn
geese giːs
Geeson (i) 'giːs ³n, (ii) 'dʒiːs ³n
Geevor 'giːv ə ‖ -ʲr
Ge'ez 'giː ez
geezer 'giːz ə ‖ -ʲr **~s** z
Geffrye 'dʒef ri
gefilte gə 'fɪlt ə
Gehenna gɪ 'hen ə gə-
Gehrig 'geər ɪg ‖ 'ger-
Gehry 'geər i ‖ 'ger i
Geiger 'gaɪg ə ‖ -ʲr
   'Geiger ˌcounter
Geikie 'giːk i
geisha 'geɪʃ ə —Jp [ge,e ça] **~s** z
Geissler 'gaɪs lə ‖ -lʲr —Ger ['gais lɐ]
gel 'girl' gel **gels** gelz
gel 'jell, jelly' dʒel **gelled** dʒeld **gelling**
   'dʒel ɪŋ **gels** dʒelz
gelada dʒɪ 'lɑːd ə dʒə-, dʒe- **~s** z
gelatin 'dʒel ət ɪn §-ən
gelatine 'dʒel ə tiːn ˌ‧'‧
gelatinous dʒə 'læt ɪn əs dʒɪ-, dʒe-, -ən-
   ‖ -'læt ³n_əs **~ly** li **~ness** nəs nɪs
geld geld **gelded** 'geld ɪd -əd **gelding**
   'geld ɪŋ **gelds** geldz **gelt** gelt
Geldart 'geld ɑːt ‖ -ɑːrt
gelding 'geld ɪŋ **~s** z
Geldof 'geld ɒf -ɔːf ‖ -ɔːf -ɑːf
gelid 'dʒel ɪd §-əd
gelignite 'dʒel ɪg naɪt -əg-
Gell (i) dʒel, (ii) gel
Geller 'gel ə ‖ -ʲr
Gelligaer ˌgeɬ li 'geə ˌgeɬ i-, -'gaɪə ‖ -'geʲr
   -'gaɪʲr —Welsh [ˌge ɬi 'gair, -'gair]
Gell-Mann ˌgel 'mæn
gelt gelt
gem dʒem **gems** dʒemz
Gemara gə 'mɑːr ə ge-
gemeinschaft gə 'maɪn ʃɑːft -ʃæft —Ger
   [gə 'main ʃaft]
geminate n, adj 'dʒem ɪn ət -ən-, -ɪt; -ɪ neɪt,
   -ə- **~s** s

gemi|nate *v* 'dʒem ɪ |neɪt -ə- **~nated** neɪt ɪd
-əd ‖ neɪt̬ əd **~nates** neɪts **~nating** neɪt ɪŋ
‖ neɪt̬ ɪŋ
gemination ˌdʒem ɪ 'neɪʃ ᵊn -ə- **~s** z
Gemini 'dʒem ɪ naɪ -ə-, -niː **~s** z
Geminian ˌdʒem ɪ 'naɪ ən -ə-, -'niː ~s z
Gemm|a, gemm|a 'dʒem |ə **~ae** iː **~as, ~a's**
əz
Gemmell, Gemmill 'gem ᵊl
gemmology, gemology dʒe 'mɒl ədʒ i
‖ -'mɑːl-
gemot, gemote gɪ 'məʊt gə- ‖ -'moʊt **~s** s
gemsbok 'gemz bɒk 'hems-, -bʌk ‖ -bɑːk **~s** s
gemstone 'dʒem stəʊn ‖ -stoʊn **~s** z
-gen dʒən, dʒen — **glycogen** 'glaɪk ədʒ ən
-əʊ dʒen
gen dʒen **genned** dʒend **genning** 'dʒen ɪŋ
gens dʒenz
gendarme 'ʒɒnd ɑːm 'ʒɒ̃d- ‖ 'ʒɑːnd ɑːrm —*Fr*
[ʒɑ̃ daʁm] **~s** z
gender 'dʒend ə ‖ -ᵊr **~s** z
gender-bender 'dʒend ə ˌbend ə
‖ -ᵊr ˌbend ᵊr **~s** z
gender-neutral ˌdʒend ə 'njuːtr əl ◂ §-'nuːtr-
‖ -ᵊr 'nuːtr- -'njuːtr-
gender-specific ˌdʒend ə spə 'sɪf ɪk ◂ -spɪ-‥
‖ ˌˌ-ᵊr-
gene, Gene dʒiːn **genes, Gene's** dʒiːnz
'gene pool
genealogical ˌdʒiːn i‿ə 'lɒdʒ ɪk ᵊl ◂ ‖ -'lɑːdʒ-
~ly ᵢi
genealogist ˌdʒiːn i 'æl ədʒ ɪst △-'ɒl-, §-əst
‖ -'ɑːl- **~s** s
genealog|y ˌdʒiːn i 'æl ədʒ |i △-'ɒl- ‖ -'ɑːl-
~ies iz
genera 'dʒen ər ə
general 'dʒen ᵊr_əl **~s** z
ˌgeneral de'livery; ˌgeneral e'lection;
ˌgeneral 'knowledge; ˌgeneral
prac'titioner; ˌgeneral 'staff; ˌgeneral
'strike
generalis... —*see* **generaliz...**
generalissimo ˌdʒen ᵊr_ə 'lɪs ɪ məʊ -'·ə-
‖ -moʊ **~s** z
generalist 'dʒen ᵊr_əl ɪst §-əst **~s** s
generalit|y ˌdʒen ə 'ræl ət |i -ɪt i ‖ -ət̬ |i **~ies**
iz
generalization ˌdʒen ᵊr_əl aɪ 'zeɪʃ ᵊn əl ɪ-
‖ -əl ə- **~s** z
generaliz|e 'dʒen ᵊr_ə laɪz **~ed** d **~es** ɪz əz
~ing ɪŋ
generally 'dʒen ᵊr_əl i
general-purpose ˌdʒen ᵊr_əl 'pɜːp əs ◂
‖ -'pɜːp-
generalship 'dʒen ᵊr_əl ʃɪp **~s** s
gene|rate 'dʒen ə |reɪt **~rated** reɪt ɪd -əd
‖ reɪt̬ əd **~rates** reɪts **~rating** reɪt ɪŋ ‖ reɪt̬ ɪŋ
generation ˌdʒen ə 'reɪʃ ᵊn **~s** z
ˌgene'ration gap
generational ˌdʒen ə 'reɪʃ ᵊn ᵊl ◂ **-ly** i
generativ|e 'dʒen ᵊr_ət ɪv ‖ -ᵊr_ət̬ ɪv -ə reɪt̬ ɪv
~ely li **~eness** nəs nɪs **-ist/s** ɪst/s §əst/s
generator 'dʒen ə reɪt ə ‖ -reɪt̬ ᵊr **~s** z

generic dʒə 'ner ɪk dʒɪ- **~ally** ᵊl_i **~s** s
generosity ˌdʒen ə 'rɒs ət i -ɪt i ‖ -'rɑːs ət̬ i
generous 'dʒen ᵊr_əs **-ly** li **~ness** nəs nɪs
Genese dʒə 'niːs dʒɪ-
Genesee ˌdʒen ə 'siː -ɪ-
genesis, G~ 'dʒen əs ɪs -ɪs-, -ɪz, §-əs
-genesis dʒen əs ɪs -ɪs-, §-əs —
morphogenesis ˌmɔːf əʊ 'dʒen əs ɪs -ɪs ɪs,
§-əs ‖ ˌmɔːrf oʊ-
genet *animal* 'dʒen ɪt §-ət **~s** s
Genet *French writer* ʒə 'neɪ —*Fr* [ʒə nɛ]
genetic dʒə 'net ɪk dʒɪ- ‖ -'net̬ ɪk **~ally** ᵊl_i **~s**
s
ge,netic 'code; ge,netic ,engi'neering
geneticist dʒə 'net ɪs ɪst dʒɪ-, -əs-, §-əst
‖ -'net̬- **~s** s
Geneva dʒə 'niːv ə dʒɪ-
Ge,neva con'vention
Genevan dʒə 'niːv ᵊn dʒɪ- **~s** z
Genevieve 'dʒen ə viːv -ɪ-, ˌ·'·‥ —*Fr*
Geneviève [ʒən vjɛːv]
Genghis 'dʒeŋ gɪs 'gen-, -gɪz, §-gəs, §-gəz
genial *'cheerful'* 'dʒiːn i_əl ‖ 'dʒiːn jəl **-ly** i
~ness nəs nɪs
genial *'of the chin'* dʒə 'niː əl dʒɪ-, -'naɪ_əl
geniality ˌdʒiːn i 'æl ət i -ɪt i ‖ -ət̬ i
-genic 'dʒen ɪk 'dʒiːn ɪk — **mutagenic**
ˌmjuːt ə 'dʒen ɪk ◂ ‖ ˌmjuːt̬-
genie, Genie 'dʒiːn i **genies, Genie's**
'dʒiːn iz
genii 'dʒiːn i aɪ
genip 'gɪn ep **~s** s
genital 'dʒen ɪt ᵊl -ət- ‖ -ət̬ ᵊl **-ly** ᵢi **~s** z
genitalia ˌdʒen ɪ 'teɪl i_ə -ə-
genitival ˌdʒen ə 'taɪv ᵊl ◂ -ɪ- **-ly** i **~s** z
genitive 'dʒen ət ɪv -ɪt- ‖ -ət̬- **~s** z
genitourinary ˌdʒen ɪ təʊ 'jʊər ɪn ər_i ˌ·ə-,
-'jɔːr-, -'·ən- ‖ ˌdʒen ə toʊ 'jʊr ə ner i
geni|us 'dʒiːn i_|əs **~i** aɪ **~uses** əs ɪz -əz
ˌgenius 'loci
genned-up ˌdʒend ʌp ◂
Gennesaret, Gennesareth gə 'nez ər ɪt gɪ-,
ge-, -ət; -ə ret ‖ -'nes-
Genoa 'dʒen əʊ ə dʒə 'nəʊ ə, dʒɪ-, dʒe- ‖ -oʊ ə
—*It* Genova ['dʒɛː no va]
genocidal ˌdʒen ə 'saɪd ᵊl ◂ -əʊ-
genocide 'dʒen ə saɪd -əʊ-
Genoese ˌdʒen əʊ 'iːz ◂ ‖ -oʊ- -'iːs ◂
genome 'dʒiːn əʊm ‖ -oʊm **~s** z
genomic dʒi 'nəʊm ɪk ‖ -'noʊm-
genotype 'dʒen ə taɪp 'dʒiːn- **~s** s
-genous *stress-imposing* dʒən əs —
androgenous æn 'drɒdʒ ən əs ‖ -'drɑːdʒ-
genre 'ʒɒn rə 'ʒɑːn-, 'ʒɒ̃-, 'dʒɒn- ‖ 'ʒɑːn- —*Fr*
[ʒɑ̃ːʁ]
gent, Gent dʒent **gents** dʒents
genteel dʒen 'tiːᵊl dʒən- **-ly** li **~ness** nəs nɪs
gentian 'dʒenᵗʃ ᵊn 'dʒenᵗʃ i ən **~s** z
gentile, G~ 'dʒent aɪᵊl **~s** z
gentility dʒen 'tɪl ət i -ɪt- ‖ -ət̬ i
gentle, G~ 'dʒent ᵊl ‖ 'dʒent̬ ᵊl **gentler**
'dʒent lə ‖ -lᵊr **gentlest** 'dʒent lɪst -ləst
gentlefolk 'dʒent ᵊl fəʊk ‖ 'dʒent̬ ᵊl foʊk **~s** s

gentle|man, G~ 'dʒent ᵊl |mən ‖ 'dʒenṭ-
~men mən men —*in rapid casual AmE also*
'dʒen əm ən
,gentleman 'farmer; ,gentleman's
a'greement; ,gentleman's 'gentleman
gentle|man-at-arms ,dʒent ᵊl |mən ət 'ɑːmz
‖ ,dʒenṭ ᵊl |mən əṭ 'ɑːrmz **~men-at-arms**
mən- men-
gentlemanly 'dʒent ᵊl mən li ‖ 'dʒenṭ-
gentleness 'dʒent ᵊl nəs -nɪs ‖ 'dʒenṭ-
gentle|woman 'dʒent ᵊl |,wʊm ən ‖ 'dʒenṭ-
~women ,wɪm ɪn -ən
gently 'dʒent li
Gentoo, g~ 'dʒent uː dʒen 'tuː **~s** z
gentrification ,dʒentr ɪf ɪ 'keɪʃ ᵊn ,-əf-, §-ə'-
~s z
gentri|fy 'dʒentr ɪ |faɪ -ə- **~fied** faɪd **~fier/s**
faɪ ə/z ‖ faɪ ᵊr/z **~fies** faɪz **~fying** faɪ ɪŋ
gentry, G~ 'dʒentr i
genuflect 'dʒen ju flekt -jə- ‖ -jə- **~ed** ɪd əd
~ing ɪŋ **~s** s
genuflection, genuflexion
,dʒen ju 'flek ʃᵊn -jə- ‖ -jə- **~s** z
genuine 'dʒen ju ɪn §,ən, △-aɪn **~ly** li **~ness**
nəs nɪs
genus 'dʒiːn əs 'dʒen- **genera** 'dʒen ər ə
-geny *stress-imposing* dʒən i — **phylogeny**
faɪ 'lɒdʒ ən i ‖ -'lɑːdʒ-
geo- *comb. form*
with stress-neutral suffix |dʒiː əʊ ‖ |dʒiː oʊ —
geothermal ,dʒiː əʊ 'θɜːm ᵊl ◄ ‖ -oʊ 'θɝːm-
with stress-imposing suffix dʒi 'ɒ+ ‖ dʒi 'ɑː+
— **geophagy** dʒi 'ɒf ədʒ i ‖ -'ɑːf-
geocentric ,dʒiː əʊ 'sentr ɪk ◄ -oʊ- **~ally** ᵊl i
GeoCities *tdmk* ,dʒiː əʊ 'sɪt iz ‖ -oʊ 'sɪṭ-
geode 'dʒiː əʊd ‖ -oʊd **~s** z
geodesic ,dʒiː əʊ 'diːs ɪk ◄ -'des-; dʒɪə 'diːs ɪk
‖ -ə 'des- -'diːs-
,geo,desic 'dome
geodesist dʒi 'ɒd əs ɪst -ɪs-, -əz-, -ɪz-, §-əst
‖ -'ɑːd- **~ists** ɪsts §əsts **~y** i
geodetic ,dʒiː əʊ 'det ɪk ◄ dʒɪə 'det-
‖ ,dʒiː ə 'det̬ ɪk ◄ **~ally** ᵊl i
Geoff dʒef **Geoff's** dʒefs
Geoffrey 'dʒef ri
Geoghegan *(i)* 'geɪg ən, *(ii)* gɪ 'heɪg ən
geographer dʒi 'ɒg rəf ə ‖ -'ɑːg rəf ᵊr **~s** z
geographic ,dʒiː ə 'græf ɪk dʒɪə 'græf- **~al** ᵊl
~ally ᵊl i
geograph|y dʒi 'ɒg rəf |i 'dʒɒg- ‖ -'ɑːg- **~ies**
iz
geologic ,dʒiː ə 'lɒdʒ ɪk ◄ dʒɪə 'lɒdʒ- ‖ -'lɑːdʒ-
~al ᵊl **~ally** ᵊl i
geologist dʒi 'ɒl ədʒ ɪst §-əst ‖ -'ɑːl- **~s** s
geolog|y dʒi 'ɒl ədʒ |i ‖ -'ɑːl- **~ies** iz
geomanc|y 'dʒiː ə mæn�percentᵗs| i **~er/s** ə/z ‖ ᵊr/z
geomatic ,dʒiː ə 'mæt ɪk ◄ -əʊ- ‖ -'mæt̬ ɪk **~s** s
geometer dʒi 'ɒm ɪt ə -ət- ‖ -'ɑːm əṭ ᵊr **~s** z
geometric ,dʒiː ə 'metr ɪk ◄ -əʊ-; dʒɪə 'metr-
~al ᵊl **~ally** ᵊl i
,geo,metric pro'gression
geometrician ,dʒiː ə me 'trɪʃ ᵊn -mə'-;
dʒi ,ɒm ə- ‖ dʒi ,ɑːm ə- **~s** z

geometr|y dʒi 'ɒm ətr |i 'dʒɒm-, -ɪtr- ‖ -'ɑːm-
~ies iz
geophysical ,dʒiː əʊ 'fɪz ɪk ᵊl ◄ ‖ ,-ə- **~ly** i
geophysicist ,dʒiː əʊ 'fɪz ɪs ɪst -əs ɪst, §-əst
‖ ,dʒiː ə- **~s** s
geophysics ,dʒiː əʊ 'fɪz ɪks ‖ -ə-
geopolitical ,dʒiː əʊ pə 'lɪt ɪk ᵊl ◄ -ə pə 'lɪt̬-
~ly i
geopolitics ,dʒiː əʊ 'pɒl ə tɪks -'ɪ- ‖ -ə 'pɑːl-
Geordie 'dʒɔːd i ‖ 'dʒɔːrd i **~s** z
George dʒɔːdʒ ‖ dʒɔːrdʒ **George's** 'dʒɔːdʒ ɪz
-əz ‖ 'dʒɔːrdʒ əz
,George 'Cross
Georges ʒɔːʒ dʒɔːdʒ ‖ ʒɔːrʒ dʒɔːrdʒ —*Fr*
[ʒɔʁʒ]
Georgetown 'dʒɔːdʒ taʊn ‖ 'dʒɔːrdʒ- —*in*
Guyana locally -tʌŋ
georgette, G~ ₍ᵢ₎dʒɔː 'dʒet ‖ ₍ᵢ₎dʒɔːr- **~s** s
Georgia 'dʒɔːdʒ ə 'dʒɔːdʒ i ə ‖ 'dʒɔːrdʒ ə
Georgian 'dʒɔːdʒ ən 'dʒɔːdʒ i ‿ən ‖ 'dʒɔːrdʒ ən
~s z
georgic 'dʒɔːdʒ ɪk ‖ 'dʒɔːrdʒ- **~s** s
Georgie 'dʒɔːdʒ i ‖ 'dʒɔːrdʒ i
Georgina dʒɔː 'dʒiːn ə ‖ dʒɔːr-
geostationary ,dʒiː əʊ 'steɪʃ ᵊn ər i ◄ -ᵊn ᵊr-
‖ -oʊ 'steɪʃ ə ner i
geosynchronous ,dʒiː əʊ 'sɪŋk rən əs ◄
‖ ,dʒiː oʊ-
Gephardt 'gep hɑːt ‖ -hɑːrt
Geraint 'ger aɪnt ∙ː ∙ —*Welsh* ['ge raɪnt]
Gerald 'dʒer əld
Geraldine 'dʒer əl diːn —*but* **-daɪn** *in*
Coleridge
Geraldo dʒə 'ræld əʊ ‖ hə 'rɑːld oʊ —*Sp*
[xe 'ral do]
Geraldton 'dʒer əld tən
geranium dʒə 'reɪn i‿əm dʒɪ- **~s** z
Gerard 'dʒer ɑːd -əd; dʒe 'rɑːd, dʒə-
‖ dʒə 'rɑːrd
Gerber *(i)* 'dʒɜːb ə ‖ 'dʒɜːːb ᵊr, *(ii)* 'gɜːb ə
‖ 'gɜːb ᵊr —*The tdmk for baby food is usually*
(ii).
gerbera 'dʒɜːb ər ə 'gɜːb- ‖ 'dʒɜːb- 'gɜːb- **~s** s
gerbil 'dʒɜːb ᵊl -ɪl ‖ 'dʒɜːːb- **~s** z
Gerda 'gɜːd ə ‖ 'gɜːd ə
Gere gɪə ‖ gɪᵊr
Gerhardi, Gerhardie dʒə 'hɑːd i
‖ dʒɝ 'hɑːrd i
geriatric ,dʒer i 'ætr ɪk ◄ ‖ ,dʒɪr- **~s** s
geriatrician ,dʒer i ə 'trɪʃ ᵊn ‖ ,dʒɪr- **~s** z
Gericault, Géricault 'ʒer ɪ kəʊ -ə-, ∙ ∙ː
‖ ,ʒeɪ rɪ 'koʊ —*Fr* [ʒe ʁi ko]
Geritol *tdmk* 'dʒer ɪ tɒl -ə- ‖ -tɑːl
germ dʒɜːm ‖ dʒɝːm **germs** dʒɜːmz ‖ dʒɝːmz
'germ cell; ,germ 'warfare
Germaine dʒɜː 'meɪn ₍ᵢ₎dʒɜː- ‖ dʒᵊr-
German, g~ 'dʒɜːm ən ‖ 'dʒɝːm- **~s** z
,German 'measles; ,German 'shepherd
germander dʒɜː 'mænd ə dʒə- ‖ dʒᵊr 'mænd ᵊr **~s** z
germane dʒɜː 'meɪn ∙ ∙ ‖ dʒᵊr- **~ly** li **~ness**
nəs nɪs
Germanic, g~ dʒɜː 'mæn ɪk dʒə- ‖ dʒᵊr-

Germanicus dʒɜː 'mæn ɪk əs dʒə- ‖ dʒɚr-
germanium dʒɜː 'meɪn i‿əm dʒə- ‖ dʒɚr-
German|y 'dʒɜːm ən |i ‖ 'dʒɝːm- **~ies, ~ys, ~y's** iz
germicidal ‚dʒɜːm ɪ 'saɪd ᵊl ◂ -ə- ‖ ‚dʒɝːm-
germicide 'dʒɜːm ɪ saɪd -ə- ‖ 'dʒɝːm- **~s** z
germinal 'dʒɜːm ɪn ᵊl -ən- ‖ 'dʒɝːm-
germi|nate 'dʒɜːm ɪ |neɪt -ə- ‖ 'dʒɝːm-
  ~nated neɪt ɪd -əd ‖ neɪt̬ əd **~nates** neɪts
  ~nating neɪt ɪŋ ‖ neɪt̬ ɪŋ
germination ‚dʒɜːm ɪ 'neɪʃ ᵊn -ə- ‖ ‚dʒɝːm- **~s** z
Germiston 'dʒɜːm ɪst ən §-əst- ‖ 'dʒɝːm-
Germolene tdmk 'dʒɜːm ə liːn ‖ 'dʒɝːm-
Gerona dʒə 'rəʊn ə ‖ -'roʊn- —Sp [xe 'ro na], Catalan Girona [ʒi 'ro nə]
Geronimo dʒə 'rɒn ɪ məʊ dʒɪ-, dʒe-, -ə- ‖ -'rɑːn ə moʊ
Gerontius gə 'rɒnt i‿əs dʒɪ-, dʒə-, -'rɒnʧ- ‖ -'rɑːnt-
gerontocrac|y ‚dʒer ɒn 'tɒk rəs |i ‚-ən- ‖ -ən 'tɑːk- **~ies** iz
gerontocratic dʒə ‚rɒnt ə 'kræt ɪk ◂ ‚dʒer ɒnt-, ‚-ənt- ‖ dʒə ‚rɑːnt ə 'kræt̬ ɪk ◂
gerontological dʒə ‚rɒnt ə 'lɒdʒ ɪk ᵊl ◂ ‚dʒer ɒnt-, ‚-ənt- ‖ dʒə ‚rɑːnt ə 'lɑːdʒ-
gerontologist ‚dʒer ɒn 'tɒl ədʒ ɪst ‚-ən-, §-əst ‖ -ən 'tɑːl- **~s** s
gerontology ‚dʒer ɒn 'tɒl ədʒ i ‚-ən- ‖ -ən 'tɑːl-
-gerous stress-imposing dʒər əs —
  dentigerous den 'tɪdʒ ər əs
Gerrard 'dʒer ɑːd -əd; dʒe 'rɑːd, dʒə- ‖ dʒə 'rɑːrd
Gerry 'dʒer i
gerrymander 'dʒer i mænd ə ‚·'·· ‖ -ᵊr **~ed** d
  gerrymandering 'dʒer i mænd ᵊr ɪŋ ‚·'··· **~s** z
Gershwin 'gɜːʃ wɪn §-wən ‖ 'gɝːʃ-
Gertie 'gɜːt i ‖ 'gɝːt̬ i
Gertrude 'gɜːtr uːd ‖ 'gɝːtr- -ʊd
Gerty 'gɜːt i ‖ 'gɝːt̬ i
gerund 'dʒer ənd -ʌnd **~s** z
gerundival ‚dʒer ən 'daɪv ᵊl ◂ -ʌn-
gerundive dʒə 'rʌnd ɪv dʒɪ-, dʒe- **~s** z
Gervais dʒə 'veɪs ‖ dʒɚr-
Gervaise, Gervase 'dʒɜːv eɪz -ɪz, -əs; dʒɜː 'veɪz, -'veɪs ‖ 'dʒɝːv-
Geryon 'ger i‿ən
gesellschaft gə 'zel ʃɑːft -ʃæft —Ger G~ [gə 'zɛl ʃaft]
gesso 'dʒes əʊ ‖ -oʊ
Gest gest
gestalt gə 'ʃtælt -'ʃtɑːlt; 'dʒest ælt ‖ gə 'ʃtɑːlt —Ger G~ [gə 'ʃtalt] **~en** ən **~s** s
gestapo, G~ ge 'stɑːp əʊ ‖ gə 'stɑːp oʊ —Ger G~ [ge 'sta: po]
gest|ate dʒe 'st|eɪt 'dʒest |eɪt ‖ 'dʒest |eɪt
  ~ated eɪt ɪd -əd ‖ eɪt̬ əd **~ates** eɪts **~ating** eɪt ɪŋ ‖ eɪt̬ ɪŋ
gestation dʒe 'steɪʃ ᵊn **~s** z
  ge'station ‚period
gestatorial ‚dʒest ə 'tɔːr i‿əl ◂ ‖ -'toʊr-

gestatory dʒe 'steɪt ər i 'dʒest ə ‚tər i ‖ 'dʒest ə tɔːr i -tour i
Gestetner tdmk ge 'stet nə gɪ-, gə- ‖ -nᵊr
gesticu|late dʒe 'stɪk jʊ |leɪt -jə- ‖ -jə- **~lated** leɪt ɪd -əd ‖ leɪt̬ əd **~lates** leɪts **~lating** leɪt ɪŋ ‖ leɪt̬ ɪŋ
gesticulation dʒe ‚stɪk jʊ 'leɪʃ ᵊn -jə- ‖ -jə- **~s** z
gestural 'dʒes tʃər əl
ges|ture 'dʒes |tʃə →'dʒeʃ- ‖ -|tʃᵊr **~tured** tʃəd ‖ tʃᵊrd **~tures** tʃəz ‖ tʃᵊrz **~turing** tʃər ɪŋ
gesundheit gə 'zʊnd haɪt —Ger G~ [gə 'zʊnt haɪt]
get get **gets** gets **getting** 'get ɪŋ ‖ 'get̬ ɪŋ **got** gɒt ‖ gɑːt **gotten** 'gɒt ᵊn ‖ 'gɑːt ᵊn
get-at-able get 'æt əb ᵊl ‖ get̬ 'æt̬-
getaway 'get ə ‚weɪ ‖ 'get̬- **~s** z
get-go 'get gəʊ ‖ -goʊ
Gethin 'geθ ɪn
Gething 'geθ ɪŋ
Gethsemane geθ 'sem ən i
getout 'get aʊt ‖ 'get̬- **~s** s
get-rich-quick ‚get rɪtʃ 'kwɪk ◂
get-together 'get tə ‚geð ə ‖ -ᵊr **~s** z
Getty 'get i ‖ 'get̬ i
Gettysburg 'get ɪz bɜːg ‖ 'get̬ ɪz bɝːg
  ‚Gettysburg Ad'dress
getup 'get ʌp ‖ 'get̬- **~s** s
get-up-and-go ‚get ʌp ən 'gəʊ →-ᵊŋ'·, →-m'· ‖ ‚get̬ ʌp ən 'goʊ
geum 'dʒiː‿əm **~s** z
gewgaw 'gjuː gɔː 'guː- ‖ -gɑː **~s** z
Gewurztraminer, Gewürztraminer gə 'vʊəts trə ‚miːn ə ‖ -'vɝːts trə ‚miːn ᵊr —Ger [gə 'vʏʁts tʁa ‚miːn ɐ]
geyser 'giːz ə 'gaɪz ə ‖ 'gaɪz ᵊr (*) —In BrE, 'gaɪz ə (if at all) particularly for the meaning 'hot spring'; the water heater is always 'giːz- **~s** z
Ghan in Australia gæn
Ghana 'gɑːn ə
Ghanaian gɑː 'neɪ ən gə- ‖ -'naɪ- **~s** z
gharry 'gær i ‖ 'ger-
ghast|ly 'gɑːst |li §'gæst- ‖ 'gæst- **~lier** li‿ə ‖ li‿ᵊr **~liest** li‿ɪst əst **~liness** li nəs -nɪs
ghat, ghaut gɑːt gɔːt, gʌt ‖ gɔːt **ghats, Ghats, ghauts** gɑːts gɔːts, gʌts ‖ gɔːts
ghee giː
Ghent gent —Flemish Gent [ɣɛnt]
gherkin 'gɜːk ɪn §-ən ‖ 'gɝːk- **~s** z
ghetto 'get əʊ ‖ 'get̬ oʊ **~s** z
  'ghetto ‚blaster
ghettois|e, ghettoiz|e 'get əʊ aɪz ‖ 'get̬ oʊ- **~ed** d **~es** ɪz əz **~ing** ɪŋ
ghi giː
Ghia 'giː‿ə —It ['giː a]
Ghibelline 'gɪb ə liːn -laɪn ‖ -ᵊl ən
ghillie 'gɪl i **~s** z
Ghosh gəʊʃ ‖ goʊʃ

ghost gəʊst ‖ goʊst **ghosted** 'gəʊst ɪd -əd
‖ 'goʊst əd **ghosting** 'gəʊst ɪŋ ‖ 'goʊst ɪŋ
ghosts gəʊsts ‖ goʊsts
  '**ghost town**
Ghostbusters 'gəʊst ˌbʌst əz ‖ 'goʊst ˌbʌst ³rz
ghost|ly 'gəʊst |li ‖ 'goʊst |li **~lier** li ə ‖ li ³r
  ~liest li ɪst əst **~liness** li nəs nɪs
ghost|write 'gəʊst |raɪt ‖ 'goʊst- **~writer/s**
  ˌraɪt ə/z ‖ ˌraɪt̮ ³r/z **~writes** raɪts **~writing**
  ˌraɪt ɪŋ ‖ ˌraɪt̮ ɪŋ
ghoul guːl **ghouls** guːlz
ghoulish 'guːl ɪʃ **~ly** li **~ness** nəs nɪs
GHQ ˌdʒiː eɪtʃ 'kjuː §-heɪtʃ-
ghyll gɪl **ghylls** gɪlz
GI ˌdʒiː 'aɪ ◂ **~s, ~'s** z
Gianni dʒi 'ɑːn i 'dʒɑːn i —*It* ['dʒan ni]
giant 'dʒaɪ ənt **~s, ~'s** s
  ˌGiant's 'Causeway; 'giant ˌkiller; ˌgiant
  'panda
giantess 'dʒaɪ ənt es -ɪs, -əs; ˌdʒaɪ ən 'tes
  ‖ 'dʒaɪ ənt̮ əs **~es** ɪz əz
giantism 'dʒaɪ ənt ˌɪz əm
giant-size 'dʒaɪ ənt saɪz
giaour, G~ 'dʒaʊ ə ‖ 'dʒaʊ ³r **giaours, G~**
  'dʒaʊ əz ‖ 'dʒaʊ ³rz
giardiasis ˌdʒiː ɑː 'daɪ əs ɪs §-əs ‖ -ɑːr-
Gib '*Gibraltar*' dʒɪb
Gibb gɪb
gibber '*speak incoherently*' 'dʒɪb ə ‖ -³r **~ed** d
  gibbering 'dʒɪb ər ɪŋ **~s** z
Gibberd 'gɪb əd ‖ -³rd
gibberelic ˌdʒɪb ə 'rel ɪk ◂

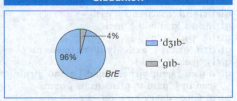

GIBBERISH

96%   —4%
  ■ 'dʒɪb-
  ■ 'gɪb-
BrE

gibberish 'dʒɪb ər ɪʃ 'gɪb- — *Preference poll,*
  BrE: 'dʒɪb- 96%, 'gɪb- 4%.
Gibbes gɪbz
gibbet 'dʒɪb ɪt -ət **~s** s
gibbon, G~ 'gɪb ən **~s** z
Gibbons 'gɪb ənz
gibbosit|y gɪ 'bɒs ət |i -ɪt- ‖ -'bɑːs ət̮ |i **~ies**
  iz
gibbous 'gɪb əs **~ly** li **~ness** nəs nɪs
Gibbs gɪbz
gibe dʒaɪb (= *jibe*) **gibed** dʒaɪbd **gibes** dʒaɪbz
  gibing/ly 'dʒaɪb ɪŋ /li
Gibeon 'gɪb i ən
Gibeonite 'gɪb i ə naɪt **~s** s
giblets 'dʒɪb ləts -lɪts
Gibraltar dʒɪ 'brɔːlt ə dʒə-, -'brɒlt- ‖ -³r
  -'brɑːlt-
Gibraltarian ˌdʒɪb rɔːl 'teər i ən ◂ ˌrɒl-;
  dʒɪ ˌbrɔːl-, dʒə-, -ˌbrɒl- ‖ -'ter-, ˌrɑːl-, -'tær- **~s**
  z
Gibran ʒɪ 'brɑːn

Gibson 'gɪb sᵊn
gid gɪd
Giddens 'gɪd ᵊnz
Gidding 'gɪd ɪŋ
gidd|y, Giddy 'gɪd |i **~ied** id **~ier** i ə ‖ i ³r
  ~ies iz **~iest** i ɪst i əst **~ily** ɪ li əl i **~iness**
  i nəs i nɪs **~ying** i ɪŋ
Gide ʒiːd —*Fr* [ʒid]
Gidea 'gɪd i ə
Gideon 'gɪd i ən **~s** z
Gielgud 'giː³l gʊd
Gieve giːv
GIF, gif gɪf dʒɪf **GIFs, gifs** gɪfs dʒɪfs
Giffard, Gifford (i) 'dʒɪf əd ‖ -³rd, (ii) 'gɪf-
gift gɪft **gifted** 'gɪft ɪd -əd **gifting** 'gɪft ɪŋ
  gifts gɪfts
  'gift horse; 'gift ˌtoken
gifted 'gɪft ɪd -əd **~ly** li **~ness** nəs nɪs
giftwrap 'gɪft ræp **~ped** t **~ping** ɪŋ **~s** s
gig gɪg **gigs** gɪgz

GIGA-

84%   16%
  ■ 'gɪg-
  ■ dʒ-, -aɪ-, -iː-
BrE

giga- ¦gɪg ə — **gigabyte** 'gɪg ə baɪt
  — *Preference poll, BrE:* 'gɪg- 84%, *others*
  (dʒ-, -aɪ-, -iː-) *16%.*
gigabit 'gɪg ə bɪt **~s** s
gigabyte 'gɪg ə baɪt **~s** s
gigahertz 'gɪg ə hɜːts ‖ -hɝːts
gigantic dʒaɪ 'gænt ɪk ‖ -'gænt̮ ɪk **~ally** ³l_i
giggl|e 'gɪg ³l **~ed** d **~er/s** ə/z ‖ ³r/z **~es** z
  ~ing/ly ˌɪŋ /li
Giggleswick 'gɪg ³lz wɪk
giggl|y 'gɪg ³l_|i **~ier** i ə ‖ i ³r **~iest** i ɪst i əst
  ~iness i nəs i nɪs
Giggs gɪgz
Gigha 'giː ə
Gigi 'ʒiː ʒiː
Gigli 'dʒiːl jiː -iː —*It* ['dʒiʎ ʎiy]
gigolo 'dʒɪg ə ləʊ 'ʒɪg- ‖ -loʊ **~s** z
gigot 'dʒɪg ət 'ʒɪg-, -əʊ ‖ ʒiː 'goʊ —*Fr* [ʒi go]
gigue ʒiːg —*Fr* [ʒig] **gigues** ʒiːgz
Gijón hi 'hɒn ‖ -'hoʊn —*Sp* [xi 'xon]
Gikuyu gɪ 'kuː juː
Gil gɪl
Gila 'hiːl ə —*but in BrE a spelling*
  pronunciation 'giːl ə *is also heard*
Gilbert, g~ 'gɪlb ət ‖ -³rt **~s, ~'s** s
Gilbertian gɪl 'bɜːt i ən -'bɜːʃ ³n ‖ -'bɝːt̮- **~s** z
Gilbey 'gɪlb i
Gilchrist 'gɪl krɪst
gild gɪld (= *guild*) **gilded** 'gɪld ɪd -əd **gilding**
  'gɪld ɪŋ **gilds** gɪldz **gilt** gɪlt
Gildersleeve 'gɪld ə sliːv ‖ -³r-
Gilead 'gɪl i æd ‖ -əd
Giles dʒaɪ³lz

G

gilet 'ʒiːl eɪ ‖ ʒə 'leɪ ~s z —Fr [ʒi le]
gilgai 'gɪlg aɪ
Gilgamesh 'gɪlg ə meʃ
Gilhooley gɪl 'huːl i
Gilkes, Gilks dʒɪlks
gill 'organ of breathing', 'wattle', 'ravine', 'stream' gɪl **gills** gɪlz
gill 'liquid measure' dʒɪl **gills** dʒɪlz
Gill name (i) gɪl, (ii) dʒɪl
Gillespie gɪ 'lesp i gə-
Gillette dʒɪ 'let dʒə-
Gilliam 'gɪl i‿əm
Gillian 'dʒɪl i‿ən
Gilliat, Gilliatt 'gɪl i‿ət
Gillick 'gɪl ɪk
gillie, G~ 'gɪl i ~s z
Gillies 'gɪl iz
gilliflower 'dʒɪl i ˌflaʊ‿ə ‖ -ˌflaʊˌə'r ~s z
Gilligan 'gɪl ɪg ən
Gillingham (i) 'dʒɪl ɪŋ əm, (ii) 'gɪl- —The place in Kent is (i); those in Dorset and Norfolk are (ii). The family name may be either.
Gillow 'gɪl əʊ ‖ -oʊ
Gillray 'gɪl reɪ
gilly 'gɪl i
gillyflower 'dʒɪl i ˌflaʊ‿ə ‖ -ˌflaʊˌə'r ~s z
Gilman 'gɪl mən
Gilmore, Gilmour 'gɪl mɔː -mə ‖ -mɔːr -moʊr
Gilpin 'gɪlp ɪn §-ən
Gilroy 'gɪl rɔɪ
gilt gɪlt (= guilt) **gilts** gɪlts
gilt-edged ˌgɪlt 'edʒd ◄
Gilwell 'gɪl wəl -wel
gimbals 'dʒɪm bᵊlz 'gɪm-
gimcrack 'dʒɪm kræk
gimlet 'gɪm lət -lɪt ~s s
gimlet-eyed ˌgɪm lət 'aɪd ◄ -lɪt- ‖ -ləṭ-
gimme 'gɪm i
gimmick 'gɪm ɪk ~s s
gimmickry 'gɪm ɪk ri
gimmicky 'gɪm ɪk i
gimp gɪmp **gimped** gɪmpt **gimping** 'gɪmp ɪŋ **gimps** gɪmps
gimpy 'gɪmp i
Gimson (i) 'gɪmᵖs ᵊn, (ii) 'dʒɪmᵖs- —The late Prof. A.C.Gimson, phonetician, was (i).
gin dʒɪn **ginned** dʒɪnd **ginning** 'dʒɪn ɪŋ **gins** dʒɪnz
ˌgin 'rummy; ˌgin 'sling; 'gin trap
Gina 'dʒiːn ə
Gingell 'gɪndʒ ᵊl
ginger, G~ 'dʒɪndʒ ə ‖ -ᵊr ~ed d **gingering** 'dʒɪndʒ ər ɪŋ ~s z
ˌginger 'ale; ˌginger 'beer; 'ginger group; 'ginger nut
gingerbread 'dʒɪndʒ ə bred ‖ -ᵊr-
ginger|ly 'dʒɪndʒ ə |li ‖ -ᵊr- ~liness li nəs -nɪs
gingersnap 'dʒɪndʒ ə snæp ‖ -ᵊr- ~s s
gingery 'dʒɪndʒ ər i
gingham 'gɪŋ əm ~s z
gingival dʒɪn 'dʒaɪv ᵊl 'dʒɪndʒ ɪv-
gingivitis ˌdʒɪndʒ ɪ 'vaɪt ɪs -ə- ‖ -'vaɪṭ əs

Gingold 'gɪŋ gəʊld →-gɒʊld ‖ -goʊld
Gingrich 'gɪŋ grɪtʃ
ginkgo 'gɪŋk əʊ -gəʊ ‖ -oʊ ~es z
Ginn gɪn
ginner|y 'dʒɪn ər| i ~ies iz
Ginnie, Ginny 'dʒɪn i
Gino 'dʒiːn əʊ ‖ -oʊ
ginormous dʒaɪ 'nɔːm əs ‖ -'nɔːrm əs ~ly li
Ginsberg, Ginsburg 'gɪnz bɜːg ‖ -bɜːɡ
ginseng 'dʒɪn seŋ
Gioconda ˌdʒiːˌə 'kɒnd ə ‖ -'kɑːnd- —It [dʒo 'kon da]
Giotto 'dʒɒt əʊ 'ʒɒt-; dʒi 'ɒt- ‖ 'dʒɑːṭ oʊ 'dʒɔːṭ- —It ['dʒɔt to]
Giovanni dʒəʊ 'vɑːn i ˌdʒiːˌə'--, -'væn- ‖ dʒoʊ- dʒə- —It [dʒo 'van ni]
gip 'cheat' dʒɪp **gipped** dʒɪpt **gipping** 'dʒɪp ɪŋ **gips** dʒɪps
gippo 'dʒɪp əʊ ‖ -oʊ ~s z
Gippsland 'gɪps lænd -lənd
gippy 'dʒɪp i
ˌgippy 'tummy
gips|y, Gips|y 'dʒɪps |i ~ies, ~y's iz
giraffe dʒə 'rɑːf dʒɪ-, §-'ræf ‖ -'ræf ~s s
Giraldus dʒɪ 'ræld əs dʒə-
Giˌraldus Cam'brensis kæm 'bren's ɪs §-əs
gird gɜːd ‖ gɜːd **girded** 'gɜːd ɪd -əd ‖ 'gɜːd əd
girding 'gɜːd ɪŋ ‖ 'gɜːd ɪŋ **girds** gɜːdz ‖ gɜːdz **girt** gɜːt ‖ gɜːt
girder 'gɜːd ə ‖ 'gɜːd ᵊr ~s z
girdl|e 'gɜːd ᵊl ‖ 'gɜːd ᵊl ~ed d ~es z ~ing ɪŋ
'girdle cake
girl gɜːl ‖ gɜːl **girls** gɜːlz ‖ gɜːlz
ˌgirl 'Friday; ˌgirl 'guide; ˌgirl 'scout ‖ '· ·
girlfriend 'gɜːl frend ‖ 'gɜːl- ~s z
girlhood 'gɜːl hʊd ‖ 'gɜːl-
girlie 'gɜːl i ‖ 'gɜːl i
girlish 'gɜːl ɪʃ ‖ 'gɜːl- ~ly li ~ness nəs nɪs
girly 'gɜːl i ‖ 'gɜːl i
girn gɜːn ‖ gɜːn **girned** gɜːnd ‖ gɜːnd **girning** 'gɜːn ɪŋ ‖ 'gɜːn ɪŋ **girns** gɜːnz ‖ gɜːnz
giro, Giro 'dʒaɪᵊr əʊ ‖ -oʊ ~s z
Girobank tdmk 'dʒaɪᵊr əʊ bæŋk ‖ -oʊ-
girt gɜːt ‖ gɜːt
girth gɜːθ ‖ gɜːθ **girthed** gɜːθt ‖ gɜːθt
girthing 'gɜːθ ɪŋ ‖ 'gɜːθ ɪŋ **girths** gɜːθs ‖ gɜːθs
Girton 'gɜːt ᵊn ‖ 'gɜːt ᵊn
Girtonian gɜː 'təʊn i‿ən ‖ gᵊr- ~s z
Girvan 'gɜːv ᵊn ‖ 'gɜːv ᵊn
Gisborne, Gisbourne 'gɪz bən -bɔːn ‖ -bɔːrn -boʊrn
Giscard d'Estaing ˌʒiːsk ɑː de 'stæ -'stæŋ ‖ -ɑːr- —Fr [ʒis kaʁ dɛs tæ̃]
Giselle ʒɪ 'zel dʒɪ-, dʒə- —Fr [ʒi zɛl]
Gish gɪʃ
gismo 'gɪz məʊ ‖ -moʊ ~s z
gissa nonstd 'give us a' 'gɪs ə
Gissing 'gɪs ɪŋ
gist dʒɪst
git gɪt **gits** gɪts
Gitane tdmk ʒɪ 'tɑːn ‖ -'tæn ~s z —Fr [ʒi tan]
gite, gîte ʒiːt —Fr [ʒit] **gites, gîtes** ʒiːts

Gittins 'gɪt ɪnz §-ᵊnz ‖ 'gɪt ᵊnz
Giuliani ˌdʒuːl i 'ɑːn i
Giulietta ˌdʒuːl i 'et ə ‖ -'eţ ə —*It*
[dʒu 'ljet ta]
Giuseppe dʒu 'sep i —*It* [dʒu 'zεp pe]
give gɪv **gave** geɪv **given** 'gɪv ᵊn **gives** gɪvz
giving 'gɪv ɪŋ —*The phrase* give me *also has
a non-standard casual form* 'gɪm i, *sometimes
written* gimme; *similarly* give us a, *see* gissa
give-and-take ˌgɪv ᵊn 'teɪk
giveaway 'gɪv ə ˌweɪ ~s z
giveback 'gɪv bæk ~s s
given 'gɪv ᵊn
'given name
Givenchy *tdmk* ʒiː 'vɒnˈʃ i ‖ 'ʒiːv ɑːn ʃiː ˌ·'·ˈ·
giver 'gɪv ə ‖ -ᵊr ~s z
Giza 'giːz ə
gizmo 'gɪz məʊ ‖ -moʊ ~s z
gizzard 'gɪz əd ‖ -ᵊrd ~s z
glabell|a glə 'bel |ə ~ae iː
glabrous 'gleɪb rəs
glace, glacé 'glæs eɪ 'glɑːs-, -i ‖ glæ 'seɪ ~ed
d ~ing ɪŋ ~s z
glacial 'gleɪʃ ᵊl 'gleɪʃ i ᵊl, 'gleɪs i ᵊl ~ly i
glaci|ate 'gleɪs i |eɪt 'gleɪʃ- ‖ 'gleɪʃ i |eɪt
~ated eɪt ɪd -əd ‖ eɪţ əd ~ates eɪts ~ating
eɪt ɪŋ ‖ eɪţ ɪŋ
glaciation ˌgleɪs i 'eɪʃ ᵊn ˌgleɪʃ- ‖ ˌgleɪʃ- ~s z
glacier 'glæs i ə 'gleɪs- ‖ 'gleɪʃ ᵊr (*) ~s z
glaciology ˌgleɪs i 'ɒl ədʒ i ‖ ˌgleɪʃ i 'ɑːl-
glacis 'glæs i -ɪs ˌ§-əs ‖ glæ 'siː ~ *pl* z
glad glæd **gladder** 'glæd ə ‖ -ᵊr **gladdest**
'glæd ɪst -əst **glads** glædz
ˌglad 'eye, ˈ· ·; ˌglad 'hand, ˈ· ·; 'glad rags
gladden 'glæd ᵊn ~ed d ~ing ˏɪŋ ~s z
glade gleɪd **glades** gleɪdz
glad-hand ˌglæd 'hænd ˈ· · ~ed ɪd əd ~er/s
ə/z ‖ ᵊr/z ~ing ɪŋ ~s z
gladiator 'glæd i eɪt ə ‖ -eɪţ ᵊr ~s z
gladiatorial ˌglæd i ə 'tɔːr i ᵊl ◂ ‖ -'toʊr-
gladiol|us ˌglæd i 'əʊl |əs ‖ -'oʊl- ~i aɪ ~uses
əs ɪz -əz
glad|ly 'glæd |li ~ness nəs nɪs
gladsome 'glæd səm ~ly li ~ness nəs nɪs
Gladstone 'glæd stən ‖ -stoʊn -stən
ˌGladstone 'bag ‖ ˈ· ·
Gladwin 'glæd wɪn §-wən
Gladys 'glæd ɪs §-əs
Glagolitic, g~ ˌglæg əʊ 'lɪt ɪk ◂ ‖ -ə 'lɪţ ɪk ◂
glair gleə ‖ gleᵊr glæᵊr
glair|y 'gleər |i ‖ 'gler |i 'glær- ~iness i nəs
i nɪs
Glaisher 'gleɪʃ ə ‖ -ᵊr
Glaister 'gleɪst ə ‖ -ᵊr
glam, Glam glæm
Glamis 'glɑːmz (*!*)
glamor 'glæm ə ‖ -ᵊr
Glamorgan glə 'mɔːg ən ‖ -'mɔːrg-
glamoris... —*see* **glamoriz...**
glamorization ˌglæm ər aɪ 'zeɪʃ ᵊn -ər ɪ-
‖ -ər ə-
glamoriz|e 'glæm ə raɪz ~ed d ~es ɪz əz ~ing
ɪŋ

glamorous 'glæm ər əs ~ly li ~ness nəs nɪs
glamour 'glæm ə ‖ -ᵊr
glance glɑːnˈs §glænˈs ‖ glænˈs **glanced**
glɑːnˈst §glænˈst ‖ glænˈst **glances** 'glɑːnˈs ɪz
§'glænˈs-, -əz ‖ 'glænˈs əz **glancing/ly**
'glɑːnˈs ɪŋ/ li §'glænˈs- ‖ 'glænˈs-
gland glænd **glands** glændz
glanders 'glænd əz 'glɑːnd- ‖ -ᵊrz
glandular 'glænd jʊl ə 'glændʒ əl ə
‖ 'glændʒ əl ᵊr
ˌglandular 'fever
glans glænz **glandes** 'glænd iːz
Glanvill, Glanville 'glæn vɪl -vᵊl
Glanyrafon, Glan-yr-Afon ˌglæn ər 'æv ᵊn
—*Welsh* [glan ər 'a von]
Glaramara ˌglær ə 'mɑːr ə ‖ ˌgler-
glare gleə ‖ gleᵊr glæᵊr **glared** gleəd ‖ gleᵊrd
glæᵊrd **glares** gleəz ‖ gleᵊrz glæᵊrz
glaring/ly 'gleər ɪŋ /li ‖ 'gleᵊr ɪŋ /li 'glæᵊr-
Glaser 'gleɪz ə ‖ -ᵊr

GLASGOW

BrE

Glasgow 'glɑːz gəʊ 'glæz-, 'glɑːs-, 'glæs-;
'glɑːsk əʊ, 'glæsk- ‖ 'glæs goʊ 'glæz-
—— *Preference poll, BrE:* z *forms* 85%, s *forms*
15%.
Glaslyn 'glæs lɪn
glasnost 'glæs nɒst 'glɑːz- ‖ 'glɑːs noʊst
—*Russ* ['głas nəsʲtʲ]
glass, Glass glɑːs §glæs ‖ glæs **glassed** glɑːst
§glæst ‖ glæst **glasses** 'glɑːs ɪz §'glæs-, -əz
‖ 'glæs əz
ˌglass 'eye, ˌglass 'fibre ◂
glassblower 'glɑːs ˌbləʊ ə §'glæs-
‖ 'glæs ˌbloʊ ᵊr ~s z
glasscutter 'glɑːs ˌkʌt ə §'glæs- ‖ 'glæs ˌkʌţ ᵊr
~s z
glassed-in ˌglɑːst 'ɪn ◂ §ˌglæst- ‖ ˌglæst-
glassful 'glɑːs fʊl §'glæs- ‖ 'glæs- ~s z
glass|house 'glɑːs |haʊs §'glæs- ‖ 'glæs-
~houses haʊz ɪz -əz
glassine 'glɑːs iːn §'glæs- ‖ glæ 'siːn
glasspaper 'glɑːs ˌpeɪp ə §'glæs-
‖ 'glæs ˌpeɪp ᵊr
glassware 'glɑːs weə §'glæs- ‖ 'glæs wer -wær
glassworks 'glɑːs wɜːks §'glæs- ‖ 'glæs wɜːks
glasswort 'glɑːs wɜːt §'glæs-, §-wɔːt
‖ 'glæs wɜːt -wɔːrt ~s s
glass|y 'glɑːs |i §'glæs- ‖ 'glæs |i ~ier i ə ‖ i ᵊr
~iest i ɪst i əst ~ily ɪ li əl i ~iness i nəs i nɪs
glassy-eyed ˌglɑːs i 'aɪd ◂ §ˌglæs- ‖ ˌglæs-
Glastonbury 'glæst ən bər i 'glɑːst-, →ˈ·əm-,
§-ˌber i ‖ -ˌber i
Glaswegian glɑːz 'wiːdʒ ᵊn glæz-, glɑːs-,
glæs-, ˌ·- ‖ glæs- ~s z

Glauber 'glaʊb ə 'glɔːb ə, 'glɔːb ə ‖ -ᵊr ~'s z
glaucoma glɔː 'kəʊm ə glaʊ- ‖ glaʊ 'koʊm ə
glɔː-, glɑː-
glaucomatous glɔː 'kəʊm ət əs glaʊ-, -'kɒm-
‖ glaʊ 'koʊm əʈ əs glɔː-, glɑː-, -'kɑːm-
glaucous 'glɔːk əs ‖ 'glɑːk-
Glaxo tdmk 'glæks əʊ ‖ -oʊ
GlaxoSmithKline tdmk
ˌglæks əʊ ˌsmɪθ 'klaɪn ‖ -oʊ-
glaze gleɪz **glazed** gleɪzd **glazes** 'gleɪz ɪz -əz
glazing 'gleɪz ɪŋ
Glazebrook 'gleɪz brʊk
glazier, G~ 'gleɪz i‿ə 'gleɪʒ ə, 'gleɪʒ i‿ə
‖ 'gleɪʒ ᵊr ~s z
Glazunof, Glazunov 'glæz u nɒf ‖ -ə noʊf
-ə nɑːf, -ə nɔːf —Russian [ɡɫə zu 'nɔf]
GLC ˌdʒiː el 'siː
gleam gliːm **gleamed** gliːmd **gleaming**
'gliːm ɪŋ **gleams** gliːmz
glean gliːn **gleaned** gliːnd **gleaner/s**
'gliːn ə/z ‖ -ᵊr/z **gleaning/s** 'gliːn ɪŋ/z
gleans gliːnz
Gleason 'gliːs ᵊn
Gleave gliːv
glebe gliːb **glebes** gliːbz
glee gliː
glee club
gleeful 'gliː fᵊl -fʊl ~**ly** i ~**ness** nəs nɪs
gleet gliːt
glen, Glen glen **glens, Glen's** glenz
Glencoe ˌ₍ˌ₎glen 'kəʊ →₍ˌ₎gleŋ- ‖ -'koʊ
Glenda 'glend ə
Glendale 'glen deɪᵊl
Glendaruel ˌglen də 'ruː əl
Glendenning glen 'den ɪŋ
Glendinning glen 'dɪn ɪŋ
Glendower glen 'daʊ ə ‖ -'daʊ ᵊr
Gleneagles glen 'iːg ᵊlz
Glenelg glen 'elg
Glenfiddich glen 'fɪd ɪk -ɪx
glengarr|y, G~ glen 'gær |i →gleŋ- ‖ -'ger-,
'·· ~**ies** iz
Glengormley glen 'gɔːm li →gleŋ- ‖ -'gɔːrm-
Glenice 'glen ɪs §-əs
Glenlivet glen 'lɪv ɪt -ət
Glenmorangie ˌglen mə 'rændʒ i →ˌglem-;
ˌ·'mɒr əndʒ i
Glenn glen
Glenrothes glen 'rɒθ ɪs §-əs ‖ -'rɑːθ əs
Glenville 'glen vɪl
Glenys 'glen ɪs §-əs
gley gleɪ **gleys** gleɪz
glia 'gliː‿ə 'glaɪ‿
glial 'gliː‿əl 'glaɪ‿
glib glɪb **glibber** 'glɪb ə ‖ -ᵊr **glibbest** 'glɪb ɪst
-əst **glibly** 'glɪb li **glibness** 'glɪb nəs -nɪs
glide glaɪd **glided** 'glaɪd ɪd -əd **glides** glaɪdz
gliding 'glaɪd ɪŋ
glide path
glider 'glaɪd ə ‖ -ᵊr ~s z
glimmer 'glɪm ə ‖ -ᵊr ~**ed** d **glimmering**
'glɪm ᵊr ɪŋ ~s z
glimmering 'glɪm ᵊr ɪŋ ~**ly** li ~s z

glimpse glɪmps **glimpsed** glɪmpst **glimpses**
'glɪmps ɪz -əz **glimpsing** 'glɪmps ɪŋ
Glinka 'glɪŋk ə —Russian ['glʲin kə]
glint glɪnt **glinted** 'glɪnt ɪd -əd ‖ 'glɪnʈ əd
glinting 'glɪnt ɪŋ ‖ 'glɪnʈ ɪŋ **glints** glɪnts
glioma glaɪ 'əʊm ə ‖ -'oʊm ə ~**s** z
glissad|e n, v glɪ 'sɑːd -'seɪd ~**ed** ɪd əd ~**es** z
~**ing** ɪŋ
glissand|o glɪ 'sænd |əʊ ‖ -'sɑːnd |oʊ ~**i** iː
~**os** əʊz ‖ oʊz
glisten 'glɪs ᵊn ~**ed** d ~**ing** ˌ ɪŋ ~s z
glister 'glɪst ə ‖ -ᵊr ~**ed** d **glistering**
'glɪst ᵊr ɪŋ ~s z
glitch glɪtʃ **glitches** 'glɪtʃ ɪz -əz
glitter 'glɪt ə ‖ 'glɪʈ ᵊr ~**ed** d **glittering/ly**
'glɪt ᵊr ɪŋ/ li ‖ 'glɪʈ ᵊr ɪŋ ~s z
glitterati ˌglɪt ə 'rɑːt iː -i ‖ ˌglɪʈ ə 'rɑːʈ i
glitz glɪts **glitzed** glɪtst **glitzes** 'glɪts ɪz -əz
glitzing 'glɪts ɪŋ
glitz|y 'glɪts |i ~**ier** i‿ə ‖ i‿ᵊr ~**iest** i‿ɪst i‿əst
~**iness** i nəs i nɪs
Gloag gləʊg ‖ gloʊg
gloaming 'gləʊm ɪŋ ‖ 'gloʊm ɪŋ
gloat gləʊt ‖ gloʊt **gloated** 'gləʊt ɪd -əd
‖ 'gloʊʈ əd **gloating/ly** 'gləʊt ɪŋ /li
‖ 'gloʊʈ ɪŋ /li **gloats** gləʊts ‖ gloʊts
glob glɒb ‖ glɑːb **globs** glɒbz ‖ glɑːbz
global 'gləʊb ᵊl ‖ 'gloʊb ᵊl ~**ism** ˌɪz əm ~**ist/s**
ɪst/s §əst/s ~**ly** i
ˌglobal 'warming
globalisation, globalization
ˌgləʊb ᵊl aɪ 'zeɪʃ ᵊn -ɪ'·· ‖ ˌgloʊb ᵊl ə-
globalis|e, globaliz|e 'gləʊb ə laɪz -ᵊl aɪz
‖ 'gloʊb- ~**ed** d ~**es** ɪz əz ~**ing** ɪŋ
globe gləʊb ‖ gloʊb **globes** gləʊbz ‖ gloʊbz
ˌglobe 'artichoke
globefish 'gləʊb fɪʃ ‖ 'gloʊb- ~**es** ɪz əz
globeflower 'gləʊb ˌflaʊ ə ‖ 'gloʊb ˌflaʊ ᵊr ~**s**
z
globetrott|er 'gləʊb ˌtrɒt |ə
‖ 'gloʊb ˌtrɑːʈ |ᵊr ~**ers** əz ‖ ᵊrz ~**ing** ɪŋ
globose 'gləʊb əʊs gləʊ 'bəʊs ‖ 'gloʊb oʊs
~**ly** li ~**ness** nəs nɪs
globosity gləʊ 'bɒs ət i -ɪt- ‖ gloʊ 'bɑːs əʈ i
globular 'glɒb jʊl ə -jəl- ‖ 'glɑːb jᵊl ᵊr ~**ly** li
~**ness** nəs nɪs
globule 'glɒb juːl ‖ 'glɑːb- ~**s** z
globulin 'glɒb jʊl ɪn -jəl-, §-ən ‖ 'glɑːb jᵊl ən
~**s** z
glocal 'gləʊk ᵊl ‖ 'gloʊk ᵊl
glocalization ˌgləʊk əl aɪ 'zeɪʃ ᵊn -əl ɪ-
‖ ˌgloʊk əl ə-
glockenspiel 'glɒk ən spiː ᵊl →-ŋ-, -ʃpiː ᵊl
‖ 'glɑːk- —Ger ['glɔk ᵊn ʃpiːl] ~**s** z
glom glɒm ‖ glɑːm **glommed** glɒmd ‖ glɑːmd
glomming 'glɒm ɪŋ ‖ 'glɑːm ɪŋ **gloms**
glɒmz ‖ glɑːmz
gloom gluːm
gloom|y 'gluːm |i ~**ier** i‿ə ‖ i‿ᵊr ~**iest** i‿ɪst i‿əst
~**ily** ɪ li əl i ~**iness** i nəs i nɪs
gloop gluːp
glop glɒp ‖ glɑːp
gloppy 'glɒp i ‖ 'glɑːp i

Gloria, g~ 'glɔːr i ə ‖ 'glour- **~s** z
  ˌgloria in ex'celsis ek 'sels ɪs ɪk-; eks 'tʃels-,
  ek 'ʃels-, -iːs; ˌGloria 'Patri 'pɑːtr iː 'pætr-, -i
Gloriana ˌglɔːr i 'ɑːn ə ‖ ˌglour-, -ˌæn-
glorie... —*see* **glory**
glorification ˌglɔːr ɪf ɪ 'keɪʃ ᵊn ˌ-əf-, §-ə'-
  ‖ ˌglour- **~s** z
glori|fy 'glɔːr ɪ |faɪ -ə- ‖ 'glour- **~fied** faɪd
  ~fier/s faɪˌə/z ‖ faɪˌᵊr/z **~fies** faɪz **~fying**
  faɪ ɪŋ
glorious 'glɔːr i əs ‖ 'glour- **~ly** li **~ness** nəs
  nɪs
glor|y 'glɔːr |i ‖ 'glour- **~ied** id **~ies** iz **~ying**
  i ɪŋ
  'glory hole
gloss glɒs ‖ glɑːs glɔːs **glossed** glɒst ‖ glɑːst
  glɔːst **glosses** 'glɒs ɪz -əz ‖ 'glɑːs əz 'glɔːs-
  glossing 'glɒs ɪŋ ‖ 'glɑːs ɪŋ 'glɔːs-
glossal 'glɒs ᵊl ‖ 'glɑːs ᵊl 'glɔːs-
glossar|y 'glɒs ər ˌ|i ‖ 'glɑːs- 'glɔːs- **~ies** iz
glossectomy glɒ 'sekt əm i ‖ glɑː- glɔː-
glossematic ˌglɒs ɪ 'mæt ɪk ◂ -ə-
  ‖ ˌglɑːs ə 'mæt̬ ɪk ◂ ˌglɔːs- **~s** s
glossi... —*see* **glossy**
glossolalia ˌglɒs əʊ 'leɪl i ə ‖ ˌglɑːs ə- ˌglɔːs-
Glossop 'glɒs əp ‖ 'glɑːs-
glossopharyngeal ˌglɒs əʊ ˌfær ɪn 'dʒiːˌəl
  -fə 'rɪndʒ iˌəl ‖ ˌglɑːs oʊ ˌfær ən 'dʒiː əl
  ˌglɔːs-, -ˌfer-
gloss|y 'glɒs |i ‖ 'glɑːs |i 'glɔːs- **~ier** iˌə ‖ iˌᵊr
  ~iest iˌɪst iˌəst **~ily** ɪ li əl i **~iness** i nəs i nɪs
Gloster 'glɒst ə 'glɔːst- ‖ 'glɑːst ᵊr 'glɔːst-
glottal 'glɒt ᵊl ‖ 'glɑːt̬ ᵊl **~ly** i **~s** z
  ˌglottal 'stop
glottalic glɒ 'tæl ɪk ‖ glɑː-
glottalis... —*see* **glottaliz...**
glottalization ˌglɒt ᵊl aɪ 'zeɪʃ ᵊn -ɪ'-
  ‖ ˌglɑːt̬ ᵊl ə- **~s** z
glottaliz|e 'glɒt ᵊl aɪz -ə laɪz ‖ 'glɑːt̬ ᵊl aɪz **~ed**
  d **~es** ɪz əz **~ing** ɪŋ
glottis 'glɒt ɪs §-əs ‖ 'glɑːt̬ əs **~es** ɪz əz
glottochronology ˌglɒt əʊ krə 'nɒl ədʒ i
  ‖ ˌglɑːt̬ oʊ krə 'nɑːl-
Gloucester 'glɒst ə 'glɔːst- ‖ 'glɑːst ᵊr 'glɔːst-
  ~s z **~shire** ʃə ʃɪə ‖ ʃᵊr ʃɪr
glove glʌv **gloved** glʌvd **gloves** glʌvz
  gloving 'glʌv ɪŋ
  'glove comˌpartment; 'glove ˌpuppet
glover, G~ 'glʌv ə ‖ -ᵊr **~s** z
glow gləʊ ‖ gloʊ **glowed** gləʊd ‖ gloʊd
  glowing/ly 'gləʊ ɪŋ /li ‖ 'gloʊ ɪŋ /li **glows**
  gləʊz ‖ gloʊz
glower 'glaʊˌə ‖ 'glaʊˌᵊr **~ed** d **glowering/ly**
  'glaʊ ər ɪŋ /li ‖ 'glaʊˌᵊr ɪŋ /li **~s** z
glowstick 'gləʊ stɪk ‖ 'gloʊ- **~s** s
glow-worm 'gləʊ wɜːm ‖ 'gloʊ wɜːm **~s** z
gloxinia glɒk 'sɪn iˌə ‖ glɑːk- **~s** z
Gloy *tdmk* glɔɪ
gloze gləʊz ‖ gloʊz **glozed** gləʊzd ‖ gloʊzd
  glozes 'gləʊz ɪz -əz ‖ 'gloʊz əz **glozing**
  'gləʊz ɪŋ ‖ 'gloʊz ɪŋ
Glubb glʌb
Gluck glʊk —*Ger* [glʊk]

gluco- *comb. form*
  with stress-neutral suffix ˌglu:k əʊ ‖ -oʊ —
  glucocorticoid ˌglu:k əʊ 'kɔːt ɪ kɔɪd -'-ə-
  ‖ -oʊ 'kɔːrt̬-
glucose 'glu:k əʊz -əʊs ‖ -oʊs -oʊz
glucoside 'glu:k əʊ saɪd ‖ -ə- **~s** z
glue glu: **glued** glu:d **glues** glu:z **gluing**
  'glu:ˌɪŋ
gluer 'glu:ˌə ‖ ᵊr **~s** z
glue-sniff|er 'glu: ˌsnɪf |ə ‖ -|ᵊr **~ers** əz ‖ ᵊrz
  ~ing ɪŋ
gluey 'glu:ˌi
gluhwein, glühwein 'glu: vaɪn -*Ger* **G~**
  'gly: vaɪn
gluing 'glu:ˌɪŋ
glum glʌm **glummer** 'glʌm ə ‖ -ᵊr **glummest**
  'glʌm ɪst -əst
glume glu:m (= *gloom*) **~s** z
glum|ly 'glʌm |li **~ness** nəs nɪs
gluon 'glu: ɒn ‖ -ɑːn **~s** z
glut glʌt **gluts** glʌts **glutted** 'glʌt ɪd -əd
  ‖ 'glʌt̬ əd **glutting** 'glʌt ɪŋ ‖ 'glʌt̬ ɪŋ
glutamate 'glu:t ə meɪt ‖ 'glu:t̬- **~s** s
glutamic glu: 'tæm ɪk
glutamine 'glu:t ə mi:n -mɪn ‖ 'glu:t̬-
gluteal 'glu:t iˌəl ‖ 'glu:t̬-
gluten 'glu:t ᵊn -ɪn
gluteus 'glu:t iˌəs ‖ 'glu:t̬-
  ˌgluteus 'maximus
glutinous 'glu:t ɪn əs -ᵊn- ‖ 'glu:t ᵊn əs **~ly** li
  ~ness nəs nɪs
glutton 'glʌt ᵊn **~s** z
gluttonous 'glʌt ᵊn əs **~ly** li
gluttony 'glʌt ᵊn i
glyceride 'glɪs ə raɪd **~s** z
glycerin, glycerine 'glɪs ər ɪn §-ᵊr ən; -ə ri:n,
  ˌglɪs ə 'ri:n
glycerol 'glɪs ə rɒl ‖ -roʊl -rɑːl, -rɔːl
glycine 'glaɪs i:n
glyco- *comb. form*
  with stress-neutral suffix ˌglaɪk əʊ ‖ -oʊ —
  glycopeptide ˌglaɪk əʊ 'pept aɪd ‖ -oʊ-
  with stress-imposing suffix glaɪ 'kɒ+
  ‖ glaɪ 'kɑː+ — **glycogeny** glaɪ 'kɒdʒ ən i
  ‖ -'kɑːdʒ-
glycogen 'glaɪk ədʒ ən -əʊ dʒen ‖ -oʊ dʒen
glycol 'glaɪk ɒl ‖ -oʊl -ɑːl, -ɔːl
glycoside 'glaɪk əʊ saɪd ‖ -ə- **~s** z
Glyder 'glɪd ə ‖ -ᵊr —*Welsh* ['glə der] **~s** z
Glyn glɪn
Glynde glaɪnd
Glyndebourne 'glaɪnd bɔːn →'glaɪm- ‖ -bɔːrn
  -boʊrn
Glynis 'glɪn ɪs §-əs
Glynn, Glynne glɪn
Glynwed *tdmk* 'glɪn wed
glyph glɪf **glyphs** glɪfs
glyptodont 'glɪpt əʊ dɒnt ‖ -ə dɑːnt **~s** s
GM ˌdʒiː 'em ◂
G-man 'dʒiː mæn **G-men** 'dʒiː men
GMT ˌdʒiː em 'tiː
gnarled nɑːld ‖ nɑːrld
gnarly 'nɑːl i ‖ 'nɑːrl i

G

gnash næʃ **gnashed** næʃt **gnasher/s** 'næʃ ə/z
‖ -ᵊr/z **gnashes** 'næʃ ɪz -əz **gnashing** 'næʃ ɪŋ
gnat næt **gnats** næts
gnaw nɔː ‖ nɑː **gnawed** nɔːd ‖ nɑːd **gnawing**
'nɔː ɪŋ ‖ 'nɔː ɪŋ 'nɑː- **gnawn** nɔːn ‖ nɑːn
gnaws nɔːz ‖ nɑːz
gneiss naɪs gə 'naɪs —Ger Gneis [gnais]
gnocchi 'nɒk i 'njɒk i, gə 'nɒk i ‖ 'nɑːk i
'njɑːk i, 'noʊk i —It ['nɔk ki]
gnome nəʊm ‖ noʊm **gnomes** nəʊmz
‖ noʊmz
gnomic 'nəʊm ɪk ‖ 'noʊm- **~ally** ᵊl i
gnomish 'nəʊm ɪʃ ‖ 'noʊm-
gnomon 'nəʊm ɒn -ən ‖ 'noʊm ɑːn **~s** z
Gnosall 'nəʊs ᵊl ‖ 'noʊs-
gnostic, G~ 'nɒst ɪk ‖ 'nɑːst- **~s** s
gnosticism, G~ 'nɒst ɪ ˌsɪz əm -ə- ‖ 'nɑːst-
-gnosy stress-imposing gnəs i —
pharmacognosy ˌfɑːm ə 'kɒg nəs i
‖ ˌfɑːrm ə 'kɑːg-
GNP ˌdʒiː en 'piː
gnu nuː njuː; gə 'nuː, -'njuː —*The forms with*
gə- are jocular, as generally is the entire word.
In serious discourse this animal is called a
wildebeest. **gnus** nuːz njuːz; gə 'nuːz, -'njuːz
go gəʊ ‖ goʊ —*There are nonstandard weak*
forms §gə, §gu **goes** gəʊz ‖ goʊz —*There are*
nonstandard weak forms §gəz, §gʊz **going**
'gəʊ ɪŋ ‖ 'goʊ ɪŋ —*The phrase going to,*
when used as a modal (showing the future),
has a casual weak form (')gən ə, *also*
(')gəʊ ɪn ə, (')gən ə, (')gəʊ ɪnt ə ‖ (')goʊ ᵊn ə,
ˌənt ə. *In RP these are used, if at all, only*
before words beginning with a consonant
sound, being replaced before a vowel sound by
(')gən u *or other forms with final* u *rather*
than ə. *See* gonna. **gone** gɒn §gɔːn, §gɑːn
‖ gɔːn gɑːn **went** went
Goa, goa 'gəʊ ə ‖ 'goʊ ə **~s** z
goad gəʊd ‖ goʊd **goaded** 'gəʊd ɪd -əd
‖ 'goʊd əd **goading** 'gəʊd ɪŋ ‖ 'goʊd ɪŋ
goads gəʊdz ‖ goʊdz
go-ahead *adj* 'gəʊ ə ˌhed ˌ· ·'·◂ ‖ 'goʊ-
go-ahead *n* 'gəʊ ə ˌhed ‖ 'goʊ-
goal gəʊl →gɒʊl ‖ goʊl **goals** gəʊlz →gɒʊlz
‖ goʊlz
'goal line
goalie 'gəʊl i →'gɒʊl- ‖ 'goʊl i **~s** z
goalkeep|er 'gəʊl ˌkiːp| ə →'gɒʊl-
‖ 'goʊl ˌkiːp| ᵊr **~ers** əz ‖ ᵊrz **~ing** ɪŋ
goalless 'gəʊl ləs →'gɒʊl-, -lɪs ‖ 'goʊl-
goalmouth 'gəʊl maʊθ →'gɒʊl- ‖ 'goʊl-
goal-oriented 'gəʊl ˌɔːr i ent ɪd →'gɒʊl-, -ˌɒr-
‖ 'goʊl ˌɔːr i ent əd -ˌoʊr-
goalpost 'gəʊl pəʊst →'gɒʊl- ‖ 'goʊl poʊst **~s**
s
goaltend|er 'gəʊl tend| ə →'gɒʊl-
‖ 'goʊl tend ᵊr **~ers** əz ‖ ᵊrz **~ing** ɪŋ
Goan 'gəʊ ən ‖ 'goʊ ən **~s** z
Goanese ˌgəʊ ə 'niːz ◂ ‖ ˌgoʊ- -'niːs ◂
goanna gəʊ 'æn ə ‖ goʊ- **~s** z
go-as-you-please ˌgəʊ əz ju 'pliːz →ˌ·əʒ-
‖ ˌgoʊ-

goat gəʊt ‖ goʊt **goats** gəʊts ‖ goʊts
goatee ˌgəʊ 'tiː ◂ ‖ ˌgoʊ- **~s** z
goatherd 'gəʊt hɜːd ‖ 'goʊt hɜːd **~s** z
Goathland 'gəʊθ lənd ‖ 'goʊθ-
goatsbeard 'gəʊts bɪəd ‖ 'goʊts bɪrd **~s** z
goatskin 'gəʊt skɪn ‖ 'goʊt- **~s** z
goatsucker 'gəʊt ˌsʌk ə ‖ 'goʊt ˌsʌk ᵊr **~s** z
gob gɒb ‖ gɑːb **gobbed** gɒbd ‖ gɑːbd
gobbing 'gɒb ɪŋ ‖ 'gɑːb ɪŋ **gobs** gɒbz
‖ gɑːbz
gobbet 'gɒb ɪt §-ət ‖ 'gɑːb- **~s** s
gobbl|e 'gɒb ᵊl ‖ 'gɑːb ᵊl **~ed** d **~es** z **~ing**
ɪŋ
gobbledegook, gobbledygook
'gɒb ᵊl di guːk -gʊk ‖ 'gɑːb-
gobbler 'gɒb lə ‖ 'gɑːb lᵊr **~s** z
Gobelin 'gəʊb əl ɪn 'gɒb-, §-ən ‖ 'goʊb- —*Fr*
[gɔb læ̃] **~s** z
go-between 'gəʊ bɪ ˌtwiːn -bə-, §-biː- ‖ 'goʊ-
~s z
Gobi 'gəʊb i ‖ 'goʊb i —*Chi* Gēbì [¹kɤ ⁴pi]
gobie... —*see* **goby**
goblet 'gɒb lət -lɪt ‖ 'gɑːb- **~s** s
goblin 'gɒb lɪn -lən ‖ 'gɑːb- **~s** z
gobo 'gəʊb əʊ ‖ 'goʊb oʊ **~s** z
Gobowen gɒ 'bəʊ ɪn -ən ‖ gɑː 'boʊ-
gobsmack 'gɒb smæk ‖ 'gɑːb- **~ed** t **~ing** ɪŋ
~s s
gobstopper 'gɒb ˌstɒp ə ‖ 'gɑːb ˌstɑːp ᵊr **~s** z
go-by *'snub'* 'gəʊ baɪ ‖ 'goʊ-
gob|y *'fish'* 'gəʊb |i ‖ 'goʊb |i **~ies** iz
go-cart 'gəʊ kɑːt ‖ 'goʊ kɑːrt **~s** s
god, God gɒd ‖ gɑːd **gods, God's** gɒdz
‖ gɑːdz
Godalming 'gɒd ᵊl mɪŋ ‖ 'gɑːd-
Godard 'gɒd ɑː -ɑːd ‖ goʊ 'dɑːr —*Fr* [gɔ daʁ]
god-awful ˌgɒd 'ɔːf ᵊl ◂ ‖ ˌgɑːd- -'ɑːf-
Godber 'gɒd bə →'gɒb- ‖ 'gɑːd bᵊr
god|child 'gɒd |tʃaɪᵊld ‖ 'gɑːd- **~children**
ˌtʃɪldr ən ˌtʃʊldr-
goddam, goddamn 'gɒd æm ‖ ˌgɑːd 'dæm ◂
~ed d
goddammit gɒ 'dæm ɪt §-ət ‖ ˌgɑːd-
Goddard 'gɒd ɑːd -əd ‖ 'gɑːd ᵊrd -ɑːrd
goddaughter 'gɒd ˌdɔːt ə ‖ 'gɑːd ˌdɔːt̬ ᵊr
-ˌdɑːt̬- **~s** z
goddess 'gɒd es -ɪs, -əs ‖ 'gɑːd əs **~es** ɪz əz
Godel, Gödel 'gɜːd ᵊl 'gəʊd- ‖ 'goʊd- —*Ger*
['gøː dᵊl]
godet 'gəʊd eɪ -et; gəʊ 'det ‖ goʊ 'deɪ -'det
godetia gəʊ 'diːʃ ə -'diːʃ i ə ‖ gə- **~s** z
godfather 'gɒd ˌfɑːð ə ‖ 'gɑːd ˌfɑːð ᵊr **~s** z
god-fearing 'gɒd ˌfɪər ɪŋ ‖ 'gɑːd ˌfɪr ɪŋ
godforsaken 'gɒd fə ˌseɪk ən ˌ· ·'· · ‖ 'gɑːd fᵊr-
Godfrey 'gɒd fri ‖ 'gɑːd-
God-given 'gɒd ˌgɪv ᵊn →'gɑːg- ‖ 'gɑːd-
godhead, G~ 'gɒd hed ‖ 'gɑːd-
Godiva gə 'daɪv ə
godless 'gɒd ləs -lɪs ‖ 'gɑːd- **~ness** nəs nɪs
Godley 'gɒd li ‖ 'gɑːd-
godlike 'gɒd laɪk ‖ 'gɑːd-
god|ly 'gɒd |li ‖ 'gɑːd- **~liness** li nəs -nɪs
Godmanchester 'gɒd mən ˌtʃest ə ˌ· ·'· ·
‖ 'gɑːd mən ˌtʃest ᵊr

Glottal stop

A **glottal stop**, symbolized ʔ, is a PLOSIVE made at the glottis (= made by the vocal folds). In English it is sometimes used as a kind of t-sound, and sometimes has other functions.

1   In certain positions ʔ may be used as an allophone of the phoneme t, as when **pointless** ˈpɔɪnt ləs is pronounced ˈpɔɪnʔ ləs. This is known as **glottalling** or **glottal replacement** of t. It is condemned by some people; nevertheless, it is increasingly heard, especially in BrE. Sometimes the glottal articulation accompanies a simultaneous alveolar articulation.

2   ʔ is found as an allophone of t only
   - at the **end** of a syllable, and
   - if the preceding sound is a vowel or SONORANT.

Provided these conditions are satisfied, it is widely used in both BrE and AmE where the following sound is an obstruent
football ˈfʊt bɔːl → ˈfʊʔ bɔːl
outside ˌaʊt ˈsaɪd → ˌaʊʔ ˈsaɪd
that faint buzz ˌðæt ˌfeɪnt ˈbʌz → ˌðæʔ ˌfeɪnʔ ˈbʌz

or a nasal
atmospheric ˌæt məs ˈfer ɪk → ˌæʔ məs ˈfer ɪk
button ˈbʌt ᵊn → ˈbʌʔ n
that name ˌðæt ˈneɪm → ˌðæʔ ˈneɪm

or a semivowel or non-syllabic l
Gatwick ˈɡæt wɪk → ˈɡæʔ wɪk
quite well ˌkwaɪt ˈwel → ˌkwaɪʔ ˈwel
brightly ˈbraɪt li → ˈbraɪʔ li

Some speakers of BrE also use it at the end of a word under other circumstances as well:
not only this ˌnɒʔ əʊn li ˈðɪs **but also that** bəʔ ˌɔːl səʊ ˈðæʔ.

Compare AmE ˌnɑːt̬ oʊn li ˈðɪs, bət̬ ˌɔːl soʊ ˈðæt; in this position t̬ is also heard in casual BrE.

3   ʔ is also optionally used as a way of adding emphasis to a syllable that begins with a vowel sound (see HARD ATTACK). It can be used to separate adjacent vowel sounds in successive syllables (= to avoid **hiatus**). In BrE this can be a way of avoiding r (see R-LIAISON), as in one pronunciation of **underexpose** ˌʌnd ə ɪk ˈspəʊz (-ə ʔɪk-).

4   ʔ also forms an essential part of certain interjections, e.g. AmE **uh-uh** ˌʔʌʔ ˈʌʔ.

5   A glottal stop is sometimes used, especially in BrE, to strengthen tʃ or tr at the end of a syllable, and also p, t, k if followed by a consonant or at the end of a word. This is known as **glottal reinforcement**: **teaching** ˈtiːtʃ ɪŋ → ˈtiːʔtʃ ɪŋ, **April** ˈeɪp rəl → ˈeɪʔp rəl, **right!** raɪt → raɪʔt.

Glottal stop ▶

> **Glottal stop** continued
>
> Learners of English should be careful not to apply glottal reinforcement (as opposed to glottal replacement) in words such as **pretty** ˈprɪt i and **jumping** ˈdʒʌmp ɪŋ.

godmother ˈɡɒd ˌmʌð ə →ˈɡɒb- ‖ ˈɡɑːd ˌmʌð ᵊr ~s z
Godolphin ɡə ˈdɒlf ɪn §-ᵊn ‖ ɡə ˈdɑːlf-
Godot ˈɡɒd əʊ ‖ ɡɑː ˈdoʊ ɡə- —*Fr* [ɡɔ do]
godown ˈɡəʊ daʊn ‖ ˈɡoʊ- ~s z
godparent ˈɡɒd ˌpeər ənt →ˈɡɒb- ‖ ˈɡɑːd ˌper- -ˌpær- ~s s
godsend ˈɡɒd send ‖ ˈɡɑːd- ~s z
godson ˈɡɒd sʌn ‖ ˈɡɑːd- ~s z
godspeed, G~ ˌɡɒd ˈspiːd ‖ ˌɡɑːd-
Godthaab, Godthab ˈɡɒt hɑːb -hɔːb ‖ ˈɡɑːt hɑːb ˈɡoʊt- —*Danish* [ˈɡɔd hoːʔb]
Godunov ˈɡɒd ə nɒf ˈɡʊd-, -u- ‖ ˈɡʊd ə nɔːf -nɑːf —*Russ* [ɡə dʊ ˈnɔf]
Godwin ˈɡɒd wɪn §-wən ‖ ˈɡɑːd-
godwit ˈɡɒd wɪt ‖ ˈɡɑːd- ~s s
Godzilla ɡɒd ˈzɪl ə ‖ ɡɑːd-
Goebbels ˈɡɜːb ᵊlz -ᵊls ‖ ˈɡʊb- ˈɡɜːb- —*Ger* [ˈɡœb ᵊls]
goer ˈɡəʊ ə ‖ ˈɡoʊ ᵊr ~s z
-goer ˌɡəʊ ə ‖ ˌɡoʊ ᵊr — **party-goer** ˈpɑːt i ˌɡəʊ ə ‖ ˈpɑːrt̬ i ˌɡoʊ ᵊr
Goering ˈɡɜːr ɪŋ ‖ ˈɡer- ˈɡɜː- —*Ger* [ˈɡøː ʀɪŋ]
goes ɡəʊz ‖ ɡoʊz —*There are nonstandard weak forms* §ɡəz, §ɡʊz
goest ˈɡəʊ ɪst -əst ‖ ˈɡoʊ-
goeth ˈɡəʊ ɪθ -əθ ‖ ˈɡoʊ-
Goethals ˈɡəʊθ ᵊlz ‖ ˈɡoʊθ-
Goethe ˈɡɜːt ə ‖ ˈɡeɪt ə ˈɡɜːt̬-, -i —*Ger* [ˈɡøː tə]
gofer ˈɡəʊf ə ‖ ˈɡoʊf ᵊr ~s z
Goff, Goffe ɡɒf ‖ ɡɑːf
goffer ˈɡəʊf ə ‖ ˈɡɑːf ᵊr *(*)* ~**ed** d **goffering** ˈɡəʊf ər ɪŋ ‖ ˈɡɑːf ər ɪŋ ~s z
Gog ɡɒɡ ‖ ɡɑːɡ
Gogarty ˈɡəʊɡ ət i ‖ ˈɡoʊɡ ᵊrt̬ i
go-gett|er ˈɡəʊ ˌɡet| ə ‚·ˈ·· ‖ ˈɡoʊ ˌɡet̬| ᵊr ~**ers** əz ‖ ᵊrz ~**ing** ɪŋ
goggl|e ˈɡɒɡ ᵊl ‖ ˈɡɑːɡ ᵊl ~**ed** d ~**es** z ~**ing** ɪŋ ˈgoggle box
goggle-eyed ˌɡɒɡ ᵊl ˈaɪd ◂ ···· ‖ ˌɡɑːɡ-
Gogmagog ˌɡɒɡ mə ˈɡɒɡ ◂ ‖ ˌɡɑːɡ mə ˈɡɑːɡ ◂ ˌGogmagog ˈHills
go-go ˈɡəʊ ɡəʊ ‖ ˈɡoʊ ɡoʊ ˈgo-go ˌdancer
Gogol ˈɡəʊɡ ɒl ‖ ˈɡoʊɡ ɑːl -ᵊl —*Russ* [ˈɡɔ ɡəlʲ]
Goidel ˈɡɔɪd ᵊl
Goidelic, Goidhelic ɡɔɪ ˈdel ɪk
going ˈɡəʊ ɪŋ ‖ ˈɡoʊ ɪŋ ~s z —*see note at* go
-going ˌɡəʊ ɪŋ ‖ ˌɡoʊ ɪŋ — **party-going** ˈpɑːt i ˌɡəʊ ɪŋ ‖ ˈpɑːr t̬i ˌɡoʊ ɪŋ
going-over ˌɡəʊ ɪŋ ˈəʊv ə ˈ··ˌ·· ‖ ˌɡoʊ ɪŋ ˈoʊv ᵊr
goings-on ˌɡəʊ ɪŋz ˈɒn ‖ ˌɡoʊ ɪŋz ˈɑːn -ˈɔːn

goiter, goitre ˈɡɔɪt ə ‖ ˈɡɔɪt̬ ᵊr ~s z
goitrous ˈɡɔɪtr əs
goji ˈɡəʊdʒ i ‖ ˈɡoʊdʒ i —*Chi* gǒuqǐ [³kou ³tɕ ʰi]
go-kart ˈɡəʊ kɑːt ‖ ˈɡoʊ kɑːrt ~s s
Golan ˈɡəʊl æn -ɑːn; ɡəʊ ˈlɑːn ‖ ˈɡoʊl ɑːn ˌGolan ˈheights
Golborne ˈɡəʊl bɔːn →ˈɡɒʊl- ‖ ˈɡoʊl bɔːrn -boʊrn
Golconda ɡɒl ˈkɒnd ə ‖ ɡɑːl ˈkɑːnd ə
gold ɡəʊld →ɡɒʊld ‖ ɡoʊld **golds** ɡəʊldz →ɡɒʊldz ‖ ɡoʊldz
ˈGold Coast; ˈgold ˌdigger; ˈgold dust; ˌgold ˈleaf; ˌgold ˈmedal; ˌgold ˈplate; ˈgold reˌserve; ˈgold rush; ˈgold ˌstandard
Golda ˈɡəʊld ə →ˈɡɒʊld- ‖ ˈɡoʊld ə
goldbeater ˈɡəʊld ˌbiːt ə →ˈɡɒʊld- ‖ ˈɡoʊld ˌbiːt̬ ᵊr ~s z
Goldberg ˈɡəʊld bɜːɡ →ˈɡɒʊld- ‖ ˈɡoʊld bɜːɡ
Goldblum ˈɡəʊld bluːm →ˈɡɒʊld- ‖ ˈɡoʊld-
goldbrick ˈɡəʊld brɪk →ˈɡɒʊld- ‖ ˈɡoʊld- ~**ed** t ~**ing** ɪŋ ~s s
goldcrest ˈɡəʊld krest →ˈɡɒʊld- ‖ ˈɡoʊld- ~s s
golden ˈɡəʊld ən →ˈɡɒʊld- ‖ ˈɡoʊld- ~**ly** li ~**ness** nəs nɪs
ˈgolden age, ‚·ˈ·; ˌgolden ˈeagle; ˌGolden ˈFleece; ˌGolden ˈGate◂, ˌGolden Gate ˈBridge; ˌgolden ˈhandshake; ˌgolden ˈjubilee; ˌgolden ˈmean; ˌgolden ˈoldie; ˌgolden ˈrule; ˌgolden ˈsyrup; ˌgolden ˈwedding
goldeneye ˈɡəʊld ən aɪ →ˈɡɒʊld- ‖ ˈɡoʊld- ~s z
goldenrod ˈɡəʊld ən rɒd →ˈɡɒʊld-, ‚·ˈ· ‖ ˈɡoʊld ən rɑːd
goldfield ˈɡəʊld fiːᵊld →ˈɡɒʊld- ‖ ˈɡoʊld- ~s z
goldfinch ˈɡəʊld fɪntʃ →ˈɡɒʊld- ‖ ˈɡoʊld- ~**es** ɪz əz
goldfish ˈɡəʊld fɪʃ →ˈɡɒʊld- ‖ ˈɡoʊld- ~**es** ɪz əz
ˈgoldfish bowl
Goldie ˈɡəʊld i →ˈɡɒʊld- ‖ ˈɡoʊld i
Goldilocks, g~ ˈɡəʊld i lɒks →ˈɡɒʊld- ‖ ˈɡoʊld i lɑːks
Golding ˈɡəʊld ɪŋ →ˈɡɒʊld- ‖ ˈɡoʊld-
goldmin|e ˈɡəʊld maɪn →ˈɡɒʊld- ‖ ˈɡoʊld- ~**er/s** ə/z ‖ ᵊr/z ~**es** z ~**ing** ɪŋ
gold-plated ˌɡəʊld ˈpleɪt ɪd ◂ →ˌɡɒʊld-, -əd ‖ ˌɡoʊld ˈpleɪt̬ əd ◂
gold-rimmed ˌɡəʊldˈrɪmd ◂ →ˌɡɒʊld- ‖ ˌɡoʊld-
Goldschmidt ˈɡəʊld ʃmɪt →ˈɡɒʊld- ‖ ˈɡoʊld-

goldsmith, G~ 'gəʊld smɪθ →'gɒʊld-
 ‖ 'goʊld- **~s** s

Goldwater 'gəʊld ˌwɔːt ə →'gɒʊld-
 ‖ 'goʊld ˌwɔːt̬ ʳr -ˌwɑːt̬ ʳr

Goldwyn 'gəʊld wɪn →'gɒʊld- ‖ 'goʊld-

golem 'gəʊl əm ‖ 'goʊl- **~s** z

golf gɒlf gɒf, gɔːf, §gəʊlf ‖ 'gɑːlf gɔːlf
 'golf ball; **'golf club**; **'golf course**; **'golf
 links**

golfer 'gɒlf ə -gɒf-, -gɔːf-, §'gəʊlf- ‖ 'gɑːlf ʳr
 'gɔːlf- **~s** z

golfing 'gɒlf ɪŋ -gɒf-, -gɔːf-, §'gəʊlf- ‖ 'gɑːlf ɪŋ
 'gɔːlf-

Golgi 'gɒldʒ i ‖ 'gɔːldʒ i 'gɑːldʒ i —*It*
 ['gɔl dʒi]

Golgotha 'gɒlg əθ ə ‖ 'gɑːlg-

Goliath, g~ gə 'laɪ əθ goʊ- **~s, ~'s** s

Golightly gəʊ 'laɪt li ‖ goʊ-

Gollancz 'gɒl æŋks -ənts; gə 'lænts, -'læŋks
 ‖ gə 'lænts

golliwog, golliwogg 'gɒl i wɒg
 ‖ 'gɑːl i wɑːg **~s** z

Gollum 'gɒl əm ‖ 'gɑːl-

golly 'gɒl i ‖ 'gɑːl i

gollywog 'gɒl i wɒg ‖ 'gɑːl i wɑːg **~s** z

Gomer 'gəʊm ə ‖ 'goʊm ʳr

Gomes 'gəʊm ez ‖ 'goʊm- —*Port* ['go mɪʃ],
 BrPort ['go mis]

Gomez 'gəʊm ez ‖ 'goʊm- —*Sp* Gómez
 ['go meθ, -mes]

Gomm, Gomme gɒm ‖ gɑːm

Gomorrah gə 'mɒr ə ‖ -'mɔːr ə -'mɑːr-

Gompers 'gɒmp əz ‖ 'gɑːmp ʳrz

Gomperts, Gompertz 'gɒmp əts
 ‖ 'gɑːmp ʳrts

Gomshall 'gɒm ʃ°l 'gʌm- ‖ 'gɑːm-

-gon gən gɒn ‖ gɑːn — **hexagon** 'heks əg ən
 -ə gɒn ‖ -ə gɑːn

gonad 'gəʊn æd 'gɒn- ‖ 'goʊn- **~s** z

gonadotrophin ˌgəʊn əd əʊ 'trəʊf ɪn ˌgɒn-,
 -'trɒf-, -°n ‖ ˌgoʊn əd ə 'troʊf- **~s** z

-gonal *stress-imposing* g°n əl — **isogonal**
 aɪ 'sɒg °n əl ‖ -'sɑːg-

Goncourt ˌgɒŋ 'kʊə '·· ‖ ˌgoʊn 'kʊ°r —*Fr*
 [gɔ̃ kuːʁ]

Gond gɒnd ‖ gɑːnd **Gonds** gɒndz ‖ gɑːndz

Gondi 'gɒnd i ‖ 'gɑːnd i

gondola 'gɒnd əl ə ‖ 'gɑːnd- **~s** z

gondolier ˌgɒnd ə 'lɪə -°l 'ɪə ‖ ˌgɑːnd ə 'lɪ°r **~s**
 z

Gondwana gɒn 'dwɑːn ə ‖ gɑːn- **~land** lænd

gone gɒn §gɔːn, §gɑːn ‖ gɔːn gɑːn — *Preference
 poll, AmE:* gɔːn 76 %, gɑːn 24% (*of those who
 distinguish these two vowels*).

goner 'gɒn ə ‖ 'gɔːn °r 'gɑːn- **~s** z

Goneril 'gɒn ʳr ɪl -°l ‖ 'gɑːn-

gonfalon 'gɒn fəl ən ‖ 'gɑːn- **~s** z

gong gɒŋ ‖ gɔːŋ gɑːŋ **gongs** gɒŋz ‖ gɔːŋz
 gɑːŋz

goniometer ˌgəʊn i 'ɒm ɪt ə -ət ə
 ‖ ˌgoʊn i 'ɑːm ət̬ °r **~s** z

goniometric ˌgəʊn i ə 'metr ɪk ◂ ‖ ˌgoʊn- **~al**
 °l **~ally** °l̩ i

GONE

76% gɔːn
24% gɑːn

AmE

gonk gɒŋk ‖ gɑːŋk **gonks** gɒŋks ‖ gɑːŋks

gonna *contracted weak form before a consonant*
 (')gən ə —*There is no real RP strong form for
 this informal contraction of going to, although
 spelling pronunciations* 'gɒn ə, 'gʌn ə *are
 sometimes used in reading. There is an AmE
 strong form* 'gɔːn ə, 'gɑːn ə. —*Before a vowel
 sound, the contracted weak form* (')gən u *is
 sometimes used (see discussion at to).*

gonococ|cus ˌgɒn əʊ 'kɒk |əs
 ‖ ˌgɑːn ə 'kɑːk |əs **~ci** saɪ siː, aɪ

gonorrhea, gonorrhoea ˌgɒn ə 'rɪə
 ‖ ˌgɑːn ə 'riː ə

Gonville 'gɒn vɪl -v°l ‖ 'gɑːn-

-gony *stress-imposing* gən i — **cosmogony**
 kɒz 'mɒg ən i ‖ kɑːz 'mɑːg-

Gonzales, Gonzalez gɒn 'zɑːl ɪz gən-, -ez, -əz
 ‖ gən 'zɑːl əs gɑːn-, gɔːn-, -'sɑːl-, -es —*Sp*
 González [gon 'θa leθ, -'sa les]

gonzo 'gɒnz əʊ ‖ 'gɑːnz oʊ **~s** z

goo guː

goober 'guːb ə ‖ -°r **~s** z

Gooch guːtʃ

good, Good gʊd **better** 'bet ə ‖ 'bet̬ °r **best**
 best **goods** gʊdz —*In the phrase a good deal
 ('quite a lot')* a d *is often lost in RP (providing
 deal is unstressed), thus a good deal better*
 ə ˌgʊd iː°l 'bet ə.

 good ˌafter'noon, ·ˈ ·ˈ·ˈ; **ˌgood 'book;**
 ₍ˌ₎**good 'day;** ₍ˌ₎**good 'evening; ˌGood
 'Friday; ˌgood 'looker; ˌgood 'looks;**
 ₍ˌ₎**good 'morning; ˌgood 'offices; ˌgood
 Sa'maritan**

Goodall 'gʊd ɔːl ‖ -ɑːl

Goodbody 'gʊd ˌbɒd i →'gʊb- ‖ -ˌbɑːd i

good-by, good-bye, goodbye ˌgʊd 'baɪ ◂
 →ˌgʊb- **~s** z

Goodchild 'gʊd tʃaɪ°ld

Goode gʊd

Goodenough 'gʊd ɪ ˌnʌf -ə-, -°n ˌʌf

Goodfellow 'gʊd ˌfel əʊ ‖ -oʊ

good-for-nothing ˌgʊd fə 'nʌθ ɪŋ ◂ ·ˈ·,·ˈ
 ‖ -fʳr-

Goodge guːdʒ gʊdʒ

Goodhart 'gʊd hɑːt ‖ -hɑːrt

good-hearted ˌgʊd 'hɑːt ɪd ◂ -əd ‖ -'hɑːrt̬-

good-humored, good-humoured
 ˌgʊd 'hjuːm əd ◂ -°rd ◂ -'juːm- **~ly** li **~ness**
 nəs nɪs

goodie 'gʊd i **~s** z

goodish 'gʊd ɪʃ

Goodison 'gʊd ɪs ən -əs-

goodli... —*see* **goodly**

Goodliffe ˈgʊd lɪf
good-looking ˌgʊd ˈlʊk ɪŋ ◂
good|ly ˈgʊd |li **~lier** li‿ə ‖ li‿ᵊr **~liest** li‿ɪst əst **~liness** li nəs -nɪs
Goodman ˈgʊd mən →ˈgʊb-
good-natured ˌgʊd ˈneɪtʃ əd ◂ ‖ -ᵊrd **~ly** li **~ness** nəs nɪs
goodness ˈgʊd nəs -nɪs
goodnight ₍ˌ₎gʊd ˈnaɪt ◂ gə- **~s** s
good-o, good-oh ˌgʊd ˈəʊ ‖ -ˈoʊ
Goodrich ˈgʊd rɪtʃ
goods gʊdz
good-tempered ˌgʊd ˈtemp əd ◂ ‖ -ᵊrd ◂ **~ly** li **~ness** nəs nɪs
good|wife ˈgʊd |waɪf **~wives** waɪvz
goodwill ˌgʊd ˈwɪl ◂
ˌgoodwill ˈvisit
Goodwin ˈgʊd wɪn §-wən
Goodwood ˈgʊd wʊd
Goodwright ˈgʊd raɪt
good|y ˈgʊd |i **~ies** iz
Goodyear ˈgʊd jə -jɪə, -jɜː ‖ -jᵊr -jɪr; ˈgʊdʒ ɪr
goody-good|y ˈgʊd i ˌgʊd |i ˌ· ·ˈ· · **~ies** iz
goody-two-shoes ˌgʊd i ˈtuː ʃuːz
goo|ey ˈguː‿|i **~ier** i ə ‖ i ᵊr **~iest** i ɪst i əst **~iness** i nəs i nɪs
goof guːf **goofed** guːft **goofing** ˈguːf ɪŋ **goofs** guːfs
goofball ˈguːf bɔːl ‖ -bɑːl **~s** z
goof-off ˈguːf ɒf ‖ -ɔːf -ɑːf
goof|y ˈguːf |i **~ier** i‿ə ‖ i‿ᵊr **~iest** i‿ɪst i‿əst **~ily** ɪ li əl i **~iness** i nəs i nɪs
Googie ˈguːg i
Googl|e *tdmk* ˈguːg ᵊl **~ed** d **~es** z **~ing** ‿ɪŋ
googlewhack ˈguːg ᵊl wæk -hwæk **~ed** t **~ing** ɪŋ **~s** s
goog|ly ˈguːg |li **~lies** liz
googol ˈguːg ɒl -ᵊl ‖ -ɔːl -ɑːl, -ᵊl **~s** z
googolplex ˈguːg ɒl pleks -ᵊl- ‖ -ɔːl- -ɑːl-, -ᵊl-
goo-goo ˈguː guː
gooi... —*see* **gooey**
gook *'sludge'* gʊk guːk
gook *'SE Asian'* guːk **gooks** guːks
Goole guːl
gool|ie, ~y ˈguːl i **~ies** z
goon guːn **goons** guːnz
gooner|y ˈguːn ər |i **~ies** iz
Goonhilly gʊn ˈhɪl i ˌguːn-, ˈ·ˌ· ·
goop guːp
goosander guː ˈsænd ə ‖ -ᵊr **~s** z
goose guːs **geese** giːs **goosed** guːst **gooses, goose's** ˈguːs ɪz -əz **goosing** ˈguːs ɪŋ
ˈgoose egg; **ˈgoose ˌpimples**
gooseberr|y ˈgʊz bər‿|i §ˈgʊs-, §ˈguːs-, §ˈguːz- ‖ ˈguːs ˌber |i ˈguːz-, -bər‿|i **~ies** iz
goosebumps ˈguːs bʌmps
goosedown ˈguːs daʊn
gooseflesh ˈguːs fleʃ
goosefoot ˈguːs fʊt **~s** s
goosegog ˈgʊz gɒg ‖ -gɑːg **~s** z
gooseneck ˈguːs nek **~s** s
goosestep ˈguːs step **~ped** t **~ping** ɪŋ **~s** s
Goosnargh ˈguːs nə ‖ -nᵊr
Goossens ˈguːs ᵊnz
GOP ˌdʒiː əʊ ˈpiː ‖ -oʊ-
gopher ˈgəʊf ə ‖ ˈgoʊf ᵊr **~s** z
Gorazde gə ˈræʒ deɪ gɔː-, -də —*Serbian* Goražde [ˈgɔ raʒ dɛ]
Gorbachev, Gorbachov ˈgɔːb ə tʃɒf -tʃɒv, ˌ· ·ˈ· ‖ ˈgɔːrb ə tʃɔːf -tʃɑːf —*Russ* [gər bʌ ˈtʃɔf]
Gorbals ˈgɔːb ᵊlz ‖ ˈgɔːrb-
gorblimey ₍ˌ₎gɔː ˈblaɪm i ‖ gɔːr-
Gordian ˈgɔːd i‿ən ‖ ˈgɔːrd-
ˌGordian ˈknot
Gordimer ˈgɔːd ɪm ə §-əm ə ‖ ˈgɔːrd əm ᵊr
Gordon ˈgɔːd ᵊn ‖ ˈgɔːrd ᵊn
Gordonstoun ˈgɔːd ᵊnz tən -ᵊnᵗst ən ‖ ˈgɔːrd-
gore, Gore gɔː ‖ gɔːr goʊr **gored** gɔːd ‖ gɔːrd goʊrd **gores** gɔːz ‖ gɔːrz goʊrz **goring** ˈgɔːr ɪŋ ‖ ˈgoʊr-
Gorecki, Górecki gɔː ˈret ski gə- —*Polish* [gu ˈrets ki]
Gore-Tex *tdmk* ˈgɔː teks ‖ ˈgɔːr-
gorge gɔːdʒ ‖ gɔːrdʒ **gorged** gɔːdʒd ‖ gɔːrdʒd **gorges** ˈgɔːdʒ ɪz -əz ‖ ˈgɔːrdʒ əz **gorging** ˈgɔːdʒ ɪŋ ‖ ˈgɔːrdʒ ɪŋ
gorgeous ˈgɔːdʒ əs ‖ ˈgɔːrdʒ- **~ly** li **~ness** nəs nɪs
gorget ˈgɔːdʒ ɪt -ət ‖ ˈgɔːrdʒ- **~s** s
Gorgias ˈgɔːdʒ i‿əs -æs ‖ ˈgɔːrdʒ-
gorgon, G~ ˈgɔːg ən ‖ ˈgɔːrg- **~s, ~'s** z
Gorgonzola ˌgɔːg ən ˈzəʊl ə ◂ →-ŋ- ‖ ˌgɔːrg ən ˈzoʊl ə —*It* [gor gon ˈdzɔː la]
Gorham ˈgɔːr əm
gori... —*see* **gory**
gorilla gə ˈrɪl ə **~s** z
Goring ˈgɔːr ɪŋ
Gorki, Gorky ˈgɔːk i ‖ ˈgɔːrk i —*Russ* [ˈgɔrʲ kʲɪj]
Gorleston ˈgɔːlst ən ‖ ˈgɔːrlst-
Gorman ˈgɔːm ən ‖ ˈgɔːrm-
gormandis|e, gormandiz|e ˈgɔːm ən daɪz ‖ ˈgɔːrm- **~ed** d **~er/s** ə/z ‖ ᵊr/z **~es** ɪz əz **~ing** ɪŋ
Gormanston ˈgɔːm ənᵗst ən ‖ ˈgɔːrm-
Gormenghast ˈgɔːm ən gɑːst →-əŋ-, §-gæst ‖ ˈgɔːrm ən gæst
gormless ˈgɔːm ləs -lɪs ‖ ˈgɔːrm- **~ly** li **~ness** nəs nɪs
Gormley ˈgɔːm li ‖ ˈgɔːrm-
Goronwy gə ˈrɒn wi gɒ- ‖ -ˈrɑːn- —*Welsh* [go'ro nui, -nwi]
Gorran ˈgɒr ən ‖ ˈgɔːr-
Gor-Ray *tdmk* ˈgɔː reɪ ‖ ˈgɔːr-
Gorringe ˈgɒr ɪndʒ -əndʒ ‖ ˈgɔːr- ˈgɑːr-
gorse gɔːs ‖ gɔːrs
Gorsedd ˈgɔːs eð ‖ ˈgɔːrs- —*Welsh* [ˈgor seð]
Gorseinon gɔː ˈsaɪn ən ‖ gɔːr- —*Welsh* [gor ˈsəi non]
Gorst gɔːst ‖ gɔːrst
Gorton ˈgɔːt ᵊn ‖ ˈgɔːrt ᵊn
gor|y ˈgɔːr |i ‖ ˈgoʊr- **~ier** i‿ə ‖ i‿ᵊr **~iest** i‿ɪst i‿əst **~ily** əl i ɪ li **~iness** i nəs i nɪs
Gosforth ˈgɒs fəθ -fɔːθ ‖ ˈgɑːs fɔːrθ -foʊrθ
gosh gɒʃ ‖ gɑːʃ
goshawk ˈgɒs hɔːk ‖ ˈgɑːs- -hɑːk **~s** s

Goshen 'gəʊʃ ³n ‖ 'goʊʃ ³n
gosling, G~ 'gɒz lɪŋ ‖ 'gɑːz- **~s** z
go-slow ˌgəʊ 'sləʊ ◂ · · · ‖ 'goʊ sloʊ **~s** z
gospel, G~ 'gɒsp ³l ‖ 'gɑːsp ³l **~s** z
  'gospel ˌmusic; ˌgospel 'truth
gospeler, gospeller 'gɒsp əl ə ‖ 'gɑːsp ³l ər
  ~s z
Gosport, g~ 'gɒs pɔːt ‖ 'gɑːs pɔːrt -poʊrt **~s** s
Goss gɒs ‖ gɔːs gɑːs
Gossage 'gɒs ɪdʒ ‖ 'gɑːs-
gossamer 'gɒs əm ə ‖ 'gɑːs əm ³r 'gɑːz- **~ed** d
Gosse gɒs ‖ gɔːs gɑːs
gossip 'gɒs ɪp §-əp ‖ 'gɑːs əp **~ed** t **~er/s** ə/z
  ‖ ³r/z **~ing** ɪŋ **~s** s
gossipmonger 'gɒs ɪp ˌmʌŋ gə §-əp-
  ‖ 'gɑːs əp ˌmʌŋ g³r -ˌmɑːŋ- **~s** z
gossipy 'gɒs ɪp i §-əp- ‖ 'gɑːs-
gossypol 'gɒs i pɒl ‖ 'gɑːs ə poʊl -pɑːl, -pɔːl
got gɒt ‖ gɑːt
gotcha 'gɒtʃ ə ‖ 'gɑːtʃ ə **~s** z
Goth gɒθ ‖ gɑːθ **Goths** gɒθs ‖ gɑːθs
Gotha 'gəʊθ ə 'gəʊt- ‖ 'goʊθ ə —Ger ['goː ta]
Gotham nickname for NYC 'gɒθ əm 'gəʊθ-
  ‖ 'gɑːθ-
Gotham place in Notts 'gəʊt əm 'gɒt- ‖ 'goʊt̬-
  'gɑːt̬-
Gothard 'gɒθ ɑːd ‖ 'gɑːθ ɑːrd
Gothenburg 'gɒθ ³n bɜːg 'gɒt- ‖ 'gɑːθ ³n bɜːg
  'gɑːt- —Swedish Göteborg [ˌjœt ə 'bɔrj]
Gothic 'gɒθ ɪk ‖ 'gɑːθ ɪk **~ally** ³l̬_i
Gothicism 'gɒθ ɪ ˌsɪz əm -ə- ‖ 'gɑːθ-
gotta 'gɒt ə ‖ 'gɑːt̬ ə —Although this spelling
  is nonstandard, particularly in BrE, the
  pronunciation given is quite usual not only in
  GenAm but also in informal RP for got to
  ('must') before a word beginning with a
  consonant sound. Before a vowel, the
  corresponding pronunciation is usually 'gɒt u
  ‖ 'gɑːt̬ ə —see discussion at to
gotten 'gɒt ³n ‖ 'gɑːt ³n
gotterdammerung ˌgɒt ə 'dæm ə rʊŋ ˌgɜːt-,
  -'dem-, -rʌŋ ‖ ˌgɑːt̬ ³r- —Ger
  Götterdämmerung ['gœ tɐ ˌdɛ mə ʁʊŋ]
Gottfried 'gɒt friːd ‖ 'gɑːt- —Ger ['gɔt fʁiːt]
Gotti 'gɒt i ‖ 'gɑːt̬ i
Gottingen, Göttingen 'gɜːt ɪŋ ən 'gɒt- ‖ 'get̬-
  'goʊt̬-, 'gɜːt̬- —Ger ['gœt ɪŋ ṇe]
gouach|e gu 'ɑːʃ gwɑːʃ —Fr [gwaʃ] **~es** ɪz əz
Gouda 'gaʊd ə ‖ 'guːd ə —Dutch ['xɔu daː]
Goudge guːdʒ gʊdʒ
Goudhurst 'gaʊd hɜːst ‖ -hɜːst
gouge gaʊdʒ **gouged** gaʊdʒd **gouges**
  'gaʊdʒ ɪz -əz **gouging** 'gaʊdʒ ɪŋ
Gough gɒf ‖ gɑːf
goujon 'guːdʒ ən 'guːʒ-, -ɒn, -ɒ̃ ‖ gu 'ʒoʊn
  —Fr [gu ʒɔ̃] **~s** z
goulash 'guːl æʃ ‖ -ɑːʃ -æʃ **~es** ɪz əz
Gould guːld gəʊld
Gounod 'guːn əʊ ‖ -oʊ —Fr [gu no]
gourami, gouramy gʊ 'rɑːm i 'gʊər əm i **~s** z
gourd, gourde gʊəd gɔːd ‖ gɔːrd gourd, gʊ³rd
  gourds, gourdes gʊədz gɔːdz ‖ gɔːrdz
  goʊrdz, gʊ³rdz

Gourlay, Gourley 'gʊəl i ‖ 'gʊrl i
gourmand 'gʊəm ənd 'gɔːm- ‖ 'gʊrm ɑːnd
  -ənd; gʊr 'mɑːnd —Fr [guʁ mɑ̃] **~s** z
gourmet 'gʊəm eɪ 'gɔːm- ‖ 'gʊrm eɪ gʊr 'meɪ
  —Fr [guʁ mɛ] **~s** z
Gourock 'gʊər ək ‖ 'gʊr-
gout gaʊt **gouts** gaʊts
goutweed 'gaʊt wiːd
gout|y 'gaʊt |i ‖ 'gaʊt̬ |i **~ier** i ə ‖ i ³r **~iest**
  i ɪst i_əst **~ily** ɪ li əl i **~iness** i nəs i nɪs
Govan 'gʌv ³n
gov|ern 'gʌv |³n ‖ -|³rn **~erned** ³nd ‖ ³rnd
  ~erning ³n_ɪŋ ‖ ³rn ɪŋ **~erns** ³nz ‖ ³rnz
governance 'gʌv ³n_ən⁀s ‖ -³rn ən⁀s
governess 'gʌv ³n_əs -ɪs, -es ‖ -³rn əs **~es** ɪz əz
government 'gʌv ³n mənt →-³m-, -ə- ‖ -³rn-
  —There are also casual forms 'gʌb m mənt,
  'gʌm mənt **~s** s
governmental ˌgʌv ³n 'ment ³l ◂ -→³m-, -ə-
  ‖ ˌgʌv ³rn 'ment̬ ³l ◂ **~ly** i
governor 'gʌv ³n ə ‖ 'gʌv ³n ³r -³rn ³r **~s** z
governor-general ˌgʌv ³n ə 'dʒen rəl
  -'dʒen ³r əl ‖ -³n ³r- **governors-general**
  ˌgʌv ³n əz- -³n ³rz-
governorship 'gʌv ³n ə ʃɪp ‖ -³n ³r- -³rn ³r- **~s**
  s
Govett 'gʌv ɪt -ət
Gow gaʊ
Gowan, gowan 'gaʊ ən **~s** z
Gower (i) 'gaʊ ə ‖ 'gaʊ ³r, (ii) gɔː ‖ gɔːr -The
  peninsula in Wales, and the London street, are
  (i). The family name is sometimes (ii).
Gowing 'gaʊ ɪŋ **~s** z
gown gaʊn **gowned** gaʊnd **gowning**
  'gaʊn ɪŋ **gowns** gaʊnz
Gowrie 'gaʊ³r i
goy gɔɪ **goyim** 'gɔɪ ɪm -jɪm, §-əm **goys** gɔɪz
Goya 'gɔɪ ə —Sp ['go ja] **~s, ~'s** z
Goyt gɔɪt
Gozo 'gəʊz əʊ ‖ 'goʊz oʊ
GP ˌdʒiː 'piː **~s, ~'s** z
G-Plan tdmk 'dʒiː plæn
GPO ˌdʒiː piː 'əʊ ◂ ‖ -'oʊ ◂
Graafian 'grɑːf i ən 'græf-
grab græb **grabbed** græbd **grabbing** 'græb ɪŋ
  grabs græbz
  'grab ˌbag
grabber 'græb ə ‖ -³r **~s** z
grabby 'græb i
graben 'grɑːb ən **~s** z
Gracch|us 'græk |əs **~i** iː aɪ
grace, Grace greɪs **graced** greɪst **graces,**
  Graces, Grace's 'greɪs ɪz -əz **gracing**
  'greɪs ɪŋ
  'grace ˌnote
grace-and-favour ˌgreɪs ³n 'feɪv ə ◂ -³nd- ‖ -³r
Gracechurch 'greɪs tʃɜːtʃ ‖ -tʃɜːtʃ
graceful 'greɪs f³l -fʊl **~ly** _i **~ness** nəs nɪs
Graceland 'greɪs lænd -lənd
graceless 'greɪs ləs -lɪs **~ly** li **~ness** nəs nɪs
Gracey, Gracie 'greɪs i
gracious 'greɪʃ əs **~ly** li **~ness** nəs nɪs
grackle 'græk ³l **~s** z

G

grad græd **grads** grædz
gradability ˌɡreɪd ə 'bɪl ət i -ɪt i ‖ -ət̬ i
gradable 'ɡreɪd əb ᵊl
gradate ɡrə 'd|eɪt ‖ 'ɡreɪd |eɪt **~ated** eɪt ɪd
-əd ‖ eɪt̬ əd **~ates** eɪts **~ating** eɪt ɪŋ ‖ eɪt̬ ɪŋ
gradation ɡrə 'deɪʃ ᵊn ɡreɪ-, græ- **~al** ᵊl **~s** z
grade, Grade ɡreɪd **graded** 'ɡreɪd ɪd -əd
  grades ɡreɪdz **grading** 'ɡreɪd ɪŋ
  'grade ˌcrossing; **'grade school**
Gradgrind 'ɡræd ɡraɪnd →'ɡræɡ-
gradience 'ɡreɪd i‿ənˢs
gradient 'ɡreɪd i‿ənt **~s** s

GRADUAL

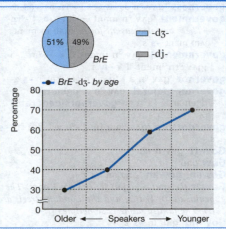

-dʒ-
-dj-

51% 49%
BrE

● BrE -dʒ- by age

Percentage
80
70
60
50
40
30
0

Older ◄— Speakers —► Younger

---

gradual 'ɡrædʒ u‿əl 'ɡræd ju‿əl; 'ɡrædʒ ᵊl **~ly**
i **~ness** nəs nɪs — *Preference poll, BrE*
(gradually): dʒ *51%*, dj *49%; born since 1973,*
dʒ *70%,* dj *30%.*
graduate *adj, n* 'ɡrædʒ u‿ət 'ɡræd ju‿, ɪt, -eɪt
~s s
gradu|ate *v* 'ɡrædʒ u |eɪt 'ɡræd ju- **~ated**
eɪt ɪd -əd ‖ eɪt̬ əd **~ates** eɪts **~ating** eɪt ɪŋ
‖ eɪt̬ ɪŋ
graduation ˌɡrædʒ u 'eɪʃ ᵊn ˌɡræd ju- **~s** z
gradus 'ɡræd əs 'ɡreɪd- **~es** ɪz əz
Grady 'ɡreɪd i
Graeco- ˌɡriːk əʊ ‖ -oʊ — **Graeco-Roman**
  ˌɡriːk əʊ 'rəʊm ən ◄ ‖ -oʊ 'roʊm-
Graeme 'ɡreɪ əm ɡreɪm
Graf ɡrɑːf ɡræf —*Ger* [ɡʁaːf]
graffit|i ɡrə 'fiːt |i ɡræ- ‖ -'fiːt̬ |i **-o** əʊ ‖ oʊ
Grafham, Graffham 'ɡræf əm —*but* Grafham
  in Cambridgeshire is 'ɡrɑːf-
graft ɡrɑːft §græft ‖ græft **grafted** 'ɡrɑːft ɪd
  §'græft-, -əd ‖ 'græft əd **grafting** 'ɡrɑːft ɪŋ
  §'græft- ‖ 'græft ɪŋ **grafts** ɡrɑːfts §græfts
  ‖ græfts
grafter 'ɡrɑːft ə §'græft- ‖ 'græft ᵊr **~s** z
Grafton 'ɡrɑːft ən §'græft- ‖ 'græft-
Graham, g~, Grahame 'ɡreɪ əm
Grahamstown 'ɡreɪ əmz taʊn
Graig ɡraɪɡ —*Welsh* [ɡraiɡ]
Grail, grail ɡreɪᵊl **grails** ɡreɪᵊlz

grain ɡreɪn **grained** ɡreɪnd **graining**
  'ɡreɪn ɪŋ **grains** ɡreɪnz
  'grain ˌelevator
Grainger 'ɡreɪndʒ ə ‖ -ᵊr
Grainne, Gráinne 'ɡrɔːn jə ‖ 'ɡrɑːn-
grain|y 'ɡreɪn |i **~ier** i‿ə ‖ i‿ᵊr **~iest** i‿ɪst i‿əst
  ~iness i nəs i nɪs
-gram ɡræm — **gorillagram** ɡə 'rɪl ə ɡræm
gram, Gram ɡræm **grams** ɡræmz
gramercy, G~ ɡrə 'mɜːs i ‖ -'mɜːs i —*but in*
  NYC G~ Park *is* 'ɡræm əs i ‖ -ᵊrs i
graminaceous ˌɡræm ɪ 'neɪʃ əs ◄ -ə-
grammalogue 'ɡræm ə lɒɡ ‖ -lɔːɡ -lɑːɡ **~s** z
grammar 'ɡræm ə ‖ -ᵊr **~s** z
  'grammar school
grammarian ɡrə 'meər i‿ən ‖ -'mer- -'mær- **~s**
  z
grammatical ɡrə 'mæt ɪk ᵊl ‖ -'mæt̬- **~ly** i
grammaticality ɡrə ˌmæt ɪ 'kæl ət i §-ˌ-ə-,
  -ɪt i ‖ -ˌmæt̬ ə 'kæl ət̬ i
gramme ɡræm **grammes** ɡræmz
Gramm|y 'ɡræm |i **~ies, ~ys** iz
Gram-negative ˌɡræm 'neɡ ət ɪv ◄ ‖ -ət̬-
gramophone 'ɡræm ə fəʊn ‖ -foʊn **~s** z
  'gramophone ˌrecord
Grampian 'ɡræmp i‿ən **~s** z
Gram-positive ˌɡræm 'pɒz ət ɪv ◄ -ət-
  ‖ -'pɑːz ət̬-
Gramps ɡræmps
grampus 'ɡræmp əs **~es** ɪz əz
gran, Gran ɡræn —*See also phrases with this*
  word **grans, Gran's** ɡrænz
Granada ɡrə 'nɑːd ə —*Sp* [ɡra 'na ða]
granadilla ˌɡræn ə 'dɪl ə ‖ -'diː ə **~s** z
Granados ɡrə 'nɑːd ɒs ‖ -oʊs —*Sp*
  [ɡra 'na ðos]
granar|y 'ɡræn ər |i ‖ 'ɡren- **~ies** iz
Granby 'ɡræn bi →'ɡræm-
Gran Canaria ˌɡræn kə 'neər i‿ə →ˌɡræŋ-,
  -'nɑːr- ‖ ˌɡrɑːn kə 'nɑːr i‿ə -'nær-, -'ner- —*Sp*
  [ɡraŋ ka 'na rja]
grand, Grand ɡrænd —*but in French*
  expressions ɡrɒn, ɡrɒ̃ ‖ ɡrɑːn —*Fr* [ɡrɑ̃]
  —*See also phrases with this word* **grander**
  'ɡrænd ə ‖ -ᵊr **grandest** 'ɡrænd ɪst -əst
  grands ɡrændz
  ˌGrand 'Canyon; **ˌgrand 'jury**; **ˌgrand**
  'opera; **ˌgrand pi'ano**; **ˌGrand 'Rapids**;
  ˌgrand 'slam
grandad, G~ 'ɡræn dæd **~s, ~'s** z
grandadd|y 'ɡræn ˌdæd |i **~ies, ~y's** iz
grandchild 'ɡræn tʃaɪᵊld 'ɡrænd- **~'s** z
grandchildren 'ɡræn ˌtʃɪldr ən 'ɡrænd-,
  -ˌtʃʊldr- **~'s** z
Grand Coulee ˌɡrænd 'kuːl i
granddad 'ɡræn dæd **~s** z
granddadd|y 'ɡræn ˌdæd| i **~ies** iz
granddaughter 'ɡræn ˌdɔːt ə 'ɡrænd-
  ‖ -ˌdɔːt̬ ᵊr -ˌdɑːt̬- **~s** z
grandduke ˌɡrænd 'djuːk ◄ →-'dʒuːk ‖ -'duːk
  -'djuːk **~s** s
grande dame ˌɡrɑːn 'dæm ‖ -'dɑːm —*Fr*
  [ɡʁɑ̃d dam]

grandee græn ˈdiː ~s z
grandeur ˈgrændʒ ə ˈgræn djʊə, ˈgrɒ̃-, -djə
‖ -ᵊr -ʊr
grandfather, G~ ˈgrænd ˌfɑːð ə ‖ -ᵊr ~s, ~'s z
ˌgrandˌfather 'clock
Grand Guignol ˌgrɒn ˈgiːn jɒl ˌgrɒ̃-
‖ ˌgrɑːn giːn 'jʊʊl -ˈjɔːl, -ˈjɑːl —Fr [-gi njɔl]
grandiloquence græn ˈdɪl ək wənts
grandiloquent græn ˈdɪl ək wənt ~ly li
grandiose ˈgrænd i əʊs -əʊz ‖ -oʊs ˌ·ˈ· ~ly li
~ness nəs nɪs
grandiosity ˌgrænd i ˈɒs ət i -ɪt i ‖ -ˈɑːs ət i
Grandison ˈgrænd ɪs ən -əs-
grandly ˈgrænd li
grandma, G~ ˈgræn mɑ: ˈgrænd-, →ˈgræm- -mɔ: ~s, ~'s z
grand mal ˌgrɒn ˈmæl ˌgrɒ̃- ‖ ˌgræn ˈmɑːl
ˌgrɑːn-, -ˈmæl, ˈ··—Fr [-mal]
grandmama, grandmamma ˈgrænd mə ˌmɑ:
→ˈgræm- ~s, ~'s z
Grand Marnier tdmk ˌgrɒn ˈmɑːn i eɪ ˌgrɒ̃-
‖ ˌgrɑːn mɑːrn ˈjeɪ —Fr [-maʁ nje]
grandmaster ˈgrænd ˌmɑːst ə →ˈgræm-,
§-ˌmæst-, ˌ·ˈ·· ‖ -ˌmæst ᵊr ~s z
grandmother, G~ ˈgræn ˌmʌð ə ˈgrænd-,
→ˈgræm- ‖ -ᵊr ~s, ~'s z
grandness ˈgrænd nəs -nɪs
grandpa, G~ ˈgræn pɑ: →ˈgræm- ‖ -pɔ: ~s,
~'s z
grandparent ˈgrænd ˌpeər ənt →ˈgræm-
‖ -ˌper- -ˌpær- ~s s
grand prix ˌgrɒn ˈpriː ˌgrɒ̃-, ˌgrɑːn-, ˌgrɔːn-,
→ˌgrɒm-, →ˌgrɑːm-, →ˌgrɔːm- ‖ ˌgrɑːn- —Fr
[gʁɑ̃ pʁi] **grands prix** —as sing. or with
added z
grandsire ˈgrænd ˌsaɪ ə ‖ -ˌsaɪ ᵊr ~s z
grandson ˈgræn sʌn ˈgrænd- ~s z
grands prix ˌgrɒn ˈpriː ˌgrɒ̃-, ˌgrɑːn-, ˌgrɔːn-,
→ˌgrɒm-, →ˌgrɑːm-, →ˌgrɔːm-, -ˈpriːz ‖ ˌgrɑːn-
—Fr [gʁɑ̃ pʁi]
grandstand ˈgrænd stænd ~ing ɪŋ ~s z
grange, G~ greɪndʒ **granges** ˈgreɪndʒ ɪz -əz
Grangemouth ˈgreɪndʒ maʊθ -məθ
Grange-over-Sands ˌgreɪndʒ əʊv ə ˈsændz
‖ -oʊv ᵊr-
Granger ˈgreɪndʒ ə ‖ -ᵊr
granite ˈgræn ɪt -ət ~s s
granitic grə ˈnɪt ɪk græ- ‖ -ˈnɪt ɪk
grannie, granny, G~ ˈgræn i ~s, ~'s z
ˈgranny flat; ˈgranny knot; ˌGranny
'Smith
granola grə ˈnəʊl ə greɪ- ‖ -ˈnoʊl ə
granolithic ˌgræn ə ˈlɪθ ɪk ◄
grant, Grant grɑːnt §grænt ‖ grænt **granted**
ˈgrɑːnt ɪd §ˈgrænt-, -əd ‖ ˈgrænt̬ əd **granting**
ˈgrɑːnt ɪŋ §ˈgrænt- ‖ ˈgrænt̬ ɪŋ **grants**
grɑːnts §grænts ‖ grænts
Granta ˈgrɑːnt ə ˈgrænt- ‖ ˈgrænt̬ ə
grant-aided ˌgrɑːnt ˈeɪd ɪd ◄ §ˌgrænt-, -əd
‖ ˌgrænt̬-
Grantchester ˈgrɑːn tʃɪst ə ˈgræn-, -tʃəst-,
§-ˌtʃest- ‖ ˈgræn ˌtʃest ᵊr
grantee ₍ˌ₎grɑːn ˈtiː §₍ˌ₎græn- ‖ ₍ˌ₎græn- ~s z

Granth grʌnt —Hindi [grənt̪ʰ]
Grantham ˈgrænθ əm
grant-in-aid ˌgrɑːnt ɪn ˈeɪd §ˌgrænt-
‖ ˌgrænt ᵊn-
Grantley, Grantly ˈgrɑːnt li §ˈgrænt-
‖ ˈgrænt-
grant-maintaned ˌgrɑːnt meɪn ˈteɪnd ◄
§ˌgrænt-, -men-, -mən- ‖ ˌgrænt-
grantor ₍ˌ₎grɑːn ˈtɔː §₍ˌ₎græn-; ˈgrɑːnt ə,
§ˈgrænt- ‖ ₍ˌ₎græn ˈtɔːr ˈgrænt̬ ᵊr ~s z
Grantown-on-Spey ˌgræn taʊn ɒn ˈspeɪ
ˌgrænt ən- ‖ -ɑːn ˈspeɪ -ɔːnˈ·
gran turismo ˌgræn tʊə ˈrɪz məʊ -tuᵊ-
‖ ˌgrɑːn tʊ ˈrɪz moʊ -ˈriːz- —It
[gran tu ˈriz mo]
granular ˈgræn jʊl ə -jəl- ‖ -jəl ᵊr
granularity ˌgræn jʊ ˈlær ət i ˌjə-, -ɪt i
‖ -jə ˈlær ət̬ i -ˈler-
granu|late ˈgræn jʊ |leɪt -jə- ‖ -jə- ~**lated**
leɪt ɪd -əd ‖ leɪt̬ əd ~**lates** leɪts ~**lating**
leɪt ɪŋ ‖ leɪt̬ ɪŋ
granulation ˌgræn jʊ ˈleɪʃ ᵊn -jə- ‖ -jə- ~s z
granule ˈgræn juːl ~s z
Granville ˈgræn vɪl -vᵊl
grape greɪp **grapes** greɪps
grapefruit ˈgreɪp fruːt ~s s
Grapelli grə ˈpel i
grapeshot ˈgreɪp ʃɒt ‖ -ʃɑːt
grapevine ˈgreɪp vaɪn ~s z

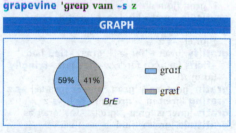

BrE

graph grɑːf græf ‖ græf — Preference poll, BrE:
grɑːf 59% (English southerners 77%), græf
41% (English southerners 23%). **graphed**
grɑːft græft ‖ græft **graphing** ˈgrɑːf ɪŋ ˈgræf-
‖ ˈgræf ɪŋ **graphs** grɑːfs græfs ‖ græfs
ˈgraph ˌpaper
-graph grɑːf græf ‖ græf — **photograph**
ˈfəʊt ə grɑːf -græf ‖ ˈfoʊt̬ ə græf
grapheme ˈgræf iːm ~s z
graphemic græ ˈfiːm ɪk grə- ~**ally** ᵊl̩ i
-grapher stress-imposing grəf ə ‖ -ᵊr —
photographer fəʊ ˈtɒg rəf ə ‖ fə ˈtɑːg rəf ᵊr
-graphic ˈgræf ɪk — **photographic**
ˌfəʊt ə ˈgræf ɪk ◄ ‖ ˌfoʊt̬-
graphic ˈgræf ɪk ~**al** ᵊl ~**ally** ᵊl̩ i ~s s
ˌgraphic deˈsign; ˌgraphic deˈsigner
graphite ˈgræf aɪt
graphological ˌgræf ə ˈlɒdʒ ɪk ᵊl ◄ ‖ -ˈlɑːdʒ-
~**ly** _i
graphologist græ ˈfɒl ədʒ ɪst grə-, §-əst
‖ -ˈfɑːl- ~s s
graphology græ ˈfɒl ədʒ i grə- ‖ -ˈfɑːl-
-graphy stress-imposing grəf i — **photography**
fəʊ ˈtɒg rəf i ‖ fə ˈtɑːg-

G

grapnel 'græp nᵊl ~s z
grappa 'græp ə ‖ 'grɑːp ə —*It* ['grɑp pa]
Grappelli grə 'pel i —*Fr* [gra pɛ li]
grappl|e 'græp ᵊl ~ed d ~es z ~ing ɪŋ
  'grappling hook; 'grappling ˌiron
graptolite 'græpt əʊ laɪt ‖ -ə- ~s s
Grasmere 'grɑːs mɪə §'græs- ‖ 'græs mɪr
grasp grɑːsp §græsp ‖ græsp grasped grɑːspt
  §græspt ‖ græspt grasping/ly 'grɑːsp ɪŋ /li
  §'græsp- ‖ 'græsp ɪŋ /li
grass, Grass grɑːs §græs ‖ græs —*Ger* [gras]
  grassed grɑːst §græst ‖ græst grasses
  'grɑːs ɪz §'græs-, -əz ‖ 'græs əz grassing
  'grɑːs ɪŋ §'græs- ‖ 'græs ɪŋ
  ˌgrass 'roots; ˌgrass 'widow; ˌgrass
  'widower
grasshopper 'grɑːs ˌhɒp ə §'græs-
  ‖ 'græs ˌhɑːp ᵊr ~s z
Grassington 'grɑːs ɪŋ tən §'græs- ‖ 'græs-
grassland 'grɑːs lænd §'græs-, -lənd ‖ 'græs-
  ~s z
grass|y 'grɑːs |i §'græs- ‖ 'græs |i ~ier i ə
  ‖ iᵊr ~iest i ɪst i əst ~iness i nəs i nɪs
grate greɪt grated 'greɪt ɪd -əd ‖ 'greɪt̬ əd
  grates greɪts grating 'greɪt ɪŋ ‖ 'greɪt̬ ɪŋ
grateful 'greɪt fᵊl -fʊl ~ly ˌi ~ness nəs nɪs
grater 'greɪt ə ‖ 'greɪt̬ ᵊr ~s z
Gratiano ˌgræʃ i 'ɑːn əʊ ˌgrɑː-ʃ-
  ‖ ˌgrɑːʃ 'jɑːn oʊ
graticule 'græt ɪ kjuːl -ə- ‖ 'græt̬ ə- ~s z
gratification ˌgræt ɪf ɪ 'keɪʃ ᵊn ˌ-əf-, §-ə'--
  ‖ ˌgræt̬- ~s z
grati|fy 'græt ɪ |faɪ -ə- ‖ 'græt̬- ~fied faɪd
  ~fier/s faɪ ə/z ‖ faɪ ᵊr/z ~fies faɪz ~fying/ly
  faɪ ɪŋ /li
gratin 'græt æn ‖ 'grɑːt ᵊn —*Fr* [gʁa tæ̃] ~s z
grating 'greɪt ɪŋ ‖ 'greɪt̬ ɪŋ ~ly li ~s z
gratis 'græt ɪs 'greɪt-, 'grɑːt-, -əs ‖ 'græt̬ əs
gratitude 'græt ɪ tjuːd -ə-, →-tʃuːd
  ‖ 'græt̬ ə tuːd -tjuːd
Grattan, Gratton 'græt ᵊn
gratuitous grə 'tjuː ɪt əs →-'tʃuː;
  △ˌgrætʃ u 'ɪʃ əs ‖ -'tuː ət̬ əs -'tjuː- ~ly li
  ~ness nəs nɪs
gratuit|y grə 'tjuː ət |i →-'tʃuːˌ, ɪt- ‖ -'tuː ət̬ |i
  -'tjuː- ~ies iz
graupel 'graʊp ᵊl
gravadlax 'græv əd læks ‖ 'grɑːv əd lɑːks
gravamen grə 'veɪm en -'vɑːm-, -ən; 'græv əm-
  ‖ -ən
grave *n* 'burial place'; *adj* 'serious'; *v* greɪv
  graved greɪvd graver 'greɪv ə ‖ -ᵊr graves
  greɪvz gravest 'greɪv ɪst -əst graving
  'greɪv ɪŋ
  'graving dock
grave *accent mark* grɑːv ‖ greɪv grɑːv graves
  grɑːvz ‖ greɪvz grɑːvz
grave *mus* 'grɑːv eɪ —*It* ['gra: ve]
gravedigger 'greɪv ˌdɪg ə ‖ -ᵊr ~s z
gravel 'græv ᵊl ~ed, ~led d ~ing, ~ling ɪŋ ~s
  z
Graveley 'greɪv li
gravelly, G~ 'græv ᵊl i

gravely 'greɪv li
graven 'greɪv ᵊn
graveness 'greɪv nəs -nɪs
Graveney 'greɪv ni
graver 'greɪv ə ‖ -ᵊr ~s z
graves *pl* 'burial places' greɪvz
graves *pl* 'accent marks' grɑːvz ‖ greɪvz grɑːvz
Graves *wine* grɑːv —*Fr* [gʁɑːv]
Graves *family name* greɪvz
Gravesend ˌgreɪvz 'end ◄
graveside 'greɪv saɪd
gravesite 'greɪv saɪt ~s s
gravestone 'greɪv stəʊn ‖ -stoʊn ~s z
graveyard 'greɪv jɑːd ‖ -jɑːrd ~s z
gravid 'græv ɪd §-əd ~ly li ~ness nəs nɪs
gravie... —*see* gravy
gravitas 'græv ɪ tæs -ə-, -tɑːs
gravi|tate 'græv ɪ |teɪt -ə- ~tated teɪt ɪd -əd
  ‖ teɪt̬ əd ~tates teɪts ~tating teɪt ɪŋ ‖ teɪt̬ ɪŋ
gravitation ˌgræv ɪ 'teɪʃ ᵊn -ə- ~al ᵊl ~ally
  ᵊl i
gravitative 'græv ɪ teɪt ɪv '·ə- ‖ -teɪt̬ ɪv
gravit|y 'græv ət |i -ɪt- ‖ -ət̬ |i ~ies iz
gravlaks 'græv læks ‖ 'grɑːv lɑːks 'græv-
  —*Swedish* ['grav laks]
gravure grə 'vjʊə -'vjɔː ‖ -'vjʊᵊr
grav|y 'greɪv |i ~ies iz
  'gravy boat, 'gravy train
gray, Gray greɪ grayed greɪd grayer 'greɪ ə
  ‖ -ᵊr grayest 'greɪ ɪst -əst graying 'greɪ ɪŋ
  grays, Grays, Gray's greɪz
  ˌgray 'area; 'gray ˌmatter; ˌGray's 'Inn
graybeard 'greɪ bɪəd ‖ -bɪrd ~s z
grayhound 'greɪ haʊnd ~s z
grayish 'greɪ ɪʃ
graylag 'greɪ læg ~s z
grayling 'greɪl ɪŋ ~s z
gray|ly 'greɪ |li ~ness nəs nɪs
grayscale 'greɪ skeɪᵊl
Grayson 'greɪs ᵊn
graywacke 'greɪ ˌwæk ə
Graz grɑːts —*Ger* [gʁaːts]
graze greɪz grazed greɪzd grazes 'greɪz ɪz -əz
  grazing 'greɪz ɪŋ
grazer 'greɪz ə ‖ -ᵊr ~s z
grazier 'greɪz i ə 'greɪʒ ə, 'greɪʒ i ə ‖ 'greɪʒ ᵊr
  (*) ~s z
Grealey 'griːl i
grease *n* griːs
  'grease gun
grease *v* griːs griːz greased griːst griːzd
  greases 'griːs ɪz 'griːz-, -əz greasing
  'griːs ɪŋ 'griːz-
  ˌgreased 'lightning
greasepaint 'griːs peɪnt
greaseproof 'griːs pruːf §-prʊf
greaser *v* 'griːs ə 'griːz- ‖ -ᵊr ~s z

GREASY

86% 'griːs-
14% 'griːz-

AmE

greas|y 'griːs |i 'griːz- — *Preference poll, AmE:*
'griːs- *86%,* 'griːz- *14%.* **~ier** i ə ‖ i_ᵊr **~iest**
i_ɪst i_əst **~ily** ɪ li əl i **~iness** i nəs i nɪs
,greasy 'spoon

great greɪt *(= grate)* **greater** 'greɪt ə
‖ 'greɪt̬ ᵊr **greatest** 'greɪt ɪst -əst ‖ 'greɪt̬ əst
greats greɪts
,Great 'Barrier Reef; ,Great 'Bear; ,Great
'Britain; ,great 'circle; ,Great 'Dane;
,Greater 'London◂, ,Greater ,London
'Council; ,Great 'Lakes; ,Great 'Plains

great- |greɪt —*Compounds in great- are usually*
late-stressed: ,great-'grand,daughter. *However*
great-aunt *and* great-uncle, *which are regularly*
subject to stress-shifting in names
(,great-'aunt◂, ,Great-Aunt 'Mary), *are by*
some people always given early stress.

great-aunt ,greɪt 'ɑːnt ◂ §-'ænt, '··
‖ ,greɪt̬ 'ænt ◂ -'ɑːnt **~s** s

greatcoat 'greɪt kəʊt ‖ -koʊt **~s** s

great|ly 'greɪt |li **~ness** nəs nɪs

Greatorex 'greɪt ə reks ‖ 'greɪt̬-

great-uncle ,greɪt 'ʌŋk ᵊl ◂ '·,·· ‖ ,greɪt̬- **~s** z

greave, G~ griːv *(= grieve)* **greaves** griːvz

Greaves *(i)* greɪvz, *(ii)* griːvz

grebe griːb **grebes** griːbz

Grecian 'griːʃ ᵊn **~s** z

Greco 'grek əʊ ‖ -oʊ

Greco- |'griːk əʊ |grek- ‖ -oʊ — **Greco-Roman**
,griːk əʊ 'rəʊm ən ◂ ,grek- ‖ -oʊ 'roʊm-

Greece griːs

greed griːd

greed|y 'griːd |i **~ier** i ə ‖ i_ᵊr **~iest** i_ɪst i_əst
~ily ɪ li əl i **~iness** i nəs i nɪs

greedy-guts 'griːd i gʌts

Greek, greek griːk **greeked** 'griːk ɪŋ
greeking 'griːk ɪŋ **Greeks, greeks** griːks
,Greek 'Orthodox

Greeley, Greely 'griːl i

green, Green griːn **greened** griːnd **greener**
'griːn ə ‖ -ᵊr **greenest** 'griːn ɪst -əst
greening 'griːn ɪŋ **greens, G~** griːnz
,green 'bean; 'green belt; ,green 'fingers;
,green 'light; ,Green 'Paper; ,green
'pepper; ,green 'tea; ,green 'thumb

Greenaway 'griːn ə weɪ

greenback 'griːn bæk →'griːm- **~s** s

Greenbaum *(i)* 'griːn baʊm →'griːm-,
(ii) -bɔːm ‖ -bɑːm, *(iii)* -bəʊm ‖ -boʊm —*The*
late Prof. Sidney G~, grammarian, claimed
not to care which variant people used for his
name; he was generally known as (i)

Greenberg 'griːn bɜːg →'griːm- ‖ -bɜːg

Greene griːn

greener|y 'griːn ər |i **~ies** iz

green-eyed ,griːn 'aɪd ◂ ‖ '··
,green-eyed 'monster

Greenfield, g~ 'griːn fiːᵊld

greenfinch 'griːn fɪntʃ **~es** ɪz əz

green|fly 'griːn |flaɪ **~flies** flaɪz

Greenford 'griːn fəd ‖ -fᵊrd

greengag|e 'griːn geɪdʒ →'griːn- **~es** ɪz əz

greengrocer 'griːn ,grəʊs ə →'griːn-
‖ -,groʊs ᵊr **~s** z

greengrocer|y 'griːn ,grəʊs ᵊr |i →'griːn-
‖ -,groʊs- **~ies** iz

Greengross 'griːn grɒs →'griːn- ‖ -grɑːs

Greenhalgh 'griːn hælʃ -hɔːlʃ, -hɒlʃ, -hældʒ,
-hɔːl

Greenham 'griːn əm

Greenhill 'griːn hɪl

greenhorn 'griːn hɔːn ‖ -hɔːrn **~s** z

Greenhough 'griːn ɒf -hɒf, -həʊ, -haʊ, -hʌf
‖ -hoʊ

green|house 'griːn |haʊs **~houses** haʊz ɪz -əz
'greenhouse ef,fect

greenish 'griːn ɪʃ

Greenland 'griːn lənd -lænd **~er/s** ə/z ‖ ᵊr/z

Greenlandic ₍ᵢ₎griːn 'lænd ɪk

green|ly 'griːn |li **~ness** nəs nɪs

Greenock 'griːn ək

Greenough 'griːn əʊ ‖ -oʊ

Greenpeace 'griːn piːs →'griːm-, ,·'·

greenroom 'griːn ruːm -rʊm **~s** z

greensand 'griːn sænd **~s** z

greenshank 'griːn ʃæŋk **~s** s

Greenslade 'griːn sleɪd

Greensleeves 'griːn sliːvz

greenstick 'griːn stɪk

greenstone 'griːn stəʊn ‖ -stoʊn

Greenstreet 'griːn striːt

greenstuff 'griːn stʌf

greensward 'griːn swɔːd ‖ -swɔːrd **~s** z

Greenville 'griːn vɪl -vᵊl

greenwash 'griːn wɒʃ ‖ -wɑːʃ -wɔːʃ **~ed** t **~es**
ɪz əz **~ing** ɪŋ

Greenwell 'griːn wəl -wel

Greenwich 'gren ɪtʃ 'grɪn-, -ɪdʒ —*This applies*
both to the London borough, location of the
meridian, and to G~ Village *in NYC; also to*
the town in CT, though this is sometimes
'griːn wɪtʃ
,Greenwich 'Mean Time, ,··,·'·;
,Greenwich 'Village

greenwood, G~ 'griːn wʊd **~s** z

Greer grɪə ‖ grɪᵊr

greet, Greet griːt **greeted** 'griːt ɪd -əd
‖ 'griːt̬ əd **greeting** 'griːt ɪŋ ‖ 'griːt̬ ɪŋ
greets griːts

greeter 'griːt ə ‖ 'griːt̬ ᵊr **~s** z

Greg greg

gregarious grɪ 'geər i_əs grə- ‖ -'ger- -'gær-
~ly li **~ness** nəs nɪs

Gregg greg

Gregor 'greg ə ‖ -ᵊr

G

G

Gregorian grɪ 'gɔːr i̯ ən grə-, gre- ‖ -'gour- ~s
z
Gregory 'greg ər i
Gregson 'greg sən
Gregynog grɪ 'gʌn ɒg grə-, gre- ‖ -ɑːg
—Welsh [gre 'gə nog]
Greig (i) greg, (ii) griːg
gremlin 'grem lɪn §-lən ~s z
grenache grə 'næʃ gre- ‖ -'nɑːʃ
Grenada grɪ 'neɪd ə grə-, gre-
grenade grɪ 'neɪd grə- ~s z
Grenadian grɪ 'neɪd i̯ ən grə-, gre- ~s z
grenadier ˌgren ə 'dɪə ◄ ‖ -'dɪ²r ◄ ~s z
grenadilla ˌgren ə 'dɪl ə ~s z
grenadine, G~ ˌgren ə diːn ˌ·'·· ~s z
Grendel 'grend ²l
Grendon 'grend ən
Grenfell 'gren f²l -fel
Grenoble grɪ 'nəʊb ²l grə- ‖ -'noʊb- —Fr
[gʁə nɔbl]
Grenville 'gren vɪl -v²l
Gresham 'greʃ əm 'gres-
Gresley 'grez li
Greta (i) 'griːt ə ‖ 'griːt̬ ə, (ii) 'gret ə ‖ 'gret̬ ə
Gretchen 'gretʃ ən —Ger ['gʁɛːt çən]
Gretel 'gret ²l ‖ 'gret̬ ²l —Ger ['gʁeː t²l]
Gretna 'gret nə
ˌGretna 'Green
Gretzky 'gret ski
Greville 'grev ɪl -²l
grew, Grew gruː
grey, Grey greɪ greyed greɪd greyer 'greɪ ə
‖ -²r greyest 'greɪ ɪst -əst greying 'greɪ ɪŋ
greys greɪz
ˌgrey 'area; ˌgrey 'matter
greybeard 'greɪ bɪəd ‖ -bɪrd ~s z
greyhound 'greɪ haʊnd ~s z
greyish 'greɪ ɪʃ
greylag 'greɪ læg ~s z
grey|ly 'greɪ |li ~ness nəs nɪs
greyscale 'greɪ skeɪ²l
Greystoke 'greɪ stəʊk ‖ -stoʊk
greywacke 'greɪ ˌwæk ə
Gribble, g~ 'grɪb ²l
Grice graɪs
Gricean 'graɪs i̯ ən
gricer 'graɪs ə ‖ -²r ~s z
grid grɪd grids grɪdz
griddl|e 'grɪd ²l ~ed d ~es z ~ing ˌɪŋ
griddlecake 'grɪd ²l keɪk ~s s
gridiron 'grɪd ˌaɪ ən ‖ -ˌaɪ ²rn ~ed d ~ing ɪŋ
~s z
Gridley 'grɪd li
gridlock 'grɪd lɒk ‖ -lɑːk ~ed t ~s s
grief griːf
grief-stricken 'griːf ˌstrɪk ən
Grieg griːg —Norw [griːg]
Grierson 'grɪəs ²n ‖ 'grɪ²rs ²n
grievanc|e 'griːv ²nts §-i̯ ²nts ~es ɪz əz
grieve, G~ griːv grieved griːvd grieves
griːvz grieving/ly 'griːv ɪŋ /li

grievous 'griːv əs △'griːv i̯ əs ~ly li ~ness
nəs nɪs
ˌgrievous ˌbodily 'harm
griff, griffe grɪf griffes, griffs grɪfs
griffin, G~ 'grɪf ɪn -²n ~s z
Griffith 'grɪf ɪθ §-əθ
Griffiths 'grɪf ɪθs §-əθs
griffon 'grɪf ²n ~s z
grift grɪft grifted 'grɪft ɪd -əd grifting
'grɪft ɪŋ grifts grɪfts
grifter 'grɪft ə ‖ -²r ~s z
grig, Grig, Grigg grɪg grigs, Grigg's grɪgz
Grignard 'griːn jɑː ‖ griːn 'jɑːrd —Fr
[gʁi njaːʁ]
Grigson 'grɪg s²n
grike graɪk grikes graɪks
grill grɪl grilled grɪld grilling 'grɪl ɪŋ grills
grɪlz
grille grɪl (= grill) grilles grɪlz
grillroom 'grɪl ruːm -rʊm ~s z
grilse grɪls
grim grɪm grimmer 'grɪm ə ‖ -²r grimmest
'grɪm ɪst -əst
ˌgrim 'reaper
grimac|e v, n grɪ 'meɪs grə-; 'grɪm əs ~ed t ~es
ɪz əz ~ing ɪŋ
Grimaldi grɪ 'mɔːld i grə-, -'mɒld- ‖ -'mɑːld-
grimalkin grɪ 'mælk ɪn grə-, -'mɔːlk-, §-ən
‖ -'mɔːlk- ~s z
grime graɪm grimed graɪmd grimes graɪmz
griming 'graɪm ɪŋ
Grimes graɪmz
Grimethorpe 'graɪm θɔːp ‖ -θɔːrp
grimi... —see grimy
grimly 'grɪm li
Grimm grɪm Grimm's grɪmz
grimness 'grɪm nəs -nɪs
Grimond 'grɪm ənd
Grimsargh 'grɪmz ə ‖ -²r
Grimsby 'grɪmz bi
Grimshaw 'grɪm ʃɔː ‖ -ʃɑː
Grimston 'grɪmᵖst ən
grim|y 'graɪm |i ~ier i ə ‖ i ²r ~iest i ɪst i əst
~ily ɪ li əl i ~iness i nəs i nɪs
grin grɪn grinned grɪnd grinning 'grɪn ɪŋ
grins grɪnz
grind graɪnd grinding 'graɪnd ɪŋ grinds
graɪndz ground graʊnd
'grinding wheel
Grindelwald 'grɪnd ²l vɑːld -væld, -wɔːld
—Ger ['grɪn d²l valt]
grinder 'graɪnd ə ‖ -²r ~s z
Grindon 'grɪnd ən
grindstone 'graɪnd stəʊn ‖ -stoʊn ~s z
gringo 'grɪŋ gəʊ ‖ -goʊ ~s z
Grinstead, Grinsted 'grɪn stɪd -sted
Grinton 'grɪnt ən ‖ -²n
griot 'griː əʊ ‖ -oʊ —Fr [gʁi o] ~s z
grip grɪp gripped grɪpt gripping/ly
'grɪp ɪŋ /li grips grɪps
gripe graɪp griped graɪpt gripes graɪps
griping/ly 'graɪp ɪŋ /li
griper 'graɪp ə ‖ -²r ~s z

gripp... —*see* **grip**
grippe grɪp griːp
Griqua 'griːk wə 'grɪk- **~land** lænd
grisaille grɪ 'zeɪ^əl grə-, griː-, -'zaɪ, -'zaɪ^əl
‖ -'zaɪ -'zeɪ^əl —*Fr* [gʁi zaj]
Griselda grɪ 'zeld ə grə-
griseofulvin ˌgrɪz i əʊ 'fʊlv ɪn ˌgrɪs-, -'fʌlv-,
§-^ən ‖ -i̯ə-
grisette grɪ 'zet **~s** s
Grisewood 'graɪz wʊd
gris|ly 'grɪz |li (= grizzly) **~lier** li̯ə ‖ li̯^ər
~liest li̯ɪst li̯əst
grison 'graɪs ^ən 'grɪz- **~s** z
grissini grɪ 'siːn i grə- —*It* [gris 'siː ni]
grist, Grist grɪst
gristle 'grɪs ^əl
grist|ly 'grɪs |^əl̯i **~liness** ^əl̯i nəs -nɪs
Griswold 'grɪz w^əld -wəʊld, →-wɒʊld ‖ -woʊld
grit grɪt **grits** grɪts **gritted** 'grɪt ɪd -əd
‖ 'grɪt̮ əd **gritting** 'grɪt ɪŋ ‖ 'grɪt̮ ɪŋ
gritter 'grɪt ə ‖ 'grɪt̮ ^ər **~s** z
gritt|y 'grɪt |i ‖ 'grɪt̮ |i **~ier** i̯ə ‖ i̯^ər **~iest**
i̯ɪst i̯əst **~ily** ɪ li əl i **~iness** i nəs i nɪs
Grizedale 'graɪz deɪ^əl
grizzl|e 'grɪz ^əl **~ed** d **~es** z **~ing** ɪŋ
grizz|ly 'grɪz |li **~lier** li̯ə ‖ li̯^ər **~lies** liz
~liest li̯ɪst li̯əst
ˌgrizzly 'bear ‖ '· · ·
groan grəʊn ‖ groʊn **groaned** grəʊnd
‖ groʊnd **groaning** 'grəʊn ɪŋ ‖ 'groʊn ɪŋ
groans grəʊnz ‖ groʊnz
groaner 'grəʊn ə ‖ 'groʊn ^ər **~s** z
groaning 'grəʊn ɪŋ ‖ 'groʊn ɪŋ **~ly** li **~s** z
groat grəʊt ‖ groʊt **groats** grəʊts ‖ groʊts
Gro-Bag *tdmk* 'grəʊ bæg ‖ 'groʊ- **~s** z
grocer 'grəʊs ə ‖ 'groʊs ^ər **~s** z
grocer|y 'grəʊs ə |i →'grəʊʃ r|i ‖ 'groʊs-
→'groʊʃ r|i **~ies** iz
grockle 'grɒk ^əl ‖ 'graːk- **~s** z
Grocott 'grəʊ kɒt ‖ 'groʊ kaːt
Groening *cartoonist* 'greɪn ɪŋ
grog grɒg ‖ graːg
Grogan 'grəʊg ən ‖ 'groʊg-
grogg|y 'grɒg |i ‖ 'graːg |i **~ier** i̯ə ‖ i̯^ər **~iest**
i̯ɪst i̯əst **~ily** ɪ li əl i **~iness** i nəs i nɪs
grogram 'grɒg rəm ‖ 'graːg-
groin grɔɪn **groining** 'grɔɪn ɪŋ **groins** grɔɪnz
Grolier 'grəʊl i̯ə ‖ 'groʊl i̯^ər —*Fr* [gʁɔ lje]
grommet 'grɒm ɪt 'grʌm-, -ət ‖ 'graːm- **~s** s
gromwell 'grɒm w^əl -wel ‖ 'graːm- **~s** z
Gromyko grə 'miːk əʊ ‖ -oʊ —*Russ*
[grʌ 'mɨ kə]
Groningen 'grəʊn ɪŋ ən 'grɒn- ‖ 'groʊn-
—*Dutch* ['xroː nɪŋ ən]
groom, Groom gruːm grʊm **groomed** gruːmd
grooms gruːmz grʊmz **grooming** 'gruːm ɪŋ
Groombridge 'gruːm brɪdʒ
grooms|man 'gruːmz |mən |mən 'grʊmz- **~men**
mən men
Groote Eylandt 'gruːt ˌaɪl ənd ‖ 'gruːt̮-
groove gruːv **grooved** gruːvd **groover/s**
'gruːv ə/z ‖ -^ər/z **grooves** gruːvz **grooving**
'gruːv ɪŋ

groov|y 'gruːv |i **~ier** i̯ə ‖ i̯^ər **~iest** i̯ɪst i̯əst
grope grəʊp ‖ groʊp **groped** grəʊpt ‖ groʊpt
gropes grəʊps ‖ groʊps **groping/ly**
'grəʊp ɪŋ /li ‖ 'groʊp-
groper 'grəʊp ə ‖ 'groʊp ^ər **~s** z
Gropius 'grəʊp i̯əs ‖ 'groʊp-
grosbeak 'grəʊs biːk 'grɒs- ‖ 'groʊs- **~s** s
groschen 'grɒʃ ^ən 'grəʊʃ- ‖ 'groʊʃ- —*Ger*
['gʁɔʃ ^ən]
grosgrain 'grəʊ greɪn ‖ 'groʊ-
Grosmont (*i*) 'grəʊ mənt -mɒnt ‖ 'groʊ maːnt,
(*ii*) 'grəʊs- ‖ 'groʊs-, (*iii*) 'grɒs- ‖ 'graːs-
—*The place in North Yks is (i) or (ii), that in
Gwent (iii)*
gros point ˌgrəʊ 'pɔɪnt ‖ 'groʊ pɔɪnt
gross grəʊs ‖ groʊs **grossed** grəʊst ‖ groʊst
grosser 'grəʊs ə ‖ 'groʊs ^ər (= grocer)
grosses 'grəʊs ɪz -əz ‖ 'groʊs əz **grossest**
'grəʊs ɪst -əst ‖ 'groʊs əst **grossing**
'grəʊs ɪŋ ‖ 'groʊs ɪŋ
Gross (*i*) grəʊs ‖ groʊs, (*ii*) grɒs ‖ graːs
Grosseteste 'grəʊs teɪt -test ‖ 'groʊs-
grossly 'grəʊs li ‖ 'groʊs li
Grossman 'grəʊs mən ‖ 'groʊs-
Grossmith 'grəʊs mɪθ ‖ 'groʊs-
grossness 'grəʊs nəs -nɪs ‖ 'groʊs-
gross-out 'grəʊs aʊt ‖ 'groʊs-
Grosvenor 'grəʊv nə 'grəʊv ən ə; §'grɒv-
‖ 'groʊv n^ər
grosz grɒʃ ‖ graːʃ —*Polish* [grɔʃ] **groszy**
'grɒʃ i ‖ 'graːʃ i —*Polish* ['grɔ ʃi]
Grosz grəʊs ‖ groʊs
grot grɒt ‖ graːt **grots** grɒts ‖ graːts
Grote grəʊt ‖ groʊt
grotesque grəʊ 'tesk ‖ groʊ- **~ly** li **~ness** nəs
nɪs **~s** s
grotesquer|ie, grotesquer|y grəʊ 'tesk ər |i
‖ groʊ- **~ies** iz
Grotius 'grəʊt i̯əs ‖ 'groʊʃ-
grotto 'grɒt əʊ ‖ 'graːt̮ oʊ **~es, ~s** z
grott|y 'grɒt |i ‖ 'graːt̮ |i **~ier** i̯ə ‖ i̯^ər **~iest**
i̯ɪst i̯əst **~iness** i nəs i nɪs
grouch graʊtʃ **grouched** graʊtʃt **grouches**
'graʊtʃ ɪz -əz **grouching** 'graʊtʃ ɪŋ
Groucho 'graʊtʃ əʊ ‖ -oʊ
grouch|y 'graʊtʃ |i **~ier** i̯ə ‖ i̯^ər **~iest** i̯ɪst
i̯əst **~ily** ɪ li əl i **~iness** i nəs i nɪs
ground graʊnd **grounded** 'graʊnd ɪd -əd
grounding/s 'graʊnd ɪŋ/z **grounds** graʊndz
ˌground 'bait; ˌground con'trol; 'ground
crew; ˌground 'floor◂; ˌground 'glass◂;
'ground plan; ˌground 'rent; ˌground 'rule;
'ground speed; 'ground staff; 'ground
stroke
groundbreaking 'graʊnd ˌbreɪk ɪŋ
grounder 'graʊnd ə ‖ -^ər **~s** z
groundhog 'graʊnd hɒg ‖ -haːg -hɔːg **~s** z
groundless 'graʊnd ləs -lɪs **~ly** li **~ness** nəs
nɪs
groundling 'graʊnd lɪŋ **~s** z
groundnut 'graʊnd nʌt **~s** s
groundsel 'graʊnd s^əl **~s** z
groundsheet 'graʊnd ʃiːt **~s** s

grounds|keeper 'graʊn*dz*| ˌkiːp ə ‖ -ᵊr
 ~keepers ˌkiːp əz ‖ -ᵊrz **~man** mən mæn
 ~men mən men
groundswell 'graʊn*d* swel **~s** z
groundwater 'graʊn*d* ˌwɔːt ə ‖ -ˌwɔːt̮ ᵊr
 -ˌwɑːt̮ᵊr
groundwork 'graʊn*d* wɜːk ‖ -wɜːk
group gruːp **grouped** gruːpt **grouping**
 'gruːp ɪŋ **groups** gruːps
 ˌgroup 'captain◂; ˌgroup 'practice; ˌgroup
 'therapy
grouper 'gruːp ə ‖ -ᵊr **~s** z
groupie 'gruːp i **~s** z
grouse graʊs **groused** graʊst **grouses**
 'graʊs ɪz -əz **grousing** 'graʊs ɪŋ
grout graʊt **grouted** 'graʊt ɪd -əd ‖ 'graʊt̮ əd
 grouting 'graʊt ɪŋ ‖ 'graʊt̮ ɪŋ **grouts** graʊts
grove, Grove grəʊv ‖ groʊv **groves** grəʊvz
 ‖ groʊvz
grovel 'grɒv ᵊl 'grʌv- ‖ 'grʌv- 'grɑːv- **~ed,
 ~led** d **~ing, ~ling** ˌɪŋ **~s** z
Grover 'grəʊv ə ‖ 'groʊv ᵊr
Groves grəʊvz ‖ groʊvz
grow grəʊ ‖ groʊ **grew** gruː **growing**
 'grəʊ ɪŋ ‖ 'groʊ ɪŋ **grown** grəʊn §'grəʊ ən
 ‖ groʊn **grows** grəʊz ‖ groʊz
 'growing pains; 'growing ˌseason
growbag 'grəʊ bæg ‖ 'groʊ- **~s** z
grower 'grəʊ ə ‖ 'groʊ ᵊr **~s** z
growl graʊl **growled** graʊld **growling**
 'graʊl ɪŋ **growls** graʊlz
growler 'graʊl ə ‖ -ᵊr **~s** z
Growmore *tdmk* 'grəʊ mɔː ‖ 'groʊ mɔːr -moʊr
grown grəʊn §'grəʊ ən ‖ groʊn
grown-up *adj* ˌgrəʊn 'ʌp ◂ ‖ ˌgroʊn-
 ˌgrown-up 'sons
grown-up *n* 'grəʊn ʌp ˌ·'· ‖ 'groʊn- **~s** s
growth grəʊθ ‖ groʊθ **growths** grəʊθs
 ‖ groʊθs
 'growth ˌhormone
groyne grɔɪn (= *groin*) **groynes** grɔɪnz
Grozny 'grɒz ni ‖ 'groʊz- —*Also, misguidedly,*
 'grɒʒ- ‖ 'groʊʒ- —*Russ* ['grɔz nij]
grub grʌb **grubbed** grʌbd **grubbing** 'grʌb ɪŋ
 grubs grʌbz
grubber 'grʌb ə ‖ -ᵊr **~s** z
grubb|y 'grʌb |i **~ier** i ə ‖ i ᵊr **~iest** i ɪst i əst
 ~ily ɪ li əl i **~iness** i nəs i nɪs
grubstak|e 'grʌb steɪk **~ed** t **~es** s **~ing** ɪŋ
grudge grʌdʒ **grudged** grʌdʒd **grudges**
 'grʌdʒ ɪz -əz **grudging/ly** 'grʌdʒ ɪŋ /li
gruel 'gruː əl §gruːl **~ing, ~ling** ɪŋ
gruesome 'gruːs əm **~ly** li **~ness** nəs nɪs
gruff grʌf **gruffer** 'grʌf ə ‖ -ᵊr **gruffest**
 'grʌf ɪst -əst **gruffly** 'grʌf li **gruffness**
 'grʌf nəs -nɪs
Gruffydd 'grɪf ɪð —*Welsh* ['grɪ fɪð, 'grɪ fɪð]
Gruinard 'grɪn jəd ‖ -jᵊrd —*There is also a
 spelling pronunciation* 'gruːˌɪ nɑːd ‖ -nɑːrd
grumbl|e 'grʌm bᵊl **~ed** d **~es** z **grumbling/ly**
 'grʌm blɪŋ /li
grumbler 'grʌm blə ‖ -blᵊr **~s** z
grummet 'grʌm ɪt -ət **~s** s

grump grʌmp **grumps** grʌmps
grump|y 'grʌmp |i **~ier** i ə ‖ i ᵊr **~iest** i ɪst
 i əst **~ily** ɪ li əl i **~iness** i nəs i nɪs
Grundig *tdmk* 'grʌnd ɪg 'grʊnd-
Grundy 'grʌnd i
Grundyism 'grʌnd i ˌɪz əm
grunge grʌndʒ
grung|y 'grʌndʒ| i **~ier** i ə ‖ i ᵊr **~iest** i ɪst
 i əst
grunt grʌnt **grunted** 'grʌnt ɪd -əd ‖ 'grʌnt̮ əd
 grunting 'grʌnt ɪŋ ‖ 'grʌnt̮ ɪŋ **grunts**
 grʌnts
Grunwell 'grʌn wel
Gruyere, Gruyère 'gruː jeə -jə; gru 'jeə
 ‖ gru 'jeᵊr grɪ- —*Fr* [gʁy jɛːʁ]
gryphon 'grɪf ᵊn **~s** z
g-spot 'dʒiː spɒt ‖ -spɑːt **~s** s
Gstaad gə 'ʃtɑːd -'stɑːd —*Ger* [kʃtaːt]
G-string 'dʒiː strɪŋ **~s** z
GTI ˌdʒiː tiː 'aɪ **~s, ~'s** z
guacamole ˌgwɑːk ə 'məʊl i -'moʊl i —*Sp*
 [gwa ka 'mo le]
Guadalajara ˌgwɑːd ᵊl ə 'hɑːr ə —*Sp*
 [gwa ða la 'xa ɾa]
Guadalcanal ˌgwɑːd ᵊl kə 'næl —*Sp*
 [gwa ðal ka 'nal]
Guadalquivir ˌgwɑːd ᵊl kwɪ 'vɪə -'kwɪv ə
 ‖ -'kwɪv ᵊr -kiː 'vɪᵊr —*Sp* [gwa ðal ki 'βiɾ]
Guadeloupe ˌgwɑːd ə 'luːp -ᵊl 'uːp, '···—*Fr*
 [gwad lup]
guaiacol 'gwaɪ‿ə kɒl ‖ -koʊl -kɔːl, -kɑːl
guaiacum 'gwaɪ‿ək əm **~s** z
Guam gwɑːm
guanabana gwə 'nɑːb ən ə ˌgwɑːn ə 'bɑːn ə
 —*Sp* guanábana [gwa 'na βa na]
guanaco gwə 'nɑːk əʊ gwɑː- ‖ -oʊ **~s** z
Guangdong ˌgwæŋ 'dʊŋ ‖ ˌgwɑːŋ- —*Chi*
 Guǎngdōng [³kwaŋ ¹tʊŋ]
Guangxi ˌgwæŋ 'ʃiː —*Chi* Guǎngxī [³kwaŋ ¹ɕi]
Guangzhou ˌgwæŋ 'dʒəʊ ‖ ˌgwɑːŋ 'dʒoʊ
 —*Chi* Guǎngzhōu [³kwaŋ ¹tʂou]
guanidine 'gwɑːn ɪ diːn -ə-, -dɪn; §-ɪd ən, -əd-
guanine 'gwɑːn iːn 'gu‿ə niːn
guano 'gwɑːn əʊ ‖ -oʊ
guanosine 'gwɑːn əʊ siːn -ziːn, -sɪn, §-sᵊn
 ‖ -ə-
Guantanamo gwæn 'tæn ə məʊ gwɑːn-, -'tɑːn-
 ‖ gwɑːn 'tɑːn ə moʊ —*Sp* Guantánamo
 [gwan 'ta na mo]
guar gu‿ɑː gwɑː ‖ gwɑːr —*In India,* gwɑː(r)
Guarani, Guaraní, g- ˌgwɑːr ə 'niː:
 'gwɑːr ən i —*Sp* [gwa ɾa 'ni] **~s** z
guarantee ˌgær ən 'tiː ◂ ‖ ˌger-, ˌgɑːr- **~d** d
 ~ing ɪŋ **~s** z
guarantor ˌgær ən 'tɔː ‖ -'tɔːr ˌger-, ˌgɑːr- **~s** z
guar|anty 'gær |ən ti -|ənt i ‖ 'ger-, 'gɑːr-
 ~anties ən tiːz ənt iz
guard, Guard gɑːd ‖ gɑːrd **guarded** 'gɑːd ɪd
 -əd ‖ 'gɑːrd əd **guarding** 'gɑːd ɪŋ ‖ 'gɑːrd ɪŋ
 guards gɑːdz ‖ gɑːrdz
 'guard's van
guarded 'gɑːd ɪd -əd ‖ 'gɑːrd əd **~ly** li **~ness**
 nəs nɪs

guard|house 'gɑːd |haʊs ‖ 'gɑːrd- **~houses**
  haʊz ɪz əz
guardian, G~ 'gɑːd i‿ən ‖ 'gɑːrd- **~s** z **~ship**
  ʃɪp
  ,guardian 'angel
guardrail 'gɑːd reɪəl ‖ 'gɑːrd- **~s** z
guardroom 'gɑːd ruːm -rʊm ‖ 'gɑːrd- **~s** z
guards|man 'gɑːdz |mən -mæn ‖ 'gɑːrdz-
  ~men mən men
Guatemal|a ,gwɑːt ə 'mɑːl |ə ,gwæt-, ,gwʌt-,
  -ɪ- ‖ ,gwɑːt̬ ə- **~an/s** ən/z
guava 'gwɑːv ə 'gwɔːv- **~s** z
Guayaquil ,gwaɪ ə 'kiːəl -'kɪl —Sp
  [gwa ja 'kil]
Gubba 'gʌb ə
Gubbins, g~ 'gʌb ɪnz §-ənz
gubernatorial ,guːb ən ə 'tɔːr i əl ◂ ,gjuːb-
  ‖ ,guːb ³rn ə- -'toʊr-
Gucci tdmk 'guːtʃ i
guck gʌk gʊk
gudgeon 'gʌdʒ ən **~s** z
  'gudgeon pin
Gudgin 'gʌdʒ ɪn -ən
Gudrun 'gʊdr uːn
Gue gjuː
guelder-ros|e 'geld ə rəʊz ,·'· ‖ -roʊz **~es** ɪz
  əz
Guelf, Guelph gwelf **Guelfs, Guelphs** gwelfs
guenon 'gwen ən -ɒn; gə 'nɒn, -'nɔ̃; 'giːn ən
  ‖ gə 'noʊn -'nɑːn **~s** z
guerdon 'gɜːd ³n ‖ 'gɝːd ³n **~s** z
guerilla gə 'rɪl ə ge- —Normally = gorilla. The
  ge- pronunciation aims explicitly to avoid this
  homophony. —Sp guerrilla [ge 'rri ʎa, -ja]
Guerin 'geər ɪn §-ən ‖ 'ger-
Guernica 'gɜːn ɪk ə 'gwɜːn-, gɜː 'niːk ə
  ‖ 'gwern- —Sp [ger 'ni ka]
Guernsey, g~ 'gɜːnz i ‖ 'gɝːnz i **~s** z
guerrilla gə 'rɪl ə ge- —see **guerilla**
guess ges **guessed** gest (= guest) **guesses**
  'ges ɪz -əz **guessing** 'ges ɪŋ
guesser 'ges ə ‖ -³r **~s** z
guessti|mate v 'gest ɪ |meɪt -ə- **~mated**
  meɪt ɪd -əd ‖ meɪt̬ əd **~mates** meɪts **~mating**
  meɪt ɪŋ ‖ meɪt̬ ɪŋ
guesstimate n 'gest ɪm ət -əm-, -ɪt, -eɪt **~s** s
guesswork 'ges wɜːk ‖ -wɝːk
guest, Guest gest **guested** 'gest ɪd -əd
  guesting 'gest ɪŋ **guests** gests
  'guest ,worker
guest|house 'gest |haʊs **~houses** haʊz ɪz -əz
guestroom 'gest ruːm -rʊm **~s** z
Guevara gə 'vɑːr ə gɪ-, ge- —Sp [ge 'βa ɾa]
guff gʌf
guffaw gʌ 'fɔː gə- ‖ -'fɑː; 'gʌf ɔː, -ɑː **~ed** d
  guffawing gʌ 'fɔːˑ ɪŋ gə- ‖ -'fɔː ɪŋ -'fɑː ɪŋ;
  'gʌf ɔːˑ ɪŋ, -ɑː- **~s** z
Guggenheim 'gʊg ən haɪm 'guːg-
GUI 'guː i
Guiana gi 'ɑːn ə gaɪ-, -'æn- ‖ -'æn ə -'ɑːn ə **~s**
  z -This is appropriate for the name of the
  general region. Compare **Guyana**, formerly
  British Guiana.

Guianese ,gaɪ ə 'niːz ◂ ,giː- ‖ -'niːs
guid gɪd —or, in Scots dialect pronunciation
  (perhaps simulated), [gyd, gʏd]
guidance 'gaɪd ³n⟨ts⟩
guide, Guide gaɪd **guided** 'gaɪd ɪd -əd
  guides gaɪdz **guiding** 'gaɪd ɪŋ
  ,guided 'missile
guidebook 'gaɪd bʊk →'gaɪb-, §-buːk **~s** s
guideline 'gaɪd laɪn **~s** z
guider, G~ 'gaɪd ə ‖ -³r **~s** z
Guido 'gwiːd əʊ 'giːd- ‖ -oʊ —It ['gwiː do]
guidon 'gaɪd ³n **~s** z
guild gɪld (= gild) **guilds** gɪldz
Guildenstern 'gɪld ən stɜːn ‖ -stɝːn
guilder 'gɪld ə ‖ -³r **~s** z
Guildford 'gɪl fəd ‖ -f³rd
guildhall, G~ 'gɪld hɔːl ◂ ,·'· ‖ -hɔːl -hɑːl **~s** z
guile gaɪəl
guileful 'gaɪəl f³l -fʊl **~ly** i **~ness** nəs nɪs
guileless 'gaɪəl ləs -lɪs **~ly** li **~ness** nəs nɪs
Guilford 'gɪl fəd ‖ -f³rd
Guilin ,gweɪ 'lɪn —Chi Guìlín [⁴kweɪ ²lɪn]
Guillain-Barré ,giː læn 'bær eɪ →-læm-, -jæn-,
  -lən-, -jən- ‖ gi ˌæ bə 'reɪ -ˌæm- —Fr
  [gi læ ba ʁe]
Guillaume 'giː əʊm ‖ giː 'joʊm —Fr [gi joːm]
guillemot 'gɪl ɪ mɒt -ə- ‖ -mɑːt **~s** s
guillotin|e 'gɪl ə tiːn 'giː-, -jə-, ,·'· **~ed** d **~es**
  z **~ing** ɪŋ
guilt gɪlt
guiltless 'gɪlt ləs -lɪs **~ly** li **~ness** nəs nɪs
guilt-ridden 'gɪlt ,rɪd ³n
guilt|y 'gɪlt |i **~ier** i ə ‖ i ³r **~iest** i ɪst i əst
  ~ily ɪ li əl i **~iness** i nəs i nɪs
guinea, G~ 'gɪn i **~s** z
  'guinea fowl; 'guinea pig; 'guinea worm
Guinea-Bissau ,gɪn i bɪ 'saʊ
Guinean 'gɪn i‿ən **~s** z
Guinevere 'gwɪn ɪ vɪə 'gɪn-, -ə- ‖ -vɪr
Guinness 'gɪn ɪs -əs; gɪ 'nes **~es** ɪz əz
guipure gɪ 'pjʊə §gə- ‖ -'pjʊ³r -'pʊ³r
Guisborough 'gɪz bər ə ‖ -,bɝ: oʊ
guise, Guise gaɪz (= guys) —but the French
  name is giːz **guises** 'gaɪz ɪz -əz
Guiseley 'gaɪz li
guitar gɪ 'tɑː gə- ‖ -'tɑːr **~s** z
guitarist gɪ 'tɑːr ɪst §-əst **~s** s
Guizhou ,gweɪ 'dʒəʊ ‖ -'dʒoʊ —Chi Guìzhōu
  [⁴kweɪ ¹tʂoʊ]
Gujarat, Gujerat ,gʊdʒ ə 'rɑːt ,guːdʒ-
  —Hindi [gʊdʒ raːt̪]
Gujarati, Gujerati ,gʊdʒ ə 'rɑːt i ◂ ,guːdʒ-
  —Hindi [gʊdʒ raː t̪i]
Gulag 'guːl æg -ɑːg ‖ -ɑːg
gular 'gjuːl ə 'guːl- ‖ -³r
Gulbenkian gʊl 'beŋk i ən
gulch gʌltʃ **gulches** 'gʌltʃ ɪz -əz
gulden 'gʊld ən **~s** z
gules gjuːlz
gulf, Gulf gʌlf **gulfs** gʌlfs
  'Gulf Stream
gull gʌl **gulled** gʌld **gulling** 'gʌl ɪŋ **gulls**
  gʌlz

Gullah 'gʌl ə ~s z
Gullane (i) 'gɪl ən, (ii) 'gʌlən
gullet 'gʌl ɪt -ət ~s s
Gullett 'gʌl ɪt -ət
gulley 'gʌl i ~s z
gullibility ˌgʌl ə 'bɪl ət i ˌ-ɪ-, -ɪt i ‖ -ət i
gullib|le 'gʌl əb |əl -ɪb- **~ly** li
Gulliford 'gʌl i fəd ‖ -fərd
Gullit 'hʊl ɪt 'huːl-, §-ət —Dutch ['xʏl ɪt]
Gulliver 'gʌl ɪv ə -əv- ‖ -ər
gull|y, Gully 'gʌl |i ~ies iz
gulp gʌlp **gulped** gʌlpt **gulping** 'gʌlp ɪŋ
  gulps gʌlps
gum gʌm **gummed** gʌmd **gumming** 'gʌm ɪŋ
  gums gʌmz
  ˌgum 'arabic; 'gum tree
gumball 'gʌm bɔːl ‖ -bɑːl ~s z
Gumbel 'gʌm bəl
gumbo, Gumbo 'gʌm bəʊ ‖ -boʊ ~s z
gumboil 'gʌm bɔɪəl ~s z
gumboot 'gʌm buːt ~s s
Gumbs gʌmz
gumdrop 'gʌm drɒp ‖ -drɑːp ~s s
gumma 'gʌm ə ~s z
Gummer 'gʌm ə ‖ -ər
Gummidge 'gʌm ɪdʒ
gumm|y 'gʌm |i ~ier i ə ‖ i ər ~ies iz ~iest
  i ɪst i əst
gumption 'gʌmp ʃən
gumshield 'gʌm ʃiːəld ~s z
gumshoe 'gʌm ʃuː ~ing ɪŋ ~s z
gun gʌn **gunned** gʌnd **gunning** 'gʌn ɪŋ **guns**
  gʌnz
  'gun ˌcarriage; 'gun ˌcotton
gunboat 'gʌn bəʊt →'gʌm- ‖ -boʊt ~s s
gundog 'gʌn dɒg ‖ -dɔːg -dɑːg ~s z
gundy, Gundy 'gʌnd i
gunfight 'gʌn faɪt ~s s
gunfighter 'gʌn ˌfaɪt ə ‖ -ˌfaɪt ər ~s z
gunfire 'gʌn ˌfaɪ ə ‖ -ˌfaɪ ər
Gunga Din ˌgʌŋ gə 'dɪn
gunge gʌndʒ
gung-ho ˌgʌŋ 'həʊ ◄ ‖ -'hoʊ
gungy 'gʌndʒ i
gunk gʌŋk
gun|man 'gʌn |mən →'gʌm-, -mæn **~men**
  mən men
gunmetal 'gʌn ˌmet əl →'gʌm- ‖ -ˌmeţ əl
Gunn gʌn
gunnel 'gʌn əl ~s z
Gunnell 'gʌn əl
gunner 'gʌn ə ‖ -ər ~s z
gunnera 'gʌn ər ə ~s z
Gunnersbury 'gʌn əz bər i ‖ -ərz ˌber i
gunnery 'gʌn ər i
Gunnison 'gʌn ɪs ən
gunny 'gʌn i
gunnysack 'gʌn i sæk
gunpoint 'gʌn pɔɪnt →'gʌm-
gunpowder 'gʌn ˌpaʊd ə →'gʌm- ‖ -ər
gunrunn|er 'gʌn ˌrʌn |ə ‖ -|ər ~ers əz ‖ ərz
  ~ing ɪŋ
gunship 'gʌn ʃɪp ~s s

gunshot 'gʌn ʃɒt ‖ -ʃɑːt
gunshy 'gʌn ʃaɪ
gunslinger 'gʌn ˌslɪŋ ə ‖ -ər ~s z
gunsmith 'gʌn smɪθ ~s s
Gunter 'gʌnt ə ‖ -ər —but as a German name,
  'gʊnt ə ‖ -ər —Ger Gunter ['gʊn tɐ], Günter
  ['gʏn tɐ]
Gunther 'gʌnᵗθ ə ‖ -ər —but as a German
  name, 'gʊnt ə ‖ -ər —Ger Gunther ['gʊn tɐ],
  Günther ['gʏn tɐ]
gun-toting 'gʌn ˌtəʊt ɪŋ ‖ -ˌtoʊţ-
gunwale 'gʌn əl ~s z
gunyah 'gʌn jə ~s z
guoyu ˌgwɔː 'uː -'juː —Chi guóyǔ [²kwɔ ³jy]
gupp|y, Guppy 'gʌp |i ~ies iz
Gupta 'gʊpt ə 'gʌpt- —Hindi [gʊp ʈaː]
Gur gʊə ‖ gʊʳr
gurdwara gɜː 'dwɑːr ə gʊə-,'··;
  ˌgʊr ə 'dwɑːr ə ‖ 'gɜːd- ~s z
gurgl|e 'gɜːg əl ‖ 'gɜːg əl ~ed d ~es z ~ing ɪŋ
Gurkha 'gɜːk ə 'gʊək- ‖ 'gɜːk ə ~s z
Gurkhali ˌ(ˌ)gɜː 'kɑːl i ˌgʊə- ‖ ˌ(ˌ)gɜː-
Gurmukhi 'gʊə mʊk i ‖ 'gʊr-
gurnard 'gɜːn əd ‖ 'gɜːn ərd ~s z
gurnet 'gɜːn ɪt §-ət ‖ 'gɜːn- ~s s
Gurney, g~ 'gɜːn i ‖ 'gɜːn i ~'s, ~s z
guru 'gʊr uː 'gʊər-; 'guː ruː ‖ 'guː ruː —Hindi
  [gʊ ruː] ~s z
Gus gʌs
gush gʌʃ **gushed** gʌʃt **gushes** 'gʌʃ ɪz -əz
  gushing/ly 'gʌʃ ɪŋ /li
gusher 'gʌʃ ə ‖ -ər ~s z
gush|y 'gʌʃ |i ~ier i ə ‖ i ər ~iest i ɪst i əst
  ~ily ɪ li əl i ~iness i nəs i nɪs
guss|et 'gʌs |ɪt §-ət ‖ -ət ~eted ɪt ɪd §ət-, -əd
  ‖ əţ əd ~eting ɪt ɪŋ §ət- ‖ əţ ɪŋ ~ets ɪts §əts
  ‖ əts
Gussie, Gussy, gussy 'gʌs i **gussied** 'gʌs id
gust gʌst **gusted** 'gʌst ɪd -əd **gusting** 'gʌst ɪŋ
  gusts 'gʌsts
gustation gʌ 'steɪʃ ən
gustatory 'gʌst ət ər i gʌs 'teɪt ər i ‖ -ə tɔːr i
  -tour i
Gustav, Gustave 'gʊst ɑːv 'gʌst- ‖ 'gʌst-
Gustavus gʊ 'stɑːv əs gʌ-, gə-
gusto 'gʌst əʊ ‖ -oʊ
gust|y 'gʌst |i ~ier i ə ‖ i ər ~iest i ɪst i əst
  ~ily ɪ li əl i ~iness i nəs i nɪs
gut gʌt **guts** gʌts **gutted** 'gʌt ɪd -əd ‖ 'gʌţ əd
  gutting 'gʌt ɪŋ ‖ 'gʌţ ɪŋ
Gutenberg 'guːt ən bɜːg ‖ -bɜːg —Ger
  ['guː tᵊn bɛʁk]
Guthrie 'gʌθ ri
gutless 'gʌt ləs -lɪs ~ly li ~ness nɪs nəs
Guto 'gɪt əʊ ‖ 'gɪt oʊ —Welsh ['gɪt o]
guts|y 'gʌts |i ~ier i ə ‖ i ər ~iest i ɪst i əst
  ~ily ɪ li əl i ~iness i nəs i nɪs
gutta 'gʌt ə 'gʊt- ‖ 'gʌţ ə 'gʊţ- **guttae** 'gʌt iː
  'gʊt-
gutta-percha ˌgʌt ə 'pɜːtʃ ə ‖ ˌgʌţ ə 'pɜːtʃ ə
gutter ˌgʌt ə ‖ 'gʌţ ər **~ed** d **guttering**
  'gʌt ər ɪŋ ‖ 'gʌţ ər ɪŋ ~s z
  'gutter press, ˌ·'·.

Gutteridge 'gʌt̬ ər ɪdʒ ‖ 'gʌt̬ ər-
guttersnipe 'gʌt̬ ə snaɪp ‖ 'gʌt̬ ʳr- ~s s
guttural 'gʌt̬ ər əl ‖ 'gʌt̬ ər əl →'gʌtr əl ~ism
   ‚ɪz əm ~ly i ~ness nəs nɪs ~s z
gutturality ‚gʌt̬ ə 'ræl ət i -ɪt i
   ‖ ‚gʌt̬ ə 'ræl ət̬ i
guv, Guv gʌv
guvnor, guv'nor, G~ 'gʌv nə ‖ -nʳr ~s z
guy, Guy gaɪ —See also phrases with this word
   guyed gaɪd **guying** 'gaɪ ɪŋ **guys** gaɪz
   'guy line; 'guy rope
Guyana gaɪ 'æn ə -'ɑːn-
Guyanese ‚gaɪ ə 'niːz ◂
Guy Fawkes ‚gaɪ 'fɔːks ◂ '·· ‖ -'fɑːks
   ‚Guy 'Fawkes night, '· · ·
Guyler 'gaɪl ə ‖ -ʳr
guzzl|e 'gʌz ᵊl ~ed d ~es z ~ing ɪŋ
Gwalia 'gwɑːl i ə
Gwalior 'gwɑːl i ɔː ‖ -ɔːr —Hindi [gʋɑːl jər]
Gwatkin 'gwɒt kɪn ‖ 'gwɑːt-
Gwaun-cae-Gurwen ‚gwaɪn kə 'gɜː wən
   →-‚gwaɪn- ‖ -'gɜːː- —Welsh
   [gwain kai 'gɪr wen]
Gwbert 'gʊb ət ‖ -ʳrt
gweilo ‚gweɪ 'ləʊ ‖ -'loʊ —Cantonese
   [²kwej ²low]
Gwen gwen
Gwenda 'gwend ə
Gwendolin, Gwendoline, Gwendolyn
   'gwend ə lɪn -ᵊl ɪn, §-ən ‖ -ᵊl ɪn -ən
Gwendraeth 'gwen draɪθ
Gwenllian 'gwen ɬi ən -li‚ən ‖ -li‚ən —Welsh
   ['gwen ɬjan]
Gwent gwent
Gwilym 'gwɪl ɪm
Gwydir, Gwydyr (i) 'gwɪd ə -ɪə ‖ -ɪr, (ii)
   'gwaɪd-
Gwyn gwɪn
Gwynant 'gwɪn ænt
Gwynedd 'gwɪn əð -ɪð, -eð —Welsh ['gwi neð]
Gwyneth 'gwɪn əθ -ɪθ, -eθ
Gwynfor 'gwɪn və -vɔː ‖ -vʳr -vɔːr —Welsh
   ['gwin vor]
gwyniad 'gwɪn i æd ~s z
Gwynn, Gwynne gwɪn
Gwynneth 'gwɪn əθ -ɪθ, -eθ
Gwyther (i) 'gwaɪð ə ‖ -ʳr, (ii) 'gwɪð ə ‖ -ʳr
gybe dʒaɪb **gybed** dʒaɪbd **gybes** dʒaɪbz
   gybing 'dʒaɪb ɪŋ
Gyle gaɪᵊl
Gyles dʒaɪᵊlz
gym dʒɪm **gyms** dʒɪmz
   'gym shoe
gymkhana dʒɪm 'kɑːn ə ~s z
gymnasi|um 'hall for gymnastics'
   dʒɪm 'neɪz i‚əm ~a ə ~ums əmz
gymnasium 'secondary school' gɪm 'nɑːz i‚əm
   -ʊm —Ger G~ [gym 'nɑː zjʊm] ~s z

gymnast 'dʒɪm næst ‖ -nəst ~s s
gymnastic dʒɪm 'næst ɪk ~ally ᵊl‚i ~s s
gymnosophist dʒɪm 'nɒs əf ɪst §-əst ‖ -'nɑːs-
   ~s s
gymnosperm 'dʒɪm nəʊ spɜːm ‖ -nə spɜːm ~s
   z
gymslip 'dʒɪm slɪp ~s s
gynaec... —see **gynec...**
gyneciu|um, gynoeci|um gaɪ 'niːs i‚əm
   dʒaɪ- ~a ə
gynecological ‚gaɪn ɪk ə 'lɒdʒ ɪk ᵊl ◂ ‚-ək-
   ‖ -'lɑːdʒ- ‚dʒaɪn- ~ly i
gynecologist ‚gaɪn ɪ 'kɒl ədʒ ɪst ‚-ə-, §-əst
   ‖ -'kɑːl- ‚dʒaɪn- ~s s
gynecology ‚gaɪn ɪ 'kɒl ədʒ i ‚-ə- ‖ -'kɑːl-
   ‚dʒaɪn-
Gyngell 'gɪndʒ ᵊl
-gynous stress-imposing dʒɪn əs dʒən əs —
   androgynous æn 'drɒdʒ ɪn əs -ən-
   ‖ -'drɑːdʒ-
gyp dʒɪp **gypped** dʒɪpt **gypping** 'dʒɪp ɪŋ
   gyps dʒɪps
gypsophila dʒɪp 'sɒf ɪl ə -əl-,
   △‚dʒɪps ə 'fɪl i‚ə ‖ -'sɑːf-
gypsum 'dʒɪps əm
gyps|y, Gyps|y 'dʒɪps |i ~ies iz
gyr|ate v dʒaɪʳ 'r|eɪt dʒɪ-, dʒə-; 'dʒaɪʳr |eɪt
   ‖ 'dʒaɪʳr |eɪt ~ated eɪt ɪd -əd ‖ eɪt̬ əd ~ates
   eɪts ~ating eɪt ɪŋ ‖ eɪt̬ ɪŋ
gyration dʒaɪʳ 'reɪʃ ᵊn dʒɪ-, dʒə- ~s z
gyratory dʒaɪʳ 'reɪt ər i dʒə-; 'dʒaɪʳr ət‚ər i
   ‖ 'dʒaɪʳr ə tɔːr i -toʊr i
gyre 'dʒaɪ ə ‖ 'dʒaɪ‚ʳr **gyred** 'dʒaɪ‚əd
   ‖ 'dʒaɪ‚ʳrd **gyres** 'dʒaɪ‚əz ‖ 'dʒaɪ‚ʳrz **gyring**
   'dʒaɪ‚ər ɪŋ ‖ 'dʒaɪ‚ʳr ɪŋ
gyrfalcon 'dʒɜː ‚fɔːlk ən 'dʒɪə-, -‚fɔːk-, -‚fælk-
   ‖ 'dʒɜːː ‚fælk ən -‚fɔːlk-, -‚fɑːlk- ~s z
gyri 'dʒaɪʳr aɪ
gyro 'meat sandwich' 'ʒɪʳr əʊ 'gɪʳr-
   ‖ 'dʒaɪʳr oʊ ~s z —ModGk ['ji ro]
gyro 'gyroscope, gyrocompass' 'dʒaɪʳr əʊ ‖ -oʊ
   ~s z
gyro- comb. form
   with stress-neutral suffix ¦dʒaɪʳr əʊ ‖ -ə —
   gyrostatic ‚dʒaɪʳr əʊ 'stæt ɪk ◂
   ‖ -ə 'stæt̬ ɪk ◂
gyrocompass 'dʒaɪʳr əʊ ‚kʌmp əs ‖ -oʊ-
   -‚kɑːmp- ~es ɪz əz
gyromagnetic ‚dʒaɪʳr əʊ mæg 'net ɪk ◂
   -məg'·- ‖ -oʊ mæg 'net̬-
gyroscope 'dʒaɪʳr ə skəʊp ‖ -skoʊp ~s s
gyroscopic ‚dʒaɪʳr ə 'skɒp ɪk ◂ ‖ -'skɑːp-
   ~ally ᵊl‚i
gyr|us 'dʒaɪʳr |əs ~i aɪ
Gytha 'gɪθ ə
gyve dʒaɪv **gyved** dʒaɪvd **gyves** dʒaɪvz
   gyving 'dʒaɪv ɪŋ

Hh

h Spelling-to-sound

1 Where the spelling is **h**, the pronunciation is regularly h as in **house** haʊs. The letter **h** may also form part of one of the digraphs **ch, gh, ph, rh, sh, th, wh** (see under **c, g, p, r, s, t, w** respectively).

2 **h** is silent in a number of cases:
- at the beginning of the exceptional words **heir** eə ‖ er, **honest** ˈɒn ɪst ‖ ˈɑːn əst, **hono(u)r** ˈɒn ə ‖ ˈɑːn ᵊr, **hour** ˈaʊ ə ‖ ˈaʊ ᵊr and their derivatives; also, in AmE only, in **herb** ɜːb
- at the end of a word after a vowel letter, as in **oh** əʊ ‖ oʊ, **hurrah** hə ˈrɑː
- in most cases where it is at the beginning of a weak-vowelled syllable, as in the WEAK FORMs of **he, her, him, his, has, have**; in words such as **annihilate, vehicle**; and sometimes also in words such as **hotel, historic**.

3 The sound h is also occasionally written **wh** as in **who** huː.

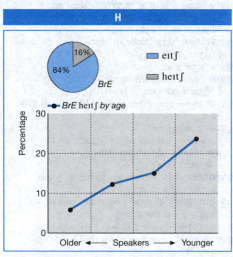

H, h eɪtʃ §heɪtʃ —*The form* heɪtʃ *is standard in Irish English, but traditionally not in BrE or AmE. It is, however, spreading in BrE. Preference poll, BrE:* eɪtʃ *84%,* heɪtʃ *16% (born since 1982, 24%).* **H's, h's** ˈeɪtʃ ɪz §ˈheɪtʃ-, -əz —*Communications code name:* Hotel
H₂O eɪtʃ tuː -ˈəʊ §ˌheɪtʃ- ‖ -ˈoʊ
ha *interjection* hɑː
ha *measure* —*see* **hectare**

Haagen-Dazs, Häagen-Dazs *tdmk* ˌhɑːg ən ˈdɑːz -ˈdɑːs, ˈ··· ‖ ˈhɑːg ən dæs
Haakon ˈhɔːk ɒn ˈhɑːk-, -ən ‖ -ɑːn ˈhɑːk-, -ən —*Norwegian* [ˈˈhoː kɔn]
Haarlem ˈhɑːl əm -em ‖ ˈhɑːrl- —*Dutch* [ˈhaːr lɛm]
Habakkuk ˈhæb ək ək -ə kʌk; hə ˈbæk-
habeas corpus ˌheɪb i əs ˈkɔːp əs -iː æs- ‖ -ˈkɔːrp-
haberdasher ˈhæb ə dæʃ ə ‖ -ᵊr dæʃ ᵊr **~s** z
haberdasher|y ˈhæb ə dæʃ ərˌi ‖ ˈhæb ᵊr- **~ies** iz
Habgood ˈhæb gʊd
Habibie hæ ˈbiːb i hə- ‖ hɑː-
habiliment hə ˈbɪl ɪ mənt hæ-, -ə- **~s** s
habili|tate hə ˈbɪl ɪ |teɪt hæ-, -ə- **~tated** teɪt ɪd -əd ‖ teɪt əd **~tates** teɪts **~tating** teɪt ɪŋ ‖ teɪt ɪŋ
habilitation hə ˌbɪl ɪ ˈteɪʃ ᵊn hæ-, -ə-
habit ˈhæb ɪt §-ət **~s** s
habitability ˌhæb ɪt ə ˈbɪl ət i -ɪt i ‖ -əṭ ə ˈbɪl əṭ i
habitab|le ˈhæb ɪt əb |ᵊl -ət əb- ‖ -əṭ əb- **~ly** li
habitant *French settler or descendant* ˌæb i ˈtɒ̃ ˌhæb- ‖ -ˈtɑːn **~s** z
habitat, H~ *tdmk* ˈhæb ɪ tæt -ə- **~s** s
habitation ˌhæb ɪ ˈteɪʃ ᵊn -ə- **~s** z
habit-forming ˈhæb ɪt ˌfɔːm ɪŋ §-ət- ‖ -ˌfɔːrm-
habitual hə ˈbɪtʃ u əl hæ-, -ˈbɪt juˌ **~ly** i **~ness** nəs nɪs

habitu|ate hə ˈbɪtʃ u |eɪt hæ-, -ˈbɪt ju- **~ated**
eɪt ɪd -əd ‖ eɪtʃ əd **~ates** eɪts **~ating** eɪt ɪŋ
‖ eɪtʃ ɪŋ
habituation hə ˌbɪtʃ u ˈeɪʃ ᵊn hæ-, -ˌbɪt ju-
habitue, habitué hə ˈbɪtʃ u eɪ ə-, hæ-, -ˈbɪt ju-
‖ ˌ·ˌ·ˈ· —Fr [a bi tɥe] **~s** z
Habsburg ˈhæps bɜːg ‖ -bɝːg —Ger
[ˈhaːps bʊʁk] **~s** z
hacek, háček ˈhɑːtʃ ek **~s** s
hachure hæ ˈʃʊə -ˈʃjʊə ‖ -ˈʃʊˣr **~s** z
hacienda ˌhæs i ˈend ə ‖ ˌhɑːs- ˌɑːs- —AmSp
[a ˈsjen da] **~s** z
hack, Hack hæk **hacked** hækt **hacking**
ˈhæk ɪŋ **hacks** hæks
ˌhacking ˈcough; ˈhacking ˌjacket
hackamore ˈhæk ə mɔː ‖ -mɔːr -moʊr **~s** z
hackberr|y ˈhæk bər |i -ˌber |i ‖ -ˌber |i **~ies**
iz
hacker, H~ ˈhæk ə ‖ -ᵊr **~s** z
Hackett ˈhæk ɪt §-ət
hackette ˌhæk ˈet **~s** s
hackle ˈhæk ᵊl **~s** z
Hackman ˈhæk mən
hackney, H~ ˈhæk ni **~ed** d **~ing** ɪŋ **~s** z
ˌhackney ˈcarriage, ˈ·ˌ·ˌ·
hacksaw ˈhæk sɔː ‖ -sɑː **~s** z
hackwork ˈhæk wɜːk ‖ -wɝːk
had strong form **hæd**, weak forms **həd, əd, d**
—The contracted weak form **d** is used mainly
after a vowel (and is often written 'd); at the
beginning of a sentence the usual weak form is
həd, or in rapid speech **d**.
Haddington ˈhæd ɪŋ tən
haddock ˈhæd ək **~s** s
Haddon ˈhæd ᵊn
hade heɪd **haded** ˈheɪd ɪd -əd **hades** heɪdz
hading ˈheɪd ɪŋ
Hadeeth —see **Hadith**
Haden ˈheɪd ᵊn
Hades 'god of underworld'; 'hell' ˈheɪd iːz
Hadfield ˈhæd fiːᵊld
Hadith hə ˈdiːθ hæ- ‖ hɑː- —Arabic [ˈha ˈdiːθ]
hadj hædʒ hɑːdʒ
hadji ˈhædʒ i ˈhɑːdʒ-, -iː **~s** z
Hadlee, Hadley ˈhæd li
hadn't ˈhæd ᵊnt
Hadrian ˈheɪdr i ən **~'s** z
ˌHadrian's ˈWall
hadron ˈhædr ɒn ‖ -ɑːn **~s** z
hadrosaur ˈhædr əʊ sɔː ‖ -ə sɔːr **~s** z
hadst strong form **hædst**, weak forms **hədst,
ədst**
hae heɪ
haecceity hek ˈsiːˌət i hiːk-, haɪk-, -ɪt- ‖ -əẗ i
haem hiːm
haematite ˈhiːm ə taɪt
haematologist ˌhiːm ə ˈtɒl ədʒ ɪst §-əst
‖ -ˈtɑːl- **~s** s
haematology ˌhiːm ə ˈtɒl ədʒ i ‖ -ˈtɑːl-

haematom|a ˌhiːm ə ˈtəʊm| ə ‖ -ˈtoʊm| ə **~as**
əz **~ata** ət ə ‖ əẗ ə
haemo- comb. form
with stress-neutral suffix ˌhiːm əʊ ‖ -oʊ —
haemodialysis ˌhiːm əʊ daɪ ˈæl əs ɪs -ɪs ɪs,
§-əs ‖ ˌ·oʊ-
with stress-imposing suffix hiː ˈmɒ+ hɪ-
‖ -ˈmɑː+ — **haemolysis** hiː ˈmɒl əs ɪs hɪ-,
-ɪs-, §-əs ‖ -ˈmɑːl-
haemoglobin ˌhiːm ə ˈgləʊb ɪn §-ən, ˈ·ˌ··
‖ ˈhiːm ə gloʊb ən
haemophilia ˌhiːm ə ˈfɪl i ə -ˈfiːl-
haemophiliac ˌhiːm ə ˈfɪl i æk ◂ -ˈfiːl- **~s** s
haemorrhag|e ˈhem ər ɪdʒ **~ed** d **~es** ɪz əz
~ing ɪŋ
haemorrhoid ˈhem ə rɔɪd **~s** z
haemorrhoidal ˌhem ə ˈrɔɪd ᵊl ◂
Haffner, Hafner ˈhæf nə ‖ -nᵊr
hafiz ˈhɑːf ɪz
hafnium ˈhæf ni əm
Hafod ˈhæv ɒd ‖ -ɑːd —Welsh [ˈha vod]
haft hɑːft §hæft ‖ hæft **hafted** ˈhɑːft ɪd §ˈhæft-,
-əd ‖ ˈhæft əd **hafting** ˈhɑːft ɪŋ §ˈhæft-
‖ ˈhæft ɪŋ **hafts** hɑːfts §hæfts ‖ hæfts
hag hæg **hags** hægz
HAG, Hag tdmk hɑːg
Hagan ˈheɪg ən
Hagar ˈheɪg ɑː -ə ‖ -ɑːr -ᵊr
Hagerstown ˈheɪg əz taʊn ‖ -ᵊrz-
hagfish ˈhæg fɪʃ
Haggai ˈhæg aɪ ˈhæg i aɪ, -eɪ-
haggard, H~ ˈhæg əd ‖ -ᵊrd **~ly** li **~ness** nəs
nɪs
Haggerston ˈhæg əst ən ‖ -ᵊrst-
haggis ˈhæg ɪs §-əs **~es** ɪz əz
haggl|e ˈhæg ᵊl **~ed** d **~es** z **~ing** ɪŋ
hagio- comb. form
with stress-neutral suffix ˌhæg i ə ˌheɪdʒ i ə
— **hagioscope** ˈhæg i ə skəʊp ˈheɪdʒ-
‖ -skoʊp with stress-imposing suffix
ˌhæg i ˈɒ+ ˌheɪdʒ- ‖ -ˈɑː+ — **hagiolatry**
ˌhæg i ˈɒl ətr i ˌheɪdʒ- ‖ -ˈɑːl-
hagiograph|y ˌhæg i ˈɒg rəf |i ˌheɪdʒ- ‖ -ˈɑːg-
~ies iz
Hagman ˈhæg mən
Hagrid ˈhæg rɪd
hag-ridden ˈhæg ˌrɪd ᵊn
Hague heɪg —Dutch Haag [haːx]
hah hɑː
ha-ha interj ⦅ı⦆ hɑː ˈhɑː hʌ-
ha-ha n ˈhɑː hɑː **~s** z
Hahn hɑːn
hahnium ˈhɑːn i əm
Haida ˈhaɪd ə
Haifa ˈhaɪf ə
Haig heɪg
Haigh placename heɪ
Haigh family name heɪg
Haight (i) haɪt, (ii) heɪt
Haight-Ashbury ˌheɪt ˈæʃ bər i ‖ -ˌber i
Hai Karate tdmk ˌhaɪ kə ˈrɑːt i ‖ -ˈrɑːẗ i
haiku ˈhaɪk u —Jp [ha̠ˌi kɯ] **~s** z

H

hail heɪ^əl **hailed** heɪ^əld **hailing** ˈheɪ^əl ɪŋ **hails**
heɪ^əlz
  ˌHail ˈMary
hailer ˈheɪ^əl ə ‖ ^ər ~**s** z
Hailes ˈheɪ^əlz
Haile Selassie ˌhaɪl i sə ˈlæs i -sɪˈ-
Hailey ˈheɪl i
Haileybury ˈheɪl i bər‿i ‖ -ˌber i
hail-fellow-well-met ˌheɪ^əl ˌfel əʊ ˌwel ˈmet
  ‖ -oʊ- -ə-
Hailsham ˈheɪ^əl ʃəm
hailstone ˈheɪ^əl stəʊn ‖ -stoʊn ~**s** z
hailstorm ˈheɪ^əl stɔːm ‖ -stɔːrm ~**s** z
Hailwood ˈheɪ^əl wʊd
Hain heɪn
Hainan ˌhaɪ ˈnæn ‖ -ˈnɑːn —*Chi* Hǎinán
  [³hai ²nan]
Hainault ˈheɪn ɔːt -ɒlt, -ɒlt ‖ -ɔːlt -ɑːlt
Haines heɪnz
Haiphong ˌhaɪ ˈfɒŋ ‖ -ˈfɔːŋ -ˈfɑːŋ —*Vietnamese*
  [⁴hai ³fɔŋ]
hair heə ‖ he^ər hæ^ər **hairs** heəz ‖ he^ərz hæ^ərz
  ˈhair's breadth; ˌhair ˈshirt; ˈhair slide;
  ˌhair ˈtrigger◄
hairball ˈheə bɔːl ‖ ˈher- ˈhær-, -bɑːl ~**s** z
hairband ˈheə bænd ‖ ˈher- ˈhær- ~**s** z
hairbreadth ˈheə bredθ -bretθ ‖ ˈher- ˈhær-
hairbrush ˈheə brʌʃ ‖ ˈher- ˈhær- ~**es** ɪz əz
haircare ˈheə keə ‖ ˈher ker ˈhær kær
haircut ˈheə kʌt ‖ ˈher- ˈhær- ~**s** s
hairdo ˈheə duː ‖ ˈher- ˈhær- ~**s** z
hairdresser ˈheə ˌdres ə ‖ ˈher ˌdres ^ər ˈhær-
  ~**s**, ~ˈ**s** z
hairdressing ˈheə ˌdres ɪŋ ‖ ˈher- ˈhær-
hairdryer ˈheə ˌdraɪ‿ə ‖ ˈher ˌdraɪ‿^ər ~**s** z
-haired ˈheəd ‖ he^ərd hæ^ərd — **fair-haired**
  ˌfeə ˈheəd ◄ ‖ ˈfer ˈhe^ərd ˈfær hæ^ərd
hairgrip ˈheə grɪp ‖ ˈher- ˈhær- ~**s** s
hairi... —*see* **hairy**
hairless ˈheə ləs -lɪs ‖ ˈher- ˈhær- ~**ness** nəs
  nɪs
hairline ˈheə laɪn ‖ ˈher- ˈhær- ~**s** z
hairnet ˈheə net ‖ ˈher- ˈhær- ~**s** s
hairpiec|e ˈheə piːs ‖ ˈher- ˈhær- ~**es** ɪz əz
hairpin ˈheə pɪn ‖ ˈher- ˈhær- ~**s** z
  ˌhairpin ˈbend
hair-raising ˈheə ˌreɪz ɪŋ ‖ ˈher- ˈhær-
hair-restorer ˈheə rɪ ˌstɔːr ə -rə-
  ‖ ˈher rɪ ˌstɔːr ^ər ˈhær-, -ˌstoʊr- ~**s** z
hair-splitting ˈheə ˌsplɪt ɪŋ ‖ ˈher ˌsplɪt̬ ɪŋ
  ˈhær-
hairspray ˈheə spreɪ ‖ ˈher- ˈhær-
hairspring ˈheə sprɪŋ ‖ ˈher- ˈhær- ~**s** z
hairstreak ˈheə striːk ‖ ˈher- ˈhær- ~**s** s
hairstyle ˈheə staɪ^əl ‖ ˈher- ˈhær- ~**s** z
hairstylist ˈheə ˌstaɪ^əl ɪst §-əst ‖ ˈher- ˈhær- ~**s**
  s
hair|y ˈheər |i ‖ ˈher |i ˈhær- ~**ier** i‿ə ‖ i‿^ər
  ~**iest** i‿ɪst i‿əst ~**iness** i nəs i nɪs
Haiti ˈheɪt i ˈhaɪt-; haɪ ˈiːt i, hɑː- ‖ ˈheɪt̬ i
Haitian ˈheɪʃ ^ən ˈhaɪʃ-, ˈ‿i‿ən; ˈheɪt i‿ən;
  haɪ ˈiːʃ ^ən, hɑː-, -ˈiːʃ i‿ən ~**s** z
Haitink ˈhaɪt ɪŋk —*Dutch* [ˈhaːi tɪŋk]

haj, hajj hædʒ hɑːdʒ
haji, hajji ˈhædʒ i ˈhɑːdʒ-, -iː ~**s** z
haka ˈhaːk ə ~**s** s
hake heɪk **hakes** heɪks
hakim *'judge, ruler'* ˈhaːk ɪm hɑː ˈkiːm ~**s** s
hakim *'physician'* hə ˈkiːm hæ-, hɑː- ~**s** z
Hakka ˈhæk ə
Hakluyt ˈhæk luːt ˈhæk ^əl wɪt
Hal hæl
halal hə ˈlɑːl ˈhæl æl, hæ ˈlæl —*Arabic*
  [ħa ˈlaːl]
halation hə ˈleɪʃ ^ən ~**s** z
halberd ˈhæl bəd ˈhɔːl-, -bɜːd ‖ -b^ərd ~**s** z
halberdier ˌhæl bə ˈdɪə ˌhɔːl- ‖ -b^ər ˈdɪ^ər ~**s** z
halcyon ˈhæls i‿ən ~**s** z
  ˌhalcyon ˈdays
Halcyone hæl ˈsaɪ‿ən i
Haldane ˈhɔːld eɪn ˈhɒld- ‖ ˈhɑːld-
hale, Hale heɪ^əl (= *hail*) **haler** ˈheɪ^əl ə ‖ -^ər
  halest ˈheɪ^əl ɪst -əst
Haleakala ˌhaːl i aːk ə ˈlaː
haleness ˈheɪ^əl nəs -nɪs
Hales heɪ^əlz
Halesowen ⒤heɪ^əlz ˈəʊ ɪn -ən ‖ -ˈoʊ-
Halesworth ˈheɪ^əlz wɜːθ ‖ -w^ərθ
Halewood ˌheɪ^əl ˈwʊd ◄
Halex *tdmk* ˈheɪl eks
Haley ˈheɪl i
half hɑːf §hæf ‖ hæf —*See also phrases with*
  this word **halves** hɑːvz §hævz ‖ hævz
  ˌhalf a ˈcrown; ˌhalf ˈboard; ˌhalf ˈcock;
  ˌhalf ˈcrown; ˌhalf ˈmoon; ˈhalf note;
  ˌhalf ˈterm; ˌhalf ˈvolley
half- ⒤hɑːf §⒤hæf ‖ ⒤hæf
half-a-dozen ˌhɑːf ə ˈdʌz ^ən ◄ §ˌhæf- ‖ ˌhæf-
half-and-half ˌhɑːf ^ən ˈhɑːf ◄ §ˌhæf ^ən ˈhæf ◄
  ‖ ˌhæf ^ən ˈhæf ◄
half-arsed ˌhɑːf ˈɑːst ◄ §ˌhæf- ‖ ˌhæf ˈɑːrst ◄
  —*See the next entry*
half-assed ˌhɑːf ˈɑːst ◄ §ˌhæf-, -ˈæst
  ‖ ˌhæf ˈæst ◄
halfback ˈhɑːf bæk §ˈhæf- ‖ ˈhæf- ~**s** s
half-baked ˌhɑːf ˈbeɪkt ◄ §ˌhæf- ‖ ˌhæf-
half-breed ˈhɑːf briːd §ˈhæf- ‖ ˈhæf- ~**s** z
half-brother ˈhɑːf ˌbrʌð ə §ˈhæf-
  ‖ ˈhæf ˌbrʌð ^ər ~**s** z
half-caste ˈhɑːf kɑːst §ˈhæf-, §-kæst
  ‖ ˈhæf kæst ~**s** s
half-close ˌhɑːf ˈkləʊs ◄ §ˌhæf- ‖ ˌhæf ˈkloʊs
half-cocked ˌhɑːf ˈkɒkt ◄ §ˌhæf-
  ‖ ˌhæf ˈkɑːkt ◄
half-crazed ˌhɑːf ˈkreɪzd ◄ §ˌhæf- ‖ ˌhæf-
half-cup ˌhɑːf ˈkʌp §ˌhæf- ‖ ˌhæf- ~**s** s
half-cut ˌhɑːf ˈkʌt ◄ §ˌhæf- ‖ ˌhæf-
half-day *adj* ˌhɑːf ˈdeɪ ◄ §ˌhæf- ‖ ˌhæf-
  ˌhalf-day ˈclosure
half-day *n* ˈhɑːf deɪ §ˈhæf- ‖ ˈhæf- ~**s** z
half-gallon ˌhɑːf ˈgæl ən ◄ §ˌhæf- ‖ ˌhæf- ~**s** z
half-hardy ˌhɑːf ˈhɑːd i ◄ §ˌhæf-
  ‖ ˌhæf ˈhɑːrd i ◄
half-hearted ˌhɑːf ˈhɑːt ɪd ◄ §ˌhæf-, -əd
  ‖ ˌhæf ˈhɑːrt̬ əd ◄ ~**ly** li ~**ness** nəs nɪs

half-holiday ˌhɑːf ˈhɒl ə deɪ §ˌhæf-, -ɪ-, -di
‖ ˌhæf ˈhɑːl- ~s z
half-hour ˌhɑːf ˈaʊˌə ◄ §ˌhæf- ‖ ˌhæf ˈaʊˌər ◄
~ly li ~s z
half-inch ˌhɑːf ˈɪntʃ §ˌhæf- ‖ ˌhæf- ~ed t ~es ɪz
əz ~ing ɪŋ
half-length ˌhɑːf ˈleŋkθ ◄ §ˌhæf-, §-ˈlenˈθ
‖ ˌhæf-
half-|life ˈhɑːf |laɪf §ˈhæf- ‖ ˈhæf- ~lives laɪvz
half-light ˈhɑːf laɪt §ˈhæf- ‖ ˈhæf-
half-marathon ˌhɑːf ˈmær əθ ən §ˌhæf-,
-ə θɒn ‖ ˌhæf ˈmær ə θɑːn -ˈmer- ~s z
half-mast ˌhɑːf ˈmɑːst §ˌhæf-, §-ˈmæst
‖ ˌhæf ˈmæst
half-measures ˈhɑːf ˌmeʒ əz §ˈhæf-, ˌ·ˈ·ˌ
‖ ˈhæf ˌmeʒ ˈrz -ˌmeɪʒ-
half-mile ˌhɑːf ˈmaɪˈl ◄ §ˌhæf- ‖ ˌhæf-
half-nelson ˌhɑːf ˈnels ˈn §ˌhæf- ‖ ˌhæf- ˈ·ˌ·· ~s
z
half-open ˌhɑːf ˈəʊp ən ◄ §ˌhæf-
‖ ˌhæf ˈoʊp ən
Halford ˈhæl fəd ˈhɔːl-, ˈhɒl- ‖ -fˈrd ~'s z
half past *in expressions of time* ˌhɑːf ˈpɑːst ◄
ˌhɑː-, -hʌ-, §ˌhæf-, §-ˈpæst ‖ ˌhæf ˈpæst ◄
ˌhalf past ˈten
halfpence ˈheɪp ənˈts →mˈps
halfpenn|y *n* ˈheɪp nˌi ˈheɪp ən ˌi —*For the
British coin in use 1971-85, also*
ˌhɑːf ˈpen ˌi ◄, §ˌhæf- ‖ ˌhæf- ~ies iz
Halfpenny *surname* ˈhɑːf pən i §ˈhæf- ‖ ˈhæf-
halfpennyworth ˈheɪp ni wɜːθ -wəθ; ˈheɪp əθ;
ˌhɑːf ˈpen əθ, §ˌhæf- ‖ ˈheɪp ən i wɜːθ —*See*
hap'orth
half-pound ˌhɑːf ˈpaʊnd ◄ §ˌhæf- ‖ ˌhæf-
half-price ˌhɑːf ˈpraɪs ◄ §ˌhæf- ‖ ˌhæf-
half-sister ˈhɑːf ˌsɪst ə §ˈhæf- ‖ ˈhæf ˌsɪst ˈr ~s
z
half-size ˌhɑːf ˈsaɪz ◄ §ˌhæf- ‖ ˌhæf-
half-timbered ˌhɑːf ˈtɪm bəd ◄ §ˌhæf-
‖ ˌhæf ˈtɪm bˈrd ◄
half time ˌhɑːf ˈtaɪm ◄ §ˌhæf- ‖ ˈhæf taɪm
ˌhalf-time ˈscore
halftone ˌhɑːf ˈtəʊn §ˌhæf-, ˈ·· ‖ ˈhæf toʊn ~s
z
half-track *adj* ˌhɑːf ˈtræk ◄ §ˌhæf- ‖ ˌhæf-
half-track *n* ˈhɑːf træk §ˈhæf- ‖ ˈhæf- ~ed t ~s
s
half-|truth ˈhɑːf |truːθ §ˈhæf-, ˌ·ˈ· ‖ ˈhæf-
~truths truːðz truːθs
halfway ˌhɑːf ˈweɪ ◄ §ˌhæf- ‖ ˌhæf-
ˌhalfway ˈhouse
half-wit ˈhɑːf wɪt §ˈhæf- ‖ ˈhæf- ~s s
half-witted ˌhɑːf ˈwɪt ɪd ◄ §ˌhæf-, -əd
‖ ˌhæf ˈwɪt əd ◄ ~ly li ~ness nəs nɪs
half-yearly ˌhɑːf ˈjɪə li ◄ §ˌhæf- ‖ ˌhæf ˈjɪr li
halibut ˈhæl ɪb ət -əb- ~s s
Halicarnassus ˌhæl ɪ kɑː ˈnæs əs ˌ·ə- ‖ -kɑːrˈ-
halide ˈheɪl aɪd ˈhæl- ~s z
Halifax ˈhæl ɪ fæks -ə-
halitosis ˌhæl ɪ ˈtəʊs ɪs -ə-, §-əs ‖ -ˈtoʊs-
hall, Hall hɔːl ‖ hɑːl (= *haul*) **halls** hɔːlz
‖ hɑːlz
ˌhall of ˈresidence; ˌhall ˈporter

hallal hə ˈlɑːl ˈhæl æl, hæˈlæl —*Arabic*
[ħa ˈlaːl]
Hallam ˈhæl əm
Halle, Hallé ˈhæl eɪ -i ‖ ˈhɑːl ə
halleluja, hallelujah ˌhæl ɪ ˈluː jə -ə- ~s z
Halley *(i)* ˈhæl i; *(ii)* ˈhɔːl i ‖ ˈhɑːl i —*The
astronomer and the comet named after him are
usually (i) in educated speech, although some
claim that only (ii) is correct. In AmE there is
also a popular pronunciation* ˈheɪl i
halliard ˈhæl jəd ‖ -jˈrd ~s z
Halliday ˈhæl ɪ deɪ -ə-
Halliwell ˈhæl ɪ wel
hallmark ˈhɔːl mɑːk ‖ -mɑːrk ˈhɑːl- ~ed t ~ing
ɪŋ ~s s
hallo hə ˈləʊ ˌhæ-, ˌhe-, ˌhʌ- ‖ -ˈloʊ ~es z
halloo hə ˈluː ~ed d ~ing ɪŋ ~s z
Halloran ˈhæl ər ən
hallow ˈhæl əʊ ‖ -oʊ ~ed d —*but in the Lord's
Prayer also sometimes* ed, ɪd, əd ~ing ɪŋ ~s z
Hallowe'en ˌhæl əʊ ˈiːn ◄ ‖ -oʊ- ˌhɑːl-
Hallowes, Hallows ˈhæl əʊz ‖ -oʊz
hallstand ˈhɔːl stænd ‖ ˈhɑːl- ~s z
halluci|nate hə ˈluːs ɪ |neɪt -ˈljuːs-, -ə- ~nated
neɪt ɪd -əd ‖ neɪt əd ~nates neɪts ~nating
neɪt ɪŋ ‖ neɪt ɪŋ
hallucination hə ˌluːs ɪ ˈneɪʃ ən -ˌljuːs-, -ə- ~s z
hallucinatory hə ˈluːs ɪn ət ər i -ˈljuːs-, -ˈˈˈn;
·ˈ·ɪ ˈneɪt ər i ◄, ·ˌ·ə-, ˈˈ·· · · ‖ -ˈnˌə tɔːr i
-tour i
hallucinogen ˌhæl uː ˈsɪn ədʒ ən -ə dʒen;
hə ˈluːs ɪn-, -ˈˈˈn- ~s z
hallucinogenic hə ˌluːs ɪn ə ˈdʒen ɪk ◄
-ˌljuːs-, -ˌˈn-
hallux ˈhæl əks ~es ɪz əz
hallway ˈhɔːl weɪ ‖ ˈhɑːl- ~s z
halma ˈhælm ə
Halmahera ˌhælm ə ˈhɪər ə -ˈhɜːr- ‖ -ˈhɜː ə
ˌhɑːlm ə-
halo ˈheɪl əʊ ‖ -oʊ ~ed d ~es, ~s z ~ing ɪŋ
halo- *comb. form*
with stress-neutral suffix ˌhæl əʊ ‖ -ə —
halophyte ˈhæl əʊ faɪt ‖ -ə-
with stress-imposing suffix hæ ˈlɒ+ ‖ -ˈlɑː+
— **halogenous** hæ ˈlɒdʒ ən əs ‖ -ˈlɑːdʒ-
halogen ˈhæl ə dʒen ˈheɪl-, -ədʒ ən ~s z
halon ˈheɪl ɒn ‖ -ɑːn ~s z
haloperidol ˌhæl əʊ ˈper ɪ dɒl ˌheɪl-, -ə-
‖ ˌhæl oʊ ˈper ə dɔːl -dɑːl, -doʊl
halophyte ˈhæl ə faɪt ˈheɪl- ~s s
halothane ˈhæl əʊ θeɪn ˈheɪl- ‖ -ə-
Halpern ˈhælp ən ‖ -ˈrn
Hals hæls hælz ‖ hɑːls hɑːlz —*Dutch* [hɑls]
Halsbury ˈhɔːlz bər i ˈhɒlz- ‖ ˈhɔːlz ˌber i
ˈhɑːlz-
Halse hæls hɔːls, hɒls ‖ hɑːls, hɔːls
Halstead, Halsted *(i)* ˈhæl sted -stɪd, *(ii)*
ˈhɔːl- ˈhɒl- ‖ ˈhɑːl-
halt hɔːlt hɒlt ‖ hɑːlt **halted** ˈhɔːlt ɪd ˈhɒlt-, -əd
‖ ˈhɑːlt- **halting/ly** ˈhɔːlt ɪŋ /li ˈhɒlt- ‖ ˈhɑːlt-
halts hɔːlts hɒlts ‖ hɑːlts — *Preference poll,
BrE:* hɒlt 52%, hɔːlt 48%. *See chart on p. 364.*
Haltemprice ˈhɔːlt əm praɪs ˈhɒlt- ‖ ˈhɑːlt-

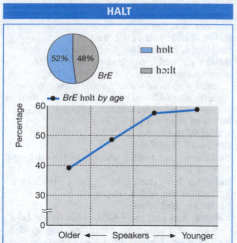

HALT

52% 48%

BrE

- ◼ hɒlt
- ◼ hɔːlt

BrE hɒlt by age

Percentage — Older ← Speakers → Younger

halter 'hɔːlt ə 'hɒlt- ‖ -ᵊr 'hɑːlt- ~s z
haltere 'hælt ɪə 'hɔːlt-, 'hɒlt- ‖ -ɪr 'hɔːlt-, 'hɑːlt- ~s z
halterneck 'hɔːlt ə nek 'hɒlt- ‖ -ᵊr- 'hɑːlt- ~s s
Halton 'hɔːlt ən 'hɒlt- 'hɑːlt-
halva, halvah 'hælv ə -ɑː ‖ hɑːl 'vɑː ' · ·
halve hɑːv ‖ hæv **halved** hɑːvd ‖ hævd **halves** hɑːvz ‖ hævz **halving** 'hɑːv ɪŋ ‖ 'hæv ɪŋ
halves from **half, halve** hɑːvz ‖ hævz
halyard 'hæl jəd ‖ -jᵊrd ~s z
ham, Ham hæm **hammed** hæmd **hamming** 'hæm ɪŋ **hams** hæmz
hamadryad ˌhæm ə 'draɪ ‿əd -æd ~s z
hamadryas ˌhæm ə 'draɪ ‿əs -æs ~es ɪz əz
Haman 'heɪm ən -æn
Hamas 'hæm æs hə 'mæs, hæ-, -'mɑːs —Arabic [ħa 'maːs]
Hamble 'hæm bᵊl
Hambledon 'hæm bᵊl dən
Hambletonian ˌhæm bᵊl 'təʊn i ‿ən ‖ -'toʊn- ~s z
Hambro 'hæm brəʊ -brə ‖ -broʊ 'hɑːm-
Hamburg 'hæm bɜːɡ ‖ -bɜːɡ —Ger ['ham bʊʁk, -bʊɐ̯k]
hamburger, H~ 'hæm ˌbɜːɡ ə ‖ -ˌbɜːɡ ᵊr ~s z
Hamelin 'hæm lɪn 'hæm əl ɪn, -ɪl- —Ger Hameln ['haː mᵊln]
Hamersley 'hæm əz li ‖ -ᵊrz-
ham-fisted ˌhæm 'fɪst ɪd ◂ -əd ~ly li ~ness nəs nɪs
ham-handed ˌhæm 'hænd ɪd ◂ -əd ~ly li ~ness nəs nɪs
Hamilcar hæ 'mɪl kɑː hə-; 'hæm ᵊl-, -ɪl- ‖ -kɑːr
Hamill 'hæm ᵊl -ɪl
Hamilton 'hæm ᵊl tən -ɪl-
Hamiltonian ˌhæm ᵊl 'təʊn i ‿ən ◂ ˌ·ɪl- ‖ 'toʊn- ~s z
Hamish 'heɪm ɪʃ
Hamite 'hæm aɪt ~s s
Hamitic hæ 'mɪt ɪk hə- ‖ -'mɪt̬ ɪk
Hamito-Semitic ˌhæm ɪ təʊ sə 'mɪt ɪk ◂ ˌ·ə-, -sɪ'·- ‖ ˌhæm ə toʊ sə 'mɪt̬ ɪk ◂

hamlet, H~ 'hæm lət -lɪt ~s s
Hamley 'hæm li
Hamlin, Hamlyn 'hæm lɪn §-lən
Hammarskjold 'hæm ə ʃəʊld →-ʃɒʊld ‖ -ᵊr ʃoʊld 'hɑːm- —Swedish Hamarskjöld ['ˈhaː mar ɧœld]
hammer, H~ 'hæm ə ‖ -ᵊr ~ed d **hammering** 'hæm ᵊr ɪŋ ~s z
  'hammer ˌdrill
hammerbeam 'hæm ə biːm ‖ -ᵊr- ~s z
Hammerfest 'hæm ə fest ‖ -ᵊr- 'hɑːm- —Norw ['ˈham ər fɛst]
hammerhead 'hæm ə hed ‖ -ᵊr- ~s z
Hammersley 'hæm əz li ‖ -ᵊrz-
Hammersmith 'hæm ə smɪθ ‖ -ᵊr-
Hammerstein (i) 'hæm ə staɪn ‖ -ᵊr-, (ii) -stiːn
Hammett 'hæm ɪt §-ət
hammock 'hæm ək ~s s
Hammond 'hæm ənd
Hammurabi ˌhæm u 'rɑːb i
hammy 'hæm i
Hampden 'hæm dən 'hæmp-
hamper 'hæmp ə ‖ -ᵊr ~ed d **hampering** 'hæmp ᵊr ɪŋ ~s z
Hampshire 'hæmp ʃə -ʃɪə ‖ -ʃᵊr -ʃɪr
Hampstead 'hæmp stɪd -sted, §-stəd
  ˌHampstead 'Heath
Hampton 'hæmp tən
  ˌHampton 'Court
hamster 'hæmᵖst ə ‖ -ᵊr ~s z
hamstring 'hæm strɪŋ ~ing ɪŋ ~s z
hamstrung 'hæm strʌŋ
Hamtramck hæm 'træm ɪk (!)
hamza, hamzah 'hæmz ə ~s z
Han hæn ‖ hɑːn —Chi hàn [⁴xan]
Hanbury 'hæn bər ‿i →'hæm-
Hancock 'hæn kɒk →'hæŋ- ‖ -kɑːk
hand hænd **handed** 'hænd ɪd -əd **handing** 'hænd ɪŋ **hands** hændz
  'hand ˌbaggage; 'hand greˌnade; 'hand ˌluggage; ˌhands 'off; ˌhands 'up; 'hand ˌtowel
handbag 'hænd bæɡ →'hæm- ~s z
handball 'hænd bɔːl →'hæm- ‖ -bɑːl ~s z
handbarrow 'hænd ˌbær əʊ →'hæm- ‖ -oʊ -ˌber- ~s z
handbasin 'hænd ˌbeɪs ᵊn →'hæm- ~s z
handbasket 'hænd ˌbɑːsk ɪt →'hæm-, §-ˌbæsk-, -ət ‖ -ˌbæsk- ~s s
handbell 'hænd bel →'hæm- ~s z
handbill 'hænd bɪl →'hæm- ~s z
handbook 'hænd bʊk →'hæm-, §-buːk ~s s
handbrake 'hænd breɪk →'hæm- ~s s
handcar 'hænd kɑː ‖ -kɑːr ~s z
handcart 'hænd kɑːt →'hæŋ- ‖ -kɑːrt ~s s
handclap 'hænd klæp →'hæŋ- ~s s
hand-crafted ˌhænd 'krɑːft ɪd ◂ §-'kræft-, -əd ‖ -'kræft-
handcuff 'hænd kʌf →'hæŋ- ~ed t ~ing ɪŋ ~s s
-handed 'hænd ɪd ◂ -əd
handedness 'hænd ɪd nəs -əd-, -nɪs
Handel 'hænd ᵊl —Ger Händel ['ˈhɛn dᵊl]

Handelian hæn ˈdiːl i ən **~s** z
hand-eye ˌhænd ˈaɪ
    ˌhand-ˌeye coordiˈnation
handful ˈhænd fʊl **~s** z
handgun ˈhænd gʌn →ˈhæŋ- **~s** z
hand-held ˈhænd held **~s** z
handhold ˈhænd həʊld →-ˈhɒʊld ‖ -hoʊld **~s** z
handicap ˈhænd i kæp **~ped** t **~per/s** ə/z
    ‖ ˀr/z **~ping** ɪŋ **~s** s
handicraft ˈhænd i krɑːft §-kræft ‖ -kræft **~s** s
handie... —*see* **handy**
handily ˈhænd ɪ li -əl i
handiwork ˈhænd i wɜːk ‖ -wɜːk

HANDKERCHIEF

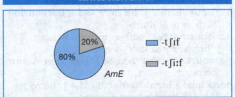

AmE

handker|chief ˈhæŋk ə |tʃɪf -tʃəf, -tʃiːf ‖ -ˀr-
    — *Preference poll, AmE:* -tʃɪf *80%,* -tʃiːf *20%.*
    ~chiefs tʃɪfs tʃəfs, tʃiːfs, tʃiːvz **~chieves** tʃiːvz
handle ˈhænd ˀl **~d** d **~s** z **handling**
    ˈhænd lɪŋ ˈhænd ˀl ɪŋ
handlebar ˈhænd ˀl bɑː ‖ -bɑːr **~s** z
handler ˈhænd lə ˈhænd ˀl ə ‖ -lˀr -ˀl ər **~s** z
hand-lettered ˌhænd ˈlet əd ◄ ‖ -ˈleṭ ˀrd ◄
Handley ˈhænd li
handloom ˈhænd luːm **~s** z
handmade ˌhænd ˈmeɪd ◄ →ˌhæm-
handmaid ˈhænd meɪd →ˈhæm- **~s** z
handmaiden ˈhænd ˌmeɪd ˀn →ˈhæm- **~s** z
hand-me-down ˈhænd mi daʊn →ˈhæm- **~s** z
handout ˈhænd aʊt **~s** s
handover ˈhænd ˌəʊv ə ‖ -ˌoʊv ˀr **~s** z
handpick v ˌhænd ˈpɪk ◄ →ˌhæm- **~ed** t **~ing**
    ɪŋ **~s** s
handplant ˈhænd plɑːnt §-plænt ‖ -plænt **~s** s
handrail ˈhænd reɪˀl **~s** z
handsaw ˈhænd sɔː ‖ -sɑː **~s** z
handset ˈhænd set **~s** s
hands-free ˌhændz ˈfriː ◄ ˈ· ·
handshak|e ˈhænd ʃeɪk **~es** s **~ing** ɪŋ
hands-off ˌhændz ˈɒf ◄ -ˈɔːf ‖ -ˈɔːf ◄ -ˈɑːf ◄
handsome ˈhæn⸳s əm **~ly** li **~ness** nəs nɪs
hands-on ˌhændz ˈɒn ◄ ‖ -ˈɑːn ◄ -ˈɔːn ◄
handspring ˈhænd sprɪŋ **~s** z
handstand ˈhænd stænd **~s** z
hand-to-hand ˌhænd tə ˈhænd ◄
hand-to-mouth ˌhænd tə ˈmaʊθ ◄
handwash ˈhænd wɒʃ ‖ -wɑːʃ -wɔːʃ **~ed** t **~es**
    ɪz əz **~ing** ɪŋ
handwork ˈhænd wɜːk ‖ -wɜːk
hand-wringing ˈhænd ˌrɪŋ ɪŋ
handwriting ˈhænd ˌraɪt ɪŋ ‖ -ˌraɪt ɪŋ
handwritten ˌhænd ˈrɪt ˀn ◄
hand|y, Handy ˈhænd |i **~ier** i ə ‖ i ˀr **~iest**
    i ɪst i əst
handy-dandy ˌhænd i ˈdænd i ◄

handy|man ˈhænd i |mæn **~men** men
hang hæŋ **hanged** hæŋd **hanging/s** ˈhæŋ ɪŋ/z
    hangs hæŋz **hung** hʌŋ
    ˌHang ˈSeng (ˌindex) seŋ —*Cantonese*
    [⁴hɐŋ ¹sɐŋ]
hangar ˈhæŋ ə -gə ‖ -ˀr -gˀr (*usually* = *hanger*)
    ~s z
Hangchow ˌhæŋ ˈtʃaʊ —*Chi* Hángzhōu
    [²xaŋ ¹ʈʂou]
hangdog ˈhæŋ dɒg ‖ -dɔːg -dɑːg **~s** z
hanger ˈhæŋ ə ‖ -ˀr s z
hang|er-on ˌhæŋ |ər ˈɒn ‖ -|ər ˈɑːn -ˈɔːn
    ~ers-on əz ˈɒn ‖ ˀrz ˈɑːn -ˈɔːn
hang-glider ˈhæŋ ˌglaɪd ə ‖ -ˀr **~s** z
hang-gliding ˈhæŋ ˌglaɪd ɪŋ
hang|man ˈhæŋ |mən **~men** mən
hangnail ˈhæŋ neɪˀl **~s** z
hangout ˈhæŋ aʊt **~s** s
hangover ˈhæŋ ˌəʊv ə ‖ -ˌoʊv ˀr **~s** z
hangul, H~ ˈhæŋ gʊl ‖ ˈhɑːn- —*Korean* hangŭl
    [han gul]
hang-up ˈhæŋ ʌp **~s** s
Hangzhou ˌhæŋ ˈdʒəʊ ‖ -ˈdʒoʊ —*Chi*
    Hángzhōu [²xaŋ ¹ʈʂou]
Hanif hə ˈnɪf
hank, Hank hæŋk **hanks** hæŋks
hanker ˈhæŋk ə ‖ -ˀr **~ed** d **hankering**
    ˈhæŋk ər ɪŋ **~s** z
hankie ˈhæŋk i **~s** z
Hanks hæŋks
hank|y ˈhæŋk |i **~ies** iz
hanky-panky ˌhæŋk i ˈpæŋk i
Hanley ˈhæn li
Hann hæn
Hanna, Hannah ˈhæn ə
Hannay ˈhæn eɪ
Hannibal ˈhæn ɪb ˀl -əb-
Hannington ˈhæn ɪŋ tən
Hanoi ⒮hæ ˈnɔɪ hə- ‖ hɑː- —*Vietnamese* Hà
    Nôi [³ha ⁶noi]
Hanover ˈhæn əʊv ə ‖ -oʊv ˀr —*Ger* Hannover
    [ha ˈno: fɐ]
Hanoverian ˌhæn əʊ ˈvɪər i ən ◄ -ˈveər-
    ‖ -ə ˈvɪr- -ˈver- **~s** z
Hanrahan ˈhæn rə hən -hæn
Hanratty hæn ˈræt i ‖ -ˈræṭ i ˈ· · ·
Hans hæn⸳s hænz —*Ger* [hans]
Hansa ˈhæn⸳s ə ˈhænz- —*Ger* [ˈhan za]
Hansard ˈhæn⸳s ɑːd -əd ‖ -ˀrd
Hanseatic, h~ ˌhæn⸳s i ˈæt ɪk ◄ ˌhænz-
    ‖ -ˈæṭ ɪk ◄
Hansel, Hänsel ˈhæn⸳s ˀl —*Ger* [ˈhan zˀl,
    ˈhen-]
Hansen ˈhæn⸳s ˀn
hansom, H~ ˈhæn⸳s əm (= *handsome*) **~s** z
Hanson ˈhæn⸳s ˀn
Hants hænts -*or as* Hampshire
Hanukah, Hanukkah ˈhɑːn ək ə ˈhɒn-, ˈhæn-,
    -ʊk-, -uːk-, -ɑː- —*Hebrew* [xa nu ˈka]
hanuman, H~ ˌhʌn u ˈmɑːn ˌhɑːn- **~s** z
    —*Hindi* [hə ɳu mɑːɳ]
Hanway ˈhæn weɪ
Hanwell ˈhæn wˀl -wel

hap hæp **happed** hæpt **happing** 'hæp ɪŋ **haps** hæps

hapax 'hæp æks
  ,hapax le'gomenon lɪ 'gɒm ɪn ən lə-, le-, -ən ən, -ə nɒn ‖ -'gɑːm ə nɑːn

ha'penny 'heɪp ni 'heɪp ən i **ha'pennies** 'heɪp niz 'heɪp ən iz

haphazard ₍ₗ₎hæp 'hæz əd ◄ ‖ -ərd **~ly** li **~ness** nəs nɪs

hapless 'hæp ləs -lɪs

haplography ₍ₗ₎hæp 'lɒg rəf i ‖ -'lɑːg-

haploid 'hæp lɔɪd **~y** i

haplolog|y ₍ₗ₎hæp 'lɒl ədʒ |i ‖ -'lɑːl- **~ies** iz

haply 'hæp li

hap'orth, ha'p'orth 'heɪp əθ ‖ -ərθ **~s** s

happen 'hæp ən **happened** 'hæp ənd →-md **happening/s** 'hæp ən ɪŋ/z **happens** 'hæp ənz →-mz

happenstance 'hæp ən stæn's →-m-, -stɑːn's

happie... —see **happy**

happily 'hæp ɪ li -əl i

happiness 'hæp i nəs -nɪs

Happisburgh 'heɪz bər ə (!)

happ|y, Happy 'hæp |i **~ier** i ə ‖ i ᵊr **~iest** i ɪst i əst
  ,happy e'vent; 'happy ,hour; ,happy 'hunting ground; ,happy 'medium

happy-clappy ,hæp i 'klæp i ◄

happy-go-lucky ,hæp i gəʊ 'lʌk i ◄ ‖ -goʊ'--

Hapsburg 'hæps bɜːg ‖ -bɜːɡ —Ger Habsburg ['haːps bʊʁk] **~s** z

haptic 'hæpt ɪk

hara-kiri ,hær ə 'kɪr i -'kɪər-, △-i 'kær i, △-i 'kɑːr i ‖ ,hɑːr- —Jp [ha ,ra ki 'ri]

haram hæ 'rɑːm hə-, hɑː- —Arabic [ha 'raːm]

harangu|e hə 'ræŋ **~ed** d **~es** z **~ing** ɪŋ

Harare hə 'rɑːr i hɑː-, -eɪ

HARASS

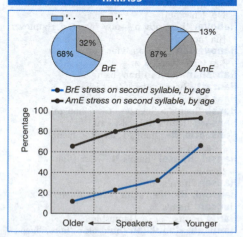

' .. | .·.

13%

32%
68%
BrE

87%
AmE

• BrE stress on second syllable, by age
• AmE stress on second syllable, by age

Percentage
100
80
60
40
20
0

Older ◄—— Speakers ——► Younger

harass 'hær əs hə 'ræs ‖ hə 'ræs 'hær əs, 'her- —The traditional RP form is 'hær əs. The pronunciation hə 'ræs, which originated in the US, was seemingly first heard in Britain in the 1970s. In time it may predominate in BrE, as

it already does in AmE. Meanwhile, it evokes negative feelings among those who use the traditional form. Preference polls, BrE: ' ·· 68%, ·˙· 32%; AmE: ·˙· 87%, ' ·· 13%. **~ed** t **~er/s** ə/z ‖ ᵊr/z **~es** ɪz əz **~ing** ɪŋ **~ment** mənt ‖ mənt

Harben 'hɑːb ən ‖ 'hɑːrb-

Harbin 'hɑː bɪn ,hɑː 'bɪn ‖ 'hɑːrb ən ,hɑːr 'bɪn —Chi Hā'erbīn [¹xa ₃ ¹pɪn]

harbinger 'hɑːb ɪndʒ ə §-əndʒ- ‖ -ᵊr **~s** z

harbor 'hɑːb ə ‖ 'hɑːrb ᵊr **~ed** d **harboring** 'hɑːb ᵊr ɪŋ ‖ 'hɑːrb- **~s** z

harbormaster 'hɑːb ə ,mɑːst ə §-,mæst- ‖ 'hɑːrb ᵊr ,mæst ᵊr **~s** z

Harborough 'hɑːb ər ə ‖ 'hɑːr ,bɜː oʊ

harbour 'hɑːb ə ‖ 'hɑːrb ᵊr **~ed** d **harbouring** 'hɑːb ᵊr ɪŋ ‖ 'hɑːrb- **~s** z

harbourmaster 'hɑːb ə ,mɑːst ə §-,mæst- ‖ 'hɑːrb ᵊr ,mæst ᵊr **~s** z

Harcourt 'hɑː kɔːt 'hɑːk ət ‖ 'hɑːr kɔːrt -koʊrt; 'hɑːrk ᵊrt

hard hɑːd ‖ hɑːrd **harder** 'hɑːd ə ‖ 'hɑːrd ᵊr **hardest** 'hɑːd ɪst -əst ‖ 'hɑːrd-
  ,hard 'by◄; ,hard 'cash; ,hard 'cider; ,hard 'copy, ' · ,·˙·; ,hard 'core 'nucleus'; 'hard core 'broken stones'; ,hard 'currency; ,hard 'disk; ,hard 'drink; ,hard 'drugs; ,hard 'feelings; ,hard 'labour; ,hard 'line; ,hard 'liquor; ,hard 'luck; ,hard 'luck ,story, · · ·˙·; ,hard of 'hearing; ,hard 'palate; ,hard 'rock; ,hard 'sell; ,hard 'shoulder; ,hard 'up◄

hard-and-fast ,hɑːd ᵊn 'fɑːst ◄ §-'fæst ‖ ,hɑːrd ᵊn 'fæst ◄

hardback 'hɑːd bæk →'hɑːb- ‖ 'hɑːrd- **~s** s

hardball 'hɑːd bɔːl →'hɑːb- ‖ 'hɑːrd- -bɑːl

hard-bitten ,hɑːd 'bɪt ᵊn ◄ →,hɑːb- ‖ ,hɑːrd-

hardboard 'hɑːd bɔːd →'hɑːb- ‖ 'hɑːrd bɔːrd -boʊrd

hard-boiled ,hɑːd 'bɔɪᵊld ◄ →,hɑːb- ‖ ,hɑːrd-
  ,hard-boiled 'egg

hardbound 'hɑːd baʊnd →'hɑːb- ‖ 'hɑːrd-

Hardcastle 'hɑːd ,kɑːs ᵊl →'hɑːg-, §-,kæs- ‖ 'hɑːrd ,kæs ᵊl

hard-core ,hɑːd 'kɔː ◄ →,hɑːg-, ' ·· ‖ ,hɑːrd 'kɔːr ◄ -'koʊr
  ,hard-core 'porn

hardcover 'hɑːd ,kʌv ə →'hɑːg- ‖ 'hɑːrd ,kʌv ᵊr

hard-done-by ,hɑːd 'dʌn baɪ →-'dʌm- ‖ ,hɑːrd-

hard-drinking ,hɑːd 'drɪŋk ɪŋ ◄ ‖ ,hɑːrd-

hard-earned ,hɑːd 'ɜːnd ◄ ‖ ,hɑːrd 'ɜːnd ◄

hard-edged ,hɑːd 'edʒd ◄ ‖ ,hɑːrd-

harden 'hɑːd ᵊn ‖ 'hɑːrd ᵊn **~ed** d **~ing** ɪŋ **~s** z

hard-fought ,hɑːd 'fɔːt ◄ ‖ ,hɑːrd- -fɑːt ◄

hard-hat 'hɑːd hæt ‖ 'hɑːrd- **~s** s

hardheaded ,hɑːd 'hed ɪd ◄ -əd ‖ ,hɑːrd- **~ly** li **~ness** nəs nɪs

hardhearted ,hɑːd 'hɑːt ɪd ◄ -əd ‖ ,hɑːrd 'hɑːrt əd ◄ **~ly** li **~ness** nəs nɪs

hard-hitting ,hɑːd 'hɪt ɪŋ ◄ ‖ ,hɑːrd 'hɪt ɪŋ ◄

Hard attack

When a word or syllable begins with a vowel sound, it is possible to start the vowel from a position where the vocal folds are first held closed, then burst open for the vowel: that is, to precede the vowel by a GLOTTAL STOP. This way of starting a vowel is called **hard attack**.

In English, hard attack is not customary. But it is sometimes used for special effect, as a way of emphasizing the importance of a word.

When hard attack is used, and the word in question is preceded by **to**, then the weak form appropriate before a consonant is often used, namely tə. Thus **to eat** is usually tu ˈiːt but sometimes tə ˈʔiːt.

H

Hardicanute ˈhɑːd ɪ kə ˌnjuːt ˈ·ə-, ˌ· ·ˈ·
  ‖ ˌhɑːrd ə kə ˈnuːt -ˈnjuːt
Hardie ˈhɑːd i ‖ ˈhɑːrd i
hardihood ˈhɑːd i hʊd ‖ ˈhɑːrd-
hardily ˈhɑːd ɪ li -əl i ‖ ˈhɑːrd-
hardiness ˈhɑːd i nəs -nɪs ‖ ˈhɑːrd-
Harding ˈhɑːd ɪŋ ‖ ˈhɑːrd-
Hardinge (i) ˈhɑːd ɪŋ ‖ ˈhɑːrd-, (ii) -ɪndʒ
hard-line ˌhɑːd ˈlaɪn ◄ ‖ ˌhɑːrd-
hard-liner ˌhɑːd ˈlaɪn ə ◄ ˈ· · ·
  ‖ ˌhɑːrd ˈlaɪn ᵊr ◄ ~**s** z
hard-luck stor|y ˌhɑːd ˈlʌk ˌstɔːr| i ‖ ˌhɑːrd-
  -ˌstoʊr| i ~**ies** iz
hard|ly ˈhɑːd |li ‖ ˈhɑːrd- ~**ness** nəs nɪs
hard-nosed ˌhɑːd ˈnəʊzd ◄ ‖ ˌhɑːrd ˈnoʊzd ◄
hard-on ˈhɑːd ɒn ‖ ˈhɑːrd ɑːn -ɔːn ~**s** z
hardpan ˈhɑːd pæn →ˈhɑːb- ‖ ˈhɑːrd-
hard-pressed ˌhɑːd ˈprest ◄ →ˌhɑːb- ‖ ˌhɑːrd-
hard-scrabble ˈhɑːd ˌskræb ᵊl ‖ ˈhɑːrd-
hard-shell ˈhɑːd ʃel ‖ ˈhɑːrd- ~**s** z
hardship ˈhɑːd ʃɪp ‖ ˈhɑːrd- ~**s** s
hardtack ˈhɑːd tæk ‖ ˈhɑːrd-
hardtop ˈhɑːd tɒp ‖ ˈhɑːrd tɑːp ~**s** s
hardware ˈhɑːd weə ‖ ˈhɑːrd wer -wær ~**s** z
hardwearing ˌhɑːd ˈweər ɪŋ ◄
  ‖ ˌhɑːrd ˈwer ɪŋ ◄ -ˈwær-
  ˌhard- ˌwearing ˈfabric
Hardwick, Hardwicke ˈhɑːd wɪk ‖ ˈhɑːrd-
hard-wired ˌhɑːd ˈwaɪ‿əd ◄ ‖ ˌhɑːrd ˈwaɪ‿ᵊrd ◄
hard-won ˌhɑːd ˈwʌn ◄ ‖ ˌhɑːrd-
hardwood ˈhɑːd wʊd ‖ ˈhɑːrd- ~**s** z
hard-working ˌhɑːd ˈwɜːk ɪŋ ◄
  ‖ ˌhɑːrd ˈwɜːk ɪŋ ◄
hard|y, Hard|y ˈhɑːd |i ‖ ˈhɑːrd |i ~**ier** i‿ə
  ‖ i‿ᵊr ~**ies**, ~**y's** iz ~**iest** i‿ɪst i‿əst
hare, Hare heə ‖ heᵊr hæᵊr (= hair) **hared**
  heəd ‖ heᵊrd hæᵊrd **hares** heəz ‖ heᵊrz hæᵊrz
  haring ˈheər ɪŋ ‖ ˈher ɪŋ ˈhær- —see also
  phrases with this word
  ˈhare ˌcoursing
harebell ˈheə bel ‖ ˈher- ˈhær- ~**s** z
harebrained ˈheə breɪnd ‖ ˈher- ˈhær-
harecloth ˈheə klɒθ -klɔːθ ‖ ˈher klɔːθ ˈhær-,
  -klɑːθ

Harefield ˈheə fiː‿ᵊld ‖ ˈher-
Hare Krishna ˌhær i ˈkrɪʃ nə ˌhɑːr- ‖ ˌhɑːr-
  ˌhær-, ˌher-
harelip ˌheə ˈlɪp ˈ· · ‖ ˈher lɪp ˈhær- ~**ped** t ◄
  ~**s** s
harem ˈhɑːr iːm ˈheər-, -əm, ₍₎hɑː ˈriːm
  ‖ ˈhær əm ˈher- ~**s** z
Harewood ˈheə wʊd ‖ ˈher- ˈhær- —but
  ˈhɑː- ‖ ˈhɑːr- for the Earl of H~, and for H~
  House
Harford ˈhɑː fəd ‖ ˈhɑːr fᵊrd
Hargraves ˈhɑː greɪvz ‖ ˈhɑːr-
Hargreaves (i) ˈhɑː griːvz ‖ ˈhɑːr-, (ii) -greɪvz
haricot ˈhær ɪ kəʊ -ə- ‖ -koʊ ˈher- ~**s** z
  ˌharicot ˈbean, ˈ· · ·
Harijan ˈhʌr ɪdʒ ən ˈhɑːr-, §-ədʒ-; -ɪ dʒɑːn, -ə-
  ‖ ˈhɑːr ɪ dʒɑːn ˈhær-, ˈher-, -dʒæn ~**s** z
Haringey ˈhær ɪŋ geɪ -gi ‖ ˈher-
hark hɑːk ‖ hɑːrk **harked** hɑːkt ‖ hɑːrkt
  harking ˈhɑːk ɪŋ ‖ ˈhɑːrk ɪŋ **harks** hɑːks
  ‖ hɑːrks
harken ˈhɑːk ən ‖ ˈhɑːrk- ~**ed** d ~**ing** ɪŋ ~**s** z
Harkness ˈhɑːk nəs -nɪs ‖ ˈhɑːrk-
Harlan ˈhɑːl ən ‖ ˈhɑːrl-
Harland ˈhɑːl ənd ‖ ˈhɑːrl-
Harlech ˈhɑːl ək -əx, -ek, -ex ‖ ˈhɑːrl- —Welsh
  [ˈhar lex]
Harlem ˈhɑːl əm ‖ ˈhɑːrl-
Harlemite ˈhɑːl ə maɪt ‖ ˈhɑːrl- ~**s** s
harlequin ˈhɑːl ə kwɪn -ɪ-, -kɪn ‖ ˈhɑːrl- ~**s** z
harlequinade ˌhɑːl ə kwɪ ˈneɪd ˌ-ɪ-, -kwə·,
  -kɪ· ‖ ˌhɑːrl- ~**s** z
Harlesden ˈhɑːlz dən ‖ ˈhɑːrlz-
Harley ˈhɑːl i ‖ ˈhɑːrl i
  ˈHarley Street
Harley-Davidson ˌhɑːl i ˈdeɪv ɪd sən -əd·
  ‖ ˌhɑːrl-
harlot ˈhɑːl ət ‖ ˈhɑːrl- ~**s** s
harlot|ry ˈhɑːl ət |ri ‖ ˈhɑːrl- ~**ries** riz
Harlow, Harlowe ˈhɑːl əʊ ‖ ˈhɑːrl oʊ
harm hɑːm ‖ hɑːrm **harmed** hɑːmd ‖ hɑːrmd
  harming ˈhɑːm ɪŋ ‖ ˈhɑːrm ɪŋ **harms** hɑːmz
  ‖ hɑːrmz
Harman ˈhɑːm ən ‖ ˈhɑːrm-

harmattan hɑː ˈmæt ᵊn ‖ hɑːr- ˌhɑːrm ə ˈtɑːn
~s z

Harmer ˈhɑːm ə ‖ ˈhɑːrm ᵊr

harmful ˈhɑːm fᵊl -fʊl ‖ ˈhɑːrm- **~ly** ˌi **~ness**
nəs nɪs

harmless ˈhɑːm ləs -lɪs ‖ ˈhɑːrm- **~ly** li **~ness**
nəs nɪs

Harmon ˈhɑːm ən ‖ ˈhɑːrm ən

Harmondsworth ˈhɑːm əndz wɜːθ
‖ ˈhɑːrm əndz wᵊrθ

harmonic hɑː ˈmɒn ɪk ‖ hɑːr ˈmɑːn ɪk **~ally**
ᵊl ˌi **~s** s

harmonica hɑː ˈmɒn ɪk ə ‖ hɑːr ˈmɑːn- **~s** z

harmonie... —*see* **harmony**

harmonious hɑː ˈməʊn i_əs ‖ hɑːr ˈmoʊn- **~ly**
li **~ness** nəs nɪs

harmonis... —*see* **harmoniz...**

harmonist ˈhɑːm ən ɪst §-əst ‖ ˈhɑːrm- **~s** s

harmonium hɑː ˈməʊn i_əm ‖ hɑːr ˈmoʊn- **~s**
z

harmonization ˌhɑːm ən aɪ ˈzeɪʃ ᵊn -ən ɪ-
‖ ˌhɑːrm ən ə- **~s** z

harmoniz|e ˈhɑːm ə naɪz ‖ ˈhɑːrm- **~ed** d **~es**
ɪz əz **~ing** ɪŋ

harmon|y ˈhɑːm ən |i ‖ ˈhɑːrm- **~ies** iz

Harmsworth ˈhɑːmz wɜːθ -wəθ
‖ ˈhɑːrmz wᵊrθ

harness ˈhɑːn ɪs -əs ‖ ˈhɑːrn- **~ed** t **~es** ɪz əz
~ing ɪŋ

Harold ˈhær əld ‖ ˈher-

harp hɑːp ‖ hɑːrp **harped** hɑːpt ‖ hɑːrpt
harping ˈhɑːp ɪŋ ‖ ˈhɑːrp ɪŋ **harps** hɑːps
‖ hɑːrps

Harpenden ˈhɑːp ənd ən →-md-

Harper, h~ ˈhɑːp ə ‖ ˈhɑːrp ᵊr **~s** z
ˌHarpers ˈFerry

Harpic *tdmk* ˈhɑːp ɪk ‖ ˈhɑːrp-

harpie... —*see* **harpy**

harpist ˈhɑːp ɪst §-əst ‖ ˈhɑːrp- **~s** s

harpoon ₍ₗ₎hɑː ˈpuːn ◂ ‖ ₍ₗ₎hɑːr- **~ed** d **~ing** ɪŋ
~s z

harpsichord ˈhɑːps ɪ kɔːd -ə- ‖ ˈhɑːrps ɪ kɔːrd
~s z

harp|y ˈhɑːp |i ‖ ˈhɑːrp |i **~ies** iz

harquebus ˈhɑːk wɪb əs -wəb- ‖ ˈhɑːrk- **~es** ɪz
əz

Harrap ˈhær əp ‖ ˈher-

harridan ˈhær ɪd ən -əd- ‖ ˈher- **~s** z

harrie... —*see* **harry**

harrier ˈhær i_ə ‖ ᵊr ˈher- **~s** z

Harries ˈhær ɪs -iz ‖ ˈher-

Harriet ˈhær i_ət ‖ ˈher-

Harrietsham ˈhær i_ət ʃəm ‖ ˈher-

Harriman ˈhær ɪ mən -ə- ‖ ˈher-

Harrington ˈhær ɪŋ tən ‖ ˈher-

Harriot, Harriott ˈhær i_ət ‖ ˈher-

Harris ˈhær ɪs §-əs ‖ ˈher-
ˌHarris ˈTweed

Harrisburg ˈhær ɪs bɜːg -əs- ‖ -bɜːg ˈher-

Harrison ˈhær ɪs ən -əs- ‖ ˈher-

Harrod ˈhær əd ‖ ˈher- **~s, ~ʼs** z

Harrogate ˈhær əg ət -əʊg-, -ɪt; -əʊ geɪt
‖ -oʊ geɪt ˈher-

Harrold ˈhær əld ‖ ˈher-

Harrovian hə ˈrəʊv i_ən hæ- ‖ -ˈroʊv- **~s** z

harrow, H~ ˈhær əʊ ‖ -oʊ ˈher- **~ed** d **~ing/ly**
ɪŋ /li **~s** z

harrumph hə ˈrʌmpf **~ed** t **~ing** ɪŋ **~s** s

harr|y ˈhær |i ‖ ˈher- **~ied** id **~ies** iz **~ying** i_ɪŋ

Harry ˈhær i ‖ ˈher- **~ʼs** z

harsh hɑːʃ ‖ hɑːrʃ **harsher** ˈhɑːʃ ə ‖ ˈhɑːrʃ ᵊr
harshest ˈhɑːʃ ɪst -əst ‖ ˈhɑːrʃ- **harshly**
ˈhɑːʃ li ‖ ˈhɑːrʃ- **harshness** ˈhɑːʃ nəs -nɪs
‖ ˈhɑːrʃ-

hart, Hart hɑːt ‖ hɑːrt **harts** hɑːts ‖ hɑːrts

hartal hɑː ˈtɑːl hɜː-; ˈhɑːt ɑːl ‖ hɑːr- **~s** z

Harte hɑːt ‖ hɑːrt

hartebeest ˈhɑːt i biːst -ə-, -bɪəst ‖ ˈhɑːrṭ ə-
ˈhɑːrt biːst **~s** s

Hartfield ˈhɑːt fiːᵊld ‖ ˈhɑːrt-

Hartford ˈhɑːt fəd ‖ ˈhɑːrt fᵊrd

Hartland ˈhɑːt lənd ‖ ˈhɑːrt-

Hartlepool ˈhɑːt li puːl -lə- ‖ ˈhɑːrt-

Hartley ˈhɑːt li ‖ ˈhɑːrt-

Hartnell ˈhɑːt nəl ‖ ˈhɑːrt-

Hartree, h~ ˈhɑː triː ‖ ˈhɑːr- **~s** z

hartshorn, H~, Hartshorne ˈhɑːts hɔːn
‖ ˈhɑːrts hɔːrn

hartʼs-tongue ˈhɑːts tʌŋ §-tɒŋ ‖ ˈhɑːrts- **~s** z

harum-scarum ˌheər əm ˈskeər əm
‖ ˌher əm ˈsker əm ˌhær əm ˈskær əm

Harun al-Rashid hæ ˌruːn æl ræ ˈʃiːd hɑː-
‖ hɑː ˌruː n ɑːl rɑː ˈʃiːd

haruspex hə ˈrʌsp eks hæ-; ˈhær ə speks

Harvard ˈhɑːv əd ‖ ˈhɑːrv ᵊrd

harvest ˈhɑːv ɪst -əst ‖ ˈhɑːrv- **~ed** ɪd əd **~er/s**
ə/z ‖ ᵊr/z **~ing** ɪŋ **~s** s
ˌharvest ˈfestival; ˌharvest ˈhome;
ˈharvest mite; ˌharvest ˈmoon; ˈharvest
mouse

harvest|man ˈhɑːv ɪst |mən -əst-, -mæn
‖ ˈhɑːrv- **~men** mən men

Harvey, Harvie ˈhɑːv i ‖ ˈhɑːrv i

Harwell ˈhɑː wəl -wel ‖ ˈhɑːr-

Harwich ˈhær ɪdʒ -ɪtʃ ‖ ˈher-

Harwood ˈhɑː wʊd ‖ ˈhɑːr-

Haryana ˌhær i ˈɑːn ə ˌhʌr- ‖ ˌhɑːr- —*Hindi*
[hər ˈjɑː ɳə]

Harz hɑːts ‖ hɑːrts —*Ger* [haːʁts]

has *strong form* **hæz**, *weak forms* həz, əz, z, s
—*Of the weak forms,* əz *is not used
clause-initially, and* s, z *are used in that
position only in very fast speech; in other
environments* həz, əz *are more formal than the
contracted forms* s, z. *The most usual weak
forms are* əz *after a word ending in* s, z, ʃ, ʒ,
tʃ, dʒ; s *after one ending in* p, t, k, f, θ; *and*
z *otherwise. The latter two are sometimes
shown in writing as the contraction* ʼs. *See
note at* have *concerning the choice between
strong and weak form.*

has-been ˈhæz biːn -bɪn ‖ -bɪn **~s** z

Hasdrubal ˈhæz drʊb ᵊl -druːb-; -dru bæl

Haseldine ˈheɪz ᵊl daɪn

hash hæʃ **hashed** hæʃt **hashes** 'hæʃ ɪz -əz
　hashing 'hæʃ ɪŋ
　ˌhash 'browns; 'hash mark
Hashemite 'hæʃ ɪ maɪt -ə- **~s** s
Hashimoto ˌhæʃ i 'məʊt əʊ ‖ -'moʊt̬ oʊ
hashish 'hæʃ ɪʃ -iːʃ; hæ 'ʃiːʃ
Hasid 'hæs ɪd 'xɑːs-, -əd **Hasidim** 'hæs ɪd ɪm
　'xɑːs-, -əd-; hæ'sɪd-
Hasidic hæ 'sɪd ɪk hɑː-
Hasidism 'hæs ɪd ˌɪz əm hæ 'sɪd-
Haslam 'hæz ləm
Haslemere 'heɪz ᵊl mɪə ‖ -mɪr
haslet 'heɪz lət 'hæz-, -lɪt
Haslett (i) 'heɪz lət -lɪt, (ii) 'hæz-
Haslingden 'hæz lɪŋ dən
Hasmonaean, Hasmonean ˌhæs mə 'niː ən
hasn't 'hæz ᵊnt
hasp hɑːsp hæsp ‖ hæsp **hasped** hɑːspt hæspt
　‖ hæspt **hasping** 'hɑːsp ɪŋ 'hæsp- ‖ 'hæsp ɪŋ
　hasps hɑːsps hæsps ‖ hæsps
Hassan hə 'sɑːn hæ-; 'hæs ᵊn ‖ 'hɑːs ɑːn
Hasselblad tdmk 'hæs ᵊl blæd ‖ 'hɑːs ᵊl blɑːd
Hasselhoff 'hæs ᵊl hɒf ‖ -hɔːf -hɑːf
hassium ˌhæs i əm
hassl|e 'hæs ᵊl **~ed** d **~es** z **~ing** ˌɪŋ
hassock 'hæs ək **~s** s
hast strong form hæst, weak forms həst, əst, st
hasta la vista ˌæst ə lə 'vɪst ə -'læ'--, -lɑː'--
　‖ ˌɑːst ə lə 'viːst ə —Sp [ˌas ta la 'βis ta]
hasta mañana ˌæst ə mə 'njɑːn ə -mæ'--
　‖ ˌɑːst ə mɑː- —Sp [ˌas ta ma 'ɲa na]
haste heɪst
hasten 'heɪs ᵊn **~ed** d **~ing** ˌɪŋ **~s** z
hasti... —see **hasty**
Hastings 'heɪst ɪŋz
hast|y 'heɪst |i **-ier** i ə ‖ i ᵊr **-iest** i ɪst i ̩əst
　-ily ɪ li əl i **-iness** i nəs i nɪs
hat hæt **hats** hæts **hatted** 'hæt ɪd -əd
　‖ 'hæt̬ əd **hatting** 'hæt ɪŋ ‖ 'hæt̬ ɪŋ
　'hat trick
hatband 'hæt bænd **~s** z
hatbox 'hæt bɒks ‖ -bɑːks
hatch, Hatch hætʃ **hatched** hætʃt **hatches**
　'hætʃ ɪz -əz **hatching** 'hætʃ ɪŋ
hatchback 'hætʃ bæk **~s** s
hatcheck ˌhæt tʃek
Hatcher 'hætʃ ə ‖ -ᵊr
hatcher|y 'hætʃ ər |i **-ies** iz
hatchet 'hætʃ ɪt §-ət **~s** s
　'hatchet job; 'hatchet man
hatchet-faced ˌhætʃ ɪt 'feɪst ◂ §-ət-, '···
hatchling 'hætʃ lɪŋ **~s** z
hatchment 'hætʃ mənt **~s** s
hatchway 'hætʃ weɪ **~s** z
hate heɪt **hated** 'heɪt ɪd -əd ‖ 'heɪt̬ əd **hates**
　heɪts **hating** 'heɪt ɪŋ ‖ 'heɪt̬ ɪŋ
hateful 'heɪt fᵊl -fʊl **-ly** i **-ness** nəs nɪs
hatemonger 'heɪt ˌmʌŋ gə ‖ -gᵊr -ˌmɑːŋ- **~s** z
hater 'heɪt ə ‖ 'heɪt̬ ᵊr **~s** z
Hatfield 'hæt fiːᵊld
hath strong form hæθ, weak forms həθ, əθ
hatha 'hæθ ə 'hʌt- —Hindi [hə t̪ʰə]
Hathaway 'hæθ ə weɪ

Hatherleigh 'hæð ə li -liː ‖ -ᵊr-
Hatherley 'hæð ə li ‖ -ᵊr-
Hathern 'hæð ᵊn ‖ -ᵊrn
Hathersage 'hæð ə seɪdʒ -sɪdʒ, -sedʒ ‖ -ᵊr-
Hathor 'hæθ ɔː ‖ -ɔːr
hatpin 'hæt pɪn **~s** z
hatred 'heɪtr ɪd -əd **~s** z
Hatshepsut hæt 'ʃep suːt
hatter 'hæt ə ‖ 'hæt̬ ᵊr **~s** z
Hatteras 'hæt ər əs ‖ 'hæt̬-
Hattersley 'hæt əz li ‖ 'hæt̬ ᵊrz-
Hattie 'hæt i ‖ 'hæt̬ i
Hatton 'hæt ᵊn
Hatty 'hæt i ‖ 'hæt̬ i
hauberk 'hɔː bɜːk ‖ -bɜːk 'hɑː- **~s** s
Haugh (i) hɔː ‖ hɑː, (ii) hɒf ‖ hɑːf, (iii) hɑːx
　‖ hɑːk
Haughey 'hɔː hi 'hɒ- ‖ 'hɔːk i 'hɑːk-
haughti... —see **haughty**
Haughton 'hɔːt ᵊn ‖ 'hɑːt-
haught|y 'hɔːt |i ‖ 'hɔːt̬ |i 'hɑːt̬- **-ier** i ə ‖ i ᵊr
　-iest i ɪst i ̩əst **-ily** ɪ li əl i **-iness** i nəs i nɪs
haul hɔːl ‖ hɑːl **hauled** hɔːld ‖ hɑːld **hauling**
　'hɔːl ɪŋ ‖ 'hɑːl- **hauls** hɔːlz ‖ hɑːlz
haulage 'hɔːl ɪdʒ ‖ 'hɑːl-
　'haulage conˌtractor
hauler 'hɔːl ə ‖ -ᵊr 'hɑːl- **~s** z
haulier 'hɔːl i ə ‖ -ᵊr 'hɑːl- **~s** z
haulm hɔːm ‖ hɑːm **haulms** hɔːmz ‖ hɑːmz
haunch hɔːntʃ ‖ hɑːntʃ **haunches** 'hɔːntʃ ɪz -əz
　‖ 'hɑːntʃ-
haunt hɔːnt ‖ hɑːnt **haunted** 'hɔːnt ɪd -əd
　‖ 'hɔːnt̬ əd 'hɑːnt̬- **haunting/ly** 'hɔːnt ɪŋ /li
　‖ 'hɔːnt̬ ɪŋ /li 'hɑːnt̬- **haunts** hɔːnts ‖ hɑːnts
Hausa 'haʊs ə 'haʊz ə
hausfrau, H~ 'haʊs fraʊ —Ger ['haʊs fʁaʊ]
　-en ən **~s** z
haut|bois sing. 'əʊ |bɔɪ 'həʊ-, 'hɔːt- ‖ 'hoʊ-
　'oʊ- **-bois** pl bɔɪz **-boy** bɔɪ **-boys** bɔɪz
haute əʊt ‖ oʊt —Fr [oːt]
　ˌhaute cou'ture; ˌhaute cui'sine
hauteur əʊ 'tɜː '·· ‖ hoʊ 'tɜː hɔː-, hɑː- —Fr
　[o tœːʁ]
Havana hə 'væn ə -'vɑːn ə —Sp Habana
　[a 'βa na]
Havant 'hæv ᵊnt
Havasupai ˌhɑːv ə 'suːp aɪ ◂
have strong form hæv, weak forms həv, əv, v
　—The weak form v is used only after a vowel
　(when it is often written as the contraction
　've), or in very fast speech at the beginning of
　a sentence; əv is not used at the beginning of
　a sentence. Weak forms of have, has, had are
　used only when the word functions as the
　perfective auxiliary, or is the equivalent of
　have got and is used with an object that is not
　a pronoun, or in the constructions had
　better/best/rather. **had** hæd (see) **hadn't**
　'hæd ᵊnt **has** hæz (see) **hasn't** 'hæz ᵊnt
　haven't 'hæv ᵊnt **haves** hævz **having**
　'hæv ɪŋ
Havel 'hɑːv ᵊl —Czech ['ha vel]
Havelock, h~ 'hæv lɒk ‖ -lɑːk

H

haven 'heɪv ᵊn ~s z
have-not 'hæv nɒt ˌ·'· ‖ -nɑːt —*contrastively always* ˌ·'· ~s s
haven't 'hæv ᵊnt
haver 'heɪv ə ‖ -ᵊr ~ed d **havering** 'heɪv ər_ɪŋ ~s z
Haverfordwest ˌhæv ə fəd 'west ˌhɑː fəd 'west ‖ ˌhæv ᵊr fᵊrd-
Havergal 'hæv əg ᵊl ‖ -ᵊrg-
Haverhill 'heɪv ər_ɪl ᵊr_əl, 'heɪv ə hɪl ‖ -ᵊr-
Havering 'heɪv ər_ɪŋ
Havers 'heɪv əz ‖ -ᵊrz
haversack 'hæv ə sæk ‖ -ᵊr- ~s s
Haversian, h~ hə 'vɜːʃ ᵊn hæ-, -'vɜːʒ- ‖ -'vɜːʒ ᵊn
haversine 'hæv ə saɪn ‖ -ᵊr- ~s z
Haverstock 'hæv ə stɒk ‖ -ᵊr stɑːk
haves hævz
Haviland 'hæv ɪ lənd -ə-
Havisham 'hæv ɪʃ əm -əʃ-
havoc 'hæv ək
Havre *place in MT* 'hæv ə ‖ -ᵊr
Havre *place in France* 'ɑːv rə —*Fr* Le Havre [lə ɑːvʁ]
Havre de Grace *place in MD* ˌhæv ə də 'græs -'greɪs ‖ ˌ·ᵊr-
haw, Haw hɔː ‖ hɑː **hawed** hɔːd ‖ hɑːd **hawing** 'hɔːʳ ɪŋ ‖ 'hɔː ɪŋ 'hɑː- **haws** hɔːz ‖ hɑːz
Hawaii, Hawai'i hə 'waɪ i hɑː-, -iː ‖ -'wɑː- —*Hawaiian* [ha waɪ ʔi]
Hawaiian, Hawai'ian hə 'waɪ ən -'waɪ i ən ‖ -'wɑː jən ~s z
Hawarden (i) 'hɑːd ᵊn ‖ 'hɑːrd ᵊn; (ii) 'heɪ ˌwɔːd ᵊn ‖ -ˌwɔːrd- —*The place in Clwyd is* (i); *Viscount H~ and the place in Iowa are* (ii)
Hawes hɔːz ‖ hɑːz
hawfinch 'hɔː fɪntʃ ‖ 'hɑː- ~es ɪz əz
haw-haw, H~ 'hɔː hɔː ‖ 'hɑː hɑː
Hawick 'hɔː ɪk hɔɪk ‖ 'hɑː-
hawk hɔːk ‖ hɑːk **hawked** hɔːkt ‖ hɑːkt **hawking** 'hɔːk ɪŋ ‖ 'hɑːk- **hawks** hɔːks ‖ hɑːks
'hawk moth
hawkbit 'hɔːk bɪt ‖ 'hɑːk- ~s s
Hawke hɔːk ‖ hɑːk
hawker 'hɔːk ə ‖ -ᵊr 'hɑːk- ~s s
Hawker-Siddeley *tdmk* ˌhɔːk ə 'sɪd ᵊl i ‖ -ᵊr- ˌhɑːk-
Hawkes hɔːks ‖ hɑːks
hawk-eye 'hɔːk aɪ ‖ 'hɑːk- ~d d
Hawking 'hɔːk ɪŋ ‖ 'hɑːk-
Hawkinge 'hɔːk ɪndʒ ‖ 'hɑːk-
Hawkins 'hɔːk ɪnz ‖ 'hɑːk-
hawkish 'hɔːk ɪʃ ‖ 'hɑːk- ~ness nəs nɪs
hawk-nosed ˌhɔːk 'nəʊzd ◂ ‖ -noʊzd ◂ 'hɑːk-
Hawks hɔːks ‖ hɑːks
hawk's-beard 'hɔːks bɪəd ‖ -bɪrd 'hɑːks- ~s z
hawksbill 'hɔːks bɪl ‖ 'hɑːks- ~s z
Hawksmoor 'hɔːks mʊə -mɔː ‖ -mʊr 'hɑːks-
hawkweed 'hɔːk wiːd ‖ 'hɑːk- ~s z
Hawley 'hɔːl i ‖ 'hɑːl i

Hawn hɔːn ‖ hɑːn
Haworth 'haʊ_əθ 'hɔː- ‖ 'hɔː wᵊrθ 'hɑː-
hawse, Hawse hɔːz ‖ hɑːz **hawses** 'hɔːz ɪz -əz ‖ 'hɑːz-
hawser 'hɔːz ə ‖ -ᵊr 'hɑːz- ~s z
hawthorn, H~, Hawthorne 'hɔː θɔːn ‖ -θɔːrn 'hɑː- ~s z
Hawthornden 'hɔː θɔːn dən ‖ -θɔːrn- 'hɑː-
Hawthorne 'hɔː θɔːn ‖ -θɔːrn 'hɑː-
Hawtrey 'hɔːtr i ‖ 'hɑːtr i
Haxey 'hæks i
hay, Hay heɪ **hayed** heɪd **haying** 'heɪ ɪŋ **hays** heɪz
'hay ˌfever, ˌ·'·
Hayakawa ˌhaɪ ə 'kɑː wə ‖ ˌhɑː jə-
haycock, H~ 'heɪ kɒk ‖ -kɑːk ~s s
Hayden 'heɪd ᵊn
Haydn *Austrian composer* 'haɪd ᵊn —*Ger* ['haɪ dᵊn] ~'s z
Haydn *English or Welsh name* 'heɪd ᵊn
Haydock 'heɪ dɒk ‖ -dɑːk
Haydon 'heɪd ᵊn
Hayek 'haɪ ek 'hɑː jek
Hayes heɪz
hayfork 'heɪ fɔːk ‖ -fɔːrk ~s s
Hayle heɪᵊl
Hayley 'heɪl i
Hayling 'heɪl ɪŋ
hayloft 'heɪ lɒft -lɔːft ‖ -lɔːft -lɑːft ~s s
haymak|er 'heɪ ˌmeɪk |ə ‖ -|ᵊr ~ers əz ‖ ᵊrz ~ing ɪŋ
Hayman 'heɪ mən
Haymarket 'heɪ ˌmɑːk ɪt §-ət ‖ -ˌmɑːrk-
Haynes heɪnz
hayrick 'heɪ rɪk ~s s
hayride 'heɪ raɪd ~s z
Hays heɪz
hayseed 'heɪ siːd ~s z
haystack 'heɪ stæk ~s s
Hayter 'heɪt ə ‖ 'heɪt ᵊr
haywain 'heɪ weɪn ~s z
Hayward 'heɪ wəd ‖ -wᵊrd
haywire 'heɪ ˌwaɪ_ə ‖ -ˌwaɪ_ᵊr
Haywood 'heɪ wʊd
Hayworth 'heɪ wəθ -wɜːθ ‖ -wᵊrθ
Hazan hə 'zæn
hazard 'hæz əd ‖ -ᵊrd ~ed ɪd əd ~ing ɪŋ ~s z
hazardous 'hæz əd əs ‖ -ᵊrd- ~ly li ~ness nəs nɪs
Hazchem 'hæz kem
haze heɪz **hazed** heɪzd **hazes** 'heɪz ɪz -əz **hazing** 'heɪz ɪŋ
hazel, Hazel, Hazell 'heɪz ᵊl ~s z
hazelnut 'heɪz ᵊl nʌt ~s s
hazi... —*see* hazy
Hazlerigg 'heɪz ᵊl rɪg
Hazlett, Hazlitt 'hæz lɪt 'heɪz-, -lət
hazmat, HazMat 'hæz mæt
haz|y 'heɪz |i ~ier i‿ə ‖ i‿ᵊr ~iest i‿ɪst i‿əst ~ily ɪ li əl i ~iness i nəs i nɪs
Hazzard 'hæz əd ‖ -ᵊrd
H-block 'eɪtʃ blɒk §'heɪtʃ- ‖ -blɑːk ~s s
H-bomb 'eɪtʃ bɒm §'heɪtʃ- ‖ -bɑːm ~s z

HBOS 'eɪtʃ bɒs §'heɪtʃ- ‖ -bɔːs -baːs
he *n* hiː
he *pronoun*strong form hiː, *weak forms* hi, i
—*The form i is not used at the beginning of a sentence or clause.*
he- 'hiː — **he-goat** 'hiː gəʊt ‖ -goʊt
Heacham 'hetʃ əm 'hiːtʃ-
head, Head hed **headed** 'hed ɪd -əd **heading** 'hed ɪŋ **heads** hedz
,head 'start; ,head 'waiter
headache 'hed eɪk ~s s
headachy 'hed eɪk i
headband 'hed bænd →'heb- ~s z
headbang|er 'hed ˌbæŋ| ə →'heb- ‖ -ᵊr ~ers əz ‖ ᵊrz ~ing ɪŋ
headboard hed bɔːd →'heb- ‖ -bɔːrd -boʊrd ~s z
head|butt 'hed| bʌt →'heb- ~butted bʌt ɪd -əd ‖ bʌt̬- ~butting bʌt ɪŋ ‖ bʌt̬- ~butts bʌts
headcas|e 'hed keɪs →'heg- ~es ɪz əz
headcheese 'hed tʃiːz
headdress 'hed dres ~es ɪz əz
-headed 'hed ɪd -əd — **bullet-headed** ˌbʊl ɪt 'hed ɪd ◂ -ət-, -əd
header 'hed ə ‖ -ᵊr ~s z
headfirst ˌhed 'fɜːst ◂ ‖ -'fɜːst ◂
headgear 'hed ɡɪə →'heg- ‖ -ɡɪr
head|hunt 'hed |hʌnt ~hunted hʌnt ɪd -əd ‖ hʌnt̬ əd ~hunting hʌnt ɪŋ ‖ hʌnt̬ ɪŋ ~hunts hʌnts
headhunter 'hed ˌhʌnt ə ‖ -ˌhʌnt̬ ᵊr
headi... —*see* **heady**
heading 'hed ɪŋ ~s z
Headingley 'hed ɪŋ li
Headlam 'hed ləm
headlamp 'hed læmp ~s s
headland 'hed lənd -lænd ~s z
headless 'hed ləs -lɪs
Headley 'hed li
headlight 'hed laɪt ~s s
headlin|e 'hed laɪn ~ed d ~er/s ə/z ‖ ᵊr/z ~es z ~ing ɪŋ
headline-grabbing 'hed laɪn ˌɡræb ɪŋ
headlock 'hed lɒk ‖ -laːk
headlong 'hed lɒŋ ˌ·'· ‖ -lɔːŋ -laːŋ
head|man 'hed |mən →'heb-, -mæn ~men mən men
headmaster ˌhed 'maːst ə ◂ →,heb-, §-'mæst-, '·ˌ·· ‖ -'mæst ᵊr ◂ ~s z
headmistress ˌhed 'mɪs trəs ◂ →,heb-, -trɪs, '·ˌ·· ~es ɪz əz
head-on ˌhed 'ɒn ◂ ‖ -'aːn ◂ -'ɔːn ◂
headphone 'hed fəʊn ‖ -foʊn ~s z
headpiec|e 'hed piːs →'heb- ~es ɪz əz
headquarter ˌhed 'kwɔːt ə ◂ →,heg-, '·ˌ·· ‖ -ˌkwɔːrt̬ ᵊr -ˌkwɔːt̬- ~ed d ~s z
headrest 'hed rest ~s s
headroom 'hed ruːm -rʊm
headrush 'hed rʌʃ
head|scarf 'hed |skaːf ‖ -|skaːrf ~scarves skaːvz ‖ skaːrvz
headset 'hed set ~s s
headship 'hed ʃɪp ~s s

headshrinker 'hed ˌʃrɪŋk ə ‖ -ᵊr ~s z
headstall 'hed stɔːl ‖ -staːl ~s z
headstand 'hed stænd ~s z
headstone, H~ 'hed stəʊn ‖ -stoʊn ~s z
headstrong 'hed strɒŋ ‖ -strɔːŋ -straːŋ
heads-up 'hedz ʌp ˌ·'·
head-to-head ˌhed tə 'hed ◂
head-up *adj, adv* ˌhed 'ʌp ◂
headwaters 'hed ˌwɔːt əz ‖ -ˌwɔːt̬ ᵊrz -ˌwaːt̬-
headway 'hed weɪ
headwind 'hed wɪnd ~s z
headword 'hed wɜːd ‖ -wɜːd ~s z
head|y 'hed |i ~ier i ə ‖ i ᵊr ~iest i ɪst i əst ~ily ɪ li əl i ~iness i nəs i nɪs
heal, Heal hiːᵊld **healing** 'hiːᵊl ɪŋ **heals, Heal's** hiːᵊlz
Healaugh 'hiːl ə
Healdsburg 'hiːᵊldz bɜːɡ ‖ -bɜːɡ
healer 'hiːᵊl ə ‖ -ᵊr ~s z
Healey 'hiːl i
health helθ
'health ˌcare; 'health ˌcentre; 'health ˌfarm; 'health ˌfood; ˌhealth 'maintenance ˌorganiˌzation; 'health ˌvisitor
healthful 'helθ fᵊl -fʊl ~ly i ~ness nəs nɪs
health|y 'helθ |i ~ier i ə ‖ i ᵊr ~iest i ɪst i əst ~ily ɪ li əl i ~iness i nəs i nɪs
Healy 'hiːl i
Heaney 'hiːn i
Heanor 'hiːn ə 'hem ə ‖ -ᵊr
heap hiːp **heaped** hiːpt **heaping** 'hiːp ɪŋ **heaps** hiːps
hear hɪə ‖ hɪᵊr (= *here*) **heard** hɜːd ‖ hɜːd (!) **hearing** 'hɪər ɪŋ ‖ 'hɪr ɪŋ **hears** hɪəz ‖ hɪᵊrz
heard, Heard hɜːd ‖ hɜːd (= *herd*)
hearer 'hɪər ə ‖ 'hɪr ᵊr ~s z
hearing 'hɪər ɪŋ ‖ 'hɪr ɪŋ ~s z
'hearing aid
hearing-impaired ˌhɪər ɪŋ ɪm 'peəd ◂ '···ˌ· ‖ ˌhɪr ɪŋ ɪm 'peᵊrd ◂ -'pæᵊrd ◂
hearken 'haːk ən ‖ 'haːrk ən ~ed d ~ing ɪŋ ~s z
Hearn, Hearne hɜːn ‖ hɜːn
hearsay 'hɪə seɪ ˌ·'· ‖ 'hɪr-
hearse hɜːs ‖ hɜːs **hearses** 'hɜːs ɪz -əz ‖ 'hɜːs əz
Hearst hɜːst ‖ hɜːst
heart haːt ‖ haːrt (= *hart*) **hearted** 'haːt ɪd -əd ‖ 'haːrt̬ əd **hearting** 'haːt ɪŋ ‖ 'haːrt̬ ɪŋ **hearts** haːts ‖ haːrts
'heart atˌtack; 'heart diˌsease; 'heart ˌfailure
heartache 'haːt eɪk ‖ 'haːrt̬- ~s s
heartbeat 'haːt biːt ‖ 'haːrt̬- ~s s
heartbreak 'haːt breɪk ‖ 'haːrt̬- ~s s
heartbreaking 'haːt ˌbreɪk ɪŋ ‖ 'haːrt̬- ~ly li
heartbroken 'haːt ˌbrəʊk ən ‖ 'haːrt̬ ˌbroʊk ən ~ly li ~ness nəs nɪs
heartburn 'haːt bɜːn ‖ 'haːrt̬ bɜːn
-hearted 'haːt ɪd ◂ -əd ‖ 'haːrt̬ əd — **tender-hearted** ˌtend ə 'haːt ɪd ◂ -əd ‖ -ᵊr 'haːrt̬ əd ◂

H

hearten 'haːt ᵊn ‖ 'haːrt ᵊn **~ed** d **~ing/ly**
ɪŋ /li **~s** z
heartfelt 'haːt felt ‖ 'haːrt-
hearth haːθ ‖ haːrθ **hearths** haːθs haːðz
‖ haːrθs
hearthrug 'haːθ rʌg ‖ 'haːrθ- **~s** z
hearti... —*see* **hearty**
heartland 'haːt lænd ‖ 'haːrt- **~s** z
heartless 'haːt ləs **~ly** li **~ness** nəs nɪs
heart-lung ˌhaːt 'lʌŋ ‖ ˌhaːrt-
ˌheart-'lung maˌchine
heartrending 'haːt ˌrend ɪŋ ‖ 'haːrt- **~ly** li
heart-searching 'haːt ˌsɜːtʃ ɪŋ
‖ 'haːrt ˌsɜːtʃ ɪŋ **~s** z
heartsease 'haːts iːz ‖ 'haːrts-
heart-shaped 'haːt ʃeɪpt ‖ 'haːrt-
heartsick 'haːt sɪk ‖ 'haːrt- **~ness** nəs nɪs
heart-stopping 'haːt ˌstɒp ɪŋ
‖ 'haːrt ˌstaːp ɪŋ
heartstrings 'haːt strɪŋz ‖ 'haːrt-
heartthrob 'haːt θrɒb ‖ 'haːrt θraːb **~s** z
heart-to-heart ˌhaːt tə 'haːt ◄ -tu-
‖ ˌhaːrt tə 'haːrt ◄
ˌheart-to-heart 'chat
heartwarming 'haːt ˌwɔːm ɪŋ
‖ 'haːrt ˌwɔːrm ɪŋ **~ly** li
heartwood 'haːt wʊd ‖ 'haːrt-
heartworm 'haːt wɜːm ‖ 'haːrt wɜːrm **~s** z
heart|y 'haːt |i ‖ 'haːrt̬ |i **~ier** i ə ‖ i ᵊr **~iest**
i ɪst i əst **~ily** ɪ li əl i **~iness** i nəs i nɪs
heat hiːt **heated/ly** 'hiːt ɪd /li -əd /li
‖ 'hiːt̬ əd /li **heating** 'hiːt ɪŋ ‖ 'hiːt̬ ɪŋ **heats**
hiːts
'heat exˌchanger; 'heat exˌhaustion;
'heat pump; 'heat rash; 'heat shield;
'heat wave
heater 'hiːt ə ‖ 'hiːt̬ ᵊr **~s** z
heath, Heath hiːθ **heaths** hiːθs
ˌHeath 'Robinson
Heathcliff, Heathcliffe 'hiːθ klɪf
Heathcoat, Heathcote (i) 'heθ kət, (ii) 'hiːθ-
heathen 'hiːð ᵊn **~dom** dəm **~ish** ɪʃ **~ism**
ˌɪz əm
heather, H~ 'heð ə ‖ -ᵊr —*but the place in*
Leics is 'hiːð- **~s** z
heather-mixture 'heð ə ˌmɪks tʃə ˌ·'··
‖ -ᵊr ˌmɪks tʃᵊr
heathery 'heð ər i
Heathfield 'hiːθ fiːᵊld
Heathrow ˌhiːθ 'rəʊ ◄ '·· ‖ 'hiːθ roʊ
ˌHeathrow 'Airport
Heaton 'hiːt ᵊn
heatproof 'hiːt pruːf §-prʊf
heat-resistant 'hiːt ri ˌzɪst ənt -rə-
heat-seeking 'hiːt ˌsiːk ɪŋ
heatstroke 'hiːt strəʊk ‖ -stroʊk
heave hiːv **heaved** hiːvd **heaves** hiːvz
heaving 'hiːv ɪŋ **hove** həʊv ‖ hoʊv
heave-ho ˌhiːv 'həʊ ‖ -'hoʊ
heaven, H~ 'hev ᵊn **~s** z
heavenly 'hev ᵊn li
heaven-sent ˌhev ᵊn 'sent ◄ '··
heavenward 'hev ᵊn wəd ‖ -wᵊrd **~s** z

heavi... —*see* **heavy**
Heaviside 'hev i saɪd
heav|y 'hev |i **~ier** i ə ‖ i ᵊr **~iest** i ɪst i əst
~ily ɪ li əl i **~iness** i nəs i nɪs
ˌheavy 'hydrogen; ˌheavy 'industry;
ˌheavy 'metal; ˌheavy 'petting; ˌheavy
'water
heavy-duty ˌhev i 'djuːt i ◄ →-'dʒuːt i ◄
‖ -'duːt̬ i ◄ -'djuːt̬ i ◄
heavy-handed ˌhev i 'hænd ɪd ◄ -əd **~ly** li
~ness nəs nɪs
heavy-hearted ˌhev i 'haːt ɪd ◄ -əd
‖ -'haːrt̬ əd ◄
heavy-laden ˌhev i 'leɪd ᵊn ◄
heavy-set ˌhev i 'set ◄
heavyweight 'hev i weɪt **~s** s
Hebburn 'heb ɜːn -ən ‖ -ᵊrn
Hebden 'heb dən
hebdomadal heb 'dɒm əd ᵊl ‖ -'daːm- **~ly** i
Hebe 'hiːb i
Hebei ˌhɜː 'beɪ ‖ ˌhʌ- —*Chi* Héběi [²ɣɤ ³peɪ]
hebephrenia ˌhiːb ɪ 'friːn i ə ˌheb-, ˌ-ə-
Heber 'hiːb ə ‖ -ᵊr
Hebraic hɪ 'breɪ ɪk hə-, hiː-
Hebraist 'hiːb reɪ ɪst -rɪ-, §-əst **~s** s
Hebrew 'hiːb ruː **~s** z
Hebridean ˌheb rə 'diː ən ◄ -rɪ- **~s** z
Hebrides 'heb rə diːz -rɪ-
Hebron 'heb rɒn 'hiːb-, -rən ‖ -rən
Hecate 'hek ət i ‖ -ət̬ i —*in Shakespeare also*
'hek ət
hecatomb 'hek ə tuːm -təʊm ‖ -toʊm **~s** z
Hecht hekt
heck, Heck hek
heckelphone 'hek ᵊl fəʊn ‖ -foʊn **~s** z
heckl|e 'hek ᵊl **~ed** d **~er/s** ə/z ‖ ᵊr/z **~es** z
~ing ɪŋ
Heckmondwike 'hek mənd waɪk
heckuva 'hek əv ə
hectare 'hekt eə -ə, -aː ‖ -er -ær **~s** z
hectic 'hekt ɪk **~ally** ᵊl_i
hecto- ˌhekt ə -əʊ — **hectogram**
'hekt ə græm
hectograph 'hekt ə graːf -əʊ-, -græf ‖ -græf **~s**
s
hector, H~ 'hekt ə ‖ -ᵊr **~ed** d **hectoring**
'hekt ər ɪŋ **~s** z
Hecuba 'hek jʊb ə
he'd *strong form* hiːd, *weak forms* hid, id
—*The weak form* id *is not used at the*
beginning of a sentence or clause.
heddle, H~ 'hed ᵊl **~s** z
Hedex *tdmk* 'hed eks
hedge hedʒ **hedged** hedʒd **hedges** 'hedʒ ɪz
-əz **hedging** 'hedʒ ɪŋ
'hedge ˌsparrow
hedgehog 'hedʒ hɒg -ɒg ‖ -hɔːg -haːg **~s** z
hedgehop 'hedʒ hɒp ‖ -haːp **~ped** t **~per/s**
ə/z ‖ ᵊr/z **~ping** ɪŋ **~s** s
Hedgerley 'hedʒ ə li ‖ -ᵊr-
hedgerow 'hedʒ rəʊ ‖ -roʊ **~s** z
Hedges 'hedʒ ɪz -əz
Hedley 'hed li

hedonic hi: ˈdɒn ɪk hɪ- ‖ -ˈdɑːn ɪk **~s** s
hedonism ˈhiːd ᵊn ˌɪz əm ˈhed-
hedonist ˈhiːd ᵊn ɪst ˈhed-, §-əst **~s** s
hedonistic ˌhiːd ə ˈnɪst ɪk ◂ ˌhed-, -ᵊn ˈɪst-
  ~ally ᵊl i
Hedy ˈhed i
heebie-jeebies ˌhiːb i ˈdʒiːb iz
heed hiːd **heeded** ˈhiːd ɪd -əd **heeding**
  ˈhiːd ɪŋ **heeds** hiːdz
heedful ˈhiːd fᵊl -fʊl **~ly** li **~ness** nəs nɪs
heedless ˈhiːd ləs -lɪs **~ly** li **~ness** nəs nɪs
hee-haw ˈhiː hɔː ˌˈ ‖ -hɑː **~s** z
heel hiː ᵊl **heeled** hiː ᵊld **heeling** ˈhiː ᵊl ɪŋ **heels**
  hiː ᵊlz
heelball ˈhiː ᵊl bɔːl ‖ -bɑːl **~s** z
heelbar ˈhiː ᵊl bɑː ‖ -bɑːr **~s** z
heelflip ˈhiːl flɪp **~s** s
Heenan ˈhiːn ən
Heep hiːp
HEFCE ˈhef si -ki, -kə
Heffer ˈhef ə ‖ -ᵊr
Hefner ˈhef nə ‖ -nᵊr
heft heft **hefted** ˈheft ɪd -əd **hefting** ˈheft ɪŋ
  hefts hefts
heft|y ˈheft |i **~ier** i ə ‖ i ᵊr **~iest** i ɪst i əst
  ~ily ɪ li əl i **~iness** i nəs i nɪs
Hegarty ˈheg ət i ‖ -ᵊrt i
Hegel ˈheɪg ᵊl —Ger [ˈheː gᵊl]
Hegelian hɪ ˈɡeɪl i ən heɪ-, -ˈɡiːl- **~s** z
hegemonic ˌheg ə ˈmɒn ɪk ◂ ˌhiːg-, ˌhedʒ-, -ɪ-
  ‖ -ˈmɑːn ɪk ◂
hegemon|y hɪ ˈgem ən |i hiː-, -ˈdʒem-;
  ˈheg ɪm-, ˈhedʒ-, ˈ-əm- ‖ hə ˈdʒem ən |i hɪ-,
  -ˈgem-; ˈhedʒ ə moʊn |i **~ies** iz
hegira, H~ ˈhedʒ ɪr ə -ər-; hɪ ˈdʒaɪᵊr ə, he- **~s**
  z
Heidegger ˈhaɪd eg ə -ɪg- ‖ -ᵊr —Ger
  [ˈhai dɛg ɐ]
Heidelberg ˈhaɪd ᵊl bɜːg ‖ -bɜːg —Ger
  [ˈhai dᵊl bɛʁk]
Heidi ˈhaɪd i
heifer ˈhef ə ‖ -ᵊr **~s** z
heigh-ho ˌheɪ ˈhəʊ ˌˈ ‖ -ˈhoʊ —Usually said
  with a low-rise nuclear tone.
height haɪt △haɪtθ **heights** haɪts △haɪtθs
heighten ˈhaɪt ᵊn **~ed** d **~ing** ɪŋ **~s** z
Heighway (i) ˈhaɪ weɪ, (ii) ˈheɪ-
Heilbron, Heilbronn ˈhaɪ ᵊl brɒn ‖ -brɑːn
  —Ger [hail ˈbʁɔn]
Heilongjiang ˌheɪ lɒŋ ˈdʒæŋ -lʊŋ-, -dʒi æŋ
  ‖ -lʊŋ dʒi ˈɑːŋ —Chi Hēilóngjiāng
  [¹xei ²lʊŋ ¹tɕjɑŋ]
Heimlich ˈhaɪm lɪk -lɪx —Ger [ˈhaɪm lɪç]
  ˈHeimlich maˌnoeuvre/maˌneuver
Heine ˈhaɪn ə —Ger [ˈhai nə]
Heineken tdmk ˈhaɪn ɪk ən -ək-
Heinemann ˈhaɪn ə mən
Heiney ˈhaɪn i
Heinkel ˈhaɪŋk ᵊl
Heinlein ˈhaɪn laɪn
heinous ˈheɪn əs §ˈhiːn-, △ˈˈi əs **~ly** li **~ness**
  nəs nɪs
Heinz tdmk haɪnz haɪnts

heir eə ‖ eᵊr æᵊr (= air) **heirs** eəz ‖ eᵊrz æᵊrz
  ˌheir apˈparent; ˌheir preˈsumptive
heiress ˈeər es -ɪs, -əs; ˌeər ˈes ‖ ˈer əs ˈær- **~es**
  ɪz əz
heirless ˈeə ləs -lɪs ‖ ˈer- ˈær- **~ness** nəs nɪs
heirloom ˈeə luːm ‖ ˈer- ˈær- **~s** z
heirship ˈeə ʃɪp ‖ ˈer- ˈær- (= airship) **~s** s
Heisenberg ˈhaɪz ᵊn bɜːg ‖ -bɜːg —Ger
  [ˈhai zᵊn bɛʁk]
heist haɪst **heisted** ˈhaɪst ɪd -əd **heisting**
  ˈhaɪst ɪŋ **heists** haɪsts
hejira, H~ ˈhedʒ ɪr ə -ər-; hɪ ˈdʒaɪᵊr ə, he- **~s** z
Hekla ˈhek lə —Icelandic [ˈhɛhk la]
held held
Helen ˈhel ən -ɪn
Helena (i) ˈhel ən ə -ɪn-, (ii) hə ˈliːn ə hɪ- -The
  place in Montana is (i); the personal name
  was formerly (ii) but is now usually (i). See
  also St H~.
Helene he ˈleɪn hə-, hɪ- ‖ -ˈliːn (*)
helenium hə ˈliːn i əm hɪ-
Helensburgh ˈhel ənz bər ə ˈ-ɪnz-, §-ˌbʌr ə
  ‖ ˈhel ənz bɜːg
Helfgott ˈhelf gɒt ‖ -gɑːt
Helga ˈhelg ə
helianthus ˌhiːl i ˈænˈθ əs ˌhel- **~es** ɪz əz
helical ˈhel ɪk ᵊl ˈhiːl- **~ly** i
helices ˈhel ɪ siːz ˈhiːl-, -ə-
helicoid ˈhel ɪ kɔɪd -ə- **~s** z
Helicon, h~ ˈhel ɪk ən -ək-; -ɪ kɒn, -ə- ‖ -ə kɑːn
  -ɪk ən **~s** z
heliconia ˌhel ɪ ˈkəʊn i ə ‖ -ˈkoʊn-
helicopter ˈhel ɪ kɒpt ə ˈ-ə-, ˈ-i-; ˌˈˈˈ
  ‖ -ə kɑːpt ᵊr ˈhiːl- **~s** z
helideck ˈhel i dek **~s** s
Helier ˈhel i ə ‖ ᵊr
Heligoland ˈhel ɪ gəʊ lænd ˈ-ə-, -ɪg ə- ‖ -goʊ-
helio- comb. form
  with stress-neutral suffix ˌhiːl i əʊ ‖ -oʊ
  — **heliocentric** ˌhiːl i əʊ ˈsentr ɪk ◂ ‖ -i oʊ-
  with stress-imposing suffix ˌhiːl i ˈɒ+ ‖ -ˈɑː+
  — **heliometer** ˌhiːl i ˈɒm ɪt ə -ət ə
  ‖ -ˈɑːm ət ᵊr
Heliogabalus ˌhiːl i ə ˈgæb əl əs -i ɒl- ‖ -i oʊ-
heliograph ˈhiːl i ə grɑːf -græf ‖ -græf **~ed** t
  ~ing ɪŋ **~s** s
Heliopolis ˌhiːl i ˈɒp əl ɪs §-əs ‖ -ˈɑːp-
Helios ˈhiːl i ɒs ‖ -ɑːs
heliotrope ˈhiːl i ə trəʊp ˈhel- ‖ -troʊp **~s** s
heliotropic ˌhiːl i ə ˈtrɒp ɪk ◂ ‖ -ˈtrɑːp ɪk ◂
  ~ally ᵊl i
heliotropism ˌhiːl i ˈɒtr ə ˌpɪz əm
  ˈhiːl i ə trəʊp ˌɪz-, ˌˈˈˌˈˈ, ˌˈˈˈˈˈ ‖ -ˈɑːtr-
helipad ˈhel i pæd §-ə- ‖ ˈhiːl- **~s** z
heliport ˈhel i pɔːt §-ə- ‖ -pɔːrt ˈhiːl-, -poʊrt **~s**
  s
heli-ski|ing ˈhel i ˌskiː| ɪŋ **~er/s** ə/z ‖ ᵊr/z
helium ˈhiːl i əm
helix ˈhiːl ɪks **helices** ˈhel ɪ siːz ˈhiːl-, -ə- **~es**
  ɪz əz
hell, Hell hel **hells, Hell's** helz
  ˌHell's ˈAngel

he'll *strong form* hiːᵊl, *weak forms* hiᵊl, ᵊl
—*The weak form* iᵊl *is not used at the beginning of a sentence or clause.*

hellacious he ˈleɪʃ əs **~ly** li
Helladic he ˈlæd ɪk
Hellas ˈhel æs
hell-bent ˌhel ˈbent ◀
hellcat ˈhel kæt **~s** s
hellebore ˈhel ɪ bɔː -ə- ‖ -bɔːr -bour **~s** z
helleborine ˈhel ɪ bə raɪn ˈ-ə-, -riːn; ˌ··ˈbɔːr iːn **~s** z
Hellene ˈhel iːn **~s** z
Hellenic he ˈlen ɪk hɪ-, hə-, -ˈliːn-
Hellenism ˈhel ɪn ˌɪz əm -ən- **~s** z
Hellenistic ˌhel ɪ ˈnɪst ɪk ◀ -ə-
Heller ˈhel ə ‖ -ᵊr
Hellespont ˈhel ɪ spɒnt -ə- ‖ -spaːnt
hellfire ˌhel ˈfaɪ‿ə ˈ·· ‖ ˈhel ˌfaɪ‿ᵊr
hell-hole ˈhel həʊl →-hɒʊl ‖ -hoʊl **~s** z
Hellicar ˈhel ɪ kɑː -ə- ‖ -kɑːr
hellion ˈhel jən **~s** z
hellish ˈhel ɪʃ **~ly** li **~ness** nəs nɪs
Hellman ˈhel mən
hello hə ˈləʊ he- ‖ -ˈloʊ **~ed** d **~es** z **~ing** ɪŋ
helluva ˈhel əv ə
helm helm **helms** helmz
helm|et ˈhelm |ɪt -ət ‖ -|ət **~eted** ɪt ɪd ət-, -əd ‖ əʈ əd **~ets** ɪts əts ‖ əts
Helmholtz ˈhelm həʊlts →-hɒʊlts ‖ -hoʊlts
—*Ger* [ˈhɛlm hɔlts]
helminth ˈhelm ɪnᵗθ **~s** s
helminthiasis ˌhelm ɪn ˈθaɪ əs ɪs §-ən-, §-əs
helminthological ˌhelm ɪnᵗθ ə ˈlɒdʒ ɪk ᵊl ◀ §ˌ-ənᵗθ- ‖ -ˈlɑːdʒ- **~ly** ˌi
helmintholog|ist ˌhelm ɪn ˈθɒl ədʒ |ɪst §ˌ-ən-, §-əst ‖ -ˈθɑːl- **~ists** ɪsts §əsts **~y** i
Helmsdale ˈhelmz deɪᵊl
Helmsley ˈhelmz li ˈhemz-
helms|man ˈhelmz |mən **~men** mən men
Heloise, Héloïse ˈel əʊ iːz ˌ·ˈ· ‖ ˈhel oʊ iːz ˈel- —*Fr* [e lɔ iːz]
helot ˈhel ət **~s** s
helotry ˈhel ət ri
help help **helped** helpt **helping/s** ˈhelp ɪŋ/z **helps** helps
ˌhelping ˈhand
helpdesk ˈhelp desk **~s** s
helper ˈhelp ə ‖ -ᵊr **~s** z
helpful ˈhelp fᵊl -ful **~ly** i **~ness** nəs nɪs
helpless ˈhelp ləs -lɪs **~ly** li
helpline ˈhelp laɪn **~s** z
Helpmann ˈhelp mən
helpmate ˈhelp meɪt **~s** s
helpmeet ˈhelp miːt **~s** s
Helsinki hel ˈsɪŋk i ˈhels ɪŋk i —*Finnish* [ˈhel siŋ ki]
Helston ˈhelst ən
helter-skelter ˌhelt ə ˈskelt ə ‖ -ᵊr ˈskelt ᵊr **~s** z
helve helv **helves** helvz
Helvellyn hel ˈvel ɪn -ən
Helvetia hel ˈviːʃ ə -ˈviːʃ i‿ə
Helvetic hel ˈvet ɪk ‖ -ˈveʈ ɪk

hem hem **hemmed** hemd **hemming** ˈhem ɪŋ **hems** hemz
hemal ˈhiːm ᵊl
he-|man ˈhiː |mæn **~men** men
hematite ˈhiːm ə taɪt ˈhem-
hemato- *comb. form*
with stress-neutral suffix ˌhiːm ə təʊ ˌhem- ‖ -əʈ ə — **hematogenesis** ˌhiːm ət əʊ ˈdʒen əs ɪs ˌhem-, -ɪs ɪs, §-əs ‖ -əʈ ə-
with stress-imposing suffix ˌhiːm ə ˈtɒ + ˌhem- ‖ -ˈtɑː + — **hematogenous** ˌhiːm ə ˈtɒdʒ ən əs ˌhem- -ˈtɑːdʒ-
hematologist ˌhiːm ə ˈtɒl ədʒ ɪst §-əst ‖ -ˈtɑːl- **~s** z
hematology ˌhiːm ə ˈtɒl ədʒ i ‖ -ˈtɑːl-
hematoma ˌhiːm ə ˈtəʊm ə ‖ -ˈtoʊm ə **~s** z
heme hiːm
Hemel Hempstead ˌhem ᵊl ˈhemp stɪd -stəd, -sted
he-men ˈhiː men
hemi- ˌhem i — **hemihydrate** ˌhem i ˈhaɪdr eɪt
hemidemisemiquaver ˌhem i ˌdem i ˈsem i ˌkweɪv ə ‖ -ᵊr **~s** z
Heming ˈhem ɪŋ
Hemingway ˈhem ɪŋ weɪ
hemiplegia ˌhem i ˈpliːdʒ i‿ə -ˈpliːdʒ ə
hemiplegic ˌhem i ˈpliːdʒ ɪk ◀ **~s** s
hemipterous hɪ ˈmɪpt ər əs he-, hə-
hemisphere ˈhem ɪ sfɪə -ə- ‖ -sfɪr **~s** z
hemispheric ˌhem i ˈsfer ɪk ◀ ‖ -ˈsfɪr- **~al** ᵊl **~ally** ᵊl i
hemistich ˈhem i stɪk **~s** s
hemline ˈhem laɪn **~s** z
hemlock ˈhem lɒk ‖ -lɑːk **~s** s
Hemmings ˈhem ɪŋz
hemo- *comb. form*
with stress-neutral suffix ˌhiːm əʊ ‖ -oʊ — **hemodialysis** ˌhiːm əʊ daɪ ˈæl əs ɪs -ɪs ɪs, §-əs ‖ ˌ-oʊ-
with stress-imposing suffix hiː ˈmɒ + hɪ- ‖ -ˈmɑː + — **hemolysis** hiː ˈmɒl əs ɪs hɪ-, -ɪs-, §-əs ‖ -ˈmɑːl-
hemoglobin ˌhiːm ə ˈgləʊb ɪn §-ən, ˈ···· ‖ ˈhiːm ə gloʊb ən
hemophilia ˌhiːm ə ˈfɪl i‿ə -ˈfiːl-
hemophiliac ˌhiːm ə ˈfɪl i æk ◀ -ˈfiːl- **~s** s
hemorrhag|e ˈhem ᵊr ˌɪdʒ **~ed** d **~es** ɪz əz **~ing** ɪŋ
hemorrhoid ˈhem ə rɔɪd **~s** z
hemorrhoidal ˌhem ə ˈrɔɪd ᵊl ◀
hemp hemp
ˈhemp ˌnettle
Hempel ˈhemp ᵊl
hempen ˈhemp ən
Hempstead ˈhempst ed -ɪd, §-əd
hemstitch ˈhem stɪtʃ **~ed** t **~es** ɪz əz **~ing** ɪŋ
hen hen **hens** henz
ˈhen house; ˈhen ˌparty
Henan hɜː ˈnæn ‖ hə ˈnɑːn —*Chi* Hénán [²xɤ ²nan]
henbane ˈhen beɪn →ˈhem-

henbit 'hen bɪt →'hem-
hence hen's
henceforth ˌhen's 'fɔːθ '·· ‖ -'fɔːrθ -'fourθ
henceforward ˌhen's 'fɔː wəd ‖ -'fɔːr wərd
hench|man 'hentʃ |mən **~men** mən
hendeca- *comb. form* ˌhen dek ə ·| ··
— **hendecasyllabic** ˌhen dek ə sɪ 'læb ɪk ◂
·| ··, -sə'--
hendecagon ˌhen 'dek əg ən ‖ -ə gɑːn **~s** z
Henderson 'hend əs ən ‖ -ərs-
hendiadys hen 'daɪ‿əd ɪs §-əs
Hendon 'hend ən
Hendricks, Hendrix 'hendr ɪks
Hendry 'hendr i
Heneage 'hen ɪdʒ
Heneghan 'hen ɪg ən
henge hendʒ **henges** 'hendʒ ɪz -əz
Hengist 'heŋ gɪst -gəst, -dʒɪst
Henley 'hen li
Henman 'hen mən →'hem-
henna 'hen ə **hennaed** 'hen əd **hennaing**
'hen ə‿ ɪŋ ‖ -ə ɪŋ **hennas** 'hen əz
Hennessey, Hennessy 'hen əs i -ɪs-
Henning 'hen ɪŋ
henpecked 'hen pekt →'hem-
Henri ˌɒn 'riː ˌɒ̃-, '·· ‖ ɑːn 'riː —*Fr* [ɑ̃ ʁi] —*but as an American family name,* 'hen ri
henries —*see* **henry**
Henrietta ˌhen ri 'et ə ◂ ‖ -'eţ ə ◂
Henriques hen 'riːk ɪz §-əz
Hen|ry, hen|ry 'hen |ri —*but as a French name,* ˌɒn 'riː ‖ ˌɑːn- —*Fr* [ɑ̃ ʁi] **~ries, ~rys, ~ry's** riz
Henryson 'hen rɪs ən -rəs-
Henslow, Henslowe 'henz ləʊ ‖ -loʊ
Henson 'hen's ən
Henton 'hent ən ‖ -ən
Henty 'hent i ‖ 'henţ i
hep hep
heparin 'hep ər ɪn §-ən
hepatic hɪ 'pæt ɪk he-, hə- ‖ -'pæţ ɪk **~s** s
hepatica hɪ 'pæt ɪk ə he-, hə- ‖ -'pæţ- **~s** z
hepatitis ˌhep ə 'taɪt ɪs ◂ -əs ‖ -'taɪţ əs ◂ ˌhepaˌtitis 'B
Hepburn (i) 'hep bɜːn ‖ -bɜ˞ːn; (ii) 'heb ɜːn -ən ‖ -ərn
Hephaestus hɪ 'fiːst əs he-, hə- ‖ -'fest- (*)
Hephzibah 'hefs ɪ bɑː 'heps-, -ə- ‖ -əb ə
Heppenstall 'hep ən stɔːl →-m- ‖ -stɑːl
Hepplewhite 'hep ᵊl waɪt -hwaɪt
hepta- *comb. form*
with stress-neutral suffix ˌhept ə
— **heptastich** 'hept ə stɪk
with stress-imposing suffix hep 'tæ+
— **heptamerous** hep 'tæm ər əs
heptagon 'hept əg ən -ə gɒn ‖ -ə gɑːn **~s** z
heptagonal hep 'tæg ən ᵊl **~ly** i
heptane 'hept eɪn
heptarch|y 'hept ɑːk |i ‖ -ɑːrk |i **~ies** iz
Heptateuch 'hept ə tjuːk →-tʃuːk ‖ -tuːk -tjuːk
heptathlete hep 'tæθ liːt **~s** s
heptathlon hep 'tæθ lən -lɒn ‖ -lɑːn **~s** z
Hepworth 'hep wɜːθ -wəθ ‖ -wᵊrθ

her *strong form* hɜː ‖ hɜ˞ː, *weak forms* hə, ɜː, ə ‖ hᵊr, ɜ˞ː, ᵊr —*The weak forms* ɜː, ə ‖ ɜ˞ː, ᵊr *are not used at the beginning of a sentence or clause.*
Hera 'hɪər ə ‖ 'hɪr ə
Heraclean ˌher ə 'kliː ən ◂
Heracles, Herakles 'her ə kliːz
Heraclitus ˌher ə 'klaɪt əs ˌhɪər- ‖ -'klaɪţ əs
Heraklion he 'ræk li‿ən hɪ-, hə- —*ModGk* [i 'rak ljon]
herald 'her əld **~ed** ɪd əd **~ing** ɪŋ **~s** z
heraldic hə 'ræld ɪk he-, hɪ- **~ally** ᵊl‿i
herald|ry 'her əld |ri **~ries** riz

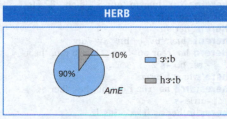

HERB

10% ɜ˞ːb
90% hɜ˞ːb
AmE

herb hɜːb ‖ ɜ˞ːb hɜ˞ːb — *Preference poll, AmE:* ɜ˞ːb *90%,* hɜ˞ːb *10%.* **herbs** hɜːbz ‖ ɜ˞ːbz hɜ˞ːbz
ˌherb 'bennet; ˌherb 'Paris; ˌherb 'Robert
Herb *personal name* hɜːb ‖ hɜ˞ːb
herbaceous hə 'beɪʃ əs hɜː- ‖ hɜ˞ː- ɜ˞ː-
herˌbaceous 'border
herbage, H~ 'hɜːb ɪdʒ ‖ 'ɜ˞ːb- 'hɜ˞ːb-
herbal 'hɜːb ᵊl ‖ 'ɜ˞ːb ᵊl 'hɜ˞ːb- **~s** z
herbalist 'hɜːb ᵊl ɪst §-əst ‖ 'ɜ˞ːb- 'hɜ˞ːb- **~s** s
herbari|um hɜː 'beər i‿|əm ‖ hɜ˞ː 'ber- ɜ˞ː-, -'bær- **~a** ə **~ums** əmz
Herbert 'hɜːb ət ‖ 'hɜ˞ːb ᵊrt
herbicide 'hɜːb ɪ saɪd -ə- ‖ 'hɜ˞ːb- 'ɜ˞ːb- **~s** z
Herbie 'hɜːb i ‖ 'hɜ˞ːb i
herbivore 'hɜːb ɪ vɔː -ə- ‖ 'ɜ˞ːb ə vɔːr 'hɜ˞ːb-, -voʊr **~s** z
herbivorous hɜː 'bɪv ər‿əs hə- ‖ ɜ˞ː- hɜ˞ː- **~ly** li
Hercegovina ˌhɜːts ə 'gɒv ɪn ə ˌheəts-, -ˌɪ-, -ən ə; -gəʊ 'viːn ə ‖ ˌherts ə 'goʊv- —*Serbian* [''hɛr tsɛ ɡɔ vi na]
Herceptin *tdmk* hɜː 'sept ɪn ‖ hɜ˞ː-
Herculaneum ˌhɜːk ju 'leɪn i‿əm ‖ ˌhɜ˞ːk jə-
Herculean ˌhɜːk ju 'liː ən ◂ -jə-; hɜː 'kjuːl i‿ən ‖ ˌhɜ˞ːk jə-
Hercules 'hɜːk ju liːz -jə- ‖ 'hɜ˞ːk jə-
herd, Herd hɜːd ‖ hɜ˞ːd **herded** 'hɜːd ɪd -əd ‖ 'hɜ˞ːd əd **herding** 'hɜːd ɪŋ ‖ 'hɜ˞ːd ɪŋ **herds** hɜːdz ‖ hɜ˞ːdz
herds|man 'hɜːdz |mən ‖ 'hɜ˞ːdz- **~men** mən
Herdwick 'hɜːd wɪk ‖ 'hɜ˞ːd-
here hɪə ‖ hɪᵊr (= *hear*) **here's** hɪəz ‖ hɪᵊrz
hereabout ˌhɪər ə 'baʊt '··· ‖ 'hɪr ə ˌbaʊt **~s** s
hereafter ˌhɪər 'ɑːft ə §-'æft- ‖ hɪr 'æft ᵊr
hereby ˌhɪə 'baɪ ◂ '·· ‖ ˌhɪr 'baɪ ◂
hereditability hɪ ˌred ɪt ə 'bɪl ət i hə-, he-, -ɪt i ‖ -əţ ə 'bɪl əţ i
hereditab|le hɪ 'red ɪt əb |ᵊl hə-, he-, -'·ət- ‖ -'red əţ- **~ly** li
hereditament ˌher ɪ 'dɪt ə mənt ˌ·ə- ‖ -'dɪţ- **~s** s

H

hereditarily hə ˈred ət ˌər əl i hɪ-, he-, -ˈɪt ̣-,
-ɪ li; ·ˌ·ə ˈter-, -ɪ ˈter- ‖ hə ˌred ə ˈter əl i

hereditar|y hə ˈred ət ˌər |i hɪ-, he-, -ˈɪt ̣-
‖ -ə ter |i **~iness** i nəs i nɪs

heredit|y hə ˈred ət |i hɪ-, he-, -ɪt- ‖ -ət ̣ |i **~ies**
iz

Hereford (i) ˈher ɪ fəd -ə- ‖ -fᵊrd, (ii) ˈhɜː fəd
‖ ˈhɜː fᵊrd —*The city and former county in
England are (i); the town in TX is (ii). For the
breed of cattle or pigs, and for street names,
etc., (i) in BrE, usually (ii) in AmE.* **~shire** ʃə
ʃɪə ‖ ʃᵊr

herein ˌhɪər ˈɪn ◂ ‖ hɪr-

hereinafter ˌhɪər ɪn ˈɑːft ə ◂ §-ən-, §-ˈæft-
‖ ˌhɪr ən ˈæft ᵊr ◂

Heren ˈher ən

hereof ˌhɪər ˈɒv ◂ ‖ hɪr ˈʌv -ˈɑːv

Herero hə ˈreər əʊ -ˈrɪər-; ˈhɪər ə rəʊ, ˈheər-
‖ -ˈrer oʊ **~s** z

here's hɪəz ‖ hɪᵊrz

heresiarch hə ˈriːz i ɑːk hɪ-, he-; ˈher əs-
‖ -ɑːrk **~s** s

heres|y ˈher əs |i -ɪs- **~ies** iz

heretic ˈher ə tɪk -ɪ- **~s** s

heretical hə ˈret ɪk ᵊl hɪ-, he- ‖ -ˈret ̣- **~ly** ˌi

hereto ˌhɪə ˈtuː ◂ ‖ hɪr-

heretofore ˌhɪə tu ˈfɔː ◂ -tə-, -tuː- ‖ ˈhɪrt ̣ ə fɔːr
-four, ˌ·ˈ·

hereunder ˌhɪər ˈʌnd ə ◂ ‖ hɪr ˈʌnd ᵊr

hereupon ˌhɪər ə ˈpɒn ◂ ‖ hɪr ə pɑːn -pɔːn,
ˌ·ˈ·

Hereward ˈher ɪ wəd -ə- ‖ -wᵊrd

herewith ˌhɪə ˈwɪð ◂ -ˈwɪθ ‖ hɪr-

Herford ˈhɜː fəd ‖ ˈhɜː fᵊrd

Hergé ˌeə ˈʒeɪ ‖ ˌer- —*Fr* [ɛʁ ʒe]

heriot, H~, Heriott ˈher i ət **~s**, **~'s** s

Heriot-Watt ˌher i ət ˈwɒt ‖ -ˈwɑːt

heritable ˈher ɪt əb ᵊl ˈ·ət- ‖ ˈher ət ̣-

heritag|e ˈher ɪt ɪdʒ -ət- ‖ -ət ̣- **~es** ɪz əz

herm hɜːm ‖ hɜːm **herms** hɜːmz ‖ hɜːmz

Herman ˈhɜːm ən ‖ ˈhɜːm-

Hermann ˈhɜːm ən ‖ ˈhɜːm- —*Ger* [ˈhɛʁ man]

hermaphrodite hɜː ˈmæf rə daɪt hə- ‖ hᵊr- **~s**
s

hermaphroditic hɜː ˌmæf rə ˈdɪt ɪk ◂ hə-
‖ hᵊr ˌmæf rə ˈdɪt ̣ ɪk ◂ **~ally** ᵊl i

hermeneutic ˌhɜːm ə ˈnjuːt ɪk ◂ -ˈɪ-
‖ ˌhɜːm ə ˈnuːt ̣ ɪk ◂ -ˈnjuːt ̣- **~al** ᵊl **~ally** ᵊl i **~s**
s

Hermes ˈhɜːm iːz ‖ ˈhɜːm-

Hermès tdmk ˌeə ˈmes ‖ ˌer- —*Fr* [ɛʁ mɛs]

Hermesetas tdmk ˌhɜːm ɪ ˈsiːt əs -ə-, ˌ, -əz, -æs
‖ ˌhɜːm ə ˈsiːt ̣ əs -əz

hermetic hɜː ˈmet ɪk hə- ‖ hᵊr ˈmet ̣ ɪk **~ally**
ᵊl i

Hermia ˈhɜːm i ə ‖ ˈhɜːm-

Hermione hɜː ˈmaɪ ən i hə- ‖ hᵊr-

hermit ˈhɜːm ɪt §-ət ‖ ˈhɜːm- **~s** s
'hermit crab

hermitag|e ˈhɜːm ɪt ɪdʒ -ət- ‖ ˈhɜːm ət ̣ ɪdʒ
—*but the* H~ *in St Petersburg is usually*
ˌeəm ɪ ˈtɑːʒ, -ə- ‖ ˌerm- **~es** ɪz əz

Hermon ˈhɜːm ən ‖ ˈhɜːm-

hern, Hern, Herne hɜːn ‖ hɜːn

hernia ˈhɜːn i ə ‖ ˈhɜːn- **~s** z

'hi: roʊ
'hɪr oʊ
AmE

hero, Hero ˈhɪər əʊ ‖ ˈhiː roʊ ˈhɪr oʊ —
Preference poll, AmE: ˈhi: roʊ 57%, ˈhɪr oʊ
43%. **~es** z
'hero ˌworship

Herod ˈher əd

Herodias hə ˈrəʊd i æs hɪ-, he-, -əs ‖ -ˈroʊd-

Herodotus hə ˈrɒd ət əs hɪ-, he- ‖ -ˈrɑːd ət ̣ əs

heroic hə ˈrəʊ ɪk hɪ-, he- ‖ -ˈroʊ ɪk **~al** ᵊl **~ally**
ᵊl i **~s** s
heˌroic ˈcouplet

heroin ˈher əʊ ɪn §-ən ‖ -oʊ ən

heroine ˈher əʊ ɪn ˈhɪər-, -iːn, §-ən ‖ -oʊ ən
(usually = heroin) **~s** z

heroism ˈher əʊ ˌɪz əm ‖ -oʊ-

heron, Heron ˈher ən **~s** z

heron|ry ˈher ən |ri **~ries** riz

hero-worship n, v ˈhɪər əʊ ˌwɜːʃ ɪp §-əp
‖ ˈhi: roʊ ˌwɜːʃ əp ˈhɪr oʊ- **~ed, ~ped** t **~ing,
~ping** ɪŋ **~s** s

herpes ˈhɜːp iːz ‖ ˈhɜːp-

herpetological ˌhɜːp ɪt ə ˈlɒdʒ ɪk ᵊl ◂ ˌ·ət-
‖ ˌhɜːp ət ̣ ə ˈlɑːdʒ- **~ly** ˌi

herpetologist ˌhɜːp ɪ ˈtɒl ədʒ ɪst ˌ·ə-, §-əst
‖ ˌhɜːp ə ˈtɑːl- **~s** s

herpetology ˌhɜːp ɪ ˈtɒl ədʒ i ˌ·ə-
‖ ˌhɜːp ə ˈtɑːl-

Herr heə ‖ heᵊr hæᵊr —*Ger* [hɛʁ]

herrenvolk, H~ ˈher ən fəʊk -fɒlk ‖ -foʊk
-fɔːlk, -fɑːlk —*Ger* [ˈhɛʁ ən fɔlk]

Herrick ˈher ɪk

Herries ˈher ɪs -ɪz, §-əs, §-əz

herring, H~ ˈher ɪŋ **~s** z
'herring gull

herringbone ˈher ɪŋ bəʊn ‖ -boʊn **~s** z

Herriot ˈher i ət

hers hɜːz ‖ hɜːz

Herschel, Herschell ˈhɜːʃ ᵊl ‖ ˈhɜːʃ-

herself strong form hɜː ˈself ‖ hɜː-, weak forms
hə-, ɜː-, ə- ‖ hᵊr-, ᵊr- —*The forms* ɜː-, ə- ‖ ᵊr-
*are not used at the beginning of a sentence or
clause.*

Hersham ˈhɜːʃ əm ‖ ˈhɜːʃ-

Hershey ˈhɜːʃ i ‖ ˈhɜːʃ i
'Hershey bar

Herstmonceux ˌhɜːst mən ˈsjuː ◂ -ˈsuː-
‖ ˌhɜːst mən ˈsuː

Herter ˈhɜːt ə ‖ ˈhɜːt ̣ ᵊr

Hertford (i) ˈhɑː fəd ‖ ˈhɑːr fᵊrd, (ii) ˈhɑːt-
‖ ˈhɑːrt-, (iii) ˈhɜːt- ‖ ˈhɜːt- —*The traditional
pronunciation for the English county town and
the Oxford college, (i), has been largely*

superseded by the spelling pronunciation (ii).
As an American name, (iii). **~shire** ʃə ʃɪə ‖ ʃᵊr
ʃɪr
Herts hɑːts ‖ hɑːrts
hertz, Hertz hɜːts ‖ hɜːts —*Ger* [hɛʀts]
Hertzian 'hɜːts i̯ ən 'heəts- ‖ 'hɜːts- 'herts-
Hertzog 'hɜːts ɒg ‖ 'hɜːts ɑːg
Hervey (i) 'hɑːv i ‖ 'hɑːrv i, (ii) 'hɜːv i
‖ 'hɜːv i
Herzegovina ˌhɜːts ə 'gɒv ɪn ə ˌheəts-, -ˌɪ-,
-ən ə; -gəʊ 'viːn ə ‖ ˌherts ə 'gouv- —*Serbian*
Hercegovina ['hɛr tsɛ gɔ vi na]
Herzl 'hɜːts ᵊl ‖ 'herts- —*Ger* ['hɛʀts ᵊl]
he's *strong form* hiːz, *weak forms* hiz, iːz, iz
—*At the beginning of a sentence or clause,*
only the forms with h *are used.*
Heseltine 'hes ᵊl taɪn 'hez-
Heselwood 'hes ᵊl wʊd 'hez-
Hesiod 'hiːs i̯ əd 'hes-, -ɒd
hesitance 'hez ɪt ən̩ts -ət- ‖ -ᵊn̩ts
hesitanc|y 'hez ɪt ən̩ts |i 'ˑət- ‖ -ᵊn̩ts |i ~ies iz
hesitant 'hez ɪt ənt -ət- ‖ -ᵊnt ~ly li
hesi|tate 'hez ɪ |teɪt -ə- ~**tated** teɪt ɪd -əd
‖ teɪt̬ əd ~**tates** teɪts ~**tating/ly** teɪt ɪŋ/ li
‖ teɪt̬ ɪŋ/ li
hesitation ˌhez ɪ 'teɪʃ ᵊn -ə- ~**s** z
Hesketh 'hesk əθ -ɪθ
Hesperia he 'spɪər i̯ ə ‖ -'spɪr-
Hesperian he 'spɪər i̯ ən ‖ -'spɪr-
Hesperides hɪ 'sper ɪ diːz he-, hə-, -ə-
Hesperus 'hesp ər əs
Hess hes
Hessayon 'hes i̯ ən
Hesse hes 'hes ə —*Ger* ['hɛs ə]
hessian, H~ 'hes i̯ ən ‖ 'heʃ ᵊn *(*)* ~**s** z
Hessle *place in Humberside* 'hez ᵊl
Hester 'hest ə ‖ -ᵊr
Heston 'hest ən
Heswall 'hez wəl ‖ -wɔːl -wɑːl
het het **hets** hets
ˌhet 'up
hetaer|a, hetair|a hɪ 'taɪᵊr |ə he- ‖ -'tɪr |ə ~**ae**
iː aɪ ~**ai** aɪ ~**as** əz
heterarch|y 'het ə rɑːk |i ‖ 'het̬ ə rɑːrk |i
~**ies** iz
hetero 'het ər əʊ ‖ 'het̬ ə roʊ ~**s** z
hetero- *comb. form*
with stress-neutral suffix ˌhet ər əʊ
‖ ˌhet̬ ə roʊ — **heterographic**
ˌhet ər əʊ 'græf ɪk ◄ ‖ ˌhet̬ ə roʊ-
with stress-imposing suffix ˌhet ə 'rɒ+
‖ ˌhet̬ ə 'rɑː+ — **heterography**
ˌhet ə 'rɒg rəf i ‖ ˌhet̬ ə 'rɑːg-
heteroclite 'het ər əʊ klaɪt ‖ 'het̬ ər ə- ~**s** s
heterocyclic ˌhet ər əʊ 'saɪk lɪk ◄ -'sɪk-
‖ ˌhet̬ ə roʊ-
heterodox 'het ər əʊ dɒks ‖ 'het̬ ər ə dɑːks
→'hetr ə dɑːks
heterodox|y 'het ər əʊ dɒks |i
‖ 'het̬ ər ə dɑːks |i →'hetr ə dɑːks |i ~**ies** iz
heterodyne 'het ər əʊ daɪn ‖ 'het̬ ər ə-
→'hetr ə daɪn

heterogeneity ˌhet ər əʊ dʒə 'niː ət i
ˌhet ə ˌrɒdʒ ə-, -dʒɪ'-, -'neɪ-, -ɪt i
‖ ˌhet̬ ə rou dʒə 'niː ət̬ i →ˌhetr ou dʒə'--
heterogeneous ˌhet ər əʊ 'dʒiːn i̯ əs ◄
‖ ˌhet̬ ə rou- →ˌhetr ou'--, -ə'-- ~**ly** li ~**ness**
nəs nɪs
heteronym 'het ər əʊ nɪm ‖ 'het̬ ə rou-
→'hetr ou nɪm, -ə nɪm ~**s** z
heteronymous ˌhet ə 'rɒn ɪm əs ◄ -əm əs
‖ ˌhet̬ ə 'rɑːn-
heterorganic ˌhet ər ɔː 'gæn ɪk ◄ ‖ ˌhet̬ ər ɔːr-
heterosexism ˌhet ər əʊ 'seks ˌɪz əm
‖ ˌhet̬ ə rou-
heterosexist ˌhet ər əʊ 'seks ɪst ◄ §-əst
‖ ˌhet̬ ə rou- ~**s** s
heterosexual ˌhet ər əʊ 'sek ʃu̯ əl ◄
-'seks ju̯ əl, -'sekʃ ᵊl ‖ ˌhet̬ ə rou- -ər ə- ~**ly** i
~**s** z
heterosexuality ˌhet ər əʊ ˌsek ʃu 'æl ət i
-ˌseks ju- ‖ ˌhet̬ ə rou ˌsekʃ u 'æl ət̬ i -ər ə-
heterozygote ˌhet ər əʊ'zaɪg əʊt
‖ ˌhet̬ ə rou 'zaɪg out ~**s** s
heterozygous ˌhet ər əʊ 'zaɪg əs ‖ ˌhet̬ ə rou-
Hetherington 'heð ər ɪŋ tən
Hettie 'het i ‖ 'het̬ i
Hetton-le-Hole ˌhet ᵊn lɪ 'həʊl -lə'-, →-'hɒʊl
‖ -'hoʊl
Hetty 'het i ‖ 'het̬ i
Heugh *family name* hjuː
Heugh *village in Northumberland* hjuːf
Heulwen 'haɪᵊl wen —*Welsh* ['həɪl wen, 'həɪl-]
heuristic hjuᵊ 'rɪst ɪk ~**ally** ᵊl i ~**s** s
Hever 'hiːv ə ‖ -ᵊr
hew, Hew hjuː ‖ juː **hewed** hjuːd ‖ juːd
hewing 'hjuː ɪŋ ‖ 'juː **hewn** hjuːn ‖ juːn
hews hjuːz ‖ juːz
hewer 'hjuː ə ‖ ᵊr 'juː ~**s** z
Hewett, Hewitt 'hjuː ɪt §ˌət ‖ 'juː-
Hewlett 'hjuːl ɪt §-ət ‖ 'juːl-
hewn hjuːn ‖ juːn
Hewson 'hjuːs ᵊn ‖ 'juːs-
hex heks **hexed** hekst **hexes** 'heks ɪz -əz
hexing 'heks ɪŋ
hexa- *comb. form*
with stress-neutral suffix ˌheks ə — **hexapod**
'heks ə pɒd ‖ -pɑːd
with stress-imposing suffix hek 'sæ+
— **hexapody** hek 'sæp əd i
hexachlorophene ˌheks ə 'klɔːr ə fiːn -'klɒr-
‖ -'klour-
hexad 'heks æd ~**s** z
hexadecimal ˌheks ə 'des ɪm ᵊl ◄ -əm ᵊl ~**ly** i
~**s** z
hexagon 'heks əg ən ‖ -ə gɑːn ~**s** z
hexagonal hek 'sæg ən ᵊl ~**ly** i
hexagram 'heks ə græm ~**s** z
hexahedron ˌheks ə 'hiːdr ən -'hedr- ~**s** z
hexameter hek 'sæm ɪt ə -ət- ‖ -ət̬ ᵊr ~**s** z
hexamine 'heks ə miːn
hexane 'heks eɪn
Hexham 'heks əm
hey heɪ *(= hay)*
heyday 'heɪ deɪ

Heyer 'heɪ ə ‖ -ʲr
Heyerdahl 'heɪ ə dɑːl 'haɪˌ ‖ 'haɪˌʲr-
— *Norwegian* ['heɪ ər dɑːl]
Heyes heɪz
Heyford 'heɪ fəd ‖ -fʲrd
Heyhoe 'heɪ həʊ ‖ -hoʊ
Heys heɪz
Heysel 'haɪs ʲl 'heɪs- — *Du* ['heɪ sʲl]
Heysham 'hiːʃ əm — *Often* 'heɪʃ- *by those not
familiar with the name.*
Heythrop 'hiːθ rəp -rɒp ‖ -rɑːp
Heywood 'heɪ wʊd
Hezbollah ˌhez bɒ 'lɑː ˌhɪz- ‖ -bə-
Hezekiah ˌhez ɪ 'kaɪˌə -ə-
hi haɪ (= *high*)
Hialeah ˌhaɪ ə 'liː ə
hiatus haɪ 'eɪt əs hi- ‖ -'eɪt̬- **~es** ɪz əz
hi ˌatus 'hernia
Hiawatha ˌhaɪ ə 'wɒθ ə ‖ -'wɔːθ ə ˌhiː-, -'wɑːθ-
hibachi hɪ 'bɑːtʃ i — *Jp* ['çi ba tɕi] **~s** z
Hibberd 'hɪb əd ‖ -ʲrd
Hibbert 'hɪb ət ‖ -ʲrt
hibernacul|um ˌhaɪb ə 'næk jʊl ‖əm -jəl əm
‖ -ʲr 'næk jəl- **~a** ə
hiber|nate 'haɪb ə |neɪt ‖ -ʲr- **~nated** neɪt ɪd
-əd ‖ neɪt̬ əd **~nates** neɪts **~nating** neɪt ɪŋ
‖ neɪt̬ ɪŋ
hibernation ˌhaɪb ə 'neɪʃ ʲn ‖ -ʲr- **~s** z
Hibernia haɪ 'bɜːn i ə hɪ- ‖ -'bɜːn-
Hibernian haɪ 'bɜːn i ən hɪ- ‖ -'bɜːn- — *The
football team is* hɪ- **~s** z
Hibernicism haɪ 'bɜːn ɪ ˌsɪz əm -ə- ‖ -'bɜːn- **~s**
z
hibiscus haɪ 'bɪsk əs hɪ-, hə- **~es** ɪz əz
Hibs hɪbz
hic hɪk
ˌhic 'jacet ◂ 'jæk et ɪ 'dʒeɪs-
hiccough, hiccup 'hɪk ʌp -əp **~ed** t **~ing** ɪŋ **~s**
s
hick, Hick hɪk **hicks** hɪks
Hickey, h~ 'hɪk i **~s** z
Hickok 'hɪk ɒk ‖ -ɑːk
hickor|y 'hɪk ər |i **~ies** iz
Hicks hɪks
Hickson 'hɪks ən
hid hɪd
hidalgo hɪ 'dælg əʊ ‖ -oʊ — *Sp* [i 'ðal ɣo] **~s** z
Hidatsa hɪ 'dæts ə ‖ -'dɑːts-
Hidcote 'hɪd kət →'hɪg-
hidden 'hɪd ʲn
hide haɪd **hidden** 'hɪd ʲn **hides** haɪdz **hiding**
'haɪd ɪŋ
hide-and-seek ˌhaɪd ʲn 'siːk
hideaway 'haɪd ə ˌweɪ **~s** z
hidebound 'haɪd baʊnd →'haɪb-
hi-de-hi ˌhaɪ di 'haɪ
hideous 'hɪd i əs **~ly** li **~ness** nəs nɪs
hideout 'haɪd aʊt **~s** s
hidey-hole 'haɪd i həʊl →-hɒʊl ‖ -hoʊl **~s** z
hiding 'haɪd ɪŋ **~s** z
hie haɪ (= *high*) **hied** haɪd **hieing, hying**
'haɪ ɪŋ **hies** haɪz
hierarch 'haɪˌʲr ɑːk ‖ -ɑːrk **~s** s

hierarchic ˌ(ˌ)haɪˌʲr 'ɑːk ɪk ‖ -'rɑːrk- **~al** ʲl **~ally**
ʲl i
hierarch|y 'haɪˌʲr ɑːk |i ‖ -ɑːrk |i **~ies** iz
hieratic ˌ(ˌ)haɪˌʲr 'ræt ɪk ‖ -'ræt̬ ɪk **~al** ʲl **~ally**
ʲl i
hierocratic ˌhaɪˌʲr əʊ 'kræt ɪk ◂ ‖ -ə 'kræt̬ ɪk ◂
~al ʲl **~ally** ʲl i
hieroglyph 'haɪˌʲr ə glɪf **~s** s
hieroglyphic ˌhaɪˌʲr ə 'glɪf ɪk ◂ **~al** ʲl **~ally** ʲl i
~s s
Hieronymus ˌhaɪˌʲr 'rɒn ɪm əs ˌhɪə- ‖ -'rɑːn-
hierophant 'haɪˌʲr əʊ fænt ‖ -ə- haɪ 'er ə fænt
~s s
hifalutin, hifalutin' ˌhaɪ fə 'luːt ɪn ◂ -ʲn ‖ -ʲn
hi-fi 'haɪ faɪ ˌ·'· **~s** z
Higginbotham *(i)* 'hɪg ɪn ˌbɒt əm -ən-, →-ɪm-
‖ -ˌbɑːt̬ əm, *(ii)* -ˌbɒθ əm ‖ -ˌbɑː θ əm
Higginbottom 'hɪg ɪn ˌbɒt əm -ən-, →-ɪm-
‖ -ˌbɑːt̬ əm
Higgins 'hɪg ɪnz §-ənz
higgl|e 'hɪg ʲl **~ed** d **~es** z **~ing** ɪŋ
higgledy-piggledy ˌhɪg ʲld i 'pɪg ʲld i ◂
higgler 'hɪg ʲl.ə ‖ ər **~s** z
Higgs hɪgz
-high 'haɪ haɪ — **knee-high** ˌniː 'haɪ ◂ '· ·
high haɪ **higher** 'haɪˌə ‖ 'haɪˌʲr **highest**
'haɪ ɪst əst **highs** haɪz
ˌhigh 'chair, '· · ‖ '· ·; ˌHigh 'Church; ˌHigh
Com'mission; ˌHigh Com'missioner, ˌHigh
'Court◂; ˌhigh ex'plosive; ˌhigh fi'delity;
ˌHigh 'German; ˌhigh 'horse; ˌhigh 'jinks,
'· ·; ˌhigh 'jump; ˌhigh 'jumper; 'high life;
ˌhigh 'mass; ˌhigh 'point; ˌhigh 'priest;
ˌhigh 'priestess; ˌhigh 'profile; ˌhigh
re'lief; ˌhigh 'road; ˌhigh 'school; ˌhigh
'seas; ˌhigh 'season; ˌHigh 'Sheriff; 'high
spot; ˌhigh 'street; ˌhigh 'table; ˌhigh
'tea; ˌhigh tech'nology; ˌhigh 'tide; ˌhigh
'time; ˌhigh 'treason; ˌhigh 'water; ˌhigh
'water mark; ˌHigh 'Wycombe
Higham 'haɪˌəm — *but the place in S. Yorks. is
locally also* 'hɪk-
high-and-mighty ˌhaɪˌən 'maɪt i ◂ →-əm-
‖ -'maɪt̬ i
highball 'haɪ bɔːl ‖ -bɑːl **~s** z
highborn 'haɪ bɔːn ˌ·'· ‖ -bɔːrn
highboy 'haɪ bɔɪ **~s** z
highbrow 'haɪ braʊ **~s** z
Highbury 'haɪ bər i ‖ -ˌber i
highchair ˌhaɪ 'tʃeə ‖ 'haɪ tʃer **~s** z
high-class ˌhaɪ 'klɑːs ◂ §-'klæs ‖ -'klæs ◂
Highclere 'haɪ klɪə ‖ -klɪr
Highcliffe 'haɪ klɪf
high-definition ˌhaɪ def ə 'nɪʃ ʲn ◂ -ɪ'·-
high-density ˌhaɪ 'den^ts ət i ◂ -ɪt- ‖ -ət̬ i
high-end ˌhaɪ 'end ◂
higher 'haɪˌə ‖ 'haɪˌʲr
ˌhigher ˌedu'cation
higher-end ˌhaɪˌʲr'end ◂ ‖ ˌhaɪˌʲr-
higher-up ˌhaɪˌʲr 'ʌp ◂ ‖ ˌhaɪˌʲr-
highest 'haɪ ɪst əst
highfalutin, highfalutin' ˌhaɪ fə 'luːt ɪn ◂
-ʲn ‖ -ʲn

highfaluting ˌhaɪ fə ˈluːt ɪŋ ◂
high-five ˌhaɪ ˈfaɪv
high-flier, high-flyer ˌhaɪ ˈflaɪˌə ‖ -ˈflaɪˌʳr ~s z
high-flown ˌhaɪ ˈfləʊn ◂ ‖ -ˈfloʊn ◂
  ˌhigh-flown ˈlanguage
high-flying ˌhaɪ ˈflaɪ ɪŋ ◂
Highgate ˈhaɪ geɪt -gɪt, -gət
high-grade ˌhaɪ ˈgreɪd ◂
Highgrove ˈhaɪ grəʊv ‖ -groʊv
high-handed ˌhaɪ ˈhænd ɪd ◂ -əd ~ly li ~ness
  nəs nɪs
high-|hat ˈhaɪ |hæt -hats hæts -hatted
  hæt ɪd -əd ‖ hæt̬ əd ~hatting hæt ɪŋ
  ‖ hæt̬ ɪŋ
high-heeled ˌhaɪ ˈhiːʳld ◂
high-keyed ˌhaɪ ˈkiːd ◂
highland, H~ ˈhaɪl ənd ~s z
  ˌHighland ˈfling
highlander, H~ ˈhaɪl ənd ə ‖ -ʳr ~s z
high-level ˌhaɪ ˈlev ᵊl ◂
high|light ˈhaɪ |laɪt ~lighted laɪt ɪd -əd
  ‖ laɪt̬ əd ~lighting laɪt ɪŋ ‖ laɪt̬ ɪŋ ~lights
  laɪts
highlighter ˈhaɪ laɪt ə ‖ -laɪt̬ ʳr ~s z
highly ˈhaɪ li
highly-strung ˌhaɪ li ˈstrʌŋ ◂
high-maintenance ˌhaɪ ˈmeɪnt ən‿ənᵗs ◂ ‖ -ᵊn‿
high-minded ˌhaɪ ˈmaɪnd ɪd ◂ -əd ~ly li ~ness
  nəs nɪs
highness ‘quality of being high’ ˈhaɪ nəs -nɪs
Highness title ˈhaɪn əs -ɪs ~es ɪz əz
high-octane ˌhaɪ ˈɒkt eɪn ◂ ‖ -ˈɑːkt-
high-pass ˌhaɪ ˈpɑːs ◂ §-ˈpæs ‖ -ˈpæs ◂
high-performance ˌhaɪ pə ˈfɔːm ənᵗs ◂
  ‖ -pʳr ˈfɔːrm-
high-pitched ˌhaɪ ˈpɪtʃt ◂
high-powered ˌhaɪ ˈpaʊ‿əd ◂ ‖ -ˈpaʊ‿ʳrd
high-pressure ˌhaɪ ˈpreʃ ə ◂ ‖ -ʳr ◂
high-priced ˌhaɪ ˈpraɪst ◂
high-principled ˌhaɪ ˈprɪnᵗs ɪp ᵊld ◂ -əp-
high-profile ˌhaɪ ˈprəʊf aɪʳl ◂ ‖ -ˈproʊf-
high-ranking ˌhaɪ ˈræŋk ɪŋ ◂
high-res ˌhaɪ ˈrez ◂
high-ris|e ˈhaɪ raɪz ˌ·ˈ·◂ ~es ɪz əz
high-risk ˌhaɪ ˈrɪsk ◂
high-sounding ˌhaɪ ˈsaʊnd ɪŋ ◂
high-speed ˌhaɪ ˈspiːd ◂
  ˌhigh-speed ˈtrain
high-spirited ˌhaɪ ˈspɪr ɪt ɪd ◂ §-ət-, -əd
  ‖ -ət̬ əd ◂ ~ly li ~ness nəs nɪs
high-strung ˌhaɪ ˈstrʌŋ ◂
hightail ˈhaɪ teɪʳl ~ed d ~ing ɪŋ ~s z
high-tech ˌhaɪ ˈtek ◂
high-tension ˌhaɪ ˈtenᵗʃ ᵊn ◂
high-toned ˌhaɪ ˈtəʊnd ◂ ‖ -ˈtoʊnd ◂
high-top ˈhaɪ tɒp ‖ -tɑːp ~s s
high-up n ˈhaɪ ʌp ~s s
high-voltage ˌhaɪ ˈvəʊlt ɪdʒ ◂ →‖-ˈvɒʊlt-
  ‖ -ˈvoʊlt-
highway ˈhaɪ weɪ ~s z
  ˌHighway ˈCode
highway|man ˈhaɪ weɪ |mən ~men mən

high-wire ˌhaɪ ˈwaɪ‿ə ◂ ‖ ˈhaɪ waɪʳr
high-yield ˌhaɪ ˈjiːʳld ◂ ~er/s ə/z ◂ ‖ ʳr/z ~ing
  ɪŋ ◂
hijab hɪ ˈdʒɑːb —Arabic [hɪ dʒɑːb]
hijack ˈhaɪ dʒæk ~ed t ~er/s ə/z ‖ ʳr/z ~ing
  ɪŋ ~s s
hijinks ˈhaɪ dʒɪŋks
hike haɪk hiked haɪkt hikes haɪks hiking
  ˈhaɪk ɪŋ
hiker ˈhaɪk ə ‖ -ʳr ~s z
hila ˈhaɪl ə
Hilaire hɪ ˈleə ˈhɪl eə ‖ -ˈleʳr —Fr [i lɛːʁ]
hilar ˈhaɪl ə ‖ -ʳr
hilarious hɪ ˈleər i‿əs hə- ‖ -ˈler- haɪ-, -ˈlær- ~ly
  li ~ness nəs nɪs
hilarity hɪ ˈlær ət i hə-, -ɪt- ‖ -ət̬ i -ˈler-
Hilary ˈhɪl ər i
Hilbert ˈhɪlb ət ‖ -ʳrt —Ger [ˈhɪl bɐt], Czech
  [ˈfiil bert]
Hilbre ˈhɪlb ri
Hilda ˈhɪld ə
Hildebrand ˈhɪld ə brænd
Hildegarde ˈhɪld ə gɑːd ‖ -gɑːrd
Hildenborough ˈhɪld ən ˌbʌr ə -bər‿ə
  ‖ -ˌbɝː oʊ
Hilfiger tdmk ˈhɪlf ɪg ə ‖ -ʳr
hill, Hill hɪl hills hɪlz
Hillary ˈhɪl ər i
hillbill|y ˈhɪl ˌbɪl |i ~ies iz
Hillel ˈhɪl el -əl; hɪ ˈleʳl
Hiller ˈhɪl ə ‖ -ʳr
Hillery ˈhɪl ər i
Hillhead ˌhɪl ˈhed
Hilliard ˈhɪl i‿əd -ɑːd ‖ ʳrd -ɑːrd
Hillingdon ˈhɪl ɪŋ dən
Hillman ˈhɪl mən
hillock ˈhɪl ək ~s s
Hills hɪlz
Hillsboro, Hillsborough ˈhɪlz bər‿ə §-ˌbʌr ə
  ‖ -ˌbɝː oʊ
hillside ˈhɪl saɪd ˌ·ˈ· ~s z
hilltop ˈhɪl tɒp ‖ -tɑːp ~s s
hill-walk|er ˈhɪl ˌwɔːk| ə ‖ -ʳr -ˌwɑːk- ~ers əz
  ‖ ʳrz ~ing ɪŋ
hilly ˈhɪl i
Hilo place in Hawaii ˈhiːl əʊ ‖ -oʊ
hilt hɪlt hilted ˈhɪlt ɪd -əd hilts hɪlts
Hilton ˈhɪlt ən
hil|um ˈhaɪl |əm ~a ə ~i aɪ ~us əs
Hilversum ˈhɪlv ə səm -sʊm ‖ -ʳr- —Dutch
  [ˈhɪl vər sʏm]
him strong form hɪm, weak forms həm, ɪm
  §həm, §əm —In the rare instances where this
  word occurs after a pause or at the beginning
  of a clause, it is always hɪm.
Himalaya ˌhɪm ə ˈleɪ ə hɪ ˈmɑːl i‿ə —Hindi
  [hɪ mɑː ləj] ~s z
Himalayan ˌhɪm ə ˈleɪ ən hɪ ˈmɑːl i‿ən
Himmler ˈhɪm lə ‖ -lʳr —Ger [ˈhɪm lɐ]
himself strong form hɪm ˈself §həm-, weak form
  ɪm- §əm- —The weak form is not used at the
  beginning of a sentence or clause.
Himyaritic ˌhɪm jə ˈrɪt ɪk ◂ ‖ -ˈrɪt̬-

Hinayana ˌhiːn ə ˈjɑːn ə ˌhɪn-, -ɪ-
Hinchcliffe ˈhɪntʃ klɪf
Hinchinbrook ˈhɪntʃ ɪn brʊk →-ɪm-; -ən-, →-əm-
Hinchingbrooke ˈhɪntʃ ɪŋ brʊk
Hinchley ˈhɪntʃ li
Hinchliffe ˈhɪntʃ lɪf
Hinckley ˈhɪŋk li
hind haɪnd **hinds** haɪndz
Hind *(i)* haɪnd, *(ii)* hɪnd
hindbrain ˈhaɪnd breɪn →ˈhaɪm- **~s** z
Hinde haɪnd
Hindemith ˈhɪnd ə mɪt -mɪθ, §-məθ —*Ger* [ˈhɪn də mɪt]
Hindenburg ˈhɪnd ən bɜːg →-əm- ‖ -bɜːg —*Ger* [ˈhɪn dᵊn bʊʀk]
hinder *adj* ˈhaɪnd ə ‖ -ᵊr **~most** məʊst ‖ moʊst
hinder *v* ˈhɪnd ə ‖ -ᵊr **~ed** d **hindering** ˈhɪnd ᵊr ɪŋ **~s** z
hinderer ˈhɪnd ᵊr ə ‖ -ər **~s** z
Hindhead ˈhaɪnd hed
Hindi ˈhɪnd i -iː
Hindle ˈhɪnd ᵊl
Hindley *(i)* ˈhɪnd li, *(ii)* ˈhaɪnd li —*The town in Greater Manchester is (i). Otherwise, (ii) is more usual.*
Hindmarsh ˈhaɪnd mɑːʃ →ˈhaɪm- ‖ -mɑːrʃ
hindmost ˈhaɪnd məʊst →ˈhaɪm- ‖ -moʊst
hindquarter ˌhaɪnd ˈkwɔːt ə →ˌhaɪm-, -ˈkɔːt-, ˈ·ˌ·· ‖ ˈhaɪnd ˌkwɔːrt̬ ᵊr -ˌkwɔːt̬ ᵊr **~s** z
hindrance ˈhɪndr ənᵗs **~es** ɪz əz
hindsight ˈhaɪnd saɪt
Hindu ˌhɪn ˈduː ◄ ˈ· · ‖ ˈhɪn duː **~s** z ˌHindu ˈKush kʊʃ kuːʃ
Hinduism ˈhɪn du ˌɪz əm ˌ·ˈduː-
Hindustani ˌhɪn du ˈstɑːn i ◄ ‖ -ˈstæn i ◄ -ˈstɑːn i
Hine haɪn
Hines haɪnz
hinge hɪndʒ **hinged** hɪndʒd **hinges** ˈhɪndʒ ɪz -əz **hinging** ˈhɪndʒ ɪŋ
hinn|y ˈhɪn |i **~ied** id **~ies** iz **~ying** i ɪŋ
Hinshelwood ˈhɪnʃ ᵊl wʊd
hint hɪnt **hinted** ˈhɪnt ɪd -əd ‖ ˈhɪnt̬ əd **hinting** ˈhɪnt ɪŋ ‖ ˈhɪnt̬ ɪŋ **hints** hɪnts
hinterland ˈhɪnt ə lænd -lənd ‖ ˈhɪnt̬ ᵊr-
Hinton ˈhɪnt ən
hip hɪp **hipped** hɪpt **hipper** ˈhɪp ə ‖ -ᵊr **hippest** ˈhɪp ɪst -əst ˈhip flask; ˈhip joint; ˌhip ˈpocket
hip|bath ˈhɪp |bɑːθ §-bæθ ‖ -|bæθ **~baths** bɑːðz §bɑːθs, §bæðz, §bæθz ‖ bæðz bæθs
hipbone ˈhɪp bəʊn ‖ -boʊn **~s** z
hip-hop ˈhɪp hɒp ‖ -hɑːp
hiphuggers ˈhɪp ˌhʌg əz ‖ -ᵊrz
hipness ˈhɪp nəs -nɪs
Hipparchus hɪ ˈpɑːk əs ‖ -ˈpɑːrk-
hippeastrum ˌhɪp i ˈæs trəm **~s** z
hipped hɪpt
Hippias ˈhɪp i æs -iˌəs
hippie ˈhɪp i **~s** z
hippo, Hippo ˈhɪp əʊ ‖ -oʊ **~s** z
hippocamp|us ˌhɪp ə ˈkæmp |əs **~i** aɪ

Hippocrates hɪ ˈpɒk rə tiːz ‖ -ˈpɑːk-
Hippocratic ˌhɪp əʊ ˈkræt ɪk ◄ ‖ -ə ˈkræt̬ ɪk ◄ ˌHippoˌcratic ˈoath
Hippocrene ˈhɪp əʊ kriːn ˌ· ·ˈkriːn iː, -i ‖ -ə-
Hippodrome, h~ ˈhɪp ə drəʊm ‖ -droʊm **~s** z
Hippolyta hɪ ˈpɒl ɪt ə -ət- ‖ -ˈpɑːl ət̬ ə
Hippolyte hɪ ˈpɒl ɪ tiː -ə- ‖ -ˈpɑːl-
Hippolytus hɪ ˈpɒl ɪt əs -ət- ‖ -ˈpɑːl ət̬ əs
hippopot|amus ˌhɪp ə ˈpɒt |əm əs ‖ -ˈpɑːt̬- **~ami** ə maɪ **~amuses** əm əs ɪz -əz
hipp|y ˈhɪp |i **~ies** iz
hipster ˈhɪpst ə ‖ -ᵊr **~s** z
hiragana ˌhɪər ə ˈgɑːn ə ˌhɪr-, ˌhiː rə- —*Jp* [çi ˌra ˈŋa na, -ˈga-, -ŋa-]
Hiram ˈhaɪᵊr əm
hircine ˈhɜːs aɪn -ɪn, §-ᵊn ‖ ˈhɜːs-
Hird hɜːd ‖ hɜːd
hire ˈhaɪ ə ‖ ˈhaɪ ᵊr **hired** ˈhaɪ əd ‖ ˈhaɪ ᵊrd **hires** ˈhaɪ əz ‖ ˈhaɪ ᵊrz **hiring/s** ˈhaɪ ᵊr ɪŋ/z ‖ ˈhaɪ ᵊr ɪŋ/z ˌhire ˈpurchase
hireling ˈhaɪ ə lɪŋ ‖ ˈhaɪ ᵊr- **~s** z
Hirnant ˈhɜː nænt ‖ ˈhɜː- —*Welsh* [ˈhir nant]
Hirohito ˌhɪr əʊ ˈhiːt əʊ ‖ -oʊ ˈhiːt oʊ —*Jp* [çi ˈro çi to]
Hiroshima hɪ ˈrɒʃ ɪm ə hə-, -əm-; ˌhɪr ə ˈʃiːm ə, -ɒ- ‖ ˌhɪr oʊ ˈʃiːm ə hə ˈroʊʃ əm ə —*Jp* [çi ˌro çi ma]
Hirst hɜːst ‖ hɜːst
hirsute ˈhɜːs juːt -uːt; hɜː ˈsjuːt, -ˈsuːt ‖ ˈhɜːs uːt **~ness** nəs nɪs
hirundine hɪ ˈrʌnd aɪn -ɪn, §-ən
Hirwain, Hirwaun ˈhɪə waɪn ‖ ˈhɪr- —*locally also* ˈhɜː wɪn —*Welsh* [ˈhir waɪn]
his *strong form* hɪz, *weak forms* hɪz, ɪz §həz, §əz —*The forms* ɪz, §əz *are not used at the beginning of a sentence or clause.*
Hiscock *(i)* ˈhɪs kɒk ‖ -kɑːk, *(ii)* -kəʊ ‖ -koʊ
Hislop ˈhɪz ləp -lɒp ‖ -lɑːp
his'n'hers ˌhɪz ᵊn ˈhɜːz ‖ -ˈhɜːz
Hispanic, h~ hɪ ˈspæn ɪk **~s** s
Hispanicism hɪ ˈspæn ɪ ˌsɪz əm -ə- **~s** z
Hispaniola ˌhɪsp æn i ˈəʊl ə hɪ ˌspæn-; ˌhɪsp æn ˈjəʊl ə ‖ ˌhɪsp ən ˈjoʊl ə
Hispano- hɪ ˈspæn əʊ -ˈspɑːn-; ˈhɪsp ən- ‖ -oʊ
Hispano-Suiza *tdmk* hɪ ˌspæn əʊ ˈswiːz ə ‖ -oʊ-
hispid ˈhɪsp ɪd §-əd
hiss hɪs **hissed** hɪst **hisser/s** ˈhɪs ə/z ‖ -ᵊr/z **hisses** ˈhɪs ɪz -əz **hissing** ˈhɪs ɪŋ
hissy fit ˈhɪs i fɪt **~s** s
hist hɪst —*or e.g.* [sːt]
histamine ˈhɪst ə miːn -mɪn
histo- *comb. form* *with stress-neutral suffix* ˌhɪst əʊ ‖ -oʊ — **histocompatible** ˌhɪst əʊ kəm ˈpæt əb ᵊl ◄ -ɪb ᵊl ‖ -oʊ kəm ˈpæt̬- *with stress-imposing suffix* hɪ ˈstɒ + ‖ -ˈstɑː + — **histolysis** hɪ ˈstɒl əs ɪs -ɪs-, §-əs ‖ -ˈstɑːl-
histogram ˈhɪst ə græm **~s** z
histological ˌhɪst ə ˈlɒdʒ ɪk ᵊl ◄ ‖ -ˈlɑːdʒ- **~ly** i
histology hɪ ˈstɒl ədʒ i ‖ -ˈstɑːl-
Histon ˈhɪst ən

historian hɪ ˈstɔːr i_ən ‖ -ˈstoʊr- —*sometimes without h when after the indefinite article* an
~**s** z

HISTORIC

94% with h
6% without h

BrE

historic hɪ ˈstɒr ɪk ‖ -ˈstɔːr ɪk -ˈstɑːr-
—*sometimes without h when after the indefinite article* an — *Preference poll, BrE: with h 94%, without h 6%.*
historical hɪ ˈstɒr ɪk ᵊl ‖ -ˈstɔːr- -ˈstɑːr-
—*sometimes without h when after the indefinite article* an ~**ly** i
historicism hɪ ˈstɒr ɪ ˌsɪz əm -ə- ‖ -ˈstɔːr-
-ˈstɑːr-
historicity ˌhɪst ə ˈrɪs ət i ˌˈɒ-, -ɪt i ‖ -ət̬ i
historie... —*see* **history**
historiographer hɪ ˌstɒr i ˈɒgr əf ə ə -ˌstɔːr-;
ˌhɪst ɔːr-, -ˌɒr- ‖ -ˌstɔːr i ˈɑːg rəf ᵊr ~**s** z
historiography hɪ ˌstɒr i ˈɒgr əf i -ˌstɔːr-;
ˌhɪst ɔːr-, -ˌɒr- ‖ -ˌstɔːr i ˈɑːg-
his|tory ˈhɪs |tri ˈ· |tər i ~**tories** triz tər iz
histrionic ˌhɪs tri ˈɒn ɪk ◄ ‖ -ˈɑːn ɪk ◄ ~**al** ᵊl
~**ally** ᵊl i ~**s** s
hit hɪt **hits** hɪts **hitting** ˈhɪt ɪŋ ‖ ˈhɪt̬ ɪŋ
ˈhit ˌlist; ˈhit ˌman; ˈhit paˌrade
Hitachi *tdmk* hɪ ˈtɑːtʃ i -ˈtætʃ i —*Jp* [ˈçi ta tɕi]
hit-and-miss ˌhɪt ᵊn ˈmɪs ◄ -ᵊnd-
hit-and-run ˌhɪt ᵊn ˈrʌn ◄ -ᵊnd-
hitch, Hitch hɪtʃ **hitched** hɪtʃt **hitches** ˈhɪtʃ ɪz
-əz **hitching** ˈhɪtʃ ɪŋ
ˈhitching post
Hitchcock ˈhɪtʃ kɒk ‖ -kɑːk
Hitchens ˈhɪtʃ ɪnz -ənz
hitchhik|e ˈhɪtʃ haɪk ~**ed** t ~**er/s** ə/z ‖ ᵊr/z
~**es** s ~**ing** ɪŋ
Hitchin ˈhɪtʃ ɪn §-ən
Hite haɪt
hitech, hi-tech ˌhaɪ ˈtek ◄
hither, H~ ˈhɪð ə ‖ -ᵊr
ˌHither ˈGreen
hitherto ˌhɪð ə ˈtuː ◄ ‖ -ᵊr-
Hitler ˈhɪt lə ‖ -lᵊr —*Ger* [ˈhɪt lɐ]
Hitlerian hɪt ˈlɪər i_ən ‖ -ˈlɪr-
Hitlerism ˈhɪt lər ˌɪz əm ‖ ˈhɪt lᵊr-
hi-top ˈhaɪ tɒp ‖ -tɑːp ~**s** s
hit-or-miss ˌhɪt ɔː ˈmɪs ◄ ‖ ˌhɪt̬ ᵊr-
hitt... —*see* **hit**
hitter ˈhɪt ə ‖ ˈhɪt̬ ᵊr ~**s** z
Hittite ˈhɪt aɪt ~**s** s
HIV ˌeɪtʃ aɪ ˈviː §ˌheɪtʃ-
ˌHIˈV inˌfection; ˌHIˌV ˈpositive
hive haɪv **hived** haɪvd **hives** haɪvz **hiving**
ˈhaɪv ɪŋ
hiway ˈhaɪ weɪ ~**s** z
Hixon ˈhɪks ᵊn

hiya ˈhaɪ jə
Hizbollah ˌhɪz bɒ ˈlɑː ‖ -bə- ˌhez-
Hluhluwe ʃlu ˈʃluː weɪ ɬu ˈɬuː- —*Zulu*
[ɬu ˈɬuː wɛ]
h'm m, hm —*or e.g.* [mm̩m]
HMO ˌeɪtʃ em ˈəʊ ‖ -ˈoʊ ~**s** z
HMS ˌeɪtʃ em ˈes ◄ △ ˌheɪtʃ-
ˌHMS ˈHood
ho həʊ ‖ hoʊ
Hoad həʊd ‖ hoʊd
Hoadley, Hoadly ˈhəʊd li ‖ ˈhoʊd-
hoag|ie, hoag|y ˈhəʊg |i ‖ ˈhoʊg |i ~**ies** iz
hoar, Hoar hɔː ‖ hɔːr hour
hoard hɔːd ‖ hɔːrd hourd **hoarded** ˈhɔːd ɪd -əd
‖ ˈhɔːrd əd ˈhourd- **hoarding** ˈhɔːd ɪŋ
‖ ˈhɔːrd ɪŋ ˈhourd- **hoards** hɔːdz ‖ hɔːrdz
hourdz
hoarder ˈhɔːd ə ‖ ˈhɔːrd ᵊr ˈhourd- ~**s** z
hoarding ˈhɔːd ɪŋ ‖ ˈhɔːrd ɪŋ ˈhourd- ~**s** z
Hoare hɔː ‖ hɔːr hour
hoar-frost ˌhɔː ˈfrɒst -ˈfrɔːst, ˈ· · ‖ ˈhɔːr frɔːst
ˈhour-, -frɑːst
hoarse hɔːs ‖ hɔːrs hours **hoarsely** ˈhɔːs li
‖ ˈhɔːrs li ˈhours- **hoarseness** ˈhɔːs nəs -nɪs
‖ ˈhɔːrs- ˈhours- **hoarser** ˈhɔːs ə ‖ ˈhɔːrs ᵊr
ˈhours- **hoarsest** ˈhɔːs ɪst -əst ‖ ˈhɔːrs əst
ˈhours-
hoar|y ˈhɔːr |i ‖ ˈhour- ~**ier** i_ə ‖ i_ᵊr ~**iest** i_ɪst
i_əst ~**iness** i nəs i nɪs
hoatzin həʊ ˈæts ɪn ˌwaɪt ˈsiːn ‖ hoʊ- ~**s** z
hoax həʊks ‖ hoʊks **hoaxed** həʊkst ‖ hoʊkst
hoaxer/s ˈhəʊks ə/z ‖ ˈhoʊks ᵊr/z **hoaxes**
ˈhəʊks ɪz -əz ‖ ˈhoʊks əz **hoaxing** ˈhəʊks ɪŋ
‖ ˈhoʊks ɪŋ
hob hɒb ‖ hɑːb **hobs** hɒbz ‖ hɑːbz
Hobart *(i)* ˈhəʊb ɑːt ‖ ˈhoʊb ɑːrt, *(ii)* -ət ‖ -ᵊrt,
(iii) ˈhʌb ət ‖ -ᵊrt —*The place in Tasmania is (i), that in IN (ii); the 17th-century judge Sir Henry H~ is believed to have been (iii).*
Hobbes hɒbz ‖ hɑːbz
hobbit ˈhɒb ɪt §-ət ‖ ˈhɑːb- ~**s** s
hobbl|e ˈhɒb ᵊl ‖ ˈhɑːb- ~**ed** d ~**es** z ~**ing** ɪŋ
hobbledehoy ˌhɒb ᵊl dɪ ˈhɔɪ ˈ· · · ·
‖ ˈhɑːb ᵊl dɪ hɔɪ ~**s** z
Hobbs hɒbz ‖ hɑːbz
hobb|y ˈhɒb |i ‖ ˈhɑːb |i ~**ies** iz
hobbyhors|e ˈhɒb i hɔːs ‖ ˈhɑːb i hɔːrs ~**es** ɪz
əz
hobbyist ˈhɒb i ɪst §-əst ‖ ˈhɑːb- ~**s** s
Hobday, h~ ˈhɒb deɪ ‖ ˈhɑːb-
hobgoblin ₍ₐ₎hɒb ˈgɒb lɪn §-lən, ˈ· ˌ· ·
‖ ˈhɑːb ˌgɑːb- ~**s** z
Hobley ˈhəʊb li ‖ ˈhoʊb-
hobnail ˈhɒb neᵊl ‖ ˈhɑːb- ~**ed** d ~**s** z
hobnob ˈhɒb nɒb ₍ₐ₎ˈ·ˈ· ‖ ˈhɑːb nɑːb ~**bed** d
~**bing** ɪŋ ~**s** z
hobo ˈhəʊb əʊ ‖ ˈhoʊb oʊ ~**es**, ~**s** z
Hoboken ˈhəʊ bəʊk ən ‖ ˈhoʊ boʊk- —*Dutch*
[ˈhoː boː kən]
Hobsbawm ˈhɒbz bɔːm ‖ ˈhɑːbz- -bɑːm
Hobson ˈhɒb sᵊn ‖ ˈhɑːb- ~'**s** z
ˌHobson's ˈchoice

Hobson-Jobson ˌhɒb sᵊn 'dʒɒb sᵊn
‖ ˌhɑːb sᵊn 'dʒɑːb sᵊn
Ho Chi Minh ˌhəʊ ˌtʃi: 'mɪn ◄ ‖ ˌhoʊ-
—*Vietnamese* [³ho ²tʃi ¹miɲ]
ˌHo Chi ˌMinh 'City
Ho Chi Minh ˌhəʊ tʃi: 'mɪn ◄ ‖ ˌhoʊ-
ˌHo Chi ˌMinh 'City
hock hɒk ‖ hɑːk **hocked** hɒkt ‖ hɑːkt **hocking**
'hɒk ɪŋ ‖ 'hɑːk ɪŋ **hocks** hɒks ‖ hɑːks
hockey 'hɒk i ‖ 'hɑːk i
'hockey stick
Hockney 'hɒk ni ‖ 'hɑːk- ~**s** ~'**s** z
hocus-pocus ˌhəʊk əs 'pəʊk əs
‖ ˌhoʊk əs 'poʊk əs
hod hɒd ‖ hɑːd **hods** hɒdz ‖ hɑːdz
Hodder 'hɒd ə ‖ 'hɑːd ᵊr
Hoddesdon 'hɒdz dən 'hɒd ɪz dən, -əz-
‖ 'hɑːdz-
Hoddinott 'hɒd ɪ nɒt -ə- ‖ 'hɑːd ᵊn ɑːt
Hoddle 'hɒd ᵊl ‖ 'hɑːd-
Hodge hɒdʒ ‖ hɑːdʒ
hodge-podge 'hɒdʒ pɒdʒ ‖ 'hɑːdʒ pɑːdʒ
Hodges 'hɒdʒ ɪz -əz ‖ 'hɑːdʒ-
Hodgkin 'hɒdʒ kɪn §-kən ‖ 'hɑːdʒ- ~'**s** z
'Hodgkin's di,sease
Hodgkinson 'hɒdʒ kɪn sən §-kən- ‖ 'hɑːdʒ-
Hodgson 'hɒdʒ sᵊn ‖ 'hɑːdʒ-
hodometer hɒ 'dɒm ɪt ə -ət- ‖ hoʊ 'dɑːm ət̬ ᵊr
Hodson 'hɒd sᵊn ‖ 'hɑːd-
hoe, Hoe həʊ ‖ hoʊ **hoed** həʊd ‖ hoʊd
hoeing 'həʊ ɪŋ ‖ 'hoʊ ɪŋ **hoes** həʊz ‖ hoʊz
Hoechst hɜːkst ‖ hoʊkst —*Ger* Höchst [høːçst]
hoedown 'həʊ daʊn ‖ 'hoʊ- ~**s** z
hoer 'həʊ ə ‖ 'hoʊ ᵊr ~**s** z
Hoey 'həʊ i ‖ 'hoʊ i
Hoffa 'hɒf ə ‖ 'hɑːf ə
Hoffman, Hoffmann 'hɒf mən ‖ 'hɑːf-
Hoffnung 'hɒf nʊŋ ‖ 'hɑːf-
Hofmannsthal 'hɒf mənz tɑːl ‖ 'hoʊf- —*Ger*
['hoːf mans taːl]
Hofmeister 'hɒf ˌmaɪst ə ‖ 'hɑːf ˌmaɪst ᵊr
—*Ger* ['hoːf ˌmai stɐ]
hog hɒg ‖ hɔːg hɑːg **hogged** hɒgd ‖ hɔːgd
hɑːgd **hogging** 'hɒg ɪŋ ‖ 'hɔːg ɪŋ 'hɑːg ɪŋ
hogs hɒgz ‖ hɔːgz hɑːgz
Hogan, hogan 'həʊg ən ‖ 'hoʊg- ~**s** z
Hogarth (i) 'həʊ gɑːθ ‖ 'hoʊ gɑːrθ,
(ii) 'hɒg ət ‖ 'hɑːg ᵊrt
Hogarthian həʊ 'gɑːθ iˌən ‖ hoʊ 'gɑːrθ- ~**s** z
Hogben 'hɒg bən ‖ 'hɔːg- 'hɑːg-
Hogg, hogg hɒg ‖ hɔːg hɑːg
hogg... —*see* **hog**
Hoggart 'hɒg ət ‖ 'hɔːg ᵊrt 'hɑːg-
hogget 'hɒg ɪt §-ət ‖ 'hɔːg- 'hɑːg- ~**s** s
hoggish 'hɒg ɪʃ ‖ 'hɔːg- 'hɑːg- ~**ly** li ~**ness**
nəs nɪs
Hogmanay 'hɒg mə neɪ ˌ· ·' · ‖ 'hɑːg-
hogshead 'hɒgz hed ‖ 'hɔːgz- 'hɑːgz- ~**s** z
hog|tie 'hɒg |taɪ ‖ 'hɔːg- 'hɑːg- ~**tied** taɪd
~**tieing**, ~**tying** taɪ ɪŋ ~**ties** taɪz
Hogwarts 'hɒg wɔːts ‖ 'hɔːg wɔːrts 'hɑːg-
hogwash 'hɒg wɒʃ ‖ 'hɔːg wɑːʃ 'hɑːg-, -wɔːʃ
hogweed 'hɒg wiːd ‖ 'hɔːg- 'hɑːg- ~**s** z

Hohenlinden ˌhəʊ ən 'lɪnd ən ‖ ˌhoʊ- '· ·ˌ · ·
—*Ger* [hoː ən 'lɪn dᵊn]
Hohenzollern ˌhəʊ ən 'zɒl ən
‖ ˌhoʊ ən ˌzɑːl ᵊrn —*Ger* [hoː ən 'tsɔl ɐn] ~**s**
z
Hohner *tdmk* 'həʊn ə ‖ 'hoʊn ᵊr —*Ger*
['hoː nɐ]
ho-ho ˌhəʊ 'həʊ ‖ ˌhoʊ 'hoʊ
ho-hum ˌhəʊ 'hʌm ‖ ˌhoʊ-
hoick, hoik hɔɪk **hoicked, hoiked** hɔɪkt
hoicking, hoiking 'hɔɪk ɪŋ **hoicks, hoiks**
hɔɪks
hoi polloi ˌhɔɪ pə 'lɔɪ -pɒ-, -'pɒl ɔɪ
hoisin hɔɪ 'sɪn ◄ '· ·
hoist hɔɪst **hoisted** 'hɔɪst ɪd -əd **hoisting**
'hɔɪst ɪŋ **hoists** hɔɪsts
hoity-toity ˌhɔɪt i 'tɔɪt i ‖ ˌhɔɪt̬ i 'tɔɪt̬ i
hok|ey 'həʊk |i ‖ 'hoʊk |i ~**ier** iˌə ‖ iˌᵊr ~**iest**
i ɪst iˌəst ~**eyness**, ~**iness** i nəs i nɪs
ˌhokey 'cokey 'kəʊk i ‖ 'koʊk i
hoki 'həʊk i ‖ 'hoʊk i
Hokkaido hɒ 'kaɪd əʊ ‖ hoʊ 'kaɪd oʊ hɑː-
—*Jp* [hok 'kai doo]
Hokonui, h~ ˌhəʊk ə 'nuː i ‖ ˌhoʊk-
hokum 'həʊk əm ‖ 'hoʊk-
Hokusai 'hɒk u saɪ ‖ 'hoʊk- —*Jp* ['ho kɯ sai]
Holbeach, Holbech, Holbeche 'hɒl biːtʃ
'hɑːl- ‖ 'hoʊl-
Holbeck 'hɒl bek 'həʊl- ‖ 'hoʊl-
Holbein 'hɒl baɪn ‖ 'hoʊl- —*Ger* ['hɔl bain]
~**s** z
Holborn, Holborne 'həʊb ən 'həʊlb-
‖ 'hoʊl bɔːrn —*as a family name, also*
'hɒlb-; *the place in Scotland is*
həʊl 'bɔːn ‖ hoʊl 'bɔːrn
Holbrook, Holbrooke 'həʊl brʊk →'hɒʊl-
‖ 'hoʊl-
Holby 'həʊl bi →'hɒʊl- ‖ 'hoʊl-
Holcomb, Holcombe 'həʊl kəm →'hɒʊl-;
'hɒl-, 'həʊ- ‖ 'hoʊl-
hold həʊld →hɒʊld ‖ hoʊld **held** held **holding**
'həʊld ɪŋ →'hɒʊld- ‖ 'hoʊld ɪŋ **holds** həʊldz
→hɒʊldz ‖ hoʊldz
'holding ˌcompany; 'holding opeˌration;
'holding ˌpattern
holdall 'həʊld ɔːl →'hɒʊld- ‖ 'hoʊld- -ɑːl ~**s** z
Holden, h~ 'həʊld ən →'hɒʊld- ‖ 'hoʊld-
holder, H~ 'həʊld ə →'hɒʊld- ‖ 'hoʊld ᵊr ~**s** z
-holder ˌhəʊld ə →ˌhɒʊld- ‖ ˌhoʊld ᵊr —
kettle-holder 'ket ᵊl ˌhəʊld ə →-ˌhɒʊld-
‖ 'ket̬ ᵊl ˌhoʊld ᵊr
Holderness 'həʊld ə nəs →'hɒʊld-, -nɪs
‖ 'hoʊld ᵊr-
holdfast 'həʊld fɑːst →'hɒʊld-, §-fæst
‖ 'hoʊld fæst ~**s** s
holding 'həʊld ɪŋ →'hɒʊld- ‖ 'hoʊld ɪŋ ~**s** z
holdover 'həʊld ˌəʊv ə →'hɒʊld-
‖ 'hoʊld ˌoʊv ᵊr ~**s** z
holdup 'həʊld ʌp →'hɒʊld- ‖ 'hoʊld- ~**s** s
hole həʊl →hɒʊl ‖ hoʊl **holed** həʊld →hɒʊld
‖ hoʊld (= *hold*) **holes** həʊlz →hɒʊlz ‖ hoʊlz
holing 'həʊl ɪŋ →'hɒʊl- ‖ 'hoʊl ɪŋ
ˌhole in 'one

hole-and-corner ˌhəʊl ən ˈkɔːn ə →ˌhɒʊl-,
-ənd-, →-əŋ- ‖ ˌhoʊl ən ˈkɔːrn ᵊr
hole-in-the-wall ˌhəʊl ɪn ðə ˈwɔːl →ˌhɒʊl-
‖ ˌhoʊl- -ˈwɑːl
holey ˈhəʊl i →ˈhɒʊl- ‖ ˈhoʊl i
Holford ˈhəʊl fəd →ˈhɒʊl-, ˈhɒl- ‖ ˈhoʊl fᵊrd
holi... —see **holy**
holiday, H~ ˈhɒl ə deɪ -ɪ-, -di ‖ ˈhɑːl- **~ed** d
~ing ɪŋ **~s** z
ˌholiday ˈcamp; ˌHoliday ˈInn *tdmk*
holidaymaker ˈhɒl ə deɪ ˌmeɪk ə ˈ·ɪ-, ˈ· ·di-
‖ ˈhɑːl ə deɪ ˌmeɪk ᵊr **~s** z
holier-than-thou ˌhəʊl i ə ðən ˈðaʊ ◂
‖ ˌhoʊl iᵊr-
holiness, H~ ˈhəʊl i nəs -nɪs ‖ ˈhoʊl-
Holinshed ˈhɒl ɪn ʃed ‖ ˈhɑːl- —*This is the
usual pronunciation for the 16th-c. chronicler,
though he may well actually have been
-ɪnz hed.*
holism ˈhəʊl ˌɪz əm →ˈhɒʊl-, ˈhɒl- ‖ ˈhoʊl-
holistic həʊ ˈlɪst ɪk hɒ- ‖ hoʊ- **~ally** ᵊl i
Holland, h~ ˈhɒl ənd ‖ ˈhɑːl- —*Dutch*
[ˈhɔl ɑnt]
hollandaise ˌhɒl ən ˈdeɪz ◂ ‖ ˌhɑːl- ˈ···
ˌhollandaise ˈsauce, ‖ ˌ·· ˈ·, ˈ··· ·
holl|er ˈhɒl |ə ‖ ˈhɑːl |ᵊr **~ered** əd ‖ ᵊrd
~ering ər ɪŋ **~ers** əz ‖ ᵊrz
Holles ˈhɒl ɪs §-əs ‖ ˈhɑːl-
Hollick ˈhɒl ɪk ‖ ˈhɑːl-
Holliday ˈhɒl ə deɪ -ɪ-, -di ‖ ˈhɑːl-
Hollie ˈhɒl i ‖ ˈhɑːl i
Hollinghurst ˈhɒl ɪŋ hɜːst ‖ ˈhɑːl ɪŋ hɜːst
Hollingsworth ˈhɒl ɪŋz wɜːθ -wəθ
‖ ˈhɑːl ɪŋz wɜːθ
Hollins ˈhɒl ɪnz §-ənz ‖ ˈhɑːl-
Hollis ˈhɒl ɪs §-əs ‖ ˈhɑːl-
hollow ˈhɒl əʊ ‖ ˈhɑːl oʊ **~ed** d **~ing** ɪŋ **~ly** li
~ness nəs nɪs **~s** z
Holloway ˈhɒl ə weɪ ‖ ˈhɑːl-
hollowed-out ˌhɒl əʊd ˈaʊt ◂ ‖ ˌhɑːl-
hollowware ˈhɒl əʊ weə ‖ ˈhɑːl oʊ wer -wær
holl|y, Holly ˈhɒl |i ‖ ˈhɑːl |i **~ies** iz
hollyhock ˈhɒl i hɒk ‖ ˈhɑːl i hɑːk -hɔːk **~s** s
Hollywood ˈhɒl i wʊd ‖ ˈhɑːl-
ˌHollywood ˈstars
holm həʊm ‖ hoʊm (= *home*) **holms** həʊmz
‖ hoʊmz
Holm həʊm §həʊlm ‖ hoʊm hoʊlm
Holman ˈhəʊl mən →ˈhɒʊl- ‖ ˈhoʊl-
Holme həʊm §həʊlm ‖ hoʊm hoʊlm
Holmes həʊmz §həʊlmz ‖ hoʊmz hoʊlmz
Holmesdale ˈhəʊmz deɪᵊl ‖ ˈhoʊmz-
Holmfirth ˌhəʊm ˈfɜːθ ‖ ˌhoʊm ˈfɜːθ
holmium ˈhəʊlm i əm →ˈhɒʊlm-, ˈhɒlm-
‖ ˈhoʊlm-
holm-oak ˈhəʊm əʊk ˌ·ˈ· ‖ ˈhoʊm oʊk **~s** s
Holmwood ˈhəʊm wʊd ‖ ˈhoʊm-
Holness ˈhəʊl nəs →ˈhɒʊl-, -nɪs, -nes ‖ ˈhoʊl-
holo- *comb. form*
with stress-neutral suffix ˌhɒl əʊ ‖ ˌhoʊl ə
ˌhɑːl ə — **holoblastic** ˌhɒl əʊ ˈblæst ɪk ◂
‖ ˌhoʊl ə- ˌhɑːl-

with stress-imposing suffix hɒ ˈlɒ+ həʊ-
‖ hoʊ ˈlɑː+ hə- — **holopathy** hɒ ˈlɒp əθ i
həʊ- ‖ hoʊ ˈlɑːp-
holocaust ˈhɒl ə kɔːst ˈhəʊl- ‖ ˈhoʊl- ˈhɑːl-,
-kɑːst **~s** s
Holocene ˈhɒl əʊ siːn ‖ ˈhoʊl ə- ˈhɑːl-
Holofernes ˌhɒl ə ˈfɜːn iːz hə ˈlɒf ə niːz
‖ ˌhɑːl ə ˈfɜːn iːz ˌhoʊl-
hologram ˈhɒl ə græm ‖ ˈhoʊl- ˈhɑːl- **~s** z
holograph ˈhɒl ə grɑːf -græf ‖ ˈhoʊl ə græf
ˈhɑːl- **~s** s
holography hɒ ˈlɒg rəf i həʊ- ‖ hoʊ ˈlɑːg rəf i
holophras|e ˈhɒl əʊ freɪz ‖ ˈhoʊl ə- ˌhɑːl ə-
~es ɪz əz
holophrastic ˌhɒl əʊ ˈfræst ɪk ◂ ‖ ˌhoʊl ə-
ˌhɑːl ə-
holothurian ˌhɒl əʊ ˈθjʊər i ən -ˈθjɔːr-, -ˈθʊər-
‖ ˌhoʊl ə ˈθʊr- ˌhɑːl-, -ˈθjʊr- **~s** z
holp həʊlp →hɒʊlp ‖ hoʊlp
holpen ˈhəʊlp ən →ˈhɒʊlp- ‖ ˈhoʊlp-
Holroyd ˈhɒl rɔɪd ˈhəʊl- ‖ ˈhɑːl- ˈhoʊl-
hols '*holidays*' hɒlz ‖ hɑːlz
Holst həʊlst →hɒʊlst ‖ hoʊlst
Holstein, h~ ˈhɒl staɪn ˈhəʊl- ‖ ˈhoʊl stiːn
-staɪn —*Ger* [ˈhɔl ʃtaɪn] **~s** z
holster ˈhəʊlst ə →ˈhɒʊlst- ‖ ˈhoʊlst ᵊr **~ed** d
~s z
Holt həʊlt →hɒʊlt ‖ hoʊlt
Holtby ˈhəʊlt bi →ˈhɒʊlt- ‖ ˈhoʊlt-
holus-bolus ˌhəʊl əs ˈbəʊl əs
‖ ˌhoʊl əs ˈboʊl əs
hol|y ˈhəʊl |i ‖ ˈhoʊl |i **~ier** i ə ‖ iᵊr **~iest**
i ɪst i əst **~ily** əl i ɪ i **~iness** i nəs i nɪs
ˌHoly ˈBible; ˌHoly Comˈmunion; ˌHoly
ˈFamily; ˌHoly ˈGhost; ˌHoly ˈGrail; the
ˈHoly Land; ˌholy of ˈholies; ˌholy
ˈorders; ˌHoly ˌRoman ˈEmpire; ˌHoly
ˈScripture; ˌHoly ˈSee; ˌHoly ˈSpirit; ˈholy
ˌwater, ˌ·· ˈ·· ·; ˈHoly Week; ˌHoly ˈWrit
Holyhead *place in Gwynedd* ˌhɒl i ˈhed ◂ ˈ···
‖ ˈhɑːl i hed
Holyoak, Holyoake, Holyoke ˈhəʊl i əʊk
‖ ˈhoʊl i oʊk —*but Holyoke, MA, is usually*
ˈhoʊl joʊk
Holyport *place in Berks* ˈhɒl i pɔːt
‖ ˈhɑːl i pɔːrt -poʊrt
Holyrood ˈhɒl i ruːd ‖ ˈhoʊl-
holyston|e ˈhəʊl i stəʊn ‖ ˈhoʊl i stoʊn **~ed** d
~es z **~ing** ɪŋ
Holywell ˈhɒl i wel -wəl ‖ ˈhɑːl-
homage ˈhɒm ɪdʒ ‖ ˈhɑːm-
hombre ˈɒm breɪ -bri ‖ ˈɑːm bri ˈʌm-, -breɪ
—*Sp* [ˈom bre] **~s** z
homburg, H~ ˈhɒm bɜːg ‖ ˈhɑːm bɜːg —*Ger*
[ˈhɔm bʊʁk] **~s** z
home həʊm ‖ hoʊm **homed** həʊmd ‖ hoʊmd
homes həʊmz ‖ hoʊmz **homing** ˈhəʊm ɪŋ
‖ ˈhoʊm ɪŋ —*The phrase* at home *formerly
had an RP variant* ə ˈtəʊm, *now obsolete.*
ˌhome ˈbrew; ˌHome ˈCounties; ˌhome
ˌecoˈnomics; ˌhome ˈfront; ˌHome ˈGuard;
ˌhome ˈhelp; ˌhome ˈmovie; ˈHome
ˌOffice; ˌhome ˈrule; ˌhome ˈrun; ˌHome

'Secretary; ˌhome 'straight; ˌhome
'stretch; ˌhome 'truth
Home *family name* (i) həʊm ‖ hoʊm, (ii) hjuːm
—*The Earls of Home are* (ii).
home-baked ˌhəʊm 'beɪkt ◂ ‖ ˌhoʊm-
Homebase *tdmk* 'həʊm beɪs ‖ 'hoʊm-
homebod|y 'həʊm ˌbɒd |i ‖ 'hoʊm ˌbɑːd |i
~ies iz
home-bound 'həʊm baʊnd
homeboy 'həʊm bɔɪ ‖ 'hoʊm- **~s** z
home-brewed ˌhəʊm 'bruːd ◂ ‖ ˌhoʊm-
ˌhome-brewed 'beer
homebuyer 'həʊm ˌbaɪ ə ‖ -baɪ ʳr **~s** z
homecoming 'həʊm ˌkʌm ɪŋ ‖ 'hoʊm- **~s** z
homegirl 'həʊm ɡɜːl ‖ -ɡɜːl **~s** z
homegrown ˌhəʊm 'ɡrəʊn ◂
‖ ˌhoʊm 'ɡroʊn ◂
ˌhomegrown 'cucumbers
homeland 'həʊm lænd -lənd ‖ 'hoʊm- **~s** z
homeless 'həʊm ləs -lɪs ‖ 'hoʊm- **~ness** nəs
nɪs
homelike 'həʊm laɪk ‖ 'hoʊm-
home|ly 'həʊm |li ‖ 'hoʊm- **~lier** li ə ‖ li ʳr
~liest li ɪst li əst **~liness** li nəs li nɪs
homemade ˌhəʊm 'meɪd ◂ ‖ 'hoʊm meɪd -eɪd
homemaker 'həʊm ˌmeɪk ə ‖ 'hoʊm ˌmeɪk ʳr
~s z
homeo- *comb. form*
with stress-neutral suffix ˌhəʊm i əʊ ˌhɒm-
‖ ˌhoʊm i ə — **homeomorphism**
ˌhəʊm i əʊ 'mɔːf ˌɪz əm ˌhɒm-
‖ ˌhoʊm i ə 'mɔːrf-
with stress-imposing suffix ˌhəʊm i 'ɒ+ ˌhɒm-
‖ ˌhoʊm i 'ɑː+ — **homeology**
ˌhəʊm i 'ɒl ədʒ i ˌhɒm- ‖ ˌhoʊm i 'ɑːl-
homeopath 'həʊm i ə pæθ 'hɒm- ‖ 'hoʊm- **~s**
s
homeopathic ˌhəʊm i ə 'pæθ ɪk ◂ ˌhɒm-
‖ ˌhoʊm- **~ally** ʲl i
homeopathist ˌhəʊm i 'ɒp əθ ɪst ˌhɒm-, §-əst
‖ ˌhoʊm i 'ɑːp- **~s** s
homeopathy ˌhəʊm i 'ɒp əθ i ˌhɒm-
‖ ˌhoʊm i 'ɑːp- ˌhɑːm-
homeostasis ˌhəʊm i əʊ 'steɪs ɪs §-əs;
ˌhəʊm i 'ɒst əs ɪs, -əs ‖ ˌhoʊm i oʊ-
homeostatic ˌhəʊm i əʊ 'stæt ɪk ◂
‖ ˌhoʊm i oʊ 'stæt ɪk ◂ **~ally** ʲl i
homeotic ˌhəʊm i 'ɒt ɪk ◂ ˌhɒm-
‖ ˌhoʊm i 'ɑːt ɪk ◂
homeowner 'həʊm ˌəʊn ə ‖ 'hoʊm ˌoʊn ʳr **~s**
z
homepag|e 'həʊm peɪdʒ ‖ 'hoʊm- **~es** ɪz əz
Homepride *tdmk* 'həʊm praɪd ‖ 'hoʊm-
Homer, homer 'həʊm ə ‖ 'hoʊm ʳr **~s, ~'s** z
Homeric həʊ 'mer ɪk ‖ hoʊ- **~ally** ʲl i
Homerton 'hɒm ət ən ‖ 'hɑːm ʳrt ʰn
homeschool 'həʊm skuːl ‖ 'hoʊm- **~ed** d **~ing**
ɪŋ **~s** z
homesick 'həʊm sɪk ‖ 'hoʊm- **~ness** nəs nɪs
homespun 'həʊm spʌn ‖ 'hoʊm-
homestay 'həʊm steɪ ‖ 'hoʊm- **~s** z
homestead *n* 'həʊm sted -stɪd, -stəd ‖ 'hoʊm-
~s z

homestead *v* 'həʊm sted ‖ 'hoʊm- **~ed** ɪd əd
~er/s ə/z ‖ ʳr/z **~ing** ɪŋ **~s** z
hometown ˌhəʊm 'taʊn ◂ ‖ ˌhoʊm-
homeward 'həʊm wəd ‖ 'hoʊm wʳrd **~s** z
homework 'həʊm wɜːk ‖ 'hoʊm wɜːk **~er/s**
ə/z ‖ ʳr/z **~ing** ɪŋ
hom|ey 'həʊm |i ‖ 'hoʊm |i **~ier** i ə ‖ i ʳr
~iest i ɪst i əst
homicidal ˌhɒm ɪ 'saɪd ʲl ◂ -ə- ‖ ˌhaːm- ˌhoʊm-
~ly i
homicide 'hɒm ɪ saɪd -ə- ‖ 'haːm- 'hoʊm- **~s** z
homiletic ˌhɒm ɪ 'let ɪk ◂ -ə-, ⚠-'lekt-
‖ ˌhaːm ə 'leʈ ɪk ◂ **~ally** ʲl i **~s** s
homil|y 'hɒm əl |i -ɪl- ‖ 'haːm- **~ies** iz
homing 'həʊm ɪŋ ‖ 'hoʊm ɪŋ
'homing ˌpigeon
hominid 'hɒm ə nɪd -ɪ-; §-ən əd ‖ 'haːm- **~s** z
hominoid 'hɒm ə nɔɪd -ɪ- ‖ 'haːm- **~s** z
hominy 'hɒm ən i -ɪn- ‖ 'haːm-
homo, Homo 'həʊm əʊ ‖ 'hoʊm oʊ **~s** z
ˌHomo 'sapiens 'sæp i enz 'seɪp-, -i ənz
homo- *comb. form*
with stress-neutral suffix ˌhəʊm əʊ ˌhɒm-
‖ ˌhoʊm ə — **homotaxis** ˌhəʊm əʊ 'tæks ɪs
ˌhɒm-, §-əs ‖ ˌhoʊm ə-
with stress-imposing suffix hə 'mɒ+ hɒ-
‖ hə 'maː+ hoʊ- — **homogonous**
hə 'mɒɡ ən əs hɒ- ‖ hə 'maːɡ- hoʊ-
homoeo... —*see* **homeo...**
homoerotic ˌhəʊm əʊ ɪ 'rɒt ɪk ◂ ˌhɒm-, -ə'--
‖ ˌhoʊm oʊ ɪ 'raːʈ ɪk ◂
homoeroticism ˌhəʊm əʊ ɪ 'rɒt ɪ ˌsɪz əm
ˌhɒm-, -ə'--, -'-ə- ‖ ˌhoʊm oʊ ɪ 'raːʈ ə-
homogeneity ˌhəʊm əʊ dʒə 'niː ət i ˌhɒm-,
-dʒɪ'--, -'neɪ-, -ɪt i ‖ ˌhoʊm ə dʒə 'niː əʈ i
-'neɪ-

HOMOGENEOUS

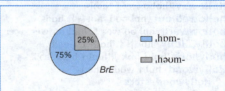

75% | ˌhɒm-
25% | ˌhəʊm-
BrE

homogeneous ˌhɒm əʊ 'dʒiːn i əs ◂ ˌhəʊm-
‖ ˌhoʊm ə- — *Preference poll, BrE:* ˌhɒm-
75%, ˌhəʊm- *25%.* **~ly** li **~ness** nəs nɪs
homogenis... —*see* **homogeniz...**
homogenization hə ˌmɒdʒ ən aɪ 'zeɪʃ ʰn hɒ-,
-'-ɪn-, -ɪ'-- ‖ -ˌmaːdʒ ən ə- hoʊ-
homogeniz|e hə 'mɒdʒ ə naɪz hɒ-, -ɪ-
‖ -'maːdʒ- hoʊ- **~ed** d **~es** ɪz əz **~ing** ɪŋ
homogenous hə 'mɒdʒ ən əs hɒ-, -ɪn-
‖ hoʊ 'maːdʒ-
homograph 'hɒm ə ɡraːf 'həʊm-, -ɡræf
‖ 'haːm ə ɡræf 'hoʊm- **~s** s
homographic ˌhɒm ə 'ɡræf ɪk ◂ ‖ ˌhaːm-
ˌhoʊm-
homolog 'hɒm ə lɒɡ ‖ 'hoʊm ə lɔːɡ 'haːm-,
-laːɡ **~s** z

homologous hə ˈmɒl əg əs hɒ- ‖ hoʊ ˈmɑːl-
hə-
homologue ˈhɒm ə lɒg ‖ ˈhoʊm ə lɔːg ˈhɑːm-,
-lɑːg **~s** z
homolog|y hə ˈmɒl ədʒ |i hɒ- ‖ hoʊ ˈmɑːl-
hə- **~ies** iz
homonym ˈhɒm ə nɪm ˈhəʊm- ‖ ˈhɑːm- ˈhoʊm-
~s z
homonymous hə ˈmɒn ɪm əs hɒ-, -əm-
‖ hoʊ ˈmɑːn- hə- **~ly** li
homonymy hə ˈmɒn ɪm i hɒ-, -əm-
‖ hoʊ ˈmɑːn- hə-
homophile ˈhəʊm əʊ faɪəl ˈhɒm- ‖ ˈhoʊm ə-
~s z
homophobe ˈhəʊm əʊ fəʊb ˈhɒm-
‖ ˈhoʊm ə foʊb **~s** z
homophobia ˌhəʊm əʊ ˈfəʊb i ə ˌhɒm-
‖ ˌhoʊm ə ˈfoʊb-
homophobic ˌhəʊm əʊ ˈfəʊb ɪk ◄ ˌhɒm-
‖ ˌhoʊm ə ˈfoʊb-
homophone ˈhɒm ə fəʊn ˈhəʊm-
‖ ˈhɑːm ə foʊn ˈhoʊm- **~s** z
homophonic ˌhɒm ə ˈfɒn ɪk ◄ ˌhəʊm-
‖ ˌhɑːm ə ˈfɑːn ɪk ◄ ˌhoʊm-, -ˈfoʊn-
homophonous hə ˈmɒf ən əs hɒ- ‖ hoʊ ˈmɑːf-
hə-
homophony hə ˈmɒf ən i hɒ- ‖ hoʊ ˈmɑːf- hə-
homorganic ˌhɒm ɔː ˈgæn ɪk ◄ ˌhəʊm-
‖ ˌhoʊm ɔːr- ˌhɑːm-

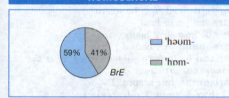
homosexual ˌhəʊm əʊ ˈsek ʃu əl ◄ ˌhɒm-,
-ˈseks ju əl, -ˈsek ʃəl ‖ ˌhoʊm ə ˈsekʃ u əl ◄
-ˈʃəl — *Preference poll, BrE:* ˌhəʊm- *59%,*
ˌhɒm- *41%.* **~s** z
homosexuality ˌhəʊm əʊ ˌsekʃ u ˈæl ət i
ˌhɒm-, -ˌseks ju-, -ɪt i
‖ ˌhoʊm ə ˌsekʃ u ˈæl əṯ i
homozygous ˌhɒm ə ˈzaɪg əs ◄ ˌhəʊm-
‖ ˌhoʊm- ˌhɑːm-
homunc|ulus hɒ ˈmʌŋk |jʊl əs hə-
‖ hoʊ ˈmʌŋk |jəl əs **~uli** jʊ laɪ ‖ jə laɪ
hom|y ˈhəʊm |i ‖ ˈhoʊm |i **~ier** i ə ‖ iᵊr **~iest**
i ɪst i əst
Hon. *'Honourable'; 'Honorary'* ɒn ‖ ɑːn **Hons**
ɒnz ‖ ɑːnz
Hon *'Honey'* hʌn
honcho ˈhɒntʃ əʊ ‖ ˈhɑːntʃ oʊ **~s** z
Honda *tdmk* ˈhɒnd ə ‖ ˈhɑːnd ə —*Jp* [ho͜n da]
~s z
Honddu ˈhɒn ði ‖ ˈhɑːn-
Hondur|an hɒn ˈdjʊər |ən -ˈdʊər-, →-ˈdʒʊər-
‖ hɑːn ˈdʊr- -ˈdjʊr- **~ans** ənz **~as** əs æs

hone, Hone həʊn ‖ hoʊn **honed** həʊnd
‖ hoʊnd **hones** həʊnz ‖ hoʊnz **honing**
ˈhəʊn ɪŋ ‖ ˈhoʊn ɪŋ
Honecker ˈhɒn ek ə -ɪk- ‖ ˈhɑːn ɪk ᵊr —*Ger*
[ˈhɔn ɛk ɐ]
Honegger ˈhɒn ɪg ə -eg- ‖ ˈhɑːn ɪg ᵊr —*Fr*
[ɔ nɛ gɛːʁ]
honest ˈɒn ɪst -əst ‖ ˈɑːn əst **~ly** li
honest-to-goodness ˌɒn ɪst tə ˈgʊd nəs ◄
ˌ-əst-, -tuˈ--, -nɪs ‖ ˌɑːn əst-
honesty ˈɒn əst i -ɪst- ‖ ˈɑːn-
honey, Honey ˈhʌn i **~ed** d **~s** z
honeybee ˈhʌn i bi: **~s** z
honeybun ˈhʌn i bʌn **~s** z
honeybunch ˈhʌn i bʌntʃ **~es** ɪz əz
honeycomb ˈhʌn i kəʊm ‖ -koʊm **~ed** d **~ing**
ɪŋ **~s** z
Honeycomb, Honeycombe ˈhʌn i kəʊm
‖ -koʊm
honeydew ˈhʌn i dju: →-dʒu: ‖ -du: -dju:
ˌhoneydew ˈmelon
honeyed ˈhʌn id
honeymoon ˈhʌn i mu:n **~ed** d **~er/s** ə/z
‖ ᵊr/z **~ing** ɪŋ **~s** z
ˈhoneymoon ˌcouple
honeypot ˈhʌn i pɒt ‖ -pɑːt **~s** s
honeysuckle ˈhʌn i ˌsʌk ᵊl **~s** z
Hong Kong ˌhɒŋ ˈkɒŋ ◄ ‖ ˈhɑːŋ kɑːŋ ˈhɔːŋ-,
-kɔːŋ, ˌ·ˈ· —*Chi* Xiānggǎng [¹ɕjaŋ ³kaŋ],
Cantonese [¹hœːŋ ²kɔːŋ]
Honiara ˌhəʊn i ˈɑːr ə ˌhɒn- ‖ ˌhoʊn-
honied ˈhʌn id
honi soit qui mal y pense
ˌɒn i ˌswɑː ki: ˌmæl i ˈpɒ̃s
‖ ˌɑːn i ˌswɑː ki: ˌmɑːl i: ˈpɑːns ˌɔːn-, ˌoʊn-
—*Fr* [ɔ ni swa ki ma li pɑ̃ːs]
Honiton ˈhʌn ɪt ən ˈhɒn-, -ət-
honk hɒŋk ‖ hɑːŋk hɔːŋk **honked** hɒŋkt
‖ hɑːŋkt hɔːŋkt **honking** ˈhɒŋk ɪŋ
‖ ˈhɑːŋk ɪŋ ˈhɔːŋk- **honks** hɒŋks ‖ hɑːŋks
hɔːŋks
honk|ie, honk|y ˈhɒŋk |i ‖ ˈhɑːŋk |i ˈhɔːŋk-
~ies iz
honky-tonk ˈhɒŋk i tɒŋk ˌ·ˈ· ‖ ˈhɑːŋk i tɑːŋk
ˈhɔːŋk i tɔːŋk **~s** s
Honolulu ˌhɒn ə ˈluːl uː -ˈl ˈuːl- ‖ ˌhɑːn-
honor, Honor ˈɒn ə ‖ ˈɑːn ᵊr **~ed** d **honoring**
ˈɒn ər ɪŋ ‖ ˈɑːn ər ɪŋ **~s** z
ˈhonor roll
honorab|le, H~ ˈɒn ər əb |ᵊl ‖ ˈɑːn- ˈ·ᵊrb |ᵊl
~leness ᵊl nəs -nɪs **~ly** li
ˌhonorable ˈmention
honorari|um ˌɒn ə ˈreər i |əm -ˈrɑːr-
‖ ˌɑːn ə ˈrer- **~a** ə **~ums** əmz
honorary ˈɒn ᵊr_ər i △ˈɒn ər_i ‖ ˈɑːn ə rer i
honoree ˌɒn ə ˈriː ‖ ˌɑːn- **~s** z
honorific ˌɒn ə ˈrɪf ɪk ◄ ‖ ˌɑːn- **~ally** ᵊl_i **~s** s
honoris causa hɒ ˌnɔːr ɪs ˈkaʊz ɑː ɒ-, -ˈkaʊs-,
-ə ‖ oʊ ˌnɔːr əs ˈkaʊs ɑː ɑː-, -, ˌnoʊr-, -ə
honour, H~ ˈɒn ə ‖ ˈɑːn ᵊr **~ed** d **honouring**
ˈɒn ər ɪŋ ‖ ˈɑːn ər ɪŋ **~s** z
ˈhonours list

H

honourab|le, H~ 'ɒn ər‚əb |ᵊl ‖ 'ɑːn- ‚-ᵊrb |ᵊl
~leness ᵊl nəs -nɪs **~ly** li
‚honourable 'mention
Honshu 'hɒn ʃuː ‖ 'hɑːn- —*Jp* ['hon ɕɯɯ]
Hoo huː
hooch huːtʃ
hoochie 'huːtʃ i **~s** z
hood hʊd **hooded** 'hʊd ɪd -əd **hooding**
'hʊd ɪŋ **hoods** hʊdz
-hood hʊd — **fatherhood** 'fɑːð ə hʊd ‖ -ᵊr-
hoodie 'hʊd i **~s** z
hoodlum 'huːd ləm ‖ 'hʊd- 'huːd- **~s** z
hoodoo 'huː duː **~ed** d **~ing** ɪŋ **~s** z
hood|wink 'hʊd |wɪŋk **~winked** wɪŋkt
~winking wɪŋk ɪŋ **~winks** wɪŋks
hooey 'huː i
hoof huːf hʊf **hoofed** huːft hʊft **hoofing**
'huːf ɪŋ 'hʊf- **hoofs** huːfs hʊfs **hooves** huːvz
hʊvz
hoofer 'huːf ə 'hʊf- ‖ -ᵊr **~s** z
Hoogly, Hooghly 'huːg li
hoo-ha 'huː hɑː **~s** z
hook, Hook hʊk §huːk **hooked** hʊkt §huːkt
hooking 'hʊk ɪŋ §'huːk- **hooks** hʊks §huːks
hooka, hookah 'hʊk ə **~s** z
Hooke hʊk §huːk
hooker, H~ 'hʊk ə §'huːk- ‖ -ᵊr **~s** z
hookey 'hʊk i
hook-nosed ‚hʊk 'nəʊzd ◂ §‚huːk-, '‚· ·
‖ 'hʊk noʊzd
hookup 'hʊk ʌp §'huːk- **~s** s
hookworm 'hʊk wɜːm §'huːk- ‖ -wɜːm **~s** z
hooky 'hʊk i
Hooley 'huːl i
hooligan 'huːl ɪg ən -əg- **~s** z
hooliganism 'huːl ɪg ən ‚ɪz əm '·əg-
Hoon huːn
hoop huːp §hʊp **hooped** huːpt §hʊpt **hooping**
'huːp ɪŋ §'hʊp- **hoops** huːps §hʊps
Hooper 'huːp ə §'hʊp- ‖ -ᵊr
hoop-la 'huːp lɑː 'hʊp-
hoopoe 'huːp uː -əʊ **~s** z
hooray hu 'reɪ hə-, ‚huː- **~ed** d **~ing** ɪŋ **~s** z
hoo‚ray 'Henry, ‚· · '‚· ·
hoosegow 'huːs gaʊ **~s** z
Hoosier, h~ 'huːʒ ə ‖ -ᵊr **~s** z
Hooson 'huːs ᵊn
hoot huːt **hooted** 'huːt ɪd -əd ‖ 'huːt̬ əd
hooting 'huːt ɪŋ ‖ 'huːt̬ ɪŋ **hoots** huːts
hootch, H~ *tdmk* huːtʃ
hootenann|y 'huːt ᵊn æn |i **~ies** iz
hooter 'huːt ə ‖ 'huːt̬ ᵊr **~s** z
Hooton 'huːt ᵊn
hoover, H~ 'huːv ə ‖ -ᵊr **~ed** d **hoovering**
'huːv ər ɪŋ **~s** z
hooves huːvz §hʊvz
hop hɒp ‖ hɑːp **hopped** hɒpt ‖ hɑːpt **hopping**
'hɒp ɪŋ ‖ 'hɑːp ɪŋ **hops** hɒps ‖ hɑːps
Hopcraft 'hɒp krɑːft §-kræft ‖ 'hɑːp kræft
Hopcroft 'hɒp krɒft -krɔːft ‖ 'hɑːp krɔːft -krɑːft

hope, Hope həʊp ‖ hoʊp **hoped** həʊpt
‖ hoʊpt **hopes** həʊps ‖ hoʊps **hoping**
'həʊp ɪŋ ‖ 'hoʊp ɪŋ
'hope chest
hoped-for 'həʊptfɔː ‖ -fɔːr
hopeful 'həʊp fᵊl -fʊl ‖ 'hoʊp- **~ly** ‚i **~ness**
nəs nɪs **~s** z
hopeless 'həʊp ləs -lɪs ‖ 'hoʊp- **~ly** li **~ness**
nəs nɪs
Hopi 'həʊ pi 'həʊp i ‖ 'hoʊ pi **~s** z
Hopkin 'hɒp kɪn ‖ 'hɑːp-
Hopkins 'hɒp kɪnz ‖ 'hɑːp-
Hopkinson 'hɒp kɪn sən ‖ 'hɑːp-
hoplite 'hɒp laɪt ‖ 'hɑːp- **~s** s
hopp... —*see* **hop**
hopped-up ‚hɒpt 'ʌp ◂ ‖ ‚hɑːpt-
hopper, H~ 'hɒp ə ‖ 'hɑːp ᵊr **~s** z
hop-picker 'hɒp ‚pɪk ə ‖ 'hɑːp ‚pɪk ᵊr **~s** z
Hoppus 'hɒp əs ‖ 'hɑːp-
hopsack 'hɒp sæk ‖ 'hɑːp- **~ing** ɪŋ
hopscotch 'hɒp skɒtʃ ‖ 'hɑːp skɑːtʃ
Hopton 'hɒpt ən ‖ 'hɑːpt-
Hopwood 'hɒp wʊd ‖ 'hɑːp-
hora 'hɔːr ə ‖ 'hoʊr- **~s** z
Horabin 'hɒr ə bɪn ‖ 'hɔːr-
Horace 'hɒr əs -ɪs ‖ 'hɔːr- 'hɑːr-
Horatian hə 'reɪʃ ᵊn hɒ-, -'reɪʃ i ən
Horatio hə 'reɪʃ i əʊ hɒ- ‖ oʊ -'reɪʃ oʊ
Horatius hə 'reɪʃ i əs hɒ-, -'reɪʃ əs
Horbury 'hɔː bər i ‖ 'hɔːr ‚ber i
horde hɔːd ‖ hɔːrd hoʊrd *(= hoard)* **hordes**
hɔːdz ‖ hɔːrdz hoʊrdz
Hordern 'hɔːd ᵊn ‖ 'hɔːrd ᵊrn
Hore hɔː ‖ hɔːr hoʊr
Horeb 'hɔːr eb ‖ 'hoʊr-
horehound 'hɔː haʊnd ‖ 'hɔːr-
horizon hə 'raɪz ᵊn —*sometimes* ə- *after the
indefinite article* an **~s** z
horizontal ‚hɒr ɪ 'zɒnt ᵊl ◂ -ə-
‖ ‚hɔːr ə 'zɑːnt̬ ᵊl ◂ ‚hɑːr- **~ly** i **~s** z
Horley 'hɔːl i ‖ 'hɔːrl i
Horlick 'hɔːl ɪk ‖ 'hɔːrl-
Horlicks *tdmk* 'hɔːl ɪks ‖ 'hɔːrl-
hormonal ₍₁₎hɔː 'məʊn ᵊl ‖ hɔːr 'moʊn ᵊl
hormone 'hɔːm əʊn ‖ 'hɔːrm oʊn **~s** z
Hormuz ‚hɔː 'muːz 'hɔːm əz ‖ ‚hɔːr- 'hɔːrm əz
horn, Horn hɔːn ‖ hɔːrn **horned** hɔːnd
‖ hɔːrnd **horning** 'hɔːn ɪŋ ‖ 'hɔːrn ɪŋ **horns**
hɔːnz ‖ hɔːrnz
hornbeam 'hɔːn biːm →'hɔːm- ‖ 'hɔːrn- **~s** z
hornbill 'hɔːn bɪl →'hɔːm- ‖ 'hɔːrn- **~s** z
hornblende 'hɔːn blend →'hɔːm- ‖ 'hɔːrn- **~s**
z
Hornblower 'hɔːn ‚bləʊ ə →'hɔːm-
‖ 'hɔːrn ‚bloʊ ᵊr
Hornby 'hɔːn bi →'hɔːm- ‖ 'hɔːrn-
Horncastle 'hɔːn ‚kɑːs ᵊl →'hɔːŋ-, §-‚kæs-
‖ 'hɔːrn ‚kæs ᵊl
Hornchurch 'hɔːn tʃɜːtʃ ‖ 'hɔːrn tʃɜːtʃ
Horne hɔːn ‖ hɔːrn
horned *adj* hɔːnd 'hɔːn ɪd, -əd ‖ hɔːrnd
'hɔːrn əd
Horner 'hɔːn ə ‖ 'hɔːrn ᵊr

hornet 'hɔːn ɪt -ət ‖ 'hɔːrn- **~s** s
  'hornet's nest
Horney 'hɔːn i ‖ 'hɔːrn i
horni... —see horny
Horniman 'hɔːn ɪ mən -ə- ‖ 'hɔːrn-
hornpipe 'hɔːn paɪp →'hɔːm- ‖ 'hɔːrn- **~s** s
horn-rimmed ˌhɔːn 'rɪmd ◀ ‖ ˌhɔːrn-
Hornsby 'hɔːnz bi ‖ 'hɔːrnz-
Hornsea 'hɔːn siː ‖ 'hɔːrn-
Hornsey 'hɔːnz i ‖ 'hɔːrnz i
hornswoggl|e 'hɔːn ˌswɒɡ ᵊl
  ‖ 'hɔːrn ˌswɑːɡ ᵊl **~ed** d **~es** z **~ing** ɪŋ
horn|y 'hɔːn |i ‖ 'hɔːrn |i **~ier** i ə ‖ i ᵊr **~iest**
  i ɪst i əst **~ily** ɪ li əl i **~iness** i nəs i nɪs
horologist hə 'rɒl ədʒ ɪst hɒ-, hɔː-, §-əst
  ‖ hə 'rɑːl- **~s** s
horologium, H~ ˌhɒr ə 'ləʊdʒ i əm ˌhɔːr-
  ‖ ˌhɔːr ə 'loʊdʒ-
horology hə 'rɒl ədʒ i hɒ-, hɔː- ‖ hə 'rɑːl-
horoscope 'hɒr ə skəʊp ‖ 'hɔːr ə skoʊp 'hɑːr-
  ~s s
Horowitz 'hɒr ə wɪts -vɪts ‖ 'hɔːr- 'hɑːr-
horrendous hɒ 'rend əs hə- ‖ hɔː- hɑː- **~ly** li
  ~ness nəs nɪs
horrib|le 'hɒr əb |ᵊl -ɪb- ‖ 'hɔːr- 'hɑːr- **~leness**
  ᵊl nəs -nɪs **~ly** li
horrid 'hɒr ɪd §-əd ‖ 'hɔːr əd 'hɑːr- **~ly** li
  ~ness nəs nɪs
horrific hɒ 'rɪf ɪk hə- ‖ hɔː- hɑː- **~ally** ᵊl i
horri|fy 'hɒr ɪ |faɪ -ə- ‖ 'hɔːr- 'hɑːr- **~fied/ly**
  faɪd /li **~fies** faɪz **~fying/ly** faɪ ɪŋ /li
horripilation hɒ ˌrɪp ɪ 'leɪʃ ᵊn -ə-; ˌhɒr ɪp-,
  ˌ·əp- ‖ hɔː- hɑː-
Horrocks 'hɒr əks ‖ 'hɔːr- 'hɑːr-
horror 'hɒr ə ‖ 'hɔːr ᵊr 'hɑːr- **~s** z
  'horror film; 'horror ˌmovie; 'horror
  ˌstory
horror-stricken 'hɒr ə ˌstrɪk ən ‖ 'hɔːr ᵊr-
  'hɑːr-
horror-struck 'hɒr ə strʌk ‖ 'hɔːr ᵊr- 'hɑːr-
Horsa 'hɔːs ə ‖ 'hɔːrs ə
Horsbrugh 'hɔːs brə 'hɔːz- ‖ 'hɔːrz-
hors de combat ˌɔː də 'kɒm bɑː -'kõ-, -bæt
  ‖ ˌɔːr də koʊm 'bɑː —Fr [ɔʁ də kõ ba]
hors-d'oeuvre, ~s ˌɔː 'dɜːv ‖ ˌɔːr 'dɜːv —Fr
  [ɔʁ dœːvʁ]
horse hɔːs ‖ hɔːrs horsed hɔːst ‖ hɔːrst horses
  'hɔːs ɪz -əz ‖ 'hɔːrs əz horsing 'hɔːs ɪŋ
  ‖ 'hɔːrs ɪŋ
  'horse brass; ˌhorse 'chestnut ‖ '· ˌ· ·;
  'horse ˌopera; 'horse sense
horse-and-buggy ˌhɔːs ᵊn 'bʌɡ i -ᵊnd-, →-ᵊm-
  ‖ ˌhɔːrs-
horse-and-cart ˌhɔːs ᵊn 'kɑːt -ᵊnd-, →-ᵊŋ-
  ‖ ˌhɔːrs ᵊn 'kɑːrt
horseback 'hɔːs bæk ‖ 'hɔːrs-
horsebox 'hɔːs bɒks ‖ 'hɔːrs bɑːks **~es** ɪz əz
horsedrawn 'hɔːs drɔːn ‖ 'hɔːrs- -drɑːn
Horseferry 'hɔːs ˌfer i -fər i ‖ 'hɔːrs-
horseflesh 'hɔːs fleʃ ‖ 'hɔːrs-
horse|fly 'hɔːs |flaɪ ‖ 'hɔːrs- **~flies** flaɪz
Horseguard 'hɔːs ɡɑːd ‖ 'hɔːrs ɡɑːrd **~s** z
horsehair 'hɔːs heə ‖ 'hɔːrs her -hær

horsehide 'hɔːs haɪd ‖ 'hɔːrs-
horselaugh 'hɔːs lɑːf §-læf ‖ 'hɔːrs læf **~s** s
horse|man 'hɔːs |mən ‖ 'hɔːrs- **~manship**
  mən ʃɪp **~men** mən men
horsemastership 'hɔːs ˌmɑːst ə ʃɪp §-ˌmæst-
  ‖ 'hɔːrs ˌmæst ᵊr-
horseplay 'hɔːs pleɪ ‖ 'hɔːrs-
horsepower 'hɔːs ˌpaʊ ə ‖ 'hɔːrs ˌpaʊ ᵊr
horseracing 'hɔːs ˌreɪs ɪŋ ‖ 'hɔːrs-
horseradish 'hɔːs ˌræd ɪʃ ‖ 'hɔːrs- **~es** ɪz əz
horse-rid|ing 'hɔːs ˌraɪd| ɪŋ ‖ 'hɔːrs- **~er/s** ə/z
  ‖ ᵊr/z
horseshit 'hɔːs ʃɪt →'hɔːʃ- ‖ 'hɔːrs- →'hɔːrʃ-,
  'hɔːr-
horseshoe 'hɔːs ʃuː →'hɔːʃ- ‖ 'hɔːrs- →'hɔːrʃ-,
  'hɔːr- **~s** z
horsetail 'hɔːs teɪᵊl ‖ 'hɔːrs- **~s** z
horse-trading 'hɔːs ˌtreɪd ɪŋ ‖ 'hɔːrs-
horsewhip 'hɔːs wɪp -hwɪp ‖ 'hɔːrs- **~ped** t
  ~ping ɪŋ **~s** s
horse|woman 'hɔːs |ˌwʊm ən ‖ 'hɔːrs-
  ~women ˌwɪm ɪn §-ən
hors|ey, H~ 'hɔːs |i ‖ 'hɔːrs |i **~ier** i ə ‖ i ᵊr
  ~iest i ɪst i əst
Horsfall 'hɔs fɔːl ‖ 'hɔːrs fɑːl -fɔːl
Horsforth 'hɔːs fəθ ‖ 'hɔːrs fᵊrθ
Horsham 'hɔːʃ əm ‖ 'hɔːrʃ-
horsi... —see horsey, horsy
Horsley 'hɔːz li ‖ 'hɔːrz-
Horsmonden ˌhɔːz mən 'den ‖ ˌhɔːrz-
Horsted Keynes ˌhɔːst ɪd 'keɪnz -əd- ‖ ˌhɔːrst-
hors|y 'hɔːs |i ‖ 'hɔːrs |i **~ier** i ə ‖ i ᵊr **~iest**
  i ɪst i əst
hortative 'hɔːt ət ɪv hɔː- 'teɪt- ‖ 'hɔːrt ət ɪv **~ly**
  li
hortatory 'hɔːt ət ər i hɔː- 'teɪt ər i
  ‖ 'hɔːrt ə tɔːr i -tour i
Hortensia, h~ hɔː 'tenˡs i ə -'tenˡʃ-
  ‖ hɔːr 'tenˡʃə **~s** z
horticultural ˌhɔːt ɪ 'kʌltʃ ᵊr əl ◀ ˌ·ə-
  ‖ ˌhɔːrt ə- **~ist/s** ɪst/s §əst/s **~ly** i
horticulture 'hɔːt ɪ ˌkʌltʃ ə -ə-; §ˌ·ˡ··
  ‖ 'hɔːrt ə ˌkʌltʃ ᵊr
horticulturist ˌhɔːt ɪ 'kʌltʃ ər ɪst ˌ·ə-, §-əst
  ‖ ˌhɔːrt ə- **~s** s
Horton 'hɔːt ᵊn ‖ 'hɔːrt ᵊn
Horus 'hɔːr əs ‖ 'hour-
Horwich 'hɒr ɪtʃ -ɪdʒ ‖ 'hɔːr-
Horwood 'hɔː wʊd ‖ 'hɔːr-
hosanna həʊ 'zæn ə ‖ hoʊ- **~s** z
hose, Hose həʊz ‖ hoʊz hosed həʊzd ‖ hoʊzd
  hoses 'həʊz ɪz -əz ‖ 'hoʊz əz hosing
  'həʊz ɪŋ ‖ 'hoʊz ɪŋ
Hosea həʊ 'zɪə ‖ hoʊ 'ziː ə
Hoseason (i) həʊ 'siːz ᵊn '·ˌ· ·‖ hoʊ-,
  (ii) ˌhəʊs i 'eɪs ᵊn -'æs- ‖ ˌhoʊs-
hosel 'həʊz ᵊl ‖ 'hoʊz ᵊl **~s** z
hosepipe 'həʊz paɪp ‖ 'hoʊz- **~s** s
hoser 'həʊz ə ‖ -ᵊr **~s** z
Hosey 'həʊz i ‖ 'hoʊz i
hosier, H~ 'həʊz i ə 'həʊʒ jə, -ə ‖ 'hoʊʒ ᵊr **~s** z
hosiery 'həʊz i ər i 'həʊʒ jər i, -ər i
  ‖ 'hoʊʒ ər i

Hoskins, Hoskyns 'hɒsk ɪnz §-ənz ‖ 'hɑːsk-
hospic|e 'hɒsp ɪs §-əs ‖ 'hɑːsp- **~es** ɪz əz

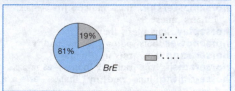

HOSPITABLE

19%
81%
■ .ˈ...
■ ˈ....
BrE

hospitab|le hɒ 'spɪt əb |ᵊl hə-; 'hɒsp ɪt-, '·ət-
‖ 'hɑːsp əţ- hɑː 'spɪt- — *Preference poll, BrE:*
.ˈ··· *81%*, ˈ···· *19%*. **~ly** li
hospital 'hɒsp ɪt ᵊl ‖ 'hɑːsp ɪţ ᵊl **~s** z
hospitalis... —*see* **hospitaliz...**
hospitalit|y ˌhɒsp ɪ 'tæl ət |i ˌ·ə-, -ɪt i
‖ ˌhɑːsp ə 'tæl əţ |i **~ies** iz
hospitalization ˌhɒsp ɪt ᵊl aɪ 'zeɪʃ ᵊn ˌ·ət-, -ɪ'··
‖ ˌhɑːsp ɪţ ᵊl ə-
hospitaliz|e 'hɒsp ɪt ᵊl aɪz '·ət-, -ə laɪz
‖ 'hɑːsp ɪţ- **~ed** d **~es** ɪz əz **~ing** ɪŋ
host, Host həʊst ‖ hoʊst **hosted** 'həʊst ɪd -əd
‖ 'hoʊst əd **hosting** 'həʊst ɪŋ ‖ 'hoʊst ɪŋ
hosts həʊsts ‖ hoʊsts
hosta 'hɒst ə 'həʊst- ‖ 'hoʊst ə 'hɑːst- **~s** z
hostag|e 'hɒst ɪdʒ ‖ 'hɑːst- **~es** ɪz əz
hostel 'hɒst ᵊl ‖ 'hɑːst- **~ing, ~ling** ɪŋ **~s** z
hosteler, hosteller 'hɒst ᵊl ə ‖ 'hɑːst ᵊl ər **~s**
z
hostel|ry 'hɒst ᵊl |ri ‖ 'hɑːst- **~ries** riz
hostess 'həʊst ɪs -əs, -es; ˌhəʊs 'tes ‖ 'hoʊst əs
~es ɪz əz
hostile 'hɒst aɪᵊl ‖ 'hɑːst ᵊl -aɪᵊl **~ly** li
hostilit|y hɒ 'stɪl ət |i §hə-, -ɪt- ‖ hɑː 'stɪl əţ |i
~ies iz
hostler 'ɒs lə 'hɒs- ‖ 'ɑːs lᵊr 'hɑːs- **~s** z
hot hɒt ‖ hɑːt **hots** hɒts ‖ hɑːts **hotted**
'hɒt ɪd -əd ‖ 'hɑːţ əd **hotting** 'hɒt ɪŋ
‖ 'hɑːţ ɪŋ
ˌhot 'air; ˌhot 'air balˌloon; ˌhot cross
'bun; ˌhot 'dog *'frankfurter roll'* ‖ '· ·; ˌhot
'flash, ˌhot 'flush; ˌhot po'tato; 'hot rod;
'hot seat; 'hot spot; ˌhot 'stuff; ˌhot
'water
hotbed 'hɒt bed ‖ 'hɑːt- **~s** z
hot-blooded ˌhɒt 'blʌd ɪd ◂ -əd ‖ ˌhɑːt- **~ness**
nəs nɪs
Hotbot *tdmk* 'hɒt bɒt ‖ 'hɑːt bɑːt
hot cake, hotcake ˌhɒt 'keɪk ‖ 'hɑːt keɪk **~s**
s
Hotchkiss 'hɒtʃ kɪs ‖ 'hɑːtʃ-
hotchpot 'hɒtʃ pɒt ‖ 'hɑːtʃ pɑːt **~s** s
hotchpotch 'hɒtʃ pɒtʃ ‖ 'hɑːtʃ pɑːtʃ **~es** ɪz əz
hot-dog *v* 'hɒt dɒg ‖ 'hɑːt dɔːg -dɑːg **~ged** d
~ging ɪŋ **~s** z
hotel ˌhəʊ 'tel ◂ həʊ-, əʊ- ‖ ˌhoʊ- **~s** z
hotelier həʊ 'tel i eɪ əʊ-, -iˌə ‖ ˌoʊt ᵊl 'jeɪ
hoʊ 'tel jᵊr, ˌhoʊţ ᵊl 'rᵊr **~s** z
hot|foot ˌhɒt '|fʊt ◂ '·· ‖ 'hɑːt |fʊt **~footed**
fʊt ɪd -əd ‖ fʊţ əd **~footing** fʊt ɪŋ ‖ fʊţ ɪŋ
~foots fʊts

hot-gospel|er, hot-gospell|er
ˌhɒt 'gɒsp əl |ə ‖ ˌhɑːt 'gɑːsp ᵊl |ᵊr **~ers** əz
‖ ᵊrz **~ing** ɪŋ
Hotham *(i)* 'hʌð əm, *(ii)* 'hɒθ əm ‖ 'hɑːθ-,
(iii) 'hɒt əm ‖ 'hɑːţ əm
hothead 'hɒt hed ‖ 'hɑːt- **~s** z
hotheaded ˌhɒt 'hed ɪd ◂ -əd ‖ ˌhɑːt- **~ly** li
~ness nəs nɪs
hot|house 'hɒt |haʊs ‖ 'hɑːt- **~houses**
haʊz ɪz -əz
hotline 'hɒt laɪn ‖ 'hɑːt- **~s** z
hotlink 'hɒt lɪŋk ‖ 'hɑːt- **~s** s
hotly 'hɒt li ‖ 'hɑːt-
Hotmail *tdmk* 'hɒt meɪᵊl ‖ 'hɑːt-
hotplate 'hɒt pleɪt ‖ 'hɑːt- **~s** s
Hotpoint *tdmk* 'hɒt pɔɪnt ‖ 'hɑːt-
hotpot 'hɒt pɒt ‖ 'hɑːt pɑːt **~s** s
hotrod 'hɒt rɒd ‖ 'hɑːt rɑːd **~ded** ɪd əd **~der/s**
ə/z -ᵊr/z **~ding** ɪŋ **~s** z
hotshot 'hɒt ʃɒt ‖ 'hɑːt ʃɑːt **~s** s
hotspur, H~ 'hɒt spɜː -spə ‖ 'hɑːt spɜː **~s** z
hott... —*see* **hot**
hot-tempered ˌhɒt 'temp əd ◂
‖ ˌhɑːt 'temp ᵊrd ◂
Hottentot 'hɒt ᵊn tɒt ‖ 'hɑːt ᵊn tɑːt **~s** s
hottie 'hɒt i ‖ 'hɑːt i **~s** z
hot-water bottle ˌhɒt 'wɔːt ə ˌbɒt ᵊl
‖ ˌhɑːt 'wɔːţ ᵊr ˌbɑːţ ᵊl -'wɑːţ- **~s** z
hot-wire *v* ˌhɒt 'waɪ_ə ‖ ˌhɑːt 'waɪ_ᵊr **~d** d **~s**
z **hot-wiring** ˌhɒt 'waɪ_ər ɪŋ
‖ ˌhɑːt 'waɪ_ᵊr ɪŋ
Houdini hu 'diːn i
hough hɒk ‖ hɑːk **houghed** hɒkt ‖ hɑːkt
houghing 'hɒk ɪŋ ‖ 'hɑːk ɪŋ **houghs** hɒks
‖ hɑːks
Hough *(i)* hʌf, *(ii)* hɒf, *(iii)* hɔːf hɑːf, *(iii)* haʊ
Houghall 'hɒf ᵊl ‖ 'hɑːf ᵊl
Hougham 'hʌf əm
Houghton *(i)* 'hɔːt ᵊn ‖ 'hɑːt-, *(ii)* 'haʊt ᵊn,
(iii) 'hoʊt ᵊn ‖ 'hoʊt-
Houghton-le-Spring ˌhəʊt ᵊn li 'sprɪŋ -lə'·
‖ ˌhoʊt-
Houlihan 'huːl ɪ hən -ə-
houmous 'hʊm ʊs 'huːm-, -əs
hound haʊnd **hounded** 'haʊnd ɪd -əd
hounding 'haʊnd ɪŋ **hounds** haʊndz
Houndsditch 'haʊndz dɪtʃ
hound's-tooth 'haʊndz tuːθ §-tʊθ, ˌ·'·
Hounslow 'haʊnz ləʊ ‖ -loʊ
hour 'aʊ_ə ‖ 'aʊᵊr *(= our)* **hours** 'aʊ_əz
‖ 'aʊ_ᵊrz
'hour hand
hourglass 'aʊ_ə glɑːs §-glæs ‖ 'aʊ_ᵊr glæs **~es**
ɪz əz
houri 'hʊər i ‖ 'hʊr i **~s** z
hourly 'aʊ_ə li ‖ 'aʊ_ᵊr li
Housatonic ˌhuːs ə 'tɒn ɪk ◂ ˌhuːz- ‖ -'tɑːn-
house *n, adj* haʊs **houses** 'haʊz ɪz -əz *(!)*
'house ˌagent; 'house arˌrest, ˌ· ·'·; 'house
ˌhusband; 'house lights; 'house ˌmartin;
ˌHouse of 'Commons; ˌHouse of 'Lords;

,House of ,Repre'sentatives; 'house
,party; ,Houses of 'Parliament; 'house
,sparrow

house v haʊz housed haʊzd houses 'haʊz ɪz
-əz housing 'haʊz ɪŋ

House family name haʊs

houseboat 'haʊs bəʊt ‖ -boʊt ~s s

housebound 'haʊs baʊnd

houseboy 'haʊs bɔɪ ~s z

housebreak 'haʊs breɪk ~er/s ə/z ‖ ᵊr/z ~ing
ɪŋ housebroken 'haʊs ˌbrəʊk ən
‖ -ˌbroʊk ən

housebuy|er 'haʊs ˌbaɪ|ə ‖ -ˌbaɪ|ᵊr ~ers əz
‖ ᵊrz ~ing ɪŋ

housecoat 'haʊs kəʊt ‖ -koʊt ~s s

housecraft 'haʊs krɑːft §-kræft ‖ -kræft

housedog 'haʊs dɒg ‖ -dɔːg -dɑːg ~s z

housefather 'haʊs ˌfɑːð ə ‖ -ᵊr ~s z

house|fly 'haʊs |flaɪ ~flies flaɪz

houseful 'haʊs fʊl ~s z

Housego 'haʊs gəʊ ‖ -goʊ

household 'haʊs həʊld →-hɒʊld, -əʊld
‖ -hoʊld ~s z

,household 'name

householder, H~ 'haʊs həʊld ə →-hɒʊld-,
-əʊld- ‖ -hoʊld ᵊr ~s z

housekeeper 'haʊs ˌkiːp ə ‖ -ᵊr ~s z

housekeeping 'haʊs ˌkiːp ɪŋ

houseleek 'haʊs liːk ~s s

housemaid 'haʊs meɪd ~s z

,housemaid's 'knee

house|man 'haʊs |mən -mæn ~men mən men

housemaster 'haʊs ˌmɑːst ə §-ˌmæst-
‖ -ˌmæst ᵊr ~ship/s ʃɪp/s ~s z

housemate 'haʊs meɪt ~s s

housemistress 'haʊs ˌmɪs trəs -trɪs ~es ɪz əz

housemother 'haʊs ˌmʌð ə ‖ -ᵊr ~s z

houseparent 'haʊs ˌpeər ənt ‖ -ˌper- -ˌpær- ~s
s

housephone 'haʊs fəʊn ‖ -foʊn ~s z

houseplant 'haʊs plɑːnt §-plænt ‖ -plænt ~s s

house-proud 'haʊs praʊd

houseroom 'haʊs ruːm -rʊm

houses from house n, v 'haʊz ɪz -əz (!)

house-|sit 'haʊs| sɪt ~sitter/s ˌsɪt ə/z
‖ ˌsɪt ᵊr/z ~sitting ˌsɪt ɪŋ ‖ ˌsɪt ɪŋ

house-to-house ˌhaʊs tə 'haʊs ◂ -tu-

housetop 'haʊs tɒp ‖ -tɑːp ~s s

house-train 'haʊs treɪn ~ed d ~ing ɪŋ ~s z

houseware 'haʊs weə ‖ -wer ~s z

housewarming 'haʊs ˌwɔːm ɪŋ ‖ -ˌwɔːrm ɪŋ
~s z

house|wife 'haʊs |waɪf —formerly also 'hʌz ɪf
~wifely waɪf li ~wives waɪvz

housewifery 'haʊs wɪf ər i 'haʊs waɪf ər i
(*) —formerly also 'hʌz ɪf ri, -əf-

housework 'haʊs wɜːk ‖ -wɜːk

housey-housey, housie-housie
ˌhaʊz i 'haʊz i

housing 'haʊz ɪŋ ~s z
'housing associ,ation; 'housing e,state;
'housing ,project

Housman 'haʊs mən

Houston (i) 'huːst ən, (ii) 'hjuːst ən §'juːst-,
(iii) 'haʊst ən —The Scottish name is (i), the
Texan (ii), the NYC street and GA county
(iii).

Houtman Abrolhos ˌhaʊt mən ə 'brɒl əs
‖ -'brɑːl- -'broʊl-

Houyhnhnm 'huːˌɪn əm hu 'ɪn- ‖ 'hwɪn əm
hu 'ɪn əm

hove, Hove həʊv ‖ hoʊv

hovel 'hɒv ᵊl 'hʌv- ‖ 'hʌv ᵊl 'hɑːv- ~s z

hov|er 'hɒv |ə 'hʌv- ‖ 'hʌv |ᵊr 'hɑːv- ~ered əd
‖ ᵊrd ~ering ᵊr ɪŋ ~ers əz ‖ ᵊrz
'hover fly

hovercraft 'hɒv ə krɑːft 'hʌv-, §-kræft
‖ 'hʌv ᵊr kræft 'hɑːv- ~s s

hover|fly 'hɒv ə |flaɪ 'hʌv- ‖ 'hʌv ᵊr- 'hɑːv-
~flies flaɪz

Hoveringham 'hɒv ᵊr ɪŋ əm ‖ 'hʌv- 'hɑːv-

hoverport 'hɒv ə pɔːt 'hʌv- ‖ 'hʌv ᵊr pɔːrt
'hɑːv-, -poʊrt ~s s

hovertrain 'hɒv ə treɪn 'hʌv- ‖ 'hʌv ᵊr- 'hɑːv-
~s z

Hovis tdmk 'həʊv ɪs §-əs ‖ 'hoʊv-

how haʊ
,How 'are you? (greeting); ('Fine.) ,How are
'you? (reply); ,How do you 'do?

Howard 'haʊ əd ‖ 'haʊ ᵊrd ~s, ~'s z

howdah 'haʊd ə ~s z

Howden 'haʊd ᵊn

how-do-you-do n ˌhaʊ dju 'duː -djə-, -dʒu-,
-dʒə-, -di-, -də ju-; '····~s z

howdy 'haʊd i

how-d'ye-do n ˌhaʊ djə 'duː -dʒə-, -di-; '····~s
z

Howe, howe haʊ

howe'er haʊ 'eə ‖ -'eᵊr

Howell 'haʊ əl haʊl ‖ 'haʊ əl

Howells 'haʊ əlz haʊlz ‖ 'haʊ əlz

Howerd 'haʊ əd ‖ 'haʊ ᵊrd

however haʊ 'ev ə ˌ-- ‖ -ᵊr

Howie 'haʊ i

Howitt 'haʊ ɪt §-ət

howitzer 'haʊ ɪts ə §ˌəts- ‖ -ᵊr ~s z

howl haʊl howled haʊld howling 'haʊl ɪŋ
howls haʊlz

Howland 'haʊ lənd

howler 'haʊl ə ‖ -ᵊr ~s z

howsoever ˌhaʊ səʊ 'ev ə ◂ ‖ -soʊ 'ev ᵊr ◂

Howth place in Co. Dublin həʊθ ‖ hoʊθ

how-to 'haʊ tuː

howzat ˌhaʊ 'zæt

Hoxha 'hɒdʒ ə ‖ 'hoʊdʒ ɑː 'hɑːdʒ-,-ə
—Albanian ['ho dʒa]

Hoxton 'hɒkst ən ‖ 'hɑːkst-

hoy, Hoy hɔɪ hoys hɔɪz

hoya 'hɔɪ ə ~s z

hoyden 'hɔɪd ᵊn ~s z

hoydenish 'hɔɪd ən ɪʃ

Hoylake 'hɔɪ leɪk

Hoyle hɔɪᵊl

HP ˌeɪtʃ 'piː ◂ §ˌheɪtʃ-

HQ ˌeɪtʃ 'kjuː §ˌheɪtʃ-

HRH ˌeɪtʃ ɑːr 'eɪtʃ §ˌheɪtʃ ɑː 'heɪtʃ ‖ -ɑːr-

HRT ˌeɪtʃ ɑː 'tiː §ˌheɪtʃ- ‖ -ɑːr-
hryvna, hryvnia 'rɪv ni ə 'riːv-, -nə
—*Ukrainian* [ˈfiriu nʲə]
HTML ˌeɪtʃ tiː em 'el §ˌheɪtʃ-
Hu *Chinese name* huː: —*Chi* Hú [²xu]
hub hʌb hubs hʌbz
Hubbard 'hʌb əd ‖ -ᵊrd
hubbi... —*see* hubby
Hubble 'hʌb ᵊl
hubble-bubble 'hʌb ᵊl ˌbʌb ᵊl ~s z
hubbub 'hʌb ʌb ~s z
hubb|y 'hʌb |i ~ies iz
hubcap 'hʌb kæp ~s s
Hubei ˌhuː 'beɪ —*Chi* Húběi [²xu ³bei]
Hubert 'hjuːb ət ‖ -ᵊrt
hubris 'hjuːb rɪs 'huːb-, §-rəs
hubristic hju 'brɪst ɪk hu- ~ally ᵊl_i
Huck hʌk
huckaback 'hʌk ə bæk
huckleberr|y, H~ 'hʌk ᵊl bər |i -ˌber |i
‖ -ˌber |i ~ies iz
Hucknall 'hʌk nᵊl
huckster 'hʌkst ə ‖ -ᵊr huckstering
'hʌkst ər ɪŋ ~s z
hucksterism 'hʌkst ər ˌɪz əm
Huckvale 'hʌk verᵊl
Hudd hʌd
Huddersfield 'hʌd əz fiːᵊld ‖ -ᵊrz-
huddl|e 'hʌd ᵊl ~ed d ~es z ~ing ɪŋ
Huddleston 'hʌd ᵊl stən
Hudibras 'hjuːd ɪ bræs -ə-
hudibrastic, H~ ˌhjuːd ɪ 'bræst ɪk ◄ -ə-
Hudnott 'hʌd nɒt ‖ -nɑːt
Hudson 'hʌd sᵊn
ˌHudson 'Bay; ˌHudson 'River
hue hjuː (= *hew, Hugh*) hued hjuːd hues hjuːz
ˌhue and 'cry
huevos rancheros ˌweɪv ɒs ræn 'tʃeər ɒs
‖ -oʊs ræn 'tʃer oʊs —*Sp* [ˌwe βos
ran 'tʃe ros, -βoɾ-]
Huey 'hjuː i
huff, Huff hʌf huffed hʌft huffing 'hʌf ɪŋ
huffs hʌfs
huffish 'hʌf ɪʃ ~ly li ~ness nəs nɪs
huff|y 'hʌf |i ~ier i_ə ‖ i_ᵊr ~iest i_ɪst i_əst ~ily
ɪ li əl i ~iness i nəs i nɪs
hug hʌg hugged hʌgd hugging 'hʌg ɪŋ hugs
hʌgz
huge hjuːdʒ §juːdʒ huger 'hjuːdʒ ə §'juːdʒ-
‖ -ᵊr hugest 'hjuːdʒ ɪst §'juːdʒ-, -əst
huge|ly 'hjuːdʒ |li §'juːdʒ- ~ness nəs nɪs
huggable 'hʌg əb ᵊl
hugger 'hʌg ə ‖ -ᵊr ~s z
hugger-mugger 'hʌg ə ˌmʌg ə ‖ -ᵊr ˌmʌg ᵊr
Huggies *tdmk* 'hʌg iz
Huggins 'hʌg ɪnz §-ənz
Hugh hjuː
Hughenden 'hjuː ən dən
Hughes hjuːz
Hughey, Hughie 'hjuː i
Hugo 'hjuːg əʊ ‖ -oʊ
Hugon 'hjuːg ən -ɒn ‖ -ɑːn

Hugue|not, h~ 'hjuːg ə |nəʊ 'huːg-, -nɒt
‖ -|nɑːt (*) ~nots nəʊz nɒts ‖ nɑːts
huh hʌ hʌh
huh-uh ˌhʌʔ 'ʌ —*The first syllable is
higher-pitched than the second.*
Huhne hjuːn
Huish 'hjuː ɪʃ
hula 'huːl ə ~s z
hula-hoop, Hula-Hoop *tdmk* 'huːl ə huːp ~s s
hula-hula ˌhuːl ə 'huːl ə ~s z
Hulbert 'hʌl bət ‖ -bᵊrt
hulk hʌlk hulked hʌlkt hulking 'hʌlk ɪŋ
hulks hʌlks
hull, Hull hʌl hulled hʌld hulling 'hʌl ɪŋ
hulls hʌlz
hullabaloo ˌhʌl ə bə 'luː ˈ···· ~s z
hullo hə 'ləʊ ₍ᵢ₎hʌ- ‖ -'loʊ ~s z
Hulme (i) hjuːm, (ii) hʌlm —*In Britain (i), in
the US (ii).*
Hulot 'uːl əʊ ‖ uː 'loʊ —*Fr* [y lo]
Hulse hʌls
Hulsean hʌl 'siː ən
hum hʌm hummed hʌmd humming 'hʌm ɪŋ
hums hʌmz
human 'hjuːm ən §'juːm- ~ly li ~ness nəs nɪs
~s z
ˌhuman 'being; ˌhuman 'race; ˌhuman
'rights
humana, Humana *tdmk* hju 'mɑːn ə
humane hju 'meɪn ˌhjuː- ~ly li ~ness nəs nɪs
humanis... —*see* humaniz...
humanism 'hjuːm ə ˌnɪz əm §'juːm-
humanist 'hjuːm ən ɪst §'juːm-, §-əst ~s s
humanistic ˌhjuːm ə 'nɪst ɪk ◄ §ˌjuːm- ~ally
ᵊl_i
humanitarian hju ˌmæn ɪ 'teər i_ən §ju-,
ˌhjum æn-, -ə'-- ‖ -'ter- ~ism ˌɪz əm
humanit|y hju 'mæn ət |i §ju-, -ɪt i ‖ -əţ |i
~ies iz
humanization ˌhjuːm ən aɪ 'zeɪʃ ᵊn §ˌjuːm-,
-ən ɪ- ‖ -ən ə-
humaniz|e 'hjuːm ə naɪz §'juːm- ~ed d ~es ɪz
əz ~ing ɪŋ
humankind ˌhjuːm ən 'kaɪnd §ˌjuːm-, →-əŋ-
humanly 'hjuːm ən li §'juːm-
humanoid 'hjuːm ə nɔɪd §'juːm- ~s z
Humber 'hʌm bə ‖ -bᵊr
Humberside 'hʌm bə saɪd ‖ -bᵊr-
Humbert 'hʌm bət ‖ -bᵊrt
humble 'hʌm bᵊl humbled 'hʌm bᵊld
humbler 'hʌm blə ‖ -blᵊr humbles
'hʌm bᵊlz humblest 'hʌm blɪst -bləst
humbling 'hʌm bᵊl ɪŋ
ˌhumble 'pie
humbleness 'hʌm bᵊl nəs -nɪs
humbly 'hʌm bli
Humboldt 'hʌm bəʊlt 'hʊm-, →-bɒʊlt ‖ -boʊlt
—*Ger* [ˈhʊm bɔlt]
humbug 'hʌm bʌg ~ged d ~ging ɪŋ ~s z
humbuggery 'hʌm bʌg ər i
humdinger ˌhʌm 'dɪŋ ə ‖ -ᵊr ~s z
humdrum 'hʌm drʌm
Hume hjuːm

humectant hju ˈmekt ənt ~s s
humeral ˈhjuːm ər əl ~s z
hum|erus ˈhjuːm |ər əs (= humorous) ~eri
  ə raɪ
humic ˈhjuːm ɪk
humid ˈhjuːm ɪd §ˈjuːm-, §-əd
humidex ˈhjuːm ɪ deks §ˈjuːm-, -ə-
humidification hju ˌmɪd ɪf ɪ ˈkeɪʃ ən §ju-,
  ·,əf-, §-ə'··
humidifier hju ˈmɪd ɪ |faɪ ə ǁ ˌ°r ~s z
humidi|fy hju ˈmɪd ɪ |faɪ §ju-, -ə- ~fied faɪd
  ~fies faɪz ~fying faɪ ɪŋ
humidity hju ˈmɪd ət i §ju-, -ɪt- ǁ -ət̬ i
humid|ly ˈhjuːm ɪd |li §ˈjuːm-, §-əd- ~ness nəs
  nɪs
humidor ˈhjuːm ɪ dɔː §ju:m-, -ə- ǁ -dɔːr ~s z
humili|ate hju ˈmɪl i |eɪt §ju- ~ated eɪt ɪd -əd
  ǁ eɪt̬ əd ~ates eɪts ~ating/ly eɪt ɪŋ /li
  ǁ eɪt̬ ɪŋ /li
humiliation hju ˌmɪl i ˈeɪʃ ən ˌhjuːm ɪl-; §ju- ~s
  z
humility hju ˈmɪl ət i §ju-, -ɪt- ǁ -ət̬ i
humm... —see hum
hummingbird ˈhʌm ɪŋ bɜːd ǁ -bɜːd ~s z
hummock ˈhʌm ək ~s s
hummus ˈhʊm ʊs ˈhʌm-, -əs
humongous hju ˈmʌŋ gəs
humor ˈhjuːm ə §ˈjuːm- ǁ -ʳr ~ed d **humoring**
  hjuːm ər ɪŋ §ˈjuːm- ~s z
humoral ˈhjuːm ər əl
humoresque ˌhjuːm ə ˈresk ~s s
humorist ˈhjuːm ər ɪst §ˈjuːm-, §-əst ~s s
humoristic ˌhjuːm ə ˈrɪst ɪk ◂ §ˈjuːm- ~al ᵊl
humorless ˈhjuːm ə ləs §ˈjuːm-, -lɪs ǁ -ʳr- ~ly li
  ~ness nəs nɪs
humorous ˈhjuːm ər əs §ˈjuːm- ~ly li ~ness
  nəs nɪs
humour ˈhjuːm ə §ˈjuːm- ǁ -ʳr ~ed d
  humouring hjuːm ər ɪŋ §ˈjuːm- ~s z
humourless ˈhjuːm ə ləs §ˈjuːm-, -lɪs ǁ -ʳr- ~ly
  li ~ness nəs nɪs
hump hʌmp **humped** hʌmpt **humping**
  ˈhʌmp ɪŋ **humps** hʌmps
humpback ˈhʌmp bæk ~ed t
  ˌhumpbacked ˈbridge
Humperdinck German composer ˈhʊmp ə dɪŋk
  ˈhʌmp- ǁ -ʳr- —Ger [ˈhʊm pɐ dɪŋk]
Humperdinck British pop singer ˈhʌmp ə dɪŋk
  ǁ -ʳr-
humph hʌmᵖf or e.g. m̩m, m̩m̩m̩, həm̩m̩ with
  falling pitch
Humphrey ˈhʌmᵖf ri
Humphreys, Humphries, Humphrys
  ˈhʌmᵖf riz
humpt|y ˈhʌmpt |i ~ies iz
  ˌHumpty ˈDumpty ˈdʌmpt i
hump|y ˈhʌmp| i ~ier i_ə ǁ i_ʳr ~ies iz ~iest
  i_ɪst _əst
humungous hju ˈmʌŋ gəs
humus ˈhjuːm əs §ˈjuːm-
Humvee, h~ tdmk ˌhʌm ˈviː ˈ··~s z
Hun hʌn **Huns** hʌnz

Hunan ˌhuː ˈnæn ǁ -ˈnɑːn -ˈnæn —Chi Húnán
  [²xu ²nan]
hunch hʌntʃ **hunched** hʌntʃt **hunches**
  ˈhʌntʃ ɪz -əz **hunching** ˈhʌntʃ ɪŋ
hunchback ˈhʌntʃ bæk ~ed t ~s s
hundred ˈhʌndr əd -ɪd ǁ ˈhʌnd ʳrd ~s z
  ˌhundreds and ˈthousands
hundredfold ˈhʌndr əd fəʊld -ɪd-, -»-fɒʊld
  ǁ -foʊld ˈhʌnd ʳrd-
hundredth ˈhʌndr ədθ -ɪdθ, -ətθ, -ɪtθ
  ǁ ˈhʌnd ʳrdθ ~s s
hundredweight ˈhʌndr əd weɪt -ɪd-
  ǁ ˈhʌnd ʳrd- ~s s
hung hʌŋ
Hungarian hʌŋ ˈgeər i_ən ǁ -ˈger- -ˈgær- ~s z
Hungary ˈhʌŋ gər i
hunger ˈhʌŋ gə ǁ -gʳr ~ed d **hungering**
  ˈhʌŋ gər ɪŋ ~s z
  ˈhunger march; ˈhunger ˌmarcher;
  ˈhunger strike; ˈhunger ˌstriker
Hungerford ˈhʌŋ gə fəd -fɔːd ǁ -gʳr fʳrd
hungover ˌhʌŋ ˈəʊv ə ◂ -ˈoʊv ʳr ◂
hun|gry ˈhʌŋ |gri ~grier gri_ə ǁ gri_ʳr ~griest
  gri_ɪst əst ~grily grəl i grɪ li
hung-up ˌhʌŋ ˈʌp ◂
hunk hʌŋk **hunks** hʌŋks
hunker, H~ ˈhʌŋk ə ǁ -ʳr ~ed d **hunkering**
  ˈhʌŋk ər ɪŋ ~s z
hunk|y ˈhʌŋk| i ~ier i_ə ǁ i_ʳr ~iest i_ɪst _əst
hunky-dory ˌhʌŋk i ˈdɔːr i ǁ -ˈdoʊr-
Hunniford ˈhʌn i fəd §-fɔːd ǁ -fʳrd
Hunnish, h~ ˈhʌn ɪʃ ~ness nəs nɪs
Hunslet ˈhʌnz lət -lɪt
Hunstanton hʌn ˈstænt ən —locally also
  ˈhʌnˌst ən
hunt hʌnt **hunted** ˈhʌntɪd -əd ǁ ˈhʌnt̬ əd
  hunting ˈhʌnt ɪŋ ǁ ˈhʌnt̬ ɪŋ **hunts** hʌnts
  ˈhunting ground
Hunt, Hunte hʌnt
hunter, H~ ˈhʌnt ə ǁ ˈhʌnt̬ ʳr ~s z
hunter-gatherer ˌhʌnt ə ˈgæð ər_ə
  ǁ ˌhʌnt̬ ʳr ˈgæð ʳr_ər ~s z
hunter-killer ˌhʌnt ə ˈkɪl ə ǁ ˌhʌnt̬ ʳr ˈkɪl ʳr ~s
  z
Huntingdon ˈhʌnt ɪŋ dən ǁ ˈhʌnt̬- ~shire ʃə
  ʃɪə ǁ ʃʳr ʃɪr
Huntingford ˈhʌnt ɪŋ fəd ǁ ˈhʌnt̬ ɪŋ fʳrd
Huntington ˈhʌnt ɪŋ tən ǁ ˈhʌnt̬- ~'s z
  ˌHuntington ˈBeach; ˌHuntington's
  cho'rea
Huntley, Huntly ˈhʌnt li
huntress ˈhʌntr əs -ɪs, -es ~es ɪz əz
hunts|man ˈhʌnts |mən ~men mən men
Huntsville ˈhʌnts vɪl
Huon ˈhjuː ɒn ǁ -ɑːn
Hurd hɜːd ǁ hɜːd
hurdl|e ˈhɜːd ᵊl ǁ ˈhɜːd ᵊl ~ed d ~es z ~ing ɪŋ
hurdler ˈhɜːd lə ǁ ˈhɜːd lʳr ~s z
hurdy-gurd|y ˈhɜːd i ˌgɜːd |i ˌ·ˈ··
  ǁ ˈhɜːd i ˌgɜːd |i ~ies iz
Hurford ˈhɜː fəd ǁ ˈhɜː fʳrd
hurl hɜːl ǁ hɜːl **hurled** hɜːld ǁ hɜːld **hurling**
  ˈhɜːl ɪŋ ǁ ˈhɜːl ɪŋ **hurls** hɜːlz ǁ hɜːlz

H

hurler ˈhɜːl ə ‖ ˈhɝːl ᵊr **~s** z
hurley, H~ ˈhɜːl i ‖ ˈhɝːl i **~s** z
Hurlingham ˈhɜːl ɪŋ əm ‖ ˈhɝːl-
hurly-burl|y ˈhɜːl i ˌbɜːl |i ˌ· ·ˈ· · ‖ ˌhɝːl i ˈbɝːl |i ˈ· ·ˌ· · **~ies** iz
Hurn hɜːn ‖ hɝːn
Huron ˈhjʊər ən §ˈjʊər-, §ˈhjuːr-, -ɒn ‖ ˈhjʊr ən ˈjʊr-, -ɑːn
hurrah hə ˈrɑː hʊ- ‖ -ˈrɔː **~s** z
hurray hə ˈreɪ hʊ- **~s** z
Hurrell *(i)* ˈhʌr əl ‖ ˈhɝː‿, *(ii)* ˈhʊər əl ‖ ˈhʊr-

HURRICANE

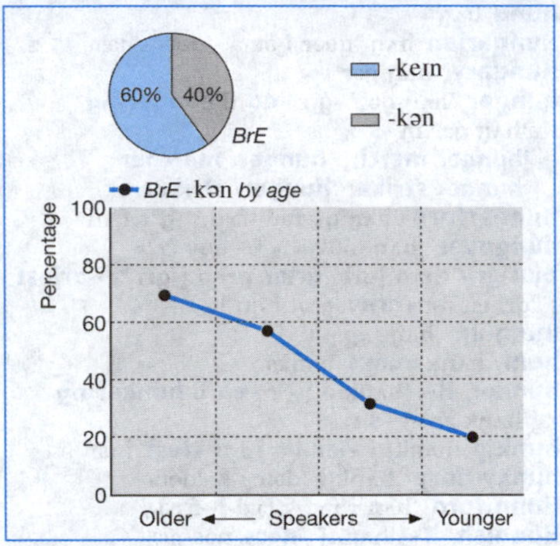
60%
40%
BrE
-keɪn
-kən
BrE -kən by age
Percentage
100
80
60
40
20
0
Older
Speakers
Younger

hurricane ˈhʌr ɪk ən -ək-; -ɪ keɪn, -ə- ‖ ˈhɝː ə keɪn — *Preference poll, BrE:* -kən *40% (born before 1942, 70%),* -keɪn *60%.* **~s** z
ˈhurricane lamp
hurr|y ˈhʌr |i ‖ ˈhɝː |i **~ied/ly** id /li **~ies** iz **~ying** i ɪŋ
Hurst hɜːst ‖ hɝːst
Hurstmonceux ˌhɜː*st* mən ˈsjuː -ˈsuː, -ˈzuː ‖ ˌhɝː*st* mən ˈsuː
Hurstpierpoint ˌhɜː*st* pɪə ˈpɔɪnt ‖ ˌhɝː*st* pɪr-
hurt, Hurt hɜːt ‖ hɝːt **hurting** ˈhɜːt ɪŋ ‖ ˈhɝːţ ɪŋ **hurts** hɜːts ‖ hɝːts
hurtful ˈhɜːt fᵊl -fʊl ‖ ˈhɝːt- **~ly** ‿i **~ness** nəs nɪs
hurtl|e ˈhɜːt ᵊl ‖ ˈhɝːţ ᵊl **~ed** d **~es** z **~ing** ‿ɪŋ
husband ˈhʌz bənd **~ed** ɪd əd **~ing** ɪŋ **~s** z
husband|man ˈhʌz bənd |mən →-bəm- **~men** mən men
husbandry ˈhʌz bənd ri
hush hʌʃ **hushed** hʌʃt **hushes** ˈhʌʃ ɪz -əz **hushing** ˈhʌʃ ɪŋ
ˈhush ˌmoney; **ˈHush ˌPuppies** *tdmk*
hushaby, hushabye, hush-a-bye ˈhʌʃ ə baɪ
hush-hush ˌhʌʃ ˈhʌʃ ◂ ˈ· · ‖ ˈhʌʃ hʌʃ
hush-up *n* ˈhʌʃ ʌp
husk hʌsk **husked** hʌskt **husking** ˈhʌsk ɪŋ **husks** hʌsks
huski... —*see* **husky**
Huskisson ˈhʌsk ɪs ən -əs-
husk|y ˈhʌsk |i **~ier** i‿ə ‖ i‿ᵊr **~ies** iz **~iest** i‿ɪst i‿əst **~ily** ɪ li əl i **~iness** i nəs i nɪs

huss hʌs
Huss hʌs hʊs —*German, Czech* [hʊs]
Hussain hu ˈseɪn
hussar hu ˈzɑː hə- ‖ -ˈzɑːr **~s** z
Hussein hu ˈseɪn
Hussey ˈhʌs i
Hussite ˈhʌs aɪt ˈhʊs- **~s** s
huss|y, Hussy ˈhʌs |i ˈhʌz- **~ies** iz
hustings ˈhʌst ɪŋz
hustl|e ˈhʌs ᵊl **~ed** d **~es** z **~ing** ‿ɪŋ
hustler ˈhʌs lə ˈhʌs ᵊl‿ə ‖ -lᵊr **~s** z
Huston ˈhjuːst ən
hut hʌt **hutted** ˈhʌt ɪd -əd ‖ ˈhʌţ əd **hutting** ˈhʌt ɪŋ ‖ ˈhʌţ ɪŋ **huts** hʌts
hutch, Hutch hʌtʃ **hutches** ˈhʌtʃ ɪz -əz
Hutchence ˈhʌtʃ ənᵗs
Hutcheson ˈhʌtʃ ɪs ən -əs-
Hutchings ˈhʌtʃ ɪŋz
Hutchins ˈhʌtʃ ɪnz
Hutchinson ˈhʌtʃ ɪn sən -ən-
Hutchison ˈhʌtʃ ɪs ən -əs-
hutment ˈhʌt mənt **~s** s
Hutterite ˈhʌt ə raɪt ˈhʊt-, ˈhuːt- ‖ ˈhʌţ- ˈhʊţ-, ˈhuːţ- **~s** s
Hutton ˈhʌt ᵊn
Hutu ˈhuːt uː **~s** z
Huw hjuː —*Welsh* [hiu, hɪu]
Huxley ˈhʌks li
Huxtable ˈhʌkst əb ᵊl
Huygens ˈhaɪɡ ənz —*Dutch* [ˈhœy xəns]
Huyton ˈhaɪt ᵊn *(= heighten)*
huzza, huzzah hu ˈzɑː hʌ-, hə- **~s** z
Hwang-Ho ˌhwæŋ ˈhəʊ ‖ -ˈhoʊ —*Chi* Huáng Hé [²xwɑŋ ²xɤ]
hwyl ˈhuː‿ɪl əl —*Welsh* [huil, huɨl]
Hy haɪ
hyacinth, H~ ˈhaɪ‿ə sɪnᵗθ **~s** s
hyacinthine ˌhaɪ‿ə ˈsɪnᵗθ aɪn -iːn
Hyacinthus ˌhaɪ‿ə ˈsɪnᵗθ əs
Hyades ˈhaɪ‿ə diːz
hyaena haɪ ˈiːn ə **~s** z
hyalin ˈhaɪ‿ə lɪn
hyaline ˈhaɪ‿ə lɪn -liːn, -laɪn
hyalo- *comb. form*
with stress-neutral suffix ¦haɪ‿əl əʊ haɪ ¦æl ə ‖ -oʊ haɪ ¦æl ə — **hyaloplasm** ˈhaɪ‿əl əʊ ˌplæz əm haɪ ˈæl ə- ‖ -oʊˌ-
with stress-imposing suffix ˌhaɪ‿ə ˈlɒ+ ‖ -ˈlɑː+ — **hyalophagy** ˌhaɪ‿ə ˈlɒf ədʒ i ‖ -ˈlɑːf-
hyaloid ˈhaɪ‿ə lɔɪd
Hyannis haɪ ˈæn ɪs §-əs
Hyatt ˈhaɪ‿ət
hybrid ˈhaɪb rɪd §-rəd **~s** z
ˌhybrid ˈvigour
hybridis... —*see* **hybridiz...**
hybridism ˈhaɪb rɪ ˌdɪz əm ‖ -rə-
hybridity haɪ ˈbrɪd ət i -ɪt i ‖ -əţ i
hybridization ˌhaɪb rɪd aɪ ˈzeɪʃ ᵊn ˌ·rəd-, -ɪˈ-- ‖ -rəd ə- **~s** z
hybridiz|e ˈhaɪb rɪ daɪz -rə- **~ed** d **~es** ɪz əz **~ing** ɪŋ
hydatid ˈhaɪd ət ɪd haɪ ˈdæt-, §-əd ‖ -əţ əd **~s** z

Hyde haɪd
 ˌHyde 'Park◂, ˌHyde ˌPark 'Corner
Hyder *tdmk* 'haɪd ə ‖ -ᵊr —*Welsh* ['hə der]
Hyderabad 'haɪd ər ə bæd -bɑːd, ˌ·· ·ˈ·
hydr|a, Hydra 'haɪdr |ə ~**ae** iː ~**as** əz
hydrangea haɪ 'dreɪndʒ ə -'dreɪndʒ i ə
 ‖ -'drændʒ ə ~**s** z
hydrant 'haɪdr ənt ~**s** s
hydrate *n* 'haɪdr eɪt ~**s** s
hydr|ate *v* haɪ 'dr|eɪt 'haɪdr |eɪt ‖ 'haɪdr |eɪt
 ~**ated** eɪt ɪd -əd ‖ eɪt̬ əd ~**ates** eɪts ~**ating**
 eɪt ɪŋ ‖ eɪt̬ ɪŋ
hydration haɪ 'dreɪʃ ᵊn
hydraulic haɪ 'drɔːl ɪk -'drɒl- ‖ -'drɑːl- ~**ally**
 ᵊl_i ~**s** s
hydrazine 'haɪdr ə ziːn -zɪn, -zaɪn
hydric 'haɪdr ɪk
hydride 'haɪdr aɪd ~**s** z
hydro 'haɪdr əʊ ‖ -oʊ ~**s** z
hydro- *comb. form*
 with stress-neutral suffix ˌhaɪdr əʊ ‖ -ə
 — **hydrotaxis** ˌhaɪdr əʊ 'tæks ɪs §-əs ‖ -ə-
 with stress-imposing suffix haɪ 'drɒ +
 ‖ -'drɑː + — **hydrophanous** haɪ 'drɒf ən əs
 ‖ -'drɑːf-
hydrocarbon ˌhaɪdr əʊ 'kɑːb ən ‖ -ə 'kɑːrb-
 ~**s** z
hydrocele 'haɪdr əʊ siːᵊl ‖ -ə- ~**s** z
hydrocephalus ˌhaɪdr əʊ 'kef əl əs -'sef-
 ‖ -oʊ 'sef-
hydrochloric ˌhaɪdr əʊ 'klɒr ɪk ◂ -'klɔːr-
 ‖ -ə 'klɔːr- -'kloʊr-
 ˌhydroˌchloric 'acid
hydrochloride ˌhaɪdr əʊ 'klɔːr aɪd ‖ -ə-
 -'kloʊr- ~**s** z
hydrocortisone ˌhaɪdr əʊ 'kɔːt ɪ zəʊn -'·ə-
 ‖ -ə 'kɔːrt̬ ə zoʊn -soʊn
hydrodynamic ˌhaɪdr əʊ daɪ 'næm ɪk ◂ -dɪ'--
 ‖ ˌhaɪdr oʊ- ~**ally** ᵊl_i ~**s** s
hydroelectric ˌhaɪdr əʊ ɪ 'lek trɪk ◂ -ə'--
 ‖ ˌhaɪdr oʊ- ~**ally** ᵊl_i
hydroelectricity ˌhaɪdr əʊ i ˌlek 'trɪs ət i
 -əʊ ə-, -əʊ ˌel ek-, -əʊ ˌɪl ek-, -əʊ ˌiː lek-, -'trɪz-,
 -ɪt i ‖ -oʊ i ˌlek 'trɪs ət̬ i
hydrofoil 'haɪdr əʊ fɔɪᵊl ‖ -ə- ~**s** z
hydrogen 'haɪdr ədʒ ən -ɪdʒ-, -ɪn
 'hydrogen ˌbomb; ˌhydrogen per'oxide;
 ˌhydrogen 'sulphide
hydroge|nate 'haɪdr ədʒ ə |neɪt -ədʒ ɪ-;
 haɪ 'drɒdʒ- ‖ haɪ 'drɑːdʒ- 'haɪdr ədʒ- ~**nated**
 neɪt ɪd -əd ‖ neɪt̬ əd ~**nates** neɪts ~**nating**
 neɪt ɪŋ ‖ neɪt̬ ɪŋ
hydrographer haɪ 'drɒg rəf ə ‖ -'drɑːg rəf ᵊr
 ~**s** z
hydrographic ˌhaɪdr əʊ 'græf ɪk ◂ ‖ -ə- ~**ally**
 ᵊl_i
hydrography haɪ 'drɒg rəf i ‖ -'drɑːg-
hydroid 'haɪdr ɔɪd ~**s** z
hydrologic ˌhaɪdr ə 'lɒdʒ ɪk ‖ -'lɑːdʒ- ~**al** ᵊl
 ~**ally** ᵊl_i
hydrologist haɪ 'drɒl ədʒ ɪst §-əst ‖ -'drɑːl- ~**s**
 s
hydrology haɪ 'drɒl ədʒ i ‖ -'drɑːl-

hydrolys|e 'haɪdr ə laɪz ~**ed** d ~**es** ɪz əz ~**ing**
 ɪŋ
hydrolysis haɪ 'drɒl əs ɪs -ɪs-, §-əs ‖ -'drɑːl-
hydrolytic ˌhaɪdr ə 'lɪt ɪk ◂ ‖ -'lɪt̬ ɪk ◂ ~**ally**
 ᵊl_i
hydrolyz|e 'haɪdr ə laɪz ~**ed** d ~**es** ɪz əz ~**ing**
 ɪŋ
hydrometer haɪ 'drɒm ɪt ə -ət- ‖ -'drɑːm ət̬ ᵊr
 ~**s** z
hydropathy haɪ 'drɒp əθ i ‖ -'drɑːp-
hydrophilic ˌhaɪdr əʊ 'fɪl ɪk ◂ ‖ -ə-
hydrophob|ia ˌhaɪdr əʊ 'fəʊb| i ə ‖ -ə 'foʊb|-
 ~**ic** ɪk ◂
hydrophone 'haɪdr ə fəʊn ‖ -foʊn ~**s** z
hydrophyte 'haɪdr ə faɪt ~**s** s
hydroplane 'haɪdr əʊ pleɪn ‖ -ə- ~**s** z
hydroponic ˌhaɪdr əʊ 'pɒn ɪk ◂ ‖ -ə 'pɑːn- ~**s**
 s
hydrostatic ˌhaɪdr əʊ 'stæt ɪk ◂ ‖ -ə 'stæt̬ ɪk ◂
 ~**ally** ᵊl_i ~**s** s
hydrotherapy ˌhaɪdr əʊ 'θer əp i ‖ ˌhaɪdr ə-
hydrotropic ˌhaɪdr əʊ 'trɒp ɪk ◂
 ‖ -ə 'trɑːp ɪk ◂ -'troʊp-
hydrotropism haɪ 'drɒtr ə ˌpɪz əm ‖ -'drɑːtr-
hydrous 'haɪdr əs
hydroxide haɪ 'drɒks aɪd ‖ -'drɑːks- ~**s** z
hydroxy haɪ 'drɒks i ‖ -'drɑːks i
hydroxyl haɪ 'drɒks ɪl -ᵊl ‖ -'drɑːks-
hydrozoan ˌhaɪdr əʊ 'zəʊ ən ‖ -ə 'zoʊ- ~**s** z
Hydrus 'haɪdr əs
hyena haɪ 'iːn ə ~**s** z
hyetograph 'haɪ ət əʊ grɑːf '·ɪt-, -græf; haɪ 'et-
 ‖ -ət̬ ə græf haɪ 'et̬- ~**s** s
Hygeia haɪ 'dʒiː ə
Hygena *tdmk* haɪ 'dʒiːn ə
hygiene 'haɪdʒ iːn
hygienic haɪ 'dʒiːn ɪk ‖ ˌhaɪdʒ i 'en ɪk ◂
 haɪ 'dʒen ɪk (*) ~**ally** ᵊl_i
hygienist 'haɪdʒ iːn ɪst haɪ 'dʒiːn-, §-əst
 ‖ haɪ 'dʒiːn əst -'dʒen-; 'haɪdʒ iːn əst ~**s** s
hygrometer haɪ 'grɒm ɪt ə -ət- ‖ -'grɑːm ət̬ ᵊr
 ~**s** z
hygroscopic ˌhaɪg rə 'skɒp ɪk ◂ ‖ -'skɑːp-
Hylas 'haɪl əs -æs
Hylda 'hɪld ə
Hylton 'hɪlt ən
Hyman 'haɪm ən
hymen, Hymen 'haɪm en ‖ -ən ~**s** z
hymeneal ˌhaɪm e 'niː əl ◂ -ɪ-, -ə- ‖ -ə-
hymenopterous ˌhaɪm ə 'nɒpt ər əs ◂ ˌ·ɪ-, ˌ·e-
 ‖ -'nɑːpt-
Hymettus haɪ 'met əs ‖ -'met̬ əs
Hymie 'haɪm i
hymn hɪm (= *him*) **hymned** hɪmd **hymning**
 'hɪm ɪŋ **hymns** hɪmz
 'hymn ˌbook
hymnal 'hɪm nəl ~**s** z
hymnodist 'hɪm nəd ɪst §-əst ~**s** s
hymnod|y 'hɪm nəd |i ~**ies** iz
hymnology hɪm 'nɒl ədʒ i ‖ -'nɑːl-
Hynd haɪnd
hyoid 'haɪ ɔɪd
hyoscine 'haɪ əʊ siːn ‖ -ə-

hyoscyamine ˌhaɪ əʊ 'saɪˌə miːn -mɪn, §-mən
‖ ˌhaɪ ə-

hypallage haɪ 'pæl ədʒ i -əg-, -iː **~s** z

Hypatia haɪ 'peɪʃ ə -'peɪʃ i ̩ə

hype haɪp **hyped** haɪpt **hypes** haɪps **hyping**
'haɪp ɪŋ

hyped 'up

hyper- comb. form
  with stress-neutral suffix ˌhaɪp ə ‖ ˌhaɪp ᵊr
  —but before a vowel sound, -ər ‖ -ᵊr;
  — **hyperpyrexia** ˌhaɪp ə paɪᵊ 'reks i ̩ə
  ‖ ˌhaɪp ᵊr-; — **hyperacidity**
  ˌhaɪp ər ə 'sɪd ət i -æ'--, -ɪt i ‖ -ər ə 'sɪd əṭ i
  with stress-imposing suffix haɪ 'pɜː+
  ‖ haɪ 'pɜː+ — **hypergamy** haɪ 'pɜːg əm i
  ‖ -'pɜːg-

hyperactive ˌhaɪp ər 'ækt ɪv ◄ ‖ -ər- **~ly** li

hyperactivity ˌhaɪp ər æk 'tɪv ət i -ɪt i
  ‖ -ər æk 'tɪv əṭ i

hyperbaric ˌhaɪp ə 'bær ɪk ◄ ‖ -ᵊr- -'ber-

hyperbaton haɪ 'pɜːb ə tɒn ‖ -'pɜːb ə taːn

hyperb|ola haɪ 'pɜːb| əl ə ‖ -'pɜːb|- **~olae**
  ə liː **~olas** əl əz

hyperbole haɪ 'pɜːb əl i ⚠ 'haɪp ə bəʊl
  ‖ -'pɜːb- **~s** z

hyperbolic ˌhaɪp ə 'bɒl ɪk ◄ ‖ -ᵊr 'baːl ɪk ◄
  ~ally ᵊl̩i
  ˌhyper|bolic 'function

hyperboloid haɪ 'pɜːb ə lɔɪd ‖ -'pɜːb- **~s** z

hyperborean, H~ ˌhaɪp ə 'bɔːr i ̩ən
  -bɔː 'riːˌən, -bɒ'-- ‖ ˌhaɪp ᵊr- -'bour- **~s** z

hypercoristic ˌhaɪp ə kɔː 'rɪst ɪk ◄ -kɒ'--, -kə'--
  ‖ -ᵊr kə- **~ally** ᵊl̩i **~s** s

hypercorrect ˌhaɪp ə kə 'rekt ◄ ‖ ˌhaɪp ᵊr- **~ly**
  li **~ness** nəs nɪs

hypercorrection ˌhaɪp ə kə 'rek ʃᵊn
  ‖ ˌhaɪp ᵊr- **~s** z

hypercritical ˌhaɪp ə 'krɪt ɪk ᵊl ◄
  ‖ ˌhaɪp ᵊr 'krɪṭ- **~ly** ̩i

hypercube 'haɪp ə kjuːb ‖ -ᵊr- **~s** z

hyperglycaemia, hyperglycemia
  ˌhaɪp ə glaɪ 'siːm i ̩ə ‖ ˌhaɪp ᵊr-

hypericum haɪ 'per ɪk əm **~s** z

Hyperides haɪ 'per ə diːz -ə-; ˌhaɪp ə 'raɪd iːz

hyperinflation ˌhaɪp ər ɪn 'fleɪʃ ᵊn

Hyperion haɪ 'pɪər i ̩ən -'per- ‖ -'pɪr-

hyperlink 'haɪp ə lɪŋk ‖ -ᵊr- **~s** s

hypermarket 'haɪp ə ˌmaːk ɪt §-ət
  ‖ -ᵊr ˌmaːrk- **~s** s

hyperpituitarism ˌhaɪp ə pɪ 'tjuːˌɪt ə ˌrɪz əm
  -pə'--, →-'tʃuːˌ, §-'·ət- ‖ -ᵊr pə 'tuː əṭ- -'tjuː-

hypersensitive ˌhaɪp ə 'sents ət ɪv ◄ -ɪt ɪv
  ‖ -ᵊr 'sents əṭ ɪv ◄ **~ness** nəs nɪs

hypersensitivity ˌhaɪp ə ˌsents ə 'tɪv ət i -ˌ·ɪ-,
  -ɪt i ‖ -ᵊr ˌsents ə 'tɪv əṭ i

hypersonic ˌhaɪp ə 'sɒn ɪk ◄ ‖ -ᵊr 'saːn ɪk ◄ **~s**
  s

hyperspace 'haɪp ə speɪs ̩·ˈ· ‖ -ᵊr-

hypertension ˌhaɪp ə 'tenᵗʃ ᵊn ‖ -ᵊr-

hypertensive ˌhaɪp ə 'tents ɪv ◄ ‖ -ᵊr-

hypertext 'haɪp ə tekst ‖ -ᵊr-

hyperthyroid ˌhaɪp ə 'θaɪᵊr ɔɪd ◄ ‖ -ᵊr- **~ism**
  ˌɪz əm

hypertroph|y haɪ 'pɜːtr əf |i ‖ -'pɜːtr- **~ied** id
  ~ies iz **~ying** i ɪŋ

hyperventi|late ˌhaɪp ə 'vent ɪ |leɪt -ə leɪt,
  -ᵊl|eɪt ‖ -ᵊr 'venṭ ᵊl|eɪt **~lated** leɪt ɪd -əd
  ‖ leɪṭ əd **~lates** leɪts **~lating** leɪt ɪŋ ‖ leɪṭ ɪŋ

hyperventilation ˌhaɪp ə ˌvent ɪ 'leɪʃ ᵊn -ə'--,
  -ᵊl 'eɪʃ- ‖ -ᵊr ˌvenṭ ᵊl 'eɪʃ ᵊn

hyph|a 'haɪf |ə **~ae** iː

hyphen 'haɪf ᵊn **~s** z

hyphe|nate 'haɪf ə |neɪt **~nated** neɪt ɪd -əd
  ‖ neɪṭ əd **~nates** neɪts **~nating** neɪt ɪŋ
  ‖ neɪṭ ɪŋ

hyphenation ˌhaɪf ə 'neɪʃ ᵊn **~s** z

hypnagogic, hypnogogic ˌhɪp nə 'gɒdʒ ɪk ◄
  -'gəʊdʒ- ‖ -'gaːdʒ ɪk ◄ -'goʊdʒ- **~s** s

hypno- comb. form
  with stress-neutral suffix ˌhɪp nəʊ ‖ -nou
  — **hypnotherapy** ˌhɪp nəʊ 'θer əp i
  ‖ ˌhɪp noʊ-
  with stress-imposing suffix hɪp 'nɒ+ ‖ -'naː+
  — **hypnology** hɪp 'nɒl ədʒ i ‖ -'naːl-

Hypnos 'hɪp nɒs ‖ -naːs -noʊs, -nəs

hypnos|is hɪp 'nəʊs |ɪs §-əs ‖ -'noʊs- **~es** iːz

hypnothera|pist ˌhɪp nəʊ 'θer ə pɪst ‖ ˌ·noʊ-
  ~ists ɪsts §əsts **~py** i

hypnotic hɪp 'nɒt ɪk ‖ -'naːṭ ɪk **~ally** ᵊl̩i **~s** s

hypnotis... —see **hypnotiz...**

hypnotism 'hɪp nə ˌtɪz əm

hypnotist 'hɪp nət ɪst §-əst ‖ -nəṭ- **~s** s

hypnotiz|e 'hɪp nə taɪz **~ed** d **~es** ɪz əz **~ing**
  ɪŋ

hypo 'haɪp əʊ ‖ -oʊ

hypo- comb. form
  with stress-neutral suffix ˌhaɪp əʊ ‖ -ə —but
  before a vowel ˌhaɪp əʊ ‖ -oʊ —
  hypochlorous ˌhaɪp əʊ 'klɔːr əs ◄ ‖ -ə-
  -'klour- — **hypoallergenic**
  ˌhaɪp əʊ ˌæl ə 'dʒen ɪk -ɜː'-- ‖ -oʊ ˌæl ᵊr-
  —The fact that RP ˌhaɪp ə is ambiguous as
  between hypo- and hyper- means that for
  clarity it is arguably better to avoid reducing
  the second syllable and therefore always to say
  ˌhaɪp əʊ
  with stress-imposing suffix haɪ 'pɒ+ ‖ -'paː+
  — **hypogynous** haɪ 'pɒdʒ ɪn əs -ən-
  ‖ -'paːdʒ-

hypocaust 'haɪp əʊ kɔːst ‖ -ə- -kaːst **~s** s

hypocenter, hypocentre 'haɪp əʊ ˌsent ə
  ‖ -ə ˌsenṭ ᵊr **~s** z

hypochondria ˌhaɪp əʊ 'kɒndr i ̩ə
  ‖ -ə 'kaːndr-

hypochondriac ˌhaɪp əʊ 'kɒndr i æk
  ‖ -ə 'kaːndr- **~s** s

hypochondriacal ˌhaɪp əʊ kɒn 'draɪˌək ᵊl ◄
  -kən'-- ‖ -oʊ kaːn-

hypocorism haɪ 'pɒk ə ˌrɪz əm
  ˌhaɪp ə 'kɔːr ɪz əm ‖ -'paːk-

hypocris|y hɪ 'pɒk rəs |i §haɪ-, -rɪs- ‖ -'paːk-
  ~ies iz

hypocrite 'hɪp ə krɪt **~s** s

hypocritical ˌhɪp ə 'krɪt ɪk ᵊl ◄ ‖ -'krɪṭ- **~ly** ̩i

hypodermic ˌhaɪp əʊ 'dɜːm ɪk ◄
‖ -ə 'dɜːm ɪk ◄ **~ally** ᵊl̩ i **~s** s
    ˌhypo͵dermic 'needle
hypodermis ˌhaɪp əʊ 'dɜːm ɪs §-əs
‖ -ə 'dɜːm əs
hypogeal ˌhaɪp əʊ 'dʒiː əl ◄ ‖ -oʊ-
hypoglossal ˌhaɪp əʊ 'glɒs ᵊl ◄ ‖ -ə 'glɑːs ᵊl ◄
hypoglycaem|ia, hypoglycem|ia
    ˌhaɪp əʊ glaɪ 'siːm| i ə ‖ ˌhaɪp oʊ- **~ic** ɪk ◄
hypoid 'haɪp ɔɪd **~s** z
hyponym 'haɪp əʊ nɪm ‖ -ə- **~s** z
hyponymy haɪ 'pɒn əm i -ɪm i ‖ -'paːn-
hypostasis haɪ 'pɒst əs ɪs §-əs ‖ -'pɑːst-
hypostatic ˌhaɪp ə 'stæt ɪk ◄ ‖ -'stæt̬ ɪk ◄
    ˌhypo͵static 'union
hypostatis... —*see* **hypostatiz...**
hypostatization haɪ ˌpɒst ət aɪ 'zeɪʃ ᵊn -ɪt ɪ-
‖ -ˌpɑːst ət̬ ə-
hypostatiz|e haɪ 'pɒst ə taɪz ‖ -'pɑːst- **~ed** d
    ~es ɪz əz **~ing** ɪŋ
hypostyle 'haɪp əʊ staɪᵊl ‖ -oʊ-
hyposulfite, hyposulphite ˌhaɪp əʊ 'sʌlf aɪt
‖ -oʊ-
hypotactic ˌhaɪp əʊ 'tækt ɪk ◄ ‖ -ə- -oʊ- **~ally**
    ᵊl̩ i
hypotaxis ˌhaɪp əʊ 'tæks ɪs §-əs ‖ -ə- -oʊ-
hypo|tension ˌhaɪp əʊ 'tenᵗʃ ᵊn ‖ ˌhaɪp oʊ-
    ~tensive 'tenᵗs ɪv
hypotenuse haɪ 'pɒt ə njuːz -ɪ-, -ᵊn juːz
‖ -'pɑːt ᵊn uːs -juːs *(*)*
hypothalamic ˌhaɪp əʊ θə 'læm ɪk ◄
‖ ˌhaɪp oʊ-
hypothalamus ˌhaɪp əʊ 'θæl əm əs
‖ ˌhaɪp oʊ-

hypothe|cate haɪ 'pɒθ ə |keɪt -ɪ- ‖ -'pɑːθ- hɪ-
    ~cated keɪt ɪd -əd ‖ keɪt̬ əd **~cates** keɪts
    ~cating keɪt ɪŋ ‖ keɪt̬ ɪŋ
hypothecation haɪ ˌpɒθ ə 'keɪʃ ᵊn -ɪ- ‖ -ˌpɑːθ-
    hɪ- **~s** z
hypothermia ˌhaɪp əʊ 'θɜːm i ə ‖ -oʊ 'θɜːm-
hypoth|esis haɪ 'pɒθ |əs ɪs -ɪs-, §-əs **~eses**
    ə siːz ɪ-
hypothesiz|e, hypothesiz|e haɪ 'pɒθ ə saɪz
‖ -'pɑːθ- **~ed** d **~es** ɪz əz **~ing** ɪŋ
hypothetical ˌhaɪp ə 'θet ɪk ᵊl ◄ ‖ -'θet̬- **~ly** i
hypothyroid ˌhaɪp əʊ 'θaɪᵊr ɔɪd ◄ ‖ -oʊ- **~ism**
    ˌɪz əm
hypoxia haɪ 'pɒks i ə ‖ -'pɑːks-
hypsometer hɪp 'sɒm ɪt ə -ət- ‖ -'saːm ət̬ ᵊr **~s**
    z
hypsometry hɪp 'sɒm ətr i -ɪtr- ‖ -'saːm-
hyrax 'haɪᵊr æks **~es** ɪz əz
Hyrcania hɜː 'keɪn i ə ‖ hɜː-
Hyslop 'hɪz ləp
hyssop 'hɪs əp
hysterectom|y ˌhɪst ə 'rekt əm |i **~ies** iz
hysteresis ˌhɪst ə 'riːs ɪs §-əs
hysteria hɪ 'stɪər i ə ‖ -'stɪr- -'ster- **~s** z
hysteric hɪ 'ster ɪk **~s** s
hysterical hɪ 'ster ɪk ᵊl **~ly** i
hysteron proteron ˌhɪst ə rɒn 'prɒt ə rɒn
    →-rɒm'-- ‖ ˌhɪst ə raːn 'praːt̬ ə raːn
Hythe haɪð
Hyundai *tdmk* 'haɪ ən daɪ -ʌn-, -ʊn-, -deɪ;
‖ 'hʌnd eɪ —*Korean* [hjəːn dɛ]
Hywel 'haʊ ᵊl —*Welsh* ['hə wel]
Hz hɜːts ‖ hɜːts

i Spelling-to-sound

1 Where the spelling is **i**, the pronunciation differs according to whether the vowel is short or long, followed or not by **r**, and strong or weak.

2 The 'strong' pronunciation is regularly

ɪ as in **bit** bɪt ('short I'), or

aɪ as in **time** taɪm ('long I').

3 Where **i** is followed by **r**, the 'strong' pronunciation is

ɜː ‖ ɝː as in **firm** fɜːm ‖ fɝːm

aɪ(ə) as in **fire** faɪ‿ə ‖ ˈfaɪ‿ᵊr, **virus** ˈvaɪᵊr əs

or, indeed, the regular 'short' pronunciation ɪ as in **miracle** ˈmɪr ək ᵊl.

4 Less frequently, the 'strong' pronunciation is

iː as in **machine** mə ˈʃiːn.

5 The 'weak' pronunciation is

ɪ as in **rabbit** ˈræb ɪt (although some speakers, especially of AmE, use ə instead, thus ˈræb ət) or

ə as in **admiral** ˈæd mər əl.

Where the following sound is a vowel, the 'weak' pronunciation is

i as in **medium** ˈmiːd i‿əm (see COMPRESSION) or the **i** is silent, serving only to indicate the pronunciation of the consonant as in **special** ˈspeʃ ᵊl (see **c, s, t**).

6 In the rare cases where **i** is found at the end of a word, the pronunciation is either strong aɪ as in **hi** haɪ or

weak i as in **spaghetti** spə ˈget i ‖ spə ˈget̬ i.

7 **i** also forms part of the digraphs **ai, ei, ie, oi, ui**.

ie Spelling-to-sound

1 Where the spelling is the digraph **ie**, the pronunciation is regularly

iː as in **piece** piːs (especially in the middle of a word) or

aɪ as in **tie** taɪ (especially at the end of a word) or

ɪə ‖ ɪ as in **fierce** fɪəs ‖ fɪrs (before **r**).

2 The 'weak' pronunciation in **-ied**, **-ies** is usually
i as in **buried** ˈber id. Thus the spelling change from **y** to **ie** in inflected forms of
words written with **y** at the end does not imply any change in pronunciation.

3 Note the exceptional **friend** frend and **sieve** sɪv; also the usual pronunciation
of **handkerchief**, -tʃɪf.

4 **ie** is not a digraph in **science**, **pliers**, **society**, **acquiesce**, **Viennese**, **happiest**.

I, i *name of letter* aɪ *(= eye)* **I's, i's** aɪz
—*Communications code name:* India

I *pronoun* aɪ *This word has no true weak form in
RP, though in rapid casual speech it may
become monophthongal* a. *In GenAm it is
sometimes weakened to* ə.

I-5 ˌaɪ ˈfaɪv —*and similarly for the names of
other US interstate highways*

Iacoca ˌaɪ ə ˈkɒk ə ‖ ˌaɪ ə ˈkɑːk ə

Iago i ˈɑːg əʊ ‖ -oʊ —*but as a Welsh personal
name,* ˈjɑːg əʊ ‖ -oʊ —, —*Welsh* [ˈja go]

Iain ˈiː ən

-ial *stress-imposing* i‿əl —*This suffix sometimes
causes a change in the stressed vowel:*
ˌmanaˈgerial* -ˈdʒɪər i‿əl ‖ -ˈdʒɪr-

iamb ˈaɪ æm -æmb **~s** z

iambic aɪ ˈæm bɪk **~s** s

iam|bus aɪ ˈæm |bəs **~bi** baɪ **~buses** bəs ɪz -əz

Ian ˈiː ən —*In AmE sometimes* ˈaɪ ən

-ian *stress-imposing* i‿ən —*This suffix sometimes
causes a change in the stressed vowel:*
₍₎Peckˈsniffian ₍₎Chauˈcerian -ˈsɪər i‿ən
‖ -ˈsɪr i‿ən

Ianthe aɪ ˈænθ i

Ianucci jæ ˈnuːtʃ i jə-

Iapetus aɪ ˈæp ɪt əs -ət- ‖ -əţ əs

IATA i ˈɑːt ə aɪ-

IATEFL ˌaɪ ə ˈtef ᵊl

iatrogenic aɪ ˌætr əʊ ˈdʒen ɪk ◄ ˌ‿ -- ‖ -ə-

Ibadan ɪ ˈbæd ᵊn ‖ iː ˈbɑːd ᵊn -ɑːn —*Yoruba*
[i ba dɔ̃]

Ibbotson ˈɪb əts ən

Ibcol *tdmk* ˈɪb kɒl ‖ -koʊl -kɔːl, -kɑːl

I-beam ˈaɪ biːm **~s** z

Iberi|a aɪ ˈbɪər i‿|ə ‖ -ˈbɪr- **~an/s** ən/z

ibex ˈaɪb eks **~es** ɪz əz

Ibibio ɪ ˈbɪb i‿əʊ -ˈbiːb- ‖ -oʊ **~s** z

ibid ˈɪb ɪd §-əd

ibidem ˈɪb ɪ dem -ə-; ɪ ˈbaɪd em

-ibility ə ˈbɪl ət i ɪ-, -ɪt- ‖ -əţ i — **visibility**
ˌvɪz ə ˈbɪl ət i -ɪˈ--, -ɪt i ‖ -əţ i

ibis ˈaɪb ɪs §-əs **~es** ɪz əz

Ibiza ɪ ˈbiːθ ə aɪ-, iː-, -ˈbiːz-, -ˈbiːts- —*Sp*
[i ˈβi θa], *Catalan* [i ˈβi sa, əi-]

-ible əb ᵊl ɪb ᵊl — **visible** ˈvɪz əb ᵊl -ɪb-

IBM *tdmk* ˌaɪ biː ˈem
ˌIBM comˈpatible

ibn, Ibn *in Arabic names* ˈɪb ən

Ibo ˈiːb əʊ ‖ -oʊ —*Ibo* [i gbo] **~s** z

Ibrahim ˈɪb rə hiːm -hɪm, ˌ‿ ‿ˈ‿ —*Arabic*
[i bra ˈhiːm]

Ibrox ˈaɪb rɒks ‖ -rɑːks

Ibsen ˈɪb sən —*Norwegian* [ˈip sən]

Ibstock ˈɪb stɒk ‖ -stɑːk

ibuprofen ˌaɪb juː ˈprəʊf en -ᵊn;
aɪ ˈbjuːp rəʊ fen ‖ -ˈproʊf ᵊn

-ic *stress-imposing* ɪk — **periodic**
ˌpɪər i ˈɒd ɪk ◄ ‖ ˌpɪr i ˈɑːd ɪk ◄

IC ˌaɪ ˈsiː **ICs** ˌaɪ ˈsiːz

-ical *stress-imposing* ɪk ᵊl — **periodical**
ˌpɪər i ˈɒd ɪk ᵊl ◄ ‖ ˌpɪr i ˈɑːd ɪk ᵊl ◄

-ically *stress-imposing* ɪk li ɪk əl i —
periodically ˌpɪər i ˈɒd ɪk li -ˈɒd ɪk əl i
‖ ˌpɪr i ˈɑːd- —*shown in entries simply as*
ɪk ᵊl i

Icaria ɪ ˈkeər i‿ə aɪ- ‖ -ˈker-

Icarus ˈɪk ər əs ˈaɪk-

ICBM ˌaɪ siː biː ˈem **~s** z

ICE CREAM

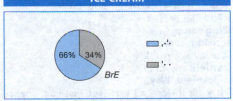

66%   34%

BrE

---

ice aɪs **iced** aɪst **ices** ˈaɪs ɪz -əz **icing** ˈaɪs ɪŋ
ˈice age; ˈice axe; ˈice ˌbucket; ˌice
ˈcream ◄, ˈ‿ ‿ ‖ ˈ‿ ‿ —*Preference poll, BrE:*
ˌ‿ ˈ‿ 66%, ˈ‿ ‿ 34%; ˌice-cream ˈsoda; ˈice
field; ˈice floe; ˈice ˌhockey; ˌice ˈlolly,
ˈ‿ ˌ‿ ‿; ˈice pack; ˈice pick; ˈice rink; ˈice
sheet; ˈice ˌwater

iceball ˈaɪs bɔːl ‖ -bɑːl

iceberg ˈaɪs bɜːg ‖ -bɜːːg **~s** z
ˌiceberg ˈlettuce, ˈ‿ ‿ ˌ‿

ice-blue ˌaɪs ˈbluː ◄

icebound ˈaɪs baʊnd

icebox ˈaɪs bɒks ‖ -bɑːks **~es** ɪz əz

icebreaker ˈaɪs ˌbreɪk ə ‖ -ᵊr **~s** z

icecap ˈaɪs kæp **~s** s

ice-cold ˌaɪs ˈkəʊld ◄ →-ˈkɒʊld ‖ -ˈkoʊld ◄

icefall ˈaɪs fɔːl ‖ -fɑːl **~s** z

ice|house ˈaɪs |haʊs **~houses** haʊz ɪz -əz

Iceland 'aɪs lənd §-lænd
Icelander 'aɪs lənd ə -lænd- ‖ -ᵊr ~s z
Icelandic aɪs 'lænd ɪk
icemaker 'aɪs ˌmeɪk ə ‖ -ᵊr ~s z
ice|man 'aɪs |mæn -mən **~men** men mən
Iceni aɪ 'siːn aɪ -i
ice-|skate 'aɪs |skeɪt 'aɪ|s keɪt **~skated** skeɪt ɪd
-əd ‖ skeɪʈ əd **~skater/s** skeɪt ə/z ‖ skeɪʈ ᵊr/z
~skates skeɪts **~skating** skeɪt ɪŋ ‖ skeɪʈ ɪŋ
Ice-T ˌaɪs 'tiː
ice-tray 'aɪs treɪ **~s** z
Ichabod 'ɪk ə bɒd 'ɪx- ‖ -bɑːd
ich dien ˌɪx 'diːn ˌɪk- ‖ ˌɪk- —*Ger* [ʔɪç 'diːn];
 Welsh eich dyn [əχ 'diːn, əiχ-, -'diːn]
I Ching ˌiː 'tʃɪŋ ˌaɪ-, -'dʒɪŋ —*Chi* yì jīng
 [⁴i ¹tɕiŋ]
ich-laut 'ɪx laʊt 'ɪk- ‖ 'ɪk- —*Ger* Ich-Laut
 ['ʔɪç laʊt] **~s** s
ichneumon ɪk 'njuːm ən ‖ -'nuːm- -'njuːm- **~s**
 z
 ich'neumon fly
ichor 'aɪk ɔː ‖ -ɔːr
ichthyo- *comb. form*
 with stress-neutral suffix |ɪkθ i ə -əʊ ‖ -oʊ
 — **ichthyophobia** ˌɪkθ i ə 'fəʊb i ə -i əʊ-
 ‖ -'foʊb- -i oʊ-
 with stress-imposing suffix ˌɪkθ i 'ɒ+ ‖ -'ɑː+
 — **ichthyophagous** ˌɪkθ i 'ɒf əg əs ◂ ‖ -'ɑːf-
ichthyological ˌɪkθ i ə 'lɒdʒ ɪk ᵊl ◂ -i əʊ-
 ‖ -'lɑːdʒ- -i oʊ- **~ly** i
ichthyolog|ist ˌɪkθ i 'ɒl ədʒ |ɪst -§əst ‖ -'ɑːl-
 ~ists ɪsts §əsts **~y** i
ichthyosaurus ˌɪkθ i ə 'sɔːr əs **~es** ɪz əz
ichthyosis ˌɪkθ i 'əʊs ɪs §-əs ‖ -'oʊs-
ICI *tdmk* ˌaɪ siː 'aɪ
ici... —*see* **icy**
-ician 'ɪʃ ᵊn — **musician** mju 'zɪʃ ᵊn
icicle 'aɪs ɪk ᵊl **~s** z
icing 'aɪs ɪŋ **~s** z
 'icing ˌsugar
Icke (i) aɪk, (ii) ɪk
Icknield 'ɪk niːᵊld
 ˌIcknield 'Way
ick|y 'ɪk |i **~ier** i ə ‖ i ᵊr **~iest** i ɪst i əst **~iness**
 i nəs -nɪs
icon 'aɪk ɒn -ən ‖ -ɑːn **~s** z
iconic aɪ 'kɒn ɪk ‖ -'kɑːn-
Iconium aɪ 'kəʊn i əm ‖ -'koʊn-
icono- *comb. form*
 with stress-neutral suffix aɪ |kɒn ə |aɪk ɒn ə
 ‖ aɪ |kɑːn ə |aɪk ɑːn ə — **iconographic**
 aɪ ˌkɒn ə 'græf ɪk ◂ ˌaɪk ɒn- ‖ aɪ ˌkɑːn-
 ˌaɪk ɑːn-
 with stress-imposing suffix ˌaɪk ə 'nɒ+ -ɒ-
 ‖ -'nɑː+ — **iconology** ˌaɪk ə 'nɒl ədʒ i -ɒ-
 ‖ -'nɑːl-
iconoclasm aɪ 'kɒn ə ˌklæz əm ‖ -'kɑːn-
iconoclast aɪ 'kɒn ə klæst -klɑːst ‖ -'kɑːn- **~s** s
iconoclastic aɪ ˌkɒn ə 'klæst ɪk ◂ ˌaɪk ɒn-
 ‖ aɪ ˌkɑːn- ˌaɪk ɑːn- **~ally** ᵊl̩ i
iconograph|y ˌaɪk ə 'nɒg rəf |i ‖ -'nɑːg- **~ies**
 iz

iconost|asis ˌaɪk ə 'nɒst |əs ɪs ˌ·ɒ-, §-əs
 ‖ -'nɑːst- **~ases** ə siːz
icosahedr|on ˌaɪk əs ə 'hiːdr |ən ˌ·ɒs-, aɪ ˌkɒs-,
 -'hedr- ‖ aɪ ˌkoʊs- -ˌkɑːs-; ˌaɪk oʊs-, ˌ·ɑːs- **~a** ə
 ~ons ənz
ictal 'ɪkt ᵊl
icteric ɪk 'ter ɪk
icterus 'ɪkt ər əs
ictus 'ɪkt əs **~es** ɪz əz
icy 'aɪs i **icier** 'aɪs i ə ‖ ᵊr **iciest** 'aɪs i ɪst əst
 icily 'aɪs ɪ li -əl i **iciness** 'aɪs i nəs -nɪs
-id ɪd §əd — **acarid** 'æk ər ɪd §-əd **arachnid**
 ə 'ræk nɪd §-nəd
id *in psychology* ɪd **ids** ɪdz
ID, id *'(proof of) identity'* ˌaɪ 'diː
 ˌI'D ˌcard
I'd aɪd
Ida 'aɪd ə
Idaho 'aɪd ə həʊ ‖ -hoʊ
Idahoan 'aɪd ə həʊ ən ◂ ˌ·ᵊ'·· ‖ -hoʊ ən **~s** z
Idd *Moslem festival* iːd
Iddesleigh 'ɪdz li
-ide aɪd — **lanthanide** 'lænᵗθ ə naɪd

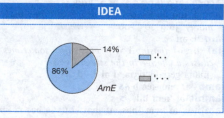

IDEA

AmE

idea aɪ 'dɪə ˌaɪ-, §-'diː ə ‖ ₍ᵢ₎aɪ 'diː ə '···
 — *Preference poll, AmE:* '···86%, '···14%. **~s** z
ideal ₍ᵢ₎aɪ 'dɪəl -'diː əl ‖ ₍ᵢ₎aɪ 'diː əl **~ly** i li **~s** z
idealis... —*see* **idealiz...**
idealism aɪ 'dɪəl ˌɪz əm ˌaɪ-, -'diː ə ˌlɪz-;
 'aɪd i ə ˌlɪz ᵊm ‖ aɪ 'diː ə ˌlɪz əm **~s** z
idealist aɪ 'dɪəl ɪst ˌaɪ-, -'diː əl-, 'aɪd i əl-, §-əst
 ‖ aɪ 'diː əl əst **~s** s
idealistic aɪ ˌdɪə 'lɪst ɪk ◂ ˌaɪd i ə 'lɪst ɪk◂,
 aɪ ˌdiː ə- ‖ aɪ ˌdiː ə 'lɪst ɪk ◂ ˌaɪd i ə- **~ally** ᵊl̩ i
idealization aɪ ˌdɪəl aɪ 'zeɪʃ ᵊn ˌaɪ ˌdɪəl-,
 aɪ ˌdiː əl aɪ'··, §ˌaɪd i əl-, -ɪ'··
 ‖ aɪ ˌdiː əl ə 'zeɪʃ ᵊn **~s** z
idealiz|e aɪ 'dɪəl aɪz ˌaɪ-; -'diː ə laɪz, §'aɪd i ə-
 ‖ aɪ 'diː ə laɪz **~ed** d **~es** ɪz əz **~ing** ɪŋ
ideally ₍ᵢ₎aɪ 'dɪəl i -'diː əl i, -li ‖ ₍ᵢ₎aɪ 'diː əl i -li
ideate 'aɪd i ǀeɪt **~ated** eɪt ɪd -əd ‖ eɪʈ əd
 ~ates eɪts **~ating** eɪt ɪŋ ‖ eɪʈ ɪŋ
ideation ˌaɪd i 'eɪʃ ᵊn **~al** ᵊl **~ally** ᵊl i
idee, idée 'iːd eɪ iː 'deɪ —*Fr* [i de] **idees,**
 idées *as sing., or* z
 ˌidee 'fixe, ˌidée 'fixe fiːks fiːks —*Fr* [fiks];
 ˌidée re'çue rə 'suː —*Fr* [ʁə sy]
idem 'ɪd em 'aɪd-, 'iːd-
ident 'aɪd ent **~s** s
identical aɪ 'dent ɪk ᵊl ɪ-, ə- ‖ -'denʈ- **~ly** i
 i,dentical 'twin
identifiab|le aɪ 'dent ɪ faɪ əb |ᵊl -'ə-, § ·ˌ·'··
 ‖ -'denʈ ə- **~ly** li

identification aɪ ˌdent ɪf ɪ 'keɪʃ ᵊn ɪ-, ə-, -ˌəf-,
§-ə'- ‖ -ˌdenṯ- **~s** z
identi|fy aɪ 'dent ɪ |faɪ ɪ-, ə-, -ə- ‖ -'denṯ ə |faɪ
~fied faɪd **~fier/s** faɪ ə/z ‖ faɪ ᵊr/z **~fies** faɪz
~fying faɪ ɪŋ
identikit, I~ *tdmk* aɪ 'dent ɪ kɪt ɪ-, ə- ‖ -'denṯ-
identit|y aɪ 'dent ət |i ɪ-, ə-, -ɪt- ‖ -'denṯ əṯ |i
~ies iz
   i'dentity card; **i'dentity ˌcrisis**
ideogram 'ɪd i ə græm 'aɪd-, -i əʊ- **~s** z
ideograph 'ɪd i ə grɑːf 'aɪd-, -i əʊ-, -græf
‖ -græf **~s** s
ideographic ˌɪd i ə 'græf ɪk ◄ ˌaɪd-, -i əʊ- **~ally**
ᵊl i
ideography ˌɪd i 'ɒgr əf i ˌaɪd- ‖ -'ɑːg-
ideological ˌaɪd i ə 'lɒdʒ ɪk ᵊl ◄ ˌɪd- ‖ -'lɑːdʒ-
~ly i
ideologist ˌaɪd i 'ɒl ədʒ ɪst ˌɪd-, §-əst ‖ -'ɑːl-
~s s
ideologue 'aɪd i ə lɒg -lɔːg -lɑːg **~s** z

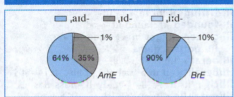

IDEOLOGY

Legend: ˌaɪd- ‖ ˌɪd- ‖ ˌiːd-

AmE: 64%, 35%, 1%
BrE: 90%, 10%

ideolog|y ˌaɪd i 'ɒl ədʒ |i ˌɪd- ‖ -'ɑːl-
— *Preference polls, AmE:* ˌaɪd- 64%, ˌɪd- 35%,
ˌiːd- 1%; *BrE:* ˌaɪd- 90%, ˌɪd- 10%. **~ies** iz
ideophone 'ɪd i ə fəʊn 'aɪd-, -i əʊ- ‖ -foʊn **~s** z
ides, Ides aɪdz
idio- *comb. form*
   with stress-neutral suffix ¦ɪd i əʊ ¦ -ə
   — **idioglossia** ˌɪd i əʊ 'glɒs i ə ‖ -ə 'glɑːs-
   -'gloʊs-
   with stress-imposing suffix ˌɪd i 'ɒ+ ‖ -'ɑː+
   — **idiopathy** ˌɪd i 'ɒp əθ i ‖ -'ɑːp-
idioc|y 'ɪd i əs |i **~ies** iz
idiolect 'ɪd i ə lekt -i əʊ- **~s** s
idiolectal ˌɪd i ə 'lekt ᵊl ◄ -i əʊ- **~ly** i
idiom 'ɪd i əm **~s** z
idiomatic ˌɪd i ə 'mæt ɪk ◄ -i əʊ- ‖ -'mæṯ-
~ally ᵊl i
idiosyncras|y ˌɪd i əʊ 'sɪŋk rəs |i ‖ -i ə- **~ies**
iz
idiosyncratic ˌɪd i əʊ sɪŋ 'kræt ɪk -sɪn'-
‖ ə sɪn 'kræṯ ɪk **~ally** ᵊl i
idiot 'ɪd i əṯ **~s** s
   idiot savant ˌiːd i əʊ sæ 'vɒ̃ ˌɪd i əṯ 'sæv ᵊnt
   ‖ ˌiːd joʊ sɑː 'vɑːn -sæ'- —*Fr* [i djo sa vɑ̃]
idiotic ˌɪd i 'ɒt ɪk ◄ ‖ -'ɑːṯ ɪk ◄ **~ally** ᵊl i
idiot-proof 'ɪd i əṯ pruːf §-prʊf
Idist 'iːd ɪst §-əst **~s** s
Iditarod *place in AK* aɪ 'dɪt ə rɒd
‖ aɪ 'dɪṯ ə rɑːd
idle, Idle 'aɪd ᵊl **idleness** 'aɪd ᵊl nəs -nɪs
   idler/s 'aɪd lə/z ‖ -lᵊr/z **idlest** 'aɪd lɪst -ləst
idly 'aɪd li
Ido 'iːd əʊ ‖ -oʊ

idol 'aɪd ᵊl (= *idle*) **~s** z
idolater, idolator aɪ 'dɒl ət ə ‖ -'dɑːl əṯ ᵊr **~s**
z
idolatrous aɪ 'dɒl ətr əs ‖ -'dɑːl- **~ly** li **~ness**
nəs nɪs
idolatr|y aɪ 'dɒl ətr |i ‖ -'dɑːl- **~ies** iz
idolis... —*see* **idoliz...**
idolization ˌaɪd ᵊl aɪ 'zeɪʃ ᵊn -ᵊl ɪ-, -ə laɪ-
‖ -ᵊl ə-
idoliz|e 'aɪd ᵊl aɪz -ə laɪz **~ed** d **~er/s** ə/z
‖ ᵊr/z **~es** ɪz əz **~ing** ɪŋ
Idomeneo ɪ ˌdɒm ə 'neɪ əʊ
‖ ˌiːd oʊm ə 'neɪ oʊ
Idomeneus aɪ 'dɒm ɪ njuːs ɪ-, -ə-
‖ -'dɑːm ə nuːs -njuːs
Idris 'ɪdr ɪs -aɪdr-, §-əs
Idwal 'ɪd wəl
idyl, idyll 'ɪd ᵊl 'aɪd-, -ɪl ‖ 'aɪd ᵊl **~s** z
idyllic ɪ 'dɪl ɪk aɪ- ‖ aɪ- **~ally** ᵊl i
-ie i — **sweetie** 'swiːt i ‖ 'swiːṯ i
i.e. ˌaɪ 'iː
iechyd da ˌjæk i 'dɑ: —*Welsh* [ˌje χid 'dɑː,
-χịd-]
-ier *comparative of* **-y** i ə ‖ i ᵊr — **dirtier**
'dɜːt i ə ‖ 'dɜːṯ i ᵊr
-ier *suffix forming nouns* 'ɪə ‖ 'ɪᵊr — **brigadier**
ˌbrɪg ə 'dɪə ‖ -'dɪᵊr
-ies *pl of* **-y** iz — **doggies** 'dɒg iz ‖ 'dɔːg iz
'dɑːg-
-iest *superlative of* **-y** ɪ ɪst əst — **dirtiest**
'dɜːt i ɪst əst ‖ 'dɜːṯ i əst
Iestyn 'jest ɪn —*Welsh* ['je sdin, -sdin]
Ieuan 'jaɪ ən -æn —*Welsh* ['jə jan]
if ɪf §ɪv —*In RP this word has no separate weak
form; but in some other varieties, including
GenAm, it may have a weak form* əf **ifs** ɪfs
Ife *place in Nigeria* 'iː feɪ —*Yoruba* [i fe]
Ife *family name* aɪf
-iferous 'ɪf ər əs — **carboniferous**
ˌkɑːb ə 'nɪf ər əs ‖ ˌkɑːrb-
iff ɪf —*Since iff is pronounced identically with
plain if, its use ('if and only if') is in practice
restricted to writing.*
iff|y 'ɪf |i **~iness** i nəs i nɪs
Ifield 'aɪ fiːᵊld
Ifor 'aɪv ə 'aɪf-; 'iː vɔː ‖ -ᵊr —*Welsh* ['i vor]
-iform ɪ fɔːm ə- ‖ ə fɔːrm — **cruciform**
'kruːs ɪ fɔːm -ə- ‖ -ə fɔːrm
iftar, I~ 'ɪft ɑː ‖ -ɑːr —*Arabic* [ʔif 'tˤɑːr]
-ify *stress-imposing* ɪ faɪ ə- — **solidify**
sə 'lɪd ɪ faɪ sɒ-, -ə-
Igbo 'iːb əʊ ‖ -oʊ —*Ibo* [i gbo] **~s** z
Iggy 'ɪg i
Ightham 'aɪt əm ‖ 'aɪṯ-
igitur 'ɪg ɪ tʊə 'ɪdʒ-, §-ə; -ɪt ə, §-ət ə ‖ -tʊr
Iglesias i 'gleɪz i əs —*Sp* [i 'ɣle sjas]
igloo 'ɪg luː **~s** z
Ignatian ɪg 'neɪʃ i ən -'neɪʃ ᵊn **~s** z
Ignatieff ɪg 'næt i ef ‖ -'næṯ-
Ignatius ɪg 'neɪʃ əs -'neɪʃ i əs
igneous 'ɪg ni əs
ignimbrite 'ɪg nɪm braɪt §-nəm-

ignis fatuus ˌɪg nɪs ˈfæt ju‿əs §ˌ·nəs-, -ˈfætʃ u‿
 ‖ -ˈfætʃ u‿əs **ignes fatui** ˌɪg neɪz ˈfæt ju iː
ˌ·niːz-, -ˈfætʃ u-, -aɪ ‖ -niːz ˈfætʃ u aɪ

ig|nite ɪg ˈnaɪt **~nited** ˈnaɪt ɪd -əd ‖ ˈnaɪţ əd
 ~nites ˈnaɪts **~niting** ˈnaɪt ɪŋ ‖ ˈnaɪţ ɪŋ

ignition ɪg ˈnɪʃ ᵊn **~s** z

ignitron ɪg ˈnaɪtr ɒn ˈɪg nɪ trɒn, -nə- ‖ -ɑːn **~s**
z

ignob|le ɪg ˈnəʊb |ᵊl ˌɪg- ‖ -ˈnoʊb- **~ly** li

ignominious ˌɪg nə ˈmɪn i ̯əs ◂ ˌ·nəʊ- **~ly** li
 ~ness nəs nɪs

ignomin|y ˈɪg nəm ɪn |i -ən i **~ies** iz

ignoramus ˌɪg nə ˈreɪm əs **~es** ɪz əz

ignorance ˈɪg nər ᵊnⁱs

ignorant ˈɪg nər ənt **~ly** li

ignore ɪg ˈnɔː ‖ -ˈnɔːr -ˈnoʊr **~d** d **~s** z
 ignoring ɪg ˈnɔːr ɪŋ ‖ -ˈnoʊr-

ignotum per ignotius
 ɪg ˌnəʊt əm ˌpɜːr ɪg ˈnəʊt i ̯əs -ˌ·ˈpər ·ˈ·-, -ʊs
 ‖ ɪg ˌnoʊt əm ˌpɜː ɪg ˈnoʊt-

Igoe ˈaɪg əʊ ‖ -oʊ

Igor ˈiːg ɔː ‖ -ɔːr —*Russ* [ˈi gər ʲ]

Igorot ˌiːg ə ˈrəʊt ˌɪg- ‖ -ˈroʊt **~s** s

Iguaçu, Iguaçú ˌɪg wə ˈsuː —*Port* [i gwa ˈsu]

iguana ɪ ˈgwɑːn ə ˌɪg ju ˈɑːn ə **~s** z

iguanodon ɪ ˈgwɑːn ə dɒn ˌɪg ju ˈɑːn-, -əd ən
 ‖ -dɑːn **~s** z

Iguazu, Iguazú ˌɪg wə ˈsuː —*Sp* [i ɣwa ˈsu]

IKBS ˌaɪ keɪ biː ˈes

Ike aɪk

IKEA *tdmk* aɪ ˈkiːⸯ ə i ˈkeɪ ə

ikebana ˌiːk eɪ ˈbɑːn ə ˌɪk-, -i- —*Jp*
 [i ˈke ba na]

ikon ˈaɪk ɒn -ən ‖ -ɑːn **~s** z

il- ₍ᵢ₎ɪ, ˌɪl — **illiberal** ɪ ˈlɪb ᵊr‿əl ˌɪ-, ˌɪl-

Ilchester ˈɪl tʃɪst ə ‖ -ˌtʃest ᵊr

-ile aɪᵊl ‖ əl (*) —*This BrE-AmE difference is a
general tendency; there are several exceptions.*
 — **agile** ˈædʒ aɪᵊl ‖ ˈædʒ əl

ILEA ˈɪl i ə ˌaɪ el i ˈeɪ ◂

ileac ˈɪl i æk (= *iliac*)

Ile de France ˌiːᵊl də ˈfrɒs ‖ -ˈfrɑːⁿs —*Fr*
 Île-de-France [il də fʁɑ̃ːs]

ileostom|y ˌɪl i ˈɒst əm |i ‖ -ˈɑːst- **~ies** iz

Iles aɪᵊlz

ileum ˈɪl i əm (= *ilium*)

ileus ˈɪl i ̯əs

ilex ˈaɪl eks **~es** ɪz əz

Ilford ˈɪl fəd ‖ -fᵊrd

Ilfracombe ˈɪlf rə kuːm

ilia ˈɪl i ə

iliac ˈɪl i æk

Iliad ˈɪl i əd -i æd

Iliffe ˈaɪl ɪf

ili|um ˈɪl i ̯əm **~a** ə

Ilium *'Troy'* ˈaɪl i ̯əm ˈɪl- ‖ ˈɪl-

ilk ɪlk

Ilkeston ˈɪlk ɪst ən -əst-

Ilkley ˈɪlk li

ill ɪl **ills** ɪlz **worse** wɜːs ‖ wɜːs **worst** wɜːst
 ‖ wɜːst
 ˌill at ˈease; ˌill ˈfeeling; ˌill ˈwill

I'll aɪᵊl

ill-ad|vised ˌɪl əd |ˈvaɪzd ◂ §-æd- **~visedly**
 ˈvaɪz ɪd li -əd-

ill-assorted ˌɪl ə ˈsɔːt ɪd ◂ -əd ‖ -ˈsɔːrţ əd ◂

illative ɪ ˈleɪt ɪv ˈɪl ət- ‖ ˈɪl əţ ɪv ɪ ˈleɪţ-

Illawarra ˌɪl ə ˈwɒr ə ‖ -ˈwɔːr ə

ill-bred ˌɪl ˈbred ◂

ill-conceived ˌɪl kən ˈsiːvd ◂ §-kɒn-

ill-considered ˌɪl kən ˈsɪd əd ◂ §-kɒn- ‖ -ᵊrd ◂

ill-defined ˌɪl di ˈfaɪnd ◂

ill-disposed ˌɪl dɪ ˈspəʊzd ◂ ‖ -ˈspoʊzd ◂

illegal ɪ ˈliːg ᵊl ˌɪ-, ˌɪl- **~ly** i

illegalit|y ˌɪl iː ˈgæl ət i |i ˌ·ɪ-, ˌ·liː-, -ɪt i **~ies** iz

illegibility ɪ ˌledʒ ə ˈbɪl ət i ˌɪ-, ˌɪl-, -ɪˈ·-, -ɪt i
 ‖ -əţ i

illegib|le ɪ ˈledʒ əb |ᵊl ˌɪ-, ˌɪl-, -ɪb- **~ly** li

illegitimac|y ˌɪl ə ˈdʒɪt əm əs |i ˌ·ɪ-, -ˈ·ɪm-
 ‖ -ˈdʒɪţ əm- **~ies** iz

illegitimate ˌɪl ə ˈdʒɪt əm ət ◂ ˌ·ɪ-, -ɪm ət, -ɪt
 ‖ -ˈdʒɪţ əm- **~ly** li

ill-equipped ˌɪl ɪ ˈkwɪpt ◂ -ə-

ill-fated ˌɪl ˈfeɪt ɪd ◂ -əd ‖ -ˈfeɪţ əd

ill-favored, ill-favoured ˌɪl ˈfeɪv əd ◂ ‖ -ᵊrd ◂

ill-fitting ˌɪl ˈfɪt ɪŋ ◂ ‖ -ˈfɪţ-

ill-founded ˌɪl ˈfaʊnd ɪd ◂ -əd

ill-gotten ˌɪl ˈgɒt ᵊn ◂ ‖ -ˈgɑːt ᵊn ◂
 ˌill-ˌgotten ˈgains

illiberal ɪ ˈlɪb ᵊr‿əl ˌɪ-, ˌɪl- **~ly** i

illiberality ˌɪl ɪb ə ˈræl ət i ˌɪl lɪb-, -ɪt i ‖ -əţ i

illicit ɪ ˈlɪs ɪt ˌ·ɪ-, ˌɪl-, §-ət ~**ly** li **~ness** nəs nɪs

illimitab|le ɪ ˈlɪm ɪt əb |ᵊl ˌ·ɪ-, ˌɪl-, §-ət əb-
 ‖ -əţ əb- **~ly** li

ill-informed ˌɪl ɪn ˈfɔːmd ◂ ‖ -ˈfɔːrmd ◂

Illingworth ˈɪl ɪŋ wəθ -wɜːθ ‖ -wɜːθ

illinium ɪ ˈlɪn i əm

Illinois ˌɪl ə ˈnɔɪ -ɪ-, -ˈnɔɪz

Illinoisan ˌɪl ə ˈnɔɪ ən ◂ -ɪ-, -ˈnɔɪz ᵊn **~s** z

illiquid ɪ ˈlɪk wɪd ˌɪl-, §-wəd

illiterac|y ɪ ˈlɪt ᵊr əs |i ˌ·ɪ-, ˌɪl- ‖ -ˈlɪţ ər əs |i
 →-ˈlɪtr əs i **~ies** iz

illiterate ɪ ˈlɪt ᵊr ət ˌ·ɪ-, ˌɪl-, -ɪt ‖ -ˈlɪţ ər ət
 →-ˈlɪtr ət **~ly** li **~ness** nəs nɪs **~s** s

ill-judged ˌɪl ˈdʒʌdʒd ◂

ill-mannered ˌɪl ˈmæn əd ◂ ‖ -ᵊrd ◂ **~ly** li

ill-natured ˌɪl ˈneɪtʃ əd ◂ ‖ -ᵊrd◂ **~ly** li **~ness**
 nəs nɪs

illness ˈɪl nəs -nɪs **~es** ɪz əz

illocution ˌɪl ə ˈkjuːʃ ᵊn **~s** z

illocutionary ˌɪl ə ˈkjuːʃ ᵊn ər_i ◂ -ᵊn_ər i
 ‖ -ə ner i

illogical ɪ ˈlɒdʒ ɪk ᵊl ˌ·ɪ-, ˌɪl- ‖ -ˈlɑːdʒ- **~ly** _i
 ~ness nəs nɪs

illogicality ɪ ˌlɒdʒ ɪ ˈkæl ət i ˌɪ,·ˈ·-, ˌɪl-; -əˈ·-,
 -ɪt i ‖ ɪ ˌlɑːdʒ ə ˈkæl əţ i

ill-omened ˌɪl ˈəʊm end ◂ -ənd ‖ -ˈoʊm-

ill-prepared ˌɪl pri ˈpeəd ◂ -prə- ‖ -ˈpeᵊrd ◂

ill-served ˌɪl ˈsɜːvd ◂ ‖ -ˈsɜːvd ◂

ill-starred ˌɪl ˈstɑːd ◂ ‖ -ˈstɑːrd ◂

ill-suited ˌɪl ˈsuːt ɪd ◂ -ˈsjuːt-, -əd ‖ -ˈsuːţ-

ill-tempered ˌɪl ˈtemp əd ◂ ‖ -ᵊrd ◂ **~ly** li

ill-timed ˌɪl ˈtaɪmd ◂

ill-|treat ₍ᵢ₎ɪl |ˈtriːt **~treated** ˈtriːt ɪd -əd
 ‖ ˈtriːţ əd **~treating** ˈtriːt ɪŋ ‖ ˈtriːţ ɪŋ
 ~treatment ˈtriːt mənt **~treats** ˈtriːts

Illtud 'ɪlt ɪd —*Welsh* ['ɾɬ tɪd, -tɪd]
illumin|ance ɪ 'luːm ɪn |ənᵗs -'ljuːm-, -ən- **~ant**
   ənt
illumi|nate ɪ 'luːm ɪ |neɪt -'ljuːm-, -ə- **~nated**
   neɪt ɪd -əd ‖ neɪt̬ əd **~nates** neɪts **~nating**
   neɪt ɪŋ ‖ neɪt̬ ɪŋ
Illuminati, i~ ɪ ˌluːm ɪ 'nɑːt iː -ə-
illumination ɪ ˌluːm ɪ 'neɪʃ ᵊn -ˌljuːm-, -ə- **~s** z
illumin|e ɪ 'luːm ɪn -'ljuːm-, ən **~ed** d **~es** z
   ~ing ɪŋ
ill-us|e v ˌɪl 'juːz **~ed** d **~es** ɪz əz **~ing** ɪŋ
ill-use n ˌɪl 'juːs
illusion ɪ 'luːʒ ᵊn -'ljuːʒ- **~s** z
illusionist ɪ 'luːʒ ən ɪst -'ljuːʒ-, ᵊn̩-, §-əst **~s** s
illusive ɪ 'luːs ɪv -'ljuːs-, §-'luːz- **~ly** li **~ness**
   nəs nɪs
illusory ɪ 'luːs ər̩ i -'ljuːs-, -'luːz-, -'ljuːz-

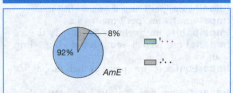

92%   8%
       '···
       ·'··
    AmE

illu|strate 'ɪl ə |streɪt -ju- ‖ ɪ 'lʌs treɪt
   — *Preference poll, AmE:* '··· 92%, ·'·· 8%.
   ~strated streɪt ɪd -əd ‖ streɪt̬ əd **~strates**
   streɪts **~strating** streɪt ɪŋ ‖ streɪt̬ ɪŋ
illustration ˌɪl ə 'streɪʃ ᵊn **~s** z
illustrative 'ɪl ə strət ɪv -streɪt-; ɪ 'lʌs trət ɪv
   ‖ ɪ 'lʌstr ət̬ ɪv 'ɪl ə streɪt̬ ɪv **~ly** li
illustrator 'ɪl ə streɪt ə ‖ -streɪt̬ ᵊr **~s** z
illustrious ɪ 'lʌs tri əs **~ly** li **~ness** nəs nɪs
Illyria ɪ 'lɪr i ə -'lɪᵊr-
Illyrian ɪ 'lɪr i ən -'lɪᵊr- **~s** z
Illyricum ɪ 'lɪr ɪk əm -'lɪᵊr-
ilmenite 'ɪl mə naɪt -mɪ-
Ilminster 'ɪl mɪnst ə ‖ -ᵊr
Ilocano, Ilokano ˌiːl əʊ 'kɑːn əʊ
   ‖ -oʊ 'kɑːn oʊ **~s** z
Ilona ɪ 'ləʊn ə ‖ -'loʊn ə
Ilson 'ɪls ən
Ilyushin ɪl 'juːʃ ɪn -ᵊn —*Russ* [ɪlʲ 'ju ʃɪn]
I'm aɪm —*In casual speech the phrase* I'm going
   to *before a verb is also* aɪŋ ən ə, aɪm ən ə
im- ɪm —*but before* m *usually* ɪ; *generally*
   stressed only for emphasis or if the following
   syllable is unstressed: im'possible,
   ˌimme'morial
iMac *tdmk* 'aɪ mæk **~s** s
image 'ɪm ɪdʒ **imaged** 'ɪm ɪdʒd **images**
   'ɪm ɪdʒ ɪz -əz **imaging** 'ɪm ɪdʒ ɪŋ
image-maker 'ɪm ɪdʒ ˌmeɪk ə ‖ -ᵊr **~s** z
imager 'ɪm ɪdʒ ə -ədʒ- ‖ -ᵊr **~s** z
imager|y 'ɪm ɪdʒ ər̩ |i **~ies** iz
imaginab|le ɪ 'mædʒ ɪn əb |ᵊl -ən əb- **~ly** li
imaginar|y ɪ 'mædʒ ɪn ᵊr̩ |i -ᵊn̩ ər |i ‖ -ə ner |i
   ~ies iz **~ily** əl i ɪ li **~iness** i nəs i nɪs
imagination ɪ ˌmædʒ ɪ 'neɪʃ ᵊn -ə- **~s** z

imaginative ɪ 'mædʒ ɪn ət ɪv -ən̩ ət-
   ‖ -ən̩ ət̬ ɪv -ə neɪt̬ ɪv **~ly** li **~ness** nəs nɪs
imagin|e ɪ 'mædʒ ɪn -ən **~ed** d **~es** z **~ingIs**
   ɪŋ|z
imagines *from* **imagine** ɪ 'mædʒ ɪnz -ənz
imagines *n pl of* **imago** ɪ 'meɪdʒ ɪ niːz
   -'mædʒ-, -'mɑːg-, -ə-
imaging 'ɪm ɪdʒ ɪŋ
imago ɪ 'meɪg əʊ -'mɑːg- ‖ -oʊ **~es** z
imam ɪ 'mɑːm 'iː mɑːm **~s** z
Imax, IMAX *tdmk* 'aɪ mæks
imbalanc|e ⑴ɪm 'bæl ənᵗs **~es** ɪz əz
imbecile 'ɪm bə siːᵊl -bɪ-, -saɪᵊl ‖ -bəs ᵊl -ɪl (*)
   ~s z
imbecilic ˌɪm bə 'sɪl ɪk ◂ -bɪ-
imbecilit|y ˌɪm bə 'sɪl ət i |i -ˌbɪ-, -ɪt i ‖ -ət̬ |i
   ~ies iz
imbed ɪm 'bed **~ded** ɪd əd **~ding** ɪŋ **~s** z
Imbert 'ɪm bət ‖ -bᵊrt
imbib|e ɪm 'baɪb **~ed** d **~es** z **~ing** ɪŋ
Imbrium 'ɪm bri əm
imbroglio ɪm 'brəʊl i əʊ ‖ -'broʊl joʊ **~s** z
Imbros 'ɪm brɒs ‖ -brɑːs
imbru|e ɪm 'bruː **~ed** d **~es** z **~ing** ɪŋ
imbu|e ɪm 'bjuː **~ed** d **~es** z **~ing** ɪŋ
Imelda ɪ 'meld ə
IMF ˌaɪ em 'ef
Imhof 'ɪm həʊf ‖ -hoʊf
imide 'ɪm aɪd **~s** z
imine 'ɪm iːn ɪ 'miːn **~s** z
imi|tate 'ɪm ɪ |teɪt -ə- **~tated** teɪt ɪd -əd
   ‖ teɪt̬ əd **~tates** teɪts **~tating** teɪt ɪŋ ‖ teɪt̬ ɪŋ
imitation ˌɪm ɪ 'teɪʃ ᵊn -ə- **~s** z
imitative 'ɪm ɪt ət ɪv '·ət-; ɪ teɪt-, -ə teɪt-
   ‖ -ə teɪt̬ ɪv **~ly** li **~ness** nəs nɪs
imitator 'ɪm ɪ teɪt ə '·ə- ‖ -teɪt̬ ᵊr **~s** z
immaculate ɪ 'mæk jʊl ət ə-, -jəl-, -ɪt ‖ -jəl-
   ~ly li **~ness** nəs nɪs
   Im,maculate Con'ception
immanenc|e 'ɪm ən ənᵗs **~y** i
immanent 'ɪm ən ənt **~ly** li
Immanuel ɪ 'mæn ju əl ə-
immaterial ˌɪm ə 'tɪər i əl ◂ ‖ -'tɪr- **~ly** i
   ~ness nəs nɪs
immature ˌɪm ə 'tjʊə ◂ -'tʃʊə, -'tjɔː, -'tʃɔː
   ‖ -'tʊᵊr -'tʃʊᵊr, -'tjʊᵊr **~ly** li **~ness** nəs nɪs
immaturity ˌɪm ə 'tjʊər ət i -'tʃʊər-, -'tjɔːr-,
   -'tʃɔːr-, -ɪt i ‖ -'tʊr ət̬ i -'tʃʊr-, -'tjʊr-
immeasurab|le ɪ 'meʒ ər əb |ᵊl ˌɪ-, ˌɪm- **~ly** li
immediac|y ɪ 'miːd i əs |i ə-, -'miːdʒ əs |i **~ies**
   iz
immediate ɪ 'miːd i ət ə-, -'miːdʒ ət, -ɪt **~ly** li
   ~ness nəs nɪs
Immelmann 'ɪm ᵊl mæn -mən ‖ -mən -mɑːn
   —*Ger* ['ʔɪm ᵊl man]
immemorial ˌɪm ə 'mɔːr i əl ◂ ˌɪ- ‖ -'moʊr- **~ly**
   i
immense ɪ 'menᵗs ə- **~ly** li **~ness** nəs nɪs
immensit|y ɪ 'menᵗs ət i |i ə-, -ɪt- ‖ -ət̬ |i **~ies** iz
immers|e ɪ 'mɜːs ə- ‖ ɪ 'mɜːs **~ed** t **~es** ɪz əz
   ~ing ɪŋ

immersion ɪ ˈmɜːʃ ᵊn ə-, -ˈmɜːʒ- ‖ ɪ ˈmɜːʒ ᵊn
-ˈmɜːʃ- **~s** z
  im'mersion ˌheater
immigrant ˈɪm ɪg rənt -əg- **~s** s
immi|grate ˈɪm ɪ |greɪt -ə- **~grated** greɪt ɪd
-əd ‖ greɪt̬ əd **~grates** greɪts **~grating**
greɪt ɪŋ ‖ greɪt̬ ɪŋ
immigration ˌɪm ɪ ˈgreɪʃ ᵊn -ə- **~s** z
imminenc|e ˈɪm ɪn ən̩t s -ən- **~y** i
imminent ˈɪm ɪn ənt -ən- **~ly** li
Immingham ˈɪm ɪŋ əm §-həm
immiscib|le ɪ ˈmɪs əb |ᵊl -ɪb- **~ly** li
immobile ɪ ˈməʊb aɪᵊl ‖ ɪ ˈmoʊb ᵊl -iːᵊl *(*)*
immobilis... —*see* **immobiliz...**
immobility ˌɪm əʊ ˈbɪl ət i -ɪt i ‖ -oʊ ˈbɪl ət̬ i
immobilization ɪ ˌməʊb əl aɪ ˈzeɪʃ ᵊn -ˌɪl-, -ɪˈ-
‖ ɪ ˌmoʊb əl ə- **~s** z
immobiliz|e ɪ ˈməʊb ə laɪz -ɪ-, -ᵊl aɪz
‖ ɪ ˈmoʊb- **~ed** d **~er/s** ə/z ‖ ᵊr/z **~es** ɪz əz
~ing ɪŋ
immoderate ɪ ˈmɒd ᵊr ət ‖-, ˌɪm-, -ɪt
‖ ɪ ˈmɑːd̬- **~ly** li **~ness** nəs nɪs
immodest ɪ ˈmɒd ɪst ‖-, ˌɪm-, -əst ‖ ɪ ˈmɑːd-
~ly li
immodesty ɪ ˈmɒd əst i ‖-, ˌɪm-, -ɪst-
‖ ɪ ˈmɑːd-
immo|late ˈɪm əʊ |leɪt ‖-ə- **~lated** leɪt ɪd -əd
‖ leɪt̬ əd **~lates** leɪts **~lating** leɪt ɪŋ ‖ leɪt̬ ɪŋ
immolation ˌɪm əʊ ˈleɪʃ ᵊn ‖-ə- **~s** z
immoral ɪ ˈmɒr əl ə-, ‖-, ˌɪm- ‖ ɪ ˈmɔːr əl
ɪ ˈmɑːr- **~ly** i
immoralit|y ˌɪm ə ˈræl ət i ‖i ˌ-ɒ-, ˌ-ɔː-, -ɪt i
‖ -ət̬ i ‖i **~ies** iz
immortal ɪ ˈmɔːt ᵊl ə-, ‖-, ˌɪm- ‖ ɪ ˈmɔːrt̬ ᵊl **~ly**
i **~s** z
immortalis... —*see* **immortaliz...**
immortality ˌɪm ɔː ˈtæl ət i -ɪt i ‖ -ɔːr ˈtæl ət̬ i
immortaliz|e ɪ ˈmɔːt ᵊl aɪz -ə laɪz
‖ ɪ ˈmɔːrt̬ ᵊl aɪz **~ed** d **~es** ɪz əz **~ing** ɪŋ
immortelle ˌɪm ɔː ˈtel ‖ -ɔːr- **~s** z
immovab|le ɪ ˈmuːv əb |ᵊl ə-, ‖-, ˌɪm- **~ly** li
immune ɪ ˈmjuːn ə-, ‖-ɪ-
  im'mune reˌsponse; im'mune ˌsystem
immunis... —*see* **immuniz...**
immunit|y ɪ ˈmjuːn ət i ‖i ə-, -ɪt- ‖ -ət̬ i ‖i **~ies** iz
immunization ˌɪm ju naɪ ˈzeɪʃ ᵊn ˌ-jə-, -ɪˈ-
‖ ˌɪm jən ə- ɪ ˌmjuːn ə- **~s** z
immuniz|e ˈɪm ju naɪz -jə- ‖ -jə- **~ed** d **~es** ɪz
əz **~ing** ɪŋ
immuno- *comb. form*
  with stress-neutral suffix ˈɪm ju nəʊ
  ɪ ˈmjuːn əʊ ‖ ˈɪm jə noʊ ɪ ˈmjuːn oʊ —
  immunodeficiency ˌɪm ju nəʊ dɪ ˈfɪʃ ᵊn̩t s i
  ɪ ˌmjuːn əʊ-, -dəˈ-- ‖ ˌɪm jə noʊ-
immunological ˌɪm jʊn ə ˈlɒdʒ ɪk ᵊl ◄
  ɪ ˌmjuːn-, -ə ə ˈlɑːdʒ- **~ly** i
immunologist ˌɪm ju ˈnɒl ədʒ ɪst §-əst
  ‖ ˌɪm jə ˈnɑːl- **~s** s
immunology ˌɪm ju ˈnɒl ədʒ i ‖ ˌɪm jə ˈnɑːl-
immunosuppression ˌɪm ju nəʊ sə ˈpreʃ ᵊn
  ɪ ˌmjuːn- ‖ ˌɪm jə noʊ-
immunosuppressive ˌɪm ju nəʊ sə ˈpres ɪv
  ɪ ˌmjuːn- ‖ ˌɪm jə noʊ- **~s** z

immure ɪ ˈmjʊə -ˈmjɔː ‖ ɪ ˈmjʊᵊr **~d** d **~s** z
  immuring ɪ ˈmjʊər ɪŋ -ˈmjɔːr- ‖ ɪ ˈmjʊr ɪŋ
immutability ɪ ˌmjuːt ə ˈbɪl ət i ˌɪ,-, ˌɪm,-,
  -ɪt i ‖ -ˌmjuːt̬ ə ˈbɪl ət̬ i
immutab|le ɪ ˈmjuːt əb |ᵊl ˌɪ-, ˌɪm- ‖ -ˈmjuːt̬-
~ly li
I-mode ˈaɪ məʊd ‖ -moʊd
Imogen ˈɪm ədʒ ən -ɪn, -ə dʒen ‖ -ə dʒen
  -ədʒ ən
Imogene ˈɪm ə dʒiːn
imp ɪmp **imps** ɪmps
impact *n* ˈɪm pækt **~s** s
impact *v* ɪm ˈpækt ˈ·· **~ed** ɪd əd **~ing** ɪŋ **~s** s
impair ɪm ˈpeə ‖ -ˈpeᵊr -ˈpæᵊr **~ed** d
  impairing ɪm ˈpeər ɪŋ ‖ -ˈper ɪŋ -ˈpær ɪŋ **~s**
  z
impairment ɪm ˈpeə mənt ‖ -ˈper- -ˈpær- **~s** s
impala ɪm ˈpɑːl ə ‖ -ˈpæl ə —*Zulu* [i ˈmpˈaː la]
  ~s z
impal|e ɪm ˈpeɪᵊl **~ed** d **~es** z **~ing** ɪŋ
impalement ɪm ˈpeɪᵊl mənt **~s** s
impalpab|le ɪm ˈpælp əb |ᵊl ˌɪm- **~ly** li
impanel ɪm ˈpæn ᵊl **~ed, ~led** d **~ing, ~ling**
  ɪŋ **~s** z
imparisyllabic ˌɪm ˌpær ɪ sɪ ˈlæb ɪk -ˌ-ə-, -sə'--
  ‖ -ˌper-
imparit|y ɪm ˈpær ət |i ˌɪm-, -ɪt- ‖ -ət̬ |i -ˈper-
  ~ies iz
im|part ɪm |ˈpɑːt ‖ -|ˈpɑːrt **~parted** ˈpɑːt ɪd
  -əd ‖ ˈpɑːrt̬ əd **~parting** ˈpɑːt ɪŋ ‖ ˈpɑːrt̬ ɪŋ
  ~parts ˈpɑːts ‖ ˈpɑːrts
impartial ɪm ˈpɑːʃ ᵊl ˌɪm- ‖ -ˈpɑːrʃ ᵊl **~ly** i
impartiality ˌɪm ˌpɑːʃ i ˈæl ət i ˌ-, ˌ·ˈ-, -ɪt i
  ‖ ɪm ˌpɑːrʃ i ˈæl ət̬ i ˌ·, ˌ·ˈ-
impassab|le ɪm ˈpɑːs əb |ᵊl ˌɪm-, §-ˈpæs-
  -ˈpæs- **~leness** ᵊl nəs -nɪs **~ly** li
impasse æm ˈpɑːs ɪm-, ɒm-, -ˈpæs, ˈ··
  ‖ ˈɪm pæs ·ˈ· —*Fr* [æ̃ pas] **~es** ɪz əz
impassibility ɪm ˌpæs ə ˈbɪl ət i -ˌ-ɪ-, -ɪt i
  ‖ -ət̬ i
impassib|le ɪm ˈpæs əb |ᵊl ˌɪm-, -ɪb- **~ly** li
impassion ɪm ˈpæʃ ᵊn **~ed** d **~ing** ɪŋ **~s** z
impassive ɪm ˈpæs ɪv **~ly** li **~ness** nəs nɪs
impassivity ˌɪm pæ ˈsɪv ət i -ɪt i ‖ -ət̬ i
impasto ɪm ˈpæst əʊ -ˈpɑːst- ‖ -oʊ
impatience ɪm ˈpeɪʃ ᵊn̩t s
impatiens ɪm ˈpeɪʃ i enz -ˈpæt- ‖ -ˈpeɪʃ ᵊnz
  -ᵊn̩t s
impatient ɪm ˈpeɪʃ ᵊnt **~ly** li
impeach ɪm ˈpiːtʃ **~ed** t **~es** ɪz əz **~ing** ɪŋ
  ~ment/s mənt/s
impeccab|le ɪm ˈpek əb |ᵊl **~ly** li
impecuniosity ˌɪm pɪ ˌkjuːn i ˈɒs ət i -ɪt i
  ‖ -ˈɑːs ət̬ i
impecunious ˌɪm pɪ ˈkjuːn i ̩əs ◄ ˌ-pə- **~ly** li
  ~ness nəs nɪs
impedanc|e ɪm ˈpiːd ᵊn̩t s **~es** ɪz əz
imped|e ɪm ˈpiːd **~ed** ɪd əd **~es** z **~ing** ɪŋ
impediment ɪm ˈped ɪ mənt -ə- **~s** s
impedimenta ɪm ˌped ɪ ˈment ə -ə- ‖ -ˈment̬ ə
impel ɪm ˈpel **~led** d **~ling** ɪŋ **~s** z
impeller ɪm ˈpel ə ‖ -ᵊr **~s** z
impend ɪm ˈpend **~ed** ɪd əd **~ing** ɪŋ **~s** z

impenetrability ɪm ˌpen ɪtr ə ˈbɪl ət i ˌ·ˌ· · ·ˈ·-, -ətr ·ˈ·-, -ɪt i ‖ -əʈ i

impenetrab|le ɪm ˈpen ɪtr əb |ᵊl ˌɪm-, -ˈ·ətr- ~**ly** li

impenitence ɪm ˈpen ɪt ənᵗs ˌɪm-, -ət- ‖ -ᵊnᵗs

impenitent ɪm ˈpen ɪt ənt ˌɪm-, -ət- ‖ -ᵊnt ~**ly** li ~**s** s

imperatival ɪm ˌper ə ˈtaɪv ᵊl ◂ ~**ly** i

imperative ɪm ˈper ət ɪv ‖ -əʈ ɪv ~**ly** li ~**ness** nəs nɪs ~**s** z

imperator ˌɪmp ə ˈrɑːt ɔː -ˈreɪt- ‖ -ɔːr -ˈrɑːʈ ᵊr

imperceptibility ˌɪm pə ˌsept ə ˈbɪl ət i -ˌ·ɪ-, -ɪt i ‖ ˌɪm pᵊr ˌsept ə ˈbɪl əʈ i

imperceptib|le ˌɪm pə ˈsept əb |ᵊl -ɪb ᵊl ‖ ˌɪm pᵊr- ~**ly** li

imperfect ɪm ˈpɜːf ɪkt ˌɪm-, -əkt, -ekt ‖ -ˈpɜːf- ~**ly** li ~**ness** nəs nɪs ~**s** s

imperfection ˌɪm pə ˈfek ʃᵊn ‖ ˌɪm pᵊr- ~**s** z

imperfective ˌɪm pə ˈfekt ɪv ‖ ˌɪm pᵊr- ~**ly** li ~**s** z

imperforate ɪm ˈpɜːf ər ət ˌɪm-, ɪt, -ə reɪt ‖ -ˈpɜːf- ~**s** s

imperial ɪm ˈpɪər i əl ‖ -ˈpɪr- ~**s** z

imperialism ɪm ˈpɪər i ə ˌlɪz əm ‖ -ˈpɪr- ~**s** z

imperialist ɪm ˈpɪər i əl ɪst §-əst ‖ -ˈpɪr- ~**s** s

imperialistic ɪm ˌpɪər i əl ˈɪst ɪk ◂ ‖ -ˌpɪr- ~**ally** ᵊl i

imperially ɪm ˈpɪər i əl i ‖ -ˈpɪr-

imperil ɪm ˈper əl -ɪl ~**ed, ~led** d ~**ing, ~ling** ɪŋ ~**s** z

imperious ɪm ˈpɪər i əs ‖ -ˈpɪr- ~**ly** li ~**ness** nəs nɪs

imperishab|le ɪm ˈper ɪʃ əb |ᵊl ~**ly** li

imperium ɪm ˈpɪər i əm ‖ -ˈpɪr-

impermanenc|e ɪm ˈpɜːm ən ənᵗs ˌɪm- ‖ -ˈpɜːm- ~**y** i

impermanent ɪm ˈpɜːm ən ənt ˌɪm- ‖ -ˈpɜːm- ~**ly** li

impermeability ɪm ˌpɜːm i ə ˈbɪl ət i ˌ·ˌ·- ‖ -ˌpɜːm i ə ˈbɪl əʈ i

impermeab|le ɪm ˈpɜːm i əb |ᵊl ˌɪm- ‖ -ˈpɜːm- ~**leness** ᵊl nəs -nɪs ~**ly** li

impermissibility ˌɪm pə ˌmɪs ə ˈbɪl ət i -ɪ·-, -ɪt i ‖ -pᵊr ˌmɪs ə ˈbɪl əʈ i

impermissib|le ˌɪm pə ˈmɪs əb |ᵊl ◂ -ɪb ᵊl ‖ ˌɪm pᵊr- ~**ly** li

impersonal ɪm ˈpɜːs ᵊn əl ˌɪm- ‖ -ˈpɜːs- ~**ly** i ~**s** z

imperso|nate ɪm ˈpɜːs ə |neɪt ‖ -ˈpɜːs- ~**nated** neɪt ɪd -əd ‖ neɪʈ əd ~**nates** neɪts ~**nating** neɪt ɪŋ ‖ neɪʈ ɪŋ

impersonation ɪm ˌpɜːs ə ˈneɪʃ ᵊn ‖ -ˌpɜːs- ~**s** z

impersonator ɪm ˈpɜːs ə neɪt ə ‖ -ˈpɜːs ə neɪʈ ᵊr ~**s** z

impertinenc|e ɪm ˈpɜːt ɪn ənᵗs -ᵊn‿ ‖ -ˈpɜːt ᵊn‿ənᵗs ~**es** ɪz əz ~**y** i

impertinent ɪm ˈpɜːt ɪn ənt -ᵊn‿ ‖ -ˈpɜːt ᵊn‿ənt ~**ly** li

imperturbability ˌɪm pə ˌtɜːb ə ˈbɪl ət i -ɪt i ‖ -pᵊr ˌtɜːb ə ˈbɪl əʈ i

imperturbab|le ˌɪm pə ˈtɜːb əb |ᵊl ◂ ‖ ˌɪm pᵊr ˈtɜːb- ~**ly** li

impervious ɪm ˈpɜːv i‿əs ˌɪm- ‖ -ˈpɜːv- ~**ly** li ~**ness** nəs nɪs

impetigo ˌɪm pɪ ˈtaɪg əʊ -pə-, -pe- ‖ -oʊ

impetuosit|y ɪm ˌpet ju ˈɒs ət |i -ˌpetʃ u- ‖ -ˌpetʃ u ˈɑːs əʈ |i ~**ies** iz

impetuous ɪm ˈpetʃ u‿əs -ˈpet ju ~**ly** li ~**ness** nəs nɪs

impetus ˈɪmp ɪt əs -ət- ‖ -əʈ- ~**es** ɪz əz

Impex ˈɪmp eks

impi ˈɪmp i —*Zulu* [ˈiː mpˈi] ~**s** z

impiet|y ɪm ˈpaɪ ət |i ˌɪm-, -ɪt- ‖ -əʈ |i ~**ies** iz

imping|e ɪm ˈpɪndʒ ~**ed** d ~**ement** mənt ~**es** ɪz əz ~**ing** ɪŋ

IMPIOUS

53% 47%

☐ -ˈpaɪ-
☐ ˈɪmp-

BrE

---

impious ˈɪmp i əs ₍ₜ₎ɪm ˈpaɪ əs — *Preference poll, BrE:* ˈɪmp- *47% (born before 1942, 63%),* -ˈpaɪ- *53%. The traditional, irregular pronunciation* ˈɪmp i əs *has lost ground in favour of* ₍ₜ₎ɪm ˈpaɪ əs ~**ly** li ~**ness** nəs nɪs

impish ˈɪmp ɪʃ ~**ly** li ~**ness** nəs nɪs

implacability ɪm ˌplæk ə ˈbɪl ət i ˌɪm plæk-, -ɪt i ‖ -əʈ i

implacab|le ɪm ˈplæk əb |ᵊl ~**leness** ᵊl nəs -nɪs ~**ly** li

im|plant v ɪm |ˈplɑːnt §-ˈplænt, ·· ‖ -|ˈplænt ~**planted** ˈplɑːnt ɪd §ˈplænt-, -əd ‖ ˈplænʈ əd ~**planting** ˈplɑːnt ɪŋ §ˈplænt- ‖ ˈplænʈ ɪŋ ~**plants** ˈplɑːnts §ˈplænts ‖ ˈplænts

implant n ˈɪm plɑːnt §-plænt ‖ -plænt ~**s** s

implantation ˌɪm plɑːn ˈteɪʃ ᵊn -plæn- ‖ -plæn- ~**s** z

implausibilit|y ɪm ˌplɔːz ə ˈbɪl ət |i ˌ·ˌ· ·ˈ·-, -ɪt i ‖ -əʈ i -ˌplɑːz-, ˌ·ˌ·ˈ·-

implausib|le ɪm ˈplɔːz əb |ᵊl ˌɪm-, -ɪb- ‖ -ˈplɑːz- ~**ly** li

implement n ˈɪmp lɪ mənt -lə- ~**s** s

imple|ment v ˈɪmp lɪ |ment -lə-, -mənt, §·ˌ·ˈment —*See note at* -ment ~**mented** ment ɪd mənt-, -əd ‖ menʈ əd ~**menting** ment ɪŋ mənt- ‖ menʈ ɪŋ ~**ments** ments mənts

implementation ˌɪmp lɪ men ˈteɪʃ ᵊn ˌ·lə-, -mən·- ~**s** z

impli|cate ˈɪmp lɪ |keɪt -lə- ~**cated** keɪt ɪd -əd ‖ keɪʈ əd ~**cates** keɪts ~**cating** keɪt ɪŋ ‖ keɪʈ ɪŋ

implication ˌɪmp lɪ ˈkeɪʃ ᵊn -lə- ~**s** z

implicative ɪm ˈplɪk ət ɪv ˈɪmp lɪ keɪt-, ·ˈ·lə- ‖ ˈɪmp lə keɪt ɪv ɪm ˈplɪk əʈ- ~**ly** li

implicature ɪm ˈplɪk ətʃ ə -ə tjʊə ‖ -ᵊr ~**s** z

implicit ɪm ˈplɪs ɪt §-ət ~**ly** li ~**ness** nəs nɪs

implie... —*see* **imply**

implod|e ɪm ˈpləʊd ‖ -ˈploʊd ~**ed** ɪd əd ~**es** z ~**ing** ɪŋ

implore ɪm 'plɔː ‖ -'plɔːr -'plour ~d d ~s z
  imploring/ly ɪm 'plɔːr ɪŋ /li ‖ -'plour-
implosion ɪm 'pləʊʒ ³n ‖ -'plouʒ- ~s z
implosive ɪm 'pləʊs ɪv ͵ɪm-, -'pləʊz- ‖ -'plous-
  -'plouz- ~ly li ~s z
im|ply ɪm |'plaɪ ~plied 'plaɪd ~plies 'plaɪz
  ~plying 'plaɪ ɪŋ
impolite ͵ɪm pə 'laɪt ◂ ~ly li ~ness nəs nɪs
impolitic ɪm 'pɒl ə tɪk ͵ɪm-, -ɪ- ‖ -'pɑːl- ~ly li
  ~ness nəs nɪs
imponderab|le ɪm 'pɒnd ər əb |³l ͵ɪm-
  ‖ -'pɑːnd ~leness ³l nəs -nɪs ~les ³lz ~ly li
im|port v ɪm |'pɔːt ͵-, ˈ·· ‖ -|'pɔːrt -'pourt
  ~ported 'pɔːt ɪd -əd ‖ 'pɔːrt̬ əd 'pourt̬-
  ~porting 'pɔːt ɪŋ ‖ 'pɔːrt̬ ɪŋ -'pourt̬- ~ports
  'pɔːts ‖ 'pɔːrts 'pourts
import n 'ɪm pɔːt ‖ -pɔːrt -pourt ~s s
importance ɪm 'pɔːt ³nts ‖ -'pɔːrt-
important ɪm 'pɔːt ³nt ‖ -'pɔːrt- ~ly li
importation ͵ɪm pɔː 'teɪʃ ³n ‖ -pɔːr- -pour- ~s
  z
importer ɪm 'pɔːt ə ͵-, ˈ··· ‖ -'pɔːrt̬ ³r -'pourt̬-
  ~s z
import-export ͵ɪm pɔːt 'eks pɔːt
  ‖ -pɔːrt 'eks pɔːrt -pourt 'eks pourt
importunate ɪm 'pɔːt jʊn ət -'pɔːtʃ ən ͵·, -ɪt
  ‖ -'pɔːrtʃ ən ət ~ly li ~ness nəs nɪs
importun|e ͵ɪmp ə 'tjuːn ͵ɪm pɔː-, →-'tʃuːn;
  ɪm 'pɔːt juːn, -'pɔːtʃ uːn ‖ ͵ɪmp ³r 'tuːn -'tjuːn;
  ɪm 'pɔːrtʃ ən ~ed d ~es z ~ing ɪŋ
importunit|y ͵ɪmp ə 'tjuːn ət |i ͵ɪm pɔː-,
  →-'tʃuːn-, -ɪt i ‖ ͵ɪmp ³r 'tuːn ət |i ͵ɪm pɔːr-,
  -'tjuːn- ~ies iz
impos|e ɪm 'pəʊz ‖ -'pouz ~ed d ~es ɪz əz
  ~ing ɪŋ
imposing ɪm 'pəʊz ɪŋ ‖ -'pouz ɪŋ ~ly li ~ness
  nəs nɪs
imposition ͵ɪm pə 'zɪʃ ³n ~s z
impossibilit|y ɪm ͵pɒs ə 'bɪl ət |i ͵·,͵·· ·'·-, -ɪt i
  ‖ -͵pɑːs ə 'bɪl ət̬ |i ~ies iz
impossible ɪm 'pɒs əb ³l ͵ɪm-, -ɪb- ‖ -'pɑːs-
impossibly ɪm 'pɒs əb li -ɪb- ‖ -'pɑːs-
impost 'ɪm pəʊst -pɒst ‖ -poust ~s s
imposter, impostor ɪm 'pɒst ə ‖ -'pɑːst ³r ~s
  z
imposture ɪm 'pɒs tʃə ‖ -'pɑːs tʃ³r ~s z
impotenc|e 'ɪmp ət ³n‿s ‖ -³n‿ts ~y i
impotent 'ɪmp ət ənt ‖ -³nt ~ly li
impound ɪm 'paʊnd ~ed ɪd əd ~ing ɪŋ ~s z
impoverish ɪm 'pɒv ər ɪʃ ‖ -'pɑːv- ~ed t ~es
  ɪz əz ~ing ɪŋ
impoverishment ɪm 'pɒv ər ɪʃ mənt ‖ -'pɑːv-
  ~s s
impracticability ɪm ͵prækt ɪk ə 'bɪl ət i
  ͵ɪm,·· ·'·-, -ɪt i ‖ -ət̬ i
impracticab|le ɪm 'prækt ɪk əb |³l ͵ɪm-
  ~leness ³l nəs -nɪs ~ly li
impractical ɪm 'prækt ɪk ³l ͵ɪm- ~ness nəs nɪs
  ~ly i
impracticality ɪm ͵prækt ɪ 'kæl ət i ͵ɪm,··'·-,
  -ɪt i ‖ -ət̬ i
imprecation ͵ɪmp rə 'keɪʃ ³n ͵ɪmp ri-, ͵ɪm pre-
  ~s z

imprecatory 'ɪmp rə keɪt ər i '·ri-, ͵··'··-;
  ɪm 'prek ət ͵ər i ‖ 'ɪmp rɪk ə tɔːr i ɪm 'prek-,
  -tour i
imprecise ͵ɪm prə 'saɪs ◂ -pri- ~ly li
imprecision ͵ɪm prə 'sɪʒ ³n -pri-
impregnability ɪm ͵preg nə 'bɪl ət i ͵ɪm,··'·-,
  -ɪt i ‖ -ət̬ i
impregnab|le ɪm 'preg nəb |³l ͵ɪm- ~ly li
impreg|nate v 'ɪm preg |neɪt ·'··
  ‖ ɪm 'preg |neɪt ·'·· ~nated neɪt ɪd -əd
  ‖ neɪt̬ əd ~nates neɪts ~nating neɪt ɪŋ
  ‖ neɪt̬ ɪŋ
impregnation ͵ɪm preg 'neɪʃ ³n ͵·,·'·· ~s z
impresario ͵ɪmp rə 'sɑːr i əʊ ·'ri-, ͵ɪm pre-
  ‖ -oʊ -'ser-, -'sær- ~s z
impress n 'ɪm pres ~es ɪz əz
impress v ɪm 'pres ~ed t ~es ɪz əz ~ing ɪŋ
impression ɪm 'preʃ ³n ~s z
impressionability ɪm ͵preʃ ³n ə 'bɪl ət i -ɪt i
  ‖ -ət̬ i
impressionable ɪm 'preʃ ³n əb ³l ~ness nəs
  nɪs
impressionism ɪm 'preʃ ³n ͵ɪz əm -ə ͵nɪz-
impressionist ɪm 'preʃ ³n ɪst §-əst ~s s
impressionistic ɪm ͵preʃ ə 'nɪst ɪk ◂ ~ally ³l_i
impressive ɪm 'pres ɪv ~ly li ~ness nəs nɪs
imprest 'ɪm prest ·'· ~s s
imprimatur ͵ɪm prɪ 'mɑːt ə -prə-, -praɪ-, -'meɪt-
  ‖ -ʊr -³r ~s z
im|print v ɪm |'prɪnt ·'· ~printed 'prɪnt ɪd -əd
  ‖ 'prɪnt̬ əd ~printing 'prɪnt ɪŋ ‖ 'prɪnt̬ ɪŋ
  ~prints 'prɪnts
imprint n 'ɪm prɪnt ~s s
imprison ɪm 'prɪz ³n ~ed d ~ing ͵ɪŋ ~s z
imprisonment ɪm 'prɪz ³n mənt →-'·əm-
improbabilit|y ɪm ͵prɒb ə 'bɪl ət i |i ͵·,͵· ·'·-, -ɪt i
  ‖ -͵prɑːb ə 'bɪl ət̬ |i ~ies iz
improbab|le ɪm 'prɒb əb |³l ͵ɪm- ‖ -'prɑːb-
  ~leness ³l nəs -nɪs ~ly li
impromptu ɪm 'prɒmp tjuː -'prɒmp tʃuː
  ‖ -'prɑːmp uː -juː ~s z
improper ɪm 'prɒp ə ͵ɪm- ‖ -'prɑːp ³r ~ly li
  ~ness nəs nɪs
  im͵proper 'fraction, ͵im͵proper 'fraction
impropriet|y ͵ɪm prə 'praɪ_ət |i △,·pə-, -ɪt i
  ‖ -ət̬ |i ~ies iz
improv 'ɪm prɒv ‖ -prɑːv
improvability ɪm ͵pruːv ə 'bɪl ət i -ɪt i ‖ -ət̬ i
improvable ɪm 'pruːv əb ³l
improv|e ɪm 'pruːv ͵ɪm- ~ed d ~es z ~ing ɪŋ
improvement ɪm 'pruːv mənt ~s s
improver ɪm 'pruːv ə ‖ -³r ~s z
improvidence ɪm 'prɒv ɪd ³nts ͵ɪm-, -əd-
  ‖ -'prɑːv- -ə denᵗs
improvident ɪm 'prɒv ɪd ənt ͵ɪm-, -əd-
  ‖ -'prɑːv- -ə dent ~ly li
improvisation ͵ɪm prə vaɪ 'zeɪʃ ³n -prə vɪ-,
  -prɒv ɪ- ‖ ͵ɪm ͵prɑːv ə- ͵·͵··, ͵ɪm prəv- ~al ³l ~s
  z
improvisatory ͵ɪm prə 'vaɪz ət ͵ər i ◂ -'vɪz-;
  -vaɪ 'zeɪt ər i ‖ -ə tɔːr i -tour i
improvis|e 'ɪm prə vaɪz ‖ ͵·'·· ~ed d ~es ɪz əz
  ~ing ɪŋ

imprudence ɪm ˈpruːd ənts ˌɪm-
imprudent ɪm ˈpruːd ənt ˌɪm- **~ly** li
impudenc|e ˈɪmp jʊd ənts ‖ -jəd- **~y** i
impudent ˈɪmp jʊd ənt ‖ -jəd- **~ly** li
impugn ɪm ˈpjuːn **~ed** d **~ing** ɪŋ **~s** z
impuls|e ˈɪm pʌls **~es** ɪz əz
   ˈimpulse ˌbuying
impulsion ɪm ˈpʌl ʃᵊn **~s** z
impulsive ɪm ˈpʌls ɪv **~ly** li **~ness** nəs nɪs
impunit|y ɪm ˈpjuːn ət i -ɪt- ‖ -əʈ i **~ies** iz
impure ˌɪm ˈpjʊə ◂ ɪm-, -ˈpjɔː ‖ -ˈpjʊᵊr **~ly** li
   ~ness nəs nɪs
impurit|y ɪm ˈpjʊər ət i ˌɪm-, -ɪt- ‖ -ˈpjʊr əʈ i
   ~ies iz
imputable ɪm ˈpjuːt əb ᵊl ‖ -ˈpjuːʈ-
imputation ˌɪm pju ˈteɪʃ ᵊn ‖ -pjə- -pju- **~s** z
imputation ˌɪm pju ˈteɪʃ ᵊn ‖ -pjə- **~s** z
im|pute ɪm ‖ˈpjuːt **~puted** ˈpjuːt ɪd -əd
   ‖ ˈpjuːʈ əd **~putes** ˈpjuːts **~puting** ˈpjuːt ɪŋ
   ‖ ˈpjuːʈ ɪŋ
Imran ˈɪm ræn -rɑːn ‖ -rɑːn
Imus ˈaɪm əs
in ɪn *There is no separate weak form in RP. In*
   some other accents, including GenAm, there is
   a weak form §ən
in- ɪn —*but before* n *usually* ɪ; *before* k *or* g
   assimilates to ɪŋ; *generally stressed only (i) if*
   meaning 'in' rather than 'not'; or (ii) for
   emphasis; or (iii) if the following syllable is
   unstressed: inˈcredible, ˌinˈside, ˌinatˈtentive
-in ɪn —*but in scientific senses also* §ən
   — **tannin** ˈtæn ɪn §-ən ‖ -ən — **teach-in**
   ˈtiːtʃ ɪn
-in' *nonstandard form of* **-ing** ɪn ən —*but after* t
   or d *usually* ᵊn — **likin'** ˈlaɪk ɪn -ən — **eatin'**
   ˈiːt ᵊn -ɪn
Ina ˈiːn ə ˈaɪn ə
inability ˌɪn ə ˈbɪl ət i -ɪt i ‖ -əʈ i
in absentia ˌɪn əb ˈsent i ə -ˈsenʃ-, -i ɑː
   ‖ -ˈsenʃ ə
inaccessibility ˌɪn ək ˌses ə ˈbɪl ət i ˌæk-,
   ˌˌɪk-, -ˌˌɪ-, -ɪt i ‖ -əʈ i
inaccessib|le ˌɪn ək ˈses əb ‖ᵊl ◂ ˌæk-, ˌˌɪk-,
   -ɪb ᵊl **~ly** li
inaccurac|y ɪn ˈæk jər əs ‖i ˌɪn-, -ˈjʊr-, -ɪs i
   ~ies iz
inaccurate ɪn ˈæk jər ət ˌɪn-, -jʊr-, -ɪt **~ly** li
   ~ness nəs nɪs
inaction ɪn ˈæk ʃᵊn ˌɪn-
inacti|vate ɪn ˈækt ɪ ‖veɪt -ə- **~vated** veɪt ɪd
   -əd ‖ veɪʈ əd **~vates** veɪts **~vating** veɪt ɪŋ
   ‖ veɪʈ ɪŋ
inactivation ɪn ˌækt ɪ ˈveɪʃ ᵊn ˌˌˌˌˌ-, -ə-ˌ-- **~s** z
inactive ɪn ˈækt ɪv ˌɪn- **~ly** li **~ness** nəs nɪs
inactivity ˌɪn æk ˈtɪv ət i -ɪt i ‖ -əʈ i
inadequac|y ɪn ˈæd ɪk wəs ‖i ˌɪn-, -ˈ-ək- **~ies**
   iz
inadequate ɪn ˈæd ɪk wət ˌɪn-, -ək-, -wɪt **~ly** li
inadmissibility ˌɪn əd ˌmɪs ə ˈbɪl ət i ˌæd-,
   -ˌ-ɪ-, -ɪt i ‖ -əʈ i
inadmissib|le ˌɪn əd ˈmɪs əb ‖ᵊl ◂ ˌæd-, -ɪb ᵊl
   ~ly li

inadvertenc|e ˌɪn əd ˈvɜːt ᵊnts §-æd- ‖ -ˈvɜːt-
   ~es ɪz əz **~ies** ɪz **~y** i
inadvertent ˌɪn əd ˈvɜːt ᵊnt ◂ §-æd- ‖ -ˈvɜːt-
   ~ly li
inadvisability ˌɪn əd ˌvaɪz ə ˈbɪl ət i §ˌæd-,
   -ɪt i ‖ -əʈ i
inadvisable ˌɪn əd ˈvaɪz əb ᵊl ◂ §ˌæd-
inalienability ɪn ˌeɪl i ən ə ˈbɪl ət i ˌɪn-, ˌˌˌˌˌ--,
   -ɪt i ‖ -əʈ i
inalienab|le ɪn ˈeɪl i ən əb ‖ᵊl ˌɪn- **~ly** li
inamorata ɪn ˌæm ə ˈrɑːt ə ˌˌˌˌ-- ‖ -ˈrɑːʈ ə **~s**
   z
inamorato ɪn ˌæm ə ˈrɑːt əʊ ˌˌˌˌ-- ‖ -ˈrɑːʈ oʊ
   ~s z
inane ɪ ˈneɪn **~ly** li
inanimate ɪn ˈæn ɪm ət -əm- **~ly** li **~ness** nəs
   nɪs
inanition ˌɪn ə ˈnɪʃ ᵊn
inanit|y ɪ ˈnæn ət i ‖i -ɪt- ‖ -əʈ ‖i **~ies** iz
inapplicability ˌɪn ə ˌplɪk ə ˈbɪl ət i -ɪt i;
   ˌˌˌ æp lɪk-, ˌˌˌˌ- ‖ ɪn ˌæp lɪk ə ˈbɪl əʈ i ˌˌˌˌ-
inapplicab|le ˌɪn ə ˈplɪk əb ‖ᵊl (ˌ)ɪn ˌæp lɪk-
   ‖ ɪn ˈæp lɪk- ˌɪn- **~ly** li
inappropriate ˌɪn ə ˈprəʊp ri ət -ɪt ‖ -ˈproʊpr-
   ~ly li **~ness** nəs nɪs
inapt ɪn ˈæpt ˌɪn- **~ly** li **~ness** nəs nɪs
inaptitude ɪn ˈæpt ɪ tjuːd ˌɪn-, -ə-, →-tʃuːd
   ‖ -ə tuːd -tjuːd
inarticulac|y ˌɪn ɑː ˈtɪk jʊl əs ‖i -ˈ-jəl-
   ‖ -ɑːr ˈtɪk jəl- **~ies** iz
inarticulate ˌɪn ɑː ˈtɪk jʊl ət ◂ -jəl ət, -ɪt
   ‖ -ɑːr ˈtɪk jəl- **~ly** li **~ness** nəs nɪs
inartistic ˌɪn ɑː ˈtɪst ɪk ◂ ‖ -ɑːr- **~ally** ᵊl‿i
inasmuch ˌɪn əz ˈmʌtʃ
inattention ˌɪn ə ˈtenʃ ᵊn **~s** z
inattentive ˌɪn ə ˈtent ɪv ◂ ‖ -ˈtenʈ ɪv ◂ **~ly** li
   ~ness nəs nɪs
inaudibility ɪn ˌɔːd ə ˈbɪl ət i ˌɪn,ˌˌˌ‿ˌˌ--, -ɪ-ˌ--, -ɪt i
   ‖ -əʈ i -ˌɑːd-
inaudib|le ɪn ˈɔːd əb ‖ᵊl ˌɪn-, -ɪb- ‖ -ˈɑːd- **~ly** li
inaugural ɪ ˈnɔːg jʊr əl -jər-, -ᵊr‿əl ‖ -jər əl
   ɪ ˈnɑːg-, -ᵊr‿əl **~s** z
inaugu|rate ɪ ˈnɔːg jə ‖reɪt -juᵊ-, -ə- ‖ ɪ ˈnɑːg-
   ~rated reɪt ɪd -əd ‖ reɪʈ əd **~rates** reɪts
   ~rating reɪt ɪŋ ‖ reɪʈ ɪŋ
inauguration ɪ ˌnɔːg jə ˈreɪʃ ᵊn ɪn ˌɔːg-, -juᵊ-,
   -ə- ‖ ɪ ˌnɑːg- **~s** z
inauspicious ˌɪn ɔː ˈspɪʃ əs ◂ -ɒ- ‖ -ɑː- **~ly** li
   ~ness nəs nɪs
in-between ˌɪn bi ˈtwiːn ◂ →ˌ-ɪm-, -bə- **~s** z
inboard ˈɪn bɔːd →ˈɪm- ‖ -bɔːrd -boʊrd
inborn ˌɪn ˈbɔːn ◂ →ˌ-ɪm- ‖ -ˈbɔːrn
   ˌinborn aˈbility
inbound ˈɪn baʊnd →ˈɪm-
in-bounds ˌɪn ˈbaʊndz
inbox ˈɪn bɒks →ˈɪm- ‖ -bɑːks **~es** ɪz əz
inbred ˌɪn ˈbred ◂ →ˌ-ɪm-
   ˌinbred ˈcourtesy
inbreeding ˈɪn ˌbriːd ɪŋ →ˈɪm-
in-built ˌɪn ˈbɪlt ◂ →ˌ-ɪm-, ˈ‿ˌ-
Inc ɪŋk —*see also* **Incorporated**
Inca ˈɪŋk ə **~s** z

incalculab|le ɪn 'kælk jʊl əb |ᵊl ˌ-ɪn-, →ˌ(ˌ)ɪŋ-,
  -'·jəl | -'kælk jəl- ~ly li
incandesc|e ˌɪn kæn 'des →ˌɪŋ-, -kən- | -kən-
  ~ed t ~es ɪz əz ~ing ɪŋ
incandesc|ence ˌɪn kæn 'des |ᵊnᵗs →ˌɪŋ-, -kən-
  | -kən- ~ent/ly ᵊnt /li
incantation ˌɪn kæn 'teɪʃ ᵊn →ˌɪŋ- ~s z
incantatory ˌɪn kæn 'teɪt ər i →ˌɪŋ-;
  ɪn 'kænt ət ˌər i | ɪn 'kænt ə tɔːr i -tour i
incapability ɪn ˌkeɪp ə 'bɪl ət i →ɪŋ-, ·ˌ·, ·'·-,
  -ɪt i | -ət i
incapab|le ɪn 'keɪp əb |ᵊl →ɪŋ-, ˌ·- ~leness
  ᵊl nəs -nɪs ~ly li
incapaci|tate ˌɪn kə 'pæs ɪ |teɪt →ˌɪŋ-, -'·ə-
  ~tated teɪt ɪd -əd | teɪt̬ əd ~tates teɪts
  ~tating teɪt ɪŋ | teɪt̬ ɪŋ
incapacitation ˌɪn kə ˌpæs ɪ 'teɪʃ ᵊn →ˌɪŋ-,
  -ə'·-
incapacit|y ˌɪn kə 'pæs ət |i →ˌɪŋ-, -ɪt i | -ət̬ |i
  ~ies iz
incapsul... —see encapsul...
in-car ˌɪn 'kɑː ◄ →ˌɪŋ- | -'kɑːr ◄
incarce|rate ɪn 'kɑːs ə |reɪt →ɪŋ- | -'kɑːrs-
  ~rated reɪt ɪd -əd | reɪt̬ əd ~rates reɪts
  ~rating reɪt ɪŋ | reɪt̬ ɪŋ
incarceration ɪn ˌkɑːs ə 'reɪʃ ᵊn →ɪŋ-, ˌɪn, ·'·-,
  | -ˌkɑːrs- ~s z
incarnadin|e ɪn 'kɑːn ə daɪn →ɪŋ-, -diːn
  | -'kɑːrn- ~ed d ~es z ~ing ɪŋ
incarnate adj ɪn 'kɑːn ət →ɪŋ-, -ɪt, -eɪt
  | -'kɑːrn-
incarn|ate v 'ɪn kɑːn |eɪt →'ɪŋ-, ·'·· | -kɑːrn-
  ~ated eɪt ɪd -əd | eɪt̬ əd ~ates eɪts ~ating
  eɪt ɪŋ | eɪt̬ ɪŋ
incarnation ˌɪn kɑː 'neɪʃ ᵊn →ˌɪŋ- | -kɑːr- ~s z
incautious ɪn 'kɔːʃ əs ˌ·ɪn-, →ˌ(ˌ)ɪŋ- | -'kɑːʃ- ~ly
  li ~ness nəs nɪs
Ince ɪnᵗs
incendiarism ɪn 'send i ə ˌrɪz əm
  §-'sendʒ ə ˌrɪz əm
incendiar|y ɪn 'send i ər |i §-'sendʒ ər i
  | -'send i er |i ~ies iz
incens|e v 'enrage' ɪn 'senᵗs ~ed t ~es ɪz əz
  ~ing ɪŋ
incense n 'ɪn senᵗs
incentive ɪn 'sent ɪv | -'sent̬ ɪv ~s z
incentivis|e, incentiviz|e ɪn 'sent ɪ vaɪz -ə-
  | -'sent̬- ~ed d ~es ɪz əz ~ing ɪŋ
inception ɪn 'sep ʃᵊn ~s z
inceptive ɪn 'sept ɪv ~s z
incertitude ɪn 'sɜːt ɪ tjuːd ˌɪn-, -ə-, →-tʃuːd
  | -'sɜːt̬ ə tuːd -tjuːd ~s z
incessant ɪn 'ses ᵊnt ~ly li ~ness nəs nɪs
incest 'ɪn sest
incestuous ɪn 'sest ju_əs | -'ses tʃu- ~ly li
  ~ness nəs nɪs
inch ɪntʃ inched ɪntʃt inches 'ɪntʃ ɪz -əz
  inching 'ɪntʃ ɪŋ
Inchcape 'ɪntʃ keɪp ˌ(ˌ)·'·
inchoate adj ɪn 'kəʊ ət →ɪŋ-, -ɪt, -eɪt; 'ɪŋ kəʊ-
  | -'koʊ- ~ly li
inchoative ɪn 'kəʊ ət ɪv →ɪŋ- | -'koʊ ət̬- ~s z

Inchon ˌɪn 'tʃɒn ◄ | -'tʃɑːn ·· ··Korean Inchŏ n
  [in tʃˌŽɔn]
inchworm 'ɪntʃ wɜːm | -wɝːm ~s z
incidenc|e 'ɪnᵗs ɪd ənᵗs -əd- | -ə denᵗs ~es ɪz əz
incident 'ɪnᵗs ɪd ənt -əd- | -ə dent ~s s
incidental ˌɪnᵗs ɪ 'dent ᵊl ◄ -ə- | -'dent̬ ᵊl ~ly ˌi
  ~s z
  ˌinci,dental 'comments
incidential ˌɪnᵗs ɪ 'denᵗʃ ᵊl ◄ -ə-
incine|rate ɪn 'sɪn ə |reɪt ~rated reɪt ɪd -əd
  | reɪt̬ əd ~rates reɪts ~rating reɪt ɪŋ | reɪt̬ ɪŋ
incineration ɪn ˌsɪn ə 'reɪʃ ᵊn ~s z
incinerator ɪn 'sɪn ə reɪt ə | -reɪt̬ ᵊr ~s z
incipienc|e ɪn 'sɪp i_ənᵗs ~y i
incipient ɪn 'sɪp i_ənt ~ly li
incis|e ɪn 'saɪz ~ed d ~es ɪz əz ~ing ɪŋ
incision ɪn 'sɪʒ ᵊn ~s z
incisive ɪn 'saɪs ɪv §-'saɪz- ~ly li ~ness nəs nɪs
incisor ɪn 'saɪz ə | -ᵊr ~s z
in|cite ɪn |'saɪt ~cited 'saɪt ɪd -əd | 'saɪt̬ əd
  ~cites 'saɪts ~citing 'saɪt ɪŋ | 'saɪt̬ ɪŋ
incitement ɪn 'saɪt mənt ~s s
incivilit|y ˌɪn sə 'vɪl ət |i ˌ·sɪ-, -ɪt i | -ət̬ |i ~ies
  iz
inclemency ɪn 'klem ᵊnᵗs i ˌɪn-, →ˌ(ˌ)ɪŋ-
inclement ɪn 'klem ənt ˌɪn-, →ˌ(ˌ)ɪŋ-,
  △'ɪŋk ᵊl mənt ~ly li
inclination ˌɪn klɪ 'neɪʃ ᵊn →ˌɪŋ-, -klə- ~s z
incline n 'ɪn klaɪn →'ɪŋ- ~s z
inclin|e v ɪn 'klaɪn →ɪŋ- ~ed d ~es z ~ing ɪŋ
inclinometer ˌɪn klɪ 'nɒm ɪt ə →ˌɪŋ-, ˌ·klə-
  | -'nɑːm ət̬ ᵊr ~s z
inclos|e ɪn 'kləʊz →ɪŋ- | -'kloʊz ~ed d ~es ɪz
  əz ~ing ɪŋ
inclosure ɪn 'kləʊʒ ə →ɪŋ- | -'kloʊʒ ᵊr ~s z
includ|e ɪn 'kluːd →ɪŋ- ~ed ɪd əd ~es z ~ing
  ɪŋ
inclusion ɪn 'kluːʒ ᵊn →ɪŋ- ~s z
inclusive ɪn 'kluːs ɪv →ɪŋ-, §-'kluːz- ~ly li
  ~ness nəs nɪs
incognito ˌɪn kɒg 'niːt əʊ ◄ →ˌ·ɪŋ-;
  ɪn 'kɒg nɪ təʊ, →ɪŋ-, -nə- | ˌɪn kɑːg 'niːt oʊ
  ɪn 'kɑːg nə toʊ
incogniz|ance ɪn 'kɒg nɪz |ənᵗs §-'·nəz-
  | -'kɑːg- ~ant ənt
incoherenc|e ˌɪn kəʊ 'hɪər ənᵗs →ˌɪŋ-
  | -koʊ 'hɪr- -'her- ~y i
incoherent ˌɪn kəʊ 'hɪər ənt ◄ →ˌɪŋ-
  | -koʊ 'hɪr- -'her- ~ly li ~ness nəs nɪs
incombustib|le ˌɪn kəm 'bʌst əb |ᵊl ◄ →ˌɪŋ-,
  §ˌ·kɒm-, -ɪb ᵊl ~ly li
income 'ɪn kʌm →'ɪŋ-, -kəm ~s z
  'income tax
incomer 'ɪn ˌkʌm ə | -ᵊr ~s z
incoming 'ɪn ˌkʌm ɪŋ →'ɪŋ-
incommensurab|le ˌɪn kə 'menᵗʃ ər_əb |ᵊl ◄
  →ˌɪŋ-, -'menᵗs-, -'·jər- ~ly li
incommensurate ˌɪn kə 'menᵗʃ ər_ət ◄ →ˌɪŋ-,
  -'menᵗs-, -'·jər-, ɪt ~ly li ~ness nəs nɪs
incommod|e ˌɪn kə 'məʊd →ˌɪŋ- | -'moʊd ~ed
  ɪd əd ~es z ~ing ɪŋ
incommodious ˌɪn kə 'məʊd i_əs ◄ →ˌɪŋ-
  | -'moʊd- ~ly li ~ness nəs nɪs

incommunicab|le ˌɪn kə ˈmjuːn ɪk əb |ᵊl ◂
→ˌɪŋ- **~ly** li

incommunicado ˌɪn kə ˌmjuːn ɪ ˈkɑːd əʊ
→ˌɪŋ-, -ˌ-ə- ‖ -oʊ

incommunicative ˌɪn kə ˈmjuːn ɪ kət ɪv ◂
-ˈ-ə-, -keɪt ɪv ‖ -ə keɪţ ɪv -ɪk əţ- **~ly** li **~ness**
nəs nɪs

incomparability ɪn ˌkɒmp ər ə ˈbɪl ət i →ˌɪŋ-,
-ˌ-ˌ-, -ɪt i; ˌɪn kəm ˌpær ə-, →ˌɪŋ-, §-ˌpeər-
‖ ɪn ˌkɑːmp ər ə ˈbɪl əţ i -ˌ-ˌ-; ˌɪn kəm ˌpær-,
-ˌper-

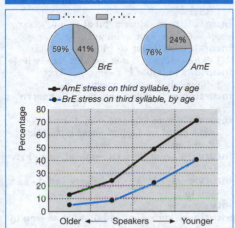
incomparab|le ɪn ˈkɒmp ər əb |ᵊl →ˌɪŋ-, -ˌ-;
ˌɪn kəm ˈpær-, →ˌɪŋ-, §-kɒm-, §-ˈpeər-
‖ ɪn ˈkɑːmp ər əb |ᵊl ɪn-; ˌɪn kəm ˈper-, -ˈpær-
— *Preference polls, AmE:* ·ˈ···· *76%,* ˌ·ˈ···
24%; BrE: ·ˈ···· *59%,* ˌ·ˈ··· *41%.* **~leness**
ᵊl nəs -nɪs **~ly** li

incompatibilit|y ˌɪn kəm ˌpæt ə ˈbɪl ət |i
→ˌɪŋ-, §,kɒm-, -ˌ-ɪ-, -ɪt i ‖ -ˌpæţ ə ˈbɪl əţ |i
~ies iz

incompatib|le ˌɪn kəm ˈpæt əb |ᵊl ◂ →ˌɪŋ-,
§,kɒm-, -ɪb ᵊl ‖ -ˈpæţ- **~les** ᵊlz **~ly** li

incompetenc|e ɪn ˈkɒmp ɪt ən¹s →ˌɪŋ-, ˌ-, -ət-
‖ -ˈkɑːmp ət ᵊn¹s **~y** i

incompetent ɪn ˈkɒmp ɪt ənt →ˌɪŋ-, ˌ-, -ət-
‖ -ˈkɑːmp ət ᵊnt **~ly** li **~s** s

incomplete ˌɪn kəm ˈpliːt ◂ →ˌɪŋ-, §-kɒm- **~ly**
li **~ness** nəs nɪs

incomprehensibility
ɪn ˌkɒmp rɪ ˌhen¹s ə ˈbɪl ət i →ˌɪŋ-, -ˌ-ˌ-, -rə-ˌ-
-ˌ-ɪ-, -ɪt i ‖ ɪn ˌkɑːmp rɪ ˌhen¹s ə ˈbɪl əţ i -ˌ-ˌ-

incomprehensib|le
ɪn ˌkɒmp rɪ ˈhen¹s əb |ᵊl ◂ →ˌɪŋ-, -ˌ-ˌ-, -rə¹-ˌ-
-ɪb ᵊl ‖ ɪn ˌkɑːm- -ˌ-ˌ- **~ly** li

incomprehension ɪn ˌkɒmp rɪ ˈhen¹ʃ ᵊn →ˌɪŋ-,
-ˌ-ˌ-, -rə¹-ˌ- ‖ ɪn ˌkɑːmp- -ˌ-ˌ-

inconceivability ˌɪn kən ˌsiːv ə ˈbɪl ət i →ˌɪŋ-,
§,kɒn-, -ɪt i ‖ -əţ i

inconceivab|le ˌɪn kən ˈsiːv əb |ᵊl ◂ →ˌɪŋ-,
§,kɒn- **~leness** ᵊl nəs -nɪs **~ly** li

inconclusive ˌɪn kən ˈkluːs ɪv ◂ →ˌɪŋ-, →-kəŋ-,
§-kɒn-, §-ˈkluːz- **~ly** li **~ness** nəs nɪs

incongruit|y ˌɪn kən ˈgruː ət |i →ˌɪŋ-, →,-kəŋ-,
ˌ-kɒn-, →-ˌkɒŋ-, ɪt i ‖ -əţ |i **~ies** iz

incongruous ɪn ˈkɒŋ gru əs →ˌɪŋ- ‖ -ˈkɑːŋ- **~ly**
li **~ness** nəs nɪs

inconsequence ɪn ˈkɒn¹s ɪk wən¹s →ˌɪŋ-, ˌ-,
-ək-; §-ə kwen¹s ‖ -ˈkɑːn¹s-

inconsequent ɪn ˈkɒn¹s ɪk wənt →ˌɪŋ-, ˌɪn-,
-ək-; §-ə kwent ‖ -ˈkɑːn¹s- **~ly** li

inconsequential ɪn ˌkɒn¹s ɪ ˈkwen¹ʃ ᵊl ◂ →ˌɪŋ-,
ˌɪn-, -ˌ-, -ə¹-ˌ- ‖ -ˌkɑːn¹s- **~ly** i **~ness** nəs nɪs

inconsequentiality
ɪn ˌkɒn¹s ɪ ˌkwen¹ʃ i ˈæl ət i →ˌɪŋ-, -ˌ-ˌ-, -ə-ˌ-,
-ɪt i ‖ -ˌkɑːn¹s i ˌkwen¹ʃ i ˈæl əţ i

inconsiderab|le ˌɪn kən ˈsɪd ər əb |ᵊl ◂ →ˌɪŋ-,
§,kɒn- **~ly** li

inconsiderate ˌɪn kən ˈsɪd ər ət ◂ →ˌɪŋ-,
§,kɒn-, -ɪt **~ly** li **~ness** nəs nɪs

inconsideration ˌɪn kən ˌsɪd ə ˈreɪʃ ᵊn →ˌɪŋ-,
§,kɒn-

inconsistenc|y ˌɪn kən ˈsɪst ən¹s |i →ˌɪŋ-,
§,kɒn- **~ies** iz

inconsistent ˌɪn kən ˈsɪst ənt ◂ →ˌɪŋ-, §-kɒn-
~ly li

inconsolab|le ˌɪn kən ˈsəʊl əb |ᵊl ◂ →ˌɪŋ-,
§,kɒn- ‖ -ˈsoʊl- **~leness** ᵊl nəs -nɪs **~ly** li

inconspicuous ˌɪn kən ˈspɪk ju əs →ˌɪŋ-,
§,kɒn- **~ly** li **~ness** nəs nɪs

inconstanc|y ɪn ˈkɒn¹st ən¹s |i →ˌɪŋ-, ˌ-
‖ -ˈkɑːn¹st- **~ies** iz

inconstant ɪn ˈkɒn¹st ənt →ˌɪŋ-, ˌ- ‖ -ˈkɑːn¹st-
~ly li

incontestability ˌɪn kən ˌtest ə ˈbɪl ət i →ˌɪŋ-,
§,kɒn-, -ɪt i ‖ -əţ i

incontestab|le ˌɪn kən ˈtest əb |ᵊl ◂ →ˌɪŋ-,
§,kɒn- **~ly** li

incontinence ɪn ˈkɒnt ɪn ən¹s →ˌɪŋ-, ˌ-, -ən̩
‖ -ˈkɑːnt ᵊn¹ən¹s

incontinent ɪn ˈkɒnt ɪn ənt →ˌɪŋ-, ˌ-, -ən̩
‖ -ˈkɑːnt ᵊn¹ənt **~ly** li

incontrovertib|le ˌɪn ˌkɒntr ə ˈvɜːt əb |ᵊl
→ˌɪŋ-, -ˌ-ˌ- ‖ ˌɪn ˌkɑːntr ə ˈvɜːţ- **~leness** ᵊl nəs
-nɪs **~ly** li

inconvenienc|e ˌɪn kən ˈviːn i ən¹s →ˌɪŋ-,
§,kɒn- **~ed** t **~es** ɪz əz **~ing** ɪŋ

inconvenient ˌɪn kən ˈviːn i ənt ◂ →ˌɪŋ-,
§,kɒn- **~ly** li

incorpo|rate *v* ɪn ˈkɔːp ə |reɪt →ˌɪŋ- ‖ -ˈkɔːrp-
~rated reɪt ɪd -əd ‖ reɪţ əd **~rates** reɪts
~rating reɪt ɪŋ ‖ reɪţ ɪŋ

incorporate *adj* ɪn ˈkɔːp ər ət →ˌɪŋ-, -ɪt, -ə reɪt
‖ -ˈkɔːrp-

incorporation ɪn ˌkɔːp ə ˈreɪʃ ᵊn →ˌɪŋ-
‖ -ˌkɔːrp- **~s** z

incorporeal ˌɪn kɔː ˈpɔːr i əl ◂ →ˌɪŋ- ‖ ˌɪn kɔːr-
-ˈpoʊr- **~ly** li

incorrect ˌɪn kə ˈrekt ◂ →ˌɪŋ- **~ly** li **~ness** nəs
nɪs

incorrigibility ɪn ˌkɒr ɪdʒ ə ˈbɪl ət i →ˌɪŋ-, -ˌ-ˌ-,
-ədʒ ə-, -ɪt i ‖ ɪn ˌkɔːr ədʒ ə ˈbɪl əţ i -ˌkɑːr-,
-ˌ-ˌ-

incorrigib|le ɪn ˈkɒr ɪdʒ əb |ᵊl →ˌɪŋ-, ˌ-, -ˈ-ədʒ-
‖ -ˈkɔːr- -ˈkɑːr- **~les** ᵊlz **~ly** li

incorrupt ‚ɪn kə 'rʌpt →‚ɪŋ- **~ly** li **~ness** nəs
nɪs
incorruptibility ‚ɪn kə ‚rʌpt ə 'bɪl ət i →‚ɪŋ-,
-‚-‚-, -ɪt i ‖ -əţ i
incorruptib|le ‚ɪn kə 'rʌpt əb |ᵊl ◄ →‚ɪŋ-,
-ɪb ᵊl **~les** ᵊlz **~ly** li
incorruption ‚ɪn kə 'rʌp ʃᵊn →‚ɪŋ-

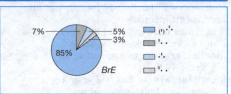

INCREASE (noun)

7% — 5%
3%
85%
BrE

increas|e n 'ɪŋ kriːs 'ɪn-, ₍ᵢ₎'·—*The stress
distinction between verb* ·'· *and noun* '·· *is not
always made consistently. Nevertheless, in a
BrE preference poll 85% preferred to make this
distinction (as against 7% preferring* '·· *for
both verb and noun, 5%* ·'· *for both, and 3%*
'·· *for the verb,* ·'· *for the noun).* **~es** ɪz əz
increas|e v ɪn 'kriːs →‚ɪŋ-, ‚-, '·· *(not -'kriːz)*
~ed t **~es** ɪz əz **~ing/ly** ɪŋ /li
incredibility ɪn ‚kred ə 'bɪl ət i →‚ɪŋ-, ‚‚-, -ɪ'--,
-ɪt i ‖ -əţ i
incredib|le ɪn 'kred əb |ᵊl →‚ɪŋ-, ‚-, -ɪb- **~ly** li
incredulity ‚ɪn krə 'djuːl ət i →‚ɪŋ-, ‚krɪ-,
‚kre-, →-'dʒuːl-, -ɪt i ‖ -'duːl əţ i -'djuːl-
incredulous ɪn 'kred jʊl əs →‚ɪŋ-, -jəl-
‖ -'kredʒ əl əs **~ly** li **~ness** nəs nɪs
incre|ment v 'ɪŋ krɪ |ment 'ɪn-, -krə- —*See
note at* -ment **~mented** ment ɪd -əd
‖ menţ əd **~menting** ment ɪŋ ‖ menţ ɪŋ
~ments ments
increment n 'ɪŋ krɪ mənt 'ɪn-, -krə- **~s** s
incremental ‚ɪŋ krɪ 'ment ᵊl ◄ ‚ɪn-, -krə-
‖ -'menţ ᵊl ◄ **~ly** i
incrimi|nate ɪn 'krɪm ɪ |neɪt →‚ɪŋ-, -ə- **~nated**
neɪt ɪd -əd ‖ neɪţ əd **~nates** neɪts **~nating**
neɪt ɪŋ ‖ neɪţ ɪŋ
incrimination ɪn ‚krɪm ɪ 'neɪʃ ᵊn →‚ɪŋ-, -ə-
incriminatory ɪn 'krɪm ɪn ət ˌər i →‚ɪŋ-, -'·ən-;
-'krɪm ɪ neɪt ər i, -'·ə-, ‚·‚·'·· ‖ -ə tɔːr i
-toʊr i
in-crowd 'ɪn kraʊd
incrust ɪn 'krʌst →‚ɪŋ- **~ed** ɪd əd **~ing** ɪŋ **~s** s
incrustation ‚ɪn krʌ 'steɪʃ ᵊn →‚ɪŋ- **~s** z
incu|bate 'ɪŋ kju |beɪt 'ɪn- ‖ -kjə- **~bated**
beɪt ɪd -əd ‖ beɪţ əd **~bates** beɪts **~bating**
beɪt ɪŋ ‖ beɪţ ɪŋ
incubation ‚ɪŋ kju 'beɪʃ ᵊn ‚ɪn- ‖ -kjə- **~s** z
incubator 'ɪŋ kju beɪt ə 'ɪn- ‖ -kjə beɪţ ᵊr **~s** z
in|cubus 'ɪŋ |kjʊb əs 'ɪn- **~cubi** kju baɪ
~cubuses kjʊb əs ɪz -əz
inculc|ate 'ɪn kʌlk |eɪt →'ɪŋ-, -kᵊl k|eɪt;
ɪn 'kʌlk-, →‚ɪŋ- ‖ ɪn 'kʌlk |eɪt '··· **~ated**
eɪt ɪd -əd ‖ eɪţ əd **~ates** eɪts **~ating** eɪt ɪŋ
‖ eɪţ ɪŋ
inculcation ‚ɪn kʌl 'keɪʃ ᵊn →‚ɪŋ-, -kᵊl- **~s** z

inculp|ate 'ɪn kʌlp |eɪt →'ɪŋ-; ·'··
‖ ɪn 'kʌlp |eɪt '··· **~ated** eɪt ɪd -əd ‖ eɪţ əd
~ates eɪts **~ating** eɪt ɪŋ ‖ eɪţ ɪŋ
inculpation ‚ɪn kʌl 'peɪʃ ᵊn →‚ɪŋ- **~s** z
inculpatory ɪn 'kʌlp ət ˌər i →‚ɪŋ-;
'ɪn kʌlp eɪt ər i, →'ɪŋ-; ‚ɪn kʌl 'peɪt-, →‚ɪŋ-
‖ -'kʌlp ə tɔːr i -toʊr i
incumbenc|y ɪn 'kʌm bən's |i →‚ɪŋ- **~ies** iz
incumbent ɪn 'kʌm bənt →‚ɪŋ- **~ly** li **~s** s
incunabul|um ‚ɪn kju 'næb jʊl |əm →‚ɪŋ- **~a**
ə **~ar** ə ‖ ᵊr
in|cur ɪn |'kɜː →‚ɪŋ- ‖ -|'kɜː: **~curred** 'kɜːd
‖ 'kɜːd **~curring** 'kɜːr ɪŋ ‖ 'kɜː: ɪŋ **~curs** 'kɜːz
‖ 'kɜː:z
incurability ɪn ‚kjʊər ə 'bɪl ət i →‚ɪŋ-, -‚kjɔːr-,
‚·‚-, -ɪt i ‖ ɪn ‚kjʊr ə 'bɪl əţ i ‚·‚-
incurab|le ɪn 'kjʊər əb |ᵊl →‚ɪŋ-, ‚-, -'kjɔːr-
‖ -'kjʊr- **~leness** ᵊl nəs -nɪs **~les** ᵊlz **~ly** li
incurious ɪn 'kjʊər i ˌəs →‚ɪŋ-, ‚-, -'kjɔːr-
‖ -'kjʊr- **~ly** li **~ness** nəs nɪs
incursion ɪn 'kɜːʃ ᵊn →‚ɪŋ-, -'kɜːʒ- ‖ -'kɜː:ʒ ᵊn **~s**
z
incurv|ate v 'ɪn kɜːv |eɪt →'ɪŋ- ‖ -kɜː:v- ·'··
~ated eɪt ɪd -əd ‖ eɪţ əd **~ates** eɪts **~ating**
eɪt ɪŋ ‖ eɪţ ɪŋ
incurvate adj ɪn 'kɜːv et →‚ɪŋ-, -ət, -ɪt ‖ -'kɜː:v-
·'·;
incurv|e ‚ɪn 'kɜːv ◄ → ‚ɪŋ- ‖ -'kɜː:v **~ed** d **~es** z
~ing ɪŋ
incus 'ɪŋk əs
incus|e ɪn 'kjuːz →‚ɪŋ- **~ed** d **~es** ɪz əz **~ing** ɪŋ
Ind ɪnd aɪnd
Ind 'Coope tdmk kuːp
indaba ɪn 'dɑːb ə —*Zulu* [i 'ndaː ɓa] **~s** z
indebted ɪn 'det ɪd -əd ‖ -'deţ əd **~ness** nəs
nɪs
indecenc|y ɪn 'diːs ᵊn's |i ‚ɪn- **~ies** iz
indecent ɪn 'diːs ᵊnt ‚ɪn- **~ly** li
in‚decent as'sault, ‚‚·· ·'·; in‚decent
ex'posure
indecipherability ‚ɪn di ‚saɪf ər ˌə 'bɪl ət i
‚·də-, -ɪt i ‖ -əţ i
indecipherab|le ‚ɪn di 'saɪf ər əb |ᵊl ◄ ‚·də-
~leness ᵊl nəs -nɪs **~ly** li
indecision ‚ɪn di 'sɪʒ ᵊn -də-, -'zɪʃ-
indecisive ‚ɪn di 'saɪs ɪv ◄ -də-, -'saɪz- **~ly** li
~ness nəs nɪs
indeclinab|le ‚ɪn di 'klaɪn əb |ᵊl ◄ ‚·də-
~leness ᵊl nəs -nɪs **~ly** li
indecorous ɪn 'dek ər əs ‚ɪn-, §‚ɪn dɪ 'kɔːr əs ◄,
-də- ‖ ‚ɪn dɪ 'kɔːr əs, -'koʊr- **~ly** li **~ness** nəs
nɪs
indecorum ‚ɪn di 'kɔːr əm -də- ‖ -'koʊr-
indeed ɪn 'diːd ‚ɪn-
indefatigab|le ‚ɪn di 'fæt ɪg əb |ᵊl ◄ ‚·də-
‖ -'fæţ- **~leness** ᵊl nəs -nɪs **~ly** li
indefeasibility ‚ɪn di ‚fiːz ə 'bɪl ət i ‚·də-
‖ -əţ i
indefeasib|le ‚ɪn di 'fiːz əb |ᵊl ◄ ‚·də-, -ɪb · **~ly**
li
indefensib|le ‚ɪn di 'fen's əb |ᵊl ◄ ‚·də-, -ɪb ·
~leness ᵊl nəs -nɪs **~ly** li

indefinab|le ˌɪn di 'faɪn əb |ᵊl ◂ ˌ-də- **~leness**
ᵊl nəs -nɪs **~ly** li
indefinite ɪn 'def ən‿ət ˌɪn-, -ɪn-, -ɪt **~ly** li
~ness nəs nɪs
in ˌdefinite 'article, ˌ·ˌ·· ˈ··
indelib|le ɪn 'del əb |ᵊl ˌɪn-, -ɪb- **~leness**
ᵊl nəs -nɪs **~ly** li
indelicac|y ɪn 'del ɪk əs |i ˌɪn-, -'ək- **~ies** iz
indelicate ɪn 'del ɪk ət ˌɪn-, -ək-, -ɪt **~ly** li
~ness nəs nɪs
indemnification ɪn ˌdem nɪf ɪ 'keɪʃ ᵊn -ˌnəf-,
§-ə'· **~s** z
indemni|fy ɪn 'dem nɪ |faɪ -nə- **~fied** faɪd
~fier/s faɪ‿ə/z ‖ faɪ‿ᵊr/z **~fies** faɪz **~fying**
faɪ ɪŋ
indemnit|y ɪn 'dem nət |i -nɪt- ‖ -nət̬ |i **~ies**
iz
indene 'ɪnd iːn
indent *n* 'ɪn dent ·ˈ· **~s** s
in|dent *v* ɪn |'dent ˌ·'·◂ **~dented** 'dent ɪd -əd
‖ 'dent̬ əd **~denting** 'dent ɪŋ ‖ 'dent̬ ɪŋ
~dents 'dents
indentation ˌɪn den 'teɪʃ ᵊn **~s** z
indent|ure *n, v* ɪn 'dentʃ |ə ‖ -|ᵊr **~ured** əd
‖ ᵊrd **~ures** əz ‖ ᵊrz **~uring** ər ɪŋ
independence ˌɪn di 'pend ən‿s ◂ -də-
ˌInde'pendence Day; ˌInde,pendence 'Hall
independent, I~ ˌɪn di 'pend ənt ◂ -də- **~ly** li
~s s
ˌinde,pendent 'clause
in-depth ˌɪn 'depθ ◂
indescribability ˌɪn di ˌskraɪb ə 'bɪl ət i ˌ·də-,
-ɪt i ‖ -ət̬ i
indescribab|le ˌɪn di 'skraɪb əb |ᵊl ◂ ˌ·də-
~leness ᵊl nəs -nɪs **~ly** li
Indesit *tdmk* 'ɪnd ɪ sɪt -ə-, -e-
indestructibility ˌɪn di ˌstrʌkt ə 'bɪl ət i ˌ·də-,
-ˌ·ɪ-, -ɪt i ‖ -ət̬ i
indestructib|le ˌɪn di 'strʌkt əb |ᵊl ◂ ˌ·də-,
-ɪb- ᵊl **~leness** ᵊl nəs -nɪs **~ly** li
indeterminab|le ˌɪn di 'tɜːm ɪn əb |ᵊl ◂ ˌ·də-,
-ən‿əb- ‖ -'tɜːm- **~ly** li
indeterminac|y ˌɪn di 'tɜːm ɪn əs |i ˌ·də-,
-ən‿əs- ‖ -'tɜːm- **~ies** iz
indeterminate ˌɪn di 'tɜːm ɪn ət ◂ ˌ·də-, -ən‿,
-ɪt ‖ -'tɜːm- **~ly** li **~ness** nəs nɪs
index *n, v* 'ɪnd eks **~ed** t **~es** ɪz əz **~ing** ɪŋ
indices 'ɪnd ɪ siːz -ə-
'index ˌfinger; 'index ˌnumber
indexation ˌɪnd ek 'seɪʃ ᵊn **~s** z
indexer 'ɪnd eks ə ‖ -ᵊr **~s** z
indexical ɪn 'deks ɪk ᵊl **~ly** ˌi
index-|linked ˌɪnd eks |'lɪŋkt ◂ **~linking**
'lɪŋk ɪŋ
India, india 'ɪnd i‿ə
ˌindia 'rubber◂, ˌindia-,rubber 'ball
Indian 'ɪnd i‿ən **~s** z
ˌIndian 'corn; ˌIndian 'ink; ˌIndian 'Ocean;
ˌIndian 'summer
Indiana ˌɪnd i 'æn‿ə -'ɑːn-
Indianan ˌɪnd i 'æn ən ◂ -'ɑːn- **~s** z
Indianapolis ˌɪnd i‿ə 'næp əl ɪs §-əs
Indianian ˌɪnd i 'æn i‿ən ◂ -'ɑːn- **~s** z

Indic 'ɪnd ɪk
indi|cate 'ɪnd ɪ |keɪt -ə- **~cated** keɪt ɪd -əd
‖ keɪt̬ əd **~cates** keɪts **~cating** keɪt ɪŋ
‖ keɪt̬ ɪŋ
indication ˌɪn dɪ 'keɪʃ ᵊn -də- **~s** z
indicative ɪn 'dɪk ət ɪv ‖ -ət̬ ɪv **~ly** li **~s** z
indicator 'ɪnd ɪ keɪt ə '·ə- ‖ -keɪt̬ ᵊr **~s** z
'indicator board
indices 'ɪnd ɪ siːz -ə-
in|dict ɪn |'daɪt *(! = indite)* **~dicted** 'daɪt ɪd
-əd ‖ 'daɪt̬ əd **~dicting** 'daɪt ɪŋ ‖ 'daɪt̬ ɪŋ
~dicts 'daɪts
indictable ɪn 'daɪt əb ᵊl ‖ -'daɪt̬-
indiction ɪn 'dɪk ʃᵊn **~s** z
indictment ɪn 'daɪt mənt **~s** s
indie 'ɪnd i **~s** z
Indies 'ɪnd iz
indifference ɪn 'dɪf rən‿s -'dɪf ər ən‿s
indifferent ɪn 'dɪf rənt -'dɪf ər ənt **~ly** li
indigence 'ɪnd ɪdʒ ən‿s
indigene 'ɪnd ɪ dʒiːn §-ə- **~s** z
indigenous ɪn 'dɪdʒ ən‿əs -ɪn- **~ly** li **~ness**
nəs nɪs
indigent 'ɪnd ɪdʒ ənt **~ly** li **~s** s
indigestibility ˌɪn dɪ ˌdʒest ə 'bɪl ət i ˌ·də-,
ˌ·daɪ-, -ˌ·ɪ-, -ɪt i ‖ -ət̬ i
indigestib|le ˌɪn dɪ 'dʒest əb |ᵊl ◂ ˌ·də-, ˌ·daɪ-,
-ɪb ᵊl **~ly** li
indigestion ˌɪn dɪ 'dʒes tʃən -də-, →-'dʒeʃ-
indignant ɪn 'dɪg nənt **~ly** li
indignation ˌɪn dɪg 'neɪʃ ᵊn
indignit|y ɪn 'dɪg nət |i -nɪt- ‖ -nət̬ |i **~ies** iz
indigo 'ɪnd ɪ ɡəʊ ‖ -ɡoʊ **~es, ~s** z
Indio 'ɪnd i‿əʊ ‖ -oʊ
Indira 'ɪnd ɪr ə -ər-; ɪn 'dɪər ə ‖ -'dɪr-
indirect ˌɪn də 'rekt ◂ -dɪ-, -daɪ- **~ly** li **~ness**
nəs nɪs
ˌindi,rect 'object; ˌindi,rect 'speech
indirection ˌɪn də 'rek ʃᵊn -dɪ-, -daɪ-
indiscernib|le ˌɪn dɪ 'sɜːn əb |ᵊl ◂ ˌ·də-,
-'zɜːn-, -ɪb ᵊl ‖ -'sɜːn- -'zɜːn- **~ly** li
indiscipline ɪn 'dɪs əp lɪn ˌɪn-, -'·ɪp-, -lən;
§ˌɪn dɪ 'sɪp-
indiscreet ˌɪn dɪ 'skriːt ◂ -də- **~ly** li **~ness** nəs
nɪs
indiscretion ˌɪn dɪ 'skreʃ ᵊn -də- **~s** z
indiscriminate ˌɪn dɪ 'skrɪm ɪn ət ◂ ˌ·də-,
-'·ən‿, -ɪt **~ly** li **~ness** nəs nɪs
indispensability ˌɪn dɪ ˌspen‿s ə 'bɪl ət i ˌ·də-,
-ɪt i ‖ -ət̬ i
indispensab|le ˌɪn dɪ 'spen‿s əb |ᵊl ◂ ˌ·də-
~les ᵊlz **~ly** li
indispose ˌɪn dɪ 'spəʊz -də- ‖ -'spoʊz **~ed** d ◂
indisposition ɪn ˌdɪsp ə 'zɪʃ ᵊn ˌ·ˌ·· -ˈ··· **~s** z
indisputability ˌɪn dɪ ˌspjuːt ə 'bɪl ət i -ɪt i;
ɪn ˌdɪs pjuːt-, ˌ·ˌ· ‖ -ˌspjuːt̬ ə 'bɪl ət̬ i
indisputab|le ˌɪn dɪ 'spjuːt əb |ᵊl ◂ ˌ·də-;
ₗ(ₗ)ɪn 'dɪs pjuːt- ‖ -'spjuːt̬- **~ly** li
indissolubility ˌɪn dɪ ˌsɒl ju 'bɪl ət i ˌ·də-,
-ˌ·jə-, -ɪt i ‖ -ˌsaːl jə 'bɪl ət̬ i
indissolub|le ˌɪn dɪ 'sɒl jʊb |ᵊl ◂ ˌ·də-, -jəb ᵊl
‖ -'saːl jəb |ᵊl **~leness** ᵊl nəs -nɪs **~ly** li

I

indistinct ˌɪn dɪ ˈstɪŋkt ◄ -də- **~ly** li **~ness** nəs
nɪs

indistinguishab|le ˌɪn dɪ ˈstɪŋ gwɪʃ əb |ᵊl ◄
ˌ-də- **~ly** li

in|dite ɪn |ˈdaɪt **~dited** ˈdaɪt ɪd -əd ‖ ˈdaɪʈ əd
~dites ˈdaɪts **~diting** ˈdaɪt ɪŋ ‖ ˈdaɪʈ ɪŋ

indium ˈɪnd i əm

individual ˌɪnd ɪ ˈvɪdʒ u‿əl ◄ ˌ-ə-, -ˈvɪd ju‿ **~ly** i
~s z

individualis... —see **individualiz...**

individualism ˌɪnd ɪ ˈvɪdʒ u ə ˌlɪz əm ˌ-ə-,
-ˈvɪd ju‿; -ˈvɪdʒ u ˌlɪz əm **~s** z

individualist ˌɪnd ɪ ˈvɪdʒ u‿əl ɪst ˌ-ə-, -ˈvɪd ju‿,
§-əst; -ˈvɪdʒ ʊl ɪst, -əst **~s** s

individualistic ˌɪnd ɪ ˌvɪdʒ u‿ə ˈlɪst ɪk ˌ-ə-,
-ˌvɪd ju‿, -ˌvɪdʒ u'-- **~ally** ᵊl i

individualit|y ˌɪnd ɪ ˌvɪdʒ u ˈæl ət |i ˌ-ə-,
-ˌvɪd ju-, -ɪt i ‖ -əʈ |i **~ies** iz

individualization ˌɪnd ɪ ˌvɪdʒ u‿əl aɪ ˈzeɪʃ ᵊn
ˌ-ə-, -ˌvɪd ju-, -ɪ'-- ‖ -ə'-- **~s** z

individualiz|e ˌɪnd ɪ ˈvɪdʒ u‿ə laɪz ˌ-ə-,
-ˈvɪd ju‿; -ˈvɪdʒ u laɪz **~ed** d **~es** ɪz əz **~ing** ɪŋ

individu|ate ˌɪnd ɪ ˈvɪdʒ u |eɪt ˌ-ə-, -ˈvɪd ju-
~ated eɪt ɪd -əd ‖ eɪʈ əd **~ates** eɪts **~ating**
eɪt ɪŋ ‖ eɪʈ ɪŋ

individuation ˌɪnd ɪ ˌvɪdʒ u ˈeɪʃ ᵊn ˌ-ə-,
-ˌvɪd ju- **~s** z

indivisibility ˌɪn dɪ ˌvɪz ə ˈbɪl ət i ˌ-də-, -ˌ-ɪ-,
-ɪt i ‖ -əʈ i

indivisib|le ˌɪn dɪ ˈvɪz əb |ᵊl ◄ ˌ-də-, -ɪb ᵊl
~leness ᵊl nəs -nɪs **~ly** li

Indo- ˌɪnd əʊ ‖ -oʊ — **Indo-Pacific**
ˌɪnd əʊ pə ˈsɪf ɪk ◄ ‖ ˌ-oʊ-

Indo-Aryan ˌɪnd əʊ ˈeər i‿ən ◄ ‖ -oʊ ˈer- -ˈær-

Indo-China ˌɪnd əʊ ˈtʃaɪn ə ◄ ‖ -oʊ-

Indo-Chinese ˌɪnd əʊ ˌtʃaɪ ˈniːz ‖ -oʊ-

indoctri|nate ɪn ˈdɒk trɪ |neɪt -trə- ‖ -ˈdɑːk-
~nated neɪt ɪd -əd ‖ neɪʈ əd **~nates** neɪts
~nating neɪt ɪŋ ‖ neɪʈ ɪŋ

indoctrination ɪn ˌdɒk trɪ ˈneɪʃ ᵊn ˌ·,·-, -trə'--
‖ -ˌdɑːk- **~s** z

Indo-European ˌɪnd əʊ ˌjʊər ə ˈpiːˌən ◄ -ˌjɔːr-
‖ -oʊ ˌjʊr- **~ist/s** ɪst/s -əst/s
ˌIndo-Euroˌpean ˈlanguages

Indo-Germanic ˌɪnd əʊ dʒɜː ˈmæn ɪk ◄
-əʊ dʒɜ- ‖ -oʊ dʒɝː- -oʊ dʒɝr-

Indo-Iranian ˌɪnd əʊ ɪ ˈreɪn i‿ən ◄ ‖ ˌ-oʊ-

indole ˈɪnd əʊl →-ɒʊl ‖ -oʊl

indolence ˈɪnd əl ən's

indolent ˈɪnd əl ənt **~ly** li

indomitab|le ɪn ˈdɒm ɪt əb |ᵊl ◄ -'-ət-
‖ -ˈdɑːm əʈ- **~ly** li

Indonesia ˌɪnd əʊ ˈniːʒ ə -ˈniːz i‿ə, -ˈniːs-;
-ˈniːʃ ə

Indonesian ˌɪnd əʊ ˈniːʒ ᵊn ◄ -ˈniːz i‿ən,
-ˈniːs-; -ˈniːʃ ᵊn **~s** z

indoor ɪn ˈdɔː ◄ ‖ -ˈdɔːr ◄ -ˈdoʊr **~s** z
ˌindoor ˈgames

Indore ˌ(ˌ)ɪn ˈdɔː ‖ -ˈdɔːr —Hindi Indaur
[ɪŋ ˌdəʊr]

indors|e ɪn ˈdɔːs ən- ‖ -ˈdɔːrs **~ed** t **~es** ɪz əz
~ement/s mənt/s **~ing** ɪŋ

Indra ˈɪndr ə

indrawn ˌɪn ˈdrɔːn ◄ ‖ -ˈdrɑːn
ˌindrawn ˈbreath

indri ˈɪndr i **~s** z

indubitab|le ɪn ˈdjuːb ɪt əb |ᵊl ˌɪn-, →-ˈdʒuːb-,
-ˈ-ət- ‖ -ˈduːb əʈ- -ˈdjuːb- **~ly** li

induc|e ɪn ˈdjuːs →-ˈdʒuːs ‖ -ˈduːs -ˈdjuːs **~ed** t
~es ɪz əz **~ing** ɪŋ

inducement ɪn ˈdjuːs mənt →-ˈdʒuːs- ‖ -ˈduːs-
-ˈdjuːs- **~s** s

induct ɪn ˈdʌkt **~ed** ɪd əd **~ing** ɪŋ **~s** s

inductanc|e ɪn ˈdʌkt ən's **~es** ɪz əz

inductee ˌɪn dʌk ˈtiː **~s** z

induction ɪn ˈdʌk ʃᵊn **~s** z
inˈduction coil

inductive ɪn ˈdʌkt ɪv **~ly** li **~ness** nəs nɪs

indu|e ɪn ˈdjuː ən-, →-ˈdʒuː ‖ -ˈduː -ˈdjuː **~ed** d
~es z **~ing** ɪŋ

indulg|e ɪn ˈdʌldʒ **~ed** d **~es** ɪz əz **~ing** ɪŋ

indulgenc|e ɪn ˈdʌldʒ ən's **~es** ɪz əz

indulgent ɪn ˈdʌldʒ ənt **~ly** li

indurate adj ˈɪn djʊᵊr ət →-ˈdʒʊᵊr-, -ɪt, -eɪt
‖ -dər- -djər-

indu|rate v ˈɪn djʊᵊ |reɪt →-ˈdʒuᵊ- ‖ -də- -djə-
~rated reɪt ɪd -əd ‖ reɪʈ əd **~rates** reɪts
~rating reɪt ɪŋ ‖ reɪʈ ɪŋ

induration ˌɪn djuᵊ ˈreɪʃ ᵊn →-dʒuᵊ- ‖ ˌɪn də-
-djə-

Indus ˈɪnd əs

industrial ɪn ˈdʌs tri‿əl **~ly** i **~s** z
inˌdustrial ˈaction; inˌdustrial
ˌarchaeˈology; inˌdustrial deˈsign;
inˌdustrial eˈstate; inˌdustrial
ˌrevoˈlution

industrialis... —see **industrializ...**

industrialism ɪn ˈdʌs tri‿əl ˌɪz əm

industrialist ɪn ˈdʌs tri‿əl ɪst §-əst **~s** s

industrialization ɪn ˌdʌs tri‿əl aɪ ˈzeɪʃ ᵊn -ɪ'--
‖ -ə'-- **~s** z

industrializ|e ɪn ˈdʌs tri‿ə laɪz **~ed** d **~es** ɪz
əz **~ing** ɪŋ

industrial-strength ɪn ˈdʌs tri‿əl streŋᵏθ
§-streŋθ

industrious ɪn ˈdʌs tri‿əs **~ly** li **~ness** nəs nɪs

indus|try ˈɪnd əs |tri §-ʌs- **~tries** triz

industry-wide ˌɪnd əs tri ˈwaɪd ◄ §-ʌs-

in|dwell ˌ(ˌ)ɪn |ˈdwel **~dwelling** ˈdwel ɪŋ
~dwells ˈdwelz **~dwelt** ˈdwelt

Indy ˈɪnd i

-ine aɪn, iːn, ɪn §ən —As a suffix, iːn in
chemical senses ('bromine, 'caffeine), otherwise
usually aɪn ('bovine, 'crystalline). When not
felt as a suffix, often ɪn, §ən ('discipline,
'famine), sometimes stressed iːn (rou'tine).

inebri|ate v ɪ ˈniːb ri |eɪt **~ated** eɪt ɪd -əd
‖ eɪʈ əd **~ates** eɪts **~ating** eɪt ɪŋ ‖ eɪʈ ɪŋ

inebriate adj, n ɪ ˈniːb ri‿ət -ɪt, -eɪt **~s** s

inebriation ɪ ˌniːb ri ˈeɪʃ ᵊn

inebriety ˌɪn i ˈbraɪ‿ət i §ˌ-ə-, ˌɪt i ‖ -əʈ i

inedibility ɪn ˌed ə ˈbɪl ət i ˌɪn,·-, -ɪ'--, -ɪt i
‖ -əʈ i

inedible ɪn ˈed əb ᵊl ˌɪn-, -ɪb ᵊl

ineducable ɪn ˈed jʊk əb ᵊl ˌɪn-, -ˈjuːk-;
-ˈedʒ ʊk-, -ˈ-ək- ‖ -ˈedʒ ək-

ineffability ɪn ˌef ə ˈbɪl ət i -ɪt i ‖ -ət̬ i
ineffab|le ɪn ˈef əb |ᵊl **~leness** ᵊl nəs -nɪs **~ly**
li
ineffaceab|le ˌɪn i ˈfeɪs əb ᵊl ◄ ˌ-e-, ˌ-ə- **~ly** li
ineffective ˌɪn ə ˈfekt ɪv ◄ -i- **~ly** li **~ness** nəs
nɪs
ineffectual ˌɪn ə ˈfek tʃu ᵊl ◄ ˌ-i-, -tju ᵊl, -ʃu ᵊl
~ly i **~ness** nəs nɪs
inefficacy ɪn ˈef ɪkəs i
inefficienc|y ˌɪn ə ˈfɪʃ ᵊnᵗs |i ˌ-i- **~ies** iz
inefficient ˌɪn ə ˈfɪʃ ᵊnt ◄ -i- **~ly** li
inelastic ˌɪn i ˈlæst ɪk ◄ -ə-, -ˈlɑːst-
inelasticity ˌɪn i læ ˈstɪs ət i ˌ-ə-, -lɑːˈ--;
ˌɪn ˌiːl æˈ--, ˌɪn ˌel æˈ--, -ɑːˈ--, -ɪt i ‖ -ət̬ i
inelegance ɪn ˈel ɪg ənᵗs ˌɪn-, -əg-
inelegant ɪn ˈel ɪg ənt ˌɪn-, -əg- **~ly** li
ineligibility ɪn ˌel ɪdʒ ə ˈbɪl ət i -ˌədʒ-, ˌ‚--,
-ɪˈ--, -ɪt i ‖ -ət̬ i
ineligib|le ɪn ˈel ɪdʒ əb |ᵊl ˌɪn-, -ˈədʒ-, -ɪb ᵊl
~ly li
ineluctab|le ˌɪn i ˈlʌkt əb |ᵊl ◄ ˌ-ə- **~ly** li
inept ɪ ˈnept ˌɪn ˈept ◄ **~ly** li **~ness** nəs nɪs
ineptitude ɪ ˈnept ɪ tjuːd -ə-, →-tʃuːd ‖ **-tuːd**
-tjuːd
inequalit|y ˌɪn i ˈkwɒl ət |i ˌ-ə-, -ɪt i
‖ -ˈkwɑːl ət̬ |i **-ies** iz
inequitab|le ɪn ˈek wɪt əb |ᵊl ˌɪn-, -ˈwət-
‖ -ˈek wət̬- **~leness** ᵊl nəs -nɪs **~ly** li
inequit|y ɪn ˈek wət |i ˌɪn-, -ɪt- ‖ -wət̬ |i **~ies**
iz
ineradicab|le ˌɪn i ˈræd ɪk əb |ᵊl ◄ ˌ-ə-
~leness ᵊl nəs -nɪs **~ly** li
inert ɪ ˈnɜːt ‖ ɪ ˈnɜːt **~ly** li **~ness** nəs nɪs
inertance ɪ ˈnɜːt ᵊnᵗs ‖ -ˈnɜːt-
inertia ɪ ˈnɜːʃ ə -ˈnɜːʃ i ə ‖ ɪ ˈnɜːʃ ə
i**ˈnertia reel**; i**ˌnertia ˈselling**, ⸳⸳ ⸳⸳
inertial ɪ ˈnɜːʃ ᵊl -ˈnɜːʃ i əl ‖ ɪ ˈnɜːʃ ᵊl
inescapab|le ˌɪn ɪ ˈskeɪp əb |ᵊl ◄ ˌ-ə- **~ly** li
inessential ˌɪn ɪ ˈsenᵗʃ ᵊl ◄ -ə- **~s** z
inessive ɪn ˈes ɪv ˌɪn- **~s** z
inestimab|le ɪn ˈest ɪm əb |ᵊl ˌɪn-, -ˈəm- **~ly** li
inevitability ɪn ˌev ɪt ə ˈbɪl ət i ˌ‚--, -ət ə-, -ɪt i
‖ -ət̬ ə ˈbɪl ət̬ i
inevitab|le ɪn ˈev ɪt əb |ᵊl ˌ‚-, -ˈət- ‖ -ˈev ət̬-
~leness ᵊl nəs -nɪs **~ly** li
inexact ˌɪn ɪg ˈzækt ◄ -eg-, -əg-, -ɪk-, -ek-, -ək-
~ly li **~ness** nəs nɪs
inexactitude ˌɪn ɪg ˈzækt ɪ tjuːd ˌeg-, ˌəg-,
ˌɪk-, ˌek-, ˌək-, -ə ⸳, →-tʃuːd ‖ -ə tuːd -tjuːd **~s**
z
inexcusab|le ˌɪn ɪk ˈskjuːz əb |ᵊl ◄ ˌ-ek-, ˌ-ək-
~leness ᵊl nəs -nɪs **~ly** li
inexhaustib|le ˌɪn ɪg ˈzɔːst əb |ᵊl ◄ ˌeg-, ˌəg-,
ˌɪk-, ˌek-, ˌək-, -ɪb ᵊl ‖ -ˈzɑːst- **leness** ᵊl nəs
-nɪs **~ly** li
inexorability ɪn ˌeks ər ə ˈbɪl ət i §-ˌegz-, -ɪt i
‖ -ət̬ i
inexorab|le ɪn ˈeks ər əb |ᵊl §-ˈegz- **leness**
ᵊl nəs -nɪs **~ly** li
inexpedienc|e ˌɪn ɪk ˈspiːd i ənᵗs ˌ-ek-, ˌ-ək- **~y**
i
inexpedient ˌɪn ɪk ˈspiːd i ənt ◄ ˌ-ek-, ˌ-ək- **~ly**
li

inexpensive ˌɪn ɪk ˈspenᵗs ɪv ◄ -ek-, -ək- **~ly** li
~ness nəs nɪs
inexperience ˌɪn ɪk ˈspɪər i ənᵗs ˌ-ek-, ˌ-ək-
‖ -ˈspɪr- **~d** t
inexpert ɪn ˈeks pɜːt ˌɪn-; ˌɪn ek ˈspɜːt ◄, -ɪk-,
-ək- ‖ ɪn ˈeks pɜːt ˌɪn-; ˌɪn ɪk ˈspɜːt ◄ **~ly** li
~ness nəs nɪs
inexpiab|le ɪn ˈeks pi əb |ᵊl ˌɪn- **~leness**
ᵊl nəs -nɪs **~ly** li
inexplicability ˌɪn ɪk ˌsplɪk ə ˈbɪl ət i ˌ-ek-,
ˌ-ək-, -ɪt i; ɪn ˌeks plɪk-, ˌ‚,-- ‖ -ət̬ i
inexplicab|le ˌɪn ɪk ˈsplɪk əb |ᵊl ◄ ˌ-ek-, ˌ-ək-;
₍₎ɪn ˈeks plɪk- **~leness** ᵊl nəs -nɪs **~ly** li
inexplicit ˌɪn ɪk ˈsplɪs ɪt -ek-, -ək-, §-ət **~ly** li
~ness nəs nɪs
inexpressib|le ˌɪn ɪk ˈspres əb |ᵊl ◄ ˌ-ek-,
ˌ-ək-, -ɪb ᵊl **~leness** ᵊl nəs -nɪs **~ly** li
inexpressive ˌɪn ɪk ˈspres ɪv ◄ -ek-, -ək- **~ly** li
~ness nəs nɪs
inextinguishab|le ˌɪn ɪk ˈstɪŋ gwɪʃ əb |ᵊl ◄
ˌ-ek-, ˌ-ək-, -ˈ‚wɪʃ- **~leness** ᵊl nəs -nɪs **~ly** li
in extremis ˌɪn ɪk ˈstriːm ɪs -ek-, -ək-, §-əs
inextricability ˌɪn ɪk ˌstrɪk ə ˈbɪl ət i ˌ-ek-,
ˌ-ək-, -ɪt i; ɪn ˌeks trɪk-, ˌ‚,-- ‖ -ət̬ i
inextricab|le ˌɪn ɪk ˈstrɪk əb |ᵊl ◄ ˌ-ek-, ˌ-ək-;
₍₎ɪn ˈeks trɪk- **~leness** ᵊl nəs -nɪs **~ly** li
Inez ˈiːn ez ˈaɪn- ‖ ˈaɪn ez aɪ ˈnez, ˈiːn ez;
iː ˈnez, ɪ- —*Sp* [ˈi neθ]
infallibility ɪn ˌfæl ə ˈbɪl ət i ˌ‚,--, -ɪˈ--, -ɪt i
‖ -ət̬ i
infallib|le ɪn ˈfæl əb |ᵊl ˌɪn-, -ɪb- **~leness**
ᵊl nəs -nɪs **~ly** li
infamous ˈɪn fəm əs *(!)* **~ly** li **~ness** nəs nɪs
infam|y ˈɪn fəm |i **~ies** iz
infanc|y ˈɪnᵗf ənᵗs |i **~ies** iz
infant ˈɪnᵗf ənt **~s** s
ˌinfant ˈprodigy; ˈinfant school
infanta ɪn ˈfænt ə —*Sp* [in ˈfan ta] **~s** z
infante ɪn ˈfænt i —*Sp* [in ˈfan te] **~s** z
infanticidal ɪn ˌfænt ɪ ˈsaɪd ᵊl ◄ ˌ-ə- ‖ -ˌfænt̬ ə-
infanticide ɪn ˈfænt ɪ saɪd -ə- ‖ -ˈfænt̬ ə- **~s** z
infantile ˈɪnᵗf ən taɪᵊl ‖ -tᵊl
ˌinfantile ˈparalysis
infantilism ɪn ˈfænt ɪ ˌlɪz əm -ˈ-ə- ‖ -ˈfænt̬ ə-
infantr|y ˈɪnᵗf əntr |i **~ies** iz
infantry|man ˈɪnᵗf əntr i |mən -mæn **~men**
mən men
infarct ˈɪn fɑːkt ⸳ˈ⸳ ‖ -ˈfɑːrkt **~s** s
infarction ɪn ˈfɑːk ʃᵊn ‖ -ˈfɑːrk- **~s** z
infatu|ate ɪn ˈfæt ju |eɪt -ˈfætʃ u- ‖ ɪn ˈfætʃ u-
~ated eɪt ɪd -əd ‖ eɪt̬ əd **~ates** eɪts **~ating**
eɪt ɪŋ ‖ eɪt̬ ɪŋ
infatuation ɪn ˌfæt ju ˈeɪʃ ᵊn -ˌfætʃ u-
‖ ɪn ˌfætʃ u- **~s** z
infect ɪn ˈfekt **~ed** ɪd əd **~ing** ɪŋ **~s** s
infection ɪn ˈfek ʃᵊn **~s** z
infectious ɪn ˈfek ʃəs **~ly** li **~ness** nəs nɪs
infective ɪn ˈfekt ɪv **~ness** nəs nɪs
infectivity ˌɪn fek ˈtɪv ət i -ɪt i ‖ -ət̬ i
infelicitous ˌɪn fə ˈlɪs ɪt əs ◄ ˌ-fɪ-, ˌ-fe-, -ət əs
‖ -ət̬ əs **~ly** li
infelicit|y ˌɪn fə ˈlɪs ət |i ˌ-fɪ-, ˌ-fe-, -ɪt i ‖ -ət̬ |i
~ies iz

infer ɪn ˈfɜː ‖ -ˈfɝː **~red** d **inferring** ɪn ˈfɜːr ɪŋ ‖ ɪn ˈfɝː ɪŋ **~s** z

inferab|le ɪn ˈfɜːr əb |ᵊl ˈɪnf ər‿əb |ᵊl ‖ -ˈfɝː- **~ly** li

inferenc|e ˈɪnᵊf ᵊr‿ənᵗs **~es** ɪz əz

inferential ˌɪnᵊf ə ˈrenᵗʃ ᵊl ◄ **~ly** i

inferior ɪn ˈfɪər i‿ə ˌɪn- ‖ -ˈfɪr i‿ᵊr **~s** z

inferiorit|y ɪn ˌfɪər i ˈɒr ət i ˌˌˌˌ-, -ɪt i ‖ ɪn ˌfɪr i ˈɔːr ət̬ i ˌ-ˈɑːr- **~ies** iz
  in ˌferi'ority ˌcomplex

infernal ɪn ˈfɜːn ᵊl ‖ -ˈfɝːn- **~ly** i

inferno, I~ ɪn ˈfɜːn əʊ ‖ -ˈfɝːn oʊ **~s** z

inferrab|le ɪn ˈfɜːr əb |ᵊl ˈɪnf ər‿əb |ᵊl ‖ -ˈfɝː- **~ly** li

infertile ɪn ˈfɜːt aɪᵊl ˌɪn- ‖ -ˈfɝːt̬ ᵊl (*)

infertility ˌɪnf ə ˈtɪl ət i ˌfɜː-, -ɪt i ‖ -ˈfᵊr ˈtɪl ət̬ i

infest ɪn ˈfest **~ed** ɪd əd **~ing** ɪŋ **~s** s

infestation ˌɪn fe ˈsteɪʃ ᵊn **~s** z

infibu|late ɪn ˈfɪb ju |leɪt -jə- ‖ -jə- **~lated** leɪt ɪd -əd ‖ leɪt̬ əd **~lates** leɪts **~lating** leɪt ɪŋ ‖ leɪt̬ ɪŋ

infibulation ɪn ˌfɪb ju ˈleɪʃ ᵊn -jə- ‖ -jə- **~s** z

infidel ˈɪn fɪd ᵊl -fəd-; -fɪ del, -fə- **~s** z

infidelit|y ˌɪn fɪ ˈdel ət |i ˌfə-, -ɪt i ‖ -ət̬ |i **~ies** iz

infield ˈɪn fiːᵊld **~s** z

infielder ˈɪn ˌfiːᵊld ə ‖ -ᵊr **~s** z

infight|er ˈɪn ˌfaɪt |ə ‖ -ˌfaɪt̬ |ᵊr **~ers** əz ‖ ᵊrz **~ing** ɪŋ

infill ˈɪn fɪl **~ed** d **~ing** ɪŋ **~s** z

infil|trate ˈɪn fɪl |treɪt -fᵊl- ‖ ɪn ˈfɪl|tr eɪt ˈɪn fᵊl |treɪt (*) **~trated** treɪt ɪd -əd ‖ treɪt̬ əd **~trates** treɪts **~trating** treɪt ɪŋ ‖ treɪt̬ ɪŋ

infiltration ˌɪn fɪl ˈtreɪʃ ᵊn -fᵊl- **~s** z

infiltrator ˈɪn fɪl treɪt ə ‖-ᵊl- ‖ ɪn ˈfɪltr eɪt̬ ᵊr ˈɪn fᵊl treɪt̬-

infinite ˈɪn fɪn ət -ɪt; ˈɪnf ən‿ət, ɪt —*but in church music usually* ˈɪn fɪ naɪt, -fə-, -faɪ- **~ly** li **~ness** nəs nɪs

infinitesimal ˌɪn fɪn ɪ ˈtes ɪm ᵊl ◄ -əˈ-, -əm ᵊl; ˌɪnf ən‿, -ˈtez- **~ly** i

infiniti... —*see* **infinity**

infinitival ɪn ˌfɪn ɪ ˈtaɪv ᵊl ◄ ˌˌˌˌ-, -əˈ-

infinitive ɪn ˈfɪn ət ɪv -ɪt- ‖ -ət̬ ɪv **~s** z

infinitude ɪn ˈfɪn ɪ tjuːd -ə-, →-tʃuːd ‖ -tuːd -tjuːd **~s** z

infinit|y ɪn ˈfɪn ət |i -ɪt- ‖ -ət̬ |i **~ies** iz

infirm ɪn ˈfɜːm ˌɪn- ‖ -ˈfɝːm **~ly** li **~ness** nəs nɪs

infirmar|y ɪn ˈfɜːm ᵊr |i ‖ -ˈfɝːm- **~ies** iz

infirmit|y ɪn ˈfɜːm ət i ‖i -ɪt- ‖ -ˈfɝːm ət̬ |i **~ies** iz

infix *n* ˈɪn fɪks **~es** ɪz əz

infix *v* ˈɪn fɪks ₍ₒ₎ˈ· **~ed** t **~es** ɪz əz **~ing** ɪŋ

in flagrante ˌɪn flə ˈɡrænt i -eɪ ‖ -ˈɡrɑːnt-
  in fla,grante de'licto dɪ ˈlɪkt əʊ də-, diː-, deɪ- ‖ -oʊ

inflam|e ɪn ˈfleɪm **~ed** d **~es** z **~ing** ɪŋ

inflammab|le ɪn ˈflæm əb |ᵊl **~leness** ᵊl nəs -nɪs **~ly** li

inflammation ˌɪn flə ˈmeɪʃ ᵊn **~s** z

inflammatory ɪn ˈflæm ət‿ᵊr i ‖ -ə tɔːr i -toʊr i

inflatable ɪn ˈfleɪt əb ᵊl ‖ -ˈfleɪt̬- **~s** z

in|flate ɪn |ˈfleɪt **~flated** ˈfleɪt ɪd -əd ‖ ˈfleɪt̬ əd **~flates** ˈfleɪts **~flating** ˈfleɪt ɪŋ ‖ ˈfleɪt̬ ɪŋ

inflation ɪn ˈfleɪʃ ᵊn **~ism** ˌɪz əm **~s** z

inflationary ɪn ˈfleɪʃ ᵊn ər i -ᵊn‿ər- ‖ -ə ner i
  in,flationary 'spiral

inflation-proof ɪn ˈfleɪʃ ᵊn pruːf §-prʊf

inflator ɪn ˈfleɪt ə ‖ ɪn ˈfleɪt̬ ᵊr **~s** z

inflect ɪn ˈflekt **~ed** ɪd əd **~ing** ɪŋ **~s** s

inflection ɪn ˈflek ʃᵊn **~al** ᵊl **~s** z

inflexibility ɪn ˌfleks ə ˈbɪl ət i ˌˌˌˌ-, -ɪˈ-, -ɪt i ‖ -ət̬ i

inflexib|le ɪn ˈfleks əb |ᵊl ˌɪn-, -ɪb- **~leness** ᵊl nəs -nɪs **~ly** li

inflexion ɪn ˈflek ʃᵊn **~al** ᵊl **~s** z

inflict ɪn ˈflɪkt **~ed** ɪd əd **~ing** ɪŋ **~s** s

infliction ɪn ˈflɪk ʃᵊn

in-flight ˌɪn ˈflaɪt ◄
  ,in-flight 'movies

inflorescenc|e ˌɪn flə ˈres ᵊnᵗs -flɔː-, -flɒ- ‖ -flɔː-, -flɑː- **~es** ɪz əz

inflow ˈɪn fləʊ ‖ -floʊ **~s** z

influenc|e ˈɪnᵊf lu‿ənᵗs **~es** ɪz əz

influence-peddling ˈɪnf lu‿ənᵗs ˌped ᵊl ɪŋ

influential ˌɪnᵊf lu ˈenᵗʃ ᵊl ◄ **~ly** i

influenza ˌɪnᵊf lu ˈenz ə

influx ˈɪn flʌks **~es** ɪz əz

info ˈɪn fəʊ ‖ -foʊ

infobahn ˈɪn fəʊ bɑːn ‖ -oʊ-

infocom ˈɪn fəʊ kɒm ‖ -oʊ kɑːm **~s** z

infomediary ˌɪn fəʊ ˈmiːd i‿ər i ‖ ˌɪn foʊ ˈmiːd i er i

infomercial ˌɪn fəʊ ˈmɜːʃ ᵊl ‖ ˈɪn foʊ mɝːʃ ᵊl ˈ-fə- **~s** z

inform ɪn ˈfɔːm ‖ -ˈfɔːrm **~ed** d **~ing** ɪŋ **~s** z

informal ɪn ˈfɔːm ᵊl ˌɪn- ‖ -ˈfɔːrm- **~ly** i

informalit|y ˌɪn fɔː ˈmæl ət |i -ɪt i ‖ -fɔːr ˈmæl ət̬ |i ˌ-fᵊr- **~ies** iz

informant ɪn ˈfɔːm ənt ‖ -ˈfɔːrm- **~s** s

informatics ˌɪnᵊf ə ˈmæt ɪks -ɔː- ‖ -ᵊr ˈmæt̬-

information ˌɪnᵊf ə ˈmeɪʃ ᵊn ‖ -ᵊr- **~al** əl ◄
  ,infor'mation re,trieval; ,infor'mation tech,nology, ˌ·ˌ·ˌ· ·ˈ·ˌ··

informative ɪn ˈfɔːm ət ɪv ‖ -ˈfɔːrm ət̬ ɪv **~ly** li **~ness** nəs nɪs

informer ɪn ˈfɔːm ə ‖ -ˈfɔːrm ᵊr **~s** z

Infoseek *tdmk* ˈɪn fəʊ siːk ‖ -foʊ-

infotainment ˌɪn fəʊ ˈteɪn mənt →-ˈteɪm- ‖ -foʊ- ˈ···

infowar ˈɪn fəʊ wɔː ‖ -foʊ wɔːr

infra ˈɪnᵊf rə
  ,infra 'dig

infra- ¦ɪnᵊf rə — **infrasonic** ˌɪnᵊf rə ˈsɒn ɪk ◄ ‖ -ˈsɑːn-

infraction ɪn ˈfræk ʃᵊn **~s** z

infralapsarian ˌɪnᵊf rə læp ˈseər i‿ən ◄ ‖ -ˈser- -ˈsær- **~ism** ˌɪz əm **~s** z

infrared ˌɪnᵊf rə ˈred ◄

infrastructure ˈɪnᵊf rə ˌstrʌk tʃə ‖ -tʃᵊr **~s** z

infrequency ɪn ˈfriːk wənᵗs i ˌɪn-

infrequent ɪn ˈfriːk wənt ˌɪn- **~ly** li

infring|e ɪn ˈfrɪndʒ **~ed** d **~er/s** ə/z ‖ ˀr/z **~es**
ɪz əz **~ing** ɪŋ
infringement ɪn ˈfrɪndʒ mənt **~s** s
infundibul|um ˌɪn fʌn ˈdɪb jʊl |əm -jəl əm
‖ -jəl |əm **~a** ə **~ar** ə ‖ ˀr
infuri|ate ɪn ˈfjʊər i |eɪt -ˈfjɔːr- ‖ -ˈfjʊr- **~ated**
eɪt ɪd -əd ‖ eɪt̬ əd **~ates** eɪts **~ating/ly**
eɪt ɪŋ /li ‖ eɪt̬-
infus|e ɪn ˈfjuːz **~ed** d **~er/s** ə/z ‖ ˀr/z **~es** ɪz
əz **~ing** ɪŋ
infusion ɪn ˈfjuːʒ ˀn **~s** z
infusori|a ˌɪn fju ˈzɔːr i |ə ◂ -ˈsɔːr- ‖ -ˈzʊr-,
-ˈsʊr- **~al** əl **~an/s** ən/z
-ing ɪŋ —For △m, △ən, see at -in'. —Note the
typical late/early stress difference between
phrases, such as a ˌsinging caˈnary, where the
-ing word is a participial adjective, and
compounds, such as a ˈsinging ˌlesson, where
the -ing word is a verbal noun (gerund).
Inga (i) ˈɪŋ ə, (ii) ˈɪŋ gə
Ingamells ˈɪŋ gə melz
Ingatestone ˈɪŋ gət stəʊn -geɪt- ‖ -stoʊn
ingathering ˈɪn ˌgæð ər ɪŋ →ˈɪŋ-
Inge family name (i) ɪŋ, (ii) ɪndʒ —In Britain
usually (i), in the US usually (ii).
Inge personal name, (i) ˈɪŋ ə, (ii) ˈɪŋ gə
ingenious ɪn ˈdʒiːn i ˌəs ˌɪn- **~ly** li **~ness** nəs
nɪs
ingenue, ingénue ˈæ̃ʒ ə njuː ˈ5ʒ-, -e-, -eɪ-,
-nuː, ˌ·ˈ· ‖ ˈændʒ ə nuː ˈɑːndʒ-, -njuː —Fr
[æ̃ ʒe ny] **~s** z
ingenuit|y ˌɪndʒ ə ˈnjuːˌət |i ˌ·ɪ-, §-ˈnuːˌ, ɪt i
‖ -ˈnuː ət̬ |i -ˈnjuː- **~ies** iz
ingenuous ɪn ˈdʒen ju ˌəs **~ly** li **~ness** nəs nɪs
Ingersoll tdmk ˈɪŋ gə sɒl ‖ -gˀr sɔːl -sɑːl, -sˀl
ingest ɪn ˈdʒest ˌɪn- **~ed** ɪd əd **~ing** ɪŋ **~s** s
ingestion ɪn ˈdʒes tʃən ˌɪn-, →-ˈdʒeʃ- **~s** z
Ingham ˈɪŋ əm
ingle, Ingle ˈɪŋ gˀl **~s** z
Ingleborough ˈɪŋ gˀl bər̩ə §-ˌbʌr ə ‖ -ˌbɜː oʊ
inglenook ˈɪŋ gˀl nʊk §-nuːk **~s** s
Ingleton ˈɪŋ gˀl tən
Inglewood ˈɪŋ gˀl wʊd
Inglis ˈɪŋ glɪs -gˀlz —in Scotland, -gˀlz
inglorious ɪn ˈglɔːr i ˌəs →ɪŋ-, ˌ·- ‖ -ˈgloʊr- **~ly**
li **~ness** nəs nɪs
Ingmar ˈɪŋ mɑː ‖ -mɑːr
ingoing ˈɪn ˌgəʊ ɪŋ →ˈɪŋ- ‖ -ˌgoʊ- **~s** z
Ingold ˈɪŋ gəʊld →-gɒʊld ‖ -goʊld
Ingoldsby ˈɪŋ gˀldz bi
ingot ˈɪŋ gət -gɒt **~s** s
ingraft ɪn ˈgrɑːft ən-, →ɪŋ-, →əŋ-, §-ˈgræft
‖ -ˈgræft **~ed** ɪd əd **~ing** ɪŋ **~s** s
ingrain ɪn ˈgreɪn →ɪŋ-, ˌ·- **~ed** d **~ing** ɪŋ **~s** s
Ingram ˈɪŋ grəm
Ingrams ˈɪŋ grəmz
ingrate ˈɪn greɪt →ˈɪŋ-, ·ˈ· **~s** s
ingrati|ate ɪn ˈgreɪʃ i |eɪt →ɪŋ- **~ated** eɪt ɪd
-əd ‖ eɪt̬ əd **~ates** eɪts **~ating/ly** eɪt ɪŋ /li
‖ eɪt̬ ɪŋ /li
ingratitude ɪn ˈgræt ɪ tjuːd →ɪŋ-, ˌ·-, -ˈ·ə-,
→§-tʃuːd ‖ -ˈgræt̬ ə tuːd -tjuːd
Ingrebourne ˈɪŋ grɪ bɔːn -grə- ‖ -bɔːrn -boʊrn

ingredient ɪn ˈgriːd i ˌənt →ɪŋ- **~s** s
Ingres ˈæ̃ŋgr ˈæŋ grə —Fr [ɑ̃ːgʁ]
ingress ˈɪn gres →ˈɪŋ- **~es** ɪz əz
ingressive ɪn ˈgres ɪv →ɪŋ-, ˌ·- **~ly** li **~s** z
Ingrid ˈɪŋ grɪd -grəd
in-group n ˈɪn gruːp →ˈɪŋ- **~s** s
ingrowing ˌɪn ˈgrəʊ ɪŋ ◂ →ˌɪŋ-, ˈ·ˌ··
‖ ˈɪn ˌgroʊ ɪŋ
ingrown ˌɪn ˈgrəʊn ◂ →ˌɪŋ- ‖ -ˈgroʊn
inguinal ˈɪŋ gwɪn ˀl §-gwən-
Ingush ˈɪŋ gʊʃ
Ingushetia ˌɪŋ gʊ ˈʃet i ˌə -ˈʃiːʃ ə
Ingvar ˈɪŋ vɑː ‖ -vɑːr
inhab|it ɪn ˈhæb |ɪt §-ət ‖ -|ət **~ited** ɪt ɪd §ət-,
-əd ‖ ət̬ əd **~iting** ɪt ɪŋ §ət- ‖ ət̬ ɪŋ **~its** ɪts
§əts ‖ əts
inhabitable ɪn ˈhæb ɪt əb ˀl §-ət əb- ‖ -ət̬ əb-
inhabitant ɪn ˈhæb ɪt ənt §-ət- ‖ -ət̬ ˀnt **~s** s
inhalant ɪn ˈheɪl ənt **~s** s
inhalation ˌɪn hə ˈleɪʃ ˀn -ə- **~s** z
inhalator ˈɪn hə leɪt ə ‖ -leɪt̬ ˀr ˈɪn ˀl eɪt̬- **~s** z
inhal|e ɪn ˈherˀl ˌɪn- **~ed** d **~er/s** ə/z ‖ ˀr/z **~es**
z **~ing** ɪŋ
inharmonious ˌɪn hɑː ˈməʊn i ˌəs ◂
‖ -hɑːr ˈmoʊn- **~ly** li **~ness** nəs nɪs
inhere ɪn ˈhɪə ‖ -ˈhɪˀr **~d** d **~s** z **inhering**
ɪn ˈhɪər ɪŋ ‖ -ˈhɪr ɪŋ

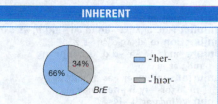

INHERENT

66% ▪ -ˈher-
34% ▪ -ˈhɪər-
BrE

inherent ɪn ˈher ənt -ˈhɪər- ‖ -ˈhɪr-
— Preference poll, BrE: -ˈher- 66%, -ˈhɪər-
34%. **~ly** li
inher|it ɪn ˈher |ɪt -ət ‖ -|ət **~ited** ɪt ɪd ət-, -əd
‖ ət̬ əd **~iting** ɪt ɪŋ ət- ‖ ət̬ ɪŋ **~its** ɪts əts ‖ əts
inheritability ɪn ˌher ɪt ə ˈbɪl ət i -ət ə-, -ɪt i
‖ -ət̬ ə ˈbɪl ət̬ i
inheritable ɪn ˈher ɪt əb ˀl -ət- · · ‖ -ət̬ əb ˀl
inheritanc|e ɪn ˈher ɪt ən's -ət- ‖ -ət̬ ˀn's **~es**
ɪz əz
inheritor ɪn ˈher ɪt ə -ət- ‖ -ət̬ ˀr **~s** z
inhib|it ɪn ˈhɪb |ɪt §-ət ‖ -|ət **~ited/ly** ɪt ɪd /li
§ət-, -əd /li ‖ ət̬ əd /li **~iting** ɪt ɪŋ §ət- ‖ ət̬ ɪŋ
~its ɪts §əts ‖ əts
inhibition ˌɪn hɪ ˈbɪʃ ˀn -ɪ-, -ə- **~s** z
inhibitor ɪn ˈhɪb ɪt ə §-ət- ‖ -ət̬ ˀr **~s** z
inhibitory ɪn ˈhɪb ɪt̩ər i -ˈ·ət̩ ‖ -ə tɔːr i -toʊr i
inhospitab|le ˌɪn hɒ ˈspɪt əb |ˀl ◂
ˌ(ˌ)ɪn ˈhɒsp ɪt-, -ˈ·ət- ‖ ˌɪn hɑː ˈspɪt̬-
ˌ(ˌ)ɪn ˈhɑːsp ət̬- **~leness** ˀl nəs -nɪs **~ly** li
in-house ˌɪn ˈhaʊs ◂
inhuman ɪn ˈhjuːm ən ˌɪn-, §-ˈjuːm- **~ly** li
~ness nəs nɪs
inhumane ˌɪn hju ˈmeɪn ◂ §-ju- **~ly** li
inhumanit|y ˌɪn hju ˈmæn ət |i §ˌ·ju-, -ɪt i
‖ -ət̬ |i **~ies** iz

Inigo 'ɪn ɪ gəʊ -ə- ‖ -goʊ
inimical ɪ 'nɪm ɪk ᵊl
inimitab|le ɪ 'nɪm ɪt əb |ᵊl -ət əb- ‖ -əţ əb- **~ly**
li
iniquitous ɪ 'nɪk wɪt əs -wət- ‖ -wəţ əs **~ly** li
~ness nəs nɪs
iniquit|y ɪ 'nɪk wət |i -wɪt- ‖ -wəţ |i **~ies** iz
initial ɪ 'nɪʃ ᵊl **~ed, ~led** d **~ing, ~ling** ɪŋ **~ly**
i **~s** z
initialis... —*see* **initializ...**
initialization ɪ ˌnɪʃ əl ˌaɪ 'zeɪʃ ᵊn -əl ɪ- ‖ -əl ə-
~s z
initializ|e ɪ 'nɪʃ ə laɪz -ᵊl aɪz **~ed** d **~es** ɪz əz
~ing ɪŋ
initiate *n* ɪ 'nɪʃ i ət ɪt, -eɪt **~s** s
initi|ate *v* ɪ 'nɪʃ i |eɪt **~ated** eɪt ɪd -əd ‖ eɪţ əd
~ates eɪts **~ating** eɪt ɪŋ ‖ eɪţ ɪŋ
initiation ɪ ˌnɪʃ i 'eɪʃ ᵊn **~s** z
initiative ɪ 'nɪʃ ət ɪv -'nɪʃ i ˌət ɪv ‖ -əţ ɪv **~s** z
initiator ɪ 'nɪʃ i eɪt ə ‖ -eɪţ ᵊr **~s** z
initiatory ɪ 'nɪʃ i ə ˌtər i ɪ ˌnɪʃ i 'eɪt ˌər i ◄
‖ ə tɔːr i ə toʊr i
inject ɪn 'dʒekt **~ed** ɪd əd **~ing** ɪŋ **~s** s
injection ɪn 'dʒek ʃᵊn **~s** z
injector ɪn 'dʒekt ə ‖ -ᵊr **~s** z
in-joke 'ɪn dʒəʊk ‖ -dʒoʊk **~s** s
injudicious ˌɪn dʒu 'dɪʃ əs ◄ **~ly** li **~ness** nəs
nɪs
Injun 'ɪndʒ ən **~s** z
injunct *v* ɪn 'dʒʌŋkt **~ed** ɪd əd **~ing** ɪŋ **~s** s
injunction ɪn 'dʒʌŋk ʃᵊn **~s** z
injure 'ɪndʒ ə ‖ -ᵊr **~d** d **~s** z **injuring**
'ɪndʒ ər ɪŋ
injurious ɪn 'dʒʊər i ˌəs △'ɪndʒ ər əs
‖ ɪn 'dʒʊr- **~ly** li **~ness** nəs nɪs
injur|y 'ɪndʒ ər ˌi **~ies** iz
'**injury time**
injustic|e ɪn 'dʒʌst ɪs ˌɪn-, -əs **~es** ɪz əz
ink ɪŋk **inked** ɪŋkt **inking** 'ɪŋk ɪŋ **inks** ɪŋks
Inkatha ɪn 'kɑːt ə →ɪŋ- —*Zulu* [iŋ kʼaː tha]
inkblot 'ɪŋk blɒt ‖ -blɑːt **~s** s
inkbottle 'ɪŋk ˌbɒt ᵊl ‖ -ˌbɑːţ ᵊl **~s** z
ink-cap 'ɪŋk kæp **~s** s
Inkerman 'ɪŋk ə mən ‖ -ᵊr- -mɑːn —*Russ*
[ɪn kʲɪr ˈman]
inkhorn 'ɪŋk hɔːn ‖ -hɔːrn **~s** z
inkjet 'ɪŋk dʒet
inkling 'ɪŋk lɪŋ **~s** z
inkpad 'ɪŋk pæd **~s** z
Inkpen 'ɪŋk pen
inkpot 'ɪŋk pɒt ‖ -pɑːt **~s** s
inkstand 'ɪŋk stænd **~s** z
inkwell 'ɪŋk wel **~s** z
ink|y 'ɪŋk |i **~ier** i ə ‖ i ᵊr **~iest** i ɪst i əst
~iness i nəs i nɪs
INLA ˌaɪ en el 'eɪ
inlaid ˌɪn 'leɪd ◄
inland *adj* 'ɪn lənd -lænd
ˌInland 'Revenue
inland *adv* ₍ₗ₎ɪn 'lænd '··
in-laws 'ɪn lɔːz ‖ -lɑːz
in|lay *v* ˌɪn |'leɪ '·· **~laid** 'leɪd ◄ **~laying**
'leɪ ɪŋ **~lays** 'leɪz

inlay *n* 'ɪn leɪ **~s** z
inlet 'ɪn lət -lɪt, -let **~s** s
in-line ˌɪn 'laɪn ◄
ˌin-line 'skates
in loco parentis ɪn ˌləʊk əʊ pə 'rent ɪs §-əs
‖ ɪn ˌloʊk oʊ pə 'renţ əs
inly 'ɪn li
Inman 'ɪn mən →'ɪm-
Inmarsat 'ɪn mɑː sæt →'ɪm- ‖ -mɑːr-
inmate 'ɪn meɪt →'ɪm- **~s** s
in medias res ɪn ˌmiːd i æs 'reɪz →ɪm-,
-ˌmeɪd-, -ˌmed-, -ɑːsˈ-, əsˈ-, -ˈreɪs
in memoriam ˌɪn mɪ 'mɔːr i ˌæm →ˌɪm-, ˌˌmə-,
-æm ‖ -'moʊr-
in-migrant 'ɪn ˌmaɪg rənt →'ɪm- **~s** s
inmost 'ɪn məʊst →'ɪm-, -məst ‖ -moʊst
inn ɪn *(= in)* **inns** ɪnz
ˌInns of 'Court
innards 'ɪn ədz ‖ ᵊrdz
innate ɪ 'neɪt ◄ ɪ-, ˌɪn- **~ly** li **~ness** nəs nɪs
ˌinnate 'knowledge, ˌ·ˌ·ˈ··
inner 'ɪn ə ‖ -ᵊr **~s** z
ˌinner 'city; ˌInner 'Hebrides; ˌinner 'man;
'inner tube, ˌ·ˈ·
inner-city ˌɪn ə 'sɪt i ◄ ‖ ˌɪn ᵊr 'sɪţ i ◄
innermost 'ɪn ə məʊst ‖ -ᵊr moʊst
innerv|ate 'ɪn ɜːv |eɪt ɪ 'nɜːv |eɪt ‖ ɪ 'nɜːv |eɪt
'ɪn ᵊr v|eɪt **~ated** eɪt ɪd -əd ‖ eɪţ əd **~ates**
eɪts **~ating** eɪt ɪŋ ‖ eɪţ ɪŋ
innervation ˌɪn ɜː 'veɪʃ ᵊn -ə- ‖ ˌɪn ᵊr- **~s** z
Innes 'ɪn ɪs -ɪz, -əs, -əz
inning 'ɪn ɪŋ **~s** z **~ses** zɪz zəz
Innisfail ˌɪn ɪs 'feɪᵊl -əs-
Innisfree ˌɪn ɪs 'friː -əs-
innit *nonstd form of* **isn't it** 'ɪn ɪt -ət
innkeeper 'ɪn ˌkiːp ə →'ɪŋ- ‖ -ᵊr **~s** z
innocence 'ɪn əs ənts -əʊs-
innocent, I~ 'ɪn əs ənt -əʊs- **~ly** li **~s** s
innocuous ɪ 'nɒk ju əs ə- ‖ ɪ 'nɑːk- **~ly** li
~ness nəs nɪs
innominate ɪ 'nɒm ɪn ət ə-, -ən-, -ɪt; -ɪ neɪt, -ə-
‖ ɪ 'nɑːm-
inno|vate 'ɪn ə ʊ |veɪt ‖ -ə- **~vated** veɪt ɪd -əd
‖ veɪţ əd **~vates** veɪts **~vating** veɪt ɪŋ
‖ veɪţ ɪŋ
innovation ˌɪn ə ʊ 'veɪʃ ᵊn ‖ -ə- **~al** ᵊl ◄ **~s** z

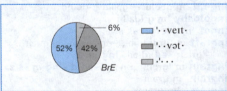

INNOVATIVE

— 6%

52% 42%

□ '··veɪt·
■ '··vət·
▨ ·ˈ···

BrE

innovative 'ɪn ə ʊ veɪt ɪv -vət ɪv; ɪ 'nəʊv ət ɪv
‖ 'ɪn ə veɪţ ɪv — *Preference poll, BrE:* '··veɪt·
52%, '··vət· 42%, ·ˈ···6%. **~ly** li **~ness** nəs
nɪs
innovator 'ɪn ə veɪt ə ‖ -veɪţ ᵊr **~s** z
innovatory ˌɪn ə veɪt ər i -vət ˌər i
‖ 'ɪn əv ə tɔːr i -toʊr i

Innoxa _tdmk_ ɪ ˈnɒks ə ‖ ɪ ˈnɑːks ə
Innsbruck ˈɪnz brʊk —_Ger_ [ˈʔɪnˢs bʀʊk]
innuendo ˌɪn ju ˈend əʊ ‖ -oʊ ~**es** z
Innuit ˈɪn u ɪt -ju-, §-ət
innumerab|le ɪ ˈnjuːm ər‿əb |ᵊl ə-, §ɪ ˈnuːm-
‖ ɪ ˈnuːm- ɪ ˈnjuːm- ~**leness** ᵊl nəs -nɪs ~**ly** li
innumeracy ɪ ˈnjuːm ər‿əs i §ɪ ˈnuːm-
‖ ɪ ˈnuːm- ɪ ˈnjuːm-
innumerate ɪ ˈnjuːm ər‿ət §ɪ ˈnuːm-, ˌɪt
‖ ɪ ˈnuːm- ɪ ˈnjuːm- ~**s** s
inocu|late ɪ ˈnɒk ju |leɪt ə-, -jə- ‖ ɪ ˈnɑːk jə-
~**lated** leɪt ɪd -əd ‖ leɪt̬ əd ~**lates** leɪts
~**lating** leɪt ɪŋ ‖ leɪt̬ ɪŋ
inoculation ɪ ˌnɒk ju ˈleɪʃ ᵊn ə-, -jə-
‖ ɪ ˌnɑːk jə- ~**s** z
inoculator ɪ ˈnɒk ju leɪt ə ə-, -jə-
‖ ɪ ˈnɑːk jə leɪt̬ ᵊr ~**s** z
inoffensive ˌɪn ə ˈfenˢ ɪv ◂ ~**ly** li ~**ness** nəs
nɪs
inoperab|le ɪn ˈɒp ər‿əb |ᵊl ˌɪn- ‖ ɪn ˈɑːp- ~**ly**
li
inoperative ɪn ˈɒp ər‿ət ɪv ˌɪn-, -ə reɪt ɪv
‖ ɪn ˈɑːp ər‿ət̬ ɪv -ə reɪt̬ ɪv ~**ness** nəs nɪs
inopportune ɪn ˈɒp ə tjuːn ˌɪn-, →-tʃuːn; -ˌ· ·ˈ·
‖ ɪn ˌɑːp ᵊr ˈtuːn ◂ -ˈtjuːn ~**ly** li ~**ness** nəs nɪs
inordinate ɪn ˈɔːd ɪn ət ən-, -ᵊn‿, -ɪt
‖ -ˈɔːrd ᵊn‿ət ~**ly** li ~**ness** nəs nɪs
inorganic ˌɪn ɔː ˈgæn ɪk ◂ ‖ -ɔːr- ~**ally** ᵊl i
ˌinorˌganic ˈchemistry
Inouye ɪ ˈnuː eɪ
in-patient ˈɪn ˌpeɪʃ ᵊnt →ˈɪm- ~**s** s
in|put _v, n_ ˈɪn |pʊt →ˈɪm- ~**puts** pʊts ~**putted**
pʊt ɪd -əd ‖ pʊt̬ əd ~**putting** pʊt ɪŋ ‖ pʊt̬ ɪŋ
input/output, input-output ˌɪn pʊt ˈaʊt pʊt
→ˌɪm- ‖ -pʊt̬-
inquest ˈɪŋ kwest ˈɪn- ~**s** s
inquietude ɪn ˈkwaɪ‿ə tjuːd →ɪŋ-, ɪ tjuːd,
→§-tʃuːd ‖ -tuːd -tjuːd
inquire ɪn ˈkwaɪ‿ə →ɪŋ-, ən- ‖ -ˈkwaɪ‿ʳr ~**d** d
~**s** z **inquiring/ly** ɪn ˈkwaɪ‿ər ɪŋ /li →ɪŋ-, ən-
‖ -ˈkwaɪ‿ʳr ɪŋ /li
inquirer ɪn ˈkwaɪ‿ʳr ə →ɪŋ-, ən- ‖ -ᵊr ~**s** z

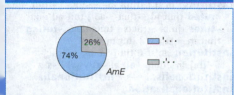

26%
74%
‖ ˈ· · ·
‖ ˌ· ˈ· ·
AmE

inquir|y ɪn ˈkwaɪ‿ʳr |i →ɪŋ-, ən- ‖ ˈɪn kwər |i ,
→ˈɪŋ-, -kwaɪ‿ʳr-; ɪn ˈkwaɪ‿ʳr i, →ɪŋ- —
Preference poll, AmE: ˈ· · · _74%,_ ˌ· ˈ· · _26%._ ~**ies**
iz
inquisition, I~ ˌɪŋ kwɪ ˈzɪʃ ᵊn ˌɪn-, -kwə- ~**s** z
inquisitive ɪn ˈkwɪz ət ɪv →ɪŋ-, -ɪt- ‖ -ət̬ ɪv ~**ly**
li ~**ness** nəs nɪs
inquisitor ɪn ˈkwɪz ɪt ə →ɪŋ-, -ət- ‖ -ət̬ ᵊr ~**s** z
inquisitorial ɪn ˌkwɪz ə ˈtɔːr i‿əl ◂ →ɪŋ-, ˌ·ˌ·-,
-ɪˈ·- ‖ -ˈtoʊr- ~**ly** i

inquorate ˌɪn ˈkwɔːr eɪt ◂ →ˌɪŋ-, -ət, -ɪt
‖ -ˈkwoʊr-
in re ₍ₗ₎ɪn ˈriː -ˈreɪ
in-residence ₍ₗ₎ɪn ˈrez ɪd ən<s -əd-
inroad ˈɪn rəʊd ‖ -roʊd ~**s** z
inrush ˈɪn rʌʃ ~**es** ɪz əz
insalubrious ˌɪn sə ˈluːb ri‿əs ◂ -ˈljuːb- ~**ly** li
~**ness** nəs nɪs
ins and outs ˌɪnz ᵊn ˈaʊts -ᵊnd-
insane ɪn ˈseɪn ˌɪn- ~**ly** li
insanitar|y ɪn ˈsæn ə tər |i ˌɪn-, -ˈ·ɪ‿ ‖ -ə ter |i
~**iness** i nəs i nɪs
insanit|y ɪn ˈsæn ət |i ˌɪn-, -ɪt i ‖ -ət̬ |i ~**ies** iz
insatiab|le ɪn ˈseɪʃ əb |ᵊl -ˈseɪʃ i‿əb |ᵊl ~**leness**
ᵊl nəs -nɪs ~**ly** li
insatiate ɪn ˈseɪʃ i‿ət ɪt, -eɪt ~**ly** li ~**ness** nəs
nɪs
inscape ˈɪn skeɪp ~**d** t ~**s** s
inscrib|e ɪn ˈskraɪb ~**ed** d ~**es** z ~**ing** ɪŋ
inscription ɪn ˈskrɪp ʃᵊn ~**s** z
inscrutability ɪn ˌskruːt ə ˈbɪl ət i ˌ·ˌ·-, -ɪt i
‖ ɪn ˌskruːt̬ ə ˈbɪl ət̬ i
inscrutab|le ɪn ˈskruːt əb |ᵊl ˌɪn- ‖ -ˈskruːt̬-
~**leness** ᵊl nəs -nɪs ~**ly** li
inseam ˈɪn siːm ~**s** z
insect ˈɪn sekt ~**s** s
insecticidal ɪn ˌsekt ɪ ˈsaɪd ᵊl ◂ -ə-
insecticide ɪn ˈsekt ɪ saɪd -ə- ~**s** z
insectivore ɪn ˈsekt ɪ vɔː -ə- ‖ -vɔːr -voʊr ~**s** z
insectivorous ˌɪn sek ˈtɪv ər‿əs ◂
insecure ˌɪn sɪ ˈkjʊə ◂ -sə-, -ˈkjɔː ‖ -ˈkjʊᵊr ~**ly** li
~**ness** nəs nɪs
insecurit|y ˌɪn sɪ ˈkjʊər ət |i ˌ·sə-, -ˈkjɔːr-, -ɪt i
‖ -ˈkjʊr ət̬ |i ~**ies** iz
insemi|nate ɪn ˈsem ɪ |neɪt -ə- ~**nated** neɪt ɪd
-əd ‖ neɪt̬ əd ~**nates** neɪts ~**nating** neɪt ɪŋ
‖ neɪt̬ ɪŋ
insemination ɪn ˌsem ɪ ˈneɪʃ ᵊn ˌɪn-, -ə- ~**s** z
inseminator ɪn ˈsem ɪ neɪt ə -ˈ·ə- ‖ -ə neɪt̬ ᵊr
~**s** z
insensate ɪn ˈsenˢ eɪt ˌɪn-, -ət, -ɪt ~**ly** li
insensibility ɪn ˌsenˢ ə ˈbɪl ət i ˌ·ˌ· ·ˈ·-, -ɪˈ·-,
-ɪt i ‖ -ət̬ i
insensib|le ɪn ˈsenˢ əb |ᵊl ˌɪn-, -ɪb- ~**ly** li
insensitive ɪn ˈsenˢ ət ɪv ˌɪn-, -ɪt- ‖ -ət̬ ɪv ~**ly**
li ~**ness** nəs nɪs
insensitivity ɪn ˌsenˢ ə ˈtɪv ət i ˌ·ˌ· ·ˈ·-, -ɪˈ·-,
-ɪt i ‖ -ət̬ i
insenti|ence ɪn ˈsenʃ |ən<s -ˈsenʃ i‿|ən<s ~**ent**
ənt
inseparability ɪn ˌsep ər‿ə ˈbɪl ət i ˌ·ˌ·-, -ɪt i
‖ -ət̬ i
inseparab|le ɪn ˈsep ər‿əb |ᵊl ˌɪn- ~**leness**
ᵊl nəs -nɪs ~**ly** li
in|sert _v_ ɪn |ˈsɜːt -ˈzɜːt ‖ -|ˈsɜːt ~**serted** ˈsɜːt ɪd
ˈzɜːt-, -əd ‖ ˈsɜːt̬ əd ~**serting** ˈsɜːt ɪŋ ˈzɜːt-
‖ ˈsɜːt̬ ɪŋ ~**serts** ˈsɜːts ˈzɜːts ‖ ˈsɜːts
insert _n_ ˈɪn sɜːt -zɜːt ‖ -sɜːt ~**s** s
insertion ɪn ˈsɜːʃ ᵊn -ˈzɜːʃ- ‖ -ˈsɜːʃ- ~**s** z
in-service ˌɪn ˈsɜːv ɪs ◂ -əs ‖ -ˈsɜːv-
ˌin-ˌservice ˈtraining
in|set _v_ ɪn |ˈset ˈ· · ~**sets** ˈsets ~**setting** ˈset ɪŋ
‖ ˈset̬ ɪŋ

I

inset _n_ 'ɪn set ~**s** s
inshallah, insha'allah ɪn 'ʃæl ə -'ʃɑːl-
‖ ˌɪn ʃɑ: 'lɑ: —_Arabic_ [ɪn ˌʃa: ʔaɫ 'ɫa:h,
ɪn ʃɑ: 'ɫɑ:h]
inshore ˌɪn 'ʃɔː ◄ ‖ -'ʃɔːr ◄ -'ʃour
ˌinshore 'fishing
inside ˌɪn 'saɪd ◄ —_but_ '·· _when contrasted_
with outside ~**s** z
ˌinside 'job, '·· ·; ˌinside 'left; ˌinside
'out; ˌinside 'track
insider ˌɪn 'saɪd ə ◄ ‖ -ᵊr ~**s** z
inˌsider 'trading, ·ˌ·· '··
insidious ɪn 'sɪd i̯əs ~**ly** li ~**ness** nəs nɪs
insight 'ɪn saɪt ~**s** s
insightful 'ɪn saɪt fʊl ·'·· ~**ly** i
insignia ɪn 'sɪg ni̯ə ~**s** z
insignificanc|e ˌɪn sɪg 'nɪf ɪk ən⁀s ~**y** i
insignificant ˌɪn sɪg 'nɪf ɪk ənt ◄ ~**ly** li
insincere ˌɪn sɪn 'sɪə ◄ -sᵊn- ‖ -'sɪᵊr ~**ly** li
insincerity ˌɪn sɪn 'ser ət i ˌ-sᵊn-, -ɪt i ‖ -əṭ i
insinu|ate ɪn 'sɪn ju |eɪt ~**ated** eɪt ɪd -əd
‖ eɪṭ əd ~**ates** eɪts ~**ating** eɪt ɪŋ ‖ eɪṭ ɪŋ
insinuation ɪn ˌsɪn ju 'eɪʃ ᵊn ·ˌ·- ~**s** z
insipid ɪn 'sɪp ɪd §-əd ~**ly** li ~**ness** nəs nɪs
insipidity ˌɪn sɪ 'pɪd ət i §ˌ-sə-, -ɪt i ‖ -əṭ i
insist ɪn 'sɪst ~**ed** ɪd əd ~**ing** ɪŋ ~**s** s
insistenc|e ɪn 'sɪst ən⁀s ~**y** i
insistent ɪn 'sɪst ənt ~**ly** li
in situ ₍ᵢ₎ɪn 'sɪt juː -'sɪtʃ uː, -'saɪt juː, -'saɪtʃ u:
‖ -'saɪt uː -'siːt-, -'sɪt-, -juː
insobriety ˌɪn səʊ 'braɪ ət i ɪt i
‖ ˌɪn sə 'braɪ əṭ i
insofar ˌɪn səʊ 'fɑ: ◄ ‖ -sə 'fɑːr
insolation ˌɪn səʊ 'leɪʃ ᵊn ‖ -soʊ-
insole 'ɪn səʊl →-sɒʊl ‖ -soʊl ~**s** z
insolence 'ɪn⁀s əl ən⁀s
insolent 'ɪn⁀s əl ənt ~**ly** li
insolubility ɪn ˌsɒl ju 'bɪl ət i ·ˌ·ˌ-·, -ɪt i
‖ ɪn ˌsɑːl jə 'bɪl əṭ i ·ˌ·ˌ-
insolub|le ɪn 'sɒl jʊb |ᵊl ˌɪn- ‖ -'sɑːl jəb |ᵊl
~**leness** ᵊl nəs -nɪs ~**ly** li
insolvab|le ɪn 'sɒlv əb |ᵊl ˌɪn-, §-'səʊlv-
‖ -'sɑːlv- ~**ly** li
insolvenc|y ɪn 'sɒlv ən⁀s |i ˌɪn- ‖ -'sɑːlv- ~**ies**
iz
insolvent ɪn 'sɒlv ənt ˌɪn- ‖ -'sɑːlv- ~**s** s
insomnia ɪn 'sɒm ni̯ə ‖ -'sɑːm-
insomniac ɪn 'sɒm ni æk ‖ -'sɑːm- ~**s** s
insomuch ˌɪn səʊ 'mʌtʃ ◄ ‖ -sə-
insouciance ɪn 'suːs i̯ən⁀s -ð̃s —_Fr_
[æ̃ su sjɑ̃ːs]
insouciant ɪn 'suːs i̯ənt -ð̃ —_Fr_ [æ̃ su sjɑ̃] ~**ly**
li
inspan 'ɪn spæn ·'· ~**ned** d ~**ning** ɪŋ ~**s** z
inspect ɪn 'spekt ~**ed** ɪd əd ~**ing** ɪŋ ~**s** s
inspection ɪn 'spek ʃᵊn ~**s** z
inspector ɪn 'spekt ə ‖ -ᵊr ~**s** z
inspectorate ɪn 'spekt ər‿ət ɪt ~**s** s
inspectorship ɪn 'spekt ə ʃɪp ‖ -ᵊr- ~**s** s
inspiration ˌɪn spə 'reɪʃ ᵊn -spɪ-, -spɑːr- ~**s** z
inspirational ˌɪn spə 'reɪʃ ᵊn‿əl ◄ ·ˌspɪ-, ·ˌspɑːr-
~**ly** i

inspiratory ɪn 'spaɪᵊr ət‿ər i -'spɪr- ‖ -ə tɔːr i
-touri
inspire ɪn 'spaɪ‿ə ‖ -'spaɪ‿ᵊr ~**d** d ~**s** z
inspiring/ly ɪn 'spaɪ‿ər ɪŋ /li ‖ -'spaɪ‿ᵊr ɪŋ /li
inspirer ɪn 'spaɪ‿ər ə ‖ -'spaɪ‿ᵊr ər ~**s** z
inspir|it ɪn 'spɪr |ɪt -ət ‖ -|ət ~**ited** ɪt ɪd ət-, -əd
‖ əṭ əd ~**iting** ɪt ɪŋ ət- ‖ əṭ ɪŋ ~**its** ɪts əts ‖ əts
inspiss|ate ɪn 'spɪs |eɪt '··· ~**ated** eɪt ɪd -əd
‖ eɪṭ əd ~**ates** eɪts ~**ating** eɪt ɪŋ ‖ eɪṭ ɪŋ
inst ɪn⁀st _or as_ instant, institute
instabilit|y ˌɪn stə 'bɪl ət |i -ɪt i ‖ -əṭ |i ~**ies** iz
instal, instal|l ɪn 'stɔːl ‖ -'stɑːl ~**led** d ~**ling**
ɪŋ **instals, installs** ɪn 'stɔːlz ‖ -'stɑːlz
installation ˌɪn⁀st ə 'leɪʃ ᵊn ~**s** z
installer ɪn 'stɔːl ə ‖ -ᵊr -'stɑːl- ~**s** z
instalment, installment ɪn 'stɔːl mənt
‖ -'stɑːl- ~**s** s
in'stallment plan
Instamatic _tdmk_ ˌɪn⁀st ə 'mæt ɪk ◄ ‖ -'mæṭ ɪk
~**s** s
instanc|e 'ɪn⁀st ən⁀s ~**ed** t ~**es** ɪz əz ~**ing** ɪŋ
instant 'ɪn⁀st ənt ~**ly** li
instantaneous ˌɪn⁀st ən 'teɪn i̯əs ◄ ~**ly** li
~**ness** nəs nɪs
instanter ɪn 'stænt ə ‖ -'stænṭ ᵊr
instanti|ate ɪn 'stæn⁀ʃ i |eɪt ~**ated** eɪt ɪd -əd
‖ eɪṭ əd ~**ates** eɪts ~**ating** eɪt ɪŋ ‖ eɪṭ ɪŋ
instantiation ɪn ˌstæn⁀ʃ i 'eɪʃ ᵊn ~**s** z
instead ɪn 'sted
instep 'ɪn step ~**s** s
insti|gate 'ɪn⁀st ɪ |geɪt -ə- ~**gated** geɪt ɪd -əd
‖ geɪṭ əd ~**gates** geɪts ~**gating** geɪt ɪŋ
‖ geɪṭ ɪŋ
instigation ˌɪn⁀st ɪ 'geɪʃ ᵊn -ə- ~**s** z
instigator 'ɪn⁀st ɪ geɪt ə '·ə- ‖ -geɪṭ ᵊr ~**s** z
instil, instil|l ɪn 'stɪl ~**led** d ~**ling** ɪŋ **instils,
instills** ɪn 'stɪlz
instillation ˌɪn⁀st ɪ 'leɪʃ ᵊn -ə-
instiller ɪn 'stɪl ə ‖ -ᵊr ~**s** z
instilment, instillment ɪn 'stɪl mənt
instinct 'ɪn stɪŋkt ~**s** s
instinctive ɪn 'stɪŋkt ɪv ~**ly** li ~**ness** nəs nɪs
instinctual ɪn 'stɪŋkt ju‿əl -'stɪŋk tʃu‿əl
‖ -'stɪŋk tʃu‿əl ~**ly** li
insti|tute 'ɪn⁀st ɪ |tjuːt -ə-, →-tʃuːt ‖ -|tuːt -tjuːt
~**tuted** tjuːt ɪd →tʃuːt-, -əd ‖ tuːṭ əd tjuːṭ-
~**tutes** tjuːts →tʃuːts ‖ tuːts tjuːts ~**tuting**
tjuːt ɪŋ →§tʃuːt- ‖ tuːṭ ɪŋ tjuːṭ-
institution ˌɪn⁀st ɪ 'tjuːʃ ᵊn -ə-, →-'tʃuːʃ-
‖ -'tuːʃ ᵊn -'tjuːʃ- ~**al** ᵊl ~**ally** ᵊl i ~**s** z
institutionalis... —_see_ **institutionaliz...**
institutionalization
ˌɪn⁀st ɪ ˌtjuːʃ ᵊn‿əl aɪ 'zeɪʃ ᵊn ·ˌ·ə-, →-ˌtʃuːʃ-,
-ɪ'·- ‖ -ˌtuːʃ ᵊn‿əl ə-
institutionaliz|e ˌɪn⁀st ɪ 'tjuːʃ ᵊn‿ə laɪz ·ˌ·ə-,
→-'tʃuːʃ-, əl aɪz ‖ -'tuːʃ- -'tjuːʃ- ~**ed** d ~**es** ɪz
əz ~**ing** ɪŋ
in-store ˌɪn 'stɔː ◄ ‖ -'stɔːr ◄ -'stoʊr
ˌin-store 'banking
Instow 'ɪn stəʊ ‖ -stoʊ
instruct ɪn 'strʌkt ~**ed** ɪd əd ~**ing** ɪŋ ~**s** s
instruction ɪn 'strʌk ʃᵊn ~**s** z
instructional ɪn 'strʌk ʃᵊn‿əl ~**ly** i

instructive ɪn 'strʌkt ɪv ~**ly** li ~**ness** nəs nɪs
instructor ɪn 'strʌkt ə ‖ -ᵊr ~**s** z ~**ship/s** ʃɪp/s
instructress ɪn 'strʌk trəs -trɪs, -tres ~**es** ɪz əz
instru|ment ν 'ɪnˢ trə |ment -tru-, ˌ·'·— *see note at* -ment ~**mented** ment ɪd -əd ‖ menţ əd ~**menting** ment ɪŋ ‖ menţ ɪŋ ~**ments** ments
instrument n 'ɪnˢ trə mənt -tru- ~**s** s
  '**instrument** ˌpanel
instrumental ˌɪnˢ trə 'ment ᵊl ◄ -tru- ‖ -'menţ ᵊl ~**ly** i ~**s** z
instrumentalist ˌɪnˢ trə 'ment ᵊl ɪst -tru-, §-əst ‖ -'menţ- ~**s** s
instrumentalit|y ˌɪnˢ trə mən 'tæl ət |i ˌ-tru-, -mən'--, -ɪt i ‖ -əţ |i ~**ies** iz
instrumentation ˌɪnˢ trə mən 'teɪʃ ᵊn ˌ-tru-, -mən'--
insubordinate ˌɪn sə 'bɔːd ɪn ət ◄ -ᵊn̩ˌ·, -ɪt ‖ -'bɔːrd ᵊn̩ ət ~**ly** li ~**s** s
insubordination ˌɪn sə ˌbɔːd ɪ 'neɪʃ ᵊn -ˌɪ- ‖ -ˌbɔːrd ᵊn 'eɪʃ ᵊn
insubstantial ˌɪn səb 'stænʃ ᵊl ◄ §-sʌb-, -'stɑːnʃ- ~**ly** i
insufferab|le ɪn 'sʌf ᵊr_əb |ᵊl ~**leness** ᵊl nəs -nɪs ~**ly** li
insufficienc|y ˌɪn sə 'fɪʃ ᵊn'ts |i ~**ies** iz
insufficient ˌɪn sə 'fɪʃ ᵊnt ◄ ~**ly** li
insuf|flate 'ɪn sə |fleɪt ɪn 'sʌ|f leɪt, '·· ~**flated** fleɪt ɪd -əd ‖ fleɪţ əd ~**flates** fleɪts ~**flating** fleɪt ɪŋ ‖ fleɪţ ɪŋ
insufflation ˌɪn sə 'fleɪʃ ᵊn -sʌ- ~**s** z
insular 'ɪnˢ jʊl ə -jəl-; §'ɪnᵗʃ ʊl ə, §-əl- ‖ 'ɪnˢ əl ᵊr -jəl-; 'ɪnᵗʃ- ~**ly** li
insularism 'ɪnˢ jʊl ə ˌrɪz əm '·jəl-; §'ɪnᵗʃ ʊl-, §'·əl- ‖ 'ɪnˢ əl- '·jəl-; 'ɪnᵗʃ-
insularity ˌɪnˢ jʊ 'lær ət i ˌ·jə-, -ɪt i; §ˌɪnᵗʃ u- ‖ ˌɪnˢ ə 'lær əţ i ˌ·jə-, -'ler-; ˌɪnᵗʃ-
insu|late 'ɪnˢ ju |leɪt -jə-; §'ɪnᵗʃ u- ‖ -ə- (*) ~**lated** leɪt ɪd -əd ‖ leɪţ əd ~**lates** leɪts ~**lating** leɪt ɪŋ ‖ leɪţ ɪŋ
  '**insulating** ˌtape
insulation ˌɪnˢ ju 'leɪʃ ᵊn -jə-; §ˌɪnᵗʃ u- ‖ -ə-
insulator 'ɪnˢ ju leɪt ə '·jə-; §'ɪnᵗʃ u- ‖ -ə leɪţ ᵊr ~**s** z
insulin 'ɪnˢ jʊl ɪn -jəl-, §-ən; §'ɪnᵗʃ ʊl-, -əl- ‖ -əl ən
insult ν ɪn 'sʌlt ~**ed** ɪd əd ~**ing** ɪŋ ~**s** s
insult n 'ɪn sʌlt ~**s** s
insuperability ɪn ˌsuːp ᵊr_ə 'bɪl ət i -ˌsjuːp-, ˌ·ˌ·-, -ɪt i ‖ -əţ i
insuperab|le ɪn 'suːp ᵊr_əb |ᵊl ˌɪn-, -'sjuːp- ~**leness** ᵊl nəs -nɪs ~**ly** li
insupportab|le ˌɪn sə 'pɔːt əb |ᵊl ◄ ‖ -'pɔːrţ- -'poʊrţ- ~**leness** ᵊl nəs -nɪs ~**ly** li
insurable ɪn 'ʃʊər əb ᵊl -'ʃɔːr- ‖ -'ʃʊr- -'ʃɜː-
insuranc|e ɪn 'ʃʊər ən'ts -'ʃɔːr-, -'ʃɜːr- ‖ -'ʃʊr- -'ʃɜː-; 'ɪn ʃʊr- — *Preference poll, AmE:* ·'·· 88%, '··· 12%. ~**es** ɪz əz
  in'**surance** ˌpolicy
insure ɪn 'ʃʊə -'ʃɔː ‖ -'ʃʊᵊr -'ʃɜː ~**d** d ~**s** z
  insuring ɪn 'ʃʊər ɪŋ -'ʃɔːr- ‖ -'ʃʊr ɪŋ -'ʃɜː-
insurer ɪn 'ʃʊər ə -'ʃɔːr ə ‖ -'ʃʊr ᵊr -'ʃɜː- ~**s** z
insurgenc|e ɪn 'sɜːdʒ ən'ts ‖ -'sɜːdʒ- ~**y** i

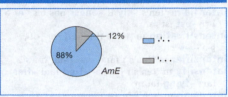

INSURANCE

88%   12% ·'··   '···
AmE

insurgent ɪn 'sɜːdʒ ənt ‖ -'sɜːdʒ- ~**s** s
insurmountab|le ˌɪn sə 'maʊnt əb |ᵊl ◄ ‖ ˌɪn sᵊr 'maʊnţ- ~**ly** li
insurrection ˌɪn sə 'rek ʃᵊn ~**s** z
insurrectionar|y ˌɪn sə 'rek ʃᵊn_ər |i -ʃᵊn ər_|i ‖ -ʃə ner |i ~**ies** iz
inswing 'ɪn swɪŋ ~**s** z
inswinger 'ɪn ˌswɪŋ ə ‖ -ᵊr ~**s** z
intact ɪn 'tækt ˌɪn- ~**ness** nəs nɪs
intaglio ɪn 'tɑːl i_əʊ -'tæl- ‖ ɪn 'tæl joʊ -'tɑːl- —*It* [in 'taʎ ʎo] ~**s** z
intake, I~ 'ɪn teɪk ~**s** s
intangibility ɪn ˌtændʒ ə 'bɪl ət i ˌ·ˌ·-, -ɪ'--, -ɪt i ‖ -əţ i
intangib|le ɪn 'tændʒ əb |ᵊl ˌɪn-, -ɪb- ~**leness** ᵊl nəs -nɪs ~**ly** li
Intasun *tdmk* 'ɪnt ə sʌn
integer 'ɪnt ɪdʒ ə -ədʒ- ‖ -ᵊr ~**s** z
integral 'ɪnt ɪg rəl -əg-; ɪn 'teg-; ⚠ 'ɪntr ɪg ᵊl, -əg- ‖ 'ɪnţ ɪg rəl ɪn 'teg- ~**ly** i ~**s** z
  ˌintegral 'calculus
inte|grate 'ɪnt ɪ |greɪt -ə- ‖ 'ɪnţ ə- ~**grated** greɪt ɪd -əd ‖ greɪţ əd ~**grates** greɪts ~**grating** greɪt ɪŋ ‖ greɪţ ɪŋ
  ˌintegrated 'circuit
integration ˌɪnt ɪ 'greɪʃ ᵊn -ə- ‖ ˌɪnţ ə- ~**s** z
integrative 'ɪnt ɪ greɪt ɪv '·ə-, -grət- ‖ 'ɪnţ ə greɪţ ɪv
integrator 'ɪnt ɪ greɪt ə '·ə- ‖ 'ɪnţ ə greɪţ ᵊr ~**s** z
integrity ɪn 'teg rət i -rɪt- ‖ -rəţ i
integument ɪn 'teg ju mənt ‖ -jə- ~**s** s
Intel *tdmk* 'ɪn tel
intellect 'ɪnt ə lekt -ɪ-, -ᵊl ekt ‖ 'ɪnţ ᵊl ekt ~**s** s
intellectual ˌɪnt ə 'lek tʃu_əl ◄ ˌ·ɪ-, -ᵊl 'ek-, -tju-, -ʃu· ‖ ˌɪnţ ᵊl 'ek- ~**ly** i ~**s** z
intellectualis|e, intellectualiz|e ˌɪnt ə 'lek tʃu_ə laɪz ˌ·ɪ-, -ᵊl 'ek-, -tju_ə-, -ʃu_ə- ‖ ˌɪnţ ᵊl 'ek- ~**ed** d ~**es** ɪz əz ~**ing** ɪŋ
intelligenc|e ɪn 'tel ɪdʒ ən'ts -ədʒ- ~**es** ɪz əz
  in'**telligence** ˌofficer; in'**telligence** ˌquotient; in'**telligence** ˌtest
intelligent ɪn 'tel ɪdʒ ənt -ədʒ- ~**ly** li
intelligentsia ɪn ˌtel ɪ 'dʒent si_ə ˌ·ˌ·-, -'gent- ~**s** z
intelligibility ɪn ˌtel ɪdʒ ə 'bɪl ət i -ˌ·ədʒ-, -ɪ'--, -ɪt i ‖ -əţ i
intelligib|le ɪn 'tel ɪdʒ əb |ᵊl -ˌ·ədʒ-, -ɪb ᵊl ~**ly** li
Intelsat 'ɪn tel sæt
intemperance ɪn 'temp ᵊr_ən'ts ˌɪn-
intemperate ɪn 'temp ər_ət ˌɪn-, -ɪt ~**ly** li ~**ness** nəs nɪs

intend ɪn 'tend ~**ed** ɪd əd ~**ing** ɪŋ ~**s** z
intendant ɪn 'tend ənt ~**s** s
intens|e ɪn 'ten^ts ~**ely** li ~**eness** nəs nɪs ~**er** ə
‖ ʰr ~**est** ɪst əst
intensification ɪn ˌten^ts ɪf ɪ 'keɪʃ ᵊn -ˌəf-,
§-ə'-- ~**s** z
intensifier ɪn 'ten^ts ɪ faɪ ə -'-ə- ‖ -faɪ ʰr ~**s** z
intensi|fy ɪn 'ten^ts ɪ |faɪ -ə- ~**fied** faɪd ~**fies**
faɪz ~**fying** faɪ ɪŋ
intension ɪn 'ten^tʃ ᵊn (= intention) ~**s** z
intensional ɪn 'ten^tʃ ᵊn əl (= intentional)
intensit|y ɪn 'ten^ts ət |i -ɪt- ‖ -əṯ |i ~**ies** iz
intensive ɪn 'ten^ts ɪv ~**ly** li ~**ness** nəs nɪs ~**s** z
in͵tensive 'care
intent n, adj ɪn 'tent ~**ly** li ~**ness** nəs nɪs ~**s** s
intention ɪn 'ten^tʃ ᵊn ~**s** z
intentional ɪn 'ten^tʃ ᵊn əl ~**ly** i
inter prep, Lat 'ɪnt ə ‖ 'ɪnṯ ʰr
inter v 'bury' ɪn 't₃ː ‖ -'t₃ː ~**red** d **interring**
ɪn 't₃ːr ɪŋ ‖ -'t₃ː ɪŋ ~**s** z
inter- ¦ɪnt ə ‖ ¦ɪnṯ ʰr, but before a vowel sound
¦ɪnt ər ‖ ¦ɪnṯ ər — **intermesh** v ˌɪnt ə 'meʃ
‖ ˌɪnṯ ʰr- — **interurban** ˌɪnt ər 'ɜːb ən ◂
‖ ˌɪnṯ ər 'ɜːb-
interact v ˌɪnt ər 'ækt ‖ ˌɪnṯ ər- ~**ed** ɪd əd ~**ing**
ɪŋ ~**s** s
interaction ˌɪnt ər 'æk ʃᵊn ‖ ˌɪnṯ ər- ~**s** z
interactive ˌɪnt ər 'ækt ɪv ◂ ‖ ˌɪnṯ ər- ~**ly** li
interactivity ˌɪnt ər æk 'tɪv ət i
‖ ˌɪnṯ ʰr æk 'tɪv əṯ i
interagency ˌɪnt ər 'eɪdʒᵊn^ts i ◂ ‖ ˌɪnṯ ʰr-
inter alia ˌɪnt ər 'eɪl i ə -'ɑːl-, -'æl- ‖ ˌɪnṯ ər-
inter|breed v ˌɪnt ə |'briːd ‖ ˌɪnṯ ʰr- ~**bred**
'bred ~**breeding** 'briːd ɪŋ ~**breeds** 'briːdz
intercalary ɪn 't₃ːk ᵊl ər i ˌɪnt ə 'kæl ər i◂,
-'keɪl- ‖ ɪn 't₃ːk ə ler i ˌɪnṯ ʰr 'kæl ər i ◂
interca|late ɪn 't₃ːk ə |leɪt ‖ -ᵊl eɪt;
ˌɪnt ə kə '|leɪt ‖ ɪn 't₃ːk ə |leɪt
ˌɪnṯ ʰr kə '|leɪt ~**lated** leɪt ɪd -əd ‖ leɪt əd
~**lates** leɪts ~**lating** leɪt ɪŋ ‖ leɪt ɪŋ
intercalation ɪn ˌt₃ːk ə 'leɪʃ ᵊn ˌɪnt ə kə-
‖ ɪn ˌt₃ːk ə- ˌɪnṯ ʰr kə- ~**s** z
interced|e ˌɪnt ə 'siːd ‖ ˌɪnṯ ʰr- ~**ed** ɪd əd ~**er/s**
ə/z ‖ ʰr/z ~**es** z ~**ing** ɪŋ
intercept v ˌɪnt ə 'sept '··· ‖ ˌɪnṯ ʰr- ~**ed** ɪd əd
~**ing** ɪŋ ~**s** s
intercept n 'ɪnt ə sept ‖ 'ɪnṯ ʰr- ~**s** s
interception ˌɪnt ə 'sep ʃᵊn ‖ ˌɪnṯ ʰr- ~**s** z
interceptor ˌɪnt ə 'sept ə ‖ ˌɪnṯ ʰr 'sept ʰr ~**s** z
intercession ˌɪnt ə 'seʃ ᵊn ‖ ˌɪnṯ ʰr- ~**al** əl ◂
~**s** z
intercessor ˌɪnt ə 'ses ə '···· ‖ ˌɪnṯ ʰr 'ses ʰr
~**s** z
intercessory ˌɪnt ə 'ses ər i ◂ ‖ ˌɪnṯ ʰr-
interchang|e v ˌɪnt ə 'tʃeɪndʒ ◂ ‖ ˌɪnṯ ʰr- ~**ed**
d ~**es** ɪz əz ~**ing** ɪŋ
interchang|e n 'ɪnt ə tʃeɪndʒ ‖ 'ɪnṯ ʰr- ~**es** ɪz
əz
interchangeability ˌɪnt ə ˌtʃeɪndʒ ə 'bɪl ət i
-ɪt i ‖ ˌɪnṯ ʰr ˌtʃeɪndʒ ə 'bɪl əṯ i
interchangeab|le ˌɪnt ə 'tʃeɪndʒ əb |ᵊl ◂
‖ ˌɪnṯ ʰr- ~**leness** ᵊl nəs -nɪs ~**ly** li

inter-city, intercity ˌɪnt ə 'sɪt i ◂
‖ ˌɪnṯ ʰr 'sɪṯ i ◂
intercollegiate ˌɪnt ə kə 'liːdʒ ət ◂ -ɪt,
-'liːdʒ i ˌət, ɪt ‖ ˌɪnṯ ʰr-
intercom 'ɪnt ə kɒm ‖ 'ɪnṯ ʰr kɑːm ~**s** z
intercommuni|cate ˌɪnt ə kə 'mjuːn ɪ |keɪt
-'-ə- ‖ ˌɪnṯ ʰr- ~**cated** keɪt ɪd -əd ‖ keɪṯ əd
~**cates** keɪts ~**cating** keɪt ɪŋ ‖ keɪṯ ɪŋ
intercommunication
ˌɪnt ə kə ˌmjuːn ɪ 'keɪʃ ᵊn -ˌ-ə- ‖ ˌɪnṯ ʰr- ~**s** z
intercommunion ˌɪnt ə kə 'mjuːn i ən
‖ ˌɪnṯ ʰr-
interconnect ˌɪnt ə kə 'nekt ◂ ‖ ˌɪnṯ ʰr- ~**ed** ɪd
əd ~**ing** ɪŋ ~**s** s
interconnection ˌɪnt ə kə'nek ʃᵊn ‖ ˌɪnṯ ʰr-
intercontinental ˌɪnt ə ˌkɒnt ɪ 'nent ᵊl ◂ -ˌ-ə-
‖ ˌɪnṯ ʰr ˌkɑːnt ᵊn 'enṯ ᵊl ◂
ˌinterconti͵nental bal͵listic 'missile
intercostal ˌɪnt ə 'kɒst ᵊl ◂ ‖ ˌɪnṯ ʰr 'kɑːst ᵊl ◂
intercourse 'ɪnt ə kɔːs ‖ 'ɪnṯ ʰr kɔːrs -kours
intercultural ˌɪnt ə 'kʌltʃ ʰr əl ◂ ‖ ˌɪnṯ ʰr-
intercurrent ˌɪnt ə 'kʌr ənt ◂ ‖ ˌɪnṯ ʰr 'k₃ː-
~**ly** li
inter|cut v ˌɪnt ə |'kʌt ‖ ˌɪnṯ ʰr- ~**cuts** 'kʌts
~**cutting** 'kʌt ɪŋ ‖ 'kʌṯ ɪŋ
interdenominational
ˌɪnt ə dɪ ˌnɒm ɪ 'neɪʃ ᵊn əl ◂ -də,·-, -,·ə-
‖ ˌɪnṯ ʰr dɪ ˌnɑːm ə- ~**ism** ˌɪz əm
interdental ˌɪnt ə 'dent ᵊl ◂ ‖ ˌɪnṯ ʰr 'denṯ ᵊl ◂
~**ly** i ~**s** z
interdepartmental ˌɪnt ə ˌdiː pɑːt 'ment ᵊl ◂
-ˌ·dɪ,·ˈ··, -ˌ·də,·ˈ·· ‖ ˌɪnṯ ʰr ˌdiː pɑːrt 'menṯ ᵊl ◂
-ˌ·dɪ,·ˈ·· ~**ly** i
ˌinterdepart͵mental 'rivalry
interdependence ˌɪnt ə dɪ 'pend ən^ts -də'--,
§-diː'-- ‖ ˌɪnṯ ʰr-
interdependent ˌɪnt ə dɪ 'pend ənt ◂ -də'--,
§-diː'-- ‖ ˌɪnṯ ʰr- ~**ly** li
interdict v ˌɪnt ə 'dɪkt -'daɪt ‖ ˌɪnṯ ʰr- ~**ed** ɪd
əd ~**ing** ɪŋ ~**s** s
interdict n 'ɪnt ə dɪkt -daɪt ‖ 'ɪnṯ ʰr- ~**s** s
interdiction ˌɪnt ə 'dɪk ʃᵊn ‖ ˌɪnṯ ʰr- ~**s** z
interdisciplinarity ˌɪnt ə ˌdɪs ə plɪ 'nær ət i
-ˌ·ɪ-, -ɪt i ‖ ˌɪnṯ ʰr ˌdɪs ə plə 'nær əṯ i -'ner-
interdisciplinary ˌɪnt ə 'dɪs ə plɪn ər i ◂ -'·ɪ-,
-plən··, -ˌ·ˌ·ˈ·· ‖ ˌɪnṯ ʰr 'dɪs ə plə ner i ◂
interest 'ɪntr əst -ɪst, -est; 'ɪnt ə rest
‖ 'ɪnṯ ə rest ~**ed** ɪd əd ~**ing** ɪŋ ~**s** s
'interest ˌgroup
interested 'ɪntr əst ɪd -ɪst-, 'ɪnt ə rest ɪd, -əd
‖ 'ɪnṯ ə rest əd ~**ly** li ~**ness** nəs nɪs
interest-free ˌɪntr əst 'friː ◂ -ɪst-, -est;
ˌɪnt ə rest- ‖ ˌɪnṯ ə rest-
interesting 'ɪntr əst ɪŋ -ɪst-, -est-; 'ɪnt ə rest ɪŋ
‖ 'ɪnṯ ə rest ɪŋ ~**ly** li
interfac|e v 'ɪnt ə feɪs ˌ·'· ‖ 'ɪnṯ ʰr- ~**ed** t ~**es**
ɪz əz ~**ing** ɪŋ
interfac|e n 'ɪnt ə feɪs ‖ 'ɪnṯ ʰr- ~**es** ɪz əz
interfaith ˌɪnt ə 'feɪθ ◂ ‖ ˌɪnṯ ər-
inter|fere ˌɪnt ə |'fɪə ‖ ˌɪnṯ ʰr |'fɪʰr -ə- ~**fered**
'fɪəd ‖ 'fɪʰrd ~**feres** 'fɪəz ‖ 'fɪʰrz ~**fering**
'fɪər ɪŋ ◂ ‖ 'fɪr ɪŋ ◂
interference ˌɪnt ə 'fɪər ən^ts ‖ ˌɪnṯ ʰr 'fɪr- -ə-

interferometer ˌɪnt ə fə 'rɒm ɪt ə -ət- ə
‖ ˌɪnt̬ ªr fə 'rɑːm ət̬ ªr ˌ-ə-, -fɪ'-- **~s** z
interferometric ˌɪnt ə ˌfer əʊ 'metr ɪk ◄ -ˌfɪər-
‖ ˌɪnt̬ ªr ˌfɪr ə- **~ally** ªl i
interferon ˌɪnt ə 'fɪər ɒn ‖ ˌɪnt̬ ªr 'fɪr ɑːn -ə-
Interflora *tdmk* ˌɪnt ə 'flɔːr ə ‖ ˌɪnt̬ ªr- -'flour-
intergalactic ˌɪnt ə gə 'lækt ɪk ◄ ‖ ˌɪnt̬ ªr-
intergenerational ˌɪnt ə ˌdʒen ə 'reɪʃ ªn ªl ◄
‖ ˌɪnt̬ ªr-
interglacial ˌɪnt ə 'gleɪs i̯ əl ◄ -'gleɪʃ-,
-'gleɪʃ ªl ‖ ˌɪnt̬ ªr 'gleɪʃ ªl ◄
intergovernmental ˌɪnt ə ˌgʌv ªn 'ment ªl ◄
-ˌgʌv ªm-, -ˌgʌb ªm-, -ˌgʌv ə-, -ˌgʌm 'ment-
‖ ˌɪnt̬ ªr ˌgʌv ªrn 'ment̬ ª l ◄
interim 'ɪnt ər ɪm §-əm ‖ 'ɪnt̬-
interior ɪn 'tɪər i̯ ə ‖ -'tɪr i̯ ªr **~ly** li **~s** z
   in̩terior 'decorator
interioris|e, interioriz|e ɪn 'tɪər i̯ ə raɪz
‖ -'tɪr- **~ed** d **~es** ɪz əz **~ing** ɪŋ
interject ˌɪnt ə 'dʒekt ‖ ˌɪnt̬ ªr- **~ed** ɪd əd **~ing**
   ɪŋ **~s** s
interjection ˌɪnt ə 'dʒek ʃªn ‖ ˌɪnt̬ ªr- **~s** z
interlac|e ˌɪnt ə 'leɪs ‖ ˌɪnt̬ ªr- **~ed** t **~es** ɪz əz
~ing ɪŋ
Interlaken ˈɪnt ə ˌlɑːk ən ˌ·'·· ‖ 'ɪnt̬ ªr- —*Ger*
   ['ʔɪn tɐ lak ªn]
interlanguag|e 'ɪnt ə ˌlæŋ gwɪdʒ -wɪdʒ
‖ 'ɪnt̬ ªr- **~es** ɪz əz
interlard ˌɪnt ə 'lɑːd ‖ ˌɪnt̬ ªr 'lɑːrd **~ed** ɪd əd
~ing ɪŋ **~s** z
inter|leaf *n* 'ɪnt ə ‖liːf ‖ 'ɪnt̬ ªr- **~leaves** liːvz
interleav|e *v* ˌɪnt ə 'liːv ‖ ˌɪnt̬ ªr- **~ed** d **~es** z
~ing ɪŋ
interleaves *n pl* 'ɪnt ə liːvz ‖ 'ɪnt̬ ªr-
interleaves *from v* ˌɪnt ə 'liːvz ‖ ˌɪnt̬ ªr-
interleukin ˌɪnt ə 'luːk ɪn -'ljuːk-, §-ən
‖ ˌɪnt̬ ªr-
interlin|e *v* ˌɪnt ə 'laɪn ‖ ˌɪnt̬ ªr- **~ed** d **~es** z
~ing ɪŋ
interlinear ˌɪnt ə 'lɪn i̯ ə ◄ ‖ ˌɪnt̬ ªr 'lɪn i̯ ªr
Interlingua, i~ ˌɪnt ə 'lɪŋ gwə ˌ·'·· ‖ ˌɪnt̬ ªr-
Interlingue ˌɪnt ə 'lɪŋ gweɪ ‖ ˌɪnt̬ ªr-
interlink *v* ˌɪnt ə 'lɪŋk ‖ ˌɪnt̬ ªr- **~ed** t **~ing** ɪŋ
~s s
interlock *v* ˌɪnt ə 'lɒk ‖ ˌɪnt̬ ªr 'lɑːk **~ed** t **~ing**
   ɪŋ **~s** s
interlock *n* 'ɪnt ə lɒk ‖ 'ɪnt̬ ªr lɑːk **~s** s
interlocutor ˌɪnt ə 'lɒk jut ə -jət ə
‖ ˌɪnt̬ ªr 'lɑːk jət̬ ªr **~s** z
interlocutor|y ˌɪnt ə 'lɒk jut ər |i -'jət-
‖ ˌɪnt̬ ªr 'lɑːk jə tɔːr |i -tour i **~ies** iz
interloper 'ɪnt ə ləʊp ə ˌ·'·· ‖ 'ɪnt̬ ªr loʊp ªr
   ˌ·'·· **~s** z
interlude 'ɪnt ə luːd -ljuːd; -ªl uːd, -juːd
‖ 'ɪnt̬ ªr- **~s** z
intermarriage ˌɪnt ə 'mær ɪdʒ ‖ ˌɪnt̬ ªr- -'mer-
intermarr|y ˌɪnt ə 'mær |i ‖ ˌɪnt̬ ªr- -'mer-
~ied id **~ies** iz **~ying** i̯ ɪŋ
intermediar|y ˌɪnt ə 'miːd i̯ ər |i ◄
‖ ˌɪnt̬ ªr 'miːd i er |i **~ies** iz
intermediate ˌɪnt ə 'miːd i̯ ət ◄ -ɪt ‖ ˌɪnt̬ ªr-
~ly li **~ness** nəs nɪs **~s** s
interment ɪn 'tɜː mənt ‖ -'tɜː- **~s** s

intermezz|o ˌɪnt ə 'mets |əʊ -'medz-
‖ ˌɪnt̬ ªr 'mets |oʊ **~i** i i: **~os** əʊz ‖ oʊz
interminab|le ɪn 'tɜːm ɪn əb |ªl |ªl ˌɪn-, -ən̩əb-
‖ -'tɜːm- **~ly** li
intermingl|e ˌɪnt ə 'mɪŋ gªl ‖ ˌɪnt̬ ªr- **~ed** d
~es z **~ing** ɪŋ
intermission ˌɪnt ə 'mɪʃ ªn ‖ ˌɪnt̬ ªr- **~s** z
inter|mit ˌɪnt ə ‖'mɪt ‖ ˌɪnt̬ ªr- **~mits** 'mɪts
~mitted 'mɪt ɪd -əd ‖ 'mɪt̬ əd **~mitting**
   'mɪt ɪŋ ‖ 'mɪt̬ ɪŋ
intermittent ˌɪnt ə 'mɪt ªnt ◄ ‖ ˌɪnt̬ ªr- **~ly** li
intermix ˌɪnt ə 'mɪks ‖ ˌɪnt̬ ªr- **~ed** t **~es** ɪz əz
~ing ɪŋ
intern *v 'confine'* ɪn 'tɜːn ‖ -'tɜːn '·· **~ed** d
~ing ɪŋ **~s** z
intern *n* 'ɪn tɜːn ‖ -tɜːn **~s** z
intern *v 'act as an intern(e)'* 'ɪn tɜːn ‖ -tɜːn
~ed d **~ing** ɪŋ **~s** z
internal ɪn 'tɜːn ªl ˌɪn- ‖ -'tɜːn- **~ly** i **~s** z
   in̩ternal com'bustion; In̩ternal 'Revenue
   ˌService
internalis... —*see* **internaliz...**
internalization ɪn ˌtɜːn əl aɪ 'zeɪʃ ªn ˌˌˌ-, -ɪ'--
‖ ɪn ˌtɜːn ªl ə- **~s** z
internaliz|e ɪn 'tɜːn ə laɪz -ªl aɪz ‖ -'tɜːn ªl aɪz
~ed d **~es** ɪz əz **~ing** ɪŋ
international, I~ ˌɪnt ə 'næʃ ªn ªl ◄ ‖ ˌɪnt̬ ªr-
~ly i **~s** z
   ˌinter̩national 'date line; ˌinter̩national
   'law
Internationale ˌɪnt ə ˌnæʃ ə 'nɑːl
   -ˌnæʃ i̯ ə 'nɑːl ‖ ˌɪnt̬ ªr-
internationalis... —*see* **internationaliz...**
international|ism ˌɪnt ə 'næʃ ªn ªl |ˌɪz əm
‖ ˌɪnt̬ ªr- **~ist/s** ɪst/s §əst/s
internationalization
   ˌɪnt ə ˌnæʃ ªn ªl aɪ 'zeɪʃ ªn -ɪ'--
‖ ˌɪnt̬ ªr ˌnæʃ ªn ªl ə-
internationaliz|e ˌɪnt ə 'næʃ ªn ə laɪz
‖ ˌɪnt̬ ªr- **~ed** d **~es** ɪz əz **~ing** ɪŋ
interne 'ɪn tɜːn ‖ -tɜːn **~s** z
internecine ˌɪnt ə 'niːs aɪn ◄
‖ ˌɪnt̬ ªr 'niːs ªn ◄ -'nes-, -iːn, -aɪn
internee ˌɪn tɜː 'niː ‖ -tɜː- **~s** z
Internet, i~ ˌɪnt ə net ‖ 'ɪnt̬ ªr-
internist 'ɪn tɜːn ɪst §-əst; ˌ·'·· ‖ -tɜːn- **~s** s
internment ɪn 'tɜːn mənt →-'tɜːm- ‖ -'tɜːn- **~s**
   s
internship 'ɪn tɜːn ʃɪp ˌ·'·· ‖ -tɜːn- **~s** s
interoffice ˌɪnt ər 'ɒf ɪs ◄ ‖ ˌɪnt̬ ªr-
interpel|late ɪn 'tɜːp ə |leɪt -eː-; ˌɪnt ə 'pe|l eɪt
‖ ˌɪnt̬ ªr 'pe|l eɪt ɪn 'tɜːp ə |leɪt **~lated** leɪt ɪd
   -əd ‖ leɪt̬ əd **~lates** leɪts **~lating** leɪt ɪŋ
   ‖ leɪt̬ ɪŋ
interpellation ɪn ˌtɜːp ə 'leɪʃ ªn -eː-; ˌɪnt ə pə-,
   -pe'-- ‖ ˌɪnt̬ ªr pə- ɪn ˌtɜːp ə- **~s** z
interpene|trate ˌɪnt ə 'pen ɪ |treɪt -'ə-
‖ ˌɪnt̬ ªr- **~trated** treɪt ɪd -əd ‖ treɪt̬ əd
~trates treɪts **~trating** treɪt ɪŋ ‖ treɪt̬ ɪŋ
interpenetration ˌɪnt ə ˌpen ɪ 'treɪʃ ªn -ˌə-
‖ ˌɪnt̬ ªr- **~s** z
interpersonal ˌɪnt ə 'pɜːs ªn ªl ◄
‖ ˌɪnt̬ ªr 'pɜːs-

I

interplanetary ˌɪnt ə 'plæn ɪt‿ər i ◂ -'ət‿
‖ ˌɪnt̮ ᵊr 'plæn ə ter i
interplay 'ɪnt ə pleɪ ‖ 'ɪnt̮ ᵊr-
Interpol 'ɪnt ə pɒl ‖ 'ɪnt̮ ᵊr poʊl (*)
interpo|late ɪn 'tɜːp ə |leɪt ‖ -'tɜːp- **~lated**
leɪt ɪd -əd ‖ leɪt̮ əd **~lates** leɪts **~lating**
leɪt ɪŋ ‖ leɪt̮ ɪŋ
interpolation ɪn ˌtɜːp ə 'leɪʃ ᵊn ‖ -ˌtɜːp- **~s** z
interpos|e ˌɪnt ə 'pəʊz ‖ ˌɪnt̮ ᵊr 'poʊz **~ed** d
~es ɪz əz **~ing** ɪŋ
interposition ˌɪnt ə pə 'zɪʃ ᵊn ɪn ˌtɜːp ə-
‖ ˌɪnt̮ ᵊr
interp|ret ɪn 'tɜːp |rɪt -rət ‖ -'tɜːp |rət **~reted**
rɪt ɪd rət-, -əd ‖ rət̮ əd **~reting** rɪt ɪŋ rət-
‖ rət̮ ɪŋ **~rets** rɪts rəts ‖ rəts
interpretation ɪn ˌtɜːp rɪ 'teɪʃ ᵊn -rə- ‖ -ˌtɜːp-
~s z
interpretative ɪn 'tɜːp rɪt ət ɪv -'·rət-; -rɪ teɪt-,
-rə teɪt- ‖ -'tɜːp rə teɪt̮ ɪv -rət̮ ət̮- **~ly** li
interpreter ɪn 'tɜːp rɪt ə -rət- ‖ -'tɜːp rət̮ ᵊr **~s**
z
interpretive ɪn 'tɜːp rɪt ɪv -rət- ‖ -'tɜːp rət̮ ɪv
~ly li
interquartile ˌɪnt ə 'kwɔːt aɪᵊl ◂
‖ ˌɪnt̮ ᵊr 'kwɔːrt- -'kwɔːrt̮ ᵊl ◂ **~s** z
interracial ˌɪnt ə 'reɪʃ ᵊl ◂ ‖ ˌɪnt̮ ᵊr- **~ly** i
Inter-Rail 'ɪnt ə reɪᵊl ‖ ˌɪnt̮ ᵊr-
interreg|num ˌɪnt ə 'reg |nəm ‖ ˌɪnt̮ ᵊr- **~na**
nə **~nums** nəmz
interre|late ˌɪnt ə rɪ |'leɪt -rəˈ, §-riːˈ ‖ ˌɪnt̮ ᵊr-
~lated 'leɪt ɪd -əd ‖ 'leɪt̮ əd **~lates** 'leɪts
~lating 'leɪt ɪŋ ‖ 'leɪt̮ ɪŋ
interrelation ˌɪnt ə ri 'leɪʃ ᵊn -rə'- ‖ ˌɪnt̮ ᵊr- **~s**
z **~ship/s** ʃɪp/s
interro|gate ɪn 'ter ə |geɪt **~gated** geɪt ɪd -əd
‖ geɪt̮ əd **~gates** geɪts **~gating** geɪt ɪŋ
‖ geɪt̮ ɪŋ
interrogation ɪn ˌter ə 'geɪʃ ᵊn **~s** z
in ˌterro'gation mark
interrogative ˌɪnt ə 'rɒg ət ɪv ◂
‖ ˌɪnt̮ ə 'rɑːg ət̮ ɪv ◂ **~ly** li **~s** z
interrogator ɪn 'ter ə geɪt ə ‖ -geɪt̮ ᵊr **~s** z
interrogator|y ˌɪnt ə 'rɒg ət‿ər |i ◂
‖ ˌɪnt̮ ə 'rɑːg ə tɔːr |i -tour i **~ies** iz
interrupt v ˌɪnt ə 'rʌpt ‖ ˌɪnt̮ ə- **~ed** ɪd əd **~ing**
ɪŋ **~s** s
interrupt n 'ɪnt ə rʌpt ˌ·'· ‖ 'ɪnt̮ ə- **~s** s
interruption ˌɪnt ə 'rʌp ʃᵊn ‖ ˌɪnt̮ ə- **~s** z
interscholastic ˌɪnt ə skə 'læst ɪk ◂ -skɒˈ-
‖ ˌɪnt̮ ᵊr-
inter se ˌɪnt ə 'seɪ -'siː ‖ ˌɪnt̮ ᵊr-
intersect ˌɪnt ə 'sekt ‖ ˌɪnt̮ ᵊr- **~ed** ɪd əd **~ing**
ɪŋ **~s** s
intersection ˌɪnt ə 'sek ʃᵊn '·ˌ··
‖ 'ɪnt̮ ᵊr ˌsek ʃᵊn ˌ·'·· **~s** z
intersession 'ɪnt ə ˌseʃ ᵊn ‖ ˌɪnt̮ ᵊr- **~s** z
intersex 'ɪnt ə seks ‖ 'ɪnt̮ ᵊr- **~es** ɪz əz
interspac|e v ˌɪnt ə 'speɪs '·'· ‖ ˌɪnt̮ ᵊr- **~ed** t
~es ɪz əz **~ing** ɪŋ
interspac|e n 'ɪnt ə speɪs ˌ·'· ‖ 'ɪnt̮ ᵊr- **~es** ɪz
əz
interspers|e ˌɪnt ə 'spɜːs ‖ ˌɪnt̮ ᵊr 'spɜːs **~ed** t
~es ɪz əz **~ing** ɪŋ

interspersion ˌɪnt ə 'spɜːʃ ᵊn §-'spɜːʒ-
‖ ˌɪnt̮ ᵊr 'spɜːʒ ᵊn
interstate n 'ɪnt ə steɪt ‖ 'ɪnt̮ ᵊr- **~s** s
interstate adj ˌɪnt ə 'steɪt ◂ '·· ‖ ˌɪnt̮ ᵊr-
ˌinterstate 'highway
interstellar ˌɪnt ə 'stel ə ◂ ‖ ˌɪnt̮ ᵊr 'stel ᵊr
ˌinterˌstellar 'dust
interstic|e ɪn 'tɜːst ɪs -əs ‖ -'tɜːst- **~es** ɪz əz
interstitial ˌɪnt ə 'stɪʃ ᵊl ◂ ‖ ˌɪnt̮ ᵊr- **~ly** i **~s** z
intertextuality ˌɪnt ə ˌteks tju 'æl ət i -tʃu'--,
-ɪt i ‖ ˌɪnt̮ ᵊr ˌteks tʃu 'æl ət̮ i
intertidal ˌɪnt ə 'taɪd ᵊl ◂ ‖ ˌɪnt̮ ᵊr-
intertribal ˌɪnt ə 'traɪb ᵊl ◂ ‖ ˌɪnt̮ ᵊr-
intertwin|e ˌɪnt ə 'twaɪn ‖ ˌɪnt̮ ᵊr- **~ed** d **~es**
z **~ing** ɪŋ
interurban ˌɪnt ər 'ɜːb ən ◂ ‖ ˌɪnt̮ ər 'ɜːb-
interval 'ɪnt əv ᵊl ‖ 'ɪnt̮ ᵊrv ᵊl **~s** z
interven|e ˌɪnt ə 'viːn ‖ ˌɪnt̮ ᵊr- **~ed** d **~es** z
~ing ɪŋ
intervention ˌɪnt ə 'venʃ ᵊn ‖ ˌɪnt̮ ᵊr- **~ism**
ˌɪz əm **~ist/s** ɪst/s §əst/s ‖ əst/s **~s** z
inter|view n, v 'ɪnt ə |vjuː ‖ 'ɪnt̮ ᵊr- **~viewed**
vjuːd **~viewing** vjuː ɪŋ **~views** vjuːz
interviewee ˌɪnt ə vju 'iː ‖ ˌɪnt̮ ᵊr- **~s** z
interviewer 'ɪnt ə vjuː ə ‖ 'ɪnt̮ ᵊr vjuː ᵊr **~s** z
intervocalic ˌɪnt ə vəʊ 'kæl ɪk ◂ ‖ ˌɪnt̮ ᵊr voʊ-
~ally ᵊl i
interwar ˌɪnt ə 'wɔː ◂ ‖ ˌɪnt̮ ᵊr 'wɔːr ◂
inter|weave ˌɪnt ə |'wiːv ‖ ˌɪnt̮ ᵊr- **~weaves**
'wiːvz **~weaving** 'wiːv ɪŋ **~wove** 'wəʊv
‖ 'woʊv **~woven** 'wəʊv ᵊn ◂ ‖ 'woʊv ᵊn ◂
intestacy ɪn 'test əs i
intestate ɪn 'test eɪt -ət, -ɪt **~s** s
intestinal ɪn 'test ɪn ᵊl -ənˌᵊl; ˌɪnt e 'staɪn ᵊl ◂
intestine ɪn 'test ɪn -iːn, -ən **~s** z
in-thing ˌɪn 'θɪŋ
intifada ˌɪnt ɪ 'fɑːd ə —Arabic [in ti 'fɑː dˤa]
intimac|y 'ɪnt ɪm əs |i '-əm- ‖ 'ɪnt̮ əm- **~ies** iz
inti|mate v 'ɪnt ɪ |meɪt -ə- ‖ 'ɪnt̮ ə- **~mated**
meɪt ɪd -əd ‖ meɪt̮ əd **~mates** meɪts **~mating**
meɪt ɪŋ ‖ meɪt̮ ɪŋ
intimate adj, n 'ɪnt ɪm ət -əm-, -ɪt ‖ 'ɪnt̮ əm ət
~ly li **~ness** nəs nɪs **~s** s
intimation ˌɪnt ɪ 'meɪʃ ᵊn -ə- ‖ ˌɪnt̮ ə- **~s** z
intimi|date ɪn 'tɪm ɪ |deɪt ˌɪn-, -ə- **~dated**
deɪt ɪd -əd ‖ deɪt̮ əd **~dates** deɪts **~dating**
deɪt ɪŋ ‖ deɪt̮ ɪŋ
intimidation ɪn ˌtɪm ɪ 'deɪʃ ᵊn ˌ·ˌ·-, -ə'--
intimidatory ɪn ˌtɪm ɪ 'deɪt ər i ◂ -ˌ·ə-; ·'·····
‖ ɪn 'tɪm əd ə tɔːr i -tour i
into strong form 'ɪn tuː -tu, weak forms (')ɪnt ə
(especially before a consonant), (')ɪnt u
(especially before a vowel)
intolerab|le ɪn 'tɒl ər_əb |ᵊl ‖ -'tɑːl- **~leness**
ᵊl nəs -nɪs **~ly** li
intoleranc|e ɪn 'tɒl ər ən¹s ˌɪn- ‖ -'tɑːl- **~es** ɪz
əz
intolerant ɪn 'tɒl ər ənt ˌɪn- ‖ -'tɑːl- **~ly** li
into|nate 'ɪn təʊ |neɪt ‖ -tə- **~nated** neɪt ɪd
-əd ‖ neɪt̮ əd **~nates** neɪts **~nating** neɪt ɪŋ
‖ neɪt̮ ɪŋ
intonation ˌɪn tə 'neɪʃ ᵊn -təʊ- **~s** z
ˌinto'nation ˌpatterns

intonational ˌɪn tə ˈneɪʃ ᵊn‿əl ˌ-təʊ-
intonative ˈɪn təʊ neɪt ɪv ‖ -tə neɪt ɪv
inton|e ɪn ˈtəʊn ‖ -ˈtoʊn **~ed** d **~es** z **~ing** ɪŋ
in toto ɪn ˈtəʊt əʊ ‖ -ˈtoʊt oʊ
Intourist *tdmk* ˈɪn ˌtʊər ɪst -ˌtɔːr-, §-əst ‖ -ˌtʊr-
intoxicant ɪn ˈtɒks ɪk ənt -ək- ‖ -ˈtɑːks- **~s** s
intoxi|cate ɪn ˈtɒks ɪ |keɪt ə- ‖ -ˈtɑːks- **~cated**
  keɪt ɪd -əd ‖ keɪt̬ əd **~cates** keɪts **~cating**
  keɪt ɪŋ ‖ keɪt̬ ɪŋ
intoxication ɪn ˌtɒks ɪ ˈkeɪʃ ᵊn -ə- ‖ -ˌtɑːks- **~s**
  z
intra- ¦ɪntr ə — **intracardiac**
  ˌɪntr ə ˈkɑːd i æk ◂ ‖ -ˈkɑːrd-
intractability ɪn ˌtrækt ə ˈbɪl ət i ˌ-,-, -ɪt i
  ‖ -ət̬ i
intractab|le ɪn ˈtrækt əb ¦ᵊl ˌɪn- **~leness**
  ᵊl nəs -nɪs **~ly** li
intrados ɪn ˈtreɪd ɒs ‖ ˈɪntr ə dɑːs -doʊ
intramural ˌɪntr ə ˈmjʊər əl ◂ -ˈmjɔːr- ‖ -ˈmjʊr-
  ~ly i
intramuscular ˌɪntr ə ˈmʌsk jʊl ə ◂ -jᵊl ə
  ‖ -jəl ᵊr
intranet ˈɪntr ə net **~s** s
intransigenc|e ɪn ˈtræn⹁ɪdʒ ənᵗs -ˈtrænz-,
  -ˈtrɑːnᵗs-, -ˈtrɑːnz-, -ədʒ- **~y** i
intransigent ɪn ˈtræn⹁ɪdʒ ənt -ˈtrænz-,
  -ˈtrɑːnᵗs-, -ˈtrɑːnz-, -ədʒ- **~ly** li **~s** s
intransitive ɪn ˈtræn⹁ət ɪv ˌɪn-, -ˈtrænz-,
  -ˈtrɑːnᵗs-, -ˈtrɑːnz-, -ɪt- ‖ -ət̬ ɪv **~ly** li **~ness**
  nəs nɪs **~s** z
intransitivity ɪn ˌtræn⹁ə ˈtɪv ət i -ˌtrænz-,
  -ˌtrɑːnᵗs-, -ˌtrɑːnz-, ˌ-,-, -əˈ-, -ət i ‖ -ət̬ i
intrapersonal ˌɪntr ə ˈpɜːs ᵊn əl ◂ ‖ -ˈpɜːs-
intrapreneur ˌɪntr ə prə ˈnɜː -preˈ-, -ˈnjʊə
  ‖ -ˈnɜː -ˈnʊᵊr **~s** z
intrastate ˌɪntr ə ˈsteɪt ◂
intrauterine ˌɪntr ə ˈjuːt ə raɪn ◂ ‖ -ˈjuːt̬ ər ən
  -ə raɪn
  ˌintra ˌuterine deˈvice
intrava|sate ɪn ˈtræv ə |seɪt ˌ-ˈ- **~sated** seɪt ɪd
  -əd ‖ seɪt̬ əd **~sates** seɪts **~sating** seɪt ɪŋ
  ‖ seɪt̬ ɪŋ
intravasation ɪn ˌtræv ə ˈseɪʃ ᵊn ˌ-,-,- **~s** z
intravenous ˌɪntr ə ˈviːn əs ◂ △-ˈvin i əs **~es**
  ɪz əz **~ly** li
in-tray ˈɪn treɪ **~s** z
intrench ɪn ˈtrentʃ ən- **~ed** t **~es** ɪz əz **~ing** ɪŋ
  ~ment/s mənt/s
intrepid ɪn ˈtrep ɪd §-əd **~ly** li **~ness** nəs nɪs
intrepidity ˌɪn trə ˈpɪd ət i ˌ-trɪ-, ˌ-tre-, -ɪt i
  ‖ -ət̬ i
intricac|y ˈɪntr ɪk əs |i ˈ-ək- **~ies** iz
intricate ˈɪntr ɪk ət -ək-, -ɪt **~ly** li **~ness** nəs
  nɪs
intrigu|e *v* ɪn ˈtriːg **~ed** d **~es** z **~ing** ɪŋ
intrigue *n* ˈɪn triːg ·ˈ· **~s** z
intrinsic ɪn ˈtrɪnᵗs ɪk ˌɪn-, -ˈtrɪnz- **~ally** ᵊl‿i
intro ˈɪntr əʊ ‖ -oʊ **~s** z
intro- ¦ɪntr əʊ ‖ -ə — **introgression**
  ˌɪntr əʊ ˈgreʃ ᵊn ‖ -ə-
introduc|e ˌɪntr ə ˈdjuːs →-ˈdʒuːs ‖ -ˈduːs
  -ˈdjuːs **~ed** t **~es** ɪz əz **~ing** ɪŋ
introduction ˌɪntr ə ˈdʌk ʃᵊn **~s** z

introductor|y ˌɪntr ə ˈdʌkt̬ ᵊr |i ◂ **~ily** əl i ɪ li
  ˌintro₁ductory ˈoffer
introit ˈɪn trɔɪt ɪn ˈtrəʊ ɪt, §-ət ‖ ɪn ˈtroʊ ət, ˈ···
  ~s s
introject ˌɪntr əʊ ˈdʒekt ‖ -ə- **~ed** ɪd əd **~ing**
  ɪŋ **~s** s
introjection ˌɪntr əʊ ˈdʒek ʃᵊn ‖ -ə-
intromission ˌɪntr əʊ ˈmɪʃ ᵊn ‖ -ə- **~s** z
intro|mit ˌɪntr əʊ ¦ˈmɪt ‖ -ə- **~mits** ˈmɪts
  ~mitted ˈmɪt ɪd -əd ‖ ˈmɪt̬ əd **~mitting**
  ˈmɪt ɪŋ ‖ ˈmɪt̬ ɪŋ
introspect ˌɪntr əʊ ˈspekt ‖ -ə- **~ed** ɪd əd **~ing**
  ɪŋ **~s** s
introspection ˌɪntr əʊ ˈspek ʃᵊn ‖ -ə- **~s** z
introspective ˌɪntr əʊ ˈspekt ɪv ◂ ‖ -ə- **~ly** li
  ~ness nəs nɪs
introversion ˌɪntr əʊ ˈvɜːʃ ᵊn -ˈvɜːʒ-
  ‖ -ə ˈvɜːʒ ᵊn
introvert *n* ˈɪntr əʊ vɜːt ‖ -ə vɜːt **~s** s
introvert *v* ˌɪntr əʊ ˈvɜːt ‖ -ə ˈvɜːt **~verted**
  ˈvɜːt ɪd -əd ‖ ˈvɜːt̬ əd **~verting** ˈvɜːt ɪŋ
  ‖ ˈvɜːt̬ ɪŋ **~verts** ˈvɜːts ‖ ˈvɜːts
intrud|e ɪn ˈtruːd **~ed** ɪd əd **~es** z **~ing** ɪŋ
intruder ɪn ˈtruːd ə ‖ -ᵊr **~s** z
intrusion ɪn ˈtruːʒ ᵊn **~s** z
intrusive ɪn ˈtruːs ɪv §-ˈtruːz- **~ly** li **~ness** nəs
  nɪs
intrust ɪn ˈtrʌst ən- **~ed** ɪd əd **~ing** ɪŋ **~s** s
intu|bate ˈɪn tju |beɪt →-tʃu- ‖ -tu- -tju-
  ~bated beɪt ɪd -əd ‖ beɪt̬ əd **~bates** beɪts
  ~bating beɪt ɪŋ ‖ beɪt̬ ɪŋ
intu|it ɪn ˈtjuː ¦ɪt §→-ˈtʃuː⹁, §ˌət ‖ -ˈtuː ¦ət
  -ˈtjuː- **~ited** ɪt ɪd §ət-, -əd ‖ ət̬ əd **~iting** ɪt ɪŋ
  §ət- ‖ ət̬ ɪŋ **~its** ɪts §əts ‖ əts
intuition ˌɪn tju ˈɪʃ ᵊn →-tʃu- ‖ -tu- -tju- **~s** z
intuitive ɪn ˈtjuː ət ɪv →-ˈtʃuː⹁, ɪt ɪv
  ‖ -ˈtuː ət̬ ɪv -ˈtjuː- **~ly** li **~ness** nəs nɪs
intumesc|e ˌɪn tju ˈmes →-tʃu- ‖ -tu- -tju- **~ed**
  t **~es** ɪz əz **~ing** ɪŋ
intumesc|ence ˌɪn tju ˈmes ¦ᵊnᵗs -tʃu- ‖ -tu-
  -tju- **~ent** ᵊnt
intussuscept ˌɪnt ə sə ˈsept -əs sə- ‖ ˌɪnt̬- **~ed**
  ɪd əd **~ing** ɪŋ **~s** s
intussusception ˌɪnt ə sə ˈsep ʃᵊn -əs sə-
  ‖ ˌɪnt̬-
Inuit ˈɪn u ɪt -ju-, §-ət **~s** s
Inuk ˈɪn ʊk
Inuktitut ɪ ˈnʊk tɪ tʊt -tə-
inun|date ˈɪn ʌn |deɪt -ən- **~dated** deɪt ɪd -əd
  ‖ deɪt̬ əd **~dates** deɪts **~dating** deɪt ɪŋ
  ‖ deɪt̬ ɪŋ
inundation ˌɪn ʌn ˈdeɪʃ ᵊn -ən- **~s** z
Inupiaq ɪ ˈnuːp i æk
inure ɪ ˈnjʊə ə-, -ˈnjɔː ‖ ɪn ˈjʊᵊr ɪ ˈnʊᵊr **~d** d **~s**
  z **inuring** ɪ ˈnjʊər ɪŋ ə-, -ˈnjɔːr- ‖ ɪn ˈjʊr ɪŋ
  ɪ ˈnʊr-
inurn ɪn ˈɜːn ‖ ɪn ˈɜːn **~ed** d **~ing** ɪŋ **~ment**
  mənt **~s** z
in utero ɪn ˈjuːt ə rəʊ ‖ ɪn ˈjuːt̬ ə roʊ
in vacuo ɪn ˈvæk ju əʊ ‖ -oʊ
invad|e ɪn ˈveɪd **~ed** ɪd əd **~er/s** ə/z ‖ ᵊr/z **~es**
  z **~ing** ɪŋ

invalid adj 'not valid' ɪn ˈvæl ɪd ˌɪn-, §-əd **~ly** li

invalid n, v, adj 'ill, infirm' ˈɪn və liːd -lɪd ‖ -vəl əd **~ed** ɪd əd **~ing** ɪŋ **~s** z

invali|date ɪn ˈvæl ɪ |deɪt ˌɪn-, -ə- **~dated** deɪt ɪd -əd ‖ deɪt̬ əd **~dates** deɪts **~dating** deɪt ɪŋ ‖ deɪt̬ ɪŋ

invalidation ɪn ˌvæl ɪ ˈdeɪʃ ən -ə-, ˌ•ˌ•-

invalidity ˌɪn və ˈlɪd ət i -ɪt i ‖ -ət̬ i

invaluab|le ɪn ˈvæl ju əb |əl -ˈvæl jub |əl **~ly** li

Invar tdmk ɪn ˈvɑː ˈ• •; ˈɪn və ‖ -ˈvɑːr ˈ• •

invariability ɪn ˌveər i ə ˈbɪl ət i ˌ•ˌ•-, -ɪt i ‖ ɪn ˌver i ə ˈbɪl ət̬ i -ˌvær-

invariab|le ɪn ˈveər i əb |əl ˌɪn- ‖ -ˈver- -ˈvær- **~leness** əl nəs -nɪs **~ly** li

invariance ɪn ˈveər i ən¹s ˌɪn- ‖ -ˈver- -ˈvær-

invariant ɪn ˈveər i ənt ˌɪn- ‖ -ˈver- -ˈvær- **~s** s

invasion ɪn ˈveɪʒ ən **~s** z

invasive ɪn ˈveɪs ɪv §-ˈveɪz- **~ly** li

invective ɪn ˈvekt ɪv **~ly** li **~ness** nəs nɪs

inveigh ɪn ˈveɪ **~ed** d **~ing** ɪŋ **~s** z

inveigl|e ɪn ˈveɪg əl -ˈviːg- **~ed** d **~ement** mənt **~es** z **~ing** ɪŋ

in|vent ɪn |ˈvent **~vented** ˈvent ɪd -əd ‖ ˈvent̬ əd **~venting** ˈvent ɪŋ ‖ ˈvent̬ ɪŋ **~vents** ˈvents

invention ɪn ˈvenᵗʃ ən **~s** z

inventive ɪn ˈvent ɪv ‖ -ˈvent̬ ɪv **~ly** li **~ness** nəs nɪs

inventor ɪn ˈvent ə ‖ ˈvent̬ ər **~s** z

inventor|y n, v ˈɪn vənt ər |i ɪn ˈvent ər |i ‖ ˈɪn vən tɔːr |i -tour i **~ies** iz

Inver ˈɪn və ‖ -vᵊr

Inveraray ˌɪn vər ˈeər i -ə ‖ -ˈer i -ˈær i

Invercargill ˌɪn və ˈkɑːg ɪl -ᵊl; -kɑː ˈgɪl ‖ -vᵊr ˈkɑːrg ᵊl

Invergarry ˌɪn və ˈgær i ‖ -vᵊr- -ˈger-

Invergordon ˌɪn və ˈgɔːd ᵊn ‖ -vᵊr ˈgɔːrd ᵊn

Inverkeithing ˌɪn və ˈkiːð ɪŋ ‖ -vᵊr-

Invermoriston ˌɪn və ˈmɒr ɪst ən -ˈ•əst- ‖ -vᵊr ˈmɔːr- -ˈmɑːr-

Inverness ˌɪn və ˈnes ◂ ‖ -vᵊr-
ˌInverness ˈTerrace

invers|e adj, n ˌɪn ˈvɜːs ◂ ɪn- ‖ -ˈvɜːs ˈ• • **~ely** li **~es** ɪz əz
ˌinverse proˈportion

inversion ɪn ˈvɜːʃ ᵊn §-ˈvɜːʒ- ‖ -ˈvɜːʒ ᵊn **~s** z

invert adj, n ˈɪn vɜːt ‖ -vɜːt **~s** s

in|vert v ɪn |ˈvɜːt ˌɪn- ‖ -|ˈvɜːt **~verted** ˈvɜːt ɪd -əd ‖ ˈvɜːt̬ əd **~verting** ˈvɜːt ɪŋ ‖ ˈvɜːt̬ ɪŋ **~verts** ˈvɜːts ‖ ˈvɜːts
in ˌverted ˈcomma; in ˌverted ˈsnob

invertebrate ɪn ˈvɜːt ɪb rət ˌɪn-, -əb-, -rɪt; -ɪ breɪt, -ə- ‖ -ˈvɜːt̬- **~s** s

Inverurie ˌɪn vər ˈʊər i ‖ -ˈʊr i

invest ɪn ˈvest **~ed** ɪd əd **~ing** ɪŋ **~s** s

investi|gate ɪn ˈvest ɪ |geɪt -ə- **~gated** geɪt ɪd -əd ‖ geɪt̬ əd **~gates** geɪts **~gating** geɪt ɪŋ ‖ geɪt̬ ɪŋ

investigation ɪn ˌvest ɪ ˈgeɪʃ ᵊn -ˌ•ə- **~s** z

investigative ɪn ˈvest ɪg ət ɪv -ˈ•əg-; -ɪ geɪt ɪv, -ə • • ‖ -ə geɪt̬ ɪv

investigator ɪn ˈvest ɪ geɪt ə -ˈ•ə- ‖ -geɪt̬ ᵊr **~s** z

investigatory ɪn ˈvest ɪg ət ᵊr i ɪn ˌvest ɪ ˈgeɪt ər i ◂ -ˌ•ə-; ˌ•ˌ•••• ‖ ɪn ˈvest ɪg ə tɔːr i -tour i

investiture ɪn ˈvest ɪtʃ ə -ətʃ ə; -ɪ tjʊə, -ə- ‖ -ətʃ ᵊr -ə tʃʊr **~s** z

investment ɪn ˈvest mənt **~s** s

investor ɪn ˈvest ə ‖ -ᵊr **~s** z

inveterate ɪn ˈvet ər ət -ɪt ‖ ɪn ˈvet̬ ər ət →ɪn ˈvetr ət **~ly** li **~ness** nəs nɪs

invidious ɪn ˈvɪd i əs **~ly** li **~ness** nəs nɪs

invigi|late ɪn ˈvɪdʒ ə |leɪt -ɪ- **~lated** leɪt ɪd -əd ‖ leɪt̬ əd **~lates** leɪts **~lating** leɪt ɪŋ ‖ leɪt̬ ɪŋ

invigilation ɪn ˌvɪdʒ ə ˈleɪʃ ᵊn -ɪ- **~s** z

invigilator ɪn ˈvɪdʒ ə leɪt ə -ˈ•ɪ- ‖ -leɪt̬ ᵊr **~s** z

invigo|rate ɪn ˈvɪg ə |reɪt **~rated** reɪt ɪd -əd ‖ reɪt̬ əd **~rates** reɪts **~rating** reɪt ɪŋ ‖ reɪt̬ ɪŋ

invigoration ɪn ˌvɪg ə ˈreɪʃ ᵊn

invincibility ɪn ˌvɪnᵗs ə ˈbɪl ət i ˌ•ˌ•-, -ɪˈ•-, -ɪt i ‖ -ət̬ i

invincib|le ɪn ˈvɪnᵗs əb |əl ˌɪn-, -ɪb- **~leness** əl nəs -nɪs **~ly** li

inviolability ɪn ˌvar əl ə ˈbɪl ət i ˌ•ˌ•-, -ɪt i ‖ -ət̬ i

inviolab|le ɪn ˈvar əl əb |əl ˌɪn- **~leness** əl nəs -nɪs **~ly** li

inviolate ɪn ˈvar əl ət -ɪt, ə leɪt **~ly** li **~ness** nəs nɪs

invisibility ɪn ˌvɪz ə ˈbɪl ət i ˌ•ˌ•-, -ɪˈ•-, -ɪt i ‖ -ət̬ i

invisib|le ɪn ˈvɪz əb |əl ˌɪn-, -ɪb- **~leness** əl nəs -nɪs **~ly** li

invitation ˌɪn vɪ ˈteɪʃ ᵊn -və- **~s** z

in|vite v ɪn |ˈvaɪt **~vited** ˈvaɪt ɪd -əd ‖ ˈvaɪt̬ əd **~vites** ˈvaɪts **~viting/ly** ˈvaɪt ɪŋ /li ‖ ˈvaɪt̬-

invite n ˈɪn vaɪt **~s** s

invitee ˌɪn vaɪ ˈtiː -vɪ- ‖ -və- **~s** z

in vitro ɪn ˈviːtr əʊ -ˈvɪtr- ‖ -oʊ

in vivo ɪn ˈviːv əʊ -ˈvaɪv- ‖ -oʊ

invocation ˌɪn vəʊ ˈkeɪʃ ᵊn -və- **~s** z

invoic|e n, v ˈɪn vɔɪs **~ed** t **~es** ɪz əz **~ing** ɪŋ

invok|e ɪn ˈvəʊk ‖ -ˈvoʊk **~ed** t **~es** s **~ing** ɪŋ

involucre ˈɪn və luːk ə -ljuːk ə, ˌ•ˈ•• ‖ -ᵊr **~s** z

involuntar|ily ɪn ˈvɒl ən ˌtər |əl i ˌɪn-, -ən ter əl i, -ɪ li; ˌ•ˌ• •ˈter əl i, -ˈtær-, -ɪ li ‖ ɪn ˌvɑːl ən ˈter əl i ˌ•ˌ•-, -ˈtær- **~iness** i nəs i nɪs

involuntar|y ɪn ˈvɒl ənt ər |i ˌɪn-, §-ən ter i ‖ -ˈvɑːl ən ter |i

involute ˈɪn və luːt -ljuːt, ˌ•ˈ• **~s** s

involution ˌɪn və ˈluːʃ ᵊn -ˈljuːʃ- **~s** z

involv|e ɪn ˈvɒlv §-ˈvəʊlv, →§-ˈvɒʊlv ‖ -ˈvɑːlv
— Preference poll, BrE: -ˈvɒlv 86%, -ˈvəʊlv/-ˈvɒʊlv 14%. **~ed** d **~ement/s** mənt/s **~es** z **~ing** ɪŋ

invulnerability ɪn ˌvʌln ər ə ˈbɪl ət i -ˌvʌn-, ˌ•ˌ•-, -ɪt i ‖ -ət̬ i

invulnerab|le ɪn ˈvʌln ər əb |əl ˌɪn-, -ˈvʌn- **~leness** əl nəs -nɪs **~ly** li

inward, I~ ˈɪn wəd ‖ -wᵊrd **~ly** li **~ness** nəs nɪs **~s** z

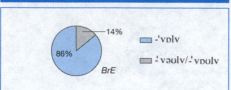

INVOLVE

14%
86%

■ -'vɒlv
▨ -'vəʊlv/-'vɒlv

BrE

inward-looking 'ɪn wəd ˌlʊk ɪŋ §-ˌluːk-; ˌ·'·· ◄
‖ -wᵊrd-
Inwood 'ɪn wʊd
in-word 'ɪn wɜːd ‖ -wɜːd ~s z
inwrought ˌɪn 'rɔːt ◄ ‖ -'rɑːt
INXS ɪn 'eks es
in-your-face, in-yer-face ˌɪn jə 'feɪs ◄ -jɔː-
‖ -jᵊr-
I/O ˌaɪ 'əʊ ◄ ‖ -'oʊ ◄ *or as* input/output
Io 'aɪ əʊ ‖ -oʊ
Ioan 'jəʊ ən ‖ 'joʊ- —*Welsh* ['jo an]
iodate 'aɪˌə deɪt -əʊ- ~s s
iodic aɪ 'ɒd ɪk ‖ -'ɑːd ɪk
iodide 'aɪˌə daɪd -əʊ- ~s z
iodin 'aɪˌəd ɪn -əʊd-, §-ən
iodine 'aɪˌə diːn -əʊ-, -daɪn ‖ -daɪn əd ən
iodis... —*see* **iodiz...**
iodization ˌaɪˌə daɪ 'zeɪʃ ᵊn əd ɪ- ‖ -əd ə-
iodiz|e 'aɪˌə daɪz -əʊ- ~ed d ~es ɪz əz ~ing ɪŋ
iodoform aɪ 'ɒd ə fɔːm ‖ aɪ 'oʊd ə fɔːrm -'ɑːd-
(*)
iodopsin ˌaɪ əʊ 'dɒps ɪn §-ən ‖ -ə 'dɑːps-
iodous aɪ 'ɒd əs 'aɪˌəd- ‖ aɪ 'oʊd- -'ɑːd-, 'aɪ əd-
Iolanthe ˌaɪˌə 'lænᵗθ i -əʊ-
Iolo 'jəʊl əʊ 'joʊl oʊ —*Welsh* ['jo lo]
ion 'aɪ ən —*Also occasionally* 'aɪ ɒn ‖ -ɑːn, *in
RP mainly to avoid confusion with* iron ~s z
-ion *stress-imposing* jən, ən, ən, ᵊn —*often with
changes to a stem-final consonant:* in'jection
ɪn 'dʒek ʃᵊn
Iona aɪ 'əʊn ə ‖ -'oʊn ə
Ione aɪ 'əʊn i ‖ -'oʊn i
Ionesco ˌiːˌə 'nesk əʊ -ɒ-; jɒ 'nesk- ‖ -oʊ —*Fr*
[jɔ nɛs ko]
Ionia aɪ 'əʊn iˌə ‖ -'oʊn-
Ionian aɪ 'əʊn iˌən ‖ -'oʊn- ~s z
Ionic aɪ 'ɒn ɪk ‖ -'ɑːn- ~s s
ionis... —*see* **ioniz...**
ionization ˌaɪˌən aɪ 'zeɪʃ ᵊn -ɪ'·- ‖ -ə 'zeɪʃ- ~s z
ioniz|e 'aɪˌə naɪz ~ed d ~er/s ə/z ‖ ᵊr/z ~es ɪz
əz ~ing ɪŋ
ionosphere aɪ 'ɒn ə sfɪə ‖ -'ɑːn ə sfɪr
Iorwerth 'jɔː wɜːθ -weəθ ‖ 'jɔːr wᵊrθ —*Welsh*
['jor werθ]
iota aɪ 'əʊt ə ‖ -'oʊt̬ ə ~s z
IOU ˌaɪ əʊ 'juː ‖ -oʊ- ~s, ~'s z
Iowa 'aɪ əʊ ə 'aɪˌə wə ‖ 'aɪ ə wə
Iowan 'aɪ əʊ ən 'aɪˌə wən ‖ 'aɪ ə wən ~s z
IPA ˌaɪ piː 'eɪ
ipecac 'ɪp ɪ kæk -ə-
ipecacuanha ˌɪp ɪ kæk ju 'æn ə ˌ·ə-, -'ɑːn-
Iphigenia ˌaɪf ɪdʒ ɪ 'naɪˌə ˌɪf-, ɪ ˌfɪdʒ-, -ə'·ˌ
iPhone *tdmk* 'aɪ fəʊn ‖ -foʊn ~s z

iPod *tdmk* 'aɪ pɒd ‖ -pɑːd ~s z
Ipoh 'iːp əʊ ‖ -oʊ
ipomoea ˌɪp ə 'miːˌə ˌaɪp- ~s z
ipse dixit ˌɪps i 'dɪks ɪt -eɪ, §-ət
ipsilateral ˌɪps ɪ 'læt̬ˌᵊr əl ◄ ‖ -'læt̬ ər əl
→-'lætr əl
ipso facto ˌɪps əʊ 'fækt əʊ ◄ ‖ -oʊ 'fækt oʊ ◄
Ipsus 'ɪps əs
Ipswich 'ɪps wɪtʃ
IQ ˌaɪ 'kjuː ~s, ~'s z
ˌI'Q test
Iqbal 'ɪk bæl 'ɪg-, -bɑːl —*Arabic* [ɪq 'baːl]
ir- ɪ —*generally stressed only for emphasis or if
the following syllable is unstressed:* ˌɪrre'spective
Ira 'aɪᵊr ə
IRA ˌaɪ ɑːr 'eɪ ‖ -ər-
Irak ɪ 'rɑːk -'ræk
Iraki ɪ 'rɑːk i -'ræk- ~s z
Iran ɪ 'rɑːn -'ræn
Iranian ɪ 'reɪn iˌən aɪᵊ-, -'rɑːn- ~s z
Iraq ɪ 'rɑːk -'ræk ‖ aɪ- —*Arabic* [ʕi 'rɑːq]
Iraqi ɪ 'rɑːk i -'ræk- ‖ aɪ- ~s z
irascibility ɪ ˌræs ə 'bɪl ət i -ˌ·ɪ-, -ɪt i ‖ -ət̬ i
irascib|le ɪ 'ræs əb |ᵊl -ɪb- ~leness ᵊl nəs -nɪs
~ly li
irate aɪᵊ 'reɪt ˌ·'· ◄ ~ly li
ire 'aɪ ə ‖ 'aɪᵊr
ireful 'aɪˌə fᵊl -fʊl ‖ 'aɪˌᵊr- ~ly ̣i ~ness nəs nɪs
Ireland 'aɪˌə lənd ‖ 'aɪˌᵊr-
Iremonger 'aɪˌə ˌmʌŋ gə ‖ 'aɪˌᵊr ˌmʌŋ gᵊr
-ˌmɑːŋ-
Irene 'aɪᵊ riːn aɪᵊ 'riːn i ‖ aɪ 'riːn ˌ·· —*but the
name of the Greek goddess is always* -'riːn i
irenic aɪᵊ 'riːn ɪk -'ren- ~ally ᵊl i
Ireton 'aɪᵊr ə tən ‖ 'aɪˌᵊrt ᵊn
Irian 'New Guinea' 'ɪr iˌən 'ɪər-, -ɑːn
ˌIrian 'Jaya 'dʒaɪˌə 'dʒɑː jə
iridaceous ˌɪr ɪ 'deɪʃ əs ◄ ˌaɪᵊr-, -ə-
iridesc|ence ˌɪr ɪ 'des |ᵊnᵗs -ə- ~ent ᵊnt
iridium ɪ 'rɪd iˌəm aɪᵊ-
iridolog|ist ˌɪr ɪ 'dɒl ədʒ |ɪst ˌ·ə-, §-əst
‖ -'dɑːl- ~ists ɪsts §əsts ~y i
irie 'aɪᵊr i
iris, Iris 'aɪᵊr ɪs §-əs **irises, Iris's** 'aɪᵊr ɪs ɪz
§-əs-, -əz
Irish 'aɪᵊr ɪʃ ~ism ˌɪz əm
ˌIrish 'coffee; ˌIrish 'Sea; ˌIrish 'stew
Irish|man 'aɪᵊr ɪʃ |mən ~men mən men ~ness
nəs nɪs ~ry ri ~woman ˌwʊm ən ~women
ˌwɪm ɪn §-ən
iritis aɪᵊ 'raɪt ɪs §-əs ‖ -'raɪt̬ əs
irk ɜːk ‖ ɜːk **irked** ɜːkt ‖ ɜːkt **irking** 'ɜːk ɪŋ
‖ 'ɜːk ɪŋ **irks** ɜːks ‖ ɜːks
irksome 'ɜːk səm ‖ 'ɜːk- ~ly li ~ness nəs nɪs
Irkutsk ɜː 'kʊtsk ɪə- ‖ ɪr- —*Russ* [ɪr 'kutsk]
Irlam 'ɜːl əm ‖ 'ɜːl-
Irma 'ɜːm ə ‖ 'ɜːm ə
Irnbru *tdmk* 'aɪˌən bruː → ˌəm- ‖ 'aɪˌᵊrn-
iron 'aɪˌən ‖ 'aɪˌᵊrn **ironed** 'aɪˌənd ‖ 'aɪˌᵊrnd
ˌironing 'aɪˌən ɪŋ ‖ 'aɪˌᵊrn ɪŋ **irons** 'aɪˌənz
‖ 'aɪˌᵊrnz

'Iron Age; ,Iron 'Curtain; 'ironing board; 'iron mold, 'iron mould; ,iron 'rations
Ironbridge 'aɪ ən brɪdʒ →-əm- ‖ 'aɪ ˌərn-
ironclad 'aɪ ən klæd →-əŋ- ‖ 'aɪ ˌərn- ~s z
iron-gray, iron-grey ˌaɪ ən 'greɪ ◄ →-əŋ- ‖ ˌaɪ ˌərn-
ironic aɪ ˈrɒn ɪk ‖ -'rɑːn- ~al ᵊl ~ally ᵊl ̩i
ironie... —see **irony**
ironist 'user of irony' 'aɪ ˈr ən ɪst §-əst ~s s
ironmaster 'aɪ ən ˌmɑːst ə →-əm-, §-ˌmæst- ‖ 'aɪ ˌərn ˌmæst ᵊr ~s z
ironmonger 'aɪ ən ˌmʌŋ gə →-əm- ‖ 'aɪ ˌərn ˌmʌŋ gᵊr -ˌmɑːŋ- ~s z
ironmonger|y 'aɪ ən ˌmʌŋ gər ̩i →-əm- ‖ 'aɪ ˌərn- ˌmɑːŋ- ~ies iz
iron-on ˌaɪ ən ɒn ̩·ˈ·◄ ‖ 'aɪ ˌərn ɑːn -ɔːn- ~s z
Ironside 'aɪ ən saɪd ‖ 'aɪ ˌərn- ~s z
ironstone 'aɪ ən stəʊn ‖ 'aɪ ˌərn stoʊn
ironware 'aɪ ən weə ‖ 'aɪ ˌərn wer -wær
ironwood 'aɪ ən wʊd ‖ 'aɪ ˌərn-
ironwork 'aɪ ən wɜːk ‖ 'aɪ ˌərn wɜːk ~s s
irony adj 'like iron' 'aɪ ən i ‖ 'aɪ ˌərn i
iron|y n 'aɪ ˈr ən ̩i ~ies iz
Iroquoian ˌɪr ə 'kwɔɪ ən ◄ ~s z
Iro|quois sing. 'ɪr ə |kwɔɪ -kwɔɪz ~quois pl kwɔɪz kwɔɪ
irradi|ate ɪ 'reɪd i |eɪt ~ated eɪt ɪd -əd ‖ eɪt̬ əd ~ates eɪts ~ating eɪt ɪŋ ‖ eɪt̬ ɪŋ
irradiation ɪ ˌreɪd i 'eɪʃ ᵊn ~s z
irrational ɪ 'ræʃ ᵊn ᵊl ̩ɪ- ‖ ̩ɪr- ~ly i
irrationalit|y ɪ ˌræʃ ə 'næl ət i ̩i ̩ɪ,--, -ɪt i ‖ -ət̬ i ̩i ̩ɪr,-- ~ies iz
Irrawaddy ˌɪr ə 'wɒd i ‖ -'wɑːd i
irrealis ˌɪr i 'ɑːl ɪs §-əs
irreconcilability ɪr ˌek ən ˌsaɪl ə 'bɪl ət i ̩ɪ,--, -ŋ,--, -ɪt i ‖ -ət̬ i
irreconcilab|le ̩ɪr ˌek ən 'saɪl əb |ᵊl ◄ ɪ,--, ̩·'····, →-ŋ'·- ~ly li
irrecoverab|le ˌɪr i 'kʌv ər əb |ᵊl ◄ ̩·ə- ~leness ᵊl nəs -nɪs ~ly li
irredeemability ˌɪr i ˌdiːm ə 'bɪl ət i ̩·ə-, -ɪt i ‖ -ət̬ i
irredeemab|le ˌɪr i 'diːm əb |ᵊl ◄ ̩·ə- ~les ᵊlz ~ly li
irredentism, I~ ̩ɪr i 'dent ̩ɪz əm ̩·ə-
irredentist, I~ ̩ɪr i 'dent ɪst ◄ -ə-, §-əst ‖ -'dent̬ əst ~s s
irreducibility ̩ɪr i ˌdjuː s ə 'bɪl ət i ̩·ə-, →-,dʒuː s-, -ɪt i ‖ -,duː s ə 'bɪl ət̬ i ̩·ə-,djuːs-
irreducib|le ̩ɪr i 'djuː s əb |ᵊl ◄ ̩·ə-, →-'dʒuː s- ‖ -'duː s- -'djuː s- ~leness ᵊl nəs -nɪs ~ly li
irrefutab|le ̩ɪr i 'fjuː t əb |ᵊl ◄ ̩·ə-; ɪ 'ref jʊt-, -'·jət- ‖ ̩ɪr i 'fjuː t̬ əb |ᵊl ◄ i 'ref jət̬-, ̩·ɪ-, ̩ɪr-
— Preference poll, BrE: ·ˈ····· 93%, ·ˈ····· 7%.
~ly li
irregardless ̩ɪr i 'gɑːd ləs ◄ -ə-, -lɪs ‖ -'gɑːrd-
irregular ɪ 'reg jʊl ə ̩ɪ-, -jəl-, §-əl- ‖ -jəl ᵊr ̩ɪr- ~ly li ~s z
irregularit|y ɪ ˌreg jʊ 'lær ət |i ̩i ̩ɪr eg-, -jə'·-, -ɪt i ‖ ɪ ˌreg jə 'lær ət̬ |i ̩i ̩ɪr,--, -'ler- ~ies iz
irrelevanc|e ɪ 'rel əv ᵊn̩ts ̩ɪ-, -'·ɪv- ‖ ̩ɪr- ~ies iz ~y i
irrelevant ɪ 'rel əv ənt ̩ɪ-, -ɪv- ‖ ̩ɪr- ~ly li

IRREFUTABLE

7%
93%
BrE

---

irreligion ̩ɪr i 'lɪdʒ ən ◄ -ə-
irreligious ̩ɪr i 'lɪdʒ əs ◄ -ə- ~ly li ~ness nəs nɪs
irremediab|le ̩ɪr i 'miːd i əb |ᵊl ◄ ̩·ə- ~ly li
irremovab|le ̩ɪr i 'muːv əb |ᵊl ◄ ̩·ə- ~ly li
irreparab|le ̩ɪr i 'rep ər əb |ᵊl §ˌɪr i 'peər əb |ᵊl ◄, ̩·ə- ‖ ̩ɪr-; ̩ɪr i 'per-, -'pær- ~leness ᵊl nəs -nɪs ~ly li
irreplaceable ̩ɪr i 'pleɪs əb |ᵊl ◄ ̩·ə-
irrepressib|le ̩ɪr i 'pres əb |ᵊl ◄ ̩·ə-, -ɪb ᵊl ~leness ᵊl nəs -nɪs ~ly li
irreproachab|le ̩ɪr i 'prəʊtʃ əb |ᵊl ◄ ̩·ə- ‖ -'proʊtʃ- ~leness ᵊl nəs -nɪs ~ly li
irresistibility ̩ɪr i ˌzɪst ə 'bɪl ət i ̩·ə-, -ɪt i ‖ -ət̬ i
irresistib|le ̩ɪr i 'zɪst əb |ᵊl ◄ ̩·ə-, -ɪb ᵊl ~leness ᵊl nəs -nɪs ~ly li
irresolute ɪ 'rez ə luːt ̩ɪ-, -ljuːt ‖ -əl ət ~ly li ~ness nəs nɪs
irresolution ɪ ˌrez ə 'luːʃ ᵊn ̩ɪ rez ə'·-, -'ljuːʃ-
irrespective ̩ɪr i 'spekt ɪv ◄ -ə- ~ly li
irresponsibility ̩ɪr i ˌspɒn̩ts ə 'bɪl ət i ̩·ə-, -ɪ'·-, -ɪt i ‖ -ˌspɑːn̩ts ə 'bɪl ət̬ i
irresponsib|le ̩ɪr i 'spɒn̩ts əb |ᵊl ◄ ̩·ə-, -ɪb ᵊl ‖ -'spɑːn̩ts- ~leness ᵊl nəs -nɪs ~ly li
irretrievab|le ̩ɪr i 'triːv əb |ᵊl ◄ ̩·ə- ~leness ᵊl nəs -nɪs ~ly li
irreverence ɪ 'rev ᵊr ən̩ts ̩ɪ- ‖ ̩ɪr-
irreverent ɪ 'rev ᵊr ənt ̩ɪ- ‖ ̩ɪr- ~ly li
irreversibility ̩ɪr i ˌvɜːs ə 'bɪl ət i ̩·ə-, -ɪ'·-, -ɪt i ‖ -ˌvɜːs ə 'bɪl ət̬ i
irreversib|le ̩ɪr i 'vɜːs əb |ᵊl ◄ ̩·ə-, -ɪb ᵊl ‖ -'vɜːs- ~leness ᵊl nəs -nɪs ~ly li
irrevocability ̩ɪ ˌrev ək ə 'bɪl ət i ̩ɪr i ˌvəʊk-, -ɪt i ‖ -ət̬ i ̩ɪr ˌrev ək ə'·-
irrevocab|le ɪ 'rev ək əb |ᵊl ̩ɪr i 'vəʊk-, ̩·ə- ‖ ̩ɪr-; ̩ɪr i 'voʊk- ~leness ᵊl nəs -nɪs ~ly li
irrigable 'ɪr ɪg əb ᵊl -əg-
irri|gate 'ɪr ɪ |geɪt -ə- ~gated geɪt ɪd -əd ‖ geɪt̬ əd ~gates geɪts ~gating geɪt ɪŋ ‖ geɪt̬ ɪŋ
irrigation ̩ɪr ɪ 'geɪʃ ᵊn -ə- ~al ᵊl ◄
irritability ̩ɪr ɪt ə 'bɪl ət i ̩·ət-, -ɪt i ‖ ̩ɪr ət̬ ə 'bɪl ət̬ i
irritab|le 'ɪr ɪt əb |ᵊl -ət əb- ‖ -ət̬ əb- ~leness ᵊl nəs -nɪs ~ly li
irritant 'ɪr ɪt ənt -ət- ‖ -ət ᵊnt ~s s
irri|tate 'ɪr ɪ |teɪt -ə- ~tated teɪt ɪd -əd ‖ teɪt̬ əd ~tates teɪts ~tating/ly teɪt ɪŋ /li ‖ teɪt̬ ɪŋ /li
irritation ̩ɪr ɪ 'teɪʃ ᵊn -ə- ~s z
irrupt ɪ 'rʌpt ̩ɪ- ‖ ̩ɪr- (usually = erupt) ~ed ɪd əd ~ing ɪŋ ~s s

irruption ɪ ˈrʌp ʃ⁰n ˌɪ- ‖ ˌɪr- **~s** z
irruptive ɪ ˈrʌpt ɪv ˌɪ- ‖ ˌɪr-
Irvine (i) ˈɜːv ɪn §-⁰n ‖ ˈɜːv-, (ii) -aɪn —*The place in Strathclyde is (i), that in CA (ii). As a personal name, usually (i).*
Irving ˈɜːv ɪŋ ‖ ˈɜːv-
Irwell ˈɜː wel ‖ ˈɜː-
Irwin ˈɜː wɪn §-wən ‖ ˈɜː-
is strong form ɪz, weak forms z, s —*After a word ending in* s, z, ʃ, ʒ, tʃ, dʒ *there is no distinct weak form in RP, though in some varieties* §əz *is used. Otherwise, the contracted form* s *may be used after a word ending in* p, t, k, f, θ, *while* z *may be used after one ending in a vowel sound or* b, d, g, v, ð, m, n, ŋ, l *and AmE* r; s *and* z *may be shown in orthography as 's. No contraction is possible when this word is stranded:* is *is always strong and uncontracted in* Tell me what it is.
ISA ˈaɪs ə **ISAs, ISA's** ˈaɪs əz
Isaac ˈaɪz ək
Isaacs ˈaɪz əks
Isabel ˈɪz ə bel
Isabella ˌɪz ə ˈbel ə
Isador, Isadore ˈɪz ə dɔː ‖ -dɔːr -doʊr
Isadora ˌɪz ə ˈdɔːr ə ‖ -ˈdoʊr-
isagogic ˌaɪs ə ˈgɒdʒ ɪk ◂ ‖ -ˈgɑːdʒ- **~s** s
Isaiah aɪ ˈzaɪ ə §-ˈzeɪ ə ‖ aɪ ˈzeɪ ə (*)
Isambard ˈɪz əm bɑːd ‖ -bɑːrd
-isation aɪ ˈzeɪʃ ⁰n ɪ- ‖ ə ˈzeɪʃ ⁰n (*)
— **canonisation** ˌkæn ən aɪ ˈzeɪʃ ⁰n -ən ɪ- ‖ -ən ə-
Isbister (i) ˈaɪz bɪst ə ‖ -ər, (ii) ˈɪz-
ISBN ˌaɪ es bi: ˈen
Iscariot ɪ ˈskær i ət ə- ‖ ɪ ˈsker-
ischaem|ia, ischem|ia ɪ ˈskiːm |i ə ~**ic** ɪk
ischi|um ˈɪsk i |əm **~a** ə **~al** əl
ISDN ˌaɪ es di: ˈen
-ise aɪz —*see also* **-ize**
isenthalpic ˌaɪs en ˈθælp ɪk ◂ ˌaɪz-, -ɪn-, -⁰n-
isentropic ˌaɪs en ˈtrɒp ɪk ◂ ˌaɪz-, -ɪn-, -⁰n- ‖ -ˈtrɑːp ɪk -ˈtroʊp-
Iseult i ˈzuːlt -ˈsuːlt
-ish ɪʃ — **boyish** ˈbɔɪ ɪʃ —*also informally as a separate word, 'approximately, to a certain extent'* ish ɪʃ
Isham ˈaɪʃ əm
Isherwood ˈɪʃ ə wʊd ‖ -⁰r-
Ishiguro ˌɪʃ i ˈgʊər əʊ ‖ -ˈgʊr oʊ
Ishihara ˌɪʃ i ˈhɑːr ə
Ishmael ˈɪʃ meɪ⁰l -mi əl
Ishmaelite ˈɪʃ mi ə laɪt ˈɪʃ meɪ⁰l aɪt; ˈɪʃ mə laɪt, -mɪ- **~s** s
Ishtar ˈɪʃt ɑː ‖ -ɑːr
Isidor, Isidore ˈɪz ə dɔː -ɪ- ‖ -dɔːr -doʊr
isinglass ˈaɪz ɪŋ glɑːs §-glæs ‖ -⁰n glæs -ɪŋ-
Isis ˈaɪs ɪs §-əs
Isla ˈaɪl ə
Islam ˈɪs lɑːm ˈɪz-, -læm, -ləm; ɪs ˈlɑːm, ɪz-, -ˈlæm —*Arabic* [ɪs ˈlɑːm]
Islamabad ɪs ˈlɑːm ə bæd ɪz-, -ˈlæm-, -bɑːd
Islamic ɪs ˈlæm ɪk ɪz-, -ˈlɑːm-

Islam|ism ˈɪs ləm ˌɪz əm ˈɪz-, -lɑːm-, -læm- **~ist/s** ɪst/s §əst/s
Islamophobia ɪs ˌlæm əʊ ˈfəʊb i ə ɪz-, -ˌlɑːm-; ˌ·ˈ·· ‖ -ˈfoʊb-
island ˈaɪl ənd **~ed** ɪd əd **~ing** ɪŋ **~s** z
islander ˈaɪl ənd ə ‖ -⁰r **~s** z
Islay ˈaɪl ə -eɪ
isle aɪ⁰l **isles** aɪ⁰lz
ˌIsle of ˈMan; ˌIsle of ˈWight
islet ˈaɪl ət -ɪt **~s** s
Isleworth ˈaɪz ⁰l wɜːθ -wəθ ‖ -w⁰rθ
Islington ˈɪz lɪŋ tən
Islip (i) ˈaɪs lɪp, (ii) ˈɪz- —*The places in England and NY are (i); the family name is usually (ii)*
Islwyn ˈɪs lu ɪn ɪz ˈluː‿, ɪs- —*Welsh* [ˈɪs lʊɪn, -lu‿ɪn]
ism ˈɪz əm **isms** ˈɪz əmz
-ism ˌɪz əm — **Darwinism** ˈdɑː wɪ ˌnɪz əm -wə- ‖ ˈdɑːr-
Ismaili, Isma'ili ˌɪz mɑː ˈiːl i ◂ ɪz ˈmaɪl i ‖ ˌɪs meɪ ˈɪl i ˌɪz- —*Arabic* [ɪs mɑː ˈʕi liː] **~s** z
Ismailia, Ismailiya ˌɪz maɪ ˈliː‿ə ˌɪs- ‖ ˌɪz meɪ ə ˈliː ə
Ismay ˈɪz meɪ
isn't contracted form ˈɪz ⁰nt
ISO ˌaɪ es ˈəʊ ‖ -ˈoʊ
iso- comb. form
with stress-neutral suffix ˌaɪs əʊ ‖ -oʊ
— **isoseismal** ˌaɪs əʊ ˈsaɪz m⁰l ◂ ‖ -oʊ-
with stress-imposing suffix aɪ ˈsɒ+ ‖ aɪ ˈsɑː+
— **isogonal** aɪ ˈsɒg ən ⁰l ‖ -ˈsɑːg-
isobar ˈaɪs əʊ bɑː ‖ -ə bɑːr **~s** z
isobaric ˌaɪs əʊ ˈbær ɪk ◂ ‖ -ə- -ˈber-
isobath ˈaɪs əʊ bæθ -bɑː θ ‖ ə bæθ **~s** s
Isobel ˈɪz ə bel
isochromatic ˌaɪs əʊ krəʊ ˈmæt ɪk ◂ ‖ ˌaɪs ə kroʊ ˈmæt̬ ɪk ◂
isochronal aɪ ˈsɒk rən ⁰l ‖ -ˈsɑːk- **~ly** i
isochronicit|y aɪ ˌsɒk rə ˈnɪs ət |i ˌaɪs əʊ krə-, -ɪt i ‖ aɪ ˌsɑːk rə ˈnɪs ət̬ |i **~ies** iz
isochronis|e, isochroniz|e aɪ ˈsɒk rə naɪz ‖ -ˈsɑːk- **~ed** d **~es** ɪz əz **~ing** ɪŋ
isochronous aɪ ˈsɒk rən əs ‖ -ˈsɑːk- **~ly** li
isochron|y aɪ ˈsɒk rən |i ‖ -ˈsɑːk- **~ies** iz
isoclinal ˌaɪs əʊ ˈklaɪn ⁰l ◂ ‖ -ə-
isocline ˈaɪs əʊ klaɪn ‖ -ə- **~s** z
isoclinic ˌaɪs əʊ ˈklɪn ɪk ◂ ‖ -ə-
Isocrates aɪ ˈsɒk rə tiːz ‖ -ˈsɑːk-
isogloss ˈaɪs əʊ glɒs ‖ -ə glɑːs -glɔːs **~es** ɪz əz
isohyet ˌaɪs əʊ ˈhaɪ ət -ɪt ‖ -oʊ- **~s** s
iso|late v ˈaɪs ə |leɪt ‖ ˈɪs- **~lated** leɪt ɪd -əd ‖ leɪt̬ əd **~lates** leɪts **~lating** leɪt ɪŋ ‖ leɪt̬ ɪŋ
isolate n, adj ˈaɪs əl ət -ɪt; -ə leɪt ‖ ˈɪs- **~s** s
isolation ˌaɪs ə ˈleɪʃ ⁰n ‖ ˌɪs- **~ism** ɪz əm **~ist/s** ɪst/s §əst/s
isolative ˈaɪs əl ət ɪv -ə leɪt- ‖ ˈaɪs ə leɪt̬ ɪv ˈɪs- **~ly** li
Isolda ɪ ˈzɒld ə ‖ ɪ ˈsoʊld ə -ˈzoʊld ə
Isolde ɪ ˈzɒld ə ‖ ɪ ˈsoʊld ·ˈ·ə —*Ger* [ʔi ˈzɔl də]
isomer ˈaɪs əm ə ‖ -⁰r **~s** z
isomeric ˌaɪs əʊ ˈmer ɪk ◂ ‖ -ə-

isomerism aɪ 'sɒm ə ˌrɪz əm ‖ -'saːm- **~s** z
isometric ˌaɪs əʊ 'met rɪk ◄ ‖ -ə- **~s** s
isomorph 'aɪs əʊ mɔːf ‖ -ə mɔːrf **~s** s
isomorphic ˌaɪs əʊ 'mɔːf ɪk ◄ ‖ -ə 'mɔːrf- **~ally**
ᵊl i
isomorphism ˌaɪs əʊ 'mɔːf ɪz əm ‖ -ə 'mɔːrf-
~s z
Ison 'aɪs ᵊn
isophone 'aɪs əʊ fəʊn ‖ -ə foʊn **~s** z
isopleth 'aɪs əʊ pleθ ‖ -ə- **~s** s
isoprene 'aɪs əʊ priːn ‖ -ə-
isopropyl ˌaɪs əʊ 'prəʊp ɪl ◄ -ᵊl
‖ -ə 'proʊp ᵊl ◄
isosceles aɪ 'sɒs ə liːz -ɪ- ‖ -'saːs-
isospora aɪ 'sɒs ər ə ‖ -'saːsp- **~s** z
isotherm 'aɪs əʊ θɜːm ‖ -ə θɜːm **~s** z
isotonic ˌaɪs əʊ 'tɒn ɪk ◄ ‖ -ə 'taːn-
isotope 'aɪs ə təʊp -əʊ- ‖ -ə toʊp **~s** s
isotopic ˌaɪs əʊ 'tɒp ɪk ◄ ‖ -ə 'taːp- **~ally** ᵊl i
ISP ˌaɪ es 'piː **~s** z
I-Spy, I-spy ˌaɪ 'spaɪ
Israel 'ɪz reɪᵊl 'ɪz riˌəl ‖ 'ɪz riˌəl —in singing
usually 'ɪz reɪ el
Israeli ɪz 'reɪl i **~s** z
Israelite 'ɪz riˌə laɪt 'ɪz reɪᵊl aɪt; 'ɪz rə laɪt, -rɪ-
~s s
Issigonis ˌɪs ɪ 'gəʊn ɪs -ə-, §-əs ‖ -'goʊn-
issuable 'ɪʃ uˌəb ᵊl 'ɪs juˌ, 'ɪʃ juˌ
issuance 'ɪʃ uˌənˤs 'ɪs juˌ, 'ɪʃ juˌ

ISSUE

'ɪʃ uː
'ɪs juː
'ɪʃ juː

BrE

● BrE 'ɪʃ(j)uː by age

Older ◄— Speakers —► Younger

issue 'ɪʃ uː 'ɪs juː, 'ɪʃ juː — Preference poll, BrE:
'ɪʃ uː: 49%, 'ɪs juː: 30%, 'ɪʃ juː: 21%. In AmE
always 'ɪʃ uː. **issued** 'ɪʃ uːd 'ɪs juːd, 'ɪʃ- **issues**
'ɪʃ uːz 'ɪs juːz, 'ɪʃ- **issuing** 'ɪʃ uː ɪŋ 'ɪs juː ɪŋ,
'ɪʃ-
issuer 'ɪʃ uːˌə 'ɪs juːˌə, 'ɪʃ- ‖ ˌ°r **~s** z
Issus 'ɪs əs
Issy 'ɪs i
-ist ɪst §-əst ‖ əst — **machinist** mə 'ʃiːn ɪst
§-əst ‖ -əst
-istan ɪ 'staːn ə-, -'stæn — **Londonistan**
ˌlʌnd ən ɪ 'staːn -ən ə-, -'stæn

Istanbul ˌɪst æn 'bʊl ◄ -aːn-, →-æm-, -'buːl
‖ '··· —Turkish İstanbul [is 'tɑn bul]
Isthmian 'ɪsθ miˌən 'ɪs-, 'ɪst-
isthmus 'ɪs məs 'ɪsθ-, 'ɪst- **~es** ɪz əz
-istic 'ɪst ɪk — **impressionistic**
ɪm ˌpreʃ ə 'nɪst ɪk ◄
istle 'ɪst li
Istria 'ɪs triˌə
Isuzu tdmk i 'suːz uː aɪ- —Jp [i ˌsɯ dzɯ]
it strong form ɪt —There is no distinct weak
form in RP, but in some other varieties,
including most GenAm, there is a weak form
§ət. —The phrases it is, it isn't are often
syllabified irregularly, as ɪ 'tɪz, ɪ 'tɪz ᵊnt.
IT 'information technology' ˌaɪ 'tiː
ITA, i.t.a. ˌaɪ tiː 'eɪ ◄
Italian ɪ 'tæl jən ə- **~s** z
italianate, I~ ɪ 'tæl jə neɪt ə-
italic, I~ ɪ 'tæl ɪk ə-, aɪ- **~s** s
italicis... —see **italiciz...**
italicization ɪ ˌtæl ɪ saɪ 'zeɪʃ ᵊn ə-, aɪ-, -ˌ-ə-,
-sɪ'-- ‖ -ə sə- **~s** z
italiciz|e ɪ 'tæl ɪ saɪz ə-, aɪ-, -ə- **~ed** d **~es** ɪz əz
~ing ɪŋ
Italo- ɪ ˌtæl əʊ ə-; ¦ɪt əl əʊ ‖ ɪ ˌtæl oʊ ¦ɪʈ ᵊl oʊ
— **Italo-German** ɪ ˌtæl əʊ 'dʒɜːm ən ◄
— ¦ɪt əl əʊ- ‖ -oʊ 'dʒɜːm ən ◄ ˌɪʈ ᵊl oʊ-
Italy 'ɪt əl i ‖ 'ɪʈ ᵊl i
Itasca lake in MN aɪ 'tæsk ə
itch ɪtʃ **itched** ɪtʃt **itches** 'ɪtʃ ɪz -əz **itching**
'ɪtʃ ɪŋ
Itchen 'ɪtʃ ɪn -ən
itch|y 'ɪtʃ |i **~ier** iˌə ‖ iˌᵊr **~iest** iˌɪst iˌəst
~iness i nəs i nɪs
ˌitchy 'feet; ˌitchy 'palm
it'd 'it would', 'it had' ɪt əd ‖ ɪʈ əd
-ite aɪt — **Luddite** 'lʌd aɪt
item 'aɪt əm -ɪm, -em ‖ 'aɪʈ əm **~s** z
itemis|e, itemiz|e 'aɪt ə maɪz -ɪ- ‖ 'aɪʈ- **~ed** d
~es ɪz əz **~ing** ɪŋ
ite|rate 'ɪt ə |reɪt ‖ 'ɪʈ- **~rated** reɪt ɪd -əd
‖ reɪʈ əd **~rates** reɪts 'ɪʈ- **~rating** reɪt ɪŋ ‖ reɪʈ ɪŋ
iteration ˌɪt ə 'reɪʃ ᵊn ‖ ˌɪʈ- **~s** z
iterative 'ɪt̬ ˌər ət ɪv 'ɪt ə reɪt- ‖ 'ɪʈ ə reɪʈ ɪv
-ər əʈ- **~ly** li **~ness** nəs nɪs
iterativity ˌɪt̬ ˌər ə 'tɪv ət i -ɪt i
‖ ˌɪʈ ər ə 'tɪv əʈ i
Ithaca 'ɪθ ək ə
Ithon 'aɪθ ɒn ‖ -aːn —Welsh ['əj θon]
ithyphallic ˌɪθ i 'fæl ɪk ◄ ˌaɪθ- **~s** s
-itides pl of **-itis** 'ɪt ɪ diːz -ə- ‖ -'ɪʈ ə diːz
— **meningitides** ˌmen ɪn 'dʒɪt ɪ diːz §ˌ-ən-,
§-'-ə- ‖ -'dʒɪʈ ə diːz
itinerancy aɪ 'tɪn ər ənˤs i ɪ-
itinerant aɪ 'tɪn ər ənt ɪ- **~s** s
itinerar|y aɪ 'tɪn ᵊrˌər |i △-'tɪn ərˌ|i ‖ -ə rer |i
~ies ɪz
-ition 'ɪʃ ᵊn — **opposition** ˌɒp ə 'zɪʃ ᵊn ‖ ˌaːp-
-itious 'ɪʃ əs — **adventitious** ˌæd vən 'tɪʃ əs ◄
-ven-
-itis 'aɪt ɪs §-əs ‖ 'aɪʈ əs — **enteritis**
ˌent ə 'raɪt ɪs §-əs ‖ ˌenʈ ə 'raɪʈ əs

-itive *stress-imposing* ət ɪv ɪt- ‖ əţ ɪv
— **competitive** kəm 'pet ət ɪv -ɪt-
‖ -'peţ əţ ɪv
it'll *'it will'* ɪt ᵊl ‖ ɪţ ᵊl
Itma 'ɪt mɑː
ITN ˌaɪ tiː 'en
-itory *stress-imposing* ət̬ˌər i ɪt̬ˌɪɛ i ‖ ə tɔːr i
ə toʊr i *(*)* — **territory** 'ter ət̬ˌər i '-ɪt̬ˌ
‖ 'ter ə tɔːr i -toʊr i
its ɪts —*non-RP weak form* əts
it's *'it is'; 'it has'* ɪts —*non-RP weak form* əts
itself ɪt 'self §ət-
itsy-bitsy ˌɪts i 'bɪts i ◄
itty-bitty ˌɪt i 'bɪt i ◄ ‖ ˌɪţ i 'bɪţ i ◄
iTunes *tdmk* ˌaɪ tjuːnz →-tʃuːnz, §-tuːnz ‖ -tuːnz
-tjuːnz
ITV ˌaɪ tiː 'viː ◄
-ity *stress-imposing* ət i ɪt i ‖ əţ i — **modernity**
mɒ 'dɜːn ət i mə-, -ɪt i ‖ mɑː 'dɜːn əţ i
IUD ˌaɪ juː 'diː ~s, ~'s z
Ivan 'aɪv ᵊn —*but as a foreign name also*
ˌiː 'væn ◄, ɪ-, -'vɑːn
Ivana ɪ 'vɑːn ə -'væn-
Ivanhoe 'aɪv ᵊn həʊ ‖ -hoʊ
-ive ɪv — **prohibitive** prəʊ 'hɪb ɪt ɪv -ət-
‖ proʊ 'hɪb əţ ɪv
I've *'I have'* aɪv
Iveagh 'aɪv ə -eɪ
Iveco *tdmk* ɪ 'veɪk əʊ aɪ 'viːk- ‖ -oʊ

Ivens 'aɪv ᵊnz
Iver 'aɪv ə ‖ -ᵊr
Ives aɪvz
ivi... —*see* **ivy**
ivied 'aɪv id
Ivor 'aɪv ə ‖ -ᵊr
Ivorian aɪ 'vɔːr i ən ɪ- ~s z
ivor|y, Ivor|y 'aɪv ᵊr ˌi ~ies, ~y's iz
ˌIvory 'Coast; ˌivory 'tower
ivy, Ivy 'aɪv i **ivied** 'aɪv id **ivies** 'aɪv iz
'Ivy ˌLeague
Iwan 'juː ən —*Welsh* ['i wan]
Iwo 'iː wəʊ ‖ -woʊ -wə
ˌIwo 'Jima 'dʒiːm ə —*Jp* [i ˌoo dʑi ma]
ixia 'ɪks i ə ~s z
Ixion ɪk 'saɪ ən
Izaak 'aɪz ək
Izal *tdmk* 'aɪz ᵊl
izard, Izard 'ɪz əd ‖ -ᵊrd ~s z
-ization aɪ 'zeɪʃ ᵊn ɪ- ‖ ə 'zeɪʃ ᵊn *(*)*
— **velarization** ˌviːl ər aɪ 'zeɪʃ ᵊn -ɪ'--
‖ -ə 'zeɪʃ ᵊn
-ize aɪz —*This suffix is unstressed (though
strong) in RP and GenAm, but sometimes
stressed in other varieties* — **velarize**
'viːl ə raɪz §ˌ· ·'·
Izzard, i~ *(i)* 'ɪz əd ‖ -ᵊrd, *(ii)* -ɑːd ‖ -ɑːrd
Izzy 'ɪz i

I

Jj

j Spelling-to-sound

1 Where the spelling is **j**, the pronunciation is regularly dʒ as in **jump** dʒʌmp.

2 Occasionally, in words of foreign origin, it is
ʒ as in **jabot** ˈʒæb əʊ ‖ ʒæ ˈboʊ or
j as in **hallelujah** ˌhæl ɪ ˈluː jə.

3 The sound dʒ is also regularly written **dg** or **g**, as in **hedge** hedʒ,
large lɑːdʒ ‖ lɑːrdʒ.

J

J, j dʒeɪ **Js, J's, j's** dʒeɪz —*Communications
code name:* Juliet
jab dʒæb **jabbed** dʒæbd **jabbing** ˈdʒæb ɪŋ
jabs dʒæbz
jabber ˈdʒæb ə ‖ -ʳr **~ed** d **jabbering**
ˈdʒæb ər ɪŋ **~s** z
jabberer ˈdʒæb ər ə ‖ -ʳr **~s** z
Jabberwock, j~ ˈdʒæb ə wɒk ‖ -ʳr wɑːk **~y** i
Jabez ˈdʒeɪb ez -ɪz
jabiru ˌdʒæb ə ˈruː -ɪ-, ˈ· · ·- **~s** z
jaborandi ˌdʒæb ə ˈrænd i ˌʒæb-, -ræn ˈdiː **~s**
z
jabot ˈʒæb əʊ ‖ ʒæ ˈboʊ —*Fr* [ʒa bo] **~s** z
jacamar ˈdʒæk ə mɑː ˈʒæk- ‖ -mɑːr **~s** z
jacana dʒə ˈkɑːn ə ˈdʒæk ən ə; ˌdʒæs ə ˈnɑː,
ˌʒæs- —*Port* jaçanã [ʒɐ sɐ ˈnɐ̃] **~s** z
jacaranda ˌdʒæk ə ˈrænd ə **~s** z
Jacinta dʒə ˈsɪnt ə —*but as a foreign name also*
hæ- —*Sp* [xa ˈθin ta, -ˈsin-]
jacinth, J~ ˈdʒæs ɪntθ ˈdʒeɪs-, §-ᵊntθ ‖ ˈdʒeɪs-
ˈdʒæs- **~s** s
Jacintha dʒə ˈsɪntθ ə dʒæ-
jack, Jack dʒæk **jacked** dʒækt **jacking**
ˈdʒæk ɪŋ **jacks, Jack's** dʒæks
ˌJack ˈFrost; ˈjack knife; ˈjack plug; ˌJack
ˈRobinson; ˌJack ˈRussell; ˌjack ˈtar; ˌJack
the ˈLad
jackal ˈdʒæk ɔːl -ᵊl ‖ -ᵊl -ɔːl, -ɑːl **~s** z
jackanapes ˈdʒæk ə neɪps
jackaroo ˌdʒæk ə ˈruː **~ed** d **~ing** ɪŋ **~s** z
jackass ˈdʒæk æs -ɑːs **~es** ɪz əz
jack|boot ˈdʒæk| buːt **~booted** buːt ɪd -əd
‖ -buːt̬- **~boots** buːts
jackdaw ˈdʒæk dɔː ‖ -dɑː **~s** z
jackeroo ˌdʒæk ə ˈruː **~ed** d **~ing** ɪŋ **~s** z
jacket ˈdʒæk ɪt §-ət **~s** s
jackfruit ˈdʒæk fruːt **~s** s
jackhammer ˈdʒæk ˌhæm ə ‖ -ʳr **~s** z

Jackie ˈdʒæk i
jack-in-office ˈdʒæk ɪn ˌɒf ɪs §-ən-, §-əs
‖ -ˌɑːf əs -ˌɔːf-
jack-in-the-box ˈdʒæk ɪn ðə ˌbɒks §ˈ·ən-
‖ -ˌbɑːks **~es** ɪz əz
jack-in-the-pulpit ˌdʒæk ɪn ðə ˈpʊlp ɪt
§-ˈpʌlp-, §-ət
jack|knife *n, v* ˈdʒæk |naɪf **~knifed** naɪft
~knifes naɪfs **~knifing** naɪf ɪŋ
Jacklin ˈdʒæk lɪn §-lən
Jackman ˈdʒæk mən
Jacko ˈdʒæk əʊ ‖ -oʊ
jack-of-all-trades ˌdʒæk əv ˈɔːl treɪdz ˌ·ˌ·ˈ·
‖ -ˈɑːl-
jack-o'-lantern ˈdʒæk ə ˌlænt ən ˈ·ˌ·ˌ· ‖ -ʳrn
~s z
jackpot ˈdʒæk pɒt ‖ -pɑːt **~s** s
jackrabbit ˈdʒæk ˌræb ɪt §-ət **~s** s
jacksnipe ˈdʒæk snaɪp **~s** s
Jackson ˈdʒæks ən
Jacksonian dʒæk ˈsəʊn i ˌən ‖ -ˈsoʊn- **~s** z
Jacksonville ˈdʒæks ən vɪl
jack-the-lad ˌdʒæk ðə ˈlæd **~s** z
Jacky ˈdʒæk i
Jacob ˈdʒeɪk əb -ʌb **~'s** z
Jacobean ˌdʒæk əʊ ˈbiː ən ◄ -ə- **~s** z
Jacobethan ˌdʒæk əʊ ˈbiːθ ᵊn ◄ ‖ -ə-
Jacobi *(i)* ˈdʒæk əb i, *(ii)* dʒə ˈkəʊb i
‖ -ˈkoʊb i
jacobian, J~ dʒə ˈkəʊb i ən ‖ -ˈkoʊb- **~s** z
Jacobin ˈdʒæk əb ɪn §-ən **~ism** ˌɪz əm **~s** z
Jacobite ˈdʒæk ə baɪt **~s** s
Jacobs ˈdʒeɪk əbz -ʌbz
Jacobson ˈdʒeɪk əb sən
jacobus, J~ dʒə ˈkəʊb əs ‖ -ˈkoʊb- **~es** ɪz əz
Jacoby *(i)* dʒə ˈkəʊb i ‖ -ˈkoʊb-,
(ii) ˈdʒæk əb i

Jacquard 'dʒæk ɑːd dʒə 'kɑːd ‖ -ɑːrd —Fr [ʒa kaːʁ] **~s** z

Jacqueline 'dʒæk ə liːn -lɪn; 'dʒæk liːn, 'ʒæk-, -lɪn

Jacquelyn 'dʒæk əl ɪn §-ən

Jacques dʒeɪks dʒæks, ʒæk ‖ ʒɑːk —Fr [ʒak]

Jacqui 'dʒæk i

jacuzzi, J~ tdmk dʒə 'kuːz i dʒæ- **~s** z

jade, Jade dʒeɪd **jaded** 'dʒeɪd ɪd -əd **jades** dʒeɪdz **jading** 'dʒeɪd ɪŋ

jadeite 'dʒeɪd aɪt **~s** s

j'adoube ʒæ 'duːb ʒə-, ʒɑː-

jaeger, J~ tdmk 'jeɪg ə 'dʒeɪg- ‖ -ər **~s** z

Jael 'dʒeɪ əl -el

Jaffa, jaffa 'dʒæf ə **jaffas** 'dʒæf əz
  ˌJaffa 'orange

jaffle 'dʒæf əl **~s** z

Jaffna 'dʒæf nə

jag, Jag dʒæg **jagged** v dʒægd **jagging**
  'dʒæg ɪŋ **jags, Jags** dʒægz

Jagan 'dʒeɪg ən

jagged adj 'dʒæg ɪd -əd **~ly** li **~ness** nəs nɪs

Jagger 'dʒæg ə ‖ -ər

jagg|y 'dʒæg |i **~ier** i ə ‖ i ər **~iest** i ɪst i əst

Jago 'dʒeɪg əʊ ‖ -oʊ

jaguar, J~ 'dʒæg ju ə §-ɑː ‖ 'dʒæg wɑːr
  'dʒæg ju ɑːr **~s** z

jaguarondi ˌdʒæg wə 'rɒnd i ˌʒæg- ‖ -'rɑːnd i
  ˌdʒɑːg-, ˌʒɑːg- **~s** z

jaguarundi ˌdʒæg wə 'rʌnd i ˌʒæg- ‖ ˌdʒɑːg-,
  ˌʒɑːg- **~s** z

Jah dʒɑː

jai dʒaɪ —Hindi [dʒæ]

jai alai ˌhaɪ ə 'laɪ ···; ˌhaɪ 'laɪ, ·· ‖ 'haɪ laɪ
  ˌhaɪ ə 'laɪ

jail dʒeɪəl **jailed** dʒeɪəld **jailing** 'dʒeɪəl ɪŋ **jails**
  dʒeɪəlz

jailbait 'dʒeɪəl beɪt

jailbird 'dʒeɪəl bɜːd ‖ -bɜːd **~s** z

jailbreak 'dʒeɪəl breɪk **~er/s** ə/z ‖ ər/z **~s** s

jailer, jailor 'dʒeɪl ə ‖ -ər **~s** z

jailhouse 'dʒeɪəl haʊs

Jaime 'dʒeɪm i —but as a Spanish name,
  'haɪm i —Sp ['xai me]

Jain dʒaɪn dʒeɪn **~ism** ˌɪz əm **~s** z

Jaipur ˌdʒaɪ 'pʊə -'pɔː ‖ 'dʒaɪ pʊr —Hindi
  [dʒəi pʊr]

Jairus 'dʒaɪər əs dʒeɪ 'aɪər əs

Jakarta dʒə 'kɑːt ə ‖ -'kɑːrt ə

Jake, jake dʒeɪk **Jake's, jakes, Jakes** dʒeɪks

Jakobson 'jɑːk əb sən

JAL tdmk dʒæl dʒɑːl

Jalalabad dʒə 'lɑːl ə bɑːd -'læl-, -bæd, ·ˌ··ˈ·
  —Hindi [dʒə lɑː lɑː bɑːd̪]

jalap 'dʒæl əp 'dʒɒl- ‖ 'dʒɑːl-

jalapeno, jalapeño ˌhæl ə 'peɪn jəʊ
  ‖ ˌhɑːl ə 'peɪn joʊ ˌhæl- —Sp [xa la 'pe ɲo]
  ~s z

jalfrezi dʒæl 'freɪz i

jalop|y dʒə 'lɒp |i ‖ -'lɑːp |i **~ies** iz

jalousie 'ʒæl u ziː, ·ˌ·ˈ·; §dʒə 'luːs i ‖ 'dʒæl əs i
  (*) **~s** z

jam dʒæm **jammed** dʒæmd **jamming**
  'dʒæm ɪŋ **jams** dʒæmz
  'jam ˌsession

Jamaica dʒə 'meɪk ə

Jamaican dʒə 'meɪk ən **~s** z

Jamal dʒə 'mɑːl

jamb dʒæm dʒæmb (usually = jam) **jambs**
  dʒæmz dʒæmbz

jambalaya ˌdʒæm bə 'laɪ ə ˌdʒʌm- **~s** z

jamboree ˌdʒæm bə 'riː ◂ **~s** z

Jamelia dʒə 'miːl i ə

James dʒeɪmz **James', James's** 'dʒeɪmz ɪz -əz;
  dʒeɪmz

Jamesian 'dʒeɪm zi ən **~s** z

Jameson 'dʒeɪm sən 'dʒem ɪs ən, 'dʒɪm-,
  'dʒæm-, 'dʒeɪm-, -əs-

Jamestown 'dʒeɪmz taʊn

Jamie 'dʒeɪm i

Jamieson 'dʒeɪm ɪs ən 'dʒem-, 'dʒɪm-, 'dʒæm-

Jamiroquai dʒə 'mɪr ə kwaɪ

jamm... —see jam

jammer 'dʒæm ə ‖ -ər **~s** z

jammies 'dʒæm iz

Jammu 'dʒæm uː 'dʒʌm-

jamm|y 'dʒæm |i **~ier** i ə ‖ i ər **~iest** i ɪst i əst

jam-packed ˌdʒæm 'pækt ◂

Jamshid, Jamshyd ˌdʒæm 'ʃiːd ··, -ʃɪd

Jan dʒæn —but as a male name also jæn ‖ jɑːn
  —and by confusion also ʒɒ̃, ʒæn —Polish,
  Czech, Swedish, Norwegian [jan], Dutch [jɑn]

Jan. dʒæn —see also **January**

Janacek, Janáček 'jæn ə tʃek -ɑː- —Czech
  ['ja naː tʃek]

Jancis 'dʒænˢs ɪs §-əs

Jane dʒeɪn

Janet 'dʒæn ɪt -ət

Janette dʒə 'net dʒæ-

jangl|e 'dʒæŋ gəl **~ed** d **~es** z **~ing** ɪŋ

Janice 'dʒæn ɪs -əs

Janie 'dʒeɪn i

Janine dʒə 'niːn

Janis 'dʒæn ɪs -əs

janissar|y 'dʒæn ɪs ər |i --əs- ‖ -ə ser |i **~ies** iz

janitor 'dʒæn ɪt ə -ət- ‖ -ət ər **~s** z

janitorial ˌdʒæn ɪ 'tɔːr i əl ◂ ˌ-ə- ‖ -'toʊr-

janizar|y 'dʒæn ɪz ər |i '-əz- ‖ -ə zer |i **~ies** iz

Jansen 'dʒænˢs ən **~ism** ˌɪz əm **~ist/s** ɪst/s
  §əst/s

Jansky, j~ 'dʒænˢs ki

Janson 'dʒænˢs ən

Jantzen tdmk 'dʒænts ⁿn 'jænts-

January 'dʒæn ju ər i 'dʒæn jur i,
  §'dʒæn ju er i ‖ -ju er i

Janus 'dʒeɪn əs

Janvrin 'dʒæn vrɪn -vrən

Jap dʒæp **Japs** dʒæps

Japan, japan dʒə 'pæn **~ned** d **~ning** ɪŋ **~s,
  ~'s** z

Japanese ˌdʒæp ə 'niːz ◂
  ˌJapanese 'lantern; ˌJapanese 'maple;
  ˌJapanese 'people

jape dʒeɪp **japes** dʒeɪps

Japhet 'dʒeɪf et -ɪt, §-ət

J

Japheth 'dʒeɪf eθ -ɪθ, §-əθ
Japhetic dʒeɪ 'fet ɪk dʒə- ǁ -'feţ ɪk
japonica dʒə 'pɒn ɪk ə ǁ -'pɑːn- ~s z
Jaques (i) dʒeɪks, (ii) dʒæks —but in
  Shakespeare 'dʒeɪk wɪz
jar dʒɑː ǁ dʒɑːr **jarred** dʒɑːd ǁ dʒɑːrd **jarring**
  'dʒɑːr ɪŋ **jars** dʒɑːz ǁ dʒɑːrz
Jardine 'dʒɑːd iːn ǁ dʒɑːr 'diːn
jardiniere, jardinière ˌʒɑːd ɪn i 'eə
  ˌʒɑːd ɪn ɪ 'jeə ǁ ˌdʒɑːrd ⁱn 'ɪⁱr ˌʒɑːrd-, -'jeⁱr
  —Fr [ʒaʁ di njɛːʁ] ~s z
Jared 'dʒær əd ǁ 'dʒer-
jargon 'dʒɑːg ən ǁ 'dʒɑːrg- -aːn ~s z
jargonistic ˌdʒɑːg ə 'nɪst ɪk ◂ ǁ ˌdʒɑːrg-
jarhead 'dʒɑː hed ǁ 'dʒɑːr- ~s z
Jarlsberg tdmk 'jɑːlz bɜːg ǁ 'jɑːrlz bɜːg
Jarman 'dʒɑːm ən ǁ 'dʒɑːrm-
Jarndyce 'dʒɑːnd aɪs ǁ 'dʒɑːrnd-
Jarrad 'dʒær əd ǁ 'dʒer-
jarrah 'dʒær ə ǁ 'dʒer- ~s z
Jarratt, Jarrett 'dʒær ət -ɪt ǁ 'dʒer-
Jarrold 'dʒær əld ǁ 'dʒer-
Jarrow 'dʒær əʊ ǁ -oʊ 'dʒer-
Jaruzelski ˌjær u 'zel ski ǁ ˌjɑːr- —Polish
  [ja ru 'zel ski]
Jarvik 'dʒɑːv ɪk ǁ 'dʒɑːrv-
Jarvis 'dʒɑːv ɪs §-əs ǁ 'dʒɑːrv-
Jas. dʒæs —see also **James**
jasmine, J~ 'dʒæz mɪn 'dʒæs-, §-mən ~s, ~'s z
Jason 'dʒeɪs ⁿn
jasper, J~ 'dʒæsp ə ǁ -ⁿr ~s, ~'s z
jaundice 'dʒɔːnd ɪs §-əs ǁ 'dʒɑːnd- ~d t
jaunt dʒɔːnt ǁ dʒɑːnt **jaunted** 'dʒɔːnt ɪd -əd
  ǁ 'dʒɔːnţ əd 'dʒɑːnţ- **jaunting** 'dʒɔːnt ɪŋ
  ǁ 'dʒɔːnţ ɪŋ 'dʒɑːnţ- **jaunts** dʒɔːnts ǁ dʒɑːnts
  'jaunting car
jaunt|y 'dʒɔːnt |i ǁ 'dʒɔːnţ |i 'dʒɑːnţ- ~ier i ə
  ǁ i ⁿr ~iest i ɪst i əst ~ily ɪ li əl i ~iness i nəs
  i nɪs
Java 'dʒɑːv ə ǁ 'dʒæv ə —in AmE the computer
  language is 'dʒɑːv ə, and this is also the most
  usual pronunciation for the island; but coffee
  is often 'dʒæv ə, while the places in NY are
  'dʒeɪv ə
Javan 'dʒɑːv ⁿn ǁ 'dʒæv- ~s z
Javanese ˌdʒɑːv ə 'niːz ◂ ǁ ˌdʒæv- ˌdʒɑːv-,
  -'niːs ◂
JavaScript 'dʒɑːv ə skrɪpt ǁ 'dʒæv-
javelin 'dʒæv əl ɪn § ən ~s z
Javits 'dʒæv ɪts §-əts
jaw dʒɔː ǁ dʒɑː **jawed** dʒɔːd ǁ dʒɑːd **jawing**
  'dʒɔːˑ ɪŋ ǁ 'dʒɔːˑ ɪŋ 'dʒɑːˑ
jawbone 'dʒɔː bəʊn ǁ -boʊn 'dʒɑː- ~s z
jawbreaker 'dʒɔː ˌbreɪk ə ǁ -ⁿr 'dʒɑː- ~s z
jawline 'dʒɔː laɪn ǁ 'dʒɑː-
jay, Jay dʒeɪ **jays, Jay's** dʒeɪz
jaybird 'dʒeɪ bɜːd ǁ -bɜːd
Jaycee ˌdʒeɪ 'siː
Jayne dʒeɪn
jaywalk 'dʒeɪ wɔːk ǁ -wɑːk ~ed t ~er/s ə/z
  ǁ ⁿr/z ~ing ɪŋ ~s s
Jaywick 'dʒeɪ wɪk

jazz dʒæz **jazzed** dʒæzd **jazzes** 'dʒæz ɪz -əz
  jazzing 'dʒæz ɪŋ
jazzed-up ˌdʒæzd 'ʌp ◂
jazz|man 'dʒæz| mæn ~men men
jazz|y 'dʒæz |i ~ier i ə ǁ i ⁿr ~iest i ɪst i əst
  ~ily ɪ li əl i ~iness i nəs i nɪs
JCB tdmk ˌdʒeɪ siː 'biː ~s, ~'s z
jealous 'dʒel əs ~ly li ~ness nəs nɪs
jealous|y 'dʒel əs |i ~ies iz
Jean male name, French ʒɒ̃ ǁ ʒɑːn —Fr [ʒɑ̃]
Jean female name dʒiːn
Jeanette dʒɪ 'net dʒə-
Jeanie, Jeannie 'dʒiːn i
Jeannine dʒɪ 'niːn dʒə-
jeans, Jeans dʒiːnz
Jeavons 'dʒev ⁿnz
Jeb, Jebb dʒeb
Jebusite 'dʒeb ju zaɪt ǁ -jə saɪt ~s s
Jed dʒed
Jedburgh 'dʒed bər ə →'dʒeb-
Jedda, Jeddah 'dʒed ə —Arabic ['dʒed da]
Jedediah ˌdʒed ɪ 'daɪ ə ◂ -ə-
Jedi 'dʒed aɪ
jeep, Jeep tdmk dʒiːp **jeeps** dʒiːps
jeepers 'dʒiːp əz ǁ -ⁿrz
jeepney 'dʒiːp ni ~s z
Jeeps dʒiːps
jeer dʒɪə ǁ dʒɪⁿr **jeered** dʒɪəd ǁ dʒɪⁿrd **jeering**
  'dʒɪər ɪŋ ǁ 'dʒɪr ɪŋ **jeers** dʒɪəz ǁ dʒɪⁿrz
Jeeves dʒiːvz
jeez dʒiːz
Jeff dʒef
Jefferies 'dʒef riz
Jeffers 'dʒef əz ǁ -ⁿrz
Jefferson 'dʒef əs ən ǁ -ⁿrs-
Jeffersonian ˌdʒef ə 'səʊn i ən ◂ ǁ -ⁿr 'soʊn-
  ~s z
Jeffery, Jeffrey 'dʒef ri
Jeffreys, Jeffries 'dʒef riz
Jeger 'dʒeɪg ə ǁ -ⁿr
Jehoshaphat dʒɪ 'hɒʃ ə fæt dʒə-, -'hɒs-
  ǁ -'hɑːs-
Jehovah dʒɪ 'həʊv ə dʒə- ǁ -'hoʊv ə ~'s z
  Je,hovah's 'Witness
Jehu 'dʒiː hju: ǁ -hu:
jejune dʒɪ 'dʒuːn dʒə- ~ly li ~ness nəs nɪs
jejunum dʒɪ 'dʒuːn əm dʒə- ~s z
Jekyll (i) 'dʒek ⁿl -ɪl, (ii) 'dʒiːk-
jell dʒel **jelled** dʒeld **jelling** 'dʒel ɪŋ **jells**
  dʒelz
jellaba, jellabah 'dʒel əb ə dʒə 'lɑːb ə ~s z
Jellicoe 'dʒel ɪ kəʊ -ə- ǁ -koʊ
jellie... —see **jelly**
jello, Jello, Jell-O tdmk 'dʒel əʊ ǁ -oʊ ~s z
jell|y 'dʒel |i ~ied id ~ies iz ~ying i ɪŋ
  ˌjellied 'eels; 'jelly ˌbaby; 'jelly bean;
  'jelly roll
jellyfish 'dʒel i fɪʃ ~es ɪz əz
Jemima dʒɪ 'maɪm ə dʒə-
jemm|y, Jemmy 'dʒem |i ~ied id ~ies iz
  ~ying i ɪŋ
Jena 'jeɪn ə —Ger ['je: na]

je ne sais quoi ˌʒə nə seɪ ˈkwɑː —*Fr*
[ʒən sɛ kwa]
jenga ˈdʒeŋ gə
Jenifer ˈdʒen ɪf ə -əf- ‖ -ᵊr
Jenkin ˈdʒeŋk ɪn §-ən
Jenkins ˈdʒeŋk ɪnz §-ənz
Jenkinson ˈdʒeŋk ɪn sən §-ən-
Jenks dʒeŋks
Jenner ˈdʒen ə ‖ -ᵊr
jennet ˈdʒen ɪt §-ət ~**s** s
Jennie ˈdʒen i
jennie... —*see* **jenny**
Jennifer ˈdʒen ɪf ə -əf- ‖ -ᵊr
Jennings ˈdʒen ɪnz
jenny, Jenny ˈdʒen i **jennies, Jenny's**
ˈdʒen iz
Jensen ˈdʒenᵗs ən —*but as a non-English name
also* ˈjenᵗs- —*Danish* [ˈjɛn sən], *German*
[ˈjɛn zᵊn]
Jenůfa ˈjen uːf ə —*Czech* [ˈje nu: fa]
jeopardis|e, jeopardiz|e ˈdʒep ə daɪz ‖ -ᵊr-
~**ed** d ~**es** ɪz əz ~**ing** ɪŋ
jeopardy ˈdʒep əd i ‖ -ᵊrd i
Jephthah ˈdʒefθ ə
jequirity dʒɪ ˈkwɪr ət i dʒə-, -ɪt- ‖ -əṭ i
je'quirity bean
jerboa dʒɜː ˈbəʊ ə dʒə- ‖ dʒᵊr ˈboʊ ə ~**s** z
jeremiad ˌdʒer ɪ ˈmaɪ əd -ə-, -æd ~**s** z
Jeremiah ˌdʒer ɪ ˈmaɪ ə ◀ -ə- ~**s**, ~**'s** z
Jeremy ˈdʒer əm ɪ -ɪm-
Jerez hə ˈrez he-, -ˈreθ, -ˈres —*Sp* [xe ˈreθ]
Jericho ˈdʒer ɪ kəʊ ‖ -koʊ
jerk dʒɜːk ‖ dʒɜːk **jerked** dʒɜːkt ‖ dʒɜːkt
jerking ˈdʒɜːk ɪŋ ‖ ˈdʒɜːk ɪŋ **jerks** dʒɜːks
‖ dʒɜːks
jerkin ˈdʒɜːk ɪn §-ən ‖ ˈdʒɜːk- ~**s** z
jerkwater ˈdʒɜːk ˌwɔːt ə ‖ ˈdʒɜːk ˌwɔːṭ ᵊr
-ˌwɑːṭ ᵊr
jerk|y ˈdʒɜːk |i ‖ ˈdʒɜːk |i ~**ier** i ə ‖ i ᵊr ~**iest**
i ɪst i əst ~**ily** ɪ li əl i ~**iness** i nəs i nɪs
Jermaine dʒə ˈmeɪn ‖ dʒᵊr-
Jermyn ˈdʒɜːm ɪn §-ən ‖ ˈdʒɜːm-
jeroboam, J~ ˌdʒer ə ˈbəʊ əm ‖ -ˈboʊ- ~**s** z
Jerome dʒə ˈrəʊm dʒɪ-, dʒe- ‖ -ˈroʊm
Jerrold ˈdʒer əld
jerr|y, Jerr|y ˈdʒer |i ~**ies, ~y's** iz
ˈjerry can
jerry-|build ˈdʒer i |bɪld ~**builder/s** bɪld ə/z
‖ -ᵊrz ~**building** bɪld ɪŋ ~**builds** bɪldz ~**built**
bɪlt
jersey, J~ ˈdʒɜːz i ‖ ˈdʒɜːz i ~**s** z
ˌJersey ˈCity
Jerusalem dʒə ˈruːs əl əm dʒɪ-, dʒe- ‖ -ˈruːz-
Jeˌrusalem ˈartichoke
Jervaulx ˈdʒɜːv əʊ ‖ ˈdʒɜːv oʊ —*but as a
family name* -ɪs, -əs
Jervis ˈdʒɜːv ɪs ˈdʒɑːv-, §-əs ‖ ˈdʒɜːv-
Jerwood ˈdʒɜː wʊd ‖ ˈdʒɜː-
Jespersen ˈjesp əs ən ˈdʒesp- ‖ -ᵊrs- —*Danish*
[ˈjes bɛ sən]
Jess, jess dʒes **jessed** dʒest (= *jest*) **jesses**
ˈdʒes ɪz -əz **jessing** ˈdʒes ɪŋ
jessamine, J~ ˈdʒes əm ɪn §-ən

Jesse ˈdʒes i —*sometimes also* dʒes
Jessel ˈdʒes ᵊl
Jessica ˈdʒes ɪk ə
Jessie ˈdʒes i
Jessop ˈdʒes əp
jest dʒest **jested** ˈdʒest ɪd -əd **jesting/ly**
ˈdʒest ɪŋ /li **jests** dʒests
jester ˈdʒest ə ‖ -ᵊr ~**s** z
Jesu ˈdʒiːz juː ‖ -uː —*in singing also* ˈjeɪz uː,
ˈjeɪs- ~**'s** z
Jesuit ˈdʒez ju ɪt ˈdʒeʒ-, -u , § ət ‖ ˈdʒeʒ u ət
ˈdʒez- ~**s** s
jesuitic, J~ ˌdʒez ju ˈɪt ɪk ◀ ˈdʒeʒ-, -u-
‖ ˌdʒeʒ u ˈɪt ɪk ◀ ˌdʒez- ~**al** ᵊl ~**ally** ᵊl i
Jesus ˈdʒiːz əs ‖ -əz **Jesus'** ˈdʒiːz əs ‖ -əz
ˌJesus ˈChrist
jet dʒet **jets** dʒets **jetted** ˈdʒet ɪd -əd
‖ ˈdʒeṭ əd **jetting** ˈdʒet ɪŋ ‖ ˈdʒeṭ ɪŋ
ˈjet ˌengine; ˈjet lag; ˌjet proˈpulsion; ˈjet
set; ˈjet stream
jet-black ˌdʒet ˈblæk ◀
jete, jeté ʒə ˈteɪ —*Fr* [ʒə te, ʃte] ~**s** z
jetfoil ˈdʒet fɔɪᵊl ~**s** z
Jethro ˈdʒeθ rəʊ ‖ -roʊ
jet-lagged ˈdʒet lægd
jetliner ˈdʒet ˌlaɪn ə ‖ -ᵊr ~**s** z
jet-propelled ˌdʒet prə ˈpeld ◀
jetsam ˈdʒet səm -sæm
jet-setter ˈdʒet set ə ‖ -seṭ ᵊr
jet-ski, jetski, Jet Ski *tdmk* ˈdʒet ski: ~**ed** d
~**es** z ~**ing** ɪŋ ~**s** z
jettison ˈdʒet ɪs ən -ɪz-, -əs-, -əz- ‖ ˈdʒeṭ- ~**ed**
d ~**ing** ɪŋ ~**s** z
jett|y ˈdʒet |i ‖ ˈdʒeṭ |i ~**ies** iz
Jeuda ˈdʒuːd ə
jeu d'esprit, jeux d'esprit ˌʒɜː de ˈspriː
‖ ˌʒuː- —*Fr* [ʒø dɛs pʀi]
jeunesse dor|ee, ~ée ˌʒɜːn es ˈdɔːr eɪ
ʒɜː ˌnes dɔː ˈreɪ ‖ ʒuː ˌnes dɔː ˈreɪ —*Fr*
[ʒœ nɛs dɔ ʀe, -nɛz-]
Jevons ˈdʒev ᵊnz
Jew dʒuː **Jews** dʒuːz
jewel ˈdʒuː əl dʒuːᵊl ~**led, ~ed** d ~**s** z
Jewel, Jewell ˈdʒuː əl dʒuːᵊl
jeweller, jeweler ˈdʒuː əl ə ˈdʒuːᵊl ə ‖ -ᵊr ~**s** z
jewellery, jewelry ˈdʒuː əl ri ˈdʒuːᵊl ri;
§ˈdʒuːᵊl ər i
Jewess ˈdʒuː es -ɪs, -əs, ˌdʒuː ˈes ‖ -əs ~**es** ɪz əz
Jewett ˈdʒuː ɪt § ət
Jewish ˈdʒuː ɪʃ ~**ness** nəs nɪs
Jewry ˈdʒʊər i §ˈdʒuː ri ‖ ˈdʒuː ri
jew's-harp ˌdʒuːz ˈhɑːp ‖ ˈdʒuːz hɑːrp ˈdʒuːs-
Jewson ˈdʒuːs ᵊn
Jeyes dʒeɪz
Jezebel ˈdʒez ə bel -ɪ-, -bᵊl
Jezreel ˈdʒez ri əl dʒez ˈriːᵊl
Jiang Qing ˌdʒæŋ ˈtʃɪŋ dʒi ˌæŋ- ‖ ˌdʒi ˌɑːŋ-
—*Chi* Jiāng Qīng [¹tɕjaŋ ¹tɕʰiŋ]
Jiangsu ˌdʒæŋ ˈsu: dʒi ˌæŋ- ‖ ˌdʒi ˌɑːŋ- —*Chi*
Jiāngsū [¹tɕjaŋ ¹su]
Jiangxi ˌdʒæŋ ˈʃi: dʒi ˌæŋ- ‖ ˌdʒi ˌɑːŋ- —*Chi*
Jiāngxī [¹tɕjaŋ ¹ɕi]

J

Jiang Zemin ˌdʒæŋ zə ˈmɪn dʒi ˌæŋ-, -zi-
‖ ˌdʒɑːŋ- ˌʒɑːŋ-, dʒi ˌɑːŋ- —*Chi* Jiāng Zémín
[¹tɕjaŋ ²tsɤ ²mɪn]

jib dʒɪb **jibbed** dʒɪbd **jibbing** ˈdʒɪb ɪŋ **jibs**
dʒɪbz

jibe dʒaɪb **jibed** dʒaɪbd **jibes** dʒaɪbz **jibing**
ˈdʒaɪb ɪŋ

jicama ˈhiːk əm ə ˈhɪk-

JICTAR ˈdʒɪkt ɑː ‖ -ɑːr

Jif *tdmk* dʒɪf

jiff dʒɪf **jiffs** dʒɪfs

Jiffi *tdmk* ˈdʒɪf i

jiffy ˈdʒɪf i **jiffies** ˈdʒɪf iz

jig dʒɪg **jigged** dʒɪgd **jigging** ˈdʒɪg ɪŋ **jigs**
dʒɪgz

jigger ˈdʒɪg ə ‖ -ᵊr **~ed** d **~s** z

jiggery-pokery ˌdʒɪg ər i ˈpəʊk ər i ‖ -ˈpoʊk-

jiggl|e ˈdʒɪg ᵊl **~ed** d **~es** z **~ing** ɪŋ

jiggly ˈdʒɪg ᵊl̩ i

jiggy ˈdʒɪg i

jigsaw ˈdʒɪg sɔː ‖ -sɑː **~s** z
ˈjigsaw ˌpuzzle

jihad dʒɪ ˈhæd dʒə-, -ˈhɑːd ‖ -ˈhɑːd **~i/z** i/z
—*Arabic* [dʒɪ ˈhɑːd] **~s** z

jilbab dʒɪl ˈbæb -ˈbɑːb **~s** z —*Arabic*
[dʒɪl ˈbaːb]

Jilin ˌdʒiː ˈlɪn ˈdʒɪl ɪn —*Chi* Jílín [²tɕi ²lɪn]

Jill dʒɪl

jilt dʒɪlt **jilted** ˈdʒɪlt ɪd -əd **jilting** ˈdʒɪlt ɪŋ
jilts dʒɪlts

Jim dʒɪm
ˌjim ˈcrow, Jim ˈCrow law

jim-dandy ˌdʒɪm ˈdænd i ◂

jiminy ˈdʒɪm ən i -ɪm-

jimjams ˈdʒɪm dʒæmz

Jimmi, Jimmie, Jimmy, jimm|y ˈdʒɪm |i
~ies iz

jimson weed ˈdʒɪmᵖs ən wiːd **~s** z

Jin *dynasty* dʒɪn —*Chi* Jīn [³tɕɪn]

Jinan ˌdʒiː ˈnæn ‖ -ˈnɑːn —*Chi* Jínán
[⁴tɕi ²nan]

Jindiworobak ˌdʒɪnd i ˈwɒr ə bæk ‖ -ˈwɔːr-
~s s

jingl|e ˈdʒɪŋ gᵊl **~ed** d **~es** z **~ing** ɪŋ

jingo ˈdʒɪŋ gəʊ ‖ -goʊ **~es** z **~ism** ˌɪz əm
~ist/s ɪst/s §əst/s ‖ əst/s

jingoistic ˌdʒɪŋ gəʊ ˈɪst ɪk ◂ ‖ -goʊ- **~ally** ᵊl̩ i

jinks dʒɪŋks

jinn dʒɪn

Jinnah ˈdʒɪn ə

jinni ˈdʒɪn i dʒɪ ˈniː

Jinnie, Jinny ˈdʒɪn i

jinricksha, jinrikisha dʒɪn ˈrɪk ʃə ˌ-ˌ-, -ˈʃɔː
‖ -ʃə: -ʃɑː —*Jp* [dʒi̥n ri ˈki ça, -ˈri ki-] **~s** z

jinx dʒɪŋks **jinxed** dʒɪŋkst **jinxes** ˈdʒɪŋks ɪz
-əz **jinxing** ˈdʒɪŋks ɪŋ

jipijapa ˌhɪp i ˈhaːp ə **~s** z

jitney ˈdʒɪt ni **~s** z

jitter ˈdʒɪt ə ‖ ˈdʒɪt̬ ᵊr **~ed** d **jittering**
ˈdʒɪt ər ɪŋ ‖ ˈdʒɪt̬ ər ɪŋ **~s** z

jitterbug ˈdʒɪt ə bʌg ‖ ˈdʒɪt̬ ᵊr- **~ged** d **~ging**
ɪŋ **~s** z

jittery ˈdʒɪt ər i ‖ ˈdʒɪt̬-

jiujitsu ˌdʒuː ˈdʒɪts uː —*Jp* [ˈdʒɯɯ dʒɯ tsɯ]

jive dʒaɪv **jived** dʒaɪvd **jives** dʒaɪvz **jiving**
ˈdʒaɪv ɪŋ

jizz dʒɪz

Jnr —*see* **Junior**

Jo, jo dʒəʊ ‖ dʒoʊ

Joab ˈdʒəʊ æb ‖ ˈdʒoʊ-

Joachim ˈjəʊ ə kɪm ‖ ˈjoʊ- —*Ger* [jo ˈʔax ɪm,
ˈjoː ax ɪm]

Joad dʒəʊd ‖ dʒoʊd

Joan dʒəʊn ‖ dʒoʊn

Joanna dʒəʊ ˈæn ə ‖ dʒoʊ-

Joanne ˌ(ˌ)dʒəʊ ˈæn ‖ ˌ(ˌ)dʒoʊ-

job *'employment, task'* dʒɒb ‖ dʒɑːb **jobbed**
dʒɒbd ‖ dʒɑːbd **jobbing** ˈdʒɒb ɪŋ ‖ ˈdʒɑːb ɪŋ
jobs dʒɒbz ‖ dʒɑːbz
ˌjob ˈlot, ˈˌ- ˌ-; ˈjob share

Job *name* dʒəʊb ‖ dʒoʊb **Job's** dʒəʊbz
‖ dʒoʊbz
ˌJob's ˈcomforter; ˌJob's ˈtears

jobber ˈdʒɒb ə ‖ ˈdʒɑːb ᵊr **~s** z

jobbery ˈdʒɒb ər i ‖ ˈdʒɑːb-

Jobcentre ˈdʒɒb ˌsent ə ‖ ˈdʒɑːb ˌsent̬ ᵊr **~s** z

jobholder ˈdʒɒb ˌhəʊld ə →-ˌhʊuld-
‖ ˈdʒɑːb ˌhoʊld ᵊr **~s** z

job-hunt|er/s ˈdʒɒb ˌhʌnt| ə/z
‖ ˈdʒɑːb ˌhʌnt̬ ᵊr/z **~ing** ɪŋ

jobless ˈdʒɒb ləs -lɪs ‖ ˈdʒɑːb- **~ness** nəs nɪs

Jobs *(i)* dʒəʊbz ‖ dʒoʊbz *(ii)* dʒɒbz ‖ dʒɑːbz

job-sharing ˈdʒɒb ˌʃeər ɪŋ ‖ ˈdʒɑːb ˌʃer ɪŋ
-ˌʃær-

Jobson ˈdʒɒb sᵊn ‖ ˈdʒɑːb-

jobsworth ˈdʒɒbz wɜːθ ‖ ˈdʒɑːbz wɜːθ **~s** s

Jo'burg ˈdʒəʊ bɜːg ‖ ˈdʒoʊ bɜːg

Jocasta dʒəʊ ˈkæst ə ‖ dʒoʊ-

Jocelyn ˈdʒɒs lɪn -lən; ˈdʒɒs əl ɪn, -ən
‖ ˈdʒɑːs-

Jock, jock dʒɒk ‖ dʒɑːk **Jock's, jocks** dʒɒks
‖ dʒɑːks

jockey ˈdʒɒk i ‖ ˈdʒɑːk i **~ed** d **~ing** ɪŋ **~s** z

jockstrap ˈdʒɒk stræp ‖ ˈdʒɑːk- **~s** s

jocose dʒəʊ ˈkəʊs ‖ dʒoʊ ˈkoʊs dʒə- **~ly** li

jocosity dʒəʊ ˈkɒs ət i -ɪt- ‖ dʒoʊ ˈkɑːs ət̬ i
dʒə-

jocular ˈdʒɒk jʊl ə -jəl- ‖ ˈdʒɑːk jəl ᵊr **~ly** li

jocularity ˌdʒɒk jʊ ˈlær ət i ˌ-jə-, -ɪt i
‖ ˌdʒɑːk jə ˈlær ət̬ i -ˈler-

jocund ˈdʒɒk ənd ˈdʒəʊk-, -ʌnd ‖ ˈdʒɑːk-
ˈdʒoʊk- **~ly** li

jocundity dʒə ˈkʌnd ət i dʒɒ-, dʒəʊ-, -ɪt-
‖ dʒoʊ ˈkʌnd ət̬ i dʒɑː-

jod jɒd ‖ jɑːd jɔːd, jʊd **jods** jɒdz ‖ jɑːdz jɔːdz,
jʊdz

jodhpurs ˈdʒɒd pəz ‖ ˈdʒɑːd pᵊrz

Jodi, Jodie ˈdʒəʊd i ‖ ˈdʒoʊd i

Jodrell ˈdʒɒdr əl ‖ ˈdʒɑːdr-
ˌJodrell ˈBank

Jody ˈdʒəʊd i ‖ ˈdʒoʊd i

Joe, joe dʒəʊ ‖ dʒoʊ
ˌJoe ˈBloggs; ˌJoe ˈpublic

Joel ˈdʒəʊ əl -el ‖ ˈdʒoʊ-

Joey, joey ˈdʒəʊ i ‖ ˈdʒoʊ i **~s, ~'s** z

jog dʒɒg ‖ dʒɑːg **jogged** dʒɒgd ‖ dʒɑːgd
   jogging 'dʒɒg ɪŋ ‖ 'dʒɑːg ɪŋ **jogs** dʒɒgz
   ‖ dʒɑːgz
   'jog trot

jogger 'dʒɒg ə ‖ 'dʒɑːg ᵊr **~s** z

joggl|e 'dʒɒg ᵊl ‖ 'dʒɑːg- **~ed** d **~es** z **~ing** ɪŋ

Johannesburg dʒəʊ 'hæn ɪs bɜːg §-'hɒn-, -ɪz-
   ‖ dʒoʊ 'hæn əs bɜːg

Johannine dʒəʊ 'hæn aɪn ‖ -ən

John, john dʒɒn ‖ dʒɑːn **John's, johns** dʒɒnz
   ‖ dʒɑːnz
   ,John 'Bull; ,John 'Doe

Johnian 'dʒəʊn i ən ‖ 'dʒoʊn- **~s** z

Johnnie 'dʒɒn i ‖ 'dʒɑːn i

johnn|y, J~ 'dʒɒn |i ‖ 'dʒɑːn |i **~ies** iz

johnnycake 'dʒɒn i keɪk ‖ 'dʒɑːn- **~s** s

johnny-come-late|ly ,dʒɒn i kʌm 'leɪt |li
   ‖ ,dʒɑːn- **~lies** liz

Johnny-on-the-spot ,dʒɒn i ɒn ðə 'spɒt
   ‖ ,dʒɑːn i ɑːn ðə 'spɑːt -ɔːn-·

John o'Groats ,dʒɒn ə 'grəʊts
   ‖ ,dʒɑːn ə 'groʊts

Johns dʒɒnz ‖ dʒɑːnz

Johnson 'dʒɒnᵗs ᵊn ‖ 'dʒɑːnᵗs-

Johnsonian dʒɒn 'səʊn i ən ‖ dʒɑːn 'soʊn-

Johnston *(i)* 'dʒɒnᵗst ən ‖ 'dʒɑːnᵗst-,
   (ii) 'dʒɒnᵗs ᵊn ‖ 'dʒɑːnᵗs-

Johnstone *(i)* 'dʒɒnᵗst ən ‖ 'dʒɑːnᵗst-,
   (ii) 'dʒɒnᵗs ᵊn ‖ 'dʒɑːnᵗs-, *(iii)* 'dʒɒn stəʊn
   ‖ 'dʒɑːn stoʊn

Johor, Johore dʒəʊ 'hɔː ‖ dʒə 'hɔːr -'hoʊr

joie de vivre ,ʒwɑː də 'viːv rə -'viːv —*Fr*
   [ʒwad viːvʁ]

join dʒɔɪn **joined** dʒɔɪnd **joining** 'dʒɔɪn ɪŋ
   joins dʒɔɪnz

joined-up ,dʒɔɪnd 'ʌp ◂

joiner 'dʒɔɪn ə ‖ -ᵊr **~s** z

joinery 'dʒɔɪn ər i

joint dʒɔɪnt **jointed** 'dʒɔɪnt ɪd -əd ‖ 'dʒɔɪn̬t əd
   jointing 'dʒɔɪnt ɪŋ ‖ 'dʒɔɪn̬t ɪŋ **jointly**
   'dʒɔɪnt li

joint-stock ,dʒɔɪnt 'stɒk ·· ‖ -'stɑːk
   ,joint-'stock ,company

joist dʒɔɪst **joists** dʒɔɪsts

Jojo, jo-jo 'dʒəʊ dʒəʊ ‖ 'dʒoʊ dʒoʊ

jojoba həʊ 'həʊb ə ‖ hoʊ 'hoʊb ə —*Sp*
   [xo 'xo βa]

joke dʒəʊk ‖ dʒoʊk **joked** dʒəʊkt ‖ dʒoʊkt
   jokes dʒəʊks ‖ dʒoʊks **joking/ly**
   'dʒəʊk ɪŋ /li ‖ 'dʒoʊk ɪŋ /li

joker 'dʒəʊk ə ‖ 'dʒoʊk ᵊr **~s** z

jok|ey, jok|y 'dʒəʊk |i ‖ 'dʒoʊk |i **~ily** i li əl i
   ~iness i nəs i nɪs

Jolie ʒəʊ 'liː ‖ ʒoʊ-

Joliet *place in IL* ,dʒəʊl i 'et ·· · ‖ ,dʒoʊl-

Jolley, Jollie 'dʒɒl i ‖ 'dʒɑːl i

jolli... —*see* **jolly**

Jolliffe 'dʒɒl ɪf §-əf ‖ 'dʒɑːl-

jollification ,dʒɒl ɪf ɪ 'keɪʃ ᵊn ,-əf-, §-ə'-·
   ‖ ,dʒɑːl- **~s** z

jollity 'dʒɒl ət i -ɪt- ‖ 'dʒɑːl ət̬ i

joll|y, Jolly 'dʒɒl |i ‖ 'dʒɑːl |i **~ied** id **~ier** i ə
   ‖ i ᵊr **~ies** iz **~iest** i ɪst i əst **~ily** ɪ li əl i
   ~iness i nəs i nɪs **~ying** i ɪŋ
   ,Jolly 'Roger

jollyboat 'dʒɒl i bəʊt ‖ 'dʒɑːl i boʊt **~s** s

Jolson 'dʒəʊl sən →'dʒɒʊl-; 'dʒɒl- ‖ 'dʒoʊl-

jolt dʒəʊlt →dʒɒʊlt ‖ dʒoʊlt **jolted** 'dʒəʊlt ɪd
   →'dʒɒʊlt-, -əd ‖ 'dʒoʊlt əd **jolting** 'dʒəʊlt ɪŋ
   →'dʒɒʊlt- ‖ 'dʒoʊlt ɪŋ

jolty 'dʒəʊlt i →'dʒɒʊlt- ‖ 'dʒoʊlt i

Jolyon 'dʒɒl i ən 'dʒɒl- ‖ 'dʒoʊl jən

Jon dʒɒn ‖ dʒɑːn

Jonah, jonah 'dʒəʊn ə ‖ 'dʒoʊn ə

Jonas 'dʒəʊn əs ‖ 'dʒoʊn-

Jonathan 'dʒɒn əθ ən ‖ 'dʒɑːn-

Jones dʒəʊnz ‖ dʒoʊnz **Joneses** 'dʒəʊnz ɪz -əz
   ‖ 'dʒoʊnz əz

Jonesian 'dʒəʊnz i ən ‖ 'dʒoʊnz- **~s** z

Jonestown 'dʒəʊnz taʊn ‖ 'dʒoʊnz-

Jong jɒŋ ‖ jɑːŋ

jongleur ,ʒɒŋ 'glɜː ,dʒɒŋ- ‖ 'dʒɑːŋ glᵊr **~s** z *or
   as sing.* —*Fr* [ʒɔ̃ glœːʁ]

Joni 'dʒəʊn i ‖ 'dʒoʊn i

jonquil 'dʒɒŋk wɪl -wəl ‖ 'dʒɑːŋk- 'dʒɑːn kwəl
   ~s z

Jonson, Jonsson 'dʒɒnᵗs ən ‖ 'dʒɑːnᵗs-

Jools dʒuːlz

Joplin 'dʒɒp lɪn §-lən ‖ 'dʒɑːp-

Jopling 'dʒɒp lɪŋ ‖ 'dʒɑːp-

Joppa 'dʒɒp ə ‖ 'dʒɑːp ə

Jopson 'dʒɒps ən ‖ 'dʒɑːps-

Jordan 'dʒɔːd ᵊn ‖ 'dʒɔːrd-

Jordanhill ,dʒɔːd ᵊn 'hɪl ◂ ‖ ,dʒɔːrd-

Jordanian dʒɔː 'deɪn i ən ‖ dʒɔːr- **~s** z

Jorge 'hɔː heɪ ‖ 'hɔːr- —*Sp* ['xor xe]

Jorrocks 'dʒɒr əks ‖ 'dʒɔːr- 'dʒɑːr-

jorum 'dʒɔːr əm ‖ 'dʒoʊr- **~s** z

José *(i)* həʊ 'zeɪ -'seɪ ‖ hoʊ- —*Sp* [xo 'se], *(ii)*
   'ʒəʊs eɪ 'ʒoʊ 'seɪ —*Fr* [ʒo se]

Joseph 'dʒəʊz ɪf §'dʒəʊs-, -əf ‖ 'dʒoʊz əf
   'dʒoʊs-

Josephine 'dʒəʊz ɪ fiːn §'dʒəʊs-, -ə-
   ‖ 'dʒoʊz ə- 'dʒoʊs-

Josephson 'dʒəʊz ɪf sən 'dʒəʊs-, -əf- ‖ 'dʒoʊz-
   'dʒoʊs-

Josephus dʒəʊ 'siːf əs ‖ dʒoʊ-

josh, Josh dʒɒʃ ‖ dʒɑːʃ **joshed** dʒɒʃt ‖ dʒɑːʃt
   joshes 'dʒɒʃ ɪz -əz ‖ 'dʒɑːʃ əz **joshing**
   'dʒɒʃ ɪŋ ‖ 'dʒɑːʃ ɪŋ

Joshua 'dʒɒʃ ju ə -u ə ‖ 'dʒɑːʃ u ə
   'Joshua tree

Josiah dʒəʊ 'saɪ ə -'zaɪ ə ‖ dʒoʊ-

Josie 'dʒəʊz i ‖ 'dʒoʊz i

joss, Joss dʒɒs ‖ dʒɑːs
   'joss stick

jostl|e 'dʒɒs ᵊl ‖ 'dʒɑːs- **~ed** d **~es** z **~ing** ɪŋ

Jost van Dyke ,jəʊst væn 'daɪk ‖ ,joʊst-

jot dʒɒt ‖ dʒɑːt **jots** dʒɒts ‖ dʒɑːts **jotted**
   'dʒɒt ɪd -əd ‖ 'dʒɑːt̬ əd **jotting** 'dʒɒt ɪŋ
   ‖ 'dʒɑːt̬ ɪŋ

jotter 'dʒɒt ə ‖ 'dʒɑːt̬ ᵊr **~s** z

jotting 'dʒɒt ɪŋ ‖ 'dʒɑːt̬ ɪŋ **~s** z

joule, Joule dʒuːl dʒaʊl, dʒəʊl **~s, ~'s** z

J

jounce dʒaʊnˢs **jounced** dʒaʊnˢst **jounces**
'dʒaʊnˢs ɪz -əz **jouncing** 'dʒaʊnˢs ɪŋ
journal 'dʒɜːn ᵊl ‖ 'dʒɜ˞ːn- ~s z
journalese ˌdʒɜːn ə 'liːz -ᵊl 'iːz ‖ ˌdʒɜ˞ːn ᵊl 'iːz
-'iːs
journalism 'dʒɜːn ə ˌlɪz əm -ᵊl ˌɪz- ‖ 'dʒɜ˞ːn-
journalist 'dʒɜːn əl ɪst §-əst ‖ 'dʒɜ˞ːn- ~s s
journalistic ˌdʒɜːn ə 'lɪst ɪk ◂ -ᵊl 'ɪst-
‖ ˌdʒɜ˞ːn ᵊl 'ɪst ɪk ◂ **~ally** ᵊl i
journey 'dʒɜːn i ‖ 'dʒɜ˞ːn i **~ed** d **~ing/s** ɪŋ/z
~s z
journey|man 'dʒɜːn i |mən ‖ 'dʒɜ˞ːn- **~men**
mən men
journo 'dʒɜːn əʊ ‖ 'dʒɜ˞ːn oʊ **~s** z
joust dʒaʊst **jousted** 'dʒaʊst ɪd -əd **jousting**
'dʒaʊst ɪŋ **jousts** dʒaʊsts
Jove dʒəʊv ‖ dʒoʊv
jovial 'dʒəʊv i əl ‖ 'dʒoʊv- **~ly** i
joviality ˌdʒəʊv i 'æl ət i -ɪt i
‖ ˌdʒoʊv i 'æl ət̬ i
Jovian 'dʒəʊv i ən ‖ 'dʒoʊv-
Jowell (i) 'dʒaʊ əl (ii) 'dʒəʊ əl ‖ 'dʒoʊ- —The
British politician Tessa J~ is (i)
Jowett, Jowitt (i) 'dʒaʊ ɪt -ət, (ii) 'dʒəʊ-
‖ 'dʒoʊ-
jowl dʒaʊl **jowls** dʒaʊlz
-jowled 'dʒaʊld
joy, Joy dʒɔɪ **joys** dʒɔɪz
Joyce dʒɔɪs
joyful 'dʒɔɪf ᵊl 'dʒɔɪ fʊl **~ly** i **~ness** nəs nɪs
joyless 'dʒɔɪ ləs -lɪs **~ly** li **~ness** nəs nɪs
Joyner 'dʒɔɪn ə ‖ -ᵊr
Joynson 'dʒɔɪnˢs ən
joyous 'dʒɔɪ əs **~ly** li **~ness** nəs nɪs
joyrid|e 'dʒɔɪ raɪd **~er/s** ə/z ‖ ᵊr/z **~ing** ɪŋ **~s**
z
joystick 'dʒɔɪ stɪk **~s** s
JP ˌdʒeɪ 'piː- **~s, ~'s** z
jpeg, jpg 'dʒeɪ peg **~s, ~'s** z
Jr —see **Junior**
Juan wɑːn hwɑːn, 'dʒuː ən ‖ hwɑːn —Sp
[xwan]
Juanita wə 'niːt ə xwə-; ˌdʒuː ə 'niːt ə
‖ hwɑː 'niːt̬ ə —Sp [xwa 'ni ta]
jubilant 'dʒuːb ɪl ənt -əl- **~ly** li
Jubilate ˌdʒuːb ɪ 'lɑːt i ˌjuːb-, -ə-, -eɪ ‖ -'leɪt̬ i
~s z
jubilation ˌdʒuːb ɪ 'leɪʒ ᵊn -ə- **~s** z
jubilee 'dʒuːb ɪ liː -ə-, ˌ·'· **~s** z
Judaea dʒu 'dɪə -'diː ə ‖ dʒu 'diː ə
Judaean dʒu 'dɪən -'diː ən ‖ dʒu 'diː ən **~s** z
Judaeo- dʒu ¦diː əʊ -¦deɪ- ‖ -oʊ —
Judaeo-Spanish dʒu ˌdiː əʊ 'spæn ɪʃ ◂ -ˌdeɪ-
‖ -oʊ-
Judah 'dʒuːd ə
Judaic dʒu 'deɪ ɪk **~a** ə **~ally** ᵊl i
judais... —see **judaiz...**
Judaism 'dʒuːd eɪ ˌɪz əm -i-; 'dʒuːd ˌɪz əm
‖ -ə-
judaiz|e 'dʒuːd eɪ aɪz **~ed** d **~es** ɪz əz **~er/s**
ə/z ‖ -ᵊr/z **~ing** ɪŋ
Judas, judas 'dʒuːd əs **~es, 's** ɪz əz
'Judas tree

Judd dʒʌd
judder 'dʒʌd ə ‖ -ᵊr **~ed** d **juddering**
'dʒʌd ər ɪŋ **~s** z
Jude dʒuːd **Jude's** dʒuːdz
Judea dʒu 'dɪə -'diː ə ‖ dʒu 'diː ə
Judean dʒu 'dɪən -'diː ən ‖ dʒu 'diː ən **~s** z
Judeo- dʒu ¦diː əʊ -¦deɪ- ‖ -oʊ
— **Judeo-Spanish** dʒu ˌdiː əʊ 'spæn ɪʃ ◂
-ˌdeɪ- ‖ -oʊ-
judge dʒʌdʒ **judged** dʒʌdʒd **judges** 'dʒʌdʒ ɪz
-əz **judging** 'dʒʌdʒ ɪŋ
judgement 'dʒʌdʒ mənt **~s** s
judgemental dʒʌdʒ 'ment ᵊl ‖ -'ment̬ ᵊl **~ly** i
judgeship 'dʒʌdʒ ʃɪp **~s** s
judgment 'dʒʌdʒ mənt **~s** s
'judgment day
judgmental dʒʌdʒ 'ment ᵊl ‖ -'ment̬ ᵊl **~ly** i
Judi 'dʒuːd i
judicative 'dʒuːd ɪk ət ɪv '·ək- ‖ -ɪ keɪt̬ ɪv
judicature 'dʒuːd ɪk ə tʃə -tjʊə; dʒu 'dɪk-
‖ -ɪ keɪtʃ ᵊr -ɪk ə tʃʊr **~s** z
judicial dʒu 'dɪʃ ᵊl **~ly** i
judiciar|y dʒu 'dɪʃ ər |i -'dɪʃ i ər |i
‖ -'dɪʃ i er |i **~ies** iz
judicious dʒu 'dɪʃ əs **~ly** li **~ness** nəs nɪs
Judith 'dʒuːd ɪθ -əθ
judo 'dʒuːd əʊ ‖ -oʊ —Jp ['dʑɯᵚdo͜o]
Jud|y, jud|y 'dʒuːd |i **~y's, ~ies** iz
jug dʒʌg **jugged** dʒʌgd **jugging** 'dʒʌg ɪŋ
jugs dʒʌgz
jug-eared ˌdʒʌg 'ɪəd ◂ ‖ 'dʒʌg ɪrd
jugful 'dʒʌg fʊl **~s** z
juggernaut, J~ 'dʒʌg ə nɔːt ‖ -ᵊr- -nɑːt **~s** s
juggins 'dʒʌg ɪnz §-ənz
juggl|e 'dʒʌg ᵊl **~ed** d **~es** z **~ing** ɪŋ
juggler 'dʒʌg lə 'dʒʌg ᵊl ə ‖ 'dʒʌg lᵊr -ᵊl ər **~s**
z
jugglery 'dʒʌg lər i
Jugoslav 'juːg əʊ slɑːv ˌ·'· ‖ -oʊ slɑːv -slæv **~s**
z
Jugoslavi|a ˌjuːg əʊ 'slɑːv i |ə ‖ ˌ·oʊ- **~an/s**
ən/z
jugular 'dʒʌg jʊl ə -jəl- ‖ -jəl ᵊr **~s** z
ˌjugular 'vein
Jugurtha dʒu 'gɜːθ ə ju- ‖ -'gɜ˞ːθ ə
juice dʒuːs **juiced** dʒuːst **juices** 'dʒuːs ɪz -əz
juicing 'dʒuːs ɪŋ
juicer 'dʒuːs ə ‖ -ᵊr **~s** z
juic|y 'dʒuːs |i **~ier** i ə ‖ i ᵊr **~iest** i ɪst i əst
~ily ɪ li əl i **~iness** i nəs i nɪs
Juilliard 'dʒuːl i ɑːd ‖ -ɑːd
jujitsu dʒu 'dʒɪts uː ˌdʒuː- —Jp
['dʑɯᵚ dʑi tsɯᵚ]
juju 'dʒuː dʒuː **~ism** ˌɪz əm **~s** z
jujube 'dʒuː dʒuːb uːb i '·ʊb i **~s** z
juke dʒuːk **juked** dʒuːkt **jukes** dʒuːks **juking**
'dʒuːk ɪŋ
jukebox 'dʒuːk bɒks ‖ -bɑːks **~es** ɪz əz
Jukes dʒuːks
julep 'dʒuːl ɪp -ep, -əp **~s** s
Jules dʒuːlz —Fr [ʒyl]
Julia 'dʒuːl i ə ‖ 'dʒuːl jə
Julian 'dʒuːl i ən ‖ 'dʒuːl jən

Juliana ˌdʒuːl i ˈɑːn ə ‖ -ˈæn ə
Julie ˈdʒuːl i
Julien ˈdʒuːl i ən ‖ ˈdʒuːl jən
julienne ˌdʒuːl i ˈen ◂ ˌʒuːl- —*Fr* [ʒy ljɛn]
Juliet *(i)* ˈdʒuːl i ət ‖ ˈdʒuːl jət, *(ii)* ˌdʒuːl i ˈet
ˈ··· —*In Shakespeare, traditionally (i)*
Juliette ˌdʒuːl i ˈet
Julius ˈdʒuːl i əs ‖ ˈdʒuːl jəs
July dʒu ˈlaɪ dʒə-, ˌdʒuː- ~**s** z
jumbl|e ˈdʒʌm bᵊl ~**ed** d ~**es** z ~**ing** ɪŋ
ˈ**jumble sale**
jum|bly ˈdʒʌm |bli ~**blies** bliz
jumbo, Jumbo ˈdʒʌm bəʊ ‖ -boʊ ~**s** z
ˈ**jumbo jet**, ˌ··ˈ·
jumbo-sized ˈdʒʌm bəʊ saɪzd ‖ -boʊ-
JumboTron *tdmk* ˈdʒʌm bəʊ trɒn ‖ -boʊ trɑːn
jumbuck ˈdʒʌm bʌk ~**s** s

JUMPED

               24%   □ dʒʌmpt

    76%

                      □ dʒʌmt

              BrE

---

jump dʒʌmp **jumped** dʒʌmpt — *Preference
poll, BrE* dʒʌmpt *76%,* dʒʌmt *24%.* **jumping**
ˈdʒʌmp ɪŋ **jumps** dʒʌmps
ˈ**jump jet**; ˈ**jump leads**; ˈ**jump seat**
jumped-up ˌdʒʌmpt ˈʌp ◂
jumper ˈdʒʌmp ə ‖ -ᵊr ~**s** z
jumping-off ˌdʒʌmp ɪŋ ˈɒf -ˈɔːf ‖ -ˈɔːf -ˈɑːf
ˌjumping-ˈoff place
jump-off ˈdʒʌmp ɒf -ɔːf ‖ -ɔːf -ɑːf ~**s** s
jump-|start ˈdʒʌmp| stɑːt ˌ·ˈ· ‖ -stɑːrt
~**started** stɑːt ɪd -əd ‖ stɑːrt̬ əd ~**starting**
stɑːt ɪŋ ‖ stɑːrt̬ ɪŋ ~**starts** stɑːts ‖ stɑːrts
jumpsuit ˈdʒʌmp suːt -sjuːt ~**s** s
jump-up ˈdʒʌmp ʌp ~**s** s
jump|y ˈdʒʌmp |i ~**ier** i ə ‖ i ᵊr ~**iest** i ɪst i əst
~**ily** ɪ li əl i ~**iness** i nəs i nɪs
junction ˈdʒʌŋk ʃən ~**s** z
ˈ**junction box**
juncture ˈdʒʌŋk tʃə -ʃə ‖ -tʃᵊr ~**s** z
June dʒuːn **Junes, June's** dʒuːnz
Juneau ˈdʒuːn əʊ dʒu ˈnəʊ ‖ -oʊ
Jung jʊŋ —*Ger* [jʊŋ]
Jungfrau ˈjʊŋ fraʊ —*Ger* [ˈjʊŋ fʀaʊ]
Jungian ˈjʊŋ i ən ~**s** z
jungle ˈdʒʌŋ gᵊl ~**s** z
ˈ**jungle gym**
Juninho dʒu ˈniːn jəʊ ‖ -joʊ —*Port*
[ʒu ˈni ɲu]
junior, J~ ˈdʒuːn i ə ‖ ˈdʒuːn jᵊr ~**s** z
ˌ**Junior ˈCollege**; ˈ**junior school**
juniper ˈdʒuːn ɪp ə -əp- ‖ -ᵊr ~**s** z
Junipero hu ˈniːp ə rəʊ ‖ -roʊ —*Sp* Junípero
[xu ˈni pe ɾo]
Junius ˈdʒuːn i əs ‖ ˈdʒuːn jəs

---

junk dʒʌŋk **junked** dʒʌŋkt **junking** ˈdʒʌŋk ɪŋ
junks dʒʌŋks
ˈ**junk bond**; ˈ**junk food**; ˈ**junk mail**; ˈ**junk
shop**
Junker ˈjʊŋk ə ‖ -ᵊr —*Ger* [ˈjʊŋ kɐ] ~**s** z
junk|et ˈdʒʌŋk |ɪt §-ət ‖ -|ət ~**eted** ɪt ɪd §ət-,
-əd ‖ ət̬ əd ~**eting** ɪt ɪŋ §ət- ‖ ət̬ ɪŋ ~**ets** ɪts
§əts ‖ əts
junkie ˈdʒʌŋk i ~**s** z
Junkin ˈdʒʌŋk ɪn §-ən
junk|y ˈdʒʌŋk |i ~**ies** iz
junkyard ˈdʒʌŋk jɑːd ‖ -jɑːrd ~**s** z
Juno ˈdʒuːn əʊ ‖ -oʊ
Junoesque ˌdʒuːn əʊ ˈesk ◂ ‖ -oʊ-
Junor ˈdʒuːn ə ‖ -ᵊr
junta ˈdʒʌnt ə ˈhʊnt-, ˈdʒʊnt- ‖ ˈhʊnt ə —*Sp*
[ˈxun ta] ~**s** z
Jupiter ˈdʒuːp ɪt ə -ət- ‖ -ət̬ ᵊr
Jura, jura ˈdʒʊər ə ‖ ˈdʒʊr ə —*Fr* [ʒy ʁa]
Jurassic dʒuᵊ ˈræs ɪk
Jurgen, Jürgen ˈjɜːg ən ˈjʊəg- ‖ ˈjɜːg ən —*Ger*
[ˈjʏʁ gᵊn]
juridical dʒuᵊ ˈrɪd ɪk ᵊl ~**ly** i
jurie... —*see* jury
jurisdiction ˌdʒʊər ɪs ˈdɪk ʃᵊn ˈdʒɜːr-, ˈdʒɔːr-,
-əs-, -ɪz-, -əz- ‖ ˌdʒʊr- ~**s** z
jurisprudence ˌdʒʊər ɪs ˈpruːd ᵊn̩ts ˈdʒɜːr-,
ˈdʒɔːr-, -əs-, ˈ·ˌ·· ‖ ˌdʒʊr-
jurist ˈdʒʊər ɪst ˈdʒɜːr-, ˈdʒɔːr-, §-əst ‖ ˈdʒʊr- ~**s**
s
juror ˈdʒʊər ə ˈdʒɜːr-, ˈdʒɔːr- ‖ ˈdʒʊr ᵊr ~**s** z

JURY

                    10%   □ -ʊə-
                    13%   ■ -ɜː-
    77%   □ -ɔː-

             BrE

BrE by age: -●- -ʊə-   -●- -ɔː-   -●- -ɜː-

Percentage (y-axis: 0, 20, 40, 60, 80, 100)

Older ◄——— Speakers ———► Younger

---

jur|y, Jury ˈdʒʊər |i ˈdʒɜːr-, ˈdʒɔːr- ‖ ˈdʒʊr |i
— *Preference poll, BrE* -ʊə- *77%,* -ɜː- *13%,*
-ɔː- *10%.* ~**ies** iz
jury|man ˈdʒʊər i |mən ˈdʒɜːr-, ˈdʒɔːr- ‖ ˈdʒʊr-
~**men** mən men
jurymast ˈdʒʊər i mɑːst ˈdʒɜːr-, ˈdʒɔːr-, -məst,
§-mæst ‖ ˈdʒʊr i mæst —*naut* -məst
jury|men ˈdʒʊər i |mən ˈdʒɜːr-, ˈdʒɔːr-, -men
‖ ˈdʒʊr- ~**woman** ˌwʊm ən ~**women**
ˌwɪm ɪn -ən
jus *'law'* dʒʌs juːs

jussive 'dʒʌs ɪv ~s z
just *advstrong form* dʒʌst dʒəst, dʒest, *weak form* dʒəst §dʒɪst
just *adj* dʒʌst
justic|e, J~ 'dʒʌst ɪs §-əs ~**es** ɪz əz
   ,Justice of the 'Peace
justiciable dʒʌ 'stɪʃ i_əb ᵊl -'stɪʃ əb ᵊl
justiciar|y dʒʌ 'stɪʃ i ər |i -'stɪʃ ər |i ‖ -i er |i ~**ies** iz
justifiability ,dʒʌst ɪ faɪ ə 'bɪl ət i -ɪt i ‖ -əţ i

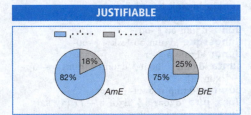

JUSTIFIABLE

18%
82%
AmE

25%
75%
BrE

justifiab|le ,dʒʌst ɪ 'faɪ əb |ᵊl ,-ə-, '·····
— *Preference polls: AmE,* ·'····· *82%,* '·····
18%; BrE, ·'···· *75%,* '····· *25%.* ~**ly** li
justification ,dʒʌst ɪf ɪ 'keɪʃ ᵊn ,-əf-, §-ə-'·· ~**s** z
justificatory 'dʒʌst ɪf ɪ keɪt ər i '-əf-, §'· -ə-,
  ·'···, '·· ɪk ət ər i ‖ dʒʌ 'stɪf ɪk ə tɔːr i
  -tour i; 'dʒʌst əf ə keɪţ ər i
justi|fy 'dʒʌst ɪ |faɪ -ə- ~**fied** faɪd ~**fier/s**
  faɪ ə/z ‖ faɪ ᵊr/z ~**fies** faɪz ~**fying** faɪ ɪŋ
Justin 'dʒʌst ɪn §-ən
Justine 'dʒʌst iːn dʒʌ 'stiːn ‖ dʒʌ 'stiːn —*Fr* [ʒy stin]

Justinian dʒʌ 'stɪn i ən
just-in-time ,dʒʌst ɪn 'taɪm ◄ §-ən-
just|ly 'dʒʌst |li ~**ness** nəs nɪs
jut dʒʌt **juts** dʒʌts **jutted** 'dʒʌt ɪd -əd
  ‖ 'dʒʌţ əd **jutting** 'dʒʌt ɪŋ ‖ 'dʒʌţ ɪŋ
jute, Jute dʒuːt **jutes, Jutes** dʒuːts
Jutland 'dʒʌt lənd —*Danish* Jylland
  ['jyl an?]
Juvenal 'dʒuːv ᵊn əl -ɪn-

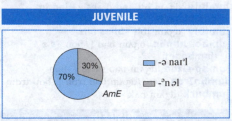

JUVENILE

30%
70%
AmE

⬛ -ə naɪᵊl
⬛ -ᵊn əl

juvenile 'dʒuːv ə naɪᵊl -ɪ- ‖ -ᵊn əl — *Preference poll, AmE:* -ə naɪᵊl *70%,* -ᵊnəl *30%.* ~**s** z
  ,juvenile de'linquent
juvenil|ia ,dʒuːv ə 'nɪl| i ə ,-ɪ- ~**ity** ət i ɪt i
  ‖ əţ i
Juventus ju 'vent əs
juxtapos|e ,dʒʌkst ə 'pəʊz '···
  ‖ 'dʒʌkst ə poʊz ~**ed** d ~**es** ɪz əz ~**ing** ɪŋ
juxtaposition ,dʒʌkst ə pə 'zɪʃ ᵊn ~**s** z
JVC *tdmk* ,dʒeɪ viː 'siː
Jyväskylä 'juːv ə skjuːl ə —*Finnish*
  ['jy væs ky læ]

Kk

K, k keɪ **k's, Ks, K's** keɪz —*Communications code name:* Kilo
Kaaba 'kɑːb ə 'kɑː əb ə
kabaddi kə 'bæd i —*Hindi* [kə bəd̪ d̪i]
Kabaka kə 'bɑːk ə
kabala kæ 'bɑːl ə kə-
Kabardian kə 'bɑɪd i ən ‖ -'bɑːrd-
kabbala, Kabbalah kæ 'bɑːl ə kə-
kabob kə 'bɒb ‖ -'bɑːb ~s z
kaboom kə 'buːm
kabuki kə 'buːk i kæ- —*Jp* [ka ˌbɯ ki]
Kabul 'kɑːb ʊl 'kɔːb-, -ᵊl; kə 'bʊl
Kabyle kə 'baɪᵊl
Kaddish, k~ 'kæd ɪʃ ‖ 'kɑːd-
Kadett *tdmk* kə 'det
Kadima kə 'diːm ə
kaffeeklatsch 'kæf i klætʃ ‖ 'kɔːf- 'kɑːf-
Kaffir 'kæf ə ‖ -ᵊr ~s z
Kaffraria kæ 'freər i ə kə- ‖ -'frer-
Kafir 'kæf ə ‖ -ᵊr ~s z
Kafka 'kæf kə ‖ 'kɑːf- —*Czech, Ger* ['kaf ka]
Kafkaesque ˌkæf kəʳ 'esk ◂ ‖ ˌkɑːf kə-
kaftan 'kæft æn -ɑːn ‖ -ən kæf 'tæn ~s z
Kagan 'keɪg ən
kagoul, kagoule kə 'guːl ~s z
Kahan kə 'hɑːn
Kahlo 'kɑːl əʊ ‖ -oʊ
Kahlua, Kahlúa *tdmk* kə 'luː ə kɑː-
Kahn kɑːn
kahuna kə 'huːn ə ~s z
Kai kaɪ
　Kai 'Tak tæk ‖ tɑːk —*Cantonese* [²kʰəj ¹tɛk]
kail keɪᵊl
kailyard 'keɪᵊl jɑːd ‖ -jɑːrd
kainite 'kaɪn aɪt 'keɪn-
Kaiser 'kaɪz ə ‖ -ᵊr —*Ger* ['kai zɐ] ~s z
Kaiserslautern ˌkaɪz əz 'laʊt ɜːn -ᵊn, '····
　‖ -ᵊrz 'laʊt ᵊrn —*Ger* [kai zɐs 'lau tɐn]
kaka 'kɑːk ɑː -ə ~s z
Kakadu ˌkæk ə 'duː ◂ '···

kakapo 'kɑːk ə pəʊ ‖ -poʊ ~s z
kakemono ˌkæk ɪ 'məʊn əʊ
　‖ ˌkɑːk ə 'moʊn oʊ —*Jp* [ka 'ke mo no]
kala-azar ˌkæl əʳ ə 'zɑː ˌkɑːl- ‖ ˌkɑːl ə ə 'zɑɪr
　kæl-
Kalahari ˌkæl ə 'hɑːr i ◂ ‖ ˌkɑːl-
Kalamazoo, k~ ˌkæl əm ə 'zuː ◂
kalanchoe ˌkæl ən 'kəʊ i →-ᵊn- ‖ -'koʊ i
　kə 'læŋk u i ~s z
Kalashnikov *tdmk* kə 'læʃ nɪ kɒf -nə-
　‖ -'lɑːʃ nɪ kɑːf ~s s
kale keɪᵊl
kaleidoscope kə 'laɪd ə skəʊp ‖ -skoʊp ~s s
kaleidoscopic kə ˌlaɪd ə 'skɒp ɪk ◂ ‖ -'skɑːp-
　~ally ᵊl i
kalends 'kæl endz -ɪndz, -əndz
Kalevala ˌkɑːl ɪ 'vɑːl ə ˌkæl-, -ə-, -ɑː, '····
　—*Finnish* ['ka le va lɑ]
Kalgoorlie kæl 'gʊəl i ‖ -'gʊrl i
kali *plant* 'keɪl aɪ 'kæl i
Kali *Hindu goddess of destruction* 'kɑːl i —*Skt*
　['kɑː liː]
Kalimantan ˌkæl ɪ 'mænt ən -æn
　‖ ˌkɑːl ɪ 'mɑːnt ɑːn
Kalispel, Kalispell 'kæl ə spel -ɪ-, ˌ·'·
kalmia 'kælm i ə ~s z
Kalmuck 'kæl mʌk -mək ~s s
Kalmyk 'kæl mɪk ~s s
Kama 'kɑːm ə
Kamasutra ˌkɑːm ə 'suːtr ə
Kamchatka kæm 'tʃæt kə ‖ kɑːm-, -'tʃɑːt-
　—*Russ* [kʌm 'tʃat kə]
kameez kə 'miːz
Kamen 'keɪm ən
kamikaze ˌkæm ɪ 'kɑːz i ◂ -ə- ‖ ˌkɑːm- —*Jp*
　[ka 'mi ka dze] ~s z
Kampala kæm 'pɑːl ə ‖ kɑːm-
kampong, K~ 'kæm pɒŋ ˌ·'· ‖ 'kɑːm pɔːŋ -pɑːŋ
Kampuche|a ˌkæmp u 'tʃiːˌ|ə **~an/s** ən/z
kana 'kɑːn ə —*Jp* [ka ˌna]

Kanak kə ˈnɑːk -ˈnæk **~s** s
kanaka, K~ kə ˈnæk ə -ˈnɑːk ə; ˈkæn ək ə **~s** z
Kanarese ˌkæn ə ˈriːz ◄ ‖ -ˈriːs ◄
kanban ˈkæn bæn →ˈkæm- —*Jp* [ka͜ˌm baɴ]
Kanchenjunga ˌkæntʃ ən ˈdʒʊŋ gə -ˈdʒʌŋ- ‖ ˌkɑːntʃ-
Kandahar ˌkænd ə ˈhɑː ‖ -ˈhɑːr ˈ· · ·
Kandinsky kæn ˈdɪnᵗsk i —*Russ* [kʌn ˈdʲin skʲij]
Kandy ˈkænd i ‖ ˈkɑːnd i
Kane keɪn
Kanga, kanga ˈkæŋ gə
kangaroo ˌkæŋ gə ˈruː ◄ **~s** z
ˌkangaroo ˈcourt, · ·ˈ· ·
kanji ˈkændʒ i ˈkɑːndʒ i ‖ ˈkɑːndʒ i —*Jp* [ka͜ˌn dʑi] **~s** z
Kannada ˈkɑːn əd ə ˈkæn-
Kano ˈkɑːn əʊ ‖ -oʊ
Kansan ˈkænz ən **~s** z
Kansas ˈkænz əs ˈkænᵗs-
ˌKansas ˈCity ◄, ˌKansas ˌCity ˈsteak
Kant kænt ‖ kɑːnt —*Ger* [kant]
Kantian ˈkænt i ən ‖ ˈkɑːnt- ˈkænt- **~s** z
Kaohsiung ˌkaʊ ˈʃʊŋ -ʃi ˈʊŋ —*Chi* Gāoxióng [¹kɛu ²çjʊŋ]
kaolin ˈkeɪ əl ɪn §-ən
kaon ˈkeɪ ɒn -ɑːn **~s** z
kapellmeister kə ˈpel ˌmaɪst ə kæ- ‖ -ᵊr **~s** z
Kaplan ˈkæp lən
kapok ˈkeɪp ɒk ‖ -ɑːk
Kapoor kə ˈpʊə ‖ kə ˈpʊᵊr
Kaposi kə ˈpəʊz i kæ-, kɑː-, -ˈpəʊs-; ˈkɑːp əʃ i, ˈkæp- ‖ kə ˈpoʊs i ˈkæp əs i —*Hungarian* [ˈkɒ po ʃi]
kappa ˈkæp ə **~s** z
kaput kə ˈpʊt kæ- ‖ kɑː-, -ˈpuːt
kara ˈkʌr ə —*Punjabi* [kə raː]
karabiner ˌkær ə ˈbiːn ə ‖ -ᵊr ˌker- **~s** z
Karachi kə ˈrɑːtʃ i
Karadzic ˈkær ə dʒɪtʃ ‖ ˈkɑːr- —*Serbian* Karadžić [ˈka ɾa dʒitɕ]
Karajan ˈkær ə jɑːn ‖ ˈkɑːr- -jən —*Ger* [ˈka: ʁa jan, ˈka-]
Karakoram, Karakorum ˌkær ə ˈkɔːr əm ‖ ˌkɑːr- -ˈkoʊr-
karakul ˈkær ək ᵊl -ə kʊl ‖ ˈker- **~s** z
karaoke ˌkær i ˈəʊk i -eɪ-, -ə- ‖ -ˈoʊk- ˌker- —*Jp* [ka͜ˌra o ke]
karat ˈkær ət ‖ ˈker- (= *carrot*) **~s** s
karate kə ˈrɑːt i ‖ -ˈrɑːt̬ i —*Jp* [ka͜ˌra te]
Kardomah *tdmk* kɑː ˈdəʊm ə ‖ kɑːr ˈdoʊm ə
karela kə ˈrel ə **~s** z
Kareli|a kə ˈriːl i i |ə **~an/s** ən/z
Karen *female name (i)* ˈkær ən ‖ ˈker-, *(ii)* ˈkɑːr ən
Karen *Myanmar people* kə ˈren ˌkæ- **~s** z
Karenina kə ˈren ɪn ə §-ən- —*Russ* [kʌ ˈrʲe nʲi nə]
Kariba kə ˈriːb ə kæ-
Karin *(i)* ˈkær ɪn -ən ‖ ˈker-, *(ii)* ˈkɑːr-
Karl kɑːl ‖ kɑːrl
Karla ˈkɑːl ə ‖ ˈkɑːrl ə
Karloff ˈkɑːl ɒf ‖ ˈkɑːrl ɔːf -ɑːf

Karlsruhe ˈkɑːlz ruː ə ‖ ˈkɑːrlz- —*Ger* [ˈkaʁls ʁuː ə]
karm|a ˈkɑːm| ə ˈkɜːm|- ‖ ˈkɑːrm| ə —*Hindi* [kərm] **~ic** ɪk
Karnataka kə ˈnɑːt ək ə ‖ kə ˈr ˈnɑːt̬-
Karno ˈkɑːn əʊ ‖ ˈkɑːrn oʊ
Karol ˈkær əl ‖ ˈker-
Karoo kə ˈruː
Karpeles ˈkɑːp ə liːz -ɪ- ‖ ˈkɑːrp-
Karpov ˈkɑːp ɒf -ɒv ‖ ˈkɑːrp ɑːf —*Russ* [ˈkar pəf]
karst kɑːst ‖ kɑːrst
kart kɑːt ‖ kɑːrt **karting** ˈkɑːt ɪŋ ‖ ˈkɑːrt̬ ɪŋ **karts** kɑːts ‖ kɑːrts
karyo- *comb. form*
with stress-neutral suffix ¦kær i əʊ ‖ -ə ¦ker-
— **karyotype** ˈkær i əʊ taɪp ‖ -i ə- ˈker-
with stress-imposing suffix ˌkær i ˈɒ+ ‖ -ˈɑː+ ˌker- — **karyogamy** ˌkær i ˈɒg əm i ‖ -ˈɑːg- ˌker-
kasbah ˈkæz bɑː -bə ‖ ˈkɑːz-
kasha ˈkæʃ ə ˈkɑːʃ- ‖ ˈkɑːʃ ə
Kashmir ˌkæʃ ˈmɪə ◄ ‖ -ˈmɪᵊr ˌkæʒ-; ˈ· ·
Kashmiri kæʃ ˈmɪər i ‖ -ˈmɪr i ˌkæʒ- **~s** z
Kasparov kæ ˈspɑːr ɒf -ɒv; ˈkæsp ə rɒf ‖ -ɑːf -ɔːf —*Russ* [kʌ ˈspa rəf]
kat kæt kɑːt ‖ kɑːt
kata... —*see* **cata...**
katabatic ˌkæt ə ˈbæt ɪk ◄ ‖ ˌkæt̬ ə ˈbæt̬ ɪk ◄ **~s** s
katakana ˌkæt ə ˈkɑːn ə ‖ ˌkɑːt̬- —*Jp* [ka͜ˌta ˈka na, -ˈta ka-]
Katanga kə ˈtæŋ gə ‖ -ˈtɑːŋ-
Katarina ˌkæt ə ˈriːn ə ‖ ˌkæt̬-
Kate keɪt
Katerina ˌkæt ə ˈriːn ə ‖ ˌkæt̬-
Kath kæθ
Katharevousa, Katharevusa, k~ ˌkæθ ə ˈrev ʊs ə -əs ə ‖ ˌkɑːθ- —*ModGk* [ka θa ˈre vu sa]
Katharine, Katherine ˈkæθ ᵊr ɪn §-ᵊr ən
—*but the river and town in N. Terr, Australia, are* -ə raɪn
Kathie ˈkæθ i
Kathleen ˈkæθ liːn ‖ ˌ·ˈ· —*formerly* ˌ·ˈ· *in BrE too*
Kathmandu ˌkæt mæn ˈduː ◄ ˌkɑːt-, -mən-, -mɑːn-
Kathryn ˈkæθ rɪn -rən
Kathy ˈkæθ i
Katie ˈkeɪt i ‖ ˈkeɪt̬ i
Katin ˈkeɪt ɪn §-ᵊn ‖ -ᵊn
Katmai ˈkæt maɪ
Katmandu ˌkæt mæn ˈduː ◄ ˌkɑːt-, -mən-, -mɑːn-
Katowice ˌkæt əʊ ˈviːts ə -ˈvɪts-, -eɪ ‖ -oʊ- -ə- —*Polish* [ka to ˈvi tse]
Katrina kə ˈtriːn ə
Katrine *name of loch* ˈkætr ɪn §-ən
Katy ˈkeɪt i ‖ ˈkeɪt̬ i
katydid ˈkeɪt i dɪd ‖ ˈkeɪt̬- **~s** z
Katyn ˈkæt ɪn ‖ kɑː ˈtiːn kə- —*Russ* [kʌ ˈtinʲ]
Katyusha kə ˈtjuːʃ ə kæ-

Katz kæts
Kauai, Kaua'i kaʊ ˈɑː i —*Hawaiian* [kau a ʔi]
Kaufman ˈkɔːf mən ˈkaʊf- ‖ ˈkɑːf-
Kaunas ˈkaʊn əs —*Lith* [ˈˈkau nas]
Kaunda kɑː ˈʊnd ə -ˈuːnd-
Kaur kɔː ˈkaʊ‿ə ‖ kɔːr ˈkaʊ‿ər
kauri ˈkaʊər i ~**s** z
kava ˈkɑːv ə
Kavanagh *(i)* ˈkæv ən ə, *(ii)* kə ˈvæn ə, *(iii)* ˈkæv ə nɑː
Kawasaki, k~ ˌkaʊ ə ˈsɑːk i ˌkɑː wə- —*Jp* [ka ˌɰa sa ki]
Kay keɪ
kayak ˈkaɪ æk ~**er/s** ə/z ‖ ər/z ~**s** s
Kaye keɪ
kayo ˌkeɪ ˈəʊ ‖ -ˈoʊ ~**ed** d ~**ing** ɪŋ ~**s** z
Kayser Bondor *tdmk* ˌkeɪz ə ˈbɒnd ə ‖ -ər ˈbɑːnd ər
Kazakh kə ˈzæk -ˈzɑːk, ˈkæz æk ‖ kə ˈzɑːk ~**s** s
Kazakhstan ˌkæz æk ˈstɑːn ˌkɑːz-, -ɑːk-, kə ˌzɑːk-, -ˈstæn
Kazan kə ˈzæn -ˈzɑːn —*Russ* [kʌ ˈzanʲ]
kazi ˈkɑːz i ~**s** z
kazoo kə ˈzuː ~**s** z
kbyte ˈkɪl əʊ baɪt ‖ -ə- ~**s** s
KC ˌkeɪ ˈsiː ~**s** z
kea ˈkiː ə ˈkeɪ- ~**s** z
Keady ˈkiːd i
Kean, Keane *(i)* kiːn, *(ii)* keɪn
Keanu ki ˈɑːn uː
Kearney, Kearny *(i)* ˈkɑːn i ‖ ˈkɑːrn i, *(ii)* ˈkɜːn i ‖ ˈkɜːrn i —*The places in NB and NJ are (i); the places in Co. Down and CA are (ii); as family names, both pronunciations are found.*
Keating ˈkiːt ɪŋ ‖ ˈkiːt̬ ɪŋ ~**'s** z
Keaton ˈkiːt ᵊn
Keats kiːts
Keatsian ˈkiːts i ən ~**s** z
Keays kiːz
kebab kɪ ˈbæb kə- ‖ -ˈbɑːb ~**s** z
Keble ˈkiːb ᵊl
kebob kɪ ˈbɒb kə- ‖ -ˈbɑːb ~**s** z
ked ked **keds** kedz
kedge kedʒ **kedged** kedʒd **kedges** ˈkedʒ ɪz -əz **kedging** ˈkedʒ ɪŋ
kedgeree ˌkedʒ ə ˈriː · · · ‖ ˈkedʒ ə riː ~**s** z
Kedleston ˈked ᵊlst ən —*locally also* -ləst-
Kedron ˈkedr ɒn ˈkiːdr-, -ən ‖ ˈkiːdr ən
Keds *tdmk* kedz
Keeble ˈkiːb ᵊl
Keeffe kiːf
Keegan ˈkiːg ən
keel kiːᵊl **keeled** kiːᵊld **keeling** ˈkiːᵊl ɪŋ **keels** kiːᵊlz
Keele kiːᵊl
Keeler ˈkiːl ə ‖ -ər
Keeley ˈkiːl i
keelhaul ˈkiːᵊl hɔːl ‖ -hɑːl ~**ed** d ~**ing** ɪŋ ~**s** z
Keeling ˈkiːl ɪŋ
keelson ˈkels ᵊn ˈkiːᵊls- ~**s** z
keema ˈkiːm ə

keen, Keen kiːn **keened** kiːnd **keener** ˈkiːn ə ‖ -ər **keenest** ˈkiːn ɪst -əst **keening** ˈkiːn ɪŋ **keens** kiːnz
Keenan ˈkiːn ən
Keene kiːn
keenly ˈkiːn li **keenness** ˈkiːn nəs -nɪs
keep kiːp **keeping** ˈkiːp ɪŋ **keeps** kiːps **kept** kept
keep-away ˈkiːp ə ˌweɪ
keeper ˈkiːp ə ‖ -ər ~**s** z
keepie-uppie ˌkiːp i ˈʌp i
keepnet ˈkiːp net ~**s** s
keepsake ˈkiːp seɪk ~**s** s
keeshond ˈkeɪs hɒnd ‖ -hɑːnd ~**s** z
Keewatin ki ˈweɪt ɪn §-ᵊn
kef kef keɪf
keffiya ke ˈfiː ə
Keflavik ˈkef lə vɪk —*Icelandic* Keflavík [ˈcɛp la viːk]
keg keg **kegs** kegz
Kegan ˈkiːg ən
kegger ˈkeg ə ‖ -ər ~**s** z
kegler ˈkeg lə ‖ -lᵊr ~**s** z
Keig kiːg
Keighley *(i)* ˈkiːθ li, *(ii)* ˈkiː li —*The place in WYks is (i); the family or personal name may be either (i) or (ii).*
Keigwin ˈkeg wɪn
Keiller, Keillor ˈkiːl ə ‖ -ər
Keir kɪə ‖ kɪᵊr
Keira ˈkɪər ə ‖ ˈkɪr ə
keister ˈkiːst ə ˈkaɪst ə ‖ -ər ~**s** z
Keitel ˈkaɪt ᵊl
Keith kiːθ
Kekule, Kekulé ˈkek ju leɪ -jə- ‖ ˈkeɪk ə- —*Ger* [ˈkeː ku le]
Kekwick ˈkek wɪk
Keller, k~ ˈkel ə ‖ -ər ~**s** z
Kellett ˈkel ɪt §-ət
Kelley, Kellie ˈkel i
Kellogg ˈkel ɒg ‖ -ɔːg -ɑːg ~**'s** *tdmk* z
Kells kelz
Kelly ˈkel i
keloid ˈkiːl ɔɪd ~**s** z
kelp kelp
kelper ˈkelp ə ‖ -ər ~**s** z
kelp|ie, kelp|y ˈkelp |i ~**ies** iz
Kelsey ˈkels i
Kelso ˈkels əʊ ‖ -oʊ
Kelton ˈkelt ən
Kelvin, k~ ˈkelv ɪn §-ᵊn
Kelvinator *tdmk* ˈkelv ɪ neɪt ə ‖ -ˈə- ‖ -ə neɪt̬ ər
Kelvinside ˌkelv ɪn ˈsaɪd -ᵊn-
Kemble ˈkem bᵊl
Kemp, kemp kemp
'Kemp Town
Kempis ˈkemp ɪs §-əs
Kempson ˈkemps ən
kempt kempt
Kemsley ˈkemz li
ken, Ken ken
Kenco *tdmk* ˈken kəʊ →ˈkeŋ- ‖ -koʊ
Kendal, Kendall ˈkend ᵊl

K

kendo ˈkend əʊ ‖ -oʊ —*Jp* [ˈken doo]
Kendrick ˈkendr ɪk
Keneally kɪ ˈniːl i i kə-, ke-
Kenelm ˈken elm
Kenilworth ˈken ᵊl wɜːθ -ɪl-, -wəθ ‖ -wɜːθ
Kenmare ken ˈmeə ‖ -ˈmeᵊr
Kennebunkport ˌken ə ˈbʌŋk pɔːt ‖ -pɔːrt
   -poʊrt
Kennedy ˈken əd i -ɪd- **~s, ~ˈs** z
kennel ˈken ᵊl **~ed, ~led** d **~ing, ~ling** ɪŋ **~s** z
Kennelly ˈken əl i
Kennet ˈken ɪt -ət
Kenneth ˈken ɪθ -əθ
kenning, K~ ˈken ɪŋ **~s** z
Kennington ˈken ɪŋ tən
Kenny ˈken i
keno ˈkiːn əʊ ‖ -oʊ
Kenosha kɪ ˈnəʊʃ ə kə- ‖ kə ˈnoʊʃ ə
kenosis ke ˈnəʊs ɪs kɪ-, §-əs ‖ -ˈnoʊs-
Kenrick ˈken rɪk
Kensal ˈkens ᵊl ˈkenz-
Kenshole (i) ˈken ʃəʊl →-ʃɒʊl ‖ -ʃoʊl,
   (ii) ˈkenz həʊl →-hɒʊl ‖ -hoʊl
Kensington ˈkenz ɪŋ tən
Kensit ˈkenz ɪt ˈkenˈs-, §-ət
Kensitas *tdmk* ˈkenz ɪ tæs
Kent kent
kentia ˈkent i‿ə **~s** z
Kentigern ˈkent ɪg ən -ɪ gɜːn ‖ ˈkenţ ɪ gɜːrn
Kentish ˈkent ɪʃ
Kenton ˈkent ən ‖ -ᵊn
Kentucky ken ˈtʌk i ˌ-- ‖ kən- (*)
Kenwood ˈken wʊd
Kenworthy ˈken ˌwɜːð i ‖ -ˌwɜːð i
Kenya ˈken jə ˈkiːn- —*Mostly* ˈkiːn- *before
   independence,* ˈken- *since.*
Kenyan ˈken jən ˈkiːn- **~s** z
Kenyatta ken ˈjæt ə ‖ -ˈjɑːţ ə
Kenyon ˈken jən
Keogh, Keough ˈkiː əʊ kjəʊ ‖ ˈkiː oʊ
Keown ˈkiː əʊn kjəʊn, ki ˈəʊn ‖ ki ˈoʊn kjoʊn,
   ˈkiː oʊn
kepi ˈkeɪp i —*Fr* képi [ke pi] **~s** z
Kepler ˈkep lə ‖ -lᵊr —*Ger* [ˈkɛp lɐ]
Keppel ˈkep ᵊl
kept kept
Ker (i) kɜː ‖ kɜːt, (ii) kɑː ‖ kɑːr, (iii) keə ‖ keᵊr
   —*In the US,* (i); *in Scotland,* kɛːr (= iii).
Kerala ˈker əl ə kə ˈrɑːl ə
keratin ˈker ət ɪn §-ən ‖ -ᵊn
keratitis ˌker ə ˈtaɪt ɪs §-əs ‖ -ˈtaɪţ əs
kerato- *comb. form*
   with stress-neutral suffix ˈker ət əʊ ‖ -əţ oʊ
   — **keratoplasty** ˈker ət əʊ ˌplæst i ‖ -əţ oʊ-
   with stress-imposing suffix ˌker ə ˈtɒ +
   ‖ -ˈtɑː + — **keratogenous**
   ˌker ə ˈtɒdʒ ən əs ◄ ‖ -ˈtɑːdʒ-
keratosis ˌker ə ˈtəʊs ɪs §-əs ‖ -ˈtoʊs əs
kerb kɜːb ‖ kɜːb **kerbed** kɜːbd ‖ kɜːbd
   kerbing ˈkɜːb ɪŋ ‖ ˈkɜːb ɪŋ **kerbs** kɜːbz
   ‖ kɜːbz
   ˈkerb ˌcrawler, ˈkerb ˌcrawling
kerbstone ˈkɜːb stəʊn ‖ ˈkɜːb stoʊn **~s** z

kerchief ˈkɜː tʃɪf -tʃəf, -tʃiːf ‖ ˈkɜː- **~s** s
kerching kə ˈtʃɪŋ ‖ kᵊr-
Kerenski, Kerensky kə ˈren sk i —*Russ*
   [ˈkʲe rʲɪn skʲɪj]
kerf kɜːf ‖ kɜːf **kerfs** kɜːfs ‖ kɜːfs
kerfuffle kə ˈfʌf ᵊl ‖ kᵊr-
Kerguelen ˈkɜːg əl ɪn -ɪl-, -ən ‖ ˈkɜːg-
Kermadec ˈkɜːm ə dek ‖ ˈkɜːm-
kermes ˈkɜːm iːz -ɪz ‖ ˈkɜːm-
kermess ˈkɜːm es ‖ ˈkɜːm əs kᵊr ˈmes
kermis ˈkɜːm ɪs §-əs ‖ ˈkɜːm-
Kermit ˈkɜːm ɪt §-ət ‖ ˈkɜːm-
Kermode (i) ˈkɜːm əʊd ‖ ˈkɜːm oʊd,
   (ii) kɜː ˈməʊd ‖ kɜː ˈmoʊd
kern, Kern kɜːn ‖ kɜːn **kerned** kɜːnd ‖ kɜːnd
   kerning ˈkɜːn ɪŋ ‖ ˈkɜːn ɪŋ **kerns** kɜːnz
   ‖ kɜːnz
kernel ˈkɜːn ᵊl ‖ ˈkɜːn ᵊl **~s** z
kerosene, kerosine ˈker ə siːn ˌ·ˈ·
Kerouac ˈker u æk
Kerr (i) kɜː ‖ kɜːt, (ii) kɑː ‖ kɑːr, (iii) keə ‖ keᵊr
   —*In the US,* (i).
kerria ˈker i‿ə **~s** z
Kerrigan ˈker ɪg ən §-əg-
Kerrin ˈker ɪn §-ən
Kerry ˈker i
kersey, K~ ˈkɜːz i ‖ ˈkɜːz i **~s** z
Kershaw ˈkɜː ʃɔː ‖ ˈkɜː- -ʃɑː
kerygma kə ˈrɪg mə
Kes kes
kesh *'Sikh beard and hair'* keɪʃ
Kesh keʃ
Kesteven ke ˈstiːv ᵊn kɪ-; ˈkest ɪv ən, -əv-
Keston ˈkest ən
kestrel ˈkes trəl **~s** z
Keswick *place in Cumbria* ˈkez ɪk
Keswick *family name(i)* ˈkez ɪk, (ii) -wɪk
ketamine ˈket ə miːn ‖ ˈkeţ-
ketch, Ketch ketʃ **ketches** ˈketʃ ɪz -əz
Ketchikan ˈketʃ ɪ kæn -ə-
ketchup ˈketʃ əp -ʌp **~s** s
ketone ˈkiːt əʊn ‖ -oʊn **~s** z
ketonuria ˌkiːt əʊ ˈnjʊər i ə ‖ -oʊ ˈnʊr- -ˈnjʊr-
ketosis kiː ˈtəʊs ɪs kɪ-, §-əs ‖ -ˈtoʊs əs
Kettering ˈket ər ɪŋ ‖ ˈkeţ ər ɪŋ
kettle, K~ ˈket ᵊl ‖ ˈkeţ ᵊl **~s** z
kettledrum ˈket ᵊl drʌm ‖ ˈkeţ- **~s** z
Kettley ˈket li
Ketton ˈket ᵊn
Kev kev
Kevin ˈkev ɪn §-ᵊn
kevlar, K~ *tdmk* ˈkev lɑː ‖ -lɑːr
Kevorkian kə ˈvɔːk i_ən ‖ -ˈvɔːrk-
Kew kjuː
   ˌKew ˈGardens
kewpie, K~ *tdmk* ˈkjuːp i
kex keks
key, Key kiː **keyed** kiːd **keying** ˈkiː ɪŋ **keys**
   kiːz
   ˌkeyed ˈup ◄; ˈkey ˌmoney; ˈkey ring; ˈkey
   ˌsignature; ˌKey ˈWest

keyboard 'kiː bɔːd ‖ -bɔːrd -boʊrd **~ed** ɪd əd **~er/s** ə/z ‖ ³r/z **~ing** ɪŋ **~ist/s** ɪst/s §əst/s **~s** z

Keyes kiːz

keyholder 'kiː ˌhəʊld ə →-ˌhɒʊld ə ‖ -ˌhoʊld ³r **~s** z

keyhole 'kiː həʊl →-hɒʊl ‖ -hoʊl **~s** z

keylog|ger 'kiː ˌlɒg ə ‖ -ˌlɔːg ³r -ˌlɑːg- **~gers** əz ‖ ³rz **~ging** ɪŋ

Keynes (i) keɪnz, (ii) kiːnz —as a family name, and for the economist, usually (i); in the placename Horsted K~, (i), but in Milton K~, (ii).

Keynesian 'keɪnz i ən **~ism** ˌɪz əm **~s** z

keynote 'kiː nəʊt ‖ -noʊt **~s** s

Keynsham 'keɪn ʃəm

Keyonna ki 'ɒn ə ‖ -'ɑːn ə

keypad 'kiː pæd **~s** z

keypal 'kiː pæl **~s** z

keypunch 'kiː pʌntʃ **~ed** t **~es** ɪz əz **~ing** ɪŋ

Keyser (i) 'kiːz ə ‖ -³r, (ii) kaɪz-

keystone 'kiː stəʊn ‖ -stoʊn **~s** z

keystroke 'kiː strəʊk ‖ -stroʊk **~s** s

keyword 'kiː wɜːd ‖ -wɜːd **~s** z

kg sing. 'kɪl ə græm ~ pl z

Khachaturian ˌkætʃ ə 'tʊər i ən ˌkɑːtʃ-, -'tjʊər- ‖ ˌkɑːtʃ ə 'tʊr- —Russ [xə tʃɪ tu 'rʲan]

khaki 'kɑːk i ‖ 'kæk i **~s** z

Khalid 'kɑːl ɪd —Arabic ['xaː lɪd]

khalif 'keɪl ɪf 'kæl-, §-əf; kæ 'liːf **~s** s

khalifate 'kæl ɪ feɪt 'keɪl-, -ə- **~s** s

Khalsa 'kʌls ə —Hindi-Urdu [kʰəl saː]

Khamenei, Khamene'i ˌkɑːm ə 'neɪ -neɪ 'iː —Farsi [xɑː me neʔ 'iː]

khan, Khan kɑːn **khans** kɑːnz

khanate 'kɑːn eɪt **~s** s

Khartoum, Khartum ˌkɑː 'tuːm kɑː- ‖ ₍ˌ₎kɑːr- —Arabic [xɑr 'tˤuːm]

Khayyam kaɪ 'æm -'ɑːm ‖ -'jɑːm

khazi 'kɑːz i **~s** z

khedive, K~ kɪ 'diːv kə-, ke- **~s** z

Khmer kmeə kə 'meə ‖ kə 'me³r **Khmers** kmeəz kə 'meəz ‖ kə 'me³rz

Khoisan ˌkɔɪ 'saːn -'sæn

Khomeini kɒ 'meɪn i kəʊ-, həʊ- ‖ koʊ- kə-

Khrushchev 'krʊs tʃɒf 'krʊʃ-, ·'· ‖ 'kruːs tʃef -tʃɔːf, -tʃɑːf, ·'· —Russ [xru 'ɕtɕɵf]

Khyber 'kaɪb ə ‖ -³r
   ˌKhyber 'Pass

kHz 'kɪl əʊ hɜːts ‖ -ə hɜːts

kiang ki 'æŋ 'kiː æŋ ‖ -'ɑːŋ 'kiː æŋ, -ɑŋ **~s** z

Kia-Ora tdmk ˌkiː ə 'ɔːr ə

kibbl|e 'kɪb ³l **~ed** d **~es** z **~ing** ɪŋ

kibbutz kɪ 'bʊts **kibbutzim** ˌkɪb ʊt 'siːm

kibitz 'kɪb ɪts **~ed** t **~er/s** ə/z ‖ ³r/z **~es** ɪz əz **~ing** ɪŋ

kibla, kiblah 'kɪb lə —Arabic ['qɪb lah]

kibosh 'kaɪ bɒʃ ‖ -bɑːʃ

kick kɪk **kicked** kɪkt **kicking/s** 'kɪk ɪŋ/z **kicks** kɪks

kickabout 'kɪk ə ˌbaʊt **~s** s

Kickapoo 'kɪk ə puː **~s** z

kick-ass 'kɪk æs

kickback 'kɪk bæk **~s** s

kickball 'kɪk bɔːl ‖ -baːl

kickbox|er 'kɪk ˌbɒks| ə ‖ -ˌbɑːks| ³r **~ers** əz ‖ ³rz **~ing** ɪŋ

kickdown 'kɪk daʊn

kicker 'kɪk ə ‖ -³r **~s** z

kickflare 'kɪk fleə ‖ -fler **~s** z

kickflip 'kɪk flɪp **~s** s

kick-off 'kɪk ɒf -ɔːf ‖ -ɔːf -ɑːf **~s** s

kickshaw 'kɪk ʃɔː ‖ -ʃɑː **~s** z

kickstand 'kɪk stænd **~s** z

kick-|start 'kɪk |stɑːt ˌ·'· ‖ -|stɑːrt **~started** stɑːt ɪd -əd ‖ stɑːrt̬ əd **~starting** stɑːt ɪŋ ‖ stɑːrt̬ ɪŋ **~starts** stɑːts ‖ stɑːrts

kicky 'kɪk i

kid kɪd **kidded** 'kɪd ɪd -əd **kidding** 'kɪd ɪŋ **kids** kɪdz
   ˌkid 'gloves

Kidd kɪd

kidder 'kɪd ə ‖ -³r **~s** z

Kidderminster 'kɪd ə ˌmɪnst ə ‖ -³r ˌmɪn'st ³r

kiddie 'kɪd i **~s** z

kiddie-cam 'kɪd i kæm

kiddo 'kɪd əʊ

kidd|y 'kɪd |i **~ies** iz

kid-glove ˌkɪd 'glʌv ◂ →ˌkɪg-

Kidlington 'kɪd lɪŋ tən

Kidman 'kɪd mən

kidnap 'kɪd næp **~ed, ~ped** t **~er/s, ~per/s** ə/z ‖ ³r/z **~ing, ~ping** ɪŋ **~s** s

kidney 'kɪd ni **~s** z
   'kidney bean; 'kidney maˌchine; 'kidney stone

kidney-shaped 'kɪd ni ʃeɪpt

Kidsgrove 'kɪdz grəʊv ‖ -groʊv

kidskin 'kɪd skɪn

kidult 'kɪd ʌlt **~s** s

Kidwelly kɪd 'wel i

Kiel kiː³l —Ger [kiːl]

kielbasa kiː³l 'baːs ə kɪl-, -'bæs- —Polish kiełbasa [kʲew 'ba sa]

Kielder 'kiː³ld ə ‖ -³r

Kieran, Kieron 'kɪər ən ‖ 'kɪr-

Kierkegaard 'kɪək ə gɑːd ‖ 'kɪrk ə gɑːrd -ɪ- —Danish ['kiʁ gə gɔːʔʁ]

kieselguhr 'kiːz ³l gʊə ‖ -gʊr

Kiev, ki|ev 'kiː |ev -|ef, ·'· **~s** evz efs —Russ ['kʲi jɪf], Ukrainian Kyiv ['kɪ jɪf]

Kigali kɪ 'gaːl i kə-

kike kaɪk **kikes** kaɪks

Kikuyu kɪ 'kuː juː **~s** z

Kilauea ˌkɪl ə 'weɪ ə ˌkiːl aʊ 'eɪ ə

Kilbracken kɪl 'bræk ən

Kilbride kɪl 'braɪd

Kilburn 'kɪlb ən 'kɪl bɜːn ‖ -³rn

Kildare kɪl 'deə ‖ -'de³r -'dæ³r

kilderkin 'kɪld ək ɪn §-ən ‖ -³rk- **~s** z

Kilfedder kɪl 'fed ə ‖ -³r

Kilian 'kɪl i ən

kilim, K~ kɪ 'liːm

Kilimanjaro ˌkɪl ɪm ən 'dʒɑːr əʊ ˌ·ə-, -ɪ mæn-, -ə mæn- ‖ -oʊ

Kilkenny kɪl 'ken i

kill kɪl **killed** kɪld **killing** 'kɪl ɪŋ **kills** kɪlz
Killamarsh 'kɪl ə mɑːʃ ‖ -mɑːrʃ
Killanin kɪ 'læn ɪn kə-, §-ən
Killarney kɪ 'lɑːn i kə- ‖ -'lɑːrn i
killdeer 'kɪl dɪə ‖ -dɪˀr ~s z
killer 'kɪl ə ‖ -ˀr ~s z
  ˌkiller 'whale, '··
Killiecrankie ˌkɪl i 'kræŋk i
Killin kɪ 'lɪn kə-
Killiney kɪ 'laɪn i kə-
killing 'kɪl ɪŋ ~ly li ~s z
killjoy 'kɪl dʒɔɪ ~s z
Kilmainham kɪl 'meɪn əm
Kilmarnock kɪl 'mɑːn ək -ɒk ‖ -'mɑːrn ək
Kilmuir kɪl 'mjʊə ‖ -'mjʊˀr
kiln kɪln kɪl **kilns** kɪlnz kɪlz
Kilner, k~ 'kɪl nə ‖ -nˀr
Kilnsey 'kɪlnz i
kilo 'kiːl əʊ ‖ -oʊ 'kɪl- ~s z
kilo- 'kɪl əʊ- ‖ 'kɪl ə 'kiːl ə — **kilocalorie**
  'kɪl əʊ ˌkæl ər i ‖ '·ə- 'kiːl-
kilobyte 'kɪl əʊ baɪt ‖ -ə- ~s s
kilocycle 'kɪl əʊ ˌsaɪk ˀl ‖ -ə- ~s z
kilogram, kilogramme 'kɪl ə græm 'kiːl- ~s z
kilohertz 'kɪl əʊ hɜːts ‖ -ə hɜːts
kilojoule 'kɪl ə dʒuːl ~s z
kiloliter, kilolitre 'kɪl əʊ ˌliːt ə ‖ -ə ˌliːt̮ ˀr ~s z

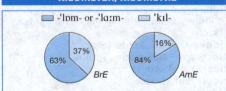

KILOMETER, KILOMETRE

■ -'lɒm- or -'lɑːm-   ■ 'kɪl-

BrE: 63% / 37%
AmE: 84% / 16%

kilometer, kilometre kɪ 'lɒm ɪt ə kə-, -ət-;
  'kɪl ə ˌmiːt ə ‖ kə 'lɑːm ət̮ ˀr kɪ-; 'kɪl ə ˌmiːt̮ ˀr
  —On the analogy of 'centiˌmetre, 'milliˌmetre,
  it is clear that the stressing 'kiloˌmetre is
  logical and might be expected to predominate.
  Nevertheless, it does not. Preference polls, BrE:
  -'lɒm- 63%, 'kɪl- 37%; AmE: -'lɑːm- 84%, 'kɪl-
  16% -'lɒm- 57%. ~s z
kiloton 'kɪl əʊ tʌn ‖ -ə- ~s z
kilovolt 'kɪl əʊ vəʊlt →·-vɒʊlt ‖ -ə voʊlt ~s s
kilowatt 'kɪl ə wɒt ‖ -ə wɑːt ~s s
kilowatt-hour ˌkɪl ə wɒt 'aʊ ə
  ‖ ˌkɪl ə wɑːt̮ 'aʊ ˀr ~s z
Kilpatrick kɪl 'pætr ɪk
Kilroy ˌkɪl 'rɔɪ '··
Kilsby 'kɪlz bi
kilt kɪlt **kilted** 'kɪlt ɪd -əd **kilts** kɪlts
kilter 'kɪlt ə ‖ -ˀr
Kim kɪm
Kimball 'kɪm bˀl
Kimber 'kɪm bə ‖ -bˀr
Kimberley 'kɪm bə li ‖ -bˀr-
kimberlite 'kɪm bə laɪt ‖ -bˀr-
Kimberly 'kɪm bə li ‖ -bˀr-

Kimbolton kɪm 'bəʊlt ən →·-'bɒʊlt-
  ‖ -'boʊlt ˀn
kimchee, kimchi, kimch'i 'kɪm tʃi: —Korean
  [ğim tʃʰi]
Kimmeridge 'kɪm ə rɪdʒ
kimono kɪ 'məʊn əʊ kə-; §'kɪm ə nəʊ
  ‖ -'moʊn ə -oʊ —Jp [ki ˌmo no]
kin kɪn
-kin kɪn §kən — **lambkin** 'læm kɪn §-kən
kina 'kiːn ə
Kinabalu ˌkɪn ə 'bɑːl u: -bə 'lu:
kinaesthesia ˌkɪn iːs 'θiːz i ə ə ˌkaɪn-, ·ɪs-, ·əs-
  ‖ ˌkɪn əs 'θiːʒ ə
kinaesthetic ˌkɪn iːs 'θet ɪk ◄ ˌkaɪn-, -ɪs-, -əs-
  ‖ -əs 'θet̮- ~ally ˀl i
Kincaid kɪn 'keɪd →kɪŋ-
Kincardine kɪn 'kɑːd ɪn →kɪŋ-, -ˀn ‖ -'kɑːrd ˀn
Kincora kɪn 'kɔːr ə →kɪŋ-
kind kaɪnd **kinds** kaɪndz
kinda 'kaɪnd ə
Kinder 'kɪnd ə ‖ -ˀr
kindergarten 'kɪnd ə ˌgɑːt ˀn ‖ -ˀr ˌgɑːrt ˀn
  ~s z
kindergartner 'kɪnd ə ˌgɑːt nə ‖ -ˀr ˌgɑːrt nˀr
  -ˌgɑːrd- ~s z
Kindersley 'kɪnd əz li ‖ -ˀrz-
kind-hearted ˌkaɪnd 'hɑːt ɪd ◄ -əd
  ‖ -'hɑːrt̮ əd ◄ ~ly li ~ness nəs nɪs
kindle 'kɪnd ˀl ~ed d ~es z ~ing ɪŋ
kindling n 'kɪnd lɪŋ
kind|ly 'kaɪnd |li ~lier li ə ‖ li ˀr ~liest li ɪst
  əst ~liness li nəs -nɪs
kindness 'kaɪnd nəs -nɪs ~es ɪz əz
kindred 'kɪndr əd -ɪd ~ness nəs nɪs
kine kaɪn
kinematic ˌkɪn ɪ 'mæt ɪk ◄ ˌkaɪn-, -ə- ‖ -'mæt̮-
  ~s s
kinesics kaɪ 'niːs ɪks kɪ-, -'niːz-
kinesiology kɪˌniːz i 'ɒl ədʒ | i ‖ -'ɑːl ~ist | s
  ɪst | s ‖ əst | s
kinesthesia ˌkɪn iːs 'θiːz i ə ə ˌkaɪn-, ·ɪs-, ·əs-
  ‖ ˌkɪn əs 'θiːʒ ə
kinesthetic ˌkɪn iːs 'θet ɪk ◄ ˌkaɪn-, -ɪs-, -əs-
  ‖ -əs 'θet̮- ~ally ˀl i
kinetic kaɪ 'net ɪk kɪ-, kə- ‖ kə 'net̮ ɪk kɪ-, kaɪ-
  ~ally ˀl i ~s s
  kiˌnetic 'energy
kinfolk 'kɪn fəʊk ‖ -foʊk ~s s
king, King kɪŋ **kings, King's** kɪŋz
  ˌKing 'George; King ˌJames 'version,
  ˌ·' '· ·'·; ˌKing 'Lear; ˌKing's 'Bench,
  ˌKing's 'Bench Diˌvision; ˌKing's 'Counsel;
  ˌKings 'Cross◄; ˌKing's 'English; ˌking's
  'evidence; ˌking's 'evil; ˌKing's 'Lynn
kingcup 'kɪŋ kʌp ~s s
kingdom 'kɪŋ dəm ~s z
Kingdon 'kɪŋ dən
kingfisher 'kɪŋ ˌfɪʃ ə ‖ -ˀr ~s z
Kingham 'kɪŋ əm
kinglet 'kɪŋ lət -lɪt ~s s
king|ly 'kɪŋ |li ~lier li ə ‖ li ˀr ~liest li ɪst əst
  ~liness li nəs -nɪs
kingmaker 'kɪŋ ˌmeɪk ə ‖ -ˀr ~s z

kingpin ˈkɪŋ pɪn ˌ·ˈ· **~s** z
Kingsbridge ˈkɪŋz brɪdʒ
Kingsbury ˈkɪŋz bər i ‖ -ˌber i
Kingsford ˈkɪŋz fəd ‖ -fᵊrd
kingship ˈkɪŋ ʃɪp **~s** s
king-size ˈkɪŋ saɪz **~d** d
Kingsley ˈkɪŋz li
Kingston ˈkɪŋᵏst ən ˈkɪŋz tən
  ˌKingston upon ˈThames
Kingstown ˈkɪŋz taʊn
Kingsway ˈkɪŋz weɪ
Kingswear ˈkɪŋz wɪə ‖ -wɪr
Kingswinford kɪŋ ˈswɪn fəd ‖ -fᵊrd
Kingswood ˈkɪŋz wʊd
Kington ˈkɪŋ tən
Kingussie kɪŋ ˈjuːs i (!)
kink kɪŋk **kinked** kɪŋkt **kinking** ˈkɪŋk ɪŋ
  kinks kɪŋks
kinkajou ˈkɪŋk ə dʒuː **~s** z
kink|y ˈkɪŋk |i **~ier** i ə ‖ i ᵊr **~iest** i ɪst i əst
  ~ily ɪ li əl i **~iness** i nəs i nɪs
Kinloch ˌkɪn ˈlɒk -ˈlɒx ‖ -ˈlɑːk
Kinloss ˌkɪn ˈlɒs ‖ -ˈlɔːs -ˈlɑːs
Kinnear kɪ ˈnɪə -ˈneə ‖ -ˈnɪᵊr
Kinnock ˈkɪn ək
Kinross ˌkɪn ˈrɒs ‖ -ˈrɔːs -ˈrɑːs
Kinsale ˌkɪn ˈseᵊl
Kinsella (i) ˌkɪn ˈsel ə, (ii) ˈkɪnˢ əl ə
Kinsey ˈkɪnz i
kinsfolk ˈkɪnz fəʊk ‖ -foʊk
Kinshasa kɪn ˈʃɑːs ə -ˈʃæs-, -ˈʃɑːz-
kinship ˈkɪn ʃɪp
kins|man ˈkɪnz |mən **~men** mən men
  ~woman ˌwʊm ən **~women** ˌwɪm ɪn §-ən
Kintyre ˌkɪn ˈtaɪ ə ‖ kɪn ˈtaɪ ᵊr
kiosk ˈkiː ɒsk §ˈkaɪ- ‖ kiː ˈɑːsk ki ˈɑːsk **~s** s
Kiowa ˈkiː ə wɑː -wə, -weɪ **~s** z
kip kɪp **kipped** kɪpt **kipping** ˈkɪp ɪŋ **kips** kɪps
Kipling ˈkɪp lɪŋ
Kiplingesque ˌkɪp lɪŋ ˈesk ◄
Kipp kɪp
kippa, kippah kɪ ˈpɑː **kippot** kɪ ˈpəʊt ‖ -ˈpoʊt
Kippax ˈkɪp əks -æks
kipper ˈkɪp ə ‖ -ᵊr **~ed** d **kippering** ˈkɪp ər ɪŋ
  ~s z
Kipps kɪps
kir kɪə ‖ kɪᵊr —Fr [kiːʁ]
Kirbigrip tdmk ˈkɜːb i grɪp ‖ ˈkɜːb- **~s** s
Kirby ˈkɜːb i ‖ ˈkɜːb i
Kirchhoff ˈkɜːk ɒf -hɒf ‖ ˈkɪrk hɔːf ˈkɜːk-, -hɑːf
  —Ger [ˈkɪʁç hɔf]
Kirghiz, Kirgiz ˈkɜː gɪz ˈkɪə- ‖ kɪr ˈgiːz
Kirghizia kɜː ˈgɪz i ə kɪə- ‖ kɪr ˈgiːʒ ə -i ə
Kiribati ˌkɪr ɪ ˈbɑːt i ˌkɪər-, -ə-, -ˈbæt i; ˌ·ˈbæs,
  ˈ··· —The pronunciation recommended by all
  reference books is -bæs, -ˈbæs; but the influence
  of orthography is such that this form has not
  established itself in the face of spelling
  pronunciations.
Kiri Te Kanawa ˌkɪr i ti ˈkɑːn ə wə ˌkɪər-,
  -ˈkæn-
kirk, Kirk kɜːk ‖ kɜːk **kirks, Kirk's** kɜːks
  ‖ kɜːks

Kirkbride ˌkɜːk ˈbraɪd ‖ ˌkɜːk-
Kirkby (i) ˈkɜːk bi ‖ ˈkɜːk-, (ii) ˈkɜːb i ‖ ˈkɜːb i
  —The place in Merseyside is (ii) (!), as are
  other places in the north of England; places in
  the Midlands are (i); the family name may be
  either.
Kirkcaldy kə ˈkɒd i kɜː-, -ˈkɔːd- ‖ kᵊr ˈkɑːd i
  -ˈkɔːd-, -ˈkɑːld-, -ˈkɔːld- (!)
Kirkcudbright kə ˈkuːb ri kɜː- ‖ kᵊr- (!)
Kirkdale ˈkɜːk derᵊl ‖ ˈkɜːk-
Kirkgate streets in Leeds, Bradford ˈkɜːg ət
  ˈkɜː geɪt ‖ ˈkɜːk geɪt
Kirkham ˈkɜːk əm ‖ ˈkɜːk-
Kirkland ˈkɜːk lənd ‖ ˈkɜːk-
Kirklees ˌkɜːk ˈliːz ‖ ˌkɜːk-
Kirkpatrick ˌkɜːk ˈpætr ɪk ‖ ˌkɜːk-
Kirkstall place in W Yks ˈkɜːk stɔːl -stəl
  ‖ ˈkɜːk- -stɑːl
Kirkstone ˈkɜːk stən -stəʊn ‖ ˈkɜːk stoʊn
Kirkuk kɪə ˈkʊk kɜː- ‖ kɪr- kᵊr- —Arabic
  [kɪr ˈkuːk]
Kirkup ˈkɜːk əp -ʌp ‖ ˈkɜːk-
Kirkwall ˈkɜːk wɔːl ‖ ˈkɜːk- -wɑːl
Kirov ˈkɪər ɒv -ɒf ‖ ˈkɪr ɔːf -ɑːf —Russ [ˈkʲi rəf]
kirpan kɪə ˈpɑːn kɜː- ‖ kɪr- —Punjabi [kɪr paːn]
  ~s z
Kirriemuir ˌkɪr i ˈmjʊə ‖ -ˈmjʊᵊr
kirsch kɪəʃ kɜːʃ ‖ kɪrʃ —Ger [kɪʁʃ]
Kirsten ˈkɜːst ɪn -ən ‖ ˈkɜːst- —but as a foreign
  name also ˈkɪəst- ‖ ˈkɪrst-
Kirstie, Kirsty ˈkɜːst i ‖ ˈkɜːst i
kirtle ˈkɜːt ᵊl ‖ ˈkɜːt ᵊl **~s** z
Kirton ˈkɜːt ᵊn ‖ ˈkɜːt-
Kisangani ˌkɪs æŋ ˈgɑːn i ‖ ˌkiːs ɑːn-
kish, Kish kɪʃ
Kishinev ˈkɪʃ ɪ nev -ə-, -nef Moldovan Chişinău
  [ki ʃi ˈnəu]
kishke ˈkɪʃ kə **~s** z
kismet ˈkɪz met ˈkɪs-, -mɪt, -mət
kiss kɪs **kissed** kɪst **kisses** ˈkɪs ɪz -əz **kissing**
  ˈkɪs ɪŋ
  ˈkissing bug; ˈkissing gate; ˌkiss of
  ˈdeath; ˌkiss of ˈlife
kissable ˈkɪs əb ᵊl
kissagram ˈkɪs ə græm **~s** z
kisser ˈkɪs ə ‖ -ᵊr **~s** z
Kissimmee kɪ ˈsɪm i
Kissinger ˈkɪs ɪndʒ ə -əndʒ-; ˈ·ɪŋ ə ‖ -ᵊr
kiss-me-quick ˌkɪs mi ˈkwɪk ◄
kissoff ˈkɪs ɒf -ɔːf ‖ -ɔːf -ɑːf
kissogram ˈkɪs ə græm **~s** z
kit, Kit kɪt **kits** kɪts **kitted** ˈkɪt ɪd -əd ‖ ˈkɪt̬ əd
  kitting ˈkɪt ɪŋ ‖ ˈkɪt̬ ɪŋ
Kitaj kɪ ˈtaɪ
kitbag ˈkɪt bæg **~s** z
Kit-Cat, kit-cat ˈkɪt kæt **~s** s
kitchen, K~ ˈkɪtʃ ən -ɪn **~s** z
  ˌkitchen ˈgarden
Kitchener ˈkɪtʃ ən ə -ɪn- ‖ -ᵊn ər
kitchenette ˌkɪtʃ ə ˈnet -ɪ- **~s** s
kitchen-sink ˌkɪtʃ ən ˈsɪŋk ◄ -ɪn-
kitchenware ˈkɪtʃ ən weə -ɪn- ‖ -wer

K

kite, Kite kaɪt **kited** 'kaɪt ɪd -əd ‖ 'kaɪt̬- **kites**
kaɪts **kiting** 'kaɪt ɪŋ ‖ 'kaɪt̬-
kite-flying 'kaɪt ˌflaɪ ɪŋ
Kit-E-Kat tdmk 'kɪt i kæt ‖ 'kɪt̬-
Kitemark 'kaɪt mɑːk ‖ -mɑːrk
kith kɪθ
  ˌkith and 'kin
kiting 'kaɪt ɪŋ ‖ 'kaɪt̬ ɪŋ
Kit-Kat tdmk 'kɪt kæt ~s s
kitsch kɪtʃ
Kitson 'kɪts ən
Kitt kɪt
kitten 'kɪt ᵊn ~ed d ~ing ɪŋ ~s z
kittenish 'kɪt ᵊn ɪʃ ~ly li ~ness nəs nɪs
Kittitian kɪ 'tɪʃ ᵊn ~s z
kittiwake 'kɪt i weɪk ‖ 'kɪt̬- ~s s
Kitto 'kɪt əʊ ‖ 'kɪt̬ oʊ
Kitts kɪts
kitt|y, Kitt|y 'kɪt |i ‖ 'kɪt̬ |i ~ies, ~y's iz
  'Kitty Hawk
kitty-corner 'kɪt i ˌkɔːn ə ‖ 'kɪt̬ i ˌkɔːr nᵊr
  -ˌkɔːn-
Kitzbuehel, Kitzbuhel, Kitzbühel
  'kɪts bju əl -bu əl; '·bjuːl, -buːl —Ger
  ['kɪts byː əl]
kiva 'kiːv ə ~s z
Kiveton place in SYks 'kɪv ɪt ən -ət-
Kiwanian ki 'wɑːn i ən §kə- ~s z
Kiwanis kɪ 'wɑːn ɪs §kə-, §-əs
kiwi, Kiwi 'kiː wiː ~s z
  'kiwi fruit
Kizzy 'kɪz i
Klamath 'klæm əθ ~s s
  ˌKlamath 'Falls; 'Klamath weed
klan, Klan klæn
Klans|man 'klænz |mən ~men mən men
klatsch klætʃ
Klatt klæt
Klaus klaʊs —Ger [klaʊs]
klavier klæ 'vɪə klə- ‖ -'vɪᵊr ~s z
klaxon, K~ tdmk 'klæks ən ~s z
Klebs-Loffler, Klebs-Löffler ˌklebz 'lʌf lə
  -'lɜːf- ‖ -'lef lᵊr —Ger [ˌkleːps 'lœf lɐ]
Klee kleɪ —Ger [kleː]
Kleenex tdmk 'kliːn eks ~es ɪz əz
Klein klaɪn
Kleinwort 'klaɪn wɔːt ‖ -wɔːrt
Klemperer 'klemp ər ə ‖ -ᵊr ər —Ger
  ['klɛmp ɐʁ ɐ]
klepht kleft (= cleft) **klephts** klefts
kleptomania ˌklept əʊ 'meɪn i ə ‖ ˌ·ə-
kleptomaniac ˌklept əʊ 'meɪn i æk ◀ ‖ ˌ·ə- ~s
  s
klezmer 'klez mə ‖ -mᵊr
klieg kliːg
  'klieg light
Klim tdmk klɪm
Klimt klɪmᵖt
Kline klaɪn
Klinefelter 'klaɪn felt ə ‖ -ᵊr ~'s z
Klingon 'klɪŋ ɒn ‖ -ɑːn -ɔːn
klipspringer 'klɪp ˌsprɪŋ ə ‖ -ᵊr ~s z
Klondike 'klɒnd aɪk ‖ 'klɑːnd-

kloof kluːf **kloofs** kluːfs
Klosters 'kləʊst əz 'klɒst- ‖ 'kloʊst ᵊrz —Ger
  ['kloː stɐs]
kludge kluːdʒ klʌdʒ **kludged** kluːdʒd klʌdʒd
  kludging 'kluːdʒ ɪŋ 'klʌdʒ- **kludges**
  'kluːdʒ ɪz 'klʌdʒ-, -əz
kludgey, kludgy 'kluːdʒ i 'klʌdʒ i
klutz klʌts **klutzes** 'klʌts ɪz -əz
klutz|y 'klʌts |i ~ier i ə ‖ i ᵊr ~iest i ɪst i əst
  ~iness i nəs i nɪs
klystron, K~ tdmk 'klaɪs trɒn 'klɪs- ‖ -trɑːn ~s
  z
km —see **kilometre**
K-Mart tdmk 'keɪ mɑːt ‖ -mɑːrt
knack næk **knacks** næks
knacker 'næk ə ‖ -ᵊr ~ed d **knackering**
  'næk ər ɪŋ ~s z
  'knacker's yard
knackwurst 'næk vʊəst ‖ 'nɑːk wɜːst -wʊrst
  —Ger ['knak vʊʁst]
knap næp (= nap) **knapped** næpt **knapping**
  'næp ɪŋ **knaps** næps
Knapp næp
knapsack 'næp sæk ~s s
knapweed 'næp wiːd ~s z
Knaresborough 'neəz bər ə ‖ 'nerz ˌbɜːː oʊ
Knatchbull 'nætʃ bʊl
knave neɪv (= nave) **knaves** neɪvz
knaver|y 'neɪv ər |i ~ies iz
knavish 'neɪv ɪʃ ~ly li ~ness nəs nɪs
knawel nɔːl 'nɔː əl ‖ nɑːl
knead niːd (= need) **kneaded** 'niːd ɪd -əd
  kneading 'niːd ɪŋ **kneads** niːdz
Knebworth 'neb wəθ -wɜːθ ‖ -wᵊrθ
knee niː **kneed** niːd (= need) **kneeing** 'niː ɪŋ
  knees niːz
  'knee ˌbreeches
Kneebone 'niː bəʊn ‖ -boʊn
kneecap 'niː kæp ~ped t ~ping ɪŋ ~s s
knee-deep ˌniː 'diːp ◀
knee-high ˌniː 'haɪ ◀
kneehole 'niː həʊl →-hɒʊl ‖ -hoʊl ~s z
knee-jerk 'niː dʒɜːk ‖ -dʒɜːk
kneel niːᵊl **kneeled** niːᵊld **kneeling** 'niːᵊl ɪŋ
  kneels niːᵊlz **knelt** nelt
knee-length 'niː leŋᵏθ -lenᵗθ
kneeler 'niːᵊl ə ‖ -ᵊr ~s z
knees-up 'niːz ʌp
knell nel **knells** nelz
Kneller 'nel ə ‖ -ᵊr
knelt nelt
Knesset 'knes et -ɪt, -ət; kə 'nes·
knew njuː ‖ nuː njuː (= new)
K'nex tdmk kə 'neks
knicker 'nɪk ə ‖ -ᵊr ~s z
knickerbocker, K~ 'nɪk ə bɒk ə ‖ -ᵊr bɑːk ᵊr
  ~s z
  ˌknickerbocker 'glory
knick-knack 'nɪk næk ~s s
Knieval kə 'niːv ᵊl
knife naɪf **knifed** naɪft **knifes** naɪfs **knifing**
  'naɪf ɪŋ **knives** naɪvz
knife-edge 'naɪf edʒ

knife-point 'naɪf pɔɪnt

knight, K~ naɪt (= *night*) **knighted** 'naɪt ɪd
-əd ‖ 'naɪt̬ əd **knighting** 'naɪt ɪŋ ‖ 'naɪt̬ ɪŋ
knights, Knight's naɪts

knight-errant ˌnaɪt 'er ənt ‖ ˌnaɪt̬-
knights-errant ˌnaɪts 'er ənt

knighthood 'naɪt hʊd ~**s** z

knight|ly 'naɪt |li (= *nightly*) ~**liness** li nəs
-nɪs

Knighton 'naɪt ᵊn

Knightsbridge 'naɪts brɪdʒ

kniphofia nɪ 'fəʊf i ə naɪ- ‖ -'foʊf- ~**s** z

knish kə 'nɪʃ knɪʃ **knishes** kə 'nɪʃ ɪz -əz; 'knɪʃ·

knit nɪt (= *nit*) **knits** nɪts **knitted** 'nɪt ɪd -əd
‖ 'nɪt̬ əd **knitter** 'nɪt ə ‖ 'nɪt̬ ʳr ~**s** z **knitting**
'nɪt ɪŋ ‖ 'nɪt̬ ɪŋ
  'knitting ˌneedle

knitwear 'nɪt weə ‖ -wer

knives naɪvz

knob nɒb ‖ nɑːb **knobbed** nɒbd ‖ nɑːbd
  knobs nɒbz ‖ nɑːbz

knobbly 'nɒb ᵊl i ‖ 'nɑːb-

knobby 'nɒb i ‖ 'nɑːb i

knobkerrie 'nɒb ˌker i -kər- ‖ 'nɑːb- ~**s** z

knock, Knock nɒk ‖ nɑːk **knocked** nɒkt
  ‖ nɑːkt **knocking** 'nɒk ɪŋ ‖ 'nɑːk ɪŋ **knocks**
  nɒks ‖ nɑːks

knockabout 'nɒk ə ˌbaʊt ‖ 'nɑːk- ~**s** s

knockback 'nɒk bæk ‖ 'nɑːk- ~**s** s

knockdown 'nɒk daʊn ‖ 'nɑːk- ~**s** z

knock-down-drag-out
  ˌnɒk daʊn 'dræg aʊt ◂ ‖ ˌnɑːk-

knocker 'nɒk ə ‖ 'nɑːk ʳr ~**s** z

knock|er-up ˌnɒk |ər ˈʌp ‖ ˌnɑːk ʳr- ~**ers-up**
əz ˈʌp ‖ ʳrz ˈʌp

knock-for-knock ˌnɒk fə 'nɒk ◂
  ‖ ˌnɑːk fʳr 'nɑːk ◂

knock-forward ˌnɒk 'fɔː wəd
  ‖ ˌnɑːk 'fɔːr wʳrd ~**s** z

Knockholt 'nɒk həʊlt →-hɒʊlt ‖ 'nɑːk hoʊlt

knock-knee ˌnɒk 'niː ‖ ˌnɑːk- ~**d** d ◂

knock-knock ˌnɒk 'nɒk ‖ ˌnɑːk 'nɑːk
  ˌknock-'knock joke

knockoff 'nɒk ɒ-ɔːf ‖ 'nɑːk ɔːf -ɑːf ~**s** s

knock-on ˌnɒk 'ɒn ˈ·· ‖ ˌnɑːk 'ɑːn -'nɔːn
  ˌknock-'on efˌfect, ˌknock-on ef'fect,
  'knock-on efˌfect

knockout 'nɒk aʊt ‖ 'nɑːk- ~**s** s

knock-up 'nɒk ʌp ‖ 'nɑːk- ~**s** s

knockwurst 'nɒk wɜːst ‖ 'nɑːk wɜːst -vʊrst

Knole nəʊl →nɒʊl ‖ noʊl

knoll, Knoll nəʊl →nɒʊl ‖ noʊl **knolls** nəʊlz
  →nɒʊlz ‖ noʊlz

Knollys nəʊlz →nɒʊlz ‖ noʊlz

Knopf knɒpf ‖ knɑːpf

Knorr nɔː ‖ nɔːr

Knossos 'knɒs ɒs 'nɒs-, -əs ‖ 'nɑːs əs

knot nɒt ‖ nɑːt (= *not*) **knots** nɒts ‖ nɑːts
  knotted 'nɒt ɪd -əd ‖ 'nɑːt̬ əd **knotting**
  'nɒt ɪŋ ‖ 'nɑːt̬ ɪŋ

knotgrass 'nɒt grɑːs §-græs ‖ 'nɑːt græs

knothole 'nɒt həʊl →-hɒʊl ‖ 'nɑːt hoʊl ~**s** z

Knott nɒt ‖ nɑːt

knott... —*see* **knot**

Knottingley 'nɒt ɪŋ li ‖ 'nɑːt̬-

knott|y 'nɒt |i ‖ 'nɑːt̬ |i ~**ier** i ə ‖ i ʳr ~**iest**
  i ɪst i əst ~**iness** i nəs i nɪs

knout naʊt **knouts** naʊts

know nəʊ ‖ noʊ (= *no*) **knew** njuː ‖ nuː njuː
  knowing 'nəʊ ɪŋ ‖ 'noʊ ɪŋ **known** nəʊn
  §'nəʊ ən ‖ noʊn **knows** nəʊz ‖ noʊz

knowable 'nəʊ əb ᵊl ‖ 'noʊ-

know-all 'nəʊ ɔːl ‖ 'noʊ- -ɑːl ~**s** z

know-how 'nəʊ haʊ ‖ 'noʊ-

knowing 'nəʊ ɪŋ ‖ 'noʊ ɪŋ ~**ly** li ~**ness** nəs nɪs

know-it-all 'nəʊ ɪt ɔːl §-ət- ‖ 'noʊ ət̬- -ɑːl ~**s** z

Knowle nəʊl →nɒʊl ‖ noʊl

knowledge 'nɒl ɪdʒ ‖ 'nɑːl- (!)

knowledgeab|le 'nɒl ɪdʒ əb |ᵊl ‖ 'nɑːl- ~**ly** li

Knowles nəʊlz →nɒʊlz ‖ noʊlz

known nəʊn §'nəʊ ən ‖ noʊn

know-nothing 'nəʊ ˌnʌθ ɪŋ ‖ 'noʊ- ~**s** z

Knowsley 'nəʊz li ‖ 'noʊz-

Knox nɒks ‖ nɑːks

Knoxville 'nɒks vɪl ‖ 'nɑːks-

Knoydart 'nɔɪd ɑːt -ət- ‖ -ɑːrt

knuckl|e 'nʌk ᵊl ~**ed** d ~**es** z ~**ing** ɪŋ

knuckleball 'nʌk ᵊl bɔːl ‖ -bɑːl ~**s** z

knucklebone 'nʌk ᵊl bəʊn ‖ -boʊn ~**s** z

knuckle-dragger 'nʌk ᵊl ˌdræg ə ‖ -ʳr ~**s** z

knuckle-duster 'nʌk ᵊl ˌdʌst ə ‖ -ʳr ~**s** z

knucklehead 'nʌk ᵊl hed ~**s** z

knurl nɜːl ‖ nɜːl **knurled** nɜːld ‖ nɜːld **knurls**
  nɜːlz ‖ nɜːlz

Knuston 'nʌst ən

Knutsford 'nʌts fəd ‖ -fʳrd

KO, k.o. ˌkeɪ 'əʊ ‖ -'oʊ ~**'d** d ~**'ing** ɪŋ ~**'s** z

koa 'kəʊ ə ‖ 'koʊ ə ~**s** z

koala kəʊ 'ɑːl ə ‖ koʊ- ~**s** z

koan 'kəʊ æn -ən, -ɑːn ‖ 'koʊ ɑːn —*Jp*
  [ko‚o an] ~**s** z

Kobe *American personal name* kəʊb ‖ koʊb

Kobe *place in Japan* 'kəʊb eɪ -i ‖ 'koʊb eɪ —*Jp*
  ['ko‧o be]

Koblenz kəʊ 'blents ‖ 'koʊ blents —*Ger*
  ['koː blents]

Koch (i) kəʊk ‖ koʊk, (ii) kɒtʃ ‖ kɑːtʃ, (iii) kɒx
  ‖ kɔːk kɑːk —*Ger* [kɔx]

Kochel, Köchel 'kɜːk ᵊl 'kɜːx- ‖ 'kɜːʃ ᵊl 'kɜːk-
  —*Ger* ['kœç ᵊl]
  'Köchel ˌnumber

Kodachrome *tdmk* 'kəʊd ə krəʊm
  ‖ 'koʊd ə kroʊm

Kodak, kodak *tdmk* 'kəʊd æk ‖ 'koʊd- ~**s, ~'s**
  s

Kodaly, Kodály 'kəʊd aɪ ‖ koʊ 'daɪ —*Hung*
  ['ko daːj]

Kodiak 'kəʊd i æk ‖ 'koʊd-

Koestler 'kɜːst lə ‖ 'kest lʳr

Kofi 'kəʊf i ‖ 'koʊf i

Koh-i-noor ˌkəʊ i 'nʊə ◂ -'nɔː, ˈ··
  ‖ 'koʊ ə nʊr

kohl, Kohl kəʊl →kɒʊl ‖ koʊl —*Ger* [koːl]

kohlrabi ˌkəʊl 'rɑːb i →ˌkɒʊl- ‖ ˌkoʊl-

koi kɔɪ —*Jp* ['ko i]

koine, koiné 'kɔɪn eɪ -iː, -i ~**s** z

Kojak ˈkəʊdʒ æk ‖ ˈkoʊdʒ-
Kokomo ˈkəʊk ə məʊ ‖ ˈkoʊk ə moʊ
Kokoschka kəʊ ˈkɒʃ kə ‖ kə ˈkɑːʃ- -ˈkɔːʃ-
—*Ger* [ko ˈkɔʃ ka, ˈkɔ kɔʃ ka]
kola, Kola ˈkəʊl ə ‖ ˈkoʊl ə
Kolkata kɒl ˈkʌt ə -ˈkæt- ‖ kɔːl- kɑːl-, koʊl-
—*Bengali* [ˈkol ka ʈa]
kolkhoz ˌkɒl ˈkɒz -ˈkɔːz, -ˈhɔːz ‖ kɑːl ˈkɑːz
-ˈkɔːz —*Russ* [kʌɫ ˈxɒs] **~es** ɪz əz
Kolynos *tdmk* ˈkɒl ɪ nɒs -ə- ‖ ˈkɑːl ə nɑːs
Komi ˈkəʊm i ‖ ˈkoʊm i **~s** z
Komodo kə ˈməʊd əʊ ‖ -ˈmoʊd oʊ
Ko‚modo ˈdragon
Komsomol ˈkɒm sə mɒl ‚·ˈ· ‖ ˈkɑːm sə mɑːl
-mɔːl, ‚·ˈ· —*Russ* [kəm sʌ ˈmɔɫ]
Kondratieff, Kondratiev kɒn ˈdræt i ef
‖ kɑːn ˈdrɑːt- —*Russ* [kʌn ˈdra tʲɪf]
Kongo ˈkɒŋ gəʊ ‖ ˈkɑːŋ goʊ
Konica *tdmk* ˈkɒn ɪk ə ˈkəʊn- ‖ ˈkɑːn- ˈkoʊn-
—*Jp* [ˈko ɲi ka]
Konigsberg, Königsberg ˈkɜːn ɪgz bɜːg
ˈkəʊn-, -beəg ‖ ˈkeɪn ɪgz bɜːg ˈkʊn- —*Ger*
[ˈkøː nɪçs bɛʁk]
Konkani ˈkɒŋk ən i ‖ ˈkɑːŋk-
Konrad ˈkɒn ræd ‖ ˈkɑːn-
Kon-Tiki ˌkɒn ˈtiːk i -ˈtɪk- ‖ ˌkɑːn-
Koo ku:
kook ku:k **kooks** ku:ks
kookaburra ˈkʊk ə bʌr ə ‖ -bɜː ə **~s** z
Kookai, Kookaï *tdmk* ˈkuː kaɪ
kook|y ˈkuːk |i **~ier** i ə ‖ i ᵊr **~iest** i ɪst i əst
~iness i nəs i nɪs
Kool *tdmk* ku:l
Kool-Aid *tdmk* ˈkuːl eɪd
Koontz ku:nts
Kootenay ˈkuːt ə neɪ -ᵊn eɪ ‖ -ᵊn eɪ
kop, Kop kɒp ‖ kɑːp *(= cop)* **kops** kɒps
‖ kɑːps
kopeck, kopek ˈkəʊp ek ˈkɒp- ‖ ˈkoʊp- **~s** s
kopje ˈkɒp i ‖ ˈkɑːp i **~s** z
koppa ˈkɒp ə ‖ ˈkɑːp ə **~s** z
Koppel ˈkɒp ᵊl ‖ ˈkɑːp ᵊl
koppie ˈkɒp i ‖ ˈkɑːp i **~s** z
Koran kɔː ˈrɑːn kɒ-, kə- ‖ kə- —*Arabic*
[qur ˈʔɑːn]
Koranic kɔː ˈræn ɪk kɒ-, kə- ‖ kə-
Kordofan ˌkɔːd əʊ ˈfæn -ˈfɑːn ‖ ˌkɔːrd oʊ ˈfɑːn
Kordofanian ˌkɔːd əʊ ˈfeɪn i ən ◂ -ˈfɑːn-
‖ ˌkɔːrd oʊ ˈfæn-
Korea kə ˈrɪə kɒ-, §-ˈriː ə ‖ kə ˈriː ə
Korean kə ˈrɪən kɒ-, §-ˈriː ən ‖ kə ˈriː ən **~s** z
korfball ˈkɔːf bɔːl ‖ ˈkɔːrf- -bɑːl
korma ˈkɔːm ə ‖ ˈkɔːrm ə **~s** z
Korsakoff, Korsakov, Korsakow ˈkɔːs ə kɒf
‖ ˈkɔːrs ə kɑːf -kɔːf —*Russ* [ˈkɔr sə kəf]
Kos *Greek island* kɒs ‖ kɑːs kɔːs, koʊs
kos *Indian measure of distance* kəʊs ‖ koʊs
Kosciusko *name of mountain* ˌkɒs i ˈʌsk əʊ
-ˈʊsk- ‖ ˌkɑːs i ˈʌsk oʊ ˌkɑːsk- —*Polish*
Kościuszko [kɔɕ ˈt͡ɕuʃ kɔ]
kosher ˈkəʊʃ ə ‖ ˈkoʊʃ ᵊr
Kosovar ˈkɒs ə vɑː ‖ ˈkoʊs ə vɑːr ˈkɑːs-, ˈkɔːs-
~s z

Kosovo ˈkɒs ə vəʊ ‖ ˈkoʊs ə voʊ ˈkɑːs-, ˈkɔːs-
—*Serbian* [ˈkɔ sɔ vɔ], *Albanian* Kosova
[ˈkɔ sɔ va]
Kosset *tdmk* ˈkɒs ɪt §-ət ‖ ˈkɑːs-
Kossoff ˈkɒs ɒf ‖ ˈkɑːs ɔːf -ɑːf
Kotex *tdmk* ˈkəʊt eks ‖ ˈkoʊt-
kotow ˌkəʊ ˈtaʊ ‖ koʊ ˈtoʊ ˈ·· **~ed** d **~ing** ɪŋ
~s z
koumis, koumiss ˈkuːm ɪs -əs
kour|os ˈkʊər ɒs ‖ ˈkʊr- **~oi** ɔɪ
Kowloon ˌkaʊ ˈluːn ◂ —*Cantonese* [²kɐw ⁴lɔŋ]
kowtow ˌkaʊ ˈtaʊ ‖ ˈ·· **~ed** d **~ing** ɪŋ **~s** z
Koštunica kɒʃ ˈtuːn ɪts ə ‖ kɔːʃ-, kɑːʃ-, koʊʃ-
—*Serbian* [ko ˈʃtu ni tsa]
kraal krɑːl krɔːl —*in South African English,*
krɔːl **kraals** krɑːlz krɔːlz
Kraft *tdmk* krɑːft §kræft ‖ kræft
krait kraɪt **kraits** kraɪts
Krakatoa ˌkræk ə ˈtəʊ ə ˌkrɑːk- ‖ -ˈtoʊ ə
kraken ˈkrɑːk ən ˈkreɪk-, ˈkræk- **~s** z
Krakow ˈkræk aʊ -əʊ, -ɒf ‖ ˈkrɑːk aʊ —*Polish*
Kraków [ˈkra kuf]
Kramer ˈkreɪm ə ‖ -ᵊr
kraut, Kraut kraʊt **krauts** kraʊts
Kray kreɪ
Krebs krebz
Kremlin, k~ ˈkrem lɪn §-lən
Kreutzer ˈkrɔɪts ə ‖ -ᵊr —*Ger* [ˈkʁɔy tsɐ]
krill krɪl
krimmer ˈkrɪm ə ‖ -ᵊr
Kringle ˈkrɪŋ gᵊl
Krio ˈkriː əʊ ‖ -oʊ **~s** z
kris *'knife'* kriːs krɪs
Kris *personal name* krɪs
Krishna ˈkrɪʃ nə
Krishnamurti ˌkrɪʃ nə ˈmɜːt i -ˈmʊət i
‖ -ˈmɜːt̬ i
Krispie ˈkrɪsp i **~s** z
Krista ˈkrɪst ə
Kristen ˈkrɪst ən
Kristi, Kristie ˈkrɪst i
Kristle ˈkrɪst ᵊl
Kristy ˈkrɪst i
Krona *tdmk*, **krona** ˈkrəʊn ə ‖ ˈkroʊn ə
—*Swedish* [ˈkruː na] **kronor** ˈkrəʊn ɔː
‖ ˈkroʊn ɔːr —*Swedish* [ˈkruː nʊr]
krone ˈkrəʊn ə ‖ ˈkroʊn ə —*Danish* [ˈkʁoː nə]
kroner ˈkrəʊn ə ‖ ˈkroʊn ᵊr —*Danish*
[ˈkʁoː nɒ]
Kru kru: **Krus** kru:z
Kruger ˈkruːg ə ‖ -ᵊr —*Afrikaans* [ˈkry xər]
Krugerrand, k~ ˈkruːg ə rænd **~s** z
Krupp krʊp krʌp —*Ger* [kʁʊp] **Krupp's** krʊps
krʌps
Kruschen *tdmk* ˈkrʊʃ ᵊn ˈkrʌʃ-
Krushchev ˈkrʊs tʃɒf ˈkrʊʃ-, ‚·ˈ· ‖ ˈkruːs tʃef
-tʃɔːf, -tʃɑːf, ‚·ˈ· —*Russ* [xru ˈɕt͡ɕɔf]
krypton ˈkrɪpt ɒn -ən ‖ -ɑːn
kryptonite ˈkrɪpt ə naɪt
Kshatriya ˈkʃætr i ə
Kuala Lumpur ˌkwɑːl ə ˈlʊmp ʊə ˌkwɒl-,
-ˈlʌmp-, -ə ‖ -lʊm ˈpʊᵊr
Kublai ˈkuːb lə ˈkʊb-, -laɪ

Kubla Khan ˌkuːb lə ˈkɑːn ˌkʊb-
Kubrick ˈkjuːb rɪk
kuccha ˈkʌtʃ ə —*Punjabi* [kət tʃə]
kudos ˈkjuːd ɒs ‖ -oʊz ˈkuːd-, -oʊs, -ɑːs
kudu ˈkuːd uː ˈkʊd- ~s z
kudzu ˈkʊd zuː —*Jp* [ˈkɯ dzɯ]
Kufic ˈkuːf ɪk ˈkjuːf-
Kuhn kuːn
Kuhnian ˈkuːn i̯ ən
Kuiper ˈkaɪp ə ‖ -ᵊr
Ku Klux Klan ˌkuː klʌks ˈklæn ˌkjuː-, △ˌkluː-
kukri ˈkʊk ri ~s z
kulak ˈkuːl æk ‖ ku ˈlɑːk -ˈlæk; ˈkuːl ɑːk, -æk —*Russ* [ku ˈłak] ~s s
Kultur kʊl ˈtʊə ‖ -ˈtʊᵊr —*Ger* [kʊl ˈtuːɐ]
kumis, kumiss ˈkuːm ɪs §-əs
kummel, kümmel ˈkʊm ᵊl ‖ ˈkɪm- *(*)* —*Ger* [ˈkʏm ᵊl]
kumquat ˈkʌm kwɒt ‖ -kwɑːt ~s s
!Kung, !xū kʊŋ —*In the language so named, the exclamation mark denotes a post-alveolar ('palatal') click. This accompanies a voiceless velar affricate* [kx]. *The vowel is a nasalized* [ũ]. *The syllable is said on a low rising tone.*
kung fu ˌkʌŋ ˈfuː ˌkʊŋ- —*Chi* gōngfū [¹kʊŋ ¹fu]
Kunming ˌkʊn ˈmɪŋ —*Chi* Kūnming [¹kʰuən ²miŋ]
Kuomintang ˌkwəʊ mɪn ˈtæŋ ˌgwəʊ- ‖ ˌkwoʊ mɪn ˈtɑːŋ ˌgwoʊ-, -ˈtæŋ —*Chi* Guómíndǎng [²kwɔ ²mɪn ³taŋ]
Kuoni *tdmk* ku ˈəʊn i ‖ -ˈoʊn i
Kurath ˈkjʊər æθ ‖ ˈkjʊr-
Kurd kɜːd kʊəd ‖ kɜːd kʊᵊrd **Kurds** kɜːdz kʊədz ‖ kɜːdz kʊᵊrdz
Kurdish ˈkɜːd ɪʃ ‖ ˈkɜːd-
Kurdistan ˌkɜːd ɪ ˈstɑːn -ə-, -ˈstæn ‖ ˈkɜːd ə stæn
Kureishi ku ˈreʃ i -ˈreɪʃ-
Kuril, Kurile kʊ ˈriːᵊl kju- ‖ ˈkʊr ɪl ˈkjʊr-
Kurosawa ˌkʊər əʊ ˈsɑː wə ‖ ˌkʊr oʊ- —*Jp* [ku ˌro sa wa]
kursaal ˈkɜːz ᵊl ˈkɜːs-; ˈkɜː sɑːl, ˈkʊə-, -sᵊl, -zɑːl ‖ ˈkʊr sɑːl
Kursk kʊəsk ‖ kʊᵊrsk —*Russ* [kursk]
Kurt kɜːt kʊət ‖ kɜːt —*Ger* [kʊʁt]
kurtosis kɜː ˈtəʊs ɪs kə-, §-əs ‖ kɜː ˈtoʊs əs
kuru ˈkʊr uː
kurus ku ˈrʊʃ -ˈruːʃ *Turkish* kuruş [ku ˈrʊʃ]
kurus kʊ ˈrʊʃ -ˈruːʃ

Kurzweil ˈkɜːz waɪᵊl ˈkɜːts-, -vaɪᵊl ‖ ˈkɜːz-
Kutch kʌtʃ
Kuwait ku ˈweɪt kju-, kə- —*Arabic* [ku ˈweːt]
Kuwaiti ku ˈweɪt i kju-, kə- ‖ -ˈweɪt i ~s z
Kvaerner, Kværner kə ˈvɜːn ə -ˈvɑːn- ‖ -ˈvɜːn ᵊr
kvas, kvass kvɑːs kvæs ‖ kwɑːs
kvetch kvetʃ **kvetched** kvetʃt **kvetches** ˈkvetʃ ɪz -əz **kvetching** ˈkvetʃ ɪŋ
Kwa kwɑː
Kwajalein ˈkwɑːdʒ ə leɪn -əl ən
Kwakiutl ˌkwɑːk i ˈuːt ᵊl ◄ ‖ -ˈuːt̬-
Kwandebele, KwaNdebele ˌkwɒnd ɪ ˈbel i ˌkwɑːnd-, -ˈbeɪl-, -eɪ ‖ ˌkwɑːnd-
Kwanza, Kwanzaa ˈkwɑːnz ə ˈkwænz-, -ɑː
kwashiorkor ˌkwɒʃ i ˈɔːk ɔː ˌkwæʃ-, -ə ‖ ˌkwɑːʃ i ˈɔːrk ᵊr -ːɔː
kwatcha ˈkwɑːtʃ ə
KwaZulu kwɑː ˈzuːl uː
kwela ˈkweɪl ə
Kwells *tdmk* kwelz
KWIC kwɪk
Kwik-Fit *tdmk* ˈkwɪk fɪt
Kwiksave *tdmk* ˈkwɪk seɪv
Kyd kɪd
Kyle, kyle kaɪᵊl
Kyleakin ˌ(ˌ)kaɪᵊl ˈæk ɪn
Kylie ˈkaɪl i
kymogram ˈkaɪm əʊ græm ‖ -ə- ~s z
kymograph ˈkaɪm əʊ grɑːf -græf ‖ -ə græf ~s s
kymographic ˌkaɪm əʊ ˈgræf ɪk ◄ ‖ -ə- ~ally ᵊl i
Kynance ˈkaɪn ænᵗs
Kynaston ˈkɪn əst ən
Kyocera *tdmk* ˌkaɪ ə ˈsɪər ə ‖ -ˈsɪr ə —*Jp* [kjo ˌo se ɾa]
Kyoto ki ˈəʊt əʊ ‖ -ˈoʊt oʊ —*Jp* [ˈkjoo to]
kyphosis kaɪ ˈfəʊs ɪs §-əs ‖ -ˈfoʊs-
kyphotic kaɪ ˈfɒt ɪk ‖ -ˈfɑːt̬-
Kyrgyz ˈkɜːg ɪz ˈkɪəg- ‖ ˈkɜːg- ˈkɪrg-
Kyrgyzstan ˌkɜːg ɪ ˈstɑːn ˌkɪəg-, -ˈstæn ‖ ˌkɜːg- ˌkɪrg-, ˈ···
kyrie ˈkɪr i eɪ ˈkɪər-, -iː
kyrie e'leison ɪ ˈleɪs ɒn e-, -ᵊn; -ˈleɪ ə sɒn ‖ -ɑːn
Kyushu ki ˈuːʃ uː ˈkjuːʃ uː —*Jp* [ˈkjɯɯ ɕɯɯ]
Kyzyl Kum kə ˌzɪl ˈkuːm -ˈkʊm —*Russ* [kɨ ˌzɨł ˈkum]

Ll

L

L, l el (= *ell*) **Ls, l's, L's** elz —*Communications code name:* Lima 'liːm ə
ˌL'1; ˌL'2

la lɑː —*but in French, Italian, and Spanish expressions also* lə, læ — *Fr, It, Sp* [la]; *in family names usually* lə —*See also phrases with this word*

LA ˌel 'eɪ ◄ —*see also* **Los Angeles**
ˌLA 'Law

laager 'lɑːg ə ‖ -ᵊr (= *lager*) **~ed** d **~s** z

Laa-Laa 'lɑː lɑː

lab læb **labs** læbz

Laban (i) 'leɪb ən -æn, (ii) 'lɑːb-, (iii) lə 'bæn —*The biblical figure is (i), the dance notation system and its inventor (ii).*

label 'leɪb ᵊl **~ed, ~led** d **~ing, ~ling** ɪŋ **~s** z

labia 'leɪb i ə
ˌlabia ma'jora mə 'dʒɔːr ə ‖ -'dʒoʊr-; ˌlabia mi'nora mɪ 'nɔːr ə mə- ‖ -'noʊr-

labial 'leɪb i ᵊl **~ly** i **~s** z

labialis... —*see* **labializ...**

labiality ˌleɪb i 'æl ət i -ɪt i ‖ -əţ i

labialization ˌleɪb i ᵊl aɪ 'zeɪʃ ᵊn -ɪ'-- ‖ -ə 'zeɪʃ- **~s** z

labializ|e 'leɪb i ə laɪz **~ed** d **~es** ɪz əz **~ing** ɪŋ

labial-velar ˌleɪb i ᵊl 'viːl ə ◄ ‖ -ᵊr ◄ **~s** z

labiate 'leɪb i eɪt -ət, -ɪt **~s** s

labile 'leɪb aɪᵊl ‖ -ᵊl

lability leɪ 'bɪl ət i lə-, -ɪt i ‖ -əţ i

labiodental ˌleɪb i əʊ 'dent ᵊl ◄
‖ -oʊ 'denţ ᵊl ◄ **~ly** i **~s** z

labiopalatal ˌleɪb i əʊ 'pæl ət ᵊl ◄
‖ -oʊ 'pæl əţ ᵊl ◄ **~ly** i **~s** z

labiovelar ˌleɪb i əʊ 'viːl ə ◄ ‖ -oʊ 'viːl ᵊr ◄ **~s** z

labiovelaris... —*see* **labiovelariz...**

labiovelarization ˌleɪb i əʊ ˌviːl ər aɪ 'zeɪʃ ᵊn -ɪ'-- ‖ -i oʊ ˌviːl ər ə- **~s** z

labiovelariz|e ˌleɪb i əʊ 'viːl ə raɪz ‖ -i oʊ- **~ed** d **~es** ɪz əz **~ing** ɪŋ

labi|um 'leɪb i ˌjəm **~a** ə

La Boheme, La Bohème ˌlɑː bəʊ 'em ˌlæ-, -'eɪm ‖ -boʊ- —*Fr* [la bo ɛm]

labor 'leɪb ə ‖ -ᵊr **~ed** d **laboring** 'leɪb ər ɪŋ **~s** z
ˈlabor camp; ˈLabor Day; ˈlabor exˌchange; ˈlabor ˌmarket; ˌlabor of ˈlove; ˈLabor ˌParty; ˈlabor ˌunion

laborator|y lə 'bɒr ət ər |i ‖ 'læb ᵊr ə tɔːr |i -tour i (*) —*In BrE formerly also* 'læb ər əţ ər i **~ies** iz

laborer 'leɪb ər ə ‖ -ᵊr ər **~s** z

labor-intensive ˌleɪb ər ɪn 'tenᵗs ɪv ◄ ‖ ˌ-ᵊr-

laborious lə 'bɔːr i əs ‖ -'boʊr- **~ly** li **~ness** nəs nɪs

Laborite 'leɪb ə raɪt **~s** s

labor-saving 'leɪb ə ˌseɪv ɪŋ ‖ -ᵊr-

Labouchere ˌlæb uː 'ʃeə '··· ‖ -'ʃeᵊr

labour 'leɪb ə ‖ -ᵊr **~ed** d **labouring** 'leɪb ər ɪŋ **~s** z
ˈlabour camp; ˈLabour Day; ˈlabour exˌchange; ˈlabour ˌmarket; ˌlabour of ˈlove; ˈLabour ˌParty; ˈlabour ˌunion

labourer 'leɪb ər ə ‖ -ᵊr ər **~s** z

labour-intensive ˌleɪb ər ɪn 'tenᵗs ɪv ◄ ‖ ˌ-ᵊr-

Labourite 'leɪb ə raɪt **~s** s

labour-saving 'leɪb ə ˌseɪv ɪŋ ‖ -ᵊr-

Labov lə 'bɒv -'bəʊv ‖ -'boʊv

Labovian lə 'bəʊv i ən ‖ -'boʊv-

Labrador 'læb rə dɔː ‖ -dɔːr **~s** z
ˌLabrador re'triever

Labuan lə 'buː ən ‖ ˌlɑːb u 'ɑːn

laburnum lə 'bɜːn əm ‖ -'bɝːn- ~s z
labyrinth 'læb ə rɪnᶿ -ɪ- ~s s
labyrinthine ˌlæb ə 'rɪnᶿ aɪn ◂ -ɪ- ‖ -ən -iːn,
  -aɪn
labyrinthitis ˌlæb ər ɪn 'θaɪt ɪs -ᵊrˌən-, §-əs
  ‖ -'θaɪt̬ əs
lac '100 000' lɑːk læk lacs lɑːks læks
lac 'resin' læk (= lack) lacs læks
Lacan læ 'kɒ̃ -'kɑːn ‖ lə 'kɑːn —Fr [la kɑ̃]
Laccadive 'læk əd ɪv 'lɑːk-, ə diːv, -daɪv
lace leɪs laced leɪst laces 'leɪs ɪz -əz lacing
  'leɪs ɪŋ
Lacedaemon ˌlæs ə 'diːm ən -ɪ-
Lacedaemonian ˌlæs ə dɪ 'məʊn i̯ən ◂ ˌ-ɪ-,
  -də'-- ‖ -'moʊn- ~s z
lace|rate v 'læs ə |reɪt ~rated reɪt ɪd -əd
  ‖ reɪt̬ əd ~rates reɪts ~rating reɪt ɪŋ ‖ reɪt̬ ɪŋ
laceration ˌlæs ə 'reɪʃ ᵊn ~s z
Lacert|a lə 'sɜːt |ə ‖ -'sɝːt̬ |ə ~ae iː
lace-up 'leɪs ʌp ~s s
lacewing 'leɪs wɪŋ ~s z
Lacey 'leɪs i
laches 'lætʃ ɪz 'leɪtʃ-, -əz
Lachesis 'læk ɪs ɪs △'lætʃ-, -əs-, §-əs
Lachlan 'lɒk lən 'læk- ‖ 'lɑːk-
lachryma Christi ˌlæk rɪm ə 'krɪst i ˌ-rəm-
lachrymal 'læk rɪm əl -rəm- ~s z
lachrymator 'læk rɪ meɪt ə 'ˌ-rə- ‖ -meɪt̬ ᵊr ~s z
lachrymator|y ˌlæk rɪ 'meɪt ər |i ◂ ˌ-rə-, 'ˌ-·-,
  'ˌ··mət̬ ᵊr |i ‖ 'læk rəm ə tɔːr |i -toʊr i ~ies iz
lachrymose 'læk rɪ məʊs -rə-, -məʊz ‖ -moʊs
  ~ly li
La Cienega ˌlɑː si 'en əg ə
lack læk lacked lækt lacking 'læk ɪŋ lacks
  læks
lackadaisical ˌlæk ə 'deɪz ɪk ᵊl ◂ ~ly ᵢ ~ness
  nəs nɪs
Lackawanna ˌlæk ə 'wɒn ə ‖ -'wɑːn ə
lackey 'læk i ~s z
lackluster, lacklustre 'læk ˌlʌst ə ˌ·'·· ‖ -ᵊr
Lacock 'leɪk ɒk ‖ -ɑːk
Laconia lə 'kəʊn i̯ə ‖ -'koʊn-
laconic lə 'kɒn ɪk ‖ -'kɑːn- ~ally ᵊl̩ ᵢ
lacquer 'læk ə ‖ -ᵊr ~ed d lacquering
  'læk ᵊr ɪŋ ~s z
lacrim... —see lachrym...
lacrosse lə 'krɒs ‖ -'krɔːs -'krɑːs
lacrymal 'læk rɪm əl -rəm- ~s z
lact|ate v ₍ˌ₎læk 't|eɪt 'læk |eɪt ‖ 'lækt |eɪt
  ~ated eɪt ɪd -əd ‖ eɪt̬ əd ~ates eɪts ~ating
  eɪt ɪŋ ‖ eɪt̬ ɪŋ
lactate n 'lækt eɪt ~s s
lactation ₍ˌ₎læk 'teɪʃ ᵊn ~s z
lacteal 'lækt i̯əl ~s z
lactic 'lækt ɪk
  ˌlactic 'acid
lactobacill|us ˌlækt əʊ bə 'sɪl |əs ‖ ˌ-oʊ- ~i aɪ
lactose 'lækt əʊs -əʊz ‖ -oʊs -oʊz
lacun|a lə 'kjuːn |ə læ-, -'kuːn- ~ae iː aɪ
lac|y, Lacy 'leɪs |i ~ier i̯ə ‖ i̯ᵊr ~iest i̯ɪst i̯əst
  ~iness i nəs i nɪs
lad læd lads lædz
Lada tdmk 'lɑːd ə ~s z

Ladakh lə 'dɑːk -'dɔːk
Ladbroke 'læd brʊk →'læb-, -brəʊk ‖ -broʊk
  ~'s s
Ladd læd
ladder 'læd ə ‖ -ᵊr ~ed d laddering 'læd ər ɪŋ
  ~s z
ladd|ie, ladd|y 'læd |i ~ies iz
ladd|ish 'læd |ɪʃ ~ism ˌɪz əm
lade leɪd (= laid) laded 'leɪd ɪd -əd laden
  'leɪd ᵊn lades leɪdz lading 'leɪd ɪŋ
Ladefoged 'læd ɪ fəʊg ɪd 'ˌ-ə-, -əd ‖ -foʊg-
laden 'leɪd ᵊn
Laden 'lɑːd ᵊn —Arabic ['laː dɪn]
ladette læ'det ~s s
Ladhar Bheinn ˌlɑː 'ven ‖ ˌlɑːr- —ScG
  [ˌɬaar 'vjeɲ]
la-di-da ˌlɑː di 'dɑː ◂
ladies 'leɪd iz
ladies-in-waiting ˌleɪd iz ɪn 'weɪt ɪŋ §-ᵊn'--
  ‖ -ᵊn 'weɪt̬ ɪŋ
ladieswear 'leɪd iz weə ‖ -wer -wær
Ladin læ 'diːn lə-
lading 'leɪd ɪŋ
Ladino, l~ lə 'diːn əʊ læ- ‖ -oʊ
ladl|e 'leɪd ᵊl ~ed d ~es z ~ing ɪŋ
lad|y, Lad|y 'leɪd |i ~ies, ~ies', ~y's iz
  'ladies' man; 'ladies' room; 'Lady
  ˌChapel; 'Lady Day; 'lady's ˌfingers, ˌ·· '··
ladybird 'leɪd i bɜːd ‖ -bɝːd ~s z
ladybug 'leɪd i bʌg ~s z
ladyfinger 'leɪd i ˌfɪŋ gə ‖ -gᵊr ~s z
lady|-in-waiting ˌleɪd i|ˌ ɪn 'weɪt ɪŋ §-ən'--
  ‖ -ən 'weɪt̬ ɪŋ ladies~ ˌleɪd iz-
lady-killer 'leɪd i ˌkɪl ə ‖ -ᵊr ~s z
ladylike 'leɪd i laɪk
ladyship 'leɪd i ʃɪp ~s s
Ladysmith 'leɪd i smɪθ
lady's-slipper ˌleɪd iz 'slɪp ə ‖ -ᵊr ~s z
Lae leɪ 'leɪ i, 'lɑː eɪ
Laertes leɪ 'ɜːt iːz ‖ -'ɝːt iːz
Laetitia li 'tɪʃ ə lə-, -'tɪʃ i̯ə
laetrile, L~ tdmk 'leɪ ə traɪᵊl -trɪl; -ətr əl
  ‖ -ətr əl -ə trɪl
laevo- ¦liːv əʊ ‖ -ə — laevorotation
  ˌliːv əʊ rəʊ 'teɪʃ ᵊn ‖ -ə roʊ-
laevulose 'liːv jʊ ləʊz 'lev-, -jə-, -ləʊs
  ‖ -jə loʊs -loʊz
Lafayette ˌlɑː faɪ 'et -feɪ- ‖ ˌlæf i- ˌlɑːf-, -eɪ-
  —Fr [la fa jɛt]
Lafcadio læf 'kɑːd i əʊ ‖ lɑːf 'kɑːd i oʊ
Laffan lə 'fæn
Laffer 'læf ə ‖ -ᵊr
  'Laffer curve
Lafford 'læf əd ‖ -ᵊrd
LaFontaine ˌlæf ɒn 'ten ˌlɑː fɒn-, -'teɪn
  ‖ ˌlɑː fɔːn 'ten -foʊn- —Fr [la fɔ̃ tɛn]
lag læg lagged lægd lagging 'læg ɪŋ lags
  lægz
Lagan, lagan 'læg ən
lager 'lɑːg ə ‖ -ᵊr 'lɔːg- ~s z
Lagerfeld 'lɑːg ə felt ‖ -ᵊr-
laggard 'læg əd ‖ -ᵊrd ~ly li ~s z
lagnappe, lagniappe 'læn jæp ˌ·'· ~s s

lagomorph 'læg ə mɔːf ‖ -mɔːrf **~s** s
Lagonda *tdmk* lə 'gɒnd ə ‖ -'gɑːnd ə **~s** z
lagoon lə 'guːn **~s** z
Lagos *in Nigeria* 'leɪg ɒs ‖ -aːs —*Those not familiar with Nigeria also sometimes say* 'lɑːg ɒs ‖ -ous
Lagrange lə 'grɒ̃ʒ læ-, lɑː-, -'grɑːnʒ, -'greɪndʒ ‖ -'grɑːndʒ —*Fr* [la gʁɑ̃ːʒ]
La Guardia lə 'gwɑːd i ə ‖ -'gwɑːrd-
Laguna *tdmk* lə 'guːn ə
  La ˌguna 'Beach
lahar 'lɑː hɑː ‖ -hɑːr **~s** z
lah-di-dah ˌlɑː di 'dɑː ◄
Lahnda 'lɑːnd ə
Lahore lə 'hɔː ‖ -'hɔːr -'hour —*Urdu* [la: hoːr]
laic 'leɪ ɪk **~al** ᵊl **~ally** ᵊl_i **~s** s
laicis... —*see* **laiciz...**
laicization ˌleɪ ɪs aɪ 'zeɪʃ ᵊn ˌ-əs-, -ɪ'-- ‖ -əs ə- **~s** z
laiciz|e 'leɪ ɪ saɪz -ə- **~ed** d **~es** ɪz əz **~ing** ɪŋ
laid leɪd
laid-back ˌleɪd 'bæk ◄ →ˌleɪb-
Laidlaw 'leɪd lɔː ‖ -lɑː
lain leɪn (= *lane*)
Laindon 'leɪnd ən
Laing (i) læŋ, (ii) leɪŋ
Laingian 'læŋ i ən **~s** z
lair leə ‖ 'leᵊr læᵊr **lairs** leəz ‖ 'leᵊrz læᵊrz
laird, Laird leəd ‖ leᵊrd læᵊrd **lairds** leədz ‖ leᵊrdz læᵊrdz
Lairg leəg ‖ leᵊrg læᵊrg
lairy 'leər i ‖ 'ler i
laisser-faire, laissez-faire ˌleɪs eɪ 'feə ˌles- ‖ -'feᵊr -'fæᵊr —*Fr* [lɛ se fɛːʁ]
lait|y 'leɪ ət ‖ i -ɪt- ‖ -ət̬ ‖ i **~ies** iz
Laius 'leɪ i_əs 'laɪˌəs, 'leɪ- ‖ 'leɪ əs 'leɪ i_əs
La Jolla lə 'hɔɪ ə
lake, Lake leɪk **lakes** leɪks
  Lake 'Charles; 'Lake ˌDistrict; 'Lake ˌPoets; ˌLake Suc'cess
lakebed 'leɪk bed **~s** z
lakeland, L~ 'leɪk lənd -lænd **~s** z
Lakenheath 'leɪk ən hiːθ
Laker 'leɪk ə ‖ -ᵊr
Lakesha lə 'keʃ ə
lakeside, L~ 'leɪk saɪd
lakh lɑːk læk —*Hindi* [laːkh] **lakhs** lɑːks læks
Lakme, Lakmé 'læk meɪ -mi
Lakshadweep læk 'ʃæd wiːp
Lakshmi 'lʌk ʃmi 'læk-, 'lɑːk- —*Sanskrit* [lək ʂmiː]
Lalage 'læl əg i -ədʒ-
la-la land 'lɑː lɑː lænd
Laleham 'leɪl əm
-lalia 'leɪl i_ə — **coprolalia** ˌkɒp rəʊ 'leɪl i_ə ‖ ˌkɑːp rə-
Lalique *tdmk* læ 'liːk lə- ‖ lɑː- —*Fr* [la lik]
Lallans 'læl ənz
lallation læ 'leɪʃ ᵊn **~s** z
lalling 'læl ɪŋ
Lalo 'lɑːl əʊ ‖ -ou —*Fr* [la lo]
lam læm **lammed** læmd **lamming** 'læm ɪŋ **lams** læmz

lama 'lɑːm ə **~s** z
Lamaism 'lɑːm əʳ ˌɪz əm ‖ -ə-
Lamarck lə 'mɑːk læ-, lɑː- ‖ -'mɑːrk —*Fr* [la maʁk]
Lamarckian lə 'mɑːk i ən læ-, lɑː- ‖ -'mɑːrk- **~s** z
Lamarr lə 'mɑː ‖ -'mɑːr
lamaser|y 'lɑːm əs ər ‖i ‖ -ə ser ‖i **~ies** iz
Lamaze lə 'meɪz
Lamaze lə 'meɪz —*Fr* [la maz]
lamb, Lamb læm (= *lam*) **lambed** læmd
  lambing 'læm ɪŋ **lambs, Lamb's** læmz
  ˌlamb 'chop ‖ 'lamb chop
lambad|a læm 'bɑːd ‖ ə ‖ lɑːm- **~aed** əd **~aing** əʳ ɪŋ ‖ ə ɪŋ **~as** əz
Lambarene ˌlæm bə 'riːn i ‖ ˌlɑːm- —*Fr* Lambaréné [lɑ̃ ba ʁe ne]
lambast læm 'bæst -'bɑːst **~ed** ɪd əd **~ing** ɪŋ **~s** s
lambast|e læm 'beɪst **~ed** ɪd əd **~ing** ɪŋ **~es** s
lambda 'læmd ə **~s** z
lambdacism 'læmd ə ˌsɪz əm **~s** z
Lambeg, l~ læm 'beg **~s** z
lambent 'læm bənt **~ly** li
Lambert, l~ 'læm bət ‖ -bᵊrt **~s, ~'s** s
Lambeth 'læm bəθ
  ˌLambeth 'Conference; ˌLambeth 'Palace; ˌLambeth 'Walk
lambkin 'læm kɪn §-kən **~s** z
lamblike 'læm laɪk
Lamborghini *tdmk* ˌlæm bɔː 'giːn i -bə- ‖ ˌlɑːm bɔːr- -bᵊr- —*It* [lam bor 'gi ni] **~s** z
Lamborn, Lambourne 'læm bɔːn ‖ -bɔːrn -bourn
Lambretta *tdmk* læm 'bret ə ‖ -'bret̬ ə **~s** z
Lambrusco, l~ læm 'brʊsk əʊ ‖ -'bruːsk ou —*It* [lam 'brus ko]
lambskin 'læm skɪn **~s** z
lambswool 'læmz wʊl
Lambton 'læmᵖt ən
LAMDA 'læmd ə
lame leɪm **lamed** leɪmd **lamer** 'leɪm ə ‖ -ᵊr **lames** leɪmz **lamest** 'leɪm ɪst -əst **laming** 'leɪm ɪŋ
  ˌlame 'duck
lamé 'lɑːm eɪ 'læm- ‖ lɑː 'meɪ læ-
lamebrain 'leɪm breɪn **~ed** d **~s** z
lamell|a lə 'mel ‖ə **~ae** iː **~as** əz
lamellibranch lə 'mel ɪ bræŋk §-'ə-
lame|ly 'leɪm ‖li **~ness** nəs nɪs
lament *v, n* lə 'ment **lamented** lə 'ment ɪd -əd ‖ lə 'men̬t əd **lamenting** lə 'ment ɪŋ ‖ lə 'men̬t ɪŋ **laments** lə 'ments
lamentab|le lə 'ment əb ‖ᵊl 'læm ənt-, -ˌɪnt- ‖ lə 'men̬t- 'læm ən̬t- — *Preference poll, BrE:* -'ment- 72%, 'læm- 28% (born before 1942, 44%). **~ly** li
lamentation ˌlæm ən 'teɪʃ ᵊn -ɪn-, -en- **~s, L~s** z
lame-o 'leɪm əʊ ‖ -ou **~s** z
La Mesa *place in CA* lə 'meɪs ə
lamin|a 'læm ɪn ‖ə -ən- **~ae** iː **~as** əz
laminal 'læm ɪn ᵊl -ən- **~s** z

LAMENTABLE

Pie chart: 72% / 28%, BrE. Legend: ☐ -'ment-, ☐ 'læm-

Graph: ● BrE -'ment- by age. Percentage axis 0–90. Older ◄— Speakers —► Younger

laminar 'læm ɪn ə -ən- ‖ -ᵊr
ˌlaminar 'flow
laminaria ˌlæm ɪ 'neər i‿ə ˌ·ə- ‖ -'ner- -'nær-
lami|nate v 'læm ɪ |neɪt -ə- **~nated** neɪt ɪd -əd
‖ neɪt̬ əd **~nates** neɪts **~nating** neɪt ɪŋ
‖ neɪt̬ ɪŋ
laminate n, adj 'læm ɪ neɪt -ə-; -ən ət, -ɪt **~s** s
lamination ˌlæm ɪ 'neɪʃ ᵊn -ə- **~s** z
laminator 'læm ɪ neɪt ə '·ə- ‖ -neɪt̬ ᵊr **~s** z
Laming (i) 'leɪm ɪŋ, (ii) 'læm-
Lamington, l~ 'læm ɪŋ tən **~s** z
Lammas 'læm əs
lammergeier, lammergeyer 'læm ə gaɪˌə
‖ -ᵊr gaɪˌᵊr **~s** z
Lammermoor 'læm ə mʊə -mɔː, ˌ··'· ‖ -mʊr
-mɔːr, -mʊʊr
Lammermuir 'læm ə mjʊə -mjɔː ‖ -ᵊr mjʊr
ˌLammermuir 'Hills
Lamond 'læm ənd
Lamont (i) 'læm ənt, (ii) lə 'mɒnt ‖ -'mɑːnt
—In AmE, (ii).
Lamorna lə 'mɔːn ə ‖ -'mɔːrn ə
lamp læmp **lamps** læmps
lamp-black 'læmp blæk
Lampedusa ˌlæmp ɪ 'djuːz ə -ə-, →-'dʒuːz-,
-'duːz- ‖ -ə 'duːz ə -'duːs- —It
[lam pe 'du: za]
lampern 'læmp ən ‖ -ᵊrn **~s** z
Lampeter 'læmp ɪt ə -ət- ‖ -ət̬ ᵊr
lamplight 'læmp laɪt
lamplighter 'læmp ˌlaɪt ə ‖ -ˌlaɪt̬ ᵊr **~s** z
Lamplugh 'læmp luː -lə
lampoon ₍ₗ₎læm 'puːn **~ed** d **~ing** ɪŋ **~s** z
lamp-post 'læmp pəʊst ‖ -poʊst **~s** s
lamprey 'læmp ri **~s** z
lampshade 'læmp ʃeɪd **~s** z
LAN læn or as local area network
Lana 'lɑːn ə ‖ 'læn ə
Lanagan 'læn əg ən
Lanai, lanai lə 'naɪ lɑː-, -'nɑː i **~s** z
Lanark 'læn ək ‖ -ᵊrk **~shire** ʃə ʃɪə, ˌʃaɪˌə ‖ ʃᵊr
ʃɪr

Lancashire 'læŋk ə ʃə -ʃɪə ‖ -ʃᵊr -ʃɪə
Lancaster 'læŋk əst ə 'læŋ kɑːst ə, -kæst- ‖ -ᵊr
'læŋ kæst ᵊr
Lancastrian læŋ 'kæs tri‿ən **~s** z
lance, Lance lɑːnⁿs §lænⁿs ‖ lænⁿs **lanced**
lɑːnⁿst §lænⁿst ‖ lænⁿst **lances, Lance's**
'lɑːnⁿs ɪz §'lænⁿs-, -əz ‖ 'lænⁿs əz **lancing**
'lɑːnⁿs ɪŋ §'lænⁿs- ‖ 'lænⁿs ɪŋ
ˌlance 'corporal ◄
lancelet 'lɑːnⁿs lət §'lænⁿs-, -lɪt ‖ 'lænⁿs- **~s** s
Lancelot 'lɑːnⁿs ə lɒt §'lænⁿs-, -əlˌət
‖ 'lænⁿs ə lɑːt -əlˌət
lanceolate 'lɑːnⁿs i‿ə leɪt §'lænⁿs-, -lət, -lɪt
‖ 'lænⁿs-
lancer 'lɑːnⁿs ə §'lænⁿs- ‖ 'lænⁿs ᵊr **~s** z
lancet 'lɑːnⁿs ɪt §'lænⁿs-, -ət ‖ 'lænⁿs ət **~s** s
Lanchester 'lɑːntʃ ɪst ə 'læntʃ-, -əst-,
§'læn ˌtʃest ə ‖ 'læn ˌtʃest ᵊr
Lancia tdmk 'lɑːnⁿs i‿ə §'lænⁿs- —It ['lan tʃa]
~s z
lanci|nate 'lænⁿs ɪ |neɪt 'lɑːnⁿs-, -ə- **~nated**
neɪt ɪd -əd ‖ neɪt̬ əd **~nates** neɪts **~nating**
neɪt ɪŋ ‖ neɪt̬ ɪŋ
Lancing 'lɑːnⁿs ɪŋ §'lænⁿs- ‖ 'lænⁿs ɪŋ
Lancome, Lancôme tdmk 'lɒŋ kəʊm
‖ 'lɑːŋ 'koʊm lɔːŋ-
Lancs. læŋks
land, Land lænd **landed** 'lænd ɪd -əd **landing**
'lænd ɪŋ **lands** lændz
'land ˌagent; 'land crab; ˌlanded 'gentry;
ˌLand's 'End
landau, L~ 'lænd ɔː -aʊ ‖ -aʊ -ɔː, -ɑː **~s** z
landaulet, landaulette ˌlænd ɔː 'let ‖ -ɑː- **~s**
s
landbank 'lænd bæŋk →'læmb-
land-based 'lænd beɪst →'læmb-
lander, L~ 'lænd ə ‖ -ᵊr **~s** z
Landers 'lænd əz ‖ -ᵊrz
landfall 'lænd fɔːl ‖ -fɑːl **~s** z
landfill 'lænd fɪl **~s** z
land-form 'lænd fɔːm ‖ -fɔːrm **~s** z
land-hold|er/s 'lænd ˌhəʊld ə/z →ˌhɒʊld-
‖ -ˌhoʊld ᵊr/z **~ing** ɪŋ
landing 'lænd ɪŋ **~s** z
'landing craft; 'landing field; 'landing
gear; 'landing net; 'landing stage;
'landing strip
Landis 'lænd ɪs §-əs
landlad|y 'lænd leɪd |i **~ies** iz
landless 'lænd ləs -lɪs
landline 'lænd laɪn **~s** z
landlocked 'lænd lɒkt ‖ -lɑːkt
landlord 'lænd lɔːd ‖ -lɔːrd **~ism** ˌɪz əm **~s** z
landlubber 'lænd ˌlʌb ə ‖ -ᵊr **~ly** li **~s** z
landmark 'lænd mɑːk →'læm- ‖ -mɑːrk **~s** s
landmass 'lænd mæs →'læm- **~es** ɪz əz
landmine 'lænd maɪn →'læm- **~s** z
Landor 'lænd ɔː -ə ‖ -ɔːr -ᵊr
landowner 'lænd ˌəʊn ə ‖ -ˌoʊn ᵊr **~s** z
landrail 'lænd reɪᵊl **~s** z
land rover, Land-Rover tdmk 'lænd ˌrəʊv ə
‖ -ˌroʊv ᵊr **~s** z
Landsat 'lænd sæt

landscap|e 'lænd skeıp **~ed** t **~er/s** ə/z ‖ ˀr/z
~es s **~ing** ıŋ
ˌlandscape 'gardening; 'landscape mode
Landseer 'lænd sıə ‖ -sır
landslide 'lænd slaıd **~s** z
landslip 'lænd slıp **~s** s
landward 'lænd wəd ‖ -wˀrd **~s** z
Landy 'lænd i
lane, Lane leın **lanes** leınz
Lanfranc 'læn fræŋk
Lang læŋ
Langan 'læŋ ən
Langbaurgh 'læŋ baːf -baː ‖ -baːrf -baːr
Langdale 'læŋ derˀl
Lange (i) læŋ i (ii) 'lɒŋ ‖ 'laːŋ i -The NZ
politician is (ii)
Langer 'læŋ ə ‖ -ˀr
Langerhans 'læŋ ə hænz -hænˢs
‖ 'laːŋ ˀr haːnz -haːnˢs —Ger ['laŋ ɐ hanˢs]
Langford 'læŋ fəd ‖ -fˀrd
Langham 'læŋ əm
Langholm place in Dumfries & Galloway
'læŋ əm —often called -həʊm ‖ -hoʊm by
those not familiar with the name
Langland 'læŋ lənd
langlauf 'læŋ laʊf ‖ 'laːŋ- **~er/s** ə/z ‖ -ˀr/z
Langley 'læŋ li
Langmuir 'læŋ mjʊə ‖ -mjʊr
Langobardic ˌlæŋ gəʊ 'baːd ık ◂ ‖ -ə 'baːrd-
langouste ˌlɒŋ 'guːst '·· ‖ ˌlaːŋ- —Fr [lɑ̃ gust]
~s s
langoustine ˌlɒŋ gu 'stiːn ‖ ˌlaːŋ- —Fr
[lɑ̃ gu stin] **~s** z
langsyne, lang syne (ˌ)læŋ 'saın
Langton 'læŋkt ən
Langtry 'læŋ tri
languag|e 'læŋ gwıdʒ §'læŋ wıdʒ **~es** ız əz
'language la,boratory ‖ - ,laboratory;
'language ,teaching
langue lɒŋg laːŋg, laːŋ, lõg ‖ laːŋg —Fr [lɑ̃ːg]
,langue de 'chat də 'ʃaː —Fr [də ʃa]
Languedoc ˌlɒŋ gə 'dɒk ˌlaːŋ-, '···
‖ ˌlaːŋ gə 'daːk -'dɔːk, -'doʊk —Fr [lɑ̃g dɔk]
languid 'læŋ gwıd §-gwəd **~ly** li **~ness** nəs nıs
languish, L~ 'læŋ gwıʃ **~ed** t **~es** ız əz **~ing/ly**
ıŋ/li **~ment** mənt
languor 'læŋ gə ‖ -gˀr
languorous 'læŋ gər əs **~ly** li **~ness** nəs nıs
langur læŋ 'gʊə lʌŋ-; 'læŋ gə ‖ -'gʊˀr **~s** z
Lanigan 'læn ıg ən -əg-
La Niña lə 'niːn jə laː-, læ- ‖ laː- —Sp
[la 'ni ɲa]
lank læŋk
Lankester 'læŋk ıst ə -əst- ‖ -ˀr
lank|ly 'læŋk |li **~ness** nəs nıs
lank|y 'læŋk |i **~ier** i ə ‖ i ˀr **~iest** i ıst i əst
~ily ı lı əl i **~iness** i nəs i nıs
lanner 'læn ə ‖ -ˀr **~s** z
lanolin 'læn əl ın §-ən
lanoline 'læn ə liːn -lın
Lansbury 'lænz bər i ‖ -,ber i
Lansdown, Lansdowne 'lænz daʊn
Lansing 'laːnˢs ıŋ §'lænˢs- ‖ 'lænˢs ıŋ

lansker, L~ 'læn skə ‖ -skˀr
lantern 'lænt ən ‖ -ˀrn **~s** z
lantern-jawed ˌlænt ən 'dʒɔːd ◂ ‖ -ˀrn-
-'dʒaːd
lanternslide 'lænt ən slaıd ‖ -ˀrn- **~s** z
lanthanide 'lænˀθ ə naıd **~s** z
lanthanum 'lænˀθ ən əm
lanyard 'læn jəd -jaːd ‖ -jˀrd **~s** z
Lanza 'lænz ə ‖ 'laːnz ə
Lanzarote ˌlænz ə 'rɒt i ‖ ˌlaːnˢts ə 'roʊt i
—Sp [lan θa 'ro te, -sa-]
Lao laʊ
Laocoon, Laocoön leı 'ɒk əʊ ɒn -ən
‖ -'aːk oʊ aːn
Laodamia ˌleı əʊ də 'maı,ə ‖ leı ˌaːd ə-
Laodice|a ˌleı əʊ dı 'siː,ə -əd ə- ‖ -əd ə-
leı ˌaːd ə- **~an/s** ən/z
Laoighis, Laois liːʃ —Irish [ɫiːʃ]
Laomedon leı 'ɒm ıd ən -əd- ‖ -'aːm ə daːn
Laos laʊs laʊz; 'laː ɒs ‖ 'laː oʊs laʊs; 'leı aːs
Laotian 'laʊʃ ˀn 'laʊʃ i ən; leı 'əʊʃ ˀn,
-'əʊʃ i ən ‖ leı 'oʊʃ ˀn 'laʊʃ ˀn **~s** z
Lao-tse, Lao-tsze, Lao-tzu ˌlaʊ 'tseı -'tsiː,
-'tsu: —Chi Lǎo Zǐ [³lɐu ³tsɯ]
lap læp **lapped** læpt **lapping** 'læp ıŋ **laps**
læps
laparoscope 'læp ər ə skəʊp ‖ -skoʊp **~s** s
laparoscop|y ˌlæp ə 'rɒsk əp |i ‖ -'raːsk- **~ies**
iz
laparotom|y ˌlæp ə 'rɒt əm |i ‖ -'raːt əm |i
~ies iz
La Paz lə 'pæz ‖ lə 'paːz —AmSp [la 'pas]
lapdanc|er/s 'læp ˌdaːnˢs ə/z §-ˌdænˢs-
‖ -ˌdænˢs ˀr/z **~ing** ıŋ
lapdog 'læp dɒg ‖ -dɔːg -daːg **~s** z
lapel lə 'pel læ- **~s** z
lap-held 'læp held
Laphroaig lə 'frɔıg laː-, læ-
lapidar|y 'læp ıd ˀr i ‖ -'əd ‖ -ə der |i **~ies** iz
lapilli lə 'pıl aı
lapis lazuli ˌlæp ıs 'læz jʊl i §,-əs-, -jəl i, -aı
‖ -ə liː -'læʒ-
Lapith 'læp ıθ **~s** s
Laplace lə 'plaːs læ-, laː-, -'plæs —Fr [la plas]
Lapland 'læp lænd -lənd
Laplander 'læp lænd ə -lənd- ‖ -ˀr **~s** z
Lapotaire ˌlæp ɒ 'teə -ə- ‖ -oʊ 'teˀr -'tæˀr
Lapp læp
lappet 'læp ıt -ət **~s** s
Lappin 'læp ın §-ən
Lappish 'læp ıʃ
Lapsang Souchong ˌlæp sæŋ su: 'ʃɒŋ -'tʃɒŋ
‖ ˌlaːp saːŋ 'su: ʃaːŋ
lapse læps (= laps) **lapsed** læpst **lapses**
'læps ız -əz **lapsing** 'læps ıŋ
lapsus linguae ˌlæps əs 'lıŋ gwaı -gwi:
laptop 'læp tɒp ‖ -taːp **~s** s
Laputa lə 'pjuːt ə ‖ -'pjuːt̬ ə
Laputan lə 'pjuːt ˀn **~s** z
lapwing 'læp wıŋ **~s** z
Lar, lar laː ‖ laːr **lares** 'laːr eız 'leər iːz
‖ 'lær iːz 'ler-
lars laːz ‖ laːrz

Lara ˈlɑːr ə
Laramie ˈlær əm i ‖ ˈler-
Larbert ˈlɑːb ət ‖ ˈlɑːrb ᵊrt
larboard ˈlɑːb əd ˈlɑː bɔːd ‖ ˈlɑːrb ᵊrd
larcenous ˈlɑːs ən əs -ɪn- ‖ ˈlɑːrs- **~ly** li
larcen|y ˈlɑːs ən |i -ɪn- ‖ ˈlɑːrs- **~ies** iz
larch lɑːtʃ ‖ lɑːrtʃ **larches** ˈlɑːtʃ ɪz -əz
 ‖ ˈlɑːrtʃ əz
lard lɑːd ‖ lɑːrd **larded** ˈlɑːd ɪd -əd ‖ ˈlɑːrd əd
 larding ˈlɑːd ɪŋ ‖ ˈlɑːrd ɪŋ **lards** lɑːdz
 ‖ lɑːrdz
lard-ass ˈlɑːd ɑːs -æs ‖ ˈlɑːrd æs **~es** ɪz əz
larder ˈlɑːd ə ‖ ˈlɑːrd ᵊr **~s** z
Lardner ˈlɑːd nə ‖ ˈlɑːrd nᵊr
lardy ˈlɑːd i ‖ ˈlɑːrd i
 ˈlardy cake
Laredo lə ˈreɪd əʊ ‖ -oʊ
lares ˈlɑːr eɪz ˈleər iːz ‖ ˈlær iːz ˈler-
Largactil, l~ tdmk lɑː ˈgækt ɪl -ᵊl ‖ ˈlɑːr-
large, Large lɑːdʒ ‖ lɑːrdʒ **larger** ˈlɑːdʒ ə
 ‖ ˈlɑːrdʒ ᵊr **largest** ˈlɑːdʒ ɪst -əst ‖ ˈlɑːrdʒ-
large-hearted ˌlɑːdʒ ˈhɑːt ɪd ◂ -əd
 ‖ ˌlɑːrdʒ ˈhɑːrt̮ əd ◂ **~ness** nəs nɪs
largely ˈlɑːdʒ li ‖ ˈlɑːrdʒ li
large-minded ˌlɑːdʒ ˈmaɪnd ɪd ◂ -əd ‖ ˌlɑːrdʒ-
 ~ness nəs nɪs
largeness ˈlɑːdʒ nəs -nɪs ‖ ˈlɑːrdʒ-
large-scale ˌlɑːdʒ ˈskeɪᵊl ◂ ‖ ˌlɑːrdʒ-
largess, largesse ₍ᵢ₎lɑː ˈdʒes -ˈʒes; ˈlɑːdʒ es
 ‖ ₍ᵢ₎lɑːr-
larghetto lɑː ˈget əʊ ‖ lɑːr ˈget̮ oʊ **~s** z
largish ˈlɑːdʒ ɪʃ ‖ ˈlɑːrdʒ-
largo ˈlɑːg əʊ ‖ ˈlɑːrg oʊ **~s** z
Largs lɑːgz ‖ lɑːrgz
lariat ˈlær i ət ‖ ˈler- **~s** s
Larisa, Larissa lə ˈrɪs ə
Larium, l~ ˈleər i əm ‖ ˈler- ˈlær-
lark, Lark lɑːk ‖ lɑːrk **larked** lɑːkt ‖ lɑːrkt
 larking ˈlɑːk ɪŋ ‖ ˈlɑːrk ɪŋ **larks** lɑːks
 ‖ lɑːrks
Larkhall ˈlɑːk hɔːl ‖ ˈlɑːrk- -hɑːl
Larkin ˈlɑːk ɪn §-ən ‖ ˈlɑːrk-
larkspur ˈlɑːk spɜː ‖ ˈlɑːrk spɜː **~s** z
larky ˈlɑːk i ‖ ˈlɑːrk i
Larmor ˈlɑːm ə -ɔː ‖ ˈlɑːrm ᵊr -ɔːr
larn lɑːn ‖ lɑːrn **larned** lɑːnd ‖ lɑːrnd **larning**
 ˈlɑːn ɪŋ ‖ ˈlɑːrn ɪŋ **larns** lɑːnz ‖ lɑːrns —This
 is a non-standard variant of learn, sometimes
 used humorously.
Larnaca ˈlɑːn ək ə ‖ ˈlɑːrn-
Larne lɑːn ‖ lɑːrn
Larousse læ ˈruːs ‖ lɑː- —Fr [la ʁus]
larrikin ˈlær ɪk ɪn -ək-, §-ən ‖ ˈler- **~s** z
larrup ˈlær əp ‖ ˈler- **~ed** t **~ing** ɪŋ **~s** s
Larry ˈlær i ‖ ˈler-
Lars lɑːz ‖ lɑːrz lɑːrs —Swedish [lɑːʂ]
 ˌLars ˈPorsena ˈpɔːs ɪn ə -ən- ‖ ˈpɔːrs-
LARSP lɑːsp ‖ lɑːrsp
larv|a ˈlɑːv |ə ‖ ˈlɑːrv |ə **~ae** iː eɪ **~al** ᵊl
Larwood ˈlɑː wʊd ‖ ˈlɑːr-
laryngal lə ˈrɪŋ gᵊl læ- **~s** z

laryngeal lə ˈrɪndʒ əl læ-, -ˈrɪndʒ i əl;
 ˌlær ɪn ˈdʒiː əl ◂, -ən- ‖ ˌlær ən ˈdʒiː əl, ˌler-
 ~s z
laryngealis... —see **laryngealiz...**
laryngealization lə ˌrɪndʒ əl aɪ ˈzeɪʃ ᵊn læ-,
 -əl ɪ- ‖ -əl ə-
laryngealiz|e lə ˈrɪndʒ ə laɪz læ- **~ed** d **~es** ɪz
 əz **~ing** ɪŋ
laryngectomee ˌlær ɪn ˈdʒekt ə miː ˌ-ən-,
 ˌ·ˌ·ˌ·ˈ· ‖ ˌler- **~s** z
laryngectom|y ˌlær ɪn ˈdʒekt əm |i ˌ-ən-
 ‖ ˌler- **~ies** iz
larynges læ ˈrɪndʒ iːz lə-
laryngitis ˌlær ɪn ˈdʒaɪt ɪs -ən-, §-əs
 ‖ -ˈdʒaɪt̮ əs ˌler-
laryngo- comb. form
 with stress-neutral suffix lə ˌrɪŋ gəʊ ‖ -goʊ
 — **laryngophantom** lə ˌrɪŋ gəʊ ˈfænt əm
 ‖ -goʊ ˈfænt̮-
 with stress-imposing suffix ˌlær ɪŋ ˈgɒ +
 ‖ ˌlær ən ˈgɑː+ ˌler-, →-ɪŋ- — **laryngopathy**
 ˌlær ɪŋ ˈgɒp əθ i ‖ -ən ˈgɑːp əθ i ˌler-, →ˌ-ɪŋ-
laryngograph, L~ tdmk lə ˈrɪŋ gəʊ grɑːf læ-,
 -græf ‖ -gə græf **~s** s
laryngographic lə ˌrɪŋ gəʊ ˈgræf ɪk ◂ læ-
 ‖ -gə- **~ally** ᵊl i
laryngography ˌlær ɪŋ ˈgɒg rəf i
 ‖ ˌlær ən ˈgɑːg-, ˌler-, →ˌ-ɪŋ-
laryngological lə ˌrɪŋ gə ˈlɒdʒ ɪk ᵊl ◂ læ-
 ‖ -ˈlɑːdʒ- **~ly** i
laryngolog|ist/s ˌlær ɪŋ ˈgɒl ədʒ |ɪst/s §-əst/s
 ‖ ˌlær ən ˈgɑːl-, ˌler-, →ˌ-ɪŋ- **~y** i
laryngoscope lə ˈrɪŋ gə skəʊp læ- ‖ -skoʊp **~s**
 s
laryngoscopic lə ˌrɪŋ gə ˈskɒp ɪk ◂ læ-
 ‖ -ˈskɑːp ɪk ◂ **~ally** ᵊl i
laryngoscop|y ˌlær ɪŋ ˈgɒsk əp |i
 ‖ ˌlær ən ˈgɑːsk- ˌler-, →ˌ-ɪŋ- **~ies** iz
larynx ˈlær ɪŋks ‖ ˈler- **~es** ɪz əz **larynges**
 læ ˈrɪndʒ iːz lə-
Las Spanish article læs ‖ lɑːs —usually
 unstressed. See also phrases with this word
 —Sp [las]
lasagn|a lə ˈzæn |jə -ˈsæn-, -ˈzɑːn-, -ˈsɑːn-
 ‖ -ˈzɑːn- —It [la ˈzaɲ ɲa] **~e** jə jeɪ —It [-ɲe]
lascar, L~ ˈlæsk ə ‖ -ᵊr **~s** z
Lascaux ˈlæsk əʊ læ ˈskəʊ ‖ lɑː ˈskoʊ læ- —Fr
 [las ko]
Lascelles ˈlæs ᵊlz lə ˈselz
lascivious lə ˈsɪv i əs **~ly** li **~ness** nəs nɪs
Lasdun ˈlæzd ən
laser ˈleɪz ə ‖ -ᵊr **~s** z
 ˈlaser ˌprinter
laserjet ˈleɪz ə dʒet ‖ -ᵊr- **~s** s
lash læʃ **lashed** læʃt **lashes** ˈlæʃ ɪz -əz
 lashing/s ˈlæʃ ɪŋ/z
Lasham ˈlæʃ əm —locally also ˈlæs-
lash-up ˈlæʃ ʌp **~s** s
LASIK ˈleɪz ɪk
Laski ˈlæsk i
Las Palmas læs ˈpæl məs ˌ-ˌ-, -ˈpɑːl-
 ‖ lɑːs ˈpɑːlm əs —Sp [las ˈpal mas]
lass, Lass læs **lasses** ˈlæs ɪz -əz

Lassa 'læs ə 'lɑːs-
  ˌLassa 'fever
Lassen 'læs ᵊn
lassi 'læs i 'lʌs- ‖ lɑ: 'si: —*Hindi* [lə si]
lassie, L~ 'læs i ~s z
lassitude 'læs ɪ tjuːd -ə-, →-tʃuːd ‖ -tuːd -tjuːd
lasso lə 'suː læː-; 'læs əʊ ‖ 'læs oʊ læ 'suː *(*)*
  ~ed d ~ing ɪŋ ~es, ~s z
last, Last lɑːst §læst ‖ læst **lasted** 'lɑːst ɪd
  §'læst-, -əd ‖ 'læst əd **lasting** 'lɑːst ɪŋ §'læst-
  ‖ 'læst ɪŋ **lasts** lɑːsts §læsts ‖ læsts
  ˌlast 'judgment; ˌlast 'minute; 'last name,
  ˌ· '·; ˌlast 'night; ˌlast 'post; ˌlast 'straw;
  ˌlast 'week; ˌlast 'word
last-ditch ˌlɑːst 'dɪtʃ ◂ §ˌlæst- ‖ ˌlæst-
last-gasp ˌlɑːst'gɑːsp ◂ §ˌlæst-, §-'gæsp
  ‖ ˌlæst 'gæsp ◂
lasting 'lɑːst ɪŋ §'læst- ‖ 'læst ɪŋ ~ly li ~ness
  nəs nɪs
lastly 'lɑːst li §'læst- ‖ 'læst li
last-minute ˌlɑːst 'mɪn ɪt ◂ §-ət ‖ ˌlæst-
Las Vegas læs 'veɪg əs ˌ·- ‖ lɑːs-
lat læt **lats** læts
Latakia ˌlæt ə 'kiːˌə ‖ ˌlæt̬- ˌlɑːt̬-
Latasha lə 'tæʃ ə
latch lætʃ **latched** lætʃt **latches** 'lætʃ ɪz -əz
  latching 'lætʃ ɪŋ
latchet 'lætʃ ɪt -ət ~s s
latchkey 'lætʃ kiː ~s z
  'latchkey child
late leɪt **later** 'leɪt ə ‖ 'leɪt̬ ᵊr **latest** 'leɪt ɪst
  -əst ‖ 'leɪt̬ əst
late-breaking 'leɪt ˌbreɪk ɪŋ
latecomer 'leɪt ˌkʌm ə ‖ -ᵊr ~s z
lateen lə 'tiːn ~s z
lately 'leɪt li
latenc|y 'leɪt ᵊnᵗs |i ~ies iz
lateness 'leɪt nəs -nɪs ~es ɪz əz
late-night 'leɪt naɪt
latent 'leɪt ᵊnt ~ly li
  ˌlatent 'heat
later 'leɪt ə ‖ 'leɪt̬ ᵊr
lateral 'læt̬ᵊr əl ‖ 'læt̬ ər əl →'lætr əl ~ly i ~s
  z
  ˌlateral 'fricative; ˌlateral 'thinking
laterality ˌlæt ə 'ræl ət i -ɪt i ‖ ˌlæt̬ ə 'ræl ət̬ i
Lateran 'læt ər ən ‖ 'læt̬-
laterite 'læt ə raɪt ‖ 'læt̬-
latest 'leɪt ɪst -əst ‖ 'leɪt̬-
latex 'leɪt eks ~es ɪz əz
LaTeX, LaTEX *computing* 'leɪ tek
lath lɑːθ læθ ‖ læθ **laths** lɑːθs lɑːðz; læθs, læðz
  ‖ læðz læθs
Latham *(i)* 'leɪð əm, *(ii)* 'leɪθ-
lathe leɪð **lathes** leɪðz
lath|er 'lɑːð |ə 'læð- ‖ 'læð |ᵊr — *Preference
  poll, BrE:* 'lɑːð- *72% (southerners 88%),* 'læð-
  28% (southerners 12%). ~ered əd ‖ ᵊrd
  ~ering ər ɪŋ ~ers əz ‖ ᵊrz
lathery 'lɑːð ər i 'læð- ‖ 'læð-
lathi 'lɑːt i —*Hindi* [laː ʈʰi] ~s z
Lathom *(i)* 'leɪð əm, *(ii)* 'leɪθ-
Latimer 'læt ɪm ə -əm- ‖ 'læt̬ əm ᵊr

LATHER

'lɑːð- 72%
'læð- 28%
BrE

Latin 'læt ɪn §-ᵊn ‖ 'læt ᵊn ~s z
  ˌLatin A'merican◂
Latina læ 'tiːn ə lə- ‖ lɑː-, -ɑː: ~s z s
Latinate 'læt ɪ neɪt §-ə- ‖ -ᵊn eɪt
latinis... —*see* **latiniz...**
latin|ism 'læt ɪn |ˌɪz əm §-ᵊn- ‖ 'læt̬ ᵊn- ~ist/s
  ɪst/s §əst/s ‖ əst/s
latinization ˌlæt ɪn aɪ 'zeɪʃ ᵊn §ˌ·ᵊn-, -ɪ'·-
  ‖ ˌlæt̬ ᵊn ə-
latiniz|e 'læt ɪ naɪz §-ᵊn aɪz ‖ -ᵊn aɪz ~ed d
  ~es ɪz əz ~ing ɪŋ
Latino læ 'tiːn əʊ lə- ‖ -oʊ ~s z s
latish 'leɪt ɪʃ ‖ 'leɪt̬ ɪʃ
latitude 'læt ɪ tjuːd -ə-, →-tʃuːd ‖ 'læt̬ ə tuːd
  -tjuːd ~s z
latitudinal ˌlæt ɪ 'tjuːd ɪn ᵊl ◂ ·ə-, →-'tʃuːd-,
  -ᵊn ᵊl ‖ ˌlæt̬ ə 'tuːd ᵊn ᵊl ◂ -'tjuːd-
latitudinarian ˌlæt ɪ ˌtjuːd ɪ 'neər iˌən ·ə-,
  →-ˌtʃuːd-, -ˌ·ə- ‖ ˌlæt̬ ə ˌtuːd ᵊn 'er iˌən -ˌtjuːd-
  ~s z
Latium 'leɪʃ iˌəm
latke 'lɑːt kə ~s z
Latona lə 'təʊn ə ‖ -'toʊn ə
Latoya lə 'tɔɪ ə
latria lə 'traɪˌə
latrine lə 'triːn ~s z
Latrobe, La Trobe lə 'trəʊb ‖ -'troʊb
-latry *stress-imposing* lətr i — **hagiolatry**
  ˌhæg i 'ɒl ətr i ˌheɪdʒ- ‖ -'ɑːl-
latte 'læt eɪ 'lɑːt- ‖ 'lɑːt eɪ ~s z —*It* ['lat te]
latter 'læt ə ‖ 'læt̬ ᵊr
latter-day ˌlæt ə 'deɪ ◂ ‖ ˌlæt̬ ᵊr-
  ˌlatter-day 'hero
latterly 'læt ə li -ᵊl i ‖ 'læt̬ ᵊr li
lattic|e 'læt ɪs -əs ‖ 'læt̬ əs ~ed t ~es ɪz əz
  ~ework wɜːk ‖ wɜːk ~ing ɪŋ
Lattimore 'læt ɪ mɔː: -ə- ‖ 'læt̬ ə mɔːr -moʊr
Latvi|a 'læt vi |ə ‖ 'lɑːt- ~an/s ən/z
laud, Laud lɔːd ‖ lɑːd **lauded** 'lɔːd ɪd -əd
  ‖ 'lɑːd- **lauding** 'lɔːd ɪŋ ‖ 'lɑːd- **lauds, Lauds**
  lɔːdz ‖ lɑːdz
Lauda 'laʊd ə —*Ger* ['lau da]
laudability ˌlɔːd ə 'bɪl ət i -ɪt i ‖ -ət̬ i ˌlɑːd-
laudab|le 'lɔːd əb |ᵊl ‖ 'lɑːd- ~ly li
laudanum 'lɔːd ᵊn_əm 'lɒd- ‖ 'lɑːd-
laudatory 'lɔːd ət ᵊr i ‖ -ə tɔːr i 'lɑːd-, -toʊri
Lauder 'lɔːd ə ‖ -ᵊr 'lɑːd-
Lauderdale 'lɔːd ə derᵊl ‖ -ᵊr- 'lɑːd-
laugh lɑːf §læf ‖ læf **laughed** lɑːft §læft ‖ læft
  laughing 'lɑːf ɪŋ §'læf- ‖ 'læf ɪŋ **laughs** lɑːfs
  §læfs ‖ læfs
  'laughing gas; ˌlaughing 'jackass
laughab|le 'lɑːf əb |ᵊl §'læf- ‖ 'læf- ~ly li

Laugharne lɑːn ‖ lɑːrn
laughingly 'lɑːf ɪŋ li §'læf- ‖ 'læf ɪŋ li
laughingstock 'lɑːf ɪŋ stɒk '§læf-
‖ 'læf ɪŋ stɑːk
laughter 'lɑːft ə §'lɑːft- ‖ 'læft ᵊr
Laughton 'lɔːt ᵊn ‖ 'lɑːt-
Launceston 'lɔːnˢst ən 'lɑːnˢs ᵊn,
'lɔːnˢs- ‖ 'lɔːnˢs əst ən 'lɑːnˢs- —*but in*
Tasmania, 'lɒnˢs əst ən ‖ 'lɑːnˢs-
launch lɔːntʃ ‖ lɑːntʃ —*In RP formerly also*
'lɑːntʃ. **launched** lɔːntʃt ‖ lɑːntʃt **launcher/s**
'lɔːntʃ ə/z ‖ -ᵊr/z 'lɑːntʃ- **launches** 'lɔːntʃ ɪz
-əz ‖ 'lɑːntʃ- **launching** 'lɔːntʃ ɪŋ ‖ 'lɑːntʃ-
'**launching pad, 'launch pad**; '**launch
,vehicle**
laund|er 'lɔːnd| ə ‖ -ᵊr 'lɑːnd|- **~ered** əd ‖ ᵊrd
~ering ᵊr ɪŋ **~ers** əz ‖ ᵊrz
launderette, L~ *tdmk* ,lɔːnd ə 'ret ,lɒːn 'dret
‖ ,lɑːnd- **~s** s
laundress 'lɔːndr es -əs, -ɪs ‖ 'lɑːndr- **~es** ɪz əz
laundrette ,lɔːn 'dret ‖ ,lɑːn- **~s** s
laundromat, L~ *tdmk* 'lɔːndr ə mæt ‖ 'lɑːndr-
~s s
laundr|y 'lɔːndr |i ‖ 'lɑːndr- **~ies** iz
'**laundry ,basket**
Lauper 'laʊp ə ‖ -ᵊr
Laura 'lɔːr ə
lauraceous lɒ 'reɪʃ əs lɔː- ‖ lɔː- lɑː-
Laurasia lɔː 'reɪʃ ə -'reɪʒ-, -'reɪʒ i ə ‖ lɔː 'reɪʒ ə
lɑː-, -'reɪʃ-
Laurasian lɔː 'reɪʃ ᵊn -'reɪʒ-, -'reɪʒ i ən
‖ lɔː 'reɪʒ ᵊn lɑː-, -'reɪʃ-
laureate 'lɔːr i ət 'lɒr-, -ɪt ‖ 'lɑːr- **~s** s **~ship**
ʃɪp
laurel, L~ 'lɒr əl ‖ 'lɔːr- 'lɑːr- **~s** z
Lauren 'lɔːr ən 'lɒr- ‖ 'lɑːr-
Laurence 'lɒr ᵊnˢs ‖ 'lɔːr- 'lɑːr-
Laurentian lɒ 'ren'ʃ ᵊn lɔː- ‖ lɔː- lɑː- **~s** z
Lauretta lə 'ret ə lɔː- ‖ -'reţ ə
lauric 'lɔːr ɪk 'lɒr- ‖ 'lɑːr-
Laurie 'lɒr i ‖ 'lɔːr i
Laurier 'lɒr i ə -eɪ ‖ 'lɔːr i ᵊr ,lɒr i ei
Lauriston 'lɒr ɪst ən -əst- ‖ 'lɔːr- 'lɑːr-
laurustinus ,lɒr ə 'staɪn əs ,lɔːr- ‖ ,lɔːr-
lauryl 'lɒr ɪl 'lɔːr-, -əl ‖ 'lɔːr əl 'lɑːr-
Lausanne ləʊ 'zæn ‖ loʊ- —*Fr* [lo zan, -ɛ-]
lav læv **lavs** lævz
lava 'lɑːv ə
lavabo lə 'vɑːb əʊ -'veɪb- ‖ -oʊ **~es** z
lavage 'læv ɪdʒ -ɑːʒ; læ 'vɑːʒ ‖ lə 'vɑːʒ
'læv ɪdʒ
Laval lə 'væl læ- —*Fr* [la val]
lavaliere lə ,væl i 'eə ‖ ,læv ə 'lɪᵊr ,lɑːv- **~s** z
lavatorial ,læv ə 'tɔːr i əl ◄ ‖ -'tour-
lavator|y 'læv ət ᵊr |i ‖ -ə tɔːr |i -tour i **~ies** iz
lave leɪv **laved** leɪvd **laves** leɪvz **laving**
'leɪv ɪŋ
lavender, L~ 'læv ənd ə -ɪnd- ‖ -ᵊr **~s** z
Lavengro lə 'veŋ grəʊ ‖ -groʊ
Lavenham 'læv ən ᵊm
laver '*basin*' 'leɪv ə ‖ -ᵊr **~s** z
laver '*seaweed*' 'lɑːv ə ‖ -ᵊr 'leɪv-
Laver *family name* 'leɪv ə ‖ -ᵊr

Lavern, Laverne lə 'vɜːn ‖ -'vɝːn
Lavers 'leɪv əz ‖ -ᵊrz
Lavinia lə 'vɪn i ə
lavish 'læv ɪʃ **~ed** t **~es** ɪz əz **~ing** ɪŋ **~ly** li
~ness nəs nɪs
Lavoisier lə 'vwɑːz i eɪ læ-, -'vwɑːz-
‖ ,læv wɑː zi 'eɪ —*Fr* [la vwa zje]
lavv|y 'læv |i **~ies** iz
law, Law lɔː ‖ lɑː **laws** lɔːz ‖ lɑːz
law-abiding 'lɔː ˌə ,baɪd ɪŋ ‖ -ɪ:- 'lɑː-
law-breaker 'lɔː ,breɪk ə ‖ -ᵊr 'lɑː- **~s** z
Lawes lɔːz ‖ lɑːz
Lawford 'lɔː fəd ‖ -fᵊrd 'lɑː-
lawful 'lɔː fᵊl -fʊl ‖ 'lɑː- **~ly** i **~ness** nəs nɪs
Lawler 'lɔːl ə ‖ -ᵊr 'lɑːl-
lawless, L~ 'lɔː ləs -lɪs ‖ 'lɑː- **~ly** li **~ness** nəs
nɪs
Lawley 'lɔː li ‖ 'lɑː-
lawmaker 'lɔː ,meɪk ə ‖ -ᵊr 'lɑː- **~s** z
law|man 'lɔː| mæn ‖ 'lɑː- **~men** men
lawn lɔːn ‖ lɑːn **lawns** lɔːnz ‖ lɑːnz
'**lawn ,party**; '**lawn 'tennis** ‖ '·,··
lawnmower 'lɔːn ,məʊ ə ‖ -,moʊ ᵊr 'lɑːn- **~s** z
Lawrance, Lawrence 'lɒr ənˢs ‖ 'lɔːr- 'lɑːr-
lawrencium lə 'renˢs i əm lɔː-, lɒ- ‖ lɔː- lɑː-
Lawrentian lɒ 'ren'ʃ ᵊn lɔː:-, -'ren'ʃ i ən ‖ lɔː-
lɑː- **~s** z
Lawrie, Lawry 'lɒr i ‖ 'lɔːr i 'lɑːr i
Lawson 'lɔːs ᵊn ‖ 'lɑːs-
lawsuit 'lɔː suːt -sjuːt ‖ 'lɑː- **~s** s
Lawton 'lɔːt ᵊn ‖ 'lɑːt-

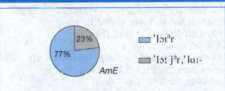

LAWYER

	'lɔɪ ᵊr
77%	23%
	'lɔː jᵊr, 'lɑː-

AmE

lawyer 'lɔː jə -ɪ 'lɔɪ ə ‖ 'lɔɪ ᵊr 'lɔː jᵊr, 'lɑː- **~s** z
— *Preference poll, AmE:* 'lɔɪ ᵊr 77%, 'lɔː jᵊr,
'lɑː jᵊr 23%.
lax læks **laxed** lækst **laxer** 'læks ə ‖ -ᵊr **laxes**
'læks ɪz -əz **laxest** 'læks ɪst -əst **laxing**
'læks ɪŋ
Laxalt 'læks ɔːlt ‖ -ɑːlt
laxative 'læks ət ɪv ‖ -əţ ɪv **~s** z
Laxey 'læks i
laxity 'læks ət i -ɪt- ‖ -əţ i
lax|ly 'læks |li **~ness** nəs nɪs
lay leɪ **laid** leɪd **laying** 'leɪ ɪŋ **lays** leɪz
,**lay 'brother**; ,**lay 'figure** ‖ '· ,· ·; ,**lay
'reader**; ,**lay 'sister**
layabout 'leɪ ə ,baʊt **~s** s
layaway 'leɪ ə,weɪ
lay-by 'leɪ baɪ **~s** z
Laycock 'leɪ kɒk ‖ -kɑːk
layer 'leɪ ə leə ‖ -ᵊr leᵊr **~ed** d **layering**
'leɪ ᵊr ɪŋ 'leᵊr ɪŋ ‖ 'leɪ ɪŋ **~s** z
'**layer cake**
layette leɪ 'et **~s** s

L

lay|man 'leɪ |mən **~men** mən
lay-off 'leɪ ɒf -ɔːf ‖ -ɔːf -ɑːf **~s** s
layout 'leɪ aʊt **~s** s
layover 'leɪ ˌəʊv ə ‖ -ˌoʊv ᵊr **~s** z
layperson 'leɪ ˌpɜːs ᵊn ‖ -ˌpɜːs- **~s** z
layshaft 'leɪ ʃɑːft §-ʃæft ‖ -ʃæft **~s** s
Layton 'leɪt ᵊn
lay-up 'leɪ ʌp **~s** s
lay|woman 'leɪ ˌwʊm ən **~women** ˌwɪm ɪn §-ən
Lazard 'læz ɑːd ‖ -lə 'zɑːrd **~s** z
lazaretto ˌlæz ə 'ret əʊ ‖ -'reṭ oʊ **~s** z
Lazarus 'læz ᵊr ᵊs
laze leɪz (= lays) **lazed** leɪzd **lazes** 'leɪz ɪz -əz
lazing 'leɪz ɪŋ
Lazenby 'leɪz ᵊn bi →-ᵊm-
lazi... —see **lazy**
Lazio 'læts i əʊ ‖ 'lɑːts i oʊ —It ['lat tsjo]
Lazonby 'leɪz ᵊn bi →-ᵊm-
lazulite 'læz ju laɪt 'læʒ-, -jə- ‖ 'læʒ ə- (*)
laz|y 'leɪz |i **~ier** i ə ‖ i ᵊr **~iest** i ɪst i əst **~ily**
ɪ li əl i **~iness** i nəs i nɪs
lazybones 'leɪz i bəʊnz ‖ -boʊnz
lb sing. paʊnd **lb** pl paʊndz **lbs** paʊndz
lbw ˌel biː 'dʌb ᵊl ju
LCD ˌel siː 'diː **~s, ~'s** z
LCM ˌel siː 'em **~s, ~'s** z
LDC ˌel diː 'siː **~s, ~'s** z
L-dopa, L-Dopa ˌel 'dəʊp ə ‖ -'doʊp ə
L-driver 'el ˌdraɪv ə ‖ -ᵊr **~s** z
Le, le in family names lə —See also phrases
with this word—and note occasional
exceptions, e.g. Le Fanu
-le- in place names li lə — **Stanford-le-Hope**
ˌstæn fəd li 'həʊp ‖ -fᵊrd li 'hoʊp
lea, Lea liː (= lee) **leas** liːz
LEA ˌel i: 'eɪ **~s, ~'s** z
leach, Leach liːtʃ (= leech) **leached** liːtʃt
leaches 'liːtʃ ɪz -əz **leaching** 'liːtʃ ɪŋ
Leacock 'liː kɒk 'leɪ- ‖ -kɑːk
lead n 'metal' led **leaded** 'led ɪd -əd **leading**
'led ɪŋ **leads** ledz
lead v; n 'guiding, first place/act/actor, leash,
cord, flex' liːd **leading** 'liːd ɪŋ **leads** liːdz
led led
Leadbetter 'led ˌbet ə →-'leb-; ˌ·'·· ‖ -ˌbeṭ ᵊr
Leadbitter 'led ˌbɪt ə →-'leb- ‖ -ˌbɪṭ ᵊr
leaded 'led ɪd -əd
leaden 'led ᵊn **~ly** li **~ness** nəs nɪs
Leadenhall 'led ᵊn hɔːl ‖ -hɑːl
leader 'liːd ə ‖ -ᵊr **~s** z
leadership 'liːd ə ʃɪp ‖ -ᵊr- **~s** s
lead-free ˌled 'friː ◂
lead-in 'liːd ɪn ˌ·'· **~s** z
leading adj 'main', 'guiding' 'liːd ɪŋ **~ly** li
ˌleading 'article; ˌleading 'edge; ˌleading
'lady; ˌleading 'light; ˌleading 'question
leading n 'metal', 'space between rows of type'
'led ɪŋ
lead-off 'liːd ɒf -ɔːf ‖ -ɔːf -ɑːf
lead poisoning ˌled 'pɔɪz ᵊn ɪŋ
lead time 'liːd taɪm **~s** z
lead-up 'liːd ʌp **~s** s

leaf liːf **leafed** liːft **leafing** 'liːf ɪŋ **leafs** liːfs
leaves liːvz
'leaf mould
leafage 'liːf ɪdʒ
leafi... —see **leafy**
leafless 'liːf ləs -lɪs **~ness** nəs nɪs
leaf|let 'liːf |lət -lɪt **~leted, ~letted** lət ɪd lɪt-,
-əd ‖ lət əd **~leting, ~letting** lət ɪŋ lɪt-
‖ lət ɪŋ **~lets** ləts lɪts ‖ ləts
leaf|y 'liːf |i **~ier** i ə ‖ i ᵊr **~iest** i ɪst i əst
~iness i nəs i nɪs
Leagrave 'liː greɪv
league liːg —In AmE there is also a
non-standard pronunciation lɪg. **leagued** liːgd
leagues liːgz **leaguing** 'liːg ɪŋ
Leah liː ə
Leahy 'liː hi 'leɪ-, -i
leak liːk (= leek) **leaked** liːkt **leaking** 'liːk ɪŋ
leaks liːks
leakag|e 'liːk ɪdʒ **~es** ɪz əz
Leakey 'liːk i
leak|y 'liːk |i **~ier** i ə ‖ i ᵊr **~iest** i ɪst i əst
~iness i nəs i nɪs
Leamington (i) 'lem ɪŋ tən, (ii) 'liːm- —The
place in England is (i); that in Canada, (ii).
ˌLeamington 'Spa
lean, Lean liːn **leaned** liːnd lent **leaning**
'liːn ɪŋ **leans** liːnz **leant** lent
Leander li 'ænd ə ‖ -ᵊr
Leane liːn
leaned liːnd lent
LeAnn, Leanne li 'æn
leanness 'liːn nəs -nɪs
leant lent (= lent)
lean-to 'liːn tuː ˌ·'· **~s** z
leap liːp **leaped** liːpt lept ‖ liːpt **leaping**
'liːp ɪŋ **leaps** liːps **leapt** lept
'leap year
leaped lept liːpt ‖ liːpt
leapfrog 'liːp frɒg ‖ -frɔːg -frɑːg **~ged** d **~ging**
ɪŋ **~s** z
leapt lept
Lear lɪə ‖ lɪᵊr
Learjet tdmk 'lɪə dʒet ‖ 'lɪr- **~s** s
learn lɜːn ‖ lɜːn **learned** lɜːnd lɜːnt ‖ lɜːnd
learning 'lɜːn ɪŋ ‖ 'lɜːn ɪŋ **learns** lɜːnz
‖ lɜːnz **learnt** lɜːnt ‖ lɜːnt
learned past & pp of learn; adj 'acquired by
experience' lɜːnd lɜːnt ‖ lɜːnd
learned adj 'scholarly', 'well-informed' 'lɜːn ɪd
-əd ‖ 'lɜːn əd **~ly** li **~ness** nəs nɪs
learner 'lɜːn ə ‖ 'lɜːn ᵊr **~s** z
ˌlearner 'driver
learnt lɜːnt ‖ lɜːnt
Leary 'lɪər i ‖ 'lɪr i
leasable 'liːs əb ᵊl
lease liːs **leased** liːst **leases** 'liːs ɪz -əz **leasing**
'liːs ɪŋ
leaseback 'liːs bæk **~s** s
leasehold 'liːs həʊld →-hɒʊld ‖ -hoʊld **~er/s**
ə/z ‖ ᵊr/z **~s** z
leash liːʃ **leashed** liːʃt **leashes** 'liːʃ ɪz -əz
leashing 'liːʃ ɪŋ

Leason 'liːs ᵊn
least liːst
leastways 'liːst weɪz
leastwise 'liːst waɪz
leat liːt **leats** liːts
Leatham (i) 'liːθ əm, (ii) 'liːð-
leather, L~ 'leð ə ‖ -ᵊr **~ed** d **leathering**
  'leð ər_ɪŋ **~s** z
leatherback 'leð ə bæk ‖ -ᵊr- **~s** s
leatherette, L~ tdmk ˌleð ə 'ret ◂
Leatherhead 'leð ə hed ‖ -ᵊr-
leatherjacket 'leð ə ˌdʒæk ɪt §-ət ‖ -ᵊr- **~s** s
leatherneck 'leð ə nek ‖ -ᵊr- **~s** s
leather|y 'leð ər_|i **~iness** i nəs i nɪs
leave liːv **leaves** liːvz **leaving** 'liːv ɪŋ **left** left
  'leave ˌtaking
leaved liːvd
leaven 'lev ᵊn **~ed** d **~ing** _ɪŋ **~s** z
Leavenworth 'lev ᵊn wɜːθ -wəθ ‖ -wɝːθ
leaves liːvz
leave-taking 'liːv ˌteɪk ɪŋ
leaving 'liːv ɪŋ **~s** z
Leavis 'liːv ɪs -əs
Leavisite 'liːv ɪ saɪt -ə- **~s** s
Leavitt 'lev ɪt §-ət
Lebanese ˌleb ə 'niːz ◂ ‖ -'niːs ◂
Lebanon 'leb ən ən -ə nɒn ‖ -ə nɑːn
lebensraum, L~ 'leɪb ənz raʊm →-mz-, -ənˈs-
  —Ger ['leː bəns ʀaʊm, -bms-]
Le Bon lə 'bɒn ‖ -'bɑːn -'bɔːn
Lebon 'liːb ən
Lebowa lə 'bəʊ ə ‖ -'boʊ ə
Lec tdmk lek
Le Carré lə 'kær eɪ ‖ lə kɑː 'reɪ
leccy 'electricity' 'lek i
lech letʃ **leched** letʃt **leches** 'letʃ ɪz -əz
  leching 'letʃ ɪŋ
lecher 'letʃ ə ‖ -ᵊr **~s** z
lecherous 'letʃ ər_əs **~ly** li **~ness** nəs nɪs
lecher|y 'letʃ ər |i **~ies** iz
Lechlade 'letʃ leɪd
Lechmere 'letʃ mɪə 'leʃ- ‖ -mɪr
lecithin 'les ɪθ ɪn -əθ-, -ən
Leckhampton 'lek ˌhæmᵖt ən
Lecky 'lek i
Leconfield 'lek ən fiːᵊld
Le Corbusier lə kɔː 'buːz i eɪ -'bjuːz-
  ‖ lə ˌkɔːrb uːz 'jeɪ -uːs- —Fr [lə kɔʁ by zje]
Le Creuset tdmk lə 'kruːz eɪ ‖ lə kruː 'zeɪ
  —Fr [lə kʁø zɛ]
lect lekt **lects** lekts
lectal 'lekt ᵊl
lectern 'lekt ən -ɜːn ‖ -ᵊrn **~s** z
lectionar|y 'lek ʃᵊn ər_|i -ʃᵊn_ər |i ‖ -ʃəˌner |i
  ~ies iz
lector 'lekt ɔː ‖ -ɔːr -ᵊr **~s** z
lecture 'lek tʃə -ʃə ‖ -tʃᵊr -ʃᵊr **~d** d **~s** z
  lecturing 'lek tʃər ɪŋ -ʃər ɪŋ
lecturer 'lek tʃər ə -ʃər ə ‖ -tʃᵊr ər -ʃᵊr ər **~s** z
lectureship 'lek tʃə ʃɪp -ʃə- ‖ -tʃᵊr- -ʃᵊr- **~s** s
led led
LED ˌel iː 'diː **~s**, **~'s** z
Leda 'liːd ə 'leɪd ə

Ledbury 'led bər_i →'leb- ‖ -ˌber i
lederhosen 'leɪd ə ˌhəʊz ᵊn ‖ -ᵊr ˌhoʊz ᵊn
  —Ger ['leː dɐ ˌhoːz ᵊn]
Ledgard 'ledʒ ɑːd ‖ -ɑːrd
ledge ledʒ **ledged** ledʒd **ledges** 'ledʒ ɪz -əz
ledger, L~ 'ledʒ ə ‖ -ᵊr **~s** z
lee, Lee liː **lees, Lee's** liːz
  ˌlee 'shore ‖ '· ·; ˌlee 'tide ‖ '· ·
leech, Leech liːtʃ **leeched** liːtʃt **leeches**
  'liːtʃ ɪz -əz **leeching** 'liːtʃ ɪŋ
Leeds liːdz
Lee-Enfield ˌliː 'en fiːᵊld
leek, Leek liːk **leeks** liːks
Leeming 'liːm ɪŋ
leer lɪə ‖ lɪᵊr **leered** lɪəd ‖ lɪᵊrd **leering**
  'lɪər ɪŋ ‖ 'lɪr ɪŋ **leers** lɪəz ‖ lɪᵊrz
leer|y 'lɪər |i ‖ 'lɪr |i **~ier** i ə ‖ i ᵊr **~iest** i ɪst
  i_əst **~ily** əl i i li **~iness** i nəs i nɪs
lees, Lees liːz
Leeson 'liːs ᵊn
leet liːt **leets** liːts
leeward, L~ 'liː wəd ‖ -wᵊrd —also nautical
  'luː əd, 'ljuː ‖ _ᵊrd **~s** z
  'Leeward ˌIslands ‖ ˌ· '·◂
leeway 'liː weɪ
Lefanu, Le Fanu (i) 'lef ə njuː -nuː ‖ -nuː
  -njuː, (ii) lə 'fɑːn uː
Lefevre lə 'fiːv ə ‖ -ᵊr —but as a French name,
  lə 'fev —Fr Lefebvre, Lefèvre [lə fɛːvʁ]
left left
  ˌleft 'luggage ˌoffice; ˌleft 'wing◂
left-click ˌleft'klɪk ◂ **~ed** t **~ing** ɪŋ **~s** s
left-hand ˌleft 'hænd ◂
  ˌleft-hand 'side
left-handed ˌleft 'hænd ɪd ◂ -əd **~ly** li **~ness**
  nəs nɪs
left-hander ˌleft 'hænd ə ‖ -ᵊr **~s** z
leftie... —see **lefty**
leftist 'left ɪst §-əst **~s** s
left-of-centre, left-of-center
  ˌleft əv 'sent ə ◂ ‖ -'sent ᵊr
leftover 'left ˌəʊv ə ‖ -ˌoʊv ᵊr **~s** z
leftward 'left wəd ‖ -wᵊrd **~s** z
left-winger ˌleft 'wɪŋ ə ‖ -ᵊr **~s** z
left|y 'left |i **~ies** iz
leg leg **legged** legd **legging** 'leg ɪŋ **legs** legz
  ˌleg 'side
legac|y 'leg əs |i **~ies** iz
legal 'liːg ᵊl **~ly** i
  ˌlegal 'aid; ˌlegal 'tender
legalese ˌliːg ə 'liːz -ᵊl 'iːz ‖ -'liːs
legalis... —see **legaliz...**
legalism 'liːg ə ˌlɪz əm -ᵊl ˌɪz-
legalistic ˌliːg ə 'lɪst ɪk ◂ -ᵊl 'ɪst- **-ally** ᵊl_i
legalit|y lɪ 'gæl ət i |i liː-, -ɪt- ‖ -əţ |i **~ies** iz
legalization ˌliːg əl aɪ 'zeɪʃ ᵊn -əl ɪ- ‖ -əl ə- **~s**
  z
legaliz|e 'liːg ə laɪz -ᵊl aɪz **~ed** d **~es** ɪz əz
  ~ing ɪŋ
legal-size 'liːg ᵊl saɪz
Legard 'ledʒ əd ‖ -ᵊrd
legate n 'leg ət -ɪt, -eɪt **~s** s
legatee ˌleg ə 'tiː **~s** z

legation lɪ ˈgeɪʃ ᵊn lə- **~s** z
legato lɪ ˈgɑːt əʊ lə-, le- ‖ -oʊ **~s** z
legator lɪ ˈgeɪt ə lə-, le- ‖ -ˈgeɪt ᵊr **~s** z
LegCo ˈledʒ kəʊ ‖ -koʊ
legend ˈledʒ ənd -ɪnd **~s** z
legendary ˈledʒ ənd ᵊr i ˈ· ɪnd- ‖ -ən der i
leger, Leger ˈledʒ ə ‖ -ᵊr **~s** z
　ˈleger line
legerdemain ˌledʒ ə də ˈmeɪn ‖ ˌ·ᵊr-
Legg, Legge leg
Leggatt ˈleg ət
legged adj ˈleg ɪd -əd; legd
leggings ˈleg ɪŋz
legg|y ˈleg |i **~ier** i ə ‖ i ᵊr **~iest** i ɪst i əst
　~iness i nəs i nɪs
Legh liː
leghorn 'straw; hat; breed of fowl' le ˈgɔːn
　ˌleg ˈhɔːn, ˈ· · ‖ ˈleg hɔːrn -ᵊrn
Leghorn place: old name for Livorno ˈleg hɔːn
　ˌ·ˈ· ‖ -hɔːrn
legibility ˌledʒ ə ˈbɪl ət i ˌ·ɪ-, -ɪt i ‖ -əţ i
legib|le ˈledʒ əb |ᵊl -ɪb- **~ly** li
legion ˈliːdʒ ən **~s** z
legionar|y ˈliːdʒ ən ᵊr ˌi ‖ -ə ner ˌi **~ies** iz
legionell|a ˌliːdʒ ə ˈnel |ə **~ae** iː **~as** əz
legionnaire ˌliːdʒ ə ˈneə ‖ -ˈneᵊr -ˈnæᵊr **~s** z
　ˌlegionˈnaires' diˌsease
legi|slate ˈledʒ ɪ |sleɪt -ə- **~slated** sleɪt ɪd -əd
　‖ sleɪţ əd **~slates** sleɪts **~slating** sleɪt ɪŋ
　‖ sleɪţ ɪŋ
legislation ˌledʒ ɪ ˈsleɪʃ ᵊn -ə-
legislative ˈledʒ ɪs lət ɪv ˈ·əs-; -ɪ sleɪt-, -ə sleɪt-
　‖ -ə sleɪţ ɪv -əs ləţ ɪv **~ly** li **~s** z
legislator ˈledʒ ɪ sleɪt ə ˈ·ə- -ə sleɪţ ᵊr **~s** z
legislature ˈledʒ ɪs ləţ ə ˈ·əs-; -lə tʃʊəz;
　-ɪ sleɪtʃ ə, -ə · · ‖ -ə sleɪtʃ ᵊr ˌ·ˈ·· **~s** z
legit lɪ ˈdʒɪt lə-
legitimacy lɪ ˈdʒɪt əm əs i lə-, -ˈɪm- ‖ -ˈdʒɪţ-
legiti|mate v lɪ ˈdʒɪt ə |meɪt lə-, -ɪ- ‖ -ˈdʒɪţ-
　~mated meɪt ɪd -əd ‖ meɪţ əd **~mates** meɪts
　~mating meɪt ɪŋ ‖ meɪţ ɪŋ
legitimate adj lɪ ˈdʒɪt əm ət lə-, -ɪm-, -ɪt
　‖ -ˈdʒɪţ- **~ly** li
legitimation lɪ ˌdʒɪt ə ˈmeɪʃ ᵊn lə-, -ɪ- ‖ -ˌdʒɪţ-
legitimatis... —see **legitimatiz...**
legitimatization lɪ ˌdʒɪt əm ət aɪ ˈzeɪʃ ᵊn lə-,
　-ˌ·ɪm-, -ɪˈ·-- ‖ -ˌdʒɪţ əm əţ ə-
legitimatiz|e lɪ ˈdʒɪt əm ə taɪz lə-, -ˈ·ɪm-
　‖ -ˈdʒɪţ- **~ed** d **~es** ɪz əz **~ing** ɪŋ
legitimis... —see **legitimiz...**
legitimization lɪ ˌdʒɪt əm aɪ ˈzeɪʃ ᵊn lə-,
　-ˌ·ɪm-, -ɪˈ·-- ‖ -ˌdʒɪţ əm ə-
legitimiz|e lɪ ˈdʒɪt ə maɪz lə-, -ɪ- ‖ -ˈdʒɪţ- **~ed**
　d **~es** ɪz əz **~ing** ɪŋ
legless ˈleg ləs -lɪs
Lego tdmk ˈleg əʊ ‖ -oʊ —Danish [ˈleː go]
leg-of-mutton ˌleg əv ˈmʌt ᵊn ◂
leg-over ˈleg ˌəʊv ə ‖ -ˌoʊv ᵊr
leg-pull ˈleg pʊl **~ing** ɪŋ **~s** z
Legree lɪ ˈgriː lə-
legroom ˈleg ruːm -rʊm
legume ˈleg juːm lɪ ˈgjuːm, lə- **~s** z
leguminous lɪ ˈgjuːm ɪn əs lə-, le-, -ən-

leg-up ˈleg ʌp
leg-warmer ˈleg ˌwɔːm ə ‖ -ˌwɔːrm ᵊr
legwork ˈleg wɜːk ‖ -wɜːk
Lehar, Lehár leɪ ˈhɑː lɪ-, lə-, ˈleɪ hɑː ‖ ˈleɪ hɑːr
　—Hungarian [ˈlɛ hɑːr]
Le Havre lə ˈɑːv rə -ˈhɑːv-, -ə ‖ -ᵊr —Fr
　[lə aːvʁ]
Lehigh ˈliː haɪ
Lehman, Lehmann (i) ˈleɪ mən, (ii) ˈliː-
　—Usually (i).
Lehrer ˈleər ə ˈlɪər- ‖ ˈlɪr ᵊr
lei leɪ ˈleɪ i **leis** leɪz ˈleɪ iz
Leibnitz, Leibniz ˈlaɪb nɪts ˈliːb- —Ger
　[ˈlaib nɪts]
Leica tdmk ˈlaɪk ə —Ger [ˈlai ka] **~s** z
Leicester ˈlest ə ‖ -ᵊr (!) —Sometimes called
　ˈlaɪ sest ᵊr by those not familiar with the
　name.
Leicestershire, Leics., Leics. ˈlest ə ʃə -ʃɪə
　‖ -ᵊr ʃᵊr -ʃɪr
Leiden ˈlaɪd ᵊn ˈleɪd- —Dutch [ˈlɛi dən]
Leif liːf
Leigh (i) liː, (ii) laɪ —Usually (i); but some
　places in the south of England are (ii).
Leighton ˈleɪt ᵊn
Leila ˈliːl ə ˈleɪl ə
Leinster ˈlen|st ə ‖ -ᵊr —but the Duke of L~ is
　ˈlɪn|st-
Leintwardine ˈlent wə daɪn -diːn; ˈlænt ə diːn
　‖ -wᵊr-
Leipzig ˈlaɪp sɪg -sɪk —Ger [ˈlaip tsɪç]
Leishman ˈliːʃ mən ˈlɪʃ-
leishmania ₍ᵢ₎liːʃ ˈmeɪn i ə
leishmaniasis ˌliːʃ mə ˈnaɪ əs ɪs §-əs
leister 'spear' ˈliːst ə ‖ -ᵊr
Leister name ˈlest ə ‖ -ᵊr
leisure ˈleʒ ə ‖ ˈliːʒ ᵊr ˈleʒ-, ˈleɪʒ- **~d** d **~liness**
　li nəs -nɪs **~ly** li
leisurewear ˈleʒ ə weə ‖ ˈliːʒ ᵊr wer ˈleʒ-,
　ˈleɪʒ-, -wær
Leith liːθ
leitmotif, leitmotiv, leitmotive
　ˈlaɪt məʊ ˌtiːf ˈ·ˌməʊt ɪv ‖ -moʊ- —Ger
　[ˈlait mo ˌtiːf]
Leitrim ˈliːtr ɪm §-əm
Leix liːʃ
lek lek **lekked** lekt **lekking** ˈlek ɪŋ **leks** leks
lekker ˈlek ə ‖ -ᵊr
Leland ˈliːl ənd
Lely ˈliːl i
leman ˈlem ən ˈliːm- **~s** z
Leman surname; street name in London ˈlem ən
　ˈliːm-
Le Mans lə ˈmɒ̃ ‖ -ˈmɑːn —Fr [lə mɑ̃]
Lemesurier lə ˈmeʒ ər ə ‖ -ᵊr ᵊr
　lə ˌmeʒ ər i ˈeɪ
lemm|a ˈlem |ə **~as** əz **~ata** ət ə ‖ əţ ə
lemmatis... —see **lemmatiz...**
lemmatization ˌlem ət aɪ ˈzeɪʃ ᵊn -ət ɪ- ‖ -əţ ə-
　~s z
lemmatiz|e ˈlem ə taɪz **~ed** d **~es** ɪz əz **~ing**
　ɪŋ

lemme 'lem i —*This is a non-standard or casual form of* let me
lemming 'lem ɪŋ ~s z
lemming-like 'lem ɪŋ laɪk
Lemmon 'lem ən
lem|niscus lem |'nɪsk əs ~**nisci** 'nɪs aɪ 'nɪsk-, -i:
Lemnos 'lem nɒs ‖ -nɑːs -noʊs
lemon, Lemon 'lem ən ~s z
  ,lemon 'curd; 'lemon grass; ,lemon
  me,ringue 'pie; ,lemon 'sole; ,lemon
  'squash; ,lemon 'yellow◄
lemonade ,lem ə 'neɪd ◄ ~s z
Le Monde lə 'mɒnd ‖ -'mɔːnd -'mɑːnd —*Fr*
  [lə mɔ̃ːd]
lemony 'lem ən i
Lempert 'lemp ət ‖ -ᵊrt
Lempriere 'lemp ri eə ‖ ,lemp ri 'eᵊr
Lemsip *tdmk* 'lem sɪp
Lemuel 'lem ju əl
lemur 'liːm ə -juə ‖ -ᵊr ~s z
Len len
Lena *river* 'leɪn ə 'liːn- —*Russ* ['lʲɛ nə]
Lena *personal name* 'liːn ə
lend lend **lending** 'lend ɪŋ **lends** lendz **lent**
  lent
  'lending ,library
lender 'lend ə ‖ -ᵊr ~s z
lend-lease, Lend-Lease ,lend 'liːs ‖ ' ·
lenes 'liːn iːz 'leɪn-, -eɪz

LENGTH

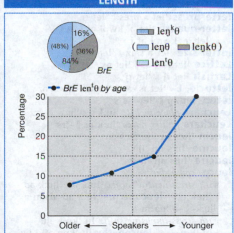

BrE

● *BrE* lenᵗθ *by age*

Percentage

Older ◄——— Speakers ———► Younger

length lenᵏθ §lenᵗθ — *Preference poll, BrE:*
  lenᵏθ *84%* (lenθ *48%*, lenᵏθ *36%*), lenᵗθ *16%*.
  lengths lenᵏθs §lenᵗθs
lengthen 'lenᵏθ ən §'lenᵗθ- ~**ed** d ~**ing** ɪŋ ~**s** z
length|ways 'lenᵏθ |weɪz §'lenᵗθ- ~**wise** waɪz
length|y 'lenᵏθ |i §'lenᵗθ- ~**ier** i ə ‖ i ᵊr ~**iest**
  i ɪst i əst ~**ily** ɪ li əl i ~**iness** i nəs i nɪs
lenienc|e 'liːn i ənᵗs ~**y** i
lenient 'liːn i ənt ~**ly** li
Lenihan 'len ə hən
Lenin 'len ɪn §-ən —*Russ* ['lʲe nʲɪn]

Leningrad 'len ɪn græd →-ɪŋ-, §-ən- —*Russ*
  [lʲɪ nʲɪn 'grat]
Lenin|ism 'len ɪn |,ɪz əm §-ən- ~**ist/s** ɪst/s
  §əst/s ‖ əst/s
lenis 'liːn ɪs 'leɪn-, §-əs **lenes** 'liːn iːz 'leɪn-, -eɪz
le|nite lɪ |'naɪt lə- ~**nited** 'naɪt ɪd -əd
  ‖ 'naɪt̬ əd ~**nites** 'naɪts ~**niting** 'naɪt ɪŋ
  ‖ 'naɪt̬ ɪŋ
lenition lɪ 'nɪʃ ᵊn lə- ~s z
lenity 'len ət i 'liːn-, -ɪt- ‖ -ət̬ i
Lennie 'len i
Lennon 'len ən
Lennox 'len əks
Lenny 'len i
leno 'liːn əʊ ‖ -oʊ ~s z
Leno *(i)* 'liːn əʊ ‖ -oʊ, *(ii)* 'len- —*Jay Leno,
  TV personality, is (ii)*
Lenor *tdmk* lɪ 'nɔː lə- ‖ -'nɔːr
Lenore lɪ 'nɔː lə- ‖ -'nɔːr -'noʊr
Lenox 'len əks
lens lenz **lenses** 'lenz ɪz -əz
lent, Lent lent
lenten 'lent ən ‖ -ᵊn
Lentheric, Lenthéric *tdmk* 'lɒntᵊθ ər ɪk 'lɒ̃θ-
  ‖ 'lɑːntᵊθ-
lenticel 'lent ɪ sel §-ə- ‖ 'lent̬ ə- ~s z
lenticular len 'tɪk jʊl ə -jəl- ‖ -jəl ᵊr
lentigo len 'taɪg əʊ ‖ -oʊ
lentil 'lent ɪl -ᵊl ‖ 'lent̬ ᵊl ~s z
lentivirus 'lent i ,vaɪ ər əs ‖ 'lent̬ ə ,vaɪrᵊ əs
  ~**es** ɪz əz
lento 'lent əʊ ‖ -oʊ ~s z
Leo 'liː əʊ ‖ 'liː oʊ
Leofric 'lef rɪk 'leɪ əf rɪk ‖ li 'ɑːf rɪk
Leominster *(i)* 'lemᵖst ə ‖ -ᵊr, *(ii)* 'lem ɪnᵗst ə
  ‖ -ənᵗst ᵊr —*The place in England is (i), that
  in MA (ii).*
Leon *personal name* 'liː ən 'leɪ-, -ɒn ‖ -ɑːn
León *place in Spain* leɪ 'ɒn ‖ -'oʊn —*Sp*
  [le 'on]
Leona li 'əʊn ə ‖ -'oʊn ə
Leonard 'len əd ‖ -ᵊrd
Leonardo ,liː əʊ 'nɑːd əʊ ,leɪ- ‖ ,liː ə 'nɑːrd oʊ
Leonid 'liː əʊn ɪd 'leɪ-, §-əd ‖ -ən-
Leonidas li 'ɒn ɪ dæs -ə- ‖ -'ɑːn əd əs
Leonie *(i)* 'liː ən i, *(ii)* li 'əʊn i ‖ -'oʊn i
leonine, L~ 'liː əʊ naɪn ‖ -ə-
Leonora ,liː ə 'nɔːr ə ‖ -'noʊr-
Leontes li 'ɒnt iːz leɪ- ‖ -'ɑːnt-
leopard 'lep əd ‖ -ᵊrd ~s z
leopardess 'lep əd es -ɪs, -əs ‖ -ᵊrd əs ~**es** ɪz
  əz
leopard-skin 'lep əd skɪn ‖ -ᵊrd-
Leopold 'liː ə pəʊld →-pɒʊld ‖ -poʊld —*but as
  a foreign name also* 'leɪ-
leotard 'liː ə tɑːd 'leɪ-, -əʊ- ‖ -tɑːrd ~s z
Lepanto lɪ 'pænt əʊ lə- ‖ -oʊ —*It* ['lɛ pan to]
Le Pen lə 'pen —*Fr* [lə pɛn]
leper 'lep ə ‖ -ᵊr ~s z
lepidopter|a, L~ ,lep ɪ 'dɒpt ər ə |ə ,-ə-
  ‖ -'dɑːpt- ~**ist/s** ɪst/s §əst/s ‖ əst/s ~**ous** əs
Lepidus 'lep ɪd əs -əd-
Lepontine lə 'pɒnt aɪn lɪ- ‖ -'pɑːnt-

Leppard 'lep ɑːd ‖ -ɑːrd
leprechaun 'lep rə kɔːn -rɪ-, -hɔːn ‖ -kɑːn **~s** z
leprosari|um ˌlep rə 'seər i ‿|əm ‖ -'ser- **~a** ə **~ums** əmz
leprosy 'lep rəs i
leprous 'lep rəs **~ly** li **~ness** nəs nɪs
Lepsius 'leps i ‿əs
leptokurtic ˌlept əʊ 'kɜːt ɪk ◄ ‖ -ə 'kɜːt̬ ɪk ◄
lepton 'lept ɒn ‖ -ɑːn **~s** z
leptospirosis ˌlept əʊ spaɪ° 'rəʊs ɪs §-əs ‖ -ə spaɪ 'roʊs əs
Lepus 'liːp əs 'lep-
Lermontov 'leə mɒnt ɒf ‖ 'ler mɑːnt ɔːf —*Russ* ['lʲer mən təf]
Lerner 'lɜːn ə ‖ 'lɜːn °r
Leroy (i) 'liː rɔɪ, (ii) lə 'rɔɪ —*As a family name, (ii).*
Lerwick 'lɜː wɪk ‖ 'lɜː-
Les *personal name* (i) *short for* **Leslie** lez, (ii) *short for* **Lester** les
les *French plural 'the'* leɪ —*but before a vowel sound* leɪz —*See also phrases with this word.* —*Fr* [le, lez]
Le Saux lə 'səʊ ‖ -'soʊ
Lesbia 'lez bi ‿ə
lesbian, L~ 'lez bi ‿ən **~ism** ˌɪz əm **~s** z
lesbo 'lez bəʊ ‖ -boʊ **~s** z
Lesbos 'lez bɒs ‖ -bɑːs -boʊs
lèse-majesté ˌleɪz 'mædʒ ə steɪ ˌliːz-, -'mæʒ-, -ɪ-, -e- ‖ ˌliːz 'mædʒ əst i —*Fr* [lɛz ma ʒɛs te]
lese-majesty ˌliːz 'mædʒ əst i ˌleɪz-, -ɪst-
lesion 'liːʒ °n **~s** z
Lesley, Leslie 'lez li ‖ 'les-
Lesmahagow ˌles mə 'heɪg əʊ ‖ -oʊ
Lesney *tdmk* 'lez ni
Lesotho lə 'suːt uː lɪ-, leɪ-, -'səʊt əʊ ‖ -'soʊt oʊ —*Sotho* [lɪ 'sʊ: tʰʊ]
less les

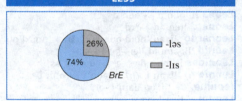

-LESS

26%
74%
■ -ləs
■ -lɪs
BrE

-less ləs lɪs —*In singing, a strong-vowelled form* les *is usual.* — *Preference poll, BrE (for the word* careless, *disregarding votes for* -les *and from respondents who do not distinguish* ɪ *from* ə *in this position):* -ləs 74%, -lɪs 26% — **faithless** 'feɪθ ləs -lɪs, *in singing* -les
lessee ˌ(ˌ)le 'siː **~s** z
lessen 'les °n (= *lesson*) **~ed** d **~ing** ˌɪŋ **~s** z
Lesseps 'les əps -eps —*Fr* [lɛ sɛps]
lesser, L~ 'les ə ‖ -°r
Lessing 'les ɪŋ
lesson 'les °n **~s** z
lessor ˌ(ˌ)le 'sɔː 'les ɔː ‖ ˌ(ˌ)le 'sɔːr 'les ɔːr **~s** z
lest lest
Lester 'lest ə ‖ -°r

Lestrange, L'Estrange lɪ 'streɪndʒ lə-
let let —*The phrase* let me *has a non-standard casual form* 'lem i, *sometimes written* lemme
lets, let's lets **letting** 'let ɪŋ ‖ 'let̬ ɪŋ
-let lət lɪt — **leaflet** 'liːf lət -lɪt
letch letʃ **letched** letʃt **letches** 'letʃ ɪz -əz **letching** 'letʃ ɪŋ
Letchworth 'letʃ wəθ -wɜːθ ‖ -wɜːθ
letdown 'let daʊn **~s** z
lethal 'liːθ °l
lethality liː 'θæl ət i -ɪt- ‖ -ət̬ i
lethally 'liːθ əl i
lethargic lə 'θɑːdʒ ɪk lɪ-, le- ‖ -'θɑːrdʒ- **~ally** °l i
lethargy 'leθ ədʒ i ‖ -°rdʒ i
Lethbridge 'leθ brɪdʒ
Lethe 'liːθ i -iː
Le Tissier lə 'tɪs i eɪ
Letitia lə 'tɪʃ ə lɪ-, -'tɪʃ i ‿ə ‖ -'tiːʃ ə
Letraset *tdmk* 'letr ə set
let's *contracted form* lets
Lett let **Letts, Lett's** lets
letter 'let ə ‖ 'let̬ °r **~ed** d **lettering** 'let ər ɪŋ ‖ 'let̬ ər ɪŋ **~s** z
  'letter bomb; **ˌletter of 'credit**; **'letter ˌopener**
letterbox 'let ə bɒks ‖ 'let̬ °r bɑːks **~es** ɪz əz **~ing** ɪŋ
letterhead 'let ə hed ‖ 'let̬ °r- **~s** z
Letterman 'let ə mən ‖ 'let̬ °r-
letter-perfect ˌlet ə 'pɜːf ɪkt ◄ -ekt, §-əkt ‖ ˌlet̬ °r 'pɜːf ɪkt ◄
letterpress 'let ə pres ‖ 'let̬ °r-
letter-quality 'let ə ˌkwɒl ət i -ɪt i ‖ 'let̬ °r ˌkwɑːl ət̬ i
letter-size 'let ə saɪz ‖ 'let̬ °r-
Lettice 'let ɪs §-əs ‖ 'let̬ əs
Lettish 'let ɪʃ ‖ 'let̬ ɪʃ
lettuc|e, L~ 'let ɪs -əs ‖ 'let̬ əs **~es** ɪz əz
letup 'let ʌp ‖ 'let̬- **~s** z
Leuchars *place in Fife* 'luːk əz 'luːx- ‖ -°rz
Leuchars *family name* 'luːk əs ‖ -°rs
leucin 'luːs ɪn 'ljuːs-, §-ən
leucine 'luːs iːn 'ljuːs-
leucite 'luːs aɪt 'ljuːs-
leuco- *comb. form*
  with stress-neutral suffix ˌluːk əʊ ˌljuːk əʊ ‖ ˌluːk ə — **leucoderma** ˌluːk əʊ 'dɜːm ə ˌljuːk- ‖ -ə 'dɜːm ə
  with stress-imposing suffix lu 'kɒ+ lju- ‖ lu 'kɑː+ — **leucopathy** lu 'kɒp əθ i lju- ‖ -'kɑːp-
leucocyte 'luːk əʊ saɪt 'ljuːk- ‖ -ə- **~s** s
leucopenia ˌluːk əʊ 'piːn i ‿ə ˌljuːk-, ˌ-ə-
leucotomis|e, leucotomiz|e lu 'kɒt ə maɪz lju- ‖ lu 'kɑːt̬- **~ed** d **~es** ɪz əz **~ing** ɪŋ
leucotom|y lu 'kɒt əm i lju- ‖ lu 'kɑːt̬- **~ies** iz
leukaemia, leukemia lu 'kiːm i ‿ə lju- **~s** z
leuko... —*see* **leuco...**
le|vant, L~ lə ˌ|'vænt lɪ- **~vanted** 'vænt ɪd -əd ‖ 'vænt̬ əd **~vanting** 'vænt ɪŋ ‖ 'vænt̬ ɪŋ **~vants** 'vænts

Levantine 'lev ³n taɪn -tiːn ‖ lə 'vænt ³n, -aɪn
~s z
levator lə 'veɪt ə lɪ-, -ɔː ‖ -'veɪʈ ³r ~s z
levee, levée 'lev i -eɪ ~s z
level 'lev ³l ~ed, ~led d ~ing, ~ling ɪŋ ~s z
ˌlevel 'crossing
leveler, L~ 'lev ³l ə ‖ -³r ~s z
level-headed ˌlev ³l 'hed ɪd ◄ ‖ '·ˌ·ˌ· ~ly li
~ness nəs nɪs
leveller, L~ 'lev ³l ə ‖ -³r ~s z
level-pegging ˌlev ³l 'peg ɪŋ
Leven (i) 'lev ³n, (ii) 'liːv ³n —Most rivers of
this name, and the Loch, are (ii), but the river
in Cumbria is (i). The family name may be
either.
Levens 'lev ³nz
lev|er 'liːv |ə ‖ 'lev |³r 'liːv- ~ered əd ‖ ³rd
~ering ³r ɪŋ ~ers əz ‖ ³rz
Lever 'liːv ə ‖ -³r
leverag|e 'liːv ³r ˌɪdʒ 'lev- ‖ 'lev- ~ed d ~es ɪz
əz ~ing ɪŋ
leveret 'lev ³r ət -ɪt ~s s
Leverhulme 'liːv ə hjuːm ‖ -³r-
Levett 'lev ɪt -ət
Levi personal or family name, (i) 'lev i,
(ii) 'liːv i
Levi biblical name 'liːv aɪ
levi... —see levy
leviathan, L~ lə 'vaɪ_əθ ən lɪ- ~s z
Levin, levin 'lev ɪn §-³n ~s z
Levine lə 'viːn
levirate 'liːv ³r ət 'lev-, -ɪr-, -ɪt; -ə reɪt
Levi's tdmk, Levis 'jeans' 'liːv aɪz
Levi Strauss clothing manufacturer
ˌliːv aɪ 'strɔːs -'straus
Levi-Strauss, Lévi-Strauss French
anthropologist ˌlev i 'straus ˌleɪv- —Fr
[le vi strɔːs]
levi|tate 'lev ɪ |teɪt -ə- ~tated teɪt ɪd -əd
‖ teɪʈ əd ~tates teɪts ~tating teɪt ɪŋ ‖ teɪʈ ɪŋ
levitation ˌlev ɪ 'teɪʃ ³n -ə- ~s z
Levite 'liːv aɪt ~s s
Levitic|us lə 'vɪt ɪk |əs lɪ- ‖ -'vɪʈ- ~al ³l
Levitra tdmk lə 'viːtr ə le-
Levittown 'lev ɪt taʊn -ət-
levit|y 'lev ət |i -ɪt- ‖ -əʈ |i ~ies iz
levodopa ˌliːv əʊ 'dəʊp ə ˌlev- ‖ -ə 'doʊp ə
'·ˌ··
lev|y v, n 'lev |i ~ied id ~ies iz ~ying i_ɪŋ
Levy name, (i) 'liːv i, (ii) 'lev i
Lew luː ljuː
lewd luːd ljuːd lewder 'luːd ə 'ljuːd- ‖ -³r
lewdest 'luːd ɪst 'ljuːd-, -əst
lewd|ly 'luːd |li 'ljuːd- ~ness nəs nɪs
Lewes 'luː_ɪs §-əs
Lewin 'luː_ɪn §-ən
Lewinsky lə 'wɪn ski
Lewis, lewis 'luː_ɪs §-əs
Lewisham 'luː_ɪʃ əm
lewisite 'luː_ɪ saɪt §-ə-
Lex, lex leks
lexeme 'leks iːm ~s z
lexemic lek 'siːm ɪk

lexical 'leks ɪk ³l ~ly ˌi
lexico- comb. form
with stress-neutral suffix ˌleks ɪ kəʊ ‖ -koʊ
— lexicostatistics ˌleks ɪ kəʊ stə 'tɪst ɪks
‖ -ˌ· koʊ-
with stress-imposing suffix ˌleks ɪ 'kɒ + -ə-
‖ -'kɑː + — lexicology ˌleks ɪ 'kɒl ədʒ i ˌ·ə-
‖ -'kɑːl-
lexicographer ˌleks ɪ 'kɒg rəf ə ˌ·ə-
‖ -'kɑːg rəf ³r ~s z
lexicographic ˌleks ɪk ə 'græf ɪk ◄ ˌ·ək- ~ally
³l_i
lexicography ˌleks ɪ 'kɒg rəf i ˌ·ə- ‖ -'kɑːg-
lexicological ˌleks ɪk ə 'lɒdʒ ɪk ³l ◄ ˌ·ək-
‖ -'lɑːdʒ- ~ly ˌi
lexicologist ˌleks ɪ 'kɒl ədʒ ɪst ˌ·ə-, §-əst
‖ -'kɑːl- ~s s
lexicology ˌleks ɪ 'kɒl ədʒ i ˌ·ə- ‖ -'kɑːl-
lexicon 'leks ɪk ən -ək-; -ɪ kɒn, -ə- ‖ -ə kɑːn ~s
z
Lexington 'leks ɪŋ tən
lexis 'leks ɪs §-əs
Lexmark tdmk 'leks mɑːk ‖ -mɑːrk
Lexus tdmk 'leks əs
ley leɪ liː
Ley (i) liː, (ii) leɪ
Leyburn 'leɪ bɜːn ‖ -bɝːn
Leyden 'laɪd ³n
Leyland 'leɪ lənd
leylandii leɪ 'lænd i aɪ ·'·· aɪ
Leys liːz
Leysdown 'leɪz daʊn
Leystonstone 'leɪt ³n stəʊn ‖ -stoʊn
Leyton 'leɪt ³n
lezzie 'lez i ~s z
Lhasa 'lɑːs ə 'læs- —Chi Lāsà ['la ⁴sa]
ˌLhasa 'apso 'æps əʊ ‖ 'ɑːps oʊ
li liː
LI ˌel 'aɪ —see also Long Island
liabilit|y ˌlaɪ_ə 'bɪl ət |i -ɪt i ‖ -əʈ |i ~ies iz
liable 'laɪ_əb ³l
liais|e li 'eɪz laɪ- ~ed d ~es ɪz əz ~ing ɪŋ
liaison li 'eɪz ³n laɪ-, -ɒn, -ɒ̃ ‖ 'liː ə zɑːn ˌ·'·;
△'leɪ-; li 'eɪz ɑːn —Fr [ljɛ zɔ̃] ~s z
Liam 'liː_əm
liana li 'ɑːn ə -'æn- ~s z
liane li 'ɑːn -'æn ~s z
Lianne li 'æn
Liao dynasty li 'aʊ —Chi Liáo [²ljau]
Liaoning li ˌaʊ 'nɪŋ —Chi Liáoníng
[²ljau ²niŋ]
liar 'laɪ_ə ‖ 'laɪ_³r ~s z
Lias, lias 'laɪ_əs
liassic, L~ laɪ 'æs ɪk
LIAT airline 'liː æt 'liː_ət
lib, Lib lɪb
ˌLib 'Dem/s dem/z
Libanus 'lɪb ən əs
libation laɪ 'beɪʃ ³n lɪ- ~s z
libber 'lɪb ə ‖ -³r ~s z
Libbie, Libby 'lɪb i
Lib-Dem, Libdem ˌlɪb 'dem ◄ ~s z
libel 'laɪb ³l ~ed, ~led d ~ing, ~ling ɪŋ ~s z

libellous, libelous ˈlaɪb əl əs ~ly li
Liberace ˌlɪb ə ˈrɑːtʃ i
liberal, L~ ˈlɪb ər_əl ~ly i ~s z
  ˌliberal ˈarts; ˌLiberal ˈDemocrat; ˈLiberal
  ˌParty; ˌliberal ˈstudies
liberalis... —see liberaliz...
liberalism ˈlɪb ər_əl ˌɪz əm
liberalit|y ˌlɪb ə ˈræl ət |i -ɪt i ‖ -əţ |i ~ies iz
liberalization ˌlɪb ər_əl aɪ ˈzeɪʃ ən -ɪˈ- ‖ -əˈ- ~s
  z
liberaliz|e ˈlɪb ər_ə laɪz ~ed d ~es ɪz əz ~ing
  ɪŋ
liberally ˈlɪb ər_əl i
libe|rate ˈlɪb ə |reɪt ~rated reɪt ɪd -əd
  ‖ reɪţ əd ~rates reɪts ~rating reɪt ɪŋ ‖ reɪţ ɪŋ
liberation ˌlɪb ə ˈreɪʃ ən ◂ ~ist/s ɪst/s §_əst/s
  ‖ _əst/s
  libeˌration theˈology, ˌ·ˈ··ˌ··
liberator ˈlɪb ə reɪt ə ‖ -reɪţ ᵊr ~s z
Liberi|a laɪ ˈbɪər i_|ə ‖ -ˈbɪr- ~an/s ən/z
libertarian ˌlɪb ə ˈteər i_ən ◂ ‖ -ᵊr ˈter- ~s z
liberti... —see liberty
libertine ˈlɪb ə tiːn -taɪn ‖ -ᵊr- ~s z
Liberton ˈlɪb ət ən ‖ -ᵊrt ən
libert|y, L~ ˈlɪb ət |i ‖ ᵊrţ |i ~ies iz
Libeskind ˈliːb ə skɪnd
libidinal lɪ ˈbɪd ɪn əl lə-, -ˈbɪd ᵊn_əl ‖ -ᵊn_əl
libidinous lɪ ˈbɪd ɪn əs lə-, -ən_əs ‖ -ən_əs
libido lɪ ˈbiːd əʊ lə- ‖ -oʊ ˈlɪb ə doʊ ~s z
LIBOR ˈlaɪb ɔː ‖ -ɔːr
Libra ˈliːb rə ˈlɪb-, ˈlaɪb-
Libran ˈliːb rən ˈlɪb-, ˈlaɪb- ~s z
librarian laɪ ˈbreər i_ən lɪ-, lə- ‖ -ˈbrer- ~s z
  ~ship ʃɪp
librar|y ˈlaɪb rər |i ˈlaɪb ər_i ‖ ˈlaɪb rer |i
  -rər i, △-er i, -ər_i ~ies iz —The awkwardness
  of two r s in the same unstressed syllable
  makes people tend to drop the first of them.
  While perhaps condemned by the speech-
  conscious, such reduced pronunciations are
  nevertheless often heard from educated
  speakers. Where in AmE the second syllable
  has a strong vowel, the reduction is more
  noticeable, hence less frequently heard and
  more strongly disapproved of.
librate laɪ ˈb|reɪt ˈlaɪb |reɪt ‖ ˈlaɪb |reɪt ~rated
  reɪt ɪd -əd ‖ reɪţ əd ~rates reɪts ~rating
  reɪt ɪŋ ‖ reɪţ ɪŋ
libration laɪ ˈbreɪʃ ən ~s z
librettist lɪ ˈbret ɪst lə-, §-əst ‖ -ˈbreţ əst ~s s
librett|o lɪ ˈbret |əʊ lə- ‖ -ˈbreţ |oʊ ~i iː ~os
  əʊz ‖ oʊz
Libreville ˈliːb rə vɪl -viːl
Librium tdmk ˈlɪb ri_əm
Liby|a ˈlɪb i_|ə ~an/s ən/z
lice laɪs
licenc|e, licens|e ˈlaɪs ᵊn|ts ~ed t ~es ɪz əz
  ~ing ɪŋ
  ˌlicensed ˈpremises; ˌlicensed ˌpractical
  ˈnurse; ˌlicensed ˈvictualler; ˈlicense
  plate; ˈlicensing laws
licensee ˌlaɪs ᵊn ˈsiː ~s z
licenser, licensor ˈlaɪs ᵊn|ts ə ‖ -ᵊr ~s z

licentiate laɪ ˈsen|ʃ i_ət lɪ-, -ˈsen|ts-, ɪt ~s s
licentious laɪ ˈsen|ʃ əs ~ly li ~ness nəs nɪs
lichee ˌlaɪ ˈtʃiː ˈlɪtʃ iː, ˈliːtʃ-, -i ‖ ˈliːtʃ i ˈlaɪtʃ i ~s
  z
lichen ˈlaɪk ən ˈlɪtʃ ᵊn, -ɪn ~s z
Lichfield ˈlɪtʃ fiːˑld
Lichtenstein family name ˈlɪkt ən staɪn -stiːn
  —Ger [ˈli çᵊn ʃtaɪn]
licit ˈlɪs ɪt §-ət ~ly li ~ness nəs nɪs
lick lɪk licked lɪkt licking ˈlɪk ɪŋ licks lɪks
lickerish ˈlɪk ᵊr ɪʃ
lickety-split ˌlɪk ət i ˈsplɪt -ɪt i- ‖ -əţ i-
lickspittle ˈlɪk ˌspɪt ᵊl ‖ -ˌspɪţ ᵊl ~s z
licorice ˈlɪk ᵊr ɪs ˌɪʃ, §_əs
lictor ˈlɪkt ə -ɔː ‖ -ᵊr ~s z
lid lɪd lidded ˈlɪd ɪd -əd lids lɪdz
Liddell (i) ˈlɪd ᵊl, (ii) lɪ ˈdel
Liddle ˈlɪd ᵊl
Liddon ˈlɪd ᵊn
Lidl tdmk ˈlɪd ᵊl
lido ˈliːd əʊ ‖ -oʊ ~s z
lie laɪ lain leɪn lay leɪ lied laɪd lies laɪz lying
  ˈlaɪ ɪŋ
  ˈlie deˌtector
Liebfraumilch, l~ ˈliːb fraʊ mɪlk -mɪlx, -mɪlʃ
  —Ger Liebfrauenmilch [liːp ˈfʁaʊ ən mɪlç]
Liebig ˈliːb ɪg —Ger [ˈliː bɪç]
Liechtenstein ˈlɪkt ən staɪn ˈlɪxt- —Ger
  [ˈlɪçt ᵊn ʃtaɪn] ~er/s ə/z ‖ ᵊr/z
lied ˈmusical setting' liːd —Ger [liːt] lieder
  ˈliːd ə ‖ -ᵊr —Ger [ˈliː dɐ]
lied past and pp of lie laɪd
lie-down ˌlaɪ ˈdaʊn ˈ·· ~s z
lief liːf (= leaf)
liege liːdʒ liːʒ lieges ˈliːdʒ ɪz ˈliːʒ-, -əz
  ˌliege ˈlord; ˈliege man
Liege, Liège li ˈeɪʒ -ˈeʒ —Fr [ljɛːʒ]
lie-in ˌlaɪ ˈɪn ˈ·· ~s z
lien ˈliːˑən liːn liens ˈliːˑənz liːnz
lieu luː ljuː
lieutenanc|y lef ˈten ən|ts |i ləf- ‖ luː- (*) ~ies
  iz
lieutenant lef ˈten ənt ləf- ‖ luː- (*) ~s s
life laɪf life's laɪfs lives laɪvz
  ˈlife belt; ˈlife ˌcycle; ˌlife exˈpectancy,
  ˈ· ·ˌ··; ˌlife imˈprisonment; ˌlife
  inˈsurance; ˈlife ˌjacket; ˈlife ˌpeer, ˌlife
  ˈpeeress; ˈlife preˌserver; ˈlife raft; ˌlife
  ˈsavings; ˈlife ˌstory; ˈlife ˌwork, ˌlife's
  ˈwork
life-affirming ˈlaɪf ə ˌfɜːm ɪŋ ‖ -ˌfɜːm-
life-and-death ˌlaɪf ᵊn ˈdeθ ◂
lifeblood ˈlaɪf blʌd
lifeboat ˈlaɪf bəʊt ‖ -boʊt ~s s
lifebuoy ˈlaɪf bɔɪ ~s z
life-giving ˈlaɪf ˌgɪv ɪŋ
lifeguard ˈlaɪf gɑːd ‖ -gɑːrd ~s z
lifeless ˈlaɪf ləs -lɪs ~ly li ~ness nəs nɪs
lifelike ˈlaɪf laɪk
lifeline ˈlaɪf laɪn ~s z
lifelong ˈlaɪf lɒŋ ˌ·ˈ· ‖ -lɔːŋ -lɑːŋ
lifer ˈlaɪf ə ‖ -ᵊr ~s z

life-sav|er 'laɪf ˌseɪv| ə ‖ -ᵊr **~ers** əz ‖ ᵊrz **~ing**
ɪŋ
life-size 'laɪf saɪz ˌ·'·◂ **~d** d
lifespan 'laɪf spæn **~s** z
lifestyle 'laɪf staɪᵊl **~s** z
life-support 'laɪf sə ˌpɔːt ˌ· ·'· ‖ -ˌpɔːrt -ˌpoʊrt
life-threatening 'laɪf ˌθret ᵊn ɪŋ
lifetime 'laɪf taɪm **~s** z
lifework ˌlaɪf 'wɜːk '· · ‖ -'wɜːk
LIFFE laɪf
Liffey 'lɪf i
Lifford 'lɪf əd ‖ -ᵊrd
lift lɪft **lifted** 'lɪftɪd -əd **lifting** 'lɪft ɪŋ **lifts**
lɪfts
liftboy 'lɪft bɔɪ **~s** z
lift|man 'lɪft |mæn **~men** men
liftoff 'lɪft ɒf -ɔːf ‖ -ɔːf -ɑːf **~s** s
ligament 'lɪg ə mənt **~s** s
ligamental ˌlɪg ə 'ment ᵊl ◂ ‖ -'ment̬ ᵊl ◂
ligand 'lɪg ənd 'laɪg- **~s** z
lig|ate 'laɪg |eɪt **~ated** eɪt ɪd -əd ‖ eɪt̬ əd
~ates eɪts **~ating** eɪt ɪŋ ‖ eɪt̬ ɪŋ
ligature 'lɪg ətʃ ə -ə tjʊə, -ə tʃʊə ‖ -ə tʃʊr
-ətʃ ᵊr, -ə tʊr **~s** z
liger 'laɪg ə ‖ -ᵊr **~s** z
ligger 'lɪg ə ‖ -ᵊr **~s** z
light laɪt **lighted** 'laɪt ɪd -əd ‖ 'laɪt̬ əd **lighter**
'laɪt ə ‖ 'laɪt̬ ᵊr **lightest** 'laɪt ɪst -əst
‖ 'laɪt̬ əst **lighting** 'laɪt ɪŋ ‖ 'laɪt̬ ɪŋ **lights**
laɪts **lit** lɪt
   ˌlight 'aircraft; ˌlight 'ale; 'light bulb;
   ˌlight 'heavyweight; 'lighting-'up time;
   'light ˌmeter; 'light pen; 'light year
lighten 'laɪt ᵊn **~ed** d **~ing** ɪŋ **~s** z
lighter 'laɪt ə ‖ 'laɪt̬ ᵊr **~s** z
lighterage 'laɪt ər ɪdʒ ‖ 'laɪt̬-
lighter|man 'laɪt ə mən ‖ 'laɪt̬ ᵊr- **~men** mən
men
lightface 'laɪt feɪs
light-fingered ˌlaɪt 'fɪŋ gəd ◂ ‖ -gᵊrd ◂ **~ness**
nəs nɪs
Lightfoot 'laɪt fʊt
light-headed ˌlaɪt 'hed ɪd ◂ -əd **~ly** li **~ness**
nəs nɪs
light-hearted ˌlaɪt 'hɑːt ɪd ◂ -əd ‖ -'hɑːrt̬ əd ◂
~ly li **~ness** nəs nɪs
light|house 'laɪt |haʊs **~houses** haʊz ɪz -əz
lightly 'laɪt li
light-minded ˌlaɪt 'maɪnd ɪd ◂ -əd **~ly** li
~ness nəs nɪs
lightness 'laɪt nəs -nɪs **~es** ɪz əz
lightning 'laɪt nɪŋ
   'lightning bug; 'lightning conˌductor;
   ˌlightning 'strike 'sudden stoppage';
   'lightning strike 'atmospheric discharge'
lightship 'laɪt ʃɪp **~s** s
lights-out ˌlaɪts 'aʊt '· ·
lightstick 'laɪt stɪk **~s** s
lightweight 'laɪt weɪt **~s** s
ligneous 'lɪg ni əs
lignification ˌlɪg nɪf ɪ 'keɪʃ ᵊn ˌnəf-, §-ə'-·-
ligni|fy 'lɪg nɪ |faɪ -nə- **~fied** faɪd **~fies** faɪz
~fying faɪ ɪŋ

lignin 'lɪg nɪn §-nən
lignite 'lɪg naɪt
lignocaine 'lɪg nəʊ keɪn ‖ -ə-
lignum vitae ˌlɪg nəm 'vaɪt i -'viːt aɪ ‖ -'vaɪt̬ i
-ə
Liguri|a lɪ 'gjʊər i |ə ‖ -'gjʊr- **~an/s** ən/z
likable 'laɪk əb ᵊl **~ness** nəs nɪs
like laɪk **liked** laɪkt **likes** laɪks **liking** 'laɪk ɪŋ
-like laɪk — **springlike** 'sprɪŋ laɪk
likeable 'laɪk əb ᵊl **~ness** nəs nɪs
likelihood 'laɪk li hʊd **~s** z
likely 'laɪk li
like-minded ˌlaɪk 'maɪnd ɪd ◂ -əd **~ly** li **~ness**
nəs nɪs
liken 'laɪk ən **~ed** d **~ing** ɪŋ **~s** z
likeness 'laɪk nəs -nɪs **~es** ɪz əz
likewise 'laɪk waɪz
liking 'laɪk ɪŋ **~s** z
Likud lɪ 'kʊd -'kuːd ‖ -'kuːd
lilac, Lilac 'laɪl ək ‖ -ɑːk, -æk **~s** s
Lilburne 'lɪl bɜːn ‖ -bɜːrn
Lilian 'lɪl i ən
Lilias 'lɪl i əs
Liliburlero ˌlɪl i bə 'leər əʊ ‖ -bᵊr 'ler oʊ
lilie... —see **lily**
Lilith 'lɪl ɪθ -əθ
Lille liːᵊl —Fr [lil]
Lillee 'lɪl i
Lillehammer 'lɪl ɪ hæm ə ‖ -ə hɑːm ᵊr -hæm-
   —Norw ['ˈlɪ lə ha mər]
Lil-lets tdmk lɪ 'lets
Lilley 'lɪl i
Lillian 'lɪl i ən
Lillibullero ˌlɪl i bə 'leər əʊ ‖ -'ler oʊ
Lillie 'lɪl i
Lilliput 'lɪl ɪ pʌt -ə-, -pʊt; -ɪp ət, -əp-
lilliputian, L~ ˌlɪl ɪ 'pjuːʃ ᵊn ◂ -ə-, -'pjuːʃ i ən
~s z
Lilly 'lɪl i
Lillywhite 'lɪl i waɪt -hwaɪt
lilo, li-lo, Lilo, Li-lo tdmk 'laɪ ləʊ ‖ -loʊ **~s** z
Lilongwe lɪ 'lɒŋ weɪ ‖ -'lɔːŋ- -'lɑːŋ-
lilt, Lilt tdmk lɪlt **lilted** 'lɪlt ɪd -əd **lilting**
'lɪlt ɪŋ **lilts** lɪlts
lilting 'lɪlt ɪŋ **~ly** li **~ness** nəs nɪs
lil|y, Lil|y 'lɪl |i **~ies, ~y's** iz
   ˌlily of the 'valley
lily-livered ˌlɪl i 'lɪv əd ◂ ‖ -ᵊrd ◂
lily-white ˌlɪl i 'waɪt ◂ -'hwaɪt
Lima, lima (i) 'liːm ə, (ii) 'laɪm ə *The place in
Peru —Sp* ['li ma] —*and the communications
code name for the letter* L *are* (i); *the place in
Ohio is* (ii); *the bean is* (ii) *in AmE, either in
BrE.*
   'lima bean
limacon, limaçon 'lɪm ə sɒn ‖ -sɑːn
   ˌliːm ə 'soʊn —Fr [li ma sɔ̃] **~s** z
Limassol 'lɪm ə sɒl ‖ -sɔːl -sɑːl, -soʊl, ˌ· ·'·
Limavady ˌlɪm ə 'væd i
limb lɪm **limbs** lɪmz
Limbaugh 'lɪm bɔː ‖ -bɑː
limber 'lɪm bə ‖ -bᵊr **~ed** d **limbering**
'lɪm bər ɪŋ **~s** z

limbic 'lɪm bɪk
limbless 'lɪm ləs -lɪs
limbo, Limbo 'lɪm bəʊ ‖ -boʊ ~s z
Limburger 'lɪm bɜːg ə ‖ -bɜːg ʳr
lim|bus 'lɪm |bəs ~bi baɪ
lime laɪm **limed** laɪmd **limes** laɪmz **liming**
'laɪm ɪŋ
,lime 'green◂; 'lime ,tree
limeade ,laɪm 'eɪd ~s z
Limehouse 'laɪm haʊs
limejuic|e 'laɪm dʒuːs ~es ɪz əz
limekiln 'laɪm kɪln -kɪl ~s z
limelight 'laɪm laɪt ~s s
limen 'laɪm en -ən ~s z **limina** 'lɪm ɪn ə §-ən ə
limerick, L~ 'lɪm ər ɪk ~s s
limescale 'laɪm skeɪ°l
limestone 'laɪm stəʊn ‖ -stoʊn
limey, Limey 'laɪm i ~s z
limin|a 'lɪm ɪn |ə §-ən- ~**al** °l
lim|it 'lɪm |ɪt §-ət | -|ət ~**ited** ɪt ɪd §ət-, -əd
‖ əṭ əd ~**iting** ɪt ɪŋ §ət- ‖ əṭ ɪŋ ~**its** ɪts §əts
‖ əts
,limited ,lia'bility
limitation ,lɪm ɪ 'teɪʃ ³n -ə- ~s z
limitless 'lɪm ɪt ləs §-ət-, -lɪs ~**ly** li ~**ness** nəs
nɪs
limn lɪm (= limb) **limned** lɪmd **limning**
'lɪm ɪŋ -nɪŋ **limns** lɪmz
limo 'lɪm əʊ ‖ -oʊ ~s z
Limoges lɪ 'məʊʒ ‖ -'moʊʒ —Fr [li mɔːʒ]
Limousin ,lɪm u 'zæn -'zæ̃ —Fr [li mu zæ̃]
limousine ,lɪm ə 'ziːn '···‖ 'lɪm ə ziːn ,··◂ ~s
z
limp lɪmp **limped** lɪmpt **limping** 'lɪmp ɪŋ
limps lɪmps
limpet 'lɪmp ɪt §-ət ~s s
limpid 'lɪmp ɪd §-əd ~**ly** li ~**ness** nəs nɪs
limpidity lɪm 'pɪd ət i -ɪt- ‖ -əṭ i
limp|ly 'lɪmp |li ~**ness** nəs nɪs
Limpopo lɪm 'pəʊp əʊ ‖ -'poʊp oʊ
limp-wristed ,lɪmp 'rɪst ɪd ◂ -əd ◂
lim|y 'laɪm |i ~**ier** i ə ‖ i ʳr ~**iest** i ɪst i əst
Linacre 'lɪn ək ə ‖ -ʳr
linage 'laɪn ɪdʒ
Lin Biao ,lɪn bi 'aʊ —Chi Lín Biāo [²lɪn ¹pjau]
Linch lɪntʃ
linchpin 'lɪntʃ pɪn ~s z
Lincoln 'lɪŋk ən ~'s z ~**shire** ʃə ʃɪə ‖ ʃʳr ʃɪr
,Lincoln's 'Inn
Lincs, Lincs. lɪŋks
linctus 'lɪŋkt əs ~**es** ɪz əz
Lind lɪnd
Linda 'lɪnd ə
lindane 'lɪnd eɪn
Lindbergh 'lɪnd bɜːg ‖ -bɜːg
linden, L~ 'lɪnd ən ~s z
Lindisfarne 'lɪnd ɪs fɑːn -əs- ‖ -fɑːrn
Lindley 'lɪnd li
Lindo 'lɪnd əʊ ‖ -oʊ
Lindon 'lɪnd ən
Lindsay, Lindsey 'lɪndz i
Lindwall 'lɪnd wɔːl ‖ -wɑːl
Lindy 'lɪnd i

line, Line laɪn **lined** laɪnd **lines** laɪnz **lining**
'laɪn ɪŋ
'line ,drawing; 'line ,printer
lineag|e 'descent' 'lɪn i ˌɪdʒ ~**es** ɪz əz
lineag|e 'number of lines' 'laɪn ɪdʒ
lineal 'lɪn i əl ~**ly** i
lineament 'lɪn i ə mənt ~s s
linear 'lɪn i ə ‖ ʳr ~**ly** li
,Linear 'B; ,linear 'programming
linearit|y ,lɪn i 'ær ət i |i -ɪt i ‖ -əṭ |i -'er- ~**ies**
iz
lineation ,lɪn i 'eɪʃ ³n ~s z
linebacker 'laɪn ,bæk ə ‖ -ʳr ~s z
Lineker 'lɪn ɪk ə -ək- ‖ -ʳr
line|man 'laɪn |mən ~**men** mən
linen 'lɪn ɪn §-ən ~s z
'linen ,basket
lineout 'laɪn aʊt ~s s
liner 'laɪn ə ‖ -ʳr ~s z
linertrain 'laɪn ə treɪn ‖ -ʳr- ~s z
lineshoot|er 'laɪn ,ʃuːt |ə ‖ -,ʃuːt |ʳr ~**ers** əz
‖ ʳrz ~**ing** ɪŋ
lines|man 'laɪnz |mən ~**men** mən men
lineup 'laɪn ʌp ~s s
Linford 'lɪn fəd ‖ -fʳrd
-ling lɪŋ — **underling** 'ʌnd ə lɪŋ ‖ -ʳr-
ling, Ling lɪŋ **lings** lɪŋz
Lingala lɪŋ 'gɑːl ə
lingam 'lɪŋ gəm ~s z
linger 'lɪŋ gə ‖ -gʳr ~**ed** d **lingering/ly**
'lɪŋ gər ɪŋ /li ~s z
lingerie 'lændʒ ər i 'lɒndʒ-; -ə reɪ
‖ ,lɑːndʒ ə 'reɪ -'riː, '···—Fr [læʒ ʁi]
Lingfield 'lɪŋ fiː°ld
lingo 'lɪŋ gəʊ ‖ -goʊ ~**es** z
lingua 'lɪŋ gwə
,lingua 'franca 'fræŋk ə
lingual 'lɪŋ gwəl §-gju əl ~s z
Linguaphone tdmk 'lɪŋ gwə fəʊn ‖ -foʊn
Linguarama tdmk ,lɪŋ gwə 'rɑːm ə ‖ -'ræm-
-'rɑːm-
linguine, linguini lɪŋ 'gwiːn i —It
[liŋ 'gwiː ne]
linguist 'lɪŋ gwɪst §-gwəst ~s s
linguistic lɪŋ 'gwɪst ɪk ~**ally** ³l_i ~s s
liniment 'lɪn ə mənt -ɪ- ~s s
lining 'laɪn ɪŋ ~s z
link, Link lɪŋk **linked** lɪŋkt **linking** 'lɪŋk ɪŋ
links lɪŋks
linkag|e 'lɪŋk ɪdʒ ~**es** ɪz əz
Linklater (i) 'lɪŋk ,leɪt ə ‖ -leɪṭ ʳr, (ii) -lət ə
‖ -ləṭ ʳr —The author Eric L~ and his son
Magnus L~ are (ii).
link|man 'lɪŋk |mæn —but in the obsolete
sense 'torchbearer' was usually -mən ~**men**
men
linkup 'lɪŋk ʌp ~s s
Linley 'lɪn li
Linlithgow lɪn 'lɪθ gəʊ ‖ -goʊ
Linnae|us, Linne|us lɪ 'niː |əs -'neɪ |əs ~**an/s**
ən/z
linnet 'lɪn ɪt §-ət ~s s
Linnhe 'lɪn i

Liquids

The English **liquids** are l and r. Both are usually voiced APPROXIMANTS. The difference between them is that

- l is ALVEOLAR and **lateral** (= the air escapes over one or both sides of the tongue, passing round the tongue tip)

- r is POST-ALVEOLAR and **median** (= the air escapes over the tongue tip, while the sides of the tongue are pressed firmly against the roof of the mouth).

In both cases there is some ALLOPHONIC variation:

- Both may be voiceless because of the ASPIRATION of a preceding plosive, e.g. **play** pleɪ, **pray** preɪ.

- In RP l is **clear** (= has e-resonance) before a vowel sound or j, but **dark** (= has ʊ-resonance; allophonic symbol ɫ) elsewhere. Hence **like** laɪk, **value** ˈvæl juː (clear), **milk** mɪlk (= mɪɫk), **fall** fɔːl (= fɔːɫ). In AmE, l may be fairly dark everywhere.

- In a consonant cluster after t or d, r is made FRICATIVE instead of approximant. The result is that tr and dr form AFFRICATES, e.g. **train** treɪn, **drain** dreɪn.

L

lino ˈlaɪn əʊ ‖ -oʊ ~s z
linocut ˈlaɪn əʊ kʌt ‖ -oʊ- ~s s
linoleic ˌlɪn əʊ ˈliː ɪk ◂ -ˈleɪ- ‖ -ə-
linoleum lɪ ˈnəʊl i‿əm lə- ‖ -ˈnoʊl- ~s z
Linotype tdmk ˈlaɪn əʊ taɪp ‖ -ə-
linseed ˈlɪn siːd
    'linseed oil, ·ˌ·ˈ·.
linsey-woolsey ˌlɪnz i ˈwʊlz i ~s z
lint lɪnt
lintel ˈlɪnt ᵊl ~s z
Linton ˈlɪnt ən ‖ -ᵊn
Lintott ˈlɪn tɒt ‖ -tɑːt
Linus ˈlaɪn əs
Linux ˈlɪn əks ˈlaɪn-
Linwood ˈlɪn wʊd
Linz lɪnts —Ger [lɪnts]
lion ˈlaɪ ən ~s z
Lionel ˈlaɪ ən ᵊl
lioness ˈlaɪ ən es -ɪs, -əs; ˌlaɪ ə ˈnes ‖ -əs ~es ɪz əz
Lionheart ˈlaɪ ən hɑːt ‖ -hɑːrt
lion-hearted ˌlaɪ ən ˈhɑːt ɪd ◂ -əd, ˈ·ˌ·ˈ· ‖ -ˈhɑːrt̬ əd ◂
lionis... —see **lioniz...**
lionization ˌlaɪ ən aɪ ˈzeɪʃ ᵊn ən ɪ- ‖ -ən ə-
lioniz|e ˈlaɪ ə naɪz ~ed d ~er/s ə/z ‖ ᵊr/z ~es ɪz əz ~ing ɪŋ
lip lɪp **lipped** lɪpt **lipping** ˈlɪp ɪŋ **lips** lɪps
    'lip gloss; 'lip ˌservice
Lipari ˈlɪp ər i —It [ˈliː pa ri]
lipase ˈlaɪp eɪs ˈlɪp-, -eɪz
lipid ˈlɪp ɪd §-əd ~s z
Lipitor tdmk ˈlɪp ɪ tɔː -ə- ‖ -tɔːr
Lipman, Lipmann ˈlɪp mən

lipo- comb. form
    with stress-neutral suffix ˌlɪp əʊ ˌlaɪp- ‖ -ə
    — **lipochrome** ˈlɪp əʊ krəʊm ˈlaɪp- ‖ -ə kroʊm
    with stress-imposing suffix lɪ ˈpɒ + laɪ- ‖ -ˈpɑː + — **lipolysis** lɪ ˈpɒl əs ɪs -ɪs-, §-əs ‖ -ˈpɑːl-
lipoid ˈlɪp ɔɪd ˈlaɪp- ~s z
lipom|a lɪ ˈpəʊm |ə lə-, laɪ- ‖ -ˈpoʊm |ə ~as əz ~ata ət ə ‖ ət̬ ə
liposome ˈlɪp əʊ səʊm ˈlaɪp- ‖ -ə soʊm ~s z
liposuction ˈlɪp əʊ ˌsʌk ʃᵊn ˈlaɪp- ‖ -oʊ- -ə-
Lippizaner ˌlɪp ɪt ˈsɑːn ə ◂ -ət- ‖ -ᵊr ◂ ~s z
Lippmann ˈlɪp mən
lipp|y ˈlɪp |i ~ier i ə ‖ i ᵊr ~iest i ɪst i əst
lip-|read present ˈlɪp |riːd ~read past, pp red ~reader/s riːd ə/z ‖ -ᵊr/z ~reading riːd ɪŋ ~reads riːdz
lip-smacking ˈlɪp ˌsmæk ɪŋ
lipstick ˈlɪp stɪk ~s s
lip-sync, lip-synch ˈlɪp sɪŋk
Lipton ˈlɪpt ən
liquefaction ˌlɪk wɪ ˈfæk ʃᵊn -wə-
lique|fy ˈlɪk wɪ |faɪ -wə- ~fied faɪd ~fier/s faɪ ə/z ‖ faɪ ᵊr/z ~fies faɪz ~fying faɪ ɪŋ
liquescenc|e lɪ ˈkwes ᵊn̩ts ~y i
liquescent lɪ ˈkwes ᵊnt
liqueur lɪ ˈkjʊə lə-, -ˈkjɔː, -ˈkjɜː ‖ -ˈkɜː- ˈkjʊr —Fr [li kœːʁ] ~s z
liquid ˈlɪk wɪd §-wəd ~ly li ~s z
    ˌliquid 'crystal; ˌliquid 'oxygen
liquidambar ˌlɪk wɪd ˈæm bə §-wəd-, ˈ··ˌ·· ‖ -bᵊr ~s z

liqui|date 'lɪk wɪ |deɪt -wə- **~dated** deɪt ɪd -əd
‖ deɪt̮ əd **~dates** deɪts **~dating** deɪt ɪŋ
‖ deɪt̮ ɪŋ
liquidation ˌlɪk wɪ 'deɪʃ ᵊn -wə- **~s** z
liquidator 'lɪk wɪ deɪt ə ˌ·wə- ‖ -deɪt̮ ᵊr **~s** z
liquidis|e, liquidiz|e 'lɪk wɪ daɪz -wə- **~ed** d
~er/s ə/z ‖ ᵊr/z **~es** ɪz əz **~ing** ɪŋ
liquidity lɪ 'kwɪd ət i lə-, -ɪt- ‖ -ət̮ i
liquitab 'lɪk wɪ tæb §-wə- **~s** z
liquor 'lɪk ə ‖ -ᵊr —*also (med, pharm)* 'laɪk-,
-wɔː ‖ -wɔːr **~ed** d **liquoring** 'lɪk ᵊr ɪŋ **~s** z

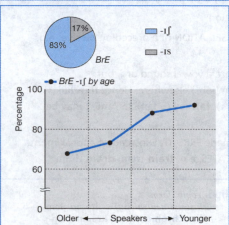

LIQUORICE

-ɪʃ 83%, -ɪs 17% (BrE pie chart)

BrE -ɪʃ by age (line graph, Older ← Speakers → Younger, Percentage)

liquorice 'lɪk ᵊr ɪʃ ˌɪs, §ˌəs *Preference poll, BrE:*
-ɪʃ 83% (born since 1981, 92%), -ɪs 17%.
ˌliquorice 'allsorts
lira 'lɪər ə ‖ 'lɪr ə —*It* ['liː ra] **lire** 'lɪər ə -eɪ, -i
‖ 'lɪr eɪ —*It* ['liː re]
liriodendron ˌlɪr i ˌəʊ 'dendr ən ‖ -iˌə- **~s** z
liripipe 'lɪr i paɪp -ə- **~s** s
Lisa (i) 'liːs ə, (ii) 'liːz ə, (iii) 'laɪz ə
Lisbet 'lɪz bət -bet, -bɪt
Lisbeth 'lɪz bəθ -beθ, -bɪθ
Lisbon 'lɪz bən —*Port* Lisboa [liʒ 'βɔʌ]
Lisburn 'lɪz bɜːn ‖ -bᵊrn
lisle, Lisle laɪᵊl —*but as a French name,* liːᵊl
—*Fr* [lil]
lisp, LISP lɪsp **lisped** lɪspt **lisping** 'lɪsp ɪŋ
lisps lɪsps
lisper 'lɪsp ə ‖ -ᵊr **~s** z
Lissajous 'liːs ə ʒuː 'lɪs-; ˌ· ·'· —*Fr* [li sa ʒu]
lissom, lissome 'lɪs əm **~ly** li **~ness** nəs nɪs
Lisson 'lɪs ᵊn
list lɪst **listed** 'lɪst ɪd -əd **listing** 'lɪst ɪŋ **lists**
lɪsts
'list ˌprice
listel 'lɪst ᵊl **~s** z
listen 'lɪs ᵊn **~ed** d **~ing** ˌɪŋ **~s** z
listenable 'lɪs ᵊn ˌəb ᵊl
listener 'lɪs ᵊn ˌə ‖ ᵊr **~s** z
Lister, l~ 'lɪst ə ‖ -ᵊr **~s,** **~'s** z
listeria lɪ 'stɪər i ə ‖ -'stɪr- **~s** z
Listerine *tdmk* 'lɪst ə riːn ‖ ˌ· ·'·

listeriosis lɪ ˌstɪər i 'əʊs ɪs -əs; ˌlɪst ɪər·'· ·
‖ lɪ ˌstɪr i 'oʊs əs
listing 'lɪst ɪŋ **~s** z
'listing ˌpaper
listless 'lɪst ləs -lɪs **~ly** li **~ness** nəs nɪs
Liston 'lɪst ən
Listowel lɪ 'stəʊ əl ‖ -'stoʊ-
listserv 'lɪst sɜːv ‖ -sɜːv **~s** z
Liszt lɪst —*Hung* [list]
lit lɪt
Lita 'liːt ə ‖ 'liːt̮ ə
Li Tai Po ˌliː ˌtaɪ 'pəʊ ‖ -'poʊ —*Chi* Lǐ Dài Bái
[³li ⁴tai ²pai]
litan|y 'lɪt ən |i ‖ -ᵊn |i **~ies** iz
Litchfield 'lɪtʃ fiːᵊld
litchi ˌlaɪ 'tʃiː 'lɪtʃ iː, 'liːtʃ-, -i ‖ 'liːtʃ i 'laɪtʃ i **~s**
z
lit crit ˌlɪt 'krɪt
lite laɪt
-lite laɪt — **chrysolite** 'krɪs ə laɪt
liter 'liːt ə ‖ 'liːt̮ ᵊr **~s** z
literacy 'lɪt ᵊr əs i ‖ 'lɪt̮ ər- →'lɪtr əs i
literal 'lɪt ᵊr əl ‖ 'lɪt̮ ər əl →'lɪtr əl **~ism** ˌɪz əm
~ist/s ɪst/s §əst/s ‖ əst/s **~ly** i **~ness** nəs nɪs
~s z
literar|y 'lɪt ᵊr ər ‖i △'lɪtr ‖i ‖ 'lɪt̮ ə rer ‖i **~ily**
əl i ɪ li **~iness** i nəs -nɪs
literate 'lɪt ᵊr ət -ɪt ‖ 'lɪt̮ ər ət →'lɪtr ət **~s** s
literati ˌlɪt ə 'rɑːt iː ‖ ˌlɪt̮ ə 'rɑːt̮ i
literatim ˌlɪt ə 'rɑːt ɪm -'reɪt-, §-əm
‖ ˌlɪt̮ ə 'reɪt̮ əm -'rɑːt̮-
literature 'lɪtr ətʃ ə -ɪtʃ-; -ə tjʊə, -ɪ-; 'lɪt ər· ·
‖ 'lɪt̮ ər ətʃ ᵊr -ə tʃʊr, →'lɪtr· · **~s** z
-lith lɪθ — **megalith** 'meg ə lɪθ
litharge 'lɪθ ɑːdʒ ‖ -ɑːrdʒ lɪ 'θɑːrdʒ
lithe laɪð ‖ laɪθ
lithe|ly 'laɪð |li ‖ 'laɪθ- **~ness** nəs nɪs
lithesome 'laɪð səm ‖ 'laɪθ-
Lithgow 'lɪθ gəʊ ‖ -goʊ
lithia 'lɪθ i ə
lithic 'lɪθ ɪk
-lithic 'lɪθ ɪk — **megalithic** ˌmeg ə 'lɪθ ɪk ◄
lithium 'lɪθ iˌəm
litho 'laɪθ əʊ ‖ -oʊ
litho- *comb. form*
with stress-neutral suffix ¦lɪθ əʊ ‖ -ə
— **lithosphere** 'lɪθ əʊ sfɪə ‖ -ə sfɪr
with stress-imposing suffix lɪ 'θɒ+ ‖ -'θɑː+
— **lithotomy** lɪ 'θɒt əm i ‖ -'θɑːt̮-
lithograph 'lɪθ əʊ grɑːf 'laɪθ-, -græf ‖ -ə græf
~s s
lithographer lɪ 'θɒg rəf ə laɪ- ‖ -'θɑːg rəf ᵊr
~s z
lithographic ˌlɪθ əʊ 'græf ɪk ◄ ˌlaɪθ- ‖ -ə-
~ally ᵊl i
lithography lɪ 'θɒg rəf i laɪ- ‖ -'θɑːg-
Lithuania ˌlɪθ ju 'eɪn iˌə ˌ·u- ‖ ˌlɪθ u-
Lithuanian ˌlɪθ ju 'eɪn iˌən ◄ ˌ·u- ‖ ˌlɪθ u- **~s** z
litigant 'lɪt ɪg ənt -əg- ‖ 'lɪt̮ ɪg- **~s** s
liti|gate 'lɪt ɪ |geɪt -ə- ‖ 'lɪt̮ ə- **~gated** geɪt ɪd
-əd ‖ geɪt̮ əd **~gates** geɪts **~gating** geɪt ɪŋ
‖ geɪt̮ ɪŋ
litigation ˌlɪt ɪ 'geɪʃ ᵊn -ə- ‖ ˌlɪt̮- **~s** z

litigious lɪ ˈtɪdʒ əs lə- **~ly** li **~ness** nəs nɪs
litmus ˈlɪt məs
   ˈlitmus ˌpaper; ˈlitmus test
litotes ˈlaɪt əʊ tiːz laɪ ˈtəʊt iːz ‖ ˈlaɪt̬ ə tiːz ˈlɪt̬-;
   laɪ ˈtoʊt iːz
litre ˈliːt ə ‖ ˈliːt̬ ᵊr **~s** z
litter ˈlɪt ə ‖ ˈlɪt̬ ᵊr **~ed** d **littering** ˈlɪt ər ɪŋ
   ‖ ˈlɪt̬ ər ɪŋ **~s** z
litterateur, littérateur ˌlɪt ᵊr ə ˈtɜː
   ‖ ˌlɪt̬ ər ə ˈtɜː- -ˈtʊᵊr; → ˌlɪtr ə· —Fr
   [li te ʁa tœːʁ] **~s** z
litterbag ˈlɪt ə bæg ‖ ˈlɪt̬ ᵊr- **~s** z
litterbin ˈlɪt ə bɪn ‖ ˈlɪt̬ ᵊr- **~s** z
litterbug ˈlɪt ə bʌg ‖ ˈlɪt̬ ᵊr- **~s** z
litterlout ˈlɪt ə laʊt ‖ ˈlɪt̬ ᵊr- **~s** s
little, L~ ˈlɪt ᵊl ‖ ˈlɪt̬ ᵊl **least** liːst **less** les
   littler ˈlɪt ᵊl ə ‖ ᵊr
   ˌlittle ˈfinger; ˈlittle ˌpeople; ˈLittle Rock
   place in AR; ˌlittle ˈwoman
Littlehampton ˌlɪt ᵊl ˈhæmp tən ◂ ˈ·· ˌ·· ‖ ˌlɪt̬-
Littlejohn ˈlɪt ᵊl dʒɒn ‖ ˈlɪt̬ ᵊl dʒɑːn
Littler ˈlɪt lə ‖ -ᵊr
Littlestone ˈlɪt ᵊl stən -stəʊn ‖ ˈlɪt̬ ᵊl stoʊn
Littleton ˈlɪt ᵊl tən ‖ ˈlɪt̬-
Litton ˈlɪt ᵊn
littoral ˈlɪt ər əl ‖ ˈlɪt̬- ˌlɪt̬ ə ˈræl, -ˈrɑːl **~s** z
liturgic lɪ ˈtɜːdʒ ɪk lə- ‖ -ˈtɜːdʒ- **~al** ᵊl **~ally**
   ᵊl i **~s** s
liturgist ˈlɪt ədʒ ɪst §-əst ‖ ˈlɪt̬ ᵊrdʒ- **~s** s
liturg|y ˈlɪt ədʒ |i ‖ ˈlɪt̬ ᵊrdʒ |i **~ies** iz
livability ˌlɪv ə ˈbɪl ət i -ɪt i ‖ -ət̬ i
livable ˈlɪv əb ᵊl
live adj, adv laɪv
   ˌlive perˈformance; ˌlive ˈwire
live vlɪv **lived** lɪvd **lives** lɪvz **living** ˈlɪv ɪŋ
liveability ˌlɪv ə ˈbɪl ət i -ɪt i ‖ -ət̬ i
liveable ˈlɪv əb ᵊl
lived-in ˈlɪvd ɪn
live-in ˌlɪv ˈɪn ◂
   ˌlive-in ˈlover
livelihood ˈlaɪv li hʊd **~s** z
livelong ˈlɪv lɒŋ ˈlaɪv- ‖ -lɔːŋ -lɑːŋ
live|ly, L~ ˈlaɪv |li **~lier** li ə ‖ li ᵊr **~liest** li ɪst
   li ˌəst **~liness** li nəs -nɪs
liven ˈlaɪv ᵊn **~ed** d **~ing** ɪŋ **~s** z
Livens ˈlɪv ᵊnz
liver ˈlɪv ə ‖ -ᵊr **~s** z
   ˈliver salts; ˈliver ˌsausage; ˈliver spot
Liver Building, bird, symbol of Liverpool ˈlaɪv ə
   ‖ -ᵊr
liverie... —see **livery**
liverish ˈlɪv ər ɪʃ **~ness** nəs nɪs
Livermore ˈlɪv ə mɔː ‖ -ᵊr mɔːr -moʊr
Liverpool ˈlɪv ə puːl ‖ -ᵊr-
Liverpudlian ˌlɪv ə ˈpʌd li ən ◂ ‖ ˌ·ᵊr- **~s** z
Liversedge ˈlɪv ə sedʒ ‖ -ᵊr-
liverwort ˈlɪv ə wɜːt §-wɔːt ‖ -ᵊr wɜːt -wɔːrt **~s**
   s
liverwurst ˈlɪv ə wɜːst ‖ -ᵊr wɜːst -wʊrst, -wʊʃt
liver|y ˈlɪv ər |i **~ied** id **~ies** iz
   ˈlivery ˌcompany; ˈlivery ˌstable
livery|man ˈlɪv ər i |mən **~men** mən men
lives pl of **life** laɪvz

lives 3 sing. of **live** lɪvz
Livesey (i) ˈlɪv si, (ii) -zi
livestock ˈlaɪv stɒk ‖ -stɑːk
Livia ˈlɪv i ə
livid ˈlɪv ɪd §-əd **~ly** li **~ness** nəs nɪs
living ˈlɪv ɪŋ **~s** z
   ˌliving ˈfossil; ˌliving ˈmemory; ˈliving
   room; ˈliving ˌstandard; ˌliving ˈwage
Livings ˈlɪv ɪŋz
Livingston ˈlɪv ɪŋ stən
Livingstone ˈlɪv ɪŋ stən -stəʊn ‖ -stoʊn
Livoni|a lɪ ˈvəʊn i ˌə ‖ -ˈvoʊn- **~an/s** ən/z
Livy ˈlɪv i
lixivi|ate lɪk ˈsɪv i |eɪt **~ated** eɪt ɪd -əd
   ‖ eɪt̬ əd **~ates** eɪts **~ating** eɪt ɪŋ ‖ eɪt̬ ɪŋ
Liz lɪz
Liza (i) ˈlaɪz ə (ii) ˈliːz ə
lizard, L~ ˈlɪz əd ‖ -ᵊrd **~s** z
Lizzie ˈlɪz i
Ljubljana ˌlʊb li ˈɑːn ə ‖ ˌluːb- —Slovene
   [lʲu ˈblʲa na]
'll ᵊl, əl —Following a word other than a
   pronoun, this contracted form is pronounced as
   a separate syllable, thus Jim'll do it
   ˈdʒɪm ᵊl ˌduː ɪt, Lucy'll do it ˈluːs i ᵊl ˌduː ɪt.
   See, however, the entries I'll, he'll, she'll,
   there'll, they'll, we'll, you'll.
llama ˈlɑːm ə **~s** z
Llan prefix in Welsh names læn θlæn, ɬæn —In
   Welsh this is ɬan, usually anglicized as læn or,
   when unstressed, lən. The Welsh sound (a
   voiceless alveolar lateral fricative) is however
   sometimes imitated by the non-Welsh as the
   cluster θl, or even as xl. No AmE forms are
   given for the Welsh names that follow.
Llanberis læn ˈber ɪs θlæn- —Welsh
   [ɬan ˈbe ris]
Llandaff ˈlænd əf ˈɬæn dæf, ˈθlæn-, ˌ·ˈ· —Welsh
   Llandaf [ɬan ˈdaːv]
Llandeilo læn ˈdaɪl əʊ ˈθlæn- ‖ -oʊ —Welsh
   [ɬan ˈdəi lo]
Llandovery læn ˈdʌv ər i θlæn- —Welsh
   Llanymddyfri [ˌɬan əm ˈðəv ri]
Llandrindod læn ˈdrɪn dɒd θlæn- ‖ -dɑːd
   —Welsh [ɬan ˈdrin dod]
Llandudno læn ˈdɪd nəʊ θlæn-, -ˈdʌd- ‖ -noʊ
   —Welsh [ɬan ˈdïd no, -ˈdid-]
Llanelli lə ˈneθ li ɬə-, læ-, θlæ-, θlə- —Welsh
   [ɬan ˈeɬ i]
Llanfairfechan ˌlæn feə ˈfek ən ˌθlæn-, -fə-,
   ˌ·ˌvaɪ ə·◂ · ‖ -fer- —Welsh [ˌɬan vair ˈve χan]
Llanfairpwll ˌlæn feə ˈpuɬ ˌvaɪ ə-, -ˈpuɬ
   ‖ -fer- Also **Llanfairpwllgwyngyll**
   ˌlæn vaɪ ə puɬ ˈgwɪn gɪɬ →-ˈgwɪŋ- ‖ ˌ·vaɪᵊr-
   —usually called **Llanfair P.G.**
   ˌlæn feə ˌpi: ˈdʒiː θlæn-, ˌ·ˌvaɪ ə·ˈ· ‖ -fer-
   —The full form, famous for its length, is
   Llanfairpwllgwyngyllgogerychwyrndrobwll-
   llandysiliogogogoch —Welsh
   [ˌɬan vair puɬ ˌgwin gɪɬ go ˌger ə ˌχwərn
   ˌdro buɬ ˌɬan də ˌsil jo ˌgo go ˈgoːχ -puɬ-,
   -ˌgwin gɪɬ-, -buɬ-]

Llangollen læn ˈgɒθ lən θlæn-, →læŋ- ‖ -ˈgɔːθ- —*Welsh* [ɬan ˈgɔ ɬen]

Llangranog læn ˈgræn ɒg θlæn-, →læŋ-, -əg ‖ -ɔːg —*Welsh* [ɬan ˈgra nog]

Llangurig læn ˈgɪr ɪg θlæn-, →læŋ- —*Welsh* [ɬan ˈgɨ rɪg, -ˈgi-]

Llanrwst læn ˈruːst θlæn- —*Welsh* [ɬan ˈruːst]

Llantrisant læn ˈtrɪs ᵊnt

Llanuwchllyn læn ˈjuːk lɪn θlæn-, lən-, θlən-, -ˈjuːx- —*Welsh* [ɬan ˈiuχ ɬɪn, -ˈiuχ ɬɪn]

Llanwrtyd læn ˈʊət ɪd θlæn- ‖ -ˈʊrt- —*Welsh* [ɬan ˈʊr tɪd, -tɪd]

Llareggub lə ˈreg əb læ-, θlə-, θlæ-, -ʌb —*not a real Welsh name*

Llewelyn lə ˈwel ɪn θlə-; lu ˈel-, θlu- —*Welsh* [ˈɬwe lɪn; ɬe ˈwe lɪn, -lɪn]

Lleyn liːn θliːn, leɪn, θleɪn —*Welsh* Llŷn [ɬɨːn, ɬiːn]

Lloret lə ˈret —*Sp* [ʎo ˈret, jo-], *Catalan* [ʎu ˈret]

Lloyd lɔɪd

Llywelyn lə ˈwel ɪn θlə-, §-ən; lu ˈel-, θlu- —*Welsh* [ɬə ˈwe lɪn, -lɪn]

lo ləʊ ‖ loʊ

lo and beˈhold

loach, Loach ləʊtʃ ‖ loʊtʃ **loaches** ˈləʊtʃ ɪz -əz ‖ ˈloʊtʃ əz

load ləʊd ‖ loʊd **loaded** ˈləʊd ɪd -əd ‖ ˈloʊd əd **loading** ˈləʊd ɪŋ ‖ ˈloʊd ɪŋ **loads** ləʊdz ‖ loʊdz

ˈload ˌfactor

load-bearing ˈləʊd ˌbeər ɪŋ ‖ ˈloʊd ˌber ɪŋ

loadmaster ˈləʊd ˌmɑːst ə §-ˌmæst- ‖ -ˌmæst ᵊr ~**s** z

loadsamoney ˈləʊdz ə ˌmʌn i ‖ ˈloʊdz-

loadstar ˈləʊd stɑː ‖ ˈloʊd stɑːr ~**s** z

loadstone ˈləʊd stəʊn ‖ ˈloʊd stoʊn ~**s** z

loaf ləʊf ‖ loʊf **loafed** ləʊft ‖ loʊft **loafing** ˈləʊf ɪŋ ‖ ˈloʊf ɪŋ **loafs** ləʊfs ‖ loʊfs **loaves** ləʊvz ‖ loʊvz

loafer ˈləʊf ə ‖ ˈloʊf ᵊr ~**s** z

loafsugar ˈləʊf ˌʃʊg ə ‖ ˈloʊf ˌʃʊg ᵊr

loam ləʊm ‖ loʊm

loamy ˈləʊm i ‖ ˈloʊm i

loan ləʊn ‖ loʊn **loaned** ləʊnd ‖ loʊnd **loaning** ˈləʊn ɪŋ ‖ ˈloʊn ɪŋ **loans** ləʊnz ‖ loʊnz

loaner ˈləʊn ə ‖ ˈloʊn ᵊr ~**s** z

loanword ˈləʊn wɜːd ‖ ˈloʊn wɜːd ~**s** z

loath ləʊθ △ləʊð ‖ loʊθ loʊð

loathe ləʊð ‖ loʊð **loathed** ləʊðd ‖ loʊðd **loather/s** ˈləʊð ə/z ‖ ˈloʊð ᵊr/z **loathes** ləʊðz ‖ loʊðz **loathing/ly** ˈləʊð ɪŋ /li ‖ ˈloʊð ɪŋ /li

loathsome ˈləʊð səm ˈləʊθ- ‖ ˈloʊð- ˈloʊθ- ~**ly** li ~**ness** nəs nɪs

loaves ləʊvz ‖ loʊvz

lob lɒb ‖ lɑːb **lobbed** lɒbd ‖ lɑːbd **lobbing** ˈlɒb ɪŋ ‖ ˈlɑːb ɪŋ **lobs** lɒbz ‖ lɑːbz

lobate ˈləʊb eɪt ‖ ˈloʊb-

lobb|y ˈlɒb |i ‖ ˈlɑːb |i ~**ied** id ~**ies** iz ~**ying** i ɪŋ

lobbyist ˈlɒb i ɪst -əst ‖ ˈlɑːb- ~**s** s

lobe ləʊb ‖ loʊb **lobed** ləʊbd ‖ loʊbd **lobes** ləʊbz ‖ loʊbz

lobelia lə ˈbiːl i ə ‖ loʊ- ~**s** z

lobeline ˈləʊb ə liːn ‖ ˈloʊb-

lobloll|y ˈlɒb ˌlɒl |i ‖ ˈlɑːb ˌlɑːl |i ~**ies** iz

lobotomis|e, lobotomiz|e lə ˈbɒt ə maɪz ‖ loʊ ˈbɑːt̬ lə- ~**ed** d ~**es** ɪz əz ~**ing** ɪŋ

lobotom|y lə ˈbɒt əm |i ‖ loʊ ˈbɑːt̬- lə- ~**ies** iz

lobscouse ˈlɒb skaʊs ‖ ˈlɑːb-

lobster ˈlɒb stə ‖ ˈlɑːb stᵊr ~**s** z

lobster|man ˈlɒb stə| mən -mæn ‖ ˈlɑːb stᵊr|- ~**men** mən men

lobsterpot ˈlɒb stə pɒt ‖ ˈlɑːb stᵊr pɑːt ~**s** s

lobular ˈlɒb jʊl ə ‖ ˈlɑːb jəl ᵊr

lobule ˈlɒb juːl ‖ ˈlɑːb- ~**s** z

local, Local ˈləʊk ᵊl ‖ ˈloʊk ᵊl ~**ly** i ~**s** z

ˌlocal ˌarea ˈnetwork; ˌlocal auˈthority; ˌlocal ˈcolour; ˌlocal ˈderby; ˌlocal ˈoption; ˈlocal time, · · ˈ.

lo-cal *'low-calorie'* ˌləʊ ˈkæl ◄ ‖ ˌloʊ-

locale ləʊ ˈkɑːl ‖ loʊ ˈkæl ~**s** z

localis... —*see* **localiz...**

localism ˈləʊk ᵊl ˌɪz əm ‖ ˈloʊk- ~**s** z

localit|y ləʊ ˈkæl ət |i -ɪt- ‖ loʊ ˈkæl ət̬ |i ~**ies** iz

localization ˌləʊk ᵊl aɪ ˈzeɪʃ ᵊn -əl ɪ- ‖ ˌloʊk ᵊl ə- ~**s** z

localiz|e ˈləʊk ə laɪz -ᵊl aɪz ‖ ˈloʊk- ~**ed** d ~**es** ɪz əz ~**ing** ɪŋ

locally ˈləʊk ᵊl i ‖ ˈloʊk-

lo-carb ˌləʊ ˈkɑːb ◄ ‖ ˌloʊ ˈkɑːrb ◄

Locarno ləʊ ˈkɑːn əʊ lɒ- ‖ loʊ ˈkɑːrn oʊ —*It* [lo ˈkar no]

loc|ate ləʊ ˈk|eɪt ‖ ˈloʊk |eɪt loʊ ˈk|eɪt ~**ated** eɪt ɪd -əd ‖ eɪt̬ əd ~**ates** eɪts ~**ating** eɪt ɪŋ ‖ eɪt̬ ɪŋ

location ləʊ ˈkeɪʃ ᵊn ‖ loʊ- ~**s** z

locative ˈlɒk ət ɪv ‖ ˈlɑːk ət̬ ɪv ~**s** z

loch lɒx lɒk ‖ lɑːk lɑːx **lochs** lɒxs lɒks ‖ lɑːks lɑːxs

Lochearnhead lɒx ˌɜːn ˈhed lɒk- ‖ lɑːk ˌɜːn- lɑːx-

Lochgilphead lɒx ˈgɪlp hed lɒk- ‖ lɑːk- lɑːx-

Lochinvar ˌlɒx ɪn ˈvɑː ˌlɒk- ‖ ˌlɑːk ən ˈvɑːr

Lochinver lɒ ˈxɪn və -ˈkɪn- ‖ lɑː ˈkɪn vᵊr

loci ˈləʊs aɪ ˈləʊk-, ˈlɒk-, -iː ‖ ˈloʊs aɪ ˈloʊk-, -iː

lock, Lock lɒk ‖ lɑːk **locked** lɒkt ‖ lɑːkt **locking** ˈlɒk ɪŋ ‖ ˈlɑːk ɪŋ **locks** lɒks ‖ lɑːks

ˈlock ˌkeeper

lockable ˈlɒk əb ᵊl ‖ ˈlɑːk-

Locke lɒk ‖ lɑːk

locker ˈlɒk ə ‖ ˈlɑːk ᵊr ~**s** z

ˈlocker room

Lockerbie ˈlɒk əb i ‖ ˈlɑːk ᵊrb i

locker-room ˈlɒk ə ruːm -rʊm ‖ ˈlɑːk ᵊr-

locket ˈlɒk ɪt §-ət ‖ ˈlɑːk- ~**s** s

Lockhart *(i)* ˈlɒk ət ‖ ˈlɑːk ᵊrt, *(ii)* -hɑːt ‖ -hɑːrt

Lockheed ˈlɒk hiːd ‖ ˈlɑːk-

lockjaw ˈlɒk dʒɔː ‖ ˈlɑːk- -dʒɑː

locknut ˈlɒk nʌt ‖ ˈlɑːk- ~**s** s

lockout ˈlɒk aʊt ‖ ˈlɑːk- ~**s** s

Locksley 'lɒks li ‖ 'lɑːks-
locksmith 'lɒk smɪθ ‖ 'lɑːk- ~s s
lockstep 'lɒk step ‖ 'lɑːk-
lockstitch 'lɒk stɪtʃ ‖ 'lɑːk- ~ed t ~es ɪz əz
  ~ing ɪŋ
lockup 'lɒk ʌp ‖ 'lɑːk- ~s s
Lockwood 'lɒk wʊd ‖ 'lɑːk-
Lockyer 'lɒk jə ‖ 'lɑːk jʲr
loco 'ləʊk əʊ ‖ 'loʊk oʊ ~s z
locomotion ˌləʊk ə 'məʊʃ ᵊn
  ‖ ˌloʊk ə 'moʊʃ ᵊn
locomotive ˌləʊk ə 'məʊt ɪv ◂ '····
  ‖ ˌloʊk ə 'moʊt ɪv ◂ ~s z
locomotor ˌləʊk əʊ 'məʊt ə ◂
  ‖ ˌloʊk ə 'moʊt ᵊr ◂
  ˌloco ˌmotor a'taxia
locoweed 'ləʊk əʊ wiːd ‖ 'loʊk oʊ-
Locris 'ləʊk rɪs 'lɒk-, -rəs ‖ 'loʊk-
locum 'ləʊk əm 'lɒk- ‖ 'loʊk- ~s z
  ˌlocum 'tenens 'ten enz 'tiːn- ‖ -ənz
locus 'ləʊk əs 'lɒk- ‖ 'loʊk-
  ˌlocus 'classicus 'klæs ɪk əs; ˌlocus 'standi
  'stænd aɪ
locust 'ləʊk əst ‖ 'loʊk- ~s s
locution ləʊ 'kjuːʃ ᵊn lɒ- ‖ loʊ- ~s z
locutionary ləʊ 'kjuːʃ ᵊn ər i -ᵊn ˌr i
  ‖ loʊ 'kjuːʃ ə ner i
Lod lɒd ‖ loʊd
lode, Lode ləʊd ‖ loʊd (= load) **lodes** ləʊdz
  ‖ loʊdz
loden 'ləʊd ᵊn ‖ 'loʊd ᵊn
lodestar 'ləʊd stɑː ‖ 'loʊd stɑːr ~s z
lodestone 'ləʊd stəʊn ‖ 'loʊd stoʊn ~s z
lodge, Lodge lɒdʒ ‖ lɑːdʒ **lodged** lɒdʒd
  ‖ lɑːdʒd **lodges** 'lɒdʒ ɪz -əz ‖ 'lɑːdʒ- **lodging**
  'lɒdʒ ɪŋ ‖ 'lɑːdʒ ɪŋ
lodger 'lɒdʒ ə ‖ 'lɑːdʒ ᵊr ~s z
lodging 'lɒdʒ ɪŋ ‖ 'lɑːdʒ ɪŋ ~s z
  'lodging house
lodgment 'lɒdʒ mənt ‖ 'lɑːdʒ- ~s s
Lodi places in US 'ləʊd aɪ ‖ 'loʊd-
Lodore ləʊ 'dɔː ‖ loʊ 'dɔːr
Lodz wʊdʒ wuːtʃ ‖ loʊdz lɑːdz, wuːdʒ —Polish
  Łódź [wutɕ]
Loeb ləʊb lɜːb ‖ loʊb —Ger [løːp]
loess, löss 'ləʊ es -ɪs, -əs; lɜːs ‖ les lʌs, 'loʊ əs,
  lɜːs —Ger [lœs, løːs]
Loewe 'ləʊ i ‖ loʊ
Lofoten ləʊ 'fəʊt ᵊn '·ˌ·· ‖ 'loʊ foʊt ᵊn —Norw
  ['luː fut ən]
loft lɒft ‖ lɔːft lɑːft **lofts** lɒfts ‖ lɔːfts lɑːfts
Lofthouse 'lɒft haʊs -əs ‖ 'lɔːft- lɑːft-
Lofting 'lɒft ɪŋ ‖ 'lɔːft ɪŋ 'lɑːft-
Loftus 'lɒft əs ‖ 'lɔːft- 'lɑːft-
loft|y 'lɒft |i ‖ 'lɔːft |i 'lɑːft- ~ier i ə ‖ i ʲr
  ~iest i ɪst i əst ~ily ɪ li əl i ~iness i nəs i nɪs
log lɒg ‖ lɔːg lɑːg **logged** lɒgd ‖ lɔːgd lɑːgd
  logging 'lɒg ɪŋ ‖ 'lɔːg ɪŋ 'lɑːg-
  ˌlog 'cabin
-log lɒg ‖ lɔːg lɑːg — **catalog** 'kæt ə lɒg
  -ᵊl ɒg ‖ 'kæt̬ ᵊl ɔːg -ɑːg
Logan 'ləʊg ən ‖ 'loʊg-

loganberr|y 'ləʊg ən bər ˌ|i →'-ŋ-, →'-əm-,
  -ˌber |i ‖ 'loʊg ən ˌber |i ~ies iz
logarithm 'lɒg ə rɪð əm -rɪθ əm ‖ 'lɔːg- 'lɑːg-
  ~s z
logarithmic ˌlɒg ə 'rɪð mɪk ◂ -'rɪθ- ‖ ˌlɔːg-
  ˌlɑːg- ~al ᵊl ~ally ᵊl_i
logbook 'lɒg bʊk §-buːk ‖ 'lɔːg- 'lɑːg- ~s s
loge ləʊʒ ‖ loʊʒ **loges** 'ləʊʒ ɪz -əz ‖ 'loʊʒ-
logg... —see **log**
logger 'lɒg ə ‖ 'lɔːg ᵊr 'lɑːg- ~s z
loggerhead 'lɒg ə hed ‖ 'lɔːg ᵊr- 'lɑːg- ~s z
loggia 'lɒdʒ i ə 'ləʊdʒ- ‖ 'loʊdʒ ə 'loʊdʒ i ə ~s
  z
logi... —see **logy**
logic 'lɒdʒ ɪk ‖ 'lɑːdʒ- ~s s
Logica tdmk 'lɒdʒ ɪk ə ‖ 'lɑːdʒ-
logical 'lɒdʒ ɪk ᵊl ‖ 'lɑːdʒ- ~ly_i ~ness nəs nɪs
-logical 'lɒdʒ ɪk ᵊl ‖ 'lɑːdʒ- — **cytological**
  ˌsaɪt əʊ 'lɒdʒ ɪk ᵊl ◂ ‖ ˌsaɪt̬ ə 'lɑːdʒ-
logicality ˌlɒdʒ ɪ 'kæl ət i §ˌ·ə-, -ɪt i
  ‖ ˌlɑːdʒ ə 'kæl ət̬ i
logician ləʊ 'dʒɪʃ ᵊn lɒ- ‖ loʊ- ~s z
Logie 'ləʊg i ‖ 'loʊg i
-logist stress-imposing lədʒ ɪst §-əst
  — **physiologist** ˌfɪz i 'ɒl ədʒ ɪst §-əst ‖ -'ɑːl-
logistic ləʊ 'dʒɪst ɪk lɒ- ‖ loʊ- ~al ᵊl ~ally ᵊl_i
  ~s s
logjam 'lɒg dʒæm ‖ 'lɔːg- 'lɑːg- ~s z
loglog 'lɒg 'lɒg ‖ 'lɔːg 'lɔːg, 'lɑːg 'lɑːg
logo, Logo, LOGO 'ləʊg əʊ 'lɒg- ‖ 'loʊg oʊ ~s
  z
logo- comb. form
  with stress-neutral suffix ˌlɒg əʊ ‖ ˌlɔːg ə
  'lɑːg ə — **logographic** ˌlɒg əʊ 'græf ɪk ◂
  ‖ ˌlɔːg ə- ˌlɑːg-
  with stress-imposing suffix lɒ 'gɒ +
  ‖ loʊ 'gɑː+ — **logography** lɒ 'gɒg rəf i
  ‖ loʊ 'gɑːg-
logogram 'lɒg ə græm ‖ 'lɔːg- 'lɑːg- ~s z
logon ˌlɒg 'ɒn ‖ ˌlɔːg 'ɑːn ˌlɑːg-, -'ɔːn ~s z
logopaed|ic, logoped|ic ˌlɒg ə 'piːd| ɪk ◂
  ‖ ˌlɔːg- ˌlɑːg- ~ics ɪks ~ist/s ɪst/s əst/s
logorrhea, logorrhoea ˌlɒg ə 'riː ə ‖ ˌlɔːg-
  ˌlɑːg-
Logos, logos 'lɒg ɒs 'ləʊg- ‖ 'loʊg ɑːs -ɔːs,
  -oʊs
logotype 'lɒg əʊ taɪp ‖ 'lɔːg- 'lɑːg- ~s s
logroll|er 'lɒg ˌrəʊl |ə →-ˌrɒʊl-
  ‖ 'lɔːg ˌroʊl |ᵊr 'lɑːg- ~ers əz ‖ ᵊrz ~ing ɪŋ
Logue ləʊg ‖ loʊg
-logue lɒg ‖ lɔːg lɑːg — **monologue**
  'mɒn ə lɒg ‖ 'mɑːn ə lɔːg -lɑːg
logwood 'lɒg wʊd ‖ 'lɔːg- 'lɑːg-
log|y 'ləʊg |i ‖ 'loʊg |i ~ier i ə ‖ i ʲr ~iest
  i ɪst i əst ~ily ɪ li əl i ~iness i nəs i nɪs
-logy stress-imposing lədʒ i — **analogy**
  ə 'næl ədʒ i
Lohengrin 'ləʊ ən grɪn -ɪn-, →-əŋ- ‖ 'loʊ-
  —Ger ['loː ən gʁiːn]
loin lɔɪn **loins** lɔɪnz
loin|cloth 'lɔɪn |klɒθ →'lɔɪŋ-, -klɔːθ ‖ -|klɔːθ
  -klɑːθ ~cloths klɒθs klɒðz, klɔːðz, klɔːθs
  ‖ klɔːðz klɔːθs, klɑːðz, klɑːθs

L

Loire lwɑː ‖ lwɑːr —*Fr* [lwaːʁ]
Lois 'ləʊ ɪs §-əs ‖ 'loʊ-
loiter 'lɔɪt ə ‖ 'lɔɪt̬ ᵊr **~ed** d **loitering**
'lɔɪt̬ ər ɪŋ ‖ 'lɔɪt̬ ər ɪŋ **~s** z
loiterer 'lɔɪt ər ə ‖ 'lɔɪt̬ ər ᵊr **~s** z
Loki 'ləʊk i ‖ 'loʊk i
Lola 'ləʊl ə ‖ 'loʊl ə
Lolita lɒ 'liːt ə ləʊ- ‖ loʊ 'liːt̬ ə **~s** z
loll lɒl ‖ lɑːl **lolled** lɒld ‖ lɑːld **lolling** 'lɒl ɪŋ
‖ 'lɑːl ɪŋ **lolls** lɒlz ‖ lɑːlz
Lollard 'lɒl əd -ɑːd ‖ 'lɑːl ᵊrd **~s** z
lollie... —*see* **lolly**
lollipop 'lɒl i pɒp ‖ 'lɑːl i pɑːp **~s** s
'lollipop man, 'lollipop ,woman
lollop 'lɒl əp ‖ 'lɑːl- **~ed** t **~ing** ɪŋ **~s** s
lollo rosso ,lɒl əʊ 'rɒs əʊ ‖ ,lɑːl oʊ 'rɑːs oʊ
,loʊl-, -'roʊs- —*It* [,lol lo 'ros so]
loll|y 'lɒl |i ‖ 'lɑːl |i **~ies** iz
lollygag 'lɒl i gæg ‖ 'lɑːl- **~ged** d **~ging** ɪŋ **~s**
z
lollypop 'lɒl i pɒp ‖ 'lɑːl i pɑːp **~s** s
Loma Prieta ,ləʊm ə pri 'et ə
‖ ,loʊm ə pri 'eɪt̬ ə -'et̬ ə
Lomas 'ləʊm əs -æs ‖ 'loʊm æs
Lomax 'ləʊm æks -əks ‖ 'loʊm-
Lombard 'lɒm bəd 'lʌm-, -bɑːd ‖ 'lɑːm bᵊrd
-bɑːrd **~s** z
'Lombard Street
Lombardi lɒm 'bɑːd i ‖ lɑːm 'bɑːrd i
Lombardo lɒm 'bɑːd əʊ ‖ lɑːm 'bɑːrd oʊ —*It*
[lom 'bar do]
Lombardy 'lɒm bəd i 'lʌm- ‖ 'lɑːm bᵊrd i
-bɑːrd i
,Lombardy 'poplar
Lombok 'lɒm bɒk ‖ 'lɑːm bɑːk ·'·
Lombrosian lɒm 'brəʊz i ᵊn ‖ lɑːm 'broʊz-
-'broʊz ᵊn **~s** z
Lombroso lɒm 'brəʊz əʊ ‖ lɑːm 'broʊz oʊ
—*It* [lom 'bro: so]
Lome, Lomé 'ləʊ meɪ ‖ loʊ 'meɪ —*Fr* [lɔ me]
Lomond 'ləʊm ənd ‖ 'loʊm-
Lomu 'ləʊm uː ‖ 'loʊm-
London 'lʌnd ən *(!)*
,London 'Airport; ,London 'Bridge;
,London 'pride
Londonderry 'lʌnd ən ,der i -ənd ,ᵊr i;
,lʌnd ən 'der i◀ —*Lord L~ iss* 'lʌnd ənd ,ər i
Londoner 'lʌnd ən ə ‖ -ᵊr **~s** z
lone ləʊn ‖ loʊn
,Lone 'Ranger; ,lone 'wolf
lone|ly 'ləʊn |li ‖ 'loʊn- **~lier** li ə ‖ li ᵊr **~liest**
li ɪst li ᵊst **~liness** li nəs li nɪs
,lonely 'hearts, ·'· ·
loner 'ləʊn ə ‖ 'loʊn ᵊr **~s** z
lonesome 'ləʊn səm ‖ 'loʊn- **~ly** li **~ness** nəs
nɪs
long, Long lɒŋ ‖ lɔːŋ lɑːŋ **longed** lɒŋd ‖ lɔːŋd
lɑːŋd **longer** 'lɒŋ gə ‖ 'lɔːŋ gᵊr 'lɑːŋ- **longest**
'lɒŋ gɪst -gəst ‖ 'lɔːŋ gəst 'lɑːŋ- **longing**
'lɒŋ ɪŋ ‖ 'lɔːŋ ɪŋ 'lɑːŋ- **longs** lɒŋz ‖ lɔːŋz
lɑːŋz
'Long Beach; ,long di'vision; ,long 'haul;
₍ᵢ₎Long 'Island, Long ,Island 'Sound,

·' , ·' ·'; 'long johns; 'long jump, 'long
,jumper; 'long shot; ,long 'suit; ,long
'ton; ,long 'vac, ,long va'cation; ,long
'wave, '· ·
Longannet lɒŋ 'æn ɪt -ət ‖ lɔːŋ- lɑːŋ-
long-awaited ,lɒŋ ə 'weɪt ɪd ◀ -əd
‖ ,lɔːŋ ə 'weɪt̬ əd ◀ ,lɑːŋ-
longboat 'lɒŋ bəʊt ‖ 'lɔːŋ boʊt 'lɑːŋ- **~s** s
longbow 'lɒŋ bəʊ ‖ 'lɔːŋ boʊ 'lɑːŋ- **~s** z
Longbridge 'lɒŋ brɪdʒ ‖ 'lɔːŋ- 'lɑːŋ-
long-distance ,lɒŋ 'dɪst ᵊnᵗs ◀ ‖ ,lɔːŋ- ,lɑːŋ-
long-drawn-out ,lɒŋ drɔːn 'aʊt ◀ ‖ ,lɔːŋ-
,lɑːŋ drɑːn-
longed-for 'lɒŋd fɔː ‖ 'lɔːŋd fɔːr 'lɑːŋd-
longer *comparative adj* 'lɒŋ gə ‖ 'lɔːŋ gᵊr 'lɑːŋ-
—*But the agent noun* longer *'one that longs',*
if ever used, is pronounced without g, *as*
-ə ‖ -ᵊr
longeron 'lɒndʒ ər ən ‖ 'lɑːndʒ ə rɑːn **~s** z
longest 'lɒŋ gɪst -gəst ‖ 'lɔːŋ- 'lɑːŋ-
longevity lɒn 'dʒev ət i lɒŋ-, -ɪt-
‖ lɑːn 'dʒev ət̬ i lɔːn-
long-expected ,lɒŋ ɪk 'spekt ɪd ◀ -ek-, -ək-,
-əd ‖ ,lɔːŋ- ,lɑːŋ-
Longfellow 'lɒŋ ,fel əʊ ‖ 'lɔːŋ ,fel oʊ 'lɑːŋ-
Longford 'lɒŋ fəd ‖ 'lɔːŋ fᵊrd 'lɑːŋ-
longhair 'lɒŋ heə ‖ 'lɔːŋ her 'lɑːŋ- **~s** z
long-haired ,lɒŋ 'heəd ◀ ‖ ,lɔːŋ 'heᵊrd ◀ ,lɑːŋ-
longhand 'lɒŋ hænd ‖ 'lɔːŋ- 'lɑːŋ-
long-haul ,lɒŋ 'hɔːl ◀ ·'· ‖ ,lɔːŋ- ,lɑːŋ 'hɑːl ◀
long-headed ,lɒŋ 'hed ɪd ◀ -əd ‖ ,lɔːŋ- ,lɑːŋ-
longhop 'lɒŋ hɒp ‖ 'lɔːŋ hɑːp 'lɑːŋ- **~s** s
longhorn 'lɒŋ hɔːn ‖ 'lɔːŋ hɔːrn 'lɑːŋ- **~s** z
long|house 'lɒŋ| haʊs ‖ 'lɔːŋ- 'lɑːŋ- **~houses**
haʊz ɪz -əz
Longhurst 'lɒŋ hɜːst ‖ 'lɔːŋ hɜːst 'lɑːŋ-
Longines *tdmk* 'lɒndʒ iːn ‖ lɑːn 'dʒiːn
longing 'lɒŋ ɪŋ ‖ 'lɔːŋ ɪŋ 'lɑːŋ- **~ly** li **~s** z
Longinus lɒn 'dʒaɪn əs lɒŋ 'giːn- ‖ lɑːn-
longish 'lɒŋ ɪʃ 'lɒŋg- ‖ 'lɔːŋ- 'lɑːŋ-

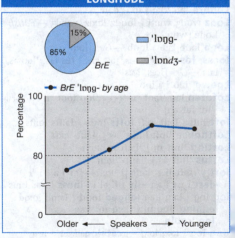

LONGITUDE

BrE
85%
15%
☐ 'lɒŋg-
☐ 'lɒndʒ-

●— BrE 'lɒŋg- by age

Percentage

100

80

0

Older ◀— Speakers —▶ Younger

longitude 'lɒŋ gɪ tjuːd -gə-, -dɪ-, -tɪ-, →-tʃuːd;
'lɒndʒ ɪ-, -ə- ‖ 'lɑːndʒ ə tuːd -tjuːd

— *Preference poll, BrE:* 'lɒŋ- *85%,* 'lɒndʒ-
*15%. Several respondents spontaneously
mentioned* 'lɒŋ dɪ-, *which was not given as an
option in the questionnaire.* **~s** z
longitudinal ˌlɒŋ gɪ 'tjuːd ɪn ᵊl ◄ ˌ·gə-,
ˌlɒndʒ ɪ-, ˌ·ə-, →-'tʃuːd-, -ᵊn || ˌlɑːŋ-
|| ˌlɑːndʒ ə 'tuːd ᵊn ◄ -'tjuːd- **~ly** i
Longland 'lɒŋ lənd || 'lɔːŋ- 'lɑːŋ-
long-lasting ˌlɒŋ 'lɑːst ɪŋ ◄ §-'læst-
|| ˌlɔːŋ 'læst ɪŋ ◄ ˌlɑːŋ-
Longleat 'lɒŋ liːt || 'lɔːŋ- 'lɑːŋ-
long-life ˌlɒŋ 'laɪf ◄ || ˌlɔːŋ- ˌlɑːŋ-
long-lived ˌlɒŋ 'lɪvd ◄ || ˌlɔːŋ 'laɪvd ◄ ˌlɑːŋ-,
-'lɪvd ◄ *(*)*
long-lost ˌlɒŋ 'lɒst ◄ -'lɔːst ◄ || ˌlɔːŋ 'lɔːst ◄
ˌlɑːŋ-, -'lɑːst ◄
Longman 'lɒŋ mən || 'lɔːŋ- 'lɑːŋ-
Longobardi ˌlɒŋ gəʊ 'bɑːd i -iː
|| ˌlɔːŋ gə 'bɑːrd i ˌlɑːŋ-, -aɪ
long-playing ˌlɒŋ 'pleɪ ɪŋ ◄ || ˌlɔːŋ- ˌlɑːŋ-
ˌlong-ˌplaying 'record
long-range ˌlɒŋ 'reɪndʒ ◄ || ˌlɔːŋ- ˌlɑːŋ-
ˌlong-range 'missiles
Longridge 'lɒŋ grɪdʒ -rɪdʒ || 'lɔːŋ- 'lɑːŋ-
long-running ˌlɒŋ 'rʌn ɪŋ ◄ || ˌlɔːŋ- ˌlɑːŋ-
long-serving ˌlɒŋ 'sɜːv ɪŋ ◄ || ˌlɔːŋ 'sɜːv- ˌlɑːŋ-
longship 'lɒŋ ʃɪp || 'lɔːŋ- 'lɑːŋ- **~s** s
longshore|man 'lɒŋ ʃɔː |mən || 'lɔːŋ ʃɔːr-
'lɑːŋ-, -ʃoʊr- **~men** mən men
longsighted ˌlɒŋ 'saɪt ɪd ◄ -əd
|| ˌlɔːŋ 'saɪt əd ◄ ˌlɑːŋ- **~ness** nəs nɪs
longstanding ˌlɒŋ 'stænd ɪŋ ◄ || ˌlɔːŋ- ˌlɑːŋ-
long-stay ˌlɒŋ 'steɪ ◄ || ˌlɔːŋ- ˌlɑːŋ-
longstop 'lɒŋ stɒp || 'lɔːŋ stɑːp 'lɑːŋ- **~s** s
longsuffering ˌlɒŋ 'sʌf ər ɪŋ ◄ || ˌlɔːŋ- ˌlɑːŋ-
~ly li
long-term ˌlɒŋ 'tɜːm ◄ || ˌlɔːŋ 'tɜːm ◄ ˌlɑːŋ-
long-time, longtime 'lɒŋ taɪm || 'lɔːŋ- 'lɑːŋ-
Longton 'lɒŋ tən || 'lɔːŋ- 'lɑːŋ-
Longtown 'lɒŋ taʊn || 'lɔːŋ- 'lɑːŋ-
longueur ₍ₒ₎lɒŋ 'gɜː || loun 'gɜː: —*Fr* [lɔ̃ gœːʁ]
~s z
Longus 'lɒŋ gəs || 'lɔːŋ- 'lɑːŋ-
longways 'lɒŋ weɪz || 'lɔːŋ- 'lɑːŋ-
longwearing ˌlɒŋ 'weər ɪŋ ◄ || ˌlɔːŋ 'wer ɪŋ ◄
ˌlɑːŋ-
longwinded ˌlɒŋ 'wɪnd ɪd ◄ -əd || ˌlɔːŋ- ˌlɑːŋ-
~ly li **~ness** nəs nɪs
longwise 'lɒŋ waɪz || 'lɔːŋ- 'lɑːŋ-
Longyearbyen 'lɒŋ jɪə ˌbjuː ən '-jɜː, -, buː-
|| 'lɔːŋ jɜːr- 'lɑːŋ- —*Norw* ['lɔŋ jiːr byː ən]
lonicera lɒ 'nɪs ər ə lə- || loʊ-
Lonnie 'lɒn i || 'lɑːn i
Lonrho *tdmk* 'lɒn rəʊ 'lʌn- || 'lɑːn roʊ
Lonsdale 'lɒnz deɪᵊl || 'lɑːnz-
loo luː **loos** luːz
Looe luː
loofa, loofah 'luːf ə **~s** z
loogie 'luːg i
look lʊk §luːk **looked** lʊkt §luːkt **looking**
'lʊk ɪŋ §'luːk- **looks** lʊks §luːks
'looking glass
look-alike 'lʊk ə ˌlaɪk §'luːk- **~s** s

looker 'lʊk ə §'luːk- || -ᵊr **~s** z
looker-on ˌlʊk ər 'ɒn §ˌluːk- || -ᵊr 'ɑːn -'ɔːn
lookers-on ˌlʊk əz 'ɒn §ˌluːk- || -ᵊrz 'ɑːn -'ɔːn
look-in 'lʊk ɪn §'luːk-
lookit 'lʊk ɪt §-ət
lookout 'lʊk aʊt §'luːk- **~s** s
look-over 'lʊk ˌəʊv ə §'luːk- || -ˌoʊv ᵊr
look-see ˌlʊk 'siː §ˌluːk-, '· ·
lookup 'lʊk ʌp §'luːk- **~s** s
loom luːm **loomed** luːmd **looming** 'luːm ɪŋ
looms luːmz
loon luːn **loons** luːnz
loon|ey, loon|ie, loon|ly 'luːn |i ~**ier** i ə
|| i ᵊr ~**ies** iz ~**eys** iz ~**iest** i ɪst i əst
'loony bin
looong, loooong *emphatic version of* long lɒŋ
|| lɔːŋ lɑːŋ *with the vowel considerably
extended*
loop luːp **looped** luːpt **looper/s** 'luːp ə/z
|| -ᵊr/z **looping** 'luːp ɪŋ **loops** luːps
loophole 'luːp həʊl →-hɒʊl || -hoʊl **~s** z
loop-the-loop ˌluːp ðə 'luːp
loopy 'luːp i
loose luːs **loosed** luːst **looser** 'luːs ə || -ᵊr
looses 'luːs ɪz -əz **loosest** 'luːs ɪst -əst
loosing 'luːs ɪŋ
ˌloose 'change; ˌloose 'end
loosebox 'luːs bɒks || -bɑːks **~es** ɪz əz
loose-fitting ˌluːs 'fɪt ɪŋ ◄ || -'fɪt ɪŋ ◄
loose-jointed ˌluːs 'dʒɔɪnt ɪd ◄ -də-
|| -'dʒɔɪnt əd ◄
loose-knit ˌluːs 'nɪt ◄
loose-leaf ˌluːs 'liːf ◄
loose-limbed ˌluːs 'lɪmd ◄
loosely 'luːs li
loosen 'luːs ᵊn **~ed** d **~ing** ɪŋ **~s** z
looseness 'luːs nəs -nɪs
loosestrife 'luːs straɪf -traɪf **~s** s
loosey-goosey ˌluːs i 'guːs i ◄
loot luːt **looted** 'luːt ɪd -əd || 'luːt̬ əd **looting**
'luːt ɪŋ || 'luːt̬ ɪŋ **loots** luːts
looter 'luːt ə || 'luːt̬ ᵊr **~s** z
lop lɒp || lɑːp **lopped** lɒpt || lɑːpt **lopping**
'lɒp ɪŋ || 'lɑːp ɪŋ **lops** lɒps || lɑːps
lope ləʊp || loʊp **loped** ləʊpt || loʊpt **lopes**
ləʊps || loʊps **loping** 'ləʊp ɪŋ || 'loʊp ɪŋ
lop-eared ˌlɒp 'ɪəd ◄ || ˌlɑːp 'ɪᵊrd ◄
loperamide ləʊ 'per ə maɪd || loʊ-
Lopez, López 'ləʊp ez || 'loʊp- —*Sp* ['lo peθ,
-pes]
Lop Nur ˌlɒp 'nʊə || ˌlɔːp 'nʊᵊr ˌlɑːp-, ˌloʊp-
—*Chi* Luóbùbó [²lwɔ ⁴pu ²pɔ]
lop-sided ˌlɒp 'saɪd ɪd ◄ -əd || ˌlɑːp- **~ly** li
~ness nəs nɪs
loquacious ləʊ 'kweɪʃ əs lɒ- || loʊ- **~ly** li
~ness nəs nɪs
loquacity ləʊ 'kwæs ət i lɒ-, -ɪt-
|| loʊ 'kwæs ət̬ i
loquat 'ləʊ kwɒt -kwæt || 'loʊ kwɑːt **~s** s
lor lɔː || lɔːr
Lora 'lɔːr ə
Loraine lə 'reɪn lɒ-
Loram 'lɔːr əm

loran 'lɔːr ən ~s z
Lorca 'lɔːk ə ‖ 'lɔːrk ə —*Sp* ['lor ka]
Lorcan 'lɔːk ən ‖ 'lɔːrk-
lord, Lord lɔːd ‖ lɔːrd —*but as a vocative in a court of law, my lord is also* mɪ 'lʌd, mə-
  lorded 'lɔːd ɪd -əd ‖ 'lɔːrd əd **lording** 'lɔːd ɪŋ ‖ 'lɔːrd ɪŋ **lords, Lords, Lord's** lɔːdz ‖ lɔːrdz
  ˌLord 'Chancellor; ˌLord Chief 'Justice; ₍ˌ₎Lord 'Mayor; ˌLord's 'Prayer
lordling 'lɔːd lɪŋ ‖ 'lɔːrd- ~s z
lord|ly 'lɔːd |li ‖ 'lɔːrd- ~**lier** li ə ‖ li ᵊr ~**liest** li ɪst li əst ~**liness** li nəs li nɪs
lordosis lɔː 'dəʊs ɪs §-əs ‖ lɔːr 'doʊs əs
lordship, L~ 'lɔːd ʃɪp ‖ 'lɔːrd- ~s s
lordy 'lɔːd i ‖ 'lɔːrd i
lore lɔː ‖ lɔːr loʊr
L'Oréal *tdmk* ˌlɒr i 'æl '·· ‖ ˌrɔːl i 'æl -'ɑːl
Lorelei, Loreley 'lɒr ə laɪ 'lɔːr- ‖ 'lɔːr- —*Ger* [lo: ʁə 'laɪ]
Loren 'lɔːr en -ən; lɔː 'ren, lə- ‖ 'lɔːr ən —*It* ['lɔː ren]
Lorentz 'lɒr ənts 'lɔːr- ‖ 'lɔːr- 'loʊr- —*Dutch* ['loː rənts]
Lorenz 'lɒr ənz ‖ 'lɔːr- 'loʊr- —*but as a German name,* 'lɔːr ənts, 'lɒr- —*Ger* ['loː ʁents]
Lorenzo lə 'renz əʊ lɒ- ‖ -oʊ lɔː-
Loretta lə 'ret ə lɒ-, lɔː- ‖ lə 'reţ ə lɔː-
Loretto lə 'ret əʊ lɔː- ‖ lə 'reţ oʊ lɔː-
lorgnette ₍ˌ₎lɔːn 'jet ‖ lɔːrn- —*Fr* [lɔʁ njɛt] ~s s
Lorie 'lɒr i ‖ 'lɔːr i
lorie... —*see* **lory**
lorikeet 'lɒr ɪ kiːt -ə-, ˌ·'· ‖ 'lɔːr- 'lɑːr- ~s s
lorimer, L~ 'lɒr ɪm ə -əm- ‖ 'lɔːr əm ᵊr ~s z
loris, Loris 'lɔːr ɪs §-əs ‖ 'loʊr- ~**es** ɪz əz
lorn lɔːn ‖ lɔːrn
Lorna 'lɔːn ə ‖ 'lɔːrn ə
Lorne lɔːn ‖ lɔːrn
Lorraine lə 'reɪn lɒ-, lɔː- —*Fr* [lɔ ʁɛn]
lorr|y 'lɒr |i §'lʌr- ‖ 'lɔːr |i 'lɑːr- ~**ies** iz
  'lorry park
lor|y 'lɔːr |i ‖ 'loʊr- ~**ies** iz
Los Alamos lɒs 'æl ə mɒs ‖ lɔːs 'æl ə moʊs lɑːs-
Los Angeles lɒs 'ændʒ ə liːz -ɪ-, -lɪs, -ləs ‖ lɔːs 'ændʒ əl əs lɑːs-, -'æŋ gəl-, -ə liːz
lose luːz **loses** 'luːz ɪz -əz **losing** 'luːz ɪŋ **lost** lɒst lɔːst ‖ lɔːst lɑːst
Loseley 'ləʊz li ‖ 'loʊz-
loser 'luːz ə ‖ -ᵊr ~s z
Losey 'ləʊz i ‖ 'loʊz i
Los Gatos lɒs 'gæt əʊs ‖ loʊs 'gɑːţ oʊs lɔːs-, lɑːs-
loss lɒs lɔːs ‖ lɔːs lɑːs **losses** 'lɒs ɪz 'lɔːs-, -əz ‖ 'lɔːs əz 'lɑːs-
  'loss adˌjuster; 'loss ˌleader
Lossiemouth ˌlɒs i 'maʊθ ‖ ˌlɔːs- ˌlɑːs-
loss-making 'lɒs ˌmeɪk ɪŋ 'lɔːs- ‖ 'lɔːs- 'lɑːs-
lossy 'lɒs i ‖ 'lɔːs i 'lɑːs-
lost lɒst lɔːst ‖ lɔːst lɑːst
  ˌlost 'cause; ˌlost 'property

lost-and-found ˌlɒst ən 'faʊnd ˌlɔːst- ‖ ˌlɔːst- 'lɑːst-
Lostwithiel lɒst 'wɪθ i əl ‖ lɔːst- lɑːst-
lot, Lot lɒt ‖ lɑːt **lots** lɒts ‖ lɑːts
loth ləʊθ ‖ loʊθ
Lothario ləʊ 'θɑːr i əʊ lɒ-, -'θeər- ‖ loʊ 'θer i oʊ -'θær-
Lothbury 'ləʊθ bər i 'lɒθ- ‖ 'loʊθ ˌber i
Lothian 'ləʊð i ən ‖ 'loʊð- ~s z
lotic 'ləʊt ɪk ‖ 'loʊţ ɪk
lotion 'ləʊʃ ᵊn ‖ 'loʊʃ- ~s z
lotsa *'lots of'* 'lɒts ə ‖ 'lɑːts ə
lotta *'lot of'* 'lɒt ə ‖ 'lɑːţ ə
lotter|y 'lɒt ər |i ‖ 'lɑːţ ər |i →'lɑːtr |i ~**ies** iz
Lottie, Lotty 'lɒt i ‖ 'lɑːţ i
lotto, Lotto 'lɒt əʊ ‖ 'lɑːţ oʊ
lotus 'ləʊt əs ‖ 'loʊţ əs ~**es** ɪz əz
lotus-eater 'ləʊt əs ˌiːt ə ‖ 'loʊţ əs ˌiːţ ᵊr ~s z
Lou luː
louche luːʃ
loud laʊd **louder** 'laʊd ə ‖ -ᵊr **loudest** 'laʊd ɪst -əst
Loudan, Loudon, Loudoun 'laʊd ᵊn
louden 'laʊd ᵊn ~**ed** d ~**ing** ɪŋ ~s z
loudhailer ˌlaʊd 'heɪl ə ‖ -ᵊr ~s z
loudly 'laʊd li
loud|mouth 'laʊd |maʊθ ~**mouths** maʊðz maʊθs
loudmouthed ˌlaʊd 'maʊðd ◂ -'maʊθt, '··
loudness 'laʊd nəs -nɪs ~**es** ɪz əz
loudspeaker ˌlaʊd 'spiːk ə '·ˌ·· ‖ -ᵊr ~s z
Loudwater 'laʊd ˌwɔːt ə ‖ -ˌwɔːt ᵊr -ˌwɑːţ-
Louella lu 'el ə
lough, Lough lɒx lɒk ‖ lɑːk lɑːx —*but as a family name also* lʌf, ləʊ ‖ loʊ **loughs** lɒxs lɒks ‖ lɑːks lɑːxs
Loughboro', Loughborough 'lʌf bər ə §-, ˌbʌr- ‖ -ˌbɝ oʊ
Loughlin 'lɒx lɪn 'lɒk-, -lən ‖ 'lɑːf- 'lɑːk-
Loughor 'lʌx ə ‖ 'lʌk ᵊr
Loughton 'laʊt ᵊn
Louie 'luː i
Louis *(i)* 'luː i, *(ii)* ɪs §-əs —*Fr* [lwi, lu i]
  ˌLouis Qua'torze kə 'tɔːz kæ- ‖ -'tɔːrz —*Fr* [ka tɔʁz]; ˌLouis 'Quinze kænz —*Fr* [kɛ̃z]; ˌLouis 'Seize sez seɪz —*Fr* [sɛːz]; ˌLouis 'Treize trez treɪz —*Fr* [tʁɛːz]
Louisa lu 'iːz ə
Louisburg 'luː ɪs bɜːg §-əs- ‖ -bɝːg
louis d'or ˌluː i 'dɔː ‖ -'dɔːr ~s z
Louise lu 'iːz
Louisiana lu ˌiːz i 'æn ə ˌluː ɪz-, -'ɑːn-
Louisville 'luː i vɪl §-ə-
lounge laʊndʒ **lounged** laʊndʒd **lounges** 'laʊndʒ ɪz -əz **lounging** 'laʊndʒ ɪŋ
  'lounge bar, ˌ· '·; 'lounge suit
lounger 'laʊndʒ ə ‖ -ᵊr ~s z
Lounsbury 'laʊnz bər i ‖ -ˌber i
loupe luːp (= *loop*) **loupes** luːps
lour 'laʊ ə ‖ 'laʊ ᵊr ~**ed** d **louring** 'laʊ ər ɪŋ ‖ 'laʊ ᵊr ɪŋ ~s z
Lourdes lʊəd lʊədz, lɔːdz ‖ lʊᵊrd —*Fr* [luʁd]

louse *v* laʊz laʊs **loused** laʊzd laʊst **louses**
'laʊz ɪz 'laʊs-, -əz **lousing** 'laʊz ɪŋ 'laʊs-
louse *n* laʊs **lice** laɪs
lous|y 'laʊz |i ~ier i‿ə ‖ i‿ᵊr ~iest i‿ɪst i‿əst
~ily ɪ li əl i ~iness i nəs i nɪs
lout laʊt **louts** laʊts
Louth (i) laʊθ, (ii) laʊð —*The place in*
England is (i), *the place in Ireland* (ii)
loutish 'laʊt ɪʃ ‖ 'laʊt̬ ɪʃ ~ly li ~ness nəs nɪs
Louvain lu 'væn -'væ̃; 'lu:v æn, -æ̃ —*Fr*
[lu væ̃]
louv|er, louv|re 'lu:v |ə ‖ -|ᵊr ~ered, ~red əd
‖ ᵊrd ~ers, ~res əz ‖ ᵊrz
Louvre *museum* 'lu:v rə lu:v ‖ 'lu:v ᵊr —*Fr*
[lu:vʁ]
lovab|le 'lʌv əb |ᵊl ~leness ᵊl nəs -nɪs ~ly li
lovage 'lʌv ɪdʒ
lovat, Lovat 'lʌv ət
love, Love lʌv **loved** lʌvd **loves** lʌvz **loving**
'lʌv ɪŋ
'love af,fair; 'love match; 'love nest;
'love ,story
loveab|le 'lʌv əb |ᵊl ~leness ᵊl nəs -nɪs ~ly li
lovebird 'lʌv bɜːd ‖ -bɜːd ~s z
lovebite 'lʌv baɪt ~s s
love|child 'lʌv |tʃaɪᵊld ~children ,tʃɪldr ən
Loveday 'lʌv deɪ
loved-up ,lʌvd 'ʌp ◂
lovefest 'lʌv fest ~s s
love-hate ,lʌv 'heɪt
,love-'hate re,lationship
love-in-a-mist ,lʌv ɪn ə 'mɪst §,·ən-
Lovejoy 'lʌv dʒɔɪ
Lovelace 'lʌv leɪs
loveless 'lʌv ləs -lɪs ~ly li ~ness nəs nɪs
loveli... —*see* lovely
love-lies-bleeding ,lʌv laɪz 'bli:d ɪŋ
Lovell 'lʌv ᵊl
lovelock, L~ 'lʌv lɒk ‖ -lɑːk ~s s
lovelorn 'lʌv lɔːn ‖ -lɔːrn
love|ly 'lʌv |li ~lier li‿ə ‖ li‿ᵊr ~lies liz ~liest
li‿ɪst li‿əst ~liness li nəs -nɪs
lovemaking 'lʌv ,meɪk ɪŋ
lover 'lʌv ə ‖ -ᵊr ~ly li ~s z
Loveridge 'lʌv rɪdʒ
lovesick 'lʌv sɪk ~ness nəs nɪs
lovey 'lʌv i ~s z
lovey-dovey ,lʌv i 'dʌv i ◂ '·,·· ·
Lovibond 'lʌv i bɒnd ‖ -bɑːnd
loving 'lʌv ɪŋ ~ly li
'loving cup; ,loving 'kindness
low, Low ləʊ ‖ loʊ (*= lo*) **lowed** ləʊd ‖ loʊd
lower 'ləʊ ə ‖ 'loʊ ᵊr **lowest** 'ləʊ ɪst -əst
‖ 'loʊ əst **lowing** 'ləʊ ɪŋ ‖ 'loʊ ɪŋ **lows** ləʊz
‖ loʊz
,Low 'Church; ,Low 'German; 'low life;
,low 'profile; 'low ,season; ,low 'tide;
,low 'water, ,low 'water mark
lowborn ,ləʊ 'bɔːn ◂ ‖ ,loʊ bɔːrn
lowboy 'ləʊ bɔɪ ‖ 'loʊ-
lowbred ,ləʊ 'bred ◂ ‖ ,loʊ- '· ·
lowbrow 'ləʊ braʊ ‖ 'loʊ- ~s z
low-budget ,ləʊ 'bʌdʒ ɪt ◂ §-ət ‖ ,loʊ-

low-cal ,ləʊ 'kæl ◂ ‖ ,loʊ-
low-class ,ləʊ 'klɑːs ◂ §-'klæs ‖ ,loʊ 'klæs ◂
low-cost ,ləʊ 'kɒst ◂ -'kɔːst ‖ ,loʊ 'kɔːst ◂
-'kɑːst ◂
low-cut ,ləʊ 'kʌt ◂ ‖ ,loʊ-
low-down *adj* ,ləʊ 'daʊn ◂ ‖ ,loʊ-
lowdown *n* 'ləʊ daʊn ‖ 'loʊ-
Lowe ləʊ ‖ loʊ
Lowell 'ləʊ əl ‖ 'loʊ əl
Lowenbrau, Löwenbräu *tdmk* 'ləʊ ən braʊ
‖ 'loʊ- —*Ger* ['lø: vᵊn bʁɔy]
low-end ,ləʊ 'end ◂ ‖ ,loʊ-
lower *v* '*threaten*' 'laʊ ə ‖ 'laʊ‿ᵊr ~ed d
lowering 'laʊ ər ɪŋ ‖ 'laʊ‿ᵊr ɪŋ ~s z
lower *adj, comp of* low 'ləʊ ə ‖ 'loʊ ᵊr
,lower 'case◂; ,lower 'class◂; ,Lower East
'Side; ,Lower 'House
lower *v* '*bring down*' 'ləʊ ə ‖ 'loʊ ᵊr ~ed d
lowering 'ləʊ ər ɪŋ ‖ 'loʊ ᵊr ɪŋ ~s z
lower-end ,ləʊ ᵊr 'end ◂ ‖ ,loʊ-
lowermost 'ləʊ ə məʊst ‖ 'loʊ ᵊr moʊst
Lowestoft 'ləʊst ɒft 'ləʊ ɪst ɒft, -əst-; -əft, -əf
‖ 'loʊst ɔːft -ɑːft, -əf
low-fat ,ləʊ 'fæt ◂ ‖ ,loʊ-
low-flying ,ləʊ 'flaɪ ɪŋ ◂ ‖ ,loʊ-
low-grade ,ləʊ 'greɪd ◂ ‖ ,loʊ-
low-income ,ləʊ 'ɪn kʌm ◂ →'·ŋ-, -kəm
‖ ,loʊ-
low-key ,ləʊ 'ki: ◂ ‖ ,loʊ-
lowland, L~ 'ləʊ lənd ‖ 'loʊ- ~s z
lowlander 'ləʊ lənd ə ‖ 'loʊ lənd ᵊr ~s z
low-level ,ləʊ 'lev ᵊl ◂ ‖ ,loʊ-
low-life 'ləʊ laɪf ‖ 'loʊ- ~s s
lowlight 'ləʊ laɪt ‖ 'loʊ- ~s s
low-loader ,ləʊ 'ləʊd ə ‖ ,loʊ 'loʊd ᵊr ~s z
low|ly 'ləʊ |li ‖ 'loʊ |li ~lier li‿ə ‖ li‿ᵊr ~liest
li‿ɪst li‿əst ~liness li nəs li nɪs
low-lying ,ləʊ 'laɪ ɪŋ ◂ ‖ ,loʊ-
Lowman 'ləʊ mən ‖ 'loʊ-
low-minded ,ləʊ 'maɪnd ɪd ◂ -əd ‖ ,loʊ- ~ly li
~ness nəs nɪs
Lowndes laʊndz
low-necked ,ləʊ 'nekt ◂ ‖ ,loʊ-
lowness 'ləʊ nəs -nɪs ‖ 'loʊ-
low-paid ,ləʊ 'peɪd ◂ ‖ ,loʊ-
low-pass ,ləʊ 'pɑːs ◂ §-'pæs ‖ ,loʊ 'pæs ◂
low-paying ,ləʊ 'peɪ ɪŋ ◂ ‖ ,loʊ-
low-pitched ,ləʊ 'pɪtʃt ◂ ‖ ,loʊ-
low-powered ,ləʊ 'paʊ əd ◂ ‖ ,loʊ 'paʊ‿ᵊrd ◂
low-price ,ləʊ 'praɪs ◂ ‖ ,loʊ-
low-profile ,ləʊ 'prəʊf aɪᵊl ◂ ‖ ,loʊ 'proʊf-
low-ranking ,ləʊ 'ræŋk ɪŋ ◂ ‖ ,loʊ-
low-rent ,ləʊ 'rent ◂ ‖ ,loʊ-
lowrider 'ləʊ ,raɪd ə ‖ 'loʊ ,raɪd ᵊr ~s z
Lowrie, Lowry 'laʊᵊr i
low-rise '.ləʊ 'raɪz ◂ ‖ ,loʊ-
low-risk ,ləʊ 'rɪsk ◂ ‖ ,loʊ-
low-slung ,ləʊ 'slʌŋ◂ ‖ ,loʊ-
low-spirited ,ləʊ 'spɪr ɪt ɪd ◂ -ət-, -əd
‖ ,loʊ 'spɪr ət̬ əd ◂
low-tech ,ləʊ 'tek ◂ ‖ ,loʊ-
Lowther 'laʊð ə ‖ -ᵊr —*but as a family name*
sometimes 'ləʊð- ‖ 'loʊð-

L

Lowton 'ləʊt ᵊn ‖ 'loʊt ᵊn
lox lɒks ‖ lɑːks
Loxene *tdmk* 'lɒks iːn ‖ 'lɑːks-
Loxley 'lɒks li ‖ 'lɑːks-
loxodromic ˌlɒks ə 'drɒm ɪk ◂ ‖ ˌlɑːks ə 'drɑːm ɪk ◂ **~ally** ᵊl‿i
Loy lɔɪ
loyal 'lɔɪ‿əl
loyalism 'lɔɪ ə ˌlɪz əm
loyalist, L~ 'lɔɪ əl ɪst §-əst
loyally 'lɔɪ əl i
loyal|ty 'lɔɪ‿əl |ti **~ties** tiz
Loyd lɔɪd
Loyola 'lɔɪ əl ə lɔɪ 'əʊl- ‖ lɔɪ 'oʊl ə —*Sp* [lo 'jo la]
Lozells ləʊ 'zelz ‖ loʊ-
lozeng|e 'lɒz ɪndʒ -əndʒ ‖ 'lɑːz- **~es** ɪz əz
LP ˌel 'piː **~s, ~'s** z
LPC ˌel piː 'siː
LPG ˌel piː 'dʒiː
L-plate 'el pleɪt **~s** s
LSD ˌel es 'diː
LSE ˌel es 'iː
Ltd —*see* **Limited**
Luanda lu 'ænd ə ‖ -'ɑːnd- —*Port* ['lwen dɐ]
luau 'luː aʊ *Hawaiian* lūʻau ['luː ʔau]
Luba 'luːb ə
Lubavitcher 'luːb ə vɪtʃ ə ‖ -ᵊr **~s** z
lubber 'lʌb ə ‖ -ᵊr **~s** z
Lubbock 'lʌb ək
lube luːb **lubed** luːbd **lubes** luːbz **lubing** 'luːb ɪŋ
Lubeck, Lübeck 'luː bek 'ljuː- —*Ger* ['lyː bɛk, -beːk]
lubricant 'luːb rɪk ənt 'ljuːb-, -rək- **~s** s
lubri|cate 'luːb rɪ |keɪt 'ljuːb-, -rə- **~cated** keɪt ɪd -əd ‖ keɪţ əd **~cates** keɪts **~cating** keɪt ɪŋ ‖ keɪţ ɪŋ
lubrication ˌluːb rɪ 'keɪʃ ᵊn ˌljuːb-, -rə- **~s** z
lubricator 'luːb rɪ keɪt ə 'ljuːb-, '·rə- ‖ -keɪţ ᵊr **~s** z
lubricious luː 'brɪʃ əs ljuː- **~ly** li **~ness** nəs nɪs
lubricity luː 'brɪs ət i ljuː-, -ɪt- ‖ -əţ i
Lucan 'luːk ən
Lucas 'luːk əs
Luce luːs
Lucent *tdmk* 'luːs ᵊnt
lucerne, L~ lu 'sɜːn ‖ -'sɜːn —*Fr* [ly sɛʁn]
Lucia 'luːs i‿ə 'luːʃ-, 'luːʃ ə —*but as an Italian name* lu 'tʃiː‿ə —*It* [lu 'tʃiː a] —*see also* **St Lucia**
Lucian 'luːs i‿ən 'luːʃ- ‖ 'luːʃ ᵊn
lucid 'luːs ɪd 'ljuːs-, §-əd **~ly** li **~ness** nəs nɪs
lucidity luː 'sɪd ət i ljuː-, -ɪt- ‖ -əţ i
Lucie 'luːs i
Lucifer, l~ 'luːs ɪf ə -əf- ‖ -ᵊr **~s** z
luciferin luː 'sɪf ər ɪn §-ən
Lucille lu 'siːᵊl
Lucinda luː 'sɪnd ə
Lucite *tdmk* 'luːs aɪt
Lucius 'luːs i‿əs 'luːʃ- ‖ 'luːʃ əs
luck, Luck lʌk **lucked** lʌkt **lucking** 'lʌk ɪŋ **lucks** lʌks
luckless 'lʌk ləs -lɪs **~ly** li **~ness** nəs nɪs
Lucknow 'lʌk naʊ ˌ·'· —*Hindi* [ləkʰ nəw]
luck|y, Lucky 'lʌk |i **~ier** i‿ə ‖ i‿ᵊr **~iest** i‿ɪst i‿əst **~ily** ɪ li əl i **~iness** i nəs i nɪs
ˌlucky 'dip
Lucozade *tdmk* 'luːk əʊ zeɪd ‖ -ə-
lucrative 'luːk rət ɪv 'ljuːk- ‖ -rəţ ɪv
lucre 'luːk ə 'ljuːk- ‖ -ᵊr
Lucrece lu 'kriːs lju-
Lucretia lu 'kriːʃ ə lju-, -'kriːʃ i‿ə
Lucretius lu 'kriːʃ əs lju-, -'kriːʃ i‿əs
lucu|brate 'luːk ju |breɪt 'ljuːk- ‖ -jə- **~brated** breɪt ɪd -əd ‖ breɪţ əd **~brates** breɪts **~brating** breɪt ɪŋ ‖ breɪţ ɪŋ
lucubration ˌluːk ju 'breɪʃ ᵊn ‖ -jə- **~s** z
Lucull|us lu 'kʌl |əs lju- **~an** ən
Lucy 'luːs i
Lud, lud lʌd
Luddite, l~ 'lʌd aɪt **~s** s
lude luːd **ludes** luːdz
Ludgate 'lʌd gət -gɪt, -geɪt
ludic 'luːd ɪk 'ljuːd-
ludicrous 'luːd ɪk rəs 'ljuːd-, -ək- **~ly** li **~ness** nəs nɪs
Ludlow 'lʌd ləʊ ‖ -loʊ
Ludlum 'lʌd ləm
Ludmila, Ludmilla lʊd 'mɪl ə
ludo, Ludo 'luːd əʊ ‖ -oʊ
Ludovic 'luːd ə vɪk
Ludwig 'lʊd vɪg 'luːd- ‖ 'lʌd wɪg 'lʊd-, -vɪg —*Ger* ['luːt vɪç]
luff lʌf **luffed** lʌft **luffing** 'lʌf ɪŋ **luffs** lʌfs
Lufthansa *tdmk* 'lʊft ˌhænz ə -ˌhænᵗs- ‖ -ˌhɑːnz ə —*Ger* ['lʊft ˌhan za]
Luftwaffe 'lʊft ˌwæf ə -ˌvæf-, -ˌwɑːf-, -ˌvɑːf- ‖ -ˌvɑːf ə —*Ger* ['lʊft ˌvaf ə]
lug lʌg **lugged** lʌgd **lugging** 'lʌg ɪŋ **lugs** lʌgz
Luganda lu 'gænd ə -'gɑːnd- ‖ -'gɑːnd ə
Lugano luː 'gɑːn əʊ lə- ‖ -oʊ —*It* [lu 'gaː no]
Lugard 'luː gɑːd ˌ·'· ‖ -gɑːrd
luge luːʒ luːdʒ **luged** luːʒd luːdʒd **luges** 'luːʒ ɪz 'luːdʒ-, -əz **luging** 'luːʒ ɪŋ 'luːdʒ-
Luger *tdmk* 'luːg ə ‖ -ᵊr —*Ger* ['luː gɐ] **~s** z
lugg... —*see* **lug**
luggage 'lʌg ɪdʒ
'luggage ˌlabel; **'luggage rack**; **'luggage van**
lugger 'lʌg ə ‖ -ᵊr **~s** z
Lughnasa, Lughnasadh 'luːn əs ə
lughole 'lʌg həʊl →-hɒʊl ‖ -hoʊl —*humorously also BrE* -əʊl **~s** z
Lugosi lu 'gəʊs i ‖ -'goʊs-
lugsail 'lʌg seɪᵊl —*naut* -sᵊl **~s** z
lugubrious lə 'guːb ri‿əs lu-, -'gjuːb- **~ly** li **~ness** nəs nɪs
lugworm 'lʌg wɜːm ‖ -wɜːm **~s** z
Luigi lu 'iːdʒ i
Lukacs, Lukács 'luːk ætʃ ‖ -ɑːtʃ —*Hungarian* ['lu kaːtʃ]
Luke luːk
lukewarm ˌluːk 'wɔːm ◂ '· · ‖ -'wɔːrm **~ly** li **~ness** nəs nɪs
lull lʌl **lulled** lʌld **lulling** 'lʌl ɪŋ **lulls** lʌlz

lulla|by ˈlʌl ə |baɪ ~bied baɪd ~bies baɪz
~bying baɪ ɪŋ
Lulu, lulu ˈluːl uː ~s, ~'s z
Lulworth ˈlʌl wəθ -wɜːθ ‖ -wɜːθ
lum lʌm lumz lʌmz
lumbago lʌm ˈbeɪg əʊ ‖ -oʊ
lumbar ˈlʌm bə -bɑː ‖ -bᵊr -bɑːr
lumber ˈlʌm bə ‖ -bᵊr ~ed d lumbering
ˈlʌm bər ɪŋ ~s z
lumberjack ˈlʌm bə dʒæk ‖ -bᵊr- ~s s
lumber|man ˈlʌm bə |mən -mæn ‖ -bᵊr- ~men
mən men
lumbermill ˈlʌm bə mɪl ‖ -bᵊr- ~s z
lumber-room ˈlʌm bə ruːm -rum ‖ -bᵊr- ~s z
lumberyard ˈlʌm bə jɑːd ‖ -bᵊr jɑːrd ~s z
lumen ˈluːm ɪn -ən, -en ‖ -ən ~s z
lumiere, lumière, L~ ˈluːm i eə ˌ·ˈ·
‖ ˌluːm i ˈeᵊr —Fr [ly mjɛːʁ]
luminanc|e ˈluːm ɪn ən⁺s ˈljuːm-, -ən- ~es ɪz əz
luminar|y ˈlum ɪn ər ˌi ˈljuːm-, ˈ-ən- ‖ -ə ner ˌi
~ies iz
luminesc|e ˌluːm ɪ ˈnes ˌljuːm-, -ə- ~ed t ~es
ɪz əz ~ing ɪŋ
luminescence ˌluːm ɪ ˈnes ᵊn⁺s ˌljuːm-, -ə-
luminescent ˌluːm ɪ ˈnes ᵊnt ◄ ˌljuːm-, -ə-
luminosit|y ˌluːm ɪ ˈnɒs ət ˌi ˌljuːm-, ˌ·ə-, -ɪt i
‖ -ˈnɑːs ət ˌi ~ies iz
luminous ˈluːm ɪn əs ˈljuːm-, -ən- ~ly li ~ness
nəs nɪs
Lumley ˈlʌm li
lumme ˈlʌm i
lummox ˈlʌm əks ~es ɪz əz
lummy ˈlʌm i
lump lʌmp lumped lʌmpt lumping ˈlʌmp ɪŋ
lumps lʌmps
ˌlump ˈsum
lumpectom|y ˌlʌmp ˈekt əm |i ~ies iz
lumpen ˈlʌmp ən ˈlump-
lumpenproletariat
ˌlʌmp ən ˌprəʊl ə ˈteər i ət ˌlump-, →ˌ·əm-,
-ˌ·ɪ-, -æt ‖ -ˌprəʊl ə ˈter-
lumpfish ˈlʌmp fɪʃ ~es ɪz əz
lumpish ˈlʌmp ɪʃ ~ly li ~ness nəs nɪs
Lumpkin ˈlʌmp kɪn §-kən
lump|y ˈlʌmp |i ~ier i ə ‖ i ᵊr ~iest i ɪst i əst
Lumsden ˈlʌmz dən
Lumumba lu ˈmʊm bə -ˈmuːm-
Luna, luna ˈluːn ə ˈljuːn-
ˈluna moth
lunac|y ˈluːn əs |i ~ies iz
lunar ˈluːn ə ‖ -ᵊr
lunate ˈluːn eɪt -ət, -ɪt
lunatic ˈluːn ə tɪk ~s s
ˈlunatic aˌsylum; ˌlunatic ˈfringe
lunation lu ˈneɪʃ ᵊn ~s z
lunch lʌntʃ lunched lʌntʃt lunches ˈlʌntʃ ɪz
-əz lunching ˈlʌntʃ ɪŋ
lunchbox ˈlʌntʃ bɒks ‖ -bɑːks ~es ɪz əz
luncheon ˈlʌntʃ ən ~s z
ˈluncheon meat; ˈluncheon ˌvoucher
luncheonette ˌlʌntʃ ə ˈnet ~s s
lunchroom ˈlʌntʃ ruːm -rʊm ~s z
lunchtime ˈlʌntʃ taɪm ~s z

Lund family name lʌnd
Lund place in Sweden lʊnd —Swedish [lʊnd],
Danish [lɒnʔ]
Lundy ˈlʌnd i
lune, Lune luːn ljuːn lunes luːnz ljuːnz
Luneburg ˈluːn ə bɜːg ‖ -bɝːg —Ger Lüneburg
[ˈlyː nə bʊʁk]
lunette ⁽ˌ⁾luː ˈnet ⁽ˌ⁾ljuː- ~s s
lung lʌŋ lunged lʌŋd lungs lʌŋz
lunge lʌndʒ lunged lʌndʒd lunges ˈlʌndʒ ɪz
-əz lunging ˈlʌndʒ ɪŋ
lunged 'having lungs' lʌŋd
lunged past & pp of lunge lʌndʒd
lungfish ˈlʌŋ fɪʃ ~es ɪz əz
lungful ˈlʌŋ fʊl ~s z
lungi ˈlʊŋ gi ~s z
lungpower ˈlʌŋ ˌpaʊ ə ‖ -ˌpaʊ ᵊr
lunkhead ˈlʌŋk hed ~s z
Lunn lʌn
Lunt lʌnt
Luo ˈluː əʊ ‖ -oʊ
lupanar lu ˈpeɪn ə -ˈpɑːn-, -ɑː ‖ -ᵊr ~s z
Lupercal ˈluːp ə kæl ˈljuːp-, -ɜː- ‖ -ᵊr-
Lupercalia ˌluːp ə ˈkeɪl i ə ˌljuːp-, ˌ·ɜː- ‖ ˌ·ᵊr-
lupin, lupine n, flower ˈluːp ɪn §-ən ~s z
lupine adj ˈluːp aɪn ˈljuːp-
lupus, Lupus ˈluːp əs ˈljuːp-
lur lʊə lɜː ‖ lʊᵊr lurs lʊəz lɜːz ‖ lʊᵊrz
lurch lɜːtʃ ‖ lɜːtʃ lurched lɜːtʃt ‖ lɜːtʃt lurches
ˈlɜːtʃ ɪz -əz ‖ ˈlɜːtʃ əz lurching ˈlɜːtʃ ɪŋ
‖ ˈlɜːtʃ ɪŋ
lurcher ˈlɜːtʃ ə ‖ ˈlɜːtʃ ᵊr ~s z

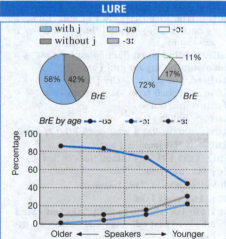

LURE

lure ljʊə lʊə, ljɜː, ljɔː ‖ lʊᵊr — Preference poll,
BrE: with j 58%, without j 42%; -ʊə 72%, -ɜː
17%, -ɔː 11%. lured ljʊəd lʊəd, ljɜːd, ljɔːd
‖ lʊᵊrd lures ljʊəz lʊəz, ljɜːz, ljɔːz ‖ lʊᵊrz
luring ˈljʊər ɪŋ ˈlʊər-, ˈljɜːr-, ˈljɔːr- ‖ ˈlʊr ɪŋ
Lurex tdmk ˈljʊər eks ˈlʊər-, ˈljɜːr-, ˈljɔːr- ‖ ˈlʊr-
Lurgan ˈlɜːg ən ‖ ˈlɜːg-
lurgy ˈlɜːg i ‖ ˈlɜːg i
lurid ˈljʊər ɪd ˈlʊər-, ˈljɜːr-, ˈljɔːr-, §-əd ‖ ˈlʊr əd
~ly li ~ness nəs nɪs

lurk lɜːk ‖ lɝːk **lurked** lɜːkt ‖ lɝːkt **lurking**
  'lɜːk ɪŋ ‖ 'lɝːk ɪŋ **lurks** lɜːks ‖ lɝːks
lurker 'lɜːk ə ‖ 'lɝːk ²r **~s** z
Lurpak *tdmk* 'lɜː pæk ‖ 'lɝː-
Lusaka lu 'sɑːk ə lʊ-, -'zɑːk-
Lusatia lu 'seɪʃ ə -'seɪʃ iˌə
Lusatian lu 'seɪʃ ²n -'seɪʃ i‿ə‿i **~s** z
luscious 'lʌʃ əs **~ly** li **~ness** nəs nɪs
lush, Lush lʌʃ **lusher** 'lʌʃ ə ‖ -²r **lushes** 'lʌʃ ɪz
  -əz **lushest** 'lʌʃ ɪst -əst
Lushington 'lʌʃ ɪŋ tən
lush|ly 'lʌʃ |li **~ness** nəs nɪs
Lusiad 'luːs i æd 'ljuːs- **~s** z
Lusitani|a ˌluːs ɪ 'teɪn iˌə ˌ‿ə- **~an/s** ən/z
lust lʌst **lusted** 'lʌst ɪd -əd **lusting** 'lʌst ɪŋ
  lusts lʌsts
luster 'lʌst ə ‖ -²r **~s** z
lustful 'lʌst fəl -fʊl **~ly** li **~ness** nəs nɪs
lusti... —*see* **lusty**
lustral 'lʌs trəl
lus|trate lʌ 's|treɪt 'lʌs |treɪt ‖ 'lʌs |treɪt
  ~trated treɪt ɪd -əd ‖ treɪt̬ əd **~trates** treɪts
  ~trating treɪt ɪŋ ‖ treɪt̬ ɪŋ
lustration lʌ 'streɪʃ ²n **~s** z
lustre 'lʌst ə ‖ -²r **~s** z
lustrous 'lʌs trəs **~ly** li **~ness** nəs nɪs
lus|trum 'lʌs |trəm **~tra** trə **~trums** trəmz
lust|y 'lʌst |i **~ier** iˌə ‖ iˌ²r **~iest** iˌɪst iˌəst **~ily**
  ɪ li əl i **~iness** i nəs i nɪs
lutanist 'luːt ən ɪst 'ljuːt-, §-əst ‖ -²n̩ əst **~s** s
lute luːt ljuːt **lutes** luːts ljuːts
luteal 'luːt iˌəl 'ljuːt- ‖ 'luːt̬-
luteinis|e, luteiniz|e 'luːt iˌɪ naɪz 'ljuːt-, -iˌə-;
  'ˌɪ naɪz, -ə-, -iː-, -²n aɪz ‖ 'luːt̬- **~ed** d **~es** ɪz
  əz **~ing** ɪŋ
lutenist 'luːt ən ɪst 'ljuːt-, §-əst ‖ -²n̩ əst **~s** s
lutetium lu 'tiːʃ əm -'tiːʃ iˌəm
Luther 'luːθ ə ‖ -²r —*Ger* ['lʊt ɐ]
Lutheran 'luːθ ²rˌən **~ism** ˌɪz əm **~s** z
Lutine ˌluː 'tiːn ◂
Luton 'luːt ²n
Lutterworth 'lʌt ə wəθ -wɜːθ ‖ 'lʌt̬ ²r wɝːθ
Lutyens 'lʌt jənz 'lʌtʃ ənz
lutz, Lutz lʊts luːts **lutzes** 'lʊts ɪz 'luːts-, -əz
luv lʌv **luvs** lʌvz
luvv|ie, luvv|y 'lʌv |i **~ies** iz
lux, Lux *tdmk* lʌks
lux|ate lʌk 's|eɪt 'lʌks |eɪt ‖ 'lʌks |eɪt **~ated**
  eɪt ɪd -əd ‖ eɪt̬ əd **~ates** eɪts **~ating** eɪt ɪŋ
  ‖ eɪt̬ ɪŋ
luxation lʌk 'seɪʃ ²n **~s** z
luxe lʌks lʊks, luːks ‖ lʊks lʌks, luːks —*Fr*
  [lyks]
Luxemburg, Luxembourg 'lʌks əm bɜːg
  ‖ -bɝːg —*Ger* ['lʊks ²m bʊʁk], *Fr*
  Luxembourg [lyk sã buːʁ] **~er/s** ə/z ‖ ²r/z
Luxor 'lʌks ɔː ‖ -ɔːr
luxuri|ance lʌg 'zjʊər iˌ|ən͡ts ləg-, lʌk-, -'ʒʊər-;
  lʌk 'sjʊər-, -'ʃʊər- ‖ lʌg 'ʒʊr- lʌk 'ʃʊr- **~ant/ly**
  ənt /li

luxuri|ate lʌg 'zjʊər i |eɪt ləg-, lʌk-, -'ʒʊər-;
  lʌk 'sjʊər-, -'ʃʊər- ‖ lʌg 'ʒʊr- lʌk 'ʃʊr- **~ated**
  eɪt ɪd -əd ‖ eɪt̬ əd **~ates** eɪts **~ating** eɪt ɪŋ
  ‖ eɪt̬ ɪŋ

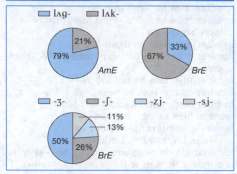

LUXURIOUS

— lʌg-   — lʌk-

| AmE | BrE |
| 79% / 21% | 67% / 33% |

— ʒ-   — ʃ-   — zj-   — sj-

BrE: 50% / 26% / 13% / 11%

luxurious lʌk 'ʒʊər iˌəs lək-, lʌg-, ləg-, -'ʃʊər-,
  -'zjʊər-, -'sjʊər- ‖ lʌg 'ʒʊr- lʌk 'ʃʊr-
— *Preference polls, AmE:* lʌg- 79%, lʌk- 21%;
BrE: lʌk- 67%, lʌg- 33%; -ʒ- 50%, -ʃ- 26%,
-zj- 13%, -sj- 11%. **~ly** li **~ness** nəs nɪs

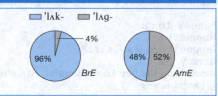

LUXURY

— 'lʌk-   — 'lʌg-

| BrE | AmE |
| 96% / 4% | 48% / 52% |

luxur|y 'lʌk ʃərˌ|i §'lʌg ʒərˌ|i ‖ 'lʌg ʒərˌ|i
  'lʌk ʃərˌ|i — *Preference polls, BrE:* 'lʌk- 96%,
  'lʌg- 4%; *AmE:* 'lʌk- 48%, 'lʌg- 52%. **~ies** iz
Luzon ˌluː 'zɒn ‖ -'zɑːn
Lvov lə 'vɒf ‖ -'vɑːf -'vɔːf —*Ukrainian* Lviv
  [lʲvʲiw], *Polish* Lwów [lvuf], *Russian* [lʲvof]
-ly li —*After a stem ending in* l, *one* l *is usually
  lost, together with any* ə, *thus* fully 'fʊl i,
  gently 'dʒent li.
Lyall 'laɪ əl
Lybrand 'laɪ brænd
lycanthrope 'laɪk ən θrəʊp laɪ 'kæn²θ rəʊp
  ‖ -θroʊp **~s** s
lycanthropy laɪ 'kæn²θ rəp i
lycee, lycée 'liːs eɪ ‖ liː 'seɪ —*Fr* [li se] **~s** z
Lyceum laɪ 'siːˌəm
lychee ˌlaɪ 'tʃiː ' ‧; 'lɪtʃ i ‖ 'liːtʃ i **~s** z
lychgate 'lɪtʃ geɪt **~s** s
lychnis 'lɪk nɪs §-nəs
Lyci|a 'lɪs iˌ|ə ‖ 'lɪʃ- **~an/s** ən/z
Lycidas 'lɪs ɪ dæs -ə-
lycopene 'laɪk əʊ piːn ‖ -oʊ-
lycopodium ˌlaɪk ə 'pəʊd iˌəm ‖ -'poʊd-
Lycos *tdmk* 'laɪk ɒs ‖ -ɑːs
Lycra *tdmk* 'laɪk rə
Lycurgus laɪ 'kɜːg əs ‖ -'kɝːg-
Lydd lɪd

lyddite 'lɪd aɪt
Lydgate 'lɪd geɪt →'lɪg-, -gɪt —*but in Sheffield,*
'lɪdʒ ɪt
Lydi|a 'lɪd i‿|ə **~an/s** ən/z
lye laɪ *(= lie)*
Lyell 'laɪ‿əl
Lygon 'lɪg ən
lying 'laɪ‿ɪŋ
lying-in ˌlaɪ‿ɪŋ 'ɪn **lyings-in** ˌlaɪ‿ɪŋz 'ɪn
Lyle laɪəl
Lyly 'lɪl i
Lyme laɪm
lyme-grass 'laɪm grɑːs §-græs ‖ -græs
Lymeswold *tdmk* 'laɪmz wəʊld →-wɒʊld
‖ -wəʊld
Lymington 'lɪm ɪŋ tən
Lymm lɪm
Lympany 'lɪmp ən i
lymph lɪmᵖf **lymphs** lɪmᵖfs
'**lymph node**
lymphadenopath|y ˌlɪmᵖf ˌæd ɪ 'nɒp əθ |i
-ˌ‿ə-, -ᵊn 'ɒp- ‖ -ᵊn 'ɑːp- **~ies** iz
lymphatic lɪm 'fæt ɪk ‖ -'fæt̬- **~s** s
lympho- *comb. form*
with stress-neutral suffix ˈlɪmᵖf əʊ ‖ -ə
— **lymphocyte** 'lɪmᵖf əʊ saɪt ‖ -ə-
with stress-imposing suffix lɪm 'fɒ+ ‖ -'fɑː+
— **lymphopathy** lɪm 'fɒp əθ i ‖ -'fɑːp-
lymphoma lɪm 'fəʊm ə ‖ -'foʊm ə **~s** z
Lympne lɪm
Lynam 'laɪn əm
lynch, Lynch lɪntʃ **lynched** lɪntʃt **lynches**
'lɪntʃ ɪz -əz **lynching** 'lɪntʃ ɪŋ
'**lynch law**; '**lynch mob**
Lynchburg 'lɪntʃ bɜːg ‖ -bɜːɡ
lynchpin 'lɪntʃ pɪn **~s** z
Lyndhurst 'lɪnd hɜːst ‖ -hɜːst
Lyndon 'lɪnd ən
Lyneham 'laɪn əm
Lynette lɪ 'net
Lynmouth 'lɪn məθ →'lɪm-
Lynn, Lynne lɪn
Lynton 'lɪnt ən ‖ -ᵊn
lynx, Lynx lɪŋks **lynxes** 'lɪŋks ɪz -əz
lynx-eyed ˌlɪŋks 'aɪd ◂ '‿·

lyo- *comb. form*
with stress-neutral suffix ˈlaɪ əʊ ‖ -ə
— **lyophilic** ˌlaɪ əʊ 'fɪl ɪk ◂ ‖ -ə-
with stress-imposing suffix laɪ 'ɒ+ ‖ -'ɑː+
— **lyophilize** laɪ 'ɒf ɪ laɪz -ə- ‖ -'ɑːf ə-
Lyon *surname* 'laɪ‿ən
Lyonesse ˌlaɪ‿ə 'nes
lyonnaise ˌliː‿ə 'neɪz ◂ ˌlaɪ‿ —*Fr* [ljɔ nɛːz]
Lyonnesse ˌlaɪ‿ə 'nes
Lyons *place in France* 'liː‿ɒ̃ -ɒn; 'laɪ‿ənz
‖ liː 'ɑːn -'ɔːn —*Fr* Lyon [ljɔ̃]
Lyons *family name* 'laɪ‿ənz
Lyra 'laɪ‿ᵊr ə
lyre 'laɪ‿ə ‖ 'laɪ‿ᵊr *(= liar)* **lyres** 'laɪ‿əz
‖ 'laɪ‿ᵊrz
lyrebird 'laɪ‿ə bɜːd ‖ 'laɪ‿ᵊr bɜːd **~s** z
lyric 'lɪr ɪk **~al** ᵊl **~ally** ᵊlɪ i **~s** s
lyricism 'lɪr ɪ ˌsɪz əm -ə-
lyricist 'lɪr ɪs ɪst -əs-, §-əst **~s** s
lyrist *'lyric poet'* 'lɪr ɪst §-əst **~s** s
lyrist *'lyre player'* 'laɪ‿ər ɪst 'lɪr ɪst; §-əst **~s** s
Lysander laɪ 'sænd ə ‖ -ᵊr
-lyse laɪz — **paralyse** 'pær ə laɪz ‖ 'per-
Lysenko lɪ 'seŋk əʊ lə- ‖ -oʊ —*Russian*
[lʲ 'sʲen kə]
lysergic laɪ 'sɜːdʒ ɪk lɪ-, lə- ‖ -'sɜːdʒ-
lyˌsergic 'acid
Lysias 'lɪs i æs ‖ -əs
lysis 'laɪs ɪs §-əs
-lysis *stress-imposing* ləs ɪs lɪs-, §-əs
— **paralysis** pə 'ræl əs ɪs -ɪs-, §-əs
Lysistrata laɪ 'sɪs trət ə ˌlɪs ɪ 'strɑːt ə, ˌlɪz-
‖ ˌlɪs ə 'strɑːt ə laɪ 'sɪs trət̬ ə
lysol, Lysol *tdmk* 'laɪs ɒl ‖ -ɔːl -ɑːl, -oʊl
lysosome 'laɪs əʊ səʊm ‖ -ə soʊm -zoʊm **~s** z
lysozyme 'laɪz əʊ zaɪm ‖ -ə zaɪm
Lystra 'lɪs trə
lystrosaur 'lɪs trəʊ sɔː ‖ -trə sɔːr
-lyte laɪt — **electrolyte** ɪ 'lek trəʊ laɪt ə-
‖ -trə-
Lytham 'lɪð əm
-lytic 'lɪt ɪk ‖ 'lɪt̬ ɪk — **electrolytic**
ɪ ˌlek trəʊ 'lɪt ɪk ◂ ‖ -trə 'lɪt̬ ɪk ◂
Lyttelton 'lɪt ᵊl tən ‖ 'lɪt̬-
Lytton 'lɪt ᵊn

L

Mm

M, m em **M's, m's, Ms** emz —*Communications code name:* Mike

'm m —*see* **I'm**

M'..., M'... *in this dictionary listed alphabetically as if written* **Mac...**

M1 ˌem ˈwʌn §-ˈwɒn **M25** ˌem ˌtwent i ˈfaɪv ⚠-ˌtwen i- ‖ -ˌtwenṭ i- **M40** ˌem ˈfɔːt i ‖ -ˈfɔːrṭ i —*and similarly for other British motorway numbers*

ma, Ma mɑː **mas, Ma's** mɑːz

MA —*see* **Massachusetts**

MA *'master of arts'* ˌem ˈeɪ

Maalox *tdmk* ˈmeɪ lɒks ‖ -lɑːks

ma'am *strong form* **mæm** mɑːm, *weak form* **məm** —*After* yes *there is also a weak form* əm.

Maas mɑːs —*Dutch* [maːs]

Maastricht ˈmɑːs trɪkt -trɪxt —*Dutch* [maː ˈstrɪxt]

Mab, Mabb mæb

Mabel ˈmeɪb ᵊl

Mabinogion ˌmæb ɪ ˈnɒg i ɒn ˌ-ə-, -i‿ən ‖ -ˈnoʊg i ɑːn —*Welsh* [ma bi ˈnog jon]

Mablethorpe ˈmeɪb ᵊl θɔːp ‖ -θɔːrp

Mableton ˈmeɪb ᵊl tən

Mabley *(i)* ˈmeɪb li, *(ii)* ˈmæb li

Mabon *(i)* ˈmeɪb ən, *(ii)* ˈmæb ən

Mac, mac mæk

Mac-, Mc- *prefix in names:(i) usually, unstressed* **mək**, *or sometimes* **mæk** *(perhaps depending on degree of formality):* McˈDonald, MacˈDonald, Macˈdonald; *but (ii)* ¦mæk *before an unstressed syllable:* ˈMcEnroe, ˈMacEnroe; *(iii)* **mə** *before* **k, g**: McˈGill, MacˈGill, Macˈgill, MacˈGill. *This prefix is spelt sometimes Mac, sometimes Mc, sometimes M' or Mᶜ, and the stem which follows may be spelt with a capital letter or with a small one. Particularly in Ireland, the prefix is sometimes written as a separate word. To save repetition, many entries below are shown only in the Mc- form, with a capital*

letter for the stem, all written as one word. Mc- is in any case listed here alphabetically as if it were Mac-.

macabre mə ˈkɑːb_rə -ə ‖ -ᵊr **~ly** li

macadam, McAdam mə ˈkæd əm

macadamia ˌmæk ə ˈdeɪm i‿ə **~s** z
   ˌmacaˈdamia nut

macadamis|e, macadamiz|e
   mə ˈkæd ə maɪz **~ed** d **~es** ɪz əz **~ing** ɪŋ

Macafee, McAfee *(i)* ˌmæk ə ˈfiː ◂ ˈ·‿·,
   (ii) mə ˈkæf i -ˈkɑːf-

McAleese ˌmæk ə ˈliːs

McAlery ˌmæk ə ˈlɪər i ‖ -ˈlɪr i

McAlinden, McAlindon ˌmæk ə ˈlɪnd ən

McAlister, McAllister mə ˈkæl ɪst ə -əst- ‖ -ᵊr

McAloon ˌmæk ə ˈluːn

McAlpine mə ˈkælp aɪn -ɪn, §-ən

McAnally ˌmæk ə ˈnæl i

McAnespie ˌmæk ə ˈnesp i

McAnulty ˌmæk ə ˈnʌlt i

Macao mə ˈkaʊ —*Port* Macáu [mɐ ˈkau], *Chi* Ào Mén [⁴au ²mən]

macaque mə ˈkɑːk -ˈkæk; ˌmæk æk **~s** s

McArdle mə ˈkɑːd ᵊl ‖ -ˈkɑːrd-

macarena ˌmæk ə ˈreɪn ə ‖ ˌmɑːk- —*Sp* macareña [ma ka ˈre ɲa]

macaroni ˌmæk ə ˈrəʊn i ◂ ‖ -ˈroʊn i ◂ **~es, ~s** z
   ˌmacaˌroni ˈcheese

macaronic ˌmæk ə ˈrɒn ɪk ◂ ‖ -ˈrɑːn ɪk ◂ **~s** s

macaroon ˌmæk ə ˈruːn **~s** z

McArthur mə ˈkɑːθ ə ‖ -ˈkɑːrθ ᵊr

Macassar, m~ mə ˈkæs ə ‖ -ᵊr
   Maˈcassar oil

McAteer ˌmæk ə ˈtɪə ˈ·‿·· ‖ -ˈtɪᵊr

Macau, Macáu mə ˈkaʊ —*Port* [mɐ ˈkau], *Chi* Ào Mén [⁴au ²mən]

Macaulay, McAulay, McAuley mə ˈkɔːl i ‖ -ˈkɑːl-

McAuliffe mə ˈkɔːl ɪf §-əf ‖ -ˈkɑːl-

Macavity mə ˈkæv ət i -ɪt- ‖ -əṭ i

McAvoy ˈmæk ə vɔɪ

macaw mə ˈkɔː ‖ -ˈkɑː **~s** z

McBain mək ˈbeɪn §mæk-
McBeal mək ˈbiːᵊl
Macbeth, McBeth mək ˈbeθ mæk-
McBrain, McBrayne mək ˈbreɪn §mæk-
McBrearty mək ˈbrɪət i §mæk- ‖ -ˈbrɪrt̬ i
McBride mək ˈbraɪd §mæk-
Macca ˈmæk ə
Maccabae|an, Maccabe|an ˌmæk ə ˈbiː ̩|ən ◂
  -ˈbeɪ- **~us** əs
McCabe mə ˈkeɪb
Maccabees ˈmæk ə biːz
Maccabeus ˌmæk ə ˈbiː ̩əs ◂ -ˈbeɪ-
McCaffray, McCaffrey mə ˈkæf ri
McCain mə ˈkeɪn
McCall mə ˈkɔːl ‖ -ˈkɑːl
McCallum mə ˈkæl əm
McCambridge mə ˈkeɪm brɪdʒ
McCanlis mə ˈkæn lɪs -ləs
McCann mə ˈkæn
McCarran mə ˈkær ən ‖ -ˈker-
McCarthy mə ˈkɑːθ i ‖ -ˈkɑːrθ i **~ism** ˌɪz əm
McCarthyite mə ˈkɑːθ i aɪt ‖ -ˈkɑːrθ- **~s** s
McCartney mə ˈkɑːt ni ‖ -ˈkɑːrt-
McCaskill mə ˈkæsk ᵊl -ɪl
McCavish mə ˈkæv ɪʃ
macchiato ˌmæk i ˈɑːt əʊ ‖ ˌmɑːk i ˈɑːt̬ oʊ
  —*It* [mak ˈkja: to]
McCleary, McCleery mə ˈklɪər i ‖ -ˈklɪr i
McClellan mə ˈklel ən
McClelland mə ˈklel ənd
Macclesfield ˈmæk ᵊlz fiːᵊld
McClintock mə ˈklɪnt ɒk -ək ‖ -ɑːk
McCloskey mə ˈklɒsk i ‖ -ˈklɑːsk i
McClure mə ˈkluə ‖ -ˈkluᵊr
McCluskie mə ˈklʌsk i
Maccoby ˈmæk əb i
McColl mə ˈkɒl ‖ -ˈkɑːl
McConachie, McConachy, McConaghy,
  McConochie mə ˈkɒn ək i -ɒx i, -ə hi
  ‖ -ˈkɑːn-
McCool mə ˈkuːl
McCormack mə ˈkɔːm ək -æk ‖ -ˈkɔːrm-
McCormick mə ˈkɔːm ɪk §-ək ‖ -ˈkɔːrm-
McCorquodale mə ˈkɔːk ə deɪᵊl ‖ -ˈkɔːrk-
McCowan mə ˈkaʊ ən
McCoy mə ˈkɔɪ
McCrae, McCrea mə ˈkreɪ
McCreadie, McCready *(i)* mə ˈkriːd i,
  (ii) mə ˈkred i
McCrindell, McCrindle mə ˈkrɪnd ᵊl
McCrum mə ˈkrʌm
McCullers mə ˈkʌl əz ‖ -ᵊrz
McCulloch, McCullough mə ˈkʌl ək -ɒx
McCurtain, McCurtin mə ˈkɜːt ɪn -ᵊn
  ‖ -ˈkɜːt̬ ᵊn
McCusker mə ˈkʌsk ə ‖ -ᵊr
McDade mək ˈdeɪd
McDermot, McDermott mək ˈdɜːm ət
  ‖ -ˈdɜːm-
McDiarmid mək ˈdɜːm ɪd §mæk-, -ˈdeəm-, §-əd
  ‖ -ˈdɜːm-
McDonagh mək ˈdɒn ə ‖ -ˈdɑːn ə

McDonald, Macdonald mək ˈdɒn ᵊld mæk-
  ‖ -ˈdɑːn- **~'s** *tdmk* z
McDonnell *(i)* ˌmæk də ˈnel, *(ii)* mək ˈdɒn ᵊl
  §mæk- ‖ -ˈdɑːn-
McDougal, McDougall mək ˈduːg ᵊl mæk-
McDowall, McDowell *(i)* mək ˈdaʊ əl
  ‖ -ˈdaʊ ᵊl, *(ii)* -ˈdəʊ- ‖ -ˈdoʊ-
McDuff, Macduff mək ˈdʌf mæk-
mace, Mace meɪs **Maced** meɪst **maces,**
  Maces ˈmeɪs ɪz -əz **Macing** ˈmeɪs ɪŋ
mace-bearer ˈmeɪs ˌbeər ə ‖ -ˌber ᵊr -ˌbær- **~s**
  z
macedoine, macédoine ˌmæs ɪ ˈdwɑːn -ə-,
  ˈ· · · **~s** z
Macedon ˈmæs ɪd ən -əd- ‖ -ə dɑːn
Macedoni|a ˌmæs ɪ ˈdəʊn i ̩|ə ˌ·ə- ‖ -ˈdoʊn-
  ~an/s ən/z
McElderry, McEldery ˈmæk ᵊl ˌder i ˌ·ˈ··
McElhone ˈmæk ᵊl həʊn ‖ -hoʊn
McElligott mə ˈkel ɪg ət -əg-
McElroy ˈmæk ᵊl rɔɪ —*but in AmE also*
  mə ˈkel-
McElwain *(i)* ˈmæk ᵊl weɪn, *(ii)* mə ˈkel weɪn
  mæk-
McEnroe ˈmæk ɪn rəʊ -ən- ‖ -roʊ
mace|rate ˈmæs ə |reɪt **~rated** reɪt ɪd -əd
  ‖ reɪt̬ əd **~rates** reɪts **~rating** reɪt ɪŋ ‖ reɪt̬ ɪŋ
maceration ˌmæs ə ˈreɪʃ ᵊn **~s** z
macerator ˈmæs ə reɪt ə ‖ -reɪt̬ ᵊr **~s** z
McEvoy ˈmæk ɪ vɔɪ -ə-
McEwan, McEwen mə ˈkjuː ən
McFadden mək ˈfæd ᵊn
McFadyean, McFadyen, McFadzean
  mək ˈfæd jən §mæk-
McFarland mək ˈfɑːl ənd ‖ -ˈfɑːrl-
McFarlane mək ˈfɑːl ɪn §mæk-, -ən ‖ -ˈfɑːrl-
McFee, McFie mək ˈfiː mæk-
McGahey mə ˈgɑː hi -ˈgæ-, -ˈgæx i
McGee mə ˈgiː
McGill mə ˈgɪl
McGillicuddy *(i)* ˈmæg lɪ ˌkʌd i,
  (ii) mə ˈgɪl i ˌkʌd i
McGilligan mə ˈgɪl ɪg ən -əg-
McGillivray mə ˈgɪl ɪv ri -əv-, -reɪ
McGillycuddy *(i)* ˈmæg lɪ ˌkʌd i,
  (ii) mə ˈgɪl i ˌkʌd i
  ˌMacgilly ˌcuddy's ˈReeks
McGinn mə ˈgɪn
McGinty mə ˈgɪnt i ‖ -ˈgɪnt̬ i
McGlashan mə ˈglæʃ ᵊn
McGoldrick mə ˈgəʊld rɪk →-ˈgɒʊld-
  ‖ -ˈgoʊld-
McGonagall mə ˈgɒn əg ᵊl ‖ -ˈgɑːn-
McGoohan mə ˈguː ən -hən
McGough mə ˈgɒf ‖ -ˈgɑːf -ˈgɔːf
McGovern mə ˈgʌv ᵊn ‖ -ᵊrn
McGowan mə ˈgaʊ ən
McGrady mə ˈgræd i *(!)*
McGrath mə ˈgrɑːθ -ˈgræθ, -ˈgrɑː ‖ -ˈgræθ —*In*
  Ireland also -ˈgræh
McGraw mə ˈgrɔː ‖ -ˈgrɑː
McGregor mə ˈgreg ə ‖ -ᵊr
McGuffey mə ˈgʌf i

M

McGuffin mə ˈɡʌf ɪn §-ᵊn

McGuigan mə ˈɡwiːɡ ən -ˈɡwɪɡ-

McGuinness mə ˈɡɪn ɪs §-əs

McGuire mə ˈɡwaɪ‿ə ‖ -ˈɡwaɪ‿ᵊr

McGurk mə ˈɡɜːk ‖ -ˈɡɜːk

McGwire mə ˈɡwaɪ‿ə ‖ -ˈɡwaɪ‿ᵊr

Mach, mach maːk mæk, mɒk —*Ger* [max]

McHale mək ˈheɪᵊl

Macheath mək ˈhiːθ mæk-

Machen *(i)* ˈmeɪtʃ ɪn -ən, *(ii)* ˈmæk-, *(iii)* ˈmæx- —*The place in Gwent is (iii)*

McHenry mək ˈhen ri

machete mə ˈʃet i -ˈtʃet-, -ˈʃeɪt-; mə ˈʃet ‖ mə ˈʃeṭ i -ˈtʃet-; mə ˈʃet **machetes** mə ˈʃet iz -ˈtʃet-, -ˈʃeɪt-; mə ˈʃets ‖ mə ˈʃeṭ iz -ˈtʃeṭ-; mə ˈʃets

Machiavelli ˌmæk iˌə ˈvel i —*It* [ma kja ˈvɛl li]

Machiavellian ˌmæk iˌə ˈvel iˌən ◂ **~ism** ˌɪz əm **~s** z

machico|late mə ˈtʃɪk əʊ |leɪt mæ- ‖ -ə- **~lated** leɪt ɪd -əd ‖ leɪṭ əd **~lates** leɪts **~lating** leɪt ɪŋ ‖ leɪṭ ɪŋ

machicolation mə ˌtʃɪk əʊ ˈleɪʃ ᵊn mæ- ‖ -ə- **~s** z

Machin ˈmeɪtʃ ɪn §-ən

machi|nate ˈmæk ɪ |neɪt ˈmæʃ-, -ə- **~nated** neɪt ɪd -əd ‖ neɪṭ əd **~nates** neɪts **~nating** neɪt ɪŋ ‖ neɪṭ ɪŋ

machination ˌmæk ɪ ˈneɪʃ ᵊn ˌmæʃ-, -ə- **~s** z

machine mə ˈʃiːn **machined** mə ˈʃiːnd **machines** mə ˈʃiːnz **machining** mə ˈʃiːn ɪŋ maˈchine code; maˈchine ˌgunner; maˈchine tool

machinegun mə ˈʃiːn ɡʌn →-ˈʃiːŋ- **~ned** d **~ning** ɪŋ **~s** z

machine-head mə ˈʃiːn hed **~s** z

machine-made mə ˈʃiːn meɪd →-ˈʃiːm-

machine-readable mə ˌʃiːn ˈriːd əb ᵊl ◂

machiner|y mə ˈʃiːn ər‿i **~ies** iz

machine-wash mə ˌʃiːn ˈwɒʃ ‖ -ˈwɔːʃ -ˈwɑːʃ **~ed** t **~es** ɪz əz **~ing** ɪŋ

machine-washable mə ˌʃiːn ˈwɒʃ əb ᵊl ‖ -ˈwɔːʃ- -ˈwɑːʃ-

machinist mə ˈʃiːn ɪst §-əst **~s** s

machismo mə ˈtʃɪz məʊ mæ-, △-ˈkɪz- ‖ maː ˈtʃiːz moʊ mə-, -ˈtʃɪz- —*Sp* [ma ˈtʃis mo]

macho ˈmætʃ əʊ ˈmɑːtʃ- ‖ ˈmɑːtʃ oʊ △ˈmaːk- **~s** z

Machrihanish ˌmæk rɪ ˈhæn ɪʃ ˌmæx-, -rə-

Machu Picchu ˌmætʃ uː ˈpɪk tʃuː ˌmɑːtʃ-, -ˈpiːk- ‖ ˌmɑːtʃ uː ˈpiːk tʃu —*Sp* [ˈma tʃu ˈpik tʃu]

Machynlleth mə ˈkʌn ɬəθ ‖ -ləθ —*Welsh* [ma ˈχən ɬeθ]

McIlroy ˈmæk ɪl rɔɪ -ᵊl-, ˌ·ˈ·-

McIlvaney ˌmæk ᵊl ˈveɪn i -ɪl-

McIlvenny ˌmæk ᵊl ˈven i -ɪl-

McIlwain ˈmæk ᵊl weɪn -ɪl-

McIlwraith ˈmæk ᵊl reɪθ -ɪl-

McIndoe ˈmæk ɪn dəʊ -ən- ‖ -doʊ

McInnes, McInnis mə ˈkɪn ɪs §-əs

McIntosh, macintosh ˈmæk ɪn tɒʃ §-ən- ‖ -tɑːʃ **~es** ɪz əz

McIntyre ˈmæk ɪn taɪ‿ə §ˈ·ən- ‖ -taɪ‿ᵊr

McIver, McIvor *(i)* mə ˈkaɪv ə ‖ -ᵊr, *(ii)* mə ˈkiːv ə ‖ -ᵊr

MacJob ⁽ˌ⁾mək ˈdʒɒb ‖ -ˈdʒɑːb —*also* ˈ· ·, *when in contrast to* (real) job **~s** z

mack, Mack mæk **macks** mæks

Mackay, McKay *(i)* mə ˈkaɪ, *(ii)* mə ˈkeɪ —*In BrE usually (i).*

McKechnie mə ˈkex ni -ˈkek- ‖ -ˈkek-

McKee mə ˈkiː

McKellar mə ˈkel ə ‖ -ᵊr

McKellen mə ˈkel ən

McKendrick mə ˈkendr ɪk

McKenna mə ˈken ə

Mackenzie, McKenzie mə ˈkenz i

McKeown mə ˈkjəʊn ‖ -ˈkjoʊn

mackerel ˈmæk rəl ˈmæk ər əl **~s** z

McKern mə ˈkɜːn ‖ -ˈkɜːn

McKerras mə ˈker əs

Mackeson ˈmæk ɪs ən -əs-

Mackie ˈmæk i

McKie *(i)* mə ˈkaɪ, *(ii)* mə ˈkiː

Mackin ˈmæk ɪn §-ən

Mackinac, Mackinaw, m~ ˈmæk ɪ nɔː -ə- ‖ -nɑː **~s** z

McKinlay, McKinley mə ˈkɪn li

McKinnon mə ˈkɪn ən

mackintosh, M~ ˈmæk ɪn tɒʃ §-ən- ‖ -tɑːʃ **~es**, **~'s** ɪz əz

McKittrick mə ˈkɪtr ɪk

McLachlan mə ˈklɒx lən -ˈklɒk- ‖ -ˈklɑːk-

MacLaine mə ˈkleɪn

Maclaren, McLaren mə ˈklær ən ‖ -ˈkler-

McLaughlin mə ˈklɒx lɪn -ˈklɒk-, -ˈɡlɒx-, §-lən ‖ -ˈklɑːk-

McLaurin mə ˈklɔːr ɪn -ˈklɒr-, §-ən

McLean, Maclean *(i)* mə ˈkleɪn, *(ii)* mə ˈkliːn

Macleans *tdmk* mə ˈkliːnz

McLehose ˈmæk ᵊl həʊz -lɪ-, -lə- ‖ -hoʊz

McLeish, MacLeish mə ˈkliːʃ mæk ˈliːʃ

McLennan mə ˈklen ən

Macleod, McLeod mə ˈklaʊd (!)

McLiammoir mə ˈkliəm ɔː ‖ -ˈkliː ə mɔːr

McLintock mə ˈklɪnt ɒk -ək ‖ -ɑːk

McLoughlin mə ˈklɒx lɪn -ˈklɒk-, -ˈɡlɒx-, §-lən ‖ -ˈklɑːk-

McLuhan mə ˈkluː‿ən

McLysaght mə ˈklaɪs ət -ə, -əkt

McMahon mək ˈmɑːn §mæk-, -ˈmɑː ən, -ˈmæ hən ‖ -ˈmæn

McManaman mək ˈmæn əm ən

McManus mək ˈmæn əs §mæk-, -ˈmɑːn-, -ˈmeɪn-

McMartin mək ˈmɑːt ɪn mæk-, §-ᵊn ‖ -ˈmɑːrt ᵊn

McMaster mək ˈmɑːst ə mæk-, §-ˈmæst- ‖ -ˈmæst ᵊr

McMenemey, McMenemy mək ˈmen əm i

McMichael mək ˈmaɪk ᵊl

Macmillan, McMillan mək ˈmɪl ən mæk-

McMullan, McMullen mək ˈmʌl ən

McMurdo mək ˈmɜːd əʊ ‖ -ˈmɜːd oʊ
McMurray mək ˈmʌr i ‖ -ˈmɜː i
McMurtry mək ˈmɜːtr i ‖ -ˈmɜːtr i
McNab mək ˈnæb §mæk-
McNaghten, McNaghton mək ˈnɔːt ᵊn mæk-
‖ -ˈnɑːt-
McNair mək ˈneə ‖ -ˈneᵊr
McNally mək ˈnæl i
Macnamara, McNamara ˌmæk nə ˈmɑːr ə
‖ ˈmæk nə ˌmær ə -ˌmer ə
McNamee ˌmæk nə ˈmiː
McNaughten, McNaughton mək ˈnɔːt ᵊn
mæk- ‖ -ˈnɑːt-
McNeice mək ˈniːs
McNeil mək ˈniːᵊl
McNeilage mək ˈniːl ɪdʒ
McNeill mək ˈniːᵊl
McNestry mək ˈnes tri
MacNugget *tdmk* mək ˈnʌg ɪt mæk-, §-ət ~**s** s
Macon *place in France; wine* ˈmɑːk ɒ̃ ˈmæk-,
-ɒn ‖ ˈmɑː ˈkoʊn —*Fr* Mâcon [mɑ kɔ̃]
Macon *place in Georgia* ˈmeɪk ən
Maconachie mə ˈkɒn ək i -əx i, -ə hi ‖ -ˈkɑːn-
Maconchy mə ˈkɒŋk i ‖ -ˈkɑːŋk i
Maconochie mə ˈkɒn ək i -əx- ‖ -ˈkɑːn-
McPhail mək ˈfeɪᵊl
McPhee mək ˈfiː
McPherson mək ˈfɜːs ᵊn mæk-, -ˈfɪəs- ‖ -ˈfɜːs ᵊn
McQuade mə ˈkweɪd
Macquarie, McQuarrie mə ˈkwɒr i
‖ -ˈkwɔːr i -ˈkwɑːr i
McQueen mə ˈkwiːn
McRae mə ˈkreɪ
macrame, macramé mə ˈkrɑːm i -eɪ
‖ ˈmæk rə meɪ *(*)*
Macready, McReady mə ˈkriːd i
macro ˈmæk rəʊ ‖ -roʊ ~**s** z
macro- *comb. form*
  with stress-neutral suffix ˌmæk rəʊ ‖ -roʊ
  — **macroclimatic** ˌmæk rəʊ klaɪ ˈmæt ɪk ◄
  ‖ ˌmæk roʊ klaɪ ˈmæt̬ ɪk ◄
  with stress-imposing suffix mæ ˈkrɒ +
  ‖ mæ ˈkrɑː+ — **macropterous**
  mæ ˈkrɒpt ər əs ‖ -ˈkrɑːpt-
macrobiotic ˌmæk rəʊ baɪ ˈɒt ɪk ◄ -bi-ˈ--
‖ -rə baɪ ˈɑːt̬ ɪk ◄ ~**ally** ᵊl̩_i ~**s** s
macrocarpa ˌmæk rəʊ ˈkɑːp ə ‖ -roʊ ˈkɑːrp ə
macrocosm ˈmækr əʊ ˌkɒz əm ‖ -ə ˌkɑːz əm
macroeconomic ˌmæk rəʊ ˌiːk ə ˈnɒm ɪk ◄
-ˌek- ‖ -roʊ ˌek ə ˈnɑːm- -ˌiːk- ~**s** s
macron ˈmæk rɒn ˈmeɪk-, -rən ‖ -rɑːn ~**s** z
macrophag|e ˈmæk rəʊ feɪdʒ ‖ -rə- —**es** ɪz əz
macroscopic ˌmækr əʊˈskɒp ɪk ◄ ‖ -oʊ ˈskɑːp-
Macrossan mə ˈkrɒs ᵊn ‖ -ˈkrɔːs- -ˈkrɑːs-
McShea mək ˈʃeɪ §mæk-
McSorley mək ˈsɔːl i ‖ -ˈsɔːrl i
McSwiney mək ˈswiːn i mæk-, -ˈswɪn-
McTaggart mək ˈtæg ət mæk- ‖ -ᵊrt
McTavish mək ˈtæv ɪʃ mæk-
McTeague mək ˈtiːg mæk-
McTeer mək ˈtɪə mæk-, mə- ‖ -ˈtɪᵊr

mac|ula ˈmæk |jʊl ə -jəl- ‖ -|jəl ə ~**ulae** ju liː
  jə- ‖ jə liː
  ˌmacula ˈlutea ˈluːt i_ə ‖ ˈluːt̬-
McVay, McVeagh, McVeigh, McVey
  mək ˈveɪ
McVicar mək ˈvɪk ə ‖ -ᵊr
McVitie, McVittie mək ˈvɪt i mæk- ‖ -ˈvɪt̬ i
McWhirter mək ˈwɜːt ə mæk-, -ˈhwɜːt-
  ‖ -ˈʰwɜːt̬ ᵊr
McWilliams mək ˈwɪl jəmz mæk-
Macy ˈmeɪs i **Macy's** *tdmk* ˈmeɪs iz
mad, Mad mæd **madder** ˈmæd ə ‖ -ᵊr
  maddest ˈmæd ɪst -əst
Madagascan ˌmæd ə ˈgæsk ən ◄ ~**s** z
Madagascar ˌmæd ə ˈgæsk ə ‖ -ᵊr
madam, Madam ˈmæd əm ~**s**, ~**'s** z
Madame, m~ ˈmæd əm ‖ mə ˈdɑːm, -ˈdæm
  —*Fr* [ma dam] ~**s**, ~**'s** z
Madang mə ˈdæŋ ‖ mɑː ˈdɑːŋ
madcap ˈmæd kæp →ˈmæg- ~**s** s
madden, M~ ˈmæd ᵊn ~**ed** d ~**ing/ly** ɪŋ /li ~**s**
  z
madder ˈmæd ə ‖ -ᵊr
Maddie ˈmæd i
madding ˈmæd ɪŋ
Maddison ˈmæd ɪs ən -əs-
Maddock ˈmæd ək
Maddocks, Maddox ˈmæd əks
made meɪd
Madeira mə ˈdɪər ə ‖ -ˈdɪr ə —*Port*
  [mɐ ˈdeɪ ɾɐ, ma ˈdeɪ ɾa]
  Maˈdeira cake
Madejski mə ˈdeɪsk i
Madeleine, m~ ˈmæd ᵊl ɪn §-ən; -ə leɪn,
  -ᵊl eɪn ~**s** z
Madeley ˈmeɪd li
Madeline ˈmæd əl ɪn §_ən —*formerly also*
  -ə laɪn
mademoiselle, M~ ˌmæd əm wə ˈzel ◄ -əˈ-;
  ˌmæm wə ˈzel —*Fr* [mad mwa zɛl, man-] ~**s**
  z
made-to-measure ˌmeɪd tə ˈmeʒ ə ◄ ‖ -ᵊr ◄
made-to-order ˌmeɪd tu ˈɔːd ə ◄ -tə-
  ‖ -ˈɔːrd ᵊr ◄
made-up ˌmeɪd ˈʌp
  ˌmade-up ˈstory
Madge mædʒ
mad|house ˈmæd |haʊs ~**houses** haʊz ɪz -əz
Madingley ˈmæd ɪŋ li
Madison ˈmæd ɪs ən -əs-
  ˌMadison ˈAvenue
Madley ˈmæd li
madly ˈmæd li
mad|man ˈmæd |mən →ˈmæb- ~**men** mən
  men
madness ˈmæd nəs -nɪs ~**es** ɪz əz
madonna, M~ mə ˈdɒn ə ‖ -ˈdɑːn ə —*It*
  [ma ˈdɔn na] ~**s**, ~**'s** z
madras *'cotton'* ˈmædr əs mə ˈdrɑːs -ˈdræs
Madras mə ˈdrɑːs -ˈdræs —*but the place in OR*
  is ˈmædr əs
madrasa, madrasah, madrassa mə ˈdræs ə
  ~**s** z

madrepore 'mædr ɪ pɔː -ə-, ˌ·'·ˌ ‖ -pɔːr -poʊr ~s z

Madrid mə 'drɪd —*Sp* [ma 'ðrið]

madrigal 'mædr ɪg ᵊl -əg- ~s z

madrilene, madrilène ˌmædr ɪ 'len -ə-, -'leɪn, '··· —*Fr* [ma dʁi lɛn] ~s z

madrona, madrone mə 'drəʊn ə ‖ -'droʊn ə ~s z

mad|woman 'mæd ˌwʊm ən ~women ˌwɪm ɪn -ən

Mae meɪ
 ˌMae 'West

Maecenas maɪ 'siːn æs miː-, -əs ‖ -əs

Maelor 'maɪl ɔː ‖ -ɔːr —*Welsh* ['məi lor, 'məi-]

maelstrom, M~ 'meɪᵊl strɒm -strəm, -strəʊm ‖ -strəm -strɑːm ~s z

maenad 'miːn æd ~s z

Maendy 'meɪnd i 'maɪnd- —*Welsh* ['məin di]

Maentwrog maɪn 'tʊər ɒg ‖ -'tʊr ɑːg —*Welsh* [məin 'tu rog, məi-n-]

Maerdy 'mɑːd i ‖ 'mɑːrd i —*but some places of this name have an alternative pronunciation* 'meɪ əd i ‖ -ᵊrd i *or* 'maɪ əd i ‖ 'maɪᵊrd i

Maersk, Mærsk meəsk ‖ meᵊrsk

Maesteg ˌmaɪs 'teɪg —*Welsh* [mais 'teːg, maːs-]

maestoso maɪ 'stəʊs əʊ -'stəʊz- ‖ -'stoʊs oʊ -'stoʊz- —*It* [ma es 'toː so]

maestro 'maɪs trəʊ ‖ -troʊ —*It* [ma 'ɛs tro, -'es-] ~s z

Maeterlinck 'meɪt ə lɪŋk ‖ 'meɪt ᵊr- —*Fr* [mɛ tɛʁ lɛ̃ːk]

Maev, Maeve meɪv

Mafeking 'mæf ɪk ɪŋ -ək-

maffia, mafia, Mafia 'mæf i ə 'mɑːf- ‖ 'mɑːf- 'mæf-

mafios|o ˌmæf i 'əʊs |əʊ ˌmɑːf-, -'əʊz- ‖ ˌmɑːf i 'oʊs |oʊ ˌmæf-, -'oʊz- ~i iː

mag mæg **mags** mægz

Magarshack 'mæg ə ʃæk ‖ -ᵊr-

magazine ˌmæg ə 'ziːn '···‖ 'mæg ə ziːn ˌ·'· ~s z

Magda 'mægd ə

Magdala 'mægd əl ə mæg 'dɑːl ə

Magdalen 'mægd əl ɪn -ən —*but the Oxford college is* 'mɔːd lɪn, -lən ‖ 'mɔːd-, 'mɑːd-

Magdalene ˌmægd ə 'liːn i 'mægd ə liːn, -lɪn —*but the Cambridge college is* 'mɔːd lɪn, -lən ‖ 'mɔːd-, 'mɑːd-

Magdalenian ˌmægd ə 'liːn i ən ◄

mage meɪdʒ **mages** 'meɪdʒ ɪz -əz

Magee mə 'giː

Magellan mə 'gel ən -'dʒel- ‖ -'dʒel ən

Magellanic ˌmæg ɪ 'læn ɪk ◄ ˌmædʒ-, -ə- ‖ ˌmædʒ-
 ˌMagelˌlanic 'cloud

magenta, M~ mə 'dʒent ə ‖ -'dʒenţ ə

Maggie, m~ 'mæg i

maggot 'mæg ət ~s s

maggoty 'mæg ət i ‖ -əţ i

Maggs mægz

Maghera ˌmæk ə 'rɑː ˌmæ hə-

Magherafelt ˌmæk ər ə 'felt ˌmæ hərˌ

Maghreb 'mɑːg reb 'mæg-, 'mʌg-, -rɪb, -rəb; mɑː 'greb, mə-

Maghull mə 'gʌl

magi, Magi 'meɪdʒ aɪ 'meɪg-

magic 'mædʒ ɪk ~ked t ~king ɪŋ ~s s
 ˌmagic 'carpet; ˌmagic 'eye; ˌmagic 'lantern; ˌMagic 'Marker *tdmk*; ˌmagic 'square; ˌmagic 'wand

magical 'mædʒ ɪk ᵊl ~ly i

magician mə 'dʒɪʃ ᵊn ~s z

Magilligan mə 'gɪl ɪg ən

Maginnis mə 'gɪn ɪs §-əs

Maginot 'mæʒ ɪ nəʊ 'mædʒ-, -ə- ‖ -noʊ —*Fr* [ma ʒi 'no]
 'Maginot Line

magisteri|al ˌmædʒ ɪ 'stɪər i |əl ◄ ˌ·ə- ‖ -'stɪr- ~ally ᵊl̩ i ~um əm

magistrac|y 'mædʒ ɪs trəs |i '·əs- ~ies iz

magistral 'mædʒ ɪs trəl -əs-; mə 'dʒɪs-, mæ-

magistrate 'mædʒ ɪ streɪt -ə-; -əs trət, -trɪt ~s s

maglev, M~ 'mæg lev

mag|ma 'mæg |mə ~mas məz ~mata mət ə ‖ -məţ ə

Magna, magna 'mæg nə
 ˌMagna 'Carta, ˌMagna 'Charta 'kɑːt ə ‖ -'kɑːrţ ə

magna cum laude ˌmæg nə kʊm 'laʊd eɪ ˌ·nɑː-

magnanimity ˌmæg nə 'nɪm ət i -ɪt i ‖ -əţ i

magnanimous mæg 'næn ɪm əs məg-, -əm- ~ly li ~ness nəs nɪs

magnate 'mæg neɪt -nət, -nɪt ~s s

magnesia, M~ mæg 'niːʃ ə məg-, -'niːs i ə, -'niːʒ ə, -'niːz i ə

magnesite 'mæg nɪ saɪt -nə-

magnesium mæg 'niːz i əm məg-, -'niːʒ əm, -'niːs i əm, -'niːʃ əm
 magˌnesium hy'droxide

magnet 'mæg nɪt -nət ~s s

magnetic mæg 'net ɪk məg- ‖ -'neţ ɪk ~ally ᵊl̩ i
 magˌnetic 'field; magˌnetic 'north; magˌnetic 'pole; magˌnetic 'tape

magnetis... —*see* **magnetiz...**

magnetism 'mæg nə ˌtɪz əm -nɪ-

magnetite 'mæg nə taɪt -nɪ-

magnetization ˌmæg nət aɪ 'zeɪʃ ᵊn ˌ·nɪt-, -ɪ'·- ‖ -nət ə- ~s z

magnetiz|e 'mæg nə taɪz -nɪ- ~ed d ~es ɪz əz ~ing ɪŋ

magneto mæg 'niːt əʊ məg- ‖ -'niːţ oʊ ~s z

magneto- *comb. form*
 with stress-neutral suffix mæg ˌniːt əʊ ‖ -ˌniːţ ə — **magnetosphere** mæg 'niːt əʊ sfɪə ‖ -'niːţ ə sfɪr
 with stress-imposing suffix ˌmæg nə 'tɒ+ -nɪ- ‖ -'tɑː+ — **magnetometer** ˌmæg nə 'tɒm ɪt ə ˌ·nɪ-, -ət ə ‖ -'tɑːm əţ ᵊr

magnetron 'mæg nə trɒn -nɪ- ‖ -trɑːn ~s z

Magnificat mæg 'nɪf ɪ kæt məg-, -ə- ~s s

magnification ˌmæg nɪf ɪ ˈkeɪʃ ᵊn ˌ-nəf-, §-ə'-- ~s z

magnificence mæg ˈnɪf ɪs ənᵗs məg-, -əs-

magnificent mæg ˈnɪf ɪs ənt məg-, -əs- ~ly li

magnifico mæg ˈnɪf ɪ kəʊ §-ə- ‖ -koʊ ~s z

magnifier ˈmæg nɪ faɪ̯ə ˈ·nə- ‖ -faɪ̯ᵊr ~s z

magni|fy ˈmæg nɪ |faɪ -nə- ~**fied** faɪd ~**fies** faɪz ~**fying** faɪ ɪŋ

  ˈmagnifying glass

magniloquence mæg ˈnɪl ək wənᵗs

magniloquent mæg ˈnɪl ək wənt ~ly li

magnitude ˈmæg nɪ tjuːd -nə-, →-tʃuːd ‖ -tuːd -tjuːd ~s z

magnolia, M~ mæg ˈnəʊl i̯ə məg- ‖ -ˈnoʊl- ~s z

Magnox, m~ ˈmæg nɒks ‖ -nɑːks

magnum ˈmæg nəm ~s z

  ˌmagnum ˈopus

Magnus ˈmæg nəs

  ˈMagnus hitch

Magnusson ˈmæg nəs ən

Magog ˈmeɪ gɒg ‖ -gɑːg

Magoo mə ˈguː

magpie ˈmæg paɪ ~s z

Magrath mə ˈgrɑː -ˈgrɑːθ, -ˈgræθ

Magraw mə ˈgrɔː ‖ -ˈgrɑː

Magri ˈmæg ri

Magritte mæ ˈgriːt mə- ‖ mɑː- —*Fr* [ma gʁit]

Magruder mə ˈgruːd ə ‖ -ᵊr

magstripe ˈmæg straɪp ~s s

maguey mə ˈgeɪ ˈmæg weɪ

Maguire mə ˈgwaɪ̯ə ‖ -ˈgwaɪ̯ᵊr

magus, Magus ˈmeɪg əs **magi, Magi** ˈmeɪdʒ aɪ ˈmeɪg-

Magwitch ˈmæg wɪtʃ

Magyar ˈmæg jɑː ‖ -jɑːr ~s z —*Hung* [ˈmɒ jɒr]

Mahabharata mə ˌhɑː ˈbɑːr ət ə ˌmɑː hə-, ˌmæ hə-,-ˈbær- —*Hindi* [mə ha: bʱa: rət]

Mahaffy mə ˈhæf i

Mahalia mə ˈheɪl i̯ə

maharaja, maharajah ˌmɑː hə ˈrɑːdʒ ə -ə- —*Hindi* [mə ha: ra: dʒa:, ma:-] ~s z

maharanee, maharani ˌmɑː hə ˈrɑːn i -ə- —*Hindi* [mə ha: ra: ni, ma:-] ~s z

Maharashtra ˌmɑː hə ˈræʃ trə -ə-, -ˈrɑːʃ- —*Hindi* [mə ha: raʃtr]

Maharishi ˌmɑː hə ˈrɪʃ i -ə- —*Hindi* [mə hər ʃi]

Mahathir ˌmæ hə ˈtɪə ˌmɑː- ‖ ˌmɑː hə ˈtɪᵊr

mahatma, M~ mə ˈhɑːt mə -ˈhæt- —*Hindi* [mə ha:ṭ ma:] ~s z

Mahayana ˌmɑː hə ˈjɑːn ə mə ˌhɑːˑ·· —*Hindi* [mə ha: jən]

Mahdi ˈmɑːd i -iː

Mahé ˈmɑː eɪ -heɪ —*Fr* [ma e]

Maher *(i)* mɑː ‖ mɑːr, *(ii)* ˈmeɪ ə ‖ ᵊr

Mahfouz mɑː ˈfuːz —*Arabic* [mah ˈfuːzˤ]

mah-jong, mah-jongg ˌmɑː ˈdʒɒŋ ‖ -ˈʒɑːŋ -ˈdʒɑːŋ, -ˈʒɔːŋ, -ˈdʒɔːŋ; ˈ··

Mahler ˈmɑːl ə ‖ -ᵊr —*Ger* [ˈmaː lɐ]

mahlstick ˈmɔːl stɪk ‖ ˈmɑːl- ˈmɔːl- ~s s

Mahmud mɑː ˈmuːd

mahoe ˈmɑː həʊ i ‖ mə ˈhoʊ ˈmɑː hoʊ

mahogan|y mə ˈhɒg ən |i ‖ -ˈhɑːg- ~**ies** iz

Mahomet mə ˈhɒm ɪt -et, §-ət ‖ -ˈhɑːm-

Mahommed mə ˈhɒm ɪd -ed, §-ət ‖ -ˈhɑːm-

Mahommedan mə ˈhɒm ɪd ən -əd- ‖ -ˈhɑːm- ~s z

Mahon *family name* mɑːn ˈmæ hən ‖ mæn

Mahoney, Mahony *(i)* ˈmɑː ən i, *(ii)* mə ˈhəʊn i ‖ -ˈhoʊn i

mahonia mə ˈhəʊn i̯ə ‖ -ˈhoʊn- ~s z

Mahood mə ˈhʊd

mahout mə ˈhaʊt mɑː-, -ˈhuːt ~s s

Mai *(i)* meɪ, *(ii)* maɪ

Maia ˈmaɪ̯ə ˈmeɪ ə

maid meɪd *(= made)* **maids** meɪdz

  ˌMaid ˈMarian

Maida ˈmeɪd ə

maidan maɪ ˈdɑːn mæ- ~s z

maiden, M~ ˈmeɪd ᵊn ~s z

  ˈmaiden name; ˌmaid of ˈhonour; ˌmaiden ˈover

maidenhair ˈmeɪd ᵊn heə ‖ -her -hær

maidenhead, M~ ˈmeɪd ᵊn hed ~s z

maidenhood ˈmeɪd ᵊn hʊd

maiden|ly ˈmeɪd ᵊn |li ~**liness** li nəs -nɪs

Maidment ˈmeɪd mənt →ˈmeɪb-

maidservant ˈmeɪd ˌsɜːv ᵊnt ‖ -ˌsɜːv- ~s s

Maidstone ˈmeɪd stən -stəʊn ‖ -stoʊn

maieutic meɪ ˈjuːt ɪk maɪ- ‖ -ˈjuːt̬-

maigre ˈmeɪg ə ‖ -ᵊr

Maigret ˈmeɪg reɪ ‖ ˌmeɪ ˈgreɪ —*Fr* [mɛ gʁɛ]

mail meᵊl *(= male)* **mailed** meᵊld **mailing** ˈmeᵊl ɪŋ **mails** meᵊlz

  ˈmailing list; ˌmail ˈorder◂; ˈmail train

mailbag ˈmeᵊl bæg ~s z

mailbomb ˈmeᵊl bɒm ‖ -bɑːm ~s z

mailbox ˈmeᵊl bɒks ‖ -bɑːks ~**es** ɪz əz

Mailer ˈmeɪl ə ‖ -ᵊr

Mailgram *tdmk* ˈmeᵊl græm ~s z

mail|man ˈmeᵊl |mæn ~**men** men

mailshot ˈmeᵊl ʃɒt ‖ -ʃɑːt ~s s

maim meɪm **maimed** meɪmd **maiming** ˈmeɪm ɪŋ **maims** meɪmz

Maimonides maɪ ˈmɒn ɪ diːz -ə- ‖ -ˈmɑːn-

main meɪn **mains** meɪnz

  ˌmain ˈchance; ˌmain ˈclause; ˌmain ˈdrag; ˌmain ˈline◂; ˈMain Street; ˌmain ˈverb

Main *river in Germany* maɪn meɪn —*Ger* [main]

Maine meɪn

mainframe ˈmeɪn freɪm ~s z

Maingay ˈmeɪn geɪ →ˈmeɪŋ-

mainland ˈmeɪn lənd -lænd

mainlin|e ˈmeɪn laɪn ˌ·ˈ· ~**ed** d ~**er/s** ə/z ‖ ᵊr/z ~**es** z ~**ing** ɪŋ

mainly ˈmeɪn li

mainmast ˈmeɪn mɑːst →ˈmeɪm-, §-mæst, -məst ‖ -mæst —*naut* -məst ~s s

mainsail ˈmeɪn seᵊl -sᵊl —*naut* -sᵊl ~s z

mainspring ˈmeɪn sprɪŋ ~s z

mainstay ˈmeɪn steɪ ~s z

mainstream ˈmeɪn striːm

M

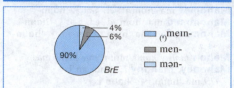

MAINTAIN

4%
6%
90%
(ˌ)meɪn-
men-
mən-

BrE

maintain (ˌ)meɪn ˈteɪn men-, mən-
— *Preference poll, BrE:* (ˌ)meɪn- *90%,* men-
6%, mən- *4%.* **~ed** d **~ing** ɪŋ **~s** z
maintenance ˈmeɪnt ən ən ˈs -ɪn-;
△(ˌ)meɪn ˈteɪn- ‖ -ᵊn
  ˈmaintenance ˌorder
Mainwaring *(i)* ˈmæn ər ɪŋ, *(ii)*
  ˈmeɪn ˌweər ɪŋ -wər-; ˌ·ˈ·· ‖ -ˌwer-
Mainz maɪnts —*Ger* [maɪnts]
Mair ˈmaɪ ə ‖ ˈmaɪ ᵊr —*Welsh* [maɪr] —*but as*
  a family name, meə ‖ meᵊr
Maire ˈmær i ‖ ˈmer- —*but as a family name,*
  meə ‖ meᵊr
Mairead mə ˈreɪd
Maisie ˈmeɪz i
maisonette, maisonnette ˌmeɪz ə ˈnet
  ˌmeɪs-, -ᵊn ˈet **~s** s
Maitland ˈmeɪt lənd
maitre d', maître d' ˌmeɪtr ə ˈdiː ˌmetr-
  ‖ ˌmeɪt ᵊr- **~s** z
maitre d'hotel, maître d'hôtel
  ˌmeɪtr ə dəʊ ˈtel ◄ ˌmetr- ‖ -doʊ ˈtel ˌmeɪt ᵊr-
  —*Fr* [mɛ tʁə do tɛl] **maitres d'hotel,**
  maîtres d'hôtel ˌmeɪtr əz- ˌmetr əz-
  ‖ ˌmeɪt ᵊrz-
maize meɪz *(= maze)*
majestic, M~ mə ˈdʒest ɪk **~al** ᵊl **~ally** ᵊl i
majest|y, M~ ˈmædʒ əst |i -ɪst- **~ies** iz
majolica mə ˈdʒɒl ɪk ə -ˈjɒl- ‖ -ˈdʒɑːl-
major, Major ˈmeɪdʒ ə ‖ -ᵊr **~ed** d **majoring**
  ˈmeɪdʒ ər ɪŋ **~s** z
  ˌmajor ˈgeneral◄; ˌmajor ˈkey; ˌmajor
  ˈleague◄; ˌmajor ˈsuit
Majorc|a mə ˈjɔːk |ə maɪ ˈɔːk-, mə ˈdʒɔːk-
  ‖ -ˈjɔːrk |ə -ˈdʒɔːrk ə —*Sp* Mallorca
  [ma ˈʎor ka, -ˈjor-] **~an/s** ən/z
majordomo ˌmeɪdʒ ə ˈdəʊm əʊ
  ‖ -ᵊr ˈdoʊm oʊ **~s** z
majorette ˌmeɪdʒ ə ˈret **~s** s
majoritarian mə ˌdʒɒr ɪ ˈteər i ən ◄ -ˌə-
  ‖ -ˌdʒɔːr ə ˈter- -ˌdʒɑːr- **~s** z
majorit|y mə ˈdʒɒr ət |i -ɪt- ‖ -ˈdʒɔːr ət |i
  -ˈdʒɑːr- **~ies** iz
  maˈjority ˌleader
majorly ˈmeɪdʒ ə li ‖ -ᵊr-
Majuro mə ˈdʒʊər əʊ ‖ mə ˈdʒʊr oʊ
majuscule ˈmædʒ ə skjuːl ‖ mə ˈdʒʌsk juːl **~s** z
Makarios mə ˈkɑːr i ɒs -ˈkær- ‖ -oʊs -ɑːs, əs
Makaton *tdmk* ˈmæk ə tɒn ˈmɑːk- ‖ -tɑːn -toʊn
make meɪk **made** meɪd **makes** meɪks **making**
  ˈmeɪk ɪŋ
make-believe ˈmeɪk bɪ ˌliːv -bə-, -§biː-, ˌ·ˈ·
make-or-break ˌmeɪk ɔː ˈbreɪk ◄ ‖ -ᵊr-

makeover ˈmeɪk ˌəʊv ə ‖ -ˌoʊv ᵊr **~s** z
Makepeace ˈmeɪk piːs
maker, Maker ˈmeɪk ə ‖ -ᵊr **~s** z
Makerere mə ˈker ər i
makeshift ˈmeɪk ʃɪft
make-up ˈmeɪk ʌp **~s** s
makeweight ˈmeɪk weɪt **~s** s
make-work ˈmeɪk wɜːk ‖ -wɜːk
making ˈmeɪk ɪŋ **~s** z
-making ˌmeɪk ɪŋ — **sick-making**
  ˈsɪk ˌmeɪk ɪŋ
Makins ˈmeɪk ɪnz §-ənz
mako ˈmɑːk əʊ ˈmeɪk- ‖ -oʊ **~s** z
mal- mæl — **maladaptive** ˌmæl ə ˈdæpt ɪv ◄
Malabar ˈmæl ə bɑː ˌ··ˈ·◄ ‖ -bɑːr
malacca, M~ mə ˈlæk ə ‖ -ˈlɑːk ə **~s** z
Malachi ˈmæl ə kaɪ
malachite ˈmæl ə kaɪt
Malachy ˈmæl ək i
maladi... —*see* **malady**
maladjust|ed ˌmæl ə ˈdʒʌst |ɪd ◄ -əd **~ment**
  mənt
maladministration ˌmæl əd ˌmɪn ɪ ˈstreɪʃ ᵊn
  ˌæd-, -ə-ˈ--
maladroit ˌmæl ə ˈdrɔɪt ◄ **~ly** li **~ness** nəs nɪs
malad|y ˈmæl əd |i **~ies** iz
Malaga ˈmæl əg ə —*Sp* Málaga [ˈma la ɣa]
Malagasy ˌmæl ə ˈgæs i ◄ -ˈgɑːz i
Malahide ˈmæl ə haɪd
malaise mæ ˈleɪz mə-
Malamud ˈmæl ə mʊd
malamute ˈmæl ə mjuːt -muːt **~s** s
Malaprop, m~ ˈmæl ə prɒp ‖ -prɑːp
malapropism ˈmæl ə prɒp ˌɪz əm ‖ ˈ·ˌprɑːp-
  ~s z
malapropos ˌmæl ˌæp rə ˈpəʊ ˌ·ˈ··· ‖ -ˈpoʊ
malar ˈmeɪl ə ‖ -ᵊr
malaria mə ˈleər i ə ‖ -ˈler-
malari|al mə ˈleər i |əl ‖ -ˈler- **~ous** əs
malarkey, malarky mə ˈlɑːk i ‖ -ˈlɑːrk i
Malathion *tdmk* ˌmæl ə ˈθaɪ ən
Malawi, Malawì i mə ˈlɑː wi **~an/s** ən/z
Malay mə ˈleɪ ‖ ˈmeɪ leɪ mə ˈleɪ **~s** z
Malaya mə ˈleɪ ə
Malayalam ˌmæl eɪ ˈɑːl əm ◄ -i-, -ə ˈjɑːl-
Malayan mə ˈleɪ ən **~s** z
Malayo-Polynesian
  mə ˌleɪ əʊ ˌpɒl i ˈniːz i ən -ˈniːʒ-, -ˈniːʒ ᵊn
  ‖ -oʊ ˌpɑːl ə ˈniːʒ ᵊn -ˈniːʃ ᵊn
Malaysia mə ˈleɪz i ə -ˈleɪʒ-, -ˈleɪʒ ə
  ‖ mə ˈleɪʒ ə -ˈleɪʃ ə
Malaysian mə ˈleɪz i ən -ˈleɪʒ-, -ˈleɪʒ ᵊn
  ‖ mə ˈleɪʒ ᵊn -ˈleɪʃ ᵊn **~s** z
Malcolm ˈmælk əm —*rarely also* ˈmɔːlk-
malcontent ˈmæl kən ˌtent §-kɒn-
  ‖ ˌmæl kən ˈtent **~s** s
malcontented ˌmæl kən ˈtent ɪd ◄ §-kɒn-, -əd
  ‖ -ˈtenṯ əd ◄
mal de mer ˌmæl də ˈmeə ‖ -ˈmeᵊr —*Fr*
  [mal də mɛːʁ]
Malden ˈmɔːld ən ˈmɒld- ‖ ˈmɑːld-
Maldive ˈmɔːld iːv ˈmɒld-, ˈmɑːld-, -ɪv, -aɪv
  ‖ ˈmɑːld-, ˈmæld- **~s** z

M

Maldivian mɔːl ˈdɪv i ən mɒl-, maːl- ‖ maːl-,
mæl- **~s** z
Maldon ˈmɔːld ən ˈmɒld- ‖ ˈmaːld-
Maldwyn (i) ˈmæld wɪn, (ii) ˈmɔːld- ˈmɒld-
‖ ˈmaːld-
male, Male meɪəl **males** meɪəlz
ˌmale ˈchauvinist◄, ˌmale ˌchauvinist ˈpig
Male, Malé capital of Maldives ˈmaːl eɪ
malediction ˌmæl ɪ ˈdɪk ʃən -ə- **~s** z
male-dominated ˌmeɪəl ˈdɒm ɪ neɪt ɪd ◄ -ˈə-
‖ -ˈdaːm ə neɪt-
malefactor ˈmæl ɪ fækt ə ˈ·ə- ‖ -ər **~s** z
malefic mə ˈlef ɪk
malefic|ence mə ˈlef ɪs |ənˈs mæ-, §-əs- **~ent**
ənt
maleic mə ˈleɪ ɪk -ˈliː-
maleness ˈmeɪəl nəs -nɪs
Malet ˈmæl ɪt -ət
male-voice ˈmeɪəl vɔɪs
malevolence mə ˈlev əl ənˈs mæ-
malevolent mə ˈlev əl ənt mæ- **~ly** li
malfeasance (ˌ)mæl ˈfiːz ənˈts
Malfi ˈmælf i
malformation ˌmæl fɔː ˈmeɪʃ ən -fə- ‖ -fɔːr-
-fˀr- **~s** z
malformed ˌmæl ˈfɔːmd ◄ ‖ -ˈfɔːrmd ◄
malfunction ˌmæl ˈfʌŋk ʃən **~ed** d **~ing** ɪŋ **~s**
z
Malham ˈmæl əm
Malhotra məl ˈhəʊtr ə ‖ -ˈhoʊtr-
Mali ˈmaːl i
Malian ˈmaːl i ən **~s** z
Malibu ˈmæl ɪ buː -ə-
malic ˈmæl ɪk ˈmeɪl-
malice ˈmæl ɪs §-əs-
malicious mə ˈlɪʃ əs **~ly** li **~ness** nəs nɪs
malign mə ˈlaɪn **~ed** d **~ing** ɪŋ **~ly** li **~s** z
malignanc|y mə ˈlɪg nənˈts |i **~ies** iz
malignant mə ˈlɪg nənt **~ly** li
maligner mə ˈlaɪn ə ‖ -ər **~s** z
malignit|y mə ˈlɪg nət |i -nɪt- ‖ -nət |i **~ies** iz
Malik ˈmæl ɪk
Malin ˈmæl ɪn §-ən
malinger mə ˈlɪŋ gə ‖ -gˀr **~ed** d **malingering**
mə ˈlɪŋ gər ɪŋ **~s** z
malingerer mə ˈlɪŋ gər ə ‖ -gˀr ər
Malinowski ˌmæl ɪ ˈnɒf ski -ə- ‖ -ˈnaːf- -ˈnɔːf-
malkin, M~ ˈmɔːk ɪn ˈmɔːlk-, ˈmɒlk-, §-ən
‖ ˈmaːk-, ˈmælk- **~s** z
mall, Mall mɔːl mæl, mɒl ‖ maːl — Preference
poll, BrE, in the sense 'shopping centre': mɔːl
50% (born since 1973: 76%), mæl 50%.
Several respondents voted for mɒl, not an
option offered. Always mæl in the London
place names The Mall, Chiswick Mall, Pall
Mall. **malls** mɔːlz mælz ‖ maːlz
Mallaig ˈmæl eɪg
Mallalieu ˈmæl ə ljuː -ljɔː, -luː ‖ -luː
Mallam ˈmæl əm
mallard ˈmæl aːd -əd ‖ -ˀrd **~s** z
Mallarmé ˈmæl aː meɪ ‖ ˌmæl aːr ˈmeɪ —Fr
[ma laʁ me]
malleability ˌmæl i ə ˈbɪl ət i -ɪt i ‖ -əṱ i

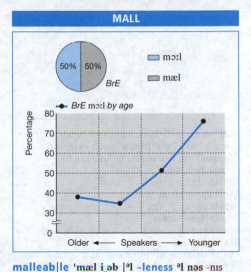

MALL

50% / 50% BrE
☐ mɔːl
☐ mæl

BrE mɔːl by age

Percentage (vertical axis: 0, 30, 40, 50, 60, 70, 80)
Older ←— Speakers —→ Younger

malleab|le ˈmæl i əb |əl ~**leness** əl nəs -nɪs
~ly li
mallee ˈmæl i **~s** z
mallei ˈmæl i aɪ
malle|olus mə ˈliːˌ|əl əs **~oli** ə laɪ
Malleson ˈmæl ɪs ən -əs-
mallet ˈmæl ɪt -ət **~s** s
Mallet, Mallett ˈmæl ɪt -ət
malle|us ˈmæl i|əs **~i** aɪ
Malling places in Kent ˈmɔːl ɪŋ ‖ ˈmaːl-
—Occasionally also, inappropriately, ˈmæl-
Mallinson ˈmæl ɪn sən -ən-
Mallorca mə ˈjɔːk ə məl- ‖ -ˈjɔːrk ə
Mallory ˈmæl ər i
mallow, M~ ˈmæl əʊ ‖ -oʊ **~s** z
mall-rat ˈmɔːl ræt ‖ ˈmaːl- **~s** s
Malmesbury ˈmaːmz bər i §ˈmɒlmz- ‖ -ˌber i
Malmo, Malmö, Malmoe ˈmælm əʊ ‖ -oʊ
—Swed Malmö [ˈˈmalm ø:]
malmsey ˈmaːmz i §ˈmɒlmz-
malnourished ˌmæl ˈnʌr ɪʃt ◄ ‖ -ˈnɜː-
malnutrition ˌmæl nju ˈtrɪʃ ən ‖ -nuː- -nju-
malodorous mæl ˈəʊd ər əs ‖ -ˈoʊd- **~ly** li
~ness nəs nɪs
Malone mə ˈləʊn ‖ -ˈloʊn
Malory ˈmæl ər i
Malpas (i) ˈmɔːlp əs ˈmɔːp- ‖ ˈmaːlp-,
(ii) ˈməʊp əs ‖ ˈmoʊp-, (iii) ˈmælp əs —The
place in Cheshire is (i) or (iii), that in
Cornwall (ii), that in Gwent (iii); the family
name is usually (iii).
Malpighi mæl ˈpiːg i —It [mal ˈpiː gi]
Malpighian mæl ˈpɪg i ən -ˈpiːg-
Malplaquet ˈmæl plə keɪ ˌ·ˈ· —Fr
[mal pla kɛ]
malpractice ˌmæl ˈprækt ɪs §-əs, ˈ·ˌ··
— Preference poll, AmE: ˌ·ˈ·· 75%, ˈ·ˌ·· 25%.
See chart on p.486.
ˌmalˈpractice inˌsurance
Malraux ˌmæl ˈrəʊ ‖ -ˈroʊ ˌmaːl- —Fr
[mal ʁo]

MALPRACTICE

75% 25%

AmE

malt mɔːlt mɒlt ‖ mɑːlt **malted** 'mɔːlt ɪd 'mɒlt,
-əd ‖ 'mɑːlt- **malting/s** 'mɔːlt ɪŋ/z 'mɒlt-
‖ 'mɑːlt- **malts** mɔːlts mɒlts ‖ mɑːlts
,malted 'milk
Malta 'mɔːlt ə 'mɒlt- ‖ 'mɑːlt-
Maltby 'mɔːlt bi 'mɒlt- ‖ 'mɑːlt-
Maltese ˌmɔːl 'tiːz ◄ ˌmɒl- ‖ ˌmɑːl-, -'tiːs ◄
,Maltese 'cross
Malteser *tdmk* mɔːl 'tiːz ə mɒl- ‖ -ᵊr mɑːl- **~s** z
Malthus 'mælθ əs
Malthusian mæl 'θjuːz iˌən mɔːl-, mɒl-, -'θuːz-
‖ -'θuːʒ ᵊn mɔːl-, mɑːl- **~s** z
Malton 'mɔːlt ən 'mɒlt- ‖ 'mɑːlt-
Maltravers mæl 'træv əz ‖ -ᵊrz
mal|treat ˌmæl |'triːt **~treated** 'triːt ɪd -əd
‖ 'triːʈ əd **~treating** 'triːt ɪŋ ‖ 'triːʈ ɪŋ
~treatment 'triːt mənt **~treats** 'triːts
maltster 'mɔːlt stə 'mɒlt- ‖ -stᵊr 'mɑːlt- **~s** z
Malvern *(i)* 'mɔːlv ən 'mɔːv-, 'mɒlv- ‖ -ᵊrn
'mɑːlv-, *(ii)* 'mælv ən ‖ -ᵊrn —*In England (i),
in the US (ii).*
malversation ˌmæl vɜː 'seɪʃ ᵊn -və- ‖ -vᵊr-
Malvinas mæl 'viːn əz mɔːl-, mɒl- —*AmSp*
[mal 'βi nas, -nah]
Malvolio mæl 'vəʊl iˌəʊ ‖ -'voʊl iˌoʊ
malware 'mæl weə ‖ -wer
Malyon 'mæl jən
mam, Mam mæm **mams, Mam's** mæmz
mama, Mama mə 'mɑː 'mæm ə ‖ 'mɑːm ə *(*)*
~s, ~'s z
'Mama's boy
Mamaroneck mə 'mær ə nek ‖ -'mer-
mamba 'mæm bə ‖ 'mɑːm- 'mæm-, -bɑː **~s** z
mambo 'mæm bəʊ ‖ 'mɑːm boʊ **~ed** d **~es, ~s**
z **~ing** ɪŋ
Mameluke 'mæm ɪ luːk -ə-, -ljuːk
Mamet 'mæm ɪt -ət
Mamie 'meɪm i
mamm|a *'breast'* 'mæm |ə **~ae** iː
mamma, Mamma *'mother'* mə 'mɑː
‖ 'mɑːm ə **~s, ~'s** z
mammal 'mæm ᵊl **~s** z
mammalian mə 'meɪl iˌən mæ- **~s** z
mammar|y 'mæm ər |i **~ies** iz
'mammary gland
mammee mæ 'miː -'meɪ ‖ mɑː-
mammogram 'mæm ə græm **~s** z
mammography mæ 'mɒg rəf i ‖ -'mɑːg-
mammon, M~ 'mæm ən
mammoth 'mæm əθ **~s** s
mamm|y, Mammy 'mæm |i **~ies** iz
man, Man mæn **manned** mænd **manning**

'mæn ɪŋ **man's** mænz **men** men **men's**
menz
,man 'Friday; ,man in the 'moon; ,man in
the 'street; ,man 'jack; ,man of 'letters;
,man of 'straw
-man mən, mæn —*This suffix may be weak or
strong. (i) In most well-established formations,
written as one word, it is weak,* mən:
policeman pə 'liːs mən. *(ii) Where written
hyphenated or as two words, and in new
formations, it is usually strong,* mæn:
spaceman 'speɪs mæn. *Note* batman *'army
servant'* 'bæt mən, *but* Batman *(cartoon
character)* 'bæt mæn
mana 'mɑːn ə
man-about-town ˌmæn ə baʊt 'taʊn
men-about-town ˌmen-
manacl|e 'mæn ək ᵊl **~ed** d **~es** z **~ing** ɪŋ
manag|e 'mæn ɪdʒ -ədʒ **~ed** d **~es** ɪz əz **~ing**
ɪŋ
manageability ˌmæn ɪdʒ ə 'bɪl ət i ˌ-ədʒ-, -ɪt i
‖ -əʈ i
manageab|le 'mæn ɪdʒ əb |ᵊl '-ədʒ- **~ly** li
management 'mæn ɪdʒ mənt -ədʒ- **~s** s
manager 'mæn ɪdʒ ə -ədʒ- ‖ -ᵊr **~s** z
manageress ˌmæn ɪdʒ ə 'res ˌ-ədʒ-, '· · ·
‖ 'mæn ɪdʒ ər əs *(*)* **~es** ɪz əz
managerial ˌmæn ə 'dʒɪər iˌəl ◄ ‖ -'dʒɪr- **~ly** i
managership 'mæn ɪdʒ ə ʃɪp '-ədʒ- ‖ -ᵊr- **~s** s
Managua mə 'næg wə -'nɑːg- ‖ -'nɑːg- —*Sp*
[ma 'na ɣwa]
manana, mañana mæn 'jɑːn ə mən- ‖ mən-
mɑːn- —*Sp* [ma 'ɲa na]
Manasseh mə 'næs iˌ-ə ‖ -ə
man-at-arms ˌmæn ət 'ɑːmz ‖ -əʈ 'ɑːrmz
men-at-arms ˌmen-
manatee ˌmæn ə 'tiː ‖ 'mæn ə tiː **~s** z
man-bag 'mæn bæg **~s** z
-mancer ˌmæn⸲s ə ‖ -ᵊr — **necromancer**
'nek rə ˌmæn⸲s ə ‖ -ᵊr
Manchester 'mæntʃ ɪst ə -əst-; 'mæn ˌtʃest-
‖ -ᵊr
manchineel ˌmæntʃ ɪ 'niːᵊl -ə- **~s** z
Manchu ˌmæn 'tʃuː ◄ —*Chi* Mǎn Zhōu
[³man ¹tʂou]
Manchukuo ˌmæn tʃuː 'kwəʊ ‖ -'kwoʊ —*Chi*
Mǎn Zhōu Guó [³man ¹tʂou ²kwɔ]
Manchuri|a mæn 'tʃʊər iˌ|ə ‖ -'tʃʊr- **~an/s**
ən/z
manciple 'mæn⸲s ɪp ᵊl -əp- **~s** z
mancozeb 'mæŋk əʊ zeb ‖ -ə-
Mancunian mæn 'kjuːn iˌən →mæŋ- **~s** z
-mancy ˌmæn⸲s i — **necromancy**
'nek rə ˌmæn⸲s i
Manda 'mænd ə
mandala 'mænd əl ə 'mʌnd-; mæn 'dɑːl ə **~s** z
Mandalay ˌmænd ə 'leɪ ◄ -ᵊl 'eɪ; '· · ·
mandamus mæn 'deɪm əs **~es** ɪz əz
mandarin, M~ 'mænd ər ɪn §-ən,
ˌmænd ə 'rɪn **~s** z
,mandarin 'duck; ,mandarin 'orange
mandarinate 'mænd⸲ər ɪ neɪt ər ə- **~s** s

mandatar|y 'mænd ət̬‿ər |i '‧ɪt̬‿,
mæn 'deɪt ər |i ‖ -ə ter |i ~**ies** iz

mand|ate *v* ˌmæn 'd|eɪt 'mænd |eɪt
‖ 'mænd |eɪt ~**ated** eɪt ɪd -əd ‖ eɪt̬ əd ~**ates**
eɪts ~**ating** eɪt ɪŋ ‖ eɪt̬ ɪŋ

mandate *n* 'mænd eɪt -ɪt, -ət ~**s** s

mandator|y 'mænd ət̬‿ər |i '‧ɪt̬‿,
mæn 'deɪt ər |i ‖ -ə tɔːr |i -toʊr i ~**ies** iz

man-day 'mæn deɪ ‚·‧ ~**s** z

Mande 'mænd eɪ 'mɑːnd- ‖ 'mɑːnd eɪ
mɑːn 'deɪ ~**s** z

Mandela mæn 'del ə -'deɪl- —*Xhosa*
[ma 'ndɛː la]

Mandelbaum 'mænd ᵊl baʊm

Mandelbrot 'mænd ᵊl brəʊt ‖ 'mɑːnd ᵊl broʊt
'mænd-

Mandelson 'mænd ᵊl sən

Mandelstam 'mænd ᵊl stæm -stəm

Mandeville 'mænd ə vɪl -ɪ-

mandible 'mænd ɪb ᵊl -əb- ~**s** z

Mandingo mæn 'dɪŋ gəʊ ‖ -goʊ ~**s** z

mandolin, mandoline ˌmænd ə 'lɪn -ᵊl 'ɪn;
'mænd ᵊl ɪn, §-ən ~**s** z

mandorla mæn 'dɔːl ə ‖ -'dɔːrl ə ~**s** z

mandragora mæn 'dræg ər ə

mandrake 'mændr eɪk ~**s** s

mandrax, M~ *tdmk* 'mændr æks ~**es** ɪz əz

mandrel, mandril 'mændr əl -ɪl ~**s** z

mandrill 'mændr ɪl -əl ~**s** z

Mandy 'mænd i

mane meɪn (= *main*) **maned** meɪnd **manes**
meɪnz

Manea 'meɪn i

man-eat|er 'mæn ‚iːt |ə ‖ -‚iːt̬ |ᵊr ~**ers** əz ‖ ᵊrz
~**ing** ɪŋ

maneb 'mæn eb

maneg|e, manèg|e mæ 'neɪʒ -'neʒ —*Fr*
[ma nɛːʒ] ~**es** ɪz əz

manes, Manes *'shades of the dead'* 'mɑːn eɪz
-eɪs; 'meɪn iːz

Manet 'mæn eɪ ‖ mæ 'neɪ mə- —*Fr* [ma nɛ]
~**s**, ~**'s** z

maneuvrability, maneuverability
mə ˌnuːv ər‿ə 'bɪl ət i -ɪt i ‖ -ət̬ i

maneuvrable, maneuverable
mə 'nuːv ər‿əb ᵊl

maneuv|re, maneuv|er mə 'nuːv |ə ‖ -|ᵊr
~**ered, ~red** əd ‖ ᵊrd ~**ering, ~ring** ər‿ɪŋ
~**ers, ~res** əz ‖ ᵊrz

Manfred 'mæn frɪd -frəd, -fred

manful 'mæn fᵊl -fʊl ~**ly** i ~**ness** nəs nɪs

manga 'mæŋ gə ‖ 'mɑːŋ- —*Jp* [ma‚ŋ ŋa]

mangabey 'mæŋ gə beɪ -biː ~**s** z

manganate 'mæŋ gə neɪt ~**s** s

manganese 'mæŋ gə niːz ‚·‧‚·‧ ‖ -niːs

manganic mæn 'gæn ɪk →mæŋ-

manganous 'mæŋ gən əs mæn 'gæn əs,
→mæŋ-

mange meɪndʒ

mangel-wurzel 'mæŋ gᵊl ˌwɜːz ᵊl ‖ -ˌwɜ·z- ~**s**
z

manger 'meɪndʒ ə ‖ -ᵊr ~**s** z

mangetout ˌmɒndʒ 'tuː ‚mɑːndʒ-, ˌmɒ̃ʒ-; '‧‧
‖ ˌmɑːndʒ- —*Fr* [mɑ̃ʃ tu]

mangl|e 'mæŋ gᵊl ~**ed** d ~**es** z ~**ing** ˌɪŋ

mango 'mæŋ gəʊ ‖ -goʊ ~**es**, ~**s** z

mangold, M~ 'mæŋ gəʊld →-gɒʊld ‖ -goʊld
~**s** z

mangosteen 'mæŋ gəʊ stiːn ~**s** z

Mangotsfield 'mæŋ gəts fiːᵊld

mangrove 'mæŋ grəʊv 'mæn- ‖ -groʊv ~**s** z
'mangrove ˌswamp

mang|y 'meɪndʒ |i ~**ier** i ə ‖ i ᵊr ~**iest** i ˌɪst
i ˌəst ~**ily** ɪ li əl i ~**iness** i nəs i nɪs

manhandl|e 'mæn ˌhænd ᵊl ‚·'‧‧ ~**ed** d ~**es** z
~**ing** ˌɪŋ

Manhattan, m~ mæn 'hæt ᵊn mən- ~**s**, ~**'s** z

manhole 'mæn həʊl →-hɒʊl ‖ -hoʊl ~**s** z
'manhole ˌcover

manhood 'mæn hʊd

manhour 'mæn ˌaʊ‿ə ‖ -ˌaʊ‿ᵊr ~**s** z

manhunt 'mæn hʌnt ~**s** s

mania 'meɪn i ə ~**s** z

-mania 'meɪn i‿ə — **pyromania**
ˌpaɪᵊr‿ə 'meɪn i‿ə

maniac 'meɪn i æk ~**s** s

-maniac 'meɪn i æk — **pyromaniac**
ˌpaɪᵊr‿ə 'meɪn i æk

maniacal mə 'naɪ‿ək ᵊl ~**ly** i

manic 'mæn ɪk ~**s** s

manic-depressive ˌmæn ɪk di 'pres ɪv ◂ -də'‧-
~**s** z

Manichaean, Manichean ˌmæn ɪ 'kiː ən ◂ -ə-
~**s** z

Manichaeism, Manicheism
ˌmæn ɪ 'kiː ˌɪz əm -ə-

manicure 'mæn ɪ kjʊə -ə-, -kjɔː ‖ -kjʊr -kjɜ· ~**d**
d ~**s** z **manicuring** 'mæn ɪ kjʊər ɪŋ '‧ə-,
-kjɔːr ɪŋ ‖ -kjʊr ɪŋ -kjɜ·ː ɪŋ

manicurist 'mæn ɪ kjʊər ɪst '‧ə-, -kjɔːr ɪst, §-əst
‖ -kjʊr əst ~**s** s

manifest *adj, n, v* 'mæn ɪ fest -ə- ~**ed** ɪd əd
~**ing** ɪŋ ~**s** s

manifestation ˌmæn ɪ fe 'steɪʃ ᵊn ‚·ə-, -fə'‧- ~**s**
z

manifestly 'mæn ɪ fest li '‧ə-

manifesto ˌmæn ɪ 'fest əʊ -ə- ‖ -oʊ ~**es**, ~**s** z

manifold, M~ 'mæn ɪ fəʊld -ə-, →-fɒʊld
‖ -foʊld ~**ed** ɪd əd ~**ing** ɪŋ ~**ly** li ~**ness** nəs
nɪs ~**s** z

manikin 'mæn ɪk ɪn -ək-, §-ən ~**s** z

manila, M~, manilla mə 'nɪl ə ~**s** z
Ma‚nila 'hemp

Manilow 'mæn ɪ ləʊ -əl əʊ ‖ -loʊ

manioc 'mæn i ɒk ‖ -ɑːk

maniple 'mæn ɪp ᵊl -əp- ~**s** z

manipulability mə ˌnɪp jʊl ə 'bɪl ət i -ˌjəl-,
-ɪt i ‖ -ˌjəl ə 'bɪl ət̬ i

manipulab|le mə 'nɪp jʊl əb |ᵊl -jəl əb-
‖ -jəl əb- ~**ly** li

manipu|late mə 'nɪp ju |leɪt -jə- ‖ -jə- ~**lated**
leɪt ɪd -əd ‖ leɪt̬ əd ~**lates** leɪts ~**lating**
leɪt ɪŋ ‖ leɪt̬ ɪŋ

manipulation mə ˌnɪp ju 'leɪʃ ᵊn -jə- ‖ -jə- ~**s**
z

M

manipulative mə ˈnɪp jʊl ət ɪv -jəl ət-;
-ju leɪt-, -jə leɪt- ‖ -jə leɪt̬ ɪv -jə lət̬- **~ly** li
~ness nəs nɪs
manipulator mə ˈnɪp ju leɪt ə -jə- ‖ -jə leɪt̬ ᵊr
~s z
Manitoba ˌmæn ɪ ˈtəʊb ə -ə- ‖ -ˈtoʊb ə
manitou ˈmæn ɪ tu: §-ə-
Manitoulin ˌmæn ɪ ˈtu:l ɪn -ə-, §-ən
mankind mæn ˈkaɪnd →mæŋ-, ˌ·- —but in the
rare sense 'men as distinct from women', ˈ· ·
mank|y ˈmæŋk |i **~ier** i ə ‖ i ᵊr **~iest** i ɪst i əst
Manley, Manly ˈmæn li
man|ly ˈmæn |li **~lier** li ə ‖ li ᵊr **~liest** li ɪst
əst **~liness** li nəs -nɪs
man-made ˌmæn ˈmeɪd ◄ →ˌmæm-
ˌman-made ˈfibres
Mann mæn
manna ˈmæn ə
mannequin ˈmæn ɪk ɪn -ək-, §-ən **~s** z
manner ˈmæn ə ‖ -ᵊr **~ed** d **~s** z
mannerism ˈmæn ər ˌɪz əm **~s** z
manner|ly ˈmæn ə |li ‖ -ᵊr- **~liness** li nəs -nɪs
Manners ˈmæn əz ‖ -ᵊrz
Mannheim ˈmæn haɪm —Ger [ˈman haɪm]
mannikin ˈmæn ɪk ɪn -ək-, §-ən **~s** z
Manning ˈmæn ɪŋ
Manningham ˈmæn ɪŋ əm
mannish ˈmæn ɪʃ **~ly** li **~ness** nəs nɪs
mannitol ˈmæn ɪ tɒl §-ə- ‖ -toʊl -tɑːl, -tɔːl
Manny ˈmæn i
mano a mano ˌmæn əʊ ɑː ˈmæn əʊ
‖ ˌmɑːn oʊ ɑː ˈmɑːn oʊ —Sp
[ˌma no a ˈma no]
manoeuvrability mə ˌnuːv ər ə ˈbɪl ət i -ɪt i
‖ -ət̬ i
manoeuvrable mə ˈnuːv ər əb ᵊl
manoeuv|re, maneuv|er mə ˈnuːv |ə ‖ -|ᵊr
~ered, ~red əd ‖ ᵊrd **~ering, ~ring** ər ɪŋ
~ers, ~res əz ‖ ᵊrz
man-of-war ˌmæn əv ˈwɔː -ə- ‖ -ˈwɔːr
men-of-war ˌmen-
manometer mə ˈnɒm ɪt ə mæ-, §-ət-
‖ -ˈnɑːm ət̬ ᵊr **~s** z
manometric ˌmæn əʊ ˈmetr ɪk ◄ -ə- **~al** ᵊl
~ally ᵊl i
Manon Lescaut mæ ˌnɒ̃ le ˈskəʊ
‖ mɑː ˌnoʊn le ˈskoʊ —Fr [ma nɔ̃ lɛs ko]
manor ˈmæn ə ‖ -ᵊr (= manner) **~s** z
ˈmanor house
Manorbier ˌmæn ə ˈbɪə ‖ -ᵊr ˈbɪᵊr
manorial mə ˈnɔːr i əl mæ- ‖ -ˈnoʊr-
man-o'-war ˌmæn ə ˈwɔː ‖ -ˈwɔːr **men-o'-war**
ˌmen-
manpower ˈmæn ˌpaʊ ə →ˈmæm- ‖ -ˌpaʊ ᵊr
manque, manqué ˈmɒŋk eɪ ˈmɑːŋk-
‖ mɑːŋ ˈkeɪ —Fr [mɑ̃ ke]
Manresa mæn ˈreɪs ə -ˈreɪz- ‖ mɑːn- mæn-
—Sp [man ˈrre sa]
mansard ˈmæn̩s ɑːd -əd ‖ -ɑːrd -ᵊrd **~s** z
manse mæn̩s **manses** ˈmæn̩s ɪz -əz
Mansel, Mansell ˈmæn̩s ᵊl
manservant ˈmæn ˌsɜːv ᵊnt ‖ -ˌsɜːv- **~s** s
Mansfield ˈmæn̩s fiːᵊld

-manship mən ʃɪp — **gamesmanship**
ˈɡeɪmz mən ʃɪp
mansion ˈmænʧ ᵊn **~s** z
ˌMansion ˈHouse, ˈ· · ·
man-size ˈmæn saɪz **~d** d
manslaughter ˈmæn ˌslɔːt ə ‖ -ˌslɔːt̬ ᵊr -ˌslɑːt̬-
Manson ˈmæn̩s ᵊn
Manston ˈmæn̩st ən
manta, Manta ˈmænt ə ‖ ˈmænt̬ ə **~s** z
mantel ˈmænt ᵊl ‖ ˈmænt̬ ᵊl (= mantle) **~s** z
mantelpiec|e ˈmænt ᵊl piːs ‖ ˈmænt̬- **~es** ɪz əz
mantel|shelf ˈmænt ᵊl |ʃelf ‖ ˈmænt̬ ᵊl-
~shelves ʃelvz
mantic ˈmænt ɪk ‖ ˈmænt̬ ɪk
mantilla mæn ˈtɪl ə ‖ -ˈtiː ə —Sp [man ˈti ʎa,
-ja] **~s** z
Mantinea ˌmænt ɪ ˈniː ə -ə-, -ˈneɪ-
mantis ˈmænt ɪs §-əs ‖ ˈmænt̬ əs **~es** ɪz əz
mantissa mæn ˈtɪs ə **~s** z
mantl|e ˈmænt ᵊl ‖ ˈmænt̬ ᵊl **~ed** d **~es** z **~ing**
ɪŋ
man-to-man ˌmæn tə ˈmæn ◄
Mantovani ˌmænt ə ˈvɑːn i
mantra ˈmæntr ə ˈmʌntr- **~s** z
mantrap ˈmæn træp **~s** s
Mantu|a, m~ ˈmænt ju |ə -uˌ-; ˈmænʧ u |ə
‖ ˈmænʧ u |ə **~an/s** ən/z
manual ˈmæn ju əl **~ly** i **~s** z
Manuel forename ˌmæn ˈwel ˈ· ·; ˈmæn ju əl
‖ mæn ˈwel —Sp [ma ˈnwel]
Manuel family name ˈmæn ju əl -el
manufac|ture ˌmæn ju ˈfæk |ʧə -jə-, -ə-, -ʃə
‖ -jə ˈfæk |ʧᵊr -ʃᵊr **~tured** ʧəd ‖ ʧᵊrd **~tures**
ʧəz ‖ ʧᵊrz **~turing** ʧər ɪŋ
manufacturer ˌmæn ju ˈfæk ʧər ə ˌ-jə-, ˌ-ə-,
-ʃər ə ‖ -jə ˈfæk ʧᵊr ər -ʃᵊr ər **~s** z
manumission ˌmæn ju ˈmɪʃ ᵊn -jə- ‖ -jə- **~s** z
manu|mit ˌmæn ju |ˈmɪt -jə- ‖ -jə- **~mits** ˈmɪts
~mitted ˈmɪt ɪd -əd ‖ ˈmɪt̬ əd **~mitting**
ˈmɪt ɪŋ ‖ ˈmɪt̬ ɪŋ
manure mə ˈnjʊə -ˈnjɔː ‖ -ˈnʊᵊr -ˈnjʊᵊr **~d** d
manuring mə ˈnjʊər ɪŋ -ˈnjɔːr- ‖ -ˈnʊr ɪŋ
-ˈnjʊər- **~s** z
manuscript ˈmæn ju skrɪpt -jə- ‖ -jə- **~s** s
Manwaring ˈmæn ər ɪŋ ‖ -wɔːr-
Manx mæŋks
ˌManx ˈcat
Manx|man ˈmæŋks |mən -mæn **~men** mən
men
many ˈmen i —There are occasional weak forms
mən i, mni (esp. in how many); in AmE also
ˈmɪn i. —In Ireland often ˈmæn i **more** mɔː
‖ mɔːr moʊr **most** məʊst ‖ moʊst
man-year ˈmæn jɪə ˌ·ˈ· ‖ -jɪᵊr **~s** z
many-faceted ˌmen i ˈfæs ɪt ɪd -ət-, -et ·, -əd
‖ -ət̬·
many-sided ˌmen i ˈsaɪd ɪd ◄ -əd **~ness** nəs
nɪs
manzanilla, M~ ˌmænz ə ˈnɪl ə ‖ -ˈniː ə —Sp
[man θa ˈni ʎa, -ja] **~s** z

Mao maʊ
  Mao Tsetung ˌmaʊt sɪ ˈtʊŋ -tseɪ-; **Mao
  Zedong** ˌmaʊd zə ˈdʊŋ —*Chi* Máo Zédōng
  [²meu ²tsɤ ¹tʊŋ]
Maoism ˈmaʊ ˌɪz əm
Maoist ˈmaʊ ɪst §-əst **~s** s
Maori ˈmaʊᵊr i —*Maori* [ˈma o ɾi] **~s** z
map mæp **mapped** mæpt **mapping/s**
  ˈmæp ɪŋ/z **maps** mæps
maple ˈmeɪp ᵊl **~s** z
  ˈmaple leaf; ˌmaple ˈsyrup
Maplin ˈmæp lɪn -lən
Mapp mæp
Mappin ˈmæp ɪn §-ən
Mapplethorpe ˈmeɪp ᵊl θɔːp ˈmæp- ‖ -θɔːrp
map-read|er ˈmæp ˌriːd |ə ‖ -|ᵊr **~ers** əz ‖ ᵊrz
  ~ing ɪŋ
Maputo mə ˈpuːt əʊ ‖ -oʊ
maquette mæ ˈket **~s** s
maquillage ˌmæk i ˈɑːʒ -ˈjɑːʒ —*Fr*
  [ma ki jaːʒ]
maquis mæ ˈkiː mɑː-; ˈmæk iː, ˈmɑːk- —*Fr*
  [ma ki]
mar, Mar mɑː ‖ mɑːr **marred** mɑːd ‖ mɑːrd
  marring ˈmɑːr ɪŋ **mars** mɑːz ‖ mɑːrz
Mar. —*see* **March**
marabou, marabout ˈmær ə buː ‖ ˈmer- **~s** z
maraca mə ˈræk ə ‖ -ˈrɑːk ə -ˈræk- **~s** z
Maradona ˌmær ə ˈdɒn ə ‖ -ˈdɑːn- ˌmer- —*Sp*
  [ma ɾa ˈðo na]
maraschino, M~ ˌmær ə ˈskiːn əʊ ◄ -ˈʃiːn-
  ‖ -oʊ ◄ ˌmer-, -ˈʃiːn- **~s** z
maras|mus mə ˈræz |məs **~mic** mɪk
Marat ˈmær ɑː ‖ mə ˈrɑː —*Fr* [ma ʁa]
Marathi mə ˈrɑːt i ‖ -ˈrɑːt̬ i —*Hindi*
  [mə ra: ʈʰi] **~s** z
marathon, M~ ˈmær əθ ən -ə θɒn ‖ -ə θɑːn
  ˈmer- **~er/s** ə/z ‖ -ᵊr/z **~s** z
maraud mə ˈrɔːd ‖ -ˈrɑːd **~ed** ɪd əd **~er/s** ə/z
  ‖ ᵊr/z **~ing** ɪŋ **~s** z
Marazion ˌmær ə ˈzaɪ ən ‖ ˌmer-
Marbella *place in Spain* mɑː ˈbeɪ ə -jə ‖ mɑːr-
  —*There is also a spelling pronunciation*
  △-ˈbel ə —*Sp* [mar ˈβe ʎa, -ja]
marbl|e ˈmɑːb ᵊl ‖ ˈmɑːrb- **~ed** d **~es** z **~ing**
  ɪŋ
Marblehead ˈmɑːb ᵊl hed ˌ·ˈ· ‖ ˈmɑːrb-
Marburg ˈmɑː bɜːg ‖ ˈmɑːr bɜːg —*Ger*
  [ˈmaːʁ bʊʁk]
marc, Marc mɑːk ‖ mɑːrk *(= mark)*
Marcan ˈmɑːk ən ‖ ˈmɑːrk-
marcasite ˈmɑːk ə saɪt ‖ ˈmɑːrk-
Marceau ˌmɑː ˈsəʊ ‖ ˌmɑːr ˈsoʊ —*Fr* [maʁ so]
Marcel, m~ ₍ₗ₎mɑː ˈsel ‖ ₍ₗ₎mɑːr- **~led** d **~ling**
  ɪŋ **~s** z
Marcella ₍ₗ₎mɑː ˈsel ə ‖ ₍ₗ₎mɑːr-
Marcelle ₍ₗ₎mɑː ˈsel ‖ ₍ₗ₎mɑːr-
Marcellus mɑː ˈsel əs ‖ mɑːr-
march, March mɑːtʃ ‖ mɑːrtʃ **marched** mɑːtʃt
  ‖ mɑːrtʃt **marches, March's** ˈmɑːtʃ ɪz -əz
  ‖ ˈmɑːrtʃ əz **marching** ˈmɑːtʃ ɪŋ ‖ ˈmɑːrtʃ ɪŋ
  ˈmarching ˌorders
Marchant ˈmɑːtʃ ənt ‖ ˈmɑːrtʃ-

marcher ˈmɑːtʃ ə ‖ ˈmɑːrtʃ ᵊr **~s** z
marchioness ˌmɑː ʃ ə ˈnes ˈmɑː ʃ ən ɪs, əs
  ‖ ˈmɑːrʃ ən əs **~es** ɪz əz
Marchmont ˈmɑːtʃ mənt ‖ ˈmɑːrtʃ-
march-past ˈmɑːtʃ pɑːst §-pæst ‖ ˈmɑːrtʃ pæst
  ~s s
Marcia ˈmɑːs i ə ˈmɑːʃ ə ‖ ˈmɑːrʃ ə
Marciano ˌmɑːs i ˈɑːn əʊ ‖ ˌmɑːrs i ˈæn oʊ
Marco ˈmɑːk əʊ ‖ ˈmɑːrk oʊ
Marconi mɑː ˈkəʊn i ‖ mɑːr ˈkoʊn i —*It*
  [mar ˈkoː ni]
Marcos ˈmɑːk ɒs ‖ ˈmɑːrk oʊs
Marcus ˈmɑːk əs ‖ ˈmɑːrk-
Marcuse mɑː ˈkuːz ə ‖ mɑːr-
Marden ˈmɑːd ᵊn ‖ ˈmɑːrd- —*The place in
  Kent is sometimes* ₍ₗ₎mɑː ˈden ‖ ₍ₗ₎mɑːr-
Mardi Gras ˌmɑːd i ˈgrɑː ‖ ˈmɑːrd i grɑː -grɔː;
  ˌ·ˈ·
mardy ˈmɑːd i ‖ ˈmɑːrd i
mare *'lunar plain', 'sea'* ˈmɑːr eɪ ˈmær-, -i
  maria ˈmɑːr i ə ˈmær-
mare *'she-horse'* meə ‖ meᵊr mæᵊr **mares,
  mare's** meəz ‖ meᵊrz mæᵊrz
  ˈmare's nest
Maree mə ˈriː
Marengo mə ˈreŋ gəʊ ‖ -goʊ —*It*
  [ma ˈreŋ go]
mare's-tail ˈmeəz teɪᵊl ‖ ˈmerz- ˈmærz- **~s** z
marg mɑːdʒ ‖ mɑːrdʒ
Margach ˈmɑːg ə ‖ ˈmɑːrg ə
Margam ˈmɑːg əm ‖ ˈmɑːrg-
Margaret ˈmɑːg rət -rɪt; ˈmɑːg ər ət, -ɪt
  ‖ ˈmɑːrg-
Margaretting ˌmɑːg ə ˈret ɪŋ
  ‖ ˌmɑːrg ə ˈret̬ ɪŋ
margarine ˌmɑːdʒ ə ˈriːn ˌmɑːg-, ˈ···
  ‖ ˈmɑːrdʒ ᵊr ən -ə riːn *(*)*
Margarita, m~ ˌmɑːg ə ˈriːt ə
  ‖ ˌmɑːrg ə ˈriːt̬ ə **~s, ~'s** z
margarite ˈmɑːg ə raɪt ‖ ˈmɑːrg-
Margary ˈmɑːg ər i ‖ ˈmɑːrg-
Margate ˈmɑː geɪt -gɪt, -gət ‖ ˈmɑːr-
margay ˈmɑːg eɪ ‖ ˈmɑːrg- mɑːr ˈgeɪ **~s** z
marge mɑːdʒ ‖ mɑːrdʒ
Margerison *(i)* ˈmɑːdʒ ər ɪs ən əs ən
  ‖ ˈmɑːrdʒ-, *(ii)* mɑː ˈdʒer- ‖ mɑːr-
margin ˈmɑːdʒ ɪn §-ən ‖ ˈmɑːrdʒ- **~s** z
marginal ˈmɑːdʒ ɪn ᵊl -ᵊn əl ‖ ˈmɑːrdʒ- **~ly** i
marginalia ˌmɑːdʒ ɪ ˈneɪl i ə ˌ·ə- ‖ ˌmɑːrdʒ-
marginalis... —*see* **marginaliz...**
marginality ˌmɑːdʒ ɪ ˈnæl ət i ˌ·ə-, -ɪt i
  ‖ ˌmɑːrdʒ ə ˈnæl ət̬ i
marginalization ˌmɑːdʒ ɪn ᵊl aɪ ˈzeɪʃ ᵊn
  ˌ·ᵊn ᵊl-, -ɪˈ-- ‖ ˌmɑːrdʒ ᵊn ᵊl ə-
marginaliz|e ˈmɑːdʒ ɪn ə laɪz -ᵊn ə-, -ᵊl aɪz
  ~ed d **~es** ɪz əz **~ing** ɪŋ
Margo ˈmɑːg əʊ ‖ ˈmɑːrg oʊ
Margolis mɑː ˈgəʊl ɪs §-əs ‖ mɑːr ˈgoʊl-
Margot ˈmɑːg əʊ -ət ‖ ˈmɑːrg oʊ
margrave ˈmɑː greɪv ‖ ˈmɑːr- **~s** z
marguerite, M~ ˌmɑːg ə ˈriːt ‖ ˈmɑːrg- **~s, ~'s**
  s

M

Marham *(i)* 'mær əm ‖ 'mer-, *(ii)* 'mɑːr əm
—*Both (i) and (ii) are heard for the place in
Norfolk.*
Mari 'mɑːr i ~s z
Maria *personal name(i)* mə 'riː ə, *(ii)* mə 'raɪ ə
—*Always (ii) in the phrase* Black Maria
maria, Maria *Latin pl of* mare 'mɑːr i ə 'mær-
mariachi ˌmær i 'ɑːtʃ i ‖ ˌmɑːr- ˌmær- —*Sp*
[ma 'rja tʃi]
Marian *adj, n* 'meər i ən ‖ 'mer-
Marian *forename* 'mær i ən §-æn ‖ 'mer-
Mariana ˌmær i 'ɑːn ə ◂ ˌmeər-, -'æn-
‖ -'æn ə ◂ ˌmer-; ˌmɑːr i 'ɑːn ə ~s z
ˌMariana 'Trench
Marianne ˌmær i 'æn ‖ ˌmer- —*Fr* [maʁ jan]
Marie *(i)* mə 'riː, *(ii)* 'mɑːr i, *(iii)* 'mær i —*In
AmE (i).*
ˌMarie ˌAntoi'nette ‖ Maˌrie-
Marienbad 'mær i ən bæd mə 'riː ən-, →ˌəm·
‖ 'mer- —*Ger* [ma 'ʁiː ən baːt]
Marietta ˌmær i 'et ə ‖ -'eṱ ə ˌmer-
marigold, M~ 'mær i gəʊld §-ə-, →-gɒʊld
‖ -ə goʊld 'mer- ~s z
marihuana, marijuana ˌmær ɪ 'wɑːn ə -ə-,
-'hwɑːn-; ˌmær i ju 'ɑːn ə ‖ ˌmer-
Marilyn 'mær əl ɪn -ɪl-, -iːn ‖ 'mer-
marimba mə 'rɪm bə ~s z
Marin *(i)* 'mɑːr ɪn §-ən, *(ii)* 'mær- ‖ 'mer-,
(iii) mə 'rɪn —*The county in CA is (iii).*
marina, M~ mə 'riːn ə ~s z
marinad|e ˌmær ɪ 'neɪd -ə-, '··· ‖ ˌmer- ~ed ɪd
əd ~es z ~ing ɪŋ
marinara ˌmær ɪ 'nɑːr ə -ə- ‖ -'ner ə ˌmer-,
ˌmɑːr-, -'nɑːr-, -'nær- —*It* [ma ri 'na: ra]
mari|nate 'mær ɪ |neɪt -ə- ‖ 'mer- ~**nated**
neɪt ɪd -əd ‖ neɪṱ əd ~**nates** neɪts ~**nating**
neɪt ɪŋ ‖ neɪṱ ɪŋ
marine mə 'riːn ~s z
Ma'rine Corps
mariner, M~ 'mær ɪn ə -ən- ‖ -ᵊn ər 'mer- ~s z
mariniere ˌmær ɪn 'jeə ‖ ˌmɑːr ən 'jeᵊr ˌmær-,
ˌmer- —*Fr* marinière [ma ʁi njɛːʁ]
Marino mə 'riːn əʊ ‖ -oʊ
Mario 'mær i əʊ 'mɑːr- ‖ 'mɑːr i oʊ 'mær-,
'mer-
mariolatry, M~ ˌmeər i 'ɒl ətr i ˌmær-
‖ ˌmer i 'ɑːl- ˌmær-
Mariology ˌmeər i 'ɒl ədʒ i ˌmær-
‖ ˌmer i 'ɑːl- ˌmær-
Marion 'mær i ən 'meər- ‖ 'mer-
marionette ˌmær i ə 'net ‖ ˌmer- ~s s
mariposa ˌmær ɪ 'pəʊz ə ‖ -'poʊz ə ˌmer-,
-'poʊs-
ˌmari'posa ˌlily
Marischal 'mɑːʃ ᵊl ‖ 'mɑːrʃ-
Marist 'meər ɪst §-əst ‖ 'mer- 'mær- ~s s
marital 'mær ɪt ᵊl -ət- ‖ -əṱ ᵊl 'mer- —*In BrE
formerly also* mə 'raɪt- ~**ly** i
maritime, M~ 'mær ɪ taɪm -ə- ‖ 'mer- ~s z
Marius 'mær i əs 'mɑːr-, 'meər- ‖ 'mer-, 'mɑːr-
marjoram, M~ 'mɑːdʒ ər əm ‖ 'mɑːrdʒ-
Marjoribanks 'mɑːtʃ bæŋks ‖ 'mɑːrtʃ-
Marjorie, Marjory 'mɑːdʒ ər i ‖ 'mɑːrdʒ-

mark, Mark mɑːk ‖ mɑːrk **marked** mɑːkt
‖ mɑːrkt **marking** 'mɑːk ɪŋ ‖ 'mɑːrk ɪŋ
marks mɑːks ‖ mɑːrks
₍ᵢ₎Mark 'Antony
markdown 'mɑːk daʊn ‖ 'mɑːrk- ~s z
marked|ly 'mɑːk ɪd |li -əd- ‖ 'mɑːrk- ~**ness**
nəs nɪs
marker, M~ 'mɑːk ə ‖ 'mɑːrk ᵊr ~s z
mark|et 'mɑːk |ɪt §-ət ‖ 'mɑːrk |ət ~**eted** ɪt ɪd
§ət-, -əd ‖ əṱ əd ~**eting** ɪt ɪŋ §ət- ‖ əṱ ɪŋ ~**ets**
ɪts §əts ‖ əts
ˌmarket 'forces; ˌmarket 'garden ‖ '·· ˌ··;
~**er/s**, ~**ing**; ˌmarket 'price ‖ '·· ·; ˌmarket
re'search, -'research ‖ '·· ·ˌ·, -ˌ·ˌ·; 'market
town; ˌmarket 'value, '·· ˌ··
marketability ˌmɑːk ɪt ə 'bɪl ət i §ˌ·ət-, -ɪt i
‖ ˌmɑːrk əṱ ə 'bɪl əṱ i
marketable 'mɑːk ɪt əb ᵊl §'·ət- ‖ 'mɑːrk əṱ-
market-driven 'mɑːk ɪt ˌdrɪv ᵊn -ət- ‖ 'mɑːrk-
marketeer ˌmɑːk ɪ 'tɪə -ə- ‖ ˌmɑːrk ə 'tɪᵊr ~s z
market-maker 'mɑːk ɪt ˌmeɪk ə -ət-
‖ 'mɑːrk əṱ ˌmeɪk ᵊr ~s z
market-oriented 'mɑːk ɪt ˌɔːr i ent ɪd '·ət-,
ˌɒr-, -əd ‖ 'mɑːrk əṱ ˌɔːr i enṱ əd -ˌoʊr-
marketplac|e 'mɑːk ɪt pleɪs §-ət- ‖ 'mɑːrk-
~**es** ɪz əz
Market Rasen ˌmɑːk ɪt 'reɪz ᵊn §-ət- ‖ ˌmɑːrk-
Markey 'mɑːk i ‖ 'mɑːrk i
Markham 'mɑːk əm ‖ 'mɑːrk-
marking 'mɑːk ɪŋ ‖ 'mɑːrk ɪŋ ~s z
'marking ink
markka 'mɑːk ə ‖ 'mɑːrk ə —*Finnish*
['mark ka]
Markov 'mɑːk ɒv -ɒf ‖ 'mɑːrk ɑːf -ɔːf —*Russ*
['mar kəf]
ˌMarkov 'process ‖ '·· ˌ··
Markova mɑː 'kəʊv ə ‖ mɑːr 'koʊv ə —*Russ*
['mar kə və]
Marks mɑːks ‖ mɑːrks
ˌMarks and 'Spencer *tdmk*
marks|man 'mɑːks |mən ‖ 'mɑːrks- ~**manship**
mən ʃɪp ~**men** mən men ~**woman** ˌwʊm ən
~**women** ˌwɪm ɪn §-ən
markup 'mɑːk ʌp ‖ 'mɑːrk- ~s s
marl mɑːl ‖ mɑːrl
Marlboro *tdmk* 'mɑːl bər ə 'mɔːl-
‖ 'mɑːrl ˌbɝː oʊ
Marlboro, Marlborough *place name, family
name* 'mɔːl bər ə 'mɑːl- ‖ 'mɑːrl ˌbɝː oʊ
'mɔːrl-, -ə
Marlene *(i)* 'mɑːl iːn ˌmɑː 'liːn ‖ mɑːr 'liːn,
(ii) mɑː 'leɪn ə ‖ mɑːr- —*As an English
name, (i); as a German name, (ii).* —*Ger*
[maʁ 'leː nə]
Marler 'mɑːl ə ‖ 'mɑːrl ᵊr
Marley 'mɑːl i ‖ 'mɑːrl i
marlin, marline 'mɑːl ɪn §-ən ‖ 'mɑːrl- ~s z
marlinespike, marlinspike 'mɑːl ɪn spaɪk
-ən- ‖ 'mɑːrl- ~s s
Marlon 'mɑːl ən -ɒn ‖ 'mɑːrl-
Marlow, Marlowe 'mɑːl əʊ ‖ 'mɑːrl oʊ
Marmaduke 'mɑːm ə djuːk →-dʒuːk
‖ 'mɑːrm ə duːk -djuːk

marmalade 'mɑːm ə leɪd ‖ 'mɑːrm- ~s z
  ,marmalade 'cat
Marmara 'mɑːm ər ə ‖ 'mɑːrm-
Marmion 'mɑːm i ˌən ‖ 'mɑːrm-
marmite, M~ *tdmk* 'mɑːm aɪt ‖ 'mɑːrm-
Marmora 'mɑːm ər ə ‖ 'mɑːrm-
marmoreal mɑː 'mɔːr i ˌəl ‖ mɑːr- -'moʊr-
marmoset 'mɑːm ə zet -set, ˌ· ·ˈ· ‖ 'mɑːrm- ~s
  s
marmot 'mɑːm ət ‖ 'mɑːrm- ~s s
Marn, Marne mɑːn ‖ mɑːrn
Marner 'mɑːn ə ‖ 'mɑːrn ᵊr
Marnie 'mɑːn i ‖ 'mɑːrn i
marocain 'mær ə keɪn ˌ· ·ˈ· ‖ 'mer-
Maronite 'mær ə naɪt ‖ 'mer- ~s s
maroon mə 'ruːn ~ed d ~ing ɪŋ ~s z
Marplan *tdmk* 'mɑː plæn ‖ 'mɑːr-
Marple 'mɑːp ᵊl ‖ 'mɑːrp ᵊl
Marprelate 'mɑː ˌprel ət -ɪt ‖ 'mɑːr-
Marquand 'mɑːk wənd ‖ ˌmɑːr 'kwɑːnd
marque mɑːk ‖ mɑːrk *(= mark)* **marques**
  mɑːks ‖ mɑːrks
marquee ˌmɑː 'kiː ‖ ˌmɑːr- ~s z
Marquesan mɑː 'keɪz ᵊn -'keɪs- ‖ mɑːr- ~s z
Marquesas mɑː 'keɪz əz -'keɪs əs, -æs ‖ mɑːr-
marquess 'mɑːk wɪs -wəs ‖ 'mɑːrk- ɪz əz
marquetry 'mɑːk ɪtr i -ətr- ‖ 'mɑːrk-
marquis, M~ 'mɑːk wɪs -wəs; ˌmɑː 'kiː
  ‖ 'mɑːrk wəs ˌmɑːr 'kiː- **es** ɪz əz
marquis|e ˌmɑː 'kiːz ‖ ˌmɑːr- **es** ɪz əz
Marr mɑː ‖ mɑːr
Marrakech, Marrakesh ˌmær ə 'keʃ
  mə 'ræk eʃ ‖ ˌmer-
marram 'mær əm ‖ 'mer-
  'marram grass
marriag|e 'mær ɪdʒ ‖ 'mer- **es** ɪz əz
  'marriage ˌbroker; ˌmarriage 'guidance;
  'marriage lines
marriageability ˌmær ɪdʒ ə 'bɪl ət i ˌˌ·ədʒ,
  -ɪt i ‖ -ət i ˌmer-
marriageable 'mær ɪdʒ əb ᵊl '·ədʒ- ‖ 'mer-
  ness nəs nɪs
married 'mær id ‖ 'mer- ~s z
Marriner 'mær ɪn ə -ən- ‖ -ᵊr
Marriott 'mær i ˌət ‖ 'mer-, -ɑːt
marron 'mær ən -ɒ̃ ‖ 'mer-; mə 'roʊn, mæ-
  —*Fr* [ma ʁɔ̃] ~s z —*or as sing.*
marrow 'mær əʊ ‖ -oʊ 'mer- ~s z
marrowbone 'mær əʊ bəʊn ‖ -ə boʊn 'mer-,
  -oʊ- ~s z
marrowfat 'mær əʊ fæt ‖ -oʊ- 'mer-, -ə-
  ,marrowfat 'pea
marr|y 'mær |i ‖ 'mer- — *Preference poll,*
  AmE: 'mer- *53%,* 'mær- *47%.* **ied** id **ies** iz
  ying i ˌɪŋ
Marryat 'mær i ˌət ‖ 'mer-
Mars mɑːz ‖ mɑːrz
Marsala, m~ mɑː 'sɑːl ə ‖ mɑːr- —*It*
  [mar 'sa: la]
Marsden 'mɑːz dən ‖ 'mɑːrz-
Marseillaise ˌmɑːs eɪ 'eɪz -'jeɪz, -'ez; -ᵊl-;
  -ə 'leɪz, -'lez ‖ ˌmɑːrs- —*Fr* [maʁ sɛ jɛːz]

Marseilles ˌˌmɑː 'seɪ -'seɪlz ‖ ˌˌmɑːr- —*Fr*
  Marseille [maʁ sɛj]
marsh, Marsh mɑːʃ ‖ mɑːrʃ **marshes** 'mɑːʃ ɪz
  -əz ‖ 'mɑːrʃ əz
  'marsh gas; ˌmarsh 'marigold
Marsha 'mɑːʃ ə ‖ 'mɑːrʃ ə
marshal 'mɑːʃ ᵊl ‖ 'mɑːrʃ ᵊl **ed, led** d **ing,**
  ling ˌɪŋ ~s z
  'marshalling yard; ˌmarshal of the ˌRoyal
  'Air Force
Marshall 'mɑːʃ ᵊl ‖ 'mɑːrʃ ᵊl
  'Marshall Plan
Marshalsea 'mɑːʃ ᵊl si -siː ‖ 'mɑːrʃ-
Marsham 'mɑːʃ əm ‖ 'mɑːrʃ-
marshiness 'mɑːʃ i nəs -nɪs ‖ 'mɑːrʃ-
marshland 'mɑːʃ lænd -lənd ‖ 'mɑːrʃ- ~s z
marshmallow ˌmɑːʃ 'mæl əʊ
  ‖ 'mɑːrʃ ˌmel oʊ -ˌmæl-, -ə *(*)* ~s z
marshy 'mɑːʃ i ‖ 'mɑːrʃ i
Marsilius mɑː 'sɪl i ˌəs ‖ mɑːr-
Marson 'mɑːs ᵊn ‖ 'mɑːrs ᵊn
Marston 'mɑːst ən ‖ 'mɑːrst ən
  ˌMarston 'Moor
marsupial mɑː 'suːp i ˌəl -'sjuːp- ‖ mɑːr- ~s z
marsupi|um mɑː 'suːp i ˌ|əm -'sjuːp- ‖ mɑːr- ~a
  ə
mart mɑːt ‖ mɑːrt **marts** mɑːts ‖ mɑːrts
martagon 'mɑːt əg ən ‖ 'mɑːrt̬- ~s z
Martel, Martell mɑː 'tel ‖ mɑːr-
martello, M~ mɑː 'tel əʊ ‖ mɑːr 'tel oʊ ~s z
  Mar,tello 'tower
marten 'mɑːt ɪn -ᵊn ‖ 'mɑːrt ᵊn ~s z
Martens *(i)* 'mɑːt ɪnz -ᵊnz ‖ 'mɑːrt ᵊnz,
  (ii) mɑː 'tenz ‖ mɑːr-
Martha 'mɑːθ ə ‖ 'mɑːrθ ə
Marti 'mɑːt i ‖ 'mɑːrt̬ i
martial, M~ 'mɑːʃ ᵊl ‖ 'mɑːrʃ ᵊl *(= marshal)*
  ly i
  ˌmartial 'arts; ˌmartial 'law
Martian, m~ 'mɑːʃ ᵊn 'mɑːʃ i ˌən ‖ 'mɑːrʃ- ~s z
Martin, m~ 'mɑːt ɪn §-ᵊn ‖ 'mɑːrt ᵊn ~s, ~'s z
Martina mɑː 'tiːn ə ‖ mɑːr-
Martineau 'mɑːt ɪ nəʊ -ə-, -ᵊn əʊ
  ‖ 'mɑːrt ᵊn oʊ
martinet ˌmɑːt ɪ 'net -ə-, -ᵊn 'et ‖ ˌmɑːrt ᵊn 'et
  ~s s
Martinez mɑː 'tiːn ez ‖ mɑːr 'tiːn es -əs —*Sp*
  Martínez [mar 'ti neθ, -nes]
martingale 'mɑːt ɪn geɪᵊl →-ɪŋ-, §-ᵊn-
  ‖ 'mɑːrt ᵊn geɪᵊl ~s z
martini, M~ *tdmk* mɑː 'tiːn i ‖ mɑːr- ~s z
Martinique ˌmɑːt ɪ 'niːk -ə-, -ᵊn 'iːk
  ‖ ˌmɑːrt ᵊn 'iːk

Martinmas 'mɑːt ɪn məs →-ɪm-, §-ᵊn-, -mæs
‖ 'mɑːrt ᵊn-
Martinu 'mɑːt ɪ nuː §-ə- ‖ 'mɑːrt ᵊn uː —*Czech*
Martinů ['mar ci nuː]
Martland 'mɑːt lənd ‖ 'mɑːrt-
martlet 'mɑːt lət -lɪt ‖ 'mɑːrt- ~s s
Marty 'mɑːt i ‖ 'mɑːrt̬ i
Martyn 'mɑːt ɪn §-ᵊn ‖ 'mɑːrt ᵊn
martyr 'mɑːt ə ‖ 'mɑːrt̬ ᵊr ~ed d **martyring**
'mɑːt ər ɪŋ ‖ 'mɑːrt̬ ər ɪŋ ~s z
martyrdom 'mɑːt ə dəm ‖ 'mɑːrt̬ ᵊr- ~s z
martyrolog|y ˌmɑːt ə 'rɒl ədʒ |i
‖ ˌmɑːrt̬ ə 'rɑːl- ~ies iz
marvel 'mɑːv ᵊl ‖ 'mɑːrv ᵊl ~ed, ~led d ~ing,
~ling ɪŋ ~s z
Marvell 'mɑːv ᵊl ‖ 'mɑːrv ᵊl
marvellous, marvelous 'mɑːv ləs 'mɑːv əl əs
‖ 'mɑːrv- ~ly li ~ness nəs nɪs
Marvin 'mɑːv ɪn §-ᵊn ‖ 'mɑːrv ᵊn
Marwick 'mɑː wɪk ‖ 'mɑːr-
Marx mɑːks ‖ mɑːrks **Marx's** 'mɑːks ɪz -əz
‖ 'mɑːrks əz
'Marx ˌBrothers
Marxian 'mɑːks i ən ‖ 'mɑːrks-
Marxism 'mɑːks ˌɪz əm ‖ 'mɑːrks-
Marxism-Leninism
ˌmɑːks ˌɪz əm 'len ɪn ˌɪz əm §-'ᵊn- ‖ ˌmɑːrks-
Marxist 'mɑːks ɪst §-əst ‖ 'mɑːrks- ~s s
Marxist-Leninist ˌmɑːks ɪst 'len ɪn ɪst
§-əst 'len ɪn əst, §-ən- ‖ ˌmɑːrks- ~s s
Mary 'meər i ‖ 'mer i 'mær i
ˌMary ˌQueen of 'Scots
Maryland 'meər ɪ lənd 'mer-, -ə-, -lænd
‖ 'mer əl ənd 'mær-
Marylebone 'mær əl ə bən '-ɪ-, -lɪ ·, -bəun;
'mær ɪb ən, 'mɑːl-, -əb- ‖ 'mer əl ə boun
'mær-
Maryport 'meər i pɔːt ‖ 'mer i pɔːrt -pourt
marzipan 'mɑːz ɪ pæn -ə-, ˌ·'·, 'mɑːrz-
'mɑːrts-, -pɑːn
Masada mə 'sɑːd ə
Masai 'mɑː saɪ ˌ·'·, mə 'saɪ
masala mə 'sɑːl ə
Mascagni mæ 'skæn ji -'skɑːn- ‖ mɑː 'skɑːn ji
mæ- —*It* [ma 'skaɲ ɲi]
Mascall 'mæsk ᵊl
mascara mæ 'skɑːr ə mə- ‖ -'skær ə -'sker- (*)
~'d, ~ed d ~s z
Mascarene, m~ ˌmæsk ə 'riːn ◂ ~s z
mascarpone ˌmæsk ɑː 'pəʊn i -ə-, -eɪ; -'pəʊn
‖ ˌmɑːsk ɑːr 'poʊn eɪ —*It* [ma skar 'po: ne]
mascot 'mæsk ət -ɒt ‖ -ɑːt -ət ~s s
masculine 'mæsk jʊl ɪn 'mɑːsk-, -jəl-, §-ən,
§-ju laɪn, -jə- ‖ -jəl ən ~ly li ~ness nəs nɪs ~s
z
masculinis... —*see* **masculiniz...**
masculinity ˌmæsk ju 'lɪn ət i ˌmɑːsk-, ˌˌjə-,
-ɪt i ‖ -jə 'lɪn ət̬ i
masculinization ˌmæsk jʊl ɪn aɪ 'zeɪʒ ᵊn
ˌmɑːsk-, ˌˌjəl-, ˌˌ-ən-, -ɪ'·- ‖ ˌmæsk jəl ən ə-
masculiniz|e 'mæsk jʊl ɪ naɪz 'mɑːsk-, '·jəl-,
§-ə · ‖ 'mæsk jəl ə- ~ed d ~es ɪz əz ~ing ɪŋ
Masefield 'meɪs fiːᵊld 'meɪz-

maser 'meɪz ə ‖ -ᵊr ~s z
Maserati *tdmk* ˌmæz ə 'rɑːt i ‖ ˌmɑːs ə 'rɑːt̬ i
ˌmæz ə- ~s z
Maseru mə 'sɪər uː -'seər- ‖ ˌmæz ə ru 'mɑːs-
mash mæʃ **mashed** mæʃt **mashes** 'mæʃ ɪz -əz
mashing 'mæʃ ɪŋ
Masham (i) 'mæs əm, (ii) 'mæʃ əm —*The
place in NYks. is* (i), *the breed of sheep and
the family name either* (i) *or* (ii).
masher 'mæʃ ə ‖ -ᵊr ~s z
mashie 'mæʃ i ~s z
Mashonaland mə 'ʃɒn ə lænd -'ʃəʊn- ‖ -'ʃɑːn-
-'ʃoʊn-
masjid 'mæs dʒɪd 'mʌs-
mask mɑːsk §mæsk ‖ mæsk **masked** mɑːskt
§mæskt ‖ mæskt **masking** 'mɑːsk ɪŋ §'mæsk-
‖ 'mæsk ɪŋ **masks** mɑːsks §mæsks ‖ mæsks
'masking ˌtape
Maskall, Maskell 'mæsk ᵊl
masochism 'mæs ə ˌkɪz əm 'mæz-
masochist 'mæs ək ɪst 'mæz-, §-əst ~s s
masochistic ˌmæs ə 'kɪst ɪk ◂ ˌmæz- ~ally ᵊl i
mason, Mason 'meɪs ᵊn ~s z
'Mason ˌjar
Mason-Dixon ˌmeɪs ᵊn 'dɪks ᵊn
ˌMason-'Dixon ˌline
masonic, M~ mə 'sɒn ɪk -'zɒn- ‖ -'sɑːn-
Masonite *tdmk* 'meɪs ə naɪt
mason|ry 'meɪs ᵊn |ri ~ries riz
Masora, Masorah mə 'sɔːr ə ‖ -'sour-
Masorete 'mæs ə riːt ~s s
Masoretic ˌmæs ə 'ret ɪk ◂ ‖ -'ret̬-
masque mɑːsk mæsk ‖ mæsk (= *mask*)
masques mɑːsks mæsks ‖ mæsks

MASQUERADE

masquerad|e *n, v* ˌmæsk ə 'reɪd ˌmɑːsk-
— *Preference poll, BrE:* ˌmæsk- 62% (*English
southerners* 48%), ˌmɑːsk- 38% (*English
southerners* 52%). *In AmE always* ˌmæsk-.
~ed ɪd əd ~er/s ə/z ‖ ᵊr/z ~es z ~ing ɪŋ
mass *common n, v, adj* mæs **massed** mæst
masses 'mæs ɪz -əz **massing** 'mæs ɪŋ
ˌmass 'media; ˌmass pro'duction
Mass '*eucharist*', '*music for the Mass*' mæs mɑːs
Masses 'mæs ɪz 'mɑːs-, -əz
Mass. '*Massachusetts*' mæs —*or as*
Massachusetts
Massachusetts ˌmæs ə 'tʃuːs ɪts -'tʃuːz-, -əts
— *Preference poll, AmE:* -'tʃuːs- 87%, -'tʃuːz-
13%.
massacre 'mæs ək ə -ɪk- ‖ -ᵊr ~d d ~s z
massacring 'mæs ək ər ˌɪŋ

MASSACHUSETTS

13%
87%
-'t ʃuːs-
-'t ʃuːz-
AmE

massag|e 'mæs ɑːʒ -aːdʒ ‖ mə 'sɑːʒ -'saːdʒ *(*)*
~ed d **~es** ɪz əz **~ing** ɪŋ
'massage ˌparlour ‖ masˈsage ˌparlor
Massapequa ˌmæs ə 'piːk wə ◂
ˌMassaˌpequa 'Park
massasauga ˌmæs ə 'sɔːɡ ə ‖ -'saːɡ- **~s** z
Masscomp *tdmk* 'mæs kɒmp ‖ -kaːmp **~s** s
massé 'mæs i ‖ mæ 'seɪ **~s** z
Massenet 'mæs ə neɪ ‖ ˌmæs ə 'neɪ —*Fr*
[mas nɛ]
Massereene 'mæs ə riːn
masseter mæ 'siːt ə mə-; 'mæs ɪt ə, -ət-
‖ -'siːt̬ ³r **~s** z
masseur mæ 'sɜː mə- ‖ -'sʊ³r **~s** z
masseus|e mæ 'sɜːz mə- ‖ -'suːz -'suːs, -'sʊz
~es ɪz əz
Massey, Massie 'mæs i
massif 'mæs iːf mæ 'siːf ‖ mæ 'siːf —*Fr*
[ma sif] **~s** s
massiness 'mæs i nəs -nɪs
Massinger 'mæs ɪndʒ ə -əndʒ- ‖ -³r
massive 'mæs ɪv **~ly** li **~ness** nəs nɪs
massless 'mæs ləs -lɪs **~ness** nəs nɪs
mass-market 'mæs ˌmaːk ɪt -ət ‖ -ˌmaːrk-
Masson 'mæs ³n
mass-produc|e ˌmæs prə 'djuːs ◂ →-'dʒuːs
‖ -'duːs -'djuːs **~ed** t **~es** ɪz əz **~ing** ɪŋ
massy 'mæs i
mast maːst §mæst ‖ mæst **masts** maːsts
§mæsts ‖ mæsts
mastectom|y mæ 'stekt əm |i mə- **~ies** iz
master, M~ 'maːst ə §'mæst- ‖ 'mæst ³r **~ed** d
mastering 'maːst ər ɪŋ →'maːs trɪŋ;
§'mæst ər ɪŋ, →§'mæs trɪŋ ‖ 'mæst ər ɪŋ
→'mæs trɪŋ **~s**, **~'s** z
'master ˌcard; 'master ˌkey, ˌ·'·; ˌMaster
of 'Arts; ˌmaster of 'ceremonies; ˌMaster
of 'Science; 'master ˌrace; 'master's
deˌgree; ˌmaster 'sergeant◂
master-at-arms ˌmaːst ər ət 'aːmz §ˌmæst-
‖ ˌmæst ər ət̬ 'aːrmz **masters-at-arms** -əz ət-
‖ -³rz ət̬-
MasterCard *tdmk* 'maːst ə kaːd §'mæst-
‖ 'mæst ³r kaːrd **~s** z
masterclass 'maːst ə klaːs §'mæst ə klæs
‖ 'mæst ³r klæs
masterful 'maːst ə f³l §'mæst-, -fʊl ‖ 'mæst ³r-
~ly ˌi **~ness** nəs nɪs
master|ly 'maːst ə |li §'mæst-, -³|l i
‖ 'mæst ³r- **~liness** li nəs li nɪs
Masterman 'maːst ə mən §'mæst- ‖ 'mæst ³r-
mastermind *n*, *v* 'maːst ə maɪnd §'mæst-, ˌ·'·
‖ 'mæst ³r- **~ed** ɪd əd **~ing** ɪŋ **~s** z

masterpiec|e 'maːst ə piːs §'mæst- ‖ 'mæst ³r-
~es ɪz əz
Masters 'maːst əz §'mæst- ‖ 'mæst ³rz
masterstroke 'maːst ə strəʊk §'mæst-
‖ 'mæst ³r stroʊk **~s** s
masterwork 'maːst ə wɜːk §'mæst-
‖ 'mæst ³r wɜːk **~s** s
mastery 'maːst ər |i →'maːs tr|i; §'mæst ər |i,
→§'mæs tr|i ‖ 'mæst ər |i →'mæs tr|i **~ies** iz
masthead 'maːst hed §'mæst- ‖ 'mæst- **~s** z
mastic 'mæst ɪk
masti|cate 'mæst ɪ |keɪt §-ə- **~cated** keɪt ɪd
-əd ‖ keɪt̬ əd **~cates** keɪts **~cating** keɪt ɪŋ
‖ keɪt̬ ɪŋ
mastication ˌmæst ɪ 'keɪʃ ³n §-ə- **~s** z
masticator|y 'mæst ɪ kət ər |i -keɪt ər |i,
ˌ·ˌ·'keɪt ər |i ‖ -kə tɔːr |i -tour i **~ies** iz
mastiff 'mæst ɪf 'maːst-, §-əf **~s** s
mastitis mæ 'staɪt ɪs mə-, §-əs ‖ -'staɪt̬ əs
mastodon 'mæst ə dɒn -əd ³n ‖ -daːn **~s** z
mastoid 'mæst ɔɪd **~s** z
mastoiditis ˌmæst ɔɪ 'daɪt ɪs §-əs ‖ -'daɪt̬ əs
Mastroianni ˌmæs trəʊ 'jaːn i ˌmaːs-, -'jæn-
‖ -trə- -troʊ- —*It* [mas tro 'jan ni]
mastur|bate 'mæst ə |beɪt 'maːst- ‖ -³r-
~bated beɪt ɪd -əd ‖ beɪt̬ əd **~bates** beɪts
~bating beɪt ɪŋ ‖ beɪt̬ ɪŋ
masturbation ˌmæst ə 'beɪʃ ³n ˌmaːst- ‖ -³r- **~s**
z
masturbatory ˌmæst ə 'beɪt ər i ◂ ˌmaːst-,
'·····‖ 'mæst ³rb ə tɔːr i -tour i
mat mæt **mats** mæts **matted** 'mæt ɪd -əd
‖ 'mæt̬ əd **matting** 'mæt ɪŋ ‖ 'mæt̬ ɪŋ
Matabele ˌmæt ə 'biːl i ◂ -'bel- ‖ ˌmæt̬- **~land**
lænd **~s** z
matador 'mæt ə dɔː ‖ 'mæt̬ ə dɔːr **~s** z
Mata Hari ˌmaːt ə 'haːr i ‖ ˌmaːt̬-
Matapan 'mæt ə pæn ˌ·ˌ·'· ‖ 'mæt̬-
match mætʃ **matched** mætʃt **matches**
'mætʃ ɪz -əz **matching** 'mætʃ ɪŋ
ˌmatch 'point ‖ '· ·
matchboard 'mætʃ bɔːd ‖ -bɔːrd -bourd
matchbook 'mætʃ bʊk §-buːk **~s** s
matchbox 'mætʃ bɒks ‖ -baːks **~es** ɪz əz
match-fit ˌmætʃ 'fɪt ◂ **~ness** nəs nɪs
matchless 'mætʃ ləs -lɪs **~ly** li **~ness** nəs nɪs
matchlock 'mætʃ lɒk ‖ -laːk **~s** s
matchmaker 'mætʃ ˌmeɪk |ə ‖ -|³r **~ers** əz
‖ ³rz **~ing** ɪŋ
matchplay 'mætʃ pleɪ
matchstick 'mætʃ stɪk **~s** s
matchwood 'mætʃ wʊd
mate meɪt **mated** 'meɪt ɪd -əd ‖ 'meɪt̬ əd
mates meɪts **mating** 'meɪt ɪŋ ‖ 'meɪt̬ ɪŋ
maté 'mæt eɪ 'maːt- ‖ 'maːt eɪ maː- 'teɪ
matelot 'mæt ləʊ ‖ 'mæt̬ əl əʊ ‖ -loʊ **~s** z
mater, Mater 'meɪt ə 'maːt- ‖ 'meɪt̬ ³r 'maːt̬-
~s, **~'s** z
ˌMater ˌDolo'rosa ˌdɒl ə 'rəʊs ə -'rəʊz-
‖ ˌdoʊl ə 'roʊs ə -aː-
materia mə 'tɪər i ə ‖ -'tɪr-
maˌteria 'medica 'med ɪk ə
material mə 'tɪər i ˌəl ‖ -'tɪr- **~s** z

M

materialis... —*see* **materializ...**
materialism mə 'tɪər i‿ə ˌlɪz əm ‖ -'tɪr-
materialist mə 'tɪər i‿əl ɪst §-əst ‖ -'tɪr- ~**s** s
materialistic mə ˌtɪər i‿ə 'lɪst ɪk ◂ ‖ -ˌtɪr-
  ~**ally** ᵊl i
materialization mə ˌtɪər i‿əl aɪ 'zeɪʃ ᵊn -ɪ'--
  ‖ mə ˌtɪr i‿əl ə- ~**s** z
materializ|e mə 'tɪər i‿ə laɪz ‖ -'tɪr- ~**ed** d ~**es**
  ɪz əz ~**ing** ɪŋ
material|ly mə 'tɪər i‿əl |i ‖ -'tɪr- ~**ness** nəs
  nɪs
materiel, matériel mə ˌtɪər i 'el -'tɪər i‿əl
  ‖ -ˌtɪr- —*Fr* [ma te ʁjɛl]
maternal mə 'tɜːn ᵊl ‖ -'tɜːn ᵊl ~**ly** i
maternity mə 'tɜːn ət i -ɪt- ‖ -'tɜːn ət̬ i
mateship 'meɪt ʃɪp
matey 'meɪt i ‖ 'meɪt̬ i ~**ness** nəs nɪs
math mæθ
mathematical ˌmæθ ə 'mæt ɪk ᵊl ◂ ˌ-ɪ-;
  mæθ 'mæt- ‖ -'mæt̬- ~**ly** ˌi
mathematician ˌmæθ əm‿ə 'tɪʃ ᵊn ˌɪm- ~**s** z
mathematics ˌmæθ ə 'mæt ɪks -ɪ-; mæθ 'mæt-
  ‖ -'mæt̬ ɪks
Mather *(i)* 'meɪð ə ‖ -ᵊr, *(ii)* 'mæð-,
  (iii) 'meɪθ-
Matheson 'mæθ ɪs ən -əs-
Mathew 'mæθ ju:
Mathias mə 'θaɪ‿əs
Mathis 'mæθ ɪs §-əs
maths mæθs
Matilda mə 'tɪld ə
matinee, matinée 'mæt ɪ neɪ §-ə-, §-ᵊn eɪ
  ‖ ˌmæt ᵊn 'eɪ *(*)* ~**s** z
  '**matinee ˌidol** ‖ ˌmati'nee ˌidol**
matins 'mæt ɪnz §-ᵊnz ‖ -ᵊnz
Matisse mæ 'ti:s —*Fr* [ma tis]
Matlock 'mæt lɒk ‖ -lɑːk
Mato Grosso ˌmæt əʊ 'grɒs əʊ ˌmɑːt-
  ‖ ˌmæt̬ ə 'groʊs oʊ —*Port* [ˌma tu 'gro su]
matriarch 'meɪtr i ɑːk 'mætr- ‖ -ɑːrk ~**s** s
matriarch|al ˌmeɪtr i 'ɑːk ᵊl ◂ ˌmætr-, '····
  ‖ -'ɑːrk ᵊl ◂ ~**ic** ɪk ◂
matriarch|y 'meɪtr i ɑːk |i 'mætr- ‖ -ɑːrk |i
  ~**ies** iz
matric mə 'trɪk
matrices 'meɪtr ɪ siːz 'mætr-, -ə-
matricide 'meɪtr ɪ saɪd 'mætr-, -ə- ‖ 'mætr-
  'meɪtr- ~**s** z
matriculant mə 'trɪk jʊl ənt -jəl- ‖ -jəl- ~**s** s
matricu|late mə 'trɪk ju |leɪt -jə- ‖ -jə- ~**lated**
  leɪt ɪd -əd ‖ leɪt̬ əd ~**lates** leɪts ~**lating**
  leɪt ɪŋ ‖ leɪt̬ ɪŋ
matriculation mə ˌtrɪk ju 'leɪʃ ᵊn -jə- ‖ -jə- ~**s**
  z
matrilineal ˌmætr ɪ 'lɪn i‿əl ◂ ˌmeɪtr-, ˌ‿ə- ~**ly** i
matrilocal ˌmætr ɪ 'ləʊk ᵊl ◂ ˌmeɪtr-, -ə-, '··ˌ··
  ‖ -ə 'loʊk ᵊl ◂ ~**ly** i
matrimonial ˌmætr ɪ 'məʊn i‿əl ◂ ˌ‿ə-
  ‖ -'moʊn- ~**ly** i
matrimon|y 'mætr ɪm ən |i '·ˌəm- ‖ -ə moʊn |i
  (*) ~**ies** iz
matrix 'meɪtr ɪks —*in printing also* 'mætr- ~**es**
  ɪz əz

matron, M~ 'meɪtr ən ~**liness** li nəs -nɪs ~**ly**
  li ~**s** z
Matsu ˌmæt 'su: ‖ ˌmɑːt- —*Chi* Mǎzǔ
  [³ma ³tsu]
Matsui *tdmk* mæt 'su: i —*Jp* [ma ˌtsɯ i]
Matsushita *tdmk* ˌmæt su 'ʃiːt ə
  ‖ ˌmɑːt su 'ʃiːt̬ ə —*Jp* [ma ˌtsɯ 'ɕi ta]
matt mæt **matts** mæts
Mattachine ˌmæt ə 'ʃiːn ‖ ˌmæt̬-
matte mæt **mattes** mæts
matted 'mæt ɪd -əd ‖ 'mæt̬ əd ~**ly** li ~**ness**
  nəs nɪs
Mattel mə 'tel mæ-
matter 'mæt ə ‖ 'mæt̬ ᵊr ~**ed** d ~**s** z
Matterhorn 'mæt ə hɔːn ‖ 'mæt̬ ᵊr hɔːrn
matter-of-course ˌmæt ər əv 'kɔːs ◂
  ‖ ˌmæt̬ ər əv 'kɔːrs ◂ -'koʊrs ◂
matter-of-fact ˌmæt ər əv 'fækt ◂ -ə'·
  ‖ ˌmæt̬ ər- ~**ly** li ~**ness** nəs nɪs
Matthäus mə 'teɪ əs —*Ger* [ma 'tɛː ʊs]
Matthean mæ 'θiː ən mə-
Matthes 'mæθ ɪz -əz, -əs
Matthew 'mæθ ju:
Matthews 'mæθ ju:z
Matthey 'mæθ i 'mæt- ‖ 'mæt̬-
Matthias mə 'θaɪ əs
Matthiessen 'mæθ ɪs ən §-əs-
Mattie 'mæt i ‖ 'mæt̬ i
matting 'mæt ɪŋ ‖ 'mæt̬ ɪŋ
mattins 'mæt ɪnz §-ᵊnz ‖ -ᵊnz
mattock 'mæt ək ‖ 'mæt̬- ~**s** s
mattress 'mætr əs -ɪs ~**es** ɪz əz
matu|rate 'mætʃ u |reɪt -ə-; 'mæt juᵊ-, -jə-
  ‖ -ə- ~**rated** reɪt ɪd -əd ‖ reɪt̬ əd ~**rates** reɪts
  ~**rating** reɪt ɪŋ ‖ reɪt̬ ɪŋ
maturation ˌmætʃ u 'reɪʃ ᵊn -ə-; ˌmæt juᵊ-,
  -jə- ‖ -ə- ~**s** z
mature *adj, v* mə 'tʃʊə -'tjʊə, -'tjɔː, -'tʃɔː
  ‖ -'tʊᵊr -'tʃʊᵊr, -'tjʊᵊr ~**d** d ~**ly** li ~**ness** nəs
  nɪs **maturer** mə 'tʃʊər ə -'tjʊər-, -'tʃɔːr-,
  -'tʃɔːr- ‖ -'tʊr ᵊr -'tʃʊr-, -'tjʊr- ~**s** z **maturest**
  mə 'tʃʊər ɪst -'tjʊər-, -'tʃɔːr-, -'tʃɔːr-, -əst
  ‖ -'tʊr əst -'tʃʊr-, -'tjʊr- **maturing**
  mə 'tʃʊər ɪŋ -'tjʊər-, -'tʃɔːr-, -'tʃɔːr- ‖ -'tʊr ɪŋ
  -'tʃʊr-, -'tjʊr-
  ma ˌture 'student**
maturit|y mə 'tʃʊər ət |i -'tjʊər-, -'tʃɔːr-,
  -'tʃɔːr-, -ɪt- ‖ -'tʊr ət̬ |i -'tʃʊr-, -'tjʊr- ~**ies** iz
matutinal ˌmætʃ u 'taɪn ᵊl ◂ ˌmætʃ u-, §-ə-;
  mə 'tjuːt ɪn-, -ᵊnəl ‖ ˌmætʃ u- mə 'tuːt ᵊn əl,
  -'tjuːt- ~**ly** i
matza, matzah 'mɒts ə 'mɑːts-, 'mæts-
  ‖ 'mɑːts ə ~**s** z
matzo, matzoh 'mɒts ə 'mɑːts-, 'mæts-, -əʊ
  ‖ 'mɑːts ə -oʊ ~**s** z
mauby 'mɔːb i ‖ 'mɑːb-
Maud, maud, Maude mɔːd ‖ mɑːd **mauds,**
  Maud's mɔːdz ‖ mɑːdz
maudlin 'mɔːd lɪn §-lən ‖ 'mɑːd- ~**ly** li
Maudling 'mɔːd lɪŋ ‖ 'mɑːd-
Maudsley 'mɔːdz li ‖ 'mɑːdz-
Maufe mɔːf ‖ mɑːf
Mauger 'meɪdʒ ə ‖ -ᵊr

Maugham mɔːm ‖ mɑːm *(!)* —*occasionally also* ˈmɒf əm ‖ ˈmɔːf-, ˈmɑːf-

Maughan mɔːn ‖ mɑːn

Maui ˈmaʊ i

maul mɔːl ‖ mɑːl **mauled** mɔːld ‖ mɑːld **mauling** ˈmɔːl ɪŋ ‖ ˈmɑːl-

Mauleverer mə ˈlev ər ə mɔː- ‖ -ᵊr ər

maulstick ˈmɔːl stɪk ‖ ˈmɑːl- **~s** s

Mau Mau ˈmaʊ maʊ ˌ·ˈ· **~s** z

Maumee mɔː ˈmiː ˈ·· ‖ mɑː-

Mauna Kea ˌmaʊn ə ˈkeɪ ə

Mauna Loa ˌmaʊn ə ˈləʊ ə ‖ -ˈloʊ ə

maunder, M~ ˈmɔːnd ə ‖ -ᵊr ˈmɑːnd- **~ed** d **maundering** ˈmɔːnd ər ɪŋ ‖ ˈmɑːnd- **~s** z

Maundy, m~ ˈmɔːnd i ‖ ˈmɑːnd- ˌMaundy ˌmoney; ˌMaundy ˈThursday

Maupassant ˈməʊp ə sɒ̃ -æ- ‖ ˈmoʊp ə sɑːnt ˌ·ˈ· —*Fr* [mo pa sɑ̃]

Maupin ˈmɔːp ɪn -ən ‖ ˈmɑːp-

Maureen ˈmɔːr iːn mɔː ˈriːn ‖ mɔː ˈriːn mɑː-

Mauretani|a ˌmɒr ɪ ˈteɪn i ˌ|ə ˌmɔːr-, ˌ·ə- ‖ ˌmɔːr ə- **~an/s** ən/z

Mauriac ˈmɔːr i æk ˈməʊ ri- ‖ ˌmɔːr i ˈɑːk —*Fr* [mɔ ʁjak]

Maurice *(i)* ˈmɒr ɪs §-əs ‖ ˈmɔːr əs ˈmɑːr-, *(ii)* mɒ ˈriːs mə- ‖ mɔː- mɑː-

Mauritani|a ˌmɒr ɪ ˈteɪn i ˌ|ə ˌmɔːr-, ˌ·ə- ‖ ˌmɔːr ə- **~an/s** ən/z

Maurit|ian mə ˈrɪʃ ǀᵊn mɒ-, mɔː- ‖ mɔː- mɑː-, -ˈrɪʃ ǀi ən **~ians** ᵊnz i ˌənz **~ius** əs ‖ i ˌəs

Mauser ˈmaʊz ə ‖ -ᵊr —*Ger* [ˈmau zɐ] **~s** z

mausoleum ˌmɔːs ə ˈliː əm ˌmɔːz-, ˌmaʊz-, -ˈleɪ- ‖ ˌmɑːs-, ˌmɔːz-, ˌmɑːz- **~s** z

mauve məʊv ‖ moʊv mɔːv, mɑːv *(!)*

maven ˈmeɪv ᵊn **~s** z

maverick ˈmæv ər ˌɪk **~s** s

Mavis, mavis ˈmeɪv ɪs §-əs **~es, ~'s** ɪz əz

Mavor ˈmeɪv ə ‖ -ᵊr

maw, Maw mɔː ‖ mɑː **maws** mɔːz ‖ mɑːz

Mawddach ˈmaʊð əx -ək ‖ -ᵊk —*Welsh* [ˈmau ðaχ]

Mawdesley, Mawdsley ˈmɔːdz li ‖ ˈmɑːdz-

Mawer ˈmɔː· ə ‖ ˈmɔː·ᵊr ˈmɑː·

Mawgan ˈmɔːg ən ‖ ˈmɑːg-

Mawhinny mə ˈwɪn i -ˈhwɪn- ‖ -ˈhwɪn-

mawkish ˈmɔːk ɪʃ ‖ ˈmɑːk- **~ly** li **~ness** nəs nɪs

Mawson ˈmɔːs ᵊn ‖ ˈmɑːs-

Max, max mæks **Max's** ˈmæks ɪz -əz ˌMax ˈFactor *tdmk*

Maxell *tdmk* ˈmæks el mæk ˈsel

maxi ˈmæks i **~s, ~'s** z

maxill|a mæk ˈsɪl ǀə **~ae** iː

maxillary mæk ˈsɪl ər i ‖ ˈmæks ə ler i *(*)*

maxim, Maxim ˈmæks ɪm §-əm **~s** z

maxima ˈmæks ɪm ə -əm-

maximal ˈmæks ɪm ᵊl -ᵊm ˌəl **~ly** i

maximalist ˈmæks ɪm əl ɪst ˈ·ᵊm-, §-əst **~s** s

Maximilian ˌmæks ɪ ˈmɪl i ən ˌ·ə- ‖ ˌmæks ə ˈmɪl jən

maximin ˈmæks i mɪn ˌ·ˈ· ‖ -ə-

maximis... —*see* **maximiz...**

maximization ˌmæks ɪm aɪ ˈzeɪʃ ᵊn ˌ·əm-, -ɪˈ·- ‖ -əm ə- **~s** z

maximiz|e ˈmæks ɪ maɪz -ə- **~ed** d **~es** ɪz əz **~ing** ɪŋ

maxim|um ˈmæks ɪm ǀəm -əm- **~a** ə **~ums** əmz

Maximus, m~ ˈmæks ɪm əs -əm-

Maxine ˌmæks ˈiːn ˈ··

Maxton ˈmækst ən

Maxwell, m~ ˈmæks wel -wəl **~s** z

may, May meɪ ˈMay Day

Maya *Central American people* ˈmaɪ ˌə ˈmɑː jə **~s** z

Maya *Hindu deity,* **maya** *'illusion'* ˈmaɪ ə ˈmɑː jə

Maya *personal name (i)* ˈmeɪ ə, *(ii)* ˈmaɪ ˌə

Mayall ˈmeɪ ɔːl əl ‖ -ɑːl

Mayan ˈmaɪ ˌən **~s** z

maybe ˈmeɪb i ˈmeɪ biː, ˌ(ˌ)·ˈ· —*There is also a casual form* ˈmeb i. *The stress pattern* ˌ(ˌ)·ˈ· *is usual only when the word is at the end of a clause or sentence, with a concessive meaning:* They will try, ˌ(ˌ)mayˈbe; but they will not succeed.

maybeetle ˈmeɪ ˌbiːt ᵊl ‖ -ˌbiːt̬- **~s** z

Maybelline *tdmk* ˈmeɪb ə liːn -e-, ˌ··ˈ·

maybug ˈmeɪ bʌg **~s** z

mayday, M~ ˈmeɪ deɪ

Mayer *(i)* ˈmeɪ ə meə ‖ -ᵊr, *(ii)* ˈmaɪ ˌə ‖ -ᵊr —*(i) is an English form, (ii) a German form* —*Ger* [ˈmaɪ ɐ]

mayest ˈmeɪ ɪst -əst; meɪst

Mayfair ˈmeɪ feə ‖ -fer -fær

Mayfield ˈmeɪ fiːᵊld

Mayflower, m~ ˈmeɪ ˌflaʊ ˌə ‖ -ˌflaʊ ˌᵊr **~s** z

may|fly ˈmeɪ ǀflaɪ **~flies** flaɪz

mayhem ˈmeɪ hem

Mayhew ˈmeɪ hjuː

Maynard ˈmeɪn əd -ɑːd ‖ -ᵊrd -ɑːrd

Mayne meɪn

Maynooth mə ˈnuːθ meɪ-

mayn't meɪnt ˈmeɪ ənt

Mayo, mayo ˈmeɪ əʊ ‖ -oʊ —*in Irish English the placename is also* ·ˈ·

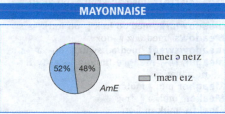

MAYONNAISE

52% 48% — ˈmeɪ ə neɪz — ˈmæn eɪz

AmE

mayonnaise ˌmeɪ ə ˈneɪz ◂ ‖ ˈmeɪ ə neɪz ˌ·ˈ·; ˈmæn eɪz — *Preference poll, AmE:* ˈmeɪ ə- 52%, ˈmæ- 48%.

mayor, Mayor meə ‖ ˈmeɪ ᵊr meᵊr **mayors, Mayor's** meəz ‖ ˈmeɪ ˌᵊrz meᵊrz

mayoral ˈmeər əl meɪ ˈɔːr əl ‖ ˈmeɪ ər əl

mayoralty ˈmeər əl ti ‖ ˈmeɪ ər əl ti ˈmer əl ti

mayoress ˌmeər ˈes ˈ· ·; ˈmeər ɪs, -əs ‖ ˈmeɪ ər əs ˈmer əs

mayorship ˈmeə ʃɪp ‖ ˈmeɪ ˌᵊr ʃɪp ˈmeᵊr- **~s** s

M

Mayotte maɪ ˈɒt -ˈjɒt ‖ -ˈjɑːt —*Fr* [ma jɔt]
maypole ˈmeɪ pəʊl →-pɒʊl ‖ -poʊl ~s z
Mays meɪz
mayst meɪst
may've ˈmeɪ əv
mayweed ˈmeɪ wiːd ~s z
mazard ˈmæz əd ‖ -ᵊrd ~s z
Mazarin ˈmæz ə rɪn -ræn —*Fr* [ma za ʁæ̃]
mazarine ˈmæz ə riːn ˌ·ˈ·◄
Mazawattee *tdmk* ˌmæz ə ˈwɒt i ‖ -ˈwɑːʧ i
Mazda *tdmk* ˈmæz də
Mazdaism ˈmæz dəʳ ˌɪz əm ‖ -ə-
maze meɪz **mazes** ˈmeɪz ɪz -əz
mazel tov ˈmæz ᵊl tɒf -tɒv ‖ ˈmɑːz ᵊl tɑːf -tɑːv
Mazeppa mə ˈzep ə
Mazola *tdmk* mə ˈzəʊl ə ‖ mə ˈzoʊl ə
mazuma mə ˈzuːm ə
mazurka mə ˈzɜːk ə ‖ -ˈzɝːk ə -ˈzʊrk- —*Polish*
  [ma ˈzur ka] ~s z
maz|y ˈmeɪz |i ~ier i ə ‖ i ᵊr ~iest i ɪst i əst
  ~ily ɪ li əl i ~iness i nəs i nɪs
MBA ˌem biː ˈeɪ
Mbabane ˌem bə ˈbɑːn i əm ˌbæ-, -bæˈ·ˌ·,
  -bɑːˈ·· —*siSwati* [mba ˈbaː ne]
MBE ˌem biː ˈiː
Mbeki əm ˈbek i —*Xhosa* [ˈmbeː ki]
mbyte, Mbyte ˈmeg ə baɪt ~s s
MC ˌem ˈsiː ~'d d ~'ing ɪŋ ~'s z
Mc... —*see* **Mac...** —*Names beginning Mc- are*
  listed in this dictionary as if written Mac-
MCC ˌem siː ˈsiː
m-commerce ˈem ˌkɒm ɜːs ‖ -ˌkɑːm ᵊrs
MCP ˌem siː ˈpiː ~s, ~'s z
MD ˌem ˈdiː
me miː, *weak form* mi
  ˈme ˌgene ˈration
ME *medical condition* ˌem ˈiː
Meacham ˈmiːʧ əm
Meacher ˈmiːʧ ə ‖ -ᵊr
mea culpa ˌmeɪ ə ˈkʊlp ə -ɑː ˈkʊlp ɑː
mead miːd
Mead, Meade miːd
meadow ˈmed əʊ ‖ -oʊ ~s z
Meadowcroft ˈmed əʊ krɒft ‖ -oʊ krɔːft
  -krɑːft
meadowlark ˈmed əʊ lɑːk ‖ -oʊ lɑːrk ~s s
Meadows ˈmed əʊz ‖ -oʊz
meadowsweet ˈmed əʊ swiːt ‖ -oʊ- -ə- ~s s
meager, M~, meagre ˈmiːg ə ‖ -ᵊr ~ly li
  ~ness nəs nɪs
Meagher mɑː ‖ mɑːr
Meaker ˈmiːk ə ‖ -ᵊr
Meakin ˈmiːk ɪn §-ən
meal miːᵊl **meals** miːᵊlz
  ˈmeal ˌticket
mealie ˈmiːl i ~s z
meals-on-wheels ˌmiːᵊlz ɒn ˈwiːᵊlz -ˈhwiːlz
  ‖ -ɑːn ˈhwiːᵊlz -ɔːn-
mealtime ˈmiːᵊl taɪm ~s z
mealworm ˈmiːᵊl wɜːm ‖ -wɝːm ~s z
meal|y ˈmiːl |i ~ier i ə ‖ i ᵊr ~iest i ɪst i əst
  ~iness i nəs i nɪs
mealybug ˈmiːl i bʌg ~s z

mealy-mouthed ˌmiːl i ˈmaʊðd ◄ ‖ -ˈmaʊθt ◄
mean miːn **meaner** ˈmiːn ə ‖ -ᵊr **meanest**
  ˈmiːn ɪst -əst **meaning** ˈmiːn ɪŋ **means** miːnz
  meant ment (!)
  ˈmeans test; ˌmean ˈtime
meander, M~ mi ˈænd ə ‖ -ᵊr ~ed d
  meandering/ly mi ˈænd ˌər ɪŋ /li ~s z
meanie ˈmiːn i ~s z
meaning ˈmiːn ɪŋ ~s z
meaningful ˈmiːn ɪŋ fᵊl -fʊl ~ly i ~ness nəs
  nɪs
meaningless ˈmiːn ɪŋ ləs -lɪs ~ly li ~ness nəs
  nɪs
mean|ly ˈmiːn |li ~ness nəs nɪs
mean-spirited ˌmiːn ˈspɪr ɪt ɪd ◄ -ət-, -əd ‖ -əʧ-
meant ment (!)
meantime ˈmiːn taɪm ˌ·ˈ·
meanwhile ˈmiːn waɪᵊl -hwaɪᵊl, ˌ·ˈ· ‖ -hwaɪᵊl
mean|y ˈmiːn| i ~ies iz
Meara (i) ˈmɪər ə ‖ ˈmɪr ə, (ii) ˈmɑːr ə
Mearns *place in Grampian* meənz ‖ meᵊrnz
Mears mɪəz ‖ mɪᵊrz
Measham ˈmiːʃ əm
measles ˈmiːz ᵊlz
meas|ly ˈmiːz |li ˈmiːz ᵊl i ~liness li nəs -nɪs
measurable ˈmeʒ ər_əb ᵊl ‖ ˈmeɪʒ-

MEASURE	
95%	5%
	■ ˈmeʒ-
	▨ ˈmeɪʒ-
	AmE

meas|ure ˈmeʒ |ə ‖ -|ᵊr ˈmeɪʒ- — *Preference*
  poll, AmE: ˈmeʒ- 95%, ˈmeɪʒ- 5%. ~ured əd
  ‖ ᵊrd ~uring ər_ɪŋ ~ures əz ‖ ᵊrz
  ˈmeasuring jug
measureless ˈmeʒ ə ləs -lɪs ‖ -ᵊr- ˈmeɪʒ- ~ly li
measurement ˈmeʒ ə mənt ‖ -ᵊr- ˈmeɪʒ- ~s s
measurer ˈmeʒ ər ə ‖ -ər ˈmeɪʒ- ~s z
meat miːt (= *meet*) **meats** miːts
  ˌmeat ˈloaf ‖ ˈ· ·
meat-and-potatoes ˌmiːt ᵊn pə ˈteɪt əʊz ◄
  -əm pə- ‖ -ˈteɪʧ oʊz ◄
meat-ax, meat-ax|e ˈmiːt æks ‖ ˈmiːʧ- ~ed t
  ~es ɪz əz ~ing ɪŋ
meatball ˈmiːt bɔːl ‖ -bɑːl ~s z
Meath *county in Ireland* miːð —*but by*
  outsiders often called miːθ
meati... —*see* **meaty**
meatless ˈmiːt ləs -lɪs
meat-packing ˈmiːt ˌpæk ɪŋ
meatus mi ˈeɪt əs ‖ -ˈeɪʧ- ~es ɪz əz
meat|y ˈmiːt |i ‖ ˈmiːʧ |i ~ier i ə ‖ i ᵊr ~iest
  i ɪst i əst ~ily ɪ li əl i ~iness i nəs i nɪs
Mebyon Kernow ˌmeb i ən ˈkɜːn əʊ
  ‖ -ˈkɝːn oʊ
Mecca, mecca ˈmek ə —*Arabic* [ˈmak ka]
meccano, M~ *tdmk* mɪ ˈkɑːn əʊ mə-, me- ‖ -oʊ
Mecham ˈmiːk əm

mechanic mɪ ˈkæn ɪk mə- **~s** s
mechanical mɪ ˈkæn ɪk ᵊl mə- **~ly** ͵i **~ness**
   nəs nɪs **~s** z
   me͵chanical ͵engiˈneering
mechanis... —*see* **mechaniz...**
mechanism ˈmek ə ͵nɪz əm **~s** z
mechanist ˈmek ən ɪst §-əst **~s** s
mechanistic ͵mek ə ˈnɪst ɪk ◄ **~ally** ᵊl ͵i
mechanization ͵mek ən aɪ ˈzeɪʃ ᵊn -ən ɪ-
   ‖ -ən ə-
mechaniz|e ˈmek ə naɪz **~ed** d **~es** ɪz əz **~ing**
   ɪŋ
Mechlin ˈmek lɪn §-lən —*Dutch* Mechelen
   [ˈmɛ xə lən], *French* Malines [ma lin]
Mecklenburg ˈmek lən bɜːg -lɪn-, ͵→-ləm-
   ‖ -bɜːɡ —*Ger* [ˈmeː klən bʊʁk, ˈmɛ-]
meconium mɪ ˈkəʊn i ͵əm mə- ‖ -ˈkoʊn-
Med, med med **meds** medz
MEd ͵em ˈed
medal ˈmed ᵊl **~s** z
medalist ˈmed ᵊl ɪst §-əst **~s** s
medallion mə ˈdæl i ən mɪ- ‖ -ˈdæl jən **~s** z
medallist ˈmed ᵊl ɪst §-əst **~s** s
Medan ˈmeɪd æn -ɑːn ‖ meɪ ˈdɑːn
Medau ˈmed aʊ
Medawar ˈmed ə wə ‖ -wᵊr
meddl|e ˈmed ᵊl (= *medal*) **~ed** d **~er/s** ͵ə/z
   ‖ ᵊr/z **~es** z **~ing** ɪŋ
meddlesome ˈmed ᵊl səm **~ly** li **~ness** nəs nɪs
Mede miːd **Medes** miːdz
Medea mə ˈdɪə mɪ-, -ˈdiː ə ‖ mə ˈdiː ə
Medellin, Medellín ͵med əl ˈjiːn ◄ -el- —*Sp*
   [me ðe ˈʎin, -ˈjiːn]
Medevac ˈmed ɪ ͵væk -ə-
medfly ˈmed flaɪ
media *other senses; Latin adj* ˈmiːd i ə ˈmed-
media *pl of* **medium**; *'means of*
   communication' ˈmiːd i ə
Media *'country of the Medes'* ˈmiːd i ə
mediaeval ͵med i ˈiːv ᵊl ◄ me ˈdiːv ᵊl ‖ ͵miːd-
   ͵med-, ͵mɪd-; mɪ ˈdiːv ᵊl (*) **~ism** ͵ɪz əm
   ~ist/s ɪst/s §əst/s ‖ əst/s **~ly** i
medial ˈmiːd i əl **~ly** i
median ˈmiːd i ən **~ly** i **~s** z
mediant ˈmiːd i ənt **~s** s
mediastin|um ͵miːd i ə ˈstaɪn |əm **~a** ə **~al**
   ᵊl ◄
medi|ate *v* ˈmiːd i |eɪt **~ated** eɪt ɪd -əd
   ‖ eɪt̬ əd **~ates** eɪts **~ating** eɪt ɪŋ ‖ eɪt̬ ɪŋ
mediation ͵miːd i ˈeɪʃ ᵊn **~s** z
mediator ˈmiːd i eɪt ə ‖ -eɪt̬ ᵊr **~s** z
medic ˈmed ɪk **~s** s
Medicaid, m~ ˈmed ɪ keɪd
medical ˈmed ɪk ᵊl **~ly** ͵i **~s** z
   ˈmedical ͵card; ˈmedical cer͵tificate
medicament mə ˈdɪk ə mənt mɪ-, me-;
   ˈmed ɪk- **~s** s
Medicare, m~ ˈmed ɪ keə ‖ -ker -kær
medi|cate ˈmed ɪ |keɪt §-ə- **~cated** keɪt ɪd -əd
   ‖ keɪt̬ əd **~cates** keɪts **~cating** keɪt ɪŋ
   ‖ keɪt̬ ɪŋ
medication ͵med ɪ ˈkeɪʃ ᵊn §-ə- **~s** z

Medici ˈmed ɪtʃ i §-ətʃ-; me ˈdiːtʃ i, mə-, mɪ-
   —*It* [ˈmeː di tʃi]
medicinal mə ˈdɪs ᵊn ᵊl mɪ-, me-, -ɪn-
   —*formerly also* ͵med ɪ ˈsaɪn ᵊl, ˈmed sᵊn-͵əl **~ly**
   i
medicine ˈmed sᵊn -sɪn, ˈmed ɪs ən, -əs-, -ɪn **~s**
   z
   ˈmedicine chest; ˈmedicine man
medick ˈmed ɪk **~s** s
medico ˈmed ɪ kəʊ ‖ -koʊ **~s** z
medieval ͵med i ˈiːv ᵊl ◄ me ˈdiːv ᵊl ‖ ͵miːd-
   ͵med-, ͵mɪd-; mɪ ˈdiːv ᵊl (*) **~ism** ͵ɪz əm
   ~ist/s ɪst/s §əst/s ‖ əst/s **~ly** i
Medina, m~ (i) me ˈdiːn ə mə-, mɪ-,
   (ii) -ˈdaɪn ə —*The place in Saudi Arabia is*
   (i) —*Arabic* [me ˈdiː na]; *that in OH,* (ii).
mediocre ͵miːd i ˈəʊk ə ◄ ͵med-, ˈ· · · ·
   ‖ -ˈoʊk ᵊr
mediocrit|y ͵miːd i ˈɒk rət |i ͵med-, -ɪt i
   ‖ -ˈɑːkr ət̬ |i **~ies** iz
medi|tate ˈmed ɪ |teɪt -ə- **~tated** teɪt ɪd -əd
   ‖ teɪt̬ əd **~tates** teɪts **~tating** teɪt ɪŋ ‖ teɪt̬ ɪŋ
meditation ͵med ɪ ˈteɪʃ ᵊn -ə- **~s** z
meditative ˈmed ɪt ət ɪv -ət ət-; -ɪ teɪt-, -ə teɪt-
   ‖ -ə teɪt̬ ɪv **~ly** li **~ness** nəs nɪs
Mediterranean ͵med ɪ tə ˈreɪn i ən ◄ ͵·ə- **~s** z
   ͵Mediter͵ranean ˈSea
medi|um ˈmiːd i |əm **~a** ə **~ums** əmz
   ͵medium ˈwave◄
medium-sized ͵miːd i əm ˈsaɪzd ◄ ˈ· · ·
medium-term ͵miːd i əm ˈtɜːm ◄ ‖ -ˈtɜːm ◄
medlar ˈmed lə ‖ -lᵊr **~s** z
medley ˈmed li **~s** z
Medlicott ˈmed lɪ kɒt ‖ -kɑːt
Medlock ˈmed lɒk ‖ -lɑːk
Medoc, Médoc ˈmed ɒk meɪ ˈdɒk ‖ meɪ ˈdɑːk
   —*Fr* [me dɔk]
Medresco me ˈdresk əʊ mə-, mɪ- ‖ -oʊ
medulla me ˈdʌl ə mə-, mɪ-
   me͵dulla ͵oblonˈgata ͵ɒb lɒŋ ˈɡaːt ə
   ‖ ͵ɑːb lɔːŋ ˈɡaːt̬ ə -lɑːŋ-
medullary me ˈdʌl ər i mə-, mɪ- ‖ ˈmed ᵊl er i
   ˈmedʒ-; mə ˈdʌl ər i (*)
Medusa, m~ mə ˈdjuːz ə me-, mɪ-, -ˈdjuːs-,
   ͵→-ˈdʒuːz- ‖ -ˈduːs ə -ˈdjuːs-, -ˈduːz-, -ˈdjuːz- **~s,**
   ~'s z
Medway ˈmed weɪ
Medwin ˈmed wɪn
Mee miː
meed miːd **meeds** miːdz
Meehan ˈmiː ən
meek, Meek miːk
meek|ly ˈmiːk |li **~ness** nəs nɪs
meerkat ˈmɪə kæt ‖ ˈmɪr- **~s** s
meerschaum ˈmɪəʃ əm ˈmɪə ʃaʊm ‖ ˈmɪrʃ əm
   ˈmɪr ʃɔːm, -ʃɑːm
Meerut ˈmɪər ət —*Hindi* [meː rətʰ]
meet miːt **meeting** ˈmiːt ɪŋ ‖ ˈmiːt̬ ɪŋ **meets**
   miːts **met** met
meet-and-greet ͵miːt ᵊn ˈɡriːt ◄
meeting ˈmiːt ɪŋ ‖ ˈmiːt̬ ɪŋ **~s** z
   ˈmeeting point

M

meeting|house 'miːt ɪŋ |haʊs ‖ 'miːtʃ-
~houses haʊz ɪz -əz
mefloquine 'mef lə kwiːn -kwɪn ‖ -kwaɪn
meg, Meg meg **megs** megz
mega 'meg ə
mega- *comb. form* |meg ə — **megastar**
'meg ə staː ‖ -staːr
megabit 'meg ə bɪt **~s** s
megabuck 'meg ə bʌk **~s** s
megabyte 'meg ə baɪt **~s** s
megacycle 'meg ə ˌsaɪk ᵊl **~s** z
megadeath 'meg ə deθ **~s** s
megahertz 'meg ə hɜːts ‖ -hɝːts
megalith 'meg ə lɪθ **~s** s
megalithic ˌmeg ə 'lɪθ ɪk ◄
megalo- *comb. form*
  with stress-neutral suffix |meg ə ləʊ -ᵊl əʊ
  ‖ -loʊ — **megaloblastic**
  ˌmeg ə ləʊ 'blæst ɪk ◄ -ᵊl əʊ- ‖ -ə loʊ-
  with stress-imposing suffix ˌmeg ə 'lɒ+
  ‖ -'laː+ — **megalopolis, M~**
  ˌmeg ə 'lɒp əl ɪs §-əs ‖ -'laːp-
megalomania ˌmeg əl əʊ 'meɪn i ə ‖ -əl ə-
megalomaniac ˌmeg əl əʊ 'meɪn i æk ‖ -əl ə-
  ~s s
megalosaur 'meg əl əʊ sɔː ‖ -ə sɔːr **~s** z
Megan (i) 'meg ən, (ii) 'miːg-, (iii) 'meɪg-
  —*In BrE always* (i).
Megane, Mégane mə 'gæn me- ‖ -'gaːn —*Fr*
  [me gan]
megaphone 'meg ə fəʊn ‖ -foʊn **~s** z
megapixel 'meg ə ˌpɪks ᵊl **~s** z
megaplex 'meg ə pleks **~es** ɪz əz
Megara, m~ 'meg ər ə
megaron 'meg ə rɒn -raːn
megastar 'meg ə staː ‖ -staːr **~s** z
megastore 'meg ə stɔː ‖ -stɔːr **~s** z
megatheri|um ˌmeg ə 'θɪər i_|əm ‖ -'θɪr- **~a** ə
megaton 'meg ə tʌn **~s** z
megawatt 'meg ə wɒt ‖ -waːt **~s** s
Megger *tdmk* 'meg ə ‖ -ᵊr
Meggeson 'meg ɪs ən -əs-
Meggezones *tdmk* 'meg ɪ zəʊnz -ə- ‖ -zoʊnz
Meggison 'meg ɪs ən -əs-
Megillah, m~ mə 'gɪl ə **~s** z
megilp mə 'gɪlp
megohm 'meg əʊm ‖ -oʊm **~s** z
megrim 'miːg rɪm -rəm **~s** z
Mehmet 'mem et —*Turkish* [mɛh 'mɛt]
Mehta 'meɪt ə
Meier 'maɪ̯ə ‖ 'maɪ̯ᵊr
Meikle 'miːk ᵊl
Meiklejohn (i) 'miːk ᵊl dʒɒn ‖ -dʒaːn,
  (ii) 'mɪk-
Mein Kampf ˌmaɪn 'kæmpf —*Ger*
  [maɪn 'kampf]
meios|is maɪ 'əʊs |ɪs meɪ-, §-əs ‖ -'oʊs- **~es** iːz
Meir mɪə ‖ mɪᵊr —*but as an Israeli name*,
  meɪ 'ɪə ‖ -'ɪᵊr
Meirion 'maɪᵊr i ɒn ‖ -aːn —*Welsh* ['məɪr jon]
Meirionnydd ˌmer i 'ɒn ɪð -ɪθ, -əθ ‖ -'aːn-
  —*Welsh* [məɪr 'jɔn i ð, -ɪð]
meishi 'meɪʃ i —*Jp* [me ˌɕi] **~s** z

Meissen 'maɪs ᵊn —*Ger* ['maɪ sᵊn]
  'Meissen ware
Meistersinger 'maɪst ə ˌsɪŋ ə ‖ -ᵊr ˌsɪŋ ᵊr
  —*Ger* ['maɪ stɐ ˌzɪŋ ɐ] **~s** z
meitnerium ˌmaɪt 'nɪər i_əm -'neər- ‖ -'nɪr-
  -'ner-
Mekka 'mek ə
Mekong ˌmiː 'kɒŋ ◄ ˌmeɪ- ‖ ˌmeɪ 'kɔːŋ ◄ -'kaːŋ
  ˌMekong 'Delta
Mel, mel mel **mels, Mel's** melz
melamine 'mel ə miːn -mɪn, -maɪn
melancholia ˌmel ən 'kəʊl i_ə →ˌ·əŋ- ‖ -'koʊl-
melancholic ˌmel ən 'kɒl ɪk ◄ →-əŋ- ‖ -'kaːl-
  ~ally ᵊl i
melancholy 'mel ən kəl i →ˈ·əŋ-, -kɒl i
  ‖ -kaːl i
Melanchthon mə 'læŋk θən mɪ-, me-, -θɒn
  ‖ -θaːn —*Ger* [me 'lançˀ tɔn]
Mela|nesia ˌmel ə| 'niːz i_ə -'niːʒ ə, -'niːs i_ə,
  -'niːʃ ə ‖ -'niːʒ ə -'niːʒ ə **~nesian/s**
  'niːz i_ən/z ◄ 'niːʒ ᵊn/z, 'niːs i_ən/z,
  'niːʃ ᵊn/z ‖ 'niːʒ ᵊn/z ◄ 'niːʃ ᵊn/z
melang|e, mélang|e meɪ 'laːnʒ me-, -'lɒ̃ʒ
  —*Fr* [me lɑ̃ːʒ] **~es** ɪz əz
Melanie 'mel ən i
melanin 'mel ən ɪn §-ən
melanism 'mel ə ˌnɪz əm
melano- *comb. form* |mel ə nəʊ ‖ -ə noʊ -ən ə
  — **melanocyte** 'mel ə nəʊ saɪt ‖ -ə noʊ-
  -ə nə-
melanoma ˌmel ə 'nəʊm ə ‖ -'noʊm ə **~s** z
melanuria ˌmel ə 'njʊər i_ə ‖ -'nʊr- -'njʊr-
melatonin ˌmel ə 'təʊn ɪn -ən ‖ -'toʊn-
Melba 'melb ə
Melbourne (i) 'mel bɔːn ‖ -bɔːrn -boʊrn,
  (ii) 'melb ən ‖ -ᵊrn —*The places in
  Cambridgeshire and Derbyshire are* (i). *The
  place in Australia is* (ii) *locally, but is often
  called* (i) *by non-Australians.*
Melchers 'meltʃ əz ‖ -ᵊrz
Melchett 'meltʃ ɪt -ət
Melchior 'melk i ɔː ‖ -ɔːr
Melchizedek mel 'kɪz ə dek
meld meld **melded** 'meld ɪd -əd **melding**
  'meld ɪŋ **melds** meldz
Meldrew 'meldr uː
Meldrum 'meldr əm
Meleager ˌmel i 'eɪg ə ‖ -'eɪdʒ ᵊr
melee, mêlée 'mel eɪ me 'leɪ ‖ 'meɪl eɪ
  meɪ 'leɪ (*) **~s** z
Melhuish (i) 'mel ɪʃ, (ii) 'mel hjuː ɪʃ -juː-, -u-,
  (iii) mel 'hjuː ɪʃ
Melia 'miːl i_ə
melic 'mel ɪk
Melilla me 'liː ə -jə —*Sp* [me 'li ja, -ʎa]
melilot 'mel ɪ lɒt -ə- ‖ -laːt **~s** s
Melina mə 'liːn ə me-, mɪ-
melinite 'mel ɪ naɪt -ə-
melio|rate 'miːl i_ə |reɪt **~rated** reɪt ɪd -əd
  ‖ reɪt̬ əd **~rates** reɪts **~rating** reɪt ɪŋ ‖ reɪt̬ ɪŋ
melioration ˌmiːl i_ə 'reɪʃ ᵊn **~s** z
meliorative 'miːl i_ər ət ɪv -ə reɪt- ‖ -ə reɪt̬ ɪv
meliorism 'miːl i_ə ˌrɪz əm

meliorist 'miːl i‿ər ɪst §-əst ~s s
melisma mə 'lɪz mə mɪ-, me- ~s z
melismatic ˌmel ɪz 'mæt ɪk ◂ §ˌ-əz-
  ‖ -'mæt̬ ɪk ◂
Melissa mə 'lɪs ə mɪ-, me-
Melksham 'melk ʃəm
melliflu|ence mə 'lɪf lu‿|ənˢs mɪ-, me- ~ent
  ənt
mellifluous mə 'lɪf lu‿əs mɪ-, me- ~ly li ~ness
  nəs nɪs
Mellish 'mel ɪʃ
Mellony 'mel ən i
Mellor 'mel ə ‖ -ᵊr
Mellors 'mel əz ‖ -ᵊrz
mellow 'mel əʊ ‖ -oʊ ~ed d ~er ə ‖ ᵊr ~est ɪst
  əst ~ing ɪŋ ~ly li ~ness nəs nɪs ~s z
Melly 'mel i
melodeon mə 'ləʊd i ən mɪ-, me- ‖ -'loʊd- ~s
  z
melodic mə 'lɒd ɪk mɪ-, me- ‖ -'lɑːd- ~ally ᵊl i
melodica mə 'lɒd ɪk ə mɪ-, me- ‖ -'lɑːd- ~s z
melodie... —see **melody**
melodion mə 'ləʊd i ən mɪ-, me- ‖ -'loʊd- ~s z
melodious mə 'ləʊd i‿əs mɪ-, me- ‖ -'loʊd- ~ly
  li ~ness nəs nɪs
melodis... —see **melodize**
melodist 'mel əd ɪst §-əst ~s s
melodiz|e 'mel ə daɪz ~ed d ~es ɪz əz ~ing ɪŋ
melodrama 'mel ə ˌdrɑːm ə -əʊ- ‖ -ˌdræm- ~s
  z
melodramatic ˌmel ə drə 'mæt ɪk ◂ ˌ-əʊ-
  ‖ -'mæt̬ ɪk ◂ ~ally ᵊl i ~s s
melod|y, M~ 'mel əd |i —Occasionally, and
  particularly in singing, also -əʊd- ‖ -oʊd- ~ies
  iz
Meloids tdmk 'mel ɔɪdz
melon 'mel ən ~s z
Melos 'miːl ɒs 'mel- ‖ -ɑːs
Melpomene mel 'pɒm ən i -ɪn i, -iː ‖ -'pɑːm-
Melrose 'mel rəʊz ‖ -roʊz
melt melt **melted** 'melt ɪd -əd **melting/ly**
  'melt ɪŋ /li **melts** melts
  'melting point; 'melting pot
meltag|e 'melt ɪdʒ ~es ɪz əz
meltdown 'melt daʊn ~s z
Melton, m~ 'melt ən
  ˌMelton 'Mowbray
Meltonian tdmk mel 'təʊn i ən ‖ -'toʊn-
meltwater 'melt ˌwɔːt ə ‖ -ˌwɔːt̬ ᵊr -ˌwɑːt̬- ~s z
Melville 'mel vɪl
Melvin, Melvyn 'melv ɪn §-ən
member 'mem bə ‖ -bᵊr ~s z
  ˌMember of 'Parliament
membership 'mem bə ʃɪp ‖ -bᵊr- ~s s
membrane 'mem breɪn ~s z
membranous 'mem brən əs mem 'breɪn-
meme miːm **memes** miːmz
memento mə 'ment əʊ mɪ-, me-, △məʊ-
  ‖ -'ment̬ oʊ ~es, ~s z
  meˌmento 'mori 'mɔr iː 'mɔːr-, -i, -aɪ
  ‖ 'mɔːr-
Memnon 'mem nɒn -nən ‖ -nɑːn

memo 'mem əʊ 'miːm- ‖ -oʊ ~s z
  'memo pad
memoir 'mem wɑː ‖ -wɑːr -wɔːr ~s z
memorabilia ˌmem ər‿ə 'bɪl i‿ə -'biːl-
memorab|le 'mem ər‿əb |ᵊl ~leness ᵊl nəs
  -nɪs ~ly li
memorand|um ˌmem ə 'rænd |əm ~a ə ~s z
memorial mə 'mɔːr i‿əl mɪ-, me- ‖ -'moʊr- ~ly
  i ~s z
memorialis|e, memorializ|e
  mə 'mɔːr i‿ə laɪz mɪ-, me- ‖ -'moʊr- ~ed d ~es
  ɪz əz ~ing ɪŋ
memorie... —see **memory**
memoris... —see **memoriz...**
memorization ˌmem ər aɪ 'zeɪʃ ᵊn -əˈ-- ‖ -əˈ--
memoriz|e 'mem ə raɪz ~ed d ~es ɪz əz ~ing
  ɪŋ
memor|y 'mem ər‿|i ~ies iz
  'memory span
memory-hogging 'mem ər‿i ˌhɒg ɪŋ
  ‖ -ˌhɑːg ɪŋ
Memphis 'memᵖf ɪs §-əs
memsahib 'mem sɑːb 'mem ˌsɑː ɪb, -hɪb ~s z
men men **men's** menz
  'men's room
-men mən, men —See note at -man. The
  pronunciation **men** is used for the plural
  rather more widely than **mæn** is for the
  singular.
menac|e 'men əs -ɪs ~ed t ~er/s ə/z ‖ ᵊr/z ~es
  ɪz əz ~ing/ly ɪŋ /li
menag|e, ménag|e ₍ᵢ₎me 'nɑːʒ ₍ᵢ₎meɪ-, mə-,
  mɪ-, -'næʒ; 'men ɑːʒ ‖ meɪ 'nɑːʒ mə- —Fr
  [me nɑːʒ] ~es ɪz əz
  méˌnage à 'trois, ˌ‧ ‧ ‧'‧ ɑː 'trwɑː —Fr
  [a tʁwa]
menagerie mə 'nædʒ ər‿i mɪ-, me-, -'næʒ-,
  -'nɑːʒ- ~s z
Menai 'men aɪ —Welsh ['me nai, -ne]
  ˌMenai 'Bridge; ˌMenai 'Strait
Menander mə 'nænd ə mɪ-, me- ‖ -ᵊr
menarche me 'nɑːk i mɪ-, mə-; 'men ɑːk
  ‖ -'nɑːrk i
men-at-arms ˌmen ət 'ɑːmz ‖ -ət̬ 'ɑːrmz
Mencap 'men kæp →'meŋ-
Mencius 'men ʃi‿əs 'menˢ əs —Chi Mèngzi
  [⁴mʌŋ tsɯ]
Mencken 'meŋk ən
mend mend **mended** 'mend ɪd -əd **mending**
  'mend ɪŋ **mends** mendz
mendacious men 'deɪʃ əs ~ly li ~ness nəs nɪs
mendacity men 'dæs ət i -ɪt- ‖ -ət̬ i
Mende 'mend eɪ
Mendel 'mend ᵊl
Mendeleev ˌmend ə 'leɪ ev ˌ·ɪ-, -ef, -əf; -ᵊl 'eɪ-
  —Russ [mʲɪnʲ dʲɪ lʲ⁽ʲ⁾e jɪf]
mendelevium ˌmend ə 'liːv i‿əm ˌ·ɪ-; -ᵊl 'iːv-
Mendeleyev ˌmend ə 'leɪ ev ˌ·ɪ-, -ef, -əf;
  -ᵊl 'eɪ- —Russ [mʲɪnʲ dʲɪ lʲ⁽ʲ⁾e jɪf]
Mendelian men 'diːl i‿ən
Mendelism 'mend ᵊl ˌɪz əm -ə ˌlɪz-
Mendelssohn 'mend ᵊl sən —Ger
  ['mɛn dᵊl zoːn, -dᵊls zoːn]

mender 'mend ə ‖ -ᵊr ~s z
Mendez, Méndez 'mend ez ‖ men 'dez —*Sp*
['men deθ, -des]
mendicant 'mend ɪk ənt §-ək- ~s s
Mendip 'mend ɪp ~s s
   ,Mendip 'Hills
Mendocino ,mend ə 'siːn əʊ ‖ -oʊ
Mendoza men 'dəʊz ə ‖ -'doʊz ə —*AmSp*
[men 'do sa]
Menelaus ,men ɪ 'leɪ əs -ə-, -ᵊl 'eɪ-
Menem 'men em
mene mene tekel upharsin
   ,miːn i 'miːn i ,tek ᵊl ju 'faːs ɪn §-ᵊn ‖ -'faːrs-
   -,tiːk-, -'fers-
Menevia mɪ 'niːv i ə mə-
menfolk 'men fəʊk ‖ -foʊk
Mengele 'meŋ əl ə —*German* [mɛŋ l ə]
Mengistu meŋ 'gɪst uː men-
menhaden men 'heɪd ᵊn mən- ~s z
menhir 'men hɪə ‖ -hɪr ~s z
menial 'miːn i‿əl ~ly i ~s z
Meniere, Ménière 'men i eə 'meɪn-, ‧ ‧ˈ‧
   ‖ mən 'jeᵊr, meɪn-; 'men jᵊr —*Fr* [me njɛːʁ]
   'Ménière's di,sease ‖ Mén'ière's-
meningeal me 'nɪndʒ i‿əl mə-, mɪ-;
   ,men ɪn 'dʒiː əl ◂, -ən-
meninges me 'nɪndʒ iːz mə-, mɪ-
meningitis ,men ɪn 'dʒaɪt ɪs -ən-, §-əs
   ‖ -'dʒaɪt̬ əs
meningococc|al mə ,nɪndʒ əʊ 'kɒk |ᵊl ◂
   -,nɪŋ gəʊ- ‖ -ə 'kaːk |ᵊl ◂ ~us əs
meninx 'men ɪŋks **meninges** me 'nɪndʒ iːz
   mə-, mɪ-
me|niscus mə |'nɪsk əs mɪ-, me- ~nisci 'nɪs aɪ
   'nɪsk-, -iː
Menlo 'men ləʊ ‖ -loʊ
Mennonite 'men ə naɪt ~s z
men-of-war ,men əv 'wɔː -ə- ‖ -'wɔːr
Menominee, Menomini, Menomonee,
   Menomonie mə 'nɒm ən i mɪ-, me-
   ‖ -'naːm- ~s z
menopausal ,men əʊ 'pɔːz ᵊl ◂ ,miːn- ‖ -ə-
   -'paːz-
menopause 'men əʊ pɔːz 'miːn- ‖ -ə- -paːz
menorah mə 'nɔːr ə mɪ- ‖ -'noʊr- ~s z
menorrhagia ,men ə 'reɪdʒ i‿ə ,miːn-;
   -'reɪdʒ ə
menorrhoea ,men ə 'riː ə ,miːn-
Menotti mə 'nɒt i mɪ-, ne- ‖ -'naːt̬ i —*It*
   [me 'nɔt ti]
mens menz
   ,mens 'rea 'riː ə 'reɪ ə; ,mens 'sana 'saːn ə
   'sæn-(in ,corpore 'sano)
   ɪn ,kɔːp ər i 'saːn əʊ →ŋ-, -,ə reɪ-, -'sæn-
   ‖ ɪn ,kɔːrp ər i 'saːn oʊ
Mensa 'menˢ ə
mensch menʃ **menschen** 'menʃ ən **mensches**
   'menʃ ɪz -əz
menses 'menˢ iːz
Menshevik 'menʃ ə vɪk -ɪ-, -viːk ~s s
Menshevism 'menʃ ə ˌvɪz əm -ɪ-
Menston 'menˢt ən

menstrual 'menˢ tru‿əl
   ,menstrual 'period
menstru|ate 'menˢ tru |eɪt ‖ 'men str|eɪt
   ~ated eɪt ɪd -əd ‖ eɪt̬ əd ~ates eɪts ~ating
   eɪt ɪŋ ‖ eɪt̬ ɪŋ
menstruation ,menˢ tru 'eɪʃ ᵊn ‖ men 'streɪʃ-
   ~s z
mensurability ,menˢʃ ər‿ə 'bɪl ət i ,menˢ-,
   -,jər-, -ɪt i ‖ -ət̬ i
mensurable 'menˢʃ ər‿əb ᵊl 'menˢs-, -,jər-
mensural 'menˢʃ ər əl 'menˢs-, -,jər-
mensuration ,menˢʃ ə 'reɪʃ ᵊn ,menˢs-, -jə-
menswear 'menz weə ‖ -wer -wær
-ment *noun ending* mənt, *verb ending* ment
   — **ornament** *n* 'ɔːn ə mənt ‖ 'ɔːrn-, *v*
   'ɔːn ə ment ‖ 'ɔːrn- —*This ending is usually*
   weak in nouns, strong in verbs (although this
   standard distinction is not always observed by
   native speakers). In most cases -ment is
   unstressed and has no effect on stress. In
   two-syllable verbs, however, it is stressed:
   compare the noun 'segment *and the verb to*
   seg'ment. *There are various exceptions,*
   including 'comment *v., n.,* la'ment *v., n.,*
   torment, ferment *(in these latter two the*
   ending is always strong, unstressed in the noun
   but stressed in the verb).
Mentadent *tdmk* 'ment ə dent ‖ 'ment̬-
mental 'ment ᵊl ‖ 'ment̬ ᵊl ~ly i
   ,mental 'age◂, a ,mental age of 'ten;
   ,mental de'fective; ,mental 'health;
   'mental ,hospital; 'mental 'note
-mental 'ment ᵊl ‖ 'ment̬ ᵊl — **ornamental**
   ,ɔːn ə 'ment ᵊl ◂ ‖ ,ɔːrn ə 'ment̬ ᵊl ◂
mentalism 'ment ᵊl ,ɪz əm -ə ,lɪz- ‖ 'ment̬-
mentalist 'ment ᵊl ɪst §-əst; -ə lɪst, §-ləst
   ‖ 'ment̬- ~s s
mentalistic ,ment ə 'lɪst ɪk ◂ ,ment ᵊl 'ɪst-
   ‖ ,ment̬ ᵊl 'ɪst ɪk ◂ ~ally ᵊl i
mentalit|y men 'tæl ət |i -ɪt- ‖ -ət̬ |i ~ies iz
mentee ,men 'tiː ~s z
menthol 'menˢθ ɒl ‖ -ɔːl -aːl
mentholated 'menˢθ ə leɪt ɪd -əd ‖ -leɪt̬ əd
mention 'menˢʃ ᵊn ~ed d ~ing ɪŋ ~s z
mentor, M~ 'ment ɔː -ə ‖ 'ment̬ ɔːr 'ment̬ ᵊr
   ~ed d **mentoring** 'ment ər ɪŋ -ɔːr-
   ‖ 'ment̬ ᵊr ɪŋ 'ment ɔːr- ~s z
menu 'men juː ‖ 'meɪn- ~s z
menu-driven 'men juː ,drɪv ᵊn ,‧‧'‧‧ ‖ 'meɪn-
Menuhin 'men juː ɪn §-ən
Menzies 'menz iz —*but in Scotland usually*
   'mɪŋ ɪs, -ɪz
Meols *(i)* miːᵊlz, *(ii)* melz —*Places near*
   Southport, Merseyside (formerly Lancs), are
   (i); that near Hoylake, Merseyside (formerly
   Cheshire), is (ii).
Meon *place in Hampshire* 'miː ən
Meopham *place in Kent* 'mep əm
meow mi 'aʊ ~ed d ~ing ɪŋ ~s z
MEP ,em iː 'piː ~s z
mepacrine 'mep ə krɪn -kriːn
Mephisto mə 'fɪst əʊ mɪ-, me- ‖ -oʊ

M

Mephistophelean, m~ ˌmef ɪst ə 'fiːl i ən ◂
ˌ·əst-; mə ˌfɪst-, mɪ-, me-; ˌmef ɪ ˌstɒf ə 'liːən
‖ -ə ˌstɑːf ə 'liːən
Mephistopheles ˌmef ɪ 'stɒf ə liːz ˌ·ə-, -'ɪ-
‖ -'stɑːf-
mephitic mɪ 'fɪt ɪk mə-, me- ‖ -'fɪt̬-
meprobamate ˌmep rəʊ 'bæm eɪt
me 'prəʊb ə meɪt, mɪ-, mə- ‖ ˌmep roʊ-
-mer mə ‖ mᵊr — **monomer** 'mɒn əʊm ə
‖ 'mɑːn əm ᵊr
Merc mɜːk ‖ mɜːk
mercantile 'mɜːk ən taɪᵊl →-ŋ- ‖ 'mɜːk ən tiːᵊl
-taɪᵊl, -tᵊl
mercantilism 'mɜːk ənt ɪ ˌlɪz əm →'·ŋt-, -ə,-,
-əl ˌɪz-, -ən taɪ ˌlɪz- ‖ 'mɜːk ən tiː ˌlɪz əm
-taɪ,-
mercantilist 'mɜːk ənt ɪl ɪst →'·ŋt-, -əl ɪst,
-aɪl ɪst, §-əst; mɜː 'kænt əl- ‖ 'mɜːk ən tiːl əst
-taɪl əst ~s s
mercaptan mɜː 'kæpt æn ‖ mᵊr-
Mercator mɜː 'keɪt ə mə-, -ɔː ‖ mᵊr 'keɪt̬ ᵊr ~'s
z
　**Mer,cator pro'jection, Mer,cator's
　pro'jection**
Merced *place in CA* mɜː 'sed ‖ mᵊr-
Mercedes mə 'seɪd ɪz mɜː-, -iːz ‖ mᵊr- —*The pl
of the tdmk is pronounced the same as the
sing., or with -iːz.*
mercenar|y 'mɜːs ᵊn ər ˌi '·ɪn- ‖ 'mɜːs ᵊn er ˌi
~**ies** iz
mercer, M~ 'mɜːs ə ‖ 'mɜːs ᵊr ~s z
merceris|e, merceriz|e 'mɜːs ə raɪz ‖ 'mɜːs-
~**ed** d ~**es** ɪz əz ~**ing** ɪŋ
merchandis|e, merchandiz|e *v*
'mɜːtʃ ən daɪz ‖ 'mɜːtʃ- ~**ed** d ~**er/s** ə/z
‖ ᵊr/z ~**es** ɪz əz ~**ing** ɪŋ
merchandise *n* 'mɜːtʃ ən daɪz -daɪs ‖ 'mɜːtʃ-
merchant, M~ 'mɜːtʃ ənt ‖ 'mɜːtʃ- ~**s** s
　ˌmerchant 'bank, ~er, ~ing; ˌmerchant
　ma'rine; ˌmerchant 'navy; ˌmerchant
　'seaman
merchantable 'mɜːtʃ ənt əb ᵊl ‖ 'mɜːtʃ ənt̬-
merchant|man 'mɜːtʃ ənt |mən ‖ 'mɜːtʃ-
~**men** mən men
Mercia 'mɜːs i ə 'mɜːʃ-, 'mɜːʃ ə ‖ 'mɜːʃ i ə
'mɜːʃ ə
Mercian 'mɜːs i ən 'mɜːʃ-, 'mɜːʃ ᵊn ‖ 'mɜːʃ i ən
'mɜːʃ ᵊn ~**s** z
mercie... —*see* **mercy**
merciful 'mɜːs ɪ fᵊl -ə-, -fʊl ‖ 'mɜːs- ~**ly** ˌi
~**ness** nəs nɪs
merciless 'mɜːs ɪ ləs -ə- ‖ 'mɜːs- ~**ly** li ~**ness**
nəs nɪs
Merck mɜːk ‖ mɜːk
mercurial mɜː 'kjʊər i əl ‖ mᵊr 'kjʊr- ~**ly** i ~s
z
mercuric mɜː 'kjʊər ɪk ‖ mᵊr 'kjʊr-
Mercurochrome *tdmk* mɜː 'kjʊər ə krəʊm
‖ mᵊr 'kjʊr ə kroʊm
mercurous 'mɜːk jʊᵊr əs -jər- ‖ 'mɜːk jər-
mercur|y, M~ 'mɜːk jʊᵊr ˌi -jər- ‖ 'mɜːk jər ˌi
~**ies, ~y's** iz
Mercutio mə 'kjuːʃ i əʊ mɜː- ‖ mᵊr 'kjuːʃ i oʊ

merc|y, Merc|y 'mɜːs ˌi ‖ 'mɜːs ˌi ~**ies, ~y's**
iz
　'mercy ˌkilling
merde meəd ‖ meᵊrd —*Fr* [mɛʁd]
mere mɪə ‖ mɪᵊr **meres** mɪəz ‖ mɪᵊrz **merest**
'mɪər ɪst -əst ‖ 'mɪr əst
Meredith 'mer əd ɪθ -ɪd-, §-əθ —*In Wales*
me 'red ɪθ
Meredydd mə 'red ɪð -ɪθ —*Welsh* [me 're dɪð]
merely 'mɪə li ‖ 'mɪr-
merest 'mɪər ɪst -əst ‖ 'mɪr-
meretricious ˌmer ə 'trɪʃ əs ◂ -ɪ- ‖ ~**ly** li ~**ness**
nəs nɪs
Merfyn 'mɜːv ɪn ‖ 'mɜːv- —*Welsh* ['mer vin,
-vin]
merganser mɜː 'gænˑs ə -'gænz-
‖ mᵊr 'gænˑs ᵊr ~**s** z
merge mɜːdʒ ‖ mɜːdʒ **merged** mɜːdʒd
‖ mɜːdʒd **merges** 'mɜːdʒ ɪz -əz ‖ 'mɜːdʒ əz
merging 'mɜːdʒ ɪŋ ‖ 'mɜːdʒ ɪŋ
merger 'mɜːdʒ ə ‖ 'mɜːdʒ ᵊr ~**s** z
Merida 'mer ɪd ə -əd- —*Sp* Mérida ['me ɾi ða]
Meriden 'mer ɪd ən -əd-
meridian mə 'rɪd i ən mɪ- ~**s** z
meridional mə 'rɪd i ən ᵊl mɪ- ~**s** z
meringue mə 'ræŋ ~**s** z
merino mə 'riːn əʊ ‖ -oʊ ~**s** z
Merioneth ˌmer i 'ɒn əθ -ɪθ, -eθ ‖ -'ɑːn-
—*Welsh* Meirionnydd [məir 'jɒn ɪð, -ɪð]
meristem 'mer i stem -ə- ~**s** z
mer|it 'mer |ɪt -ət | -|ət ~**ited** ɪt ɪd ət-, -əd
‖ ət̬ əd ~**iting** ɪt ɪŋ ət- ‖ ət̬ ɪŋ ~**its** ɪts əts ‖ əts
meritocrac|y ˌmer ɪ 'tɒk rəs ˌi ˌ·ə- ‖ -'tɑːk-
~**ies** iz
meritocrat 'mer ɪt əʊ kræt §'·ət- ‖ -ət ə- ~**s** s
meritocratic ˌmer ɪt əʊ 'kræt ɪk ◂ §ˌ·ət-
‖ -ət ə 'kræt̬- ~**ally** ᵊl ˌi
meritorious ˌmer ɪ 'tɔːr i əs ◂ ˌ·ə- ‖ -'toʊr- ~**ly**
li ~**ness** nəs nɪs
Merkel 'meək ᵊl 'mɜːk ‖ 'merk- 'mɜːk- —*Ger*
['mɛʁ kl]
merkin 'mɜːk ɪn §-ən ‖ 'mɜːk- ~**s** z
Merle, merle mɜːl ‖ mɜːl **merles, Merle's**
mɜːlz ‖ mɜːlz
merlin, M~ 'mɜːl ɪn §-ən ‖ 'mɜːl- ~**s, ~'s** z
merlot, M~ 'mɜːl əʊ 'meəl- ‖ mᵊr 'loʊ mer-
—*Fr* [mɛʁ lo]
mermaid 'mɜː meɪd ‖ 'mɜː- ~**s** z
mer|man 'mɜː |mæn ‖ 'mɜː- ~**men** men
Merman 'mɜːm ən ‖ 'mɜːm-
-merous *stress-imposing* mər əs
　— **polymerous** pə 'lɪm ər əs
Merovingian ˌmer əʊ 'vɪndʒ i ən ◂ ‖ ˌ·ə- ~**s** z
merri... —*see* **merry**
Merrick 'mer ɪk
Merrilies 'mer əl iz -ɪl-
Merrill 'mer əl -ɪl
Merrimac, Merrimack 'mer ɪ mæk -ə-
Merriman 'mer i mən
merriment 'mer i mənt
Merrion 'mer i ən
merr|y, Merry 'mer |i ~**ier** i ə ‖ i ᵊr ~**iest** i ɪst
i əst ~**ily** ɪ li əl i ~**iness** i nəs i nɪs

Merrydown *tdmk* 'mer i daʊn
merry-go-round 'mer i gəʊ ˌraʊnd ‖ -i goʊ-
 -ɪ gə- **~s** z
merrymak|er 'mer i ˌmeɪk |ə ‖ -|ᵊr **~ers** əz
 ‖ ᵊrz **~ing** ɪŋ
merrythought 'mer i θɔːt ‖ -θɑːt **~s** s
Merryweather 'mer i ˌweð ə ‖ -ᵊr
Mersey 'mɜːz i ‖ 'mɜːz i
Merseyside 'mɜːz i saɪd ‖ 'mɜːz-
Merstham 'mɜːst əm ‖ 'mɜːst-
Merthiolate *tdmk* 'mɜːθ i ə leɪt ‖ 'mɜːθ-
Merthyr 'mɜːθ ə ‖ 'mɜːθ ᵊr —*Welsh* ['mer θɪr,
 -θɪr]
 ˌMerthyr 'Tydfil 'tɪd vɪl —*Welsh* ˌMerthyr
 'Tudful ['tɪd vɪl]
Merton 'mɜːt ᵊn ‖ 'mɜːt ᵊn
Mervin, Mervyn 'mɜːv ɪn §-ᵊn ‖ 'mɜːv-
Meryl 'mer əl -ɪl
mesa, Mesa 'meɪs ə **~s** z
mesallianc|e, mésalliance|e me 'zæl i ˌənˢs
 meɪ-, -ɒ̃s ‖ meɪ- ˌmeɪz ə 'laɪ ənˢs —*Fr*
 [me za ljɑ̃ːs] **~es** ɪz əz
mescal 'mesk æl me 'skæl
mescalin, mescaline 'mesk əl ɪn §-ən, -ə liːn
Mesdames, m~ 'meɪ dæm -dæmz ‖ meɪ 'dɑːm
 —*Fr* [me dam]
mesdemoiselles ˌmeɪd əm ˌwɑ 'zel —*Fr*
 [med mwa zɛl]
meseemed mi 'siːmd **meseems** mi 'siːmz
mesembryanthemum
 mə ˌzem bri 'ænᵗθ ɪm əm mɪ-, -əmˌem **~s** z
mesencephalon ˌmes en 'kef ə lɒn ˌmez-,
 →ˌeŋ-; -'sef- ‖ -'sef ə lɑːn
mesenchyme 'mes eŋ kaɪm 'mez-
mesh meʃ **meshed** meʃt **meshes** 'meʃ ɪz -əz
 meshing 'meʃ ɪŋ
Meshach 'miːʃ æk
meshuga, meshugga mə 'ʃʊg ə
mesial 'miːz i əl 'miːs-
mesmeric mez 'mer ɪk
mesmeris... —*see* **mesmeriz...**
mesmerism 'mez mə ˌrɪz əm
mesmerist 'mez mər ɪst §-əst **~s** s
mesmeriz|e 'mez mə raɪz **~ed** d **~er/s** ə/z
 ‖ ᵊr/z **~es** ɪz əz **~ing** ɪŋ
mesne miːn (= *mean*)
meso- *comb. form*
 with stress-neutral suffix |mes əʊ |mez-,
 |miːs-, |miːz- ‖ -ə — **mesophyte** 'mes əʊ faɪt
 'mez-, 'miːs-, 'miːz- ‖ -ə-
mesolect 'mes əʊ lekt 'mez-, 'miːs-, 'miːz- ‖ -ə-
 ~s s
mesolectal ˌmes əʊ 'lekt ᵊl ◂ ˌmez-, ˌmiːs-,
 ˌmiːz- ‖ -ə- **~ly** i
Mesolithic, m~ ˌmes əʊ 'lɪθ ɪk ◂ ˌmez-, ˌmiːs-,
 ˌmiːz- ‖ -ə-
mesomorph 'mes əʊ mɔːf 'mez-, 'miːs-, 'miːz-
 ‖ -oʊ mɔːrf -ə- **~s** s
mesomorphic ˌmes əʊ 'mɔːf ɪk ◂ ˌmez-, ˌmiːs-,
 ˌmiːz- ‖ -ə 'mɔːrf- -oʊ'--
meson 'miːz ɒn 'miːs-, 'mez-, 'mes-, 'meɪz-
 ‖ -ɑːn
Mesopotamia ˌmes ə pə 'teɪm i ə ˌmesp ə'--

mesothelioma ˌmes əʊ ˌθiːl i 'əʊm ə ˌmez-,
 ˌmiːs-, ˌmiːz- ‖ -ə ˌθiːl i 'oʊm ə **~s** z
mesothelium ˌmes əʊ 'θiːl i əm ˌmez-, ˌmiːs-,
 ˌmiːz- ‖ ˌ-ə-
mesozoic ˌmes əʊ 'zəʊ ɪk ◂ ˌmez-, ˌmiːs-, ˌmiːz-
 ‖ -ə 'zoʊ-
mesquite, M~ me 'skiːt mə-, mɪ-; 'mesk iːt
mess mes **messed** mest **messes** 'mes ɪz -əz
 messing 'mes ɪŋ
 'mess ˌjacket; 'mess kit
messag|e 'mes ɪdʒ **~es** ɪz əz **~ing** ɪŋ
Messalina ˌmes ə 'liːn ə -'laɪn-
messenger, M~ 'mes ᵊndʒ ə -ɪndʒ- ‖ -ᵊr **~s** z
Messer 'mes ə ‖ -ᵊr
Messerschmidt *tdmk* 'mes ə ʃmɪt
 △'meʃ ə smɪt ‖ -ᵊr- —*Ger* ['mɛs ɐ ʃmɪt]
messi... —*see* **messy**
Messiaen 'mes jɒ̃ -jɑːn ‖ mes 'jɑːn —*Fr*
 [mɛ sjɑ̃, -sjæ̃]
messiah, M~ mə 'saɪ ə mɪ-, me- **~s** z
messianic, M~ ˌmes i 'æn ɪk ◂ **~ally** ᵊl i
Messieurs, m~ meɪ 'sjɜːz me-; 'mes əz
 ‖ meɪs 'jɜːz məs-, -'juː —*Fr* [me sjø]
Messina me 'siːn ə mə-, mɪ- —*It* [mes 'si: na]
messmate 'mes meɪt **~s** s
Messrs 'mes əz ‖ -ᵊrz
messuag|e 'mes wɪdʒ 'mes juˌɪdʒ **~es** ɪz əz
mess|y 'mes |i **~ier** i ə ‖ i ᵊr **~iest** i ɪst i əst
 ~ily ɪ li əl i **~iness** i nəs i nɪs
mestizo me 'stiːz əʊ mɪ-, mə- ‖ -oʊ -'stiːs- **~s** z
met, Met met
 'Met ˌOffice
meta *in Roman circus* 'miːt ə 'meɪt- ‖ 'miːt̬ ə
meta *fuel* 'miːt ə ‖ 'miːt̬ ə
meta- *comb. form*
 with stress-neutral suffix |met ə ‖ |met̬ ə
 — **metastatic** ˌmet ə 'stæt ɪk ◂
 ‖ ˌmet̬ ə 'stæt̬ ɪk ◂
 with stress-imposing suffix mə 'tæ+ mɪ-, me-
 — **metastasis** mə 'tæst əs ɪs mɪ-, me-, §-əs
Meta *river in Colombia* 'meɪt ə ‖ 'meɪt̬ ə —*Sp*
 ['me ta]
Meta *forename* 'miːt ə ‖ 'miːt̬ ə
metabolic ˌmet ə 'bɒl ɪk ◂ ‖ ˌmet̬ ə 'bɑːl ɪk ◂
 ~ally ᵊl i
metabolis... —*see* **metaboliz...**
metabolism mə 'tæb ə ˌlɪz əm mɪ-, me- **~s** z
metabolite mə 'tæb ə laɪt mɪ-, me- **~s** s
metaboliz|e mə 'tæb ə laɪz mɪ-, me- **~ed** d
 ~es ɪz əz **~ing** ɪŋ
metacarpal ˌmet ə 'kɑːp ᵊl ◂
 ‖ ˌmet̬ ə 'kɑːrp ᵊl ◂ **~s** z
metacarpus ˌmet ə 'kɑːp əs ‖ ˌmet̬ ə 'kɑːrp əs
metacenter, metacentre 'met ə ˌsent ə
 ‖ 'met̬ ə ˌsent̬ ᵊr **~s** z
metadata 'met ə ˌdeɪt ə -ˌdɑːt-, §-ˌdæt-
 ‖ 'met̬ ə ˌdeɪt̬ ə -ˌdæt̬-, -ˌdɑːt̬-
metal 'met ᵊl ‖ 'met̬ ᵊl **~ed, ~led** d **~ing,
 ~ling** ɪŋ **~s** z
metalanguag|e 'met ə ˌlæŋ gwɪdʒ §-wɪdʒ
 ‖ 'met̬- **~es** ɪz əz
metaldehyde me 'tæld ɪ haɪd mə-, mɪ-, -ə-

metalinguistic ˌmet ə lɪŋ 'gwɪst ɪk ◀ ‖ ˌmeţ-
~ally ᵊl_i ~s s

metallic me 'tæl ɪk mə-, mɪ- ~ally ᵊl_i

Metallica me 'tæl ɪk ə mə-, mɪ-

metalliferous ˌmet ə 'lɪf ər əs ◀ -ᵊl- 'ɪf-
‖ ˌmeţ ᵊl 'ɪf-

metalloid 'met ə lɔɪd -ᵊl- ‖ 'meţ ᵊl ɔɪd ~s z

metallurgical ˌmet ə 'lɜːdʒ ɪk ᵊl ◀ -ᵊl- 'ɜːdʒ-
‖ ˌmeţ ᵊl 'ɜːdʒ- ~ally ᵊl_i

metallurgist me 'tæl ədʒ ɪst mə-, mɪ-, §-əst;
'met ᵊl ɜːdʒ- ‖ 'meţ ᵊl ɜːdʒ əst ~s s

metallurgy me 'tæl ədʒ i mə-, mɪ-;
'met ᵊl ɜːdʒ- ‖ 'meţ ᵊl ɜːdʒ i

metalwork 'met ᵊl wɜːk ‖ 'meţ ᵊl wɜːk

metalwork|er 'met ᵊl ˌwɜːk |ə
‖ 'meţ ᵊl ˌwɜːk |ᵊr ~ers əz ‖ ᵊrz ~ing ɪŋ

metamere 'met ə mɪə ‖ 'meţ ə mɪr ~s z

metamerism me 'tæm ə ˌrɪz əm mɪ-, mə-

metamorphic ˌmet ə 'mɔːf ɪk ◀
‖ ˌmeţ ə 'mɔːrf ɪk ◀

metamorphism ˌmet ə 'mɔːf ˌɪz əm
‖ ˌmeţ ə 'mɔːrf- ~s z

metamorphos|e ˌmet ə 'mɔːf əʊz
‖ ˌmeţ ə 'mɔːrf oʊz -ous ~ed d ~es ɪz əz ~ing
ɪŋ

metamorphoses from v ˌmet ə 'mɔːf əʊz ɪz
-əz ‖ ˌmeţ ə 'mɔːrf oʊz əz -'·ous-

metamorphoses n pl ˌmet ə 'mɔːf ə siːz
-mɔː 'fəʊs iːz ‖ ˌmeţ ə 'mɔːrf-

metamorphos|is ˌmet ə 'mɔːf əs |ɪs
-mɔː 'fəʊs-, §-əs ‖ ˌmeţ ə 'mɔːrf- ~es iːz

metaphor 'met əf ə -ə fɔː ‖ 'meţ ə fɔːr -əf-ᵊr ~s
z

metaphorical ˌmet ə 'fɒr ɪk ᵊl ◀ ‖ ˌmeţ ə 'fɔːr-
-'fɑːr- ~ly_i

metaphras|e 'met ə freɪz ‖ 'meţ- ~ed d ~es ɪz
əz ~ing ɪŋ

metaphysical, M~ ˌmet ə 'fɪz ɪk ᵊl ◀ ‖ ˌmeţ-
~ly_i ~s z

metaphysics ˌmet ə 'fɪz ɪks ‖ ˌmeţ-

metastable ˌmet ə 'steɪb ᵊl ◀ ‖ ˌmeţ-

metast|asis me 'tæst |əs ɪs mɪ-, mə-, §-əs
~ases ə siːz

metastasis|e, metastasiz|e me 'tæst ə saɪz
mɪ-, mə- ~ed d ~es ɪz əz ~ing ɪŋ

metastatic ˌmet ə 'stæt ɪk ◀
‖ ˌmeţ ə 'stæţ ɪk ◀

metatarsal ˌmet ə 'tɑːs ᵊl ◀ ‖ ˌmeţ ə 'tɑːrs ᵊl ◀
~s z

metatars|us ˌmet ə 'tɑːs |əs
‖ ˌmeţ ə 'tɑːrs |əs ~i aɪ

metath|esis me 'tæθ |əs ɪs mɪ-, mə-, §-əs
~eses ə siːz

metathesis|e, metathesiz|e me 'tæθ ə saɪz
mɪ-, mə- ~ed d ~es ɪz əz ~ing ɪŋ

Metaxa tdmk me 'tæks ə mɪ-, mə-

metazoa ˌmet ə 'zəʊ ə ‖ ˌmeţ ə 'zoʊ ə

Metcalf, Metcalfe 'met kɑːf §-kæf, -kəf ‖ -kæf

mete miːt (= meet) **meted** 'miːt ɪd -əd
‖ 'miːţ əd **metes** miːts **meting** 'miːt ɪŋ
‖ 'miːţ ɪŋ

metempsychosis ˌmet emp saɪ 'kəʊs ɪs ˌ·əm-,
§-əs ‖ ˌmeţ əm saɪ 'koʊs əs mə ˌtemp ə-

meteor 'miːt i ə -ɔː ‖ 'miːţ i ᵊr -ɔːr ~s z
'meteor ˌshower

meteoric ˌmiːt i 'ɒr ɪk ◀ ‖ ˌmiːţ i 'ɔːr ɪk ◀ -'ɑːr-
~ally ᵊl_i

meteorite 'miːt i ə raɪt ‖ 'miːţ- ~s s

meteoroid 'miːt i ə rɔɪd ‖ 'miːţ- ~s z

meteorological ˌmiːt i_ər ə 'lɒdʒ ɪk ᵊl ◀
⚠ ˌmiːt ˌər ə'-- ‖ ˌmiːţ i_ər ə 'lɑːdʒ- ~ly_i

meteorologist ˌmiːt i ə 'rɒl ədʒ ɪst
⚠ ˌmiːt ə'--, §-əst ‖ ˌmiːţ i ə 'rɑːl- ~s s

meteorology ˌmiːt i ə 'rɒl ədʒ i ⚠ ˌmiːt ə'--
‖ ˌmiːţ i ə 'rɑːl-

meter 'miːt ə ‖ 'miːţ ᵊr ~ed d **metering**
'miːt ər ɪŋ ‖ 'miːţ ər ɪŋ ~s z

-meter (i) ˌmiːt ə ‖ ˌmiːţ ᵊr, (ii) mɪt ə -mət ə
‖ məţ ᵊr —Pronunciation (i) is used (a) in
units of length (also spelt -metre):
'centi ˌmeter/'centi ˌmetre, and sometimes (b)
in the meaning 'measuring device': 'volt ˌmeter.
The stress-imposing pronunciation (ii) is used
(c) with reference to versification: pen'tameter,
and sometimes (d) for 'measuring device':
ba'rometer. (Hence the different
pronunciations of the two senses of
micrometer.) In the words altimeter and
kilometer/kilometre the two types have been
confused, giving rise to competing
pronunciations with different stressings.

meth- comb. form before vowel meθ —or, in
BrE only, miːθ —see following

methacrylate meθ 'æk rɪ leɪt -'·rə-

methadone 'meθ ə dəʊn ‖ -doʊn

methamphetamine ˌmeθ æm 'fet ə miːn
-mɪn, §-mən ‖ -'feţ-

methane 'miːθ eɪn ‖ 'meθ- (*)

methanoic ˌmeθ ə 'nəʊ ɪk ◀ ‖ -'noʊ-

methanol 'meθ ə nɒl 'miːθ- ‖ -nɔːl -nɑːl, -noʊl

metheglin me 'θeg lɪn mɪ-, mə-, §-lən

methinks mi 'θɪŋks

method 'meθ əd ~s z

methodical mə 'θɒd ɪk ᵊl mɪ-, me- ‖ -'θɑːd-
~ly_i ~ness nəs nɪs

methodics mə 'θɒd ɪks mɪ-, me- ‖ -'θɑːd-

Methodism 'meθ ə ˌdɪz əm

Methodist 'meθ əd ɪst §-əst ~s s

Methodius me 'θəʊd i_əs mɪ-, mə- ‖ -'θoʊd-

methodological ˌmeθ əd ə 'lɒdʒ ɪk ᵊl ◀
‖ -'lɑːdʒ- ~ly_i

methodologist ˌmeθ ə 'dɒl ədʒ ɪst §-əst
‖ -'dɑːl- ~s s

methodolog|y ˌmeθ ə 'dɒl ədʒ |i ‖ -'dɑːl-
~ies iz

methought mi 'θɔːt ‖ -'θɑːt

meths meθs

Methuen (i) 'meθ ju_ən -u ˌ, ɪn, (ii) mə 'θjuː ən
mɪ-, me-, -'θuː ˌ, ɪn —The English family name
is (i); the place in MA is (ii).

Methuselah, m~ mə 'θjuːz əl ə mɪ-, -'θuːz-
‖ -'θuːz- ~s, -'s z

Methven 'meθ vən

methyl 'meθ ᵊl -ɪl —in BrE technical usage also
'miːθ aɪ ᵊl
ˌmethyl 'alcohol

methylamine me 'θaɪl ə miːn miː-, mɪ-, mə-;
,meθ ɪl 'æm iːn, -ᵊl- ‖ ,meθ ᵊl ə 'miːn
-'æm ən; mə 'θɪl ə miːn

methy|late *n, v* 'meθ ə |leɪt -ɪ- **~lated** leɪt ɪd
-əd ‖ leɪt̬ əd **~lates** leɪts **~lating** leɪt ɪŋ
‖ leɪt̬ ɪŋ
,methylated 'spirits

methylene 'meθ ə liːn -ɪ-

metic 'met ɪk ‖ 'met̬- **~s** s

meticulous mə 'tɪk jʊl əs mɪ-, me-, -jəl- ‖ -jəl-
~ly li **~ness** nəs nɪs

metier, métier 'met i eɪ 'meɪt- ‖ 'meɪt jeɪ ˑˑ
—*Fr* [me tje] **~s** z

metis, métis *sing.* meɪ 'tiː -'tiːs, *pl* -'tiː -'tiːs,
-'tiːz

Metonic me 'tɒn ɪk mɪ-, mə- ‖ -'tɑːn-
Me,tonic 'cycle

metonym 'met ə nɪm ‖ 'met̬- **~s** z

metonym|y me 'tɒn əm |i mə-, mɪ-, -ɪm-
‖ -'tɑːn- **~ies** iz

me-too ,miː 'tuː **~ism** ,ɪz əm

met|ope 'met |əʊp -|əp i ‖ 'met̬ |əp i **~opes**
əʊps əp iz ‖ əp iz

metre 'miːt ə ‖ 'miːt̬ ᵊr **~s** z

-metre ,miːt ə ‖ ,miːt̬ ᵊr —*see note at* **-meter**

metric 'metr ɪk **~s** s
,metric 'ton

-metric 'metr ɪk — **parametric**
,pær ə 'metr ɪk ◀ ‖ ,per-

-metrical 'metr ɪk ᵊl — **parametrical**
,pær ə 'metr ɪk ᵊl ◀ ‖ ,per-

metrical 'metr ɪk ᵊl **~ly** i

metricality ,metr ɪ 'kæl ət i ,ˑə-, -ɪt i ‖ -ət̬ i

metri|cate 'metr ɪ |keɪt -ə- **~cated** keɪt ɪd -əd
‖ keɪt̬ əd **~cates** keɪts **~cating** keɪt ɪŋ
‖ keɪt̬ ɪŋ

metrication ,metr ɪ 'keɪʃ ᵊn -ə-

metricis|e, metriciz|e 'metr ɪ saɪz -ə- **~ed** d
~es ɪz əz **~ing** ɪŋ

metro, Metro 'metr əʊ ‖ -oʊ me 'troʊ **~s** z

metro- *comb. form*
with stress-neutral suffix(i) |metr əʊ ‖ -ə,
(ii) |miːtr əʊ ‖ -ə —*(i) particularly in the
senses 'measurement', 'mother'; (ii)
particularly in the sense 'uterus'* —
metronymic ,metr əʊ 'nɪm ɪk ◀ ‖ -ə-
with stress-imposing suffix mɪ 'trɒ + mə-, me-
‖ -'trɑː + — **metrology** mɪ 'trɒl ədʒ |i mə-,
me- ‖ -'trɑːl-**~ies** iz

Metro-Goldwin-Mayer
,metr əʊ ,gəʊld wɪn 'meɪ ə →-,gɒʊld-,
→-wɪn'ˑˑ ‖ -oʊ ,goʊld wɪn 'meɪ ᵊr

Metroland 'metr əʊ lænd ‖ -oʊ-

metronidazole ,metr əʊ 'naɪd ə zəʊl
-ɒn 'aɪd-, →-zɒʊl ‖ -ə 'naɪd ə zoʊl

metronome 'metr ə nəʊm ‖ -noʊm **~s** z

metronomic ,metr ə 'nɒm ɪk ◀ ‖ -'nɑːm-

Metropole 'metr ə pəʊl →-pɒʊl ‖ -poʊl **~s** z

metropolis, M~ mə 'trɒp əl ɪs mɪ-, me-, §-əs
‖ -'trɑːp- **~es** ɪz əz

metropolitan, M~ ,metr ə 'pɒl ɪt ən ◀ -'ət-
‖ -'pɑːl ət ᵊn ◀ **~s** z

M (margin tab)

metrorrhagia ,miːtr əʊ 'reɪdʒ i ə ,metr-, ,ˑɔː-,
-'reɪdʒ ə ‖ ,ˑə-

metrosexual ,metr əʊ 'sek ʃu əl ◀ ‖ ,ˑoʊ- **~s** z

-metry *stress-imposing* mətr i mɪtr i —
chronometry krə 'nɒm ətr i -ɪtr- ‖ -'nɑːm-

Metternich 'met ə nɪk -nɪx ‖ 'met̬ ᵊr- —*Ger*
['mɛt ɐ nɪç]

mettle 'met ᵊl ‖ 'met̬ ᵊl *(= metal)*

mettlesome 'met ᵊl səm ‖ 'met̬-

Mettoy *tdmk* 'met ɔɪ

Metuchen mɪ 'tʌtʃ ᵊn mə-

Metz mets —*Fr* [mɛs]

meuniere, meunière ,mɜːn i 'eə ˑˑˑ
‖ mʌn 'jeᵊr —*Fr* [mø njɛʁ]

Meurig 'maɪᵊr ɪg —*Welsh* ['məi rig, 'məi-]

Meuse mɜːz ‖ mjuːz mʊz —*Fr* [møːz]

Meux (i) mjuːks, (ii) mjuːz, (iii) mjuː

Mevagissey ,mev ə 'gɪs i -'gɪz-

mew mjuː **mewed** mjuːd **mewing** 'mjuː ɪŋ
mews mjuːz *(= muse)*

Mewes (i) 'mev ɪs §-əs, (ii) 'mjuː ɪs § əs

mewl mjuːl *(= mule)* **mewled** mjuːld
mewling 'mjuː l ɪŋ **mewls** mjuːlz

mews mjuːz

Mexboro', Mexborough 'meks bər ə
‖ -,bɜː oʊ

Mexicali ,meks ɪ 'kæl i -'kɑːl- —*Sp*
[me xi 'ka li]

Mexican 'meks ɪk ən **~s** z

Mexico 'meks ɪk əʊ ‖ -oʊ —*Sp* México, Méjico
['me xi ko]
,Mexico 'City

Mey meɪ

Meyer (i) 'maɪ ə ‖ 'maɪ ᵊr, (ii) 'meɪ ə ‖ -ᵊr,
(iii) meə ‖ meᵊr, (iv) mɪə ‖ mɪᵊr

Meynell (i) 'men ᵊl, (ii) meɪ 'nel

Meyrick 'mer ɪk

meze 'mez eɪ ‖ me 'zeɪ 'meɪz eɪ —*Turkish*
[me 'ze]

mezereon mə 'zɪər i ən mɪ-, me- ‖ -'zɪr- **~s** z

mezuzah mə 'zʊz ə -'zuːz- **~s** z

mezzanine 'mets ə niːn 'mez- ‖ 'mez- **~s** z

mezzo 'mets əʊ 'medz- ‖ -oʊ **~s** z

mezzo-soprano ,mets əʊ sə 'prɑːn əʊ ,medz-
‖ -oʊ sə 'præn oʊ -'prɑːn- **~s** z

mezzo|tint 'mets əʊ |tɪnt 'medz- ‖ -oʊ-
~tinted tɪnt ɪd -əd ‖ tɪnt̬ əd **~tinting** tɪnt ɪŋ
‖ tɪnt̬ ɪŋ **~tints** tɪnts

mg —*see* **milligram(s)**

MGM *tdmk* ,em dʒiː 'em

Mhairi 'vɑːr i

mho məʊ ‖ moʊ **mhos** məʊz ‖ moʊz

MHz —*see* **megahertz**

mi miː

MI5 ,em aɪ 'faɪv

MI6 ,em aɪ 'sɪks

Mia 'miː ə

Miami maɪ 'æm i

miaow mi 'aʊ ,miː- **~ed** d **~ing** ɪŋ **~s** z

miasma mi 'æz mə maɪ- **~s** z

mica 'maɪk ə

micaceous maɪ 'keɪʃ əs

Micah 'maɪk ə

Micawber, m~ mə ˈkɔːb ə mɪ- ‖ -ᵊr -ˈkɑːb-
micawberish mə ˈkɔːb ər ɪʃ mɪ- ‖ -ˈkɑːb-
mice maɪs
Michael ˈmaɪk ᵊl
Michaela (i) mɪ ˈkeɪl ə mə-, (ii) maɪ-
Michaelis (i) mɪ ˈkeɪl ɪs mə-, §-əs, (ii) -ˈkaɪl-
Michaelmas ˈmɪk ᵊl məs
   ˌMichaelmas ˈdaisy
Michel mɪ ˈʃel miː- —Fr [mi ʃɛl]
Michelangelo ˌmaɪk ᵊl ˈændʒ ə ləʊ ˌmɪk-, -ˈɪ-
  ‖ -loʊ —It [mi ke ˈlan dʒe lo]
Micheldever ˈmɪtʃ ᵊl dev ə ‖ -ᵊr
Michele, Michèle mɪ ˈʃel miː- —Fr [mi ʃɛl]
Michelin tdmk ˈmɪtʃ əl ɪn ˈmɪʃ- —Fr [miʃ læ]
  —In BrE the M~ Guide is usually pronounced
  as if French.
Michelle mɪ ˈʃel miː-
Michelmore ˈmɪtʃ əl mɔː ‖ -mɔːr -moʊr
Michelob tdmk ˈmɪk ə ləʊb -ᵊl əʊb ‖ -ᵊl oʊb
Michelson (i) ˈmaɪk ᵊl sən, (ii) ˈmɪtʃ- —The
  physicist A A M~ was (i).
Michener (i) ˈmɪʃ nə ‖ -nᵊr, (ii) ˈmɪtʃ ən ə
  ‖ -ᵊn ᵊr —The novelist James M~ is (ii).
Michie ˈmɪk i ˈmɪx-, ˈmiːx-
Michigan ˈmɪʃ ɪɡ ən △ˈmɪtʃ-
Michigander ˌmɪʃ ɪ ˈɡænd ə ‖ -ᵊr ~s z
Mick, mick mɪk **micks, Mick's** mɪks
Mickey, mickey, Mickie ˈmɪk i
  ˌmickey ˈfinn; ˌMickey ˈMouse
mickle ˈmɪk ᵊl
Mickleham ˈmɪk ᵊl əm
Mickleover ˈmɪk ᵊl ˌəʊv ə ‖ -ˌoʊv ᵊr
Micklethwaite ˈmɪk ᵊl θweɪt
Micklewhite ˈmɪk ᵊl waɪt -hwaɪt ‖ -hwaɪt
Micky, micky ˈmɪk i
Micmac ˈmɪk mæk ~s s
micra, Micra tdmk ˈmaɪk rə
micro ˈmaɪk rəʊ ‖ -roʊ ~s z
micro- comb. form
  with stress-neutral suffix ˌmaɪk rəʊ ‖ -roʊ
  — **microfossil** ˌmaɪk rəʊ ˈfɒs ᵊl ‖ -ˈfɑːs-
  with stress-imposing suffix maɪ ˈkrɒ +
  ‖ -ˈkrɑː + — **micrography** maɪ ˈkrɒɡ rəf i
  ‖ -ˈkrɑːɡ-
microbe ˈmaɪk rəʊb ‖ -roʊb ~s z
microbial maɪ ˈkrəʊb i ᵊl ‖ -ˈkroʊb-
microbiological ˌmaɪk rəʊ ˌbaɪ ə ˈlɒdʒ ɪk ᵊl
  ‖ -roʊ ˌbaɪ ə ˈlɑːdʒ- ~ly i
microbiologist ˌmaɪk rəʊ baɪ ˈɒl ədʒ ɪst §-əst
  ‖ -roʊ baɪ ˈɑːl- ~s s
microbiology ˌmaɪk rəʊ baɪ ˈɒl ədʒ i
  ‖ -roʊ baɪ ˈɑːl-
microbrew ˈmaɪk rəʊ bruː ‖ -roʊ- ~s z
microbrewer|y ˈmaɪk rəʊ ˌbruː ər |i ‖ -roʊ-
  ~ies iz
microchip ˈmaɪk rəʊ tʃɪp ‖ -roʊ- ~s s
microclimate ˈmaɪk rəʊ ˌklaɪm ət -ɪt ‖ -roʊ-
  ~s s
microcline ˈmaɪk rəʊ klaɪn ‖ -roʊ- ~s z
microcomputer ˈmaɪk rəʊ kəm ˌpjuːt ə
  §-kɒm,- ‖ -roʊ kəm ˌpjuːt̬ ᵊr ~s z
microcosm ˈmaɪk rəʊ ˌkɒz əm ‖ -rə ˌkɑːz- ~s s
microcosmic ˌmaɪk rəʊ ˈkɒz mɪk ◂ ‖ -rə ˈkɑːz-

microdot ˈmaɪk rəʊ dɒt ‖ -rə dɑːt -roʊ- ~s s
microeconomic ˌmaɪk rəʊ ˌiːk ə ˈnɒm ɪk ◂
  ˌ·ˌ·,ek- ‖ -roʊ ˌek ə ˈnɑːm- -ˌiːk- ~s s
microelectronic ˌmaɪk rəʊ ɪ ˌlek ˈtrɒn ɪk
  ˌ· -ə-, -ˌel ek'--, -ˌɪl ek'--, -ˌiːl ek'--
  ‖ -roʊ ɪ ˌlek ˈtrɑːn- ~s s
microfarad ˈmaɪk rəʊ ˌfær əd -æd ‖ -roʊ- -ˌfer-
  ~s z
microfich|e ˈmaɪk rəʊ fiːʃ -fiʃ ‖ -rə- ~es ɪz əz
microfilm ˈmaɪk rəʊ fɪlm ‖ -rə- ~ed d ~ing ɪŋ
  ~s z
microgram ˈmaɪk rəʊ ɡræm ‖ -rə- ~s z
microgroove ˈmaɪk rəʊ ɡruːv ‖ -rə- -roʊ- ~s z
microlight ˈmaɪk rəʊ laɪt ‖ -rə- -roʊ- ~s s
micromanag|e ˈmaɪk rəʊ ˌmæn ɪdʒ -ədʒ
  ‖ -roʊ- ~ed d ~ement mənt ~es ɪz əz ~ing ɪŋ
micromesh ˈmaɪk rəʊ meʃ ‖ -roʊ-
micrometer, micrometre 'micron'
  ˈmaɪk rəʊ ˌmiːt ə maɪ ˈkrɒm ɪt ə, -ət ə
  ‖ -roʊ ˌmiːt̬ ᵊr ~s z
micrometer 'instrument' maɪ ˈkrɒm ɪt ə -ət-
  ‖ -ˈkrɑːm ət̬ ᵊr ~s z
microminiaturis... —see **microminiaturiz...**
microminiaturization
  ˌmaɪk rəʊ ˌmɪn ətʃ ər aɪ ˈzeɪʃ ᵊn -ˌɪtʃ-,
  -ˌi̯ ətʃ ·ˈ·-, -ˈ·-- ‖ -roʊ ˌmɪn i ˌətʃ ər ə- -ˌətʃ ·ˈ·--
microminiaturiz|e ˌmaɪk rəʊ ˈmɪn ətʃ ə raɪz
  -ˈ·ɪtʃ-, -ˈ·i̯ ətʃ ·‖-roʊ ˈmɪn i ˌətʃ- -ˈ·ətʃ ·· ~ed d
  ~es ɪz əz ~ing ɪŋ
micron ˈmaɪk rɒn -rən ‖ -rɑːn ~s z
Micronesia ˌmaɪk rəʊ ˈniːz i ə -ˈniːʒ ə,
  -ˈniːs i ə, -ˈniːʃ ə ‖ -rə -ˈniːʒ ə -ˈniːʃ-
Micronesian ˌmaɪk rəʊ ˈniːz i ən ◂ -ˈniːʒ ᵊn,
  -ˈniːs i ən, -ˈniːʃ ᵊn ‖ -rə -ˈniːʒ ᵊn -ˈniːʃ- ~s z
microorganism ˌmaɪk rəʊ ˈɔːɡ ə ˌnɪz əm
  ˈ·ˌ·,·· ‖ -roʊ ˈɔːrɡ- ~s z
Micropal ˈmaɪk rəʊ pæl ‖ -roʊ-
microphone ˈmaɪk rə fəʊn ‖ -foʊn ~s z
microprocessor ˈmaɪk rəʊ ˌprəʊs es ə -ɪs ə,
  §-əs ə; ˌ·ˈ··· ‖ -rə ˌprɑːs es ᵊr -əs ᵊr ~s z
microscope ˈmaɪk rə skəʊp ‖ -skoʊp ~s s
microscopic ˌmaɪk rə ˈskɒp ɪk ◂ ‖ -ˈskɑːp ɪk ◂
  ~ally ᵊl i
microscopy maɪ ˈkrɒsk əp i ‖ -ˈkrɑːsk-
microsecond ˈmaɪk rəʊ ˌsek ənd ˌ··ˈ·· ‖ -rə-
  -roʊ-, △-ənt ~s z
Microsoft tdmk ˈmaɪk rəʊ sɒft ‖ -rə sɔːft -sɑːft
microsurgery ˈmaɪk rəʊ ˌsɜːdʒ ər i
  ‖ -roʊ ˌsɜːdʒ-
microtome ˈmaɪk rəʊ təʊm ‖ -rə toʊm ~s z
microwav|e ˈmaɪk rə weɪv -rəʊ- ‖ -rə- -roʊ-
  ~able əb ᵊl ~ed d ~es z ~ing ɪŋ
mictu|rate ˈmɪk tjʊᵊ |reɪt -tʃə- ‖ -tʃə- -tə-
  ~rated reɪt ɪd -əd ‖ reɪt̬ əd ~rates reɪts
  ~rating reɪt ɪŋ ‖ reɪt̬ ɪŋ
micturation ˌmɪk tjʊ ˈreɪʃ ᵊn -tʃə- ‖ -tʃə- -tə-
  ~s z
micturition ˌmɪk tjʊ ˈrɪʃ ᵊn -tʃə- ‖ -tʃə- -tə- ~s
  z
mid mɪd
  ˌMid Glaˈmorgan
mid- ˌmɪd — **mid-Atlantic** ˌmɪd ət ˈlænt ɪk ◂
  ‖ -ˈlænt̬-

M

midair ˌmɪd 'eə ◄ ‖ -'eᵊr ◄ -'æᵊr
Midas 'maɪd əs -æs
mid-Atlantic ˌmɪd ət 'lænt ɪk ◄ ‖ -'lænt̬-
midbrain 'mɪd breɪn
midcourse ˌmɪd 'kɔːs ◄ →ˌmɪg- ‖ -'kɔːrs ◄ -'koʊrs
midday ˌmɪd 'deɪ ◄ ' ·
midden 'mɪd ³n ~s z
middie... —*see* **middy**
middle 'mɪd ³l ~s z
   ˌmiddle 'age; ˌMiddle 'Ages; ˌmiddle 'C;
   ˌmiddle 'class; ˌmiddle 'course, ' · ·;
   ˌmiddle 'distance; ˌmiddle 'ear; ˌMiddle
   'East; ˌMiddle 'Eastern◄; ˌMiddle 'English;
   ˌmiddle 'finger; ˌmiddle 'management;
   ˌmiddle 'name; ˌmiddle of 'nowhere;
   'middle school; ˌMiddle 'West
middle-aged ˌmɪd ³l 'eɪdʒd ◄
   ˌmiddle-aged 'spread
middlebrow 'mɪd ³l braʊ ~s z
Middlebury *place in VT* 'mɪd ³l ˌber i
middle-class ˌmɪd ³l 'klɑːs ◄ §-'klæs ‖ -'klæs ◄
middle-distance ˌmɪd ³l 'dɪst ən'̩s ◄
Middleham 'mɪd ³l əm
middle|man 'mɪd ³l |mæn ~men men
Middlemarch 'mɪd ³l mɑːtʃ ‖ -mɑːrtʃ
Middlemast 'mɪd ³l mɑːst §-mæst ‖ -mæst
middlemen 'mɪd ³l men
middle-of-the-road ˌmɪd ³lˌəv ðə 'rəʊd ◄
   -³lˌə ðə- ‖ -'roʊd ◄
middle-ranking ˌmɪd ³l 'ræŋk ɪŋ ◄
Middlesboro, Middlesborough *place in KY*
   'mɪd ³lz bər ə ‖ -ˌbɝː oʊ
Middlesbrough *place in England* 'mɪd ³lz brə
Middlesex 'mɪd ³l seks
middle-sized ˌmɪd ³l 'saɪzd ◄
Middleton 'mɪd ³l tən
Middletown 'mɪd ³l taʊn
middleweight 'mɪd ³l weɪt ~s s
Middlewich 'mɪd ³l wɪtʃ
middling 'mɪd ³lˌɪŋ ~ly li
Middx —*see* **Middlesex**
midd|y 'mɪd |i ~ies iz
Mideast ˌmɪd 'iːst
midfield 'mɪd fiːᵊld , ' · ~er/s ə/z ‖ -ᵊr/z
midge mɪdʒ **midges** 'mɪdʒ ɪz -əz
midget 'mɪdʒ ɪt §-ət ~s s
Midgley 'mɪdʒ li
midgut 'mɪd gʌt →'mɪg- ~s s
Midhurst 'mɪd hɜːst ‖ -hɝːst
midi *'mid-length (garment)'* 'mɪd i ~s z
Midi *'south of France'* mi 'di: mi:- —*Fr* [mi di]
MIDI, Midi *computer interface* 'mɪd i ~s z
Midian 'mɪd i ən
Midianite 'mɪd i ə naɪt ~s s
midinette ˌmɪd i 'net —*Fr* [mi di nɛt] ~s s
midiron 'mɪd ˌaɪ ən ‖ -ˌaɪ ᵊrn ~s z
midland, M~ 'mɪd lənd ~er/s ə/z ‖ ᵊr/z ~s z
Midler 'mɪd lə ‖ -lᵊr
mid-life ˌmɪd 'laɪf ◄
   ˌmid-life 'crisis
Midlothian mɪd 'ləʊð iˌən ‖ -'loʊð-
midmost 'mɪd məʊst →'mɪb- ‖ -moʊst

midnight 'mɪd naɪt
   ˌmidnight 'sun
mid-off ˌmɪd 'ɒf -'ɔːf ‖ -'ɔːf -'ɑːf ~s s
mid-on ˌmɪd 'ɒn ‖ -'ɑːn -'ɔːn ~s z
midpoint 'mɪd pɔɪnt →'mɪb- ~s s
mid-range ˌmɪd 'reɪndʒ ◄
midriff 'mɪd rɪf ~s s
midsection 'mɪd ˌsek ʃᵊn ~s z
midship 'mɪd ʃɪp ~s s
midship|man 'mɪd ʃɪp |mən ~men mən
midsize 'mɪd saɪz
midst mɪdst mɪtst
midstream ˌmɪd 'striːm ◄
midsummer ˌmɪd 'sʌm ə ◄ '·ˌ· · ‖ -ᵊr ~s, ~'s z
   ˌMid ˌsummer 'Day; ˌmid ˌsummer
   'madness
midterm ˌmɪd 'tɜːm ◄ ‖ -'tɜːm ◄ —*but in the
   sense* '~ *examination*' *usually* ' · ·
   — **midterms** 'mɪd tɜːmz ‖ -tɝːmz
midtown 'mɪd taʊn
midway *n,* M~ 'mɪd weɪ
midway *adj, adv* ˌmɪd 'weɪ ◄
midweek ˌmɪd 'wiːk ◄
Midwest ˌmɪd 'west
Midwestern ˌmɪd 'west ən ◄ ‖ -ᵊrn ◄
Midwesterner ˌmɪd 'west ən ə ‖ -ᵊrn ᵊr ~s z
midwicket ˌmɪd 'wɪk ɪt §-ət
mid|wife 'mɪd |waɪf ~wives waɪvz
midwifery ˌmɪd 'wɪf ər i ' · · · · ‖ ˌmɪd waɪf-
midwinter ˌmɪd 'wɪnt ə ◄ ‖ -'wɪnt̬ ᵊr ◄
midwives 'mɪd waɪvz
midyear 'mɪd jɪə ‖ -jɪr
Miele *tdmk* 'miːl ə
mien miːn (= *mean*) **miens** miːnz
Miers 'maɪˌəz ‖ 'maɪˌᵊrz
Mies van der Rohe ˌmiːz væn də 'rəʊ ə ˌmiːs-
   ‖ -dᵊr 'roʊ ə ˌvɑːn-; ' · ' · ' · ·
miff mɪf **miffed** mɪft **miffing** 'mɪf ɪŋ **miffs**
   mɪfs
MiG mɪg **MiGs, MiG's** mɪgz
might maɪt
might-have-beens 'maɪt əv biːnz -ə-, -bɪnz
   ‖ 'maɪt̬ əv bɪnz
mighti... —*see* **mighty**
mightily 'maɪt ɪ li -ᵊl i ‖ 'maɪt̬ ᵊl i
mightn't 'maɪt ᵊnt
might|y 'maɪt |i ‖ 'maɪt̬ |i ~ier iˌə ‖ iˌᵊr ~iest
   iˌɪst iˌəst ~iness i nəs i nɪs
mignon 'mɪn jɒn , '· ‖ miːn 'joʊn -'jɑːn, -'jɔːn
   —*Fr* [mi njɔ̃]
mignonette, M~ ˌmɪn jə 'net ~s s
migraine 'miːg reɪn 'maɪg-, 'mɪg- ‖ 'maɪg-
   — *Preference poll, BrE:* 'miːg- 61%, 'maɪg-
   39%. ~s z
migrant 'maɪg rənt ~s s
mig|rate ₍₎maɪ 'g|reɪt 'maɪg |reɪt ‖ 'maɪg |reɪt
   ~rated reɪt ɪd -əd ‖ reɪt̬ əd ~rates reɪts
   ~rating reɪt ɪŋ ‖ reɪt̬ ɪŋ
migration ₍₎maɪ 'greɪʃ ᵊn ~al ᵊl ~s z
migratory 'maɪg rət ər i ₍₎maɪ 'greɪt ər i
   ‖ 'maɪg rə tɔːr i -toʊr i
Miguel mi: 'gel mɪ- —*Sp, Port* [mi 'ɣel]

MIGRAINE

'mi:g-
'maɪg-

61% / 39% BrE

● BrE by 'maɪg- by age

Percentage (0–80) vs Older ◄— Speakers —► Younger

mikado, M~ mɪ 'kɑːd əʊ mə- ‖ -oʊ —*Jp*
　[mi ˌka do] ~s z
Mikardo mɪ 'kɑːd əʊ mə- ‖ -'kɑːrd oʊ
mike, Mike maɪk mikes, Mike's maɪks
Mikey 'maɪk i
Mikhail mɪ 'kaɪ²l -'xaɪ²l —*Russ* [mʲɪ xʌ 'ił]
mil mɪl (= *mill*) mils mɪlz
milad|y mɪ 'leɪd |i mə- ~ies iz
milag|e 'maɪl ɪdʒ 'maɪ²l- ~es ɪz əz
Milan mɪ 'læn mə-, -'lɑːn —*formerly* 'mɪl ən;
　but the place in IN is 'maɪl æn —*It* Milano
　[mi 'la: no]
Milanese ˌmɪl ə 'niːz ◄ -'neɪz ‖ -'niːs —*but as a
　cookery term also* ˌ· -'neɪz eɪ
milch mɪltʃ
　'milch cow
mild maɪ²ld milder 'maɪ²ld ə ‖ -²r mildest
　'maɪ²ld ɪst -əst
milden 'maɪld ²n ~ed d ~ing ɪŋ ~s z
Mildenhall 'mɪld ²n hɔːl ‖ -hɑːl
mildew 'mɪl djuː →-dʒuː ‖ -duː -djuː ~ed d
　~ing ɪŋ ~s z
mildewy 'mɪl djuːˌi →-dʒuːˌ ‖ -duːˌi -djuːˌ-
mildly 'maɪ²ld li
mild-mannered ˌmaɪld 'mæn əd ◄ ‖ -²rd ◄
Mildmay 'maɪ²ld meɪ
mildness 'maɪ²ld nəs -nɪs
Mildred 'mɪldr əd -ɪd
mile maɪ²l miles maɪ²lz
mileag|e 'maɪl ɪdʒ 'maɪ²l- ~es ɪz əz
mileometer maɪ 'lɒm ɪt ə ˌmaɪ²l 'ɒm-, -ət-
　‖ -'lɑːm ət̬ ²r ~s z
milepost 'maɪ²l pəʊst ‖ -poʊst ~s s
miler 'maɪl ə 'maɪ²l- ‖ -²r ~s z
miles *pl of* mile maɪ²lz
miles *Latin, 'soldier'* 'miːl eɪz -eɪs ‖ -eɪs
　ˌmiles ˌgloriˈosus ˌglɔːr i 'əʊs əs -ʊs ‖ -'oʊs-
　ˌgloʊr-
Miles *name* maɪ²lz
Milesian maɪ 'liːz iˌən mɪ-, -'liːʒ-, -'liːʒ ²n
　‖ -'liːʒ ²n -'liːʃ- ~s z
milestone 'maɪ²l stəʊn ‖ -stoʊn ~s z

Miletus maɪ 'liːt əs mɪ-, mə- ‖ -'liːt̬-
milfoil 'mɪl fɔɪ²l ~s z
Milford 'mɪl fəd ‖ -f²rd
　ˌMilford 'Haven
Milhaud 'miː əʊ -jəʊ ‖ miː 'oʊ -'joʊ —*Fr*
　[mi jo, -lo]
miliaria ˌmɪl i 'eər iˌə ‖ -'er- -'ær-
miliary 'mɪl iˌər i ‖ -i er i
Miliband 'mɪl ɪ bænd -ə-
milieu 'miːl jɜː ₍ˌ₎·'· ‖ miːl 'juː mɪl- —*Fr*
　[mi ljø] ~s z ~x z *or as sing.*
militancy 'mɪl ɪt ənˢts i '·ət-
militant 'mɪl ɪt ənt -ət- ~ly li ~s s
militaria ˌmɪl ɪ 'teər iˌə ˌ·ə- ‖ -'ter- -'tær-
militarily 'mɪl ɪt ²r əl i -ɪ li; ˌmɪl ɪ 'ter-, ˌ·ə-
　‖ ˌmɪl ə 'ter-
militaris... —*see* militariz...
militarism 'mɪl ɪt ə ˌrɪz əm '·ət- ‖ 'mɪl ət̬-
militarist 'mɪl ɪt ²r ɪst '·ət-, §-əst ‖ 'mɪl ət̬- ~s
　s
militaristic ˌmɪl ɪt ə 'rɪst ɪk ◄ ˌ·ət- ‖ ˌmɪl ət̬-
　~ally ²l̩i
militarization ˌmɪl ɪt ²r aɪ 'zeɪʃ ²n ˌ·ət-
　‖ -ət̬ ²r ə'·-- ~s z
militariz|e 'mɪl ɪt ə raɪz '·ət- ‖ -ət̬ ə- ~ed d ~es
　ɪz əz ~ing ɪŋ
military 'mɪl ɪ t²r i '·ə ‖ -ə ter i
　ˌmilitary po'lice
mili|tate 'mɪl ɪ |teɪt -ə- ~tated teɪt ɪd -əd
　‖ teɪt̬ əd ~tates teɪts ~tating teɪt ɪŋ ‖ teɪt̬ ɪŋ
militia mə 'lɪʃ ə mɪ- ~man mən ~men mən
　men ~s z
milk mɪlk milked mɪlkt milking 'mɪlk ɪŋ
　milks mɪlks
　ˌmilk 'chocolate; 'milk float; 'milking
　maˌchine; 'milking stool; ˌmilk 'pudding;
　'milk run; ˌmilk 'shake, ‖ '· ·; 'milk tooth
milki... —*see* milky
milkmaid 'mɪlk meɪd ~s z
milk|man 'mɪlk |mən ~men mən men
milksop 'mɪlk sɒp ‖ -sɑːp ~s s
milkweed 'mɪlk wiːd ~s z
milkwort 'mɪlk wɜːt §-wɔːt ‖ -wɜːt -wɔːrt ~s s
milk|y 'mɪlk |i -ier iˌə ‖ iˌ²r ~iest iˌɪst iˌəst
　~iness i nəs i nɪs
　ˌMilky 'Way
mill, Mill mɪl milled mɪld milling 'mɪl ɪŋ
　mills mɪlz
Millais 'mɪl eɪ mɪ 'leɪ ‖ mɪ 'leɪ
Millan 'mɪl ən
Millar 'mɪl ə ‖ -²r
Millard 'mɪl ɑːd ‖ -²rd
Millbank 'mɪl bæŋk
millboard 'mɪl bɔːd ‖ -bɔːrd -boʊrd
milldam 'mɪl dæm ~s z
millefeuille ˌmiː²l 'fɔɪ ˌmɪl-, -'fɜː jə —*Fr*
　[mil fœj]
millefiori ˌmɪl i fi 'ɔːr i ˌmɪl i 'fjɔːr i
Millen 'mɪl ən
millenarian ˌmɪl ə 'neər iˌən ◄ ˌ·ɪ- ‖ -'ner-
　-'nær- ~ism ˌɪz əm ~s z
millenni|um mɪ 'len iˌ|əm mə- ~a ə ~al əl
　~ums əmz

M

millepede 'mɪl ɪ piːd -ə- **~s** z
millepore 'mɪl ɪ pɔː -ə- ‖ -pɔːr -pour **~s** z
miller, M~ 'mɪl ə ‖ -ᵊr **~s** z
millet 'mɪl ɪt §-ət **~s** s
Millet *French name* 'miː eɪ -jeɪ ‖ miː 'jeɪ —*Fr* [mi jɛ, -lɛ]
Millett 'mɪl ɪt §-ət
milli- ¦mɪl ɪ §-ə — **millisecond** 'mɪl ɪ ˌsek ənd §-ə-, →-ŋd ‖ △-ənt
milliard 'mɪl i ɑːd 'mɪl jɑːd ‖ -ɑːrd **~s** z
millibar 'mɪl i bɑː ‖ -bɑːr **~s** z
Millicent 'mɪl ɪs ənt -əs-
Millie 'mɪl i
Milligan 'mɪl ɪg ən
milligram, milligramme 'mɪl i græm -ə- **~s** z
Millikan 'mɪl ɪk ən
milliliter, millilitre 'mɪl i ˌliːt ə -ə- ‖ -ə ˌliːt̬ ᵊr **~s** z
millimeter, millimetre 'mɪl i ˌmiːt ə -ə- ‖ -ə ˌmiːt̬ ᵊr **~s** z
milliner 'mɪl ɪn ə -ən- ‖ -ᵊr **~s** z
millinery 'mɪl ɪn ər i ˌ·ən- ‖ -ə ner i
Millington 'mɪl ɪŋ tən
million 'mɪl jən 'mɪl i ən **~s** z
millionaire ˌmɪl jə 'neə ◂ -i ə- ‖ -'neᵊr -'næᵊr; '···**~s** z
millionairess ˌmɪl jə 'neər ɪs -əs, -es; -neə 'res ‖ -'ner əs -'nær- **~es** ɪz əz
millionth 'mɪl jənᵗθ 'mɪl i ənᵗθ **~s** s
millipede 'mɪl ɪ piːd -ə- **~s** z
millisec|ond 'mɪl ɪ ˌsek |ənd -ə-, →-ŋd ‖ △-ənt **~onds** əndz →ŋdz ‖ △ənts
Millom 'mɪl əm
millpond 'mɪl pɒnd ‖ -pɑːnd **~s** z
millrace 'mɪl reɪs
Mills mɪlz
millstone 'mɪl stəʊn ‖ -stoʊn **~s** z
Millwall 'mɪl wɔːl -wəl, ˌmɪl 'wɔːl ‖ -wɑːl
millwheel 'mɪl wiːᵊl -hwiːᵊl ‖ -hwiːᵊl **~s** z
millwright 'mɪl raɪt **~s** s
Milman 'mɪl mən
Milne mɪln mɪl
Milner 'mɪln ə ‖ -ᵊr
Milnes mɪlnz mɪlz
Milngavie mɪl 'gaɪ mʌl- (!)
Milo, milo 'maɪl əʊ 'miːl- ‖ -oʊ
milometer maɪ 'lɒm ɪt ə -ət- ‖ -'lɑːm ət̬ ᵊr **~s** z
milord mi 'lɔːd mə- ‖ -'lɔːrd **~s** z
Milos 'miːl ɒs ‖ -ɑːs -oʊs
Milosevic mɪ 'lɒʃ ə vɪtʃ -'lɒs- ‖ -'loʊs- -'lɑːs- —*Serbian* Milošević [mi 'lo ʃe vitɕ]
Milport 'mɪl pɔːt ‖ -pɔːrt -pourt
milquetoast, M~ 'mɪlk təʊst ‖ -toʊst **~s** s
milt, Milt mɪlt **milted** 'mɪlt ɪd -əd **milting** 'mɪlt ɪŋ **milts** mɪlts
Miltiades mɪl 'taɪ ə diːz
Milton 'mɪlt ən
   Milton 'Keynes kiːnz
Miltonic mɪl 'tɒn ɪk ‖ -'tɑːn-
Milupa *tdmk* mi 'luːp ə
Milwaukee mɪl 'wɔːk i -iː ‖ -'wɑːk-
Mimas 'maɪm əs -æs

mime maɪm **mimed** maɪmd **mimes** maɪmz **miming** 'maɪm ɪŋ
mimeo 'mɪm i əʊ ‖ -oʊ **~ed** d **~ing** ɪŋ **~s** z
mimeograph, M~ 'mɪm i ə grɑːf -græf ‖ -græf **~ed** t **~ing** ɪŋ **~s** s
mimesis mɪ 'miːs ɪs mə-, maɪ-, §-əs
mimetic mɪ 'met ɪk mə-, maɪ- ‖ -'met̬- **~ally** ᵊl_i
Mimi 'miːm i 'mi: mi:
mimic 'mɪm ɪk **~ked** t **~king** ɪŋ **~s** s
mimic|ry 'mɪm ɪk |ri -ək- **~ries** riz
mimosa mɪ 'məʊz ə §mə-, -'məʊs- ‖ -'moʊs ə -'moʊz- **~s** z
mims|y 'mɪmz| i **~ier** i ə ‖ i ᵊr **~iest** i_ɪst _əst **~ily** ɪ li əl i **~iness** i nəs -nɪs
mimulus 'mɪm jʊl əs -jəl- ‖ -jəl-
min. —*see* (i) **minimum,** —(ii) **minute/s**
Min *river* mɪn —*Chi* Mín [²mɪn]
min|a 'maɪn |ə **~ae** i ‖ **~as** əz
minaret ˌmɪn ə 'ret '··· **~s** s
minator|y 'mɪn ət ər |i 'maɪn- ‖ -ə tɔːr |i -tour i **~ily** əl i -ɪ li
mince mɪnᵗs **minced** mɪnᵗst **minces** 'mɪnᵗs ɪz -əz **mincing/ly** 'mɪnᵗs ɪŋ /li
   ˌmince 'pie; 'mincing ma chine
mincemeat 'mɪnᵗs miːt
mincer 'mɪnᵗs ə ‖ -ᵊr **~s** z
Minch mɪntʃ **Minches** 'mɪntʃ ɪz -əz
mind maɪnd **minded** 'maɪnd ɪd -əd **minding** 'maɪnd ɪŋ **minds** maɪndz
   'mind ˌreader, 'mind ˌreading; ˌmind's 'eye
Mindanao ˌmɪnd ə 'naʊ ‖ -'nɑː: oʊ
mind-bending 'maɪnd ˌbend ɪŋ →'maɪm- **~ly** li
mind-blowing 'maɪnd ˌbləʊ ɪŋ →'maɪm- ‖ -ˌbloʊ-
mind-boggling 'maɪnd ˌbɒg ᵊl ɪŋ →'maɪm- ‖ -ˌbɑːg- **~ly** li
minder 'maɪnd ə ‖ -ᵊr **~s** z
mind-expanding 'maɪnd ɪk ˌspænd ɪŋ -ek-, -ək-
mindful 'maɪnd fᵊl -fʊl **~ly** _i **~ness** nəs nɪs
mindless 'maɪnd ləs -lɪs **~ly** li **~ness** nəs nɪs
mindset 'maɪnd set **~s** s
Mindy 'mɪnd i
mine maɪn **mined** maɪnd (= *mind*) **mines** maɪnz **mining** 'maɪn ɪŋ
   'mine de tector
minefield 'maɪn fiːᵊld **~s** z
Minehead 'maɪn hed ˌ·'·
minelayer 'maɪn ˌleɪ ə ‖ -ᵊr **~s** z
minelaying 'maɪn ˌleɪ ɪŋ
Minelli mɪ 'nel i mə-
miner 'maɪn ə ‖ -ᵊr **~s** z
mineral 'mɪn ᵊr əl **~s** z
   'mineral oil; 'mineral ˌwater
mineralogical ˌmɪn ᵊr ə 'lɒdʒ ɪk ᵊl ◂ ‖ -'lɑːdʒ- **~ly** _i
mineralogist ˌmɪn ə 'ræl ədʒ ɪst △-'rɒl-, §-əst ‖ -'rɑːl- **~s** s
mineralogy ˌmɪn ə 'ræl ədʒ i △-'rɒl- ‖ -'rɑːl-
Minerva mɪ 'nɜːv ə mə- ‖ -'nɜːv-

mineshaft 'maɪn ʃɑːft §-ʃæft ‖ -ʃæft ~s s
minestrone ˌmɪn ə 'strəʊn i -ɪ- ‖ -'stroʊn i
  ⚠ -'strəʊn
minesweeper 'maɪn ˌswiːp ə ‖ -ᵊr ~s z
minesweeping 'maɪn ˌswiːp ɪŋ
mineworker 'maɪn ˌwɜːk ə ‖ -ˌwɜːk ᵊr ~s z
ming mɪŋ **minging** 'mɪŋ ɪŋ
Ming *dynasty* mɪŋ —*Chi* Míng [²miŋ]
minge mɪndʒ
minger 'mɪŋ ə ‖ -ᵊr ~s z
Minghella mɪŋ 'gel ə
mingl|e 'mɪŋ gᵊl ~**ed** d ~**er/s** ə/z ‖ ᵊr/z ~**es** z
  ~**ing** ɪŋ
mingogram 'mɪŋ gəʊ græm ‖ -gə- ~s z
mingograph, M~ 'mɪŋ gəʊ grɑːf -græf
  ‖ -gə græf ~s s
Mingrelian mɪn 'griːl i ən →mɪŋ-
Mingulay 'mɪŋ gʊ leɪ
Mingus 'mɪŋ gəs
mingl|y 'mɪndʒ |i ~**ier** i ə ‖ i ᵊr ~**iest** i ɪst i əst
mini, Mini 'mɪn i ~**s**, ~'**s** z
mini- ˌmɪn i — **minilecture** 'mɪn i ˌlek tʃə -ʃə
  ‖ -tʃᵊr -ʃᵊr
miniature 'mɪn ətʃ ə -ɪtʃ-, -i ətʃ ə
  ‖ 'mɪn i ətʃ ᵊr ə tʃʊr; 'mɪn ɪ tʃʊr ~s z
miniaturis... —*see* **miniaturiz...**
miniaturist 'mɪn ətʃ ər ɪst -'ɪtʃ-, -'i ətʃ · ·, §-əst
  ‖ 'mɪn i ətʃ ər əst ə tʃʊr əst; 'mɪn ɪ tʃʊr əst ~**s**
  s
miniaturization ˌmɪn ətʃ ər aɪ 'zeɪʃ ᵊn
  ˌmɪn ɪtʃ-, -i ətʃ ər aɪ-, -ɪ'--
  ‖ ˌmɪn i ətʃ ər ə 'zeɪʃ ᵊn ˌmɪn ətʃ ər ə'-- ~**s** z
miniaturiz|e 'mɪn ətʃ ə raɪz '-ɪtʃ-, -i ətʃ ə-
  ‖ 'mɪn i ətʃ ə raɪz -ətʃ ə raɪz ~**ed** d ~**es** ɪz əz
  ~**ing** ɪŋ
minibar 'mɪn i bɑː ‖ -bɑːr ~s z
minibus 'mɪn i bʌs ~**ed, ~sed** t ~**es, ~ses** ɪz
  əz ~**ing, ~sing** ɪŋ
minicab 'mɪn i kæb ~s z
minicam 'mɪn i kæm ~s z
minicomputer 'mɪn i kəm ˌpjuːt ə §-kɒm,-,
  ˌ· ·'·· ‖ -ˌpjuːt̬ ᵊr ~s z
minim 'mɪn ɪm §-əm ~**s** z
minima 'mɪn ɪm ə -əm-
minimal 'mɪn ɪm ᵊl -əm- ~**ly** i
  ˌminimal 'pair
minimalism 'mɪn ɪm ᵊl ˌɪz əm
minimalist 'mɪn ɪm ᵊl ɪst '-əm-, §-əst ~**s** s
mini-mart 'mɪn i mɑːt ‖ -mɑːrt ~**s** s
minimax 'mɪn ɪ mæks -ə-
mini-me ˌmɪn i 'miː
minimis... —*see* **minimiz...**
minimization ˌmɪn ɪ maɪ 'zeɪʃ ᵊn ˌ·ə- ‖ -əm ə-
minimiz|e 'mɪn ɪ maɪz -ə- ~**ed** d ~**es** ɪz əz
  ~**ing** ɪŋ
minim|um 'mɪn ɪm |əm -əm- ~**a** ə ~**ums** əmz
  ˌminimum 'wage
minimum-security
  ˌmɪn ɪm əm sɪ 'kjʊər ət i ◂ ˌ·əm-, -sə'·, -ət i
  ‖ -'kjʊr ət̬ i
minimus 'mɪn ɪm əs -əm-
mining 'maɪn ɪŋ
minion 'mɪn jən 'mɪn i ən ~s z

mini-roundabout ˌmɪn i 'raʊnd ə ˌbaʊt ~s s
miniscule, minuscule 'mɪn ə skjuːl -ɪ- ~**s** z
miniseries 'mɪn i ˌsɪər iːz -ɪz ‖ -ˌsɪr-
minisite 'mɪn i saɪt ~**s** s
mini|skirt 'mɪn i |skɜːt ‖ -|skɜːt ~**skirted**
  skɜːt ɪd -əd ‖ skɜːt̬ əd ~**skirts** skɜːts ‖ skɜːts
minister 'mɪn ɪst ə -əst- ‖ -ᵊr ~**ed** d
  ministering 'mɪn ɪst ər ɪŋ '·əst-;
  →'mɪn ɪ strɪŋ, -ə- ~**s** z
  ˌministering 'angel
ministerial ˌmɪn ɪ 'stɪər i əl ◂ ˌ·ə- ‖ -'stɪr- ~**ly** i
ministrant 'mɪn ɪs trənt -əs- ~**s** s
ministration ˌmɪn ɪ 'streɪʃ ᵊn -ə- ~**s** z
minis|try 'mɪn ɪs |tri -əs- ~**tries** triz
minium 'mɪn i əm
minivan 'mɪn i væn ~**s** z
miniver, M~ 'mɪn ɪv ə -əv- ‖ -ᵊr
mink mɪŋk **minks** mɪŋks
minke 'mɪŋk i -ə ‖ -ə ~**s** z
Minkowski mɪŋ 'kɒf ski ‖ -'kɑːf- -'kɔːf-
Minna 'mɪn ə
Minneapolis ˌmɪn i 'æp əl ɪs §-əs
Minnehaha ˌmɪn i 'hɑː hɑː
Minnelli mɪ 'nel i mə-
minneola ˌmɪn i 'əʊl ə ‖ -'oʊl ə ~**s** z
minnesinger 'mɪn ɪ ˌsɪŋ ə -ə- ‖ -ᵊr ~**s** z
Minnesota ˌmɪn ɪ 'səʊt ə -ə- ‖ -'soʊt̬ ə
Minnesotan ˌmɪn ɪ 'səʊt ᵊn ◂ -ə- ‖ -'soʊt̬ ᵊn ◂
  ~**s** z
Minnie 'mɪn i
minnow 'mɪn əʊ ‖ -oʊ ~**s** z
Minoan mɪ 'nəʊ ən mə-, maɪ- ‖ -'noʊ ən ~**s** z
Minogue mɪ 'nəʊg mə- ‖ -'noʊg
Minolta *tdmk* mɪ 'nɒlt ə mə-, -'nəʊlt-
  ‖ -'nɑːlt ə -'noʊlt- —*Jp* [mi ˌno ɾɯ ta]
minor, Minor 'maɪn ə ‖ -ᵊr (= *miner*) ~**ed** d
  minoring 'maɪn ər ɪŋ ~**s** z
  ˌminor 'planet; ˌminor 'suit
Minorca mɪ 'nɔːk ə mə- ‖ -'nɔːrk ə —*Sp*
  Menorca [me 'nor ka]
Minories 'mɪn ər iz
minorit|y maɪ 'nɒr ət |i mɪ-, mə-, -ɪt-
  ‖ mə 'nɔːr ət̬ |i maɪ-, -'nɑːr- ~**ies** iz
minor-league ˌmaɪn ə 'liːg ‖ -ᵊr-
Minos 'maɪn ɒs ‖ -əs -ɑːs
Minotaur 'maɪn ə tɔː ‖ 'mɪn ə tɔːr maɪn- ~**s** z
Minsk mɪnsk
minster, M~ 'mɪntˢt ə ‖ -ᵊr ~**s** z
minstrel 'mɪntˢ trəl ~**s** z
minstrel|sy 'mɪntˢ trəl |si ~**sies** siz
mint mɪnt **minted** 'mɪnt ɪd -əd ‖ 'mɪnt̬ əd
  minting 'mɪnt ɪŋ ‖ 'mɪnt̬ ɪŋ **mints** mɪnts
  ˌmint 'julep; ˌmint 'sauce ‖ '· ·
mintag|e 'mɪnt ɪdʒ ‖ 'mɪnt̬- ~**es** ɪz əz
Minter 'mɪnt ə ‖ 'mɪnt̬ ᵊr
Minto 'mɪnt əʊ ‖ -oʊ
Minton 'mɪnt ən ‖ -ᵊn
minty, Minty 'mɪnt i ‖ 'mɪnt̬ i
minuend 'mɪn ju end ~**s** z
minuet ˌmɪn ju 'et ~**s** s
minus 'maɪn əs ~**es** ɪz əz
  ˌminus 'one; 'minus ˌsign
minuscule 'mɪn ə skjuː l -ɪ- ‖ mɪ 'nʌsk juː l ~**s** z

minute *adj 'tiny'* maɪ 'njuːt ˌˑˈˑ ‖ -'nuːt -'njuːt
~**ly** li

min|ute *n, v* 'mɪn |ɪt §-ət ‖ -|ət ~**uted** ɪt ɪd
§ət-, -əd ‖ əʈ əd ~**utes** ɪts §əts ‖ əts ~**uting**
ɪt ɪŋ §ət- ‖ əʈ ɪŋ
'**minute hand**; '**minute steak**

minute|man, M~ 'mɪn ɪt |mæn §-ət- ~**men**
men

minuteness maɪ 'njuːt nəs ˌ-, -nɪs ‖ -'nuːt-
-'njuːt-

minuti|a maɪ 'njuːʃ i ˌ|ə mɪ-, mə-, -'nuːʃ-,
-'njuːt-, -'nuːt- ‖ -'nuːʃ- -'njuːʃ- ~**ae** iː aɪ

minx mɪŋks **minxes** 'mɪŋks ɪz -əz

Miocene 'maɪ ə siːn

MIPS, mips mɪps

Miquelon 'miːk ə lɒn ‖ -lɑːn -lɔːn —*Fr*
[mi klɔ̃]

Mir mɪə ‖ mɪˀr —*Russ* [mʲir]

Mira 'maɪˀr ə 'mɪr-

Mirabeau 'mɪr ə bəʊ ‖ -boʊ —*Fr* [mi ʁa bo]

Mirabel 'mɪr ə bel

miracle 'mɪr ək ᵊl -ɪk- ~**s** z
'**miracle drug**; '**miracle play**

miraculous mə 'ræk jʊl əs mɪ-, -jəl- ‖ -jəl- ~**ly**
li ~**ness** nəs nɪs

mirag|e, M~ 'mɪr ɑːʒ mə 'rɑːʒ, mɪ- ‖ mə 'rɑːʒ
~**es** ɪz əz

Miranda mə 'rænd ə mɪ-

MIRAS 'maɪˀr əs -æs

mire 'maɪˌə ‖ 'maɪˌˀr **mired** 'maɪˌəd ‖ 'maɪˌˀrd
mires 'maɪˌəz ‖ 'maɪˌˀrz **miring** 'maɪˌər ɪŋ
‖ 'maɪˌˀr ɪŋ

mirepoix ˌmɪə 'pwɑː ‖ mɪr- —*Fr* [miʁ pwa]

Mirfield 'mɜː fiːˀld ‖ 'mɜː-

Mirfin 'mɜːf ɪn §-ᵊn ‖ 'mɜːf-

Miriam 'mɪr i əm

mirk mɜːk ‖ mɜːk

mirk|y 'mɜːk |i ‖ 'mɜːk |i ~**ier** i ə ‖ i ˌˀr ~**iest**
i ɪst i əst ~**ily** ɪ li əl i ~**iness** i nəs i nɪs

Miró mɪ 'rəʊ ‖ -'roʊ —*Sp, Catalan* [mi 'ro]

Mirren 'mɪr ən

Mirro *tdmk* 'mɪr əʊ ‖ -oʊ

mirror 'mɪr ə ‖ -ˀr ~**ed** d **mirroring** 'mɪr ər ɪŋ
~**s** z
ˌmirror 'image, ˑˑˌˑˑ; 'mirror ˌwriting

mirth mɜːθ ‖ mɜːθ

mirthful 'mɜːθ fᵊl -fʊl ‖ 'mɜːθ-

mirthless 'mɜːθ ləs -lɪs ‖ 'mɜːθ- ~**ly** li

MIRV mɜːv ‖ mɜːv ~**ed** d ~**ing** ɪŋ ~**s** z

mir|y 'maɪˀr |i ~**ier** i ə ‖ i ˌˀr ~**iest** i ɪst i əst
~**iness** i nəs i nɪs

mis- ˌmɪs

misadventure ˌmɪs əd 'ventʃ ə §-æd- ‖ -ˀr ~**s** z

misadvis|e ˌmɪs əd 'vaɪz §-æd- ~**ed** d ~**es** ɪz əz
~**ing** ɪŋ

misalign ˌmɪs ə 'laɪn ~**ed** d ~**ing** ɪŋ ~**ment/s**
mənt/s ~**s** z

misallianc|e ˌmɪs ə 'laɪ ən¹s ~**es** ɪz əz

misandry mɪs 'ændr i 'mɪs ᵊndr i

misanthrope 'mɪs ᵊn θrəʊp 'mɪz-, -æn-
‖ -θroʊp ~**s** s

misanthropic ˌmɪs ᵊn 'θrɒp ɪk ◂ ˌmɪz-, -æn-
‖ -'θrɑːp- ~**ally** ᵊl_i

misanthropist mɪs 'æn¹θ rəp ɪst mɪz-, §-əst ~**s**
s

misanthropy mɪs 'æn¹θ rəp i mɪz-

misapplication ˌmɪs ˌæp lɪ 'keɪʃ ᵊn -lə¹-- ~**s** z

misap|ply ˌmɪs ə |'plaɪ ~**plied** 'plaɪd ~**plies**
'plaɪz ~**plying** 'plaɪ ɪŋ

misapprehend ˌmɪs ˌæp rɪ 'hend -rə- ~**ed** ɪd
əd ~**ing** ɪŋ ~**s** z

misapprehension ˌmɪs ˌæp rɪ 'hen¹ʃ ᵊn -rə- ~**s**
z

misappropri|ate ˌmɪs ə 'prəʊp ri ˌeɪt
‖ -'proʊp- ~**ated** eɪt ɪd -əd ‖ eɪʈ əd ~**ates** eɪts
~**ating** eɪt ɪŋ ‖ eɪʈ ɪŋ

misappropriation ˌmɪs ə ˌprəʊp ri 'eɪʃ ᵊn
‖ -ˌproʊp- ~**s** z

misbegotten ˌmɪs bɪ 'gɒt ᵊn ◂ -bə- ‖ -'gɑːt ᵊn

misbehav|e ˌmɪs bɪ 'heɪv -bə- ~**ed** d ~**es** z
~**ing** ɪŋ

misbehavior, misbehaviour ˌmɪs bɪ 'heɪv jə
-bə- ‖ -jˀr ~**s** z

misc. —*see* **miscellaneous**

miscalcu|late ˌmɪs 'kælk ju |leɪt -jə- ‖ -jə-
~**lated** leɪt ɪd -əd ‖ leɪʈ əd ~**lates** leɪts
~**lating** leɪt ɪŋ ‖ leɪʈ ɪŋ

miscalculation ˌmɪs ˌkælk ju 'leɪʃ ᵊn -jə- ‖ -jə-
~**s** z

miscall ˌmɪs 'kɔːl ‖ -'kɑːl ~**ed** d ~**ing** ɪŋ ~**s** z

Miscampbell mɪ 'skæm bᵊl

miscarriag|e ₍ˌ₎mɪs 'kær ɪdʒ ◂ ˈˑˌˑˑ ‖ ˈˑˌˑˑ -ˌker-
~**es** ɪz əz
ˌmisˌcarriage of 'justice ‖ ˌˑˌˑˑ

miscarr|y ₍ˌ₎mɪs 'kær |i ˈˑˌˑˑ ‖ -'ker- ~**ied** id
~**ies** iz ~**ying** i ɪŋ

miscast ˌmɪs 'kɑːst §-'kæst ‖ -'kæst ~**ing** ɪŋ ~**s**
s

miscegenation ˌmɪs ɪdʒ ə 'neɪʃ ᵊn ˌədʒ-, -ɪ¹--;
mɪ ˌsedʒ-, mə-

miscellanea ˌmɪs ə 'leɪn i ə

miscellaneous ˌmɪs ə 'leɪn i əs ◂ ~**ly** li ~**ness**
nəs nɪs

miscellanist mɪ 'sel ən ɪst mə-, §-əst;
'mɪs ə leɪn- ‖ ˌmɪs ə leɪn- ~**s** s

miscellan|y mɪ 'sel ən |i mə-, 'mɪs ə leɪn |i
‖ 'mɪs ə leɪn |i (*) ~**ies** iz

mischance ˌmɪs 'tʃɑːn¹s →§ˌmɪʃ-, §-'tʃæn¹s, ˈˑˑ
‖ -'tʃæn¹s

mischief 'mɪs tʃɪf →§'mɪʃ-, §-tʃəf, §-tʃiːf ~**s** s

mischief-mak|er 'mɪs tʃɪf ˌmeɪk| ə →§'mɪʃ-,
§-tʃəf-, §-tʃiːf- ‖ -ˀr ~**ers** əz ‖ ˀrz ~**ing** ɪŋ

mischievous 'mɪs tʃɪv əs →§'mɪʃ-, -tʃəv-;
mɪs 'tʃiːv-, -i əs — *Preference polls, (stress)*
AmE: 'mɪs- 67%, -'tʃiːv əs 22% -'tʃiːv i əs 11%;
BrE: 'mɪs- 65% *(born since 1981: 49%)*, -'tʃiːv
əs 20% *(born since 1981: 22%)*; -'tʃiːv i əs 15%
(born since 1981: 29%); -i əs 40%. ~**ly** li
~**ness** nəs nɪs

miscible 'mɪs əb ᵊl -ɪb-

misconceiv|e ˌmɪs kən 'siːv §-kɒn- ~**ed** d ~**es**
z ~**ing** ɪŋ

misconception ˌmɪs kən 'sep ʃᵊn §-kɒn- ~**s** z

misconduct *n* ˌmɪs 'kɒn dʌkt ‖ -'kɑːn-

misconduct *v* ˌmɪs kən 'dʌkt §-kɒn- ~**ed** ɪd əd
~**ing** ɪŋ ~**s** s

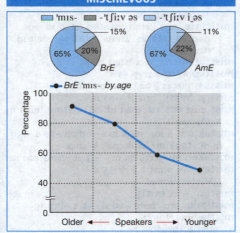

MISCHIEVOUS

☐ ˈmɪs-   ■ -ˈtʃiːv əs   ☐ -ˈtʃiːv i ˌəs

BrE: 65% 20% 15%
AmE: 67% 22% 11%

BrE ˈmɪs- by age

(graph: Percentage vs Older ← Speakers → Younger)

misconstruction ˌmɪs kən ˈstrʌk ʃᵊn §-kɒn- **~s** z
misconstru|e ˌmɪs kən ˈstruː §-kɒn- **~ed** d **~es** z **~ing** ɪŋ
miscount n ˈmɪs kaʊnt ˌ·ˈ· **~s** s
mis|count v ˌmɪs |ˈkaʊnt **~counted** ˈkaʊnt ɪd -əd ‖ ˈkaʊnt̬ əd **~counting** ˈkaʊnt ɪŋ ‖ ˈkaʊnt̬ ɪŋ **~counts** ˈkaʊnts
miscreant ˈmɪs kri ənt **~s** s
miscu|e v, n ˌmɪs ˈkjuː **~ed** d **~es** z **~ing** ɪŋ
mis|date v ˌmɪs |ˈdeɪt **~dated** ˈdeɪt ɪd -əd ‖ ˈdeɪt̬ əd **~dates** ˈdeɪts **~dating** ˈdeɪt ɪŋ ‖ ˈdeɪt̬ ɪŋ
misdeal n ˌmɪs ˈdiːᵊl ˈ·· **~s** z
misdeal v ˌmɪs ˈdiːᵊl **~ing** ɪŋ **~s** z **misdealt** ˌmɪs ˈdelt
misdeed ˌmɪs ˈdiːd ˈ·· **~s** z
misdemeanor, misdemeanour ˌmɪs dɪ ˈmiːn ə -də- ‖ -ᵊr **~s** z
misdiagnos|e ˌmɪs ˈdaɪ əg nəʊz -nəʊz, -ˌ·ˈ· ‖ -ˌdaɪ əg ˈnoʊs -ˈ··· **~ed** d **~es** ɪz əz **~ing** ɪŋ
misdirect ˌmɪs də ˈrekt -dɪ-, -daɪᵊ- **~ed** ɪd əd **~ing** ɪŋ **~s** s
misdirection ˌmɪs də ˈrek ʃᵊn -dɪ-, -daɪᵊ- **~s** z
misdoing ˌmɪs ˈduː ɪŋ ˈ·ˌ·· **~s** z
mise-en-scene, mise-en-scène ˌmiːz ɒn ˈseɪn -ˈsen ‖ -ɑːn- —Fr [mi zɑ̃ sɛn]
miser ˈmaɪz ə ‖ -ᵊr **~s** z
miserab|le ˈmɪz ər_əb |ᵊl →ˈmɪʒ rəb |ᵊl ‖ ˈmɪz ᵊrb |ᵊl **~leness** ᵊl nəs -nɪs **~ly** li
misere, misère mɪ ˈzeə §mə- ‖ -ˈzeᵊr
miserere, M~ ˌmɪz ə ˈreər i -ˈrɪər-, -eɪ ‖ -ˈrer- -ˈrɪr-
misericord mɪ ˈzer ɪ kɔːd mə-, -ə- ‖ -kɔːrd **~s** z
miserie... —see **misery**
miser|ly ˈmaɪz ə |li -ᵊ|l i ‖ -ᵊr- **~liness** li nəs li nɪs
miser|y ˈmɪz ər_|i →ˈmɪʒ r|i **~ies** iz
misfeasanc|e ₍ᵢ₎mɪs ˈfiːz ᵊnts **~es** ɪz əz
misfield n. ˌmɪs fiːᵊld **~s** z
misfield v. ˌmɪs ˈfiːᵊld **~ed** d **~ing** ɪŋ **~s** z

misfire v ˌmɪs ˈfaɪ_ə ‖ -ˈfaɪˌᵊr **~d** d **~s** z
misfiring ˌmɪs ˈfaɪ_ər ɪŋ ‖ -ˈfaɪˌᵊr ɪŋ
misfire n ˌmɪs ˈfaɪ_ə ˈ·ˌ·· ‖ -ˈfaɪˌᵊr ˈ·ˌ··· **~s** z
misfit ˈmɪs fɪt ˌ·ˈ· **~s** s
misfortune mɪs ˈfɔːtʃ ən -uːn ‖ -ˈfɔːrtʃ- **~s** z
misgiving ₍ᵢ₎mɪs ˈgɪv ɪŋ **~s** z
misgovern ˌmɪs ˈgʌv ᵊn ‖ -ᵊrn **~ed** d **~ing** ɪŋ **~s** z
misguided ₍ᵢ₎mɪs ˈgaɪd ɪd -əd **~ly** li
mishandl|e ˌmɪs ˈhænd ᵊl **~ed** d **~es** z **~ing** ɪŋ
mishap ˈmɪs hæp ₍ᵢ₎·ˈ· **~s** s
Mishcon ˈmɪʃ kɒn ‖ -kɑːn
  Mishcon de ˈReya də ˈreɪ ə
mis|hear ˌmɪs |ˈhɪə ‖ -|ˈhɪᵊr **~heard** ˈhɜːd ◄ ‖ ˈhɜːd ◄ **~hearing** ˈhɪər ɪŋ ‖ ˈhɪr ɪŋ **~hears** ˈhɪəz ‖ ˈhɪᵊrz
Mishima ˈmɪʃ ɪm ə ˈmiːʃ- —Jp [mi ˌɕi ma]
mis|hit v ˌmɪs |ˈhɪt **~hits** ˈhɪts **~hitting** ˈhɪt ɪŋ ‖ ˈhɪt̬ ɪŋ
mishit n ˈmɪs hɪt ˌ·ˈ· **~s** s
mishmash ˈmɪʃ mæʃ ‖ -mɑːʃ -mæʃ (*)
Mishna, Mishnah ˈmɪʃ nə
misinform ˌmɪs ɪn ˈfɔːm §-ᵊn- ‖ -ˈfɔːrm **~ed** d **~ing** ɪŋ **~s** z
misinformation ˌmɪs ɪn fə ˈmeɪʃ ᵊn §-ˌ·ᵊn- ‖ -ɪn fᵊr-
misinterp|ret ˌmɪs ɪn ˈtɜːp |rɪt §-ᵊn-, -rət ‖ -ˈtɜːp |rət -ət **~reted** rɪt ɪd §rət-, -əd ‖ rət̬ əd ət̬- **~reting** rɪt ɪŋ §rət- ‖ rət̬ ɪŋ ət̬- **~rets** rɪts §rəts ‖ rəts əts
misinterpretation ˌmɪs ɪn ˌtɜːp rɪ ˈteɪʃ ᵊn §-ˌᵊn-, -rə-ˈ·- ‖ -ˌtɜːp rə- -ˌtɜːp ə- **~s** z
misjudg|e ˌmɪs ˈdʒʌdʒ **~ed** d **~es** ɪz əz **~ing** ɪŋ
misjudgement, misjudgment ₍ᵢ₎mɪs ˈdʒʌdʒ mənt **~s** s
miskick v. ˌmɪs ˈkɪk **~ed** t **~ing** ɪŋ **~s** s
miskick n. ˈmɪs kɪk **~s** s
Miskin ˈmɪsk ɪn §-ən
Miskito mɪ ˈskiːt əʊ ‖ -oʊ
mis|lay ₍ᵢ₎mɪs |ˈleɪ **~laid** ˈleɪd **~laying** ˈleɪ ɪŋ **~lays** ˈleɪz
mis|lead ₍ᵢ₎mɪs |ˈliːd **~leading/ly** ˈliːd ɪŋ /li **~leads** ˈliːdz **~led** ˈled
mismanag|e ˌmɪs ˈmæn ɪdʒ **~ed** d **~es** ɪz əz **~ing** ɪŋ
mismanagement ˌmɪs ˈmæn ɪdʒ mənt
mismatch v ˌmɪs ˈmætʃ **~ed** t **~es** ɪz əz **~ing** ɪŋ
mismatch n ˈmɪs mætʃ ˌ·ˈ· **~es** ɪz əz
mismeasure ˌmɪs ˈmeʒ ə ‖ -ᵊr -ˈmeɪʒ- **~ment** mənt
misnam|e ˌmɪs ˈneɪm **~ed** d **~es** z **~ing** ɪŋ
misnomer ˌmɪs ˈnəʊm ə ‖ -ˈnoʊm ᵊr **~s** z
miso ˈmiːs əʊ ‖ -oʊ —Jp [ˈmi so]
misogynist mɪ ˈsɒdʒ ən ɪst maɪ-, mə-, -ɪn-, §-əst ‖ -ˈsɑːdʒ- **~s** s
misogynistic mɪ ˌsɒdʒ ə ˈnɪst ɪk ◄ maɪ-, mə-, -ɪn-, §-əst ‖ -ˌsɑːdʒ-
misogyny mɪ ˈsɒdʒ ən i maɪ-, mə-, -ɪn- ‖ -ˈsɑːdʒ-
misplac|e ˌmɪs ˈpleɪs **~ed** t ◄ **~es** ɪz əz **~ing** ɪŋ

M

misplacement ˌmɪs ˈpleɪs mənt
misprint n ˈmɪs prɪnt **~s** s
mis|print v ˌmɪs |ˈprɪnt **~printed** ˈprɪnt ɪd -əd
‖ ˈprɪnt̬ əd **~printing** ˈprɪnt ɪŋ ‖ ˈprɪnt̬ ɪŋ
~prints ˈprɪnts
misprision ˌmɪs ˈprɪʒ ⁿn
mispronounc|e ˌmɪs prə ˈnaʊnˀts **~ed** t **~es** ɪz
əz **~ing** ɪŋ
mispronunciation ˌmɪs prə ˌnʌnˀts i ˈeɪʃ ⁿn
△-ˌnaʊnˀts- **~s** z
misquotation ˌmɪs kwəʊ ˈteɪʃ ⁿn ‖ -kwoʊ- **~s**
z
mis|quote ˌmɪs |ˈkwəʊt ‖ -|ˈkwoʊt **~quoted**
ˈkwəʊt ɪd -əd ‖ ˈkwoʊt̬ əd **~quotes** ˈkwəʊts
‖ ˈkwoʊts **~quoting** ˈkwəʊt ɪŋ ‖ ˈkwoʊt̬ ɪŋ
mis|read v pres ˌmɪs |ˈriːd **~read** v past & pp
ˈred **~reading** ˈriːd ɪŋ **~reads** ˈriːdz
misre|port ˌmɪs ri |ˈpɔːt -rə- ‖ -|ˈpɔːrt -|ˈpoʊrt
~ported ˈpɔːt ɪd -əd ‖ ˈpɔːrt̬ əd ˈpoʊrt-
~porting ˈpɔːt ɪŋ ‖ ˈpɔːrt̬ ɪŋ ˈpoʊrt̬- **~ports**
ˈpɔːts ‖ ˈpɔːrts ˈpoʊrts
misrepre|sent ˌmɪs ˌrep ri |ˈzent -rə- ‖ ·ˌ·-
~sented ˈzent ɪd -əd ‖ ˈzent̬ əd **~senting**
ˈzent ɪŋ ‖ ˈzent̬ ɪŋ **~sents** ˈzents
misrepresentation ˌmɪs ˌrep ri zen ˈteɪʃ ⁿn
-ˌ·rə-, -zⁿn'·- ‖ ·ˌ·,·- **~s** z
misrul|e v, n ˌmɪs ˈruːl **~ed** d **~es** z **~ing** ɪŋ
miss, Miss mɪs —For the noun, when used
with a name, there is also an occasional weak
form §məs **missed** mɪst **misses** ˈmɪs ɪz -əz
missing ˈmɪs ɪŋ
ˌ(ˌ)Miss ˈAbbott; ˌmissing ˈlink
missa ˈmɪs ə
ˌmissa ˈbrevis ˈbrev ɪs ˈbreɪv-, §-əs
missal ˈmɪs ⁿl **~s** z
missel ˈmɪs ⁿl ˈmɪz-
mis-|sell ˌmɪs |ˈsel **~selling** ˈsel ɪŋ **~sells**
ˈselz **~sold** ˈsəʊld →ˈsoʊld ‖ -ˈsoʊld
Missenden ˈmɪs ⁿnd ən
misshape n ˈmɪs ʃeɪp →ˈmɪʃ- **~s** s
misshap|e v ˌmɪs ˈʃeɪp →ˌmɪʃ- **~ed** t **~en** ən
~es s **~ing** ɪŋ
missile ˈmɪs aɪⁿl -ⁿl ‖ -ⁿl **~s** z
mission ˈmɪʃ ⁿn **~s** z
missionar|y ˈmɪʃ ⁿn ər ˌi -ⁿn ˌər- ‖ -ə ner ˌi
~ies iz
ˈmissionary poˌsition
missioner ˈmɪʃ ⁿn ə ‖ ər **~s** z
missis ˈmɪs ɪz §-əz
Mississauga ˌmɪs ɪ ˈsɔːg ə -ə- ‖ -ˈsɑːg-
Mississippi ˌmɪs ɪ ˈsɪp i -ə-
ˌMississˌsippi ˈDelta
Mississippian ˌmɪs ɪ ˈsɪp i ən ◂ ˌ·ə- **~s** z
missive ˈmɪs ɪv **~s** z
Missolonghi ˌmɪs ə ˈlɒŋ gi ‖ -ˈlɔːŋ- -ˈlɑːŋ-
Missoula mɪ ˈzuːl ə mə-
Missouri mɪ ˈzʊər i mə-, -ˈsʊər- ‖ -ˈzʊr i -ˈzɜː-,
-ə
Missourian mɪ ˈzʊər i_ən mə-, -ˈsʊər- ‖ -ˈzʊr-
-ˈzɜː- **~s** z
misspell ˌmɪs ˈspel **~ed** d **~ing** ɪŋ **~s** z
misspelt ˌmɪs ˈspelt ◂

misspend ˌmɪs ˈspend **~ing** ɪŋ **~s** z **misspent**
ˌmɪs ˈspent ◂
ˌmisspent ˈyouth
mis|state ˌmɪs |ˈsteɪt **~stated** ˈsteɪt ɪd -əd
‖ ˈsteɪt̬ əd **~states** ˈsteɪts **~stating** ˈsteɪt ɪŋ
‖ ˈsteɪt̬ ɪŋ
misstatement ˌmɪs ˈsteɪt mənt **~s** s
misstep n. ˈmɪs step **~s** s
missus ˈmɪs ɪz §-əz ‖ ˈmɪs əz ˈmɪz-, -əs
miss|y, Missy ˈmɪs |i **~ies** iz
mist mɪst **misted** ˈmɪst ɪd -əd **misting** ˈmɪst ɪŋ
mists mɪsts
mistak|e v, n mɪ ˈsteɪk mə- **~en** ən **~es** s **~ing**
ɪŋ **mistook** mɪ ˈstʊk mə-, §-ˈstuːk
mistaken mɪ ˈsteɪk ən mə- **~ly** li **~ness** nəs nɪs
mister, M~ ˈmɪst ə ‖ -ᵊr **~s** z
ˌ(ˌ)Mister ˈJones
misti... —see **misty**
mistim|e ˌmɪs ˈtaɪm **~ed** d **~es** z **~ing** ɪŋ
mistle ˈmɪs ⁿl ˈmɪz-
ˈmistle thrush
mistletoe ˈmɪs ⁿl təʊ ˈmɪz- ‖ -toʊ
mistook mɪ ˈstʊk mə-, §-ˈstuːk
mistral ˈmɪs trəl -trɑːl; mɪ ˈstrɑːl, mə- —Fr
[mis tʁal]
mistrans|late ˌmɪs trænz ˈ|leɪt -trɑːnz-,
-trænˀts-, -trɑːnˀts-, -trənz-, -trənˀts- ‖ -ˈ·| ·
~lated leɪt ɪd -əd ‖ leɪt̬ əd **~lates** leɪts
~lating leɪt ɪŋ ‖ leɪt̬ ɪŋ
mistranslation ˌmɪs trænz ˈleɪʃ ⁿn -trɑːnz-,
-trænˀts-, -trɑːnˀts-, -trənz-, -trənˀts- **~s** z
mis|treat ˌmɪs |ˈtriːt **~treated** ˈtriːt ɪd -əd
‖ ˈtriːt̬ əd **~treating** ˈtriːt ɪŋ ‖ ˈtriːt̬ ɪŋ
~treats ˈtriːts
mistreatment ˌmɪs ˈtriːt mənt **~s** s
mistress, M~ ˈmɪs trəs -trɪs **~es** ɪz əz
mistrial ˌmɪs ˈtraɪ_əl ˈ·ˌ·· **~s** z
mistrust v, n ˌmɪs ˈtrʌst **~ed** ɪd əd **~ing/ly**
ɪŋ /li **~s** s
mistrustful ˌmɪs ˈtrʌst fⁿl -fʊl **~ly** i **~ness** nəs
nɪs
mist|y ˈmɪst |i **~ier** i_ə ‖ i_ᵊr **~iest** i_ɪst i_əst
~ily ɪ li əl i **~iness** i nəs i nɪs
misty-eyed ˌmɪst i ˈaɪd ◂
misunder|stand ˌmɪs ˌʌnd ə |ˈstænd ‖ -ᵊr- ·ˌ·-
~standing/s ˈstænd ɪŋ/z **~stands** ˈstændz
~stood ˈstʊd
misus|e n ˌmɪs ˈjuːs →§ˌmɪʃ- **~es** ɪz əz
misus|e v ˌmɪs ˈjuːz →§ˌmɪʃ- **~ed** d **~es** ɪz əz
~ing ɪŋ
MIT ˌem aɪ ˈtiː ◂
Mita ˈmiːt ə ‖ ˈmiːt̬ ə
Mitch, mitch mɪtʃ
Mitcham ˈmɪtʃ əm
Mitchel, Mitchell ˈmɪtʃ əl
Mitchison ˈmɪtʃ ɪs ən -əs-
Mitchum ˈmɪtʃ əm
mite maɪt (= might) **mites** maɪts
miter ˈmaɪt ə ‖ ˈmaɪt̬ ᵊr **~ed** d **mitering**
ˈmaɪt ər ɪŋ ‖ ˈmaɪt̬ ər ɪŋ **~s** z
Mitford ˈmɪt fəd ‖ -fᵊrd
Mithraic mɪ ˈθreɪ ɪk
Mithraism ˈmɪθ reɪ ˌɪz əm -rə-; mɪθ ˈreɪ··

Mithraist ˈmɪθ reɪ ɪst -rə-, §-əst; mɪθ ˈreɪ- **~s** s
Mithras ˈmɪθ ræs -rəs
Mithridates ˌmɪθ rə ˈdeɪt iːz -ɪ-
miti|gate ˈmɪt ɪ ˌɡeɪt §-ə- ‖ ˈmɪt̬ ə- **~gated**
ɡeɪt ɪd -əd ‖ ɡeɪt̬ əd **~gates** ɡeɪts **~gating**
ɡeɪt ɪŋ ‖ ɡeɪt̬ ɪŋ
mitigation ˌmɪt ɪ ˈɡeɪʃ ᵊn §-ə- ‖ ˌmɪt̬ ə-
mitochondri|on ˌmaɪt əʊ ˈkɒndr i ˌjən
‖ ˌmaɪt̬ ə ˈkɑːndr- **~a** ə **~al** əl
mitosis ₍ᵢ₎maɪ ˈtəʊs ɪs §-əs ‖ -ˈtoʊs əs
mitrailleuse ˌmɪtr aɪ ˈɜːz ‖ -ə ˈjɜːz —*Fr*
[mi tʁa jøːz]
mitral ˈmaɪtr əl
mitr|e ˈmaɪt ə ‖ ˈmaɪt̬ ᵊr **~ed** d **~es** z **mitring**
ˈmaɪt ᵊr ɪŋ ‖ ˈmaɪt̬ ᵊr ɪŋ
ˈmitre joint
Mitsubishi *tdmk* ˌmɪts u ˈbɪʃ i ‖ ˌmiːts uː ˈbiːʃ iː
—*Jp* [mi ˌtsuɯ ˈbi ɕi]
mitt mɪt **mitts** mɪts
mitten ˈmɪt ᵊn **~s** z
Mitterand ˈmiːt ə rɒ̃ ˈmɪt- ‖ -rɑːn —*Fr*
[mi tɛ ʁɑ̃]
Mitton ˈmɪt ᵊn
Mitty ˈmɪt i ‖ ˈmɪt̬ i **~ish** ɪʃ
Mitylene ˌmɪt ə ˈliːn i -ɪ-, →-ᵊl ˈiːn- ‖ ˌmɪt̬-
Mitzi ˈmɪts i
mitzvah ˈmɪts və
Miwok ˈmiː wɒk ‖ -waːk **~s** s
mix mɪks **mixed** mɪkst **mixes** ˈmɪks ɪz -əz
mixing ˈmɪks ɪŋ
ˌmixed ˈbag; ˌmixed ˈblessing; ˌmixed
ˈdoubles; ˌmixed eˈconomy; ˌmixed
ˈfarming; ˌmixed ˈgrill; ˌmixed ˈmarriage;
ˌmixed ˈmetaphor
mix-and-match ˌmɪks ᵊn ˈmætʃ ◂ -ᵊnd-
mixed-ability ˌmɪkst ə ˈbɪl ət i -ɪt i ‖ -ət̬ i
mixed up, mixed-up ˌmɪkst ˈʌp ◂
ˌmixed-up ˈkid
mixer ˈmɪks ə ‖ -ᵊr **~s** z
mixologist mɪk ˈsɒl ədʒ ɪst §-əst ‖ -ˈsɑːl- **~s** s
mixtape ˈmɪks teɪp **~s** s
Mixtec ˈmiːs tek **~s** s
mixture ˈmɪks tʃə ‖ -tʃᵊr **~s** z
mix-up ˈmɪks ʌp **~s** s
Miyake mɪ ˈjæk i ‖ mɪ ˈjaːk i —*Jp* [mi ˌja ke]
mizen, mizzen ˈmɪz ᵊn **~s** z
mizuna mɪ ˈzuːn ə
mizzenmast ˈmɪz ᵊn maːst →-ᵊm-, §-mæst
‖ -mæst **~s** s
mizzl|e ˈmɪz ᵊl **~ed** d **~es** z **~ing** ɪŋ
ml *sing.* ˈmɪl i ˌliːt ə -ə- ‖ -ə ˌliːt̬ ᵊr *pl* z
m'lady mɪ ˈleɪd i mə-
M'lord mɪ ˈlɔːd mə- ‖ -ˈlɔːrd
M'lud mɪ ˈlʌd mə-
mm *sing.* ˈmɪl i ˌmiːt ə -ə- ‖ -ə ˌmiːt̬ ᵊr *pl* z
mnemonic nɪ ˈmɒn ɪk nə-, niː-, mni- ‖ -ˈmaːn-
~ally ᵊl i **~s** s
Mnemosyne ni ˈmɒz ɪn i nə-, mni-, -ˈmɒs-,
-ən- ‖ -ˈmaːs ən i -ˈmaːz-
mo, Mo məʊ ‖ moʊ
MO ˌem ˈəʊ ‖ -ˈoʊ —*also see* Missouri
-mo məʊ ‖ moʊ — **twelvemo** ˈtwelv məʊ
‖ -moʊ

moa ˈməʊ ə ‖ ˈmoʊ ə **~s** z
Moab ˈməʊ æb ‖ ˈmoʊ-
Moabite ˈməʊ ə baɪt ‖ ˈmoʊ- **~s** s
moan məʊn ‖ moʊn **moaned** məʊnd ‖ moʊnd
moaning ˈməʊn ɪŋ ‖ ˈmoʊn ɪŋ **moans**
məʊnz ‖ moʊnz
moaner ˈməʊn ə ‖ ˈmoʊn ᵊr **~s** z
moat, Moat məʊt ‖ moʊt **moated** ˈməʊt ɪd
-əd ‖ ˈmoʊt̬ əd **moating** ˈməʊt ɪŋ ‖ ˈmoʊt̬ ɪŋ
moats məʊts ‖ moʊts
mob mɒb ‖ maːb **mobbed** mɒbd ‖ maːbd
mobbing ˈmɒbɪŋ ‖ ˈmaːb ɪŋ **mobs** mɒbz
‖ maːbz
Mobberley ˈmɒb ə li ‖ ˈmaːb ᵊr-
mobcap ˈmɒb kæp ‖ ˈmaːb- **~s** s
mobe məʊb ‖ moʊb **mobes** məʊbz ‖ moʊbz
Moberly ˈməʊb ə li ‖ ˈmoʊb ᵊr-
Mobil *tdmk* ˈməʊb ᵊl -ɪl ‖ ˈmoʊb-
mobile ˈməʊb aɪᵊl ‖ ˈmoʊb ᵊl -iːᵊl, -aɪᵊl **~s** z
ˌmobile ˈhome ‖ ˈ· · ·; ˌmobile ˈlibrary;
ˌmobile ˈphone
Mobile *place in AL* məʊ ˈbiːᵊl ˈməʊb iːᵊl
‖ moʊ ˈbiːᵊl ˈmoʊb iːᵊl
mobilis... —*see* **mobiliz...**
mobility məʊ ˈbɪl ət i -ɪt i ‖ moʊ ˈbɪl ət̬ i
mobilization ˌməʊb əl aɪ ˈzeɪʃ ᵊn ˌ-ɪl-, -ɪ-ˈ-
‖ ˌmoʊb əl ə- **~s** z
mobiliz|e ˈməʊb ə laɪz -ɪ-, -ᵊl aɪz ‖ ˈmoʊb- **~ed**
d **~es** ɪz əz **~ing** ɪŋ
Mobius, Möbius, m~ ˈmɜːb i ˌəs ˈməʊb-
‖ ˈmoʊb- ˈmeɪb- —*Ger* [ˈmøː bi ʊs]
ˌMobius ˈstrip ‖ ˈ· · ·
mobster ˈmɒb stə ‖ ˈmaːb stᵊr **~s** z
Mobutu məʊ ˈbuːt uː ‖ moʊ-
Moby ˈməʊb i ‖ ˈmoʊb i
ˌMoby ˈDick
Mocatta məʊ ˈkæt ə ‖ moʊ ˈkæt̬ ə
moccasin ˈmɒk əs ɪn §-ᵊn ‖ ˈmaːk- **~s** z
mocha, Mocha ˈmɒk ə ˈməʊk- ‖ ˈmoʊk ə
mochaccino ˌmɒk ə ˈtʃiːn əʊ
‖ ˌmoʊk ə ˈtʃiːn oʊ **~s** z
mock mɒk ‖ maːk mɔːk **mocked** mɒkt ‖ maːkt
mɔːkt **mocking/ly** ˈmɒk ɪŋ /li ‖ ˈmaːk ɪŋ /li
ˈmɔːk- **mocks** mɒks ‖ maːks mɔːks
ˌmock ˌturtle ˈsoup
mocker ˈmɒk ə ‖ ˈmaːk ᵊr ˈmɔːk- **~s** z
mocker|y ˈmɒk ᵊr |i ‖ ˈmak- ˈmɔːk- **~ies** iz
mock-heroic ˌmɒk hə ˈrəʊ ɪk ◂ -hɪ-, -he-
‖ ˌmaːk hɪ ˈroʊ ɪk ◂ ˌmɔːk- **~ally** ᵊl i **~s** s
mockingbird ˈmɒk ɪŋ bɜːd ‖ ˈmaːk ɪŋ bɜːd
ˈmɔːk- **~s** z
mockney ˈmɒk ni ‖ ˈmaːk-
mock-up ˈmɒk ʌp ‖ ˈmaːk- **~s** s
mod, Mod *'Gaelic meeting'* mɒd məʊd ‖ moʊd
—*ScG* Mòd [moːd]
mod, Mod *'modern; (adherent of, pertaining to)*
fashion style' mɒd ‖ maːd **mods** mɒdz
‖ maːdz
ˌmod ˈcon
MoD *'Ministry of Defence'* ˌem əʊ ˈdiː ◂ ‖ -oʊ-
modacrylic ˌmɒd ə ˈkrɪl ɪk ◂ ‖ ˌmaːd-
ˌmodaˌcrylic ˈfibre

M

modal 'məʊd ᵊl ‖ 'moʊd ᵊl ~s z
   ,modal au'xiliary
modalit|y məʊ 'dæl ət |i -ɪt- ‖ moʊ 'dæl əţ |i ~ies iz
modally 'məʊd ᵊl i ‖ 'moʊd ᵊl i
mode məʊd ‖ moʊd **modes** məʊdz ‖ moʊdz
model 'mɒd ᵊl ‖ 'maːd ᵊl ~ed, ~led d ~er/s, ~ler/s ə/z ‖ ᵊr/z ~ing, ~ling ɪŋ ~z z
modem 'məʊd em -əm ‖ 'moʊd- ~s z
Modena 'mɒd ɪn ə -ᵊn ə; mɒ 'deɪn ə, mə- ‖ 'moʊd ᵊn ə 'mɔːd-, 'maːd-, -aː: —*It* ['mɔː de na]
moderate *adj, n* 'mɒd ᵊr ət -ɪt ‖ 'maːd ~ly li ~ness nəs nɪs ~s s
mode|rate *v* 'mɒd ə |reɪt ‖ 'maːd- ~rated reɪt ɪd -əd ‖ reɪţ əd ~rates reɪts ~rating reɪt ɪŋ ‖ reɪţ ɪŋ
moderation ,mɒd ə 'reɪʃ ᵊn ‖ ,maːd- ~s z
moderato ,mɒd ə 'raːt əʊ ‖ ,maːd ə 'raːţ oʊ ~s z
moderator 'mɒd ə reɪt ə ‖ 'maːd ə reɪţ ᵊr ~s z
modern 'mɒd ᵊn ‖ 'maːd ᵊrn ~ly li ~ness nəs nɪs ~s z
   ,Modern 'English◄, ,Modern ,English 'Language; ,Modern 'Greek; ,modern 'jazz; ,modern pen'tathlon
modern-day ,mɒd ᵊn 'deɪ◄ ‖ ,maːd ᵊrn-
modernis... —*see* **moderniz...**
modernism 'mɒd ə ,nɪz əm -ᵊn ,ɪz- ‖ 'maːd ᵊr-
modernist 'mɒd ᵊn ɪst §-əst ‖ 'maːd ᵊrn- ~s s
modernistic ,mɒd ə 'nɪst ɪk ◄ -ᵊn 'ɪst- ‖ ,maːd ᵊr- ~ally ᵊl i
modernit|y mɒ 'dɜːn ət |i mə-, -ɪt- ‖ maː 'dɜːn əţ |i moʊ-, mə- ~ies iz
modernization ,mɒd ə naɪ 'zeɪʃ ᵊn -nɪ'--; -ᵊn ,aɪ-, -ᵊn ,ɪ- ‖ ,maːd ᵊrn ə- ~s z
moderniz|e 'mɒd ə naɪz -ᵊn aɪz ‖ 'maːd ᵊr- ~ed d ~er/s ə/z ‖ ᵊr/z ~es ɪz əz ~ing ɪŋ
modest 'mɒd ɪst §-əst ‖ 'maːd əst ~ly li
Modestine 'mɒd ɪ stiːn -ə-, ,·'· ‖ 'maːd-
Modesto mə 'dest əʊ ‖ -oʊ
modest|y, M~ 'mɒd əst |i -ɪst- ‖ 'maːd- ~ies iz
modicum 'mɒd ɪk əm -ək- ‖ 'maːd- 'moʊd- ~s z
modification ,mɒd ɪf ɪ 'keɪʃ ᵊn ,·əf-, §-ə'-- ‖ ,maːd- ~s z
modi|fy 'mɒd ɪ |faɪ -ə- ‖ 'maːd- ~fied faɪd ~fier/s faɪ ə/z ‖ faɪ ᵊr/z ~fies faɪz ~fying faɪ ɪŋ
Modigliani ,mɒd ɪl 'jaːn i ‖ ,moʊd iːl- moʊ ,diːl i 'aːn i —*It* [mo diʎ 'ʎa ni]
modiolus məʊ 'diː əl əs -'daɪ ‖ moʊ 'daɪ əl əs mə-
modish 'məʊd ɪʃ ‖ 'moʊd- ~ly li ~ness nəs nɪs
modiste məʊ 'diːst ‖ moʊ- ~s s
modular 'mɒd jʊl ə -jəl-; →'mɒdʒ ʊl ə, -əl- ‖ 'maːdʒ əl ᵊr
modularis... —*see* **modulariz...**
modularity ,mɒd jʊ 'lær ət i →,mɒdʒ u-, -ɪt i ‖ ,maːdʒ ə 'lær əţ i -'ler-
modularization ,mɒd jʊl ər aɪ 'zeɪʃ ᵊn ,·jəl-, -ɪ'--; →,mɒdʒ ʊl-, ,·əl- ‖ ,maːdʒ əl ᵊr ə-

modulariz|e 'mɒd jʊl ə raɪz '·jəl-; →'mɒdʒ ʊl-, ,·əl- ‖ 'maːdʒ əl ə raɪz ~ed d ~es ɪz əz ~ing ɪŋ
modu|late 'mɒd ju |leɪt →'mɒdʒ u-, -ə- ‖ 'maːdʒ ə- ~lated leɪt ɪd -əd ‖ leɪţ əd ~lates leɪts ~lating leɪt ɪŋ ‖ leɪţ ɪŋ
modulation ,mɒd ju 'leɪʃ ᵊn →,mɒdʒ u-, ,·ə- ‖ ,maːdʒ ə- ~s z
module 'mɒd juːl →'mɒdʒ uːl ‖ 'maːdʒ uːᵊl ~s z
modulo 'mɒd ju ləʊ -jə- ‖ 'maːdʒ ə loʊ
modulus 'mɒd jʊl əs -jəl- ‖ 'maːdʒ əl əs
   moduli mɒd ju laɪ -liː- ‖ 'maːdʒ ə laɪ
modus 'məʊd əs 'mɒd- ‖ 'moʊd əs
   ,modus ,ope'randi ,ɒp ə 'rænd i -aɪ ‖ ,aːp-;
   ,modus vi'vendi vɪ 'vend i §və-, -aɪ
Moesia 'miːs i ə 'miːz-; 'miːʃ ə, 'miːʒ ə ‖ 'miːʃ-
Moët et Chandon ,məʊ ɪt eɪ 'ʃɒd ɒ̃ ,·eɪ- ‖ ,moʊ ət eɪ ʃaːn 'dɔːn —*Fr* [mo e e ʃɑ̃ dɔ̃]
Moffat, Moffatt 'mɒf ət ‖ 'maːf-
mog, Mog mɒg ‖ maːg **mogs** mɒgz ‖ maːgz
Mogadishu ,mɒg ə 'dɪʃ uː ‖ ,maːg- ,mɔːg-, -'diːʃ-
Mogadon *tdmk* 'mɒg ə dɒn ‖ 'maːg ə daːn
Mogador ,mɒg ə 'dɔː '··· ‖ ,maːg ə 'dɔːr -'doʊr
Mogford 'mɒg fəd ‖ 'maːg fᵊrd
Mogg mɒg ‖ maːg
Moggach 'mɒg əx -ək ‖ 'maːg ək
mogg|ie, mogg|y 'mɒg |i ‖ 'maːg |i ~ies iz
Mogollon ,məʊg ə 'jəʊn ‖ ,moʊg ə 'joʊn
mogul, Mogul 'məʊg ᵊl -ʊl, -ʌl ‖ 'moʊg- moʊ 'gʌl ~s z
mohair 'məʊ heə ‖ 'moʊ her -hær
Mohamma... —*see* **Mohamme...**
Mohammed məʊ 'hæm ɪd -əd, -ed ‖ moʊ- —*Arabic* [mu 'ham mad]
Mohammedan məʊ 'hæm ɪd ən -əd- ‖ moʊ- ~ism ,ɪz əm ~s z
Mohan 'məʊ hæn -hən, -ən ‖ 'moʊ-
Mohave məʊ 'haːv i ‖ mə- moʊ- ~s z
Mohawk, m- 'məʊ hɔːk ‖ 'moʊ- -haːk ~s s
mohel 'məʊ həl ‖ 'moʊ- -əl; mɔːl ~s z
Mohican, m- məʊ 'hiːk ən 'məʊ ɪk- ‖ moʊ- mə- ~s z
Moho 'məʊ həʊ ‖ 'moʊ hoʊ
Mohole 'məʊ həʊl →-hɒʊl ‖ 'moʊ hoʊl
Mohorovicic ,məʊ hə 'rəʊv ɪ tʃɪtʃ -'·ə- ‖ ,moʊ hə 'roʊv- —*Serbo-Croat* Mohorovičić [mɔ xɔ 'rɔ vi tʃit ɕ]
Mohs məʊz ‖ moʊz —*Ger* [moːs]
Mohun (i) 'məʊ ən -hən ‖ 'moʊ hən; (ii) muːn
moi mwaː —*Fr* [mwa]
Moi *African name* mɔɪ
moidore ,mɔɪ 'dɔː: 'ɔ: bɪcm ‖ 'mɔɪd ɔːr -oʊr ~s z
moiet|y 'mɔɪ ət |i -ɪ- ‖ -əţ |i ~ies iz
Moir 'mɔɪ ə ‖ 'mɔɪᵊr
Moira 'mɔɪr ə
moire mwaː ‖ mwaːr mɔːr, moʊr
moiré 'mwaːr eɪ ‖ mwaː 'reɪ 'mɔːr eɪ, 'moʊr-
Moiseivich, Moiseiwitsch mɔɪ 'zeɪ ɪ vɪtʃ -'seɪ-

moist mɔɪst **moister** 'mɔɪst ə ‖ -ᵊr **moistest**
'mɔɪst ɪst -əst

moisten 'mɔɪs ᵊn

moist|ly 'mɔɪst |li **~ness** nəs nɪs

moisture 'mɔɪs tʃə ‖ -tʃᵊr

moisturis|e, moisturiz|e 'mɔɪs tʃə raɪz **~er/s**
ə/z ‖ ᵊr/z

moither 'mɔɪð ə ‖ -ᵊr **~ed** d **moithering**
'mɔɪð ər ɪŋ **~s** z

Mojave məʊ 'hɑːv i ‖ mə- moʊ-
Mo‚jave 'Desert

mojito məʊ 'hiːt əʊ ‖ moʊ 'hiːt̬ oʊ **~s** z s
—AmSp [mo 'hi to]

mojo 'məʊdʒ əʊ ‖ 'moʊdʒ oʊ **~s** z

moke məʊk ‖ moʊk **mokes** məʊks ‖ moʊks

molal 'məʊl əl →'mɒʊl- ‖ 'moʊl-

molar 'məʊl ə ‖ 'moʊl ᵊr **~s** z

molasses məʊ 'læs ɪz -əz ‖ mə-

mold, Mold məʊld →mɒʊld ‖ moʊld **molded**
'məʊld ɪd →'mɒʊld-, -əd ‖ 'moʊld əd
molding/s 'məʊld ɪŋ/z →'mɒʊld-
‖ 'moʊld ɪŋ/z **molds** məʊldz →mɒʊldz
‖ moʊldz

Moldavi|a mɒl 'deɪv i |ə ‖ mɑːl- **~an/s** ən/z

mold|er 'məʊld |ə →'mɒʊld- ‖ 'moʊld |ᵊr
~ered əd ‖ ᵊrd **~ering** ər ɪŋ **~ers** əz ‖ ᵊrz

Moldov|a mɒl 'dəʊv |ə ‖ mɑːl 'doʊv |ə **~an/s**
ᵊn/z

mold|y 'məʊld |i →'mɒʊld- ‖ 'moʊld |i **~ier**
i‚ə ‖ i‚ᵊr **~iest** i‚ɪst i‚əst **~iness** i nəs i nɪs

mole, Mole məʊl →mɒʊl ‖ moʊl **moles** məʊlz
→mɒʊlz ‖ moʊlz

Molech 'məʊl ek ‖ 'moʊl-

molecular mə 'lek jʊl ə məʊ-, mɒ-, -jəl-
‖ -jəl ᵊr

molecule 'mɒl ɪ kjuːl 'məʊl-, -ə- ‖ 'mɑːl- **~s** z

molehill 'məʊl hɪl →'mɒʊl- ‖ 'moʊl- **~s** z

Molesey 'məʊlz i →'mɒʊlz- ‖ 'moʊlz i

moleskin 'məʊl skɪn →'mɒʊl- ‖ 'moʊl- **~s** z

molest mə 'lest məʊ- **~ed** ɪd əd **~ing** ɪŋ **~s** s

molestation ‚məʊl e 'steɪʃ ᵊn ‚moʊl- **~s** z

molester mə 'lest ə məʊ- ‖ -ᵊr **~s** z

Molesworth 'məʊlz wɜːθ →'mɒʊlz-, -wəθ
‖ 'moʊlz wᵊrθ

Moliere, Molière 'mɒl i eə 'məʊl-
‖ moʊl 'jeᵊr —Fr [mɔ ljɛːʁ]

Molina məʊ 'liːn ə ‖ moʊ- mə-

Moline məʊ 'liːn ‖ moʊ-

moll, Moll mɒl ‖ mɑːl **molls** mɒlz ‖ mɑːlz

Mollie, mollie 'mɒl i ‖ 'mɑːl i **~s, ~'s** z

mollifiable 'mɒl ɪ faɪ‚əb ᵊl §‚·‚·'·· ‖ 'mɑːl-

mollification ‚mɒl ɪf ɪ 'keɪʃ ᵊn ‚-əf-, §-ə'·-
‖ ‚mɑːl-

molli|fy 'mɒl ɪ |faɪ -ə- ‖ 'mɑːl- **~fied** faɪd
~fier/s faɪ‚ə/z faɪ‚ᵊr/z **~fies** faɪz **~fying/ly**
faɪ ɪŋ /li

Molloy mə 'lɔɪ

mollusc, mollusk 'mɒl əsk -ʌsk ‖ 'mɑːl- **~s** s

Mollweide 'mɒl vaɪd ə ‖ 'mɔːl- 'mɑːl- —Ger
['mɔl vaɪ də]

Moll|y, moll|y 'mɒl |i ‖ 'mɑːl |i **~ies, ~y's** iz

mollycoddl|e 'mɒl i ‚kɒd ᵊl ‖ 'mɑːl i ‚kɑːd ᵊl
~ed d **~es** z **~ing** ɪŋ

Moloch, m~ 'məʊl ɒk ‖ 'moʊl ɑːk 'mɑːl ək **~s**
s

Moloney, Molony mə 'ləʊn i ‖ -'loʊn i

Molotov 'mɒl ə tɒf ‖ 'mɑːl ə tɔːf 'moʊl-,
'mɔːl-, -tɑːf —Russ ['mɔ ɫə təf]
‚Molotov 'cocktail

molt məʊlt →mɒʊlt ‖ moʊlt **molted** 'məʊlt ɪd
→'mɒʊlt-, -əd ‖ 'moʊlt əd **molting** 'məʊlt ɪŋ
→'mɒʊlt- ‖ 'moʊlt ɪŋ **molts** məʊlts →mɒʊlts
‖ moʊlts

molten 'məʊlt ən →'mɒʊlt- ‖ 'moʊlt-

molto 'mɒlt əʊ ‖ 'moʊlt oʊ —It ['mɔl to]

Molton 'məʊlt ən →'mɒʊlt- ‖ 'moʊlt-

Molucc|a məʊ 'lʌk |ə ‖ mə- **~an/s** ən/z **~as** əz

moly 'məʊl i ‖ 'moʊl i

molybdate mə 'lɪbd eɪt mɒ-, məʊ- **~s** s

molybdenum mə 'lɪbd ən əm mɒ-, məʊ-

molybdic mə 'lɪbd ɪk mɒ-, məʊ-

Molyneaux 'mɒl ɪ nəʊ -ə- ‖ 'mɑːl ə noʊ

Molyneux (i) 'mɒl ɪ njuː -ə- ‖ 'mɑːl-,
(ii) 'mʌl-, (iii) -njuːks

mom, Mom mɒm ‖ mɑːm **moms, Mom's**
mɒmz ‖ mɑːmz

mom-and-pop ‚mɒm ən 'pɒp →-əm-
‖ ‚mɑːm ən 'pɑːp

Mombasa mɒm 'bæs ə -'bɑːs- ‖ mɑːm 'bɑːs ə
-'bæs- —Swahili [mo 'mba sa]

moment 'məʊm ənt ‖ 'moʊm- **~ly** li **~s** s

momenta məʊ 'ment ə ‖ moʊ 'ment̬ ə

momentarily 'məʊm ənt‚ər əl i -ɪ li;
‚məʊm ən 'ter əl i, -ɪ li ‖ ‚moʊm ən 'ter əl i

momentar|y 'məʊm ənt‚ər |i
‖ 'moʊm ən ter |i **~iness** i nəs i nɪs

momentous məʊ 'ment əs ‖ moʊ 'ment̬ əs
mə- **~ly** li **~ness** nəs nɪs

moment|um məʊ 'ment |əm
‖ moʊ 'ment̬ |əm mə- **~a** ə

momma, Momma 'mɒm ə ‖ 'mɑːm ə **~s, ~'s**
z

momm|ie, momm|y, M~ 'mɒm |i ‖ 'mɑːm |i
~ies, ~y's iz

Momus 'məʊm əs ‖ 'moʊm-

Mon name of language or people məʊn mɒn
‖ moʊn

Mon. —see Monday

Mona, mona 'məʊn ə ‖ 'moʊn ə **~s, ~'s** z
‚Mona 'Lisa

Monacan 'mɒn ək ən mə 'nɑːk- ‖ 'mɑːn ək-
mə 'nɑːk- **~s** z

Monaco 'mɒn ə kəʊ mə 'nɑːk əʊ
‖ 'mɑːn ə koʊ mə 'nɑːk oʊ —Fr [mɔ na ko],
It ['mɔː na ko]

monad 'mɒn æd 'məʊn- ‖ 'moʊn- **~s** z

Monadhliadh ‚məʊn ə 'liː‚ə ‖ ‚moʊn-

monadic mɒ 'næd ɪk məʊ- ‖ moʊ- mə-

monadism 'mɒn ə ‚dɪz əm 'məʊn-, -æd ‚ɪz-
‖ 'moʊn æd ‚ɪz-

monadnock, M~ mə 'næd nɒk ‖ -nɑːk **~s** s

Monaghan, Monahan 'mɒn ə hən ‖ 'mɑːn-
-hæn

monandrous mɒ 'nændr əs mə- ‖ mə-

monarch 'mɒn ək §-ɑːk ‖ 'mɑːn ᵊrk -ɑːrk **~s** s

monarchal mə ˈnɑːk ᵊl mɒ- ‖ mə ˈnɑːrk- mɑː-
~ly i
monarchic mə ˈnɑːk ɪk mɒ- ‖ mə ˈnɑːrk- mɑː-
~ally ᵊl i
monarchism ˈmɒn ə ˌkɪz əm ‖ ˈmɑːn ᵊr- -ɑːr-
monarchist ˈmɒn ək ɪst §-əst ‖ ˈmɑːn ᵊrk-
-ɑːrk- ~s s
monarch|y ˈmɒn ək |i ‖ ˈmɑːn ᵊrk |i -ɑːrk-
~ies iz
Monash ˈmɒn æʃ ‖ ˈmɑːn-
monasterial ˌmɒn ə ˈstɪər i̯əl ◂
‖ ˌmɑːn ə ˈstɪr-
monastery ˈmɒn əs tər̩ i ‖ ˈmɑːn ə ster i
monastic mə ˈnæst ɪk mɒ- ~ally ᵊl i ~s s
monasticism mə ˈnæst ɪ ˌsɪz əm mɒ-, -ə-
Monastir ˌmɒn ə ˈstɪə ‖ ˌmɑːn ə ˈstɪr
monatomic ˌmɒn ə ˈtɒm ɪk ◂ ‖ ˌmɑːn ə ˈtɑːm-
monaural ˌmɒn ˈɔːr əl ◂ ‖ ˌmɑːn- ~ly i
Monbiot ˈmɒn bi əʊ →ˈmɒm- ‖ ˈmɑːn bi oʊ
Monchen-Gladbach, Mönchen-Gladbach
ˌmʌntʃ ən ˈglæd bæk →-əŋ- —*Ger*
[ˌmœn çᵊn ˈglat bax]
Monck mʌŋk
Monckton ˈmʌŋkt ən
Moncreiff, Moncreiffe, Moncrieff,
Moncrieffe mən ˈkriːf →məŋ-, mɒn- ‖ mɑːn-
Mond mɒnd ‖ mɑːnd —*Ger* [moːnt]
Mondale ˈmɒn derᵊl ‖ ˈmɑːn-
Monday ˈmʌnd eɪ -i —*See note at* **-day** ~s, ~'s
z
ˌMonday ˈmorning, that ˌMonday
ˈmorning ˌfeeling; ˈMonday Club
Mondeo *tdmk* ₍ᵢ₎mɒn ˈdeɪ əʊ ‖ ˌmɑːn ˈdeɪ oʊ
~s z
mondo, Mondo ˈmɒnd əʊ ‖ ˈmɑːnd oʊ
Mondrian ˌmɒndr i ˈɑːn ‖ ˈmɔːndr i ɑːn
ˈmɑːndr- —*Dutch* [ˈmɔn driˑ aːn]
monecious mɒ ˈniːʃ əs mə- ‖ mɑː-
Monegasque, Monégasque ˌmɒn ɪ ˈgæsk ◂
-ə- ‖ ˌmɑːn- ~s s —*Fr* [mɔ ne gask]
moneme ˈmɒn iːm ˈməʊn- ‖ ˈmoʊn- ~s z
monera, M~ mə ˈnɪər ə mɒ-, məʊ- ‖ mə ˈnɪr ə
mɑː-, moʊ-
Monet ˈmɒn eɪ ‖ moʊ ˈneɪ —*Fr* [mɔ nɛ]
monetarism ˈmʌn ɪt ə ˌrɪz əm ˈmɒn-, ˈ-ət-
‖ ˈmɑːn ə tə- ˈmʌn-
monetarist ˈmʌn ɪt̯ ər̩ ɪst ˈmɒn-, ˈ-ət̯, §-əst
‖ ˈmɑːn- ˈmʌn- ~s s
monetary ˈmʌn ɪt̯ ər i ˈmɒn-, ˈ-ət̯
‖ ˈmɑːn ə ter i ˈmʌn-
monetis|e, monetiz|e ˈmʌn ɪ taɪz ˈmɒn-, -ə-
‖ ˈmɑːn- ˈmʌn- ~ed d ~es ɪz əz ~ing ɪŋ
money, Money ˈmʌn i **moneyed, monied**
ˈmʌn id **moneys, monies** ˈmʌn iz
ˈmoney ˌmarket; ˈmoney ˌorder; ˈmoney
ˌspider; ˈmoney supˌply
moneybags ˈmʌn i bægz
moneybox ˈmʌn i bɒks ‖ -bɑːks ~es ɪz əz
moneychanger ˈmʌn i ˌtʃeɪndʒ ə ‖ -ᵊr ~s z
moneygrab|ber ˈmʌn i ˌgræb ə ‖ -ᵊr ~bers əz
‖ ᵊrz ~bing ɪŋ
moneygrub|ber ˈmʌn i ˌgrʌb |ə ‖ -|ᵊr ~bers
əz ‖ ᵊrz ~bing ɪŋ

moneylend|er ˈmʌn i ˌlend |ə ‖ -|ᵊr ~ers əz
‖ ᵊrz ~ing ɪŋ
moneymak|er ˈmʌn i ˌmeɪk |ə ‖ -|ᵊr ~ers əz
‖ ᵊrz ~ing ɪŋ
Moneypenny ˈmʌn i ˌpen i ˈmɒn- ‖ ˈmɑːn-
moneyspinner ˈmʌn i ˌspɪn ə ‖ -ᵊr ~s z
moneywort ˈmʌn i wɜːt §-wɔːt ‖ -wɜːt -wɔːrt
monger ˈmʌŋ gə ‖ ˈmɑːŋ gᵊr ˈmʌŋ- ~s z
Mongol, m~ ˈmɒŋ gᵊl -gɒl ‖ ˈmɑːŋ-
ˈmɑːn goʊl, →ˈmɑːŋ- ~s z
Mongoli|a mɒŋ ˈgəʊl i̯ə ‖ mɑːŋ ˈgoʊl- mɑːn-
~an/s ən/z
Mongolic mɒŋ ˈgɒl ɪk ‖ mɑːn ˈgɑːl ɪk →mɑːŋ-
mongolism ˈmɒŋ gə ˌlɪz əm -gɒ- ‖ ˈmɑːn-
→ˈmɑːŋ-
Mongoloid, m~ ˈmɒŋ gə lɔɪd ‖ ˈmɑːn-
→ˈmɑːŋ- ~s z
mongoos|e ˈmɒŋ guːs ˈmʌŋ- ‖ ˈmɑːn- →ˈmɑːŋ-
~es ɪz əz
mongrel ˈmʌŋ grəl ‖ ˈmɑːŋ- ~ism ˌɪz əm ~s z
mongrelis... —*see* **mongreliz...**
mongrelization ˌmʌŋ grəl aɪ ˈzeɪʃ ᵊn -ɪˈ-
‖ -əˈ-- ˌmɑːŋ-
mongreliz|e ˈmʌŋ grə laɪz ‖ ˈmɑːŋ- ~ed d ~es
ɪz əz ~ing ɪŋ
Monica ˈmɒn ɪk ə §-ək- ‖ ˈmɑːn-
monicker ˈmɒn ɪk ə ‖ ˈmɑːn ɪk ᵊr ~s z
monie... —*see* **money**
Monifieth ˌmʌn ɪ ˈfiːθ
moniker ˈmɒn ɪk ə ‖ ˈmɑːn ɪk ᵊr ~s z
monilia mɒ ˈnɪl| i̯ə mə- ‖ moʊ-
moniliform mɒ ˈnɪl ɪ fɔːm mə-, -ə-
‖ moʊ ˈnɪl ə fɔːrm
Monique mɒ ˈniːk ‖ moʊ- mə- —*Fr* [mɔ nik]
monism ˈmɒn ˌɪz əm ‖ ˈmoʊn- ˈmɑːn-
monist ˈmɒn ɪst §-əst ‖ ˈmoʊn- ˈmɑːn- ~s s
monistic mɒ ˈnɪst ɪk mə- ‖ moʊ- mɑː- ~ally
ᵊl i
monitor ˈmɒn ɪt ə -ət- ‖ ˈmɑːn ət̯ ᵊr ~ed d
monitoring ˈmɒn ɪt̯ ər ɪŋ ˈ-ət̯
‖ ˈmɑːn ət̯ ər ɪŋ →ˈmɑːn ətr ɪŋ ~s z
monk, Monk mʌŋk **monks** mʌŋks
monkey ˈmʌŋk i ~ed d ~ing ɪŋ ~s z
ˈmonkey ˌbusiness; ˈmonkey nut;
ˈmonkey wrench
monkey-puzzle ˈmʌŋk i ˌpʌz ᵊl ~s z
monkfish ˈmʌŋk fɪʃ
Mon-Khmer ˌməʊn ˈkmeə ◂ ˌməʊn kə ˈmeə
‖ ˌmoʊn ˈkmeᵊr ˌmoʊn kə ˈmeᵊr
monkhood ˈmʌŋk hʊd
Monkhouse ˈmʌŋk haʊs
monkish ˈmʌŋk ɪʃ ~ly li ~ness nəs nɪs
Monkton ˈmʌŋk tən
Monmouth ˈmɒn məθ →ˈmʌn-, →ˈmɒm-
‖ ˈmɑːn-
Monmouthshire ˈmɒn məθ ʃə →ˈmʌn-,
→ˈmɒm-, -ʃɪə ‖ ˈmɑːn məθ ʃᵊr -ʃɪr
Monnow ˈmɒn əʊ ˈmʌn- ‖ ˈmɑːn oʊ
mono ˈmɒn əʊ ‖ ˈmɑːn oʊ
Mono *lake in CA* ˈməʊn əʊ ‖ ˈmoʊn oʊ
mono- *comb. form*
with stress-neutral suffix ˌmɒn əʊ ‖ ˌmɑːn ə
-oʊ, *but before a vowel always* -əʊ ‖ -oʊ;

— **monochord** ˈmɒn əʊ kɔːd
‖ ˈmɑːn ə kɔːrd; — **monoacidic**
ˌmɒn əʊ ə ˈsɪd ɪk ◂ -æˈ-- ‖ ˌmɑːn oʊ- *with*
stress-imposing suffix mə ˈnɒ + mɒ-
‖ mə ˈnɑː + mɑː-; — **monology**
mə ˈnɒl ədʒ i mɒ- ‖ mə ˈnɑːl- mɑː-

Monoceros mə ˈnɒs ər əs ‖ -ˈnɑːs-
monochromatic ˌmɒn əʊ krə ˈmæt ɪk ◂
‖ -ˈmæt̬ ɪk ◂
monochrome ˈmɒn ə krəʊm -əʊ-
‖ ˈmɑːn ə kroʊm
monocle ˈmɒn ək ᵊl ‖ ˈmɑːn ɪk- **~d** d **~s** z
monoclonal ˌmɒn əʊ ˈkləʊn ᵊl ◂
‖ ˌmɑːn ə ˈkloʊn ᵊl ◂ -oʊ-
monocoque ˈmɒn əʊ kɒk ‖ ˈmɑːn ə koʊk
-kɑːk **~s** s
monocot ˈmɒn əʊ kɒt ‖ ˈmɑːn ə kɑːt **~s** s
monocotyledon ˌmɒn əʊ ˌkɒt ə ˈliːd ᵊn -ɪˈ--,
-ᵊl ˈiːd- ‖ ˌmɑːn ə ˌkɑːt̬ ᵊl ˈiːd ᵊn **~s** z
monocular mə ˈnɒk jʊl ə mə-, -jəl-
‖ mɑː ˈnɑːk jəl ᵊr
monoculture ˈmɒn əʊ ˌkʌltʃ ə
‖ ˈmɑːn ə ˌkʌltʃ ᵊr
monod|y ˈmɒn əd |i ‖ ˈmɑːn- **~ies** iz
monoecious mɒ ˈniːʃ əs mə- ‖ mɑː- **~ly** li
monofil ˈmɒn əʊ fɪl ‖ ˈmɑːn ə-
monogamist mə ˈnɒɡ əm ɪst mɒ-, §-əst
‖ -ˈnɑːɡ- **~s** s
monogamous mə ˈnɒɡ əm əs mɒ- ‖ -ˈnɑːɡ-
~ly li
monogamy mə ˈnɒɡ əm i mɒ- ‖ -ˈnɑːɡ-
monogenetic ˌmɒn əʊ dʒə ˈnet ɪk ◂ -dʒɪˈ--
‖ ˌmɑːn ə dʒə ˈnet̬ ɪk ◂
monoglot ˈmɒn əʊ ɡlɒt ‖ ˈmɑːn ə ɡlɑːt **~s** s
monogram ˈmɒn ə ɡræm ‖ ˈmɑːn- **~med** d **~s**
z
monograph ˈmɒn ə ɡrɑːf -ɡræf ‖ ˈmɑːn ə ɡræf
~s s
monogyny mə ˈnɒdʒ ən i mɒ-, -ɪn- ‖ -ˈnɑːdʒ-
monokini ˈmɒn əʊ ˌkiːn i ‖ ˈmɑːn ə- **~s** z
monolingual ˌmɒn əʊ ˈlɪŋ ɡwəl ◂ ˌ·ˈ·lɪŋ ɡjuˌəl
‖ ˌmɑːn ə- ˌmoʊn- **~s** z
monolith ˈmɒn ə lɪθ -ᵊl ɪθ ‖ ˈmɑːn- **~s** s
monolithic ˌmɒn ə ˈlɪθ ɪk ◂ -ᵊl ˈɪθ- ‖ ˌmɑːn-
~ally ᵊl i
monolog, monologue ˈmɒn ə lɒɡ -ᵊl
‖ ˈmɑːn ᵊl ɔːɡ -ɑːɡ **~s** z
monologuist ˈmɒn ə lɒɡ ɪst -ᵊl ɒɡ-, §-əst
‖ ˈmɑːn ᵊl ɔːɡ əst -ɑːɡ- **~s** s
monomania ˌmɒn əʊ ˈmeɪn iˌə ‖ ˌmɑːn ə-
monomaniac ˌmɒn əʊ ˈmeɪn i æk ‖ ˌmɑːn ə-
~s s
monomark, M~ *tdmk* ˈmɒn əʊ mɑːk
‖ ˈmɑːn ə mɑːrk **~s** s
monomer ˈmɒn əm ə ‖ ˈmɑːn əm ᵊr **~s** z
monomeric ˌmɒn ə ˈmer ɪk ◂ ‖ ˌmɑːn-
monomial mɒ ˈnəʊm iˌəl mə- ‖ mɑː ˈnoʊm- **~s**
z
monomorphemic ˌmɒn əʊ mɔː ˈfiːm ɪk ◂
‖ ˌmɑːn ə mɔːr-
Monongahela mə ˌnɒŋ ɡə ˈhiːl ə ◂ ‖ -ˌnɑːŋ-
Mo ˌnonga ˌhela ˈRiver

mononucleosis ˌmɒn əʊ ˌnjuːk li ˈəʊs ɪs
§-, nuːk-, §-əs ‖ ˌmɑːn oʊ ˌnuːk li ˈoʊs əs
-ˌnjuːk-
monophonic ˌmɒn əʊ ˈfɒn ɪk ◂
‖ ˌmɑːn ə ˈfɑːn ɪk ◂ -ˈfoʊn- **~ally** ᵊl i
monophthong ˈmɒn əf θɒŋ -əp-, -ə-
‖ ˈmɑːn əf θɔːŋ -ə-, -θɑːŋ **~ing** ɪŋ **~s** z
monophthongal ˌmɒn əf ˈθɒŋ ɡᵊl ◂ -əp-, -ə-
‖ ˌmɑːn əf ˈθɔːŋ ɡᵊl ◂ -ə-, -ˈθɑːŋ- **~ly** i
monophthongis... —*see* **monophthongiz...**
monophthongization
ˌmɒn əf θɒŋ ɡaɪ ˈzeɪʃ ᵊn ˌ-əp-, ˌ-ə-, -aɪˈ--, -ɡɪˈ--,
-ɪˈ-- ‖ ˌmɑːn əf θɔːŋ ɡə-, ˌ-ə-, -əˈ-- -ə z
monophthongiz|e ˈmɒn əf θɒŋ ɡaɪz ˈ-əp-, -aɪz
‖ ˈmɑːn əf θɔːŋ ɡaɪz ˈ-ə-, -θɑːŋ ·, -aɪz **~ed** d
~es ɪz əz **~ing** ɪŋ
Monophysite mə ˈnɒf ɪ saɪt -ə- ‖ mə ˈnɑːf ə-
~s s
monoplane ˈmɒn ə pleɪn ‖ ˈmɑːn- **~s** z
Monopole, m~ ˈmɒn ə pəʊl →-ppɒʊl
‖ ˈmɑːn ə poʊl **~s** z
monopolie... —*see* **monopoly**
monopolis... —*see* **monopoliz...**
monopolist mə ˈnɒp ᵊl ɪst §-əst ‖ -ˈnɑːp- **~s** s
monopolistic mə ˌnɒp ə ˈlɪst ɪk ◂ ‖ -ˌnɑːp-
~ally ᵊl i
monopolization mə ˌnɒp ə laɪ ˈzeɪʃ ᵊn -ɪˈ--
‖ -ˌnɑːp əl ə- **~s** z
monopoliz|e mə ˈnɒp ə laɪz ‖ -ˈnɑːp- **~ed** d
~es ɪz əz **~ing** ɪŋ
monopol|y, M~ *tdmk* mə ˈnɒp ᵊl |i ‖ -ˈnɑːp-
~ies iz
monopson|y mə ˈnɒps ən |i ‖ -ˈnɑːps- **~ies** iz
monorail ˈmɒn əʊ reɪᵊl ‖ ˈmɑːn ə- **~s** z
monosodium ˌmɒn əʊ ˈsəʊd iˌəm ◂
‖ ˌmɑːn ə ˈsoʊd-
ˌmono ˌsodium ˈglutamate
monospac|e ˈmɒn əʊ speɪs ‖ ˈmɑːn oʊ- **~ed** t
~es ɪz əz **~ing** ɪŋ
monosyllabic ˌmɒn əʊ sɪ ˈlæb ɪk ◂ -səˈ--
‖ ˌmɑːn ə sə- **~ally** ᵊl i
monosyllable ˈmɒn əʊ ˌsɪl əb ᵊl ˌ·ˈ·· ·
‖ ˈmɑːn ə- **~s** z
monotheism ˈmɒn əʊ θi ˌɪz əm ˈ· ·ˌθiː ɪz əm;
mə ˈnɒθ i ˌɪz əm ‖ ˈmɑːn ə-
monotheist ˈmɒn əʊ θi ɪst -ˌθiː ɪst, §-əst;
mə ˈnɒθ iˌ ‖ ˈmɑːn ə- **~s** s
monotheistic ˌmɒn əʊ θi ˈɪst ɪk ◂ ˌ· ·ˌθiːˈ· ·;
mə ˌnɒθ iˈ-- ‖ ˌmɑːn ə-
monotone ˈmɒn ə təʊn ‖ ˈmɑːn ə toʊn **~s** z
monotonous mə ˈnɒt ən əs ‖ -ˈnɑːt̬ ᵊn əs **~ly**
li **~ness** nəs nɪs
monotony mə ˈnɒt ən i ‖ -ˈnɑːt̬ ᵊn i
monotreme ˈmɒn əʊ triːm ‖ ˈmɑːn ə- **~s** z
monotype, M~ *tdmk* ˈmɒn əʊ taɪp ‖ ˈmɑːn ə-
~s s
monounsaturated
ˌmɒn əʊ ˌʌn ˈsætʃ ə reɪt ɪd ◂ -əd ‖ ˌmɑːn oʊ-
monoxide mə ˈnɒks aɪd mɒ- ‖ mə ˈnɑːks- mɑː-
~s z
Monro, Monroe mən ˈrəʊ ˌmʌn-, ˌmɒn-
‖ -ˈroʊ
Monrovia mən ˈrəʊv iˌə mɒn- ‖ -ˈroʊv-

M

mons, Mons mɒnz ‖ mɑːnz —Fr [mɔ̃ːs]
  ˌmons 'veneris 'ven ər ɪs §-əs
Monsanto tdmk mɒn 'sænt əʊ
  ‖ mɑːn 'sænt oʊ
Monsarrat 'mɒn sə ræt ˌ·ˈ· ‖ ˌmɑːn sə 'rɑːt
  -'ræt
Monsieur, m~ mə 'sjɜː 'mʊs jɜː, -jə ‖ məs 'juː
  →məʃ-, -'jɜːː; mə 'sɪ³r —There is an
  occasional weak form mə sjə —Fr [mə sjø]
Monsignor, m~ mɒn 'siːn jə ‖ mɑːn 'siːn j³r
  —It [mon siɲ 'ɲoːr]
monsoon ˌmɒn 'suːn ◂ mɒn-, mən- ‖ ˌmɑːn- ~s
  z
  ˌmonsoon 'low
monster 'mɒnᵗst ə ‖ 'mɑːnᵗst ³r ~s z
monstera mɒn 'stɪər ə 'mɒnᵗst ər ə
  ‖ 'mɑːnᵗst ər ə ~s z
monstranc|e 'mɒnᵗs trənᵗs ‖ 'mɑːnᵗs- ~es ɪz
  əz
monstrosit|y mɒn 'strɒs ət |i mən-, -ɪt-
  ‖ mɑːn 'strɑːs ət |i ~ies iz
monstrous 'mɒnᵗs trəs ‖ 'mɑːnᵗs- ~ly li ~ness
  nəs nɪs
Mont mɒnt ‖ mɑːnt —but in names of
  mountains mɔ̃, mɒn ‖ mɔːn, mɑːn, moʊn —Fr
  [mɔ̃]
  ˌMont 'Blanc blɒ̃ blɒŋ ‖ blɑːŋ —Fr [blɑ̃]
montag|e mɒn 'tɑːʒ mɔ̃-, ˈ·· ‖ mɑːn- moʊn-
  —Fr [mɔ̃ tɑːʒ] ~es ɪz əz
Montagu, Montague 'mɒnt ə gjuː ‖ 'mɑːnʈ-
  ~s, ~'s z
Montaigne mɒn 'teɪn ‖ mɑːn- moʊn- —Fr
  [mɔ̃ tɛɲ]
montan 'mɒnt ən -æn ‖ 'mɑːnt ³n
Montan|a mɒn 'tæn |ə -'tɑːn- ‖ mɑːn- ~an/s
  ən/z
montane 'mɒnt eɪn ‖ mɑːn 'teɪn ˈ··
Montauk 'mɒnt ɔːk ‖ 'mɑːnt- -ɑːk
montbretia mɒn 'briːʃ ə →mɒm- ‖ mɑːn- ~s z
Monte, monte 'mɒnt i ‖ 'mɑːnʈ i —It
  ['mon te]
  ˌMonte 'Carlo —Fr [mɔ̃ te kaʁ lo]
Montebello ˌmɒnt i 'bel əʊ -ə-
  ‖ ˌmɑːnʈ ə 'bel oʊ
Montefiore ˌmɒnt i fi 'ɔːr i -ə-, -eɪ ‖ ˌmɑːnʈ-
Montego mɒn 'tiːg əʊ ‖ mɑːn 'tiːg oʊ
  Monˌtego 'Bay
Monteith, m~ mɒn 'tiːθ ‖ mɑːn- ~s s
Montel ˌmɒn 'tel ◂ ‖ ˌmɑːn-
Montenegrin ˌmɒnt i 'niːg rɪn ◂ -ə-, -'neɪg-,
  -'neg-, §-rən ‖ ˌmɑːnʈ ə- ~s z
Montenegro ˌmɒnt i 'niːg rəʊ -ə-, -'neɪg-,
  -'neg- ‖ ˌmɑːnʈ ə 'niːg roʊ -'neg-
Monterey place in CA, **Monterrey** place in
  Mexico ˌmɒnt ə 'reɪ -ɪ- ‖ ˌmɑːnʈ- —Sp
  [mon te 'rrei]
Montesquieu ˌmɒnt e 'skjɜː -'skjuː, ˈ···
  ‖ ˌmɑːnʈ ə 'skjuː ˌmoʊnʈ- —Fr [mɔ̃ tɛs kjø]
Montessori ˌmɒnt ə 'sɔːr i -e-, -ɪ- ‖ ˌmɑːnʈ-
  -'soʊr- —It [mon tes 'sɔː ri]
Monteux mɒn 'tɜː ‖ moʊn 'tʌ —Fr [mɔ̃ tø]

Monteverdi ˌmɒnt i 'veəd i -ə-, -'vɜːd-
  ‖ ˌmɑːnʈ ə 'verd i ˌmɔːnʈ-, -'vɜːd- —It
  [mon te 'ver di]
Montevideo ˌmɒnt i vɪ 'deɪ əʊ ˌ·ə-, §-və'--,
  ˌ··'vɪd i əʊ ‖ ˌmɑːnʈ ə və 'deɪ oʊ ˌ··'vɪd i oʊ
Montezuma ˌmɒnt i 'zuːm ə -ə-, -'zjuːm-
  ‖ ˌmɑːnʈ-
Montfort 'mɒnt fət -fɔːt ‖ 'mɑːnt f³rt —Fr
  [mɔ̃ fɔːʁ]
Montgolfier, m~ mɒnt 'gɒlf i ə →mɒŋk-, -eɪ
  ‖ mɑːnt 'gɑːlf i ³r ˌ·ˌi 'eɪ —Fr [mɔ̃ gɔl fje] ~s
  z
Montgomerie, Montgomery (i)
  mənt 'gʌm ər i mən-, mɒnt-, mɒn- ‖ mɑːnt-,
  (ii) -'gɒm- ‖ -'gɑːm-
month mʌnᵗθ **months** mʌnᵗθs →mʌnᵗs
month|ly 'mʌnᵗθ |li ~lies liz
Monticello ˌmɒnt i 'tʃel əʊ -'sel-
  ‖ ˌmɑːnʈ ɪ 'tʃel oʊ -'sel-
Montmartre mɒn 'mɑːtr →mɒm-, -'mɑːtr ə
  ‖ moʊn 'mɑːr trə mɔːn- —Fr [mɔ̃ maʁtχ]
Montmorency ˌmɒnt mə 'renᵗs i ‖ ˌmɑːnt-
Montoya mɒn 'tɔɪ ə ‖ mɑːn- —Sp
  [mon 'to ja]
Montpelier, Montpellier mɒnt 'pel i ə
  mɒm-, -eɪ ‖ moʊn pel 'jeɪ ˌmɔːn-, ˌmɑːn-
  —but the place in VT is -'piːl i ə
  ‖ mɑːnt 'piːl i ³r —Fr [mɔ̃ pə lje, -pɛ-]
Montreal ˌmɒntr i 'ɔːl ◂ ‖ ˌmɑːntr- ˌmʌntr-,
  -'ɑːl —Fr Montréal [mɔ̃ ʁe al]
Montreux mɒn 'trɜː -'trəʊ ‖ moʊn 'tru -'truː
  —Fr [mɔ̃ tʁø]
Montrose mɒn 'trəʊz mən- ‖ mɑːn 'troʊz
Mont-Saint-Michel ˌmɒnt ˌsæn mɪ 'ʃel ˌmɔ̃-,
  →-ˌsæm-, -miː- ‖ ˌmoʊn- ˌmɔːn-, ˌmɑːn- —Fr
  [mɔ̃ sæ̃ mi ʃɛl]
Montserrat ˌmɒnts ə 'ræt -se-, ˈ··· ‖ ˌmɑːnts-
  -'rɑːt —In the West Indies, locally usually ˈ···
  —Catalan [munt sə 'rrat]
Montserratian ˌmɒnts ə 'reɪʃ ³n ◂ -se-
  ‖ ˌmɑːnts- ~s z
Monty 'mɒnt i ‖ 'mɑːnt i
monument, M~ 'mɒn ju mənt -jə ‖ 'mɑːn jə-
  ~s s
monumental ˌmɒn ju 'ment ³l ◂ -jə-
  ‖ ˌmɑːn jə 'menʈ ³l ~ly i
Monymusk ˌmɒn i 'mʌsk ‖ ˌmɑːn-
Monza 'mɒnz ə ‖ 'mɑːnz ə —It ['mon tsa]
Monzie mɒ 'niː mə- ‖ mɑː-
moo muː **mooed** muːd (= mood) **mooing**
  'muː ɪŋ **moos** muːz
mooch muːtʃ **mooched** muːtʃt **mooches**
  'muːtʃ ɪz -əz **mooching** 'muːtʃ ɪŋ
moocow 'muː kaʊ ~s z
mood muːd **moods** muːdz
mood-altering 'muːd ˌɔːlt ər ɪŋ -ˌɒlt-ˌ ‖ -ˌɑːlt-
Moodey, Moodie 'muːd i
mood|y, Moody 'muːd |i ~ier i ə ‖ i ³r ~iest
  i ɪst i əst ~ily ɪ li əl i ~iness i nəs i nɪs
Moog tdmk məʊg muːg ‖ moʊg —Robert M~
  preferred məʊg ‖ moʊg
  ˌMoog 'synthesizer
moola, moolah 'muːl ə

mooli 'muːl i

moon, Moon muːn **mooned** muːnd **mooning**
'muːn ɪŋ **moons** muːnz
'**moon shot**

moonbeam 'muːn biːm →'muːm- **~s** z

moon|calf 'muːn |kɑːf →'muːŋ-, §-|kæf ‖ -|kæf
~calves kɑːvz §kævz ‖ kævz

Moonee, Mooney, Moonie 'muːn i **~s** z

moon-faced 'muːn feɪst

mooni... —*see* **moony**

moonless 'muːn ləs -lɪs

moon|light 'muːn |laɪt **~lighter/s** laɪt ə/z
‖ laɪt ᵊr/z **~lighting** laɪt ɪŋ ‖ laɪt ɪŋ
,**moonlight 'flit**

moonlit 'muːn lɪt

moonrise 'muːn raɪz

moon-roof 'muːn ruːf -rʊf

moonscape 'muːn skeɪp **~s** s

moonshine 'muːn ʃaɪn

moonshiner 'muːn ʃaɪn ə ‖ -ᵊr **~s** z

moonstone 'muːn stəʊn ‖ -stoʊn **~s** z

moonstruck 'muːn strʌk

moon|y 'muːn |i **~ier** i‿ə ‖ i‿ᵊr **~iest** i‿ɪst i‿əst
~ily ɪ li əl i

moor, Moor mʊə mɔː ‖ mʊᵊr **moored** mʊəd
mɔːd ‖ mʊᵊrd **mooring** 'mʊər ɪŋ 'mɔːr-
‖ 'mʊᵊr ɪŋ

moorcock, M~ 'mʊə kɒk 'mɔː- ‖ 'mʊr kɑːk

Moorcroft 'mʊə krɒft 'mɔː- ‖ 'mʊr krɔːft
-krɑːft

Moore mʊə mɔː ‖ mʊᵊr mɔːr, mʊr

Moorgate 'mʊə geɪt 'mɔː- ‖ 'mʊr-

Moorhead 'mʊə hed 'mɔː- ‖ 'mʊr-

moorhen 'mʊə hen 'mɔː- ‖ 'mʊr- **~s** z

Moorhouse 'mʊə haʊs 'mɔː- ‖ 'mʊr-

moorings 'mʊər ɪŋz 'mɔːr- ‖ 'mʊr ɪŋz

Moorish 'mʊər ɪʃ 'mɔːr- ‖ 'mʊr ʃ

moorland, M~ 'mʊə lənd 'mɔː-, -lænd ‖ 'mʊr-
~s z

moose muːs

moot muːt **mooted** 'muːt ɪd -əd ‖ 'muːt̬ əd
mooting 'muːt ɪŋ ‖ 'muːt̬ ɪŋ **moots** muːts
,**moot 'point**; ,**moot 'question**

Moots muːts

mop mɒp ‖ mɑːp **mopped** mɒpt ‖ mɑːpt
mopping 'mɒp ɪŋ ‖ 'mɑːp ɪŋ **mops** mɒps
‖ mɑːps

mope məʊp ‖ moʊp **moped** məʊpt ‖ moʊpt
mopes məʊps ‖ moʊps **moping** 'məʊp ɪŋ
‖ 'moʊp ɪŋ

moped *n* 'məʊ ped ‖ 'moʊ- **~s** z

mopoke 'məʊp əʊk ‖ 'moʊp oʊk **~s** s

mopp... —*see* **mop**

moppet 'mɒp ɪt §-ət ‖ 'mɑːp- **~s** s

Mopsy 'mɒps i ‖ 'mɑːps i

mop-up 'mɒp ʌp ‖ 'mɑːp- **~s** s

moquette mɒ 'ket məʊ- ‖ moʊ-

mor|a 'mɔːr |ə ‖ 'moʊr- **~ae** iː **~as** əz

Morag 'mɔːr æg ‖ 'moʊr-

moraic mɔː 'reɪ ɪk ‖ moʊ-

moraine mə 'reɪn mɒ- ‖ mə- **~s** z

moral 'mɒr əl ‖ 'mɔːr əl 'mɑːr- **~s** z
,**Moral Ma'jority**; ,**Moral Re'armament**

morale mə 'rɑːl mɒ- ‖ mə 'ræl *(*)*

morale-boosting mə 'rɑːl ,buːst ɪŋ mɒ-
‖ mə 'ræl-

moralis... —*see* **moraliz...**

moralism 'mɒr ə ,lɪz əm ‖ 'mɔːr- 'mɑːr-

moralist 'mɒr əl ɪst §-əst ‖ 'mɔːr- 'mɑːr- **~s** s

moralistic ,mɒr ə 'lɪst ɪk ◄ ‖ ,mɔːr- ,mɑːr-
~ally ᵊl i

moralit|y mə 'ræl ət |i mɒ-, -ɪt- ‖ mə 'ræl ət̬ |i
mɔː- **~ies** iz
mo'rality play

moraliz|e 'mɒr ə laɪz ‖ 'mɔːr- 'mɑːr- **~ed** d
~er/s ə/z ‖ ᵊr/z **~es** ɪz əz **~ing** ɪŋ

morally 'mɒr əl i ‖ 'mɔːr- 'mɑːr-

Moran *(i)* 'mɔːr ən 'mɒr-, *(ii)* mə 'ræn mɒ-
‖ mɔː-

Morant mə 'rænt mɒ- ‖ mɔː-

morass mə 'ræs mɒ- ‖ mɔː- **~es** ɪz əz

moratori|um ,mɒr ə 'tɔːr i‿|əm ‖ ,mɔːr-
,mɑːr-, -'toʊr- **~a** ə **~ums** əmz

Moravi|a mə 'reɪv i‿|ə mɒ- ‖ **~an/s** ən/z

moray *'kind of eel'* 'mɒr eɪ 'mɔːr-; mə 'reɪ, mɒ-
‖ 'mɔːr eɪ 'moʊr-; mə 'reɪ **~s** z

Moray 'mʌr eɪ △'mɒr-, -eɪ ‖ 'mɜː i (= *Murray*)

morbid 'mɔːb ɪd §-əd ‖ 'mɔːrb- **~ly** li **~ness**
nəs nɪs

morbidezza ,mɔːb ɪ 'dets ə §-ə- ‖ ,mɔːrb- —*It*
[mor bi 'det tsa]

morbidit|y mɔː 'bɪd ət |i -ɪt- ‖ mɔːr 'bɪd ət̬ |i
~ies iz

mordancy 'mɔːd ᵊn⣂s i ‖ 'mɔːrd-

mordant 'mɔːd ᵊnt ‖ 'mɔːrd- **~ly** li **~s** s

Mordecai 'mɔːd ɪ kaɪ -ə-; ,··'keɪ aɪ, ,··'kaɪ i
‖ 'mɔːrd-

Morden 'mɔːd ᵊn ‖ 'mɔːrd-

mordent 'mɔːd ᵊnt ‖ 'mɔːrd- **~s** s

Mordor 'mɔːd ɔː ‖ 'mɔːrd ɔːr

Mordred 'mɔːdr ɪd -əd, -ed ‖ 'mɔːrdr-

Mordvin 'mɔːd vɪn ‖ 'mɔːrd-

more, More mɔː ‖ mɔːr moʊr

Morea mɔː 'rɪə mɒ-, mə- ‖ mɔː 'riː ə moʊ-

Morecambe, Morecombe 'mɔːk əm ‖ 'mɔːrk-

moreish 'mɔːr ɪʃ ‖ 'moʊr-

morel mə 'rel mɒ- ‖ mɔː- **~s** z

morello mə 'rel əʊ mɒ- ‖ -oʊ **~s** z

moreover mɔːr 'əʊv ə mər- ‖ -'oʊv ᵊr moʊr-;
'·,··

mores 'mɔːr eɪz -iːz ‖ 'moʊr-

Moresby 'mɔːz bi ‖ 'mɔːrz- 'moʊrz- —*but the*
place in Cumbria is 'mɒr ɪs bi

Moresque ⣂mɔː 'resk mə-

Moreton 'mɔːt ᵊn ‖ 'mɔːrt- 'moʊrt-

Moretonhampstead ,mɔːt ᵊn 'hæmp stɪd
-sted ‖ ,mɔːrt- ,moʊrt-

Morfa 'mɔːv ə ‖ 'mɔːrv ə —*Welsh* ['mɔr va]

Morfudd, Morfydd 'mɔːv ɪð ‖ 'mɔːrv-
—*Welsh* ['mɔr vɪð, -vɪð]

Morgan 'mɔːg ən ‖ 'mɔːrg-

morganatic ,mɔːg ə 'næt ɪk ◄
‖ ,mɔːrg ə 'næt̬ ɪk ◄ **~ally** ᵊl i

morgen 'mɔːg ən ‖ 'mɔːrg- **~s** z

Morgenthau 'mɔːg ən θɔː ‖ 'mɔːrg- -θɑː

M

morgue mɔːg ‖ mɔːrg **morgues** mɔːgz
‖ mɔːrgz
MORI 'mɔːr i 'mɒr-
Moriarty ˌmɒr i 'ɑːt i ‖ ˌmɔːr i 'ɑːrt̬ i
moribund 'mɒr ɪ bʌnd -ə-; -ɪb ənd, -əb-
‖ 'mɔːr- 'mɑːr- **~ly** li
Morison 'mɒr ɪs ən -əs- ‖ 'mɔːr- 'mɑːr-
Morissette ˌmɒr ɪ 'set -ə- ‖ ˌmɔːr- ˌmɑːr-
Morland 'mɔː lənd ‖ 'mɔːr-
Morley 'mɔːl i ‖ 'mɔːrl i
Mormon 'mɔːm ən ‖ 'mɔːrm- **~ism** ˌɪz əm **~s** z
morn mɔːn ‖ mɔːrn **morns** mɔːnz ‖ mɔːrnz
Morna 'mɔːn ə ‖ 'mɔːrn ə
mornay, M~ 'mɔːn eɪ ‖ mɔːr 'neɪ —*Fr*
[mɔʁ nɛ]
morning 'mɔːn ɪŋ ‖ 'mɔːrn ɪŋ **~s** z
'morning coat; 'morning dress, ˌˑ 'ˑ;
ˌmorning 'glory ‖ 'ˑˑ ˌˑˑ; ˌMorning 'Prayer;
'morning ˌsickness; ˌmorning 'star
morning-after ˌmɔːn ɪŋ 'ɑːft ə ◂ §-'æft-
‖ ˌmɔːrn ɪŋ 'æft ᵊr ◂
ˌmorning-'after pill
Mornington 'mɔːn ɪŋ tən ‖ 'mɔːrn-
ˌMornington 'Crescent
Moroccan mə 'rɒk ən ‖ -'rɑːk- **~s** z
Morocco, m~ mə 'rɒk əʊ ‖ -'rɑːk oʊ
moron 'mɔːr ɒn ‖ 'mɔːr ɑːn 'moʊr- **~s** z
Moroni mə 'rəʊn i ‖ -'roʊn i mɔː-
moronic mə 'rɒn ɪk mɒ-, mɔː- ‖ -'rɑːn ɪk **~ally**
ᵊl̬ i
morose mə 'rəʊs mɒ- ‖ -'roʊs mɔː- **~ly** li
~ness nəs nɪs
Morpeth 'mɔːp əθ ‖ 'mɔːrp-
morph mɔːf ‖ mɔːrf **morphed** mɔːft ‖ mɔːrft
morphing 'mɔːf ɪŋ ‖ 'mɔːrf ɪŋ **morphs** mɔːfs
‖ mɔːrfs
morph- *comb. form before vowel*
with unstressed suffix 'mɔːf ‖ 'mɔːrf
— **morphon** 'mɔːf ɒn ‖ 'mɔːrf ɑːn
with stressed suffix mɔːf ‖ mɔːrf
— **morphosis** mɔː 'fəʊs ɪs §-əs ‖ mɔːr 'foʊs-
-morph mɔːf ‖ mɔːrf — **isomorph** 'aɪs əʊ mɔːf
‖ -ə mɔːrf
morpheme 'mɔːf iːm ‖ 'mɔːrf- **~s** z
morphemic mɔː 'fiːm ɪk ‖ mɔːr- **~ally** ᵊl̬ i **~s** s
Morphett 'mɔːf ɪt §-ət ‖ 'mɔːrf ət
Morpheus 'mɔːf juːs 'mɔːf iˌəs ‖ 'mɔːrf-
morphia 'mɔːf iˌə ‖ 'mɔːrf-
-morphic 'mɔːf ɪk ‖ 'mɔːrf ɪk — **isomorphic**
ˌaɪs əʊ 'mɔːf ɪk ◂ ‖ -ə 'mɔːrf-
morphine 'mɔːf iːn ‖ 'mɔːrf-
morpho- *comb. form before cons*
with stress-neutral suffix ¦mɔːf əʊ ‖ ¦mɔːrf oʊ
— **morphotectonics** ˌmɔːf əʊ tek 'tɒn ɪks
‖ ˌmɔːrf oʊ tek 'tɑːn-
with stress-imposing suffix mɔː 'fɒ+
‖ mɔːr 'fɑː+ — **morphometry**
mɔː 'fɒm ətr i -ɪtr- ‖ mɔːr 'fɑːm-
morphological ˌmɔːf ə 'lɒdʒ ɪk ᵊl ◂
‖ ˌmɔːrf ə 'lɑːdʒ- **~ly** ˌi
morpholog|y mɔː 'fɒl ədʒ |i ‖ mɔːr 'fɑːl- **~ies**
iz

morphophoneme ˌmɔːf əʊ 'fəʊn iːm
‖ ˌmɔːrf oʊ 'foʊn- **~s** z
morphophonemic ˌmɔːf əʊ fəʊ 'niːm ɪk ◂
‖ ˌmɔːrf oʊ fə- **~ally** ᵊl̬ i **~s** s
morphophonology ˌmɔːf əʊ fəʊ 'nɒl ədʒ i
‖ ˌmɔːrf oʊ fə 'nɑːl-
morphosyntactic ˌmɔːf əʊ sɪn 'tækt ɪk ◂
‖ ˌmɔːrf oʊ-
-morphous 'mɔːf əs ‖ 'mɔːrf əs —
isomorphous ˌaɪs əʊ 'mɔːf əs ◂ ‖ -ə 'mɔːrf-
-morphy mɔːf i ‖ mɔːrf i — **isomorphy**
'aɪs əʊ mɔːf i ‖ -ə mɔːrf i
Morphy 'mɔːf i ‖ 'mɔːrf i
Morpurgo mɔː 'pɜːg əʊ ‖ mɔːr 'pɜːg oʊ
Morrell (i) mə 'rel mɒ-, (ii) 'mʌr əl ‖ 'mɜː-
Morrill 'mɒr ɪl -əl ‖ 'mɔːr- 'mɑːr-
Morris, m~ 'mɒr ɪs §-əs ‖ 'mɔːr- 'mɑːr-
'morris dance; 'morris ˌdancer; 'morris
men
Morrison 'mɒr ɪs ən §-əs- ‖ 'mɔːr- 'mɑːr-
Morrissey 'mɒr ɪs i -əs- ‖ 'mɔːr- 'mɑːr-
Morristown 'mɒr ɪs taʊn §-əs- ‖ 'mɔːr- 'mɑːr-
morrow, M~ 'mɒr əʊ ‖ 'mɔːr oʊ 'mɑːr- **~s** z
Morse, morse mɔːs ‖ mɔːrs **morses, Morse's**
'mɔːs ɪz -əz ‖ 'mɔːrs əz
ˌMorse 'code
morsel 'mɔːs ᵊl ‖ 'mɔːrs- **~s** z
Mort, mort mɔːt ‖ mɔːrt **morts, Mort's** mɔːts
‖ mɔːrts
mortadella ˌmɔːt ə 'del ə ‖ ˌmɔːrt̬ ə- **~s** z
mortal 'mɔːt ᵊl ‖ 'mɔːrt̬ ᵊl **~s** z
ˌmortal 'sin
mortalit|y mɔː 'tæl ət |i -ɪt- ‖ mɔːr 'tæl ət̬ |i
~ies iz
mortally 'mɔːt əl i ‖ 'mɔːrt̬ ᵊl i
mortar 'mɔːt ə ‖ 'mɔːrt̬ ᵊr **~ed** d **mortaring**
'mɔːt ər ɪŋ ‖ 'mɔːrt̬ ər ɪŋ **~s** z
mortarboard 'mɔːt ə bɔːd ‖ 'mɔːrt̬ ᵊr bɔːrd
-boʊrd **~s** z
Morte d'Arthur ˌmɔːt 'dɑːθ ə
‖ ˌmɔːrt 'dɑːrθ ᵊr
Mortehoe 'mɔːt həʊ ‖ 'mɔːrt hoʊ
mortem 'mɔːt əm -em ‖ 'mɔːrt̬-
mortgag|e 'mɔːg ɪdʒ ‖ 'mɔːrg- **~ed** d **~es** ɪz
əz **~ing** ɪŋ
mortgagee ˌmɔːg ɪ 'dʒiː -ə- ‖ ˌmɔːrg- **~s** z
mortgagor ˌmɔːg ɪ 'dʒɔː -ə-; 'mɔːg ɪdʒ ə, -ədʒ-
‖ ˌmɔːrg ə 'dʒɔːr 'mɔːrg ədʒ ᵊr **~s** z
mortic|e 'mɔːt ɪs §-əs ‖ 'mɔːrt̬ əs **~ed** t **~es** ɪz
əz **~ing** ɪŋ
mortician mɔː 'tɪʃ ᵊn ‖ mɔːr- **~s** z
mortification ˌmɔːt ɪf ɪ 'keɪʃ ᵊn ˌ-əf-, §-ə'--
‖ ˌmɔːrt̬ əf- **~s** z
morti|fy 'mɔːt ɪ |faɪ -ə- ‖ 'mɔːrt̬ ə- **~fied** faɪd
~fies faɪz **~fying/ly** faɪ ɪŋ /li
Mortimer 'mɔːt ɪm ə -əm- ‖ 'mɔːrt̬ əm ᵊr
mortis|e 'mɔːt ɪs §-əs ‖ 'mɔːrt̬ əs **~ed** t **~es** ɪz
əz **~ing** ɪŋ
'mortise lock
Mortlake 'mɔːt leɪk ‖ 'mɔːrt-
mortmain 'mɔːt meɪn ‖ 'mɔːrt-
Morton 'mɔːt ᵊn ‖ 'mɔːrt ᵊn

mortuar|y 'mɔːtʃ u‿ər |i ‖ 'mɔːtʃ ər |i;
'mɔːt ju‿ər i, 'mɔːt jʊr |i ‖ 'mɔːrtʃ u er |i **~ies**
iz

mosaic, M~ məʊ 'zeɪ ɪk ‖ moʊ- **~s** s

moschatel ˌmɒsk ə 'tel ‖ ˌmɑːsk- '··· **~s** z

Moscow 'mɒsk əʊ ‖ 'mɑːsk aʊ -oʊ

Moseley 'məʊz li ‖ 'moʊz-

Moselle məʊ 'zel ‖ moʊ- —Fr [mo zɛl], Ger
Mosel ['moː zᵊl]

Moses 'məʊz ɪz -əz ‖ 'moʊz-

mosey 'məʊz i ‖ 'moʊz i **~ed** d **~ing** ɪŋ **~s** z

mosh mɒʃ ‖ mɑːʃ **moshed** mɒʃt ‖ mɑːʃt
moshes 'mɒʃ ɪz -əz ‖ 'mɑːʃ əz **moshing**
'mɒʃ ɪŋ ‖ 'mɑːʃ ɪŋ

Moskva 'mɒsk və ‖ mɑːsk 'vɑː —Russ
[mʌ 'skva]

Moskvich tdmk 'mɒsk vɪtʃ ‖ 'mɑːsk- —Russ
[mʌ 'skvʲitʃ] **~es** ɪz əz

Moslem 'mɒz ləm 'mʊz-, -lɪm, -lem ‖ 'mɑːz-
'mɑːs- **~s** z

Mosley family name(i) 'məʊz li ‖ 'moʊz-,
(ii) 'mɒz- ‖ 'mɑːz-

mosque mɒsk ‖ mɑːsk **mosques** mɒsks
‖ mɑːsks

mosquito mə 'skiːt əʊ mɒ- ‖ -'skiːt̬ oʊ **~es, ~s**
z
mo'squito net

moss, Moss mɒs ‖ mɔːs mɑːs **mosses** 'mɒs ɪz
-əz ‖ 'mɔːs əz 'mɑːs-

Mossad 'mɒs æd ‖ mə 'sɑːd mɑː-, moʊ-

Mossbauer, Mössbauer 'mɒs ˌbaʊ ə
‖ 'mɔːs ˌbaʊ ᵊr 'mɑːs- —Ger ['mœs baʊ ɐ]
'Mössbauer efˌfect

moss-grown 'mɒs grəʊn ‖ 'mɔːs groʊn 'mɑːs-

Mossi 'mɒs i ‖ 'mɑːs i

Mossman 'mɒs mən ‖ 'mɔːs- 'mɑːs-

Mossop 'mɒs əp ‖ 'mɔːs- 'mɑːs-

moss|y 'mɒs |i ‖ 'mɔːs |i 'mɑːs- **~ier** i‿ə ‖ i‿ᵊr
~iest i‿ɪst i‿əst **~iness** i nəs i nɪs

most məʊst ‖ moʊst **mostly** 'məʊst li
‖ 'moʊst-
ˌmost of 'all

-most məʊst ‖ moʊst — **innermost**
'ɪn ə məʊst ‖ -ᵊr moʊst

Mostar 'mɒst ɑː ‖ 'mɑːst ɑːr 'moʊst-
—Croatian ['ˈˈmɔ stɑːr]

most-favoured, most-favored
ˌməʊst 'feɪv əd ◂ ‖ ˌmoʊst'feɪv ᵊrd ·ˈ··

Mostyn 'mɒst ɪn §-ən ‖ 'mɑːst-

Mosul 'məʊ sᵊl 'muːs- ‖ 'moʊs-

mot məʊ ‖ moʊ —Fr [mo] **mots** məʊz ‖ moʊz
ˌmot 'juste ʒuːst —Fr [ʒyst]

M.o.T., MOT ˌem əʊ 'tiː ‖ -oʊ- **~'d** d **~'ing** ɪŋ
~s, ~'s z

mote məʊt ‖ moʊt (= moat) **motes** məʊts
‖ moʊts

motel ₍ₗ₎məʊ 'tel ‖ ₍ₗ₎moʊ- **~s** z

motet ₍ₗ₎məʊ 'tet ‖ ₍ₗ₎moʊ- **~s** s

moth mɒθ ‖ mɔːθ mɑːθ **moths** mɒθs ‖ mɔːðz
mɑːðz, mɔːθs, mɑːθs

Mothaks tdmk 'mɒθ æks ‖ 'mɔːθ- 'mɑːθ-

mothball 'mɒθ bɔːl ‖ 'mɔːθ- 'mɑːθ bɑːl **~ed** d
~ing ɪŋ **~s** z

moth-eaten 'mɒθ ˌiːt ᵊn ‖ 'mɔːθ- 'mɑːθ-

mother, M~ 'mʌð ə ‖ -ᵊr **~ed** d **mothering**
'mʌð ᵊr ɪŋ **~s** z
'mother ˌcountry; ˌMother 'Goose,
ˌMother 'Goose rhyme; ˌmother 'hen;
'Mothering ˌSunday; ˌMother 'Nature;
'mother's boy; 'Mother's Day; ˌmother's
'ruin; ˌmother su'perior; ˌmother
'tongue, '···

motherboard 'mʌð ə bɔːd ‖ -ᵊr bɔːrd -boʊrd
~s z

Mothercare tdmk 'mʌð ə keə ‖ -ᵊr ker

mothercraft 'mʌð ə krɑːft §-kræft ‖ -ᵊr kræft

motherese ˌmʌð ə 'riːz

motherfuck|er 'mʌð ə ˌfʌk| ə ‖ -ᵊr ˌfʌk| ᵊr
~ers əz ‖ ᵊrz **~ing** ɪŋ

motherhood 'mʌð ə hʊd ‖ -ᵊr-

mother-in-law 'mʌð ər ɪn ˌlɔː '·ə-, -ᵊr ən-
‖ -ᵊr ən- -ˌlɑː **~s, ~'s** z **mothers-in-law**
'mʌð əz ɪn ˌlɔː §-ən ˌ· ‖ -ᵊrz ən- -ˌlɑː

motherland 'mʌð ə lænd ‖ -ᵊr-

motherless 'mʌð ə ləs -lɪs ‖ -ᵊr- **~ness** nəs nɪs

mother|ly 'mʌð ə |li ‖ -ᵊr- **~liness** li nəs -nɪs

mother-of-pearl ˌmʌð ər‿əv 'pɜːl ◂ ‖ -'pɝːl

mother-of-thousands ˌmʌð ər‿əv 'θaʊz ᵊndz

mothers- —see **mother-**

mother-to-be ˌmʌð ə tə 'biː ‖ ˌ·ᵊr-
mothers-to-be ˌmʌð əz tə 'biː ‖ ˌ·ᵊrz-

Motherwell 'mʌð ə wəl -wel ‖ -ᵊr-

mothproof 'mɒθ pruːf §-prʊf ‖ 'mɔːθ- 'mɑːθ-
~ed t **~ing** ɪŋ **~s** s

moth|y 'mɒθ |i ‖ 'mɔːθ |i 'mɑːθ- **~ier** i‿ə ‖ i‿ᵊr
~iest i‿ɪst i‿əst

motif ₍ₗ₎məʊ 'tiːf mɒ- ‖ moʊ- **~s** s

motile 'məʊt aɪᵊl ‖ 'moʊt̬ ᵊl 'moʊt aɪᵊl (*)

motility məʊ 'tɪl ət i -ɪt- ‖ moʊ 'tɪl ət̬ i

motion, M~ 'məʊʃ ᵊn ‖ 'moʊʃ ᵊn **~ed** d **~ing**
ɪŋ **~s** z
ˌmotion 'picture◂; 'motion ˌsickness

motionless 'məʊʃ ᵊn ləs -lɪs ‖ 'moʊʃ- **~ly** li
~ness nəs nɪs

moti|vate 'məʊt ɪ |veɪt -ə- ‖ 'moʊt̬ ə- **~vated**
veɪt ɪd -əd ‖ veɪt̬ əd **~vates** veɪts **~vating**
veɪt ɪŋ ‖ veɪt̬ ɪŋ

motivation ˌməʊt ɪ 'veɪʃ ᵊn -ə- ‖ ˌmoʊt̬ ə- **~s** z

motivational ˌməʊt ɪ 'veɪʃ ᵊn əl ◂ -ə- ‖ ˌmoʊt̬ ə-
~ly i

motivator 'məʊt ɪ veɪt ə -ə- ‖ 'moʊt̬ ə veɪt̬ ᵊr
~s z

motive 'məʊt ɪv ‖ 'moʊt̬ ɪv **~less** ləs lɪs **~s** z

motley, M~ 'mɒt li ‖ 'mɑːt-

motmot 'mɒt mɒt ‖ 'mɑːt mɑːt **~s** s

motocross 'məʊt əʊ krɒs -krɔːs
‖ 'moʊt̬ oʊ krɔːs -krɑːs

motor 'məʊt ə ‖ 'moʊt̬ ᵊr **~ed** d **motoring**
'məʊt ᵊr ɪŋ ‖ 'moʊt̬ ᵊr ɪŋ **~s** z
'motor lodge; 'motor ˌscooter; ˌmotor
'vehicle

motorbike 'məʊt ə baɪk ‖ 'moʊt̬ ᵊr- **~s** s

motorboat 'məʊt ə bəʊt ‖ 'moʊt̬ ᵊr boʊt **~s** s

motorcade 'məʊt ə keɪd ‖ 'moʊt̬ ᵊr- **~s** z

motorcar 'məʊt ə kɑː ‖ 'moʊt̬ ᵊr kɑːr **~s** z

M

motorcoach 'məʊt ə kəʊtʃ ‖ 'moʊt ᵊr koʊtʃ
~es ɪz əz
motorcycle 'məʊt ə ˌsaɪk ᵊl ‖ 'moʊt ᵊr- ~s z
motorcyclist 'məʊt ə ˌsaɪk lɪst §-ləst
‖ 'moʊt ᵊr- ~s s
motoris... —see **motoriz...**
motorist 'məʊt ər ɪst §-əst ‖ 'moʊt ər- ~s s
motoriz|e 'məʊt ə raɪz ‖ 'moʊt ə- ~ed d ~es
ɪz əz ~ing ɪŋ
motor|man 'məʊt ə |mən -mæn ‖ 'moʊt ᵊr-
~men mən men
motor|mouth 'məʊt ə |maʊθ ‖ 'moʊt ᵊr-
~mouths maʊðz
motorway 'məʊt ə weɪ ‖ 'moʊt ᵊr- ~s z
Motown 'məʊ taʊn ‖ 'moʊ-
Motson 'mɒts ᵊn ‖ 'maːts-
Mott mɒt ‖ maːt
motte mɒt ‖ maːt **mottes** mɒts ‖ maːts
mottl|e 'mɒt ᵊl ‖ 'maːt ᵊl ~ed d ~es z ~ing ɪŋ
motto 'mɒt əʊ ‖ 'maːt oʊ ~es, ~s z
Mottram 'mɒtr əm ‖ 'maːtr-
Motu 'məʊt uː ‖ 'moʊt-
motu proprio ˌməʊt uː 'prɒp ri əʊ -'prəʊp-
‖ ˌmoʊt uː 'proʊp ri oʊ
moue muː (= moo) —Fr [mu] **moues** muːz
moufflon, mouflon 'muːf lɒn ‖ -laːn ~s z
mouille, mouillé 'mwiː eɪ 'muː jeɪ ‖ muː 'jeɪ
—Fr [mu je]
mould, Mould məʊld →mɒʊld ‖ moʊld
moulded 'məʊld ɪd →'mɒʊld-, -əd
‖ 'moʊld əd **moulding/s** 'məʊld ɪŋ/z
→'mɒʊld- ‖ 'moʊld ɪŋ/z **moulds** məʊldz
→mɒʊldz ‖ moʊldz
mould|er 'məʊld |ə →'mɒʊld- ‖ 'moʊld |ᵊr
~ered əd ‖ ᵊrd ~ering ər ɪŋ ~ers əz ‖ ᵊrz
mould|y 'məʊld |i →'mɒʊld- ‖ 'moʊld |i ~ier
i ə ‖ i ᵊr ~iest i ɪst i əst ~iness i nəs i nɪs
Moulinex tdmk 'muːl ɪ neks -ə-
Moulin Rouge ˌmuːl æn 'ruːʒ —Fr
[mu læ ʁuːʒ]
moult, Moult məʊlt →mɒʊlt ‖ moʊlt
moulted 'məʊlt ɪd →'mɒʊlt-, -əd ‖ 'moʊlt əd
moulting 'məʊlt ɪŋ →'mɒʊlt- ‖ 'moʊlt ɪŋ
moults məʊlts →mɒʊlts ‖ moʊlts
Moulton 'məʊlt ən →'mɒʊlt- ‖ 'moʊlt-
mound maʊnd **mounds** maʊndz
mount, Mount maʊnt **mounted** 'maʊnt ɪd
-əd ‖ 'maʊnt̬ əd **mounting** 'maʊnt ɪŋ
‖ 'maʊnt̬ ɪŋ **mounts** maʊnts
ˌMount 'Everest; ˌMount 'Pleasant;
ˌMount 'Rushmore; ˌMount 'Vernon
mountain 'maʊnt ɪn -ən ‖ -ᵊn —In singing
sometimes -eɪn ~s z
'mountain ˌlion; 'mountain range;
ˌMountain 'Standard Time, 'Mountain
Time
mountaineer ˌmaʊnt ɪ 'nɪə -ə- ‖ -ᵊn 'ɪᵊr ~ed d
mountaineering ˌmaʊnt ɪ 'nɪər ɪŋ ˌ-ə-
‖ -ᵊn 'ɪr ɪŋ ~s z
mountainous 'maʊnt ɪn əs -ən- ‖ -ᵊn-
mountainside 'maʊnt ɪn saɪd -ən- ‖ -ᵊn- ~s z
mountaintop 'maʊnt ɪn tɒp -ən- ‖ -ᵊn taːp ~s
s

Mountbatten maʊnt 'bæt ᵊn ‖ 'ˌ·ˌ··
mountebank 'maʊnt ɪ bæŋk -ə- ‖ 'maʊnt̬- ~s
s
Mountford 'maʊnt fəd ‖ -fᵊrd
Mountie 'maʊnt i ‖ 'maʊnt̬ i ~s z
Mountjoy maʊnt 'dʒɔɪ 'ˌ··
Mountsorrel ˌmaʊnt 'sɒr əl ‖ -'sɔːr- -'saːr-
Mount|y 'maʊnt |i ‖ 'maʊnt̬ |i ~ies iz
Moureen 'mɔːr iːn mɔː 'riːn
Mourinho mə 'riːn jəʊ mu-, -ju —Port
[mo 'ɾi ɲu]
mourn mɔːn mʊən ‖ mɔːrn moʊrn **mourned**
mɔːnd mʊənd ‖ mɔːrnd moʊrnd **mourning**
'mɔːn ɪŋ 'mʊən- ‖ 'mɔːrn- 'moʊrn- **mourns**
mɔːnz mʊənz ‖ mɔːrnz moʊrnz
Mourne mɔːn ‖ mɔːrn moʊrn
mourner 'mɔːn ə 'mʊən- ‖ 'mɔːrn ᵊr 'moʊrn-
~s z
mournful 'mɔːn fᵊl 'mʊən-, -fʊl ‖ 'mɔːrn-
'moʊrn- ~ly i ~ness nəs nɪs
mourning 'mɔːn ɪŋ 'mʊən- ‖ 'mɔːrn ɪŋ 'moʊrn-
Mousa place in Shetland 'muːz ə
mouse v maʊz maʊs **moused** maʊzd maʊst
mouses 'maʊz ɪz 'maʊs-, -əz **mousing**
'maʊz ɪŋ 'maʊs-
mouse n maʊs **mice** maɪs **mice's** 'maɪs ɪz -əz
mouse's 'maʊs ɪz -əz
'mouse ˌmat; 'mouse pad
mousehole 'maʊs həʊl →-hɒʊl ‖ -hoʊl ~s z
Mousehole place in Cornwall 'maʊz ᵊl
mouselike 'maʊs laɪk
mouser 'maʊz ə 'maʊs- ‖ -ᵊr ~s z
mousetrap 'maʊs træp ~s s
mous|ey 'maʊs |i ~ier i ə ‖ i ᵊr ~iest i ɪst i əst
~iness i nəs i nɪs
moussaka mu 'saːk ə —ModGk [mu sa 'ka]
~s z
mousse muːs (= moose) **mousses** 'muːs ɪz -əz
Moussec tdmk ˌmuː 'sek
Moussorgsky mu 'sɔːg ski mə-, -'zɔːg-
‖ -'sɔːrg- -'zɔːrg- —Russ ['mu sərk skʲɪj]
moustach|e mə 'staːʃ mu-, §-'stæʃ, §-'stɒʃ
‖ 'mʌst æʃ mə 'stæʃ (*) ~ed t ~es ɪz əz
moustachio mə 'staːʃ i əʊ -'stæʃ-
‖ mə 'stæʃ i oʊ ~ed d ~s z
mous|y 'maʊs |i ~ier i ə ‖ i ᵊr ~iest i ɪst i əst
~iness i nəs i nɪs
mouth v maʊð **mouthed** maʊðd **mouths**
maʊðz **mouthing** 'maʊð ɪŋ
mouth n maʊθ **mouths** maʊðz §maʊθs
'mouth ˌorgan; 'mouth ˌulcer
-mouthed 'maʊðd 'maʊθt — **foul-mouthed**
ˌfaʊl 'maʊðd ◄ -'maʊθt
mouthful 'maʊθ fʊl ~s z
mouthorgan 'maʊθ ˌɔːg ən ‖ -ˌɔːrg- ~s z
mouthpart 'maʊθ paːt ‖ -paːrt ~s s
mouthpiec|e 'maʊθ piːs ~es ɪz əz
mouth-to-mouth ˌmaʊθ tə 'maʊθ ◄ -tu-
ˌmouth-to-ˌmouth reˌsusci'tation
mouthwash 'maʊθ wɒʃ ‖ -wɔːʃ -waːʃ ~es ɪz əz
mouthwatering 'maʊθ ˌwɔːt ər ɪŋ
‖ -ˌwɔːt̬ ər ɪŋ -ˌwaːt̬-

M

mouth|y 'maʊð| i 'maʊθ| i **~ier** i‿ə ‖ i‿ʰr **~iest**
i‿ɪst ‿əst
movable 'muːv əb |ᵊl
,movable 'feast
move muːv (!) **moved** muːvd **moves** muːvz
moving 'muːv ɪŋ
,moving 'picture; ,moving 'staircase;
'moving van 'removal van'
moveable 'muːv əb ᵊl
movement 'muːv mənt **~s** s
mover 'muːv ə ‖ -ʰr **~s** z
movie 'muːv i **~s** z
'movie star
moviego|er 'muːv i ,gəʊ| ə ‖ -,goʊ ʰr **~ers** əz
‖ ʰrz **~ing** ɪŋ
moviemak|er 'muːv i ,meɪk ə ‖ -ʰr **~ers** əz
‖ ʰrz **~ing** ɪŋ
Movietone tdmk 'muːv i təʊn ‖ -toʊn
moving 'muːv ɪŋ **~ly** li
mow 'stack', v 'store hay' maʊ **mowed** maʊd
mowing 'maʊ ɪŋ **mows** maʊz —but usually
məʊ ‖ moʊ in the inn name ,Barley 'Mow
mow 'grimace' maʊ **mowed** maʊd **mowing**
'maʊ ɪŋ **mows** maʊz
mow 'cut down' məʊ ‖ moʊ (= mo) **mowed**
məʊd ‖ moʊd **mowing** 'məʊ ɪŋ ‖ 'moʊ ɪŋ
mown məʊn ‖ moʊn **mows** məʊz ‖ moʊz
'mowing ma,chine
Mowat, Mowatt (i) 'məʊ ət ‖ 'moʊ-,
(ii) 'maʊ-
Mowbray 'məʊb ri -reɪ ‖ 'moʊb-
mower, Mower 'məʊ ə ‖ 'moʊ ʰr **~s** z
Mowgli 'maʊg li
Mowlam, Mowlem 'məʊl əm ‖ 'moʊl-
mown məʊn ‖ moʊn (= moan)
moxa 'mɒks ə ‖ 'mɑːks ə
moxibustion ,mɒks ɪ 'bʌs tʃən -ə- ‖ ,mɑːks-
moxie 'mɒks i ‖ 'mɑːks i
Moy mɔɪ
Moya 'mɔɪ ə
Moygashel mɔɪ 'gæʃ ᵊl 'mɔɪɡ əʃ-
Moynahan 'mɔɪn ə hən -hæn
Moyne mɔɪn
Moynihan 'mɔɪn i ən -ɪ hæn, -ə-
Moyra 'mɔɪʰr ə
Mozambican, Mozambiquan
,məʊz əm 'biːk ən ◂ -æm- ‖ ,moʊz- **~s** z
Mozambique ,məʊz əm 'biːk -æm- ‖ ,moʊz-
Mozarab məʊ 'zær əb ‖ moʊ- -'zer- **~s** z
Mozarabic məʊ 'zær əb ɪk ‖ moʊ- -'zer-
Mozart 'məʊts ɑːt ‖ 'moʊts ɑːrt —Ger
['moː tsaʁt]
Mozartian ,məʊt 'sɑːt i‿ən ◂
‖ moʊt 'sɑːrt̬ i‿ən **~s** z
mozzarella ,mɒts ə 'rel ə ◂ ‖ ,mɑːt- ,moʊt-
—It [mot tsa 'rɛl la]
mozzie 'mɒz i ‖ 'mɑːz i **~s** z
MP ,em 'piː **MPs, MP's** ,em 'piːz
mp3 ,em piː 'θriː **~s** z
MPEG, mpg 'em peg **~s** z
mph ,em piː 'eɪtʃ §-'heɪtʃ —or as miles per
hour, miles an hour
MPhil ,em 'fɪl

Mpumalanga ᵊm ,puːm ə 'læŋ gə —siSwati
[mpú má 'là: ŋgà]
Mr 'mɪst ə ‖ -ʰr
Mrs 'mɪs ɪz -əz ‖ 'mɪz-
MRSA ,em ɑːr es 'eɪ ‖ ,em ɑːr-
ms —see **manuscript**
Ms mɪz məz, məs —As a self-designation, mɪz
seems to be preferred. Those who say məz,
məs may use it in stressed as well as
unstressed position. Some claim the word is
unpronounceable.
MS 'multiple sclerosis' ,em 'es
MSc ,em es 'siː
MS-DOS tdmk ,em es 'dɒs ‖ -'dɔːs -'dɑːs
mss —see **manuscripts**
Mt —see **Mount**
MTV ,em tiː 'viː
mu mjuː (= mew)
Mubarak mu 'bɑːr æk -'bær-, -ək —Arabic
[mu 'ba: rak]
much, Much mʌtʃ **more** mɔː ‖ mɔːr moʊr
most məʊst ‖ moʊst **muchness** 'mʌtʃ nəs
-nɪs
much-heralded ,mʌtʃ 'her əld ɪd ◂ -əd
mucho 'muːtʃ əʊ ‖ -oʊ —Sp ['mu tʃo]
much-vaunted ,mʌtʃ 'vɔːnt ɪd ◂ -əd ‖ -'vɔːnt̬-
-'vɑːnt̬-
mucic 'mjuːs ɪk
mucilag|e 'mjuːs ɪl ɪdʒ -əl- **~es** ɪz əz
mucilaginous ,mjuːs ɪ 'lædʒ ɪn əs ◂ ,-ə-,
-ən əs
mucin 'mjuːs ɪn §-ᵊn **~s** z
muck, Muck mʌk **mucked** mʌkt **mucking**
'mʌk ɪŋ **mucks** mʌks
mucker 'mʌk ə ‖ -ʰr **~s** z
muckety-muck ,mʌk ət i 'mʌk ‖ -ət̬- **~s** s
muckheap 'mʌk hiːp **~s** s
muckle 'mʌk ᵊl
,Muckle 'Flugga 'flʌg ə
muckluck 'mʌk lʌk **~s** s
muckrak|er 'mʌk reɪk |ə ‖ -|ʰr **~ers** əz ‖ ʰrz
~ing ɪŋ
muck-spread|er 'mʌk ,spred| ə ‖ -ʰr **~ers** əz
‖ ʰrz **~ing** ɪŋ
muck|y 'mʌk |i **~ier** i‿ə ‖ i‿ʰr **~iest** i‿ɪst i‿əst
muco- comb. form
with stress-neutral suffix |mjuːk əʊ ‖ -oʊ
— **mucofibrous** ,mjuːk əʊ 'faɪb rəs ◂ ‖ -oʊ-
with stress-imposing suffix mju 'kɒ+ ‖ -'kɑː+
— **mucoclasis** mju 'kɒk ləs ɪs §-əs ‖ -'kɑːk-
mucous 'mjuːk əs (= mucus)
,mucous 'membrane
Mu-cron tdmk 'mjuː krɒn ‖ -krɑːn
mucus 'mjuːk əs
mud mʌd **muds** mʌdz
'mud bath; ,mud 'pie; 'mud ,puppy
mudbank 'mʌd bæŋk →'mʌb- **~s** s
mud|bath 'mʌd| bɑːθ →'mʌb-, §-bæθ ‖ -bæθ
~baths bɑːðz §bɑːθs, §bæθs, §bæðz ‖ bæðz
bæθs
Mudd mʌd
muddi... —see **muddy**
muddl|e 'mʌd ᵊl **~ed** d **~es** z **~ing** ɪŋ

muddle-headed ˌmʌd ᵊl 'hed ɪd ◀ -be- **~ly** li
~ness nəs nɪs
mudd|y 'mʌd |i **~ied** id **~ier** i ə ‖ i ᵊr **~ies** iz
~iest i ˌɪst i ˌəsi **~ily** ɪ li əl i **~iness** i nəs i nɪs
~ying i ˌɪŋ
Mudeford 'mʌd i fəd ‖ -fᵊrd (!)
mudfish 'mʌd fɪʃ **~es** ɪz əz
mudflap 'mʌd flæp ~s s
mudflat 'mʌd flæt **~s** s
Mudge mʌdʒ
mudguard 'mʌd gɑːd →'mʌg- ‖ -gɑːrd **~s** z
Mudie 'mjuːd i
mudlark 'mʌd lɑːk ‖ -lɑːrk **~s** s
mudpack 'mʌd pæk →'mʌb- **~s** s
mudskipper 'mʌd ˌskɪp ə ‖ -ᵊr **~s** z
mudslide 'mʌd slaɪd **~s** z
mudsling|er 'mʌd ˌslɪŋ |ə ‖ -|ᵊr **~ers** əz ‖ ᵊrz
~ing ɪŋ
mud-wrestling 'mʌd ˌres ᵊl ɪŋ ‖ -ˌræs-
muesli 'mjuːz li 'muːz- ‖ 'mjuːs- **~s** z —Ger
Müsli ['myːs li]
muezzin mu 'ez ɪn mju-, §-ᵊn **~s** z
muff mʌf **muffed** mʌft **muffing** 'mʌf ɪŋ
muffs mʌfs
muffin 'mʌf ɪn §-ᵊn **~s** z
muffl|e 'mʌf ᵊl **~ed** d **~es** z **~ing** ɪŋ
muffler 'mʌf lə ‖ -lᵊr **~s** z
Muffy 'mʌf i
mufti, Mufti 'mʌft i **~s** z
mug mʌg **mugged** mʌgd **mugging/s**
'mʌg ɪŋ/z **mugs** mʌgz
'mug's game
Mugabe mu 'gɑːb i -eɪ
mugful 'mʌg fʊl **~s** z
mugger 'mʌg ə ‖ -ᵊr **~s** z
Muggeridge 'mʌg ər ɪdʒ
muggins, M~ 'mʌg ɪnz §-ənz
muggle 'mʌg ᵊl **~s** z
Muggleton 'mʌg ᵊl tən
Muggletonian ˌmʌg ᵊl 'təʊn i ən ‖ -'toʊn- **~s**
z
mugg|y 'mʌg |i **~ier** i ə ‖ i ᵊr **~iest** i ˌɪst i ˌəsi
~ily ɪ li əl i **~iness** i nəs i nɪs
mugho 'mjuːg əʊ 'muːg- ‖ -oʊ **~s** z
mugshot 'mʌg ʃɒt ‖ -ʃɑːt **~s** s
mugwort 'mʌg wɜːt -wɔːt ‖ -wɜːt -wɔːt **~s** s
mugwump 'mʌg wʌmp **~s** s
Muhammed mu 'hæm ɪd -əd, -ed —Arabic
[mu 'ham mad]
Muhammedan mu 'hæm ɪd ən -əd- **~ism**
ˌɪz əm **~s** z
Muir mjʊə mjɔː ‖ mjʊᵊr
Muirhead 'mjʊə hed 'mjɔː- ‖ 'mjʊr-
mujaheddin, mujahedeen ˌmuːdʒ ə he 'diːn
ˌmʊdʒ-, ˌmuːʒ-, -ˌɑː-, -hə'· —Arabic
[mu dʒaː hi 'diːn]
Mukden 'mʊk dən
mukluk 'mʌk lʌk **~s** s
muktuk 'mʌk tʌk
mulatto mju 'læt əʊ mu-, mə- ‖ -'læt oʊ -'lɑːt̬-
~s z
mulberr|y 'mʌl bər ˌi ‖ -ˌber |i **~ies** iz
Mulcaghey mʌl 'kæ hi -'kæx i

Mulcahy mʌl 'kæ hi
mulch mʌltʃ **mulched** mʌltʃt **mulches**
'mʌltʃ ɪz -əz **mulching** 'mʌltʃ ɪŋ
mulct mʌlkt **mulcted** 'mʌlkt ɪd -əd **mulcting**
'mʌlkt ɪŋ **mulcts** mʌlkts
Mulder 'mʌld ə ‖ -ᵊr
Muldoon mʌl 'duːn
mule mjuːl **mules** mjuːlz
Mules mjuːlz
muleteer ˌmjuːl ə 'tɪə -ɪ- ‖ -'tɪᵊr **~s** z
mulga 'mʌlg ə **~s** z
Mulhearn mʌl 'hɜːn ‖ -'hɜːrn
Mulholland mʌl 'hɒl ənd ‖ -'hɑːl-
mulish 'mjuːl ɪʃ **~ly** li **~ness** nəs nɪs
mull, Mull mʌl **mulled** mʌld **mulling** 'mʌl ɪŋ
mulls mʌlz
mulla, mullah 'mʌl ə 'mʊl- **~s** z
Mullan 'mʌl ən
mullein 'mʌl ɪn -eɪn, -ən **~s** z
Muller 'mʌl ə ‖ -ᵊr —but as a German name
'mʊl-, 'muːl-, 'mjuːl- —Ger Müller ['myl ɐ]
mullet 'mʌl ɪt -ət **~s** s
Mulley 'mʌl i
Mulligan, m~ 'mʌl ɪg ən -əg- **~s** z
mulligatawny ˌmʌl ɪg ə 'tɔːn i ◀ ˌ·əg- ‖ -'tɑːn-
Mulliken 'mʌl ɪk ən
mullion 'mʌl i ən ‖ 'mʌl jən **~ed** d **~s** z
Mulroney mʌl 'rəʊn i ‖ -'roʊn i
multi- comb. form
with stress-neutral suffix ˌmʌlt i ‖ -aɪ
— **multiethnic** ˌmʌlt i 'eθ nɪk ◀ ‖ -aɪ-
with stress-imposing suffix mʌl 'tɪ+
— **multiparous** mʌl 'tɪp ər əs
multicellular ˌmʌlt i 'sel jʊl ə ◀ -jəl· ‖ -jəl ᵊr
multicolored, multicoloured 'mʌlt i ˌkʌl əd
ˌ·'··· ‖ -ᵊrd -aɪ-
multicultural ˌmʌlt i 'kʌltʃ ᵊr əl ◀ ‖ ˌ·aɪ- **~ism**
ˌɪz əm **~ist/s** ɪst/s §əst/s **~ly** i
multidimensional ˌmʌlt i daɪ 'menʃ ᵊn əl ◀
-i dɪ-, -i də- ‖ -i də-
multidirectional ˌmʌlt i daɪᵊ'rek ʃᵊn əl ◀
-i dɪ-, -i də- ‖ -i də-
multidisciplinary ˌmʌlt i 'dɪs ə plɪn ər i ◀
-'·ɪ-, -'··plən-, -,··'plɪn ər i ◀ ‖ -plə ner i
multifaceted ˌmʌlt i 'fæs ɪt ɪd ◀ -ət-, -əd ◀
‖ -ət̬ əd ◀
multi-faith ˌmʌlt i 'feɪθ ◀
multifamily ˌmʌlt i 'fæm əl i ◀ -ɪl i ◀
multifarious ˌmʌlt i 'feər i əs ◀ ˌ·ə- ‖ -'fer-
-'fær- **~ly** li **~ness** nəs nɪs
multiform 'mʌlt i fɔːm -ə- ‖ -fɔːrm
multiformity ˌmʌlt i 'fɔːm ət i ˌ·ə-, -ɪt i
‖ -'fɔːrm ət̬ i
multifunction ˌmʌlt i 'fʌŋkʃᵊn ◀ **~al** ᵊl ◀
multigrav|ida ˌmʌlt i 'græv ˌɪd ə -bə ə ◀ **~idae**
ɪ diː ə-
multilateral ˌmʌlt i 'læt ᵊr əl ◀ ‖ -'læt̬ ər əl ◀
→-'lætr əl ◀ **~ly** i
ˌmulti,lateral 'trade
multilevel ˌmʌlt i 'lev ᵊl ◀
multilingual ˌmʌlt i 'lɪŋ gwəl ◀ -'lɪŋ gju əl
‖ ˌ·aɪ- **~ism** ɪz əm **~ly** i
ˌmulti,lingual 'secretary

multimedia ˌmʌlt i 'miːd i ə ‖ ˌ-aɪ-
multimillion ˌmʌlt i 'mɪl jən ◂
multimillionaire ˌmʌlt i ˌmɪl jə 'neə ‖ -'ne²r
ˌ·aɪ-, -'næ²r; ··'··· ~s z
multinational ˌmʌlt i 'næʃ ²n_əl ◂ ‖ ˌ·aɪ- ~s z
multip|ara mʌl 'tɪp |ər ə ~arae ə riː ~arous
ər əs
multiparty ˌmʌlt i 'paːt i ◂ ‖ -'paːrt̮ i ◂
multi-player ˌmʌlt i 'pleɪ ə ◂ ‖ -²r ◂
multiple 'mʌlt ɪp ²l -əp- ~s z
  ˌmultiple scle'rosis
multiple-choice ˌmʌlt ɪp ²l 'tʃɔɪs ˌ-əp-
  ˌmultiple-'choice ˌquestion
multiplex 'mʌlt ɪ pleks -ə-, -i- ~ed t ~es ɪz əz
  ~ing ɪŋ
multiplexer, multiplexor 'mʌlt ɪ pleks ə '·ə-
  ‖ -²r ~s z
multiplicand ˌmʌlt ɪ plɪ 'kænd ˌ·ə-, §-plə'· ~s
  z
multiplication ˌmʌlt ɪ plɪ 'keɪʃ ²n ˌ·ə-, §-plə'--
  ~s z
  ˌmultipli'cation sign; ˌmultipli'cation
  ˌtable
multiplicative ˌmʌlt ɪ 'plɪk ət ɪv ˌ·ə-;
  '·· plɪ keɪt ɪv, -plə·· ‖ -'plɪk ət̮ ɪv '·· plə keɪt̮ ɪv
  ~ly li
multiplicit|y ˌmʌlt ɪ 'plɪs ət |i ˌ·ə-, -ɪt ‖ -ət̮ |i
  ~ies iz
multi|ply v 'mʌlt ɪ |plaɪ -ə- ~plied plaɪd
  ~plier/s plaɪ ə/z plaɪ ²r/z ~plies plaɪz
  ~plying plaɪ ɪŋ
multiply adv 'mʌlt əp li -ɪp-
multipolar ˌmʌlt i 'pəʊl ə ◂ ‖ -'poʊl ²r ◂
multipurpose ˌmʌlt i 'pɜːp əs ◂ ‖ -'pɜːp əs ◂
  -aɪ-
multiraci|al ˌmʌlt i 'reɪʃ |²l ◂ ‖ -aɪ- ~alism
  ə ˌlɪz əm ~ally əl i
multiskilling 'mʌlt i ˌskɪl ɪŋ
multistage 'mʌlt i steɪdʒ
multistorey, multistory ˌmʌlt i 'stɔːr i ◂
  ‖ -aɪ-, -'stoʊr-
  ˌmulti ˌstorey 'carpark
multitask 'mʌlt i taːsk §-tæsk, ·'· ‖ -'tæsk
  ~er/s ə/z ‖ ²r/z ~ing ɪŋ
multitude 'mʌlt ɪ tjuːd -ə-, →tʃuːd ‖ -tuːd
  -tjuːd ~s z
multitudinous ˌmʌlt ɪ 'tjuːd ɪn əs ◂ ·ə-,
  →'tʃuːd-, -ən əs ‖ -'tuːd ²n əs -tjuːd- ~ly li
multivitamin 'mʌlt i ˌvɪt əm ɪn -ˌvaɪt-, §-ən
  ‖ -ˌvaɪt̮- ~s z
multum in parvo ˌmʊlt ʊm ɪn 'paːv əʊ
  ˌmʌlt-, ˌ·əm-, →·ɪm'··, §-ən'·- ‖ -'paːrv oʊ
  -'paːr woʊ
mum, Mum mʌm mums, Mum's mʌmz
Mumbai ˌmʊm 'baɪ
mumbl|e 'mʌm b²l ~ed d ~es z ~ing ɪŋ
Mumbles 'mʌm b²lz
mumbling 'mʌm b²l ɪŋ ~ly li
mumbo jumbo ˌmʌm bəʊ 'dʒʌm bəʊ
  ‖ -boʊ 'dʒʌm boʊ
Mumford 'mʌm fəd ‖ -f²rd
Mumm mʌm mʊm
mummer 'mʌm ə ‖ -²r ~s z

Mummerset, m~ 'mʌm ə set ‖ -²r-
mummer|y 'mʌm ər |i ~ies iz
mummie... —see mummy
mummification ˌmʌm ɪf ɪ 'keɪʃ ²n ˌ-əf-, §-ə'--
mummi|fy 'mʌm ɪ |faɪ -ə- ~fied faɪd ~fies
  faɪz ~fying faɪ ɪŋ
mumming 'mʌm ɪŋ
mumm|y, M~ 'mʌm |i ~ies, ~y's iz
mumpish 'mʌmp ɪʃ ~ly li ~ness nəs nɪs
mumps mʌmps
mumsy, Mumsy 'mʌmz i
mum-to-be ˌmʌm tə 'biː
Muncaster 'mʌŋk əst ə §'mʌŋ ˌkaːst ə, §-ˌkæst-
  ‖ 'mʌn ˌkæst ²r
munch mʌntʃ munched mʌntʃt munches
  'mʌntʃ ɪz -əz munching 'mʌntʃ ɪŋ
Munch mʊŋk —Norwegian [mʉŋk]
Munchausen, Munchhausen,
  Münchhausen 'mʌntʃ aʊz ²n 'mʊntʃ-,
  -haʊz-; mʌn 'tʃɔːz ²n —Ger ['mʏnç hau z²n]
munchies, M~ 'mʌntʃ iz
munchkin, M~ 'mʌntʃ kɪn ~s z
Muncie 'mʌn²s i
Munda 'mʊnd ə
mundane ˌ(ˌ)mʌn 'deɪn '·· ~ly li ~ness nəs nɪs
Munday 'mʌn deɪ
Mundesley 'mʌnz li
mung mʌŋ munged mʌŋd munging 'mʌŋ ɪŋ
  mungs mʌŋz
Mungo, mungo 'mʌŋ gəʊ ‖ -goʊ
Munich 'mjuːn ɪk -ɪx —Ger München
  ['mʏn çən]
municipal mju 'nɪs ɪp ²l -əp-; §ˌmjuːn ɪ 'sɪp-,
  -ə- ~ly li
municipalis... —see municipaliz...
municipalit|y mju ˌnɪs ɪ 'pæl ət |i ˌmjuːn ɪs-,
  -ə'··, -ət i ‖ -ət̮ |i ~ies iz
municipalization mju ˌnɪs ɪp əl aɪ 'zeɪʃ ²n
  -ˌ·əp-; §ˌmjuːn ɪ ˌsɪp-, -ə- ‖ -ə'·- ~s z
municipaliz|e mju 'nɪs ɪp ə laɪz -'·əp-;
  §ˌmjuːn ɪ 'sɪp-, -ə- ~ed d ~es ɪz əz ~ing ɪŋ
munificence mju 'nɪf ɪs ən²s -əs-
munificent mju 'nɪf ɪs ənt -əs- ~ly li
muniment 'mjuːn ɪ mənt -ə- ~s s
munition mju 'nɪʃ ²n ~s z
Munn mʌn
Munro, Munroe, Munrow mən 'rəʊ mʌn-
  ‖ -'roʊ
Munsell 'mʌn²s ²l
Munster, Münster place in Germany
  'mʊn²st ə ‖ -²r —Ger ['mʏn stɐ]
Munster province of Ireland 'mʌn²st ə ‖ -²r
munt mʊnt munts mʊnts
muntjac, muntjak 'mʌnt dʒæk 'mʌntʃ æk ~s
  s
Muntz mʌnts
muon 'mjuː ɒn ‖ -aːn ~s z
muppet, M~ 'mʌp ɪt §-ət ~s s
muraena mju² 'riːn ə ~s z
mural 'mjʊər əl 'mjɔːr- ‖ 'mjʊr əl ~s z
Murchison (i) 'mɜːtʃ ɪs ən §-əs- ‖ 'mɜːtʃ-,
  (ii) 'mɜːk- ‖ 'mɜːk-

M

Murcia 'mɜːθ i ə 'mʊəθ- ‖ 'mɜːs- —*Sp*
['mur θja]
murder 'mɜːd ə ‖ 'mɜːd ᵊr ~ed d **murdering**
'mɜːd ᵊr ɪŋ ‖ 'mɜːd ᵊr ɪŋ ~s z
murderer 'mɜːd ᵊr ə ‖ 'mɜːd ər ᵊr ~s z
murderess 'mɜːd ə res -ər ɪs, -ər əs;
ˌmɜːd ə 'res ‖ 'mɜːd ər əs ~es ɪz əz
murderous 'mɜːd ᵊr əs ‖ 'mɜːd ˌ ~ly li ~ness
nəs nɪs
Murdo 'mɜːd əʊ ‖ 'mɜːd oʊ
Murdoch 'mɜːd ɒk -əx ‖ 'mɜːd ɑːk
Murdock 'mɜːd ɒk ‖ 'mɜːd ɑːk
murex 'mjʊər eks 'mjɔːr- ‖ 'mjʊr- ~es ɪz əz
Murfin 'mɜːf ɪn §-ᵊn ‖ 'mɜːf-
Murfreesboro 'mɜːf riz ˌbʌr ə
‖ 'mɜːf riz ˌbɜː oʊ -iz-, -ə
Murgatroyd 'mɜːg ə trɔɪd ‖ 'mɜːg-
Muriel 'mjʊər i əl 'mjɔːr- ‖ 'mjʊr-
Murillo mjuᵊ 'rɪl əʊ -jəʊ ‖ -oʊ —*Sp* [mu 'ri ʎo,
-jo]
murine 'mjʊər aɪn -ɪn, §-ən ‖ 'mjʊr-
murk mɜːk ‖ mɜːk
murk|y 'mɜːk |i ‖ 'mɜːk |i ~ier i ə ‖ i ᵊr ~iest
i ɪst i əst ~ily ɪ li əl i ~iness i nəs i nɪs
Murmansk mɜː 'mænˢsk mə- ‖ mʊr 'mɑːnˢsk
'·· —*Russ* ['mur mənsk]
murmur 'mɜːm ə ‖ 'mɜːm ᵊr ~ed d
murmuring/ly 'mɜːm ər ɪŋ /li
‖ 'mɜːm ər ɪŋ /li ~s z
Murph|y, murph|y 'mɜːf |i ‖ 'mɜːf |i ~ies,
~y's iz
'Murphy's Law, ·· ·.
murrain 'mʌr ɪn -ən, -eɪn ‖ 'mɜː ən ~s z
Murray 'mʌr i -eɪ ‖ 'mɜː i
Murrayfield 'mʌr i fiːᵊld ‖ 'mɜː-
murre mɜː ‖ mɜː (= *myrrh*) **murres** mɜːz
‖ mɜːz
Murrell (*i*) 'mʌr əl ‖ 'mɜː ˌəl, (*ii*) mʌ 'rel mə-
Murrow 'mʌr əʊ ‖ 'mɜː oʊ
Murrumbidgee ˌmʌr əm 'bɪdʒ i ‖ ˌmɜː əm-
Mururoa ˌmʊr ə 'rəʊ ə ‖ ˌmu: ru: 'roʊ ə
musaceous mju 'zeɪʃ əs
Muscadet, m~ 'mʌsk ə deɪ ˌ·'· —*Fr*
[my ska de] ~s z
muscadine 'mʌsk ə daɪn -əd ɪn, -əd ᵊn ~s z
muscae volitantes ˌmʌsk i ˌvɒl ɪ 'tænt iːz
ˌmʊsk-, ˌmʌs-, -ˌaɪ-, -ə'·-, -eɪz ‖ -ˌvɑːl-
muscat 'mʌsk ət -æt ~s s
Muscat 'mʌsk æt mʌ 'skæt —*Arabic*
['mas qatˁ]
muscatel ˌmʌsk ə 'tel ~s z
muscl|e 'mʌs ᵊl (= *mussel*) ~ed d ~es z ~ing
ɪŋ
muscle-bound 'mʌs ᵊl baʊnd
muscle|man 'mʌs ᵊl |mæn ~men men
muscly 'mʌs ᵊl i
muscovado ˌmʌsk ə 'vɑːd əʊ -'veɪd- ‖ -oʊ
Muscovite, m~ 'mʌsk ə vaɪt ~s s
Muscovy 'mʌsk əv i
muscular 'mʌsk jʊl ə -jəl- ‖ -jəl ᵊr ~ly li
ˌmuscular 'dystrophy
muscularity ˌmʌsk ju 'lær ət i -ɪt i
‖ -jə 'lær ət̬ i -'ler-

musculature 'mʌsk jʊl ətʃ ə '·jəl-, -ə tjʊə
‖ -jəl ə tʃʊr -ətʃ ᵊr ~s z
muse, Muse mjuːz **mused** mjuːzd **muses,**
Muses 'mjuːz ɪz -əz **musing/ly** 'mjuːz ɪŋ /li
musette mju 'zet —*Fr* [my zɛt] ~s s
museum mju 'ziː əm ˌmju:- —*Occasionally also*
-'zeɪ- ~s z
mu'seum piece
Museveni mu 'sev ən i ˌmu:s ə 'veɪn i
Musgrave 'mʌz greɪv
Musgrove 'mʌz grəʊv ‖ -groʊv
mush '*soft mass, porridge*' mʌʃ ‖ mʊʃ
mush '*face; fellow*' mʊʃ
mush '*travel by dog team*'; *interj* mʌʃ **mushed**
mʌʃt **musher/s** 'mʌʃ ə/z ‖ -ᵊr/z **mushes**
'mʌʃ ɪz -əz **mushing** 'mʌʃ ɪŋ
Musharraf mu 'ʃær əf —*Urdu* [mu ʃər əf]
mushroom 'mʌʃ rʊm -ru:m ‖ -ru:m -rʊm, -ru:n,
'mʌʃ ə- ~ed d ~ing ɪŋ ~s z
mush|y 'mʌʃ |i ‖ -mʊʃ- ~ier i ə ‖ i ᵊr ~iest i ɪst
i əst ~ily ɪ li əl i ~iness i nəs i nɪs
music 'mjuːz ɪk
'music box; 'music ˌcenter, 'music ˌcentre;
'music hall; 'music stand
musical 'mjuːz ɪk ᵊl ~ly i ~s z
'musical box; ˌmusical 'chairs; ˌmusical
'instrument
musicale ˌmjuːz ɪ 'kɑːl -'kæl ‖ -'kæl ~s z
musically 'mjuːz ɪk ᵊl i
musicassette ˌmjuːz ɪ kə 'set -kæ'- ~s s
musician mju 'zɪʃ ᵊn ~s z ~ship ʃɪp
musicological ˌmjuːz ɪk ə 'lɒdʒ ɪk ᵊl ◀ -ək-
‖ -'lɑːdʒ- ~ly i
musicolog|ist ˌmjuːz ɪ 'kɒl ədʒ |ɪst ˌ-ə-, §-əst
‖ -'kɑːl- ~ists ɪsts §əsts ~y i
musique concrète mju ˌziːk kɒŋ 'kret
‖ -koʊŋ- -kɔːŋ-, -kɑːŋ- —*Fr* [my zik kɔ̃ kʁɛt]
musk mʌsk
'musk deer
muskeg 'mʌsk eg -eɪg
muskellung|e 'mʌsk ə lʌndʒ ~es ɪz əz
musket 'mʌsk ɪt -ət ~s s
musketeer ˌmʌsk ə 'tɪə -ɪ- ‖ -'tɪᵊr ~s z
musketry 'mʌsk ɪtr i -ətr-
Muskie 'mʌsk i
muskmelon 'mʌsk ˌmel ən ~s z
Muskogean mʌ 'skəʊg i ən ‖ -'skoʊg-
Muskogee mʌ 'skəʊg i ‖ -'skoʊg i ~s z
muskrat 'mʌsk ræt ~s s
musk|y 'mʌsk |i ~ier i ə ‖ i ᵊr ~iest i ɪst i əst
~iness i nəs i nɪs
Muslim 'mʊz lɪm 'mʌz-, 'mʊs-, -ləm ‖ 'muːz-,
'muːs-, 'mʌs- — *Preference poll, BrE:* 'mʊ-
70%, 'mʌ- *30%,* -z- *89%,* -s- *11%,* -lɪm *91%,*
-ləm *9%.* ~s z
muslin 'mʌz lɪn -lən ~s z
muso 'mjuːz əʊ ‖ -oʊ ~s z
musquash 'mʌsk wɒʃ ‖ -wɑːʃ -wɔːʃ ~es ɪz əz
muss mʌs **mussed** mʌst (= *must*) **musses**
'mʌs ɪz -əz **mussing** 'mʌs ɪŋ
mussel 'mʌs ᵊl ~s z
Musselburgh 'mʌs ᵊl bər ə -ˌbʌr ə ‖ -ˌbɜː oʊ

M

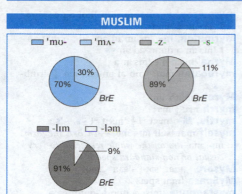

MUSLIM

◻ 'mʊ- ◻ 'mʌ- ◼ -z- ◻ -s-

30%
70%
BrE

89%
11%
BrE

◼ -lɪm ◻ -ləm

91%
9%
BrE

Mussolini ˌmʊs ə 'liːn i ˌmʌs- ‖ ˌmuːs- —*It* [mus so 'liː ni]

Mussorgsky mu 'sɔːg ski mə-, -'zɔːg- ‖ -'sɔːrg- -'zɔːrg- —*Russ* ['mu sərk skʰɪj]

must *strong form* mʌst, *weak forms* məst, məs

mustach|e mə 'stɑːʃ mʊ-, §-'stæʃ, §-'stʊʃ ‖ 'mʌst æʃ mə 'stæʃ **~ed** t **~es** ɪz əz

mustachio mə 'stɑːʃ i əʊ -'stæʃ- ‖ -i oʊ **~ed** d **~s** z

Mustafa 'mʊst əf ə 'mʌst-, -ə fɑː; mu 'stɑːf ə, mə-

mustang 'mʌst æŋ **~s** z

Mustapha 'mʊst əf ə 'mʌst-, -ə fɑː; mu 'stɑːf ə, mə-

mustard 'mʌst əd ‖ -ᵊrd **~s** z
'mustard gas; 'mustard ˌplaster

muster 'mʌst ə ‖ -ᵊr **~ed** d **mustering** 'mʌst ər ɪŋ →'mʌs trɪŋ **~s** z

musth mʌst

musti... —*see* **musty**

Mustique mu 'stiːk

mustn't 'mʌs ᵊnt →-ᵊn

must-see ˌmʌst 'siː ◂ **~s** z

must|y 'mʌst |i **~ier** i ə ‖ i ᵊr **~iest** i ɪst i əst **~ily** ɪ li əl i **~iness** i nəs i nɪs

mutability ˌmjuːt ə 'bɪl ət i -ɪt i ‖ ˌmjuːt̬ ə 'bɪl ət̬ i

mutab|le 'mjuːt əb |ᵊl ‖ 'mjuːt̬- **~leness** ᵊl nəs -nɪs **~ly** li

mutagen 'mjuːt ədʒ ən -ə dʒen ‖ 'mjuːt̬- **~s** z

mutagenic ˌmjuːt ə 'dʒen ɪk ◂ ‖ ˌmjuːt̬- **~ally** ᵊl i

mutagenicity ˌmjuːt ə dʒe 'nɪs ət i -ɪt i ‖ ˌmjuːt̬ ədʒ ə 'nɪs ət̬ i

mutant 'mjuːt ᵊnt **~s** s

mutate mju '|teɪt ‖ 'mjuː|t eɪt **~tated** teɪt ɪd -əd ‖ teɪt̬ əd **~tates** teɪts **~tating** teɪt ɪŋ ‖ teɪt̬ ɪŋ

mutation mju 'teɪʃ ᵊn **~s** z

mutatis mutandis mu ˌtɑːt ɪs mu 'tænd ɪs mju-, -ˌteɪt-, -ˌiːs-, -ˌmjuː'--, -iːs ‖ -'tɑːnd-

Mutch, mutch mʌtʃ **mutches** 'mʌtʃ ɪz -əz

mute mjuːt **muted** 'mjuːt ɪd -əd ‖ 'mjuːt̬ əd **mutely** 'mjuːt li **muteness** 'mjuːt nəs -nɪs

muter 'mjuːt ə ‖ 'mjuːt̬ ᵊr **mutes** mjuːts

mutest 'mjuːt ɪst -əst ‖ 'mjuːt̬ əst **muting** 'mjuːt ɪŋ ‖ 'mjuːt̬ ɪŋ

muti|late 'mjuːt ɪ |leɪt -ə-, -ᵊl eɪt ‖ 'mjuːt̬ ᵊl eɪt **~lated** leɪt ɪd -əd ‖ leɪt̬ əd **~lates** leɪts **~lating** leɪt ɪŋ ‖ leɪt̬ ɪŋ

mutilation ˌmjuːt ɪ 'leɪʃ ᵊn -ə-, -ᵊl 'eɪʃ- ‖ ˌmjuːt̬ ᵊl 'eɪʃ ᵊn **~s** z

mutineer ˌmjuːt ɪ 'nɪə -ə-, -ᵊn 'ɪə ‖ ˌmjuːt̬ ᵊn 'ɪᵊr **~s** z

mutini... —*see* **mutiny**

mutinous 'mjuːt ɪn əs -ən- ‖ -ᵊn̩ əs **~ly** li **~ness** nəs nɪs

mutin|y 'mjuːt ən |i -ɪn- ‖ -ᵊn |i **~ied** id **~ies** iz **~ying** i ɪŋ

mutism 'mjuːt ˌɪz əm ‖ 'mjuːt̬-

mutt mʌt **mutts** mʌts

mutter, M~ 'mʌt ə ‖ 'mʌt̬ ᵊr **~ed** d **muttering/ly** 'mʌt ər ɪŋ /li ‖ 'mʌt̬ ər ɪŋ /li →'mʌtr ɪŋ /li **~s** z

mutterer 'mʌt ər ə ‖ 'mʌt̬ ər ᵊr **~s** z

mutton 'mʌt ᵊn

muttonchop ˌmʌt ᵊn 'tʃɒp ◂ ‖ ˌmʌt̬ ᵊn tʃɑːp **~s** s
ˌmuttonchop 'whiskers

muttonhead 'mʌt ᵊn hed **~s** z

mutual 'mjuːtʃ u əl 'mjuːt ju; 'mjuːtʃ ᵊl **~ly** i **~s** z
'mutual fund

mutuality ˌmjuːtʃ u 'æl ət i ˌmjuːt ju-, -ɪt i ‖ -ət̬ i

muu-muu 'muː muː **~s** z

Muxworthy 'mʌks ˌwɜːð i ‖ -ˌwɜːð i

Muybridge 'maɪ brɪdʒ

muzak, Muzak *tdmk* 'mjuːz æk

muzz mʌz **muzzed** mʌzd **muzzes** 'mʌz ɪz -əz **muzzing** 'mʌz ɪŋ

muzzl|e 'mʌz ᵊl **~ed** d **~es** z **~ing** ɪŋ

muzzle-loader 'mʌz ᵊl ˌləʊd ə ‖ -ˌloʊd ᵊr **~s** z

muzz|y 'mʌz |i **~ier** i ə ‖ i ᵊr **~iest** i ɪst i əst **~ily** ɪ li əl i **~iness** i nəs i nɪs

mwa, mwah mwɑː mwʌ

my maɪ —*There are also weak forms* mi, mə, *found mainly in British regional (non-RP) speech (where it may be shown in spelling as* me*), but also sometimes, mainly in set phrases, in casual RP. Otherwise, there is no distinct weak form.*

myalgia maɪ 'ældʒ ə -i ə

myalgic maɪ 'ældʒ ɪk

myall, Myall 'maɪ ɔːl ‖ -ɑːl **~s** z

Myanmar 'miː ən mɑː →-əm-; mi 'æn mɑː ‖ -mɑːr mi ˌɑːn 'mɑːr

myasthenia ˌmaɪ əs 'θiːn i ə

myasthenic ˌmaɪ əs 'θen ɪk ◂

myceli|um maɪ 'siːl i ˌ|əm **~a** ə

mycella maɪ 'sel ə

Mycenae maɪ 'siːn i -iː

Mycenaean ˌmaɪs ə 'niː ən ◂ -ɪ-, -iː- **~s** z

myco- *comb. form*
with stress-neutral suffix ˌmaɪk əʊ ‖ -ə
— **mycotoxin** ˌmaɪk əʊ 'tɒks ɪn §-ᵊn ‖ -ə 'tɑːks ᵊn

mycology continued

with stress-imposing suffix maɪ ˈkɒ + ‖ -ˈkɑː +
— **mycologist** maɪ ˈkɒl ədʒ ɪst §-əst ‖ -ˈkɑːl-
mycology maɪ ˈkɒl ədʒ i ‖ -ˈkɑːl-
mycosis maɪ ˈkəʊs ɪs §-əs ‖ -ˈkoʊs əs
mydriasis mɪ ˈdraɪ əs ɪs mə-, §-əs
mydriatic ˌmɪdr i ˈæt ɪk ‖ -ˈæt̬ ɪk **~s** s
myelin ˈmaɪ əl ɪn -ɪl-, §-ən
  ˌmyelin ˈsheath
myelitis ˌmaɪ ə ˈlaɪt ɪs -ɪ-, §-əs ‖ -ˈlaɪt̬ əs
myelo- *comb. form*
  with stress-neutral suffix ˌmaɪ əl əʊ maɪ ˌel əʊ
  ‖ ˌmaɪ əl ə — **myelogram** ˈmaɪ əl əʊ græm
  maɪ ˈel- ‖ ˈmaɪ əl ə-
  with stress-imposing suffix ˌmaɪ ə ˈlɒ +
  ‖ -ˈlɑː + — **myelography** ˌmaɪ ə ˈlɒg rəf i
  ‖ -ˈlɑːg-
myeloid ˈmaɪ ə lɔɪd
myelom|a ˌmaɪ ə ˈləʊm |ə ‖ -ˈloʊm |ə **~as** əz
  ~ata ət ə ‖ ət̬ ə
Myer ˈmaɪ ə ‖ ˈmaɪ ᵊr
Myers ˈmaɪ əz ‖ ˈmaɪ ᵊrz
Myfanwy mə ˈvæn wi mɪ-, -ˈfæn- — *Welsh*
  [mə ˈvan wi, -ˈva nui]
Mykonos ˈmiːk ə nɒs ‖ -nɑːs -noʊs, -nɔːs
  — *ModGk* [ˈmi kɔ nɔs]
mylar, Mylar *tdmk* ˈmaɪl ɑː ‖ -ɑːr
Myleene ˈmaɪl iːn
Myles maɪᵊlz
mylonite ˈmaɪl ə naɪt ˈmɪl-
myna, mynah ˈmaɪn ə **~s** z
  ˈmynah bird
Mynd mɪnd
Mynett, Mynott ˈmaɪn ət
myo- *comb. form*
  with stress-neutral suffix ˌmaɪ əʊ ‖ -ə
  — **myocardial** ˌmaɪ əʊ ˈkɑːd i əl ◂
  ‖ -ə ˈkɑːrd-
  with stress-imposing suffix maɪ ˈɒ + ‖ -ˈɑː +
  — **myopathy** maɪ ˈɒp əθ i ‖ -ˈɑːp-
myocardiogram ˌmaɪ əʊ ˈkɑːd i‿ə græm
  ‖ -ə ˈkɑːrd- **~s** z
myoclonic ˌmaɪ əʊ ˈklɒn ɪk ◂ ‖ -ə ˈklɑːn ɪk ◂
  ˌmyo ˌclonic ˈspasm
myoelastic ˌmaɪ əʊ ɪ ˈlæst ɪk ◂ -ə'--, -ˈlɑːst-
  ‖ ˌmaɪ oʊ-
myope ˈmaɪ əʊp ‖ -oʊp **~s** s
myopia maɪ ˈəʊp i‿ə ‖ -ˈoʊp-
myopic maɪ ˈɒp ɪk -ˈəʊp- ‖ -ˈɑːp ɪk -ˈoʊp- **~ally**
  ᵊl i
myosin ˈmaɪ əʊ sɪn -əs ɪn ‖ -əs ən
myosotis ˌmaɪ ə ˈsəʊt ɪs §-əs ‖ -ˈsoʊt̬ əs
Myra ˈmaɪ ᵊr ə
myriad ˈmɪr i əd **~s** z
myriapod ˈmɪr i ə pɒd ‖ -pɑːd **~s** z

myrmecophagous ˌmɜːm ɪ ˈkɒf əg əs ◂ ˌ-ə-
  ‖ ˌmɜːm ə ˈkɑːf-
Myrmidon, m~ ˈmɜːm ɪd ən -əd-; -ɪ dɒn, -ə-
  ‖ ˈmɜːm ə dɑːn -əd ən **~s** z
Myrna ˈmɜːn ə ‖ ˈmɜːn ə
myrobalan maɪ ᵊ ˈrɒb əl ən mɪ-, mə- ‖ -ˈrɑːb-
  ~s z
Myron ˈmaɪ ᵊr ən
myrrh mɜː ‖ mɜː
myrtle, M~ ˈmɜːt ᵊl ‖ ˈmɜːt̬ ᵊl **~s, ~'s** z
myself maɪ ˈself mɪ-, mə- — *In BrE the forms*
  mɪ-, mə- *are on the whole restricted to very*
  casual or non-standard speech.
Mysore ₍ᵢ₎maɪ ˈsɔː ‖ -ˈsɔːr -ˈsoʊr
MySpace ˈmaɪ speɪs
mystagogue ˈmɪst ə gɒg ‖ -gɑːg -gɔːg
mysterious mɪ ˈstɪər i‿əs mə- ‖ -ˈstɪr- **~ly** li
  ~ness nəs nɪs
myster|y ˈmɪs tr|i ˈmɪst ər |i **~ies** iz
  ˈmystery play; ˈmystery tour
mystic, M~ ˈmɪst ɪk **~s** s
mystical ˈmɪst ɪk ᵊl **~ly** ‿i **~ness** nəs nɪs
mysticism ˈmɪst ɪ ˌsɪz əm -ə-
mystification ˌmɪst ɪf ɪ ˈkeɪʃ ᵊn ˌ-əf-, §-ə'-- **~s**
  z
mysti|fy ˈmɪst ɪ |faɪ -ə- **~fied** faɪd **~fier/s**
  faɪ ə/z ‖ faɪ ᵊr/z **~fies** faɪz **~fying** faɪ ɪŋ
mystique mɪ ˈstiːk ˌmɪs ˈtiːk **~s** s
myth mɪθ **myths** mɪθs
mythic ˈmɪθ ɪk **~al** ᵊl **~ally** ᵊl i
mytho- *comb. form*
  with stress-neutral suffix ˌmɪθ əʊ ‖ -ə
  — **mythopoeic** ˌmɪθ əʊ ˈpiː ɪk ◂ ‖ -ə-
  with stress-imposing suffix mɪ ˈθɒ + mə-, maɪ-
  ‖ -ˈθɑː + — **mythography** mɪ ˈθɒg rəf i mə-,
  maɪ- ‖ -ˈθɑːg-
Mytholmroyd ˌmaɪð əm ˈrɔɪd
mythological ˌmɪθ ə ˈlɒdʒ ɪk ᵊl ◂ ˌmaɪθ-
  ‖ -ˈlɑːdʒ- **~ly** ‿i
mythologist mɪ ˈθɒl ədʒ ɪst mə-, maɪ-, §-əst
  ‖ -ˈθɑːl- **~s** s
mytholog|y mɪ ˈθɒl ədʒ |i mə-, maɪ- ‖ -ˈθɑːl-
  ~ies iz
mytho|poeia ˌmɪθ əʊ |ˈpiːˌə ‖ -ə- **~poeic**
  ˈpiː ɪk ◂
Mytilene ˌmɪt ɪ ˈliːn i -ə-, -ᵊl ˈiːn-, -iː
  ‖ ˌmɪt̬ ᵊl ˈiːn i
Mytton ˈmɪt ᵊn
myxedema, myxoedema ˌmɪks i ˈdiːm ə §-ə-
myxomatosis ˌmɪks əm ə ˈtəʊs ɪs §-əs
  ‖ -ˈtoʊs əs
myxomycete ˌmɪks əʊ maɪ ˈsiːt ˌ·ˈ·· ‖ ˌ·oʊ- **~s**
  s
myxovirus ˈmɪks əʊ ˌvaɪ ᵊr əs ˌ·ˈ·· ‖ -ə- **~es** ɪz
  əz

M

Nn

n Spelling-to-sound

1 Where the spelling is **n**, the pronunciation is regularly n as in **nation** ˈneɪʃ ᵊn or ŋ as in **think** θɪŋk. **n** also forms part of the digraph **ng**.

2 The pronunciation is n everywhere *except*
- before the sound k (written **c**, **g**, **k**, **q**, **x**), and
- where the spelling is the digraph **ng** (see **ng** 2, 3 below),

in which cases the pronunciation is regularly ŋ.
Examples:
n in **net** net, **fan** fæn, **unit** ˈjuːn ɪt, **enter** ˈent ə ‖ ˈent ᵊr
ŋ in **uncle** ˈʌŋk ᵊl, **anger** ˈæŋ gə ‖ ˈæŋ gᵊr, **thanks** θæŋks,
conquer ˈkɒŋ kə ‖ ˈkɑːŋ kᵊr, **anxious** ˈæŋkʃ əs, **win** wɪŋ.

3 Where the spelling is double **nn**, the pronunciation is again regularly n as in **funny** ˈfʌn i.

4 **n** is silent when it follows **m** at the end of a word, and in the corresponding inflected forms as in **column** ˈkɒl əm ‖ ˈkɑːl əm, **condemned** kən ˈdemd (but **hymnal** ˈhɪm nəl).

ng Spelling-to-sound

1 Where the spelling is the digraph **ng**, the pronunciation is regularly
ŋ as in **singing** ˈsɪŋ ɪŋ
ŋg as in **angle** ˈæŋ gᵊl or
ndʒ as in **strange** streɪndʒ.

2 The pronunciation is ŋ when **ng** is at the end of a word or stem. Examples: **hang** hæŋ, **singer** ˈsɪŋ ə ‖ ˈsɪŋ ᵊr, **strongly** ˈstrɒŋ li ‖ ˈstrɔːŋ li. (Although in this position plain ŋ is standard in RP and GenAm, some speakers use ŋg.)

3 The pronunciation is usually ŋg when **ng** is in the middle of a word (and not at the end of a stem). Examples: **hungry** ˈhʌŋ gri, **finger** ˈfɪŋ gə ‖ ˈfɪŋ gᵊr, **single** ˈsɪŋ gᵊl.

4 The pronunciation is ndʒ
where the spelling is **nge** at the end of a word as in **challenge** ˈtʃæl ɪndʒ,
and sometimes before **e**, **i**, **y** in the middle of a word as in **danger** ˈdeɪndʒ ə ‖ ˈdeɪndʒ ᵊr.

5 The three pronunciations corresponding to the spelling **ng** are illustrated in the same context in the sets

singer ˈsɪŋ ə ‖ -ᵊr

finger ˈfɪŋ gə ‖ -gᵊr

ginger ˈdʒɪndʒ ə ‖ -ᵊr

hanger ˈhæŋ ə ‖ -ᵊr

anger ˈæŋ gə ‖ -gᵊr

danger ˈdeɪndʒ ə ‖ -ᵊr.

6 Where **n** belongs to a prefix and **g** to a stem, they do not form a digraph. Consequently, the pronunciation is usually n as in **ingenious** ɪn ˈdʒiːn i_əs. However, where the **g** is hard, then the n may become ŋ by ASSIMILATION. This is regular where the syllable containing the nasal is stressed as in **congress** ˈkɒŋ gres ‖ ˈkɑːŋ grəs, and otherwise optional as in **conclusion** kən ˈkluːʒ ᵊn → kəŋ-. (The assimilation seems to be usually made in BrE but rarely in AmE.)

N, n en **N's, n's, Ns** enz *Communications code name:* November

N —*see* **North, northerly, Northern**

'n, 'n' *conventional spelling for the weak form of* **and** ən, ən, ᵊn
  ˌfish 'n' 'chips

Naafi, NAAFI ˈnæf i

naan nɑːn næn

Naas *place in Co. Kildare* neɪs

nab næb **nabbed** næbd **nabbing** ˈnæb ɪŋ
  nabs næbz

Nabarro nə ˈbɑːr əʊ ‖ -oʊ

Nabataean, Nabatean ˌnæb ə ˈtiː ən ◂ ~s z

nabb... —*see* **nab**

Nabbs næbz

Nabisco *tdmk* nə ˈbɪsk əʊ næ- ‖ -oʊ

Nablus ˈnɑːb ləs ˈnæb-, -lʊs

nabob ˈneɪb ɒb ‖ -ɑːb ~s z

Nabokov nə ˈbəʊk ɒf ˈnæb ə kɒf ‖ -ˈbɔːk əf
  -ˈbɑːk-; ˌnæb ə kɑːf, ˈnɑːb-, -kɔːf

Naboth ˈneɪb ɒθ ‖ -ɑːθ -oʊθ

Nabucco nə ˈbuːk əʊ ‖ -oʊ —*It* [na ˈbuk ko]

nacelle nə ˈsel næ- ~s z

nacho ˈnɑːtʃ əʊ ‖ -oʊ ~s z

Nacogdoches *place in TX* ˌnæk ə ˈdəʊtʃ ɪz -əz
  ‖ -ˈdoʊtʃ əz

nacre ˈneɪk ə ‖ -ᵊr

nacreous ˈneɪk ri_əs

NACRO ˈnæk rəʊ ‖ -roʊ

nad næd **nads** nædz

nada ˈnɑːd ə —*Sp* [ˈna ða]

Na-Dene, Na-Déné ˌnɑː ˈdeɪn i -ˈden-, -eɪ;
  -də ˈneɪ; nə ˈdiːn

Nader ˈneɪd ə ‖ -ᵊr

Nadi *place in Fiji* ˈnænd i ˈnɑːnd i —*Fijian*
  [ˈna ndi]

Nadia *(i)* ˈneɪd i_ə, *(ii)* ˈnɑːd i_ə

Nadine neɪ ˈdiːn nə-

nadir ˈneɪd ɪə ˈnæd- ‖ -ɪr -ᵊr ~s z

Nadir næ ˈdɪə ‖ -ˈdɪᵊr

nae neɪ

naev|us ˈniːv |əs ~i aɪ

naff næf **naffer** ˈnæf ə ‖ -ᵊr **naffest** ˈnæf ɪst
  -əst
  ˌnaff 'off

NAFTA ˈnæft ə

nag næg **nagged** nægd **nagger/s** ˈnæg ə/z
  ‖ -ᵊr/z **nagging** ˈnæg ɪŋ **nags** nægz

Naga ˈnɑːg ə ‖ -ɑː ~s z

Nagaland ˈnɑːg ə lænd

nagana nə ˈgɑːn ə

Nagano ˈnæg ə nəʊ ˈnɑːg- ‖ -noʊ nə ˈgɑːn oʊ
  —*Jp* [ˈna ŋa no, -ga-]

Nagari ˈnɑːg ər i

Nagasaki ˌnæg ə ˈsɑːk i ˌnɑːg- ‖ -ˈsæk- —*Jp*
  [na ˈŋa sa ki, -ˈga-]

nagg... —*see* **nag**

Nagorno-Karabakh nə ˌgɔːn əʊ ˌkær ə ˈbæk
  -ˈbɑːk ‖ nə ˌgɔːrn oʊ ˌkɑːr ə ˈbɑːk —*Russ*
  [nə ˌgor nə kə rə ˈbax]

Nagoya nə ˈgɔɪ ə —*Jp* [ˈna ŋo ja, -go-]

Nagpur ˌnæg ˈpʊə ˌnɑːg-, -ˈpɔː ‖ ˌnɑːg ˈpʊᵊr

Nagy nɒdʒ ‖ nɑːdʒ —*Hung* [nɒɟ]

nah *informal, 'no'* næː nʌ ‖ nɑː

Na h-Eileanan an Iar nə ˌhɪl ən ən ən ˈjɪə
  ‖ -ˈjrᵊr

Nahuatl ˈnɑː wɑːt ᵊl ·ˈ·· ~an ᵊn ~s z

Nahum ˈneɪ həm -hʌm, -əm

naiad ˈnaɪ æd ˈnaɪ̩əd **naiades** ˈnaɪ̩ə diːz ~s z

naif, naïf naɪ ˈiːf nɑː-

nail, Nail neɪᵊl **nailed** neɪᵊld **nailing** ˈneɪᵊl ɪŋ
  nails neɪᵊlz
  ˈnail file; ˈnail ˌpolish; ˈnail ˌscissors;
  ˈnail ˌvarnish

nail-bit|er 'neɪᵊl ˌbaɪt |ə ‖ -ˌbaɪt̬ |ᵊr **~ers** əz
‖ ᵊrz **~ing/ly** ɪŋ /li
nailbrush 'neɪᵊl brʌʃ **~es** ɪz əz
nailclipper 'neɪᵊl ˌklɪp ə ‖ -ᵊr **~s** z
nailgun 'neɪᵊl gʌn **~s** z
Nailsea 'neɪᵊl siː
Nailsworth 'neɪᵊlz wəθ -wɜːθ ‖ -wᵊrθ -wɜːθ
Naipaul 'naɪ pɔːl
naira 'naɪᵊr ə
Nairn neən ‖ neᵊrn næᵊrn
Nairobi naɪᵊ 'rəʊb i ‖ -'roʊb i
Naish (i) neɪʃ, (ii) næʃ
Naismith 'neɪ smɪθ
naive, naïve naɪ 'iːv nɑː- **~ly** li **~ness** nəs nɪs
naiveté, naïveté naɪ 'iːv ə teɪ nɑː-; -'iːv teɪ
—Fr [na if te]
naivet|y, naïvet|y naɪ 'iːv ət |i nɑː-, -ɪt-;
-'iːv t|i ‖ -ət̬ |i **~ies** iz
naked 'neɪk ɪd -əd (!) **~ly** li **~ness** nəs nɪs
naker 'neɪk ə 'næk- ‖ -ᵊr **~s** z
Nakhichevan ˌnɑːk ɪ tʃɪ 'vɑːn ˌnæk-, -ˌ-ə-, -tʃə'-,
-'væn —Russ [nə xʲi tʃɪ 'vanʲ]
NALGO 'nælg əʊ ‖ -oʊ
Nam, 'Nam 'Vietnam' næm nɑːm
Nama 'nɑːm ə ‖ -ɑː **~s** z
Namaland 'nɑːm ə lænd
Namaqualand nə 'mɑːk wə lænd
Namath 'neɪm əθ
namby-pam|by ˌnæm bi 'pæm |bi ◂ **~bies**
biz
name neɪm **named** neɪmd **names** neɪmz
naming 'neɪm ɪŋ
'name day
name-calling 'neɪm ˌkɔːl ɪŋ ‖ -ˌkɑːl-
name-check 'neɪm tʃek **~ing** ɪŋ
namedrop 'neɪm drɒp **~ped** t **~per/s**
ə/z ‖ ᵊr/z **~ping** ɪŋ **~s** s
nameless 'neɪm ləs -lɪs **~ly** li **~ness** nəs nɪs
namely 'neɪm li
nameplate 'neɪm pleɪt **~s** s
namesake 'neɪm seɪk **~s** s
nametag 'neɪm tæg **~s** z
name-tape 'neɪm teɪp **~s** s
Namib 'nɑːm ɪb
Namibi|a nə 'mɪb i ̩|ə **~an/s** ən/z
Namier 'neɪm ɪə 'neɪm i ̩ə ‖ -ɪr
Namur næ 'mjʊə -'mʊə ‖ nə 'mjʊᵊr -'mʊᵊr
—Fr [na my:ʁ]
nan 'bread' 'nɑːn næn
nan 'grandmother', **Nan** personal name næn
nans, Nan's nænz
Nanaimo nə 'naɪm əʊ næ- ‖ -oʊ
Nanak 'nɑːn ək
Nancarrow næn 'kær əʊ →næŋ- ‖ -oʊ -'ker-
Nance, nance nænᵗs
Nanchang ˌnæn 'tʃæŋ ◂ ‖ ˌnɑːn 'tʃɑːŋ ◂ Chi
Nánchǎng [¹nan ³tʃaŋ]
Nanci, Nancie, Nancy personal name, **n~**
'nænᵗs i
Nancy place in France ˌnɒ̃ 'siː ˌnɑːn-, '˖ — Fr
[nɑ̃ si]
NAND nænd
'NAND gate

Nandi place in Fiji, properly Nadi 'nænd i
'nɑːnd i
nandina næn 'diːn ə **~s** z
nandrolone 'nændr ə ləʊn ‖ -loʊn
Nanette næ 'net nə-
nang næŋ
nan Gàidheal nən 'geɪᵊl
Nanga Parbat ˌnʌŋ gə 'pɜːb ət ˌnæŋ-, -'pɑːb-,
-æt ‖ -'pɜːrb- -'pɑːrb-
Nanjing ˌnæn 'dʒɪŋ ‖ nɑːn- —Chi Nánjīng
[²nan ¹tɕiŋ]
nankeen ₍ᵢ₎næn 'kiːn ◂ →næŋ-
ˌnankeen 'kestrel
Nanking ˌnæn 'kɪŋ ◂ →ˌnæŋ- ‖ ˌnɑːn- —Chi
Nánjīng [²nan ¹tɕiŋ]
nanna 'næn ə **~s** z
Nannie 'næn i
Nanning ˌnæn 'nɪŋ ◂ ‖ ˌnɑːn- —Chi Nánníng
[²nan ²niŋ]
nann|y, Nann|y 'næn |i **~ies, ~y's** iz
'nanny goat
nannygai 'næn i gaɪ **~s** z
nano 'nɑːn əʊ ‖ -oʊ
nano- ˌnæn əʊ ‖ -ə — **nanosecond**
'næn əʊ ˌsek ənd →-ŋd ‖ -ə-
nanotechnology ˌnæn əʊ tek 'nɒl ədʒ i
‖ -oʊ tek 'nɑːl-
nanobot 'næn əʊ bɒt ‖ -ə bɑːt **~s** s
nanomachine 'næn əʊ mə ˌʃiːn ‖ -oʊ mə- **~s** z
Nanook 'næn uːk -ʊk
nanopublish|er 'næn əʊ ˌpʌb lɪʃ|ə
‖ -oʊ ˌpʌb lɪʃ ᵊr **~ers** əz ‖ ᵊrz **~ing** ɪŋ
nanoscience 'næn əʊ ˌsaɪ ənᵗs ‖ -oʊ-
nanosecond 'næn əʊ ˌsek ənd ‖ -oʊ- **~s** z
Nansen 'nænᵗs ᵊn ‖ 'nɑːnᵗs-
Nant in Welsh place names nænt —Welsh
[nant]
Nantes nɑːnt nænts, nɒnt —Fr [nɑ̃:t]
Nantffrancon nænt 'fræŋk ən —Welsh
[nant 'fraŋ kon]
Nantgarw nænt 'gær uː —Welsh [nant 'ga ru]
Nantucket næn 'tʌk ɪt -ət
Nantwich 'nænt wɪtʃ
Naoise 'niːʃ ə -i
Naomi (i) 'neɪ əm i ‖ -aɪ, (ii) neɪ 'əʊm i
‖ -'oʊm i -aɪ
nap næp **napped** næpt **napping** 'næp ɪŋ **naps**
næps
Napa 'næp ə
ˌNapa 'Valley◂
napalm 'neɪp ɑːm 'næp-, §-ɑːlm **~ed** d **~ing** ɪŋ
~s z
nape neɪp **napes** neɪps
Naphtali 'næft ə laɪ
naphtha 'næfθ ə 'næpθ-
naphthalene 'næfθ ə liːn 'næpθ-
naphthol 'næfθ ɒl 'næpθ- ‖ -ɔːl -ɑːl, -oʊl
Napier 'neɪp i ̩ə ‖ ᵊr —but a few people with
this surname call it nə 'pɪə ‖ -'pɪᵊr
Napierian nə 'pɪər i ̩ən neɪ- ‖ -'pɪr-
napkin 'næp kɪn §-kən **~s** z
'napkin ring
Naples 'neɪp ᵊlz

Napoleon, n~ nə 'pəʊl i‿ən ‖ -'poʊl- **~s, ~'s** z
Napoleonic nə ˌpəʊl i 'ɒn ɪk ◂
‖ nə ˌpoʊl i 'ɑːn ɪk ◂
napolitaine, N~ næ ˌpɒl ɪ 'teɪn nə-, -ə-
‖ -ˌpɑːl- —*Fr* [na pɔ li tɛn]
nappe næp
napp|y 'næp |i **~ies** iz
'nappy rash; 'nappy ˌliner
Napster *tdmk* 'næpst ə ‖ -ᵊr
Nara 'nɑːr ə —*Jp* ['na ɾa]
Narayan nə 'raɪ‿ən
Narbonne ⑴nɑː 'bɒn ‖ ⑴nɑːr 'bɔːn -'bɑːn,
-'bʌn —*Fr* [naʁ bɔn]
narc nɑːk ‖ nɑːrk **narcs** nɑːks ‖ nɑːrks
narciss|i nɑː 'sɪs ǀaɪ -iː ‖ nɑːr- **~ism** ˌɪz əm **~ist**
ɪst §əst
narcissistic ˌnɑːs ɪ 'sɪst ɪk ◂ -ə- ‖ ˌnɑːrs- **~ally**
ᵊl‿i
narciss|us, N~ nɑː 'sɪs ǀəs ‖ nɑːr- **~i** aɪ
narcolepsy 'nɑːk əʊ leps i ‖ 'nɑːrk ə-
narcoleptic ˌnɑːk əʊ 'lept ɪk ◂ ‖ -ə-
narcos|is nɑː 'kəʊs ǀɪs §-əs ‖ nɑːr 'koʊs ǀəs
~es iːz
narcotic nɑː 'kɒt ɪk ‖ nɑːr 'kɑːt̬ ɪk **~ally** ᵊl‿i **~s**
s
narcotis... —*see* **narcotiz...**
narcotism 'nɑːk ə ˌtɪz əm ‖ 'nɑːrk-
narcotiz|e 'nɑːk ə taɪz ‖ 'nɑːrk- **~ed** d **~es** ɪz
əz **~ing** ɪŋ
nard nɑːd ‖ nɑːrd
nardoo ˌnɑː 'duː ‖ ˌnɑːr-
nareal 'neər i‿əl ‖ 'ner- 'nær-
Narelle nə 'rel
nares 'neər iːz ‖ 'ner- 'nær-
narghile, nargile, nargileh 'nɑːg ə leɪ -ɪ-, -li
‖ 'nɑːrg- **~s** z
narial 'neər i‿əl ‖ 'ner- 'nær-
Narita 'nær ɪt ə -ət-; nə 'riːt ə —*Jp* ['na ɾi ta]
nark nɑːk ‖ nɑːrk **narked** nɑːkt ‖ nɑːrkt
narking 'nɑːk ɪŋ ‖ 'nɑːrk ɪŋ **narks** nɑːks
‖ nɑːrks
nark|y 'nɑːk |i ‖ 'nɑːrk |i **~ier** i‿ə ‖ i‿ᵊr **~iest**
i‿ɪst i‿əst
Narnia 'nɑːn i‿ə ‖ 'nɑːrn-
Narraganset, Narrangansett
ˌnær ə 'gænˢs ɪt ◂ -ət ‖ ˌner-
ˌNarraˌgansett 'Bay
Narrandera *place in NSW* nə 'rænd ər ə
narrate nə 'reɪt næ- ‖ 'nær eɪt 'ner-; næ 'reɪt
narrated nə 'reɪt ɪd næ-, -əd ‖ 'nær eɪt̬ əd
'ner-; næ 'reɪt̬- **narrates** nə 'reɪts næ-
‖ 'nær eɪts 'ner-; næ 'reɪts **narrating**
nə 'reɪt ɪŋ næ- ‖ 'nær eɪt̬ ɪŋ 'ner-; næ 'reɪt̬-
narration nə 'reɪʃ ᵊn næ- ‖ næ- **~s** z
narrative 'nær ət ɪv ‖ -ət̬ ɪv 'ner- **~ly** li **~s** z
narrator nə 'reɪt ə næ-; 'nær ət ə ‖ 'nær eɪt̬ ᵊr
'ner-, -ət̬-; næ 'reɪt̬-, nə- **~s** z (*)
narrow 'nær əʊ ‖ -oʊ 'ner- **~ed** d **~er** ə ‖ ᵊr
~est ɪst əst **~ing** ɪŋ **~ly** li **~ness** nəs nɪs **~s** z
'narrow boat; ˌnarrow 'gauge◂, '·· ·;
ˌnarrow 'squeak
narrowband 'nær əʊ bænd ‖ -oʊ-

narrowcast 'nær əʊ kɑːst §-kæst ‖ -oʊ kæst
'ner- **~er/s** ə/z ‖ ᵊr/z **~ing** ɪŋ
narrow-gauge ˌnær əʊ 'geɪdʒ ◂ ‖ -oʊ-
narrow-minded ˌnær əʊ 'maɪnd ɪd ◂ -əd
‖ -oʊ- ˌner- **~ly** li **~ness** nəs nɪs
narthex 'nɑːθ eks ‖ 'nɑːrθ- **~es** ɪz əz
narwhal 'nɑː wəl ‖ 'nɑːr hwɑːl **~s** z
n-ary 'en ər i
nary 'neər i ‖ 'ner i 'nær-
NASA 'næs ə 'nɑːs-
nasal 'neɪz ᵊl **~s** z
nasalis... —*see* **nasaliz...**
nasality neɪ 'zæl ət i -ɪt- ‖ -ət̬ i
nasalization ˌneɪz əl aɪ 'zeɪʃ ᵊn -ɪ- ‖ -əl ə-
~s z
nasaliz|e 'neɪz ə laɪz -ᵊl aɪz **~ed** d **~es** ɪz əz
~ing ɪŋ
nasally 'neɪz ᵊl i
nascent 'næs ᵊnt 'neɪs-
Nasdaq, NASDAQ *tdmk* 'næz dæk
naseberr|y 'neɪz ˌber |i **~ies** iz
Naseby 'neɪz bi
Naseem ⑴næ 'siːm
Nash, Nashe næʃ
Nashua 'næʃ u‿ə
Nashville 'næʃ vɪl -vəl
nasi goreng ˌnɑːs i gə 'reŋ ˌnæs-, ˌnɑːz-,
-'gɒr eŋ, -'gɔːr eŋ —*Bahasa Ind*
[ˌna si 'go reŋ]
nasion 'neɪz i‿ən -ɒn ‖ -ɑːn **~s** z
Nasmyth (*i*) 'neɪs mɪθ (*ii*) 'neɪz- (*iii*) 'næs-
nasofrontal ˌneɪz əʊ 'frʌnt ᵊl ◂
‖ -oʊ 'frʌnt̬ ᵊl ◂
nasopharyngeal ˌneɪz əʊ ˌfær ɪn 'dʒiː əl
-ˌən-; -fə 'rɪndʒ i‿əl, -fæ'- ‖ -oʊ- -ˌfer-
nasopharynx ˌneɪz əʊ ˌfær ɪŋks ·‿·ˈ·· ‖ -oʊ-
-ˌfer- **~es** ɪz əz
Nassau *places in Bahamas and the US* 'næs ɔː
‖ -ɑː
Nassau *region of Germany* 'næs aʊ ‖ 'nɑːs-
—*Ger* ['na saʊ]
Nassau *princely family* 'næs ɔː -aʊ ‖ 'nɑːs aʊ
Nasser 'næs ə 'nɑːs- ‖ -ᵊr —*Arabic* ['nɑː sˤir]
Nastase nə 'stɑːz i næ-, -eɪ
nastic 'næst ɪk
nasturtium nə 'stɜːʃ əm ‖ næ 'stɝːʃ- nə- **~s** z
nast|y 'nɑːst |i §'næst- ‖ 'næst |i **~ier** i‿ə ‖ i‿ᵊr
~ies iz **~iest** i‿ɪst i‿əst **~ily** ɪ li əl i **~iness**
i nəs i nɪs
Nat næt **Nats, Nat's** næts
natal 'neɪt ᵊl ‖ 'neɪt̬ ᵊl
Natal *province of South Africa* nə 'tæl -'tɑːl
Natalie 'næt əl i ‖ 'næt̬ ᵊl i
natalit|y neɪ 'tæl ət i ǀi nə-, -ɪt- ‖ -ət̬ ǀi **~ies** iz
Natasha nə 'tæʃ ə ‖ -'tɑːʃ ə
natch nætʃ
Natchez 'nætʃ ɪz -əz
Natchitoches *place in Louisiana* 'næk ə tɒʃ
-ət əʃ ‖ -ə tɑːʃ -ət̬ əʃ (!)
nates 'neɪt iːz
NATFHE 'næt fi -fiː
Nathan 'neɪθ ᵊn
Nathanael, Nathaniel nə 'θæn i‿əl

Natick 'neɪt ɪk

nation 'neɪʃ ³n ~s z
  ˌnation 'state, ' · · ·

national 'næʃ ³n əl ~s z
  ˌnational 'anthem; ˌnational 'debt;
  ˌNational 'Front; ˌnational 'government;
  ˌNational 'Health ˌService; ˌNational
  In'surance; ˌnational 'park; ˌnational
  'service; ˌNational 'Trust

nationalis... —*see* **nationaliz...**

nationalism 'næʃ ³n əl ˌɪz əm ~s z

nationalist 'næʃ ³n əl ɪst §-əst ~s s

nationalistic ˌnæʃ ³n ə 'lɪst ɪk ◄ əl ˌɪst- ~ally
  ³l i

nationalit|y ˌnæʃ ə 'næl ət |i ˌnæʃ'· · ·, -ɪt i
  ‖ -ət |i ~ies iz

nationalization ˌnæʃ ³n əl aɪ 'zeɪʃ ³n -ɪ'--
  ‖ -ə 'zeɪʃ- ~s z

nationaliz|e 'næʃ ³n ə laɪz əl aɪz ~ed d ~es ɪz
  əz ~ing ɪŋ

nationally 'næʃ ³n əl i

nationhood 'neɪʃ ³n hʊd

nation-state ˌneɪʃ ³n 'steɪt ‖ ' · ·

nationwide, N~ ˌneɪʃ ³n 'waɪd ◄ ' · ·
  ˌnationwide 'broadcast

native 'neɪt ɪv ‖ 'neɪt̬ ɪv ~s z
  ˌNative 'American; ˌnative 'speaker

native-born ˌneɪt ɪv 'bɔːn ◄ ' · · ·
  ‖ ˌneɪt̬ ɪv 'bɔːrn ◄

native|ly 'neɪt ɪv |li ‖ 'neɪt̬ ɪv |li ~ness nəs
  nɪs

nativit|y, N~ nə 'tɪv ət |i -ɪt- ‖ -ət̬ |i neɪ- ~ies
  iz
  na'tivity play

NATO, Nato 'neɪt əʊ ‖ 'neɪt̬ oʊ 'neɪ toʊ

natron 'neɪtr ən -ɒn ‖ -ɑːn

NATSOPA næt 'səʊp ə ‖ -'soʊp ə

natter 'næt ə ‖ 'næt̬ ³r ~ed d **nattering**
  'næt ³r ɪŋ ‖ 'næt̬ ³r ɪŋ ~s z

natterjack 'næt ə dʒæk ‖ 'næt̬ ³r- ~s s

natt|y 'næt |i ‖ 'næt̬ |i ~ier i ə ‖ i ³r ~iest i ɪst
  i əst ~ily ɪ li əl i ~iness i nəs i nɪs

natural 'nætʃ ³r əl ~s z
  ˌnatural 'gas; ˌnatural 'history; ˌnatural
  phi'losophy; ˌnatural 'science; ˌnatural
  se'lection

natural-born ˌnætʃ ³r əl 'bɔːn ◄ ‖ -'bɔːrn ◄

naturalis... —*see* **naturaliz...**

naturalism 'nætʃ ³r ə ˌlɪz əm

naturalist 'nætʃ ³r əl ɪst §-əst ~s s

naturalistic ˌnætʃ ³r ə 'lɪst ɪk ◄ ~ally ³l i

naturalization ˌnætʃ ³r ə laɪ 'zeɪʃ ³n -³r əl aɪ-,
  -³r əl ɪ- ‖ -³r əl ə- ~s z

naturaliz|e 'nætʃ ³r ə laɪz əl aɪz ~ed d ~es ɪz
  əz ~ing ɪŋ

natural|ly 'nætʃ ³r əl |i ~ness nəs nɪs

nature 'neɪtʃ ə ‖ -³r ~d d ~s z
  'nature reˌserve; 'nature ˌstudy

naturism 'neɪtʃ ər ˌɪz əm

naturist 'neɪtʃ ər ɪst §-əst ~s s

naturopath 'neɪtʃ ər əʊ pæθ 'nætʃ- ‖ -ər ə- ~s
  s

naturopathic ˌneɪtʃ ər əʊ 'pæθ ɪk ◄ ˌnætʃ-
  ‖ -ər ə- ~ally ³l i

naturopathy ˌneɪtʃ ə 'rɒp əθ i ˌnætʃ- ‖ -'rɑːp-

NatWest *tdmk* ˌnæt 'west◄

Naucratis 'nɔːk rət ɪs §-əs ‖ -rət̬-

Naugahyde *tdmk* 'nɔːg ə haɪd ‖ 'nɑːg-

naught nɔːt ‖ nɑːt **naughts** nɔːts ‖ nɑːts

Naughtie 'nɒxt i ‖ 'nɒːkt i

naught|y 'nɔːt |i ‖ 'nɔːt̬ |i 'nɑːt̬- ~ier i ə ‖ i ³r
  ~iest i ˌɪst i əst ~ily ɪ li əl i ~iness i nəs i nɪs

Naunton 'nɔːnt ən ‖ 'nɔːnt ³n 'nɑːnt-

naupli|us 'nɔːp li əs ‖ 'nɑːp- ~i aɪ iː

Nauru nə 'ruː nɑʊ-, nɑː-, ' · ·; nɑː 'uː ruː ~an/s
  ən/z

nausea 'nɔːs i ə 'nɔːz- ‖ 'nɔːz- 'nɑːz-, 'nɔːs-,
  'nɑːs-; 'nɔːʒ ə, 'nɑːʃ-, 'nɔːʒ-, 'nɑːʒ-

nause|ate 'nɔːs i |eɪt 'nɔːz- ‖ 'nɔːz- 'nɑːz-,
  'nɔːs-, 'nɑːs-, 'nɔːʃ-, 'nɑːʃ-, 'nɔːʒ-, 'nɑːʒ- ~ated
  eɪt ɪd -əd ‖ eɪt̬ əd ~ates eɪts ~ating/ly
  eɪt ɪŋ /li ‖ eɪt̬ ɪŋ /li

nauseous 'nɔːs i əs 'nɔːz- ‖ 'ʃɔːʃ əs 'nɑːʃ-;
  'nɔːz i əs, 'nɑːz- ~ly li ~ness nəs nɪs

Nausicaa, Nausicaä nɔː 'sɪk i ə -eɪ ə ‖ nɑː-

nautch nɔːtʃ ‖ nɑːtʃ **nautches** 'nɔːtʃ ɪz -əz
  ‖ 'nɑːtʃ-

nautical 'nɔːt ɪk ³l ‖ 'nɔːt̬ ɪk ³l 'nɑːt̬- ~ly i
  ˌnautical 'mile

naut|ilus, N~ *tdmk* 'nɔːt |ɪl əs -əl- ‖ 'nɔːt̬ |³l əs
  'nɑːt̬- ~ili ɪ laɪ əl aɪ, ɪ liː, əl i: ‖ ³l aɪ ³l i:
  ~iluses ɪl əs ɪz əl-, -əz ‖ ³l əs əz

Navaho, Navajo 'næv ə həʊ ‖ -hoʊ 'nɑːv- ~s
  z

naval 'neɪv ³l

Navan 'næv ³n

navarin 'næv ər ɪn §-³r ən —*Fr* [na va ʁ̃æ] ~s
  z

Navarino ˌnæv ə 'riːn əʊ ‖ -oʊ

Navarone ˌnæv ə rəʊn ˌ· · ' ‖ -roʊn

Navarre nə 'vɑː ‖ -'vɑːr —*Fr* [na vaːʁ]

nave neɪv **naves** neɪvz

navel 'neɪv ³l (*= naval*) ~s z
  'navel ˌorange; 'navel ˌgazing

navicular nə 'vɪk jʊl ə -jəl- ‖ -jəl ³r

navie... —*see* **navy**

navigability ˌnæv ɪg ə 'bɪl ət i -ɪt i ‖ -ət̬ i

navigab|le 'næv ɪg əb |³l ~leness ³l nəs -nɪs
  ~ly li

navi|gate 'næv ɪ |geɪt -ə- ~gated geɪt ɪd -əd
  ‖ geɪt̬ əd ~gates geɪts ~gating geɪt ɪŋ
  ‖ geɪt̬ ɪŋ

navigation ˌnæv ɪ 'geɪʃ ³n -ə-

navigational ˌnæv ɪ 'geɪʃ ³n əl ◄ ˌ·ə- ~ly i

navigator 'næv ɪ geɪt ə ˌ·ə- ‖ -geɪt̬ ³r ~s z

Navratilova næv ˌræt ɪ 'ləʊv ə nəv-, ˌnæv rə-
  ‖ ˌnæv rə tɪ 'loʊv ə ˌ·ræ- —*Czech* Navratilová
  ['na vra ci lo vaː]

navv|y 'næv |i ~ies iz

nav|y 'neɪv |i ~ies iz
  ˌnavy 'blue◄

nawab nə 'wɑːb -'wɔːb ‖ -'dɔːb ~s z

Naxalite 'næks ə laɪt 'nʌks- ~s z

Naxos 'næks ɒs ‖ -ɑːs 'nɑːks-, -ous, -əs

nay neɪ **nays** neɪz

Nayland 'neɪl ənd

Nayler, Naylor 'neɪl ə ‖ -ᵊr

naysayer 'neɪ ˌseɪ ə ‖ -ᵊr **~s** z

Nazarene ˌnæz ə 'riːn '··· **~s** z

Nazareth 'næz ər əθ -ɪθ

Nazarite 'næz ə raɪt -ᵊr aɪt **~s** z

Nazca 'næz kə ‖ 'nɑːsk ə —*AmSp* ['nas ka]

Naze neɪz

Nazeing 'neɪz ɪŋ

Nazi, nazi 'nɑːts i 'næts-, 'nɑːz- **~s** z

Naziism 'nɑːts i ˌɪz əm 'næts-, 'nɑːz-

Nazism 'nɑːts ˌɪz əm 'næts-, 'nɑːz-

NB ˌen 'biː —*see also* **nota bene, Nebraska, New Brunswick**

NBA ˌen biː 'eɪ →ˌem-

NBC ˌen biː 'siː →ˌem-

NCO ˌen si 'əʊ ‖ -'oʊ **~s, ~'s** z

NCP ˌen siː 'piː

Ncube 'nuːb eɪ —*Ndebele* ['ŋǀuː ɓe]

Ndebele ᵊn dɪ 'bel i ˌen-, -də-, -deɪ-, -'beɪl-, -'biːl-, -eɪ **~s** z

N'Djamena, N'Djaména ᵊn dʒæ 'meɪn ə ‖ -dʒɑː-

Ndola ᵊn 'dəʊl ə ‖ -'doʊl-

NE —*see* **northeast, northeastern**

Neagh neɪ

Neagle 'niːg ᵊl

Neal, Neale, Neall niːᵊl

Neanderthal ni 'ænd ə tɑːl neɪ-, -θɔːl; -ət ᵊl ‖ -ᵊr θɔːl -'ɑːnd-, -tɔːl, -tɑːl —*Ger* [ne 'an dɐ taːl] **~s** z

    Ne'anderthal man, ·,····· '·

neap niːp **neaps** niːps

    'neap tide

Neapolis ni 'æp əl ɪs §-əs

neapolitan, N~ nɪə 'pɒl ɪt ən ˌniːˌə'··· ◂, -ət ən ‖ ˌniː ə 'pɑːl ət ᵊn ◂ **~s** z

near nɪə ‖ nɪᵊr **neared** nɪəd ‖ nɪᵊrd **nearer** 'nɪər ə ‖ 'nɪr ᵊr **nearest** 'nɪər ɪst -əst ‖ 'nɪr əst **nearing** 'nɪər ɪŋ ‖ 'nɪr ɪŋ **nears** nɪəz ‖ nɪᵊrz

    Near 'East, Near 'Eastern; nearest and 'dearest; near 'miss; near 'thing

nearby *adj, adv* ˌnɪə 'baɪ ◂ ‖ ˌnɪr-

    a ˌnearby 'restaurant

Nearctic ˌniː 'ɑːkt ɪk ◂ ‖ -'ɑːrkt- -'ɑːrt-

near|ly 'nɪə |li ‖ 'nɪr |li **~ness** nəs nɪs

nearside 'nɪə saɪd ˌ·'· ‖ 'nɪr-

nearsighted ˌnɪə 'saɪt ɪd ◂ -əd, '·,·· ‖ ˌnɪr 'saɪt əd ◂ **~ly** li **~ness** nəs nɪs

Neasden 'niːzd ən

neat niːt **neater** 'niːt ə ‖ 'niːt̬ ᵊr **neatest** 'niːt ɪst -əst ‖ 'niːt̬ əst

neaten 'niːt ᵊn **~ed** d **~ing** ɪŋ **~s** z

neath, 'neath niːθ

Neath niːθ

neat|ly 'niːt |li **~ness** nəs nɪs

Neave niːv

neb neb **nebs** nebz

nebbich, nebbish 'neb ɪʃ **~es** ɪz əz

Nebo *mountain in Jordan* 'niːb əʊ ‖ -oʊ

Nebo *places in Wales* 'neb əʊ ‖ -oʊ

Nebrask|a nə 'bræsk |ə nɪ- **~an/s** ən/z

Nebuchadnezzar, n~ ˌneb jʊk əd 'nez ə ˌjək- ‖ ˌneb ək əd 'nez ᵊr ˌjək- **~s** z

neb|ula 'neb |jʊl ə -jəl- ‖ -|jəl ə **~ulae** ju liː jə- ‖ jə liː **~ular** jʊl ə jəl- ‖ jəl ᵊr **~ulas** jʊl əz jəl- ‖ jəl əz

nebuliser, nebulizer 'neb ju laɪz ə ‖ -jə laɪz ᵊr **~s** z

nebulosit|y ˌneb ju 'lɒs ət |i ˌjə-, -ɪt i ‖ -jə 'lɑːs ət̬ |i **~ies** iz

nebulous 'neb jʊl əs -jəl- ‖ -jəl əs **~ly** li **~ness** nəs nɪs

NEC ˌen iː 'siː

NECESSARILY

BrE

necessarily ˌnes ə 'ser əl i ˌ·ɪ-; 'nes əs ᵊr ˌəl i, '·ɪs-, ˌɪ li — *Preference poll, BrE:* ˌ·'··· 68%, '····· 32%. *Compare* **voluntarily.**

NECESSARY

BrE

necessar|y 'nes ə ser |i '·ɪ-; 'nes əs ᵊr |i, '·ɪs- — *Preference poll, BrE:* -seri 78%, -səri 22%. **~ies** iz

    necessary 'evil

necessi|tate nə 'ses ɪ |teɪt nɪ-, ne-, -ə- **~tated** teɪt ɪd -əd ‖ teɪt̬ əd **~tates** teɪts **~tating** teɪt ɪŋ ‖ teɪt̬ ɪŋ

necessitous nə 'ses ɪt əs nɪ-, ne-, -ət- ‖ -ət̬ əs **~ly** li **~ness** nəs nɪs

necessit|y nə 'ses ɪt |i nɪ-, ne-, -ət- ‖ -ət̬ |i **~ies** iz

Nechells 'niːtʃ ᵊlz

neck nek **necked** nekt **necking** 'nek ɪŋ **necks** neks

neck-and-neck ˌnek ən 'nek ◂

Neckar 'nek ə -ɑː ‖ -ᵊr —*Ger* ['nɛk aʁ]

neckband 'nek bænd **~s** z

-necked 'nekt — **long-necked** ˌlɒŋ 'nekt ◂ ‖ ˌlɔːŋ- ˌlɑːŋ-

Necker 'nek ə ‖ -ᵊr —*Fr* [nɛ kɛːʁ]

neckerchief 'nek ə tʃɪf -tʃiːf ‖ -ᵊr- -tʃəf **~s** s

necklac|e 'nek ləs -lɪs **~ed** t **~es** ɪz əz **~ing** ɪŋ

necklet 'nek lət -lɪt **~s** s

neckline 'nek laɪn **~s** z

necktie 'nek taɪ **~s** z

neckwear 'nek weə ‖ -wer -wær

necro- *comb. form* with *stress-neutral suffix* ǀnek rəʊ ‖ -roʊ —

necrobiosis ˌnek rəʊ baɪ 'əʊs ɪs §-əs
‖ -rəʊ baɪ 'oʊs-
— *with stress-imposing suffix* ne 'krɒ + nɪ-, nə-
‖ -'krɑː + — **necrologly** ne 'krɒl ədʒ |i nɪ-,
nə- ‖ -'krɑːl-**~ies** iz

necromancer 'nek rəʊ mænˌs ə ‖ -rə mænˌs ʳr
~s z

necromancy 'nek rəʊ mænˌs i ‖ -rə mænˌs i

necrophilia ˌnek rəʊ 'fɪl iˌə -'fiːl- ‖ ˌ·rə-

necrophiliac ˌnek rəʊ 'fɪl i æk -'fiːl- ‖ ˌ·rə- ~s
s

necrophilism ne 'krɒf ɪ ˌlɪz əm nə-, nɪ-, -'·ə-
‖ -'krɑːf-

necropolis ne 'krɒp əl ɪs nə-, nɪ-, §-əs
‖ -'krɑːp- ~es ɪz əz

necrops|y 'nek rɒps |i ‖ -rɑːps- ~ies iz

necrosis ne 'krəʊs ɪs nə-, nɪ-, §-əs ‖ -'kroʊs-

necrotic ne 'krɒt ɪk nə-, nɪ- ‖ -'krɑːt ɪk

necrotis|e, necrotiz|e 'nek rə taɪz ~ed d ~es
ɪz əz ~ing ɪŋ

nectar 'nekt ə ‖ -ʳr ~s z

nectarine 'nekt ə riːn -ər ɪn, §-ər en ~s z

nectar|y 'nekt ər |i ~ies iz

ned, Ned ned neds nedz

Neddie, Neddy 'ned i ~s, ~'s z

nee, née neɪ △niː (= *nay*)

need niːd needed 'niːd ɪd -əd needing
'niːd ɪŋ needs niːdz

needful 'niːd fˀl -fʊl ~ly i ~ness nəs nɪs

Needham 'niːd əm

needl|e, N~ 'niːd ˀl ~ed d ~es z ~ing ɪŋ

needlecord 'niːd ˀl kɔːd ‖ -kɔːrd ~s z

needlecraft 'niːd ˀl krɑːft §-kræft ‖ -kræft

needlefish 'niːd ˀl fɪʃ

needlepoint 'niːd ˀl pɔɪnt

needless 'niːd ləs -lɪs ~ly li ~ness nəs nɪs

needle|woman 'niːd ˀl |ˌwʊm ən ~women
ˌwɪm ɪn -ən

needlework 'niːd ˀl wɜːk ‖ -wɜːːk

needn't 'niːd ˀnt →·-ˀn

need-to-know ˌniːd tə 'nəʊ ‖ -'noʊ

need|y 'niːd |i ~ier i ˌə ‖ i ˌʳr ~iest i ɪst i ˌəst
~ily ɪ li əl i ~iness i nəs i nɪs

neem niːm

neep niːp neeps niːps

ne'er neə ‖ neʳr næʳr

ne'er-do-well 'neə du ˌwel ‖ 'ner- 'nær- ~s z

Neeson 'niːs ˀn

Neet, NEET niːt

nefarious nɪ 'feər i ˌəs nə-, ne- ‖ -'fer- -'fær-
~ly li ~ness nəs nɪs

Nefertiti ˌnef ə 'tiːt i ‖ -ʳr 'tiːt̬ i

Neff nef

Nefyn 'nev ɪn

NEG, neg. neg

negate nɪ |'geɪt nə-, ne- ~gated 'geɪt ɪd -əd
‖ 'geɪt̬ əd ~gates 'geɪts ~gating 'geɪt ɪŋ
‖ 'geɪt̬ ɪŋ

negation nɪ 'geɪʃ ˀn nə-, ne- ~s z

negativ|e 'neg ət ɪv ‖ -ət̬ ɪv ~ed d ~ely li
~eness nəs nɪs ~es z ~ing ɪŋ

negativism 'neg ət ɪv ˌɪz əm -ət əv- ‖ -ət̬ ɪv-

negativistic ˌneg ət ɪ 'vɪst ɪk ◄ -ət ə- ‖ -ət̬ ɪ-
~ally ˀl i

negativity ˌneg ə 'tɪv ət i -ɪt i ‖ -ət̬ i

negator nɪ 'geɪt ə nə-, ne- ‖ -'geɪt̬ ʳr ~s z

Negeb 'neg eb

Negev 'neg ev nɪ 'gev, nə-

neglect *v, n* nɪ 'glekt nə-, §ˌ·ne- ~ed ɪd əd
~ing ɪŋ ~s s

neglectful nɪ 'glekt fˀl nə-, §ˌ·ne-, -fʊl ~ly i
~ness nəs nɪs

negligee, négligée 'neg lɪ ʒeɪ -lə-, -liː-
‖ ˌneg lə 'ʒeɪ ˈ·· —*Fr* négligée [ne gli ʒe] ~s
z

negligenc|e 'neg lɪdʒ ənˌs -lədʒ- ~es ɪz əz

negligent 'neg lɪdʒ ənt -lədʒ- ~ly li

negligib|le 'neg lɪdʒ əb |ˀl ˈ·lədʒ-, -ɪb ˀl
~leness ˀl nəs -nɪs ~ly li

negotiability nɪ ˌgəʊʃ i ə 'bɪl ət i nə-, -ɪt i;
-ˌgəʊʃ ə 'bɪl- ‖ nɪ ˌgoʊʃ i ə 'bɪl ət̬ i
-ˌgoʊʃ ə 'bɪl-

negotiable nɪ 'gəʊʃ iˌəb ˀl nə-, -'gəʊʃ əb ˀl
‖ -'goʊʃ- -'·əb ˀl

negoti|ate nɪ 'gəʊʃ i |eɪt nə-, -'gəʊs- ‖ -'goʊʃ-
~ated eɪt ɪd -əd ‖ eɪt̬ əd ~ates eɪts ~ating
eɪt ɪŋ ‖ eɪt̬ ɪŋ

negotiation nɪ ˌgəʊʃ i 'eɪʃ ˀn nə-, -ˌgəʊs-
‖ -ˌgoʊʃ- -ˌgoʊs- ~s z

negotiator nɪ 'gəʊʃ i eɪt ə nə-, -'gəʊs-
‖ -'goʊʃ i eɪt̬ ʳr ~s z

negress, Negress 'niːg res -rəs, -rɪs ~es ɪz əz

Negri 'neg ri

Negrillo nɪ 'grɪl əʊ nə-, ne- ‖ -oʊ -'griː-, -joʊ ~s
z

negritude, négritude 'neg rɪ tjuːd 'niːg-, -rə-,
→-tʃuːd ‖ -tuːd -tjuːd

negro, Negro *person* 'niːg rəʊ ‖ -roʊ ~es z

Negro *name of river* 'neɪg rəʊ 'neg- ‖ -roʊ

negroid, N~ 'niːg rɔɪd ~s z

negroni, N~ nɪ 'grəʊn i ne-, nə- ‖ -'groʊn i ~s
z

negus, Negus 'niːg əs ~es ɪz əz

Nehemiah ˌniːˌə 'maɪˌə ˌneɪ-, -hə-, -ɪ-, -hɪ-

Nehru 'neər uː ‖ 'neɪ ruː 'ner uː —*Hindi*
[n̪eh ruː]

neigh neɪ (= *nay*) neighed neɪd neighing
'neɪ ɪŋ neighs neɪz

neighbo... —*see* neighbou...

neighbour 'neɪb ə ‖ -ʳr ~s z

neighbourhood 'neɪb ə hʊd ‖ -ʳr- ~s z
ˌneighbourhood 'watch

neighbouring 'neɪb ər ɪŋ

neighbour|ly 'neɪb ə |li ‖ -ʳr- ~liness li nəs
-nɪs

Neil, Neill niːˀl

Neilson 'niːl sən

Neiman 'niːm ən

Neisse 'naɪs ə —*Ger* Neisse, Neiße ['nai sə]

neither 'naɪð ə 'niːð- ‖ 'niːð ʳr 'naɪð- —*See*
preference poll figures at either

Nejd nezd

Nekrasov ne 'krɑːs ɒv nɪ- ‖ -oʊv —*Russ*
[n̠ʲɪ 'kra səf]

nekton 'nekt ɒn -ən ‖ -ɑːn

Nell nel
Nellie 'nel i
Nellis 'nel ɪs §-əs
nelly, N~ 'nel i
Nelson, n~ 'nels ən **~s, ~'s** z
nematic nɪ 'mæt ɪk nə-, ne- ‖ -'mæt̬- **~s** s
nematocyst 'nem ət əʊ sɪst nɪ 'mæt-, nə-, ne-
‖ 'nem əʈ ə- nɪ 'mæʈ ə- **~s** s
nematode 'nem ə təʊd ‖ -toʊd **~s** z
nembutal, N~ *tdmk* 'nem bju tæl -bjə-, -tɒl,
-tɑːl ‖ -bjə tɔːl -tɑːl, -tæl **~s** z
nem con, nem. con. ˌnem 'kɒn ‖ -'kɑːn
Nemea nɪ 'miːˌə nə-, ne-; 'nem iˌə, 'niːm-
Nemean nɪ 'miːˌən nə-, ne-; 'nem iˌən, 'niːm- **~s**
z
nem|esis, N~ 'nem |əs ɪs -ɪs-, §-əs **~eses** ə siːz
ɪ-
Nemo 'niːm əʊ ‖ -oʊ
nemophila nɪ 'mɒf ɪl ə nə-, -əl- ‖ -'mɑːf- **~s** z
nene *kind of bird* 'neɪn eɪ **~s** z
Nene *name of river* niːn nen —*The river in the*
English midlands is known as the nen
upstream (e.g. at Northampton) but as the niːn
downstream (e.g. at Peterborough and
Wisbech).
Nennius 'nen iˌəs
neo- *comb. form*
with stress-neutral suffix ˌniː əʊ ‖ -ə -oʊ —
neophilia ˌniː əʊ 'fɪl iˌə ‖ -ˌə-
with stress-imposing suffix ni 'ɒ+ ‖ -'ɑː+ —
neophilism ni 'ɒf ɪ ˌlɪz əm -'-ə- ‖ -'ɑːf-
Neocene, n~ 'niː əʊ siːn ‖ -ə-
neoclassic ˌniː əʊ 'klæs ɪk ◄ ‖ -ˌoʊ- **~al** ᵊl ◄
neoclassicism ˌniː əʊ 'klæs ɪ ˌsɪz əm -'-ə-
‖ ˌ-oʊ-
neoclassicist ˌniː əʊ 'klæs ɪs ɪst -əs ɪst, §-əst
‖ ˌoʊ- **~s** s
neocolonialism ˌniː əʊ kə 'ləʊn iˌə ˌlɪz əm
‖ ˌniː oʊ kə 'loʊn jə ˌlɪz əm
neocolonialist ˌniː əʊ kə 'ləʊn iˌəl ɪst ◄
§-əst ◄ ‖ ˌniː oʊ kə 'loʊn jəl əst ◄ **~s** s
neocon 'niː əʊ kɒn ‖ 'niː oʊ kɑːn **~s** z
neoconservative ˌniː əʊ kən 'sɜːv ət ɪv ◄
‖ ˌniː oʊ kən 'sɜːv əʈ ɪv ◄ **~s** z
neocortex ˌniː əʊ 'kɔːt eks ‖ -oʊ 'kɔːrt-
neodymium ˌniː əʊ 'dɪm iˌəm ‖ ˌ-oʊ-
neofascist ˌniː əʊ 'fæʃ ɪst ◄ §-əst ‖ -oʊ- **~s** s
Neogaea ˌni əʊ 'dʒiːˌə ‖ -ə-
neoimpressionism ˌniː əʊ ɪm 'preʃ ᵊn ˌɪz əm
-ə ˌnɪz- ‖ ˌ-oʊ-
neoimpressionist ˌniː əʊ ɪm 'preʃ ᵊn ɪst § ˌəst
‖ ˌ-oʊ- **~s** s
Neo-Latin ˌniː əʊ 'læt ɪn ◄ §-ᵊn ‖ -oʊ 'læt ᵊn
neolithic, N~ ˌniː əʊ 'lɪθ ɪk ◄ ‖ -ə-
neologis|e, neologiz|e ni 'ɒl ə dʒaɪz ‖ -'ɑːl-
~ed d **~es** ɪz əz **~ing** ɪŋ
neologism ni 'ɒl ə ˌdʒɪz əm 'niːˌəl- ‖ -'ɑːl- **~s**
z
Neo-Melanesian ˌniː əʊ ˌmel ə 'niːz iˌən ◄
-'niːʒ ᵊn, -'niːs iˌən, -'niːʃ ᵊn ‖ ˌ-oʊ-
neomycin ˌniː əʊ 'maɪs ɪn §-ᵊn ‖ -oʊ- -ə-
neon 'niː ɒn -ən ‖ -ɑːn
'neon light

neonatal ˌniː əʊ 'neɪt ᵊl ◄ ‖ -oʊ 'neɪt̬- **~ly** i
neonate 'niː əʊ neɪt ‖ -ə- **~s** s
neo-Nazi ˌniː əʊ 'nɑːts i ◄ ‖ -oʊ- **~s** z
neophyte 'niː əʊ faɪt ‖ -ə- **~s** s
neoplasm 'niː əʊ ˌplæz əm ‖ -ə- **~s** z
neoprene 'niː əʊ priːn ‖ -ə-
Neoptolemus ˌniː ɒp 'tɒl əm əs -ɪm əs
‖ -ɑːp 'tɑːl-
neotame 'niː əʊ teɪm ‖ -ə-
neotenous ni 'ɒt ən əs ‖ -'ɑːt ᵊn əs
neoteny ni 'ɒt ən i ‖ -'ɑːt ᵊn i
neoteric ˌniː əʊ 'ter ɪk ◄ ‖ -ə- **~s** s
Neozoic ˌniː əʊ 'zəʊ ɪk ◄ ‖ -oʊ 'zoʊ-
Nepal nɪ 'pɔːl nə-, ne-, -'pɑːl ‖ nə 'pɔːl -'pɑːl,
-'pæl
Nepalese ˌnep ə 'liːz ◄ -ɔː-, -ɑː-; -ᵊl 'iːz ◄
Nepali nɪ 'pɔːl i nə-, ne-, -'pɑːl- ‖ nə 'pɔːl i
-'pɑːl-, -'pæl- **~s** z
Nepean nɪ 'piːˌən nə-
nepenthe nɪ 'penˈθ i ne-, nə-

NEPHEW

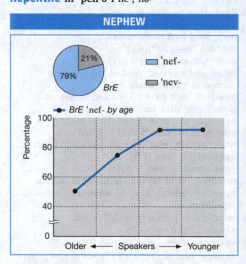

BrE 'nef- *by age*

nephew 'nef juː 'nev- — *Preference poll, BrE:*
'nef- *79%,* 'nev- *21%. It is evident that the*
traditional form with v *has been largely*
displaced by the spelling pronunciation, as has
long been the case in AmE. **~s** z
nephrite 'nef raɪt
nephritic nɪ 'frɪt ɪk nə-, ne- ‖ -'frɪt̬ ɪk
nephritis nɪ 'fraɪt ɪs nə-, ne-, §-əs ‖ -'fraɪt̬ əs
nephro- *comb. form*
with stress-neutral suffix ˌnef rəʊ ‖ -rə —
nephrolith 'nef rəʊ lɪθ ‖ -rə-
with stress-imposing suffix ne 'frɒ+ nɪ-, nə-
‖ nɪ 'frɑː+ — **nephrotomy** ne 'frɒt əm i nɪ-,
nə- ‖ nɪ 'frɑːt̬ əm i
ne plus ultra ˌneɪ plʊs 'ʊltr ɑː ˌniː-, -plʌs-,
-'ʌltr-, -ə
nepotism 'nep ə ˌtɪz əm
nepotistic ˌnep ə 'tɪst ɪk ◄ **~al** ᵊl ◄
Neptune, n~ 'nep tjuːn -tʃuːn ‖ -tuːn -tjuːn **~s,**
~'s z

Neptunian, n~ nep 'tjuːn i̯ ən →-'tʃuːn-
‖ -'tuːn- -'tjuːn-

neptunium nep 'tjuːn i̯ əm →-'tʃuːn- ‖ -'tuːn-
-'tjuːn-

nerd nɜːd ‖ nɜːd **nerds** nɜːdz ‖ nɜːdz

Nereid, n~ 'nɪər i̯ ɪd ‖ 'nɪr- **~s** z

Nereus 'nɪər i̯ uːs ˌəs ‖ 'nɪr-

Nerf, NERF tdmk nɜːf ‖ nɜːf

Nero 'nɪər əʊ ‖ 'niː roʊ 'nɪr oʊ

Neruda nə 'ruːd ə ne-, nɪ- —Sp [ne 'ru ða]

Nerurkar nɪ 'rɜːk ə nə- ‖ -'rɜːk ᵊr

Nerva 'nɜːv ə ‖ 'nɜːv ə

nerve nɜːv ‖ nɜːv **nerved** nɜːvd ‖ nɜːvd
  nerves nɜːvz ‖ nɜːvz **nerving** 'nɜːv ɪŋ
  ‖ 'nɜːv ɪŋ
  'nerve cell; **'nerve ˌcentre**; **'nerve gas**;
  'nerve ˌimpulse

nerveless 'nɜːv ləs -lɪs ‖ 'nɜːv- **~ly** li **~ness**
nəs nɪs

nerve-racking, nerve-wracking
  'nɜːv ˌræk ɪŋ ‖ 'nɜːv-

nervine 'nɜːv iːn -aɪn ‖ 'nɜːv-

nervous 'nɜːv əs ‖ 'nɜːv əs **~ly** li **~ness** nəs
nɪs
  ˌnervous 'breakdown; 'nervous ˌsystem

nervure 'nɜːv jʊə -jə ‖ 'nɜːv jʊr -jᵊr **~s** z

nerv|y 'nɜːv |i ‖ 'nɜːv |i **~ier** i̯ ə ‖ i̯ ᵊr **~lest**
i i̯ ɪst i̯ əst **~ily** ɪ li əl i **~iness** i nəs i nɪs

Nerys 'ner ɪs §-əs

Nesbit, Nesbitt 'nez bɪt

Nescafe, Nescafé tdmk 'nes kæ ˌfeɪ -ˌkæf i,
-eɪ; 'nes kæf i ˌ· ·ˋ·

nescience 'nes i̯ ənᵗs ‖ 'neʃ ᵊnᵗs 'neʃ i̯ ənᵗs

nescient 'nes i̯ ənt ‖ 'neʃ ᵊnt 'neʃ i̯ ənt **~s** s

nesh neʃ

Nesquik tdmk 'nes kwɪk

ness, Ness nes **nesses, Ness's** 'nes ɪz -əz

-ness nəs nɪs —The noun-forming suffix has no
effect upon word stress: 'careless, 'carelessness.
—In singing, a strong-vowelled form nes is
customary.

-ness in place names 'nes — **Sheerness**
ˌʃɪə 'nes ◂ ‖ ˌʃɪr-

Nesselrode, n~ 'nes ᵊl rəʊd ‖ -roʊd —Russ
[nʲi sɨl 'rɔ də]

Nessie 'nes i

Nessler 'nes lə ‖ -lᵊr —Ger ['nɛs lɐ]

nessun dorma ˌnes uːn 'dɔːm ə ‖ -'dɔːrm ə
—It [ˌnes sun 'dɔr ma]

Nessus 'nes əs

nest, Nest nest **nested** 'nest ɪd -əd **nesting**
'nest ɪŋ **nests** nests
  'nest egg

Nesta 'nest ə

nestl|e 'nes ᵊl **~ed** d **~es** z **~ing** ˌɪŋ

Nestlé tdmk 'nes leɪ -li, -ᵊl ‖ -li

nestling part of **nestle** 'nes ᵊl ɪŋ

nestling n 'young bird' 'nest lɪŋ **~s** z

Neston 'nest ən

Nestor 'nest ɔː -ə ‖ -ᵊr -ɔːr

Nestorian ne 'stɔːr i̯ ən ‖ -'stoʊr- **~ism** ˌɪz əm
~s z

Nestorius ne 'stɔːr i̯ əs ‖ -'stoʊr-

---

net net **nets** nets **netted** 'net ɪd -əd ‖ 'neţ əd
  netting 'net ɪŋ ‖ 'neţ ɪŋ

Netanyahu ˌnet ᵊn 'jɑː huː -æn-

netball 'net bɔːl ‖ -bɑːl

nether 'neð ə ‖ -ᵊr

Netherlander 'neð əl ənd ə -ə lænd ə
  ‖ -ᵊr lənd ᵊr -lænd- **~s** z

Netherlands 'neð əl əndz ‖ -ᵊr ləndz
  ˌNetherlands An'tilles

nethermost 'neð ə məʊst ‖ -ᵊr moʊst

Netherton 'neð ət ən ‖ -ᵊrt ᵊn

netherworld 'neð ə wɜːld ‖ -ᵊr wɜːld

netiquette 'net ɪ ket -ɪk ət, ˌnet ɪ 'ket
  ‖ 'neţ ɪk ət -ɪ ket

netizen 'net ɪz ən -əz- ‖ 'neţ əz ən -əs- **~s** z

Netley 'net li

netpreneur 'net prə nɜː -pre- ‖ -nɜː **~s** z

netrepreneur 'netr ə prə nɜː -ə pre- ‖ -nɜː **~s**
z

Netscape tdmk 'net skeɪp

netspeak 'net spiːk

netsuke 'net ski -skeɪ; 'nets ʊk i, -eɪ —Jp
[ne ˌtsɯ ke] **~s** z

netsurfing 'net ˌsɜːf ɪŋ ‖ -ˌsɜːf-

nett net

nett... —see **net**

Nettie 'net i ‖ 'neţ i

netting 'net ɪŋ ‖ 'neţ ɪŋ

nettl|e, N~ 'net ᵊl ‖ 'neţ ᵊl **~ed** d **~es** z **~ing**
ɪŋ
  'nettle rash

Nettlefold 'net ᵊl fəʊld →-foʊld ‖ 'neţ ᵊl foʊld

Nettleship 'net ᵊl ʃɪp ‖ -neţ-

nettlesome 'net ᵊl səm ‖ 'neţ-

network 'net wɜːk ‖ -wɜːk **~ed** t **~er/s** ə/z
  ‖ ᵊr/z **~ing** ɪŋ **~s** s

Neubrandenburg ˌnɔɪ 'brænd ən bɜːg
  ‖ -'brɑːnd ən bɜːg —Ger
  [nɔy 'bʁan dᵊn bʊʁk]

Neuchâtel, Neufchâtel ˌnɜː ʃæ 'tel ◂ -ʃə-
  ‖ ˌnuː- ˌnʊ- —Fr [nø ʃa tɛl]

neum, neume njuːm §nuːm ‖ nuːm njuːm
  neums, neumes njuːmz §nuːmz ‖ nuːmz
njuːmz

Neumann 'njuː mən §'nuː- ‖ 'nuː- 'nju: —but
as a German name, 'nɔɪ- —Ger ['nɔy man]

neural 'njʊər ə l 'njɔːr- §'nʊər- ‖ 'nʊr əl 'njʊr-,
nɜː-

neuralgia njuᵊ 'rældʒ ə njə-, njɔː-, §nuᵊ- ‖ nu-
nə-, nju-

neuralgic njuᵊ 'rældʒ ɪk njə-, njɔː-, §nuᵊ- ‖ nu-
nə-, nju-

neurasthenia ˌnjʊər əs 'θiːn i̯ ə ˌnjɔːr-,
§ˌnʊər-, -ˌæs- ‖ ˌnʊr- ˌnjʊr-

neurasthenic ˌnjʊər əs 'θen ɪk ◂ ˌnjɔːr-,
§ˌnʊər-, -ˌæs- ‖ ˌnʊr- ˌnjʊr- **~ally** ᵊl i

neuritis njuᵊ 'raɪt ɪs njə-, njɔː-, §nuᵊ-, §-əs
  ‖ nu 'raɪţ əs nə-, nju-

neuro- comb. form
  with stress-neutral suffix |njʊər əʊ |njɔːr-,
  §|nʊər- ‖ |nʊr oʊ |njʊr- — **neurobiology**
  ˌnjʊər əʊ baɪ 'ɒl ədʒ i ˌnjɔːr-, §ˌnʊər-
  ‖ ˌnʊr oʊ baɪ 'ɑːl- ˌnjʊr-

with stress-imposing suffix **njuə ˈrɒ +** njə-,
njɔː-, §nuə- ‖ **nu ˈrɑː +** nə-, nju- —
  neuropathy njuə ˈrɒp əθ i njə-, §nuə-
‖ **nu ˈrɑːp-** nə-, nju-

neuroinformatics ˌnjuər əʊ ˌɪn fə ˈmæt ɪks
ˌnjɔː.r, §ˌnuər- ‖ ˌnur oʊ ˌɪn fʳr ˈmæt̬ ɪks
ˌnjur-

neurological ˌnjuər ə ˈlɒdʒ ɪk ᵊl ◂, njɔː.r-,
§ˌnuər- ‖ ˌnur ə ˈlɑːdʒ- ˌnjur- **~ly** i

neurologist njuə ˈrɒl ədʒ ɪst njə-, njɔː-, §nuə-,
§-əst ‖ **nu ˈrɑːl-** nə-, nju- **~s** s

neurology njuə ˈrɒl ədʒ i njə-, njɔː-, §nuə-
‖ **nu ˈrɑːl-** nə-, nju-

neuroma njuə ˈrəʊm ə ‖ -ˈroʊm ə **~s** z

neuron ˈnjuər ɒn ˈnjɔː.r-, §ˈnuər- ‖ ˈnur ɑːn
ˈnjur-; ˈnjuː rɑːn **~s** z

neurone ˈnjuər əʊn ˈnjɔː.r-, §ˈnuər- ‖ ˈnur oʊn
ˈnjur-; ˈnjuː roun **~s** z

neuropath|y njuə ˈrɒp əθ |i njə-, njɔː-, §nuə-
‖ **nu ˈrɑːp-** nə-, nju- **~ies** iz

neurosci|ence ˌnjuər əʊ ˈsaɪ |ən̩s ˌnjɔː.r-,
§ˌnuər-, ˈ·ˌ·· ‖ ˌnur oʊ- ˌnjur- **~ences** ən̩s ɪz
-əz **~entist/s** ənt ɪst/s §-əst/s ‖ ənt̬ əst/s

neuros|is njuə ˈrəʊs |ɪs njə-, njɔː-, §nuə-, §-əs
‖ **nu ˈroʊs-** nə-, nju- **~es** iːz

neurosurgeon ˌnjuər əʊ ˈsɜːdʒ ən ˌnjɔː-,
§ˌnuər-, ˈ·ˌ··· ‖ ˌnur oʊ ˈsɜːdʒ ən ˌnjur- **~s** z

neurosurgery ˌnjuər əʊ ˈsɜːdʒ ər i ˌnjɔː-,
§ˌnuər-, ˈ·ˌ··· ‖ ˌnur oʊ ˈsɜːdʒ-

neurosurgical ˌnjuər əʊ ˈsɜːdʒ ɪk ᵊl ◂ ˌnjɔː-,
§ˌnuər-, ˈ·ˌ··· ‖ ˌnur oʊ ˈsɜːdʒ- **~ly** i

neurotheology ˌnjuər əʊ θi ˈɒl ədʒ i ˌnjɔː.r-,
§ˌnuər- ‖ ˌnur oʊ θi ˈɑːl- ˌnjur-

neurotic njuə ˈrɒt ɪk njə-, njɔː-, §nuə-
‖ **nu ˈrɑːt̬ ɪk** nə-, nju- **~ally** ᵊl_i **~s** s

neuroticism njuə ˈrɒt ɪ ˌsɪz əm njə-, njɔː-,
§nuə-, -ˈ·ə- ‖ **nu ˈrɑːt̬ ə-** nə-, nju-

neurotransmitter ˌnjuər əʊ trænz ˈmɪt ə
ˌnjɔː.r, §ˌnuər-, -trɑːnz·ˈ··, -trænᵗs·ˈ··,
-trɑːnᵗs·ˈ··, ˈ··ˌ·· ‖ ˌnur oʊ trænᵗs ˈmɪt̬ ʳr
-trænz·ˈ··, ˈ··ˌ··

neut|er ˈnjuːt |ə §ˈnuːt- ‖ ˈnuːt̬ |ʳr ˈnjuːt̬- **~ered**
əd ‖ ʳrd **~ering** ʳr ɪŋ **~ers** əz ‖ ʳrz

neutral ˈnjuːtr əl §ˈnuːtr- ‖ ˈnuːtr əl ˈnjuːtr- **~s**
z

neutralis... —*see* **neutraliz...**

neutralism ˈnjuːtr ə ˌlɪz əm §ˈnuːtr-, -ᵊl ˌɪz-
‖ ˈnuːtr- ˈnjuːtr-

neutralist ˈnjuːtr əl ɪst §ˈnuːtr-, §-əst ‖ ˈnuːtr-
ˈnjuːtr- **~s** s

neutrality nju ˈtræl ət i §nu-, -ɪt-
‖ **nu ˈtræl ət̬ i** nju-

neutralization ˌnjuːtr əl aɪ ˈzeɪʃ ᵊn §ˌnuːtr-,
-ɪˈ·- ‖ ˌnuːtr əl ə- ˌnjuːtr- **~s** z

neutraliz|e ˈnjuːtr ə laɪz §ˈnuːtr- ‖ ˈnuːtr-
ˈnjuːtr- **~ed** d **~es** ɪz əz **~ing** ɪŋ

neutrally ˈnjuːtr əl i §ˈnuːtr- ‖ ˈnuːtr- ˈnjuːtr-

neutrino nju ˈtriːn əʊ §nu- ‖ **nu ˈtriːn oʊ** nju-
~s z

neutron ˈnjuːtr ɒn §ˈnuːtr- ‖ ˈnuːtr ɑːn ˈnjuːtr-
~s z
  ˈ**neutron bomb**; ˈ**neutron star**

neutropenia ˌnjuːtr əʊ ˈpiːn i ə §ˌnuːtr-
‖ ˌnuːtr oʊ ˈpiːn jə ˌnjuːtr-

neutrophil ˈnjuːtr əʊ fɪl §ˈnuːtr- ‖ ˈnuːtr ə-
ˈnjuːtr-

Neva *river in USSR* ˈneɪv ə ˈniːv- —*Russ*
[nʲɪ ˈva]

Nevad|a nɪ ˈvɑːd |ə nə-, ne- ‖ nɪ ˈvæd |ə
-ˈvɑːd- —*but places in AR, IA, MO are also*
-ˈveɪd- **~an/s** ᵊn/z

Nevard nə ˈvɑːd nɪ- ‖ -ˈvɑːrd

Neve niːv

névé ˈnev eɪ ‖ neɪ ˈveɪ —*Fr* [ne ve]

never ˈnev ə ‖ -ʳr

never-ending ˌnev ʳr ˈend ɪŋ ◂ -ə-

nevermore ˌnev ə ˈmɔː ‖ -ʳr ˈmɔːr -ˈmoʊr

never-never ˌnev ə ˈnev ə ‖ -ʳr ˈnev ʳr
  ˌnever-ˈnever land

nevertheless ˌnev ə ðə ˈles ‖ ˌnev ʳr-

Nevil, Nevill, Neville ˈnev ᵊl -ɪl

Nevin ˈnev ɪn -ᵊn

Nevinson ˈnev ɪnᵗs ən -ənᵗs-

Nevis *mountain and loch in Scotland* ˈnev ɪs
§-əs

Nevis *island in West Indies* ˈniːv ɪs §-əs

nev|us ˈniːv |əs **~i** aɪ **~uses** əs ɪz -əz

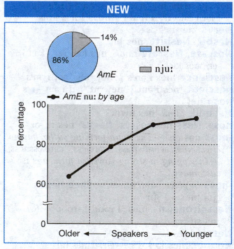

NEW

14%

86%

AmE

■ nu:

■ nju:

● *AmE nu: by age*

Percentage

100

80

60

0

Older ◄—— Speakers ——► Younger

new nju: §nu: ‖ nu: nju: — *Preference poll,
AmE:* nu: *86%,* nju: *14%.*—*See also phrases
with this word* **newer** ˈnjuːˌə ‖ ˈnuː ʳr nju:-
newest ˈnjuːˌɪst §ˈnuːˌ, əst ‖ ˈnuː əst ˈnju:-
ˌ**New** ˈ**Age**◄, **New Age** ˈ**traveller**; ˌ**new**
ˈ**blood**; ˌ**new** ˈ**broom**; ⑴**New** ˈ**Brunswick**;
ˌ**New** ˌ**Cale**ˈ**donia**; ˌ**new** ˈ**deal**, ˌ**New** ˈ**Deal**;
⑴**New** ˈ**Delhi**; ⑴**New** ˈ**England**; ˌ**New**
ˈ**Forest**◄, ˌ**New** ˌ**Forest** ˈ**pony**; ⑴**New**
ˈ**Guinea**; ⑴**New** ˈ**Hampshire**; **New** ˈ**Haven**
place in CN, also ˈ·ˌ·; ⑴**New** ˈ**Jersey**; ⑴**New**
ˈ**Mexico**; ˌ**new** ˈ**moon**; **New** ˈ**Orleans**, ˌ**New**
Orˈ**leans**; ˌ**New** ˈ**Quay** *place in Dyfed*; ˌ**New**
ˈ**Right**; ˌ**New** ˌ**Scotland** ˈ**Yard**; ˌ**New South**
ˈ**Wales**; ˌ**New** ˈ**Testament**; ˈ**new town**, ·ˈ·;
ˌ**New** ˈ**Wave**◄, ˌ**New Wave** ˈ**music**; ˌ**New**

Neutralization

1 Two PHONEMES may, in certain phonetic environments, not be distinguishable. We say the **opposition** between them is **neutralized**.

2 In most environments English p and b are in opposition: that is, they carry a potential difference in meaning. This can be seen in pairs such as **pin** pɪn and **bin** bɪn, **cup** kʌp and **cub** kʌb. After s, however, the opposition is neutralized (since p here has no ASPIRATION). Conventionally, we write **spin** phonemically as spɪn; but since there is no possible difference between p and b here we could just as well write sbɪn.

3 One type of neutralization is symbolized explicitly in LPD by the use of the symbols i and u. The opposition between iː and ɪ operates in most environments, as seen in **green** griːn and **grin** grɪn, **leap** liːp and **lip** lɪp. But there are two environments in which it is neutralized:

- when the vowel is in a WEAK syllable at the end of a word (or at the end of part of a compound word or of a stem), as in **happy** ˈhæp i, **valley** ˈvæl i, **babies** ˈbeɪb iz.

- when the vowel is in a weak syllable before another vowel, as in **radiation** ˌreɪd i ˈeɪʃ ᵊn, **glorious** ˈɡlɔːr i‿əs.

In these positions the vowel is traditionally identified with ɪ. But in fact some speakers use ɪ, some use iː, some use something intermediate or indeterminate, and some fluctuate between the two possibilities. Modern pronunciation dictionaries use the symbol i, which reflects this.

Similarly, in this dictionary the symbol u represents the neutralization of the opposition between uː and ʊ. This neutralization is found not only in i environments, but also in certain others, for example, in one pronunciation of **stimulate** ˈstɪm ju leɪt.

Do not confuse neutralization with the term **neutral vowel**, a name sometimes used for ə.

N

ˈWorld; ˌnew ˈyear◂, ˌNew Year's ˈDay, ˌNew Year's ˈEve; ⊲ₗ⟩New ˈYork, ˌNew York ˈCity, ; ⊲ₗ⟩New ˈYorker, ˌNew York ˈState

Newark ˈnjuː ək §ˈnuː- ‖ ˈnuː ᵊrk ˈnjuː- —*but the place in DE is* -ɑːk ‖ -ɑːrk

newbie ˈnjuːb i §ˈnuːb- ‖ ˈnuːb i ˈnjuːb- **~s** z

Newbiggin ˈnjuː ˌbɪɡ ɪn §ˈnuː-, §-ən ‖ ˈnuː-ˈnjuː-

Newbold ˈnjuː bəʊld §ˈnuː-, →-bɒʊld ‖ ˈnuː boʊld ˈnjuː-

Newbolt ˈnjuː bəʊlt §ˈnuː-, →-bɒʊlt ‖ ˈnuː boʊlt ˈnjuː-

newborn ˈnjuː bɔːn §ˈnuː-; ˌ·ˈ·◂ ‖ ˈnuː bɔːrn ˈnjuː-

Newbridge ˈnjuː brɪdʒ §ˈnuː- ‖ ˈnuː- ˈnjuː-

Newbrough ˈnjuː brʌf §ˈnuː- ‖ ˈnuː- ˈnjuː-

newbuild ˈnjuː bɪld §ˈnuː- ‖ ˈnuː- njuː-

Newburg, n~ ˈnjuː bɜːɡ §ˈnuː- ‖ ˈnuː bɜːɡ ˈnjuː-

Newburgh ˈnjuː bər ə §ˈnuː- ‖ ˈnuː bɜːɡ ˈnjuː-

Newbury ˈnjuː bər i §ˈnuː- ‖ ˈnuː ˌber i ˈnjuː-, -bər i

Newby ˈnjuːb i §ˈnuːb- ‖ ˈnuːb i ˈnjuːb-

Newcastle ˈnjuː ˌkɑːs ᵊl §ˈnuː-, §-ˌkæs-, §ˈ·‿· ‖ ˈnuː ˌkæs ᵊl ˈnjuː- —*In Tyne & Wear, locally* njuː ˈkæs ᵊl

ˌNewcastle-(up)on-ˈTyne, *locally* New ˌcastle-; ˌNewcastle-ˌunder-ˈLyme

Newcomb, Newcombe, Newcome ˈnjuːk əm §ˈnuːk- ‖ ˈnuːk- ˈnjuːk-

newcomer ˈnjuː ˌkʌm ə §ˈnuː- ‖ ˈnuː ˌkʌm ᵊr ˈnjuː- **~s** z

Newdigate 'njuːd ɪ geɪt §'nuːd-, -ə-, -gɪt, -gət
‖ 'nuːd- 'njuːd-
Newe njuː §nuː ‖ nuː njuː
newel 'njuː əl §'nuː- ‖ 'nuː əl 'njuː- ~s z
New Englander njuː 'ɪŋ glənd ə -lənd ə
‖ nuː 'ɪŋ glənd ʳr njuː- ~s z
newfangled ˌnjuː 'fæŋ gʰld ◂ §ˌnuː- ‖ ˌnuː-
ˌnjuː-; '·ˌ··
Newfie 'njuːf i §'nuːf- ‖ 'nuːf i 'njuːf- ~s z
new-found ˌnjuː-'faʊnd ◂ §ˌnuː- ‖ ˌnuː- ˌnjuː-
Newfoundland 'njuːf ʰnd lənd §'nuːf-, -lænd,
ˌ·'·ˌ; njuː 'faʊnd-, §nu- ‖ 'nuːf ʰnd lənd
'njuːf-, -lænd; nu 'faʊnd-, njuː- —*Locally* ˌ·'·ˌ.
The breed of dog is usually ·'··. ~s, ~'s z
Newfoundlander ˌnjuːf ʰnd 'lænd ə §ˌnuːf-;
'···ˌ, -lənd ə; njuː 'faʊnd lənd ə, §nu-
‖ 'nuːf ʰnd lənd ʳr 'njuːf-, -lænd ʳr ~s z
Newgate 'njuː geɪt §'nuː-, -gɪt, -gət ‖ 'nuː-
'njuː-
Newham 'njuː əm §'nuːˌ, -hæm; ˌ·'hæm ◂
‖ 'nuː- 'njuː-
Newhaven *place in Sussex* 'njuːˌ heɪv ʰn
§'nuː-, ·'·· ‖ 'nuː- 'njuː-
Newington 'njuːˌ ɪŋ tən §'nuː- ‖ 'nuː- 'njuː-
newish 'njuːˌ ɪʃ §'nuːˌ ‖ 'nuː- 'njuː-
new-laid ˌnjuː- 'leɪd ◂ §ˌnuː- ‖ ˌnuː- ˌnjuː-
ˌnew-laid 'eggs
Newlands 'njuː ləndz §'nuː- ‖ 'nuː- 'njuː-
new-look ˌnjuː- 'lʊk ◂ §ˌnuː- ‖ ˌnuː- ˌnjuː-
newly 'njuː li §'nuː- ‖ 'nuː- 'njuː-
Newlyn 'njuː lɪn §'nuː- ‖ 'nuː- 'njuː-
newlywed 'njuː li wed §'nuː-, ˌ·'·◂ ‖ 'nuː-
'njuː- ~s z
Newman 'njuː mən §'nuː- ‖ 'nuː- 'njuː-
Newmark 'njuː maːk §'nuː- ‖ 'nuː maːrk 'njuː-
Newmarket, n~ 'njuːˌ maːk ɪt §'nuː-, §-ət
‖ 'nuːˌ maːrk ət 'njuː-
new-mown ˌnjuː- 'məʊn ◂ §ˌnuː-
‖ ˌnuː- 'moʊn ◂ ˌnjuː-
ˌnew-mown 'hay
Newnes njuːnz §nuːnz ‖ 'nuːnz 'njuːnz
newness 'njuː nəs §'nuː-, -nɪs ‖ 'nuː- 'njuː-
Newnham 'njuːn əm §'nuːn- ‖ 'nuːn- 'njuːn-
New Orleans ˌnjuː- 'ɔːl i ˌənz §ˌnuː-, -'ɔːl ənz,
-ɔː 'liːnz ‖ ˌnuː- 'ɔːrl ənz ˌnjuː-; nuː ɔːr 'liːnz,
ˌnjuː-
Newport 'njuː pɔːt §'nuː- ‖ 'nuː pɔːrt 'njuː-,
-poʊrt
—*but in* ˌNewport 'News *place in VA,*
sometimes -pət ‖ -pʰrt
Newquay *place in Cornwall* 'njuː kiː §'nuː-
‖ 'nuː- 'njuː-
Newry 'njʊər i §'nʊər- ‖ 'nuː ri 'njuː-
news njuːz §nuːz ‖ nuːz njuːz
'news ˌagency; 'news ˌconference
newsagent 'njuːz ˌeɪdʒ ənt §'nuːz- ‖ 'nuːz-
'njuːz- ~s s
newsboy 'njuːz bɔɪ §'nuːz- ‖ 'nuːz- 'njuːz- ~s z
newscast 'njuːz kaːst §'nuːz-, §-kæst
‖ 'nuːz kæst 'njuːz- ~er/s ə/z ʳr/z ~ing ɪŋ
~s s

newsflash 'njuːz flæʃ §'nuːz- ‖ 'nuːz- 'njuːz-
~es ɪz əz
newsgroup 'njuːz gruːp §'nuːz- ‖ 'nuːz- njuːz-
~s s
newshawk 'njuːz hɔːk §'nuːz- ‖ 'nuːz- 'njuːz-,
-haːk ~s s
newshound 'njuːz haʊnd §'nuːz- ‖ 'nuːz-
'njuːz- ~s z
newsletter 'njuːz ˌlet ə §'nuːz- ‖ 'nuːz ˌleţ ʳr
'njuːz- ~s z
newsmaker 'njuːz ˌmeɪk ə §'nuːz-
‖ 'nuːz ˌmeɪk ʳr 'njuːz- ~s z
news|man 'njuːz| mæn -mən ‖ 'nuːz- 'njuːz-
~men men mən
newsmonger 'njuːz ˌmʌŋ gə §'nuːz-
‖ 'nuːz ˌmɑːŋ gʳr 'njuːz-, -ˌmʌŋ- ~s z
Newsnight 'njuːz naɪt §'nuːz- ‖ 'nuːz- 'njuːz-
Newsom, Newsome *family name* 'njuːs əm
§'nuːs- ‖ 'nuːs- 'njuːs-
Newsome *place in West Yorks.* 'njuːz əm
§'nuːz- ‖ 'nuːz- 'njuːz-

NEWSPAPER

Pie charts: AmE -z- 68%, -s- 32%; BrE -z- 57%, -s- 43%. Line graph: BrE -z- by age, Percentage axis 0–80, x-axis Older ← Speakers → Younger.

---

newspaper 'njuːz ˌpeɪp ə 'njuːs-, §'nuːz-,
§'nuːs- ‖ 'nuːz ˌpeɪp ʳr 'njuːz-, 'nuːs-, 'njuːs-
— *Preference polls, AmE:* z 68%, s 32%; *BrE:*
z 57%, s 43%. ~man mæn ~men men ~s z
~woman ˌwʊm ən ~women ˌwɪm ɪn §-ən
newspeak, N~ 'njuː spiːk §'nuː- ‖ 'nuː- 'njuː-
news|person 'njuːz ˌpɜːs ʰn §'nuːz-
‖ 'nuːz ˌpɜːs ʰn 'njuːz- ~people ˌpiːp ʰl
newsprint 'njuːz prɪnt §'nuːz- ‖ 'nuːz- 'njuːz-
newsreader 'njuːz ˌriːd ə §'nuːz-
‖ 'nuːz ˌriːd ʳr 'njuːz- ~s z
newsreel 'njuːz riːʰl §'nuːz- ‖ 'nuːz- 'njuːz- ~s
z
newsroom 'njuːz ruːm §'nuːz-, -rʊm ‖ 'nuːz-
'njuːz- ~s z
newssheet 'njuːz ʃiːt §'nuːz-, →'njuːʒ- ‖ 'nuːz-
'njuːz- ~s s
newsstand 'njuːz stænd §'nuːz- ‖ 'nuːz- 'njuːz-
~s z
Newstead 'njuːst ɪd -ed ‖ 'nuːst- 'njuːst-

newsvendor 'njuːz ˌvend ə §'nuːz-
‖ 'nuːz ˌvend ʳr 'njuːz- **~s** z
news|woman 'njuːz ˌwʊm ən §'nuːz- ‖ 'nuːz-
-'njuːz- **~women** ˌwɪm ɪn §-ən
newsworthy 'njuːz ˌwɜːð i §'nuːz-
‖ 'nuːz ˌwɜːð i 'njuːz-
newswriter 'njuːz ˌraɪt ə §'nuːz-
‖ 'nuːz ˌraɪt ʳr 'njuːz- **~s** z
news|y 'njuːz |i §'nuːz- ‖ 'nuːz |i 'njuːz- **~ier**
i‿ə ‖ i‿ʳr **~ies** iz **~iest** i ˌɪst i ˌəst **~iness** i nəs
i nɪs
newt njuːt §nuːt ‖ **nuːt** njuːt **newts** njuːts
§nuːts ‖ **nuːts** njuːts
Newton, n~ 'njuːt ʳn §'nuːt- ‖ 'nuːt ʳn 'njuːt-
~s, ~'s z
Newtonian nju 'təʊn i‿ən §nu- ‖ nu 'toʊn-
nju-
Newton-le-Willows ˌnjuːt ʳn li 'wɪl əʊz
§ˌnuːt- ‖ ˌnuːt ʳn li 'wɪl oʊz ˌnjuːt-
Newtonmore ˌnjuːt ʳn 'mɔː §ˌnuːt-
‖ ˌnuːt ʳn 'mɔːr ˌnjuː-, -'moʊr
Newtown 'njuː təʊn §'nuː- ‖ 'nuː- 'njuː- —*but
in Irish compound place-names,* ¦njuːt ʳn,
§¦nuːt- ‖ ¦nuːt ʳn, ¦njuːt- — **Newtownabbey**
ˌnjuːt ʳn 'æb i §ˌnuːt- ‖ ˌnuːt- ˌnjuːt- ,
Newtownards ˌnjuːt ʳn 'ɑːdz §ˌnuːt-
‖ ˌnuːt ʳn 'ɑːrdz ˌnjuːt-
New York ˌnjuː 'jɔːk◄ §ˌnuː- ‖ ₍ˌ₎nuː 'jɔːrk ◄
₍ˌ₎nju- **~er/s** ə/z ‖ ʳr/z
ˌNew York 'City
New Zealand nju 'ziːl ənd ˌnjuː-, §nu-, §ˌnuː-
‖ nu- nju-, ˌnuː-, ˌnjuː- —*locally sometimes*
-'zɪl-
New ˌZealand 'flax
New Zealander nju 'ziːl ənd ə ˌnjuː-,
§ˌnuː- ‖ nu 'ziːl ənd ʳr nju-, ˌnuː-, ˌnjuː- **~s** z
next nekst
next-door ˌnekst 'dɔː ◄ ‖ -'dɔːr ◄ -'doʊr ◄
ˌnext-door 'neighbour
nexus 'neks əs **~es** ɪz əz
Ney neɪ —*Fr* [nɛ]
Nez Perce, Nez Percé ˌnez 'pɜːs ˌnes-, -'peəs,
-'peəs eɪ ‖ -'pɜːs —*Fr* [ne pɛʁ se]
Ng ɪŋ eŋ —*Cantonese* [⁴ŋ, ⁴m]
Ngaio, ngaio 'naɪ əʊ ‖ -oʊ —*Maori* ['ŋai o]
~s, ~'s z
Ngiyambaa, Ngiyampaa *Australian language*
'ŋeəm bɑː ‖ 'ŋeɪ əm bɑː
Nguni ʳŋ 'guːn i
NHS ˌen eɪtʃ 'es §-heɪtʃ-
Nhulunbuy *place in Australia* 'nuːl ən bɔɪ
→-əm-
Ni '*nickel*' ˌen 'aɪ
Ni, Ní *in Irish names* niː —*Irish* [ɲi:]
niacin 'naɪ‿əs ɪn §-ʳn
Niagara naɪ 'æg ʳr‿ə ni-
Niˌagara 'Falls
Niall (i) niːʳl, (ii) 'naɪ‿əl
Niamey ni 'ɑːm eɪ ˌniə 'meɪ ‖ ˌniː ə 'meɪ —*Fr*
[nja mɛ]
Niamh niːv 'niːˌəv
nib nɪb **nibs** nɪbz
nibbl|e 'nɪb ʳl **~ed** d **~es** z **~ing** ˌɪŋ

Nibelung 'niːb ə lʊŋ —*Ger* ['niː bə lʊŋ]
Nibelungenlied 'niːb ə lʊŋ ən liːd -liːt —*Ger*
['niː bə lʊŋ ən liːt]
niblick 'nɪb lɪk **~s** s
NiCad, NiCd 'naɪ kæd
Nicaea naɪ 'siː ə
NiCam *tdmk* 'naɪ kæm
Nicarag|ua ˌnɪk ə 'ræg| ju‿ə -'rɑːg|-, -'·wə
‖ -'rɑːg| wə —*Sp* [ni ka 'ra ɣwa] **~an/s**
ən/z ◄
nice naɪs **nicer** 'naɪs ə ‖ -ʳr **nicest** 'naɪs ɪst -əst
Nice *place in France* niːs —*Fr* [nis]
nice-looking ˌnaɪs 'lʊk ɪŋ ◄ §-'luːk-
nicely 'naɪs li
Nicene ˌnaɪ 'siːn ◄
ˌNicene 'Creed
niceness 'naɪs nəs -nɪs
nicet|y 'naɪs ət |i -ɪt- ‖ -ət̮ |i **~ies** iz

NICHE

niche niːʃ nɪtʃ ‖ nɪtʃ — Preference poll, BrE: niːʃ 95%, nɪtʃ 5%. 95% niːʃ, 5% nɪtʃ BrE

niche niːʃ nɪtʃ ‖ nɪtʃ — *Preference poll, BrE:*
niːʃ *95%,* nɪtʃ *5%. In AmE only* nɪtʃ. **niches**
'niːʃ ɪz 'nɪtʃ-, 'nɪʃ-, -əz ‖ 'nɪtʃ əz
Nichiren ˌnɪtʃ ɪ 'ren ˌ· ·'; 'nɪʃ ər ən —*Jp*
['ɲi tɕi ɾen]
Nichol 'nɪk ʳl
Nichola 'nɪk əl ə
Nicholas 'nɪk əl əs
Nicholls, Nichols 'nɪk ʳlz
Nicholson 'nɪk ʳl sən
Nicias 'nɪs i‿əs
nick, Nick nɪk **nicked** nɪkt **nicking** 'nɪk ɪŋ
nicks, Nick's nɪks
nickel 'nɪk ʳl **~s** z
ˌnickel 'silver
nickel-and-dime ˌnɪk ʳl ən 'daɪm
nickelodeon ˌnɪk ə 'ləʊd i‿ən ‖ -'loʊd- **~s** z
nickel-|plate ˌnɪk ʳl |'pleɪt ◄ **~plated** 'pleɪt ɪd
-əd ‖ 'pleɪt̮ əd **~plates** 'pleɪts **~plating**
'pleɪt ɪŋ ‖ 'pleɪt̮ ɪŋ
nicker 'nɪk ə ‖ -ʳr **~ed** d **nickering** 'nɪk ər ɪŋ
~s z
Nicki 'nɪk i
Nickleby 'nɪk ʳl bi
nicknack 'nɪk næk **~s** s
nicknam|e 'nɪk neɪm **~ed** d **~es** z **~ing** ɪŋ
Nicky 'nɪk i
Nicobar 'nɪk əʊ bɑː ‖ -ə bɑːr
Nicodemus ˌnɪk ə 'diːm əs
nicoise, niçoise ₍ˌ₎niː 'swɑːz nɪ- —*Fr*
[ni swɑːz]
Nicol 'nɪk ʳl
Nicola 'nɪk əl ə
Nicole nɪ 'kəʊl →-'kɒʊl ‖ -'koʊl
Nicolette ˌnɪk ə 'let

Nicoll 'nɪk ᵊl
Nicolson 'nɪk ᵊl sən
Nicomachean naɪ ˌkɒm ə 'kiː ən ◂ ˌ·· ·ˈ· ·
‖ -ˌkɑːm-
Nicomachus ₍ᵢ₎naɪ 'kɒm ək əs ‖ -'kɑːm-
Nicosia ˌnɪk ə 'siː ə
nicotinamide ˌnɪk ə 'tɪn ə maɪd -'tiːn- ‖ -mɪd
nicotine 'nɪk ə tiːn ˌ·ˈ·
nic|tate nɪk '|teɪt ‖ 'nɪk|t eɪt **~tated** teɪt ɪd
-əd ‖ teɪt̬ əd **~tates** teɪts **~tating** teɪt ɪŋ
‖ teɪt̬ ɪŋ
nicti|tate 'nɪkt ɪ |teɪt -ə- **~tated** teɪt ɪd -əd
‖ teɪt̬ əd **~tates** teɪts **~tating** teɪt ɪŋ ‖ teɪt̬ ɪŋ
Niddrie, Niddry 'nɪdr i
nidicolous nɪ 'dɪk əl əs
nidifugous nɪ 'dɪf jʊg əs -jəg-
nid|us 'naɪd |əs **~i** aɪ **~uses** əs ɪz -əz
Niebuhr 'niː bʊə ‖ -bʊr —*Ger* ['niː buːɐ]
niece niːs **nieces** 'niːs ɪz -əz
Niedersachsen 'niːd ə ˌsæks ᵊn ‖ -ᵊr ˌsɑːks-
—*Ger* ['niː dɐ ˌzak sᵊn]
niello ni 'el əʊ ‖ -oʊ **~ed** d **~ing** ɪŋ **~s** z
Nielsen 'niːᵊls ən
Niemann 'niːm ən
Niemeyer 'niː maɪˌə ‖ -maɪˌᵊr
Niersteiner 'nɪə staɪn ə -ʃtaɪn- ‖ 'nɪr staɪn ᵊr
—*Ger* ['niːɐ ʃtain ɐ]
Nietzsche 'niːtʃ ə ‖ -i —*Ger* ['niː tʃə, 'niːts ʃə]
niff nɪf **niffed** nɪft **niffing** 'nɪf ɪŋ **niffs** nɪfs
niffy 'nɪf i
nift|y 'nɪft |i **~ier** i ə ‖ i ᵊr **~ies** iz **~iest** i ɪst
i ˌəst **~ily** ɪ li əl i
Nige naɪdʒ
Nigel 'naɪdʒ əl
nigella, N~ naɪ 'dʒel ə
Niger *country* niː 'ʒeə 'naɪdʒ ə ‖ 'naɪdʒ ᵊr —*Fr*
[ni ʒɛːʁ]
Niger *river* 'naɪdʒ ə ‖ -ᵊr
Niger-Congo ˌnaɪdʒ ə 'kɒŋ gəʊ ◂
‖ -ᵊr 'kɑːŋ goʊ
Nigeria naɪ 'dʒɪər i ə ‖ -'dʒɪr-
Nigerian naɪ 'dʒɪər i ən ‖ -'dʒɪr- **~s** z
Nigerien, Nigérien niː 'ʒeər i ən ‖ -'ʒer- —*Fr*
[ni ʒe ʁjɛ̃] **~s** z —*or as singular*
Nigerois ˌniːʒ eə 'wɑː ◂ ˌnɪʒ- ‖ -er- —*not a
French word*
niggard 'nɪg əd ‖ -ᵊrd **~s** z
niggard|ly 'nɪg əd |li ‖ -ᵊrd- **~liness** li nəs
-nɪs
nigger 'nɪg ə ‖ -ᵊr **~s** z
niggl|e 'nɪg ᵊl **~ed** d **~es** z **~ing** ɪŋ
niggler 'nɪg lə ‖ -lᵊr **~s** z
nigg|ly 'nɪg |li **~liness** li nəs -nɪs
nigh naɪ
night naɪt **nights** naɪts
'night ˌblindness, ˌ·ˈ·◂; 'night owl; 'night
school; 'night shift; 'night soil; 'night
watch, ˌ·ˈ·; ˌnight 'watchman
nightcap 'naɪt kæp **~s** s
nightclothes 'naɪt kləʊðz -kləʊz ‖ -kloʊz
-kloʊðz
nightclub 'naɪt klʌb **~bed** d **~ber/s** ə/z ‖ ᵊr/z
~bing ɪŋ **~s** z

nightcrawler 'naɪt ˌkrɔːl ə ‖ -ᵊr -ˌkrɑːl- **~s** z
nightdress 'naɪt dres **~es** ɪz əz
nightfall 'naɪt fɔːl ‖ -fɑːl
nightgown 'naɪt gaʊn **~s** z
nighthawk 'naɪt hɔːk ‖ -hɑːk **~s** s
nightie 'naɪt i 'naɪt̬ i **~s** z
nightingale, N~ 'naɪt ɪŋ geᵊl ‖ 'naɪt̬ ᵊn-
'naɪt̬ ɪŋ- **~s** z
nightjar 'naɪt dʒɑː ‖ -dʒɑːr **~s** z
nightlife 'naɪt laɪf
nightlight 'naɪt laɪt **~s** s
nightline 'naɪt laɪn **~s** z
nightlong ˌnaɪt 'lɒŋ ◂ ˈ· · ‖ -'lɔːŋ -'lɑːŋ
nightly 'naɪt li
nightmare 'naɪt meə ‖ -mer -mær **~s** z
nightmarish 'naɪt meər ɪʃ ‖ -mer- -mær- **~ly** li
~ness nəs nɪs
night-night ˌnaɪt 'naɪt
nightrider 'naɪt raɪd ə ‖ -ᵊr **~s** z
nightshade 'naɪt ʃeɪd **~s** z
nightshirt 'naɪt ʃɜːt ‖ -ʃɜ·ːt **~s** s
nightsoil 'naɪt sɔɪl
nightspot 'naɪt spɒt ‖ -spɑːt **~s** s
nightstand 'naɪt stænd **~s** z
nightstick 'naɪt stɪk **~s** s
nighttime 'naɪt taɪm
nightwear 'naɪt weə ‖ -wer
nig-nog 'nɪg nɒg ‖ -nɑːg **~s** z
nihil 'naɪ hɪl 'niː-, 'nɪ-, -həl
nihilism 'naɪ ɪ ˌlɪz əm 'niː-, -hɪ-, -ə-, -hə-;
'nɪ hɪ-, -hə-
nihilist 'naɪ ɪl ɪst 'niː-, -hɪl-, -əl-, -həl-, §-əst;
'nɪ hɪl-, -həl- **~s** s
nihilistic ˌnaɪ ɪ 'lɪst ɪk ◂ ˌniː-, -hɪ-, -ə-, -hə-;
ˌnɪ hɪ-, -hə-
nihil obstat ˌnaɪ hɪl 'ɒb stæt ˌniː-, ˌnɪ-, -həl-
‖ -'ɑːb-
Nijinsky nɪ 'dʒɪn sk i nə-, -'ʒɪn'sk- —*Russ*
[nʲɪ 'ʒin skʲɪj]
Nijmegen 'naɪ meɪg ən ·ˈ·· —*Dutch*
['nɛi meː xən]
-nik nɪk — **refusenik** rɪ 'fjuːz nɪk rə-, §rɪ-
Nike 'naɪk i naɪk
Nikita nɪ 'kiːt ə nə- ‖ -'kiːt̬ ə —*Russ* [nʲɪ'kʲi tə]
Nikkei nɪ 'keɪ 'niːk eɪ ‖ 'niːk eɪ —*Jp* [njik ˌkei,
-ˌkee]
Nikki 'nɪk i
Nikon *tdmk* 'nɪk ɒn ‖ 'naɪk ɑːn 'niːk- —*Jp*
['ɲi koɴ]
nil nɪl
ˌnil ˌdespe'randum ˌdesp ə 'rænd əm
Nile naɪᵊl
nilgai 'nɪlg aɪ **~s** z
Nilo-Saharan ˌnaɪl əʊ sə 'hɑːr ən ◂
‖ ˌnaɪl oʊ sə 'hær ən ◂ -'her-, -'hɑːr-
Nilotic naɪ 'lɒt ɪk ‖ -'lɑːt̬ ɪk
Nilsen, Nilsson 'niːᵊls ᵊn 'nɪls-
nim nɪm
nimbi 'nɪm baɪ
nim|ble 'nɪm |bᵊl **~bler** blə ‖ blᵊr **~blest** blɪst
bləst **~bleness** bᵊl nəs -nɪs **~bly** bli

nimbostratus ˌnɪm bəʊ 'streɪt əs
‖ -boʊ 'streɪʧ- -'stræʧ-
nim|bus 'nɪm |bəs **~bi** baɪ **~buses** bəs ɪz -əz
nim|by, NIM|BY 'nɪm| bi **~bies** biz **~byism**
bi ˌɪz əm
Nîmes niːm —*Fr* [nim]
nimini-piminy, niminy-piminy
ˌnɪm ən i 'pɪm ən i ◂ -ɪn i 'pɪm ɪn-
Nimitz 'nɪm ɪts §-əts
Nimmo 'nɪm əʊ ‖ -oʊ
Nimrod, n~ 'nɪm rɒd ‖ -rɑːd **~s, ~'s** z
Nin nɪn niːn
Nina 'niːn ə
nincompoop 'nɪŋk əm puːp 'nɪn kəm- **~s** s
nine naɪn —*but for clarity in communication*
code, niner 'naɪn ə ‖ -ᵊr **nines** naɪnz
ˌnine days' 'wonder
ninefold 'naɪn fəʊld →-'fʊld ‖ -foʊld
ninepin 'naɪn pɪn →'naɪm- **~s** z
nineteen ˌnaɪn 'tiːn ◂ —*occasionally, when*
stress-shifted, also 'naɪn tən **~s** z
ˌnineteen 'people; ˌnineteen ˌninety-'nine
nineteenth ˌnaɪn 'tiːnθ ◂ **~s** s
ˌnineteenth 'hole
ninetieth 'naɪnt i əθ -ɪ-θ ‖ 'naɪnʧ i əθ **~s** s
nine-to-five ˌnaɪn tə 'faɪv
Ninette nɪ 'net niː-
ninet|y 'naɪnt |i 'naɪnʧ |i **~ies** iz
ninety-nine ˌnaɪnt i 'naɪn ◂ ‖ ˌnaɪnʧ-
ninety-ninth ˌnaɪnt i 'naɪnᵗθ ◂ ‖ ˌnaɪnʧ-
Nineveh 'nɪn ɪv ə -əv-
Ningbo ˌnɪŋ 'bəʊ ‖ -'boʊ —*Chi* Níngbō
[²niŋ ¹po]
Ningxia ˌnɪŋ ʃi 'ɑː —*Chi* Níngxià [²niŋ ⁴çja]
Ninian 'nɪn i ən
ninish 'naɪn ɪʃ
ninja 'nɪnʤ ə **~s** z
ninn|y 'nɪn |i **~ies** iz
Nintendo *tdmk* nɪn 'tend əʊ ‖ -oʊ
ninth naɪnᵗθ **ninthly** 'naɪnᵗθ li **ninths** naɪnᵗθs
niobate 'naɪ əʊ beɪt ‖ -ə·
Niobe 'naɪ̮əb i -əʊb i ‖ -ə bi:
niobic naɪ 'əʊb ɪk ‖ -'oʊb-
niobium naɪ 'əʊb i̮əm ‖ -'oʊb-
nip, Nip nɪp **nipped** nɪpt **nipping/ly**
'nɪp ɪŋ /li **nips** nɪps
nipper 'nɪp ə ‖ -ᵊr **~s** z
nippi... —*see* **nippy**
nipple 'nɪp ᵊl **~s** z
nipplewort 'nɪp ᵊl wɜːt §-wɔːt ‖ -wɜːt -wɔːrt **~s**
s
Nippon 'nɪp ɒn ‖ -ɑːn nɪ 'pɑːn —*Jp* [nip 'poɴ]
Nipponese ˌnɪp ə 'niːz ◂ ‖ -'niːs ◂
nipp|y 'nɪp |i **~ier** i̮ə ‖ i̮ᵊr **~iest** i̮ɪst i̮əst **~ily**
ɪ li əl i **~iness** i nəs i nɪs
niqab nɪ 'kɑːb —*Arabic* [nɪ 'qɑːb]
NIREX, Nirex *tdmk* 'naɪᵊr eks
nirvana, N~ nɪə 'vɑːn ə nɜː- ‖ nɪr- -'væn-
—*Hindi* [nɪr vɑːn]
Nis, Niš nɪʃ niːʃ
Nisan 'naɪs æn 'nɪs-, -ɑːn ‖ 'niːs ɑːn 'nɪs ᵊn
Nisbet, Nisbett 'nɪz bət -bɪt
Nisei, nisei 'niː seɪ —*Jp* ['ɲi se:]

nisi 'naɪs aɪ 'niːs i
ˌnisi 'prius 'praɪ̮əs 'priːˌəs
Nissan *tdmk* 'nɪs æn ‖ -ɑːn 'niːs- —*Jp*
[nis ˌsaɴ]
Nissen 'nɪs ᵊn
'Nissen hut
Nistelrooy 'nɪst ᵊl rɔɪ
nit nɪt **nits** nɪts
Nita 'niːt ə ‖ 'niːʧ ə
nite naɪt
niter 'naɪt ə ‖ 'naɪʧ ᵊr
niterie 'naɪt ər i ‖ 'naɪʧ- **~s** z
nitpick 'nɪt pɪk **~ed** t **~er/s** ə/z ‖ ᵊr/z **~ing** ɪŋ
~s s
nitrate 'naɪtr eɪt -ət, -ɪt **~s** s
nitrazepam naɪ 'træz ɪ pæm -'treɪz-, -ə-
nitre 'naɪt ə ‖ 'naɪʧ ᵊr
nitric 'naɪtr ɪk
ˌnitric 'acid
nitride 'naɪtr aɪd **~s** z
nitrification ˌnaɪtr ɪf ɪ 'keɪʃ ᵊn ˌ·əf-, -ə'· ·
nitrif|y 'naɪtr ɪ faɪ -ə- **~ied** aɪd **~ies** aɪz **~ying**
aɪ ɪŋ
nitrile 'naɪtr aɪᵊl -ɪl, §-ᵊl **~s** z
nitrite 'naɪtr aɪt **~s** s
nitro 'naɪtr əʊ ‖ -oʊ
nitro- *comb. form*
with stress-neutral suffix |naɪtr əʊ ‖ -oʊ
— **nitrobenzene** ˌnaɪtr əʊ 'benz iːn ‖ -oʊ-
-ben 'ziːn
with stress-imposing suffix naɪ 'trɒ +
‖ -'trɑː + — **nitrometer** naɪ 'trɒm ɪt ə -ət-
‖ -'trɑːm əʧ ᵊr
nitrocellulose ˌnaɪtr əʊ 'sel ju ləʊs -'·jə-, -ləʊz
‖ -oʊ 'sel jə loʊs -loʊz
nitrochalk, Nitro-chalk *tdmk* 'naɪtr əʊ tʃɔːk
‖ -oʊ- -tʃɑːk
nitrogen 'naɪtr əʤ ən
nitrogenous naɪ 'trɒʤ ən əs -ɪn- ‖ -'trɑːʤ-
nitroglycerin, nitroglycerine
ˌnaɪtr əʊ 'glɪs ər ɪn ˌ·ə-, -iːn, §-ᵊn ‖ -ˌ·ə-
nitrosamine naɪ 'trəʊz ə miːn -'trəʊs-;
ˌnaɪtr əʊs ə 'miːn, -'æm iːn, '· · · · ‖ -'troʊs-
nitrous 'naɪtr əs
nitty 'nɪt i ‖ 'nɪʧ i
nitty-gritty ˌnɪt i 'grɪt i ˌnɪʧ i 'grɪʧ i
nitwit 'nɪt wɪt **~s** s
Niue 'nju: eɪ ni 'u: eɪ ‖ ni 'u: eɪ
Niu Gini (ˌ)nju: 'gɪn i
Nivea *tdmk* 'nɪv i̮ə -eɪ
Niven 'nɪv ᵊn
nix nɪks **nixed** nɪkst **nixes** 'nɪks ɪz -əz **nixing**
'nɪks ɪŋ
Nixdorf *tdmk* 'nɪks dɔːf ‖ -dɔːrf
nixie 'nɪks i **~s** z
Nixon 'nɪks ən
Nixonian nɪk 'səʊn i̮ən ‖ -'soʊn-
Nizam, nizam nɪ 'zɑːm naɪ-, -'zæm **~s** z
Nizhni Novgorod ˌnɪʒ ni 'nɒv gə rɒd
‖ -'nɑːv gə rɑːd —*Russ* [ˌnⁱiʒ nⁱi 'nɔv gə rət]
Nkomo ᵊn 'kəʊm əʊ →ᵊŋ- ‖ -'koʊm oʊ
—*Ndebele* [ŋkʼɔː mɔ]
Nkrumah ᵊn 'kruːm ə →ᵊŋ-

no nəʊ ‖ noʊ —*There is also an occasional weak form* nə **noes** nəʊz ‖ noʊz
ˌno 'ball; ˌno 'way

no., No. —*see* **number**; **North nos.** —*see* **numbers**

no-account ˌnəʊ ə 'kaʊnt ◂ ‖ ˌnoʊ-

Noachian nəʊ 'eɪk iˌən ‖ noʊ-

Noah 'nəʊ ə ‖ 'noʊ ə
ˌNoah's 'ark

Noakes nəʊks ‖ noʊks

Noam 'nəʊ əm nəʊm ‖ 'noʊ əm noʊm

nob nɒb ‖ nɑːb **nobs** nɒbz ‖ nɑːbz

no-ball ˌnəʊ 'bɔːl ‖ ˌnoʊ- ~**ed** d ~**ing** ɪŋ ~**s** z

nobbl|e 'nɒb əl ‖ 'nɑːb əl ~**ed** d ~**es** z ~**ing** ɪŋ

nobbut 'nɒb ət ‖ 'nɑːb-

nobby, Nobby 'nɒb i ‖ 'nɑːb i

Nobel (ˌ)nəʊ 'bel ‖ (ˌ)noʊ- —*Swedish* [nɔ 'bel]
No₊bel 'prize, ˌNobel 'prize

nobelium nəʊ 'biːl iˌəm ‖ noʊ- -'bel-

nobiliary nəʊ 'bɪl iˌər i ‖ noʊ 'bɪl i er i -'bɪl jər i

nobilit|y nəʊ 'bɪl ət |i -ɪt- ‖ noʊ 'bɪl ət̬ |i ~**ies** iz

noble, Noble 'nəʊb əl ‖ 'noʊb əl **nobler** 'nəʊb lə ‖ 'noʊb lər **nobles** 'nəʊb əlz ‖ 'noʊb əlz **noblest** 'nəʊb lɪst -ləst ‖ 'noʊb ləst

noble|man 'nəʊb əl |mən ‖ 'noʊb- ~**men** mən

noble-minded ˌnəʊb əl 'maɪnd ɪd ◂ -əd ‖ ˌnoʊb-

nobleness 'nəʊb əl nəs -nɪs ‖ 'noʊb-

noblesse oblige nəʊ ˌbles əʊ 'bliːʒ ˌ·◂·'· ‖ noʊ ˌbles oʊ- —*Fr* [nɔb lɛ sɔ bliːʒ]

noble|woman 'nəʊb əl |ˌwʊm ən ‖ 'noʊb- ~**women** ˌwɪm ɪn §-ən

nobly 'nəʊb li ‖ 'noʊb li

nobod|y 'nəʊb əd |i 'nəʊ ˌbɒd |i ‖ 'noʊb əd |i 'noʊ ˌbɑːd |i, -bʌd i ~**ies, ~y's** iz

no-brainer ˌnəʊ 'breɪn ə ‖ ˌnoʊ 'breɪn ər '·ˌ·· ~**s** z

nock nɒk ‖ nɑːk (= *knock*) **nocked** nɒkt ‖ nɑːkt **nocking** 'nɒk ɪŋ ‖ 'nɑːk ɪŋ **nocks** nɒks ‖ nɑːks

no-claim ˌnəʊ 'kleɪm ‖ ˌnoʊ- ~**s** z
ˌno-claim(s) 'bonus, ·'·ˌ··

no-confidence ˌnəʊ 'kɒn fɪd ənts -fəd- ‖ ˌnoʊ 'kɑːn-

no-count 'nəʊ kaʊnt ‖ 'noʊ-

noctilucent ˌnɒkt ɪ 'luːs ənt §-ə-, -'ljuːs- ‖ ˌnɑːkt ə-

noctuid 'nɒkt ju ɪd 'nɒk tʃuˌ §ˌəd ‖ 'nɑːk tʃu əd -tu- ~**s** z

nocturn 'nɒkt ɜːn ˌnɒk 'tɜːn ‖ 'nɑːkt ɜːn ~**s** z

nocturnal nɒk 'tɜːn əl ‖ nɑːk 'tɜːn əl ~**ly** i

nocturne 'nɒkt ɜːn ˌnɒk 'tɜːn ‖ 'nɑːkt ɜːn ~**s** z

nod nɒd ‖ nɑːd **nodded** 'nɒd ɪd -əd ‖ 'nɑːd əd **nodding** 'nɒd ɪŋ ‖ 'nɑːd ɪŋ **nods** nɒdz ‖ nɑːdz
ˌnodding ac'quaintance

nodal 'nəʊd əl ‖ 'noʊd əl

nodality nəʊ 'dæl ət i -ɪt- ‖ noʊ 'dæl ət̬ i

nodd... —*see* **nod**

noddle 'nɒd əl ‖ 'nɑːd əl ~**s** z

Nodd|y, nodd|y 'nɒd |i ‖ 'nɑːd |i ~**ies, ~y's** iz

node nəʊd ‖ noʊd **nodes** nəʊdz ‖ noʊdz

nodular 'nɒd jʊl ə -jəl- ‖ 'nɑːdʒ əl ər

nodule 'nɒd juːl ‖ 'nɑːdʒ uːl ~**s** z

Noel, Noël *personal name* 'nəʊˌəl -el ‖ 'noʊ-

Noel, Noël '*Christmas*' nəʊ 'el ‖ noʊ-

Noele ˌnəʊ 'el◂ ‖ ˌnoʊ-

noes *pl of* **no** nəʊz ‖ noʊz (= *nose*)

noesis nəʊ 'iːs ɪs §-əs ‖ noʊ-

noetic nəʊ 'et ɪk ‖ noʊ 'et̬ ɪk

no-fault ˌnəʊ 'fɔːlt ◂ -'fɒlt ◂ ‖ ˌnoʊ 'fɔːlt ◂ -'fɑːlt ◂

no-fly ˌnəʊ 'flaɪ ◂ ‖ ˌnoʊ-
ˌno-'fly ˌzone, ·· ·ˌ·

no-frills ˌnəʊ 'frɪlz ◂ ‖ ˌnoʊ-

nog nɒg ‖ nɑːg **nogs** nɒgz ‖ nɑːgz

noggin 'nɒg ɪn §-ən ‖ 'nɑːg- ~**s** z

no-go ˌnəʊ 'gəʊ ◂ ‖ ˌnoʊ 'goʊ
ˌno-'go ˌarea, ·· '·ˌ··

no-good ˌnəʊ 'gʊd ◂ ‖ ˌnoʊ-

Noh nəʊ ‖ noʊ —*Jp* [no,o]

no-hitter ˌnəʊ 'hɪt ə ‖ ˌnoʊ 'hɪt̬ ər ~**s** z

no-holds-barred ˌnəʊ həʊldz 'bɑːd ◂ →-hɒʊldz- ‖ ˌnoʊ hoʊldz 'bɑːrd ◂

no-hope ˌnəʊ 'həʊp ◂ ‖ ˌnoʊ 'hoʊp ◂

no-hoper ˌnəʊ 'həʊp ə ‖ ˌnoʊ 'hoʊp ər ~**s** z

nohow 'nəʊ haʊ ‖ 'noʊ-

noir nwɑː ‖ nwɑːr —*Fr* [nwaːʁ]

noise nɔɪz **noised** nɔɪzd **noises** 'nɔɪz ɪz -əz **noising** 'nɔɪz ɪŋ

noiseless 'nɔɪz ləs -lɪs ~**ly** li ~**ness** nəs nɪs

noise-maker 'nɔɪz ˌmeɪk ə ‖ -ər ~**s** z

noisette nwɑː 'zet nwæ- —*Fr* [nwa zɛt] ~**s** s —*or as singular*

noisi... —*see* **noisy**

noisome 'nɔɪs əm ~**ly** li ~**ness** nəs nɪs

nois|y 'nɔɪz |i ~**ier** iˌə ‖ iˌər ~**iest** i ɪst i əst ~**ily** ɪ li əl i ~**iness** i nəs i nɪs

Nokia *tdmk* 'nɒk iˌə ‖ 'noʊk iˌə

Nola 'nəʊl ə ‖ 'noʊl ə

Nolan 'nəʊl ən ‖ 'noʊl ən

nolens volens ˌnəʊl enz 'vəʊl enz ‖ ˌnoʊl enz 'voʊl-

noli-me-tangere, noli me tangere ˌnəʊl i ˌmeɪ 'tæŋ gər i -ˌmiː-, -'tændʒ ər-, -gə reɪ ‖ ˌnoʊl-

no-load ˌnəʊ 'ləʊd ◂ ‖ ˌnoʊ 'loʊd ◂

nolo contendere ˌnəʊl əʊ kən 'tend ər i -kɒn'·-, -ə reɪ ‖ ˌnoʊl oʊ-

nomad 'nəʊm æd ‖ 'noʊm- ~**s** z

nomadic nəʊ 'mæd ɪk ‖ noʊ- ~**ally** əl_i

nomadism 'nəʊm æd ˌɪz əm ‖ 'noʊm-

no-man's-land 'nəʊ mænz lænd ‖ 'noʊ-

nom de guerre ˌnɒm də 'geə ˌnɒ̃- ‖ ˌnɑːm də 'geər -dɪ- —*Fr* [nɔ̃d gɛːʁ] **noms de guerre** *same pronunciation*

nom de plume ˌnɒm də 'pluːm ˌnɒ̃-; '·ˌ·· ‖ ˌnɑːm- —*Fr* [nɔ̃d plym] **noms de plume** *same pronunciation*

Nome nəʊm ‖ noʊm

nomenclature nəʊ ˈmeŋk lətʃ ə;
ˈnəʊm ən kleɪtʃ ə, ˈnɒm-, →-əŋ-, ˈen-, →-eŋ-
‖ ˈnoʊm ən kleɪtʃ ᵊr noʊ ˈmen klə tʃʊr,
→-ˈmeŋ-, -klətʃ ᵊr ~s z

nominal ˈnɒm ɪn ᵊl -ən-, -ᵊn̩ əl ‖ ˈnɑːm ən ᵊl
-ᵊn̩ əl ~s z

nominally ˈnɒm ɪn əl i -ᵊn̩ əl i ‖ ˈnɑːm ən əl i
-ᵊn̩ əl-

nomi|nate ˈnɒm ɪ |neɪt -ə- ‖ ˈnɑːm- ~**nated**
neɪt ɪd -əd ‖ neɪt̬ əd ~**nates** neɪts ~**nating**
neɪt ɪŋ ‖ neɪt̬ ɪŋ

nomination ˌnɒm ɪ ˈneɪʃ ᵊn -ə- ‖ ˌnɑːm- ~s z

nominative ˈnɒm ən ət̬ ɪv ˈ·ɪn-
‖ ˈnɑːm ən ət̬ ɪv ~s z

nominator ˈnɒm ɪ neɪt ə -ə- ‖ -neɪt̬ ᵊr ~s z

nominee ˌnɒm ɪ ˈniː ◄ -ə- ‖ ˌnɑːm- ~s z

nomo- *comb. form*
with stress-neutral suffix |nɒm ə |nəʊm-
‖ |nɑːm ə |noʊm- — **nomogram**
ˈnɒm ə græm ˈnəʊm- ‖ ˈnɑːm- ˈnoʊm-
with stress-imposing suffix nɒ ˈmɒ+ nəʊ-
‖ noʊ ˈmɑː+ — **nomology** nɒ ˈmɒl ədʒ i
nəʊ- ‖ noʊ ˈmɑːl-

Nomura nəʊ ˈmjʊər ə -ˈmʊər- ‖ noʊ ˈmjʊr ə
—*Jp* [no ˌmɯ ra]

-nomy *stress-imposing* nəm i — **taxonomy**
tæk ˈsɒn əm i ‖ -ˈsɑːn-

non nɒn nəʊn ‖ nɑːn noʊn —*See also phrases
with this word*

non- |nɒn ‖ |nɑːn —*Also occasionally* |nʌn
— **nonacademic** ˌnɒn ˌæk ə ˈdem ɪk ˌnʌn-
‖ ˌnɑːn-

nonage ˈnəʊn ɪdʒ ˈnɒn- ‖ ˈnoʊn- ˈnɑːn-

nonagenarian ˌnəʊn ə dʒə ˈneər i ᵊn ◄ ˌnɒn-,
-dʒɪ-ˈ·- ‖ ˌnoʊn ə dʒə ˈner- ˌnɑːn- ~s z

nonaggression ˌnɒn ə ˈgreʃ ᵊn ‖ ˌnɑːn-

nonagon ˈnɒn əg ən ˈnəʊn-, -ə gɒn
‖ ˈnɑːn ə gɑːn ˈnoʊn- ~s z

nonalcoholic ˌnɒn ˌælk ə ˈhɒl ɪk ◄
‖ ˌnɑːn ˌælk ə ˈhɔːl ɪk ◄ -ˈhɑːl-
ˌnonalcoˌholic ˈbeverage

nonaligned ˌnɒn ə ˈlaɪnd ◄ -ᵊl ˈaɪnd ◄ ‖ ˌnɑːn-

nonalignment ˌnɒn ə ˈlaɪn mənt →-laɪm-;
-ᵊl ˈaɪn- ‖ ˌnɑːn-

no-name ˌnəʊ ˈneɪm ◄ ‖ ˌnoʊ-

nonappearanc|e ˌnɒn ə ˈpɪər ən̩ts
‖ ˌnɑːn ə ˈpɪr- ~**es** ɪz əz

nonary ˈnəʊn ər i ˈnɒn- ‖ ˈnoʊn- ˈnɑːn-

nonassertive ˌnɒn ə ˈsɜːt ɪv ◄
‖ ˌnɑːn ə ˈsɜːt̬ ɪv ◄

non-attendance ˌnɒn ə ˈtend ən̩ts ◄ ‖ ˌnɑːn-

nonbeliever ˌnɒn bi ˈliːv ə →ˌnɒm-, -bə-
‖ ˌnɑːn bi ˈliːv ᵊr ~s z

non-binding ˌnɒn ˈbaɪnd ɪŋ ◄ →ˌnɒm- ‖ ˌnɑːn-

non-biological ˌnɒn ˌbaɪ ə ˈlɒdʒ ɪk ᵊl ◄
→ˌnɒm- ‖ ˌnɑːn-

nonce nɒn̩ts ‖ nɑːn̩ts **nonces** ˈnɒn̩ts ɪz -əz
‖ ˈnɑːn̩ts əz
ˈnonce word

nonchalance ˈnɒnʃ ᵊl ən̩ts ‖ ˌnɑːn ʃə ˈlɑːn̩ts
ˈ··· (*)

nonchalant ˈnɒnʃ ᵊl ənt ‖ ˌnɑːn ʃə ˈlɑːnt ◄
ˈ··· ~**ly** li

non-com ˈnɒn kɒm →ˈnɒŋ- ‖ ˈnɑːn kɑːm ~s z

non-combat ˌnɒn ˈkɒm bæt ◄ →ˌnɒŋ-
‖ ˌnɑːn ˈkɑːm-

noncombatant ˌnɒn ˈkɒm bət ənt →ˌnɒŋ-,
-ˈkʌm-; ˌ·kəm ˈbæt ᵊnt, §-kɒm-
‖ ˌnɑːn kəm ˈbæt ᵊnt ˌ·ˈkɑːm bət ənt ~s s

noncommissioned ˌnɒn kə ˈmɪʃ ᵊnd ◄ →ˌnɒŋ-
‖ ˌnɑːn-
ˌnoncomˌmissioned ˈofficer

noncommittal ˌnɒn kə ˈmɪt ᵊl ◄ →ˌnɒŋ-
‖ ˌnɑːn kə ˈmɪt̬ ᵊl ◄ ~**ly** i

noncompetitive ˌnɒn kəm ˈpet ət ɪv ◄
→ˌnɒŋ-, §-kɒm-ˈ·, -ɪt · ‖ ˌnɑːn kəm ˈpet̬-

noncompli|ance ˌnɒn kəm ˈplaɪ |ən̩ts →ˌnɒŋ-,
§-kɒm- ‖ ˌnɑːn- ~**ant** ənt

non compos mentis ˌnɒn ˌkɒmp əs ˈment ɪs
→ˌnɒŋ-, ˌnəʊn-, -ˌɒs-
‖ ˌnɑːn ˌkɑːmp əs ˈment̬ əs noʊn-, ˌ·ˌ·ˈ··

nonconductor ˌnɒn kən ˈdʌkt ə →ˌnɒŋ-,
§-kɒn- ‖ ˌnɑːn kən ˈdʌkt ᵊr ~s z

nonconformism ˌnɒn kən ˈfɔːm ˌɪz əm
→ˌnɒŋ-, §,·kɒn- ‖ ˌnɑːn kən ˈfɔːrm-

nonconformist, N~ ˌnɒn kən ˈfɔːm ɪst ◄
→ˌnɒŋ-, §-kɒn-, §-əst ‖ ˌnɑːn kən ˈfɔːrm əst ◄
~s s

nonconformity, N~ ˌnɒn kən ˈfɔːm ət i
→ˌnɒŋ-, §,·kɒn-, -ɪt i ‖ ˌnɑːn kən ˈfɔːrm ət̬ i

noncontributory ˌnɒn kən ˈtrɪb jʊt ᵊr i ◄
→ˌnɒŋ-, §,·kɒn-; ˌ·ˌkɒn trɪ ˈbjuːt ər i, -trə-ˈ·-
‖ ˌnɑːn kən ˈtrɪb jə tɔːr i ◄ -toʊr i

non-controversial ˌnɒn ˌkɒntr ə ˈvɜːʃ ᵊl ◄
‖ ˌnɑːn ˌkɑːntr ə ˈvɜːʃ ᵊl ◄

noncooperation, non-co-operation
ˌnɒn kəʊ ˌɒp ə ˈreɪʃ ᵊn ˌnɒŋ-
‖ ˌnɑːn koʊ ˌɑːp-

non-count ˌnɒn ˈkaʊnt ◄ →ˌnɒŋ- ‖ ˌnɑːn-

noncustodial ˌnɒn kʌ ˈstəʊd i əl ◄ →ˌnɒŋ-,
-kə- ‖ ˌnɑːn-

non-dairy ˌnɒn ˈdeər i ◄ ‖ ˌnɑːn ˈder i ◄ -ˈdær-

non-deductible ˌnɒn di ˈdʌkt əb ᵊl ◄ ˌ·də-
‖ ˌnɑːn-

nondenominational
ˌnɒn di ˌnɒm ɪ ˈneɪʃ ᵊn̩ ə l ◄ ˌ·də-, -ə·ˈ·
‖ ˌnɑːn di ˌnɑːm-

nondescript ˈnɒn dɪ skrɪpt -də-, † -diː-
‖ ˌnɑːn dɪ ˈskrɪpt◄ ~s s

nondisclosure ˌnɒn dɪs ˈkləʊʒ ə -dəs-
‖ ˌnɑːn dɪs ˈkloʊʒ ᵊr

nondrip ˌnɒn ˈdrɪp ◄ ‖ ˌnɑːn-

non-durable ˌnɒn ˈdjʊər əb l ◄ →-dʒʊər-,
-ˈdjɔːr- ‖ ˌnɑːn ˈdʊr- -ˈdjʊr- ~s z

none nʌn §nɒn (= *nun*)

nonentit|y nɒ ˈnent ət |i nə-, -ɪt-
‖ nɑː ˈnent̬ ət̬ |i ~**ies** iz

nones nəʊnz ‖ noʊnz

nonessential ˌnɒn ɪ ˈsenʃ ᵊl ◄ -ə- ‖ ˌnɑːn-

nonesuch ˈnʌn sʌtʃ §ˈnɒn-

nonet ₍ᵢ₎nəʊ ˈnet nɒ- ‖ noʊ- ~s s

nonetheless ˌnʌn ðə ˈles ◄ §ˌnɒn-

non-event ˌnɒn ɪ ˈvent -ə-, §-iː-; ˈ··· ‖ ˌnɑːn-
~s s

N

non-executive ˌnɒn ɪg 'zek jʊt ɪv ◂, ˌ-eg-, ˌ-əg-, ˌ-ɪk-, ˌ-ek-, ˌ-ək-, -jət, §-ət ▪
‖ ˌnɑːn ɪg 'zek jət ɪv ◂ §-əʈ ɪv ~s z

nonexistent ˌnɒn ɪg 'zɪst ənt ◂ -eg-, -əg-, -ɪk-, -ek-, -ək- ‖ ˌnɑːn-

nonfat ˌnɒn 'fæt ◂ ‖ ˌnɑːn-

non-feasance ˌnɒn 'fiːz ᵊnˈs ‖ ˌnɑːn-

non-ferrous ˌnɒn 'fer əs ◂ ‖ ˌnɑːn-

nonfiction ˌnɒn 'fɪk ʃᵊn ‖ ˌnɑːn-

non-finite ˌnɒn 'faɪn aɪt ◂ ‖ ˌnɑːn-

nonflammable ˌnɒn 'flæm əb ᵊl ◂ ‖ ˌnɑːn-

non-governmental ˌnɒn ˌgʌv ᵊn 'ment l ◂ →ˌnɒŋ-, →ᵊ'ᵊm'ᵊ-, -ə'- ‖ ˌnɑːn ˌgʌv ᵊrn 'menʈ ᵊl ◂

non-immigrant ˌnɒn 'ɪm ɪg rənt ◂ -əg- ‖ ˌnɑːn- ~s s

noninterference ˌnɒn ˌɪnt ə 'fɪər ənˈs ‖ ˌnɑːn ˌɪnʈ ᵊr 'fɪr ənˈs

nonintervention ˌnɒn ˌɪnt ə 'venˈʃ ᵊn ‖ ˌnɑːn ˌɪnʈ ᵊr- ~ist/s ɪst/s §əst/s

noninvolvement ˌnɒn ɪn 'vɒlv mənt -ən-, §-'vəʊlv- ‖ ˌnɑːn ɪn 'vɑːlv-

non-iron ˌnɒn 'aɪ ən ◂ ‖ ˌnɑːn 'aɪ ᵊrn ◂

non-judgmental, non-judgemental ˌnɒn dʒʌdʒ 'ment ᵊl ◂ ‖ ˌnɑːn dʒʌdʒ 'menʈ ᵊl ◂

nonjuror ˌnɒn 'dʒʊər ə ‖ ˌnɑːn 'dʒʊr ᵊr ~s z

nonlinear ˌnɒn 'lɪn i̯ə ◂ ‖ ˌnɑːn 'lɪn i̯ᵊr ◂

non-member ˌnɒn 'mem bə →ˌnɒm- ‖ ˌnɑːn 'mem bᵊr ~s z

non-negotiable ˌnɒn nɪ 'gəʊʃ i̯əb ᵊl ◂, -nə-, -'·əb ᵊl ‖ ˌnɑːn nɪ 'goʊʃ-

no-no 'nəʊ nəʊ ‖ 'noʊ noʊ ~s z

nonobservance ˌnɒn əb 'zɜːv ᵊnˈs §-ɒb- ‖ ˌnɑːn əb 'zɜːv-

no-nonsense ˌnəʊ 'nɒnˈs ənˈs ◂ ‖ ˌnoʊ 'nɑːn senˈs ◂ -'nɑːnˈs ənˈs

nonoxynol nəʊ 'nɒks ɪ nɒl -ə- ‖ noʊ 'nɑːks ə nɑːl -nɔːl, -noʊl

nonpareil ˌnɒn pə 'reɪᵊl →ˌnɒm-; 'nɒn pᵊr ˌəl, →ˈnɒm- ‖ ˌnɑːn pə 'rel ◂

non-partisan ˌnɒn ˌpɑːt ɪ 'zæn ◂ →ˌnɒm- ‖ ˌnɑːn 'pɑːrʈ ə zæn ◂ -sæn ◂

nonpayment ˌnɒn 'peɪ mənt ◂ →ˌnɒm- ‖ ˌnɑːn-

non-playing ˌnɒn 'pleɪ ɪŋ ◂ →ˌnɒm- ‖ ˌnɑːn- ˌnon- ˌplaying 'captain

nonplus ˌnɒn 'plʌs →ˌnɒm-, '·· ‖ ˌnɑːn- ~sed t ~ses ɪz əz ~sing ɪŋ

non-prescription ˌnɒn pri 'skrɪp ʃᵊn ◂ →ˌnɒm-, -prə- ‖ ˌnɑːn-

non-profit ˌnɒn 'prɒf ɪt →ˌnɒm-, §-ət ‖ ˌnɑːn 'prɑːf-

non-profit-making ˌnɒn 'prɒf ɪt ˌmeɪk ɪŋ →ˌnɒm-, §-'·ət- ‖ ˌnɑːn 'prɑːf-

nonproliferation ˌnɒn prəʊ ˌlɪf ə 'reɪʃ ᵊn →ˌnɒm- ‖ ˌnɑːn prə-

non-refundable ˌnɒn ri 'fʌnd əb l ◂, ·rə- ‖ ˌnɑːn-

non-renewable ˌnɒn ri 'njuː əb ᵊl ◂ ·rə-, §-'nuː- ‖ ˌnɑːn ri 'nuː- ·rə-, -'njuː-

nonresident ˌnɒn 'rez ɪd ənt ◂ -əd- ‖ ˌnɑːn- ~s s

non-residential ˌnɒn rez ɪ 'denˈʃᵊl◂ -rez ə- ‖ ˌnɑːn- -res ə-

nonrestrictive ˌnɒn ri 'strɪkt ɪv ◂ -rə- ‖ ˌnɑːn-

nonreturnable ˌnɒn ri 'tɜːn əb ᵊl ◂, ·rə- ‖ ˌnɑːn ri 'tɜːn-

nonrhotic ˌnɒn 'rəʊt ɪk ◂ ‖ ˌnɑːn 'roʊʈ ɪk ◂

nonrhoticity ˌnɒn rəʊ 'tɪs ət i -ɪt i ‖ ˌnɑːn roʊ 'tɪs əʈ i

non-scientific ˌnɒn saɪ ən 'tɪf ɪk ◂ ‖ ˌnɑːn-

nonsectarian ˌnɒn sek 'teər i̯ ən ◂ ‖ ˌnɑːn sek 'ter- -'tær-

nonsense 'nɒnˈs ənˈs ‖ 'nɑːn senˈs 'nɑːnˈs ənˈs

nonsensical nɒn 'senˈs ɪk ᵊl ‖ ˌnɑːn- ~ly i

non sequitur ˌnɒn 'sek wɪt ə ˌnəʊn-, -wət- ‖ ˌnɑːn 'sek wəʈ ᵊr -wə tʊr ~s z

non-shrink ˌnɒn 'ʃrɪŋk ◂ ‖ ˌnɑːn-

nonskid ˌnɒn 'skɪd ◂ ‖ ˌnɑːn-

non-slip ˌnɒn 'slɪp ◂ ‖ ˌnɑːn-

nonsmok|er ˌnɒn 'sməʊk| ə ‖ ˌnɑːn 'smoʊk| ᵊr ~ers əz ‖ ᵊrz ~ing ɪŋ ◂

non-specific ˌnɒn spə 'sɪf ɪk ◂ -spɪ- ‖ ˌnɑːn- ˌnon-spe ˌcific ˌure'thritis

nonstandard ˌnɒn 'stænd əd ◂ ‖ ˌnɑːn 'stænd ᵊrd

nonstarter ˌnɒn 'stɑːt ə ‖ ˌnɑːn 'stɑːrʈ ᵊr ~s z

nonstick ˌnɒn 'stɪk ◂ ‖ ˌnɑːn- ˌnon-stick 'frying-pan

nonstop ˌnɒn 'stɒp ◂ ‖ ˌnɑːn 'stɑːp ◂

Nonsuch 'nɒn sʌtʃ 'nʌn- ‖ 'nɑːn- 'nʌn-

non-swimmer ˌnɒn 'swɪm ə ‖ ˌnɑːn 'swɪm ᵊr ~s z

nonthreatening ˌnɒn 'θret ᵊn ɪŋ ◂ ‖ ˌnɑːn-

nontoxic ˌnɒn 'tɒks ɪk ◂ ‖ ˌnɑːn 'tɑːks ɪk ◂

non-traditional ˌnɒn trə 'dɪʃ ᵊn ᵊl ◂ ‖ ˌnɑːn-

non troppo ˌnɒn 'trɒp əʊ ˌnəʊn- ‖ ˌnɑːn 'trɑːp oʊ ˌnoʊn-, -'troʊp- —*It* [non 'trɔp po]

non-U ˌnɒn 'juː ◂ ‖ ˌnɑːn-

nonunion ˌnɒn 'juːn i̯ ən ◂ ‖ ˌnɑːn- ~ised, ~ized aɪzd ◂

nonverbal ˌnɒn 'vɜːb ᵊl ◂ ‖ ˌnɑːn 'vɜːb ᵊl ◂

nonviolence ˌnɒn 'vaɪ ᵊl ənˈs ‖ ˌnɑːn-

nonviolent ˌnɒn 'vaɪ ᵊl ənt ◂ ‖ ˌnɑːn- ~ly li

nonwhite, non-White ˌnɒn 'waɪt ◂ -'hwaɪt ‖ ˌnɑːn- ~s s

noodle 'nuːd ᵊl ~s z

noogie 'nuːg i

nook nʊk §nuːk **nooks** nʊks §nuːks

nookie, nooky 'nʊk i

noon nuːn **noons** nuːnz

Noonan 'nuːn ən

noonday 'nuːn deɪ

no one *pronoun*, **no-one** 'nəʊ wʌn §-wɒn **no one's, no-one's** 'nəʊ wʌnz §-wɒnz

noontide 'nuːn taɪd

noose nuːs **noosed** nuːst **nooses** 'nuːs ɪz -əz **noosing** 'nuːs ɪŋ

Nootka 'nʊt kə 'nuːt-

nopal 'nəʊp ᵊl ‖ 'noʊp ᵊl ~s z

nope nəʊp ‖ noʊp —*usually said with the* p *unreleased*

noplace 'nəʊ pleɪs ‖ 'noʊ-

nor nɔː ‖ nɔːr —*There is also an occasional weak form* nə ‖ nᵊr

nor-, nor'- nɔː ‖ nɔːr —*but in RP before a vowel,* nɔːr — **nor'-east** ˌnɔːr 'iːst ◂ ‖ ˌnɔːr-

NOR nɔː ‖ nɔːr

Nora 'nɔːr ə

noradrenalin, noradrenaline ˌnɔːr ə 'dren əl ɪn -iːn, §-ən

Norah 'nɔːr ə

Noraid 'nɔːr eɪd

Norbert 'nɔːb ət ‖ 'nɔːrb ᵊrt

Norden 'nɔːd ᵊn ‖ 'nɔːrd ᵊn

Nordic, n~ 'nɔːd ɪk ‖ 'nɔːrd ɪk **~s** s

Nordrhein-Westfalen ˌnɔːd raɪn vest 'faːl ən ‖ ˌnɔːrd- —*Ger* [ˌnɔʁt raɪn vɛst 'faː lən]

Nordstrom *tdmk* 'nɔːd strɒm -strəm ‖ 'nɔːrd strəm -stroʊm

Nore nɔː ‖ nɔːr

nor'easter ˌnɔːr 'iːst ə -ᵊr **~s** z

Noreen 'nɔːr iːn nɔː 'riːn ‖ nɔː 'riːn

Norfolk *place in England* 'nɔːf ək ‖ 'nɔːrf- —*but places in the US are also* -ɔːk, -ɑːk. *The island off Australia is locally* 'nɔː fəʊk.
ˌNorfolk 'Broads, ˌNorfolk 'jacket; ˌNorfolk 'terrier

nori 'nɔːr i 'nɒr- —*Jp* [no 'ri]

noria 'nɔːr i ə 'noʊr- **~s** z

Noricum 'nɒr ɪk əm ‖ 'nɔːr- 'nɑːr-

Noriega ˌnɒr i 'eɪɡ ə ‖ ˌnɔːr- —*Sp* [no 'rje ɣa]

Norland, n~ 'nɔː lənd ‖ 'nɔːr-

norm, Norm nɔːm ‖ nɔːrm **norms, Norm's** nɔːmz ‖ nɔːrmz

Norma 'nɔːm ə ‖ 'nɔːrm ə

normal, N~ 'nɔːm ᵊl ‖ 'nɔːrm ᵊl **~s** z

normalcy 'nɔːm ᵊl si ‖ 'nɔːrm-

normalis... —*see* **normaliz...**

normality nɔː 'mæl ət i -ɪt- ‖ nɔːr 'mæl əţ i

normalization ˌnɔːm əl aɪ 'zeɪʃ ᵊn -əl ɪ- ‖ ˌnɔːrm əl ə- **~s** z

normaliz|e 'nɔːm ə laɪz ‖ 'nɔːrm- **~ed** d **~es** ɪz əz **~ing** ɪŋ

normally 'nɔːm əl i ‖ 'nɔːrm-

Norman 'nɔːm ən ‖ 'nɔːrm ən
ˌNorman 'Conquest

Normanby 'nɔːm ən bi →-əm- ‖ 'nɔːrm-

Normand 'nɔːm ænd -ənd ‖ 'nɔːrm-

Normandy 'nɔːm ənd i ‖ 'nɔːrm-

Normanton 'nɔːm ən tən ‖ 'nɔːrm-

normative 'nɔːm ət ɪv ‖ 'nɔːrm əţ ɪv **~ly** li **~ness** nəs nɪs

Norn nɔːn ‖ nɔːrn

Norplant *tdmk* 'nɔː plɑːnt §-plænt ‖ 'nɔːr plænt

Norrie 'nɒr i ‖ 'nɔːr i 'nɑːr-

Norris 'nɒr ɪs §-əs ‖ 'nɔːr əs 'nɑːr-

Norrköping 'nɔː tʃɜːp ɪŋ ‖ 'nɔːr tʃoʊp- —*Swed* ['nɔr çøː piŋ]

Norroy 'nɒr ɔɪ ‖ 'nɔːr- 'nɑːr-

Norse nɔːs ‖ nɔːrs

Norse|man 'nɔːs |mən ‖ 'nɔːrs- **~men** mən -men

north, North nɔːθ ‖ nɔːrθ
ˌNorth ˌCaro'lina; ˌNorth Da'kota; ˌNorth Ko'rea; ˌNorth 'Pole; ˌNorth 'Sea; ˌNorth 'Star; ˌNorth 'Yorkshire

Northallerton nɔːθ 'æl ət ən nɔːð- ‖ nɔːrθ 'æl ᵊrt ᵊn

Northampton nɔː 'θæmpt ən nə-, nɔːθ 'hæmpt- ‖ nɔːr- **~shire** ʃə ʃɪə ‖ ʃᵊr ʃɪr

Northanger nɔː 'θæŋ ɡə 'nɔːθ ˌæŋ ɡə, -ˌhæŋ-, -ə ‖ nɔːr 'θæŋ ɡᵊr 'nɔːrθ ˌæŋ-, -ˌhæŋ-

Northants 'nɔːθ ænts nɔː 'θænts ‖ 'nɔːrθ-

northbound 'nɔːθ baʊnd ‖ 'nɔːrθ-

Northbrook 'nɔːθ brʊk ‖ 'nɔːrθ-

Northcliffe 'nɔːθ klɪf ‖ 'nɔːrθ-

Northcote 'nɔːθ kət -kɒt, -kəʊt ‖ 'nɔːrθ koʊt

north-country ˌnɔːθ 'kʌntr i ◂ ‖ ˌnɔːrθ- **~men** mən men **~man** mən mæn

northeast, N~ ˌnɔːθ 'iːst ◂ ‖ ˌnɔːrθ- —*also naut* ˌnɔːr- **~er/s** ə/z ‖ ᵊr/z **~erlies** əl iz ‖ ᵊr liz **~erly** əl i ‖ ᵊr li **~ern** ən ‖ ᵊrn **~erner/s** ən ə/z ‖ ᵊrn ᵊr/z **~ward/s** wəd/z ‖ wᵊrd/z

Northenden 'nɔːð ᵊnd ən ‖ 'nɔːrð-

norther|ly 'nɔːð ə |li -əl i ‖ 'nɔːrð ᵊr |li **~lies** liz

northern, N~ 'nɔːð ᵊn ‖ 'nɔːrð ᵊrn
ˌNorthern 'Ireland; ˌnorthern 'lights; ˌNorthern 'Territory

northerner, N~ 'nɔːð ən ə ‖ 'nɔːrð ᵊrn ᵊr -ᵊn- **~s** z

northernmost 'nɔːð ᵊn məʊst →-ᵊm- ‖ -ᵊrn moʊst

Northfield 'nɔːθ fiːᵊld ‖ 'nɔːrθ- **~s** z

Northfleet 'nɔːθ fliːt ‖ 'nɔːrθ-

Northiam 'nɔːð i əm ‖ 'nɔːrð-

northing 'nɔːð ɪŋ 'nɔːθ- ‖ 'nɔːrθ ɪŋ 'nɔːrð- **~s** z

North|man 'nɔːθ mən ‖ 'nɔːrθ- **~men** mən men

north-north-|east ˌnɔːθ nɔːθ| 'iːst ‖ ˌnɔːrθ nɔːrθ- **~west** 'west

Northolt 'nɔːθ əʊlt →-ɒult ‖ 'nɔːrθ oʊlt

Northrop, Northrup 'nɔːθ rəp ‖ 'nɔːrθ-

Northumberland nɔː 'θʌm bə lənd nə- ‖ nɔːr 'θʌm bᵊr-

Northumbri|a nɔː 'θʌm bri |ə ‖ nɔːr- **~an/s** ən/z

northward 'nɔːθ wəd ‖ 'nɔːrθ wᵊrd **~s** z

northwest, N~ ˌnɔːθ 'west ◂ ‖ ˌnɔːrθ- —*also naut* ˌnɔːr- ‖ ˌnɔːrθ- **~er/s** ə/z ‖ ᵊr/z **~erlies** əl iz ‖ ᵊr liz **~erly** əl i ‖ ᵊr li **~ern** ən ‖ ᵊrn **~ward/s** wəd/z ‖ wᵊrd/z
ˌNorthwest 'Territories

Northwich 'nɔːθ wɪtʃ ‖ 'nɔːrθ-

Northwood 'nɔːθ wʊd ‖ 'nɔːrθ-

Norton 'nɔːt ᵊn ‖ 'nɔːrt ᵊn

Norvic *tdmk* 'nɔː vɪk ‖ 'nɔːr-

Norwalk 'nɔː wɔːk ‖ 'nɔːr- -wɑːk

Norway 'nɔː weɪ ‖ 'nɔːr weɪ
ˌNorway 'spruce

Norwegian nɔː 'wiːdʒ ᵊn ‖ nɔːr- **~s** z

Norwich *place in England* 'nɒr ɪdʒ -ɪtʃ ‖ 'nɔːr- 'nɑːr-

Norwich *place in CT* 'nɔː wɪtʃ ‖ 'nɔːr-

N

Norwood 'nɔː wʊd ‖ 'nɔːr-
nos, nos., Nos. 'nʌm bəz ‖ -bəʳrz
nose nəʊz ‖ noʊz **nosed** nəʊzd ‖ noʊzd **noses**
'nəʊz ɪz -əz ‖ 'noʊz əz **nosing** 'nəʊz ɪŋ
‖ 'noʊz ɪŋ
nosebag 'nəʊz bæg ‖ 'noʊz- ~s z
nosebleed 'nəʊz bliːd ‖ 'noʊz- ~s z
nosecone 'nəʊz kəʊn ‖ 'noʊz koʊn ~s z
nose|dive 'nəʊz |daɪv ‖ 'noʊz- ~dived daɪvd
~dives daɪvz ~diving daɪv ɪŋ ~dove dəʊv
‖ doʊv
no-see-um ˌnəʊ 'siː əm ‖ ˌnoʊ- ~s z
nosegay 'nəʊz geɪ ‖ 'noʊz- ~s z
nosey —see **nosy**
Nosferatu ˌnɒs fə 'rɑːt uː -fe- ‖ ˌnɑːs-
nosh nɒʃ ‖ nɑːʃ **noshed** nɒʃt ‖ nɑːʃt **noshes**
'nɒʃ ɪz -əz ‖ 'nɑːʃ əz **noshing** 'nɒʃ ɪŋ
‖ 'nɑːʃ ɪŋ
nosher|y 'nɒʃ ər |i ‖ 'nɑːʃ- ~ies iz
no-show 'nəʊ ʃəʊ ‖ 'noʊ ʃoʊ ~s z
nosh-up 'nɒʃ ʌp ‖ 'nɑːʃ- ~s s
no-side ˌnəʊ 'saɪd ‖ ˌnoʊ-
no-smoking ˌnəʊ 'sməʊk ɪŋ ‖ ˌnoʊ 'smoʊk ɪŋ
ˌno-'smoking sign
noso- comb. form
with stress-neutral suffix ˈnɒs əʊ ‖ ˈnoʊs ə
ˈnɑːs oʊ — **nosographic** ˌnɒs əʊ 'græf ɪk ◂
‖ ˌnoʊs ə- ˌnɑːs oʊ-
with stress-imposing suffix nɒ 'sɒ +
‖ noʊ 'sɑː + — **nosology** nɒ 'sɒl ədʒ i
‖ noʊ 'sɑːl-
nostalgia nɒ 'stældʒ ə -'stældʒ i ə ‖ nɑː- nə-
nostalgic nɒ 'stældʒ ɪk ‖ nɑː- nə- ~ally ᵊl i
Nostradamus ˌnɒs trə 'dɑːm əs -'deɪm-
‖ ˌnɑːs- ˌnoʊs-
Nostratic nɒ 'stræt ɪk ‖ nɑː 'stræt ɪk nɔː-
nostril 'nɒs trəl -trɪl ‖ 'nɑːs- ~s z
nostrum 'nɒs trəm ‖ 'nɑːs- ~s z
nos|y 'nəʊz |i ‖ 'noʊz |i ~ier i ə ‖ i əʳr ~iest
i ɪst i əst ~ily ɪ li əl i ~iness i nəs i nɪs
ˌnosy 'parker
not nɒt ‖ nɑːt —There is no weak form other
than the contracted n't used with certain
modals.
nota bene ˌnəʊt ə 'ben i -ɑː-, -'biːn-, -eɪ
‖ ˌnoʊt ə- -'beɪn eɪ
notabilit|y ˌnəʊt ə 'bɪl ət |i -ɪt i
‖ ˌnoʊt ə 'bɪl ət |i ~ies iz
notab|le 'nəʊt əb |ᵊl ‖ 'noʊt- ~les ᵊlz ~ly li
notarie... —see **notary**
notaris... —see **notariz...**
notarization ˌnəʊt ər aɪ 'zeɪʃ ᵊn -ər ɪ-
‖ ˌnoʊt ər ə-
notariz|e 'nəʊt ə raɪz ‖ 'noʊt- ~ed d ~es ɪz əz
~ing ɪŋ
notar|y 'nəʊt ər |i ‖ 'noʊt- ~ies iz
no|tate nəʊ 'teɪt ‖ 'noʊ|t eɪt ~tated teɪt ɪd
-əd ‖ teɪt̬ əd ~tates teɪts ~tating teɪt ɪŋ
‖ teɪt̬ ɪŋ
notation nəʊ 'teɪʃ ᵊn ‖ noʊ- ~s z
notch nɒtʃ ‖ nɑːtʃ **notched** nɒtʃt ‖ nɑːtʃt
notches 'nɒtʃ ɪz -əz ‖ 'nɑːtʃ əz **notching**
'nɒtʃ ɪŋ ‖ 'nɑːtʃ ɪŋ

note nəʊt ‖ noʊt **noted** 'nəʊt ɪd -əd ‖ 'noʊt̬ əd
notes nəʊts ‖ noʊts **noting** 'nəʊt ɪŋ
‖ 'noʊt̬ ɪŋ
notebook 'nəʊt bʊk §-buːk ‖ 'noʊt- ~s s
notecas|e 'nəʊt keɪs ‖ 'noʊt- ~es ɪz əz
noted 'nəʊt ɪd -əd ‖ 'noʊt̬ əd ~ly li ~ness nəs
nɪs
notelet 'nəʊt lət -lɪt ‖ 'noʊt- ~s s
notepad 'nəʊt pæd ‖ 'noʊt- ~s z
notepaper 'nəʊt ˌpeɪp ə ‖ 'noʊt ˌpeɪp əʳr
noteworth|y 'nəʊt ˌwɜːð |i ‖ 'noʊt ˌwɜːð |i
~ily ɪ li əl i ~iness i nəs i nɪs
not-for-profit ˌnɒt fə 'prɒf ɪt §-ət
‖ ˌnɑːt fəʳr 'prɑːf ət
nother 'nʌð ə ‖ -əʳr
nothing 'nʌθ ɪŋ §'nɒθ- ~ness nəs nɪs
ˌnothing 'doing; (there's) ˌnothing 'for it;
(there's) ˌnothing 'to it
notic|e 'nəʊt ɪs §-əs ‖ 'noʊt̬ əs ~ed t ~es ɪz əz
~ing ɪŋ
'notice board
noticeab|le 'nəʊt ɪs əb |ᵊl '-əs- ‖ 'noʊt̬ əs- ~ly
li
notifiable 'nəʊt ɪ faɪ əb |ᵊl '-ə-, ˌ·'··· ‖ 'noʊt̬-
notification ˌnəʊt ɪf ɪ 'keɪʃ ᵊn ˌ·əf-, §-ə'·-
‖ ˌnoʊt̬- ~s z
noti|fy 'nəʊt ɪ |faɪ -ə- ‖ 'noʊt̬ ə- ~fied faɪd
~fier/s faɪ ə/z ‖ faɪ əʳr/z ~fies faɪz ~fying
faɪ ɪŋ
notion 'nəʊʃ ᵊn ‖ 'noʊʃ ᵊn ~s z
notional 'nəʊʃ ᵊn_əl ‖ 'noʊʃ- ~ly i
notoriety ˌnəʊt ə 'raɪ ət i ‖ ˌnoʊt̬ ə 'raɪ ət̬ i
notorious nəʊ 'tɔːr i_əs ‖ noʊ- nə-, -'toʊr- ~ly
li ~ness nəs nɪs
Notre Dame (i) ˌnəʊtr ə 'dɑːm ◂ ˌnɒtr-
‖ ˌnoʊt̬ əʳr 'dɑːm 'noʊtr ə- (ii) -'deɪm —for the
Paris cathedral, and for the religious order in
France and Britain, (i); in the United States
(ii). —Fr [nɔ tʁə dam]
no-trump ˌnəʊ 'trʌmp ◂ ‖ ˌnoʊ- ~s s
Nott nɒt ‖ nɑːt
Nottingham 'nɒt ɪŋ əm §-həm ‖ 'nɑːt̬- -hæm
~shire ʃə ʃɪə ‖ ʃəʳr ʃɪr
Notting Hill ˌnɒt ɪŋ 'hɪl ◂ ‖ ˌnɑːt̬-
Notts nɒts ‖ nɑːts
Notus 'nəʊt əs ‖ 'noʊt̬ əs
notwithstanding ˌnɒt wɪð 'stænd ɪŋ ◂ -wɪθ-
‖ ˌnɑːt-
Nouakchott ˌnuː æk 'ʃɒt -ɑːk 'ʃɑːt —Fr
[nwak ʃɔt]
nougat 'nuːg ɑː §'nʌg ət ‖ 'nuːg ət (*)
nought nɔːt ‖ nɑːt **noughts** nɔːts ‖ nɑːts
ˌnoughts and 'crosses
Noumea, Nouméa nuː 'miː ə -'meɪ ə —Fr
[nu me a]
noumenon 'nuːm ən ən 'naʊm-, -ɪn-; -ə nɒn, -ɪ-
‖ -ə nɑːn
noun naʊn **nouns** naʊnz
nourish 'nʌr ɪʃ ‖ 'nɜː ɪʃ ~ed t ~es ɪz əz
~ing/ly ɪŋ/li ~ment mənt
nous naʊs

N

nouveau, ~x 'nu:v əʊ ‖ ,nu: 'voʊ —*Fr*
[nu vo]
,**nouveau(x) 'riche(s)** ri:ʃ —*Fr* [ʁiʃ]
nouvelle cuisine ,nu:v el kwɪ 'zi:n nu ,vel·'·,
-kwi:'· —*Fr* [nu vɛl kɥi zin]
nouvelle vague ,nu:v el 'vɑ:g —*Fr*
[nu vɛl vag]
Nov —*see* **November**
nov|a, Nov|a 'nəʊv |ə ‖ 'noʊv |ə ~**ae** i: ~**as**
əz
,**Nova 'Scotia** 'skəʊʃ ə ‖ 'skoʊʃ ə
Novartis *tdmk* nəʊ 'vɑ:t ɪs §-əs ‖ noʊ 'vɑ:r̬t əs
Novaya Zemlya ,nəʊv ə jə 'zem li̯ ə ,nɒv-,
,·ɑ:- ‖ ,noʊv- —*Russ* [,nɒ və jə zʲɪm 'lʲa]
novel 'nɒv ᵊl §'nʌv- ‖ 'nɑ:v ᵊl ~**s** z
novelette ,nɒv ə 'let ᵊl 'et ‖ ,nɑ:v- ~**s** s
novelettish ,nɒv ə 'let ɪʃ ◂ -ᵊl 'et-
‖ ,nɑ:v ə 'let̬ ɪʃ ◂ ᵊl 'et̬-
novelist 'nɒv əl ɪst §-əst ‖ 'nɑ:v- ~**s** s
novelistic ,nɒv ə 'lɪst ɪk ◂ -ᵊl 'ɪst- ‖ ,nɑ:v-
novelization, novelisation
,nɒv ᵊl aɪ 'zeɪʃ ᵊn -ɪ'·ˌ, -ə·· ‖ ,nɑ:v ᵊl ə-
novell|a nəʊ 'vel |ə ‖ noʊ- ~**as** əz ~**e** i: eɪ
Novello nə 'vel əʊ ‖ -oʊ
novelt|y 'nɒv ᵊlt |i ‖ 'nɑ:v- ~**ies** iz
November nəʊ 'vem bə ‖ noʊ 'vem bᵊr nə- ~**s**
z
novena nəʊ 'vi:n ə ‖ noʊ- ~**s** z
Novgorod 'nɒv gə rɒd ‖ 'nɑ:v gə rɑ:d —*Russ*
['nɔv gə rət]
Novial 'nəʊv i̯ əl ‖ 'noʊv-
novic|e 'nɒv ɪs §-əs ‖ 'nɑ:v əs ~**es** ɪz əz
noviciate, novitiate nəʊ 'vɪʃ i̯ ət -ɪt, -eɪt
‖ noʊ 'vɪʃ ət nə-, -'vɪʃ i̯ ət, -i eɪt ~**s** s
novocain, novocaine, N~ *tdmk*
'nəʊv əʊ keɪn 'nɒv- ‖ 'noʊv ə-
Novosibirsk ,nəʊv əʊ sɪ 'bɪəsk -sɔ'·
‖ ,noʊv ə sə 'bɪᵊrsk —*Russ* [nə və sʲɪ 'bʲirsk]
Novotel *tdmk* 'nəʊv əʊ ˌtel ‖ 'noʊv oʊ- -ə-
now naʊ
nowadays 'naʊ̯ ə deɪz
Nowell '*Christmas*' nəʊ 'el ‖ noʊ-
Nowell *personal name* 'nəʊ əl -el ‖ 'noʊ-
nowhere 'nəʊ weə -hweə ‖ 'noʊ wer -hwer,
-wær, -hwær —*Occasionally also* -wə, -hwə
‖ -wᵊr , -hwᵊr
no-win ,nəʊ 'wɪn ◂ ‖ ,noʊ-
,**no-'win situ,ation**, ·,·,·'·
nowise 'nəʊ waɪz ‖ 'noʊ-
nowt naʊt nəʊt
noxious 'nɒk ʃəs ‖ 'nɑ:k- ~**ly** li ~**ness** nəs nɪs
Noyes *family name* nɔɪz
Noyes Fludde ,nɔɪ əz 'flʊd
nozzle 'nɒz ᵊl ‖ 'nɑ:z ᵊl ~**s** z
NPR ,en pi: 'ɑ: ‖ -'ɑ:r
nr —*see* **near**
NSAID 'en sed -seɪd ~**s** z
NSPCC ,en es ,pi: si: 'si:
NSU ,en es 'ju:
-**n't** ᵊnt —*This contraction of* **not** *does not
receive stress, even for contrast:* either you DID
or you DIDN'T 'dɪd ᵊnt
nth en'θ

n-tuple 'en tjʊp ᵊl ,en 'tju:p ᵊl, →-'tʃu:p-
‖ 'en tʊp ᵊl -tjʊp-; ,en 'tu:p ᵊl, -'tju:p- ~**s** z
n-type 'en taɪp
nu *name of Greek letter* nju: §nu: ‖ nu: nju:
Nuala 'nʊəl ə ‖ 'nu:- əl ə
nuanc|e 'nju: ɑːn̩s 'nu:-, -ɒn̩s, -ɒ̃s, ,·'· ‖ 'nu:-
'nju:- —*Fr* [nɥɑ̃ːs] ~**es** ɪz əz
nub nʌb **nubs** nʌbz
Nuba 'nju:b ə §'nu:b- ‖ 'nu:b ə 'nju:b-
nubbin 'nʌb ɪn §-ən ~**s** z
nubble 'nʌb ᵊl ~**s** z
nubbly 'nʌb ᵊl̩ i
nubby 'nʌb i
Nubi|a 'nju:b i̯ |ə §'nu:b- ‖ 'nu:b- 'nju:b- ~**an/s**
ən/z
,**Nubian 'Desert**
nubile 'nju:b arᵊl §'nu:b- ‖ 'nu:b ᵊl 'nju:b-, -arᵊl

NUCLEAR

6%		■ -li̯ ə
94%		■ -jəl ə

BrE

nuclear 'nju:k li̯ ə §'nu:k-, △-jəl ə ‖ 'nu:k li̯ ᵊr
'nju:k-, △-jəl ᵊr — *Preference poll, BrE:* -li̯ ə
94%, -jələ *6%.*
,**nuclear 'energy**; ,**nuclear re'actor**;
,**nuclear 'tone**; ,**nuclear 'winter**
nuclear-free ,nju:k li̯ ə 'fri: ◂ §,nu:k-, △,·jəl-
‖ ,nu:k li̯ ᵊr- ,nju:k-, △,·jəl-
nuclei 'nju:k li aɪ §'nu:k-, -i: ‖ 'nu:k- 'nju:k-
nucleic nju 'kli: ɪk §nu-, -'kleɪ- ‖ nu- nju-
nu,cleic 'acid
nucleo- *comb. form*
with stress-neutral suffix ˌnju:k li əʊ §ˌnu:k-
‖ ˌnu:k li ə ˌnju:k- — **nucleoplasm**
'nju:k li əʊ ,plæz əm §'nu:k- ‖ 'nu:k li ə-
'nju:k-
with stress-imposing suffix ,nju:k li 'ɒ + ,nu:k-
‖ ,nu:k li 'ɑ: + ,nju:k- — **nucleofugal**
,nju:k li 'ɒf jʊg ᵊl ◂ §,nu:k-
‖ ,nu:k li 'ɑ:f jəg ᵊl ◂ ,nju:k-
nucleol|us nju 'kli: əl |əs §nu-;
,nju:k li 'əʊl |əs, §,nu:k- ‖ nu- nju- ~**i** aɪ
nucleon 'nju:k li ɒn §'nu:k- ‖ 'nu:k li ɑ:n
'nju:k- ~**s** z
nucleonic ,nju:k li 'ɒn ɪk ◂ §,nu:k-
‖ ,nu:k li 'ɑ:n ɪk ◂ ,nju:k- ~**s** s
nucleoside 'nju:k li̯ ə saɪd §'nu:k- ‖ 'nu:k-
'nju:k- ~**s** z
nucleotide 'nju:k li̯ ə taɪd §'nu:k- ‖ 'nu:k-
'nju:k- ~**s** z
nucle|us 'nju:k li̯ |əs §'nu:k-, △-jəl- ‖ 'nu:k-
'nju:k-, , △-jəl- ~**i** aɪ i:
nuclide 'nju:k laɪd §'nu:k- ‖ 'nu:k- 'nju:k- ~**s** z
nuddy 'nʌd i
nude nju:d §nu:d ‖ nu:d nju:d **nudes** nju:dz
§nu:dz ‖ nu:dz nju:dz

N

nudge nʌdʒ **nudged** nʌdʒd **nudges** 'nʌdʒ ɪz
-əz **nudging** 'nʌdʒ ɪŋ
nudibranch 'njuːd ɪ bræŋk §'nuːd-, §-ə-
‖ 'nuːd- 'njuːd- ~**s** s
nudie 'njuːd i §'nuːd i ‖ 'nuːd i 'njuːd i
nudism 'njuːd ˌɪz əm §'nuːd- ‖ 'nuːd- 'njuːd-
nudist 'njuːd ɪst §'nuːd-, §-əst ‖ 'nuːd əst
'njuːd- ~**s** s
nudit|y 'njuːd ət |i §'nuːd-, -ɪt- ‖ 'nuːd əţ |i
'njuːd- ~**ies** iz
nudnik 'nʊd nɪk ~**s** s
'nuff nʌf
Nuffield 'nʌf iːᵊld
nugatory 'njuːg ət ər i §'nuːg-; njuː 'geɪt ər i
‖ 'nuːg ə tɔːr i 'njuːg-, -toʊr-
Nugent 'njuːdʒ ənt §'nuːdʒ- ‖ 'nuːdʒ- 'njuːdʒ-
nugget 'nʌg ɪt §-ət ~**s** s
nuisanc|e 'njuːs ᵊn̩ts §'nuːs- ‖ 'nuːs- 'njuːs- ~**es**
ɪz əz
  'nuisance ˌvalue
Nuits-Saint-George ˌnwiː sæn 'ʒɔːʒ -'dʒɔːdʒ
‖ -'ʒɔːrʒ —*Fr* [nɥi sɛ̃ ʒɔʁʒ]
NUJ ˌen juː 'dʒeɪ
nuke njuːk §nuːk ‖ nuːk njuːk **nuked** njuːkt
§nuːkt ‖ nuːkt njuːkt **nukes** njuːks §nuːks
‖ nuːks njuːks **nuking** 'njuːk ɪŋ §'nuːk-
‖ 'nuːk ɪŋ 'njuːk-
Nukualofa, Nuku'alofa ˌnuː kuː ə 'ləʊf ə
‖ -'loʊf ə —*Tongan* [nu ku ʔa 'lo fa]
null nʌl
  ˌnull and 'void
nullah 'nʌl ə -ɑː ~**s** z
nulla-nulla 'nʌl ə ˌnʌl ə ~**s** z
Nullarbor 'nʌl ə bɔː ‖ -bɔːr
  ˌNullarbor 'Plain
nullification ˌnʌl ɪf ɪ 'keɪʃ ᵊn ˌ-əf-, §-əˈ-
nulli|fy 'nʌl ɪ |faɪ -ə- ~**fied** faɪd ~**fier/s** faɪ ə/z
‖ faɪ ᵊr/z ~**fies** faɪz ~**fying** faɪ ɪŋ
nullip|ara nʌ 'lɪp |ər ə ~**arae** ə riː
nullit|y 'nʌl ət |i -ɪt- ‖ -əţ |i ~**ies** iz
nul points ˌnʊl 'pwæ̃ ‖ -'pwæn —*Fr*
[nyl pwæ̃]
NUM ˌen juː 'em
Numa 'njuːm ə 'nuːm- ‖ 'nuːm ə 'njuːm-
numb nʌm **numbed** nʌmd **number** 'nʌm ə
‖ -ᵊr **numbest** 'nʌm ɪst -əst **numbing/ly**
'nʌm ɪŋ /li **numbs** nʌmz
numbat 'nʌm bæt ~**s** s
number *n, v* 'nʌm bə ‖ -bᵊr ~**ed** d **numbering**
'nʌm bər ɪŋ ~**s** z
  ˌnumber 'one◄; ˌNumber 'Ten◄, ˌNumber
  Ten 'Downing Street
number *adj 'more numb'* 'nʌm ə ‖ -ᵊr
number-crunch|er 'nʌm bə ˌkrʌntʃ |ə
‖ -bᵊr ˌkrʌntʃ |ᵊr ~**ers** əz ‖ ᵊrz ~**ing** ɪŋ
numberless 'nʌm bə ləs -lɪs ‖ -bᵊr-
numberplate 'nʌm bə pleɪt ‖ -bᵊr- ~**s** s
Numbers 'nʌm bəz ‖ -bᵊrz
numbly 'nʌm li
numbskull 'nʌm skʌl ~**s** z
numerable 'njuːm ər_əb ᵊl §'nuːm- ‖ 'nuːm-
'njuːm-

numeracy 'njuːm ər_əs i §'nuːm- ‖ 'nuːm-
'njuːm-
numeral 'njuːm ᵊr_əl §'nuːm- ‖ 'nuːm- 'njuːm-
~**s** z
numerate *adj* 'njuːm ər_ət §'nuːm-, -ɪt, -ə reɪt
‖ 'nuːm- 'njuːm-
numeration ˌnjuːm ə 'reɪʃ ᵊn §ˌnuːm- ‖ ˌnuːm-
ˌnjuːm-
numerator 'njuːm ə reɪt ə §'nuːm-
‖ 'nuːm ə reɪţ ᵊr 'njuːm- ~**s** z
numeric njuː 'mer ɪk §nuː- ‖ nuː- njuː- ~**al** ᵊl
~**ally** ᵊl_i ~**s** s
numerological ˌnjuːm ər_ə 'lɒdʒ ɪk ᵊl ◄
§ˌnuːm- ‖ ˌnuːm ər_ə 'lɑːdʒ- ˌnjuːm- ~**ly** ᵊi
numerology ˌnjuːm ə 'rɒl ədʒ i §ˌnuːm-
‖ ˌnuːm ə 'rɑːl- ˌnjuːm-
numero uno ˌnuːm ə rəʊ 'uːn əʊ njuː-
‖ ˌnuːm ə roʊ 'uːn oʊ ˌnjuːm-
numerous 'njuːm ər_əs §'nuːm- ‖ 'nuːm-
'njuːm- ~**ly** li ~**ness** nəs nɪs
Numidi|a njuː 'mɪd i |ə §nuː- ‖ nuː- njuː- ~**an/s**
ən/z
numinous 'njuːm ɪn əs §'nuːm-, -ən- ‖ 'nuːm-
'njuːm-
numismatic ˌnjuːm ɪz 'mæt ɪk ◄ §ˌnuːm-
‖ ˌnuːm əz 'mæţ ɪk ◄ ˌnjuːm-, ˌ-əs- ~**s** s
numismatist njuː 'mɪz mət ɪst §nuː-, §-əst
‖ nuː 'mɪz məţ əst njuː-, -'mɪs- ~**s** s
nummary 'nʌm ər i
nummular 'nʌm jʊl ə -jəl- ‖ -jəl ᵊr
nump|tie, nump|ty 'nʌmp| ti ~**ties** tiz
numskull 'nʌm skʌl ~**s** z
nun nʌn **nuns** nʌnz
nunatak 'nʌn ə tæk ~**s** s
Nunavut 'nuːn ə vuːt
Nunawading 'nʌn ə wɒd ɪŋ ‖ -wɑːd·
Nunc Dimittis ˌnʌŋk dɪ 'mɪt ɪs ˌnʊŋk-, -daɪ-,
-də-, §-əs ‖ -'mɪţ əs
nunchaku nʌn 'tʃæk uː ‖ -'tʃɑːk- —*Jp*
['nun tɕa kɯ] ~**s** z
nunciature 'nʌnˀts i ə tjʊə ˌətʃ ə ‖ ˌə tjʊr ˌətʃ ᵊr
~**s** z
nuncio 'nʌnˀts i əʊ 'nʌnˀtʃ-, 'nʊnˀts-, 'nʊnˀtʃ-
‖ -oʊ ~**s** z
Nuneaton nʌn 'iːt ᵊn
Nunn nʌn
nunner|y 'nʌn ər |i ~**ies** iz
Nupe *African language and people* 'nuːp eɪ
NUPE *trade union* 'njuːp i 'nuːp-
nuptial 'nʌp ʃᵊl -tʃᵊl; △'nʌp ʃu əl, △-tʃu əl ~**ly**
i ~**s** z
Nuremberg 'njʊər əm bɜːg 'njɔːr-
‖ 'nʊr əm bɜːg 'njʊr- —*Ger* Nürnberg
['nʏʁn bɛʁk]
Nureyev 'njʊər i ef njuᵊ 'reɪ-, -ev ‖ nu 'reɪ-
—*Russ* [nu 'rʲe jɪf]
Nuristan ˌnʊər ɪ 'stɑːn -'stæn ‖ ˌnʊr ɪ 'stæn
-'stɑːn
Nurofen *tdmk* 'njʊər əʊ fen §'nʊər- ‖ 'nʊr ə-
'njʊr-
nurse, Nurse nɜːs ‖ nɜːs **nursed** nɜːst ‖ nɜːst
nurses 'nɜːs ɪz -əz ‖ 'nɜːs əz **nursing** 'nɜːs ɪŋ
‖ 'nɜːs ɪŋ

nurseling 'nɜːs lɪŋ ‖ 'nɜːs- ~s z
nursemaid 'nɜːs meɪd ‖ 'nɜːs- ~s z
nurser|y 'nɜːs ²r¸|i →'nɜːʃ ri ‖ 'nɜːs ²r¸|i ~ies
   iz
   'nursery rhyme; 'nursery school
nurserymaid 'nɜːs ²r¸i meɪd →'nɜːʃ ri- ‖ 'nɜːs-
   ~s z
nursery|man 'nɜːs ²r¸i |mən →'nɜːʃ ri- ‖ 'nɜːs-
   ~men mən
nursing 'nɜːs ɪŋ ‖ 'nɜːs ɪŋ
   'nursing home; ¸nursing 'mother
nursling 'nɜːs lɪŋ ‖ 'nɜːs- ~s z
nurturance 'nɜːtʃ ²r¸ən's ‖ 'nɜːtʃ-
nurture 'nɜːtʃ ə ‖ 'nɜːtʃ ²r ~ed d ~s z
   nurturing 'nɜːtʃ ər ɪŋ ‖ 'nɜːtʃ ²r ɪŋ
NUS ¸en ju 'es
Nussbaum 'nʊs baʊm
nut nʌt **nuts** nʌts **nutted** 'nʌt ɪd -əd ‖ 'nʌt̬ əd
   nutting 'nʌt ɪŋ ‖ 'nʌt̬ ɪŋ
NUT *trades union* ¸en ju: 'ti:
nutation nju: 'teɪʃ ²n §nu:- ‖ nu:- nju:- ~s z
nut-brown ¸nʌt 'braʊn ◄
   ¸nut-brown 'hair
nutcas|e 'nʌt keɪs ~es ɪz əz
nutcracker 'nʌt ¸kræk ə ‖ -²r ~s z
nuthatch 'nʌt hætʃ ~es ɪz əz
nut|house 'nʌt |haʊs ~houses haʊz ɪz -əz
Nutkin 'nʌt kɪn
Nutley 'nʌt li
nutmeg 'nʌt meg
nutraceuticals ¸nju:tr ə 'su:t ɪk ²lz §¸nu:tr-,
   -'sju:t- ‖ ¸nu:tr ə 'su:t̬- ¸nju:tr-
Nutrasweet, NutraSweet *tdmk*
   'nju:tr ə swi:t §'nu:tr- ‖ 'nu:tr- 'nju:tr-
nutria 'nju:tr i ə §'nu:tr- ‖ 'nu:tr- 'nju:tr- ~s z
nutrient 'nju:tr i ¸ənt §'nu:tr- ‖ 'nu:tr- 'nju:tr-
   ~s s
nutrigenomics ¸nju:tr ɪ dʒi 'nəʊm ɪks
   §¸nu:tr-, -ɪ dʒə-, -'nɒm-
   ‖ ¸nu:tr ə dʒi 'noʊm ɪks ¸nju:tr-
nutriment 'nju:tr ɪ mənt §'nu:tr-, -ə- ‖ 'nu:tr-
   'nju:tr- ~s s
nutrition nju 'trɪʃ ²n §nu- ‖ nu- nju- ~al ¸əl
   ~ally ¸əl i

nutritionist nju 'trɪʃ ²n¸ɪst §nu-, §¸əst ‖ nu-
   nju- ~s s
nutritious nju 'trɪʃ əs §nu- ‖ nu- nju- ~ly li
   ~ness nəs nɪs
nutritive 'nju:tr ət ɪv §'nu:tr-, -ət-
   ‖ 'nu:tr ət̬ ɪv 'nju:tr- ~ly li ~s z
nuts nʌts
nutshell 'nʌt ʃel ~s z
Nutt nʌt
nutt... —*see* **nut**
Nuttall 'nʌt ɔːl ‖ -ɑːl
nutter, N~ 'nʌt ə ‖ 'nʌt̬ ²r ~s z
Nutting, n~ 'nʌt ɪŋ ‖ 'nʌt̬ ɪŋ
Nutton 'nʌt ²n
nutt|y 'nʌt |i ‖ 'nʌt̬ |i ~ier i¸ə ‖ i¸²r ~iest i¸ɪst
   i¸əst ~ily ɪ li əl i ~iness i nəs i nɪs
Nuuk 'nu:k
nux vomica ¸nʌks 'vɒm ɪk ə ‖ -'vɑːm-
Nuyts nɔɪts
nuzzl|e 'nʌz ²l ~ed d ~es z ~ing ¸ɪŋ
NVQ ¸en vi: 'kju: ~s z
N-word 'en wɜːd ‖ -wɜːd ~s z
NY —*see* **New York**
Nyack 'naɪ æk
Nyanja ni 'ændʒ ə
nyanza, N~ ni 'ænz ə naɪ-
Nyasaland naɪ 'æs ə lænd ni-
NYC —*see* **New York City**
Nye, nye naɪ **nyes, Nye's** naɪz
Nyerere njə 'reər i ni-, niə-, -'rer- ‖ -'rer-
nylon 'naɪl ɒn ‖ -ɑːn ~s z
nymph nɪm²f **nymphs** nɪm²fs
nymphet 'nɪm²f ɪt -ət, -et; nɪm 'fet ~s s
nympho 'nɪm²f əʊ ‖ -oʊ ~s z
nymphomania ¸nɪm²f ə 'meɪn i¸ə
nymphomaniac ¸nɪm²f ə 'meɪn i æk ~s s
Nynorsk 'ni: nɔːsk ‖ -nɔːrsk —*Norw*
   ['ny: nɔʂk]
Nyree 'naɪ²r i:
nystagmus nɪ 'stæg məs
nystatin 'nɪst ə tɪn §-ət ən
NZ ¸en 'zed ◄ ‖ -'zi: ◄ —*see* **New Zealand**

N

Oo

o Spelling-to-sound

1 Where the spelling is **o**, the pronunciation differs according to whether the vowel is
- short or long
- followed or not by **r**, and
- strong or weak.

2 The 'strong' pronunciation is regularly

ɒ ‖ ɑː as in **lot** lɒt ‖ lɑːt ('short O')

əʊ ‖ oʊ as in **nose** nəʊz ‖ noʊz ('long O').

3 Less frequently, it is

ʌ as in **come** kʌm (especially before **m, n, v, th**)

uː as in **move** muːv

ʊ as in **woman** ˈwʊm ən (note also ɪ in **women**) or

ɒ ‖ ɔː as in **cross** krɒs ‖ krɔːs (but some speakers of AmE use ɑː instead, thus krɑːs).
Note also the exceptional **gone** gɒn ‖ gɔːn.

4 Where the spelling is **or**, the 'strong' pronunciation is

ɔː as in **north** nɔːθ ‖ nɔːrθ

or, indeed, especially in BrE, the regular 'short' pronunciation

ɒ ‖ ɑː as in **moral** ˈmɒr əl (AmE ˈmɔːr əl, ˈmɑːr əl).

5 Less frequently, it is

ɜː ‖ ɝː as in **work** wɜːk ‖ wɝːk (especially after **w**) or

ʌ ‖ ɝː as in **worry** ˈwʌr i ‖ ˈwɝː i.

6 The 'weak' pronunciation is

ə as in **method** ˈmeθ əd, **Oxford** ˈɒks fəd ‖ ˈɑːks fərd.

In unstressed syllables there are often two possibilities, ə or əʊ ‖ oʊ, the second
being associated with careful speech or unfamiliar words, thus
phonetics fəʊ ˈnet ɪks ‖ foʊ ˈneṯ ɪks as a little-used word but fə ˈnet ɪks ‖ -neṯ- as
an everyday word.

7 **o** also forms part of the digraphs **oa, oe, oi, oo, ou, ow, oy** (see below).

oa Spelling-to-sound

1 Where the spelling is the digraph **oa**, the pronunciation is regularly
əʊ ‖ oʊ as in **road** rəʊd ‖ roʊd or
ɔː as in **board** bɔːd ‖ bɔːrd (before **r**).

2 Note the exceptional words **broad** brɔːd (and derivatives **abroad**, **broaden**),
cupboard ˈkʌb əd ‖ ˈkʌb ərd.

3 **oa** is not a digraph in **oasis**, **Noah**, **coalescence**, **protozoa**.

oe Spelling-to-sound

1 Where the spelling is the digraph **oe**, the pronunciation is regularly
əʊ ‖ oʊ as in **toe** təʊ ‖ toʊ.

2 Exceptionally, it is
uː in **shoe** ʃuː, **canoe** kə ˈnuː
ʌ in **does** (from **do**) dʌz
iː in **phoenix** ˈfiːn ɪks and other words of Greek origin.

3 **oe** is not a digraph in **poem**, **poetic**, **coerce**, **Noel**.

oi, oy Spelling-to-sound

1 Where the spelling is one of the digraphs **oi** and **oy**, the pronunciation is regularly
ɔɪ as in **noise** nɔɪz, **boy** bɔɪ.

2 In words of French origin, the pronunciation is often
wɑː as in **patois** ˈpæt wɑː.

3 Occasionally **oi** is weak, as in the usual pronunciation of **tortoise** ˈtɔːt əs ‖ ˈtɔːrt əs.

4 Note the exceptional words **choir** ˈkwaɪ ə ‖ ˈkwaɪ ər, **buoy** bɔɪ (AmE also ˈbuː i).

5 **oi** is not a digraph in **coincidence**, **soloist**.

oo Spelling-to-sound

1 Where the spelling is the digraph **oo**, the pronunciation is regularly either
uː as in **food** fuːd or ʊ as in **good** gʊd.
There is no rule, although ʊ is commoner before **k** (**book** bʊk). In some
words both pronunciations are in use as in **room** ruːm or rʊm.

O

2 Less frequently, the pronunciation is
ʌ as in **blood** blʌd, **flood** flʌd.

3 Where the spelling is **oor**, the pronunciation is
ɔː as in **door** dɔː ‖ dɔːr or
ʊə ‖ ʊ as in **moor** mʊə ‖ mʊr (but BrE now often mɔː).

4 Note the exceptional word **brooch** brəʊtʃ ‖ broʊtʃ (AmE also bruːtʃ).

5 **oo** is not a digraph in **zoology**, **cooperate**.

ou, ow Spelling-to-sound

1 Where the spelling is one of the digraphs **ou** and **ow**, the pronunciation is regularly
aʊ as in **round** raʊnd, **cow** kaʊ.

2 Less frequently, it is
əʊ ‖ oʊ as in **soul** səʊl ‖ soʊl, **own** əʊn ‖ oʊn
ʌ as in **touch** tʌtʃ or
uː as in **group** gruːp.

3 Note also the exceptional **could** kʊd, **should** ʃʊd, **would** wʊd.

4 Where the spelling is the notorious **ough**, the pronunciation may be any of the following:
ɔː as in **thought** θɔːt
uː as in **through** θruː
aʊ as in **bough** baʊ
əʊ ‖ oʊ as in **though** ðəʊ ‖ ðoʊ
ʌf as in **rough** rʌf
ɒf ‖ ɔːf as in **cough** kɒf ‖ kɔːf
ə ‖ oʊ as in **thorough** ˈθʌr ə ‖ ˈθɜː oʊ.
There are also other possibilities in **lough**, **hiccough** (more usually written **loch**, **hiccup**).

5 Where the spelling is **our**, the pronunciation may be strong
aʊ ə as in **flour** ˈflaʊ ə ‖ ˈflaʊ ˌʳr
ɔː as in **four** fɔː ‖ fɔːr
ɜː ‖ ɜː as in **journey** ˈdʒɜːn i ‖ ˈdʒɜːn i
ʌr ‖ ɜː as in **courage** ˈkʌr ɪdʒ ‖ ˈkɜː ɪdʒ or
ʊə ‖ ʊ as in **tourist** ˈtʊər ɪst ‖ ˈtʊr əst (BrE also ɔː); also
ʊ in the exceptional **courier**, usually ˈkʊr i ə ‖ ˈkʊr i ˌʳr.
or weak ə ‖ ʳr as in **colour** (BrE spelling) ˈkʌl ə ‖ -ʳr.

6 In the adjective ending **-ous** the pronunciation is weak əs, as in **famous** ˈfeɪm əs, **jealousy** ˈdʒel əs i.

O, o əʊ ǁ oʊ **O's, o's, Os** əʊz ǁ oʊz
—*Communications code name:* Oscar
ˈO ˌlevel; ˌO'V ˌlanguage
O, O' *in family names* əʊ ǁ oʊ —*This prefix is unstressed; it is occasionally reduced to* ə
o' ə —*weak form only; see* of
Oadby ˈəʊd bi →ˈəʊb- ǁ ˈoʊd-
oaf əʊf ǁ oʊf **oafs** əʊfs ǁ oʊfs
oafish ˈəʊf ɪʃ ǁ ˈoʊf ɪʃ **~ly** li **~ness** nəs nɪs
Oahu, O'ahu əʊ ˈɑː huː ǁ oʊ ˈɑː huː ə ˈwɑː-
—*Hawaiian* [o ˈʔa hu]
oak əʊk ǁ oʊk **oaks** əʊks ǁ oʊks
ˌOak ˈRidge; ˈoak tree
oak-apple ˈəʊk ˌæp ᵊl ǁ ˈoʊk-
oaken ˈəʊk ən ǁ ˈoʊk ən
Oakengates ˈəʊk ən ɡeɪts →-ŋ- ǁ ˈoʊk-
Oakes əʊks ǁ oʊks
Oakham ˈəʊk əm ǁ ˈoʊk-
Oakhampton ˌəʊk ˈhæmp tən ◂ ǁ ˈoʊk ˌ··
Oakland ˈəʊk lənd ǁ ˈoʊk-
Oakleigh, Oakley ˈəʊk li ǁ ˈoʊk-
Oaks əʊks ǁ oʊks
Oaksey ˈəʊks i ǁ ˈoʊks i
oakum ˈəʊk əm ǁ ˈoʊk-
Oakville ˈəʊk vɪl ǁ ˈoʊk-
Oamaru ˈɒm ə ruː ǁ ˈɑːm-
OAP ˌəʊ eɪ ˈpiː ǁ ˌoʊ- **~s, ~'s** z
oar ɔː ǁ ɔːr ʊər (= ore) **oared** ɔːd ǁ ɔːrd ʊərd
ˈoaring ˈɔːr ɪŋ ˈoʊr- **oars** ɔːz ǁ ɔːrz ʊərz
oarfish ˈɔː fɪʃ ǁ ˈɔːr- ˈoʊr-
oarlock ˈɔː lɒk ǁ ˈɔːr lɑːk ˈoʊr- **~s** s
oars|man ˈɔːz |mən ǁ ˈɔːrz- ˈoʊrz- **~manship**
mən ʃɪp **~men** mən **~woman** ˌwʊm ən
~women ˌwɪm ɪn §-ən
oarweed ˈɔː wiːd ǁ ˈɔːr- ˈoʊr-
OAS ˌəʊ eɪ ˈes ǁ ˌoʊ-
oas|is, O~ əʊ ˈeɪs |ɪs §-əs ǁ oʊ- **~es** iːz
oast əʊst ǁ oʊst
ˈoast house
oat əʊt ǁ oʊt **oats** əʊts ǁ oʊts
oatcake ˈəʊt keɪk ǁ ˈoʊt- **~s** s
oaten ˈəʊt ᵊn ǁ ˈoʊt ᵊn
Oates əʊts ǁ oʊts
oath əʊθ ǁ oʊθ **oaths** əʊðz əʊθs ǁ oʊðz oʊθs
oatmeal ˈəʊt miːᵊl ǁ ˈoʊt-
oats əʊts ǁ oʊts
OAU ˌəʊ eɪ ˈjuː ǁ ˌoʊ-
Oaxaca wə ˈhɑːk ə wɑː- —*Sp* [wa ˈxa ka]
Ob *river in USSR* ɒb ǁ oʊb ɑːb, ɔːb —*Russ* [ɔpʲ]
Obadiah ˌəʊb ə ˈdaɪ ə ǁ ˌoʊb-
Obama əʊ ˈbɑːm ə -ˈbæm- ǁ oʊ-
Oban ˈəʊb ən ǁ ˈoʊb-
obbligat|o ˌɒb lɪ ˈɡɑːt |əʊ -lə-
ǁ ˌɑːb lə ˈɡɑːt |oʊ **~i** i: **~os** əʊz ǁ oʊz
obcordate ɒb ˈkɔːd eɪt ǁ ɑːb ˈkɔːrd-

obduracy ˈɒb djʊr əs i ˈ·djər- ǁ ˈɑːb dʊr əs i
ˈ·djʊr-, ˈ·dər-, ˈ·djər-
obdurate ˈɒb djʊr ət -djər-, -ɪt ǁ ˈɑːb dʊr ət
-djʊr-, -dər-, -djər- **~ly** li **~ness** nəs nɪs
OBE ˌəʊ biː ˈiː ǁ ˌoʊ- **~s, ~'s** z
obeah ˈəʊb i ə ǁ ˈoʊb-
obedience ə ˈbiːd i ənᵗs əʊ- ǁ oʊ- ə-
obedient ə ˈbiːd i ənt əʊ- ǁ oʊ- ə- **~ly** li
obeisanc|e əʊ ˈbeɪs ᵊnᵗs -ˈbiːs- ǁ oʊ- ə- **~es** ɪz
əz
obelisk ˈɒb əl ɪsk §-əsk ǁ ˈɑːb ə lɪsk ˈoʊb- **~s** s
ob|elus ˈɒb |əl əs -ɪl- ǁ ˈɑːb- **~eli** ə laɪ ɪ-
Oberammergau ˌəʊb ər ˈæm ə ɡaʊ
ǁ ˌoʊb ər ˈɑːm ᵊr ɡaʊ —*Ger*
[ˌʔoː bɐ ˈʔam ɐ ɡaʊ]
Oberland ˈəʊb ə lænd ǁ ˈoʊb ᵊr- —*Ger*
[ˈʔoː bɐ lant]
Oberlin ˈəʊb ə lɪn ǁ ˈoʊb ᵊr- —*Fr* [ɔ bɛʁ lɛ̃]
Oberon ˈəʊb ᵊr ən -ə rɒn ǁ ˈoʊb ə rɑːn
obese əʊ ˈbiːs ǁ oʊ- **~ness** nəs nɪs
obesity əʊ ˈbiːs ət i -ɪt- ǁ oʊ ˈbiːs əţ i
obey ə ˈbeɪ əʊ- ǁ oʊ- ə- **~ed** d **~ing** ɪŋ **~s** z
obfusc|ate ˈɒb fʌsk |eɪt -fə skǀeɪt ǁ ˈɑːb-·ˈ··
~ated eɪt ɪd -əd ǁ eɪţ əd **~ates** eɪts **~ating**
eɪt ɪŋ ǁ eɪţ ɪŋ
obfuscation ˌɒb fʌ ˈskeɪʃ ᵊn -fə- ǁ ˌɑːb- **~s** z
ob-gyn, ob/gyn ˌəʊ biː ˈɡaɪn -ˈdʒɪn;
-ˌdʒiː waɪ ˈen ǁ ˌoʊb-
obi *'sash'* ˈəʊb i ǁ ˈoʊb i —*Jp* [ˈo bi] **~s** z
obi *'witchcraft'* ˈəʊb i ǁ ˈoʊb i
obit ˈəʊb ɪt ˈɒb-, §-ət ǁ ˈoʊb- —*as a shortening
of* obituary, *also* əʊ ˈbɪt ǁ oʊ- **~s** s
obiter ˈɒb ɪt ə ˈəʊb-, -ət- ǁ ˈoʊb əţ ᵊr ˈɑːb-
ˌobiter ˈdictum
obituaris|e, obituariz|e ə ˈbɪtʃ u ə raɪz əʊ-,
ɒ-, -ˈbɪt ju ̫, -ˈbɪtʃ ə raɪz **~ed** d **~es** ɪz əz **~ing**
ɪŋ
obituarist ə ˈbɪtʃ u ər ɪst əʊ-, ɒ-, -ˈbɪt ju ̫
§-əst; -ˈbɪtʃ ər ɪst ǁ -u er əst **~s** s
obituar|y ə ˈbɪtʃ u ər |i əʊ-, ɒ-, -ˈbɪt ju ̫;
-ˈbɪtʃ ər ǀi ǁ -u er ǀi **~ies** iz
object *v* əb ˈdʒekt §ˌɒb- ǁ ˌɑːb- **~ed** ɪd əd
~ing ɪŋ **~s** s
object *n* ˈɒb dʒekt -dʒɪkt ǁ ˈɑːb- **~s** s
ˈobject ˌlesson
objecti|fy *v* əb ˈdʒekt ɪ ǀfaɪ §ˌɒb-, -ə- ǁ ˌɑːb-
~fied faɪd **~fies** faɪz **~fying** faɪ ɪŋ
objection əb ˈdʒek ʃᵊn §ˌɒb- ǁ ˌɑːb- **~s** z
objectionab|le əb ˈdʒek ʃᵊn əb |ᵊl §ˌɒb-
ǁ ˌɑːb- **~ly** li
objectival ˌɒb dʒɪk ˈtaɪv ᵊl ◂ -dʒek- ǁ ˌɑːb-
objective əb ˈdʒekt ɪv ˌ··ɒb- ǁ ˌɑːb- —*When
contrastively stressed, as opposed to* subjective,
usually ˈɒb·· ǁ ˈɑːb·· **~ly** li **~ness** nəs nɪs **~s** z

O

objectivism əb 'dʒekt ɪv ˌɪz əm ₍ₜ₎ɒb-, -əv-
‖ ₍ₜ₎ɑːb-

objectivity ˌɒb dʒek 'tɪv ət i ˌdʒɪk-, -ɪt i
‖ ˌɑːb dʒek 'tɪv əţ i

objector əb 'dʒekt ə §₍ₜ₎ɒb- ‖ -ᵊr ₍ₜ₎ɑːb- **~s** z

object-oriented ˌɒb dʒekt 'ɔːr i ent ɪd ◄
-ˌdʒɪkt-, -'ɒr-, -əd ‖ ˌɑːb dʒɪkt 'ɔːr i enţəd ◄

objet, objets 'ɒb ʒeɪ ‖ ˌɔːb 'ʒeɪ ◄ ˌɑːb- —*Fr*
[ɔb ʒɛ]
ˌobjet(s) **'d'art** dɑː ‖ dɑːr —*Fr* [dɑːʁ];
ˌobjet(s) **'trouvé(s) '-trou'vé(s)** 'truːv eɪ
‖ truː 'veɪ —*Fr* [tʁu ve]

objur|gate 'ɒb dʒə ǀgeɪt -dʒɜ:- ‖ 'ɑːb dʒᵊr-
~gated geɪt ɪd -əd ‖ geɪţ əd **~gates** geɪts
~gating geɪt ɪŋ ‖ geɪţ ɪŋ

objurgation ˌɒb dʒə 'geɪʃ ᵊn -dʒɜ:-
‖ ˌɑːb dʒᵊr- **~s** z

objurgatory ɒb 'dʒɜːg ət ᵊr i əb-;
'ɒb dʒə geɪt ər i, '·dʒɜ:-, ·ˌ···
‖ əb 'dʒɜ:g ə tɔ:r i -tour i

oblast 'ɒb lɑːst -læst ‖ 'ɑːb- **~s** s —*Russ*
['ɔ bləsⁱtⁱ]

oblate *n, adj* 'ɒb leɪt əʊ 'bleɪt, ɒ- ‖ 'ɑːb leɪt
ɑː 'bleɪt, oʊ- **~ly** li **~ness** nəs nɪs **~s** s
ˌoblate **'sphere**

oblation ə 'bleɪʃ ᵊn əʊ-, ɒ- ‖ oʊ- **~s** z

obli|gate 'ɒb lɪ ǀgeɪt -lə- ‖ 'ɑːb- **~gated**
geɪt ɪd -əd ‖ geɪţ əd **~gates** geɪts **~gating**
geɪt ɪŋ ‖ geɪţ ɪŋ

obligation ˌɒb lɪ 'geɪʃ ᵊn -lə- ‖ ˌɑːb- **~s** z

obligator|y ə 'blɪg ət ᵊr ǀi ɒ- ‖ ə 'blɪg ə tɔːr ǀi
ɑː-, -tour i; 'ɑːb lɪg- **~ily** əl ɪ i li

oblig|e ə 'blaɪdʒ əʊ- **~ed** d **~es** ɪz əz **~ing** ɪŋ

obligee ˌɒb lɪ 'dʒiː -lə- ‖ ˌɑːb- **~s** z

obliging ə 'blaɪdʒ ɪŋ əʊ- **~ly** li **~ness** nəs nɪs

obligor ˌɒb lɪ 'gɔː -lə- ‖ ˌɑːb lə 'gɔːr '····**~s** z

oblique ə 'bliːk əʊ-, ɒ- ‖ oʊ-, -'blaɪk —*The*
AmE pronunciation -'blaɪk *is esp. military.* **~ly**
li **~ness** nəs nɪs **~s** s
o blique **'angle**

obliquit|y ə 'blɪk wət ǀi əʊ-, ɒ-, -ɪt- ‖ -wəţ ǀi
oʊ- **~ies** ɪz

oblite|rate ə 'blɪt ə ǀreɪt ɒ- ‖ ə 'blɪţ- oʊ-
~rated reɪt ɪd -əd ‖ reɪţ əd **~rates** reɪts
~rating reɪt ɪŋ ‖ reɪţ ɪŋ

obliteration ə ˌblɪt ə 'reɪʃ ᵊn ɒ- ‖ ə ˌblɪţ- oʊ-
~s z

oblivion ə 'blɪv i ən ɒ-, əʊ- ‖ oʊ-, ɑː-

oblivious ə 'blɪv i əs ɒ-, əʊ- ‖ oʊ-, ɑː- **~ly** li
~ness nəs nɪs

oblong 'ɒb lɒŋ ‖ 'ɑːb lɔːŋ -lɑːŋ **~s** z

obloq|uy 'ɒb lək ǀwi ‖ 'ɑːb- **~uies** wiz

obnoxious əb 'nɒk ʃəs ɒb- ‖ ɑːb 'nɑːk- əb- **~ly**
li **~ness** nəs nɪs

oboe 'əʊb əʊ ‖ 'oʊb oʊ **~s** z
ˌoboe **d'a'more** də 'mɔːr ɪ dɑː-, -eɪ

oboist 'əʊb əʊ ɪst §-əst ‖ 'oʊb oʊ- **~s** s

obol 'ɒb ɒl -ᵊl ‖ 'ɑːb ᵊl 'oʊb- **~s** z

ob|olus 'ɒb ǀəl əs ‖ 'ɑːb- **~oli** ə laɪ

Obote əʊ 'bəʊt eɪ -i ‖ oʊ 'boʊt-

O'Boyle əʊ 'bɔɪᵊl ‖ oʊ-

O'Brady (i) əʊ 'breɪd i ‖ oʊ-, (ii) əʊ 'brɔːd i
‖ oʊ- -'brɑːd- —*In AmE*, (i).

Ó Briain əʊ 'briːn ‖ oʊ- —*Irish* [oː 'brʲɪənʲ]

O'Brien, O'Bryan əʊ 'braɪ ən ‖ oʊ-

obscene əb 'siːn ₍ₜ₎ɒb- ‖ ₍ₜ₎ɑːb- **~ly** li

obscenit|y əb 'sen ət ǀi ɒb-, -'siːn-, -ɪt- ‖ -əţ ǀi
ɑːb- **~ies** iz

obscurantism ˌɒb skjʊᵊ 'rænt ˌɪz əm ˌskjə-
‖ əb 'skjʊr ən ˌtɪz əm ɑːb-; ˌɑːb skju 'ræn- (*)

obscurantist ˌɒb skjʊᵊ 'rænt ɪst ◄ -skjə-, §-əst
‖ əb 'skjʊr ənt əst ɑːb-; ˌɑːb skju 'rænţ- (*)
~s s

obscure *adj, v* əb 'skjʊə ɒb-, -'skjɔː ‖ -'skjʊᵊr
ɑːb- **~d** d **~ly** li **~ness** nəs nɪs **obscurer**
əb 'skjʊər ə ɒb-, -'skjɔːr- ‖ -'skjʊr ᵊr ɑːb-
obscures əb 'skjʊəz ɒb-, -'skjɔːz ‖ -'skjʊᵊrz
ɑːb- **obscurest** əb 'skjʊər ɪst ɒb-, -'skjɔːr-,
-əst ‖ -'skjʊr əst ɑːb- **obscuring** əb 'skjʊər ɪŋ
ɒb-, -'skjɔːr- ‖ -'skjʊr ɪŋ ɑːb-

obscurit|y əb 'skjʊər ət ǀi ɒb-, -'skjɔːr-, -ɪt-
‖ -'skjʊr əţ ǀi ɑːb- **~ies** iz

obse|crate 'ɒb sɪ ǀkreɪt -sə- ‖ 'ɑːb- **~crated**
kreɪt ɪd -əd ‖ kreɪţ əd **~crates** kreɪts
~crating kreɪt ɪŋ ‖ kreɪţ ɪŋ

obsecration ˌɒb sɪ 'kreɪʃ ᵊn -sə- ‖ ˌɑːb- **~s** z

obsequies 'ɒb sək wiz -sɪk-; ɒb 'siːk- ‖ 'ɑːb-

obsequious əb 'siːk wi əs ɒb-, △-ju əs ‖ ɑːb-
~ly li **~ness** nəs nɪs

observab|le əb 'zɜːv əb ǀᵊl §₍ₜ₎ɒb- ‖ -'zɜːv-
~les ᵊlz **~ly** li

observanc|e əb 'zɜːv ᵊnᵗs §₍ₜ₎ɒb- ‖ -'zɜːv- **~es**
ɪz əz

observant əb 'zɜːv ᵊnt §₍ₜ₎ɒb- ‖ -'zɜːv- **~ly** li

observation ˌɒbz ə 'veɪʃ ᵊn ˌɒb sə- ‖ ˌɑːbz ᵊr-
ˌɑːb sᵊr- **~al** ᵊl **~ally** ᵊl i **~s** z
ˌobser'vation car; ˌobser'vation post

observator|y əb 'zɜːv ətr ǀi §₍ₜ₎ɒb-
-'zɜːv ət ər ǀi ‖ -'zɜːv ə tɔːr ǀi -tour i **~ies** iz

observ|e əb 'zɜːv §₍ₜ₎ɒb- ‖ -'zɜːv **~ed** d **~es** z
~ing/ly ɪŋ /li

observer, O~ əb 'zɜːv ə §₍ₜ₎ɒb- ‖ -'zɜːv ᵊr **~s** z

obsess əb 'ses ɒb- ‖ ɑːb- **~ed** t **~es** ɪz əz **~ing**
ɪŋ

obsession əb 'seʃ ᵊn ɒb- ‖ ɑːb- **~al** ᵊl **~s** z

obsessive əb 'ses ɪv ɒb- ‖ ɑːb- **~ly** li **~ness**
nəs nɪs **~s** z

obsessive-compulsive
əb ˌses ɪv kəm 'pʌls ɪv ◄ ɒb-, §-kɒm-

obsidian əb 'sɪd i ən ɒb-

obsolescence ˌɒb sə 'les ᵊnᵗs ‖ ˌɑːb-

obsolescent ˌɒb sə 'les ᵊnt ◄ ‖ ˌɑːb- **~ly** li

obsolete 'ɒb sə liːt ˌ··ˈ· ‖ ˌɑːb sə 'liːt ◄ '····**~ly**
li **~ness** nəs nɪs

obstacle 'ɒb stək ᵊl -stɪk- ‖ 'ɑːb- **~s** z
'obstacle course; 'obstacle race

obstetric əb 'stetr ɪk ɒb- ‖ ɑːb- **~al** ᵊl **~ally** ᵊl i
~s s

obstetrician ˌɒb stə 'trɪʃ ᵊn -stɪ-, -ste- ‖ ˌɑːb-
~s z

obstinacy 'ɒb stɪn əs i '·stən- ‖ 'ɑːb-

obstinate 'ɒb stɪn ət -stən-, -ɪt ‖ 'ɑːb- **~ly** li
~ness nəs nɪs

obstipation ˌɒb stɪ 'peɪʃ ᵊn -stə- ‖ ˌɑːb-

obstreperous əb 'strep ᵊr əs ɒb- ‖ ɑːb- **~ly** li
~ness nəs nɪs

obstruct əb 'strʌkt §(ˌ)ɒb- ‖ (ˌ)ɑːb- **~ed** ɪd əd
~ing ɪŋ **~s** s
obstruction əb 'strʌk ʃən §(ˌ)ɒb- ‖ (ˌ)ɑːb- **~ism**
ˌɪz əm **~ist/s** ˌɪst/s §ˌəst/s ‖ əst/s **~s** z
obstructive əb 'strʌkt ɪv §(ˌ)ɒb- ‖ (ˌ)ɑːb- **~ly** li
~ness nəs nɪs
obstruent 'ɒb struˌənt ‖ 'ɑːb- **~s** s
obtain əb 'teɪn §(ˌ)ɒb- ‖ (ˌ)ɑːb- **~ed** d **~er/s** ə/z
‖ ər/z **~ing** ɪŋ **~s** z
obtainable əb 'teɪn əb əl §(ˌ)ɒb- ‖ (ˌ)ɑːb-
obtrud|e əb 'truːd ɒb- ‖ ɑːb- **~ed** ɪd əd **~es** z
~ing ɪŋ
obtrusion əb 'truːʒ ən ɒb- ‖ ɑːb- **~s** z
obtrusive əb 'truːs ɪv ɒb-, §-'truːz- ‖ ɑːb- **~ly** li
~ness nəs nɪs
obtu|rate 'ɒb tjuə |reɪt -tʃə- ‖ 'ɑːb tə |reɪt -tjə-
~rated reɪt ɪd -əd ‖ reɪt̬ əd **~rates** reɪts
~rating reɪt ɪŋ ‖ reɪt̬ ɪŋ
obturation ˌɒb tjuə 'reɪʃ ən ‖ ˌɑːb tə- -tjə- **~s** z
obturator 'ɒb tjuə reɪt ə ‖ 'ɑːb tə reɪt̬ ər -tjə-
~s z
obtuse əb 'tjuːs ɒb- ‖ əb 'tuːs ɑːb-, -'tjuːs **~ly** li
~ness nəs nɪs
obvers|e 'ɒb vɜːs ‖ 'ɑːb vɜːs ˌ·ˈ·, əb'· **~es** ɪz əz
~ely li
ob|vert ɒb |'vɜːt ‖ ɑːb |'vɜːt **~verted** 'vɜːt ɪd
-əd ‖ 'vɜːt̬ əd **~verting** 'vɜːt ɪŋ ‖ 'vɜːt̬ ɪŋ
~verts 'vɜːts ‖ 'vɜːts
obvi|ate 'ɒb vi |eɪt ‖ 'ɑːb- **~ated** eɪt ɪd -əd
‖ eɪt̬ əd **~ates** eɪts **~ating** eɪt ɪŋ ‖ eɪt̬ ɪŋ
obviative 'ɒb viˌət ɪv ‖ 'ɑːb vi eɪt̬ ɪv
obvious 'ɒb viˌəs ‖ 'ɑːb- **~ly** li **~ness** nəs nɪs
obvolute 'ɒb və luːt -ljuːt, ˌ·ˈ· ‖ 'ɑːb-
obvolution ˌɒb və 'luːʃ ən -'ljuːʃ- ‖ ˌɑːb-
O'Byrne əʊ 'bɜːn ‖ oʊ 'bɜːn
Ocado *tdmk* əʊ 'kɑːd əʊ ‖ oʊ 'kɑːd oʊ
O'Callaghan əʊ 'kæl ə hən -gən, -hæn ‖ oʊ-
ocarina ˌɒk ə 'riːn ə ‖ ˌɑːk- **~s** z
O'Casey əʊ 'keɪs i ‖ oʊ-
Occam 'ɒk əm ‖ 'ɑːk- **~s** z
  Occam's 'razor
occasion ə 'keɪʒ ən §əʊ- **~ed** d **~ing** ɪŋ **~s** z
occasional ə 'keɪʒ ən əl §əʊ- **~ly** i
Occident, o~ 'ɒks ɪd ənt -əd- ‖ 'ɑːks- -ə dent
occidental, O~ ˌɒks ɪ 'dent əl ◂ -ə-
‖ ˌɑːks ə 'dent̬ əl ◂ **~s** z
occipital ɒk 'sɪp ɪt əl -ət- ‖ ɑːk 'sɪp ət̬ əl **~s** z
occiput 'ɒks ɪ pʌt -ə-, -pət ‖ 'ɑːks- **~s** s
Occitan 'ɒks ɪt ən ‖ 'ɑːks- -ə tæn —*Fr*
[ɔk si tɑ̃]
occlud|e ə 'kluːd ɒ- ‖ ɑː- **~ed** ɪd əd **~es** z **~ing**
ɪŋ
occlusal ə 'kluːz əl ɒ-, -'kluːs- ‖ ɑː-
occlusion ə 'kluːʒ ən ɒ- ‖ ɑː- **~s** z
occlusive ə 'kluːs ɪv ɒ-, §-'kluːz- ‖ ɑː- **~s** z
occult *v* ə 'kʌlt ɒ- ‖ ɑː- **~ed** ɪd əd **~ing** ɪŋ **~s** s
occult *adj, n* 'ɒk ʌlt ɒ 'kʌlt, ə- ‖ ə 'kʌlt ɑː-,
oʊ-; 'ɑːk ʌlt
occultation ˌɒk ʌl 'teɪʃ ən -əl- ‖ ˌɑːk- **~s** z
occultism 'ɒk ʌl ˌtɪz əm -əl-; ɒ 'kʌl-, ə-
‖ ə 'kʌl- ɑː-; 'ɑːk əl-
occultist 'ɒk ʌlt ɪst -əst, §-əst; ɒ 'kʌlt-, ə-
‖ ə 'kʌlt əst ɑː-; 'ɑːk əlt- **~s** s

occupanc|y 'ɒk jʊp ənⁱs |i ·ˌjəp- ‖ 'ɑːk jəp-
~ies iz
occupant 'ɒk jʊp ənt -jəp- ‖ 'ɑːk jəp- **~s** s
occupation ˌɒk ju 'peɪʃ ən -jə- ‖ ˌɑːk jə- **~s** z
occupational ˌɒk ju 'peɪʃ ən əl ◂ ·jə- ‖ ˌɑːk jə-
~ly i
  ˌoccu'pational 'therapy
occu|py 'ɒk ju |paɪ -jə- ‖ 'ɑːk jə |paɪ **~pied**
paɪd **~pier/s** paɪ ə/z ‖ paɪ ər/z **~pies** paɪz
~pying paɪ ɪŋ
oc|cur ə |'kɜː §əʊ- ‖ ə |'kɜː **~curred** 'kɜːd
‖ 'kɜːd **~curring** 'kɜːr ɪŋ ‖ 'kɜː ɪŋ **~curs** 'kɜːz
‖ 'kɜːz
occurrenc|e ə 'kʌr ənⁱs §əʊ-, §-'kɜːr-
‖ ə 'kɜː ənⁱs **~es** ɪz əz
ocean 'əʊʃ ən ‖ 'oʊʃ ən **~s** z
oceanari|um ˌəʊʃ ə 'neər iˌ|əm ‖ ˌoʊʃ ə 'ner-
-'nær- **~a** ə **~ums** əmz
oceanfront 'əʊʃ ən frʌnt ‖ 'oʊʃ- **~s** s
oceangoing 'əʊʃ ən ˌgəʊ ɪŋ ‖ 'oʊʃ ən ˌgoʊ ɪŋ
Oceani|a ˌəʊs i 'ɑːn iˌ|ə ˌəʊʃ-, -'em-
‖ ˌoʊʃ i 'æn iˌ|ə -'ɑːn- **~an/s** ən/z ◂
oceanic, O~ ˌəʊʃ i 'æn ɪk ◂ ˌəʊs- ‖ ˌoʊʃ-
Oceanid, o~ əʊ 'siːˌən ɪd -'ʃiˌ, §-ˈəd ‖ oʊ- **~s** z
oceanographer ˌəʊʃ ə 'nɒg rəf ə ˌəʊs iˌəˈ--
‖ ˌoʊʃ ə 'nɑːg rəf ər **~s** z
oceanographic ˌəʊʃ ənˌə 'græf ɪk ◂ -iˌən ə-
‖ ˌoʊʃ-
oceanography ˌəʊʃ ə 'nɒg rəf i ˌəʊs iˌəˈ--
‖ ˌoʊʃ ə 'nɑːg rəf i
Oceanside 'əʊʃ ən saɪd ‖ 'oʊʃ-
Oceanus əʊ 'siːˌən əs -'ʃiˌ ‖ oʊ-
ocell|us əʊ 'sel |əs ‖ oʊ- **~i** aɪ iː
ocelot 'ɒs ə lɒt 'əʊs-, -ɪ- ‖ 'ɑːs ə lɑːt 'oʊs- **~s** s
och ɒx ‖ ɑːx
oche 'ɒk i ‖ 'ɑːk i **~s** z
ocher 'əʊk ə ‖ 'oʊk ər **~s** z
ocherous 'əʊk ər əs ‖ 'oʊk-
Ochil 'əʊk əl 'əʊx- ‖ 'oʊk-
Ochiltree 'ɒk əl triː 'ɒx-, 'əʊk-, 'əʊx-, -ɪl-, -tri
‖ 'ɑːk- 'oʊk-
ochlocracy ɒ 'klɒk rəs i ‖ ɑː 'klɑːk-
ochone ɒx 'əʊn ‖ ɔː 'xoʊn
Ocho Rios *place in Jamaica* ˌəʊtʃ əʊ 'riː əʊs
ˌɒtʃ- ‖ ˌoʊtʃ oʊ 'riː oʊs —*locally also* -'raɪ-
ochre 'əʊk ə ‖ 'oʊk ər **~s** z
ochreous 'əʊk riˌəs -ər- ‖ 'oʊk ər əs -riˌəs
ochry 'əʊk ər i ‖ 'oʊk-
ocker, Ocker 'ɒk ə ‖ 'ɑːk ər **~dom** dəm **~s** z
Ockham 'ɒk əm ‖ 'ɑːk-
Ockley 'ɒk li ‖ 'ɑːk-
o'clock ə 'klɒk §əʊ- ‖ ə 'klɑːk
O'Connell əʊ 'kɒn əl ‖ oʊ 'kɑːn əl
O'Conner, O'Connor əʊ 'kɒn ə ‖ oʊ 'kɑːn ər
ocotillo ˌɒk ə 'tiːl jəʊ -'tiː-, -'tiː jəʊ
‖ ˌoʊk ə 'tiːl joʊ -'tiː oʊ **~s** z
OCR ˌəʊ siː 'ɑː ‖ ˌoʊ siː 'ɑːr
Ocracoke 'əʊk rə kəʊk ‖ 'oʊk rə koʊk
oct- *comb. form before vowel* |ɒkt ‖ |ɑːkt
— **octad** 'ɒkt æd ‖ 'ɑːkt-
octa- *comb. form with stress-neutral suffix*
|ɒkt ə ‖ |ɑːkt ə — **octachord** 'ɒkt ə kɔːd
‖ 'ɑːkt ə kɔːrd *with stress-imposing suffix*

O

ɒk 'tæ+ ‖ ɑːk 'tæ+ — **octameter**
ɒk 'tæm ɪt ə -ət- ‖ ɑːk 'tæm ət ər
octad 'ɒkt æd ‖ 'ɑːkt- ~s z
octagon 'ɒkt əg ən ‖ 'ɑːkt ə gɑːn *(*)* ~s z
octagonal ɒk 'tæg ən əl ‖ ɑːk- ~ly i
octahedral ˌɒkt ə 'hiːdr əl ◂ -'hedr- ‖ ˌɑːkt-
octahedr|on ˌɒkt ə 'hiːdr |ən -'hedr- ‖ ˌɑːkt-
~a ə ~ons ənz
octal 'ɒkt əl ‖ 'ɑːkt əl
octane 'ɒkt eɪn ‖ 'ɑːkt-
Octans 'ɒkt ænz ‖ 'ɑːkt-
octant 'ɒkt ənt ‖ 'ɑːkt- ~s s
Octateuch 'ɒkt ə tjuːk §-tʃuːk ‖ 'ɑːkt ə tuːk
-tjuːk
octave 'ɒkt ɪv §-əv, -eɪv ‖ 'ɑːkt- —*Generally*
-ɪv, §-əv as a musical or literary term, but -eɪv
in the sense 'period of eight days' ~s z
Octavia ɒk 'teɪv i ə -'tɑːv- ‖ ɑːk-
Octavian ɒk 'teɪv i ən -'tɑːv- ‖ ɑːk-
Octavius ɒk 'teɪv i əs -'tɑːv- ‖ ɑːk-
octavo ɒk 'teɪv əʊ -'tɑːv- ‖ ɑːk 'teɪv oʊ -'tɑːv-
~s z
octennial ɒk 'ten i əl ‖ ɑːk-
octet ɒk 'tet ‖ ɑːk- ~s s
octo- *comb. form with stress-neutral suffix*
|ɒkt əʊ ‖ |ɑːkt ə — **octosyllable**
'ɒkt əʊ ˌsɪl əb əl ‖ ·ˌ· · ‖ 'ɑːkt ə-
October ɒk 'təʊb ə ‖ ɑːk 'toʊb ər ~s z
octodecimo ˌɒkt əʊ 'des ɪ məʊ -ə-
‖ ˌɑːkt oʊ 'des ə moʊ
octogenarian ˌɒkt əʊ dʒə 'neər i ən ◂ ·ˌ· ·dʒɪ-
‖ ˌɑːkt ə dʒə 'ner- ~s z
octopod 'ɒkt ə pɒd ‖ 'ɑːkt ə pɑːd ~s z
oct|opus 'ɒkt |əp əs -|ə pʊs ‖ 'ɑːkt- ~opi ə paɪ
~opuses əp əs ɪz -pʊs-, -əz
octoroon ˌɒkt ə 'ruːn ‖ ˌɑːkt- ~s z
octosyllabic ˌɒkt əʊ sɪ 'læb ɪk ◂ -sə'-
‖ ˌɑːkt ə-
octosyllable 'ɒkt əʊ ˌsɪl əb əl ‖ ·ˌ· · ·
‖ 'ɑːkt oʊ-
octuple 'ɒkt jʊp əl -jəp-, §-əp-; ɒk 'tjuːp əl
‖ 'ɑːkt ʊp əl -jʊp-; ɑːk 'tuːp-, -'tjuːp- ~s z
ocular 'ɒk jʊl ə -jəl- ‖ 'ɑːk jəl ər ~ly li ~s z
oculist 'ɒk jʊl ɪst -jəl-, §-əst ‖ 'ɑːk jəl əst ~s s
oculogyric ˌɒk ju ləʊ 'dʒɪr ɪk ◂ ·ˌjə-
‖ ˌɑːk jə loʊ-
oculomotor ˌɒk ju ləʊ 'məʊt ə ◂ ·ˌjə-
‖ ˌɑːk jə loʊ 'moʊt ər ◂
OD ˌəʊ 'diː ‖ ˌoʊ- ~'d, ~ed, ~'ed d ~ing, ~'ing
ɪŋ ~s, ~'s z
odalisk, odalisque 'əʊd ə lɪsk 'ɒd-, →-ºl ɪsk
‖ 'oʊd ºl ɪsk ~s s
O'Daly əʊ 'deɪl i ‖ oʊ-
odd ɒd ‖ ɑːd **odder** 'ɒd ə ‖ 'ɑːd ər **oddest**
'ɒd ɪst -əst ‖ 'ɑːd əst **odds** ɒdz ‖ ɑːdz
'odd bod; ˌodd man 'out; ˌodds and 'ends
oddball 'ɒd bɔːl →'ɒb- ‖ 'ɑːd- -bɑːl ~s z
Oddbins *tdmk* 'ɒd bɪnz →'ɒb- ‖ 'ɑːd-
Oddfellow 'ɒd ˌfel əʊ ‖ 'ɑːd ˌfel oʊ ~s z
Oddie 'ɒd i ‖ 'ɑːd i
oddish 'ɒd ɪʃ ‖ 'ɑːd ɪʃ
oddit|y 'ɒd ət |i -ɪt- ‖ 'ɑːd ət |i ~ies iz

odd-job |man ˌɒd 'dʒɒb |mæn ‖ ˌɑːd 'dʒɑːb-
~men men
oddly 'ɒd li ‖ 'ɑːd li
oddment 'ɒd mənt →'ɒb- ‖ 'ɑːd-
oddness 'ɒd nəs -nɪs ‖ 'ɑːd nəs ~es ɪz əz
oddsmaker 'ɒdz ˌmeɪk ə ‖ 'ɑːdz ˌmeɪk ər ~s z
odds-on ˌɒdz 'ɒn ◂ ‖ ˌɑːdz 'ɑːn ◂ -'ɔːn
-ode əʊd ‖ oʊd — **pentode** 'pent əʊd ‖ -oʊd
ode əʊd ‖ oʊd **odes** əʊdz ‖ oʊdz
O'Dea *(i)* əʊ 'deɪ ‖ oʊ-, *(ii)* əʊ 'diː ‖ oʊ-
Odell *(i)* 'əʊd ºl ‖ 'oʊd ºl, *(ii)* əʊ 'del ‖ oʊ-
Odense 'əʊd ºnˡs ə ‖ 'oʊd- —*Danish*
['oːʔ ðn sə]
Odeon 'əʊd i ən ‖ 'oʊd- ~s z
Oder 'əʊd ə ‖ 'oʊd ər —*Ger* ['ʔoː dɐ]
Oder-Neisse Line ˌəʊd ə 'naɪs ə laɪn
‖ ˌoʊd ər-
Odessa əʊ 'des ə ‖ oʊ- —*Russ* [ʌ 'dʲɛ sə]
Odets əʊ 'dets ‖ oʊ-
Odette əʊ 'det ‖ oʊ- —*Fr* [ɔ dɛt]
Odeum, odeum əʊ 'diː əm 'əʊd i əm
‖ oʊ 'diː əm 'oʊd i əm
Odgers 'ɒdʒ əz ‖ 'ɑːdʒ ərz
Odham 'ɒd əm ‖ 'ɑːd-
Odiham 'əʊd i əm -həm ‖ 'oʊd-
Odile əʊ 'diːºl ‖ oʊ-
Odin 'əʊd ɪn §-ºn ‖ 'oʊd-
odious 'əʊd i əs ‖ 'oʊd- ~ly li ~ness nəs nɪs
odium 'əʊd i əm ‖ 'oʊd-
Odo 'əʊd əʊ ‖ 'oʊd oʊ
Odoacer ˌɒd əʊ 'eɪs ə ˌəʊd- ‖ ˌoʊd oʊ 'eɪs ər
O'Doherty əʊ 'dɒx ət i -'dəʊ-, -'dɒ hət-
‖ oʊ 'dɑː hºrt i -'dɔːrt̬ i
odometer əʊ 'dɒm ɪt ə ɒ-, -ət-
‖ oʊ 'dɑːm ət̬ ər ~s z
O'Donnell əʊ 'dɒn ºl ‖ oʊ 'dɑːn ºl
O'Donovan əʊ 'dʌn əv ən ən -'dɒn- ‖ oʊ 'dɑːn-
odontolog|ist ˌɒd ɒn 'tɒl ədʒ ɪst ˌəʊd-, §-əst
‖ ˌoʊd ɑːn 'tɑːl- ˌɑːd- ~ists ɪsts §əsts -y i
odor 'əʊd ə ‖ 'oʊd ər ~ed d ~s z
odoriferous ˌəʊd ə 'rɪf ər əs ◂ ‖ ˌoʊd- ~ly li
~ness nəs nɪs
odorless 'əʊd ə ləs -lɪs; -ºl əs, -ɪs ‖ 'oʊd ər-
Odo-Ro-No *tdmk* ˌəʊd əʊ 'rəʊn əʊ
‖ ˌoʊd ə 'roʊn oʊ
odorous 'əʊd ər əs ‖ 'oʊd- ~ly li ~ness nəs
nɪs
odour 'əʊd ə ‖ 'oʊd ər ~ed d ~s z
odourless 'əʊd ə ləs -lɪs; -ºl əs, -ɪs ‖ 'oʊd ər-
O'Dowd əʊ 'daʊd ‖ oʊ-
O'Dwyer əʊ 'dwaɪ ə ‖ oʊ 'dwaɪ ºr
Odysseus ə 'dɪs juːs ɒ-, əʊ-, -'dɪs i əs
‖ oʊ 'dɪs i əs -'dɪʃ-, ə 'dɪs juːs
Odyssey, o~ 'ɒd əs i -ɪs- ‖ 'ɑːd- ~s z
oec... —*see* ec...
OECD ˌəʊ iː siː 'diː ‖ ˌoʊ-
oecumenic ˌiːk ju 'men ɪk ◂ ˌek- ‖ ˌek jə-
~al/ly ºl /i
OED ˌəʊ iː 'diː ‖ ˌoʊ-
oedem|a i 'diːm |ə ~as əz ~ata ət ə ‖ ət̬ ə
oedematous i 'diːm ət əs ‖ -ət̬ əs
Oedipal, o~ 'iːd ɪp ºl -əp- ‖ 'ed əp ºl 'iːd- *(*)*

Oedipus 'iːd ɪp əs -əp- ‖ 'ed əp əs 'iːd-
  '**Oedipus** ˌ**complex**

oeil-de-boeuf ˌɜː i də 'bɜːf ˌ-jə- ‖ ˌʌd ə 'bʌf
  —Fr [œj də bœf]

oenology i 'nɒl ədʒ i ‖ -'nɑːl-

Oenone i 'nəʊn i ‖ i 'noʊn i

oenophile 'iːn əʊ faɪ°l ‖ 'iːn ə- ~s z

o'er ɔː 'əʊ ə ‖ ɔːr oʊr

oersted 'ɜːst ɪd -ed, -əd ‖ 'ɜːst əd —Danish
  Ørsted ['œʁ sdeð] ~s z

oesophageal i ˌsɒf ə 'dʒiːˌəl ◂ ə-, ˌiːs ɒf ə'--
  ‖ i ˌsɑːf- ˌiːs ə 'fædʒ iˌəl ◂

oesoph|agus i 'sɒf |əg əs ə- ‖ i 'sɑːf- ~**agi**
  ə gaɪ -dʒaɪ ~**aguses** əg əs ɪz -əz

oestradiol ˌiːs trə 'daɪ ɒl ˌes-, -əl; iː 'stræd i ɒl
  ‖ ˌes trə 'daɪ ɔːl -ɑːl, -oʊl

oestrogen 'iːs trədʒ ən 'es-, -trə dʒen ‖ 'es- ~**s**
  z

oestrous, oestrus 'iːs trəs 'es- ‖ 'es- (*)

oeuvre 'ɜːv rə 'ɔːv ə ‖ 'ʊv rə 'ʊv °r —Fr
  [œːvʁ]

of strong form ɒv ‖ ʌv ɑːv (*), weak form əv
  —There is also an informal rapid-speech or
  nonstandard weak form, used before
  consonants only, ə. It is sometimes written o'.

O'Faolain, O'Faoláin əʊ 'feɪl ən -'fæl-, -ɔɪn
  ‖ oʊ-

off ɒf ɔːf ‖ ɔːf ɑːf
  '**off chance**; ˌ**off** '**colour**◂; ˌ**off** '**line**◂

off- |ɒf |ɔːf ‖ |ɔːf |ɑːf — **off-air** ˌɒf 'eə ◂
  ‖ ˌɔːf 'eºr ◂ ˌɑːf-, -'æºr

Offa 'ɒf ə ‖ 'ɔːf ə 'ɑːf-

off-air ˌɒf 'eə ◂ ˌɔːf- ‖ ˌɔːf 'eºr ◂ ˌɑːf-

offal 'ɒf °l ‖ 'ɔːf °l 'ɑːf-

Offaly 'ɒf əl i ‖ 'ɔːf- 'ɑːf-

off-balance ˌɒf 'bæl ən\`s ◂ ˌɔːf- ‖ ˌɔːf- ˌɑːf-

offbeat adj ˌɒf 'biːt ◂ ˌɔːf-, '·· ‖ ˌɔːf- ˌɑːf-

offbeat n 'ɒf biːt 'ɔːf- ‖ 'ɔːf- 'ɑːf- ~s s

off-brand 'ɒf brænd 'ɔːf- ‖ 'ɔːf- 'ɑːf- ~s z

off-Broadway ˌɒf 'brɔːd weɪ ◂ ˌɔːf- ‖ ˌɔːf- ˌɑːf-,
  -'brɑːd-

off-campus ˌɒf 'kæmp əs ◂ ˌɔːf- ‖ ˌɔːf- ˌɑːf-

off-centre, off-center ˌɒf 'sent ə ˌɔːf-
  ‖ ˌɔːf 'sen̬t ºr ˌɑːf-

off-chance 'ɒf tʃɑːn\`s 'ɔːf-, §-tʃæn\`s
  ‖ 'ɔːf tʃæn\`s 'ɑːf-

off-color, off-colour ˌɒf 'kʌl ə ◂ ˌɔːf-
  ‖ ˌɔːf 'kʌl ºr ◂ ˌɑːf-

offcut 'ɒf kʌt 'ɔːf- ‖ 'ɔːf- 'ɑːf- ~s s

off-duty ˌɒf 'djuːt i ◂ ˌɔːf-, -'dʒuːt-, §-'duːt-
  ‖ ˌɔːf 'duːt̬ i ◂ ˌɑːf-, -'djuːt̬-

Offenbach 'ɒf °n bɑːk ‖ 'ɔːf- 'ɑːf- —Fr
  [ɔ fɛn bak], Ger ['ʔɔf °n bax]

offenc|e ə 'fen\`s §əʊ- ~**eless** ləs lɪs ~**es** ɪz əz

offend ə 'fend §əʊ- ~**ed** ɪd əd ~**er/s** ə/z ºr/z
  ~**ing** ɪŋ ~**s** z

offens|e ə 'fen\`s §əʊ- —but in AmE in the
  sporting meaning 'attack, attacking side' often
  'ɑːf en\`s, 'ɔːf- ~**eless** ləs lɪs ~**es** ɪz əz

offensive ə 'fen\`s ɪv əʊ- —but in the sense
  'relating to attack' also 'ɒf en\`s ɪv ‖ 'ɔːf-, 'ɑːf-
  ~**ly** li ~**ness** nəs nɪs ~**s** z

offer 'ɒf ə ‖ 'ɔːf ºr 'ɑːf- ~**ed** d **offering/s**
  'ɒf ər ɪŋ/z ‖ 'ɔːf ər ɪŋ/z 'ɑːf- ~**s** z

offertor|y 'ɒf ət ər |i ‖ 'ɔːf ºr tɔːr |i 'ɑːf-,
  -tour i ~**ies** iz

off-glide 'ɒf glaɪd 'ɔːf- ‖ 'ɔːf- 'ɑːf- ~**s** z

off-guard ˌɒf 'gɑːd ˌɔːf- ‖ ˌɔːf 'gɑːrd ˌɑːf-

offhand ˌɒf 'hænd ◂ ˌɔːf- ‖ ˌɔːf- ˌɑːf-

offhanded ˌɒf 'hænd ɪd ˌɔːf-, -əd ‖ ˌɔːf- ˌɑːf-
  ~**ly** li ~**ness** nəs nɪs

offic|e 'ɒf ɪs §-əs ‖ 'ɑːf əs 'ɔːf- ~**es** ɪz əz
  '**office block**; '**office boy**, '**office girl**;
  '**office hours**, ˌ·ˈ·

office-bearer 'ɒf ɪs ˌbeər ə §-əs-
  ‖ 'ɑːf əs ˌbeºr ºr ~**s** z

officeholder 'ɒf ɪs ˌhəʊld ə §-əs-
  ‖ 'ɑːf əs ˌhoʊld ºr 'ɔːf- ~**s** z

officer 'ɒf ɪs ə §-əs- ‖ 'ɑːf əs ºr 'ɔːf- ~**ed** d ~**s** z

official ə 'fɪʃ °l §əʊ- ~**dom** dəm ~**s** z

officialese ə ˌfɪʃ ə 'liːz §əʊ-, ·ˈ··· ‖ -'liːs

officialis|e, officializ|e ə 'fɪʃ ə laɪz §əʊ- ~**ed**
  d ~**es** ɪz əz ~**ing** ɪŋ

officially ə 'fɪʃ əl i §əʊ-

officiant ə 'fɪʃ iˌənt §əʊ- ~**s** s

offici|ate ə 'fɪʃ i |eɪt §əʊ- ~**ated** eɪt ɪd -əd
  ‖ eɪt̬ əd ~**ates** eɪts ~**ating** eɪt ɪŋ ‖ eɪt̬ ɪŋ

officiation ə ˌfɪʃ i 'eɪʃ °n §əʊ-

officious ə 'fɪʃ əs §əʊ- ~**ly** li ~**ness** nəs nɪs

offing 'ɒf ɪŋ 'ɔːf- ‖ 'ɔːf ɪŋ 'ɑːf-

offish 'ɒf ɪʃ 'ɔːf- ‖ 'ɔːf ɪʃ 'ɑːf- ~**ly** li ~**ness** nəs
  nɪs

off-key ˌɒf 'kiː ◂ ˌɔːf- ‖ ˌɔːf- ˌɑːf-

off-kilter ˌɒf 'kɪlt ə ◂ ˌɔːf- ‖ ˌɔːf 'kɪlt ºr ◂ ˌɑːf-

off-licenc|e 'ɒf ˌlaɪs ºn\`s 'ɔːf-, ·ˈ·· ‖ 'ɔːf- 'ɑːf-
  ~**es** ɪz əz

off-load ˌɒf 'ləʊd ˌɔːf- ‖ ˌɔːf 'loʊd ˌɑːf- ~**ed** ɪd
  əd ~**ing** ɪŋ ~**s** z

off-message ˌɒf 'mes ɪdʒ ◂ ˌɔːf- ‖ ˌɔːf- ˌɑːf-

off-off-Broadway ˌɒf ɒf 'brɔːd weɪ ◂ ˌɔːf ɔːf-
  ‖ ˌɔːf ɔːf- ˌɑːf ɑːf-

off-peak ˌɒf 'piːk ◂ ˌɔːf- ‖ ˌɔːf- ˌɑːf-

off-piste ˌɒf 'piːst ◂ ˌɔːf- ‖ ˌɔːf- ˌɑːf-

offprint 'ɒf prɪnt 'ɔːf- ‖ 'ɔːf- 'ɑːf- ~**s** s

off-putting 'ɒf ˌpʊt ɪŋ 'ɔːf-, ·ˈ·· ‖ 'ɔːf ˌpʊt̬ ɪŋ
  'ɑːf-

off-ramp 'ɒf ræmp 'ɔːf- ‖ 'ɔːf- 'ɑːf- ~**s** s

off-road ˌɒf 'rəʊd ◂ ˌɔːf- ‖ ˌɔːf 'roʊd ◂ ˌɑːf-

offscouring 'ɒf ˌskaʊºr ɪŋ 'ɔːf- ‖ 'ɔːf- 'ɑːf- ~**s** z

off-screen ˌɒf 'skriːn ◂ ˌɔːf- ‖ ˌɔːf- ˌɑːf-

off-season n 'ɒf ˌsiːz ºn 'ɔːf- ‖ 'ɔːf- 'ɑːf-

off-season adj ˌɒf 'siːz ºn ◂ ˌɔːf- ‖ ˌɔːf- ˌɑːf-

offset n 'ɒf set 'ɔːf- ‖ 'ɔːf- 'ɑːf- ~**s** s

off|set v ˌɒf |'set ˌɔːf-, '·· ‖ ˌɔːf- ˌɑːf- ~**sets**
  'sets ~**setting** 'set ɪŋ ‖ 'set̬ ɪŋ

offshoot 'ɒf ʃuːt 'ɔːf- ‖ 'ɔːf- 'ɑːf- ~**s** s

offshore ˌɒf 'ʃɔː ◂ ˌɔːf- ‖ ˌɔːf 'ʃɔːr ◂ ˌɑːf-, -'ʃoʊr

offsid|e ˌɒf 'saɪd ◂ ˌɔːf- ‖ ˌɔːf- ˌɑːf- ~**er/s** ə/z
  ºr/z ~**es** z

off-site ˌɒf 'saɪt ◂ ˌɔːf- ‖ ˌɔːf- ˌɑːf-

offspring 'ɒf sprɪŋ 'ɔːf- ‖ 'ɔːf- 'ɑːf-

offstage ˌɒf 'steɪdʒ ◂ ˌɔːf- ‖ ˌɔːf- ˌɑːf-

off-street ˌɒf 'striːt ◂ ˌɔːf- ‖ ˌɔːf- ˌɑːf-
  ˌ**off-street** '**parking**

off-the-cuff ˌɒf ðə 'kʌf ◂ ˌɔːf- ‖ ˌɔːf- ˌɑːf-

off-the-peg ˌɒf ðə ˈpeg ◂ ‖ ˌɔːf- ˌɑːf-
off-the-rack ˌɒf ðə ˈræk ◂ ‖ ˌɔːf- ‖ ˌɔːf- ˌɑːf-
off-the-record ˌɒf ðə ˈrek ɔːd ◂ ˌɔːf-, §-əd
‖ ˌɔːf ðə ˈrek ərd ◂ ˌɑːf-
off-the-shelf ˌɒf ðə ˈʃelf ◂ ‖ ˌɔːf- ˌɑːf-
off-the-shoulder ˌɒf ðə ˈʃəʊld ə ◂ ˌɔːf-,
→-ˈʃʊld- ‖ ˌɔːf ðə ˈʃəʊld ᵊr ◂
off-the-wall ˌɒf ðə ˈwɔːl ◂ ˌɔːf- ‖ ˌɔːf- ˌɑːf-,
-ˈwɑːl
offtrack ˌɒf ˈtræk ◂ ˌɔːf- ‖ ˌɔːf- ˌɑːf-
off-white ˌɒf ˈwaɪt ◂ ˌɔːf-, -ˈhwaɪt
‖ ˌɔːf ˈhwaɪt ◂ ˌɑːf-
off-year ˈɒf jɪə ˌɔːf- ‖ ˈɔːf jɪr ˈɑːf- ◂
Ofgas ˈɒf gæs ‖ ˈɔːf- ˈɑːf-
Ofgem ˈɒf dʒem ‖ ˈɔːf- ˈɑːf-
O'Fiaich əʊ ˈfiː ‖ oʊ- —Irish [oː ˈfʲiə]
Ofili ə ˈfiːl i
oflag ˈɒf læg -lɑːg ‖ ˈɑːf- ˈɔːf- —Ger [ˈʔɔf laːk]
O'Flaherty əʊ ˈflɑː hət i -ˈflæ-, -ət-; -ˈfleət i
‖ oʊ ˈflæ ᵊrt̬ i -ˈflert̬ i
O'Flynn əʊ ˈflɪn ‖ oʊ-
Ofsted ˈɒf sted ‖ ˈɑːf- ˈɔːf-
oft ɒft ɔːft ‖ ɔːft ɑːft
Oftel ˈɒf tel ‖ ˈɑːf- ˈɔːf-

no t with t

27%
73%
BrE

22%
78%
AmE

often ˈɒf ᵊn ˈɒft ən, ˈɔːf ᵊn, ˈɔːft ən ‖ ˈɔːf ᵊn
ˈɑːf-; ˈɔːft ən, ˈɑːft- —Many speakers use both
the form without t and the form with it.
Preference polls, Br: no t 73%, with t 27%;
with ɒ 99%, with ɔː 1%; AmE, no t 78%, with
t 22%. ~er ə ‖ ᵊr ~est ɪst əst ~times taɪmz
ofttimes ˈɒft taɪmz ˈɔːft- ‖ ˈɔːft- ˈɑːft-
Ofwat ˈɒf wɒt ‖ ˈɑːf wɑːt
Og ɒg ‖ ɔːg ɑːg
Ogaden ˌɒg ə ˈden ‖ ˌɑːg- ˌoʊg-
ogam ˈɒg əm ˈəʊg-; mːc ‖ ˈɑːg- ˈɔːg-, ˈoʊg-
Ogbomosho ˌɒg bə ˈməʊʃ əʊ
‖ ˌɑːg bə ˈmoʊʃ oʊ
Ogden, Ogdon ˈɒgd ən ‖ ˈɔːgd- ˈɑːgd-
ogee ˈəʊdʒ iː ‖ ˈoʊdʒ iː oʊ ˈdʒiː- ~s z
Ogen ˈəʊg en ‖ ˈoʊg-
Ogg ɒg ‖ ɔːg ɑːg
ogham ˈɒg əm ˈəʊg-; ɔːm ‖ ˈɑːg- ˈɔːg-, ˈoʊg-
Ogilvie, Ogilvy ˈəʊg ᵊlv i ‖ ˈoʊg-
ogival əʊ ˈdʒaɪv ᵊl ‖ oʊ-
ogive ˈəʊdʒ aɪv ‖ ˈoʊdʒ- ~s z
og|le ˈəʊg |ᵊl ˈɒg- ‖ ˈoʊg |ᵊl ˈɑːg- — Preference
poll. BrE: ˈəʊg- 76%, ˈɒg- 24%. ~led ᵊld ~les
ᵊlz ~ling ᵊl ɪŋ
Oglethorpe ˈəʊg ᵊl θɔːp ‖ ˈoʊg ᵊl θɔːrp
Ogmore ˈɒg mɔː ‖ ˈɔːg mɔːr ˈɑːg-, -moʊr
ogonek ɒ ˈgɒn ek ə- ‖ oʊ ˈgɑːn- -ˈgoʊn- ~s s
—Polish [o ˈgo nek]
Ogoni əʊ ˈgəʊn i ‖ oʊ ˈgoʊn i ~land lænd

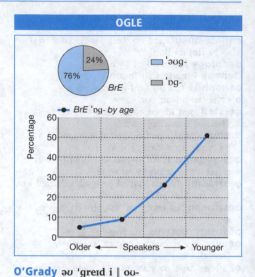

OGLE

24%
76%
BrE

▪ ˈəʊg-
▪ ˈɒg-

BrE ˈɒg- by age

Percentage
60
50
40
30
20
10
0
Older ◀— Speakers —▶ Younger

O'Grady əʊ ˈgreɪd i ‖ oʊ-
ogre ˈəʊg ə ‖ ˈoʊg ᵊr ~s z
ogreish ˈəʊg ər ɪʃ ‖ ˈoʊg-
ogress ˈəʊg rɪs -rəs, -res ‖ ˈoʊg ᵊr_əs ~es ɪz əz
Ogwen ˈɒg wen ‖ ˈɔːg- ˈɑːg-
Ogwr ˈɒg ʊə ‖ ˈɔːg ʊr ˈɑːg- —Welsh [ˈo gur]
oh əʊ ‖ oʊ (= O) oh's, ohs əʊz ‖ oʊz
OH —see Ohio
O'Hagan əʊ ˈheɪg ən ‖ oʊ-
O'Halloran əʊ ˈhæl ər ən ‖ oʊ-
O'Hanlon əʊ ˈhæn lən ‖ oʊ-
O'Hara əʊ ˈhɑːr ə ‖ oʊ ˈhær ə -ˈher-
O'Hare əʊ ˈheə ‖ oʊ ˈheᵊr -ˈhæᵊr
O'Higgins əʊ ˈhɪg ɪnz §-ənz ‖ oʊ-
Ohio əʊ ˈhaɪ əʊ ‖ oʊ ˈhaɪ oʊ ~an/s ən/z
ohm, Ohm əʊm ‖ oʊm —Ger [ˈʔoːm] ohms
əʊmz ‖ oʊmz
ohmic ˈəʊm ɪk ‖ ˈoʊm-
ohmmeter ˈəʊm ˌmiːt ə ‖ ˈoʊm ˌmiːt̬ ᵊr ~s z
OHMS ˌəʊ eɪtʃ em ˈes §,· heɪtʃ- ‖ ˌoʊ-
oho əʊ ˈhəʊ ‖ oʊ ˈhoʊ
OHP ˌəʊ eɪtʃ ˈpiː ‖ ˌoʊ- ~s z
oi ɔɪ
oick ɔɪk oicks ɔɪks
-oid ɔɪd — planetoid ˈplæn ə tɔɪd -ɪ-
oidi|um əʊ ˈɪd i_|əm ‖ oʊ- ~a ə
oik ɔɪk oiks ɔɪks
oil ɔɪᵊl oiled ɔɪᵊld oiling ˈɔɪᵊl ɪŋ oils ɔɪᵊlz
ˈoil drum; ˈoil paint; ˈoil ˌpainting; ˈoil
slick; ˈoil ˌtanker; ˈoil well
oil-based ˈɔɪᵊl beɪst
oil-bearing ˈɔɪᵊl ˌbeər ɪŋ ‖ -ˌber- -ˌbær-
oilbird ˈɔɪᵊl bɜːd ‖ -bɜːd ~s z
oilcake ˈɔɪᵊl keɪk
oilcan ˈɔɪᵊl kæn ~s z
oilcloth ˈɔɪᵊl klɒθ -klɔːθ ‖ -klɔːθ -klɑːθ
oiler ˈɔɪᵊl ə ‖ -ᵊr ~s z
oilfield ˈɔɪᵊl fiːᵊld ~s z
oil-fired ˈɔɪᵊl ˌfaɪ əd ,·' ◂ ‖ -ˌfaɪ ᵊrd
oil-free ˌɔɪᵊl ˈfriː ◂
oili... —see oily

oil|man ˈɔɪᵊl |mæn -mən **~men** men mən

oil-rich ˌɔɪᵊl ˈrɪtʃ ◂

oilrig ˈɔɪᵊl rɪg **~s** z

oilseed ˈɔɪᵊl siːd

oilskin ˈɔɪᵊl skɪn **~s** z

oilstone ˈɔɪᵊl stəʊn ‖ -stoʊn

oil|y ˈɔɪl |i **~ier** i‿ə ‖ i‿ᵊr **~iest** i‿ɪst i‿əst **~iness** i nəs i nɪs

oink ɔɪŋk **oinks** ɔɪŋks

ointment ˈɔɪnt mənt **~s** s

Oireachtas ˈer əkθ əs |ˈeər-, -əkt- —*Irish* [ˈɛ rʲəx təs]

Oise wɑːz —*Fr* [waːz]

Oistrakh ˈɔɪs traːk -traːx —*Russ* [ˈɔj strəx]

Ojibwa, Ojibway əʊ ˈdʒɪb weɪ -wə ‖ oʊ- **~s** z

OK, O.K. ₍ˌ₎əʊ ˈkeɪ ‖ ₍ˌ₎oʊ- **~'d** d **~'ing** ɪŋ **~'s** z

okapi əʊ ˈkɑːp i ‖ oʊ- **~s** z

Okavango ˌɒk ə ˈvæŋ gəʊ ◂ ‖ ˌoʊk ə ˈvæŋ goʊ ◂ -ˈvɑːŋ- ˌOka·vango "Swamp

okay ₍ˌ₎əʊ ˈkeɪ ‖ ₍ˌ₎oʊ- **~ed** d **~ing** ɪŋ **~s** z

Okayama ˌəʊk ə ˈjɑːm ə ˌɒk- ‖ ˌoʊk- —*Jp* [o ˈka ja ma]

Okazaki ˌəʊk ə ˈzɑːk i ‖ ˌoʊk- —*Jp* [o ˌka dza ki]

Okeechobee ˌəʊk ɪ ˈtʃəʊb i ‖ ˌoʊk ə ˈtʃoʊb i

O'Keefe, O'Keeffe əʊ ˈkiːf ‖ oʊ-

Okefenokee ˌəʊk ɪf ɪ ˈnəʊk i ◂ ˌəf-, -əˈ-- ‖ ˌoʊk əf ə ˈnoʊk i ˌOkefe ˌnokee 'Swamp

Okehampton ˌəʊk ˈhæmpt ən ‖ ˈoʊk ˌ··

okey-doke ˌəʊk i ˈdəʊk ‖ ˌoʊk i ˈdoʊk

okey-dokey ˌəʊk i ˈdəʊk i ‖ ˌoʊk i ˈdoʊk i

Okhotsk əʊ ˈkɒtsk ɒ-, ˈ·· ‖ oʊ ˈkɑːtsk —*Russ* [ʌ ˈxɔtsk]

Okie ˈəʊk i ‖ ˈoʊk i **~s** z

Okina|wa ˌɒk ɪ ˈnɑː |wə ˌəʊk-, -ə- ‖ ˌoʊk ə- -ˈnɑʊ ə —*Jp* [o ˌki na wa] **~wan/s** wən/z ◂

Oklahom|a ˌəʊk lə ˈhəʊm |ə ◂ ‖ ˌoʊk lə ˈhoʊm |ə **~an/s** ən/z ◂ ˌOkla ˌhoma 'City

okra ˈəʊk rə ˈɒk- ‖ ˈoʊk rə

Okri ˈɒk ri ‖ ˈɑːk-

-ol ɒl ‖ ˈɔːl ɑːl, oʊl — **glycerol** ˈglɪs ə rɒl ‖ -rɔːl -rɑːl, -roʊl

ol' *elided form of* old əʊl →ɒʊl ‖ oʊl

Olaf ˈəʊl əf -æf, -ɑːf ‖ ˈoʊl- —*Norw* [ˈˈuː laf]

Olav ˈəʊl æv -əv ‖ ˈoʊl-

Olave ˈɒl əv -ɪv, -eɪv ‖ ˈɑːl-

Olbers ˈɒlb əz ‖ ˈoʊlb ᵊrz —*Ger* [ˈʔɔl bɐs]

Olbia ˈɒlb i‿ə ‖ ˈɑːlb- —*It* [ˈɔl bja]

old əʊld →ɒʊld ‖ oʊld **older** ˈəʊld ə →ˈɒʊld- ‖ ˈoʊld ᵊr **oldest** ˈəʊld ɪst →ˈɒʊld-, -əst ‖ ˈoʊld əst

ˌold 'age◂, ˌold age 'pension, ˌold age 'pensioner; ˌOld 'Bailey; 'old boy *'former pupil'*, ˌold 'boy *'old chap'*; ˌold-'boy ˌnetwork; ˌOld 'Catholic; ˌOld Church Sla'vonic; ˌOld 'English ◂; ˌold 'flame; 'old girl ' *'former pupil'*; ˌold 'guard, '· ·; ˌold 'hand; ˌold 'hat; ˌold 'lady; ˌold 'lag; ˌold 'maid; ˌold 'man; ˌold 'master; ˌOld 'Nick; ˌold 'people's home; 'old school

'conservative attitudes', ˌold 'school ◂ *'former place of learning'*, ˌold school 'tie; ˌOld 'Testament ◂; ˌold 'wives' tale; ˌold 'woman; ˌOld 'World ◂

Oldbury ˈəʊld bər i →ˈɒʊld- ‖ ˈoʊld ˌber i

Oldcastle ˈəʊld ˌkɑːs ᵊl →ˈɒʊld-, §-ˌkæs- ‖ ˈoʊld ˌkæs ᵊl

olde ˈəʊld i →ˈɒʊld i ‖ ˈoʊld i ˌolde 'worlde ˈwɜːld i ‖ ˈwɜːld i

olden ˈəʊld ən ˈɒʊld- ‖ ˈoʊld ən

Oldenburg ˈəʊld ən bɜːg →ˈɒʊld-, →-əm- ‖ ˈoʊld ən bɜːg —*Ger* [ˈʔɔl dᵊn bʊʁk, -bʊʁç]

old-established ˌəʊld ɪ ˈstæb lɪʃt ◂ →ˌɒʊld-, -ə- ‖ ˌoʊld-

old-fashioned ˌəʊld ˈfæʃ ᵊnd ◂ →ˌɒʊld- ‖ ˌoʊld-

Oldfield ˈəʊld fiːᵊld →ˈɒʊld- ‖ ˈoʊld-

old-fogeyish, old-fogyish ˌəʊld ˈfəʊg i ɪʃ →ˌɒʊld- ‖ ˌoʊld ˈfoʊg-

old-growth ˌəʊld ˈgrəʊθ ◂ →ˌɒʊld- ‖ ˌoʊld ˈgroʊθ ◂

Oldham ˈəʊld əm →ˈɒʊld- ‖ ˈoʊld-

oldie ˈəʊld i →ˈɒʊld- ‖ ˈoʊld i **~s** z

oldish ˈəʊld ɪʃ →ˈɒʊld- ‖ ˈoʊld-

old-line ˌəʊld ˈlaɪn ◂ →ˌɒʊld- ‖ ˌoʊld-

old-maidish ˌəʊld ˈmeɪd ɪʃ ◂ →ˌɒʊld- ‖ ˌoʊld-

Oldman ˈəʊld mən →ˈɒʊld- ‖ ˈoʊld-

Oldrey ˈəʊldr i ˈɒʊldr- ‖ ˈoʊldr i

Oldsmobile *tdmk* ˈəʊldz məʊ ˌbiːᵊl →ˈɒʊldz- ‖ ˈoʊldz mə ˌbiːᵊl **~s** z

old-stager ˌəʊld ˈsteɪdʒ ə →ˌɒʊld- ‖ ˌoʊld ˈsteɪdʒ ᵊr **~s** z

oldster ˈəʊld stə →ˈɒʊld- ‖ ˈoʊld stᵊr **~s** z

old-style ˌəʊld ˈstaɪᵊl ◂ →ˌɒʊld- ‖ ˌoʊld-

old-tim|e ˌəʊld ˈtaɪm ◂ →ˌɒʊld-, ˈ·· ‖ ˌoʊld- **~er/s** ə/z ‖ ᵊr/z ˌold-time 'dancing

Olduvai ˈɒld ə vaɪ ˈəʊld-, -u-, -ju- ‖ ˈɔːld- ˈɑːld-, ˈoʊld- ˌOlduvai 'Gorge

old-womanish ˌəʊld ˈwʊm ən ɪʃ ◂ →ˌɒʊld- ‖ ˌoʊld-

old-world ˌəʊld ˈwɜːld ◂ →ˌɒʊld- ‖ ˌoʊld ˈwɜːld ◂

-ole əʊl →ɒʊl ‖ oʊl — **benzole** ˈbenz əʊl →-ɒʊl ‖ -oʊl —*but note also words such as* hyperbole, systole *with* əl i

olé əʊ ˈleɪ ‖ oʊ-

oleaginous ˌəʊl i ˈædʒ ɪn əs -ən- ‖ ˌoʊl- **~ly** li **~ness** nəs nɪs

oleander ˌəʊl i ˈænd ə ‖ ˈoʊl i ænd ᵊr ˌ·ˈ·· **~s** z

olearia ˌɒl i ˈeər i‿ə ˌəʊl- ‖ ˌoʊl i ˈer- -ˈær- **~s** z

O'Leary əʊ ˈlɪər i ‖ oʊ ˈlɪr i

oleaster ˌəʊl i ˈæst ə ‖ ˈoʊl i æst ᵊr ˌ·ˈ·· **~s** z

oleate ˈəʊl i eɪt ‖ ˈoʊl- **~s** s

olecranon əʊ ˈlek rə nɒn ˌəʊl ɪ ˈkreɪn ən, -ə- ‖ oʊ ˈlek rə nɑːn

olefin ˈəʊl ɪ fɪn -ə-, -fiːn, -fən ‖ ˈoʊl- **~s** z

olefine ˈəʊl ɪ fiːn -ə-, -fɪn ‖ ˈoʊl- **~s** z

Oleg ˈəʊl eg ˈɒl- ‖ ˈoʊl- —*Russ* [ʌ ˈlʲek]

oleic əʊ ˈliː ɪk -ˈleɪ- ‖ oʊ-

oleo ˈəʊl i əʊ ‖ ˈoʊl i oʊ

oleo- *comb. form* ˌəʊl i əʊ ‖ ˌoʊl i oʊ
— **oleoresin** ˌəʊl i əʊ 'rez ɪn §-ᵊn
‖ ˌoʊl i oʊ 'rezᵊn
oleograph 'əʊl iˌə grɑːf -græf ‖ 'oʊl iˌə græf
~**s** s
olfaction ɒl 'fæk ʃᵊn ‖ ɑːl- oʊl-
olfactory ɒl 'fækt ər i ‖ ɑːl- oʊl-
Olga 'ɒlg ə ‖ 'oʊlg ə —*Russ* ['ɔlʲ gə]
Olifant 'ɒl ɪf ənt -əf- ‖ 'ɑːl-
oligarch 'ɒl ɪ gɑːk -ə- ‖ 'ɑːl ə gɑːrk 'oʊl- ~**s** s
oligarchic ˌɒl ɪ 'gɑːk ɪk ◂ -ə-
‖ ˌɑːl ə 'gɑːrk ɪk ◂ ˌoʊl-
oligarch|y 'ɒl ɪ gɑːk |i '-ə- ‖ 'ɑːl ə gɑːrk |i
'oʊl- ~**ies** iz
oligo- *comb. form with stress-neutral suffix*
ˌɒl ɪ gəʊ -ə- ‖ ˌɑːl ɪ goʊ ˌoʊl- —
oligosaccharide ˌɒl ɪ gəʊ 'sæk ə raɪd ˌə-
‖ ˌɑːl ɪ goʊ- ˌoʊl-, -ər əd *with stress-imposing
suffix* ˌɒl ɪ 'gɒ+ -ə- ‖ ˌɑːl ə 'gɑː+ ˌoʊl-
— **oligopsony** ˌɒl ɪ 'gɒps ən i ˌ-ə-
‖ ˌɑːl ə 'gɑːps- ˌoʊl-
Oligocene 'ɒl ɪ gəʊ siːn ɒ 'lɪg əʊ- ‖ 'ɑːl ɪ goʊ-
'oʊl-; ə 'lɪg ə-
oligomer ˌɒl ɪ 'gəʊm ə ɒ 'lɪg əm ə, ə-;
'ɒl ɪg əm ə, '-əg- ‖ ə 'lɪg əm ᵊr ~**s** z
oligopol|y ˌɒl ɪ 'gɒp əl |i ˌ-ə- ‖ ˌɑːl ə 'gɑːp-
~**ies** iz
olio 'əʊl i əʊ ‖ 'oʊl i oʊ ~**s** z
Oliphant 'ɒl ɪf ənt -əf- ‖ 'ɑːl-
olivaceous ˌɒl ɪ 'veɪʃ əs ◂ -ə- ‖ ˌɑːl-
olivary 'ɒl ɪv ər i '-əv- ‖ 'ɑːl ə ver i
olive, Olive 'ɒl ɪv -əv ‖ 'ɑːl ɪv -əv ~**s**, ~'**s** z
'olive branch; ˌolive 'drab; ˌolive 'oil, '···
‖ '···
olivenite ɒ 'lɪv ə naɪt əʊ-, 'ɒl ɪv- ‖ oʊ-
Oliver 'ɒl ɪv ə -əv- ‖ 'ɑːl əv ᵊr
Olivet 'ɒl ɪ vet -ə-; -ɪv ət, -ɪt ‖ 'ɑːl-
Olivetti *tdmk* ˌɒl ɪ 'vet i -ə- ‖ ˌɑːl ə 'veʈ i —*It*
[o li 'vet ti]
Olivia ə 'lɪv iˌə ɒ-, -əʊ- ‖ oʊ-
Olivier ə 'lɪv i eɪ ɒ-, -ə ‖ oʊ-
olivine 'ɒl ɪ viːn -ə-, ˌ·'·
olla podrida ˌɒl ə pə 'driːd ə ˌ·eʲ-, -ɒɒ '··-
‖ ˌɑːl- -ɪc- —*Sp* [ˌo ʎa po 'ðri ða, ˌo ja-]
Ollerenshaw *(i)* 'ɒl ər ən ʃɔː ‖ 'ɑːl- -ʃɑː,
(ii) ˌɒl ə 'ren- ‖ ˌɑːl-
Ollerton 'ɒl ət ən ‖ 'ɑːl ᵊrt ᵊn
Ollie 'ɒl i ‖ 'ɑːl i
olm əʊlm →ɒʊlm, ɒlm ‖ oʊlm
Olmec 'ɒl mek 'əʊl-, →'ɒʊl- ‖ 'oʊl-
Olney 'əʊln i →'ɒʊln- ‖ 'oʊln i
olog|y 'ɒl ədʒ |i ‖ 'ɑːl- ~**ies** iz —*see also*
-logy
Olomouc 'ɒl ə maʊts -ɒ- ‖ 'oʊl oʊ- —*Czech*
['o lo mouts]
oloroso ˌɒl ə 'rəʊs əʊ ˌəʊl-, -'rəʊz-
‖ ˌoʊl ə 'roʊs oʊ ~**s** z —*Sp* [o lo 'ro so]
Olsen, Olson 'əʊls ᵊn →'ɒʊls- ‖ 'oʊls-
Olwen 'ɒl wen -wɪn, §-wən ‖ 'ɑːl- —*Welsh*
['ɔl wen]
Olwyn 'ɒl wɪn §-wən ‖ 'ɑːl-
Olympia ə 'lɪmp iˌə əʊ- ‖ oʊ-
Olympiad ə 'lɪmp i æd əʊ- ‖ oʊ- ~**s** z

Olympian ə 'lɪmp iˌən əʊ- ‖ oʊ- ~**s** z
Olympic ə 'lɪmp ɪk əʊ- ‖ oʊ- ~**s** s
Oˌlympic 'Games
Olympus ə 'lɪmp əs əʊ- ‖ oʊ-
Olynthus əʊ 'lɪnᵗθ əs ‖ oʊ- ə-
om, Om əʊm ɒm ‖ oʊm ɔːm, ɑːm —*Skt* [oːm]
-oma 'əʊm ə ‖ 'oʊm ə — **melanoma**
ˌmel ə 'nəʊm ə ‖ -'noʊm ə
Omagh 'əʊm ə -ɑː ‖ 'oʊm-
Omaha 'əʊm ə hɑː ‖ 'oʊm- -hɔː
O'Mahoney əʊ 'mɑː ən i ‖ oʊ- ˌoʊ mə 'hoʊn i
O'Malley *(i)* əʊ 'mæl i ‖ oʊ-, *(ii)* -'meɪl i
Oman *name of country* əʊ 'mɑːn ‖ oʊ-
—*Arabic* [ʕu 'mɑːn]
Oman *family name* 'əʊm ən ‖ 'oʊm-
Omani əʊ 'mɑːn i ‖ oʊ- ~**s** z
Omar 'əʊm ɑː ‖ 'oʊm ɑːr -ᵊr
ˌOmar Khay'yam, ˌOmar Khay'yám
kaɪ 'æm -'ɑːm ‖ kaɪ 'jɑːm -'jæm
O'Mara əʊ 'mɑːr ə ‖ oʊ-
omas|um əʊ 'meɪs |əm ‖ oʊ- ~**a** ə
ombuds|man 'ɒm bʊdz |mən -bʌdz-, -mæn
‖ 'ɑːm- ~**men** mən men
Omdurman ˌɒm dɜː 'mɑːn -də-, -'mæn;
'ɒm də mən ‖ ˌɑːm dᵊr 'mɑːn -dʊr- —*Arabic*
[um dur 'mɑːn]
-ome əʊm ‖ oʊm — **phyllome** 'fɪl əʊm ‖ -oʊm
O'Meara *(i)* əʊ 'mɑːr ə ‖ oʊ-, *(ii)* -'meər ə
‖ -'mer ə -'mær-, *(iii)* -'mɪər ə ‖ -'mɪr ə

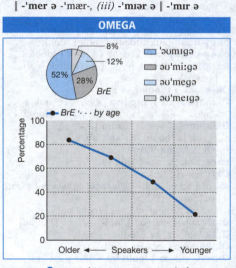

OMEGA

BrE

8%
12%
52%
28%

'əʊmɪgə
əʊ'miːgə
əʊ'megə
əʊ'meɪgə

BrE ···· by age

Percentage

Older ◂—— Speakers ——▸ Younger

omega, Omega 'əʊm ɪg ə -əg-; əʊ 'miːg ə,
-'meg-, -'meɪg- ‖ oʊ 'meɪg ə -'meg-, -'miːg-
Preference poll, BrE: 'əʊm- *52% (born before
1942, 83%)*, -'miːg- *28%*, -'meg- *12%*, -'meɪg-
8%. ~**s** z
omelet, omelette 'ɒm lət -lɪt, -let ‖ 'ɑːm-
'ɑːm əl ət ~**s** s
omen 'əʊm en -ən ‖ 'oʊm ən ~**s** z
oment|um əʊ 'ment |əm ‖ oʊ 'menʈ |əm ~**a** ə
omer, Omer 'əʊm ə ‖ 'oʊm ᵊr ~**s** z
omerta, omertà əʊ 'mɜːt ə -'meət-;
ˌəʊm ə 'tɑː ‖ oʊ 'mert ə ˌoʊm ᵊr 'tɑː —*It*
[o mer 'ta]

omicron əʊ ˈmaɪk rɒn -rən; ˈɒm ɪk-
‖ ˈɑːm ə krɑːn ˈoʊm- (*) ~s z

BrE

ominous ˈɒm ɪn əs ˈəʊm-, -ən- ‖ ˈɑːm-
— *Preference poll, BrE:* ˈɒm- *98%,* ˈəʊm- *2%.*
~**ly** li ~**ness** nəs nɪs
omissible əʊ ˈmɪs əb ᵊl -ɪb- ‖ oʊ-
omission əʊ ˈmɪʃ ᵊn ‖ oʊ- ə- ~s z
o|mit əʊ ‖ᵊmɪt ‖ oʊ- ə- ~**mits** ˈmɪts ~**mitted**
ˈmɪt ɪd -əd ‖ ˈmɪt̬ əd ~**mitting** ˈmɪt ɪŋ
‖ ˈmɪt̬ ɪŋ
ommatidi|um ˌɒm ə ˈtɪd i ̬|əm ‖ ˌɑːm- ~**a** ə
~**al** əl
omni- *comb. form*
with stress-neutral suffix ‖ɒm nɪ -nə ‖ ˌɑːm-
— **omnicompetent** ˌɒm nɪ ˈkɒmp ɪt ənt ◂
§,-nə-, -ˈət- ‖ ˌɑːm nɪ ˈkɑːmp ət ᵊnt ◂ ˌnə-
with stress-imposing suffix ɒm ˈnɪ+ ‖ ɑːm-
— **omnivorous** ɒm ˈnɪv ᵊr əs ‖ ɑːm-
omnibus ˈɒm nɪb əs -nəb-; -nɪ bʌs, -nə- ‖ ˈɑːm-
~**es** ɪz əz
omnifarious ˌɒm nɪ ˈfeər i ̬əs ◂ ˌnə-
‖ ˌɑːm nə ˈfer- -ˈfær-
omnipotence ɒm ˈnɪp ət ᵊn t s
‖ ɑːm ˈnɪp ət ᵊn t s
omnipotent ɒm ˈnɪp ət ənt ‖ ɑːm ˈnɪp ət ᵊnt
~**ly** li
omnipresence ˌɒm nɪ ˈprez ᵊn t s -nə- ‖ ˌɑːm-
omnipresent ˌɒm nɪ ˈprez ᵊnt ◂ -nə- ‖ ˌɑːm-
omniscience ɒm ˈnɪs i ̬ən t s -ˈnɪʃ-, -ˈnɪʃ ᵊn t s
‖ ɑːm ˈnɪʃ ᵊn t s
omniscient ɒm ˈnɪs i ̬ənt -ˈnɪʃ-, -ˈnɪʃ ᵊnt
‖ ɑːm ˈnɪʃ ᵊnt ~**ly** li
omnium, O~ ˈɒm ni ̬əm ‖ ˈɑːm-
omnium-gatherum ˌɒm ni ̬əm ˈgæð ər əm
‖ ˌɑːm-
omnivore ˈɒm nɪ vɔː -nə- ‖ ˈɑːm nɪ vɔːr -voʊr
~**s** z
omnivorous ɒm ˈnɪv ᵊr əs ‖ ɑːm- ~**ly** li ~**ness**
nəs nɪs
Omo *tdmk* ˈəʊm əʊ ‖ ˈoʊm oʊ
Omotic əʊ ˈmɒt ɪk ‖ oʊ ˈmɑːt̬ ɪk
omph|alos ˈɒmᵖf |ə lɒs ‖ ˈɑːmᵖf |əl əs ~**ali**
ə laɪ
Omsk ɒmᵖsk ‖ ɔːmᵖsk ɑːmᵖsk —*Russ* [ɔmsk]
on ɒn ‖ ɑːn ɔːn
'on side *'leg side'*
on- ¦ɒn ‖ ¦ɑːn ¦ɔːn — **on-going** ˌɒn ˈgəʊ ɪŋ ◂
‖ ˌɑːn ˌgoʊ ɪŋ ¦ɔːn-
-on ɒn, ən ‖ ɑːn, ən —*When this is a true*
suffix (e'lectron), *it is usually strong. When it*
is a mere ending ('common) *it is usually weak,*
but there are a number of exceptions ('coupon)
and words where speakers disagree ('lexicon).

In many cases BrE prefers a weak vowel, AmE
a strong vowel ('Amazon).
on-again off-again ˌɒn ə ˌgen ˈɒf ə ˌgen ◂
-ˌgem'- ·ˌgem, -ˈɔːf·,· ‖ ˌɑːn·,·ˈɔːf·,· -ˈɑːf·,·;
ˌɔːn·,·ˈɔːf-
onager ˈɒn ədʒ ə -əg- ‖ ˈɑːn ɪdʒ ᵊr ~**s** z **onagri**
ˈɒn ə graɪ ‖ ˈɑːn-
on-air ˌɒn ˈeə ◂ ‖ ˌɑːn ˈeᵊr ◂ ˌɔːn-, -ˈæᵊr
Onan ˈəʊn æn -ən ‖ ˈoʊn-
onanism ˈəʊn ə ˌnɪz əm -æ- ‖ ˈoʊn-
Onassis əʊ ˈnæs ɪs §-əs ‖ oʊ- -ˈnɑːs-
on-board ˈɒn bɔːd ‖ ˈɑːn bɔːrd ˈɔːn-, -boʊrd
ONC ˌəʊ en ˈsiː ‖ ˌoʊ- ~**s, ~'s** z
once wʌn t s §wɒn t s
once-over ˈwʌn t s ˌəʊv ə §'wɒn t s-, ˌ·ˈ··
‖ -ˌoʊv ᵊr
oncer ˈwʌn t s ə §'wɒn t s- ‖ -ᵊr ~**s** z
onchocerciasis ˌɒŋk əʊ sɜː ˈkaɪ əs ɪs ˌ· ·sə-,
-ˈsaɪ-, §-əs ‖ ˌɑːŋk oʊ sɜː-
onco- *comb. form with stress-neutral suffix*
¦ɒŋk əʊ ‖ ¦ɑːŋk oʊ -ə — **oncocyte**
ˈɒŋk əʊ saɪt ‖ ˈɑːŋk oʊ- -ə-
with stress-imposing suffix ɒŋ ˈkɒ+
‖ ɑːn ˈkɑː+ →ɑːŋ- — **oncology**
ɒŋ ˈkɒl ədʒ i ‖ ɑːn ˈkɑːl- →ɑːŋ-
oncogene ˈɒŋk əʊ dʒiːn ‖ ˈɑːŋk oʊ- -ə- ~**s** z
oncoming ˈɒn ˌkʌm ɪŋ →ˈɒŋ- ‖ ˈɑːn- ˈɔːn-
oncost ˈɒn kɒst →ˈɒŋ-, -kɔːst ‖ ˈɑːn kɔːst ˈɔːn-;
-ˈkɑːst ~**s** s
OND ˌəʊ en ˈdiː ‖ ˌoʊ- ~**s, ~'s** z
Ondaatje ɒn ˈdɑːtʃ ə ‖ ɑːn-
on-deck ɒn ˈdek ‖ ɑːn- ɔːn-

BrE

— BrE wɒn by age

one wʌn §wɒn — *Preference poll, BrE:* wʌn
70%, wɒn *30%. —In standard speech this*
word has no weak form. See, however, 'un.
ones, one's wʌnz §wɒnz
ˌone a'nother
one- ¦wʌn §¦wɒn — **one-tailed** ˌwʌn ˈteᵊld ◂
§,wɒn-
one-acter ˌwʌn ˈækt ə §,wɒn- ‖ -ᵊr ~**s** z
O'Neal əʊ ˈniːᵊl ‖ oʊ-

O

one-armed ˌwʌn ˈɑːmd ◄ §ˌwɒn- ‖ -ˈɑːrmd ◄
  ˌone-armed ˈbandit
one-day ˈwʌn deɪ §ˈwɒn-
one-dimensional ˌwʌn daɪ ˈmenˀʃ ᵊn̩ əl ◄
  ˌ-dɪ-, ˌ-də-
one-eyed ˌwʌn ˈaɪd ◄ §ˌwɒn-
Onega ɒ ˈneɪg ə -ˈneg- ‖ oʊ ˈneg ə -ˈniːg-;
  oʊn ˈjeɪg ə —Russ [ʌ ˈnʲɛ gə]
Onegin ɒ ˈneɪg ɪn əʊ-, ɒn ˈjeɪg-, -ᵊn ‖ oʊ- ɑː-
one-horse ˌwʌn ˈhɔːs ◄ §ˌwɒn- ‖ -ˈhɔːrs ◄
  ˌone-horse ˈtown
Oneida əʊ ˈnaɪd ə ‖ oʊ- ~s z
O'Neil, O'Neill əʊ ˈniːᵊl ‖ oʊ-
oneiromancy əʊ ˈnaɪᵊr ə mænᵗs i ‖ oʊ-
one-legged ˌwʌn ˈleg ɪd ◄ §ˌwɒn-, -əd, ˌ-ˈlegd
one-liner ˌwʌn ˈlaɪn ə §ˌwɒn- ‖ -ᵊr ~s z
one-man ˌwʌn ˈmæn ◄ →ˌwʌm-, §ˌwɒn-
  ˌone-man ˈband
oneness ˈwʌn nəs §ˈwɒn-, -nɪs
one-night ˌwʌn ˈnaɪt ◄ §ˌwɒn-
  ˌone-night ˈstand
one-off ˌwʌn ˈɒf ◄ §ˌwɒn- ‖ -ˈɔːf ◄ -ˈɑːf ~s s
one-on-one ˌwʌn ɒn ˈwʌn §ˌwɒn-ˈwɒn ‖ -ɑːn-
  -ɔːn-
Oneonta ˌəʊn i ˈɒnt ə ‖ ˌoʊn i ˈɑːnt̬ ə
one-parent ˌwʌn ˈpeᵊr ənt ◄ →ˌwʌm-, §ˌwɒn-
  ‖ -ˈper- -ˈpær-
  ˌone-ˌparent ˈfamily
one-percent ˈwʌn pə ˌsent →ˈwʌm-, §ˈwɒn-
  ‖ -pᵊr-
one-piece ˌwʌn ˈpiːs ◄ →ˌwʌm-, §ˌwɒn-
  ˌone-piece ˈsnowsuit
one-resource ˌwʌn rɪ ˈzɔːs ◄ §ˌwɒn-, -rə-,
  -ˈsɔːs ◄; ˈriː sɔːs ◄ ‖ -ˈriː sɔːrs ◄ -rɪ ˈsɔːrs ◄

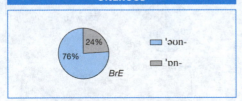

ONEROUS

24%	▢ ˈəʊn-
76%	▩ ˈɒn-
BrE	

onerous ˈəʊn ᵊr əs ˈɒn- ‖ ˈoʊn- ˈɑːn-
  — Preference poll, BrE: ˈəʊn- 76%, ˈɒn- 24%.
  ~ly li ~ness nəs nɪs
oneself wʌn ˈself wʌnz-, §wɒn-
one-shot ˈwʌn ʃɒt §ˈwɒn- ‖ -ʃɑːt
one-sided ˌwʌn ˈsaɪd ɪd ◄ §ˌwɒn-, -əd ~ly li
  ~ness nəs nɪs
  ˌone-ˌsided ˈargument
Onesimus əʊ ˈniːs ɪm əs -ˈnes-, -əm- ‖ oʊ-
one-size-fits-all ˌwʌn ˌsaɪz ˌfɪts ˈɔːc §ˌwɒn-
  ‖ -ˈɑːl
one-star ˌwʌn ˈstɑː ◄, ˌwɒn- ‖ -ˈstɑːr ◄
  ˌone-star ho'tel
one-step ˈwʌn step §ˈwɒn-
one-stop ˈwʌn stɒp §ˈwɒn- ‖ -stɑːp
onetime ˈwʌn taɪm §ˈwɒn-
one-to-one ˌwʌn tə ˈwʌn ◄ §ˌwɒn-ˈwɒn, -tu-
one-track ˌwʌn ˈtræk ◄ §ˈwɒn-
  ˌone-track ˈmind

one-two ˌwʌn ˈtuː §ˌwɒn-
one-up ˌwʌn ˈʌp §ˌwɒn- **~ping** ɪŋ
one-upmanship ₍ˌ₎wʌn ˈʌp mən ʃɪp §₍ˌ₎wɒn-
one-way ˌwʌn ˈweɪ ◄ §ˌwɒn-
  ˌone-way ˈtraffic
one-woman ˈwʌn ˌwʊm ən §ˈwɒn-
on-glide ˈɒn glaɪd →ˈɒŋ- ‖ ˈɑːn- ˈɔːn- ~s z
ongoing ˈɒn ˌgəʊ ɪŋ →ˈɒŋ-, ˌˈ· · ‖ ˈɑːn ˌgoʊ ɪŋ
  ˈɔːn-
onion ˈʌn jən ~s z
Onions (i) ˈʌn jənz, (ii) əʊ ˈnaɪˌənz ‖ oʊ-
  —The lexicographer C.T.Onions was (i).
onionskin ˈʌn jən skɪn
onium ˈəʊn iˌəm ‖ ˈoʊn-
onkaparinga, O~ ˌɒŋk ə pə ˈrɪŋ gə ‖ ˌɑːŋk-
online, on-line ˌɒn ˈlaɪn ◄ ‖ ˌɑːn- -ɔːn-
  ˌonline ˈhelp
onlooker ˈɒn ˌlʊk ə ‖ ˈɑːn ˌlʊk ᵊr ˈɔːn- ~s z
only ˈəʊn li §-i ‖ ˈoʊn li (!)
on-message ˌɒn ˈmes ɪdʒ ‖ ˌɑːn- ˌɔːn-
o.n.o. —see **or near offer**
Ono ˈəʊn əʊ ‖ ˈoʊn oʊ —Jp [o ˌno]
on-off ˌɒn ˈɒf ◄ -ˈɔːf ◄ ‖ ˌɑːn ˈɔːf ◄ ˌɔːn-, -ˈɑːf ◄
onomastic ˌɒn əʊ ˈmæst ɪk ◄ ‖ ˌɑːn oʊ- -ə- ~s
  s
onomatopoeia ˌɒn əʊ mæt ə ˈpiːˌə
  ‖ ˌɑːn ə mæt̬ ə ˈpiː ə ˌ· -mɑːt̬-
onomatopoeic ˌɒn əʊ mæt ə ˈpiː ɪk ◄
  ‖ ˌɑːn ə mæt̬- ˌ· -mɑːt̬- **~ally** ᵊl i
Onondaga ˌɒn ən ˈdɑːg ə ◄ -ˈdɔːg- ‖ ˌɑːn-
  -ˈdɔːg- ~s z
on-ramp ˈɒn ræmp ‖ ˈɑːn- ˈɔːn- ~s s
onrush ˈɒn rʌʃ ‖ ˈɑːn- ˈɔːn- ~es ɪz əz
onrushing ˈɒn ˌrʌʃ ɪŋ ‖ ˈɑːn- ˈɔːn-
on-screen ˌɒn ˈskriːn ◄ ‖ ˌɑːn- ˌɔːn-
onset ˈɒn set ‖ ˈɑːn- ˈɔːn- ~s s
onshore ˌɒn ˈʃɔː ◄ ‖ ˌɑːn ˈʃɔːr ◄ ˌɔːn-, -ˈʃoʊr
onside ˌɒn ˈsaɪd ◄ ‖ ˌɑːn- ˌɔːn-
on-site ˌɒn ˈsaɪt ◄ ‖ ˌɑːn- ˌɔːn-
onslaught ˈɒn slɔːt ‖ ˈɑːn- ˈɔːn-; -slɑːt ~s s
Onslow ˈɒnz ləʊ ‖ ˈɑːnz loʊ
on-stage ˌɒn ˈsteɪdʒ ◄ ‖ ˌɑːn- ˌɔːn-
onstream ˌɒn ˈstriːm ◄ ‖ ˌɑːn- ˌɔːn-
Ontario ɒn ˈteᵊr i əʊ ‖ ɑːn ˈter i oʊ -ˈtær-
on-the-job ˌɒn ðə ˈdʒɒb ◄ ‖ ˌɑːn ðə ˈdʒɑːb ◄
  ˌɔːn-
onto before a consonant ˈɒn tə ‖ ˈɑːn tə ˈɔːn-,
  elsewhere ˈɒn tu -tu: ‖ ˈɑːn tu ˈɔːn-, -tə
ontogenesis ˌɒnt əʊ ˈdʒen əs ɪs -ɪsˌ-, §-əs
  ‖ ˌɑːnt̬ oʊ-
ontogenetic ˌɒnt əʊ dʒə ˈnet ɪk ◄ -dʒɪˈ· ·
  ‖ ˌɑːnt̬ oʊ dʒə ˈnet̬ ɪk ◄ ~ally ᵊl i
ontogen|y ɒn ˈtɒdʒ ən |i -ɪn- ‖ ɑːn ˈtɑːdʒ-
  ~ies iz
ontological ˌɒnt ə ˈlɒdʒ ɪk ᵊl ◄ ˌɒnt ᵊl ˈɒdʒ-
  ‖ ˌɑːnt̬ ᵊl ˈɑːdʒ- ~ly_i
ontology ɒn ˈtɒl ədʒ i ‖ ɑːn ˈtɑːl-
onus ˈəʊn əs ‖ ˈoʊn əs ~es ɪz əz
onward ˈɒn wəd ‖ ˈɑːn wᵊrd ˈɔːn- ~s z
-onym stress-imposing ən ɪm §-əm ‖ ə nɪm
  — **acronym** ˈæk rən ɪm §-əm ‖ -ə nɪm
onyx ˈɒn ɪks ˈəʊn- ‖ ˈɑːn ɪks

oo-, oö- *comb. form with stress-neutral suffix*
|əʊ ə ‖ ˌoʊ ə — **oocyte, oöcyte** ˈəʊ ə saɪt
‖ ˈoʊ- *with stress-imposing suffix* əʊ ˈɒ+
‖ oʊ ˈɑː+ — **oogamy, oögamy** əʊ ˈɒg əm i
‖ oʊ ˈɑːg-

oodles ˈuːd ᵊlz

oof uːf

ooh uː **oohed** uːd **oohing** ˈuː ɪŋ **oohs** uːz

ooh-la-la, oo-la-la ˌuː lɑː ˈlɑː

oolite ˈəʊ ə laɪt ‖ ˈoʊ- **~s** s

oolith ˈəʊ ə lɪθ ˈuː ‖ ˈoʊ- **~s** s

oolitic ˌəʊ ə ˈlɪt ɪk ◄ ‖ ˌoʊ ə ˈlɪt̬ ɪk ◄

oological ˌəʊ ə ˈlɒdʒ ɪk ᵊl ◄ ‖ ˌoʊ ə ˈlɑːdʒ-

oolog|y əʊ ˈɒl ədʒ |i ‖ oʊ ˈɑːl- **~ist/s** ɪst/s
§əst/s

oolong, O~ ˈuː lɒŋ ˌ·ˈ· ‖ -lɔːŋ -lɑːŋ

oompah ˈuːm pɑː ‖ ˈʊm- **~s** z

oomph ʊmᵖf uːmᵖf

Oona, Oonagh ˈuːn ə

oops ʊps wʊps, uːps

oops-a-daisy ˌʊps ə ˈdeɪz i ˌwʊps-, ˌuːps-, ˈ·ˌ·· ·
‖ ˈ·ˌ··

Oort ɔːt ‖ ɔːrt oʊrt —*Dutch* [oːrt]

Oosterhuis ˈəʊst ə haʊs ‖ ˈoʊst ᵊr- —*Dutch*
[ˈoː stər hœys]

ooze uːz **oozed** uːzd **oozes** ˈuːz ɪz -əz **oozing**
ˈuːz ɪŋ

ooz|y ˈuːz |i **~ier** i ə ‖ iˌᵊr **~iest** i ɪst i ̩əst **~ily**
ɪ li əl i **~iness** i nəs i nɪs

op ɒp ‖ ɑːp
ˈop art

Op —*see* **Opus**

opacit|y əʊ ˈpæs ət |i -ɪt- ‖ oʊ ˈpæs ət̬ |i **~ies**
iz

opal ˈəʊp ᵊl ‖ ˈoʊp ᵊl **~s** z

opalescence ˌəʊp ə ˈles ᵊnts ˌɒp-, →ˌ·ᵊl ˈes-
‖ ˌoʊp-

opalescent ˌəʊp ə ˈles ᵊnt ◄ ˌɒp-, →ˌ·ᵊl ˈes-
‖ ˌoʊp-

opaline ˈəʊp ə laɪn -liːn, →-ᵊl aɪn, →-ᵊl iːn
‖ ˈoʊp-

opaque əʊ ˈpeɪk ‖ oʊ- **~ly** li **~ness** nəs nɪs

op. cit. ˌɒp ˈsɪt ‖ ˌɑːp-

ope əʊp ‖ oʊp **oped** əʊpt ‖ oʊpt **opes** əʊps
‖ oʊps **oping** ˈəʊp ɪŋ ‖ ˈoʊp ɪŋ

OPEC ˈəʊp ek ‖ ˈoʊp-

op-ed ˌɒp ˈed ‖ ˌɑːp-

Opel *tdmk* ˈəʊp ᵊl ‖ ˈoʊp ᵊl —*Ger* [ˈʔoː pᵊl] **~s**
z

op|en ˈəʊp |ən ‖ ˈoʊp |ən **~ened** ənd →ᵐd
~ener ən ə ‖ ᵊn ᵊr **~enest** ən ɪst əst **~ening**
ən ɪŋ **~ens** ənz →mz
ˌopen ˈday; ˌopen ˈhouse; ˌopen ˈletter;
ˌopen ˈsandwich; ˌopen ˈseason; ˌopen
ˈsecret; ˌopen ˈsesame; ˌOpen
ˈUniˈversity; ˌopen ˈverdict

open-air ˌəʊp ən ˈeə ◄ ‖ ˌoʊp ən ˈeᵊr -ˈæᵊr

open-and-shut ˌəʊp ən⸳ən ˈʃʌt ◄ -ənˌənd-
‖ ˌoʊp-

opencast ˈəʊp ən kɑːst →-m-, →-əŋ-, §-kæst
‖ ˈoʊp ən kæst

open-door ˌəʊp ən ˈdɔː ◄ →-m-
‖ ˌoʊp ən ˈdɔːr ◄ -ˈdoʊr

open-ended ˌəʊp ən ˈend ɪd ◄ -əd ‖ ˌoʊp-
~ness nəs nɪs

opener ˈəʊp ən ə ‖ ˈoʊp ᵊn ᵊr **~s** z

open-eyed ˌəʊp ən ˈaɪd ◄ ‖ ˌoʊp-

open-faced ˌəʊp ən ˈfeɪst ◄ →-m- ‖ ˌoʊp-

open-handed ˌəʊp ən ˈhænd ɪd ◄ -əd ‖ ˌoʊp-
ˈ·ˌ·· **~ly** li **~ness** nəs nɪs

open-heart ˌəʊp ən ˈhɑːt ◄ ‖ ˌoʊp ən ˈhɑːrt ◄
ˌopen-ˌheart ˈsurgery

open-hearted ˌəʊp ən ˈhɑːt ɪd ◄ -əd
‖ ˌoʊp ən ˈhɑːrt̬ əd ◄ ˈ·ˌ··

open-hearth ˌəʊp ən ˈhɑːθ ◄
‖ ˌoʊp ən ˈhɑːrθ ◄

opening ˈəʊp ən ɪŋ ‖ ˈoʊp ən ɪŋ **~s** z
ˈopening time

opening-up ˌəʊp ən ɪŋ ˈʌp ‖ ˌoʊp-

open-jaw ˌəʊp ən ˈdʒɔː ◄ ‖ ˌoʊp- -ˈdʒɑː ◄

openly ˈəʊp ən li →-m- ‖ ˈoʊp-

open-minded ˌəʊp ən ˈmaɪnd ɪd ◄ →-m-, -əd
‖ ˌoʊp- ˈ·ˌ·· **~ly** li **~ness** nəs nɪs

open-mouthed ˌəʊp ən ˈmaʊðd ◄ →-m-,
§-ˈmaʊθt ‖ ˌoʊp- ˈ·ˌ·

open-necked ˌəʊp ᵊn ˈnekt ◄ ‖ ˌoʊp-

openness ˈəʊp ən nəs →-m-, -nɪs ‖ ˈoʊp-

open-plan ˌəʊp ən ˈplæn ◄ →-m- ‖ ˌoʊp-

Openshaw ˈəʊp ən ʃɔː →-m- ‖ ˈoʊp- -ʃɑː

open-toed ˌəʊp ən ˈtəʊd ◄ ‖ ˌoʊp ən ˈtoʊd ◄

openwork ˈəʊp ən wɜːk →-m- ‖ ˈoʊp ən wɜːk

opera ˈɒp ᵊr ə ‖ ˈɑːp ᵊr ə △ i —*also as an
Italian word, It* [ˈɔː pe ɾa] *or as a French
word, Fr* opéra [ɔ pe ʁa] —*but as the plural
of* opus, *sometimes* ˈəʊp- ‖ ˈoʊp- **~s** z
ˌopéra ˈbouffe buːf —*Fr* [buf]; ˌopera
ˈbuffa ˈbuːf ə —*It* [ˈbuf fa]; ˌopéra
coˈmique kɒ ˈmiːk ‖ kɑː-; ˈopera ˌglasses;
ˈopera house; ˌopera ˈseria ˈsɪər i ə ‖ ˈsɪr-
—*It* [ˈsɛː rja]

operability ˌɒp ᵊr ə ˈbɪl ət i -ɪt i
‖ ˌɑːp ᵊr ə ˈbɪl ət̬ i

operable ˈɒp ᵊr əb ᵊl ‖ ˈɑːp-

operand ˈɒp ə rænd -ᵊr ənd ‖ ˈɑːp- **~s** z

operant ˈɒp ər ənt ‖ ˈɑːp- **~s** s

ope|rate ˈɒp ə |reɪt ‖ ˈɑːp- **~rated** reɪt ɪd -əd
‖ reɪt̬ əd **~rates** reɪts **~rating** reɪt ɪŋ ‖ reɪt̬ ɪŋ
ˈoperating ˌsystem; ˈoperating ˌtable;
ˈoperating ˌtheatre

operatic ˌɒp ə ˈræt ɪk ◄ ‖ ˌɑːp ə ˈræt̬ ɪk ◄
~ally ᵊl i **~s** s

operation ˌɒp ə ˈreɪʃ ᵊn ‖ ˌɑːp- **~s** z
ˌopeˈrations reˌsearch, -ˌresearch;
ˌopeˈrations room

operational ˌɒp ə ˈreɪʃ ᵊn ᵊl ◄ ‖ ˌɑːp- **~ly** i
ˌopeˌrational reˈsearch, -ˈresearch

operative ˈɒp ᵊr ət ɪv -ə reɪt- ‖ ˈɑːp ᵊr ət̬ ɪv
-ə reɪt̬- —*The pronunciation* -reɪt ɪv ‖ -reɪt̬ ɪv
*is heard more often for the noun than for the
adj.* **~s** z

operator ˈɒp ə reɪt ə ‖ ˈɑːp ə reɪt̬ ᵊr **~s** z

opercul|um əʊ ˈpɜːk jʊl |əm ɒ-, -jəl-
‖ oʊ ˈpɜːk jəl |əm **~a** ə

operetta ˌɒp ə ˈret ə ‖ ˌɑːp ə ˈret̬ ə **~s** z

operettist ˌɒp ə ˈret ɪst §-əst ‖ ˌɑːp ə ˈret̬ əst
~s s

O

Ophelia ə 'fi:l i‿ə əʊ-, ɒ- ‖ oʊ-
ophicleide 'ɒf ɪ klaɪd §-ə- ‖ 'ɑːf- ~s z
ophidian ɒ 'fɪd i‿ən əʊ- ‖ oʊ- ~s z
Ophir 'əʊf ə ‖ 'oʊf ᵊr
Ophiuchus ɒ 'fju:k əs ‚ɒf i 'u:k əs
‖ ‚ɑːf i 'ju:k əs ‚oʊf-
ophthalmia ɒf 'θælm i‿ə ɒp- ‖ ɑːf- ɑːp-
ophthalmic ɒf 'θælm ɪk ɒp- ‖ ɑːf- ɑːp-
ophthalmo- comb. form
  with stress-neutral suffix ɒf ¦θælm əʊ ɒp-
  ‖ ɑːf ¦θælm ə ɑːp- — ophthalmoscopic
  ɒf ‚θælm əʊ 'skɒp ɪk ◂ ɒp-
  ‖ ɑːf ‚θælm əʊ 'skɑːp ɪk ◂ ɑːp-
  with stress-imposing suffix ‚ɒfθ æl 'mɒ +
  ‚ɒpθ- ‖ ‚ɑːfθ æl 'mɑː + ‚ɑːpθ-
  — ophthalmoscopy ‚ɒfθ æl 'mɒsk əp i
  ‚ɒpθ- ‖ ‚ɑːfθ æl 'mɑːsk- ‚ɑːpθ-
ophthalmolog|ist ‚ɒfθ æl 'mɒl ədʒ |ɪst ‚ɒpθ-,
  §-əst ‖ ‚ɑːfθ æl 'mɑːl- ‚ɑːpθ- ~ists ɪsts §əsts
  ~y i
ophthalmoscope ɒf 'θælm ə skəʊp ɒp-
  ‖ ɑːf 'θælm ə skoʊp ɑːp- ~s s
Ophüls 'əʊf ᵊlz ‖ oʊ 'fʊlz —Ger ['ɔ fʏls]
-opia 'əʊp i‿ə ‖ 'oʊp i‿ə — diplopia
  dɪ 'pləʊp i‿ə ‖ -'ploʊp-
opiate 'əʊp i‿ət -ɪt, -eɪt ‖ 'oʊp- ~s s
Opie 'əʊp i ‖ 'oʊp i
opin|e əʊ 'paɪn ‖ oʊ- ~ed d ~es z ~ing ɪŋ
opinion ə 'pɪn jən §əʊ- ~s z
  o'pinion poll
opinionated ə 'pɪn jə neɪt ɪd §əʊ-, -əd
  ‖ -neɪt̬ əd
opinion-maker ə 'pɪn jən ‚meɪk ə §əʊ- ‖ -ᵊr ~s
  z
opioid 'əʊp i ɔɪd ‖ 'oʊp- ~s z
opisthobranch əʊ 'pɪs θə bræŋk ‖ ə- oʊ- ~s s
opium 'əʊp i‿əm ‖ 'oʊp-
  'opium den; 'opium ‚poppy
Opodo tdmk əʊ 'pəʊd əʊ ‖ oʊ 'poʊd oʊ
Oporto əʊ 'pɔːt əʊ ‖ oʊ 'pɔːrt̬ oʊ -'poʊrt̬-
  —Port [u 'poɾ tu]
opossum ə 'pɒs əm ‖ ə 'pɑːs əm 'pɑːs əm ~s z
Oppenheim 'ɒp ən haɪm ‖ 'ɑːp-
Oppenheimer 'ɒp ən haɪm ə
  ‖ 'ɑːp ən haɪm ᵊr
oppidan 'ɒp ɪd ən §-əd- ‖ 'ɑːp- ~s z
opponent ə 'pəʊn ənt ‖ ə 'poʊn ənt ~s s
opportune ‚ɒp ə tju:n →-tʃu:n, ‚· ·'·
  ‖ ‚ɑːp ᵊr 'tu:n ◂ -'tju:n (*) ~ly li ~ness nəs nɪs
opportun|ism ‚ɒp ə 'tju:n ‚ɪz əm →-'tʃu:n-,
  '· · ·,· · ‖ ‚ɑːp ᵊr 'tu:n- -'tju:n- ~ist/s ɪst/s ◂
  §əst/s
opportunistic ‚ɒp ə tju: 'nɪst ɪk ◂ →-tʃu:'·-
  ‖ ‚ɑːp ᵊr tu:- -tju:'·- ~ally ᵊl i
opportunit|y ‚ɒp ə 'tju:n ət |i →-'tʃu:n-, -ɪt i
  ‖ ‚ɑːp ᵊr 'tu:n ət̬ |i -'tju:n- ~ies iz
opposable ə 'pəʊz əb ᵊl ‖ ə 'poʊz-
oppos|e ə 'pəʊz ‖ ə 'poʊz ~ed d ~es ɪz əz
  ~ing ɪŋ

OPPOSITE

opposite 'ɒp əz ɪt -əs-, §-ət ‖ 'ɑːp-
  — Preference poll, BrE: -əz- 67%, -əs- 33%.
  ~ly li ~ness nəs nɪs ~s s
  ‚opposite 'number; ‚opposite 'sex
opposition ‚ɒp ə 'zɪʃ ᵊn ‖ ‚ɑːp- ~al əl ◂ ~s z
oppress ə 'pres §əʊ- ~ed t ~es ɪz əz ~ing ɪŋ
oppression ə 'preʃ ᵊn §əʊ- ~s z
oppressive ə 'pres ɪv §əʊ- ~ly li ~ness nəs nɪs
oppressor ə 'pres ə §əʊ- ‖ -ᵊr ~s z
opprobrious ə 'prəʊb ri‿əs ‖ ə 'proʊb- ~ly li
  ~ness nəs nɪs
opprobrium ə 'prəʊb ri‿əm ‖ ə 'proʊb-
oppugn ə 'pju:n ~ed d ~er/s ə/z ᵊr/z ~ing
  ɪŋ ~s z
Oprah 'əʊp rə ‖ 'oʊp rə
Opren tdmk 'əʊp rən -ren ‖ 'ɑːp- 'oʊp-
opsonic ɒp 'sɒn ɪk ‖ ɑːp 'sɑːn ɪk
opsonin 'ɒps ən ɪn §-ən ‖ 'ɑːps-
opt ɒpt ‖ ɑːpt opted 'ɒpt ɪd -əd ‖ 'ɑːpt əd
  opting 'ɒpt ɪŋ ‖ 'ɑːpt ɪŋ opts ɒpts ‖ ɑːpts
Optacon tdmk 'ɒpt ək ən ‖ 'ɑːpt ə kɑːn
optative 'ɒpt ət ɪv ɒp 'teɪt ɪv ‖ 'ɑːpt ət̬ ɪv ~s z
optic 'ɒpt ɪk ‖ 'ɑːpt ɪk ~s s
optical 'ɒpt ɪk ᵊl ‖ 'ɑːpt- ~ly i
  ‚optical 'character recog‚nition; ‚optical
  'fibre; ‚optical il'lusion
optician ɒp 'tɪʃ ᵊn ‖ ɑːp- ~s z
optim|a 'ɒpt ɪm |ə -əm- ‖ 'ɑːpt- ~al/ly ᵊl /i
optimality ‚ɒpt ɪ 'mæl ət i ‚·ə-, -ɪt i
  ‖ ‚ɑːpt ə 'mæl ət̬ i
optimis... —see optimiz...
optimism 'ɒpt ɪ ‚mɪz əm -ə- ‖ 'ɑːpt-
optimist 'ɒpt ɪm ɪst -əm-, §-əst ‖ 'ɑːpt- ~s s
optimistic ‚ɒpt ɪ 'mɪst ɪk ◂ -ə- ‖ ‚ɑːpt- ~ally
  ᵊl i
optimization ‚ɒpt ɪm aɪ 'zeɪʃ ᵊn ‚·əm-, -ɪ'·-
  ‖ ‚ɑːpt əm ə- ~s z
optimiz|e 'ɒpt ɪ maɪz -ə- ‖ 'ɑːpt- ~ed d ~es ɪz
  əz ~ing ɪŋ
optim|um 'ɒpt ɪm |əm -əm- ‖ 'ɑːpt- ~a ə
  ~ums əmz
option 'ɒp ʃᵊn ‖ 'ɑːp ʃᵊn ~s z
optional 'ɒp ʃᵊn_əl ‖ 'ɑːp- ~ly i
optoelectronic ‚ɒpt əʊ ɪ ‚lek 'trɒn ɪk -ə‚-;
  ‚· ·,el ek-, -,el ɪk-, -‚ɪl ek-, -‚iːl ek-
  ‖ ‚ɑːpt oʊ ɪ ‚lek 'trɑːn ɪk ~s s
optometr|ist ɒp 'tɒm ətr |ɪst -ɪtr-, §-əst
  ‖ ɑːp 'tɑːm- ~ists ɪsts §əsts ~y i
opt-out 'ɒpt aʊt ‖ 'ɑːpt- ~s s
Optrex tdmk 'ɒp treks ‖ 'ɑːp-
opul|ence 'ɒp jʊl |ən⁀s -jəl- ‖ 'ɑːp jəl- ~ent/ly
  ənt /li

Optional sounds

1 **Optional sounds** are sounds that are pronounced by some speakers or on some occasions, but are omitted by other speakers or on other occasions. In the *Longman Pronunciation Dictionary* (LPD) they are indicated in two ways: by **italics** and by **raised letters** in smaller type.

2 Sounds shown in **italics** are sounds which the foreign learner is recommended to include (although native speakers sometimes omit them). They denote sounds that may optionally be **elided**.

lunch　　lʌntʃ　　Some say lʌntʃ, others say lʌnʃ. LPD recommends lʌntʃ.

bacon　　'beɪk ən　　Some say 'beɪk ən, others say 'beɪk n. LPD recommends 'beɪk ən.

3 Sounds shown with **raised letters** are sounds which the foreign learner is recommended to ignore (although native speakers sometimes include them). They denote sounds that may optionally be inserted.

fence　　fenˢs　　Some say fens, others say fents. LPD recommends fens.

sadden　　'sæd ᵊn　　Some say 'sæd n, others say 'sæd ən. LPD recommends 'sæd n.

4 The number of syllables, as shown by the spacing, is not affected by omitting an optional sound. Thus there are still two syllables in **bacon**, if pronounced 'beɪk n, and in **sadden**, if pronounced 'sæd n. In such cases the n is termed **syllabic** (see SYLLABIC CONSONANTS).

5 An italic length mark, as in **agreeable** ə 'griː_əb ᵊl, means that as COMPRESSION occurs the vowel changes to the corresponding short vowel, producing a diphthong. This process is called **smoothing** — see COMPRESSION 3.

opuntia əʊ 'pʌnˈʃ i_ə ɒ- ‖ oʊ- -'pʌnʃ ə **~s** z

opus 'əʊp əs 'ɒp- ‖ 'oʊp əs **opera** 'əʊp ər ə 'ɒp- ‖ 'oʊp- 'ɑːp- **~es** ɪz əz
ˌOpus 'Dei 'deɪ iː

or ɔː ‖ ɔːr —*In AmE* ɔːr *is a strong form, paired with a weak form* ᵊr. *In BrE, however,* ɔː *normally has no weak form: there is only an occasional weak form* ə, *used chiefly in set phrases.*

-or ə ‖ ᵊr —*also occasionally for emphasis* ɔː ‖ ɔːr — **generator** 'dʒen ə reɪt ə ‖ -reɪt̬ ᵊr

ora, Ora 'ɔːr ə ‖ 'oʊr-

orach, orach|e 'ɒr ɪtʃ -ətʃ ‖ 'ɔːr ɪtʃ 'ɑːr- **~es** ɪz əz

oracle 'ɒr ək ᵊl -ɪk- ‖ 'ɔːr- 'ɑːr- **~s** z

oracular ɒ 'ræk jʊl ə ə-, ɔː-, -jəl- ‖ ɔː 'ræk jəl ᵊr oʊ-, ə- **~ly** li

oracy 'ɔːr əs i 'ɒr- ‖ 'oʊr-

Oradea ɒ 'rɑːd i_ə ɔː- ‖ ɔː- —*Romanian* [o 'ra dea]

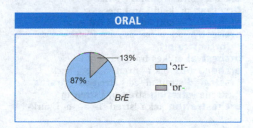

ORAL

BrE

87% 'ɔːr-
13% 'ɒr-

oral 'ɔːr əl §'ɒr- ‖ 'oʊr- — *Preference poll, BrE:* 'ɔːr- 87%, 'ɒr- 13%. **~ly** i **~s** z

Oran ə 'ræn ɔː-, -'rɑːn ‖ ɔː-, oʊ- —*Fr* [ɔ ʁɑ̃]

Orana ə 'rɑːn ə

orang|e, O~ 'ɒr ɪndʒ -əndʒ ‖ 'ɔːr- 'ɑːr- — *Preference poll, AmE:* 'ɔːr- 80%, 'ɑːr- 20%. *See chart on p. 568.* **~es** ɪz əz
'orange ˌblossom; ˌOrange Free 'State, ˌ•'••

orangeade ˌɒr ɪndʒ 'eɪd -əndʒ- ‖ ˌɔːr- ˌɑːr- **~s** z

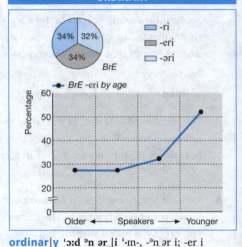

ORANGE

'ɔːr- 'ɑːr-

AmE

Orange|man 'ɒr ɪndʒ |mən -əndʒ-, -mæn
‖ 'ɔːr- 'ɑːr- **~men** mən men

oranger|y 'ɒr ɪndʒ ər‿|i '-əndʒ- ‖ 'ɔːr- 'ɑːr-
~ies iz

**orangoutan, orangoutang, orangutan,
orangutang** ɔː 'ræŋ ə tæn ɒ-, ə-, -u-, -tæŋ,
·, · ·; , · ·uː tæn, -'juː-, -tɑːn ‖ ə- **~s** z

o|rate ɔː |'reɪt ɒ-, ə- ‖ oʊ- **~rated** 'reɪt ɪd -əd
‖ 'reɪt̮ əd **~rates** 'reɪts **~rating** 'reɪt ɪŋ
‖ 'reɪt̮ ɪŋ

oration ə 'reɪʃ ᵊn ɔː-, ɒ- ‖ oʊ- **~s** z

orator 'ɒr ət ə ‖ 'ɔːr ət̮ ᵊr 'ɑːr- **~s** z

oratorical ˌɒr ə 'tɒr ɪk ᵊl ◄ ‖ ˌɔːr ə 'tɔːr-
ˌɑːr ə 'tɑːr- **~ly** ‿i

oratorio ˌɒr ə 'tɔːr i əʊ ‖ ˌɔːr ə 'tɔːr i oʊ ˌɑːr-,
-'toʊr- **~s** z

oratory, O~ 'ɒr ət̮ ər i ‖ 'ɔːr ə tɔːr i 'ɑːr-,
-toʊr i

orb ɔːb ‖ ɔːrb **orbs** ɔːbz ‖ ɔːrbz

Orbach 'ɔː bæk ‖ 'ɔːr bɑːk

orbed ɔːbd ‖ ɔːrbd —*in poetry also* 'ɔːb ɪd,
-əd ‖ 'ɔːrb-

orbicular ɔː 'bɪk jʊl ə -jəl- ‖ ɔːr 'bɪk jəl ᵊr

Orbison 'ɔːb ɪs ən -əs- ‖ 'ɔːrb-

orb|it 'ɔːb |ɪt §-ət ‖ 'ɔːrb |ət **~ited** ɪt ɪd §ət-,
-əd ‖ ət̮ əd **~iting** ɪt ɪŋ §ət- ‖ ət̮ ɪŋ **~its** ɪts
§əts ‖ əts

orbital 'ɔːb ɪt ᵊl §-ət- ‖ 'ɔːrb ət̮ ᵊl **~ly** i

orbitale ˌɔːb ɪ 'tɑːl i -ə-, -'teɪl- ‖ ˌɔːrb-

orbiter 'ɔːb ɪt ə §-ət- ‖ 'ɔːrb ət̮ ᵊr **~s** z

orc ɔːk ‖ ɔːrk **orcs** ɔːks ‖ ɔːrks

Orcadian ɔː 'keɪd i ən ‖ ɔːr- **~s** z

orchard, O~ 'ɔːtʃ əd ‖ 'ɔːrtʃ ᵊrd **~s** z

orchestra 'ɔːk ɪs trə -əs-, -es- ‖ 'ɔːrk- **~s** z
    'orchestra pit

orchestral ɔː 'kes trəl ‖ ɔːr- **~ly** i

orche|strate 'ɔːk ɪ |streɪt -ə-, -e- ‖ 'ɔːrk-
~strated streɪt ɪd -əd ‖ streɪt̮ əd **~strates**
streɪts **~strating** streɪt ɪŋ ‖ streɪt̮ ɪŋ

orchestration ˌɔːk ɪ 'streɪʃ ᵊn -ə-, -e- ‖ ˌɔːrk-
~s z

orchestrina ˌɔːk ɪ 'striːn ə -ə- ‖ ˌɔːrk- **~s** z

orchestrion ɔː 'kes tri ən ‖ ɔːr- -ɑːn **~s** z

orchid 'ɔːk ɪd §-əd ‖ 'ɔːrk əd **~s** z

orchidaceous ˌɔːk ɪ 'deɪʃ əs §-ə- ‖ ˌɔːrk-

orchidectom|y ˌɔːk ɪ 'dekt əm |i -ə- ‖ ˌɔːrk-
~ies iz

orchil 'ɔːk ɪl 'ɔːtʃ-, §-ᵊl ‖ 'ɔːrk- 'ɔːrtʃ-

orchis 'ɔːk ɪs §-əs ‖ 'ɔːrk-

orchitis ɔː 'kaɪt ɪs §əs ‖ ɔːr 'kaɪt̮ əs

Orcus 'ɔːk əs ‖ 'ɔːrk əs

Orczy 'ɔːts i 'ɔːks i, 'ɔːk zi ‖ 'ɔːrts i

Ord ɔːd ‖ ɔːrd

ordain ˌ‿ɔː 'deɪn ‖ ɔːr- **~ed** d **~ing** ɪŋ **~s** z

Orde ɔːd ‖ ɔːrd

ordeal ɔː 'diːᵊl 'ɔːd iːᵊl ‖ ɔːr- **~s** z

order 'ɔːd ə ‖ 'ɔːrd ᵊr **~ed** d **ordering**
'ɔːd ər ɪŋ ‖ 'ɔːrd ər ɪŋ **~s** z
    'order ˌpaper

order|ly 'ɔːd ə|l i ‖ 'ɔːrd ᵊr |li **~lies** liz **~liness**
li nəs -nɪs

ordinaire ˌɔːd ɪ 'neə -ə-, -ᵊn 'eə ‖ ˌɔːrd ᵊn 'eᵊr
-'æ̃ːr —*Fr* [ɔʁ di nɛːʁ]

ordinal 'ɔːd ɪn ᵊl -ᵊn̩ əl ‖ 'ɔːrd ᵊn̩ əl **~s** z

ordinanc|e 'ɔːd ɪn ənᵗs -ᵊn̩ ənᵗs ‖ 'ɔːrd ᵊn̩ ənᵗs
~es ɪz əz

ordinand 'ɔːd ɪ nænd -ə-, -ᵊn ænd, ˌ· · ˈ·
‖ 'ɔːrd ᵊn ænd ˌ· · ˈ· **~s** z

ordinarily 'ɔːd ᵊn ᵊr‿əl i '-ɪn-, '·ᵊn̩ ər əl i, -ɪ li;
ˌ· ·'er əl i, -ɪ li ‖ ˌɔːrd ᵊn 'er ə l i

ORDINARY

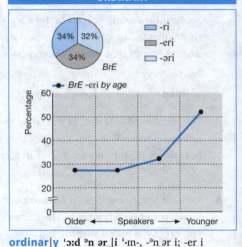

BrE -eri by age

Percentage — BrE -eri by age

Older ◄———— Speakers ————► Younger

ordinar|y 'ɔːd ᵊn ər‿|i '·ɪn-, -ᵊn̩ ər i; -er i
‖ 'ɔːrd ᵊn er |i — *Preference poll, BrE:* -ri
34%, -əri *32%,* -eri *34%.* **~ies** iz **~iness** i nəs
i nɪs
    'ordinary ˌlevel; ˌordinary 'seaman

ordinate 'ɔːd ᵊn ət -ɪn-, ɪt, -eɪt ‖ 'ɔːrd- **~s** s

ordination ˌɔːd ɪ 'neɪʃ ᵊn -ə-, -ᵊn 'eɪʃ-
‖ ˌɔːrd ᵊn 'eɪʃ ᵊn **~s** z

ordines 'ɔːd ɪ niːz -ə- ‖ 'ɔːrd-

ordnance 'ɔːd nənᵗs ‖ 'ɔːrd-
    ˌOrdnance 'Survey

ordo 'ɔːd əʊ ‖ 'ɔːrd oʊ **ordines** 'ɔːd ɪ niːz -ə-
‖ 'ɔːrd-

Ordovician ˌɔːd əʊ 'vɪʃ i ən ◄ -'vɪs-, -'vɪʃ ᵊn
‖ ˌɔːrd ə 'vɪʃ ᵊn ◄

ordure 'ɔːd jʊə ‖ 'ɔːrdʒ ᵊr 'ɔːrd jʊr

Ordzhonikidze ˌɔːdʒ ɒn i 'kɪdz i ˌ·ən-
‖ ˌɔːrdʒ ɑːn- —*Russ* [ar dʒə nʲi 'ki dzʲɪ]

ore, Ore ɔː ‖ ɔːr oʊr **ores** ɔːz ‖ ɔːrz oʊrz

öre 'ɜːr ə ‖ 'ɝː ə —*Swedish* ['øː rə]

oread 'ɔːr i æd **~s** z

Örebro 'ɜːr ə bruː ‖ 'ɝː- —*Swedish*
[œː rə 'bruː]

orectic ɒ 'rekt ɪk ə- ‖ ɔː-

oregano ˌɒr ɪ 'gɑːn əʊ -ə- ‖ ə 'reg ə noʊ ɔː- *(*)*

O

Oregon ˈɒr ɪg ən -əg- ‖ ˈɔːr- ˈɑːr-, -ə gɑːn
  ˌOregon ˈgrape; ˌOregon ˈTrail
Oregonian ˌɒr ɪ ˈgəʊn i ən ◂ ˌ-ə-
  ‖ ˌɔːr ə ˈgoʊn- ˌɑːr- ~s z
O'Reilly əʊ ˈraɪl i ‖ oʊ-
Oreo tdmk, **oreo** ˈɔːr i əʊ ‖ -oʊ ˈoʊr- ~s z
Oresteia ˌɒr ɪ ˈstaɪ ə ˌɔːr-, -ə-, -ˈsteɪ ə, -ˈstiː ə
  ‖ ˌɔːr- ˌoʊr-
Orestes ɒ ˈrest iːz ɔː-, ə- ‖ ɔː-
orfe ɔːf ‖ ɔːrf **orfes** ɔːfs ‖ ɔːrfs
Orfeo ɔː ˈfeɪ əʊ ˈɔːf i əʊ ‖ ɔːr ˈfeɪ oʊ ˈɔːrf i oʊ
  —It [or ˈfɛː o]
Orff ɔːf ‖ ɔːrf —Ger [ʔɒʁf]
Orford ˈɔːf əd ‖ ˈɔːrf ərd
org WWW and e-mail ɔːg ‖ ɔːrg
organ ˈɔːg ən ‖ ˈɔːrg ən ~s z
  ˈorgan ˌgrinder; ˈorgan ˌpipe
organa ˈɔːg ən ə ‖ ˈɔːrg-
organd|ie, organd|y ˈɔːg ənd i ‖ ˈɔːrg- ~ies
  iz
organelle ˌɔːg ə ˈnel ‖ ˌɔːrg- ~s z
organic ɔː ˈgæn ɪk ‖ ɔːr- ~ally ᵊl_i
organis... —see **organiz...**
organism ˈɔːg ə ˌnɪz əm -ən -ˌɪz- ‖ ˈɔːrg- ~s z
organist ˈɔːg ən ɪst §-əst ‖ ˈɔːrg- ~s s
organization ˌɔːg ən aɪ ˈzeɪʃ ᵊn -ɪˈ--
  ‖ ˌɔːrg ən ə-~s z
organizational ˌɔːg ən aɪ ˈzeɪʃ ᵊn_əl ◂ -ɪˈ--
  ‖ ˌɔːrg ən ə- ~ly i
organiz|e ˈɔːg ə naɪz -ən aɪz ‖ ˈɔːrg- ~ed d ~es
  ɪz əz ~ing ɪŋ
  ˌorganized ˈcrime
organizer ˈɔːg ə naɪz ə -ən -aɪz-
  ‖ ˈɔːrg ə naɪz ᵊr ~s z
organo- comb. form
  with stress-neutral suffix ɔː ǀgæn əʊ ǀɔːg ən əʊ
  ‖ ɔːr ǀgæn ə ɔːrg ən ə — **organochlorine**
  ɔː ˌgæn əʊ ˈklɔːr iːn ˌɔːg ən- ‖ ɔːr ˌgæn ə-
  ˌɔːrg ən-, -ˈkloʊr-, -ən
  with stress-imposing suffix ˌɔːg ə ˈnɒ+
  ‖ ˌɔːrg ə ˈnɑː+ — **organography**
  ˌɔːg ə ˈnɒg rəf i ‖ ˌɔːrg ə ˈnɑːg-
organogram ˈɔːg ən ə græm ‖ ɔːr- ~s z
organon ˈɔːg ə nɒn ‖ ˈɔːrg ə nɑːn ~s z **organa**
  ˈɔːg ən ə ‖ ˈɔːrg-
organ|um ˈɔːg ən ǀəm ‖ ˈɔːrg- ~a ə
organza ɔː ˈgænz ə ‖ ɔːr-
orgasm ˈɔːg æz əm ‖ ˈɔːrg- ~ed d ~ing ɪŋ ~s
  z
orgasmic ɔː ˈgæz mɪk ‖ ɔːr- ~ally ᵊl_i
orgeat ˈɔːʒ ɑː ‖ ˈɔːrʒ- —Fr [ɔʁ ʒa]
orgi... —see **orgy...**
orgiastic ˌɔːdʒ i ˈæst ɪk ◂ ‖ ˌɔːrdʒ- ~ally ᵊl_i
orgone ˈɔːg əʊn ‖ ˈɔːrg oʊn
Orgreave ˈɔː griːv ‖ ˈɔːr-
org|y ˈɔːdʒ |i ‖ ˈɔːrdʒ |i ~ies iz
Oriana ˌɔːr i ˈɑːn ə ˌɒr-
oriel, Oriel ˈɔːr i_əl ‖ ˈoʊr- ~s z
  ˌoriel ˈwindow, ˈ··ˌ··
ori|ent v ˈɔːr i ǀent ˈɒr- ‖ ˈoʊr- ~**ented** ent ɪd
  -əd ‖ enṯ əd ~**enting** ent ɪŋ ‖ enṯ ɪŋ ~**ents**
  ents

orient, O~ adj, n ˈɔːr i ənt ˈɒr- ‖ ˈoʊr-
  ˌOrient Exˈpress
oriental, O~ ˌɔːr i ˈent ᵊl ◂ ˌɒr- ‖ -ˈenṯ ᵊl ◂
  ˌoʊr- ~**ism** ˌɪz əm ~**ist/s** ɪst/s §əst/s ‖ əst/s ~**s**
  z
orien|tate ˈɔːr i ən ǀteɪt ˈɒr-, -i en- ‖ ˈoʊr-
  ~**tated** teɪt ɪd -əd ‖ teɪṯ əd ~**tates** teɪts
  ~**tating** teɪt ɪŋ ‖ teɪṯ ɪŋ
orientation ˌɔːr i ən ˈteɪʃ ᵊn ˌɒr-, -i en- ‖ ˌoʊr-
  ~**s** z
orien|teer ˌɔːr i ən ǀˈtɪə ˌɒr-, -i en|- ‖ -ˈtɪr ˌoʊr-
  ~**teering** ˈtɪər ɪŋ ‖ ˈtɪr ɪŋ ~**teered** ˈtɪəd
  ‖ ˈtɪrd ~**teers** ˈtɪəz ‖ ˈtɪrd
orific|e ˈɒr əf ɪs -ɪf-, §-əs ‖ ˈɔːr əf əs ˈɑːr- ~**es** ɪz
  əz
oriflamme ˈɒr ɪ flæm -ə- ‖ ˈɔːr ə- ˈɑːr- ~**s** z
origami ˌɒr ɪ ˈgɑːm i ˌɔːr-, -ə- ‖ ˌɔːr ə- —Jp
  [o ˈri ŋa mi, -ga-]
origanum ə ˈrɪg ən əm ɒ-; ˌɒr ɪ ˈgɑːn-, -ə-
Origen ˈɒr ɪ dʒen -ə- ‖ ˈɔːr- ˈɑːr-
origin ˈɒr ɪdʒ ɪn -ədʒ-, -ən ‖ ˈɔːr- ˈɑːr- ~**s** z
original ə ˈrɪdʒ ᵊn_əl ɒ-, -ɪn- ~**s** z
  oˌriginal ˈsin
originalit|y ə ˌrɪdʒ ə ˈnæl ət |i ɒ-, -ˌɪ-, -ɪt i
  ‖ -əṯ |i ~**ies** iz
originally ə ˈrɪdʒ ᵊn_əl i ɒ-, -ˈɪn-
origi|nate ə ˈrɪdʒ ə ǀneɪt ɒ-, -ɪ- ~**nated** neɪt ɪd
  -əd ‖ neɪṯ əd ~**nates** neɪts ~**nating** neɪt ɪŋ
  ‖ neɪṯ ɪŋ
origination ə ˌrɪdʒ ə ˈneɪʃ ᵊn ɒ-, -ɪ-
originative ə ˈrɪdʒ ə neɪt ɪv ɒ-, -ɪ- ·, -ən ət ɪv,
  -ɪn ət ɪv ‖ -neɪṯ ɪv ~**ly** li
originator ə ˈrɪdʒ ə neɪt ə ɒ-, -ˈ·ɪ- ‖ -neɪṯ ᵊr ~**s**
  z
O-ring ˈəʊ rɪŋ ‖ ˈoʊ- ~**s** z
Orinoco ˌɒr ɪ ˈnəʊk əʊ -ə- ‖ ˌɔːr ə ˈnoʊk oʊ
  ˌoʊr- —Sp [o ri ˈno ko]
Orinthia ə ˈrɪnᵗθ i_ə ɒ-
oriole ˈɔːr i əʊl →-ɒʊl, -əl ‖ -oʊl ˈoʊr- ~**s** z
Orion ə ˈraɪ ən ɒ-, ɔː- ‖ oʊ- **Orionis**
  ˌɔːr i ˈəʊn ɪs §-əs ‖ -ˈoʊn-
O'Riordan (i) əʊ ˈrɪəd ᵊn ‖ oʊ ˈrɪrd ᵊn,
  (ii) əʊ ˈraɪ_əd ᵊn ‖ oʊ ˈraɪ ᵊrd ᵊn
orison ˈɒr ɪz ən -əz- ‖ ˈɔːr əs- ˈɑːr-, -əz- ~**s** z
Orissa ɒ ˈrɪs ə ɔː-, ə- ‖ oʊ-
Oriya ɒ ˈriːə ɔː-, ə- ‖ ɔː-
ork ɔːk ‖ ɔːrk **orks** ɔːks ‖ ɔːrks
Orkney ˈɔːk ni ‖ ˈɔːrk- ~**s** z
  ˈOrkney ˌIslands ‖ ˌ··ˈ··
Orlando ɔː ˈlænd əʊ ‖ ɔːr ˈlænd oʊ
orle ɔːl ‖ ɔːrl **orles** ɔːlz ‖ ɔːrlz
Orleans, Orléans ɔː ˈliː_ənz ˈɔːl i_ˌ, ɔːl eɪ ˈɑ̃
  ‖ ˈɔːrl i_ənz ɔːr ˈliːnz —Fr [ɔʁ le ɑ̃]
Orlon, orlon tdmk ˈɔːl ɒn ‖ ˈɔːrl ɑːn
orlop ˈɔː lɒp ‖ ˈɔːr lɑːp ~**s** s
Orly ˈɔːl i ‖ ˈɔːrl i ɔːr ˈliː —Fr [ɔʁ li]
Orm, Orme ɔːm ‖ ɔːrm
Ormandy ˈɔːm ənd i ‖ ˈɔːrm-
Ormeau ˈɔːm əʊ ·ˈ· ‖ ˈɔːrm oʊ
ormer ˈɔːm ə ‖ ˈɔːrm ᵊr ~**s** z
Ormerod ˈɔːm ᵊr ɒd ‖ ˈɔːrm ᵊr ɑːd
Ormesby ˈɔːmz bi ‖ ˈɔːrmz-
ormolu ˈɔːm ə luː -lju: ‖ ˈɔːrm-

O

Ormond, Ormonde ˈɔːm ənd ‖ ˈɔːrm-
Ormrod ˈɔːm rɒd ‖ ˈɔːrm rɑːd
Ormsby ˈɔːmz bi ‖ ˈɔːrmz-
Ormskirk ˈɔːmz kɜːk ˈɔːmᵖs- ‖ ˈɔːrmz kɜːk
Ormulum ˈɔːm jʊl əm -jəl- ‖ ˈɔːrm-
orna|ment v ˈɔːn ə |ment ‖ ˈɔːrn- —*See note
at* -ment **~mented** ment ɪd -əd ‖ menʈ əd
~menting ment ɪŋ ‖ menʈ ɪŋ **~ments** ments
ornament n ˈɔːn ə mənt ‖ ˈɔːrn- **~s** s
ornamental ˌɔːn ə ˈment ᵊl ◄
‖ ˌɔːrn ə ˈmenʈ ᵊl ◄ **~ly** i
ornamentation ˌɔːn ə men ˈteɪʃ ᵊn -əm-
‖ ˌɔːrn- **~s** s
ornate ₍ˌ₎ɔː ˈneɪt ‖ ₍ˌ₎ɔːr- **~ly** li **~ness** nəs nɪs
orner|y ˈɔːn ər ˌi ‖ ˈɔːrn- -ɑːn- **~ier** i ə ‖ i ᵊr
~iest i ˌɪst i ˌəst **~iness** i nəs i nɪs
ornitho- *comb. form with stress-neutral suffix*
¦ɔːn ɪθ əʊ -əθ- ‖ ¦ɔːrn əθ ə — **ornithomancy**
ˈɔː ɪθ əʊ ˌmænᵗs i ‖ ˈɔːrn əθ ə- *with
stress-imposing suffix* ˌɔːn ɪ ˈθɒ+ -ə-
‖ ˌɔːrn ə ˈθɑː+ — **ornithoscopy**
ˌɔːn ɪ ˈθɒsk əp i ˌ-ə- ‖ ˌɔːrn ə ˈθɑːsk-
ornithological ˌɔːn ɪθ ə ˈlɒdʒ ɪk ᵊl ◄ ˌ-əθ-
‖ ˌɔːrn əθ ə ˈlɑːdʒ- **~ly** ˌi
ornitholog|ist ˌɔːn ɪ ˈθɒl ədʒ |ɪst ˌ-ə-, §-əst
‖ ˌɔːrn ə ˈθɑːl- **~ists** ɪsts §əsts **~y** i
ornithopter ˈɔːn ɪ θɒpt ə ˌ-ə- ‖ ˈɔːrn ə θɑːpt ᵊr
~s z
ornithosis ˌɔːn ɪ ˈθəʊs ɪs -ə-, §-əs
‖ ˌɔːrn ə ˈθoʊs əs
oro- *comb. form with stress-neutral suffix* ¦ɒr əʊ
¦ɔːr- ‖ ¦ɔːr ə ¦ɑːr-, ¦oʊr- — **orographic**
ˌɒr əʊ ˈgræf ɪk ◄ ˌɔːr- ‖ ˌɔːr ə- ˌɑːr-, ˌoʊr- *with
stress-imposing suffix* ɒ ˈrɒ+ ɔː- ‖ ɔː ˈrɑː+ ɑː-,
oʊ- — **orology** ɒ ˈrɒl ədʒ i ɔː- ‖ ɔː ˈrɑːl ədʒ i
ɑː-, oʊ-
oronasal ˌɔːr əʊ ˈneɪz ᵊl ◄ -oʊ- ˌoʊr-
Oronsay ˈɒr ən seɪ -zeɪ ‖ ˈɔːr-
Orontes ə ˈrɒnt iːz ɒ- ‖ ɔː ˈrɑːnt iːz ɑː-, oʊ-
oropharynx ˈɔːr əʊ ˌfær ɪŋks ˌ·ˈ··
‖ ˈɔːr oʊ ˌfær- ˈoʊr-, -ə-, -ˌfer-
orotund ˈɒr əʊ tʌnd ˈɔːr- ‖ ˈɔːr ə- ˈɑːr-, ˈoʊr-
orotundity ˌɒr əʊ ˈtʌnd ət i ˌɔːr-, -ɪt i
‖ ˌɔːr ə ˈtʌnd əʈ i ˌɑːr-, ˌoʊr-
O'Rourke əʊ ˈrɔːk -ˈrʊək ‖ oʊ ˈrɔːrk
Orphean ɔː ˈfiː ən ˈɔːf i ən ‖ ɔːr ˈfiː ən ˈɔːrf i ˌ~s
z
Orpheus ˈɔːf juːs ˈɔːf i ˌəs ‖ ˈɔːrf-
Orphic ˈɔːf ɪk ‖ ˈɔːrf-
Orphism ˈɔːf ˌɪz əm ‖ ˈɔːrf-
orphrey ˈɔːf ri ‖ ˈɔːrf- **~s** z
orpiment ˈɔːp ɪ mənt §-ə- ‖ ˈɔːrp-
orpin ˈɔːp ɪn §-ən ‖ ˈɔːrp- **~s** z
orpine ˈɔːp aɪn -ɪn, §-ən ‖ ˈɔːrp ən **~s** z
Orpington ˈɔːp ɪŋ tən ‖ ˈɔːrp- **~s** z
Orr ɔː ‖ ɔːr
Orrell ˈɒr əl ‖ ˈɔːr- ˈɑːr-
orrer|y ˈɒr ər ‖i ‖ ˈɔːr- ˈɑːr- **~ies** iz
orris ˈɒr ɪs §-əs ‖ ˈɔːr- ˈɑːr-
Orsini ɔː ˈsiːn i ‖ ɔːr- —*It* [or ˈsiː ni]

Orsino ɔː ˈsiːn əʊ ‖ ɔːr ˈsiːn oʊ
Orson ˈɔːs ᵊn ‖ ˈɔːrs ᵊn
ortanique ˌɔːt ə ˈniːk -ᵊn ˈiːk ‖ ˌɔːrt ᵊn ˈiːk **~s** s
Ortega ɔː ˈteɪg ə ‖ ɔːr- —*Sp* [or ˈte ɣa]
orthicon ˈɔːθ ɪ kɒn -ə- ‖ ˈɔːrθ ɪ kɑːn **~s** z
ortho- *comb. form with stress-neutral suffix*
¦ɔːθ əʊ ‖ ¦ɔːrθ ə -oʊ — **orthotone**
ˈɔːθ əʊ təʊn ‖ ˈɔːrθ ə toʊn -oʊ- *with
stress-imposing suffix* ɔː ˈθɒ+ ‖ ɔːr ˈθɑː+ —
orthotropous ɔː ˈθɒtr əp əs ‖ ɔːr ˈθɑːtr-
orthocenter, orthocentre ˈɔːθ əʊ ˌsent ə
‖ ˈɔːrθ ə ˌsenʈ ᵊr -oʊ- **~s** z
orthochromatic ˌɔːθ əʊ krəʊ ˈmæt ɪk ◄
‖ ˌɔːrθ ə kroʊ ˈmæʈ ɪk **~ally** ᵊl i
orthoclase ˈɔːθ əʊ kleɪz -kleɪs ‖ ˈɔːrθ ə- -oʊ-
orthodontic ˌɔːθ əʊ ˈdɒnt ɪk ◄
‖ ˌɔːrθ ə ˈdɑːnʈ ɪk ◄ **~s** s
orthodontist ˌɔːθ əʊ ˈdɒnt ɪst §-əst
‖ ˌɔːrθ ə ˈdɑːnʈ əst **~s** s
orthodox, O~ ˈɔːθ ə dɒks ‖ ˈɔːrθ ə dɑːks
ˌOrthodox ˈChurch
orthodox|y ˈɔːθ ə dɒks ‖i ‖ ˈɔːrθ ə dɑːks ‖i
~ies iz
orthoepic ˌɔːθ əʊ ˈep ɪk ‖ ˌɔːrθ oʊ-
orthoep|ist ˈɔːθ əʊ ˌep |ɪst §-əst, ˌ·ˈ··ˌ;
ɔː ˈθəʊ ɪp-, -ˈəp- ‖ ˈɔːrθ oʊ- **~ists** ɪsts §əsts **~y**
i
orthogonal ɔː ˈθɒg ən ᵊl ‖ ɔːr ˈθɑːg- **~ly** i
orthographer ɔː ˈθɒg rəf ə ‖ ɔːr ˈθɑːg rəf ᵊr
~s z
orthographic ˌɔːθ ə ˈgræf ɪk ◄ ‖ ˌɔːrθ- **~ally**
ᵊl i
orthograph|y ɔː ˈθɒg rəf ‖i ‖ ɔːr ˈθɑːg- **~ies** iz
orthopaed|ic, orthoped|ic
ˌɔːθ ə ˈpiːd ‖ɪk/s ◄ ‖ ˌɔːrθ- **~ics** ɪks **~ist** ɪst
§əst ‖ əst **~ists** ɪsts §əsts **~y** i
orthopter|a ɔː ˈθɒpt ər ‖ə ‖ ɔːr ˈθɑːpt- **~an** ən
~ous əs
orthoptic ɔː ˈθɒpt ɪk ‖ ɔːr ˈθɑːpt ɪk **~s** s
orthos|is ɔː ˈθəʊs ‖ɪs §-əs ‖ ɔːr ˈθoʊs ‖əs **~es**
iːz
orthostich|ous ɔː ˈθɒst ɪk ‖əs -ək- ‖ ɔːr ˈθɑːst-
~y i
orthotic ɔː ˈθɒt ɪk ‖ ɔːr ˈθɑːʈ ɪk **~s** s
ortolan ˈɔːt əl ən -ə læn ‖ ˈɔːrʈ ᵊl ən **~s** z
Orton ˈɔːt ᵊn ‖ ˈɔːrt ᵊn
Ortonesque ˌɔːt ə ˈnesk ◄ →-ᵊn ˈesk
‖ ˌɔːrt ᵊn ˈesk ◄
orts ɔːts ‖ ɔːrts
Orville ˈɔː vɪl ˈɔːv ᵊl ‖ ˈɔːrv ᵊl
Orwell ˈɔː wel -wəl ‖ ˈɔːr-
Orwellian ɔː ˈwel i ən ‖ ɔːr-
-ory ər i ‖ ər i, ɔːr i oʊr i —*This suffix is
usually stress-neutral when attached to a free
stem* (diˈrectory, ˈpromissory)*; otherwise it
imposes stress on one of the two preceding
syllables* (perˈfunctory, ˈrepertory). *It has a
strong vowel in AmE* (-ɔːr i) *if the preceding
vowel is weak* (ˈdormitory)*; otherwise, and
always in BrE, it has a weak vowel.*
oryx ˈɒr ɪks ‖ ˈɔːr- ˈɑːr-, ˈoʊr- **~es** ɪz əz
orzo ˈɔːz əʊ ˈɔːdz- ‖ -oʊ
os *'bone'*; *'mouth'* ɒs ‖ ɑːs

Osag|e ˌ(ˌ)əʊ ˈseɪdʒ ˈ·· ‖ ˌ(ˌ)oʊ- **~es** ɪz əz
Osaka əʊ ˈsɑːk ə ˈ···, ˈɔːs ək ə ‖ oʊ- —*Jp*
[o,o sa ka]
Osama bin Laden əʊ ˌsɑːm ə bɪn ˈlɑːd ᵊn -en
‖ oʊ- —*Arabic* [u ˈsɑː ma bin ˈlɑː dan]
Osbert ˈɒz bət -bɜːt ‖ ˈɑːz bᵊrt
Osborn, Osborne, Osbourne ˈɒz bɔːn -bən
‖ ˈɑːz bɔːrn
Oscan ˈɒsk ən ‖ ˈɑːsk-
Oscar, oscar ˈɒsk ə ‖ ˈɑːsk ᵊr
oscil|late ˈɒs ɪ |leɪt -ə-, -ᵊ|l eɪt ‖ ˈɑːs- **~lated**
leɪt ɪd -əd ‖ leɪt̬ əd **~lates** leɪts **~lating**
leɪt ɪŋ ‖ leɪt̬ ɪŋ
oscillation ˌɒs ɪ ˈleɪʃ ᵊn -ə-, -ᵊl ˈeɪʃ- ‖ ˌɑːs- **~s** z
oscillator ˈɒs ɪ leɪt ə ˈ·ə-, -ᵊl eɪt- ‖ ˈɑːs ə leɪt̬ ᵊr
~s z
oscillatory ˈɒs ɪl ət ər i ˈ·əl-; ˌɒs ɪ ˈleɪt ᵊr i,
ˌ·ə-, ˈ····· ‖ ˈɑːs əl ə tɔːr i -toʊr i
oscillo- *comb. form with stress-neutral suffix*
ə ¦sɪl əʊ ɒ- ‖ ɑː ¦sɪl ə — **oscillographic**
ə,sɪl əʊ ˈgræf ɪk ◂ ɒ- ‖ ɑː ˌsɪl ə- *with
stress-imposing suffix* ˌɒs ɪ ˈlɒ+ -ə-
‖ ˌɑːs ə ˈlɑː + — **oscillography**
ˌɒs ɪ ˈlɒg rəf i -ə- ‖ ˌɑːs ə ˈlɑːg-
oscillogram ə ˈsɪl ə græm ɒ- ‖ ɑː- **~s** z
oscillograph ə ˈsɪl ə grɑːf ɒ-, -græf ‖ -græf ɑː-
~s s
oscilloscope ə ˈsɪl ə skəʊp ɒ- ‖ -skoʊp ɑː- **~s** s
Osco-Umbrian ˌɒsk əʊ ˈʌm bri ˌən ◂
‖ ˌɑːsk oʊ-
osculant ˈɒsk jʊl ənt -jəl- ‖ ˈɑːsk jəl-
oscular ˈɒsk jʊl ə -jəl- ‖ ˈɑːsk jə lᵊr
oscu|late ˈɒsk ju |leɪt ‖ ˈɑːsk jə- **~lated** leɪt ɪd
-əd ‖ leɪt̬ əd **~lates** leɪts **~lating** leɪt ɪŋ
‖ leɪt̬ ɪŋ
osculation ˌɒsk ju ˈleɪʃ ᵊn -jə- ‖ ˌɑːsk jə- **~s** z
osculatory ˈɒsk jʊl ət ər i ˈ·jəl-,
ˌɒsk ju ˈleɪt ᵊr i ‖ ˈɑːsk jəl ə tɔːr i -toʊr i
oscul|um ˈɒsk jʊl |əm -jəl- ‖ ˈɑːsk jəl- **~a** ə
-oses ˈəʊs iːz ‖ ˈoʊs iːz — **fibroses**
faɪ ˈbrəʊs iːz ‖ -ˈbroʊs-
Osgood ˈɒz gʊd ‖ ˈɑːz-
O'Shaughnessy əʊ ˈʃɔːn əs i -ɪs- ‖ oʊ- -ˈʃɑːn-
O'Shea *(i)* əʊ ˈʃeɪ ‖ oʊ-, *(ii)* -ˈʃiː
Oshkosh ˈɒʃ kɒʃ ‖ ˈɑːʃ kɑːʃ
osier ˈəʊz i ə ˈəʊʒ ə, ˈəʊʒ i ə ‖ ˈoʊʒ ᵊr ˈoʊz i ᵊr
~s z
Osijek ˈɒs i ek ‖ oʊs- —*Croatian* [ˈɔ si jɛk]
Osiris əʊ ˈsaɪᵊr ɪs ɒ-, §-əs ‖ oʊ-
-osis ˈəʊs ɪs §-əs ‖ ˈoʊs əs — **ornithosis**
ˌɔːn ɪ ˈθəʊs ɪs -ə-, §-əs ‖ ˌɔːr nə ˈθoʊs əs
-osity ˈɒs ət i -ɪt i ‖ ˈɑːs ət̬ i **verbosity**
vɜː ˈbɒs ət i -ɪt i ‖ vɜː ˈbɑːs ət̬ i
Oslo ˈɒz ləʊ ˈɒs- ‖ ˈɑːz loʊ ˈɑːs- —*Norw*
[ˈʊs lu]
Osman ɒz ˈmɑːn ɒs-; ˈɒz mən ‖ ˈɑːz mən ˈɑːs-
Osmanli ɒz ˈmæn li ɒs-, -ˈmɑːn- ‖ ɑːz- ɑːs- **~s** z
Osmiroid *tdmk* ˈɒz mə rɔɪd -mɪ- ‖ ˈɑːz-
osmium ˈɒz mi əm ‖ ˈɑːz-
Osmond ˈɒz mənd ‖ ˈɑːz- **~s** z
osmosis ɒz ˈməʊs ɪs ɒs-, §-əs ‖ ɑːs ˈmoʊs əs
ɑːz-

Osmotherley, Osmotherly ɒz ˈmʌð ə li
‖ ɑːz ˈmʌð ᵊr-
osmotic ɒz ˈmɒt ɪk ɒs- ‖ ɑːz ˈmɑːt̬ ɪk ɑːs- **~ally**
ᵊl i
Osmund, o~ ˈɒz mənd ‖ ˈɑːz- ɑːs-
osmunda ɒz ˈmʌnd ə ‖ ɑːz- ɑːs-
Osnabruck, Osnabrück ˈɒz nə brʊk ‖ ˈɑːz-
—*Ger* [ˈʔɔs na ˈbʁʏk]
Osnaburg, Osnaburgh, o~ ˈɒz nə bɜːg
‖ ˈɑːz nə bɝːg
osprey ˈɒsp ri -reɪ ‖ ˈɑːsp- **~s** z
Ossa ˈɒs ə ‖ ˈɑːs ə
osseous ˈɒs i əs ‖ ˈɑːs- **~ly** li
Osset ˈɒs ɪt §-ət ‖ ˈɑːs- **~s** s
Ossetia ɒ ˈset i ə ɒ ˈsiːʃ ə ‖ ɑː ˈseт̬ i ə ɑː ˈsiːʃ ə
Ossetian ɒ ˈset i ən ɒ ˈsiːʃ ᵊn ‖ ɑː ˈseт̬ i ən
ɑː ˈsiːʃ ᵊn **~s** z
Ossetic ɒ ˈset ɪk ‖ ɑː ˈseт̬ ɪk
Ossett ˈɒs ɪt §-ət ‖ ˈɑːs-
Ossian ˈɒs i ən ‖ ˈɒʃ ᵊn ˈɑːs i ən
Ossianic ˌɒs i ˈæn ɪk ◂ ‖ ˌɑːs- ˌɑːʃ-
ossicle ˈɒs ɪk ᵊl ‖ ˈɑːs- **~s** z
ossification ˌɒs ɪf ɪ ˈkeɪʃ ᵊn ˌ·əf-, §-ə'- ‖ ˌɑːs-
ossifrag|e ˈɒs ɪf rɪdʒ -ə-; -ɪ freɪdʒ, -ə- ‖ ˈɑːs-
~es ɪz əz
ossi|fy ˈɒs ɪ |faɪ -ə- ‖ ˈɑːs- **~fied** faɪd **~fies** faɪz
~fying faɪ ɪŋ
Ossining ˈɒs ᵊn ɪŋ -ɪn- ‖ ˈɑːs-
osso bucco, osso buco ˌɒs əʊ ˈbʊk əʊ -ˈbuːk-
‖ ˌoʊs oʊ ˈbuːk oʊ ˌɑːs- —*It* [ˌɔs so ˈbu ko]
ossuar|y ˈɒs ju ər |i ‖ ˈɑːs ju er |i **~ies** iz
osteitis ˌɒst i ˈaɪt ɪs §-əs ‖ ˌɑːst i ˈaɪt̬ əs
Ostend ˌ(ˌ)ɒst ˈend ‖ ˌ(ˌ)ɑːst- —*Dutch* Oostende
[oːst ˈen də], *Fr* Ostende [ɔs ˈtɑ̃ːd]
ostensib|le ɒ ˈstenᵗs əb |ᵊl -ɪb- ‖ ɑː- ə- **~ly** li
ostensive ɒ ˈstenᵗs ɪv ‖ ɑː- **~ly** li
ostentation ˌɒst en ˈteɪʃ ᵊn -ən- ‖ ˌɑːst-
ostentatious ˌɒst en ˈteɪʃ əs ◂ -ən- ‖ ˌɑːst- **~ly**
li **~ness** nəs nɪs
osteo- *comb. form with stress-neutral suffix*
¦ɒst i ˌəʊ ‖ ¦ɑːst i ə — **osteoclast**
ˈɒst i ˌəʊ klæst ‖ ˈɑːst i ə- *with stress-imposing
suffix* ˌɒst i ˈɒ+ ‖ ˌɑːst i ˈɑː+ — **osteology**
ˌɒst i ˈɒl ədʒ i ‖ ˌɑːst i ˈɑːl-
osteoarthritis ˌɒst i əʊ ɑː ˈθraɪt ɪs §-əs
‖ ˌɑːst i oʊ ɑːr ˈθraɪt̬ əs
osteomalacia ˌɒst i əʊ mə ˈleɪʃ i ə -ˈleɪʃ ə
‖ ˌɑːst i oʊ-
osteomyelitis ˌɒst i əʊ ˌmaɪ ə ˈlaɪt ɪs §-əs
‖ ˌɑːst i oʊ ˌmaɪ ə ˈlaɪt̬ əs
osteopath ˈɒst i əʊ pæθ ‖ ˈɑːst i ə- **~s** s
osteopathic ˌɒst i əʊ ˈpæθ ɪk ◂ ‖ ˌɑːst i ə-
~ally ᵊl i
osteopathy ˌɒst i ˈɒp əθ i ‖ ˌɑːst i ˈɑːp-
osteoporosis ˌɒst i əʊ pɔː ˈrəʊs ɪs §-əs
‖ ˌɑːst i oʊ pə ˈroʊs əs
Osterley ˈɒst ə li →-ᵊl i ‖ ˈɑːst ᵊr-
Ostermilk *tdmk* ˈɒst ə mɪlk ‖ ˈɑːst ᵊr-
Ostia ˈɒst i ə ‖ ˈɑːst-
ostiar|y ˈɒst i ər |i ‖ ˈɑːst i er |i **~ies** iz
ostinato ˌɒst ɪ ˈnɑːt əʊ -ə- ‖ ˌɑːst ə ˈnɑːt̬ oʊ
ˌɔːst- **~s** z
osti|um ˈɒst i ˌ|əm ‖ ˈɑːst- **~a** ə

O

ostler, O~ 'ɒs lə ‖ 'ɑːs lᵊr ~s z
ostom|y 'ɒst əm| i ‖ 'ɑːst- **~ies** iz —*see also* **-stomy**
ostracis... —*see* **ostraciz...**
ostracism 'ɒs trə ˌsɪz əm ‖ 'ɑːs- **~s** z
ostraciz|e 'ɒs trə saɪz ‖ 'ɑːs- **~ed** d **~es** ɪz əz **~ing** ɪŋ
Ostrava 'ɒs trəv ə ‖ 'ɔːs- 'ɑːs-, 'oʊs- —*Czech* ['ɔ stra va]
ostrich 'ɒs trɪtʃ -trɪdʒ ‖ 'ɑːs- 'ɔːs- **~es** ɪz əz
  'ostrich egg; 'ostrich ˌfeather
Ostrogoth 'ɒs trəʊ gɒθ ‖ 'ɑːs trə gɑːθ **~s** s
Ostrogothic ˌɒs trəʊ 'gɒθ ɪk ◂ ‖ ˌɑːs trə 'gɑːθ ɪk ◂
Ostwald 'ɒst vælt ‖ 'ɑːst- —*Ger* ['ɔst valt]
Ostyak 'ɒst jæk 'ɒst i æk ‖ 'ɑːst jɑːk -i ɑːk, -æk **~s** s
O'Sullivan əʊ 'sʌl ɪv ən -əv- ‖ oʊ-
Oswald 'ɒz wɒld ‖ 'ɑːz-
Oswaldtwistle 'ɒz wɒld ˌtwɪs ᵊl -ᵊl- ‖ 'ɑːz-
Oswego ɒ 'swiːg əʊ -'zwiːg- ‖ ɑː 'swiːg oʊ
Oswestry 'ɒz wəs tri -wɪs- ‖ 'ɑːz-
Osyth 'əʊz ɪθ 'əʊs- ‖ 'oʊz-
Otago əʊ 'tɑːg əʊ ɒ- ‖ oʊ 'tɑːg oʊ
Otaheite ˌəʊt ə 'hiːt i -'heɪt- ‖ ˌoʊt̬ ə 'hiːt̬ i
otarine 'əʊt ə raɪn ‖ 'oʊt̬-
otar|y 'əʊt ər| i ‖ 'oʊt̬- **~ies** iz
O tempora! O mores
  ˌ(ˌ)əʊ 'temp ər ə ˌ(ˌ)əʊ 'mɔːr iːz -eɪz, -eɪs
  ‖ ˌ(ˌ)oʊ 'temp ər ə ˌ(ˌ)oʊ- -'moʊr-
Otford 'ɒt fəd ‖ 'ɑːt fᵊrd
Othello əʊ 'θel əʊ ɒ- ‖ ə 'θel oʊ oʊ-
other 'ʌð ə ‖ 'ʌð ᵊr **others** 'ʌð əz ‖ -ᵊrz
otherness 'ʌð ə nəs -nɪs ‖ -ᵊr-
otherwise 'ʌð ə waɪz ‖ -ᵊr-
otherworld|ly ˌʌð ə 'wɜːld |li ◂ ‖ -ᵊr 'wɝːld- **~liness** li nəs -nɪs
Othman ɒθ 'mɑːn ‖ ɑːθ-
Otho 'əʊθ əʊ ‖ 'oʊθ oʊ
-otic 'ɒt ɪk ‖ 'ɑːt̬ ɪk —*but* 'əʊt ɪk ‖ 'oʊt̬ ɪk *when not related to a noun in* -osis — **symbiotic** ˌsɪm baɪ 'ɒt ɪk ◂ ‖ -'ɑːt̬ ɪk ◂ — **periotic** ˌper i 'əʊt ɪk ◂ ‖ -'oʊt̬ ɪk ◂
otic 'əʊt ɪk 'ɒt- ‖ 'oʊt̬ ɪk 'ɑːt̬-
otiose 'əʊt i ˌəʊs 'əʊʃ-, -əʊz; 'əʊʃ i əs ‖ 'oʊʃ i oʊs 'oʊt̬- **~ly** li
otiosity ˌəʊt i 'ɒs ət i ˌəʊʃ-, -ɪt i ‖ ˌoʊʃ i 'ɑːs ət̬ i ˌoʊt̬-
Otis 'əʊt ɪs §-əs ‖ 'oʊt̬ əs
otitis əʊ 'taɪt ɪs §-əs ‖ oʊ 'taɪt̬ əs
Otley 'ɒt li ‖ 'ɑːt-
oto- *comb. form with stress-neutral suffix* |əʊt əʊ ‖ |oʊt̬ ə — **otocyst** 'əʊt əʊ sɪst ‖ 'oʊt̬ ə- *with stress-imposing suffix* əʊ 'tɒ+ ‖ oʊ 'tɑː+ — **otology** əʊ 'tɒl ədʒ i ‖ oʊ 'tɑːl-
otolaryngolog|ist ˌəʊt əʊ ˌlær ɪŋ 'gɒl ədʒ |ɪst §-əst ‖ ˌoʊt̬ oʊ ˌlær ɪŋ 'gɑːl- -ˌler- **~ists** ɪsts §əsts **~y** i
Otomanguean ˌəʊt ə 'mæŋ gi ən -geɪ ən ‖ ˌoʊt̬-
O'Toole əʊ 'tuːl ‖ oʊ-

Otranto ɒ 'trænt əʊ 'ɒtr ən təʊ ‖ oʊ 'trɑːnt oʊ —*It* ['ɔː tran to]
OTT ˌəʊ tiː 'tiː ‖ ˌoʊ-
ottar 'ɒt ə ‖ 'ɑːt̬ ᵊr
ottava əʊ 'tɑːv ə ɒ- ‖ oʊ- ot̬ˌtava 'rima 'riːm ə
Ottawa 'ɒt ə wə ‖ 'ɑːt̬ ə wə -wɑː:, -wɔː-
otter 'ɒt ə ‖ 'ɑːt̬ ᵊr **~s** z
Otterburn 'ɒt ə bɜːn ‖ 'ɑːt̬ ᵊr bɝːn
Ottery 'ɒt ər i ‖ 'ɑːt̬-
Ottfur 'ɒt fə ‖ 'ɑːt fᵊr
Otto, otto 'ɒt əʊ ‖ 'ɑːt̬ oʊ
Ottoline 'ɒt ə lɪn -ᵊl n ‖ 'ɑːt̬-
ottoman, O~ 'ɒt ə mən -əʊ- ‖ 'ɑːt̬- **~s** z
Otway 'ɒt weɪ ‖ 'ɑːt-
Ötzi 'əʊts i 'ɜːts i ‖ 'oʊts i —*Ger* ['œts i]
ouabain ˌwɑː 'beɪ ɪn -'bɑː:-, ' · ·
Ouachita 'wɒʃ ə tɔː ‖ 'wɑːʃ- -tɑː **~s** z
Ouagadougou ˌwɑːg ə 'duːg uː ˌwæg-
oubliette ˌuːb li 'et **~s** s
ouch aʊtʃ
oud uːd **ouds** uːdz
Oudenaarde, Oudenarde 'uːd ə nɑːd -ᵊn ɑːd ‖ -nɑːrd —*Dutch* ['ɔu də nɑːr də]
Oudh aʊd
ought ɔːt ‖ ɑːt —*The combination* ought to *is often pronounced with a single* t, *as* 'ɔːt ə ‖ 'ɔːt̬ ə *(esp. before a consonant sound; also, esp. BrE,* 'ɔːt u *before a vowel sound).*
oughta = ought to 'ɔːt ə ‖ 'ɔːt̬ ə 'ɑːt̬ ə
Oughtershaw 'aʊt ə ʃɔː ‖ 'aʊt̬ ᵊr- -ʃɑː
Oughterside 'aʊt ə saɪd ‖ 'aʊt̬ ᵊr-
oughtn't 'ɔːt ᵊnt →-ᵊn-t ‖ 'ɑːt-
Oughton (i) 'aʊt ᵊn, (ii) 'ɔːt ᵊn ‖ 'ɑːt-
Ouida 'wiːd ə
ouija, O~ *tdmk* 'wiːdʒ ə -ɑː:, -i 'ouija board
ould *dialectal form of* old aʊld
Ould *family name (i)* əʊld →ɒʊld ‖ oʊld, *(ii)* uːld
Oulton 'əʊlt ən →'ɒʊlt- ‖ 'oʊlt ᵊn
ounce aʊnts **ounces** 'aʊnts ɪz -əz
Oundle 'aʊnd ᵊl
our 'aʊ ə ɑː ‖ 'aʊ ᵊr ɑːr —*Some speakers use* ɑː ‖ ɑːr *as the weak form,* 'aʊ ə ‖ 'aʊ ᵊr *as the strong; others use only one or only the other. In RP the latter form in any case readily undergoes smoothing (see* COMPRESSION) *to* ɑː:, ɑː.
  ˌOur 'Father; ˌ(ˌ)Our 'Lady; ˌ(ˌ)Our 'Lord
-our ə ‖ ᵊr — **armour** 'ɑːm ə ‖ 'ɑːrm ᵊr
ours 'aʊ əz ɑːz ‖ 'aʊ ᵊrz ɑːrz
our|self ˌ(ˌ)aʊ ə |'self ɑː |'self ‖ ˌ(ˌ)aʊ ᵊr |'self ɑːr |'self **~selves** 'selvz
-ous əs — **hazardous** 'hæz əd əs ‖ -ᵊrd- **carnivorous** kɑː 'nɪv ər əs ‖ kɑːr-
Ouse uːz
ousel 'uːz ᵊl **~s** z
Ouseley, Ousley 'uːz li
Ouspensky u 'spen'sk i —*Russ* [u ˈsʲpʲenʲ sʲkʲij]
oust aʊst **ousted** 'aʊst ɪd -əd **ousting** 'aʊst ɪŋ **ousts** aʊsts

ouster 'aʊst ə ‖ -ᵊr ~s z

out aʊt **outed** 'aʊt ɪd -əd ‖ 'aʊt̬ əd **outing**
'aʊt ɪŋ ‖ 'aʊt̬ ɪŋ **outs** aʊts

out- ˌaʊt

outag|e 'aʊt ɪdʒ ‖ 'aʊt̬- ~**es** ɪz əz

out-and-out ˌaʊt ᵊn 'aʊt ◂ -ᵊnd-
ˌout-and-ˌout 'failure

outback, O~ 'aʊt bæk

outbalanc|e ˌaʊt 'bæl ən⁀s ~**ed** t ~**es** ɪz əz
~**ing** ɪŋ

outbid ˌaʊt 'bɪd ~**ding** ɪŋ ~**s** z

outboard 'aʊt bɔːd ‖ -bɔːrd -boʊrd ~**s** z
ˌoutboard 'motor

outbound 'aʊt baʊnd

outbox *n.* 'aʊt bɒks ‖ -baːks ~**es** ɪz əz

outbrav|e ˌaʊt 'breɪv ~**ed** d ~**es** z ~**ing** ɪŋ

outbreak 'aʊt breɪk ~**s** s

outbuilding 'aʊt ˌbɪld ɪŋ ~**s** z

outburst 'aʊt bɜːst ‖ -bɝːst ~**s** s

outcast, outcaste 'aʊt kɑːst §-kæst ‖ -kæst ~**s**
s

outclass ˌaʊt 'klɑːs §-'klæs ‖ -'klæs ~**ed** t ~**es**
ɪz əz ~**ing** ɪŋ

outcome 'aʊt kʌm ~**s** z

outcrop 'aʊt krɒp ‖ -krɑːp ~**ped** t ~**ping** ɪŋ ~**s**
s

out|cry 'aʊt |kraɪ ~**cries** kraɪz

out|date ˌaʊt |'deɪt ~**dated** 'deɪt ɪd ◂ -əd
‖ 'deɪt̬ əd ◂ ~**dates** 'deɪts ~**dating** 'deɪt ɪŋ
‖ 'deɪt̬ ɪŋ

outdid ˌaʊt 'dɪd

outdistanc|e ˌaʊt 'dɪst ən⁀s ~**ed** t ~**es** ɪz əz
~**ing** ɪŋ

out|do ˌaʊt |'duː ~**did** 'dɪd ~**does** 'dʌz ~**done**
'dʌn

outdoor ˌaʊt 'dɔː ◂ ‖ -'dɔːr ◂ -'doʊr ~**s** z ~**sy** zi
ˌoutdoor 'shoes

out|draw ˌaʊt| 'drɔː ‖ -'drɑː ~**drawing**
'drɔːᵊ ɪŋ ‖ 'drɔː ɪŋ 'drɑː ɪŋ ~**drawn** 'drɔːn
‖ 'drɑːn ~**draws** 'drɔːz ‖ 'drɑːz ~**drew** 'druː

outer 'aʊt ə ‖ 'aʊt̬ ᵊr
ˌOuter 'Hebrides

outermost 'aʊt ə məʊst ‖ 'aʊt̬ ᵊr moʊst

outerwear 'aʊt ə weə ‖ 'aʊt̬ ᵊr wer

outfac|e ˌaʊt 'feɪs ~**ed** t ~**es** ɪz əz ~**ing** ɪŋ

outfall 'aʊt fɔːl ‖ -fɑːl ~**s** z

outfield 'aʊt fiːᵊld

outfielder 'aʊt fiːᵊld ə ‖ -ᵊr ~**s** z

out|fight ˌaʊt |'faɪt ~**fighting** 'faɪt ɪŋ
‖ 'faɪt̬ ɪŋ ~**fights** 'faɪts ~**fought** 'fɔːt ‖ 'faːt

out|fit 'aʊt |fɪt ~**fits** fɪts ~**fitted** fɪt ɪd -əd
‖ fɪt̬ əd ~**fitting** fɪt ɪŋ ‖ fɪt̬ ɪŋ

outfitter 'aʊt fɪt ə ‖ -fɪt̬ ᵊr ~**s** z

outflank ˌaʊt 'flæŋk ~**ed** t ~**ing** ɪŋ ~**s** s

outflow *n.* 'aʊt fləʊ ‖ -floʊ ~**s** z

outflow *v.* ˌaʊt 'fləʊ ‖ -'floʊ ~**ed** d ~**ing** ɪŋ ~**s**
z

outfought ˌaʊt 'fɔːt ‖ -'faːt

outfox ˌaʊt 'fɒks ‖ -'faːks ~**ed** t ~**es** ɪz əz ~**ing**
ɪŋ

outgeneral ˌaʊt 'dʒen ᵊr əl ~**ed**, ~**led** d ~**ing**,
~**ling** ɪŋ ~**s** z

outgo *n.* 'aʊt gəʊ ‖ -goʊ ~**es** z

outgoing *n.* 'aʊt gəʊ ɪŋ ‖ -goʊ- ~**s** z

outgoing *adj.* ˌaʊt 'gəʊ ɪŋ ◂ '·ˌ·· ‖ -'goʊ-

outgrew ˌaʊt 'gruː

out-group *n.* 'aʊt gruːp ~**s** s

out|grow ˌaʊt |'grəʊ ‖ -|'groʊ ~**grew** 'gruː
~**growing** 'grəʊ ɪŋ ‖ 'groʊ ɪŋ ~**grown**
'grəʊn ‖ 'groʊn ~**grows** 'grəʊz ‖ 'groʊz

outgrowth 'aʊt grəʊθ ‖ -groʊθ ~**s** s

outguess ˌaʊt 'ges ~**ed** t ~**es** ɪz əz ~**ing** ɪŋ

outgun ˌaʊt 'gʌn ~**ned** d ~**ning** ɪŋ ~**s** z

out-Herod ˌaʊt 'her əd ~**ed** ɪd əd ~**ing** ɪŋ ~**s** z

out|house 'aʊt |haʊs ~**houses** haʊz ɪz -əz

Outhwaite *(i)* 'aʊθ weɪt, *(ii)* 'əʊθ- ‖ 'oʊθ-,
(iii) 'uːθ-

outing 'aʊt ɪŋ ‖ 'aʊt̬ ɪŋ ~**s** z

outlaid ˌaʊt 'leɪd '··

outlander, O~ 'aʊt lænd ə ‖ -ᵊr ~**s** z

outlandish ˌaʊt 'lænd ɪʃ ~**ly** li ~**ness** nəs nɪs

outlast ˌaʊt 'lɑːst §-'læst ‖ -'læst ~**ed** ɪd əd
~**ing** ɪŋ ~**s** s

outlaw *n, v* 'aʊt lɔː ‖ -lɑː ~**ed** d **outlawing**
'aʊt lɔːʳ ɪŋ ‖ -lɔːʳ ɪŋ -lɑːʳ- ~**s** z

outlaw|ry 'aʊt lɔː |ri ‖ -lɑː- ~**ries** riz

outlay *n* 'aʊt leɪ ~**s** z

out|lay *v* ˌaʊt |'leɪ '·· ~**laid** 'leɪd ~**laying**
'leɪ ɪŋ ~**lays** 'leɪz

outlet 'aʊt let -lət, -lɪt ~**s** s

outlier 'aʊt ˌlaɪ ə ‖ -ˌlaɪ ᵊr ~**s** z

outlin|e *v* 'aʊt laɪn ˌ·'· ~**ed** d ~**es** z ~**ing** ɪŋ

outline *n* 'aʊt laɪn ~**s** z

outliv|e ˌaʊt 'lɪv ~**ed** d ~**es** z ~**ing** ɪŋ

outlook 'aʊt lʊk §-luːk ~**s** s

outlying 'aʊt ˌlaɪ ɪŋ ˌ·'·

outman ˌaʊt 'mæn ~**ned** d ~**ning** ɪŋ ~**s** z

outmaneuve|r, outmanoeuv|re
ˌaʊt mə 'nuːv |ə ‖ -|ᵊr -'njuːv- ~**red** əd ‖ ᵊrd
~**res** əz ‖ ᵊrz ~**ring** ᵊr ɪŋ ‖ ᵊr ɪŋ

outmarch ˌaʊt 'mɑːtʃ ‖ -'mɑːrtʃ ~**ed** t ~**es** ɪz
əz ~**ing** ɪŋ

outmatch ˌaʊt 'mætʃ ~**ed** t ~**es** ɪz əz ~**ing** ɪŋ

outmoded ˌaʊt 'məʊd ɪd ◂ -əd ‖ -'moʊd- ~**ly**
li ~**ness** nəs nɪs

outmost 'aʊt məʊst ‖ -moʊst

outnumber ˌaʊt 'nʌm bə ‖ -bᵊr ~**ed** d
outnumbering ˌaʊt 'nʌm bər ɪŋ ~**s** z

out-of-body ˌaʊt əv 'bɒd i ◂
‖ ˌaʊt̬ əv 'baːd i ◂

out-of-court ˌaʊt əv 'kɔːt ◂ ‖ ˌaʊt̬ əv 'kɔːrt ◂
-'koʊrt ◂

out-of-date ˌaʊt əv 'deɪt ◂ ‖ ˌaʊt̬-

out-of-door ˌaʊt əv 'dɔː ◂ ‖ ˌaʊt̬ əv 'dɔːr ◂
-'doʊr

out-of-pocket ˌaʊt əv 'pɒk ɪt ◂ §-ət
‖ ˌaʊt̬ əv 'paːk-
ˌout-of-ˌpocket ex'penses

out-of-sight ˌaʊt əv 'saɪt ◂ ‖ ˌaʊt̬-

out-of-state ˌaʊt əv 'steɪt ◂ ‖ ˌaʊt̬-

out-of-the-way ˌaʊt əv ðə 'weɪ ◂ -ə ðə-
‖ ˌaʊt̬-
ˌout-of-the-ˌway 'places

out-of-town ˌaʊt əv 'taʊn ◂ ‖ ˌaʊt̬-

out-of-work ˌaʊt əv 'wɜːk ◂ ‖ ˌaʊt̬ əv 'wɝːk ◂

outpac|e ˌaʊt 'peɪs ~**ed** t ~**es** ɪz əz ~**ing** ɪŋ

O

outpatient 'aʊt ˌpeɪʃ ᵊnt ~s s
outperform ˌaʊt pə 'fɔːm ‖ -pᵊr 'fɔːrm ~ed d
~ing ɪŋ ~s z
outplacement 'aʊt ˌpleɪs mənt ~s s
outplay ˌaʊt 'pleɪ ~ed d ~ing ɪŋ ~s z
out|point ˌaʊt |'pɔɪnt ~pointed 'pɔɪnt ɪd -əd
‖ 'pɔɪn̩t əd ~pointing 'pɔɪnt ɪŋ ‖ 'pɔɪn̩t ɪŋ
~points 'pɔɪnts
outpoll ˌaʊt 'pəʊl ◂ →'pɒʊl ◂ ‖ -'poʊl ◂ ~ed d
~ing ɪŋ ~s z
outport 'aʊt pɔːt ‖ -pɔːrt -poʊrt ~s s
outpost 'aʊt pəʊst ‖ -poʊst ~s s
outpour v ˌaʊt 'pɔː ‖ -'pɔːr -'poʊr ~ed d
outpouring ˌaʊt 'pɔːr ɪŋ ‖ -'poʊr- ~s z
outpour n 'aʊt pɔː ‖ -pɔːr -poʊr ~s z
outpouring n 'aʊt ˌpɔːr ɪŋ ˌ·'·· ‖ -ˌpoʊr- ~s z
out|put n, v 'aʊt |pʊt ~puts pʊts ~putted
pʊt ɪd -əd ‖ pʊt̚ əd ~putting pʊt ɪŋ ‖ pʊt̚ ɪŋ
outrag|e v 'aʊt reɪdʒ ˌ·'· ~ed d ~es ɪz əz ~ing
ɪŋ
outrag|e n 'aʊt reɪdʒ ~es ɪz əz
outrageous ⑴aʊt 'reɪdʒ əs ~ly li ~ness nəs
nɪs
Outram (i) 'uːtr əm, (ii) 'aʊtr əm
outran ˌaʊt 'ræn
outrang|e ˌaʊt 'reɪndʒ ~ed d ~es ɪz əz ~ing
ɪŋ
out|rank ˌaʊt |'ræŋk ~ranked 'ræŋkt
~ranking 'ræŋk ɪŋ ~ranks 'ræŋks
outre, outré 'uːtr eɪ ‖ uː 'treɪ —Fr [u tʁe]
outreach n 'aʊt riːtʃ ~es ɪz əz
outreach v ˌaʊt 'riːtʃ ~ed t ~es ɪz əz ~ing ɪŋ
out|ride ˌaʊt |'raɪd ~ridden 'rɪd ᵊn ~rides
'raɪdz ~rode 'rəʊd ‖ 'roʊd
outrider 'aʊt ˌraɪd ə ‖ -ᵊr ~s z
outrigger 'aʊt ˌrɪg ə ‖ -ᵊr ~s z
outright adj 'aʊt raɪt
outright adv ⑴aʊt 'raɪt '··
outrival ˌaʊt 'raɪv ᵊl ~ed, ~led d ~ing, ~ling
ɪŋ ~s z
outrode ˌaʊt 'rəʊd ‖ -'roʊd
out|run ˌaʊt |'rʌn ~ran 'ræn ~running
'rʌn ɪŋ ~runs 'rʌnz
outrush 'aʊt rʌʃ ~es ɪz əz
out|sell ˌaʊt |'sel ~selling 'sel ɪŋ ~sells 'selz
~sold 'səʊld →'sɒʊld ‖ 'soʊld
outset 'aʊt set
out|shine ˌaʊt |'ʃaɪn ~shines 'ʃaɪnz ~shining
'ʃaɪn ɪŋ ~shone 'ʃɒn ‖ 'ʃoʊn (*)
out|shoot ˌaʊt| 'ʃuːt ◂ ~shooting 'ʃuːt̚ ɪŋ
~shoots 'ʃuːts ~shot 'ʃɒt ‖ 'ʃɑːt
outside ˌaʊt 'saɪd ◂ —stressed '·· whenever
contrasted with inside ~s z
ˌoutside 'broadcast; ˌoutside 'world
outsider ˌaʊt 'saɪd ə ‖ -ᵊr ~s z
outsize ˌaʊt 'saɪz ◂ '·· ~d d
outskirts 'aʊt skɜːts ‖ -skɜːts
out|smart ˌaʊt |'smaːt ‖ -|'smaːrt ~smarted
'smaːt ɪd -əd ‖ 'smaːrt̚ əd ~smarting
'smaːt ɪŋ ‖ 'smaːrt̚ ɪŋ ~smarts 'smaːts
‖ 'smaːrts
outsourc|e 'aʊt sɔːs ‖ -sɔːrs -soʊrs ~ed t ~es
ɪz əz ~ing ɪŋ

outspan, O~ n 'aʊt spæn ~s z
outspan v ˌaʊt 'spæn ~ned d ~ning ɪŋ ~s z
outspend ˌaʊt 'spend ~ing ɪŋ ~s z **outspent**
ˌaʊt 'spent
outspoken ⑴aʊt 'spəʊk ən ‖ -'spoʊk- ~ly li
~ness nəs nɪs
outspread v, adj ˌaʊt 'spred ◂ ~ing ɪŋ ~s z
outspread n 'aʊt spred
outstanding ⑴aʊt 'stænd ɪŋ ~ly li
outstare ⑴aʊt 'steə ‖ -'steᵊr -'stæᵊr ~d d ~s z
outstaring ˌaʊt 'steər ɪŋ ‖ -'ster ɪŋ -'stær-
outstation 'aʊt ˌsteɪʃ ᵊn ~ed d ~s z
outstay ˌaʊt 'steɪ ~ed d ~ing ɪŋ ~s z
outstretched ˌaʊt 'stretʃt ◂
outstrip ˌaʊt 'strɪp ~ped t ~ping ɪŋ ~s s
outswing 'aʊt swɪŋ ~er/s ə/z ‖ ᵊr/z ~s z
outta 'out of' 'aʊt ə ‖ 'aʊt̚ ə
out-take 'aʊt teɪk ~s s
outtalk ˌaʊt 'tɔːk ‖ -'tɑːk ~ed t ~ing ɪŋ ~s s
out-tray 'aʊt treɪ ~s z
outturn 'aʊt tɜːn ‖ -tɜːrn ~s z
out|vote ˌaʊt |'vəʊt ‖ -|'voʊt ~voted 'vəʊt ɪd
-əd ‖ 'voʊt̚ əd ~votes 'vəʊts ‖ 'voʊts
~voting 'vəʊt ɪŋ ‖ 'voʊt̚ ɪŋ
outward 'aʊt wəd ‖ -wᵊrd ~ly li ~ness nəs nɪs
~s z
ˌOutward 'Bound
out|wear ˌaʊt |'weə ‖ -|'weᵊr -'wæᵊr ~wears
'weəz ‖ 'weᵊrz 'wæᵊrz ~worn 'wɔːn ◂
‖ 'wɔːrn ◂ 'woʊrn
outweigh ˌaʊt 'weɪ ~ed d ~ing ɪŋ ~s z
out|wit ˌaʊt |'wɪt ~wits 'wɪts ~witted 'wɪt ɪd
-əd ‖ 'wɪt̚ əd ~witting 'wɪt ɪŋ ‖ 'wɪt̚ ɪŋ
outwith ˌaʊt 'wɪθ ◂ -'wɪð —Since this is
mainly a Scottish word, it tends to be said
with the θ of Scottish with
outwore ˌaʊt 'wɔː ‖ -'wɔːr -'woʊr
outwork n 'aʊt wɜːk ‖ -wɜːk ~er/s ə/z ‖ ᵊr/z
outworn ˌaʊt 'wɔːn ◂ ‖ -'wɔːrn ◂ -'woʊrn
ouzel 'uːz ᵊl ~s z
ouzo 'uːz əʊ ‖ -oʊ —Gk ['u zɔ]
ova 'əʊv ə ‖ 'oʊv ə
oval, Oval 'əʊv ᵊl ‖ 'oʊv- ~ly i ~ness nəs nɪs
~s z
ˌOval 'Office, '··, ·'·
Ovaltine tdmk 'əʊv ᵊl tiːn ‖ 'oʊv-
Ovambo əʊ 'væm bəʊ ‖ oʊ 'vɑːm boʊ
ovarian əʊ 'veər i‿ən ‖ oʊ 'ver- -'vær-
ovar|y 'əʊv ər |i ‖ 'oʊv- ~ies iz
ovate Welsh title 'ɒv ət -ɪt; 'əʊv eɪt ‖ 'ɑːv- ~s s
ovate 'egg-shaped' 'əʊv eɪt -ət, -ɪt ‖ 'oʊv- ~ly li
ovation əʊ 'veɪʃ ᵊn ‖ oʊ- ~s z
Ove Arup ˌəʊv 'ær əp ‖ ˌoʊv- -'er-
oven 'ʌv ᵊn ~s z
ovenbird 'ʌv ᵊn bɜːd →-ᵊm- ‖ -bɜːd ~s z
Ovenden (i) 'ɒv ᵊn dən ‖ 'ɑːv-, (ii) 'əʊv-
‖ 'oʊv-
ovenproof 'ʌv ᵊn pruːf →-ᵊm-, §-pruf
oven-ready ˌʌv ᵊn 'red i ◂
ˌoven-ˌready 'turkey
Ovens 'ʌv ᵊnz
ovenware 'ʌv ᵊn weə ‖ -wer -wær

over, Over ˈəʊv ə ‖ ˈoʊv ᵊr **~s** z
,**over and 'done with**
over- ˌəʊv ə ‖ ˌoʊv ᵊr —*but before a vowel sound,* ˌəʊv ər ‖ ˌoʊv ər
overabundance ˌəʊv ər ə ˈbʌnd ᵊn⸲s ˌ·ˌ·rə·· ‖ ˌoʊv ər⸲
overachiever ˌəʊv ər ə ˈtʃiːv ə ˌ·ˌ·rə·· ‖ ˌoʊv ər⸲ə ˈtʃiːv ᵊr **~s** z
overact ˌəʊv ər ˈækt ‖ ˌoʊv ər- **~ed** ɪd əd **~ing** ɪŋ **~s** s
overactive ˌəʊv ər ˈækt ɪv ‖ ˌoʊv ər-
overactivity ˌəʊv ər æk ˈtɪv ət i -ɪt i ‖ ˌoʊv ər æk ˈtɪv ət̬ i
overage *n* '*surplus*' ˈəʊv ər ɪdʒ ‖ ˈoʊv-
overage *adj* '*too old*' ˌəʊv ər ˈeɪdʒ ◀ ‖ ˌoʊv ər-
overall *n* ˈəʊv ər ɔːl ‖ ˈoʊv ər- -ɑːl **~s** z
overall *adj, adv* ˌəʊv ər ˈɔːl ◀ ‖ ˌoʊv ər- -ˈɑːl
overambitious ˌəʊv ər æm ˈbɪʃ əs ◀ ‖ ˌoʊv ər- **~ly** li
overanxiety ˌəʊv ər æŋ ˈzaɪ ət i ˌ·ˌ·æŋg-, ˌ·ɪt, i ‖ ˌoʊv ər æŋ ˈzaɪ ət̬ i
overanxious ˌəʊv ər ˈæŋk ʃəs ◀ ‖ ˌoʊv ər- **~ly** li **~ness** nəs nɪs
overarch ˌəʊv ər ˈɑːtʃ ‖ ˌoʊv ər ˈɑːrtʃ **~ed** t **~es** ɪz əz **~ing** ɪŋ
overarm ˈəʊv ər ɑːm ‖ ˈoʊv ər ɑːrm
over|awe ˌəʊv ər ˈɔː ‖ ˌoʊv ər- -ˈɑː **~awed** ɔːd ‖ ɑːd **~awes** ˈɔːz ‖ ˈɑːz **~awing** ˈɔː ɪŋ ‖ ˈɔː ɪŋ ‖ ˈɑː
overbalanc|e ˌəʊv ə ˈbæl ən⸲s ‖ ˌoʊv ᵊr- **~ed** t **~es** ɪz əz **~ing** ɪŋ
over|bear ˌəʊv ə |ˈbeə ‖ ˌoʊv ᵊr |ˈbeᵊr -ˈbæᵊr **~bearing/ly** ˈbeər ɪŋ /li ‖ ˈber ɪŋ /li ˈbær- **~bore** ˈbɔː ‖ ˈbɔːr ˈboʊr **~borne** ˈbɔːn ‖ ˈbɔːrn ˈboʊrn
overbid *n* ˈəʊv ə bɪd ‖ ˈoʊv ᵊr- **~s** z
overbid *v* ˌəʊv ə ˈbɪd ‖ ˌoʊv ᵊr- **~ding** ɪŋ **~s** z
overbite ˈəʊv ə baɪt ‖ ˈoʊv ᵊr-
over|blow *v* ˌəʊv ə |ˈbləʊ ‖ ˌoʊv ᵊr |ˈbloʊ ˌ·· **~blew** ˈbluː **~blowing** ˈbləʊ ɪŋ ‖ ˈbloʊ ɪŋ **~blown** ˈbləʊn ‖ ˈbloʊn **~blows** ˈbləʊz ‖ ˈbloʊz
overboard ˈəʊv ə bɔːd ˌ·ˌ· ‖ ˈoʊv ᵊr bɔːrd -boʊrd
overbook ˌəʊv ə ˈbʊk §-ˈbuːk ‖ ˌoʊv ᵊr- **~ed** t **~ing** ɪŋ **~s** s
overbor... —*see* **overbear**
overbridg|e ˈəʊv ə brɪdʒ ‖ ˈoʊv ᵊr- **~es** ɪz əz
overburden *v* ˌəʊv ə ˈbɜːd ᵊn ‖ ˌoʊv ᵊr ˈbɜːd ᵊn **~ed** d **~ing** ɪŋ **~s** z
overburden *n* ˈəʊv ə ˌbɜːd ᵊn ‖ ˈoʊv ᵊr ˌbɜːd ᵊn **~s** z
overcall *v* ˌəʊv ə ˈkɔːl ‖ ˌoʊv ᵊr- -ˈkɑːl **~ed** d **~ing** ɪŋ **~s** z
overcall *n* ˈəʊv ə kɔːl ‖ ˈoʊv ᵊr- -kɑːl **~s** z
overcame ˌəʊv ə ˈkeɪm ‖ ˌoʊv ᵊr-
overcapacity ˌəʊv ə kə ˈpæs ət i -ɪt i ‖ ˌoʊv ᵊr kə ˈpæs ət̬ i
overcast *adj* ˌəʊv ə ˈkɑːst ◀ §-ˈkæst, ˈ··· ‖ ˌoʊv ᵊr ˈkæst ◀
overcast *n* ˈəʊv ə kɑːst §-kæst ‖ ˈoʊv ᵊr kæst
overcautious ˌəʊv ə ˈkɔːʃ əs ◀ ‖ ˌoʊv ᵊr- -ˈkɑːʃ-

overcharg|e *v* ˌəʊv ə ˈtʃɑːdʒ ‖ ˌoʊv ᵊr ˈtʃɑːrdʒ **~ed** d **~es** ɪz əz **~ing** ɪŋ
overcharg|e *n* ˈəʊv ə tʃɑːdʒ ‖ ˈoʊv ᵊr tʃɑːrdʒ **~es** ɪz əz
overcloud ˌəʊv ə ˈklaʊd ‖ ˌoʊv ᵊr- **~ed** ɪd əd **~ing** ɪŋ **~s** z
overcoat ˈəʊv ə kəʊt ‖ ˈoʊv ᵊr koʊt **~s** s
over|come ˌəʊv ə |ˈkʌm ‖ ˌoʊv ᵊr- **~came** ˈkeɪm **~comes** ˈkʌmz **~coming** ˈkʌm ɪŋ
overcom|mit ˌəʊv ə kə |ˈmɪt ‖ ˌoʊv ᵊr- **~mits** ˈmɪts **~mitted** ˈmɪt ɪd -əd ‖ ˈmɪt̬ əd **~mitting** ˈmɪt ɪŋ ‖ ˈmɪt̬ ɪŋ
overcompen|sate ˌəʊv ə ˈkɒmp ən ⸲seɪt -en- ‖ ˌoʊv ᵊr ˈkɑːmp- **~sated** seɪt ɪd -əd ‖ seɪt̬ əd **~sates** seɪts **~sating** seɪt ɪŋ ‖ seɪt̬ ɪŋ
overcompensation ˌəʊv ə ˌkɒmp ən ˈseɪʃ ᵊn -ˌen- ‖ ˌoʊv ᵊr ˌkɑːmp- **~s** z
overconfid|ence ˌəʊv ə ˈkɒn fɪd |ən⸲s -fəd- ‖ ˌoʊv ᵊr ˈkɑːn- **~ent/ly** ənt /li
overcook ˌəʊv ə ˈkʊk ◀ §-ˈkuːk ‖ ˌoʊv ᵊr- **~ed** t **~ing** ɪŋ **~s** s
overcrop ˌəʊv ə ˈkrɒp ‖ ˌoʊv ᵊr ˈkrɑːp **~ped** t **~ping** ɪŋ **~s** s
overcrowd ˌəʊv ə ˈkraʊd ‖ ˌoʊv ᵊr- **~ed** ɪd əd **~ing** ɪŋ **~s** z
overdevelop ˌəʊv ə dɪ ˈvel əp -ə də-, §-ə diː- ‖ ˌoʊv ᵊr- **~ed** t **~ing** ɪŋ **~ment** mənt **~s** s
over|do ˌəʊv ə |ˈduː ‖ ˌoʊv ᵊr- **~did** ˈdɪd **~does** ˈdʌz **~done** ˈdʌn ◀ **~doing** ˈduː ɪŋ
overdos|e *n* ˈəʊv ə dəʊs §-dəʊz ‖ ˈoʊv ᵊr doʊs **~es** ɪz əz
overdos|e *v* ˌəʊv ə ˈdəʊs §-ˈdəʊz ‖ ˌoʊv ᵊr ˈdoʊs **~ed** t **~es** ɪz əz **~ing** ɪŋ
overdraft ˈəʊv ə drɑːft §-dræft ‖ ˈoʊv ᵊr dræft **~s** s
over|draw ˌəʊv ə| ˈdrɔː ‖ ˌoʊv ᵊr| -ˈdrɑː, ˌ··· **~drawing** ˈdrɔː ɪŋ ‖ ˈdrɔː ɪŋ ˈdrɑː- **~drawn** ˈdrɔːn ◀ ‖ ˈdrɑːn **~draws** ˈdrɔːz ‖ ˈdrɑːz **~drew** ˈdruː
overdress ˌəʊv ə ˈdres ‖ ˌoʊv ᵊr- **~ed** t ◀ **~es** ɪz əz **~ing** ɪŋ
overdrew ˌəʊv ə ˈdruː ‖ ˌoʊv ᵊr- ˌ···
overdrive *n* ˈəʊv ə draɪv ‖ ˈoʊv ᵊr-
overdue ˌəʊv ə ˈdjuː ◀ →§-ˈdʒuː ‖ ˌoʊv ᵊr ˈduː ◀ -ˈdjuː
,**overdue 'bills**
over-easy ˌəʊv ər ˈiːz i ◀ ‖ ˌoʊv ᵊr-
over|eat ˌəʊv ər| ˈiːt ‖ ˌoʊv ᵊr| ˈiːt **~ate** ˈet ˈeɪt ‖ ˈeɪt **~eaten** ˈiːt ᵊn **~eating** ˈiːt ɪŋ ‖ ˈiːt̬ ɪŋ **~eats** ˈiːts
overegg ˌəʊv ər ˈeg ‖ ˌoʊv ᵊr- **~ed** d **~ing** ɪŋ **~s** z
overempha|sis ˌəʊv ər ˈemᵖf ə |sɪs ‖ ˌoʊv ᵊr- **~ses** siːz
overemphasis|e, overemphasiz|e ˌəʊv ər ˈemᵖf ə saɪz ‖ ˌoʊv ᵊr- **~ed** d **~es** ɪz əz **~ing** ɪŋ
overesti|mate *v* ˌəʊv ər ˈest ɪ |meɪt -ˈ·ə- ‖ ˌoʊv ᵊr- **~mated** meɪt ɪd -əd ‖ meɪt̬ əd **~mates** meɪts **~mating** meɪt ɪŋ ‖ meɪt̬ ɪŋ
overestimate *n* ˌəʊv ər ˈest ɪm ət -ˈ·əm-, -ɪt; -ɪ meɪt, -ə meɪt ‖ ˌoʊv ᵊr- **~s** s

O

overex|cite ˌəʊv ər ɪk |ˈsaɪt -ek'·, -ək'·, ˌ·rɪk'·,
ˌ·rək'· ‖ ˌoʊv ər- **~cited** ˈsaɪt ɪd -əd ‖ ˈsaɪt̬ əd
~citement ˈsaɪt mənt **~cites** ˈsaɪts **~citing**
ˈsaɪt ɪŋ ‖ ˈsaɪt̬ ɪŋ

overe|xert ˌəʊv ər ɪg |ˈzɜːt -eg'·, -əg'·, -ɪk'·,
-ek'·, -ək'·, ˌ·rɪg'·, ˌ·rəg'· ‖ ˌoʊv ər ɪg |ˈzɜːt
~xerted ˈzɜːt ɪd -əd ‖ ˈzɜːt̬ əd   **~xerting**
ˈzɜːt ɪŋ ‖ ˈzɜːt̬ ɪŋ **~xerts** ˈzɜːts ‖ ˈzɜːts

overexertion ˌəʊv ər ɪg ˈzɜːʃ ᵊn -eg'·, -əg'·,
-ɪk'·, -ek'·, -ək'·, ˌ·rɪg'·, ˌ·rəg'·
‖ ˌoʊv ər ɪg ˈzɜːʃ ᵊn **~s** z

overexpos|e ˌəʊv ər ɪk ˈspəʊz -ek'·, -ək'·,
ˌ·rɪk'·, ˌ·rək'· ‖ ˌoʊv ər ɪk ˈspoʊz **~ed** d **~es** ɪz
əz **~ing** ɪŋ

overexposure ˌəʊv ər ɪk ˈspəʊʒ ə -ek'··, -ək'··,
ˌ·rɪk'·, ˌ·rək'· ‖ ˌoʊv ər ɪk ˈspoʊʒ ᵊr **~s** z

overextend ˌəʊv ər ɪk ˈstend -ek'·, -ək'·, ˌ·rɪk'·,
ˌ·rək'· ‖ ˌoʊv ər- **~ed** ɪd ◂ əd **~ing** ɪŋ **~s** z

over|feed ˌəʊv ə |ˈfiːd ‖ ˌoʊv ᵊr- **~fed** ˈfed
~feeding ˈfiːd ɪŋ **~feeds** ˈfiːdz

overfill ˌəʊv ə ˈfɪl ◂ ‖ ˌoʊv ᵊr- **~ed** d **~ing** ɪŋ
~s z

overfish ˌəʊv ə ˈfɪʃ ◂ ‖ ˌoʊv ᵊr- **~ed** t **~es** ɪz əz
~ing ɪŋ

over|flew ˌəʊv ə |ˈfluː ‖ ˌoʊv ᵊr- **~flies** ˈflaɪz

overflight ˈəʊv ə flaɪt ‖ ˈoʊv ᵊr- **~s** s

overflow v ˌəʊv ə ˈfləʊ ‖ ˌoʊv ᵊr ˈfloʊ **~ed** d
~ing ɪŋ **~s** z

overflow n ˈəʊv ə fləʊ ‖ ˈoʊv ᵊr floʊ **~s** z

over|fly ˌəʊv ə |ˈflaɪ ◂ ‖ ˌoʊv ᵊr- **~flew** ˈfluː
~flies ˈflaɪz **~flown** ˈfləʊn ‖ ˈfloʊn **~flying**
ˈflaɪ ɪŋ

overfond ˌəʊv ə ˈfɒnd ◂ ‖ ˌoʊv ᵊr ˈfɑːnd ◂

overgarment ˈəʊv ə ˌɡɑːm ənt
‖ ˈoʊv ᵊr ˌɡɑːrm ənt **~s** s

overgeneralis... —*see* **overgeneraliz...**

overgeneralization
ˌəʊv ə ˌdʒen ᵊr ᵊl aɪ ˈzeɪʃ ᵊn ˌʲəl ɪ-
‖ ˌoʊv ᵊr ˌdʒen ᵊr ᵊl ə ˈzeɪʃ ᵊn

overgeneraliz|e ˌəʊv ə ˈdʒen ᵊr ə laɪz
‖ ˌoʊv ᵊr- **~ed** d **~es** ɪz əz **~ing** ɪŋ

overgraz|e ˌəʊv ə ˈɡreɪz ‖ ˌoʊv ᵊr- **~ed** d **~es**
ɪz əz **~ing** ɪŋ

overground ˈəʊv ə ɡraʊnd ‖ ˈoʊv ᵊr-

overgrown ˌəʊv ə ˈɡrəʊn ◂ ‖ ˌoʊv ᵊr ˈɡroʊn ◂
ˌovergrown ˈgarden

overgrowth ˈəʊv ə ɡrəʊθ ‖ ˈoʊv ᵊr ɡroʊθ

overhand ˈəʊv ə hænd ‖ ˈoʊv ᵊr-

over|hang v ˌəʊv ə |ˈhæŋ ‖ ˌoʊv ᵊr- **~hanging**
ˈhæŋ ɪŋ ◂ **~hangs** ˈhæŋz **~hung** ˈhʌŋ ◂

overhang n ˈəʊv ə hæŋ ‖ ˈoʊv ᵊr- **~s** z

overhast|y ˌəʊv ə ˈheɪst |i ‖ ˌoʊv ᵊr- **~ily** ɪ li
əl i **~iness** i nəs i nɪs

overhaul v ˌəʊv ə ˈhɔːl ‖ ˌoʊv ᵊr- -ˈhɑːl **~ed** d
~ing ɪŋ **~s** z

overhaul n ˈəʊv ə hɔːl ‖ ˈoʊv ᵊr- -hɑːl **~s** z

overhead adj, adv ˌəʊv ə ˈhed ◂ ‖ ˌoʊv ᵊr-
ˌoverhead ˈcamshaft; ˌoverhead
proˈjector

overhead n ˈəʊv ə hed ‖ ˈoʊv ᵊr- **~s** z

over|hear ˌəʊv ə |ˈhɪə ‖ ˌoʊv ᵊr |ˈhɪᵊr **~heard**
ˈhɜːd ◂ ‖ ˈhɜːd ◂ (!) **~hearing** ˈhɪər ɪŋ
‖ ˈhɪr ɪŋ **~hears** ˈhɪəz ‖ ˈhɪᵊrz

over|heat ˌəʊv ə |ˈhiːt ‖ ˌoʊv ᵊr- **~heated**
ˈhiːt ɪd -əd ‖ ˈhiːt̬ əd **~heating** ˈhiːt ɪŋ
‖ ˈhiːt̬ ɪŋ **~heats** ˈhiːts

overhung ˌəʊv ə ˈhʌŋ ◂ ‖ ˌoʊv ᵊr-

overindulg|e ˌəʊv ər ɪn ˈdʌldʒ ‖ ˌoʊv ər- **~ed**
d **~ence** ən'ts **~ent/ly** ənt /li **~es** ɪz əz **~ing**
ɪŋ

overjoyed ˌəʊv ə ˈdʒɔɪd ◂ ‖ ˌoʊv ᵊr-

overkill ˈəʊv ə kɪl ‖ ˈoʊv ᵊr-

overladen ˌəʊv ə ˈleɪd ᵊn ◂ ‖ ˌoʊv ᵊr-

overlaid ˌəʊv ə ˈleɪd ◂ ‖ ˌoʊv ᵊr-

overland ˈəʊv ə lænd ˌ· ·ˈ· ◂ ‖ ˈoʊv ᵊr- **~er/s** ə/z
‖ ᵊr/z

overlap n ˈəʊv ə læp ‖ ˈoʊv ᵊr- **~s** s

overlap v ˌəʊv ə ˈlæp ‖ ˌoʊv ᵊr- **~ped** t **~ping**
ɪŋ **~s** s

overlay n ˈəʊv ə leɪ ‖ ˈoʊv ᵊr- **~s** z

over|lay v ˌəʊv ə |ˈleɪ ‖ ˌoʊv ᵊr- **~laid** ˈleɪd
~laying ˈleɪ ɪŋ **~lays** ˈleɪz

overleaf ˌəʊv ə ˈliːf ˈ· ·· ‖ ˈoʊv ᵊr liːf

over|leap ˌəʊv ə |ˈliːp ‖ ˌoʊv ᵊr- **~leaped**
ˈlept ˈliːpt ‖ ˈliːpt **~leaping** ˈliːp ɪŋ **~leaps**
ˈliːps **~leapt** ˈlept

over|lie ˌəʊv ə |ˈlaɪ ‖ ˌoʊv ᵊr- **~lain** ˈleɪn **~lay**
ˈleɪ **~lies** ˈlaɪz **~lying** ˈlaɪ ɪŋ

overload v ˌəʊv ə ˈləʊd ‖ ˌoʊv ᵊr ˈloʊd **~ed** ɪd
əd **~ing** ɪŋ **~s** z

overload n ˈəʊv ə ləʊd ‖ ˈoʊv ᵊr loʊd **~s** z

overlong ˌəʊv ə ˈlɒŋ ◂ ‖ ˌoʊv ᵊr ˈlɔːŋ -ˈlɑːŋ

overlook v ˌəʊv ə ˈlʊk §-ˈluːk ‖ ˌoʊv ᵊr- **~ed** t
~ing ɪŋ **~s** s

overlook n ˈəʊv ə lʊk §-luːk ‖ ˈoʊv ᵊr- **~s** s

overlord ˈəʊv ə lɔːd ‖ ˈoʊv ᵊr lɔːrd **~s** z **~ship**
ʃɪp

overly ˈəʊv ə li ‖ ˈoʊv ᵊr-

overlying ˌəʊv ə ˈlaɪ ɪŋ ◂ ‖ ˌoʊv ᵊr-

overman v ˌəʊv ə ˈmæn ‖ ˌoʊv ᵊr- **~ned** d
~ning nɪŋ **~s** z

overmast|er ˌəʊv ə ˈmɑːst |ə §-ˈmæst-
‖ ˌoʊv ᵊr ˈmæst |ᵊr **~ered** əd ‖ ᵊrd **~ering**
ᵊr ɪŋ **~ers** əz ‖ ᵊrz

overmuch ˌəʊv ə ˈmʌtʃ ◂ ‖ ˌoʊv ᵊr-

overnight adj, adv ˌəʊv ə ˈnaɪt ◂ ‖ ˌoʊv ᵊr-
ˌovernight ˈbag

overoptimistic ˌəʊv ər ˌɒpt ɪ ˈmɪst ɪk ◂ -ˌ·ə-
‖ ˌoʊv ər ˌɑːpt- **~ally** ᵊl i

overpaid ˌəʊv ə ˈpeɪd ◂ ‖ ˌoʊv ᵊr-

overpass ˈəʊv ə pɑːs §-pæs ‖ ˈoʊv ᵊr pæs **~es**
ɪz əz

over|pay v, ˌəʊv ə |ˈpeɪ ‖ ˌoʊv ᵊr- **~paid** ˈpeɪd ◂
~paying ˈpeɪ ɪŋ **~ment/s** mənt/s **~pays**
ˈpeɪz

overplay ˌəʊv ə ˈpleɪ ‖ ˌoʊv ᵊr- **~ed** d **~ing** ɪŋ
~s z

overplus ˈəʊv ə plʌs ‖ ˈoʊv ᵊr-

overpopu|late ˌəʊv ə ˈpɒp ju |leɪt -ˈ·jə-
‖ ˌoʊv ᵊr ˈpɑːp jə- **~lated** leɪt ɪd -əd ‖ leɪt̬ əd
~lates leɪts **~lating** leɪt ɪŋ ‖ leɪt̬ ɪŋ

overpopulation ˌəʊv ə ˌpɒp ju ˈleɪʃ ᵊn -jə'·-
‖ ˌoʊv ᵊr ˌpɑːp jə-

overpower ˌəʊv ə ˈpaʊ ə ‖ ˌoʊv ᵊr ˈpaʊ ᵊr **~ed**
d **overpowering/ly** ˌəʊv ə ˈpaʊ ər ɪŋ /li
‖ ˌoʊv ᵊr ˈpaʊ ᵊr ɪŋ /li **~s** z

O

overpressure ˈəʊv ə ˌpreʃ ə ‖ ˈoʊv ᵊr ˌpreʃ ᵊr
overpriced ˌəʊv ə ˈpraɪst ◂ ‖ ˌoʊv ᵊr-
over|print v ˌəʊv ə |ˈprɪnt ‖ ˌoʊv ᵊr- **~printed**
 ˈprɪnt ɪd -əd ‖ ˈprɪnt̬ əd **~printing** ˈprɪnt ɪŋ
 ‖ ˈprɪnt̬ ɪŋ **~prints** ˈprɪnts
overprint n ˈəʊv ə prɪnt ‖ ˈoʊv ᵊr- **~s** s
overproduc|e ˌəʊv ə prə ˈdjuːs
 §-ˈduːs §→ˈdʒuːs ‖ ˌoʊv ᵊr prə ˈduːs -ˈdjuːs
 ~ed t **~es** ɪz əz **~ing** ɪŋ
overproduction ˌəʊv ə prə ˈdʌk ʃᵊn ‖ ˌoʊv ᵊr-
overproof ˌəʊv ə ˈpruːf ‖ ˌoʊv ᵊr-
overprotect ˌəʊv ə prəʊ ˈtekt ‖ ˌoʊv ᵊr prə-
 ~ed ɪd əd **~ing** ɪŋ **~s** s
overprotective ˌəʊv ə prəʊ ˈtekt ɪv ◂
 ‖ ˌoʊv ᵊr prə-
overqualified ˌəʊv ə ˈkwɒl ɪ faɪd ◂ -ˈ-ə-
 ‖ ˌoʊv ᵊr ˈkwɑːl-
overran ˌəʊv ə ˈræn ‖ ˌoʊv ᵊr-
over|rate ˌəʊv ə |ˈreɪt ‖ ˌoʊv ᵊr- **~rated**
 ˈreɪt ɪd -əd ‖ ˈreɪt̬ əd ◂ **~rates** ˈreɪts
 ~rating ˈreɪt ɪŋ ‖ ˈreɪt̬ ɪŋ
overreach ˌəʊv ə ˈriːtʃ ‖ ˌoʊv ᵊr- **~ed** t **~es** ɪz
 əz **~ing** ɪŋ
overreact ˌəʊv ə ri ˈækt ‖ ˌoʊv ᵊr- **~ed** ɪd əd
 ~ing ɪŋ **~s** s
overreaction ˌəʊv ə ri ˈæk ʃᵊn ‖ ˌoʊv ᵊr- **~s** z
override n ˈəʊv ə raɪd ‖ ˈoʊv ᵊr- **~s** z
over|ride v ˌəʊv ə |ˈraɪd ‖ ˌoʊv ᵊr- **~ridden**
 ˈrɪd ᵊn **~rides** ˈraɪdz **~riding/ly** ˈraɪd ɪŋ /li
 ~rode ˈrəʊd ‖ ˈroʊd
overrider ˈəʊv ə raɪd ə ‖ ˈoʊv ᵊr raɪd ᵊr **~s** z
overripe ˌəʊv ə ˈraɪp ‖ ˌoʊv ᵊr- **~ness** nəs nɪs
overrul|e ˌəʊv ə ˈruːl ‖ ˌoʊv ᵊr- **~ed** d **~es** z
 ~ing ɪŋ
overrun n ˈəʊv ə rʌn ‖ ˈoʊv ᵊr- **~s** z
over|run v ˌəʊv ə |ˈrʌn ‖ ˌoʊv ᵊr- **~ran** ˈræn
 ~running ˈrʌn ɪŋ **~runs** ˈrʌnz
oversaw ˌəʊv ə ˈsɔː ‖ ˌoʊv ᵊr- -ˈsɑː
oversea ˌəʊv ə ˈsiː ◂ ‖ ˌoʊv ᵊr- **~s** z
 overseas ˈpostɪŋ
over|see v ˌəʊv ə |ˈsiː ‖ ˌoʊv ᵊr- **~saw** ˈsɔː ‖ ˈsɑː
 ~seeing ˈsiː ɪŋ **~seen** ˈsiːn **~sees** ˈsiːz
overseer ˈəʊv ə sɪə ˈ·ˌsiː ə ‖ ˈoʊv ᵊr sɪr
 ˈ·ˌsiː ᵊr **~s** z
over|sell ˌəʊv ə |ˈsel ‖ ˌoʊv ᵊr- **~selling**
 ˈsel ɪŋ **~sells** ˈselz **~sold** ˈsəʊld →ˈsɒʊld
 ‖ ˈsoʊld
oversensitive ˌəʊv ə ˈsenˢs ət ɪv -ɪt ɪv
 ‖ ˌoʊv ᵊr ˈsenˢs ət̬ ɪv
oversensitivity ˌəʊv ə ˌsenˢs ə ˈtɪv ət i -ɪ'-,
 -ɪt i ‖ ˌoʊv ᵊr ˌsenˢs ə ˈtɪv ət̬ i
oversew ˈəʊv ə səʊ ˌ·ˈ· ‖ ˈoʊv ᵊr soʊ **~ed** d
 ~ing ɪŋ **~n** n **~s** z
oversexed ˌəʊv ə ˈsekst ◂ ‖ ˌoʊv ᵊr-
overshadow ˌəʊv ə ˈʃæd əʊ ‖ ˌoʊv ᵊr ˈʃæd oʊ
 ~ed d **~ing** ɪŋ **~s** z
overshoe ˈəʊv ə ʃuː ‖ ˈoʊv ᵊr- **~s** z
overshoot n ˈəʊv ə ʃuːt ‖ ˈoʊv ᵊr- **~s** s
over|shoot v ˌəʊv ə |ˈʃuːt ‖ ˌoʊv ᵊr-
 ~shooting ˈʃuːt ɪŋ ‖ ˈʃuːt̬ ɪŋ **~shoots** ˈʃuːts
 ~shot ˈʃɒt ◂ ‖ ˈʃɑːt ◂
overside ˈəʊv ə saɪd ‖ ˈoʊv ᵊr-
oversight ˈəʊv ə saɪt ‖ ˈoʊv ᵊr- **~s** s

oversimplification ˌəʊv ə ˌsɪmp lɪf ɪ ˈkeɪʃ ᵊn
 -ˌ·ləf-, §-ə'-- ‖ ˌoʊv ᵊr- **~s** z
oversimpli|fy ˌəʊv ə ˈsɪmp lɪ |faɪ -ˈ-lə-
 ‖ ˌoʊv ᵊr- **~fied** faɪd **~fies** faɪz **~fying** faɪ ɪŋ
oversize adj ˌəʊv ə ˈsaɪz ◂ ‖ ˌoʊv ᵊr- **~d** d
 oversize ˈboots
over|sleep v ˌəʊv ə |ˈsliːp ‖ ˌoʊv ᵊr-
 ~sleeping ˈsliːp ɪŋ **~sleeps** ˈsliːps **~slept**
 ˈslept
oversold ˌəʊv ə ˈsəʊld →-ˈsɒʊld
 ‖ ˌoʊv ᵊr ˈsoʊld
overspend n ˈəʊv ə spend ‖ ˈoʊv ᵊr- **~s** z
over|spend v ˌəʊv ə |ˈspend ‖ ˌoʊv ᵊr-
 ~spending ˈspend ɪŋ **~spends** ˈspendz
 ~spent ˈspent
overspill n ˈəʊv ə spɪl ‖ ˈoʊv ᵊr- **~s** z
overstaff ˌəʊv ə ˈstɑːf §-ˈstæf ‖ ˌoʊv ᵊr ˈstæf
 ~ed t **~ing** ɪŋ **~s** s
over|state ˌəʊv ə |ˈsteɪt ‖ ˌoʊv ᵊr- **~stated**
 ˈsteɪt ɪd -əd ‖ ˈsteɪt̬ əd **~states** ˈsteɪts
 ~stating ˈsteɪt ɪŋ ‖ ˈsteɪt̬ ɪŋ
overstatement ˌəʊv ə ˈsteɪt mənt ˈ·ˌ··
 ‖ ˈoʊv ᵊr ˌsteɪt- **~s** s
overstay ˌəʊv ə ˈsteɪ ‖ ˌoʊv ᵊr- **~ed** d **~er/s**
 ə/z ‖ ᵊr/z **~ing** ɪŋ **~s** z
oversteer v ˌəʊv ə ˈstɪə ‖ ˌoʊv ᵊr ˈstɪᵊr **~ed** d
 oversteering ˌəʊv ə ˈstɪər ɪŋ
 ‖ ˌoʊv ᵊr ˈstɪr ɪŋ **~s** z
oversteer n ˈəʊv ə stɪə ‖ ˈoʊv ᵊr stɪr
overstep v ˌəʊv ə ˈstep ‖ ˌoʊv ᵊr- **~ped** t
 ~ping ɪŋ **~s** s
overstock v ˌəʊv ə ˈstɒk ‖ ˌoʊv ᵊr ˈstɑːk **~ed** t
 ~ing ɪŋ **~s** s
overstrain v ˌəʊv ə ˈstreɪn ‖ ˌoʊv ᵊr- **~ed** d
 ~ing ɪŋ **~s** z
overstrain n ˈəʊv ə streɪn ˌ·ˈ· ‖ ˈoʊv ᵊr-
overstretch ˌəʊv ə ˈstretʃ ‖ ˌoʊv ᵊr- **~ed** t **~es**
 ɪz əz **~ing** ɪŋ
overstrung ˌəʊv ə ˈstrʌŋ ◂ ˈ·ˌ·· ‖ ˌoʊv ᵊr-
overstuffed ˌəʊv ə ˈstʌft ◂ ‖ ˌoʊv ᵊr-
oversubscrib|e ˌəʊv ə səb ˈskraɪb §-sʌb'·
 ‖ ˌoʊv ᵊr- **~ed** d **~es** z **~ing** ɪŋ
oversup|ply v ˌəʊv ə sə |ˈplaɪ ‖ ˌoʊv ᵊr-
 ~plied ˈplaɪd **~plies** ˈplaɪz **~plying** ˈplaɪ ɪŋ
oversupply n ˌəʊv ə sə ˈplaɪ ˈ·ˌ··
 ‖ ˈoʊv ᵊr sə ˌplaɪ
overt əʊ ˈvɜːt ˈəʊv ɜːt ‖ oʊ ˈvɜːt oʊv ɜːt **~ly** li
overtake ˌəʊv ə ˈteɪk ‖ ˌoʊv ᵊr- **~taken**
 ˈteɪk ən ◂ **~takes** ˈteɪks **~taking** ˈteɪk ɪŋ
 ~took ˈtʊk §ˈtuːk
overtax v ˌəʊv ə ˈtæks ‖ ˌoʊv ᵊr- **~ed** t **~es** ɪz
 əz **~ing** ɪŋ
over-the-counter ˌəʊv ə ðə ˈkaʊnt ə ◂
 ‖ ˌoʊv ᵊr ðə ˈkaʊnt̬ ᵊr ◂
over-the-top ˌəʊv ə ðə ˈtɒp ◂
 ‖ ˌoʊv ᵊr ðə ˈtɑːp ◂
overthrow n ˈəʊv ə θrəʊ ‖ ˈoʊv ᵊr θroʊ **~s** z
over|throw v ˌəʊv ə |ˈθrəʊ ◂ ‖ ˌoʊv ᵊr |ˈθroʊ
 ~threw ˈθruː **~throwing** ˈθrəʊ ɪŋ ‖ ˈθroʊ ɪŋ
 ~thrown ˈθrəʊn ◂ §ˈθrəʊ ən ‖ ˈθroʊn ◂
 ~throws ˈθrəʊz ‖ ˈθroʊz
overthrust ˈəʊv ə θrʌst ‖ ˈoʊv ᵊr- **~s** s

O

overtime *n, adv* 'əʊv ə taɪm ‖ 'oʊv ᵊr-
  'overtime ban
overtire ˌəʊv ə 'taɪ‿ə ◀ ‖ ˌoʊv ᵊr 'taɪ‿ᵊr ◀ **~d** d
  overtiring ˌəʊv ə 'taɪ‿ᵊr ɪŋ
  ‖ ˌoʊv ᵊr 'taɪ‿ᵊr ɪŋ **~s** z
Overton 'əʊv ət ən ‖ 'oʊv ᵊrt ᵊn
overtone 'əʊv ə təʊn ‖ 'oʊv ᵊr toʊn **~s** z
overtook ˌəʊv ə 'tʊk §-'tuːk ‖ ˌoʊv ᵊr-
overtop ˌəʊv ə 'tɒp ‖ ˌoʊv ᵊr 'tɑːp **~ped** t
  ~ping ɪŋ **~s** s
overtrick 'əʊv ə trɪk ‖ 'oʊv ᵊr- **~s** s
overtrump ˌəʊv ə 'trʌmp ‖ ˌoʊv ᵊr- **~ed** t
  ~ing ɪŋ **~s** s
overture 'əʊv ə tjʊə -tʃʊə, -tʃə ‖ 'oʊv ᵊr tʃʊr
  -tʃᵊr, -tjʊr **~s** z
overturn *v* ˌəʊv ə 'tɜːn ‖ ˌoʊv ᵊr 'tɜːn **~ed** d
  ~ing ɪŋ **~s** z
overus|e *v* ˌəʊv ə 'juːz ‖ ˌoʊv ᵊr- **~ed** d **~es** ɪz
  əz **~ing** ɪŋ
overuse *n* ˌəʊv ə 'juːs ‖ ˌoʊv ᵊr-
overvalu|e ˌəʊv ə 'væl juː ‖ ˌoʊv ᵊr- **~ed** d
  ~es z **~ing** ɪŋ
overview 'əʊv ə vjuː ‖ 'oʊv ᵊr- **~s** z
overweening ˌəʊv ə 'wiːn ɪŋ ◀ ‖ ˌoʊv ᵊr- **~ly**
  li
overweight *n* 'əʊv ə weɪt ‖ 'oʊv ᵊr-
over|weight *v, adj* ˌəʊv ə |'weɪt ◀ ‖ ˌoʊv ᵊr-
  ~weighted 'weɪt ɪd -əd ‖ 'weɪt̬ əd
  ~weighting 'weɪt ɪŋ ‖ 'weɪt̬ ɪŋ **~weights**
  'weɪts
overwhelm ˌəʊv ə 'welm -'hwelm
  ‖ ˌoʊv ᵊr 'hwelm **~ed** d **~ing/ly** ɪŋ /li **~s** z
over|wind ˌəʊv ə 'waɪnd ‖ ˌoʊv ᵊr- **~winding**
  'waɪnd ɪŋ **~winds** 'waɪndz **~wound** 'waʊnd
overwint|er ˌəʊv ə 'wɪnt |ə ‖ ˌoʊv ᵊr 'wɪnt̬ |ᵊr
  ~ered əd ‖ ᵊrd **~ering** ᵊr ɪŋ ‖ ər ɪŋ **~ers** əz
  ‖ ᵊrz
overwork *n* ˌəʊv ə 'wɜːk '··· ‖ ˌoʊv ᵊr 'wɜːk
overwork *v* ˌəʊv ə 'wɜːk ‖ ˌoʊv ᵊr 'wɜːk **~ed** t
  ~ing ɪŋ **~s** s
overwound ˌəʊv ə 'waʊnd ◀ ‖ ˌoʊv ᵊr-
over|write ˌəʊv ə |'raɪt ‖ ˌoʊv ᵊr- **~writes**
  'raɪts **~writing** 'raɪt ɪŋ ‖ 'raɪt̬ ɪŋ **~written**
  'rɪt ᵊn **~wrote** 'rəʊt ‖ 'roʊt
overwrought ˌəʊv ə 'rɔːt ◀ ‖ ˌoʊv ᵊr- -'rɑːt
overzealous ˌəʊv ə 'zel əs ◀ ‖ ˌoʊv ᵊr- **~ly** li
  ~ness nəs nɪs
Ovett 'əʊv et əʊ 'vet ‖ 'oʊv et oʊ 'vet
Ovid *(i)* 'ɒv ɪd §-əd ‖ 'ɑːv-; *(ii)* 'əʊv ɪd §-əd
  ‖ 'oʊv- — *The Latin poet is known as (i); the
  American place name and personal name is
  (ii).*
Ovidian ɒ 'vɪd i ən əʊ- ‖ oʊ- ɑː-
oviduct 'əʊv ɪ dʌkt §-ə- ‖ 'oʊv ə- **~s** s
Oviedo ɒv i 'eɪd əʊ ˌəʊv- ‖ ˌoʊv i 'eɪd oʊ
  —*Sp* [o 'βje ðo]
oviform 'əʊv ɪ fɔːm §-ə- ‖ 'oʊv ə fɔːrm
ovine 'əʊv aɪn ‖ 'oʊv-
Oving 'əʊv ɪŋ ‖ 'oʊv-
Ovingdean 'əʊv ɪŋ diːn -ɒv- ‖ 'oʊv-
oviparous əʊ 'vɪp ər əs ‖ oʊ- **~ly** li
ovipositor ˌəʊv ɪ 'pɒz ɪt ə §ˌ-ə-, §-ət ə
  ‖ ˌoʊv ə 'pɑːz ət̬ ᵊr '··· ··· **~s** z

ovoid 'əʊv ɔɪd ‖ 'oʊv- **~s** z
ovo|lo 'əʊv ə |ləʊ ‖ 'oʊv ə |loʊ **~li** liː
ovoviviparity ˌəʊv əʊ ˌvɪv ɪ 'pær ət i -ə'--,
  -ət i ‖ ˌoʊv oʊ ˌvɪv ə 'pær ət̬ i
ovoviviparous ˌəʊv əʊ vɪ 'vɪp ᵊr əs ◀ -və'--,
  -vaɪ'-- ‖ ˌoʊv oʊ vaɪ-
ovular 'ɒv jʊl ə 'əʊv-, -jəl- ‖ 'ɑːv jəl ᵊr 'oʊv-
ovu|late *v* 'ɒv ju |leɪt 'əʊv-, -jə- ‖ 'ɑːv jə- 'oʊv-
  ~lated leɪt ɪd -əd ‖ leɪt̬ əd **~lates** leɪts
  ~lating leɪt ɪŋ ‖ leɪt̬ ɪŋ
ovulation ˌɒv ju 'leɪʃ ᵊn ˌəʊv-, -jə- ‖ ˌɑːv jə-
  ˌoʊv- **~s** z
ovule 'ɒv juːl 'əʊv- ‖ 'ɑːv- 'oʊv- **~s** z
ov|um 'əʊv |əm ‖ 'oʊv |əm **~a** ə
ow aʊ
Owain 'əʊ aɪn ‖ 'oʊ- —*Welsh* ['ə waɪn, 'o-]
Owbridge 'əʊ brɪdʒ ‖ 'oʊ-
owe əʊ ‖ oʊ (= *oh, O*) **owed** əʊd ‖ oʊd **owes**
  əʊz ‖ oʊz **owing** 'əʊ ɪŋ ‖ 'oʊ ɪŋ
Owen 'əʊ ɪn -ən ‖ 'oʊ ən
Owens 'əʊ ɪnz -ənz ‖ 'oʊ ənz
Ower *(i)* 'aʊ ə, *(ii)* 'əʊ ə ‖ 'oʊ ᵊr
  —*Usually (i).* **~s** z
owie 'aʊ i **~s** z
owing 'əʊ ɪŋ ‖ 'oʊ ɪŋ
owl aʊl **owls** aʊlz
owlet 'aʊl ət -ɪt, -et **~s** s
owlish 'aʊl ɪʃ **~ly** li **~ness** nəs nɪs
owl-like 'aʊl laɪk
own əʊn ‖ oʊn **owned** əʊnd ‖ oʊnd **owning**
  'əʊn ɪŋ ‖ 'oʊn ɪŋ **owns** əʊnz ‖ oʊnz
  ˌon your 'own; ˌown 'goal
own-brand ˌəʊn 'brænd ◀ →ˌ-, ˌəʊm-, '·· ‖ ˌoʊn-
  ~s z
owner 'əʊn ə ‖ 'oʊn ᵊr **~s** z
owner-driver ˌəʊn ə 'draɪv ə
  ‖ ˌoʊn ᵊr 'draɪv ᵊr **~s** z
owner-occu|pied ˌəʊn ər 'ɒk ju |paɪd ◀ -'jə-
  ‖ ˌoʊn ər 'ɑːk jə- **~pier/s** paɪ ə/z ‖ paɪ ᵊr/z
owner-operator ˌəʊn ər 'ɒp ə reɪt ə
  ‖ ˌoʊn ᵊr 'ɑːp ə reɪt̬ ᵊr **~s** z
ownership 'əʊn ə ʃɪp ‖ 'oʊn ᵊr-
own-label ˌəʊn 'leɪb ᵊl ◀ ‖ ˌoʊn-
owt aʊt əʊt —*This is a non-standard variant of*
  aught
ox ɒks ‖ ɑːks **oxen** 'ɒks ᵊn ‖ 'ɑːks ᵊn **ox's**
  'ɒks ɪz -əz ‖ 'ɑːks əz
oxalate 'ɒks ə leɪt →-ᵊl eɪt ‖ 'ɑːks-
oxalic ˌ(ˌ)ɒk 'sæl ɪk ‖ ˌ(ˌ)ɑːk-
oxalis ˌ(ˌ)ɒk 'sæl ɪs -'sɑːl-, 'ɒks əl-, §-əs
  ‖ ɑːk 'sæl əs 'ɑːks əl-
oxblood 'ɒks blʌd ‖ 'ɑːks-
oxbow 'ɒks bəʊ ‖ 'ɑːks boʊ **~s** z
Oxbridge 'ɒks brɪdʒ ‖ 'ɑːks-
oxcart 'ɒks kaːt ‖ 'ɑːks kaːrt **~s** s
oxen 'ɒks ᵊn ‖ 'ɑːks ᵊn
Oxenden 'ɒks ᵊnd ən ‖ 'ɑːks-
Oxenford 'ɒks ᵊn fɔːd -fəd ‖ 'ɑːks ᵊn fɔːrd -fᵊrd
Oxenham 'ɒks ᵊn əm ‖ 'ɑːks-
Oxenholme 'ɒks ᵊn həʊm ‖ 'ɑːks ᵊn hoʊm
oxer 'ɒks ə ‖ 'ɑːks ᵊr **~s** z
oxeye 'ɒks aɪ ‖ 'ɑːks- **~s** z
  ˌoxeye 'daisy

Oxfam 'ɒks fæm ‖ 'ɑːks-
Oxford, o~ 'ɒks fəd ‖ 'ɑːks fᵊrd **~shire** ʃə ʃɪə
‖ ʃᵊr ʃɪr **~s, ~'s** z
‚Oxford 'Circus; ‚Oxford 'English; 'Oxford ‚movement; 'Oxford Street
Oxhey 'ɒks i -heɪ ‖ 'ɑːks-
oxhide 'ɒks haɪd ‖ 'ɑːks-
oxidant 'ɒks ɪd ənt -əd- ‖ 'ɑːks- *(usually = occident)* **~s** s
oxidas|e 'ɒks ɪ deɪz -ə-, -deɪs ‖ 'ɑːks- **~es** ɪz əz
oxidation ‚ɒks ɪ 'deɪʃ ᵊn -ə- ‖ ‚ɑːks- **~s** z
oxidative 'ɒks ɪ deɪt ɪv '·ə- ‖ 'ɑːks ə deɪt̬ ɪv
oxide 'ɒks aɪd ‖ 'ɑːks- **~s** z
oxidis... —*see* **oxidiz...**
oxidization ‚ɒks ɪd aɪ 'zeɪʃ ᵊn ‚·əd-, -ɪ'·- ‖ ‚ɑːks əd ə- **~s** z
oxidiz|e 'ɒks ɪ daɪz -ə- ‖ 'ɑːks ə- **~ed** d **~es** ɪz əz **~ing** ɪŋ
oxime 'ɒks iːm -aɪm ‖ 'ɑːks- **~s** z
Oxley 'ɒks li ‖ 'ɑːks-
oxlip 'ɒks lɪp ‖ 'ɑːks- **~s** s
Oxnard *(i)* 'ɒks nəd ‖ 'ɑːks nᵊrd, *(ii)* -nɑːd ‖ -nɑːrd —*The place in CA is (ii).*
Oxo *tdmk* 'ɒks əʊ ‖ 'ɑːks oʊ
Oxon 'ɒks ɒn -ᵊn, ɒk 'sɒn ‖ 'ɑːks ɑːn
Oxonian ɒk 'səʊn i ən ‖ ɑːk 'soʊn- **~s** z
oxonium ɒk 'səʊn i əm ‖ ɑːk 'soʊn-
oxpecker 'ɒks ‚pek ə ‖ 'ɑːks ‚pek ᵊr **~s** z
Oxshott 'ɒk ʃɒt 'ɒks- ‖ 'ɑːk ʃɑːt
oxtail 'ɒks terᵊl ‖ 'ɑːks- **~s** z
Oxted 'ɒkst ɪd -əd, -ed ‖ 'ɑːkst əd
Oxton 'ɒkst ən ‖ 'ɑːkst-
oxtongue 'ɒks tʌŋ §-tɒŋ ‖ 'ɑːks- **~s** z
Oxus 'ɒks əs ‖ 'ɑːks əs
oxy- *comb. form with stress-neutral suffix* ‖ɒks i ‖ ‖ɑːks i — **oxychloride** ‚ɒks i 'klɔːr aɪd ‖ ‚ɑːks i 'klɔːr aɪd -'klour- *with stress-imposing suffix* ɒk 'sɪ+ ‖ ɑːk 'sɪ+ — **oxypathy** ɒk 'sɪp əθ i ‖ ɑːk-
oxyacetylene ‚ɒks i‚ə 'set ə liːn ◂ -'·ɪ-, -lɪn; -ᵊl iːn, -ɪn ‖ ‚ɑːks i ə 'set̬ ᵊl iːn ◂ -ən
Oxydol *tdmk* 'ɒks ɪ dɒl ‖ 'ɑːks ə dɑːl -dɑːl
oxygen 'ɒks ɪdʒ ən -ədʒ- ‖ 'ɑːks-
'oxygen mask; 'oxygen tent

oxyge|nate 'ɒks ɪdʒ ə |neɪt '·ədʒ-; ɒk 'sɪdʒ-
‖ 'ɑːks- **~nated** neɪt ɪd -əd ‖ neɪt̬ əd **~nates** neɪts **~nating** neɪt ɪŋ ‖ neɪt̬ ɪŋ
oxygenation ‚ɒks ɪdʒ ə 'neɪʃ ᵊn ɒk ‚sɪdʒ ə- ‖ ‚ɑːks- **~s** z
oxygenis|e, oxygeniz|e 'ɒks ɪdʒ ə naɪz '·ədʒ- ‖ 'ɑːks- **~ed** d **~es** ɪz əz **~ing** ɪŋ
oxymor|on ‚ɒks i 'mɔːr ɒn -ən ‖ ‚ɑːks i 'mɔːr |ɑːn -'moʊr- **~a** ə **~ons** ɒnz ənz ‖ ɑːnz
Oxyrhynchus ‚ɒks i 'rɪŋk əs ‖ ‚ɑːks-
oxytocic ‚ɒks i 'təʊs ɪk ◂ ‖ ‚ɑːks i 'toʊs ɪk ◂ **~s** s
oxytocin ‚ɒks i 'təʊs ɪn §-ᵊn ‖ ‚ɑːks i 'toʊs ᵊn
oxytone 'ɒks i təʊn ‖ 'ɑːks i toʊn **~s** z
oyer 'ɔɪ ə ‖ 'ɔɪ ᵊr
oyes, oyez əʊ 'jez -'jes, -'jeɪ, '·· ‖ oʊ-
oyster 'ɔɪst ə ‖ -ᵊr **~s** z
'oyster bed
oyster-catcher 'ɔɪst ə ‚kætʃ ə §-‚ketʃ- ‖ -ᵊr ‚kætʃ ᵊr **~s** z
Oystermouth 'ɔɪst ə maʊθ ‖ -ᵊr-
oz, oz. *sing.* aʊn‖s, *pl* 'aʊn‖s ɪz -əz
Oz ɒz ‖ ɑːz
Ozalid *tdmk* 'ɒz əl ɪd '·əʊ- ‖ 'ɑːz-
Ozanne əʊ 'zæn ‖ oʊ-
Ozark 'əʊz ɑːk ‖ 'oʊz ɑːrk **~s** s
ozocerite əʊ 'zəʊk ə raɪt -'zəʊs-; ‚əʊz əʊ 'sɪər aɪt ‖ oʊ 'zoʊk- -'zoʊs-; ‚oʊz oʊ 'sɪr aɪt
ozokerite əʊ 'zəʊk ə raɪt ‚əʊz əʊ 'kɪər aɪt ‖ oʊ 'zoʊk- ‚oʊz oʊ 'kɪr aɪt
ozone 'əʊz əʊn əʊ 'zəʊn ‖ 'oʊz oʊn oʊ 'zoʊn
'ozone ‚layer, ·'· ‚··
ozone-friendly ‚əʊz əʊn 'frend li ◂ ‖ ‚oʊz oʊn-
ozonic əʊ 'zɒn ɪk ‖ oʊ 'zɑːn ɪk
ozoniferous ‚əʊz əʊ 'nɪf ᵊr əs ‖ ‚oʊz ə-
ozonosphere əʊ 'zəʊn ə sfɪə -'zɒn- ‖ oʊ 'zoʊn ə sfɪr -'zɑːn-
ozs, ozs. 'aʊn‖s ɪz -əz
Ozymandias ‚ɒz i 'mænd i‚əs ‚·ə-, -æs ‖ ‚ɑːz-
Ozzie 'ɒz i ‖ 'ɑːz i

O

Pp

P

P, p piː **P's, p's, Ps** piːz —*Communications code
name:* Papa
p *'penny, pence'* piː —*See note at* **pence**
pa, Pa pɑː ‖ pɔː **pas, Pa's** pɑːz ‖ pɔːz
PA ˌpiː 'eɪ —*but see also* Pennsylvania
pa'anga pɑː 'æŋ ə -gə ‖ -'ɑːŋ-
Pablo 'pæb ləʊ ‖ 'pɑːb loʊ —*Sp* ['pa βlo]
pablum 'pæb ləm
pabulum 'pæb jʊl əm -jəl- ‖ -jəl-
PABX ˌpiː eɪ biː 'eks
paca 'pɑːk ə 'pæk ə ~**s** z
pace *n, v* **paced** peɪst **paces** 'peɪs ɪz -əz
    pacing 'peɪs ɪŋ
    'pace ˌbowler
pace *prep 'with due deference to'* 'peɪs i
    'pɑːtʃ eɪ, 'pɑːk-
Pace *family name* peɪs
pacemaker 'peɪs ˌmeɪk ə ‖ -ᵊr ~**s** z
pacer 'peɪs ə ‖ -ᵊr ~**s** z
pacesetter 'peɪs ˌset ə ‖ -ˌset ᵊr ~**s** z
pac|ey 'peɪs |i ~**ier** i ə ‖ i ᵊr ~**iest** i ɪst i əst
    ~**ily** ɪ li əl i

Pachelbel 'pæk ᵊl bel 'pæx-, 'pɑːk-, 'pɑːx-
    ‖ 'pɑːk- —*Ger* [pa 'xɛl bᵊl; 'pax ɛl-, -bɛl]
pachinko pə 'tʃɪŋk əʊ ‖ -oʊ —*Jp* [pa 'tɕiɲ ko]
pachisi pə 'tʃiːz i pæ-, -'tʃiːs-
Pachuco pə 'tʃuːk əʊ ‖ -oʊ ~**s** z —*Sp*
    [pa 'tʃu ko]
pachyderm 'pæk i dɜːm ‖ -dɜːm ~**s** z
pachydermatous ˌpæk i 'dɜːm ət əs əs ◂
    ‖ -'dɜːm ət̬ əs ◂
pacific, P~ pə 'sɪf ɪk ~**ally** ᵊl‿i
    Pa͵cific ͵North'west; Pa͵cific 'Ocean;
    Pa͵cific 'rim
pacification ˌpæs ɪf ɪ 'keɪʃ ᵊn ˌ-əf-, §-ə'-‿~**s** z
pacificatory ˌpæs ɪf ɪ 'keɪt ər i ◂ ˌ-əf-, -ə'-‿-,
    pə 'sɪf ɪk ət̬ ər i ‖ pə 'sɪf ɪk ə tɔːr i -toʊr i
pacificist pə 'sɪf ɪs ɪst pæ-, -əs-, §-əst ~**s** s
pacifier 'pæs ɪ faɪ ə ˌ-ə- ‖ faɪ ᵊr ~**s** z
pacifism 'pæs ɪ ˌfɪz əm -ə-
pacifist 'pæs ɪf ɪst -əf-, §-əst ~**s** s
paci|fy 'pæs ɪ |faɪ -ə- ~**fied** faɪd ~**fies** faɪz
    ~**fying** faɪ ɪŋ
Pacino pə 'tʃiːn əʊ ‖ -oʊ

pack pæk **packed** pækt *(= pact)* **packing**
  'pæk ɪŋ **packs** pæks
   'pack ˌanimal; 'pack ice; 'packing case
packag|e 'pæk ɪdʒ **~ed** d **~es** ɪz əz **~ing** ɪŋ
  'package deal; ˌpackage 'holiday;
  'package store; 'package tour, ˌ· · '.
Packard 'pæk ɑːd -ᵊrd ‖ -ᵊrd
packed-out ˌpækt 'aʊt ◂
packer, P~ 'pæk ə ‖ -ᵊr **~s** z
pack|et 'pæk |ɪt §-ət ‖ -|ət **~eted** ɪt ɪd §ət-, -əd
  ‖ ət̬ əd **~eting** ɪt ɪŋ §ət- ‖ ət̬ ɪŋ **~ets** ɪts §əts
  ‖ əts
packet-switching 'pæk ɪt ˌswɪtʃ ɪŋ §-ət-
packhors|e 'pæk hɔːs ‖ -hɔːrs **~es** ɪz əz
pack|man 'pæk| mən -mæn **~men** mən men
packsaddle 'pæk ˌsæd ᵊl **~s** z
Pac-man *tdmk* 'pæk mæn
pact pækt **pacts** pækts
pac|y 'peɪs |i **~ier** i ə ‖ i ᵊr **~iest** i ɪst i əst **~ily**
  ɪ li əl i
pad pæd **padded** 'pæd ɪd -əd **padding**
  'pæd ɪŋ **pads** pædz
Padang 'pɑː dæŋ -dɑːŋ
Padarn 'pæd ᵊn -ɑːn ‖ -ᵊrn -ɑːrn —*Welsh*
  ['pa darn]
padauk pə 'daʊk
Padbury 'pæd bər i →'pæb- ‖ -ˌber i
padd... —*see* **pad**
Paddick 'pæd ɪk
paddie... —*see* **paddy**
Paddington 'pæd ɪŋ tən
paddl|e 'pæd ᵊl **~ed** d **~es** z **~ing** ɪŋ
  'paddle boat; 'paddle ˌsteamer; 'paddling
  pool; 'paddle wheel
paddock, P~ 'pæd ək **~s** s
paddly, Paddly 'pæd |i **~ies, ~y's** iz
  'paddy field; 'paddy ˌwagon
paddymelon 'pæd i ˌmel ən **~s** z
paddywhack 'pæd i wæk -hwæk ‖ -hwæk **~s** s
pademelon 'pæd i ˌmel ən **~s** z
Paderborn ˌpɑː d ə 'bɔːn ˌ· · · ‖ -ᵊr 'bɔːrn —*Ger*
  [pa: dɐ 'bɔʁn]
Paderewski ˌpæd ə 'ref ski -'rev- ‖ ˌpɑːd-
  —*Polish* [pa dɛ 'rɛf ski]
Padfield 'pæd fiːᵊld
Padiham 'pæd i əm
padlock 'pæd lɒk ‖ -lɑːk **~ed** t **~ing** ɪŋ **~s** s
Padmore 'pæd mɔː →'pæb- ‖ -mɔːr -moʊr
Padraic 'pɑːdr ɪk -ɪg
Padraig 'pɑːdr ɪg —*Irish* ['pɑ rɪg]
padre 'pɑːdr i -eɪ **~s** z
padron|e pə 'drəʊn |i pæ-, -eɪ ‖ -'droʊn |i **~es**
  iz **~i** iː
padsaw 'pæd sɔː ‖ -sɑː **~s** z
Padstow 'pæd stəʊ ‖ -stoʊ
Padu|a 'pæd ju |ə ‖ 'pædʒ u |ə —*It* Padova
  ['pa: do va] **~an/s** ən/z
Paducah pə 'duːk ə -'djuːk-
paean 'piː ən **~s** z
paederast 'ped ə ræst 'piːd- **~s** s
paederastic ˌped ə 'ræst ɪk ◂ ˌpiːd- **~ally** ᵊl̩ i
paederasty 'ped ə ræst i 'piːd-
paediatric ˌpiːd i 'ætr ɪk ◂ **~ally** ᵊl̩ i **~s** s

paediatrician ˌpiːd i ə 'trɪʃ ᵊn **~s** z
paedophile 'piːd əʊ faɪᵊl ‖ 'ped ə- 'piːd- **~s** z
paedophilia ˌpiːd əʊ 'fɪl i ə ‖ ˌped ə- ˌpiːd-
paedophiliac ˌpiːd əʊ 'fɪl i æk ‖ ˌped ə- ˌpiːd-
  ~s s
paella paɪ 'el ə ‖ pɑː- -'eɪl jə, -'eɪ- —*Sp*
  [pa 'e ʎa, -ja] **~s** z
paeon 'piː ən ‖ -ɑːn **~s** z
paeon|y 'piːən |i **~ies** iz
pagan 'peɪg ən **~dom** dəm **~s** z
Paganini ˌpæg ə 'niːn i ‖ ˌpɑːg- —*It*
  [pa ga 'ni: ni]
paganism 'peɪg ən ˌɪz əm
page, Page peɪdʒ **paged** peɪdʒd **pages,**
  Page's 'peɪdʒ ɪz -əz **paging** 'peɪdʒ ɪŋ
  'page boy
pageant 'pædʒ ənt **~s** s
pageantr|y 'pædʒ əntr |i **~ies** iz
page-jack 'peɪdʒ dʒæk **~ing** ɪŋ
pager 'peɪdʒ ə ‖ -ᵊr **~s** z
Paget 'pædʒ ɪt -ət **~'s** s
  'Paget's di ˌsease
Pagham 'pæg əm
paginate 'pædʒ ɪ |neɪt -ə- **~nated** neɪt ɪd -əd
  ‖ neɪt̬ əd **~nates** neɪts **~nating** neɪt ɪŋ
  ‖ neɪt̬ ɪŋ
pagination ˌpædʒ ɪ 'neɪʃ ᵊn -ə- **~s** z
Paglia 'pɑːl jə 'pæg li ə
Pagliacci ˌpæl i 'ɑːtʃ i ‖ ˌpɑːl 'jɑːtʃ i —*It*
  [paʎ 'ʎat tʃi]
Pagnell 'pæg nᵊl
Pagnol pæn 'jɒl ‖ -'joʊl —*Fr* [pa 'njɔl]
pagoda pə 'gəʊd ə ‖ -'goʊd ə **~s** z
  pa'goda tree
Pago Pago ˌpɑːg əʊ 'pɑːg əʊ
  ˌpæŋ gəʊ 'pæŋ gəʊ, ˌpeɪg əʊ 'peɪg əʊ
  ‖ ˌpɑːŋ goʊ 'pɑːŋ goʊ ˌpɑːg oʊ 'pɑːg oʊ
pah pɑː
Pahang pə 'hʌŋ -'hæŋ ‖ -'hɑːŋ
Pahari pə 'hɑːr i
Pahlavi 'pɑːl əv i
paid peɪd
paid-up ˌpeɪd 'ʌp ◂
  ˌpaid-up 'members
Paige peɪdʒ
paigle 'peɪg ᵊl **~s** z
Paignton 'peɪnt ən ‖ -ᵊn
pail peɪᵊl **pails** peɪᵊlz
pailful 'peɪl fʊl **~s** z
paillass|e 'pæl i æs ˌ· '·· ‖ pæl 'jæs **~es** ɪz əz
paillette ₍ᵢ₎pæl 'jet ˌpæl i 'et ‖ paɪ 'jet —*Fr*
  [pa jɛt] **~s** s
pain, Pain peɪn **pained** peɪnd **paining**
  'peɪn ɪŋ **pains** peɪnz
pain au chocolat ˌpæn əʊ 'ʃɒk ə lɑː
  ‖ -oʊ ˌʃɑːk ə 'lɑː —*Fr* [pɛ̃ o ʃɔ kɔ la]
Paine peɪn
painful 'peɪn fᵊl -fʊl **~ly** i **~ness** nəs nɪs
painkill|er 'peɪn ˌkɪl |ə →'peɪn- ‖ -ᵊr **~ers** əz
  ᵊrz **~ing** ɪŋ
painless 'peɪn ləs -lɪs **~ly** li **~ness** nəs nɪs
painstaking 'peɪnz ˌteɪk ɪŋ **~ly** li
Painswick 'peɪnz wɪk

paint peɪnt **painted** ˈpeɪnt ɪd -əd ‖ ˈpeɪnt̬ əd
  painting/s ˈpeɪnt ɪŋ/z ‖ ˈpeɪnt̬ ɪŋ/z **paints**
  peɪnts
paintball ˈpeɪnt bɔːl ‖ -baːl **~er/s** ə/z ‖ ᵊr/z
  ~ing ɪŋ
paintbox ˈpeɪnt bɒks ‖ -baːks **~es** ɪz əz
paintbrush ˈpeɪnt brʌʃ **~es** ɪz əz
painter, P~ ˈpeɪnt ə ‖ ˈpeɪnt̬ ᵊr **~s** z
painterly ˈpeɪnt ə li →-ᵊl i ‖ ˈpeɪnt̬ ᵊr li
paintwork ˈpeɪnt wɜːk ‖ -wɜːk
pair peə ‖ peᵊr pæᵊr **paired** peəd ‖ peᵊrd
  pæᵊrd **pairing** ˈpeər ɪŋ ‖ ˈper ɪŋ ˈpær- **pairs**
  peəz ‖ peᵊrz pæᵊrz
pais|a ˈpaɪs aː **~as** aːz **~e** eɪ
Paish peɪʃ
Paisley, p~ ˈpeɪz li **~s, ~'s** z
Paiute ˌpaɪ ˈuːt -ˈjuːt, ˈ·· **~s** s

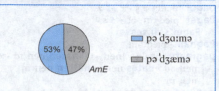

PAJAMAS

53% pə ˈdʒɑːmə
47% pə ˈdʒæmə
AmE

pajama pə ˈdʒɑːm ə △bə- ‖ -ˈdʒæm ə
  — *Preference poll, AmE:* -ˈdʒɑːm- *53%,*
  -ˈdʒæm- *47%.* **~ed** d **~s** z
pakapoo ˌpæk ə ˈpuː ◄ **~s** z
  ˌpakapoo ˈticket, ·ˈ·ˌ· ··
pak-choi ˌpæk ˈtʃɔɪ ˌpaːk- ˌbɒk- ‖ ˌpaːk- ˌbaːk-
pakeha, P~ ˈpaːk i haː -ə-, ˌ·ˈ· **~s** z
Pakenham *place in Suffolk* ˈpeɪk ən ̩əm
Pakenham *family name* ˈpæk ən ̩əm
Paki ˈpæk i ˈpaːk i **~s** z
Paki-bashing ˈpæk i ˌbæʃ ɪŋ ˈpaːk-
Pakistan ˌpaːk ɪ ˈstaːn ˌpæk-, -ə- ‖ ˈpæk ɪ stæn
  ˈpaːk ɪ staːn, ˌ·ˈ· *(*)*
Pakistani ˌpaːk ɪ ˈstaːn i ◄ -ə-, -ˈstæn-
  ‖ ˌpæk ɪ ˈstæn i ◄ ˌpaːk ɪ ˈstaːn i **~s** z
pakora pə ˈkɔːr ə ‖ -ˈkoʊr-
pal, Pal, PAL pæl **palled** pæld **palling** ˈpæl ɪŋ
  pals pælz
palac|e ˈpæl əs -ɪs **~es** ɪz əz
  ˌpalace ˌrevoˈlution
paladin ˈpæl əd ɪn §-ən **~s** z
Palaearctic ˌpæl i ˈaːkt ɪk ◄ ˌpeɪl-
  ‖ ˌpeɪl i ˈaːrkt ɪk ◄ -ˈaːrt̬-
palaeo- *comb. form with stress-neutral suffix*
  ¦pæl i əʊ ¦peɪl- ‖ ¦peɪl i oʊ —
  palaeomagnetism
  ˌpæl i əʊ ˈmæg nə ˌtɪz əm ˌpeɪl-, -ˈnɪ-
  ‖ ˌpeɪl i oʊ- *with stress-imposing suffix*
  ˌpæl i ˈɒ + ˌpeɪl- ‖ ˌpeɪl i ˈaː + —
  palaeographer ˌpæl i ˈɒg rəf ə ˌpeɪl-
  ‖ ˌpeɪl i ˈaːg rəf ᵊr **~s** z
palaeobotany ˌpæl i əʊ ˈbɒt ən i ˌpeɪl-
  ‖ ˌpeɪl i oʊ ˈbaːt ᵊn ̩i
Palaeocene, p~ ˈpæl i əʊ siːn ‖ ˈpeɪl i ə-
palaeographic ˌpæl i əʊ ˈgræf ɪk ◄ ˌpeɪl-
  ‖ ˌpeɪl i ə-

palaeography ˌpæl i ˈɒg rəf i ˌpeɪl-
  ‖ ˌpeɪl i ˈaːg-
Palaeolithic, p~ ˌpæl i əʊ ˈlɪθ ɪk ◄ ˌpeɪl-
  ‖ ˌpeɪl i ə-
palaeontological ˌpæl i ˌɒnt ə ˈlɒdʒ ɪk ᵊl
  ˌpeɪl- ‖ ˌpeɪl i ˌaːnt̬ ᵊl ˈaːdʒ ɪk ᵊl
palaeontolog|ist ˌpæl i ɒn ˈtɒl ədʒ |ɪst ˌpeɪl-,
  §-əst ‖ ˌpeɪl i aːn ˈtaːl ədʒ |əst **~ists** ɪsts §əsts
  ~y i
Palaeozoic, p~ ˌpæl i əʊ ˈzəʊ ɪk ◄ ˌpeɪl-
  ‖ ˌpeɪl i ə ˈzoʊ ɪk ◄
palaes|tra pə ˈlaɪs |trə -ˈliːs-, -ˈles- ‖ -ˈles-
  ~trae triː traɪ **~tras** trəz
palais *sing* .ˈpæl eɪ -i ‖ pæ ˈleɪ **palais** *pl*
  ˈpæl eɪz ‖ pæ ˈleɪz
  ˌpalais de ˈdanse ‖ ·ˌ·-də ˈdaːnᵗs -ˈdɒ̃s,
  §-ˈdænᵗs‖ də ˈdænᵗs
palankeen, palanquin ˌpæl ən ˈkiːn →-əŋ- **~s**
  z
palatability ˌpæl ət ə ˈbɪl ət i ˌ·ɪt-, -ɪt i
  ‖ ˌpæl ət̬ ə ˈbɪl ət̬ i
palatab|le ˈpæl ət əb |ᵊl -ɪt əb- ‖ -ət̬ əb-
  ~leness ᵊl nəs -nɪs **~ly** li
palatal ˈpæl ət ᵊl pə ˈleɪt ᵊl ‖ -ət̬ ᵊl —*In*
  phonetics ˈ···, *in anatomy (BrE) sometimes* ·ˈ··
  ~ly i **~s** z
palatalis... —*see* **palataliz...**
palatalization ˌpæl ət əl aɪ ˈzeɪʃ ᵊn pə ˌleɪt-,
  -ɪˈ-- ‖ -ət̬ ᵊl ə- **~s** z
palataliz|e ˈpæl ət ə laɪz pə ˈleɪt-, →-ᵊl aɪz
  ‖ -ət̬ ᵊl aɪz **~ed** d **~es** ɪz əz **~ing** ɪŋ
palate ˈpæl ət -ɪt **~s** s
palatial pə ˈleɪʃ ᵊl -ˈleɪʃ i ᵊl **~ly** i
palatinate, P~ pə ˈlæt ɪn ət -ən-, -ɪt ‖ -ᵊn ət **~s**
  s
palatine, P~ ˈpæl ə taɪn **~s** z
palatoalveolar ˌpæl ət əʊˌælv i ˈəʊl ə ◄
  -æl ˈviː əl ə ◄ ‖ -ət̬ oʊ æl ˈviː əl ᵊr **~s** z
palatogram ˈpæl ət əʊ græm ‖ -ət̬ ə- **~s** z
palatographic ˌpæl ət əʊ ˈgræf ɪk ◄ ‖ -ət̬ ə-
  ~ally ᵊl i
palatography ˌpæl ə ˈtɒg rəf i ‖ -ˈtaːg-
Palau pə ˈlaʊ paː-
palaver pə ˈlaːv ə ‖ -ᵊr -ˈlæv- **~s** z
Palawan pə ˈlaː wən
palazz|o pə ˈlæts |əʊ ‖ -ˈlaːts |oʊ **~i** iː **~os**
  əʊz ‖ oʊz —*It* [pa ˈlat tso]
pale peᵊl *(= pail)* **paler** ˈpeᵊl ə ‖ -ᵊr **palest**
  ˈpeᵊl ɪst -əst
  ˌpale ˈale
Pale *in eastern Ireland* peᵊl
Pale *place in Bosnia* ˈpaːl eɪ —*Serbian* [ˈpa le]
Palearctic ˌpæl i ˈaːkt ɪk ◄ ˌpeɪl-
  ‖ ˌpeɪl i ˈaːrkt ɪk ◄ -ˈaːrt̬-
palefac|e ˈpeᵊl feɪs **~es** ɪz əz
pale|ly ˈpeᵊl |li **~ness** nəs nɪs
paleo-, palaeo- *comb. form with stress-neutral*
  suffix ¦pæl i əʊ ¦peɪl- ‖ ¦peɪl i oʊ —
  paleomagnetism ˌpæl i əʊ ˈmæg nə ˌtɪz əm
  ˌpeɪl-, -ˈnɪ- ‖ ˌpeɪl i oʊ- *with stress-imposing*
  suffix ˌpæl i ˈɒ + ˌpeɪl- ‖ ˌpeɪl i ˈaː + —
  paleographer ˌpæl i ˈɒg rəf ə ˌpeɪl-
  ‖ ˌpeɪl i ˈaːg rəf ᵊr **~s** z

paleobotany ˌpæl i əʊ ˈbɒt ən i ˌpeɪl-
‖ ˌpeɪl i oʊ ˈbɑːt ᵊn‿i
Paleocene, p~ ˈpæl i əʊ siːn ˈpeɪl- ‖ ˈpeɪl i ə-
paleographic ˌpæl i əʊ ˈgræf ɪk ◄ ˌpeɪl-
‖ ˌpeɪl i ə-
paleography ˌpæl i ˈɒg rəf i ˌpeɪl-
‖ ˌpeɪl i ˈɑːg-
Paleolithic, p~ ˌpæl i əʊ ˈlɪθ ɪk ◄ ˌpeɪl-
‖ ˌpeɪl i ə-
paleontological ˌpæl i ˌɒnt ə ˈlɒdʒ ɪk ᵊl ˌpeɪl-
‖ ˌpeɪl i ˌɑːnt ᵊl ˈɑːdʒ ɪk ᵊl
paleontolog|ist ˌpæl i ɒn ˈtɒl ədʒ ɪst ˌpeɪl-,
§-əst ‖ ˌpeɪl i ɑːn ˈtɑːl ədʒ ǀəst **~ists** ɪsts §əsts
~y i
paleotype ˈpæl i əʊ taɪp ˈpeɪl- ‖ ˈpeɪl i oʊ-
Paleozoic, p~ ˌpæl i əʊ ˈzəʊ ɪk ◄ ˌpeɪl-
‖ ˌpeɪl i ə ˈzoʊ ɪk ◄
Palermo pə ˈleəm əʊ -ˈlɜːm- ‖ -ˈlerm oʊ -ˈlɜːm-
—*It* [pa ˈler mo]
Palestine ˈpæl ə staɪn -ɪ-
Palestinian ˌpæl ə ˈstɪn i‿ən ◄ ˌ-ɪ- **~s** z
pales|tra pə ˈles |trə -ˈliːs- **~trae** triː traɪ, treɪ
~tras trəz
Palestrina ˌpæl ə ˈstriːn ə -ɪ-, -e- —*It*
[pa les ˈtri: na]
Palethorp, Palethorpe ˈperᵊl θɔːp ‖ -θɔːrp
palette ˈpæl ət -ɪt, -et **~s** s
ˈpalette knife
Paley ˈpeɪl i
palfrey, P~ ˈpɔːlf ri ˈpɒlf- ‖ ˈpɑːlf- **~s** z
Palfreyman ˈpɔːlf ri mən ˈpɒlf- ‖ ˈpɑːlf-
Palgrave ˈpæl greɪv ˈpɔːl- ‖ ˈpɔːl-, ˈpɑːl-
Pali ˈpɑːl i
Palikir ˈpæl ɪk ə ‖ -ᵊr
palimony ˈpæl ɪm ən i ˈ-ə- ‖ -ə moʊn i (*)
palimpsest ˈpæl ɪmp sest -əmp- **~s** s
Palin ˈpeɪl ɪn §-ən
palindrome ˈpæl ɪn drəʊm -ən- ‖ -droʊm **~s** z
palindromic ˌpæl ɪn ˈdrɒm ɪk ◄ -ən-
ǀ-ˈdroʊm ɪk ◄ -ˈdrɑːm-
paling, P~ ˈpeɪl ɪŋ **~s** z
palingenesis ˌpæl ɪn ˈdʒen əs ɪs ˌ-ən-, -ɪs ɪs,
§-əs
palinode ˈpæl ɪ nəʊd -ə- ‖ -noʊd **~s** z
palisad|e ˌpæl ɪ ˈseɪd -ə- **~ed** ɪd əd **~es** z **~ing**
ɪŋ
palish ˈpeɪl ɪʃ
Palitoy *tdmk* ˈpæl ɪ tɔɪ -ə-
Palk pɔːk pɔːlk ‖ pɑːk, pɔːlk, pɑːlk
pall pɔːl ‖ pɑːl **palled** pɔːld ‖ pɑːld **palling**
ˈpɔːl ɪŋ ‖ ˈpɑːl- **palls** pɔːlz ‖ pɑːlz
Palladian pə ˈleɪd i‿ən -ˈlɑːd-
palladic pə ˈlæd ɪk -ˈleɪd-
Palladio pə ˈlæd i əʊ -ˈlɑːd- ‖ -ˈlɑːd i oʊ —*It*
[pal ˈla djo, -di o]
palladium, P~ pə ˈleɪd i‿əm
palladous pə ˈleɪd əs ˈpæl əd-
Pallas ˈpæl əs -æs
ˌPallas Aˈthene
pallbearer ˈpɔːl ˌbeər ə ‖ -ˌber ᵊr ˈpɑːl-, -ˌbær-
~s z
pallet ˈpæl ət -ɪt **~s** s
palletis... —*see* **palletiz...**

palletization ˌpæl ət aɪ ˈzeɪʃ ᵊn ˌ-ɪt-, -ɪˈ--
‖ -ət̬ ə-
palletiz|e ˈpæl ə taɪz -ɪ- **~ed** d **~es** ɪz əz **~ing**
ɪŋ
palliass|e ˈpæl i æs ˌ‧ˈ‧ ‖ ˌpæl ˈjæs **~es** ɪz əz
palli|ate ˈpæl i |eɪt **~ated** eɪt ɪd -əd ‖ eɪt̬ əd
~ates eɪts **~ating** eɪt ɪŋ ‖ eɪt̬ ɪŋ
palliation ˌpæl i ˈeɪʃ ᵊn **~s** z
palliative ˈpæl i‿ət ɪv ‖ -i eɪt ɪv -i‿ət̬ ɪv **~s** z
pallid ˈpæl ɪd §-əd **~ly** li **~ness** nəs nɪs
Palliser ˈpæl ɪs ə -əs- ‖ -ᵊr
palli|um ˈpæl i |əm **~a** ə **~ums** əmz
Pall Mall ˌpæl ˈmæl ◄ —*Formerly also*
ˌpel ˈmel◄
pallor ˈpæl ə ‖ -ᵊr
pally ˈpæl i

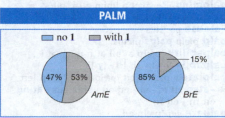

PALM

no 1   with 1

47% 53%   *AmE*

85% — 15%   *BrE*

palm pɑːm §pɑːlm, §pælm, §pɒlm ‖ pɑːlm pɑːm,
pɔːlm, pɔːm — *Preference polls, AmE: no 1*
47%, with 1 53%; BrE: no 1 85%, with 1 15%.
palmed pɑːmd §pɑːlmd, §pælmd, §pɒlmd
‖ pɑːlmd pɑːmd, pɔːlmd, pɔːmd **palming**
ˈpɑːm ɪŋ §ˈpɑːlm-, §ˈpælm-, §ˈpɒlm-
‖ ˈpɑːlm ɪŋ ˈpɑːm-, pɔːlm-, pɔːm- **palms**
pɑːmz §pɑːlmz, §pælmz, §pɒlmz ‖ pɑːlmz
pɑːmz, pɔːlmz, pɔːmz
ˌPalm ˈBeach; ˈpalm ˌoil; ˌPalm ˈSprings;
ˌPalm ˈSunday; ˌpalm ˈwine
Palma ˈpælm ə ˈpɑːm-, ˈpɑːlm-, §ˈpɒlm-
‖ ˈpɑːlm ə -ɑː- —*Sp* [ˈpal ma]
palmar ˈpælm ə §ˈpɑːlm-, §ˈpɒlm-, -ɑː- ‖ -ᵊr
palmate ˈpælm eɪt ˈpɑːm-, §ˈpɑːlm-, §ˈpɒlm-,
-ət, -ɪt **~ly** li
palmcorder ˈpɑːm ˌkɔːd ə §ˈpɑːlm-, §ˈpælm-,
§ˈpɒlm-; ˌ‧ˈ‧ ‖ ˈpɑːlm ˌkɔːrd ᵊr ˈpɑːm-, ˈpɔːlm-,
ˈpɔːm- **~s** z
Palme ˈpɑːlm ə —*Swedish* [ˈˈpal mə]
palmer, P~ ˈpɑːm ə §ˈpɑːlm-, §ˈpælm-, §ˈpɒlm-
‖ ˈpɑːlm ᵊr ˈpɑːm-, ˈpɔːlm-, ˈpɔːm- **~s, ~ˈs** z
Palmerston ˈpɑːm əst ən §ˈpɑːlm-, §ˈpælm-,
§ˈpɒlm- ‖ ˈpɑːlm ᵊrst- ˈpɑːm-, ˈpɔːlm-, ˈpɔːm-
ˌPalmerston ˈNorth
palmetto ˈpæl ˈmet əʊ pɑː-, §pɑːl-, §pɒl-
‖ -ˈmet̬ oʊ **~s** z
palmist ˈpɑːm ɪst §ˈpɑːlm-, §ˈpælm-, §ˈpɒlm-,
§-əst ‖ ˈpɑːlm ɪst ˈpɑːm-, ˈpɔːlm-, ˈpɔːm- **~s** s
palmistry ˈpɑːm ɪs tri §ˈpɑːlm-, §ˈpælm-,
§ˈpɒlm-, -əs- ‖ ˈpɑːlm əs tri ˈpɑːm-, ˈpɔːlm-,
ˈpɔːm-
palmitate ˈpælm ɪ teɪt ˈpɑːm-, §ˈpɑːlm-,
§ˈpɒlm-, -ə- **~s** s
palmitic pæl ˈmɪt ɪk pɑː-, §pɑːl-, §pɒl-
‖ -ˈmɪt̬ ɪk

P

palmitin 'pælm ɪt ɪn 'pɑːm-, §'pɑːlm-,
§'pɒlm-, -ət-, §-ən ‖ -ət ᵊn
Palmolive *tdmk* ˌpɑːm 'ɒl ɪv §ˌpɑːlm-, §'pælm-,
§'pɒlm-, §-əv ‖ ˌpɑːlm 'ɑːl ɪv ˌpɑːm-, ˌpɔːlm-,
ˌpɔːm-
palm-sized 'pɑːm saɪzd §'pɑːlm-, §'pælm-,
§'pɒlm- ‖ 'pɑːlm- 'pɑːm-, 'pɔːlm-, 'pɔːm-
palmtop 'pɑːm tɒp §'pɑːlm-, §'pælm-, §'pɒlm-
‖ 'pɑːlm tɑːp 'pɑːm-, 'pɔːlm-, 'pɔːm- **~s** s
palm|y 'pɑːm |i §'pɑːlm-, §'pælm-, §'pɒlm-
‖ 'pɑːlm |i 'pɑːm-, 'pɔːlm-, 'pɔːm- **~ier** i ə
‖ i ᵊr **~iest** i ɪst i əst
Palmyra, p~ ₍ᵢ₎pæl 'maɪᵊr ə **~s** z
Palo Alto ˌpæl əʊ 'ælt əʊ ‖ ˌpæl oʊ 'ælt oʊ
palolo pə 'ləʊl əʊ ‖ -'loʊl oʊ
Palomar 'pæl əʊ mɑː ‖ -ə mɑːr ˌ·'·
palomino, P~ ˌpæl ə 'miːn əʊ ‖ -oʊ **~s** z
palooka pə 'luːk ə **~s** z
Palouse pə 'luːs
palp pælp **palps** pælps
palpability ˌpælp ə 'bɪl ət i -ɪt i ‖ -ət i
palpab|le 'pælp əb |ᵊl **~ly** li
palp|ate *v* pæl 'p|eɪt 'pælp |eɪt ‖ 'pælp |eɪt
~ated eɪt ɪd -əd ‖ eɪt̬ əd **~ates** eɪts **~ating**
eɪt ɪŋ ‖ eɪt̬ ɪŋ
palpate *adj* 'pælp eɪt
palpation pæl 'peɪʃ ᵊn
palpebral 'pælp ɪb rəl -əb-; pæl 'piːb-, -'peb-
palpi 'pælp aɪ -iː
palpi|tate 'pælp ɪ |teɪt -ə- **~tated** teɪt ɪd -əd
‖ teɪt̬ əd **~tates** teɪts **~tating** teɪt ɪŋ ‖ teɪt̬ ɪŋ
palpitation ˌpælp ɪ 'teɪʃ ᵊn -ə- **~s** z
palsgrave, P~ 'pɔːlz greɪv ‖ 'pɑːlz-
pals|y 'pɔːlz |i 'pɒlz- ‖ 'pɑːlz- **~ied** id **~ies** iz
~ying i ɪŋ
palsy-walsy ˌpælz i 'wælz i ◂
palt|er 'pɔːlt |ə 'pɒlt- ‖ -|ᵊr 'pɑːlt- **~ered** əd
‖ ᵊrd **~ering** ᵊr ɪŋ **~ers** əz ‖ ᵊrz
Paltrow 'pæltr əʊ ‖ -oʊ
paltr|y 'pɔːltr |i 'pɒltr- ‖ 'pɑːltr- **~ier** i ə ‖ i ᵊr
~iest i ɪst i əst **~ily** ɪ li əl i **~iness** i nəs i nɪs
paludal pə 'luːd ᵊl -'ljuːd-; 'pæl jʊd-, -jəd-
Paludrine, p~ 'pæl ju drɪn -u-, -jə-, -driːn
palynolog|ist ˌpæl ɪ 'nɒl ədʒ |ɪst ˌ·ə-, §-əst
‖ -'nɑːl- **~ists** ɪsts §əsts **~y** i
Pam pæm
Pama-Nyungan ˌpɑːm ə 'njʊŋ ən ◂ -gən
Pamela 'pæm əl ə -ɪl ə
Pamir pə 'mɪə ‖ -'mɪᵊr **~s** z
Pamlico 'pæm lɪ kəʊ -lə- ‖ -koʊ
ˌPamlico 'Sound
pampa, Pampa 'pæmp ə —*Sp* ['pam pa]
pampas 'pæmp əs -əz
ˈpampas grass
pamper 'pæmp ə ‖ -ᵊr **~ed** d **pampering**
'pæmp ᵊr ɪŋ **~s** z
Pampers *tdmk* 'pæmp əz ‖ -ᵊrz
pamphlet 'pæmᵖf lət -lɪt **~s** s
pamphle|teer ˌpæmᵖf lə |'tɪə -lɪ- ‖ -|'tɪᵊr
~teered 'tɪəd ‖ 'tɪᵊrd **~teering** 'tɪər ɪŋ
‖ 'tɪr ɪŋ **~teers** 'tɪəz ‖ 'tɪᵊrz
Pamphyli|a pæm 'fɪl i |ə **~an/s** ən/z

Pamplona pæm 'pləʊn ə ‖ -'ploʊn ə — *Sp*
[pam 'plo na]
pan, Pan pæn —*but in the sense 'betel leaf'*,
pɑːn **panned** pænd **panning** 'pæn ɪŋ **pans**
pænz
ˌPan 'Am *tdmk*
pan- |pæn — **Pan-Arabism** ˌpæn 'ær əb ɪz əm
panacea ˌpæn ə 'sɪə -'siːˌə ‖ -'siː ə **~s** z
panache pə 'næʃ pæ-, -'nɑːʃ
panada pə 'nɑːd ə **~s** z
Panadol *tdmk* 'pæn ə dɒl ‖ -dɑːl **~s** z
pan-African ˌpæn 'æf rɪk ən ◂ **~ism** ɪz əm
Panama, p~ 'pæn ə mɑː ˌ·'·; -mɔː — *Sp*
Panamá [pa na 'ma] **~s, ~'s** z
ˌPanama Ca'nal; ˌPanama 'hat
Panamanian ˌpæn ə 'meɪn i ən ◂ **~s** z
Panasonic *tdmk* ˌpæn ə 'sɒn ɪk ‖ -'sɑːn ɪk
panatela, panatella ˌpæn ə 'tel ə **~s** z
Panathenaea ˌpæn ˌæθ ɪ 'niːˌə ·ˌ·'·ˌ·, -ə'--
pancak|e 'pæn keɪk 'pæŋk eɪk **~ed** t **~es** s
~ing ɪŋ
ˌPancake 'Day; ˌpancake 'landing;
ˌpancake 'roll; ˌPancake 'Tuesday
pancetta pæn 'tʃet ə ‖ -'tʃet̬- —*It*
[pan 'tʃet ta]
panchax 'pæn tʃæks **~es** ɪz əz
Pancho 'pæntʃ əʊ ‖ -oʊ —*Sp* ['pan tʃo]
panchromatic ˌpæn krəʊ 'mæt ɪk ◂ →ˌpæŋ-
‖ -kroʊ 'mæt̬ ɪk ◂ -krə-
Pancras 'pæŋk rəs
pancreas 'pæŋk ri əs -æs ‖ 'pæn kri- **~es** ɪz əz
pancreatic ˌpæŋk ri 'æt ɪk ◂ ‖ -'æt̬ ɪk
ˌpæn kri-
pancreatin 'pæŋk ri ət ɪn pæn 'kriː-, →ˌpæŋ-,
§-ən ‖ -ən
pancreatitis ˌpæŋk ri ə 'taɪt ɪs §-əs ‖ -'taɪt̬ əs
pancuronium ˌpæn kjʊ 'rəʊn i əm →ˌpæŋ-,
-kjə- ‖ -'roʊn-
panda 'pænd ə **~s** z
ˈpanda car; ˌpanda 'crossing
pandanus pæn 'deɪn əs -'dæn- **~es** ɪz əz
Pandarus 'pænd ər əs
pandect 'pæn dekt **~s** s
pandemic ₍ᵢ₎pæn 'dem ɪk **~s** s
pandemonium ˌpænd ə 'məʊn i əm ˌ·ɪ-
‖ -'moʊn-
pander 'pænd ə ‖ -ᵊr **~ed** d **pandering**
'pænd ᵊr ɪŋ **~s** z
pandialectal ˌpæn ˌdaɪ ə 'lekt ᵊl ◂
pandit, P~ 'pænd ɪt 'pʌnd-, §-ət —*Hindi*
[pən ɖɪt] **~s** s
Pandora, p~ ₍ᵢ₎pæn 'dɔːr ə ‖ -'doʊr- **~s, ~'s** z
Panˌdora's 'box
pandowd|y pæn 'daʊd |i **~ies** iz
pane, Pane peɪn (= *pain*) **paned** peɪnd **panes**
peɪnz
panegyric ˌpæn ə 'dʒɪr ɪk -ɪ- ‖ -'dʒaɪr- **~s** s
panegyris|e, panegyriz|e 'pæn ədʒ ə raɪz
-ɪdʒ-, -ɪ- **~ed** d **~es** ɪz əz **~ing** ɪŋ
panegyrist ˌpæn ə 'dʒɪr ɪst -ɪ-, §-əst, '····
‖ -'dʒaɪr- **~s** s
panel 'pæn ᵊl **~ed, ~led** d **~ing, ~ling** ɪŋ **~s** z
ˈpanel ˌbeater; ˈpanel saw

panelist, panellist 'pæn əl ɪst §-əst ~s z
Panesar 'pæn ə sɑː ‖ -sɑːr
panetton|e ˌpæn ə 'təʊn |i -ɪ- ‖ -'toʊn |i
ˌpɑːn- —It [pa net 'to: ne] ~es iz ~i iː
pan-|fry 'pæn |fraɪ ~fried fraɪd ~fries fraɪz
~frying fraɪ ɪŋ
panful 'pæn fʊl ~s z
pang pæŋ pangs pæŋz
panga 'pæŋ gə ‖ 'pɑːŋ gə ~s z
Pangaea pæn 'dʒiː ə
Pangbourne 'pæn bɔːn ‖ -bɔːrn -boʊrn
Pangloss 'pæn glɒs →'pæŋ- ‖ -glɑːs -glɔːs
Panglossian, p~ ₍ᵢ₎pæn 'glɒs i ən →₍ᵢ₎pæŋ-
‖ -'glɑːs- -'glɔːs-
pangolin pæŋ 'gəʊl ɪn §-ən; 'pæŋg əʊ lɪn,
§-lən ‖ 'pæŋ gəl ən 'pæn-, -'goʊl- ~s z
panhandl|e 'pæn ˌhænd ᵊl ~ed d ~er/s ə/z
‖ ᵊr/z ~es z ~ing ɪŋ
panhellenic ˌpæn hɪ 'len ɪk ◂ -he-, -hə-, -ɪ-, -ə-,
-'liːn-
panhellenism ˌpæn 'hel ɪn ˌɪz əm -ən-
panic 'pæn ɪk ~ked t ~king ɪŋ ~s s
'panic ˌbutton; 'panic ˌstations
panicky 'pæn ɪk i
panicle 'pæn ɪk ᵊl ~s z
panicle 'pæn ɪk ᵊl ~s z
panic-|stricken 'pæn ɪk |ˌstrɪk ən ~struck
strʌk
panini, P~ 'sandwich(es)'; 'prickly pear'; Italian
name pə 'niːn i —It [pa 'ni: ni] ~s z
Panini Sanskrit name 'pɑːn ɪ ni: -ni —Skt
['pɑː ɳɪ ɳi]
Panjab ˌpʌn 'dʒɑːb '· ·
Panjabi ₍ᵢ₎pʌn 'dʒɑːb i pən-, -iː ~s z
panjandrum pæn 'dʒændr əm pən- ~s z
Pankhurst 'pæŋk hɜːst ‖ -hɜːrst
panlectal ˌpæn 'lekt ᵊl ◂
Panmunjom ˌpæn mʊn 'dʒɒm
‖ ˌpɑːn mʊn 'dʒɑːm —Korean
[pʰan mun dʒɔm]
pannage 'pæn ɪdʒ
Pannal, Pannell 'pæn ᵊl
panne pæn (= pan)
pannier 'pæn i ə ‖ ᵊr ~ed d ~s z
pannikin 'pæn ɪ kɪn -ə-, §-kən ~s z
Pannonia pə 'nəʊn i ə pæ- ‖ -'noʊn-
panoch|a pə 'nəʊtʃ |ə ‖ -'noʊtʃ- ~e i
panop|ly 'pæn əp |li ~lied lid ~lies liz
panoptic ₍ᵢ₎pæn 'ɒpt ɪk ‖ -'ɑːpt- ~al ᵊl
panopticon ₍ᵢ₎pæn 'ɒpt ɪk ən §-ək-
‖ -'ɑːpt ə kɑːn ~s z
panorama, P~ ˌpæn ə 'rɑːm ə ‖ -'ræm ə
-'rɑːm- ~s z
panoramic ˌpæn ə 'ræm ɪk ◂ -'rɑːm- ~ally ᵊl_i
panpipes 'pæn paɪps →'pæm-
pan-roasted 'pæn ˌrəʊst ɪd -əd ‖ -ˌroʊst-
Pan-Slavism ˌpæn 'slɑːv ˌɪz əm -'slæv-
pans|y, Pans|y 'pænz |i ~ies, ~y's iz
pant pænt panted 'pænt ɪd -əd ‖ 'pænt̬ əd
panting/ly 'pænt ɪŋ /li ‖ 'pænt̬ ɪŋ /li pants
pænts

Pantagruel ˌpænt ə gru 'el '· ·ˌgru_əl
‖ pæn 'tæg ru el ˌpænt̬ ə 'gruː əl —Fr
[pɑ̃ ta gʁɥ ɛl]
Pantagruelian ˌpænt ə gru 'el i ən ◂
ˌpænt ə 'gruːl i ən ‖ ˌpænt̬ ə-
pantalette ˌpænt ə 'let -ᵊl 'et ‖ ˌpænt̬ ᵊl 'et ~s
s
pantaloon, P~ ˌpænt ə 'luːn ◂ -ᵊl 'uːn, '· · ·
‖ ˌpænt̬ ᵊl 'uːn ◂ ~s z
pantechnicon pæn 'tek nɪk ən ~s z
Pantelleria ˌpænt el ə 'riː ə ·ˌ·— —It
[pan tel le 'ri: a]
Pantene tdmk ˌpæn 'ten
pantheism 'pænᵗθ i ˌɪz əm
pantheist 'pænᵗθ i ɪst §-əst ~s s
pantheistic ˌpænᵗθ i 'ɪst ɪk ◂ ~al ᵊl ~ally ᵊl_i
pantheon 'pænᵗθ i ən pæn 'θiː·, -ɒn ‖ -ɑːn ~s
z
panther 'pænᵗθ ə ‖ -ᵊr ~s z
pantie girdle 'pænt i ˌgɜːd ᵊl
‖ 'pænt̬ i ˌgɜːd ᵊl ~s z
panties 'pænt iz ‖ 'pænt̬ iz
pantihose 'pænt i həʊz ‖ 'pænt̬ i hoʊz
pantile 'pæn taɪᵊl ~s z
panto 'pænt əʊ ‖ -oʊ ~s z
pantograph 'pænt əʊ grɑːf -græf
‖ 'pænt̬ ə græf ~s s
pantomime 'pænt ə maɪm ‖ 'pænt̬- ~s z
pantomimic ˌpænt ə 'mɪm ɪk ◂ ‖ ˌpænt̬-
pantomimist 'pænt ə maɪm ɪst §-əst, ·'··
‖ 'pænt̬- ~s s
Panton 'pænt ən ‖ -ᵊn
pantothenic ˌpænt ə 'θen ɪk ◂ ‖ ˌpænt̬-
pantr|y 'pæntr |i ~ies iz
pants pænts
pantsuit 'pænt suːt -sjuːt
pant|y 'pænt |i ‖ 'pænt̬ |i ~ies iz
'panty hose; 'panty raid
Pantycelyn ˌpænt ə 'kel ɪn —Welsh
[ˌpant ə 'ke lɪn]
pantyliner 'pænt i ˌlaɪn ə ‖ 'pænt̬ i ˌlaɪn ᵊr ~s
z
pantywaist 'pænt i weɪst ‖ 'pænt̬- ~s s
Pan Yan tdmk ˌpæn 'jæn ◂
Panza 'pænz ə —Sp ['pan θa]
panzer 'pænz ə ‖ -ᵊr —Ger ['pan tsɛ] ~s z
pap, Pap pæp paps pæps
papa, Papa pə 'pɑː ‖ 'pɑːp ə —but as code
name for the letter P, usually 'pɑːp ə even in
BrE ~s z
papabile pɑː 'pɑːb ɪ leɪ —It [pa 'pɑː bi le]
papac|y 'peɪp əs |i ~ies iz
Papadopoulos ˌpæp ə 'dɒp əl əs
‖ ˌpɑːp ə 'dɑːp- —Greek [pa pa 'ðo pu los]
papadum 'pæp əd əm 'pʌp-, 'pɒp-, -ə dʌm ~s
z
Papagen|a ˌpæp ə 'geɪn ə ~o -əʊ ‖ -oʊ
papain pə 'peɪ ɪn -'paɪ-, §-ən
papal 'peɪp ᵊl ~ly i
Papandreou ˌpæp æn 'dreɪ uː ‖ ˌpɑːp ɑːn-
—Greek [pa pan 'dre u]

paparazz|o ˌpæp ə ˈræts |əʊ -ˈrɑːts-
‖ ˌpɑːp ə ˈrɑːts |oʊ -ˈrɑːz- **~i** i -iː —*It*
[pa pa ˈrat tso]

papaverine pə ˈpæv ə riːn -ˈpeɪv-, -rɪn, -rən

papaw ˈpɔːp ɔː pə ˈpɔː ‖ ˈpɑːp-, -ɑː **~s** z

papaya pə ˈpaɪ ə **~s** z

Papeete ˌpɑːp i ˈeɪt i -ə-, -ˈiːt-; pə ˈpiːt i
‖ -ˈeɪt eɪ pə ˈpiːʧ i

paper ˈpeɪp ə ‖ -ᵊr **~ed** d **papering** ˈpeɪp ər_ɪŋ
~s z
ˌpaper ˈbag *(bag made of paper)*, ˈpaper
bag *(bag for newspapers);* ˈpaper chase;
ˈpaper clip; ˈpaper knife; ˈpaper ˌmoney;
ˌpaper ˈtiger; ˈpaper trail

paperback ˈpeɪp ə bæk ‖ -ᵊr- **~s** s

paperboard ˈpeɪp ə bɔːd ‖ -ᵊr bɔːrd -boʊrd

paperboy ˈpeɪp ə bɔɪ ‖ -ᵊr- **~s** z

paperclip ˈpeɪp ə klɪp ‖ -ᵊr- **~s** s

paperhanger ˈpeɪp ə ˌhæŋ ə ‖ -ᵊr ˌhæŋ ᵊr **~s** z

paperless ˈpeɪp ə ləs -lɪs ‖ -ᵊr-

paper-pusher ˈpeɪp ə ˌpʊʃ ə ‖ -ᵊr ˌpʊʃ ᵊr **~s** z

paper-thin ˌpeɪp ə ˈθɪn ◂ ‖ -ᵊr-

paperweight ˈpeɪp ə weɪt ‖ -ᵊr- **~s** s

paperwork ˈpeɪp ə wɜːk ‖ -ᵊr wɜːk

papery ˈpeɪp ər i

Paphlagoni|a ˌpæf lə ˈgəʊn i_|ə ‖ -ˈgoʊn-
~an/s ən/z

Paphos ˈpæf ɒs ˈpeɪf- ‖ -oʊs ˈpɑːf- —*Greek*
[ˈpa fos]

Papiament|o ˌpæp i_ə ˈment |əʊ ˌpɑːp-
‖ ˌpɑːp jə ˈment |oʊ **~u** uː

papier-mache, papier-mâché
ˌpæp i eɪ ˈmæʃ eɪ ◂ ˌpeɪp ə ˈmæʃ-
‖ ˌpeɪp ᵊr mə ˈʃeɪ ◂ -mæˈ· *(*)* —*Fr*
[pa pje ma ʃe]

papill|a pə ˈpɪl |ə **~ae** iː

papillary pə ˈpɪl ər i ‖ ˈpæp ə ler i

papillate ˈpæp ɪ leɪt -ə-, →-ᵊl eɪt, pə ˈpɪl eɪt

papillom|a ˌpæp ɪ ˈləʊm |ə -ə- ‖ -ˈloʊm |ə **~as**
əz **~ata** ət ə ‖ əʈ ə

papillon, P~ ˈpæp ɪ lɒn -ə- ‖ -lɑːn ˌpɑːp- —*Fr*
[pa pi jɔ̃] **~s** z

papillote ˈpæp ɪ lɒt -ə-, -ləʊt ‖ ˌpæp ɪ ˈjoʊt
ˌpɑːp- —*Fr* [pa pi jɔt] **~s** s

papist ˈpeɪp ɪst §-əst **~s** s

papistic peɪ ˈpɪst ɪk pə- **~al** ᵊl

papistry ˈpeɪp ɪs tri -əs-

papoos|e pə ˈpuːs ‖ pæ- pə- **~es** ɪz əz

pappardelle ˌpæp ə ˈdel eɪ -ɑː-, -i ‖ -ᵊr- -ɑːr-
—*It* [pap paɾ ˈdɛl le]

papp|ous, ~us ˈpæp |əs **~i** aɪ

papp|y ˈpæp |i **~ier** i_ə ‖ i_ᵊr **~iest** i_ɪst i_əst
~ies iz

paprika ˈpæp rɪk ə; pə ˈpriːk ə, pæ-
‖ pə ˈpriːk ə pæ- *(*)*

Papu|a ˈpæp u_|ə ˈpɑːp-, -ju- **~an/s** ən/z
ˌPapua New ˈGuinea

papule ˈpæp juːl **~s** z

Papworth ˈpæp wɜːθ -wəθ ‖ -wᵊrθ

papyr|us pə ˈpaɪᵊr |əs **~i** aɪ **~uses** əs ɪz -əz

par, Par pɑː ‖ pɑːr
ˌpar ˈvalue

para *'paratrooper', 'paragraph'* ˈpær ə ‖ ˈper ə
~s z

para *monetary unit* ˈpɑːr ə **~s** z

para- *comb. form with stress-neutral suffix*
¦pær ə ‖ ¦per ə — **parapraxis**
ˌpær ə ˈpræks ɪs §-əs ‖ ˌper- *with*
stress-imposing suffix pə ˈræ+ — **parabasis**
pə ˈræb əs ɪs §-əs

Pará *river in Brazil* pə ˈrɑː —*Port* [pɐ ˈra]

parable ˈpær əb ᵊl ‖ ˈper- **~s** z

parabola pə ˈræb əl ə **~s** z

parabolic ˌpær ə ˈbɒl ɪk ◂ ‖ ˌpær ə ˈbɑːl ɪk ◂
ˌper- **~al** ᵊl **~ally** ᵊl_i

paraboloid pə ˈræb ə lɔɪd **~s** z

Paraburdoo ˌpær ə bə ˈduː ‖ -bᵊr ˈ· ˌper-

Paracel ˌpær ə ˈsel **~s** z

Paracelsus ˌpær ə ˈsels əs ‖ ˈper-

paracetamol ˌpær ə ˈsiːt ə mɒl -ˈset-
‖ -ˈsiːt ə mɑːl ˌper-, -ˈseʈ-, -mɔːl, -moʊl **~s** z

para|chute ˈpær ə |ʃuːt ‖ ˈper- **~chuted** ʃuːt ɪd
-əd ‖ ˈʃuːʈ əd **~chutes** ʃuːts **~chuting** ʃuːt ɪŋ
‖ ˈʃuːʈ ɪŋ

parachutist ˈpær ə ʃuːt ɪst §-əst, ˌ· ·ˈ· ·
‖ -ʃuːʈ əst ˈper- **~s** s

Paraclete, p~ ˈpær ə kliːt ‖ ˈper-

parad|e pə ˈreɪd **~ed** ɪd əd **~es** z **~ing** ɪŋ
paˈrade ground

paradichlorobenzene
ˌpær ə ˌdaɪ klɔːr əʊ ˈbenz iːn ˌ· · ·ˌ-- ‖ -oʊˈ· ·
ˌper-, -klour·ˈ· ·, -ben ˈziːn

paradigm ˈpær ə daɪm ‖ ˈper-, -dɪm **~s** z

paradigmatic ˌpær ə dɪg ˈmæt ɪk ◂
‖ -ˈmæʈ ɪk ◂, ˌper- **~ally** ᵊl_i

paradisal ˌpær ə ˈdaɪs ᵊl ◂ -ˈdaɪz- ‖ ˌper-

paradise, P~ ˈpær ə daɪs ‖ ˈper-, -daɪz

paradisiac ˌpær ə ˈdɪz i æk ◂ ; -ˈdɪs-;
-dɪ ˈsaɪ ˌək, -də·ˈ-- ‖ ˌper-

paradisiacal ˌpær ə dɪ ˈsaɪ ˌək ᵊl ◂ -də·ˈ-- ‖ ˌper-

parador ˈpær ə dɔː ‖ ˌpɑːr ɑː ˈdɔːr —*Sp*
[pa ɾa ˈðoɾ] **~s** z

parados ˈpær ə dɒs ‖ -dɑːs ˈper- **~es** ɪz əz

paradox ˈpær ə dɒks ‖ -dɑːks ˈper- **~es** ɪz əz

paradoxical ˌpær ə ˈdɒks ɪk ᵊl ◂ ‖ -ˈdɑːks-
ˌper- **~ly** _i **~ness** nəs nɪs

paraffin ˈpær ə fɪn -fiːn, ˌ· ·ˈ·; §ˈpær əf ən
‖ ˈper-
ˈparaffin wax, ˌ· · ·ˈ·

paraglid|er ˈpær ə ˌglaɪd ə ‖ -ᵊr ˈper- **~ers** əz
‖ ᵊrz **~ing** ɪŋ

paragoge ˌpær ə ˈgəʊdʒ i ‖ -ˈgoʊdʒ i ˌper-

paragogic ˌpær ə ˈgɒdʒ ɪk ◂ ‖ -ˈgɑːdʒ- ˌper-

paragon ˈpær əg ən ‖ -ə gɑːn ˈper-, -əg ən *(*)*
~s z

paragraph ˈpær ə grɑːf -græf ‖ -græf ˈper- **~ed**
t **~ing** ɪŋ **~s** s

paragraphia ˌpær ə ˈgræf i_ə -ˈgrɑːf- ‖ ˌper-

Paraguay ˈpær ə gwaɪ ˌ· ·ˈ· ‖ ˈper-, -gweɪ —*Sp*
[pa ɾa ˈɣwai]

Paraguayan ˌpær ə ˈgwaɪ ˌən ◂ ‖ ˌper-, -ˈgweɪ-
~s z

parakeet ˈpær ə kiːt ˌ· ·ˈ· ‖ ˈper- **~s** s

paralanguage ˈpær ə ˌlæŋ gwɪdʒ -wɪdʒ ‖ ˈper-

paraldehyde pə ˈræld ɪ haɪd -ˈ-ə-

paralegal ˌpær ə ˈliːg ᵊl ◄ ‖ ˌper- **~s** z

paralinguistic ˌpær ə lɪŋ ˈgwɪst ɪk ◄ ‖ ˌper-
~**ally** ᵊl‿i ~**s** s

parallactic ˌpær ə ˈlækt ɪk ◄ ‖ ˌper- ~**ally** ᵊl‿i

parallax ˈpær ə læks ‖ ˈper- ~**es** ɪz əz

parallel ˈpær ə lel -əl əl ‖ ˈper- ~**ed, ~led** d
~**ing, ~ling** ɪŋ ~**s** z
ˌparallel ˈbars

parallelepiped ˌpær ə lel ə ˈpaɪp ed
ˌ‿‧‧‧ep ɪ ped, -ə- ‖ ˌper- ~**s** z

parallelism ˈpær ə lel ˌɪz əm -ləl ˌ-;
⚠ˈpær ə ˌlɪz əm ‖ ˈper- ~**s** z

parallelogram ˌpær ə ˈlel ə græm ‖ ˌper- ~**s** z

paralogism pə ˈræl ə ˌdʒɪz əm ~**s** z

Paralympics ˌpær ə ˈlɪmp ɪks ‖ ˌper-

paralysation ˌpær ə laɪ ˈzeɪʒ ᵊn ‖ -lə'-- ˌper-

paralys|e ˈpær ə laɪz ‖ ˈper- ~**ed** d ~**es** ɪz əz
~**ing/ly** ɪŋ/ li

paralyses *from v* ˈpær ə laɪz ɪz -əz ‖ ˈper-

paralyses *n pl* pə ˈræl ə siːz -ɪ-

paral|ysis pə ˈræl |əs ɪs -ɪs-, §-əs ~**yses** ə siːz
ɪ-

paralytic ˌpær ə ˈlɪt ɪk ◄ ‖ -ˈlɪt̬ ɪk ◄ ˌper- ~**ally**
ᵊl‿i ~**s** s

paralyzation ˌpær ə laɪ ˈzeɪʒ ᵊn ‖ -lə'-- ˌper-

paralyz|e ˈpær ə laɪz ‖ ˈper- ~**ed** d ~**es** ɪz əz
~**ing** ɪŋ

paramagnetic ˌpær ə mæg ˈnet ɪk ◄ -məg'--
‖ -ˈnet̬ ɪk ◄ ˌper-

paramagnetism ˌpær ə ˈmæg nə ˌtɪz əm -ˈ-nɪ-
‖ ˌper-

Paramaribo ˌpær ə ˈmær ɪ bəʊ §-ˈ-ə- ‖ -boʊ
ˌper- —*Dutch* [pɑː rɑː ˈmɑː ri boː]

paramatta ˌpær ə ˈmæt ə ‖ -ˈmæt̬ ə ˌper-

parameci|um ˌpær ə ˈmiːs i ̯|əm ‖ ˌper- -ˈmiːʃ-
~**a** ə ~**ums** əmz

paramedic ˌpær ə ˈmed ɪk ‖ ˌper- ~**al** ᵊl ◄ ~**s** s

parameter pə ˈræm ɪt ə -ət- ‖ -ət̬ ᵊr ~**s** z

parameteris... —*see* **parameteriz...**

parameterization pə ˌræm ɪt̯ ᵊr aɪ ˈzeɪʃ ᵊn
-ˌ‧ət̯, -ɪ'-- ‖ -ət̬ ᵊr ə- →-ˌ‧ətr ə'‧‧

parameteriz|e pə ˈræm ɪt ə raɪz -ˈ‧ət-;
→ ‧ˈ‧ɪ traɪz, -ə- ‖ -ət̬ ə- ~**ed** d ~**es** ɪz əz ~**ing**
ɪŋ

parametric ˌpær ə ˈmetr ɪk ◄ ‖ ˌper- ~**ally** ᵊl‿i

parametris... —*see* **parametris...**

parametrization pə ˌræm ətr aɪ ˈzeɪʃ ᵊn -ˌ‧ɪtr-,
-ɪ'-- ‖ -ə'--

parametriz|e pə ˈræm ə traɪz -ɪ- ~**ed** d ~**es** ɪz
əz ~**ing** ɪŋ

paramilitar|y ˌpær ə ˈmɪl ɪt ᵊr |i ◄ -ˈ‧ət̯
‖ -ə ter |i ˌper- ~**ies** iz

paramnesia ˌpær æm ˈniːz i ̯ə -ˈniːʒ ə
‖ -ˈniːʒ ə ˌper-

paramount ˈpær ə maʊnt ‖ ˈper- ~**cy** si ~**ly** li

paramour, P~ ˈpær ə mʊə -mɔː ‖ ˈpær ə mɔːr
ˈper- ~**s** z

Paramus pə ˈræm əs

Paraná ˌpær ə ˈnɑː ‖ ˌper-, ˌpɑːr- —*Port*
[pɐ ɾɐ ˈna], *Sp* [pa ɾa ˈna]

parang ˈpɑːr æŋ ~**s** z

paranoi|a ˌpær ə ˈnɔɪ |ə ‖ ˌper- ~**ac** æk ◄ ɪk
~**acally** æk ᵊl‿i ɪk-

paranoid ˈpær ə nɔɪd ‖ ˈper- ~**s** z

paranormal ˌpær ə ˈnɔːm ᵊl ◄ ‖ -ˈnɔːrm ᵊl ◄
ˌper- ~**ly** i

parapet ˈpær əp ɪt -ət, -ə pet ‖ ˈper- ~**s** s

paraph ˈpær æf -əf ‖ ˈper-; pə ˈræf ~**s** s

paraphernalia ˌpær ə fə ˈneɪl i ̯ə ‖ -ə fᵊr- ˌper-

paraphilia ˌpær ə ˈfɪl i ̯ə ‖ ˌper- ~**s** z

paraphras|e *n, v* ˈpær ə freɪz ‖ ˈper- ~**ed** d
~**es** ɪz əz ~**ing** ɪŋ

paraphrastic ˌpær ə ˈfræst ɪk ◄ ‖ ˌper- ~**ally**
ᵊl‿i

paraplegia ˌpær ə ˈpliːdʒ ə -ˈpliːdʒ i ̯ə ‖ ˌper-

paraplegic ˌpær ə ˈpliːdʒ ɪk ◄ ‖ ˌper- ~**s** s

paraprax|is ˌpær ə ˈpræks |ɪs ˌper- ~**es** iːz

parapsychologic ˌpær ə ˌsaɪk ə ˈlɒdʒ ɪk
-ˌpsaɪk- ‖ -ˈlɑːdʒ- ˌper- ~**al/ly** ᵊl‿i

parapsycholog|ist ˌpær ə saɪ ˈkɒl ədʒ |ɪst
-psaɪ'--, §-əst ‖ -ˈkɑːl- ˌper- ~**ists** ɪsts §əsts ~**y** i

paraquat, P~ *tdmk* ˈpær ə kwɒt -kwæt
‖ -kwɑːt ˈper-

paras ˈpær əz ‖ ˈper-

parasailing ˈpær ə ˌseɪl ɪŋ ‖ ˈper-

parasang ˈpær ə sæŋ ‖ ˈper- ~**s** z

parascend|ing ˈpær ə ˌsend| ɪŋ ‖ ˈper- ~**er/s**
ə/z ‖ ᵊr/z

para|shah, P~ ˈpær ə |ʃɑː ‖ ˈpɑːr- ~**shoth** ʃəʊt
‖ ʃoʊt

parasite ˈpær ə saɪt ‖ ˈper- ~**s** s

parasitic ˌpær ə ˈsɪt ɪk ◄ ‖ -ˈsɪt̬ ɪk ◄ ˌper- ~**al** ᵊl
~**ally** ᵊl‿i

parasitism ˈpær ə saɪt ˌɪz əm -sɪ ˌtɪz- ‖ -ə saɪt̬-
ˈper-, -sə ˌtɪz-

parasitology ˌpær ə saɪ ˈtɒl ədʒ i -sɪ ˈtɒl-
‖ -saɪ ˈtɑːl- ˌper-, -sə-

parasol ˈpær ə sɒl ˌ‧‧ˈ‧ ‖ -sɔːl ˈper-, -sɑːl ~**s** z

parasympathetic ˌpær ə ˌsɪmp ə ˈθet ɪk ◄
‖ -ˈθet̬ ɪk ◄ ˌper-

parasynthesis ˌpær ə ˈsɪnθ əs ɪs -ɪs ɪs, §-əs
‖ ˌper-

parasynthetic ˌpær ə sɪn ˈθet ɪk ◄ ‖ -ˈθet̬ ɪk ◄
ˌper- ~**ally** ᵊl‿i

paratactic ˌpær ə ˈtækt ɪk ◄ ‖ ˌper- ~**ally** ᵊl‿i

parataxis ˌpær ə ˈtæks ɪs §-əs, ˈ‧‧‧‧ ‖ ˌper-

parathion ˌpær ə ˈθaɪ ɒn -ˈθaɪ̯ ən ‖ -ɑːn ˌper-

parathyroid ˌpær ə ˈθaɪ̯ᵊr ɔɪd ◄ ‖ ˌper- ~**s** z
ˌpara'thyroid gland, ˌ‧‧ˌ‧ˈ‧

paratroop ˈpær ə truːp ‖ ˈper- ~**er/s** ə/z ‖ ᵊr/z
~**s** s

paratyphoid ˌpær ə ˈtaɪf ɔɪd ‖ ˌper-

paravane ˈpær ə veɪn ‖ ˈper- ~**s** z

parboil ˈpɑː bɔɪᵊl ‖ ˈpɑːr- ~**ed** d ~**ing** ɪŋ ~**s** z

parbuckle ˈpɑː bʌk ᵊl ‖ ˈpɑːr- ~**s** z

parcel ˈpɑːs ᵊl ‖ ˈpɑːrs ᵊl ~**ed, ~led** d ~**ing,
~ling** ɪŋ ~**s** z
ˌparcel ˈpost; ˌparcel ˈbomb

Parcelforce ˈpɑːs ᵊl fɔːs ‖ ˈpɑːrs ᵊl fɔːrs -foʊrs

parch pɑːtʃ ‖ pɑːrtʃ **parched** pɑːtʃt ‖ pɑːrtʃt
parches ˈpɑːtʃ ɪz -əz ‖ ˈpɑːrtʃ əz **parching**
ˈpɑːtʃ ɪŋ ‖ ˈpɑːrtʃ ɪŋ

parchedness ˈpɑːtʃt nəs -nɪs ‖ ˈpɑːrtʃt-

parcheesi, parchesi pɑː ˈtʃiːz i -ˈtʃiːs i ‖ pɑːr-

parchment ˈpɑːtʃ mənt ‖ ˈpɑːrtʃ- ~**s** s

pard pɑːd ‖ pɑːrd **pards** pɑːdz ‖ pɑːrdz

pardalote 'pɑːd ə ləʊt →-ᵊl əʊt ‖ 'pɑːrd ᵊl oʊt
~s s
pardner, P~ 'pɑːd nə ‖ 'pɑːrd nʳr ~s z
Pardoe 'pɑːd əʊ ‖ 'pɑːrd oʊ
pardon 'pɑːd ᵊn ‖ 'pɑːrd ᵊn ~ed d ~ing ɪŋ ~s
z
pardonab|le 'pɑːd ᵊn əb |ᵊl ‖ 'pɑːrd- ~ly li
pardoner 'pɑːd ᵊn ə ‖ 'pɑːrd ᵊn ər ~s z
pare peə ‖ peᵊr pæᵊr *(= pair)* **pared** peəd
‖ peᵊrd pæᵊrd **pares** peəz ‖ peᵊrz pæᵊrz
paring 'peər ɪŋ ‖ 'per ɪŋ 'pær-
pared-down ˌpeəd 'daʊn ◄ ‖ ˌperd- pærd-
paregoric ˌpær ə 'gɒr ɪk ◄ -ɪ- ‖ -'gɔːr ɪk ◄
ˌper-, -'gɑːr-
parenchyma pə 'reŋk ɪm ə §-əm-
par|ent *n, v* 'peər |ənt ‖ 'per |ənt 'pær-
~**ented** ənt ɪd -əd ‖ ənt̬ əd ~**enting** ənt ɪŋ
‖ ənt̬ ɪŋ ~**ents** ənts
'**parent ˌcompany,** ˌ‧‧‧'‧‧‧
parentag|e 'peər ənt ɪdʒ ‖ 'per ənt̬ ɪdʒ 'pær-
~**es** ɪz əz
parental pə 'rent ᵊl ‖ -'rent̬ ᵊl ~**ly** i
parenteral pæ 'rent ər əl pə- ‖ -'rent̬-
parenth|esis pə 'renᵗθ |əs ɪs -ɪs-, §-əs ~**eses**
ə siːz ɪ-
parenthesis|e, parenthesiz|e
pə 'renᵗθ ə saɪz ~**ed** d ~**es** ɪz əz ~**ing** ɪŋ
parenthetic ˌpær ən 'θet ɪk ◄ -en- ‖ -'θet̬ ɪk ◄
ˌper- ~**al** ᵊl ~**ally** ᵊl i
parenthood 'peər ənt hʊd ‖ 'per- 'pær-
parentless 'peər ənt ləs -lɪs ‖ 'per- 'pær-
parent-teacher ˌpeər ənt 'tiːtʃ ə
‖ ˌper ənt 'tiːtʃ ʳr ˌpær-
ˌparent-'teacher associˌation
pareo 'pɑːr eɪ əʊ pɑː 'reɪ- ‖ -oʊ ~**s** z
parer 'peər ə ‖ 'per ʳr 'pær- ~**s** z
parerg|on pə 'rɜːg |ɒn -'eəg-, -|ən ‖ -'rɜːg ɑːn
-'rerg- ~**a** ə
paresis pə 'riːs ɪs §-əs; 'pær əs-, -ɪs-
paretic pə 'ret ɪk ‖ -'ret̬-
pareu 'pɑːr eɪ uː pɑː 'reɪ- ~**s** z
par excellence ˌₚₐpɑːʳ 'eks ə lɑːnˢs -lɒ̃s,
-əl ənˢs ‖ ˌpɑːr ˌeks ə 'lɑːnˢs —*Fr*
[pa ʁɛk sɛ lɑ̃ːs]
parfait ˌpɑː 'feɪ '‧‧ ‖ ˌpɑːr- ~**s** z
Parfitt 'pɑːf ɪt §-ət ‖ 'pɑːrf-
parfum pɑː 'fʌ̃ -'fʌm ‖ pɑːr- —*Fr* [paʁ fœ̃]
parg|et 'pɑːdʒ |ɪt §-ət ‖ 'pɑːrdʒ |ət ~**eted** ɪt ɪd
§ət-, -əd ‖ ət̬ əd ~**eting** ɪt ɪŋ §ət- ‖ ət̬ ɪŋ ~**ets**
ɪts §əts ‖ əts
Pargiter 'pɑːdʒ ɪt ə §-ət- ‖ 'pɑːrdʒ ət̬ ʳr
Parham 'pær əm
parhelia pɑː 'hiːl i ə ‖ pɑːr-
parheliacal ˌpɑː hɪ 'laɪ ək ᵊl ◄ §-hə- ‖ ˌpɑːr-
parhelic ₚₐpɑː 'hiːl ɪk ‖ ₚₐpɑːr-
parheli|on pɑː 'hiːl i |ən -ɒn ‖ pɑːr- ~**a** ə
pariah pə 'raɪ ə 'pær i ə ~**s** z
Parian 'peər i ən ‖ 'per- 'pær- ~**s** z
parietal pə 'raɪ ət ᵊl -ɪt- ‖ -ət̬ ᵊl ~**s** z
pari-mutuel ˌpær i 'mjuːtʃ u əl -'mjuːt ju əl,
-'mjuːtʃ əl ‖ ˌper- ~**s** z
paring 'peər ɪŋ ‖ 'per- 'pær- ~**s** z *(= pairing)*

pari passu ˌpær i 'pæs uː ˌpɑːr-, -juː
‖ ˌpɑː r i 'pɑːs uː
paripinnate ˌpær i 'pɪn eɪt ◄ -ə- ‖ ˌper-
Paris 'pær ɪs §-əs ‖ 'per- —*Fr* [pa ʁi]
parish, P~ 'pær ɪʃ ‖ 'per- ~**es** ɪz əz
ˌparish 'clerk; ˌparish 'priest; ˌparish
'register
parishioner pə 'rɪʃ ᵊn ə ‖ ʳr ~**s** z
parish-pump ˌpær ɪʃ 'pʌmp ‖ ˌper-
Parisian pə 'rɪz i ən ‖ pə 'rɪʒ ᵊn -'riːʒ- *(*)* ~**s** z
parisyllabic ˌpær ɪ sɪ 'læb ɪk ◄ ˌ-ə-, -sə'--
‖ ˌper-
parit|y 'pær ət |i -ɪt- ‖ -ət̬ |i 'per- ~**ies** ɪz
park, Park pɑːk ‖ pɑːrk **parked** pɑːkt ‖ pɑːrkt
parking 'pɑːk ɪŋ ‖ 'pɑːrk ɪŋ **parks** pɑːks
‖ pɑːrks
ˌPark 'Avenue
parka 'pɑːk ə ‖ 'pɑːrk ə ~**s** z
park-and-ride ˌpɑːk ənd 'raɪd ‖ ˌpɑːrk-
Parke pɑːk ‖ pɑːrk
Parker 'pɑːk ə ‖ 'pɑːrk ʳr
Parkes pɑːks ‖ pɑːrks
Parkeston, Parkestone 'pɑːkst ən ‖ 'pɑːrkst-
Parkgate *(i)* 'pɑːk geɪt ‖ 'pɑːrk-, *(ii)* ˌ‧'‧ —*In
Co. Antrim, (i); in Cheshire, (ii).*
Parkhouse 'pɑːk haʊs ‖ 'pɑːrk-
Parkhurst 'pɑːk hɜːst ‖ 'pɑːrk hɜːst
parkin, P~ 'pɑːk ɪn §-ən ‖ 'pɑːrk-
parking 'pɑːk ɪŋ ‖ 'pɑːrk ɪŋ
'parking ˌgarage ‖ ˌ‧‧ ‧ˌ‧; 'parking light;
'parking lot; 'parking ˌmeter; 'parking
space; 'parking ˌticket; 'park ˌkeeper
Parkinson 'pɑːk ɪn sən §-ən- ‖ 'pɑːrk- ~**'s** z
'Parkinson's diˌsease; 'Parkinson's law
parkinsonian ˌpɑːk ɪn 'səʊn i ən ◄
‖ ˌpɑːrk ən 'soʊn-
parkinsonism 'pɑːk ɪn sə ˌnɪz əm §'-ən-,
-sən ˌɪz- ‖ 'pɑːrk-
parkland 'pɑːk lænd ‖ 'pɑːrk- ~**s** z
Parkray *tdmk* 'pɑːk reɪ ‖ 'pɑːrk-
Parks pɑːks ‖ pɑːrks
Parkstone 'pɑːkst ən ‖ 'pɑːrk stoʊn
parkway 'pɑːk weɪ ‖ 'pɑːrk- ~**s** z
park|y 'pɑːk |i ‖ 'pɑːrk |i ~**ier** i ə ‖ i ʳr ~**iest**
i ɪst i əst
parlance 'pɑːl ənᵗs ‖ 'pɑːrl-
parlando pɑː 'lænd əʊ ‖ pɑːr 'lɑːnd oʊ —*It*
[par 'lan do]
parlay 'pɑːl i ‖ 'pɑːrl eɪ -i ~**ed** d ~**ing** ɪŋ ~**s** z
parley 'pɑːl i ‖ 'pɑːrl i ~**ed** d ~**ing** ɪŋ ~**s** z
parleyvoo ˌpɑːl i 'vuː -eɪ- ‖ ˌpɑːrl-
parliament, P~ 'pɑːl ə mənt -ɪ-, -jə- ‖ 'pɑːrl-
~**s** s
parliamentarian ˌpɑːl ə men 'teər i ən ˌ-ɪ-,
ˌ-jə-, -mən'-- ‖ ˌpɑːrl ə men 'ter- -mən'-- ~**ism**
ˌɪz əm ~**s** z
parliamentary ˌpɑːl ə 'ment ər i ◄ ˌ-ɪ-, ˌ-jə-
‖ ˌpɑːrl ə 'ment̬-
Parlophone *tdmk* 'pɑːl ə fəʊn ‖ 'pɑːrl ə foʊn
parlor, parlour 'pɑːl ə ‖ 'pɑːrl ʳr ~**s** z
'parlor car; 'parlour game; 'parlour maid
parlous 'pɑːl əs ‖ 'pɑːrl əs ~**ly** li ~**ness** nəs nɪs
parlyaree ˌpɑːl i 'ɑːr i ‖ ˌpɑːrl-

Parma 'pɑːm ə ‖ 'pɑːrm ə —*It* ['par ma]
Parmenides pɑː 'men ɪ diːz -ə- ‖ pɑːr-
Parmenter 'pɑːm ɪnt ə -ənt- ‖ 'pɑːrm ənt ᵊr
Parmentier pɑː 'ment i̯ə -'mɒnt i eɪ;
   'pɑːm ənt jeɪ ‖ ˌpɑːrm ən 'tjeɪ —*Fr*
   [paʁ mɑ̃ tje] *(*)*
Parmesan ˌpɑːm ɪ 'zæn ◂ -ə- ‖ 'pɑːrm ə zɑːn
   -ʒɑːn, -zæn; -əz ən *(*)*
   ˌParmesan 'cheese
parmigiana ˌpɑːm ɪ 'dʒɑːn ə -'ʒɑːn- ‖ ˌpɑːrm-
   —*It* [par mi 'dʒɑː na]
Parminter 'pɑːm ɪnt ə -ənt- ‖ 'pɑːrm ənt ᵊr
Parmiter 'pɑːm ɪt ə -ət- ‖ 'pɑːrm ət ᵊr
Parnassian pɑː 'næs i̯ən ‖ pɑːr- ~s z
Parnassus pɑː 'næs əs ‖ pɑːr- —*ModGk*
   Parnassos [par na 'sɔs]
Parnell *(i)* pɑː 'nel ‖ pɑːr-, *(ii)* 'pɑːn ᵊl
   ‖ 'pɑːrn ᵊl
Parnes pɑːnz ‖ pɑːrnz
parochial pə 'rəʊk i̯əl ‖ -'roʊk- ~ism ˌɪz əm
   ~ly i
parodist 'pær əd ɪst §-əst ‖ 'per- ~s s
parod|y 'pær əd |i ‖ 'per- ~ied id ~ies iz
   ~ying i ɪŋ
paroecious pə 'riːʃ əs
parol 'pær əl pə 'rəʊl, →-'rʊʊl ‖ 'per-
parol|e pə 'rəʊl →-'rʊʊl ‖ -'roʊl ~ed d ~es z
   ~ing ɪŋ
parolee pə ˌrəʊ 'liː ‖ -ˌroʊ- pə 'roʊl iː ~s z
paronomasia ˌpær ən ə 'meɪz i̯ə -ə nəʊ-,
   -'meɪs- ‖ ˌpær ə noʊ 'meɪʒ ə ˌper-, -'meɪʒ i̯ə
paronychia ˌpær ə 'nɪk i̯ə ‖ ˌper-
paronym 'pær ə nɪm ‖ 'per- ~s z
paronym|ous pə 'rɒn ɪm |əs pæ-, -əm-
   ‖ -'rɑːn- ~ously əs li ~y i
Paroo 'pɑːr uː
Paros 'peər ɒs 'pær-, 'pɑːr- ‖ 'per ɑːs 'pær-
parotid pə 'rɒt ɪd §-əd ‖ -'rɑːt̬ əd
parotitis ˌpær ə 'taɪt ɪs §-əs ‖ -'taɪt̬ əs ˌper-
-parous *stress-imposing* pər əs — **oviparous**
   əʊ 'vɪp ər əs ‖ oʊ-
parousia, P~ pə 'ruːz i̯ə -'ruːs-
paroxysm 'pær ək ˌsɪz əm -ɒk-; pə 'rɒks ˌɪz-
   ‖ 'per-; pə 'rɑːks ˌɪz- ~s z
paroxysmal ˌpær ək 'sɪz məl ◂ -ɒk- ‖ ˌper- ~ly
   i
paroxytone pə 'rɒks ɪ təʊn pæ-, -ə-
   ‖ -'rɑːks ə toʊn ~s z
Parozone *tdmk* 'pær ə zəʊn ‖ -zoʊn 'per-
parquet 'pɑːk eɪ -i ‖ pɑːr 'keɪ *(*)* ~ed d ~ing
   ɪŋ ~s z
parquetr|y 'pɑːk ɪtr |i -ətr- ‖ 'pɑːrk- ~ies iz
parr, Parr pɑː ‖ pɑːr (= *par*) **parrs, Parr's** pɑːz
   ‖ pɑːrz
Parracombe 'pær ə kuːm ‖ 'per-
Parramatta, p~ ˌpær ə 'mæt ə ‖ -'mæt̬ ə ˌper-
parrel 'pær əl ‖ 'per- ~s z
Parret, Parrett 'pær ɪt §-ət ‖ 'per-
parricidal ˌpær ɪ 'saɪd ᵊl ◂ -ə- ‖ ˌper-
parricide 'pær ɪ saɪd -ə- ‖ 'per- ~s z
Parrish 'pær ɪʃ ‖ 'per-
parr|ot, P~ 'pær |ət ‖ 'per- ~oted ət ɪd -əd
   ‖ ət̬ əd ~oting ət ɪŋ ‖ ət̬ ɪŋ ~ots əts

parrot-fashion 'pær ət ˌfæʃ ᵊn ‖ 'per-
parrotfish 'pær ət fɪʃ ‖ 'per- ~es ɪz əz
Parrott 'pær ət ‖ 'per-
parr|y, Parry 'pær |i ‖ 'per- ~ied id ~ies iz
   ~ying i ɪŋ
parsable 'pɑːz əb ᵊl ‖ 'pɑːrs-
parse pɑːz ‖ pɑːrs *(*)* **parsed** pɑːzd ‖ pɑːrst
   parses 'pɑːz ɪz -əz ‖ 'pɑːrs əz **parsing**
   'pɑːz ɪŋ ‖ 'pɑːrs ɪŋ
parsec 'pɑː sek ‖ 'pɑːr- ~s s
Parsee 'pɑːs iː ˌpɑː 'siː ‖ 'pɑːrs ɪ ˌpɑːr 'siː —*In*
   India, ˌˑˈˑ ~s z
parser 'pɑːs ə ‖ 'pɑːrs ᵊr ~s z
Parsi —*see* **Parsee**
Parsifal 'pɑːs ɪf ᵊl -əf-; -ɪ fɑːl, -ə-, -fæl ‖ 'pɑːrs-
   —*Ger* ['paʁ zi fal]
parsimonious ˌpɑːs ɪ 'məʊn i̯əs ◂ ˌˑə-
   ‖ ˌpɑːrs ə 'moʊn- ~ly li ~ness nəs nɪs
parsimony 'pɑːs ɪm ən i '-əm-
   ‖ 'pɑːrs ə moʊn i *(*)*
Parsippany pə 'sɪp ən i ‖ pᵊr-
parsley 'pɑːs li ‖ 'pɑːrs li
Parsley *family name* 'pɑːz li ‖ 'pɑːrz-
Parslow 'pɑːz ləʊ ‖ 'pɑːrz loʊ 'pɑːrs-
parsnip 'pɑːs nɪp §-nəp ‖ 'pɑːrs- ~s s
parson 'pɑːs ᵊn ‖ 'pɑːrs ᵊn ~s z
   ˌparson's 'nose
parsonag|e 'pɑːs ᵊn ɪdʒ ‖ 'pɑːrs- ~es ɪz əz
parsonic pɑː 'sɒn ɪk ‖ pɑːr 'sɑːn ɪk ~al ᵊl
Parsons 'pɑːs ᵊnz ‖ 'pɑːrs-
part pɑːt ‖ pɑːrt **parted** 'pɑːt ɪd -əd ‖ 'pɑːrt̬ əd
   parting 'pɑːt ɪŋ ‖ 'pɑːrt̬ ɪŋ **parts** pɑːts
   ‖ pɑːrts
   ˌpart ex'change; ˌpart of 'speech; 'part
   work
par|take pɑː |'teɪk ‖ pɑːr- pᵊr- ~taken 'teɪk ən
   ~taker/s 'teɪk ə/z ‖ 'teɪk ᵊr/z ~takes 'teɪks
   ~taking 'teɪk ɪŋ ~took 'tʊk §'tuːk
parterre pɑː 'teə ‖ pɑːr 'teᵊr —*Fr* [paʁ tɛːʁ]
   ~s z
Parthenia pɑː 'θiːn i̯ə ‖ pɑːr-
parthenium pɑː 'θiːn i̯əm ‖ pɑːr- ~s z
parthenogenesis ˌpɑːθ ə nəʊ 'dʒen əs ɪs ˌˑɪ-,
   -ɪs ɪs, §-əs ‖ ˌpɑːrθ ə noʊ-
Parthenon 'pɑːθ ən ən -ɪn-; -ə nɒn, -ɪ-
   ‖ 'pɑːrθ ə nɑːn
Parthenope pɑː 'θen əp i ‖ pɑːr-
Parthi|a 'pɑːθ i̯ə ‖ 'pɑːrθ- ~an/s ən/z
partial 'pɑːʃ ᵊl ‖ 'pɑːrʃ ᵊl ~ness nəs nɪs ~s z
partialit|y ˌpɑːʃ i 'æl ət i |i -ɪt i
   ‖ ˌpɑːrʃ i 'æl ət̬ |i ~ies iz
partially 'pɑːʃ əl̯i ‖ 'pɑːrʃ-
participant pɑː 'tɪs ɪp ənt -əp- ‖ pᵊr- pɑːr- ~s s
partici|pate pɑː 'tɪs ɪ |peɪt -ə- ‖ pɑːr- pᵊr-
   ~pated peɪt ɪd -əd ‖ peɪt̬ əd ~pates peɪts
   ~pating peɪt ɪŋ ‖ peɪt̬ ɪŋ
participation pɑː ˌtɪs ɪ 'peɪʃ ᵊn ˌpɑːt ɪs-, -ə'-·-
   ‖ pɑːr- pᵊr-
participative pɑː 'tɪs ɪ peɪt ɪv -'ə, -·pət ɪv
   ‖ pɑːr 'tɪs ə pət̬ ɪv pᵊr-, -peɪt̬ ɪv
participator pɑː 'tɪs ɪ |peɪt ə -ə-
   ‖ pɑːr 'tɪs ə peɪt̬ ᵊr pᵊr- ~s z

participatory pɑː ˌtɪs ɪ ˈpeɪt ər i ◂ ˌpɑːt ɪs-,
-ə'--; pɑː ˈtɪs ɪ pət ̩ər i, -'-ə-
‖ pɑːr ˈtɪs əp ə tɔːr i pᵊr-, -tour i

participial ˌpɑːt ɪ ˈsɪp i ̩əl ◂ ˌ-ə- ‖ ˌpɑːrṭ ə- **~ly**
i

participle ˈpɑːt ɪs ɪp ᵊl '·əs-, -əp ·; pɑː ˈtɪs-;
ˈpɑːts ɪp ᵊl, -əp- ‖ ˈpɑːrṭ ə sɪp ᵊl **~s** z

Partick ˈpɑːt ɪk ‖ ˈpɑːrṭ ɪk

particle ˈpɑːt ɪk ᵊl ‖ ˈpɑːrṭ- **~s** z

parti-colored, parti-coloured
ˌpɑːt i ˈkʌl əd ◂ '·, ·, · ‖ ˌpɑːrṭ i ˈkʌl ᵊrd ◂

particular pə ˈtɪk jʊl ə -jəl-; △-'tɪk lə
‖ pᵊr ˈtɪk jəl ᵊr pə- **~s** z

particularis... —see **particulariz...**

particularism pə ˈtɪk jʊl ər ˌɪz əm -'·jəl-
‖ pᵊr ˈtɪk jəl- pə-, pɑːr-

particularit|y pə ˌtɪk ju ˈlær ət |i -ˌjə-, -ɪt i
‖ pᵊr ˌtɪk jə ˈlær əṭ |i pə-, ˌpɑːr ˌtɪk·'--, -'ler-
~ies iz

particularization pə ˌtɪk jʊl ər aɪ ˈzeɪʃ ᵊn
-ˌjəl-, -ɪ'-- ‖ pᵊr ˌtɪk jəl ər ə- pə-, pɑːr-

particulariz|e pə ˈtɪk jʊl ə raɪz -'·jəl-
‖ pᵊr ˈtɪk jəl- pə-, pɑːr- **~ed** d **~es** ɪz əz **~ing**
ɪŋ

particularly pə ˈtɪk jʊl ə li -'·jəl-
‖ pᵊr ˈtɪk jəl ᵊr pə- —in casual speech
sometimes also -'tɪk jəl ̩i

particulate pɑː ˈtɪk jʊl ət pə-, -ɪt, -ju leɪt
‖ pɑːr ˈtɪk jəl ət pᵊr-, -jə leɪt

parting ˈpɑːt ɪŋ ‖ ˈpɑːrṭ ɪŋ **~s** z
ˌparting ˈshot

Partington ˈpɑːt ɪŋ tən ‖ ˈpɑːrṭ-

parti pris ˌpɑːt i ˈpriː ‖ ˌpɑːrṭ- —Fr
[paʀ ti pʀi]

partisan ˌpɑːt ɪ ˈzæn ◂ -ə-, '· · · ‖ ˈpɑːrṭ əz ən
-əs-; -ə zæn (*) **~s** z **~ship** ʃɪp

partita pɑː ˈtiːt ə ‖ pɑːr ˈtiːṭ ə

-partite ˈpɑːt aɪt ‖ ˈpɑːrt- — **tripartite**
ˌ(ˌ)traɪ ˈpɑːt aɪt ‖ -'pɑːrt-

partition pɑː ˈtɪʃ ᵊn pə- ‖ pɑːr- pᵊr- **~ed** d **~ing**
ɪŋ **~s** z

partitive ˈpɑːt ət ɪv -ɪt- ‖ ˈpɑːrṭ əṭ ɪv **~ly** li **~s**
z

partiz... —see **partis...**

partly ˈpɑːt li ‖ ˈpɑːrt-

partner ˈpɑːt nə ‖ ˈpɑːrt nᵊr **~ed** d **partnering**
ˈpɑːt nər ɪŋ ‖ ˈpɑːrt nər ɪŋ **~less** ləs lɪs **~s** z
~ship/s ʃɪp/s

Parton ˈpɑːt ᵊn ‖ ˈpɑːrt ᵊn

partook pɑː ˈtʊk §-'tuːk ‖ pɑːr-

partridg|e, P~ ˈpɑːtr ɪdʒ ‖ ˈpɑːrtr ɪdʒ **~es** ɪz
əz

part-singing ˈpɑːt ˌsɪŋ ɪŋ ‖ ˈpɑːrt-

part-song ˈpɑːt sɒŋ ‖ ˈpɑːrt sɔːŋ -sɑːŋ **~s** z

part-time ˌpɑːt ˈtaɪm ◂ ‖ ˌpɑːrt-
ˌpart-time ˈjob

part-timer ˌpɑːt ˈtaɪm ə ‖ ˌpɑːrt ˈtaɪm ᵊr **~s** z

parturient pɑː ˈtjʊər i ̩ənt ‖ pɑːr ˈtʊr- -'tjʊr-

parturition ˌpɑːt jʊ ˈrɪʃ ᵊn -jə-, ˌpɑːtʃ ə-
‖ ˌpɑːrṭ ə-, ˌpɑːrtʃ ə-, ˌpɑːrt ju-

partway ˌpɑːt ˈweɪ ◂ '· · ‖ ˌpɑːrt-

part|y ˈpɑːt |i ‖ ˈpɑːrṭ |i **~ied** id **~ies** iz **~ying**
i ɪŋ

ˌparty ˈline 'political view', ˈparty line
'shared phone line'; **ˈparty piece**; ˌparty
ˈpolitics; **ˈparty ˌpooper**; ˌparty ˈwall

party-col... —see **parti-col...**

partygoer ˈpɑːt i ˌɡəʊ ə ‖ ˈpɑːrṭ i ˌɡoʊ ᵊr **~s** z

parvenu, parvenue ˈpɑːv ə nju: -nu:
‖ ˈpɑːrv ə nu: -nju: —Fr [paʀ və ny] **~s** z

parvo ˈpɑːv əʊ ‖ ˈpɑːrv oʊ **~s** z

parvovirus ˈpɑːv əʊ ˌvaɪᵊr əs ‖ ˈpɑːrv oʊ- **~es**
ɪz əz

Parzival ˈpɑːts ɪ fɑːl -ə- ‖ ˈpɑːrts- —Ger
[ˈpar tsi fal]

pas pɑː —Fr [pa] —see also phrases with this
word

Pasadena ˌpæs ə ˈdiːn ə

Pasargadae pə ˈsɑːɡ ə di: ‖ -'sɑːrɡ-

pascal unit of pressure ˈpæsk ᵊl ₍ₙ₎pæ ˈskæl
‖ ₍ₙ₎pɑː ˈskɑːl **~s** z

Pascal proper name; computer language
₍ₙ₎pæ ˈskæl -'skɑːl; ˈpæsk æl, -ɑːl, -ᵊl —Fr
[pas kal]

Pascale ₍ₙ₎pæ ˈskɑːl -'skæl

paschal ˈpæsk ᵊl ˈpɑːsk-

Pasco, Pascoe ˈpæsk əʊ ‖ -oʊ

pas de basque ˌpɑː də ˈbɑː -'bɑːsk ‖ -'bæsk
—Fr [pad bask]

pas de deux ˌpɑː də ˈdɜː ‖ -'du: -'dɜː —Fr
[pad dø]

paseo pæ ˈseɪ əʊ ‖ -oʊ pɑː- —Sp [pa ˈse o]

pash pæʃ **pashes** ˈpæʃ ɪz -əz

pasha, Pasha ˈpɑːʃ ə ˈpæʃ-, pə ˈʃɑː **~s** z

pashmina pæʃ ˈmiːn ə pʌʃ- **~s** z

Pashto ˈpʌʃt əʊ ˈpæʃt- ‖ -oʊ

pasigraph|y pə ˈsɪɡ rəf |i **~ies** iz

Pasiphae, Pasiphaë pə ˈsɪf i iː -eɪ- ‖ -ə-

Pasmore ˈpɑːs mɔː ˈpæs- ‖ ˈpæs mɔːr -mour

paso doble ˌpæs əʊ ˈdəʊb leɪ
‖ ˌpɑːs oʊ ˈdoʊb- —Sp [ˌpa so ˈðoβ le]

Pasolini ˌpæs əʊ ˈliːn i ‖ -oʊ- —It
[pa zo ˈliː ni]

pasqueflower ˈpæsk ˌflaʊ̩ə ˈpɑːsk- ‖ -ˌflaʊ̩ᵊr
~s z

pasquinad|e ˌpæsk wɪ ˈneɪd -wə- **~ed** ɪd əd
~es z **~ing** ɪŋ

pass pɑːs §pæs ‖ pæs **passed** pɑːst §pæst
‖ pæst **passes** ˈpɑːs ɪz -əz ‖ ˈpæs əz **passing**
ˈpɑːs ɪŋ §'pæs- ‖ ˈpæs ɪŋ
ˈpass deˌgree; ˌpass ˈout v; ˈpass out n

passab|le ˈpɑːs əb |ᵊl §'pæs- ‖ ˈpæs- **~leness**
ᵊl nəs -nɪs **~ly** li

passacaglia ˌpæs ə ˈkɑːl i ̩ə ‖ ˌpɑːs- -'kæl-
—Not actually an Italian word.

passade pæ ˈseɪd pə-

passag|e ˈpæs ɪdʒ —but as a move in dressage,
also pæ ˈsɑːʒ **~es** ɪz əz

passageway ˈpæs ɪdʒ weɪ **~s** z

Passaic pə ˈseɪ ɪk

Passamaquoddy ˌpæs əm ə ˈkwɒd i
‖ -'kwɑːd i

passant ˈpæs ᵊnt ˈpɑːs-, -ɒ̃t —Fr [pa sɑ̃]

Passat tdmk pæ ˈsæt -'sɑːt

passbook ˈpɑːs bʊk §'pæs-, §-buːk ‖ ˈpæs- **~s** s

Passchendaele ˈpæʃ ᵊn deɪᵊl

passe, passé, passée 'pɑːs eɪ 'pæs- ‖ pæ 'seɪ
—*Fr* [pa se] *(*)*
passel 'pæs ᵊl ~s z
passenger, P~ 'pæs ɪndʒ ə -əndʒ- ‖ -ᵊr ~s z
passe-partout ˌpæs pɑː 'tuː ˌpɑːs-, -pə-, '···
‖ -pɑːr 'tuː -pᵊr- —*Fr* [pas paʁ tu]
pass|erby 'pɑːs |ə 'baɪ §ˌpæs- ‖ ˌpæs |ᵊr 'baɪ
'··· **~ersby** əz 'baɪ ‖ 'rz 'baɪ
passerine 'pæs ə raɪn -riːn
Passfield 'pɑːs fiːᵊld 'pæs- ‖ 'pæs-
passible *'capable of feeling'* 'pæs ɪb ᵊl -əb-
passim 'pæs ɪm §-əm
passing 'pɑːs ɪŋ §'pæs- ‖ 'pæs ɪŋ
   ˌpassing 'note; ˌpassing 'off; ˌpassing
   'out; ˌpassing 'shot
passion, P~ 'pæʃ ᵊn ~s z
   'passion play; ˌPassion 'Sunday; ˌPassion
   'week
passionate 'pæʃ ᵊn ət ~ly li
passionflower 'pæʃ ᵊn ˌflaʊ ə ‖ -ˌflaʊ ᵊr ~s z
passionfruit 'pæʃ ᵊn fruːt ~s s
passionless 'pæʃ ᵊn ləs -lɪs ~ly li ~ness nəs
   nɪs
Passiontide 'pæʃ ᵊn taɪd
passive 'pæs ɪv §-əv ~ly li ~ness nəs nɪs ~s z
passivis... —*see* **passivis...**
passivity pæ 'sɪv ət i pə-, -ɪt- ‖ -ət i
passivization ˌpæs ɪv aɪ 'zeɪʃ ᵊn ˌ·əv-, -ɪ'-
   ‖ -ɪv ə-
passiviz|e 'pæs ɪ vaɪz -ə- ~ed d ~es ɪz əz ~ing
   ɪŋ
passkey 'pɑːs kiː §'pæs- ‖ 'pæs- ~s z
Passmore 'pɑːs mɔː 'pæs- ‖ 'pæs mɔːr -moʊr
passover, P~ 'pɑːs ˌəʊv ə §'pæs-
   ‖ 'pæs ˌoʊv ᵊr ~s z
passport 'pɑːs pɔːt §'pæs- ‖ 'pæs pɔːrt -poʊrt
   ~s s
password 'pɑːs wɜːd §'pæs- ‖ 'pæs wɜːd ~s z
Passy pæ 'siː ‖ pɑː- —*Fr* [pa si]
past pɑːst §pæst ‖ pæst
   ˌpast 'master; ˌpast 'participle, -'···;
   ˌpast 'perfect; ˌpast 'tense
pasta 'pæst ə ‖ 'pɑːst ə *(*)*
past|e peɪst ~ed ɪd əd ~es s ~ing ɪŋ
pasteboard 'peɪst bɔːd ‖ -bɔːrd -boʊrd
pastel 'pæst ᵊl ₍ₜ₎pæ 'stel ‖ pæ 'stel ~s z
pastelist, pastellist 'pæst ᵊl ɪst §-əst
   ‖ pæ 'stel- ~s s
pastern 'pæst ən -ɜːn ‖ -ᵊrn ~s z
Pasternak 'pæst ə næk ‖ -ᵊr- —*Russ*
   [pə sʲtʲɪr 'nak]
paste-up 'peɪst ʌp ~s s
Pasteur ₍ₜ₎pæ 'stɜː ˌpɑː- ‖ -'stɜːː —*Fr* [pa stœːʁ]
pasteuris... —*see* **pasteuriz...**
pasteurization ˌpɑːs tʃər aɪ 'zeɪʃ ᵊn ˌpæs-;
   ˌpɑːst ər-, ˌpæst-, -ˌjʊr-; -ɪ'-- ‖ ˌpæs tʃər ə-
   -ˌtər-
pasteuriz|e 'pɑːs tʃə raɪz 'pæs-; 'pɑːst ə-,
   'pæst-, -juə-, -jə- ‖ 'pæs tʃə raɪz -tə- ~ed d
   ~es ɪz əz ~ing ɪŋ
pastich|e pæ 'stiːʃ 'pæst iːʃ ‖ pɑː- ~es ɪz əz
pastil, pastille 'pæst ᵊl -ɪl; ₍ₜ₎pæ 'stiːᵊl ~s z
pastime 'pɑːs taɪm §'pæs- ‖ 'pæs- ~s z

pasting 'peɪst ɪŋ ~s z
pastis pæ 'stiːs -'stɪs —*Fr* [pa stis]
past-master 'pɑːst ˌmɑːst ə §-,mæst-, ˌ·'··
   ‖ 'pæst ˌmæst ᵊr
Paston 'pæst ən
pastor 'pɑːst ə §'pæst- ‖ 'pæst ᵊr ~s z
pastoral 'pɑːst ᵊr əl 'pæst-; §pɑː 'stɔːr əl, §pæ-
   ‖ 'pæst- —*but as a noun, sometimes* ˌ·ə 'rɑːl
   ~s z
pastorale ˌpæst ə 'rɑːl ˌpɑːst-, -'ræl; -'·i ~s z
pastoral|ism 'pɑːst ᵊr əl ‖ˌɪz əm 'pæst-
   ‖ 'pæst- ~ist/s ɪst/s §əst/s ~ly i
pastorate 'pɑːst ər ət §'pæst-, -ɪt ‖ 'pæst- ~s s
pastrami pə 'strɑːm i pæ-
pas|try 'peɪs |tri ~tries triz
pastrycook 'peɪs tri kʊk §-kuːk ~s s
pasturage 'pɑːs tʃər ɪdʒ §'pæs-, -tjʊr-, -tjər-
   ‖ 'pæs-
pasture *n, v* 'pɑːs tʃə §'pæs-, -tjə, -tjʊə
   ‖ 'pæs tʃᵊr ~d d ~s z **pasturing** 'pɑːs tʃər ɪŋ
   §'pæs-, -tjər-, -tjʊr- ‖ 'pæs tʃᵊr ɪŋ
pastureland 'pɑːs tʃə lænd §'pæs- ‖ 'pæs tʃᵊr-
   ~s z
past|y *n 'pie'* 'pæst |i 'pɑːst- ~ies iz
past|y *adj 'paste-like'* 'peɪst |i ~ier i ə ‖ i ᵊr
   ~iest i ɪst i əst ~iness i nəs i nɪs
pasty-faced 'peɪst i feɪst ˌ·'·
pat, Pat pæt **pats, Pat's** pæts **patted** 'pæt ɪd
   -əd ‖ 'pæt əd **patting** 'pæt ɪŋ ‖ 'pæt ɪŋ
pat-a-cake 'pæt ə keɪk ‖ 'pæt-
patagi|um pə 'teɪdʒ i |əm ˌpæt ə 'dʒaɪ |əm
   ‖ ˌpæt- ~a ə
Patagoni|a ˌpæt ə 'gəʊn i |ə ‖ ˌpæt ə 'goʊn-
   ~an/s ən/z ◄
pataka *'Maori storehouse'* 'pɑːt ə kɑː ‖ 'pɑːt̬-
   ~s z
Pataki pə 'tæk i
pat-ball 'pæt bɔːl ‖ -bɑːl
patch, Patch pætʃ **patched** pætʃt **patches,
   Patch's** 'pætʃ ɪz -əz **patching** 'pætʃ ɪŋ
   ˌpatch 'pocket
patchouli 'pætʃ ʊl i -əl-; pə 'tʃuːl-, -iː
patchwork 'pætʃ wɜːk ‖ -wɜːːk ~s s
patch|y 'pætʃ |i ~ier i ə ‖ i ᵊr ~iest i ɪst i əst
   ~ily ɪ li əl i ~iness i nəs i nɪs
Pate peɪt
pate *'top of the head'* peɪt **pates** peɪts
pate, paté, pâté *'meat spread'* 'pæt eɪ -i
   ‖ pɑː 'teɪ pæ- —*Fr* [pa te] *(*)* **pates, patés,
   pâtés** 'pæt eɪz -iz ‖ pɑː 'teɪz pæ- —*see also
   phrases with this word*
pâte *'paste for porcelain'* pɑːt —*Fr* [pat]
pâté de foie ˌpæt eɪ də 'fwɑː ˌ·i- ‖ pɑː ˌteɪ-
   pæ- —*Fr* [pa ted fwa]
   ˌpâté de ˌfoie 'gras 'grɑː —*Fr* [gʁa]
Patel *(i)* pə 'tel, *(ii)* pə 'teɪᵊl
Pateley 'peɪt li
patell|a pə 'tel |ə ~ae iː ~ar ə ‖ ᵊr ~as əz
paten 'pæt ᵊn ~s z
patency 'peɪt ᵊn's i
pat|ent *n, adj, v* 'peɪt |ᵊnt 'pæt- ‖ 'pæt |ᵊnt
   'peɪt- *(*)* —*In BrE the pronunciation* 'pæt- *is
   mainly restricted to technical use; in AmE the*

pronunciation 'peɪt- *is used only in the sense* '*open, obvious*'. **~ented** ᵊnt ɪd -əd ‖ ᵊnt̬ əd
~enting ᵊnt ɪŋ ‖ ᵊnt̬ ɪŋ **~ents** ᵊnts
ˌpatent 'leather◂; ˌpatent 'medicine;
'Patent ˌOffice
patentable 'peɪt ᵊnt əb ᵊl 'pæt- ‖ 'pæt ᵊnt̬-
patentee ˌpeɪt ᵊn 'tiː ˌpæt- ‖ ˌpæt- **~s** z
patently 'peɪt ᵊnt li
pater '*prayer*' 'pæt ə 'pɑːt- ‖ 'pɑːt er 'pɑːt̬ ᵊr **~s**
z
Pater, pater '*father*' 'peɪt ə ‖ 'peɪt̬ ᵊr **~s**, **~'s** z
paterfamilias ˌpeɪt ə fə 'mɪl i æs ˌpæt-, -əs
‖ ˌpɑːt̬ ᵊr fə 'miːl i ˌəs ˌpeɪt̬-, ˌpæt̬- **~es** ɪz əz
paternal pə 'tɜːn ᵊl ‖ -'tɜːn-
paternalism pə 'tɜːn əl ˌɪz əm -ə ˌlɪz- ‖ -'tɜːn-
paternalistic pə ˌtɜːn ə 'lɪst ɪk ◂ -ᵊl 'ɪst-
‖ pə ˌtɜːn ᵊl 'ɪst ɪk ◂ **~ally** ᵊl i
paternally pə 'tɜːn əl i ‖ -'tɜːn-
paternity pə 'tɜːn ət i -ɪt- ‖ -'tɜːn ət̬ i —*In
contrast with* maternity, *sometimes* 'pə,··
pa'ternity test
paternoster, P~ ˌpæt ə 'nɒst ə ◂
‖ ˌpɑːt̬ ᵊr 'nɑːst ᵊr ◂ ˌpæt̬-, -'nɔːst-, '·· ,·· **~s** z
ˌPaternoster 'Row
Paterson 'pæt əs ən ‖ 'pæt̬ ᵊrs ən
path '*way*' pɑːθ §pæθ ‖ pæθ (*) **paths** pɑːðz
§pæðz, §pɑːθs, §pæθs ‖ pæðz pæθs
path '*pathology*' pæθ
'path lab
PATH *NY-NJ subway system* pæθ
-path pæθ — **osteopath** 'ɒst i əʊ pæθ
‖ 'ɑːst i ə pæθ
Pathan pə 'tɑːn —*Hindi* [pə t̪ʰɑːn̪] **~s** z
Pathé 'pæθ eɪ
pathetic pə 'θet ɪk ‖ -'θet̬ ɪk **~ally** ᵊl i
pathfinder 'pɑːθ ˌfaɪnd ə §'pæθ-
‖ 'pæθ ˌfaɪnd ᵊr **~s** z
pathic 'pæθ ɪk **~s** s
-pathic 'pæθ ɪk — **psychopathic**
ˌsaɪk əʊ 'pæθ ɪk ◂ ‖ -ə-
pathless 'pɑːθ ləs §'pæθ-, -lɪs ‖ 'pæθ- **~ness**
nəs nɪs
Pathmark *tdmk* 'pæθ mɑːk ‖ -mɑːrk
patho- *comb. form with stress-neutral suffix*
ˌpæθ əʊ ‖ -oʊ — **pathopsychology**
ˌpæθ əʊ saɪ 'kɒl ədʒ i ‖ -ə- *with
stress-imposing suffix* pə 'θɒ+ ‖ -'θɑː+ —
patholysis pə 'θɒl əs ɪs -ɪs ɪs, §-əs ‖ -'θɑːl-
pathogen 'pæθ ədʒ ən -ə dʒen **~s** z
pathogenic ˌpæθ ə 'dʒen ɪk ◂ **~ally** ᵊl i
pathognomy pə 'θɒg nəm i ‖ -'θɑːg-
pathological ˌpæθ ə 'lɒdʒ ɪk ᵊl ◂ ‖ -'lɑːdʒ-
~ly i
pathologist pə 'θɒl ədʒ ɪst §-əst ‖ -'θɑːl- **~s** s
patholog|y pə 'θɒl ədʒ |i ‖ -'θɑːl- **~ies** ɪz
pathos 'peɪθ ɒs ‖ -ɑːs -ɔːs, -oʊs
pathway 'pɑːθ weɪ §'pæθ- ‖ 'pæθ- **~s** z
-pathy *stress-imposing* pəθ i — **telepathy**
tə 'lep əθ i tɪ-, te-
Patiala ˌpʌt i 'ɑːl ə ‖ ˌpʌt̬- —*Panjabi*
[pə t̪i aː lə]
patience, P~ 'peɪʃ ᵊn'ts
patient 'peɪʃ ᵊnt **~ly** li **~s** s

patina 'pæt ɪn ə -ən-, pə 'tiːn ə ‖ pə 'tiːn ə (*)
~s z
patio 'pæt i əʊ ‖ 'pæt̬ i oʊ 'pɑːt̬- **~s** z
patisserie, pâtisserie pə 'tiːs ər i pæ-, -'tɪs-
—*Fr* [pa tis ʁi] **~s** z
Patmore 'pæt mɔː ‖ -mɔːr -moʊr
Patmos 'pæt mɒs ‖ -məs -mɑːs, -moʊs
Patna 'pæt nə 'pʌt- —*Hindi* [pət̪ n̪aː]
pat|ois *sing.* 'pæt |wɑː ‖ 'pɑːt- —*Fr* [pa twa]
~ois *pl* wɑːz —*Fr* [pa twa]
Paton 'peɪt ᵊn
Patras 'pætr æs -əs; pə 'træs —*Gk* ['pa tras]
patrial 'peɪtr i əl 'pætr- **~s** z
patriality ˌpeɪtr i 'æl ət i ˌpætr- -ət̬ i
patriarch 'peɪtr i ɑːk 'pætr- ‖ -ɑːrk **~s** s
patriarchal ˌpeɪtr i 'ɑːk ᵊl ◂ ˌpætr- ‖ -'ɑːrk ᵊl ◂
~ism ˌɪz əm **~ly** i
patriarchate 'peɪtr i ɑːk ət 'pætr-, -ɪt, -eɪt
‖ -ɑːrk- **~s** s
patriarch|y 'peɪtr i ɑːk |i 'pætr- ‖ -ɑːrk |i **~ies**
ɪz
Patrice pə 'triːs
Patricia pə 'trɪʃ ə -'trɪʃ i ə ‖ -'triːʃ-
patrician pə 'trɪʃ ᵊn **~s** z
patriciate pə 'trɪʃ i ət -eɪt
patricide 'pætr ɪ saɪd 'peɪtr-, -ə- **~s** z
Patrick 'pætr ɪk
patriclinous pə 'trɪk lɪn əs -lən-;
ˌpætr ɪ 'klaɪn əs ◂, -ə-
Patricroft 'pætr ɪ krɒft -ə- ‖ -krɔːft -krɑːft
patrilineal ˌpætr ə 'lɪn i əl ◂ -ˌɪ-
patrilocal ˌpætr ə 'ləʊk ᵊl ◂ -ˌɪ-, '·· ,··
‖ -'loʊk ᵊl ◂
patrimonial ˌpætr ə 'məʊn i əl ◂ -ˌɪ- ‖ -'moʊn-
~ly i
patrimon|y 'pætr ɪm ən |i '·əm- ‖ -ə moʊn |i
(*) **~ies** ɪz
patriot 'pætr i ət 'peɪtr- ‖ 'peɪtr- **~s** s

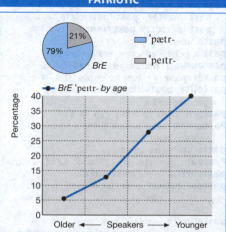

PATRIOTIC

patriotic ˌpætr i 'ɒt ɪk ◂ ˌpeɪtr-
‖ ˌpeɪtr i 'ɑːt̬ ɪk ◂ — *Preference poll, BrE:*
'pætr- *79%,* 'peɪtr- *21%.* **~ally** ᵊl i
patriotism 'pætr i ə ˌtɪz əm 'peɪtr- ‖ 'peɪtr-

patristic pə 'trɪst ɪk pæ- ~s s
Patroclus pə 'trɒk ləs ‖ -'troʊk-
patrol pə 'trəʊl →-'trɒʊl ‖ -'troʊl ~led d ~ling
ɪŋ ~s z
pa'trol car; pa'trol ˌwagon
patrol|man pə 'trəʊl |mən →-'trɒʊl-, -mæn
‖ -'troʊl- ~men mən men ~woman ˌwʊm ən
~women ˌwɪm ɪn -ən
patrology pə 'trɒl ədʒ i pæ- ‖ -'trɑːl-
patron 'peɪtr ən ~s z
ˌpatron 'saint
patronage 'pætr ən ɪdʒ
patronal pə 'trəʊn ᵊl pæ- ‖ 'peɪtr ən‿ᵊl (*)
patroness ˌpeɪtr ə 'nes '·· ·; -ən əs, -ɪs
‖ 'peɪtr ən əs ~es ɪz əz

PATRONISE

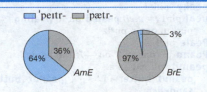

'peɪtr- ▨ 'pætr-

3%
64% | 36% | 97%
AmE | BrE

---

patronis|e, patroniz|e 'pætr ə naɪz ‖ 'peɪtr-
'pætr- — *Preference polls, AmE:* 'peɪtr- 64%,
'pætr- 36%; *BrE:* 'pætr- 97%, 'peɪtr- 3%. ~ed
d ~es ɪz əz ~ing ɪŋ
patronymic ˌpætr ə 'nɪm ɪk ◂ ~ally ᵊl̬ i ~s s
pats|y, Pats|y 'pæts |i ~ies, ~y's iz
Pattaya 'pæt eɪ ə -ɑː
patten, P~ 'pæt ᵊn ~s z
patter 'pæt ə ‖ 'pæt̬ ᵊr ~ed d pattering
'pæt ər ɪŋ ‖ 'pæt̬ ər ɪŋ ~s z
Patterdale 'pæt ə deᵊl ‖ 'pæt̬ ᵊr-
pattern 'pæt ᵊn ‖ 'pæt̬ ᵊrn ~ed d ~ing ˌɪŋ ‖ ɪŋ
~s z
Patterson 'pæt əs ən ‖ 'pæt̬ ᵊrs ən
Patti, Pattie 'pæt i ‖ 'pæt̬ i
Pattison 'pæt ɪs ən -əs- ‖ 'pæt̬-
Patton 'pæt ᵊn
patt|y, Patt|y 'pæt |i ‖ 'pæt̬ |i ~ies, ~y's iz
patulous 'pæt jʊl əs -jəl- ‖ 'pæt̬ʃ əl əs ~ly li
~ness nəs nɪs
patzer 'pɑːts ə 'pæts- ‖ -ᵊr ~s z
paua 'paʊ‿ə ~s z
paucal 'pɔːk ᵊl ‖ 'pɑːk-
paucity 'pɔːs ət i -ɪt- ‖ ᵊt̬ i 'pɑːs-
Paul pɔːl ‖ pɑːl Paul's pɔːlz ‖ pɑːlz
Paula 'pɔːl ə ‖ 'pɑːl-
Paulette ⑴pɔː 'let ‖ ⑴pɑː-
Pauli (i) 'paʊl i, (ii) 'pɔːl i ‖ 'pɑːl-
Pauline *adj 'relating to St Paul'; n 'pupil of St
Paul's School'* 'pɔːl aɪn ‖ 'pɑːl- ~s z
Pauline *forename* 'pɔːl iːn ‖ ⑴pɔː 'liːn ⑴pɑː-
(*)
Pauling 'pɔːl ɪŋ ‖ 'pɑːl-
Paulinus pɔː 'laɪn əs ‖ pɑː-
Paull pɔːl ‖ pɑːl
paulownia pɔː 'ləʊn i‿ə ‖ -'loʊn- pɑː- ~s z
Pauncefote 'pɔːn⸴s fət -fʊt ‖ 'pɑːnˌs-

paunch pɔːntʃ ‖ pɑːntʃ paunches 'pɔːntʃ ɪz -əz
‖ 'pɑːntʃ-
paunch|y 'pɔːntʃ |i ‖ 'pɑːntʃ- ~iness i nəs i nɪs
pauper 'pɔːp ə ‖ -ᵊr 'pɑːp- ~s z
pauperis... —*see* pauperiz...
pauperism 'pɔːp ər ˌɪz əm ‖ 'pɑːp-
pauperization ˌpɔːp ər aɪ 'zeɪʒ ᵊn -ɪ'·- ‖ -ər ə-
ˌpɑːp-
pauperiz|e 'pɔːp ə raɪz ‖ 'pɑːp- ~ed d ~es ɪz
əz ~ing ɪŋ
paupiette ˌpəʊp i 'et ‖ ˌpoʊp- ~s s —*or as*
singular —*Fr* [po pjɛt]
Pausanias pɔː 'seɪn i æs -əs ‖ pɑː-
pause pɔːz ‖ pɑːz paused pɔːzd ‖ pɑːzd pauses
'pɔːz ɪz -əz ‖ 'pɑːz- pausing 'pɔːz ɪŋ ‖ 'pɑːz-
pavan, pavane pə 'væn -'vɑːn, 'pæv ᵊn
‖ pə 'vɑːn -'væn ~s z
Pavarotti ˌpæv ə 'rɒt i ‖ -'rɑːt̬ i —*It*
[pa va 'rɔt ti]
pave peɪv paved peɪvd paves peɪvz paving
'peɪv ɪŋ
pavé 'pæv eɪ ‖ pæ 'veɪ —*Fr* [pa ve]
pavement 'peɪv mənt ~s s
'pavement ˌartist
Pavey 'peɪv i
pavilion pə 'vɪl i‿ən ‖ pə 'vɪl jən ~ed d ~ing
ɪŋ ~s z
paving 'peɪv ɪŋ
'paving stone
pavior, paviour, P~ 'peɪv jə ‖ -jᵊr ~s z
Pavitt 'pæv ɪt §-ət
Pavlov 'pæv lɒv ‖ -lɑːv 'pɑːv- —*Russ*
['pav ɫəf]
Pavlova, p~ pæv 'ləʊv ə 'pæv ləv ə ‖ -'loʊv ə
pɑːv- —*Russ* ['pav ɫə və] ~s z
Pavlovian ⑴pæv 'ləʊv i‿ən ‖ -'loʊv- ⑴pɑːv-
Pavlow 'pæv ləʊ ‖ -loʊ
Pavo 'pɑːv əʊ ‖ -oʊ
Pavonia pə 'vəʊn i‿ə ‖ -'voʊn-
pavonine 'pæv əʊ naɪn ‖ -ə-
paw pɔː ‖ pɑː pawed pɔːd ‖ pɑːd pawing
'pɔː ɪŋ ‖ 'pɑː- paws pɔːz ‖ pɑːz
pawk|y 'pɔːk |i ‖ 'pɑːk- ~ier i ə ‖ i‿ᵊr ~iest
i‿ɪst i‿əst ~ily ɪ li əl i ~iness i nəs i nɪs
pawl pɔːl ‖ pɑːl (= pall, Paul) pawls pɔːlz
‖ pɑːlz
pawn pɔːn ‖ pɑːn pawned pɔːnd ‖ pɑːnd
pawning 'pɔːn ɪŋ ‖ 'pɑːn- pawns pɔːnz
‖ pɑːnz
pawnbrok|er 'pɔːn ˌbrəʊk |ə ‖ -ˌbroʊk |ᵊr
'pɑːn- ~ers əz ‖ ᵊrz ~ing ɪŋ
Pawnee pɔː 'niː ‖ pɑː- ~s z
pawnshop 'pɔːn ʃɒp ‖ -ʃɑːp 'pɑːn- ~s s
pawpaw, paw-paw 'pɔː pɔː ‖ 'pɑː pɑː ~s z
Pawtucket pɔː 'tʌk ɪt pə-, §-ət ‖ pə- pɔː-, pɑː-
pax, Pax pæks ‖ pɑːks
ˌPax 'Christi 'krɪst i; ˌPax Ro'mana
rəʊ 'mɑːn ə ‖ roʊ-; ˌpax vo'biscum
vəʊ 'bɪsk əm -ʊm ‖ voʊ-
Paxman 'pæks mən
Paxo *tdmk* 'pæks əʊ ‖ -oʊ
Paxos 'pæks ɒs ‖ -oʊs —*Gk* [pa 'ksos]
Paxton 'pækst ən

pay peɪ **paid** peɪd **paying** ˈpeɪ ɪŋ **pays** peɪz
　ˈpay claim; ˈpay dirt; ˈpay ˌenvelope;
　ˌpaying ˈguest; ˈpay ˌpacket; ˈpay phone;
　ˈpay ˌstation; ˈpay train
payable ˈpeɪ əb ᵊl
pay-as-you-go ˌpeɪ əz ju ˈɡəʊ ◂ -əz jə-,
　→-əʒ ju-, →-əʒ jə, →-əʒ u-, →-əʒ ə-
　‖ -əʒ ə ˈɡoʊ ◂
payback ˈpeɪ bæk
paybed ˈpeɪ bed ~s z
paycheck, paycheque ˈpeɪ tʃek ~s s
payday ˈpeɪ deɪ ~s z
PAYE ˌpiː eɪ waɪ ˈiː
payee ˌpeɪ ˈiː ~s z
payer ˈpeɪ ə ‖ -ᵊr ~s z
paying-in ˌpeɪ ɪŋ ˈɪn
　ˌpaying ˈin slip
payload ˈpeɪ ləʊd ‖ -loʊd ~s z
paymaster ˈpeɪ ˌmɑːst ə §-ˌmæst- ‖ -ˌmæst ᵊr
　~s z
　ˌpaymaster ˈgeneral
payment ˈpeɪm ənt ~s s
Payn, Payne peɪn
paynim, P~ ˈpeɪn ɪm
Paynter ˈpeɪnt ə ‖ ˈpeɪnt̬ ᵊr
payoff ˈpeɪ ɒf -ɔːf ‖ -ɔːf -ɑːf ~s s
payola peɪ ˈəʊl ə ‖ -ˈoʊl ə
payout ˈpeɪ aʊt ~s s
Paypal tdmk ˈpeɪ pæl
pay-per-ˈclick ˌpeɪ pə ‖ˈklɪk ◂ ‖ -pᵊr- ~view
　ˈvjuː ◂
payphone ˈpeɪ fəʊn ‖ -foʊn ~s z
payroll ˈpeɪ rəʊl →-rɒʊl ‖ -roʊl ~s z
payslip ˈpeɪ slɪp ~s s
Payton ˈpeɪt ᵊn
pay-TV ˌpeɪ tiː ˈviː ˈ· ·ˌ·
Paz pæz ‖ pɑːz —AmSp [pas, pah]
pazazz pə ˈzæz
PBS ˌpiː biː ˈes
PC, P.C. ˌpiː ˈsiː ◂ ~s, ~ˈs z
PCB ˌpiː siː ˈbiː ~s z
PE ˌpiː ˈiː
pea piː **peas** piːz
　ˌpea ˈgreen◂; ˈpea ˌjacket; ˌpea ˈsouper
Peabody ˈpiː ˌbɒd i ˈpeɪ-; ˈpiːb əd i ‖ -ˌbɑːd i
pea-brained ˈpiː breɪnd
peace, Peace piːs
　ˈPeace Corps; ˈpeace ˌoffering; ˈpeace
　pipe
peaceab|le ˈpiːs əb |ᵊl ~leness ᵊl nəs -nɪs ~ly
　li
peaceful ˈpiːs fᵊl -fʊl ~ly i ~ness nəs nɪs
Peacehaven ˈpiːs ˌheɪv ᵊn
peacekeep|er ˈpiːs ˌkiːp| ə ‖ -ᵊr ~ers əz ‖ -ᵊrz
　~ing ɪŋ
peace-loving ˈpiːs ˌlʌv ɪŋ
peacemak|er ˈpiːs ˌmeɪk| ə ‖ -ᵊr ~ers əz ‖ -ᵊrz
　~ing ɪŋ
peacenik ˈpiːs nɪk ~s s
peacetime ˈpiːs taɪm
peach, Peach piːtʃ **peaches** ˈpiːtʃ ɪz -əz
　ˌPeach ˈMelba
peaches-and-cream ˌpiːtʃ ɪz ᵊn ˈkriːm ◂ →-ᵊŋ-

Peachey ˈpiːtʃ i
peachick ˈpiː tʃɪk ~s s
Peachum ˈpiːtʃ əm
peach|y ˈpiːtʃ |i ~ier i ə ‖ iˌᵊr ~iest i ɪst i əst
　~iness i nəs i nɪs
peacock, P~ ˈpiː kɒk ˈpiː kɒk ‖ ˈpiː kɑːk ~s s
　ˌpeacock ˈblue◂
peafowl ˈpiː faʊl ~s z
peahen ˈpiː hen ~s z
peak piːk (= peek) **peaked** piːkt **peaking**
　ˈpiːk ɪŋ **peaks** piːks
Peak, Peake piːk
　ˈPeak ˌDistrict; ˌpeak ˈtime◂
peaked adj ˈhaving a peak'; past and pp of
　peak piːkt
peaked adj ˈpeaky, pale' — ‖ ˈpiːk əd
Peaker ˈpiːk ə ‖ -ᵊr
peaky ˈpiːk i
peal piːᵊl (= peel) **pealed** piːᵊld **pealing**
　ˈpiːᵊl ɪŋ **peals** piːᵊlz
Peale piːᵊl
Peano pi ˈɑːn əʊ ‖ -oʊ —It [pe ˈaː no]
peanut ˈpiː nʌt ~s s
　ˌpeanut ˈbutter ◂ ‖ ˈ· ·ˌ·; ˌpeanut ˌbutter
　ˈsandwich
pear peə ‖ peᵊr pæᵊr (= pair) **pears** peəz
　‖ peᵊrz pæᵊrz
Pear family name pɪə ‖ peᵊr
Pearce pɪəs ‖ pɪᵊrs
pearl, Pearl pɜːl ‖ pɜːl **pearled** pɜːld ‖ pɜːld
　pearling ˈpɜːl ɪŋ ‖ ˈpɜːl ɪŋ **pearls** pɜːlz
　‖ pɜːlz
　ˈpearl ˌdiver; ˌPearl ˈHarbor
pearlite ˈpɜːl aɪt ‖ ˈpɜːl-
pearlwort ˈpɜːl wɜːt -wɔːt ‖ ˈpɜːl wɜːt
pearl|y ˈpɜːl |i ‖ ˈpɜːl |i ~ies i ə ‖ iˌᵊr ~ies iz
　~iest i ɪst i əst ~iness i nəs i nɪs
　ˌpearly ˈgates
pearmain, P~ ˈpeə meɪn ˈpɜː- ‖ ˈper- ~s z
Pearn pɜːn ‖ pɜːn
Pears family name (i) pɪəz ‖ pɪᵊrz, (ii) peəz
　‖ peᵊrz pæᵊrz —The singer Sir Peter Pears was
　(i), but the brand of soap is (ii)
Pearsall ˈpɪəs ᵊl -ɔːl ‖ ˈpɪrs ɔːl -ɑːl
Pearse pɪəs ‖ pɪᵊrs
pear-shaped ˈpeə ʃeɪpt ‖ ˈper- ˈpær-
Pearson ˈpɪəs ᵊn ‖ ˈpɪrs ᵊn
Peart pɪət ‖ prᵊrt
Peary ˈpɪər i ‖ ˈpɪr i
peasant ˈpez ᵊnt ~s s
　ˌPeasants' Reˈvolt
peasantry ˈpez ᵊntr i
pease, Pease piːz
　ˌpease ˈpudding
Peaseblossom ˈpiːz ˌblɒs əm ‖ -ˌblɑːs əm
peasecod ˈpiːz kɒd ‖ -kɑːd ~s z
peashooter ˈpiː ˌʃuːt ə ‖ -ˌʃuːt̬ ᵊr ~s z
pea-souper ˌpiː ˈsuːp ə ‖ -ᵊr ~s z
peat, Peat, Peate piːt
　ˈpeat bog
peat|y ˈpiːt |i ‖ ˈpiːt̬ |i ~ier i ə ‖ iˌᵊr ~iest i ɪst
　i əst ~iness i nəs i nɪs
Peaudouce tdmk ˌpəʊ ˈduːs ‖ ˌpoʊ-

peav|ey, peav|y, P~ 'piːv |i ~eys, ~ies iz
pebbl|e 'peb ᵊl ~ed d ~es z ~ing ɪŋ
pebble-dash 'peb ᵊl dæʃ ~ed t ~es ɪz əz ~ing ɪŋ
pebbly 'peb ᵊl_i
pec pek **pecs** peks
pecan pɪ 'kæn 'piːk æn, -ən ‖ pɪ 'kɑːn -'kæn; 'piːk æn ~s z
peccadillo ˌpek ə 'dɪl əʊ ‖ -oʊ ~s z
peccar|y 'pek ər |i ~ies iz
peccavi pe 'kɑːv i: —Formerly -'keɪv aɪ
peck, Peck pek **pecked** pekt **pecking** 'pek ɪŋ **pecks** peks
  'pecking ˌorder
pecker 'pek ə ‖ -ᵊr ~s z
Peckham 'pek əm
Peckinpah 'pek ɪn pɑː -ən-
peckish 'pek ɪʃ ~ly li ~ness nəs nɪs
Peckitt 'pek ɪt §-ət
Pecksniff 'pek snɪf
Pecksniffian ₍₁₎pek 'snɪf i_ən
Peconic pɪ 'kɒn ɪk ‖ -'kɑːn-
pecorino ˌpek ə 'riːn əʊ ‖ -oʊ —It [pe ko 'ri: no]
Pecos 'peɪk əs -ɒs ‖ -ɑːs -oʊs
Pécs petʃ ‖ peɪtʃ —Hungarian [peːtʃ]
pecten 'pekt ɪn -en, §-ən
pectic 'pekt ɪk
pectin 'pekt ɪn §-ən
pecti|nate 'pekt ɪ |neɪt -ə- ~nated neɪt ɪd -əd ‖ neɪt̬ əd ~nately neɪt li
pectoral 'pekt ᵊr_əl ~s z
  ˌpectoral 'cross; ˌpectoral'fin
pecu|late 'pek ju |leɪt -jə- ‖ -jə- ~lated leɪt ɪd -əd ‖ leɪt̬ əd ~lates leɪts ~lating leɪt ɪŋ ‖ leɪt̬ ɪŋ
peculation ˌpek ju 'leɪʃ ᵊn -jə- ‖ -jə- ~s z
peculator 'pek ju leɪt ə -'jə- ‖ -jə leɪt̬ ᵊr ~s z
peculiar pɪ 'kjuːl i_ə pə-, △bə- ‖ -'kjuːl jᵊr ~s z
peculiarit|y pɪ ˌkjuːl i 'ær ət |i pə-, △bə-, -ɪt i ‖ -əţ |i -'er-; ˌ·ˌ'jær-, -'jer- ~ies iz
peculiarly pɪ 'kjuːl i_ə li pə-, △bə- ‖ -'kjuːl jᵊr li
pecuniar|y pɪ 'kjuːn i_ər |i pə-, -'kjuːn ər |i ‖ -i er |i ~ily əl i ɪ li
-ped ped — biped 'baɪ ped
pedagogic ˌped ə 'gɒdʒ ɪk ◄ -'gəʊdʒ-, -'gɒg- ‖ -'gɑːdʒ ɪk -'goʊdʒ- ~al ᵊl ◄ ~ally ᵊl_i
pedagogue 'ped ə gɒg ‖ -gɑːg ~s z
pedagogy 'ped ə gɒdʒ i -gəʊdʒ-, -gɒg- ‖ -goʊdʒ i -gɑːdʒ-
pedal n, v 'ped ᵊl (= peddle) ~ed, ~led d ~ing, ~ling ˌɪŋ ~s z
pedal adj 'piːd ᵊl 'ped-
pedalo 'ped ə ləʊ → -ᵊl əʊ ‖ -ᵊl oʊ ~s z
pedant 'ped ᵊnt ~s s
pedantic pɪ 'dænt ɪk pə-, pe- ‖ -'dænţ ɪk ~ally ᵊl_i
pedantr|y 'ped ᵊntr |i ~ies iz
Pedder 'ped ə ‖ -ᵊr
peddl|e 'ped ᵊl ~ed d ~es z ~ing ˌɪŋ
peddler 'ped lə ‖ -lᵊr ~s z
-pede piːd — millipede 'mɪl ɪ piːd -ə-

Peden 'piːd ᵊn
pederast 'ped ə ræst 'piːd- ~s s
pederastic ˌped ə 'ræst ɪk ◄ ˌpiːd- ~ally ᵊl_i
pederasty 'ped ə ræst i 'piːd-
pedestal 'ped ɪst ᵊl -əst- ~s z
pedestrian pə 'des tri_ən pɪ- ~s z
  pe͵destrian 'crossing
pedestrianis... —see pedestrianiz...
pedestrianization pə ˌdes tri_ən aɪ 'zeɪʃ ᵊn pɪ-, -ɪ'·- ‖ -ə'·-
pedestrianiz|e pə 'des tri_ə naɪz pɪ- ~ed d ~es ɪz əz ~ing ɪŋ
Pedi 'ped i
pediatric ˌpiːd i 'ætr ɪk ◄ ~ally ᵊl_i ~s s
pediatrician ˌpiːd i_ə 'trɪʃ ᵊn ~s z
pedicab 'ped i kæb ~s z
pedicel 'ped i sel -ə- ~s z
pedicle 'ped ɪk ᵊl ~s z
pedicular pɪ 'dɪk jʊl ə pe-, pə-, -jəl- ‖ -jəl ᵊr
pedicure 'ped i kjʊə -ə-, -kjɔː ‖ -kjʊr ~s z
pedicurist 'ped i kjʊər ɪst '·ə-, ˌ·ə kjɔːr-, §-əst ‖ -kjʊr əst ~s s
pediform 'ped i fɔːm ‖ -fɔːrm
pedigree 'ped ɪ griː -ə- ~d d ~s z
pediment 'ped ɪ mənt -ə- ~s s
pedimented 'ped ɪ ment ɪd '·ə-, -mənt-, -əd ‖ -menţ əd
pedipalp 'ped i pælp ~s s
pedlar 'ped lə ‖ -lᵊr ~s z
pedogenesis ˌped əʊ 'dʒen əs ɪs ˌpiːd-, -ɪs ɪs, §-əs ‖ ˌ·ə-
pedometer pɪ 'dɒm ɪt ə pə-, pe-, -ət- ‖ -'dɑːm əţ ᵊr ~s z
pedophile 'piːd əʊ faɪᵊl ‖ -ə- 'ped- ~s z
pedophilia ˌpiːd əʊ 'fɪl i_ə ‖ ˌ·ə- ˌped-
pedophiliac ˌpiːd əʊ 'fɪl i æk ‖ ˌ·ə- ˌped- ~s s
Pedro, p~ 'pedr əʊ 'peɪdr-, 'piːdr- ‖ 'peɪdr oʊ —Sp ['pe ðro]
Peds tdmk pedz
peduncle pɪ 'dʌŋk ᵊl pə-, pe- ‖ 'piːd ʌŋk ᵊl ~s z
peduncular pɪ 'dʌŋk jʊl ə pə-, pe-, -jəl- ‖ -jəl ᵊr
pedunculate pɪ 'dʌŋk ju leɪt pə-, pe-, -jə-, -lət, -lɪt ‖ -jə-
pee piː **peed** piːd **peeing** 'piː ɪŋ **pees** piːz
Peeb|les 'piːb |ᵊlz ~lesshire ᵊlz ʃə →ᵊlʒ-, -ʃɪə, §-ˌʃər_ə
Pee Dee ˌpiː 'diː ◄
  ˌPee Dee 'River
peek, Peek piːk **peeked** piːkt **peeking** 'piːk ɪŋ **peeks** piːks
peekaboo ˌpiːk ə 'buː '···
peel, Peel, Peele piːᵊl **peeled** piːᵊld
  peeling/s 'piːᵊl ɪŋ/z **peels** piːᵊlz
peeler 'piːl ə ‖ -ᵊr ~s z
peen piːn
peep piːp **peeped** piːpt **peeping** 'piːp ɪŋ
  peeps piːps
  ˌpeeping 'Tom
peepbo 'piːp bəʊ -əʊ, ˌ·'· ‖ -boʊ
pee-pee 'piː piː ~s z
peeper 'piːp ə ‖ -ᵊr ~s z

peephole 'piːp həʊl →-hɒʊl ‖ -hoʊl ~s z
peepshow 'piːp ʃəʊ ‖ -ʃoʊ ~s z
peep-toe 'piːp təʊ ‖ -toʊ
peepul 'piːp ᵊl (= people) ~s z
peer pɪə ‖ pɪᵊr **peered** pɪəd ‖ pɪᵊrd **peering**
'pɪər ɪŋ ‖ 'pɪr ɪŋ **peers** pɪəz ‖ pɪᵊrz
'peer group; ˌpeer re'view
peerag|e 'pɪər ɪdʒ ‖ 'pɪr- ~es ɪz əz
peeress ˌpɪər 'es ‖ ·, -əs, -ɪs ‖ 'pɪr əs ~es ɪz əz
peerie 'pɪər i ‖ 'pɪr i
peerless 'pɪə ləs -lɪs ‖ 'pɪr- ~ly li ~ness nəs
nɪs
peer-to-peer ˌpɪə tə 'pɪə ◂ ‖ ˌpɪr tə 'pɪᵊr ◂
peeve piːv **peeved** piːvd **peeving** 'piːv ɪŋ
peeves piːvz
peevish 'piːv ɪʃ ~ly li ~ness nəs nɪs
peewee, P~ 'piː wiː ~s z
peewit 'piː wɪt ~s s
peg, Peg, Pegg peg **pegged** pegd **pegging**
'peg ɪŋ **pegs** pegz
ˌpeg 'leg ‖ '· ·
Pegasus 'peg əs əs
pegboard 'peg bɔːd ‖ -bɔːrd -boʊrd ~s z
Peggie 'peg i
Peggotty 'peg ət i ‖ -ət̬ i
Peggy 'peg i
Pegler 'peg lə ‖ -lᵊr
pegmatite 'peg mə taɪt
Pei peɪ
peignoir 'peɪn wɑː ‖ peɪn 'wɑːr —Fr
[pɛn waːʁ, pɛnj-] ~s z
Peiping ˌpeɪ 'pɪŋ
Peirce pɪəs ‖ pɪᵊrs
pejoration ˌpiːdʒ ə 'reɪʃ ᵊn ˌpedʒ-
pejorative pɪ 'dʒɒr ət ɪv pə-, -'dʒɔːr-;
'piːdʒ ər ˌət- ‖ -'dʒɔːr ət̬ ɪv -'dʒɑːr-;
'pedʒ ə reɪt̬ ɪv ~ly li ~s z
peke piːk (= peak) **pekes** piːks
Pekin ˌpiː 'kɪn ◂
Pekines|e ˌpiːk ɪ 'niːz ◂ -ə- ‖ -'niːs ~es ɪz əz
Peking ˌpiː 'kɪŋ ◂ —see also **Beijing**
Pekingese ˌpiːk ɪ 'niːz ◂ -ɪŋ 'iːz ◂, -ə- ‖ -'niːs,
-ɪŋ 'iːs, '···
pekoe 'piːk əʊ ‖ -oʊ
pelag|e 'pel ɪdʒ ~es ɪz əz
pelagian, P~ pɪ 'leɪdʒ i_ən pə-, pe-, -'leɪdʒ ᵊn
~ism ˌɪz əm ~s z
pelagic pə 'lædʒ ɪk pɪ-, pe-
Pelagius pɪ 'leɪdʒ i_əs pə-, pe-
pelargonium ˌpel ə 'gəʊn i_əm ˌɑː-
‖ -ɑːr 'goʊn- ~s z
Pelasgian pe 'læz dʒi_ən pɪ-, pə-, -gi_ən;
-'læz dʒən ~s z
Pele, Pelé, Pelee, Pelée place name,
mountain 'pel eɪ pə 'leɪ ‖ pə 'leɪ 'peɪ leɪ —Fr
[pə le]
Pele, Pelé footballer 'pel eɪ ‖ 'peɪl eɪ —Port
[pɛ 'lɛ]
pelerine 'pel ə riːn -rɪn ~s z
Peleus 'piːl juːs 'piːl i_əs, 'pel-
pelf pelf
Pelham, p~ 'pel əm ~s, ~'s z
Pelias 'piːl i æs -əs

pelican, P~ 'pel ɪk ən ~s z
ˌpelican 'crossing
Pelion 'piːl i_ən -ɒn
peliss|e pə 'liːs pe-, pɪ- ~es ɪz əz
Pella 'pel ə
pellagra pə 'læg rə pɪ-, pe-, -'leɪg-, -'lɑːg-
Pelleas, Pelléas 'pel eɪ æs -i- —Fr [pɛ le ɑːs]
Pelles 'pel iːz
pell|et 'pel |ɪt §-ət ‖ -|ət ~eted ɪt ɪd §ət-, -əd
‖ ət̬ əd ~eting ɪt ɪŋ §ət- ‖ ət̬ ɪŋ ~ets ɪts §əts
‖ əts
Pelletier 'pel ət i eɪ ˌpel ə 'tɪᵊr —Fr
[pɛl tje]
pellicle 'pel ɪk ᵊl ~s z
pellicular pə 'lɪk jʊl ə pe-, pɪ-, -jəl- ‖ -jəl ᵊr
pellitor|y 'pel ɪt ər i 'ɪ '·ət̬ ‖ ə tɔːr i 'ɪ -toʊr i
~ies iz
pell-mell ˌpel 'mel ◂
pellucid pɪ 'luːs ɪd pə-, pe-, -'ljuːs-, §-əd ~ly li
~ness nəs nɪs
Pelman 'pel mən ~ism ˌɪz əm
pelmet 'pelm ɪt -ət ~s s
Peloponnese 'pel əp ə niːs ˌ···ˈ·
‖ ˌpel əp ə 'niːz -'niːs —ModGk Peloponnesos
[pe lo 'po ni sos]
Peloponnesian ˌpel əp ə 'niːʃ ᵊn ◂ -'niːʃ i_ən
‖ -'niːʒ- ~s z
ˌPelopon nesian 'War
Peloponnesus ˌpel əp ə 'niːs əs
Pelops 'piːl ɒps 'pel- ‖ -ɑːps
pelorus pə 'lɔːr əs pɪ- ‖ -'loʊr- ~es ɪz əz
Pelosi pə 'ləʊs i ‖ -'loʊs i
pelota pə 'lɒt ə pɪ-, pe-, -'ləʊt- ‖ -'loʊt̬ ə —Sp
[pe 'lo ta]
peloton 'pel ət ən -ə tɒn ‖ -ə tɑːn ˌ·ˈ· ~s z
pelt pelt **pelted** 'pelt ɪd -əd **pelting** 'pelt ɪŋ
pelts pelts
peltast 'pelt æst ~s s
peltate 'pelt eɪt ~ly li
Peltier 'pelt i eɪ —Fr [pɛl tje]
Pelton 'pelt ən
pelvic 'pelv ɪk
pelv|is 'pelv |ɪs §-əs ~es iːz ~ises ɪs ɪz §əs ɪz,
-əz
Pemba 'pem bə
Pemberton 'pem bət ən ‖ -bᵊrt ᵊn
Pembrey ₍ᵢ₎pem 'breɪ 'pem bri
Pembridge 'pem brɪdʒ
Pembroke 'pem brʊk -brək, -brəʊk ‖ -broʊk
-brʊk ~shire ʃə ʃɪə ‖ ʃᵊr ʃɪr
Pembury 'pem bər_i
pemican, pemmican 'pem ɪk ən
pemphigus 'pemᵖf ɪg əs §-əg-; pem 'faɪg-
pen, Pen pen **penned** pend (= pend) **penning**
'pen ɪŋ **pens** penz
'pen friend; 'pen name; 'pen pal; 'pen
ˌpusher
penal 'piːn ᵊl
'penal ˌcolony
penalis... —see **penaliz...**
penalization ˌpiːn ᵊl aɪ 'zeɪʃ ᵊn -ɪ'·-- ‖ -ᵊl ə-
ˌpen- ~s z

penaliz|e 'piːn ə laɪz -ᵊl aɪz ‖ 'piːn ᵊl aɪz 'pen-
~ed d ~es ɪz əz ~ing ɪŋ
penally 'piːn əl i
penalt|y 'pen ᵊlt |i ~ies iz
'penalty ˌarea; 'penalty box; 'penalty
goal; 'penalty kick
penanc|e 'pen ən⁶s ~es ɪz əz
pen-and-ink ˌpen ən 'ɪŋk ◄ -ənd-
Penang pə 'næŋ pe-
Penarth pe 'nɑːθ pə- ‖ -'nɑːrθ —Welsh
[pe 'nɑrθ]
penates pe 'nɑːt eɪz pɪ-, pə-, -iːz, -'neɪt iːz
‖ 'neɪt- -'nɑːt-
pence pen⁶s —There is a BrE weak form pən⁶s,
but it is now fairly rare. Prices are usually
quoted with the strong form pen⁶s or with p
piː, usually stressed: **15p** ˌfɪf tiːn 'pen⁶s,
ˌfɪf tiːn 'piː
penchant 'pɒ̃ ʃɒ̃ 'pɒn ʃɒn, 'pɒŋ ʃɒŋ
‖ 'pentʃ ənt (*) —Fr [pɑ̃ ʃɑ̃] ~s z ‖ s
pencil 'pen⁶s ᵊl -ɪl ~ed, ~led d ~ing, ~ling ɪŋ
~s z
'pencil ˌcase; 'pencil ˌsharpener
pencil-thin ˌpen⁶s ᵊl 'θɪn ◄ -ɪl-
Pencoed ₍ˌ₎pen 'kɔɪd →₍ˌ₎peŋ-
pend pend pending 'pend ɪŋ
pendant 'pend ənt ~s s
Pendennis pen 'den ɪs §-əs
pendent 'pend ənt ~ly li ~s s
pendente lite pen ˌdent i 'laɪt iː -i
pendentive pen 'dent ɪv ‖ -'denṭ ɪv ~s z
Pender 'pend ə ‖ -ᵊr
Penderecki ˌpend ə 'ret ski —Polish
[pen de 'rets ki]
Pendergast 'pend ə gɑːst §-gæst ‖ -ᵊr gæst
Pendine ₍ˌ₎pen 'daɪn
pending 'pend ɪŋ
Pendle 'pend ᵊl
Pendlebury 'pend ᵊl bər ˌi ‖ -ˌber i
Pendleton 'pend ᵊl tən
Pendolino tdmk ˌpend ə 'liːn əʊ ‖ -oʊ
pendragon, P~ pen 'dræg ən ~s z
pendulous 'pend jʊl əs -jəl- ‖ 'pendʒ əl əs ~ly
li ~ness nəs nɪs
pendulum 'pend jʊl əm -jəl- ‖ 'pendʒ əl əm
~s z
Penelope pə 'nel əp i pɪ-
peneplain, peneplane 'piːn ɪ pleɪn 'pen-, -ə-,
ˌ· '· ~s z
penetrability ˌpen ətr ə 'bɪl ət i ˌɪtr-, -ɪt i
‖ -əṭ i
penetrab|le 'pen ətr əb |ᵊl '·ɪtr- ~ly li
penetralia ˌpen ə 'treɪl i ə ˌɪ-
penetrance 'pen ətr ən⁶s -ɪtr-
pene|trate 'pen ə |treɪt -ɪ- ~trated treɪt ɪd -əd
‖ treɪṭ əd ~trates treɪts ~trating/ly
treɪt ɪŋ /li ‖ treɪṭ ɪŋ /li
penetration ˌpen ə 'treɪʃ ᵊn -ɪ- ~s z
penetrative 'pen ətr ət ɪv '·ɪtr-; -ə treɪt-,
-ɪ treɪt- ‖ -ə treɪṭ ɪv -ly li ~ness nəs nɪs
Penfold 'pen fəʊld →-fɒʊld ‖ -foʊld
penfriend 'pen frend ~s z
Pengam 'peŋ gəm

Penge pendʒ
Pengelly pen 'gel i →peŋ-
penguin, P~ 'peŋ gwɪn §-gwən ~s z
Penhaligon pen 'hæl ɪg ən
penicillin ˌpen ə 'sɪl ɪn -ɪ-, §-ən
penicillium ˌpen ə 'sɪl i ˌəm ˌɪ-
Penicuik 'pen i kʊk
penile 'piːn aɪᵊl ‖ -ᵊl
penillion pe 'nɪθ li ˌən pɪ-, pə-, -'nɪl i ˌ —Welsh
[pe 'nɪɬ jon]
peninsula pə 'nɪn⁶s jʊl ə pɪ-, pe-, -'nɪn⁶tʃ ʊl ə
‖ -əl ə ~s z
peninsular pə 'nɪn⁶s jʊl ə pɪ-, pe-, -'nɪn⁶tʃ ʊl ə
‖ -ᵊl ər
penis 'piːn ɪs §-əs ~es ɪz əz
Penistone 'pen ɪst ən
penitence 'pen ɪt ən⁶s -ət- ‖ -ət ᵊn⁶s
penitent 'pen ɪt ənt -ət- ‖ -ət ᵊnt ~ly li ~s s
penitential ˌpen ɪ 'tenᵗʃ ᵊl ◄ -ə- ~ly i
penitentiar|y ˌpen ɪ 'tenᵗʃ ər |i ˌ·ə- ~ies iz
Penk peŋk
Penkhull 'peŋk ᵊl -hʌl
pen|knife 'pen |naɪf ~knives naɪvz
Penkridge 'peŋk rɪdʒ
Penlee ₍ˌ₎pen 'liː
Penmaenmawr, Penmaen-mawr
ˌpen mən 'maʊ ə →ˌpem-, →ˌ·məm-, ˌ·maɪn-;
ˌ· ·'mɔː ‖ -'maʊ ᵊr —Welsh [ˌpɛn maɪn 'maur,
-mən-]
pen|man 'pen mən →'pem- ~manship
mən ʃɪp ~men mən men
Penn pen
Penn. pen or as Pennsylvania
penn|a 'pen |ə ~ae iː
pennant, P~ 'pen ənt ~s s
penne 'pen eɪ -i —It ['pen ne]
Penney, Pennie 'pen i
penni... —see penny
penniless 'pen ɪ ləs -ə-, -lɪs; -ᵊl əs, -ɪs ~ly li
~ness nəs nɪs
Pennine 'pen aɪn ~s z
ˌPennine 'Way
Pennington 'pen ɪŋ tən
pennon 'pen ən ~ed d ~s z
pennorth, penn'orth 'pen əθ ‖ -ᵊrθ
Pennsylvania ˌpen⁶s ᵊl 'veɪn i ə ◄ ˌ·ɪl-
‖ ˌ· ·'jə ◄
ˌPennsylˌvania 'Dutch
Pennsylvanian ˌpen⁶s ᵊl 'veɪn i ən ◄ ˌ·ɪl-
‖ ˌ· ·'jən ◄ ~s z
penn|y, Penn|y 'pen |i ~ies, ~y's iz
ˌpenny 'black; ˌpenny 'dreadful; ˌpenny
'whistle
-penny adj-forming suffix pən i, ˌpen i —
tenpenny 'ten pən i 'temp ən ˌi, 'ten ˌpen i
—These are pre-1971. Since decimalization the
equivalent is pence, p thus **a 10p packet**
ə ˌten piː 'pæk ɪt : see note at pence
penny-ante ˌpen i 'ænt i ◄ ‖ -'ænṭ i ◄
pennycress 'pen i kres
Pennycuick (i) 'pen i kʊk, (ii) -kwɪk,
(iii) -kjuːk
penny-farthing ˌpen i 'fɑːð ɪŋ ‖ -'fɑːrð- ~s z

P

Pennyfeather 'pen i ˌfeð ə ‖ -ˀr
penny-halfpen|ny ˌpen i 'heɪp |ni **~nies** niz
penny-pinch|er 'pen i ˌpɪntʃ| ə ‖ ˀr **~ers** əz ‖ **rz ~ing** ɪŋ
pennyroyal ˌpen i 'rɔɪ_əl **~s** z
pennyweight 'pen i weɪt **~s** s
penny-wise ˌpen i 'waɪz ◂
pennywort 'pen i wɜːt -wɔːt ‖ -wɝːt -wɔːrt
pennyworth 'pen əθ 'pen i wɜːθ, -wəθ ‖ 'pen i wɝːθ **~s** s
Penobscot pə 'nɒb skɒt pe-, pɪ-, -skət ‖ -'nɑːb skɑːt -skət
penological ˌpiːn ə 'lɒdʒ ɪk ᵊl ‖ -'lɑːdʒ- **~ly** i
penology ₍ᵢ₎pi: 'nɒl ədʒ i pɪ- ‖ -'nɑːl-
Pen-rhos places in Gwynedd, Gwent, Powys ˌpen 'rəʊs ◂ ‖ -'roʊs —Welsh [ˌpɛn 'hroːs]
Penrhos place in Gwynedd 'pen rəʊs -rɒs ‖ -roʊs —Welsh ['pɛn hroːs]
Penrhyn 'pen rɪn —Welsh ['pɛn hrin, -hrin]
Penrhyndeudraeth ˌpen rɪn 'daɪdr əθ -aɪθ —Welsh [ˌpɛn hrin 'dəi draiθ]
Penrith place in NSW 'pen rɪθ -rəθ —locally -rəθ
Penrith place in Cumbria 'pen rɪθ ˌ·ˈ· —locally also 'pɪər ɪθ
Penrose 'pen rəʊz ₍ᵢ₎·ˈ· ‖ -roʊz
Penry 'pen ri
Penryn ₍ᵢ₎pen 'rɪn
Pensacola ˌpenˢs ə 'kəʊl ə ‖ -'koʊl ə
Pen-sarn places in Clwyd and Gwynedd pen 'saːn ‖ -'sɑːrn
Pensarn place in Dyfed 'pen saːn -sɑːrn
pensée 'põs eɪ ˌpõ 'seɪ ‖ pɑːn 'seɪ —Fr [pɑ̃ se] **~s** z or as sing.
penseroso ˌpenˢs ə 'rəʊz əʊ -'rəʊs- ‖ -'roʊs oʊ
Penshurst 'penz hɜːst ‖ -hɝːst
pensile 'penˢs aɪᵊl ‖ -ᵊl
pension 'payment' 'penᵗʃ ᵊn **~ed** d **~ing** ɪŋ **~s** z
  'pension fund
pension 'boarding-house' 'põs jõ ‖ pɑːns 'joʊn —Fr [pɑ̃ sjɔ̃] **~s** z
pensionable 'penᵗʃ ᵊn_əb ᵊl
pensioner 'penᵗʃ ᵊn ə ‖ ᵊr **~s** z
pensive 'penˢs ɪv **~ly** li **~ness** nəs nɪs
penstemon pen 'stiːm ən 'penᵗst ɪm-, -əm- **~s** z
penstock 'pen stɒk ‖ -stɑːk **~s** s
pent pent
  'pent 'up◂
pent- comb. form ¦pent — **pentoxide** ˌpent 'ɒks aɪd ‖ -'ɑːks-
penta, Penta 'pent ə ‖ 'penţ ə
penta- comb. form with stress-neutral suffix ¦pent ə ‖ ¦penţ ə — **pentaprism** 'pent ə ˌprɪz əm ‖ 'penţ ə- with stress-imposing suffix pen 'tæ+ — **pentamerous** pen 'tæm ər əs
pentacle 'pent ək ᵊl ‖ 'penţ- **~s** z
pentad 'pent æd **~s** z
pentagon, P~ 'pent əg ən -ə gɒn ‖ 'penţ ə gɑːn **~s** z
pentagonal pen 'tæg ən ᵊl

pentagram 'pent ə græm ‖ 'penţ- **~s** z
pentahedr|on ˌpent ə 'hiːdr |ən -'hedr- ‖ ˌpenţ- **~a** ə **~al** ᵊl **~ons** ənz
pentamerous pen 'tæm ər əs
pentameter pen 'tæm ɪt ə -ət- ‖ -əţ ər **~s** z
pentane 'pent eɪn
pentangle 'pent ˌæŋ gᵊl **~s** z
Pentateuch 'pent ə tjuːk →-tʃuːk ‖ 'penţ ə tuːk -tjuːk
pentathlete pen 'tæθ liːt **~s** s
pentathlon pen 'tæθ lən -lɒn ‖ -lɑːn
pentatonic ˌpent ə 'tɒn ɪk ◂ ‖ ˌpenţ ə 'tɑːn ɪk ◂
Pentax tdmk 'pent æks
Pentecost 'pent ɪ kɒst -ə- ‖ 'penţ ə kɔːst -kɑːst
pentecostal ˌpent ɪ 'kɒst ᵊl ◂ -ə- ‖ ˌpenţ ə 'kɔːst ᵊl ◂ -'kɑːst- **~ism** ˌɪz əm **~ist/s** ɪst/s §əst/s
Pentel tdmk 'pen tel
Pentelicus pen 'tel ɪk əs
Pentelikon pen 'tel ɪk ən -ɪ kɒn ‖ -ɪ kɑːn
Penthesilea ˌpenᵗθ es ɪ 'leɪ ə ˌ·əs-, -ə'·-, -'liː ə
Pentheus 'penᵗθ juːs 'penᵗθ i əs
pent|house 'pent |haʊs **~houses** haʊz ɪz -əz
pentiment|o ˌpent ɪ 'ment |əʊ -ə- ‖ ˌpenţ ə 'ment |oʊ **~i** iː —It [pɛn ti 'men t|o, -i]
Pentire pen 'taɪ ə ‖ -'taɪ ᵊr
Pentium tdmk 'pent i əm ‖ 'penţ-
Pentland 'pent lənd
  ˌPentland 'Firth
pentobarbitone ˌpent əʊ 'baːb ɪ təʊn -'·ə- ‖ ˌpenţ ə 'bɑːrb ə toʊn
pentode 'pent əʊd ‖ -oʊd **~s** z
Penton 'pent ən ‖ -ᵊn
Pentonville 'pent ən vɪl ˌ·ˈ· ‖ -ᵊn-
pentose 'pent əʊz -əʊs ‖ -oʊs -oʊz
Pentothal tdmk 'pent ə θæl -θᵊl, -θɒl ‖ 'penţ ə θɔːl -θɑːl
Pentre 'pentr ə 'pen treɪ —Welsh ['pen tre]
Pentreath pen 'triːθ
pentstemon pent 'stiːm ən pen-, -'stem-; 'penᵗst ɪm-, -əm- **~s** z
pent-up ˌpent 'ʌp ◂ ‖ ˌpenţ-
  ˌpent-up e'motions
penuche pə 'nuːtʃ i
penult pə 'nʌlt pɪ-, pe- ‖ 'piːn ʌlt (*)
penultimate pə 'nʌlt ɪm ət pɪ-, pe-, -əm ət, -ɪt **~ly** li **~s** s
penum|bra pə 'nʌm |brə pɪ-, pe- **~brae** briː **~bral** brᵊl **~bras** brəz
penurious pə 'njʊər i_əs pɪ-, pe- ‖ -'nʊr- -'njʊr- **~ly** li **~ness** nəs nɪs
penury 'pen jər i -jʊr-
Penutian pɪ 'njuːt i_ən pe-, pə-, -'nuːt-; -'njuːʃ ᵊn, -'nuːʃ- ‖ -'nuːʃ-
Penwith ₍ᵢ₎pen 'wɪθ
Penwortham 'pen wəð əm ‖ -wᵊrð-
Penybont, Pen-y-bont ˌpen ə 'bɒnt -i- ‖ -'bɑːnt —Welsh [ˌpɛn ə 'bɔnt]
Penyghent ˌpen i 'gent ˈ··ˈ
Pen-y-groes ˌpen ə 'grɔɪs -i-, -'grəʊs —Welsh [ˌpɛn ə 'grois]

Penzance pen 'zænᵗs pən-, -'zɑːnᵗs

peon 'piː ən -ɒn ‖ -ɑːn —*formerly, and in India,*
　pjuːn **~s** z

peonage 'piː ən ɪdʒ

peon|y 'piː ən |i **~ies** iz

peopl|e 'piːp ᵊl **~ed** d **~es** z **~ing** ɪŋ

people-watching 'piːp ᵊl ˌwɒtʃ ɪŋ ‖ -ˌwɑːtʃ-
　-ˌwɔːtʃ-

Peoria pi 'ɔːr i ə ‖ -'oʊr-

Peover 'piːv ə ‖ -ᵊr

pep, PEP pep **pepped** pept **pepping** 'pep ɪŋ
　peps peps
　'pep pill; 'pep talk

Pepe 'pep eɪ —*Sp* ['pe pe]

peperomia ˌpep ə 'rəʊm i ə ‖ -'roʊm- **~s** z

peperoni ˌpep ə 'rəʊn i ‖ -'roʊn i

Pepin 'pep ɪn §-ən

Pepita pe 'piːt ə pə- —*Sp* [pe 'pi ta]

peplum 'pep ləm **~s** z

pepp... —*see* **pep**

Peppard 'pep ɑːd ‖ pe 'pɑːrd

pepper, P~ 'pep ə ‖ -ᵊr **~ed** d **peppering**
　'pep ər ɪŋ **~s** z
　'pepper mill; 'pepper pot

pepper-and-salt ˌpep ᵊr ən 'sɒlt ◂ ˌ-ə-, -ᵊnd'-,
　-'sɔːlt ‖ -'sɔːlt -'sɑːlt

pepperbox 'pep ə bɒks ‖ -ᵊr bɑːks **~es** ɪz əz

peppercorn 'pep ə kɔːn ‖ -ᵊr kɔːrn **~s** z
　ˌpeppercorn 'rent

Pepperidge 'pep ə rɪdʒ

peppermint 'pep ə mɪnt ‖ -ᵊr- **~s** s

pepperoni ˌpep ə 'rəʊn i ‖ -'roʊn i

pepper|y 'pep ər |i **~iness** i nəs i nɪs

Peppiatt 'pep i ət

pepp|y 'pep |i **~iness** i nəs i nɪs

Pepsi *tdmk* 'peps i **~s** z

Pepsi-Cola *tdmk* ˌpeps i 'kəʊl ə ‖ -'koʊl ə

pepsin 'peps ɪn §-ən **~s** z

Pepsodent *tdmk* 'peps əʊ dent -əd ənt
　‖ -əd ənt

peptic 'pept ɪk
　ˌpeptic 'ulcer

peptide 'pept aɪd **~s** z

Pepto-Bismol *tdmk* ˌpept əʊ 'bɪz mɒl
　‖ -toʊ 'bɪz mɑːl

peptone 'pept əʊn ‖ -oʊn **~s** z

Pepys (i) piːps, (ii) 'pep ɪs, (iii) peps —*the
　diarist is* (i)

Pequot 'piː kwɒt ‖ -kwɑːt **~s** s

per pɜː ‖ pɜːr, *weak form* pə ‖ pᵊr —*see also
　phrases with this word*

per- pə ‖ pᵊr (*but before a vowel* pər), *or* ¦pɜː
　‖ ¦pɜː (*but in RP before a vowel* ¦pɜːr)

peradventure ˌpɜːr əd 'ventʃ ə ˌper-, pərˌ,
　§-æd- ‖ 'pɜː əd ˌventʃ ᵊr 'per-, ˌ·'· ·

Perahia pə 'raɪ ə

Perak 'peər ə 'pɪər ə ‖ 'per ə —*There are also
　spelling pronunciations* pə 'ræk, pe-,
　pɪ- ‖ -'rɑːk, 'peɪ ræk —*Malay* [pe ɾaʔ]

perambu|late pə 'ræm bju |leɪt -bjə- ‖ -bjə-
　~lated leɪt ɪd -əd ‖ leɪt əd **~lates** leɪts
　~lating leɪt ɪŋ ‖ leɪt ɪŋ

perambulation pə ˌræm bju 'leɪʃ ᵊn -bjə-
　‖ -bjə- **~s** z

perambulator pə 'ræm bju leɪt ə -'bjə-
　‖ -bjə leɪt ᵊr **~s** z

per annum pər 'æn əm ‖ pər-

perborate pə 'bɔːr eɪt pɜː-; 'pɜːb ə reɪt ‖ pᵊr-
　-'boʊr- **~s** s

percale pə 'keɪᵊl -'kɑːl ‖ pᵊr-

per capita pə 'kæp ɪt ə ˌpɜː-, §-ət-
　‖ pᵊr 'kæp əţ ə

perceivab|le pə 'siːv əb |ᵊl ‖ pᵊr- **~ly** li

perceiv|e pə 'siːv ‖ pᵊr- **~ed** d **~es** z **~ing** ɪŋ

percent, per cent pə 'sent ‖ pᵊr-

percentag|e pə 'sent ɪdʒ ‖ pᵊr 'senţ ɪdʒ **~es**
　ɪz əz

percentile pə 'sent aɪᵊl ‖ pᵊr- -'senţ ᵊl **~s** z

percept 'pɜː sept ‖ 'pɜː- **~s** s

perceptibility pə ˌsept ə 'bɪl ət i -ˌ·ɪ-, -ɪt i
　‖ pᵊr ˌsept ə 'bɪl əţ i

perceptib|le pə 'sept əb |ᵊl -'ɪb- ‖ pᵊr- **~ly** li

perception pə 'sep ʃᵊn ‖ pᵊr- **~s** z

perceptive pə 'sept ɪv ‖ pᵊr- **~ly** li **~ness** nəs
　nɪs

perceptivity ˌpɜː sep 'tɪv ət i pə ˌsep-, -ɪt i
　‖ ˌpɜː sep 'tɪv əţ i

perceptual pə 'sep tʃu əl -ʃu; -'sept ju ‖ pᵊr-
　~ly i

Perceval 'pɜːs ɪv ᵊl -əv- ‖ 'pɜːs-

perch pɜːtʃ ‖ pɜːtʃ **perched** pɜːtʃt ‖ pɜːtʃt
　perches 'pɜːtʃ ɪz -əz ‖ 'pɜːtʃ əz **perching**
　'pɜːtʃ ɪŋ ‖ 'pɜːtʃ ɪŋ

perchance pə 'tʃɑːnᵗs ˌpɒ:-, §-'tʃænᵗs
　‖ pᵊr 'tʃænᵗs

Percheron 'pɜː ʃə rɒn ‖ 'pɜːtʃ ə rɑːn 'pɜːʃ-
　—*Fr* [pɛʁ ʃə ʁɔ̃] **~s** z

percipience pə 'sɪp i ənᵗs ‖ pᵊr-

percipient pə 'sɪp i ənt ‖ pᵊr- **~ly** li **~s** s

Percival 'pɜːs ɪv ᵊl -əv- ‖ 'pɜːs-

perco|late 'pɜːk ə |leɪt △-ju-, △-jə-‖ 'pɜːk-
　~lated leɪt ɪd -əd ‖ leɪt əd **~lates** leɪts
　~lating leɪt ɪŋ ‖ leɪt ɪŋ

percolation ˌpɜːk ə 'leɪʃ ᵊn △-ju-, △-jə-
　‖ ˌpɜːk- **~s** z

percolator 'pɜːk ə leɪt ə △'·ju-, △'·jə-
　‖ 'pɜːk ə leɪţ ᵊr **~s** z

per contra ˌpɜː 'kɒntr ə pə- ‖ ˌpɜː 'kɑːntr ə

percuss pə 'kʌs ‖ pᵊr- **~ed** t **~es** ɪz əz **~ing** ɪŋ

percussion pə 'kʌʃ ᵊn ‖ pᵊr- **~s** z
　per'cussion cap

percussionist pə 'kʌʃ ᵊn ɪst §ˌ·əst ‖ pᵊr- **~s** s

percussive pə 'kʌs ɪv ‖ pᵊr- **~ly** li **~ness** nəs
　nɪs

percutaneous ˌpɜː kju 'teɪn i əs ‖ ˌpɜː- **~ly** li

Percy 'pɜːs i ‖ 'pɜːs i

per diem ˌpɜː 'diː em pə-, -'daɪ-, -əm ‖ pᵊr-
　ˌpɜː-

Perdita 'pɜːd ɪt ə §-ət- ‖ 'pɜːd əţ ə pᵊr 'diːţ ə

perdition pə 'dɪʃ ᵊn pɜː- ‖ pᵊr-

Perdue, p~ 'pɜːd juː ‖ pᵊr 'duː -'djuː

pere, père, Père peə ‖ peᵊr —*Fr* [pɛʁ]

peregri|nate 'per əg rɪ |neɪt '·ɪg-, -rə- · **~nated**
　neɪt ɪd -əd ‖ neɪţ əd **~nates** neɪts **~nating**
　neɪt ɪŋ ‖ neɪţ ɪŋ

P

peregrination ˌper əg rɪ 'neɪʃ ᵊn ˌ‑ɪg‑, ‑rə'‑‑ **~s** z

peregrine, P~ 'per əg rɪn ‑ɪg‑, §‑rən; ‑ɪ griːn, ‑ə‑ **~s** z
ˌperegrine 'falcon

pereira, P~ pə 'reər ə ‑'rɪər‑ ‖ ‑'rer ə
pe'reira bark

Perelman (i) 'per əl mən, (ii) 'pɜːl mən
‖ 'pɜːl‑ —Usually (i).

peremptor|y pə 'rempt ᵊr ˌi pɪ‑; 'per əmpt‑
—Both stressings are in use among English lawyers. **~ily** əl i ɪ ɪ li **~iness** i nəs i nɪs

perennial pə 'ren i ˌəl **~ly** i **~s** z

perentie pə 'rent i ‖ ‑'renʈ i **~s** z

Peres pə 'rez

perestroika ˌper ə 'strɔɪk ə ‑ɪ‑ — Russ [pʲɪ rʲɪ 'strɔj kə]

Pérez de Cuéllar ˌper əz də 'kweɪl jɑː ˌ‑ɪz‑, ˌ‑ez‑ ‑'kweɪ‑ ‖ ‑jɑːr —AmSp [ˌpe res de 'kwe jar, ˌ‑reh‑]

perfect v pə 'fekt pɜː‑ ‖ pᵊr‑ **~ed** ɪd əd **~ing** ɪŋ **~s** s

perfect adj, n 'pɜːf ɪkt ‑ekt, §‑əkt ‖ 'pɜːf‑ **~s** s
ˌperfect 'tense; ˌperfect 'participle

perfectibility pə ˌfekt ə 'bɪl ət i pɜː‑, ‑ˌ‑ɪ‑, ‑ɪt i
‖ pᵊr ˌfekt ə 'bɪl əʈ i

perfectib|le pə 'fekt əb |ᵊl pɜː‑, ‑'‑ɪb‑ ‖ pᵊr‑ **~ly** li

perfection pə 'fek ʃᵊn ‖ pᵊr‑ **~s** z

perfectionism pə 'fek ʃᵊn ˌɪz əm ‖ pᵊr‑

perfectionist pə 'fek ʃᵊn ɪst § ˌəst ‖ pᵊr‑ **~s** s

perfective pə 'fekt ɪv ‖ pᵊr‑ **~ly** li **~ness** nəs nɪs **~s** z

perfect|ly 'pɜːf ɪkt li ‑ekt‑, §‑əkt‑ ‖ 'pɜːf‑ **~ness** nəs nɪs

perfecto pə 'fekt əʊ ‖ pᵊr 'fekt oʊ **~s** z

perfervid pɜː 'fɜːv ɪd pə‑, §‑əd ‖ pᵊr 'fɜːv‑ **~ly** li **~ness** nəs nɪs

perfidious pə 'fɪd i ˌəs pɜː‑ ‖ pᵊr‑ **~ly** li **~ness** nəs nɪs

perfid|y 'pɜːf əd |i ‑ɪd‑ ‖ 'pɜːf‑ **~ies** iz

perfoliate pə 'fəʊl i ˌət ət, ‑eɪt ‖ pᵊr 'foʊl‑

perforate adj 'pɜːf ər ˌət ɪt, ‑ə reɪt ‖ 'pɜːf‑

perfo|rate v 'pɜːf ə |reɪt ‖ 'pɜːf‑ **~rated** reɪt ɪd ‑əd ‖ reɪʈ əd **~rates** reɪts **~rating** reɪt ɪŋ ‖ reɪʈ ɪŋ

perforation ˌpɜːf ə 'reɪʃ ᵊn ‖ ˌpɜːf‑ **~s** z

perforator 'pɜːf ə reɪt ə ‖ 'pɜːf ə reɪʈ ᵊr **~s** z

perforce pə 'fɔːs pɜː‑ ‖ pᵊr 'fɔːrs ‑'foʊrs

perform pə 'fɔːm ‖ pᵊr 'fɔːrm **~ed** d **~ing** ɪŋ **~s** z

performanc|e pə 'fɔːm ənᵗs ‖ pᵊr 'fɔːrm‑ **~es** ɪz əz

performance-enhancing
pə 'fɔːm ənᵗs ɪn ˌhɑːnᵗs ɪŋ ‑‑en‑, ‑ˌən‑, ‑ˌhænᵗs‑ ‖ pr 'fɔːrm ənᵗs ɪn ˌhænᵗs ɪŋ

performance-related
pə ˌfɔːm əns ri 'leɪt ɪd ‑rə'‑ ‖ pᵊr 'fɔːrm əns rə ˌleɪʈ əd

performative pə 'fɔːm ət ɪv ‖ pᵊr 'fɔːrm əʈ ɪv **~s** z

performer pə 'fɔːm ə ‖ pᵊr 'fɔːrm ᵊr **~s** z

perfume n 'pɜː fjuːm ‖ 'pɜː fjuːm pᵊr 'fjuːm **~s** z

perfum|e v 'pɜː fjuːm pə 'fjuːm, pɜː‑ ‖ pᵊr 'fjuːm 'pɜː fjuːm **~ed** d **~es** z **~ing** ɪŋ

perfumer pə 'fjuːm ə pɜː‑; 'pɜː fjuːm ə ‖ pᵊr 'fjuːm ᵊr 'pɜː fjuːm ᵊr **~s** z

perfumer|y pə 'fjuːm ər |i pɜː‑ ‖ pᵊr‑ **~ies** iz

perfumier pə 'fjuːm i ə pɜː‑, ‑eɪ ‖ pᵊr 'fjuːm i ᵊr **~s** z

perfunctor|y pə 'fʌŋkt ᵊr |i pɜː‑ ‖ pᵊr‑ **~ily** əl i ɪ li **~iness** i nəs i nɪs

perfus|e pə 'fjuːz pɜː‑ ‖ pᵊr‑ **~ed** d **~es** ɪz əz **~ing** ɪŋ

perfusion pə 'fjuːʒ ᵊn pɜː‑ ‖ pᵊr‑ **~s** z

Pergamon 'pɜːg əm ən ‖ 'pɜːg‑ ‑ə mɑːn

Pergamum 'pɜːg əm əm ‖ 'pɜːg‑

pergola 'pɜːg əl ə pə 'gəʊl ə ‖ 'pɜːg əl ə pᵊr 'goʊl ə **~s** z

Pergolesi ˌpɜːg əʊ 'leɪz i ‖ ˌpɜːg ə‑ ‑'leɪs‑ —It [per go 'le si]

Perham 'per əm

perhaps pə 'hæps ‖ pᵊr‑ —informally also pər 'æps, præps

peri 'pɪər i ‖ 'pɪr i **~s** z

peri- comb. form with stress-neutral suffix ˌper i —but before a consonant sound often ˌper ɪ, §ˌper ə ˌper ə — **perinatal** ˌper i 'neɪt ᵊl ◄ ‖ ˌper ə 'neɪʈ ᵊl ◄ with stress-imposing suffix pə 'rɪ+ pɪ‑, pe‑ — **pericope** pə 'rɪk əp i pɪ‑, pe‑

perianth 'per i ænᵗθ **~s** s

pericarditis ˌper i kɑː 'daɪt ɪs §‑əs ‖ ˌper ə kɑːr 'daɪʈ əs

pericardi|um ˌper i 'kɑːd i ˌəm ‖ ‑ə 'kɑːrd‑ **~a** ə **~ums** əmz

pericarp 'per i kɑːp ‑ə‑ ‖ ‑ə kɑːrp **~s** s

Periclean ˌper ɪ 'kliː ən ◄ ‑ə‑

Pericles 'per ɪ kliːz ‑ə‑

pericynthion ˌper i 'sɪnᵗθ i ˌən ‖ ‑ə 'sɪnᵗθ i ɑːn

peridot 'per i dɒt ‖ ‑ə dɑːt ‑doʊ

perigee 'per i dʒiː ‑i‑, ‑ə‑ **~s** z

Perigord, Périgord 'per ɪ gɔː ‑ə‑ ‖ ˌper ə 'gɔːr —Fr [pe ʁi gɔːʁ]

perihelio|n ˌper i 'hiːl i ˌən ˌ‑ə‑ **~a** ə

peril 'per əl ‑ɪl **~s** z

perilous 'per əl əs ‑ɪl‑ **~ly** li **~ness** nəs nɪs

perilune 'per i luːn ‑ljuːn ‖ ‑ə‑

perimeter pə 'rɪm ɪt ə pɪ‑, pe‑, ‑ət‑ ‖ ‑əʈ ᵊr **~s** z

perinatal ˌper ɪ 'neɪt ᵊl ‑ə‑ ‖ ‑'neɪʈ‑

perineal ˌper ɪ 'niː əl ‑ə‑

perine|um ˌper ɪ 'niː ˌəm ‑ə‑ **~a** ə

period 'pɪər i ˌəd ‖ 'pɪr‑ **~s** z
'period piece

periodate pər 'aɪ ə deɪt ‖ pər‑ **~s** s

periodic 'recurring at intervals' ˌpɪər i 'ɒd ɪk ◄ ‖ ˌpɪr i 'ɑːd ɪk ◄
ˌperiˌodic 'table

periodic 'derived by addition of water to I_2O_7' ˌpɜːr aɪ 'ɒd ɪk ◄ ‖ ˌpɜː aɪ 'ɑːd‑

periodical ˌpɪər i 'ɒd ɪk ᵊl ◄ ‖ ˌpɪr i 'ɑːd ɪk ᵊl ◄ **~ly** i **~s** z

periodicity ˌpɪər i ə 'dɪs ət i ‖ ˌpɪr i ə 'dɪs əʈ i

periodont|al ˌper i əʊ ˈdɒnt |ᵊl ◂
‖ ˌper i oʊ ˈdɑːnt |ᵊl ◂ -ə'- ~ic -ɪk ◂ ~ics ɪks
~ist/s ɪst/s §-əst/s
perioste|um ˌper i ˈɒst i |əm ‖ -'ɑːst- ~a ə ~al
əl
periotic ˌper i ˈəʊt ɪk ◂ -'ɒt- ‖ -'oʊt̬-
peripatetic, P~ ˌper ɪ pə ˈtet ɪk ◂ -ə-, ˌ·i-
‖ -'tet̬- ~ally ᵊl_i ~s s
peripeteia, peripetia ˌper ɪ pə ˈtiːˌə, -ə-, ˌ·i-,
-'taɪ_ə ~s z
peripet|y pə ˈrɪp ət |i pe-, pɪ- ‖ -ət̬ |i ~ies iz
peripheral pə ˈrɪf ᵊr_əl pɪ-, pe- ~s z
pe.ripheral ˈnervous ˌsystem
peripherality pə ˌrɪf ə ˈræl ət i pɪ-, pe-, -ɪt i
‖ -ət̬ i
peripherally pə ˈrɪf ᵊr_əl i pɪ-, pe-
peripher|y pə ˈrɪf ər_|i pɪ-, pe- ~ies iz
periph|rasis pə ˈrɪf |rəs ɪs pɪ-, pe-, §-əs ~rases
rə siːz
periphrastic ˌper ɪ ˈfræst ɪk ◂ -ə-, -i- ~ally ᵊl_i
perique pə ˈriːk
periscope ˈper ɪ skəʊp -ə- ‖ -skoʊp ~s s
periscopic ˌper ɪ ˈskɒp ɪk ◂ -ə- ‖ -'skɑːp ɪk ◂
perish ˈper ɪʃ ~ed t ~es ɪz əz ~ing/ly ɪŋ /li
perishability ˌper ɪʃ ə ˈbɪl ət i -ɪt i ‖ -ət̬ i
perishable ˈper ɪʃ əb ᵊl ~ness nəs nɪs ~s z
perisher ˈper ɪʃ ə ‖ -ᵊr ~s z
perispom|enon ˌper i ˈspəʊm |ə nɒn
‖ -'spoʊm |ə nɑːn ~ena ən ə
perissodactyl pə ˌrɪs əʊ ˈdækt ɪl pɪ-, pe-, §-ᵊl,
·'·ˌ·ˌ· ‖ -ə'- ~s z
peristalsis ˌper ɪ ˈstæls ɪs -ə-, §-əs ‖ -'stɔːls əs
-'staːls-, -'stæls-
peristaltic ˌper ɪ ˈstælt ɪk ◂ -ə- ‖ -'stɔːlt ɪk ◂
-'staːlt-, -'stælt-
peristyle ˈper ɪ staɪᵊl -ə-, -i- ~s z
peritone|um ˌper ɪ təʊ ˈniː |əm ˌ·ə-
‖ ˌper ət ᵊn ˈiː |əm ~a ə
peritonitis ˌper ɪ təʊ ˈnaɪt ɪs -ə-, §-əs
‖ ˌper ət ᵊn ˈaɪt̬ əs
Perivale ˈper ɪ verᵊl -i-, -ə-
periwig ˈper i wɪg ~ged d ~s z
periwinkle ˈper i ˌwɪŋk ᵊl ~s z
perjure ˈpɜːdʒ ə ‖ ˈpɜːdʒ ᵊr ~d d perjuring
ˈpɜːdʒ ər_ɪŋ ‖ ˈpɜːdʒ ər_ɪŋ ~s z
perjurer ˈpɜːdʒ ər ə ‖ ˈpɜːdʒ ᵊr_ər ~s z
perjurious pɜː ˈdʒʊər i_əs pə-, -'dʒɔːr-
‖ pɜː ˈdʒʊr- pᵊr- ~ly li ~ness nəs nɪs
perjur|y ˈpɜːdʒ ər_|i ~ies iz
perk pɜːk ‖ pɜːk perked ˈpɜːkt ‖ pɜːkt perking
ˈpɜːk ɪŋ ‖ ˈpɜːk ɪŋ perks pɜːks ‖ pɜːks
perki... —see perky
Perkin ˈpɜːk ɪn §-ən ‖ ˈpɜːk-
Perkins ˈpɜːk ɪnz §-ənz ‖ ˈpɜːk-
Perks pɜːks ‖ pɜːks
perk|y, Perky ˈpɜːk |i ‖ ˈpɜːk |i ~ier i_ə ‖ i_ᵊr
~iest i_ɪst i_əst ~ily i li əl i ~iness i nəs i nɪs
perlative ˈpɜːl ət ɪv ‖ ˈpɜːl ət̬-
Perlis ˈpɜːl ɪs §-əs ‖ ˈpɜːl- —Malay [ˈper lis]
perlite ˈpɜːl aɪt ‖ ˈpɜːl-
Perlman ˈpɜːl mən ‖ ˈpɜːl-
perlocution ˌpɜː ləʊ ˈkjuːʃ ᵊn -lɒ- ‖ ˌpɜː lə-

perlocutionary ˌpɜː ləʊ ˈkjuːʃ ᵊn ər i ◂ ˌ·lɒ-
‖ ˌpɜː lə ˈkjuːʃ ə ner i ◂
perm pɜːm ‖ pɜːm permed pɜːmd ‖ pɜːmd
perming ˈpɜːm ɪŋ ‖ ˈpɜːm ɪŋ perms pɜːmz
‖ pɜːmz
Perm place in Russia pɜːm ‖ pɜːm —Russ
[pʲermʲ]
permaculture ˈpɜːm ə ˌkʌltʃ ə
‖ ˈpɜːm ə ˌkʌltʃ ᵊr
permafrost ˈpɜːm ə frɒst -frɔːst
‖ ˈpɜːm ə frɔːst -frɑːst
permalloy ˈpɜːm ə lɔɪ pɜːm ˈæl ɪc ‖ -ᵊl ɔɪ
‖ ˌpɜːm ˈæl ɔɪ ˈpɜːm ə lɔɪ
permanenc|e ˈpɜːm ən_ənˈs ‖ ˈpɜːm- ~ies iz
~y i
permanent ˈpɜːm ən_ənt ‖ ˈpɜːm- ~ly li ~s s
ˌpermanent ˈwave; ˌpermanent ˈway
permanganate pə ˈmæŋ gə neɪt pɜː-; -gən ɪt,
-ət ‖ pᵊr- ~s s
permanganic ˌpɜː mæn ˈgæn ɪk ◂ →-mæŋ-
‖ ˌpɜː-
permeability ˌpɜːm i_ə ˈbɪl ət i -ɪt i
‖ ˌpɜːm i_ə ˈbɪl ət̬ i
permeab|le ˈpɜːm i_əb ᵊl ‖ ˈpɜːm- ~ly li
permeance ˈpɜːm i_ən's ‖ ˈpɜːm-
perme|ate ˈpɜːm i eɪt ‖ ˈpɜːm- ~ated eɪt ɪd
-əd ‖ eɪt̬ əd ~ates eɪts ~ating eɪt ɪŋ ‖ eɪt̬ ɪŋ
permeation ˌpɜːm i ˈeɪʃ ᵊn ‖ ˌpɜːm-
Permian ˈpɜːm i_ən ‖ ˈpɜːm-
permissib|le pə ˈmɪs əb ᵊl -'ɪb- ‖ pᵊr-
~leness ᵊl nəs -nɪs ~ly li
permission pə ˈmɪʃ ᵊn ‖ pᵊr- ~s z
permissive pə ˈmɪs ɪv ‖ pᵊr- ~ly li ~ness nəs
nɪs
per|mit v pə |ˈmɪt ‖ pᵊr- ~mits ˈmɪts ~mitted
ˈmɪt ɪd -əd ‖ ˈmɪt̬ əd ~mitting ˈmɪt ɪŋ
‖ ˈmɪt̬ ɪŋ
permit n ˈpɜːm ɪt ‖ ˈpɜː mɪt pᵊr ˈmɪt ~s s
permittivity ˌpɜːm ɪ ˈtɪv ət i ˌ·ə-
‖ ˌpɜːm ɪ ˈtɪv ət̬ i
permu|tate ˈpɜːm ju |teɪt -jə- ‖ ˈpɜːm-
pᵊr ˈmjuː|t eɪt ~tated teɪt ɪd -əd ‖ teɪt̬ əd
~tates teɪts ~tating teɪt ɪŋ ‖ teɪt̬ ɪŋ
permutation ˌpɜːm ju ˈteɪʃ ᵊn -jə- ‖ ˌpɜːm- ~al
ᵊl ~s z
per|mute pə |ˈmjuːt ‖ pᵊr- ~muted ˈmjuːt ɪd
-əd ‖ ˈmjuːt̬ əd ~mutes ˈmjuːts ~muting
ˈmjuːt ɪŋ ‖ ˈmjuːt̬ ɪŋ
Permutit tdmk pə ˈmjuːt ɪt §-ət; ˈpɜːm jʊt-
‖ pᵊr ˈmjuːt̬-
Pernambuco ˌpɜːn əm ˈbuːk əʊ -æm-, -ˈbjuːk-
‖ ˌpɜːn əm ˈbuːk oʊ —Port [per nɐm ˈbu ku]
pernicious pə ˈnɪʃ əs pɜː- ‖ pᵊr- ~ly li ~ness
nəs nɪs
per.nicious aˈnaemia
pernickety pə ˈnɪk ət i -ɪt- ‖ pᵊr ˈnɪk ət̬ i
Pernod tdmk ˈpɜːn əʊ ˈpeən- ‖ per ˈnoʊ —Fr
[pɛʁ no]
Peron, Perón pə ˈrɒn pe-, pɪ- ‖ -ˈroʊn —Sp
[pe ˈron]
perone|al ˌper əʊ ˈniːˌ|əl ◂ ‖ -oʊ- -ə- ~us əs

pero|rate 'per ə |reɪt -ɒ-, -ɔː- ‖ 'pɜː- **~rated**
reɪt ɪd -əd ‖ reɪţ əd **~rates** reɪts **~rating**
reɪt ɪŋ ‖ reɪţ ɪŋ
peroration ˌper ə 'reɪʃ ªn **~s** z
Perowne pə 'rəʊn pe- ‖ -'roʊn
peroxide pə 'rɒks aɪd ‖ -'rɑːks- **~s** z
pe‚roxide 'blonde

perp pɜːp ‖ pɜːp **perps** pɜːps ‖ pɜːps
perpend *n* 'pɜː pend ‖ 'pɜː- **~s** z
perpendicular ˌpɜːp ən 'dɪk jʊl ə ◂ →ˌm-,
-jəl ə ‖ ˌpɜːp ən 'dɪk jəl ªr **~ly** li **~s** z
perpendicularity ˌpɜːp ən ˌdɪk ju 'lær ət i
→ˌm-, -ˌjə-, -ɪt i ‖ ˌpɜːp ən ˌdɪk jə 'lær əţ i
-'ler-

perpe|trate 'pɜːp ə |treɪt -ɪ- ‖ 'pɜːp- **~trated**
treɪt ɪd -əd ‖ treɪţ əd **~trates** treɪts **~trating**
treɪt ɪŋ ‖ treɪţ ɪŋ

perpetration ˌpɜːp ə 'treɪʃ ªn -ɪ- ‖ ˌpɜːp- **~s** z
perpetrator 'pɜːp ə treɪt ə '-ɪ- ‖ 'pɜːp ə treɪţ ªr
~s z

PERPETUAL

perpetual pə 'pet ju ªl →-'petʃ u̬‿, -'petʃ əl
‖ pªr 'petʃ u̬ əl — *Preference poll, BrE:* -tju‿əl
57%, -tʃu‿əl *37%,* -tʃəl *6%.* **~ly** i
perpetu|ate pə 'pet ju |eɪt -'petʃ u-
‖ pªr 'petʃ u |eɪt **~ated** eɪt ɪd -əd ‖ eɪţ əd
~ates eɪts **~ating** eɪt ɪŋ ‖ eɪţ ɪŋ
perpetuation pə ˌpet ju 'eɪʃ ªn -ˌpetʃ u-
‖ pªr ˌpetʃ u-
perpetuit|y ˌpɜːp ə 'tjuː‿ət |i ˌ·ɪ-, →-'tʃuː‿, ɪt i
‖ ˌpɜːp ə 'tuː‿əţ |i -'tjuː- **~ies** iz
perpetuum mobile pə ˌpet ju‿əm 'məʊb əl i
pɜː-, -, petʃ u̬‿, -ˌpet u̬‿, -ɪl-, -eɪ
‖ pªr ˌpetʃ u əm 'moʊb-
Perpignan 'pɜːp iː njɒ̃ ‖ ˌpɜːp iː njɑ̃ːn 'jɑːn —*Fr*
[pɛʁ pi njɑ̃]
perplex pə 'pleks ‖ pªr- **~ed** t **~es** ɪz əz **~ing**
ɪŋ
perplexed|ly pə 'pleks ɪd |li -əd-; pə 'plekst |li
‖ pªr- **~ness** nəs nɪs
perplexit|y pə 'pleks ət |i -ɪt-
‖ pªr 'pleks əţ |i **~ies** iz
per pro ˌpɜː 'prəʊ ◂ ‖ ˌpɜː 'proʊ ◂

perquisite 'pɜːk wɪz ɪt -wəz-, §-ət ‖ 'pɜːk- **~s** s
Perranporth ˌper ən 'pɔːθ →-əm- ‖ -'pɔːrθ
Perrault 'per əʊ ‖ pe 'roʊ —*Fr* [pɛ ʁo]
Perrier *tdmk* 'per i eɪ ‖ ˌ·'·· —*Fr* [pɛ ʁje] **~s** z
Perrin 'per ɪn §-ən —*but as a French name,
also* -æ̃, *Fr* [pɛ ʁæ̃]
perruquier pə 'ruːk i eɪ —*Fr* [pɛ ʁy kje] **~s** z
perr|y, Perr|y 'per |i **~ies, ~y's** iz
Persaud pə 'sɔːd ‖ pªr- -'sɑːd
Perse, perse pɜːs ‖ pɜːs
per se ˌpɜː 'seɪ ‖ ˌpɜː- ˌper-, -'siː
perse|cute 'pɜːs ɪ |kjuːt -ə- ‖ 'pɜːs- **~cuted**
kjuːt ɪd -əd ‖ kjuːţ əd **~cutes** kjuːts **~cuting**
kjuːt ɪŋ ‖ kjuːţ ɪŋ
persecution ˌpɜːs ɪ 'kjuːʃ ªn -ə- ‖ ˌpɜːs- **~s** z
persecutor 'pɜːs ɪ kjuːt ə '-ə- ‖ 'pɜːs ɪ kjuːţ ªr
~s z
persecutory ˌpɜːs ɪ 'kjuːt ər i ˌ·ə-, '·····
‖ 'pɜːs ɪ kjuːţ ər i -kju tɔːr i, -kju toʊr i
Perseid 'pɜːs i ɪd §-əd ‖ pɜːs- **~s** z
Persephone pɜː 'sef ən i pə- ‖ pªr-
Persepolis pɜː 'sep əl ɪs pə-, §-əs ‖ pªr-
Perseus 'pɜːs juːs 'pɜːs i‿əs ‖ 'pɜːs i‿əs
'pɜːs juːs, -uːs
perseverance ˌpɜːs ɪ 'vɪər ªn's -ə-
‖ ˌpɜːs ə 'vɪr-
perseve|rate pə 'sev ə |reɪt ‖ pªr- **~rated**
reɪt ɪd -əd ‖ reɪţ əd **~rates** reɪts **~rating**
reɪt ɪŋ ‖ reɪţ ɪŋ
perseveration pə ˌsev ə 'reɪʃ ªn pɜː- ‖ pªr- **~s**
z
perseverative pə 'sev ər‿ət ɪv
‖ pªr 'sev ə reɪţ ɪv **~ly** li
persevere ˌpɜːs ɪ 'vɪə -ə- ‖ ˌpɜːs ə 'vɪªr **~d** d **~s**
z **persevering/ly** ˌpɜːs ɪ 'vɪər ɪŋ /li ˌ·ə-
‖ ˌpɜːs ə 'vɪr ɪŋ /li
Pershing 'pɜːʃ ɪŋ ‖ 'pɜːʃ ɪŋ
Pershore 'pɜː ʃɔː ‖ 'pɜː ʃɔːr -ʃoʊr
Persi|a 'pɜːʒ |ə 'pɜːʒ- ‖ 'pɜːʒ |ə **~an/s** ªn/z
‚Persian 'cat
persienne ˌpɜːs i 'en ‖ ˌpɜːz- —*Fr* [pɛʁ sjɛn]
~s z
persiflage 'pɜːs ɪ flɑːʒ 'peəs-, -ə-, ˌ·'· ‖ 'pɜːs-
'pers- —*Fr* [pɛʁ si flɑːʒ]
Persil *tdmk* 'pɜːs ɪl -ªl ‖ 'pɜːs-
persimmon pə 'sɪm ən pɜː- ‖ pªr- **~s** z
Persis 'pɜːs ɪs §-əs ‖ 'pɜːs-
persist pə 'sɪst ‖ pªr- -'zɪst **~ed** ɪd əd **~ing** ɪŋ
~s s
persistenc|e pə 'sɪst ªn's ‖ pªr- -'zɪst- **~y** i
persistent pə 'sɪst ənt ‖ pªr- -'zɪst- **~ly** li
persnickety pə 'snɪk ət i -ɪt- ‖ pªr 'snɪk əţ i
person 'pɜːs ªn ‖ 'pɜːs ªn **~s** z
person|a pə 'səʊn |ə pɜː- ‖ pªr 'soʊn |ə -ɑ- **~ae**
iː aɪ **~as** əz
‚persona 'grata 'grɑːt ə 'greɪt- ‖ 'grɑːţ ə
'græt-, 'greɪţ-; per‚sona ‚non 'grata nəʊn
nɒn ‖ nɑːn noʊn
personable 'pɜːs ªn‿əb ªl ‖ 'pɜːs- **~leness**
ªl nəs -nɪs
personag|e 'pɜːs ªn‿ɪdʒ ‖ 'pɜːs- **~es** ɪz əz
personal 'pɜːs ªn‿əl ‖ 'pɜːs- **~s** z
‚personal as'sistant; 'personal ‚column;

,**personal** com'**puter**; ,**personal** e'**state**;
,**personal** '**pronoun**; ,**personal** '**property**;
,**personal** '**stereo**

personalis... —*see* **personaliz...**

personalit|y ˌpɜːs ə 'næl ət |i -ɪt i
‖ ˌpɜːs ə 'næl ət̬ |i **~ies** iz
,**perso'nality cult**; ,**perso'nality test**

personalization ˌpɜːs ᵊn̩ əl aɪ 'zeɪʃ ᵊn -ɪ'‑
‖ ˌpɜːs ᵊn̩ əl ə-

personaliz|e 'pɜːs ᵊn̩ ə laɪz -əl aɪz ‖ 'pɜːs- **~ed**
d **~es** ɪz əz **~ing** ɪŋ

personally 'pɜːs ᵊn̩ əl i ‖ 'pɜːs-

perso|nate v 'pɜːs ə |neɪt -ᵊ|n eɪt ‖ 'pɜːs-
~nated neɪt ɪd -əd ‖ neɪt̬ əd **~nates** neɪts
~nating neɪt ɪŋ ‖ neɪt̬ ɪŋ

personation ˌpɜːs ə 'neɪʃ ᵊn ‖ ˌpɜːs- **~s** z

personator 'pɜːs ə neɪt ə →-ᵊn eɪt-
‖ 'pɜːs ᵊn̩ eɪt̬ ᵊr **~s** z

personification pə ˌsɒn ɪf ɪ 'keɪʃ ᵊn pɜː-, -ˌ-əf-,
§-ə'‑ ‖ pᵊr ˌsɑːn- **~s** z

personi|fy pə 'sɒn ɪ |faɪ pɜː-, -ə- ‖ pᵊr 'sɑːn-
~fied faɪd **~fier/s** faɪ ə/z ‖ faɪ ᵊr/z **~fies** faɪz
~fying faɪ ɪŋ

personnel ˌpɜːs ə 'nel -ᵊn 'el ‖ ˌpɜːs-
,**person'nel** ˌmanager

person-to-person ˌpɜːs ᵊn tə 'pɜːs ᵊn ◂ -ᵊn tu-
‖ ˌpɜːs ᵊn tə 'pɜːs ᵊn ◂

perspective pə 'spekt ɪv ‖ pᵊr- **~ly** li **~s** z

perspex, P- *tdmk* 'pɜːsp eks ‖ 'pɜːsp-

perspicacious ˌpɜːsp ɪ 'keɪʃ əs ◂ -ə- ‖ ˌpɜːsp-
~ly li **~ness** nəs nɪs

perspicacity ˌpɜːsp ɪ 'kæs ət i ˌ-ə-, -ɪt i
‖ ˌpɜːsp ə 'kæs ət̬ i

perspicuity ˌpɜːsp ɪ 'kjuː ət i ˌ-ə-, ɪt i
‖ ˌpɜːsp ə 'kjuː ət̬ i

perspicuous pə 'spɪk ju əs ‖ pᵊr- **~ly** li **~ness**
nəs nɪs

perspiration ˌpɜːsp ə 'reɪʃ ᵊn ‖ ˌpɜːsp-

perspiratory pə 'spaɪ ər ət ᵊr i -'spɪr-;
'pɜːsp ər · ·, '‑ɪr- ‖ pᵊr 'spaɪr ə tɔːr i
'pɜːsp ər ə-, -tour i

perspire pə 'spaɪ ə ‖ pᵊr 'spaɪ ᵊr **~d** d **~s** z
perspiring pə 'spaɪ ər ɪŋ ‖ pᵊr 'spaɪ ᵊr ɪŋ

persuad|e pə 'sweɪd ‖ pᵊr- **~ed** ɪd əd **~er/s** ə/z
‖ ᵊr/z **~es** z **~ing** ɪŋ

persuasion pə 'sweɪʒ ᵊn ‖ pᵊr- **~s** z

persuasive pə 'sweɪs ɪv -'sweɪz- ‖ pᵊr- **~ly** li
~ness nəs nɪs

pert pɜːt ‖ pɜːt **perter** 'pɜːt ə ‖ 'pɜːt̬ ᵊr **pertest**
'pɜːt ɪst -əst ‖ 'pɜːt̬ əst

pertain pə 'teɪn pɜː- ‖ pᵊr- **~ed** d **~ing** ɪŋ **~s** z

Perth pɜːθ ‖ pɜːθ

Perthite 'pɜːθ aɪt ‖ 'pɜːθ- **~s** s

Perthshire 'pɜːθ ʃə -ʃɪə, -ˌʃaɪ ə ‖ 'pɜːθ ʃᵊr -ʃɪr,
-ˌʃaɪ ᵊr

pertinacious ˌpɜːt ɪ 'neɪʃ əs ◂ -ə-
‖ ˌpɜːt ᵊn 'eɪʃ əs **~ly** li **~ness** nəs nɪs

pertinacity ˌpɜːt ɪ 'næs ət i ˌ-ə-, -ɪt i
‖ ˌpɜːt ᵊn 'æs ət̬ i

pertinence 'pɜːt ɪn ən̩ s -ən- ‖ 'pɜːt ᵊn̩ ən̩ s

pertinent 'pɜːt ɪn ənt -ən- ‖ 'pɜːt ᵊn̩ ənt **~ly** li

pert|ly 'pɜːt| li ‖ 'pɜːt̬ li **~ness** nəs -nɪs

perturb pə 'tɜːb pɜː- ‖ pᵊr 'tɜːb **~ed** d **~ing** ɪŋ
~s z

perturbation ˌpɜːt ə 'beɪʃ ᵊn ˌpɜː tɜː- ‖ ˌpɜːt̬ ᵊr-
ˌpɜː tɜː- **~s** z

pertussis pə 'tʌs ɪs §-əs ‖ pᵊr-

Pertwee 'pɜːt wiː ‖ 'pɜːt-

Peru pə 'ruː —*Sp* Perú [pe 'ru] **~'s** z

Perugia pə 'ruːdʒ ə pɪ-, pe-, -'ruːdʒ i ə —*It*
[pe 'ruː dʒa]

Perugino ˌper u 'dʒiːn əʊ ‖ -oʊ —*It*
[pe ɾu 'dʒi: no]

peruke pə 'ruːk pe- **~s** s

perusal pə 'ruːz ᵊl pe- **~s** z

perus|e pə 'ruːz pe- **~ed** d **~es** ɪz əz **~ing** ɪŋ

Perutz pə 'rʊts -'ruːts —*Ger* ['pɛʁ ʊts]

Peruvian pə 'ruːv i ən pe- **~s** z

Peruzzi pə 'ruːts i —*It* [pe 'rut tsi]

perv, perve pɜːv ‖ pɜːv **perved** pɜːvd ‖ pɜːvd
perves pɜːvz ‖ pɜːvz **perving** 'pɜːv ɪŋ
‖ 'pɜːv ɪŋ

pervad|e pə 'veɪd pɜː- ‖ pᵊr- **~ed** ɪd əd **~es** z
~ing ɪŋ

pervasion pə 'veɪʒ ᵊn ‖ pᵊr-

pervasive pə 'veɪs ɪv pɜː-, -'veɪz- ‖ pᵊr- **~ly** li
~ness nəs nɪs

perverse pə 'vɜːs ‖ pᵊr 'vɜːs **~ly** li **~ness** nəs
nɪs

perversion pə 'vɜːʃ ᵊn -'vɜːʒ- ‖ pᵊr 'vɜːʒ ᵊn
-'vɜːʃ- **~s** z

perversit|y pə 'vɜːs ət i -ɪt- ‖ pᵊr 'vɜːs ət̬ i
~ies iz

perversive pə 'vɜːs ɪv ‖ pᵊr 'vɜːs ɪv

per|vert v pə |'vɜːt ‖ pᵊr |'vɜːt **~verted**
'vɜːt ɪd -əd ‖ 'vɜːt̬ əd **~verting** 'vɜːt ɪŋ
‖ 'vɜːt̬ ɪŋ **~verts** 'vɜːts ‖ 'vɜːts

pervert n 'pɜː vɜːt ‖ 'pɜː vɜːt **~s** s

perverter pə 'vɜːt ə ‖ pᵊr 'vɜːt̬ ᵊr **~s** z

pervious 'pɜːv i əs ‖ 'pɜːv- **~ness** nəs nɪs

Pery (i) 'peər i ‖ 'per i 'pær-, (ii) 'pɪər i
‖ 'pɪr i, (iii) 'per i

Pesach 'peɪs ɑːk -ɑːx

Pescadores ˌpesk ə 'dɔːr iːz ‖ -'dour-

peseta pə 'seɪt ə ‖ -'seɪt̬ ə —*Sp* [pe 'se ta] **~s**
z

pesewa pe 'siː wə pɪ-, pə- **~s** z

Peshawar pə 'ʃɑː wə pe-, -'ʃɔː- ‖ -wᵊr

pesk|y 'pesk |i **~ier** i ə ‖ i ᵊr **~iest** i ɪst i əst
~ily ɪ li əl i **~iness** i nəs i nɪs

peso 'peɪs əʊ ‖ -oʊ —*Sp* ['pe so] **~s** z

pessar|y 'pes ər |i **~ies** iz

pessimism 'pes ə ˌmɪz əm 'pez-, -ɪ-

pessimist 'pes əm ɪst 'pez-, -ɪm-, §-əst **~s** s

pessimistic ˌpes ə 'mɪst ɪk ◂ ˌpez-, -ɪ- **~ally** ᵊl i

pest pest **pests** pests

Pest *place in Hungary* pest peʃt —*Hung* [pɛʃt]

Pestalozzi ˌpest ə 'lɒts i ‖ -'lɑːts i —*It*
[pes ta 'lot tsi]

pester 'pest ə ‖ -ᵊr **~ed** d **pestering**
'pest ər ɪŋ **~s** z

pesticide 'pest ɪ saɪd -ə- **~s** z

pestiferous pes 'tɪf ᵊr əs **~ly** li

pestilenc|e 'pest ɪl ən̩ s -əl-, △-jʊl- **~es** ɪz əz

pestilent 'pest ɪl ənt -əl-, △-jʊl- **~ly** li

pestilential ˌpest ɪ ˈlentʃ ᵊl ◂ -ə-, →-ᵊl ˈentʃ- **~ly** i

pestl|e ˈpes ᵊl ˈpest- **~ed** d **~es** z **~ing** ˌɪŋ

pesto ˈpest əʊ ‖ -oʊ —*It* [ˈpes to]

pet, PET pet **pets** pets **petted** ˈpet ɪd -əd ‖ ˈpet̬ əd **petting** ˈpet ɪŋ ‖ ˈpet̬ ɪŋ **'pet name,** ˌ· ˈ·; **'PET ˌscan(ner)**

Peta ˈpiːt ə ‖ ˈpiːt̬ ə

peta- ¦pet ə ‖ ¦pet̬ ə

petaflop ˈpet ə flɒp ‖ ˈpet̬ ə flɑːp **~s** s

Pétain ˈpet æ̃ ˈpeɪt- ‖ peɪ ˈtæ̃ —*Fr* [pe tæ̃]

petal ˈpet ᵊl ‖ ˈpet̬ ᵊl **~ed, ~led** d **~s** z

petanque, pétanque ˌpeɪ ˈtɒŋk ‖ -ˈtɑːŋk —*Fr* [pe tɑ̃k]

petard pe ˈtɑːd pɪ-, pə-; ˈpet ɑːd ‖ -ˈtɑːrd **~s** z

petasus ˈpet əs əs ‖ ˈpet̬- **~es** ɪz əz

Pete piːt

petechi|a pe ˈtiːk i ¦ə pɪ-, pə- **~ae** iː

Peter, peter ˈpiːt ə ‖ ˈpiːt̬ ᵊr **~ed** d **petering** ˈpiːt ᵊr ɪŋ ‖ ˈpiːt̬ ᵊr ɪŋ **~s, ~'s** z **ˌPeter 'Pan**

Peterboro', Peterborough ˈpiːt ə bər ˌə -ˌbʌr ə ‖ ˈpiːt̬ ᵊr ˌbɜː oʊ

Peterhead ˌpiːtə ˈhed ‖ ˌpiːt̬ ᵊr-

Peterkin ˈpiːt ə kɪn ‖ ˈpiːt̬ ᵊr-

Peterlee ˌpiːt ə ˈliː ˈ· · · ‖ ˌpiːt̬ ᵊr-

Peterloo ˌpiːt ə ˈluː ◂ ‖ ˌpiːt̬ ᵊr- **ˌPeterloo 'massacre**

peter|man ˈpiːt ə ¦mən -mæn ‖ ˈpiːt̬ ᵊr- **~men** mən men

Peters ˈpiːt əz ‖ ˈpiːt̬ ᵊrz

Petersburg ˈpiːt əz bɜːg ‖ ˈpiːt̬ ᵊrz bɜːg

Petersfield ˈpiːt əz fiːᵊld ‖ ˈpiːt̬ ᵊrz-

Petersham, p~ ˈpiːt əʃ əm ‖ ˈpiːt̬ ᵊrʃ- -ᵊr ʃæm

Peterson ˈpiːt əs ən ‖ ˈpiːt̬ ᵊrs ən

Petherick ˈpeθ ər ˌɪk

Pethick ˈpeθ ɪk

pethidine ˈpeθ ɪ diːn -ə-

petillant, pétillant ˈpet i ñ -ɪl ənt, §-ᵊl- ‖ ˌpet̬ ɪ ˈjɑːn —*Fr* [pe ti jɑ̃]

petiole ˈpet i əʊl ˈpiːt-, →-ɒʊl ‖ ˈpet̬ i oʊl **~s** z

petit ˈpet i pə ˈtiː ‖ ˈpet̬ i —*Fr* [pə ti] **ˌpetit 'bourgeois,** ˌ· · ˈ·; **ˌpetit ˌbourgeoi'sie; ˌpetit 'four** fʊə fɔː ‖ fɔːr four —*Fr* [fuʁ]; **ˌpetit 'mal** mæl ‖ mɑːl mæl —*Fr* [mal]; **ˌpetit 'point; ˌpetit(s) 'pois** pwɑː —*Fr* [pwa]; **ˌpetit 'pain** pæ̃ —*Fr* [pæ̃]

petite pə ˈtiːt —*Fr* [pə tit]

petition pə ˈtɪʃ ᵊn pɪ- **~ed** d **~ing** ˌɪŋ **~s** z

petitioner pə ˈtɪʃ ᵊn ˌə pɪ- ‖ ᵊr **~s** z

petitio principii pɪ ˌtɪʃ i əʊ prɪn ˈsɪp i aɪ pe-, pə-, -ˌtɪt-, -ˈkɪp-, -iː ‖ -ˌ·oʊ-

Peto ˈpiːt əʊ ‖ ˈpiːt̬ oʊ

Petofi, Petöfi ˈpet əf i -ɜːf i ‖ ˈpet̬ əf i —*Hung* Petőfi [ˈpe tø: fi]

Petra ˈpetr ə ˈpiːtr-

Petrarch ˈpetr ɑːk ‖ -ɑːrk

Petrarchan pe ˈtrɑːk ən pɪ-, pə- ‖ -ˈtrɑːrk-

petrel ˈpetr ᵊl (= *petrol*) **~s** z

Petri ˈpiːtr i ˈpetr i —*Ger* [ˈpeː tʀi]

Petrie ˈpiːtr i

petrifaction ˌpetr ɪ ˈfæk ʃᵊn -ə-

petri|fy ˈpetr ɪ ¦faɪ -ə- **~fied** faɪd **~fies** faɪz **~fying** faɪ ɪŋ

Petrine ˈpiːtr aɪn

petro- *comb. form with stress-neutral suffix* ¦petr əʊ ‖ -ə — **petrological** ˌpetr əʊ ˈlɒdʒ ɪk ᵊl ◂ ‖ -ə ˈlɑːdʒ- *with stress-imposing suffix* pe ˈtrɒ+ pɪ-, pə- ‖ -ˈtrɑː+ — **petrography** pe ˈtrɒg rəf i pɪ-, pə- ‖ -ˈtrɑːg-

Petroc ˈpetr ɒk ‖ -ɑːk

petrochemical ˌpetr əʊ ˈkem ɪk ᵊl ◂ ‖ -oʊ- **~s** z

petrodollar ˈpetr əʊ ˌdɒl ə ‖ -oʊ ˌdɑːl ᵊr **~s** z

Petrofina *tdmk* ˌpetr əʊ ˈfiːn ə ‖ -oʊ-

petroglyph ˈpetr əʊ glɪf ‖ -ə- **~s** s

Petrograd ˈpetr ə græd —*Russ* [pʲɪ trʌ ˈgrat]

petrol ˈpetr ᵊl **'petrol ˌstation; 'petrol tank**

petrolatum ˌpetr ə ˈleɪt əm ‖ -ˈleɪt̬ əm -ˈlɑːt̬-

petrol-bomb ˈpetr ᵊl bɒm ‖ -bɑːm **~ed** d **~ing** ɪŋ **~s** z

petroleum pə ˈtrəʊl i ˌəm pɪ- ‖ -ˈtroʊl- **peˌtroleum 'jelly**

petrologist pə ˈtrɒl ədʒ ɪst pɪ-, pe-, §-əst ‖ -ˈtrɑːl- **~s** s

petrology pə ˈtrɒl ədʒ i pɪ-, pe- ‖ -ˈtrɑːl-

Petronas pe ˈtrəʊn æs pɪ-, pə-, -əs ‖ -ˈtroʊn- -ɑːs

Petronella, p~ ˌpetr ə ˈnel ə

Petronius pɪ ˈtrəʊn i ˌəs pə-, pe- ‖ -ˈtroʊn-

Petropavlovsk ˌpetr əʊ ˈpæv lɒfsk ‖ -ə ˈpæv lɔːfsk -lɑːfsk —*Russ* [pʲɪ trʌ ˈpav ləfsk]

Petruchio pɪ ˈtruːtʃ i ˌəʊ pə-, pe-, -ˈtruːk- ‖ -oʊ

pe-tsai ˌpeɪt ˈsaɪ

petticoat ˈpet i kəʊt ‖ ˈpet̬ i koʊt **~s** s **ˌPetticoat 'Lane**

Pettifer ˈpet ɪf ə -əf- ‖ ˈpet̬ əf ᵊr

pettifog ˈpet i fɒg ‖ ˈpet̬ i fɔːg -fɑːg **~ged** d **~ger/s** ə/z ‖ ᵊr/z **~gery** ər i **~ging** ɪŋ **~s** z

Pettigrew ˈpet i gruː ‖ ˈpet̬-

pettish ˈpet ɪʃ ‖ ˈpet̬ ɪʃ **~ly** li **~ness** nəs nɪs

Pettit ˈpet ɪt §-ət ‖ ˈpet̬ ət

pettitoes ˈpet i təʊz ‖ ˈpet̬ i toʊz

Pettitt ˈpet ɪt §-ət ‖ ˈpet̬ ət

pett|y, Petty ˈpet ¦i ‖ ˈpet̬ ¦i **~ier** i ə ‖ i ˌᵊr **~iest** i ɪst i ˌəst **~ily** i li əl i **~iness** i nəs i nɪs **ˌpetty 'bourgeois,** ˌ· · ˈ·; **ˌpetty 'cash; ˌpetty 'larceny; ˌpetty 'officer◂**

Petula pə ˈtjuːl ə pɪ-, pe-, →-ˈtʃuːl- ‖ -ˈtuːl ə -ˈtjuːl-

petulanc|e ˈpet jʊl ən⸴s ˈpetʃ əl- ‖ ˈpetʃ əl- **~y** i

petulant ˈpet jʊl ənt ˈpetʃ əl- ‖ ˈpetʃ əl- **~ly** li

Petulengro ˌpet ju ˈleŋ grəʊ -ə-, ˌpetʃ ə- ‖ ˌpetʃ ə ˈleŋ groʊ

petunia pə ˈtjuːn i ˌə pɪ-, pe-, →-ˈtʃuːn- ‖ pɪ ˈtuːn jə -ˈtjuːn- **~s** z

petuntse ˌpeɪ ˈtʊnts ə pɪ-, -ˈtʌnts-, -i —*Chi* bái dūn zǐ [²paɪ ¹tuən ˌtsɯ]

Petworth ˈpet wɜːθ -wəθ ‖ -wᵊrθ

Peugeot *tdmk* ˈpɜːʒ əʊ ˈpjuːʒ-, ˈpjuːdʒ-, -ɒt ‖ pjuː ˈʒoʊ puː-, pɜː- —*Fr* [pø ʒo]

Pevensey 'pev ᵊnz i
Peveril 'pev ᵊr̯əl ɪl
Pevsner 'pevz nə ‖ -nᵊr
pew pju: **pews** pju:z
pewit 'pi: wɪt ‖ 'pju: ət **~s** s
Pewsey 'pju:z i
pewter 'pju:t ə ‖ 'pju:t̯ ᵊr
pewterer 'pju:t ər ə ‖ 'pju:t̯ ər ᵊr **~s** z
peyote peɪ 'əʊt i pi- ‖ -'oʊt̯ i —*Sp* [pe 'jo te]
Peyronie's 'per ən iz ‖ ,per ə 'ni:z —*Fr*
   [pɛ ʁɔ ni]
Peyton 'peɪt ᵊn
Pfeiffer 'faɪf ə 'pfaɪf ə ‖ -ᵊr
pfenn|ig 'fen |ɪg 'pfen-, -ɪk —*Ger* ['pfɛn ɪç]
   ~igs ɪgz ɪks
Pfizer 'faɪz ə ‖ -ᵊr
PG ,pi: 'dʒi: **~s, ~'s** z
PGA ,pi: dʒi: 'eɪ
pH ,pi: 'eɪtʃ §-'heɪtʃ
Phaeacian fi 'eɪʃ ᵊn **~s** z
Phaedo 'fi:d əʊ 'faɪd- ‖ -oʊ 'fed-
Phaedra 'fi:dr ə 'faɪdr- ‖ 'fedr ə
Phaedrus 'fi:dr əs 'faɪdr- ‖ 'fedr əs
phaen... —*see* **phen...**
Phaethon, Phaëthon 'feɪ əθ ᵊn -ɪθ- ‖ -ə θɑːn
phaeton 'feɪt ᵊn ‖ 'feɪ ət ᵊn **~s** z
phage feɪdʒ **phages** 'feɪdʒ ɪz -əz
phagocyte 'fæg əʊ saɪt ‖ -ə- **~s** s
phagocytosis ,fæg əʊ saɪ 'təʊs ɪs §-əs
   ‖ -oʊ saɪ 'toʊs-
-phagous *stress-imposing* fəg əs
   — **saprophagous** sæ 'prɒf əg əs ‖ -'prɑːf-
-phagy *stress-imposing* fədʒ i — **geophagy**
   dʒi 'ɒf ədʒ i ‖ -'ɑːf-
Phaidon *tdmk* 'faɪd ᵊn
phalang|e 'fæl ændʒ fə 'lændʒ ‖ 'feɪl- **~es** ɪz
   əz
phalanger fə 'lændʒ ə ‖ -ᵊr **~s** z
Phalangist fə 'lændʒ ɪst fæ-, §-əst; 'fæl əndʒ-
   ‖ feɪ- **~s** s
phalanx 'fæl æŋks ‖ 'feɪl- 'fæl- **phalanges**
   fə 'lændʒ i:z fæ- ‖ feɪ-
phalaris 'fæl ər ɪs §-əs
phalarope 'fæl ə rəʊp ‖ -roʊp **~s** s
phalli 'fæl aɪ -i:
phallic 'fæl ɪk
phallocrat 'fæl əʊ kræt ‖ -ə- **~s** s
phallocratic ,fæl əʊ 'kræt ɪk ◄ ‖ -ə 'kræt̯-
phall|us 'fæl| əs **~i** aɪ -i: **~uses** əs ɪz -əz
phanerogam 'fæn ər əʊ gæm fə 'ner- ‖ -ər ə-
   ~s z
phanerogamic ,fæn ər əʊ 'gæm ɪk ◄ ‖ -ə'--
phanerogamous ,fæn ə 'rɒg əm əs ◄ ‖ -'rɑːg-
phanerozoic, P~ ,fæn ər əʊ 'zəʊ ɪk ◄
   ‖ -ə 'zoʊ-
phantasm 'fæn ,tæz əm **~s** z
phantasmagoria ,fæn tæz mə 'gɒr i̯ə
   fæn ,tæz-, -'gɔːr- ‖ fæn ,tæz mə 'gɔːr i̯ə
   -'gour-
phantasmagoric ,fæn tæz mə 'gɒr ɪk ◄
   fæn ,tæz- ‖ fæn ,tæz mə 'gɔːr ɪk ◄ -'gɑːr- **~al**
   ᵊl
phantasmal fæn 'tæz mᵊl

phantasmic fæn 'tæz mɪk
phantas|y 'fænt əs |i ‖ 'fænt̯- **~ies** iz
phantom 'fænt əm ‖ 'fænt̯ əm **~s** z
   ,phantom 'limb
-phany *stress-imposing* fən i — **theophany**
   θi 'ɒf ən i ‖ -'ɑːf-
Pharaoh, p~ 'feər əʊ ‖ 'fer oʊ 'fær-; 'feɪ roʊ **~s**
   z
   'pharaoh ant
Pharaonic ,feər eɪ 'ɒn ɪk ◄ feə 'rɒn-
   ‖ ,fer eɪ 'ɑːn ɪk ◄ ,fær-
pharisaic, P~ ,fær ɪ 'seɪ ɪk ◄ -ə- ‖ ,fer- **~al** ᵊl
   ~ally ᵊl̯i **~alness** ᵊl nəs -nɪs
Pharisaism 'fær ɪ seɪ ,ɪz əm '·ə- ‖ 'fer-
pharisee, P~ 'fær ɪ si: -ə- ‖ 'fer- **~s** z
pharma 'fɑːm ə ‖ 'fɑːrm ə
pharmaceutic ,fɑːm ə 'suːt ɪk ◄ -'sjuːt-, -'kjuːt-
   ‖ ,fɑːrm ə 'suːt̯ ɪk ◄ **~al** ᵊl **~ally** ᵊl̯i **~s** s
pharmacist 'fɑːm əs ɪst §-əst ‖ 'fɑːrm- **~s** s
pharmaco- *comb. form with stress-neutral suffix*
   ¦fɑːm ə kəʊ ‖ ¦fɑːrm ə koʊ —
   pharmacodynamic
   ,fɑːm ə kəʊ daɪ 'næm ɪk ◄ ‖ ,fɑːrm ə koʊ-
   with stress-imposing suffix ,fɑːm ə 'kɒ +
   ‖ ,fɑːrm ə 'kɑː + — **pharmacognosy**
   ,fɑːm ə 'kɒg nəs i ‖ ,fɑːrm ə 'kɑːg-
pharmacological ,fɑːm ə kə 'lɒdʒ ɪk ᵊl ◄
   ‖ ,fɑːrm ək ə 'lɑːdʒ- **~ly** _i
pharmacologist ,fɑːm ə 'kɒl ədʒ ɪst §-əst
   ‖ ,fɑːrm ə 'kɑːl- **~s** s
pharmacology ,fɑːm ə 'kɒl ədʒ i
   ‖ ,fɑːrm ə 'kɑːl-
pharmacopoei|a, pharmacopei|a
   ,fɑːm ə kə 'piː |ə -əʊ'·- ‖ ,fɑːrm- **~al** əl **~as** əz
pharmac|y 'fɑːm əs |i ‖ 'fɑːrm- **~ies** iz
Pharos 'feər ɒs ‖ 'fer ɑːs 'fær-
Pharsalus fɑː 'seɪl əs ‖ fɑːr-
pharyngal fə 'rɪŋ gᵊl fæ- **~s** z
pharyngeal ,fær ən 'dʒiː əl ◄ -ɪn-;
   fə 'rɪndʒ i̯əl, fæ- ‖ ,fer- **~s** z
pharynges fæ 'rɪndʒ iːz fə-
pharyngitis ,fær ən 'dʒaɪt ɪs -ɪn-, §-əs
   ‖ -'dʒaɪt̯ əs ,fer-
pharyngo- *comb. form with stress-neutral suffix*
   fə ¦rɪŋ gəʊ ‖ -gə — **pharyngoscope**
   fə 'rɪŋ gəʊ skəʊp ‖ -gə skoʊp *with*
   stress-imposing suffix ,fær ɪŋ 'gɒ + ‖ -'gɑː +
   ,fer- — **pharyngotomy** ,fær ɪŋ 'gɒt əm i
   ‖ -'gɑːt̯- ,fer-
pharynx 'fær ɪŋks ‖ 'fer- **~es** ɪz əz **pharynges**
   fæ 'rɪndʒ iːz fə-
phase feɪz **phased** feɪzd **phases** 'feɪz ɪz -əz
   phasing 'feɪz ɪŋ
phase-out 'feɪz aʊt **~s** s
phaser 'feɪz ə ‖ -ᵊr **~s** z
phasmid 'fæz mɪd §-məd **~s** z
phat fæt
phat-ass 'fæt æs ‖ 'fæt̯-
phatic 'fæt ɪk ‖ 'fæt̯ ɪk
PhD ,pi: eɪtʃ 'di: §-heɪtʃ- **~s, ~'s** z
pheasant 'fez ᵊnt **~s** s
Phebe, p~ 'fiːb i **~s, ~'s** z
Phebus 'fiːb əs

Phedo 'fiːd əʊ 'faɪd- ‖ -oʊ
Phedra 'fiːdr ə 'faɪdr-
Phedrus 'fiːdr əs 'faɪdr-
Pheidippides faɪ 'dɪp ɪ diːz -ə-
Phelan (i) 'fiːl ən, (ii) 'feɪl ən
phellem 'fel em -əm
Phelps felps
phenacetin fə 'næs ət ɪn fɪ-, fe-, -ɪt ɪn, §-ən
phenetic fə 'net ɪk fɪ- ‖ -'neţ- ~s s
Phenicia fə 'nɪʃ ə fɪ-; -'nɪʃ i ə ‖ -'niːʃ-
Phenician fə 'nɪʃ ᵊn fɪ-; -'nɪʃ i ən ‖ -'niːʃ- ~s z
phenobarbital ˌfiːn əʊ 'baːb ɪt ᵊl -ə ᵊl ‖ -oʊ 'baːrb ə tɔːl -taːl
phenobarbitone ˌfiːn əʊ 'baːb ɪ təʊn -'ə- ‖ -oʊ 'baːrb ə toʊn
phenol 'fiːn ɒl ‖ -oʊl -ɔːl, -aːl ~s z
phenolic fɪ 'nɒl ɪk §fə- ‖ -'noʊl- -'naːl-
phenolphthalein ˌfiːn ɒl 'θeɪl iːn ˌ-ᵊl-, -'θæl-, -'fθæl-, -ən, -'·iːn ‖ ˌfiːn ᵊl 'θæl i ən
phenom fɪ 'nɒm fə- ‖ fɪ 'naːm fɪ 'naːm ~s z
phenomena fə 'nɒm ɪn ə fɪ-, -ən- ‖ -'naːm-
phenomenal fə 'nɒm ɪn ᵊl fɪ-, -ən- ‖ -'naːm- ~ly i
phenomenological fə ˌnɒm ɪn ə 'lɒdʒ ɪk ᵊl ◂ fɪ-, -ˌən- ‖ -ˌnaːm ən ə 'laːdʒ- ~ly i
phenomenology fə ˌnɒm ɪ 'nɒl ədʒ i fɪ-, -ˌ·ə- ‖ -ˌnaːm ə 'naːl-
phenom|enon fə 'nɒm| ɪn ən fɪ-, -ən- ‖ -'naːm| ə naːn -ən ən ~ena ən ə (*)
phenotype 'fiːn əʊ taɪp ‖ -ə- ~s s
phenotypic ˌfiːn əʊ 'tɪp ɪk ◂ ‖ -ə- ~al ᵊl ~ally ᵊl̩ i
Phensic tdmk 'fen's ɪk 'fenz-
phenyl 'fiːn arᵊl 'fen-, -ᵊl, -ɪl ‖ 'fen ᵊl 'fiːn-
phenylalanine ˌfiːn ɪl 'æl ə niːn fen-, -ˌ·ᵊl-, -aɪ-ᵊl- ‖ ˌfen ᵊl-
phenylketonuria ˌfiːn ɪl ˌkiːt əʊ 'njʊər i ə ˌfen-, -ˌ·ᵊl-, -aɪ-ᵊl- ‖ ˌfen ᵊl ˌkiːţ oʊ 'nʊr i ə -ˌkiːt ᵊn 'ʊr-, -'jʊr-
pheromonal ˌfer ə 'məʊn ᵊl ◂ ‖ -'moʊn-
pheromone 'fer ə məʊn ‖ -moʊn ~s z
phew fjuː —and non-speech sounds such as [ʍ, ʍu, ʍʊ, ɸ, pɸ:]
phi faɪ **phis** faɪz
    ˌPhi ˌBeta 'Kappa
phial 'faɪ əl ~s z
Phibbs fɪbz
Phidias 'fɪd i æs 'faɪd- ‖ -əs
Phidippides faɪ 'dɪp ɪ diːz -ə-
Phil fɪl
phil- comb. form before vowel before unstressed syllable ˌfɪl — **philatelic** ˌfɪl ə 'tel ɪk ◂ before stressed syllable əʊ 'l+ fə- ‖ fə 'l+ — **philately** fɪ 'læt əl i fə- ‖ fə 'læţ ᵊl i
-phil fɪl — **Francophil** 'fræŋk əʊ fɪl ‖ -oʊ- -ə-
Philadelphia ˌfɪl ə 'delf i ə
Philadelphian ˌfɪl ə 'delf i ən ◂ ~s z
philadelphus ˌfɪl ə 'delf əs ~es ɪz əz
philander fɪ 'lænd ə fə- ‖ -ᵊr ~ed d
    philandering fɪ 'lænd ᵊr ɪŋ fə- ~s z
philanderer fɪ 'lænd ᵊr ə fə- ‖ -ᵊr ~s z
philanthrope 'fɪl ən θrəʊp -æn- ‖ -θroʊp ~s s

philanthropic ˌfɪl ən 'θrɒp ɪk ◂ -æn- ‖ -'θraːp- ~al ᵊl ~ally ᵊl̩ i
philanthropist fɪ 'lænᵗθ rəp ɪst fə-, §-əst ~s s
philanthrop|y fɪ 'lænᵗθ rəp |i fə- ~ies iz
philatelic ˌfɪl ə 'tel ɪk ◂ ~ally ᵊl̩ i
philatelist fɪ 'læt əl ɪst fə-, §-əst ‖ fə 'læţ ᵊl əst ~s s
philately fɪ 'læt əl i fə- ‖ fə 'læţ ᵊl i
Philbin 'fɪl bɪn
Philby 'fɪl bi
-phile farᵊl — **Anglophile** 'æŋ gləʊ farᵊl ‖ -ə-
Phileas 'fɪl i əs
Philemon fɪ 'liːm ɒn faɪ-, fə-, -mən ‖ -ən
Philharmonia ˌfɪl haː 'məʊn i ə ˌ·aː-, ˌ·ə- ‖ -haːr 'moʊn-
philharmonic ˌfɪl aː 'mɒn ɪk ◂ -ə-, -haː- ‖ -haːr 'maːn- -ᵊr- ~s s
philhellene ˌfɪl 'hel iːn '·· · ~s z
philhellenic ˌfɪl he 'liːn ɪk ◂ -hə-, -'len-
philhellenism ˌfɪl 'hel ə ˌnɪz əm -ɪ-
-philia 'fɪl i ə — **necrophilia** ˌnek rəʊ 'fɪl i ə ‖ -ə-
-philiac 'fɪl i æk — **coprophiliac** ˌkɒp rəʊ 'fɪl i æk ‖ ˌkaːp rə-
-philic 'fɪl ɪk — **photophilic** ˌfəʊt əʊ 'fɪl ɪk ◂ ‖ ˌfoʊţ ə-
Philip 'fɪl ɪp §-əp
Philippa 'fɪl ɪp ə -əp-
Philippe fɪ 'liːp —Fr [fi lip]
Philippi fɪ 'lɪp aɪ fə-; 'fɪl ɪ paɪ, -ə-
Philippian fɪ 'lɪp i ən fə- ~s z
philippic fɪ 'lɪp ɪk fə- ~s s
Philippine 'fɪl ə piːn -ɪ-; ˌ·ˌ·'· ~s z
Philips 'fɪl ɪps §-əps
Philipson 'fɪl ɪps ən §-əps-
Philistia fɪ 'lɪst i ə fə-
philistine, P~ 'fɪl ɪ staɪn -ə- ‖ -stiːn fɪ 'lɪst ən, -iːn (*) ~s z
philistinism 'fɪl ɪst ɪ ˌnɪz əm '·əst-, -ə,·- ‖ 'fɪl ə stiː-
Phillip, Phillipp 'fɪl ɪp §-əp
Phillips 'fɪl ɪps §-əps
Phillis 'fɪl ɪs §-əs
Phillpot, Phillpott 'fɪl pɒt ‖ -paːt
phillumenist fɪ 'luːm ən ɪst fə-, -'ljuːm-, -ɪn-, §-əst ~s s
phillumeny fɪ 'luːm ən i fə-, -'ljuːm-, -ɪn-
Philly 'fɪl i
philo- comb. form
    with stress-neutral suffix ˌfɪl əʊ ‖ -ə
    — **philosophical** ˌfɪl əʊ 'sɒf ɪk ᵊl ◂ ‖ -ə 'saːf-
    with stress-imposing suffix fɪ 'lɒ+ ‖ -'laː+
    — **philogyny** fɪ 'lɒdʒ ən i fə-, -ɪn- ‖ -'laːdʒ-
Philo 'faɪl əʊ ‖ -oʊ
Philoctetes ˌfɪl ɒk 'tiːt iːz -ɒk-
philodendron, P~ ˌfɪl ə 'dendr ən ~s z
philological ˌfɪl əʊ 'lɒdʒ ɪk ᵊl ◂ ‖ -ə 'laːdʒ- ~ly i
philologist fɪ 'lɒl ədʒ ɪst fə-, §-əst ‖ -'laːl- ~s s
philology fɪ 'lɒl ədʒ i fə- ‖ -'laːl-
Philomel, p~ 'fɪl əʊ mel ‖ -ə- ~s z
Philomela ˌfɪl əʊ 'miːl ə ‖ -ə-
Philomena ˌfɪl əʊ 'miːn ə ‖ -ə-

philoprogenitive ˌfɪl əʊ prəʊ ˈdʒen ət ɪv ◄
-ɪt ɪv ‖ -ə prou ˈdʒen əţ ɪv **~ly** li **~ness** nəs nɪs

philosopher fə ˈlɒs əf ə fɪ- ‖ -ˈlɑːs əf ᵊr **~s** z
phiˌlosopher's ˈstone

philosophic ˌfɪl ə ˈsɒf ɪk ◄ -ˈzɒf- ‖ -ˈsɑːf- -ˈzɑːf-
~al ᵊl ◄ **~ally** ᵊl̩ i

philosophis|e, philosophiz|e fə ˈlɒs ə faɪz
fɪ- ‖ -ˈlɑːs- **~ed** d **~er/s** ə/z ᵊr/z **~es** ɪz əz
~ing ɪŋ

philosoph|y fə ˈlɒs əf |i fɪ- ‖ -ˈlɑːs- **~ies** iz

Philostratus fɪ ˈlɒs trət əs fə- ‖ -ˈlɑːs trəţ əs

-philous stress-imposing fɪl əs -fəl- ‖ fəl əs
— **acidophilous** ˌæs ɪ ˈdɒf ɪl əs ◄ §ˌ-ə-, -əl əs
‖ ˌæs ə ˈdɑːf əl əs ◄

Philp fɪlp

Philpot ˈfɪl pɒt ‖ -pɑːt

Philpotts ˈfɪl pɒts ‖ -pɑːts

philter, philtre ˈfɪlt ə ‖ -ᵊr (= filter) **~s** z

phimosis faɪ ˈməʊs ɪs §-əs ‖ -ˈmoʊs əs

Phineas ˈfɪn i əs -æs

Phipps fɪps

phish fɪʃ **phishing** ˈfɪʃ ɪŋ

phiz, Phiz fɪz (= fizz)

Phizackerley fɪ ˈzæk əl i fə- ‖ -ᵊr li

phizog ˈfɪz ɒg ‖ -ɑːg

phlebitic flɪ ˈbɪt ɪk flə- ‖ -ˈbɪţ-

phlebitis flɪ ˈbaɪt ɪs flə-, §-əs ‖ -ˈbaɪţ əs

phlebotom|y flɪ ˈbɒt əm |i flə- ‖ -ˈbɑːţ- **~ies**
iz **~ist/s** ɪst/s §əst/s

Phlegethon ˈfleg ɪθ ᵊn -əθ-; -ɪ θɒn, -ə-
‖ -ə θɑːn

phlegm flem

phlegmatic fleg ˈmæt ɪk ‖ -ˈmæţ ɪk **~ally** ᵊl̩ i

phlegmy ˈflem i

phloem ˈfləʊ ɪm -em, §-əm ‖ ˈfloʊ em

phlogistic flɒ ˈdʒɪst ɪk ‖ floʊ-

phlogiston flɒ ˈdʒɪst ən -ɒn ‖ floʊ- -ɑːn

phlox flɒks ‖ flɑːks (= flocks) **phloxes**
ˈflɒks ɪz -əz ‖ ˈflɑːks əz

Phnom Penh ˌnɒm ˈpen ˌpnɒm-, pə ˌnɒm ˈpen
‖ ˌnɑːm- —Khmer [pʰnɔm ˈpiɲ]

-phobe fəʊb ‖ foʊb — **Anglophobe**
ˈæŋ gləʊ fəʊb ‖ -glə foʊb

phobia ˈfəʊb i ə ‖ ˈfoʊb i ə **~s** z

-phobia ˈfəʊb i ə ‖ ˈfoʊb i ə — **Francophobia**
ˌfræŋ kəʊ ˈfəʊb i ə ‖ -ə ˈfoʊb-

phobic ˈfəʊb ɪk ‖ ˈfoʊb ɪk **~ally** ᵊl̩ i **~s** s

-phobic ˈfəʊb ɪk ‖ ˈfoʊb ɪk — **Russophobic**
ˌrʌs əʊ ˈfəʊb ɪk ◄ ‖ -ə ˈfoʊb-

Phobos ˈfəʊb ɒs ‖ ˈfoʊb ɑːs

Phocaea fəʊ ˈsiː ə ‖ foʊ-

Phocian ˈfəʊʃ i ən ˈfəʊs- ‖ ˈfoʊʃ- **~s** z

phocine ˈfəʊs aɪn ‖ ˈfoʊs-

Phocion ˈfəʊs i ən ‖ ˈfoʊʃ i ən -ɑːn

Phocis ˈfəʊs ɪs §-əs ‖ ˈfoʊs-

phocomelia ˌfəʊk əʊ ˈmiːl i ə ‖ ˌfoʊk oʊ-

phocomely fəʊ ˈkɒm əl i -ɪl- ‖ foʊ ˈkɑːm-

Phoebe, p~ ˈfiːb i **~s, ~'s** z

Phoebus ˈfiːb əs

Phoenicia fə ˈnɪʃ ə fɪ-; -ˈnɪʃ i ə ‖ -ˈniːʃ-
Phoenician fə ˈnɪʃ ᵊn fɪ-; -ˈnɪʃ i ən ‖ -ˈniːʃ- **~s** z

phoenix, P~ ˈfiːn ɪks **~es, ~'s** ɪz əz **~like** laɪk

phon fɒn ‖ fɑːn **phons** fɒnz ‖ fɑːnz

phon- comb. form
before vowel before unstressed syllable ¦fəʊn-
¦fɒn- ‖ ¦foʊn — **phoniatric** ˌfəʊn i ˈætr ɪk ◄
ˌfɒn- ‖ ˌfoʊn-
before stressed syllable fəʊ ˈn+ ‖ foʊ ˈn+
— **phonendoscope** fəʊ ˈnend ə skəʊp
‖ foʊ ˈnend ə skoʊp

phonaesthesia ˌfəʊn iːs ˈθiːz i ə ˌ-ɪs-, ˌ-əs-,
-ˈθiːʒ- ‖ ˌfoʊn əs ˈθiːʒ ə

phon|ate fəʊ ˈn|eɪt ‖ ˈfoʊn |eɪt **~ated** eɪt ɪd
-əd ‖ eɪţ əd **~ates** eɪts **~ating** eɪt ɪŋ ‖ eɪţ ɪŋ

phonation fəʊ ˈneɪʃ ᵊn ‖ foʊ-
phoˈnation type

phonatory fəʊ ˈneɪt ər i ˈfəʊn ət ər i
‖ ˈfoʊn ə tɔːr i -tour i

phone fəʊn ‖ foʊn **phoned** fəʊnd ‖ foʊnd
phones fəʊnz ‖ foʊnz **phoning** ˈfəʊn ɪŋ
‖ ˈfoʊn ɪŋ
ˈphone book; **ˈphone box**; **ˈphone call**

-phone fəʊn ‖ foʊn — **anglophone**
ˈæŋ gləʊ fəʊn ‖ -ə foʊn

phonecard, P~ ˈfəʊn kɑːd →ˈfəʊŋ-
‖ ˈfoʊn kɑːrd **~s** z

phone-in ˈfəʊn ɪn ‖ ˈfoʊn- **~s** z

phonematic ˌfəʊn i ˈmæt ɪk ◄ -iː-, -ə-
‖ ˌfoʊn ə ˈmæţ ɪk ◄

phoneme ˈfəʊn iːm ‖ ˈfoʊn- **~s** z

phonemic fəʊ ˈniːm ɪk ‖ fə- foʊ- **~ally** ᵊl̩ i **~s** s

phonemicis... —see **phonemiciz...**

phonemicist fəʊ ˈniːm ɪs ɪst -əs-, §-əst ‖ fə-
foʊ- **~s** s

phonemicization fəʊ ˌniːm ɪs aɪ ˈzeɪʃ ᵊn -ˌəs-,
-ɪˈ-- ‖ fə ˌniːm əs ə- foʊ- **~s** z

phonemiciz|e fəʊ ˈniːm ɪ saɪz -ə- ‖ fə- foʊ-
~ed d **~es** ɪz əz **~ing** ɪŋ

phonesthesia ˌfəʊn iːs ˈθiːz i ə ˌ-ɪs-, ˌ-əs,
-ˈθiːʒ- ‖ ˌfoʊn əs ˈθiːʒ ə

phone-tapping ˈfəʊn ˌtæp ɪŋ ‖ ˈfoʊn- **~s** z

phonetic fə ˈnet ɪk fəʊ- ‖ -ˈneţ ɪk **~ally** ᵊl̩ i **~s** s
phoˌnetic ˈsymbol

Phonetica fəʊ ˈnet ɪk ə ‖ fə ˈneţ-

phonetician ˌfəʊn ɪ ˈtɪʃ ᵊn ˌfɒn-, -ə- ‖ ˌfoʊn-
ˌfɑːn- **~s** z

phoneticis... —see **phoneticiz...**

phoneticization fəʊ ˌnet ɪs aɪ ˈzeɪʃ ᵊn -ˌəs-
‖ foʊ ˌneţ əs ə- fə-

phoneticiz|e fəʊ ˈnet ɪ saɪz -ə- ‖ foʊ ˈneţ- fə-
~ed d **~es** ɪz əz **~ing** ɪŋ

phon|ey, phon|y ˈfəʊn |i ‖ ˈfoʊn |i **~eyness,
~iness** i nəs i nɪs **~eys, ~ies** iz **~ier** i ə ‖ i ᵊr
~iest i ɪst i əst **~ily** ɪ li əl i
ˌphoney ˈwar

phoniatric ˌfəʊn i ˈætr ɪk ◄ ˌfɒn- ‖ ˌfoʊn- ˌfɑːn-
~s s

phonic ˈfɒn ɪk ˈfəʊn- ‖ ˈfɑːn ɪk ˈfoʊn- **~s** s

phono- comb. form
with stress-neutral suffix ¦fəʊn əʊ ¦fɒn-
‖ ¦foʊn ə — **phonoscope** ˈfəʊn əʊ skəʊp
ˈfɒn- ‖ ˈfoʊn ə skoʊp
with stress-imposing suffix fəʊ ˈnɒ+
‖ fə ˈnɑː+ foʊ- — **phonometer**
fəʊ ˈnɒm ɪt ə -ət- ‖ fə ˈnɑːm əţ ᵊr foʊ-

phonogram 'fəʊn ə græm ‖ 'foʊn- **~s** z

phonograph 'fəʊn ə grɑːf -græf ‖ 'foʊn ə græf **~s** s

phonographic ˌfəʊn ə 'græf ɪk ◄ ‖ ˌfoʊn- **~ally** ᵊl‿i

phonological ˌfəʊn ə 'lɒdʒ ɪk ᵊl ◄ ˌfɒn-, -ᵊl 'ɒdʒ- ‖ ˌfoʊn ᵊl 'ɑːdʒ- ˌfɑːn- **~ly** ‿i

phonologist fəʊ 'nɒl ədʒ ɪst §-əst ‖ fə 'nɑːl- foʊ- **~s** s

phonolog|y fəʊ 'nɒl ədʒ |i ‖ fə 'nɑːl- foʊ- **~ies** iz

phonotactic ˌfəʊn əʊ 'tækt ɪk ◄ ˌfɒn- ‖ ˌfoʊn- ˌfɑːn- **~ally** ᵊl‿i **~s** s

-phonous stress-imposing fən əs
— **homophonous** hə 'mɒf ən əs hɒ- ‖ hə 'mɑːf-

phon|y 'fəʊn |i ‖ 'foʊn |i **~iness** i nəs i nɪs **~ies** iz **~ier** i‿ə ‖ i‿ᵊr **~iest** i‿ɪst i‿əst **~ily** ɪ li əl i

-phony stress-imposing fən i — **cacophony** kæ 'kɒf ən i ‖ -'kɑːf-

phooey 'fuː‿i

-phore fɔː ‖ fɔːr four — **anthophore** 'ænθ əʊ fɔː ‖ -ə fɔːr -four

-phoresis fə 'riːs ɪs §-əs — **electrophoresis** ɪ ˌlek trəʊ fə 'riːs ɪs ə-, §-əs ‖ -ˌtrə-

phormium 'fɔːm i‿əm ‖ 'fɔːrm-

-phorous stress-imposing fər əs — **anthophorous** æn 'θɒf ər əs ‖ -'θɑːf-

phosgene 'fɒz dʒiːn 'fɒs- ‖ 'fɑːz-

phosphatas|e 'fɒs fə teɪz -teɪs ‖ 'fɑːs- **~es** ɪz əz

phosphate 'fɒs feɪt ‖ 'fɑːs- **~s** s

phosphatic ₍ˌ₎fɒs 'fæt ɪk ‖ ₍ˌ₎fɑːs 'fæt̬ ɪk -'feɪt-

phosphene 'fɒs fiːn ‖ 'fɑːs- **~s** z

phosphide 'fɒs faɪd ‖ 'fɑːs- **~s** z

phosphite 'fɒs faɪt ‖ 'fɑːs- **~s** s

phospho- comb. form
with stress-neutral suffix ¦fɒs fəʊ ‖ ¦fɑːs foʊ
— **phospholipid** ˌfɒs fəʊ 'lɪp ɪd §-əd ‖ ˌfɑːs foʊ-**~s** z

phosphor 'fɒs fə ‖ 'fɑːs fᵊr -fɔːr **~s** z

phosphoresc|e ˌfɒs fə 'res ‖ ˌfɑːs- **~ed** t **~es** ɪz əz **~ing** ɪŋ

phosphorescence ˌfɒs fə 'res ᵊnts ‖ ˌfɑːs-

phosphorescent ˌfɒs fə 'res ᵊnt ◄ ‖ ˌfɑːs- **~ly** li

phosphoric ₍ˌ₎fɒs 'fɒr ɪk ‖ ₍ˌ₎fɑːs 'fɔːr ɪk -'fɑːr-

phosphorous 'fɒs fər‿əs ‖ 'fɑːs-

phosphorus, P~ 'fɒs fər‿əs ‖ 'fɑːs-

phosphory|late fɒs 'fɒr ə ¦leɪt 'fɒs fər-, -ɪ- ‖ fɑːs 'fɔːr- -'fɑːr- **~lated** leɪt ɪd -əd ‖ leɪt̬ əd **~lates** leɪts **~lating** leɪt ɪŋ ‖ leɪt̬ ɪŋ

phosphorylation fɒs ˌfɒr ə 'leɪʃ ᵊn ˌ·····, ˌ·fər-, -ɪ'·- ‖ fɑːs ˌfɔːr- -ˌfɑːr-, ˌ·····

phossy 'fɒs i ‖ 'fɑːs i

photic 'fəʊt ɪk ‖ 'foʊt̬ ɪk

photo 'fəʊt əʊ ‖ 'foʊt̬ oʊ **~s** z
'**photo call**; ˌ**photo 'finish**; '**photo op**, '**photo oppor**ˌ**tunity**

photo- comb. form
with stress-neutral suffix ¦fəʊt əʊ ‖ ¦foʊt̬ oʊ
— **photomicrograph** ˌfəʊt əʊ 'maɪk rəʊ grɑːf -græf ‖ ˌfoʊt̬ oʊ 'maɪk rə græf
with stress-imposing suffix fəʊ 'tɒ + ‖ foʊ 'tɑː + — **photometry** fəʊ 'tɒm ətr i -ɪtr- ‖ foʊ 'tɑːm-

photocell 'fəʊt əʊ sel ‖ 'foʊt̬ oʊ- **~s** z

photochemical ˌfəʊt əʊ 'kem ɪk ᵊl ◄ ‖ ˌfoʊt̬ oʊ- **~ly** ‿i

photochromic ˌfəʊt əʊ 'krəʊm ɪk ◄ ‖ ˌfoʊt̬ oʊ 'kroʊm ɪk ◄ **~s** s

photocomposition ˌfəʊt əʊ ˌkɒmp ə 'zɪʃ ᵊn ‖ ˌfoʊt̬ oʊ ˌkɑːmp-

photocopier 'fəʊt əʊ ˌkɒp i‿ə ˌ·ˌ··· ‖ 'foʊt̬ oʊ ˌkɑːp i‿ᵊr ˌ·ˌ·- **~s** z

photocop|y n, v 'fəʊt əʊ ˌkɒp |i ˌ·ˌ·· ‖ 'foʊt̬ oʊ ˌkɑːp |i -ə- **~ied** id **~ies** iz **~ying** i ɪŋ

photoelectric ˌfəʊt əʊ ɪ 'lek trɪk ◄ -ə'-- ‖ ˌfoʊt̬ oʊ- **~ally** ᵊl‿i ˌphotoe ˌlectric 'cell

Photofit tdmk 'fəʊt əʊ fɪt ‖ 'foʊt̬ oʊ-

photoflood 'fəʊt əʊ flʌd ‖ 'foʊt̬ oʊ- **~s** z

photogenic ˌfəʊt əʊ 'dʒen ɪk ◄ -'dʒiːn- ‖ ˌfoʊt̬ ə- **~ally** ᵊl‿i

photogrammetr|ist ˌfəʊt əʊ 'græm ətr |ɪst -ɪtr-, §-əst ‖ ˌfoʊt̬ oʊ- **~ists** ɪsts §əsts **~y** i

photograph n, v 'fəʊt ə grɑːf -græf ‖ 'foʊt̬ ə græf **~ed** t **~ing** ɪŋ **~s** s

photographer fə 'tɒg rəf ə ‖ -'tɑːg rəf ᵊr **~s** z

photographic ˌfəʊt ə 'græf ɪk ◄ ‖ ˌfoʊt̬ ə- **~ally** ᵊl‿i ˌphoto ˌgraphic 'memory

photography fə 'tɒg rəf i ‖ -'tɑːg-

photogravure ˌfəʊt əʊ grə 'vjʊə ‖ ˌfoʊt̬ ə grə 'vjʊᵊr **~s** z

photojournalism ˌfəʊt əʊ 'dʒɜːn ᵊl ˌɪz əm ˌ·ˌ·ˌ·ˌ· ‖ ˌfoʊt̬ oʊ 'dʒɜːn-

photokinesis ˌfəʊt əʊ kaɪ 'niːs ɪs -kɪ'--, §-əs ‖ ˌfoʊt̬ oʊ-

photolitho ˌfəʊt əʊ 'laɪθ əʊ ‖ ˌfoʊt̬ oʊ 'lɪθ oʊ

photolithography ˌfəʊt əʊ lɪ 'θɒg rəf i -laɪ'--, §-lə'-- ‖ ˌfoʊt̬ oʊ lɪ 'θɑːg-

photometer fəʊ 'tɒm ɪt ə §-ət- ‖ foʊ 'tɑːm ət̬ ᵊr **~s** z

photomontag|e ˌfəʊt əʊ mɒn 'tɑːʒ ‖ ˌfoʊt̬ oʊ mɑːn- ˌ·ə- **~es** ɪz əz

photon 'fəʊt ɒn ‖ 'foʊt̬ ɑːn **~s** z

photonasty 'fəʊt əʊ ˌnæst i ‖ 'foʊt̬ oʊ-

photophobia ˌfəʊt əʊ 'fəʊb i‿ə ‖ ˌfoʊt̬ ə 'foʊb-

photo-reconnaissance ˌfəʊt əʊ ri 'kɒn ɪs ənts -rə'--, -'əs- ‖ ˌfoʊt̬ oʊ ri 'kɑːn əz ənts -'əs-

photosensitis... —see **photosensitiz...**

photosensitive ˌfəʊt əʊ 'sents ət ɪv ◄ -ɪt ɪv ‖ ˌfoʊt̬ oʊ 'sents ət̬ ɪv ◄

photosensitivity ˌfəʊt əʊ ˌsents ə 'tɪv ət i -ɪ'--, -ɪt i ‖ ˌfoʊt̬ oʊ ˌsents ə 'tɪv ət̬ i

photosensitization ˌfəʊt əʊ ˌsents ət aɪ 'zeɪʃ ᵊn -ˌ·ɪt-, -ɪ'-- ‖ ˌfoʊt̬ oʊ ˌsents ət̬ ə-

photosensitiz|e ˌfəʊt əʊ 'sents ə taɪz -'·ɪ- ‖ ˌfoʊt̬ oʊ- **~ed** d **~es** ɪz əz **~ing** ɪŋ

Phoneme and allophone

1 A **phoneme** is one of the basic distinctive units in the phonetics of a language. The actual speech sounds which represent it are its **allophones**. Phonemes have the power of distinguishing words in the language (e.g. p and b, as in **pit** pɪt and **bit** bɪt); allophones, as such, do not (e.g. clear and dark varieties of l).

2 Each language has its own phonemic system and its own rules for determining the allophones appropriate to the phonemes in various phonetic environments. In English, for example, the phoneme p comprises both aspirated and unaspirated allophones (see ASPIRATION). In some other languages, e.g. Hindi, aspirated and unaspirated plosives represent distinct phonemes. English ʃ varies according to its surroundings (see COARTICULATION). The phoneme iː comprises both clipped and unclipped allophones (see CLIPPING).

3 The allophones of a phoneme are phonetically similar to one another. More importantly, their distribution is either **complementary** (= predictable by rule from the context) or else **random** (= in free variation). When it is important to distinguish phonemic transcription from allophonic or impressionistic transcription, it is usual to enclose the former in slants / /, the latter in square brackets [ ].

4 The phonetic notation in this dictionary is phonemic, with the following minor exceptions:

- The symbols i, u are employed to reflect the NEUTRALIZATION of /iː - ɪ/ and /uː - ʊ/ in certain positions.

- For AmE, the allophone [t̬] of /t/ is symbolized explicitly.

- The optional allophone [oʊ] of /əʊ/ (BrE) is symbolized explicitly.

- For some speakers (not of RP), ʌ and ə are not in contrast.

- Italic and raised symbols show the possibility of omission or insertion of a sound.

- The marks ˌ, ◄ §, ⚠ are added.

P

---

photoset ˈfəʊt əʊ set ‖ ˈfoʊt̬ oʊ- **~s** s
photosphere ˈfəʊt əʊ sfɪə ‖ ˈfoʊt̬ oʊ sfɪr
photostat, P~ *tdmk* ˈfəʊt əʊ stæt ‖ ˈfoʊt̬ ə-
    ~ed, ~ted ɪd əd **~ing, ~ting** ɪŋ **~s** s
photostatic ˌfəʊt əʊ ˈstæt ɪk ◄
    ‖ ˌfoʊt̬ ə ˈstæt̬ ɪk ◄ **~ally** ᵊl i
photosynthesis ˌfəʊt əʊ ˈsɪntᶿ əs ɪs -ɪs ɪs, §-əs
    ‖ ˌfoʊt̬ oʊ-
photosynthesis|e, photosynthesiz|e
    ˌfəʊt əʊ ˈsɪntᶿ ə saɪz -ˈɪ- ‖ ˌfoʊt̬ oʊ- **~ed** d
    ~es ɪz əz **~ing** ɪŋ
photosynthetic ˌfəʊt əʊ sɪn ˈθet ɪk ◄
    ‖ ˌfoʊt̬ oʊ sɪn ˈθet̬ ɪk ◄ **~ally** ᵊl i
phototropic ˌfəʊt əʊ ˈtrɒp ɪk ◄ -ˈtroʊp-
    ‖ ˌfoʊt̬ ə ˈtrɑːp ɪk ◄ -ˈtroʊp- **~ally** ᵊl i
phototropism ˌfəʊt əʊ ˈtrəʊp ˌɪz əm
    fəʊ ˈtɒtr ə ˌpɪz- ‖ foʊ ˈtɑːtr ə ˌpɪz əm
    ˌfoʊt̬ oʊ ˈtroʊp ˌɪz-

phototypesett|er ˌfəʊt əʊ ˈtaɪp ˌset| ə ˈ·ˌ·ˌ·
    ‖ ˌfoʊt̬ oʊ ˈtaɪp set̬| ᵊr **~ers** əz ‖ ᵊrz **~ing** ɪŋ
photovoltaic ˌfəʊt əʊ vɒl ˈteɪ ɪk ◄
    ‖ ˌfoʊt̬ oʊ vɑːl- -voʊl-ˈ--
phrasal ˈfreɪz ᵊl **~ly** i
    phrasal ˈverb
phrase freɪz *(= frays)* **phrased** freɪzd **phrases**
    ˈfreɪz ɪz -əz **phrasing/s** ˈfreɪz ɪŋ/z
    ˈphrase ˌmarker
phrasebook ˈfreɪz bʊk §-buːk **~s** s
phraseological ˌfreɪz i ə ˈlɒdʒ ɪk ᵊl ◄
    ‖ -ˈlɑːdʒ- **~ly** ˌi
phraseolog|y ˌfreɪz i ˈɒl ədʒ |i ‖ -ˈɑːl- **~ies** iz
phrase-structure ˈfreɪz ˌstrʌk tʃə ˌ·ˈ·· ‖ -tʃᵊr
phratr|y ˈfreɪtr |i **~ies** iz
phreatic fri ˈæt ɪk ‖ -ˈæt̬-
phrenetic frə ˈnet ɪk frɪ-, fre- ‖ -ˈnet̬ ɪk **~al** ᵊl
    ~ally ᵊl i

phrenic 'fren ɪk
phrenological ˌfren ə 'lɒdʒ ɪk ᵊl ◂ ‖ -'lɑːdʒ-
phrenolog|ist frə 'nɒl ədʒ |ɪst frɪ-, fre-, §-əst
 ‖ -'nɑːl- **~ists** ɪsts §əsts **~y** i
Phrygi|a 'frɪdʒ i ˌ|ə **~an/s** ən/z
Phryne 'fraɪn i
phthalein 'θeɪl i ˌɪn 'θæl-, 'fθæl-, ən; '·iːn
 ‖ 'θæl i ˌən 'θeɪl-, '·iːn
phthalic 'θæl ɪk 'fθæl-, 'θeɪl-
phthisis 'θaɪs ɪs 'taɪs-, 'fθaɪs-, §-əs
Phuket ˌpu: 'ket —Thai [ˈphuː ᵊˈked]
phut, phutt fʌt
phwoar BrE interjection fwɔː —or various
 non-speech vocalizations such as [ɸʊɔɑ]
phyco- comb. form
 with stress-neutral suffix ˈfaɪk əʊ ‖ -oʊ —
 phycomycetous ˌfaɪk əʊ maɪ 'siːt əs ◂
 ‖ -oʊ maɪ 'siːt̮-
 with stress-imposing suffix faɪ 'kɒ + ‖ -'kɑː +
 — **phycology** faɪ 'kɒl ədʒ i ‖ -'kɑːl-
Phyfe faɪf
phyla 'faɪl ə
phylacter|y fɪ 'lækt ər |i **~ies** iz
phyletic faɪ 'let ɪk ‖ -'let̮- **~ally** ᵊl_i
Phyllida 'fɪl ɪd ə -əd-
Phyllis 'fɪl ɪs §-əs
phyllo 'fiːl əʊ ‖ 'fiːl oʊ
phyllo- comb. form with stress-neutral suffix
 ˈfɪl əʊ ‖ -ə — **phyllotaxis** ˌfɪl əʊ 'tæks ɪs
 §-əs ‖ -ə-
Phyllosan tdmk 'fɪl əʊ sæn ‖ -oʊ-
-phyllous 'fɪl əs — **monophyllous**
 ˌmɒn əʊ 'fɪl əs ◂ ‖ ˌmɑːn ə-
phylloxera fɪ 'lɒks ər ə ˌfɪl ɒk 'sɪər ə
 ‖ ˌfɪl ɑːk 'sɪr ə fɪ 'lɑːks ər ə
phylo- comb. form
 with stress-neutral suffix ˈfaɪl əʊ ‖ -oʊ —
 phylogenetic ˌfaɪl əʊ dʒə 'net ɪk ◂ -dʒɪ'--
 ‖ ˌfaɪl oʊ dʒə 'net̮ ɪk ◂
 with stress-imposing suffix faɪ 'lɒ + ‖ -'lɑː +
 — **phylogeny** faɪ 'lɒdʒ ən i -ɪn- ‖ -'lɑːdʒ-
phylogen|y faɪ 'lɒdʒ ən| i -ɪn- ‖ -'lɑːdʒ- **~ies**
 iz
phyl|um 'faɪl |əm **~a** ə
physalis faɪ 'seɪl ɪs §-əs; 'faɪs əl-
Phys. Ed. ˌfɪz 'ed
physiatrist ˌfɪz i 'ætr ɪst §-əst
physic 'fɪz ɪk **~ked** t **~king** ɪŋ **~s** s
physical 'fɪz ɪk ᵊl **~ly** ˌi **~s** z
 ˌphysical eduˈcation; ˌphysical ˈjerks;
 ˌphysical ˈtraining
physicality ˌfɪz ɪ 'kæl ət i ˌ-ə- ‖ -ət̮ i
physician fɪ 'zɪʃ ᵊn fə- **~s** z
physicist 'fɪz ɪs ɪst -əs-, §-əst **~s** s
physics 'fɪz ɪks
physio 'fɪz i əʊ ‖ -oʊ **~s** z
physio- comb. form
 with stress-neutral suffix ˈfɪz i əʊ ‖ -oʊ -ə —
 physiocrat 'fɪz i əʊ kræt ‖ -i oʊ- ˌi ə-
 with stress-imposing suffix ˌfɪz i 'ɒ + ‖ -'ɑː +
 — **physiography** ˌfɪz i 'ɒg rəf i ‖ -'ɑːg-
physiognomic ˌfɪz i ə 'nɒm ɪk ◂ ‖ -'nɑːm-
 ~ally ᵊl_i

physiognom|y ˌfɪz i 'ɒn əm |i -'ɒg nəm-
 ‖ -ˈɑːg nəm |i -i 'ɑːn əm- **~ies** iz **~ist/s** ɪst/s
 §-əst/s
physiological ˌfɪz i ə 'lɒdʒ ɪk ᵊl ◂ ‖ -'lɑːdʒ-
 ~ly i
physiologist ˌfɪz i 'ɒl ədʒ ɪst §-əst ‖ -'ɑːl- **~s** s
physiology ˌfɪz i 'ɒl ədʒ i ‖ -'ɑːl-
physiotherapist ˌfɪz i ˌəʊ 'θer əp ɪst §-əst
 ‖ ˌ·-oʊ- **~s** s
physiotherapy ˌfɪz i ˌəʊ 'θer əp i ‖ ˌ·-oʊ-
physique fɪ 'ziːk fə- **~s** s
physostigmine ˌfaɪs əʊ 'stɪg miːn ‖ -ə-
-phyte faɪt — **epiphyte** 'ep i faɪt
Phythian 'fɪð i ən
phyto- comb. form
 with stress-neutral suffix ˈfaɪt əʊ ‖ ˈfaɪt̮ oʊ —
 phytopathology ˌfaɪt əʊ pə 'θɒl ədʒ i -pæ'--
 ‖ ˌfaɪt̮ oʊ pə 'θɑːl-
 with stress-imposing suffix faɪ 'tɒ + ‖ -'tɑː +
 — **phytography** faɪ 'tɒg rəf i ‖ -'tɑːg-
pi paɪ **pis** paɪz
Piacenza ˌpiː ə 'tʃents ə —It [pja 'tʃen tsa]
Piaf 'piː æf ‖ piː 'ɑːf —Fr [pjaf]
piaff|e pi 'æf **~ed** t **~ing** ɪŋ **~s** s
piaffer pi 'æf ə ‖ -ᵊr **~s** z
Piaget pi 'æʒ eɪ -'ɑːʒ- ‖ ˌpiː ə 'ʒeɪ -ɑː- —Fr
 [pja ʒɛ]
Piagetian ˌpiː ə 'ʒet i ən ◂ ˌ·ɑː-; -'ʒeɪ ən
 ‖ -'ʒeɪ ən **~s** z
pia mater ˌpaɪ ə 'meɪt ə ˌpiː ‖ -'meɪt̮ ᵊr
 ˌpiː ə 'mɑːt̮ ᵊr, '··,··
pianissimo ˌpiː ə 'nɪs ɪ məʊ ˌ·ɑː-, -ə · ‖ -moʊ **~s**
 z
pianist 'piː ən ɪst 'pjɑːn ɪst, pi 'æn ɪst, §-əst
 ‖ pi 'æn əst 'piː ən- **~s** s
piano adv; adj; n '(passage played) softly'
 'pjɑːn əʊ pi 'ɑːn əʊ ‖ pi 'ɑːn oʊ **~s** z
piano n 'instrument' pi 'æn əʊ -'ɑːn-; 'pjæn əʊ,
 'pjɑːn- ‖ -oʊ **~s** z
 piˌano acˈcordion; piˌano duˈet; piˈano
 ˌwire
pianoforte pi ˌæn əʊ 'fɔːt i -ˌɑːn-, -eɪ; -'fɔːt;
 ˌpjæn əʊ'--, ˌpjɑːn- ‖ -oʊ 'fɔːrt eɪ -'foʊrt-, -i;
 -'·ə fɔːrt, -foʊrt **~s** z
pianola, P~ tdmk ˌpiː ə 'nəʊl ə -æ-; pɪə'··
 ‖ -'noʊl- **~s** z
piassava ˌpiː ə 'sɑːv ə
piaster, piastre pi 'æst ə -'ɑːst- ‖ -ᵊr **~s** z
piazza pi 'æts ə -'ɑːts-, -'ædz- ‖ -'ɑːz ə -'æz- (*)
 —It ['pjat tsa] **~s** z
pibroch 'piːb rɒk -rɒx, -rɒʃ ‖ -rɑːk —ScG
 piobaireachd ['piːb rɔxk] **~s** s
pic pɪk **pics** pɪks
pica 'paɪk ə **~s** z
picador 'pɪk ə dɔː ‖ -dɔːr **~s** z
Picard 'pɪk ɑːd ‖ piː 'kɑːrd —Fr [pi kaʁ]
Picardy 'pɪk əd i ‖ -ᵊrd i —Fr Picardie
 [pi kaʁ di]
picaresque ˌpɪk ə 'resk ◂
picaroon ˌpɪk ə 'ruːn **~s** z
Picasso pɪ 'kæs əʊ -'kɑːs- ‖ -'kɑːs oʊ —Sp
 [pi 'ka so]
picayune ˌpɪk ə 'juːn ◂ -eɪ-, -i-, -i 'uːn **~s** z

Phrasal verbs

1　Like other PHRASEs, a **phrasal verb** (= a verb consisting of two words, a verb word and an adverbial **particle**) is typically pronounced with late stress. So the particle has greater stress than the verb word itself.

　ˌlook ˈdown
　ˌtalk ˈover

　Don't ˌlook ˈdown!
　We must ˌtalk things ˈover.

2　A **prepositional verb** (= a verb consisting of a verb word and a prepositional particle), on the other hand, is in most cases pronounced with early stress. So the verb word has greater stress than the preposition.

　ˈlook at
　ˈtalk to

　What are you ˈlooking at?
　I ˌwant to ˈtalk to you.

3　If the preposition of a prepositional verb is **stranded** (= has no following noun or pronoun), it is pronounced in its strong form, even though unstressed.

　ˌ**What are you ˈlooking** [æt]**?**

　compare **Look** [ət] ˈ**that!**

4　Exceptionally, if the two parts of a phrasal verb are **separated** by a **noun** (not a pronoun), the main stress goes on the noun, not on the particle.

　ˌpick ˈup
　It'll be ˌpicked ˈup.
　ˌ**Pick it ˈup!**
　but ˌ**Pick your ˈbooks up!**

　ˌtake ˈoff
　The ˌplane ˌtook ˈoff.
　but **She ˌtook her ˈshoes off**.

5　Some phrasal verbs have two particles, one adverbial and one prepositional. The first is stressed, the second unstressed.

　He ˌlooked ˈdown on her.
　(How do you) **put ˈup with it?**
　(I want) **to ˌfind ˈout about it**.

Piccadilly ˌpɪk ə ˈdɪl i ◄
　ˌPiccaˌdilly ˈCircus
piccalilli ˌpɪk ə ˈlɪl i ˈ· · · ·
piccaninn|y ˌpɪk ə ˈnɪn |i ˈ· · · · ~**ies** iz
piccolo ˈpɪk ə ləʊ ‖ -loʊ ~**s** z
pice paɪs

pichiciago ˌpɪtʃ i si ˈeɪg əʊ ˌ·ə-, -ˈɑːg- ‖ -oʊ ~**s**
　z
pichiciego ˌpɪtʃ i si ˈeɪg əʊ ˌ·ə- ‖ -oʊ ~**s** z
pick, Pick pɪk **picked** pɪkt **picking** ˈpɪk ɪŋ
　picks pɪks
pickaback ˈpɪk ə bæk

pickan... —*see* **piccan...**

pick-and-mix ˌpɪk ən ˈmɪks →-əm-

pickax, pickax|e ˈpɪk æks **~ed** t **~es** ɪz əz **~ing** ɪŋ

picker ˈpɪk ə ‖ -ᵊr **~s** z

pickerel ˈpɪk ᵊr‿əl **~s** z

Pickering ˈpɪk ᵊr‿ɪŋ

picker-up ˌpɪk ər ˈʌp ‖ -ᵊr-

pick|et ˈpɪk |ɪt §-ət ‖ -|ət **~eted** ɪt ɪd §ət-, -əd ‖ əţ əd **~eting** ɪt ɪŋ §ət- ‖ əţ ɪŋ **~ets** ɪts §əts ‖ əts

  ˈpicket line

Pickett ˈpɪk ɪt §-ət

Pickford ˈpɪk fəd ‖ -fᵊrd

pickings ˈpɪk ɪŋz

pickl|e ˈpɪk ᵊl **~ed** d **~es** z **~ing** ɪŋ

Pickles ˈpɪk ᵊlz

picklock ˈpɪk lɒk ‖ -lɑːk **~s** s

pick-me-up ˈpɪk mi ʌp **~s** s

pickpocket ˈpɪk ˌpɒk ɪt §-ət ‖ -ˌpɑːk ət **~s** s

Pickthorne ˈpɪk θɔːn ‖ -θɔːrn

pick-up ˈpɪk ʌp **~s** s

Pickup *family name* ˈpɪk ʌp

Pickwick ˈpɪk wɪk

  ˌPickwick ˈPapers ‖ ˈ·· ˌ··

Pickwickian ₍ₗ₎pɪk ˈwɪk i‿ən

pick|y ˈpɪk |i **~ier** i‿ə ‖ i‿ᵊr **~iest** i‿ɪst i‿əst **~iness** i nəs i nɪs

picnic ˈpɪk nɪk **~ked** t **~king** ɪŋ **~s** s

picnicker ˈpɪk nɪk ə ‖ -ᵊr **~s** z

pico- ˈpiːk əʊ ˈpaɪk- ‖ -oʊ — **picofarad** ˈpiːk əʊ ˌfær əd ˈpaɪk-, -æd ‖ -oʊ- -ˌfer-

picot ˈpiːk əʊ pɪ ˈkəʊ ‖ -oʊ pi ˈkoʊ —*Fr* [pi ko]

picotee ˌpɪk ə ˈtiː **~s** z

picrate ˈpɪk reɪt **~s** s

picric ˈpɪk rɪk

Pict pɪkt **Picts** pɪkts

Pictish ˈpɪkt ɪʃ

pictogram ˈpɪkt əʊ græm ‖ -ə- **~s** z

pictograph ˈpɪkt əʊ grɑːf -græf ‖ -ə græf **~s** s

pictographic ˌpɪkt əʊ ˈgræf ɪk ◄ ‖ -ə- **~ally** ᵊl‿i

pictography pɪk ˈtɒg rəf i ‖ -ˈtɑːg-

Picton ˈpɪkt ən

Pictor ˈpɪkt ə ‖ -ᵊr

pictorial pɪk ˈtɔːr i‿əl ‖ -ˈtoʊr- **~ly** i

Pictoris pɪk ˈtɔːr ɪs §-əs ‖ -ˈtoʊr-

pic|ture ˈpɪk |tʃə -ʃə; △ˈpɪ|tʃ ə ‖ ˈpɪk |tʃᵊr **~tured** tʃəd ʃəd ‖ tʃᵊrd **~tures** tʃəz ʃəz ‖ tʃᵊrz **~turing** tʃər ɪŋ ʃər‿ɪŋ

  ˈpicture book; **ˈpicture frame**; **ˌpicture ˈpostcard**; **ˈpicture rail**

picture-perfect ˌpɪk tʃə ˈpɜːf ɪkt ◄ -ʃə-, -ekt, §-əkt ‖ -tʃᵊr ˈpɜːf-

picturesque ˌpɪk tʃə ˈresk ◄ -ʃə- **~ly** li **~ness** nəs nɪs

piddl|e ˈpɪd ᵊl **~ed** d **~es** z **~ing** ɪŋ

piddock ˈpɪd ək **~s** s

Pidgeon ˈpɪdʒ ən

pidgin, P~ ˈpɪdʒ ɪn -ən **~s** z

  ˌPidgin ˈEnglish

pidginis... —*see* **pidginiz...**

pidginization ˌpɪdʒ ɪn aɪ ˈzeɪʃ ᵊn ˌ·ən-, -ɪ'-- ‖ -ən ə-

pidginize ˈpɪdʒ ɪ naɪz -ə-

pie paɪ **pies** paɪz

  ˈpie chart

piebald ˈpaɪ bɔːld ‖ -bɑːld **~s** z

piece piːs (= *peace*) —*but in Fr phrases also* pi ˈes, pɪəs —*Fr* **pièce** [pjɛs] **pieced** piːst **pieces** ˈpiːs ɪz -əz **piecing** ˈpiːs ɪŋ —*see also phrases with this word*

  ˌpiece of ˈcake; **ˌpieces of ˈeight**; **ˌpiece of ˈwork**; **ˈpiece rate**

piece de resistance, pièce de résistance pi ˌes də re ˈzɪst ɒ̃s -ɪ'--, -rə'--, -riː'--; ˌpɪəs ·'--; -əⁿˈs; -ˌrez i ˈstɒ̃s ‖ pi ˌes də rɪ ˌziː ˈstɑːⁿˈs —*Fr* [pjɛs də re zis tɑ̃ːs, pjɛz-]

piecemeal ˈpiːs miːᵊl

piecework ˈpiːs wɜːk ‖ -wɜːk

piecrust ˈpaɪ krʌst **~s** s

pied paɪd

  ˌPied ˈPiper

pied-a-terre, pied-à-terre pi ˌeɪd ɑː ˈteə ˌpiː ed-, -ə'· ‖ -ˈteᵊr —*Fr* [pje ta tɛːʁ] **pieds-~** pi ˌeɪd -ˌeɪdz; ˌpiː ed, ˌpiː edz —*Fr as in sing.*

Piedmont, p~ ˈpiːd mɒnt ‖ -mɑːnt

Piedmontese ˌpiːd mən ˈtiːz ◄ -mɒn- ‖ -mɑːn- -ˈtiːs

pie-eyed ˌpaɪ ˈaɪd ◄

pie|man ˈpaɪ| mən **~men** mən men

pier pɪə ‖ pɪᵊr (= *peer*) **piers** pɪəz ‖ pɪᵊrz

  ˈpier glass

pierce, P~ pɪəs ‖ pɪᵊrs **pierced** pɪəst ‖ pɪᵊrst **pierces** ˈpɪəs ɪz -əz ‖ ˈpɪrs əz **piercing/ly** ˈpɪəs ɪŋ /li ‖ ˈpɪrs ɪŋ /li

Piercy ˈpɪəs i ‖ ˈpɪrs i

Pierian paɪ ˈɪər i‿ən pi-, -ˈer- ‖ -ˈɪr-

pieris ˈpaɪᵊr ɪs paɪ ˈɪər-, §-əs

Pierre *place in SD* pɪə ‖ pɪᵊr

Pierre *personal name* pi ˈeə ˈpiː eə ‖ -ˈeᵊr —*Fr* [pjɛːʁ]

pierrot, P~ ˈpɪər əʊ ˈpiː ə roʊ ˌ·'· —*Fr* [pjɛ ʁo] **~s** z

Piers pɪəz ‖ pɪᵊrz

pie-shaped ˈpaɪ ʃeɪpt

Piesporter ˈpiːz pɔːt ə ‖ -pɔːrţ ᵊr —*Ger* [ˈpiːs pɔʁt ɐ]

pieta, pietà ˌpiː e ˈtɑː -eɪ-, ˈ··· ‖ -eɪ- —*It* [pje ˈta]

Pietermaritzburg ˌpiːt ə ˈmær ɪts bɜːg §-ˈ·əts- ‖ ˌpiːţ ᵊr ˈmær əts bɜːg -ˈmer-

pietism, P~ ˈpaɪ ə ˌtɪz əm -ɪ-

pietist, P~ ˈpaɪ ət ɪst -əst ‖ -əţ- **~s** s

pietistic ˌpaɪ ə ˈtɪst ɪk ◄

piet|y ˈpaɪ ət |i -ɪt- ‖ -əţ |i **~ies** iz

piezo- *comb. form*

  with stress-neutral suffix ¦piːz əʊ paɪ ¦iːz əʊ, pi ¦ets əʊ, ¦paɪ ɪ zəʊ ‖ pi ¦eɪz oʊ -¦ets— **piezochemistry** ˌpiːz əʊ ˈkem ɪst ri paɪ ˌiːz əʊ'--, pi ˌets-, ˌpaɪ ɪ zəʊ-, -ˈəst- ‖ pi ˌeɪz oʊ- -ˌets-

  with stress-imposing suffix ˌpiːz ə ˈzɒ + ˌpaɪ-, -ɪ-

‖ ˌpiː ə ˈzɑː + ˌpaɪ-, -eɪ- — **piezometry**
ˌpiːˌə ˈzɒm ətr i ˌpaɪ-, ˌˌɪ-, -ɪtr i ‖ -ˈzɑːm- ˌeɪ-
piezoelectric ˌpiːz əʊ ɪ ˈlek trɪk ◂ ˌpiːts-;
paɪ ˌiːz əʊ ɪˈ--, pi ˌets-, ˌpaɪ ɪ zəʊ ɪˈ--
‖ pi ˌeɪz oʊ- -ˌeɪts-
 ˌpiezoeˌlectric ˈcrystal ‖ piˌezo-
Pifco *tdmk* ˈpɪf kəʊ ‖ -koʊ
piffl|e ˈpɪf ᵊl ~**ed** d ~**es** z ~**ing** ɪŋ
pig pɪg **pigged** pɪgd **pigging** ˈpɪg ɪŋ **pigs**
pɪgz
 ˈpig ˌiron; ˈpig ˌLatin
pigeon ˈpɪdʒ ən -ɪn ~**s** z
pigeon-chested ˌpɪdʒ ən ˈtʃest ɪd ◂ -ɪn-, -əd
‖ ˈ·ˌ··
pigeonhol|e ˈpɪdʒ ən həʊl -ɪn-, -→-hɒʊl ‖ -hoʊl
 ~**ed** d ~**es** z ~**ing** ɪŋ
pigeon-toed ˈpɪdʒ ən təʊd ˌ· ·ˈ· ‖ -toʊd
pigger|y ˈpɪg ər |i ~**ies** iz
piggi... —*see* **piggy**
piggish ˈpɪg ɪʃ ~**ly** li ~**ness** nəs nɪs
Piggott ˈpɪg ət
pigg|y ˈpɪg |i ~**ier** i ə ‖ iˌᵊr ~**ies** iz ~**iest** i ɪst
 i ˌəst
piggyback ˈpɪg i bæk ~**ed** t ~**ing** ɪŋ ~**s** s
piggybank ˈpɪg i bæŋk ~**s** s
pigheaded ˌpɪg ˈhed ɪd ◂ -əd ~**ly** li ~**ness** nəs
 nɪs
piglet ˈpɪg lət -lɪt ~**s** s
pigmeat ˈpɪg miːt
pig|ment *v* pɪg ˈ|ment ˈpɪg |mənt ~**mented**
 ment ɪd mənt-, -əd ‖ menṯ əd manṯ-
 ~**menting** ment ɪŋ mənt- ‖ menṯ ɪŋ manṯ-
 ~**ments** ments
pigment *n* ˈpɪg mənt ~**s** s
pigmentation ˌpɪg men ˈteɪʃ ᵊn -mən- ~**s** z
pig|my, Pig|my ˈpɪg |mi ~**mies** miz
pignut ˈpɪg nʌt ~**s** s
Pigott ˈpɪg ət
pigpen ˈpɪg pen ~**s** z
pigskin ˈpɪg skɪn
pigsticking ˈpɪg ˌstɪk ɪŋ
pig|sty ˈpɪg |staɪ ~**sties** staɪz
pigswill ˈpɪg swɪl
pigtail ˈpɪg teɪᵊl ~**ed** d ~**s** z
pigwash ˈpɪg wɒʃ ‖ -wɔːʃ -wɑːʃ
pigweed ˈpɪg wiːd
pika ˈpaɪk ə ˈpiːk- ~**s** z
pike, Pike paɪk **piked** paɪkt **pikes, Pike's**
 paɪks **piking** ˈpaɪk ɪŋ
 ˌPike's ˈPeak
pikelet ˈpaɪk lət -lɪt ~**s** s
pike|man ˈpaɪk |mən ~**men** mən men
pikeperch ˈpaɪk pɜːtʃ ‖ -pɜːtʃ ~**es** ɪz əz
piker ˈpaɪk ə ‖ -ᵊr ~**s** z
pikestaff ˈpaɪk stɑːf §-stæf ‖ -stæf ~**s** s
pikey ˈpaɪk i ~**s** z
pilaf, pilaff ˈpiːl æf ˈpɪl- ‖ pɪ ˈlɑːf ˈpiːl ɑːf ~**s** s
pilaster pɪ ˈlæst ə pə- ‖ -ᵊr ˈpaɪl æst- ~**ed** d ~**s**
 z
Pilate ˈpaɪl ət
Pilates pɪ ˈlɑːt iːz pə-
Pilatus pɪ ˈlɑːt əs pə- —*Ger* [pi ˈlaː tʊs]

pilau ˈpiːl aʊ ˈpɪl-; pɪ ˈlaʊ, pə- ‖ pɪ ˈloʊ -ˈlɔː,
 -ˈlɑː, -ˈlaʊ ~**s** z
pilchard ˈpɪltʃ əd ‖ -ᵊrd ~**s** z
pile paɪᵊl **piled** paɪᵊld **piles** paɪᵊlz **piling**
 ˈpaɪᵊl ɪŋ
pilea ˈpɪl i ə ˈpaɪl- ~**s** z
pileated ˈpaɪl i eɪt ɪd ˈpɪl-, -əd ‖ ˈpɪl i eɪṯ-
 ˈpaɪl-
pile-driver ˈpaɪᵊl ˌdraɪv ə ‖ -ᵊr ~**s** z
pile|um ˈpaɪl i |əm ~**a** ə
pileup ˈpaɪᵊl ʌp ~**s** s
pile|us ˈpaɪl i |əs ~**i** aɪ iː
pilfer ˈpɪlf ə ‖ -ᵊr ~**ed** d **pilfering** ˈpɪlf ər ɪŋ ~**s**
 z
pilferage ˈpɪlf ər ɪdʒ
pilferer ˈpɪlf ər ə ‖ -ᵊr ər ~**s** z
pilgrim, P~ ˈpɪl grɪm -grəm ~**s, ~'s** z
 ˌPilgrim ˈFathers
pilgrimag|e ˈpɪl grɪm ɪdʒ -grəm- ~**es** ɪz əz
Pilipino ˌpɪl ɪ ˈpiːn əʊ -ə- ‖ -oʊ
Pilkington ˈpɪlk ɪŋ tən
pill pɪl **pilled** pɪld **pilling** ˈpɪl ɪŋ **pills** pɪlz
pillag|e ˈpɪl ɪdʒ ~**ed** d ~**es** ɪz əz ~**ing** ɪŋ
pillager ˈpɪl ɪdʒ ə ‖ -ᵊr ~**s** z
pillar ˈpɪl ə ‖ -ᵊr ~**ed** d ~**s** z
 ˈpillar box; ˌpillar box ˈred◂
pillbox ˈpɪl bɒks ‖ -bɑːks ~**es** ɪz əz
Pilley ˈpɪl i
Pilling ˈpɪl ɪŋ
pillion ˈpɪl jən ˈpɪl i ən ~**s** z
pilliwinks ˈpɪl ɪ wɪŋ̠ks §-ə-
pillock ˈpɪl ək ~**s** s
pillor|y ˈpɪl ər |i ~**ied** id ~**ies** iz ~**ying** i ɪŋ
pillow ˈpɪl əʊ ‖ -oʊ ~**ed** d ~**ing** ɪŋ ~**s** z
 ˈpillow slip; ˈpillow talk
pillowcas|e ˈpɪl əʊ keɪs ‖ -ə- -oʊ- ~**es** ɪz əz
Pillsbury ˈpɪlz bər i ‖ -ˌber i
pillwort ˈpɪl wɜːt §-wɔːt ‖ -wɜːrt -wɔːrt
pilocarpine ˌpaɪl əʊ ˈkɑːp iːn -aɪn, -ɪn
 ‖ -oʊ ˈkɑːrp-
pilonidal ˌpaɪl əʊ ˈnaɪd ᵊl ◂ ‖ -ə-
pil|ot ˈpaɪl |ət ~**oted** ət ɪd -əd ‖ əṯ əd ~**oting**
 ət ɪŋ ‖ əṯ ɪŋ ~**ots** əts
 ˈpilot ˌburner; ˈpilot ˌlamp; ˈpilot ˌlight;
 ˈpilot ˌofficer
pilotage ˈpaɪl ət ɪdʒ ‖ -əṯ-
Pilsen ˈpɪlz ən ˈpɪls- —*Ger* [ˈpɪl zᵊn], *Czech*
 Plzeň [ˈpᵊl zeŋ]
pilsener, pilsner, P~ ˈpɪlz nə ˈpɪls-, ˈ·nᵊ ə
 ‖ -nᵊr ~**s** z
Pilsudski pɪl ˈsʊd ski —*Polish* Piłsudski
 [piw ˈsut ski]
Piltdown ˈpɪlt daʊn
Pilton ˈpɪlt ən
pilule ˈpɪl juːl ~**s** z
Pima ˈpiːm ə ~**s** z
Piman ˈpiːm ən
pimento pɪ ˈment əʊ pə- ‖ -ˈmenṯ oʊ ~**s** z
pimiento ˌpɪm i ˈent əʊ pɪm ˈjent-; pɪ ˈment-,
 pə- ‖ pəm ˈjenṯ oʊ pə ˈmenṯ- ~**s** z
Pimlico ˈpɪm lɪ kəʊ -lə- ‖ -koʊ
Pimm pɪm **Pimm's** pɪmz

P

pimp pɪmp **pimped** pɪmpt **pimping** ˈpɪmp ɪŋ
  pimps pɪmps
pimpernel ˈpɪmp ə nel -nᵊl ‖ -ᵊr- ~**s** z
pimple ˈpɪmp ᵊl ~**d** d ~**s** z
pimp|ly ˈpɪmp |li ~**liness** li nəs -nɪs
pimpmobile ˈpɪmp məʊ ˌbiːl ‖ -mə- -moʊ- ~**s**
  z
pin, PIN pɪn **pinned** pɪnd **pinning** ˈpɪn ɪŋ
  pins pɪnz
  ˈpin ˌmoney; ˈPIN ˌnumber; ˌpins and
  ˈneedles
pina colada, piña colada ˌpiːn ə kəʊ ˈlɑːd ə
  ˌjə- ‖ -jə kə- -ə kə- —*Sp* [ˌpi ɲa ko ˈla ða] ~**s**
  z
pinafore ˈpɪn ə fɔː ‖ -fɔːr -four ~**s** z
pinata, piñata piːn ˈjɑːt ə pɪn- ‖ -ˈjɑːt̬ ə —*Sp*
  [pi ˈɲa ta] ~**s** z
Pinatubo ˌpɪn ə ˈtuːb əʊ ‖ ˌpiːn ə ˈtuːb oʊ
pinball ˈpɪn bɔːl →ˈpɪm- ‖ -bɑːl ~**s** z
pince-nez *sing.* ˌpæn⁵s ˈneɪ ˌpɪn⁵s-, -ˈnez —*Fr*
  [pæs ne] ~ *pl* z
pincer ˈpɪn⁵s ə ‖ -ᵊr ~**s** z
  ˈpincer ˌmovement
pincerlike ˈpɪn⁵s ə laɪk ‖ -ᵊr-
pinch pɪntʃ **pinched** pɪntʃt **pinches** ˈpɪntʃ ɪz
  -əz **pinching** ˈpɪntʃ ɪŋ
pinchbeck, P~ ˈpɪntʃ bek
Pincher ˈpɪntʃ ə ‖ -ᵊr
pinch-|hit ˌpɪntʃ |ˈhɪt ~**hits** ˈhɪts ~**hitter/s**
  ˈhɪt ə/z ‖ ˈhɪt̬ ᵊr/z ~**hitting** ˈhɪt ɪŋ ‖ ˈhɪt̬ ɪŋ
pinchpenn|y ˈpɪntʃ ˌpen |i ~**ies** iz
Pinckney ˈpɪŋk ni
Pincus ˈpɪŋk əs
pincushion ˈpɪn ˌkʊʃ ᵊn →ˈpɪŋ- ~**s** z
Pindar ˈpɪnd ə -ɑː ‖ -ᵊr -ɑːr
Pindaric ₍ₗ₎pɪn ˈdær ɪk ‖ -ˈder-
pindown ˈpɪn daʊn
Pindus ˈpɪnd əs
pine, Pine paɪn **pined** paɪnd **pines** paɪnz
  pining ˈpaɪn ɪŋ
  ˈpine cone; ˈpine ˌkernel; ˈpine ˌmarten;
  ˈpine ˌneedle
pineal ˈpɪn i‿əl ₍ₗ₎paɪ ˈniː əl
  ˈpineal gland
pineapple ˈpaɪn æp ᵊl -ˌ‧‧ ~**s** z
  ˈpineapple ˌjuice
pinene ˈpaɪn iːn
Pinero pɪ ˈnɪər əʊ pə-, -ˈneər- ‖ -ˈnɪr oʊ -ˈner-
pinetree ˈpaɪn triː ~**s** z
pinet|um paɪ ˈniːt |əm ‖ -ˈniːt̬ |əm ~**a** ə
pinewood, P~ ˈpaɪn wʊd ~**s** z
piney ˈpaɪn i
pinfall ˈpɪn fɔːl ‖ -fɑːl ~**s** z
Pinfold ˈpɪn fəʊld →ˈfɒʊld ‖ -foʊld
ping pɪŋ **pinged** pɪŋd **pinging** ˈpɪŋ ɪŋ **pings**
  pɪŋz
pinger ˈpɪŋ ə ‖ -ᵊr ~**s** z
pingo ˈpɪŋ ɡəʊ ‖ -ɡoʊ ~**s** z
ping-pong, Ping-Pong *tdmk* ˈpɪŋ pɒŋ ‖ -pɑːŋ
  -pɔːŋ
Pingtung ˌpɪŋ ˈtʌŋ —*Chi* Píngdōng
  [²pʰiŋ ¹tʊŋ]
pinguid ˈpɪŋ ɡwɪd §-ɡwəd

pinhead ˈpɪn hed ~**s** z
pinhole ˈpɪn həʊl →-hɒʊl ‖ -hoʊl ~**s** z
pinion ˈpɪn jən ~**ed** d ~**ing** ɪŋ ~**s** z
pink pɪŋk **pinked** pɪŋkt **pinker** ˈpɪŋk ə ‖ -ᵊr
  pinkest ˈpɪŋk ɪst §-əst **pinking** ˈpɪŋk ɪŋ
  pinks pɪŋks
  ˌpink ˈelephant; ˌpink ˈgin; ˈpinking
  ˌscissors; ˈpinking shears
pink-collar ˌpɪŋk ˈkɒl ə ◂ ‖ -ˈkɑːl ᵊr ◂
Pinkerton ˈpɪŋk ət ən ‖ -ᵊrt ᵊn
pinkeye ˈpɪŋk aɪ
pinkie ˈpɪŋk i ~**s** z
pinkish ˈpɪŋk ɪʃ
pinkness ˈpɪŋk nəs -nɪs
pinko ˈpɪŋk əʊ ‖ -oʊ ~**es, ~s** z
pink|y ˈpɪŋk |i ~**ies** iz
pinn... —*see* **pin**
pinn|a ˈpɪn |ə ~**ae** iː ~**as** əz
pinnac|e ˈpɪn əs -ɪs ~**es** ɪz əz
pinnacl|e ˈpɪn ək ᵊl -ɪk- ~**ed** d ~**ing** ɪŋ ~**es** z
pinnate ˈpɪn eɪt -ət, -ɪt ~**ly** li
pinnatifid pɪ ˈnæt ɪ fɪd §-ə- ‖ -ˈnæt̬-
pinner, P~ ˈpɪn ə ‖ -ᵊr
Pinney ˈpɪn i
Pinnock ˈpɪn ək
pinn|y ˈpɪn |i ~**ies** iz
Pinocchio pɪ ˈnəʊk i‿əʊ pə-, -ˈnɒk-
  ‖ -ˈnoʊk i oʊ —*It* [pi ˈnɔk kjo]
Pinochet ˈpiːn əʊ ʃeɪ -tʃeɪ ‖ ˌpiːn oʊ ˈtʃet —*Sp*
  [pi no ˈtʃet]
pinochle, pinocle ˈpiː ˌnʌk ᵊl -ˌnɒk-
pinocytosis ˌpɪn əʊ saɪ ˈtəʊs ɪs §-əs
  ‖ -ə saɪ ˈtoʊs-
pinole pɪ ˈnəʊl i pə- ‖ -ˈnoʊl i
Pinot ˈpiːn əʊ ‖ -oʊ —*Fr* [pi no]
pin|point ˈpɪn |pɔɪnt →ˈpɪm- ~**pointed**
  pɔɪnt ɪd -əd ‖ pɔɪnt̬ əd ~**pointing** pɔɪnt ɪŋ
  ‖ pɔɪnt̬ ɪŋ ~**points** pɔɪnts
pinprick ˈpɪn prɪk →ˈpɪm- ~**ed** t ~**ing** ɪŋ ~**s** s
pinstripe ˈpɪn straɪp ~**d** t ~**s** s
  ˌpinstripe ˈsuit
pint paɪnt **pints** paɪnts
pinta *'pint (of milk)'* ˈpaɪnt ə ‖ ˈpaɪnt̬ ə ~**s** z
pinta *'tropical disease'*, **P~** ˈpɪnt ə ˈpiːnt-
  ‖ ˈpɪnt̬ ə ˈpɪnt ɑː —*Sp* [ˈpin ta]
pintable ˈpɪn ˌteɪb ᵊl ~**s** z
pintado pɪn ˈtɑːd əʊ ‖ -oʊ
pintail ˈpɪn teᵊl ~**s** z
Pinter ˈpɪnt ə ‖ ˈpɪnt̬ ᵊr
Pinteresque ˌpɪnt ər ˈesk ◂ ‖ ˌpɪnt̬ ə ˈresk ◂
Pinterish ˈpɪnt ər ɪʃ ‖ ˈpɪnt̬-
pintle ˈpɪnt ᵊl ‖ ˈpɪnt̬ ᵊl ~**s** z
pinto ˈpɪnt əʊ ‖ ˈpɪnt oʊ ~**s** z
  ˈpinto bean
pint-size ˈpaɪnt saɪz ~**d** d
pinup ˈpɪn ʌp ~**s** s
pinwheel ˈpɪn wiːᵊl -hwiːᵊl ‖ -ʰwiːᵊl ~**s** z
pinworm ˈpɪn wɜːm ‖ -wɜːːm ~**s** z
pinxit ˈpɪŋks ɪt §-ət
Pinxton ˈpɪŋkst ən
piny ˈpaɪn i
pinyin, P~ ˌpɪn ˈjɪn ◂ —*Chi* pīnyīn [¹pʰɪn ¹jɪn]

pinyon, piñon pɪn ˈjɒn ‖ -ˈjoʊn -ˈjɑːn; ˈ· ·
—*Sp* piñón [pi ˈɲon]
piolet ˈpiː ə leɪ ‖ ˌpiː ə ˈleɪ ~s z
pion ˈpaɪ ɒn -ən ‖ -ɑːn ~s z
pioneer, P~ ˌpaɪ ə ˈnɪə ◄ ‖ -ˈnɪᵊr ~ed d
  pioneering ˌpaɪ ə ˈnɪər ɪŋ ◄ ‖ -ˈnɪr ɪŋ ◄ ~s z
  ˌpio̱ˈneering ˈwork
pious ˈpaɪ əs ~ly li ~ness nəs nɪs
pip, Pip pɪp **pipped** pɪpt **pipping** ˈpɪp ɪŋ **pips**
  pɪps
pipal ˈpiːp ᵊl ~s z
pipe paɪp **piped** paɪpt **pipes** paɪps **piping**
  ˈpaɪp ɪŋ
  ˈpipe ˌcleaner; ˌpiped ˈmusic; ˈpipe
  dream; ˈpipe ˌorgan; ˈpipe rack; ˌpiping
  ˈhot◄
pipeclay ˈpaɪp kleɪ
pipefish ˈpaɪp fɪʃ ~es ɪz əz
pipeful ˈpaɪp fʊl ~s z
pipelin|e ˈpaɪp laɪn ~ed d ~es z ~ing ɪŋ
piper, Piper ˈpaɪp ə ‖ -ᵊr ~s z
piperaceous ˌpɪp ə ˈreɪʃ əs ˌpaɪp-
piperade ˌpɪp ə ˈrɑːd ˌpiːp- ~s z
piperazine pɪ ˈper ə ziːn paɪ-, -zɪn
piperidine pɪ ˈper ɪ diːn paɪ-, -ə-, -dɪn
pipette pɪ ˈpet ‖ paɪ- ~s s
pipework ˈpaɪp wɜːk ‖ -wɜːk
pipewort ˈpaɪp wɜːt -wɔːt ‖ -wɜːt -wɔːrt
Pipex *tdmk* ˈpaɪp eks
piping ˈpaɪp ɪŋ
pipistrelle ˌpɪp ɪ ˈstrel -ə-, ˈ· · · ~s z
pipit ˈpɪp ɪt §-ət ~s s
pipkin ˈpɪp kɪn §-kən ~s z
pipp... —*see* **pip**
Pippa ˈpɪp ə
pippin ˈpɪp ɪn §-ən ~s z
pipsqueak ˈpɪp skwiːk ~s s
piquancy ˈpiːk ənts i
piquant ˈpiːk ənt -ɑːnt -ly li
pique piːk *(= peak)* **piqued** piːkt **piques** piːks
  piquing ˈpiːk ɪŋ
piqué ˈpiːk eɪ ‖ piː ˈkeɪ —*Fr* [pi ke]
piquet *'card game'* pɪ ˈket -ˈkeɪ
Piquet ˈpiːk eɪ
pirac|y ˈpaɪᵊr əs |i ˈpɪr- ~ies iz
Piraeus ₍ᵢ₎paɪᵊ ˈriː əs pɪ ˈreɪ əs, pə- —*ModGk*
  Peiraiás [pi rɛ ˈas]
Piran ˈpɪr ən
Pirandello ˌpɪr ən ˈdel əʊ ‖ -oʊ —*It*
  [pi ran ˈdɛl lo]
piranha, piraña pə ˈrɑːn ə pɪ-, -jə ‖ -ˈræn- ~s z
  piˈranha fish
pir|ate ˈpaɪᵊr |ət -ɪt ~ated ət ɪd ɪt-, -əd ‖ əṭ əd
  ~ates əts ɪts ~ating ət ɪŋ ɪt- ‖ əṭ ɪŋ
piratical ₍ᵢ₎paɪᵊ ˈræt ɪk ᵊl pɪ-, pə- ‖ -ˈræṭ- ~ly i
Pirbright ˈpɜː braɪt ‖ ˈpɜːr-
Pirelli *tdmk* pə ˈrel i pɪ- —*It* [pi ˈrɛl li]
Pirie ˈpɪr i
Pirithous, Pirithoüs paɪᵊ ˈrɪθ əʊ əs ‖ -oʊ əs
pirog, pirogue pɪ ˈrəʊg pə- ‖ -ˈroʊg ˈpiː roʊg
  ~s z
piroshki pɪ ˈrɒʃ ki pə-; ˌpɪr əʃ ˈkiː ‖ -ˈrɔːʃ-
  -ˈrɑːʃ-, -ˈrʌʃ- —*Russ* [pʲɪ rʌ ˈʃkʲi]

pirou|ette ˌpɪr u ‖ˈet ~etted ˈet ɪd -əd ‖ ˈeṭ əd
  ~ettes ˈets ~etting ˈet ɪŋ ‖ ˈeṭ ɪŋ
pirozhki —*see* **piroshki**
Pisa ˈpiːz ə —*It* [ˈpiː sa]
pis aller ˌpiːz ˈæl eɪ ‖ -æ ˈleɪ —*Fr* [pi za le]
Pisan ˈpiːz ᵊn ~s z
piscatorial ˌpɪsk ə ˈtɔːr i əl ◄ ‖ -ˈtoʊr- ~ly i
piscatory ˈpɪsk ət ər i ‖ -ə tɔːr i -tour i
Piscean ˈpaɪs i ən ˈpɪsk-, ˈpɪs-; paɪ ˈsiː ~s z
Pisces ˈpaɪs iːz ˈpɪsk-, ˈpɪs-
pisci- *comb. form*
  with stress-neutral suffix ˌpɪs ɪ
  — **pisciculture** ˈpɪs ɪ ˌkʌltʃ ə ‖ -ᵊr
  with stress-imposing suffix pɪ ˈsɪ+ §pə-
  — **piscivorous** pɪ ˈsɪv ər əs §pə-
piscin|a pɪ ˈsiːn |ə §pə-, -ˈʃiːn-, -ˈsaɪn- ~ae iː
  ~as əz
piscine ˈpɪs aɪn ˈpɪsk-, ˈpaɪs-, -iːn ~s z
Pisgah ˈpɪz gɑː -gə
pish pɪʃ
Pisidia paɪ ˈsɪd i ə
Pisistratus paɪ ˈsɪs trət əs ‖ -trəṭ-
piss pɪs **pissed** pɪst **pisses** ˈpɪs ɪz -əz **pissing**
  ˈpɪs ɪŋ
pissant ˈpɪs ænt ~ing ɪŋ ~s s
Pissarro pɪ ˈsɑːr əʊ ‖ -oʊ —*Fr* [pi sa ʁo]
pisser ˈpɪs ə ‖ -ᵊr ~s z
pisshead ˈpɪs hed ~s z
pissoir ˈpiːs wɑː ‖ piː ˈswɑːr —*Fr* [pi swaːʁ] ~s z
piss-poor ˌpɪs ˈpɔː ◄ -ˈpʊə ◄ ‖ -ˈpʊᵊr ◄ -ˈpɔːr ◄,
  -ˈpoʊr ◄
piss-take ˈpɪs teɪk ~s s
piss-up ˈpɪs ʌp ~s s
pissy ˈpɪs i
pistachio pɪ ˈstɑːʃ i əʊ pə-, -ˈstæʃ-, -ˈstætʃ-
  ‖ -ˈstæʃ i oʊ -ˈstɑːʃ- ~s z
piste piːst **pistes** piːsts
pistil ˈpɪst ɪl -ᵊl ~s z
pistol ˈpɪst ᵊl ~s z
  ˈpistol grip
pistole pɪ ˈstəʊl ‖ -ˈstoʊl ~s z
pistol-whip ˈpɪst ᵊl wɪp -hwɪp ~ped t ~ping
  ɪŋ ~s s
piston ˈpɪst ən ~s z
  ˈpiston ring; ˈpiston rod
pit pɪt **pits** pɪts **pitted** ˈpɪt ɪd -əd ‖ ˈpɪṭ əd
  pitting ˈpɪt ɪŋ ‖ ˈpɪṭ ɪŋ
  ˈpit bull, ˌpit bull ˈterrier; ˈpit ˌpony; ˈpit
  stop
pita ˈpɪt ə ˈpiːt- ‖ ˈpiːṭ ə
pit-a-pat ˌpɪt ə ˈpæt ˈ· · · ‖ ˈpɪṭ ə pæt -ɪ-
Pitcairn ˈpɪt keən ·ˈ· ‖ -kern —*as a family
  name, usually* ·ˈ·
pitch pɪtʃ **pitched** pɪtʃt **pitches** ˈpɪtʃ ɪz -əz
  pitching ˈpɪtʃ ɪŋ
  ˈpitch pine; ˈpitch pipe
pitch-and-putt ˌpɪtʃ ən ˈpʌt -ənd-, →əm-
pitch-and-toss ˌpɪtʃ ən ˈtɒs -ənd-, -ˈtɔːs ‖ -ˈtɔːs
  -ˈtɑːs
pitch-black ˌpɪtʃ ˈblæk ◄
pitchblende ˈpɪtʃ blend
pitch-dark ˌpɪtʃ ˈdɑːk ◄ ‖ -ˈdɑːrk

pitcher 'pɪtʃ ə ‖ -ᵊr ~s z
  'pitcher plant
pitchfork 'pɪtʃ fɔːk ‖ -fɔːrk ~s s
pitch|man 'pɪtʃ| mən -mæn ~men mən men
pitchout 'pɪtʃ aʊt ~s s
pitch|y 'pɪtʃ |i ~ier i ə ‖ i ᵊr ~iest i ɪst i əst
  ~iness i nəs -nɪs
piteous 'pɪt i əs ~ly li ~ness nəs nɪs
pitfall 'pɪt fɔːl ‖ -fɑːl ~s z
pith pɪθ pithed pɪθt pithing 'pɪθ ɪŋ piths
  pɪθs
  ,pith 'helmet ‖ '·‚·
pithead 'pɪt hed ~s z
pithecanthropus, P~ ,pɪθ i 'kænᵗθ rəp əs
  -kæn 'θrəʊp- ‖ -kæn 'θroʊp-
pith|y 'pɪθ |i ~ier i ə ‖ i ᵊr ~iest i ɪst i əst ~ily
  ɪ li əl i ~iness i nəs i nɪs
pitiab|le 'pɪt i əb |ᵊl ‖ 'pɪt̬- ~leness ᵊl nəs -nɪs
  ~ly li
pitie... —see pity
pitiful 'pɪt ɪ f°l -ə-, -ʊl ‖ 'pɪt̬- ~ly ‚i ~ness nəs
  nɪs
pitiless 'pɪt ɪ ləs -ə-, -lɪs; -ᵊl əs, -ɪs ‖ 'pɪt̬- ~ly li
  ~ness nəs nɪs
Pitjantjatjara ,pɪtʃ ən tʃə 'tʃær ə
Pitlochry pɪt 'lɒx ri -'lɒk- ‖ -'lɑːk-
pit|man, P~ 'pɪt |mən ~men mən men
Pitney 'pɪt ni
piton 'piːt ɒn -ō̃ ‖ -ɑːn —Fr [pi tɔ̃] ~s z
pitot, Pitot 'piːt əʊ ‖ -oʊ ~s z
  'Pitot tube
Pitsea 'pɪt siː
Pitt pɪt
pitta 'kind of bread' 'pɪt ə 'piːt- ‖ 'pɪt̬ ə
  'pitta bread
pitta 'kind of bird' 'pɪt ə ‖ 'pɪt̬ ə ~s z
pittanc|e 'pɪt ᵊnᵗs ‖ 'pɪt̬- ~es ɪz əz
Pittenweem ,pɪt ᵊn 'wiːm
pitter-patter 'pɪt ə ,pæt ə ‚·'·‚·
  ‖ 'pɪt̬ ᵊr ,pæt̬ ᵊr -i-
pittosporum pɪ 'tɒsp ər əm ‖ -'tɑːsp-
Pittsburg, Pittsburgh 'pɪts bɜːg ‖ -bɜˑg
pituitar|y pɪ 'tjuː‿ɪ tər |i pə-, →-'tʃuː‿‚ə‚
  ‖ -'tuː‿ə ter |i -'tjuː- ~ies iz
  pi'tuitary gland
pituri 'pɪtʃ ər i
pity 'pɪt i ‖ 'pɪt̬ i pitied 'pɪt id ‖ 'pɪt̬ id pities
  'pɪt iz ‖ 'pɪt̬ iz pitying/ly 'pɪt i ɪŋ /li ‖ 'pɪt̬ i-
pityriasis ,pɪt ɪ 'raɪ‿əs ɪs ‚·ə-, §-əs ‖ ,pɪt̬-
Pius 'paɪ‿əs
piv|ot 'pɪv |ət ~oted ət ɪd -əd ‖ ət̬ əd ~oting
  ət ɪŋ ‖ ət̬ ɪŋ ~ots əts
pivotal 'pɪv ət ᵊl ‖ -ət̬ ᵊl ~ly ‚i
pix pɪks (= picks)
pixel 'pɪks ᵊl -el ~s z
pix|elate 'pɪks| ə leɪt →-ᵊl eɪt ~elated
  ə leɪt ɪd -əd ‖ -ᵊl eɪt̬ əd ~elates ə leɪts
  →ᵊl eɪts ~elating ə leɪt ɪŋ ‖ ᵊl eɪt̬ ɪŋ
pixelation ,pɪks ə 'leɪʃ ᵊn →-ᵊl 'eɪʃ-
pixie 'pɪks i ~s z
pixilated 'pɪks ɪ leɪt ɪd '‚ə- ‖ -leɪt̬ əd
pix|y 'pɪks |i ~ies iz

Pizarro pɪ 'zɑːr əʊ ‖ -oʊ —Sp [pi 'θa rro,
  -'sa-]
Piz Buin tdmk ,pɪts 'buːɪn
pizza 'piːts ə ~s z
  'Pizza Hut tdmk
pizzazz pə 'zæz pɪ-
pizzeria ,piːts ə 'riː‿ə ,pɪts- ~s z
Pizzey (i) 'pɪts i, (ii) 'pɪz i
pizzicato ,pɪts ɪ 'kɑːt əʊ -ə- ‖ -'kɑːt̬ oʊ ~s z
pizzle 'pɪz ᵊl ~s z
pj's, PJ's 'piː dʒeɪz
PL/1 ,piː el 'wʌn §-'wɒn
placab|le 'plæk əb |ᵊl ~ly li
placard v 'plæk ɑːd ‖ -ɑːrd -ᵊrd; plə 'kɑːrd,
  plæ- ~ed ɪd əd ~ing ɪŋ ~s z
placard n 'plæk ɑːd ‖ -ɑːrd -ᵊrd ~s z
pla|cate plə '|keɪt ‖ 'pleɪ|k eɪt (*) ~cated
  keɪt ɪd -əd ‖ keɪt̬ əd ~cates keɪts ~cating
  keɪt ɪŋ ‖ keɪt̬ ɪŋ
placatory plə 'keɪt ər i pleɪ-; 'plæk ət̬ ər i
  ‖ 'pleɪk ə tɔːr i 'plæk-, -toʊr i (*)
place pleɪs placed pleɪst places 'pleɪs ɪz -əz
  placing/s 'pleɪs ɪŋ/z
  'place card; 'place mat; 'place name;
  'place ,setting
placebo plə 'siːb əʊ plæ- ‖ -oʊ ~s z
  pla'cebo ef,fect
placekick 'pleɪs kɪk ~ed t ~er/s ə/z ‖ ᵊr/z
  ~ing ɪŋ ~s s
place|man 'pleɪs |mən ~men mən
placement 'pleɪs mənt ~s s
pla|centa plə '|sent ə ‖ -'|sent̬ ə ~centae
  'sent iː ~cental 'sent ᵊl ‖ 'sent̬ ᵊl ~centas
  'sent əz ‖ 'sent̬ əz
placer 'pleɪs ə ‖ -ᵊr 'plæs-
Placerville place in CA 'plæs ə vɪl ‖ -ᵊr-
placet 'pleɪs et -ɪt ~s s
placid 'plæs ɪd §-əd ~ly li ~ness nəs nɪs
placidity plə 'sɪd ət i plæ-, -ɪt- ‖ -ət̬ i
placket 'plæk ɪt §-ət ~s s
plagal 'pleɪg ᵊl
plage 'beach' plɑːʒ plages 'plɑːʒ ɪz -əz —Fr
  [plaːʒ]
plage 'bright region on the sun' plɑːʒ pleɪdʒ
  plages 'plɑːʒ ɪz 'pleɪdʒ-, -əz
plagiaris... —see plagiariz...
plagiarism 'pleɪdʒ ə ‚rɪz əm -i‚ə- ~s z
plagiarist 'pleɪdʒ ər ɪst -i‚ər-, §-əst ~s s
plagiaristic ,pleɪdʒ ə 'rɪst ɪk ◄ -i‚ə-
plagiariz|e 'pleɪdʒ ə raɪz -i‚ə- ~ed d ~es ɪz əz
  ~ing ɪŋ
plagioclas|e 'pleɪdʒ i‚ə kleɪz -kleɪs ~es ɪz əz
plague pleɪg plagued pleɪgd plagues pleɪgz
  plaguing 'pleɪg ɪŋ
plagu|ey, plagu|y 'pleɪg |i ~ily əl i ɪ li
plaice pleɪs (= place)
plaid plæd (!) plaids plædz
Plaid Cymru ,plaɪd 'kʌm ri -'kʊm-, -'kuːm-
  —Welsh [‚plaɪd 'kəm ri, -ri]
plain pleɪn (= plane) plainer 'pleɪn ə ‖ -ᵊr
  plainest 'pleɪn ɪst -əst
  ,plain 'chocolate; ,plain 'flour; ,plain
  'sailing

plainchant 'pleɪn tʃɑːnt §-tʃænt ‖ -tʃænt
plain-clothes ˌpleɪn 'kləʊðz ◄ →ˌpleɪŋ-, -kləʊz
‖ -'kloʊz -'kloʊðz
plain|ly 'pleɪn |li ~**ness** nəs nɪs
plains|man 'pleɪnz |mən ~**men** mən men
plainsong 'pleɪn sɒŋ ‖ -sɔːŋ -sɑːŋ
plainspoken ˌpleɪn 'spəʊk ən ◄ ‖ -'spoʊk ən
~**ness** nəs nɪs
plains|woman 'pleɪnz |ˌwʊm ən ~**women**
ˌwɪm ɪn -ən
plaint pleɪnt **plaints** pleɪnts
plaintiff 'pleɪnt ɪf §-əf ‖ 'pleɪnt̬ əf ~**s** s
plaintive 'pleɪnt ɪv ‖ 'pleɪnt̬ ɪv ~**ly** li ~**ness**
nəs nɪs
Plaistow (i) 'plɑːst əʊ 'plæst- ‖ -oʊ, (ii)
'pleɪst əʊ ‖ -oʊ —The places in Greater
London are (i). The family name may be
either (i) or (ii).
plait plæt ‖ pleɪt plæt (!) **plaited** 'plæt ɪd -əd
‖ 'pleɪt̬ əd 'plæt̬- **plaiting** 'plæt ɪŋ ‖ 'pleɪt̬ ɪŋ
'plæt̬- **plaits** plæts ‖ pleɪts plæts
plan plæn **planned** plænd **planning** 'plæn ɪŋ
plans plænz
   '**planning** perˌmission
planar 'pleɪn ə ‖ -ᵊr (= plainer)
planarian plə 'neər i‿ən ‖ -'ner- -'nær- ~**s** z
planchet 'plɑːntʃ ɪt §'plæntʃ-, §-ət ‖ 'plæntʃ ət
~**s** s
planchette plɑːn 'ʃet plɒ̃-, plæn- ‖ plæn- —Fr
[plɑ̃ ʃɛt] ~**s** s
Planck plæŋk ‖ plɑːŋk —Ger [plaŋk]
plane pleɪn **planned** pleɪnd **planes** pleɪnz
planing 'pleɪn ɪŋ
   '**plane tree**
planeload 'pleɪn ləʊd ‖ -loʊd ~**s** z
planer 'pleɪn ə ‖ ᵊr ~**s** z
planet 'plæn ɪt §-ət ~**s** s
planetari|um ˌplæn ə 'teər i‿|əm ˌ-ɪ- ‖ -'ter-
-'tær- ~**a** ə ~**ums** əmz
planetary 'plæn ət̬ ər i 'ˌɪt̬ ‖ -ə ter i
planetesimal ˌplæn ɪ 'tes ɪm ᵊl ◄ ˌ-ə-, -'tez-,
-əm ᵊl
planetoid 'plæn ə tɔɪd -ɪ- ~**s** z
plangency 'plændʒ ənˢi
plangent 'plændʒ ənt ~**ly** li
plani... —see **plane**
planigale 'plæn ɪ geɪᵊl -ə- ~**s** z
planimeter plæ 'nɪm ɪt ə plə-, pleɪ- ‖ -ət̬ ᵊr
~**s** z
planimetric ˌplæn ɪ 'metr ɪk ◄ -ə- ~**al/ly** ᵊl /‿i
planimetry plæ 'nɪm ətr i plə-, pleɪ-, -ɪtr-
plank plæŋk **planked** plæŋkt **planking**
'plæŋk ɪŋ **planks** plæŋks
plankton 'plæŋkt ən -ɒn ‖ ɑːn
planktonic plæŋk 'tɒn ɪk ‖ -'tɑːn ɪk
plann... —see **plan**
planner 'plæn ə ‖ -ᵊr ~**s** z
plano-concave ˌpleɪn əʊ 'kɒn keɪv ◄ →-'kɒŋ-,
ˌ··ˌ·ˈ· ‖ -oʊ 'kɑːn-
plano-convex ˌpleɪn əʊ 'kɒn veks ◄ ˌ··ˌ·ˈ·
‖ -oʊ 'kɑːn-

plant, Plant plɑːnt §plænt ‖ plænt **planted**
'plɑːnt ɪd §'plænt-, -əd ‖ 'plænt̬ əd
planting/s 'plɑːnt ɪŋ/z §'plænt- ‖ 'plænt̬ ɪŋ/z
Plantagenet plæn 'tædʒ ən‿ət -'ɪn-, -ɪt, -et ~**s**
s
plantain 'plænt ɪn 'plɑːnt-, -ən ‖ -ᵊn ~**s** z
plantar 'plænt ə -ɑː ‖ 'plænt̬ ᵊr 'plænt ɑːr
plantation plɑːn 'teɪʃ ᵊn plæn- ‖ plæn- ~**s** z
planter, P~ 'plɑːnt ə §'plænt- ‖ 'plænt̬ ᵊr ~**s** s
plantigrade 'plænt ɪ greɪd 'plɑːnt-, §-ə-
‖ 'plænt̬ ə- ~**s** z
Plantin 'plænt ɪn 'plɑːnt-, -ən ‖ plɑːn 'tæn
plantocrac|y ₍ˌ₎plɑːn 'tɒkr əs |i §₍ˌ₎plæn-
‖ plæn 'tɑːk- ~**ies** iz

PLAQUE

61% plæk
39% plɑːk
BrE

plaque plæk plɑːk, pleɪk — Preference poll,
BrE: plæk 61%, plɑːk 39%. Some people
distinguish between a plæk on a wall and
plɑːk or pleɪk on their teeth. In AmE always
plæk. **plaques** plæks plɑːks, pleɪks
plash plæʃ **plashed** plæʃt **plashes** 'plæʃ ɪz -əz
plashing 'plæʃ ɪŋ
plashy 'plæʃ i
-**plasia** 'pleɪz i‿ə ‖ 'pleɪʒ i‿ə 'pleɪʒ ə —
hypoplasia ˌhaɪp əʊ 'pleɪz i‿ə ‖ -oʊ 'pleɪʒ-
-ˈ·ə
-**plasm** ˌplæz əm — **protoplasm**
'prəʊt əʊ ˌplæz əm ‖ 'proʊt̬ ə-
plasma 'plæz mə ~**s** z
plasmapheresis ˌplæz mə 'fer əs ɪs -'fɪər-,
§-əs
plasmid 'plæz mɪd §-məd ~**s** z
plasmo- comb. form
  with stress-neutral suffix ˌplæz məʊ ‖ -mə —
  plasmosome 'plæz məʊ səʊm ‖ -mə soʊm
  with stress-imposing suffix plæz 'mɒ +
  ‖ -'mɑː + — **plasmolysis** plæz 'mɒl əs ɪs
  -ɪs ɪs, §-əs ‖ -'mɑːl-
plasmodi|um plæz 'məʊd i‿|əm ‖ -'moʊd- ~**a**
ə ~**al** əl
Plassey 'plæs i ‖ 'plɑːs-
-**plast** plæst — **chloroplast** 'klɔːr əʊ plæst
‖ -ə- 'kloʊr-
plast|er 'plɑːst |ə §'plæst- ‖ 'plæst |ᵊr ~**ered**
əd ‖ ᵊrd ~**ering** ər‿ɪŋ ~**ers** əz ‖ ᵊrz
  ˌplaster 'cast, '·· ·; ˌplaster of 'Paris
plasterboard 'plɑːst ə bɔːd §'plæst-
‖ 'plæst ᵊr bɔːrd -boʊrd
plasterer 'plɑːst ər‿ə §'plæst- ‖ 'plæst ᵊr ər ~**s**
z
plastic 'plæst ɪk 'plɑːst- — Preference poll,
BrE: 'plæst- 91% (English southerners 94%),
'plɑːst- 9% (English southerners 6%). In AmE
always 'plæst-. ~**s** s See chart on p. 618.

PLASTIC

91% | ■ 'plæst-
9% | ■ 'plɑːst-

BrE

ˌplastic 'art; ˌplastic 'bullet; ˌplastic ex'plosive; ˌplastic 'surgeon; ˌplastic 'surgery

-plastic 'plæst ɪk — **protoplastic**
ˌprəʊt əʊ 'plast ɪk ◄ ‖ ˌproʊt̬ ə-

plasticine, P~ *tdmk* 'plæst ə siːn ‖ 'plɑːst-, -ɪ-

plasticis... —*see* **plasticiz...**

plasticity plæ 'stɪs ət i plɑː-, -ɪt- ‖ -ət̬ i

plasticization ˌplæst ɪs aɪ 'zeɪʃ ᵊn ˌ-əs-, -ɪ'-- ‖ -əs ə-

plasticiz|e 'plæst ɪ saɪz -ə- ~ed d ~er/s ə/z ‖ ᵊr/z ~es ɪz əz ~ing ɪŋ

plastid 'plæst ɪd §-əd ~s z

plastron 'plæs trən ~s z

-plasty ˌplæst i — **rhinoplasty** 'raɪn əʊ ˌplæst i ‖ -oʊ-

plat plæt **plats** plæts **platted** 'plæt ɪd -əd ‖ 'plæt̬ əd **platting** 'plæt ɪŋ ‖ 'plæt̬ ɪŋ

Plata 'plɑːt ə ‖ 'plɑːt̬ ə —*Sp* ['pla ta]

Plataea plə 'tiː ə plæ-

plat du jour ˌplɑː duː 'ʒʊə -djuː-, -də- ‖ -də 'ʒʊᵊr —*Fr* [pla dy ʒuːʁ] **plats du jour** *same pronunciation*

plate, Plate pleɪt **plated** 'pleɪt ɪd -əd ‖ 'pleɪt̬ əd **plates** pleɪts **plating** 'pleɪt ɪŋ ‖ 'pleɪt̬ ɪŋ
ˌplate 'glass◄; 'plate rack; ˌplate tec'tonics

plateau 'plæt əʊ plæ 'təʊ, plə- ‖ plæ 'toʊ ~s, ~x z

plateful 'pleɪt fʊl ~s z

plate-glass ˌpleɪt 'glɑːs ◄ §-'glæs ‖ -'glæs ◄ ˌplate-glass 'window

platelayer 'pleɪt ˌleɪ ə ‖ -ᵊr ~s z

platelet 'pleɪt lət -lɪt ~s s

platen 'plæt ᵊn ~s z

plater, P~ 'pleɪt ə ‖ 'pleɪt̬ ᵊr ~s z

platform 'plæt fɔːm ‖ -fɔːrm ~s z

Plath plæθ

Platignum *tdmk* plæ 'tɪg nəm plə-

platino- *comb. form*
with stress-neutral suffix |plæt ɪn əʊ -ən- ‖ -ᵊn oʊ — **platinocyanic** ˌplæt ɪn əʊ saɪ 'æn ɪk ◄ ˌ-ən- ‖ ˌ-ən oʊ-

platinum 'plæt ɪn əm -ᵊn ‖ -ᵊn ̩əm ˌplatinum 'blonde

platitude 'plæt ɪ tjuːd -ə-, →-tʃuːd ‖ 'plæt̬ ə tuːd -tjuːd ~s z

platitudinis|e, platitudiniz|e ˌplæt ɪ 'tjuːd ɪ naɪz ˌ-ə-, →-'tʃuːd-, -ᵊn aɪz ‖ ˌplæt̬ ə 'tuːd ᵊn aɪz -'tjuːd- ~ed d ~es ɪz əz ~ing ɪŋ

platitudinous ˌplæt ɪ 'tjuːd ɪn əs ◄ ˌ-ə-, →-'tʃuːd-, -ən ̩əs ‖ ˌplæt̬ ə 'tuːd ᵊn̩əs ◄ ~ly li

Plato 'pleɪt əʊ ‖ 'pleɪt̬ oʊ

platonic, P~ plə 'tɒn ɪk ‖ -'tɑːn ɪk ~ally ᵊl ̩i

Platonism 'pleɪt ə ˌnɪz əm -ᵊn ˌɪz- ‖ 'pleɪt̬ ᵊn ˌɪz əm

Platonist 'pleɪt ᵊn ɪst §-əst ‖ -ᵊn- ~s s

platoon plə 'tuːn ~s z

Platt plæt

Plattdeutsch 'plæt dɔɪtʃ ‖ 'plɑːt- —*Ger* ['plat dɔytʃ]

Platte plæt

platter 'plæt ə ‖ 'plæt̬ ᵊr ~s z

Platting 'plæt ɪŋ ‖ 'plæt̬ ɪŋ

plat|y *'kind of fish'* 'plæt |i ‖ 'plæt̬ |i ~ies, ~ys iz

platyhelminth ˌplæt ɪ 'helm ɪntθ ‖ ˌplæt̬ i- ~s s

platykurtic ˌplæt ɪ 'kɜːt ɪk ◄ ‖ ˌplæt̬ i 'kɜːt̬ ɪk ◄

platypus 'plæt ɪp əs -əp-; -ɪ pʊs ‖ 'plæt̬- ~es ɪz əz

platyrrhine 'plæt ɪ raɪn -ə- ‖ 'plæt̬-

plaudit 'plɔːd ɪt §-ət ‖ 'plɑːd- ~s s

plausibility ˌplɔːz ə 'bɪl ət i ˌ-ɪ-, -ɪt i ‖ -ət̬ i ˌplɑːz-

plausib|le 'plɔːz əb |ᵊl -ɪb- ‖ 'plɑːz- ~leness ᵊl nəs -nɪs ~ly li

Plautus 'plɔːt əs ‖ 'plɔːt̬ əs 'plɑːt̬-

Plaxtol 'plækst ᵊl

play pleɪ **played** pleɪd **playing** 'pleɪ ɪŋ **plays** pleɪz
'play dough; 'playing card; 'playing field

playa *'player'* 'pleɪ ə ~s z

playa *'beach'* 'plaɪ ̩ə —*Sp* ['pla ja] ~s z

playable 'pleɪ əb ᵊl

play-act 'pleɪ ækt ~ed ɪd əd ~ing ɪŋ ~or/s ə/z ‖ ᵊr/z ~s s

play-action 'pleɪ ˌæk ʃᵊn

playback 'pleɪ bæk ~s s

playbill 'pleɪ bɪl ~s z

playbook 'pleɪ bʊk §-buːk ~s s

playboy 'pleɪ bɔɪ ~s z

play-by-play ˌpleɪ baɪ 'pleɪ ◄

Play-Doh *tdmk* 'pleɪ dəʊ ‖ -doʊ

played-out ˌpleɪd 'aʊt ◄

player, P~ 'pleɪ ə ‖ -ᵊr ~s, ~'s z ˌplayer pi'ano

Playfair 'pleɪ feə ‖ -fer -fær

playfellow 'pleɪ ˌfel əʊ ‖ -oʊ ~s z

Playford 'pleɪ fəd ‖ -fᵊrd

playful 'pleɪf ᵊl 'pleɪ fʊl ~ly ̩i ~ness nəs nɪs

playgoer 'pleɪ ˌgəʊ ə ‖ -ˌgoʊ ᵊr ~s z

playground 'pleɪ graʊnd ~s z

playgroup 'pleɪ gruːp ~s s

play|house 'pleɪ |haʊs ~houses haʊz ɪz -əz

playlet 'pleɪ lət -lɪt ~s s

playlist 'pleɪ lɪst ~s s

playmaker 'pleɪ ˌmeɪk ə ‖ -ᵊr ~s z

playmate 'pleɪ meɪt ~s s

play-off 'pleɪ ɒf -ɔːf ‖ -ɔːf -ɑːf ~s s

playpen 'pleɪ pen ~s z

playroom 'pleɪ ruːm -rʊm ~s z

playschool 'pleɪ skuːl ~s z
PlayStation *tdmk* 'pleɪ ˌsteɪʃ ᵊn
playsuit 'pleɪ suːt -sjuːt ~s s
Playtex *tdmk* 'pleɪ teks
plaything 'pleɪ θɪŋ ~s z
playtime 'pleɪ taɪm ~s z
playwright 'pleɪ raɪt ~s s
play-writing 'pleɪ ˌraɪt ɪŋ ‖ -ˌraɪt-
plaza, Plaza 'plɑːz ə ‖ 'plæz- —*Sp* ['pla θa,
-sa] ~s z
plc ˌpiː el 'siː
plea pliː **pleas** pliːz (= *please*)
'plea ˌbargaining
pleach pliːtʃ **pleached** pliːtʃt **pleaches**
'pliːtʃ ɪz -əz **pleaching** 'pliːtʃ ɪŋ
plead pliːd **pleaded** 'pliːd ɪd -əd **pleading**
'pliːd ɪŋ **pleads** pliːdz **pled** pled
pleader 'pliːd ə ‖ -ᵊr ~s z
pleading 'pliːd ɪŋ ~ly li ~s z
pleasanc|e, P~ 'plez ᵊn¹s ~es ɪz əz
pleas|ant 'plez| ᵊnt ~anter ᵊnt ə ‖ ᵊnt̬ ᵊr
~antest ᵊnt ɪst -əst ‖ ᵊnt̬ əst
pleasant|ly 'plez ᵊnt| li ~ness nəs nɪs
pleasantr|y 'plez ᵊntr |i ~ies iz
please pliːz **pleased** pliːzd **pleases** 'pliːz ɪz
-əz **pleasing** 'pliːz ɪŋ
Pleasence 'plez ᵊn¹s
pleaser 'pliːz ə ‖ -ᵊr ~s z
pleasing 'pliːz ɪŋ ~ly li
pleasurab|le 'pleʒ ər əb |ᵊl ~leness ᵊl nəs -nɪs
~ly li
pleas|ure 'pleʒ |ə ‖ -|ᵊr 'pleɪʒ- ~ured əd ‖ ᵊrd
~ures əz ‖ ᵊrz ~uring ər ɪŋ
'pleasure boat; 'pleasure trip
pleat pliːt **pleated** 'pliːt ɪd -əd ‖ 'pliːt̬ əd
pleating 'pliːt ɪŋ ‖ 'pliːt̬ ɪŋ **pleats** pliːts
pleather 'pleð ə ‖ -ᵊr
pleb pleb **plebs** plebz
plebby 'pleb i
plebe pliːb **plebes** pliːbz
plebeian plə 'biː ən plɪ- ~s z
plebiscite 'pleb ɪ saɪt -ə-; -ɪs ɪt, -əs-, -§ət ~s s
plebs plebz
plec|tron 'plek |trən ‖ -|traːn ~tra trə
~trum/s trəm/z
pled pled
pledge pledʒ **pledged** pledʒd **pledges**
'pledʒ ɪz -əz **pledging** 'pledʒ ɪŋ
pledgee ˌpledʒ 'iː ~s z
pledger, P~ 'pledʒ ə ‖ -ᵊr ~s z
pledget 'pledʒ ɪt §-ət ~s s
pledgor ˌpledʒ 'ɔː ‖ -'ɔːr ~s z
-plegia 'pliːdʒ ə 'pliːdʒ i ə — **paraplegia**
ˌpær ə 'pliːdʒ ə -'·i ə ‖ ˌper-
-plegic 'pliːdʒ ɪk — **quadriplegic**
ˌkwɒdr ɪ 'pliːdʒ ɪk ◂ -ə- ‖ ˌkwɑːdr-
Pleiad, p~ 'plaɪ əd ‖ 'pliː əd 'pleɪ-, -æd ~s z
—*Fr* Pléiade [ple jad]
Pleiades 'plaɪ ə diːz ‖ 'pliː- 'pleɪ-
plein-air ˌpleɪn 'eə ◂ ‖ -'eᵊr ◂ -'æᵊr —*Fr*
[plɛ nɛːʁ]
pleistocene, P~ 'plaɪst əʊ siːn ‖ -ə-
plenar|y 'pliːn ər |i 'plen- ~ies iz ~ily əl i ɪ li

plenipotentiar|y ˌplen ɪ pə 'tenᵗʃ ər |i ◂ ˌ·ə-,
-pəʊ'·-, -'·i ər |i ‖ -'tenᵗʃ i er |i ~ies iz
plenitude 'plen ɪ tjuːd -ə-, →-tʃuːd ‖ -ə tuːd
-tjuːd ~s z
plenteous 'plent i əs ‖ 'plent̬- ~ly li ~ness
nəs nɪs
plentiful 'plent ɪf ᵊl -əf-, -ʊl ‖ 'plent̬- ~ly i
~ness nəs nɪs
plenty 'plent i ‖ 'plent̬ i —*A casual-speech
form* 'plen i *is also heard in BrE*
plenum 'pliːn əm 'plen-, 'pleɪn- ~s z
pleonasm 'pliː ə næz əm ~s z
pleonastic ˌpliː ə 'næst ɪk ◂ ~ally ᵊl i
plesiosaur 'pliːs i ə sɔː 'pliːz- ‖ 'pliːz i ə sɔːr
~s z
plesiosaur|us ˌpliːs i ə 'sɔːr |əs ‖ ˌpliːz- ~i aɪ
Plessey 'ples i
plethora 'pleθ ər ə ple 'θɔːr ə, plə-, plɪ-
plethoric ple 'θɒr ɪk plə-, plɪ- ‖ -'θɔːr ɪk -'θɑːr-
~ally ᵊl i
plethysmograph plə 'θɪz məʊ grɑːf plɪ-, ple-,
-'θɪs-, -græf ‖ -ə græf ~s s
pleur|a 'plʊər |ə 'plɔːr- ‖ 'plʊr |ə ~ae iː ~al əl
(= *plural*)
pleurisy 'plʊər əs i 'plɔːr-, -ɪs- ‖ 'plʊr-
pleuritic plʊᵊ 'rɪt ɪk ‖ -'rɪt̬ ɪk
pleuropneumonia ˌplʊər əʊ nju 'məʊn i ə
§nu- ‖ ˌplʊr oʊ nu 'moʊn- nju- ~like laɪk
Plexiglas, p~, plexiglass *tdmk* 'pleks i glɑːs
§-glæs ‖ -glæs
plexor 'pleks ə ‖ -ᵊr ~s z
plexus 'pleks əs ~es ɪz əz
Pleydell (i) 'pled ᵊl, (ii) pleɪ 'del
pliability ˌplaɪ ə 'bɪl ət i -ɪt i ‖ -ət̬ i
pliab|le 'plaɪ əb |ᵊl ~leness ᵊl nəs -nɪs ~ly li
pliancy 'plaɪ ən¹s i
pliant 'plaɪ ənt ~ly li ~ness nəs nɪs
plica 'plaɪk ə **plicae** 'plaɪs iː 'plaɪk-
plié 'pliː eɪ ‖ pliː 'eɪ —*Fr* [pli e] ~s z
plie... —*see* **ply**
pliers 'plaɪ əz ‖ 'plaɪ ᵊrz
plight plaɪt **plighted** 'plaɪt ɪd -əd ‖ 'plaɪt̬ əd
plighting 'plaɪt ɪŋ ‖ 'plaɪt̬ ɪŋ **plights** plaɪts
plimsole, plimsoll, P~ 'plɪmᵖs ᵊl 'plɪm səʊl
‖ -soʊl ~s z
'Plimsoll line, 'Plimsoll mark
pling plɪŋ **plings** plɪŋz
plink plɪŋk **plinked** plɪŋkt **plinking** 'plɪŋk ɪŋ
plinks plɪŋks
Plinlimmon plɪn 'lɪm ən
plinth plɪn¹θ **plinths** plɪn¹θs
Pliny 'plɪn i
pliocene, P~ 'plaɪ əʊ siːn ‖ -ə-
plip plɪp
plisse, plissé 'pliːs eɪ 'plɪs- ‖ plɪ 'seɪ
PLO ˌpiː el 'əʊ ‖ -'oʊ
plod plɒd ‖ plɑːd **plodded** 'plɒd ɪd -əd
‖ 'plɑːd əd **plodding** 'plɒd ɪŋ ‖ 'plɑːd ɪŋ
plods plɒdz ‖ plɑːdz
plodder 'plɒd ə ‖ 'plɑːd ᵊr ~s z
Ploesti, Ploiesti plɔɪ 'eʃt i —*Romanian*
Ploieşti [plo 'jeʃtʲ]

P

Plomer *family name (i)* 'pləʊm ə ‖ 'plʊom ᵊr, *(ii)* 'pluːm ə ‖ -ᵊr —*The writer William P~ inherited the pronunciation (i), but chose to change it to (ii).*
Plomley 'plʌm li
plonk plɒŋk ‖ plaːŋk **plonked** plɒŋkt
　plonking/ly 'plɒŋk ɪŋ /li ‖ 'plaːŋk ɪŋ /li
　plonks plɒŋks ‖ plaːŋks
plonker 'plɒŋk ə ‖ 'plaːŋk ᵊr ~**s** z
plop plɒp ‖ plaːp **plopped** plɒpt ‖ plaːpt
　plopping 'plɒp ɪŋ ‖ 'plaːp ɪŋ **plops** plɒps
　‖ plaːps
plosion 'pləʊʒ ᵊn ‖ 'plʊoʒ ᵊn ~**s** z
plosive 'pləʊs ɪv 'pləʊz- ‖ 'plʊos- 'plʊoz- ~**s** z
plot plɒt ‖ plaːt **plots** plɒts ‖ plaːts **plotted**
　'plɒt ɪd -əd ‖ 'plaːt̬ əd **plotting** 'plɒt ɪŋ
　‖ 'plaːt̬ ɪŋ
Plotinus pləʊ 'taɪn əs plɒ- ‖ plʊo-
plotless 'plɒt ləs -lɪs ‖ 'plaːt-
plotter 'plɒt ə ‖ 'plaːt̬ ᵊr ~**s** z
plough, Plough plaʊ **ploughed** plaʊd
　ploughing 'plaʊ ɪŋ **ploughs** plaʊz
ploughboy 'plaʊ bɔɪ ~**s** z
ploughland 'plaʊ lænd
plough|man 'plaʊ |mən ~**men** mən men
　ˌploughman's 'lunch
ploughshare 'plaʊ ʃeə ‖ -ʃer -ʃær ~**s** z
Plouviez 'pluːv i eɪ
Plovdiv 'plɒv dɪv ‖ 'plaːv- 'plʊov- —*Bulgarian*
　['plov dif]
plover 'plʌv ə ‖ -ᵊr 'plʊov- ~**s** z
plow, Plow plaʊ **plowed** plaʊd **plowing**
　'plaʊ ɪŋ **plows** plaʊz
plowboy 'plaʊ bɔɪ ~**s** z
Plowden 'plaʊd ᵊn
plowland 'plaʊ lænd
plow|man 'plaʊ |mən ~**men** mən men
Plowright 'plaʊ raɪt
plowshare 'plaʊ ʃeə ‖ -ʃer -ʃær ~**s** z
ploy plɔɪ **ploys** plɔɪz
pluck plʌk **plucked** plʌkt **plucking** 'plʌk ɪŋ
　plucks plʌks
pluck|y 'plʌk |i ~**ier** i ə ‖ i ᵊr ~**iest** i ɪst i əst
　~**ily** ɪ li əl i ~**iness** i nəs i nɪs
plug plʌg **plugged** plʌgd **plugging** 'plʌg ɪŋ
　plugs plʌgz
plug-and-play ˌplʌg ən 'pleɪ ◂ →-əm-
plug-compatible ˌplʌg kəm 'pæt əb ᵊl ◂
　§ˌ-kɒm-, -ɪb ᵊl ‖ -'pæt̬- ~**s** z
plughole 'plʌg həʊl →-hɒʊl ‖ -hoʊl ~**s** z
plug-in 'plʌg ɪn ~**s** z
plug-ug|ly 'plʌg ˌʌg |li ~**lies** liz
plum plʌm **plums** plʌmz
　ˌplum 'cake; ˌplum 'duff; ˌplum 'pudding;
　'plum tree
plumag|e 'pluːm ɪdʒ ~**es** ɪz əz
plumb plʌm (= *plum*) **plumbed** plʌmd
　plumbing 'plʌm ɪŋ **plumbs** plʌmz
　'plumb line
plumbago plʌm 'beɪg əʊ ‖ -oʊ ~**s** z
plumber 'plʌm ə ‖ -ᵊr ~**s** z
　ˌplumber's 'friend, ˌplumber's 'helper
plumbic 'plʌm bɪk

plumbing 'plʌm ɪŋ
plumbous 'plʌm bəs
plumbum 'plʌm bəm 'plʊm-
plume pluːm **plumed** pluːmd **plumes** pluːmz
　pluming 'pluːm ɪŋ
Plummer 'plʌm ə ‖ -ᵊr
plumm|et 'plʌm |ɪt §-ət ‖ -|ət ~**eted** ɪt ɪd §ət-,
　-əd ‖ ət̬ əd ~**eting** ɪt ɪŋ §ət- ‖ ət̬ ɪŋ ~**ets** ɪts
　§əts ‖ əts
plumm|y 'plʌm |i ~**ier** i ə ‖ i ᵊr ~**iest** i ɪst i əst
　~**iness** i nəs i nɪs
plumose 'pluːm əʊs pluː 'məʊs ‖ 'pluːm oʊs
　pluː 'moʊs
plump plʌmp **plumped** plʌmpt **plumper**
　'plʌmp ə ‖ -ᵊr **plumpest** 'plʌmp ɪst -əst
　plumping 'plʌmp ɪŋ **plumply** 'plʌmp li
　plumpness 'plʌmp nəs -nɪs **plumps** plʌmps
Plumpton 'plʌmpt ən
Plumptre, Plumtre 'plʌmp triː
Plumstead 'plʌmᵖst ɪd -ed
plumule 'pluːm juːl ~**s** z
plunder 'plʌnd ə ‖ -ᵊr ~**ed** d **plundering**
　'plʌnd ᵊr ɪŋ ~**s** z
plunderer 'plʌnd ᵊr ə ‖ -ər ~**s** z
plunderous 'plʌnd ər əs
plunge plʌndʒ **plunged** plʌndʒd **plunges**
　'plʌndʒ ɪz -əz **plunging** 'plʌndʒ ɪŋ
plunger 'plʌndʒ ə ‖ -ᵊr ~**s** z
plunk plʌŋk **plunked** plʌŋkt **plunking**
　'plʌŋk ɪŋ **plunks** plʌŋks
Plunket, Plunkett 'plʌŋk ɪt §-ət
pluperfect ˌpluː 'pɜːf ɪkt ◂ -ekt, §-əkt ‖ -'pɜːf-
　'ˌ·ˌ·· ~**s** s
plural 'plʊər əl 'plɔːr- ‖ 'plʊr əl ~**s** z
pluralis... —*see* **pluraliz...**
pluralism 'plʊər ə ˌlɪz əm 'plɔːr-, -ᵊl ˌɪz-
　‖ 'plʊr-
pluralist 'plʊər əl ɪst 'plɔːr-, §-əst ‖ 'plʊr- ~**s** s
pluralistic ˌplʊər ə 'lɪst ɪk ◂ ˌplɔːr- ‖ ˌplʊr-
　~**ally** ᵊl i
pluralit|y plʊᵊ 'ræl ət |i ˌplʊə-, ˌplɔː-, -ɪt-
　‖ -ət̬ |i ~**ies** iz
pluralization ˌplʊər əl aɪ 'zeɪʃ ᵊn ˌplɔːr-, -ɪ'--
　‖ ˌplʊr əl ə-
pluraliz|e 'plʊər ə laɪz 'plɔːr- ‖ 'plʊr- ~**ed** d
　~**es** ɪz əz ~**ing** ɪŋ
pluri- |plʊər i |plɔːr i ‖ |plʊr i — **plurisyllable**
　ˌplʊər i 'sɪl əb ᵊl ˌplɔːr- ‖ ˌplʊr-
plus plʌs **pluses, plusses** 'plʌs ɪz -əz
　ˌplus 'fours; 'plus sign
plus ça change ˌpluː sɑː 'ʃɒnʒ ‖ -'ʃɑːnʒ —*Fr*
　[ply sa ʃɑ̃:ʒ]
plush plʌʃ
plush|y 'plʌʃ |i ~**ier** i ə ‖ i ᵊr ~**iest** i ɪst i əst
　~**ily** ɪ li əl i ~**iness** i nəs i nɪs
Plutarch 'pluːt ɑːk ‖ -ɑːrk
Pluto 'pluːt əʊ ‖ 'pluːt̬ oʊ
plutocrac|y pluː 'tɒk rəs |i ‖ -'tɑːk- ~**ies** iz
plutocrat 'pluːt əʊ kræt ‖ 'pluːt̬ ə- ~**s** s
plutocratic ˌpluːt əʊ 'kræt ɪk ◂
　‖ ˌpluːt̬ ə 'kræt̬ ɪk ◂ ~**ally** ᵊl i
pluton 'pluːt ɒn ‖ -ɑːn ~**s** z
Plutonian pluː 'təʊn i ən ‖ -'toʊn-

Plosive releases

1 The English plosives (see ARTICULATION) are p, t, k, b, d, g and the GLOTTAL STOP. In a plosive air is compressed for a moment behind the articulators and prevented from escaping. This stage of a plosive is called the **hold**. The movements leading up to the hold are called the **approach**, and those leading from the hold are called the **release**.

2 With the alveolar plosives t and d, to describe how the sound fits in with the surrounding sounds we sometimes need to consider the SOFT PALATE and also the sides of the tongue, since it may be their movements that constitute the approach or release stage.

3 If n is followed by d, as in **handy** ˈhænd i, the change from the nasal to the plosive is made by movin the SOFT PALATE up (to cut off the air flow through the nose), while the tongue remains in contact with the alveolar ridge. This is **nasal approach**, and usually causes no difficulty to EFL learners.

4 Conversely, if d is followed by n, as in **midnight** ˈmɪd naɪt, the change from the plosive to the nasal is made by moving the soft palate down (to allow air flow through the nose). This is known as **nasal release**, and may be difficult for some learners.

It would not sound right to release the d in **midnight** by moving the tongue tip down (**oral release**) and then moving it back up for the n. Similarly in **submit** səb ˈmɪt the lips do not move as we go from b to m – the b is released nasally.

The same applies if one word ends in a plosive and the next begins with a nasal, as in **did nothing** ˌdɪd ˈnʌθɪŋ.

5 In a word such as **suddenly**, shown in this dictionary as ˈsʌd ᵊn li, the usual pronunciation has no ə, which means that the n immediately follows d, so that the d has nasal release: ˈsʌd n li. (In the less usual pronunciation ˈsʌd ən li the d would have ordinary oral release.)

6 Where t is followed by n, as in **fitness** ˈfɪt nəs, **button** ˈbʌt ᵊn, **quite nice** ˌkwaɪt ˈnaɪs, the t may be pronounced as an alveolar plosive with nasal release. Alternatively, it may be pronounced as a glottal stop.

7 If d is followed by l, as in **sadly** ˈsæd li, **good luck** ˌɡʊd ˈlʌk, **middle** ˈmɪd l, the change from the plosive to the lateral (see LIQUIDS) is made by moving the side rims of the tongue down while keeping the tongue tip in contact with the alveolar ridge. This is known as **lateral release**.

Plosive releases ▶

Plosive releases continued

8 If t is followed by l, as in **brightly** ˈbraɪt li, **quite lucky** ˌkwaɪt ˈlʌk i, the t may be pronounced as an alveolar plosive with lateral release, or as a glottal stop. But where the l is syllabic, as in the usual pronunciation of **little** ˈlɪt l ‖ ˈlɪt l̩, it is more usual to have a laterally released alveolar t.

9 If one plosive is immediately followed by another, as in **acting** ˈækt ɪŋ, **rubbed** ˈrʌbd, the first plosive in most styles of English has **no audible release**, because its release is **masked** by the articulation of the second plosive.

10 In the case of a geminate plosive (see DOUBLE CONSONANT SOUNDS) as in **midday** ˌmɪd ˈdeɪ, the first d in this word has no release and the second d has no approach. Together they make a single long d:.

---

plutonic pluː ˈtɒn ɪk ‖ -ˈtɑːn ɪk
plutonium pluː ˈtəʊn i‿əm ‖ -ˈtoʊn-
pluvial ˈpluːv i‿əl ~s z
pluviometer ˌpluːv i ˈɒm ɪt ə -ət ə
  ‖ -ˈɑːm ət ᵊr ~s z
pluvious ˈpluːv i‿əs
ply plaɪ **plied** plaɪd **plies** plaɪz **plying** ˈplaɪ ɪŋ
Plymouth ˈplɪm əθ
  ˌPlymouth ˈBrethren; ˌPlymouth ˈRock
Plynlimon plɪn ˈlɪm ən —*Welsh* Pumlimon
  [pɪm ˈlɪm ɔn]
plywood ˈplaɪ wʊd ~s z
PM, pm ˌpiː ˈem ◂
PMT ˌpiː em ˈtiː
p-n ˌpiː ˈen
pneumatic nju ˈmæt ɪk §nu- ‖ nu ˈmæt ɪk
  nju-, nə- ~ally ᵊl‿i ~s s
  pneuˌmatic ˈdrill
pneumatophore ˈnjuːm ət əʊ fɔː §ˈnuːm-;
  nju ˈmæt-, §nu- ‖ nu ˈmæt ə fɔːr nju-, nə-,
  -foʊr; ˈnuːm ət-,ˈnjuːm- ~s z
pneumo- *comb. form*
  with stress-neutral suffix ǀnjuːm əʊ §ǀnuːm-
  ‖ ǀnuːm ə ǀnjuːm- — **pneumogastric**
  ˌnjuːm əʊ ˈgæs trɪk ◂ §ˌnuːm- ‖ ˌnuːm ə-
  ˌnjuːm-
  with stress-imposing suffix nju ˈmɒ+
  ‖ nu ˈmɑː+ nju- — **pneumography**
  nju ˈmɒɡ rəf i ‖ nu ˈmɑːɡ- nju-
pneumococ|cus ˌnjuːm əʊ ˈkɒk| əs §ˌnuːm-
  ‖ ˌnuːm ə ˈkɑːk| əs ~ci aɪ saɪ, iː, siː
pneumoconiosis ˌnjuːm əʊ ˌkəʊn i ˈəʊs ɪs
  §ˌnuːm-, §-əs ‖ ˌnuːm oʊ ˌkoʊn i ˈoʊs əs
  ˌnjuːm-
pneumocystis ˌnjuːm əʊ ˈsɪst ɪs §-əs
  ‖ ˌnuːm ə- ˌnjuːm-
  ˌpneumoˌcystis caˈrinii kə ˈraɪn i aɪ kæ-,
  -ˈriːn-
pneumonia nju ˈməʊn i‿ə §nu- ‖ nu ˈmoʊn-
  nju-, nə-
pneumonic nju ˈmɒn ɪk §nu- ‖ nu ˈmɑːn ɪk
  nju-, nə-

pneumothorax ˌnjuːm əʊ ˈθɔːr æks §ˌnuːm-
  ‖ ˌnuːm ə- -ˈθoʊr-
PNG ˌpiː en ˈdʒiː
Pnom Penh ˌpnɒm ˈpen ˌnɒm-, pə ˌnɒm ˈpen
  ‖ ˌpnɑːm- ˌnɑːm —*Khmer* [pʰnɔm ˈpiɲ]
Pnyx pnɪks nɪks
po pəʊ ‖ poʊ
Po *'polonium'* ˌpiː ˈəʊ ‖ -ˈoʊ
Po *name of river, name of Teletubby* pəʊ ‖ poʊ
  —*It* [pɔ]
PO ˌpiː ˈəʊ ◂ ‖ -ˈoʊ ◂ ~s, ~'s z
poach pəʊtʃ ‖ poʊtʃ **poached** pəʊtʃt ‖ poʊtʃt
  poaches ˈpəʊtʃ ɪz -əz ‖ ˈpoʊtʃ əz **poaching**
  ˈpəʊtʃ ɪŋ ‖ ˈpoʊtʃ ɪŋ
poacher ˈpəʊtʃ ə ‖ ˈpoʊtʃ ᵊr ~s z
Pobjoy ˈpɒb dʒɔɪ ‖ ˈpɑːb-
Pocahontas ˌpɒk ə ˈhɒnt əs -æs
  ‖ ˌpoʊk ə ˈhɑːnt əs
pochard ˈpəʊtʃ əd ˈpɒtʃ- ‖ ˈpoʊtʃ ᵊrd ~s z
pochette pɒ ˈʃet poʊ- ~s s
pock pɒk ‖ pɑːk **pocked** pɒkt ‖ pɑːkt
pock|et ˈpɒk |ɪt §-ət ‖ ˈpɑːk |ət ~eted ɪt ɪd
  §ət-, -əd ‖ ət əd ~eting ɪt ɪŋ §ət- ‖ ət ɪŋ ~ets
  ɪts §əts ‖ əts
  ˈpocket ˌmoney
pocketable ˈpɒk ɪt əb ᵊl §ˈ-ət- ‖ ˈpɑːk ət-
pocketbook ˈpɒk ɪt bʊk §-ət-, §-buːk ‖ ˈpɑːk-
  ~s s
pocketful ˈpɒk ɪt fʊl §-ət- ‖ ˈpɑːk- ~s z
pocket-handker|chief ˌpɒk ɪt ˈhæŋk ə |tʃɪf
  §ˌ-ət-, -tʃəf, -tʃiːf ‖ ˌpɑːk ət ˈhæŋk ᵊr- ~chiefs
  tʃɪfs tʃəfs, tʃiːfs, tʃiːvz
pocket|knife ˈpɒk ɪt |naɪf §-ət- ‖ ˈpɑːk-
  ~knives naɪvz
pocket-sized ˈpɒk ɪt saɪzd -ət- ‖ ˈpɑːk-
Pocklington ˈpɒk lɪŋ tən ‖ ˈpɑːk-
pockmark ˈpɒk mɑːk ‖ ˈpɑːk mɑːrk ~ed t
  ~ing ɪŋ ~s s
poco ˈpəʊk əʊ ‖ ˈpoʊk oʊ —*It* [ˈpɔː ko]
Pocock ˈpəʊ kɒk ‖ ˈpoʊ kɑːk
pococurante ˌpəʊk əʊ kjuᵊ ˈrænt i
  ‖ ˌpoʊk oʊ ku ˈrænt i -ku'-, -ˈrɑːnt̬- ~s z

Pocono 'pəʊk ə nəʊ ‖ 'poʊk ə noʊ **~s** z
pod pɒd ‖ pɑːd **podded** 'pɒd ɪd -əd ‖ 'pɑːd əd
  podding 'pɒd ɪŋ ‖ 'pɑːd ɪŋ **pods** pɒdz
  ‖ pɑːdz
-pod pɒd ‖ pɑːd — **arthropod** 'ɑːθ rəʊ pɒd
  ‖ 'ɑːrθ rə pɑːd
podagra pɒ 'dæg rə pəʊ-, 'pɒd əg- ‖ pə-
  'pɑːd əg-
podcast 'pɒd kɑːst →ˈpɒg-, §-kæst
  ‖ 'pɑːd kæst **~ing** ɪŋ **~s** s
podd|y 'pɒd |i ‖ 'pɑːd |i **~ies** iz
Podge, podge pɒdʒ ‖ pɑːdʒ
Podgorica 'pɒd gɒr ɪts ə ‖ 'pɑːd gɔːr-
  —Serbian ['pod go ri tsa]
podg|y 'pɒdʒ |i ‖ 'pɑːdʒ |i **~ier** i ə ‖ i ˌʳr **~iest**
  i ˌɪst i ˌəst **~ily** ɪ li əl i **~iness** i nəs i nɪs
Podhoretz pɒd 'hɒr ets ‖ pɑːd 'hɔːr- -'hɑːr-
podiatric ˌpəʊd i 'ætr ɪk ◂ -pɒd- ‖ ˌpoʊd-
podiatr|ist pəʊ 'daɪ ˌətr| ɪst §-əst ‖ pə- poʊ-
  ~ists ɪsts §əsts **~y** i
podi|um 'pəʊd i |əm ‖ 'poʊd- **~a** ə **~ums** əmz
Podmore 'pɒd mɔː ‖ 'pɑːd mɔːr -moʊr
-podous stress-imposing pəd əs —
  gastropodous gæ 'strɒp əd əs ‖ -'strɑːp-
podsol 'pɒd sɒl ‖ 'pɑːd sɑːl -sɔːl **~s** z
Podunk 'pəʊ dʌŋk ‖ 'poʊ-
podzol 'pɒd zɒl ‖ 'pɑːd zɑːl -zɔːl **~s** z
Poe pəʊ ‖ poʊ

POEM

68% / 32%

■ 2 syllables
■ 1 syllable

AmE

poem 'pəʊ ɪm -əm, -em; pəʊm ‖ 'poʊ əm
  poʊm **~s** z — Preference poll, AmE: two
  syllables 68%, one syllable 32%.
poes|y 'pəʊ əz |i -ɪz-, -ez- ‖ 'poʊ- -əs- **~ies** iz
poet 'pəʊ ɪt -ət, -et ‖ 'poʊ ət **~s** s
  ˌpoet 'laureate
poetaster ˌpəʊ ɪ 'tæst ə -ə-, -e-, -'teɪst-, 'ˈ· · ·
  ‖ 'poʊ ə tæst ˌʳr **~s** z
poetess ˌpəʊ ɪ 'tes -ə-, -e-; 'pəʊ ɪt ɪs, -ət-, -et-,
  -əs, -es ‖ 'poʊ əţ əs **~es** ɪz əz
poetic pəʊ 'et ɪk ‖ poʊ 'eţ ɪk **~al** ˀl **~ally** ˀl i
  ~s s
  po,etic 'justice; po,etic 'licence
poetry 'pəʊ ətr i -ɪtr- ‖ 'poʊ-
po-faced ˌpəʊ 'feɪst ◂ ·· ‖ ˌpoʊ-
pogey, pogie 'pəʊg i ‖ 'poʊg i **~s** z
pogge pɒg ‖ pɑːg **pogges** pɒgz ‖ pɑːgz
Poggenpohl tdmk 'pɒg ən pəʊl →-əm-, →-ŋ-,
  →-pɒʊl ‖ 'pɑːg ən poʊl —Ger ['pɔ gn poːl]
pogo 'pəʊg əʊ ‖ 'poʊg oʊ
  'pogo stick
pogrom 'pɒg rəm -rɒm ‖ 'poʊg rəm pə 'grɑːm,
  -'grʌm **~s** z
Pogue pəʊg ‖ poʊg **Pogues** pəʊgz ‖ poʊgz
pog|y 'pəʊg |i ‖ 'poʊg |i **~ies** iz

-poiesis pɔɪ 'iːs ɪs §-əs — **haemopoiesis**
  ˌhiːm əʊ pɔɪ 'iːs ɪs §-əs ‖ -ˌə-
-poietic pɔɪ 'et ɪk ‖ pɔɪ 'eţ ɪk
  — **haemopoietic** ˌhiːm əʊ pɔɪ 'et ɪk ◂
  ‖ -ə pɔɪ 'eţ ɪk ◂
poignancy 'pɔɪn jən¦s i -ən¦s-
poignant 'pɔɪn jənt -ənt **~ly** li
poikilotherm 'pɔɪk ɪl əʊ θɜːm '·əl-; pɔɪ 'kɪl-
  ‖ -ə θɜːm -oʊ- **~s** z
poikilothermic ˌpɔɪk ɪl əʊ 'θɜːm ɪk ◂ ˌ·əl-
  ‖ -ə 'θɜːm ɪk ◂ -oʊ-
Poincaré 'pwæŋ kæ reɪ ˌ· ·ˈ· ‖ ˌpwɑːŋ kɑː 'reɪ
  —Fr [pwɛ̃ ka ʁe]
poinciana ˌpɔɪn¦s i 'ɑːn ə -'æn- ‖ -'æn ə **~s** z
Poindexter 'pɔɪn ˌdekst ə ‖ -ˀr
poinsettia pɔɪn 'set i ə pɔɪnt- ‖ -'seţ i ə
  △-'seţ ə **~s** z
point pɔɪnt **pointed** 'pɔɪnt ɪd -əd ‖ 'pɔɪnţəd
  pointing 'pɔɪnt ɪŋ ‖ 'pɔɪnţ ɪŋ **points** pɔɪnts
  'point ˌduty; ˌpoint of 'order; ˌpoint of
  'view
point-blank ˌpɔɪnt 'blæŋk ◂
  ˌpoint-blank re'fusal
point-by-point ˌpɔɪnt baɪ 'pɔɪnt ◂
pointe pwænt —Fr [pwɛ̃t]
Pointe-à-Pitre ˌpwænt ə 'piːtr -æ-, -ɑː-,
  -'piːtr ə —Fr [pwɛ̃ ta pitʁ]
pointed 'pɔɪnt ɪd -əd ‖ 'pɔɪnţ əd **~ly** li **~ness**
  nəs nɪs
pointer 'pɔɪnt ə ‖ 'pɔɪnţ ˀr **~s** z
pointillism 'pɔɪnt ɪ ˌlɪz əm 'pwænt-, -ə-, -, -iː-,
  -ˌjɪz-; -ˀl ˌɪz- ‖ 'pɔɪnţ ˀl ˌɪz əm 'pwænţ- —Fr
  pointillisme [pwɛ̃ ti jism]
pointillist 'pɔɪnt ɪl ɪst 'pwænt-, -i-, -ˀl-, §-əst
  ‖ 'pɔɪnţ ˀl- ˌpwæn ti 'jiːst **~s** s —Fr
  pointilliste [pwɛ̃ ti jist]
pointless 'pɔɪnt ləs -lɪs **~ly** li **~ness** nəs nɪs
Pointon 'pɔɪnt ən ‖ -ˀn
points|man 'pɔɪnts |mən **~men** mən men
point-to-point ˌpɔɪnt tə 'pɔɪnt -tu-
pointy 'pɔɪnt i ‖ 'pɔɪnţ i
pointy-headed ˌpɔɪnt i 'hed ɪd ◂ -əd ◂
  ‖ ˌpɔɪnţ-
Poirot 'pwɑːr əʊ ‖ pwɑː 'roʊ —Fr [pwa ʁo]
poise pɔɪz **poised** pɔɪzd **poises** 'pɔɪz ɪz -əz
  poising 'pɔɪz ɪŋ
poison 'pɔɪz ˀn **~ed** d **~ing** ɪŋ **~s** z
  ˌpoison 'gas; '· · ·; ˌpoison 'ivy
poisonous 'pɔɪz ˀn_əs **~ly** li **~ness** nəs nɪs
poison-pen ˌpɔɪz ˀn 'pen →-ˀm-
  ˌpoison-'pen ˌletter
Poisson 'pwɑːs ɒn 'pwæs-, 'pwʌs-, -ɒ̃, -ˀn
  ‖ pwɑː 'soʊn -'sɔːn, -'sɑːn —Fr [pwa sɔ̃]
  ˌPoisson ˌdistri'bution ‖ ·ˌ· ·ˈ· ·
Poitier 'pwɒt i eɪ 'pwɑːt-, 'pɔɪt- ‖ 'pwɑːt- -jeɪ
Poitiers 'pwɑːt i eɪ 'pwɒt- ‖ ˌpwɑːt i 'eɪ —Fr
  [pwa tje]
poke pəʊk ‖ poʊk **poked** pəʊkt ‖ poʊkt **pokes**
  pəʊks ‖ poʊks **poking** 'pəʊk ɪŋ ‖ 'poʊk ɪŋ
Pokemon, Pokémon 'pəʊk ɪ mɒn 'pɒk-, -eɪ-,
  -e- ‖ 'poʊk ɪ mɑːn -eɪ- **~s** z —Jp
  [po ˌke moɴ]

P

poker 'pəʊk ə ‖ 'poʊk ᵊr ~s z
  'poker face
poker-faced 'pəʊk ə feɪst ˌ·'·◂ ‖ 'poʊk ᵊr-
pokerwork 'pəʊk ə wɜːk ‖ 'poʊk ᵊr wɜːk
pokeweed 'pəʊk wiːd ‖ 'poʊk-
pok|ey, pok|ie, pokly 'pəʊk |i ‖ 'poʊk |i
  ~eys iz ~ier iˌə ‖ iˌᵊr ~ies iz ~iest iˌɪst iˌəst
  ~ily ɪ li əl i ~iness i nəs i nɪs
pol pɒl ‖ 'pɑːl **pols** pɒlz ‖ pɑːlz
  ˌPol 'Pot
Polabian pəʊ 'leɪb iˌən -'lɑːb- ‖ poʊ-
Polack, Polak 'pəʊl æk -ək ‖ 'poʊl- ~s s
Poland 'pəʊl ənd ‖ 'poʊl-
Polanski pə 'læn'sk i pɒ- ‖ poʊ-
polar 'pəʊl ə ‖ 'poʊl ᵊr
  ˌpolar 'bear ‖ '·· ·
Polari pəʊ 'lɑːr i ‖ pə-
polarimeter ˌpəʊl ə 'rɪm ɪt ə -ət ə
  ‖ ˌpoʊl ə 'rɪm ət ᵊr ~s z
Polaris pəʊ 'lɑːr ɪs -'lær-, -'leər-, §-əs
  ‖ pə 'lær əs poʊ-, -'ler-, -'lɑːr-
polaris... —see **polariz...**
polariscope pəʊ 'lær ɪ skəʊp -'·ə-
  ‖ poʊ 'lær ə skoʊp pə-, -'ler- ~s s
polarit|y pəʊ 'lær ət |i -ɪt- ‖ poʊ 'lær ət |i pə-,
  -'ler- ~ies iz
polarization ˌpəʊl ər aɪ 'zeɪʃ ᵊn -ɪ'·-
  ‖ ˌpoʊl ər ə- ~s z
polariz|e 'pəʊl ə raɪz ‖ 'poʊl- ~ed d ~es ɪz əz
  ~ing ɪŋ
Polaroid *tdmk* 'pəʊl ə rɔɪd ‖ 'poʊl- ~s z
polder 'pəʊld ə →'pɒʊld-, 'pɒld- ‖ 'poʊld ᵊr ~s
  z
Poldhu ₍ₗ₎pɒl 'djuː →-'dʒuː ‖ ₍ₗ₎pɑːl 'duː -'dju:
pole pəʊl →pɒʊl ‖ poʊl **poled** pəʊld →pɒʊld
  ‖ poʊld **poles** pəʊlz →pɒʊlz ‖ poʊlz **poling**
  'pəʊl ɪŋ →'pɒʊl- ‖ 'poʊl ɪŋ
  'pole poˌsition; 'pole star; 'pole vault
Pole *surname (i)* pəʊl →pɒʊl ‖ poʊl, *(ii)* puːl
Pole *'Polish person'* pəʊl →pɒʊl ‖ poʊl **Poles**
  pəʊlz →pɒʊlz ‖ 'poʊlz
poleax, poleax|e 'pəʊl æks →'pɒʊl- ‖ 'poʊl-
  ~ed t ~es ɪz əz ~ing ɪŋ
polecat 'pəʊl kæt →'pɒʊl- ‖ 'poʊl- ~s s
Polegate 'pəʊl geɪt →'pɒʊl- ‖ 'poʊl-
polemarch 'pɒl ɪ mɑːk -ə- ‖ 'pɑːl ə mɑːrk ~s s
polemic pə 'lem ɪk pəʊ-, pɒ- ~al ᵊl ~ally ᵊlˌi
  ~s s
polemicist pə 'lem ɪs ɪst -əs-, §-əst ~s s
polenta pəʊ 'lent ə ‖ poʊ 'lenț ə pə-, -'lent ɑː
Polesden 'pəʊlz dən →'pɒʊlz- ‖ 'poʊlz-
  ˌPolesden 'Lacey
Polesworth 'pəʊlz wəθ →'pɒʊlz-, -wɜːθ
  ‖ 'poʊlz wᵊrθ
pole-vault 'pəʊl vɔːlt →'pɒʊl-, -vɒlt ‖ 'poʊl-
  -vɑːlt ~ed ɪd əd ~er/s ə/z ‖ ᵊr/z ~ing ɪŋ ~s s
Poliakoff ˌpɒl i 'ɑːk ɒf ‖ ˌpɑːl i 'ɑːk ɔːf -ɑːf
polic|e pə 'liːs pʊ-; pliːs; §'pəʊl iːs ~ed t ~es ɪz
  əz ~ing ɪŋ
  poˌlice 'constable◂; poˈlice dog; poˈlice
  force; poˈlice ˌofficer; poˈlice state;
  poˈlice ˌstation

police|man pə 'liːs |mən pʊ-; 'pliːs |mən;
  §'pəʊl iːs- ~men mən men ~woman ˌwʊm ən
  ~women ˌwɪm ɪn §-ən
polic|y 'pɒl əs |i -ɪs- ‖ 'pɑːl- ~ies iz
policyholder 'pɒl əs i ˌhəʊld ə '·ɪs-, →-ˌhɒʊld-
  ‖ 'pɑːl əs i ˌhoʊld ᵊr ~s z
polimerism pə 'lɪm ə ˌrɪz əm pɒ-; 'pɒl ɪm-,
  '·əm- ‖ 'pɑːl əm-
polio 'pəʊl i əʊ ‖ 'poʊl i oʊ
poliomyelitis ˌpəʊl iˌəʊ ˌmaɪ ə 'laɪt ɪs -ɪ'·-,
  §-əs ‖ ˌpoʊl i oʊ ˌmaɪ ə 'laɪț əs
polis 'pɒl ɪs §-əs ‖ 'pɑːl əs 'poʊl-
-polis *stress-imposing* pəl ɪs §-əs — **Annapolis**
  ə 'næp əl ɪs §-əs
Polisario ˌpɒl ɪ 'sɑːr i əʊ ˌ·ə-
  ‖ ˌpoʊl ə 'sɑːr i oʊ ˌpɑːl-
poli sci ˌpɒl i 'saɪ ‖ ˌpɑːl-
polish *v, n* 'pɒl ɪʃ ‖ 'pɑːl ɪʃ ~ed t ~er/s ə/z
  ‖ ᵊr/z ~es ɪz əz ~ing ɪŋ
Polish *adj* 'pəʊl ɪʃ ‖ 'poʊl ɪʃ
politburo, P~ 'pɒl ɪt ˌbjʊər əʊ pə 'liːt-,
  pə 'lɪt-, -ˌbjɔːr-, '·bjuᵊ ˌrəʊ ‖ 'pɑːl ət ˌbjʊr oʊ
po|lite pə |'laɪt ~litely 'laɪt li ~liteness
  'laɪt nəs nɪs ~liter 'laɪt ə ‖ 'laɪț ᵊr ~litest
  'laɪt ɪst -əst ‖ 'laɪț əst
politesse ˌpɒl ɪ 'tes -ə- ‖ ˌpɑːl-
politic 'pɒl ə tɪk -ɪ- ‖ 'pɑːl- ~ly li ~s s
political pə 'lɪt ɪk ᵊl ‖ -'lɪț- ~ly ˌi
  poˌlitical a'sylum; poˌlitical ge'ography;
  poˌlitical 'prisoner; poˌlitical 'science
politicalis... —see **politicaliz...**
politicalization pə ˌlɪt ɪk əl aɪ 'zeɪʃ ᵊn -ɪ'·-
  ‖ -ˌlɪț ɪk əl ə-
politicaliz|e pə ˌlɪt ɪk ə laɪz -ᵊl aɪz ‖ -'lɪț- ~ed
  d ~es ɪz əz ~ing ɪŋ
politician ˌpɒl ə 'tɪʃ ᵊn -ɪ'· ‖ ˌpɑːl- ~s z
politicis... —see **politiciz...**
politicization pə ˌlɪt ɪ saɪ 'zeɪʃ ᵊn -ˌ·ə-, -sɪ'·-
  ‖ -ˌlɪț əs ə-
politiciz|e pə 'lɪt ɪ saɪz -ə- ‖ -'lɪț- ~ed d ~es ɪz
  əz ~ing ɪŋ
politick|ing 'pɒl ə tɪk| ɪŋ '·ɪ- ‖ 'pɑːl- ~ed t
politico pə 'lɪt ɪ kəʊ ‖ -'lɪț ɪ koʊ ~s z
politico- *comb. form* pə ˌlɪt ɪ kəʊ ‖ -ˌlɪț ɪ koʊ
  — **politicoeconomic**
  pə ˌlɪt ɪk əʊ ˌiːk ə 'nɒm ɪk -ˌek-
  ‖ pə ˌlɪț ɪ koʊ ˌek ə 'nɑːm ɪk
politics 'pɒl ə tɪks -ɪ- ‖ 'pɑːl-
polit|y 'pɒl ət |i -ɪt- ‖ 'pɑːl əț |i ~ies iz
Polk pəʊk ‖ poʊk
polk|a 'pɒlk |ə 'pəʊlk- ‖ 'poʊlk |ə 'poʊk- —*In*
  polka dot, *AmE usually* 'poʊk ə ~aed əd
  ~aing ᵊr ɪŋ ‖ ə ɪŋ ~as əz
  'polka dot
Polkinghorn, Polkinghorne 'pɒlk ɪŋ hɔːn
  ‖ 'pɑːlk ɪŋ hɔːrn
poll *n, v* pəʊl →pɒʊl, §pɒl ‖ poʊl —*but in the*
  obsolete senses 'parrot', 'student taking pass
  degree' was pɒl ‖ pɑːl **polled** pəʊld →pɒʊld
  ‖ poʊld **polling** 'pəʊl ɪŋ →'pɒʊl- ‖ 'poʊl ɪŋ
  polls pəʊlz →pɒʊlz ‖ poʊlz
  'polling booth; 'polling day; 'polling
  ˌstation; 'poll tax

P

Poll *name* pɒl ‖ pɑːl
pollack 'pɒl ək ‖ 'pɑːl- ~**s** s
pollan 'pɒl ən ‖ 'pɑːl- ~**s** z
pollard 'pɒl əd -ɑːd ‖ 'pɑːl ᵊrd ~**ed** ɪd əd ~**ing**
ɪŋ ~**s** z
Pollard 'pɒl ɑːd -əd ‖ 'pɑːl ɑːrd -ᵊrd
pollen, P~ 'pɒl ən ‖ 'pɑːl-
'**pollen count**
polli|nate 'pɒl ə |neɪt -ɪ- ‖ 'pɑːl- ~**nated**
neɪt ɪd -əd ‖ neɪt̬ əd ~**nates** neɪts ~**nating**
neɪt ɪŋ ‖ neɪt̬ ɪŋ
pollination ˌpɒl ə 'neɪʃ ᵊn -ɪ- ‖ ˌpɑːl- ~**s** z
Pollit, Pollitt 'pɒl ɪt -ət ‖ 'pɑːl-
polliwog 'pɒl i wɒg ‖ 'pɑːl i wɑːg -wɔːg ~**s** z
Pollock, p~, Pollok 'pɒl ək ‖ 'pɑːl- ~**s** s
Pollokshields ˌpɒl ək 'ʃiːᵊldz ‖ ˌpɑːl-
pollster 'pəʊl stə →'pɒʊl-, §'pɒl- ‖ 'poʊl stᵊr
~**s** z
pollutant pə 'luːt ᵊnt -'ljuːt- ~**s** s
pol|lute pə |'luːt -'ljuːt ~**luted** 'luːt ɪd 'ljuːt-,
-əd ‖ 'luːt̬ əd ~**lutes** 'luːts 'ljuːts ~**luting**
'luːt ɪŋ 'ljuːt- ‖ 'luːt̬ ɪŋ
polluter pə 'luːt ə -'ljuːt- ‖ -'luːt̬ ᵊr ~**s** z
pollution pə 'luːʃ ᵊn -'ljuːʃ- ~**s** z
Pollux 'pɒl əks ‖ 'pɑːl-
Polly 'pɒl i ‖ 'pɑːl i
Pollyanna ˌpɒl i 'æn ə ‖ ˌpɑːl- ~**s**, ~'**s** z
Pollyanna|ish ˌpɒl i 'æn əʳ| ɪʃ ◄
‖ ˌpɑːl i 'æn ə| ɪʃ ◄ ~**ism** ˌɪz əm
Polmont 'pəʊl mɒnt →'pɒʊl- ‖ 'poʊl mɑːnt
—*but in Scotland, locally* -mənt
polo, Polo 'pəʊl əʊ ‖ 'poʊl oʊ
'**polo neck**
polonais|e ˌpɒl ə 'neɪz ‖ ˌpɑːl- ˌpoʊl- ~**es** ɪz əz
polonium pə 'ləʊn iˌəm ‖ -'loʊn-
Polonius pə 'ləʊn iˌəs ‖ -'loʊn-
polony pə 'ləʊn i ‖ -'loʊn i
Polperro pɒl 'per əʊ ‖ pɑːl 'per oʊ
Polson 'pəʊl sən →'pɒʊl- ‖ 'poʊl-
poltergeist 'pɒlt ə gaɪst 'pəʊlt-, △-dʒaɪst
‖ 'poʊlt ᵊr- ~**s** s
poltroon pɒl 'truːn ‖ pɑːl- ~**s** z
poltroonery pɒl 'truːn ər i ‖ pɑːl-
Polwarth 'pɒl wəθ ‖ 'pɑːl wᵊrθ
poly 'pɒl i ‖ 'pɑːl i ~**s** z
'**poly bag**
poly- *comb. form*
with stress-neutral suffix ˌpɒl i ‖ ˌpɑːl i —*but
in certain more familiar words, before a
consonant, also* ˌpɒl ə ‖ ˌpɑːl ə —
polygenesis ˌpɒl i 'dʒen əs ɪs -ɪs ɪs, §-əs
‖ ˌpɑːl-
with stress-imposing suffix pə 'lɪ + pɒ-
— **polyphagous** pə 'lɪf əg əs pɒ-
polyamide ˌpɒl i 'æm aɪd -ɪd, §-əd ‖ ˌpɑːl- ~**s**
z
polyamory ˌpɒl i 'æm ər i ‖ ˌpɑːl-
polyandrous ˌpɒl i 'ændr əs ◄ ‖ ˌpɑːl-
polyandry ˌpɒl i 'ændr i '·ˌ·· ‖ ˌpɑːl-
polyanth|a ˌpɒl i 'æn̯θ |ə ‖ ˌpɑːl- ~**as** əz
~**us/es** əs /ɪz -əz
Polybius pə 'lɪb iˌəs pɒ-

polycarbonate ˌpɒl i 'kɑːb ə neɪt -nət, -nɪt
‖ ˌpɑːl i 'kɑːrb- ~**s** s
Polycarp 'pɒl i kɑːp ‖ 'pɑːl i kɑːrp
Polycell *tdmk* 'pɒl i sel ‖ 'pɑːl-
polychaete 'pɒl i kiːt ‖ 'pɑːl- ~**s** s
polychlorinated ˌpɒl i 'klɔːr ɪ neɪt ɪd ◄ -'·ə-,
-əd ‖ ˌpɑːl i 'klɔːr ə neɪt̬ əd ◄ -'kloʊr-
polychrom|e 'pɒl i krəʊm ‖ 'pɑːl i kroʊm ~**y**
i
polyclinic ˌpɒl i 'klɪn ɪk '·ˌ·· ‖ ˌpɑːl-
polycotton ˌpɒl i 'kɒt ᵊn ◄ ‖ ˌpɑːl i 'kɑːt ᵊn ◄
Polycrates pə 'lɪk rə tiːz pɒ-
polydactyl ˌpɒl i 'dækt ɪl ◄ -ᵊl ‖ ˌpɑːl-
polyester ˌpɒl i 'est ə ◄ '·ˌ·· ‖ 'pɑːl i ˌest ᵊr
~**s** z
polyethylene ˌpɒl i 'eθ ə liːn ◄ -'·ɪ-, -ᵊl iːn
‖ ˌpɑːl-
Polyfilla *tdmk* 'pɒl i ˌfɪl ə ‖ 'pɑːl-
polygamist pə 'lɪg əm ɪst pɒ-, §-əst ~**s** s
polygamous pə 'lɪg əm əs pɒ- ~**ly** li
polygamy pə 'lɪg əm i pɒ-
polygene 'pɒl i dʒiːn ‖ 'pɑːl- ~**s** z
polygenic ˌpɒl i 'dʒen ɪk ◄ ‖ ˌpɑːl-
polyglot 'pɒl i glɒt ‖ 'pɑːl i glɑːt ~**s** s
polygon 'pɒl ɪg ən -əg-; -i gɒn ‖ 'pɑːl i gɑːn ~**s**
z
polygonal pə 'lɪg ən ᵊl pɒ- ~**ly** i
polygonum pə 'lɪg ən əm pɒ-
polygraph 'pɒl i grɑːf -græf ‖ 'pɑːl i græf ~**s** s
Polygrip *tdmk* 'pɒl i grɪp ‖ 'pɑːl-
polygynous pə 'lɪdʒ ən əs pɒ-, -ɪn-
polygyny pə 'lɪdʒ ən i pɒ-, -ɪn-
polyhedr|on ˌpɒl i 'hiːdr |ən -'hedr- ‖ ˌpɑːl-
~**a** ə ~**al** əl ~**ons** ənz
Polyhymnia ˌpɒl i 'hɪm niˌə ‖ ˌpɑːl-
polylectal ˌpɒl i 'lekt ᵊl ◄ ‖ ˌpɑːl-
polymath 'pɒl i mæθ ‖ 'pɑːl- ~**s** s
polymer 'pɒl ɪm ə -əm- ‖ 'pɑːl əm ᵊr ~**s** z
polymeras|e 'pɒl ɪm ə reɪz '·əm-; pə 'lɪm-,
-reɪs ‖ 'pɑːl əm-
polymeric ˌpɒl ɪ 'mer ɪk ◄ ‖ ˌpɑːl ə-
polymeris... —*see* **polymeriz...**
polymerization ˌpɒl ɪm ər aɪ 'zeɪʃ ᵊn ˌ·əm-,
-ɪ'·-; pə ˌlɪm- ‖ ˌpɑːl əm ər ə- pə ˌlɪm-
polymeriz|e 'pɒl ɪm ə raɪz '·əm-; pə 'lɪm-
‖ 'pɑːl- ~**ed** d ~**es** ɪz əz ~**ing** ɪŋ
polymerous pə 'lɪm ər əs pɒ-
polymorph|ic ˌpɒl ɪ 'mɔːf |ɪk ◄
‖ ˌpɑːl ɪ 'mɔːrf |ɪk ◄ ~**ism** ˌɪz əm ~**ous** əs ◄

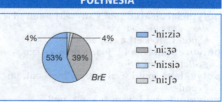

POLYNESIA

Preference poll, BrE: 4% -'niːziə, 4% -'niːʒə, 53% -'niːsiə, 39% -'niːʃə (BrE)

Polynesia ˌpɒl ɪ 'niːz iˌə ˌ·ə-, -'niːʒ ə, -'niːs iˌə,
-'niːʃ ə ‖ ˌpɑːl ə 'niːʒ ə -'niːʃ— *Preference
poll, BrE:* -'niːziə *53%,* -'niːʒə *39%,* -'niːsiə
4%, -'niːʃə *4%.*

Polynesian ˌpɒl ɪ ˈniːz i‿ən ‿ˌ-ə-, -ˈniːʒ ᵊn,
-ˈniːs i‿ən, -ˈniːʃ ᵊn ‖ ˌpɑːl ə ˈniːʒ ᵊn -ˈniːʃ- **~s**
z

Polynices ˌpɒl i ˈnaɪs iːz ‖ ˌpɑːl-

polynomial ˌpɒl i ˈnəʊm i‿əl ◂
‖ ˌpɑːl ə ˈnoʊm- **~s** z

polyp ˈpɒl ɪp -əp- ‖ ˈpɑːl əp **~s** s

polypeptide ˌpɒl i ˈpept aɪd ‖ ˌpɑːl- **~s** z

Polyphemus ˌpɒl ɪ ˈfiːm əs -ə- ‖ ˌpɑːl-

polyphonic ˌpɒl i ˈfɒn ɪk ◂ ‖ ˌpɑːl i ˈfɑːn ɪk ◂
~ally ᵊl‿i

polyphon|y pə ˈlɪf ən i ‖ i pɒ- **~ies** iz

polypi ˈpɒl ɪ paɪ -ə- ‖ ˈpɑːl-

polyploid ˈpɒl i plɔɪd ‖ ˈpɑːl- **~s** z

polypod ˈpɒl i pɒd ‖ ˈpɑːl i pɑːd **~s** z

polypod|y ˈpɒl i pəʊd ‖i ‖ ˈpɑːl ə poʊd ‖i **~ies**
iz

polypous ˈpɒl ɪp əs -əp- ‖ ˈpɑːl-

polypropylene ˌpɒl i ˈprəʊp ə liːn ◂ -ˈˌɪ-
‖ ˌpɑːl i ˈproʊp-

polypus ˈpɒl ɪp əs -əp- ‖ ˈpɑːl- **~es** ɪz əz

polysaccharide ˌpɒl i ˈsæk ə raɪd ‖ ˌpɑːl- **~s** z

polysemous pə ˈlɪs ɪm əs pɒ-, -əm-;
ˌpɒl i ˈsiːm əs ‖ ˌpɑːl i ˈsiːm əs **~ly** li

polysemy pə ˈlɪs ɪm i pɒ-, -əm-; ˈpɒl i ˌsiːm i,
ˌˌ·ˈ·ˌ ‖ ˌpɑːl i ˈsiːm i

polysorbate ˌpɒl i ˈsɔːb eɪt ◂
‖ ˌpɑːl i ˈsɔːrb eɪt

polystyrene ˌpɒl i ˈstaɪᵊr iːn ◂ ‖ ˌpɑːl-

polysyllabic ˌpɒl i sɪ ˈlæb ɪk ◂ -sə-- ‖ ˌpɑːl-
~ally ᵊl‿i

polysyllable ˈpɒl i ˌsɪl əb ᵊl ˌ·ˈ·ˌ·· ‖ ˈpɑːl- **~s** z

polysyndeton ˌpɒl i ˈsɪnd ət ən -ˈ·ɪt-
‖ ˌpɑːl i ˈsɪnd ə tɑːn

polysynthetic ˌpɒl i sɪn ˈθet ɪk ◂
‖ ˌpɑːl i sɪn ˈθeţ ɪk ◂

polysystemic ˌpɒl i sɪ ˈstiːm ɪk ◂ -sə-ˌ-, -ˈstem-
‖ ˌpɑːl-

polytechnic ˌpɒl i ˈtek nɪk -ə- ‖ ˌpɑːl- **~s** s

polytetrafluoroethylene
ˌpɒl i ˌtetr ə ˌfluər əʊ ˈeθ ə liːn -ˌflɔːr-
‖ ˌpɑːl i ˌtetr ə ˌflʊr oʊ-

polytheism ˈpɒl i θi ˌɪz əm ˈ··ˌθiː ɪz əm
‖ ˈpɑːl-

polytheist ˈpɒl i θi ɪst ˈ··ˌθiː ɪst, §-əst ‖ ˈpɑːl-
~s s

polytheistic ˌpɒl i θi ˈɪst ɪk ◂ ‖ ˌpɑːl- **~ally**
ᵊl‿i

polythene ˈpɒl ɪ θiːn -ə- ‖ ˈpɑːl-

polyunsaturate ˌpɒl i ʌn ˈsætʃ ə reɪt -ʊ-,
-ˈsæt jʊ- ‖ ˌpɑːl- **~s** s

polyunsatu|rated ˌpɒl i ʌn ˈsætʃ ə reɪt ɪd ◂
-ˈˌʊ-, -ˈsæt jʊ-, -əd
‖ ˌpɑːl i ʌn ˈsætʃ ə reɪţ əd ◂

polyurethane ˌpɒl i ˈjʊər ə θeɪn ◂ -ˈjɔːr-, -ˈˌɪ-,
△-θiːn ‖ ˌpɑːl i ˈjʊr-

polyvalent ˌpɒl i ˈveɪl ənt pə ˈlɪv əl ənt, pɒ-
‖ ˌpɑːl-

polyvinyl ˌpɒl i ˈvaɪn ᵊl ◂ -ɪl ‖ ˌpɑːl-

Polyxena pə ˈlɪks ən ə pɒ-, -ɪn-

Polzeath pɒl ˈzeθ -ˈziːθ ‖ poʊl-

pom, Pom pɒm ‖ pɑːm **poms, Poms** pɒmz
‖ pɑːmz

poma, Poma ˈpɒm ə ˈpəʊm ə ‖ ˈpɑːm ə
ˈpoʊm ə

pomace ˈpʌm ɪs ˈpɒm-, §-əs ‖ ˈpɑːm-

pomad|e pəʊ ˈmeɪd pɒ-, -ˈmɑːd ‖ poʊ- pɑː- **~ed**
ɪd əd **~es** z **~ing** ɪŋ

Pomagne *tdmk* pəʊ ˈmeɪn ‖ poʊ-

pomander pəʊ ˈmænd ə ‖ ˈpoʊm ænd ᵊr
poʊ ˈmænd ᵊr **~s** z

pome pəʊm ‖ poʊm **pomes** pəʊmz ‖ poʊmz

pomegranate ˈpɒm ɪ græn ət ˈ·ə-, -ɪt ‖ ˈpɑːm-
ˈ·græn ət, ˈpʌm- **~s** s

pomelo ˈpɒm ə ləʊ -ɪ-; pə ˈmel əʊ
‖ ˈpɑːm ə loʊ **~s** z

Pomerani|a ˌpɒm ə ˈreɪn i‿ə ‖ ˌpɑːm- **~an/s**
ən/z

Pomeroy *(i)* ˈpɒm ə rɔɪ ‖ ˈpɑːm-, *(ii)* ˈpəʊm-
‖ ˈpoʊm-

pomfret *'kind of fish'* ˈpɒm frət -frɪt ‖ ˈpɑːm-

Pomfret, p~ ˈpɒm frət ˈpʌm-, -frət ‖ ˈpɑːm-
ˌPomfret ˈcake

pomiferous pɒ ˈmɪf ᵊr əs pəʧ- ‖ poʊ-

pommel *n* ˈpɒm ᵊl ˈpʌm- ‖ ˈpʌm ᵊl ˈpɑːm- **~s** z

pommel *v* ˈpʌm ᵊl ˈpɒm- **~ed, ~led** d **~ing,
~ling** ɪŋ **~s** z

pomm|ie, pomm|y, Pomm|y ˈpɒm ‖i
‖ ˈpɑːm ‖i **~ies** iz

Pomo ˈpəʊm əʊ ‖ ˈpoʊm oʊ **~s** z

Pomona, p~ pəʊ ˈməʊn ə ‖ pə ˈmoʊn ə

pomp pɒmp ‖ pɑːmp **pomps** pɒmps ‖ pɑːmps

pompadour, P~ ˈpɒmp ə dʊə -dɔː
‖ ˈpɑːmp ə dɔːr -dʊr, -dʊr —*Fr* [pɔ̃ pa duːʁ]
~s z

pompano, P~ ˈpɒmp ə nəʊ ˈpʌmp-
‖ ˈpɑːmp ə noʊ **~s** z
ˌPompano ˈBeach

Pompeian, Pompeiian pɒm ˈpeɪ ən -ˈpiː
‖ pɑːm- **~s** z

Pompeii pɒm ˈpeɪ i -iː;; pɒm ˈpeɪ ‖ pɑːm-

Pompey ˈpɒmp i ‖ ˈpɑːmp i

Pomphrey ˈpɒmᵖf ri ‖ ˈpɑːmᵖf-

Pompidou ˈpɒmp ɪ du: -ə- ‖ ˈpɑːmp- —*Fr*
[pɔ̃ pi du]

pompom ˈpɒm pɒm ‖ ˈpɑːm pɑːm **~s** z

pompon ˈpɒm pɒn ‖ ˈpɑːm pɑːn —*Fr* [pɔ̃ pɔ̃]
~s z

pomposit|y pɒm ˈpɒs ət |i -ɪt-
‖ pɑːm ˈpɑːs əţ |i **~ies** iz

pompous ˈpɒmp əs ‖ ˈpɑːmp əs **~ly** li **~ness**
nəs nɪs

'pon pɒn ‖ pɑːn

ponce pɒnᵗs ‖ pɑːnᵗs **ponced** pɒnᵗst ‖ pɑːnᵗst
ponces ˈpɒnᵗs ɪz -əz ‖ ˈpɑːnᵗs əz **poncing**
ˈpɒnᵗs ɪŋ ‖ ˈpɑːnᵗs ɪŋ

Ponce *Spanish name; place in PR* ˈpɒnᵗs eɪ
pɒnᵗs ‖ ˈpɔːnᵗs eɪ ˈpɑːnᵗs-, ˈpoʊnᵗs- —*AmSp*
[ˈpon se]

poncey ˈpɒnᵗs i ‖ ˈpɑːnᵗs i

poncho ˈpɒntʃ əʊ ‖ ˈpɑːntʃ oʊ —*Sp* [ˈpon tʃo]
~s z

poncy ˈpɒnᵗs i ‖ ˈpɑːnᵗs i

pond, Pond pɒnd ‖ pɑːnd **ponds** pɒndz
‖ pɑːndz

pond|er 'pɒnd |ə ‖ 'pɑːnd |ᵊr ~ered əd ‖ ᵊrd
~ering/s ᵊr ɪŋ/z ~ers əz ‖ ᵊrz
ponderosa ˌpɒnd ə 'rəʊz ə -'rəʊs-
‖ ˌpɑːnd ə 'roʊs ə -'roʊz- ~s z
ponderous 'pɒnd ᵊr əs ‖ 'pɑːnd ~ly li ~ness
nəs nɪs
Ponders 'pɒnd əz ‖ 'pɑːnd ᵊrz
Pondicherry ˌpɒnd ɪ 'tʃer i §-ə-, -'ʃer-
‖ ˌpɑːnd-
Pondo 'pɒnd əʊ ‖ 'pɑːnd oʊ ~land lænd ~s z
pondweed 'pɒnd wiːd ‖ 'pɑːnd-
pone pəʊn ‖ poʊn —but in the sense 'player to
right of dealer', also 'pəʊn i ‖ 'poʊn i ~s z
pong pɒŋ ‖ pɑːŋ pɔːŋ **ponged** pɒŋd ‖ pɑːŋd
pɔːŋd **ponging** 'pɒŋ ɪŋ ‖ 'pɑːŋ ɪŋ 'pɔːŋ-
pongs pɒŋz ‖ pɑːŋz pɔːŋz
pongee ˌ(ˌ)pɒn 'dʒiː ˌˈ·· ‖ ˌ(ˌ)pɑːn-
pongid 'pɒndʒ ɪd §-əd ‖ 'pɑːndʒ- ~s z
pongo 'pɒŋ gəʊ ‖ 'pɑːŋ goʊ ~s z
pongy 'pɒŋ i ‖ 'pɑːŋ i 'pɔːŋ-
poniard 'pɒn jəd -jɑːd ‖ 'pɑːn jᵊrd ~ed ɪd əd
~ing ɪŋ ~s z
ponie... —see **pony**
pons pɒnz ‖ pɑːnz **pontes** 'pɒnt iːz
‖ 'pɑːnt iːz
ˌpons ˌasi'norum ˌæs ɪ 'nɔːr əm -ə-, -ʊm
‖ -'noʊr-
Ponson 'pɒnˈs ən ‖ 'pɑːnˈs-
Ponsonby 'pɒnˈs ən bi →-əm- ‖ 'pɑːnˈs-
Pont pɒnt ‖ pɑːnt
Pontardawe ˌpɒnt ə 'daʊ i -eɪ ‖ ˌpɑːnt̬ ᵊr-
—Welsh [ˌpɔnt ar 'dau e]
Pontardulais ˌpɒnt ə 'dɪl əs -'dʌl-, -aɪs
‖ ˌpɑːnt̬ ᵊr- —Welsh Pontarddulais
[ˌpɔnt ar 'ði laɪs]
Pontchartrain 'pɒntʃ ə treɪn ˌ·'·· ‖ 'pɑːntʃ ᵊr-
Pontefract 'pɒnt ɪ frækt -ə- ‖ 'pɑːnt̬- —locally
formerly also 'pʌmᵖf rət, 'pɒmᵖf-, -rɪt
Ponteland ˌpɒnt 'iːl ənd ‖ ˌpɑːnt-
pontes 'pɒnt iːz ‖ 'pɑːnt iːz
Pontfaen, Pont-faen ˌ(ˌ)pɒnt 'vaɪn ‖ ˌ(ˌ)pɑːnt-
Ponti 'pɒnt i ‖ 'pɑːnt̬ i
Pontiac 'pɒnt i æk ‖ 'pɑːnt̬- ~s s
Pontic 'pɒnt ɪk ‖ 'pɑːnt̬ ɪk
pontifex, P~ 'pɒnt ɪ feks -ə- ‖ 'pɑːnt̬ ə-
pontifices, P~ pɒn 'tɪf ə siːz -ɪ- ‖ pɑːn-
pontiff 'pɒnt ɪf ‖ 'pɑːnt̬ əf ~s s
pontifical pɒn 'tɪf ɪk ᵊl ‖ pɑːn- ~ally ᵊl_i ~s z
pontifi|cate v pɒn 'tɪf ɪ |keɪt -ə- ‖ pɑːn-
~cated keɪt ɪd -əd ‖ keɪt̬ əd ~cates keɪts
~cating keɪt ɪŋ ‖ keɪt̬ ɪŋ
pontificate n pɒn 'tɪf ɪk ət -ək ət, -ɪt; -ɪ keɪt,
-ə keɪt ‖ pɑːn- ~s s
pontification pɒn ˌtɪf ɪ 'keɪʃ ᵊn ˌpɒnt ɪf-, -ə-
‖ pɑːn- ~s z
Pontin 'pɒnt ɪn §-ən ‖ 'pɑːnt ᵊn ~'s z
Pontine, p~ 'pɒnt aɪn ‖ 'pɑːnt-
ˌPontine 'Marshes
Ponting 'pɒnt ɪŋ ‖ 'pɑːnt̬-
Pontius 'pɒnt i_əs 'pɒntʃ-, 'pɒntʃ əs
‖ 'pɑːntʃ əs
ˌPontius 'Pilate

Pont l'Évêque ˌpɒ̃ leɪ 'vek ‖ ˌpɑːn- ˌpɑːnt-
—Fr [pɔ̃ le vɛk]
Pontllan-fraith ˌpɒnt læn 'vraɪθ -θlæn-
‖ ˌpɑːnt- —Welsh [pɔnt ɬan 'vraiθ]
Ponton 'pɒnt ən ‖ 'pɑːnt ᵊn
pontoon ˌ(ˌ)pɒn 'tuːn ‖ ˌ(ˌ)pɑːn- ~s z
Pontop 'pɒnt ɒp ‖ 'pɑːnt ɑːp
ˌPontop 'Pike
Pontus 'pɒnt əs ‖ 'pɑːnt̬-
Pont-y-clun ˌpɒnt ə 'kliːn -i- ‖ ˌpɑːnt̬- —Welsh
[ˌpɔnt ə 'kliːn]
Pontypool ˌpɒnt ə 'puːl -i-, '··· ‖ ˌpɑːnt̬-
—Welsh [ˌpɔnt ə 'puːl]
Pontypridd ˌpɒnt ə 'priːð ˌ·i-, -'prɪd, '···
‖ ˌpɑːnt̬- —Welsh [ˌpɔnt ə 'priːð]
pon|y 'pəʊn |i ‖ 'poʊn |i ~ies iz
ˌpony ex'press
ponytail 'pəʊn i terᵊl ‖ 'poʊn- ~s z
pony-trekk|ing 'pəʊn i ˌtrek| ɪŋ ‖ 'poʊn-
~er/s ə/z ‖ ᵊr/z
Ponzi 'pɒnz i ‖ 'pɑːnz i
'Ponzi scheme
poo puː **pooed** puːd **pooing** 'puː ɪŋ **poos** puːz
pooch puːtʃ **pooches** 'puːtʃ ɪz -əz
poodle 'puːd ᵊl ~s z
poof pʊf puːf ~s s
poofter 'pʊft ə 'puːft- ‖ -ᵊr ~s z
poofy 'pʊf i 'puːf-
pooh, Pooh puː
Pooh-Bah ˌpuː 'bɑː
pooh-pooh ˌpuː 'puː ~ed d ~ing ɪŋ ~s z
Poohsticks 'puː stɪks
Pook puːk
pool puːl **pooled** puːld **pooling** 'puːl ɪŋ **pools**
puːlz
Poole puːl
Poolewe pʊl 'juː ˌ(ˌ)puːl-
Pooley 'puːl i
poolroom 'puːl ruːm -rʊm ~s z
poolside 'puːl saɪd
poon puːn **poons** puːnz
Poona 'puːn ə
poontang 'puːn tæŋ
poop puːp **pooped** puːpt **pooping** 'puːp ɪŋ
poops puːps
'poop deck
pooper 'puːp ə ‖ -ᵊr ~s z
pooper-scooper 'puːp ə ˌskuːp ə
‖ -ᵊr ˌskuːp ᵊr ~s z
poo-poo 'puː puː
poop-scoop 'puːp skuːp ~ed d ~ing ɪŋ ~s s
poopy 'puːp i
poor pɔː puə ‖ pʊᵊr pɔːr, poʊr — Preference
poll, BrE: pɔː 74%, puə 26% (born before
1942: 41%). See chart on p. 628. **poorer**
'pɔːr ə 'puər- ‖ 'pʊr ᵊr 'pɔːr-, 'poʊr- **poorest**
'pɔːr ɪst 'puər-, -əst ‖ 'pʊr əst 'pɔːr-, 'poʊr-
'poor box; 'poor law; ˌpoor re'lation;
ˌpoor 'white
Poore puə pɔː ‖ pʊᵊr pɔːr, poʊr
poor|house 'pɔː |haʊs 'puə- ‖ 'pʊr- 'pɔːr-,
'poʊr- ~houses haʊz ɪz -əz

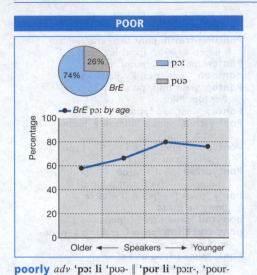

POOR

26% ▨ pɔː
74% ▨ pʊə
BrE

—●— *BrE* pɔː by age

Percentage (y-axis: 0, 20, 40, 60, 80, 100)

Older ◀— Speakers —▶ Younger

poorly *adv* 'pɔː li 'pʊə- ‖ 'pʊr li 'pɔːr-, 'pʊr-
  ,poorly 'off◀
poorly *adj* 'pɔːl i 'pʊəl i ‖ 'pʊrl i 'pɔːrl-, 'pʊrl-
poorness 'pɔː nəs 'pʊə-, -nɪs ‖ 'pʊr- 'pɔːr-,
  'pʊr-
poor-spirited ,pɔː 'spɪr ɪt ɪd ◀ ,pʊə-, §-ət-, -əd
  ‖ ,pʊr 'spɪr əţ əd ◀ ,pɔːr-, ,pʊr-
Pooter 'puːt ə ‖ 'puːţ ᵊr
Pooterish 'puːt ər ɪʃ ‖ 'puːţ-
pootl|e 'puːt ᵊl ‖ 'puːţ ᵊl **~ed** d **~es** z **~ing** ɪŋ
poove puːv **pooves** puːvz
pop, Pop pɒp ‖ pɑːp **popped** pɒpt ‖ pɑːpt
  popping 'pɒp ɪŋ ‖ 'pɑːp ɪŋ **pops** pɒps
  ‖ pɑːps
  'pop art, ,· '·◀; 'pop ,concert; 'pop group;
  'pop ,music; 'popping crease
popadam, popadom, popadum 'pɒp əd əm
  ‖ 'pɑːp- **~s** z
popcorn 'pɒp kɔːn ‖ 'pɑːp kɔːrn
pop-down 'pɒp daʊn ‖ ' pɑːp-
pope, Pope pəʊp ‖ poʊp **popes, Pope's**
  pəʊps ‖ poʊps
  ,Pope's 'nose
popemobile 'pəʊp məʊ ,biːᵊl ‖ 'poʊp mə- **~s**
  z
popery 'pəʊp ər i ‖ 'poʊp-
Popeye 'pɒp aɪ ‖ 'pɑːp-
pop-eyed ,pɒp 'aɪd ◀ '· · ‖ 'pɑːp aɪd
popgun 'pɒp gʌn ‖ 'pɑːp- **~s** z
Popham 'pɒp əm ‖ 'pɑːp-
popinjay 'pɒp ɪn dʒeɪ §-ən- ‖ 'pɑːp- **~s** z
popish 'pəʊp ɪʃ ‖ 'poʊp- **~ly** li **~ness** nəs nɪs
poplar, P~ 'pɒp lə ‖ 'pɑːp lᵊr **~s** z
poplin 'pɒp lɪn §-lən ‖ 'pɑːp- **~s** z
popliteal ,pɒp lɪ 'tiː əl ◀ -lə-; pɒ 'plɪt i əl
  ‖ ,pɑːp-
Popocatepetl ,pɒp əʊ kæt ə 'pet ᵊl -ɪ'·-;
  ,· ·'· · · · ‖ ,poʊp ə kæţ ə 'peţ ᵊl ,pɑːp- —*Sp*
  Popacatépetl [po po ka 'te petl]
popover 'pɒp ,əʊv ə ‖ 'pɑːp ,oʊv ᵊr **~s** z
popp... —*see* pop
poppa, Poppa 'pɒp ə ‖ 'pɑːp ə **~s, ~'s** z

poppadom, poppadum 'pɒp əd əm ‖ 'pɑːp-
  ~s z
Poppaea pɒ 'piː ə ‖ pɑː-
popper, P~ 'pɒp ə ‖ 'pɑːp ᵊr **~s** z
Popperian pɒ 'pɪər i ˌən ‖ pɑː 'pɪr-
poppet 'pɒp ɪt §-ət ‖ 'pɑːp- **~s** s
poppi... —*see* pop, poppy
poppl|e 'pɒp ᵊl ‖ 'pɑːp ᵊl **~ed** d **~es** z **~ing** ˌɪŋ
Poppleton 'pɒp ᵊl tən ‖ 'pɑːp-
Popplewell 'pɒp ᵊl wel ‖ 'pɑːp-
popp|y, Poppy 'pɒp |i ‖ 'pɑːp |i **~ies** iz
  'Poppy Day
poppycock 'pɒp i kɒk ‖ 'pɑːp i kɑːk
poppyseed 'pɒp i siːd ‖ 'pɑːp-
popshop 'pɒp ʃɒp ‖ 'pɑːp ʃɑːp **~s** s
popsicle, P~ *tdmk* 'pɒps ɪk ᵊl ‖ 'pɑːps- **~s** z
pops|ie, pops|y 'pɒps |i ‖ 'pɑːps |i **~ies** iz
populace 'pɒp jʊl əs -jəl-, -ɪs ‖ 'pɑːp jəl əs
popular 'pɒp jʊl ə -jəl- ‖ 'pɑːp jəl ᵊr
popularis... —*see* populariz...
popularity ,pɒp jʊ 'lær ət i ,·jə-, -ɪt i
  ‖ ,pɑːp jə 'lær əţ i -'ler-
popularization ,pɒp jʊl ər aɪ 'zeɪʃ ᵊn ,·jəl-,
  -ɪ'·- ‖ ,pɑːp jəl ər ə- **~s** z
populariz|e 'pɒp jʊl ə raɪz '·jəl- ‖ 'pɑːp jəl-
  ~ed d **~es** ɪz əz **~ing** ɪŋ
popularly 'pɒp jʊl ə li '·jəl- ‖ 'pɑːp jəl ᵊr li
popu|late 'pɒp jʊ |leɪt -jə- ‖ 'pɑːp jə- **~lated**
  leɪt ɪd -əd ‖ leɪţ əd **~lates** leɪts **~lating**
  leɪt ɪŋ ‖ leɪţ ɪŋ
population ,pɒp jʊ 'leɪʃ ᵊn -jə- ‖ ,pɑːp jə- **~s** z
  ,popu'lation ex,plosion
populism, P~ 'pɒp jʊ ,lɪz əm -jə- ‖ 'pɑːp jə-
populist, P~ 'pɒp jʊl ɪst -jəl-, §-əst ‖ 'pɑːp jəl-
  ~s s
populous 'pɒp jʊl əs -jəl- ‖ 'pɑːp jəl əs **~ly** li
  ~ness nəs nɪs
pop-under 'pɒp ,ʌnd ə ‖ 'pɑːp ,ʌnd ᵊr **~s** z
pop-up 'pɒp ʌp ‖ 'pɑːp ʌp **~s** s
porbeagle 'pɔː ,biːg ᵊl ‖ 'pɔːr- **~s** z
porcelain 'pɔːs ᵊl_ɪn ən, -eɪn ‖ 'pɔːrs- 'poʊrs- **~s**
  z
porch pɔːtʃ ‖ pɔːrtʃ poʊrtʃ **porches** 'pɔːtʃ ɪz -əz
  ‖ 'pɔːrtʃ əz 'poʊrtʃ-
Porchester 'pɔːtʃ ɪst ə -əst-, §-est-
  ‖ 'pɔːr ,tʃest ᵊr
porcine 'pɔːs aɪn ‖ 'pɔːrs-
porcin|o pɔː 'tʃiːn| əʊ ‖ pɔːr 'tʃiːn| oʊ **~i** iː
  —*It* [por 'tʃiː no]
porcupine 'pɔːk jʊ paɪn -jə- ‖ 'pɔːrk jə- **~s** z
pore, Pore pɔː pour **pored** pɔːd ‖ pɔːrd pourd
  pores pɔːz ‖ pɔːrz pourz **poring** 'pɔːr ɪŋ
  ‖ 'poʊr-
porg|y, Porg|y 'pɔːg |i ‖ 'pɔːrg |i **~ies, ~y's**
  iz
pork pɔːk ‖ pɔːrk poʊrk
  'pork ,barrel; ,pork 'chop ‖ '· ·; ,pork 'pie
porker 'pɔːk ə ‖ 'pɔːrk ᵊr 'poʊrk- **~s** z
pork|ie, Pork|ie, porkly, Porkly 'pɔːk |i
  ‖ 'pɔːrk |i 'poʊrk- **~ies, ~y's** iz **~iness** i nəs
  i nɪs
pork-pie *hat* 'pɔːk paɪ ‖ 'pɔːrk- **~s** z
Porlock 'pɔː lɒk ‖ 'pɔːr lɑːk

porn pɔːn ‖ pɔːrn
porno 'pɔːn əʊ ‖ 'pɔːrn oʊ
pornographer pɔː 'nɒg rəf ə pə-
  ‖ pɔːr 'nɑːg rəf ᵊr ~**s** z
pornographic ˌpɔːn ə 'græf ɪk ◂ ‖ ˌpɔːrn-
  ~**ally** ᵊl i
pornography pɔː 'nɒg rəf i pə- ‖ pɔːr 'nɑːg-
poromeric ˌpɔːr əʊ 'mer ɪk ◂ ˌpɒr- ‖ -ə- ˌpoʊr-
porosit|y pɔː 'rɒs ət |i -ɪt- ‖ pə 'rɑːs ət |i pɔː-,
  poʊ- ~**ies** iz
porous 'pɔːr əs ‖ 'poʊr- ~**ly** li ~**ness** nəs nɪs
porphyria pɔː 'fɪr i‿ə -'faɪᵊr- ‖ pɔːr-
porphyrin 'pɔːf ər ɪn -ɪr-, §-ən ‖ 'pɔːrf- ~**s** z
porphyr|y 'pɔːf ər |i -ɪr- ‖ 'pɔːrf- ~**ies** iz
porpois|e 'pɔːp əs ‖ 'pɔːrp- —*occasionally also*
  a spelling pronunciation 'pɔː pɔɪs, -pɔɪz ‖ 'pɔːr-
  ~**es** ɪz əz
porridge 'pɒr ɪdʒ ‖ 'pɔːr- 'pɑːr-
porringer 'pɒr ɪndʒ ə -əndʒ- ‖ 'pɔːr əndʒ ᵊr
  'pɑːr- ~**s** z
Porsche *tdmk* pɔːʃ 'pɔːʃ ə ‖ pɔːrʃ 'pɔːrʃ ə, -i
  —*Ger* ['pɔʁ ʃə] **Porsches** 'pɔːʃ ɪz -əz
  ‖ 'pɔːrʃ əz -iz
Porsena 'pɔːs ən ə -ɪn- ‖ 'pɔːrs-
Porson 'pɔːs ᵊn ‖ 'pɔːrs-
port pɔːt ‖ pɔːrt poʊrt **ported** 'pɔːt ɪd -əd
  ‖ 'pɔːrt̬ əd 'poʊrt̬- **porting** 'pɔːt ɪŋ ‖ 'pɔːrt̬ ɪŋ
  'poʊrt̬- **ports** pɔːts ‖ pɔːrts poʊrts —*see also*
  phrases with this word
  ˌPort E'lizabeth; ˌ₍ₗ₎Port 'Harcourt; ₍ₗ₎Port
  'Hedland; ₍ₗ₎Port 'Jackson; ₍ₗ₎Port 'Lincoln;
  ₍ₗ₎Port 'Moresby; ˌport of 'call; ˌport of
  'entry; ˌPort of 'Spain; ₍ₗ₎Port 'Stanley
portability ˌpɔːt ə 'bɪl ət i -ɪt i
  ‖ ˌpɔːrt̬ ə 'bɪl ət̬ i ˌpoʊrt̬-
portable 'pɔːt əb ᵊl ‖ 'pɔːrt̬- 'poʊrt̬- ~**ness** nəs
  nɪs ~**s** z
Portacrib *tdmk* 'pɔːt ə krɪb ‖ 'pɔːrt̬- 'poʊrt̬-
Portadown ˌpɔːt ə 'daʊn ‖ ˌpɔːrt̬- ˌpoʊrt̬-
portage 'pɔːt ɪdʒ pɔː 'tɑːʒ ‖ 'pɔːrt̬ ɪdʒ 'poʊrt̬-;
  pɔːr 'tɑːʒ
Portage 'pɔːt ɪdʒ ‖ 'pɔːrt̬ ɪdʒ 'poʊrt̬-
  ˌPortage la 'Prairie
Portakabin *tdmk* 'pɔːt ə ˌkæb ɪn §-ən ‖ 'pɔːrt̬-
  'poʊrt̬- ~**s** z
portal, P~ 'pɔːt ᵊl ‖ 'pɔːrt̬ ᵊl 'poʊrt̬- ~**s** z
Portaloo, p~ *tdmk* 'pɔːt ə luː ‖ 'pɔːrt̬- ~**s** z
portament|o ˌpɔːt ə 'ment |əʊ
  ‖ ˌpɔːrt̬ ə 'ment |oʊ ˌpoʊrt̬- ~**i** iː
porta-pott|y, Porta Pott|y *tdmk*
  'pɔːt ə ˌpɒt| i ‖ 'pɔːrt̬ ə ˌpɑːt| i ~**ies** iz
Port Askaig ₍ₗ₎pɔːt 'æsk eɪg ‖ ₍ₗ₎pɔːrt̬- ₍ₗ₎poʊrt̬-
portative 'pɔːt ət ɪv ‖ 'pɔːrt̬ ət̬ ɪv 'poʊrt̬-
Port-au-Prince ˌpɔːt əʊ 'prɪn⁺s ‖ ˌpɔːrt̬ oʊ
  ˌpoʊrt̬- —*Fr* [pɔ ʁo pʁɛ̃s]
Portbury 'pɔːt bər‿i ‖ 'pɔːrt ˌber i 'poʊrt-
portcullis pɔːt 'kʌl ɪs -əs ‖ pɔːrt- poʊrt- ~**es** ɪz
  əz
porte, P~ pɔːt ‖ pɔːrt poʊrt
porte-cochere, porte-cochère ˌpɔːt kɒ 'ʃeə
  ‖ ˌpɔːrt koʊ 'ʃeᵊr ˌpoʊrt- ~**s** z
portend pɔː 'tend ‖ pɔːr- poʊr- ~**ed** ɪd əd ~**ing**
  ɪŋ ~**s** z

portent 'pɔːt ent ‖ 'pɔːrt- 'poʊrt- ~**s** s
portentous pɔː 'tent əs △-'tenᵗʃ-
  ‖ pɔːr 'tent̬ əs poʊr- ~**ly** li ~**ness** nəs nɪs
Porteous 'pɔːt i‿əs ‖ 'pɔːrt̬-
porter, P~ 'pɔːt ə ‖ 'pɔːrt̬ ᵊr 'poʊrt̬- ~**s** z
porterage 'pɔːt ər ɪdʒ ‖ 'pɔːrt̬- 'poʊrt̬-
porterhouse 'pɔːt ə haʊs ‖ 'pɔːrt̬ ᵊr- 'poʊrt̬-
  ˌporterhouse 'steak
Porteus 'pɔːt i‿əs ‖ 'pɔːrt̬-
Port Eynon ₍ₗ₎pɔːt 'aɪn ən ‖ ₍ₗ₎pɔːrt̬- ₍ₗ₎poʊrt̬-
portfolio ˌpɔːt 'fəʊl i‿əʊ ‖ ˌpɔːrt 'foʊl i oʊ
  ˌpoʊrt- ~**s** z
Porth pɔːθ ‖ pɔːrθ —*see also phrases with this
  word*
Porthcawl ₍ₗ₎pɔːθ 'kɔːl -'kaʊl ‖ ₍ₗ₎pɔːrθ- -'kɑːl
Porth Dinllaen ˌpɔːθ dɪn 'θlaɪn ‖ ˌpɔːrθ-
  —*Welsh* [ˌpɔrθ dɪn 'ɬəin, -'ɬiːn]
Porthleven ₍ₗ₎pɔːθ 'lev ᵊn ‖ ₍ₗ₎pɔːrθ-
Porthmadog ₍ₗ₎pɔːθ 'mæd ɒg
  ‖ ₍ₗ₎pɔːrθ 'mæd ɔːg -ɑːg —*Welsh*
  [pɔrθ 'ma dog]
porthole 'pɔːt həʊl →-hɒʊl ‖ 'pɔːrt hoʊl
  'poʊrt- ~**s** z
Portia 'pɔːʃ ə 'pɔːʃ i‿ə ‖ 'pɔːrʃ ə 'poʊrʃ-
portico 'pɔːt ɪ kəʊ ‖ 'pɔːrt̬ ɪ koʊ 'poʊrt̬- ~**s** z
portiere, portière ˌpɔːt i 'eə ‖ ˌpɔːrt̬ i 'eᵊr
  ˌpoʊrt̬-; pɔːr 'tiᵊr, poʊr- —*Fr* [pɔʁ tjɛːʁ] ~**s** z
Portillo pɔː 'tɪl əʊ ‖ pɔːr 'tɪl oʊ
portion 'pɔːʃ ᵊn ‖ 'pɔːrʃ ᵊn 'poʊrʃ- ~**ed** d ~**ing**
  ɪŋ ~**less** ləs lɪs ~**s** z
Portishead 'pɔːt ɪs hed §-əs- ‖ 'pɔːrt̬- 'poʊrt̬-
Portland, p~ 'pɔːt lənd ‖ 'pɔːrt- 'poʊrt-
  ˌPortland ce'ment; ˌPortland 'stone
Portlaoise ˌpɔːt 'liːʃ ə ‖ ˌpɔːrt- ˌpoʊrt-
port|ly 'pɔːt |li ‖ 'pɔːrt- 'poʊrt- ~**liness** li nəs
  -nɪs
Portmadoc ˌpɔːt 'mæd ək ‖ ˌpɔːrt- ˌpoʊrt-
Portman 'pɔːt mən ‖ 'pɔːrt- 'poʊrt-
portmanteau ₍ₗ₎pɔːt 'mænt əʊ
  ‖ pɔːrt 'mænt oʊ poʊrt- ~**s, ~x** z
  ₍ₗ₎port'manteau word
Portmeirion ₍ₗ₎pɔːt 'mer i‿ən ‖ ₍ₗ₎pɔːrt-
  ₍ₗ₎poʊrt-
Portnoy 'pɔːt nɔɪ ‖ 'pɔːrt- 'poʊrt-
Porto 'pɔːt əʊ ‖ 'pɔːrt̬ oʊ 'poʊrt̬-
Porto Alegre ˌpɔːt əʊ ə 'leg ri ˌ-u- ‖ ˌpɔːrt̬ u-
  -rə —*Port* Pôrto Alegre [por tu ɐ 'lɛ gri]
Portobello ˌpɔːt əʊ 'bel əʊ ◂
  ‖ ˌpɔːrt̬ ə 'bel oʊ ◂ poʊrt̬-
Portofino ˌpɔːt əʊ 'fiːn əʊ ‖ ˌpɔːrt̬ ə 'fiːn oʊ
  —*It* [pɔr to 'fiː no]
Porton 'pɔːt ᵊn ‖ 'pɔːrt ᵊn
Porto Ric|o ˌpɔːt əʊ 'riːk |əʊ
  ‖ ˌpɔːrt̬ ə 'riːk |oʊ ˌpoʊrt̬- ~**an/s** ən/z
portrait 'pɔːtr ət -ɪt, -eɪt ‖ 'pɔːrtr ət poʊrtr- ~**s**
  s
portraitist 'pɔːtr ət ɪst -ɪt-, -eɪt-, §-əst
  ‖ 'pɔːrtr ət̬ əst 'poʊrtr- ~**s** s
portraiture 'pɔːtr ɪtʃ ə -ətʃ-; -ɪ tjʊə, -ə-
  ‖ 'pɔːrtr ə tʃʊr 'poʊrtr-, -ətʃ ᵊr
portray pɔː 'treɪ ‖ pɔːr- poʊr-, pᵊr- ~**ed** d ~**ing**
  ɪŋ ~**s** z
portrayal pɔː 'treɪ əl ‖ pɔːr- pᵊr- ~**s** z

P

portrayer pɔː 'treɪ ə ‖ pɔːr 'treɪ ᵊr pᵊr- **~s** z
Portreath pɔː 'triːθ ‖ pɔːr-
Portree pɔː 'triː ‖ pɔːr-
Portrush ₍ˌ₎pɔːt 'rʌʃ ‖ ₍ˌ₎pɔːrt- ₍ˌ₎poᵘrt-
Port Said ˌpɔːt 'saɪd -'sɑː iːd ‖ ˌpɔːrt- ˌpoᵘrt-
Port Salut ˌpɔː sæ 'luː -sə- ‖ ˌpɔːr- ˌpoᵘr- —*Fr* [pɔʁ sa ly]
Portscatho ₍ˌ₎pɔːt 'skæθ əʊ ‖ ₍ˌ₎pɔːrt 'skæθ oᵘ ₍ˌ₎poᵘrt-
Portsea 'pɔːts i 'pɔːt siː ‖ 'pɔːrt siː 'poᵘrt-
Portslade ˌpɔːt 'sleɪd ◄ ‖ ˌpɔːrt- ˌpoᵘrt-
Portsmouth 'pɔːts məθ ‖ 'pɔːrts- 'poᵘrts-
Port Talbot ₍ˌ₎pɔːt 'tɔːlb ət pɔː-, pə-, -'tælb-, -'tɒlb- ‖ ₍ˌ₎pɔːrt- ₍ˌ₎poᵘrt-, -'tɑːlb-
portugaise ˌpɔːtʃ u 'geɪz ◄ ‖ ˌpɔːrtʃ- ˌpoᵘrtʃ- —*Fr* [pɔʁ ty gɛːz]
Portugal 'pɔːtʃ ʊg ᵊl -əg-; 'pɔːt jʊg- ‖ 'pɔːrtʃ əg ᵊl 'poᵘrtʃ-
Portuguese ˌpɔːtʃ u 'giːz ◄ -ə-; ˌpɔːt ju- ‖ ˌpɔːrtʃ-, ˌpoᵘrtʃ-, -'giːs, '···
  ˌPortu,guese 'food; ,Portuguese ,man-of-'war
pose pəʊz ‖ poᵘz **posed** pəʊzd ‖ poᵘzd **poses** 'pəʊz ɪz -əz ‖ 'poᵘz əz **posing** 'pəʊz ɪŋ ‖ 'poᵘz ɪŋ
Poseidon pə 'saɪd ᵊn pɒ- ‖ poᵘ-
poser 'pəʊz ə ‖ 'poᵘz ᵊr **~s** z
poseur ₍ˌ₎pəʊ 'zɜː ‖ pou 'zɜː **~s** z
posey 'pəʊz i ‖ 'poᵘz i
posh pɒʃ ‖ pɑːʃ —*In BrE there is also a jocular form* pəʊʃ **poshly** 'pɒʃ li ‖ 'pɑːʃ- **poshness** 'pɒʃ nəs -nɪs ‖ 'pɑːʃ-
pos|it 'pɒz |ɪt §-ət ‖ 'pɑːz |ət **~ited** ɪt ɪd §ət-, -əd ‖ ət̬ əd **~iting** ɪt ɪŋ §ət- ‖ ət̬ ɪŋ **~its** ɪts §əts ‖ ət̬s
position pə 'zɪʃ ᵊn **~ed** d **~ing** ˌɪŋ **~s** z
positional pə 'zɪʃ ᵊn_əl **~ly** i
positive 'pɒz ət ɪv -ɪt-; 'pɒz tɪv ‖ 'pɑːz ət̬ ɪv 'pɑːz tɪv **~ly** li —*but as an interj in AmE, sometimes* ˌpɑːz ə 'tɪv li **~ness** nəs nɪs **~s** z
  ,positive di,scrimi'nation; ,positive 'pole
positivism 'pɒz ət ɪv ˌɪz əm '·ɪt- ‖ 'pɑːz ət̬-
positivist 'pɒz ət ɪv ɪst '·ɪt-, §-əst ‖ 'pɑːz ət̬- **~s** s
positron 'pɒz ɪ trɒn -ə- ‖ 'pɑːz ə trɑːn **~s** z
positronium ˌpɒz ɪ 'trəʊn iˌəm ˌ·ə- ‖ ˌpɑːz ə 'troᵘn- **~s** z
Posner 'pɒz nə ‖ 'pɑːz nᵊr
posological ˌpəʊs ə 'lɒdʒ ɪk ᵊl ◄ ‖ ˌpɑːs ə 'lɑːdʒ- **~ly** ˌi
posology pəʊ 'sɒl ədʒ i ‖ pə 'sɑːl- poᵘ-
poss. pɒs ‖ pɑːs
posse 'pɒs i ‖ 'pɑːs i **~s** z
possess pə 'zes **~ed** t **~es** ɪz əz **~ing** ɪŋ
possession pə 'zeʃ ᵊn **~s** z
possessive pə 'zes ɪv **~ly** li **~ness** nəs nɪs **~s** z
  pos,sessive 'pronoun
possessor pə 'zes ə ‖ -ᵊr **~s** z
possessory pə 'zes ər i
posset 'pɒs ɪt §-ət ‖ 'pɑːs ət **~s** s
possibilit|y ˌpɒs ə 'bɪl ət |i ˌ·ɪ-, -ɪt i ‖ ˌpɑːs ə 'bɪl ət̬ |i **~ies** iz
possible 'pɒs əb ᵊl -ɪb- ‖ 'pɑːs- **~s** z

possibly 'pɒs əb li -ɪb- ‖ 'pɑːs-
possum, P~ 'pɒs əm ‖ 'pɑːs- **~s** z
post, Post pəʊst ‖ poᵘst **posted** 'pəʊst ɪd -əd ‖ 'poᵘst əd **posting** 'pəʊst ɪŋ ‖ 'poᵘst ɪŋ **posts** pəʊsts ‖ poᵘsts
  'post ex,change; 'post horn; 'post house; 'post ,office; 'post office box
post- ˌpəʊst ‖ ˌpoᵘst —*if the following sound is a consonant (not h), the t can optionally be elided —* **post-Victorian** ˌpəʊst vɪk 'tɔːr i_ən ◄ ‖ ˌpoᵘst- -'toᵘr-
Posta 'pɒst ə ‖ 'poᵘst ə
postag|e 'pəʊst ɪdʒ ‖ 'poᵘst- **~es** ɪz əz
  'postage stamp
postal, P~ 'pəʊst ᵊl ‖ 'poᵘst- **~ly** i
  ,postal 'order, '·· ,··
postbag 'pəʊst bæg ‖ 'poᵘst- **~s** z
post-bellum ˌpəʊst 'bel əm ◄ ‖ ˌpoᵘst-
postbox 'pəʊst bɒks ‖ 'poᵘst bɑːks **~es** ɪz əz
postcard 'pəʊst kɑːd ‖ 'poᵘst kɑːrd **~s** z
post-chais|e 'pəʊst ʃeɪz ‖ 'poᵘst- **~es** ɪz əz
postcode 'pəʊst kəʊd ‖ 'poᵘst koᵘd **~s** z
postconsonantal ˌpəʊst ˌkɒn's ə 'nænt ᵊl ◄ ‖ ˌpoᵘst ˌkɑːn's ə 'nænt̬ ᵊl ◄ **~ly** i
post|date ˌpəʊst |'deɪt ◄ ‖ ˌpoᵘst- **~dated** 'deɪt ɪd -əd ‖ 'deɪt̬ əd **~dates** 'deɪts **~dating** 'deɪt ɪŋ ‖ 'deɪt̬ ɪŋ
postdoc 'pəʊst 'dɒk ‖ ˌpoᵘst 'dɑːk '··· **~s** s
postdoctoral ˌpəʊst 'dɒkt ər əl ◄ →·-'dɒk trəl ‖ ˌpoᵘst 'dɑːkt-
poster, P~ 'pəʊst ə ‖ 'poᵘst ᵊr **~s** z
  'poster ,colour; 'poster paint
poste restante ˌpəʊst 'rest ɒnt ‖ ˌpoᵘst re 'stɑːnt —*Fr* [pɔst ʁɛs tɑ̃ːt]
posterior pɒ 'stɪər i_ə ‖ pɑː 'stɪr i_ᵊr poᵘ- **~ly** li **~s** z
posteriority pɒ ˌstɪər i 'ɒr ət i ˌpɒst ɪər-, -ɪt i ‖ pɑː ˌstɪr i 'ɔːr ət̬ i -'ɑːr-
posterity pɒ 'ster ət i -ɪt- ‖ pɑː 'ster ət̬ i
postern 'pɒst ən 'pəʊst- ‖ 'poᵘst ᵊrn 'pɑːst- **~s** z
postfix 'pəʊst fɪks ‖ 'poᵘst-
post-free ˌpəʊst 'friː ◄ ‖ ˌpoᵘst-
postgame ˌpəʊst 'geɪm ◄ ‖ ˌpoᵘst-
Postgate 'pəʊst geɪt ‖ 'poᵘst-
postglacial ˌpəʊst 'gleɪs i_əl ◄ -'gleɪʃ i_əl, -'gleɪʃ ᵊl ‖ ˌpoᵘst 'gleɪʃ ᵊl ◄
postgrad 'pəʊst græd ˌ·'· ‖ 'poᵘst- **~s** z
postgraduate ₍ˌ₎pəʊst 'græd ju_ət -'grædʒ u_, ɪt ‖ ₍ˌ₎poᵘst 'grædʒ u_ət **~s** s
posthaste ˌpəʊst 'heɪst ‖ ˌpoᵘst-
post hoc ˌpəʊst 'hɒk -'həʊk ‖ ˌpoᵘst 'hɑːk
posthumous 'pɒst jʊm əs -jəm-; 'pɒs tʃʊm-, -tʃəm- ‖ 'pɑːs tʃəm əs -tʃʊm- **~ly** li **~ness** nəs nɪs
posthypnotic ˌpəʊst hɪp 'nɒt ɪk ◄ -ɪp- ‖ ˌpoᵘst hɪp 'nɑːt̬ ɪk ◄
postich|e pɒ 'stiːʃ ‖ pɔː- pɑː- **~es** ɪz əz
postie 'pəʊst i ‖ 'poᵘst i **~s** z
postilion, postillion pɒ 'stɪl i_ən pə- ‖ poᵘ 'stɪl jən pə- **~s** z
postimpressionism ˌpəʊst ɪm 'preʃ ᵊn ˌɪz əm -ə-, ˌnɪz- ‖ ˌpoᵘst-

postimpressionist ˌpəʊst ɪm ˈpreʃ ᵊn_ɪst ◂ əst
‖ ˌpoʊst- ~s s
postindustrial ˌpəʊst ɪn ˈdʌs tri_əl ◂ ‖ ˌpoʊst-
posting ˈpəʊst ɪŋ ‖ ˈpoʊst ɪŋ ~s z
Post-it tdmk ˈpəʊst ɪt §-ət ‖ ˈpoʊst- ~s s
Postlethwaite ˈpɒs ᵊl θweɪt ‖ ˈpɑːs-
postlude ˈpəʊst luːd -ljuːd ‖ ˈpoʊst- ~s z
post|man ˈpəʊst |mən ‖ ˈpoʊst- **~men** mən
ˌpostman's ˈknock
postmark n, v ˈpəʊst mɑːk ‖ ˈpoʊst mɑːrk ~ed
t ~ing ɪŋ ~s s
postmaster ˈpəʊst ˌmɑːst ə §-ˌmæst-
‖ ˈpoʊst ˌmæst ᵊr ◂ ‖ -
ˌPostˌmaster ˈGeneral
postmen ˈpəʊst mən ‖ ˈpoʊst-
postmenopausal ˌpəʊst men ə ˈpɔːzᵊl ◂
‖ ˌpoʊst- -ˈpɑːz-ᵊl ◂
post meridiem ˌpəʊst mə ˈrɪd i_əm -em
‖ ˌpoʊst-
postmistress ˈpəʊst ˌmɪs trəs -trɪs ‖ ˈpoʊst-
~es ɪz əz
post-modern ˌpəʊst ˈmɒd ᵊn
‖ ˌpoʊst ˈmɑːd ᵊrn **~ism** ˌɪz əm **~ist/s**
ɪst/s § əst/s
postmortem ˌpəʊst ˈmɔːt əm -em, ˈ·ˌ··
‖ ˌpoʊst ˈmɔːrt̬ əm ~s z
postnasal ˌpəʊstˈneɪz ᵊl ◂ ‖ ˌpoʊst-
postnatal ˌpəʊst ˈneɪt ᵊl ◂ ‖ ˌpoʊst ˈneɪt̬ ᵊl ◂
~ly i
post-op ˌpəʊst ˈɒp ◂ ‖ ˌpoʊst ˈɑːp ◂
postoperative ˌpəʊst ˈɒp ᵊr_ət ɪv ◂ -ə reɪt-
‖ ˌpoʊst ˈɑːp ᵊr_ət̬ ɪv ◂ **~ly** li
postpaid ˌpəʊst ˈpeɪd ◂ ‖ ˌpoʊst-
post-partum ˌpəʊst ˈpɑːt əm ◂
‖ ˌpoʊst ˈpɑːrt̬ əm ◂
postpon|e ₍ₗ₎pəʊst ˈpəʊn ◂ pəs-
‖ ₍ₗ₎poʊst ˈpoʊn **~ed** d **~es** z **~ing** ɪŋ
postpos|e ˌpəʊst ˈpəʊz ◂ ˈ·· ‖ ˌpoʊst ˈpoʊz ◂
ˈ·· **~ed** d **~es** ɪz əz **~ing** ɪŋ
postposition ˌpəʊst pə ˈzɪʃ ᵊn ‖ ˌpoʊst- **~al** ᵊl
~s z
postpositive ˌpəʊst ˈpɒz ət ɪv -ɪt-
‖ ˌpoʊst ˈpɑːz ət̬ ɪv **~ly** li **~s** z
postprandial ˌpəʊst ˈprænd i_əl ◂ ‖ ˌpoʊst-
postproduction ˌpəʊst prə ˈdʌk ʃᵊn ◂
‖ ˌpoʊst-
postscript, P~ ˈpəʊst skrɪpt ‖ ˈpoʊst- **~s** s
postseason ˌpəʊstˈsiːz ᵊn ◂ ‖ ˌpoʊst-
postsecondary ˌpəʊst ˈsek ᵊnd_ər i ◂ -ən der i
‖ ˌpoʊst ˈsek ən der i ◂
poststructural ˌpəʊst ˈstrʌk tʃᵊr_əl ◂ ˈ·ˌʃᵊr‿
‖ ˌpoʊst- **~ism** ˌɪz əm **~ist/s** ɪst/s əst/s
posttest ˈpəʊst test ‖ ˈpoʊst- **~ed** ɪd əd **~ing**
ɪŋ **~s** s
post-traumatic ˌpəʊst trɔː ˈmæt ɪk ◂ -trɑʊ-,
-trə- ‖ ˌpoʊst trɔː ˈmæt̬ ɪk ◂ -trə-
postulant ˈpɒs tjʊl ənt →-tʃʊl- ‖ ˈpɑːs tʃᵊl- **~s**
s
postulate n ˈpɒs tjʊl ət →-tʃʊl-, -ɪt; -tju leɪt,
→-tʃu- ‖ ˈpɑːs tʃᵊl ət -tʃə leɪt **~s** s
postu|late v ˈpɒs tju |leɪt -tʃu- ‖ ˈpɑːs tʃə-
~lated leɪt ɪd -əd ‖ leɪt̬ əd **~lates** leɪts
~lating leɪt ɪŋ ‖ leɪt̬ ɪŋ

postulation ˌpɒs tju ˈleɪʃ ᵊn →-tʃu- ‖ ˌpɑːs tʃə-
~s z
Postum tdmk ˈpɒst əm ˈpoʊst- ‖ ˈpɑːst-
postural ˈpɒs tʃər əl -tjʊr- ‖ ˈpɑːs-
posture ˈpɒs tʃə -tjʊə ‖ ˈpɑːs tʃᵊr **~d** d
posturing ˈpɒs tʃər ɪŋ -tjʊər- ‖ ˈpɑːs- **~s** z
postviral ˌpəʊst ˈvaɪᵊr əl ◂ ‖ ˌpoʊst-
postvocalic ˌpəʊst vəʊ ˈkæl ɪk ◂ ‖ ˌpoʊst və-
~ally ᵊl_i
postwar ˌpəʊst ˈwɔː ◂ ‖ ˌpoʊst ˈwɔːr ◂
pos|y, Pos|y ˈpəʊz |i ‖ ˈpoʊz |i **~ies, ~y's** iz
pot pɒt ‖ pɑːt **pots** pɒts ‖ pɑːts **potted** ˈpɒt ɪd
-əd ‖ ˈpɑːt̬ əd **potting** ˈpɒt ɪŋ ‖ ˈpɑːt̬ ɪŋ
ˈpot plant; ˈpotting shed
potability ˌpəʊt ə ˈbɪl ət i -ɪt i
‖ ˌpoʊt̬ ə ˈbɪl ət̬ i
potable ˈpəʊt əb ᵊl ‖ ˈpoʊt̬- **~ness** nəs nɪs
potage pɒ ˈtɑːʒ pəʊ-; ˈpɒt ɑːʒ, ˈpəʊt- ‖ poʊ-
—Fr [pɔ taːʒ]
potash ˈpɒt æʃ ‖ ˈpɑːt̬-
potassic pə ˈtæs ɪk
potassium pə ˈtæs i_əm
poˌtassium ˈcyanide
potation pəʊ ˈteɪʃ ᵊn ‖ poʊ- **~s** z
potato pə ˈteɪt əʊ △bə- ‖ pə ˈteɪt̬ oʊ pət̬ ˈeɪt-,
-ə- **~es** z
poˈtato ˌbeetle; poˈtato cake; poˈtato
chip; poˌtato ˈcrisp; poˈtato ˌpeeler
potatory ˈpəʊt ət_ər i ‖ ˈpoʊt̬ ə tɔːr i -toʊr i
pot-au-feu ˌpɒt əʊ ˈfɜː ‖ ˌpɑːt̬ oʊ ˈfʌ —Fr
[pɔ to fø]
Potawatomi ˌpɒt ə ˈwɒt əm i ‖ ˌpɑːt̬ ə ˈwɑːt̬-
~s z
potbell|ied ˌpɒt ˈbel |id ◂ ˈ·ˌ·· ‖ ˈpɑːt̬ ˌbel |id ◂
~y i
potboiler ˈpɒt ˌbɔɪl ə ‖ ˈpɑːt̬ ˌbɔɪl ᵊr **~s** z
potbound ˈpɒt baʊnd ‖ ˈpɑːt̬-
potch pɒtʃ ‖ pɑːtʃ
poteen pə ˈtʃiːn pɒ-, pəʊ-, -ˈtiːn ‖ poʊ-
Potemkin pə ˈtemᵖ kɪn §-kən ‖ poʊ- —Russ
[pʌ ˈtⁱɔm kⁱɪn]
Poˌtemkin ˈvillage
potenc|y ˈpəʊt ᵊn's |i ‖ ˈpoʊt̬- **~ies** iz
potent ˈpəʊt ᵊnt ‖ ˈpoʊt̬- **~ly** li **~ness** nəs nɪs
potentate ˈpəʊt ᵊn teɪt ‖ ˈpoʊt̬- **~s** s
potential pə ˈten'ʃ ᵊl pəʊ- **~ly** i **~s** z
potentialit|y pə ˌten'ʃ i ˈæl ət |i pəʊ-, -ɪt i
‖ -ət̬ |i **~ies** iz
potenti|ate pəʊ ˈten'ʃ i |eɪt ‖ pə- **~ated** eɪt ɪd
-əd ‖ eɪt̬ əd **~ates** eɪts **~ating** eɪt ɪŋ ‖ eɪt̬ ɪŋ
potentiation pəʊ ˌten'ʃ i ˈeɪʃ ᵊn ‖ pə- **~s** z
potentilla ˌpəʊt ᵊn ˈtɪl ə ‖ ˌpoʊt̬- **~s** z
potentiometer pə ˌten'ʃ i ˈɒm ɪt ə pəʊ-, -ət ə
‖ -ˈɑːm ət̬ ᵊr **~s** z
potful ˈpɒt fʊl ‖ ˈpɑːt̬- **~s** z
pothead ˈpɒt hed ‖ ˈpɑːt̬- **~s** z
potheen pə ˈtʃiːn pɒ-, pəʊ-, -ˈtiːn, -ˈθiːn ‖ poʊ-
poth|er ˈpɒð |ə ‖ ˈpɑːð |ᵊr **~ered** əd ‖ ᵊrd
~ering ᵊr_ɪŋ **~ers** əz ‖ ᵊrz
potherb ˈpɒt hɜːb ‖ ˈpɑːt̬ ɜːb **~s** z
potholder ˈpɒt ˌhəʊld ə →-ˌhʊʊld-
‖ ˈpɑːt̬ ˌhoʊld ᵊr **~s** z

P

pothol|e 'pɒt həʊl →-hɒʊl ‖ 'pɑːt hoʊl **~ed** d **~er/s** ə/z ‖ ᵊr/z **~es** z **~ing** ɪŋ

pothook 'pɒt hʊk §-huːk ‖ 'pɑːt- **~s** s

pot|house 'pɒt |haʊs ‖ 'pɑːt- **~houses** haʊz ɪz -əz

pothunt|er 'pɒt ˌhʌnt |ə ‖ 'pɑːt ˌhʌnt̬ |ᵊr **~ers** əz ‖ ᵊrz **~ing** ɪŋ

potich|e pɒ 'tiːʃ ‖ poʊ- —*Fr* [pɔ tiʃ] **~es** ɪz əz

Potidae|a ˌpɒt ɪ 'diː |ə -ə- ‖ ˌpɑːt̬- **~an/s** ən/z

potion 'pəʊʃ ᵊn ‖ 'poʊʃ ᵊn **~s** z

Potiphar 'pɒt ɪf ə -əf-; -ɪ fɑː, -ə- ‖ 'pɑːt əf ᵊr

potlatch 'pɒt lætʃ ‖ 'pɑːt- **~es** ɪz əz

potluck ˌpɒt 'lʌk ‖ 'pɑːt-

pot|man 'pɒt |mən ‖ 'pɑːt- **~men** mən men

Potomac pə 'təʊm æk -ək ‖ -'toʊm ək -ɪk

potoroo ˌpɒt ə 'ruː ˌpɒt- ‖ ˌpoʊt̬- **~s** z

Potosi (i) pə 'təʊs i ‖ -'toʊs i (ii) ˌpɒt əʊ 'siː ‖ ˌpoʊt̬ ə- —*Places in the US are* (i); *in Bolivia,* (ii) —*Sp* Potosí [po to 'si]

potpourri ˌpəʊ pʊ 'riː -'pʊr i, -'pʊər i ‖ ˌpoʊ- —*Fr* [po pu ʁi]

pot-roast 'pɒt rəʊst ‖ 'pɑːt roʊst **~ed** ɪd əd **~ing** ɪŋ **~s** s

Potsdam 'pɒts dæm ‖ 'pɑːts- —*Ger* ['pɔts dam]

potsherd 'pɒt ʃɜːd ‖ 'pɑːt ʃɜːd **~s** z

potshot 'pɒt ʃɒt ‖ 'pɑːt ʃɑːt **~s** s

Pott pɒt ‖ pɑːt

pott... —*see* **pot**

pottage 'pɒt ɪdʒ ‖ 'pɑːt̬-

potter, P~ 'pɒt ə ‖ 'pɑːt̬ ᵊr **~ed** d **pottering** 'pɒt ᵊr ɪŋ ‖ 'pɑːt̬ ər ɪŋ **~s, ~'s** z

ˌpotter's 'wheel

Potteries 'pɒt ər iz ‖ 'pɑːt̬-

Potterton 'pɒt ət ən ‖ 'pɑːt̬ ᵊrt ᵊn

potter|y 'pɒt ˌər |i ‖ 'pɑːt̬ ər |i **~ies** iz

Pottinger 'pɒt ɪndʒ ə -əndʒ- ‖ 'pɑːt ᵊndʒ ᵊr

potto 'pɒt əʊ ‖ 'pɑːt oʊ **~s** z

Potts pɒts ‖ pɑːts

pott|y 'pɒt |i ‖ 'pɑːt̬ |i **~ier** i ə ‖ i ᵊr **~ies** iz **~iest** i ɪst i əst **~iness** i nəs i nɪs

potty-train 'pɒt i treɪn ‖ 'pɑːt̬- **~ed** d **~ing** ɪŋ **~s** z

pouch paʊtʃ **pouched** paʊtʃt **pouches** 'paʊtʃ ɪz -əz **pouching** 'paʊtʃ ɪŋ

pouf, pouffe *derogatory slang* '*homosexual*' pʊf puːf **poufs, pouffes** pʊfs puːfs, puːvz

pouf, pouffe '*seat*', '*hairstyle*', '*padding*' puːf **poufs, pouffes** puːfs

Poughill (i) 'pɒf ɪl -ᵊl ‖ 'pɑːf-, (ii) 'pʌf-, (iii) 'paʊ-

Poughkeepsie pə 'kɪps i (!)

Pouilly-Fumé ˌpuː ji 'fuːm eɪ ‖ pu ˌjiː fu 'meɪ —*Fr* [pu ji fy me]

Poujad|ism ˌpuː 'ʒɑːd |ˌɪz əm ·ˌ·ˌ· **~ist/s** ɪst/s əst/s

Poulenc 'puːl æŋk —*Fr* [pu lɛ̃k]

Poulsen, Poulson 'pəʊl sən →'pɒʊl- ‖ 'poʊl-

poult '*chick*' pəʊlt →pɒʊlt ‖ poʊlt **poults** pəʊlts →pɒʊlts ‖ poʊlts

poult '*fabric*' puːlt pʊlt **poults** puːlts pʊlts

Poulteney 'pəʊlt ni →'pɒʊlt- ‖ 'poʊlt-

Poulter 'pəʊlt ə →'pɒʊlt- ‖ 'poʊlt ᵊr

poulterer 'pəʊlt ˌər ə →'pɒʊlt ˌ ‖ 'poʊlt ᵊr ər **~s** z,

poultic|e 'pəʊlt ɪs →'pɒʊlt-, -əs ‖ 'poʊlt əs **~ed** t **~es** ɪz əz **~ing** ɪŋ

Poultney 'pəʊlt ni →'pɒʊlt- ‖ 'poʊlt-

Poulton 'pəʊlt ən →'pɒʊlt- ‖ 'poʊlt-

Poulton-le-Fylde ˌpəʊlt ən lə 'faɪᵊld →ˌpɒʊlt-, -li- ‖ ˌpoʊlt-

poultry 'pəʊltr i →'pɒʊltr- ‖ 'poʊltr i

poultry|man 'pəʊltr i |mən →'pɒʊltr- ‖ 'poʊltr- **~men** mən men

pounce paʊn̩s **pounced** paʊn̩st **pounces** 'paʊn̩s ɪz -əz **pouncing** 'paʊn̩s ɪŋ

pound, Pound paʊnd **pounded** 'paʊnd ɪd -əd **pounding/s** 'paʊnd ɪŋ/z **pounds, Pound's** paʊndz

ˌpound 'cake; ˌpound 'sterling

poundag|e 'paʊnd ɪdʒ **~es** ɪz əz

-pounder 'paʊnd ə ‖ -ᵊr — **two-pounder** ˌtuː 'paʊnd ə ‖ -ᵊr

Pountney 'paʊnt ni

Poupart (i) 'puːp ɑːt ‖ puː- 'pɑːrt, (ii) 'pəʊp- ‖ poʊ 'pɑːrt

pour pɔː ‖ pɔːr pour (= *pore*) **poured** pɔːd ‖ pɔːrd poʊrd **pouring** 'pɔːr ɪŋ ‖ 'poʊr- **pours** pɔːz ‖ pɔːrz poʊrz

pourboire pʊə 'bwaː: '·· ‖ pʊr 'bwaːr **~s** z —*Fr* [puʁ bwaːʁ]

pourer 'pɔːr ə ‖ 'pɔːr ᵊr 'poʊr- **~s** z

pous|sette puː |'set **~setted** 'set ɪd -əd ‖ 'set̬ əd **~settes** 'sets **~setting** 'set ɪŋ ‖ 'set̬ ɪŋ

poussin, P~ 'puːs æn -ɪn, §-ᵊn ‖ puː 'sæn —*Fr* [pu sæ̃] **~s, ~'s** z

pout paʊt **pouted** 'paʊt ɪd -əd ‖ 'paʊt̬ əd **pouting** 'paʊt ɪŋ ‖ 'paʊt̬ ɪŋ **pouts** paʊts

pouter 'paʊt ə ‖ 'paʊt̬ ᵊr **~s** z

poutine ˌpuː 'tiːn

poverty 'pɒv ət i ‖ 'pɑːv ᵊrt̬ i

ˌpoverty trap

poverty-stricken 'pɒv ət i ˌstrɪk ən ‖ 'pɑːv ᵊrt̬-

Povey (i) 'pəʊv i 'poʊv i, (ii) pə 'veɪ

pow *interj* paʊ

POW ˌpiː əʊ 'dʌb ᵊl juː ‖ ˌ·oʊ- -ə jə **~s, ~'s** z

powder 'paʊd ə ‖ -ᵊr **~ed** d **powdering** 'paʊd ˌər ɪŋ **~s** z

ˌpowder 'blue◂; 'powder keg; 'powder puff; 'powder room

Powderham 'paʊd ᵊr əm

powdery 'paʊd ᵊr i

Powell (i) 'paʊ ᵊl paʊl, (ii) 'pəʊ əl ‖ 'poʊ- —*The writer* Anthony P~ *is* (ii).

power, Power 'paʊ ə ‖ 'paʊ ᵊr **powered** 'paʊ ˌəd ‖ 'paʊ ᵊrd **powering** 'paʊ ᵊr ɪŋ ‖ 'paʊ ᵊr ɪŋ **powers** 'paʊ əz ‖ 'paʊ ᵊrz

'power base; 'power ˌbroker; 'power cut; 'power dive; 'power drill; ˌpower of at'torney; 'power pack; 'power plant; 'power play; 'power point; ˌpower 'politics; 'power ˌstation; ˌpower 'steering; 'power ˌstructure

power-assisted ˌpaʊ ər ə 'sɪst ɪd ◂ ‖ ˌpaʊ ᵊr-

powerboat 'paʊ ə bəʊt ‖ 'paʊ ᵊr boʊt ~s s

-powered 'paʊ əd ‖ 'paʊ ᵊrd — **low-powered**
ˌləʊ 'paʊ əd ◂ ‖ ˌloʊ 'paʊ ᵊrd ◂

powerful 'paʊ əf ᵊl ə fʊl ‖ 'paʊ ᵊrf ᵊl ᵊr fʊl ~**ly**
ˌi ~**ness** nəs nɪs

power|house 'paʊ ə |haʊs ‖ 'paʊ ᵊr- ~**houses**
haʊz ɪz -əz

powerless 'paʊ ə ləs -lɪs ‖ 'paʊ ᵊr- ~**ly** li
~**ness** nəs nɪs

Powerpoint 'paʊ ə pɔɪnt ‖ 'paʊ ᵊr-

Powerscourt (i) 'paʊ əz kɔːt ‖ 'paʊ ᵊrz kɔːrt
-koʊrt, (ii) 'pɔːz- ‖ 'pɔːrz-

power-sharing 'paʊ ə ˌʃeər ɪŋ ‖ 'paʊ ᵊr-

Powhatan 'paʊ ə tæn ˌ· ·ˈ·; 'paʊ hæt ᵊn

Powis (i) 'paʊ ɪs §-əs, (ii) 'pəʊ- ‖ 'poʊ-

Pownall 'paʊn ᵊl

powwow n, v 'paʊ waʊ ~**ed** d ~**ing** ɪŋ ~s z

Powys (i) 'pəʊ ɪs §-əs ‖ 'poʊ-, (ii) 'paʊ-
—Welsh ['pə wɪs, 'po-] —The Welsh county
is (ii), but the family name is usually (i).

pox pɒks ‖ 'pɑːks **poxes** 'pɒks ɪz -əz
‖ 'pɑːks əz

poxy 'pɒks i ‖ 'pɑːks i

Poynings 'pɔɪn ɪŋz

Poynting 'pɔɪnt ɪŋ ‖ 'pɔɪnt̬-

Pozidriv tdmk 'pɒz ɪ draɪv -ə- ‖ 'pɑːz-

Poznan, Poznań 'pɒz næn ˌ· ·ˈ· ‖ 'poʊz nɑːn
—Polish ['pɔ znaɲ]

P-plate 'piː pleɪt ~s s

PPS ˌpiː piː 'es

PR ˌpiː 'ɑː

Praa preɪ

practicability ˌprækt ɪk ə 'bɪl ət i -ɪt i ‖ -ət̬ i

practicab|le 'prækt ɪk əb |ᵊl ~**ly** li

practical 'prækt ɪk ᵊl ~s z
ˌpractical 'joke

practicalit|y ˌprækt ɪ 'kæl ət i |i ˌ·ə-, -ɪt i
‖ -ət̬ |i ~**ies** iz

practically 'prækt ɪk li -ɪk ᵊl i

practic|e, practis|e 'prækt ɪs §-əs ~**ed** t ~**es**
ɪz əz ~**ing** ɪŋ

practicum 'prækt ɪk əm

practitioner præk 'tɪʃ ᵊn ə ‖ ᵊr ~s z

Prada 'prɑːd ə

Prader-Willi ˌprɑːd ə 'vɪl i -'wɪl i ‖ -ᵊr-

Pradesh prə 'deɪʃ -'deʃ —Hindi [prə ɖeːʃ]

Prado 'prɑːd əʊ ‖ -oʊ —Sp ['pra ðo]

praecox 'priː kɒks 'praɪ- ‖ -kɑːks

Praed preɪd

praedial 'priːd i əl

praelector ₍ᵢ₎praɪ 'lekt ə ₍ᵢ₎priː-, -ɔː ‖ -ᵊr ~s z

praemunire ˌpraɪ mjuː 'nɪər i ˌpriː-, -mjə-,
-'naɪᵊr- ‖ -'nɪr i

prae|nomen ˌpriː |'nəʊm en ˌpraɪ-
‖ -|'noʊm ən ~**nomina** 'nɒm ɪn ə 'nəʊm-,
-ən- ‖ 'noʊm-

praepostor priː 'pɒst ə ‖ -'pɑːst ᵊr ~s z

praesidi|um prɪ 'sɪd i |əm prə-, praɪ-, -'zɪd- ~**a**
ə

praetor 'priːt ə -ɔː ‖ 'priːt̬ ᵊr ~s z

praetorian priː 'tɔːr i ən praɪ- ‖ -'toʊr- ~s z

pragmatic præg 'mæt ɪk ‖ -'mæt̬ ɪk ~**ally** ᵊl i
~s s

pragmatism 'præg mə ˌtɪz əm

pragmatist 'præg mət ɪst §-əst ‖ -mət̬- ~s s

Prague prɑːg

Praia 'praɪ ə —Port ['pra ja]

prairie 'preər i ‖ 'prer i ~s z
'prairie dog; ˌprairie 'rose

praise preɪz (= prays) **praised** preɪzd **praises**
'preɪz ɪz -əz **praising** 'preɪz ɪŋ

praiser 'preɪz ə ‖ -ᵊr ~s z

praiseworth|y 'praɪz ˌwɜːd |i ‖ -ˌwɜːð |i ~**ily**
ɪ li əl i ~**iness** i nəs i nɪs

Prakrit 'prɑː krɪt ~s s

praline 'prɑːl iːn ‖ 'preɪl- 'prɑːl- ~s z

pram 'boat' prɑːm præm **prams** prɑːmz præmz

pram 'baby carriage' præm **prams** præmz

prana 'prɑːn ə

prance prɑːn⁵s §præn⁵s ‖ præn⁵s **pranced**
prɑːn⁵st §præn⁵st ‖ præn⁵st **prancer/s**
'prɑːn⁵s ə/z §'præn⁵s- ‖ 'præn⁵s ᵊr/z **prances**
'prɑːn⁵s ɪz §'præn⁵s-, -əz ‖ 'præn⁵s əz
prancing 'prɑːn⁵s ɪŋ §'præn⁵s- ‖ 'præn⁵s ɪŋ

prancer 'prɑːn⁵s ə §'præn⁵s ə ‖ 'præn⁵s ᵊr ~s z

prandial 'prænd i əl ~**ly** i

prang præŋ **pranged** præŋd **pranging**
'præŋ ɪŋ **prangs** præŋz

Prangnell 'præŋ nᵊl

prank præŋk **pranks** præŋks

prank|ish 'præŋk| ɪʃ ~**some** səm

prankster 'præŋkst ə ‖ -ᵊr ~s z

p'raps præps —see **perhaps**

prase preɪz

praseodymium ˌpreɪz i əʊ 'dɪm i əm ‖ -oʊ'-
ˌpreɪs-

prat præt **prats** præts

Pratchett 'prætʃ ɪt §-ət

prate preɪt **prated** 'preɪt ɪd -əd ‖ 'preɪt̬ əd
prates preɪts **prating** 'preɪt ɪŋ ‖ 'preɪt̬ ɪŋ

prater 'preɪt ə ‖ 'preɪt̬ ᵊr ~s z

pratfall 'præt fɔːl ‖ -fɑːl ~s z

pratincole 'præt ɪŋ kəʊl 'preɪt-, →-kɒʊl
‖ 'præt ᵊn koʊl ~s z

pratique 'præt iːk -ɪk; præ 'tiːk ‖ præ 'tiːk

Pratt præt

prattl|e 'præt ᵊl ‖ 'præt̬ ᵊl ~**ed** d ~**er/s** ə/z
‖ ᵊrz ~**es** z ~**ing** ɪŋ

Pravda 'prɑːv də —Russ ['prav də]

prawn prɔːn ‖ prɑːn **prawns** prɔːnz ‖ prɑːnz
ˌprawn 'cocktail; ˌprawn 'cracker

praxis 'præks ɪs §-əs

Praxiteles præk 'sɪt ə liːz -ɪ-; -ᵊl iːz ‖ -'sɪt̬ ᵊl iːz

pray preɪ **prayed** preɪd **praying** 'preɪ ɪŋ **prays**
preɪz (= praise)
ˌpraying 'mantis

prayer 'one that prays' 'preɪ ə ‖ -ᵊr ~s z

prayer 'act/words of praying' preə ‖ preᵊr
præᵊr ~s z
'prayer book; 'prayer ˌmeeting; 'prayer
mat; 'prayer rug; 'prayer wheel

prayerful 'preə fʊl ‖ 'prer- 'prær- ~**ly** i ~**ness**
nəs nɪs

pre- ˌpriː, pri, prə, ˌpre —Compare re- . As a
productive prefix meaning 'before' (sometimes
spelt with a hyphen), ˌpriː: (preadapt

ˌpriː_ə 'dæpt, pre-sleep ˌpriː 'sliːp◂).
Otherwise, with a vaguer meaning, **pri, prə**
before a consonant sound (prepare **pri 'peə**
prə- ‖ -'peᵊr); *but if stressed through the
operation of a stressing rule usually* ˌpre +
(preparation ˌprep ə 'reɪʃ ᵊn).

preach priːtʃ **preached** priːtʃt **preaches**
'priːtʃ ɪz -əz **preaching** 'priːtʃ ɪŋ
preacher, P~ 'priːtʃ ə ‖ -ᵊr ~s z
preachi|fy 'priːtʃ ɪ |faɪ §-ə- ~**fied** faɪd ~**fies**
faɪz ~**fying** faɪ ɪŋ
preach|y 'priːtʃ |i ~**ier** i ə ‖ i ᵊr ~**iest** i ɪst ˌəst
~**iness** i nəs -nɪs
preadamic ˌpriː ə 'dæm ɪk ◂
preadamite ˌpriː 'æd ə maɪt ◂ ~s s
preamble pri 'æm bᵊl 'priː ˌæm- ~s z
pre-amp 'priː æmp ~s s
preamplification ˌpriː ˌæmp lɪf ɪ 'keɪʃ ᵊn
ˌ·ˌ·ˈ·ˌ, -ləf ˈ·-, §-ə'-
preampli|fy ₍ₐ₎priː 'æmp lɪ |faɪ -lə- ~**fied** faɪd
~**fier/s** faɪ ə/z ‖ faɪ ᵊr/z ~**fies** faɪz ~**fying**
faɪ ɪŋ
prearrang|e ˌpriː ə 'reɪndʒ ◂ ~**ed** d ~**ement**
mənt ~**es** ɪz əz ~**ing** ɪŋ
prebend 'preb ənd ~s z
prebendar|y 'preb ənd ˌᵊr |i ‖ -ən der |i ~**ies**
iz
prebuttal ˌpriː 'bʌt ᵊl pri- ‖ -'bʌt̬- ~s z
precambrian, Pre-Cambrian
₍ₐ₎priː 'kæm bri ən
precancerous ˌpriː 'kæn⸢s ər əs
precarious pri 'keər i əs prə- ‖ -'ker- -'kær-
~**ly** li ~**ness** nəs nɪs
precast ˌpriː 'kɑːst ◂ -'kæst ‖ -'kæst ◂ '·· ~**ing**
ɪŋ ~s s
precatory 'prek ət ər i ‖ -ə tɔːr i -tour i
precaution pri 'kɔːʃ ᵊn prə- ‖ -'kɑːʃ- ~s z
precautionary pri 'kɔːʃ ᵊn ər i -ᵊn ˌər i
‖ -ə ner i -'kɑːʃ-
preced|e pri 'siːd prə- ~**ed** ɪd əd ~**es** z ~**ing** ɪŋ
precedence 'pres ɪd ən⸢s 'priːs-, -əd-;
ˌpri 'siːd ᵊn⸢s, prə-
precedent *adj* pri 'siːd ᵊnt 'pres ɪd ənt, 'priːs-,
-əd- ~**ly** li
precedent *n* 'pres ɪd ənt 'priːs-, -əd- ~s s
precedented 'pres ɪ dent ɪd 'priːs-, '·ə-,
-dənt ·, -əd ‖ -dent̬ əd
precedential ˌpres ɪ 'den⸢ʃ ᵊl ◂ ˌpriːs-, -ə-
precentor pri 'sent ə prə- ‖ -'sent̬ ᵊr ~s z
precept 'priː sept ~s s
preceptor pri 'sept ə prə- ‖ -ᵊr 'priː sept ᵊr ~s
z
precess pri 'ses prə- ~**ed** t ~**es** ɪz əz ~**ing** ɪŋ
precession pri 'seʃ ᵊn prə- ~s z
precessional pri 'seʃ ᵊn ˌəl prə-
precinct 'priː sɪŋkt ~s s
preciosity ˌpreʃ i 'ɒs ət i ˌpres-, -ɪt i ‖ -'ɑːs ət̬ i
precious 'preʃ əs ~**ly** li ~**ness** nəs nɪs
ˌprecious 'metal; ˌprecious 'stone
precipic|e 'pres əp ɪs -ɪp-, §-əs ~**es** ɪz əz
precipitant pri 'sɪp ɪt ənt prə-, -ət- ~s s

precipi|tate *v* pri 'sɪp ɪ |teɪt prə-, -ə- ~**tated**
teɪt ɪd -əd ‖ teɪt̬ əd ~**tates** teɪts ~**tating**
teɪt ɪŋ ‖ teɪt̬ ɪŋ
precipitate *n, adj* pri 'sɪp ɪt ət prə-, -ət-, -ɪt;
-ɪ teɪt, -ə- ‖ -ət̬ ət -ə teɪt ~**ly** li ~**ness** nəs nɪs
~s s
precipitation pri ˌsɪp ɪ 'teɪʃ ᵊn prə-, -ə- ~s z
precipitous pri 'sɪp ɪt əs prə-, -ət- ‖ -ət̬ əs ~**ly**
li ~**ness** nəs nɪs
precis, précis *n sing., v* 'preɪs iː ‖ preɪ 'siː (*)
~ *n pl* z ~**ed** d ~**es** z ~**ing** ɪŋ
precise pri 'saɪs prə- ~**ly** li ~**ness** nəs nɪs
precision pri 'sɪʒ ᵊn prə- ~**ist/s** ɪst/s §əst/s
‖ əst/s
precision-made pri ˌsɪʒ ᵊn 'meɪd ◂ prə-,
→-ᵊm-
preclassical ˌpriː 'klæs ɪk ᵊl ◂
preclinical ˌpriː 'klɪn ɪk ᵊl ◂
preclud|e pri 'kluːd prə- ~**ed** ɪd əd ~**es** z ~**ing**
ɪŋ
preclusion pri 'kluːʒ ᵊn prə-
preclusive pri 'kluːs ɪv prə- ‖ -'kluːz- ~**ly** li
precocial pri 'kəʊʃ ᵊl prə- ‖ -'koʊʃ-
precocious pri 'kəʊʃ əs prə- ‖ -'koʊʃ əs ~**ly** li
~**ness** nəs nɪs
precocity pri 'kɒs ət i prə-, -ɪt- ‖ -'kɑːs ət̬ i
precognition ˌpriː kɒg 'nɪʃ ᵊn ‖ -kɑːg-
pre-colonial ˌpriː kə 'ləʊn i əl ◂ ‖ -'loʊn-
pre-Columbian ˌpriː kə 'lʌm bi ən ◂
ˌpre-Coˌlumbian 'pottery
precompos|e ˌpriː kəm 'pəʊz §-kɒm- ‖ -'poʊz
~**ed** d ◂ ~**es** ɪz əz ~**ing** ɪŋ
preconceiv|e ˌpriː kən 'siːv ◂ §-kɒn- ~**ed** d
~**es** z ~**ing** ɪŋ
ˌpreconˌceived i'deas
preconception ˌpriː kən 'sep ʃᵊn §-kɒn- ~s s
precon|cert ˌpriː kən |'sɜːt §-kɒn- ‖ -|'sɜːt
~**certed** 'sɜːt ɪd -əd ‖ 'sɜːt̬ əd ~**certing**
'sɜːt ɪŋ ‖ 'sɜːt̬ ɪŋ ~**certs** 'sɜːts ‖ 'sɜːts
precondition ˌpriː kən 'dɪʃ ᵊn §-kɒn- ~s s
preconis|e, preconiz|e 'priːk ə naɪz ~**ed** d
~**es** ɪz əz ~**ing** ɪŋ
preconsonantal ˌpriː ˌkɒn⸢s ə 'nænt ᵊl ◂
‖ -ˌkɑːn⸢s ə 'nænt̬ ᵊl ◂ -'nent̬- ~**ly** i
precook ˌpriː 'kʊk §-'kuːk ~**ed** t ~**ing** ɪŋ ~s s
precursive pri 'kɜːs ɪv prə- ‖ -'kɝːs ɪv ~**ly** li
precursor pri 'kɜːs ə prə- ‖ -'kɝːs ᵊr ~s z
precursor|y pri 'kɜːs ər |i prə- ‖ -'kɝːs- ~**ily**
əl i ɪ li
predaceous, predacious pri 'deɪʃ əs prə-
~**ness** nəs nɪs
pre|date *'antedate'* ₍ₐ₎priː- |'deɪt ~**dated**
'deɪt ɪd -əd ‖ 'deɪt̬ əd ~**dates** 'deɪts ~**dating**
'deɪt ɪŋ ‖ 'deɪt̬ ɪŋ
pre|date *'prey on'* pri |'deɪt prə- ~**dated**
'deɪt ɪd -əd ‖ 'deɪt̬ əd ~**dates** 'deɪts ~**dating**
'deɪt ɪŋ ‖ 'deɪt̬ ɪŋ
predation pri 'deɪʃ ᵊn prə- ~s z
predator 'pred ət ə -ɪt- ‖ -ət̬ ᵊr -ə tɔːr ~s z
predator|y 'pred ət ˌər |i ‖ -ə tɔːr |i -tour i ~**ily**
əl i ɪ li ~**iness** i nəs i nɪs
predawn ˌpriː 'dɔːn ◂ ‖ -'dɑːn ◂

predeceas|e ˌpriː dɪ ˈsiːs -də- **~ed** t **~es** ɪz əz **~ing** ɪŋ

PREDECESSOR

'pred- 88%, ˌpred·ˈ·· 9%, 'priːd-
3%.
AmE

predecessor 'priːd ɪ ses ə ˈ·ə-, ˌ·ˈ·· ‖ 'pred ə ses ³r ˌ·ˈ··; 'priːd- — *Preference poll, AmE:* 'pred- 88%, ˌpred·ˈ·· 9%, 'priːd- 3%. **~s** z
predefin|e ˌpriː dɪ ˈfaɪn -də- §-diː- **~ed** d ◄ **~ed** z **~ing** ɪŋ
predestinate *adj* ₍ᵢ₎pri: 'dest ɪn ət prɪ-, -ən-, -ɪt; -ɪ neɪt, -ə- **~ly** li
predesti|nate *v* ₍ᵢ₎pri: 'dest ɪ |neɪt prɪ-, -ə· **~nated** neɪt ɪd -əd ‖ neɪt̬ əd **~nates** neɪts **~nating** neɪt ɪŋ ‖ neɪt̬ ɪŋ
predestination pri: ˌdest ɪ 'neɪʃ ³n prɪ-, ˌpriː-, ˌ·ˈ·-, -ə'--
predestin|e ₍ᵢ₎pri: 'dest ɪn prɪ-, -ən **~ed** d **~es** z **~ing** ɪŋ
predetermination ˌpriː dɪ ˌtɜːm ɪ 'neɪʃ ³n ˌdə-, -,ə- ‖ -,tɜːm-
predetermin|e ˌpriː di 'tɜːm ɪn ◄ -də-, -ən ‖ -'tɜːm ən **~ed** d **~es** z **~ing** ɪŋ
predeterminer ˌpriː di 'tɜːm ɪn ə ˌ·də-, -ən ə ‖ -'tɜːm ən ³r **~s** z
predial 'priːd i əl
predicability ˌpred ɪk ə 'bɪl ət i -ɪt i ‖ -ət̬ i
predicable 'pred ɪk əb ³l **~ness** nəs nɪs **~s** z
predicament pri 'dɪk ə mənt prə- —*but in the sense 'logical category', also* 'pred ɪk- **~s** s
predi|cate *v* 'pred ɪ |keɪt **~cated** keɪt ɪd -əd ‖ keɪt̬ əd **~cates** keɪts **~cating** keɪt ɪŋ ‖ keɪt̬ ɪŋ
predicate *n* 'pred ɪk ət 'priːd-, -ɪt; -ɪ keɪt **~s** s
predication ˌpred ɪ 'keɪʃ ³n -ə- **~s** z
predicative pri 'dɪk ət ɪv prə- ‖ -ət̬ ɪv 'pred ɪk-; 'pred ɪ keɪt̬ ɪv **~ly** li **~ness** nəs nɪs **~s** z
predicator 'pred ɪ keɪt ə ˈ·ə- ‖ -keɪt̬ ³r **~s** z
predict pri 'dɪkt prə- **~ed** ɪd əd **~ing** ɪŋ **~s** s
predictability pri ˌdɪkt ə 'bɪl ət i prə-, -ɪt i ‖ -ət̬ i
predictab|le pri 'dɪkt əb |³l prə- **~ly** li
prediction pri 'dɪk ʃ³n prə- **~s** z
predictive pri 'dɪkt ɪv prə- **~ly** li **~ness** nəs nɪs
predictor pri 'dɪkt ə prə- ‖ -³r **~s** z
predigest ˌpriː daɪ 'dʒest -dɪ-, -də- **~ed** ɪd əd **~ing** ɪŋ **~s** s
predilection ˌpriːd ɪ 'lek ʃ³n -ə-, -³l 'ek-; △-'lɪk- ‖ ˌpred ³l 'ek ʃ³n ˌpriːd- **~s** z
predispos|e ˌpriː dɪ 'spəʊz -də- ‖ -'spoʊz **~ed** d **~es** ɪz əz **~ing** ɪŋ
predisposition ˌpriː ˌdɪsp ə 'zɪʃ ³n **~s** z
prednisolone pred 'nɪs ə ləʊn ‖ -loʊn

prednisone 'pred nɪ səʊn -nə-, -zəʊn, -zəʊn ‖ -soʊn -zoʊn
predominanc|e pri 'dɒm ɪn ən¹s prə-, -ən- ‖ -'dɑːm- **~y** i
predominant pri 'dɒm ɪn ənt prə-, -ən- ‖ -'dɑːm- **~ly** li
predomi|nate pri 'dɒm ɪ |neɪt prə-, -ə· ‖ -'dɑːm- **~nated** neɪt ɪd -əd ‖ neɪt̬ əd **~nates** neɪts **~nating** neɪt ɪŋ ‖ neɪt̬ ɪŋ
Preece priːs
pre-echo ˌpriː 'ek əʊ ‖ -oʊ **~es** z
pre-eclampsia ˌpriː ɪ 'klæmps i ə ˌe-, ˌ·ə-
Preedy 'priːd i
preemie 'priːm i **~s** z
preeminence pri 'em ɪn ən¹s ˌpriː-, -ən-
preeminent pri 'em ɪn ənt ˌpriː-, -ən- **~ly** li
preempt pri 'empt ˌpriː- **~ed** ɪd əd **~ing** ɪŋ **~s** s
preemption pri 'emp ʃ³n ˌpriː- **~s** z
preemptive pri 'empt ɪv ˌpriː- **~ly** li
preemptor pri 'empt ə ˌpriː-, -ɔː ‖ -³r **~s** z
preen, Preen priːn **preened** priːnd **preening** 'priːn ɪŋ **preens** priːnz
preexilian ˌpriː ɪg 'zɪl i ən ◄ ˌeg-, ˌ·əg-, ˌ·ɪk-, ˌek-, ˌ·ək-
pre-exilic ˌpriː ɪg 'zɪl ɪk ◄ -eg-, -əg-, -ɪk-, -ek-, -ək-
preexist ˌpriː ɪg 'zɪst -eg-, -əg-, -ɪk-, -ek-, -ək- **~ed** ɪd əd **~ing** ɪŋ **~s** s
preexistenc|e ˌpriː ɪg 'zɪst ən¹s -eg-, -əg-, -ɪk-, -ek-, -ək- **~es** ɪz əz
preexistent ˌpriː ɪg 'zɪst ənt ◄ -eg-, -əg-, -ɪk-, -ek-, -ək- **~ly** li
prefab 'priː fæb **~s** z
prefabri|cate ˌpriː 'fæb |keɪt -rə- **~cated** keɪt ɪd -əd ‖ keɪt̬ əd **~cates** keɪts **~cating** keɪt ɪŋ ‖ keɪt̬ ɪŋ
prefabrication ˌpriː ˌfæb rɪ 'keɪʃ ³n ·ˌ·ˈ·-, -rə'-- **~s** z
prefac|e *n, v* 'pref əs -ɪs **~ed** t **~es** ɪz əz **~ing** ɪŋ
prefator|y 'pref ət ˌər |i ‖ -ə tɔːr |i -toʊr i **~ily** əl i ɪ li
prefect 'priː fekt **~s** s
prefectorial ˌpriː fek 'tɔːr i əl ◄ ‖ -'toʊr-
prefectural pri 'fek tʃər əl ₍ᵢ₎-tjʊr-; 'priː fek-
prefecture 'priː fek tʃə -tʃʊə; -fekt jʊə ‖ -tʃ³r **~s** z
prefer pri 'fɜː prə- ‖ -'fɜː **~red** d **preferring** pri 'fɜːr ɪŋ prə- ‖ -'fɜː ɪŋ **~s** z
pre͵ferred 'stock
preferability ˌpref ³r ə 'bɪl ət i △pri ˌfɜːr ə-, prə- ‖ -ət̬ i △pri ˌfɜː ə-
preferab|le 'pref ³r ̩əb |³l △pri 'fɜːr əb |³l, prə- ‖ △pri 'fɜː- **~leness** ³l nəs -nɪs **~ly** li
preferenc|e 'pref ³r ̩ən¹s **~es** ɪz əz 'preference ˌshares
preferential ˌpref ə 'ren¹ʃ ³l ◄ **~ly** i
preferment pri 'fɜː mənt prə- ‖ -'fɜː- **~s** s
prefiguration ˌpriː ˌfɪg ə 'reɪʃ ³n -jʊ³- ‖ -jə- **~s** z
prefigure ₍ᵢ₎priː 'fɪg ə ‖ -j³r *(*)* **~d** d **~s** z **prefiguring** ₍ᵢ₎priː 'fɪg ər ɪŋ ‖ -jər ɪŋ **~ment** mənt
prefix *n* 'priː fɪks **~es** ɪz əz

prefix v 'pri: fıks ₍ᵢ₎pri: 'fıks **~ed** t **~es** ız əz
~ing ıŋ
prefixal ₍ᵢ₎pri: 'fıks ᵊl 'pri: fıks- **~ly** i
preflight ˌpri: 'flaıt ◄
preformation ˌpri: fɔ: 'meıʃᵊn ‖ -fɔːr-
prefrontal ₍ᵢ₎pri: 'frʌnt ᵊl ‖ -'frʌn̪t ᵊl
pregame ˌpri: 'geım ◄
preggers 'preg əz ‖ -ᵊrz
pregnanc|y 'preg nənᵗs |i **~ies** iz
pregnant 'preg nənt **~ly** li
prehead 'pri: hed **~s** z
pre|heat ˌpri: |'hi:t ◄ **~heated** 'hi:t ıd -əd
‖ 'hi:t̪ əd **~heating** 'hi:t ıŋ ‖ 'hi:t̪ ıŋ **~heats**
'hi:ts
ˌpreˌheated 'oven
prehensile pri 'henᵗs aıᵊl prə- ‖ -ᵊl (*)
prehistoric ˌpri: hı 'stɒr ık ◄ -ı- ‖ -'stɔːr ık
-'stɑːr- **~ally** ᵊl̩i
prehistory ˌpri: 'hıs tri -tər i
pre-ignition ˌpri: ıg 'nıʃ ᵊn
prejudg|e 'dʒʌdʒ **~ed** d **~ement, ~ment**
mənt **~es** ız əz **~ing** ıŋ
prejudic|e 'predʒ u dıs -ə-, §-dəs, §-daıs
‖ -əd əs **~ed** t **~es** ız əz **~ing** ıŋ
prejudicial ˌpredʒ u 'dıʃ ᵊl ◄ -ə- ‖ -ə- **~ly** i
prelac|y 'prel əs |i **~ies** iz
prelapsarian ˌpri: læp 'seər i̯ən ◄ ‖ -'ser- **~s**
z
prelate 'prel ət -ıt **~s** s
prelim 'pri: lım prı 'lım, prə- **~s** z
preliminar|y pri 'lım ın ᵊr̩|i prə-, -ᵊn̯ər |i;
§-ı ner |i, §-ə ner i ‖ -ə ner |i **~ies** iz **~ily** əl i
ı li
prelingual ˌpri: 'lıŋ gwəl ◄ , ·'lıŋ gju̯əl ◄ **~ly** i
preliterate ₍ᵢ₎pri: 'lıt̩ər ət ◄ -ıt ‖ -'lıt̪ ər-
→-'lıtr-
pre-loved ˌpri: 'lʌvd ◄
prelude 'prel ju:d ‖ 'preıl-, -u:d; 'pri: lu:d **~s** z
prelusive pri 'lu:s ıv -'lju:s- ‖ -'lu:z- **~ly** li
Prem prem
premarital ₍ᵢ₎pri: 'mær ıt ᵊl -ət- ‖ -ət̪ ᵊl -'mer-
~ly i

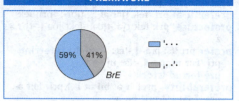

PREMATURE

— Preference poll, BrE: ' · · · 59%, ˌ · ·ˈ· 41%.

premature 'prem ət̬ʃ ə 'pri:m-; -ə tjʊə, -tʃʊə,
-tjɔ:, -tʃɔ:; ˌ ·ə 'tʃʊə, -'tʃɔ:, -'tjʊə, -'tjɔ:
‖ ˌpri:m ə 'tʊᵊr ◄ -'tʃʊᵊr, -'tjʊᵊr; ' · · ·
— Preference poll, BrE: ' · · · 59%, ˌ · ·ˈ· 41%.
(*) **~ly** li **~ness** nəs nıs
prematurity ˌprem ə 'tʃʊər ət i ˌpri:m-,
-'tjʊər-, -'tʃɔːr-, -'tʃɔːr-, -ıt i ‖ ˌpri:m ə 'tʊr ət̪ i
-'tʃʊr-, -'tjʊr-
premed ₍ᵢ₎pri: 'med **~s** z
premedical ₍ᵢ₎pri: 'med ık ᵊl
premedication ˌpri: ˌmed ı 'keıʃ ᵊn · , · ·ˈ·- **~s** z

premedi|tate ₍ᵢ₎pri: 'med ı |teıt pri-, prə-, -ə-
~tated teıt ıd -əd ‖ teıt̪ əd **~tates** teıts
~tating teıt ıŋ ‖ teıt̪ ıŋ
premeditation pri ˌmed ı 'teıʃ ᵊn prə-, -ə-;
ˌpri:, · ·ˈ--, -ə'--
premenstrual ˌpri: 'menᵗs tru̯əl ◄
ˌpreˌmenstrual 'tension
premier 'prem i̯ə 'pri:m- ‖ pri 'mıᵊr -'mjıᵊr;
'pri:m i̯ᵊr (*) **~s** z
premiere, première 'prem i eə -i̯ə, , · ·'eə
‖ pri 'mıᵊr pre-, -'mjıᵊr; prım 'jeᵊr (*) **~s** z
premiership 'prem i̯ə ʃıp 'pri:m-
‖ pri 'mıᵊr ʃıp -'mjıᵊr-; 'pri:m i̯ᵊr-
Preminger 'prem ındʒ ə ‖ -ᵊr
premis|e v 'prem ıs §-əs; prı 'maız, prə- **~ed** t
~es ız əz **~ing** ıŋ
prem|ise n 'prem| ıs §-əs **~ises** ıs ız əs-, -əz;
ı si:z, ə-
premiss 'prem ıs §-əs **~es** ız əz
premium 'pri:m i̯əm **~s** z
'premium bond, · · · '.
premodification ˌpri: ˌmɒd ıf ı 'keıʃ ᵊn -, -əf-,
§-ə'· · ‖ -ˌmɑːd-
premodi|fy ˌpri: 'mɒd ı |faı -ə- ‖ -'mɑːd-
~fied faıd **~fier/s** faı̯ə/z ‖ faı̯ᵊr/z **~fies** faız
~fying faı ıŋ
premolar ₍ᵢ₎pri: 'məʊl ə ‖ -'moʊl ᵊr **~s** z
premonition ˌprem ə 'nıʃ ᵊn ˌpri:m- **~s** z
premonitor|y pri 'mɒn ıt̬ ər |i prə-, ˌpri:-,
-'·ət̬ ‖ -'mɑːn ə tɔːr |i -toʊr i **~ily** əl i ı ı li
prenatal ˌpri: 'neıt ᵊl ◄ ‖ -'neıt̪ ᵊl ◄ **~ly** i
Prendergast 'prend ə gɑːst -gæst ‖ -ᵊr gæst
prentice, P~, Prentis, Prentiss 'prent ıs §-əs
‖ 'pren̪t əs
prenuptial ˌpri: 'nʌp ʃᵊl ◄ -tʃəl; △-'nʌp ʃu̯əl,
△-tʃu̯əl **~ly** i **~s** z —The nonstandard
pronunciations are reflected in a nonstandard
spelling prenuptial
preoccupation pri ˌɒk ju 'peıʃ ᵊn ˌpri:, · ·ˈ--,
-jə'-- ‖ -ˌɑːk jə- **~s** z
preoccu|py pri 'ɒk ju |paı ˌpri:-, -jə- ‖ -'ɑːk jə-
~pied paıd **~pies** paız **~pying** paı ıŋ
pre-op ˌpri: 'ɒp ◄ ‖ -'ɑːp ◄
preoperative ˌpri: 'ɒp ər̯ət ıv ◄
‖ -'ɑːp ər̯ət̪ ıv **~ly** li
preordain ˌpri: ɔ: 'deım ‖ -ɔːr- **~ed** d **~ing** ıŋ
~s z
preordination ₍ᵢ₎pri: ˌɔːd ı 'neıʃ ᵊn -ə'--,
-ᵊn 'eıʃ- ‖ -ˌɔːrd ᵊn 'eıʃ ᵊn **~s** z
pre-owned ˌpri: 'əʊnd ◄ ‖ -'oʊnd ◄
prep prep **prepped** prept **prepping** 'prep ıŋ
preps preps
'prep school
prepack ˌpri: 'pæk ◄ **~ed** t **~ing** ıŋ **~s** s
prepackag|e ˌpri: 'pæk ıdʒ ◄ **~ed** d **~es** ız əz
~ing ıŋ
prepaid ˌpri: 'peıd ◄
preparation ˌprep ə 'reıʃ ᵊn **~s** z
preparative pri 'pær ət ıv prə- ‖ -ət̪ ıv -'per-
~ly li **~s** z
preparator|y pri 'pær ət̬ər |i prə- ‖ -ə tɔːr |i
-'per-, -toʊr i; 'prep ər̯ə- **~ily** əl i ı li
pre'paratory school

prepare pri 'peə prə- ‖ -'pe²r -'pæ²r **~d** d
  preparing pri 'peər ɪŋ prə- ‖ -'per ɪŋ -'pær-
  ~s z
preparedness pri 'peər ɪd nəs prə-, -əd-, -nɪs;
  -'peəd nəs, -nɪs ‖ -'per əd- -'pær-; -'perd nəs,
  -'pærd-
pre|pay ˌpri: ‖ 'peɪ ◄ **~paid** 'peɪd ◄ **~paying**
  'peɪ ɪŋ **~payment** 'peɪ mənt **~pays** 'peɪz
prepense pri 'pen⁀s ˌpri:-, prə- **~ly** li
preponderanc|e pri 'pɒnd ər ən⁀s prə-
  ‖ -'pɑːnd‿ **~y** i
preponderant pri 'pɒnd‿ər ənt prə- ‖ -'pɑːnd‿
  ~ly li
preponde|rate pri 'pɒnd ə |reɪt prə-
  ‖ -'pɑːnd- **~rated** reɪt ɪd -əd ‖ reɪt̬ əd **~rates**
  reɪts **~rating** reɪt ɪŋ ‖ reɪt̬ ɪŋ
prepos|e ˌpri: 'pəʊz ◄ ‖ -'poʊz ◄ **~ed** d **~es** ɪz
  əz **~ing** ɪŋ
preposition ˌprep ə 'zɪʃ ³n **~s** z
prepositional ˌprep ə 'zɪʃ ³n‿ əl ◄ **~ly** i **~s** z
  ˌprepo'sitional 'phrase
prepositive ₍ᵢ₎pri: 'pɒz ət ɪv -ɪt- ‖ -'pɑːz ət̬ ɪv
  ~ly li **~s** z
prepossess ˌpri: pə 'zes **~ed** t **~es** ɪz əz **~ing**
  ɪŋ
prepossessing|ly ˌpri: pə 'zes ɪŋ |li **~ness**
  nəs nɪs
prepossession ˌpri: pə 'zeʃ ³n **~s** z
preposterous pri 'pɒst ər əs prə-, §pri:-
  ‖ -'pɑːst- **~ly** li **~ness** nəs nɪs
prepotency ₍ᵢ₎pri: 'pəʊt ³n⁀s i ‖ -'poʊt-
prepotent ₍ᵢ₎pri: 'pəʊt ³nt ‖ -'poʊt- **~ly** li
prepp|ie, prepp|y 'prep |i **~ier** i‿ə ‖ i‿³r **~ies**
  iz **~iest** i‿ɪst ‿əst
preprint 'pri: prɪnt **~s** s
preproduction ˌpri: prə 'dʌk ʃ³n
preprogrammed ˌpri: 'prəʊ græmd ◄
  §-grəmd ◄ ‖ -'proʊ-
prepubescent ˌpri: pju 'bes ³nt ◄
prepuc|e 'pri:p ju:s **~es** ɪz əz
prequel 'pri: kwəl **~s** z
Pre-Raphaelite ₍ᵢ₎pri: 'ræf ə laɪt ₍ᵢ₎'‿i‿ə ‿,
  ₍ᵢ₎'‿eɪ ə ‿‖ ₍ᵢ₎'reɪf- **~s** s
prerecord ˌpri: rɪ 'kɔːd ◄ -rə-, §-ri:- ‖ -'kɔːrd
  ~ed ɪd əd **~ing** ɪŋ **~s** z
preregist|er ˌpri: 'redʒ ɪst| ə -əst|- ‖ -³r **~ered**
  əd ‖ ³rd **~ering** ər‿ɪŋ **~ers** əz ‖ ³rz
prerequisite ₍ᵢ₎pri: 'rek wəz ɪt -wɪz-, §-ət **~s** s
prerogative pri 'rɒg ət ɪv prə- ‖ -'rɑːg ət̬ ɪv **~s**
  z
pres|a 'pres| ə -ɑː ‖ 'preɪs| ə **~as** əz ɑːz **~e** eɪ
  —*It* ['pre: sa]
presag|e v, n 'pres ɪdʒ -ɑːʒ; pri 'seɪdʒ **~ed** d
  ~es ɪz əz **~ing** ɪŋ
presbyopia ˌprez bi 'əʊp i‿ə ˌpres-, -baɪ-
  ‖ -'oʊp-
presbyopic ˌprez bi 'ɒp ɪk ◄ ˌpres-, -baɪ-
  ‖ -'ɑːp ɪk ◄
presbyter 'prez bɪt ə 'pres-, -bət- ‖ -bət̬ ³r **~s** z
Presbyterian, p~ ˌprez bɪ 'tɪər i‿ən ◄ ˌpres-,
  ˌ-bə- ‖ -'tɪr- **~ism** ˌɪz əm **~s** z
presbyter|y 'prez bɪt‿ər |i 'pres-, '-bət‿;
  §-bɪ ter i, §-bə ‿ ‿ ‖ -bə ter |i **~ies** iz

Prescelly, Prescely pri 'sel i prə-, pre-
  —*Welsh* Preseli [pre 'sɛ li]
preschool *adj* ˌpri: 'sku:l ◄
  ˌpreschool 'playgroup
preschool *n* 'pri: sku:l **~er/s** ə/z ‖ ³r/z **~s** z
prescience 'pres i‿ən⁀s 'preʃ- ‖ 'preʃ ³n⁀s
  'pri:ʃ-, -i‿ən⁀s
prescient 'pres i‿ənt 'preʃ- ‖ 'preʃ ³nt 'pri:ʃ-,
  -i‿ənt **~ly** li
prescientific ˌpri:, saɪ ən 'tɪf ɪk ◄
prescind pri 'sɪnd prə- **~ed** ɪd əd **~ing** ɪŋ **~s** z
Prescot, Prescott 'presk ət -ɒt ‖ -ɑːt
prescrib|e pri 'skraɪb prə- **~ed** d **~er/s** ə/z
  ‖ ³r/z **~es** z **~ing** ɪŋ
prescript *n* 'pri: skrɪpt **~s** s
prescript *adj* pri 'skrɪpt prə-; 'pri: skrɪpt
prescription pri 'skrɪp ʃ³n prə- **~s** z
  pre'scription charge; pre'scription drug
prescriptive pri 'skrɪpt ɪv prə- **~ly** li **~ness**
  nəs nɪs
  pre,scriptive 'right
prescriptiv|ism pri 'skrɪpt ɪv |ˌɪz əm prə-
  ~ist/s ɪst/s §əst/s ‖ əst/s
preseason ˌpri: 'si:z ³n ◄ **~s** z
presenc|e 'prez ³n⁀s **~es** ɪz əz
  ˌpresence of 'mind
present *adj; n 'gift'; n 'time now'* 'prez ³nt **~ly**
  li **~s** s
  ˌpresent 'participle; ˌpresent 'perfect;
  ˌpresent 'tense
pre|sent *v; n 'military stance'* pri |'zent prə-
  ~sented 'zent ɪd -əd ‖ 'zent̬ əd **~senting**
  'zent ɪŋ ‖ 'zent̬ ɪŋ **~sents** 'zents
presentab|le pri 'zent əb |³l prə- ‖ -'zent̬-
  ~leness ³l nəs -nɪs **~ly** li
presentation ˌprez ³n 'teɪʃ ³n ˌpri:z-, -en- **~s** z
  ˌpresen'tation ˌcopy
presentational ˌprez ³n 'teɪʃ ən‿³l ◄ ˌpri:z-,
  ˌ-en-
present-day ˌprez ³nt 'deɪ ◄
presenteeism ˌprez ³n 'ti: ˌɪz əm
presentencing ˌpri: 'sent ən⁀s ɪŋ ◄ ‖ -³n⁀s-
presenter pri 'zent ə prə- ‖ -'zent̬ ³r **~s** z
presentient pri 'sen⁀ʃ ³nt prə-, -'zen⁀ʃ- -'‿i‿ənt,
  -'sent i‿ənt
presentiment pri 'zent ɪ mənt prə-, -'sent-, -ə-
  ‖ -'zent̬- **~s** s
presently 'prez ³nt li
presentment pri 'zent mənt prə-
preservable pri 'zɜːv əb ³l prə- ‖ -'zɜːv-
preservation ˌprez ə 'veɪʃ ³n ‖ -³r- **~ist/s**
  ɪst/s §əst/s **~s** z
  ˌpreser'vation ˌorder
preservative pri 'zɜːv ət ɪv prə- ‖ -'zɜːv ət̬ ɪv
  ~s z
preserv|e pri 'zɜːv prə- ‖ -'zɜːv **~ed** d **~er/s**
  ə/z ‖ ³r/z **~es** z **~ing** ɪŋ
pre|set ˌpri: |'set ◄ **~sets** 'sets **~setting**
  'set ɪŋ ‖ 'set̬ ɪŋ
Preshaw 'preʃ ɔː ‖ -ɑː
preshrunk ˌpri: 'ʃrʌŋk ◄
  ˌpreshrunk 'jeans
presid|e pri 'zaɪd prə- **~ed** ɪd əd **~es** z **~ing** ɪŋ

presidenc|y 'prez ɪd ən‡s |i '·əd- ‖ -ə den‡s |i
~ies iz
president, P~ 'prez ɪd ənt -əd- ‖ -ə dent **~s** s
president-elect ˌprez ɪd ənt ɪ 'lekt ˌ·əd-, -ə'·
‖ ˌ·'·ənt̬- ˌ·ə den̬t-
presidential ˌprez ɪ 'den‡ʃ əl ◂ -ə- **~ly** i
presidio prɪ 'sɪd i əʊ prə-, -'zɪd- ‖ -oʊ -'siːd-
—*Sp* [pre 'si ðjo] **~s** z
presidi|um prɪ 'sɪd i‿|əm prə-, priː-, -'zɪd- **~a** ə

PRESLEY

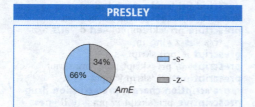

66%
34%
□ -s-
■ -z-
AmE

Presley 'pres li 'prez- — *Preference poll, AmE:*
'pres- *66%*, 'prez- *34%*.
pre-Socratic, Presocratic ˌpriː səʊ 'kræt ɪk ◂
‖ -sə 'kræt̬- -soʊ- **~s** s
press, Press pres **pressed** prest **presses**
'pres ɪz -əz **pressing** 'pres ɪŋ
'press ˌagency; 'press ˌagent; 'press
ˌbaron; 'press box; 'press ˌconference;
'press ˌcutting; 'press ˌgallery; 'press
ˌofficer; 'press reˌlease; 'press run; 'press
ˌsecretary
pressgang 'pres gæŋ **~ed** d **~ing** ɪŋ **~s** z
pressie 'prez i **~s** z
pressing 'pres ɪŋ **~ly** li **~s** z
press|man 'pres |mæn -mən **~men** men -mən
pressmark 'pres mɑːk ‖ -mɑːrk **~s** s
pressroom 'pres ruːm -rʊm **~s** z
press-stud 'pres stʌd 'prest ʌd **~s** z
press-up 'pres ʌp **~s** s
pressure 'preʃ ə ‖ -ᵊr **~d** d **pressuring**
'preʃ ər ɪŋ **~s** z
'pressure ˌcooker; 'pressure gauge;
'pressure group; 'pressure point
pressuris... —*see* **pressuriz...**
pressurization ˌpreʃ ər aɪ 'zeɪʃ ᵊn -ɪ'·- ‖ -ə'·-
~s z
pressuriz|e 'preʃ ə raɪz **~ed** d **~es** ɪz əz **~ing**
ɪŋ
Prestatyn pre 'stæt ɪn prɪ-, -ᵊn ‖ -ᵊn — *Welsh*
[pre 'sdat ɪn, -ɪn]
Prestbury 'prest bər‿i
Prestcold *tdmk* 'prest kəʊld →-kɒʊld ‖ -koʊld
Presteigne ₍ᵢ₎pre 'stiːn
Prestel *tdmk* 'pres tel
Prester 'prest ə ‖ -ᵊr
prestidigitation ˌprest ɪ dɪdʒ ɪ 'teɪʃ ᵊn ˌ·ə-,
-ə'·- **~s** z
prestidigitator ˌprest ɪ 'dɪdʒ ɪ teɪt ə ˌ·ə-, -'·ə-
‖ -teɪt̬ ᵊr **~s** z
prestige ₍ᵢ₎pre 'stiːʒ -'stiːdʒ
Prestige *family name* 'prest ɪdʒ

PRESTIGIOUS

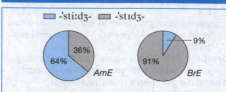

□ -'stiːdʒ- ■ -'stɪdʒ-

64% / 36% *AmE*
91% / 9% *BrE*

prestigious pre 'stɪdʒ əs prɪ-, prə-, -'stiːdʒ-,
-'·i‿əs — *Preference polls, AmE:* -'stiːdʒ- *64%*,
-'stɪdʒ- *36%*; *BrE:* -'stɪdʒ- *91%*, -'stiːdʒ- *9%*.
~ly li **~ness** nəs nɪs
prestissimo pre 'stɪs ɪ məʊ -ə- ‖ -moʊ **~s** z
presto, P~ 'prest əʊ ‖ -oʊ **~s** z
Preston 'prest ən
Prestonpans ˌprest ən 'pænz →-əm-
prestressed ˌpriː 'strest ◂
ˌprestressed 'concrete
Prestwich 'prest wɪtʃ
Prestwick 'prest wɪk
presumably prɪ 'zjuːm əb li prə-, -'zuːm-,
§-'ʒuːm- ‖ -'zuːm-

PRESUME

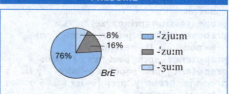

76% / 16% / 8%
□ -'zjuːm
■ -'zuːm
□ -'ʒuːm
BrE

presum|e prɪ 'zjuːm prə-, -'zuːm, §-'ʒuːm
‖ -'zuːm — *Preference poll, BrE:* -'zjuːm *76%*,
-'zuːm *16%*, -'ʒuːm *8%*. **~ed** d **~es** z **~ing** ɪŋ
presumedly prɪ 'zjuːm ɪd li prə-, -'zuːm-,
-'ʒuːm-, -əd- ‖ -'zum əd li -'zuːm ɪd li
presumption prɪ 'zʌmp ʃᵊn prə- **~s** z
presumptive prɪ 'zʌmpt ɪv prə- **~ly** li
presumptuous prɪ 'zʌmp tʃu‿əs prə-, -tju‿əs,
-ʃu‿əs; -'zʌmp tʃəs, -ʃəs -'ʃəs **~ly** li **~ness** nəs nɪs
presuppos|e ˌpriː sə 'pəʊz ‖ -'poʊz **~ed** d **~es**
ɪz əz **~ing** ɪŋ
presupposition ˌpriː ˌsʌp ə 'zɪʃ ᵊn **~s** z
Pret a Manger *tdmk* ˌpret ə 'mɒ̃ʒ eɪ -æ-
‖ ˌpret ɑː mɑː 'ʒeɪ —*Fr* prêt-à-manger
[pʁɛ ta mɑ̃ ʒe]
prêt-à-porter ˌpret ɑː 'pɔːt eɪ ◂ ‖ -pɔːr 'teɪ
—*Fr* [pʁɛ ta pɔʁ te]
pretax ˌpriː 'tæks ◂
ˌpretax 'profits
preteen ˌpriː 'tiːn ◂ **~s** z
pretenc|e prɪ 'ten‡s prə- ‖ 'priː ten‡s (*) **~es** ɪz
əz
pretend prɪ 'tend prə- **~ed** ɪd əd **~ing** ɪŋ **~s** z
pretender prɪ 'tend ə prə- ‖ -ᵊr **~s** z
pretens|e prɪ 'ten‡s prə- ‖ 'priː ten‡s (*) **~es** ɪz
əz
pretension prɪ 'ten‡ʃ ᵊn prə- **~s** z
pretentious prɪ 'ten‡ʃ əs prə- **~ly** li **~ness** nəs
nɪs

P

preterit, preterite ˈpret‿ər ɪt -ət ‖ ˈpreʈ ər ət
~s s
preterm ˌpriː ˈtɜːm ◀ ‖ -ˈtɜːm◀
pretermission ˌpriːt ə ˈmɪʃ ᵊn ‖ ˌpriːʈ ᵊr-
preter|mit ˌpriːt ə |ˈmɪt ‖ ˌpriːʈ ᵊr- **~mits**
ˈmɪts **~mitted** ˈmɪt ɪd -əd ‖ ˈmɪʈ əd **~mitting**
ˈmɪt ɪŋ ‖ ˈmɪʈ ɪŋ
preternatural ˌpriːt ə ˈnætʃ ᵊr əl ◀ ‖ ˌpriːʈ ᵊr-
~ism ˌɪz əm **~ly** i **~ness** nəs nɪs
pretest ˈpriː test **~s** s
pretext ˈpriː tekst **~s** s
pretonic ˌpriː ˈtɒn ɪk ◀ ‖ -ˈtɑːn ɪk ◀ **~ally** ᵊl i
pretor ˈpriːt ə -ɔː ‖ ˈpriːʈ ᵊr **~s** z
Pretori|a pri ˈtɔːr i |ə prə- ‖ -ˈtoʊr- **~us** əs
pretorian pri ˈtɔːr i‿ən praɪ- ‖ -ˈtoʊr- **~s** z
pretrial ˌpriː ˈtraɪ əl ◀ ‖ -ˈtraɪ əl ◀
pretti... —see **pretty**
prettification ˌprɪt ɪf ɪ ˈkeɪʃ ᵊn ˌəf-, §-ᵊˈ--
‖ ˌprɪʈ- **~s** z
pretti|fy ˈprɪt ɪ |faɪ §-ə- ‖ ˈprɪʈ- **~fied** faɪd
~fier/s faɪ‿ə/z ‖ faɪ‿ᵊr/z **~fies** faɪz **~fying**
faɪ ɪŋ
pretty ˈprɪt |i ‖ ˈprɪʈ |i (!) —In AmE there are
also casual forms ˈpɜːt i, ˈprʊʈ i **~ied** id **~ier**
i‿ə ‖ i‿ᵊr **~ies** iz **~iest** i‿ɪst i‿əst **~ily** ɪ li əl i
~iness i nəs i nɪs **~ying** i ɪŋ
ˌpretty ˈgood; a ˌpretty ˈpenny
pretty-pretty ˈprɪt i ˌprɪt i ‖ ˈprɪʈ i ˌprɪʈ i
pretzel ˈprets ᵊl **~s** z
prevail pri ˈveɪᵊl prə- **~ed** d **~ing/ly** ɪŋ /li **~s** z
prevalenc|e ˈprev əl ən‿s **~es** ɪz əz
prevalent ˈprev əl ənt **~ly** li
prevari|cate pri ˈvær ɪ |keɪt prə-, -ə- ‖ -ˈver-
~cated keɪt ɪd -əd ‖ keɪʈ əd **~cates** keɪts
~cating keɪt ɪŋ ‖ keɪʈ ɪŋ
prevarication pri ˌvær ɪ ˈkeɪʃ ᵊn prə-, -ə'--
‖ -ˌver- **~s** z
prevaricator pri ˈvær ɪ keɪt ə prə-, -ˈ-ə-
‖ -keɪʈ ᵊr -ˈver- **~s** z
prevenient pri ˈviːn i‿ənt prə- **~ly** li
pre|vent pri |ˈvent prə- —but in the obsolete
sense 'go before', ˌpriː:- **~vented** ˈvent ɪd -əd
‖ ˈvenʈ əd **~venting** ˈvent ɪŋ ‖ ˈvenʈ ɪŋ
~vents ˈvents
preventability, preventibility
pri ˌvent ə ˈbɪl ət i prə- ‖ -ˌvenʈ ə ˈbɪl əʈ i
preventab|le, preventib|le pri ˈvent əb |ᵊl
prə- ‖ -ˈvenʈ- **~ly** li
preventative pri ˈvent ət ɪv prə- ‖ -ˈvenʈ əʈ ɪv
~ly li **~ness** nəs nɪs **~s** z
preventer pri ˈvent ə prə- ‖ -ˈvenʈ ᵊr **~s** z
prevention pri ˈventʃ ᵊn prə-
preventive pri ˈvent ɪv prə- ‖ -ˈvenʈ ɪv **~ly** li
~ness nəs nɪs **~s** z
preverbal ˌpriː ˈvɜːb ᵊl ◀ ‖ -ˈvɜːb ᵊl ◀
preview ˈpriː vjuː **~ed** d **~ing** ɪŋ **~s** z
Previn ˈprev ɪn §-ᵊn
previous ˈpriːv i‿əs **~ly** li **~ness** nəs nɪs
prevision ˌpriː ˈvɪʒ ᵊn prɪ-, prə-
prevocalic ˌpriː vəʊ ˈkæl ɪk ◀ ‖ -voʊ- -və-
~ally ᵊl i
prewar ˌpriː ˈwɔː ◀ ‖ -ˈwɔːr ◀
ˌprewar ˈprices

prewash ˌpriː ˈwɒʃ ◀ ‖ -ˈwɑːʃ ◀ -ˈwɔːʃ ◀
Prewett ˈpruː ɪt §ət
prey preɪ (= pray) **preyed** preɪd **preying**
ˈpreɪ ɪŋ **preys** preɪz
preyer ˈpreɪ ə ‖ -ᵊr **~s** z
prezzie ˈprez i **~s** z
Priam ˈpraɪ‿əm -æm
priapic praɪ ˈæp ɪk -ˈeɪp-
priapism ˈpraɪ‿ə ˌpɪz əm
Priapus praɪ ˈeɪp əs ˈpraɪ‿əp əs
Pribilof ˈprɪb ɪ lɒf -ə-, -ləf ‖ -lɑːf -lɔːf
price, Price praɪs **priced** praɪst **prices, Price's**
ˈpraɪs ɪz -əz **pricing/s** ˈpraɪs ɪŋ/z
ˈprice con‿trol; ˈprice list; ˈprice tag;
ˈprice war
price-cutting ˈpraɪs ˌkʌt ɪŋ ‖ -ˌkʌʈ-
priceless ˈpraɪs ləs -lɪs **~ly** li **~ness** nəs nɪs
price-sensitive ˌpraɪs ˈsen‿s ət ɪv ◀ -ɪt- ‖ -əʈ-
PricewaterhouseCoopers
ˌpraɪs ˌwɔːt ə haʊs ˈkuːp əz
‖ -ˌwɔːʈ ᵊr haʊs ˈkuːp ᵊrz -ˌwɑːʈ-
pric|ey, pric|y ˈpraɪs |i **~ier** i‿ə ‖ i‿ᵊr **~iest**
i‿ɪst i‿əst **~ily** ɪ li əl i **~iness** i nəs i nɪs
Prichard ˈprɪtʃ əd ‖ -ᵊrd
prick prɪk **pricked** prɪkt **pricking/s** ˈprɪk ɪŋ/z
pricks prɪks
pricker ˈprɪk ə ‖ -ᵊr **~s** z
pricket ˈprɪk ɪt §-ət **~s** s
prickl|e ˈprɪk ᵊl **~ed** d **~es** z **~ing** ɪŋ
prick|ly ˈprɪk |li -ᵊl‿|i **~lier** li‿ə ‖ li‿ᵊr **~liest**
li‿ɪst li‿əst **~iness** li nəs -nɪs
ˌprickly ˈheat; ˌprickly ˈpear
pricy ˈpraɪs i —see **pricey**
pride, Pride praɪd **prided** ˈpraɪd ɪd -əd
prides, Pride's praɪdz **priding** ˈpraɪd ɪŋ
Prideaux ˈprɪd əʊ ‖ -oʊ
prideful ˈpraɪd fᵊl **~ly** ‿i **~ness** nəs nɪs
prie... —see **pry**
prie-dieu ˌpriː ˈdjɜː ˈ· · ‖ -ˈdjuː **~s, ~x** z —or as
sing. —Fr [pʁi djø]
priest priːst **priests** priːsts
priestcraft ˈpriːst krɑːft §-kræft ‖ -kræft
priestess ˌpriːst ˈes ◀ ˈpriːst es, -ɪs, -əs
‖ ˈpriːst əs **~es** ɪz əz
priesthood ˈpriːst hʊd
Priestland ˈpriːst lənd
Priestley ˈpriːst li
priest|ly ˈpriːst |li **~lier** li‿ə ‖ li‿ᵊr **~liest** li‿ɪst
li‿əst **~liness** li nəs nɪs
priest-ridden ˈpriːst ˌrɪd ᵊn
prig prɪg **prigs** prɪgz
priggery ˈprɪg ər i
priggish ˈprɪg ɪʃ **~ly** li **~ness** nəs nɪs
prim prɪm **primmer** ˈprɪm ə ‖ -ᵊr **primmest**
ˈprɪm ɪst -əst
prima ballerina ˌpriːm ə ˌbæl ə ˈriːn ə **~s** z
primac|y ˈpraɪm əs |i **~ies** iz
prima donna ˌpriːm ə ˈdɒn ə
‖ ˌprɪm ə ˈdɑːn ə ˌpriːm- **~s** z
primaeval praɪ ˈmiːv ᵊl **~ly** i
prima facie ˌpraɪm ə ˈfeɪʃ i ◀ -ˈfeɪs, -iː, -ˈ·i‿iː,
§-ˈfeɪʃ ə
primal ˈpraɪm ᵊl

P

primaquine 'praɪm ə kwiːn

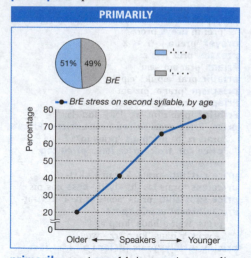

PRIMARILY

51% 49%

·.···

'.···

BrE

BrE stress on second syllable, by age

Older ◄— Speakers —► Younger

primarily praɪ 'mer əl i -'meər-, -'mær-, -ɪ li;
'praɪm ᵊr‿əl i ‖ 'praɪm er— *Preference poll,
BrE:* '···· 49%, ·'··· 51%.

Primark *tdmk* 'praɪ mɑːk ‖ -mɑːrk

primar|y 'praɪm ər |i ‖ -er |i -ər i **~ies** iz
‚primary 'accent; ‚primary 'colour;
'primary ‚school; ‚primary 'stress

primate *'higher mammal'* 'praɪm eɪt **primates**
'praɪm eɪts praɪ 'meɪt iːz

primate *'archbishop'* 'praɪm ət -ɪt, -eɪt **~s** s
~ship/s ʃɪp/s

primatolog|ist ‚praɪm ə 'tɒl ədʒ |ɪst §-əst
‖ -'tɑːl- **~ists** ɪsts §əsts **~y** i

prime, Prime praɪm —*in the phrase* prime
minister *also* ₍ᵢ₎praɪ **primed** praɪmd **primes**
praɪmz **priming/s** 'praɪm ɪŋ/z
‚prime 'cost; ‚prime me'ridian; ‚prime
'minister; ‚prime 'mover; ‚prime
'number; 'prime rate, ‚· '·; 'prime time,
‚· '·.

primer *'paint'; 'explosive'* 'praɪm ə ‖ -ᵊr **~s** z

primer *'introductory book'* 'praɪm ə ‖ 'prɪm ᵊr
(*) **~s** z

primeval praɪ 'miːv ᵊl **~ly** i

primigrav|ida ‚praɪm ɪ ' græv |ɪd ə ‚pri:m-,
‚·ə-, -'əd- **~idae** ɪ diː ə- **~idas** ɪd əz əd-

priming 'praɪm ɪŋ **~s** z

primip|ara praɪ 'mɪp |ər ə **~arae** ə riː **~aras**
ər əz **~arous** ər əs

primitive 'prɪm ət ɪv -ɪt- ‖ -əţ ɪv **~ly** li **~ness**
nəs nɪs **~s** z

primitiv|ism 'prɪm ət ɪv| ‚ɪz əm '·ɪt- ‖ '·əţ-
~ist/s ɪst/s §əst/s

primly 'prɪm li

primm... —*see* prim

primness 'prɪm nəs -nɪs

primo 'priːm əʊ ‖ -oʊ **~s** z

primogenitor ‚praɪm əʊ 'dʒen ɪt ə ‚pri:m-,
-ət ə ‖ -oʊ 'dʒen əţ ᵊr **~s** z

primogeniture ‚praɪm əʊ 'dʒen ɪtʃ ə ‚pri:m-,
-ətʃ ə, -ɪt jʊə ‖ -oʊ 'dʒen ətʃ ᵊr -ə tʃʊr

primordial praɪ 'mɔːd i‿əl ‖ -'mɔːrd- **~ly** i **~s** z

primp prɪmp **primped** prɪmpt **primping**
'prɪmp ɪŋ **primps** prɪmps

primros|e, P~ 'prɪm rəʊz ‖ -roʊz **~es** ɪz əz
‚primrose 'path; ‚primrose 'yellow◄

primula, P~ 'prɪm jʊl ə -jəl- ‖ -jəl ə **~s** z

primum mobile ‚praɪm əm 'məʊb ɪl i ‚pri:m-,
‚·ʊm-, -əl i; -ɪ leɪ, -ə · ‖ -'moʊb-

primus, P~ *tdmk* 'praɪm əs **~es** ɪz əz
‚primus ‚inter 'pares ‚ɪnt ə 'pɑːr iːz -'pær-,
-ɪz ‖ -‚ɪnţ ᵊr 'pær iːz -'per-; 'primus stove

prince, P~ prɪnᵗs **princes, Prince's** 'prɪnᵗs ɪz
-əz
₍ᵢ₎Prince 'Charming; ‚prince 'consort;
₍ᵢ₎Prince 'Edward ‚Island ‖ ·‚·'·‚·; ‚Prince
of 'Wales; ‚prince 'regent

princedom 'prɪnᵗs dəm **~s** z

princeling 'prɪnᵗs lɪŋ **~s** z

prince|ly 'prɪnᵗs |li **~lier** li‿ə ‖ li‿ᵊr **~liest**
li‿ɪst ‿əst **~liness** li nəs -nɪs

Princes Risborough ‚prɪnᵗs ɪz 'rɪz bər‿ə ‚·əz-
‖ -‚bɝː oʊ

PRINCESS

60% 40%

·‚·'·◄

·‚·'··

BrE

BrE stress on first syllable, by age

Older ◄— Speakers —► Younger

princess, P~ ‚prɪn 'ses ◄ prɪn-; 'prɪnᵗs es
‖ 'prɪnᵗs əs 'prɪn ses **~es** ɪz əz — *Preference
poll, BrE:* ‚·'·◄ 60%, '·· 40%. *The streets
named* Princess St *in Manchester and
Huddersfield, in the north of England, are
often pronounced locally as if spelt* Prince's
Street.
‚Princess 'Di; ‚princess 'royal

Princeton 'prɪnᵗs tən

Princetown 'prɪnᵗs taʊn

principal 'prɪnᵗs əp ᵊl -ɪp- (= *principle*) **~s** z
‚principal 'boy; ‚principal 'parts

principalit|y, P~ ‚prɪnᵗs ə 'pæl ət |i ‚·ɪ-, -ɪt |i
‖ -əţ |i **~ies** iz

principally 'prɪnᵗs əp ᵊl i '·ɪp-

principalship 'prɪnᵗs əp ᵊl ʃɪp '·ɪp- **~s** s

Principe, Príncipe 'prɪnᵗs ɪ peɪ -ə-; -ɪp i, -əp i,
-ə —*Port* ['prí si pə]

Principia prɪn 'sɪp i‿ə

principi|um prɪn 'sɪp i‿əm prɪŋ 'kɪp- **~a** ə

principle 'prɪnᵗs əp ᵊl -ɪp- **~d** d **~s** z
Pring prɪŋ
Pringle 'prɪŋ gᵊl **~s** z
prink prɪŋk **prinked** prɪŋkt **prinking** 'prɪŋk ɪŋ **prinks** prɪŋks
Prinknash 'prɪn ɪdʒ *(!)*
Prinn prɪn
Prinnie, Prinny 'prɪn i
Prinsep 'prɪnᵗs ep
print prɪnt **printed** 'prɪnt ɪd -əd ‖ 'prɪnţ əd **printing/s** 'prɪnt ɪŋ/z ‖ 'prɪnţ ɪŋ/z **prints** prɪnts
ˌprinted 'circuit; **'printed ˌmatter**; **'printing ink**; **'printing maˌchine**; **'printing press**; **'print run**; **'print shop**
printable 'prɪnt əb ᵊl ‖ 'prɪnţ-
Printator *tdmk* ₍ˌ₎prɪn 'teɪt ə ‖ -'teɪţ ᵊr **~s** z
printed-paper ˌprɪnt ɪd 'peɪp ə ◂ -əd-, →-ɪb- ‖ ˌprɪnţ əd 'peɪp ᵊr ◂
printer 'prɪnt ə ‖ 'prɪnţ ᵊr **~s** z
printer|y 'prɪnt ər |i ‖ 'prɪnţ- **~ies** iz
printhead 'prɪnt hed **~s** z
printmak|er 'prɪnt ˌmeɪk ə ‖ -ᵊr **~ers** əz ‖ ᵊrz **~ing** ɪŋ
printout 'prɪnt aʊt ‖ 'prɪnţ- **~s** s
print-through 'prɪnt θruː
printwheel 'prɪnt wiːᵊl -hwiːᵊl ‖ -*h*wiːᵊl **~s** z
prion *bird* 'praɪ ɒn ‖ -ɑːn **~s** z
prion *infectious particle* 'priː ɒn 'praɪ- ‖ -ɑːn **~s** z
prior, Prior 'praɪ‿ə ‖ 'praɪ‿ᵊr **~s** z
prioress ˌpraɪ‿ə 'res 'praɪ‿ər es, -əs, -ɪs ‖ 'praɪ ər əs **~es** ɪz əz
priori… —*see* **priory**
prioritisation, prioritization praɪ ˌɒr ɪ taɪ 'zeɪʃ ᵊn -ˌə-, -tɪ'--, -tə'-- ‖ -ˌɔːr əţ ə- -ˌɑːr-
prioritis|e, prioritiz|e praɪ 'ɒr ɪ taɪz -ə- ‖ -'ɔːr- -'ɑːr- **~ed** d **~es** ɪz əz **~ing** ɪŋ
priorit|y praɪ 'ɒr ət |i -ɪt- ‖ -'ɔːr əţ |i -'ɑːr- **~ies** iz
prior|y, P~ 'praɪ‿ər |i **~ies** iz
Priscian 'prɪʃ i‿ən 'prɪʃ ᵊn
Priscilla prɪ 'sɪl ə prə-
prise praɪz *(= prize)* **prised** praɪzd **prises** 'praɪz ɪz -əz **prising** 'praɪz ɪŋ
prism 'prɪz əm **~s** z
prismatic ₍ˌ₎prɪz 'mæt ɪk ‖ -'mæţ ɪk **~ally** ᵊl‿i
prison 'prɪz ᵊn **~s** z
'prison camp; **ˌprison 'visitor**
prisoner 'prɪz ᵊn‿ə ‖ ‿ər **~s** z
ˌprisoner of 'war
priss|y 'prɪs |i **~ier** i‿ə ‖ i‿ᵊr **~iest** i‿ɪst i‿əst **~ily** ɪ li əl i **~iness** i nəs i nɪs
Pristina prɪ 'stiːn ə -'ʃtiːn-; 'prɪʃt ɪn ə, 'priːʃt- —*Serbian* Priština ['priː ʃti na]
pristine 'prɪst iːn -aɪn; prɪ 'stiːn
Pritchard 'prɪtʃ əd -ɑːd ‖ -ᵊrd -ɑːrd
Pritchett 'prɪtʃ ɪt -ət
prithee 'prɪð i -iː
Pritt prɪt
Prius *tdmk* 'praɪ‿əs 'priː‿ ‖ 'priː əs

PRIVACY

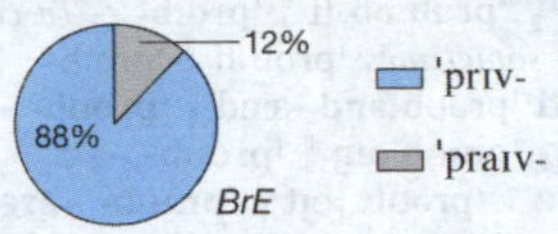

privacy 'prɪv əs i 'praɪv- ‖ 'praɪv- — *Preference poll, BrE:* 'prɪv- *88%,* 'praɪv- *12%.*
private 'praɪv ət -ɪt **~ly** li **~ness** nəs nɪs **~s** s
ˌprivate de'tective; **ˌprivate 'enterprise**; **ˌprivate 'eye**; **ˌprivate in'vestigator**; **ˌprivate 'member('s bill)**; **ˌprivate 'parts**; **ˌprivate 'school**; **ˌprivate 'sector◂**; **ˌprivate 'soldier**
privateer ˌpraɪv ə 'tɪə -ɪ- ‖ -'tɪᵊr **~s** z
privation praɪ 'veɪʃ ᵊn **~s** z
privatis… —*see* **privatiz…**
privative 'prɪv ət ɪv praɪ 'veɪt ɪv ‖ -əţ ɪv **~ly** li
privatization ˌpraɪv ət aɪ 'zeɪʃ ᵊn ˌ-ɪt-, -ɪ'-- ‖ -əţ ə- **~s** z
privatiz|e 'praɪv ə taɪz -ɪ- **~ed** d **~es** ɪz əz **~ing** ɪŋ
privet 'prɪv ɪt §-ət **~s** s
privi… —*see* **privy**
privileg|e 'prɪv əl‿ɪdʒ -ɪl- **~ed** d **~es** ɪz əz
privit|y 'prɪv ət |i -ɪt- ‖ -əţ |i **~ies** iz
priv|y 'prɪv |i **~ier** i‿ə ‖ i‿ᵊr **~ies** iz **~iest** i‿ɪst i‿əst **~ily** ɪ li əl i
ˌPrivy 'Council; **ˌPrivy 'Purse**; **ˌPrivy 'Seal**
prix fixe ˌpriː 'fɪks -'fiːks —*Fr* [pʁi fiks]
prize praɪz **prized** praɪzd **prizes** 'praɪz ɪz -əz **prizing** 'praɪz ɪŋ
ˌprize 'cattle; **'prize day**; **'prize ˌmoney**; **'prize ring**
prize|fight 'praɪz |faɪt **~fighter/s** faɪt ə/z ‖ faɪţ ᵊr/z **~fighting** faɪt ɪŋ ‖ faɪţ ɪŋ
prize-giving 'praɪz ˌgɪv ɪŋ **~s** z
prize|man 'praɪz |mən **~men** mən men
prizewinn|er 'praɪz ˌwɪn ə ‖ -ᵊr **~ers** əz ‖ ᵊrz **~ing** ɪŋ
pro prəʊ ‖ proʊ **pros** prəʊz ‖ proʊz
pro- ¦prəʊ, prə, prəʊ, ¦prɒ ‖ ¦proʊ, prə, ¦prɑː —*As a productive prefix meaning 'in favour of' (sometimes spelt with a hyphen),* ¦prəʊ ‖ ¦proʊ (pro-French ˌprəʊ 'frentʃ ◂ | ˌproʊ-). *Otherwise, with a vaguer meaning,* prə *(before a consonant sound only:* proclaim prə 'kleɪm*), or in less familiar words and slower speech* prəʊ ‖ proʊ*; but if stressed through the operation of a stressing rule usually* ¦prɒ+ ‖ ¦prɑː (proclamation ˌprɒk lə 'meɪʃ ᵊn ‖ ˌprɑːk-). *See individual entries.*
PRO *initials* ˌpiː ɑːr 'əʊ ‖ -ɑːr 'oʊ **~s, ~'s** z
PRO *grammatical term* prəʊ ‖ proʊ
proa 'prəʊ ə ‖ 'proʊ ə **~s** z
proactive ₍ˌ₎prəʊ 'ækt ɪv ‖ ₍ˌ₎proʊ-
pro-am ˌprəʊ 'æm ◂ ‖ ₍ˌ₎proʊ-
probabilistic ˌprɒb əb ə 'lɪst ɪk ◂ ˌ· ·ɪ- ‖ ˌprɑːb- **~ally** ᵊl‿i

probabilit|y ˌprɒb ə 'bɪl ət |i -ɪt i
‖ ˌprɑːb ə 'bɪl ət̬ |i **~ies** iz
probable 'prɒb əb ³l ‖ 'prɑːb- **~s** z
probably 'prɒb əb li ‖ 'prɑːb- —*In casual
speech sometimes* 'prɒb li ‖ 'prɑːb-
proband 'prəʊb ənd -ænd ‖ 'proʊb- **~s** z
probang 'prəʊb æŋ ‖ 'proʊb- **~s** z
prob|ate *v* 'prəʊb |eɪt ‖ 'proʊb- **~ated** eɪt ɪd
-əd ‖ eɪt̬ əd **~ates** eɪts **~ating** eɪt ɪŋ ‖ eɪt̬ ɪŋ
probate *n* 'prəʊb eɪt -ət, -ɪt ‖ 'proʊb-
probation prə 'beɪʃ ³n prəʊ- ‖ proʊ- **~s** z
  pro'bation of ˌficer
probationary prə 'beɪʃ ³n ˌər i prəʊ-, -ən ³r i
‖ proʊ 'beɪʃ ə ner i
probationer prə 'beɪʃ ³n ə prəʊ-
‖ proʊ 'beɪʃ ³n ˌər **~s** z
probative 'prəʊb ət ɪv ‖ 'proʊb ət̬ ɪv
probe prəʊb ‖ proʊb **probed** prəʊbd ‖ proʊbd
  probes prəʊbz ‖ proʊbz **probing** 'prəʊb ɪŋ
‖ 'proʊb ɪŋ
Probert *(i)* 'prəʊb ət ‖ 'proʊb ³rt, *(ii)* 'prɒb-
‖ 'prɑːb-
probing 'prəʊb ɪŋ ‖ 'proʊb ɪŋ **~ly** li **~s** z
probiotic ˌprəʊ baɪ 'ɒt ɪk ◂
‖ ˌproʊ baɪ 'ɑːt̬ ɪk ◂ **~s** s
probity 'prəʊb ət i -ɪt- ‖ 'proʊb ət̬ i
problem 'prɒb ləm -lɪm, -lem ‖ 'prɑːb- —*In
very casual speech also* -³m **~s** z
  'problem child
problematic ˌprɒb lə 'mæt ɪk ◂ -lɪ-
‖ ˌprɑːb lə 'mæt̬ ɪk ◂ **~al** ³l ◂ **~ally** ³l̬ i
problem-solution ˌprɒb ləm sə 'luːʃ ³n -lɪm--,
-lem --, -'ljuːʃ- ‖ ˌprɑːb-
problem-solving 'prɒb ləm ˌsɒlv ɪŋ -lɪm-,
-lem-, §-ˌsəʊlv- ‖ 'prɑːb ləm ˌsɑːlv ɪŋ
pro bono ˌprəʊ 'bəʊn əʊ ‖ ˌproʊ 'boʊn oʊ
proboscis prəʊ 'bɒs ɪs -'bɒsk-, -'bəʊs-, §-əs
‖ prə 'bɑːs əs -'bɑːsk- **-es** ɪz əz
Probyn 'prəʊb ɪn §-ən ‖ 'proʊb-
procaine 'prəʊ keɪn ·ˈ· ‖ 'proʊ-
procathedral ˌprəʊ kə 'θiːdr əl ‖ ˌproʊ- **~s** z
Procea *tdmk* 'prəʊs i̯ə prəʊ 'siː ə ‖ 'proʊs-
procedural prəʊ 'siːdʒ ³r_əl -'siːd jʊr əl ‖ prə-
  ~ly i
procedure prəʊ 'siːdʒ ə -'siːd jə ‖ prə 'siːdʒ ³r
  ~s z
proceed *v* prə 'siːd prəʊ- ‖ proʊ- **~ed** ɪd əd
  ~ing/s ɪŋ/z **~s** z
proceeds *n* 'prəʊs iːdz ‖ 'proʊs-
pro-celebrity ˌprəʊ sɪ 'leb rət i ◂ ˌˈsɪ-, -rɪt i
‖ ˌproʊ sə 'leb rət̬ i ◂

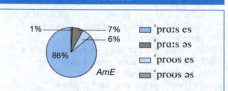

1%	'prɑːs es
7%	'prɑːs əs
6%	'proʊs es
86%	'proʊs əs
AmE	

process *n; v 'treat, submit to a ~'* 'prəʊs es
'prɒs-, -ɪs, §-əs ‖ 'prɑːs es 'proʊs-, -əs

— *Preference poll, AmE:* 'prɑːs es 86%;
'prɑːs əs 7%; 'proʊs es 6%, 'proʊs əs 1%. **~ed**
t **~es** ɪz əz ‖ iːz **~ing** ɪŋ
  ˌprocessed 'cheese
process *v 'walk in procession'* prəʊ 'ses ‖ prə-
  ~ed t **~es** ɪz əz **~ing** ɪŋ
procession prə 'seʃ ³n **~s** z
processional prə 'seʃ ³n_əl **~ly** i **~s** z
processor 'prəʊs es ə 'prɒs-, -ɪs-, §-əs-
‖ 'prɑːs es ³r **~s** z
pro-choice ˌprəʊ 'tʃɔɪs ◂ ‖ ˌproʊ-
Procktor 'prɒkt ə ‖ 'prɑːkt ³r
proclaim prə 'kleɪm prəʊ- ‖ proʊ- **~ed** d **~er/s**
ə/z ‖ ³r/z **~ing** ɪŋ **~s** z
proclamation ˌprɒk lə 'meɪʃ ³n ‖ ˌprɑːk- **~s** z
proclamatory prəʊ 'klæm ət_ər i
‖ proʊ 'klæm ə tɔːr i -toʊr i
proclitic ₍ˌ₎prəʊ 'klɪt ɪk ‖ ₍ˌ₎proʊ 'klɪt̬ ɪk **~s** s
proclivit|y prəʊ 'klɪv ət |i -ɪt-
‖ proʊ 'klɪv ət̬ |i **~ies** iz
Procne 'prɒk ni ‖ 'prɑːk-
proconsul ˌprəʊ 'kɒn⁀s ³l ‖ ˌproʊ 'kɑːn⁀s ³l **~s**
z
proconsular ˌprəʊ 'kɒn⁀s jʊl ə -jəl-
‖ ˌproʊ 'kɑːn⁀s ³l_ər
proconsulate ˌprəʊ 'kɒn⁀s jʊl ət -jəl-, -ɪt
‖ ˌproʊ 'kɑːn⁀s əl_ət **~s** s
proconsulship ˌprəʊ 'kɒn⁀s ³l ʃɪp
‖ ˌproʊ 'kɑːn⁀s- **~s** s
procrasti|nate prəʊ 'kræst ɪ |neɪt -ə- ‖ prə-
proʊ-, pə- **~nated** neɪt ɪd -əd ‖ neɪt̬ əd
~nates neɪts **~nating** neɪt ɪŋ ‖ neɪt̬ ɪŋ
procrastination prəʊ ˌkræst ɪ 'neɪʃ ³n 'prəʊ-,
-ə- ‖ prə- proʊ-, pə- **~s** z
procrastinator prəʊ 'kræst ɪ neɪt ə -'·ə-
‖ prə 'kræst ə neɪt̬ ³r proʊ-, pə- **~s** z
procre|ate 'prəʊk ri |eɪt ˌ·'·| ‖ 'proʊk- **~ated**
eɪt ɪd -əd ‖ eɪt̬ əd **~ates** eɪts **~ating** eɪt ɪŋ
‖ eɪt̬ ɪŋ
procreation ˌprəʊk ri 'eɪʃ ³n ‖ ˌproʊk-
procreative 'prəʊk ri eɪt ɪv 'prɒk-, ri_ət-;
ˌ·'·eɪt- ‖ 'proʊk ri eɪt̬ ɪv
Procrust|ean prəʊ 'krʌst |i_ən ‖ proʊ- prə-,
pə- **~es** iːz
Procter 'prɒkt ə ‖ 'prɑːkt ³r
proctitis prɒk 'taɪt ɪs §-əs ‖ prɑːk 'taɪt̬ əs
procto- *comb. form with stress-neutral suffix*
ˌprɒkt əʊ ‖ ˌprɑːkt ə — **proctotome**
'prɒkt əʊ təʊm ‖ 'prɑːkt ə toʊm *with
stress-imposing suffix* prɒk 'tɒ+
‖ prɑːk 'tɑː+ — **proctology** prɒk 'tɒl ədʒ i
‖ prɑːk 'tɑːl-
proctor, P~ 'prɒkt ə ‖ 'prɑːkt ³r **~s** z
proctorial prɒk 'tɔːr i_əl ‖ prɑːk- -'toʊr-
proctoscope 'prɒkt ə skəʊp ‖ 'prɑːkt ə skoʊp
~s s
procumbent prəʊ 'kʌm bənt ‖ proʊ-
procurable prə 'kjʊər əb ³l prəʊ-, -'kjɔːr-
‖ -'kjʊr- proʊ-
procuration ˌprɒk jʊə 'reɪʃ ³n -jə- ‖ ˌprɑːk jə-
~s z

procurator 'prɒk juˤ reɪt ə '·jə-
∥ 'prɑːk jə reɪt ˤr ~s z
,procurator 'fiscal

procure prə 'kjʊə prəʊ-, -'kjɔː ∥ -'kjʊˤr proʊ-
~d d ~ment/s mənt/s ~s z **procuring**
prə 'kjʊər ɪŋ prəʊ-, -'kjɔːr- ∥ -'kjʊr ɪŋ proʊ-

procurer prə 'kjʊər ə prəʊ-, -'kjɔːr- ∥ -'kjʊr ˤr
proʊ- ~s z

procuress prə 'kjʊər es prəʊ-, -'kjɔːr-, -ɪs, -əs;
'prɒk jʊr-, -jər- ∥ -'kjʊr əs proʊ- ~es ɪz əz

Procyon 'prəʊs i ən ∥ 'proʊs i ɑːn

prod, Prod prɒd ∥ prɑːd **prodded** 'prɒd ɪd -əd
∥ 'prɑːd əd **prodding** 'prɒd ɪŋ ∥ 'prɑːd ɪŋ
prods, Prods prɒdz ∥ prɑːdz

Prodd|ie, Prodd|y 'prɒd| i ∥ 'prɑːd| i ~ies ɪz

Prodi 'prəʊd i ∥ 'proʊd i —It ['prɔː di]

prodigal 'prɒd ɪg ˤl ∥ 'prɑːd- ~ly i ~s z
,prodigal 'son

prodigalit|y ,prɒd ɪ 'ɡæl ət |i ,-ə-, -ɪt i
∥ ,prɑːd ə 'ɡæl ət̬ |i ~ies ɪz

prodigious prə 'dɪdʒ əs ~ly li ~ness nəs nɪs

prodig|y 'prɒd ədʒ |i -ɪdʒ-; △'prɒdʒ əd i
∥ 'prɑːd- ~ies ɪz

prodromal ˌˌprəʊ 'drəʊm ˤl
∥ ˌˌproʊ 'droʊm ˤl

prodrome 'prəʊ drəʊm ∥ 'proʊ droʊm ~s z

produc|e v prə 'djuːs §-'duːs, →-'dʒuːs ∥ -'duːs
-'djuːs ~ed t ~es ɪz əz ~ing ɪŋ

produce n 'prɒd juːs 'prɒdʒ uːs ∥ 'proʊ duːs
-djuːs; 'prɑːd uːs, -juːs (*)

producer prə 'djuːs ə §-'duːs-, →'dʒuːs-
∥ -'duːs ˤr ~s z

producible prə 'djuːs əb ˤl §-'duːs-, →'dʒuːs-
∥ -'duːs- -'djuːs-

product 'prɒd ʌkt -əkt ∥ 'prɑːd- ~s s
'product line

production prə 'dʌk ʃˤn ~s z
pro'duction line

productive prə 'dʌkt ɪv ~ly li ~ness nəs nɪs

productivity ,prɒd ʌk 'tɪv ət i ,prəʊd-, ,-ək-,
-ɪt i ∥ ,proʊ dʌk 'tɪv ət̬ i proʊ ,dʌk 'tɪv-, prə-;
,prɑːd ək 'tɪv-

proem 'prəʊ em ∥ 'proʊ- ~s z

prof prɒf ∥ prɑːf **profs** prɒfs ∥ prɑːfs

Prof. prɒf ∥ prɑːf —or see Professor

profanation ,prɒf ə 'neɪʃ ˤn ∥ ,prɑːf-

profan|e v, adj prə 'feɪn prəʊ- ∥ proʊ- ~ed d
~ely li ~er/s ə/z ∥ ˤr/z ~eness nəs nɪs ~es z
~ing ɪŋ

profanit|y prə 'fæn ət |i prəʊ-, -ɪt- ∥ -ət̬ i proʊ-
~ies ɪz

profess prə 'fes prəʊ- ∥ proʊ- ~ed t ~es ɪz əz
~ing ɪŋ

professedly prə 'fes ɪd li prəʊ-, -əd- ∥ proʊ-

profession prə 'feʃ ˤn ~s z

professional prə 'feʃ ˤn_əl ~ism ,ɪz əm ~ly i

professor prə 'fes ə ∥ -ˤr ~s z

professorate prə 'fes ər ət -ɪt ~s s

professorial ,prɒf ə 'sɔːr i_əl ,·ɪ-, ,·e- ∥ ,proʊf-
,prɑːf-, -'soʊr- ~ly i

professoriate ,prɒf ə 'sɔːr i_ət ,·ɪ-, ,·e-, ɪt, -eɪt
∥ ,proʊf- ,prɑːf-

professorship prə 'fes ə ʃɪp ∥ -ˤr- ~s s

proff|er 'prɒf |ə ∥ 'prɑːf |ˤr ~ered əd ∥ ˤrd
~ering ər_ɪŋ ~ers əz ∥ ˤrz

proficienc|y prə 'fɪʃ ˤnˤs |i ~ies iz

proficient prə 'fɪʃ ˤnt ~ly li

profil|e 'prəʊf aɪˤl ∥ 'proʊf- —formerly also
-iːˤl ~ed d ~es z ~ing ɪŋ

prof|it 'prɒf |ɪt §-ət ∥ 'prɑːf |ət ~ited ɪt ɪd §ət-,
-əd ∥ ət̬ əd ~iting ɪt ɪŋ §ət- ∥ ət̬ ɪŋ ~its ɪts
§əts ∥ əts
'profit ,margin; 'profit ,sharing

profitability ,prɒf ɪt ə 'bɪl ət i ,·ət-, -ɪt i
∥ ,prɑːf ət̬ ə 'bɪl ət̬ i

profitab|le 'prɒf ɪt əb |ˤl '·ət- ∥ 'prɑːf ət̬- ~ly
li

profi|teer ,prɒf ɪ 'tɪə -ə- ∥ ,prɑːf ə |'tɪˤr
~teered 'tɪəd ∥ 'tɪˤrd ~teering 'tɪər ɪŋ
∥ 'tɪr ɪŋ ~teers 'tɪəz ∥ 'tɪˤrz

profiterole prə 'fɪt ə rəʊl prɒ-, -'fiːt-, →-rɒʊl;
'prɒf ɪt-, ,·· ·'· ∥ -'fɪt̬ ə roʊl ~s z

profitless 'prɒf ɪt ləs §-ət-, -lɪs ∥ 'prɑːf-

profit-making 'prɒf ɪt ,meɪk ɪŋ -ət- ∥ 'prɑːf-

profit-taking 'prɒf ɪt ,teɪk ɪŋ -ət- ∥ 'prɑːf-

profligacy 'prɒf lɪɡ əs i '·ləɡ- ∥ 'prɑːf-

profligate 'prɒf lɪɡ ət -ləɡ-, -ɪt ∥ 'prɑːf- ~ly li
~ness nəs nɪs

pro-form 'prəʊ fɔːm ∥ 'proʊ fɔːrm

pro forma ˌˌprəʊ 'fɔːm ə ◂ ∥ ˌˌproʊ 'fɔːrm ə

profound prə 'faʊnd prəʊ- ∥ proʊ- ~er ə ∥ ˤr
~est ɪst əst ~ly li ~ness nəs nɪs

Profumo prə 'fjuːm əʊ prəʊ- ∥ -oʊ

profundit|y prə 'fʌnd ət |i prəʊ-, -ɪt- ∥ -ət̬ |i
~ies iz

profuse prə 'fjuːs prəʊ- ∥ proʊ- ~ly li ~ness
nəs nɪs

profusion prə 'fjuːʒ ˤn prəʊ- ∥ proʊ- ~s z

prog prɒɡ ∥ prɑːɡ **progs** prɒɡz ∥ prɑːɡz

progenitor prəʊ 'dʒen ɪt ə §-ət-
∥ proʊ 'dʒen ət̬ ˤr prə- ~s z

progen|y 'prɒdʒ ən |i 'prəʊdʒ-, -ɪn- ∥ 'prɑːdʒ-
~ies iz

progesterone prəʊ 'dʒest ə rəʊn
∥ proʊ 'dʒest ə roʊn

progestogen prəʊ 'dʒest ədʒ ən -ɪn, -ə dʒen
∥ proʊ- ~s z

proglott|id prəʊ 'ɡlɒt |ɪd §-əd
∥ proʊ 'ɡlɑːt̬ |əd ~ids ɪdz §ədz ∥ ədz ~is ɪs
§əs

prognathic prɒɡ 'næθ ɪk ∥ prɑːɡ-

prognathism 'prɒɡ nə ,θɪz əm ∥ 'prɑːɡ-

prognathous prɒɡ 'neɪθ əs prɒɡ 'neɪθ-
∥ 'prɑːɡ nəθ əs prɑːɡ 'neɪθ-

prognos|is prɒɡ 'nəʊs |ɪs §-əs
∥ prɑːɡ 'noʊs |əs ~es iːz

prognostic prɒɡ 'nɒst ɪk ∥ prɑːɡ 'nɑːst ɪk ~s s

prognosti|cate prɒɡ 'nɒst ɪ |keɪt §-ə-
∥ prɑːɡ 'nɑːst- ~cated keɪt ɪd -əd ∥ keɪt̬ əd
~cates keɪts ~cating keɪt ɪŋ ∥ keɪt̬ ɪŋ

prognostication prɒɡ ,nɒst ɪ 'keɪʃ ˤn prəɡ-,
,prɒɡ· ·'·-, §-ə'·- ∥ prɑːɡ ,nɑːst- ~s z

prognosticator prɒɡ 'nɒst ɪ keɪt ə §-'·ə-
∥ prɑːɡ 'nɑːst ə keɪt̬ ˤr ~s z

program 'prəʊ ɡræm §-ɡrəm ∥ 'proʊ- ~ed,
~med d ~ing, ~ming ɪŋ ~s z

ˌprogrammed 'course; ˌprogrammed
inˈstruction; ˌprogrammed 'learning;
'programme ˌmusic
programmable prəʊ 'græm əb ᵊl 'prəʊ græm-
‖ 'proʊ græm- ˌ˙ ˌ ˙ ˙
programmatic ˌprəʊg rə 'mæt ɪk ◄
‖ ˌproʊg rə 'mæt̬ ɪk ◄ **~ally** ᵊl̬ i
programm|e 'prəʊ græm §-grəm ‖ 'proʊ- **~ed**
d **~es** z **~ing** ɪŋ
programmer 'prəʊ græm ə §-grəm-
‖ 'proʊ græm ᵊr -grəm- **~s** z
progress n 'prəʊ gres 'prɒg res ‖ 'prɑːg rəs
-res
'progress ˌchaser; 'progress reˌport
progress v prəʊ 'gres ' ˙ ˙ ‖ prə- **~ed** t **~es** ɪz əz
~ing ɪŋ
progression prəʊ 'greʃ ᵊn ‖ prə- **~al** ᵊl **~s** z
progressive prəʊ 'gres ɪv ‖ prə- **~ly** li **~ness**
nəs nɪs **~s** z
progressivism prəʊ 'gres ɪv ˌɪz əm ‖ prə-
prohib|it prəʊ 'hɪb |ɪt §-ət ‖ proʊ 'hɪb ət prə-
~ited ɪt ɪd §ət-, -əd ‖ ət̬ əd **~iting** ɪt ɪŋ §ət-
‖ ət̬ ɪŋ **~its** ɪts §əts ‖ əts
prohibition ˌprəʊ ɪ 'bɪʃ ᵊn -hɪ-, -ə-, §-hə-
‖ ˌproʊ ə- **~ism** ˌɪz əm **~ist/s** ɪst/s §əst/s
‖ əst/s **~s** z
prohibitive prəʊ 'hɪb ɪt ɪv -ət-
‖ proʊ 'hɪb ət̬ ɪv prə- **~ly** li
prohibitory prəʊ 'hɪb ɪt̬ ər i -'˙ət ˌ
‖ proʊ 'hɪb ə tɔːr i prə-, -toʊr i

PROJECT

project n 'prɒdʒ ekt -ɪkt; 'prəʊ dʒekt ‖ 'prɑːdʒ-
— *Preference poll, BrE:* ɒ 84%, əʊ 16%. **~s** s
project v prə 'dʒekt prəʊ-, prɒ- **~ed** ɪd əd **~ing**
ɪŋ **~s** s
projectile prəʊ 'dʒekt aɪᵊl 'prɒdʒ ekt-, -ɪkt-
‖ prə 'dʒekt ᵊl **~s** z
projection prə 'dʒek ʃᵊn prəʊ-, prɒ- **~s** z
projectionist prə 'dʒek ʃᵊn ˌɪst prəʊ-, prɒ-,
§ˌəst **~s** s
projective prəʊ 'dʒekt ɪv ‖ prə- **~ly** li
projector prə 'dʒekt ə prəʊ-, prɒ- ‖ -ᵊr **~s** z
prokaryote ₍ˌ₎prəʊ 'kær i əʊt -ɒt
‖ ₍ˌ₎proʊ 'kær i oʊt -'ker- **~s** s
prokaryotic prəʊ ˌkær i 'ɒt ɪk ˌ˙ˌ˙˙-
‖ proʊ ˌkær i 'ɑːt̬ ɪk ◄
Prokofiev prə 'kɒf i ef ‖ -'kɔːf i əf -'koʊf-, -ef
—*Russ* [prʌ 'kɔfʲ jɪf]
prolactin prəʊ 'lækt ɪn §-ən ‖ proʊ-
prolaps|e n 'prəʊ læps prəʊ 'læps
‖ proʊ 'læps ' ˙ ˙ **~es** ɪz əz
prolaps|e v prəʊ 'læps 'prəʊ læps ‖ proʊ- **~ed**
t **~es** ɪz əz **~ing** ɪŋ

prolate 'prəʊl eɪt prəʊ 'leɪt ‖ 'proʊl- **~ly** li
~ness nəs nɪs
prolative prəʊ 'leɪt ɪv 'prəʊl ət- ‖ proʊ 'leɪt̬ ɪv
prole prəʊl →prɒʊl ‖ proʊl **proles** prəʊlz
→prɒʊlz ‖ proʊlz
proleg 'prəʊ leg ‖ 'proʊ- **~s** z
prolegom|enon ˌprəʊl ə 'gɒm |ɪn ən ˌ-ɪ-, ˌ-e-,
-ən ən; -|ɪ nɒn, -ə ˙ ‖ ˌproʊl ɪ 'gɑːm |ə nɑːn
~ena ɪn ə ən-
prolepsis prəʊ 'liːps ɪs -'leps-, §-əs
‖ proʊ 'leps əs
proleptic prəʊ 'lept ɪk ‖ proʊ- **~ally** ᵊl̬ i
proletarian ˌprəʊl ə 'teər i ən ◄ ˌ-ɪ-, ˌ-e-
‖ ˌproʊl ə 'ter- -'tær- **~s** z
proletariat ˌprəʊl ə 'teər i ət ˌ-ɪ-, ˌ-e-, -æt
‖ ˌproʊl ə 'ter- -'tær- **~s** s
pro-life ₍ˌ₎prəʊ 'laɪf ‖ ₍ˌ₎proʊ- **~r/s** ə/z ‖ ᵊr/z
prolife|rate prəʊ 'lɪf ə |reɪt ‖ prə- **~rated**
reɪt ɪd -əd ‖ reɪt̬ əd **~rates** reɪts **~rating**
reɪt ɪŋ ‖ reɪt̬ ɪŋ
proliferation prəʊ ˌlɪf ə 'reɪʃ ᵊn ‖ prə- **~s** z
prolific prəʊ 'lɪf ɪk ‖ prə- **~acy** əs i **~ally** ᵊl̬ i
~ness nəs nɪs
prolix 'prəʊ lɪks ₍ˌ₎˙'˙ ‖ proʊ 'lɪks ' ˙ ˙ **~ly** li
prolixity prəʊ 'lɪks ət i -ɪt i ‖ proʊ 'lɪks ət̬ i
prolocutor prəʊ 'lɒk jʊt ə -jət-
‖ proʊ 'lɑːk jət̬ ᵊr **~s** z
prolog, PROLOG, prologue 'prəʊ lɒg
‖ 'proʊ lɔːg -lɑːg **~s** z
prolong prəʊ 'lɒŋ ‖ prə 'lɔːŋ -'lɑːŋ **~ed** d **~ing**
ɪŋ **~s** z
prolongation ˌprəʊ lɒŋ 'geɪʃ ᵊn ‖ ˌproʊ lɔːŋ-
-lɑːŋ-; prə,˙˙'˙ ˙ **~s** z
prom, PROM prɒm ‖ prɑːm **proms, PROMs**
prɒmz ‖ prɑːmz
promenad|e ˌprɒm ə 'nɑːd◄ -ɪ-, '˙ ˙ ˙
‖ ˌprɑːm ə 'neɪd◄ -'nɑːd (*) —*but in square
dancing,* -'neɪd◄ *even in BrE* **~ed** ɪd əd **~er/s**
ə/z ‖ ᵊr/z **~es** z **~ing** ɪŋ
ˌpromenade 'concert, ˌ˙˙'˙ ˌ˙˙; ˌprome'nade
deck
Promethean prəʊ 'miːθ i ən ‖ prə- **~s** z
Prometheus prəʊ 'miːθ juːs -'miːθ i əs ‖ prə-
promethium prəʊ 'miːθ i əm ‖ prə-
prominenc|e 'prɒm ɪn ənˈs -ən- ‖ 'prɑːm- **~es**
ɪz əz **~y** i
prominent 'prɒm ɪn ənt -ən- ‖ 'prɑːm- **~ly** li
promiscuit|y ˌprɒm ɪ 'skjuːˌət |i ˌ˙ə-, ɪt i
‖ ˌprɑːm ə 'skjuː ət̬ |i ˌproʊm- **~ies** iz
promiscuous prə 'mɪsk ju əs prɒ- ‖ proʊ- **~ly**
li **~ness** nəs nɪs
promis|e v, n 'prɒm ɪs §-əs ‖ 'prɑːm əs **~ed** t
~es ɪz əz **~ing/ly** ɪŋ /li
ˌPromised 'Land ‖ ˌ˙ ˙ ˙
promisee ˌprɒm ɪ 'siː §-ə- ‖ ˌprɑːm- **~s** z
promisor ˌprɒm ɪ 'sɔː ˌ˙ ˙ ˙ ‖ ˌprɑːm ə 'sɔːr **~s** z
promissory 'prɒm ɪs ər i prəʊ 'mɪs-
‖ 'prɑːm ə sɔːr i -soʊr i, -△ser i
prommer 'prɒm ə ‖ 'prɑːm ᵊr **~s** z
promo 'prəʊm əʊ ‖ 'proʊm oʊ **~s** z
promontor|y 'prɒm ənt ər |i
‖ 'prɑːm ən tɔːr |i -toʊr i **~ies** iz

pro|mote prə |'məʊt ‖ -|'moʊt ~**moted**
'məʊt ɪd -əd ‖ 'moʊt̬ əd ~**motes** 'məʊts
‖ 'moʊts ~**moting** 'məʊt ɪŋ ‖ 'moʊt̬ ɪŋ
promoter prə 'məʊt ə ‖ -'moʊt̬ ᵊr ~**s** z
promotion prə 'məʊʃ ᵊn ‖ -'moʊʃ ᵊn ~**s** z
promotional prə 'məʊʃ ᵊn ᵊl ‖ -'moʊʃ- ~**ly** i
prompt prɒmpt ‖ prɑːmpt **prompted**
'prɒmpt ɪd -əd ‖ 'prɑːmpt əd **prompter/s**
'prɒmpt ə/z ‖ 'prɑːmpt ᵊr/z **promptest**
'prɒmpt ɪst -əst ‖ 'prɑːmpt əst **prompting/s**
'prɒmpt ɪŋ/z ‖ 'prɑːmpt- **prompts** prɒmpts
‖ prɑːmpts
promptitude 'prɒmpt ɪ tjuːd -ə-, →-'tʃuːd
‖ 'prɑːmpt ə tuːd -tjuːd
prompt|ly '͵prɒmpt |li ‖ 'prɑːmpt- ~**ness** nəs
nɪs
promul|gate 'prɒm ᵊl |geɪt ‖ 'prɑːm-
proʊ 'mʌl|g eɪt ~**gated** geɪt ɪd -əd ‖ geɪt̬ əd
~**gates** geɪts ~**gating** geɪt ɪŋ ‖ geɪt̬ ɪŋ
promulgation ͵prɒm ᵊl 'geɪʃ ᵊn ‖ ͵prɑːm-
͵proʊm- ~**s** z
promulgator 'prɒm ᵊl geɪt ə
‖ 'prɑːm ᵊl geɪt̬ ᵊr 'proʊm- ~**s** z
pronate prəʊ 'neɪt 'prəʊn eɪt ‖ 'proʊn eɪt
pronated prəʊ 'neɪt ɪd -əd; 'prəʊn eɪt-
‖ 'proʊn eɪt̬ əd **pronates** prəʊ 'neɪts
'prəʊn eɪts ‖ 'proʊn eɪts **pronating**
prəʊ 'neɪt ɪŋ 'prəʊn eɪt- ‖ 'proʊn eɪt̬ ɪŋ
pronation prəʊ 'neɪʃ ᵊn ‖ proʊ-
pronator prəʊ 'neɪt ə ‖ 'proʊn eɪt̬ ᵊr ~**s** z
-prone prəʊn ‖ proʊn — **accident-prone**
'æks ɪd ənt prəʊn '-əd- ‖ -proʊn
prone prəʊn ‖ proʊn
prone|ly 'prəʊn |li ‖ 'proʊn- ~**ness** nəs nɪs
prong prɒŋ ‖ prɔːŋ prɑːŋ **pronged** prɒŋd
‖ prɔːŋd prɑːŋd **pronging** 'prɒŋ ɪŋ
‖ 'prɔːŋ ɪŋ 'prɑːŋ- **prongs** prɒŋz ‖ prɔːŋz
prɑːŋz
-pronged 'prɒŋd ‖ 'prɔːŋd 'prɑːŋd
— **three-pronged** ͵θriː 'prɒŋd ◄ ‖ -'prɔːŋd ◄
-'prɑːŋd
pronghorn 'prɒŋ hɔːn ‖ 'prɔːŋ hɔːrn 'prɑːŋ- ~**s**
z
pronominal prəʊ 'nɒm ɪn ᵊl -ᵊn͵ᵊl
‖ proʊ 'nɑːm ᵊn͵ᵊl ~**s** z
pronominalis... —see **pronominaliz...**
pronominalization
prəʊ ͵nɒm ɪn ᵊl aɪ 'zeɪʃ ᵊn -͵ᵊn͵, -ɪ'--
‖ proʊ ͵nɑːm ᵊn͵ᵊl ə- ~**s** z
pronominaliz|e prəʊ 'nɒm ɪn ə laɪz -'-ᵊn͵,
-ᵊl aɪz ‖ proʊ 'nɑːm- ~**ed** d ~**es** ɪz əz ~**ing** ɪŋ
pronominally prəʊ 'nɒm ɪn ᵊl i -'-ᵊn͵ᵊl-
‖ proʊ 'nɑːm ᵊn͵ᵊl i
pronoun 'prəʊ naʊn ‖ 'proʊ- ~**s** z
pronounc|e prə 'naʊnts ~**ed** t ~**es** ɪz əz ~**ing**
ɪŋ
pronounceable prə 'naʊnts əb ᵊl
pronouncedly prə 'naʊnts ɪd li -əd-
pronouncement prə 'naʊnts mənt ~**s** s
pronto 'prɒnt əʊ ‖ 'prɑːnt oʊ
pronunciamento prə ͵nʌnts i ə 'ment əʊ
-͵nʌntˢ-ʃ- ‖ proʊ ͵nʌnts i ə 'ment̬ oʊ ~**s** z

pronunciation prə ͵nʌntˢ i 'eɪʃ ᵊn ⚠-,naʊntˢ-
~**s** z
proof pruːf §prʊf **proofs** pruːfs §prʊfs
͵proof 'spirit ‖ '· ͵··
-proof pruːf §prʊf — **mothproof** 'mɒθ pruːf
§-prʊf ‖ 'mɔːθ- 'mɑːθ-
proof|read pres 'pruːf |riːd §prʊf- ~**read** past
& pp red ~**reader/s** riːd ə/z ‖ riːd ᵊr/z
~**reading** riːd ɪŋ ~**reads** riːdz
Proops pruːps
prop prɒp ‖ prɑːp **propped** prɒpt ‖ prɑːpt
propping 'prɒp ɪŋ ‖ 'prɑːp ɪŋ **props** prɒps
‖ prɑːps
'prop shaft
propaedeutic ͵prəʊ pi 'djuːt ɪk ◄ §-'duːt-,
→-'dʒuːt- ‖ ͵proʊ pɪ 'duːt̬ ɪk ◄ -'djuːt̬- ~**al** ᵊl
~**s** s
propaganda ͵prɒp ə 'gænd ə ‖ ͵prɑːp-
propagandis... —see **propagandiz...**
propagandist ͵prɒp ə 'gænd ɪst §-əst ‖ ͵prɑːp-
~**s** s
propagandiz|e ͵prɒp ə 'gænd aɪz ‖ ͵prɑːp-
~**ed** d ~**es** ɪz əz ~**ing** ɪŋ
propa|gate 'prɒp ə |geɪt ‖ 'prɑːp- ~**gated**
geɪt ɪd -əd ‖ geɪt̬ əd ~**gates** geɪts ~**gating**
geɪt ɪŋ ‖ geɪt̬ ɪŋ
propagation ͵prɒp ə 'geɪʃ ᵊn ‖ ͵prɑːp- ~**s** z
propagative 'prɒp ə geɪt ɪv ‖ 'prɑːp ə geɪt̬ ɪv
~**ly** li
propagator 'prɒp ə geɪt ə ‖ 'prɑːp ə geɪt̬ ᵊr ~**s**
z
propane 'prəʊp eɪn ‖ 'proʊp-
proparoxytone ͵prəʊ pə 'rɒks ɪ təʊn ◄ ͵·pæ-,
-'-ə- ‖ ͵proʊ pæ 'rɑːks ɪ toʊn ◄ -pə- ~**s** z
propel prə 'pel ~**led** d ~**ling** ɪŋ ~**s** z
pro'pelling ͵pencil, ͵··'··
propellant, propellent prə 'pel ənt ~**s** s
propeller prə 'pel ə ‖ -ᵊr ~**s** z
pro'peller shaft
propene 'prəʊp iːn ‖ 'proʊp-
propensit|y prəʊ 'pentˢ ət |i -ɪt-
‖ prə 'pentˢ ət̬ |i ~**ies** iz
proper 'prɒp ə ‖ 'prɑːp ᵊr
͵proper 'fraction; ͵proper 'name; ͵proper
'noun
properly 'prɒp əl i ‖ 'prɑːp ᵊr li —In RP there
is also a casual form 'prɒp li
Propertius prəʊ 'pɜːʃ əs -'pɜːʃ i͵əs
‖ proʊ 'pɜːʃ əs
propert|y 'prɒp ət |i ‖ 'prɑːp ᵊrt̬ |i ~**ied** id
~**ies** iz
'property boom
prophase 'prəʊ feɪz ‖ 'proʊ-
prophec|y n 'prɒf əs |i -ɪs- ‖ 'prɑːf- ~**ies** iz
prophe|sy v 'prɒf ə |saɪ -ɪ- ‖ 'prɑːf- ~**sied** saɪd
~**sies** saɪz ~**sying** saɪ ɪŋ
prophet, P~ 'prɒf ɪt §-ət ‖ 'prɑːf ət (= profit)
~**s** s
prophetess ͵prɒf ɪ 'tes -ə-, '·· ·; 'prɒf ɪt ɪs, -ət-,
-əs ‖ 'prɑːf ət̬ əs ~**es** ɪz əz
prophethood 'prɒf ɪt hʊd §-ət- ‖ 'prɑːf ət-
prophetic prəʊ 'fet ɪk ‖ prə 'fet̬ ɪk ~**al** ᵊl ~**ally**
ᵊl͵i

P

prophylactic ˌprɒf ə 'lækt ɪk ◂ -ɪ- ‖ ˌprouf-
ˌprɑːf- **~ally** ᵊl i **~s** s
prophylaxis ˌprɒf ə 'læks ɪs -ɪ-, §-əs ‖ ˌprouf-
ˌprɑːf-
propinquity prəʊ 'pɪŋk wət i -wɪt-
‖ prə 'pɪŋk wət i
propionate 'prəʊp i ə neɪt ‖ 'proup-
propionic ˌprəʊp i 'ɒn ɪk ◂
‖ ˌproup i 'ɑːn ɪk ◂
propiti|ate prəʊ 'pɪʃ i |eɪt ‖ prou- **~ated**
eɪt ɪd -əd ‖ eɪt̬ əd **~ates** eɪts **~ating** eɪt ɪŋ
‖ eɪt̬ ɪŋ
propitiation prəʊ ˌpɪʃ i 'eɪʃ ᵊn ‖ prou- **~s** z
propitiator prəʊ 'pɪʃ i eɪt ə ‖ prou 'pɪʃ i eɪt̬ ᵊr
~s z
propitiator|y prəʊ 'pɪʃ i ə ₜər |i -eɪt ər |i,
ˌ·ˌ··'eɪt ər |i ‖ prou 'pɪʃ i ə tɔːr |i -tour i **~ies**
iz
propitious prə 'pɪʃ əs **~ly** li **~ness** nəs nɪs
propjet 'prɒp dʒet ‖ 'prɑːp- **~s** s
propolis 'prɒp əl ɪs §-əs ‖ 'prɑːp-
proponent prə 'pəʊn ənt ‖ -'poun- **~s** s
Propontis prəʊ 'pɒnt ɪs §-əs ‖ prə 'pɑːnt̬ əs
proportion prə 'pɔːʃ ᵊn ‖ -'pɔːrʃ ᵊn pə-,
-'poʊrʃ- **~ed** d **~ing** ɪŋ **~s** z
proportionab|le prə 'pɔːʃ ᵊn əb |ᵊl ‖ -'pɔːrʃ-
pə-, -'poʊrʃ- **~leness** ᵊl nəs -nɪs **~ly** li
proportional prə 'pɔːʃ ᵊn əl ‖ -'pɔːrʃ- pə-,
-'poʊrʃ- **~s** z
   pro,portional ,represen'tation
proportionality prə ˌpɔːʃ ə 'næl ət i -ɪt i
‖ -ˌpɔːrʃ ə 'næl ət̬ i pə-, -ˌpoʊrʃ-
proportionally prə 'pɔːʃ ᵊn əl i ‖ -'pɔːrʃ- pə-,
-'poʊrʃ-
proportionate _adj_ prə 'pɔːʃ ᵊn ət -ɪt ‖ -'pɔːrʃ-
pə-, -'poʊrʃ- **~ly** li **~ness** nəs nɪs
proposal prə 'pəʊz ᵊl ‖ -'poʊz ᵊl **~s** z
propos|e prə 'pəʊz ‖ -'pouz **~ed** d **~er/s** ə/z
‖ -ᵊr/z **~es** ɪz əz **~ing** ɪŋ
proposition ˌprɒp ə 'zɪʃ ᵊn ‖ ˌprɑːp- **~ed** d
~ing ɪŋ **~s** z
propositional ˌprɒp ə 'zɪʃ ᵊn əl ◂ ‖ ˌprɑːp- **~ly**
i
propound prə 'paʊnd **~ed** ɪd əd **~ing** ɪŋ **~s** z
proppy 'prɒp i ‖ 'prɑːp i
propranolol prəʊ 'præn ə lɒl
‖ prou 'præn ə lɑːl -lɔːl, -loul
proprietar|y prə 'praɪ ət ər |i ‖ -ə ter |i **~ies**
iz **~ily** əl i -ɪ li
proprietor prə 'praɪ ət ə ‖ ət̬ ᵊr **~s** z **~ship** ʃɪp
proprietorial prə ˌpraɪ ə 'tɔːr i əl ‖ prou-,
-'tour- **~ly** i
proprietress prə 'praɪ ətr əs -ɪs, -es **~es** ɪz əz
propriet|y prə 'praɪ ət |i -ɪt- ‖ -ət̬ |i **~ies** iz
proprioception ˌprəʊp ri ə 'sep ʃᵊn ˌprɒp-,
-əʊ'-- ‖ ˌproup ri ou-
proprioceptive ˌprəʊp ri ə 'sept ɪv ◂ ˌprɒp-,
-əʊ'-- ‖ ˌproup ri ou- **~ly** li
proprioceptor ˌprəʊp ri ə 'sept ə ˌprɒp-, -əʊ'--
‖ ˌproup ri ou 'sept ᵊr **~s** z
proptosis prɒp 'təʊs ɪs §-əs ‖ prɑːp 'tous-
propulsion prə 'pʌlʃ ᵊn
propulsive prə 'pʌls ɪv

propyl 'prəʊp ɪl -əl, -aɪᵊl ‖ 'proup-
propylae|um ˌprɒp ɪ 'liː ₗəm ˌprəʊp-, -ə-
‖ ˌprɑːp- ˌproup- **~a** ə
propylene 'prəʊp ɪ liːn -ə- ‖ 'proup-
pro rata ₍ˌ₎prəʊ 'rɑːt ə -'reɪt- ‖ ₍ˌ₎prou 'reɪt̬ ə
-'rɑːt̬-, -'ræt̬-
pro|rate ˌprəʊ |'reɪt ‖ ₍ˌ₎prou- **~rated** 'reɪt ɪd
-əd ‖ 'reɪt̬ əd **~rates** 'reɪts **~rating** 'reɪt ɪŋ
‖ 'reɪt̬ ɪŋ
prorogation ˌprəʊ rəʊ 'geɪʃ ᵊn ˌprɒr ə-
‖ ˌprou rə- ˌprɔːr ə- **~s** z
prorogu|e prəʊ 'rəʊg ‖ prou 'roug prə- **~ed** d
~es z **~ing** ɪŋ
prosaic prəʊ 'zeɪ ɪk ‖ prou- **~ally** ᵊl i **~ness**
nəs nɪs
pros and cons ˌprəʊz ᵊn 'kɒnz -ᵊnd-, -→ᵊŋ-
‖ ˌprouz ᵊn 'kɑːnz
prosceni|um prəʊ 'siːn i ₗəm ‖ prou- **~a** ə
~ums əmz
prosciutto prəʊ 'ʃuːt əʊ ‖ prou 'ʃuːt̬ ou —_It_
[pro 'ʃut to]
proscrib|e prəʊ 'skraɪb ‖ prou- **~ed** d **~es** z
~ing ɪŋ
proscription prəʊ 'skrɪp ʃᵊn ‖ prou- **~s** z
proscriptive prəʊ 'skrɪpt ɪv ‖ prou- **~ly** li
~ness nəs nɪs
prose prəʊz ‖ prouz **prosed** prəʊzd ‖ prouzd
proses 'prəʊz ɪz -əz ‖ 'prouz əz **prosing**
'prəʊz ɪŋ ‖ 'prouz ɪŋ
prose|cute 'prɒs ɪ |kjuːt -ə- ‖ 'prɑːs- **~cuted**
kjuːt ɪd -əd ‖ kjuːt̬ əd **~cutes** kjuːts **~cuting**
kjuːt ɪŋ ‖ kjuːt̬ ɪŋ
prosecution ˌprɒs ɪ 'kjuːʃ ᵊn -ə- ‖ ˌprɑːs- **~s** z
prosecutor 'prɒs ɪ kjuːt ə '·ə-
‖ 'prɑːs ɪ kjuːt̬ ᵊr **~s** z
prosecutorial ˌprɒs ɪ kju: 'tɔːr i ᵊl ◂ ˌ·ə-
‖ ˌprɑːs- -'tour-
proselyte 'prɒs ə laɪt -ɪ- ‖ 'prɑːs- **~s** s
proselytis... —_see_ **proselytiz...**
proselytism 'prɒs əl ə ˌtɪz əm '·ɪl-, -ˌ·,--
‖ 'prɑːs- '·ə laɪ-
proselytiz|e 'prɒs əl ə taɪz '·ɪl-, -ɪ · ‖ 'prɑːs-
~ed d **~es** ɪz əz **~ing** ɪŋ
Proserpina prə 'sɜːp ɪn ə prɒ-, prəʊ-, §-ən-
‖ prə 'sɜːp- prou-
Proserpine 'prɒs ə paɪn ‖ 'prɑːs ᵊr-
prosimian prəʊ 'sɪm i ən ‖ prou- **~s** z
prosodic prə 'sɒd ɪk prəʊ-, -'zɒd- ‖ -'sɑːd ɪk
~ally ᵊl i
prosodist 'prɒs əd ɪst 'prɒz-, 'prəʊz-, §-əst
‖ 'prɑːs- **~s** s
prosod|y 'prɒs əd |i 'prɒz-, 'prəʊz- ‖ 'prɑːs-
~ies iz
prosopopeia, prosopopoeia
ˌprɒs əʊp əʊ 'piː ə prəʊ ˌsəʊp- ‖ ˌprɑːs əp ə-
prou ˌsoup ə-, ˌprous oup ə-
prospect _n_ 'prɒsp ekt ‖ 'prɑːsp- **~s** s
prospect _v_ prə 'spekt prɒ-; 'prɒsp ekt
‖ 'prɑːsp ekt _(*)_ **~ed** ɪd əd **~ing** ɪŋ **~s** s
prospective prə 'spekt ɪv prɒ- ‖ prɑː- **~ly** li
prospector prə 'spekt ə prɒ-; 'prɒsp ekt ə
‖ 'prɑːsp ekt ᵊr _(*)_ **~s** z
prospectus prə 'spekt əs prɒ- ‖ prɑː- **~es** ɪz əz

prosp|er 'prɒsp |ə ‖ 'prɑːsp |ᵊr **~ered** əd ‖ ᵊrd
~ering ər_ɪŋ **~ers** əz ‖ ᵊrz
prosperit|y prɒ 'sper ət |i prə-, -ɪt i
‖ prɑː 'sper ət̮ |i **~ies** iz
Prospero 'prɒsp ə rəʊ ‖ 'prɑːsp ə roʊ
prosperous 'prɒsp ər_əs ‖ 'prɑːsp- **~ly** li
~ness nəs nɪs
Prosser 'prɒs ə ‖ 'prɑːs ᵊr
Prost prɒst prəʊst ‖ proʊst
prostaglandin ˌprɒst ə 'glænd ɪn §-ən
‖ ˌprɑːst- **~s** z
prostate 'prɒst eɪt ‖ 'prɑːst- **~s** s
'prostate gland
prostatectom|y ˌprɒst ə 'tekt əm |i ‖ ˌprɑːst-
~ies iz
prostatic prɒ 'stæt ɪk prə- ‖ prɑː 'stæt̮ ɪk
prosthes|is ₍ᵢ₎prɒs 'θiːs |ɪs prəs-, §-əs;
'prɒs θəs-, -θɪs- ‖ prɑːs- **~es** iːz
prosthetic ₍ᵢ₎prɒs 'θet ɪk prəs- ‖ prɑːs 'θet̮ ɪk
~ally ᵊl_i **~s** s
prosthodont|ics ˌprɒs θəʊ 'dɒnt| ɪks
‖ ˌprɑːs θə 'dɑːnt̮| ɪks **~ist/s** ɪst/s §əst/s
prosti|tute v, n 'prɒst ɪ |tjuːt -ə-, →-tʃuːt
‖ 'prɑːst ə |tuːt -tjuːt **~tuted** tjuːt ɪd →tʃuːt-,
-əd ‖ tuːt̮ əd tjuːt̮- **~tutes** tjuːts →tʃuːts ‖ tuːts
tjuːts **~tuting** tjuːt ɪŋ →tʃuːt- ‖ tuːt̮ ɪŋ tjuːt̮-
prostitution ˌprɒst ɪ 'tjuːʃ ᵊn -ə-, →-'tʃuːʃ-
‖ ˌprɑːst ə 'tuːʃ ᵊn -'tjuːʃ-
pro|strate v prɒ '|streɪt prə- ‖ 'prɑː |s treɪt (*)
~strated streɪt ɪd -əd ‖ streɪt̮ əd **~strates**
streɪts **~strating** streɪt ɪŋ ‖ streɪt̮ ɪŋ
prostrate adj 'prɒs treɪt prɒ 'streɪt, prə-
‖ 'prɑːs-
prostration prɒ 'streɪʃ ᵊn prə- ‖ prɑː- **~s** z
prostyle 'prəʊ staɪᵊl ‖ 'proʊ-
pros|y 'prəʊz |i ‖ 'proʊz |i **~ier** i_ə ‖ i_ᵊr **~iest**
i_ɪst i_əst **~ily** ɪ li əl i **~iness** i nəs i nɪs
prot- comb. form before vowel prəʊt ‖ proʊt
— **protoxide** prəʊ 'tɒks aɪd ‖ proʊ 'tɑːks-
protactinium ˌprəʊt æk 'tɪn i_əm ‖ ˌproʊt̮-
protagonist prəʊ 'tæg ən ɪst §-əst ‖ proʊ- **~s** s
Protagoras prəʊ 'tæg ə ræs -ər əs ‖ proʊ-
protanopia ˌprəʊt ə 'nəʊp i_ə -ᵊn 'əʊp-
‖ ˌproʊt̮ ᵊn 'oʊp-
protanopic ˌprəʊt ə 'nɒp ɪk ◂ -ᵊn 'ɒp-
‖ ˌproʊt̮ ᵊn 'ɑːp ɪk ◂
prot|asis 'prɒt |əs ɪs §-əs ‖ 'prɑːt̮- **~ases** ə siːz
protea 'prəʊt i_ə ‖ 'proʊt̮ i_ə **~s** z
protean prəʊ 'tiː_ən 'prəʊt i_ən ‖ 'proʊt̮ i_ən
proʊ 'tiː ən
proteas|e 'prəʊt i eɪz -eɪs ‖ 'proʊt̮- **~es** ɪz əz
protect prə 'tekt prəʊ- ‖ proʊ- **~ed** ɪd əd **~ing**
ɪŋ **~s** s
protecting|ly prə 'tekt ɪŋ| li prəʊ- ‖ proʊ-
~ness nəs nɪs
protection prə 'tek ʃᵊn prəʊ- ‖ proʊ- **~ism**
ˌɪz əm **~ist/s** ɪst/s §əst/s ‖ əst/s
pro'tection ˌracket
protective prə 'tekt ɪv prəʊ- ‖ proʊ- **~ly** li
~ness nəs nɪs
pro ˌtective 'custody
protector, P~ prə 'tekt ə prəʊ- ‖ -ᵊr proʊ-
~ship/s ʃɪp/s **~s** z

protectorate, P~ prə 'tekt ər_ət prəʊ-, -ɪt
‖ proʊ- **~s** s
protectress prə 'tek trəs prəʊ-, -trɪs ‖ proʊ-
~es ɪz əz
protege, protégé, protegee, protégée
'prɒt ə ʒeɪ 'prəʊt-, -ɪ- ‖ 'proʊt̮- ˌ· ·ˈ· —Fr
[pʁɔ te ʒe] **~s** z
protein 'prəʊt iːn 'prəʊt i_ɪn ‖ 'proʊt̮- **~s** z
pro tem ₍ᵢ₎prəʊ 'tem ‖ ₍ᵢ₎proʊ-
proterozoic, P~ ˌprəʊt ər əʊ 'zəʊ ɪk ◂ ˌprɒt
‖ ˌprɑːt̮ ər ə 'zoʊ ɪk ◂ ˌproʊt̮-
protest v prə 'test prəʊ-, 'prəʊt est ‖ 'proʊt est
~ed ɪd əd **~ing/ly** ɪŋ /li **~s** s
protest n 'prəʊt est ‖ 'proʊt est **~s** s
protestant, P~ 'prɒt ɪst ənt -əst- ‖ 'prɑːt̮- **~s** s
protestantism, P~ 'prɒt ɪst ənt ˌɪz əm '-əst-
‖ 'prɑːt̮ əst ənt̮-
protestation ˌprɒt ɪ 'steɪʃ ᵊn ˌprəʊt-, -ə-, -e-
‖ ˌprɑːt̮ ə-, ˌproʊt̮ ə-, ˌproʊt e- **~s** z

PROTESTER

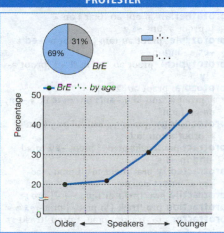

69% / 31% / BrE

BrE ⋯ by age

(pie chart and line graph: Percentage on y-axis from 0 to 50; x-axis from Older ◀— Speakers —▶ Younger)

protester prə 'test ə prəʊ-; 'prəʊt est ə
‖ 'proʊt est ᵊr prə 'test- — Preference poll,
BrE: ⋮ · 69%, ⋯ 31% (born since 1982:
45%). **~s** z
Proteus 'prəʊt juːs 'prəʊt i_əs ‖ 'proʊt̮ i_əs
'proʊt juːs
prothalami|on ˌprəʊ θə 'leɪm i_|ən ‖ ˌproʊ-
-i |ɑːn **~a** ə **~um** əm
Prothero, Protheroe 'prɒð ə rəʊ
‖ 'prɑːð ə roʊ
proth|esis 'prɒθ |əs ɪs -ɪs-, §-əs ‖ 'prɑːθ- **~eses**
ə siːz ɪ-
prothetic prəʊ 'θet ɪk ‖ prə 'θet̮ ɪk prɑː- **~ally**
ᵊl i
prothonotar|y ˌprəʊθ əʊ 'nəʊt ər| i
prəʊ 'θɒn ət ᵊr| i ‖ proʊ 'θɑːn ə ter| i
ˌproʊθ oʊ 'noʊt̮ ər| i **~ies** iz
protist 'prəʊt ɪst §-əst ‖ 'proʊt̮- **~s** s
protist|a prəʊ 'tɪst |ə ‖ proʊ- **~an/s** ən/z **~ic**
ɪk
protium 'prəʊt i_əm ‖ 'proʊt̮- 'proʊʃ-
proto- comb. form
with stress-neutral suffix ¦prəʊt əʊ

‖ ¦proʊt oʊ — **Proto-Norse** ˌproʊt əʊ 'nɔːs ◂
‖ ˌproʊt oʊ 'nɔːrs ◂
with stress-imposing suffix prəʊ 'tɒ +
‖ proʊ 'tɑː + — **protogynous**
prəʊ 'tɒdʒ ɪn əs -ən- ‖ proʊ 'tɑːdʒ-
protoceratops ˌprəʊt əʊ 'ser ə tɒps
‖ ˌproʊt oʊ 'ser ə tɑːps
protocol 'prəʊt əʊ kɒl ‖ 'proʊt ə kɑːl -kɔːl,
-koʊl ~**s** z
Proto-Indo-European
ˌprəʊt əʊ ˌɪnd əʊ jʊər ə 'piː ən -jɔːr ə'--
‖ ˌproʊt oʊ ˌɪnd oʊ jʊr-
protolanguag|e 'prəʊt əʊ ˌlæŋ gwɪdʒ -wɪdʒ,
ˌ· ·ʼ· · ‖ 'proʊt oʊ- ~**es** ɪz əz
proton, P~ 'prəʊt ɒn ‖ 'proʊt ɑːn ~**s** z
protonotar|y ˌprəʊt əʊ 'nəʊt ər| i
prəʊ 'tɒn ət ər| i ‖ proʊ 'tɑːn ə ter| i
ˌproʊt oʊ 'noʊt ər| i ~**ies** iz
protoplasm 'prəʊt əʊ ˌplæz əm ‖ 'proʊt ə-
protoplast 'prəʊt əʊ plæst -plɑːst ‖ 'proʊt ə-
~**s** s
prototherian ˌprəʊt əʊ 'θɪər i ən ◂
‖ ˌproʊt ə 'θɪr- ~**s** z
prototyp|e 'prəʊt əʊ taɪp ‖ 'proʊt ə- ~**ed** t
~**es** s ~**ing** ɪŋ
prototypical ˌprəʊt əʊ 'tɪp ɪk ᵊl ◂ ‖ ˌproʊt ə-
~**ly** ˌi
protozo|a ˌprəʊt əʊ 'zəʊ |ə ◂
‖ ˌproʊt ə 'zoʊ |ə ◂ ~**an/s** ən/z ~**ic** ɪk ◂ ~**on**
ɒn ən ‖ ɑːn
protozoology ˌprəʊt əʊ zəʊ 'ɒl ədʒ i -zu'--
‖ ˌproʊt ə zoʊ 'ɑːl-
protract prə 'trækt prəʊ- ‖ proʊ- ~**ed** ɪd əd
~**ing** ɪŋ ~**s** s
protracted|ly prə 'trækt ɪd |li prəʊ-, -əd-
‖ proʊ- ~**ness** nəs nɪs
protractile prə 'trækt aɪᵊl prəʊ- ‖ -ᵊl proʊ-
protraction prə 'træk ʃᵊn prəʊ- ‖ proʊ- ~**s** z
protractor prə 'trækt ə prəʊ- ‖ proʊ 'trækt ᵊr
'· · · ~**s** z
protrud|e prə 'truːd prəʊ- ‖ proʊ- ~**ed** ɪd əd
~**ing** ɪŋ ~**es** z
protrusion prə 'truːʒ ᵊn prəʊ- ‖ proʊ- ~**s** z
protrusive prə 'truːs ɪv prəʊ-, §-'truːz- ‖ proʊ-
~**ly** li ~**ness** nəs nɪs
protuberanc|e prə 'tjuːb ᵊr ᵊn¹s prəʊ-,
→-'tʃuːb-, △-'truːb- ‖ -'tuːb- -'tjuːb- ~**es** ɪz əz
protuberant prə 'tjuːb ᵊr ənt prəʊ-, →-'tʃuːb-,
△-'truːb- ‖ -'tuːb- -'tjuːb- ~**ly** li
Protus 'prəʊt əs ‖ 'proʊt əs
proud, Proud praʊd **prouder** 'praʊd ə ‖ -ᵊr
proudest 'praʊd ɪst -əst
Proudfoot 'praʊd fʊt
Proudhon 'pruːd ɒn ‖ pruː 'dɔːn -'dɑːn, -'doʊn
—*Fr* [pʁu dɔ̃]
Proudie 'praʊd i
proudly 'praʊd li
Proulx pruː
Proust pruːst —*Fr* [pʁust]
Proustian 'pruːst i ən ~**s** z
proustite 'pruːst aɪt
Prout praʊt
provab|le 'pruːv əb |ᵊl ~**ly** li

Provan 'prɒv ᵊn 'prəʊv- ‖ 'prɑːv-
prove pruːv *(!)* **proved** pruːvd **proven**
'pruːv ᵊn 'prəʊv- **proves** pruːvz **proving**
'pruːv ɪŋ
'**proving ground**
proven 'pruːv ᵊn 'prəʊv-
provenance 'prɒv ən ən¹s -ɪn- ‖ 'prɑːv-
-ə nɑːn¹s
Provencal, Provençal, Provencale,
Provençale ˌprɒv ɒn 'sɑːl ◂ -ð̃-, -ᵊn-
‖ ˌprɑːv ɑːn-, ˌproov- —*Fr* [pʁɔ vã sal]
Provence prɒ 'vɒ̃s prə- ‖ prə 'vɑːn¹s prooʊ-
—*Fr* [pʁɔ vãːs]
provender 'prɒv ɪnd ə -ənd- ‖ 'prɑːv ᵊnd ᵊr
provenience prə 'viːn i ən¹s prəʊ- ‖ proʊ-
proverb, P~ 'prɒv ɜːb ‖ 'prɑːv ɜːb —*but as a*
grammatical term, 'kind of pro-form',
'prəʊ vɜːb ‖ 'proʊ vɜːb ~**s** z
proverbial prə 'vɜːb i əl prɒ-, prəʊ- ‖ -'vɜːb-
~**ly** i
provid|e prə 'vaɪd prəʊ- ~**ed** ɪd əd ~**ing** ɪŋ ~**es**
z
providence, P~ 'prɒv ɪd ən¹s -əd- ‖ 'prɑːv-
-ə den¹s
provident 'prɒv ɪd ənt -əd- ‖ 'prɑːv- ~**ly** li
providential ˌprɒv ɪ 'den¹ʃ ᵊl ◂ -ə- ‖ ˌprɑːv-
~**ly** i
provider prə 'vaɪd ə §prəʊ- ‖ -ᵊr ~**s** z
provinc|e, P~ 'prɒv ɪn¹s §-ᵊn¹s ‖ 'prɑːv- ~**es** ɪz
əz
Provincetown 'prɒv ɪn¹s taʊn §-ᵊn¹s- ‖ 'prɑːv-
provincial prə 'vɪn¹ʃ ᵊl ~**ism** ˌɪz əm ~**s** z
provinciality prə ˌvɪn¹ʃ i 'æl ət i -ɪt i ‖ -əṭ i
provision prə 'vɪʒ ᵊn prəʊ- ~**ed** d ~**ing** ɪŋ ~**s**
z
provisional, P~ prə 'vɪʒ ᵊn əl prəʊ- ~**ism**
ˌɪz əm ~**ly** i ~**s** z
proviso prə 'vaɪz əʊ prəʊ- ‖ -oʊ ~**s**, ~**es** z
provisor prə 'vaɪz ə prəʊ- ‖ -ᵊr ~**s** z
provisory prə 'vaɪz ər i
Provo, p~ 'prəʊv əʊ ‖ 'proʊv oʊ ~**s** z
provocation ˌprɒv ə 'keɪʃ ᵊn -əʊ- ‖ ˌprɑːv- ~**s**
z
provocative prə 'vɒk ət ɪv prəʊ- ‖ -'vɑːk əṭ ɪv
~**ly** li ~**ness** nəs nɪs
provok|e prə 'vəʊk prəʊ- ‖ -'voʊk ~**ed** t ~**es** s
~**ing/ly** ɪŋ /li
provolone ˌprəʊv ə 'ləʊn i ‖ ˌproʊv ə 'loʊn i
—*It* [pro vo 'lo: ne]
provost 'prɒv əst 'prəʊv-, -ɒst ‖ 'proʊv oʊst
'prɑːv əst ~**s** s ~**ship/s** ʃɪp/s —*but in* p~
marshal *and other military senses,*
prə 'vəʊ ‖ 'proʊv oʊ, *with a corresponding*
plural ~**s** z
pro**vost** 'marshal ‖ ˌ· · '· ·
prow praʊ **prows** praʊz
prowess 'praʊ es 'prəʊ-, -ɪs, -əs, ·'es ‖ 'praʊ əs
prowl praʊl **prowled** praʊld **prowling**
'praʊl ɪŋ **prowls** praʊlz
'**prowl car**
prowler 'praʊl ə ‖ -ᵊr ~**s** z
Prowse *(i)* praʊs, *(ii)* praʊz
prox, prox. prɒks ‖ prɑːks

proxemic prɒk ˈsiːm ɪk ‖ prɑːk- **~s** s
proxie... —*see* **proxy**
Proxima ˈprɒks ɪm ə -əm- ‖ ˈprɑːks-
proximal ˈprɒks ɪm ᵊl -əm- ‖ ˈprɑːks- **~ly** i
proximate ˈprɒks ɪm ət -əm-, -ɪt ‖ ˈprɑːks- **~ly**
  li
proxime accessit ˌprɒks ɪm i æk ˈses ɪt ˌ· ·eɪ-,
  -ək'·-, -ə ˈkes-, §-ət ‖ ˌprɑːks- **~s** s
proximit|y prɒk ˈsɪm ət |i -ɪt-
  ‖ prɑːk ˈsɪm ət̬ |i **~ies** iz
proximo ˈprɒks ɪ məʊ -ə- ‖ ˈprɑːks ə moʊ
prox|y ˈprɒks |i ‖ ˈprɑːks |i **~ies** iz
Prozac *tdmk* ˈprəʊz æk ‖ ˈproʊz-
Pru pruː
prude pruːd **prudes** pruːdz
prudence, P~ ˈpruːd ᵊnᵗs
prudent ˈpruːd ᵊnt **~ly** li
prudential, P~ pru ˈdenᵗʃ ᵊl **~ly** i
pruder|y ˈpruːd ər |i **~ies** iz
Prudhoe (i) ˈprʌd əʊ -həʊ ‖ -oʊ, (ii) ˈpruːd-
  —*The place in Northumberland is* (i), *locally*
  §ˈprʊd-; *but* P~ Bay *in AK is* (ii).
  ˌPrudhoe ˈBay
Prud'hon pruː ˈdɒ̃ ‖ -ˈdɑːn —*Fr* [pʀy dɔ̃]
prudish ˈpruːd ɪʃ **~ly** li **~ness** nəs nɪs
Prue pruː
Prufrock ˈpruː frɒk ‖ -frɑːk
prune pruːn **pruned** pruːnd **prunes** pruːnz
  pruning ˈpruːn ɪŋ
  ˈpruning hook; ˈpruning knife
Prunella, p~ pru ˈnel ə
prunus, P~ ˈpruːn əs **~es** ɪz əz
prurienc|e ˈprʊər i ənᵗs ‖ ˈprʊr- **~y** i
prurient ˈprʊər i ənt ‖ ˈprʊr- **~ly** li
pruriginous prʊᵊ ˈrɪdʒ ɪn əs -ən-
prurigo prʊᵊ ˈraɪg əʊ ‖ -oʊ
pruritus prʊᵊ ˈraɪt əs ‖ -ˈraɪt̬ əs
  pruˌritus ˈani ˈeɪn aɪ
prusik, P~ ˈprʌs ɪk **~ed** t **~ing** ɪŋ **~s** s
Prussi|a ˈprʌʃ |ə **~an/s** ᵊn/z
  ˌPrussian ˈblue◄
prussic ˈprʌs ɪk
  ˌprussic ˈacid
pry, Pry praɪ **pried** praɪd (= *pride*) **pries** praɪz
  (= *prize*) **prying/ly** ˈpraɪ ɪŋ /li
Pryce praɪs
Prynne prɪn
Pryor ˈpraɪ̯ə ‖ ˈpraɪ̯ᵊr
prytaneum ˌprɪt ə ˈniːˌəm -ᵊn ˈiːˌ ‖ -ᵊn ˈiː əm
Przewalski prəʒ ɪ ˈvæl ski -əˈ·; ˌpɜːʒˈ·ˈ·; ʃəˈ·ˈ·;
  -ˈwɔːl-, -ˈwɒl- ‖ ʃə ˈvɑːl ski prɪz-, -ˈwɑːl-
  —*Russ* [pɾʒɪ ˈvalʲ skʲɪj] **~'s** z
  Przeˌwalski's ˈhorse
PS, P.S. ˌpiː ˈes **~'s** ɪz əz
ps... *Note: words spelt with* ps... *are occasionally*
  pronounced with initial ps, *as written, rather*
  than with the usual plain s *sound. Thus* psalm
  is occasionally pronounced psɑːm. *This is not*
  shown in individual entries.
psalm sɑːm §sɑːlm, §sɒlm **psalms** sɑːmz
  §sɑːlmz, §sɒlmz
psalmist ˈsɑːm ɪst §ˈsɑːlm-, §ˈsɒlm-, §-əst **~s** s
psalmodic sæl ˈmɒd ɪk sɑː- ‖ -ˈmɑːd-

psalmod|y ˈsɑːm əd |i ˈsælm-, §ˈsɑːlm-, §ˈsɒlm-
  ~ies iz
psalter, P~ ˈsɔːlt ə ˈsɒlt- ‖ -ᵊr ˈsɑːlt- **~s** z
psalteri|um sɔːl ˈtɪər i ˌ|əm sɒl- ‖ -ˈtɪr- sɑːl- **~a**
  ə
psalter|y ˈsɔːlt ər |i ˈsɒlt- ‖ ˈsɑːlt- **~ies** iz
psephological ˌsiːf ə ˈlɒdʒ ɪk ᵊl ◄ ˌsef-
  ‖ -ˈlɑːdʒ- **~ly** ˌi
psephologist si ˈfɒl ədʒ ɪst sə-, se-, §-əst
  ‖ -ˈfɑːl- **~s** s
psephology si ˈfɒl ədʒ i sə-, se- ‖ -ˈfɑːl-
pseud sjuːd suːd ‖ suːd **pseuds** sjuːdz suːdz
  ‖ suːdz
pseudepigrapha ˌsjuːd ɪ ˈpɪg rəf ə ˌsuːd-, ˌ·ə-,
  ˌ·e- ‖ ˌsuːd-
pseudo ˈsjuːd əʊ ˈsuːd- ‖ ˈsuːd oʊ
pseudo- *comb. form*
  with stress-neutral suffix ˌsjuːd əʊ ˌsuːd-
  ‖ ˌsuːd oʊ — **pseudo-Marxist**
  ˌsjuːd əʊ ˈmɑːks ɪst ◄ ˌsuːd-, §-əst
  ‖ ˌsuːd oʊ ˈmɑːrks əst ◄
pseudomonas ˌsjuːd əʊ ˈməʊn əs ˌsuːd-;
  sju ˈdɒm ən əs, su- ‖ ˌsuːd ə ˈmoʊn əs
  su ˈdɑːm ən əs
pseudonym ˈsjuːd ə nɪm ˈsuːd-, ᵊn ɪm
  ‖ ˈsuːd ᵊn ɪm **~s** z
pseudonymous sju ˈdɒn ɪm əs suː-, -əm-
  ‖ suː ˈdɑːn- **~ly** li
pseudopod ˈsjuːd əʊ pɒd ˈsuːd- ‖ ˈsuːd ə pɑːd
  ~s z
pseudopodi|um ˌsjuːd əʊ ˈpəʊd i ˌ|əm ˌsuːd-
  ‖ ˌsuːd oʊ ˈpoʊd- -ə- **~a** ə
pseudy ˈsjuːd i ˈsuːd- ‖ ˈsuːd i
pshaw pɸ̩ə, pɸ̩, pʃɔː, pʃɑː —*now obsolete:*
  the spelling may have represented a bilabial
  affricate with 'lip voice' (a 'raspberry', a
  'Bronx cheer').
psi psaɪ saɪ **psis** psaɪz saɪz
psilocybin ˌsaɪl əʊ ˈsaɪb ɪn ˌsɪl-, §-ən ‖ ˌ·ə-
Psion *tdmk* ˈsaɪ ɒn ‖ -ɑːn
psittacine ˈsɪt ə saɪn -sɪn ‖ ˈsɪt̬ ə-
psittacosis ˌsɪt ə ˈkəʊs ɪs §-əs ‖ ˌsɪt̬ ə ˈkoʊs əs
psoas ˈsəʊ æs -əs ‖ ˈsoʊ-
psoriasis sə ˈraɪ̯ əs ɪs sɒ-, sɔː-, §-əs ‖ soʊ-
psoriatic ˌsɔːr i ˈæt ɪk ◄ sɔː ˈraɪ̯ ət ɪk
  ‖ -ˈæt̬ ɪk ◄ ˌsoʊr-
psst ps, pst
psych, psyche *v* saɪk **psyched** saɪkt **psyches**
  v , **psychs** saɪks **psyching** ˈsaɪk ɪŋ
psyche *n*, **P~** ˈsaɪk i -iː **~s** z
psychedelia ˌsaɪk ə ˈdiːl i̯ə ˌ·ɪ-
psychedelic ˌsaɪk ə ˈdel ɪk ◄ -ɪ- **~ally** ᵊl̩i
psychiatric ˌsaɪk i ˈætr ɪk ◄ -aɪ- **~al** ᵊl **~ally**
  ᵊl̩i
psychiatrist saɪ ˈkaɪ̯ ətr ɪst sɪ-, sə-, §-əst **~s** s
psychiatry saɪ ˈkaɪ̯ ətr i sɪ-, sə-
psychic ˈsaɪk ɪk **~al** ᵊl **~ally** ᵊl̩i **~s** s
psycho ˈsaɪk əʊ ‖ -oʊ **~s** z
psycho- *comb. form*
  with stress-neutral suffix ˌsaɪk əʊ ‖ -oʊ
  — **psychosocial** ˌsaɪk əʊ ˈsəʊʃ ᵊl ◄
  ‖ -oʊ ˈsoʊʃ ᵊl ◄

with stress-imposing suffix saɪ ˈkɒ + ‖ -ˈkɑː +
— **psychometry** saɪ ˈkɒm ətr i -ɪtr- ‖ -ˈkɑːm-
psychoacoustic ˌsaɪk əʊ ə ˈkuːst ɪk ◄ ‖ ˌoʊ-
~**al** ᵊl ~**ally** ᵊl‿i ~**s** s
psychoactive ˌsaɪk əʊ ˈækt ɪv ◄ ‖ -oʊ-
psychoanalys|e ˌsaɪk əʊ ˈæn ə laɪz -ᵊl aɪz
‖ -oʊ ˈæn ᵊl aɪz ~**ed** d ~**es** ɪz əz ~**ing** ɪŋ
psychoanalysis ˌsaɪk əʊ ə ˈnæl əs ɪs -ɪs ɪs §-əs
‖ ˌoʊ-
psychoanalyst ˌsaɪk əʊ ˈæn əl ɪst §-əst ‖ ˌoʊ-
~**s** s
psychoanalytic ˌsaɪk əʊ ˌæn ə ˈlɪt ɪk ◄ -ᵊl ˈɪt-
‖ -oʊ ˌæn ᵊl ˈɪt̬ ɪk ◄ ~**al** ᵊl ~**ally** ᵊl‿i
psychoanalyz|e ˌsaɪk əʊ ˈæn ə laɪz -ᵊl aɪz
‖ -oʊ ˈæn ᵊl aɪz ~**ed** d ~**es** ɪz əz ~**ing** ɪŋ
psychobabble ˈsaɪk əʊ ˌbæb ᵊl ‖ -oʊ-
psychobiology ˌsaɪk əʊ baɪ ˈɒl ədʒ i
‖ -oʊ baɪ ˈɑːl-
psychochemical ˌsaɪk əʊ ˈkem ɪk ᵊl ◄ ‖ ˌoʊ-
~**s** z
psychodrama ˈsaɪk əʊ ˌdrɑːm ə ‖ -ə- -ˌdræm-
~**s** z
psychognosis saɪ ˈkɒg nəs ɪs §-əs ‖ -ˈkɑːg-
psychokinesis ˌsaɪk əʊ kaɪ ˈniːs ɪs -kɪˈ-, §-kəˈ-
‖ ˌoʊ-
psychokinetic ˌsaɪk əʊ kaɪ ˈnet ɪk ◄ -kɪˈ-,
§-kəˈ- ‖ -oʊ kaɪ ˈnet̬ ɪk ◄
psycholinguist ˌsaɪk əʊ ˈlɪŋ gwɪst §-gwəst
‖ -oʊ- ~**s** s
psycholinguistic ˌsaɪk əʊ lɪŋ ˈgwɪst ɪk ◄
‖ ˌoʊ- ~**ally** ᵊl‿i ~**s** s
psychological ˌsaɪk ə ˈlɒdʒ ɪk ᵊl ◄ ‖ -ˈlɑːdʒ-
~**ly** i
ˌpsycho͵logical ˈwarfare
psychologism saɪ ˈkɒl ə ˌdʒɪz əm ‖ -ˈkɑːl-
psychologist saɪ ˈkɒl ədʒ ɪst §-əst ‖ -ˈkɑːl-
psycholog|y saɪ ˈkɒl ədʒ |i ‖ -ˈkɑːl- ~**ies** iz
psychometric ˌsaɪk əʊ ˈmetr ɪk ◄ ‖ -ə- ~**ally**
ᵊl‿i ~**s** s
psychometry saɪ ˈkɒm ətr i -ɪtr- ‖ -ˈkɑːm-
psychopath ˈsaɪk əʊ pæθ ‖ -ə- ~**s** s
psychopathic ˌsaɪk əʊ ˈpæθ ɪk ◄ ‖ -ə- ~**ally**
ᵊl‿i
psychopathological
ˌsaɪk əʊ ˌpæθ ə ˈlɒdʒ ɪk ᵊl
‖ -oʊ ˌpæθ ə ˈlɑːdʒ-
psychopathology ˌsaɪk əʊ pə ˈθɒl ədʒ i
-pæˈ- ‖ -oʊ pə ˈθɑːl-
psychophysical ˌsaɪk əʊ ˈfɪz ɪk ᵊl ◄ ‖ ˌoʊ- ~**ly**
i
psychoses saɪ ˈkəʊs iːz ‖ -ˈkoʊs-
psychosexual ˌsaɪk əʊ ˈseks ju‿əl ◄ -ˈsekʃ u‿,
-ˈsekʃ ᵊl ‖ -oʊ ˈsekʃ u‿əl ◄ -ˈ-ᵊl ~**ly** i
psychos|is saɪ ˈkəʊs |ɪs §-əs ‖ -ˈkoʊs- ~**es** iːz
psychosocial ˌsaɪk əʊ ˈsəʊʃ ᵊl ◄ ‖ -oʊ ˈsoʊʃ-
~**ly** -i
psychosomatic ˌsaɪk əʊ səʊ ˈmæt ɪk ◄
‖ -ə sə ˈmæt̬ ɪk ◄ ~**ally** ᵊl‿i
psychotherapeutic ˌsaɪk əʊ ˌθer ə ˈpjuːt ɪk
‖ -oʊ ˌθer ə ˈpjuːt̬ ɪk ~**ally** ᵊl‿i ~**s** s
psychotherapist ˌsaɪk əʊ ˈθer əp ɪst §-əst
‖ ˌoʊ- ~**s** s
psychotherapy ˌsaɪk əʊ ˈθer əp i ‖ ˌoʊ-

psychotic saɪ ˈkɒt ɪk ‖ -ˈkɑːt̬ ɪk ~**ally** ᵊl‿i ~**s** s
psychotropic ˌsaɪk əʊ ˈtrɒp ɪk ◄ -ˈtrəʊp-
‖ -ə ˈtroʊp ɪk ◄ ~**ally** ᵊl‿i ~**s** s
psychrometer saɪ ˈkrɒm ɪt ə -ət-
‖ -ˈkrɑːm ət̬ ᵊr ~**s** z
psyllid ˈsɪl ɪd §-əd ~**s** z
psy ops ˈsaɪ ɒps ‖ -ɑːps
PTA ˌpiː tiː ˈeɪ
Ptah tɑː ptɑː; pə ˈtɑː
ptarmigan ˈtɑːm ɪg ən -əg- ‖ ˈtɑːrm- ~**s** z
pteridology ˌter ɪ ˈdɒl ədʒ i ˌ-ə- ‖ -ˈdɑːl-
pteridophyte ˈter ɪd ə faɪt ˈ-əd-; tə ˈrɪd- ~**s** s
pterodactyl ˌter əʊ ˈdækt ɪl -ᵊl ‖ -ə- ~**s** z
pterosaur ˈter ə sɔː ‖ -sɔːr ~**s** z
-pterous *stress-imposing* ptər əs — **dipterous**
ˈdɪpt ər əs
pterygium tə ˈrɪdʒ i‿əm
pterygoid ˈter ɪ ɡɔɪd -ə-
PTFE ˌpiː tiː ef ˈiː
PTO, pto ˌpiː tiː ˈəʊ ‖ -ˈoʊ
Ptolemaeus ˌtɒl ə ˈmiː əs -ɪ-, -ˈmeɪ- ‖ ˌtɑːl-
Ptolemaic ˌtɒl ə ˈmeɪ ɪk ◄ -ɪ- ‖ ˌtɑːl-
Ptolemy ˈtɒl əm i -ɪm- ‖ ˈtɑːl-
ptomain, ptomaine ˈtəʊm eɪn təʊ ˈmeɪn
‖ ˈtoʊm- ~**s** z
ptosed təʊzd ‖ toʊzd
ptosis ˈtəʊs ɪs §-əs ‖ ˈtoʊs-
ptotic ˈtəʊt ɪk ˈtɒt- ‖ ˈtoʊt̬-
Pty —*see* **proprietary** prə ˈpraɪ‿ət ᵊr |i
‖ -ə ter |i
ptyalin ˈtaɪ əl ɪn §-ən
p-type ˈpiː taɪp
pub pʌb **pubbed** pʌbd **pubbing** ˈpʌb ɪŋ **pubs**
pʌbz
pub-crawl ˈpʌb krɔːl ‖ -krɑːl ~**ed** d ~**er/s** ə/z
‖ ᵊr/z ~**ing** ɪŋ ~**s** z
pube pjuːb **pubes** pjuːbz
pubertal ˈpjuːb ət ᵊl ‖ -ᵊrt̬ ᵊl
puberty ˈpjuːb ət i ‖ -ᵊrt̬ i
pubes *plural of* pubis ˈpjuːb iːz
pubes *'groin; pubic hair'* ˈpjuːb iːz —*but as a
colloquial word, taken as a plural, usually*
pjuːbz
pubescence pju ˈbes ᵊnᵗs
pubescent pju ˈbes ᵊnt
pubic ˈpjuːb ɪk
pub|is ˈpjuːb |ɪs §-əs ~**es** iːz
public ˈpʌb lɪk
ˌpublic ˈbar; ˌpublic ˈcompany; ˌpublic
con͵venience; ˌpublic ˈenemy;; ˌpublic
ˈgallery; ˌpublic ˈhouse; ˌPublic ˈLending
Right; ˌpublic ˈlibrary; ˌpublic ˈnuisance;
ˌpublic ˈownership; ˌpublic oˈpinion;
ˌpublic ˈprosecutor; ˌpublic reˈlations;
ˌpublic ˈspirit; ˌpublic ˈspeaking; ˌpublic
ˈschool, ˈ···; ˌpublic ˈworks
public-address ˌpʌb lɪk ə ˈdres
ˌpublic-adˈdress ˌsystem
publican ˈpʌb lɪk ən ~**s** z
publication ˌpʌb lɪ ˈkeɪʃ ᵊn -lə- ~**s** z
publicis|e ˈpʌb lɪ saɪz -lə- ~**ed** d ~**es** ɪz əz
~**ing** ɪŋ
publicist ˈpʌb lɪs ɪst -ləs, §-əst ~**s** s

publicity pʌb ˈlɪs ət i pəb-, -ɪt- ‖ -əɟ i
publiciz|e ˈpʌb lɪ saɪz -lə- **~ed** d **~es** ɪz əz
  ~ing ɪŋ
public|ly ˈpʌb lɪk |li **~ness** nəs nɪs
public-minded ˌpʌb lɪk ˈmaɪnd ɪd ◂ -əd ◂
public-spirited ˌpʌb lɪk ˈspɪr ɪt ɪd ◂ -ət ɪd, -əd
  ‖ -ət əd ◂ **~ness** nəs nɪs
publish ˈpʌb lɪʃ **~ed** t **~es** ɪz əz **~ing** ɪŋ
  ˈpublishing house
publishable ˈpʌb lɪʃ əb ᵊl
publisher ˈpʌb lɪʃ ə ‖ -ᵊr **~s** z
Publius ˈpʌb li‿əs
Puccini pu ˈtʃiːn i —It [put ˈtʃiː ni]
puccoon pə ˈkuːn pʌ- **~s** z
puce pjuːs
puck, Puck pʌk **pucks, Puck** ˈs pʌks
pucker ˈpʌk ə ‖ -ᵊr **~ed** d **puckering**
  ˈpʌk ər ɪŋ **~s** z
Puckeridge ˈpʌk ər ɪdʒ
puckish ˈpʌk ɪʃ **~ly** li **~ness** nəs nɪs
pud pʊd **puds** pʊdz
pudding ˈpʊd ɪŋ —There is also a
  non-standard form △ˈpʊd ᵊn, sometimes
  written pudden **~s** z
puddl|e ˈpʌd ᵊl **~ed** d **~es** z **~ing** ˌɪŋ
Puddletown ˈpʌd ᵊl taʊn
puddock ˈpʌd ək **~s** s
pudend|um pju ˈdend |əm **~a** ə
pudg|y ˈpʌdʒ |i **~ier** i‿ə ‖ i‿ᵊr **~iest** i‿ɪst i‿əst
  ~ily ɪ li əl i **~iness** i nəs i nɪs
Pudsey ˈpʌd si ˈpʌdz i
pudu ˈpuːd uː **~s** z
pueblo, P~ ˈpweb ləʊ pu ˈeb ləʊ ‖ -loʊ —Sp
  [ˈpwe βlo]
puerile ˈpjʊər aɪᵊl ˈpjɔːr-; ˈpjuː‿ə raɪᵊl ‖ ˈpjʊr ᵊl
  -aɪl **~ly** li **~ness** nəs nɪs
puerilit|y pjuᵊ ˈrɪl ət i |i ₍ᵢ₎pjʊə-, ₍ᵢ₎pjɔː-,
  ˌpjuː‿ə-, -ɪt i ‖ -əɟ i **~ies** ɪz
puerperal pju ˈɜːp ᵊr əl ‖ -ˈɜːp-
puerperium ˌpjuːˌə ˈpɪər i‿əm ‖ -ᵊr ˈpɪr-
Puerto ˈpwɜːt əʊ ˈpweət- ‖ ˈpwerɟ oʊ —Sp
  [ˈpwer to] —see also phrases with this word
Puerto Rican ˌpwɜːt əʊ ˈriːk |ən ◂ ˌpweət-,
  ˌpɔːt- ‖ ˌpwerɟ ə-, ˌpɔːrɟ-, ˌpoʊrɟ- **~s** z
Puerto Rico ˌpwɜːt əʊ ˈriːk əʊ ˌpweət-, ˌpɔːt-
  ‖ ˌpwerɟ ə-, ˌpɔːrɟ-, ˌpoʊrɟ- —Sp
  [pwer to ˈrri ko]
Puerto Vallarta ˌpwɜːt əʊ vaɪ ˈɑːt ə ˌpweət-,
  -və ˈlɑːt ə ‖ ˌpwerɟ ə vaː ˈjɑːrɟ ə —Sp
  [ˌpwer to βa ˈjar ta, -ˈʎar-]
puff pʌf **puffed** pʌft **puffing** ˈpʌf ɪŋ **puffs**
  pʌfs
puffa ˈpʌf ə
  ˈpuffa ˌjacket
puffball ˈpʌf bɔːl ‖ -bɑːl **~s** z
puffer ˈpʌf ə ‖ -ᵊr **~s** z
puffery ˈpʌf ər i
puffi... —see **puffy**
puffin ˈpʌf ɪn §-ᵊn **~s** z
puffin|ry ˈpʌf ɪn |ri §-ᵊn- **~ries** riz
puff-puff ˈpʌf pʌf **~s** s
puff|y ˈpʌf |i **~ier** i‿ə ‖ i‿ᵊr **~iest** i‿ɪst i‿əst
  ~iness i nəs i nɪs

puftaloon ˌpʌft ə ˈluːn **~s** z
pug pʌg **pugged** pʌgd **pugging** ˈpʌg ɪŋ **pugs**
  pʌgz
Puget ˈpjuːdʒ ɪt §-ət
puggaree ˈpʌg ər i **~s** z
puggree ˈpʌg ri **~s** z —Hindi [pə gri:]
Pugh, Pughe pjuː
pugilism ˈpjuːdʒ ɪ ˌlɪz əm -ə-
pugilist ˈpjuːdʒ ɪl ɪst -əl-, §-əst **~s** s
pugilistic ˌpjuːdʒ ɪ ˈlɪst ɪk ◂ -ə- **~ally** ᵊl i
Pugin ˈpjuːdʒ ɪn §-ən
pug-mill ˈpʌg mɪl **~s** z
pugnacious pʌg ˈneɪʃ əs **~ly** li **~ness** nəs nɪs
pugnacity pʌg ˈnæs ət i -ɪt- ‖ -əɟ i
pug-nose ˌpʌg ˈnəʊz ˈ· · ‖ ˈpʌg noʊz **~d** d ◂
Pugwash ˈpʌg wɒʃ ‖ -wɔːʃ -wɑːʃ
puisne ˈpjuːn i
puissance ˈpwiː‿ s õs -ɒnᵗs, -ᵊnᵗs, -ænᵗs
  ‖ ˈpjuː əs ənᵗs —In poetic usage also
  ˈpjuː ɪs ᵊnᵗs, -əs-; pju ˈɪs-; ˈpwɪs ᵊnᵗs
puissant ˈpwiːs ɒnt ˈpjuː ɪs ᵊnt, -əs-; pju ˈɪs-;
  ˈpwɪs ᵊnt ‖ ˈpjuː əs ənt **~ly** li
puja ˈpuːdʒ ə -ɑː- **~s** z —Hindi [puː dʒaː]
puke pjuːk **puked** pjuːkt **pukes** pjuːks **puking**
  ˈpjuːk ɪŋ
pukeko ˈpʊk ə kəʊ ‖ -koʊ **~s** z
pukey, puky ˈpjuːk i
pukka ˈpʌk ə
pula ˈpuːl ə ˈpjuːl- ˈpʊl-
Pulaski pə ˈlæsk i pju-, pʊ-
Pulborough ˈpʊl bər ə ‖ -ˌbɜː oʊ
pulchritude ˈpʌlk rɪ tjuːd -rə-, →-tʃuːd ‖ -tuːd
  -tjuːd
pulchritudinous ˌpʌlk rɪ ˈtjuːd ɪn əs ◂ -ˌrə-,
  →-ˈtʃuːd-, -ᵊn əs ‖ -ˈtuːd ᵊn əs ◂ -ˈtjuːd-
pule pjuːl **puled** pjuːld **pules** pjuːlz **puling/ly**
  ˈpjuːl ɪŋ /li
Pulham ˈpʊl əm
puli ˈpjuːl i ˈpʊl-, ˈpuːl- **~s** z
Pulitzer ˈpʊl ɪts ə ˈpjuːl-, §-əts- ‖ -ᵊr
pull pʊl **pulled** pʊld **pulling** ˈpʊl ɪŋ **pulls**
  pʊlz
pullback ˈpʊl bæk **~s** s
pull-down ˈpʊl daʊn
Pullen ˈpʊl ɪn -ən
pullet ˈpʊl ɪt -ət **~s** s
pulley ˈpʊl i **~s** z
pull-in ˈpʊl ɪn **~s** z
Pullman, p~ ˈpʊl mən **~s** z
pull-on ˈpʊl ɒn ‖ -ɑːn -ɔːn
pullorum pʊ ˈlɔːr əm pə- ‖ -ˈloʊr-
pull-out ˈpʊl aʊt **~s** s
pullover ˈpʊl ˌəʊv ə ‖ -ˌoʊv ᵊr **~s** z
pullthrough ˈpʊl θruː **~s** z
pullu|late ˈpʌl ju |leɪt -jə- ‖ -jə- **~lated** leɪt ɪd
  -əd ‖ leɪɟ əd **~lates** leɪts **~lating** leɪt ɪŋ
  ‖ leɪɟ ɪŋ
pullulation ˌpʌl ju ˈleɪʃ ᵊn -jə- ‖ -jə- **~s** z
Pullum ˈpʊl əm
pull-up ˈpʊl ʌp **~s** s
Pulman ˈpʊl mən
pulmonary ˈpʌl mən ər_i ˈpʊl- ‖ -mə ner i

pulmonic pʌl ˈmɒn ɪk pʊl- ‖ -ˈmɑːn ɪk **~ally**
ᵊl i
pulp pʌlp **pulped** pʌlpt **pulping** ˈpʌlp ɪŋ
pulps pʌlps
pulpit ˈpʊlp ɪt §ˈpʌlp-, §-ət **~s** s
pulpwood ˈpʌlp wʊd
pulp|y ˈpʌlp |i **~ier** i ə ‖ i ᵊr **~iest** i ɪst i əst
~iness i nəs i nɪs
pulque ˈpʊlk i ˈpuːlk-, -eɪ —*Sp* [ˈpul ke]
pulsar ˈpʌls ɑː ‖ -ɑːr **~s** z
pulsate pʌl ˈseɪt ‖ ˈpʌls eɪt **pulsated**
pʌl ˈseɪt ɪd -əd ‖ ˈpʌls eɪʔ əd **pulsates**
pʌl ˈseɪts ‖ ˈpʌls eɪts **pulsating** pʌl ˈseɪt ɪŋ
‖ ˈpʌls eɪʔ ɪŋ
pulsatile ˈpʌls ə taɪᵊl ‖ -əʔ ᵊl
pulsation pʌl ˈseɪʃ ᵊn **~s** z
pulsative ˈpʌls ət ɪv ‖ -əʔ-
pulsator pʌl ˈseɪt ə ‖ ˈpʌls eɪʔ ᵊr **~s** z
pulsatory pʌl ˈseɪt ər i ˈpʌls ət ᵊr i
‖ ˈpʌls ə tɔːr i -tour i
pulse pʌls **pulsed** pʌlst **pulses** ˈpʌls ɪz -əz
pulsing ˈpʌls ɪŋ
pulsimeter pʌl ˈsɪm ɪt ə -ət- ‖ -əʔ ᵊr **~s** z
Pulteney *(i)* ˈpʌlt ən i *(ii)* ˈpəʊlt- →ˈpɒʊlt-
‖ ˈpɒʊlt-
pulu ˈpuːl uː
pulveris... —*see* **pulveriz...**
pulverization ˌpʌlv ər aɪ ˈzeɪʃ ᵊn ˌpʊlv-ˌɪˈ--
‖ -ər ə-
pulveriz|e ˈpʌlv ə raɪz ˈpʊlv- **~ed** d **~es** ɪz əz
~ing ɪŋ
pulverulent pʌl ˈver ʊl ənt -jʊl-, -əl-
pulvinar pʌl ˈvaɪn ə ‖ -ᵊr **~s** z
pulvi|nate ˈpʌlv ɪ |neɪt -ə- **~nated** neɪt ɪd -əd
‖ neɪʔ əd **~nately** neɪt li
puma ˈpjuːm ə ‖ ˈpuːm- **~s** z
pumice ˈpʌm ɪs §-əs
pumice stone ˈpʌm ɪs stəʊn -i-, §-əs- ‖ -stoʊn
~s z
pummel ˈpʌm ᵊl **~ed, ~led** d **~ing, ~ling** ɪŋ
~s z
pump pʌmp **pumped** pʌmpt **pumping**
ˈpʌmp ɪŋ **pumps** pʌmps
ˈpump room
pumpernickel ˈpʌmp ə ˌnɪk ᵊl ˈpʊmp- ‖ -ᵊr-
—*Ger* [ˈpʊm pɐ nɪk ᵊl]
Pumphrey ˈpʌmᵖf ri
pumpkin ˈpʌmp kɪn §-kən ‖ △ˈpʌŋk ən **~s** z
pun pʌn **punned** pʌnd **punning/ly** ˈpʌn ɪŋ /li
puns pʌnz
punch, Punch pʌntʃ **punched** pʌntʃt
punches, Punch's ˈpʌntʃ ɪz -əz **punching**
ˈpʌntʃ ɪŋ
ˈpunch ball; ˈpunch bowl; ˈpunch card;
ˌpunched ˈcard; ˈpunching bag; ˈpunch
line
Punch-and-Judy ˌpʌntʃ ən ˈdʒuːd i -ənd-
ˌPunch-and-ˈJudy show
punchbag ˈpʌntʃ bæg **~s** z
punch-drunk ˈpʌntʃ drʌŋk ˌ·ˈ·
puncheon ˈpʌntʃ ən **~s** z
puncher ˈpʌntʃ ə ‖ -ᵊr **~s** z

Punchinello, p~ ˌpʌntʃ ɪ ˈnel əʊ -ə- ‖ -oʊ **~s,
~es** z
punchline ˈpʌntʃ laɪn **~s** z
punch-up ˈpʌntʃ ʌp **~s** s
punch|y ˈpʌntʃ |i **~ier** i ə ‖ i ᵊr **~iest** i ɪst i əst
~ily ɪ li əl i **~iness** i nəs i nɪs
punctate *adj* ˈpʌŋkt eɪt
punctilio pʌŋk ˈtɪl i əʊ ‖ -oʊ **~s** z
punctilious pʌŋk ˈtɪl i əs **-ly** li **~ness** nəs nɪs
punctual ˈpʌŋk tʃu əl -tju əl
punctuality ˌpʌŋk tʃu ˈæl ət i ˌ·tju-, -ɪt i ‖ -əʔ i
punctually ˈpʌŋk tʃu əl i -tju əl-
punctu|ate ˈpʌŋk tʃu |eɪt -tju- **~ated** eɪt ɪd -əd
‖ eɪʔ əd **~ates** eɪts **~ating** eɪt ɪŋ ‖ eɪʔ ɪŋ
punctuation ˌpʌŋk tʃu ˈeɪʃ ᵊn -tju- **~s** z
ˌpunctuˈation mark

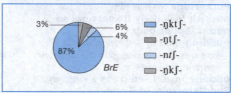

3% 6%
4%
87%
BrE

■ -ŋktʃ-
■ -ŋtʃ-
■ -ntʃ-
■ -ŋkʃ-

puncture ˈpʌŋk tʃə -ʃə; §ˈpʌntʃ ə ‖ -tʃᵊr —
Preference poll, BrE: -ŋktʃ- 87%, -ŋtʃ- 6%, -ntʃ-
4%, -ŋkʃ- 3%. **~d** d **puncturing** ˈpʌŋk tʃər ɪŋ
-ʃər ɪŋ **~s** z
pundit ˈpʌnd ɪt §-ət **~s** s
Pune ˈpuːn ə
pungency ˈpʌndʒ ᵊn[t]s i
pungent ˈpʌndʒ ənt **~ly** li
puni... —*see* **puny**
Punic ˈpjuːn ɪk
punish ˈpʌn ɪʃ **~ed** t **~er/s** ə/z ‖ -ᵊr/z **~es** ɪz əz
~ing/ly ɪŋ /li
punishable ˈpʌn ɪʃ əb ᵊl
punishment ˈpʌn ɪʃ mənt **~s** s
punitive ˈpjuːn ət ɪv -ɪt- ‖ -əʔ ɪv **~ly** li **~ness**
nəs nɪs
Punjab pʌn ˈdʒɑːb pʊn-, ˈ·· —*There is no
etymological justification for the* pʊn *forms.*
Punjabi pʌn ˈdʒɑːb i pʊn-, -iː **~s** z
punji ˈpʌndʒ i **~s** z
punk pʌŋk **punks** pʌŋks
ˌpunk ˈrock; ˌpunk ˈrocker
punka, punkah ˈpʌŋk ə **~s** z
punkin *non-standard form of* pumpkin ˈpʌŋk ɪn
-ən **~s** z
punk|y ˈpʌŋk |i **~ier** i ə ‖ i ᵊr **~iest** i ɪst i əst
~iness i nəs i nɪs
punnet ˈpʌn ɪt §-ət **~s** s
punster ˈpʌn stə ‖ -stᵊr **~s** z
punt *'boat'; 'kick'; 'gamble'; 'hollow at base of
bottle'* pʌnt **punted** ˈpʌnt ɪd -əd ‖ ˈpʌnʔ əd
punting ˈpʌnt ɪŋ ‖ ˈpʌnʔ ɪŋ **punts** pʌnts
punt *'Irish pound'* pʊnt **punts** pʊnts
punter ˈpʌnt ə ‖ ˈpʌnʔ ᵊr **~s** z
punt|y ˈpʌnt |i ‖ ˈpʌnʔ |i **~ies** iz
pun|y ˈpjuːn |i **~ier** i ə ‖ i ᵊr **~iest** i ɪst i əst
~ily ɪ li əl i **~iness** i nəs i nɪs

pup pʌp **pupped** pʌpt **pupping** 'pʌp ɪŋ **pups** pʌps

pup|a 'pjuːp |ə ~**ae** iː -**al** ᵊl ~**as** əz

pup|ate pjuː 'p|eɪt ǁ 'pjuːp |eɪt ~**ated** eɪt ɪd -əd ǁ eɪt̬ əd ~**ates** eɪts ~**ating** eɪt ɪŋ ǁ eɪt̬ ɪŋ

pupation pjuː 'peɪʃ ᵊn

pupil 'pjuːp ᵊl -ɪl ~**s** z

pupilage, pupillage 'pjuːp əl ɪdʒ -ɪl-

pupillary 'pjuːp əl ər i '·ɪl- ǁ -ə ler i

puppadum 'pʌp ə dʌm ~**s** z

puppet 'pʌp ɪt §-ət ~**s** s

puppeteer ˌpʌp ɪ 'tɪə -ə- ǁ -'tɪ°r ~**s** z

puppetry 'pʌp ɪtr i -ətr-

Puppis 'pʌp ɪs

pupp|y 'pʌp |i ~**ies** iz
 'puppy dog; 'puppy fat; 'puppy love

Purbeck 'pɜː bek ǁ 'pɜː-

purblind 'pɜː blaɪnd ǁ 'pɜː- ~**ly** li ~**ness** nəs nɪs

Purcell (i) 'pɜːs ᵊl ǁ 'pɜːs ᵊl, (ii) pɜː 'sel ǁ pɜː-
 —The composer was (i).

purchasable 'pɜːtʃ əs əb ᵊl '·ɪs- ǁ 'pɜːtʃ-

purchas|e, P~ 'pɜːtʃ əs -ɪs ǁ 'pɜːtʃ əs ~**ed** t ~**er/s** ə/z ǁ -ᵊr/z ~**es** ɪz əz ~**ing** ɪŋ
 'purchase tax; 'purchasing ˌpower

purda, purdah 'pɜːd ə -ɑː ǁ 'pɜːd ə
 —Hindi-Urdu [pər d̪aː]

Purdie 'pɜːd i ǁ 'pɜːd i

Purdon 'pɜːd ᵊn ǁ 'pɜːd ᵊn

Purdue 'pɜːd juː ǁ pᵊr 'duː

Purdy 'pɜːd i ǁ 'pɜːd i

pure pjʊə pjɔː ǁ pjʊ°r pjɜː **purer** 'pjʊər ə 'pjɔːr- ǁ 'pjʊr ᵊr 'pjɜː- **purest** 'pjʊər ɪst 'pjɔːr-, -əst ǁ 'pjʊr əst 'pjɜː-

pureblood 'pjʊə blʌd 'pjɔː- ǁ 'pjʊr- 'pjɜː-

pureblooded ˌpjʊə 'blʌd ɪd ◂ ˌpjɔː-, -əd ǁ ˌpjʊr- ˌpjɜː-

purebred 'pjʊə bred 'pjɔː- ǁ 'pjʊr- 'pjɜː- ~**s** z

puree, purée 'pjʊər eɪ 'pjɔːr- ǁ pju 'reɪ -'riː ~**s** z

pure|ly 'pjʊə| li 'pjɔː|- ǁ 'pjʊr|- 'pjɜː|- ~**ness** nəs nɪs

purfl|e 'pɜːf ᵊl ǁ 'pɜːf ᵊl ~**ed** d ~**es** z ~**ing/s** ɪŋ/z

Purfleet 'pɜː fliːt ǁ 'pɜː-

purgation pɜː 'geɪʃ ᵊn ǁ pɜː-

purgative 'pɜːg ət ɪv △'pɜːdʒ- ǁ 'pɜːg ət̬ ɪv ~**s** z

purgatorial ˌpɜːg ə 'tɔːr i ᵊl ◂ ǁ ˌpɜːg- -'toʊr-

purgator|y, P~ 'pɜːg ətr |i ǁ 'pɜːg ə tɔːr |i -toʊr i ~**ies** iz

purge pɜːdʒ ǁ pɜːdʒ **purged** pɜːdʒd ǁ pɜːdʒd **purges** 'pɜːdʒ ɪz -əz ǁ 'pɜːdʒ əz **purging** 'pɜːdʒ ɪŋ ǁ 'pɜːdʒ ɪŋ

purification ˌpjʊər ɪf ɪ 'keɪʃ ᵊn ˌpjɔːr-, ˌ·əf-, §-ə'·- ǁ ˌpjʊr- ˌpjɜː- ~**s** z

purificator 'pjʊər ɪf ɪ keɪt ə 'pjɔːr-, '·əf-, §-ə·· ǁ 'pjʊr əf ə keɪt̬ ᵊr 'pjɜː- ~**s** z

purificatory ˌpjʊər ɪf ɪ 'keɪt ər i ˌpjɔːr-, ˌ·əf-, §ˌ·ə-, '·····, '· fɪk ət ər i ǁ pju 'rɪf ɪk ə tɔːr i pjə-, -toʊr i; 'pjʊr əf ək-, 'pjɜː-

puri|fy 'pjʊər ɪ |faɪ 'pjɔːr-, -ə- ǁ 'pjʊr- 'pjɜː- ~**fied** faɪd ~**fier/s** faɪ ə/z ǁ faɪ ᵊr/z ~**fies** faɪz ~**fying** faɪ ɪŋ

Purim 'pʊər ɪm 'pjʊər-, pʊ° 'riːm ǁ 'pʊr-

Purina tdmk pjə 'riːn ə pjuː°-

purine 'pjʊər iːn 'pjɔːr-, -aɪn ǁ 'pjʊr-

purism 'pjʊər ˌɪz əm 'pjɔːr- ǁ 'pjʊr-

purist 'pjʊər ɪst 'pjɔːr-, §-əst ǁ 'pjʊr əst ~**s** s

puristic pju° 'rɪst ɪk pjɔː- ~**al** ᵊl ~**ally** ᵊl i

Puritan 'pjʊər ɪt ən 'pjɔːr-, -ət- ǁ 'pjʊr ət ᵊn ~**s** z

puritanical ˌpjʊər ɪ 'tæn ɪk ᵊl ◂ ˌpjɔːr-, ˌ·ə- ǁ ˌpjʊr- ~**ly** i ~**ness** nəs nɪs

Puritanism 'pjʊər ɪt ən ˌɪz əm 'pjɔːr-, -ət- ǁ 'pjʊr ət ᵊn-

purity 'pjʊər ət i 'pjɔːr-, -ɪt- ǁ 'pjʊr ət̬ i

purl pɜːl ǁ pɜːl (= pearl) **purled** pɜːld ǁ pɜːld **purling** 'pɜːl ɪŋ ǁ 'pɜːl ɪŋ **purls** pɜːlz ǁ pɜːlz

purler 'pɜːl ə ǁ 'pɜːl ᵊr ~**s** z

Purley 'pɜːl i ǁ 'pɜːl i

purlieu 'pɜːl juː §-luː ǁ 'pɜːl uː -juː ~**s** z

purlin, purline 'pɜːl ɪn §-ən ǁ 'pɜːl- ~**s** z

purloin pɜː 'lɔɪn '·· ǁ pɜː- ~**ed** d ~**ing** ɪŋ ~**s** z

Purnell pɜː 'nel ǁ pɜː-

purpl|e 'pɜːp ᵊl ǁ 'pɜːp ᵊl ~**ed** d ~**es** z ~**ing** ɪŋ
 ˌpurple 'heart, ˌPurple 'Heart; ˌpurple 'passage; ˌpurple 'patch

purplish 'pɜːp ᵊl ɪʃ ǁ 'pɜːp-

purport n 'pɜː pɔːt 'pɜːp ət ǁ 'pɜː pɔːrt -poʊrt ~**s** s

purport v pə 'pɔːt pɜː-; 'pɜːp ət, -ɔːt ǁ pᵊr 'pɔːrt -'poʊrt **purported** pə 'pɔːt ɪd pɜː-, -əd; 'pɜːp ət-, -ɔːt- ǁ pᵊr 'pɔːrt̬ əd -'poʊrt̬- **purporting** pə 'pɔːt ɪŋ pɜː-; 'pɜːp ət-, -ɔːt- ǁ pᵊr 'pɔːrt̬ ɪŋ -'poʊrt̬- ~**s** s

purpos|e n, v 'pɜːp əs ǁ 'pɜːp əs ~**ed** t ~**es** ɪz əz ~**ing** ɪŋ

purpose-built ˌpɜːp əs 'bɪlt ◂ ǁ ˌpɜːp-

purposeful 'pɜːp əs fᵊl -fʊl ǁ 'pɜːp- ~**ly** i ~**ness** nəs nɪs

purposeless 'pɜːpəs ləs -lɪs ǁ 'pɜːp- ~**ly** li ~**ness** nəs nɪs

purposely 'pɜːp əs li ǁ 'pɜːp-

purposive 'pɜːp əs ɪv ǁ 'pɜːp- pᵊr 'poʊs- ~**ly** li ~**ness** nəs nɪs

purpura 'pɜːp jʊr ə -jər- ǁ 'pɜːp jər ə -ɪr ə

purr pɜː ǁ pɜː **purred** pɜːd ǁ pɜːd **purring** 'pɜːr ɪŋ ǁ 'pɜː ɪŋ **purrs** pɜːz ǁ pɜːz

purse pɜːs ǁ pɜːs **pursed** pɜːst ǁ pɜːst **purses** 'pɜːs ɪz -əz ǁ 'pɜːs əz **pursing** 'pɜːs ɪŋ ǁ 'pɜːs ɪŋ
 'purse strings

purser 'pɜːs ə ǁ 'pɜːs ᵊr ~**s** z

purse-snatch|er 'pɜːs ˌsnætʃ |ə ǁ 'pɜːs ˌsnætʃ |ᵊr ~**ers** əz ǁ ᵊrz ~**ing** ɪŋ

purslane 'pɜːs lən -lɪn, -leɪn ǁ 'pɜːs- ~**s** z

pursuance pə 'sjuː ᵊn/s -'suː ǁ pᵊr 'suː-

pursuant pə 'sjuː ᵊnt -'suː ǁ pᵊr 'suː- ~**ly** li

pur|sue pə |'sjuː -'suː ǁ pᵊr |'suː ~**sued** 'sjuːd 'suːd ǁ 'suːd ~**sues** 'sjuːz 'suːz ǁ 'suːz ~**suing** 'sjuː ɪŋ 'suː ǁ 'suː ɪŋ

pursuer pə 'sjuː ə -'suː ǁ pᵊr 'suː ᵊr ~**s** z

pursuit pə 'sjuːt -'suːt ǁ pᵊr 'suːt ~**s** s

pursuivant 'pɜːs ɪv ənt -əv-, -wɪv- ‖ 'pɜːs- **~s** s
purty *non-standard form of* pretty 'pɜːt i
‖ 'pɜːt̬ i
purulenc|e 'pjʊər ʊl ən^ts -jʊl-, -əl- ‖ 'pjʊr əl-
-jəl- **~y** i
purulent 'pjʊər ʊl ən^ts -jʊl-, -əl- ‖ 'pjʊr əl-
-jəl- **~ly** li
Purves 'pɜːv ɪs §-əs ‖ 'pɜːv əs
purvey pə 'veɪ pɜː- ‖ p^ər 'veɪ 'pɜːv eɪ **~ed** d
~ing ɪŋ **~s** z
purveyance pə 'veɪ ən^ts pɜː- ‖ p^ər-
purveyor pə 'veɪ ə pɜː- ‖ p^ər 'veɪ ^ər **~s** z
purview 'pɜː vjuː ‖ 'pɜː- **~s** z
Purvis 'pɜːv ɪs §-əs ‖ 'pɜːv əs
pus pʌs
Pusan ˌpuː 'sæn ‖ -'saːn —*Korean* [pu san]
Pusey 'pjuːz i
Puseyite 'pjuːz i aɪt **~s** s
push pʊʃ **pushed** pʊʃt **pushes** 'pʊʃ ɪz -əz
pushing 'pʊʃ ɪŋ
'push ˌbutton
pushbike 'pʊʃ baɪk **~s** s
push-button 'pʊʃ ˌbʌt ^ən
pushcart 'pʊʃ kɑːt ‖ -kɑːrt **~s** s
push-chain 'pʊʃ tʃeɪn **~s** z
pushchair 'pʊʃ tʃeə ‖ -tʃer **~s** z
pushdown 'pʊʃ daʊn
pusher 'pʊʃ ə ‖ -^ər **~s** z
pushful 'pʊʃ f^əl -fʊl **~ly** i **~ness** nəs nɪs
Pushkin 'pʊʃ kɪn —*Russ* ['pʊʃ k^jɪn]
pushover 'pʊʃ ˌəʊv ə ‖ -ˌoʊv ^ər **~s** z
pushpin 'pʊʃ pɪn **~s** z
push-pull ˌpʊʃ 'pʊl ◀
pushrod 'pʊʃ rɒd ‖ -rɑːd **~s** z
push-|start 'pʊʃ |stɑːt ˌ·'· ‖ -|stɑːrt **~started**
stɑːtɪd -əd ‖ stɑːrt̬ əd **~starting** stɑːt ɪŋ
‖ stɑːrt̬ ɪŋ **~starts** stɑːts ‖ stɑːrts
Push|to 'pʌʃ| təʊ ‖ -toʊ **~tu** tuː
push-up 'pʊʃ ʌp **~s** s
push|y 'pʊʃ |i **~ier** i ə ‖ i ^ər **~iest** i ɪst i əst
~ily ɪ li əl i **~iness** i nəs i nɪs
pusillanimity ˌpjuːs ɪl ə 'nɪm ət i ˌpjuːz-, ˌ·əl-,
-æ'··, -ɪt i ‖ -ət̬ i
pusillanimous ˌpjuːs ɪ 'læn ɪm əs ◀ ˌpjuːz-,
ˌ·ə-, -əm əs **~ly** li
puss pʊs **pusses** 'pʊs ɪz -əz
'puss moth
puss|y *n* 'pʊs |i **~ies** iz
ˌpussy 'willow
pussy *adj*, *'purulent'* 'pʌs i
pussycat 'pʊs i kæt **~s** s
pussy|foot 'pʊs i |fʊt **~footed** fʊt ɪd -əd
‖ fʊt̬ əd **~footer/s** fʊt ə/z ‖ fʊt̬ ^ər/z **~footing**
fʊtɪŋ ‖ fʊt̬ ɪŋ **~foots** fʊts
pustular 'pʌst jʊl ə -jəl-; →'pʌs tʃʊl ə, -tʃəl-
‖ 'pʌs tʃəl ^ər
pustule 'pʌst juːl →'pʌs tʃuːl ‖ 'pʌs tʃuːl **~s** z
put pʊt **puts** pʊts **putting** 'pʊt ɪŋ
putative 'pjuːt ət ɪv ‖ 'pjuːt̬ ət̬ ɪv **~ly** li
put-down 'pʊt daʊn **~s** z
Putin 'puːt ɪn -^ən —*Russ* ['pu t^jɪn]
Putnam 'pʌt nəm
Putney 'pʌt ni

put-off 'pʊt ɒf -ɔːf ‖ 'pʊt̬ ɔːf -ɑːf **~s** s
put-on 'pʊt ɒn ‖ 'pʊt̬ ɑːn -ɔːn **~s** z
putonghua ˌpuː tɒŋ 'hwaː ‖ -tɔːŋ- -taːŋ-
—*Chinese* pǔtōnghuà [³pʰu ¹tʰʊŋ ⁴xwa]
put-|put 'pʌt |pʌt ˌ·'· **~puts** pʌts **~putted**
pʌt ɪd -əd ‖ pʌt̬ əd **~putting** pʌt ɪŋ ‖ pʌt̬ ɪŋ
putrefaction ˌpjuːtr ɪ 'fæk ʃ^ən -ə-
putrefactive ˌpjuːtr ɪ 'fækt ɪv ◀ -ə-
putre|fy 'pjuːtr ɪ |faɪ -ə- **~fied** faɪd **~fies** faɪz
~fying faɪ ɪŋ
putresc|ence pjuː 'tres |^ən^ts **~ent** ^ənt
putrid 'pjuːtr ɪd §-əd
putridity pjuː 'trɪd ət i -ɪt- ‖ -ət̬ i
putrid|ly 'pjuːtr ɪd |li §-əd- **~ness** nəs nɪs
putsch pʊtʃ **putsches** 'pʊtʃ ɪz -əz
putt pʌt **putted** 'pʌt ɪd -əd ‖ 'pʌt̬ əd **putting**
'pʌt ɪŋ ‖ 'pʌt̬ ɪŋ **putts** pʌts
puttanesca ˌpʊt ə 'nesk ə →-^ən 'esk-
‖ ˌpuː tɑː 'nesk ɑː —*It* [put ta 'ne ska]
puttee 'pʌt i -iː, pʌ 'tiː ‖ pʌ 'tiː **~s** z
Puttenham 'pʌt ^ən əm
putter *v; n 'golfer, golf club'* 'pʌt ə ‖ 'pʌt̬ ^ər **~s**
z
putter *n 'one that puts'* 'pʊt ə ‖ 'pʊt̬ ^ər **~s** z
putti *plural of* putto 'pʊt i -iː ‖ 'pʊːt̬ iː
puttie... —*see* **putty**
putting *pres part of* **putt** 'pʌt ɪŋ ‖ 'pʌt̬ ɪŋ
'putting ˌgreen
putting *pres ptcp of* **put** 'pʊt ɪŋ ‖ 'pʊt̬ ɪŋ
Puttnam 'pʌt nəm
putto 'pʊt əʊ ‖ 'pʊːt oʊ **putti** 'pʊt i -iː
‖ 'pʊːt̬ iː
putt|y 'pʌt |i ‖ 'pʌt̬ |i **~ied** id **~ies** iz **~ying**
i ɪŋ
put-up 'pʊt ʌp ‖ 'pʊt̬ ʌp
put-upon 'pʊt ə ˌpɒn ‖ 'pʊt̬ ə ˌpɑːn -ˌpɔːn
Put-U-Up *tdmk* 'pʊt ju ʌp →'pʊtʃ u- ‖ 'pʊt̬ʃ u-
putz pʌts pʊts **putzes** 'pʌts ɪz 'pʊts-, -əz
Puy-de-Dôme ˌpwiː də 'daʊm ‖ -'doʊm —*Fr*
[pɥi də doːm]
puzzl|e 'pʌz ^əl **~ed** d **~es** z **~ing/ly** ɪŋ /li
puzzlement 'pʌz ^əl mənt
puzzler 'pʌz ^əl ə ‖ ^ər **~s** z
PVC ˌpiː viː 'siː ◀
Pwllheli pə 'θel i pʊ-, -'ɬel-, pʊθ 'lel i —*Welsh*
[pʊɬ 'he li, pʊɬ-]
PX ˌpiː 'eks **~s** ɪz əz
pyaemia paɪ 'iːm i ə
Pybus 'paɪb əs
Pydna 'pɪd nə
Pye paɪ
Pyecombe 'paɪ kuːm
pye-dog 'paɪ dɒg ‖ -dɔːg -dɑːg **~s** z
pyelo- *comb. form*
with stress-neutral suffix |paɪ ə ləʊ
‖ |paɪ ə loʊ — **pyelogram** 'paɪ ə ləʊ græm
‖ 'paɪ ə loʊ-
with stress-imposing suffix ˌpaɪ ə 'lɒ +
‖ -'lɑː + — **pyelography** ˌpaɪ ə 'lɒg rəf i
‖ -'lɑːg-
pyemia paɪ 'iːm i ə
pygmaean pɪg 'miː[.]ən
Pygmalion pɪg 'meɪl i ən

pygmean pɪg ˈmiː ̯ən

pygmy, Pygmy ˈpɪg mi **pygmies, P~** ˈpɪg miz

pyjama pə ˈdʒɑːm ə pɪ-, △bə- ‖ -ˈdʒæm- **~s** z

Pyke paɪk

pyknic ˈpɪk nɪk (= picnic)

pylon ˈpaɪl ən -ɒn ‖ -ɑːn **~s** z

pyloric paɪ ˈlɒr ɪk -ˈlɔːr- ‖ -ˈlɔːr ɪk -ˈloʊr-

pylor|us paɪ ˈlɔːr |əs ‖ -ˈloʊr- **~i** aɪ iː

Pylos ˈpaɪl ɒs ‖ -ɑːs

Pym, Pymm pɪm

Pynchon ˈpɪntʃ ən

pyo- comb. form
with stress-neutral suffix ⸾paɪ əʊ ‖ -ə
— pyogenic ˌpaɪ əʊ ˈdʒen ɪk ◂ -ˈdʒiːn- ‖ -ə-
with stress-imposing suffix paɪ ˈɒ+ ‖ -ˈɑː+
— pyogenous paɪ ˈɒdʒ ən əs ‖ -ˈɑːdʒ-

pyoid ˈpaɪ ɔɪd

Pyongyang ˌpjɒŋ ˈjæŋ ‖ ˌpjʌŋ ˈjɑːŋ ˌpjɑːŋ-
—Korean [pʰjɔŋ jaŋ]

pyorrhea, pyorrhoea ˌpaɪ ə ˈrɪə §-ˈriː ̯ə
‖ ˌpaɪ ə ˈriː ə

pyosis paɪ ˈəʊs ɪs §-əs ‖ -ˈoʊs əs

pyracantha ˌpaɪə r ə ˈkænᵗθ ə **~s** z

Pyrah ˈpaɪə r ə

pyramid ˈpɪr ə mɪd **~ed** ɪd əd **~ing** ɪŋ **~s** z
ˈpyramid ˌselling ˌ··· ·ˈ··

pyramidal pɪ ˈræm ɪd ᵊl pə-, §-əd ᵊl;
ˈpɪr ə mɪd ᵊl, ˌ··ˈ·· ◂ **~ly** i

Pyramus ˈpɪr əm əs

pyran ˈpaɪə r æn paɪ ˈræn

pyrargyrite paɪ ˈrɑːdʒ ə raɪt -ɪ- ‖ -ˈrɑːrdʒ-

pyre ˈpaɪ ə ‖ ˈpaɪ ̯ᵊr **pyres** ˈpaɪ əz ‖ ˈpaɪ ̯ᵊrz

pyrene ˈpaɪə r iːn —but in the sense 'nutlet',
also paɪ ̯ˈriːn **~s** z

Pyrene paɪ ˈriːn i

Pyrenean ˌpɪr ə ˈniː ən ◂ -ɪ- **~s** z

Pyrenees ˌpɪr ə ˈniːz -ɪ- ‖ ˈpɪr ə niːz (*)

pyrethrin paɪə ˈriːθ rɪn §-rən ‖ -ˈreθ-

pyrethrum paɪə ˈriːθ rəm ‖ -ˈreθ-

pyretic paɪə ˈret ɪk ‖ -ˈreṭ ɪk

Pyrex tdmk ˈpaɪə r eks

pyrexia paɪə ˈreks i ə

Pyrford ˈpɜː fəd ‖ ˈpɜː fᵊrd

pyridine ˈpɪr ɪ diːn -ə-

pyriform ˈpɪr ɪ fɔːm ˈpaɪ ̯ᵊr-, -ə- ‖ -fɔːrm

pyrimidine paɪ ̯ᵊ ˈrɪm ɪ diːn -ə- ‖ pə-

pyrite ˈpaɪ ̯ᵊr aɪt

pyrites paɪə ˈraɪt iːz pɪ-, pə-; ˈpaɪ ̯ᵊr aɪts
‖ pə ˈraɪt̬ iz

pyritic paɪə ˈrɪt ɪk pɪ-. pə- ‖ -ˈrɪt̬ ɪk

pyro- comb. form
with stress-neutral suffix ⸾paɪ ̯ᵊr əʊ ‖ -ə
— pyrophosphate ˌpaɪ ̯ᵊr əʊ ˈfɒs feɪt
‖ -ə ˈfɑːs-
with stress-imposing suffix paɪə ˈrɒ+ ‖ -ˈrɑː+
— pyrolysis paɪə ˈrɒl əs ɪs -ɪs-, §-əs ‖ -ˈrɑːl-

pyroclastic ˌpaɪ ̯ᵊr əʊ ˈklæst ɪk ◂ -ə-
ˌpyro ˌclastic ˈflow

pyrogall|ic ˌpaɪ ̯ᵊr əʊ ˈgæl| ɪk ◂ ‖ -ə- **~ol** ɒl
‖ ɔːl -ɑːl, -oʊl

pyromania ˌpaɪ ̯ᵊr əʊ ˈmeɪn i ə ‖ -ə-

pyromaniac ˌpaɪ ̯ᵊr əʊ ˈmeɪn i æk ‖ -ə- **~s** s

pyrosis paɪə ˈrəʊs ɪs §-əs ‖ -ˈroʊs əs

pyrotechnic ˌpaɪ ̯ᵊr əʊ ˈtek nɪk ◂ ‖ -ə- **~al** ᵊl
~ally ᵊl i **~s** s

pyroxene paɪə ˈrɒks iːn ‖ -ˈrɑːks- pə-

Pyrrha ˈpɪr ə

Pyrrhic, p~ ˈpɪr ɪk **~s** s

Pyrrho ˈpɪr əʊ ‖ -oʊ

Pyrrhus ˈpɪr əs

pyrrole ˈpɪr əʊl →-ɒʊl; pɪ ˈrəʊl, §pə- ‖ ˈpɪr oʊl

pyruvic paɪə ˈruːv ɪk

Pytchley ˈpaɪtʃ li

Pythagoras paɪ ˈθæg ər əs -ə ræs ‖ pə- pɪ-

Pythagorean paɪ ˌθæg ə ˈriː ən ◂ ˌpaɪ θæg əˈ--
‖ pə- pɪ- **~ism** ˌɪz əm **~s** z

Pytheas ˈpɪθ i əs -æs

Pythia ˈpɪθ i ə

Pythian ˈpɪθ i ən

Pythias ˈpɪθ i æs -i əs

python, P~ ˈpaɪθ ᵊn ‖ -ɑːn -ᵊn **~s** z

Pythonesque ˌpaɪθ ə ˈnesk ◂

pythoness ˈpaɪθ ə nes -ən ɪs, -ən əs ‖ -ən əs
ˈpɪθ- **~es** ɪz əz

pythonic paɪ ˈθɒn ɪk pɪ- ‖ -ˈθɑːn-

pyuria paɪ ˈjʊər i ə ‖ -ˈjʊr-

pyx pɪks (= picks) **pyxes** ˈpɪks ɪz -əz

pyxie ˈpɪks i **~s** z

Qq

q Spelling-to-sound

1 Except in occasional words from foreign languages, the letter **q** is always followed by **u**. Where the spelling is the resultant digraph **qu**, the pronunciation is regularly

kw as in **quite** kwaɪt or

k as in **picturesque** ˌpɪk tʃə ˈresk.

2 The pronunciation is generally kw. Examples: **queen** kwiːn, **squeak** skwiːk, **equal** ˈiːk wəl, **liquid** ˈlɪk wɪd.

3 However, in the case of **que** at the end of a word, and in a minority of other words, the pronunciation is k. Examples: **clique** kliːk, **cheque** tʃek (AmE spelling: **check**), **queue** kjuː, **liquor** ˈlɪk ə ‖ ˈlɪk °r.

4 Where the spelling is **cqu**, the pronunciation is again either kw as in **acquaint** ə ˈkweɪnt or k as in **lacquer** ˈlæk ə ‖ ˈlæk °r.

Q

Q, q kjuː: **Q's, q's, Qs, qs** kjuːz
—*Communications code name:* Quebec
ˈQ ˌfever
Qaddafi, Qadhafi gə ˈdɑːf i -ˈdæf- —*Arabic*
[ɣað ˈðɑː fi]
Qaeda —*see* **Al-Qaeda**
Qantas *tdmk* ˈkwɒnt əs -æs ‖ ˈkwɑːnt-
qat kɑːt —*Arabic* [qaːt]
Qatar ˈkæt ɑː ˈgæt-, ˈkʌt-, ˈgʌt-; gæ ˈtɑː, kæ-,
kə- ‖ ˈkɑːt ɑːr kə ˈtɑːr —*Arabic* [ˈqa tˤɑr]
Qatari kæ ˈtɑːr i gæ-, kə- ~**s** z
QC, Q.C. ˌkjuː ˈsiː ~**s**, ~**'s** z
QE2 ˌkjuː iː ˈtuː
QED, q.e.d. ˌkjuː iː ˈdiː
qi tʃiː —*Chi* qì [⁴tɕʰi]
qibla, qiblah ˈkɪb lə ‖ —*Arabic* [ˈqib lah]
Qin *dynasty* tʃɪn —*Chinese* Qín [²tɕʰɪn]
Qinetiq *tdmk* kɪ ˈnet ɪk ‖ -ˈneţ-
Qing *dynasty* tʃɪŋ —*Chinese* Qīng [¹tɕʰɪŋ]
Qingdao ˌtʃɪŋ ˈdaʊ —*Chinese* Qīngdǎo
[¹tɕʰɪŋ ³tau]
Qinghai ˌtʃɪŋ ˈhaɪ —*Chinese* Qīnghǎi
[¹tɕʰɪŋ ³xai]
Qom kʊm kɒm, xʊm —*Persian* [ɢom]
qoph kɒf kɔːf, kʊf, kəʊf ‖ kɔːf kɑːf, koʊf
Q-rating ˈkjuː ˌreɪt ɪŋ ‖ -ˌreɪţ ɪŋ
qt, q.t. ˌkjuː ˈtiː
Q-Tip *tdmk* ˈkjuː tɪp ~**s** s
qua kweɪ kwɑː
Quaalude *tdmk* ˈkweɪ luːd ~**s** z

quack kwæk **quacked** kwækt **quacking**
ˈkwæk ɪŋ **quacks** kwæks
quackery ˈkwæk ər i
quad kwɒd ‖ kwɑːd **quads** kwɒdz ‖ kwɑːdz
Quadragesim|a ˌkwɒdr ə ˈdʒes ɪm |ə -əm ə
‖ ˌkwɑːdr- ~**al** °l
quadrangle ˈkwɒdr æŋ g°l ‖ ˈkwɑːdr- ~**s** z
quadrangular kwɒ ˈdræŋ gjʊl ə -gjəl-
‖ kwɑː ˈdræŋ gjəl °r
quadrant ˈkwɒdr ənt ‖ ˈkwɑːdr- ~**s** s
quadrantal kwɒ ˈdrænt °l ‖ kwɑː ˈdrænţ °l
quadraphonic ˌkwɒdr ə ˈfɒn ɪk ◂
‖ ˌkwɑːdr ə ˈfɑːn ɪk ◂ ~**ally** °l_i ~**s** s
quadraphony kwɒ ˈdrɒf ən i -ˈdræf-;
ˈkwɒdr ə fɒn i ‖ kwɑː ˈdrɑː f- ˈkwɑːdr ə fɑːn i
quadrasonic ˌkwɒdr ə ˈsɒn ɪk ◂
‖ ˌkwɑːdr ə ˈsɑːn ɪk ◂ ~**ally** °l_i ~**s** s
quadrat ˈkwɒdr ət -æt ‖ ˈkwɑːdr- ~**s** s
quadr|ate *v* kwɒ ˈdr|eɪt ‖ ˈkwɑːdr |eɪt ~**ated**
eɪt ɪd -əd ‖ eɪţ əd ~**ates** eɪts ~**ating** eɪt ɪŋ
‖ eɪţ ɪŋ
quadrate *n, adj* ˈkwɒdr eɪt -ət, -ɪt ‖ ˈkwɑːdr-
~**s** s
quadratic kwɒ ˈdræt ɪk ‖ kwɑː ˈdræţ ɪk ~**s** s
quaˌdratic eˈquation
quadrature ˈkwɒdr ətʃ ə -ɪtʃ-; -ət jʊə, -ɪt-
‖ ˈkwɑːdr ətʃ °r -ə tʃʊr, -ə tʊr ~**s** z
quadrenni|al kwɒ ˈdren i_|əl ‖ kwɑː- ~**a** ə
~**ally** əl_i ~**um** əm

quadri- *comb. form*
  with stress-neutral suffix ˌkwɒdr ɪ -ə
  ‖ ˌkwɑːdr ə — **quadrilingual**
  ˌkwɒdr ɪ ˈlɪŋ gwəl ◂ -ə-, §-ˈlɪŋ gju̯əl
  ‖ ˌkwɑːdr ə-
  with stress-imposing suffix kwɒ ˈdrɪ+ ‖ kwɑː-
  — **quadripara** kwɒ ˈdrɪp ər ə ‖ kwɑː-
quadric ˈkwɒdr ɪk ‖ ˈkwɑːdr ɪk
quadriceps ˈkwɒdr ɪ seps -ə- ‖ ˈkwɑːdr- **~es** ɪz
  əz
quadriga kwɒ ˈdriːg ə kwə-, -ˈdraɪg- ‖ kwɑː-
  ~s z
quadrilateral ˌkwɒdr ɪ ˈlæt̬ �*r əl ◂ ˌ-ə-
  ‖ ˌkwɑːdr ə ˈlæt̬ ər əl ◂ →-ˈlætr əl **~s** z
quadrilingual ˌkwɒdr ɪ ˈlɪŋ gwəl ◂ -ə-
  ‖ ˌkwɑːdr- **~ly** i **~s** z
quadrille kwə ˈdrɪl kwɒ- ‖ kwɑː- **~s** z
quadrillion kwɒ ˈdrɪl jən -i̯ən
  ‖ kwɑː ˈdrɪl jən **~s** z
quadrinomial ˌkwɒdr ɪ ˈnəʊm i̯əl ◂ ˌ-ə-
  ‖ ˌkwɑːdr ə ˈnoʊm- **~s** z
quadripartite ˌkwɒdr ɪ ˈpɑːt aɪt ◂ -ə-
  ‖ ˌkwɑːdr ə ˈpɑːrt aɪt ◂
quadriplegia ˌkwɒdr ɪ ˈpliːdʒ i̯ə ◂ ˌ-ə-,
  -ˈpliːdʒ ə ‖ ˌkwɑːdr-
quadriplegic ˌkwɒdr ɪ ˈpliːdʒ ɪk ◂ ˌ-ə-
  ‖ ˌkwɑːdr- **~s** s
quadrivium kwɒ ˈdrɪv i̯əm ‖ kwɑː-
quadroon kwɒ ˈdruːn ‖ kwɑː- **~s** z
quadrophonic ˌkwɒdr ə ˈfɒn ɪk ◂
  ‖ ˌkwɑːdr ə ˈfɑːn ɪk ◂ **~ally** �*l i̯ **~s** s
quadrophony kwɒ ˈdrɒf ən i ˈkwɒdr ə fɒn i
  ‖ kwɑː ˈdrɑːf- ˈkwɑːdr ə fɑːn i
quadrumanous kwɒ ˈdruːm ən əs ‖ kwɑː-
quadruped ˈkwɒdr u ped -ə- ‖ ˈkwɑːdr ə- **~s** z
quadrupl|e ˈkwɒdr ʊp �*l -əp-; kwɒ ˈdruːp-
  ‖ kwɑː ˈdruːp �*l -ˈdrʌp-; ˈkwɑːdr əp- **~ed** d
  ~es z **~ing** ɪŋ
quadruplet ˈkwɒdr ʊp lət -əp-, -lɪt, -let;
  kwɒ ˈdruːp-, §-ˈdrʌp- ‖ kwɑː ˈdruːp- -ˈdrʌp-;
  ˈkwɑːdr əp- **~s** s
quadruplex ˈkwɒdr u pleks -ə-;
  kwɒ ˈdruːp leks ‖ ˈkwɑːdr ə pleks
  kwɑː ˈdruːp leks
quadruplicate *adj* kwɒ ˈdruːp lɪk ət -lək ət,
  -ɪt; -lɪ keɪt, -lə- ‖ kwɑː- **~s** s
quadrupli|cate *v* kwɒ ˈdruːp lɪ |keɪt -lə-
  ‖ kwɑː- **~cated** keɪt ɪd -əd ‖ keɪt̬ əd **~cates**
  keɪts **~cating** keɪt ɪŋ ‖ keɪt̬ ɪŋ
quadruply ˈkwɒdr ʊp li -əp-; kwɒ ˈdruːp-
  ‖ kwɑː ˈdruːp li -ˈdrʌp-; ˈkwɑːdr əp-
quaestor ˈkwiːst ə ˈkwaɪst-, -ɔː ‖ ˈkwest �*r
  ˈkwiːst- **~s** z
quaff kwɒf kwɑːf ‖ kwɑːf kwæf **quaffed** kwɒft
  kwɑːft ‖ kwɑːft kwæft **quaffing** ˈkwɒf ɪŋ
  ˈkwɑːf- ‖ ˈkwɑːf ɪŋ ˈkwæf- **quaffs** kwɒfs
  kwɑːfs ‖ kwɑːfs kwæfs
quaffer ˈkwɒf ə ˈkwɑːf- ‖ ˈkwɑːf �*r ˈkwæf- **~s** z
quag kwæg kwɒg ‖ kwɑːg **quags** kwægz
  kwɒgz ‖ kwɑːgz
quagga ˈkwæg ə ˈkwɒg- ‖ ˈkwɑːg- **~s** z
quagg|y ˈkwæg |i ˈkwɒg- ‖ ˈkwɑːg- **~ier** i̯ə
  ‖ i̯�*r **~iest** i̯ɪst i̯əst **~iness** i nəs i nɪs

Quaglino's *tdmk* kwæg ˈliːn əʊz
  ‖ kwɑːg ˈliːn oʊz

QUAGMIRE

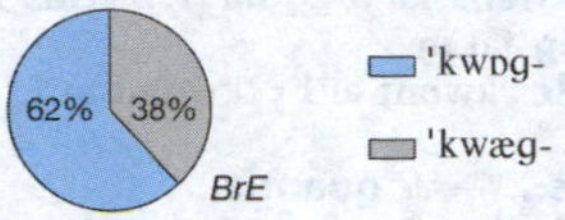

  62% 38%

■ ˈkwɒg-
■ ˈkwæg-

BrE

quagmire ˈkwɒg maɪ̯ə ˈkwæg- ‖ ˈkwæg maɪ̯�*r
  ˈkwɑːg- — *Preference poll, BrE:* ˈkwɒg- *62%,*
  ˈkwæg- *38%.* **~s** z
quahog ˈkwɑː hɒg ‖ ˈkwɔː hɔːg ˈkwɑː-, ˈkwoʊ-,
  ˈkoʊ-, -hɑːg **~s** z
Quaid kweɪd
Quai d'Orsay ˌkeɪ ˈdɔːs eɪ ‖ -dɔːr ˈseɪ —*Fr*
  [ke dɔʁ sɛ]
quail, Quail kweɪ̯l **quailed** kweɪ̯ld **quailing**
  ˈkweɪ̯l ɪŋ **quails** kweɪ̯lz
Quain kweɪn
quaint kweɪnt **quainter** ˈkweɪnt ə
  ‖ ˈkweɪnt̬ �*r **quaintest** ˈkweɪnt ɪst -əst
  ‖ ˈkweɪnt̬-
quaint|ly ˈkweɪnt |li **~ness** nəs nɪs
quake kweɪk **quaked** kweɪkt **quakes** kweɪks
  quaking ˈkweɪk ɪŋ
quake-proof ˈkweɪk pruːf §-prʊf **~ed** t **~ing** ɪŋ
  ~s s
Quaker ˈkweɪk ə ‖ -�*r **~ly** li **~s** z
Quakerism ˈkweɪk ər ˌɪz əm
quak|y ˈkweɪk |i **~ier** i̯ə ‖ i̯�*r **~iest** i̯ɪst i̯əst
  ~ily ɪ li əl i **~iness** i nəs i nɪs
Qualcast *tdmk* ˈkwɒl kɑːst -§kæst
  ‖ ˈkwɑːl kæst
Qualcomm *tdmk* ˈkwɒl kɒm ‖ ˈkwɑːl kɑːm
qualia ˈkweɪl i̯ə
qualification ˌkwɒl ɪf ɪ ˈkeɪʃ �*n ˌ-əf-, §-ə*-
  ‖ ˌkwɑːl- **~s** z
qualificative ˈkwɒl ɪf ɪk ət ɪv ˈ-əf-; -ɪ keɪt ɪv,
  -ə·; ˌ·· ˈkeɪt ɪv◂, -ə·· ‖ ˈkwɑːl əf ə keɪt̬ ɪv
qualificatory ˌkwɒl ɪf ɪ ˈkeɪt ər ˌi ˌ-əf-, §-ə*-
  ‖ ˈkwɑːl əf ɪk ə tɔːri ˈ-ɪf-, -toʊr i
quali|fy ˈkwɒl ɪ |faɪ -ə- ‖ ˈkwɑːl- **~fied** faɪd
  ~fier/s faɪ ə/z ‖ faɪ �*r/z **~fies** faɪz **~fying**
  faɪ ɪŋ
qualitative ˈkwɒl ɪt ət ɪv ˈ-ət-; -ɪ teɪt-, -ə teɪt-
  ‖ ˈkwɑːl ə teɪt̬ ɪv **~ly** li
qualit|y ˈkwɒl ət |i ˈ-ɪt- ‖ ˈkwɑːl ət̬ |i **~ies** iz
qualm kwɑːm kwɔːm, §kwɑːlm ‖ kwɔːm,
  kwɑːlm **qualms** kwɑːmz kwɔːmz, §kwɑːlmz
  ‖ kwɔːmz, kwɑːlmz
qualmish ˈkwɑːm ɪʃ ˈkwɔːm-, §ˈkwɑːlm-
  ‖ ˈkwɔːm-, ˈkwɑːlm- **~ly** li **~ness** nəs nɪs
quandar|y ˈkwɒnd ər |i ‖ ˈkwɑːnd- **~ies** iz
quandong ˈkwɒnd ɒŋ ‖ ˈkwɑːnd ɑːŋ **~s** z
quango ˈkwæŋ gəʊ ‖ -goʊ **~s** z
Quant, quant kwɒnt ‖ kwɑːnt
quant|a ˈkwɒnt |ə ‖ ˈkwɑːnt̬ |ə **~al** �*l
Quantel *tdmk* ˌkwɒn ˈtel ˌ·· ‖ ˌkwɑːn-
quantic ˈkwɒnt ɪk ‖ ˈkwɑːnt̬ ɪk

Q

quantifiable ˈkwɒnt ɪ faɪ‿əb ᵊl ˈ‧ə-, ˌ‧ᵊ‧‧‧
‖ ˈkwɑːnt̬-

quantification ˌkwɒnt ɪf ɪ ˈkeɪʃ ᵊn ˌ‧əf-, §-
‖ ˌkwɑːnt̬-

quanti|fy ˈkwɒnt ɪ |faɪ -ə- ‖ ˈkwɑːnt̬- **~fied**
faɪd **~fier/s** faɪ‿ə/z ‖ faɪ‿ᵊr/z **~fies** faɪz
~fying faɪ ɪŋ

quantile ˈkwɒnt aɪᵊl ‖ ˈkwɑːnt aɪᵊl ˈkwɑːnt̬ ᵊl
~s z

quantis... —*see* **quantiz...**

quantitative ˈkwɒnt ɪt ət ɪv ˈ‧ət-; -ɪ teɪt-,
-ə teɪt- ‖ ˈkwɑːnt̬ ə teɪt̬ ɪv **~ly** li

quantit|y ˈkwɒnt ət |i -ɪt- ‖ ˈkwɑːnt̬ ət̬ |i **~ies**
iz
ˈquantity surˌveyor, ˌ‧‧‧ ‧ˈ‧‧

quantization ˌkwɒnt aɪ ˈzeɪʃ ᵊn -ɪ-
‖ ˌkwɑːnt̬ ə-

quantiz|e ˈkwɒnt aɪz ‖ ˈkwɑːnt- **~ed** d **~es** ɪz
əz **~ing** ɪŋ

Quantock ˈkwɒnt ək -ɒk ‖ ˈkwɑːnt ɑːk **~s** s

quant|um ˈkwɒnt |əm ‖ ˈkwɑːnt̬ |əm **~a** ə
ˌquantum ˈjump; ˌquantum ˈleap;
ˌquantum meˈchanics; ˈquantum ˌtheory

quarantin|e ˈkwɒr ən tiːn ‖ ˈkwɔːr- ˈkwɑːr-
~ed d **~es** z **~ing** ɪŋ

quark *'soft cheese'* kwaːk ‖ kwɑːrk —*Ger*
[kvaʁk]

quark *'elementary particle'* kwaːk kwɔːk
‖ kwɑːrk kwɔːrk **quarks** kwaːks kwɔːks
‖ kwɑːrks kwɔːrks

QuarkXPress ˌkwaːk ɪk ˈspres -ek-, -ək-
‖ ˌkwɑːrk-, ˌkwɔːrk-

Quarles kwɔːlz kɔːlz ‖ ˈkwɔːrlz

Quarndon ˈkwɔːn dən ˈkɔːn- ‖ ˈkwɔːrn-

quarrel ˈkwɒr əl ‖ ˈkwaːr əl ˈkwɔːr- **~ed**, **~led**
d **~ing**, **~ling** ɪŋ **~s** z

quarreler, quarreller ˈkwɒr əl ə
‖ ˈkwaːr əl ᵊr ˈkwɔːr- **~s** z

quarrelsome ˈkwɒr əl səm ‖ ˈkwaːr- ˈkwɔːr-
~ly li **~ness** nəs nɪs

quarr|y, Q~ ˈkwɒr |i ‖ ˈkwaːr |i ˈkwɔːr- **~ied**
id **~ies** iz **~ying** i ɪŋ

quarry|man ˈkwɒr i mən -mæn ‖ ˈkwaːr-
ˈkwɔːr- **~men** mən men

quart *'two pints'* kwɔːt kɔːt ‖ kwɔːrt **quarts**
kwɔːts kɔːts ‖ kwɔːrts

quart *in fencing; at cards* kaːt ‖ kaːrt

quartan ˈkwɔːt ᵊn ˈkɔːt- ‖ ˈkwɔːrt ᵊn **~s** z

quarte kaːt ‖ kaːrt —*Fr* [kaʁt]

QUARTER

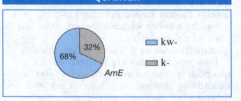

- ☐ kw-
- ☐ k-

AmE

quart|er ˈkwɔːt |ə ˈkɔːt- ‖ ˈkwɔːrt̬ |ᵊr ˈkɔːrt̬-
—*AmE also occasionally dissimilated to*
ˈkwɔːt̬ ᵊr, ˈkɔːt̬ ᵊr, *and similarly in compounds.*
— *Preference poll, AmE:* kw- 68%, k- 32%.

~ered əd ‖ ᵊrd **~ering/s** ər ɪŋ/z **~ers** əz ‖ ᵊrz
ˈquarter day; ˈquarter note; ˈquarter
ˌsessions

quarterback ˈkwɔːt ə bæk ˈkɔːt- ‖ ˈkwɔːrt̬ ᵊr-
ˈkɔːrt̬- **~s** s

quarterdeck ˈkwɔːt ə dek ˈkɔːt- ‖ ˈkwɔːrt̬ ᵊr-
~s s

quarterfinal ˌkwɔːt ə ˈfaɪn ᵊl ˌkɔːt-
‖ ˌkwɔːrt̬ ᵊr- **~ist/s** ɪst/s §əst/s **~s** z

quarterlight ˈkwɔːt ə laɪt ˈkɔːt-, -ᵊl aɪt
‖ ˈkwɔːrt̬ ᵊr- **~s** s

quarter|ly ˈkwɔːt ə|l i ˈkɔːt- ‖ ˈkwɔːrt̬ ᵊr |li
~lies liz

Quartermaine ˈkwɔːt ə meɪn ˈkɔːt-
‖ ˈkwɔːrt̬ ᵊr-

quartermaster ˈkwɔːt ə ˌmaːst ə ˈkɔːt-,
§-ˌmæst- ‖ ˈkwɔːrt̬ ᵊr ˌmæst ᵊr **~s** z
ˌquarterˌmaster ˈgeneral; ˌquarterˌmaster
ˈsergeant

quartern ˈkwɔːt ᵊn ˈkɔːt- ‖ ˈkwɔːrt̬ ᵊrn **~s** z

quarter|staff ˈkwɔːt ə |staːf ˈkɔːt-, §-stæf
‖ ˈkwɔːrt̬ ᵊr |stæf **~staves** steɪvz -staːvz

quartet, quartette ₍ˌ₎kwɔː ˈtet ₍ˌ₎kɔː-
‖ ₍ˌ₎kwɔːr- **~s** s

quartic ˈkwɔːt ɪk ˈkɔːt- ‖ ˈkwɔːrt̬ ɪk **~s** s

quartile ˈkwɔːt aɪᵊl ˈkɔːt- ‖ ˈkwɔːrt aɪᵊl
ˈkwɔːrt̬ ᵊl **~s** z

quarto ˈkwɔːt əʊ ˈkɔːt- ‖ ˈkwɔːrt̬ oʊ **~s** z

quartz kwɔːts kɔːts ‖ kwɔːrts (= *quarts*)

quartzite ˈkwɔːts aɪt ˈkɔːts- ‖ ˈkwɔːrts-

quasar ˈkweɪz aː ˈkweɪs-, ‖ -aːr **~s** z

quash kwɒʃ ‖ kwaːʃ **quashed** kwɒʃt ‖ kwaːʃt
quashes ˈkwɒʃ ɪz -əz ‖ ˈkwaːʃ əz **quashing**
ˈkwɒʃ ɪŋ ‖ ˈkwaːʃ ɪŋ

Quashi, Quashie ˈkwɒʃ i ˈkwaːʃ- ‖ ˈkwaːʃ i

quasi ˈkweɪz aɪ ˈkweɪs-, ˈkwaːz-, ˈkwæz-, -i

quasi- ˌkweɪz aɪ ˌkweɪs-, ˌkwaːz-, ˌkwæz-, -i
— **quasi-judicial** ˌkweɪz aɪ dʒu ˈdɪʃ ᵊl ◂
ˌkweɪs-, ˌkwaːz-, ˌkwæz-, ˌ-i-

Quasimodo ˌkwaːz ɪ ˈməʊd əʊ ˌkwɒz-, ˌkwæz-
‖ -ˈmoʊd oʊ —*Formerly* ˌkweɪs aɪ-. *The
Italian poet was* kwa ˈziː mo do,
kwa zi ˈmɔː do.

quassia ˈkwɒʃ ə ˈkwɒʃ i ə ‖ ˈkwaːʃ ə

quatercentenary ˌkwæt ə sen ˈtiːn ər i
ˌkwɒt-, ˌkweɪt-, -ˈten- ‖ ˌkwaːt̬ ᵊr sen ˈten ər i
-ˈsent ᵊn er i

Quatermain ˈkwɒt ə meɪn ˈkɔːt- ‖ ˈkwaːt̬ ᵊr-

Quatermass ˈkweɪt ə mæs ‖ ˈkweɪt̬ ᵊr-

quaternar|y, Q~ kwə ˈtɜːn ər |i kwɒ-
‖ ˈkwaːt̬ ᵊr nər |i kwə ˈtɜːn ər |i **~ies** iz

quaternion kwə ˈtɜːn i‿ən kwɒ- ‖ kwə ˈtɜːn-
kwaː- **~s** z

quatrain ˈkwɒtr eɪn -ən ‖ ˈkwaːtr- **~s** z

quatrefoil ˈkætr ə fɔɪᵊl ‖ ˈkæt̬ ᵊr- **~s** z

Quattro ˈkwɒtr əʊ ˈkwætr- ‖ ˈkwaːtr oʊ

quattrocento ˌkwætr əʊ ˈtʃent əʊ ˌkwɒtr-
‖ ˌkwaːtr oʊ ˈtʃent oʊ —*It*
[kwat tro ˈtʃen to]

quaver ˈkweɪv ə ‖ -ᵊr **~ed** d **quavering/ly**
ˈkweɪv ər ɪŋ /li **~s** z

quay, Quay kiː ‖ keɪ, kweɪ *(in BrE, and in AmE mostly, = key) —but as a family name, usually* kweɪ **quays** kiːz ‖ keɪz, kweɪz
quayage 'kiː ɪdʒ ‖ 'keɪ-, 'kweɪ-
Quayle kweɪ^əl
quayside 'kiː saɪd ‖ 'keɪ-, 'kweɪ-
quean kwiːn (= *queen*) **queans** kwiːnz
Queanbeyan 'kwiːn bi‿ən →'kwiːm-
queas|y 'kwiːz |i ~**ier** i‿ə | i‿^ər ~**iest** i‿ɪst i‿əst ~**ily** ɪ li əl i ~**iness** i nəs ɪ nɪs
Quebec, Québec kwɪ 'bek kwə-, kə- —*Fr* [ke bɛk]
Quebecer, Quebecker kwɪ 'bek ə kwə-, kə- ‖ -^ər ~**s** z
Quebecois, Québécois, q~ ˌkeɪb e 'kwɑː ◂ ˌkeb-, -ɪ-, -ə- —*Fr* [ke be kwa]
quebracho keɪ 'brɑːtʃ əʊ kɪ- ‖ -oʊ —*Sp* [ke 'βra tʃo] ~**s** z
Quechua 'ketʃ u‿ə ‖ -'wɑː ~**s** z
queen, Queen kwiːn **queened** kwiːnd **queening** 'kwiːn ɪŋ **queens** kwiːnz
  (₁)**Queen 'Anne**; '**queen cake**; ˌ**queen 'consort**; ˌ**Queen E'lizabeth**; ˌ**queen 'mother**; ˌ**Queen's 'Bench**, ˌ**Queen's 'Bench Di,vision**; ˌ**Queen's 'Council**; ˌ**Queen's 'English**; ˌ**queen's 'evidence**
Queenborough 'kwiːn bər‿ə ‖ -ˌbɜː oʊ
queendom 'kwiːn dəm
Queenie 'kwiːn i
queenlike 'kwiːn laɪk
queen|ly 'kwiːn |li ~**liness** li nəs -nɪs
Queens kwiːnz
Queensberry 'kwiːnz bər‿i §-ˌber i ‖ -ˌber i ˌ**Queensberry 'Rules** ‖ '··· ·
Queensferry 'kwiːnz ˌfer i
queen-size 'kwiːn saɪz
Queensland 'kwiːnz lənd -lænd —*In Australia usually* -lænd
Queenstown 'kwiːnz taʊn
Queensway 'kwiːnz weɪ
queer kwɪə ‖ kwɪ^ər **queerer** 'kwɪər ə ‖ 'kwɪr ^ər **queerest** 'kwɪər ɪst -əst ‖ 'kwɪr əst ˌ**Queer Street**
queerish 'kwɪər ɪʃ ‖ 'kwɪr-
queer|ly 'kwɪə |li ‖ 'kwɪr- ~**ness** nəs nɪs
quefrency 'kwiːf rən^ts i
quel kel —*Fr* [kɛl]
quell kwel **quelled** kweld **quelling** 'kwel ɪŋ **quells** kwelz
Quellenforschung 'kwel ən ˌfɔːʃ ʊŋ ‖ -ˌfɔːrʃ- —*Ger* ['kvɛ lən ˌfɔʁ ʃʊŋ]
Quemoy kɪ 'mɔɪ ke- —*Chinese* Jīnmén [¹tɕin ²mən]
quench kwentʃ **quenched** kwentʃt **quenches** 'kwentʃ ɪz -əz **quenching** 'kwentʃ ɪŋ
quencher 'kwentʃ ə ‖ -^ər ~**s** z
quenda 'kwend ə ~**s** z
quenelle kə 'nel ~**s** z
Quenington 'kwen ɪŋ tən
Quennell kwɪ 'nel kwə-; 'kwen ^əl
Quentin 'kwent ɪn §-ən ‖ -^ən
quercitron 'kwɜː sɪtr ən ˌ·'·· ‖ 'kwɜː- ~**s** z
queri... —*see* **query**

quern kwɜːn ‖ kwɝːn **querns** kwɜːnz ‖ kwɝːnz
querulous 'kwer ʊl əs -jʊl-, -əl- ‖ -əl əs ~**ly** li ~**ness** nəs nɪs
quer|y 'kwɪər |i ‖ 'kwɪr |i 'kwer- ~**ied** id ~**ies** iz ~**ying** i ɪŋ
quesadilla ˌkeɪs ə 'diː ə ~**s** z —*Sp* [ke sa 'ði ʎa, -ja]
quest kwest **quested** 'kwest ɪd -əd **questing** 'kwest ɪŋ **quests** kwests
Quested 'kwest ɪd -əd
question 'kwes tʃən →'kweʃ-, -tjən ~**ed** d ~**ing/ly** ɪŋ/ li ~**s** z
  '**question mark**; '**question ˌmaster**; '**question tag**; '**question time**; '**question word**
questionab|le 'kwes tʃən əb |^əl →'kweʃ-, 'tjən- ~**leness** ^əl nəs -nɪs ~**ly** li
questioner 'kwes tʃən ə 'kweʃ-, -tjən- ‖ -^ər ~**s** z

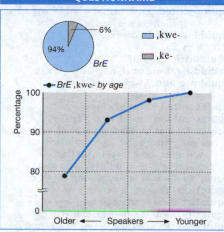

QUESTIONNAIRE

6% ▨ ˌkwe-
94% ▨ ˌke-
BrE

— ●— BrE ˌkwe- by age

Percentage: 100 / 90 / 80 / 0

Older ◄— Speakers —► Younger

---

questionnaire ˌkwes tʃə 'neə ˌkes-, →ˌkweʃ-, ˌti‿ə'·, '··· ‖ -'ne^ər -'næ^ər — *Preference poll, BrE:* 'kwe- 94% (born since 1973: 100%), 'ke- 6%. ~**s** z
questor 'kwiːst ə 'kwaɪst-, -ɔː ‖ 'kwest ^ər 'kwiːst- ~**s** z
Quetta 'kwet ə ‖ 'kweţ ə
quetzal 'kets ^əl 'kwets-; ket 'sæl ‖ ket 'sɑːl -'sæl ~**s** z
Quetzalcoatl ˌkets ^əl kəʊ 'æt ^əl ‖ ket 'sɑːl kwɑːţ ^əl ·'·koʊ ˌɑːţ ^əl
queue kjuː (! = *cue*) **queued** kjuːd **queues** kjuːz **queuing** 'kjuː ɪŋ
queue-jump 'kjuː dʒʌmp ~**ed** t ~**er/s** ə/z ‖ ^ər/z ~**ing** ɪŋ ~**s** s
Quex kweks
Quezon 'keɪz ɒn 'keɪs- ‖ -ɑːn ˌ**Quezon 'City**
Qufu ˌtʃuː 'fuː —*Chinese* Qūfù [¹tɕʰy ⁴fu]
quibbl|e 'kwɪb ^əl ~**ed** d ~**er/s** ˌə/z ‖ ˌ^ər/z ~**es** z ~**ing** ɪŋ
quiche kiːʃ **quiches** 'kiːʃ ɪz -əz

Q

quick, Quick kwɪk **quicker** 'kwɪk ə ‖ 'kwɪk ᵊr
  quickest 'kwɪk ɪst -əst
  ˌquick 'march ‖ '· ·
quick-and-dirty ˌkwɪk ən 'dɜːt i ◂ ‖ -'dɝːt i ◂
quick-change ˌkwɪk 'tʃeɪndʒ
quicken 'kwɪk ən **~ed** d **~ing** ɪŋ **~s** z
quick-fire ˌkwɪk 'faɪ ə ◂ ‖ -'faɪ ᵊr
quick-|freeze ˌkwɪk |'friːz **~freezes** 'friːz ɪz
  -əz **~froze** frəʊz ‖ 'frəʊz **~frozen** 'frəʊz ᵊn ◂
  ‖ ' frəʊz ᵊn ◂
quickie 'kwɪk i **~s** z
quicklime 'kwɪk laɪm
quickly, Q~ 'kwɪk li
quickness 'kwɪk nəs -nɪs
quicksand 'kwɪk sænd **~s** z
quickset 'kwɪk set
quicksilver 'kwɪk ˌsɪlv ə ‖ -ᵊr
quickstep 'kwɪk step **~s** s
quick-tempered ˌkwɪk 'temp əd ◂ ‖ -ᵊrd ◂
  '·ˌ· ·
quickthorn 'kwɪk θɔːn ‖ -θɔːrn
quick-witted ˌkwɪk 'wɪt ɪd ◂ -əd ‖ -'wɪt̬ əd ◂
  '·ˌ· · **~ly** li **~ness** nəs nɪs
quid kwɪd **quids** kwɪdz
  ˌquids 'in
Quidditch 'kwɪd ɪtʃ
quiddit|y 'kwɪd ət i |i -ɪt- ‖ -ət̬ |i **~ies** iz
quid pro quo ˌkwɪd prəʊ 'kwəʊ
  ‖ -proʊ 'kwoʊ **~s** z
quiescence kwi 'es ᵊn̩ts kwaɪ-
quiescent kwi 'es ᵊnt kwaɪ- **~ly** li
quiet 'kwaɪ ət **quieted** 'kwaɪ ət ɪd -əd ‖ -ət̬ əd
  quieter 'kwaɪ ət ə ‖ -ət̬ ᵊr **quietest**
  'kwaɪ ət ɪst -əst ‖ -ət̬ əst **quieting**
  'kwaɪ ət ɪŋ ‖ -ət̬ ɪŋ **quiets** 'kwaɪ əts
quieten 'kwaɪ ət ᵊn **~ed** d **~ing** ɪŋ **~s** z
quietism 'kwaɪ ət ˌɪz əm -ɪt- ‖ -ət̬-
quietist 'kwaɪ ət ɪst -ɪt-, §-əst ‖ -ət̬- **~s** s
quiet|ly 'kwaɪ ət ‖ li **~ness** nəs -nɪs
quietude 'kwaɪ ə tjuːd -ɪ-, →-tʃuːd ‖ -tuːd
  -tjuːd
quietus kwaɪ 'iːt əs kwi-, -'eɪt- ‖ -'iːt̬ əs **~es** ɪz
  əz
quiff kwɪf **quiffs** kwɪfs
Quiggin 'kwɪg ɪn §-ən
Quigley 'kwɪg li
quill kwɪl **quilled** kwɪld **quilling** 'kwɪl ɪŋ
  quills kwɪlz
Quiller-Couch ˌkwɪl ə 'kuːtʃ ‖ -ᵊr-
Quilliam 'kwɪl i_əm
Quilp kwɪlp
quilt kwɪlt **quilted** 'kwɪlt ɪd -əd **quilting**
  'kwɪlt ɪŋ **quilts** kwɪlts
Quilter, q~ 'kwɪlt ə ‖ -ᵊr
quim kwɪm **quims** kwɪmz
quin, Quin kwɪn **quins** kwɪnz
quinary 'kwaɪn ər i
Quinault family name 'kwɪn ᵊlt
quince kwɪn̩ts **quinces** 'kwɪn̩ts ɪz -əz
quincentenar|y ˌkwɪn sen 'tiːn ər |i ˌ·s²n-,
  -'ten- ‖ -'ten ər |i ˌ·'sent ᵊn er i **~ies** iz
quincentennial ˌkwɪn sen 'ten i_əl ◂ ˌ·s²n- **~s**
  z

Quincey 'kwɪn̩ts i
quincuncial kwɪn 'kʌn̩tʃ ᵊl →kwɪŋ- **~ly** i
quincunx 'kwɪŋk ʌŋks **~es** ɪz əz
Quincy 'kwɪn̩ts i
quindecagon ₍ᵢ₎kwɪn 'dek əg ən ‖ -ə gɑːn **~s**
  z
quindecennial ˌkwɪn dɪ 'sen i_əl ◂ ˌ·də-, ˌ·de-
  ~ly i
Quindlen 'kwɪnd lɪn -lən
quinine kwɪ 'niːn kwə-; 'kwɪn iːn ‖ 'kwaɪn aɪn
  'kwɪn- (*)
Quinion 'kwɪn i_ən
Quink tdmk kwɪŋk
Quinlan 'kwɪn lən
Quinn kwɪn
quinoa ki 'nəʊ ə 'kiːn wɑː ‖ -'noʊ-
quinoline 'kwɪn ə liːn -lɪn, §-lən; -ᵊl iːn, -ɪn,
  §-ən ‖ -ᵊl iːn
quinone kwɪ 'nəʊn 'kwɪn əʊn ‖ -'noʊn
  'kwaɪn oʊn
quinquagenarian ˌkwɪŋk wə dʒə 'neər i_ən ◂
  ˌ·wɪ-, ˌ· -dʒɪ- ‖ -'ner- -'nær- **~s** z
Quinquagesima ˌkwɪŋk wə 'dʒes ɪm ə ◂ ˌ·wɪ-,
  -əm ə
quinque- comb. form
  with stress-neutral suffix ˌkwɪŋk wɪ §-wə
  — **quinquepartite** ˌkwɪŋk wɪ 'pɑːt aɪt ◂
  §-wə- ‖ -'pɑːrt-
quinquenni|al kwɪŋ 'kwen i_|əl kwɪn- **~a** ə
  ~ally əl_i **~um** əm
quinquevalent ˌkwɪŋk wɪ 'veɪl ənt ◂ §-wə-;
  kwɪn 'kwev əl-, →kwɪŋ-
quinsy 'kwɪnz i
quint kwɪnt kɪnt **quints** kwɪn̩ts kɪn̩ts
quintain 'kwɪnt ən -ɪn ‖ -ᵊn **~s** z
quintal 'kwɪnt ᵊl ‖ -s z
quintan 'kwɪnt ən ‖ -ᵊn **~s** z
quintessence kwɪn 'tes ᵊn̩ts
quintessential ˌkwɪnt ɪ 'sen̩tʃ ᵊl ◂ -ə-
  ‖ ˌkwɪnt̬ ə- **~ly** i
quintet, quintette ₍ᵢ₎kwɪn 'tet **~s** s
quintic 'kwɪnt ɪk ‖ 'kwɪnt̬ ɪk
quintile 'kwɪnt aɪᵊl **~s** z
Quintilian kwɪn 'tɪl i_ən
quintillion kwɪn 'tɪl jən -i_ən **~s** z
Quintin 'kwɪnt ɪn §-ən ‖ -ᵊn
Quinton 'kwɪnt ən ‖ -ᵊn
quintupl|e 'kwɪnt jʊp ᵊl -əp-; kwɪn 'tjuːp-
  ‖ kwɪn 'tuːp ᵊl -'tjuːp-, -'tʌp-; 'kwɪnt̬ əp- **~ed**
  d **~es** z **~ing** ɪŋ
quintuplet 'kwɪnt jʊp lət -əp-, -lɪt, -let;
  kwɪn 'tjuːp-, §-'tʌp- ‖ kwɪn 'tʌp lət -'tuːp-,
  -'tjuːp-; 'kwɪnt̬ əp- **~s** s
Quintus 'kwɪnt əs ‖ 'kwɪnt̬ əs
quinze kænz —Fr [kɛ̃ːz]
quip kwɪp **quipped** kwɪpt **quipping** 'kwɪpɪŋ
  quips kwɪps
quipster 'kwɪps tə ‖ -tᵊr **~s** z
quipu 'kiːp uː 'kwɪp-
quire 'kwaɪ_ə ‖ 'kwaɪ_ᵊr (= choir) **quires**
  'kwaɪ_əz ‖ 'kwaɪ_ᵊrz
Quirinal 'kwɪr ɪn ᵊl -ən-
Quirinus kwɪ 'raɪn əs kwə-

quirk kwɜːk ‖ kwɜːk **quirks** ˈkwɜːks ‖ kwɜːks
Quirk, Quirke kwɜːk ‖ kwɜːk
quirk|y ˈkwɜːk |i ‖ ˈkwɜːk |i **~ier** i‿ə ‖ i‿ᵊr
   ~iest i‿ɪst i‿əst **~ily** ɪ li əl i **~iness** i nəs i nɪs
quirt kwɜːt ‖ kwɜːt **quirts** kwɜːts ‖ kwɜːts
quisling ˈkwɪz lɪŋ **~s** z
quit kwɪt **quits** kwɪts **quitted** ˈkwɪt ɪd -əd
   ‖ ˈkwɪt̬ əd **quitting** ˈkwɪt ɪŋ ‖ ˈkwɪt̬ ɪŋ
quitch kwɪtʃ
quite kwaɪt
Quito ˈkiːt əʊ ‖ -oʊ —*Sp* [ˈki to]
quitrent ˈkwɪt rent
quits kwɪts
quittanc|e ˈkwɪt ᵊn⁔s **~es** ɪz əz
quitter ˈkwɪt ə ‖ ˈkwɪt̬ ᵊr **~s** z
quittor ˈkwɪt ə ‖ ˈkwɪt̬ ᵊr
quiver ˈkwɪv ə ‖ -ᵊr **~ed** d **quivering/ly**
   ˈkwɪv ər‿ɪŋ /li **~s** z
quiverful ˈkwɪv ə fʊl ‖ -ᵊr- **~s** z
qui vive ˌkiː ˈviːv
Quix *tdmk* kwɪks
Quixote ˈkwɪks ət -əʊt; kɪ ˈhəʊt i ‖ kiː ˈhoʊt i
   —*Sp* [ki ˈxo te]
quixotic kwɪk ˈsɒt ɪk ‖ -ˈsɑːt̬ ɪk **~al** ᵊl **~ally**
   ᵊl‿i
quixotism ˈkwɪks ə ˌtɪz əm
quiz kwɪz **quizzed** kwɪzd **quizzes** ˈkwɪz ɪz -əz
   quizzing ˈkwɪz ɪŋ
quizmaster ˈkwɪz ˌmɑːst ə §-ˌmæst-
   ‖ -ˌmæst ᵊr **~s** z
quizzical ˈkwɪz ɪk ᵊl **~ly** ‿i
quo kwəʊ ‖ kwoʊ
   ˌquo ˈvadis ˈvɑːd ɪs ˈwɑːd-, §-əs
quod kwɒd ‖ kwɑːd
quodlibet ˈkwɒd lɪ bet -lə- ‖ ˈkwɑːd- **~s** s

quoin kɔɪn kwɔɪn **quoined** kɔɪnd kwɔɪnd
   quoining ˈkɔɪn ɪŋ ˈkwɔɪn- **quoins** kɔɪnz
   kwɔɪnz
quoit kɔɪt kwɔɪt **quoits** kɔɪts kwɔɪts
quokka ˈkwɒk ə ‖ ˈkwɑːk ə **~s** z
quoll kwɒl ‖ kwɑːl **quolls** kwɒlz ‖ kwɑːlz
quondam ˈkwɒnd æm -əm ‖ ˈkwɑːnd-
Quonset *tdmk* ˈkwɒn⁔s ɪt -ət, -et ‖ ˈkwɑːn⁔s ət
   ˈkwɑːnz-
   ˈQuonset hut
quorate ˈkwɔːr eɪt -ət, -ɪt ‖ ˈkwoʊr-
Quorn kwɔːn ‖ kwɔːrn
quorum ˈkwɔːr əm ‖ ˈkwoʊr- **~s** z
Quosh *tdmk* ˈkwɒʃ ‖ kwɑːʃ
quota ˈkwəʊt ə §ˈkəʊt- ‖ ˈkwoʊt̬ ə **~s** z
quotability ˌkwəʊt ə ˈbɪl ət i §ˌkəʊt-, -ɪt i
   ‖ ˌkwoʊt̬ ə ˈbɪl ət̬ i ˌkoʊt̬-
quotab|le ˈkwəʊt əb |ᵊl §ˈkəʊt- ‖ ˈkwoʊt̬-
   ˈkoʊt̬- **~ly** li
quotation kwəʊ ˈteɪʃ ᵊn kwə-, §kəʊ- ‖ kwoʊ-
   koʊ- **~s** z
   quoˈtation mark
quote kwəʊt §kəʊt ‖ kwoʊt koʊt **quoted**
   ˈkwəʊt ɪd §ˈkəʊt- ‖ ˈkwoʊt̬ əd ˈkoʊt̬- **quotes**
   kwəʊts §kəʊts ‖ kwoʊts koʊts **quoting**
   ˈkwəʊt ɪŋ §ˈkəʊt- ‖ ˈkwoʊt̬ ɪŋ ˈkoʊt̬-
quoth kwəʊθ §kəʊθ ‖ kwoʊθ
quotha ˈkwəʊθ ə §ˈkəʊθ- ‖ ˈkwoʊθ ə
quotidian kwəʊ ˈtɪd i ən kwɒ-, §kəʊ- ‖ kwoʊ-
quotient ˈkwəʊʃ ᵊnt §ˈkəʊʃ- ‖ ˈkwoʊʃ ᵊnt **~s** s
Qur'an, Quran kɔː ˈrɑːn kə-, kɒ-, -ˈræn
   ‖ kə ˈrɑːn -ˈræn; kuᵊr ˈɑːn, -ˈæn —*Arabic*
   [qur ˈʔɑːn]
Quy kwaɪ
q.v. ˌkjuː ˈviː
Qwaqwa ˈkwɑːk wə
qwerty, QWERTY ˈkwɜːt i ‖ ˈkwɜːt̬ i ˈkwert̬-

Q

Rr

r Spelling-to-sound

1   Where the spelling is **r**, the pronunciation is regularly r as in **run** rʌn.

2   Where the spelling is double **rr**, the pronunciation is again regularly r as in **merry** ˈmer i.

3   When the spelling is **r** followed by a consonant letter or a silent **e**, or when **r** is at the end of a word, then the pronunciation differs in different varieties of English:

   • In RP, the **r** is silent. The same applies to most varieties of English English, to Australian English, and to the other 'non-rhotic' accents. In connected speech, however, r may be pronounced at the end of a word if the next word begins with a vowel sound (see R-LIAISON).

   • In GenAm, the pronunciation is r. The same applies to Scottish English, to Irish English, and to the other 'rhotic' accents. In GenAm, the r coalesces with a preceding ɜ vowel to give ɜː.

   • Examples:

	RP	GenAm
farm	fɑːm	fɑːrm
more	mɔː	mɔːr
stir	stɜː	stɜː
murder	ˈmɜːd ə	ˈmɜːd ər

4   In the middle or at the end of a word, **r** frequently affects the preceding vowel. Consequently **ar**, **er**, **ir**, **or**, **ur**, **yr** could be regarded as digraphs, and **air**, **are**, **ear**, **eer**, **eir**, **ere**, **eur**, **ier**, **ire**, **oar**, **oor**, **ore**, **our**, **ure** as trigraphs (see individual entries).

5   The sound r may also appear in non-rhotic accents in certain cases where no corresponding letter **r** is written, as when **thawing** is pronounced ˈθɔːr ɪŋ. This is known as 'intrusive r', see R-LIAISON. Note also the exceptional word **colonel** ˈkɜːn əl ‖ ˈkɜːn əl.

6   The exceptional word **iron** is pronounced as if written **iorn**, namely ˈaɪ ən ‖ ˈaɪ ərn.

rh Spelling-to-sound

Where the spelling is the digraph **rh** or its doubled form **rrh**, the pronunciation is regularly the same as that of the letter **r**:

r as in **rhythm** ˈrɪð əm, **rhapsody** ˈræps əd i or
BrE silent, AmE r as in **catarrh** kə ˈtɑː ‖ kə ˈtɑːr.

R-liaison

1 In BrE (RP) and other **non-rhotic** accents, a word in isolation never ends in r. But in connected speech an r may be pronounced in some cases if the next word begins with a vowel sound.

2 This typically happens with a word that ends in one of the following vowels: ə, ɑː, ɔː, ɜː, ɪə, eə, ʊə.

far	fɑː ‖ fɑːr	In isolation, or before a consonant sound, this word is pronounced fɑː. But in a phrase such as **far away, far out** it is usually pronounced fɑːr.
near	nɪə ‖ nɪ^ər	In isolation, the RP form is nɪə. But in a phrase such as **near enough** it is usually pronounced nɪər.

3 Usually, as in the cases just mentioned, the spelling includes **r**. The added r-sound is then known as **linking r**. It corresponds to a historical r, now lost before a consonant or pause. (In **rhotic** accents, such as GenAm, this r is still always present, and is therefore not 'linking'.)

4 In RP, however, as in other non-rhotic accents, the sound r is frequently added even if there is no letter **r** in the spelling. This **intrusive r** does not correspond to historical r, and there is no corresponding r in AmE.

comma	ˈkɒm ə ‖ ˈkɑːm ə	In isolation, the RP form is ˈkɒm ə. But in a phrase such as **put a comma in**, it is often pronounced ˈkɒm ər. (In GenAm it is always ˈkɑːm ə, whatever the environment.)
thaw	θɔː ‖ θɒː	In isolation, RP **thaw** is θɔː. In the phrase **thaw out**, intrusive r may be added, giving θɔːr ˈaʊt. (In GenAm there is no r.)

5 In principle, this dictionary shows the CITATION pronunciation of words. Therefore it does not indicate places where r-liaison is likely across a word boundary. They can be inferred from the rules given above. However, it *does* show r-liaison within a word, both linking and intrusive. Linking r within a word, being obligatory, is shown in ordinary type; intrusive r, being optional (and disapproved of by some) is shown in raised type.

storing ˈstɔːr ɪŋ
thawing ˈθɔː^r ɪŋ

R

R, r ɑː ‖ ɑːr **R's, r's, Rs, rs** ɑːz ‖ ɑːrz
—*Communications code name:* Romeo
RA ˌɑːr ˈeɪ ‖ ˌɑːr-
Ra rɑː
Raasay ˈrɑːs eɪ
Rab ræb
Raban ˈreɪb ən

Rabat rə ˈbɑːt rɑː-, -ˈbæt —*Arabic* [rɑ ˈbɑːtˤ], *Fr* [ʁa ba]
Rabaul rə ˈbaʊl
rabb|et ˈræb |ɪt §-ət ‖ -|ət **~eted** ɪt ɪd §ət-, -əd ‖ əţ əd **~eting** ɪt ɪŋ §ət- ‖ əţ ɪŋ **~ets** ɪts §əts ‖ əts
rabbi ˈræb aɪ **~s** z

Rabbie ˈræb i
rabbinate ˈræb ɪn ət §-ən-, -ɪt; -ɪ neɪt, -ə- **~s** s
rabbinic, R~ rə ˈbɪn ɪk ræ- **~al** ᵊl **~ally** ᵊl‿i
rabbinistic ˌræb ɪ ˈnɪst ɪk ◂ -ə-
rabb|it ˈræb |ɪt §-ət ‖ -|ət **~ited** ɪt ɪd §ət-, -əd ‖ əţ əd **~iting** ɪt ɪŋ §ət- ‖ əţ ɪŋ **~its** ɪts §əts ‖ əts
ˈ**rabbit hutch**; ˈ**rabbit punch**; ˈ**rabbit ˌwarren**
rabbitfish ˈræb ɪt fɪʃ §-ət-
rabble ˈræb ᵊl **~s** z
rabble-rouser ˈræb ᵊl ˌraʊz ə ‖ -ᵊr **~s** z
rabble-rousing ˈræb ᵊl ˌraʊz ɪŋ
Rabelais ˈræb ə leɪ -ᵊl eɪ ‖ ˌ··ˈ· —*Fr* [ʁa blɛ]
Rabelaisian ˌræb ə ˈleɪz i‿ən ◂ -ˈleɪʒ ᵊn ‖ -ˈleɪʒ ᵊn ◂
rabid ˈræb ɪd ˈreɪb-, §-əd **~ly** li **~ness** nəs nɪs
rabidity rə ˈbɪd ət i -ɪt i ‖ -əţ i
rabies ˈreɪb iːz -iz
rabietic ˌreɪb i ˈet ɪk ◂ ‖ -ˈeţ ɪk ◂
Rabin ˈreɪb ɪn §-ən —*but as an Israeli name,* ræ ˈbiːn ‖ rɑː-
Rabindranath rə ˈbɪndr ə nɑːθ -nɑːt —*Hindi* [rə ʋɪn̪ d̪rə n̪aːtʰ], *Bengali* [ro bin̪ d̪rɔ natʰ]
Rabinowitz rə ˈbɪn ə wɪts ræ-, -vɪts
RAC ˌɑːr eɪ ˈsiː
Racal *tdmk* ˈreɪk ɔːl -ᵊl ‖ -ɑːl
raccoon rə ˈkuːn ræ- ‖ ræ- **~s** z
race reɪs **raced** reɪst **races** ˈreɪs ɪz -əz **racing** ˈreɪs ɪŋ
ˈ**race card**; ˈ**race ˌmeeting**; ˌ**race reˈlations**; ˈ**race ˌriot**
racecours|e ˈreɪs kɔːs ‖ -kɔːrs -koʊrs **~es** ɪz əz
racegoer ˈreɪs ˌgəʊ ə ‖ -ˌgoʊ ᵊr **~s** z
racehors|e ˈreɪs hɔːs ‖ -hɔːrs **~es** ɪz əz
raceme ˈræs iːm ˈreɪs-; ræ ˈsiːm, rə- ‖ reɪ ˈsiːm rə- **~s** z
racemic rə ˈsiːm ɪk ræ-, reɪ-, -ˈsem-
racer ˈreɪs ə ‖ -ᵊr **~s** z
racetrack ˈreɪs træk **~s** s **~s** z
raceway ˈreɪs weɪ
Rachael, Rachel ˈreɪtʃ əl —*but as a French name,* ræ ˈʃel —*Fr* [ʁa ʃɛl]
Rachelle rə ˈʃel ˈreɪtʃ əl
rachis ˈreɪk ɪs §-əs
rachitis rə ˈkaɪt ɪs ræ-, §-əs ‖ -ˈkaɪţ əs
Rachman ˈræk mən
Rachmaninoff, Rachmaninov ræk ˈmæn ɪn ɒf ‖ rɑːk ˈmɑːn ə nɔːf -nɑːf —*Russ* [rʌx ˈma nʲɪ nəf]
Rachmanism, r~ ˈræk mən ˌɪz əm
racial ˈreɪʃ ᵊl ˈreɪʃ i‿əl, ˈreɪs i‿əl
racialism ˈreɪʃ ə ˌlɪz əm -ᵊl ˌɪz-; ˈreɪʃ i‿əl ˌɪz əm, ˈreɪs-
racialist ˈreɪʃ əl ɪst ˈreɪʃ i‿əl ɪst, ˈreɪs-, §-əst **~s** s
racially ˈreɪʃ ᵊl i ˈreɪʃ i‿əl i, ˈreɪs-
Racine *French writer* ræ ˈsiːn rə- —*Fr* [ʁa sin]
Racine *place in Wisconsin* rə ˈsiːn reɪ-
racism ˈreɪs ˌɪz əm
racist ˈreɪs ɪst ˈreɪʃ-, §-əst **~s** s
rack ræk **racked** rækt **racking** ˈræk ɪŋ **racks** ræks
rack-and-pinion ˌræk ən ˈpɪn jən →-əm-
rack|et ˈræk |ɪt §-ət ‖ -|ət **~eted** ɪt ɪd §ət-, -əd ‖ əţ əd **~eting** ɪt ɪŋ §ət- ‖ əţ ɪŋ **~ets** ɪts §əts ‖ əts
racketball ˈræk ɪt bɔːl §-ət- ‖ -bɑːl
racke|teer ˌræk ə |ˈtɪə -ɪ- ‖ -|ˈtɪᵊr **~teered** ˈtɪəd ‖ ˈtɪᵊrd **~teering** ˈtɪər ɪŋ ‖ ˈtɪr ɪŋ **~teers** ˈtɪəz ‖ ˈtɪᵊrz
rackety ˈræk ət i -ɪt- ‖ -əţ i
Rackham ˈræk əm
rack-rail ˈræk reɪᵊl
rack-|rent ˈræk |rent **~ rented** rent ɪd -əd ‖ renţ əd **~renter/s** rent ə/z ‖ renţ ᵊr/z **~renting** rent ɪŋ ‖ renţ ɪŋ **~rents** rents
raclette ræ ˈklet —*Fr* [ʁa klɛt]
raconteur ˌræk ɒn ˈtɜː ‖ -ɑːn ˈtɜː -ən- —*Fr* [ʁa kɔ̃ tœːʁ] **~s** z
racoon rə ˈkuːn ræ- ‖ ræ- **~s** z
racquet ˈræk ɪt §-ət **~s** s
racquetball ˈræk ɪt bɔːl -ət- ‖ -bɑːl
rac|y ˈreɪs |i **~ier** i‿ə ‖ i‿ᵊr **~iest** i‿ɪst i‿əst **~ily** ɪ li əl i **~iness** i nəs i nɪs
rad ræd **rads** rædz
RADA ˈrɑːd ə
radar ˈreɪd ɑː ‖ -ɑːr **~s** z
Radbourne ˈræd bɔːn →ˈræb- ‖ -bɔːrn -boʊrn
Radburn ˈræd bɜːn →ˈræb- ‖ -bɜːn
Radcliff, Radcliffe, Radclyffe ˈræd klɪf →ˈræg-
raddle ˈræd ᵊl **~d** d
Radetzky rə ˈdet ski ræ- ‖ rɑː- —*Ger* [ʁa ˈdɛts ki]
Radford ˈræd fəd ‖ -fᵊrd
radial ˈreɪd i‿əl **~ly** i **~s** z
ˌ**radial ˈtyre**
radial-ply ˌreɪd i‿əl ˈplaɪ ◂ ˈ····
radian ˈreɪd i‿ən **~s** z
radiance ˈreɪd i‿ənᵗs
radiant ˈreɪd i‿ənt **~ly** li **~s** s
radi|ate ˈreɪd i |eɪt **~ated** eɪt ɪd -əd ‖ eɪţ əd **~ates** eɪts **~ating** eɪt ɪŋ ‖ eɪţ ɪŋ
radiation ˌreɪd i ˈeɪʃ ᵊn **~s** z
ˌ**radiˈation ˌsickness**
radiator ˈreɪd i eɪt ə ‖ -eɪţ ᵊr **~s** z
radical ˈræd ɪk ᵊl **~s** z
radicalis... —*see* **radicaliz...**
radicalism ˈræd ɪk ᵊl ˌɪz əm
radicaliz|e ˈræd ɪk ə laɪz **~ed** d **~es** ɪz əz **~ing** ɪŋ
radically ˈræd ɪk ᵊl‿i
radicand ˈræd ɪ kænd -ə- **~s** z
radicchio rə ˈdɪk i əʊ ræ-, -ˈdiːtʃ- ‖ rə ˈdiːk i‿oʊ rɑː- —*It* [ra ˈdik kjo]
Radice rə ˈdiːtʃ i -eɪ
radices ˈreɪd ɪ siːz ˈræd-, §-ə-
radicle ˈræd ɪk ᵊl *(= radical)* **~s** z
radii ˈreɪd i aɪ
radio ˈreɪd i əʊ ‖ -oʊ **~ed** d **~ing** ɪŋ **~s** z
ˌ**radio aˈlarm**, ˈ··· ·ˌ·; ˌ**radio aˈstronomy**, ˈ··· ·ˌ··· ; ˈ**radio ˌbeacon**; ˈ**radio car**; ˈ**radio ˌfrequency**; ˌ**radio ˈtelescope**; ˈ**radio wave**
radio- *comb. form*
with stress-neutral suffix ¦reɪd i əʊ ‖ -oʊ

— **radionuclide** ˌreɪd i əʊ 'nju:k laɪd
§-'nu:k- ‖ -oʊ 'nu:k- -'nju:k-
with stress-imposing suffix ˌreɪd i 'ɒ+ ‖ -'ɑ:+
— **radioscopy** ˌreɪd i 'ɒsk əp i ‖ -'ɑ:sk-
radioactive ˌreɪd i ̩əʊ 'ækt ɪv ◂ ‖ ˌ· ·oʊ- ~**ly** li
ˌradio ˌactive de'cay
radioactivity ˌreɪd i ̩əʊ æk 'tɪv ət i -ɪt i
‖ -oʊ æk 'tɪv ət̬ i
radiocarbon ˌreɪd i əʊ 'kɑ:b ən ◂
‖ -oʊ 'kɑ:rb ən ◂
ˌradio ˌcarbon 'dating
radio-cassette ˌreɪd i ̩əʊ kə 'set -kæ'· ‖ -i oʊ-
radio-controlled ˌreɪd i ̩əʊ kən 'trəʊld ◂
§-kɒn'·, →-'trʊʊld ◂ ‖ -oʊ kən 'troʊld ◂
radiogram 'reɪd i ̩əʊ græm ‖ -i ̩oʊ- ~**s** z
radiograph 'reɪd i ̩əʊ grɑːf -græf ‖ -oʊ græf ~**s**
s
radiographer ˌreɪd i 'ɒg rəf ə ‖ -'ɑ:g rəf ər ~**s**
z
radiographic ˌreɪd i ̩əʊ 'græf ɪk ◂ ‖ -i ̩ə- ~**ally**
əl i
radiography ˌreɪd i 'ɒg rəf i ‖ -'ɑ:g-
Radiohead 'reɪd i ̩əʊ hed ‖ -i oʊ-
radioisotope ˌreɪd i ̩əʊ 'aɪs əʊ təʊp
‖ -oʊ 'aɪs ə toʊp ~**s** s
radiolarian ˌreɪd i əʊ 'leər i ̩ən ‖ -oʊ 'ler-
-'lær- ~**s** z
radiolocation ˌreɪd i ̩əʊ ləʊ 'keɪʃ ən
‖ -i ̩oʊ loʊ-
radiological ˌreɪd i ̩əʊ 'lɒdʒ ɪk əl ◂ ‖ -ə 'lɑ:dʒ-
~**ly** i
radiologist ˌreɪd i 'ɒl ədʒ ɪst §-əst ‖ -'ɑ:l- ~**s** s
radiology ˌreɪd i 'ɒl ədʒ i ‖ -'ɑ:l-
radionic ˌreɪd i 'ɒn ɪk ◂ ‖ -'ɑ:n- ~**s** s
radiopag|e ˌreɪd i əʊ 'peɪdʒ ‖ -i oʊ- ~**ed** d
~**er/s** ə/z ‖ -ər/z ~**es** ɪz əz ~**ing** ɪŋ
radiopaque ˌreɪd i əʊ 'peɪk ◂ ‖ -i oʊ-
radiophonic ˌreɪd i ̩əʊ 'fɒn ɪk ◂
‖ -oʊ 'fɑ:n ɪk ◂
radioscopy ˌreɪd i 'ɒsk əp i ‖ -'ɑ:sk-
radiosonde 'reɪd i əʊ sɒnd ‖ -oʊ sɑ:nd ~**s** z
radiotherapist ˌreɪd i ̩əʊ 'θer əp ɪst §-əst
‖ ˌ· ·oʊ- ~**s** s
radiotherapy ˌreɪd i ̩əʊ 'θer əp i ‖ ˌ· ·oʊ-
radish 'ræd ɪʃ ~**es** ɪz əz
radium 'reɪd i əm
radi|us 'reɪd i ̩|əs ~**i** aɪ ~**uses** əs ɪz -əz
radix 'reɪd ɪks **radices** 'reɪd i si:z 'ræd-, §-ə-
radixes 'reɪd ɪks ɪz -əz
Radlett 'ræd lət -lɪt
Radley 'ræd li
Radnor 'ræd nə ‖ -nər -nɔːr ~**shire** ʃə ʃɪə ‖ ʃər
ʃɪr
radome 'reɪd əʊm ‖ -oʊm ~**s** z
radon 'reɪd ɒn ‖ -ɑːn
Radovan 'ræd ə væn ‖ 'rɑːd ə vɑːn —*Serbian*
['ra do van]
Radox *tdmk* 'reɪd ɒks ‖ -ɑːks
radula 'ræd jʊl ə §'rædʒ əl- ‖ 'rædʒ əl ə
radulae 'ræd ju li: §'rædʒ ə- ‖ 'rædʒ ə li:
radwaste 'ræd weɪst
Rae reɪ
Raeburn 'reɪ bɜːn ‖ -bɜːn

Rael-Brook *tdmk* ˌreɪəl 'brʊk
Raelene 'reɪ li:n
RAF ˌɑːr eɪ 'ef —*also, informally,* ræf
Rafe reɪf
Rafferty, r~ 'ræf ət i ‖ -ərt̬ i
raffia 'ræf i ə
raffinose 'ræf ɪ nəʊz -ə-, -nəʊs ‖ -noʊs
raffish 'ræf ɪʃ ~**ly** li ~**ness** nəs nɪs
raffl|e 'ræf əl ~**ed** d ~**es** z ~**ing** ɪŋ
Raffles 'ræf əlz
rafflesia ræ 'fli:z i ə -'fli:ʒ- ‖ rə 'fli:ʒ ə ræ- ~**s**
z
Rafsanjani ˌræf sæn 'dʒɑːn i -sɑːn- ‖ ˌrɑːf sən-
ˌrʌf-, -sɑːn- —*Farsi* [ræf sæn dʒɑ 'ni:]
raft, Raft rɑːft §ræft ‖ ræft **rafted** rɑːft ɪd
§'ræft-, -əd ‖ 'ræft əd **rafting** 'rɑːft ɪŋ §'ræft-
‖ 'ræft ɪŋ **rafts** rɑːfts §ræfts ‖ ræfts
rafter 'rɑːft ə §'ræft- ‖ 'ræft ər ~**s** z
rafts|man 'rɑːfts |mən §'ræfts- ‖ 'ræfts- ~**men**
mən -men
rag ræg **ragged** *past & pp* rægd **ragging**
'ræg ɪŋ **rags** rægz
ˌrag 'doll ‖ '· ·; 'rag trade
raga 'rɑːg ə rɑːg ~**s** z
ragamuffin 'ræg ə ˌmʌf ɪn §-ən ~**s** z
rag-and-bone |man ˌræg ən 'bəʊn |mæn
-ənd-, →-əm-, →-'bəʊm- ‖ -'boʊn- ~**men**
men
ragbag 'ræg bæg ~**s** z
rage reɪdʒ **raged** reɪdʒd **rages** 'reɪdʒ ɪz -əz
raging 'reɪdʒ ɪŋ
ragg... —*see* **rag**
ragga 'ræg ə
ragged *adj* 'ræg ɪd -əd ~**ly** li ~**ness** nəs nɪs
ˌragged 'robin
raggedy 'ræg əd i -ɪd-
raggle-taggle ˌræg əl 'tæg əl ◂ '·· ˌ··
ragi... —*see* **rage**
raglan, R~ 'ræg lən ~**s** z
Rag|man, r~ 'ræg |mən ~**men** men mən
ragout ræ 'gu: 'ræg u: ~**s** z
ragpicker 'ræg ˌpɪk ə ‖ -ər ~**s** z
ragstone 'ræg stəʊn ‖ -stoʊn
rags-to-riches ˌrægz tə 'rɪtʃ ɪz -əz
ragtag 'ræg tæg
ragtime 'ræg taɪm
ragtop 'ræg tɒp ‖ -tɑːp ~**s** s
Ragu *tdmk* ræ 'gu: 'ræg u:
ragweed 'ræg wiːd
ragworm 'ræg wɜːm ‖ -wɜːm ~**s** z
ragwort 'ræg wɜːt §-wɔːt ‖ -wɜːt -wɔːrt ~**s** s
rah rɑː
rah-rah ˌrɑː rɑː ‖ ˌrɔː rɔː
Rahway *place in NJ* 'rɔː weɪ 'rɑː-
raid reɪd **raided** 'reɪd ɪd -əd **raiding** 'reɪd ɪŋ
raids reɪdz
raider 'reɪd ə ‖ -ər ~**s** z
Raif reɪf
Raikes reɪks
rail reɪəl **railed** reɪəld **railing** 'reɪəl ɪŋ **rails**
reɪəlz
'rail ˌticket
railcar 'reɪəl kɑː ‖ -kɑːr ~**s** z

R

railcard 'reɪᵊl kɑːd ‖ -kɑːrd ~s z
railhead 'reɪᵊl hed ~s z
railing 'reɪl ɪŋ ~s z
railler|y 'reɪl ər |i ~ies iz
railroad 'reɪᵊl rəʊd ‖ -roʊd ~ed ɪd əd ~ing ɪŋ ~s z
Railton 'reɪᵊlt ən
Railtrack *tdmk* 'reɪᵊl træk
railway 'reɪᵊl weɪ ~s z
　'railway ˌstation; 'railway train
railway|man 'reɪᵊl weɪ |mən -wi- ~men mən men
raiment 'reɪm ənt
rain reɪn **rained** reɪnd **raining** 'reɪn ɪŋ **rains** reɪnz
　'rain check; 'rain ˌforest; 'rain gauge
Raina *(i)* raɪ 'iːn ə, *(ii)* 'reɪn ə
rainbird 'reɪn bɜːd ‖ -bɜːd ~s z
rainbow, R~ 'reɪn bəʊ →'reɪm- ‖ -boʊ ~s z
raincoat 'reɪn kəʊt →'reɪn- ‖ -koʊt ~s s
raindrop 'reɪn drɒp ‖ -drɑːp ~s s
Raine reɪn
rainfall 'reɪn fɔːl ‖ -fɑːl
Rainford 'reɪn fəd ‖ -fᵊrd
Rainhill ˌreɪn 'hɪl
Rainier *Mount* 'reɪn i ə rə 'nɪə, reɪ- ‖ rə 'nɪᵊr reɪ-; 'reɪn ɪr
Rainier *prince of Monaco* 'reɪn i eɪ ‖ rə 'nɪᵊr reɪ-; ren 'jeɪ —*Fr* [ʁɛ nje]
rainless 'reɪn ləs -lɪs
rainmaker 'reɪn ˌmeɪk ə →'reɪm- ‖ -ᵊr ~s z
rainproof 'reɪn pruːf →'reɪm-, §-prʊf ~ed t ~ing ɪŋ ~s s
rainstorm 'reɪn stɔːm ‖ -stɔːrm ~s z
rainwater 'reɪn ˌwɔːt ə ‖ -ˌwɔːt̬ ᵊr -ˌwɑːt̬-
rainwear 'reɪn weə ‖ -wer -wær
rain|y 'reɪn |i ~ier i ə ‖ i ᵊr ~iest i ɪst i əst ~ily ɪ li əl i ~iness i nəs i nɪs
Raisa raɪ 'iːs ə rɑː- ‖ rɑː- —*Russ* [rʌ 'i sə]
raise reɪz **raised** reɪzd **raises** 'reɪz ɪz -əz **raising** 'reɪz ɪŋ
raiser 'reɪz ə ‖ -ᵊr ~s z
raisin 'reɪz ᵊn ~s z
Raison 'reɪz ᵊn
raison d'etre, raison d'être ˌreɪz ɔ̃ 'detr ə -ɒn- ‖ -oʊn- —*Fr* [ʁɛ zɔ̃ dɛtʁ]
Raistrick 'reɪs trɪk
raita 'raɪt ə -ɑː
raj rɑːdʒ rɑːʒ —*There is no justification in Hindi for the pronunciation* rɑːʒ *often heard in English.* —*Hindi* [rɑːdʒ]
raja, rajah 'rɑːdʒ ə ~s z
Rajasthan ˌrɑːdʒ ə 'stɑːn
Rajasthani ˌrɑːdʒ ə 'stɑːn i ◂
Rajneesh ˌrɑːdʒ 'niːʃ
Rajpoot, Rajput 'rɑːdʒ pʊt ~s s —*Hindi* [rɑːdʒ puːt̪]
Rajputana ˌrɑːdʒ pʊ 'tɑːn ə
rake reɪk **raked** reɪkt **rakes** reɪks **raking** 'reɪk ɪŋ
rake-off 'reɪk ɒf ‖ -ɔːf -ɑːf ~s s
raki 'rɑːk i 'ræk-; rɑː 'kiː
rakish 'reɪk ɪʃ ~ly li ~ness nəs nɪs

rale, râle rɑːl ræl **rales, râles** rɑːlz rælz
Ralegh, Raleigh *(i)* 'rɑːl i, *(ii)* 'rɔːl i ‖ 'rɑːl i, *(iii)* 'ræl i —*Sir Walter R~ was probably (ii), as is the place in NC; R~ bicycles are (ii) in AmE, (iii) in BrE.*
Ralf *(i)* rælf, *(ii)* reɪf
rallentando ˌræl ən 'tænd əʊ -en- ‖ ˌrɑːl ən 'tɑːnd oʊ *(*)* —*It* [ral len 'tan do] ~s z
rall|y 'ræl |i ~ied id ~ies iz ~ying i ɪŋ
rallycross 'ræl i krɒs -krɔːs ‖ -krɔːs -krɑːs
Ralph *(i)* rælf, *(ii)* reɪf —*In AmE, (i).*
Ralston 'rɔːlst ən 'rɒlst- ‖ 'rɑːlst-
ram, Ram, RAM ræm **rammed** ræmd **ramming** 'ræm ɪŋ **rams** ræmz
Rama 'rɑːm ə
Ramachandra ˌrɑːm ə 'tʃʌndr ə -'tʃændr-
ramada, R~ *tdmk* rə 'mɑːd ə ~s z
Ramadan ˌræm ə 'dɑːn ˌrɑːm-, ˌrʌm-, -'dæn, '...
Ramadge, Ramage 'ræm ɪdʒ
Ramakrishna ˌrɑːm ə 'krɪʃ nə
Raman 'rɑːm ən
Ramayana rə 'maɪ ən ə -'mɑː jən- —*Hindi* [raː ma: jən]
Rambert 'rɒm beə 'rɒ̃- ‖ rɑːm 'beᵊr
rambl|e 'ræm bᵊl ~ed d ~es z ~ing ɪŋ
rambler 'ræm blə ‖ -blᵊr ~s z
rambling *adj, n* 'ræm blɪŋ ~ly li ~s z
Rambo 'ræm bəʊ ‖ -boʊ
Ramboesque ˌræm bəʊ 'esk ◂ ‖ -boʊ-
Rambouillet rɒm 'buː jeɪ ræm-, -leɪ; '... ‖ ˌrɑːm bu 'jeɪ ˌræm-, -'leɪ —*Fr* [ʁɑ̃ bu jɛ]
rambunctious ræm 'bʌŋk ʃəs ~ly li ~ness nəs nɪs
rambutan ræm 'buːt ᵊn ˌræm bu 'tæn, -'tɑːn ~s z
Rameau 'rɑːm əʊ 'ræm- ‖ ræ 'moʊ rɑː- —*Fr* [ʁa mo]
ramekin 'ræm ɪ kɪn -ə-, 'ræm kɪn, §-kən ~s z
Ramelson 'ræm ᵊl sən
ramen 'rɑːm en -ən —*Jp* ['raa meɴ]
Rameses 'ræm ɪ siːz -ə-
ramie 'ræm i 'rɑːm-
ramification ˌræm ɪf ɪ 'keɪʃ ᵊn ˌ·əf-, §-ə'·- ~s z
rami|fy 'ræm ɪ |faɪ -ə- ~fied faɪd ~fies faɪz ~fying faɪ ɪŋ
Ramillies 'ræm ɪl iz -əl- —*Fr* [ʁa mi ji]
Ramirez, Ramírez rə 'mɪər ez ‖ -'mɪr- —*Sp* [rra 'mi reθ, -res]
ramjet 'ræm dʒet ~s s
rammer 'ræm ə ‖ -ᵊr ~s z
rammish 'ræm ɪʃ ~ly li ~ness nəs nɪs
Ramon, Ramón rə 'mɒn ræ- ‖ -'moʊn —*Sp* [rra 'mon]
Ramona rə 'məʊn ə ræ- ‖ -'moʊn ə
Ramos 'rɑːm ɒs ‖ rɑː 'moʊs 'reɪm oʊs —*Sp* ['rra mos], *Port* ['ʁʁɐ muʃ, -mus]
ramose 'reɪm əʊs -əʊz; ræ 'məʊs ‖ -oʊs
ramp ræmp **ramped** ræmpt **ramping** 'ræmp ɪŋ **ramps** ræmps
rampag|e *n* 'ræmp eɪdʒ ræm 'peɪdʒ ~es ɪz əz

rampag|e *v* ræm 'peɪdʒ 'ræmp eɪdʒ **~ed** d **~es**
ɪz əz **~ing** ɪŋ
rampageous ræm 'peɪdʒ əs **~ly** li **~ness** nəs
nɪs
rampant 'ræmp ənt **~ly** li
rampart 'ræmp ɑːt -ət ‖ -ɑːrt -ᵊrt **~s** s
rampion 'ræmp i‿ən **~s** z
Ramprakash 'ræm prə kæʃ
Rampton 'ræmpt ən
ram-raid 'ræm reɪd **~ed** ɪd əd **~er/s** ə/z ‖ ᵊr/z
~ing ɪŋ **~s** z
ramrod 'ræm rɒd ‖ -rɑːd **~s** z
Ramsaran 'rɑːmᵖs ər ən
Ramsay 'ræmz i
Ramsbotham 'ræmz ˌbɒθ əm -ˌbɒt- ‖ -ˌbɑː θ-
Ramsbottom 'ræmz ˌbɒt əm -ˌbɑːt̬-
Ramsden 'ræmz dən
Ramses 'ræm siːz
Ramsey 'ræmz i
Ramsgate 'ræmz geɪt -gɪt
ramshackle 'ræm ˌʃæk ᵊl
ramshorn 'ræmz hɔːn ‖ -hɔːrn
ramson 'ræmz ən 'ræmᵖs- **~s** z
ram|us 'reɪm |əs **~i** aɪ
ran ræn
Ranby 'ræn bi →'ræm-
Rance ræn's rɑːn's ‖ ræn's
ranch rɑːntʃ §ræntʃ ‖ ræntʃ **ranched** rɑːntʃt
§ræntʃt ‖ ræntʃt **ranches** 'rɑːntʃ ɪz §'ræntʃ-,
-əz ‖ 'ræntʃ əz **ranching** 'rɑːntʃ ɪŋ §'ræntʃ-
‖ 'ræntʃ ɪŋ
'ranch house
rancher 'rɑːntʃ ə §'ræntʃ- ‖ 'ræntʃ ᵊr **~s** z
ranchero rɑːn 'tʃeər əʊ ræn- ‖ -'tʃer oʊ **~s** z
rancho, R~ 'rɑːntʃ əʊ §'ræntʃ- ‖ -oʊ **~s** z
rancid 'ræn's ɪd §-əd **~ness** nəs nɪs
rancidity ræn 'sɪd ət i -ɪt- ‖ -ət̬ i
rancor 'ræŋk ə ‖ -ᵊr
rancorous 'ræŋk ər əs **~ly** li **~ness** nəs nɪs
rancour 'ræŋk ə ‖ -ᵊr (= *ranker*)
rand, Rand rænd rɑːnt, rɒnt —*Afrikaans*
[rant]
Randal, Randall 'rænd ᵊl
Randalstown 'rænd ᵊlz taʊn
R and B, R & B ˌɑːr ən 'biː →-əm-, -ənd-
‖ ˌɑːr-
R and D, R & D ˌɑːr ən 'diː -ənd- ‖ ˌɑːr-
randi... —*see* **randy**
Randolph 'rænd ɒlf -ᵊlf ‖ -ɑːlf
random 'rænd əm
randomis... —*see* **randomiz...**
randomization ˌrænd əm aɪ 'zeɪʃ ᵊn -əm ɪ-
‖ -əm ə- **~s** z
randomiz|e 'rænd ə maɪz §ˌ·'·· **~ed** d **~es** ɪz
əz **~ing** ɪŋ
random|ly 'rænd əm |li **~ness** nəs nɪs
R and R, R & R ˌɑːr ənd 'ɑː ‖ ˌɑːr ənd 'ɑːr
rand|y, Randy 'rænd |i **~ier** i‿ə ‖ i‿ᵊr **~iest**
i‿ɪst i‿əst **~ily** ɪ li əl i **~iness** i nəs i nɪs
ranee 'rɑːn i ⍩rɑː 'niː **~s** z
Ranelagh 'ræn ɪl ə -əl-, -i; -ə lɔː
Ranfurly 'rænf əl i ræn 'fɜːl i ‖ -ᵊrl i
rang ræŋ

range reɪndʒ **ranged** reɪndʒd **ranges**
'reɪndʒ ɪz -əz **ranging** 'reɪndʒ ɪŋ
'range ˌfinder
ranger, R~ 'reɪndʒ ə ‖ -ᵊr **~s** z
rangi... —*see* **range**
Rangoon ⍩ræŋ 'guːn ‖ ⍩ræn-
rang|y 'reɪndʒ |i **~ier** i‿ə ‖ i‿ᵊr **~iest** i‿ɪst i‿əst
~iness i nəs i nɪs
rani 'rɑːn i ⍩rɑː 'niː **~s** z
ranitidine rə 'nɪt ɪ diːn ræ-, -ə- ‖ -'nɪt̬-
Ranjit 'rʌn dʒɪt 'ræn-
rank, Rank ræŋk —*but as a German name in*
AmE, rɑːŋk **ranked** ræŋkt **ranking** 'ræŋk ɪŋ
ranks ræŋks
ˌrank and 'file
ranker 'ræŋk ə ‖ -ᵊr **~s** z
Rankin, Rankine 'ræŋk ɪn §-ən
rankl|e 'ræŋk ᵊl **~ed** d **~es** z **~ing** ɪŋ
rank|ly 'ræŋk| li **~ness** nəs nɪs
rankshift 'ræŋk ʃɪft **~ed** ɪd əd **~ing** ɪŋ **~s** s
Rannoch 'ræn ək -əx
ransack 'ræn sæk **~ed** t **~er/s** ə/z ‖ ᵊr/z **~ing**
ɪŋ **~s** s
ransom 'ræn's əm **~ed** d **~er/s** ə/z ‖ ᵊr/z **~ing**
ɪŋ **~s** z
Ransom, Ransome 'ræn's əm
rant rænt **ranted** 'rænt ɪd -əd ‖ 'rænt̬ əd
ranting/ly 'rænt ɪŋ /li ‖ 'rænt̬- **rants** rænts
rantings 'rænt ɪŋz ‖ 'rænt̬-
Rantzen 'rænts ᵊn
Ranulph 'ræn ʌlf -ᵊlf
ranunc|ulus rə 'nʌŋk |jʊl əs -jəl- ‖ -|jəl əs
~uli ju laɪ jə- ‖ jə laɪ **~uluses** jʊl əs ɪz jəl-,
-əz ‖ jəl əs əz
Raoul raʊ 'uːl rɑː- ‖ rɑː- —*Fr* [ʁa ul]
rap ræp **rapped** ræpt **rapping** 'ræp ɪŋ **raps**
ræps
rapacious rə 'peɪʃ əs **~ly** li **~ness** nəs nɪs
rapacity rə 'pæs ət i -ɪt- ‖ -ət̬ i
Rapallo rə 'pæl əʊ ‖ -'pɑːl oʊ —*It* [ra 'pal lo]
rape reɪp **raped** reɪpt **rapes** reɪps **raping**
'reɪp ɪŋ
'rape oil
Raper 'reɪp ə ‖ -ᵊr
rapeseed 'reɪp siːd
raphae 'reɪf iː
Raphael 'ræf eɪ əl 'ræf eᵊl, 'ræf i‿əl —*These*
forms may be heard for the angel, the
surname, and the artist (*It* Raffaello
[raf fa 'ɛl lo]). *The angel and surname, though*
not the artist, are further sometimes
pronounced 'reɪf ᵊl, -jəl. *The artist is*
sometimes 'ræf aɪ el ‖ ˌrɑːf aɪ 'el.
raph|e 'reɪf |i -iː **~ae** iː
rapid 'ræp ɪd §-əd **~ly** li **~ness** nəs nɪs **~s** z
ˌrapid 'transit
Rapidan ˌræp ɪ 'dæn -ə-
rapid-fire ˌræp ɪd 'faɪ‿ə ◂ §-əd-
‖ ˌræp əd 'faɪ‿ᵊr ◂
rapidity rə 'pɪd ət i ræ-, -ɪt- ‖ -ət̬ i
rapid-response ˌræp ɪd rɪ 'spɒn's ◂ ˌ-əd-, -rə'·
‖ -'spɑːn's-
rapier 'reɪp i‿ə ‖ -ᵊr **~s** z

rapine 'ræp aɪn -ɪn, §-ən
rapist 'reɪp ɪst §-əst ~s s
Rapoport 'ræp əʊ pɔːt ‖ -ə pɔːrt
Rappahannock ˌræp ə 'hæn ək ◂
rapparee ˌræp ə 'riː ~s z
rappel ræ 'pel rə- ˌ-ed, ~led d ~ing, ~ling ɪŋ
~s z
rapper 'ræp ə ‖ -ᵊr ~s z
rapport ræ 'pɔː rə-; 'ræp ɔː ‖ -'pɔːr -'poʊr —Fr
[ʁa pɔːʁ]
rapporteur ˌræp ɔː 'tɜː ‖ -ɔːr 'tɝː —Fr
[ʁa pɔʁ tœːʁ] ~s z
rapprochement ræ 'prɒʃ mɒ̃ rə-, -'prəʊʃ-,
-mɒ̃ ‖ ˌræp roʊʃ 'maːn —Fr [ʁa pʁɔʃ mɑ̃]
rapscallion ræp 'skæl i ən ~s z
rapt ræpt
raptor 'ræpt ə -ɔː ‖ -ᵊr -ɔːr ~s z
raptorial ræp 'tɔːr i əl ‖ -'toʊr-
rapture 'ræp tʃə ‖ -tʃᵊr ~s z
rapturous 'ræp tʃər əs ~ly li ~ness nəs nɪs
Rapunzel rə 'pʌnz ᵊl
Raquel ræ 'kel rə- ‖ raː- —Sp [rra 'kel]
rara avis ˌreər ə ᵊr 'eɪv ɪs ˌraːr ər ' æv-, -'aːv-,
§-əs; -'ɑː wɪs ‖ ˌrer ə- ˌrær-
rare reə ‖ reᵊr ræᵊr **rarer** 'reər ə ‖ 'rer ᵊr 'rær-
 rarest 'reər ɪst -əst ‖ 'rer əst 'rær-
 ˌrare 'earth, ˌrare 'earth ˌelement
rarebit 'reə bɪt 'ræb ɪt, §-ət ‖ 'rer- 'rær-
rarefaction ˌreər ɪ 'fæk ʃᵊn -ə- ‖ ˌrer- ˌrær-
rare|fy 'reər ɪ |faɪ -ə- ‖ 'rer- 'rær- ~fied faɪd
 ~fies faɪz ~fying faɪ ɪŋ
rarely 'reə li ‖ 'rer li 'rær-
rareness 'reə nəs -nɪs ‖ 'rer- 'rær-
rareripe 'reə raɪp ‖ 'rer- 'rær-
raring 'reər ɪŋ ‖ 'rer ɪŋ 'rær-
Raritan 'rær ɪt ən -ət- ‖ -ət ᵊn
rarit|y 'reər ət |i -ɪt- ‖ 'rer ət |i 'rær- ~ies iz
Rarotonga ˌreər ə 'tɒŋ gə -'tɒŋ ə
 ‖ ˌrær ə 'taːŋ gə ˌrer-, ˌraːr-, -'tɔːŋ-
rasbora ræz 'bɔːr ə ‖ -'boʊr- ~s z
rascal 'raːsk ᵊl §'ræsk- ‖ 'ræsk ᵊl ~s z
rascalit|y raː 'skæl ət |i ræ-, -ɪt-
 ‖ ræ 'skæl ət |i ~ies iz
rascally 'raːsk əl i §'ræsk- ‖ 'ræsk-
rash ræʃ **rasher** 'ræʃ ə ‖ -ᵊr **rashes** 'ræʃ ɪz -əz
 rashest 'ræʃ ɪst -əst
rasher 'ræʃ ə ‖ -ᵊr ~s z
Rashid ræ 'ʃiːd ‖ raː-
rash|ly 'ræʃ |li ~ness nəs nɪs
Rask ræsk —Danish [ʁasg]
Rasmus 'ræz məs
rasp raːsp §ræsp ‖ ræsp **rasped** raːspt §ræspt
 ‖ ræspt **rasping** 'raːsp ɪŋ §'ræsp- ‖ 'ræsp ɪŋ
 rasps raːsps §ræsps ‖ ræsps
raspberr|y, R~ 'raːz bər ˌi 'raːs-, §'ræz-
 ‖ 'ræz ˌber ˌi -bər ˌi (*) ~ies iz
Rasputin ræ 'spjuːt ɪn -'spuː-, §-ᵊn ‖ -ᵊn
 —Russ [rʌ 'spu tʲɪn]
rasp|y 'raːsp| i §'ræsp| i ‖ 'ræsp| i ~ier i ə
 ‖ i ᵊr ~iest i ɪst i əst
Rasta 'ræst ə 'rʌst- ‖ 'raːst- ~s z
Ras Tafari, Rastafari ˌræs tə 'faːr i —in
 Jamaica also -fə 'raɪ

Rastafarian, r~ ˌræst ə 'feər i ən ◂ ˌrʌst-,
 -'faːr- ‖ -'fer- ~ism ˌɪz əm ~s z
Rasta|man 'ræst ə| mæn 'rʌst- ‖ 'raːst- ~men
 men
raster 'ræst ə ‖ -ᵊr ~s z
rasteris|e, rasteriz|e 'ræst ə raɪz ~ed d ~er/s
 ə/z ‖ ᵊr/z ~es ɪz əz ~ing ɪŋ
Rastrick 'ræs trɪk
Rastus 'ræst əs
rat ræt **rats** ræts **ratted** 'ræt ɪd -əd ‖ 'ræt əd
 ratting 'ræt ɪŋ ‖ 'ræt ɪŋ
 'rat race; 'rat run; 'rat trap
rata tree 'raːt ə ‖ 'raːt ə ~s z —see also **pro
 rata**
ratable 'reɪt əb ᵊl ‖ 'reɪt-
ratafia ˌræt ə 'fiə -'fiː ə ‖ ˌræt ə 'fiː ə ~s z
rataplan ˌræt ə 'plæn ‖ ˌræt- ~ned d ~ning ɪŋ
 ~s z
rat-arsed 'ræt aːst ‖ -æst -aːrst
rat-a-tat ˌræt ə 'tæt '·· ‖ ˌræt-
rat-a-tat-tat ˌræt ə ˌtæt 'tæt ‖ ˌræt-
ratatouille ˌræt ə 'twiː -æ-, -'tuː i ‖ ˌræt- —Fr
 [ʁa ta tuj]
ratbag 'ræt bæg ~s z
rat-catcher 'ræt ˌkætʃ ə ‖ -ᵊr ~s z
ratchet 'rætʃ ɪt §-ət ~s s
Ratcliff, Ratcliffe 'ræt klɪf
rate reɪt **rated** 'reɪt ɪd -əd ‖ 'reɪt əd **rates**
 reɪts **rating** 'reɪt ɪŋ ‖ 'reɪt ɪŋ
 ˌrate of ex'change
rateable 'reɪt əb ᵊl ‖ 'reɪt-
 ˌrateable 'value
rate-cap 'reɪt kæp ~ped t ~ping ɪŋ ~s s
ratel 'reɪt ᵊl 'raːt-, -el ‖ 'reɪt ᵊl 'raːt- ~s z
ratepayer 'reɪt ˌpeɪ ə ‖ -ᵊr ~s z
ratfink 'ræt fɪŋk ~s s
Rathbone 'ræθ bəʊn ‖ -boʊn
rathe reɪð
rather 'raːð ə §'ræð- ‖ 'ræð ᵊr —As a BrE
 interjection, 'certainly', also ˌraː 'ðɜː
Rather family name 'ræð ə ‖ -ᵊr
Rathfarnham ræθ 'faːn əm ‖ -'faːrn-
Rathgar ræθ 'gaː ‖ -'gaːr
Rathlin 'ræθ lɪn §-lən
Rathmines ræθ 'maɪnz
ratification ˌræt ɪf ɪ 'keɪʃ ᵊn ˌ-əf-, §-ə'·- ‖ ˌræt-
 ~s z
rati|fy 'ræt ɪ |faɪ -ə- ‖ 'ræt ə |faɪ ~fied faɪd
 ~fier/s faɪ ə/z ‖ faɪ ᵊr/z ~fies faɪz ~fying
 faɪ ɪŋ
rating 'reɪt ɪŋ ‖ 'reɪt ɪŋ ~s z
ratio 'reɪʃ i əʊ ‖ oʊ 'reɪʃ oʊ ~s z
ratioci|nate ˌræt i 'ɒs ɪ |neɪt ˌræʃ-, -'əʊs-,
 -ə neɪt, ᵊn eɪt ‖ ˌræʃ i 'aːs ᵊn eɪt ˌræt-, -'oʊs-
 ~nated neɪt ɪd -əd ‖ neɪt əd ~nates neɪts
 ~nating neɪt ɪŋ ‖ neɪt ɪŋ
ratiocination ˌræt i ˌɒs ɪ 'neɪʃ ᵊn ˌræʃ-, -ˌəʊs-,
 -ə'·- ‖ ˌræʃ i ˌaːs- ˌræt-, -ˌoʊs- ~s z
ration 'ræʃ ᵊn ‖ 'reɪʃ- ~ed d ~ing ˌɪŋ ~s z
rational 'ræʃ ᵊn_əl
rationale ˌræʃ ə 'naːl -'næl; -'naːl eɪ ‖ -'næl ~s
 z
rationalis... —see **rationaliz...**

rationalism 'ræʃ ⁿn_ə ˌlɪz əm -ⁿn̩_əl ˌɪz-
rationalist 'ræʃ ⁿn_əl ɪst §-əst ~s s
rationalistic ˌræʃ ⁿn_ə 'lɪst ɪk ◄ -ally ᵊl_i
rationalit|y ˌræʃ ə 'næl ət |i -ɪt i || -ət |i ~ies
iz
rationalization ˌræʃ ⁿn_əl aɪ 'zeɪʃ ⁿn -əl ɪ-
|| -əl ə- ~s z
rationaliz|e 'ræʃ ⁿn_ə laɪz -ən̩_əl aɪz ~ed d ~es
ɪz əz ~ing ɪŋ
rationally 'ræʃ ⁿn_əl i
Ratisbon 'ræt ɪz bɒn -ɪs-, -əz-, -əs-
|| 'ræt̬ əs bɑːn
ratite 'ræt aɪt ~s s
ratlin, ratline 'ræt lɪn §-lən ~s z
Ratner 'ræt nə || -nᵊr
ratoon rə 'tuːn ræ- ~ed d ~ing ɪŋ ~s z
ratpack 'ræt pæk
Ratskeller 'ræts ˌkel ə || 'rɑːts ˌkel ᵊr —Ger
['ʁaːts ˌkɛl ɐ] ~s z
ratt... —see **rat**
rat-tail 'ræt teiᵊl ~s z
rattan rə 'tæn ræ- ~s z
rat-tat ˌræt 'tæt
rat-tat-tat ˌræt ə 'tæt -æt- || ˌræt̬-
Rattenbury 'ræt ⁿn bər_i || -ˌber i
ratter 'ræt ə || 'ræt̬ ᵊr ~s z
Rattigan 'ræt ɪg ən -əg- || 'ræt̬-
rattl|e, R~ 'ræt ᵊl || 'ræt̬ ᵊl ~ed d ~es z ~ing
ɪŋ
rattle-brained 'ræt ᵊl breɪnd || 'ræt̬-
rattler 'ræt ᵊl_ə || 'ræt ᵊlᵊr 'ræt̬ ᵊl ər ~s z
rattlesnake 'ræt ᵊl sneɪk || 'ræt̬- ~s s
rattletrap 'ræt ᵊl træp || 'ræt̬- ~s s
rattling 'ræt ᵊl_ɪŋ || 'ræt lɪŋ 'ræt̬ ᵊl ɪŋ
rattly 'ræt ᵊl_i || 'ræt̬ li 'ræt̬ ᵊl i
rattoon —see **ratoon**
rat-trap 'ræt træp ~s s
Rattray 'rætr i -eɪ
ratt|y 'ræt |i || 'ræt̬ |i ~ier i_ə || i_ᵊr ~iest i_ɪst
i_əst ~ily ɪ li əl i ~iness i nəs -nɪs
Ratzinger 'ræts ɪŋ ə || -ᵊr
raucous 'rɔːk əs || 'rɑːk- ~ly li ~ness nəs nɪs
Raul raʊ 'uːl rɑː- || rɑː- —Sp [ʁʁa 'ul]
raunch rɔːntʃ || rɑːntʃ
raunch|y 'rɔːntʃ |i || 'rɑːntʃ- ~ier i_ə || i_ᵊr ~iest
i_ɪst i_əst ~ily ɪ li əl i ~iness i nəs i nɪs
Raunds rɔːndz || rɑːndz
Rauschenberg 'raʊʃ ⁿn bɜːg || -bɜːg
rauwolfia rɔː 'wʊlf i_ə raʊ-, -'wɒlf- || rɑː-
ravag|e 'ræv ɪdʒ ~ed d ~es ɪz əz ~ing ɪŋ
rave reɪv **raved** reɪvd **raves** reɪvz **raving**
'reɪv ɪŋ
ravel 'ræv ᵊl ~ed, ~led d ~ing, ~ling ɪŋ ~s z
Ravel ræ 'vel rə- || rɑː- —Fr [ʁa vɛl]
ravelin 'ræv lɪn §-lən ~s z
raven n, adj, **Raven** 'reɪv ⁿn ~s z
raven v 'ræv ⁿn ~ed d ~ing_ɪŋ ~s z
Ravenglass 'reɪv ⁿn glɑːs →-ᵊŋ-, §-glæs
|| -glæs
raven-haired ˌreɪv ⁿn 'heəd ◄ || -'heᵊrd ◄
-'hæᵊrd
ravening 'ræv ⁿn_ɪŋ ~ly li
Ravenna rə 'ven ə —It [ra 'ven na]

ravenous 'ræv ⁿn_əs ~ly li ~ness nəs nɪs
Ravensbourne 'reɪv ⁿnz bɔːn || -bɔːrn -boʊrn
raver 'reɪv ə || -ᵊr ~s z
Raverat 'rɑːv ə rɑː
rave-up 'reɪv ʌp ~s s
Ravilious rə 'vɪl i_əs
ravin 'ræv ɪn §-ⁿn
ravine rə 'viːn ~s z
raving 'reɪv ɪŋ ~ly li ~s z
ravioli ˌræv i 'əʊl i -'oʊl i ˌrɑːv-
ravish 'ræv ɪʃ ~ed t ~es ɪz əz ~ing/ly ɪŋ /li
raw rɔː || rɑː **rawer** 'rɔːʳ ə || 'rɔː ᵊr 'rɑː- **rawest**
'rɔːʳ ɪst -əst || 'rɔː əst 'rɑː-
ˌraw 'deal; ˌraw ma'terials
Rawalpindi ˌrɔːl 'pɪnd i ˌrɑː wəl'-- || ˌrɑː wəl'--
raw-boned ˌrɔː 'bəʊnd ◄ || -'boʊnd ◄ ˌrɑː-
Rawdon 'rɔːd ⁿn || 'rɑːd-
rawhide 'rɔː haɪd || 'rɑː-
Rawle rɔːl || rɑːl
Rawlings 'rɔːl ɪŋz || 'rɑːl-
Rawlins 'rɔːl ɪnz §-ənz || 'rɑːl-
Rawlinson 'rɔːl ɪn's ən §-ən's- || 'rɑːl-
Rawlplug, r~ tdmk 'rɔːl plʌg || 'rɑːl-
raw|ly 'rɔː |li || 'rɑː- ~ness nəs nɪs
Rawmarsh 'rɔː mɑːʃ || -mɑːrʃ 'rɑː-
Rawson 'rɔːs ⁿn || 'rɑːs-
Rawsthorne 'rɔːs θɔːn || -θɔːrn 'rɑːs-, 'rɔːz-,
'rɑːz-
Rawtenstall 'rɒt ⁿn stɔːl 'rɔːt- || 'rɔːt-
'rɑːt ⁿn stɑːl
ray, Ray reɪ **rays** reɪz
Ray-Bans tdmk 'reɪ bænz
Raybould 'reɪ bəʊld →-bɒʊld || -boʊld
Rayburn 'reɪ bɜːn || -bᵊrn
Rayleen 'reɪ liːn
Rayleigh 'reɪl i
rayless 'reɪ ləs -lɪs
Rayment 'reɪm ənt
Raymond 'reɪm ənd
Raynaud 'reɪn əʊ || reɪ 'noʊ —Fr [ʁɛ no]
Rayner 'reɪn ə || -ᵊr
Raynes reɪnz
rayon 'reɪ ɒn || -ɑːn ~s z
raze reɪz (= raise) **razed** reɪzd **razes** 'reɪz ɪz
-əz **razing** 'reɪz ɪŋ
razoo rɑː 'zuː rə-
razor 'reɪz ə || -ᵊr ~ed d **razoring** 'reɪz ər ɪŋ ~s
z
'razor blade; ˌrazor 'edge, ˌrazor's 'edge
razorback 'reɪz ə bæk || -ᵊr- ~s s
razorbill 'reɪz ə bɪl || -ᵊr- ~s z
razor-sharp ˌreɪz ə 'ʃɑːp ◄ || -ᵊr 'ʃɑːrp ◄
razorshell 'reɪz ə ʃel || -ᵊr- ~s z
razor-thin ˌreɪz ə 'θɪn ◄ || -ᵊr-
razz ræz **razzed** ræzd **razzes** 'ræz ɪz -əz
razzing 'ræz ɪŋ
razzamatazz ˌræz əm_ə 'tæz '····
razzia 'ræz i_ə ~s z
razzle 'ræz ᵊl
razzle-dazzle ˌræz ᵊl 'dæz ᵊl '··ˌ··
razzmatazz ˌræz mə 'tæz '····
RC ˌɑː 'siː || ˌɑːr-

R

r-colored, r-coloured 'ɑ: ˌkʌl əd
‖ 'ɑːr ˌkʌl ᵊrd
Rd —see **Road**
're ə ‖ ᵊr → **they're, we're, you're**
re note in music reɪ
re prep 'regarding' riː
RE 'religious education' ˌɑːr 'iː ‖ ˌɑːr-
re- ¦riː; ri, rə —(i) As a productive prefix
meaning 'again' (sometimes spelt with a
hyphen), ¦ri: (refill v ˌriː 'fɪl, n 'riː fɪl). Any
words in re- not included below may be
assumed to involve this productive prefix. (ii)
Otherwise, with a vaguer meaning, ri before a
vowel sound (react ri 'ækt), and ri, rə before a
consonant (return ri 'tɜːn, rə- ‖ -'tɜːn); but if
stressed through the operation of a stressing
rule usually ¦re+ (recommend
ˌrek ə 'mend).
Rea (i) reɪ, (ii) riː
reach riːtʃ **reached** riːtʃt **reaches** 'riːtʃ ɪz -əz
reaching 'riːtʃ ɪŋ
reachable 'riːtʃ əb ᵊl
reach-me-down 'riːtʃ mi daʊn ~s z
reac|quaint ˌriː ə| 'kweɪnt ~**quainted**
'kweɪnt ɪd -əd ‖ 'kweɪnṯ- ~**quainting**
'kweɪnt ɪŋ ‖ 'kweɪnṯ ɪŋ ~**quaints** 'kweɪnts
react ri 'ækt ~**ed** ɪd əd ~**ing** ɪŋ ~**s** s
reactance ri 'ækt ənts
reactant ri 'ækt ənt ~**s** s
reaction ri 'æk ʃᵊn ~**s** z
re'action time
reactionar|y ri 'æk ʃᵊn ər_|i -ʃᵊn ər |i
‖ -ʃə ner |i ~**ies** iz
reacti|vate ri 'ækt ɪ |veɪt ˌriː-, -ə- ~**vated**
veɪt ɪd -əd ‖ veɪṯ əd ~**vates** veɪts ~**vating**
veɪt ɪŋ ‖ veɪṯ ɪŋ
reactivation ri ˌækt ɪ 'veɪʃ ᵊn ˌriː-, ·'--, -ə'-- ~**s**
z
reactive ri 'ækt ɪv ~**ly** li ~**ness** nəs nɪs
reactor ri 'ækt ə ‖ -ᵊr ~**s** z
read v pres; n riːd (= reed) **read** v past, pp red
(= red) **reading** 'riːd ɪŋ **reads** riːdz
'reading ˌmatter; **'reading room**
Read riːd
readability ˌriːd ə 'bɪl ət i -ɪt i ‖ -əṯ i
readab|le 'riːd əb |ᵊl ~**ly** li
readdress ˌriː ə 'dres ~**ed** t ~**es** ɪz əz ~**ing** ɪŋ
Reade riːd
reader, R~ 'riːd ə ‖ -ᵊr ~**s** z
readership 'riːd ə ʃɪp ‖ -ᵊr- ~**s** s
readi... —see **ready**
reading 'riːd ɪŋ ~**s** z
Reading name 'red ɪŋ
readjust ˌriː ə 'dʒʌst ~**ed** ɪd əd ~**ing** ɪŋ
~**ment/s** mənt/s ~**s** s
Readman (i) 'red mən, (ii) 'riːd-
readmission ˌriː əd 'mɪʃ ᵊn → -əb-, -æd- ~**s** z
read|mit ˌriː əd |'mɪt → -əb-, -æd- ~**mits** 'mɪts
~**mitted** 'mɪt ɪd -əd ‖ 'mɪṯ əd ~**mitting**
'mɪt ɪŋ ‖ 'mɪṯ ɪŋ
readmittanc|e ˌriː əd 'mɪt ᵊnts → -əb-, -æd- ~**es**
ɪz əz
read-only ˌriːd 'əʊn li ◄ ‖ -'oʊn-

readout 'riːd aʊt ~**s** s
readthrough 'riːd θruː ~**s** z
read|y 'red |i ~**ied** id -**ier** i‿ə ‖ i‿ᵊr ~**ies** iz
~**iest** i‿ɪst i‿əst ~**ily** ɪ li ᵊl i ~**iness** i nəs i nɪs
~**ying** i ɪŋ
ˌready 'cash; **ˌready 'money**
ready-made ˌred i 'meɪd ◄ · · · ~**s** z
ready-mix ˌred i 'mɪks ◄ · · · ~**ed** t
ready-to-wear ˌred i tə 'weə ◄ -tu- ‖ -'weᵊr
-'wæᵊr
reaffirm ˌriː ə 'fɜːm ‖ -'fɜːm ~**ed** d ~**ing** ɪŋ ~**s**
z
reaffirmation ˌriː ˌæf ə 'meɪʃ ᵊn ·ˌ· ·'-- ‖ -ᵊr'--
~**s** z
reafforest ˌriː ə 'fɒr ɪst -əst ‖ -'fɔːr əst -'fɑːr-
~**ed** ɪd əd ~**ing** ɪŋ ~**s** s
reafforestation ˌriː ə ˌfɒr ɪ 'steɪʃ ᵊn -ˌ·ə-
‖ -ˌfɔːr- -ˌfɑːr- ~**s** z
Reagan 'reɪg ən
Reaganomics ˌreɪg ə 'nɒm ɪks ‖ -'nɑːm-
reagent ri 'eɪdʒ ənt ~**s** s

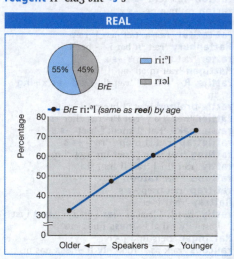

REAL

Preference poll: ri:ᵊl 55%, rɪəl 45%.

BrE ri:ᵊl *(same as reel) by age*

real adj, adv, n 'reality' rɪəl ri:ᵊl ‖ ri:ᵊl 'ri:əl
— Preference poll, BrE: ri:ᵊl (i.e. same as reel)
55%, rɪəl 45%.
'real eˌstate; **'real estate ˌagent**; **ˌreal**
'property
real n 'coin', **Real** name of football team
₍ᵢ₎reɪ 'ɑːl 'reɪ əl —Sp, Port [ˌrːe 'al] ~**s** z
realgar ri 'ælg ə -ɑː ‖ -ᵊr -ɑːr
realia reɪ 'ɑːl i ə ri 'eɪl-
realign ˌriː ə 'laɪn ~**ed** d ~**ing** ɪŋ ~**ment/s**
mənt/s ~**s** z
realis... —see **realiz...**
realism 'rɪəl ˌɪz əm 'ri:ᵊl- ‖ 'ri: ə ˌlɪz əm
realist 'rɪəl ɪst 'ri:ᵊl-, §-əst ‖ 'ri: əl əst ~**s** s
realistic ₍ᵢ₎rɪə 'lɪst ɪk ◄ ˌri: ə- ‖ ˌri: ə 'lɪst ɪk ◄
~**ally** ᵊl_i
realit|y ri 'æl ət i -ɪt i ‖ -əṯ |i ~**ies** iz
realizable 'rɪəl aɪz əb ᵊl 'ri:ᵊl- ‖ 'ri: ə laɪz əb ᵊl
realization ˌrɪəl aɪ 'zeɪʃ ᵊn ˌri:ᵊl-, -ɪ'--
‖ ˌri: əl ə 'zeɪʃ ᵊn ~**s** z

realiz|e 'rɪəl aɪz 'riː°l- ‖ 'riː ə laɪz **~ed** d **~es** ɪz
əz **~ing** ɪŋ
real-life ˌrɪəl 'laɪf ◂ ˌriː°l- ‖ ˌriː°l-
reallo|cate ˌriː 'æl əʊ |keɪt ‖ -ə |keɪt **~cated**
keɪt ɪd -əd ‖ keɪt̮ əd **~cates** keɪts **~cating**
keɪt ɪŋ ‖ keɪt̮ ɪŋ
reallocation ˌriː ˌæl əʊ 'keɪʃ °n ‖ -ə-

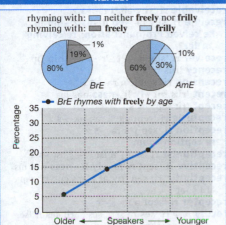

REALLY

rhyming with: ▨ neither **freely** nor **frilly**
rhyming with: ▨ **freely** ☐ **frilly**

BrE   *AmE*

BrE rhymes with **freely** by age

Older ◄—— Speakers ——► Younger

really 'rɪəl i 'riː°l i, 'reəl i ‖ 'riːl i 'rɪl i, 'riːˌəl i
— *Preference polls, BrE: rhyming with neither*
freely *nor* frilly *80%; rhyming with* freely *19%,*
rhyming with frilly *1%; AmE: rhyming with*
freely *60%, rhyming with* frilly *30%, rhyming*
with neither freely *nor* frilly *10%.*
realm relm **realms** relmz
realpolitik reɪ 'ɑːl pɒl ɪ ˌtiːk -əˌ·, ·ˌ··' ·ˌ·
‖ -'poʊl- —*Ger* [ʁe 'aːl po li ˌtiːk]
real-time ˌrɪəl 'taɪm ◂ ˌriː°l- ‖ ˌriː°l-
realtor, R~ *tdmk* 'rɪəl tə 'riː°l-, -tɔː ‖ 'riː°lt °r
⚠ 'riːl ət̮ °r **~s** z
realty 'rɪəl ti 'riː°l- ‖ 'riːˌəlt i
ream riːm **reamed** riːmd **reaming** 'riːm ɪŋ
reams riːmz
reamer 'riːm ə ‖ -°r **~s** z
reani|mate ₍ᵢ₎ri 'æn ɪ |meɪt -ə- **~mated**
meɪt ɪd -əd ‖ meɪt̮ əd **~mates** meɪts **~mating**
meɪt ɪŋ ‖ meɪt̮ ɪŋ
reap riːp **reaped** riːpt **reaping** 'riːp ɪŋ **reaps**
riːps
reaper 'riːp ə ‖ -°r **~s** z
reap|pear ˌriːˌə |'pɪə ‖ -|'pɪ°r **~peared** 'pɪəd
‖ 'pɪ°rd **~pearing** 'pɪər ɪŋ ‖ 'pɪr ɪŋ **~pears**
'pɪəz ‖ 'pɪ°rz
reappearanc|e ˌriːˌə 'pɪər ən°s ‖ -'pɪr- **~es** ɪz
əz
reapplication ˌriː æp lɪ 'keɪʃ °n ri ˌæp- **~s** z
reap|ply ˌriːˌə |'plaɪ **~plied** 'plaɪd **~plies**
'plaɪd **~plying** 'plaɪ ɪŋ
reap|point ˌriːˌə |'pɔɪnt **~pointment/s**
'pɔɪnt mənt/s **~pointed** 'pɔɪnt ɪd -əd
‖ 'pɔɪnt̮ əd **~pointing** 'pɔɪnt ɪŋ ‖ 'pɔɪnt̮ ɪŋ
~points 'pɔɪnts

reapportion ˌriː ə 'pɔːʃ °n ‖ -'pɔːrʃ- **~ment**
mənt
reappraisal ˌriːˌə 'preɪz °l **~s** z
reapprais|e ˌriːˌə 'preɪz **~ed** d **~es** ɪz əz **~ing**
ɪŋ
rear rɪə ‖ rɪ°r **reared** rɪəd ‖ rɪ°rd **rearing**
'rɪər ɪŋ ‖ 'rɪr ɪŋ **rears** rɪəz ‖ rɪ°rz
ˌrear ad'miral◂; ˌrear 'end
Rearden, Reardon 'rɪəd °n ‖ 'rɪrd °n
rear-end ˌrɪər 'end ‖ ˌrɪr- **~ed** ɪd əd **~er/s** ə/z
‖ °r/z **~ing** ɪŋ **~s** z
rearguard 'rɪə gɑːd ‖ 'rɪr gɑːrd **~s** z
ˌrearguard 'action
rearm ri 'ɑːm ˌriː- ‖ -'ɑːrm **~ed** d **~ing** ɪŋ **~s** z
rearmament ri 'ɑːm ə mənt ˌriː- ‖ -'ɑːrm-
rearmost 'rɪə məʊst ‖ 'rɪr moʊst
rearrang|e ˌriːˌə 'reɪndʒ **~ed** d **~ement/s**
mənt/s **~es** ɪz əz **~ing** ɪŋ
rearrest ˌriː ə 'rest **~ed** ɪd əd **~ing** ɪŋ **~s** s
rearview 'rɪə vjuː ‖ 'rɪr-
ˌrearview 'mirror
rearward 'rɪə wəd ‖ 'rɪr w°rd **~s** z
reason, R~ 'riːz °n **~ed** d **~ing/s** ɪŋ/z **~s** z
reasonab|le 'riːz °n‿əb |°l **~ly** li **~ness** nəs nɪs
reasoner 'riːz °n‿ə ‖ -ər **~s** z
reasonless 'riːz °n ləs -lɪs **~ly** li **~ness** nəs nɪs
reassembl|e ˌriːˌə 'sem b°l **~ed** d **~es** z **~ing**
ɪŋ
reassembly ˌriːˌə 'sem bli
reas|sert ˌriːˌə |'sɜːt ‖ -|'sɜːt **~serted** 'sɜːt ɪd
-əd ‖ 'sɜːt̮ əd **~serting** 'sɜːt ɪŋ ‖ 'sɜːt̮ ɪŋ
~serts 'sɜːts ‖ 'sɜːts
reassess ˌriːˌə 'ses **~ed** t **~es** ɪz əz **~ing** ɪŋ
~ment/s mənt/s
reassign ˌriːˌə 'saɪn **~ed** d **~ing** ɪŋ **~s** z
reassuranc|e ˌriːˌə 'ʃʊər ən°s -'ʃɔːr- ‖ -|'ʃʊr-
-'ʃɜː- **~es** ɪz əz
reas|sure ˌriːˌə |'ʃɔː -'ʃʊə; rɪə· ‖ -|'ʃʊ°r -'ʃɜː
~sured 'ʃɔːd 'ʃʊəd ‖ 'ʃʊ°rd 'ʃɜːd **~sures** 'ʃɔːz
'ʃʊəz ‖ 'ʃʊ°rz 'ʃɜːz **~suring/ly** 'ʃɔːr ɪŋ /li
'ʃʊər- ‖ 'ʃʊr ɪŋ /li 'ʃɜː-
Reaumur, Réaumur 'reɪ əʊ mjʊə
‖ ˌreɪ oʊ 'mjʊ°r —*Fr* [ʁe o myːʁ]
Reave riːv
reawaken ˌriːˌə 'weɪk ən **~ed** d **~ing** ˌɪŋ **~s** z
Reay reɪ
reb, Reb reb **rebs, Rebs** rebz
rebarbative rɪ 'bɑːb ət ɪv rə-, §riː-
‖ -'bɑːrb ət̮ ɪv
re|bate *v 'deduct'; 'form rebate in'* ri '|beɪt rə-;
'riː |beɪt **~bated** beɪt ɪd -əd ‖ beɪt̮ əd **~bates**
beɪts **~bating** beɪt ɪŋ ‖ beɪt̮ ɪŋ
rebate *n 'deduction'* 'riː beɪt ri 'beɪt, rə- **~s** s
rebate *n 'groove, joint'* 'riː beɪt 'ræb ɪt, §-ət **~s**
s
rebec, rebeck 'riːb ek 'reb- **~s** s
Rebecca, Rebekah ri 'bek ə rə-
rebel *v* rɪ 'bel rə-, §riː- **~led** d **~ling** ɪŋ **~s** z
rebel *n, adj* 'reb °l **~s** z
rebellion ri 'bel jən rə-, -i ən **~s** z
rebellious ri 'bel jəs rə-, -i əs **~ly** li **~ness** nəs
nɪs

R

rebind ˌriː ˈbaɪnd **~ing** ɪŋ **~s** z **rebound**
ˌriː ˈbaʊnd

rebirth ˌriː ˈbɜːθ ‖ -ˈbɜːθ **~er/s** ə/z ‖ -ʳr/z **~ing**
ɪŋ **~s** s

reboot *n* ˈriː buːt ˌ·ˈ· **~s** s

re|boot *v* ˌriː |ˈbuːt **~booted** ˈbuːt ɪd -əd
‖ ˈbuːt̬ əd **~booting** ˈbuːt ɪŋ ‖ ˈbuːt̬ ɪŋ
~boots ˈbuːts

rebore *v* ˌriː ˈbɔː ‖ -ˈbɔːr -ˈboʊr **~d** d **~s** z
reboring ˌriː ˈbɔːr ɪŋ ‖ -ˈboʊr-

rebore *n* ˈriː bɔː ‖ -bɔːr -boʊr **~s** z

reborn ˌriː ˈbɔːn ‖ -ˈbɔːrn

rebound *n* ˈriː baʊnd **~s** z

rebound *v* 'bounce back; have unexpected effect'
ri ˈbaʊnd rə- **~ed** ɪd əd **~ing** ɪŋ **~s** z

rebound *adj* 'again subjected to binding'
ˌriː ˈbaʊnd ◂

rebozo rɪ ˈbəʊz əʊ rə- ‖ -ˈboʊz oʊ -ˈboʊs-
—*AmSp* [ɾɾe ˈβo so] **~s** z

rebrand ˌriː ˈbrænd **~ed** ɪd əd **~ing** ɪŋ **~s** z

rebuff *n* ri ˈbʌf rə-; ˈriː bʌf **~s** s

rebuff *v* ri ˈbʌf rə- **~ed** t **~ing** ɪŋ **~s** s

rebuild *n* ˌriː ˈbɪld ˈ· · **~s** z

rebuild *v* ˌriː ˈbɪld **~ing** ɪŋ **~s** z **rebuilt**
ˌriː ˈbɪlt ◂

rebuk|e *v, n* ri ˈbjuːk rə- **~ed** t **~es** s **~ing** ɪŋ

rebus ˈriːb əs **~es** ɪz əz

re|but ri |ˈbʌt rə- **~buts** ˈbʌts **~butted** ˈbʌt ɪd
-əd ‖ ˈbʌt̬ əd **~butting** ˈbʌt ɪŋ ‖ ˈbʌt̬ ɪŋ

rebuttal ri ˈbʌt ᵊl rə- ‖ -ˈbʌt̬ ᵊl **~s** z

rebutter ri ˈbʌt ə rə- ‖ -ˈbʌt̬ ᵊr **~s** z

rec rek

recalcitranc|e ri ˈkæls ɪtr ən̩ts rə-, -ətr- **~y** i

recalcitrant ri ˈkæls ɪtr ənt rə-, -ətr- **~ly** li **~s**
s

recalcu|late ˌriː ˈkælk ju |leɪt -jə- ‖ -jə-
~lated leɪt ɪd -əd ‖ leɪt̬ əd **~lating** leɪt ɪŋ
‖ leɪt̬ ɪŋ

recall *v* ri ˈkɔːl rə- ‖ -ˈkɑːl **~ed** d **~ing** ɪŋ **~s** z

recall *n* ri ˈkɔːl rə-; ˈriː kɔːl ‖ -ˈkɑːl **~s** z

recallable ri ˈkɔːl əb ᵊl rə- ‖ -ˈkɑːl-

re|cant ri |ˈkænt rə- **~canted** ˈkænt ɪd -əd
‖ ˈkænt̬ əd **~canting** ˈkæntɪŋ ‖ ˈkænt̬ ɪŋ
~cants ˈkænts

recantation ˌriː kæn ˈteɪʃ ᵊn **~s** z

recap *v* 'retread' ˌriː ˈkæp **~ped** t **~ping** ɪŋ **~s** s

recap *n* 'retread' ˈriː kæp **~s** s

recap *v* 'recapitulate', *n* 'recapitulation'
ˈriː kæp ˌriː ˈkæp, rɪ-, rə- **~ped** t **~ping** ɪŋ
~s s

recapitalisation, recapitalization
ˌriː ˌkæp ɪt ᵊl aɪ ˈzeɪʃ ᵊn -ˈət-, -ɪˈ· ·
‖ -ˌkæp ɪt̬ ᵊl ə-

recapitalis|e, recapitaliz|e ˌriː ˈkæp ɪt ə laɪz
-ˈət-, -ᵊl aɪz ‖ -ət̬ ᵊl aɪz

recapitu|late ˌriː kə ˈpɪtʃ u |leɪt -ˈpɪt ju-
‖ -ˈpɪtʃ ə- **~lated** leɪt ɪd -əd ‖ leɪt̬ əd **~lates**
leɪts **~lating** leɪt ɪŋ ‖ leɪt̬ ɪŋ

recapitulation ˌriː kə ˌpɪtʃ u ˈleɪʃ ᵊn -ˌpɪt ju-
‖ -ˌpɪtʃ ə- **~s** z

recapitulatory ˌriː kə ˈpɪtʃ ʊl ət ᵊr i -ˈpɪt ʊl-;
-pɪtʃ u ˈleɪt ᵊr i, -pɪt ju- ‖ -əl ə tɔːr i -toʊr i

recap|ture ˌriː ˈkæp |tʃə -ʃə ‖ -|tʃᵊr **~tured**
tʃəd ʃəd ‖ tʃᵊrd **~tures** tʃəz ʃəz ‖ tʃᵊrz
~turing tʃər ɪŋ ʃər ɪŋ

recast ˌriː ˈkɑːst §-ˈkæst ‖ -ˈkæst **~ing** ɪŋ **~s** s

recce ˈrek i **~d, ~ed** d **~ing** ɪŋ **~s** z

reced|e ri ˈsiːd rə- **~ed** ɪd əd **~es** z **~ing** ɪŋ

re|ceipt ri |ˈsiːt rə- **~ceipted** ˈsiːt ɪd -əd
‖ ˈsiːt̬ əd **~ceipting** ˈsiːt ɪŋ ‖ ˈsiːt̬ ɪŋ **~ceipts**
ˈsiːts

receivable ri ˈsiːv əb ᵊl rə- **~s** z

receiv|e ri ˈsiːv rə- **~ed** d **~es** z **~ing** ɪŋ
**Re,ceived Pro,nunci'ation; re'ceiving
,order**

receiver ri ˈsiːv ə rə- ‖ -ᵊr **~s** z **~ship** ʃɪp

recency ˈriːs ᵊn̩ts i

recension ri ˈsen̩tʃ ᵊn rə- **~s** z

recent ˈriːs ᵊnt **~ly** li **~ness** nəs nɪs

recept ˈriː sept **~s** s

receptacle ri ˈsept ək ᵊl rə-, -ɪk- **~s** z

reception ri ˈsep ʃᵊn rə- **~s** z
re'ception room

receptionist ri ˈsep ʃᵊn ɪst rə-, §-əst **~s** s

receptive ri ˈsept ɪv rə- **~ly** li **~ness** nəs nɪs

receptivity ˌriː sep ˈtɪv ət i ˌres ep-, ri ˌsep-,
-ɪt i ‖ -ət̬ i

receptor ri ˈsept ə rə- ‖ -ᵊr **~s** z

recess *n, v* ri ˈses rə-; ˈriː ses ‖ ˈriː ses ri ˈses
—*Some speakers may distinguish the verb* ·ˈ·
from the noun ˈ· · **~ed** t **~es** ɪz əz **~ing** ɪŋ

recession ri ˈseʃ ᵊn rə- **~s** z

recessional ri ˈseʃ ᵊn̩ əl rə- **~s** z

recessive ri ˈses ɪv rə- **~ly** li **~ness** nəs nɪs **~s**
z

Rechabite ˈrek ə baɪt **~s** s

recharg|e *n* ˈriː tʃɑːdʒ ‖ -tʃɑːrdʒ **~es** ɪz əz

recharg|e *v* ˌriː ˈtʃɑːdʒ ‖ -ˈtʃɑːrdʒ **~ed** d **~er/s**
ə/z ‖ ᵊr/z **~es** ɪz əz **~ing** ɪŋ

recherche, recherché rə ˈʃeəʃ eɪ ‖ -ˌʃer ˈʃeɪ
—*Fr* [ʀə ʃɛʀ ʃe]

re-chip ˌriː ˈtʃɪp **~ped** t **~ping** ɪŋ **~s** s

recidivism ri ˈsɪd ɪ ˌvɪz əm rə-, -ˈə-

recidivist ri ˈsɪd ɪv ɪst rə-, -əv-, §-əst **~s** s

Recife rə ˈsiːf i re-, -ə —*BrPort* [ɾɾe ˈsi fi, xe-]

recipe ˈres əp i -ɪp- (!) **~s** z

recipient ri ˈsɪp i̯ənt rə- **~s** s

reciprocal ri ˈsɪp rək ᵊl rə- **~ly** i **~s** z

reciprocality ri ˌsɪp rə ˈkæl ət i rə- ‖ -ət̬ i

recipro|cate ri ˈsɪp rə |keɪt rə- **~cated** keɪt ɪd
-əd ‖ keɪt̬ əd **~cates** keɪts **~cating** keɪt ɪŋ
‖ keɪt̬ ɪŋ

reciprocation ri ˌsɪp rə ˈkeɪʃ ᵊn rə- **~s** z

reciprocit|y ˌres ɪ ˈprɒs ət |i ˌ·ə-, -ɪt i
‖ -ˈprɑːs ət̬ |i **~ies** iz

recision ri ˈsɪʒ ᵊn rə- **~s** z

recital ri ˈsaɪt ᵊl rə- ‖ -ˈsaɪt̬ ᵊl **~ist/s** ɪst/s §əst/s
‖ əst/s **~s** z

recitation ˌres ɪ ˈteɪʃ ᵊn -ə- **~s** z

recitative *n* ˌres ɪt ə ˈtiːv ˌ·ət- ‖ -ət̬ ə- **~s** z

re|cite ri |ˈsaɪt rə- **~cited** ˈsaɪt ɪd -əd ‖ ˈsaɪt̬ əd
~cites ˈsaɪts **~citing** ˈsaɪt ɪŋ ‖ ˈsaɪt̬ ɪŋ

reciter ri ˈsaɪt ə rə- ‖ -ˈsaɪt̬ rᵊ **~s** z

reck rek **recked** rekt **recking** ˈrek ɪŋ **recks**
reks

reckless 'rek ləs -lɪs **~ly** li **~ness** nəs nɪs
reckon 'rek ən **~ed** d **~ing/s** ɪŋ/z **~s** z
reckoner 'rek ən_ə ‖ -ᵊn_ər **~s** z
reclaim n ri 'kleɪm rə-, ˌriː-; 'riː kleɪm **~s** z
reclaim v ri 'kleɪm rə-, ˌriː- **~able** əb ᵊl **~ed** d **~ing** ɪŋ **~s** z
reclamation ˌrek lə 'meɪʃ ᵊn **~s** z
reclassi|fy ˌriː 'klæs ɪ| faɪ -ə- **~fied** faɪd **~fies** faɪz **~fying** faɪ ɪŋ
reclin|e ri 'klaɪn rə- **~ed** d **~er/s** ə/z ‖ ᵊr/z **~es** z **~ing** ɪŋ
reclus|e ri 'kluːs rə-; 'rek luːs ‖ 'rek luːs ri 'kluːs **~es** ɪz əz
reclusive ri 'kluːs ɪv rə-, -'kluːz- **~ly** li **~ness** nəs nɪs
recognis... —*see* **recogniz...**
recognition ˌrek əg 'nɪʃ ᵊn △-ə- **~s** z
recognizability ˌrek əg ˌnaɪz ə 'bɪl ət i △,·ə-, -ɪt i ‖ -əṭ i
recognizab|le 'rek əg naɪz əb |ᵊl △'·ə-, ˌ·'·- **~ly** li
recognizanc|e ri 'kɒg nɪz ᵊn's rə-, -'kɒn ɪz - ‖ -'kɑːg nɪz ᵊn's -'kɑːn ɪz- **~es** ɪz əz
recogniz|e 'rek əg naɪz △-ə naɪz; §,·'· **~ed** d **~es** ɪz əz **~ing** ɪŋ
recoil n 'riː kɔɪᵊl ri 'kɔɪᵊl, rə- **~s** z
recoil v ri 'kɔɪᵊl rə- **~ed** d **~ing** ɪŋ **~s** z
recoilless ri 'kɔɪᵊl ləs rə-, -lɪs ‖ 'riː·-·
recollect ˌrek ə 'lekt **~ed** ɪd əd **~ing** ɪŋ **~s** s
recollection ˌrek ə 'lek ʃᵊn **~s** z
recombinant ˌ(ˌ)riː 'kɒm bɪn ənt rɪ-, rə-, -'·bən- ‖ -'kɑːm- **~s** s
recombination ˌriː ˌkɒm bɪ 'neɪʃ ᵊn ·,·'·, ·, -bə'- ‖ -ˌkɑːm- **~s** z
recombin|e ˌriː kəm 'baɪn §-kɒm- **~ed** d **~es** z **~ing** ɪŋ
recommenc|e ˌriː kə 'men's **~ed** t **~ement** mənt **~es** ɪz əz **~ing** ɪŋ
recommend ˌrek ə 'mend **~ed** ɪd əd **~ing** ɪŋ **~s** z
recommendation ˌrek ə men 'deɪʃ ᵊn -mən'-- **~s** z
recompens|e v, n 'rek əm pen's **~ed** t **~es** ɪz əz **~ing** ɪŋ
recon 'riː kɒn ‖ -kɑːn
reconcilab|le 'rek ən saɪᵊl əb |ᵊl →'·ŋ-, ˌ·'·'·· **~leness** ᵊl nəs -nɪs **~ly** li
reconcil|e 'rek ən saɪᵊl →-ŋ-, ˌ·'·' **~ed** d **~er/s** ə/z ‖ ᵊr/z **~es** z **~ing** ɪŋ
reconciliation ˌrek ən sɪl i 'eɪʃ ᵊn →ˌ·ŋ- **~s** z
reconciliatory ˌrek ən 'sɪl i ət ər i →ˌ·ŋ-, §,····'eɪt ər i ‖ ə tɔːr i -tour i
recondite 'rek ən daɪt →-ŋ-; ri 'kɒnd aɪt, rə- ‖ ri 'kɑːnd aɪt **~ly** li **~ness** nəs nɪs
recondition ˌriː kən 'dɪʃ ᵊn §-kɒn- **~ed** d **~ing** ɪŋ **~s** z
reconnaissance ri 'kɒn ɪs ᵊn's rə-, -əs- ‖ -'kɑːn əz ᵊn's -əs-
reconnect ˌriː kə 'nekt **~ed** ɪd əd **~ing** ɪŋ **~s** s
recon|noiter, recon|noitre ˌrek ə |'nɔɪt ə ‖ ˌriːk ə |'nɔɪt ᵊr rek- (*) **~noitered, ~noitred** 'nɔɪt əd ‖ 'nɔɪt ᵊrd **~noitering,**

~noitring 'nɔɪt_ər ɪŋ ‖ 'nɔɪt ər ɪŋ →-'nɔɪtr ɪŋ
~noiters, ~noitres 'nɔɪt əz ‖ 'nɔɪt ᵊrz
reconqu|er ˌriː 'kɒŋk | ə ‖ -'kɑːŋk| ᵊr **~ered** əd ‖ ᵊrd **~ering** ər ɪŋ **~ers** əz ‖ ᵊrz
reconquest ˌriː 'kɒŋk west ‖ -'kɑːn kwest →-'kɑːŋ-, -kwəst **~s** s
reconsid|er ˌriː kən 'sɪd |ə §-kɒn- ‖ -|ᵊr **~ered** əd ‖ ᵊrd **~ering** ər ɪŋ **~ers** əz ‖ ᵊrz
reconsideration ˌriː kən ˌsɪd ə 'reɪʃ ᵊn §-kɒn-
reconsti|tute ˌriː 'kɒn'st ɪ |tjuːt -ə-, →-tʃuːt ‖ -'kɑːn'st ə |tuːt -tjuːt **~tuted** tjuːt ɪd →tʃuːt-, -əd ‖ tuːṭ əd tjuːṭ- **~tutes** tjuːts →tʃuːts ‖ tuːts tjuːts **~tuting** tjuːt ɪŋ →tʃuːt- ‖ tuːṭ ɪŋ tjuːṭ-
reconstitution ˌriː ˌkɒn'st ɪ 'tjuːʃ ᵊn -ˌ·ə-, →-'tʃuːʃ- ‖ -ˌkɑːn'st ə 'tuːʃ ᵊn -'tjuːʃ- **~s** z
reconstruct ˌriː kən 'strʌkt §-kɒn- **~ed** ɪd əd **~ing** ɪŋ **~s** s
reconstruction ˌriː kən 'strʌk ʃᵊn §-kɒn- **~s** z
reconstructive ˌriː kən 'strʌkt ɪv ◂ §-kɒn-
reconven|e ˌriː kən 'viːn §-kɒn- **~ed** d **~es** z **~ing** ɪŋ
record v ri 'kɔːd rə- ‖ -'kɔːrd **~ed** ɪd əd **~ing/s** ɪŋ/z **~s** z
re,corded de'livery; re'cording ˌstudio
record n, adj 'rek ɔːd -əd ‖ -ᵊrd **~s** z
'record ˌlibrary; 'record ˌplayer
record-break|er 'rek ɔːd ˌbreɪk |ə §-əd-, →-'·ɔːb- ‖ -ᵊrd ˌbreɪk |ᵊr **~ers** əz ‖ ᵊrz **~ing** ɪŋ
recorder ri 'kɔːd ə rə- ‖ -'kɔːrd ᵊr **~s** z **~ship** ʃɪp
record-holder 'rek ɔːd ˌhəʊld ə §-əd-, →-ˌhɒʊld- ‖ -ᵊrd ˌhoʊld ᵊr **~s** z
recordist ri 'kɔːd ɪst rə-, §-əst ‖ -'kɔːrd- **~s** s
record-keeping 'rek ɔːd ˌkiːp ɪŋ §-əd- ‖ -ᵊrd-
re|count v 'tell' ri |'kaʊnt rə- **~counted** 'kaʊnt ɪd -əd ‖ 'kaʊnṭ əd **~counting** 'kaʊnt ɪŋ ‖ 'kaʊnṭ ɪŋ **~counts** 'kaʊnts
re|count v 'count again' ˌriː |'kaʊnt **~counted** 'kaʊnt ɪd -əd ‖ 'kaʊnṭ əd **~counting** 'kaʊnt ɪŋ ‖ 'kaʊnṭ ɪŋ **~counts** 'kaʊnts
recount n 'riː kaʊnt ˌ·'· **~s** s
recoup ri 'kuːp rə- **~ed** t **~ing** ɪŋ **~ment** mənt **~s** s
recourse ri 'kɔːs rə- ‖ 'riː kɔːrs -koʊrs; ri '·, rə- (*)
recov|er 'regain; find again; get better' ri 'kʌv |ə rə- ‖ -|ᵊr **~ered** əd ‖ ᵊrd **~ering** ər ɪŋ **~ers** əz ‖ ᵊrz
recov|er 'cover again' ˌriː 'kʌv |ə ‖ -|ᵊr **~ered** əd ‖ ᵊrd **~ering** ər ɪŋ **~ers** əz ‖ ᵊrz
recoverability ri ˌkʌv ər ə 'bɪl ət i rə-, -ɪt i ‖ -əṭ i
recoverable ri 'kʌv ər əb ᵊl rə-
recover|y ri 'kʌv ər |i rə- **~ies** iz
re'covery room
recreant 'rek ri ənt **~s** s
recre|ate 'create anew' ˌriː kri |'eɪt **~ated** 'eɪt ɪd -əd ‖ 'eɪṭ əd **~ates** 'eɪts **~ating** 'eɪt ɪŋ ‖ 'eɪṭ ɪŋ
recreation 'creating anew' ˌriː kri 'eɪʃ ᵊn
recreation 'amusement' ˌrek ri 'eɪʃ ᵊn **~s** z
ˌrecre'ation ground; ˌrecre'ation room

R

recreational ˌrek ri ˈeɪʃ ᵊn‿əl
recrimi|nate ri ˈkrɪm ɪ |neɪt rə-, -ə- **~nated** neɪt ɪd -əd ‖ neɪţ əd **~nates** neɪts **~nating** neɪt ɪŋ ‖ neɪţ ɪŋ
recrimination ri ˌkrɪm ɪ ˈneɪʃ ᵊn rə-, -ə- **~s** z
recriminatory ri ˈkrɪm ɪn ət‿ər i rə-, -ˈ·ən‿; ·ˌ·ˈneɪt ər i ◂, -əˈ·- ‖ -ən‿ə tɔːr i -toʊr i
recrudesc|e ˌriː kruː ˈdes ˌrek ruː- **~ed** t **~es** ɪz əz **~ing** ɪŋ
recrudescenc|e ˌriː kruː ˈdes ᵊnᵗs ˌrek ruː- **~es** ɪz əz
recrudescent ˌriː kruː ˈdes ᵊnt ◂ ˌrek ruː-
re|cruit *v, n* ri |ˈkruːt rə- **~cruited** ˈkruːt ɪd -əd ‖ ˈkruːţ əd **~cruiting** ˈkruːt ɪŋ ‖ ˈkruːţ ɪŋ **~cruits** ˈkruːts
recruiter ri ˈkruːt ə rə- ‖ -ˈkruːţ ᵊr **~s** z
recruitment ri ˈkruːt mənt rə-
rectal ˈrekt ᵊl **~ly** i
rectangle ˈrek tæŋ gᵊl **~s** z
rectangular rek ˈtæŋ gjʊl ə -gjəl- ‖ -gjəl ᵊr **~ly** li
rectifiable ˈrekt ɪ faɪ‿əb ᵊl ˌ·ə-, ˌ·ˈ·· · ·
rectification ˌrekt ɪf ɪ ˈkeɪʃ ᵊn ˌ·əf-, §-əˈ·- **~s** z
recti|fy ˈrekt ɪ |faɪ -ə- **~fied** faɪd **~fier/s** faɪ‿ə/z ‖ faɪ‿ᵊr/z **~fies** faɪz **~fying** faɪ ɪŋ
rectilinear ˌrekt ɪ ˈlɪn i‿ə ◂ §ˌ·ə- ‖ ᵊr **~ly** li
rectitude ˈrekt ɪ tjuːd -ə-, →-tʃuːd ‖ -tuːd -tjuːd
recto ˈrekt əʊ ‖ -oʊ **~s** z
rector ˈrekt ə ‖ -ᵊr **~s** z **~ship/s** ʃɪp/s
rectorial rek ˈtɔːr i‿əl ‖ -ˈtoʊr-
rector|y ˈrekt ər‿|i **~ies** iz
rectrix ˈrek trɪks **rectrices** ˈrek trɪ siːz -trə-; rek ˈtraɪs iːz
rectum ˈrekt əm **~s** z
Reculver ri ˈkʌlv ə rə- ‖ -ᵊr
recumbent ri ˈkʌm bənt rə- **~ly** li
recupe|rate ri ˈkjuːp ə |reɪt rə-, -ˈkuːp- **~rated** reɪt ɪd -əd ‖ reɪţ əd **~rates** reɪts **~rating** reɪt ɪŋ ‖ reɪţ ɪŋ
recuperation ri ˌkjuːp ə ˈreɪʃ ᵊn rə-, ˌkuːp-
recuperative ri ˈkjuːp ər‿ət ɪv rə-, -ˈkuːp-, -ə reɪt- ‖ -ə reɪţ ɪv -ər‿əţ ɪv
recur ri ˈkɜː rə- ‖ -ˈkɝː **~red** d **recurring** ri ˈkɜːr ɪŋ rə- ‖ -ˈkɝː ɪŋ **~s** z
recurrenc|e ri ˈkʌr ənᵗs rə-, §-ˈkɜːr- ‖ -ˈkɝː ənᵗs **~es** ɪz əz
recurrent ri ˈkʌr ənt rə-, §-ˈkɜːr- ‖ -ˈkɝː ənt **~ly** li
recursion ri ˈkɜːʃ ᵊn rə-, §-ˈkɜːʒ- ‖ -ˈkɝːʒ ᵊn **~s** z
recursive ri ˈkɜːs ɪv rə- ‖ -ˈkɝːs ɪv **~ly** li **~ness** nəs nɪs
recurved ˌriː ˈkɜːvd ri-, rə- ‖ -ˈkɝːvd
recusancy ˈrek jʊz ənᵗs i ri ˈkjuːz-, rə- ‖ -jəz-
recusant ˈrek jʊz ənt ri ˈkjuːz-, rə- ‖ -jəz- **~s** s
recus|e ri ˈkjuːz rə- **~ed** d **~es** ɪz əz **~ing** ɪŋ
recyclable ˌriː ˈsaɪk ᵊl‿əb ᵊl ◂
recycl|e ˌriː ˈsaɪk ᵊl **~ed** d **~es** z **~ing** ‿ɪŋ
red, Red red **redder** ˈred ə ‖ -ᵊr **reddest** ˈred ɪst -əst **reds, Reds** redz
₍ˌ₎red ˈadmiral; **ˌred aˈlert**; **ˌred ˈblood cell**; **ˌred ˈcarpet**; **ˌRed ˈCrescent**; **ˌRed ˈCross**; **ˌred ˈdeer**; **ˌred ˈdwarf**; **₍ˌ₎Red ˈEnsign**; **ˌred ˈflag**; **ˌred ˈgiant**; **ˌred ˈherring**; **ˌRed ˈIndian**; **ˌred ˈlight**; **ˌred ˈmeat**; **ˌred ˈpepper**; **ˌRed ˈSea**; **ˌred ˈsetter**; **ˌred ˈtape**
redact ri ˈdækt rə- **~ed** ɪd əd **~ing** ɪŋ **~s** s
redaction ri ˈdæk ʃᵊn rə- **~s** z
redan ri ˈdæn rə- **~s** z
redback ˈred bæk →ˈreb- **~s** s
red-blooded ˌred ˈblʌd ɪd ◂ →ˌreb-, -əd **~ness** nəs nɪs
Redbourn, Redbourne ˈred bɔːn →ˈreb- ‖ -bɔːrn -boʊrn
redbreast ˈred brest →ˈreb- **~s** s
redbrick ˈred brɪk →ˈreb-, ˌ·ˈ· **~s** s
Redbridge ˈred brɪdʒ →ˈreb-
redbud ˈred bʌd →ˈreb- **~s** z
redcap ˈred kæp →ˈreg- **~s** s
Redcar ˈred kɑː →ˈreg- ‖ -kɑːr
Redcliffe ˈred klɪf →ˈreg-
redcoat ˈred kəʊt →ˈreg- ‖ -koʊt **~s** s
redcurrant ˌred ˈkʌr ənt ◂ →ˌreg-, ˈ·ˌ· · ‖ -ˈkɝː ənt **~s** s
Reddaway ˈred ə weɪ
redden ˈred ᵊn **~ed** d **~ing** ‿ɪŋ **~s** z
Redding ˈred ɪŋ
reddish, R~ ˈred ɪʃ **~ness** nəs nɪs
Redditch ˈred ɪtʃ
redeco|rate ₍ˌ₎riː ˈdek ə |reɪt **~rated** reɪt ɪd -əd ‖ reɪţ əd **~rates** reɪts **~rating** reɪt ɪŋ ‖ reɪţ ɪŋ
redecoration ₍ˌ₎riː ˌdek ə ˈreɪʃ ᵊn **~s** z
redeem ri ˈdiːm rə- **~ed** d **~ing** ɪŋ **~s** z
redeemable ri ˈdiːm əb ᵊl rə-
redeemer, R~ ri ˈdiːm ə rə- ‖ -ᵊr **~s** z
redefin|e ˌriː di ˈfaɪn -də- **~ed** d **~es** z **~ing** ɪŋ
redemption ri ˈdem*p* ʃᵊn rə-- **~s** z
redemptive ri ˈdem*p*t ɪv rə- **~ly** li
Redemptorist ri ˈdem*p*t ər‿ɪst rə-, §‿əst **~s** s
redeploy riː di ˈplɔɪ -də- **~ed** d **~ing** ɪŋ **~ment** mənt **~s** z
Redesdale ˈriːdz deɪᵊl
redevelop ˌriː di ˈvel əp -də- **~ed** t **~ing** ɪŋ **~ment/s** mənt/s **~s** s
redeye ˈred aɪ **~s** z
red-faced ˌred ˈfeɪst ◂
red-facedly ˌred ˈfeɪs ɪd li -əd-; -ˈfeɪst li
Redfearn, Redfern ˈred fɜːn ‖ -fɝːn
redfin ˈred fɪn **~s** z
Redford ˈred fəd ‖ -fᵊrd
Redgrave ˈred greɪv →ˈreg-
red-handed ˌred ˈhænd ɪd ◂ -əd **~ly** li
redhead, R~ ˈred hed **~s** z
Redheugh *(i)* ˈred hjuːf, *(ii)* -juːf, *(iii)* -jəf
Redhill ˌred ˈhɪl
red-hot ˌred ˈhɒt ◂ ‖ -ˈhɑːt ◂ **ˌred-hot ˈpoker**
redi|a ˈriːd i‿|ə **~ae** iː
redial ˌriː ˈdaɪ‿əl ◂ **~ed, ~led** d **~ing, ~ling** ɪŋ **~s** z
redid ˌriː ˈdɪd
Rediffusion *tdmk* ˌriː dɪ ˈfjuːʒ ᵊn -də-
redirect ˌriː də ˈrekt -dɪ-, -daɪᵊ- **~ed** ɪd əd **~ing** ɪŋ **~s** s

redirection ˌriː də ˈrek ʃən -dɪ-, -daɪə-

redistribute ˌriː dɪ ˈstrɪb juːt -də-;
ˌriː ˈdɪs trɪ bjuːt, -trə- ‖ -jət **redistributed**
ˌriː dɪ ˈstrɪb jut ɪd ˌ-də-, -əd; -ˈdɪs trɪ bjuːt-,
-ˈ-trə- ‖ -jəṭ əd **redistributes**
ˌriː dɪ ˈstrɪb juːts -də-; -ˈdɪs trɪ bjuːts, -trə-
redistributing ˌriː dɪ ˈstrɪb jut ɪŋ ˌ-də-;
-ˈdɪs trɪ bjuːt- ‖ -jəṭ ɪŋ

redistribution ˌriː ˌdɪs trɪ ˈbjuː ʃ ən -trə- **~s** z

redivivus ˌred ɪ ˈvaɪv əs -ə-, -ˈviːv-

red-letter ˌred ˈlet ə ‖ -ˈleṭ ər ◂
ˌred-ˈletter day

red-light ˌred ˈlaɪt
ˌred-ˈlight ˌdistrict

red-lin|e ˈred laɪn **~ed** d **~es** z **~ing** ɪŋ

redly ˈred li

Redman ˈred mən →ˈreb-

Redmond ˈred mənd →ˈreb-

redneck ˈred nek **~s** s

redness ˈred nəs -nɪs **~es** ɪz əz

redo ˌriː ˈduː **redid** ˌriː ˈdɪd **redoes** ˌriː ˈdʌz
redoing ˌriː ˈduː ɪŋ **redone** ˌriː ˈdʌn

redolenc|e ˈred əl ənts -əʊl- **~y** i

redolent ˈred əl ənt -əʊl-; →-əl ənt **~ly** li

redoubl|e ˌriː ˈdʌb əl ri-, rə- **~ed** d **~es** z **~ing**
ɪŋ

redoubt ri ˈdaʊt rə- **~s** s

redoubtab|le ri ˈdaʊt əb əl rə- ‖ -ˈdaʊṭ- **~ly** li

redound ri ˈdaʊnd rə- **~ed** ɪd əd **~ing** ɪŋ **~s** z

redox ˈriːd ɒks ˈred- ‖ -ɑːks

Redpath ˈred pɑːθ →ˈreb-, §-pæθ ‖ -pæθ

redpoll ˈred pəʊl →ˈreb-, →-pɒul, -pɒl ‖ -poʊl
~s z

redraft n ˈriː drɑːft §-dræft ‖ -dræft **~s** s

redraft v ˌriː ˈdrɑːft §-ˈdræft ‖ -ˈdræft **~ed** ɪd
əd **~ing** ɪŋ **~s** s

re|draw ˌriː ˈdrɔː ‖ -ˈdrɑː **~drawing** ˈdrɔːˑ ɪŋ
‖ ˈdrɔː ɪŋ ˈdrɑː- **~drawn** ˈdrɔːn ‖ ˈdrɑːn
~draws ˈdrɔːz ˈdrɑːz **~drew** ˈdruː

redress n 'satisfaction' ri ˈdres rə-; ˈriː dres

redress v 'put right' ri ˈdres rə- **~ed** t **~es** ɪz əz
~ing ɪŋ

Redruth ˌred ˈruːθ ˈ· ·

redshank ˈred ʃæŋk **~s** s

redshirt ˈred ʃɜːt ‖ -ʃɝːt **~s** s

redskin ˈred skɪn **~s** z

redstart ˈred stɑːt ‖ -stɑːrt **~s** s

red-top ˈred tɒp ‖ -tɑːp **~s** s

reduc|e ri ˈdjuːs rə-, →-ˈdʒuːs ‖ -ˈduːs -ˈdjuːs
~ed t **~es** ɪz əz **~ing** ɪŋ
reˌduced ˈcircumstances

reducer ri ˈdjuːs ə rə-, →-ˈdʒuːs- ‖ -ˈduːs ər
-ˈdjuːs- **~s** z

reducibility ri ˌdjuːs ə ˈbɪl ət i rə-, →-ˌdʒuːs-,
-ɪt i ‖ rɪ ˌduːs ə ˈbɪl əṭ i -ˌdjuːs-

reducib|le ri ˈdjuːs əb əl rə-, →-ˈdʒuːs-, -ɪb-
‖ -ˈduːs- -ˈdjuːs- **~ly** li

reductase ri ˈdʌkt eɪz rə-, -eɪs

reductio ad absurdum
ri ˌdʌkt i əʊ ˌæd əb ˈsɜːd əm rə-, -ˌdʌkʃ-,
-æb'- ‖ -oʊ ˌæd əb ˈsɝːd əm

reduction ri ˈdʌk ʃ ən rə- **~ism** ˌɪz əm **~ist/s**
ɪst/s §əst/s ‖ əst/s **~s** z

reductive ri ˈdʌkt ɪv rə-

redundanc|y ri ˈdʌnd ənts ‖i rə- **~ies** iz

redundant ri ˈdʌnd ənt rə- **~ly** li

redupli|cate ri ˈdjuːp lɪ ‖keɪt rə-, ˌriː-,
→-ˈdʒuːp-, -lə- ‖ -ˈduːp- -ˈdjuːp- **~cated**
keɪt ɪd -əd ‖ keɪṭ əd **~cates** keɪts **~cating**
keɪt ɪŋ ‖ keɪṭ ɪŋ

reduplication ri ˌdjuːp lɪ ˈkeɪʃ ən rə-,
→-ˌdʒuːp-, ˌriː-ˌ·ˈ·ˑ·, -lə- ‖ -ˌduːp- -ˌdjuːp- **~s** z

reduplicative ri ˈdjuːp lɪk ət ɪv rə-, →-ˈdʒuːp-,
-lək- ·; -lɪ keɪt ɪv, -lə · · ‖ ri ˈduːp lə keɪṭ ɪv
-ˈdjuːp-

redux ˈriː dʌks ri ˈdʌks

Redvers ˈred vəz ‖ -vərz

redwing, R~ ˈred wɪŋ **~s** z

redwood, R~ ˈred wʊd **~s** z

Ree riː

Rée reɪ

reebok, R~ tdmk ˈriː bɒk -bʌk ‖ -bɑːk **~s** s

Reece riːs

reecho ri ˈek əʊ ˌriː- ‖ -oʊ **~ed** d **~es** z **~ing** ɪŋ

reed, Reed riːd **reeded** ˈriːd ɪd -əd **reeding/s**
ˈriːd ɪŋ/z **reeds** riːdz
ˈreed ˌorgan

re-ed|it ˌriː ˈed ‖ ɪt §-ət **~ited** ɪt ɪd §-ət-, -əd
‖ -əṭ- **~iting** ɪt ɪŋ §ət- ‖ -əṭ- **~its** ɪts §əts

reedling ˈriːd lɪŋ **~s** z

reedu|cate ˌriː ˈed ju ‖keɪt -ˈedʒ u-, §-ˈedʒ ə-
‖ -ˈedʒ ə- **~cated** keɪt ɪd -əd ‖ keɪṭ əd **~cates**
keɪts **~cating** keɪt ɪŋ ‖ keɪṭ ɪŋ

reeducation ˌriː ˌed ju ˈkeɪʃ ən -ˌedʒ u-,
§-ˌedʒ ə- ‖ -ˌedʒ ə-ˌ·ˈ·ˑ·

reed|y ˈriːd ‖i **~ier** i ə ‖ i ʳr **~iest** i ɪst i əst
~iness i nəs i nɪs

reef riːf **reefed** riːft **reefing** ˈriːf ɪŋ **reefs** riːfs
ˈreef knot

reefer ˈriːf ə ‖ -ʳr **~s** z
ˈreefer ˌjacket

reek riːk **reeked** riːkt **reeking** ˈriːk ɪŋ **reeks**
riːks

Reekie ˈriːk i

reel riːəl **reeled** riːəld **reeling** ˈriːəl ɪŋ **reels**
riːəlz

reelect ˌriː ɪ ˈlekt -ə- **~ed** ɪd əd **~ing** ɪŋ **~s** s

reelection ˌriː ɪ ˈlek ʃ ən -ə- **~s** z

reel-to-reel ˌriːəl tə ˈriːəl ◂

re-emergence ˌriː i ˈmɜːdʒ ənts ˌ·ə- ‖ -ˈmɝːdʒ-

re-enact ˌriː ɪn ˈækt -en-, -ən **~ed** ɪd əd **~ing**
ɪŋ **~ment/s** mənt/s -s

reengi|neer ˌriː ˌendʒ ɪ ‖ˈnɪə §-ˌɪndʒ-, -ə‖-
‖ -ˈnɪʳr **~neered** ˈnɪəd ‖ ˈnɪʳrd **~neering**
ˈnɪər ɪŋ ‖ ˈnɪr ɪŋ **~neers** ˈnɪəz ‖ ˈnɪʳrz

reenter, re-enter ri ˈent ə ˌriː- ‖ -ˈenṭ ʳr **~ed**
d **reentering, re-entering** ri ˈent ʳr ɪŋ ˌriː-
‖ -ˈenṭ ʳr ɪŋ →-ˈentr ɪŋ

reentrant, re-entrant ri ˈentr ənt **~s** s

reentr|y, re-entr|y ri ˈentr ‖i ˌriː- **~ies** iz

Reepham ˈriːf əm

Rees, Reese riːs (!)

reestablish ˌriː ɪ ˈstæb lɪʃ -ə- **~ed** t **~es** ɪz əz
~ing ɪŋ **~ment** mənt

re-evalu|ate ˌriː i ˈvæl ju eɪt ˌ·ə- **~ated** eɪt ɪd
-əd ‖ eɪṭ əd **~ates** eɪts **~ating** eɪt ɪŋ ‖ eɪṭ ɪŋ

R

reeve, Reeve riːv **reeved** riːvd **reeves** riːvz
reeving ˈriːv ɪŋ **rove** rəʊv ‖ roʊv
Reeves riːvz
reexamination ˌriː ɪg ˌzæm ɪ ˈneɪʃ ᵊn ˌeg-,
ˌəg-, ˌɪk-, ˌek-, ˌək-, -ə'- ~**s** z
reexamin|e ˌriː ɪg ˈzæm ɪn -eg-, -əg-, -ɪk-, -ek-,
-ək-, §-ən ~**ed** d ~**es** z ~**ing** ɪŋ
ref ref **refs** refs
refac|e ˌˌriː ˈfeɪs ~**ed** t ~**es** ɪz əz ~**ing** ɪŋ
refashion ˌˌriː ˈfæʃ ᵊn ~**ed** d ~**ing** ˌɪŋ ~**s** z
refector|y rɪ ˈfekt ər |i rə-; ˈref ɪkt-, ˈref əkt-
~**ies** iz
refer rɪ ˈfɜː rə- ‖ -ˈfɜː ~**red** d **referring**
rɪ ˈfɜːr ɪŋ rə- ‖ -ˈfɜː ɪŋ ~**s** z
referable rɪ ˈfɜːr əb ᵊl rə-; ˈref ᵊr əb ᵊl ‖ -ˈfɜːː-
referee ˌref ə ˈriː ~**d** d ~**ing** ɪŋ ~**s** z
referenc|e ˈref ᵊr ənᵗs ~**ed** t ~**es** ɪz əz ~**ing** ɪŋ
ˈreference book; ˈreference ˌlibrary
referend|um ˌref ə ˈrend |əm ~**a** ə ~**ums** əmz
referent ˈref ᵊr ənt ~**s** s
referential ˌref ə ˈrenᵗʃ ᵊl ◂ ~**ly** i
referrab... —*see* **referab...**
referral rɪ ˈfɜːr əl rə- ‖ -ˈfɜːː əl ~**s** z
reffo ˈref əʊ ‖ -oʊ ~**s** z
refill v ˌˌriː ˈfɪl ~**ed** d ~**ing** ɪŋ ~**s** z
refill n ˈriː fɪl ˌˈ· ~**s** z
refinement rɪ ˈfaɪn mənt rə-, →-ˈfaɪm- ~**s** s
refiner|y rɪ ˈfaɪn ər |i rə- ~**ies** iz
refinish ˌriː ˈfɪn ɪʃ ~**ed** t ~**es** ɪz əz ~**ing** ɪŋ
re|fit v ˌˌriː |ˈfɪt ~**fits** ˈfɪts ~**fitted** ˈfɪt ɪd -əd
‖ ˈfɪt̬ əd ~**fitting** ˈfɪt ɪŋ ‖ ˈfɪt̬ ɪŋ
refit n ˈriː fɪt ˌˈ· ~**s** s
re|flate ˌˌriː |ˈfleɪt ~**flated** ˈfleɪt ɪd -əd
‖ ˈfleɪt̬ əd ~**flates** ˈfleɪts ~**flating** ˈfleɪt ɪŋ
‖ ˈfleɪt̬ ɪŋ
reflation ˌˌriː ˈfleɪʃ ᵊn ~**s** z
reflationary ˌˌriː ˈfleɪʃ ᵊn ər_i -ᵊn̩ ər i
‖ -ə ner i
reflect rɪ ˈflekt rə- ~**ed** ɪd əd ~**ing** ɪŋ ~**s** s
re·flecting ˌtelescope
reflection rɪ ˈflek ʃᵊn rə- ~**s** z
reflective rɪ ˈflekt ɪv rə- ~**ly** li ~**ness** nəs nɪs
reflectivit|y ˌˌriː flek ˈtɪv ət i |i rɪ,ˈ·· ·, rə-; -ɪt i
‖ -ət̬ |i ~**ies** iz
reflector rɪ ˈflekt ə rə- ‖ -ᵊr ~**s** z
reflet rə ˈfleɪ rɪ- ~**s** z —*Fr* [ʁə flɛ]
reflex n, adj ˈriː fleks ~**es** ɪz əz
reflex v rɪ ˈfleks rə-, ˌriː-, ˈriː fleks ~**ed** t ~**es** ɪz
əz ~**ing** ɪŋ
reflexion rɪ ˈflek ʃᵊn rə- ~**s** z
reflexive rɪ ˈfleks ɪv rə- ~**ly** li ~**ness** nəs nɪs ~**s**
z
re·flexive ˈpronoun
reflexivis... —*see* **reflexiviz...**
reflexivity ˌˌriː flek ˈsɪv ət i rɪ,ˈ·· ·, rə- -ɪt i
‖ -ət̬ i
reflexivization rɪ ˌfleks ɪv aɪ ˈzeɪʃ ᵊn rə-,
-,əv-, -ɪ'- ‖ -ə'- ~**s** z
reflexiviz|e rɪ ˈfleks ɪ vaɪz rə-, -ə- ~**ed** d ~**es**
ɪz əz ~**ing** ɪŋ
reflexology ˌˌriː flek ˈsɒl ədʒ i ‖ -ˈsɑːl-

re|float ˌˌriː |ˈfləʊt ‖ -|ˈfloʊt ~**floated** ˈfləʊt ɪd
-əd ‖ ˈfloʊt̬ əd ~**floating** ˈfləʊt ɪŋ ‖ ˈfloʊt̬ ɪŋ
~**floats** ˈfləʊts ‖ ˈfloʊts
refluent ˈref lu ənt
reflux n ˈriː flʌks ~**es** ɪz əz
reforest ˌˌriː ˈfɒr ɪst -əst ‖ -ˈfɔːr əst -ˈfɑːr- ~**ed**
ɪd əd ~**ing** ɪŋ ~**s** s
reforestation ˌˌriː ˌfɒr ɪ ˈsteɪʃ ᵊn ˌ·ˌ·'·· ·, -ə'--
‖ -ˌfɔːr- -ˌfɑːr- ~**s** z
reform v 'improve, rectify'; n rɪ ˈfɔːm rə-
‖ -ˈfɔːrm ~**ed** d ~**ing** ɪŋ ~**s** z
reform, re-form v 'form again' ˌˌriː ˈfɔːm
‖ -ˈfɔːrm ~**ed** d ~**ing** ɪŋ ~**s** z
reform|at ˌˌriː ˈfɔːm |æt ‖ -ˈfɔːrm- ~**ats** æts
~**atted** æt ɪd -əd ‖ æt̬ əd ~**atting** æt ɪŋ
‖ æt̬ ɪŋ
reformation, R~ ˌref ə ˈmeɪʃ ᵊn ˌɔː- ‖ -ᵊr- ~**s** z
reformative rɪ ˈfɔːm ət ɪv rə- ‖ -ˈfɔːrm ət̬ ɪv
reformator|y rɪ ˈfɔːm ət̬ˌər |i rə-
‖ -ˈfɔːrm ə tɔːr |i -toʊr i ~**ies** iz
reformism rɪ ˈfɔːm ˌɪz əm rə- ‖ -ˈfɔːrm-
reformist rɪ ˈfɔːm ɪst rə-, §-əst ‖ -ˈfɔːrm- ~**s** s
reformu|late ˌˌriː ˈfɔːm ju leɪt -jə- ‖ -ˈfɔːrm jə-
~**lated** leɪt ɪd -əd ‖ leɪt̬ əd ~**lates** leɪts
~**lating** leɪt ɪŋ ‖ leɪt̬ ɪŋ
refract rɪ ˈfrækt rə- ~**ed** ɪd əd ~**ing** ɪŋ ~**s** s
re·fracting ˌtelescope
refraction rɪ ˈfræk ʃᵊn rə- ~**s** z
refractive rɪ ˈfrækt ɪv rə- ~**ly** li ~**ness** nəs nɪs
re·fractive ˈindex
refractivity ˌˌriː fræk ˈtɪv ət i rɪ,ˈ·· ·, rə-, -ɪt i
‖ -ət̬ i
refractometer ˌˌriː fræk ˈtɒm ɪt ə rɪ,ˈ·· ·, rə-,
-ət ə ‖ -ˈtɑːm ət̬ ᵊr ~**s** z
refractor rɪ ˈfrækt ə rə- ‖ -ᵊr ~**s** z
refractor|y rɪ ˈfrækt ᵊr |i rə- ~**ies** iz ~**ily** əl i
ɪ li ~**iness** i nəs i nɪs
refrain v, n rɪ ˈfreɪn rə- ~**ed** d ~**ing** ɪŋ ~**s** z
re|freeze ˌˌriː| ˈfriːz ~**freezes** ˈfriːz ɪz -əz
~**froze** ˈfrəʊz ‖ ˈfroʊz ~**frozen** ˈfrəʊz ᵊn
‖ ˈfroʊz ᵊn
refresh rɪ ˈfreʃ rə- ~**ed** t ~**er/s** ə/z ᵊr/z ~**es** ɪz
əz ~**ing/ly** ɪŋ /li
re·fresher course
refreshment rɪ ˈfreʃ mənt rə- ~**s** s
refried ˌˌriː ˈfraɪd ◂
refrigerant rɪ ˈfrɪdʒ ᵊr ənt rə- ~**s** s
refrige|rate rɪ ˈfrɪdʒ ə |reɪt rə- ~**rated** reɪt ɪd
-əd ‖ reɪt̬ əd ~**rates** reɪts ~**rating** reɪt ɪŋ
‖ reɪt̬ ɪŋ
refrigeration rɪ ˌfrɪdʒ ə ˈreɪʃ ᵊn rə-
refrigerator rɪ ˈfrɪdʒ ə reɪt ə rə- ‖ -reɪt̬ ᵊr ~**s** z
re·frigerator-ˈfreezer, ·ˈ···,··
reft reft
refuel ˌˌriː ˈfjuː əl ˌˈfjuːl ~**ed**, ~**led** d ~**ing**,
~**ling** ɪŋ ~**s** z
refug|e ˈref juːdʒ -juːʒ ~**es** ɪz əz
refugee ˌref ju ˈdʒiː ~**s** z
refulgence rɪ ˈfʌldʒ ənᵗs rə-, -ˈfʊldʒ-
refulgent rɪ ˈfʌldʒ ənt rə-, -ˈfʊldʒ- ~**ly** li
refund v rɪ ˈfʌnd rə-, ˌriː-, ˈriː fʌnd ~**ed** ɪd əd
~**ing** ɪŋ ~**s** z
refund n ˈriː fʌnd ~**s** z

R

refundable ri ˈfʌnd əb ᵊl rə-, ˌriː-
refurbish ˌriː ˈfɜːb ɪʃ ‖ ri-, -ˈfɜːb ɪʃ **~ed** t **~es**
ɪz əz **~ing** ɪŋ **~ment/s** mənt/s
refusal ri ˈfjuːz ᵊl rə- **~s** z
refus|e *v* ri ˈfjuːz rə- **~ed** d **~es** ɪz əz **~ing** ɪŋ
refuse *n* ˈref juːs (!)
  ˈrefuse ˌdump
refusenik ri ˈfjuːz nɪk rə- **~s** s
refutable ri ˈfjuːt əb ᵊl rə-; ˈref jut- ‖ ri ˈfjuːt̬-
refutation ˌref ju ˈteɪʃ ᵊn **~s** z
re|fute ri |ˈfjuːt rə- **~futed** ˈfjuːt ɪd -əd
  ‖ ˈfjuːt̬ əd **~futes** ˈfjuːts **~futing** ˈfjuːt ɪŋ
  ‖ ˈfjuːt̬ ɪŋ
Reg redʒ (!) **Reg's** ˈredʒ ɪz -əz
-reg *BrE stress-neutral suffix relating to age of*
  cars redʒ **S-reg** ˈes redʒ
regain ri ˈgeɪn rə-, ˌriː- **~ed** d **~ing** ɪŋ **~s** z
regal ˈriːg ᵊl
regal|e ri ˈgeɪᵊl rə- **~ed** d **~es** z **~ing** ɪŋ
regalia ri ˈgeɪl i‿ə rə- ‖ -ˈ-jə
regalit|y riː ˈgæl ət i ri-, -ɪt- ‖ -ət̬ |i **~ies** iz
regally ˈriːg ᵊl i
Regan ˈriːg ən
regard *v, n* ri ˈgɑːd rə- ‖ -ˈgɑːrd **~ed** ɪd əd
  ~ing ɪŋ **~s** z
regardful ri ˈgɑːd fᵊl rə-, -fʊl ‖ -ˈgɑːrd- **~ly** ˌi
  ~ness nəs nɪs
regardless ri ˈgɑːd ləs rə-, -lɪs ‖ -ˈgɑːrd- **~ly** li
  ~ness nəs nɪs
regatta ri ˈgæt ə rə- ‖ -ˈgæt̬ ə -ˈgɑːt̬- **~s** z
regenc|y, R~ ˈriːdʒ ən‿ts |i **~ies** iz
regenerate *adj* ri ˈdʒen ər‿ət rə-, ˌriː-, -ɪt,
  -ə reɪt **~ness** nəs nɪs
regene|rate *v* ri ˈdʒen ə |reɪt rə-, ˌriː- **~rated**
  reɪt ɪd -əd ‖ reɪt̬ əd **~rates** reɪts **~rating**
  reɪt ɪŋ ‖ reɪt̬ ɪŋ
regeneration ri ˌdʒen ə ˈreɪʃ ᵊn rə-, ˌriː,·ˌ·ˈ·-
  ~s z
regenerative ri ˈdʒen ər‿ət ɪv rə-, ˌriː-,
  -ə reɪt ɪv ‖ -ər‿ət̬ ɪv -ə reɪt̬ ɪv **~ly** li
Regensburg ˈreɪg ənz bɜːg -bʊəg ‖ -bɜːg
  —*Ger* [ˈʁeːg ᵊns bʊʁk]
regent, R~ ˈriːdʒ ənt **~s**, **~'s** s **~ship/s** ʃɪp/s
  ˌRegent's ˈPark; ˈRegent ˌStreet
Reger ˈreɪg ə ‖ -ᵊr
reggae ˈreg eɪ
Reggie ˈredʒ i
Reggio ˈredʒ i əʊ ‖ -oʊ —*It* [ˈred dʒo]
regicide ˈredʒ ɪ saɪd -ə- **~s** z
regime, régime reɪ ˈʒiːm re-, rɪ-, rə-, §-ˈdʒiːm;
  ˈreɪʒ iːm ‖ rə- —*Fr* [ʁe ʒim] **~s** z
regimen ˈredʒ ɪm ən -əm-; -ɪ men, -ə- **~s** z
regi|ment *v* ˈredʒ ɪ |ment -ə-, ˌ·ˈ·|· —*See note*
  at -ment **~mented** ment ɪd -əd ‖ menţ əd
  ~menting ment ɪŋ ‖ menţ ɪŋ **~ments** ments
regiment *n* ˈredʒ ɪ mənt -ə- **~s** s
regimental ˌredʒ ɪ ˈment ᵊl ◂ -ə- ‖ -ˈmenţ ᵊl ◂
  ~ly i **~s** z
regimentation ˌredʒ ɪ men ˈteɪʃ ᵊn ˌ·ə-,
  -mən'-
Regina rɪ ˈdʒaɪn ə rə-, §riː- —*but as a personal*
  name, sometimes -ˈdʒiːn-
Reginald ˈredʒ ɪn ᵊld -ᵊn‿əld

region ˈriːdʒ ən **~s** z
regional ˈriːdʒ ᵊn‿əl
regionalism ˈriːdʒ ən‿ə ˌlɪz əm
regionality ˌriːdʒ ə ˈnæl ət i -ɪt i ‖ -ət̬ i
regionally ˈriːdʒ ᵊn‿əl i
Regis ˈriːdʒ ɪs §-əs
register ˈredʒ ɪst ə -əst- ‖ -ᵊr **~ed** d
  registering ˈredʒ ɪst ər‿ɪŋ '-əst- **~s** z
  ˌRegistered ˌGeneral ˈNurse; ˌRegistered
  ˈNurse; ˌregistered ˈmail; ˌregistered
  ˈpost; ˈregister ˌoffice
registrable ˈredʒ ɪs trəb ᵊl '-əs-
registrant ˈredʒ ɪs trənt -əs- **~s** s
registrar ˌredʒ ɪ ˈstrɑː -ə-, ˈ·· · ‖ ˈredʒ ə strɑːr
  ~s z
registrar|y ˈredʒ ɪs trər |i '-əs- ‖ -trer |i **~ies**
  iz
registration ˌredʒ ɪ ˈstreɪʃ ᵊn -ə- **~s** z
  ˌregiˈstration ˌdocument; ˌregiˈstration
  ˌnumber
regis|try ˈredʒ ɪs |tri -əs- **~tries** triz
  ˈregistry ˌoffice
Regius ˈriːdʒ i‿əs ˈriːdʒ əs
reglet ˈreg lət -lɪt **~s** s
regnal ˈreg nᵊl
regnant ˈreg nənt
rego *'registration'* ˈredʒ əʊ ‖ -oʊ
regress *v* ri ˈgres rə-, ˌriː- **~ed** t **~es** ɪz əz **~ing**
  ɪŋ
regress *n* ˈriː gres
regression ri ˈgreʃ ᵊn rə-, ˌriː- **~s** z
  reˈgression aˌnalysis
regressive ri ˈgres ɪv rə-, ˌriː- **~ly** li **~ness** nəs
  nɪs
re|gret *v, n* ri |ˈgret rə- **~grets** ˈgrets
  ~gretted ˈgret ɪd -əd ‖ ˈgret̬ əd **~gretting**
  ˈgret ɪŋ ‖ ˈgret̬ ɪŋ
regretful ri ˈgret fᵊl rə-, -fʊl **~ly** ˌi **~ness** nəs
  nɪs
regrett... —*see* **regret...**
regrettab|le ri ˈgret əb ᵊl rə- ‖ -ˈgret̬- **~ly** li
regroup ˌriː ˈgruːp **~ed** t **~ing** ɪŋ **~s** s
regs *'regulations'* regz
regular ˈreg jʊl ə -jəl-, △-əl̩ ə ‖ -jəl ᵊr **~s** z
regularis... —*see* **regulariz...**
regularit|y ˌreg ju ˈlær ət |i ˌ·jə-, △ˌ·ə-, -ɪt i
  ‖ -jə ˈlær ət̬ |i -ˈler- **~ies** iz
regularization ˌreg jʊl ər aɪ ˈzeɪʃ ᵊn ˌ·jəl-,
  △ˌ·əl̩, -ɪˈ- ‖ -jəl ər ə- **~s** z
regulariz|e ˈreg jʊl ə raɪz '·jəl-, △ˌ·əl̩ ‖ -jəl-
  ~ed d **~es** ɪz əz **~ing** ɪŋ
regularly ˈreg jʊl ə li '·jəl-, △ˈ·əl̩ əl i
  ‖ -jəl ᵊr li
regu|late ˈreg ju |leɪt -jə-, §-ə- ‖ -jə- **~lated**
  leɪt ɪd -əd ‖ leɪt̬ əd **~lates** leɪts **~lating**
  leɪt ɪŋ ‖ leɪt̬ ɪŋ
regulation ˌreg ju ˈleɪʃ ᵊn -jə-, △-ə- ‖ -jə- **~s** z
regulative ˈreg jʊl ət ɪv '·jəl-; -ju leɪt ɪv
  ‖ -jə leɪt̬ ɪv -jəl ət-
regulator ˈreg ju leɪt ə '·jə-, △ˈ·ə- ‖ -jə leɪt̬ ᵊr
  ~s z

R

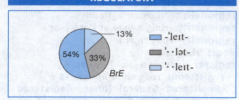

REGULATORY

- ■ -'leɪt- — 13%
- ■ '··lət- — 33%
- □ '··leɪt- — 54%

BrE

regulatory ˌreg ju 'leɪt ər i ˌ·jə-, △ˌ·ə-,
'·····, '··lət ər i ‖ 'reg jəl ə tɔːr i -toʊr i
— *Preference poll, BrE:* -'leɪt- *54%,* '··lət-
33%, '··leɪt ·· *13%.*

regulo 'reg ju ləʊ -jə-, △-ə- ‖ -jə loʊ
regulus, R~ 'reg jʊl əs -jəl-, §-əl- ‖ -jəl-
regurgi|tate ri 'gɜːdʒ ɪ |teɪt rə-, ˌriː-, -ə-
‖ -'gɜːdʒ- **~tated** teɪt ɪd -əd ‖ teɪt̬ əd **~tates**
teɪts **~tating** teɪt ɪŋ ‖ teɪt̬ ɪŋ
regurgitation ri ˌgɜːdʒ ɪ 'teɪʃ ᵊn rə-, ˌriː,·····,
-ə'-- ‖ -ˌgɜːdʒ- **~s** z
rehab 'riː hæb
rehabili|tate ˌriːə 'bɪl ɪ |teɪt ˌ·hə-, -'·ə- **~tated**
teɪt ɪd -əd ‖ teɪt̬ əd **~tates** teɪts **~tating**
teɪt ɪŋ ‖ teɪt̬ ɪŋ
rehabilitation ˌriːə ˌbɪl ɪ 'teɪʃ ᵊn ˌ·hə-, -ə'- **~s**
z
rehash *n* 'riː hæʃ ˌ·'· **~es** ɪz əz
rehash *v* ˌ(ˌ)riː 'hæʃ **~ed** t **~es** ɪz əz **~ing** ɪŋ
re|hear ˌriː |'hɪə ‖ -|'hɪʳr **~heard** 'hɜːd ‖ 'hɜːd
~hearing 'hɪər ɪŋ ‖ 'hɪr ɪŋ **~hears** 'hɪəz
‖ 'hɪʳrz
rehearsal ri 'hɜːs ᵊl rə- ‖ -'hɜːs ᵊl **~s** z
rehears|e ri 'hɜːs rə- ‖ -'hɜːs **~ed** t **~es** ɪz əz
~ing ɪŋ
reheat *n* 'riː hiːt **~s** s
re|heat *v* ˌriː |'hiːt **~heated** 'hiːt ɪd -əd
‖ 'hiːt̬ əd **~heating** 'hiːt ɪŋ ‖ 'hiːt̬ ɪŋ **~heats**
'hiːts
Rehnquist 'ren kwɪst →'reŋ-
Rehoboam, r~ ˌriːə 'bəʊ əm -hə- ‖ -'boʊ əm
~s z
rehous|e ˌriː 'haʊz **~ed** d **~es** ɪz əz **~ing** ɪŋ
re|hydrate ˌriː| haɪ 'dreɪt ‖ -'haɪdr eɪt
~hydrated haɪ 'dreɪt ɪd əd ‖ 'haɪdr eɪt̬ əd
~hydrates haɪ 'dreɪts ‖ 'haɪdr eɪts
~hydrating haɪ 'dreɪt ɪŋ ‖ 'haɪdr eɪt̬ ɪŋ
rehydration ˌriː haɪ 'dreɪʃ ᵊn
Reich raɪk raɪʃ —*Ger* [ʁaɪç]
Reichstag 'raɪks tɑːg 'raɪxs, 'raɪʃ- —*Ger*
[ˈʁaɪçs tɑːk]
Reid riːd
reification ˌreɪ ɪf ɪ 'keɪʃ ᵊn ˌriː-, -əf-, §-ə'--
rei|fy 'reɪ ɪ |faɪ 'riː-, -ə- **~fied** faɪd **~fies** faɪz
~fying faɪ ɪŋ
Reigate 'raɪ geɪt -gɪt
reign reɪn (= *rain*) **reigned** reɪnd **reigning**
'reɪn ɪŋ **reigns** reɪnz
ˌreign of 'terror
reiki 'reɪk i —*Jp* [ˈɾee ki]
Reilly 'raɪl i
reimburs|e ˌriː ɪm 'bɜːs -əm- ‖ -'bɜːs **~ed** t
~ement/s mənt/s **~es** ɪz əz **~ing** ɪŋ

Reims riːmz —*Fr* [ʁɛ̃ːs]
rein reɪn (= *rain*) **reined** reɪnd **reining**
'reɪn ɪŋ **reins** reɪnz
reincarn|ate *v* ˌriː ɪn 'kɑːn |eɪt →-ɪŋ-; ˌ·'··;
-kɑː 'n|eɪt ‖ -'kɑːrn |eɪt **~ated** eɪt ɪd -əd
‖ eɪt̬ əd **~ates** eɪts **~ating** eɪt ɪŋ ‖ eɪt̬ ɪŋ
reincarnate *adj* ˌriː ɪn 'kɑːn ət ◂ →-ɪŋ-, -ɪt, -eɪt
‖ -'kɑːrn ət
reincarnation ˌriː ɪn kɑː 'neɪʃ ᵊn →ˌ·ɪŋ-
‖ -kɑːr'-- **~s** z
reindeer 'reɪn dɪə ‖ -dɪr
reinforc|e ˌriː ɪn 'fɔːs §-ən- ‖ -'fɔːrs -'foʊrs **~ed**
t **~ement/s** mənt/s **~es** ɪz əz **~ing** ɪŋ
ˌreinforced 'concrete
Reinhardt, Reinhart 'raɪn hɑːt ‖ -hɑːrt
reinstal, reinstal|l ˌriː ɪn 'stɔːl ‖ -'stɑːl **~led** d
~ling ɪŋ **~s** z
rein|state ˌriː ɪn |'steɪt **~stated** 'steɪt ɪd -əd
‖ 'steɪt̬ əd **~statement** 'steɪt mənt **~states**
'steɪts **~stating** 'steɪt ɪŋ ‖ 'steɪt̬ ɪŋ
reinsurance ˌriː ɪn 'ʃʊər ᵊn⁺s -'ʃɔːr- ‖ -'ʃʊr ᵊn⁺s
-'ʃɜː-
reinsure ˌriː ɪn 'ʃʊə -'ʃɔː ‖ -'ʃʊʳr -'ʃɜː- **~d** d
reinsuring ˌriː ɪn 'ʃʊər ɪŋ -'ʃɔːr- ‖ -'ʃʊr ɪŋ
-'ʃɜː- **~s** z
reinterp|ret ˌriː ɪn 'tɜːp |rɪt -rət ‖ -'tɜːp |rət
~reted rɪt ɪd rət əd ‖ rət̬ əd **~reting** rɪt ɪŋ
rət ɪŋ ‖ rət̬ ɪŋ **~rets** rɪts rəts ‖ rəts
reinterpretation ˌriː ɪn ˌtɜːp rɪ 'teɪʃ ᵊn -rə'--
‖ -ˌtɜːp- **~s** z
reintroduc|e ˌriː ɪntr ə 'djuːs →-'dʒuːs, §-'duːs
‖ -'duːs -'djuːs **~ed** t **~es** ɪz əz **~ing** ɪŋ
reintroduction ˌriː ɪntrə 'dʌk ʃᵊn **~s** z
rein|vent ˌriː ɪn| 'vent **~vented** 'vent ɪd -əd
‖ 'vent̬ ɪŋ **~venting** 'vent ɪŋ ‖ 'vent̬ ɪŋ
~vents 'vents
reinvest ˌriː ɪn 'vest **~ed** ɪd əd **~ing** ɪŋ **~s** s
reinvigo|rate ˌriː ɪn 'vɪg ə |reɪt **~rated** reɪt ɪd
-əd ‖ reɪt̬ əd **~rates** reɪts **~rating** reɪt ɪŋ
‖ reɪt̬ ɪŋ
reinvigoration ˌriː ɪn ˌvɪg ə 'reɪʃ ᵊn
reissu|e *v, n* ˌriː 'ɪʃ uː -'ɪs juː, -'ɪʃ juː **~ed** d **~es**
z **~ing** ɪŋ
reite|rate ri 'ɪt ə |reɪt ˌriː- ‖ -'ɪt̬- **~rated** reɪt ɪd
-əd ‖ reɪt̬ əd **~rates** reɪts **~rating** reɪt ɪŋ
‖ reɪt̬ ɪŋ
reiteration ri ˌɪt ə 'reɪʃ ᵊn ˌriː,·'·· ‖ -ˌɪt̬- **~s** z
Reith riːθ
reject *v* ri 'dʒekt rə- **~ed** ɪd əd **~ing** ɪŋ **~s** s
reject *n* 'riː dʒekt **~s** s
rejection ri 'dʒek ʃᵊn rə- **~s** z
rejig ˌriː 'dʒɪg **~ged** d **~ger/s** ə/z ‖ ᵊr/z **~ging**
ɪŋ **~s** z
rejoic|e ri 'dʒɔɪs rə- **~ed** t **~es** ɪz əz **~ing/ly**
ɪŋ /li
rejoin *'join again'*, **re-join** ˌriː 'dʒɔɪn **~ed** d
~ing ɪŋ **~s** z
rejoin *'reply'* ri 'dʒɔɪn rə- **~ed** d **~ing** ɪŋ **~s** z
rejoinder ri 'dʒɔɪnd ə rə- ‖ -ᵊr **~s** z
rejuve|nate ri 'dʒuːv ə |neɪt rə-, -ɪ- **~nated**
neɪt ɪd -əd ‖ neɪt̬ əd **~nates** neɪts **~nating**
neɪt ɪŋ ‖ neɪt̬ ɪŋ

R

rejuvenation ri ˌdʒuːv ə 'neɪʃ ᵊn rə-, ˌriː.ˌ·ˈ·, -ɪ'-- ~s z

rejuvenesc|ence ˌriː. ˌdʒuːv ə 'nes |ᵊn's ri,·ˈ·-, rə-, -ɪ'-- ~ent ᵊnt

rekindl|e ˌ(ˌ)riː 'kɪnd ᵊl ~ed d ~es z ~ing ɪŋ

relaid ˌriː 'leɪd ◄

relaps|e v ri 'læps rə- ~ed t ~es ɪz əz ~ing ɪŋ

relaps|e n ri 'læps rə-; 'riː læps ~es ɪz əz

re|late, R~ ri |'leɪt rə- ~lated 'leɪt ɪd -əd ‖ 'leɪt̬ əd ~lates 'leɪts ~lating 'leɪt ɪŋ ‖ 'leɪt̬ ɪŋ

related ri 'leɪt ɪd -əd ‖ -'leɪt̬ əd ~ness nəs nɪs

relation ri 'leɪʃ ᵊn rə- ~s z

relational ri 'leɪʃ ᵊn əl rə-

relationship ri 'leɪʃ ᵊn ʃɪp rə- ~s s

relatival ˌrel ə 'taɪv ᵊl ◄

relative 'rel ət ɪv ‖ -ət̬ ɪv ~ly li ~ness nəs nɪs ~s z

ˌrelative 'clause; ˌrelative 'pronoun

relativis... —see **relativiz...**

relativism 'rel ət ɪv ˌɪz əm ‖ 'rel ət̬-

relativistic ˌrel ət ɪv 'ɪst ɪk ◄ -əv'-- ‖ ˌrel ət̬- ~ally ᵊl i

relativity, R~ ˌrel ə 'tɪv ət i -ɪt i ‖ -ət̬ i

relativization ˌrel ət ɪv aɪ 'zeɪʃ ᵊn -ɪ'-- ‖ ˌrel ət̬ ɪv ə- ~s z

relativiz|e 'rel ət ɪv aɪz ‖ 'rel ət̬- ~ed d ~es ɪz əz ~ing ɪŋ

relator ri 'leɪt ə rə- ‖ -'leɪt̬ ᵊr ~s z

relaunch n 'riː lɔːntʃ ‖ -lɑːntʃ ~es ɪz əz

relaunch v ˌriː 'lɔːntʃ ‖ -'lɑːntʃ ~ed t ~es ɪz əz ~ing ɪŋ

relax ri 'læks rə- ~ed t ~es ɪz əz ~ing ɪŋ

relaxant ri 'læks ᵊnt rə- ~s s

relaxation ˌriː læk 'seɪʃ ᵊn ˌrel ək- ~s z

re|lay v 'lay again' ˌriː |'leɪ ~laid 'leɪd ~laying 'leɪ ɪŋ ~lays 'leɪz

relay n 'riː leɪ ~s z

'relay race; 'relay ˌstation

relay v 'send by relay' 'riː leɪ ri 'leɪ, rə- ~ed d ~ing ɪŋ ~s z

releas|e v, n ri 'liːs rə- ~ed t ~es ɪz əz ~ing ɪŋ

rele|gate 'rel ɪ |geɪt -ə- ~gated geɪt ɪd -əd ‖ geɪt̬ əd ~gates geɪts ~gating geɪt ɪŋ ‖ geɪt̬ ɪŋ

relegation ˌrel ɪ 'geɪʃ ᵊn -ə- ~s z

re|lent ri |'lent rə- ~lented 'lent ɪd -əd ‖ 'lent̬ əd ~lenting 'lent ɪŋ ‖ 'lent̬ ɪŋ ~lents 'lents

relentless ri 'lent ləs rə-, -lɪs ~ly li ~ness nəs nɪs

relevanc|e 'rel əv ᵊn's -ɪv-; △'rev ᵊl- ~y i

relevant 'rel əv ənt -ɪv-; △'rev ᵊl- ~ly li

reliability ri ˌlaɪ ə 'bɪl ət i rə-, -ɪt i ‖ -ət̬ i

reliab|le ri 'laɪ əb |ᵊl rə- ~ly li

reliance ri 'laɪ ən's rə-

reliant ri 'laɪ ənt rə- ~ly li

relic 'rel ɪk ~s s

relict 'rel ɪkt ~s s

relie... —see **rely**

relief ri 'liːf rə- ~s s

re'lief map; re'lief road

reliev|e ri 'liːv rə- ~ed d ~es z ~ing ɪŋ

reliever ri 'liːv ə rə- ‖ -ᵊr ~s z

relievo ri 'liːv əʊ rə-; ˌrel i 'eɪv əʊ ‖ -oʊ ~s z

religion ri 'lɪdʒ ən rə- ~s z

religiose ri 'lɪdʒ i əʊs rə-, -əʊz ‖ -oʊs

religiosity ri ˌlɪdʒ i 'ɒs ət i rə-, -ɪt i; ˌrel ɪ 'dʒɒs· ·, ˌ·ə- ‖ -'ɑːs ət̬ i

religious ri 'lɪdʒ əs rə- ~ly li ~ness nəs nɪs

relin|e ˌriː 'laɪn ~ed d ~es z ~ing ɪŋ

relinquish ri 'lɪŋk wɪʃ rə- ~ed t ~es ɪz əz ~ing ɪŋ ~ment mənt

reliquar|y 'rel ɪk wər |i '·ək- ‖ -ə kwer |i ~ies iz

relish n, v 'rel ɪʃ ~ed t ~es ɪz əz ~ing ɪŋ

reliv|e ˌriː 'lɪv ~ed d ~es z ~ing ɪŋ

reload ˌriː 'ləʊd ‖ -'loʊd ~ed ɪd əd ~ing ɪŋ ~s z

reloc|ate ˌriː ləʊ 'k|eɪt ‖ ˌriː 'loʊk |eɪt -loʊ 'k|eɪt ~ated eɪt ɪd -əd ‖ eɪt̬ əd ~ates eɪts ~ating eɪt ɪŋ ‖ eɪt̬ ɪŋ

relocation ˌriː ləʊ 'keɪʃ ᵊn ‖ -loʊ- ~s z

reluctance ri 'lʌkt ən's rə-

reluctant ri 'lʌkt ənt rə- ~ly li

reluctivity ˌrel ʌk 'tɪv ət i ˌriː lʌk-, ri ˌlʌk-, rə ˌlʌk-, -ɪt i ‖ -ət̬ i

re|ly ri |'laɪ rə- ~lied 'laɪd ~lies 'laɪz ~lying 'laɪ ɪŋ

rem rem

REM rem ˌɑːr iː 'em ‖ ˌɑːr iː 'em

remade ˌriː 'meɪd

remain ri 'meɪn rə- ~ed d ~ing ɪŋ ~s z

remaind|er n, v ri 'meɪnd |ə rə- ‖ -|ᵊr ~ered əd ‖ ᵊrd ~ering ᵊr ɪŋ ~ers əz ‖ ᵊrz

remake n 'riː meɪk ~s s

re|make v ˌriː |'meɪk ~made 'meɪd ~makes 'meɪks ~making 'meɪk ɪŋ

remand ri 'mɑːnd rə-, §-'mænd ‖ -'mænd ~ed ɪd əd ~ing ɪŋ ~s z

remanence 'rem ən ən's

remark ri 'mɑːk rə- ‖ -'mɑːrk ~ed t ~ing ɪŋ ~s s

remarkab|le ri 'mɑːk əb |ᵊl rə- ‖ -'mɑːrk- ~ly li

remarque, R~ ri 'mɑːk rə- ‖ -'mɑːrk

remarriag|e ˌriː 'mær ɪdʒ ‖ -'mer- ~es ɪz əz

remarr|y ˌriː 'mær |i ‖ -'mer- ~ied id ~ies iz ~ying i ɪŋ

remaster ˌriː 'mɑːst ə §-'mæst- ‖ -'mæst ᵊr ~ed d ~ing ɪŋ ~s z

rematch n 'riː mætʃ ~es ɪz əz

Rembrandt 'rem brænt -brənt —Dutch ['rɛm brɑnt] ~s, ~'s s

REME 'riːm i

remediab|le ri 'miːd i əb |ᵊl rə- ~leness ᵊl nəs -nɪs ~ly li

remedial ri 'miːd i əl rə- ~ly i

remediation ri ˌmiːd i 'eɪʃ ᵊn rə-

remed|y 'rem əd |i -ɪd- ~ied id ~ies iz ~ying i ɪŋ

remem|ber ri 'mem |bə rə- ‖ -|bᵊr ~bered bəd ‖ bᵊrd ~bering bər ɪŋ ~bers bəz ‖ bᵊrz

R

remembranc|e ri 'mem brən¦s
rə- △-'mem b³r ən¦s **~er/s** ə/z ‖ -³r/z **~es** ɪz
əz
Re'membrance Day; **Re,membrance
'Sunday**
Remick 'rem ɪk
remilitaris... —*see* **remilitariz...**
remilitarization ˌriː ˌmɪl ɪt ³r aɪ 'zeɪʃ ³n -ˌət-,
·ˌ· · · ·'· ·, -ɪ'-- ‖ -əʈ ³r ə-
remilitariz|e (ˌ)riː 'mɪl ɪt ə raɪz -'-ət-
‖ -əʈ ə raɪz **~ed** d **~es** ɪz əz **~ing** ɪŋ
remind ri 'maɪnd rə- **~ed** ɪd əd **~ing** ɪŋ **~s** z
reminder ri 'maɪnd ə rə- ‖ -³r **~s** z
Remington 'rem ɪŋ tən
reminisc|e ˌrem ɪ 'nɪs -ə- **~ed** t **~es** ɪz əz **~ing**
ɪŋ
reminiscenc|e ˌrem ɪ 'nɪs ³n¦s -ə- **~es** ɪz əz
reminiscent ˌrem ɪ 'nɪs ³nt ◂ -ə- **~ly** li
remiss ri 'mɪs rə- **~ness** nəs nɪs
remission ri 'mɪʃ ³n rə- **~s** z
re|mit v ri ‖'mɪt rə- **~mits** 'mɪts **~mitted**
'mɪt ɪd -əd ‖ 'mɪʈ əd **~mitting** 'mɪt ɪŋ
‖ 'mɪʈ ɪŋ
remit n 'riː mɪt ri 'mɪt, rə- **~s** s
remittanc|e ri 'mɪt ³n¦s rə- **~es** ɪz əz
remittee ri ˌmɪt 'iː rə- **~s** z
remittent ri 'mɪt ³nt rə- **~ly** li
remitter ri 'mɪt ə rə- ‖ -'mɪʈ ³r **~s** z
remix n 'riː mɪks **~es** ɪz əz
remnant, R~ 'rem nənt **~s** s
remodel (ˌ)riː 'mɒd ³l ‖ -'mɑːd ³l **~ed, ~led** d
~ing, ~ling ɪŋ **~s** z
remold v ˌriː 'məʊld →-'mɒʊld ‖ -'moʊld **~ed**
ɪd əd **~ing** ɪŋ **~s** z
remold n 'riː məʊld →-mɒʊld ‖ -moʊld **~s** z
remonstranc|e ri 'mɒn¦s trən¦s rə- ‖ -'mɑːn¦s-
~es ɪz əz
remonstrant, R~ ri 'mɒn¦s trənt rə-
‖ -'mɑːn¦s- **~s** s
remons|trate ˌrem ən s|treɪt ri 'mɒn-, rə-
‖ ri 'mɑːn¦s |treɪt **~trated** treɪt ɪd -əd
‖ treɪʈ əd **~trates** treɪts **~trating** treɪt ɪŋ
‖ treɪʈ ɪŋ
remonstration ˌrem ən 'streɪʃ ³n ‖ ri ˌmɑːn-
~s z
remonstrative ri 'mɒn¦s trət ɪv rə-
‖ -'mɑːn¦s trəʈ ɪv
remontant ri 'mɒnt ənt rə- ‖ -'mɑːnt ³nt **~s** s
remora 'rem ³r ə ri 'mɔːr ə, rə- **~s** z
remorse ri 'mɔːs rə- ‖ -'mɔːrs
remorseful ri 'mɔːs f³l rə-, -fʊl ‖ -'mɔːrs- **~ly** i
~ness nəs nɪs
remorseless ri 'mɔːs ləs rə-, -lɪs ‖ -'mɔːrs- **~ly**
li **~ness** nəs nɪs
remortgag|e ˌriː 'mɔːg ɪdʒ ‖ -'mɔːrg- **~ed** d
~es ɪz əz **~ing** ɪŋ
re|mote ri ‖'məʊt rə- ‖ -ˌ'moʊt **~moter**
'məʊt ə ‖ 'moʊʈ ³r **~motest** 'məʊtɪst -əst
‖ 'moʊʈ əst
re,mote con'trol
remote-controlled ri ˌməʊt kən 'trəʊld ◂ rə-,
§-kɒn- ‖ -ˌmoʊt kən 'troʊld ◂

remote|ly ri 'məʊt |li rə- ‖ -'moʊt- **~ness** nəs
nɪs
remoulade, rémoulade ˌrem ə 'leɪd -u-,
-'lɑːd ‖ ˌreɪm ə 'lɑːd -u- **~s** z
remould v ˌriː 'məʊld →-'mɒʊld ‖ -'moʊld **~ed**
ɪd əd **~ing** ɪŋ **~s** z
remould n 'riː məʊld →-mɒʊld ‖ -moʊld **~s** z
re|mount v ˌriː ‖'maʊnt **~mounted** 'maʊnt ɪd
-əd ‖ 'maʊnʈ əd **~mounting** 'maʊnt ɪŋ
‖ 'maʊnʈ ɪŋ **~mounts** 'maʊnts
remount n 'riː maʊnt ˌ·'· **~s** s
removability ri ˌmuːv ə 'bɪl ət i rə- ‖ -əʈ i
removab|le ri 'muːv əb |³l rə- **~leness** ³l nəs
-nɪs **~ly** li
removal ri 'muːv ³l rə- **~s** z
re'moval van
remov|e ri 'muːv rə- **~ed** d **~es** z **~ing** ɪŋ
-remover ri ˌmuːv ə rə- ‖ -³r — **stain-remover**
'steɪn ri ˌmuːv ə -rə- ‖ -³r
remover ri 'muːv ə rə- ‖ -³r **~s** z
Remploy *tdmk* 'rem plɔɪ
remune|rate ri 'mjuːn ə |reɪt rə- **~rated**
reɪt ɪd -əd ‖ reɪʈ əd **~rates** reɪts **~rating**
reɪt ɪŋ ‖ reɪʈ ɪŋ
remuneration ri ˌmjuːn ə 'reɪʃ ³n
rə- △-'njuːm- **~s** z
remunerative ri 'mjuːn ³r ət ɪv rə-,
△-'njuːm-, -ə reɪt- ‖ -ər ̩əʈ ɪv -ə reɪʈ- **~ly** li
~ness nəs nɪs
Remus 'riːm əs
Remy, Rémy 'reɪm i ‖ reɪ 'miː —*Fr* [ʁə mi,
ʁe-]
renaissanc|e, R~ ri 'neɪs ³n¦s rə-, -ɒ̃s;
ˌren eɪ 'sɒ̃s ‖ ˌren ə 'saːn¦s -'zaːn¦s, '· · · (*)
—*Fr* [ʁə nɛ sɑ̃ːs] **~es** ɪz əz
renal 'riːn ³l
renam|e (ˌ)riː 'neɪm **~ed** d **~es** z **~ing** ɪŋ
renascenc|e ri 'næs ³n¦s rə-, -'neɪs- **~es** ɪz əz
renascent ri 'næs ³nt rə-, -'neɪs-
Renata ri 'nɑːt ə rə- ‖ -'nɑːʈ ə
Renault 'ren əʊ ‖ rə 'nɔːlt -'nɑːlt, -'noʊ (*)
—*Fr* [ʁə no] **~s** z
rend rend **rending** 'rend ɪŋ **rends** rendz **rent**
rent
Rendall, Rendell 'rend ³l
render 'rend ə ‖ -³r **~ed** d **rendering/s**
'rend ³r ɪŋ/z **~s** z
rendezvous v, n sing. 'rɒnd ɪ vuː- -ə-, -eɪ-
‖ 'rɑːnd eɪ- —*Fr* [ʁɑ̃ de vu] **~** n pl; v 3rd
sing. z **~ed** d **~ing** ɪŋ
rendition ren 'dɪʃ ³n **~s** z
rendzina rend 'ziːn ə **~s** z
Rene, René *man's name(i)* 'ren eɪ 'rən-, -i,
(ii) rə 'neɪ —*in AmE* (ii)
Renee, Renée *woman's name(i)* 'ren eɪ 'rən-,
(ii) rə 'neɪ, (iii) 'riːn i —*in AmE* (ii)
Rene *woman's name, short for* **Irene** 'riːn i
renegade 'ren ɪ geɪd -ə- **~s** z
reneg|e, renegu|e ri 'niːg rə-, -'neɪg, -'neg
‖ -'nɪg -'neg, -'niːg **~ed** d **~es** z **~ing** ɪŋ
renegotiable ˌriː nɪ 'gəʊʃ i̩ əb ³l ˌnə-,
'gəʊʃ əb ³l ‖ -'goʊʃ- -'goʊʃəb ³l

R

renegoti|ate ˌriː nɪ 'gəʊʃ i eɪt ˌ·nə- ‖ -'goʊʃ-
~ated eɪt ɪd -əd ~ates eɪts ~ating eɪt ɪŋ
‖ eɪt̬ ɪŋ

renew ri 'njuː rə-, ˌriː-, §-'nuː ‖ -'nuː -'njuː ~ed
d ~ing ɪŋ ~s z

renewability ri ˌnjuː ə 'bɪl ət i rə-, §-'nuː ˌ,
-ɪt i ‖ -ˌnuː- ə 'bɪl ət̬ i -ˌnjuː-

renewable ri 'njuː əb ᵊl rə-, ˌriː-, §-'nuː ˌ
‖ -'nuː əb ᵊl -'njuː- ~s z

renewal ri 'njuː əl rə-, ˌriː-, -'njuːl, §-'nuː ˌ,
§-'nuːl ‖ -'nuː əl -'njuː- ~s z

renewer ri 'njuː ə rə-, §-'nuː ˌ ‖ -'nuː ᵊr -'njuː ˌ
~s z

Renfrew 'ren fruː

reniform 'ren ɪ fɔːm 'riːn-, -ə- ‖ -fɔːrm

renin 'riːn ɪn §-ən

Renishaw 'ren ɪ ʃɔː §-ə- ‖ -ʃɑː

renminbi ˌren mɪn 'biː →ˌrem-, →-mɪm —Chi
rénmínbì [²ʐən ²mɪn ⁴pi]

Rennell 'ren ᵊl ‖ rə 'nel

Rennes ren —Fr [ʁɛn]

rennet 'ren ɪt §-ət

Rennie 'ren i ~s tdmk z

rennin 'ren ɪn §-ən

Reno 'riːn əʊ ‖ -oʊ

Renoir 'ren wɑː 'rən-; rə 'nwɑː ‖ rən 'wɑːr
'ren· —Fr [ʁə nwaːʁ] ~s, ~'s z

renounc|e ri 'naʊnts rə- ~ed t ~es ɪz əz ~ing
ɪŋ ~ement mənt

reno|vate 'ren əʊ |veɪt ‖ -ə- ~vated veɪt ɪd
-əd ‖ veɪt̬ əd ~vates veɪts ~vating veɪt ɪŋ
‖ veɪt̬ ɪŋ

renovation ˌren əʊ 'veɪʃ ᵊn ‖ -ə- ~s z

renown ri 'naʊn rə- ~ed d

Renshaw 'ren ʃɔː ‖ -ʃɑː

Rensselaer ˌren⁀s ə 'lɪə ‖ -'lɪʳr

rent rent rented 'rent ɪd -əd ‖ 'rent̬ əd
renting 'rent ɪŋ ‖ 'rent̬ ɪŋ rents rents
'rent boy; 'rent strike

rentable 'rent əb ᵊl ‖ 'rent̬-

rent-a-car 'rent ə kɑː ‖ 'rent̬ ə kɑːr

rent-a-crowd 'rent ə kraʊd ‖ 'rent̬-

rental 'rent ᵊl ‖ 'rent̬ ᵊl ~s z

rent-a-mob 'rent ə mɒb ‖ 'rent̬ ə mɑːb

rent-a-quote 'rent ə kwəʊt ‖ 'rent̬ ə kwoʊt

renter 'rent ə ‖ 'rent̬ ᵊr ~s z

rent-free ˌrent 'friː ◂

rentier 'rɒnt i eɪ 'rɑːnt- ‖ rɑːn 'tjeɪ —Fr
[ʁɑ̃ tje] ~s z

Rentokil tdmk 'rent əʊ kɪl ‖ 'rent̬ ə-

Renton 'rent ən ‖ -ᵊn

renumber ˌriː 'nʌm bə ‖ -bᵊr ~ed d
renumbering/s ˌriː 'nʌm bər ɪŋ/z ~s z

renunciation ri ˌnʌn⁀s i 'eɪʃ ᵊn rə- ~s z

Renwick (i) 'ren ɪk, (ii) -wɪk

reop|en ri 'əʊp |ən ˌriː- ‖ -'oʊp |ən ~ened ənd
→md ~ening ən ɪŋ ~ens ənz →mz

reorder ˌriː 'ɔːd ə ‖ -'ɔːrd ᵊr ~ed d reordering
ˌriː 'ɔːd ər ɪŋ ~s z

reorganis... —see reorganiz...

reorganization ri ˌɔːg ən aɪ 'zeɪʃ ᵊn ˌriː,··'··,
-ɪ'- ‖ -ˌɔːrg ən̬ə- ~s z

reorganiz|e ri 'ɔːg ə naɪz ˌriː- ‖ -'ɔːrg- ~ed d
~es ɪz əz ~ing ɪŋ

rep rep reps reps

repackag|e ˌriː 'pæk ɪdʒ ~ed d ~es ɪz əz ~ing
ɪŋ

repaid ri 'peɪd rə-, ₍ˌ₎riː-

re|paint ˌriː| 'peɪnt ~painted 'peɪnt ɪd -əd
‖ 'peɪnt̬ əd ~painting 'peɪnt ɪŋ ‖ 'peɪnt̬ ɪŋ
~paints 'peɪnts

repair ri 'peə rə- ‖ -'peᵊr -'pæᵊr ~ed d
repairing ri 'peər ɪŋ rə- ‖ -'per ɪŋ -'pær- ~s z

repairable ri 'peər əb ᵊl rə- ‖ -'per- -'pær-

repairer ri 'peər ə rə- ‖ -'per ᵊr -'pær- ~s z

repair|man ri 'peə |mæn rə-, -mən ‖ -'per-
-'pær- ~men men mən

reparab|le 'rep ər əb ᵊl ~ly li

reparation ˌrep ə 'reɪʃ ᵊn ~s z

reparative ri 'pær ət ɪv rə-; 'rep ᵊr ˌ ‖ -ət̬ ɪv
-'per-

repartee ˌrep ɑː 'tiː ‖ -ɑːr 'teɪ -ᵊr-, -'tiː

repast ri 'pɑːst rə-, §-'pæst; 'riː pɑːst, §-pæst
‖ -'pæst ~s s

repatri|ate ˌriː 'pætr i |eɪt rə- ‖ -'peɪtr- (*)
~ated eɪt ɪd -əd ‖ eɪt̬ əd ~ates eɪts ~ating
eɪt ɪŋ ‖ eɪt̬ ɪŋ

repatriation ˌriː ˌpætr i 'eɪʃ ᵊn ri,·'·, rə-
‖ ˌriː ˌpeɪtr- ,·'·· ~s z

re|pay ri |'peɪ rə- ~paid 'peɪd ~paying 'peɪ ɪŋ
~pays 'peɪz

repayable ri 'peɪ əb ᵊl rə-, ˌriː-

repayment ri 'peɪ mənt rə- ~s s

repeal v, n ri 'piːᵊl rə- ~ed d ~ing ɪŋ ~s z

re|peat v, n ri |'piːt rə- ~peated/ly 'piːt ɪd /li
-əd /li ‖ 'piːt̬ əd /li ~peating 'piːt ɪŋ
‖ 'piːt̬ ɪŋ ~peats 'piːts

repeatable ri 'piːt əb ᵊl rə- ‖ -'piːt̬-

repeater ri 'piːt ə rə- ‖ -'piːt̬ ᵊr ~s z

repechage, repêchage 'rep ə ʃɑːʒ -ɪ-, ,·'··
—Fr [ʁə pɛ ʃaːʒ]

repel ri 'pel rə- ~led d ~ling ɪŋ ~s z

repellant, repellent ri 'pel ənt rə- ~s s

repellor ri 'pel ə rə- ‖ -ᵊr ~s z

re|pent ri |'pent rə- ~pented 'pent ɪd -əd
‖ 'pent̬ əd ~penting 'pent ɪŋ ‖ 'pent̬ ɪŋ
~pents 'pents

repentanc|e ri 'pent ən⁀s rə- ‖ -ᵊn⁀s ~es ɪz əz

repentant ri 'pent ənt rə- ‖ -ᵊnt ~ly li

repercussion ˌriːp ə 'kʌʃ ᵊn ‖ -ᵊr- ˌrep- ~s z

repertoire 'rep ə twɑː ‖ -ᵊr twɑːr -ə- ~s z

repertor|y 'rep ət ər |i ‖ -ᵊr tɔːr |i '·ə-, -toʊr i
~ies iz
'repertory ˌcompany

repetend 'rep ɪ tend -ə-, ,·'·· ~s z

repetiteur, répétiteur ri ˌpet ɪ 'tɜː rə-, -,·ə-;
ˌrep ə tiː'· ‖ ˌreɪ peɪt ɪ 'tɜː ˌ·pet- —Fr
[ʁe pe ti tœːʁ] ~s z

repetition ˌrep ə 'tɪʃ ᵊn -ɪ- ~s z

repetitious ˌrep ə 'tɪʃ əs ◂ -ɪ- ~ly li ~ness nəs
nɪs

repetitive ri 'pet ət ɪv rə-, -ɪt- ‖ -'pet̬ ət̬ ɪv ~ly
li ~ness nəs nɪs

rephras|e ˌriː 'freɪz ~ed d ~es ɪz əz ~ing ɪŋ

repin|e ri 'paɪn rə- ~ed d ~es z ~ing ɪŋ

replac|e ri 'pleɪs rə-, ˌriː- **~ed** t **~es** ɪz əz **~ing** ɪŋ

replaceable ri 'pleɪs əb ᵊl rə-, ˌriː-

replacement ri 'pleɪs mənt rə-, ˌriː- **~s** s

replay v ˌriː 'pleɪ **~ed** d **~ing** ɪŋ **~s** z

replay n 'riː pleɪ **~s** z

replenish ri 'plen ɪʃ rə- **~ed** t **~es** ɪz əz **~ing** ɪŋ **~ment/s** mənt/s

replete ri 'pliːt rə- **~ness** nəs nɪs

repletion ri 'pliːʃ ᵊn rə-

replevin ri 'plev ɪn rə- §-ᵊn

replev|y ri 'plev |i rə- **~ied** id **~ies** iz **~ying** i ɪŋ

replica 'rep lɪk ə **~s** z

replicability ˌrep lɪk ə 'bɪl ət i -ɪt i ‖ -ət̬ i

replicable 'rep lɪk əb ᵊl

repli|cate v 'rep lɪ |keɪt -lə- **~cated** keɪt ɪd -əd ‖ keɪt̬ əd **~cates** keɪts **~cating** keɪt ɪŋ ‖ keɪt̬ ɪŋ

replication ˌrep lɪ 'keɪʃ ᵊn -lə- **~s** z

re|ply ri |'plaɪ rə- **~plied** 'plaɪd **~plies** 'plaɪz **~plying** 'plaɪ ɪŋ

reply-paid ri ˌplaɪ 'peɪd ◂ rə-

repo 'riː pəʊ ‖ -poʊ **~s** z

répondez s'il vous plaît ri ˌpɒnd eɪ ˌsiː vuː 'pleɪ rə-, reɪ-, -ˌsɪl- ‖ -ˌpɔːnd- -ˌpɑːnd- —Fr [ʁe pɔ̃ de sil vu plɛ]

re|port v, n ri |'pɔːt rə- ‖ -|'pɔːrt -'poʊrt **~ported/ly** 'pɔːt ɪd /li -əd- ‖ 'pɔːrt̬- 'poʊrt̬- **~porting** 'pɔːt ɪŋ ‖ 'pɔːrt̬ ɪŋ 'poʊrt̬- **~ports** 'pɔːts ‖ 'pɔːrts 'poʊrts **re**ˌ**ported 'speech**

reportage ˌrep ɔː 'tɑːʒ ri 'pɔːt ɪdʒ, rə- ‖ ri 'pɔːrt̬ ɪdʒ -'poʊrt̬-; ˌrep ɔːr 'tɑːʒ, -ᵊr-

reporter ri 'pɔːt ə rə- ‖ -'pɔːrt̬ ᵊr -'poʊrt̬- **~s** z

reportorial ˌrep ɔː 'tɔːr i əl ◂ ˌriːp-, -ə- ‖ ˌrep ᵊr- -'toʊr- **~ly** i

repos|e v, n ri 'pəʊz rə- ‖ -'poʊz **~ed** d **~es** ɪz əz **~ing** ɪŋ

reposeful ri 'pəʊz fᵊl rə-, -fʊl ‖ -'poʊz- **~ly** i **~ness** nəs nɪs

reposition ˌriː pə 'zɪʃ ᵊn **~ed** d **~ing** ɪŋ **~s** z

repositor|y ri 'pɒz ɪt̬ ᵊr |i rə-, -ᵊt̬- ‖ -'pɑːz ə tɔːr |i -toʊr i **~ies** iz

repossess ˌriː pə 'zes **~ed** t **~es** ɪz əz **~ing** ɪŋ

repossession ˌriː pə 'zeʃ ᵊn **~s** z

repousse, repoussé rə 'puːs eɪ ri- ‖ -ˌpuː 'seɪ —Fr [ʁə pu se]

repp rep

reprehend ˌrep ri 'hend -rə- **~ed** ɪd əd **~ing** ɪŋ **~s** z

reprehensibility ˌrep ri ˌhen's ə 'bɪl ət i ˌrə-, -ˌɪ-, -ɪt i ‖ -ət̬ i

reprehensib|le ˌrep ri 'hen's əb |ᵊl ◂ ˌrə-, -ɪb ᵊl **~ly** li

reprehension ˌrep ri 'hen'ʃ ᵊn -rə-

re-pre|sent ˌriː pri |'zent -prə- **~sented** 'zent ɪd -əd ‖ 'zent̬ əd **~senting** 'zent ɪŋ ‖ 'zent̬ ɪŋ **~sents** 'zents

repre|sent ˌrep ri |'zent -rə- **~sented** 'zent ɪd -əd ‖ 'zent̬ əd **~senting** 'zent ɪŋ ‖ 'zent̬ ɪŋ **~sents** 'zents

representation ˌrep ri zen 'teɪʃ ᵊn ˌ·rə-, -zən'- **~s** z

representational ˌrep ri zen 'teɪʃ ᵊn ˌəl ◂ ˌ·rə-, -zən'- **~ism** ˌɪz əm

representative ˌrep ri 'zent ət ɪv ◂ ˌ·rə- ‖ -'zent̬ ət̬ ɪv ◂ **~ly** li **~ness** nəs nɪs **~s** z

repress ri 'pres rə- **~ed** t **~es** ɪz əz **~ing** ɪŋ

repression ri 'preʃ ᵊn rə- **~s** z

repressive ri 'pres ɪv rə- **~ly** li **~ness** nəs nɪs

repressor ri 'pres ə rə- ‖ -ᵊr **~s** z

repriev|e ri 'priːv rə- **~ed** d **~es** ɪz əz **~ing** ɪŋ

reprimand v 'rep ri mɑːnd -rə-, ˌ·ˈ· ‖ -mænd **~ed** ɪd əd **~ing** ɪŋ **~s** z

reprimand n 'rep ri mɑːnd -rə- ‖ -mænd **~s** z

reprint n 'riː prɪnt ˌ·ˈ· **~s** s

re|print v ˌriː |'prɪnt **~printed** 'prɪnt ɪd -əd ‖ 'prɪnt̬ əd **~printing** 'prɪnt ɪŋ ‖ 'prɪnt̬ ɪŋ **~prints** 'prɪnts

reprisal ri 'praɪz ᵊl rə- **~s** z

repris|e ri 'priːz rə-, -'praɪz **~ed** d **~es** ɪz əz **~ing** ɪŋ

repro 'riː prəʊ ‖ -proʊ **~s** z

reproach n, v ri 'prəʊtʃ rə- ‖ -'proʊtʃ **~ed** t **~es** ɪz əz **~ing** ɪŋ

reproachful ri 'prəʊtʃ fᵊl rə-, -fʊl ‖ -'proʊtʃ- **~ly** i **~ness** nəs nɪs

repro|bate 'rep rəʊ |beɪt ‖ -rə- **~bated** beɪt ɪd -əd ‖ beɪt̬ əd **~bates** beɪts **~bating** beɪt ɪŋ ‖ beɪt̬ ɪŋ

reprobation ˌrep rəʊ 'beɪʃ ᵊn ‖ -rə-

reprocess ˌriː 'prəʊs es -'prɒs-, -ɪs, §-əs ‖ -'prɑːs- **~ed** t **~es** ɪz əz **~ing** ɪŋ

reproduc|e ˌriː p rə 'djuːs ˌrep-, →-'dʒuːs ‖ -'duːs -'djuːs **~ed** t **~er/s** ə/z ‖ ᵊr/z **~es** ɪz əz **~ing** ɪŋ

reproducible ˌriː p rə 'djuːs əb ᵊl ◂ ˌrep-, →-'dʒuːs-, -ɪb ᵊl ‖ -'duːs- -'djuːs-

reproduction ˌriː p rə 'dʌk ʃᵊn ˌrep- **~s** z

reproductive ˌriː p rə 'dʌkt ɪv ◂ ˌrep- **~ly** li **~ness** nəs nɪs

reprographer rɪ 'prɒg rəf ə riː- ‖ -'prɑːg rəf ᵊr **~s** z

reprographic ˌriː p rə 'græf ɪk ◂ ˌrep- **~ally** ᵊl i **~s** s

reprography rɪ 'prɒg rəf i riː- ‖ -'prɑːg-

reproof v, 'proof again' ˌriː 'pruːf §-'prʊf **~ed** t **~ing** ɪŋ **~s** s

reproof n, 'rebuke' ri 'pruːf rə-, §-'prʊf **~s** s

reprov|e ri 'pruːv rə- **~ed** d **~es** z **~ing/ly** ɪŋ /li

reptile 'rept aɪᵊl ‖ -ᵊl -aɪᵊl **~s** z

reptilian rep 'tɪl i ən **~s** z

Repton 'rept ən

republic, R~ ri 'pʌb lɪk rə- **~s** s

republican, R~ ri 'pʌb lɪk ən rə- **~s** z

republicanism, R~ ri 'pʌb lɪk ən ˌɪz əm rə-

repudi|ate ri 'pjuːd i |eɪt rə- **~ated** eɪt ɪd -əd ‖ eɪt̬ əd **~ates** eɪts **~ating** eɪt ɪŋ ‖ eɪt̬ ɪŋ **~ator/s** eɪt ə/z ‖ eɪt̬ ᵊr/z

repudiation ri ˌpjuːd i 'eɪʃ ᵊn rə- **~s** z

repugnance ri 'pʌg nən's rə-

repugnant ri 'pʌg nənt rə- **~ly** li

R

repuls|e *v, n* ri ˈpʌls rə- **~ed** t **~es** ɪz əz **~ing** ɪŋ
repulsion ri ˈpʌlʃ ᵊn rə- **~s** z
repulsive ri ˈpʌls ɪv rə- **~ly** li **~ness** nəs nɪs
repurpos|e ˌriː ˈpɜːp əs ‖ -ˈpɝːp- **~ed** t **~es** ɪz əz **~ing** ɪŋ
reputability ˌrep jʊt ə ˈbɪl ət i §ˌ·jət-, -ɪt i ‖ -jəţ ə ˈbɪl əţ i
reputab|le ˈrep jʊt əb |ᵊl §ˈ·jət-; §ri ˈpjuːt-, §rə- ‖ ˈrep jəţ- **~ly** li
reputation ˌrep ju ˈteɪʃ ᵊn §-jə- ‖ -jə- **~s** z
repute ri ˈpjuːt rə-
reputed ri ˈpjuːt ɪd rə-, -əd ‖ -ˈpjuːţ əd **~ly** li
request ri ˈkwest rə- **~ed** ɪd əd **~ing** ɪŋ **~s** s
reˈquest stop
requiem ˈrek wi‿əm -em **~s** z
ˌrequiem ˈmass
requiescat ˌrek wi ˈesk æt ‖ ˌreɪk-, -ɑːt
require ri ˈkwaɪ‿ə rə- ‖ -ˈkwaɪ‿ᵊr **~d** d **~ment/s** mənt/s **~s** z **requiring** ri ˈkwaɪ‿ər ɪŋ rə- ‖ -ˈkwaɪ‿ᵊr ɪŋ
requisite ˈrek wɪz ɪt -wəz-, §-ət **~s** s
requisition ˌrek wɪ ˈzɪʃ ᵊn -wə- **~ed** d **~ing** ‿ɪŋ **~s** z
requital ri ˈkwaɪt ᵊl rə- ‖ -ˈkwaɪţ ᵊl **~s** z
re|quite ri |ˈkwaɪt rə- **~quited** ˈkwaɪt ɪd -əd ‖ ˈkwaɪţ əd **~quites** ˈkwaɪts **~quiting** ˈkwaɪt ɪŋ ‖ ˈkwaɪţ ɪŋ
reran ₍ˌ₎riː ˈræn
re|read *pres* ˌriː ˈriːd **~read** *past, pp* ˈred **~reading/s** ˈriːd ɪŋ/z **~reads** ˈriːdz
reredos ˈrɪə dɒs ‖ ˈrɪr dɑːs ˈrer ə dɑːs **~es** ɪz əz
rereleas|e *n* ˈriː ri liːs -rə-, ˌ· ·ˈ· **~es** ɪz əz
rereleas|e *v* ˌriː ri ˈliːs ◂ -rə- **~ed** t **~es** ɪz əz **~ing** ɪŋ
re|route ˌriː| ˈruːt -ˈraʊt *—see note at* route.
~routed ˈruːt ɪd -əd ‖ ˈruːţ əd ˈraʊţ-
~routeing, ~routing ˈruːt ɪŋ ‖ ˈruːţ ɪŋ ˈraʊţ-
~routes ˈruːts ˈraʊts
rerun *n* ˈriː rʌn **~s** z
re|run *v* ₍ˌ₎riː |ˈrʌn **~ran** ˈræn **~running** ˈrʌn ɪŋ **~runs** ˈrʌnz
res reɪz reɪs, riːz ‖ reɪs riːz *—see also phrases with this word*
resale ˈriː seɪᵊl ˌ·ˈ· **~s** z
reschedul|e ˌriː ˈʃed juːl -ˈʃedʒ uːl, -ˈsked juːl, -ˈskedʒ uːl ‖ -ˈskedʒ ʊl -uːl, -ᵊl **~ed** d **~es** z **~ing** ɪŋ
rescind ri ˈsɪnd rə- **~ed** ɪd əd **~ing** ɪŋ **~s** z
rescission ri ˈsɪʒ ᵊn rə- **~s** z
rescript ˈriː skrɪpt **~s** s
resc|ue ˈresk |juː **~ued** juːd **~ues** juːz **~uing** juː‿ɪŋ
rescuer ˈresk juː‿ə ‖ ·ᵊr **~s** z
research *v, n* ri ˈsɜːtʃ rə-, §-ˈzɜːtʃ; ˈriː sɜːtʃ ‖ ri ˈsɝːtʃ ˈriː sɝːtʃ *—the* -ˈsɜːtʃ ‖ -ˈsɝːtʃ *form appears still to predominate in universities, although* ˈriː sɜːtʃ ‖ -sɝːtʃ *has increasingly displaced it in general usage both in Britain and in America. Some speakers may distinguish between the verb* ·ˈ· *and the noun* ˈ· ·. *—Preferences polls, BrE:* ·ˈ· *80%*

RESEARCH

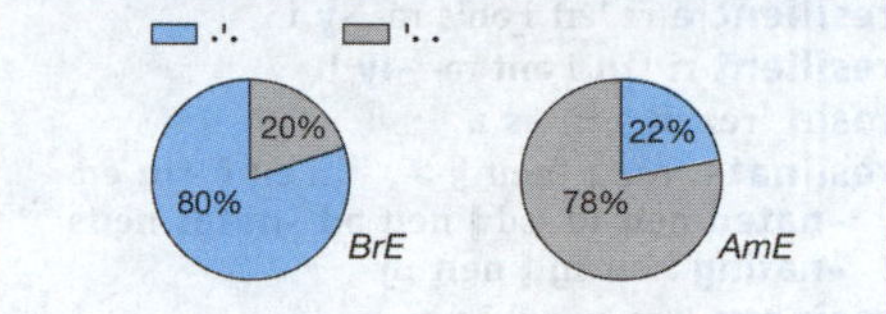

(university teachers: 95%), ˈ· · *20%; AmE, n:* ˈ· · *78%,* ·ˈ· *22%.* **~ed** t **~es** ɪz əz **~ing** ɪŋ
researcher ri ˈsɜːtʃ ə rə-, §-ˈzɜːtʃ-; ˈriː sɜːtʃ ə ‖ ri ˈsɝːtʃ ᵊr ˈriː sɝːtʃ ᵊr **~s** z
resect ri ˈsekt rə- **~ed** ɪd əd **~ing** ɪŋ **~s** s
resection ri ˈsek ʃᵊn rə- **~s** z
reseda ˈres ɪd ə -əd-; rɪ ˈsiːd ə, rə- ‖ rɪ ˈsiːd ə ˈreɪz ə dɑː
reseed ˌriː ˈsiːd **~ed** ɪd əd **~ing** ɪŋ **~s** z
reselect ˌriː sə ˈlekt -sɪ- **~ed** ɪd əd **~ing** ɪŋ **~s** s
reselection ˌriː sə ˈlek ʃᵊn -sɪ- **~s** z
resemblanc|e ri ˈzem blənᵗs rə- **~es** ɪz əz
resembl|e ri ˈzem bᵊl rə- **~ed** d **~es** z **~ing** ‿ɪŋ
re|sent ri |ˈzent rə- **~sented** ˈzent ɪd -əd ‖ ˈzenţ əd **~senting** ˈzent ɪŋ ‖ ˈzenţ ɪŋ **~sents** ˈzents
resentful ri ˈzent fᵊl rə-, -fʊl **~ly** ‿i **~ness** nəs nɪs
resentment ri ˈzent mənt rə- **~s** s
reserpine ˈres ə piːn -pɪn; ri ˈsɜːp iːn, rə-, -ɪn, §-ən ‖ ˈres ᵊr- ri ˈsɝːp iːn
reservation ˌrez ə ˈveɪʃ ᵊn ‖ -ᵊr- **~s** z
reserv|e *v, n* ri ˈzɜːv rə- ‖ -ˈzɝːv **~ed** d **~es** z **~ing** ɪŋ
reservedly ri ˈzɜːv ɪd li rə-, -əd- ‖ -ˈzɝːv-
reservist ri ˈzɜːv ɪst rə-, §-əst ‖ -ˈzɝːv- **~s** s
reservoir ˈrez əv wɑː §-ə vɔː ‖ -ᵊrv wɑːr -əv-, -wɔːr, -ɔːr **~s** z
re|set ˌriː |ˈset **~sets** ˈsets **~setting/s** ˈset ɪŋ/z ‖ ˈseţ ɪŋ/z
resettl|e ₍ˌ₎riː ˈset ᵊl ‖ -ˈseţ ᵊl **~ed** d **~es** z **~ing** ‿ɪŋ
resettlement ₍ˌ₎riː ˈset ᵊl mənt
res gestae ˌreɪz ˈgest aɪ ˌreɪs-, ˌriːz- -ˈdʒest-, -iː ‖ ˌreɪs- ˌriːz-
reshuffle *n* ˈriː ˌʃʌf ᵊl ˌ·ˈ· · **~s** z
reshuffl|e *v* ₍ˌ₎riː ˈʃʌf ᵊl **~ed** d **~es** z **~ing** ‿ɪŋ
resid|e ri ˈzaɪd rə- **~ed** ɪd əd **~es** z **~ing** ɪŋ
residenc|e ˈrez ɪd ənᵗs -əd- ‖ -ə denᵗs **~es** ɪz əz **~ies** iz **~y** i
resident ˈrez ɪd ənt -əd- ‖ -ə dent **~s** s
residential ˌrez ɪ ˈdenᵗʃ ᵊl ◂ -ə- **~ly** i
residentiar|y ˌrez ɪ ˈdenᵗʃ ər |i ˌ·ə-, -ˈ·i‿ər |i ‖ -ˈ·i er |i **~ies** iz
residual ri ˈzɪd ju‿əl rə-, -ˈzɪdʒ u‿əl ‖ -ˈzɪdʒ u‿əl -ˈzɪdʒ ᵊl **~ly** i **~s** z
residuary ri ˈzɪd ju‿ər i rə-, -ˈzɪd jʊr i; -ˈzɪdʒ uᵊr i ‖ -ˈzɪdʒ u er i
residue ˈrez ɪ djuː -ə-, →-dʒuː ‖ -duː -djuː **~s** z
residu|um ri ˈzɪd ju‿|əm rə-, -ˈzɪdʒ u‿ ‖ -ˈzɪdʒ u‿|əm **~a** ə
resign ri ˈzaɪn rə- **~ed** d **~ing** ɪŋ **~s** z
resignation ˌrez ɪg ˈneɪʃ ᵊn **~s** z

resignedly ri ˈzaɪn ɪd li rə-, -əd-
resil|e ri ˈzaɪəl rə- **~ed** d **~es** z **~ing** ɪŋ
resilienc|e ri ˈzɪl i ənᵗs rə- **~y** i
resilient ri ˈzɪl i ənt rə- **~ly** li
resin ˈrez ɪn §-ən **~s** z
resi|nate ˈrez ɪ |neɪt §-ə-, -ᵊ|n eɪt ‖ -ᵊ|n eɪt
    ~nated neɪt ɪd -əd ‖ neɪt əd **~nates** neɪts
    ~nating neɪt ɪŋ ‖ neɪt ɪŋ
resinous ˈrez ɪn əs -ᵊn əs
res ipsa loquitur ˌreɪz ˌɪps ə ˈlɒk wɪt ə ˌreɪs-,
    ˌriːz-, -ˌɑː-, §-wət ·, -ʊə
    ‖ ˌreɪs ˌɪps ə ˈloʊk wət ᵊr ˌriːz-
resist ri ˈzɪst rə- **~ed** ɪd əd **~ing** ɪŋ **~s** s
resistanc|e ri ˈzɪst ənᵗs rə- **~es** ɪz əz
resistant ri ˈzɪst ənt rə- **~ly** li
resistib|le ri ˈzɪst əb |ᵊl rə-, -ɪb- **~ly** li
resistive ri ˈzɪst ɪv rə- **~ly** li
resistivity ˌriːz ɪ ˈstɪv ət i ˌrez-, §ˌ·ə-, -ɪt ·;
    ri ˌzɪ ˈstɪv-, rə- ‖ -ət̬ i
resistor ri ˈzɪst ə rə- ‖ -ᵊr **~s** z
resit n ˈriː sɪt **~s** s
re|sit v ˌriː ˈsɪt **~sat** ˈsæt **~sits** ˈsɪts **~sitting**
    ˈsɪt ɪŋ ‖ ˈsɪt̬ ɪŋ
Resnais rə ˈneɪ re- —Fr [ʁɛ nɛ]
resol|e ˌriː ˈsəʊl →-ˈsɒʊl ‖ -ˈsoʊl **~ed** d **~es** z
    ~ing ɪŋ
resoluble ri ˈzɒl jʊb ᵊl rə- ‖ -ˈzɑːl jəb ᵊl -ˈsɑːl-
    ~ness nəs nɪs
resolute ˈrez ə luːt -ljuːt **~ly** li **~ness** nəs nɪs
resolution ˌrez ə ˈluːʃ ᵊn -ˈljuːʃ- **~s** z
resolvability ri ˌzɒlv ə ˈbɪl ət i rə-, -ˌzəʊlv-,
    -ɪt i ‖ -ˌzɑːlv ə ˈbɪl ət̬ i
resolvable ri ˈzɒlv əb ᵊl rə-, -ˈzəʊlv-
    ‖ ri ˈzɑːlv- **~ness** nəs nɪs
resolv|e ri ˈzɒlv rə- §-ˈzəʊlv ‖ -ˈzɑːlv **~ed** d
    ~es z **~ing** ɪŋ
Resolven ri ˈzɒlv ən ‖ -ˈzɑːlv-
resolvent ri ˈzɒlv ᵊnt rə-, §-ˈzəʊlv- ‖ -ˈzɑːlv- **~s**
    s
resonanc|e ˈrez ᵊn ənᵗs **~es** ɪz əz
resonant ˈrez ᵊn ənt **~ly** li **~s** s
reso|nate ˈrez ə |neɪt **~nated** neɪt ɪd -əd
    ‖ neɪt əd **~nates** neɪts **~nating** neɪt ɪŋ
    ‖ neɪt̬ ɪŋ
resonation ˌrez ə ˈneɪʃ ᵊn
resonator ˈrez ə neɪt ə ‖ -neɪt̬ ᵊr **~s** z
resorb ri ˈsɔːb rə-, ˌriː-, -ˈzɔːb ‖ -ˈsɔːrb -ˈzɔːrb
    ~ed d **~ing** ɪŋ **~s** z
resorcinol ri ˈzɔːs ɪ nɒl rə-, re-, -ə-
    ‖ -ˈzɔːrs ᵊn ɔːl -ɑːl
resorption ri ˈsɔːp ʃᵊn rə-, ˌriː-, -ˈzɔːp- ‖ -ˈsɔːrp-
    -ˈzɔːrp-
resorptive ri ˈsɔːpt ɪv rə-, ˌriː-, -ˈzɔːpt-
    ‖ -ˈsɔːrpt- -ˈzɔːrpt-
re|sort v, n ri |ˈzɔːt rə- ‖ -|ˈzɔːrt **~sorted**
    ˈzɔːt ɪd -əd ‖ ˈzɔːrt̬ əd **~sorting** ˈzɔːt ɪŋ
    ‖ ˈzɔːrt̬ ɪŋ **~sorts** ˈzɔːts ‖ ˈzɔːrts
resound ri ˈzaʊnd rə- **~ed** ɪd əd **~ing/ly** ɪŋ /li
    ~s z

RESOURCE

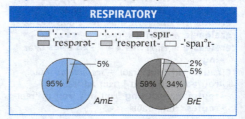

resourc|e ri ˈzɔːs rə-, -ˈsɔːs; ˈriː sɔːs, -zɔːs
    ‖ ˈriː sɔːrs -soʊrs — Preference poll, BrE: -ˈzɔːs
    49%, -ˈsɔːs 45%, ˈ· · 6%. **~ed** t **~es** ɪz əz **~ing**
    ɪŋ
resourceful ri ˈzɔːs fᵊl rə-, -ˈsɔːs-, -fʊl
    ‖ rɪ ˈsɔːrs- -soʊrs-, -ˈzɔːrs-, -ˈzoʊrs- **~ly** i
    ~ness nəs nɪs
respect v, n ri ˈspekt rə- **~ed** ɪd əd **~ing** ɪŋ **~s**
    s
respectability ri ˌspekt ə ˈbɪl ət i rə-, -ɪt i
    ‖ -ət̬ i
respectab|le ri ˈspekt əb |ᵊl rə- **~leness** ᵊl nəs
    -nɪs **~ly** li
respecter ri ˈspekt ə rə- ‖ -ᵊr **~s** z
respectful ri ˈspekt fᵊl rə-, -fʊl **~ly** i **~ness**
    nəs nɪs
respective ri ˈspekt ɪv rə- **~ly** li **~ness** nəs nɪs
Respighi re ˈspiːg i ri-, rə- —It [re ˈspiː gi]
respiration ˌresp ə ˈreɪʃ ᵊn -ɪ-
respirator ˈresp ə reɪt ə ‖ -reɪt̬ ᵊr **~s** z

RESPIRATORY

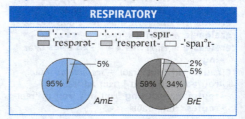

respiratory ri ˈspɪr ət ᵊr i rə-, re-, -ˈspaɪᵊr-;
    ˈresp ᵊr ət̬; ˈresp ə reɪt ᵊr i, ˌ··ˈ···
    ‖ ˈresp ᵊrˌə tɔːr i ri ˈspaɪr ə-, -tour i —
    Preference polls, AmE: ˈ· · · · · 95%, ˈ· · · · · 5%;
    BrE: -ˈspɪr- 59%, ˈrespərət- 34%, ˈrespəreɪt-
    5%, -ˈspaɪᵊr- 2%.
respire ri ˈspaɪ ə rə- ‖ -ˈspaɪ ᵊr **~d** d **~s** z
    respiring ri ˈspaɪ ᵊr ɪŋ rə- ‖ -ˈspaɪ ᵊr ɪŋ
respite ˈresp aɪt -ɪt, §-ət ‖ -ət ri ˈspaɪt **~s** s
resplendenc|e ri ˈsplend ənᵗs rə- **~y** i
resplendent ri ˈsplend ənt rə- **~ly** li
respond ri ˈspɒnd rə- ‖ -ˈspɑːnd **~ed** ɪd əd
    ~ing ɪŋ **~s** z
respondent ri ˈspɒnd ənt rə- ‖ -ˈspɑːnd- **~s** s
respons|e ri ˈspɒnᵗs rə- ‖ -ˈspɑːnᵗs **~es** ɪz əz
responsibilit|y ri ˌspɒnᵗs ə ˈbɪl ət |i rə-, -ˌ·ɪ-,
    -ɪt i ‖ -ˌspɑːnᵗs ə ˈbɪl ət̬ |i **~ies** iz
responsib|le ri ˈspɒnᵗs əb |ᵊl rə-, -ɪb-
    ‖ ri ˈspɑːnᵗs- **~ly** li
responsive ri ˈspɒnᵗs ɪv rə- ‖ -ˈspɑːnᵗs ɪv **~ly** li
    ~ness nəs nɪs
responsor|y ri ˈspɒnᵗs ᵊr |i rə- ‖ ri ˈspɑːnᵗs-
    ~ies iz

respray n 'riː spreɪ ~s z
respray v ˌriː 'spreɪ ~ed d ~ing ɪŋ ~s z
rest rest **rested** 'rest ɪd -əd **resting** 'rest ɪŋ
  rests rests
  'rest cure; 'rest home; 'resting place;
  'rest ˌperiod; 'rest room
restage|e riː 'steɪdʒ ~ed d ~es ɪz əz ~ing ɪŋ
re|state ˌriː |'steɪt ~stated 'steɪt ɪd -əd
  ‖ 'steɪt əd ~statement/s 'steɪt mənt/s
  ~states 'steɪts ~stating 'steɪt ɪŋ ‖ 'steɪt ɪŋ

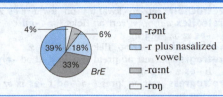

RESTAURANT

— Preference poll, BrE: -ɒnt 39% (born since
1973: 72%), -rənt 33%, -r plus nasalized vowel
18%, -ɑːnt 6%, -rɒŋ 4%. ~rants rɒnts rɑːnts,
rɒŋz, rɔ̃z, rɑ̃ːz, rɔ̃ːz, rənts ‖ rənts rɑːnts
  'restaurant car
restau|rant 'rest ə |rɒnt -rɑːnt, -rɒŋ, -rɔ̃, -rɑ̃ː,
  -rɔ̃ː; -ə|r ənt; 'res t|rɒnt, -t|rɑːnt, -t|rɔ̃, -t|rɑ̃nt
  ‖ 'rest ə|r ənt -ə |rɑːnt; 'res t|rənt, -t|rɑːnt
restaurateur ˌrest ər ə 'tɜː -ɒr ə-, -ɔːr ə-,
  ⚠-ə rɒn- ‖ -'tɜː -'tʊər —Fr [ʁɛs tɔ ʁa tœːʁ]
  ~s z
restful 'rest fᵊl -fʊl ~ly i ~ness nəs nɪs
restharrow 'rest ˌhær əʊ ‖ -oʊ -ˌher-
restitution ˌrest ɪ 'tjuːʃ ᵊn -ə-, →-tʃuːʃ-
  ‖ -'tuːʃ ᵊn -'tjuːʃ- ~s z
restive 'rest ɪv ~ly li ~ness nəs nɪs
restless 'rest ləs -lɪs ~ly li ~ness nəs nɪs
restock ˌriː 'stɒk ‖ -'stɑːk ~ed t ~ing ɪŋ ~s s
Reston 'rest ən
restoration, R~ ˌrest ə 'reɪʃ ᵊn ~s z
restorative ri 'stɔːr ət ɪv rə-, -'stɒr-;
  'rest ə reɪt- ‖ -ət ɪv -'stoʊr- ~s z
restore ri 'stɔː rə- ‖ -'stɔːr -stoʊr ~d d ~s z
  restoring ri 'stɔːr ɪŋ rə- ‖ -'stoʊr-
restorer ri 'stɔːr ə rə- ‖ -ᵊr -'stoʊr- ~s z
restrain ri 'streɪn rə- ~ed d ~er/s ə/z ‖ -ᵊr/z
  ~ing ɪŋ ~s z
restraint ri 'streɪnt rə- ~s s
restrict ri 'strɪkt rə- ~ed ɪd əd ~ing ɪŋ ~s s
restriction ri 'strɪk ʃᵊn rə- ~s z
restrictive ri 'strɪkt ɪv rə- ~ly li ~ness nəs nɪs
  reˌstrictive 'practice
restructure ˌriː 'strʌk tʃə -ʃə ‖ -tʃᵊr ~d d ~s z
  restructuring ˌriː 'strʌk tʃər ɪŋ -ʃər ɪŋ
result v, n ri 'zʌlt rə- ~ed ɪd əd ~ing ɪŋ ~s s
resultant ri 'zʌlt ənt rə- ‖ -ᵊnt ~s s
resultative ri 'zʌlt ət ɪv rə- ‖ -ət ɪv ~s z
resum|e v ri 'zjuːm rə-, -'zuːm, §-'ʒuːm
  ‖ -'zuːm ~ed d ~es z ~ing ɪŋ
resume n, résumé, resumé 'rez ju meɪ 'reɪz-,
  -u-; rɪ 'zjuːm eɪ, rə-, §riː-, -'zuːm- ‖ 'rez ə meɪ
  'reɪz-, -u-, ˌ·'· ~s z
resumption ri 'zʌmp ʃᵊn rə- ~s z

resumptive ri 'zʌmpt ɪv rə- ~ly li ~s z
resurfac|e ˌriː 'sɜːf ɪs -əs ‖ -'sɜːf əs ~ed t ~es
  ɪz əz ~ing ɪŋ
resurg|e ri 'sɜːdʒ rə- ‖ -'sɜːdʒ ~ed d ~es ɪz əz
  ~ing ɪŋ
resurgenc|e ri 'sɜːdʒ ᵊn⁀s rə- ‖ ri 'sɜːdʒ- ~es
  ɪz əz
resurgent ri 'sɜːdʒ ənt rə- ‖ ri 'sɜːdʒ-
resurrect ˌrez ə 'rekt ~ed ɪd əd ~ing ɪŋ ~s s
resurrection, R~ ˌrez ə 'rek ʃᵊn ~s z
resusci|tate ri ˌsʌs ɪ |teɪt rə-, -ə- ~tated
  teɪt ɪd -əd ‖ teɪt əd ~tates teɪts ~tating
  teɪt ɪŋ ‖ teɪt ɪŋ
resuscitation ri ˌsʌs ɪ 'teɪʃ ᵊn rə-, ˌriː·ˌ·'·-, -ə'·-
  ~s z
ret ret **rets** rets **retted** 'ret ɪd -əd ‖ 'ret əd
  retting 'ret ɪŋ ‖ 'ret ɪŋ
retable n ri 'teɪb ᵊl rə-; 'riː·ˌ·· ~s z
retail n, adj 'riː teᵊl
  'retail ˌprice ˌindex
retail v 'sell' 'riː teᵊl ₍₁₎·'· ~ed d ~ing ɪŋ ~s z
retail v 'pass on, relate' ri 'teᵊl rə- ~ed d ~ing
  ɪŋ ~s z
retailer 'riː teᵊl ə ‖ -ᵊr ~s z
retain ri 'teɪn rə- ~ed d ~ing ɪŋ ~s z
retainer ri 'teɪn ə rə- ‖ -ᵊr ~s z
retake n 'riː teɪk ~s s
re|take v ₍₁₎riː |'teɪk ~taken 'teɪk ən ~takes
  'teɪks ~taking 'teɪk ɪŋ ~took 'tʊk §'tuːk
retali|ate ri 'tæl i |eɪt rə- ~ated eɪt ɪd -əd
  ‖ eɪt əd ~ates eɪts ~ating eɪt ɪŋ ‖ eɪt ɪŋ
retaliation ri ˌtæl i 'eɪʃ ᵊn rə- ~s z
retaliatory ri 'tæl i ə ˌtər i rə-; -eɪt ər i, ˌ·,·ˌ·'eɪt-
  ‖ -ə tɔːr i -toʊr i
Retallack ri 'tæl ək rə-
retard v; n 'slowdown' ri 'tɑːd rə- ‖ -'tɑːrd ~ed
  ɪd əd ~ing ɪŋ ~s z
retard n 'mentally retarded person' 'riː tɑːd
  ‖ -tɑːrd ~s z
retardant ri 'tɑːd ᵊnt rə- ‖ rɪ 'tɑːrd- ~s s
retardate ri 'tɑːd eɪt rə- ‖ -'tɑːrd- ~s s
retardation ˌriː tɑː 'deɪʃ ᵊn ‖ -tɑːr- ri ˌ·ˌ·· ~s z
retch retʃ riːtʃ **retched** retʃt riːtʃt **retches**
  retʃ ɪz 'riːtʃ-, -əz **retching** 'retʃ ɪŋ 'riːtʃ-
rete 'riːt i ‖ 'riːt̬ i 'reɪt i **retia** 'riːt i ə 'riːʃ-
  ‖ 'riːt̬ i ə 'reɪt̬-
re|tell ˌriː |'tel ~telling 'tel ɪŋ ~tells 'telz
  ~told 'təʊld →'tɒʊld ‖ 'toʊld
retention ri 'tenᵗʃ ᵊn rə- ~s z
  re'tention fee
retentive ri 'tent ɪv rə- ‖ -'tent̬ ɪv ~ly li ~ness
  nəs nɪs
Retford 'ret fəd ‖ -fᵊrd
rethink n 'riː θɪŋk ˌ·'· ~s s
re|think v ˌriː |'θɪŋk ~thinking 'θɪŋk ɪŋ
  ~thinks 'θɪŋks ~thought 'θɔːt ‖ 'θɑːt
retiari|us ˌret i 'eər i |əs ˌriːt-, ˌriːʃ-, -'ɑːr-
  ‖ ˌret̬ i 'er- ~i aɪ iː
reticence 'ret ɪs ᵊn⁀s -əs- ‖ 'ret̬ əs-
reticent 'ret ɪs ənt -əs- ‖ 'ret̬ əs- ~ly li
reticle 'ret ɪk ᵊl ‖ 'ret̬- ~s z
reticular ri 'tɪk jʊl ə rə-, -jəl- ‖ -jəl ᵊr

reticu|late *v* rɪ ˈtɪk ju |leɪt rə-, -jə- ‖ -jə-
 ~lated leɪt ɪd -əd ‖ leɪt̬ əd **~lates** leɪts
 ~lating leɪt ɪŋ ‖ leɪt̬ ɪŋ
reticulate *adj* rɪ ˈtɪk jʊl ət rə-, -jəl-, -ɪt
reticulation rɪ ˌtɪk ju ˈleɪʃ ᵊn rə-, -jə- ‖ -jə- **~s**
 z
reticule ˈret ɪ kjuːl -ə- ‖ ˈret̬- **~s** z
reticul|um, R~ rɪ ˈtɪk jʊl |əm rə-, -jəl- ‖ -jəl-
 ~a ə
ret|ina ˈret |ɪn ə §-ᵊn̩ ə ‖ -|ᵊn̩ ə **~inae** ɪ niː
 §ən iː ‖ -ᵊn iː **~inas** ɪn əz ᵊn̩ əz ‖ ᵊn̩ əz
retinal ˈret ɪn ᵊl §-ᵊn̩ əl ‖ ˈret̬ ᵊn̩ əl
retinitis ˌret ɪ ˈnaɪt ɪs -ə-, -ᵊn ˈaɪt-, §-əs
 ‖ ˌret̬ ᵊn ˈaɪt̬ əs
 ˌreti,nitis ˌpigmen'tosa ˌpɪg men ˈtəʊs ə
 -ˈtəʊz- ‖ -ˈtoʊs ə
retino- *comb. form*
 with stress-neutral suffix |ˌret ɪn əʊ -ən-
 ‖ |ˌret ᵊn ə — **retinoscope** ˈret ɪn əʊ skəʊp
 ‖ -ᵊn ə skoʊp
 with stress-imposing suffix ˌret ɪ ˈnɒ + -ə-
 ‖ ˌret ᵊn ˈɑː + — **retinopathy**
 ˌret ɪ ˈnɒp əθ i ˌ-ə- ‖ ˌret̬ ᵊn ˈɑːp-
retinol ˈret ɪ nɒl -ə- ‖ ˈret̬ ᵊn ɔːl -ɑːl, -oʊl
retinue ˈret ɪ njuː §-ə-; §-ᵊn juː, -uː ‖ ˈret̬ ᵊn uː
 -juː **~s** z
retire rɪ ˈtaɪə rə- ‖ -ˈtaɪ ᵊr **~d** d **~s** z
 retiring/ly rɪ ˈtaɪ ər ɪ ŋ /li ‖ -ˈtaɪ ᵊr ɪŋ /li
retiree rɪ ˌtaɪ ə ˈriː rə-, ˌriː-; ˈ·· ‖ rɪ ˌtaɪ ᵊ ˈriː
 ~s z
retirement rɪ ˈtaɪ ə mənt rə- ‖ -ˈtaɪ ᵊr mənt **~s**
 s
 re'tirement age; re'tirement ,pension
re|tort *v, n* rɪ |ˈtɔːt rə- ‖ -|ˈtɔːrt **~torted**
 ˈtɔːt ɪd -əd ‖ ˈtɔːrt̬ əd **~torting** ˈtɔːt ɪŋ
 ‖ ˈtɔːrt̬ ɪŋ **~torts** ˈtɔːts ‖ ˈtɔːrts
retortion rɪ ˈtɔːʃ ᵊn rə- ‖ -ˈtɔːrʃ-
retouch *v* ˌriː ˈtʌtʃ **~ed** t **~es** ɪz əz **~ing** ɪŋ
retouch *n* ˈriː tʌtʃ ˌ·ˈ· **~es** ɪz əz
retrac|e rɪ ˈtreɪs rə-, ˌriː- **~ed** t **~es** ɪz əz **~ing**
 ɪŋ
retract rɪ ˈtrækt rə- **~ed** ɪd əd **~ing** ɪŋ **~s** s
retractable, retractible rɪ ˈtrækt əb ᵊl rə-
retractile rɪ ˈtrækt aɪᵊl rə- ‖ -ᵊl
retraction rɪ ˈtræk ʃᵊn rə- **~s** z
retractor rɪ ˈtrækt ə rə- ‖ -ᵊr **~s** z
retread *n* ˈriː tred **~s** z
retread *v* ˌriː ˈtred **~ed** ɪd əd **~ing** ɪŋ **~s** z
 retrod ˌriː ˈtrɒd ‖ -ˈtrɑːd **retrodden**
 ˌriː ˈtrɒd ᵊn ‖ -ˈtrɑːd ᵊn
re|treat *v, n* rɪ |ˈtriːt rə- **~treated** ˈtriːt ɪd -əd
 ‖ ˈtriːt̬ əd **~treating** ˈtriːt ɪŋ ‖ ˈtriːt̬ ɪŋ
 ~treats ˈtriːts
retrench rɪ ˈtrentʃ rə- **~ed** t **~es** ɪz əz **~ing** ɪŋ
 ~ment/s mənt/s
retri... —*see* **retry**
retrial ˌriː ˈtraɪ əl ˈ·ˌ·· ‖ -ˈtraɪ əl ˈ·ˌ·· **~s** z
retribution ˌretr ɪ ˈbjuː ʃᵊn -ə-
retributive rɪ ˈtrɪb jʊt ɪv rə-, -jət-;
 §ˈretr ɪ bjuːt-, ˈ-ə- ‖ -jət̬ ɪv **~ly** li
retributory rɪ ˈtrɪb jʊt̬ ᵊr i rə-, -jət̬ ‖ -jə tɔːr i
 -toʊr-
retrievability rɪ ˌtriːv ə ˈbɪl ət i rə-, -ɪt i ‖ -ət̬ i

retrievable rɪ ˈtriːv əb ᵊl rə-
retrieval rɪ ˈtriːv ᵊl rə- **~s** z
retriev|e rɪ ˈtriːv rə- **~ed** d **~es** z **~ing** ɪŋ
retriever rɪ ˈtriːv ə rə- ‖ -ᵊr **~s** z
retro ˈretr əʊ ‖ -oʊ
retro- |retr əʊ ‖ -oʊ —*formerly also* |riːtr-
 — **retrobronchial** ˌretr əʊ ˈbrɒŋk i əl ◂
 ‖ -oʊ ˈbrɑːŋk-
retroactive ˌretr əʊ ˈækt ɪv ◂ ‖ -oʊ- **~ly** li
retroced|e ˌretr əʊ ˈsiːd ‖ -oʊ- **~ed** ɪd əd **~es** z
 ~ing ɪŋ
retrocession ˌretr əʊ ˈseʃ ᵊn ‖ -oʊ-
retrochoir ˈretr əʊ ˌkwaɪ ə ‖ -oʊ ˌkwaɪ ᵊr **~s** z
retroflex *adj, n, v* ˈretr əʊ fleks ‖ -ə- **~ed** t
 ~es ɪz əz **~ing** ɪŋ
retroflexion ˌretr əʊ ˈflek ʃᵊn ‖ -ə- **~s** z
retrograd|e ˈretr əʊ greɪd ‖ -ə- **~ed** ɪd əd **~ely**
 li **~es** z **~ing** ɪŋ
retrogress ˌretr əʊ ˈgres ‖ -ə- **~ed** t **~es** ɪz əz
 ~ing ɪŋ
retrogression ˌretr əʊ ˈgreʃ ᵊn ‖ -ə- **~s** z
retrogressive ˌretr əʊ ˈgres ɪv ◂ ‖ -ə- **~ly** li
retrorocket ˈretr əʊ ˌrɒk ɪt §-ət ‖ -oʊ ˌrɑːk ət
 ~s s
retrospect ˈretr əʊ spekt ‖ -ə-
retrospection ˌretr əʊ ˈspek ʃᵊn ‖ -ə-
retrospective ˌretr əʊ ˈspekt ɪv ◂ ‖ -ə- **~ly** li
 ~ness nəs nɪs **~s** z
 ˌretro,spective ,exhi'bition
retrousse, retroussé rə ˈtruːs eɪ rɪ-
 ‖ rə ˌtruː ˈseɪ ˌretr u- *(*)* —*Fr* [ʁə tʁu se]
retroversion ˌretr əʊ ˈvɜːʃ ᵊn -ˈvɜːʒ-
 ‖ -oʊ ˈvɜːʒ ᵊn **~s** z
Retrovir *tdmk* ˈretr əʊ vɪə ‖ -oʊ vɪr
retrovirus ˈretr əʊ ˌvaɪᵊr əs ˌ·ˈ·· ‖ -ə- **~es** ɪz
 əz
re|try ˌriː |ˈtraɪ **~tried** ˈtraɪd **~tries** ˈtraɪz
 ~trying ˈtraɪ ɪŋ
retsina ret ˈsiːn ə ˈrets ɪn ə, -ən- —*ModGk*
 [ʁɛ ˈtsi na] **~s** z
Rett ret
return *v, n* rɪ ˈtɜːn rə- ‖ -ˈtɜːn **~ed** d **~ing** ɪŋ **~s**
 z
 re'turning ,officer
returnable rɪ ˈtɜːn əb ᵊl rə- ‖ -ˈtɜːn- **~s** z
returnee rɪ ˌtɜː ˈniː rə-, -ˈtɜːn iː ‖ rɪ ˌtɜːr ˈniː **~s**
 z
returner rɪ ˈtɜːn ə rə- ‖ -ˈtɜːn ᵊr **~s** z
retuse rɪ ˈtjuːs rə-, §-ˈtuːs, →-ˈtʃuːs ‖ -ˈtuːs
 -ˈtjuːs **~ness** nəs nɪs
Reuben ˈruːb ən -ɪn
reunification ˌriː ˌjuːn ɪf ɪ ˈkeɪʃ ᵊn ·ˌ··ˈ·ˌ·,
 -əf ·ˈ·-, §-ə'- **~s** z
reuni|fy ⸤ˌriː ˈjuːn ɪ |faɪ -ə- **~fied** faɪd **~fies**
 faɪz **~fying** faɪ ɪŋ
reunion ⸤ˌriː ˈjuːn i_ən ‖ -ˈjuːn jən **~s** z
Reunion, Réunion *island* ⸤ˌriː ˈjuːn i_ən
 ‖ -ˈjuːn jən —*Fr* [ʁe y njɔ̃]
reu|nite ˌriː ju |ˈnaɪt **~nited** ˈnaɪt ɪd -əd
 ‖ ˈnaɪt̬ əd **~nites** naɪts **~niting** ˈnaɪt ɪŋ
 ‖ ˈnaɪt̬ ɪŋ
reusable ⸤ˌriː ˈjuːz əb ᵊl ◂
reuse *n* ˌriː ˈjuːs

reus|e *v* ˌriː 'juːz ~ed d ~es ɪz əz ~ing ɪŋ
Reuter 'rɔɪt ə ‖ 'rɔɪt̬ ᵊr ~s z
rev rev revs revz revved revd revving 'rev ɪŋ
    'rev ˌcounter
Rev rev *or as* Reverend
revaluation ˌriː ˌvæl ju 'eɪʃ ᵊn ·ˌ· ·'· · ~s z
reval|ue ₍ˌ₎riː 'væl |juː ~ued juːd ~ues juːz
    ~uing ju ɪŋ
revamp *v* ₍ˌ₎riː 'væmp ~ed t ~ing ɪŋ ~s s
revamp *n* 'riː væmp ·'· ~s s
revanch|ism ri 'væntʃ |ˌɪz əm rə-, -'vɑːntʃ-,
    -'võʃ- ~ist/s ɪst/s §əst/s ‖ əst/s
Revd —*see* Reverend
reveal *v, n* ri 'viːᵊl rə- ~ed d ~ing/ly ɪŋ /li ~s
    z
reveille ri 'væl i rə-, -'vel- ‖ 'rev əl i (*) ~s z
revel *v, n* 'rev ᵊl ~ed, ~led d ~ing, ~ling ɪŋ ~s
    z
revelation, R~ ˌrev ə 'leɪʃ ᵊn ~s z
revelatory ˌrev ə 'leɪt̬ ər i 'rev əl ˌət̬ ər i
    ‖ 'rev əl ə tɔːr i ri 'vel ə-
reveler, reveller 'rev ᵊl ə ‖ -ᵊl ər ~s z
Revell 'rev ᵊl
revel|ry 'rev ᵊl |ri ~ries riz
Revelstoke 'rev ᵊl stəʊk ‖ -stoʊk
reven|ant 'rev ən |ənt -ɪn-; -ə n|ænt, -n|ɑ̃ː
    ~ants ənts ænts, ɑ̃ːz
reveng|e *v, n* ri 'vendʒ rə- ~ed d ~es ɪz əz
    ~ing ɪŋ
revengeful ri 'vendʒ fᵊl rə- ~ly _i ~ness nəs
    nɪs
revenue 'rev ə njuː -ɪ-, §-nuː ‖ -nuː —*formerly*
    also ri 'ven juː, rə- ~s z
reverb 'riː vɜːb ri 'vɜːb, rə- ‖ 'riː vɜːb ri 'vɜːb
    ~s z
reverberant ri 'vɜːb ᵊr ənt rə- ‖ -'vɜːb- ~ly li
reverbe|rate ri 'vɜːb ə |reɪt rə- ‖ -'vɜːb-
    ~rated reɪt ɪd -əd ‖ reɪt̬ əd ~rates reɪts
    ~rating reɪt ɪŋ ‖ reɪt̬ ɪŋ
reverberation ri ˌvɜːb ə 'reɪʃ ᵊn rə- ‖ -ˌvɜːb-
    ~s z
reverberator|y ri 'vɜːb ər ˌət̬ ər |i rə-, -reɪt ər |i
    ‖ ri 'vɜːb ər ə tɔːr |i -tour i; △·'·ə · · ~ies iz
revere, R~ ri 'vɪə rə- ‖ -'vɪᵊr ~d d ~s z
    revering ri 'vɪər ɪŋ rə- ‖ -'vɪr ɪŋ
reverenc|e 'rev ᵊr_ᵊn's ~ed t ~es ɪz əz ~ing ɪŋ
rever|end, R~ 'rev ᵊr_|ənd △-ənt ~ends əndz
    △-ənts
    ˌReverend 'Mother
reverent 'rev ᵊr_ənt ~ly li
reverential ˌrev ə 'renʃ ᵊl ◂ ~ly i
reverie 'rev ər i ~s z
revers *sing.* ri 'vɪə rə-, -'veə ‖ -'vɪᵊr -'veᵊr (!) ~
    pl z
reversal ri 'vɜːs ᵊl rə- ‖ -'vɜːs ᵊl ~s z
revers|e *adj, n, v* ri 'vɜːs rə- ‖ -'vɜːs ~ed t
    ~ely li ~es ɪz əz ~ing ɪŋ
    re ˌverse di ˌscrimi'nation; re'versing light
reversi ri 'vɜːs i rə- ‖ -'vɜːs i
reversibility ri ˌvɜːs ə 'bɪl ət i rə-, -ˌɪ-, -ɪt i
    ‖ -ˌvɜːs ə 'bɪl ət̬ i
reversib|le ri 'vɜːs əb |ᵊl rə-, -ɪb- ‖ -'vɜːs-
    ~leness ᵊl nəs -nɪs ~ly li

reversion ri 'vɜːʃ ᵊn rə-, -'vɜːʒ- ‖ -'vɜːʒ ᵊn
    -'vɜːʃ- ~s z
reversionary ri 'vɜːʃ ᵊn_ər i rə-, -'vɜːʒ-, -ən ᵊr_i
    ‖ ri 'vɜːʒ ə ner i -'vɜːʃ-
re|vert ri |'vɜːt rə- ‖ -|'vɜːt ~verted 'vɜːt ɪd
    -əd ‖ 'vɜːt̬ əd ~verting 'vɜːt ɪŋ ‖ 'vɜːt̬ ɪŋ
    ~verts 'vɜːts ‖ 'vɜːts
re|vet ri |'vet rə- ~vets 'vets ~vetted 'vet ɪd
    -əd ‖ 'vet̬ əd ~vetting 'vet ɪŋ ‖ 'vet̬ ɪŋ
revetment ri 'vet mənt rə- ~s s
Revie 'riːv i
review *n, v* ri 'vjuː rə- ~ed d ~ing ɪŋ ~s z
reviewer ri 'vjuː‿ə rə- ‖ -ᵊr ~s z
revil|e ri 'vaɪᵊl rə- ~ed d ~er/s ə/z -ᵊr/z ~es
    ~ing ɪŋ
Revill 'rev ᵊl -ɪl
revis|e ri 'vaɪz rə- ~ed d ~er/s ə/z ‖ -ᵊr/z ~es
    ɪz əz ~ing ɪŋ
    Re ˌvised 'Version
revision ri 'vɪʒ ᵊn rə- ~s z
revisionism ri 'vɪʒ ᵊn ˌɪz əm rə-
revisionist ri 'vɪʒ ᵊn_ɪst rə-, §-əst ~s s
revis|it ˌriː 'vɪz |ɪt §-ət ‖ -|ət ~ited ɪt ɪd §ət-,
    -əd ‖ ət̬ əd ~iting ɪt ɪŋ §ət- ‖ ət̬ ɪŋ ~its ɪts
    §əts ‖ əts
revitalis... —*see* revitaliz...
revitalization ˌriː ˌvaɪt ᵊl aɪ 'zeɪʃ ᵊn ·ˌ· ·'· ·
    ‖ ri ˌvaɪt̬ ᵊl ə 'zeɪʃ ᵊn ·ˌ· ·'· ·
revitaliz|e ₍ˌ₎riː 'vaɪt ə laɪz -ᵊl aɪz ‖ -'vaɪt̬ ᵊl aɪz
    ~ed d ~es ɪz əz ~ing ɪŋ
revival ri 'vaɪv ᵊl rə- ~s z
revivalism ri 'vaɪv ᵊl ˌɪz əm rə-
revivalist ri 'vaɪv ᵊl ɪst rə-, §-əst ~s s
reviv|e ri 'vaɪv rə- ~ed d ~es z ~ing ɪŋ
revivi|fy ₍ˌ₎riː 'vɪv ɪ |faɪ rə-, -ə- ~fied faɪd
    ~fies faɪz ~fying faɪ ɪŋ
reviviscence ˌrev ɪ 'vɪs ᵊn's -ə-
Revlon *tdmk* 'rev lɒn ‖ -lɑːn
revocab|le 'rev ək əb |ᵊl rɪ 'vəʊk-, rə-, §riː-
    ‖ rɪ 'voʊk- ~leness ᵊl nəs -nɪs ~ly li
revocation ˌrev əʊ 'keɪʃ ᵊn ‖ -ə- ~s z
revok|e ri 'vəʊk rə- ‖ -'voʊk ~ed t ~es s ~ing
    ɪŋ
revolt *v, n* ri 'vəʊlt rə-, →-'vɒʊlt ‖ -'voʊlt ~ed
    ɪd əd ~ing/ly ɪŋ /li ~s s
revolution ˌrev ə 'luːʃ ᵊn -'ljuːʃ- ~s z
revolutionar|y ˌrev ə 'luːʃ ən ᵊr_|i ◂ -'ljuːʃ-,
    -ᵊn ˌər |i ‖ -ə ner |i ~ies iz
revolutionis|e, revolutioniz|e
    ˌrev ə 'luːʃ ə naɪz -'ljuːʃ- ~ed d ~es ɪz əz
    ~ing ɪŋ
revolv|e ri 'vɒlv rə-, §-'vəʊlv ‖ -'vɑːlv ~ed d
    ~es z ~ing ɪŋ
    re ˌvolving 'credit; re ˌvolving 'door
revolver ri 'vɒlv ə rə-, §-'vəʊlv- ‖ -'vɑːlv ᵊr ~s
    z
revue ri 'vjuː rə- (= *review*) ~s z
revulsion ri 'vʌlʃ ᵊn rə- ~s z
Rew ruː
reward *n, v* ri 'wɔːd rə- ‖ -'wɔːrd ~ed ɪd əd
    ~ing/ly ɪŋ /li ~s z
rewind *v* ₍ˌ₎riː 'waɪnd ~ing ɪŋ ~s z rewound
    ₍ˌ₎riː 'waʊnd

R

rewind n 'ri: waɪnd ‿(‿)' - **~s** z
rewire ˌri: 'waɪ‿ə ‖ -'waɪ‿ʰr **~d** d **~s** z
  rewiring/s ˌri: 'waɪ‿ər ɪŋ/z ‖ -'waɪ‿ʰr ɪŋ/z
reword ˌri: 'wɜːd ‖ -'wɜːd **-ed** ɪd əd **~ing/s**
  ɪŋ/z **~s** z
rework ˌri: 'wɜːk ‖ -'wɜːk **-ed** t **~ing/s** ɪŋ/z **~s**
  s
re|write v ˌri: |'raɪt **~writes** 'raɪts **~written**
  'rɪt ʰn ◄ **~wrote** 'rəʊt ‖ 'roʊt
rewrite n 'ri: raɪt ˌ·' - **~s** s
Rex, rex reks **Rex's** 'reks ɪz -əz
rexine, R~ tdmk 'reks iːn
Rey reɪ
Reye raɪ reɪ **Reye's** raɪz reɪz
  'Reye's ˌsyndrome
Reyes raɪz reɪz
Reykjavik 'reɪk jə vɪk 'rek-, 'raɪk-, -viːk
  —Icelandic Reykjavík ['reːi ca viːk]
Reynard, r~ 'ren ɑːd 'rem-, -əd ‖ -ɑːrd -ʰrd
Reynold 'ren ʰld
Reynolds 'ren ʰldz
Rh ˌɑːr 'eɪtʃ ◄ §ˌɑː 'heɪtʃ ‖ ˌɑːr 'eɪtʃ ◄ —or as
  'Rhesus
  ˌR'h factor; ˌRh 'negative; ˌRh 'positive
rhabdo- comb. form ¦ræbd əʊ ‖ -oʊ —
  rhabdovirus 'ræbd əʊ ˌvaɪ‿ʰr əs ‖ -oʊ-
Rhadamanth|us ˌræd ə 'mæn'θ |əs **~ine** aɪn ◄
  ‖ ʰn ◄ aɪn ◄ **~ys** ɪs §əs
Rhaet|ia 'ri:ʃ |ə -|i‿ə **~an/s** ʰn/z i‿ən/z
Rhaetic 'ri:t ɪk ‖ 'ri:t̬ ɪk
Rhaeto-Romance ˌri:t əʊ rəʊ 'mæn's ◄
  ‖ ˌri:t̬ oʊ roʊ-
Rhaeto-Romanic ˌri:t əʊ rəʊ 'mæn ɪk ◄
  ‖ ˌri:t̬ oʊ roʊ-
rhapsodic ræp 'sɒd ɪk ‖ -'saːd ɪk **~ally** ʰl_i
rhapsodis|e, rhapsodiz|e 'ræps ə daɪz **~ed** d
  ~es ɪz əz **~ing** ɪŋ
rhapsod|y 'ræps əd |i **~ies** iz
rhatan|y 'ræt ən |i ‖ 'ræt ʰn |i **~ies** iz
Rhayader 'raɪ‿əd ə ‖ -ʰr
rhea, Rhea rɪə 'ri:‿ə ‖ 'ri: ə **rheas, Rhea's** rɪəz
  'ri:‿əz ‖ 'ri: əz
rhebok 'ri: bɒk ‖ -baːk **~s** s
Rhee ri:
Rhees ri:s
Rheidol 'raɪd ɒl ‖ -aːl -ɔːl, -oʊl —Welsh
  ['hraɪ dɔl]
Rheims ri:mz —French Reims [ʁɛ̃ːs]
rhematic ri: 'mæt ɪk ‖ -'mæt̬-
rheme ri:m (= ream) **rhemes** ri:mz
Rhenish 'ren ɪʃ 'ri:n-
rhenium 'ri:n i‿əm
rheo- comb. form
  with stress-neutral suffix ¦ri:‿ə -əʊ ‖ -oʊ
  — **rheoscope** 'ri:‿ə skəʊp -əʊ- ‖ -skoʊp
  with stress-imposing suffix ri 'ɒ+ ‖ ri 'aː+
  — **rheology** ri 'ɒl ədʒ i ‖ ri 'aːl-
rheostat 'ri:‿ə stæt -əʊ- **~s** s
rhesus, R~ 'ri:s əs
  'Rhesus ˌfactor; 'rhesus ˌmonkey; ˌRhesus
  'negative
Rhet... —see **Rhaet...**
rhetoric 'ret ə rɪk ‖ 'ret̬- (!)

rhetorical ri 'tɒr ɪk ʰl rə- ‖ ri 'tɔːr- -'taːr- **~ly**
  _i
  rhe,torical 'question
rhetorician ˌret ə 'rɪʃ ʰn ‖ ˌret̬- **~s** z
Rhett ret
rheum ru:m
rheumatic ru 'mæt ɪk ‖ -'mæt̬ ɪk **~s** s
  rheu,matic 'fever
rheumaticky ru 'mæt ɪk i ‖ -'mæt̬-
rheumatism 'ru:m ə tɪz əm
rheumatoid 'ru:m ə tɔɪd
rheumatological ˌru:m ət ə 'lɒdʒ ɪk ʰl ◄
  ‖ -ət̬ ə 'laːdʒ- **~ly** _i
rheumatologist ˌru:m ə 'tɒl ədʒ ɪst §-əst
  ‖ -'taːl- **~s** s
rheumatology ˌru:m ə 'tɒl ədʒ i ‖ -'taːl-
rheumy 'ru:m i
Rhian 'ri:‿ən —Welsh ['hri: an]
Rhiannon ri 'æn ən —Welsh [hri 'an on]
Rhianydd ri 'æn ɪð —Welsh [hri 'a nɪð, -nið]
Rhine raɪn —Ger Rhein [ʁaɪn]
Rhineland 'raɪn lænd -lənd —Ger Rheinland
  ['ʁaɪn lant]
rhinestone 'raɪn stəʊn ‖ -stoʊn **~s** z
rhinitis raɪ 'naɪt ɪs §-əs ‖ -'naɪt̬ əs
Rhinns rɪnz
rhino 'raɪn əʊ ‖ -oʊ **~s** z
rhino- comb. form
  with stress-neutral suffix ¦raɪn əʊ ‖ -oʊ
  — **rhinoplasty** 'raɪn əʊ ˌplæst i ‖ -oʊ-
  with stress-imposing suffix raɪ 'nɒ+ ‖ -'naː+
  — **rhinologist** raɪ 'nɒl ədʒ ɪst §-əst ‖ -'naːl-
rhinoceros raɪ 'nɒs ʰr əs -'naːs- **~es** ɪz əz
Rhinog 'ri:n ɒg 'rɪn- ‖ -aːg —Welsh ['hri: nog]
Rhiwbina ru 'baɪn ə —Welsh [hrɪu 'bəi na]
rhizo- comb. form
  with stress-neutral suffix ¦raɪz əʊ ‖ -oʊ —
  rhizocarpous ˌraɪz əʊ 'kaːp əs ◄
  ‖ -oʊ 'kaːrp-
  with stress-imposing suffix raɪ 'zɒ+ ‖ -'zaː+
  — **rhizotomy** raɪ 'zɒt əm i ‖ -'zaːt̬-
rhizome 'raɪz əʊm ‖ -oʊm **~s** z
rho rəʊ ‖ roʊ (= roe) **rhos** rəʊz ‖ roʊz
Rhoda 'rəʊd ə ‖ 'roʊd ə
rhodamine 'rəʊd ə mi:n ‖ 'roʊd-
Rhode Island 'rəʊd ˌaɪl ənd ˌ·'· -
  ‖ roʊd 'aɪl ənd ˌ·- **~er/s** ə/z ‖ ʰr/z
  ˌRhode ˌIsland 'Red ‖ ·ˌ·ˌ·'·
Rhodes rəʊdz ‖ roʊdz
  ˌRhodes 'scholar, ·ˌ· ˌ··
Rhodesi|a rəʊ 'di:ʃ |ə -'di:ʒ-, -i‿ə; -'di:s |i‿ə,
  -'di:z- ‖ roʊ 'di:ʒ |ə **~an/s** ʰn/z i‿ən/z
Rhodian 'rəʊd i‿ən ‖ 'roʊd- **~s** z
rhodium 'rəʊd i‿əm ‖ 'roʊd-
rhododendron ˌrəʊd ə 'dendr ən -ɪ- ‖ ˌroʊd-
  ~s z
rhodolite 'rɒd ə laɪt 'rəʊd-, -ʰl aɪt
  ‖ 'roʊd ʰl aɪt **~s** s
Rhodope 'rɒd əp i rɒ 'dəʊp i, rəʊ- ‖ 'raːd-
rhodopsin rəʊ 'dɒps ɪn §-ən ‖ roʊ 'daːps ən
rhodora rəʊ 'dɔːr ə ‖ roʊ- -'doʊr- **~s** z
Rhodri 'rɒdr i ‖ 'raːdr i —Welsh ['hrod ri]

rhomb rɒm rɒmb ‖ rɑːm rɑːmb **rhombs** rɒmz
rɒmbz ‖ rɑːmz rɑːmbz

rhombohedr|on ˌrɒm bəʊ ˈhiːdr |ən -ˈhedr-
‖ ˌrɑːm boʊ- -bə- **~a** ə **~ons** ənz

rhomboid ˈrɒm bɔɪd ‖ ˈrɑːm- **~s** z

rhom|bus ˈrɒm |bəs ‖ ˈrɑːm- **-bi** baɪ **~buses**
bəs ɪz -əz

Rhona ˈrəʊn ə ‖ ˈroʊn ə

rhonch|us ˈrɒŋk |əs ‖ ˈrɑːŋk- **~i** aɪ

Rhonda ˈrɒnd ə ‖ ˈrɑːnd ə

Rhondda ˈrɒnd ə ˈrɒn ðə ‖ ˈrɑːnd ə —*Welsh*
[ˈhrɒn ða]
ˌRhondda 'Valley

Rhone, Rhône rəʊn ‖ roʊn —*French* [ʁoːn]

Rhonwen ˈrɒn wɪn -wən, -wen ‖ ˈrɑːn-
—*Welsh* [ˈhron wen]

Rhoose ruːs

Rhos rəʊs ‖ roʊs —*Welsh* [hroːs]

Rhosllanerchrugog ˌrəʊs ˌlæn ə ˈkriːg ɒg
‖ ˌroʊs ˌlæn ᵊr ˈkriːg ɑːg —*Welsh*
[ˌhroːs ˌɬa nerχ ˈri gog, -ˈri-]

Rhosneigr ˌrəʊs ˈnaɪg ə ‖ ˌroʊs ˈnaɪg ᵊr
—*Welsh* [ˌhroːs ˈnəigr, -ˈnəi gir]

Rhossili rɒ ˈsɪl i ‖ rɑː-

rhotacis... —*see* **rhotaciz...**

rhotacism ˈrəʊt ə ˌsɪz əm ‖ ˈroʊt- **~s** z

rhotacization ˌrəʊt əs aɪ ˈzeɪʒ ᵊn -ɪˈ--
‖ ˌroʊt əs ə- **~s** z

rhotaciz|e ˈrəʊt ə saɪz ‖ ˈroʊt- **~ed** d **~es** ɪz əz
~ing ɪŋ

rhotic ˈrəʊt ɪk ‖ ˈroʊt ɪk **~s** s

rhoticity rəʊ ˈtɪs ət i -ɪt- ‖ roʊ ˈtɪs ət i

rhubarb ˈruːb ɑːb ‖ -ɑːrb

Rhuddlan ˈrɪð lən ˈrʌð-, -læn —*Welsh*
[ˈhrɪð lan, ˈhrɪð-]

Rhum rʌm

rhumb rʌm (= *rum*) **rhumbs** rʌmz

Rhyd-ddu ˌriːd ˈði: —*Welsh* [ˌhriːd ˈði:,
ˌhriːd ˈði:]

Rhydderch ˈrʌð ək -əx ‖ -ᵊrk —*Welsh*
[ˈhrə ðerχ]

Rhydding ˈrɪd ɪŋ

Rhyl rɪl —*Welsh* [hril, hrɪl]

rhyme raɪm (= *rime*) **rhymed** raɪmd **rhymes**
raɪmz **rhyming** ˈraɪm ɪŋ
'rhyming ˌslang, ˌ·ˈ·

rhymer ˈraɪm ə ‖ -ᵊr **~s** z

rhymester ˈraɪmᵖst ə ‖ -ᵊr **~s** z

Rhymney ˈrʌm ni

rhyolite ˈraɪ ə laɪt **~s** s

rhyolitic ˌraɪ ə ˈlɪt ɪk ◄ ‖ -ˈlɪt ɪk ◄

Rhys (i) riːs; (ii) raɪs —*Welsh* [hriːs, hri:s]
—*The writer Jean Rhys is* (i).

rhythm ˈrɪð əm **~s** z
ˌrhythm and 'blues; 'rhythm ˌmethod;
'rhythm ˌsection

rhythmic ˈrɪð mɪk **~ally** ᵊl_i

ria ˈriː ə **~s** z

rial ri ˈɑːl ˈri: ɑːl ‖ -ˈɔːl —*but as an obsolete
English coin,* ˈraɪ əl **~s** z

Rialto ri ˈælt əʊ ‖ -oʊ —*It* [ri ˈal to]

rib rɪb **ribbed** rɪbd **ribbing** ˈrɪb ɪŋ **ribs** rɪbz
'rib ˌcage

ribald ˈrɪb ᵊld ˈraɪb-, -ɔːld ‖ -ɔːld, -ɑːld **~ly** li **~s**
z

ribaldr|y ˈrɪb ᵊldr |i ˈraɪb-, -ɔːldr- **~ies** iz

riband ˈrɪb ənd **~s** z

Ribbentrop ˈrɪb ən trɒp →-m- ‖ -trɑːp —*Ger*
[ˈʁɪb n tʁɔp]

Ribble ˈrɪb ᵊl

ribb|on ˈrɪb |ən **~oned** ənd →md **~oning**
ən ɪŋ **~ons** ənz →mz
ˌribbon deˈvelopment

Ribena *tdmk* raɪ ˈbiːn ə

riboflavin, riboflavine ˌraɪb əʊ ˈfleɪv ɪn -iːn,
§-ᵊn ‖ -oʊ- ˈ· ·ˌ··

ribonucleic ˌraɪb əʊ nju ˈkliːˌɪk ◄ §-nuˈ--,
-ˈkleɪ- ‖ -oʊ nu- -njuˈ--

ribosomal ˌraɪb əʊ ˈsəʊm ᵊl ◄ ‖ -ə ˈsoʊm ᵊl ◄

ribosome ˈraɪb əʊ səʊm ‖ -ə soʊm -zoʊm **~s** z

Rib|ston ˈrɪb stən **~stone** stəʊn ‖ stoʊn

ribwort ˈrɪb wɜːt -wɔːt ‖ -wɜːt **~s** s

Ricard|o rɪ ˈkɑːd |əʊ ‖ -ˈkɑːrd |oʊ **~ian** i ən

Riccarton ˈrɪk ət ən ‖ -ᵊrt ᵊn

Ricci ˈriːtʃ i —*It* [ˈrit tʃi]

rice, Rice raɪs **riced** raɪst **rices** ˈraɪs ɪz -əz
ricing ˈraɪs ɪŋ
'rice ˌbowl; ˌRice 'Krispies *tdmk*; 'rice
ˌpaddy; 'rice ˌpaper; ˌrice 'pudding

Rice-a-Roni *tdmk* ˌraɪs ə ˈrəʊn i ‖ -ˈroʊn i

ricer ˈraɪs ə ‖ -ᵊr **~s** z

rich, Rich rɪtʃ **richer** ˈrɪtʃ ə ‖ -ᵊr **richest**
ˈrɪtʃ ɪst -əst

Richard ˈrɪtʃ əd ‖ -ᵊrd

Richards ˈrɪtʃ ədz ‖ -ᵊrdz

Richardson ˈrɪtʃ əd sən ‖ -ᵊrd-

Richelieu ˈriːʃ ljɜː ˈrɪʃ-, -ljuː; ˈ·ə· ‖ ˈrɪʃ luː ˈriːʃ-,
-ljuː, ˌ· ·ˈ·; ˈ·ə ·, ˌ·ᵊ·- —*Fr* [ʁi ʃə ljø]

riches, R~ ˈrɪtʃ ɪz -əz

Richey, Richie ˈrɪtʃ i

Richfield ˈrɪtʃ fiːᵊld

Richland ˈrɪtʃ lənd

richly ˈrɪtʃ li

Richmal ˈrɪtʃ mᵊl

Richmond ˈrɪtʃ mənd
ˌRichmond 'Hill; ˌRichmond-u(ˌ)pon-
'Thames; ˌRichmond, Vir'ginia;
ˌRichmond, 'Yorks

richness ˈrɪtʃ nəs -nɪs

Richter ˈrɪkt ə ˈrɪxt- ‖ -ᵊr —*Ger* [ˈʁɪç tɐ], *Russ*
[ˈrʲix tʲɪr] —*Charles R~, the seismologist, was
an American; it is therefore appropriate for the*
Richter scale *he devised to be pronounced in an
English way, with* [k]. *Nevertheless, in BrE it
is often said with* [x].

Richthofen ˈrɪxt əʊf ᵊn ˈrɪkt- ‖ ˈrɪkt oʊf ᵊn
—*Ger* [ˈʁɪçt hoːf n]

ricin ˈraɪs ɪn ˈrɪs-, §-ᵊn

ricinoleate ˌraɪs ɪ ˈnəʊl i eɪt ˌrɪs-, ˌ·ə- ‖ -ˈnoʊl-

ricinoleic ˌrɪs ɪn əʊ ˈliː ɪk ◄ ˌraɪs-, ˌ·ən-, -ˈleɪ-;
-ˈəʊl i ɪk ‖ -ᵊn oʊ-

rick, Rick rɪk **ricked** rɪkt **ricking** ˈrɪk ɪŋ **ricks**
rɪks

Rickard ˈrɪk ɑːd ‖ -ɑːrd

Rickards ˈrɪk ɑːdz ‖ -ɑːrdz

Rickenbacker ˈrɪk ən bæk ə ‖ -ᵊr

R

rickets 'rɪk ɪts §-əts
Rickett 'rɪk ɪt §-ət
Ricketts 'rɪk ɪts §-əts
rickettsi|a rɪ 'kets i̯ə ~ae iː ~al əl ~as əz
rickety 'rɪk ət i -ɪt- ‖ -əţ i
Rickey, r~, Ricki, Rickie 'rɪk i
Rickmansworth 'rɪk mənz wɜːθ -wəθ ‖ -wɜːθ
Rickover 'rɪk əʊv ə ‖ -oʊv ər
rickrack 'rɪk ræk
Ricks rɪks
ricksha, rickshaw 'rɪk ʃɔː ‖ -ʃɑː ~s z
Ricky 'rɪk i
Rico 'riːk əʊ ‖ -oʊ
rico|chet 'rɪk ə |ʃeɪ -ʃet, ‚·ˈ·|· ~cheted,
~chetted ʃeɪd ʃet ɪd, -əd ~cheting,
~chetting ʃeɪ ɪŋ ʃet ɪŋ ~chets ʃeɪz ʃets —The
-tt- spellings are used, if at all, only by the
minority, if it still exists, who pronounce -ʃet,
-'ʃet. It is very possible that both this spelling
and this pronunciation are now obsolete.
Ricoh tdmk 'riːk əʊ ‖ -oʊ —Jp [ɾi ‚koo]
ricotta rɪ 'kɒt ə rə- ‖ -'kɔːţ ə -'kɑːţ- —It
[ri 'kɔt ta]
rictus 'rɪkt əs ~es ɪz əz
rid rɪd ridded 'rɪd ɪd -əd ridding 'rɪd ɪŋ rids
rɪdz
riddance 'rɪd ᵊnts
Riddell (i) 'rɪd ᵊl (ii) rɪ 'del rə-
ridden 'rɪd ᵊn
-ridden ‚rɪd ᵊn — damp-ridden 'dæmp ‚rɪd ᵊn
Ridding 'rɪd ɪŋ
riddl|e, R~ 'rɪd ᵊl ~ed d ~es z ~ing ɪŋ
ride raɪd ridden 'rɪd ᵊn rides raɪdz riding
'raɪd ɪŋ rode rəʊd ‖ roʊd
Rideout 'raɪd aʊt
rider, Rider 'raɪd ə ‖ -ᵊr ~s z
riderless 'raɪd ə ləs -lɪs; -ᵊl əs, -ɪs ‖ -ᵊr-
ridge, Ridge rɪdʒ ridged rɪdʒd ridges
'rɪdʒ ɪz -əz ridging 'rɪdʒ ɪŋ
ridgel 'rɪdʒ ᵊl ~s z
ridgeling 'rɪdʒ lɪŋ ~s z
ridgepole 'rɪdʒ pəʊl →-pɒʊl ‖ -poʊl ~s z
ridgeway, R~, Ridgway 'rɪdʒ weɪ ~s z
ridicul|e n, v 'rɪd ɪ kjuːl -ə- ~ed d ~es z ~ing
ɪŋ
ridiculous rɪ 'dɪk jʊl əs rə-, -jəl- ‖ -jəl- ~ly li
~ness nəs nɪs
riding, R~ 'raɪd ɪŋ ~s z
Ridley 'rɪd li
Ridout (i) 'raɪd aʊt (ii) 'rɪd aʊt
Ridpath 'rɪd pɑːθ →'rɪb-, §-pæθ ‖ -pæθ
Riefenstahl 'riːf ᵊn ʃtɑːl -stɑːl —Ger
['ʁiːf n ʃtɑːl]
Riegger 'riːg ə ‖ -ᵊr
Riemann 'riː mən ‖ -mɑːn —Ger ['ʁiː man]
riesling, R~ 'riːz lɪŋ 'riːs- —Ger ['ʁiːs lɪŋ] ~s z
Rieu ri 'uː 'riː uː
Rievaulx 'riːv əʊ -əʊz; 'rɪv əz ‖ -oʊ
rife raɪf rifer 'raɪf ə ‖ -ᵊr rifest 'raɪf ɪst -əst
riff, Riff rɪf riffs rɪfs
riffl|e 'rɪf ᵊl ~ed d ~es z ~ing ɪŋ
riffraff 'rɪf ræf
Rifkind 'rɪf kɪnd

rifl|e 'raɪf ᵊl ~ed d ~es z ~ing ɪŋ
'rifle range
rifle|man 'raɪf ᵊl |mən -mæn ~men mən men
rift rɪft rifted 'rɪft ɪd -əd rifting 'rɪft ɪŋ rifts
rɪfts
'rift ‚valley, ‚·ˈ··
rig rɪg rigged rɪgd rigging/s 'rɪg ɪŋ/z rigs
rɪgz
Riga 'riːg ə —formerly also 'raɪg ə —Latvian
Rīga ['riː ga]
rigadoon ‚rɪg ə 'duːn ~s z
rigamarole 'rɪg əm ə rəʊl →-rɒʊl ‖ -roʊl ~s z
rigatoni ‚rɪg ə 'təʊn i ‖ -'toʊn i
Rigby 'rɪg bi
Rigel 'raɪg ᵊl 'raɪdʒ-
Rigg rɪg
rigg... —see rig
rigger 'rɪg ə ‖ -ᵊr ~s z
right raɪt (= rite, write) righted 'raɪt ɪd -əd
‖ 'raɪţ əd righter 'raɪt ə ‖ 'raɪţ ᵊr rightest
'raɪt ɪst -əst ‖ 'raɪţ əst righting 'raɪt ɪŋ
‖ 'raɪţ ɪŋ rights raɪts
'right ‚angle, ‚·ˈ··; ‚right a'way; ‚right of
'way; 'rights ‚issue; ‚right 'triangle;
‚right 'whale; ‚right 'wing ◂
right-about 'raɪt ə ‚baʊt ‖ 'raɪţ-
right-angled 'raɪt ‚æŋ gᵊld, ‚·ˈ·· ‖ 'raɪţ-
right-branching 'raɪt ‚brɑːntʃ ɪŋ §-‚bræntʃ-,
‚·ˈ·· ‖ -‚bræntʃ ɪŋ
right-click ‚raɪt 'klɪk ~ed t ~ing ɪŋ ~s s
righteous 'raɪtʃ əs 'raɪt i̯əs ~ly li ~ness nəs
nɪs
rightful 'raɪt fᵊl -fʊl ~ly i ~ness nəs nɪs
right-hand ‚raɪt 'hænd ◂ ‖ '··
‚right-hand 'bend; ‚right-hand 'man
right-handed ‚raɪt 'hænd ɪd ◂ -əd ~ly li ~ness
nəs nɪs
right-hander ‚raɪt 'hænd ə ‖ -ᵊr ~s z
rightism 'raɪt ‚ɪz əm ‖ 'raɪţ-
rightist 'raɪt ɪst §-əst ‖ 'raɪţ əst ~s s
rightly 'raɪt li
right-minded ‚raɪt 'maɪnd ɪd ◂ -əd ~ly li
~ness nəs nɪs
rightness 'raɪt nəs -nɪs
righto ‚raɪt 'əʊ ‖ ‚raɪţ 'oʊ
right-of-centre, right-of-center
‚raɪt əv 'sent ə ◂ ‖ ‚raɪţ əv 'senţ ᵊr ◂
right-on ‚raɪt 'ɒn ◂ ‖ ‚raɪţ 'ɑːn ◂
right-size v 'raɪt saɪz ~ing ɪŋ
right-thinking ‚raɪt 'θɪŋk ɪŋ ‚·ˈ··
right-to-die ‚raɪt tə 'daɪ
right-to-lif|e ‚raɪt tə 'laɪf ~er/s ə/z ‖ ᵊr/z
right-to-work ‚raɪt tə 'wɜːk ‖ -'wɜːk
rightward 'raɪt wəd -wᵊrd ~s z
right-wing ‚raɪt 'wɪŋ ◂ ~er/s ə/z ‖ ᵊr/z
righty 'raɪt i ‖ 'raɪţ i
righty-ho ‚raɪt i 'həʊ ‖ ‚raɪţ i 'hoʊ
rigid 'rɪdʒ ɪd §-əd
rigidit|y rɪ 'dʒɪd ət i |ɪ rə-, -ɪt- ‖ -əţ |i ~ies iz
rigid|ly 'rɪdʒ ɪd li |li §-əd- ~ness nəs nɪs
Rigil 'raɪdʒ ᵊl -ɪl
rigmarole 'rɪg mə rəʊl →-rɒʊl ‖ -roʊl ~s z

Rigoletto ˌrɪg ə 'let əʊ ‖ -'leṱ oʊ —*It*
[ri go 'let to]
rigor 'rɪg ə ‖ -ᵊr —*but as a medical term, also*
'raɪg ɔː ‖ -ɔːr **~s** z
rigor mortis 'mɔːt ɪs §-əs ‖ 'mɔːrṱ əs
ˌrigor 'mortis
rigorous 'rɪg ər_əs **~ly** li **~ness** nəs nɪs
rigour 'rɪg ə ‖ -ᵊr **~s** z
rig-out 'rɪg aʊt **~s** s
Rigsby 'rɪgz bi
Rig-Veda ˌrɪg 'veɪd ə
Rihanna ri 'æn ə ‖ -'ɑːn-
Riis riːs
Rijeka ri 'ek ə -'eɪk- —*Croatian* [rri ''ɛ ka]
Rikers 'raɪk əz ‖ -ᵊrz
Rikki 'rɪk i
Rikki-Tiki-Tavi ˌrɪk i tɪk i 'tɑːv i -'teɪv- ‖ -'tæv-
rile raɪᵊl **riled** raɪᵊld **riles** raɪᵊlz **riling** 'raɪᵊl ɪŋ
Riley 'raɪl i
riliev|o ˌrɪl i 'eɪv |əʊ ‖ rɪl 'jeɪv |oʊ —*It*
[ri 'ljeː vo] **~i** iː
Rilke 'rɪlk ə —*Ger* ['ʁɪl kə]
rill rɪl **rills** rɪlz
rillettes ₍ᵣ₎riː 'et —*Fr* [ʁi jɛt]
rim rɪm **rimmed** rɪmd **rimming** 'rɪm ɪŋ **rims**
rɪmz
Rimbaud 'ræm bəʊ ‖ ræm 'boʊ —*Fr* [ʁɛ̃ bo]
Rimbault *English family name* 'rɪm bəʊlt
→-bɒʊlt ‖ -boʊlt
rime raɪm **rimed** raɪmd **rimes** raɪmz **riming**
'raɪm ɪŋ —*see also phrases with this word*
rime riche ˌriːm 'riːʃ **rimes riches** *same*
pronunciation
rimester 'raɪmᵖst ə ‖ -ᵊr **~s** z
Rimington 'rɪm ɪŋ tən
Rimini 'rɪm ən i -ɪn- —*It* ['riː mi ni]
rimless 'rɪm ləs -lɪs
-rimmed 'rɪmd — **plastic-rimmed**
ˌplæst ɪk 'rɪmd ◂ ˌplɑːst-
Rimmer 'rɪm ə ‖ -ᵊr
Rimmington 'rɪm ɪŋ tən
Rimsky-Korsakov ˌrɪmᵖ ski 'kɔːs ə kɒf -kɒv
‖ -'kɔːrs ə kɔːf -kɑːf —*Russ*
[ˌrʲim skʲɪj 'kɔr sə kəf]
Rinaldo rɪ 'næld əʊ rə- ‖ -'nɑːld oʊ -'næld-
rind raɪnd **rinds** raɪndz
rinderpest 'rɪnd ə pest ‖ -ᵊr-
rindless 'raɪnd ləs -lɪs
ring, Ring rɪŋ **rang** ræŋ **ringed** rɪŋd **ringing**
'rɪŋ ɪŋ **rings** rɪŋz **rung** rʌŋ
'ring ˌbinder, ˌ· '· ·; 'ring ˌfinger; 'ring
main; 'ring road; 'ring ˌspanner
ringbark 'rɪŋ bɑːk ‖ -bɑːrk **~ed** t **~ing** ɪŋ **~s** s
ringbolt 'rɪŋ bəʊlt →-bɒʊlt ‖ -boʊlt **~s** s
ringer, R~ 'rɪŋ ə ‖ -ᵊr **~s** z
ring-fenc|e ˌrɪŋ 'fenᵗs **~ed** t ◂ **~es** ɪz əz **~ing**
ɪŋ
ringgit 'rɪŋ gɪt §-gət **~s** s
ringhals 'rɪŋ hæls -hɑːls
ringleader 'rɪŋ ˌliːd ə ‖ -ᵊr **~s** z
ringlet 'rɪŋ lət -lɪt **ringleted** 'rɪŋ lət ɪd -lɪt-,
-əd ‖ -ləṱ əd **~s** s

ringmaster 'rɪŋ ˌmɑːst ə §-,mæst- ‖ -,mæst ᵊr
~s z
ringneck 'rɪŋ nek **~s** s
ring-pull 'rɪŋ pʊl **~s** z
ringside 'rɪŋ saɪd
ring-tailed 'rɪŋ teɪᵊld
ringtone 'rɪŋ təʊn ‖ -toʊn **~s** z
Ringway 'rɪŋ weɪ
Ringwood 'rɪŋ wʊd
ringworm 'rɪŋ wɜːm ‖ -wɜːm
rink rɪŋk **rinks** rɪŋks
rinkhals 'rɪŋk hæls -hɑːls
rinky-dink 'rɪŋk i dɪŋk
rinse rɪnᵗs **rinsed** rɪnᵗst **rinses** 'rɪnᵗs ɪz -əz
rinsing 'rɪnᵗs ɪŋ
Rintoul rɪn 'tuːl '· ·
Rio 'riː əʊ ‖ -oʊ —*Sp* ['rri o], *Port* ['rri u,
'xi u]
ˌRio de Ja'neiro də ʒə 'nɪər əʊ deɪ-, di-,
-dʒə'-, -'neər- ‖ deɪ ʒə 'ner oʊ -'nɪr- —*Port*
[ˌxiu di ʒɐ 'nei ru]; ˌRio 'Grande grænd
'grænd i —*Sp* ['gran de]; ˌRio 'Tinto
'tɪnt əʊ ‖ -oʊ —*Sp* ['tin to]
Rioja ri 'ɒk ə -'ɒx-, -'əʊk-, -'əʊx- ‖ -'oʊ hɑː
—*Sp* ['rrjo xa]
Riordan 'rɪəd ᵊn ‖ 'rɪrd ᵊn
riot 'raɪ_ət **rioted** 'raɪ_ət ɪd -əd ‖ -əṱ əd **rioting**
'raɪ_ət ɪŋ ‖ -əṱ ɪŋ **riots** 'raɪ_əts
'riot act
rioter 'raɪ_ət ə ‖ -əṱ ᵊr **~s** z
riotous 'raɪ_ət əs ‖ -əṱ əs **~ly** li **~ness** nəs nɪs
rip, Rip rɪp **ripped** rɪpt **ripping** 'rɪp ɪŋ **rips**
rɪps
ˌRip Van 'Winkle
RIP ˌɑːr aɪ 'piː ‖ ˌɑːr-
riparian raɪ 'peər i ᵊn rɪ- -'per- **~s** z
ripcord 'rɪp kɔːd ‖ -kɔːrd **~s** z
ripe raɪp **riper** 'raɪp ə ‖ -ᵊr **ripest** 'raɪp ɪst -əst
ripely 'raɪp li
ripen 'raɪp ən **~ed** d **~ing** ɪŋ **~s** z
ripeness 'raɪp nəs -nɪs
ripieno ˌrɪp i 'eɪn əʊ ‖ -oʊ —*It* [ri 'pjeː no] **~s**
z
Ripley 'rɪp li
Ripman 'rɪp mən
rip-off 'rɪp ɒf -ɔːf ‖ -ɔːf -ɑːf **~s** s
Ripon 'rɪp ən
ripost, ripost|e *n, v* rɪ 'pɒst -'pəʊst ‖ -'poʊst
~ed ɪd əd **~ing** ɪŋ **~es, ~s** s
ripp... —*see* **rip**
ripper 'rɪp ə ‖ -ᵊr **~s** z
ripping 'rɪp ɪŋ **~ly** li
rippl|e 'rɪp ᵊl **~ed** d **~es** z **~ing/ly** ɪŋ /li
ripplet 'rɪp lət -lɪt **~s** s
Rippon 'rɪp ən
riprap 'rɪp ræp **~ped** t **~ping** ɪŋ **~s** s
rip-roaring ˌrɪp 'rɔːr ɪŋ ◂ ‖ -'roʊr-
ripsaw 'rɪp sɔː ‖ -sɑː **~s** z
ripsnort|er 'rɪp snɔːt ə ‖ -snɔːrṱ ᵊr **~ers** əz
‖ ᵊrz **~ing/ly** ɪŋ /li
riptide 'rɪp taɪd **~s** z
ripuarian, R~ ˌrɪp ju 'eər i_ən ◂ -'er- **~s** z
Risborough, Risboro' 'rɪz bər_ə ‖ -ˌbɜː oʊ

R

RISC, risc rɪsk
Risca 'rɪsk ə
Risdon 'rɪz dən
rise raɪz **risen** 'rɪz ᵊn (!) **rises** 'raɪz ɪz -əz
　rising 'raɪz ɪŋ **rose** rəʊz ‖ roʊz
riser 'raɪz ə ‖ -ᵊr **~s** z
risibility ˌrɪz ə 'bɪl ət i ˌraɪz-, ˌ·ɪ-, -ɪt i ‖ -əţ i
risib|le 'rɪz əb |ᵊl 'raɪz-, -ɪb- **~ly** li
rising 'raɪz ɪŋ **~s** z
　ˌrising 'damp
risk rɪsk **risked** rɪskt **risking** 'rɪsk ɪŋ **risks**
　rɪsks
risk-tak|ing 'rɪsk ˌteɪk |ɪŋ **~er/s** ə/z ‖ ᵊr/z
risk|y 'rɪsk |i **~ier** i ə ‖ i ᵊr **~iest** i ɪst i əst **~ily**
　ɪ li əl i **~iness** i nəs i nɪs
Risley 'rɪz li
Risorgimento rɪ ˌsɔːdʒ ɪ 'ment əʊ rə-, riː-, -ˌ·ə-
　‖ rɪ ˌsɔːrdʒ ɪ 'ment oʊ -ˌzɔːrdʒ-; ˌriː· ·ʹ· · —It
　[ˌri sor dʒi 'men to]
risotto rɪ 'zɒt əʊ -'sɒt- ‖ -'sɔːt oʊ -'saːţ-, -'zaːţ-
　—It [ˌri 'sɔt to] **~s** z
risque, risqué 'rɪsk eɪ ‖ rɪ 'skeɪ —Fr [ʁis ke]
Riss rɪs
rissole 'rɪs əʊl →-ɒʊl ‖ -oʊl rɪ 'soʊl **~s** z
Rita 'riːt ə ‖ 'riːţ ə
Ritalin tdmk 'rɪt ᵊl ɪn ‖ 'rɪţ-
ritardando ˌrɪt ɑ: 'dænd əʊ
　‖ ˌriː tɑːr 'daːnd oʊ rɪ ˌtɑːr- **~s** z
Ritchie 'rɪtʃ i
rite raɪt —but as a French word, riːt —Fr [ʁit]
　rites raɪts
ritenuto ˌrɪt ə 'njuːt əʊ -'nuːt- ‖ ˌriːt ə 'nuːt oʊ
ritornell|o ˌrɪt ə 'nel |əʊ -ɔː-; -ᵊn 'el-
　‖ ˌrɪţ ᵊr 'nel |oʊ **~i** iː **~os** əʊz ‖ oʊz
Ritson 'rɪts ən
ritual 'rɪtʃ u̞ əl 'rɪt ju̞ əl ‖ 'rɪtʃ ᵊl **~s** z
ritualis... —see **ritualiz...**
ritualism 'rɪtʃ u̞ əl ˌɪz əm 'rɪt ju̞ ‖ 'rɪtʃ əl· · ·
ritualist 'rɪtʃ u̞ əl ɪst 'rɪt ju̞, §-əst ‖ 'rɪtʃ əl· **~s** s
ritualistic ˌrɪtʃ u̞ ə 'lɪst ɪk ◄ ˌrɪt ju-, ˌrɪtʃ u 'lɪst-
　‖ ˌrɪtʃ ə 'lɪst- **~ally** ᵊl i
ritualization ˌrɪtʃ u̞ əl aɪ 'zeɪʃ ᵊn ˌrɪt ju̞, -ɪ'--
　‖ ə'-- ˌ·əl·' · ·
ritualiz|e 'rɪtʃ u̞ ə laɪz 'rɪt ju̞, 'rɪtʃ u̞·
　‖ 'rɪtʃ ə laɪz **~ed** d **~es** ɪz əz **~ing** ɪŋ
ritually 'rɪtʃ u̞ əl i 'rɪt ju̞, 'rɪtʃ əl i
Ritz rɪts
ritz|y 'rɪts |i **~ier** i ə ‖ i ᵊr **~iest** i ɪst i əst **~ily**
　ɪ li əl i **~iness** i nəs i nɪs
rival 'raɪv ᵊl **~ed, ~led** d **~ing, ~ling** ɪŋ **~s** z
rival|ry 'raɪv ᵊl |ri ‖ **~ries** riz
rive raɪv **rived** raɪvd **riven** 'rɪv ᵊn (!) **rives**
　raɪvz **riving** 'raɪv ɪŋ
Rivelin 'rɪv ᵊl ɪn
riven 'rɪv ᵊn
river, River 'rɪv ə ‖ -ᵊr **~s** z
　'river ˌbasin; 'river ˌblindness
Rivera rɪ 'veər ə ‖ -'ver ə —Sp [ˌrri 'βe ɾa]
riverbank 'rɪv ə bæŋk ‖ -ᵊr- **~s** s
riverbed 'rɪv ə bed ‖ -ᵊr- **~s** z
riverboat 'rɪv ə bəʊt ‖ -ᵊr boʊt **~s** s
riverfront 'rɪv ə frʌnt ‖ -ᵊr- **~s** s
Riverina ˌrɪv ə 'riːn ə

riverine 'rɪv ə raɪn -riːn, -rɪn
Rivers 'rɪv əz ‖ -ᵊrz
riverside, R~ 'rɪv ə saɪd ‖ -ᵊr-
riv|et 'rɪv |ɪt §-ət ‖ -|ət **~eted** ɪt ɪd §ət-, -əd
　‖ əţ əd **~eting** ɪt ɪŋ §ət- ‖ əţ ɪŋ **~ets** ɪts §əts
　‖ əts
riveter 'rɪv ɪt ə -ət- ‖ -əţ ᵊr **~s** z
Rivett rɪ 'vet
riviera, R~ ˌrɪv i 'eər ə ‖ -'er ə **~s** z
Rivington 'rɪv ɪŋ tən
rivulet 'rɪv jʊl ət -ɪt, -ju let ‖ -jəl- **~s** s
Rix rɪks
Riyadh 'riː æd -ɑːd, ·'· ‖ riː 'jɑːd —Arabic
　[ri 'jɑːðˤ]
riyal ri 'ɑːl -'jɑːl, -'æl, '· · **~s** z
Rizla tdmk 'rɪz lə
RN ˌɑːr 'en
RNA ˌɑːr en 'eɪ
Roaccutane tdmk rəʊ 'æk ju teɪn ‖ roʊ 'æk jə-
roach, Roach rəʊtʃ ‖ roʊtʃ **roaches, Roach's**
　'rəʊtʃ ɪz -əz ‖ 'roʊtʃ əz
road rəʊd ‖ roʊd **roads** rəʊdz ‖ roʊdz
　'road hog; 'road ˌmanager; 'road
　ˌmender; 'road ˌroller; 'road sense; 'road
　tax; 'road test; 'road works
roadbed 'rəʊd bed →'rəʊb- ‖ 'roʊd-
roadblock 'rəʊd blɒk →'rəʊb- ‖ 'roʊd blɑːk **~s**
　s
roadbook 'rəʊd bʊk →'rəʊb-, §-buːk ‖ 'roʊd-
　~s s
roadholding 'rəʊd ˌhəʊld ɪŋ →-ˌhɒʊld-
　‖ 'roʊd ˌhoʊld ɪŋ
road|house 'rəʊd |haʊs ‖ 'roʊd- **~houses**
　haʊz ɪz -əz
roadie 'rəʊd i ‖ 'roʊd i **~s** z
roadkill 'rəʊd kɪl →'rəʊg- ‖ 'roʊd-
road|man 'rəʊd |mən →'rəʊb-, -mæn ‖ 'roʊd-
　~men mən men
roadrunner 'rəʊd ˌrʌn ə ‖ 'roʊd ˌrʌn ᵊr **~s** z
roadshow 'rəʊd ʃəʊ ‖ 'roʊd ʃoʊ **~s** z
roadside 'rəʊd saɪd ‖ 'roʊd- **~s** z
roadstead 'rəʊd sted ‖ 'roʊd- **~s** z
roadster 'rəʊd stə ‖ 'roʊd stᵊr **~s** z
road-test 'rəʊd test ‖ 'roʊd- **~ed** ɪd əd **~ing** ɪŋ
　~s s
roadway 'rəʊd weɪ ‖ 'roʊd- **~s** z
roadwork 'rəʊd wɜːk ‖ 'roʊd wɜːk **~s** s
roadworth|y 'rəʊd ˌwɜːð |i ‖ 'roʊd ˌwɜːð |i
　~iness i nəs i nɪs
Roald 'rəʊ əld ‖ 'roʊ- —Norw ['rɾu al]
roam rəʊm ‖ roʊm **roamed** rəʊmd ‖ roʊmd
　roaming 'rəʊm ɪŋ ‖ 'roʊm ɪŋ **roams** rəʊmz
　‖ roʊmz
roamer 'rəʊm ə ‖ 'roʊm ᵊr **~s** z
roan rəʊn ‖ roʊn
Roanoke 'rəʊ ə nəʊk 'rəʊn əʊk ‖ 'roʊ ə noʊk
　'roʊn oʊk
roar rɔː ‖ rɔːr roʊr **roared** rɔːd ‖ rɔːrd roʊrd
　roaring 'rɔːr ɪŋ ‖ 'roʊr- **roars** rɔːz ‖ rɔːrz
　roʊrz
　ˌroaring 'forties
roarer 'rɔːr ə ‖ -ᵊr 'roʊr- **~s** z

roast rəʊst ‖ roʊst **roasted** 'rəʊst ɪd -əd
‖ 'roʊst əd **roasting/s** 'rəʊst ɪŋ/z
‖ 'roʊst ɪŋ/z **roasts** rəʊsts ‖ roʊsts
roaster 'rəʊst ə ‖ 'roʊst ᵊr ~s z
Roatan, Roatán ˌrəʊ ə 'tæn ‖ ˌroʊ ə 'tɑːn
—*Sp* [ro a 'tan]
Roath rəʊθ ‖ roʊθ
rob, Rob rɒb ‖ rɑːb **robbed** rɒbd ‖ rɑːbd
robbing 'rɒb ɪŋ ‖ 'rɑːb ɪŋ **robs** rɒbz ‖ rɑːbz
ˌRob 'Roy
robalo rəʊ 'bɑːl əʊ ‖ roʊ 'bɑːl oʊ ~s z
Robb rɒb ‖ rɑːb
robb... —*see* **rob**
Robbe-Grillet ˌrɒb griː 'eɪ ‖ ˌroʊb- ˌrɑːb- —*Fr*
[ʁɔb ɡʁi jɛ]
Robben 'rɒb ɪn -ən ‖ 'rɑːb ən
robber 'rɒb ə ‖ 'rɑːb ᵊr ~s z
ˌrobber 'baron, ˈ·· ··
robber|y 'rɒb ᵊr |i ‖ 'rɑːb- ~ies iz
Robbialac *tdmk* 'rɒb i̯ə læk ‖ 'rɑːb-
Robbie 'rɒb i ‖ 'rɑːb i
Robbin 'rɒb ɪn §-ən ‖ 'rɑːb ən
Robbins 'rɒb ɪnz §-ənz ‖ 'rɑːb ənz
robe, Robe rəʊb ‖ roʊb **robed** rəʊbd ‖ roʊbd
robes rəʊbz ‖ roʊbz **robing** 'rəʊb ɪŋ
‖ 'roʊb ɪŋ
Robens 'rəʊb ɪnz -ənz ‖ 'roʊb ənz
Robert 'rɒb ət ‖ 'rɑːb ᵊrt
Roberta rə 'bɜːt ə rɒ-, rəʊ- ‖ rə 'bɜːt̬ ə roʊ-
Roberto rə 'bɜːt əʊ rɒ- ‖ rə 'bɜːt̬ oʊ roʊ-
—*It* [ro 'bɛr to], *Sp* [rro 'ßer to]
Roberts 'rɒb əts ‖ 'rɑːb ᵊrts
Robertson 'rɒb ət sən ‖ 'rɑːb ᵊrt-
Robeson 'rəʊb sən ‖ 'roʊb-
Robespierre 'rəʊbz pɪə 'rəʊbz pi̯eə
‖ 'roʊbz pɪr 'roʊbz pi er —*Fr* [ʁɔ bɛs pjɛːʁ]
Robey 'rəʊb i ‖ 'roʊb i
robin, Robin 'rɒb ɪn §-ən ‖ 'rɑːb ən ~s z
ˌRobin 'Hood ‖ ˈ· ··
Robina rɒ 'biːn ə rəʊ- ‖ rə 'biːn ə
robinia, R~ rə 'bɪn i̯ə rɒ-, rəʊ- ~s z
Robinne 'rɒb ɪn §-ən ‖ 'rɑːb ən
Robins (*i*) 'rɒb ɪnz §-ənz ‖ 'rɑːb ənz, (*ii*) 'rəʊb-
‖ 'roʊb-
Robinson 'rɒb ɪn sən §-ən- ‖ 'rɑːb-
ˌRobinson 'Crusoe
Robitussin *tdmk* ˌrəʊb i 'tʌs ɪn -ᵊn ‖ ˌroʊb-
roble 'rəʊb leɪ ‖ 'roʊb- ~s z
robocop 'rəʊb əʊ kɒp ‖ 'roʊb oʊ kɑːp ~s s
robot 'rəʊb ɒt -ət ‖ 'roʊb ɑːt -ət ~s s
robotic rəʊ 'bɒt ɪk ‖ roʊ 'bɑːt̬ ɪk ~s s
Robson 'rɒb sən ‖ 'rɑːb-
robust rəʊ 'bʌst 'rəʊ bʌst ‖ roʊ 'bʌst '·· ~ly li
~ness nəs nɪs
robusta rəʊ 'bʌst ə ‖ roʊ- ~s z
Roby 'rəʊb i ‖ 'roʊb i
Robyn 'rɒb ɪn §-ən ‖ 'rɑːb ən
roc rɒk ‖ rɑːk (= *rock*)
rocaille rɒ 'kaɪ rəʊ- ‖ roʊ- rɑː- —*Fr* [ʁɔ kaj]
rocambole 'rɒk əm bəʊl →-bɒʊl
‖ 'rɑːk əm boʊl
Rocco 'rɒk əʊ ‖ 'rɑːk oʊ —*It* ['rɔk ko]
Rocester 'rəʊst ə ‖ 'roʊst ᵊr

Rochdale 'rɒtʃ deɪᵊl ‖ 'rɑːtʃ-
Roche (*i*) rəʊtʃ ‖ roʊtʃ, (*ii*) rəʊʃ ‖ roʊʃ,
(*iii*) rɒʃ ‖ rɑːʃ
Rochelle rɒ 'ʃel rə- ‖ roʊ-
roche moutonnée ˌrɒʃ muː 'tɒn eɪ
-ˌmuːt ɒ 'neɪ ‖ ˌrɔː ʃ ˌmuːt ᵊn 'eɪ ˌroʊʃ- **roches
moutonnées** *same pronunciation, or* -z
Rochester 'rɒtʃ ɪst ə -əst- ‖ 'rɑːtʃ est ᵊr -əst-
rochet 'rɒtʃ ɪt -ət ‖ 'rɑːtʃ ət ~s s
Rochford 'rɒtʃ fəd ‖ 'rɑːtʃ fᵊrd
rock, Rock rɒk ‖ rɑːk **rocked** rɒkt ‖ rɑːkt
rocking 'rɒk ɪŋ ‖ 'rɑːk ɪŋ **rocks** rɒks ‖ rɑːks
ˌrock 'bottom ◂; 'rock cake; 'rock dash;
'rock dove; 'rock ˌgarden; 'rock ˌhopper;
'rocking chair; 'rocking horse; 'rock
ˌmusic; 'rock muˌsician; 'rock plant; 'rock
ˌsalmon; 'rock salt
rockabilly 'rɒk ə ˌbɪl i ‖ 'rɑːk-
rockbound 'rɒk baʊnd ‖ 'rɑːk-
rock-climb|er 'rɒk ˌklaɪm |ə ‖ 'rɑːk ˌklaɪm |ᵊr
~ers əz ‖ ᵊrz ~ing ɪŋ
rock-crystal 'rɒk ˌkrɪst ᵊl ‖ 'rɑːk-
Rockefeller 'rɒk ə ˌfel ə -ɪ- ‖ 'rɑːk ə ˌfel ᵊr
'Rockefeller ˌCenter ‖ ˌ··· '··
rocker 'rɒk ə ‖ 'rɑːk ᵊr ~s z
rocker|y 'rɒk ᵊr |i ‖ 'rɑːk- ~ies iz
rock|et 'rɒk |ɪt §-ət ‖ 'rɑːk |ət ~eted ɪt ɪd §ət-,
-əd ‖ ət̬ əd ~eting ɪt ɪŋ §ət- ‖ ət̬ ɪŋ ~ets ɪts
§əts ‖ əts
'rocket ˌengine; 'rocket ˌlauncher; 'rocket
range
rocketry 'rɒk ɪt ri §-ət- ‖ 'rɑːk-
Rockettes rɒ 'kets ‖ rɑː-
rockfall 'rɒk fɔːl ‖ 'rɑːk- -fɑːl ~s z
rockfish 'rɒk fɪʃ ‖ 'rɑːk- ~es ɪz əz
Rockford 'rɒk fəd ‖ 'rɑːk fᵊrd
Rockhampton rɒk 'hæmp tən ‖ rɑːk-
rock-hard ˌrɒk 'hɑːd ◂ ‖ ˌrɑːk 'hɑːrd ◂
Rockies 'rɒk iz ‖ 'rɑːk iz
Rockingham 'rɒk ɪŋ əm ‖ 'rɑːk-
Rockley 'rɒk li ‖ 'rɑːk li
rockling 'rɒk lɪŋ ‖ 'rɑːk-
Rockne 'rɒk ni ‖ 'rɑːk wʊl
rock 'n' roll, rock'n'roll ˌrɒk ən 'rəʊl →-ŋ-,
→-'rɒʊl ‖ ˌrɑːk ən 'roʊl ~er/s ə/z ‖ ᵊr/z
rockros|e 'rɒk rəʊz ‖ 'rɑːk roʊz ~es ɪz əz
rock-solid ˌrɒk 'sɒl ɪd ◂ §-əd ‖ ˌrɑːk 'sɑːl-
rock-steady ˌrɒk 'sted i ◂ ‖ ˌrɑːk-
Rockwell 'rɒk wəl -wel ‖ 'rɑːk-
rock-wool 'rɒk wʊl ‖ 'rɑːk-
rock|y, Rock|y 'rɒk |i ‖ 'rɑːk |i ~ier i̯ə ‖ i̯ᵊr
~ies, ~y's iz ~iest i̯ɪst i̯əst ~iness i nəs i nɪs
ˌRocky ˌMountain 'goat; ˌRocky
'Mountains
rococo rə 'kəʊk əʊ rəʊ- ‖ -'koʊk oʊ
ˌroʊk ə 'koʊ
rod rɒd ‖ rɑːd **rods** rɒdz ‖ rɑːdz
Rod, Rodd rɒd ‖ rɑːd
Roddick 'rɒd ɪk ‖ 'rɑːd ɪk
Roddy 'rɒd i ‖ 'rɑːd i
rode rəʊd ‖ roʊd (= *road*)
rodent 'rəʊd ᵊnt ‖ 'roʊd ᵊnt ~s s
ˌrodent 'ulcer

rodeo rəʊ ˈdeɪ əʊ ˈrəʊd i- ‖ roʊ ˈdeɪ oʊ ˈroʊd i-
~s z
Roderic, Roderick ˈrɒd ər ɪk ‖ ˈrɑːd-
Rodger ˈrɒdʒ ə ‖ ˈrɑːdʒ ər
Rodgers ˈrɒdʒ əz ‖ ˈrɑːdʒ ərz
Rodin ˈrəʊd æn -æ̃ ‖ roʊ ˈdæn —Fr [ʁɔ dæ̃]
Roding ˈrəʊd ɪŋ ‖ ˈroʊd ɪŋ —Locally also
ˈruːð-, ˈruːd-
Rodman ˈrɒd mən ‖ ˈrɑːd-
Rodney ˈrɒd ni ‖ ˈrɑːd ni
rodomontad|e ˌrɒd ə mɒn ˈtɑːd ˌrəʊd-, -ˈteɪd
‖ ˌrɑːd ə mɑːn ˈteɪd ˌroʊd-, -əm ən-, -ˈtɑːd
~**ed** ɪd əd ~**es** z ~**ing** ɪŋ
Rodrigues, Rodriguez (i) rɒ ˈdriːgz ‖ rɑː-,
(ii) rɒ ˈdriːg ez ‖ rɑː- —Port [ʁɾu ˈðɾi ɣɪʃ,
xo ˈdɾi gis], Span [rro ˈðɾi ɣeθ, -ɣes] —In
AmE usually (ii).
Rodway ˈrɒd weɪ ‖ ˈrɑːd-
roe, Roe rəʊ ‖ roʊ **roes** rəʊz ‖ roʊz (= rose)
ˈroe deer
Roebling ˈrəʊb lɪŋ ‖ ˈroʊb-
roebuck, R~ ˈrəʊ bʌk ‖ ˈroʊ- ~**s** s
Roedean ˈrəʊ diːn ‖ ˈroʊ-
Roeg rəʊg ‖ roʊg
Roehampton ˌrəʊ ˈhæmp tən ˈ··· ‖ roʊ-
roentgen, R~ ˈrɒnt gən ˈrʌnt-, ˈrɜːnt-, -jən
‖ ˈrent gən ˈrʌnt-, ˈrʊnt-, -dʒən —Ger
[ˈʁœnt gən] ~**s** z
roentgenium ˌrɒnt ˈdʒiːn i‿əm ˌrʌnt-,
-ˈgiːn- ‖ ˌroʊnt- rent-
Roethke ˈret ki ˈrɜːθ- ‖ ˈreθ-, -kə
Roff, Roffe rɒf ‖ rɔːf rɑːf
Roffey ˈrɒf i ‖ ˈrɔːf i ˈrɑːf-
rogan josh ˌrəʊg ən ˈdʒəʊʃ -ˈdʒɒʃ
‖ ˌroʊg ən ˈdʒoʊʃ
rogation, R~ rəʊ ˈgeɪʃ ən ‖ roʊ-
Roˈgation Days
Roger, roger ˈrɒdʒ ə ‖ ˈrɑːdʒ ər ~**ed** d
rogering ˈrɒdʒ ər ɪŋ ~**s** z
Rogers ˈrɒdʒ əz ‖ ˈrɑːdʒ ərz
Roget ˈrɒʒ eɪ ˈrəʊʒ- ‖ roʊ ˈʒeɪ ˈ··· ~**'s** z
rogue rəʊg ‖ roʊg **rogued** rəʊgd ‖ roʊgd
rogues rəʊgz ‖ roʊgz **roguing** ˈrəʊg ɪŋ
‖ ˈroʊg ɪŋ
ˌrogues' ˈgallery
roguer|y ˈrəʊg ər |i ‖ ˈroʊg- ~**ies** iz
roguish ˈrəʊg ɪʃ ‖ ˈroʊg- ~**ly** li ~**ness** nəs nɪs
Rohan ˈrəʊ ən ‖ ˈroʊ-
Rohypnol tdmk rəʊ ˈhɪp nɒl ‖ roʊ ˈhɪp nɔːl
-nɑːl
roil rɔɪəl **roiled** rɔɪəld **roiling** ˈrɔɪəl ɪŋ **roils**
rɔɪəlz
Roisin, Roisín rʌ ˈʃiːn rɒ-
roister ˈrɔɪst ə ‖ -ər ~**ed** d **roistering**
ˈrɔɪst ər ɪŋ ~**s** z
roisterer ˈrɔɪst ər ə ‖ -ər ~**s** z
Rokeby ˈrəʊk bi ‖ ˈroʊk-
Roker ˈrəʊk ə ‖ ˈroʊk ər
Rolaids tdmk ˈrəʊl eɪdz →ˈrɒʊl- ‖ ˈroʊl-
Roland ˈrəʊl ənd ‖ ˈroʊl-
role, rôle rəʊl →rɒʊl ‖ roʊl (= roll) **roles,**
rôles rəʊlz →rɒʊlz ‖ roʊlz
ˈrole ˌmodel; ˈrole play, ˈrole ˌplaying

role-play ˈrəʊl pleɪ →ˈrɒʊl- ‖ ˈroʊl- ~**ed** d
~**ing** ɪŋ ~**s** z
Rolex tdmk ˈrəʊl eks ‖ ˈroʊl- ~**es** ɪz əz
Rolf, rolf rɒlf ‖ rɑːlf rɔːlf **rolfed** rɒlft ‖ rɑːlft
rɔːlft **rolfing** ˈrɒlf ɪŋ ‖ ˈrɑːlf ɪŋ ˈrɔːlf- **rolfs,**
Rolf's rɒlfs ‖ rɑːlfs rɔːlfs
Rolfe (i) rəʊf ‖ roʊf, (ii) rɒlf ‖ rɑːlf rɔːlf
roll rəʊl →rɒʊl ‖ roʊl **rolled** rəʊld →rɒʊld
‖ roʊld **rolling** ˈrəʊl ɪŋ →ˈrɒʊl- ‖ ˈroʊl ɪŋ
ˈroll bar; ˈroll call; ˌrolled ˈgold ◂;
ˈrolling mill; ˈrolling pin; ˈrolling stock;
ˌrolling ˈstone, ˌRolling ˈStones; ˌroll of
ˈhonour
rollaway ˈrəʊl ə ˌweɪ →ˈrɒʊl- ‖ ˈroʊl- ~**s** z
rollback ˈrəʊl bæk →ˈrɒʊl- ‖ ˈroʊl- ~**s** s
Rollei tdmk ˈrəʊl aɪ ‖ ˈroʊl- —Ger [ˈʁɔl aɪ]
roller ˈrəʊl ə →ˈrɒʊl- ‖ ˈroʊl ər ~**s** z
ˈroller ˌbearing; ˈroller blind; ˈroller
ˌcoaster; ˈRoller ˌDerby, ˌ··ˈ·· tdmk; ˈroller
skate; ˈroller ˌtowel
Rollerblad|e tdmk, r~ ˈrəʊl ə bleɪd →ˈrɒʊl-
‖ ˈroʊl ər- ~**ed** ɪd əd ~**er/s** ə/z ‖ -ər/z ~**es** z
~**ing** ɪŋ
roller-|skate ˈrəʊl ə |skeɪt →ˈrɒʊl- ‖ ˈroʊl ər-
~**skated** skeɪt ɪd -əd ‖ skeɪt əd ~**skater/s**
skeɪt ə/z ‖ skeɪt ər/z ~**skates** skeɪts
~**skating** skeɪt ɪŋ ‖ skeɪt ɪŋ
Rolleston ˈrəʊlst ən →ˈrɒʊlst- ‖ ˈroʊlst-
rollick ˈrɒl ɪk ‖ ˈrɑːl ɪk ~**ed** t ~**ing/ly** ɪŋ /li ~**s**
s
Rollins ˈrɒl ɪnz §-ənz ‖ ˈrɑːl-
rollmop ˈrəʊl mɒp →ˈrɒʊl- ‖ ˈroʊl mɑːp ~**s** s
rollneck ˈrəʊl nek →ˈrɒʊl- ‖ ˈroʊl- ~**s** s
Rollo ˈrɒl əʊ ‖ ˈrɑːl oʊ
roll-on ˈrəʊl ɒn →ˈrɒʊl- ‖ ˈroʊl ɑːn -ɔːn ~**s** z
ˌroll-on ˌroll-ˈoff◂, ˌrəʊl ˈɒf ◂ →ˌrɒʊl-, -ˈɔːf
‖ ˌroʊl ˈɔːf ◂ -ˈɑːf; ˌroll-on ˌroll-off ˈcar
ˌferry
roll-out ˈrəʊl aʊt →ˈrɒʊl- ‖ ˈroʊl- ~**s** s
rollover ˈrəʊl ˌəʊv ə →ˈrɒʊl- ‖ ˈroʊl ˌoʊv ər
Rolls rəʊlz →rɒʊlz ‖ roʊlz ~**es** ɪz əz
Rolls-Royc|e tdmk ˌrəʊlz ˈrɔɪs →ˌrɒʊlz-
‖ ˌroʊlz- ~**es** ɪz əz
rolltop ˈrəʊl tɒp →ˈrɒʊl- ‖ ˈroʊl tɑːp ~**s** s
rollup ˈrəʊl ʌp →ˈrɒʊl- ‖ ˈroʊl- ~**s** s
Rolo tdmk ˈrəʊl əʊ →ˈrɒʊl- ‖ ˈroʊl oʊ ~**s** z
Rolodex tdmk ˈrəʊl ə deks →ˈrɒʊl- ‖ ˈroʊl-
Rolph rɒlf ‖ rɑːlf
Rolston ˈrəʊlst ən →ˈrɒʊlst- ‖ ˈroʊlst-
Rolt rəʊlt →rɒʊlt ‖ roʊlt
roly-pol|y ˌrəʊl i ˈpəʊl |i ◂ →ˌrɒʊl i ˈpɒʊl i
‖ ˌroʊl i ˈpoʊl |i ◂ ~**ies** iz
ˌroly-ˌpoly ˈpudding
ROM 'computer memory' rɒm ‖ rɑːm
Rom 'gypsy' rɒm rəʊm ‖ roʊm
Roma city; people and language ˈrəʊm ə
‖ ˈroʊm ə —It [ˈroːm a]
Romagna rəʊ ˈmɑːn jə ‖ roʊ- —It
[ro ˈmaɲ ɲa]
Romaic rəʊ ˈmeɪ ɪk ‖ roʊ-
Romaine, r~ rəʊ ˈmeɪn ‖ roʊ-
roˌmaine ˈlettuce

Roman, roman 'rəʊm ən ‖ 'roʊm ən —*but as a French word,* rəʊ ˈm̃ɔ ‖ roʊ 'mɑːn —*Fr* [ʁɔ mɑ̃] *(see phrases)* ~**s** z
  ˌRoman 'alphabet; ˌRoman 'candle; ˌRoman 'Catholic; ˌRoman Ca'tholiˌcism; ˌRoman 'Empire; ˌRoman 'law; ˌRoman 'nose; ˌRoman 'numeral

roman à clef rəʊ ˌm̃ɔ ɑː 'kleɪ -ˌmɑːn- ‖ roʊ ˌmɑːn- **romans à clef** *same pronunciation* —*Fr* [ʁɔ mɑ̃ a kle]

romanc|e, R~ rəʊ 'mæn^ts 'rəʊm æn^ts ‖ roʊ 'mæn^ts 'roʊm æn^ts ~**ed** t ~**er/s** ə/z ‖ ᵊr/z ~**es** ɪz əz ~**ing** ɪŋ

Romanes *family name* rəʊ 'mɑːn ɪz -ɪs, -es ‖ roʊ-

Romanes *language* 'rɒm ə nes -ən ɪs, §-əs ‖ 'rɑːm-

Romanesque ˌrəʊm ə 'nesk ◂ ‖ ˌroʊm-

roman fleuve rəʊ ˌm̃ɔ 'flɜːv ‖ roʊ ˌmɑːn 'flʌv **romans fleuve** *same pronunciation* —*Fr* [ʁɔ mɑ̃ flœːv]

Romani|a ru 'meɪn i ˌ|ə rəʊ- ‖ roʊ- ~**an/s** ən/z

romanic, R~ rəʊ 'mæn ɪk ‖ roʊ-

romanis... —*see* **romaniz...**

Romanism 'rəʊm ən ˌɪz əm ‖ 'roʊm-

Romanist 'rəʊm ən ɪst §-əst ‖ 'roʊm- ~**s** s

romanization ˌrəʊm ən aɪ 'zeɪʃ ᵊn -ˈ-ˈ-- ‖ ˌroʊm ən ə- ~**s** z

romaniz|e 'rəʊm ə naɪz ‖ 'roʊm- ~**ed** d ~**er/s** ə/z ‖ ᵊr/z ~**es** ɪz əz ~**ing** ɪŋ

Romano, r~ rəʊ 'mɑːn əʊ ‖ roʊ 'mɑːn oʊ

Romano- rəʊ ˌmɑːn əʊ -ˌmæn- ‖ rə ˌmɑːn oʊ
  — **Romano-British** rəʊ ˌmɑːn əʊ 'brɪt ɪʃ ◂ -ˌmæn- ‖ rə ˌmɑːn oʊ 'brɪt̬ ɪʃ ◂

Roma|nov 'rəʊm ə ˌnɒf -nɒv ‖ 'roʊm ə ˌnɔːf -nɑːf —*Russ* [rʌ 'ma nəf] ~**novs** nɒfs nɒvz ‖ nɔːfs nɑːfs

Romansch, Romansh rəʊ 'mæn^tʃ ru- ‖ roʊ- -'mɑːn^tʃ

romantic rəʊ 'mæn ɪk ‖ roʊ 'mæn̬ ɪk rə- ~**ally** ᵊl i ~**s** s

romanticis... —*see* **romanticiz...**

romanticism rəʊ 'mæn t ɪ ˌsɪz əm -ə- ‖ roʊ 'mæn̬ ə- rə-

romanticist rəʊ 'mæn ɪs ɪst -əs-, §-əst ‖ roʊ 'mæn̬ ɪ- rə-

romanticization rəʊ ˌmæn t ɪs aɪ 'zeɪʃ ᵊn -ˌ-əs-, -ɪˈ-- ‖ roʊ ˌmæn̬ əs ə-

romanticiz|e rəʊ 'mæn t ɪ saɪz -ə- ‖ roʊ 'mæn̬ ə- rə- ~**ed** d ~**es** ɪz əz ~**ing** ɪŋ

Roman|y 'rɒm ən ˌ|i 'rəʊm- ‖ 'rɑːm- 'roʊm- ~**ies** iz

Rombauer 'rɒm baʊ ə ‖ 'rɑːm baʊ ˌᵊr

Romberg 'rɒm bɜːg ‖ 'rɑːm bɜːg

rom com 'rɒm kɒm ‖ 'rɑːm kɑːm ~**s** z

Rome rəʊm ‖ roʊm —*Formerly also* ruːm
  Rome's rəʊmz ‖ roʊmz —*It* Roma ['rɔ ma]

Romeo 'rəʊm i ˌəʊ ‖ 'roʊm i ˌoʊ ~**s**, ~**'s** z

romer 'rəʊm ə ‖ 'roʊm ᵊr ~**s** z

Romero rəʊ 'meər əʊ ‖ roʊ 'mer oʊ rə- —*Sp* [rːo 'me ro]

Romford 'rɒm fəd 'rʌm- ‖ 'rɑːm fᵊrd

romic, Romic 'rəʊm ɪk ‖ 'roʊm-

Romiley, Romilly 'rɒm əl i -ɪl- ‖ 'rɑːm-

Romish 'rəʊm ɪʃ ‖ 'roʊm ɪʃ

Rommel 'rɒm ᵊl ‖ 'rɑːm ᵊl 'rʌm- —*Ger* ['ʁɒm ᵊl]

Romney 'rɒm ni 'rʌm- ‖ 'rɑːm-

romneya 'rɒm ni ˌə ‖ 'rɑːm- ~**s** z

romp rɒmp ‖ rɑːmp **romped** rɒmpt ‖ rɑːmpt **romping** 'rɒmp ɪŋ ‖ 'rɑːmp ɪŋ **romps** rɒmps ‖ rɑːmps

romper 'rɒmp ə ‖ 'rɑːmp ᵊr ~**s** z
  'romper suit

Romsey 'rɒm zi 'rʌm- ‖ 'rɑːm zi

Romulus 'rɒm jʊl əs ‖ 'rɑːm jᵊl əs

Ron rɒn ‖ rɑːn

Rona 'rəʊn ə ‖ 'roʊn ə

Ronald 'rɒn ᵊld ‖ 'rɑːn ᵊld

Ronaldinho ˌrɒn ᵊl 'diːn jəʊ ‖ ˌrɑːn ᵊl 'diːn oʊ —*BrPort* [ʁɔ nal 'dʒi ɲu]

Ronaldo rɒ 'næld əʊ rə- ‖ roʊ 'nɑːld oʊ —*BrPort* [ʁɔ 'nal du]

Ronaldsay 'rɒn ᵊld seɪ -ʃeɪ ‖ 'rɑːn-

Ronaldsway 'rɒn ᵊldz weɪ ‖ 'rɑːn-

Ronan 'rəʊn ən ‖ 'roʊn-

rondavel 'rɒnd ə vel rɒn 'dɑːv ᵊl ‖ 'rɑːnd- ~**s** z

rondeau 'rɒnd əʊ ‖ 'rɑːnd oʊ rɑːn 'doʊ ~**s**, ~**x** z —*or as sing.*

rondel 'rɒnd ᵊl ‖ 'rɑːnd ᵊl rɑːn 'del ~**s** z

rondo 'rɒnd əʊ ‖ 'rɑːnd oʊ rɑːn 'doʊ ~**s** z

roneo, R~ *tdmk* 'rəʊn i ˌəʊ ‖ 'roʊn i ˌoʊ ~**ed** d ~**ing** ɪŋ ~**s** z

Ronnie 'rɒn i ‖ 'rɑːn i

Ronsard 'rɒn sɑː ‖ roʊn 'sɑːr —*Fr* [ʁɔ̃ saːʁ]

Ronson 'rɒn^ts ən ‖ 'rɑːn^ts ən

Ronstadt 'rɒn stæt ‖ 'rɑːn-

röntgen, R~ 'rɒnt gən 'rʌnt-, 'rɜːnt-, -jən ‖ 'rent gən 'rʌnt-, 'rʊnt-, -dʒən —*Ger* ['ʁœnt gᵊn] ~**s** z

Ronuk *tdmk* 'rɒn ək 'rəʊn-, -ʌk ‖ 'rɑːn-

roo, Roo ru: **roos** ru:z

rood ru:d (= *rude*) **roods** ru:dz
  'rood loft; 'rood screen

roof ru:f rʊf **roofed** ru:ft rʊft, ru:vd **roofing** 'ru:f ɪŋ 'rʊf-, 'ru:v- **roofs** ru:fs ru:vz, rʊfs
  'roof ˌgarden; 'roof rack

roofer 'ru:f ə 'rʊf- ‖ -ᵊr ~**s** z

roofies 'ru:f iz

roofless 'ru:f ləs 'rʊf-, -lɪs

rooftop 'ru:f tɒp 'rʊf- ‖ -tɑːp ~**s** s

rooftree 'ru:f tri: 'rʊf- ~**s** z

rooibos 'rɔɪ bɒs ‖ -bɔːs -bɑːs

rooinek 'rɔɪ nek ~**s** s

rook rʊk §ru:k **rooked** rʊkt §ru:kt **rooking** 'rʊk ɪŋ §'ru:k- **rooks** rʊks §ru:ks

Rook, Rooke rʊk §ru:k

rooker|y 'rʊk ər ˌ|i §'ru:k- ~**ies** iz

rook|ie, rook|y 'rʊk ˌ|i ~**ies** iz

R

ROOM

room ■ ru:m   rʊm ■

19%
81%
BrE

7%
93%
AmE

room ru:m rʊm — *Preference polls, BrE:* ru:m
81%, rʊm 19%; AmE: ru:m *93%, rʊm 7%.*
Some who say ru:m *for this word on its own*
nevertheless say rʊm *in compounds: see*
bedroom. **roomed** ru:md rʊmd **rooming**
'ru:m ɪŋ 'rʊm- **rooms** ru:mz rʊmz
'**rooming house**; '**room** ˌservice
Room, Roome ru:m
-roomed 'ru:md 'rʊmd — **three-roomed**
ˌθri: 'ru:md ◄ -'rʊmd
roomer 'ru:m ə 'rʊm- ‖ -ᵊr ~s z
roomette ˌru:m 'et ˌrʊm- ~s s
roomful 'ru:m fʊl 'rʊm- ~s z
roomie 'ru:m i 'rʊm i ~s z
roommate 'ru:m meɪt 'rʊm- ~s s
room|y 'ru:m |i 'rʊm- ~**ier** i ə ‖ iˌᵊr ~**iest** iˌɪst
iˌəst ~**ily** ɪ li əl ɪ ~**iness** i nəs i nɪs
Rooney 'ru:n i
Roope ru:p
Roosevelt 'rəʊz ə velt 'rəʊs-, -vᵊlt; 'ru:s-
‖ 'rouz- ~s, ~'s s
roost ru:st **roosted** 'ru:st ɪd -əd **roosting**
'ru:st ɪŋ **roosts** ru:sts
rooster 'ru:st ə ‖ -ᵊr ~s z
root, Root ru:t §rʊt **rooted** 'ru:t ɪd §'rʊt-, -əd
‖ 'ru:t̬ əd 'rʊt̬- **rooting** 'ru:t ɪŋ §'rʊt-
‖ 'ru:t̬ ɪŋ 'rʊt̬- **roots** ru:ts §rʊts
'**root beer**, ˌ· '·; '**root** caˌnal; ˌroot ˌmean
'**square**; '**root crop**; '**root** ˌvegetable,
ˌ· '· · ·
Rootes ru:ts
rootl|e 'ru:t ᵊl ‖ 'ru:t̬ ᵊl ~**ed** d ~**es** z ~**ing** ɪŋ
rootless 'ru:t ləs §'rʊt-, -lɪs ~**ness** nəs nɪs
rootlet 'ru:t lət §'rʊt-, -lɪt ~s s
rootstock 'ru:t stɒk §'rʊt- ‖ -sta:k ~s s
rootsy 'ru:ts i
rope rəʊp ‖ roup **roped** rəʊpt ‖ roupt **ropes**
rəʊps ‖ roups **roping** 'rəʊp ɪŋ ‖ 'roup ɪŋ
ˌrope 'ladder, '· ˌ· ·
ropedancer 'rəʊp ˌda:n⁀ts ə -ˌdæn⁀ts-
‖ 'roup ˌdæn⁀ts ᵊr ~s z
Roper 'rəʊp ə ‖ 'roup ᵊr
ropewalk 'rəʊp wɔ:k ‖ 'roup- -wa:k ~**ed** t
~**ing** ɪŋ ~s s
ropewalker 'rəʊp ˌwɔ:k ə ‖ 'roup ˌwɔ:k ᵊr
-ˌwa:k- ~s z
ropeway 'rəʊp weɪ ‖ 'roup- ~s z
rop|ey, rop|y 'rəʊp |i ‖ 'roup |i- ~**ier** i ə ‖ iˌᵊr
~**iest** iˌɪst iˌəst ~**ily** ɪ li əl ɪ ~**iness** i nəs i nɪs
Roquefort, r~ 'rɒk fɔ: ‖ 'rouk fᵊrt —*Fr*
[ʁɔk fɔːʁ]
roquet 'rəʊk i -eɪ ‖ rou 'keɪ ~**ed** d ~**ing** ɪŋ ~s
z

roquette rɒ 'ket ‖ rou- —*Fr* [ʁɔ kɛt]
Rorke rɔ:k ‖ rɔ:rk rourk
ro-ro 'rəʊ rəʊ ‖ 'rou rou ~**s, ~'s** z
rorqual 'rɔ:k wəl -ᵊl ‖ 'rɔ:rk- ~s z
Rorschach 'rɔ: ʃa:k -ʃæk ‖ 'rɔ:r- 'rour- —*Ger*
['ʁɔʁ ʃax]
'**Rorschach test**
rort rɔ:t ‖ rɔ:rt **rorts** rɔ:ts ‖ rɔ:rts
Rory 'rɔ:r i ‖ 'rour-
Ros *short for* **Rosalind** *etc* rɒz ‖ ra:z
Ros *family name* rɒs ‖ rɔ:s ra:s
Rosa 'rəʊz ə ‖ 'rouz ə
rosacea rəʊ 'zeɪʃ ə -iˌə ‖ rou-
rosaceous rəʊ 'zeɪʃ əs ‖ rou-
Rosaleen *(i)* 'rɒz ə li:n ‖ 'ra:z-, *(ii)* 'rəʊz-
‖ 'rouz-
Rosalie *(i)* 'rɒz ə li ‖ 'ra:z-, *(ii)* 'rəʊz- ‖ 'rouz-
Rosalind 'rɒz ə lɪnd ‖ 'ra:z-
Rosaline 'rɒz ə lɪn -li:n, -laɪn ‖ 'ra:z-
Rosamond, Rosamund 'rɒz ə mənd ‖ 'ra:z-
'rouz-
rosaniline rəʊ 'zæn ə li:n -laɪn; -ᵊl i:n, -aɪn;
-əl ɪn, §-ən ‖ rou 'zæn ᵊl ən -aɪn
Rosanna rəʊ 'zæn ə ‖ rou-
Rosanne rəʊ 'zæn ‖ rou-
Rosario rəʊ 'za:r i əʊ -'sa:r- ‖ rou 'sa:r i ou
-'za:r- —*Sp* [ɾɾo 'sa ɾjo]
rosari|um rəʊ 'zeər iˌ|əm ‖ rou 'zer- -'zær- ~**a**
ə ~**ums** əmz
rosar|y 'rəʊz ər |i ‖ 'rouz- ~**ies** iz
Roscoe, r~ 'rɒsk əʊ ‖ 'ra:sk ou ~**s, ~'s** z
Roscommon rɒs 'kɒm ən ‖ ra:s 'ka:m ən
rose, Rose rəʊz ‖ rouz **roses** 'rəʊz ɪz -əz
‖ 'rouz əz
'**rose** ˌgarden; ˌrose 'window, '· ˌ· ·
rosé 'rəʊz eɪ rəʊ 'zeɪ ‖ rou 'zeɪ ~s z
Roseanne *(i)* rəʊ 'zæn ‖ rou-, *(ii)* ˌrəʊz i 'æn
‖ ˌrouz-
roseate 'rəʊz iˌət -ɪt, -eɪt ‖ 'rouz- ~**ly** li
Roseau rəʊ 'zəʊ ‖ rou 'zou
rosebay ˌrəʊz 'beɪ '· · ‖ 'rouz beɪ ~s z
Roseberry, Rosebery 'rəʊz bər i
‖ 'rouz ˌber i
rosebud 'rəʊz bʌd ‖ 'rouz- ~s z
rose-colored, rose-coloured 'rəʊz ˌkʌl əd
‖ 'rouz ˌkʌl ᵊrd
Rosecrans 'rəʊz krænz 'rəʊz ə krænz ‖ 'rouz-
Rosedale 'rəʊz deɪ³l ‖ 'rouz-
rose hip, rosehip 'rəʊz hɪp ‖ 'rouz- ~s s
rosella rəʊ 'zel ə ‖ rou- ~s z
roselle, R~ rəʊ 'zel ‖ rou- ~s, ~'s z
Rosemarie ˌrəʊz mə 'ri: ‖ ˌrouz- '· · ·
rosemar|y, R~ 'rəʊz mər |i ‖ 'rouz ˌmer |i
~**ies** iz
Rosen 'rəʊz ᵊn ‖ 'rouz ᵊn
Rosenberg 'rəʊz ᵊn bɜ:g ‖ 'rouz ᵊn bɜ:g ~s z
Rosencrantz 'rəʊz ᵊn krænts ‖ 'rouz-
Rosenthal *(i)* 'rəʊz ᵊn θɔ:l ‖ 'rouz- -θa:l, *(ii)*
-ta:l
roseola rəʊ 'zi:ˌəl ə ˌrəʊz i 'əʊl ə ‖ rou 'zi: əl ə
ˌrouz i 'oul ə ~s z
roseroot 'rəʊz ru:t §-rʊt ‖ 'rouz-
rose-tinted ˌrəʊz ˌtɪnt ɪd -əd ‖ 'rouz ˌtɪnt̬ əd

Rosetta rəʊ ˈzet ə ‖ roʊ ˈzeʈ ə
  Ro͵setta ˈstone ‖ ·ˈ·· ·
rosette rəʊ ˈzet ‖ roʊ- **~s** s
Rosewall ˈrəʊz wɔːl ‖ ˈroʊz- -wɑːl
Rosewarne ˈrəʊz wɔːn ‖ ˈroʊz wɔːrn
rosewater ˈrəʊz ͵wɔːt ə ‖ ˈroʊz ͵wɔːʈ ʰr -ˌwɑːt-
rosewood ˈrəʊz wʊd ‖ ˈroʊz-
Rosheen rɒ ˈʃiːn ‖ roʊ-
Rosh Hashana, Rosh Hashanah
  ͵rɒʃ hə ˈʃɑːn ə -hæ- ‖ ͵roʊʃ hɑː ˈʃɔːn ə ͵rɔːʃ-,
  ͵rɑːʃ-, -hə-, -ˈʃɑːn-, -ˈʃoʊn-
Rosicrucian ͵rəʊz ɪ ˈkruːʃ ʰn ͵rɒz-, -ˈkruːʃ i ən
  ‖ ͵roʊz ə- **~s** z
Rosie ˈrəʊz i ‖ ˈroʊz i
rosin ˈrɒz ɪn §-ʰn ‖ ˈrɑːz- **~ed** d **~ing** ɪŋ **~s** z
Rosinante ͵rɒz ɪ ˈnænt i -ə- ‖ ͵rɑːz- —*Sp*
  [͵rro si ˈnan te]
Roskilde ˈrɒsk ɪld ə ‖ ˈrɑːsk- ˈroʊsk- —*Danish*
  [ˈʁɒs ki lə]
Roslea rɒs ˈleɪ ‖ rɔːs- rɑːs-
Roslin, Roslyn ˈrɒz lɪn §-lən ‖ ˈrɑːz-
ROSPA, RoSPA ˈrɒsp ə ‖ ˈrɑːsp ə
Ross rɒs ‖ rɔːs rɑːs
  ͵Ross ˈSea
Rossall ˈrɒs ʰl ‖ ˈrɔːs- ˈrɑːs-
Rossendale ˈrɒs ʰn deɪ ʰl ‖ ˈrɔːs- ˈrɑːs-
Rossetti (*i*) rə ˈzet i rɒ- ‖ roʊ ˈzeʈ i, (*ii*) -ˈset i
  ‖ -ˈseʈ i
Rossini rɒ ˈsiːn i rə- ‖ roʊ- —*It* [ros ˈsi: ni]
Rossiter ˈrɒs ɪt ə -ət- ‖ ˈrɔːs əʈ ʰr ˈrɑːs-
Rosslare ˈrɒs ˈleə ·ˈ· ‖ ͵rɔːs ˈleʰr ͵rɑːs-, -ˈlæʰr
Rosslyn ˈrɒs lɪn §-lən ‖ ˈrɔːs- ˈrɑːs-
Ross-on-Wye ͵rɒs ɒn ˈwaɪ ‖ ͵rɔːs ɑːn- ͵rɑːs-,
  -ɔːn-
Rostand rɒ ˈstɒ̃ ‖ roʊ ˈstɑːnd —*Fr* [ʁɒs tɑ̃]
roster ˈrɒst ə ‖ ˈrɑːst ʰr **~ed** d **rostering**
  ˈrɒst ʰr ɪŋ ‖ ˈrɑːst ʰr ɪŋ **~s** z
Rostock ˈrɒst ɒk ‖ ˈrɑːst ɑːk —*Ger* [ˈʁɒs tɔk]
Rostov ˈrɒst ɒv -ɒf ‖ ˈrɑːst ɑːv -ɑːf —*Russ*
  [ʌvs ˈtɔf]
  ͵Rostov-on-ˈDon
ros|tra ˈrɒs |trə ‖ ˈrɑːs- **~tral** trəl **~trate** treɪt
Rostrevor rɒs ˈtrev ə ‖ rɑːs ˈtrev ʰr
Rostropovich ͵rɒs trə ˈpəʊv ɪtʃ
  ‖ ͵rɑːs trə ˈpoʊv ɪtʃ —*Russ* [ʁəs trʌ ˈpɔ vʲɪtʃ]
ros|trum ˈrɒs |trəm ‖ ˈrɑːs- **~tra** trə **~trums**
  trəmz
Roswell ˈrɒz wel ‖ ˈrɑːz-
ros|y ˈrəʊz |i ‖ ˈroʊz |i **~ier** i ə ‖ i ʰr **~iest** i ɪst
  i əst **~ily** ɪ li əl i **~iness** i nəs i nɪs
Rosyth rə ˈsaɪθ rɒ-
rot rɒt ‖ rɑːt **rots** rɒts ‖ rɑːts **rotted** ˈrɒt ɪd
  -əd ‖ ˈrɑːʈ əd **rotting** ˈrɒt ɪŋ ‖ ˈrɑːʈ ɪŋ
rota, Rota ˈrəʊt ə ‖ ˈroʊʈ ə **~s** z
Rotarian rəʊ ˈteər i ən ‖ roʊ ˈter- **~s** z
rotar|y, R~ ˈrəʊt ər |i ‖ ˈroʊʈ- **~ies** iz
  ˈRotary Club; ͵rotary ˈtiller
rotatab|le rəʊ ˈteɪt əb |ʰl ‖ ˈroʊt eɪʈ- **~ly** li
rotate rəʊ ˈteɪt ‖ ˈroʊt eɪt **rotated** rəʊ ˈteɪt ɪd
  -əd ‖ ˈroʊt eɪʈ əd **rotates** rəʊ ˈteɪts
  ‖ ˈroʊt eɪts **rotating** rəʊ ˈteɪt ɪŋ
  ‖ ˈroʊt eɪʈ ɪŋ
rotation rəʊ ˈteɪʃ ʰn ‖ roʊ- **~al** ʰl ◄ **~s** z

rotative rəʊ ˈteɪt ɪv ˈrəʊt ət- ‖ ˈroʊʈ əʈ ɪv **~ly** li
rotator rəʊ ˈteɪt ə ‖ ˈroʊt eɪʈ ʰr **~s** z
rotatory rəʊ ˈteɪt ər i ˈrəʊt ət͵ər i
  ‖ ˈroʊʈ ə tɔːr i -toʊr i (*)
Rotavator —*see* **Rotovator**
rotavirus ˈrəʊt ə ͵vaɪʰr əs ‖ ˈroʊʈ- **~es** ɪz əz
rote rəʊt ‖ roʊt (= *wrote*)
rotenone ˈrəʊt ə nəʊn -ɪ-, -ʰn əʊn
  ‖ ˈroʊt ʰn oʊn
rotgut ˈrɒt gʌt ‖ ˈrɑːt-
Roth (*i*) rɒθ ‖ rɔːθ rɑːθ, (*ii*) rəʊθ ‖ roʊθ
Rothamsted ˈrɒθ əm sted ‖ ˈrɑːθ-
Rothay ˈrɒθ eɪ ‖ ˈrɑːθ-
Rothbury ˈrɒθ bər i ‖ ˈrɑːθ-
Rothenstein ˈrəʊθ ʰn staɪn ˈrəʊt-, ˈrɒθ-
  ‖ ˈrɑːθ-
Rother ˈrɒð ə ‖ ˈrɑːð ʰr
Rotherfield ˈrɒð ə fiː ʰld ‖ ˈrɑːð ʰr-
Rotherham ˈrɒð ʰr əm ‖ ˈrɑːð-
Rotherhithe ˈrɒð ə haɪð ‖ ˈrɑːð ʰr-
Rothermere ˈrɒð ə mɪə ‖ ˈrɑːð ʰr mɪr
Rothersthorpe ˈrɒð əz θɔːp ‖ ˈrɑːð ʰrz θɔːrp
  —*In Northants, locally also* -θrəp
Rotherwick ˈrɒð ə wɪk ‖ ˈrɑːð ʰr- —*formerly*
  also -ʰr ɪk
Rothes ˈrɒθ ɪz -ɪs, §-əz, §-əs ‖ ˈrɑːθ-
Rothesay ˈrɒθ si -seɪ ‖ ˈrɑːθ-
Rothko ˈrɒθ kəʊ ‖ ˈrɑːθ koʊ
Rothman ˈrɒθ mən ‖ ˈrɔːθ- ˈrɑːθ-
Rothschild ˈrɒθs tʃaɪ ʰld ˈrɒθ- ‖ ˈrɔːθs- ˈrɑːθs-,
  ˈrɔːθ-, ˈrɑːθ- **~s, ~'s** z
Rothwell ˈrɒθ wel -wəl ‖ ˈrɑːθ- —*In*
  Northants, locally also ˈrəʊ əl
roti ˈrəʊt i ‖ ˈroʊʈ i **~s** z —*Hindi* [roː ʈi]
rotifer ˈrəʊt ɪf ə §-əf- ‖ ˈroʊʈ əf ʰr **~s** z
rotifer|a rəʊ ˈtɪf ʰr |ə ‖ roʊ- **~al** ʰl **~ous** əs
rotisserie rəʊ ˈtɪs ər i -ˈtiːs- ‖ roʊ- **~s** z
roto ˈrəʊt əʊ ‖ ˈroʊʈ oʊ **~s** z
Rotodyne ˈrəʊt əʊ daɪn ‖ ˈroʊʈ ə-
rotogravure ͵rəʊt əʊ grə ˈvjʊə
  ‖ ͵roʊʈ ə grə ˈvjʊʰr
rotor ˈrəʊt ə ‖ ˈroʊʈ ʰr **~s** z
Roto-rooter *tdmk* ˈrəʊt əʊ ͵ruːt ə
  ‖ ˈroʊʈ oʊ ͵ruːʈ ʰr
Rotorua ͵rəʊt ə ˈruːʰ ə ‖ ͵roʊʈ-
rototill ˈrəʊt əʊ tɪl ‖ ˈroʊʈ- **~ed** d **~ing** ɪŋ **~s** z
rototiller, R~ *tdmk* ˈrəʊt ə ͵tɪl ə
  ‖ ˈroʊʈ ə ͵tɪl ʰr **~s** z
roto|vate ˈrəʊt ə |veɪt ‖ ˈroʊʈ- **~vated** veɪt ɪd
  -əd ‖ veɪʈ əd **~vates** veɪts **~vating** veɪt ɪŋ
  ‖ veɪʈ ɪŋ
rotovator, R~ *tdmk* ˈrəʊt ə veɪt ə
  ‖ ˈroʊʈ ə veɪʈ ʰr **~s** z
rotten ˈrɒt ʰn ‖ ˈrɑːt ʰn **~er** ə ‖ ʰr **~est** ɪst əst
  ~ly li **~ness** nəs nɪs
  ͵rotten ˈborough
rottenstone ˈrɒt ʰn stəʊn ‖ ˈrɑːt ʰn stoʊn
rotter ˈrɒt ə ‖ ˈrɑːʈ ʰr **~s** z
Rotterdam ˈrɒt ə dæm ·ˈ· ‖ ˈrɑːʈ ʰr- —*Dutch*
  [rɒt ər ˈdɑm]
Rottingdean ˈrɒt ɪŋ diːn ‖ ˈrɑːʈ- —*locally also*
  ·ˈ·.

R

Rottweiler, r~ 'rɒt waɪl ə -vaɪl- ‖ 'rɑːt waɪl ᵊr
~s z
rotund rəʊ 'tʌnd 'rəʊt ʌnd ‖ roʊ 'tʌnd
'roʊt ʌnd
rotunda, R~ rəʊ 'tʌnd ə ‖ roʊ- ~s z
rotundity rəʊ 'tʌnd ət i -ɪt- ‖ roʊ 'tʌnd əţ i
rotund|ly rəʊ 'tʌnd |li 'rəʊt ʌnd- ‖ roʊ 'tʌnd-
'roʊt ʌnd- ~**ness** nəs nɪs
rouble 'ruːb ᵊl ~s z
roué 'ruː eɪ ‖ ru 'eɪ ~s z
Rouen 'ruː ɒ̃ ‖ ru 'ɑːn —Fr [ʁwɑ̃]
rouge ruːʒ **rouged** ruːʒd **rouges** 'ruːʒ ɪz -əz
rouging 'ruːʒ ɪŋ —Fr [ʁuʒ]
,**rouge et 'noir** eɪ 'nwɑː ‖ -'nwɑːr —Fr
[e nwaːʁ]
rough rʌf (= ruff) **roughed** rʌft **rougher**
'rʌf ə ‖ -ᵊr **roughest** 'rʌf ɪst -əst **roughing**
'rʌf ɪŋ **roughs** rʌfs
,**rough 'diamond**; ,**rough 'paper**; 'rough
stuff; ,**rough 'trade**
Rough rʌf —but Rough Tor in Cornwall is raʊ
roughage 'rʌf ɪdʒ
rough-and-ready ,rʌf ᵊn 'red i ◂ -ᵊnd-
rough-and-tumble ,rʌf ᵊn 'tʌm bᵊl -ᵊnd-
roughcast 'rʌf kɑːst §-kæst ‖ -kæst ~**ing** ɪŋ ~**s**
s
rough-|dry 'rʌf |draɪ ,·'· ~**dried** draɪd ~**dries**
draɪz ~**drying** draɪ ɪŋ
roughen 'rʌf ᵊn ~**ed** d ~**ing** _ɪŋ ~**s** z
rough-|hew ,rʌf |'hjuː ~**hewed** 'hjuːd
~**hewing** 'hjuː ɪŋ ~**hewn** 'hjuːn ◂ ~**hews**
'hjuːz
roughhouse n 'rʌf haʊs
roughish 'rʌf ɪʃ ~**ness** nəs nɪs
roughly 'rʌf li
roughneck 'rʌf nek ~**s** s
roughness 'rʌf nəs -nɪs ~**es** ɪz əz
roughrider ,rʌf 'raɪd ə '·,·· ‖ -ᵊr ~**s** z
roughshod 'rʌf ʃɒd ‖ -ʃɑːd
Roughton (i) 'raʊt ᵊn, (ii) 'ruːt ᵊn
roulade ru 'lɑːd ~**s** z
rouleau 'ruːl əʊ ‖ ru 'loʊ ~**s**, ~**x** z
rou|lette ru |'let ~**letted** 'let ɪd -əd ‖ 'leţ əd
~**lettes** 'lets ~**letting** 'let ɪŋ ‖ 'leţ ɪŋ
Roumani|a ru 'meɪn i‿|ə ~**an/s** ən/z
round raʊnd **rounded** 'raʊnd ɪd -əd **rounder**
'raʊnd ə ‖ -ᵊr **roundest** 'raʊnd ɪst -əst
rounding 'raʊnd ɪŋ **rounds** raʊndz
,**round 'bracket**; ,**round 'robin**; ,**Round**
'**Table**; ,**round 'trip**
roundabout n, adj, prep 'raʊnd ə ,baʊt ~**s** s
round-arm 'raʊnd ɑːm ‖ -ɑːrm
rounded 'raʊnd ɪd -əd ~**ly** li ~**ness** nəs nɪs
roundel 'raʊnd ᵊl ~**s** z
roundelay 'raʊnd ə leɪ -ɪ-, -ᵊl eɪ ~**s** z
rounders 'raʊnd əz ‖ -ᵊrz
round-eyed ,raʊnd 'aɪd ◂
roundhand 'raʊnd hænd
Roundhay 'raʊnd eɪ -i —There is also a
spelling pronunciation -heɪ.
Roundhead 'raʊnd hed ~**s** z
round|house 'raʊnd |haʊs ~**houses** haʊz ɪz
-əz

roundish 'raʊnd ɪʃ ~**ness** nəs nɪs
round|ly 'raʊnd |li ~**ness** nəs nɪs
round-shouldered ,raʊnd 'ʃəʊld əd ◂
→-'ʃɒld- ‖ -'ʃoʊld ᵊrd ◂
rounds|man 'raʊndz |mən ~**men** mən -men
round-table ,raʊnd 'teɪb ᵊl ◂
,**round-,table di'scussions**
round-the-clock ,raʊnd ðə 'klɒk ◂ ‖ -'klɑːk ◂
round-trip ,raʊnd 'trɪp ◂
,**round-trip 'ticket**
roundup 'raʊnd ʌp ~**s** s
roundwood, R~ 'raʊnd wʊd
roundworm 'raʊnd wɜːm ‖ -wɜːm ~**s** z
Rountree 'raʊn triː
roup bird disease ruːp
Rourke rɔːk ‖ rɔːrk roʊrk
Rous raʊs
rouse raʊz **roused** raʊzd **rouses** 'raʊz ɪz -əz
rousing/ly 'raʊz ɪŋ /li
Rouse raʊs
Rousseau 'ruːs əʊ ‖ ruː 'soʊ —Fr [ʁu so]
Roussillon ,ruːs iː 'ɒ̃ -'jɒ̃ ‖ -'joʊn —Fr
[ʁu si jɔ̃]
roust raʊst **rousted** 'raʊst ɪd -əd **rousting**
'raʊst ɪŋ **rousts** raʊsts
roustabout 'raʊst ə ,baʊt ~**s** s
rout, Rout raʊt **routed** 'raʊt ɪd -əd ‖ 'raʊţ əd
routing 'raʊt ɪŋ ‖ 'raʊţ ɪŋ **routs** raʊts

ROUTE

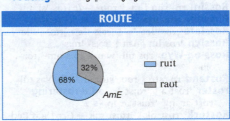

route ruːt raʊt —in BrE the form raʊt is
confined to army usage, but in AmE it is more
widespread. — Preference poll, AmE: ruːt
68%, raʊt 32%. **routed** 'ruːt ɪd -əd ‖ 'ruːţ əd
'raʊţ- **routeing/s, routing/s** 'ruːt ɪŋ/z
‖ 'ruːţ ɪŋ/z 'raʊţ- **routes** ruːts raʊts
'**route march**
router 'tool for hollowing' 'raʊt ə ‖ 'raʊţ ᵊr ~**s**
z
router 'computer networking device' 'ruːt ə
‖ 'ruːţ ᵊr 'raʊţ- ~**s** z
Routh raʊθ
routine ,ruː 'tiːn ◂ ru- ~**ly** li ~**s** z
Routledge 'raʊt lɪdʒ 'rʌt-, -ledʒ
roux sing. ruː (= rue) **roux** pl ruːz or as sing.
rove, Rove rəʊv ‖ roʊv **roved** rəʊvd ‖ roʊvd
roves rəʊvz ‖ roʊvz **roving** 'rəʊv ɪŋ
‖ 'roʊv ɪŋ
,**roving com'mission**; ,**roving 'eye**
rover, Rover 'rəʊv ə ‖ 'roʊv ᵊr ~**s**, ~'**s** z
row 'quarrel' raʊ **rowed** raʊd **rowing** 'raʊ ɪŋ
rows raʊz (= rouse)
row v 'use oars', n 'line', 'trip in rowing boat',
Row name of thoroughfare rəʊ ‖ roʊ (= roe)

rowed rəʊd ‖ roʊd (= *road*) **rowing** ˈrəʊ ɪŋ
‖ ˈroʊ ɪŋ **rows** rəʊz ‖ roʊz (= *rose*)
ˈrow house; ˈrowing boat; ˈrowing
maˌchine
Rowallan rəʊ ˈæl ən ‖ roʊ-
rowan, Rowan ˈrəʊ ən ˈraʊ‿ən ‖ ˈroʊ ən ~s z
ˈrowan tree
rowanberr|y ˈrəʊ ən ˌber |i ˈraʊ‿ən-, →-əm-
‖ ˈroʊ- ~ies iz
Rowant ˈraʊ‿ənt
rowboat ˈrəʊ bəʊt ‖ ˈroʊ boʊt ~s s
Rowbotham, Rowbottom ˈrəʊ ˌbɒt əm
‖ ˈroʊ ˌbɑːt̬ əm
rowd|y ˈraʊd |i ~ier i ə ‖ i ᵊr ~ies iz ~iest
i ˌɪst i ˌəst ~ily ɪ li əl i ~iness i nəs i nɪs ~yism
i ˌɪz əm
Rowe rəʊ ‖ roʊ
rowel ˈraʊ‿əl raʊl ‖ ˈraʊ‿əl ~ed, ~led d ~ing,
~ling ɪŋ ~s z
Rowena rəʊ ˈiːn ə ‖ roʊ-
Rowenta *tdmk* rəʊ ˈent ə ‖ roʊ ˈenṱ ə
rower ˈrəʊ ə ‖ ˈroʊ ᵊr ~s z
Rowland ˈrəʊl ənd ‖ ˈroʊl-
Rowlands ˈrəʊl əndz ‖ ˈroʊl-
Rowlandson ˈrəʊl ənd sən ‖ ˈroʊl-
Rowley ˈrəʊl i ‖ ˈroʊl i —*but* R~ Regis *in*
WMids is ˈraʊl i
Rowling ˈrəʊl ɪŋ →ˈrɒʊl- ‖ ˈroʊl ɪŋ —*This is*
appropriate for J. K. Rowling, author of the
Harry Potter series.
rowlock ˈrɒl ək ˈrʌl- ‖ ˈrɑːl- —*Also, but not*
among sailors, ˈrəʊ lɒk ‖ ˈroʊ lɑːk ~s s
Rowney (i) ˈraʊn i, (ii) ˈrəʊn i ‖ ˈroʊn i
Rowntree rəʊn triː
ˌRowntree ˈMackintosh *tdmk*
Rowridge ˈraʊ rɪdʒ
Rowse raʊs
Rowsley ˈrəʊz li ‖ ˈroʊz-
Rowton ˈraʊt ᵊn
Roxana rɒk ˈsɑːn ə ‖ rɑːk ˈsæn ə
Roxanna rɒk ˈsæn ə ‖ rɑːk-
Roxanne, r~ rɒk ˈsæn ‖ rɑːk-
Roxburgh ˈrɒks bər ə ‖ ˈrɑːks ˌbɝː oʊ
Roxy ˈrɒks i ‖ ˈrɑːks i
Roy rɔɪ
royal ˈrɔɪ‿əl ~s z
ˌroyal ˈblue ◂; ˌroyal ˈflush; ˌRoyal
ˈHighness; ˌroyal preˈrogative
royale, R~ rɔɪ ˈɑːl -ˈæl ‖ -ˈæl
royalism ˈrɔɪ‿əl ˌɪz əm
royalist ˈrɔɪ‿əl ɪst §-əst ~s s
royally ˈrɔɪ‿əl i
royalty ˈrɔɪ‿əl ti
Royce rɔɪs
Royden, Roydon ˈrɔɪd ᵊn
Royle rɔɪᵊl
Royston ˈrɔɪst ən
Royton ˈrɔɪt ᵊn
Roz rɒz ‖ rɑːz
rozzer ˈrɒz ə ‖ ˈrɑːz ᵊr ~s z
RP ˌɑː ˈpiː ‖ ˌɑːr-
rpm ˌɑː piː ˈem ‖ ˌɑːr-

-**rrhagia** ˈreɪdʒ i ə ˈreɪdʒ ə ‖ ˈreɪdʒ ə ˈreɪʒ ə
— **menorrhagia** ˌmen ə ˈreɪdʒ i ə ˌ·ˈ·ə
‖ -ˈreɪdʒ ə -ˈreɪʒ-
-**rrhaphy** *stress-imposing* rəf i — **colporrhaphy**
kɒl ˈpɒr əf i ‖ kɑːl ˈpɔːr- -ˈpɑːr-
-**rrhea, -rrhoea** ˈrɪə ˈriː ə ‖ ˈriː ə —
blenorrhea, blennorrhoea ˌblen ə ˈrɪə
-ˈriː ə ‖ -ˈriː ə
RSJ ˌɑːr es ˈdʒeɪ ~s z
RSVP ˌɑːr es viː ˈpiː
Ruabon ru ˈæb ən —*Welsh* [riu ˈa bon]
Ruanda ru ˈænd ə ‖ -ˈɑːnd ə
Ruane ru ˈen
Ruaridh ˈruər i ˈrɔːr- ‖ ˈrʊr i
rub rʌb **rubbed** rʌbd **rubbing/s** ˈrʌb ɪŋ/z **rubs**
rʌbz
rub-a-dub ˈrʌb ə dʌb
rub-a-dub-dub ˌrʌb ə dʌb ˈdʌb
rubaiyat, rubáiyát, R~ ˈruː baɪ æt -ɑːt,
-jɑːt, ˌ·ˈ·· ‖ -jɑːt
rubato ru ˈbɑːt əʊ ‖ -oʊ ~s z
rubb... —*see* **rub**
rubber ˈrʌb ə ‖ ˈrʌb ᵊr ~s z
ˌrubber ˈband; ˈrubber boot; ˌrubber
ˈdinghy; ˈrubber plant; ˌrubber ˈstamp;
ˈrubber tree
rubberis|e, rubberiz|e ˈrʌb ə raɪz ~ed d ~es
ɪz əz ~ing ɪŋ
rubberneck ˈrʌb ə nek ‖ -ᵊr- ~ed t ~er/s ə/z
‖ ᵊr/z ~ing ɪŋ ~s s
rubber-stamp ˌrʌb ə ˈstæmp ‖ -ᵊr- ~ed t ~ing
ɪŋ ~s s
rubbery ˈrʌb ər i
rubbish ˈrʌb ɪʃ ~ed t ~es ɪz əz ~ing ɪŋ
ˈrubbish bin
rubbishy ˈrʌb ɪʃ i
rubble ˈrʌb ᵊl
Rubbra ˈrʌb rə
rubdown ˈrʌb daʊn ~s z
rube, Rube ruːb **rubes, Rube's** ruːbz
rubella ru ˈbel ə
Ruben ˈruːb ɪn -ən
Rubens ˈruːb ɪnz -ənz —*Dutch* [ˈry: bəns]
rubeola ru ˈbiː‿əl ə ˌruːb i ˈəʊl ə ‖ ˌruːb i ˈoʊl ə
Rubery ˈruːb ər i
rubesc|ence ru ˈbes |ᵊnᵗs ~ent ᵊnt
Rubicon ˈruːb ɪk ən -ɪ kɒn, §-ə- ‖ -ɪ kɑːn
rubicund ˈruːb ɪk ənd §-ək-, -ɪ kʌnd, §-ə-
rubicundity ˌruːb ɪ ˈkʌnd ət i §-ə-, -ɪt i ‖ -ət̬ i
rubidium ru ˈbɪd i‿əm
rubie... —*see* **ruby**
Rubik ˈruːb ɪk ~'s s
Rubin ˈruːb ɪn §-ən
Rubinstein ˈruːb ɪn staɪn -ən-
ruble ˈruːb ᵊl ~s z
rubric ˈruːb rɪk ~s s
ruby, Ruby ˈruːb i **rubies** ˈruːb iz
RUC ˌɑː juː ˈsiː ‖ ˌɑːr-
ruche ruːʃ **ruched** ruːʃt **ruches** ˈruːʃ ɪz -əz
ruching ˈruːʃ ɪŋ
ruck rʌk **rucked** rʌkt **rucking** ˈrʌk ɪŋ **rucks**
rʌks
ruckle ˈrʌk ᵊl ~s z

rucksack 'rʌk sæk 'rʊk- ~s s
ruckus 'rʌk əs ~es ɪz əz
rucola 'ruːk əl ə
ruction 'rʌk ʃⁿ ~s z
rudbeckia rʌd 'bek i ə →rʌb-, ˌruːd- ~s z
Rudd, rudd rʌd rudds rʌdz
rudder 'rʌd ə ‖ -ᵊr ~ed d ~s z
rudderless 'rʌd ə ləs -lɪs, -ᵊl əs ‖ -ᵊr-
Ruddigore 'rʌd ɪ gɔː ‖ -gɔːr
ruddl|e 'rʌd ᵊl ~ed d ~es z ~ing ɪŋ
Ruddock, r~ 'rʌd ək ~s s
rudd|y 'rʌd |i ~ier i ə ‖ i ᵊr ~iest i ɪst i əst
  ~ily ɪ li əl i ~iness i nəs i nɪs
rude ruːd rudely 'ruːd li rudeness 'ruːd nəs
  -nɪs ruder 'ruːd ə ‖ -ᵊr rudest 'ruːd ɪst -əst
Rudge rʌdʒ
Rudgwick 'rʌdʒ wɪk -ɪk
Rudi 'ruːd i
rudiment 'ruːd ɪ mənt -ə- ~s s
rudi|mentary ˌruːd ɪ |'ment ər i ◂ ˌ-ə-
  ~mentarily 'ment ər əl i -ɪ li; men 'ter ə l i
  ~mentariness 'ment ər i nəs -nɪs
Rudolf, Rudolph 'ruːd ɒlf ‖ -ɑːlf
Rudy 'ruːd i
Rudyard 'rʌd jəd -jɑːd; 'rʌdʒ əd ‖ -jᵊrd -jɑːrd
rue ruː rued ruːd (= rude) rues ruːz ruing
  'ruː ɪŋ
rueful 'ruː fᵊl -fʊl ~ly i ~ness nəs nɪs
ruff, Ruff rʌf ruffed rʌft ruffing 'rʌf ɪŋ ruffs
  rʌfs
ruffian 'rʌf i ən ~ism ˌɪz əm ~ly li ~s z
ruffl|e 'rʌf ᵊl ~ed d ~es z ~ing ɪŋ
Rufflette tdmk ˌrʌf 'let ˌrʌf ᵊl 'et
Rufford 'rʌf əd ‖ -ᵊrd
rufous 'ruːf əs
Rufus 'ruːf əs
rug rʌg rugs rʌgz
Rugbeian rʌg 'biː ən ~s z
rugby, Rugby 'rʌg bi
  ˌrugby 'football; ˌRugby 'League; ˌRugby
  'Union
Rugeley 'ruːdʒ li 'ruːʒ-
rugged 'rʌg ɪd §-əd ~ly li ~ness nəs nɪs
rugger 'rʌg ə ‖ -ᵊr
  'rugger ball; 'rugger ˌplayer
rugose 'ruːg əʊs -əʊz; ruː 'gəʊs ‖ 'ruːg oʊs ~ly
  li
rugosity ruː 'gɒs ət i -ɪt- ‖ -'gɑːs əṭ i
rugrat 'rʌg ræt ~s s
Ruhr rʊə ‖ rʊᵊr —Ger [ʁuːɐ]
ruin 'ruː ɪn §ən ~ed d ~ing ɪŋ ~s z
ruination ˌruː ɪ 'neɪʃ ⁿ §ə-
ruinous 'ruː ɪn əs §ən- ~ly li ~ness nəs nɪs
Ruisdael 'raɪz dɑːl 'riːz-, -derᵊl —Dutch
  ['rœyz dɑːl]
Ruislip 'raɪs lɪp
rule, Rule ruːl ruled ruːld rules ruːlz ruling
  'ruːl ɪŋ
  ˌrule of 'thumb
rulebook 'ruːl bʊk §-buːk ~s s
ruler 'ruːl ə ‖ -ᵊr ~s z
ruling 'ruːl ɪŋ ~s z
  ˌruling 'class

rum rʌm rummer 'rʌm ə ‖ -ᵊr rummest
  'rʌm ɪst -əst rums rʌmz
Rumani|a ru 'meɪn i |ə ~an/s ən/z
rumba 'rʌm bə 'rʊm- ‖ 'ruːm- ~ed d rumbaing
  'rʌm bəʳ ɪŋ 'rʊm- ‖ -bə ɪŋ 'ruːm- ~s z
Rumbelow 'rʌm bə ləʊ ‖ -loʊ
rumbl|e 'rʌm bᵊl ~ed d ~es z ~ing ɪŋ
rumbling 'rʌm blɪŋ ~ly li ~s z
Rumbold 'rʌm bəʊld →-bɒʊld ‖ -boʊld
rumbustious rʌm 'bʌs tʃəs -'bʌs ti ‿əs,
  △-'bʌs tʃu ‿əs ~ly li ~ness nəs nɪs
Rumelia ru 'miːl i ə
rum|en 'ruːm |en -ɪn, -ən ~ens enz ɪnz, ənz
  ~ina ɪn ə ən ə
Rumford 'rʌm fəd ‖ -fᵊrd
ruminant 'ruːm ɪn ənt -ən- ~s s
rumi|nate 'ruːm ɪ |neɪt -ə- ~nated neɪt ɪd -əd
  ‖ neɪṭ əd ~nates neɪts ~nating/ly neɪt ɪŋ /li
  ‖ neɪṭ ɪŋ /li
rumination ˌruːm ɪ 'neɪʃ ⁿ -ə- ~s z
ruminative 'ruːm ɪ nət ɪv '-ə-, -neɪt ɪv
  ‖ -ə neɪṭ ɪv ~ly li
rumly 'rʌm li
rummag|e 'rʌm ɪdʒ ~ed d ~er/s ə/z ‖ ᵊr/z ~es
  ɪz əz ~ing ɪŋ
  'rummage sale
rummer 'rʌm ə ‖ -ᵊr ~s z
rumm|y 'rʌm |i ~ier i ə ‖ i ᵊr ~ies iz ~iest
  i ɪst əst
rumness 'rʌm nəs -nɪs
rumor, rumour 'ruːm ə ‖ -ᵊr ~ed d rumoring,
  rumouring 'ruːm ər ɪŋ ~s z
rumormonger, rumourmonger
  'ruːm ə ˌmʌŋ gə §-ˌmɒŋ- ‖ -ᵊr ˌmʌŋ gᵊr
  -ˌmɑːŋ- ~s z
rump rʌmp rumps rʌmps
  ˌrump 'steak
Rumpelstiltskin ˌrʌmp ᵊl 'stɪlt skɪn
rumpl|e 'rʌmp ᵊl ~ed d ~es z ~ing ɪŋ
Rumpole 'rʌmp əʊl →-ɒʊl ‖ -oʊl
rumpus 'rʌmp əs ~es ɪz əz
  'rumpus room
Rumsfeld 'rʌmz feld -felt
run rʌn ran ræn running 'rʌn ɪŋ runs rʌnz
runabout 'rʌn ə ˌbaʊt ~s s
runagate 'rʌn ə geɪt ~s s
run-around 'rʌn ə ˌraʊnd
runaway 'rʌn ə ˌweɪ ~s z
runcible 'rʌnᵗs əb ᵊl -ɪb-
Runcie 'rʌnᵗs i
Runciman 'rʌnᵗs ɪ mən
runcinate 'rʌnᵗs ɪn ət -ⁿn-, -ɪt; -ɪ neɪt, -ə-
Runcorn 'rʌn kɔːn →'rʌŋ- ‖ -kɔːrn
Rundall, Rundell, Rundle 'rʌnd ᵊl
run-down adj ˌrʌn 'daʊn ◂
rundown n 'rʌn daʊn ~s z
rune ruːn runes ruːnz
rung rʌŋ rungs rʌŋz
runic 'ruːn ɪk
run-in n 'rʌn ɪn ~s z
runnel 'rʌn ᵊl ~s z
runner 'rʌn ə ‖ -ᵊr ~s z
  'runner bean, ˌ· '·

runn|er-up ˌrʌn |ər 'ʌp ◂ || -|ər 'ʌp **~ers-up**
  əz 'ʌp || -ᵊrz 'ʌp
running 'rʌn ɪŋ
  'running board; ˌrunning 'jump; 'running
  light; 'running mate; ˌrunning 'water
runn|y 'rʌn |i **~ier** i ə || i ᵊr **~iest** i ɪst i ̩əst
  ~iness i nəs -nɪs
Runnymede 'rʌn i miːd
runoff, run-off 'rʌn ɒf -ɔːf || -ɔːf -ɑːf **~s** s
run-of-the-mill ˌrʌn əv ðə 'mɪl ◂ -ə ðə-
run-on 'rʌn ɒn || -ɑːn -ɔːn **~s** z
run-out 'rʌn aʊt **~s** s
runt rʌnt **runts** rʌnts
run-through 'rʌn θruː **~s** z
runtish 'rʌnt ɪʃ || 'rʌnt̬ ɪʃ
runt|y 'rʌnt |i || 'rʌnt̬ |i **~iness** i nəs i nɪs
run-up 'rʌn ʌp **~s** s
runway 'rʌn weɪ **~s** z
Runyon 'rʌn jən
rupee ˌruː 'piː ru- || 'ruːp iː ru 'piː **~s** z
Rupert 'ruːp ət || -ᵊrt
rupiah ru 'piːə **~s** z
rupture 'rʌp tʃə -ʃə || -tʃᵊr **~d** d **~s** z **rupturing**
  'rʌp tʃər ɪŋ -ʃər ɪŋ
rural 'rʊər əl || 'rʊr əl
  ˌrural 'dean
rurality rʊᵊ 'ræl ət i -ɪt- || -ət̬ i
rurally 'rʊər əl i || 'rʊr əl i
ruridecanal ˌrʊər ɪ dɪ 'keɪn ᵊl ◂ ˌ-ə-, -də'--
  || ˌrʊr-
Ruritani|a ˌrʊər ɪ 'teɪn i ̩ə ˌ-ə- || ˌrʊr- **~an/s**
  ən/z
ruse ruːz || ruːs ruːz **ruses** 'ruːz ɪz -əz || 'ruːs-
  'ruːz-
rusé 'ruːz eɪ || ru: 'zeɪ —*Fr* [ʁy ze]
Rusedski ru 'zet ski -'sed-, -'set-
rush, Rush rʌʃ **rushed** rʌʃt **rushes** 'rʌʃ ɪz -əz
  rushing/ly 'rʌʃ ɪŋ /li
  'rush hour
Rushdie 'rʊʃ di —*This is reportedly the writer*
  Salman R~'s *preference, though he is often*
  referred to as 'rʌʃ di
rusher 'rʌʃ ə || -ᵊr **~s** z
rushlight 'rʌʃ laɪt **~s** s
Rushmere 'rʌʃ mɪə || -mɪr
Rushmore 'rʌʃ mɔː || -mɔːr -moʊr
Rusholme 'rʌʃ həʊm -əm || -hoʊm
Rushton 'rʌʃt ən
Rushworth 'rʌʃ wɜːθ || -wɜːθ
rush|y 'rʌʃ |i **~ier** i ə || i ᵊr **~iest** i ɪst i ̩əst
  ~iness i nəs i nɪs
rusk, Rusk rʌsk **rusks** rʌsks
Ruskin 'rʌsk ɪn §-ən
Rusper 'rʌsp ə || -ᵊr
Russ rʌs
russe ruːs
Russel, Russell 'rʌs ᵊl
russet 'rʌs ɪt §-ət **~s** s
Russia 'rʌʃ ə **~s,** **~'s** z
Russian 'rʌʃ ᵊn **~s** z
  ˌRussian rou'lette
Russianis... —*see* **Russianiz...**

Russianization, r~ ˌrʌʃ ᵊn aɪ 'zeɪʃ ᵊn -ɪ'--
  || -ə'--
Russianiz|e, r~ 'rʌʃ ə naɪz -ᵊn aɪz **~ed** d **~er/s**
  ə/z || ᵊr/z **~es** ɪz əz **~ing** ɪŋ
Russianness 'rʌʃ ᵊn nəs -nɪs
Russification ˌrʌs ɪf ɪ 'keɪʃ ᵊn ˌ-əf-, §-ə'--
Russi|fy 'rʌs ɪ |faɪ -ə- **~fied** faɪd **~fies** faɪz
  ~fying faɪ ɪŋ
Russk|i, Russk|y 'rʌsk i **~ies** iz
Russo- |ˈrʌs əʊ || -oʊ — **Russo-Japanese**
  ˌrʌs əʊ ˌdʒæp ə 'niːz || ˌrʌs oʊ-
rust, Rust rʌst **rusted** 'rʌst ɪd -əd **rusting**
  'rʌst ɪŋ **rusts** rʌsts
  'rust belt
rustbucket 'rʌst ˌbʌk ɪt §-ət **~s** s
rustic 'rʌst ɪk **~s** s
rusti|cate 'rʌst ɪ |keɪt §-ə- **~cated** keɪt ɪd -əd
  || keɪt̬ əd **~cates** keɪts **~cating** keɪt ɪŋ
  || keɪt̬ ɪŋ
rustication ˌrʌst ɪ 'keɪʃ ᵊn §-ə- **~s** z
rusticity rʌ 'stɪs ət i -ɪt i || -ət̬ i
rustl|e 'rʌs ᵊl **~ed** d **~es** z **~ing** ɪŋ
rustler 'rʌs lə 'rʌs ᵊl ə || -ᵊl ᵊr **~s** z
rustless 'rʌst ləs -lɪs
rustling 'rʌs ᵊl ɪŋ **~ly** li
Ruston 'rʌst ən
rustproof 'rʌst pruːf §-prʊf **~ed** t **~ing** ɪŋ **~s** s
rust|y, Rusty 'rʌst |i **~ier** i ə || i ᵊr **~iest** i ɪst
  i ̩əst **~ily** ɪ li əl i **~iness** i nəs i nɪs
Ruswarp 'rʌs əp || -ᵊrp
rut rʌt **ruts** rʌts **rutted** 'rʌt ɪd -əd || 'rʌt̬ əd
  rutting 'rʌt ɪŋ || 'rʌt̬ ɪŋ
rutabaga ˌruːt ə 'beɪg ə ˌrʊt-, '···· || ˌruːt̬- **~s** z
Rutgers 'rʌt gəz || -gᵊrz
Ruth, ruth ruːθ
Rutheni|a ru 'θiːn i ̩ə **~an/s** ən/z
ruthenic ru 'θen ɪk -'θiːn-
ruthenium ru 'θiːn i ̩əm
Rutherford, r~ 'rʌð ə fəd || -ᵊr fᵊrd **~s,** **~'s** z
rutherfordium ˌrʌð ə 'fɔːd i ̩əm || ˌ-ᵊr 'fɔːrd-
  -'fɔʊrd-
Rutherglen 'rʌð ə glen || -ᵊr- —*locally* -glən
Ruthie 'ruːθ i
Ruthin 'rɪθ ɪn —*also, from those unfamiliar*
  with the name, a spelling pronunciation 'ruːθ-.
  —*Welsh* Rhuthun ['hrɪ θɪn, 'hri θɪn]
ruthless 'ruːθ ləs -lɪs **~ly** li **~ness** nəs nɪs
Ruthven *(i)* 'rɪv ᵊn, *(ii)* 'ruːθ v ən, *(iii)*
  'rʌθ vən —*The place in Tayside, and the*
  Baron, are (i); *the place in Grampian and the*
  loch are (iii).
rutilant 'ruːt ɪl ənt -əl- || 'ruːt̬ ᵊl-
rutile 'ruːt aɪᵊl || -iːᵊl -aɪᵊl
Rutland 'rʌt lənd
Rutledge 'rʌt lɪdʒ
rutt... —*see* **rut, rutty**
Rutter 'rʌt ə || 'rʌt̬ ᵊr
ruttish 'rʌt ɪʃ || 'rʌt̬ ɪʃ **~ly** li **~ness** nəs nɪs
rutt|y 'rʌt |i || 'rʌt̬ |i **~ier** i ə || i ᵊr **~iest** i ɪst
  i ̩əst **~iness** i nəs -nɪs
Ruud ruːd —*Dutch* [ʁyːt]
Ruwenzori ˌruː ən 'zɔːr i -en- || -'zoʊr-

R

Ruysdael 'raɪz dɑːl 'riːz-, -derᵊl —*Dutch*
['rœyz daːl]
Ruyter 'raɪt ə ‖ 'rɔɪʈ ᵊr —*Dutch* ['rœy tər]
Rwand|a ru 'ænd |ə -ᵊnd- ‖ -'ɑːnd- **~an/s**
ən/z
-ry +ri — **heraldry** 'her əldr i
Ryan 'raɪ ən
Ryanair *tdmk* 'raɪ ən eə ˌ·ˈ· ‖ -eᵊr
Rycroft 'raɪ krɒft ‖ -krɔːft -krɑːft
Rydal 'raɪd ᵊl
Ryde raɪd
Ryder 'raɪd ə ‖ -ᵊr

rye, Rye raɪ **ryes** raɪz
rye-grass 'raɪ grɑːs §-græs ‖ -græs **~es** ɪz əz
Ryeland, Ryland 'raɪ lənd
Rylands 'raɪ ləndz
Ryle raɪᵊl
Ryman 'raɪm ən
ryot 'raɪ ət (= *riot*) **~s** s
Ryton 'raɪt ᵊn
Ryukyu ri 'uː kjuː —*Jp* [ɾjɯˌɯ 'kjɯɯ] **~s** z
Ryvita *tdmk* ˌ₍₎raɪ 'viːt ə ‖ -'viːʈ ə
Rzeszów 'ʒeʃ uːv —*Polish* ['ʒɛ ʃuf]

Ss

s Spelling-to-sound

1 Where the spelling is **s**, the pronunciation is regularly

s as in **sense** sen's ('voiceless S') or

z as in **rises** 'raɪz ɪz ('voiced S').

Less frequently, it is

ʒ as in **pleasure** 'pleʒ ə ‖ 'pleʒ °r.

s may also form part of the digraphs **sh** or **si**, and of **sc** or **sch** (see under **c**).

2 At the beginning of a word, the pronunciation is regularly s as in **say** seɪ, **sleep** sliːp, **stand** stænd. (In this position, with spelling **s**, the pronunciation is never z.) This also applies in compounds, for example **insight** 'ɪn saɪt.

Exceptionally, the pronunciation is ʃ at the beginning of the words **sure** ʃɔː ʃʊə ‖ ʃʊ°r ʃɜː and **sugar** 'ʃʊg ə ‖ 'ʃʊg °r and their derivatives (for example: **assurance**, **sugary**).

3 In the middle of a word, it is necessary to take account of the letters on either side of the **s**.

- Where **s** is between a vowel letter and a consonant letter, the pronunciation is usually s if the following consonant sound is voiceless, z if it is voiced. Thus:

    s in **taste** teɪst

    z in **wisdom** 'wɪz dəm.

    Before silent **t**, however, the pronunciation is s as in **listen** 'lɪs °n.

- Where **s** is between two vowel letters, the pronunciation may be either

    s as in **basin** 'beɪs °n, **crisis** 'kraɪs ɪs or

    z as in **poison** 'pɔɪz °n, **easy** 'iːz i.

    There is no rule: each word must be considered separately.

    Where the spelling is **s** between a vowel and **ion**, **ual**, **ure**, the pronunciation is mostly ʒ as in **explosion** ɪk 'spləʊʒ °n ‖ ɪk 'splouʒ °n (silent **i**), **usual** 'juːʒ °l, **pleasure** 'pleʒ ə ‖ 'pleʒ °r.

    Where the spelling is **s** between a vowel and **ia**, **ian**, speakers vary: some use ʃ, some use ʒ as in **Asia** 'eɪʃ ə or 'eɪʒ ə (silent **i**).

- Where **s** follows a consonant letter, the pronunciation is usually s in **ls**, **ns**, **rs** or if the preceding sound is voiceless, but z otherwise. Thus:

    s in **consider** kən 'sɪd ə ‖ -°r, **cursor** 'kɜːs ə ‖ 'kɜːs °r, **gipsy** 'dʒɪps i

    z in **clumsy** 'klʌmz i, **observe** əb 'zɜːv ‖ əb 'zɜːv.

    Compare **insist** ɪn 'sɪst and **resist** rɪ 'zɪst. However, in some words both pronunciations are in use, for example

absorb -'sɔːb ‖ -'sɔːrb or -'zɔːb ‖ -'zɔːrb, **translate** -ns- or -nz-.

Where the spelling has **s** between **l, n, r** and **ion, ial, ure**, the pronunciation is correspondingly ʃ (with **i** silent) as in **expulsion** ɪk 'spʌlʃ ᵊn, **tension** 'tenʃ ᵊn, **controversial** ˌkɒntr ə 'vɜːʃ ᵊl ‖ ˌkɑːntr ə 'vɜːʃ ᵊl. However, in **-ersion, -ersia(n)** AmE has ʒ as in **Persian** 'pɜːʃ ᵊn ‖ 'pɜːʒ ᵊn.

4   Where the spelling has **s** at the end of a word, or before silent **e** at the end of a word, the pronunciation may be either

s as in **gas** gæs, **loose** luːs, **case** keɪs or

z as in **has** hæz, **choose** tʃuːz, **phrase** freɪz.

For **s** in **lse, nse, rse**, the pronunciation is usually

s as in **else** els, **immense** ɪ 'men's, **horse** hɔːs ‖ hɔːrs.

Beyond this, there is no rule: each word must be considered separately. Sometimes there is a distinction between related parts of speech that are spelled identically, as with **use** (juːs noun, juːz verb) and **close** (kləʊs ‖ kloʊs adjective, kləʊz ‖ kloʊz verb). (But there are also cases with no such distinction as in **promise** and **base**, always with s.) There is a BrE–AmE difference in the word **erase** ɪ 'reɪz ‖ ɪ 'reɪs.

5   The inflectional endings **-s, -es** are discussed in their alphabetic places.

6   Where the spelling has double **ss**, the pronunciation is regularly

s as in **lesson** 'les ᵊn, **kiss** kɪs.

Exceptionally, it is

z, notably in the words **dessert** dɪ 'zɜːt ‖ dɪ 'zɜːt, **possess** pə 'zes, **scissors** 'sɪz əz ‖ 'sɪz ᵊrz and their derivatives.

In **ssion, ssia, ssian, ssure**, it is

ʃ as in **mission** 'mɪʃ ᵊn, **pressure** 'preʃ ə ‖ 'preʃ ᵊr.

7   **s** is silent in various words, including **island** 'aɪl ənd and several words of French origin, among them **corps** kɔː ‖ kɔːr, **aisle** aɪl, **debris** 'deb riː ‖ də 'briː, **précis** 'preɪs iː ‖ preɪ 'siː, **viscount** 'vaɪ kaʊnt, **Grosvenor** 'grəʊv nə ‖ 'groʊv nᵊr, **Illinois** -'nɔɪ.

8   The sound s is also often written **c, sc** before **e, i, y**.

sh Spelling-to-sound

1   Where the spelling is the digraph **sh**, the pronunciation is regularly ʃ as in **sheep** ʃiːp, **fish** fɪʃ.

2   **sh** is not a digraph in words such as **mishap** 'mɪs hæp. The spelling of certain proper names has been reinterpreted in pronunciation so as to make **sh** a digraph: **Lewisham** was once **Lewis** plus **ham**, but is now 'luː ɪʃ əm.

S

3 ∫ is also written in a number of other ways, including those represented in the examples **ocean, machine, precious, sugar, conscience, compulsion, pressure, mission, creation**.

S, s es **S's, s's, Ss** 'es ɪz -əz —*Communications code name:* Sierra

ˌS'I ˌunit; ˌS₍ₗ₎V'O ˌlanguage

-s, -es *pl ending; 3rd sing. present ending, -'s possessive sing. ending; -s', -es' possessive pl ending* s, z, ɪz əz —*There are three regular pronunciations: After a sibilant (*s, z, ∫, ʒ, t∫, dʒ*), the pronunciation is* ɪz *or, less commonly in BrE but usually in AmE,* əz, *as* faces 'feɪs ɪz -əz, Mitch's 'mɪt∫ ɪz -əz. *(In singing, exceptionally, a strong-vowelled variant* ez *is usual if the spelling is* es, *as* 'feɪs ez.*) Otherwise, after a voiced consonant (*b, d, g, v, ð, m, n, ŋ, l, *AmE* r*) or a vowel sound, the pronunciation is* z, *as* names, name's **neɪmz;** *after a voiceless consonant (*p, t, k, f, θ*), the pronunciation is* s, *as* cats, cat's **kæts.** —*Certain nouns whose last sound is a voiceless fricative switch it to a voiced fricative before the plural and plural possessive endings. The ending naturally then takes the form* z. *The change is shown in spelling in the case of* **f —v** *(*wife **waɪf** — wives, wives' **waɪvz**), *but not for* θ —ð, s —z *(*mouth **maʊθ** — mouths, mouths' **maʊðz**). *In the possessive sing. and with the contracted forms of* is *and* has, *there is no such change (*wife's **waɪfs**, mouth's **maʊθs**). —*With proper names ending in a sibilant, usage varies. Usually, the possessive is pronounced regularly, though the spelling may vary:* Jones' , Jones's **'dʒəʊnz ɪz ‖ 'dʒoʊnz əz.** *Less commonly, the possessive ending is unpronounced (*dʒəʊnz ‖ dʒoʊnz*); the corresponding spelling is then* Jones'.

-'s *contracted form of* **is** s, z, ɪz —*The rules are identical to those for the 3rd sing. present ending (except that it is not usually used after a sibilant and that there is no strong-vowelled variant):* the boy's asleep ðə ˌbɔɪz ə 'sliːp

-'s *contracted form of* **has** s, z, əz —*The rules are identical to those for the 3rd sing. present ending:* the boy's begun ðə ˌbɔɪz bɪ 'gʌn —*except that on the rare occasions when it is used after a sibilant the pronunciation is* əz: the bus's arrived ðə ˌbʌs əz ə 'raɪvd

s.a.e. ˌes eɪ 'iː
Saab *tdmk* sɑːb **Saabs** sɑːbz
saag sɑːg
Saami 'sɑːm i
Saar sɑː ‖ sɑːr —*Ger* [zaːɐ]
Saarbrücken ˌsɑː 'brʊk ən '··· ‖ ˌsɑːr- '··· —*Ger* [zaːɐ 'bʁʏk ᵊn]

Saarland 'sɑː lænd ‖ 'sɑːr- —*Ger* ['zaːɐ lant]
Saatchi 'sɑːt∫ i
Saba *ancient kingdom in Arabia* 'seɪb ə 'sɑːb ə
Saba *island in the Caribbean* 'seɪb ə —*though some reference books wrongly claim it is* 'sɑːb ə *or* 'sæb ə
sabadilla ˌsæb ə 'dɪl ə
Sabaean sə 'biː ən ~s z
Sabah *territory in Malaysia* 'sɑːb ə -ɑː
Sabaoth 'sæb eɪ ɒθ -i-; sæ 'beɪ ɒθ, sə-, -əθ ‖ -ɑːθ -ɔːθ
Sabatier sə 'bæt i eɪ ‖ ˌsɑːb ɑː 'tjeɪ —*Fr* [sa ba tje]
Sabatini ˌsæb ə 'tiːn i
sabbatarian, S~ ˌsæb ə 'teər i ən ◂ ‖ -'ter- ~s z
Sabbath 'sæb əθ ~s s
sabbatical, S~ sə 'bæt ɪk ᵊl ‖ -'bæt̬- ~s z
  sab,batical 'year
Sabean sə 'biː ən ~s z
Sabellian sə 'bel i ən ~s z
Sabena *tdmk* sə 'biːn ə sæ- —*Fr* [sa be na]
saber... —*see* **sabre...**
Sabian 'seɪb i ən ~s z
sabin 'seɪb ɪn §-ən ~s z
Sabin *(i)* 'seɪb ɪn §-ən, *(ii)* 'sæb-
Sabina sə 'biːn ə
Sabine *family name(i)* 'sæb aɪn, *(ii)* 'seɪb aɪn -ɪn, §-ən —*Usually (i) in Britain, (ii) in US*
Sabine *ancient people and language* 'sæb aɪn ‖ 'seɪb- ~s z
Sabine *river, lake and pass in the US* sə 'biːn
sabir, Sabir sə 'bɪə sæ- ‖ -'bɪᵊr
sable 'seɪb ᵊl ~s z
sabot 'sæb əʊ ‖ -oʊ sæ 'boʊ, sə- —*Fr* [sa bo] ~s z
sabotag|e *n, v* 'sæb ə tɑːʒ -tɑːdʒ ~ed d ~es ɪz əz ~ing ɪŋ
saboteur ˌsæb ə 'tɜː '··· ‖ -'tɝː -'tʊᵊr ~s z
sabra, Sabra 'sɑːb rə ~s z
sab|re, sab|er 'seɪb |ə ‖ -|ᵊr ~red, ~ered əd ‖ ᵊrd ~res, ~ers əz ‖ ᵊrz ~ring, ~ering ər ɪŋ
sabre-rattling, saber-rattling 'seɪb ə ˌræt ᵊl ɪŋ ‖ -ᵊr ˌræt̬-
sabretach|e 'sæb ə tæ∫ -tɑː∫ ~es ɪz əz
sabre-toothed, saber-toothed ˌseɪb ə 'tuːθt ◂ §-'tʊθt ‖ -ᵊr- ˌsabre-toothed 'tiger
Sabrina sə 'briːn ə -'braɪn-
sac sæk (= *sack*) **sacs** sæks
Sacajawea ˌsæk ədʒ ə 'wiː ə
saccade sæ 'kɑːd sə-, -'keɪd ~s z
saccharide 'sæk ə raɪd ~s z

S

saccharin, saccharine *n* 'sæk ər‚ɪn §-ʰr‚ən, -ə riːn **~s** z
saccharine *adj* 'sæk ə riːn -raɪn, -ər‚ɪn, §-ʰr‚ən **~ly** li
Sacco 'sæk əʊ ‖ -oʊ
saccule 'sæk juːl **~s** z
sacerdotal ‚sæs ə 'dəʊt ʰl ◄ ‚sæk- ‖ -ʰr 'doʊt̮ ʰl ◄ **~ly** i
Sacha 'sæʃ ə
sachem 'seɪtʃ əm
sachet 'sæʃ eɪ ‖ sæ 'ʃeɪ (*) **~s** z
Sacheverell sə 'ʃev ʰr‚əl
Sachs sæks —*but as a German name,* zæks ‖ zɑːks —*Ger* [zaks]
sack sæk **sacked** sækt **sacking** 'sæk ɪŋ **sacks** sæks
'sack race
sackbut 'sæk bʌt **~s** s
sackcloth 'sæk klɒθ -klɔːθ ‖ -klɔːθ -klɑːθ
Sacker 'sæk ə ‖ -ʰr
sackful 'sæk fʊl **~s** z **sacksful** 'sæks fʊl
sacking 'sæk ɪŋ **~s** z
sackload 'sæk ləʊd **~s** z
Sacks sæks
Sackville 'sæk vɪl -vʰl
‚Sackville-'West
sacral 'seɪk rəl 'sæk- —*Some speakers (esp. AmE) distinguish between* 'seɪk- '*holy*' *and* 'sæk- '*of the sacrum*'.
sacrament, S~ 'sæk rə mənt **~s** s
sacramental ‚sæk rə 'ment ʰl ◄ ‖ -'ment̮ ʰl ◄ **~ly** i
Sacramento ‚sæk rə 'ment əʊ ‖ -'ment̮ oʊ
sacred 'seɪk rɪd -rəd **~ly** li **~ness** nəs nɪs
‚sacred 'cow; ‚Sacred 'Heart
sacrific|e *n, v* 'sæk rɪ faɪs -rə- **~ed** t **~es** ɪz əz **~ing** ɪŋ
sacrificial ‚sæk rɪ 'fɪʃ ʰl ◄ -rə- **~ly** i
sacrilege 'sæk rəl ɪdʒ -rɪl-
sacrilegious ‚sæk rə 'lɪdʒ əs ◄ -rɪ- **~ly** li **~ness** nəs nɪs
sacring 'seɪk rɪŋ
sacristan 'sæk rɪst ən -rəst- **~s** z
sacrist|y 'sæk rɪst |i -rəst- **~ies** iz
sacroiliac ‚seɪk rəʊ 'ɪl i æk ‚sæk- ‖ ‚roʊ-
sacrosanct 'sæk rəʊ sæŋkt ‖ -roʊ- **~ness** nəs nɪs
sacrosanctity ‚sæk rəʊ 'sæŋkt ət i -ɪt i ‖ -roʊ 'sæŋkt ət̮ i
sac|rum 'seɪk |rəm 'sæk- ‖ 'sæk- 'seɪk- **~ra** rə
sad sæd **sadder** 'sæd ə ‖ -ʰr **saddest** 'sæd ɪst -əst
Sadat sə 'dæt ‖ -'dɑːt sɑː- —*Arabic* [sa: dɑːt]
Saddam sə 'dæm ₍ₜ₎sæ-, -'dɑːm, 'sæd əm —*Arabic* [sadˤ 'dˤɑm]
sadden 'sæd ʰn **~ed** d **~ing/ly** ɪŋ /li **~s** z
saddl|e 'sæd ʰl **~ed** d **~es** z **~ing** ɪŋ
'saddle soap; 'saddle stitch
saddleback 'sæd ʰl bæk **~s** s
saddlebag 'sæd ʰl bæg **~s** z
saddlecloth 'sæd ʰl klɒθ -klɔːθ ‖ -klɔːθ -klɑːθ
saddler, S~ 'sæd lə ‖ -lʰr **~s** z
saddlery 'sæd lər i

saddle-sore 'sæd ʰl sɔː ‖ -sɔːr -soʊr
saddo 'sæd əʊ ‖ -oʊ **~s** z
Sadducee 'sæd ju si: ‖ 'sædʒ ə si: 'sæd jə- **~s** z
Sade *French writer* sɑːd —*Fr* [sad]
Sade *singer* 'ʃɑː deɪ
sadhu 'sɑːd u: **~s** z
Sadie 'seɪd i
‚Sadie 'Hawkins Day
sadiron 'sæd ‚aɪ ən ‖ -‚aɪ ʰrn **~s** z
sadism 'seɪd ‚ɪz əm ‖ 'sæd-
sadist 'seɪd ɪst §-əst ‖ 'sæd- **~s** s
sadistic sə 'dɪst ɪk **~ally** ʰl‚i
Sadleir, Sadler 'sæd lə ‖ -lʰr
‚Sadler's 'Wells
sad|ly 'sæd |li **~ness** nəs nɪs
sadomasochism ‚seɪd əʊ 'mæs ə ‚kɪz əm -'mæz- ‖ ‚oʊ- ‚sæd-
sadomasochistic ‚seɪd əʊ ‚mæs ə 'kɪst ɪk -‚mæz- ‖ ‚oʊ- ‚sæd-
safari sə 'fɑːr i **~s** z
sa'fari park; sa'fari suit
safe seɪf **safer** 'seɪf ə ‖ -ʰr **safes** seɪfs **safest** 'seɪf ɪst -əst
‚safe 'house; 'safe ‚period; ‚safe 'sex
safebreaker 'seɪf ‚breɪk ə ‖ -ʰr **~s** z
safe-conduct ‚seɪf 'kɒn dʌkt -dəkt ‖ -'kɑːn- **~s** s
safe-cracker 'seɪf ‚kræk ə ‖ -ʰr **~s** z
safe-deposit 'seɪf di ‚pɒz ɪt -də-, §-ət, ‚···· ‖ -‚pɑːz ət **~s** s
'safe-de‚posit ‚box
safeguard 'seɪf gɑːd ‖ -gɑːrd **~ed** ɪd əd **~ing** ɪŋ **~s** z
safekeeping ‚seɪf 'kiːp ɪŋ
safely 'seɪf li
safe|ty 'seɪf |ti §'seɪf ə|t i **~ties** tiz
'safety belt; 'safety catch; 'safety ‚curtain; 'safety-de‚posit ‚box; 'safety glass; 'safety ‚helmet; 'safety ‚island; 'safety lamp; 'safety match; 'safety net; 'safety pin; 'safety ‚razor; 'safety valve
safety-first ‚seɪf ti 'fɜːst ◄ ‖ -'fɜːst ◄
Safeway *tdmk* 'seɪf weɪ **~'s** z
Saffa 'sæf ə **~s** z
safflower 'sæf lau‚ə ‖ -lau‚ʰr
saffron, S~ 'sæf rən
Safire 'sæf aɪ‚ə ‖ 'sæf aɪ‚ʰr
sag sæg **sagged** sægd **sagging** 'sæg ɪŋ **sags** sægz
saga 'sɑːg ə **~s** z
sagacious sə 'geɪʃ əs **~ly** li **~ness** nəs nɪs
sagacity sə 'gæs ət i -ɪt- ‖ -ət̮ i
sagamore 'sæg ə mɔː ‖ -mɔːr -moʊr **~s** z
Sagan *British / American family name* 'seɪg ən —*but the French name is* [sa gɑ̃]
Sagar 'seɪg ə ‖ -ʰr
sage seɪdʒ **sager** 'seɪdʒ ə ‖ -ʰr **sages** 'seɪdʒ ɪz -əz **sagest** 'seɪdʒ ɪst -əst
‚sage 'green◄
sagebrush 'seɪdʒ brʌʃ
sagely 'seɪdʒ li
Sager 'seɪg ə ‖ -ʰr

saggar, sagger 'sæg ə ‖ -ᵊr ~s z
sagg|y 'sæg |i ~ier i‿ə ‖ i‿ᵊr ~iest i‿ɪst i‿əst
~iness i nəs i nɪs
Saginaw 'sæg ɪ nɔː -ə- ‖ -nɑː
sagitta, S~ sə 'dʒɪt ə -'gɪt- ‖ -'dʒɪt̬ ə
sagittal 'sædʒ ɪt ᵊl §-ət-; sə 'dʒɪt ᵊl ‖ -ət̬ ᵊl ~ly
i
Sagittari|us ˌsædʒ ɪ 'teər i‿|əs ˌ·ə- ‖ -'ter-
~an/s ən/z
sago 'seɪg əʊ ‖ -oʊ
saguaro sə 'gwɑːr əʊ -'wɑːr- ‖ -oʊ -ə ~s z
Saguenay ˌsæg ə 'neɪ ◄
Sahaptin sɑː 'hæpt ɪn sə-, §-ᵊn ~s z
Sahar|a sə 'hɑːr |ə ‖ -'hær |ə -'her-, -'hɑːr- ~an
ən
Sahel sə 'hel sɑː-
sahib sɑːb 'sɑː hɪb, -ɪb, -iːb ~s z
said sed §seɪd (!)
Said place saɪd sɑː 'iːd —Arabic [sɑ ʕiːd]
saiga 'saɪg ə
Saigon ˌsaɪ 'gɒn ‖ -'gɑːn
sail seɪᵊl **sailed** seɪᵊld **sailing/s** 'seɪᵊl ɪŋ/z
sails seɪᵊlz
'sailing boat; 'sailing ship
sailboard 'seɪᵊl bɔːd ‖ -bɔːrd -boʊrd ~ing ɪŋ ~s
z
sailboat 'seɪᵊl bəʊt ‖ -boʊt ~s s
sailcloth 'seɪᵊl klɒθ -klɔːθ ‖ -klɔːθ -klɑːθ
sailfish 'seɪᵊl fɪʃ
sailor 'seɪl ə 'seɪᵊl- ‖ -ᵊr ~s z
'sailor suit
sailplane 'seɪᵊl pleɪn ~s z
sainfoin 'sæn fɔɪn 'seɪn-
Sainsbury 'seɪnz bər‿i ‖ -ˌber i ~'s z
saint, Saint strong form seɪnt, weak form sᵊnt
—but in French names sæ̃ —Fr [sɛ̃]. —For
the common noun and family name, only the
strong form is used. For the title before a name
the weak form is usual in BrE but not in
AmE. **sainted** 'seɪnt ɪd -əd ‖ 'seɪnt̬ əd
saints, Saints seɪnts —For names beginning
Saint —see under **St-**
'saint's day
Saint-Etienne, Saint-Étienne ˌsænt et i 'en
ˌ·eɪ- —Fr [sɛ̃ te tjɛn]
sainthood 'seɪnt hʊd
Saint John place in New Brunswick
seɪnt 'dʒɒn ‖ -'dʒɑːn
saint|ly 'seɪnt |li ~lier |li‿ə ‖ li‿ᵊr ~liest li‿ɪst
‿əst ~liness li nəs -nɪs
saintpaulia sᵊnt 'pɔːl i‿ə →sᵊm-, ˌseɪnt-
‖ ˌseɪnt- -'pɑːl- ~s z
Saint-Saens, Saint-Saëns ˌsæ̃ 'sɒ̃s -'sɔ̃
‖ ˌsæn 'sɑːn -'sɑːns —Fr [sɛ̃ sɑ̃s]
Saintsbury 'seɪnts bər‿i ‖ -ˌber i
Saipan ˌsaɪ 'pæn
Saisho tdmk 'seɪʃ əʊ ‖ -oʊ
saith seθ seɪθ; 'seɪ ɪθ, -əθ
saithe seɪθ seɪð
sake 'advantage, purpose' seɪk **sakes** seɪks
for ˌgoodness 'sake, ·'··
sake 'alcoholic drink' 'sɑːk i -eɪ —Jp [sa ˌke]
saker 'seɪk ə ‖ -ᵊr ~s z

Sakhalin 'sæk ə liːn 'sɑːk-, -lɪn, ˌ·'· —Russ
[sə xʌ 'lʲin]
Sakharov 'sæk ə rɒf -rɒv ‖ 'sɑːk ə rɔːf 'sæk-,
-rɑːf —Russ ['sa xə rəf, sʌ 'xa rəf] —The
physicist Andrei S~ was ['sa xə rəf]
saki, Saki 'sɑːk i ~s z
Saks sæks
sal, Sal sæl
ˌsal am'moniac
salaam sə 'lɑːm sæ- ~ed d ~ing ɪŋ ~s z
salable 'seɪl əb ᵊl
salacious sə 'leɪʃ əs ~ly li ~ness nəs nɪs
salacity sə 'læs ət i -ɪt- ‖ -ət̬ i
salad 'sæl əd ~s z
'salad bar; 'salad cream; 'salad days;
ˌsalad 'dressing, ‖ '··‚·; 'salad oil
Saladin 'sæl əd ɪn §-ən
Salaman 'sæl ə mæn -mən
Salamanca ˌsæl ə 'mæŋk ə —Sp
[sa la 'maŋ ka]
salamander 'sæl ə mænd ə ‖ -ᵊr ~s z
salami sə 'lɑːm i ~s z
Salamis 'sæl əm ɪs §-əs
salariat sə 'leər i‿æt -i‿ət ‖ -'lær- -'ler-
salar|y 'sæl ər |i ~ied id ~ies iz ~yman
i mæn ~ymen i men
Salazar ˌsæl ə 'zɑː ‖ -'zɑːr —Port [sɐ lɐ 'zar]
salbutamol sæl 'bjuːt ə mɒl ‖ -'bjuːt̬ ə mɔːl
-mɑːl, -moʊl
salchow 'sælk əʊ 'sɔːlk-, 'sɒlk- ‖ -oʊ ~s z
Salcombe 'sɔːlk əm 'sɒlk- ‖ 'sɑːlk-
sale, Sale seɪᵊl (= sail) **sales** seɪᵊlz
'sales pitch; 'sales repreˌsentative; 'sales
reˌsistance; 'sales slip; 'sales staff; 'sales
talk; 'sales tax
saleable 'seɪl əb ᵊl
Salem 'seɪl əm -em
Salerno sə 'lɜːn əʊ -'leən- ‖ -'lern oʊ -'lɜːn-
—It [sa 'lɛr no]
saleroom 'seɪᵊl ruːm -rʊm ~s z
salesclerk 'seɪᵊlz klɑːk ‖ -klɜːk ~s s
salesgirl 'seɪᵊlz gɜːl ‖ -gɜːl ~s z
Salesian sə 'liːz i‿ən -'liːʒ- ‖ sə 'liːʒ ᵊn -'liːʃ- ~s
z
saleslad|y 'seɪᵊlz ˌleɪd |i ~ies iz
sales|man 'seɪᵊlz |mən ~manship mən ʃɪp
~men mən men ~people ˌpiːp ᵊl ~person/s
ˌpɜːs ᵊn/z ‖ ˌpɜːs ᵊn/z
salesroom 'seɪᵊlz ruːm -rʊm ~s z
sales|woman 'seɪᵊlz ˌwʊm ən ~women
ˌwɪm ɪn §-ən
Salford 'sɔːl fəd 'sɒl- ‖ -fᵊrd 'sɑːl- —A spelling
pronunciation 'sæl- is sometimes heard.
Salfords 'sæl fədz 'sɔːl-, 'sɒl- ‖ -fᵊrdz
Salian 'seɪl i‿ən ~s z
Salic, salic 'sæl ɪk 'seɪl-
salicylate sə 'lɪs ɪ leɪt -ə-, -ᵊl eɪt ~s s
salicylic ˌsæl ɪ 'sɪl ɪk ◄ -ə-
salienc|e 'seɪl i‿ən's ~y i
salient 'seɪl i‿ənt ~ly li ~ness nəs nɪs ~s s
Salieri ˌsæl i 'eər i ‖ sɒl 'jer i sæl- —It
[sa 'ljɛː ri]
saliferous sə 'lɪf ər‿əs sæ-

S

sali|fy 'sæl ɪ |faɪ §-ə- ~fied faɪd ~fies faɪz
~fying faɪ ɪŋ
Salina *place in KS* sə 'laɪn ə
Salinas *place in CA* sə 'liːn əs
saline 'seɪl aɪn -iːn ‖ -iːn -aɪn
Saline *place in Fife* 'sæl ɪn §-ən
Saline *place in MI* sə 'liːn
Salinger 'sæl ɪndʒ ə §-əndʒ- ‖ -ᵊr
salinity sə 'lɪn ət i sæ-, -ɪt- ‖ -ət i
salinometer ˌsæl ɪ 'nɒm ɪt ə ˌ-ə-, -ət ə
‖ -'nɑːm ət̬ ᵊr ~s z
Salisbury 'sɔːlz bər̬ i 'sɒlz- ‖ 'sɑːlz-, -ˌber i (!)
ˌSalisbury 'Plain
Salish 'seɪl ɪʃ ~an ən
saliva sə 'laɪv ə
salivary 'sæl ɪv ər̬ i '·əv-; sə 'laɪv ər i
‖ 'sæl ə ver i
sali|vate 'sæl ɪ |veɪt -ə- ~vated veɪt ɪd -əd
‖ veɪt̬ əd ~vates veɪts ~vating veɪt ɪŋ
‖ veɪt̬ ɪŋ
salivation ˌsæl ɪ 'veɪʃ ᵊn -ə-
Salk sɔːlk sɔːk ‖ sɑːlk, sɔːk, sɑːk
Salkeld 'sɔːlk ᵊld 'sɒlk- ‖ 'sɑːlk- —*locally also*
'sæf ᵊld
sallet 'sæl ɪt -ət ~s s
Sallis 'sæl ɪs §-əs
sallow 'sæl əʊ ‖ -oʊ ~ed d ~ing ɪŋ ~ly li
~ness nəs nɪs ~s z ~y i
Sallust 'sæl əst
sall|y, Sall|y 'sæl |i ~ied id ~ies, ~y's iz
~ying i ɪŋ
Sally-Ann, Sally-Anne ˌsæl i 'æn
salmagundi ˌsælm ə 'gʌnd i ~s z
salmanazar, S~ ˌsælm ə 'neɪz ə -'næz- ‖ -ᵊr ~s
z
salmi, salmis 'sælm i -iː
salmon, S~ 'sæm ən ~s z
ˌsalmon 'pink◂; 'salmon trout
Salmond 'sæm ənd
salmonell|a ˌsælm ə 'nel |ə ˌsæm- ~ae iː ~as
əz
Salome sə 'ləʊm i -eɪ ‖ -'loʊm-
salon 'sæl ɒn -ð, §-ɒŋ ‖ sə 'lɑːn 'sæl ɑːn ~s z
Salonica, Salonika sə 'lɒn ɪk ə ˌsæl ə 'naɪk ə,
-'niːk- ‖ sə 'lɑːn- —*Gk* Thessaloniki
[θɛ sa lɔ 'ni ci]
saloon sə 'luːn ~s z
sa'loon bar
Salop 'sæl əp -ɒp
salopettes ˌsæl ə 'pets
Salopian sə 'ləʊp i ən ‖ -'loʊp- ~s z
salpingectom|y ˌsælp ɪn 'dʒekt əm |i ~ies iz
salpingitis ˌsælp ɪn 'dʒaɪt ɪs §-əs ‖ -'dʒaɪt̬ əs
salpingo- *comb. form*
  with stress-neutral suffix sæl |pɪŋ gəʊ ‖ -gə
  — salpingogram sæl 'pɪŋ gəʊ græm
  ‖ -ə græm
  with stress-imposing suffix ˌsælp ɪŋ 'gɒ+
  ‖ -'gɑː+ — salpingoscopy
  ˌsælp ɪŋ 'gɒsk əp i ‖ -'gɑːsk-
salsa 'sæls ə ‖ 'sɑːls ə 'sɔːls- —*Sp* ['sal sa]
salsify 'sæls əf i '·ɔːls-, 'sɒls-, -ɪf-; -ə faɪ, -ɪ-

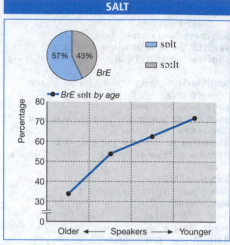

SALT

57% 43% BrE
■ sɒlt
■ sɔːlt

BrE sɒlt by age

[Graph: Percentage (y-axis 0–80) vs. Older ← Speakers → Younger (x-axis)]

salt, Salt, SALT sɔːlt sɒlt ‖ sɑːlt — *Preference
poll, BrE:* sɔːlt *43%,* sɒlt *57%.* salted 'sɔːlt ɪd
'sɒlt-, -əd ‖ 'sɔːlt əd 'sɑːlt- salting 'sɔːlt ɪŋ
'sɒlt- ‖ 'sɑːlt- salts sɔːlts sɒlts ‖ sɑːlts
'salt dome; ˌSalt Lake 'City; 'salt marsh;
'salt ˌshaker
Saltaire ₍ₗ₎sɔːlt 'eə ₍ₗ₎sɒlt- ‖ -'eᵊr ₍ₗ₎sɑːlt-, -'æᵊr
salt-and-pepper ˌsɔːlt ən 'pep ə ˌsɒlt-, ―›-əm-
‖ -ᵊr ˌsɑːlt
saltant 'sælt ənt 'sɔːlt-, 'sɒlt- ‖ 'sɔːlt-, 'sɑːlt-
saltarell|o ˌsælt ə 'rel |əʊ ˌsɔːlt-, ˌsɒlt- ‖ -|oʊ
ˌsɑːlt- ~i iː
Saltash 'sɔːlt æʃ 'sɒlt- ‖ 'sɔːlt- 'sɑːlt-
saltation sæl 'teɪʃ ᵊn sɔːl-, sɒl- ‖ sɔːl-, sɑːl- ~s z
saltbox, salt-box 'sɔːlt bɒks 'sɒlt- ‖ -bɑːks
'sɑːlt- ~es ɪz əz
Saltburn 'sɔːlt bɜːn 'sɒlt- ‖ -bɜːn 'sɑːlt-
saltbush 'sɔːlt bʊʃ 'sɒlt- ‖ 'sɑːlt-
saltcellar 'sɔːlt ˌsel ə 'sɒlt- ‖ -ᵊr 'sɑːlt- ~s z
Saltcoats 'sɔːlt kəʊts 'sɒlt- ‖ -koʊts 'sɑːlt-
Salter, s~ 'sɔːlt ə 'sɒlt- ‖ -ᵊr 'sɑːlt- ~s, ~'s z
Salterton 'sɔːlt ət ən 'sɒlt- ‖ -ᵊ ˀrt ᵊn 'sɑːlt-
saltfish 'sɔːlt fɪʃ 'sɒlt- ‖ 'sɑːlt-
Salthouse 'sɔːlt haʊs 'sɒlt- ‖ 'sɑːlt-
saltimbocca ˌsælt ɪm 'bɒk ə ˌsɔːlt-, ˌsɒlt-
‖ ˌsɑːlt ɪm 'boʊk ə ˌsɔːlt-, ˌsɑːlt-, -'bɑːk- —*It*
[sal tim 'bok ka] ~s z
saltine sɔːl 'tiːn sɒl- ‖ sɑːl- ~s z
saltire 'sɔːlt ar̬ ə 'sɒlt- ‖ -aɪ ᵊr 'sɑːlt- ~s z
Saltley 'sɔːlt li 'sɒlt- ‖ 'sɑːlt-
saltlick 'sɔːlt lɪk 'sɒlt- ‖ 'sɑːlt- ~s s
Saltmarsh 'sɔːlt mɑːʃ 'sɒlt- ‖ -mɑːrʃ 'sɑːlt-
Salton 'sɔːlt ən 'sɒlt- ‖ 'sɑːlt-
ˌSalton 'Sea
Saltoun 'sɔːlt ən 'sælt-, 'sɒlt- ‖ 'sɑːlt-
saltpan 'sɔːlt pæn 'sɒlt- ‖ 'sɑːlt- ~s z
saltpeter, saltpetre ˌsɔːlt 'piːt ə ˌsɒlt-, '·,· ·
‖ -'piːt̬ ᵊr 'sɑːlt-
saltwater 'sɔːlt ˌwɔːt ə 'sɒlt- ‖ -ˌwɔːt̬ ᵊr 'sɑːlt-,
-ˌwɑːt̬-
saltworks 'sɔːlt wɜːks 'sɒlt- ‖ -wɜːks 'sɑːlt-

S

saltwort 'sɔːlt wɜːt 'sɒlt-, §-wɔːt ‖ -wɝːt 'sɑːlt-, -wɔːrt **~s** s

salt|y 'sɔːlt |i 'sɒlt- ‖ 'sɑːlt- **~ier** i ə ‖ i ²r **~iest** i ɪst i əst **~ily** ɪ li əl i **~iness** i nəs i nɪs

salubrious sə 'luːb ri əs -'ljuːb- **~ly** li **~ness** nəs nɪs

salubrity sə 'luːb rət i -'ljuːb-, -rɪt- ‖ -rət i

Saluki, s~ sə 'luːk i **~s** z

salutar|y 'sæl jʊt ər |i ‖ -jə ter |i **~iness** i nəs i nɪs

salutation ˌsæl ju 'teɪʃ ²n ˌ-jə- **~s** z

salutatorian sə ˌluːt ə 'tɔːr i ən -ˌljuːt- ‖ -ˌluːt̬- **~s** z

sa|lute sə |'luːt -'ljuːt **~luted** 'luːt ɪd 'ljuːt-, -əd ‖ 'luːt̬ əd **~lutes** 'luːts 'ljuːts **~luting** 'luːt ɪŋ 'ljuːt- ‖ 'luːt̬ ɪŋ

Salvador 'sælv ə dɔː ˌ·'· ‖ -dɔːr —Sp [sal βa 'ðor]

Salvadorean, Salvadorian ˌsælv ə 'dɔːr i ən ◄ **~s** z

salvag|e 'sælv ɪdʒ **~ed** d **~es** ɪz əz **~ing** ɪŋ

salvageable 'sælv ɪdʒ əb ²l

salvarsan 'sælv ə sæn -əs ən ‖ -²r-

salvation sæl 'veɪʃ ²n ˌsæl- **~s** z

　Sal'vation 'Army, ˌ·'· '··

salvationist, S~ sæl 'veɪʃ ²n ɪst § əst **~s** s

salve n, v 'soothe' sælv sɑːv ‖ sæv (*) **salved** sælvd sɑːvd ‖ sævd **salves** sælvz sɑːvz ‖ sævz **salving** 'sælv ɪŋ 'sɑːv- ‖ 'sæv ɪŋ

salve v 'salvage' sælv **salved** sælvd **salves** sælvz **salving** 'sælv ɪŋ

salve Latin interj 'sælv eɪ -i; 'sæl weɪ ‖ 'sɑːl weɪ **~s** z

salver 'sælv ə ‖ -²r **~s** z

Salvesen, Salveson 'sælv ɪs ən -əs-

salvia 'sælv i ə **~s** z

salvo 'sælv əʊ ‖ -oʊ **~s, ~es** z

sal volatile ˌsæl və 'læt əl i vɒ- ‖ -'læt̬ ²l i

salwar sʌl 'wɑː ‖ -'wɑːr **~s** z

Salyut sæl 'juːt səl- ‖ sɑːl- —Russ [sʌ 'lʲut]

Salzburg 'sælts bɜːg 'sɔːlts-, 'sɒlts- ‖ 'sɔːlz bɝːg 'sɑːlz- —Ger ['zalts buʁk]

Sam sæm

SAM sæm ˌes eɪ 'em

Samantha sə 'mæn ²θ ə

samara 'sæm ər ə sə 'mɑːr ə **~s** z

Samara sə 'mɑːr ə —Russ [sʌ 'ma rə]

Samaranch 'sæm ə ræn —Catalan [sə mə 'rank]

Samaria sə 'meər i ə ‖ sə 'mer- -'mær-

Samaritan sə 'mær ɪt ən -ət- ‖ -ət ²n -'mer- **~s** z

samarium sə 'meər i əm ‖ sə 'mer- -'mær-

Samarkand ˌsæm ɑː 'kænd -ə-, '··· ‖ -²r- —Russ [sə mʌr 'kant]

samarskite 'sæm ɑːsk aɪt -ə skaɪt; sə 'mɑːsk aɪt ‖ 'sæm ɑːrsk- sə 'mɑːrsk-

sam|ba 'sæm |bə ‖ 'sɑːm- **~baed** bəd **~baing** bə² ɪŋ ‖ bə ɪŋ **~bas** bəz

sambal 'sæm b²l —Malay ['sam bal]

sambar, sambur 'sæm bə 'sɑːm- ‖ -b²r **~s** z

sambo, Sambo 'sæm bəʊ ‖ -boʊ **~s, ~'s** z

same seɪm

same-day ˌseɪm 'deɪ ◄

sameness 'seɪm nəs nɪs

same-sex ˌseɪm 'seks ◄

samey 'seɪm i

Samhain saʊn 'sɑː wɪn, 'saʊ ən —Irish [saunʲ]

Sami 'sæm i 'sɑːm i ‖ 'sɑːm i

Samian 'seɪm i ən **~s** z

samisen 'sæm ɪ sen §-ə- **~s** z

samite 'sæm aɪt 'seɪm-

samizdat ˌsæm ɪz 'dæt '···· ‖ 'sɑːm iːz dɑːt —Russ [sə mʲɪ 'zdat]

Samlesbury 'sæmz bər i 'sɑːmz- ‖ -ˌber i

Sammie, Sammy 'sæm i

Samnite 'sæm naɪt **~s** s

Samnium 'sæm ni əm

Samo|a sə 'məʊ |ə sɑː- ‖ -'moʊ |ə **~an/s** ən/z

Samos 'seɪm ɒs 'sæm- ‖ -ɑːs 'sæm oʊs —ModGk ['sa mɔs]

samosa sə 'məʊs ə sæ-, -'məʊz- ‖ -'moʊs ə **~s** z

Samothrace 'sæm əʊ θreɪs ‖ -ə-

samovar 'sæm ə vɑː ˌ·'· ‖ -vɑːr —Russ [sə mʌ 'var] **~s** z

Samoyed, Samoyede sə 'mɔɪ ed -ɪd; ˌsæm ɔɪ 'ed, -ə 'jed **~s** z

samp sæmp

sampan 'sæm pæn **~s** z

Sampford 'sæmp fəd ‖ -f²rd

samphire 'sæmᵖf aɪ ə ‖ -aɪ ²r

sampl|e 'sɑːmp ²l §'sæmp- ‖ 'sæmp ²l **~ed** d **~es** z **~ing** ɪŋ

sampler 'sɑːmp lə §'sæmp- ‖ 'sæmp l²r **~s** z

Sampras 'sæmp rəs

Sampson 'sæmᵖs ən

Samson 'sæmᵖs ən

Samsonite tdmk 'sæmᵖs ən aɪt

Samsung tdmk 'sæm sʌŋ —Korean ['sam sʊŋ]

Samuel 'sæm ju əl

Samuels 'sæm ju əlz

samurai 'sæm uᵊ raɪ -ə-, -juᵊ- ‖ -ə- —Jp [sa ˌmɯ rai] **~s** z

San, san sæn —but in foreign names, AmE sɑːn —It, Sp [san]

San'a, Sanaa sə 'nɑː sɑː-, 'sɑːn ə —Arabic [sˤan 'ʕaːʔ]

San Andreas ˌsæn æn 'dreɪ əs ◄

　ˌSan And'reas 'Fault

San Antonio ˌsæn æn 'təʊn i əʊ ‖ -'toʊn i oʊ

sanatari|um ˌsæn ə 'teər i |əm ‖ -'ter- -'tær- **~a** ə **~ums** əmz

Sanatogen tdmk sə 'næt ədʒ ən -ə dʒen ‖ -'næt̬-

sanatori|um ˌsæn ə 'tɔːr i |əm ‖ -'tour- **~a** ə **~ums** əmz

San Bernardino ˌsæn ˌbɜːn ə 'diːn əʊ →ˌsæm- ‖ -ˌbɝːn ²r 'diːn oʊ -ˌ-ə-

　ˌSan Bernar'dino 'Mountains

San Carlos ₍ˌ₎sæn 'kɑːl ɒs →₍ˌ₎sæŋ-, -əs ‖ -'kɑːrl əs

Sancerre sɒ̃ 'seə sæn- ‖ sɑːn 'se²r —Fr [sɑ̃ sɛːʁ]

Sanchez 'sæntʃ ez —Sp Sánchez ['san tʃeθ, -tʃes]

Sancho 'sæntʃ əʊ ‖ 'sɑːntʃ oʊ —*Sp* ['san tʃo]
  Sancho 'Panza 'pænz ə ‖ 'pɑːnz ə —*Sp*
  ['pan θa, -sa]
San Clemente ˌsæn klə 'ment i →ˌsæŋ-, -klɪ-
  ‖ -'menţ i
sanctification ˌsæŋktɪf ɪf ɪ 'keɪʃ ᵊn ˌ-əf-, §-ə'-‑
sancti|fy 'sæŋkt ɪ |faɪ -ə- **~fied** faɪd **~fier/s**
  faɪ‿ə/z ‖ faɪ‿ᵊr/z **~fies** faɪz **~fying** faɪ ɪŋ
sanctimonious ˌsæŋkt ɪ 'məʊn iəs ◂ ˌ-ə-
  ‖ 'moʊn- **~ly** li **~ness** nəs nɪs
sanctimony 'sæŋkt ɪ mən i '‑ə-, -məʊn i
  ‖ -moʊn i
sanction 'sæŋkʃ ᵊn **~ed** d **~ing** ɪŋ **~s** z
sanctit|y 'sæŋkt ət |i -ɪt- ‖ -əţ |i **~ies** iz
sanctuar|y, S~ 'sæŋktʃ u‿ər |i 'sæŋkt ju‿
  ‖ -er |i **~ies** iz
sanct|um 'sæŋkt |əm **~a ə ~ums** əmz
  ˌsanctum 'sanctorum sæŋk 'tɔːr əm
Sanctus 'sæŋkt əs -ʊs
  'Sanctus bell
sand sænd sanded 'sænd ɪd -əd **sanding**
  'sænd ɪŋ **sands sændz**
  'sand ˌdollar; **'sand dune**; **'sand fly**; **'sand**
  ˌmartin; **'sand ˌtable**; **'sand trap**; **'sand**
  yacht
Sand *name of novelist* sɒd ‖ sɑːnd —*Fr* [sɑ̃ːd]
sandal 'sænd ᵊl **~ed, ~led** d **~s** z
sandalwood 'sænd ᵊl wʊd **~s** z
sandarac, sandarach 'sænd ə ræk **~s** s
Sanday 'sænd eɪ -i
Sandbach 'sænd bætʃ →'sæm-
sandbag 'sænd bæg →'sæm- **~ged** d **~ger/s**
  ə/z ‖ -ᵊr/z **~ging** ɪŋ **~s** z
sandbank 'sænd bæŋk →'sæm- **~s** s
sandbar 'sænd bɑː →'sæm- ‖ -bɑːr **~s** z
sandblast 'sænd blɑːst →'sæm-, §-blæst
  ‖ -blæst **~ed** ɪd əd **~er/s** ə/z ‖ -ᵊr/z **~ing** ɪŋ
  ~s s
sandboard 'sænd bɔːd →'sæm- ‖ -bɔːrd -boʊrd
  ~ing ɪŋ **~s** z
sandbox 'sænd bɒks →'sæm- ‖ -bɑːks **~es** ɪz
  əz
  'sandbox tree
sandboy 'sænd bɔɪ →'sæm- **~s** z
Sandburg 'sænd bɜːg ‖ -bɝːg
sandcastle 'sænd ˌkɑːs ᵊl →'sæŋ-, §-ˌkæs-
  ‖ -ˌkæs ᵊl **~s** z
Sandell *(i)* 'sænd ᵊl, *(ii)* sæn 'del
Sandeman 'sænd ɪ mən -ə-; 'sænd mən
sander 'sænd ə ‖ -ᵊr **~s** z
sanderling 'sænd ə lɪŋ -dᵊl ɪŋ ‖ -ᵊr- **~s** z
Sanders 'sɑːnd əz §'sænd- ‖ 'sænd ᵊrz
Sanderson 'sɑːnd əs ən §'sænd- ‖ 'sænd ᵊr sən
Sanderstead 'sɑːnd ə sted §'sænd-, -stɪd
  ‖ 'sænd ᵊr-
Sandes sændz
sand|fly 'sænd |flaɪ **~flies** flaɪz
Sandford 'sænd fəd -fɔːd ‖ -fᵊrd -fɔːrd, -foʊrd
Sandgate 'sænd geɪt →'sæŋ-, -gɪt
sandglass 'sænd glɑːs →'sæŋ-, §-glæs ‖ -glæs
  ~es ɪz əz
sandhi 'sænd i 'sʌnd-, -hiː —*Hindi* [sən ḍʰi]
  'sandhi pheˌnomena

Sandhurst 'sænd hɜːst ‖ -hɝːst
Sandiacre 'sænd i ˌeɪk ə ‖ -ᵊr
Sandie, s~ 'sænd i
San Diego ˌsæn di 'eɪg əʊ ‖ -oʊ
Sandinista ˌsænd ɪ 'niːst ə ◂ -ə- **~s** z
sandlot 'sænd lɒt ‖ -lɑːt
sandman 'sænd mæn →'sæm-
San Domingo ˌsæn də 'mɪŋ gəʊ ‖ -goʊ —*Sp*
  [san do 'miŋ go]
Sandor 'sænd ə ‖ -ᵊr —*but as a Hungarian*
  name also 'ʃɑːnd-, -ɔː ‖ -ɔːr —*Hung* Sándor
  ['ʃaːn dor]
Sandown 'sænd aʊn
Sandoz *tdmk* 'sænd ɒz ‖ -ɑːz —*Fr* [sɑ̃ do]
sandpaper 'sænd ˌpeɪp ə →'sæm- ‖ -ᵊr **~ed** d
  sandpapering 'sænd ˌpeɪp ᵊr‿ɪŋ **~s** z
sandpiper 'sænd ˌpaɪp ə →'sæm- ‖ -ᵊr **~s** z
sandpit 'sænd pɪt →'sæm- **~s** s
Sandra 'sændr ə 'sɑːndr-
Sandringham 'sændr ɪŋ əm §-həm
Sands sændz
sandshoe 'sænd ʃuː **~s** z
sandstone 'sænd stəʊn ‖ -stoʊn **~s** z
sandstorm 'sænd stɔːm ‖ -stɔːrm **~s** z
Sandusky sæn 'dʌsk i sᵊn-

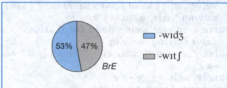

SANDWICH

BrE: 53% -wɪdʒ, 47% -wɪtʃ

sandwich, S~ 'sæn wɪdʒ 'sænd-, 'sæm-, -wɪtʃ
  — *Preference poll, BrE:* -wɪdʒ 53%, -wɪtʃ 47%.
  sandwiched 'sæn wɪdʒd 'sænd-, 'sæm-, -wɪtʃt
  ~es ɪz əz **~ing** ɪŋ
  'sandwich board; **'sandwich course**;
  'sandwich man
sandworm 'sænd wɜːm ‖ -wɝːm **~s** z
sandwort 'sænd wɜːt §-wɔːt ‖ -wɝːt **~s** s
sand|y, Sand|y 'sænd |i **~ier** i‿ə ‖ i‿ᵊr **~iest**
  i‿ɪst i‿əst **~iness** i nəs i nɪs **S~y's** iz
  ˌSandy 'Hook
sandyacht 'sænd jɒt ‖ -jɑːt **~s** s
Sandys sændz
sane seɪn saner 'seɪn ə ‖ -ᵊr **sanest** 'seɪn ɪst
  -əst
sane|ly 'seɪn |li **~ness** nəs nɪs
San Fernando ˌsæn fə 'nænd əʊ
  ‖ -fᵊr 'nænd oʊ
Sanford 'sæn fəd ‖ -fᵊrd
Sanforis|e, Sanforiz|e *tdmk* 'sæn fə raɪz **~ed**
  d **~es** ɪz əz **~ing** ɪŋ
San Francisco ˌsæn frən 'sɪsk əʊ -fræn- ‖ -oʊ
  ˌSan Franˌcisco 'Bay
San Gabriel sæn 'geɪb ri‿əl →sæŋ-
sangaree ˌsæŋ gə 'riː
Sanger 'sæŋ ə ‖ -ᵊr
sangfroid ˌsɒŋ 'frwɑː ˌsæŋ-, ˌsɑːŋ- ‖ ˌsɑːŋ-
  —*Fr* [sɑ̃ fʁwa]

S

Sango 'sæŋ gəʊ 'sɑːŋ- ‖ 'sɑːŋ goʊ
Sangre de Cristo ˌsæŋ gri də 'krɪst əʊ ◂
‖ -oʊ ◂
sangria sæn 'griːˌə →sæŋ-; 'sæŋ griˌə —*Sp*
san g ría [saŋ 'gri a]
Sangster 'sæŋᵏst ə ‖ -ᵊr
sanguinary 'sæŋ gwɪn ər i '·gwən-
‖ -gwə ner i
sanguine 'sæŋ gwɪn §-gwən- **~ly** li **~ness** nəs
nɪs
sanguineous sæŋ 'gwɪn iˌəs sæn-
sanguinity sæŋ 'gwɪn ət i sæn-, -ɪt- ‖ -əʈ i
Sanhedrin 'sæn ə drɪn -ɪ-, §-ədr ən;
sæn 'hedr ɪn, -'hiːdr-, §-ən ‖ sæn 'hedr ən
sanicle 'sæn ɪk ᵊl **~s** z
sanitarily 'sæn ət ˌər əl i '·ɪt, -ˌɪ li; ˌsæn ə 'ter-,
ˌ·ɪ- ‖ ˌsæn ə 'ter-
sanitari|um ˌsæn ə 'teər iˌ|əm ˌ·ɪ- ‖ -'ter-
-'tær- **~a** ə **~ums** əmz
sanitary 'sæn ət ˌər i ˌ·ɪtˌ ‖ -ə ter i
ˌsanitary 'napkin; ˌsanitary ˌtowel
sanitation ˌsæn ɪ 'teɪʃ ᵊn ə-
ˌsani'tation ˌworker
sanitis|e, sanitiz|e 'sæn ɪ taɪz -ə- **~ed** d **~es**
ɪz əz **~ing** ɪŋ
sanitori|um ˌsæn ə 'tɔːr iˌ|əm ˌ·ɪ- ‖ -'toʊr- **~a**
ə **~ums** əmz
sanity 'sæn ət i -ɪt- ‖ -əʈ i
San Jacinto (i) ˌsæn dʒə 'sɪnt əʊ ‖ -'sɪnʈ oʊ
-'siːnt-, (ii) -hə- —*in TX (i), in CA (ii)*
San Joaquin *river and valley in CA*
ˌsæn wɑː 'kiːn ‖ -wɔː-
San Jose *place in CA*, **San José** *place in Costa
Rica* ˌsæn həʊ 'zeɪ -əʊ- ‖ -ə 'zeɪ -hoʊ-, -oʊ-,
-'seɪ —*Sp* [saŋ xo 'se]
San Juan ˌsæn 'wɑːn -'hwɑːn
ˌSan ˌJuan Capi'strano ˌkæp ɪ 'strɑːn əʊ -ə-
‖ -oʊ
sank sæŋk
Sankey 'sæŋk i
San Leandro ˌsæn li 'ændr əʊ ‖ -oʊ
San Luis Obispo ˌsæn ˌluːˌɪs ə 'bɪsp əʊ ·ˌˌ
əs ə-, i ə- ‖ -oʊ -'biːsp-
San Marcos sæn 'mɑːk əs →sæm- ‖ -'mɑːrk əs
San Marino ˌsæn mə 'riːn əʊ →ˌsæm- ‖ -oʊ
San Mateo ˌsæn mə 'teɪ əʊ ‖ -oʊ
San Miguel ˌsæn mɪ 'gel →ˌsæm- —*Sp*
[sam mi 'gel]
San Pedro (i) sæn 'pedr əʊ →sæm- ‖ -oʊ,
(ii) sæn 'piːdr əʊ →sæm- ‖ -oʊ —*The suburb
of Los Angeles CA, and the river in AZ, are
usually (i); all other places are (ii).* —*Sp*
[sam 'pe ðɾo]
San Quentin sæn 'kwent ɪn →sæŋ-, §-ən ‖ -ᵊn
Sanquhar 'sæŋk ə ‖ -ᵊr
San Rafael *place in CA* ˌsæn rə 'fel
San Remo ˌ₍ₗ₎sæn 'reɪm əʊ -'riːm- ‖ -oʊ —*It*
[san 'rɛː mo]
sans sænz —*Fr* [sɑ̃]
San Salvador ˌ₍ₗ₎sæn 'sælv ə dɔː ‖ -dɔːr
sans-culotte ˌsænz kju 'lɒt -ku- ‖ -'lɑːt —*Fr*
[sɑ̃ ky lɔt] **~s** s

San Sebastian, San Sebastián
ˌsæn sə 'bæst iˌən ˌsɪ- ‖ -'bæs tʃən —*Sp*
[san se βas 'tjan]
sansei 'sæn seɪ ‖ 'sɑːn- —*Jp* ['saɴ see]
sanserif ˌsæn 'ser ɪf ˌsænz-, -əf
sansevieria ˌsæn sɪ 'vɪər iˌə ˌ·sə- ‖ -'vɪr- **~s** z
Sanskrit 'sænᵏs krɪt -krət
Sanskritic sæn 'skrɪt ɪk ‖ -'skrɪʈ ɪk
Sansom 'sænᵏs əm
Sanson 'sænᵏs ᵊn
sans serif, sanserif ˌsæn 'ser ɪf ˌsænz-, -əf
Santa 'sænt ə 'sɑːnt- ‖ 'sænʈ ə —*and in AmE,
but only for saints' names treated as Italian or
Spanish (not for place names in the US, not
for Santa Claus), also* 'sɑːnt ə — *It, Sp*
['san ta] **~s, 's** z
Santa Ana ˌsænt əʳ 'æn ə ‖ ˌsænʈ ə-
Santa Barbara ˌsænt ə 'bɑːb ərˌə
‖ ˌsænʈ ə 'bɑːrb-
Santa Catalina ˌsænt ə ˌkæt ə 'liːn ə
→ -ᵊl 'iːn ə ‖ ˌsænʈ ə ˌkæt-
Santa Claus 'sænt ə klɔːz 'sɑːnt-, ˌ·'· ‖ 'sænʈ-
-i-, -klɑːz
Santa Cruz *place in CA* ˌsænt ə 'kruːz
‖ 'sænʈ ə kruːz ˌ·'· —*locally usually* '· · ·
Santa Fe, Santa Fé ˌsænt ə 'feɪ '· ·
‖ 'sænʈ ə feɪ ˌ·'·
Santali sʌn 'tɑːl i sᵊn-, sæn-
Santa Maria ˌsænt ə mə 'riːˌə ‖ ˌsænʈ- —*Sp*
[san ta ma 'ri a]
Santa Monica ˌsænt ə 'mɒn ɪk ə §-ək ə
‖ ˌsænʈ ə 'mɑːn-
Santander ˌsænt ən 'deə ˌsæn tæn-,
△ˌsæn 'tænd ə ‖ ˌsɑːn tɑːn 'deᵊr —*Sp*
[san tan 'der]
Santa Rosa ˌsænt ə 'rəʊz ə ‖ ˌsænʈ ə 'roʊz ə
Santayana ˌsænt ə 'jɑːn ə -aɪ 'ɑːn-
‖ ˌsænʈ i 'æn ə -'ɑːn ə
Santee ₍ₗ₎sæn 'tiː '· ·
Santer 'sænt ə ‖ 'sænʈ ᵊr —*Fr* [sɑ̃ tɛːʁ]
santeria, S~ ˌsænt ə 'riːˌə ‖ ˌsænʈ- ˌsɑːnʈ- —*Sp*
santería [san te 'ri a]
Santiago ˌsænt i 'ɑːg əʊ ‖ ˌsænʈ i 'ɑːg oʊ
ˌsɑːnʈ- —*Sp* [san 'tja ɣo]
Santo, santo 'sænt əʊ ‖ 'sænʈ oʊ 'sɑːnt- —*It,
Sp* ['san to] **~s** z
Santo Domingo ˌsænt əʊ də 'mɪŋ gəʊ
‖ ˌsænʈ ə də 'mɪŋ goʊ —*Sp*
[san to ðo 'miŋ go]
santolina ˌsænt ə 'liːn ə -ᵊl 'iːn-
‖ ˌsænʈ ᵊl 'iːn ə
santonica sæn 'tɒn ɪk ə ‖ -'tɑːn-
santonin 'sænt ən ɪn §-ən
Santorini ˌsænt ə 'riːn i ‖ ˌsæn tə-
Santos 'sænt ɒs ‖ 'sænʈ əs —*Port* ['sɐn tuʃ,
-tus]
Sanyo *tdmk* 'sæn jəʊ ‖ -joʊ —*Jp* [sa,ɴ joo,
sa,ĩ-]
Saoirse 'seəʃ ə ‖ 'serʃ ə —*Irish* ['seːrʲ [ə]
Saône səʊn ‖ soʊn —*Fr* [soːn]
São Paulo sɑʊm 'paʊl əʊ saʊ-, -u ‖ -oʊ —*Port*
[sɐ̃um 'paulu]

S

São Tomé ˌsaʊn tə ˈmeɪ ˌsaʊ- —*Port*
[sɐ̃un tu ˈmɛ]
sap sæp sapped sæpt sapping ˈsæp ɪŋ saps
sæps
sapele, S~ sə ˈpiːl i
saphen|a sə ˈfiːn |ə ~ae iː
saphenous sə ˈfiːn əs ˈsæf ɪn əs, -ən-
sapid ˈsæp ɪd §-əd
sapience ˈseɪp i ˌən's ˈsæp-
sapiens ˈsæp i enz ˈseɪp-
sapient ˈseɪp i ˌənt ˈsæp- ~ly li
Sapir sə ˈpɪə ˈseɪ pɪə ‖ sə ˈpɪˀr
sapling ˈsæp lɪŋ ~s z
sapodilla ˌsæp ə ˈdɪl ə ~s z
saponaceous ˌsæp ə ˈneɪʃ əs ◂ ~ness nəs nɪs
saponification sə ˌpɒn ɪf ɪ ˈkeɪʃ ᵊn -ˌ-əf-, §-əˈ--
‖ sə ˌpɑːn-
saponi|fy sə ˈpɒn ɪ |faɪ -ə- ‖ sə ˈpɑːn- ~fied
faɪd ~fier/s faɪ ə/z ‖ faɪ ˀr/z ~fies faɪz
~fying faɪ ɪŋ
saponin ˈsæp ən ɪn §-ən ~s z
sapp... —*see* sap
sapper ˈsæp ə ‖ -ˀr ~s z
sapphic, S~ ˈsæf ɪk ~s s
Sapphira sə ˈfaɪˀr ə sæ-
sapphire ˈsæf aɪ ə ‖ ˈsæf aɪ ˀr ~s z
sapphism ˈsæf ˌɪz əm
Sappho ˈsæf əʊ ‖ -oʊ
Sapporo sə ˈpɔːr əʊ sæ- ‖ -oʊ —*Jp*
[sap ˌpo ɾo]
sapp|y ˈsæp |i ~ier i ə ‖ i ˀr ~iest i ɪst i əst
~ily ɪ li əl i ~iness i nəs i nɪs
sapro- *comb. form*
with stress-neutral suffix |sæp rəʊ ‖ -rə
— saprophyte ˈsæp rəʊ faɪt ‖ -rə-
with stress-imposing suffix sæ ˈprɒ +
‖ sæ ˈprɑː + — saprophagous
sæ ˈprɒf əg əs ‖ sæ ˈprɑːf-
saprobe ˈsæp rəʊb ‖ -roʊb ~s z
sapwood ˈsæp wʊd
Sara (i) ˈsɑːr ə, (ii) ˈseər ə ‖ ˈser ə ˈsær-
saraband, sarabande ˈsær ə bænd ‖ ˈser- ~s
z
Saracen ˈsær əs ən ‖ ˈser- ~s z
Saracenic ˌsær ə ˈsen ɪk ◂ ‖ ˌser-
Saragossa ˌsær ə ˈgɒs ə ‖ -ˈgɑːs ə ˌser- —*Sp*
Zaragoza [θa ɾa ˈɣo θa]
Sarah ˈseər ə ‖ ˈser ə ˈsær-
Sarah-Jane ˌseər ə ˈdʒeɪn ‖ ˌser- ˌsær-
Sarajevo ˌsær ə ˈjeɪv əʊ ‖ -oʊ ˌser- —*S-Cr*
[sa ɾa ˈjɛ vɔ]
saran, Saran sə ˈræn
Saranac ˈsær ə næk ‖ ˈser-
Sarandon sə ˈrænd ən
Sarasota ˌsær ə ˈsəʊt ə ‖ -ˈsoʊt ə ˌser-
Saratoga ˌsær ə ˈtəʊg ə ‖ -ˈtoʊg ə ˌser-
ˌSaraˌtoga ˈSprings
Saratov sə ˈrɑːt ɒv ‖ -ɑːv —*Russ* [sʌ ˈra təf]
Sarawak sə ˈrɑː wæk -wə, -wæk; ˈsær ə- ‖ -wɑːk
sarcasm ˈsɑːk ˌæz əm ‖ ˈsɑːrk-
sarcastic sɑː ˈkæst ɪk ‖ sɑːr- ~ally ᵊl i
sarcenet ˈsɑːs nət -nɪt -net ‖ ˈsɑːrs-

sarco- *comb. form*
with stress-neutral suffix |sɑːk əʊ ‖ |sɑːrk ə
— sarcocele ˈsɑːk əʊ siːᵊl ‖ ˈsɑːrk ə-
with stress-imposing suffix sɑː ˈkɒ +
‖ sɑːr ˈkɑː + — sarcolysis sɑː ˈkɒl əs ɪs -ɪs-,
§-əs ‖ sɑːr ˈkɑːl-
sarcoma sɑː ˈkəʊm ə ‖ sɑːr ˈkoʊm ə ~s z
sarcoph|agus sɑː ˈkɒf |əg əs ‖ sɑːr ˈkɑːf- ~agi
ə gaɪ -dʒaɪ
sard sɑːd ‖ sɑːrd sards sɑːdz ‖ sɑːrdz
Sardanapalus ˌsɑːd ə ˈnæp əl əs ˌsɑːd ᵊn ˈæp-;
ˌsɑːd ən ə ˈpɑːl əs ‖ ˌsɑːrd ᵊn ˈæp-
sardine *fish* ˌsɑː ˈdiːn ◂ ‖ ˌsɑːr- ~s z
ˌsardine ˈsandwich
sardine *gemstone* ˈsɑːd aɪn ‖ ˈsɑːrd- ~s z
Sardini|a sɑː ˈdɪn i ˌə ‖ sɑːr- ~an/s ən/z
Sardis ˈsɑːd ɪs §-əs ‖ ˈsɑːrd-
sardius ˈsɑːd i ˌəs ‖ ˈsɑːrd- ~es ɪz əz
sardonic sɑː ˈdɒn ɪk ‖ sɑːr ˈdɑːn ɪk ~ally ᵊl i
sardonyx ˈsɑːd ə nɪks -ᵊn ɪks; ˌsɑː ˈdɒn ɪks
‖ sɑːr ˈdɑːn ɪks ˈsɑːrd ᵊn- ~es ɪz əz
saree ˈsɑːr i —*Hindi* [ˈsɑː ɽi] ~s z
Sargant ˈsɑːdʒ ənt ‖ ˈsɑːrdʒ-
sargasso, S~ sɑː ˈgæs əʊ ‖ sɑːr ˈgæs oʊ ~s z
Sarˌgasso ˈSea
sarge sɑːdʒ ‖ sɑːrdʒ
Sargeant, Sargent ˈsɑːdʒ ənt ‖ ˈsɑːrdʒ-
Sargon ˈsɑːg ɒn ‖ ˈsɑːrg ɑːn
sari ˈsɑːr i —*Hindi* [ˈsɑː ɽi] ~s z
Sarille *tdmk* sə ˈrɪl
sarin ˈsɑːr ɪn ˈsær-, §-ən
Sark, sark sɑːk ‖ sɑːrk Sark's, sarks sɑːks
‖ sɑːrks
sarking ˈsɑːk ɪŋ ‖ ˈsɑːrk ɪŋ
Sarkozy sɑː ˈkəʊz i ‖ ˌsɑːrk oʊ ˈziː —*Fr*
[saʁ ko zi]
sark|y ˈsɑːk |i ‖ ˈsɑːrk |i ~ier i ə ‖ i ˀr ~iest
i ɪst i əst ~ily ɪ li əl i ~iness i nəs i nɪs
Sarmatia sɑː ˈmeɪʃ ə -ˈmeɪʃ i ə ‖ sɑːr-
Sarmatian sɑː ˈmeɪʃ ᵊn -ˈmeɪʃ i ˌən ‖ sɑːr- ~s z
Sarnia ˈsɑːn i ə ‖ ˈsɑːrn i ə
sarnie *'sandwich'* ˈsɑːn i ‖ — ~s z
sarong sə ˈrɒŋ ‖ -ˈrɔːŋ -ˈrɑːŋ ~s z
Saronic, s~ sə ˈrɒn ɪk ‖ -ˈrɑːn ɪk
saros ˈseər ɒs ˈseɪ rɒs ‖ ˈser ɑːs ˈsær- ~es ɪz əz
Saro-Wiwa ˌsær əʊ ˈwiː wə ˌsɑːr- ‖ ˌsɑːr oʊ-
ˌsær-
Saroyan sə ˈrɔɪ ən
Sarpedon sɑː ˈpiːd ᵊn -ɒn ‖ sɑːr- -ɑːn
sarracenia ˌsær ə ˈsiːn i ə -ˈsen- ‖ ˌser- ~s z
Sarre sɑː ‖ sɑːr
Sars, SARS sɑːz ‖ sɑːrz
sarsaparilla ˌsɑːsp ə ˈrɪl ə ◂ ˌsɑːs əp ə ˈrɪl ə
‖ ˌsæsp- ˌsɑːrsp-, -ˈrel-
sarsen ˈsɑːs ᵊn ‖ ˈsɑːrs ᵊn ~s z
sarsenet ˈsɑːs nət -nɪt, -net ‖ ˈsɑːrs-
Sarson ˈsɑːs ᵊn ‖ ˈsɑːrs ᵊn
sartor, S~ ˈsɑːt ə -ɔː ‖ ˈsɑːrt̬ ˀr
sartorial sɑː ˈtɔːr i ˌəl ‖ sɑːr- -ˈtoʊr- ~ly i
sartorius sɑː ˈtɔːr i ˌəs ‖ sɑːr- -ˈtoʊr-
Sartre ˈsɑːtr ˈsɑːtr ə ‖ ˈsɑːrtr ə —*Fr* [saʁtχ]
Sarum ˈseər əm ‖ ˈser əm ˈsær-
SAS ˌes eɪ ˈes

sash sæʃ **sashed** sæʃt **sashes** 'sæʃ ɪz -əz
  sashing 'sæʃ ɪŋ
  'sash cord; ˌsash 'window, '· ˌ· ·
Sasha 'sæʃ ə ‖ 'sɑːʃ ə
sashay 'sæʃ eɪ sæ 'ʃeɪ ‖ sæ 'ʃeɪ **~ed** d **~ing** ɪŋ
  ~s z
sashimi sæ 'ʃiːm i sə- ‖ sɑː- —*Jp* [sa ˌɕi 'mi]
Saskatchewan sæ 'skætʃ ə wən sə-, -ɪ-, -wɒn
  ‖ -wɑːn
Saskatoon, s~ ˌsæsk ə 'tuːn
Saskia 'sæsk i‿ə
Sasquatch, s~ 'sæsk wætʃ -wɒtʃ ‖ -wɑːtʃ
sass sæs **sassed** sæst **sasses** 'sæs ɪz -əz
  sassing 'sæs ɪŋ
sassab|y 'sæs əb |i **~ies** iz
sassafras 'sæs ə fræs **~es** ɪz əz
Sassanid 'sæs ən ɪd §-əd **~s** z
Sassanidae sə 'sæn ɪ diː -ə-
Sasse sæs
Sassenach 'sæs ə næk -næx; -ən ək, -ən əx
  —*ScG and Ir* ['sa sə nəx] **~s** s
Sassoon sə 'suːn sæ-
sass|y 'sæs |i **~ier** i‿ə ‖ i‿ʰr **~iest** i‿ɪst i‿əst **~ily**
  ɪ li əl i **~iness** i nəs i nɪs
sat sæt
Satan 'seɪt ʰn —*formerly also* 'sæt-
satanic sə 'tæn ɪk **~al** ʰl **~ally** ʰl‿i
Satanism 'seɪt ʰn ˌɪz əm
Satanist 'seɪt ʰn ɪst §-əst **~s** s
satay 'sæt eɪ 'sɑːt- ‖ 'sɑːt-
satchel 'sætʃ əl **~s** z
sate seɪt **sated** 'seɪt ɪd -əd ‖ 'seɪt̬ əd **sates**
  seɪts **sating** 'seɪt ɪŋ ‖ 'seɪt̬ ɪŋ
saté 'sæt eɪ 'sɑːt- ‖ 'sɑːt-
sateen sə 'tiːn sæ- **~s** z
satellite 'sæt ə laɪt -ɪ-, →-ʰl aɪt ‖ 'sæt̬ ʰl aɪt **~s**
  s
satem 'sɑːt əm 'sæt-, 'seɪt-, -em ‖ 'sɑːt̬ əm
satiab|le 'seɪʃ əb |ʰl 'seɪʃ i‿əb |ʰl **~leness**
  ʰl nəs -nɪs **~ly** li
sati|ate *v* 'seɪʃ i |eɪt **~ated** eɪt ɪd -əd ‖ eɪt̬ əd
  ~ates eɪts **~ating** eɪt ɪŋ ‖ eɪt̬ ɪŋ
satiation ˌseɪʃ i 'eɪʃ ʰn
Satie 'sæt i 'sɑːt i ‖ sæ 'tiː sɑː- —*Fr* [sa ti]
satiety sə 'taɪ ət i 'seɪʃ i, -ɪt i ‖ -ət̬ i
satin 'sæt ɪn §-ʰn ‖ -ʰn **~s** z
satinet, satinette ˌsæt ɪ 'net §-ə-, -ʰn 'et
  ‖ -ʰn 'et
satinwood 'sæt ɪn wʊd §-ʰn- ‖ -ʰn-
satiny 'sæt ɪn i §-ʰn- ‖ -ʰn i
satire 'sæt aɪ‿ə ‖ 'sæt̬ aɪ‿ʰr **~s** z
satiric sə 'tɪr ɪk **~al** ʰl **~ally** ʰl‿i **~alness** ʰl nəs
  -nɪs
satiris... —*see* **satiriz...**
satirist 'sæt ər ɪst -ɪr-, §-əst ‖ 'sæt̬- **~s** s
satirization ˌsæt ər aɪ 'zeɪʃ ʰn ˌ·ɪr-, -ɪ'·-
  ‖ ˌsæt̬ ər ə-
satiriz|e 'sæt ə raɪz -ɪ- ‖ 'sæt̬- **~ed** d **~es** ɪz əz
  ~ing ɪŋ
satisfaction ˌsæt ɪs 'fæk ʃʰn -əs- ‖ ˌsæt̬- **~s** z
satisfactor|y ˌsæt ɪs 'fækt ər |i ◂ ˌ·əs-, ‖ ˌsæt̬-
  ~ily əl i ɪ li **~iness** i nəs i nɪs

satis|fy 'sæt ɪs |faɪ -əs- ‖ 'sæt̬- **~fied** faɪd
  ~fier/s faɪ‿ə/z ‖ faɪ‿ʰr/z **~fies** faɪz **~fying/ly**
  faɪ ɪŋ /li
sat-nav 'sæt næv
satori sə 'tɔːr i —*Jp* [sa ˌto ɾi]
satphone 'sæt fəʊn ‖ -foʊn **~s** z
satrap 'sætr æp -əp ‖ 'seɪtr- **~s** s
satrap|y 'sætr əp |i ‖ 'seɪtr- **~ies** iz
satsuma, S~ sæt 'suːm ə 'sæts əm ə, -u mɑː
  —*Jp* ['sa tsɯ ma] **~s** z
Satterthwaite 'sæt ə θweɪt ‖ 'sæt̬ ʰr-
satu|rate 'sætʃ ə |reɪt -ʊ-; 'sæt jʊ- **~rated**
  reɪt ɪd -əd ‖ reɪt̬ əd **~rates** reɪts **~rating**
  reɪt ɪŋ ‖ reɪt̬ ɪŋ
saturation ˌsætʃ ə 'reɪʃ ʰn -ʊ-; ˌsæt jʊ-
  ˌsatu'ration point
Saturday 'sæt ə deɪ -di; △'sæt di ‖ 'sæt̬ ʰr-
  —*See note at* -**day** **~s** z
  ˌSaturday 'night
Saturn 'sæt ɜːn -ʰn ‖ 'sæt̬ ʰrn **~'s** z
saturnalia, S~ ˌsæt ə 'neɪl i‿ə -ˌɜː- ‖ ˌsæt̬ ʰr-
Saturnian, s~ sæ 'tɜːn i‿ən sə- ‖ -'tɝːn-
saturnine 'sæt ə naɪn ‖ 'sæt̬ ʰr-
satyagraha, S~ sʌt 'jɑːg rə hə 'sʌt jəg rə hə,
  -jə grɑː hə, -hɑː: —*Hindi* [sə tjə grəh]
satyr 'sæt ə ‖ 'seɪt̬ ʰr 'sæt̬- **~s** z
satyriasis ˌsæt ə 'raɪ‿əs ɪs ˌ·ɪ-, §-əs ‖ ˌseɪt̬- ˌsæt̬-
satyric sə 'tɪr ɪk ‖ seɪ-
sauce sɔːs **sauced** sɔːst ‖ sɑːst **sauces**
  'sɔːs ɪz -əz ‖ 'sɑːs- **saucing** 'sɔːs ɪŋ ‖ 'sɑːs-
saucepan 'sɔːs pən §'sɒs-, §-pæn ‖ -pæn 'sɑːs-
  ~s z
saucer 'sɔːs ə ‖ -ʰr 'sɑːs- **~s** z
Sauchiehall ˌsɒk i 'hɔːl ˌsɔːk-, ˌsɒx-, ˌsɔːx-
  ‖ ˌsɑːk i 'hɔːl ˌsɔːk-, -'hɑːl
Saucony *tdmk* sɔː 'kəʊn i ‖ -'koʊn i sɑː-
sauc|y 'sɔːs |i ‖ 'sɑːs- **~ier** i‿ə ‖ i‿ʰr **~iest** i‿ɪst
  i‿əst **~ily** ɪ li əl i **~iness** i nəs i nɪs
Saud saʊd sɑː 'uːd —*Arabic* [sa 'ʕuːd]
Saudi 'saʊd i 'sɔːd-; sɑː 'uːd i ‖ 'sɔːd-, 'saːd-
  —*Arabic* [sa 'ʕuː diː] **~s** z
  ˌSaudi A'rabia
sauerbraten 'saʊ‿ə brɑːt ʰn ‖ 'saʊ‿ʰr- —*Ger*
  ['zaʊ ɐ ˌbʁɑː tn̩]
sauerkraut 'saʊ‿ə kraʊt ‖ 'saʊ‿ʰr- —*Ger*
  ['zaʊ ɐ kʁaʊt]
sauger 'sɔːg ə ‖ -ʰr 'sɑːg- **~s** z
Saughall 'sɔːk ʰl ‖ 'sɑːk-
Saughton 'sɒxt ən ‖ 'sɔːkt ən 'sɑːkt-
Saugus 'sɔːg əs ‖ 'sɑːg-
Sauk sɔːk ‖ sɑːk **Sauks** sɔːks ‖ sɑːks
Saul sɔːl ‖ sɑːl
Sault Sainte Marie, Sault Ste Marie
  ˌsuː ˌseɪnt mə 'riː
sauna 'sɔːn ə 'saʊn- ‖ 'saːn-, 'saʊn- —*Finnish*
  ['sɑʊ nɑ] **~s** z
Saunders (i) 'sɔːnd əz ‖ -ʰrz, (ii) 'sɑːnd-
Saundersfoot 'sɔːnd əz fʊt ‖ -ʰrz- 'sɑːnd-
Saunderson (i) 'sɔːnd əs ən ‖ -ʰrs-, (ii) 'sɑːnd-
saunter 'sɔːnt ə ‖ 'sɔːnt̬ ʰr 'sɑːnt̬- **~ed** d
  sauntering 'sɔːnt ər ɪŋ ‖ 'sɔːnt̬ ər ɪŋ 'sɑːnt̬-
  ~s z
Saunton 'sɔːnt ən ‖ 'sɑːnt-

S

-saur sɔː ‖ sɔːr — **stegosaur** 'steg ə sɔː ‖ -sɔːr
saurian 'sɔːr i̯ ən ~**s** z
sauropod 'sɔːr əʊ pɒd ‖ -ə paːd ~**s** z
-saurus 'sːrs əs — **stegosaurus**
 ˌsteg ə 'sɔːr əs
sausag|e 'sɒs ɪdʒ ‖ 'sɔːs ɪdʒ 'saːs- (!) ~**es** ɪz əz
 'sausage dog; 'sausage meat; ˌsausage
 'roll
Saussure səʊ 'sjʊə -'sʊə ‖ soʊ 'sʊˀr -'sjʊˀr
 —*Fr* [so syːʁ]
Saussurean, Saussurian səʊ 'sjʊər i̯ ən
 -'sʊər- ‖ soʊ 'sʊr- -'sjʊr- ~**s** z
saute, sauté 'səʊt eɪ 'sɔːt-, -i ‖ soʊ 'teɪ sɔː-,
 saː- ~**d, ~ed d ~ing** ɪŋ ~**s** z
Sauterne, Sauternes səʊ 'tɜːn -'teən
 ‖ soʊ 'tɜːn -'teˀrn —*Fr* Sauternes [so tɛʁn]
sauve qui peut ˌsəʊv kiː 'pɜː ‖ ˌsoʊv kiː 'pʊ
 —*Fr* [sov ki pø]
Sauvignon 'səʊv iːn jɒn -ɪn-, -jɒ̃, ˌ·'·
 ‖ ˌsoʊv iːn 'joʊn —*Fr* [so vi njɔ̃]
savag|e, S~ 'sæv ɪdʒ ~**ed** d ~**ely** li ~**eness**
 nəs nɪs ~**es** ɪz əz ~**ing** ɪŋ
savager|y 'sæv ɪdʒ ər‿|i ~**ies** iz
savanna, savannah, S~ sə 'væn ə ~**s** z
savant 'sæv ᵊnt ‖ sə 'vaːnt sæ- (*) —*Fr* [sa vɑ̃]
 ~**s** s
savarin, S~ 'sæv ə ræ̃ -rɪn; -ər ən —*Fr*
 [sa va ʁæ̃] ~**s** z
save seɪv **saved** seɪvd **saves** seɪvz **saving**
 'seɪv ɪŋ
 ˌsaving 'grace
saveloy 'sæv ə lɔɪ -ɪ-, ˌ··'· ~**s** z
saver 'seɪv ə ‖ -ᵊr ~**s** z
Savernake 'sæv ə næk ‖ -ᵊr- —*There is also a
 spelling pronunciation* △-neɪk.
Savile, Savill 'sæv ᵊl -ɪl
savings 'seɪv ɪŋz
 'savings ac₊count; ˌsavings and 'loan,
 ˌsavings and 'loan associ₊ation; 'savings
 bank
savior, saviour, S~ 'seɪv jə ‖ -jᵊr ~**s** z
Savlon *tdmk* 'sæv lɒn ‖ -laːn
savoir-faire ˌsæv wɑː 'feə ˌsʌv- ‖ -wɑːr 'feˀr
 -'fæˀr —*Fr* [sa vwaʁ fɛːʁ]
savoir-vivre ˌsæv wɑː 'viːv rə ˌsʌv- ‖ -wɑːr-
 —*Fr* [sa vwaʁ viːvʁ]
Savonarola ˌsæv ən̩ə 'rəʊl ə ‖ -'roʊl ə —*It*
 [sa vo na 'rɔː la]
savor, savour 'seɪv ə ‖ -ᵊr ~**ed** d **savoring,
 savouring** 'seɪv ər‿ɪŋ ~**s** z
savor|y, savour|y, Savory 'seɪv ər‿|i ~**ies** iz
Savoy, savoy sə 'vɔɪ ~**s**, ~'**s** z
Savoyard sə 'vɔɪ ɑːd ˌsæv ɔɪ 'ɑːd
 ‖ ˌsæv ɔɪ 'ɑːrd ~**s** z
savv|y 'sæv |i ~**ied** id ~**ies** iz ~**ying** i̯ɪŋ
saw sɔː ‖ saː **sawed** sɔːd ‖ saːd **sawing** 'sɔːˑ ɪŋ
 ‖ 'sɔː ɪŋ 'saː- **sawn** sɔːn ‖ saːn **saws** sɔːz
 ‖ saːz
 'saw at₊tachment
Saward 'seɪ wəd ‖ -wᵊrd
Sawatch sə 'wɒtʃ ‖ -'waːtʃ
sawbones 'sɔː bəʊnz ‖ -boʊnz 'saː-

Sawbridgeworth 'sɔː brɪdʒ wɜːθ -wəθ ‖ -wɜːθ
 'saː- —*Formerly locally also* 'sæps wəθ
sawbuck 'sɔː bʌk ‖ 'saː- ~**s** s
sawdust 'sɔː dʌst ‖ 'saː-
sawed-off ˌsɔːd 'ɒf ◂ -'ɔːf ‖ -'ɔːf ◂ ˌsaːd 'aːf◂
 ˌsawed-off 'shotgun
sawfish 'sɔː fɪʃ ‖ 'saː-
saw|fly 'sɔː |flaɪ ‖ 'saː- ~**flies** flaɪz
sawhors|e 'sɔː hɔːs ‖ -hɔːrs 'saː- ~**es** ɪz əz
sawmill 'sɔː mɪl ‖ 'saː- ~**s** z
sawn sɔːn ‖ saːn
sawn-off ˌsɔːn 'ɒf ◂ -'ɔːf ‖ -'ɔːf ◂ ˌsaːn 'aːf◂
 ˌsawn-off 'shotgun
sawpit 'sɔː pɪt ‖ 'saː- ~**s** s
Sawston 'sɔːst ən ‖ 'saːst-
sawtooth 'sɔː tuːθ §-tʊθ ‖ 'saː- ~**ed** t
Sawtry 'sɔːtr i ‖ 'saːtr-
saw-wort 'sɔː wɜːt -wɔːt ‖ -wɜːt 'saː-, -wɔːrt
sawyer, S~ 'sɔː jə ‖ -jᵊr 'saː-; 'sɔɪ‿ᵊr ~**s** z
sax sæks **saxes** 'sæks ɪz -əz
Saxa *tdmk* 'sæks ə
Saxby 'sæks bi
saxe, Saxe sæks
 ˌsaxe 'blue◂
Saxe-Coburg-Gotha ˌsæks ˌkəʊ bɜːg 'gəʊθ ə
 -'gəʊt- ‖ -ˌkoʊ bɜːg 'goʊθ ə
saxhorn 'sæks hɔːn ‖ -hɔːrn ~**s** z
saxifrag|e 'sæks ɪ freɪdʒ -ə-, -frɪdʒ, -freɪʒ ~**es**
 ɪz əz
Saxin *tdmk* 'sæks ɪn §-ən
Saxmundham sæks 'mʌnd əm
Saxo 'sæks əʊ ‖ -oʊ
 ˌSaxo Gram'maticus grə 'mæt ɪk əs
 ‖ -'mæt̬-
Saxon 'sæks ᵊn ~**s** z
Saxone *tdmk* ˌsæk 'səʊn ‖ -'soʊn
Saxony, s~ 'sæks ən i
saxophone 'sæks ə fəʊn ‖ -foʊn ~**s** z
saxophonist sæks 'ɒf ən ɪst 'sæks ə fəʊn-,
 §-əst ‖ 'sæks ə foʊn əst
Saxton 'sækst ən

SAYS		

 —16%

☐ sez
☐ seɪz

84%

BrE

say seɪ **said** sed (!) **saying/s** 'seɪ ɪŋ/z **says** sez
 §seɪz — *Preference poll, BrE*: sez 84%, seɪz
 16%.
Saybolt 'seɪ bəʊlt →-bɒʊlt ‖ -boʊlt
Sayce seɪs
Sayer, s~ 'seɪ ə ‖ -ᵊr
Sayers 'seɪ əz ‖ -ᵊrz
Sayle seɪᵊl
says sez §seɪz (!)
say-so 'seɪ səʊ ‖ -soʊ ~**s** z
sazarac, sazerac, S~ *tdmk* 'sæz ə ræk ~**s** s
S-bend 'es bend ~**s** z

scab skæb **scabbed** skæbd **scabbing** 'skæb ɪŋ
  scabs skæbz
scabbard 'skæb əd ‖ -ᵊrd **~s** z
scabb|y 'skæb |i **~ier** i ə ‖ i ᵊr **~iest** i ɪst i əst
  ~ily ɪ li əl i **~iness** i nəs i nɪs
scabies 'skeɪb iːz 'skeɪb i ˌiːz
scabious 'skeɪb i əs **~es** ɪz əz
scabrous 'skeɪb rəs 'skæb- ‖ 'skæb- **~ly** li
  ~ness nəs nɪs
scad skæd **scads** skædz
Scafell ˌskɔː 'fel ◄ ˌskɑː-
  ˌScafell 'Pike
scaffold 'skæf əʊld →-ɒʊld, -ᵊld ‖ -ᵊld -oʊld
  ~ed ɪd əd **~er/s** ə/z ‖ -ᵊr/z **~ing** ɪŋ **~s** z
scag skæg
scagliola skæl 'jəʊl ə ‖ -'joʊl ə —It
  [skaʎ 'ʌːɔː la]
scala, Scala 'skɑːl ə —In anatomy, also
  'skeɪl ə
scalability ˌskeɪᵊl ə 'bɪl ət i -ɪt i ‖ -əṭ i
scalable 'skeɪl ᵊl əb ᵊl
scalar 'skeɪl ə -ɑː ‖ -ᵊr -ɑːr **~s** z
scalawag 'skæl ə wæg -i- **~s** z
scald skɔːld §skɒld ‖ skɑːld **scalded** 'skɔːld ɪd
  §'skɒld-, -əd ‖ 'skɑːld- **scalding/s** 'skɔːld ɪŋ/z
  §'skɒld- ‖ 'skɑːld- **scalds** skɔːldz §skɒldz
  ‖ skɑːldz
scale skeɪᵊl **scaled** skeɪᵊld **scales** skeɪᵊlz
  scaling 'skeɪᵊl ɪŋ
scalene 'skeɪl iːn ˌskeɪ 'liːn ◄
scalen|us skeɪ 'liːn |əs skə- **~i** aɪ
scaler 'skeɪl ə ‖ -ᵊr **~s** z
Scalextric tdmk ˌskeɪ 'leks trɪk
Scaliger 'skæl ɪdʒ ə -§ədʒ- ‖ -ᵊr
scallion 'skæl i ən ‖ 'skæl jən **~s** z

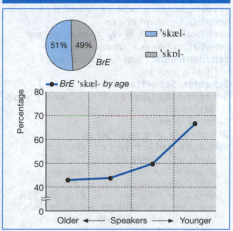

SCALLOP

51% 49%
BrE
■ 'skɒl-
■ 'skæl-

BrE 'skæl- by age
Percentage
80 70 60 50 40 0
Older ◄— Speakers —► Younger

scallop 'skɒl əp 'skæl- ‖ 'skæl əp 'skɑːl- —
  Preference poll, BrE: 'skɒl- *49%,* 'skæl- *51%.*
  ~ed t **~ing** ɪŋ **~s** s
scall|y 'skæl |i **~ies** iz
scallywag 'skæl i wæg **~s** z
scaloppin|e ˌskæl ə 'piːn |i ‖ ˌskɑːl- **~i** iː i

scalp skælp **scalped** skælpt **scalping**
  'skælp ɪŋ **scalps** skælps
Scalpay 'skælp eɪ -i
scalpel 'skælp ᵊl **~s** z
scalper 'skælp ə ‖ -ᵊr **~s** z
scal|y 'skeɪl |i **~ier** i ə ‖ i ᵊr **~iest** i ɪst i əst
  ~iness i nəs i nɪs
scam skæm **scammed** skæmd **scamming**
  'skæm ɪŋ **scams** skæmz
Scammell 'skæm ᵊl
scammer 'skæm ə ‖ -ᵊr **~s** z
scammon|y 'skæm ən |i **~ies** iz
scamp skæmp **scamped** skæmpt **scamping**
  'skæmp ɪŋ **scamps** skæmps
scamper 'skæmp ə ‖ -ᵊr **~ed** d **scampering/s**
  'skæmp ər ɪŋ/z **~s** z
scampi 'skæmp i
scampish 'skæmp ɪʃ **~ly** li **~ness** nəs nɪs
scan skæn **scanned** skænd **scanning** 'skæn ɪŋ
  scans skænz
scandal 'skænd ᵊl **~s** z
scandalis|e, scandaliz|e 'skænd ᵊl aɪz -ə laɪz
  ~ed d **~es** ɪz əz **~ing** ɪŋ
scandalmonger 'skænd ᵊl ˌmʌŋ gə -ˌmɒŋ-
  ‖ -gᵊr -ˌmɑːŋ- **~s** z
scandalous 'skænd ᵊl əs **~ly** li **~ness** nəs nɪs
scandent 'skænd ənt
Scanderbeg 'skænd ə beg ‖ -ᵊr-
Scandi|a, s~ 'skænd i |ə **~an** ən
Scandic 'skænd ɪk
Scandinavi|a ˌskænd ɪ 'neɪv i |ə ˌ-ə- **~an/s**
  ən/z
scandium 'skænd i əm
Scania tdmk 'skæn i ə
Scanlan, Scanlon 'skæn lən
scann... —see **scan**
scanner 'skæn ə ‖ -ᵊr **~s** z
scansion 'skænʃ ᵊn **~s** z
scansorial skæn 'sɔːr i əl ‖ -'soʊr-
scant skænt **scanter** 'skænt ə ‖ 'skænṭ ᵊr
  scantest 'skænt ɪst -əst ‖ 'skænṭ əst
scanti... —see **scanty**
scantling 'skænt lɪŋ **~s** z
scant|ly 'skænt |li **~ness** nəs nɪs
scant|y 'skænt |i ‖ 'skænṭ |i **~ier** i ə ‖ i ᵊr **~ies**
  iz **~iest** i ɪst i əst **~ily** ɪ li əl i **~iness** i nəs
  i nɪs
Scapa 'skɑːp ə 'skæp-
  ˌScapa 'Flow
-scape skeɪp — **seascape** 'siː skeɪp
scape|goat 'skeɪp |gəʊt ‖ -|goʊt **~goated**
  gəʊt ɪd -əd ‖ goʊṭ əd **~goating** gəʊt ɪŋ
  ‖ goʊṭ ɪŋ **~goats** gəʊts ‖ goʊts
scapegrac|e 'skeɪp greɪs **~es** ɪz əz
scaphoid 'skæf ɔɪd **~s** z
scapolite 'skæp əʊ laɪt ‖ -ə-
scap|ula 'skæp |jʊl ə §-jᵊl- ‖ -|jəl ə **~ulae**
  ju liː jə- ‖ jə liː **~ulas** jʊl əz jəl- ‖ jəl əz
scapular 'skæp jʊl ə §-jəl- ‖ -jəl ᵊr **~s** z
scar skɑː ‖ skɑːr **scarred** skɑːd ‖ skɑːrd
  scarring 'skɑːr ɪŋ **scars** skɑːz ‖ skɑːrz
  'scar ˌtissue
scarab 'skær əb ‖ 'sker- **~s** z

S

scarabae|us ˌskær ə 'biː |əs ‖ ˌsker- **~i** aɪ
Scaramouch, Scaramouche 'skær ə muːʃ
ˌmuːʃ, -maʊtʃ ‖ 'sker-
Scarboro', Scarborough 'skɑː bᵊr ə
‖ 'skɑːr ˌbɝː oʊ
Scarbrough 'skɑː brə ‖ 'skɑːr- -broʊ
scarce skeəs ‖ skeᵊrs skæᵊrs **scarcer** 'skeəs ə
‖ 'skeᵊrs ᵊr 'skæᵊrs- **scarcest** 'skeəs ɪst -əst
‖ 'skeᵊrs əst 'skæᵊrs-
scarce|ly 'skeəs |li ‖ 'skeᵊrs |li 'skæᵊrs- **~ness**
nəs nɪs
scarcit|y 'skeəs ət |i -ɪt- ‖ 'skers əţ |i 'skærs-
~ies iz
scare skeə ‖ skeᵊr skæᵊr **scared** skeəd ‖ skeᵊrd
skæᵊrd **scares** skeəz ‖ skeᵊrz skæᵊrz **scaring**
'skeər ɪŋ ‖ 'sker ɪŋ 'skær-
scarecrow 'skeə krəʊ ‖ 'sker kroʊ 'skær- **~s** z
scaredy-cat, scaredy cat 'skeəd i kæt
‖ 'skerd- 'skærd- **~s** s
scaremonger 'skeə ˌmʌŋ gə ə -ˌmɒŋ-
‖ 'sker ˌmʌŋ gᵊr 'skær-, -ˌmɑːŋ- **~s** z
scaremongering 'skeə ˌmʌŋ gər ɪŋ -ˌmɒŋ-
‖ -ˌmɑːŋ-
scarer 'skeər ə ‖ 'sker ᵊr **~s** z
scar|ey 'skeər |i ‖ 'sker |i 'skær- **~ier** i ə ‖ i ᵊr
~iest i ɪst i əst **~ily** əl i i li **~iness** i nəs i nɪs
scarf skɑːf ‖ skɑːrf **scarfed** skɑːft ‖ skɑːrft
scarfing 'skɑːf ɪŋ ‖ 'skɑːrf ɪŋ **scarfs** skɑːfs
‖ skɑːrfs **scarves** skɑːvz ‖ skɑːrvz
Scarface 'skɑː feɪs 'skɑːr-
Scarfe skɑːf ‖ skɑːrf
Scargill 'skɑː gɪl 'skɑːg ᵊl ‖ 'skɑːr-
scari... —*see* **scary**
scarification ˌskær ɪf ɪ 'keɪʃ ᵊn ˌskeər-, ˌ-əf-,
§-ə'- ‖ ˌsker- **~s** z
scarificator 'skær ɪf ɪ keɪt ə 'skeər-, '-əf-, §'· -ə-
‖ -keɪţ ᵊr 'sker- **~s** z
scari|fy 'skær ɪ |faɪ 'skeər-, -ə- ‖ 'sker- **~fied**
faɪd **~fier/s** faɪ ə/z ‖ faɪ ᵊr/z **~fies** faɪz
~fying faɪ ɪŋ
Scarisbrick 'skeəz brɪk ‖ 'skerz- 'skærz-
scarlatina ˌskɑːl ə 'tiːn ə ‖ ˌskɑːrl-
Scarlatti skɑː 'læt i ‖ skɑːr 'lɑːţ i —*It*
[skar 'lat ti]
scarlet 'skɑːl ət -ɪt ‖ 'skɑːrl-
ˌscarlet 'fever; ˌscarlet 'pimpernel;
ˌscarlet 'runner; ˌscarlet 'woman
Scarlett 'skɑːl ət -ɪt ‖ 'skɑːrl-
Scarman 'skɑː mən ‖ 'skɑːr-
scarp skɑːp ‖ skɑːrp **scarped** skɑːpt ‖ skɑːrpt
scarping 'skɑːp ɪŋ ‖ 'skɑːrp ɪŋ **scarps** skɑːps
‖ skɑːrps
scarper 'skɑːp ə ‖ 'skɑːrp ᵊr **~ed** d **scarpering**
'skɑːp ər ɪŋ ‖ 'skɑːrp- **~s** z
scarr... —*see* **scar**
SCART skɑːt skɑːrt
scarves skɑːvz ‖ skɑːrvz
scar|y 'skeər |i ‖ 'sker |i 'skær- **~ier** i ə ‖ i ᵊr
~iest i ɪst i əst **~ily** əl i i li **~iness** i nəs i nɪs
Scase skeɪs
scat skæt **scats** skæts **scatted** 'skæt ɪd -əd
‖ 'skæţ əd **scatting** 'skæt ɪŋ ‖ 'skæţ ɪŋ
scathing 'skeɪð ɪŋ **~ly** li

scatological ˌskæt ə 'lɒdʒ ɪk ᵊl ◂ lᵉ- 'ɒdʒ-
‖ ˌskæţ ᵊl 'ɑːdʒ- **~ly** i
scatology skæ 'tɒl ədʒ i ‖ -'tɑːl-
scatter 'skæt ə ‖ 'skæţ ᵊr **~ed** d **scattering**
'skæt ər ɪŋ ‖ 'skæţ ər ɪŋ **~s** z
'scatter ˌcushion; 'scatter ˌdiagram
scatterbrain 'skæt ə breɪn ‖ 'skæţ ᵊr- **~ed** d
~s z
Scattergood 'skæt ə gʊd ‖ 'skæţ ᵊr-
scatter-gun 'skæt ə gʌn ‖ 'skæţ ᵊr- **~s** z
scattershot 'skæt ə ʃɒt ‖ 'skæţ ᵊr ʃɑːt
scatt|y 'skæt |i ‖ 'skæţ |i **~ier** i ə ‖ i ᵊr **~iest**
i ɪst i əst **~ily** ɪ li əl i **~iness** i nəs i nɪs
scaup skɔːp ‖ skɑːp **scaups** skɔːps ‖ skɑːps
scaveng|e 'skæv ɪndʒ -ᵊndʒ **~ed** d **~es** ɪz əz
~ing ɪŋ
scavenger 'skæv ɪndʒ ə -ᵊndʒ- ‖ -ᵊr **~s** z
scena 'ʃeɪn ə ‖ -ɑː —*It* ['ʃɛ na]
scenario sə 'nɑːr i əʊ sɪ-, se-, -'neər-
‖ sə 'nær i oʊ -'ner-, -'nɑːr- **~s** z
scenarist 'siːn ər ɪst sə 'nɑːr-, sɪ-, se-, §-əst
‖ sə 'nær əst -'ner-, -'nɑːr-
scene siːn (= *seen*) **scenes** siːnz
scenery 'siːn ər i
sceneshifter 'siːn ˌʃɪft ə ‖ -ᵊr **~s** z
scenic 'siːn ɪk 'sen- **~ally** ᵊl_i
scenographer si: 'nɒg rəf ə ‖ -'nɑːg rəf ᵊr **~s**
z
scenographic ˌsiːn əʊ 'græf ɪk ◂ ‖ -ə- **~ally**
ᵊl_i
scenography si: 'nɒg rəf i ‖ -'nɑːg-
scent sent (= *cent, sent*) **scented** 'sent ɪd -əd
‖ 'senţ əd **scenting** 'sent ɪŋ ‖ 'senţ ɪŋ **scents**
sents
'scent mark
scentless 'sent ləs -lɪs
scepter, sceptre 'sept ə ‖ -ᵊr **~ed** d **~s** z
sceptic, S~ 'skept ɪk **~s** s
sceptical 'skept ɪk ᵊl **~ly** i **~ness** nəs nɪs
scepticism 'skept ɪ ˌsɪz əm -ə-
schadenfreude 'ʃɑːd ᵊn ˌfrɔɪd ə —*Ger* S~
['ʃaːd n ˌfʀɔyd ə]
Schaefer, Schaeffer, Schafer 'ʃeɪf ə ‖ -ᵊr
Schaghticoke 'skæt i kʊk 'ʃæt-, -kəʊk ‖ 'skæţ-
'ʃæţ-, -koʊk
Schama 'ʃɑːm ə
Schapiro ʃə 'pɪər əʊ ‖ -'pɪr oʊ
schedul|e 'ʃed juːl 'ʃedʒ uːl; 'sked juːl,
'skedʒ uːl ‖ 'skedʒ uːl -ᵊl —*The AmE
pronunciation with* sk- *is increasingly heard in
BrE. Preference poll, BrE:* ʃ- 70%, sk- 30%
(*born since 1973, 65%*); -dj- 79%, -dʒ- 21%.
~ed d **~es** z **scheduling** 'ʃed jʊl ɪŋ 'ʃedʒ ʊl-;
'sked jʊl-, 'skedʒ ʊl- ‖ 'skedʒ uːl ɪŋ -ᵊl-
scheelite 'ʃiːᵊl aɪt
Scheherazade ʃə ˌher ə 'zɑːd ə ʃɪ-, -ˌhɪər-,
-'zɑːd
Scheldt ʃelt skelt —*Dutch* Schelde ['sxɛl də]
Schelling 'ʃel ɪŋ —*Ger* ['ʃɛl ɪŋ]
schema 'skiːm ə **~s** z **schemata** 'skiːm ət ə
skiː 'mɑːt ə ‖ 'skiːm əţ ə skiː 'mɑːţ ə —*The*

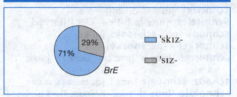

SCHEDULE

◼ ʃ-   ◻ sk-   ◼ -dj-   ◻ -dʒ-

70% / 30% *BrE*

79% / 21% *BrE*

BrE sk- by age

Percentage (80 70 60 50 40 30 20 10 0)

Older ◄——— Speakers ———► Younger

---

classically correct plural form, with initial stress, is being displaced by a new form with penultimate stress.

schematic ski: 'mæt ɪk skɪ- ‖ -'mæt̬ ɪk **~ally**
ᵊl i **~s** s
schematis... —*see* **schematiz...**
schematism 'skiːm ə ˌtɪz əm **~s** z
schematization ˌskiːm ət aɪ 'zeɪʃ ᵊn -ɪ'-‖ -ət ə- **~s** z
schematiz|e 'skiːm ə taɪz **~ed** d **~es** z **~ing** ɪŋ
scheme skiːm **schemed** skiːmd **schemes**
skiːmz **scheming** 'skiːm ɪŋ
schemer 'skiːm ə ‖ -ᵊr **~s** z
Schenectady skɪ 'nekt əd i skə-
Schengen 'ʃeŋ ən —*Ger* ['ʃeŋ ən]
Schering 'ʃɪər ɪŋ ‖ 'ʃɪr- —*Ger* ['ʃeːr ɪŋ]
scherzando skeət 'sænd əʊ sk3ːt-
‖ skert 'saːnd oʊ —*It* [sker 'tsan do] **~s** z
scherz|o 'skeəts |əʊ 'sk3ːt- ‖ 'skerts |oʊ —*It*
['sker tso] **~i** iː **~os** əʊz ‖ oʊz
Scheveningen 'skeɪv ən ɪŋ ən —*Dutch*
['sxe: və nɪŋ ən]
Schiaparelli ˌskæp ə 'rel i ˌʃæp- ‖ ˌskjɑːp- —*It*
[skja pa 'rɛl li]
Schick ʃɪk
Schiedam 'skiː dæm ˌ·'· skɪ- —*Dutch*
[sxi 'dɑm]
Schiffer 'ʃɪf ə ‖ -ᵊr —*Ger* ['ʃɪf ɐ]
Schiller, s~ 'ʃɪl ə ‖ -ᵊr —*Ger* ['ʃɪl ɐ]
schilling 'ʃɪl ɪŋ **~s** z
Schindler 'ʃɪnd lə ‖ -l³r —*Ger* ['ʃɪnd lɐ]
Schiphol 'skɪp ɒl ‖ -oʊl —*Dutch* [sxɪp 'hɔl, '··]
schipperke 'ʃɪp ək i 'skɪp- ‖ -ᵊrk i **~s** z
schism 'skɪz əm 'sɪz- —*The traditional* 'sɪz- *is being displaced, except perhaps among the clergy, by* 'skɪz-. *Preference poll, BrE:* 'skɪz-*71%,* 'sɪz- *29%.* **~s** z
schismatic skɪz 'mæt ɪk sɪz- ‖ -'mæt̬ ɪk **~ally**
ᵊl i **~s** s
schist ʃɪst **schists** ʃɪsts
schistosome 'ʃɪst ə səʊm ‖ -soʊm -zoʊm **~s** z

SCHISM

◼ 'skɪz-   ◼ 'sɪz-

71% / 29% *BrE*

---

schistosomiasis ˌʃɪst ə səʊ 'maɪ əs ɪs §-əs
‖ -ə soʊ-
schizandra skɪt 'sændr ə
schizanthus, S~ skɪt 'sæn'θ əs skɪ 'zæn'θ- **~es**
ɪz əz
schizo 'skɪts əʊ ‖ -oʊ **~s** z
schizo- *comb. form*
with stress-neutral suffix 'skɪts əʊ 'skɪz-,
'skaɪz- — **schizocarp** 'skɪts əʊ kɑːp 'skɪz-,
'skaɪz- ‖ -ə kɑːrp
with stress-imposing suffix skɪt 'sɒ+ skɪ 'zɒ+,
skaɪ- ‖ -'sɑː+ — **schizogony** skɪt 'sɒg ən i
skɪ 'zɒg-, skaɪ- ‖ skɪ 'zɑːg- skɪt 'sɑːg-
schizoid 'skɪts ɔɪd 'skɪdz- **~s** z
schizont 'skɪts ɒnt 'skaɪz-, 'skɪz- ‖ -ɑːnt **~s** s
schizophrenia ˌskɪts əʊ 'friːn i̯ə ‖ ˌ·ə- -'fren-
~s z
schizophrenic ˌskɪts əʊ 'fren ɪk ◄ -'friːn- ‖ -ə-
~ally ᵊl i **~s** s
Schlegel 'ʃleɪg ᵊl —*Ger* ['ʃleː gᵊl]
Schleicher 'ʃlaɪk ə 'ʃlaɪx- ‖ -ᵊr —*Ger* ['ʃlaɪ çɐ]
schlemiel ʃlə 'miːᵊl **~s** z
schlep, schlepp ʃlep **schlepped** ʃlept
schlepping 'ʃlep ɪŋ **schleps, schlepps** ʃleps
Schlesinger 'ʃles ɪndʒ ə 'sles-, -əndʒ- ‖ -ᵊr
Schleswig 'ʃlez vɪg 'ʃles-, -wɪg —*Ger*
['ʃleːs vɪç]
Schleswig-Holstein ˌʃlez vɪg 'hɒl staɪn ˌʃles-,
-wɪg-, -'həʊl- ‖ -'hoʊl- —*Ger*
[ˌʃleːs vɪç 'hɔl ʃtaɪn]
Schliemann 'ʃliː mən -mæn —*Ger* ['ʃliː man]
schlieren 'ʃlɪər ən ‖ 'ʃlɪr ən
Schlitz ʃlɪts
schlock ʃlɒk ‖ ʃlɑːk
schlock|y 'ʃlɒk |i ‖ 'ʃlɑːk |i **~ier** i̯ə ‖ i̯ᵊr **~iest**
i ɪst i̯əst
schlong ʃlɒŋ ‖ ʃlɑːŋ ʃlɔːŋ **schlongs** ʃlɒŋz
‖ ʃlɑːŋz ʃlɔːŋz
schmaltz, schmalz ʃmɔːlts ʃmɒlts, ʃmælts
‖ ʃmɑːlts ʃmɔːlts
schmaltzy, schmalzy 'ʃmɔːlts i 'ʃmɒlts-,
'ʃmælts- ‖ 'ʃmɑːlts i 'ʃmɔːlts-
Schmeichel 'smaɪk ᵊl —*Danish* ['smaɪ g̊l]
Schmidt ʃmɪt
schmo, schmoe ʃməʊ ‖ ʃmoʊ **schmoes** ʃməʊz
‖ ʃmoʊz
schmooze ʃmuːz **schmoozed** ʃmuːzd
schmoozes 'ʃmuːz ɪz -əz **schmoozing**
'ʃmuːz ɪŋ
schmuck ʃmʌk **schmucks** ʃmʌks
Schnabel 'ʃnɑːb ᵊl
schnapps, schnaps ʃnæps
schnauzer 'ʃnaʊts ə ‖ -ᵊr 'ʃnaʊz- **~s** z

S

Schneider, s~ 'ʃnaɪd ə ‖ -ər —Ger ['ʃnai də]
~s z
schnitzel 'ʃnɪts əl △ 'snɪtʃ- ~s z
Schnitzler 'ʃnɪts lə ‖ -lər —Ger ['ʃnɪts lɐ]
schnook ʃnʊk schnooks ʃnʊks
schnorkel —see snorkel
schnorrer 'ʃnɒr ə 'ʃnɔːr ə ‖ 'ʃnɔːr ər 'ʃnʊər ər
~s z
schnoz, schnoz|z ʃnɒz ‖ ʃnɑːz ~zes ɪz əz
schnozzle 'ʃnɒz əl 'snɒz- ‖ 'ʃnɑːz əl ~s z
Schoenberg, Schönberg 'ʃɜːn bɜːg
‖ 'ʃoʊn bɜːg 'ʃɜːn- —Ger ['ʃøːn bɛʁk]
Schofield 'skəʊ fiːəld ‖ 'skoʊ-
schola cantorum ˌskəʊl ə kæn 'tɔːr əm
‖ ˌskoʊl- -'toʊr-
scholar 'skɒl ə ‖ 'skɑːl ər ~s z
scholar|ly 'skɒl ə |li ‖ 'skɑːl ər |li ~liness
li nəs -nɪs
scholarship 'skɒl ə ʃɪp ‖ 'skɑːl ər-
   'scholarship boy
scholastic skə 'læst ɪk skɒ- ~ally əl i ~s s
scholasticism skə 'læst ɪ ˌsɪz əm skɒ-, -'ə-
Scholefield 'skəʊl fiːəld →'skɒʊl- ‖ 'skoʊl-
Scholes skəʊlz →skɒʊlz ‖ skoʊlz
Scholey 'skəʊl i ‖ 'skoʊl i
Scholfield (i) 'skəʊ fiːəld ‖ 'skoʊ-, (ii) 'skəʊl-
→'skɒʊl- ‖ 'skoʊl-
scholiast 'skəʊl i æst əst ‖ 'skoʊl- ~s s
scholi|um 'skəʊl i ˌ|əm ‖ 'skoʊl- ~a ə ~ums
əmz
Scholl (i) ʃɒl ‖ ʃɑːl ʃɔːl, (ii) ʃəʊl →ʃɒʊl ‖ ʃoʊl
Schonberg, Schönberg 'ʃɜːn bɜːg -beəg
‖ 'ʃoʊn bɜːg 'ʃɜːn- —Ger ['ʃøːn bɛʁk]
Schonfield 'skɒn fiːəld ‖ 'skɑːn-
school skuːl schooled skuːld schooling
   'skuːl ɪŋ schools skuːlz
   'school board; ˌschool 'tie; ˌschool
   'uniform; ˌschool 'year
schoolboy 'skuːl bɔɪ ~s z
school|child 'skuːl |tʃaɪəld ~children
   ˌtʃɪldr ən ˌtʃʊldr-
schoolday 'skuːl deɪ ~s z
schoolfellow 'skuːl ˌfel əʊ ‖ -oʊ ~s z
schoolgirl 'skuːl gɜːl ‖ -gɝːl ~s z
school|house 'skuːl |haʊs ~houses ˌhaʊz ɪz
   -əz
schoolkid 'skuːl kɪd ~s z
school-leaver ˌskuːl 'liːv ə '·ˌ·· ‖ -ər ~s z
school-leaving ˌskuːl 'liːv ɪŋ '·ˌ··
school|man 'skuːl |mæn -mən ~men men mən
schoolmarm 'skuːl mɑːm ‖ -mɑːrm ~ish ɪʃ ~s
   z
schoolmast|er 'skuːl ˌmɑːst |ə §-ˌmæst-
   ‖ -ˌmæst |ər ~ering ər ɪŋ ~ers əz ‖ ərz
schoolmate 'skuːl meɪt ~s s
schoolmen 'skuːl men -mən
schoolmistress 'skuːl ˌmɪs trəs -trɪs ~es ɪz əz
schoolmistressy 'skuːl ˌmɪs trəs i -trɪs-
schoolroom 'skuːl ruːm -rʊm ~s z
schoolteacher 'skuːl ˌtiːtʃ ə ‖ -ər ~s z
schoolteaching 'skuːl ˌtiːtʃ ɪŋ
schoolwork 'skuːl wɜːk ‖ -wɝːk
schoolyard 'skuːl jɑːd ‖ -jɑːrd ~s z

schooner 'skuːn ə ‖ -ər ~s z
Schopenhauer 'ʃəʊp ən haʊ ə 'ʃɒp-
   ‖ 'ʃoʊp ən haʊ ˌər —Ger ['ʃoːp n̩ hau ɐ]
schorl ʃɔːl ‖ ʃɔːrl
schottisch|e ʃɒ 'tiːʃ ‖ 'ʃɑːt ɪʃ ~es ɪz əz
Schottky 'ʃɒt ki ‖ 'ʃɑːt ki
Schreiber 'ʃraɪb ə ‖ -ər
Schreiner 'ʃraɪn ə ‖ -ər
Schroder 'ʃrəʊd ə ‖ 'ʃroʊd ər
Schröder 'ʃrɜːd ə ‖ 'ʃroʊd ər 'ʃreɪd- —Ger
   ['ʃʁøː də]
Schrodinger, Schrödinger 'ʃrɜːd ɪŋ ə
   ‖ 'ʃroʊd ɪŋ ər 'ʃreɪd- —Ger ['ʃʁøː dɪŋ ɐ]
Schroeder 'ʃrɜːd ə ‖ 'ʃroʊd ər 'ʃreɪd- —Ger
   ['ʃʁøː də]
schtick ʃtɪk
schtuck ʃtʊk
schtum, schtoom ʃtʊm
schtup ʃtʊp schtupped ʃtʊpt schtupping
   'ʃtʊp ɪŋ schtups ʃtʊps
Schubert 'ʃuːb ət -ɜːt ‖ -ərt —Ger ['ʃu: bɐt]
Schultz, Schulz ʃʊlts
Schumacher 'ʃuː ˌmæk ə ‖ -ər -ˌmɑːk- —Ger
   ['ʃu: ˌmax ɐ]
Schuman 'ʃuːm ən —Fr [ʃu man]
Schumann 'ʃuːm ən -æn, -ɑːn ‖ -ɑːn —Ger
   ['ʃu: man]
schuss ʃʊs ʃuːs, ʃuːʃ —Ger [ʃʊs] schussed ʃʊst
   ʃuːst, ʃuːʃt schusses 'ʃʊs ɪz 'ʃuːs-, 'ʃuːʃ-, -əz
   schussing 'ʃʊs ɪŋ 'ʃuːs-, 'ʃuːʃ-
Schuyler 'skaɪl ə ‖ -ər
Schuylerville 'skaɪl ə vɪl ‖ -ər-
Schuylkill river in PA 'skuːl kɪl 'skuːk əl
schwa ʃwɑː ʃvɑː schwas ʃwɑːz ʃvɑːz
Schwab ʃwɑːb
Schwann ʃwɒn ʃvæn ‖ ʃwɑːn ʃvɑːn —Ger
   [ʃvan]
Schwartz ʃwɔːts ‖ ʃwɔːrts —but as a German
   name, ʃvɑːts ‖ ʃvɑːrts —Ger [ʃvaʁts]
Schwartzenegger 'ʃwɔːts ə neg ə
   ‖ 'ʃwɔːrts ə neg ər —Ger ['ʃvaʁts ən ɛg ɐ]
Schwartzschild 'ʃwɔːts ʃɪld →'ʃwɔːtʃ-; -tʃaɪəld
   ‖ 'ʃwɔːrts- —Ger ['ʃvaʁts ʃɪlt]
Schwarzkopf 'ʃvɑːts kɒpf 'ʃwɑːts-, 'ʃwɔːts-
   ‖ 'ʃwɔːrts kɑːpf 'ʃvɑːrts- —Ger ['ʃvaʁts kɔpf]
Schwarzwald 'ʃvɑːts væld 'ʃwɑːts-, -wæld
   ‖ 'ʃvɑːrts vɑːld —Ger ['ʃvaʁts valt]
Schweitzer 'ʃwaɪts ə 'ʃvaɪts- ‖ -ər —Ger
   ['ʃvai tsɐ]
Schweppes tdmk ʃweps
sciatic saɪ 'æt ɪk ‖ -'æt ɪk
sciatica saɪ 'æt ɪk ə ‖ -'æt-
Scicon tdmk 'saɪ kɒn ‖ -kɑːn
science 'saɪ ənts sciences 'saɪ ənts ɪz -əz
   ˌscience 'fiction; 'science park
scientific ˌsaɪ ən 'tɪf ɪk ◀ ~ally əl i
   ˌscien tific 'method
scientism 'saɪ ən ˌtɪz əm
scientist 'saɪ ənt ɪst §-əst ‖ 'saɪ ənt əst ~s s
scientologist, S~ ˌsaɪ ən 'tɒl ədʒ ɪst §-əst
   ‖ -'tɑːl- ~s s
Scientology tdmk ˌsaɪ ən 'tɒl ədʒ i ‖ -'tɑːl-
sci-fi ˌsaɪ 'faɪ ◀

S

scilicet 'sɪl ɪ set 'saɪl-, -ə-; 'skiːl ɪ ket
scilla, S~ 'sɪl ə ~s z
Scillies 'sɪl iz
Scillonian sɪ 'ləʊn i ən sə- ‖ -'loʊn- ~s z
Scill|y 'sɪl |i ~ies iz
scimitar 'sɪm ɪt ə -ət-; -ɪ tɑː, -ə- ‖ -əţ ᵊr -ə tɑːr ~s z
scintilla sɪn 'tɪl ə ~s z
scintill|ate 'sɪnt ɪ l|eɪt -ə-, -ᵊl |eɪt ‖ 'sɪnţ ᵊl |eɪt ~ated eɪt ɪd -əd ‖ eɪţ əd ~ates eɪts ~ating eɪt ɪŋ ‖ eɪţ ɪŋ
scintillation ˌsɪnt ɪ 'leɪʃ ᵊn -ə-, -ᵊl 'eɪʃ- ‖ ˌsɪnţ ᵊl 'eɪʃ ᵊn ~s z
scintillator 'sɪnt ɪ leɪt ə '-ə-, -ᵊl eɪt ə ‖ 'sɪnţ ᵊl eɪţ ᵊr ~s z
scintillometer ˌsɪnt ɪ 'lɒm ɪt ə ˌ-ə-, -ᵊl 'ɒm-, -ət ə ‖ ˌsɪnţ ᵊl 'ɑːm əţ ᵊr ~s z
sciolism 'saɪ ə ˌlɪz əm -əʊ-
sciolist 'saɪ əl ɪst -əʊl-, §-əst ~s s
sciolistic ˌsaɪ ə 'lɪst ɪk ◂ -əʊ-
scion 'saɪ ən ~s z
Scioto river in OH saɪ 'əʊt əʊ ‖ -'oʊţ ə -'oʊţ oʊ
Scipio 'skɪp i əʊ 'sɪp- ‖ -oʊ
scire facias ˌsaɪᵊr i 'feɪʃ i æs -əs
scirocco, S~ sɪ 'rɒk əʊ sə-, ʃɪ- ‖ -'rɑːk oʊ —It [ʃi 'rɔk ko] ~s z
scirrh|us 'sɪr |əs 'skɪr- ~i aɪ ~ous əs ~uses əs ɪz -əz
scission 'sɪʒ ᵊn 'sɪʃ- ~s z
scissor 'sɪz ə ‖ -ᵊr (!) ~ed d **scissoring** 'sɪz ᵊr ɪŋ ~s z
scissors-and-paste ˌsɪz əz ən 'peɪst →-əm'--, -ənd'-- ‖ ˌsɪz ᵊrz- ˌscissors-and-'paste job
Scituate 'sɪtʃ u eɪt
sclaff sklæf **sclaffed** sklæft **sclaffing** 'sklæf ɪŋ **sclaffs** sklæfs
sclera 'sklɪᵊr ə ‖ 'sklɪr ə 'skler-
sclero- comb. form
　with stress-neutral suffix ¦sklɪᵊr əʊ ¦skler- ‖ ¦sklɪr ə ¦skler- — **scleroderma** ˌsklɪᵊr əʊ 'dɜːm ə ˌskler- ‖ ˌsklɪr ə 'dɜːm ə ˌskler-
　with stress-imposing suffix sklə 'rɒ + sklɪ-, sklɪə-, skle- ‖ sklə 'rɑː + sklɪ- — **sclerotomy** sklə 'rɒt əm i sklɪ-, sklɪə-, skle- ‖ -'rɑːţ-
sclerom|a sklə 'rəʊm |ə sklɪ-, sklɪə-, skle- ‖ -'roʊm |ə ~as əz ~ata ət ə ‖ əţ ə
scleros|is sklə 'rəʊs |ɪs sklɪ-, sklɪə-, skle-, §-əs ‖ -'roʊs |əs ~es iːz
sclerotic sklə 'rɒt ɪk sklɪ-, sklɪə-, skle- ‖ -'rɑːţ ɪk
sclerous 'sklɪᵊr əs 'skler- ‖ 'sklɪr əs 'skler-
Scobell ₍₁₎skəʊ 'bel ‖ 'skoʊ bel
Scobie, Scoby 'skəʊb i ‖ 'skoʊb i
scoff skɒf ‖ skɑːf skɔːf **scoffed** skɒft ‖ skɑːft skɔːft **scoffing/ly** 'skɒf ɪŋ /li ‖ 'skɑːf- 'skɔːf- **scoffs** skɒfs ‖ skɑːfs skɔːfs
scoffer 'skɒf ə ‖ 'skɑːf ᵊr 'skɔːf- ~s z
scofflaw 'skɒf lɔː ‖ 'skɑːf- -lɑː ~s z
Scofield 'skəʊ fiːᵊld ‖ 'skoʊ-
scold skəʊld →skɒʊld ‖ skoʊld **scolded** 'skəʊld ɪd →'skɒʊld-, -əd ‖ 'skoʊld əd

scolding/s 'skəʊld ɪŋ/z →'skɒʊld- ‖ 'skoʊld ɪŋ/z **scolds** skəʊldz →skɒʊldz ‖ skoʊldz
scoliosis ˌskɒl i 'əʊs ɪs ˌskəʊl-, §-əs ‖ ˌskoʊl i 'oʊs əs ˌskɑːl-
scoliotic ˌskɒl i 'ɒt ɪk ◂ ˌskəʊl- ‖ ˌskoʊl i 'ɑːţ ɪk ◂ ˌskɑːl-
scollop 'skɒl əp ‖ 'skɑːl əp ~ed t ~ing ɪŋ ~s s
scombroid 'skɒm brɔɪd ‖ 'skɑːm- ~s z
sconce skɒnˡs ‖ skɑːnˡs **sconced** skɒnˡst ‖ skɑːnˡst **sconces** 'skɒnˡs ɪz -əz ‖ 'skɑːnˡs əz **sconcing** 'skɒnˡs ɪŋ ‖ 'skɑːnˡs ɪŋ

SCONE

65% skɒn
35% skəʊn
BrE

scone skɒn skəʊn ‖ skoʊn skɑːn — Preference poll, BrE: skɒn 65%, skəʊn 35%. **scones** skɒnz skəʊnz ‖ skoʊnz skɑːnz
Scone place in Tayside skuːn
Scooby-doo ˌskuːb i 'duː
scoop skuːp **scooped** skuːpt **scooping** 'skuːp ɪŋ **scoops** skuːps
scooper 'skuːp ə ‖ -ᵊr ~s z
scoot skuːt **scooted** 'skuːt ɪd -əd ‖ 'skuːţ əd **scooting** 'skuːt ɪŋ ‖ 'skuːţ ɪŋ **scoots** skuːts
scoot|er 'skuːt |ə ‖ 'skuːţ |ᵊr ~ered əd ‖ ᵊrd ~ering ᵊr ɪŋ ~ers əz ‖ ᵊrz
-scope skəʊp ‖ skoʊp — **microscope** 'maɪk rə skəʊp ‖ -skoʊp
scope skəʊp ‖ skoʊp **scopes** skəʊps ‖ skoʊps **scoping** 'skəʊp ɪŋ ‖ 'skoʊp ɪŋ
Scopes skəʊps ‖ skoʊps
-scopic 'skɒp ɪk ‖ 'skɑːp ɪk — **microscopic** ˌmaɪk rəʊ 'skɒp ɪk ◂ -rə 'skɑːp ɪk
scopolamine skəʊ 'pɒl ə miːn -mɪn, §-mən ‖ skə 'pɑːl-; ˌskoʊp ə 'læm ən
scopoline 'skəʊp ə liːn -lɪn, §-lən ‖ 'skoʊp-
scops skɒps ‖ skɑːps
Scopus 'skəʊp əs ‖ 'skoʊp əs
-scopy stress-imposing + skəp i — **microscopy** maɪ 'krɒsk əp i ‖ -'krɑːsk-
scorbutic skɔː 'bjuːt ɪk ‖ skɔːr 'bjuːţ ɪk ~ally ᵊl i
scorch skɔːtʃ ‖ skɔːrtʃ **scorched** skɔːtʃt ‖ skɔːrtʃt **scorches** 'skɔːtʃ ɪz -əz ‖ 'skɔːrtʃ əz **scorching/ly** 'skɔːtʃ ɪŋ /li ‖ 'skɔːrtʃ ɪŋ /li ˌscorched 'earth, ˌscorched 'earth ˌpolicy
scorcher 'skɔːtʃ ə ‖ 'skɔːrtʃ ᵊr ~s z
score skɔː ‖ skɔːr skoʊr **scored** skɔːd ‖ skɔːrd skoʊrd **scores** skɔːz ‖ skɔːrz skoʊrz **scoring** 'skɔːr ɪŋ ‖ 'skoʊr- 'score draw
scoreboard 'skɔː bɔːd ‖ 'skɔːr bɔːrd 'skoʊr boʊrd ~s z
scorebook 'skɔː bʊk §-buːk ‖ 'skɔːr- 'skoʊr- ~s s

scorecard 'skɔː kɑːd ‖ 'skɔːr kɑːrd 'skoʊr- ~s z
scorekeeper 'skɔː ˌkiːp ə ‖ 'skɔːr ˌkiːp ᵊr
  'skoʊr- ~s z
scoreless 'skɔː ləs -lɪs ‖ 'skɔːr- 'skoʊr-
scoreline 'skɔː laɪn ‖ 'skɔːr- ~s z
scorer 'skɔːr ə ‖ -ᵊr 'skoʊr- ~s z
scoresheet 'skɔː ʃiːt ‖ 'skɔːr- 'skoʊr- ~s s
scoria 'skɔːr i ə skə 'riː ə ‖ 'skoʊr-
scoriaceous ˌskɔːr i 'eɪʃ əs ◄ ‖ ˌskoʊr-
scorn skɔːn ‖ skɔːrn **scorned** skɔːnd ‖ skɔːrnd
  scorning 'skɔːn ɪŋ ‖ 'skɔːrn ɪŋ **scorns** skɔːnz
  ‖ skɔːrnz
scornful 'skɔːn fᵊl -fʊl ‖ 'skɔːrn- **~ly** ˌi **~ness**
  nəs nɪs
Scorpian 'skɔːp i ən ‖ 'skɔːrp- ~s z
Scorpio 'skɔːp i əʊ ‖ 'skɔːrp i oʊ ~s z
scorpion 'skɔːp i ən ‖ 'skɔːrp- ~s z
Scorpius 'skɔːp i əs ‖ 'skɔːrp-
Scorsese skɔː 'seɪz i ‖ skɔːr-
scorzonera ˌskɔːz ə 'nɪər ə ‖ ˌskɔːrz ə 'ner ə
Scot, scot skɒt ‖ skɑːt **Scots** skɒts ‖ skɑːts
Scotcade tdmk 'skɒt keɪd ‖ 'skɑːt-
Scotch, s~ skɒtʃ ‖ skɑːtʃ **scotched** skɒtʃt
  ‖ skɑːtʃt **scotches** 'skɒtʃ ɪz -əz ‖ 'skɑːtʃ əz
  scotching 'skɒtʃ ɪŋ ‖ 'skɑːtʃ ɪŋ
  ˌScotch 'broth; ˌScotch 'egg; ˌScotch
  'mist; ˌScotch 'pancake; ˌScotch 'tape
  tdmk, '· ·; ˌScotch 'whisky
Scotchgard tdmk 'skɒtʃ gɑːd ‖ 'skɑːtʃ gɑːrd
Scotch-Irish ˌskɒtʃ 'aɪᵊr ɪʃ ◄ ‖ ˌskɑːtʃ-
Scotch|man 'skɒtʃ |mən ‖ 'skɑːtʃ- **~men** mən
  ~woman ˌwʊm ən **~women** ˌwɪm ɪn §-ən
scoter 'skəʊt ə ‖ 'skoʊt̬ ᵊr ~s z
scot-free ˌskɒt 'friː ‖ ˌskɑːt-
Scotia, s~ 'skəʊʃ ə ‖ 'skoʊʃ ə
Scotland 'skɒt lənd ‖ 'skɑːt-
  ˌScotland 'Yard
scotoma skɒ 'təʊm ə skəʊ- ‖ skə 'toʊm ə
  skoʊ- ~s z
Scots skɒts ‖ skɑːts
  ˌScots 'pine
Scots|man 'skɒts |mən ‖ 'skɑːts- **~men** mən
Scotstoun 'skɒts tən ‖ 'skɑːts-
Scots|woman 'skɒts |ˌwʊm ən ‖ 'skɑːts-
  ~women ˌwɪm ɪn §-ən
Scott skɒt ‖ skɑːt
Scotticism 'skɒt ɪ ˌsɪz əm -ə- ‖ 'skɑːt̬ ə- ~s z
Scottie, s~ 'skɒt i ‖ 'skɑːt̬ i ~s z
Scottish 'skɒt ɪʃ ‖ 'skɑːt̬ ɪʃ **~ness** nəs nɪs
  ˌScottish 'Gaelic; ˌScottish 'terrier
Scottsdale 'skɒts deɪᵊl ‖ 'skɑːts-
Scott|y, s~ 'skɒt |i ‖ 'skɑːt̬ |i **~ies, ~y's** iz
Scotus 'skəʊt əs ‖ 'skoʊt̬ əs
scoundrel 'skaʊndr əl ~s z
scoundrelly 'skaʊndr əl i
scour 'skaʊ ə ‖ skaʊ ᵊr **scoured** skaʊ əd
  ‖ skaʊ ᵊrd **scouring** 'skaʊ ər ɪŋ ‖ 'skaʊ ᵊr ɪŋ
  scours 'skaʊ əz ‖ skaʊ ᵊrz
scourer 'skaʊ ər ə ‖ 'skaʊ ᵊr ᵊr ~s z
scourge skɜːdʒ ‖ skɜːːdʒ **scourged** skɜːdʒd
  ‖ skɜːːdʒd **scourges** 'skɜːdʒ ɪz -əz
  ‖ 'skɜːːdʒ əz **scourging** 'skɜːdʒ ɪŋ
  ‖ 'skɜːːdʒ ɪŋ

Scouse, s~ skaʊs
Scouser 'skaʊs ə ‖ -ᵊr ~s z
scout, Scout skaʊt **scouted** 'skaʊt ɪd -əd
  ‖ 'skaʊt̬ əd **scouting** 'skaʊt ɪŋ ‖ skaʊt̬ ɪŋ
  scouts skaʊts
scouter, S~ 'skaʊt ə ‖ 'skaʊt̬ ᵊr ~s z
scoutmaster 'skaʊt ˌmɑːst ə §-ˌmæst-
  ‖ -ˌmæst ᵊr ~s z
scow skaʊ **scows** skaʊz
scowl skaʊl **scowled** skaʊld **scowler/s**
  'skaʊl ə/z ‖ -ᵊr/z **scowling/ly** 'skaʊl ɪŋ /li
  scowls skaʊlz
scrabbl|e, S~ tdmk 'skræb ᵊl **~ed** d **~es** z **~ing**
  ɪŋ
scrabbl|y 'skræb ᵊl |i **~ier** i ə ‖ i ᵊr **~iest** i ɪst
  i əst
scrag skræg **scragged** skrægd **scragging**
  'skræg ɪŋ **scrags** skrægz
  ˌscrag 'end
scraggl|y 'skræg ᵊl |i **~ier** i ə ‖ i ᵊr **~iest** i ɪst
  i əst **~iness** i nəs i nɪs
scragg|y 'skræg |i **~ier** i ə ‖ i ᵊr **~iest** i ɪst
  i əst **~ily** ɪ li əl i **~iness** i nəs i nɪs
scram skræm **scrammed** skræmd **scramming**
  'skræm ɪŋ **scrams** skræmz
scrambl|e 'skræm bᵊl **~ed** d **~es** z **~ing** ɪŋ
  ˌscrambled 'egg
scrambler 'skræm blə ‖ -blᵊr ~s z
scramjet 'skræm dʒet ~s s
scran skræn
Scranton 'skrænt ən ‖ -ᵊn
scrap skræp **scrapped** skræpt **scrapping**
  'skræp ɪŋ **scraps** skræps
  'scrap heap; 'scrap ˌiron; 'scrap ˌpaper,
  ˌ ·'· ·
scrapbook 'skræp bʊk §-buːk ~s s
scrape skreɪp **scraped** skreɪpt **scrapes** skreɪps
  scraping/s 'skreɪp ɪŋ/z
scrapeover 'skreɪp ˌəʊv ə ‖ -ˌoʊv ᵊr ~s z
scraper 'skreɪp ə ‖ -ᵊr ~s z
scraperboard 'skreɪp ə bɔːd ‖ -ᵊr bɔːrd -boʊrd
  ~s z
scrapheap 'skræp hiːp ~s s
scrapie 'skreɪp i
scraping 'skreɪp ɪŋ ~s z
scrapp... —see **scrap**
scrapple 'skræp ᵊl
scrapp|y 'skræp |i **~ier** i ə ‖ i ᵊr **~iest** i ɪst
  i əst **~ily** ɪ li əl i **~iness** i nəs i nɪs
scratch skrætʃ **scratched** skrætʃt **scratches**
  'skrætʃ ɪz -əz **scratching/s** 'skrætʃ ɪŋ/z
  'scratch ˌpaper; 'scratch sheet; 'scratch
  test
scratch-and-sniff ˌskrætʃ ən 'snɪf ◄
scratchcard 'skrætʃ kɑːd ‖ -kɑːrd ~s z
scratcher 'skrætʃ ə ‖ -ᵊr ~s z
scratchmaster 'skrætʃ ˌmɑːst ə §-ˌmæst-
  ‖ -ˌmæst ᵊr ~s z
scratchpad 'skrætʃ pæd ~s z
Scratchwood 'skrætʃ wʊd
scratch|y 'skrætʃ |i **~ier** i ə ‖ i ᵊr **~iest** i ɪst
  i əst **~ily** ɪ li əl i **~iness** i nəs i nɪs

S

scrawl skrɔːl ‖ skrɑːl **scrawled** skrɔːld ‖ skrɑːld
  scrawling ˈskrɔːl ɪŋ ‖ ˈskrɑːl- **scrawls** skrɔːlz
  ‖ skrɑːlz
scrawler ˈskrɔːl ə ‖ -ᵊr ˈskrɑːl- **~s** z
scrawl|y ˈskrɔːl |i ‖ ˈskrɑːl- **~ier** i ə ‖ i ᵊr **~iest**
  i ɪst i əst **~iness** i nəs i nɪs
scrawn|y ˈskrɔːn |i ‖ ˈskrɑːn- **~ier** i ə ‖ i ᵊr
  ~iest i ɪst i əst **~ily** ɪ li əl i **~iness** i nəs i nɪs
scream skriːm **screamed** skriːmd
  screaming/ly ˈskriːm ɪŋ /li **screams** skriːmz
screamer ˈskriːm ə ‖ -ᵊr **~s** z
scree skriː **screes** skriːz
screech skriːtʃ **screeched** skriːtʃt **screeches**
  ˈskriːtʃ ɪz -əz **screeching** ˈskriːtʃ ɪŋ
  ˈscreech owl
screecher ˈskriːtʃ ə ‖ -ᵊr **~s** z
screech|y ˈskriːtʃ| i **~ier** i ə ‖ i ᵊr **~iest** i ɪst
  i əst
screed skriːd **screeds** skriːdz
screen skriːn **screened** skriːnd **screening/s**
  ˈskriːn ɪŋ/z **screens** skriːnz
  ˈscreen ˌprinting; **ˈscreen ˌsaver**; **ˈscreen
  test**
screengrab ˈskriːn græb →ˈskriːn- **~s** z
screenplay ˈskriːn pleɪ →ˈskriːm- **~s** z
screenshot ˈskriːn ʃɒt ‖ -ʃɑːt **~s** s
screenwrit|er ˈskriːn ˌraɪt |ə ‖ -ˌraɪt |ᵊr **~ers**
  əz ‖ ᵊrz **~ing** ɪŋ
screw skruː **screwed** skruːd **screwing**
  ˈskruː ɪŋ **screws** skruːz
  ˈscrew cap; **ˈscrew jack**; **ˈscrew pine**;
  ˈscrew thread; **ˈscrew top** n ˌ · ˈ·
screwball ˈskruː bɔːl ‖ -bɑːl **~s** z
screwdriver ˈskruː ˌdraɪv ə ‖ -ᵊr **~s** z
screw-top adj ˌskruː ˈtɒp ◄ ' ·· ‖ -ˈtɑːp ◄
  ˌscrew-top ˈjar
screw-up ˈskruː ʌp **~s** s
screwworm ˈskruː wɜːm ‖ -wɜːm **~s** z
screw|y ˈskruː |i **~ier** i ə ‖ i ᵊr **~iest** i ɪst i əst
Scriabin skri ˈæb ɪn §-ən; ˈskriːəb ɪn ‖ -ˈɑːb ən
  —Russ [ˈskrʲæ bʲɪn]
scribal ˈskraɪb ᵊl
scribbl|e ˈskrɪb ᵊl **~ed** d **~es** z **~ing/s** ɪŋ/z
scribbler ˈskrɪb ᵊl ə ‖ ᵊr **~s** z
scribe skraɪb **scribed** skraɪbd **scribes** skraɪbz
  scribing ˈskraɪb ɪŋ
scriber ˈskraɪb ə ‖ -ᵊr **~s** z
Scribner ˈskrɪb nə ‖ -nᵊr
scrim skrɪm **scrims** skrɪmz
Scrimgeour, Scrimger ˈskrɪm dʒə ‖ -dʒᵊr
scrimmag|e ˈskrɪm ɪdʒ **~ed** d **~es** ɪz əz **~ing**
  ɪŋ
scrimp skrɪmp **scrimped** skrɪmpt **scrimping**
  ˈskrɪmp ɪŋ **scrimps** skrɪmps
scrimshank ˈskrɪm ʃæŋk **~ed** t **~er/s** ə/z
  ‖ ᵊr/z **~ing** ɪŋ **~s** s
scrimshaw ˈskrɪm ʃɔː ‖ -ʃɑ: **~ed** d
  scrimshawing ˈskrɪm ʃɔːʳ ɪŋ ‖ -ʃɔː ɪŋ -ʃɑː- **~s**
  z
scrip skrɪp **scrips** skrɪps
  ˈscrip ˌissue
Scripps skrɪps
scripsit ˈskrɪps ɪt §-ət

script skrɪpt **scripted** ˈskrɪpt ɪd -əd **scripting**
  ˈskrɪpt ɪŋ **scripts** skrɪpts
scriptori|um skrɪp ˈtɔːr i ˌ|əm ‖ -ˈtour- **~a** ə
  ~ums əmz
scriptural ˈskrɪp tʃᵊr əl -ʃᵊr ˌ **~ly** i
scripture, S~ ˈskrɪp tʃə -ʃə ‖ -tʃᵊr **~s** z
scriptwriter ˈskrɪpt ˌraɪt ə ‖ -ˌraɪt ᵊr **~s** z
scrivener, S~ ˈskrɪv ᵊn ə ‖ ᵊr **~s** z
scrod skrɒd ‖ skrɑːd **scrods** skrɒdz ‖ skrɑːdz
scrofula ˈskrɒf jʊl ə §-jəl- ‖ ˈskrɑːf jəl ə ˈskrɔːf-
scrofulous ˈskrɒf jʊl əs §-jəl- ‖ ˈskrɑːf jəl əs
  ˈskrɔːf- **~ly** li **~ness** nəs nɪs
scroggin ˈskrɒg ɪn -ən ‖ ˈskrɑːg ən
scroll skrəʊl →skrɒʊl ‖ skroʊl **scrolled**
  skrəʊld →skrɒʊld ‖ skroʊld **scrolling**
  ˈskrəʊl ɪŋ →ˈskrɒʊl- ‖ ˈskroʊl ɪŋ **scrolls**
  skrəʊlz →skrɒʊlz ‖ skroʊlz
scrollwork ˈskrəʊl wɜːk →ˈskrɒʊl-
  ‖ ˈskroʊl wɜːk
Scrooby ˈskruːb i
Scrooge, s~ skruːdʒ **Scrooges, s~** ˈskruːdʒ ɪz
  -əz
scrot|um ˈskrəʊt |əm ‖ ˈskroʊt |əm **~a** ə **~al**
  ᵊl **~ums** əmz
scrounge skraʊndʒ **scrounged** skraʊndʒd
  scrounges ˈskraʊndʒ ɪz -əz **scrounging**
  ˈskraʊndʒ ɪŋ
scrounger ˈskraʊndʒ ə ‖ -ᵊr **~s** z
scrub skrʌb **scrubbed** skrʌbd **scrubbing**
  ˈskrʌb ɪŋ **scrubs** skrʌbz
  ˈscrubbing brush, **ˈscrub brush**
scrubber ˈskrʌb ə ‖ -ᵊr **~s** z
scrubb|y ˈskrʌb |i **~ier** i ə ‖ i ᵊr **~iest** i ɪst i əst
  ~iness i nəs i nɪs
scrubland ˈskrʌb lənd -lænd ‖ -lænd
scruff skrʌf **scruffs** skrʌfs
scruff|y ˈskrʌf |i **~ier** i ə ‖ i ᵊr **~iest** i ɪst i əst
  ~ily ɪ li əl i **~iness** i nəs i nɪs
scrum skrʌm **scrummed** skrʌmd **scrumming**
  ˈskrʌm ɪŋ **scrums** skrʌmz
scrumcap ˈskrʌm kæp **~s** s
scrum|half ˌskrʌm |ˈhɑːf §-ˈhæf ‖ -|ˈhæf
  ~halves ˈhɑːvz §ˈhævz ‖ ˈhævz
scrummag|e ˈskrʌm ɪdʒ **~ed** d **~es** ɪz əz **~ing**
  ɪŋ
scrump skrʌmp **scrumped** skrʌmpt
  scrumping ˈskrʌmp ɪŋ **scrumps** skrʌmps
scrumptious ˈskrʌmp ʃəs **~ly** li **~ness** nəs nɪs
scrumpy ˈskrʌmp i
scrunch skrʌntʃ **scrunched** skrʌntʃt
  scrunches ˈskrʌntʃ ɪz -əz **scrunching**
  ˈskrʌntʃ ɪŋ
scrunch|ie, scrunch|y ˈskrʌntʃ| i **~ies** iz
scrupl|e ˈskruːp ᵊl **~ed** d **~es** z **~ing** ɪŋ
scrupulosit|y ˌskruːp jʊ ˈlɒs ət |i ˌ·jə-
  ‖ -jə ˈlɑːs əţ| i **~ies** iz
scrupulous ˈskruːp jʊl əs -jəl- ‖ -jəl əs **~ly** li
  ~ness nəs nɪs
scrutable ˈskruːt əb ᵊl ‖ ˈskruːţ-
scrutator skruː ˈteɪt ə ‖ -ˈteɪt ᵊr **~s** z
scrutineer ˌskruːt ɪ ˈnɪə -ə-, -ᵊn ˈɪə
  ‖ ˌskruːt ᵊn ˈɪᵊr **~s** z

S

scrutinis|e, scrutiniz|e 'skruːt ɪ naɪz -ə-, -ᵊn aɪz ‖ -ᵊn aɪz **~ed** d **~es** ɪz əz **~ing** ɪŋ
scrutin|y 'skruːt ɪn |i -ən‿i ‖ -ᵊn‿|i **~ies** iz
Scruton 'skruːt ᵊn
scry skraɪ **scried** skraɪd **scries** skraɪz **scrying** 'skraɪ ɪŋ
Scrymgeour 'skrɪm dʒə ‖ -dʒᵊr
SCSI 'skʌz i
scuba 'skuːb ə
  'scuba ˌdiving
scud skʌd **scudded** 'skʌd ɪd -əd **scudding** 'skʌd ɪŋ **scuds** skʌdz
Scudamore 'skjuːd ə mɔː 'skuːd- ‖ -mɔːr -muᵊr
scuff skʌf **scuffed** skʌft **scuffing** 'skʌf ɪŋ **scuffs** skʌfs
scuffl|e 'skʌf ᵊl **~ed** d **~es** z **~ing** ‿ɪŋ
scuffmark 'skʌf mɑːk ‖ -mɑːrk **~s** s
scull skʌl (= skull) **sculled** skʌld **sculling** 'skʌl ɪŋ **sculls** skʌlz
sculler 'skʌl ə ‖ -ᵊr **~s** z
sculler|y 'skʌl ər‿|i **~ies** iz
Sculley 'skʌl i
Scullin 'skʌl ɪn §-ən
scullion 'skʌl i ən ‖ 'skʌl jən **~s** z
Scully 'skʌl i
sculpsit 'skʌlps ɪt §-ət
sculpt skʌlpt **sculpted** 'skʌlpt ɪd -əd **sculpting** 'skʌlpt ɪŋ **sculpts** skʌlpts
sculptor 'skʌlpt ə ‖ -ᵊr **~s** z
sculptress 'skʌlp trəs -trɪs, -tres **~es** ɪz əz
sculptural 'skʌlp tʃᵊr‿əl -ʃᵊr- **~ly** li
sculp|ture 'skʌlp |tʃə -ʃə ‖ -|tʃᵊr **~tured** tʃəd ʃəd ‖ tʃᵊrd **~tures** tʃəz ʃəz ‖ tʃᵊrz **~turing** tʃər ɪŋ ʃər‿ɪŋ
sculpturesque ˌskʌlp tʃə 'resk ◄ -ʃə- **~ly** li **~ness** nəs nɪs
scum skʌm **scummed** skʌmd **scumming** 'skʌm ɪŋ **scums** skʌmz
scumbag 'skʌm bæg **~s** z
scumbl|e 'skʌm bᵊl **~ed** d **~es** z **~ing** ‿ɪŋ
scummy 'skʌm i
scuncheon 'skʌntʃ ən **~s** z
scunge skʌndʒ
scung|y 'skʌndʒ |i **~ier** i ə ‖ i ᵊr **~ies** iz **~iest** i ɪst ‿əst
scunner 'skʌn ə ‖ -ᵊr **~ed** d **scunnering** 'skʌn ər‿ɪŋ **~s** z
Scunthorpe 'skʌn θɔːp ‖ -θɔːrp
scup skʌp
scupper 'skʌp ə ‖ -ᵊr **~ed** d **scuppering** 'skʌp ər‿ɪŋ **~s** z
Scuppernong, s~ 'skʌp ə nɒŋ ‖ -ᵊr nɑːŋ -nɔːŋ **~s** z
scurf skɜːf ‖ skɜːf
scurf|y 'skɜːf |i ‖ 'skɜːf |i **~iness** i nəs i nɪs
scurri... —see **scurry**
scurrilit|y skə 'rɪl ət |i skʌ-, -ɪt- ‖ -əṭ |i **~ies** iz
scurrilous 'skʌr əl əs -ɪl- ‖ 'skɜ·ː- **~ly** li **~ness** nəs nɪs
scurr|y 'skʌr |i ‖ 'skɜ·ː |i **~ied** id **~ies** iz **~ying** i‿ɪŋ
S-curve 'es kɜːv ‖ -kɜ·ːv **~s** z

scurv|y 'skɜːv |i ‖ 'skɜ·ːv |i **~ier** i ə ‖ i ᵊr **~iest** i ɪst i əst **~ily** ɪ li əl i **~iness** i nəs i nɪs
'scuse skjuːz
scut skʌt **scuts** skʌts
scuta —see **scutum**
Scutari 'skuːt ər i sku 'tɑːr i ‖ 'skuːṭ ər i —It ['sku: ta ɾi]
scutch skʌtʃ **scutched** skʌtʃt **scutches** 'skʌtʃ ɪz -əz **scutching** 'skʌtʃ ɪŋ
scutcheon 'skʌtʃ ən **~s** z
scute skjuːt skuːt **scutes** skjuːts skuːts
scutell|um skju 'tel |əm sku- **~a** ə
scutt|er 'skʌt |ə ‖ 'skʌṭ |ᵊr **~ered** əd ‖ -ᵊrd **~ering** ər ɪŋ ‖ ᵊr ɪŋ **~ers** əz ‖ -ᵊrz
scuttl|e 'skʌt ᵊl ‖ 'skʌṭ ᵊl **~ed** d **~es** z **~ing** ‿ɪŋ
scuttlebutt 'skʌt ᵊl bʌt ‖ 'skʌṭ- **~s** s
scut|um, S~ 'skjuːt |əm 'skuːt- ‖ 'skjuːṭ |əm 'skuːṭ- **~a** ə
scuzz skʌz
scuzz|y 'skʌz |i **~ier** i ə ‖ i ᵊr **~iest** i ɪst i əst
Scylla 'sɪl ə
scythe saɪð §saɪθ **scythed** saɪðd §saɪθt **scythes** saɪðz §saɪθs **scything** 'saɪð ɪŋ §'saɪθ-
Scythi|a 'sɪð i‿|ə 'sɪθ- ‖ 'sɪθ- **~an/s** ən/z
SDI ˌes di: 'aɪ
SDLP ˌes di el 'piː
SDP ˌes di: 'piː
se in Latin expressions seɪ siː, in French expressions sə —see also phrases with this word
SE ˌes 'iː ◄ —see southeast, southeastern
sea siː (= see) **seas** siːz
  'sea aˌnemone; 'sea breeze, ˌ· '·; 'sea ˌcaptain; 'sea change; 'sea cow; 'sea dog; ˌsea 'green◄; ˌsea ˌisland 'cotton; 'sea king; 'sea legs; 'sea ˌlevel; 'sea ˌlion; 'sea mile; 'sea mist; 'sea ˌpower; 'Sea Scout; 'sea ˌserpent; 'sea slug; 'sea ˌurchin
seabed 'siː bed
Seabee 'siː biː **~s** z
seabird 'siː bɜːd ‖ -bɜ·ːd **~s** z
seaboard 'siː bɔːd ‖ -bɔːrd -bourd
Seaborg 'siː bɔːg ‖ -bɔːrg
seaborne 'siː bɔːn ‖ -bɔːrn -bourn
seacoast 'siː kəʊst ‖ -koʊst **~s** s
seafarer 'siː ˌfeər ə ‖ -ˌfer ᵊr -ˌfær- **~s** z
seafaring 'siː ˌfeər ɪŋ ‖ -ˌfer ɪŋ -ˌfær-
seafood 'siː fuːd
Seaford (i) 'siːf əd ‖ -ᵊrd, (ii) ˌsiː 'fɔːd ‖ -'fɔːrd -'fourd —Both (i) and (ii) are used for the place in East Sussex; the place in Long Island, NY is (i)
Seaforth 'siː fɔːθ ‖ -fɔːrθ -fourθ
seafront 'siː frʌnt **~s** s
Seaga si 'ɑːg ə
Seagal 'siːg ᵊl
seagirt 'siː gɜːt ‖ -gɜ·ːt
seagoing 'siː ˌgəʊ ɪŋ ‖ -ˌgoʊ ɪŋ
sea-green ˌsiː 'griːn ◄
seagull 'siː gʌl **~s** z
seahors|e 'siː hɔːs ‖ -hɔːrs **~es** ɪz əz
seakale 'siː keɪᵊl

seal, Seal siːᵊl **sealed** siːᵊld **sealing** 'siːᵊl ɪŋ
  seals siːᵊlz
  'sealing wax
sealant 'siːᵊl ənt ~s s
Seale siːᵊl
sealer 'siːᵊl ə ‖ -ᵊr ~s z
Sealey 'siːl i
sealift 'siː lɪft ~s s
Sealink *tdmk* 'siː lɪŋk
sealskin 'siːᵊl skɪn
Sealyham 'siːl i‿əm ‖ -hæm ~s z
seam siːm *(= seem)* **seamed** siːmd **seaming**
  'siːm ɪŋ **seams** siːmz
sea|man, S~ 'siː |mən ~men mən men
seaman|like 'siː mən |laɪk ~ship ʃɪp
Seamas 'ʃeɪm əs
seamen 'siː mən -men
seamer, S~ 'siːm ə ‖ -ᵊr ~s z
seamless 'siːm ləs -lɪs ~ly li ~ness nəs nɪs
seamstress 'semᵖs trəs 'siːmᵖs-, -trɪs ‖ 'siːmᵖs-
  ~es ɪz əz
Seamus 'ʃeɪm əs
seam|y 'siːm |i ~ier i‿ə ‖ i‿ᵊr ~iest i‿ɪst i‿əst
  ~iness i nəs i nɪs
Sean ʃɔːn ‖ ʃɑːn —*Irish* Seán [ʃɑːn]
Seanad 'ʃæn əd -əð —*Irish* ['ʃa nəd]
seanc|e, séanc|e 'seɪ ɒ̃s -ɑːn¹s, -ɒn¹s ‖ -ɑːn¹s
  —*Fr* [se ɑ̃ːs] ~es ɪz əz
seaplane 'siː pleɪn ~s z
seaport 'siː pɔːt ‖ -pɔːrt -poʊrt ~s s
sear sɪə ‖ sɪʳr **seared** sɪəd ‖ sɪʳrd **searing/ly**
  'sɪər ɪŋ /li ‖ 'sɪr ɪŋ /li **sears** sɪəz ‖ sɪʳrz
search sɜːtʃ ‖ sɜːtʃ **searched** sɜːtʃt ‖ sɜːtʃt
  searches 'sɜːtʃ ɪz -əz ‖ 'sɜːtʃ əz **searching/ly**
  'sɜːtʃ ɪŋ /li ‖ 'sɜːtʃ ɪŋ /li
  'search ,party; 'search ,warrant
searcher 'sɜːtʃ ə ‖ 'sɜːtʃ ᵊr ~s z
searchlight 'sɜːtʃ laɪt ‖ 'sɜːtʃ- ~s s
Searcy *(i)* 'sɪəs i ‖ 'sɪrs i, *(ii)* 'sɜːs i ‖ 'sɜːs i
  —*The place in AL is (ii)*
Searle sɜːl ‖ sɜːl
Sears sɪəz ‖ sɪʳrz
Seascale 'siː skeɪᵊl
seascape 'siː skeɪp ~s s
seashell 'siː ʃel ~s z
seashore 'siː ʃɔː ‖ -ʃɔːr -ʃoʊr ~s z
seasick 'siː sɪk
seasickness 'siː sɪk nəs -,sɪk-, -nɪs
seaside 'siː saɪd ,·'·
season 'siːz ᵊn ~ed d ~ing ɪŋ ~s z
  'season ,ticket ‖ ,·'··
seasonab|le 'siːz ᵊn‿əb |ᵊl ~ly li
seasonal 'siːz ᵊn‿əl ~ly i
seasonality ,siːz ə 'næl ət i -ɪt i ‖ -ət i
seasoning 'siːz ᵊn‿ɪŋ ~s z
seat siːt **seated** 'siːt ɪd -əd ‖ 'siːt̬ əd **seating**
  'siːt ɪŋ ‖ 'siːt̬ ɪŋ **seats** siːts
  'seat belt
SEAT *tdmk* 'seɪ æt -ət ‖ -ɑːt
-seater 'siːt ə ‖ 'siːt̬ ᵊr — **three-seater**
  ,θriː 'siːt ə ◄ ‖ -'siːt̬ ᵊr ◄
Seathwaite 'siː θweɪt
seating 'siːt ɪŋ ‖ 'siːt̬ ɪŋ ~s z

seatmate 'siːt meɪt ~s s
SEATO 'siːt əʊ ‖ -oʊ
seat-of-the-pants ,siːt əv ðə 'pænts ‖ ,siːt̬-
Seaton 'siːt ᵊn
Seattle si 'æt ᵊl ‖ -'æt̬ ᵊl
seawall ,siː 'wɔːl '·· ‖ -wɑːl ~s z
seaward 'siː wəd ‖ -wᵊrd ~s z
seawater 'siː ,wɔːt ə ‖ -,wɔːt̬ ᵊr -,wɑːt̬-
seaway 'siː weɪ ~s z
seaweed 'siː wiːd
seaworth|y 'siː ,wɜːð |i ‖ -,wɜːð |i ~iness
  i nəs i nɪs
Seb seb
sebaceous sə 'beɪʃ əs sɪ-
Sebastian sə 'bæst i‿ən sɪ- ‖ sə 'bæs tʃən
Sebastopol sə 'bæst ə pɒl sɪ-, -pᵊl ‖ -poʊl
  —*Russ* Sevastopol [sʲɪ vʌ 'sto pəlʲ]
Sebba 'seb ə
seborrhea, seborrhoea ,seb ə 'riː‿ə
Sebring 'siːb rɪŋ
sebum 'siːb əm
sec sek
SECAM 'siː kæm
secant 'siːk ᵊnt 'sek- -ænt ~s s
secateurs 'sek ət əz -ə tɜːz, ,sek ə 'tɜːz
  ‖ ,sek ə 'tɜːz
Secaucus sɪ 'kɔːk əs sə- ‖ -'kɑːk-
secco 'sek əʊ ‖ -oʊ —*It* ['sek ko] ~s z
Seccotine *tdmk* 'sek ə tiːn
seced|e sɪ 'siːd sə- ~ed ɪd əd ~es z ~ing ɪŋ
secession sɪ 'seʃ ᵊn sə- ~ism ,ɪz əm ~ist/s ɪst/s
  §əst/s ‖ əst/s ~s z
sech *'hyperbolic secant'* seʃ setʃ, ʃek —*or as* sec
  h
Secker 'sek ə ‖ -ᵊr
seclud|e sɪ 'kluːd sə- ~ed ɪd əd ~es z ~ing ɪŋ
secluded|ly sɪ 'kluːd ɪd |li -əd- ~ness nəs nɪs
seclusion sɪ 'kluːʒ ᵊn sə-
seclusive sɪ 'kluːs ɪv sə-, §-'kluːz- ~ly li ~ness
  nəs nɪs
Secombe 'siːk əm
second *adj; n; number; adv; determiner; v*
  'support' 'sek ənd △-ᵊnt ~ed ɪd əd ~ing ɪŋ
  ~s z
  ,second 'best◄; ,second 'childhood;
  ,second 'class; ,Second 'Coming; ,second
  'cousin; ,second 'hand *(on a clock)*; at
  ,second 'hand *'indirectly'*; ,second
  'helping; ,second lieu'tenant◄; ,second
  'mortgage; ,second 'nature; ,second
  'person◄, ,second ,person 'plural; ,second
  'sight; ,second 'thoughts; ,second 'wind;
  ,Second ,World 'War
second *v 'move to special duty'* sɪ 'kɒnd sə-
  ‖ -'kɑːnd ~ed ɪd əd ~ing ɪŋ ~s z
secondarily 'sek ənd ᵊr əl i ,·ᵊn 'der əl i,
  '···· ‖ ,sek ən 'der əl i '·····
secondar|y 'sek ənd ᵊr |i §-ᵊn der- ‖ -ᵊn der |i
  ~ies iz ~iness i nəs i nɪs
  ,secondary 'modern; ,secondary 'accent,
  ,secondary'stress

S

second-class ˌsek ənd ˈklɑːs ◄ →-ŋ-, §-ˈklæs ‖ -ˈklæs ◄
ˌsecond-classˈcitizen
second-degree ˌsek ənd dɪ ˈgriː ◄ →ˌˈŋ-, -də-, §-diː-ˈ
ˌsecond-deˌgree ˈburn
seconder ˈsek ənd ə ‖ -ᵊr ~s z
second-generation
ˌsek ənd ˌdʒen ə ˈreɪʃ ᵊn ◄ →ˌ-ŋ-
ˌsecond-geneˌration Auˈstralian
second-guess ˌsek ənd ˈges →-ŋ- ~ed t ~er/s ə/z ‖ ᵊr/z ~es ɪz əz ~ing ɪŋ
secondhand, second-hand adj
ˌsek ənd ˈhænd ◄
ˌsecond-hand ˈfurniture
second-in-command ˌsek ənd ɪn kə ˈmɑːnd →-ˌ-ŋ-ˈ, §-ˈmænd ‖ -ˈmænd ~s z
secondly ˈsek ənd li
secondment sɪ ˈkɒnd mənt sə- ‖ -ˈkɑːnd- ~s s
second|o se ˈkɒnd |əʊ sɪ-, sə- ‖ sɪ ˈkoʊnd |oʊ -ˈkɑːnd- ~i iː
second-rate ˌsek ənd ˈreɪt ◄ →-ŋ- ~ness nəs nɪs
ˌsecond-rate perˈformance
second-rater ˌsek ənd ˈreɪt ə ‖ -ˈreɪt ᵊr ~s z
second-string ˌsek ənd ˈstrɪŋ ◄ →-ŋ-
secrecy ˈsiːk rəs i -rɪs-
secret ˈsiːk rət -rɪt ~s s
ˌsecret ˈagent; ˌsecret poˈlice; ˌsecret ˈservice
secretaire ˌsek rə ˈteə -rɪ- ‖ -ˈteᵊr ~s z
secretarial ˌsek rə ˈteər i əl ◄ -rɪ- ‖ -ˈter-
secretariat ˌsek rə ˈteər i ət -rɪ-, -æt ‖ -ˈter- ~s s
secretar|y ˈsek rət̬ ər |i ˈ-rɪt̬ˌ, Δˈjʊt̬ˌ, Δˈət̬; -rə ter |i, -rɪ-ˌ, Δˌ-ju-ˌ, Δ-ə-ˌ ‖ -rə ter |i Δ-ə-ˌ ~ies iz
secretary-general ˌsek rət̬ ər i ˈdʒen ᵊr əl ˌ-rɪt̬ˌ, Δˌjʊt̬ˌ, Δˌət̬; -rə ter i-, -rɪ-, Δ-ju-, Δˌ-ə- ‖ ˌrə ter-
secrete sɪ ˈkriːt sə- **secreted** sɪ ˈkriːt ɪd sə-, -əd; Δˈsiːk rət-, Δ-rɪt- ‖ -ˈkriːt̬ əd **secretes** sɪ ˈkriːts sə- **secreting** sɪ ˈkriːt ɪŋ sə-; Δˈsiːk rət ɪŋ, Δ-rɪt- ‖ -ˈkriːt̬ ɪŋ
secretion sɪ ˈkriːʃ ᵊn sə- ~s z
secretive ˈsiːk rət ɪv -rɪt-; sɪ ˈkriːt ɪv, sə- ‖ ˈsiːk rət̬ ɪv sɪ ˈkriːt̬ ɪv ~ly li ~ness nəs nɪs
secretly ˈsiːk rət li -rɪt-
secretor|y sɪ ˈkriːt̬ ər |i sə- ~ies iz
sect sekt **sects** sekts
sectarian sek ˈteər i ən ‖ -ˈter- ~ism ˌɪz əm ~s z
sectar|y ˈsekt ər |i ~ies iz
section ˈsek ʃᵊn ~ed d ~ing ˌɪŋ ~s z
sectional ˈsek ʃᵊn əl ~ly i
sectionalis... —see **sectionaliz...**
sectionalism ˈsek ʃᵊn əl ˌɪz əm
sectionalization ˌsek ʃᵊn əl aɪ ˈzeɪʃ ᵊn -ɪ-ˈ ‖ -əˈ-
sectionaliz|e ˈsek ʃᵊn ə laɪz ~ed d ~es ɪz əz ~ing ɪŋ
sector ˈsekt ə ‖ -ᵊr ~s z
sectoral ˈsekt ər əl

secular ˈsek jʊl ə -jəl- ‖ -jəl ᵊr ~ly li ~s z
secularis... —see **seculariz...**
secularism ˈsek jʊl ə ˌrɪz əm -jəl ə- ‖ -jəl ə-
secularist ˈsek jʊl ər ɪst -jəl ər-, §-əst ‖ -jəl ər-
secularity ˌsek ju ˈlær ət i ˌjə-, -ɪt i ‖ -jə ˈlær ət̬ i -ˈler-
secularization ˌsek jʊl ər aɪ ˈzeɪʃ ᵊn ˌjəl-, -ɪ-ˈ ‖ -jəl ər ə-
seculariz|e ˈsek jʊl ə raɪz -jəl ə- ‖ -jəl ə- ~ed d ~es ɪz əz ~ing ɪŋ
secure sɪ ˈkjʊə sə-, -ˈkjɔː ‖ -ˈkjʊᵊr ~d d ~s z
securing sɪ ˈkjʊər ɪŋ sə-, -ˈkjɔːr- ‖ -ˈkjʊr ɪŋ
securely sɪ ˈkjʊə li sə-, -ˈkjɔː- ‖ -ˈkjʊᵊr li
Securicor tdmk sɪ ˈkjʊər ɪ kɔː sə-, -ˈkjɔːr-, -ə- ‖ -ˈkjʊr ə kɔːr
securitis... —see **securitiz...**
securitization sɪ ˌkjʊər ɪt aɪ ˈzeɪʃ ᵊn sə-, -ˌkjɔːr-, -ˌət-, -ɪ-ˈ ‖ -ˌkjʊr ət̬ ə-
securitiz|e sɪ ˈkjʊər ɪ taɪz sə-, -ˈkjɔːr-, -ə- ‖ -ˈkjʊr ə taɪz ~ed d ~es ɪz əz ~ing ɪŋ
securit|y sɪ ˈkjʊər ət |i sə-, -ˈkjɔːr-, -ɪt i ‖ -ˈkjʊr ət̬ |i ~ies iz
seˈcurity ˌblanket; seˈcurity ˌclearance; Seˈcurity ˌCouncil; seˈcurity risk
Sedaka sə ˈdɑːk ə sɪ-
sedan, Sedan sɪ ˈdæn sə- —Fr [sə dɑ̃] ~s z
seˌdan ˈchair ‖ ˈ· ·
sedate adj, v sɪ ˈdeɪt sə- **sedated** sɪ ˈdeɪt ɪd sə-, -əd ‖ -ˈdeɪt̬ əd ~ly li ~ness nəs nɪs ~s s
sedating sɪ ˈdeɪt ɪŋ sə- ‖ -ˈdeɪt̬ ɪŋ
sedation sɪ ˈdeɪʃ ᵊn sə- ~s z
sedative ˈsed ət ɪv ‖ -ət̬ ɪv ~s z
Sedbergh ˈsed bə →ˈseb-, -bɜːg, ˈsed bər ə ‖ -bɜːg
Seddon ˈsed ᵊn
sedentarily ˈsed ᵊnt ər əl i ˈsed ᵊn ter əl i, -ɪ li, ˌ·ˈ·ˌ·; §sɪ ˈdent̬ˌ, sə- ‖ ˌsed ᵊn ˈter əl i
sedentar|y ˈsed ᵊnt ər |i §-ᵊn ter |i; §sɪ ˈdent ər |i, §sə- ‖ -ᵊn ter |i ~iness i nəs i nɪs
Seder ˈseɪd ə ‖ -ᵊr
sedge sedʒ **sedges** ˈsedʒ ɪz -əz
Sedgefield ˈsedʒ fiːᵊld
Sedgemoor ˈsedʒ mɔː -mʊə ‖ -mʊr
Sedgewick, Sedgwick ˈsedʒ wɪk
sedgy ˈsedʒ i
sedilia sɪ ˈdɪl i ə -ˈdiːl-, -ˈdaɪl-
sediment ˈsed ɪ mənt -ə- ~s s
sedimentary ˌsed ɪ ˈment ər i ◄ ˌ-ə-
sedimentation ˌsed ɪ men ˈteɪʃ ᵊn ˌ-ə-, -mən-ˈ
sedition sɪ ˈdɪʃ ᵊn sə-
seditious sɪ ˈdɪʃ əs sə- ~ly li ~ness nəs nɪs
Sedlescombe ˈsed ᵊlz kəm
Sedley ˈsed li
seduc|e sɪ ˈdjuːs sə-, →-ˈdʒuːs ‖ -ˈduːs -ˈdjuːs ~ed t ~er/s ə/z ‖ -ᵊr/z ~es ɪz əz ~ing ɪŋ
seduction sɪ ˈdʌk ʃᵊn sə- ~s z
seductive sɪ ˈdʌkt ɪv sə- ~ly li ~ness nəs nɪs
seductress sɪ ˈdʌk trəs sə-, -trɪs ~es ɪz əz
sedulity sɪ ˈdjuːl ət i sə-, →-ˈdʒuːl-, -ɪt- ‖ -ˈduːl ət̬ i -ˈdjuːl-
sedulous ˈsed jʊl əs §-jəl-; ˈsedʒ ʊl- ‖ ˈsedʒ əl əs ~ly li ~ness nəs nɪs

sedum 'siːd əm ~s z

see si: **saw** sɔː ‖ sɑ: **seeing** 'siː ɪŋ **seen** siːn
  sees siːz
  ˌSeeing 'Eye dog

Seear 'siːˌə ‖ -ᵊr

Seebeck 'siː bek —Ger ['zeː bɛk]
  'Seebeck efˌfect

seed, Seed siːd **seeded** 'siːd ɪd -əd **seeding**
  'siːd ɪŋ **seeds** siːdz

seedbed 'siːd bed →'siːb- ~s z

seedcake 'siːd keɪk →'siːg- ~s s

seedcorn 'siːd kɔːn →'siːg- ‖ -kɔːrn

seed-eater 'siːd ˌiːt ə ‖ -ˌiːt̬ ᵊr ~s z

seeder 'siːd ə ‖ -ᵊr ~s z

seedless 'siːd ləs -lɪs

seedling 'siːd lɪŋ ~s z

seeds|man 'siːdz |mən ~**men** mən men

seedtime 'siːd taɪm ~s z

seed|y 'siːd |i ~**ier** i ə ‖ iˌᵊr ~**iest** i ɪst i ᵊst
  ~**ily** ɪ li əl i ~**iness** i nəs i nɪs

Seeger 'siːg ə ‖ -ᵊr

seek siːk **seeking** 'siːk ɪŋ **seeks** siːks **sought**
  sɔːt ‖ sɑːt

seeker 'siːk ə ‖ -ᵊr ~s z

Seeley, Seely 'siːl i

seem siːm **seemed** siːmd **seeming/ly**
  'siːm ɪŋ /li **seems** siːmz

seem|ly 'siːm |li ~**lier** li ə ‖ liˌᵊr ~**liest** li ɪst
  li ᵊst ~**liness** li nəs li nɪs

seen siːn

seep siːp **seeped** siːpt **seeping** 'siːp ɪŋ **seeps**
  siːps

seepag|e 'siːp ɪdʒ ~**es** ɪz əz

seer sɪə 'siːˌə ‖ sɪᵊr 'siː ᵊr **seers** sɪəz 'siːˌəz
  ‖ sɪᵊrz 'siː ᵊrz

seersucker 'sɪə ˌsʌk ə ‖ 'sɪr ˌsʌk ᵊr

seesaw 'siː sɔː ‖ -sɑ: ~**ed** d **seesawing**
  'siː sɔːʳ ɪŋ ‖ -sɔː ɪŋ -sɑ:- ~**s** z

seethe siːð **seethed** siːðd **seethes** siːðz
  seething 'siːð ɪŋ

see-through 'siː θruː

Seferis se 'feər ɪs sɪ-, sə-, §-əs —Greek
  [sɛ 'fɛ rɪs]

Sefton 'seft ən

Sega tdmk 'siːg ə 'seɪg ə

Segal 'siːg ᵊl

Seggie 'seg i

segment n 'seg mənt ~s s

seg|ment v ₍ˌ₎seg '|ment sɪg-, səg- ‖ '· ·
  ~**mented** ment ɪd -əd ‖ menţ əd ~**menting**
  ment ɪŋ ‖ menţ ɪŋ ~**ments** ments

segmental seg 'ment ᵊl sɪg-, səg- ‖ -'menţ- ~**ly**
  i ~s z

segmentation ˌseg men 'teɪʃ ᵊn -mən- ~**s** z

segno 'seg nəʊ 'sen jəʊ, 'sem- ‖ 'seɪn joʊ —It
  ['sen ɲo]

sego 'siːg əʊ ‖ -oʊ ~**s** z
  ˌsego 'lily

Ségolène ˌseg əʊ 'leɪn ‖ ˌseɪg oʊ- —Fr
  [se ɡɔ lɛn]

Segovia sɪ 'gəʊv iˌə sə-, se- ‖ -'goʊv- —Sp
  [se 'ɣo βja]

Segrave 'siː greɪv

segre|gate 'seg rɪ |geɪt -rə- ~**gated** geɪt ɪd -əd
  ‖ geɪţ əd ~**gates** geɪts ~**gating** geɪt ɪŋ
  ‖ geɪţ ɪŋ

segregation ˌseg rɪ 'geɪʃ ᵊn -rə- ~**ist/s** ɪst/s
  §əst/s ‖ əst/s

segue 'seg weɪ 'seɪg-, -wi —It ['seː gwe] ~**d** d
  ~**ing** ɪŋ ~**s** z

seguidilla ˌseg i 'diːl jə -'diː- —Sp
  [se ɣi 'ði ʎa, -ja] ~**s** z

sei seɪ (= say)
  'sei whale

seiche seɪʃ **seiches** 'seɪʃ ɪz -əz

Seidlitz 'sed lɪts §-ləts

Seifert 'siːf ət ‖ -ᵊrt

seigneur sen 'jɜː sem-; 'seɪn jə ‖ seɪn 'jɜː siːn-
  —Fr [sɛ njœːʁ] ~**s** z

seigneurial sen 'jɜːr iˌəl sem- ‖ seɪn 'jɜː- -'jʊr-

seignior 'seɪn jə ‖ -jɔːr ·'· ~**s** z

seigniorage 'seɪn jər ɪdʒ

seigniorial ₍ˌ₎seɪn 'jɔːr iˌəl ‖ -'jour-

seignior|y 'seɪn jər |i ~**ies** iz

Seiko tdmk 'seɪk əʊ 'siːk- ‖ -oʊ —Jp [se̞ɪ koo,
  se̞,e-]

seine, Seine seɪn —Fr [sɛn] **seined** seɪnd
  seines seɪnz **seining** 'seɪn ɪŋ
  'seine net

Seinfeld 'saɪn feld

Seiriol 'saɪʳr i ɒl əl ‖ -ɑːl -ɔːl —Welsh
  ['səɪr jɔl]

seise siːz (= seize, sees, seas) **seised** siːzd

seisin 'siːz ɪn §-ᵊn

seismic 'saɪz mɪk ~**ally** ᵊl i

seismicity ₍ˌ₎saɪz 'mɪs ət i -ɪt i ‖ -əţ i

seismograph 'saɪz mə grɑːf -græf ‖ -græf ~**s** s

seismographic ˌsaɪz mə 'græf ɪk ◂ ~**ally** ᵊl i

seismography saɪz 'mɒg rəf i ‖ -'mɑːg-

seismologist saɪz 'mɒl ədʒ ɪst §-əst ‖ -'mɑːl-
  ~**s** s

seismology saɪz 'mɒl ədʒ i ‖ -'mɑːl-

seismometer ₍ˌ₎saɪz 'mɒm ɪt ə -ət ə
  ‖ -'mɑːm əţ ᵊr ~**s** z

seitan 'seɪ tæn ‖ -tɑːn

seize siːz (= sees, seas) **seized** siːzd **seizes**
  'siːz ɪz -əz **seizing** 'siːz ɪŋ

seizure 'siːʒ ə 'siːz jə ‖ -ᵊr ~**s** z

sejant 'siːdʒ ənt

Sejanus sɪ 'dʒeɪn əs sə-

selah, Selah 'siːl ə -ɑː

Selangor sə 'læŋ ə sɪ-, -ɔː ‖ -ᵊr -'lɑːŋ-, -ɔːr, -gɔːr

Selassie sə 'læs i sɪ- ‖ -'lɑːs i

Selborne, Selbourne 'sel bɔːn ‖ -bɔːrn -bourn

Selby 'sel bi

Selden 'seld ən

seldom 'seld əm

select sə 'lekt sɪ- ~**ed** ɪd əd ~**ing** ɪŋ ~**ness** nəs
  nɪs ~**s** s
  seˌlect comˈmittee

selectee sə ˌlek 'tiː sɪ- ~**s** z

selection sə 'lek ʃᵊn sɪ- ~**s** z

selective sə 'lekt ɪv sɪ- ~**ly** i ~**ness** nəs nɪs

selectivity sə ˌlek 'tɪv ət i sɪ-, ˌsɪl ek-, ˌsiːl ek-,
  ˌsel ek-, -ɪt i ‖ -əţ i

selector sə 'lekt ə sɪ- ‖ -ᵊr ~**s** z

Selena sə ˈliːn ə sɪ-
Selene sə ˈliːn i sɪ-
selenic sə ˈliːn ɪk sɪ-, -ˈlen-
selenite ˈsel ə naɪt -ɪ-
selenium sə ˈliːn i‿əm
seleno- *comb. form*
　with stress-neutral suffix sə ˌliːn əʊ sɪ- ‖ -oʊ -ə
　— **selenographic** sə ˌliːn əʊ ˈɡræf ɪk ◂
　‖ -oʊ- -ə-
　with stress-imposing suffix ˌsiːl ə ˈnɒ+ -ɪ-
　‖ ˌsel ə ˈnɑː+ — **selenology**
　ˌsiːl ə ˈnɒl ədʒ i -ɪ- ‖ ˌsel ə ˈnɑːl-
Seles ˈsel ez -əs —*Serbian* Seleš [ˈsɛ lɛʃ]
Seleucia sə ˈluːs i‿ə sɪ-, -ˈluːʃ-, -ˈljuːs-, -ˈljuːʃ-
Seleucid sə ˈluːs ɪd sɪ-, -ˈljuːs-, §-əd ~**s** z
Seleucus sə ˈluːk əs sɪ-, -ˈljuːk-
self, Self self **selves** selvz
self- ¦self —*Words with this prefix normally
　have late stress.* — **self-abasement**
　ˌself ə ˈbeɪs mənt
self-abnegation ˌself ˌæb nɪ ˈɡeɪʃ ᵊn -ne¹--,
　-nə¹--
self-absorbed ˌself əb ˈsɔːbd ◂ -æb-, -ˈzɔːbd
　‖ -ˈsɔːrbd ◂ -ˈzɔːrbd
self-abuse *n* ˌself ə ˈbjuːs
self-access ˌself ˈæk ses
self-acting ˌself ˈækt ɪŋ ◂
self-actualization, self-actualisation
　ˌself ˌæk tʃu‿ə laɪ ˈzeɪʃ ᵊn -tju‿, ˌə‿l -ɪ- ‖ ˌə‿l ə-
self-addressed ˌself ə ˈdrest ◂
self-adhesive ˌself əd ˈhiːs ɪv ◂ §-æd-
self-administered ˌself əd ˈmɪn ɪst əd §ˌæd-,
　-əst- ‖ -ᵊrd
self-aggrandizement ˌself ə ˈɡrænd ɪz mənt
　-əz-, -aɪz ·
self-aggrandizing ˌself ə ˈɡrænd aɪz ɪŋ ◂
self-appointed ˌself ə ˈpɔɪnt ɪd ◂ -əd
　‖ -ˈpɔɪnt̬ əd ◂
self-assembly ˌself ə ˈsem bli
self-assertion ˌself ə ˈsɜːʃ ᵊn ‖ -ˈsɜːʃ ᵊn
self-assertive ˌself ə ˈsɜːt ɪv ‖ -ˈsɜːt̬ ɪv ~**ly** li
　~**ness** nəs nɪs
self-assessment ˌself ə ˈses mənt ~**s** s
self-assurance ˌself ə ˈʃɔːr ən�t s -ˈʃʊər-
　‖ -ˈʃʊr ənˑt s -ˈʃɜː-
self-assured ˌself ə ˈʃɔːd ◂ -ˈʃʊəd ‖ -ˈʃʊᵊrd ◂
　-ˈʃɜːd
self-awareness ˌself ə ˈweə nəs -nɪs ‖ -ˈwer-
　-ˈwær-
self-build ˌself ˈbɪld ◂
self-catering ˌself ˈkeɪt ər ɪŋ ‖ -ˈkeɪt̬-
self-centered, self-centred ˌself ˈsent əd
　‖ -ˈsent̬ ᵊrd ~**ly** li ~**ness** nəs nɪs
self-certification ˌself ˌsɜːt ɪf ɪ ˈkeɪʃ ᵊn -əf-¹· ·,
　-ə¹· · ‖ -ˌsɜːt̬-
self-command ˌself kə ˈmɑːnd §-ˈmænd
　‖ -ˈmænd
self-concept ˌself ˈkɒn sept ‖ -ˈkɑːn- ~**s** s
self-confessed ˌself kən ˈfest ◂ §-kɒn-
　ˌself-conˌfessed ˈliar
self-confid|ence ˌself ˈkɒn fɪd |ənᵗ s §-fəd-
　‖ -ˈkɑːn- ~**ent/ly** ənt /li

self-congratulation
　ˌself kən ˌɡrætʃ u ˈleɪʃ ᵊn →ˌ·kəŋ-, §→ˌ·kɒŋ-,
　-ˌɡræt ju¹· · ‖ -ˌɡrætʃ ə- -ˌɡrædʒ ə-
self-congratulatory
　ˌself kən ˌɡrætʃ u ˈleɪt ər i ◂ →ˌ·kəŋ-,
　§ˌ·kɒn-, -ˌ·ə-, -ˌɡræt ju-; ˌ· ·¹· ·lət ᵊr i
　‖ ˌself kən ˈɡrætʃ əl ə tɔːr i -ˈɡrædʒ-, -toʊr i
self-conscious ˌself ˈkɒnᵗ ʃ əs ◂ ‖ -ˈkɑːnᵗ ʃ əs
　~**ly** li ~**ness** nəs nɪs
self-contained ˌself kən ˈteɪnd ◂ §-kɒn-
self-contradictory ˌself ˌkɒntr ə ˈdɪkt ər i
　‖ -ˌkɑːntr-
self-control ˌself kən ˈtrəʊl §-kɒn-, →-ˈtrɒʊl
　‖ -ˈtroʊl ~**led** d
self-correcting ˌself kə ˈrekt ɪŋ ◂
self-critical ˌself ˈkrɪt ɪk ᵊl ‖ -ˈkrɪt̬-
self-criticism ˌself ˈkrɪt ɪ ˌsɪz əm -ə- ‖ -ˈkrɪt̬-
self-deception ˌself dɪ ˈsep ʃᵊn -də-
self-defeating ˌself dɪ ˈfiːt ɪŋ ◂ -də-
　‖ -ˈfiːt̬ ɪŋ ◂
self-defence, self-defense ˌself dɪ ˈfenᵗ s -də-
self-denial ˌself dɪ ˈnaɪ‿əl -də- ~**s** z
self-deprecating ˌself ˈdep rə keɪt ɪŋ ◂
　‖ -keɪt̬ ɪŋ ◂
self-described ˌself dɪ ˈskraɪbd ◂ -də-
self-destruct ˌself dɪ ˈstrʌkt -də- ~**ed** ɪd əd
　~**ing** ɪŋ ~**s** s
self-destruction ˌself dɪ ˈstrʌk ʃᵊn -də-
self-destructive ˌself dɪ ˈstrʌkt ɪv ◂ -də- ~**ly** li
　~**ness** nəs nɪs
self-determination ˌself dɪ ˌtɜːm ɪ ˈneɪʃ ᵊn
　ˌ·də-, -ə¹·-- ‖ -ˌtɜːm-
self-directed ˌself də ˈrekt ɪd ◂ -dɪ-, -daɪᵊ-
self-discipline ˌself ˈdɪs ə plɪn -ɪ-, §ˌ·dɪ ˈsɪp lɪn
　~**d** d ◂
self-|doubt ˌself ¦ˈdaʊt ~**doubting** ˈdaʊt ɪŋ
　‖ ˈdaʊt̬ ɪŋ
self-drive ˌself ˈdraɪv ◂
self-educated ˌself ˈed ju keɪt ɪd ◂ -ˈedʒ u-,
　§-ˈedʒ ə- ‖ -ˈedʒ ə keɪt̬ əd ◂
self-effac|ement ˌself ɪ ˈfeɪs |mənt -ə- ~**ing**
　ɪŋ ◂
self-em|ployed ˌself ɪm ¦ˈplɔɪd ◂ §-əm-
　~**ployment** ˈplɔɪ mənt
self-esteem ˌself ɪ ˈstiːm §-ə-
self-evident ˌself ˈev ɪd ənt ◂ -əd-, §-ə dent
　~**ly** li
self-examination ˌself ɪɡ ˌzæm ɪ ˈneɪʃ ᵊn
　ˌeɡ-, ˌəɡ-, ˌɪk-, ˌek-, ˌək-, -ə¹·--
self-explanatory ˌself ɪk ˈsplæn ət ər i ◂ ˌek-,
　ˌək- ‖ -ə tɔːr i -toʊr i
self-expression ˌself ɪk ˈspreʃ ᵊn -ek-, -ək-
self-fulfilling ˌself fʊl ˈfɪl ɪŋ ◂
　ˌself-fulˌfilling ˈprophecy
self-governing ˌself ˈɡʌv ᵊn ɪŋ ◂ ‖ -ᵊrn ɪŋ ◂
self-government ˌself ˈɡʌv ᵊn mənt →-ᵊm-
　‖ -ᵊrn-
self-hatred ˌself ˈheɪtr ɪd -əd
selfheal ˈself hiːᵊl ~**s** z
self-help ˌself ˈhelp
selfhood ˈself hʊd
self-imag|e ˌself ˈɪm ɪdʒ ~**es** ɪz əz

S

self-import|ance ˌself ɪm ˈpɔːt |ᵊnˈs
‖ -ˈpɔːrt |ᵊnˈs **~ant/ly** ᵊnt /li
self-imposed ˌself ɪm ˈpəʊzd ◄ ‖ -ˈpoʊzd ◄
ˌself-imˌposed ˈtask
self-improvement ˌself ɪm ˈpruːv mənt
self-induced ˌself ɪn ˈdjuːst ◄ →-ˈdʒuːst,
§-ˈduːst ‖ -ˈduːst ◄ -ˈdjuːst
self-indulg|ence ˌself ɪn ˈdʌldʒ |ᵊnˈs **~ent/ly**
ənt /li
self-inflicted ˌself ɪn ˈflɪkt ɪd ◄ -əd
self-interest ˌself ˈɪntr əst -ɪst, -est; ˈɪnt ə rest
‖ ˈɪnt̬ ə rest **~ed** ɪd əd
selfish ˈself ɪʃ **~ly** li **~ness** nəs nɪs
self-knowledge ˌself ˈnɒl ɪdʒ ‖ -ˈnɑːl-
selfless ˈself ləs -lɪs **~ly** li **~ness** nəs nɪs
self-locking ˌself ˈlɒk ɪŋ ◄ ‖ -ˈlɑːk ɪŋ ◄
self-made ˌself ˈmeɪd ◄
ˌself-made ˈman
self-opinionated ˌself ə ˈpɪn jə neɪt ɪd ◄
§-ˌəʊ-, -əd ‖ -neɪt̬-
self-perpetuating ˌself pə ˈpetʃ u eɪt ɪŋ ◄
-ˈpet ju- ‖ -pᵊr ˈpetʃ u eɪt̬ ɪŋ ◄
self-pity ˌself ˈpɪt i ‖ -ˈpɪt̬ i **~ing/ly** ɪŋ /li
self-possessed ˌself pə ˈzest ◄ **~ly** li
self-possession ˌself pə ˈzeʃ ᵊn
self-preservation ˌself ˌprez ə ˈveɪʒ ᵊn ‖ -ᵊr-
self-proclaimed ˌself prəʊˈkleɪmd ◄
self-raising ˌself ˈreɪz ɪŋ
ˌself-ˈraising flour, ‿‿ · ‿ ·
self-regulating ˌself ˈreg ju leɪt ɪŋ ◄ -ˈjə-
‖ -jə leɪt̬ ɪŋ ◄
self-regulation ˌself ˌreg ju ˈleɪʃ ᵊn -jə-
self-regulatory ˌself ˌreg ju ˈleɪt ər i -jə·-,
-ˈ‿‿‿, ˈ· -lət ᵊr i ‖ -ˈreg jəl ə tɔːr i -tour i
self-reli|ance ˌself ri ˈlaɪ |ᵊnˈs -rə- **~ant/ly**
ənt /li
self-respect ˌself ri ˈspekt -rə- **~ing** ɪŋ ◄
self-restraint ˌself ri ˈstreɪnt -rə-
Selfridg|e ˈself rɪdʒ **~es** ɪz əz
self-righteous ˌself ˈraɪtʃ əs ◄ -ˈraɪt i̯ əs **~ly** li
~ness nəs nɪs
self-rising ˌself ˈraɪz ɪŋ ◄
self-rule ˌself ˈruːl
self-sacrific|e ˌself ˈsæk rɪ faɪs -rə- **~ing** ɪŋ
selfsame ˈself seɪm ˌ·ˈ·
self-satisfied ˌself ˈsæt ɪs faɪd ◄ -əs-
‖ -ˈsæt̬ əs-
self-seek|er ˌself ˈsiːk |ə ‖ -|ᵊr **~ers** əz ‖ ᵊrz
~ing ɪŋ ◄
self-service ˌself ˈsɜːv ɪs ◄ §-əs ‖ -ˈsɜːrv əs ◄
self-serving ˌself ˈsɜːv ɪŋ ◄ ‖ -ˈsɜːrv-
self-starter ˌself ˈstɑːt ə ‖ -ˈstɑːrt̬ ᵊr **~s** z
self-styled ˌself ˈstaɪᵊld ◄
self-suffici|ency ˌself sə ˈfɪʃ |ᵊnˈs i **~ent/ly**
ᵊnt /li
self-supporting ˌself sə ˈpɔːt ɪŋ ‖ -ˈpɔːrt̬ ɪŋ
-ˈpoʊrt̬-
self-sustaining ˌself sə ˈsteɪn ɪŋ ◄
self-taught ˌself ˈtɔːt ◄ ‖ -ˈtɑːt ◄
self-titled ˌself ˈtaɪt ᵊld ◄ ‖ -ˈtaɪt̬-
self-will ˌself ˈwɪl **~ed** d ◄
self-winding ˌself ˈwaɪnd ɪŋ ◄
self-worth ˌself ˈwɜːθ ‖ -ˈwɜːrθ

Selhurst ˈsel hɜːst ‖ -hɜːrst
Seligman, Seligmann ˈsel ɪg mən
Selina sə ˈliːn ə sɪ-
Seljuk ˌsel ˈdʒuːk ˈ· ·
Selkirk ˈsel kɜːk ‖ -kɜːrk
sell sel **selling** ˈselɪŋ **sells** selz **sold** səʊld
→sɒʊld ‖ soʊld
ˈselling point
Sellafield ˈsel ə fiːᵊld
Sellar ˈsel ə ‖ -ᵊr
Sellars ˈsel əz ‖ -ᵊrz
sell-by date ˈsel baɪ deɪt
seller ˈsel ə ‖ -ᵊr **~s** z
ˈseller's ˈmarket
Sellers ˈsel əz ‖ -ᵊrz
Sellick ˈsel ɪk
Sellinge ˈsel ɪndʒ
sell-off ˈsel ɒf -ɔːf ‖ -ɔːf -ɑːf
sellotap|e, S~ tdmk ˈsel əʊ teɪp ‖ -ə- **~ed** t
~es s **~ing** ɪŋ
sell-out ˈsel aʊt **~s** s
Selly ˈsel i
Selma ˈselm ə
Selous sə ˈluː
Selsey ˈsels i
seltzer, S~ ˈselts ə ‖ -ᵊr **~s** z
selvag|e, selvedg|e ˈselv ɪdʒ **~es** ɪz əz
selves selvz
Selwyn ˈsel wɪn
Selznick ˈselz nɪk
semanteme sə ˈmænt iːm sɪ- **~s** z
semantic sə ˈmænt ɪk sɪ- ‖ -ˈmænt̬ ɪk **~ally** ᵊl‿i
~s s
semantician sə ˌmæn ˈtɪʃ ᵊn sɪ- **~s** z
semanticist sə ˈmænt əs ɪst sɪ-, -ɪs-, §-əst
‖ -ˈmænt̬- **~s** s
semaphore ˈsem ə fɔː ‖ -fɔːr -four **~d** d **~s** z
semaphoring ˈsem ə fɔːr ɪŋ ‖ -four ɪŋ
semaphoric ˌsem ə ˈfɒr ɪk ◄ ‖ -ˈfɔːr ɪk ◄ -ˈfɑːr-
~ally ᵊl‿i
semasiology sə ˌmeɪz i ˈɒl ədʒ i sɪ-, -ˌmeɪs-
‖ -ˈɑːl-
sematic sə ˈmæt ɪk sɪ- ‖ -ˈmæt̬ ɪk
semblanc|e ˈsem blənˈs **~es** ɪz əz
semeio... —see **semio...**
Semele ˈsem əl i -ɪl-; -ə leɪ, -ɪ-
sememe ˈsiːm iːm **~s** z
semen ˈsiːm ən -en (= seamen)
Semer Water ˈsem ə ˌwɔːt ə ‖ -ᵊr ˌwɔːt̬ ᵊr
-ˌwɑːt̬-
semester sə ˈmest ə sɪ- ‖ -ᵊr **~s** z
semi ˈsem i ‖ -aɪ **~s** z
semi- |ˌsem i ‖ -aɪ —Words with this prefix
mostly have late stress; certain exceptions are
found in the list below. — Preference poll,
AmE: -i 60%, -aɪ 40%. See chart on p. 728.
— **semiblind** ˌsem i ˈblaɪnd ◄ ‖ -aɪ-
semiannual ˌsem i ˈæn ju əl ◄ ‖ ˌsem aɪ- **~ly** i
semi-arid ˌsem i ˈær ɪd ◄ §-əd ‖ -ar-, -ˈer-
semi-autobiographical
ˌsem i ˌɔːt əʊbaɪ ə ˈgræf ɪk ᵊl ◄ ‖ -ˌɔːt̬ ə-
ˌsem aɪ-, -ˌɑːt̬ ə-

S

SEMI-

60% -i
40% -aɪ

AmE

---

semiautomatic ˌsem i ˌɔːt ə ˈmæt ɪk ◂
‖ -ˌɔːt̬ ə ˈmæt̬ ɪk ◂ -ˌɑː- **~ally** ᵊl i
semibreve ˈsem i briːv ‖ -aɪ-, -brev **~s** z
semicircle ˈsem i ˌsɜːk ᵊl ‖ -ˌsɜːk ᵊl **~s** z
semicircular ˌsem i ˈsɜːk jʊl ə ◂ -jəl ə
‖ -ˈsɜːk jəl ᵊr ◂
semicolon ˌsem i ˈkəʊl ən -ɒn, ˈ· ·ˌ· ·
‖ ˈsem i ˌkoʊl ən **~s** z
semiconduct|ing ˌsem i kən ˈdʌkt |ɪŋ §-kɒn-'-
‖ -ˌaɪ- **~or/s** ə/z ‖ -ᵊr/z
semiconscious ˌsem i ˈkɒnʃ əs ◂ ‖ -ˈkɑːnᵗʃ-
-aɪ-
semiconsonant ˌsem i ˈkɒnˈsən ənt ˈ· ·ˌ· ·
‖ -ˈkɑːnᵗs- ˌsem aɪ- **~s** s
semiconsonantal ˌsem i ˌkɒnᵗs ə ˈnænt ᵊl ◂
‖ -ˌkɑːnᵗs ə ˈnænt̬ ᵊl ◂ ˌsem aɪ-
semidarkness ˌsem i ˈdɑːk nəs -nɪs ‖ -ˈdɑːrk-
-aɪ-
semidetached ˌsem i di ˈtætʃt ◂ -i də-
‖ ˌsem aɪ-
ˌsemideˌtached ˈbungalow
semifinal ˌsem i ˈfaɪn ᵊl ◂ ‖ -aɪ- **~s** z
semifinalist ˌsem i ˈfaɪn ᵊl ɪst §-əst ‖ -ˌaɪ- **~s** s
semigloss ˈsem i glɒs ‖ -glɔːs -aɪ-, -glɑːs
semillon, S~ ˈsem i ɒ̃ ˈseɪm- ‖ -ˌ· i ˈjoʊn —*Fr*
Sémillon [se mi jɔ̃]
seminal ˈsem ɪn ᵊl ˈsiːm-, -ən- **~ly** i
seminar ˈsem ɪ nɑː -ə- ‖ -nɑːr **~s** z
seminarian ˌsem ɪ ˈneər i ᵊn ˌ·ə- ‖ -ˈner- **~s** z
seminarist ˈsem ɪn ər ɪst ˈ·ən-, §-əst **~s** s
seminar|y ˈsem ɪn ər ˌi ˈ·ən- ‖ -ə ner |i **~ies** iz
Seminole ˈsem ɪ nəʊl -ə-, →-nɒʊl ‖ -noʊl **~s** z
seminomadic ˌsem i nəʊ ˈmæd ɪk ◂ ‖ -noʊ-ˈ· ·
ˌ·aɪ-
semiolog|ist ˌsem i ˈɒl ədʒ |ɪst ˌsiːm-, §-əst
‖ -ˈɑːl- **~ists** ɪsts §əsts **~y** i
semiology ˌsem i ˈɒl ədʒ i ˌsiːm- ‖ -ˈɑːl- ˌ·aɪ-
semiotic ˌsem i ˈɒt ɪk ◂ ˌsiːm- ‖ -ˈɑːt̬ ɪk ◂ -aɪ-
~s s
semiotician ˌsem i ə ˈtɪʃ ᵊn ˌsiːm- **~s** z
Semipalatinsk ˌsem i pə ˈlæt ɪnsk ‖ -ˈlɑːt-
—*Russ* [sʲɪ mʲi pə ˈɫa tʲinsk]
semipermeable ˌsem i ˈpɜːm i ˌəb ᵊl ◂
‖ -ˈpɜːm- ˌsem aɪ-
semiprecious ˌsem i ˈpreʃ əs ◂ -aɪ-
semiprivate ˌsem i ˈpraɪv ət ◂ -ɪt ‖ -aɪ-
semiprofessional ˌsem i prə ˈfeʃ ᵊn ᵊl ◂ ˌ·aɪ-
~s z
semiquaver ˈsem i ˌkweɪv ə ‖ -ᵊr **~s** z
Semiramide ˌsem i ˈrɑːm ɪd i -əd i; -ɪ deɪ
Semiramis sə ˈmɪr ə mɪs sɪ-, se-, §-əm əs
semi-retired ˌsem i ri ˈtaɪˌəd ◂ -rə·ˈ· ·
‖ -ˈtaɪ ᵊrd ◂ ˌsem aɪ-

---

semiskilled ˌsem ɪ ˈskɪld ◂ ‖ -aɪ-
semi-skimmed ˌsem i ˈskɪmd ◂ ‖ -aɪ-
semisweet ˌsem i ˈswiːt ◂ ‖ -aɪ-
Semite ˈsiːm aɪt ˈsem- ‖ ˈsem aɪt **~s** s
Semitic sə ˈmɪt ɪk sɪ- ‖ -ˈmɪt̬ ɪk **~s** s
semitone ˈsem i təʊn ‖ -toʊn -aɪ- **~s** z
semitrailer ˈsem i ˌtreɪl ə ‖ ˈsem aɪ ˌtreɪl ᵊr -i-
~s z
semitropical ˌsem i ˈtrɒp ɪk ᵊl ◂ ‖ -ˈtrɑːp- ˌ·aɪ-
semivocalic ˌsem i vəʊ ˈkæl ɪk ◂ ‖ -voʊ'-
semivowel ˈsem i ˌvaʊ əl ˈ· -vaʊl **~s** z
semiweek|ly ˌsem i ˈwiːk |li ◂ ‖ -aɪ- **~lies** liz
semolina ˌsem ə ˈliːn ə
ˌsemoˌlina ˈpudding
Semper, s~ ˈsemp ə ‖ -ᵊr
sempiternal ˌsemp ɪ ˈtɜːn ᵊl ◂ -ə- ‖ -ˈtɜːn ᵊl ◂
~ly i
Semple ˈsemp ᵊl
semplice ˈsemp lɪtʃ i -lɪ tʃeɪ —*It* [ˈsem pli tʃe]
sempre ˈsemp ri -reɪ —*It* [ˈsɛm pre]
sempstress ˈsemps trəs -trɪs **~es** ɪz əz
Semtex *tdmk* ˈsem teks
sen *unit of currency* sen
Sen., sen. —*see* **senator, senior**
SEN ˌes iː ˈen **~s** z
senary ˈsiːn ər i ˈsen-
senate, S~ ˈsen ət -ɪt **~s** s
senator, S~ ˈsen ət ə ‖ -ət̬ ᵊr —*In AmE, as a
title also* ˈsent ᵊr **~s** z
senatorial ˌsen ə ˈtɔːr i əl ◂ ‖ -ˈtoʊr- **~ly** i
send, Send send **sending** ˈsend ɪŋ **sends**
sendz **sent** sent
Sendai ˈsend aɪ —*Jp* [ˈsen dai]
Sendak ˈsend æk
sender ˈsend ə ‖ -ᵊr **~s** z
send-off ˈsend ɒf -ɔːf ‖ -ɔːf -ɑːf **~s** s
send-up ˈsend ʌp **~s** s
Senec|a ˈsen ɪk |ə -ək- **~an** ən **~as** əz
ˌSeneca ˈFalls; ˌSeneca ˈLake
Senedd ˈsen eð -ɪð, -əð
Senegal ˌsen ɪ ˈgɔːl -ə-, -ˈgɑːl
Senegalese ˌsen ɪg ə ˈliːz ◂ -ɔː'-
Senegambia ˌsen ɪ ˈgæm bi ə ˌ·ə-
senescence sɪ ˈnes ᵊnᵗs sə-
senescent sɪ ˈnes ᵊnt sə-
seneschal ˈsen ɪʃ ᵊl -əʃ-; -ɪ ʃɑːl, -ə- **~s** z
Senghenydd seŋ ˈhen ɪð
Senhor, s~ sen ˈjɔː ‖ seɪn ˈjɔːr —*Port* [sɪ ˈɲor]
Senhora, s~ sen ˈjɔːr ə ‖ seɪn- -ˈjoʊr- —*Port*
[sɪ ˈɲo ɾɐ]
Senhorita, s~ ˌsen jɔː ˈriːt ə -jə-
‖ ˌseɪn jə ˈriːt̬ ə —*Port* [sɪ ɲo ˈri tɐ] **~s** z
senile ˈsiːn aɪᵊl ‖ ˈsen-, -ᵊl **~ly** li
senility sə ˈnɪl ət i sɪ-, -ɪt- ‖ -ət̬ i
senior, S~ ˈsiːn i ə ‖ ˈsiːn jᵊr **~s** z
ˌsenior ˈcitizen
seniorit|y ˌsiːn i ˈɒr ət i |i -ɪt i ‖ ˌsiːn ˈjɔːr ət̬ |i
-ˈjɑːr- **~ies** iz
Senlac ˈsen læk
senna, Senna ˈsen ə
Sennacherib se ˈnæk ər ɪb sə-, sɪ-, §-əb
sennet ˈsen ɪt §-ət **~s** s
Sennett ˈsen ɪt §-ət

sennight, se'nnight 'sen aɪt ~s s
Senor, Señor, s~ sen 'jɔː ‖ seɪn 'jɔːr —*Sp*
[se 'ɲoɾ]
Senora, Señora, s~ sen 'jɔːr ə ‖ seɪn- -'jouɾ-
—*Sp* [se 'ɲo ɾa]
Senorita, Señorita, s~ ˌsen jɔː 'riːt ə -jə-
‖ ˌseɪn jə 'riːt̬ ə —*Sp* [se ɲo 'ɾi ta] ~**s** z
sensate 'sen⁺s eɪt -ət, -ɪt
sensation sen 'seɪʃ ⁿn sⁿn- ~**s** z
sensational sen 'seɪʃ ⁿn ‿əl sⁿn- ~**ly** i
sensationalis|e, sensationaliz|e
sen 'seɪʃ ⁿn ‿ə laɪz sⁿn- ~**ed** d ~**es** ɪz əz ~**ing**
ɪŋ
sensational|ism sen 'seɪʃ ⁿn ‿əl| ˌɪz əm sⁿn-
~**ist/s** ɪst/s §əst/s ‖ əst/s
sense sen⁺s **sensed** sen⁺st **senses** 'sen⁺s ɪz -əz
sensing 'sen⁺s ɪŋ
'**sense organ**
senseless 'sen⁺s ləs -lɪs ~**ly** li ~**ness** nəs nɪs
sensibilit|y ˌsen⁺s ə 'bɪl ət |i ˌ-ɪ-, -ɪt i ‖ -ət̬ |i
~**ies** iz
sensib|le 'sen⁺s əb |ᵊl -ɪb- ~**leness** ᵊl nəs -nɪs
~**ly** li
Sensimetrics *tdmk* ˌsen⁺s ɪ 'metr ɪks -ə-
sensitis... —*see* **sensitiz...**
sensitive 'sen⁺s ət ɪv -ɪt- ‖ -ət̬ ɪv ~**ly** li ~**ness**
nəs nɪs ~**s** z
sensitivit|y ˌsen⁺s ə 'tɪv ət |i ˌ-ɪ-, -ɪt i ‖ -ət̬ |i
~**ies** iz
sensitization ˌsen⁺s ət aɪ 'zeɪʃ ⁿn ˌ-ɪt-, -ɪ'--
‖ -ət̬ ə- ~**s** z
sensitiz|e 'sen⁺s ə taɪz -ɪ- ~**ed** d ~**es** ɪz əz ~**ing**
ɪŋ
Sensodyne *tdmk* 'sen⁺s əʊ daɪn ‖ -ə-
sensor 'sen⁺s ə ‖ -ᵊr (= *censor*) ~**s** z
sensorimotor ˌsen⁺s ər i 'məʊt ə ◂ ‖ -'moʊt̬ ᵊr
sensory 'sen⁺s ər i
sensual 'sen⁺s ju ‿əl 'senʧ u ‿əl ‖ 'senʧ u ‿əl
'senʧ əl ~**ism** ˌɪz əm ~**ist/s** ɪst/s §əst/s
‖ əst/s ~**ly** i
sensualit|y ˌsen⁺s ju 'æl ət |i ˌsenʧ u-, -ɪt i
‖ ˌsenʧ u 'æl ət̬ |i ~**ies** iz
sensuous 'sen⁺s ju ‿əs 'senʧ u ‿əs ‖ 'senʧ u ‿əs
~**ly** li ~**ness** nəs nɪs
sent sent
Sentamu 'sent ə mu:
sentenc|e 'sent ən⁺s ‖ -ᵊn⁺s ~**ed** t ~**es** ɪz əz
~**ing** ɪŋ
'**sentence ˌstructure**
sentential sen 'tenʧ ᵊl ~**ly** i
sententious sen 'tenʧ əs ~**ly** li ~**ness** nəs nɪs
sentience 'senʧ ⁿn⁺s 'senʧ i ‿ən⁺s; 'sent i ‿ən⁺s
‖ 'senʧ i ‿ən⁺s
sentient 'senʧ ⁿnt 'senʧ i ‿ənt; 'sent i ‿ənt
‖ 'senʧ i ‿ənt ~**ly** li ~**s** s
sentiment 'sent ɪ mənt -ə- ‖ 'senţ ə- ~**s** s
sentimental ˌsent ɪ 'ment ᵊl ◂ -ə-
‖ ˌsenţ ə 'menţ ᵊl ◂
sentimentalis... —*see* **sentimentaliz...**
sentimentalism ˌsent ɪ 'ment ə ˌlɪz əm ˌ-ə-,
-ᵊl ˌɪz- ‖ ˌsenţ ə 'menţ ᵊl ˌɪz əm
sentimentalist ˌsent ɪ 'ment ᵊl ɪst ˌ-ə-
‖ ˌsenţ ə 'menţ- ~**s** s

sentimentality ˌsent ɪ men 'tæl ət i ˌ-ə-,
-mən'--, -ɪt i ‖ ˌsenţ ə men 'tæl əţ i -mən'--
sentimentalization
ˌsent ɪ ˌment əl aɪ 'zeɪʃ ⁿn ˌ-ə-
‖ ˌsenţ ə ˌmenţ ᵊl ə-
sentimentaliz|e ˌsent ɪ 'ment ə laɪz ˌ-ə-,
-ᵊl aɪz ‖ ˌsenţ ə 'menţ ᵊl aɪz ~**ed** d ~**es** ɪz əz
~**ing** ɪŋ
sentimentally ˌsent ɪ 'ment ᵊl i ˌ-ə-
‖ ˌsenţ ə 'menţ ᵊl i
sentinel 'sent ɪn ᵊl -ən- ‖ 'sent ᵊn ‿əl ~**s** z
sentr|y 'sentr |i ~**ies** iz
'**sentry box**
sentry-go 'sentr i gəʊ ‖ -goʊ
senza 'sents ə -ɑː —*It* ['sent tsa]
Seonaid ʃə 'neɪd —*ScG* ['ʃo nidʒ]
Seoul səʊl →soul ‖ soʊl —*Korean* ['sə ul]
sepal 'sep ᵊl 'siːp- ~**s** z
-sepalous 'sep əl əs — **polysepalous**
ˌpɒl i 'sep əl əs ◂ ‖ ˌpɑːl-
-sepaly 'sep əl i — **polysepaly** ˌpɒl i 'sep əl i
‖ ˌpɑːl-
separability ˌsep ər ə 'bɪl ət i -ɪt i ‖ -əţ i
separab|le 'sep ər əb |ᵊl ~**ly** li
separate *adj, n* 'sep ᵊr ət ɪt ~**ly** li ~**ness** nəs
nɪs ~**s** s
sepa|rate *v* 'sep ə |reɪt ~**rated** reɪt ɪd -əd
‖ reɪt̬ əd ~**rates** reɪts ~**rating** reɪt ɪŋ ‖ reɪt̬ ɪŋ
separation ˌsep ə 'reɪʃ ⁿn ~**s** z
separatism, S~ 'sep ᵊr ət ˌɪz əm ɪt,-- ‖ əţ,--
separatist, S~ 'sep ᵊr ət ɪst ɪt ɪst, §-əst ‖ əţ əst
~**s** s
separative 'sep ᵊr ət ɪv ‖ əţ ɪv -ə reɪt̬ ɪv
separator 'sep ə reɪt ə ‖ -reɪt̬ ᵊr ~**s** z
Sephard|i sɪ 'fɑːd |i sə-, se- ‖ -'fɑːrd |i ~**ic** ɪk
~**im** ɪm §əm ‖ əm
sepia 'siːp i ‿ə ~**s** z
sepiolite 'siːp i ‿ə laɪt
sepoy 'siːp ɔɪ ~**s** z
sepsis 'seps ɪs §-əs
sept sept **septs** septs
September sep 'tem bə sɪp-, səp- ‖ -bᵊr ~**s** z
septennial sep 'ten i ‿əl ~**ly** i
septet, septette ₍ᵢ₎sep 'tet ~**s** s
septic 'sept ɪk
ˌ**septic 'tank** '···
septicaemia, septicemia ˌsept ɪ 'siːm i ‿ə
§ˌ-ə-
Septimus 'sept ɪm əs -əm-
septuagenarian ˌsept ju ‿ə dʒə 'neər i ‿ən ◂
ˌsep tʃu, -dʒɪ'-- ‖ ˌsep tʃu ‿ə dʒə 'ner- ˌsept u,
ˌsept ju, ~**s** z
Septuagesima ˌsept ju ‿ə 'dʒes ɪm ə ˌsep tʃu,
-əm ə ‖ ˌsep tʃu, ˌsept u, ˌsept ju,
Septuagint 'sept ju ‿ə dʒɪnt 'sep tʃu, ‖ -u ‿ə-
'sep tʃu, 'sept ju,
sept|um 'sept |əm ~**a** ə
sepulcher 'sep ᵊlk ə ‖ -ᵊr ~**s** z
sepulchral sə 'pʌlk rəl sɪ-, se- ~**ly** i
sepulchre 'sep ᵊlk ə ‖ -ᵊr ~**s** z
sepulture 'sep ᵊlʧ ə -ᵊl tjʊə ‖ -ᵊlʧ ᵊr -ᵊl tʃʊr
Sepulveda sə 'pʌlv əd ə -'pʊlv- —*Also,
inappropriately,* ˌsep ᵊl 'veɪd ə

S

sequel 'siːk wəl **~s** z
sequel|a sɪ 'kwiːl |ə sə-, se-, -'kwel- **~ae** iː
sequenc|e 'siːk wənᵗs **~ed** t **~er/s** ə/z ‖ ᵊr/z
  ~es ɪz əz **~ing** ɪŋ
sequent 'siːk wənt **~s** s
sequential sɪ 'kwenᵗʃ ᵊl sə- **~ly** i
sequester sɪ 'kwest ə sə- ‖ -ᵊr **~ed** d
  sequestering sɪ 'kwest ər ɪŋ **~s** z
sequestrant 'siːk wəs trənt 'sek-, -wɪs-, -wes-;
  sɪ 'kwes-, sə- **~s** s
seque|strate 'siːk wə |streɪt 'sek-, -wɪ-, -we-;
  sɪ 'kwe|s treɪt, sə- **~strated** streɪt ɪd -əd
  ‖ streɪt əd **~strates** streɪts **~strating**
  streɪt ɪŋ ‖ streɪt ɪŋ
sequestration ˌsiːk wə 'streɪʃ ᵊn ˌsek-, -wɪ-,
  -we- **~s** z
seques|trum sɪ 'kwes trəm sə- **~tra** trə
sequin 'siːk wɪn §-wən **~ed, ~ned** d **~s** z
sequoia, S~, Sequoya, Sequoyah sɪ 'kwɔɪ ə
  sə-, se- **~s** z
sera 'sɪər ə ‖ 'sɪr ə
seraglio sə 'rɑːl i əʊ sɪ-, se- ‖ -'ræl joʊ -'rɑːl-
  ~s z
serape sə 'rɑːp i sɪ-, se-, -'ræp-, -eɪ **~s** z
ser|aph 'ser |əf **~aphim** ə fɪm **~aphs** əfs
seraphic sə 'ræf ɪk sɪ-, se- **~ally** ᵊl i
seraphim 'ser ə fɪm
Seraphina ˌser ə 'fiːn ə
Serapis 'ser əp ɪs §-əs ‖ sə 'reɪp-
Serb sɜːb ‖ sɜːːb **Serbs** sɜːbz ‖ sɜːːbz
Serbi|a 'sɜːb i |ə ‖ 'sɜːːb- **~an/s** ən/z
Serbo-Croat ˌsɜːb əʊ 'krəʊ æt ◂
  ‖ ˌsɜːːb oʊ 'kroʊ æt ◂
Serbo-Croatian ˌsɜːb əʊ krəʊ 'eɪʃ ᵊn ◂
  ‖ ˌsɜːːb oʊ kroʊ 'eɪʃ ᵊn ◂
sere sɪə ‖ sɪᵊr (= sear)
Serena sə 'riːn ə sɪ-, se-, -'reɪn-
serenad|e ˌser ə 'neɪd -ɪ-, '··· **~ed** ɪd əd **~es** z
  ~ing ɪŋ
serendipitous ˌser ən 'dɪp ət əs ˌen-, -ɪt əs
  ‖ -əţ əs **~ly** li
serendipity ˌser ən 'dɪp ət i ˌen-, -ɪt i ‖ -əţ i
serene sə 'riːn sɪ- **~ly** li **~ness** nəs nɪs
Serengeti ˌser ən 'get i →-əŋ-, -ɪn-, →-ɪŋ-
  ‖ -'geţ i
serenit|y sə 'ren ət |i sɪ-, -ɪt- ‖ -əţ |i **~ies** ɪz
serf sɜːf ‖ sɜːːf (= surf) **serfs** sɜːfs ‖ sɜːːfs
serf|dom 'sɜːf |dəm ‖ 'sɜːːf- **~hood** hʊd
serge sɜːdʒ ‖ sɜːːdʒ
Serge sɜːdʒ ‖ sɜːːdʒ —Fr [sɛʁʒ]
sergeant 'sɑːdʒ ənt ‖ 'sɑːrdʒ ənt **~s** s
  ˌsergeant 'major
sergeant|-at-arms ˌsɑːdʒ ənt| ət 'ɑːmz
  ‖ ˌsɑːrdʒ ənţ| əţ 'ɑːrmz **sergeants~** ˌənts
Sergei 'seə geɪ 'sɜːg-,·'· ‖ ser 'geɪ —Russ
  ['sʲɪr gʲej]
Sergio 'sɜːdʒ i əʊ ‖ 'sɜːːdʒ i oʊ —It ['sɛr dʒo]
serial 'sɪər i əl ‖ 'sɪr- **~s** z
  'serial ˌnumber; ˌserial mo'nogamy;
  'serial rights
serialis... —see **serializ...**
serialization ˌsɪər i əl aɪ 'zeɪʃ ᵊn -ɪ'··
  ‖ ˌsɪr i əl ə- **~s** z

serializ|e 'sɪər i ə laɪz ‖ 'sɪr- **~ed** d **~es** ɪz əz
  ~ing ɪŋ
serially 'sɪər i əl i ‖ 'sɪr-
seriatim ˌsɪər i 'eɪt ɪm ˌser-, -'ɑːt-, §-əm
  ‖ ˌsɪr ɪ 'eɪţ əm -'æţ-
sericulture 'sɪər ɪ ˌkʌltʃ ə 'ser-, §-ə-
  ‖ 'ser ə ˌkʌltʃ ᵊr
seriema ˌser i 'iːm ə **~s** z
series sing., pl 'sɪər iːz -ɪz ‖ 'sɪr iːz —Some BrE
  speakers pronounce the sing. with **-ɪz**, the pl
  with **-iːz**
serif 'ser ɪf -əf **~s** s
serin 'ser ɪn §-ən **~s** z
Seringapatam sə ˌrɪŋ gə pə 'tɑːm sɪ-, -'tæm
seriocomic ˌsɪər i əʊ 'kɒm ɪk ◂
  ‖ ˌsɪr i oʊ 'kɑːm ɪk ◂ **~ally** ᵊl̩ i
serious 'sɪər i əs ‖ 'sɪr- **~ly** li **~ness** nəs nɪs
serjeant 'sɑːdʒ ənt ‖ 'sɑːrdʒ ənt **~s** s
serjeant|-at-arms ˌsɑːdʒ ənt| ət 'ɑːmz
  ‖ ˌsɑːrdʒ ənţ| əţ 'ɑːrmz **serjeants~** ˌənts
Serle sɜːl ‖ sɜːːl
sermon 'sɜːm ən ‖ 'sɜːːm ən **~s** z
sermonette ˌsɜːm ə 'net ‖ ˌsɜːːm- **~s** s
sermonis|e, sermoniz|e 'sɜːm ə naɪz ‖ 'sɜːːm-
  ~ed d **~er/s** ə/z ‖ ᵊr/z **~es** ɪz əz **~ing** ɪŋ
serocon|vert ˌsɪər əʊ kən |'vɜːt §-kɒn|·
  ‖ ˌsɪr oʊ kən |'vɜːt **~verted** 'vɜːt ɪd -əd
  ‖ 'vɜːţ əd **~verting** 'vɜːt ɪŋ ‖ 'vɜːţ ɪŋ **~verts**
  'vɜːts ‖ 'vɜːːts
serological ˌsɪər ə 'lɒdʒ ɪk ᵊl ◂ ‖ ˌsɪr ə 'lɑːdʒ-
  ~ly i
serology sɪ 'rɒl ədʒ i sɪə- ‖ -'rɑːl-
seronegative ˌsɪər əʊ 'neg ət ɪv ◂
  ‖ ˌsɪr oʊ 'neg əţ ɪv ◂
seropositive ˌsɪər əʊ 'pɒz ət ɪv ◂ -ɪt ɪv
  ‖ ˌsɪr oʊ 'pɑːz əţ ɪv ◂
seropositivity ˌsɪər əʊ ˌpɒz ə 'tɪv ət i -ɪ'··,
  -ɪt i ‖ ˌsɪr oʊ ˌpɑːz ə 'tɪv əţ i
Serota sə 'rəʊt ə sɪ- ‖ -'roʊţ ə
serotine 'ser əʊ taɪn ‖ -ə- -tɪn **~s** z
serotonin ˌsɪər əʊ 'təʊn ɪn ˌser-, §-ən
  ‖ ˌsɪr ə 'toʊn ən ˌser-
serous 'sɪər əs ‖ 'sɪr əs
serow 'ser əʊ ‖ -oʊ sə 'roʊ **~s** z
Seroxat tdmk sə 'rɒks æt sɪ- ‖ -'rɑːks-
Serpell 'sɜːp ᵊl ‖ 'sɜːːp ᵊl
Serpens 'sɜːp enz -ənz ‖ 'sɜːːp-
serpent 'sɜːp ənt →-mt ‖ 'sɜːːp- **~s** s
serpentine, S~ 'sɜːp ən taɪn →-m-
  ‖ 'sɜːːp ən tiːn -taɪn
SERPS sɜːps ‖ sɜːːps
Serra 'ser ə —Sp ['se rra]
serrated sə 'reɪt ɪd sɪ-, se-, -əd ‖ -'reɪţ əd
serration sə 'reɪʃ ᵊn sɪ-, se- **~s** z
serried 'ser id
ser|um 'sɪər |əm ‖ 'sɪr |əm **~a** ə **~ums** əmz
serval 'sɜːv ᵊl ‖ 'sɜːːv ᵊl **~s** z
servant 'sɜːv ᵊnt ‖ 'sɜːːv ᵊnt **~s** s
serve sɜːv ‖ sɜːːv **served** sɜːvd ‖ sɜːːvd **serves**
  sɜːvz ‖ sɜːːvz **serving** 'sɜːv ɪŋ ‖ 'sɜːːv ɪŋ
server 'sɜːv ə ‖ 'sɜːːv ᵊr **~s** z
server|y 'sɜːv ər |i ‖ 'sɜːːv- **~ies** ɪz

servic|e, S~ 'sɜːv ɪs §-əs ‖ 'sɜːᵛv əs **~ed** t **~es** ɪz əz **~ing** ɪŋ
  'service charge; 'service flat; 'service road; 'service ˌstation

serviceability ˌsɜːv ɪs ə 'bɪl ət i §ˌ-əs-, -ɪt i ‖ ˌsɜːᵛv əs ə 'bɪl ət̬ i

serviceab|le 'sɜːv ɪs əb |ᵊl §'-əs- ‖ 'sɜːᵛv əs- **~leness** ᵊl nəs -nɪs **~ly** li

serviceberr|y 'sɜːᵛv ɪs ˌber |i -əs- ‖ 'sɜːᵛv əs- **~ies** iz

service|man 'sɜːv ɪs |mən §-əs- ‖ 'sɜːᵛv əs- -mæn **~men** mən men **~woman** ˌwʊm ən **~women** ˌwɪm ɪn §-ən

serviette ˌsɜːv i 'et ‖ ˌsɜːᵛv- **~s** s

servile 'sɜːv aɪᵊl ‖ 'sɜːv ᵊl -aɪᵊl **~ly** li **~ness** nəs nɪs

servility sɜː 'vɪl ət i -ɪt- ‖ sɜː 'vɪl ət̬ i

serving 'sɜːv ɪŋ ‖ 'sɜːᵛv ɪŋ **~s** z
  'serving spoon

Servis tdmk 'sɜːv ɪs §-əs ‖ 'sɜːᵛv-

Servite 'sɜːv aɪt ‖ 'sɜːᵛv- **~s** s

servitor 'sɜːv ɪt ə -ət- ‖ 'sɜːᵛv ət̬ ᵊr **~s** z

servitude 'sɜːv ɪ tjuːd -ə-, →-tʃuːd ‖ 'sɜːᵛv ə tuːd -tjuːd

servo 'sɜːv əʊ ‖ 'sɜːᵛv oʊ **~s** z

servomechanism 'sɜːv əʊ ˌmek ə nɪz əm ‖ 'sɜːᵛv oʊ- **~s** z

servomotor 'sɜːv əʊ ˌməʊt ə ‖ 'sɜːᵛv oʊ ˌmoʊt̬ ᵊr **~s** z

sesame 'ses əm i
  'sesame seeds

Sesotho sɪ 'suːt uː sə-, se-

sesqui- |sesk wi — **sesquioxide** ˌsesk wi 'ɒks aɪd ‖ -'ɑːks-

sesquicentennial ˌsesk wi sen 'ten i əl **~s** z

sesquipedalian ˌsesk wi pɪ 'deɪl i ən ◂ ˌ-wə-, -pə'-, -pe'- **~s** z

sessile 'ses aɪᵊl -ᵊl, -ɪl

session 'seʃ ᵊn **~s** z

sessional 'seʃ ᵊn_əl **~ly** i **~s** z

Sessions 'seʃ ᵊnz

sest|erce 'sest |ɜːs ‖ -|ɜːs **~erces** ɜːs ɪz əs-, -əz; ə siːz ‖ ɜːs əz

sesterti|um se 'stɜːt i |əm -'stɜːʃ-ᵊ ‖ -'stɜːᵗʃ- -stɜːʃ |əm **~a** ə

sestet ₍ᵢ₎ses 'tet **~s** s

set set **sets** sets **setting** 'set ɪŋ ‖ 'set̬ ɪŋ
  ˌset 'book; ˌset 'piece; ˌset 'point; ˌset 'theory

seta 'siːt ə ‖ 'siːt̬ ə **setae** 'siːt iː -eɪ, -aɪ

setaceous sɪ 'teɪʃ əs sə-, siː-

Setanta se 'tænt ə sɪ-, sə-

setaside 'set ə ˌsaɪd ‖ 'set̬-

setback 'set bæk **~s** s

set-down 'set daʊn

se-tenant sə 'ten ənt sɪ-, siː- ‖ ˌset ᵊn 'ɑːn —Fr [sə tə nɑ̃]

Seth seθ —but as an Indian name, seɪt

Seton, s~ 'siːt ᵊn

setscrew 'set skruː **~s** z

setsquare 'set skweə ‖ -skwer -skwær **~s** z

sett set **setts** sets

settee se 'tiː sə- **~s** z

setter, S~ 'set ə ‖ 'set̬ ᵊr **~s** z

setting 'set ɪŋ ‖ 'set̬ ɪŋ **~s** z

settl|e 'set ᵊl ‖ 'set̬ ᵊl **~ed** d **~es** z **~ing** ɪŋ

settlement 'set ᵊl mənt **~s** s

settler 'set ᵊl ə ‖ 'set̬ ᵊl ᵊr **~s** z

set-to 'set tuː ˌ·'· **~s** z

set-top 'set tɒp ‖ -tɑːp

Setubal, Setúbal sə 'tuːb ᵊl se-, -æl —Port [sə 'tu βɐl]

set-up, setup 'set ʌp ‖ 'set̬ ʌp **~s** s

Seumas 'ʃuːm əs —ScG ['ʃu məs]

Seurat 'sɜːr ɑː ‖ sʊ 'rɑː —Fr [sœ ʁa]

Seuss sjuːs suːs ‖ suːs

Sevastopol sə 'væst ə pɒl sɪ-, -pᵊl ‖ -poʊl —Russ Sevastopol [sᵊɪ vʌ 'sto pəlʲ]

seven 'sev ᵊn —In casual speech also →'seb m (not before a vowel sound) **~s** z

sevenfold 'sev ᵊn fəʊld →'seb m-, →fɒʊld ‖ -foʊld

sevenish 'sev ᵊn ɪʃ

Sevenoaks 'sev ᵊn əʊks ‖ -oʊks

seventeen ˌsev ᵊn 'tiːn ◂ —In casual speech also →ˌseb m- **~s** z **~th/s** θ/s

seventh 'sev ᵊnᵗθ —Casually also →'seb mᵖθ **~s** s
  ˌseventh 'heaven

Seventh-Day ˌsev ᵊnᵗθ 'deɪ ◂

seventh-inning ˌsev nᵗθ 'ɪn ɪŋ ◂

seventieth 'sev ᵊnt i əθ ɪθ ‖ 'sev ᵊnt̬- —Casually also →'seb mᵖt i əθ **~s** s

sevent|y 'sev ᵊnt |i ‖ -ᵊnt̬ |i —Casually also →'seb mᵖt |i **~ies** iz

seventy-eight ˌsev ᵊnt i 'eɪt ◂ ‖ ˌsev ᵊnt̬- —Casually also →ˌseb mᵖt- **~s** s

Seven-Up, 7-Up tdmk ˌsev ᵊn 'ʌp **~s** s

seven-year ˌsev ᵊn 'jɪə ◂ -'jɜː ‖ -'jɪᵊr ◂ —Casually also →ˌseb m-
  ˌseven-year 'itch

sever 'sev ə ‖ -ᵊr **~ed** d **severing** 'sev ᵊr ɪŋ **~s** z

several 'sev rəl 'sev ᵊr_əl **~ly** i

severanc|e 'sev ᵊr_ᵊnᵗs **~es** ɪz əz
  'severance pay

severe sɪ 'vɪə sə- ‖ -'vɪᵊr **severer** sɪ 'vɪər ə sə- ‖ -'vɪr ᵊr **severest** sɪ 'vɪər ɪst sə-, -əst ‖ -'vɪr əst **~ly** li **~ness** nəs nɪs

severed 'sev əd ‖ -ᵊrd

severit|y sɪ 'ver ət i |i sə-, -ɪt i ‖ -ət̬ |i **~ies** iz

Severn 'sev ᵊn ‖ -ᵊrn

Severus sɪ 'vɪər əs sə- ‖ -'vɪr əs

seviche sɪ 'viːtʃ eɪ sə-, seɪ-, -i —AmSp [se 'vi tʃe]

Seville sə 'vɪl sɪ-, se- —Sp Sevilla [se 'βi ʎa, -ja] —but usually 'sev ᵊl, -ɪl in the expression ˌSeville 'orange

Sevres, Sèvres 'seɪv rə 'sev- ‖ 'sev rə —Fr [sɛːvʁ]

sew səʊ ‖ soʊ (= so) **sewed** səʊd ‖ soʊd **sewing** 'səʊ ɪŋ ‖ 'soʊ ɪŋ **sews** səʊz ‖ soʊz
  'sewing maˌchine

sewage 'suː ɪdʒ 'sjuː
  'sewage farm

S

Seward *(i)* 'siː wəd ‖ -wᵊrd, *(ii)* 'sjuː əd 'suː
‖ 'suːᵊrd

Sewell 'sjuː əl 'suː ; 'sjuːl, 'suːl ‖ 'suː əl

sewer *'drain'; 'servant'* 'suː ə 'sjuː ‖ ᵊr ~s z

sewer *'one that sews'* 'səʊ ə ‖ 'soʊ ᵊr ~s z

sewerage 'suː ər ɪdʒ 'sjuː

sewn səʊn ‖ soʊn

sex seks sexed sekst *(= sext)* sexes 'seks ɪz
-əz sexing 'seks ɪŋ
'sex ap‚peal; 'sex ‚hormone; 'sex ‚object;
'sex ‚organ

sexagenarian ‚seks ə dʒə 'neər i ‚ən ◄ -dʒɪ'--,
-dʒeˈ-- ‖ -'ner- ~s z

Sexagesima ‚seks ə 'dʒes ɪm ə -əm ə

-sexed 'sekst — highly-sexed ‚haɪ li 'sekst ◄

sexi... —*see* sexy

sexism 'seks ‚ɪz əm

sexist 'seks ɪst §-əst ~s s

sexless 'seks ləs -lɪs ~ly li ~ness nəs nɪs

sex-linked ‚seks 'lɪŋkt ◄ '· ·

sexological ‚seks ə 'lɒdʒ ɪk ᵊl ◄ ‖ -'laːdʒ-

sexologist sek 'sɒl ədʒ ɪst §-əst ‖ -'saːl- ~s s

sexology sek 'sɒl ədʒ i ‖ -'saːl-

sexploitation ‚seks plɔɪ 'teɪʃ ᵊn

sexpot 'seks pɒt ‖ -paːt ~s s

sex-starved 'seks staːvd ‚·'· ‖ -staːrvd

sext, Sext sekst

Sextans 'sekst ənz

sextant 'sekst ənt ~s s

sextet ₍ˌ₎seks 'tet ~s s

sextile 'sekst aɪᵊl

sextodecimo ‚sekst əʊ 'des ɪ məʊ -ə·
‖ -oʊ 'des ə moʊ

sexton, S~ 'sekst ən ~s z

sextupl|e 'sekst jʊp ᵊl -jəp-; sek 'stjuːp-
‖ sek 'stuːp ᵊl -'stʊp-, -'stʌp-; 'sekst əp- ~ed d
~es z ~ing ɪŋ

sextuplet 'seks tjʊp lət seks 'tjuːp-, §-'tʌp-, -lɪt,
-let ‖ sek 'stʌp- -'stuːp-, -'stjuːp-; 'sekst əp- ~s
s

sexual 'sek ʃu əl 'seks ju əl, 'sek ʃᵊl ~ly i
‚sexual 'intercourse

sexualit|y ‚sek ʃu 'æl ət |i ‚seks ju-, -ɪt i
‖ -əţ |i ~ies iz

sexualization, sexualisation
‚sek ʃu əl aɪ 'zeɪʃ ᵊn ‚seks ju ‚-ɪ'-· ‖ -ə'· ·

sexualiz|e, sexualis|e 'sek ʃu ə laɪz 'seks ju
~ed d ~es ɪz əz ~ing ɪŋ

Sexwale se 'kwaːl eɪ —*Venda* [se 'xwaː le]

sex|y 'seks |i ~ier i ə ‖ i ᵊr ~iest i ɪst i əst ~ily
ɪ li əl i ~iness i nəs i nɪs

Seychelles ₍ˌ₎seɪ 'ʃelz -'ʃel, '· ·

Seychellois ‚seɪ ʃel 'waː ◄

Seyfert 'saɪf ət 'siːf- ‖ -ᵊrt

Seymour *(i)* 'siː mɔː ‖ -mɔːr -moʊr, *(ii)* 'siːm ə
‖ -ᵊr, *(iii)* 'seɪm ə ‖ -ᵊr

sez *non-standard spelling of* says sez

SF ‚es 'ef

sforzand|o ₍ˌ₎sfɔːt 'sænd |əʊ
‖ ₍ˌ₎sfɔːrt 'saːnd |oʊ -'sænd- ~i iː

sgian-dhu ‚skiː ən 'duː ‚skiːn'·

SGML ‚es dʒiː em 'el

sgraffit|o skræ 'fiːt| əʊ ‖ -oʊ —*It*
[zgraf 'fiː to] ~i iː i

Sgurr skʊə ‖ skʊᵊr —*ScG* [skur]

sh, shh, ssh ʃ

Shaanxi ‚ʃɑːn 'ʃiː —*Chi* Shǎnxī [³ʂan ¹çi]

Shabbat ʃə 'bæt -'baːt ‖ -'baːt 'ʃaːb əs

shabb|y 'ʃæb |i ~ier i ə ‖ i ᵊr ~iest i ɪst i əst
~ily ɪ li əl i ~iness i nəs i nɪs

shack ʃæk shacked ʃækt shacking 'ʃæk ɪŋ
shacks ʃæks

shackl|e 'ʃæk ᵊl ~ed d ~es z ~ing ‚ɪŋ

Shackleton 'ʃæk ᵊl tən ~s, ~'s z

shad ʃæd shads ʃædz

Shadbolt 'ʃæd bəʊlt →'ʃæb-, →-bɒʊlt ‖ -boʊlt

shadbush 'ʃæd bʊʃ ~es ɪz əz

shaddock, S~ 'ʃæd ək ~s s

shade ʃeɪd shaded 'ʃeɪd ɪd -əd shades ʃeɪdz
shading/s 'ʃeɪd ɪŋ/z

shadoof ʃə 'duːf ʃæ- ~s s

shadow 'ʃæd əʊ ‖ -oʊ ~ed d ~ing ɪŋ ~s z
‚shadow 'cabinet; 'shadow play

shadowbox 'ʃæd əʊ bɒks ‖ -oʊ baːks ~ed t
~es ɪz əz ~ing ɪŋ

shadow|y 'ʃæd əʊ |i ‖ -oʊ |i ~ier i ə ‖ i ᵊr
~iest i ɪst i əst ~iness i nəs i nɪs

Shadrach 'ʃædr æk 'ʃeɪdr-, -aːx

Shadwell 'ʃæd wel -wəl

shad|y 'ʃeɪd |i ~ier i ə ‖ i ᵊr ~iest i ɪst i əst
~ily ɪ li əl i ~iness i nəs i nɪs

SHAEF ʃeɪf

Shaeffer 'ʃeɪf ə ‖ -ᵊr

Shafaye ʃə 'feɪ

Shaffer 'ʃæf ə ‖ -ᵊr

shaft ʃaːft §ʃæft ‖ ʃæft shafted 'ʃaːft ɪd §'ʃæft-,
-əd ‖ 'ʃæft əd shafting/s 'ʃaːft ɪŋ/z §'ʃæft-
‖ 'ʃæft ɪŋ/z shafts ʃaːfts §ʃæfts ‖ ʃæfts

Shaftesbury 'ʃaːfts bər i §'ʃæfts- ‖ 'ʃæfts ‚ber i

Shafto, Shaftoe 'ʃaːft əʊ §'ʃæft- ‖ 'ʃæft oʊ

shag ʃæg shagged ʃægd shagging 'ʃæg ɪŋ
shags ʃægz
‚shagged 'out

shagbark 'ʃæg baːk ‖ -baːrk ~s s

shagger 'ʃæg ə ‖ -ᵊr ~s z

shagg|y 'ʃæg |i ~ier i ə ‖ i ᵊr ~iest i ɪst i əst
~ily ɪ li əl i ~iness i nəs i nɪs

shaggy-dog ‚ʃæg i 'dɒg ‖ -'dɔːg -'daːg
‚shaggy-'dog ‚story

shagreen ʃə 'griːn ʃæ-

shah, Shah ʃaː shahs ʃaːz

shaheed, shahid ʃə 'hiːd ʃæ- —*Arabic*
[ʃa 'hiːd]

Shairp *(i)* ʃaːp ‖ ʃaːrp, *(ii)* ʃeəp ‖ ʃeᵊrp

Shaka 'ʃaːk ə 'ʃaːg-

shake ʃeɪk shaken 'ʃeɪk ən shakes ʃeɪks
shaking/s 'ʃeɪk ɪŋ/z shook ʃʊk §ʃuːk

shakedown 'ʃeɪk daʊn ~s z

shaken 'ʃeɪk ən

shake-out, shakeout 'ʃeɪk aʊt ~s s

shaker, S~ 'ʃeɪk ə ‖ -ᵊr ~s z

Shakerley 'ʃæk ə li ‖ -ᵊr-

Shakeshaft 'ʃeɪk ʃaːft §-ʃæft ‖ -ʃæft

Shakespear, Shakespeare 'ʃeɪk spɪə ‖ -spɪr

Shakespearean ₍ˌ₎ʃeɪk 'spɪər i ən ‖ -'spɪr- ~s z

Shakespeareana (ˌ)ʃeɪk ˌspɪər i ˈɑːn ə
‖ -ˌspɪr i ˈæn ə -ˈɑːn-, -ˈeɪn-
Shakespearian (ˌ)ʃeɪk ˈspɪər i ˌən ‖ -ˈspɪr- ~s z
Shakespeariana (ˌ)ʃeɪk ˌspɪər i ˈɑːn ə
‖ -ˌspɪr i ˈæn ə -ˈɑːn-, -ˈeɪn-
shake-up ˈʃeɪk ʌp ~s s
shako ˈʃæk əʊ ˈʃeɪk-, ˈʃɑːk- ‖ -oʊ ~s z
shak|y ˈʃeɪk |i ~ier i ə ‖ i ᵊr ~iest i ɪst i ˌəst
~ily ɪ li əl i ~iness i nəs i nɪs
Shalden, Shaldon ˈʃɔːld ən ˈ ʃɒld- ‖ ˈʃɑːld-
shale ʃeɪᵊl **shales** ʃeɪᵊlz
Shalford ˈʃæl fəd ‖ -fᵊrd
shall strong form ʃæl, weak form ʃᵊl —There are
also weak forms ʃə, ʃ, used only before a
following word beginning with a consonant.
shallop ˈʃæl əp ~s s
shallot ʃə ˈlɒt ‖ -ˈlɑːt ˈʃæl ət ~s s
shallow ˈʃæl əʊ ‖ -oʊ ~ed d ~er ə ‖ ᵊr ~est ɪst
əst ~ing ɪŋ ~ly li ~ness nəs nɪs ~s z
shalom ʃæ ˈlɒm ʃə-, -ˈləʊm ‖ ʃɑː ˈloʊm ʃə-
sha,lom a'leichem ə ˈleɪx əm
shalt strong form ʃælt, weak form ʃᵊlt
shalwar ʃʌl ˈwɑː ‖ -ˈwɑːr ~s z
shal,war ka'meez
sham ʃæm **shammed** ʃæmd **shamming**
ˈʃæm ɪŋ **shams** ʃæmz
shaman ˈʃæm ən ˈʃeɪm-, ˈʃɑːm- ‖ ˈʃɑːm ən
ˈʃeɪm-, ˈʃæm- ~ism ˌɪz əm ~s z
shamanistic ˌʃæm ə ˈnɪst ɪk ◄ ˌʃɑːm-, ˌʃeɪm-
‖ ˌʃɑːm- ˌʃeɪm-, ˌʃæm-
shamateur ˈʃæm ət ə -ə tʃʊə, -tʃə, -tjʊə;
ˌʃæm ə ˈtɜː ◄ ‖ ˈʃæm ə tʃʊr -əṭ ᵊr, -ə tjʊr ~s z
shamateurism ˈʃæm ət ər ˌɪz əm -ət ʃə ər-,
-ə tɜːr-, -ə tʃʊər-, -ə tjʊər- ‖ ˈʃæm ə tʃʊr-
-əṭ ᵊr-, -ə tjʊr-
shambl|e ˈʃæm bᵊl ~ed d ~es z ~ing ᵊŋ
shambolic ʃæm ˈbɒl ɪk ‖ -ˈbɑːl ɪk ~ally ᵊl i
shame ʃeɪm **shamed** ʃeɪmd **shames** ʃeɪmz
shaming ˈʃeɪm ɪŋ
shamefaced ˌʃeɪm ˈfeɪst ◄
shamefaced|ly ˌʃeɪm ˈfeɪst |li -ˈfeɪs ɪd |li, -əd-
~ness nəs nɪs
shameful ˈʃeɪm fᵊl -fʊl ~ly ˌi ~ness nəs nɪs
shameless ˈʃeɪm ləs -lɪs ~ly li ~ness nəs nɪs
shaming ˈʃeɪm ɪŋ ~ly li
shamisen ˈʃæm ɪ sen ‖ ˈʃɑːm- —Jp
[ça ˌmi sen] ~s z
shamm... —see sham
shamm|y ˈʃæm |i ~ies iz
shampoo (ˌ)ʃæm ˈpuː ~ed d ~ing ɪŋ ~s z
shamrock ˈʃæm rɒk ‖ -rɑːk ~s s
shamus ˈʃɑːm əs ˈʃeɪm- ~es ɪz əz
Shan ʃɑːn —for the people and language, also
ʃæn **Shans** ʃɑːnz ʃænz
Shandong ˌʃæn ˈdɒŋ ‖ ˌʃɑːn ˈdɔːŋ —Chi
Shāndōng [¹ʂan ¹tʊŋ]
shand|y ˈʃænd |i ~ies iz
shandygaff ˈʃænd i gæf ~s s
Shane ʃeɪn
Shang dynasty ʃæŋ ‖ ʃɑːŋ —Chi Shāng [¹ʂaŋ]
Shangaan ʃæn ˈgɑːn ~s z
Shanghai, s~ ˌʃæŋ ˈhaɪ ˙ · ·—Chi Shànghǎi
[⁴ʂaŋ ³xai] ~ed d ~ing ɪŋ ~s z

Shango ˈʃæŋ gəʊ ‖ -goʊ
Shangri-La ˌʃæŋ gri ˈlɑː
Shanita ʃə ˈniːt ə ‖ -ˈniːṭ ə
shank ʃæŋk **shanks** ʃæŋks
ˌshank's ˈmare
Shankill ˈʃæŋk ɪl -ᵊl
Shanklin ˈʃæŋk lɪn §-lən
Shankly ˈʃæŋk li
Shanks ʃæŋks
shanks's ˈʃæŋks ɪz -əz
ˌshanks's ˈpony
Shannon ˈʃæn ən
shan't ʃɑːnt ‖ ʃænt
Shantou ˌʃæn ˈtəʊ ‖ ˌʃɑːn ˈtoʊ —Chi Shàntóu
[⁴ʂan ²tʰoʊ]
shantung, S~ ˌʃæn ˈtʌŋ —Chi Shāndōng
[¹ʂan ¹tʊŋ]
shant|y ˈʃænt |i ‖ ˈʃænṭ |i ~ies iz
shanty-town ˈʃænt i taʊn ‖ ˈʃænṭ- ~s z
Shanxi ˌʃæn ˈʃiː —Chi Shǎnxī [¹ʂan ¹ɕi]
Shap ʃæp
shape ʃeɪp **shaped** ʃeɪpt **shapes** ʃeɪps
shaping ˈʃeɪp ɪŋ
SHAPE ʃeɪp
-shaped ʃeɪpt — **pear-shaped** ˈpeə ʃeɪpt
‖ ˈper-
shapeless ˈʃeɪp ləs ~ly li ~ness nəs nɪs
shape|ly ˈʃeɪp |li ~lier li ə ‖ li ᵊr ~liest li ɪst
əst ~liness li nəs -nɪs
Shapiro ʃə ˈpɪər əʊ ‖ -ˈpɪr oʊ
shard ʃɑːd ‖ ʃɑːrd **shards** ʃɑːdz ‖ ʃɑːrdz
share ʃeə ‖ ʃeᵊr ʃæᵊr **shared** ʃeəd ‖ ʃeᵊrd ʃæᵊrd
shares ʃeəz ‖ ʃeᵊrz ʃæᵊrz **sharing** ˈʃeər ɪŋ
‖ ˈʃer ɪŋ ˈʃær-
ˈshare cerˌtificate
sharecropper ˈʃeə krɒp ə ‖ ˈʃer krɑːp ᵊr ˈʃær-
~s z
shareholder ˈʃeə ˌhəʊld ə →-ˌhɒʊld-
‖ ˈʃer ˌhoʊld ᵊr ˈʃær- ~s z
shareholding ˈʃeə ˌhəʊld ɪŋ →-ˌhɒʊld-
‖ ˈʃer ˌhoʊld ɪŋ ~s z
share-out ˈʃeər aʊt ‖ ˈʃer aʊt ˈʃær- ~s s
shareware ˈʃeə weə ‖ ˈʃer wer ˈʃær wær
sharia, shari'ah ʃə ˈriː ə ʃɑː- —Ar [ʃa ˈri: ʕa]
Sharif, s~ ʃə ˈriːf ʃɑː-, ʃæ-
Sharjah ˈʃɑːdʒ ɑː ˈʃɑːʒ-, -ə ‖ ˈʃɑːrdʒ-
shark ʃɑːk ‖ ʃɑːrk **sharks** ʃɑːks ‖ ʃɑːrks
sharkskin ˈʃɑːk skɪn ‖ ˈʃɑːrk-
Sharman ˈʃɑːm ən ‖ ˈʃɑːrm-
Sharm el-Sheikh ˌʃɑːm el ˈʃeɪk -ᵊl- ‖ ˌʃɑːrm-
—Arabic [ˌʃarm aʃ ˈʃeix]
Sharon personal name ˈʃær ən ‖ ˈʃer-
Sharon Israeli politician ʃə ˈrɒn -ˈrəʊn ‖ -ˈroʊn
Sharon place name; (rose of ~) ˈʃeər ən ‖ ˈʃɑːr-,
ˈʃær-, -ɒn ‖ ˈʃær ən ˈʃer-
ˈSharon fruit
sharp ʃɑːp ‖ ʃɑːrp **sharped** ʃɑːpt ‖ ʃɑːrpt
sharper ˈʃɑːp ə ‖ ˈʃɑːrp ᵊr **sharpest** ˈʃɑːp ɪst
-əst ‖ ˈʃɑːrp əst **sharping** ˈʃɑːp ɪŋ ‖ ˈʃɑːrp ɪŋ
sharps ʃɑːps ‖ ʃɑːrps
ˌsharp ˈend; ˌsharp ˈpractice
Sharp, Sharpe ʃɑːp ‖ ʃɑːrp
sharp-eared ˌʃɑːp ˈɪəd ◄ ‖ ˌʃɑːrp ˈɪᵊrd ◄

shar pei ˌʃɑː ˈpeɪ ‖ ˌʃɑːr- ~s z —*Chi* shā pí
[¹ʂa ²pʰi]
sharpen ˈʃɑːp ən ‖ ˈʃɑːrp ən ~ed d ~ing ɪŋ ~s
z
sharpener ˈʃɑːp nə ˈʃɑːp ən ̩ə ‖ ˈʃɑːrp ən ̩ər
sharper ˈʃɑːp ə ‖ ˈʃɑːrp ər ~s z
Sharpeville ˈʃɑːp vɪl ‖ ˈʃɑːrp-
sharp-eyed ˌʃɑːp ˈaɪd ◄ ‖ ˌʃɑːrp-
sharpie ˈʃɑːrp i ‖ ˈʃɑːrp i ~s z
sharpish ˈʃɑːp ɪʃ ‖ ˈʃɑːrp ɪʃ ~ly li
Sharples ˈʃɑːp ᵊlz ‖ ˈʃɑːrp ᵊlz
sharp|ly ˈʃɑːp |li ‖ ˈʃɑːrp |li ~ness nəs nɪs
Sharpness ˌʃɑːp ˈnes ‖ ˌʃɑːrp-
sharp-set ˌʃɑːp ˈset ◄ ‖ ˌʃɑːrp-
sharpshooter ˈʃɑːp ˌʃuːt ə ‖ ˈʃɑːrp ˌʃuːt ᵊr ~s z
sharp-sighted ˌʃɑːp ˈsaɪt ɪd ◄ -əd
‖ ˌʃɑːrp ˈsaɪt əd ◄
sharp-tongued ˌʃɑːp ˈtʌŋd ◄ ‖ ˌʃɑːrp-
sharp-witted ˌʃɑːp ˈwɪt ɪd ◄ -əd
‖ ˌʃɑːrp ˈwɪt əd ◄
Sharwood ˈʃɑː wʊd ‖ ˈʃɑːr-
shashlik ˈʃæʃ lɪk ˈʃɑːʃ- ‖ ˈʃɑːʃ- ˌˑˈˑ ~s s
Shasta ˈʃæst ə
ˌShasta ˈdaisy
shat ʃæt
Shatner ˈʃæt nə ‖ -nᵊr
shatter ˈʃæt ə ‖ ˈʃæt ᵊr ~ed d **shattering/ly**
ˈʃæt ̩ər ɪŋ /li ‖ ˈʃæt ̩ər ɪŋ /li ~s z
shatterproof ˈʃæt ə pruːf §-pruf ‖ ˈʃæt ᵊr-
Shaughnessy ˈʃɔːn əs i ‖ ˈʃɑːn-
Shaun ʃɔːn ‖ ʃɑːn
shave ʃeɪv **shaved** ʃeɪvd **shaves** ʃeɪvz
shaving ˈʃeɪv ɪŋ
ˈshaving cream; ˈshaving foam
shaveling ˈʃeɪv lɪŋ ~s z
shaven ˈʃeɪv ᵊn
shaver ˈʃeɪv ə ‖ -ᵊr ~s z
Shavian ˈʃeɪv i ən ~s z
shaving ˈʃeɪv ɪŋ ~s z
Shaw, shaw ʃɔː ‖ ʃɑː
Shawcross ˈʃɔː krɒs -krɔːs ‖ -krɔːs ˈʃɑː krɑːs
shawl ʃɔːl ‖ ʃɑːl **shawls** ʃɔːlz ‖ ʃɑːlz
shawm ʃɔːm ‖ ʃɑːm **shawms** ʃɔːmz ‖ ʃɑːmz
Shawn ʃɔːn ‖ ʃɑːn
Shawnee ˌʃɔː ˈniː ‖ ₍ₗ₎ʃɑː- ~s z
shay ʃeɪ **shays** ʃeɪz
Shayler ˈʃeɪl ə ‖ -ᵊr
s/he ˌʃiː ɔː ˈhiː ‖ -ᵊr-
she *strong form* ʃiː, *weak form* ʃi
she- ˈʃiː — **she-cat** ˈʃiː kæt
shea *tree* ʃiː ˈʃiː ə
ˈshea nut
Shea *name* ʃeɪ
sheaf ʃiːf **sheaves** ʃiːvz
Sheaffer ˈʃeɪf ə ‖ -ᵊr
shear ʃɪə ‖ ʃɪᵊr *(= sheer)* **sheared** ʃɪəd ‖ ʃɪᵊrd
shearing ˈʃɪər ɪŋ ‖ ˈʃɪr ɪŋ **shears** ʃɪəz ‖ ʃɪᵊrz
shorn ʃɔːn ‖ ʃɔːrn ʃoʊrn
Sheard *(i)* ʃeəd ‖ ʃeᵊrd, *(ii)* ʃɪəd ‖ ʃɪᵊrd, *(iii)*
ʃɜːd ‖ ʃɜːd
shearer, S~ ˈʃɪər ə ‖ ˈʃɪr ᵊr ~s z
shearling ˈʃɪə lɪŋ ‖ ˈʃɪr- ~s z
Shearman ˈʃɪə mən ‖ ˈʃɪr-

shears ʃɪəz ‖ ʃɪᵊrz
shearwater ˈʃɪə ˌwɔːt ə ‖ ˈʃɪr ˌwɔːt ᵊr -ˌwɑːt̬-
~s z
sheath *n* ʃiːθ **sheaths** ʃiːðz ʃiːθs
ˈsheath knife
sheathe *v* ʃiːð **sheathed** ʃiːðd **sheathes** ʃiːðz
sheathing ˈʃiːð ɪŋ
sheave ʃiːv **sheaved** ʃiːvd **sheaves** ʃiːvz
sheaving ˈʃiːv ɪŋ
Sheba ˈʃiːb ə
shebang ʃɪ ˈbæŋ ʃə-
she-bear ˈʃiː beə ‖ -ber ~s z
shebeen ʃɪ ˈbiːn ʃə- ~s z
Sheboygan ʃɪ ˈbɔɪɡ ən ʃə-
shed ʃed **shedding** ˈʃed ɪŋ **sheds** ʃedz
she'd *strong form* ʃiːd, *occasional weak form* ʃid
she-devil ˈʃiː ˌdev ᵊl -ɪl ~s z
shedload ˈʃed ləʊd ‖ -loʊd ~s z
Sheehan ˈʃiː hən
Sheelagh ˈʃiːl ə
sheen, Sheen ʃiːn
Sheena, Sheenagh, Sheenah ˈʃiːn ə
Sheene ʃiːn
sheep ʃiːp **sheep's** ʃiːps
ˈsheep's eyes; ˈsheep tick
sheepdip ˈʃiːp dɪp ~s s
sheepdog ˈʃiːp dɒg ‖ -dɔːg -dɑːg ~s z
sheepfold ˈʃiːp fəʊld →-fɒʊld ‖ -foʊld ~s z
sheepish ˈʃiːp ɪʃ ~ly li ~ness nəs nɪs
sheepmeat ˈʃiːp miːt
sheep-pen ˈʃiːp pen ~s z
sheepsbit ˈʃiːps bɪt ~s s
sheepshank ˈʃiːp ʃæŋk ~s s
sheepskin ˈʃiːp skɪn ~s z
sheer ʃɪə ‖ ʃɪᵊr **sheered** ʃɪəd ‖ ʃɪᵊrd **sheerer**
ˈʃɪər ə ‖ ˈʃɪr ᵊr **sheerest** ˈʃɪər ɪst -əst ‖ ˈʃɪr əst
sheering ˈʃɪər ɪŋ ‖ ˈʃɪr ɪŋ **sheers** ʃɪəz ‖ ʃɪᵊrz
Sheerness ˌʃɪə ˈnes ◄ ‖ ˌʃɪr-
sheesh ʃiːʃ
sheesha ˈʃiːʃ ə —*Arabic* [ˈʃiː ʃah]
sheet ʃiːt **sheeting** ˈʃiːt ɪŋ ‖ ˈʃiːt̬ ɪŋ **sheets**
ʃiːts
ˈsheet ˌanchor; ˈsheet ˌfeeder; ˌˑˈˌˑˌsheet
ˈlightning, ˈˌˑˈˑ; ˌsheet ˈmusic, ˈˌˑˈˑ
Sheetrock *tdmk* ˈʃiːt rɒk ‖ -rɑːk
Sheffer ˈʃef ə ‖ -ᵊr
Sheffield ˈʃef iːld
ˌSheffield ˈplate
Shefford ˈʃef əd ‖ -ᵊrd
Sheherazade ʃə ˌher ə ˈzɑːd ə ʃɪ-, -ˌhɪər-,
-ə ˈzɑːd ‖ -ˌhɪr-
sheikh, sheik, S~ ʃeɪk ʃiːk **sheikhs, sheiks**
ʃeɪks ʃiːks
sheikhdom, sheikdom ˈʃeɪk dəm ˈʃiːk- ~s z
Sheila, s~ ˈʃiːl ə ~s, ~'s z
shekel ˈʃek ᵊl ~s z
Shelagh ˈʃiːl ə
Shelburne ˈʃel bən -bɜːn ‖ -bɜːn
Shelby ˈʃel bi
Sheldon ˈʃeld ən
Sheldonian ʃel ˈdəʊn i ən ‖ -ˈdoʊn-
sheldrake, S~ ˈʃel dreɪk ~s s
shelduck ˈʃel dʌk ~s s

shelf ʃelf **shelves** ʃelvz
 'shelf life
Shelford 'ʃel fəd ‖ -fᵊrd
shell, Shell ʃel **shelled** ʃeld **shelling** 'ʃel ɪŋ
 shells, Shell's ʃelz
she'll strong form ʃiːl, occasional weak form ʃil
shellac ʃə 'læk ʃe-; 'ʃel æk ~ked t ~king ɪŋ ~s
 s
shellback 'ʃel bæk ~s s
Shelley 'ʃel i
shellfire 'ʃel ˌfaɪ ə ‖ -ˌfaɪ ᵊr
shellfish 'ʃel fɪʃ ~es ɪz əz
shell-like 'ʃel laɪk
Shell-Mex tdmk ˌʃel 'meks
shellshock 'ʃel ʃɒk ‖ -ʃɑːk ~ed t
Shelta 'ʃelt ə
shelter 'ʃelt ə ‖ -ᵊr ~ed d **sheltering**
 'ʃelt ᵊr ɪŋ ~s z
shelt|ie, shelt|y 'ʃelt |i ~ies iz
Shelton 'ʃelt ən
shelve ʃelv **shelved** ʃelvd **shelves** ʃelvz
 shelving 'ʃelv ɪŋ
Shem ʃem
shemozzle ʃɪ 'mɒz ᵊl ʃə- ‖ -'mɑːz-
Shena 'ʃiːn ə
Shenandoah ˌʃen ən 'dəʊ ə ◂ ‖ -'doʊ ə ◂
 ˌShenanˌdoah 'Valley
shenanigan ʃɪ 'næn ɪg ən ʃə-, §-əg- ~s z
Shenfield 'ʃen fiːᵊld
Shenyang ˌʃen 'jæŋ ˌʃʌn- ‖ -'jɑːŋ —Chi
 Shěnyáng [³ʂən ²jaŋ]
Shenzhen ˌʃen 'dʒen ˌʃʌn 'dʒʌn —Chi
 Shēnzhèn [¹ʂən ⁴tʂən]
Sheol, She'ol 'ʃiː ɒl -əʊl ‖ -oʊl ·'·
Shepard 'ʃep əd ‖ -ᵊrd
shepherd, S~ 'ʃep əd ‖ -ᵊrd ~ed ɪd əd ~ing ɪŋ
 ~s z
 ˌshepherd's 'pie
shepherdess ˌʃep ə 'des '···, -dɪs ‖ 'ʃep ᵊrd əs
 ~es ɪz əz
shepherd's-purse ˌʃep ədz 'pɜːs ‖ -ᵊrdz 'pɜːs
Sheppard 'ʃep əd ‖ -ᵊrd
 ˌSheppard's cor'rection
Sheppey 'ʃep i
Shepreth 'ʃep rəθ
Shepshed 'ʃep ʃed
Shepton 'ʃept ən
 ˌShepton 'Mallet
Sher (i) ʃɜː ‖ ʃɜːʳ, (ii) ʃeə ‖ ʃeᵊr
Sheraton 'ʃer ət ən ‖ -ᵊn ~s z
sherbert, sherbet 'ʃɜːb ət ‖ 'ʃɜːb- -ᵊrt ~s s
Sherborne, Sherbourne 'ʃɜː bən -bɔːn
 ‖ 'ʃɜː bɔːrn
Sherbrooke 'ʃɜː brʊk ‖ 'ʃɜː-
sherd ʃɜːd ‖ ʃɜːd **sherds** ʃɜːdz ‖ ʃɜːdz
Shere ʃɪə ‖ ʃɪᵊr
Sheree, Sheri 'ʃer i
sheria ʃə 'riː ə
Sheridan 'ʃer ɪd ən -əd- ‖ -ᵊn
sheriff 'ʃer ɪf -əf ~s s
Sheringham 'ʃer ɪŋ əm
Sherlaw 'ʃɜː lɔː ‖ 'ʃɜː- -lɑː
Sherley 'ʃɜːl i ‖ 'ʃɜːl i

Sherlock 'ʃɜː lɒk ‖ 'ʃɜː lɑːk
 ˌSherlock 'Holmes
Sherlockian ʃɜː 'lɒk i ən ‖ ʃɜː 'lɑːk- ~s z
Sherman 'ʃɜː mən ‖ 'ʃɜː mən
Sherpa, s~ 'ʃɜːp ə ‖ 'ʃɜːp ə ~s z
Sherratt 'ʃer ət
Sherree, Sherri 'ʃer i
Sherrin 'ʃer ɪn §-ən
Sherrington 'ʃer ɪŋ tən
sherr|y, S~ 'ʃer |i ~ies iz
Sherwin 'ʃɜː wɪn -wən ‖ 'ʃɜː-
Sherwood 'ʃɜː wʊd ‖ 'ʃɜː-
 ˌSherwood 'Forest
Sheryl 'ʃer ɪl -əl
she's strong form ʃiːz, occasional weak form ʃiz
Shetland 'ʃet lənd ~s z
 ˌShetland 'pony
Shetlander 'ʃet lənd ə ‖ -ᵊr ~s z
Shettleston 'ʃet ᵊls tən ‖ 'ʃet̬-
Shevardnadze ˌʃev əd 'nɑːd zeɪ -zi ‖ -ᵊrd-
Shevington 'ʃev ɪŋ tən
Shevon, Shevonne ʃə 'vɒn ʃɪ- ‖ -'vɑːn
Shew ʃuː
shew... —see **show...**
shewbread 'ʃəʊ bred ‖ 'ʃoʊ-
Shewell 'ʃuː əl ʃuːl
she-|wolf 'ʃiː wʊlf ~wolves wʊlvz
shh interjection ʃ
Shia, Shi'a, Shi'a, Shiah 'ʃiː ə
shiatsu ʃi 'æts uː -'ɑːts- ‖ -'ɑːts- —Jp
 [çi ˌa tsɯ]
shibboleth 'ʃɪb ə leθ -əl əθ, -əl ɪθ ~s s
shicker 'ʃɪk ə ‖ -ᵊr ~ed d
shie... —see **shy**
shield, Shield ʃiːᵊld **shielded** 'ʃiːᵊld ɪd -əd-
 shielding 'ʃiːᵊld ɪŋ **shields** 'ʃiːᵊldz
 Shields ʃiːᵊldz
shieling 'ʃiːl ɪŋ ~s z
shift ʃɪft **shifted** 'ʃɪft ɪd -əd **shifting** 'ʃɪft ɪŋ
 shifts ʃɪfts
 'shift key; 'shift stick; 'shift ˌworker;
 'shift ˌworking
shifter 'ʃɪft ə ‖ -ᵊr ~s z
shiftless 'ʃɪft ləs -lɪs ~ly li ~ness nəs nɪs
shiftwork 'ʃɪft wɜːk ‖ -wɜːk ~er/s ə/z ‖ -ᵊr/z
shift|y 'ʃɪft |i ~ier i ə ‖ i ᵊr ~iest i ɪst i əst ~ily
 ɪ li əl i ~iness i nəs i nɪs
shigell|a ʃɪ 'gel |ə ~ae iː ~as əz
shigellosis ˌʃɪg ə 'ləʊs ɪs -e-, §-əs ‖ -'loʊs əs
shih-tzu, shih tzu, shih tzu, S~ ˌʃiːt 'zuː ˌʃɪt-,
 -'suː —Chi shīzi [¹ʂɨˡ·dzɯ] ~s z
Shiism 'ʃiː ˌɪz əm
shiitake ʃɪ 'tɑːk eɪ ˌʃiːˌɪ·'·, -i —Jp ['çii ta ke]
Shiite, Shi'ite, Shi'ite 'ʃiː aɪt ~s s
Shijiazhuang ˌʃiː dʒiː ə dʒu 'æŋ ‖ -'ɑːŋ —Chi
 Shíjiāzhuāng [²ʂɨˡ ¹tɕja ¹tʂwaŋ]
shikaree, shikari ʃɪ 'kɑːr i ʃə-, -'kær- ~s z
Shikoku 'ʃiːk əʊ kuː ‖ -oʊ- —Jp [çi̥ 'ko kɯ]
shiksa, shikse 'ʃɪks ə ~s z
shill ʃɪl **shilled** ʃɪld **shilling** 'ʃɪl ɪŋ **shills** ʃɪlz
shillelagh ʃɪ 'leɪl ə ʃə-, -i ~s z
Shillibeer 'ʃɪl ɪ bɪə -ə- ‖ -bɪr
shilling, S~ 'ʃɪl ɪŋ ~s z

S

Shillong ʃɪ 'lɒŋ ‖ -'lɔːŋ -'lɑːŋ
Shilluk ʃɪ 'lʊk ‖ -'luːk ~s s
shilly-shall|y 'ʃɪl i ˌʃæl |i ~ied id ~ies iz
  ~ying i ɪŋ
Shiloh 'ʃaɪl əʊ ‖ -oʊ
Shilton 'ʃɪlt ən
shim ʃɪm **shimmed** ʃɪmd **shimming** 'ʃɪm ɪŋ
  shims ʃɪmz
shimmer 'ʃɪm ə ‖ -ᵊr ~ed d **shimmering**
  'ʃɪm ər ɪŋ ~s z
shimm|y 'ʃɪm |i ~ied id ~ies iz ~ying i ɪŋ
shin ʃɪn **shinned** ʃɪnd **shinning** 'ʃɪn ɪŋ **shins**
  ʃɪnz
shinbone 'ʃɪn bəʊn →'ʃɪm- ‖ -boʊn ~s z
shindig 'ʃɪn dɪg ~s z
shind|y 'ʃɪnd |i ~ies iz
shine ʃaɪn **shined** ʃaɪnd **shines** ʃaɪnz **shining**
  'ʃaɪn ɪŋ **shone** ʃɒn ‖ ʃoʊn (*)
shiner 'ʃaɪn ə ‖ -ᵊr ~s z
shingl|e 'ʃɪŋ gᵊl ~ed d ~es z ~ing ɪŋ
shingly 'ʃɪŋ gli
shining 'ʃaɪn ɪŋ ~ly li
shinn|y 'ʃɪn |i ~ied id ~ies iz ~ying i ɪŋ
Shinto 'ʃɪnt əʊ ‖ -oʊ —Jp ['ɕin to] ~ism
  ˌɪz əm ~ist/s ɪst/s §əst/s ‖ əst/s
shinty 'ʃɪnt i ‖ 'ʃɪnt i
Shinwell 'ʃɪn wel -wəl
shin|y 'ʃaɪn |i ~ier i ə ‖ i ᵊr ~iest i ɪst i əst
  ~ily ɪ li əl i ~iness i nəs i nɪs
-ship ʃɪp — **workmanship** 'wɜːk mən ʃɪp
  ‖ 'wɜːk-
ship ʃɪp **shipped** ʃɪpt **shipping** 'ʃɪp ɪŋ **ships**
  ʃɪps
  'ship ˌbiscuit; 'ship ca,nal; ˌship's
  'chandler
shipboard 'ʃɪp bɔːd ‖ -bɔːrd -boʊrd
shipbroker 'ʃɪp ˌbrəʊk ə ‖ -ˌbroʊk ᵊr ~s z
shipbuild|er 'ʃɪp ˌbɪld |ə ‖ -|ᵊr ~ers əz ‖ ᵊrz
  ~ing ɪŋ
Shiplake 'ʃɪp leɪk
Shipley 'ʃɪp li
shipload 'ʃɪp ləʊd ‖ -loʊd ~s z
Shipman 'ʃɪp mən
shipmate 'ʃɪp meɪt ~s s
shipment 'ʃɪp mənt ~s s
shipowner 'ʃɪp ˌəʊn ə ‖ -ˌoʊn ᵊr ~s z
Shippam 'ʃɪp əm
shipper 'ʃɪp ə ‖ -ᵊr ~s z
shipping 'ʃɪp ɪŋ
  'shipping ˌforecast; 'shipping lane
shipshape 'ʃɪp ʃeɪp
Shipston 'ʃɪpst ən
Shipton 'ʃɪpt ən
ship-to-shore ˌʃɪp tə 'ʃɔː -tu- ‖ -'ʃɔːr -'ʃoʊr
shipway 'ʃɪp weɪ ~s z
shipworm 'ʃɪp wɜːm ‖ -wɜːm ~s z
shipwreck 'ʃɪp rek ~ed t ~ing ɪŋ ~s s
shipwright 'ʃɪp raɪt ~s s
shipyard 'ʃɪp jɑːd ‖ -jɑːrd ~s z
Shiraz, s~ ʃɪ 'ræz ʃɪə-, 'rɑːz ‖ -'rɑːz
-shire ʃə ʃɪə ‖ ᵊr ʃɪr — **Lincolnshire**
  'lɪŋk ən ʃə -ʃɪə ‖ -ʃᵊr -ʃɪr

shire 'ʃaɪ ə ‖ 'ʃaɪ ᵊr **shires** 'ʃaɪ əz ‖ 'ʃaɪ ᵊrz
  'shire ˌcounties; 'shire horse
Shire, Shiré river and region in Malawi 'ʃɪər eɪ
  -ə ‖ 'ʃɪr-
shirk ʃɜːk ‖ ʃɜːk **shirked** ʃɜːkt ‖ ʃɜːkt **shirking**
  'ʃɜːk ɪŋ ‖ 'ʃɜːk ɪŋ **shirks** ʃɜːks ‖ ʃɜːks
shirker 'ʃɜːk ə ‖ 'ʃɜːk ᵊr ~s z
Shirley 'ʃɜːl i ‖ 'ʃɜːl i
shirr ʃɜː ‖ ʃɜː **shirred** 'ʃɜːd ‖ ʃɜːd **shirring**
  'ʃɜːr ɪŋ ‖ 'ʃɜː ɪŋ **shirrs** ʃɜːz ‖ ʃɜːz
shirt, Shirt ʃɜːt ‖ ʃɜːt **shirts** ʃɜːts ‖ ʃɜːts
shirtdress 'ʃɜːt dres ‖ 'ʃɜːt- ~es ɪz əz
shirtfront 'ʃɜːt frʌnt ‖ 'ʃɜːt- ~s s
shirting 'ʃɜːt ɪŋ ‖ 'ʃɜːt ɪŋ ~s z
shirtsleeve 'ʃɜːt sliːv ‖ 'ʃɜːt- ~d d ~s z
shirttail 'ʃɜːt terᵊl ‖ 'ʃɜːt- ~s z
shirtwaist 'ʃɜːt weɪst ˌ·'· ‖ 'ʃɜːt- ~er/s ə/z
  ‖ ᵊr/z ~s s
shirt|y 'ʃɜːt |i ‖ 'ʃɜːt̬ |i ~ier i ə ‖ i ᵊr ~iest i ɪst
  i əst ~iness i nəs i nɪs
shish kebab ˌʃɪʃ kə 'bæb ˌʃiːʃ-, -kɪ-, '···
  ‖ 'ʃɪʃ kə bɑːb ~s z
shit ʃɪt **shat** ʃæt **shits** ʃɪts **shitted** 'ʃɪt ɪd -əd
  ‖ 'ʃɪt̬ əd **shitting** 'ʃɪt ɪŋ ‖ 'ʃɪt̬ ɪŋ
shitake, shitaki ʃɪ 'tɑːk i ˌʃiːˌɪ'·ˌ·, -eɪ —Jp
  ['ɕii ta ke]
shitbag 'ʃɪt bæg ~s z
shite ʃaɪt
shitfaced 'ʃɪt feɪst
shithead 'ʃɪt hed ~s z
shithole 'ʃɪt həʊl →-hɒʊl ‖ -hoʊl ~s z
shit-hot ˌʃɪt 'hɒt ◂ ‖ -'hɑːt ◂
shithouse 'ʃɪt haʊs
shitless 'ʃɪt ləs -lɪs
shit-scared ˌʃɪt 'skeəd ◂ ‖ -'skeᵊrd ◂
Shittim, s~ 'ʃɪt ɪm §-əm ‖ 'ʃɪt̬ əm
shitt|y 'ʃɪt |i ‖ 'ʃɪt̬ |i ~ier i ə ‖ i ᵊr ~iest i ɪst
  i əst ~ily ɪ li əl i ~iness i nəs i nɪs
shitzu ˌʃiːt 'zu: ˌʃɪt-, -'su: —Chi shīzi ['ʂɻ̩˩dzɿ]
  ~s z
shiv ʃɪv **shivs** ʃɪvz
Shiva 'ʃiːv ə 'ʃɪv- —Hindi [ʃɪʋ]
shivaree ˌʃɪv ə 'riː '···· ~s z
shiver 'ʃɪv ə ‖ -ᵊr ~ed d **shivering/ly**
  'ʃɪv ər ɪŋ /li ~s z
shivery 'ʃɪv ər i
shl... —see **schl...**
Shloer tdmk ʃlɜː ‖ ʃlɜː
shmuck ʃmʌk **shmucks** ʃmʌks
shmutter, schmatte 'ʃmʌt ə ‖ 'ʃmɑːt̬ ə
Shoah 'ʃəʊ ɑː ‖ 'ʃoʊ-
shoal ʃəʊl →ʃɒʊl ‖ ʃoʊl **shoaled** ʃəʊld →ʃɒʊld
  ‖ ʃoʊld **shoaling** 'ʃəʊl ɪŋ →'ʃɒʊl- ‖ 'ʃoʊl ɪŋ
  shoals ʃəʊlz →ʃɒʊlz ‖ ʃoʊlz
shoat ʃəʊt ‖ ʃoʊt **shoats** ʃəʊts ‖ ʃoʊts
shock ʃɒk ‖ ʃɑːk **shocked** ʃɒkt ‖ ʃɑːkt
  shocking/ly 'ʃɒk ɪŋ /li ‖ 'ʃɑːk ɪŋ /li **shocks**
  ʃɒks ‖ ʃɑːks
  'shock ab,sorber; ˌshocking 'pink◂;
  'shock ˌtreatment; 'shock troops; 'shock
  wave
shocker 'ʃɒk ə ‖ 'ʃɑːk ᵊr ~s z
Shockey 'ʃɒk i ‖ 'ʃɑːk i

shockheaded ˌʃɒk ˈhed ɪd ◂ -əd ‖ ˌʃɑːk-
shockproof ˈʃɒk pruːf §-prʊf ‖ ˈʃɑːk-
shod ʃɒd ‖ ʃɑːd
shodd|y ˈʃɒd |i ‖ ˈʃɑːd |i ~ier i‿ə ‖ i‿ʳr ~ies iz
   ~iest i‿ɪst i‿əst ~ily ɪ li ə l i ~iness i nəs i nɪs
shoe ʃuː (= shoo) shod ʃɒd ‖ ʃɑːd shoed ʃuːd
   shoeing ˈʃuː ɪŋ shoes ʃuːz
shoebill ˈʃuː bɪl ~s z
shoeblack ˈʃuː blæk ~s s
shoebox ˈʃuː bɒks ‖ -baːks ~es ɪz əz
Shoeburyness ˌʃuː bər i ˈnes
shoehorn ˈʃuː hɔːn ‖ -hɔːrn ~ed d ~ing ɪŋ ~s
   z
shoelace ˈʃuː leɪs ~es ɪz əz
shoeless ˈʃuː ləs -lɪs
shoemaker, S~ ˈʃuː ˌmeɪk ə ‖ -ʳr ~s z
shoeshine ˈʃuː ʃaɪn
shoestring ˈʃuː strɪŋ ~s z
shoetree ˈʃuː triː ~s z
shogun ˈʃəʊ gʌn -guːn, -gən ‖ ˈʃoʊ- —Jp
   [ço̞ o̞ ŋɯ̃ːn, -gɯ̃ːn] ~s z
shogunate ˈʃəʊ gə neɪt -gu-, -gʌ-; -gən ət, -ɪt
   ‖ ˈʃoʊ- ~s z
Sholokhov ˈʃɒl ə kɒf ‖ ˈʃɔːl ə kɔːf ˈʃɑːl ə kɑːf
   —Russian [ˈʃo lə xəf]
Sholto ˈʃɒlt əʊ ‖ ˈʃɑːlt oʊ
Shona Zimbabwean language and people ˈʃɒn ə
   ˈʃəʊn- ‖ ˈʃoʊn ə ~s z
Shona personal name ˈʃəʊn ə ‖ ˈʃoʊn ə
shone ʃɒn ‖ ʃoʊn (*)
shonk|y ˈʃɒŋk| i ‖ ˈʃɑːŋk| i ~ier i‿ə ‖ i‿ʳr ~iest
   i‿ɪst ‿əst
shoo ʃuː shooed ʃuːd shooing ˈʃuː ɪŋ shoos
   ʃuːz
shoofly ˈʃuː flaɪ
   ˌshooflyˈpie ‖ ˌ· ·
shoo-in ˈʃuː ɪn ~s z
shook ʃʊk §ʃuːk
shoot ʃuːt shooting/s ˈʃuːt ɪŋ/z ‖ ˈʃuːt̬ ɪŋ/z
   shoots ʃuːts shot ʃɒt ‖ ʃɑːt
   ˈshooting box; ˈshooting brake;
   ˈshooting ˌgallery; ˈshooting ˌmatch;
   ˌshooting ˈstar; ˈshooting stick
shoot-'em-up ˈʃuːt əm ʌp ‖ ˈʃuːt̬- ~s s
-shooter ˌʃuːt ə ‖ ˌʃuːt̬ ʳr — duck-shooter
   ˈdʌk ˌʃuːt ə ‖ -ˌʃuːt̬ ʳr
shooter, S~ ˈʃuːt ə ‖ ˈʃuːt̬ ʳr ~s z
shoot-out ˈʃuːt aʊt ‖ ˈʃuːt̬- ~s s
shop ʃɒp ‖ ʃɑːp shopped ʃɒpt ‖ ʃɑːpt
   shopping ˈʃɒp ɪŋ ‖ ˈʃɑːp ɪŋ shops ʃɒps
   ‖ ʃɑːps
   ˈshop asˌsistant; ˌshop ˈfloor, ˈ· ·;
   ˈshopping ˌbasket; ˈshopping ˌcentre;
   ˈshopping mall; ˌshop ˈsteward ‖ ˈ· ˌ· ·;
   ˌshop ˈwindow
shopaholic ˌʃɒp ə ˈhɒl ɪk ‖ ˌʃɑːp ə ˈhɔːl ɪk
   -ˈhɑːl- ~s s
shop-bought ˈʃɒp bɔːt ‖ ˈʃɑːp- -baːt
shopfitt|er ˈʃɒp ˌfɪt| ə ‖ ˈʃɑːp ˌfɪt̬| ʳr ~ers əz
   ‖ -ʳrz ~ing ɪŋ
shopfront ˈʃɒp frʌnt ‖ ˈʃɑːp- ~s s
shophar ˈʃəʊf ɑː ‖ ˈʃoʊf ɑːr -ʳr ~s z
shopkeeper ˈʃɒp ˌkiːp ə ‖ ˈʃɑːp ˌkiːp ʳr ~s z

shoplift ˈʃɒp lɪft ‖ ˈʃɑːp- ~ed ɪd əd ~er/s ə/z
   ‖ ʳr/z ~ing ɪŋ ~s s
shopp... —see shop
shoppe ʃɒp ‖ ʃɑːp —jocularly also
   ˈʃɒp i ‖ ˈʃɑːp i
shopper ˈʃɒp ə ‖ ˈʃɑːp ʳr ~s z
shopsoiled ˈʃɒp sɔɪʳld ‖ ˈʃɑːp-
shopwalker ˈʃɒp ˌwɔːk ə ‖ ˈʃɑːp ˌwɔːk ʳr
   -ˌwaːk- ~s z
shopworn ˈʃɒp wɔːn ‖ ˈʃɑːp wɔːrn -woʊrn
shore, Shore ʃɔː ‖ ʃɔːr ʃoʊr shored ʃɔːd ‖ ʃɔːrd
   ʃoʊrd shores ʃɔːz ‖ ʃɔːrz ʃoʊrz shoring
   ˈʃɔːr ɪŋ ‖ ˈʃoʊr-
   ˈshore leave
Shoreditch ˈʃɔː dɪtʃ ‖ ˈʃɔːr- ˈʃoʊr-
Shoreham ˈʃɔːr əm ‖ ˈʃoʊr-
shoreline ˈʃɔː laɪn ‖ ˈʃɔːr- ˈʃoʊr- ~s z
shorn ʃɔːn ‖ ʃɔːrn ʃoʊrn
short, Short ʃɔːt ‖ ʃɔːrt shorted ˈʃɔːt ɪd -əd
   ‖ ˈʃɔːrt̬ əd shorter ˈʃɔːt ə ‖ ˈʃɔːrt̬ ʳr shortest
   ˈʃɔːt ɪst -əst ‖ ˈʃɔːrt̬ əst shorting ˈʃɔːt ɪŋ
   ‖ ˈʃɔːrt̬ ɪŋ shorts ʃɔːts ‖ ʃɔːrts
   ˌshort ˌback and ˈsides; ˌshort ˈcircuit;
   ˈshort cut, ˌ· ˈ· — Preference poll, BrE: ˈ· ·
   59%, ˌ· ˈ· 41%; ˈshort list; ˌshort ˈshrift;
   ˌshort ˈstory; ˌshort ˈterm; ˌshort ˈtime;
   ˌshort ˈwave
shortag|e ˈʃɔːt ɪdʒ ‖ ˈʃɔːrt̬- ~es ɪz əz
shortbread ˈʃɔːt bred ‖ ˈʃɔːrt̬- ~s z
shortcake ˈʃɔːt keɪk ‖ ˈʃɔːrt- ~s s
short-chang|e ˌʃɔːt ˈtʃeɪndʒ ‖ ˌʃɔːrt- ~ed d ~es
   ɪz əz ~ing ɪŋ
short-circu|it ˌʃɔːt ˈsɜːk |ɪt §-ət
   ‖ ˌʃɔːrt ˈsɜːk |ət ~ited ɪt ɪd §ət-, -əd ‖ ət̬ əd
   ~iting ɪt ɪŋ §ət- ‖ ət̬ ɪŋ ~its ɪts §əts ‖ əts
shortcoming ˈʃɔːt ˌkʌm ɪŋ ˌ· ˈ· · ‖ ˈʃɔːrt- ~s z
shortcrust ˈʃɔːt krʌst ‖ ˈʃɔːrt-

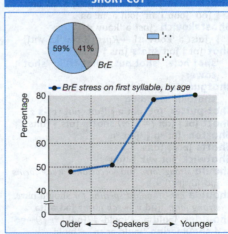

SHORT CUT

59% 41%

BrE

BrE stress on first syllable, by age

Percentage (y-axis: 0, 40, 50, 60, 70, 80)

Older ← Speakers → Younger

shortcut ˈʃɔːt kʌt ˌ· ˈ· ‖ ˈʃɔːrt- ~s s
short-dated ˌʃɔːt ˈdeɪt ɪd ◂ -əd
   ‖ ˌʃɔːrt ˈdeɪt̬ əd ◂
short-day ˈʃɔːt deɪ ‖ ˈʃɔːrt-
short-eared ˌʃɔːt ˈɪəd ◂ ‖ ˌʃɔːrt̬ ɪrd

shorten ˈʃɔːt ᵊn ‖ ˈʃɔːrt ᵊn **~ed** d **~ing** ɪŋ **~s** z
Shorter ˈʃɔːt ə ‖ ˈʃɔːrt̬ ᵊr
shortfall ˈʃɔːt fɔːl ‖ ˈʃɔːrt- -fɑːl **~s** z
shorthand ˈʃɔːt hænd ‖ ˈʃɔːrt-
  ˌshorthand ˈtypist
shorthanded ˌʃɔːt ˈhænd ɪd ◄ -əd ‖ ˌʃɔːrt-
short-haul ˈʃɔːt hɔːl ˌ·ˈ· ‖ ˈʃɔːrt- -hɑːl
shorthold ˈʃɔːt həʊld →-hɒʊld ‖ ˈʃɔːrt hoʊld
  ~s z
shorthorn, S~ ˈʃɔːt hɔːn ‖ ˈʃɔːrt hɔːrn **~s** z
shortie ˈʃɔːt i ‖ ˈʃɔːrt̬ i **~s** z
shortish ˈʃɔːt ɪʃ ‖ ˈʃɔːrt̬ ɪʃ
Shortland ˈʃɔːt lənd ‖ ˈʃɔːrt-
short-list ˈʃɔːt lɪst ‖ ˈʃɔːrt- **~ed** ɪd əd **~ing** ɪŋ
  ~s s
short-lived ˌʃɔːt ˈlɪvd ◄ ‖ ˌʃɔːrt ˈlaɪvd ◄ -ˈlɪvd
short|ly ˈʃɔːt |li ‖ ˈʃɔːrt̬ |li **~ness** nəs nɪs
Shorto ˈʃɔːt əʊ ‖ ˈʃɔːrt̬ oʊ
short-order ˈʃɔːt ˌɔːd ə ˌ·ˈ·· ‖ ˈʃɔːrt̬ ˌɔːrd ᵊr
short-range ˌʃɔːt ˈreɪndʒ ◄ ‖ ˌʃɔːrt-
short-|sheet ˈʃɔːt |ʃiːt ‖ ˈʃɔːrt- **~sheeted**
  ʃiːt ɪd -əd ‖ ʃiːt̬ əd **~sheeting** ʃiːt ɪŋ ‖ ʃiːt̬ ɪŋ
  ~sheets ʃiːts
shortsighted ˌʃɔːt ˈsaɪt ɪd ◄ -əd
  ‖ ˌʃɔːrt ˈsaɪt̬ əd ◄ **~ly** li **~ness** nəs nɪs
short-sleeved ˌʃɔːt ˈsliːvd ◄ ‖ ˌʃɔːrt-
short-staffed ˌʃɔːt ˈstɑːft ◄ §-ˈstæft
  ‖ ˌʃɔːrt ˈstæft ◄
short-stay ˌʃɔːt ˈsteɪ ◄ ‖ ˌʃɔːrt-
shortstop ˈʃɔːt stɒp ‖ ˈʃɔːrt stɑːp **~s** s
short-tempered ˌʃɔːt ˈtemp əd ◄
  ‖ ˌʃɔːrt ˈtemp ᵊrd ◄
short-term ˌʃɔːt ˈtɜːm ◄ ‖ ˌʃɔːrt ˈtɜːm ◄ **~ism**
  ɪz əm
shortwave ˌʃɔːt ˈweɪv ◄ ˈ·· ‖ ˌʃɔːrt-
short-winded ˌʃɔːt ˈwɪnd ɪd ◄ -əd ‖ ˌʃɔːrt-
short|y ˈʃɔːt |i ‖ ˈʃɔːrt̬ |i **~ies** iz
Shoshone ʃəʊ ˈʃəʊn i ‖ ʃoʊ ˈʃoʊn i ʃə- **~s** z
Shoshonean ʃəʊ ˈʃəʊn i_ən ˌʃəʊʃ ə ˈniː ən
  ‖ ʃoʊ ˈʃoʊn i_ən ˌʃoʊʃ ə ˈniː ən
Shostakovich ˌʃɒst ə ˈkəʊv ɪtʃ
  ‖ ˌʃɑːst ə ˈkoʊv ɪtʃ —Russ [ʃɨ stʌ ˈkɔ vʲɪtʃ]
shot ʃɒt ‖ ʃɑːt **shots** ʃɒts ‖ ʃɑːts
  ˈshot hole; ˈshot put; ˌshot ˈsilk; ˈshot
  ˌtower
shotgun ˈʃɒt ɡʌn ‖ ˈʃɑːt- **~s** z
  ˌshotgun ˈwedding
shot-putter ˈʃɒt ˌpʊt ə ‖ ˈʃɑːt ˌpʊt̬ ᵊr **~s** z
shott ʃɒt ‖ ʃɑːt *(= shot)* **shotts** ʃɒts ‖ ʃɑːts
Shotton ˈʃɒt ᵊn ‖ ˈʃɑːt ᵊn
Shotts ʃɒts ‖ ʃɑːts
Shotwick ˈʃɒt wɪk ‖ ˈʃɑːt-
should *strong form* ʃʊd, *occasional weak forms*
  ʃəd ʃd, ʃt *(!)*
shoulda *non-standard spelling for* should have:
  strong form ˈʃʊd ə, *weak forms* ʃəd ə ʃtə
shoulder ˈʃəʊld ə →ˈʃɒʊld- ‖ ˈʃoʊld ᵊr *(!)* **~ed**
  d **shouldering** ˈʃəʊld ᵊr ɪŋ →ˈʃɒʊld̬
  ‖ ˈʃoʊld ᵊr ɪŋ **~s** z
  ˈshoulder bag; ˈshoulder blade; ˈshoulder
  strap
shoulder-high ˌʃəʊld ə ˈhaɪ ◄ →ˌʃɒʊld-
  ‖ ˌʃoʊld ᵊr-

shoulder-length ˈʃəʊld ə leŋkθ →ˈʃɒʊld-,
  -lenᵗθ ‖ ˈʃoʊld ᵊr-
shouldn't ˈʃʊd ᵊnt
shouldst *strong form* ʃʊdst ʃʊtst, *occasional*
  weak form ʃədst ʃətst
should've *strong form* ˈʃʊd əv, *occasional weak*
  form ʃtəv
shout ʃaʊt **shouted** ˈʃaʊt ɪd -əd ‖ ˈʃaʊt̬ əd
  shouting ˈʃaʊt ɪŋ ‖ ˈʃaʊt̬ ɪŋ **shouts** ʃaʊts
shove ʃʌv **shoved** ʃʌvd **shoves** ʃʌvz **shoving**
  ˈʃʌv ɪŋ
shove-halfpenny, shove-ha'penny
  ˌʃʌv ˈheɪp ni
shovel ˈʃʌv ᵊl **~ed, ~led** d **~ing, ~ling** ɪŋ **~s** z
shovelboard ˈʃʌv ᵊl bɔːd ‖ -bɔːrd -boʊrd
shoveler, shoveller ˈʃʌv ᵊl_ə ‖ ᵊr **~s** z
shovelful ˈʃʌv ᵊl fʊl **~s** z
shovelware ˈʃʌv ᵊl weə ‖ -wer -wær
show ʃəʊ ‖ ʃoʊ **showed** ʃəʊd ‖ ʃoʊd **showing**
  ˈʃəʊ ɪŋ ‖ ˈʃoʊ ɪŋ **shown** ʃəʊn ‖ ʃoʊn **shows**
  ʃəʊz ‖ ʃoʊz
  ˈshow ˌbusiness; ˈshow ˌjumper; ˈshow
  ˌjumping; ˌshow of ˈhands; ˈshow ˌtrial
showband ˈʃəʊ bænd ‖ ˈʃoʊ- **~s** z
showbiz ˈʃəʊ bɪz ‖ ˈʃoʊ-
showboat ˈʃəʊ bəʊt ‖ ˈʃoʊ boʊt **~s** s
showcas|e ˈʃəʊ keɪs ‖ ˈʃoʊ- **~es** ɪz əz
showdown ˈʃəʊ daʊn ‖ ˈʃoʊ- **~s** z
shower *'one that shows'* ˈʃəʊ ə ‖ ˈʃoʊ ᵊr **~s** z
shower *v; n 'sudden rain; ~ bath; etc.'* ˈʃaʊ ə
  ‖ ˈʃaʊ ᵊr **~ed** d **showering** ˈʃaʊ ᵊr ɪŋ
  ‖ ˈʃaʊ ᵊr ɪŋ **~s** z
  ˈshower bath; ˈshower gel
showerproof ˈʃaʊ ə pruːf -§prʊf ‖ ˈʃaʊ ᵊr pruːf
  ~ed t **~ing** ɪŋ **~s** s
showery ˈʃaʊ ᵊr i ‖ ˈʃaʊ ᵊr i
showgirl ˈʃəʊ ɡɜːl ‖ ˈʃoʊ ɡɜːl **~s** z
showground ˈʃəʊ ɡraʊnd ‖ ˈʃoʊ- **~s** z
showi... —*see* **showy**
show|man ˈʃəʊ |mən ‖ ˈʃoʊ- **~manship**
  mən ʃɪp **~men** mən men
shown ʃəʊn §ˈʃəʊ ən ‖ ʃoʊn
show-off ˈʃəʊ ɒf -ɔːf ‖ ˈʃoʊ ɔːf -ɑːf **~s** s
showpiec|e ˈʃəʊ piːs ‖ ˈʃoʊ- **~es** ɪz əz
showplac|e ˈʃəʊ pleɪs ‖ ˈʃoʊ- **~es** ɪz əz
showroom ˈʃəʊ ruːm -rʊm ‖ ˈʃoʊ- **~s** z
show-stopper ˈʃəʊ ˌstɒp ə ‖ ˈʃoʊ ˌstɑːp ᵊr **~s**
  z
show-stopping ˈʃəʊ ˌstɒp ɪŋ ‖ ˈʃoʊ ˌstɑːp ɪŋ
showtime ˈʃəʊ taɪm ‖ ˈʃoʊ-
show|y ˈʃəʊ |i ‖ ˈʃoʊ |i **~ier** i_ə ‖ i_ᵊr **~iest**
  i_ɪst i_əst **~ily** ɪ li əl i **~iness** i nəs i nɪs
shoyu ˈʃɔɪ uː —*Jp* [ço̞o̞ jɯ]
shrank ʃræŋk
shrapnel, S~ ˈʃræp nᵊl
shred ʃred **shredded** ˈʃred ɪd -əd **shredding**
  ˈʃred ɪŋ **shreds** ʃredz
shredder ˈʃred ə ‖ -ᵊr **~s** z
Shreveport ˈʃriːv pɔːt ‖ -pɔːrt -poʊrt
shrew ʃruː **shrews** ʃruːz
  ˈshrew mole

Short vowel, long vowel

IN SPELLING

1   To each vowel letter in English spelling there correspond two vowel sounds, the vowel letter then traditionally being known as 'short' or 'long' respectively (see **a**, **e**, **i**, **o**, **u**). (There are also other possibilities that have no traditional names.) The following guidelines are to help you decide whether the short or long pronunciation is likely to be appropriate.

2   A single vowel letter generally counts as **short**

- in a word of one syllable, ending in a consonant (**back**, **red**, **tip**, **rod**, **cut**, **hymn**)
- in a stressed penultimate syllable, where the vowel is followed by two or more consonant letters (**battle**, **jelly**, **middle**, **doctor**, **system**).

3   A single vowel letter generally counts as **long**

- before one consonant letter plus silent **e** (**take**, **complete**, **time**, **rope**, **rude**, **type**). However, there are several exceptions, including **have**, **give**, **one**, **come**, **love**.
- in a word of one syllable, where the vowel is not followed by a consonant (**me**, **hi**, **go**, **flu**, **try**).
- in a stressed penultimate syllable, where the vowel is followed by only one consonant letter, or by a vowel letter (**potato**, **thesis**, **item**, **over**, **tribunal**, **asylum**; **chaos**, **neon**, **triumph**, **heroic**, **ruin**, **dying**).

4   There are many cases not covered by these guidelines. Furthermore, the guidelines have exceptions. That is why you need a pronunciation dictionary.

IN PHONETICS

5   The English vowels can also be divided into short and long on the basis of their pronunciation. Other things being equal, a long vowel has greater duration than a short vowel. However, vowel duration is strongly influenced by the phonetic environment. In general, the difference between short and long vowels is less noticeable in AmE than in BrE.

6   The **short** vowels are ɪ, e, æ, ɒ, ʊ, ʌ, together with the WEAK vowels ə, i, u. Of these, æ is a special case: it is not similar in quality to any long vowel, and many speakers lengthen it (particularly before certain consonants, notably b and d).

7   The **long** vowels are iː, uː, ɑː, ɔː, together with BrE ɜː and AmE ɝː. In the phonetic transcription system used in this dictionary, long vowels are always written with the length mark ː, in accordance with the PHONEME principle; but long vowels may in certain environments be phonetically quite short (see CLIPPING).

8   The duration of **diphthongs** is like that of long vowels.

Short vowel, long vowel ▶

S

Short vowel, long vowel continued

9   With one exception, the 'short' vowels of spelling correspond to phonetically short vowels. The exception is AmE ɑː, which is phonetically long, yet is associated with the traditional 'short O'. (The corresponding BrE ɒ is phonetically short.) The 'long vowels' of spelling correspond to three phonetic diphthongs (eɪ, aɪ, əʊ‖oʊ), one long vowel (iː), and one sequence of semivowel plus long vowel (juː).

---

shrewd ʃruːd **shrewder** ʃruːd ə ‖ -ᵊr
  shrewdest ʃruːd ɪst -əst **shrewdly** ʃruːd li
  shrewdness ʃruːd nəs -nɪs
shrewish ʃruː ɪʃ **~ly** li **~ness** nəs nɪs
Shrewsbury (i) ʃrəʊz bər‿i ‖ ʃroʊz ˌber i, (ii)
  ʃruːz- —*The place in England is usually* (i),
  though locally also (ii). *The places in the US*
  are (ii).
shriek ʃriːk **shrieked** ʃriːkt **shrieking/ly**
  ʃriːk ɪŋ /li **shrieks** ʃriːks
shrift ʃrɪft
shrike ʃraɪk **shrikes** ʃraɪks
shrill ʃrɪl **shrilled** ʃrɪld **shriller** ʃrɪl ə ‖ -ᵊr
  shrillest ʃrɪl ɪst -əst **shrilling** ʃrɪl ɪŋ **shrills**
  ʃrɪlz
shrillness ʃrɪl nəs -nɪs
shrilly *adv* ʃrɪl li -i
shrimp ʃrɪmp **shrimped** ʃrɪmpt **shrimping**
  ʃrɪmp ɪŋ **shrimps** ʃrɪmps
shrimper ʃrɪmp ə ‖ -ᵊr **~s** z
Shrimpton ʃrɪmpt ən
shrine ʃraɪn **shrines** ʃraɪnz
Shriner ʃraɪn ə ‖ -ᵊr **~s** z
shrink ʃrɪŋk **shrank** ʃræŋk **shrinking/ly**
  ʃrɪŋk ɪŋ /li **shrinks** ʃrɪŋks **shrunk** ʃrʌŋk
  shrunken ʃrʌŋk ən
  ˌshrinking 'violet
shrinkag|e ʃrɪŋk ɪdʒ **~es** ɪz əz
shrink-wrap ʃrɪŋk ræp ˌ·'· **~ped** t **~ping** ɪŋ **~s**
  s
shrive ʃraɪv **shrived** ʃraɪvd **shriven** ʃrɪv ᵊn (!)
  shrives ʃraɪvz **shriving** ʃraɪv ɪŋ **shrove**
  ʃrəʊv ‖ ʃroʊv
shrivel ʃrɪv ᵊl **~ed, ~led** d **~ing, ~ling** ɪŋ **~s** z
shriven ʃrɪv ᵊn
Shrivenham ʃrɪv ᵊn‿əm
Shriver ʃraɪv ə ‖ -ᵊr
shroff ʃrɒf ‖ ʃrɑːf **shroffed** ʃrɒft ‖ ʃrɑːft
  shroffing ʃrɒf ɪŋ ‖ ʃrɑːf ɪŋ **shroffs** ʃrɒfs
  ‖ ʃrɑːfs
ˈshroom ʃruːm ʃrʊm ˈshrooms ʃruːmz ʃrʊmz
Shropshire ʃrɒp ʃə -ʃɪə ‖ ʃrɑːp ʃᵊr -ʃɪr
shroud ʃraʊd **shrouded** ʃraʊd ɪd -əd
  shrouding ʃraʊd ɪŋ **shrouds** ʃraʊdz
shroud-waving ʃraʊd ˌweɪv ɪŋ
shrove, S~ ʃrəʊv ‖ ʃroʊv
  ˌShrove 'Tuesday
Shrovetide ʃrəʊv taɪd ‖ ʃroʊv-
shrub ʃrʌb **shrubs** ʃrʌbz
shrubber|y ʃrʌb ər |i **~ies** iz

shrubb|y ʃrʌb |i **~ier** i‿ə ‖ i‿ᵊr **~iest** i‿ɪst i‿əst
  ~iness i nəs i nɪs
shrug ʃrʌg **shrugged** ʃrʌgd **shrugging**
  ʃrʌg ɪŋ **shrugs** ʃrʌgz
shrunk ʃrʌŋk
shrunken ʃrʌŋk ən
shtetl ʃtet ᵊl ʃteɪt- **~s** z
shtick ʃtɪk **shticks** ʃtɪks
shtook, shtuck ʃtʊk
shtum ʃtʊm
shtup ʃtʊp **shtupped** ʃtʊpt **shtupping**
  ʃtʊp ɪŋ **shtups** ʃtʊps
shubunkin ʃu ˈbʌŋk ɪn §-ən **~s** z
shuck ʃʌk **shucked** ʃʌkt **shucking** ʃʌk ɪŋ
  shucks ʃʌks
Shuckburgh ʃʌk bər ə ‖ ʃʌk bɜːg
shudder ʃʌd ə ‖ -ᵊr **~ed** d **shuddering/ly**
  ʃʌd ər ɪŋ /li **~s** z
shuffl|e ʃʌf ᵊl **~ed** d **~es** z **~ing** ɪŋ
shuffleboard ʃʌf ᵊl bɔːd ‖ -bɔːrd -boʊrd
Shufflebottom ʃʌf ᵊl ˌbɒt əm ‖ -ˌbɑːʈ əm
shuffler ʃʌf ᵊl‿ə ‖ -ᵊr **~s** z
Shufflewick ʃʌf ᵊl wɪk
shufti, shufty ʃʊft i **shuftis** ʃʊft iz
Shughie ʃuː‿i
shul ʃuːl ʃʊl **shuln** ʃuːln ʃʊln
Shula ʃuːl ə
Shulamite ʃuːl ə maɪt **~s** s
Shulman ʃuːl mən
shun ʃʌn **shunned** ʃʌnd **shunning** ʃʌn ɪŋ
  shuns ʃʌnz
'shun *military command: 'attention'* ʃʌn
shunt ʃʌnt **shunted** ʃʌntɪd -əd ‖ ʃʌnʈ əd
  shunting ʃʌnt ɪŋ ‖ ʃʌnʈ ɪŋ **shunts** ʃʌnts
  ˈshunting ˌengine
shush ʃʊʃ ʃʌʃ **shushed** ʃʊʃt ʃʌʃt **shushes** ʃʊʃ ɪz
  ʃʌʃ-, -əz **shushing** ʃʊʃ ɪŋ ʃʌʃ-
Shuster ʃʊst ə ʃuːst- ‖ -ᵊr
Shuswap ʃʊs wɒp ʃʊʃ- ‖ -wɑːp
shut ʃʌt **shuts** ʃʌts **shutting** ʃʌt ɪŋ ‖ ʃʌʈ ɪŋ
shutdown ʃʌt daʊn **~s** z
Shute ʃuːt
Shuter ʃuːt ə ‖ ʃuːʈ ᵊr
shut-eye ʃʌt aɪ ‖ ʃʌʈ aɪ
shut-in *n* ʃʌt ɪn ‖ ʃʌʈ- **~s** z
shut-in *adj* ˌʃʌt 'ɪn ◂ ‖ ˌʃʌʈ-
shutoff *n* ʃʌt ɒf -ɔːf ‖ ʃʌʈ ɔːf -ɑːf **~s** s
shutout *n* ʃʌt aʊt ‖ ʃʌʈ- **~s** s
shutter ʃʌt ə ‖ ʃʌʈ ᵊr **~ed** d **shuttering**
  ʃʌt ᵊr ɪŋ ‖ ʃʌʈ ər ɪŋ **~s** z

shutterbug 'ʃʌt ə bʌg ‖ -r̩- ~s z
shuttl|e 'ʃʌt ᵊl ‖ 'ʃʌt̬ ᵊl ~ed d ~es z ~ing ɪŋ
  'shuttle di,plomacy
shuttlecock 'ʃʌt ᵊl kɒk ‖ 'ʃʌt̬ ᵊl kɑːk ~s s
Shuttleworth 'ʃʌt ᵊl wɜːθ -wəθ ‖ 'ʃʌt̬ ᵊl wɜːθ
Shuy ʃaɪ
shwa ʃwɑː ʃvɑː: **shwas** ʃwɑːz ʃvɑːz
-shy ʃaɪ — **work-shy** 'wɜːk ʃaɪ ‖ 'wɜːk-
shy ʃaɪ **shied** ʃaɪd **shier, shyer** 'ʃaɪ ə ‖ 'ʃaɪ ᵊr
  shies ʃaɪz **shiest, shyest** 'ʃaɪ ɪst -əst **shying**
  'ʃaɪ ɪŋ
Shylock 'ʃaɪ lɒk ‖ -lɑːk
shy|ly 'ʃaɪ |li ~ness nəs nɪs
shyster 'ʃaɪst ə ‖ -ᵊr ~s z
si siː
SI ,es 'aɪ
sial 'saɪ əl
sialagogue, sialogogue saɪ 'æl ə gɒg 'saɪ əl-
  ‖ -gɑːg ~s z
Siam ,saɪ 'æm ·ᐧ·
siamang 'siː ə mæŋ 'saɪ ~s z
Siamese ,saɪ ə 'miːz ◄ ‖ -'miːs
  ,Siamese 'cat; ,Siamese 'twin
Sian, Siân ʃɑːn
sib sɪb **sibs** sɪbz
Sibelius sɪ 'beɪl i əs sə- —Swed, Finnish
  [sɪ 'beː li us]
Siberi|a saɪ 'bɪər i |ə ‖ -'bɪr- ~an/s ən/z
sibilanc|e 'sɪb ɪl ən⁀s -əl- ~y i
sibilant 'sɪb ɪl ənt -əl- ~ly li ~s s
sibi|late 'sɪb ɪ |leɪt -ə- ~lated leɪt ɪd -əd
  ‖ leɪt̬ əd ~lates leɪts ~lating leɪt ɪŋ ‖ leɪt̬ ɪŋ
sibilation ,sɪb ɪ 'leɪʃ ᵊn -ə- ~s z
Sibley 'sɪb li
sibling 'sɪb lɪŋ ~s z
sibyl, Sibyl 'sɪb ɪl -ᵊl ~s, ~'s z
sibylline, S~ 'sɪb ɪ laɪn -ə-; sɪ 'bɪl aɪn, sə- ‖ -liːn
sic sɪk siːk —see also phrases with this word
  sicced sɪkt **siccing** 'sɪk ɪŋ **sics** sɪks
siccative 'sɪk ət ɪv ‖ -ət̬- ~s z
Sichuan ,sɪtʃ 'wɑːn —Chi Sìchuān
  [⁴suɪ ¹tʂʰwan]
Sicilian sɪ 'sɪl i ən sə- ~s z
Sicil|y 'sɪs əl |i -ɪl- ~ies iz
sick sɪk **sicker** 'sɪk ə ‖ 'sɪk ᵊr **sickest** 'sɪk ɪst
  -əst
  'sick call; ,sick 'headache; 'sick leave;
  'sick pa,rade; 'sick pay
sickbag 'sɪk bæg ~s z
sickbay 'sɪk beɪ ~s z
sickbed 'sɪk bed ~s z
sicken 'sɪk ən ~ed d ~ing/ly ɪŋ /li ~s z
Sickert 'sɪk ət ‖ -ᵊrt
sickie 'sɪk i ~s z
sickl|e 'sɪk ᵊl ~ed d ~es z ~ing ɪŋ
sickle-cell 'sɪk ᵊl sel
  ,sickle-cell a'naemia
sick|ly 'sɪk |li ~lier li ə ‖ li ᵊr ~liest li ɪst li əst
  ~liness li nəs li nɪs
sickness 'sɪk nəs -nɪs ~es ɪz əz
  'sickness ,benefit
sicko 'sɪk əʊ ‖ -oʊ ~s z
sickout 'sɪk aʊt ~s s

sickroom 'sɪk ruːm -rʊm ~s z
sic transit gloria mundi
  ,sɪk 'trænz ɪt ,glɔːr i ə 'mʊnd i ,siːk-,
  -'træn⁀s-, -'trɑːnz-, -'trɑːn⁀s-, §-'·ət-, -ɑː'·-, -iː
  ‖ -,glʊr-
Sid sɪd
Sidcup 'sɪd kʌp →'sɪg-, -kəp
Siddall 'sɪd ɔːl ‖ -ɑːl
Siddeley 'sɪd ᵊl i
Siddhartha sɪ 'dɑːt ə ‖ -'dɑːrt̬ ə
Siddons 'sɪd ᵊnz
side saɪd **sided** 'saɪd ɪd -əd **sides** saɪdz **siding**
  'saɪd ɪŋ
  'side dish; 'side ef,fect; 'side ,issue; 'side
  ,order; 'side street
sidearm 'saɪd ɑːm ‖ -ɑːrm ~s z
sideband 'saɪd bænd →'saɪb-
sidebar 'saɪd bɑː →'saɪb- ‖ -bɑːr ~s z
sideboard 'saɪd bɔːd →'saɪb- ‖ -bɔːrd -boʊrd ~s
  z
Sidebotham, Sidebottom 'saɪd ,bɒt əm
  →'saɪb- ‖ -,bɑːt̬ əm —Some bearers of these
  names insist on fanciful pronunciations such
  as 'siːd-, -,bəʊθ əm ‖ -,boʊθ-, or even
  ,sɪd ɪ bə 'tɑːm, -'təʊm ‖ -'toʊm
sideburn 'saɪd bɜːn →'saɪb- ‖ -bɜːn ~s z
sidecar 'saɪd kɑː →'saɪg- ‖ -kɑːr ~s z
-sided 'saɪd ɪd -əd — **many-sided**
  ,men i 'saɪd ɪd ◄ -əd
sidekick 'saɪd kɪk →'saɪg- ~s s
sidelight 'saɪd laɪt ~s s
sidelin|e 'saɪd laɪn ~ed d ~es z ~ing ɪŋ
sidelong 'saɪd lɒŋ ‖ -lɔːŋ -lɑːŋ
side|man 'saɪd |mən →'saɪb-, -mæn ~men
  men mən
side-on ,saɪd 'ɒn ◄ ‖ -'ɑːn -'ɔːn
sidereal saɪ 'dɪər i əl sɪ- ‖ -'dɪr-
siderite 'saɪd ə raɪt 'sɪd- ‖ 'sɪd-
siderostat 'sɪd ər əʊ stæt ~s s
sidesaddle 'saɪd ,sæd ᵊl ~s z
sideshow 'saɪd ʃəʊ ‖ -ʃoʊ ~s z
sideslip 'saɪd slɪp ~ped t ~ping ɪŋ ~s s
sides|man 'saɪdz |mən ~men mən men
sidesplitting 'saɪd ,splɪt ɪŋ ‖ -,splɪt̬ ɪŋ ~ly li
sidestep 'saɪd step ~ped t ~ping ɪŋ ~s s
sidestroke 'saɪd strəʊk ‖ -stroʊk
sideswip|e 'saɪd swaɪp ~ed t ~es s ~ing ɪŋ
sidetrack 'saɪd træk ~ed t ~ing ɪŋ ~s s
side-view 'saɪd vjuː
sidewalk 'saɪd wɔːk ‖ -wɑːk ~s s
  'sidewalk ,artist
sidewall 'saɪd wɔːl ‖ -wɑːl ~s z
sideward 'saɪd wəd ‖ -wᵊrd ~s z
sideways 'saɪd weɪz
side-wheeler 'saɪd wiːᵊl ə -hwiːᵊl- ‖ -ᵊr
sidewinder 'saɪd ,waɪnd ə ‖ -ᵊr ~s z
Sidgwick 'sɪdʒ wɪk
siding 'saɪd ɪŋ ~s z
sidl|e 'saɪd ᵊl ~ed d ~es z ~ing ɪŋ
Sidmouth 'sɪd məθ →'sɪb-
Sidney 'sɪd ni
Sidon 'saɪd ᵊn
Sidonian saɪ 'dəʊn i ən ‖ -'doʊn- ~s z

S

Sidonie sɪ 'dəʊn i ‖ -'doʊn i
SIDS sɪdz
Sieff siːf
siege siːdʒ siːʒ **sieges** 'siːdʒ ɪz 'siːʒ-, -əz
Siegel 'siːg əl
Siegfried 'siːg friːd —*Ger* ['ziːk fʁiːt]
Sieg Heil ˌsiːg 'haɪəl —*Ger* [ˌziːk 'haɪl]
Sieglinde siː 'glɪnd ə sɪ- —*Ger* [ziːk 'lɪn də]
Siemens, s~ 'siːm ənz —*Ger* ['ziː məns, -mɛns]
Siena si 'en ə —*It* ['sjɛː na]
Sienese ˌsiː e 'niːz ◂ -ə- ‖ -'niːs
sienna si 'en ə
sierra, S~ si 'er ə -'eər-; 'sɪər ə —*Sp* ['sje rra]
   ~s z —*see also phrases with this word*
   Si,erra Ne'vada
Sierra Leone si ˌer ə li 'əʊn -ˌeər-, -'əʊn i; ˌsɪər· ·'· ‖ -'oʊn -'oʊn i
Sierra Leonean, Sierra Leonian
   si ˌer ə li 'əʊn i ən ◂ -ˌeər-; ˌsɪər· ·'·- ‖ -'oʊn- s z
Sierra Madre si ˌer ə 'mɑːdr eɪ -ˌeər-, -i —*Sp* ['mað re]
siesta si 'est ə ~s z
sieve sɪv (!) **sieved** sɪvd **sieves** sɪvz **sieving** 'sɪv ɪŋ
sievert, S~ 'siːv ət ‖ -ərt ~s s
sift sɪft **sifted** 'sɪft ɪd -əd **sifting/s** 'sɪft ɪŋ/z **sifts** sɪfts
Sifta *tdmk* 'sɪft ə
sifter 'sɪft ə ‖ -ər ~s z
Sigal 'siːg əl
sigh saɪ **sighed** saɪd (= side) **sighing** 'saɪ ɪŋ **sighs** saɪz (= size)
sight saɪt (= site, cite) **sighted** 'saɪt ɪd -əd ‖ 'saɪţ əd **sighting** 'saɪt ɪŋ ‖ 'saɪţ ɪŋ **sights** saɪts
-sighted 'saɪt ɪd -əd ‖ 'saɪţ əd — **far-sighted** ˌfɑː 'saɪt ɪd ◂ -əd ‖ ˌfɑːr 'saɪţ əd ◂
sightless 'saɪt ləs -lɪs **~ly** li **~ness** nəs nɪs
sightline 'saɪt laɪn ~s z
sight|ly 'saɪt |li **~lier** li ə ‖ li ər **~liest** li ɪst li əst
sight-|read *pres* 'saɪt |riːd **~read** *past & pp* red **~reader/s** riːd ə/z ‖ -ər/z **~reading** riːd ɪŋ **~reads** riːdz
sightscreen 'saɪt skriːn ~s z
sightseeing 'saɪt ˌsiː ɪŋ
sightseer 'saɪt ˌsiː ə ‖ ər ~s z
sigint, SIGINT 'sɪg ɪnt
Sigismond, Sigismund 'sɪg ɪs mənd 'sɪdʒ-, -ɪz-
sig|lum 'sɪg |ləm **~la** lə
sigma 'sɪg mə ~s z
sigmatic sɪg 'mæt ɪk ‖ -'mæţ ɪk
sigmoid 'sɪg mɔɪd
Sigmund 'sɪg mənd —*Ger* ['ziːk mʊnt]
sign saɪn (= sine) **signed** saɪnd **signing** 'saɪn ɪŋ **signs** saɪnz
   'sign ˌlanguage
signage 'saɪn ɪdʒ
signal 'sɪg nəl **~ed, ~led** d **~ing, ~ling** ɪŋ **~s** z
   'signal box; **'signal ˌtower**

signaler 'sɪg nəl ə ‖ -ər **~s** z
signalis|e, signaliz|e 'sɪg nə laɪz -nəl aɪz **~ed** d **~es** ɪz əz **~ing** ɪŋ
signaller 'sɪg nəl ə ‖ -ər **~s** z
signally 'sɪg nəl i
signal|man 'sɪg nəl |mən -mæn **~men** mən men
signalment 'sɪg nəl mənt **~s** s
signal-to-noise ˌsɪg nəl tə 'nɔɪz
   ˌsignal-to-'noise ˌratio
signator|y 'sɪg nət ər |i ‖ -nə tɔːr |i -toʊr i **~ies** iz
signature 'sɪg nətʃ ə -nɪtʃ- ‖ -ər -nə tʃʊr **~s** z
   'signature tune
signboard 'saɪn bɔːd →'saɪm- ‖ -bɔːrd -boʊrd **~s** z
signer 'saɪn ə ‖ -ər **~s** z
signet 'sɪg nɪt -nət **~s** s
   'signet ring
significance sɪg 'nɪf ɪk ən's -ək-
significant sɪg 'nɪf ɪk ənt -ək- **~ly** li
signification ˌsɪg nɪf ɪ 'keɪʃ ən ˌ-nəf-, §-ə'·- **~s** z
significative sɪg 'nɪf ɪk ət ɪv -'·ək-; -ɪ keɪt-, -ə keɪt- ‖ -ə keɪţ ɪv **~ly** li **~ness** nəs nɪs
signi|fy 'sɪg nɪ |faɪ -nə- **~fied** faɪd **~fier/s** faɪ ə/z ‖ faɪ ər/z **~fies** faɪz **~fying** faɪ ɪŋ
Signor, s~ 'siːn jɔː -'·· ‖ -jɔːr [ˌɲor]
Signora, s~ siːn 'jɔːr ə —*It* [sin 'ɲo: ra]
Signorina, s~ ˌsiːn jɔː 'riːn ə ◂ -jə- —*It* [sin ɲo 'ri: na]
signpost 'saɪn pəʊst →'saɪm- ‖ -poʊst **~ed** ɪd əd **~ing** ɪŋ **~s** s
signwrit|er 'saɪn ˌraɪt| ə ‖ -ˌraɪţ| ər **~ers** əz ‖ -ərz **~ing** ɪŋ
Sigourney sɪ 'gɔːn i -'gʊən- ‖ -'gʊrn i
Sigurd 'sɪg ʊəd 'siːg-, -ɜːd ‖ -ərd
Sihanouk 'siː ə nuːk
sika 'siːk ə ~s z
sike, Sike saɪk **sikes, Sikes** saɪks
Sikh siːk sɪk —*Hindi* [sɪkʰ] **Sikhs** siːks sɪks
Sikhism 'siːk ˌɪz əm 'sɪk-
Sikkim 'sɪk ɪm sɪ 'kɪm
Sikkimese ˌsɪk ɪ 'miːz ◂ ‖ -'miːs ◂
Sikorsky sɪ 'kɔːsk i ‖ -'kɔːrsk-
silage 'saɪl ɪdʒ
silane 'sɪl eɪn 'saɪl-
Silas 'saɪl əs
Silbury 'sɪl bər i ‖ -ˌber i
   ˌSilbury 'Hill
Silchester 'sɪltʃ ɪst ə -əst-; 'sɪl tʃest ə ‖ -ər
Silcox 'sɪl kɒks ‖ -kɑːks
sild sɪld **silds** sɪldz
sildenafil sɪl 'den ə fɪl
Sile, Síle *personal name* 'ʃiːl ə
Sileby 'saɪəl bi
silenc|e 'saɪl ən's **~ed** t **~es** ɪz əz **~ing** ɪŋ
silencer 'saɪl ən's ə ‖ -ər **~s** z
silent 'saɪl ənt **~ly** li **~ness** nəs nɪs
   ˌsilent 'partner
Silenus saɪ 'liːn əs sɪ-, -'leɪn-
Silesia, s~ saɪ 'liːz i ə sɪ-, -'liːs-; -'liːʒ ə, -'liːʃ- ‖ saɪ 'liːʒ ə sɪ-, -'liːʃ-

Silesian saɪ ˈliːz i ən sɪ-, -ˈliːs-; -ˈliːʒ ən, -ˈliːʃ-
 ‖ saɪ ˈliːʒ ən sɪ-, -ˈliːʃ- **~s** z
silex ˈsaɪl eks
silhou|ette ˌsɪl u ˈet -ju-, ˈ··· **~etted** et ɪd -əd
 ‖ et əd **~ettes** ets **~etting** et ɪŋ ‖ et ɪŋ
silica ˈsɪl ɪk ə
silicate ˈsɪl ɪ keɪt -ə-; -ɪk ət, -ɪt **~s** s
silicic sɪ ˈlɪs ɪk sə-
silicon ˈsɪl ɪk ən -ək-; -ɪ kɒn, -ə-, △-kəʊn
 ‖ -ɪ kɑːn
 ˌsilicon ˈchip; ˌSilicon ˈValley
silicone ˈsɪl ɪ kəʊn -ə- ‖ -koʊn **~s** z
silicosis ˌsɪl ɪ ˈkəʊs ɪs -ə-, §-əs ‖ -ˈkoʊs əs
silicotic ˌsɪl ɪ ˈkɒt ɪk ◂ -ə- ‖ -ˈkɑːṭ- **~s** s
silk, Silk sɪlk **silks** sɪlks
silken ˈsɪlk ən
silki... —*see* **silky**
Silkin ˈsɪlk ɪn §-ən
silkscreen ˈsɪlk skriːn **~ing** ɪŋ
silkworm ˈsɪlk wɜːm ‖ -wɜ˞ːm **~s** z
silk|y ˈsɪlk |i **~ier** i ə ‖ i ə˞r **~iest** i ɪst i əst **~ily**
 ɪ li əl i **~iness** i nəs i nɪs
sill sɪl **sills** sɪlz
sillabub ˈsɪl ə bʌb **~s** z
Sillars ˈsɪl əz ‖ -ə˞rz
Sillery ˈsɪl ər i
silli... —*see* **silly**
sillimanite ˈsɪl ɪm ə naɪt ˈ-əm-
Sillito, Sillitoe ˈsɪl ɪ təʊ -ə- ‖ -toʊ
Silloth ˈsɪl əθ
Sills sɪlz
sill|y ˈsɪl |i **~ier** i ə ‖ i ə˞r **~ies** iz **~iest** i ɪst
 i əst **~iness** i nəs i nɪs
 ˌsilly ˈbilly, ˈ··ˌ··; ˈsilly ˌseason
silo ˈsaɪl əʊ ‖ -oʊ **~s** z
Siloam saɪ ˈləʊ əm sɪ-, -æm ‖ -ˈloʊ-
siloxane sɪ ˈlɒks eɪn saɪ-, sə- ‖ -ˈlɑːks-
Silsoe ˈsɪls əʊ ‖ -oʊ
silt sɪlt **silted** ˈsɪlt ɪd -əd **silting** ˈsɪlt ɪŋ **silts**
 sɪlts
siltation sɪl ˈteɪʃ ən
silty ˈsɪlt i
Silures saɪ ˈlʊər iːz sɪ-, -ˈljʊər-, -ˈljɔːr- ‖ ˈsɪl jə˞r-
Silurian saɪ ˈlʊər i ən sɪ-, -ˈljʊər-, -ˈljɔːr- ‖ -ˈlʊr-
Silva ˈsɪlv ə
silvan ˈsɪlv ən
Silvanus sɪl ˈveɪn əs
silver, S~ ˈsɪlv ə ‖ -ə˞r **~ed** d **silvering**
 ˈsɪlv ər ɪŋ **~s** z
 ˌsilver ˈbirch; ˈsilver foil, ˌ·ˈ·; ˌsilver
 ˈjubilee, ˌ··ˈ·, ˈ··ˌ·; ˌsilver ˈmedal; ˌsilver
 ˈnitrate; ˌsilver ˈpaper; ˌsilver ˈplate◂;
 ˌsilver ˈwedding, ˌsilver ˈwedding
 anniˌversary
silverfish ˈsɪlv ə fɪʃ ‖ -ə˞r- **~es** ɪz əz
silveri... —*see* **silvery**
Silverman ˈsɪlv ə mən ‖ -ə˞r-
Silvers ˈsɪlv əz ‖ -ə˞rz
silverside ˈsɪlv ə saɪd ‖ -ə˞r- **~s** z
silversmith ˈsɪlv ə smɪθ ‖ -ə˞r- **~ing** ɪŋ **~s** s
Silverstone ˈsɪlv ə stəʊn ‖ -ə˞r stoʊn
silver-tongued ˌsɪlv ə ˈtʌŋd ◂ §-ˈtɒŋd ‖ -ə˞r-
Silvertown ˈsɪlv ə taʊn ‖ -ə˞r-

silverware ˈsɪlv ə weə ‖ -ə˞r wer -wær
silverweed ˈsɪlv ə wiːd ‖ -ə˞r-
silver-Y ˌsɪlv ə ˈwaɪ ‖ -ə˞r-
 ˌsilver-ˈY moth
silver|y ˈsɪlv ər |i **~iness** i nəs i nɪs
Silvester sɪl ˈvest ə ‖ -ə˞r
Silvia ˈsɪlv i ə
silviculture ˈsɪlv ɪ ˌkʌltʃ ə §-ə- ‖ -ə˞r
Silvie ˈsɪlv i
Silvikrin *tdmk* ˈsɪlv ɪ krɪn -ə-
s'il vous plait, s'il vous plaît ˌsi vuː ˈpleɪ
 ˌsiːəl- —*Fr* [sil vu plɛ]
Sim, sim sɪm
sima ˈsaɪm ə
simazine ˈsaɪm ə ziːn
simba, Simba ˈsɪm bə
Simca *tdmk* ˈsɪm kə **~s** z
Simcox ˈsɪm kɒks ‖ -kɑːks
Simenon ˈsiːm ə nɒ̃ ˈsɪm-, -nɒn ‖ ˌsiːm ə ˈnɔːn
 -ˈnoʊn, -ˈnɑːn —*Fr* [sim nɔ̃]
Simeon ˈsɪm i ən
Simes saɪmz
Simey ˈsaɪm i
Simi sɪ ˈmiː ˈsiːm i
simian ˈsɪm i ən **~s** z
similar ˈsɪm əl ə -ɪl ə ‖ -ə˞l ə˞r
similarit|y ˌsɪm ə ˈlær ət |i ˌ-ɪ-, -ɪt |i ‖ -əṭ |i
 -ˈler- **~ies** iz
similarly ˈsɪm əl ə li -ɪl ə li ‖ -ə˞l ə˞r li
simile ˈsɪm əl i -ɪl- **~s** z
similitude sɪ ˈmɪl ɪ tjuːd sə-, -ə-, →-tʃuːd
 ‖ -ə tuːd -tjuːd **~s** z
Simla ˈsɪm lə
Simm sɪm
simmer ˈsɪm ə ‖ -ə˞r **~ed** d **simmering**
 ˈsɪm ər ɪŋ **~s** z
Simmonds ˈsɪm əndz
Simmons ˈsɪm ənz
Simms sɪmz
simnel, S~ ˈsɪm n̩l
Simon ˈsaɪm ən —*but as a French name,*
 siː ˈmɒ̃ ‖ -ˈmoʊn —*Fr* [si mɔ̃]
 ˌSimon ˈsays
Simonds *(i)* ˈsɪm əndz, *(ii)* ˈsaɪm əndz
Simone sɪ ˈməʊn sə- ‖ -ˈmoʊn
simoniacal ˌsaɪm ə ˈnaɪ ək ᵊl ◂
Simonides saɪ ˈmɒn ɪ diːz -ə- ‖ -ˈmɑːn-
simon-pure ˌsaɪm ən ˈpjʊə ◂ -ˈpjɔː ‖ -ˈpjʊə˞r ◂
Simons ˈsaɪm ənz
Simonsbath ˈsɪm ənz bɑːθ §-bæθ ‖ -bæθ
Simonstown ˈsaɪm ənz taʊn
simony ˈsaɪm ən i ˈsɪm-
simoom sɪ ˈmuːm §sə- **~s** z
simpatico sɪm ˈpæt ɪ kəʊ -ˈpɑːt- ‖ -ˈpɑːṭ ɪ koʊ
 -ˈpæṭ- —*It* [sim ˈpa ti ko]
simper ˈsɪmp ə ‖ -ə˞r **~ed** d **simpering/ly**
 ˈsɪmp ər ɪŋ /li **~s** z
Simpkin ˈsɪmp kɪn
Simpkins ˈsɪmp kɪnz
Simpkinson ˈsɪmp kɪn sən
simple ˈsɪmp ᵊl **simpler** ˈsɪmp lə ‖ -l̩ə˞r
 ˌsimples ˈsɪmp ᵊlz **simplest** ˈsɪmp lɪst -ləst

S

,simple 'fracture; ,simple 'interest;
,simple 'life; ,simple ma'chine; ,simple
'time

simple-hearted ,sɪmp ᵊl 'hɑːt ɪd ◀ -əd
‖ -'hɑːrt̬ əd ◀

simple-minded ,sɪmp ᵊl 'maɪnd ɪd ◀ -əd- **~ly** li
~ness nəs nɪs

simpleness 'sɪmp ᵊl nəs -nɪs

simpleton 'sɪmp ᵊl tən **~s** z

simplex 'sɪm pleks

simplicit|y sɪm 'plɪs ət |i -ɪt- ‖ -ət̬ |i **~ies** iz

simplification ,sɪmp lɪf ɪ 'keɪʃ ᵊn ˌ-ləf-, §-ə'-
~s z

simpli|fy 'sɪmp lɪ |faɪ -lə- **~fied** faɪd **~fier/s**
faɪ ə/z ‖ faɪ ᵊr/z **~fies** faɪz **~fying** faɪ ɪŋ

simplistic sɪm 'plɪst ɪk **~ally** ᵊl i

Simplon 'sæm plɒn 'sɪm- ‖ -plɑːn —Fr
[sæ plɔ̃]

simply 'sɪmp li

Simpson 'sɪmps ᵊn **~s** z
　　,Simpson 'Desert

Sims sɪmz

Simson 'sɪmᵖ sᵊn

simulac|rum ,sɪm ju 'leɪk |rəm §-jə-, -'læk-
‖ ,sɪm jə- **~ra** rə

simu|late 'sɪm ju |leɪt -jə- ‖ -jə- **~lated** leɪt ɪd
-əd ‖ leɪt̬ əd **~lates** leɪts **~lating** leɪt ɪŋ
‖ leɪt̬ ɪŋ

simulation ,sɪm ju 'leɪʃ ᵊn -jə- ‖ -jə- **~s** z

simulator 'sɪm ju leɪt ə '-jə- ‖ -jə leɪt̬ ᵊr **~s** z

simulcast 'sɪm ᵊl kɑːst §-kæst ‖ 'saɪm ᵊl kæst
(*) **~ed** ɪd əd **~ing** ɪŋ **~s** s

simultaneity ,sɪm ᵊl tə 'neɪ ət i -'niː-, -ɪt i
‖ ,saɪm ᵊl tə 'niː ət̬ i (*)

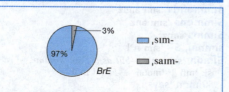

SIMULTANEOUS

3%

97%

■ ,sɪm-
■ ,saɪm-

BrE

simultaneous ,sɪm ᵊl 'teɪn i əs ◀ ‖ ,saɪm- (*)
— Preference poll, BrE: ,sɪm- 97%, ,saɪm- 3%.
~ly li **~ness** nəs nɪs

simvastatin ,sɪm və 'stæt ɪn §-ᵊn ‖ -ᵊn

sin 'do wrong' sɪn **sinned** sɪnd **sinning** 'sɪn ɪŋ
sins sɪnz

sin in trigonometry saɪn

Sinai 'saɪn aɪ 'saɪn i̩ aɪ, 'saɪn eɪ aɪ

Sinatra sɪ 'nɑːtr ə sə-

Sinbad 'sɪn bæd →'sɪm-

sin-bin 'sɪn bɪn →'sɪm- **~s** z

since sɪn's

sin|cere sɪn |'sɪə sᵊn- ‖ -|'sɪʳr **~cerely** 'sɪə li
‖ 'sɪr li **~cerer** 'sɪər ə ‖ 'sɪr ᵊr **~cerest**
'sɪər ɪst -əst ‖ 'sɪr əst

sincerity sɪn 'ser ət i sᵊn-, -ɪt i ‖ -ət̬ i

Sinclair (i) 'sɪn kleə →'sɪŋ-, §-klə ‖ -kler -klær,
(ii) sɪn 'kleə →sɪŋ- ‖ -'kleʳr -'klæʳr

Sind, Sindh sɪnd —Hindi [sɪɳdʱ]

Sindbad 'sɪnd bæd

Sinden 'sɪnd ən

Sindhi 'sɪnd i -hi —Hindi [sɪŋ d̪ʱi] **~s** z

Sindy tdmk 'sɪnd i

sine prep, Latin 'sɪn i 'saɪn-, 'siːn-, -eɪ —see also
phrases with this word

sine n, in trigonometry **saɪn sines** saɪnz
　　'sine wave

Sinead, Sinéad ʃɪ 'neɪd -'neəd

sinecure 'sɪn ɪ kjʊə 'saɪn-, -§ə-, -kjɔː- **~s** z

sine die ,saɪn i 'daɪ iː -i; ,sɪn i 'diː eɪ, -eɪ-;
　　⚠ ,saɪn i 'daɪ

sine qua non ,sɪn i ˌkwɑː 'nɒn ˌsiːn-, -eɪ-,
-'nəʊn; ,saɪn i ˌkweɪ- ‖ -'nɑːn -'nəʊn

sinew 'sɪn juː **~s** z

sinewy 'sɪn juː i

sinfonia, S~ ,sɪn fə 'nɪə sɪn 'fəʊn i̩ə
‖ ,sɪn fə 'niː ə -foʊ- **~s** z

sinfonietta ,sɪn fəʊn i 'et ə ˌ-fən-, ˌ-fɒn-;
　·'jet ə ‖ ,sɪn fən 'jet̬ ə -foʊn- **~s** z

sinful 'sɪn fᵊl -ful **~ly** i **~ness** nəs nɪs

sing sɪŋ **sang** sæŋ **singing** 'sɪŋ ɪŋ **sings** sɪŋz
sung sʌŋ
　　'Sing Sing

singable 'sɪŋ əb ᵊl

singalong 'sɪŋ ə lɒŋ ‖ -lɔːŋ -lɑːŋ **~s** z

Singapore ,sɪŋ ə 'pɔː ◀ -gə-, '· · · ‖ 'sɪŋ gə pɔːr
-ə-, -poʊr

Singaporean ,sɪŋ ə 'pɔːr i̩ ən ◀ -gə-,
-pɔː 'riː ən ‖ -'poʊr- **~s** z

singe sɪndʒ **singed** sɪndʒd **singeing** 'sɪndʒ ɪŋ
singes 'sɪndʒ ɪz -əz

singer, S~ 'sɪŋ ə ‖ -ᵊr **~s** z

singer-songwriter ,sɪŋ ə 'sɒŋ ˌraɪt ə
‖ ,sɪŋ ᵊr 'sɔːŋ ˌraɪt̬ᵊr -'sɑːŋ- **~s** z

Singh sɪŋ

Singhala 'sɪŋ həl ə

Singhalese ,sɪŋ ə 'liːz ◀ -hə-, -gə- ‖ -gə- -'liːs

singing 'sɪŋ ɪŋ

singl|e 'sɪŋ gᵊl **~ed** d **~es** z **~ing** ɪŋ
　　,single 'file; ,single 'parent

single-action ,sɪŋ gᵊl 'æk ʃᵊn ◀

single-breasted ,sɪŋ gᵊl 'brest ɪd ◀ -əd

single-decker ,sɪŋ gᵊl 'dek ə ◀ ‖ -ᵊr **~s** z

single-family ,sɪŋ gᵊl 'fæm li ◀ -'fæm əl i, -ɪl i

single-handed ,sɪŋ gᵊl 'hænd ɪd ◀ -əd **~ly** li
~ness nəs nɪs

single-lens ,sɪŋ gᵊl 'lenz ◀
　　,single-lens 'reflex (,camera)

single-minded ,sɪŋ gᵊl 'maɪnd ɪd ◀ -əd **~ly** li
~ness nəs nɪs

singleness 'sɪŋ gᵊl nəs -nɪs

single-sex ,sɪŋ gᵊl 'seks ◀

single-spac|ed ,sɪŋ gᵊl 'speɪs|t ◀ **~ing** ɪŋ

singlestick 'sɪŋ gᵊl stɪk **~s** s

singlet 'sɪŋ glət -glɪt **~s** s

singleton, S~ 'sɪŋ gᵊl tən **~s** z

single-track ,sɪŋ gᵊl 'træk ◀

single-user ,sɪŋ gᵊl 'juːz ə ◀ ‖ -ᵊr

singly 'sɪŋ gli

singsong 'sɪŋ sɒŋ ‖ -sɔːŋ -sɑːŋ **~s** z

singular 'sɪŋ gjʊl ə -gjəl- ‖ -gjəl ᵊr **~ly** li **~ness**
nəs nɪs **~s** z

S

singularit|y ˌsɪŋ gju 'lær ət |i ˌgjə-, -ɪt i
∥ -gjə 'lær ət̬ |i -'ler- **~ies** iz
singulary 'sɪŋ gjʊl ər i ∥ -gjə ler i
sinh ʃaɪn sɪn'ʃ, ˌsaɪn 'eɪtʃ ∥ sɪnʃ
Sinhala 'sɪn həl ə 'sɪŋ-
Sinhalese ˌsɪn hə 'liːz ◂ ˌsɪŋ-, -ə- ∥ -'liːs
sinister 'sɪn ɪst ə §-əst- ∥ -ər **~ly** li **~ness** nəs
nɪs
sinistral 'sɪn ɪs trəl -əs- **~ly** i **~s** z
sinistrorse 'sɪn ɪ strɔːs -ə-, ˌ· ·'· ∥ -strɔːrs **~ly** li
Sinitic saɪ 'nɪt ɪk sɪ- ∥ -'nɪt̬-
Sinitta sɪ 'niːt ə sə- ∥ -'niːt̬-
sink sɪŋk **sank** sæŋk **sinking** 'sɪŋk ɪŋ **sinks**
sɪŋks **sunk** sʌŋk **sunken** 'sʌŋk ən
‚**sinking** ˌfeeling; **'sinking fund**
sinkable 'sɪŋk əb ᵊl
sinker 'sɪŋk ə ∥ -ᵊr **~s** z
sinkhole 'sɪŋk həʊl →-hɒʊl ∥ -hoʊl **~s** z
sinless 'sɪn ləs -lɪs **~ly** li **~ness** nəs nɪs
Sinnatt 'sɪn ət
sinner 'sɪn ə ∥ -ᵊr **~s** z
Sinn Fein ˌʃɪn 'feɪn —Ir Sinn Féin
[ˌʃiːnʲ 'heːnʲ] **~er/s** ə/z ∥ -ᵊr/z
Sinnott 'sɪn ət
Sino- ˌsaɪn əʊ ∥ -oʊ — **Sino-Japanese**
ˌsaɪn əʊ ˌdʒæp ə 'niːz ∥ ˌoʊ- -'niːs
sinological ˌsaɪn əʊ 'lɒdʒ ɪk ᵊl ◂ ˌsɪn-
∥ -ə 'lɑːdʒ-
sinologist saɪ 'nɒl ədʒ ɪst sɪ-, §sə-, §-əst
∥ -'nɑːl- **~s** s
sinologue 'saɪn əʊ lɒg 'sɪn-, -ᵊl ɒg ∥ -ᵊl ɔːg
-ɑːg **~s** z
sinology saɪ 'nɒl ədʒ i sɪ-, §sə- ∥ -'nɑːl-
Sino-Tibetan ˌsaɪn əʊ tɪ 'bet ᵊn ◂ ˌsɪn-, -tə'--
∥ ˌoʊ-
sinsemilla ˌsɪnˈs ə 'mɪl ə -ɪ-, -'miːl-, -'miː-, -jə
sinter 'sɪnt ə ∥ 'sɪnt̬ ᵊr **~ed** d **sintering**
'sɪnt ər ɪŋ ∥ 'sɪnt̬- **~s** z
sinuosit|y ˌsɪn ju 'ɒs ət |i -ɪt i ∥ -'ɑːs ət̬ |i **~ies**
iz
sinuous 'sɪn ju‚əs **~ly** li **~ness** nəs nɪs
sinus 'saɪn əs **~es** ɪz əz
sinusitis ˌsaɪn ə 'saɪt ɪs §-əs ∥ -'saɪt̬ əs
sinusoid 'saɪn ə sɔɪd **~s** z
sinusoidal ˌsaɪn ə 'sɔɪd ᵊl ◂ **~ly** i
Siobhan, Siobhán ʃə 'vɔːn ʃɪ- ∥ -'vɑːn
Sion 'Zion' 'saɪ ən 'zaɪ‚
Sion, Siôn male personal name, Welsh ʃɔːn
∥ ʃɑːn
Sion place in Switzerland si 'ɒ̃ ∥ -'ɔːn -'ɑːn,
-'oʊn —Fr [sjɔ̃]
Siouan 'suː ən
Sioux sing. suː **Sioux** pl suːz suː
Siouxsie 'suːz i
sip sɪp **sipped** sɪpt **sipping** 'sɪp ɪŋ **sips** sɪps
siphon 'saɪf ᵊn **~ed** d **~ing** ‚ɪŋ **~s** z
siphonic saɪ 'fɒn ɪk ∥ -'fɑːn-
siphonophore saɪ 'fɒn ə fɔː 'sɪf ən ə-
∥ -'fɑːn ə fɔːr -four **~s** z
Siple 'saɪp ᵊl
Siqueiros sɪ 'keər ɒs ∥ -'keɪ roʊs —Sp
[si 'kei ɾos]

sir, Sir strong form sɜː ∥ sɜːr, weak form sə ∥ sᵊr
—The weak form is customary in BrE
whenever this word is used with a name, as Sir
John; Sir Peter Smith. Otherwise the strong
form is usual: yes, sir. In AmE the weak form
is little used. **sirs** sɜːz ∥ sɜːz —There is no
weak form of the plural.
sirdar, S~ 'sɜːd ɑː sɜː 'dɑː ∥ 'sɜːd ɑːr **~s** z
sire 'saɪ‚ə ∥ 'saɪ‚ᵊr **sired** 'saɪ‚əd ∥ 'saɪ‚ᵊrd **sires**
'saɪ‚əz ∥ 'saɪ‚ᵊrz **siring** 'saɪ‚ər ɪŋ ∥ 'saɪ‚ᵊr ɪŋ
siree ˌsɜː 'riː sə 'riː ∥ sə 'riː ˌsɜː 'iː
siren 'saɪ‚ᵊr ən -ɪn **~s** z
sirenian saɪ‚ 'riːn i‚ən **~s** z
Sirhowy sɜː 'haʊ i ∥ sɜː-
Sirius 'sɪr i‚əs 'saɪ‚ᵊr-
sirloin 'sɜː lɔɪn ∥ 'sɜː- **~s** z
‚**sirloin 'steak**
sirocco sɪ 'rɒk əʊ sə- ∥ -'rɑːk oʊ **~s** z
Siros 'sɪər ɒs ∥ 'sɪr ɑːs —Gk ['si ɾos]
sirrah 'sɪr ə
sirree ˌsɜː 'riː sə- ∥ sə 'riː ˌsɜː 'iː
sis sɪs
sisal 'saɪs ᵊl 'saɪz-
siskin 'sɪsk ɪn §-ən **~s** z
Sisley 'sɪz li
Sissie 'sɪs i
sissified 'sɪs ɪ faɪd -ə-
Sissinghurst 'sɪs ɪŋ hɜːst ∥ -hɜːst
Sisson 'sɪs ᵊn
Sissons 'sɪs ᵊnz
siss|y 'sɪs |i **~ies** iz
sister, S~ 'sɪst ə ∥ -ᵊr **~s** z
sisterhood 'sɪst ə hʊd ∥ -ᵊr- **~s** z
sister-|in-law 'sɪst ər |ɪn ˌlɔː 'sɪs tə-, §ˌən‚·
∥ -ᵊr- ˌlɑː: **sisters-~** 'sɪst əz ∥ 'sɪst ᵊrz
sist|erly 'sɪst |ə li -|ᵊl i ∥ -|ᵊr li **~erliness**
ə li nəs ᵊl i-, -nɪs ∥ ᵊr li nəs
Sistine 'sɪst iːn -aɪn
sis|trum 'sɪs |trəm **~tra** trə **~troid** trɔɪd
~trums trəmz
siSwati sɪ 'swaːt i
Sisyphean ˌsɪs ɪ 'fiː ən ◂ -ə-
Sisyphus 'sɪs ɪf əs -əf-
sit sɪt **sat** sæt **sits** sɪts **sitting** 'sɪt ɪŋ ∥ 'sɪt̬ ɪŋ
sitar sɪ 'tɑː 'sɪt ɑː ∥ sɪ 'tɑːr —Hindi [sɪ t̪aːr] **~s**
z
sitcom 'sɪt kɒm ∥ -kɑːm **~s** z
sit-down 'sɪt daʊn
site saɪt (= sight, cite) **sited** 'saɪt ɪd -əd
∥ 'saɪt̬ əd **sites** saɪts **siting** 'saɪt ɪŋ ∥ 'saɪt̬ ɪŋ
site-specific ˌsaɪt spə 'sɪf ɪk ◂ -spɪ-
sit-in 'sɪt ɪn ∥ 'sɪt̬ ɪn **~s** z
Sitka, sitka 'sɪt kə
sitrep 'sɪt rep **~s** s
sitter 'sɪt ə ∥ 'sɪt̬ ᵊr **~s** z
sitting 'sɪt ɪŋ ∥ 'sɪt̬ ɪŋ **~s** z
‚**Sitting 'Bull**; ‚**sitting 'duck**; '**sitting
room**; ‚**sitting 'target**; ‚**sitting 'tenant**
Sittingbourne 'sɪt ɪŋ bɔːn ∥ 'sɪt̬ ɪŋ bɔːrn
-boʊrn
situ|ate v 'sɪtʃ u |eɪt 'sɪt ju-, §'sɪt u- **~ated**
eɪt ɪd -əd ∥ eɪt̬ əd **~ates** eɪts **~ating** eɪt ɪŋ
∥ eɪt̬ ɪŋ

S

situate *adj* 'sɪtʃ u eɪt 'sɪt ju-, §'sɪt u-, -ət, -ɪt

SITUATION

1% — 35%
□ -tj-
64%
■ -tʃ-
□ -t-
BrE

BrE -tʃ- by age

Percentage
50
40
30
20
10
0
Older ◄—— Speakers ——► Younger

situation ˌsɪtʃ u 'eɪʃ ᵊn ˌsɪt ju-, §ˌsɪt u- —
Preference poll, BrE tʃ *35%,* tj *64%,* t *1%.* **~al**
ᵊl **~ally** ᵊl i **~s** z
ˌsitu.ation 'comedy, ˌ·'·· ˌ·,··; ˌsitu'ation
room
sit-up 'sɪt ʌp ‖ 'sɪţ ʌp **~s** s
sit-upon 'sɪt ə ˌpɒn ‖ 'sɪţ ə ˌpɑːn **~s** z
Sitwell 'sɪt wəl -wel **~s** z
sitz sɪts (= *sits*)
'sitz bath
Siva 'ʃiːv ə 'ʃɪv-, 'siːv-, 'sɪv- —*Hindi* [ʃɪʊ]
Siwash, s~ 'saɪ wɒʃ ‖ -wɑːʃ -wɔːʃ
six sɪks **sixes** 'sɪks ɪz -əz
ˌSix 'Counties; ˌSix ˌDay 'War
sixer 'sɪks ə ‖ -ᵊr **~s** z
six-figure 'sɪks ˌfɪg ə ‖ -jᵊr
sixfold 'sɪks fəʊld →-fɒʊld ‖ -foʊld
six-footer ˌsɪks 'fʊt ə ‖ -'fʊţ ᵊr **~s** z
sixgun 'sɪks gʌn **~s** z
sixish 'sɪks ɪʃ
six-pack 'sɪks pæk **~s** s
sixpenc|e 'sɪks pən's **~es** ɪz əz
sixpenny 'sɪks pən i
six-shooter 'sɪks ˌʃuːt ə →'sɪkʃ-, ˌ·'·· ‖ -ˌʃuːţ ᵊr
~s z
sixte sɪkst
sixteen ˌsɪks 'tiːn ◄ **~s** z
sixteenmo, 16mo ˌsɪks 'tiːn məʊ →-'tiːm-
‖ -moʊ
sixteenth ˌsɪks 'tiːntᶿ ◄ **~ly** li **~s** s
ˌsix'teenth note
sixth sɪksᶿ sɪkstᶿ, △sɪkᶿ **sixths** sɪksᶿs sɪkstᶿs,
△sɪkᶿs —*but in casual speech both sing. and
pl are sometimes* sɪks *or* sɪkst
'sixth form; ˌsixth 'sense
sixties 'sɪkst iz
sixtieth 'sɪkst i‿əθ ɪθ **~s** s
Sixtus 'sɪkst əs
sixt|y 'sɪkst |i **~ies** iz

sixty-four ˌsɪkst i 'fɔː ◄ ‖ -'fɔːr ◄ -'foʊr
ˌsixty-four ˌthousand ˌdollar 'question,
ˌ·'·· ˌ··
sixty-fourth ˌsɪkst i 'fɔːθ ◄ ‖ -'fɔːrθ ◄ -'foʊrθ
~s s
sixty-nine ˌsɪkst i 'naɪn ◄
sizab|le 'saɪz əb |ᵊl **~leness** ᵊl nəs -nɪs **~ly** li
sizar 'saɪz ə ‖ -ᵊr **~s** z
size saɪz **sized** saɪzd **sizes** 'saɪz ɪz -əz **sizing**
'saɪz ɪŋ
sizeab|le 'saɪz əb |ᵊl **~leness** ᵊl nəs -nɪs **~ly** li
-sized ˌsaɪzd saɪzd — **medium-sized**
ˌmiːd i‿əm 'saɪzd ◄
Sizer, Sizergh 'saɪz ə ‖ -ᵊr
Sizewell 'saɪz wəl -wel
sizz|le 'sɪz ᵊl **~ed** d **~es** z **~ing/ly** ɪŋ /li
sizzler 'sɪz ᵊl‿ə ‖ ᵊr **~s** z
sjambok 'ʃæm bɒk -bʌk ‖ ʃæm 'bɑːk -'bʌk
—*Afrikaans* ['ʃam bok] **~s** s
ska skɑː
skag skæg
Skagerrak 'skæg ə ræk —*Danish*
['sga: jə ʁak, 'sga-]
Skagway 'skæg weɪ
skank skæŋk
skanky 'skæŋk i
Skara Brae ˌskær ə 'breɪ ‖ ˌsker-
skat skæt ‖ skɑːt skæt —*Ger* [skaːt]
skate skeɪt **skated** 'skeɪt ɪd -əd ‖ 'skeɪţ əd
skates skeɪts **skating** 'skeɪt ɪŋ ‖ 'skeɪţ ɪŋ
skateboard 'skeɪt bɔːd ‖ -bɔːrd -boʊrd **~er/s**
ə/z ‖ ᵊr/z **~ing** ɪŋ **~s** z
skater 'skeɪt ə ‖ 'skeɪţ ᵊr **~s** z
skatole 'skæt əʊl →-ɒʊl ‖ -oʊl
skean skiːn 'skiː ən **skeans** skiːnz 'skiː ənz
ˌskean 'dhu duː
Skeat skiːt
skedaddl|e skɪ 'dæd ᵊl skə- **~ed** d **~es** z **~ing**
ɪŋ
skeet skiːt
'skeet ˌshooting
skeeter 'skiːt ə ‖ 'skiːţᵊr **~s** z
skeeve skiːv **skeeved** skiːvd **skeeves** skiːvz
skeeving 'skiːv ɪŋ
Skeffington 'skef ɪŋ tən
skeg skeg **skegs** skegz
Skegness ˌskeg 'nes ◄
skein skeɪn **skeins** skeɪnz
skeletal 'skel ɪt ᵊl -ət-; skɪ 'liːt-, skə-
‖ 'skel əţ ᵊl skə 'liːţ ᵊl **~ly** i
skeleton 'skel ɪt ən -ət-, △-ɪnt- ‖ -ᵊn **~s** z
'skeleton key
Skelmersdale 'skelm əz deɪᵊl ‖ -ᵊrz- —*locally
also* 'skem-
Skelton 'skelt ən
skep skep **skeps** skeps
skeptic, S~ 'skept ɪk **~s** s
skeptical 'skept ɪk ᵊl **~ly** ‿i **~ness** nəs nɪs
skepticism 'skept ɪ ˌsɪz əm -ə-
Skerritt 'sker ɪt §-ət
skerr|y 'sker |i **~ies** iz
sketch sketʃ **sketched** sketʃt **sketches**
'sketʃ ɪz -əz **sketching** 'sketʃ ɪŋ

sketchbook 'sketʃ bʊk §-buːk
sketchi... —*see* **sketchy**
Sketchley 'sketʃ li
sketchpad 'sketʃ pæd ~s z
sketch|y 'sketʃ |i ~**ier** i ə ‖ i ²r ~**iest** i ɪst i əst
   ~**ily** ɪ li əl i ~**iness** i nəs i nɪs
skew skju: **skewed** skju:d **skewing** 'skju: ɪŋ
   skews skju:z
skewbald 'skju: bɔːld ‖ -bɑːld ~s z
Skewen 'skjuː ɪn §ˌən
skewer 'skjuː ə ‖ ²r ~**ed** d **skewering**
   'skjuː ər ɪŋ ~s z
skewness 'skju: nəs -nɪs
skew-whiff ˌskjuː 'wɪf ◄ -'hwɪf
ski ski: —*In 1935 BBC announcers were
   recommended to say ʃi:. Yet this form is now
   entirely obsolete.* **skied** ski:d **skiing** 'ski: ɪŋ
   skis ski:z
   'ski jump; 'ski ˌjumping; 'ski lift; 'ski
   plane; 'ski pole; 'ski stick
skibob 'ski: bɒb ‖ -bɑːb ~**ber/s** ə/z ‖ ²r/z
   ~**bing** ɪŋ ~s z
skid skɪd **skidded** 'skɪd ɪd -əd **skidding**
   'skɪd ɪŋ **skids** skɪdz
   ˌskid 'row
Skiddaw 'skɪd ɔː ‖ -ɑː
skiddoo skɪ 'duː ~**ed** d ~**ing** ɪŋ ~s z
skidlid 'skɪd lɪd ~s z
Skidmore 'skɪd mɔː ‖ -mɔːr
skidoo skɪ 'duː ~**ed** d ~**ing** ɪŋ ~s z
skidpan 'skɪd pæn →'skɪb- ~s z
skidproof 'skɪd pru:f §-prʊf
skied *past of* **sky** skaɪd
skied *past of* **ski** ski:d
skier 'ski: ə ‖ ²r ~s z
skies skaɪz
skiff skɪf **skiffs** skɪfs
skiffle 'skɪf ²l
skijoring 'ski: ˌdʒɔ:r ɪŋ ˌ·'·· ‖ -ˌdʒʊr-
skilful 'skɪl f²l -fʊl ~**ly** _i ~**ness** nəs nɪs
skill skɪl **skilled** skɪld **skills** skɪlz
skillet 'skɪl ɪt -ət ~s s
skillful 'skɪl f²l -fʊl ~**ly** _i ~**ness** nəs nɪs
skilly 'skɪl i
skim skɪm **skimmed** skɪmd **skimming/s**
   'skɪm ɪŋ/z **skims** skɪmz
   ˌskimmed 'milk, ˌskim 'milk
skimmer 'skɪm ə ‖ ²r ~s z
skimmia 'skɪm i ə ~s z
skimp skɪmp **skimped** skɪmpt **skimping**
   'skɪmp ɪŋ **skimps** skɪmps
skimp|y 'skɪmp |i ~**ier** i ə ‖ i ²r ~**iest** i ɪst i əst
   ~**ily** ɪ li əl i ~**iness** i nəs i nɪs
skin skɪn **skinned** skɪnd **skinning** 'skɪn ɪŋ
   skins skɪnz
   'skin ˌdiver; 'skin ˌdiving; 'skin flick;
   'skin graft
skincare 'skɪn keə →'skɪŋ- ‖ -ker
skin-deep ˌskɪn 'di:p ◄
skin-|dive 'skɪn |daɪv ~**dived** daɪvd ~**dives**
   daɪvz ~**diving** daɪv ɪŋ ~**dove** dəʊv ‖ doʊv
skinflint 'skɪn flɪnt ~s s
skinful 'skɪn fʊl ~s z

skinhead 'skɪn hed ~s z
skink skɪŋk **skinks** skɪŋks
skinless 'skɪn ləs -lɪs
skinlike 'skɪn laɪk
skinn... —*see* **skin**
-skinned 'skɪnd — **thick-skinned**
   ˌθɪk 'skɪnd ◄
Skinner, s~ 'skɪn ə ‖ -²r ~**s**, ~'**s** z
Skinnerian skɪ 'nɪər i ən ‖ -'nɪr- -'ner- ~s z
skinn|y 'skɪn |i ~**ier** i ə ‖ i ²r ~**iest** i ɪst i əst
   ~**iness** i nəs i nɪs
skinny-dip 'skɪn i dɪp ~**ped** t ~**per/s** ə/z
   ‖ ²r/z ~**ping** ɪŋ ~s s
skint skɪnt
skin-tight ˌskɪn 'taɪt ◄
skip skɪp **skipped** skɪpt **skipping** 'skɪp ɪŋ
   skips skɪps
skipjack 'skɪp dʒæk ~s s
skipper 'skɪp ə ‖ -²r ~**ed** d **skippering**
   'skɪp ər ɪŋ ~s z
skipping-rope 'skɪp ɪŋ rəʊp ‖ -roʊp ~s s
Skippy 'skɪp i
Skipton 'skɪp tən
skirl skɜːl ‖ skɜ·l **skirled** skɜːld ‖ skɜ·ld
   skirling 'skɜːl ɪŋ ‖ 'skɜ·l ɪŋ **skirls** skɜːlz
   ‖ skɜ·lz
skirmish 'skɜːm ɪʃ ‖ 'skɜ·m- ~**ed** t ~**er/s** ə/z
   ‖ -²r/z ~**es** ɪz əz ~**ing** ɪŋ
skirret 'skɪr ɪt -ət
skirt skɜːt ‖ skɜ·t **skirted** 'skɜːt ɪd -əd
   ‖ 'skɜ·t̬ əd **skirting/s** 'skɜːt ɪŋ/z ‖ 'skɜ·t̬ ɪŋ/z
   skirts skɜːts ‖ skɜ·ts
   'skirting board
skis ski:z
skit skɪt **skits** skɪts
skite skaɪt **skited** 'skaɪt ɪd -əd ‖ 'skaɪt̬- **skites**
   skaɪts **skiting** 'skaɪt ɪŋ ‖ 'skaɪt̬-
skitter 'skɪt ə ‖ 'skɪt̬ ²r ~**ed** d **skittering**
   'skɪt ər ɪŋ ‖ 'skɪt̬ ər ɪŋ ~s z
skittish 'skɪt ɪʃ ‖ 'skɪt̬ ɪʃ ~**ly** li ~**ness** nəs nɪs
skittl|e 'skɪt ²l ‖ 'skɪt̬ ²l ~**ed** d ~**es** z ~**ing** ˌɪŋ
skive skaɪv **skived** skaɪvd **skives** skaɪvz
   skiving 'skaɪv ɪŋ
skiver 'skaɪv ə ‖ -²r ~s z
skivv|y 'skɪv |i ~**ied** id ~**ies** iz ~**ying** i ˌɪŋ
skiwear 'ski: weə ‖ -wer -wær
skoal skəʊl →skɒʊl ‖ skoʊl
Skoda, Škoda *tdmk* 'skəʊd ə 'ʃkəʊd-
   ‖ 'skoʊd ə —*Czech* ['ʃko da] ~s z
Skokholm 'skɒk həʊm 'skəʊk əm
   ‖ 'skɑːk hoʊm
Skokie 'skəʊk i ‖ 'skoʊk i
skol, Skol *tdmk* skɒl skəʊl ‖ skoʊl
Skomer 'skəʊm ə ‖ 'skoʊm ²r
Skopje 'skɒp ji -jeɪ ‖ 'skɑːp- 'skɔːp-, skoʊp-
   —*Macedonian* ['skɔp jɛ], *Serbian* Skoplje
   ['skɔp lʲɛ]
Skrine (*i*) skri:n, (*ii*) skraɪn
skua 'skjuː ə ~s z
Skues skju:z
skulduggery skʌl 'dʌg ər i
skulk skʌlk **skulked** skʌlkt **skulking** 'skʌlk ɪŋ
   skulks skʌlks

S

skull skʌl skulls skʌlz
skullcap 'skʌl kæp ~s s
skullduggery skʌl 'dʌg ər i
skunk skʌŋk skunks skʌŋks
  'skunk ˌcabbage
skunkworks 'skʌŋk wɜ:ks ‖ -wɜ:ks
sky skaɪ skied skaɪd skies skaɪz skying
  'skaɪ ɪŋ
sky-blue ˌskaɪ 'blu: ◄
skycap 'skaɪ kæp ~s s
skydiv|er/s 'skaɪ ˌdaɪv |ə/z ‖ -|ᵊr/z ~ing ɪŋ
Skye skaɪ
sky-high ˌskaɪ 'haɪ ◄
skyhook 'skaɪ hʊk ~s s
skyjack 'skaɪ dʒæk ~ed t ~er/s ə/z ‖ ᵊr/z ~ing
  ɪŋ ~s s
Skylab 'skaɪ læb
skylark 'skaɪ lɑ:k ‖ -lɑ:rk ~ed t ~ing ɪŋ ~s s
skylight 'skaɪ laɪt ~s s
skyline 'skaɪ laɪn
Skype skaɪp
skyrock|et 'skaɪ ˌrɒk |ɪt §-ət ‖ -ˌrɑ:k |ət ~eted
  ɪt ɪd §ət-, -əd ‖ ət əd ~eting ɪt ɪŋ §ət- ‖ ət ɪŋ
  ~ets ɪts §əts ‖ əts
skyscape 'skaɪ skeɪp ~s s
skyscraper 'skaɪ ˌskreɪp ə ‖ -ᵊr ~s z
Skywalker 'skaɪ ˌwɔ:k ə ‖ -ᵊr -ˌwɑ:k-
skyward 'skaɪ wəd ‖ -wᵊrd ~s z
skywriting 'skaɪ ˌraɪt ɪŋ ‖ -ˌraɪt ɪŋ
slab slæb slabbed slæbd slabbing 'slæb ɪŋ
  slabs slæbz
  'slab cake
Slabbert 'slæb ət ‖ -ᵊrt
slack, Slack slæk slacked slækt slacker
  'slæk ə ‖ -ᵊr slackest 'slæk ɪst -əst slacking
  'slæk ɪŋ slacks slæks
slacken 'slæk ən ~ed d ~ing ˌɪŋ ~s z
slacker 'slæk ə ‖ -ᵊr ~s z
slack-jawed ˌslæk 'dʒɔ:d ◄ ‖ -'dʒɑ:d ◄
slack|ly 'slæk |li ~ness nəs nɪs
Slade sleɪd
slag slæg slagged slægd slagging 'slæg ɪŋ
  slags slægz
slagg|y 'slæg| i ~ier i ə ‖ i ᵊr ~iest i ɪst i əst
slagheap 'slæg hi:p ~s s
slain sleɪn
slainte, slàinte 'slɑ:ntʃ ə 'slɑ:ndʒ ə, 'slɑ:n jə
  —ScG ['s̺ta: ɲə]
  ˌslàinte 'mhath vɑ: —ScG [va]
Slaithwaite 'slæθ weɪt —locally also 'slaʊ ɪt
slake sleɪk slaked sleɪkt slakes sleɪks slaking
  'sleɪk ɪŋ
slalom 'slɑ:l əm ~s z
slam slæm slammed slæmd slamming
  'slæm ɪŋ slams slæmz
slam-bang ˌslæm 'bæŋ
slammer 'slæm ə ‖ -ᵊr ~s z
slander 'slɑ:nd ə §'slænd- ‖ 'slænd ᵊr ~ed d
  slandering 'slɑ:nd ᵊr ɪŋ §'slænd̩
  ‖ 'slænd̩ ᵊr ɪŋ ~s z
slanderer 'slɑ:nd ᵊr ə §'slænd̩ ‖ 'slænd̩ ᵊr ᵊr
  ~s z

slanderous 'slɑ:nd ᵊr əs §'slænd̩
  ‖ 'slænd̩ ᵊr əs ~ly li ~ness nəs nɪs
slang slæŋ slanged slæŋd slanging 'slæŋ ɪŋ
  slangs slæŋz
  'slanging match
slang|y 'slæŋ |i ~ily ɪ li əl i ~iness i nəs i nɪs
slant slɑ:nt §slænt ‖ slænt slanted 'slɑ:nt ɪd
  §'slænt-, -əd ‖ 'slænt̩ əd slanting/ly
  'slɑ:nt ɪŋ /li §'slænt- ‖ 'slænt̩ ɪŋ /li slants
  slɑ:nts §slænts ‖ slænts
slant|ways 'slɑ:nt weɪz §'slænt- ‖ 'slænt-
  ~wise waɪz
slap slæp slapped slæpt slapping 'slæp ɪŋ
  slaps slæps
slap-bang ˌslæp 'bæŋ
slapdash 'slæp dæʃ ˌ·'·
slaphapp|y 'slæp ˌhæp |i ˌ·'·· ~ier i ə ‖ i ᵊr
  ~iest i ɪst i əst
slaphead 'slæp hed ~s z
slapjack 'slæp dʒæk ~s s
slapper 'slæp ə ‖ -ᵊr ~s z
slapstick 'slæp stɪk ~s s
slap-up 'slæp ʌp ˌ·'·
slash slæʃ slashed slæʃt slashes 'slæʃ ɪz -əz
  slashing 'slæʃ ɪŋ
  'slash mark
slash-and-burn ˌslæʃ ᵊn 'bɜ:n →-ᵊm- ‖ -'bɜ:n
slasher 'slæʃ ə ‖ -ᵊr ~s z
slat slæt slats slæts slatted 'slæt ɪd -əd
  ‖ 'slæt̩ əd slatting 'slæt ɪŋ ‖ 'slæt̩ ɪŋ
slate sleɪt slated 'sleɪt ɪd -əd ‖ 'sleɪt̩ əd slates
  sleɪts slating 'sleɪt ɪŋ ‖ 'sleɪt̩ ɪŋ
slater, S~ 'sleɪt ə ‖ 'sleɪt̩ ᵊr ~s z
slather 'slæð ə ‖ -ᵊr ~ed d slathering
  'slæð ᵊr ɪŋ ~s z
slattern 'slæt ᵊn -ɜ:n ‖ 'slæt̩ ᵊrn ~liness li nəs
  -nɪs ~ly li ~s z
Slattery 'slæt ər i ‖ 'slæt̩-
slaty 'sleɪt i ‖ 'sleɪt̩ i
slaughter, S~ 'slɔ:t ə ‖ 'slɔ:t̩ ᵊr 'slɑ:t̩- ~ed d
  slaughtering 'slɔ:t ᵊr ɪŋ ‖ 'slɔ:t̩ ᵊr ɪŋ 'slɑ:t̩-
  ~s z
slaughterer 'slɔ:t ᵊr ə ‖ 'slɔ:t̩ ᵊr ᵊr 'slɑ:t̩- ~s z
slaughter|house 'slɔ:t ə |haʊs ‖ 'slɔ:t̩ ᵊr-
  'slɑ:t̩- ~houses ˌhaʊz ɪz -əz
Slav slɑ:v ‖ slæv Slavs slɑ:vz ‖ slævz
slave sleɪv slaved sleɪvd slaves sleɪvz slaving
  'sleɪv ɪŋ
  'slave ˌdriver; ˌslave 'labour; 'slave
  ˌtrade; 'slave ˌtraffic
slaver v 'drool'; n 'saliva' 'slæv ə 'sleɪv-
  ‖ 'slæv ᵊr 'sleɪv-, 'slɑ:v- ~ed d slavering
  'slæv ᵊr ɪŋ 'sleɪv- ‖ 'sleɪv-, 'slɑ:v- ~s z
slaver n 'one dealing in slaves' 'sleɪv ə ‖ -ᵊr ~s
  z
slavery 'sleɪv ᵊr i
slavey 'sleɪv i ~s z
Slavic 'slɑ:v ɪk 'slæv-
slavish 'sleɪv ɪʃ ~ly li ~ness nəs nɪs
Slavo- |slɑ:v əʊ |slæv- ‖ -oʊ — Slavophile
  'slɑ:v əʊ faɪᵊl 'slæv-, -fɪl ‖ -oʊ-
Slavonia slə 'vəʊn i ə ‖ -'voʊn-
Slavonic slə 'vɒn ɪk slæ- ‖ -'vɑ:n ɪk

slaw slɔː ‖ slɑː

slay sleɪ **slain** sleɪn **slayed** sleɪd **slaying**
'sleɪ ɪŋ **slays** sleɪz **slew** sluː

slayer 'sleɪ ə ‖ -ʰr ~s z

Slazenger tdmk 'slæz ɪndʒ ə -əndʒ- ‖ -ʰr

Sleaford 'sliː fəd ‖ -fʰrd

sleaze sliːz

sleaze|bag/s 'sliːz| bæg/z **~ball/s** bɔːl/z
‖ bɑːl/z

sleaz|y 'sliːz |i ~ier i_ə ‖ i_ʰr ~iest i_ɪst i_əst
~ily ɪ li əl i ~iness i nəs i nɪs

sled sled **sledded** 'sled ɪd -əd **sledding**
'sled ɪŋ **sleds** sledz

sledge sledʒ **sledged** sledʒd **sledges**
'sledʒ ɪz -əz **sledging** 'sledʒ ɪŋ

sledgehammer 'sledʒ ˌhæm ə ‖ -ʰr ~s z

sleek sliːk **sleeked** sliːkt **sleeker** 'sliːk ə ‖ -ʰr
sleekest 'sliːk ɪst -əst **sleeking** 'sliːk ɪŋ
sleeks sliːks

sleek|ly 'sliːk |li ~ness nəs nɪs

sleep sliːp **sleeping** 'sliːp ɪŋ **sleeps** sliːps
slept slept
'sleeping bag; 'sleeping car; 'sleeping
draught; ˌsleeping 'partner 'inactive
business partner'; 'sleeping pill; ˌsleeping
po'liceman; 'sleeping ˌsickness

Sleepeezee tdmk ˌsliːp 'iːz i

sleeper 'sliːp ə ‖ -ʰr ~s z

sleepi... —see **sleepy**

sleepless 'sliːp ləs -lɪs ~ly li ~ness nəs nɪs

sleepover 'sliːp ˌəʊv ə ‖ -ˌoʊv ʰr ~s z

sleepwalk 'sliːp wɔːk ‖ -wɑːk **~ed** t **~er/s** ə/z
‖ ʰr/z **~ing** ɪŋ ~s s

sleepwear 'sliːp weə ‖ -wer -wær

sleep|y 'sliːp |i ~ier i_ə ‖ i_ʰr ~iest i_ɪst i_əst
~ily ɪ li əl i ~iness i nəs i nɪs

sleepyhead 'sliːp i hed ~s z

sleet sliːt **sleeted** 'sliːt ɪd -əd ‖ 'sliːt̬ əd
sleeting 'sliːt ɪŋ ‖ 'sliːt̬ ɪŋ **sleets** sliːts

sleety 'sliːt i ‖ 'sliːt̬ i

sleeve sliːv **sleeved** sliːvd **sleeves** sliːvz
sleeving 'sliːv ɪŋ

-sleeved 'sliːvd — **short-sleeved**
ˌʃɔːt 'sliːvd ◂ ‖ ˌʃɔːrt-

sleeveless 'sliːv ləs -lɪs

sleigh sleɪ (= slay) **sleighed** sleɪd **sleighing**
'sleɪ ɪŋ **sleighs** sleɪz

sleighbell 'sleɪ bel ~s z

sleight slaɪt (= slight)

slend|er 'slend |ə ‖ -|ʰr **~erer** ər ə ‖ ʰr ər
~erest ər ɪst -əst

slenderis|e, slenderiz|e 'slend ə raɪz ~ed d
~es ɪz əz ~ing ɪŋ

slender|ly 'slend ə |li ‖ -ʰr- ~ness nəs nɪs

slept slept

Slessor 'sles ə ‖ -ʰr

sleuth sluːθ sljuːθ **sleuthed** sluːθt sljuːθt
sleuthing 'sluːθ ɪŋ 'sljuːθ- **sleuths** sluːθs
sljuːθs

sleuthhound 'sluːθ haʊnd 'sljuːθ- ~s z

slew sluː sljuː **slewed** sluːd sljuːd **slewing**
'sluː ɪŋ 'sljuː- **slews** sluːz sljuːz

slice slaɪs **sliced** slaɪst **slices** 'slaɪs ɪz -əz
slicing 'slaɪs ɪŋ
ˌsliced 'bread

slice-of-life ˌslaɪs əv 'laɪf

slicer 'slaɪs ə ‖ -ʰr ~s z

slick slɪk **slicked** slɪkt **slicker** 'slɪk ə ‖ 'slɪk ʰr
slickest 'slɪk ɪst -əst **slicking** 'slɪk ɪŋ **slicks**
slɪks

slickenside 'slɪk ən saɪd →-ŋ- ~s z

slicker 'slɪk ə ‖ -ʰr ~s z

slick|ly 'slɪk |li ~ness nəs nɪs

slide slaɪd **slid** slɪd **slides** slaɪdz **sliding**
'slaɪd ɪŋ
'slide rule; 'slide valve; ˌsliding 'door;
ˌsliding 'scale

slider 'slaɪd ə ‖ -ʰr ~s z

Slieve sliːv

slight slaɪt **slighted** 'slaɪt ɪd -əd ‖ 'slaɪt̬ əd
slighter 'slaɪt ə ‖ 'slaɪt̬ ʰr **slightest** 'slaɪt ɪst
-əst ‖ 'slaɪt̬ əst **slighting/ly** 'slaɪt ɪŋ /li
‖ 'slaɪt̬ ɪŋ /li **slights** slaɪts

slightly 'slaɪt li

Sligo 'slaɪg əʊ ‖ -oʊ

slily 'slaɪ li

slim, Slim slɪm **slimmed** slɪmd **slimmer**
'slɪm ə ‖ -ʰr **slimmest** 'slɪm ɪst -əst
slimming 'slɪm ɪŋ **slims** slɪmz

Slimbridge 'slɪm brɪdʒ

Slimcea tdmk 'slɪm si_ə

slime slaɪm **slimed** slaɪmd **slimes** slaɪmz
sliming 'slaɪm ɪŋ

slimeball 'slaɪm bɔːl ‖ -bɑːl ~s z

slimi... —see **slimy**

slimline 'slɪm laɪn

slim|ly 'slɪm |li ~ness nəs nɪs

slimm... —see **slim**

slimmed-down ˌslɪmd 'daʊn ◂

slimmer 'slɪm ə ‖ -ʰr ~s z

slim|y 'slaɪm |i ~ier i_ə ‖ i_ʰr ~iest i_ɪst i_əst
~ily ɪ li əl i ~iness i nəs i nɪs

sling slɪŋ **slinging** 'slɪŋ ɪŋ **slings** slɪŋz **slung**
slʌŋ

slingback 'slɪŋ bæk ~s s

slinger 'slɪŋ ə ‖ -ʰr ~s z

slingshot 'slɪŋ ʃɒt ‖ -ʃɑːt ~s s

slink slɪŋk **slinking** 'slɪŋk ɪŋ **slinks** slɪŋks
slunk slʌŋk

slink|y 'slɪŋk |i ~ier i_ə ‖ i_ʰr ~iest i_ɪst i_əst
~ily ɪ li əl i ~iness i nəs i nɪs

slip slɪp **slipped** slɪpt **slipping** 'slɪp ɪŋ **slips**
slɪps
ˌslipped 'disc; 'slip road

slipcas|e 'slɪp keɪs ~es ɪz əz

slipcover 'slɪp ˌkʌv ə ‖ -ʰr ~s z

slipknot 'slɪp nɒt ‖ -nɑːt ~s s

slip-on 'slɪp ɒn ‖ -ɑːn -ɔːn ~s z

slipover 'slɪp ˌəʊv ə ‖ -ˌoʊv ʰr ~s z

slipp... —see **slip**

slippag|e 'slɪp ɪdʒ ~es ɪz əz

slipper 'slɪp ə ‖ -ʰr ~s z

slipper|y 'slɪp ər_|i ~ier i_ə ‖ i_ʰr ~iest i_ɪst
i_əst ~ily əl i ɪ li ~iness i nəs i nɪs

S

slipp|y 'slɪp |i ~**ier** i ə || i ʲr ~**iest** i ɪst i əst
~**iness** i nəs i nɪs
slipshod 'slɪp ʃɒd || -ʃɑːd
slipstitch 'slɪp stɪtʃ ~**ed** t ~**es** ɪz əz ~**ing** ɪŋ
slipstream 'slɪp striːm ~**s** z
slip-up 'slɪp ʌp ~**s** s
slipway 'slɪp weɪ ~**s** z
slit slɪt **slits** slɪts **slitting** 'slɪt ɪŋ || 'slɪt̬ ɪŋ
slither 'slɪð ə || -ʲr ~**ed** d **slithering** 'slɪð ər ɪŋ
~**s** z
slithery 'slɪð ər i
sliver 'slɪv ə || -ʲr —*but in some rare technical
senses* 'slaɪv- ~**ed** d **slivering** 'slɪv ər ɪŋ ~**s** z
slivovitz 'slɪv ə vɪts 'sliːv-
Sliwa 'sliː wə
Sloan, Sloane sləʊn || sloʊn **Sloanes, Sloan's**
sləʊnz || sloʊnz
ˌSloane 'Ranger; ˌSloane 'Square
slob slɒb || slɑːb **slobs** slɒbz || slɑːbz
slobber 'slɒb ə || 'slɑːb ʲr ~**ed** d **slobbering**
'slɒb ər ɪŋ || 'slɑːb- ~**s** z
slobberer 'slɒb ər ə || 'slɑːb ʲr ər ~**s** z
slobber|y 'slɒb ər |i || 'slɑːb- ~**iness** i nəs i nɪs
slobbish 'slɒb ɪʃ || 'slɑːb-
Slocombe, Slocum 'sləʊk əm || 'sloʊk-
sloe sləʊ || sloʊ (= *slow*) **sloes** sləʊz || sloʊz
sloe-eyed ˌsləʊ 'aɪd ◄ ·· || ˌsloʊ-
slog slɒg || slɑːg **slogged** slɒgd || slɑːgd
slogging 'slɒg ɪŋ || 'slɑːg ɪŋ **slogs** slɒgz
|| slɑːgz
slogan 'sləʊg ən || 'sloʊg ən ~**s** z
sloganeer ˌsləʊg ə 'nɪə || ˌsloʊg ə 'nɪʲr ~**ed** d
sloganeering ˌsləʊg ə 'nɪər ɪŋ
|| ˌsloʊg ə 'nɪr ɪŋ ~**s** z
slogger 'slɒg ə || 'slɑːg ʲr ~**s** z
Sloman 'sləʊ mən || 'sloʊ-
slo-mo ˌsləʊ 'məʊ || ˌsloʊ 'moʊ
sloop sluːp **sloops** sluːps
slop slɒp || slɑːp **slopped** slɒpt || slɑːpt
slopping 'slɒp ɪŋ || 'slɑːp ɪŋ **slops** slɒps
|| slɑːps
slope sləʊp || sloʊp **sloped** sləʊpt || sloʊpt
slopes sləʊps || sloʊps **sloping/ly**
'sləʊp ɪŋ /li || 'sloʊp ɪŋ /li
slopp|y 'slɒp |i || 'slɑːp |i ~**ier** i ə || i ʲr ~**iest**
i ɪst i əst ~**ily** ɪ li əl i ~**iness** i nəs i nɪs
slosh slɒʃ || slɑːʃ **sloshed** slɒʃt || slɑːʃt **sloshes**
'slɒʃ ɪz -əz || 'slɑːʃ əz **sloshing** 'slɒʃ ɪŋ
|| 'slɑːʃ ɪŋ
slosh|y 'slɒʃ |i || 'slɑːʃ |i ~**ier** i ə || i ʲr ~**iest**
i ɪst i əst ~**ily** ɪ li əl i ~**iness** i nəs i nɪs
slot slɒt || slɑːt **slots** slɒts || slɑːts **slotted**
'slɒt ɪd -əd || 'slɑːt̬ əd **slotting** 'slɒt ɪŋ
|| 'slɑːt̬ ɪŋ
ˌslot maˌchine
sloth sləʊθ §slɒθ || slɔːθ slɑːθ, sloʊθ **sloths**
sləʊθs §slɒθs || slɔːθs slɑːθs, sloʊθs
slothful 'sləʊθ fʰl 'slɒθ-, -fʊl || 'slɔːθ- 'slɑːθ-,
'sloʊθ- ~**ly** ˌi ~**ness** nəs nɪs
slouch slaʊtʃ **slouched** slaʊtʃt **slouches**
'slaʊtʃ ɪz -əz **slouching/ly** 'slaʊtʃ ɪŋ /li
ˌslouch 'hat

slouch|y 'slaʊtʃ |i ~**ily** ɪ li əl i ~**iness** i nəs
i nɪs
slough v; n *'cast-off skin'* slʌf **sloughed** slʌft
sloughing 'slʌf ɪŋ **sloughs** slʌfs
slough n *'mud, marsh, swamp'* sləʊ || sluː slaʊ
(*) —*Some Americans make a distinction
between* sluː *in the literal sense and* slaʊ *in the
figurative (*slough of de'spond). **sloughs**
sləʊz || sluːz slaʊz
Slough *place in Berks (formerly Bucks)* slaʊ
Slovak 'sləʊv æk -ɑːk || 'sloʊv- ~**s** s
Slovakia sləʊ 'væk i ə -'vɑːk- || sloʊ-
sloven 'slʌv ʰn ~**s** z
Slovene 'sləʊv iːn sləʊ 'viːn || 'sloʊv- ~**s** z
Sloveni|a sləʊ 'viːn i |ə || sloʊ- ~**an/s** ən/z
sloven|ly 'slʌv ʰn |li ~**liness** li nəs -nɪs
Slovo 'sləʊv əʊ || 'sloʊv oʊ
slow sləʊ || sloʊ **slowed** sləʊd || sloʊd **slower**
'sləʊ ə || 'sloʊ ʲr **slowest** 'sləʊ ɪst -əst
|| 'sloʊ əst **slowing** 'sləʊ ɪŋ || 'sloʊ ɪŋ **slows**
sləʊz || sloʊz
ˌslow 'motion
slowcoach 'sləʊ kəʊtʃ || 'sloʊ koʊtʃ ~**es** ɪz əz
slowdown 'sləʊ daʊn || 'sloʊ- ~**s** z
slowly 'sləʊ li || 'sloʊ li
slow-motion ˌsləʊ 'məʊʃ ʰn ◄
|| ˌsloʊ 'moʊʃ ʰn ◄
slow-moving ˌsləʊ 'muːv ɪŋ ◄ || ˌsloʊ-
slowness 'sləʊ nəs -nɪs || 'sloʊ nəs
slowpitch 'sləʊ pɪtʃ || 'sloʊ-
slowpoke 'sləʊ pəʊk || 'sloʊ poʊk ~**s** s
slow-witted ˌsləʊ 'wɪt ɪd ◄ -əd-
|| ˌsloʊ 'wɪt̬ əd ◄
slowworm 'sləʊ wɜːm || 'sloʊ wɜːm ~**s** z
slub slʌb **slubbed** slʌbd **slubbing** 'slʌb ɪŋ
slubs slʌbz
sludge slʌdʒ
sludgy 'slʌdʒ i
slue sluː **slued** sluːd **slues** sluːz **sluing** 'sluː ɪŋ
slug slʌg **slugged** slʌgd **slugging** 'slʌg ɪŋ
slugs slʌgz
slugfest 'slʌg fest ~**s** s
sluggard 'slʌg əd || -ʲrd ~**ly** li ~**s** z
slugger 'slʌg ə || -ʲr ~**s** z
sluggish 'slʌg ɪʃ ~**ly** li ~**ness** nəs nɪs
sluice sluːs **sluiced** sluːst **sluices** 'sluːs ɪz -əz
sluicing 'sluːs ɪŋ
sluicegate 'sluːs geɪt ~**s** s
sluiceway 'sluːs weɪ ~**s** z
slum slʌm **slummed** slʌmd **slumming**
'slʌm ɪŋ **slums** slʌmz
ˌslum 'clearance; ˌslum 'dweller
slumber 'slʌm bə || -bʲr ~**ed** d **slumbering**
'slʌm bər ɪŋ ~**s** z
slumberer 'slʌm bər ə || -bʲr ər ~**s** z
slumberland, S~ *tdmk* 'slʌm bə lænd || -bʲr-
slumberous 'slʌm bər əs ~**ly** li ~**ness** nəs nɪs
slumberwear 'slʌm bə weə || -bʲr wer
slumbrous 'slʌm brəs ~**ly** li ~**ness** nəs nɪs
slumlord 'slʌm lɔːd || -lɔːrd ~**s** z
slumm|y 'slʌm |i ~**ier** i ə || i ʲr ~**iest** i ɪst i əst
~**iness** i nəs i nɪs

S

slump slʌmp **slumped** slʌmpt **slumping**
'slʌmp ɪŋ **slumps** slʌmps
slung slʌŋ
slunk slʌŋk
slur slɜː ‖ slɜ: **slurred** slɜːd ‖ slɜ:d **slurring**
'slɜːr ɪŋ ‖ 'slɜ: ɪŋ **slurs** slɜːz ‖ slɜ:z
slurp slɜːp ‖ slɜ:p **slurped** slɜːpt ‖ slɜ:pt
slurping 'slɜːp ɪŋ ‖ 'slɜ:p ɪŋ **slurps** slɜːps
‖ slɜ:ps
slurr... —*see* **slur**
slurr|y 'slʌr |i ‖ 'slɜ: |i **~ies** iz
slush slʌʃ **slushed** slʌʃt **slushes** 'slʌʃ ɪz -əz
slushing 'slʌʃ ɪŋ
'**slush fund**
slush|y 'slʌʃ |i **~ier** i ə ‖ i ʲr **~iest** i ɪst i əst
~ily ɪ li əl i **~iness** i nəs i nɪs
slut slʌt **sluts** slʌts
sluttish 'slʌt ɪʃ ‖ 'slʌt̬ ɪʃ **~ly** li **~ness** nəs nɪs
slutty 'slʌt i ‖ 'slʌt̬ i
sly, Sly slaɪ **slier, slyer** 'slaɪ ə ‖ 'slaɪ ʲr **sliest,**
slyest 'slaɪ ɪst -əst
sly|ly 'slaɪ |li **~ness** nəs nɪs
slype slaɪp **slypes** slaɪps
smack smæk **smacked** smækt **smacking/s**
'smæk ɪŋ/z **smacks** smæks
smack-dab ˌsmæk 'dæb
smacker 'smæk ə ‖ -ʲr **~s** z
smackeroo ˌsmæk ə 'ruː **~s** z
Smail, Smale smeɪʲl
Smails, Smales smeɪʲlz
small smɔːl ‖ smɑːl **smaller** 'smɔːl ə ‖ -ʲr
'smɑːl- **smallest** 'smɔːl ɪst -əst ‖ 'smɑːl-
smalls smɔːlz ‖ smɑːlz
'**small ad**; '**small arms** ˌ· '·; ˌ**small 'beer**;
ˌ**small 'capital**; ˌ**small 'change**; ˌ**small**
'**fortune**; '**small fry**; '**small hours**; ˌ**small**
in'testine; ˌ**small 'print**, '· ·; ˌ**small**
'**screen**, '· ·; '**small talk**
small-boned ˌsmɔːl 'bəʊnd ◄ ‖ -'boʊnd ◄
ˌsmɑːl-
small-calibre, small-caliber
ˌsmɔːl 'kæl ɪb ə ə ◄ ‖ -ʲr ◄ ˌsmɑːl-
Smalley 'smɔːl i ‖ 'smɑːl-
smallholder 'smɔːl ˌhəʊld ə →-ˌhɒʊld-
‖ -ˌhoʊld ʲr 'smɑːl- **~s** z
smallholding 'smɔːl ˌhəʊld ɪŋ →-ˌhɒʊld-
‖ -ˌhoʊld ɪŋ 'smɑːl- **~s** z
smallish 'smɔːl ɪʃ ‖ 'smɑːl-
small-minded ˌsmɔːl 'maɪnd ɪd ◄ -əd ‖ ˌsmɑːl-
~ly li **~ness** nəs nɪs
smallness 'smɔːl nəs -nɪs ‖ 'smɑːl-
Smallpiece 'smɔːl piːs ‖ 'smɑːl-
smallpox 'smɔːl pɒks ‖ -pɑːks 'smɑːl-
small-scale ˌsmɔːl 'skeɪʲl ◄ ‖ ˌsmɑːl-
small-tim|e ˌsmɔːl 'taɪm ◄ ‖ ˌsmɑːl- **~er/s** ə/z
‖ ʲr/z
ˌ**small-time 'gangsters**
small-town ˌsmɔːl 'taʊn ◄ ‖ ˌsmɑːl-
Smallwood 'smɔːl wʊd ‖ 'smɑːl-
smalt smɔːlt smɒlt ‖ smɑːlt
smaltite 'smɔːlt aɪt 'smɒlt- ‖ 'smɑːlt-
Smarden 'smɑːd ʲn -en ‖ 'smɑːrd ʲn

smarm smɑːm ‖ smɑːrm **smarmed** smɑːmd
‖ smɑːrmd **smarming** 'smɑːm ɪŋ
‖ 'smɑːrm ɪŋ **smarms** smɑːmz ‖ smɑːrmz
smarm|y 'smɑːm |i ‖ 'smɑːrm |i **~ier** i ə ‖ i ʲr
~iest i ɪst i əst
smart, Smart smɑːt ‖ smɑːrt **smarted**
'smɑːt ɪd -əd ‖ 'smɑːrt̬ əd **smarter** 'smɑːt ə
‖ 'smɑːrt̬ ʲr **smartest** 'smɑːt ɪst -əst
‖ 'smɑːrt̬ əst **smarting** 'smɑːt ɪŋ ‖ 'smɑːrt̬ ɪŋ
smarts smɑːts ‖ smɑːrts —*see also phrases*
with this word
'**smart card**
smart aleck 'smɑːt ˌæl ɪk -ek, ˌ·'· · ‖ 'smɑːrt̬-
-ˌel- **~s** s
smart-alecky 'smɑːt ˌæl ɪk i ◄ -ek i, -ək i, ˌ·'· · ·
‖ 'smɑːrt̬- -ˌel-
smart-arse, smart-ass 'smɑːt ɑːs -æs
‖ 'smɑːrt̬ æs
smarten 'smɑːt ʲn ‖ 'smɑːrt ʲn **~ed** d **~ing** ɪŋ
~s z
Smartie *tdmk* 'smɑːt i ‖ 'smɑːrt̬ i **~s** z
smartish 'smɑːt ɪʃ ‖ 'smɑːrt̬ ɪʃ
smart|ly 'smɑːt |li ‖ 'smɑːrt̬ |li **~ness** nəs nɪs
smart-mouthed ˌsmɑːt 'maʊðd ◄ -'maʊθt ◄
‖ ˌsmɑːrt̬-
smartphone 'smɑːt fəʊn ‖ 'smɑːrt foʊn **~s** z
smart|y 'smɑːt |i ‖ 'smɑːrt̬ |i **~ies** iz
smarty-pants 'smɑːt i pænts ‖ 'smɑːrt̬-
smash smæʃ **smashed** smæʃt **smashes**
'smæʃ ɪz -əz **smashing** 'smæʃ ɪŋ
smash-and-grab ˌsmæʃ ʲnd 'græb →-ʲ-ŋ-
ˌsmash-and-'grab raid
smasher 'smæʃ ə ‖ -ʲr **~s** z
smash-up 'smæʃ ʌp **~s** s
smatana 'smæt ən ə ‖ -ʲn ə
smattering 'smæt ʲr ɪŋ ‖ 'smæt̬ ʲr ɪŋ **~s** z
smear smɪə ‖ smɪʲr **smeared** smɪəd ‖ smɪʲrd
smearing 'smɪər ɪŋ ‖ 'smɪr ɪŋ **smears** smɪəz
‖ smɪʲrz
'**smear test**
smeary 'smɪər i ‖ 'smɪr i
Smeaton 'smiːt ʲn
smectic 'smekt ɪk **~s** s
Smedley 'smed li
Smee smiː
smegma 'smeg mə
smell smel **smelled** smeld **smelling** 'smel ɪŋ
smells smelz **smelt** smelt
'**smelling salts**
Smellie 'smel i
smell|y 'smel |i **~ier** i ə ‖ i ʲr **~iest** i ɪst i əst
~iness i nəs i nɪs
smelt smelt **smelted** 'smelt ɪd -əd **smelting**
'smelt ɪŋ **smelts** smelts
smelter 'smelt ə ‖ -ʲr **~s** z
Smetana 'smet ən ə ‖ -ʲn ə —*Czech*
['sme ta na]
Smethurst 'smeθ ɜːst -hɜːst ‖ -hɜːst
Smethwick 'smeð ɪk
smew smjuː **smews** smjuːz
smidgen, smidgin 'smɪdʒ ən -ɪn **~s** z
Smike smaɪk
smilax 'smaɪl æks

smile smaɪəl **smiled** smaɪəld **smiles** smaɪəlz
  smiling/ly 'smaɪl ɪŋ /li
Smiles smaɪəlz
smiley 'smaɪl i ~s z
Smiley, Smily 'smaɪl i
Smillie 'smaɪl i
smirch smɜːtʃ ‖ smɜːtʃ **smirched** smɜːtʃt
  ‖ smɜːtʃt **smirches** 'smɜːtʃ ɪz -əz ‖ 'smɜːtʃ əz
  smirching 'smɜːtʃ ɪŋ ‖ 'smɜːtʃ ɪŋ
smirk smɜːk ‖ smɜːk **smirked** smɜːkt ‖ smɜːkt
  smirking/ly 'smɜːk ɪŋ /li ‖ 'smɜːk- **smirks**
  smɜːks ‖ smɜːks
Smirke smɜːk ‖ smɜːk
Smirnoff tdmk 'smɜːn ɒf ‖ 'smɜːn ɔːf 'smɪr-,
  -nɑːf —Russ [smʲɪr 'nɔf]
smite smaɪt **smit** smɪt **smites** smaɪts **smiting**
  'smaɪt ɪŋ ‖ 'smaɪt̬ ɪŋ **smitten** 'smɪt ən **smote**
  sməʊt ‖ smoʊt
smith, Smith smɪθ **smiths, Smith's** smɪθs
smithereens ˌsmɪð ə 'riːnz
Smithers 'smɪð əz ‖ -əʳz
Smithfield 'smɪθ fiːəld
Smithson 'smɪθ sən
Smithsonian smɪθ 'səʊn i ən ‖ -'soʊn-
smithsonite 'smɪθ sə naɪt
smith|y 'smɪð |i 'smɪθ- ~**ies** iz
smitten 'smɪt ən
smock smɒk ‖ smɑːk **smocked** smɒkt
  ‖ smɑːkt **smocking** 'smɒk ɪŋ ‖ 'smɑːk ɪŋ
  smocks smɒks ‖ smɑːks
smog smɒg ‖ smɑːg smɔːg **smogs** smɒgz
  ‖ smɑːgz smɔːgz
smogg|y 'smɒg |i ‖ 'smɑːg |i 'smɔːg- ~**ier** i ə
  ‖ i ʳr ~**iest** i ɪst i əst
smoke sməʊk ‖ smoʊk **smoked** sməʊkt
  ‖ smoʊkt **smokes** sməʊks ‖ smoʊks
  smoking 'sməʊk ɪŋ ‖ 'smoʊk ɪŋ
  'smoking ˌjacket; 'smoking comˌpartment
smoke-filled 'sməʊk fɪld ‖ 'smoʊk-
smoke-free ˌsməʊk 'friː ◂ ‖ ˌsmoʊk-
smokeless 'sməʊk ləs -lɪs ‖ 'smoʊk-
smoker, S~ 'sməʊk ə ‖ 'smoʊk ʳr ~s z
smokescreen 'sməʊk skriːn ‖ 'smoʊk- ~s z
smokestack 'sməʊk stæk ‖ 'smoʊk- ~s s
  'smokestack ˌindustry
Smokey 'sməʊk i ‖ 'smoʊk i
smoko 'sməʊk əʊ ‖ 'smoʊk oʊ ~s z
smok|y 'sməʊk |i ‖ 'smoʊk |i ~**ier** i ə ‖ i ʳr
  ~**iest** i ɪst i əst ~**ily** ɪ li əl i ~**iness** i nəs i nɪs
smold|er 'sməʊld |ə →'smɒʊld- ‖ 'smoʊld |ʳr
  ~**ered** əd ‖ ʳrd ~**ering** ˌər ɪŋ ~**ers** əz ‖ ʳrz
Smolensk smɒ 'len¹sk smə- ‖ smoʊ- —Russ
  [smʌ 'lʲensk]
Smollett 'smɒl ɪt §-ət ‖ 'smɑːl-
smolt sməʊlt →smɒʊlt ‖ smoʊlt **smolts**
  sməʊlts →smɒʊlts ‖ smoʊlts
smooch smuːtʃ **smooched** smuːtʃt **smooches**
  'smuːtʃ ɪz -əz **smooching** 'smuːtʃ ɪŋ
smoochy 'smuːtʃ i
smooth smuːð **smoothed** smuːðd **smoother**
  'smuːð ə ‖ -ʳr **smoothes** smuːðz **smoothest**
  'smuːð ɪst -əst **smoothing** 'smuːð ɪŋ
smoothbore 'smuːð bɔː ‖ -bɔːr -boʊr ~s z

smoothe smuːð **smoothed** smuːðd **smoothes**
  smuːðz **smoothing** 'smuːð ɪŋ
smoothie 'smuːð i ~s z
smooth|ly 'smuːð |li ~**ness** nəs nɪs
smooth-talking ˌsmuːð 'tɔːk ɪŋ ◂ ‖ -'tɑːk-
smooth|y 'smuːð |i ~**ies** iz
smorgasbord 'smɔːg əs bɔːd 'smɜːg-, -əz-
  ‖ 'smɔːrg əs bɔːrd -boʊrd —Swedish
  smörgåsbord ['smœr ɡɔs buʈ]
smote sməʊt ‖ smoʊt
smother 'smʌð ə ‖ -ʳr ~**ed** d **smothering**
  'smʌð ər ɪŋ ~**s** z
smould|er 'sməʊld |ə →'smɒʊld- ‖ 'smoʊld |ʳr
  ~**ered** əd ‖ ʳrd ~**ering** ˌər ɪŋ ~**ers** əz ‖ ʳrz
smudge smʌdʒ **smudged** smʌdʒd **smudges**
  'smʌdʒ ɪz -əz **smudging** 'smʌdʒ ɪŋ
smudgepot 'smʌdʒ pɒt ‖ -pɑːt ~s s
smudg|y 'smʌdʒ |i ~**ily** ɪ li əl i ~**iness** i nəs
  i nɪs
smug smʌg **smugger** 'smʌg ə ‖ -ʳr **smuggest**
  'smʌg ɪst -əst
smuggl|e 'smʌg ʳl ~**ed** d ~**er/s** ˌə/z ‖ ʳr/z ~**es**
  z ~**ing** ɪŋ
smug|ly 'smʌg |li ~**ness** nəs nɪs
smurf smɜːf ‖ smɜːf **smurfs** smɜːfs ‖ smɜːfs
smut smʌt **smuts, Smuts** smʌts
smutt|y 'smʌt |i ‖ 'smʌt̬ |i ~**ier** i ə ‖ i ʳr ~**iest**
  i ɪst i əst ~**ily** ɪ li əl i ~**iness** i nəs i nɪs
Smyrna 'smɜːn ə ‖ 'smɜːn ə —Turkish İzmir
  ['iz mir]
Smyth (i) smɪθ, (ii) smaɪθ, (iii) smaɪð
Smythe (i) smaɪð, (ii) smaɪθ
snack snæk **snacked** snækt **snacking**
  'snæk ɪŋ **snacks** snæks
  'snack bar
Snaefell ˌsneɪ 'fel
snaffl|e 'snæf ʳl ~**ed** d ~**es** z ~**ing** ɪŋ
  'snaffle bit
snafu snæ 'fuː ~**ed** d ~**ing** ɪŋ ~**s** z
snag snæg **snagged** snægd **snagging**
  'snæg ɪŋ **snags** snægz
Snagge snæg
snaggletooth 'snæg ʳl tuːθ §-tʊθ ~**ed** t
snail sneɪəl **snails** sneɪəlz
  'snail's pace
Snaith sneɪθ
snake, Snake sneɪk **snaked** sneɪkt **snakes**
  sneɪks **snaking** 'sneɪk ɪŋ
  'snake ˌcharmer; ˌsnakes and 'ladders
snakebite 'sneɪk baɪt ~s s
snakeroot 'sneɪk ruːt ‖ -rʊt ~**s** s
snakeskin 'sneɪk skɪn ~s z
snak|y 'sneɪk |i ~**ier** i ə ‖ i ʳr ~**iest** i ɪst i əst
  ~**ily** ɪ li əl i ~**iness** i nəs i nɪs
snap snæp **snapped** snæpt **snapping** 'snæp ɪŋ
  snaps snæps
  'snap ˌfastener
snapdragon 'snæp ˌdræg ən ~s z
Snape sneɪp
snap-on 'snæp ɒn ‖ -ɑːn -ɔːn
snapper 'snæp ə ‖ -ʳr ~s z
snappish 'snæp ɪʃ ~**ly** li ~**ness** nəs nɪs
Snapple tdmk 'snæp ʳl

S

snapp|y 'snæp |i **~ier** i ə ‖ i ə‿r **~iest** i ɪst i əst
   ~ily ɪ li əl i **~iness** i nəs i nɪs
snapshot 'snæp ʃɒt ‖ -ʃɑːt **~s** s
snare sneə ‖ sne ə‿r **snared** sneəd ‖ sne ə‿rd
   snares sneəz ‖ sne ə‿rz **snaring** 'sneər ɪŋ
   ‖ 'sner ɪŋ
   'snare drum
snarf snɑːf ‖ snɑːrf **snarfed** snɑːft ‖ snɑːrft
   snarfing 'snɑːf ɪŋ ‖ 'snɑːrf ɪŋ **snarfs** snɑːfs
   ‖ snɑːrfs
snark snɑːk ‖ snɑːrk **snarks** snɑːks ‖ snɑːrks
snarky 'snɑːk i ‖ 'snɑːrk i
snarl snɑːl ‖ snɑːrl **snarled** snɑːld ‖ snɑːrld
   snarling/ly 'snɑːl ɪŋ /li ‖ 'snɑːrl ɪŋ /li
   snarls snɑːlz ‖ snɑːrlz
snarl-up 'snɑːl ʌp ‖ 'snɑːrl- **~s** z
snatch snætʃ **snatched** snætʃt **snatches**
   'snætʃ ɪz -əz **snatching** 'snætʃ ɪŋ
snatcher 'snætʃ ə ‖ -ə‿r **~s** z
snazz|y 'snæz |i **~ier** i ə ‖ i ə‿r **~iest** i ɪst i əst
   ~ily ɪ li əl i **~iness** i nəs i nɪs
Snead sniːd
sneak sniːk **sneaked** sniːkt **sneaking** 'sniːk ɪŋ
   sneaks sniːks **snuck** snʌk
   ˌsneak 'preview; 'sneak thief
sneaker 'sniːk ə ‖ -ə‿r **~s** z
sneaking 'sniːk ɪŋ **~ly** li **~ness** nəs nɪs
sneak|y 'sniːk |i **~ier** i ə ‖ i ə‿r **~iest** i ɪst i əst
   ~ily ɪ li əl i **~iness** i nəs i nɪs
sneer snɪə ‖ snɪ ə‿r **sneered** snɪəd ‖ snɪ ə‿rd
   sneering/ly 'snɪər ɪŋ /li ‖ 'snɪr ɪŋ /li **sneers**
   snɪəz ‖ snɪ ə‿rz
sneeze sniːz **sneezed** sniːzd **sneezes** 'sniːz ɪz
   -əz **sneezing** 'sniːz ɪŋ
sneezeweed 'sniːz wiːd **~s** z
sneezewort 'sniːz wɜːt -wɔːt ‖ -wɜ˞ːt -wɔːrt **~s**
   s
Sneezum 'sniːz əm
Sneinton 'snent ən ‖ -ᵊn
Snelgrove, Snellgrove 'snel grəʊv ‖ -groʊv
snell, Snell snel
Snetterton 'snet ət ən ‖ 'snet̬ ᵊrt ᵊn
Sneyd sniːd
snib snɪb **snibbed** snɪbd **snibbing** 'snɪb ɪŋ
   snibs snɪbz
snick snɪk **snicked** snɪkt **snicking** 'snɪk ɪŋ
   snicks snɪks
snicker 'snɪk ə ‖ -ə‿r **~ed** d **snickering/ly**
   'snɪk ər ɪŋ /li **~s** z
Snickers tdmk 'snɪk əz ‖ -ə‿rz
snickersnee ˌsnɪk ə 'sniː '··· ‖ -ə‿r- **~s** z
snicket 'snɪk ɪt §-ət **~s** s
snide snaɪd **snider** 'snaɪd ə ‖ -ə‿r **snidest**
   'snaɪd ɪst -əst
snide|ly 'snaɪd |li **~ness** nəs nɪs
sniff snɪf **sniffed** snɪft **sniffing** 'snɪf ɪŋ **sniffs**
   snɪfs
sniffer 'snɪf ə ‖ -ə‿r **~s** z
   'sniffer dog
sniffl|e 'snɪf ᵊl **~ed** d **~es** z **~ing** ɪŋ
sniffl|y 'snɪf |i **~ier** i ə ‖ i ə‿r **~iest** i ɪst i əst
   ~ily ɪ li əl i **~iness** i nəs i nɪs
snifter 'snɪft ə ‖ -ə‿r **~s** z

snigger 'snɪg ə ‖ -ə‿r **~ed** d **sniggering/ly**
   'snɪg ər ɪŋ /li **~s** z
snip snɪp **snipped** snɪpt **snipping** 'snɪp ɪŋ
   snips snɪps
snipe snaɪp **sniped** snaɪpt **snipes** snaɪps
   sniping 'snaɪp ɪŋ
sniper 'snaɪp ə ‖ -ə‿r **~s** z
snipper 'snɪp ə ‖ -ə‿r **~s** z
snippet 'snɪp ɪt §-ət **~s** s
snippy 'snɪp i
snit snɪt **snits** snɪts
snitch snɪtʃ **snitched** snɪtʃt **snitches** 'snɪtʃ ɪz
   -əz **snitching** 'snɪtʃ ɪŋ
snivel 'snɪv ᵊl **~ed, ~led** d **~er/s, ~ler/s** ə/z
   ‖ ᵊr/z **~ing, ~ling** ɪŋ **~s** z
snob snɒb ‖ snɑːb **snobs** snɒbz ‖ snɑːbz
snobbery 'snɒb ər i ‖ 'snɑːb-
snobbish 'snɒb ɪʃ ‖ 'snɑːb- **~ly** li **~ness** nəs
   nɪs
snobbism 'snɒb ˌɪz əm ‖ 'snɑːb-
snobb|y 'snɒb |i ‖ 'snɑːb |i **~ier** i ə ‖ i ə‿r **~iest**
   i ɪst i əst **~ily** ɪ li əl i **~iness** i nəs i nɪs
SNOBOL 'snəʊb ɒl ‖ 'snoʊb ɔːl
Sno-Cat tdmk 'snəʊ kæt ‖ 'snoʊ- **~s** s
Snodgrass 'snɒd grɑːs §-græs ‖ 'snɑːd græs
Snodland 'snɒd lənd ‖ 'snɑːd-
snoek snuːk snʊk (= snook)
snog snɒg ‖ snɑːg **snogged** snɒgd ‖ snɑːgd
   snogging 'snɒg ɪŋ ‖ 'snɑːg ɪŋ **snogs** snɒgz
   ‖ snɑːgz
snood snuːd snʊd **snoods** snuːdz snʊdz
snook 'gesture of defiance' snuːk snʊk ‖ snʊk
   snuːk **snooks** snuːks snʊks ‖ snʊks snuːks
snook fish snuːk snʊk
snooker 'snuːk ə ‖ 'snʊk ə‿r (*) **~ed** d
   snookering 'snuːk ər ɪŋ ‖ 'snʊk ər ɪŋ **~s** z
snoop snuːp **snooped** snuːpt **snooping**
   'snuːp ɪŋ **snoops** snuːps
snooper 'snuːp ə ‖ -ə‿r **~s** z
Snoopy, snoop|y 'snuːp |i **~ier** i ə ‖ i ə‿r **~iest**
   i ɪst i əst
snoot snuːt **snoots** snuːts
snoot|y 'snuːt |i ‖ 'snuːt̬ |i **~ier** i ə ‖ i ə‿r **~iest**
   i ɪst i əst **~ily** ɪ li əl i **~iness** i nəs i nɪs
snooze snuːz **snoozed** snuːzd **snoozes**
   'snuːz ɪz -əz **snoozing** 'snuːz ɪŋ
snore snɔː ‖ snɔːr snoʊr **snored** snɔːd ‖ snɔːrd
   snoʊrd **snores** snɔːz ‖ snɔːrz snoʊrz **snoring**
   'snɔːr ɪŋ ‖ 'snoʊr-
snorer 'snɔːr ə ‖ -ə‿r 'snoʊr- **~s** z
snorkel 'snɔːk ᵊl ‖ 'snɔːrk ᵊl **~ed, ~led** d **~ing,**
   ~ling ɪŋ **~s** z
snort snɔːt ‖ snɔːrt **snorted** 'snɔːt ɪd -əd
   ‖ 'snɔːrt̬ əd **snorting** 'snɔːt ɪŋ ‖ 'snɔːrt̬ ɪŋ
   snorts snɔːts ‖ snɔːrts
snorter 'snɔːt ə ‖ 'snɔːrt̬ ə‿r
snot snɒt ‖ snɑːt
snott|y 'snɒt |i ‖ 'snɑːt̬ |i **~ier** i ə ‖ i ə‿r **~iest**
   i ɪst i əst **~ily** ɪ li əl i **~iness** i nəs i nɪs
snotty-nosed ˌsnɒt i 'nəʊzd ◂ '···
   ‖ ˌsnɑːt̬ i 'noʊzd
snout snaʊt **snouts** snaʊts

S

snow, Snow snəʊ ‖ snoʊ **snowed** snəʊd
‖ snoʊd **snowing** 'snəʊ ɪŋ ‖ 'snoʊ ɪŋ **snows**
snəʊz ‖ snoʊz
'snow ˌblindness; ˌSnow 'White
snowball, S~ 'snəʊ bɔːl ‖ 'snoʊ- -bɑːl **~ed** d
~ing ɪŋ **~s** z
snowberr|y 'snəʊ bər ˌi '·ˌber |i
‖ 'snoʊ ˌber |i **~ies** iz
snowbird 'snəʊ bɜːd ‖ 'snoʊ bɜːd **~s** z
snow-blind 'snəʊ blaɪnd ‖ 'snoʊ-
snowblower 'snəʊ ˌbləʊ ə ‖ 'snoʊ ˌbloʊ ᵊr **~s**
z
snowbound 'snəʊ baʊnd ‖ 'snoʊ-
snow-capped 'snəʊ kæpt ‖ 'snoʊ-
ˌsnow-capped 'peaks
Snowcem *tdmk* 'snəʊ sem ‖ 'snoʊ-
snow-clad 'snəʊ klæd ‖ 'snoʊ-
Snowden, Snowdon 'snəʊd ᵊn ‖ 'snoʊd ᵊn
Snowdonia snəʊ 'dəʊn i ə ‖ snoʊ 'doʊn-
Snowdown 'snəʊ daʊn ‖ 'snoʊ-
snowdrift 'snəʊ drɪft ‖ 'snoʊ- **~s** s
snowdrop 'snəʊ drɒp ‖ 'snoʊ drɑːp **~s** s
snowfall 'snəʊ fɔːl ‖ 'snoʊ- -fɑːl **~s** z
snowfield 'snəʊ fiːᵊld ‖ 'snoʊ- **~s** z
snowflake 'snəʊ fleɪk ‖ 'snoʊ- **~s** s
snowline 'snəʊ laɪn ‖ 'snoʊ- **~s** z
snow|man 'snəʊ |mæn ‖ 'snoʊ- **~men** men
snowmobile 'snəʊ mə ˌbiːᵊl -moʊ- ‖ 'snoʊ-
-moʊ- **~s** z
snowplough, snowplow 'snəʊ plaʊ ‖ 'snoʊ-
~s z
snowshoe 'snəʊ ʃuː ‖ 'snoʊ- **~s** z
snowstorm 'snəʊ stɔːm ‖ 'snoʊ stɔːrm **~s** z
snow-white ˌsnəʊ 'waɪt ◄ -'hwaɪt
‖ ˌsnoʊ 'hwaɪt ◄
snow|y, Snowy 'snəʊ |i ‖ 'snoʊ |i **~ier** i ə
‖ i ᵊr **~iest** i ɪst i əst **~ily** ɪ li əl i **~iness** i nəs
i nɪs
ˌSnowy 'Mountains
SNP ˌes en 'piː →-em-
snr, Snr —*see* **senior**
snub snʌb **snubbed** snʌbd **snubbing** 'snʌb ɪŋ
snubs snʌbz
snubb|y 'snʌb |i **~ier** i ə ‖ i ᵊr **~iest** i ɪst i əst
~iness i nəs i nɪs
snub-nosed ˌsnʌb 'nəʊzd ◄ '·· ‖ -'noʊzd ◄
snuck snʌk
snuff snʌf **snuffed** snʌft **snuffing** 'snʌf ɪŋ
snuffs snʌfs
snuffbox 'snʌf bɒks ‖ -bɑːks **~es** ɪz əz
snuffer 'snʌf ə ‖ -ᵊr **~s** z
snuffl|e 'snʌf ᵊl **~ed** d **~er/s** ə/z ‖ ᵊr/z **~es** z
~ing ɪŋ
snug, Snug snʌg **snugger** 'snʌg ə ‖ -ᵊr
snuggest 'snʌg ɪst -əst
snugger|y 'snʌg ər |i **~ies** iz
snuggl|e 'snʌg ᵊl **~ed** d **~es** z **~ing** ɪŋ
snug|ly 'snʌg |li **~ness** nəs nɪs
so səʊ ‖ soʊ —*There is an occasional weak form*
sə
soak səʊk ‖ soʊk **soaked** səʊkt ‖ soʊkt
soaking 'səʊk ɪŋ ‖ 'soʊk ɪŋ **soaks** səʊks
‖ soʊks

soakage 'səʊk ɪdʒ ‖ 'soʊk-
soakaway 'səʊk ə ˌweɪ ‖ 'soʊk- **~s** z
Soames səʊmz ‖ soʊmz
so-and-so 'səʊ ən səʊ -ənd- ‖ 'soʊ ən soʊ **~s** z
Soane səʊn ‖ soʊn
soap səʊp ‖ soʊp **soaped** səʊpt ‖ soʊpt
soaping 'səʊp ɪŋ ‖ 'soʊp ɪŋ **soaps** səʊps
‖ soʊps
'soap ˌbubble; 'soap ˌopera
soapberr|y 'səʊp ˌber |i ‖ 'soʊp- **~ies** iz
soapbox 'səʊp bɒks ‖ 'soʊp bɑːks **~es** ɪz əz
soapflakes 'səʊp fleɪks ‖ 'soʊp-
soapi... —*see* **soapy**
soapstone 'səʊp stəʊn ‖ 'soʊp stoʊn
soapsuds 'səʊp sʌdz ‖ 'soʊp-
soapwort 'səʊp wɜːt §-wɔːt ‖ 'soʊp wɜːt -wɔːrt
~s s
soap|y 'səʊp |i ‖ 'soʊp |i **~ier** i ə ‖ i ᵊr **~iest**
i ɪst i əst **~ily** ɪ li əl i **~iness** i nəs i nɪs
soar sɔː ‖ sɔːr sour (*= sore*) **soared** sɔːd ‖ sɔːrd
sourd **soaring/ly** 'sɔːr ɪŋ /li ‖ 'sour- **soars**
sɔːz ‖ sɔːrz sourz
Soar *river* sɔː ‖ sɔːr sour
Soar *place in Wales* 'səʊ ɑː ‖ 'soʊ ɑːr
soaraway 'sɔːr ə ˌweɪ ‖ 'sour-
Soares 'swɑːr eʃ —*Port* [swarʃ, 'swariʃ]
SOAS 'səʊ æs -æz; ˌes əʊ eɪ 'es ‖ 'soʊ-
Soave 'swɑːv eɪ —*It* [so 'aː ve]
Soay 'səʊ eɪ -ə ‖ 'soʊ-
sob sɒb ‖ sɑːb **sobbed** sɒbd ‖ sɑːbd **sobbing**
'sɒb ɪŋ ‖ 'sɑːb ɪŋ **sobs** sɒbz ‖ sɑːbz
'sob ˌstory
sobeit səʊ 'biː ɪt ‖ soʊ-
Sobell 'səʊ bel ‖ 'soʊ-
sober 'səʊb ə ‖ 'soʊb ᵊr **sobered** 'səʊb əd
‖ 'soʊb ᵊrd **soberer** 'səʊb ər ə ‖ 'soʊb ᵊr ᵊr
soberest 'səʊb ər ɪst əst ‖ 'soʊb-
sobering/ly 'səʊb ər ɪŋ /li ‖ 'soʊb- **~ly** li
~ness nəs nɪs
Sobers 'səʊb əz ‖ 'soʊb ᵊrz
Sobranie *tdmk* səʊ 'brɑːn i ‖ soʊ-
sobriety səʊ 'braɪ ət i ɪt i ‖ soʊ 'braɪ əṭ i
sobriquet 'səʊb rɪ keɪ -rə- ‖ 'soʊb- ˌ·'· **~s** z
soca 'səʊk ə ‖ 'soʊk ə
socage 'sɒk ɪdʒ ‖ 'sɑːk-
so-called ˌsəʊ 'kɔːld ◄ ‖ ˌsoʊ- -'kɑːld ◄
soccer 'sɒk ə ‖ 'sɑːk ᵊr
sociability ˌsəʊʃ ə 'bɪl ət i -ɪt i
‖ ˌsoʊʃ ə 'bɪl əṭ i
sociab|le 'səʊʃ əb |ᵊl ‖ 'soʊʃ- **~leness** ᵊl nəs
-nɪs **~ly** li
social 'səʊʃ ᵊl ‖ 'soʊʃ ᵊl **~s** z
ˌsocial ˌanthro'pology; ˌsocial 'climber;
ˌSocial 'Democrat; 'social diˌsease; ˌsocial
'distance; ˌSocial 'Register *tdmk*; ˌsocial
'science; ˌsocial se'curity; ˌsocial
'services; ˌsocial 'studies; ˌsocial work
socialis... —*see* **socializ...**
socialism 'səʊʃ ə ˌlɪz əm -ᵊl ˌɪz- ‖ 'soʊʃ-
socialist 'səʊʃ əl ɪst §-əst ‖ 'soʊʃ- **~s** s
socialistic ˌsəʊʃ ə 'lɪst ɪk ◄ ‖ ˌsoʊʃ- **~ally** ᵊl i
socialite 'səʊʃ ə laɪt ‖ 'soʊʃ- **~s** s

socialization ˌsəʊʃ əl aɪ ˈzeɪʃ ᵊn -ɪ'-- ‖ ˌsoʊʃ əl ə-

socializ|e ˈsəʊʃ ə laɪz ‖ ˈsoʊʃ- ~ed d ~es ɪz əz ~ing ɪŋ
socialized 'medicine

socially ˈsəʊʃ əl i ‖ ˈsoʊʃ-

societal sə ˈsaɪ ət ᵊl -əʈ ᵊl ~ly i

societ|y sə ˈsaɪ ət |i ‖ -əʈ |i ~ies iz

Socinian səʊ ˈsɪn i ᵊn ‖ soʊ- sə- ~s z

Socinus səʊ ˈsaɪn əs ‖ soʊ- sə-

socio- comb. form
with stress-neutral suffix ˌsəʊʃ i ˌəʊ ˌsəʊs- ‖ ˌsoʊs i ˌoʊ — sociobiology ˌsəʊʃ i ˌəʊ baɪ ˈɒl ədʒ i ˌsəʊs- ‖ ˌsoʊs i ˌoʊ baɪ ˈɑːl-
with stress-imposing suffix ˌsəʊs i ˈɒ + ˌsəʊʃ- ‖ ˌsoʊs i ˈɑː + — sociometry ˌsəʊs i ˈɒm ətr i ˌsəʊʃ-, -ɪtr i ‖ ˌsoʊs i ˈɑːm-

sociocultural ˌsəʊʃ i ˌəʊ ˈkʌltʃ ᵊr_əl ◂ ˌsəʊs- ‖ ˌsoʊs i ˌoʊ-

socioeconomic ˌsəʊʃ i ˌəʊ ˌiːk ə ˈnɒm ɪk ˌsəʊs-, -ˌek- ‖ ˌsoʊs i ˌoʊ ˌek ə ˈnɑːm ɪk -ˌiːk- ~ally ᵊl i

sociolect ˈsəʊʃ i ˌəʊ lekt ˈsəʊs- ‖ ˈsoʊs i ˌoʊ- ~s s

sociolectal ˌsəʊʃ i ˌəʊ ˈlekt ᵊl ◂ ˌsəʊs- ‖ ˌsoʊs i ˌoʊ-

sociolinguist ˌsəʊʃ i ˌəʊ ˈlɪŋ gwɪst ˌsəʊs- ‖ ˌsoʊs i ˌoʊ- ~s s

sociolinguistic ˌsəʊʃ i ˌəʊ lɪŋ ˈgwɪst ɪk ◂ ˌsəʊs- ‖ ˌsoʊs i ˌoʊ- ~ally ᵊl i ~s s

sociological ˌsəʊʃ i ə ˈlɒdʒ ɪk ᵊl ◂ ˌsəʊs- ‖ ˌsoʊs i ə ˈlɑːdʒ- ~ly i

sociologist ˌsəʊʃ i ˈɒl ədʒ ɪst ˌsəʊs-, §-əst ‖ ˌsoʊs i ˈɑːl- ~s s

sociology ˌsəʊʃ i ˈɒl ədʒ i ˌsəʊs- ‖ ˌsoʊs i ˈɑːl-

sociopath ˈsəʊʃ i ˌəʊ pæθ ˈsəʊs- ‖ ˈsoʊs i ˌoʊ- ~s s

sociopolitical ˌsəʊʃ i ˌəʊ pə ˈlɪt ɪk ᵊl ◂ ˌsəʊs- ‖ ˌsoʊs i ˌoʊ pə ˈlɪʈ-

sock sɒk ‖ saːk socked sɒkt ‖ saːkt socking ˈsɒk ɪŋ ‖ ˈsaːk ɪŋ socks sɒks ‖ saːks

sockdolager, sockdologer ˌsɒk ˈdɒl ədʒ ə ‖ saːk ˈdɑːl ɪdʒ ᵊr ~s z

sock|et ˈsɒk |ɪt §-ət ‖ ˈsaːk |ət ~eted ɪt ɪd §ət-, -əd ‖ əʈ əd ~eting ɪt ɪŋ §ət- ‖ əʈ ɪŋ ~ets ɪts §əts ‖ əts

sockeye ˈsɒk aɪ ‖ ˈsaːk aɪ ~s z

Socotra səʊ ˈkəʊtr ə sɒ- ‖ soʊ ˈkoʊtr ə sə-

Socrates ˈsɒk rə tiːz ‖ ˈsaːk-

Socratic sɒ ˈkræt ɪk səʊ- ‖ sə ˈkræʈ ɪk soʊ- ~ally ᵊl i

sod sɒd ‖ saːd sods sɒdz ‖ saːdz
sod's 'law, ' · ·

soda ˈsəʊd ə ‖ ˈsoʊd ə ~s z
'soda bread; 'soda ˌfountain; 'soda ˌwater

sodality səʊ ˈdæl ət |i -ɪt- ‖ soʊ ˈdæl əʈ |i ~ies iz

sodden ˈsɒd ᵊn ‖ ˈsaːd ᵊn ~ed d ~ing ɪŋ ~ly li ~ness nəs nɪs ~s z

sodding ˈsɒd ɪŋ ‖ ˈsaːd ɪŋ

Soddy ˈsɒd i ‖ ˈsaːd i

sodium ˈsəʊd i əm ‖ ˈsoʊd-
ˌsodium 'chloride

Sodom ˈsɒd əm ‖ ˈsaːd əm

sodomis|e ˈsɒd ə maɪz ‖ ˈsaːd- ~ed d ~es ɪz əz ~ing ɪŋ

sodomite ˈsɒd ə maɪt ‖ ˈsaːd- ~s s

sodomiz|e ˈsɒd ə maɪz ‖ ˈsaːd- ~ed d ~es ɪz əz ~ing ɪŋ

sodomy ˈsɒd əm i ‖ ˈsaːd-

Sodor ˈsəʊd ə ‖ ˈsoʊd ᵊr

soever səʊ ˈev ə ‖ soʊ ˈev ᵊr

sofa ˈsəʊf ə ‖ ˈsoʊf ə ~s z

sofabed ˈsəʊf ə bed ‖ ˈsoʊf- ~s z

Sofer ˈsəʊf ə ‖ ˈsoʊf ᵊr

soffit ˈsɒf ɪt §-ət ‖ ˈsaːf ət ~s s

Sofia ˈsəʊf i ə ˈsɒf-; səʊ ˈfiː ə, -ˈfaɪ ə ‖ ˈsoʊf i ə —Bulgarian [ˈso fi ja]

soft sɒft ‖ sɔːft saːft softer ˈsɒft ə ˈsɔːft- ‖ ˈsɔːft ᵊr ˈsaːft- softest ˈsɒft ɪst ˈsɔːft-, -əst ‖ ˈsɔːft əst ˈsaːft-
ˌsoft 'fruit; ˌsoft 'furnishings; ˌsoft 'landing; ˌsoft 'option; ˌsoft 'palate; ˌsoft 'sell; ˌsoft 'soap; 'soft spot; ˌsoft 'touch

softball ˈsɒft bɔːl ˈsɔːft- ‖ ˈsɔːft- ˈsaːft bɑːl ~s z

soft-boiled ˌsɒft ˈbɔɪld ◂ ˌsɔːft- ‖ ˌsɔːft- ˌsaːft-
ˌsoft-boiled 'eggs

soft-centered, soft-centred ˌsɒft ˈsent əd ◂ ˌsɔːft- ‖ ˌsɔːft ˈsent ᵊrd ◂ ˌsaːft-

soft-core ˌsɒft ˈkɔː ◂ ˌsɔːft- ‖ ˌsɔːft ˈkɔːr ◂ ˌsaːft-, -ˈkoʊr
ˌsoft-core 'porn

soft-cover ˌsɒft ˈkʌv ə ˌsɔːft- ‖ ˌsɔːft ˈkʌv ᵊr ◂ ˌsaːft-

soften ˈsɒf ᵊn ˈsɔːf- ‖ ˈsɔːf ᵊn ˈsaːf- ~ed d ~ing ɪŋ ~s z

softener ˈsɒf ᵊn ə ˈsɔːf- ‖ ˈsɔːf ᵊn ᵊr ˈsaːf- ~s z

softhearted ˌsɒft ˈhaːt ɪd ◂ ˌsɔːft-, §-əd ‖ ˌsɔːft ˈhaːrʈ əd ◂ ˌsaːft- ~ness nəs nɪs

softie ˈsɒft i ˈsɔːft- ‖ ˈsɔːft i ˈsaːft- ~s z

softish ˈsɒft ɪʃ ˈsɔːft- ‖ ˈsɔːft- ˈsaːft-

soft|ly ˈsɒft |li ˈsɔːft- ‖ ˈsɔːft |li ˈsaːft- ~ness nəs nɪs

softly-softly ˌsɒft li ˈsɒft li ˌsɔːft li ˈsɔːft- ‖ ˌsɔːft li ˈsɔːft li ˌsaːft li ˈsaːft-

softly-spoken ˌsɒft li ˈspəʊk ən ◂ ˌsɔːft- ‖ ˌsɔːft li ˈspoʊk ən ◂ ˌsaːft-

soft-pedal ˌsɒft ˈped ᵊl ˌsɔːft- ‖ ˌsɔːft- ˌsaːft- ~ed, ~led d ~ing, ~ling ɪŋ ~s z

soft-shoe ˈsɒft ʃuː ‖ ˈsɔːft- ˈsɔːft- ˈsaːft-

soft-soap ˌsɒft ˈsəʊp ˌsɔːft- ‖ ˌsɔːft ˈsoʊp ˌsaːft- ~ed t ~ing ɪŋ ~s s

soft-spoken ˌsɒft ˈspəʊk ən ◂ ˌsɔːft- ‖ ˌsɔːft ˈspoʊk ən ◂ ˌsaːft-

soft-top ˈsɒft tɒp ˈsɔːft- ‖ ˈsɔːft- ˈsaːft-

software ˈsɒft weə ˈsɔːft- ‖ ˈsɔːft wer ˈsaːft-, -wær
'software house

softwood ˈsɒft wʊd ˈsɔːft- ‖ ˈsɔːft- ˈsaːft- ~s z

soft|y ˈsɒft |i ˈsɔːft- ‖ ˈsɔːft |i ˈsaːft- ~ies iz

SOGAT ˈsəʊ gæt ‖ ˈsoʊ-

Sogdian ˈsɒgd i ᵊn ‖ ˈsaːgd- ~s z

Sogdiana ˌsɒgd i ˈaːn ə -ˈeɪn ə ‖ ˌsaːgd i ˈæn ə

soggy 'sɒg |i ‖ 'saːg |i ‖ 'sɔːg- **~ier** i‿ə ‖ i‿ər
~iest i‿ɪst i‿əst **~ily** ɪ li əl i **~iness** i nəs i nɪs
soh səʊ ‖ soʊ (= *so*)
Soham 'səʊ əm ‖ 'soʊ-
Soho, SoHo 'səʊ həʊ ˌ·'· ‖ 'soʊ hoʊ
　ˌSoho 'Square
soi-disant ˌswɑː 'diːz ɒ̃ ◂ -diː 'zɒ̃ ‖ -diː 'zɑːn ◂
　—*Fr* [swa di zɑ̃]
soigne, soigné, soignee, soignée
　'swɑːn jeɪ ·'· ‖ swɑːn 'jeɪ —*Fr* [swan je]
soil sɔɪºl **soiled** sɔɪºld **soiling** 'sɔɪºl ɪŋ **soils**
　sɔɪºlz
soilpipe 'sɔɪºl paɪp **~s** s
soiree, soirée 'swɑːr eɪ ‖ swɑː 'reɪ —*Fr*
　[swa ʁe] **~s** z
soixante-neuf ˌswæs ɒnt 'nɜːf ˌswʌs-
　‖ ˌswɑːs ɑːnt 'nʌf -'nɑːf —*Fr* [swa sɑ̃t nœf]
sojourn 'sɒdʒ ən 'sʌdʒ-, -ɜːn ‖ soʊ 'dʒɜːn ·'·
　(*)—*Some speakers of AmE make a stress
　difference between the noun* '·· *and the verb* ·'·
　~ed d **~ing** ɪŋ **~s** z
sojourner 'sɒdʒ ən ə 'sʌdʒ-, -ɜːn-
　‖ soʊ 'dʒɜːn ər '··· **~s** z
soke səʊk ‖ soʊk (= *soak*)
Sokoto 'səʊk ə təʊ ‖ 'soʊk oʊ toʊ
sol, Sol sɒl ‖ saːl sɔːl —*but as the name of a
　coin, in AmE also* soʊl **sols** sɒlz ‖ saːlz
sola 'səʊl ə ‖ 'soʊl ə
　ˌsola 'topi
solac|e 'sɒl əs -ɪs ‖ 'saːl əs **~ed** t **~es** ɪz əz
　~ing ɪŋ
solan 'səʊl ən ‖ 'soʊl ən **~s** z
Solana sə 'lɑːn ə sɒ-, səʊ- ‖ soʊ- —*Sp*
　[so 'la na]
solanaceous ˌsɒl ə 'neɪʃ əs ◂ ˌsəʊl- ‖ ˌsoʊl-
solanum səʊ 'leɪn əm ‖ sə-
solar, Solar 'səʊl ə §-ɑː ‖ 'soʊl ªr
　ˌsolar 'cell; ˌsolar 'panel; ˌsolar 'plexus;
　ˌsolar ˌsystem; ˌsolar 'wind; ˌsolar ˌyear
solari|um sə 'leər i‿|əm səʊ- ‖ -'lær- soʊ-, -'ler-
　~a ə **~ums** əmz
solati|um səʊ 'leɪʃ i‿|əm -'leɪʃ |əm ‖ soʊ- **~a** ə
　~ums əmz
sold səʊld →sɒʊld ‖ soʊld (= *soled*)
sold|er 'sɒld |ə 'səʊld-, §'sɒd-, §'sɔːd-
　‖ 'saːd |ªr (*) **~ered** əd ‖ ªrd **~ering** ªr ɪŋ
　~ers əz ‖ ªrz
　'soldering ˌiron
soldier 'səʊldʒ ə →'sɒʊldʒ- ‖ 'soʊldʒ ªr
　—*There is also an occasional spelling
　pronunciation* 'səʊld i‿ə ‖ 'soʊld i‿ªr **~ed** d
　soldiering 'səʊldʒ ər ɪŋ →'sɒʊldʒ-
　‖ 'soʊldʒ ªr ɪŋ **~s** z
　ˌsoldier of 'fortune
soldierlike 'səʊldʒ ə laɪk →'sɒʊldʒ-
　‖ 'soʊldʒ ªr-
soldierly 'səʊldʒ ə li →'sɒʊldʒ- ‖ 'soʊldʒ ªr-
soldier|y 'səʊldʒ ər |i →'sɒʊldʒ- ‖ 'soʊldʒ-
　~ies iz
sole səʊl →sɒʊl ‖ soʊl **soled** səʊld sɒʊld
　‖ soʊld **soles** səʊlz →sɒʊlz ‖ soʊlz **soling**
　'səʊl ɪŋ →'sɒʊl- ‖ 'soʊl ɪŋ

solecism 'sɒl ɪ ˌsɪz əm 'səʊl-, -ə- ‖ 'saːl- 'soʊl-
　~s z
Soledad 'sɒl ɪ dæd -ə- ‖ 'saːl- —*Sp*
　[so le 'ðað]
solely 'səʊl li →'sɒʊl- ‖ 'soʊl li
solemn 'sɒl əm ‖ 'saːl əm **~ly** li **~ness** nəs nɪs
solemnis... —*see* **solemniz...**
solemnit|y sə 'lem nət |i sɒ-, -nɪt i ‖ -nət̬ |i
　~ies iz
solemnization ˌsɒl əm naɪ 'zeɪʃ ªn -nɪ'--
　‖ ˌsaːl əm nə- **~s** z
solemniz|e 'sɒl əm naɪz ‖ 'saːl- **~ed** d **~es** ɪz
　əz **~ing** ɪŋ
solenoid 'sɒl ə nɔɪd 'səʊl-, -ɪ- ‖ 'soʊl- 'saːl- **~s**
　z
Solent 'səʊl ənt ‖ 'soʊl-
solera sə 'leər ə -'lɪər- ‖ -'ler- -'lær- —*Sp*
　[so 'le ɾa]
Soley 'səʊl i ‖ 'soʊl i
sol-fa ˌsɒl 'fɑː §ˌsəʊl- ‖ ˌsoʊl-
solfatara ˌsɒlf ə 'tɑːr ə ‖ ˌsoʊlf- **~s** z
solfegg|io sɒl 'fedʒ |i əʊ →'fedʒ |əʊ
　‖ saːl 'fedʒ |oʊ **~i** iː
solferino, S~ ˌsɒlf ə 'riːn əʊ ‖ ˌsaːlf ə 'riːn oʊ
solic|it sə 'lɪs |ɪt §sə-, §-ət ‖ -|ət **~ited** ɪt ɪd
　§ət-, -əd ‖ ət̬ əd **~iting** ɪt ɪŋ §ət- ‖ ət̬ ɪŋ **~its**
　ɪts §əts ‖ əts
solicitation sə ˌlɪs ɪ 'teɪʃ ªn §sə-, -ˌə- **~s** z
solicitor sə 'lɪs ɪt ə §sə-, -ət- ‖ -ət̬ ªr **~s** z
　Soˌlicitor 'General
solicitous sə 'lɪs ɪt əs §sə-, -ət- ‖ -ət̬ əs **~ly** li
　~ness nəs nɪs
solicitude sə 'lɪs ɪ tjuːd §sə-, -ə-, →-tʃuːd
　‖ -tuːd -tjuːd
solid 'sɒl ɪd §-əd ‖ 'saːl əd **~s** z
solidago ˌsɒl ɪ 'deɪg əʊ -ə- ‖ ˌsaːl ə 'deɪg oʊ
solidarity ˌsɒl ɪ 'dær ət i ˌ-ə-, -ɪt i
　‖ ˌsaːl ə 'dær ət̬ i -'der-
solidi 'sɒl ɪ daɪ -ə-, -diː ‖ 'saːl-
solidification sə ˌlɪd ɪf ɪ 'keɪʃ ªn sɒ-, -ˌəf-,
　§-ə'--
solidify sə 'lɪd ɪ faɪ sɒ-, -'ə-
solidity sə 'lɪd ət i sɒ-, -ɪt i ‖ -ət̬ i
solid|ly 'sɒl ɪd |li §-əd- ‖ 'saːl əd- **~ness** nəs
　nɪs
solid-state ˌsɒl ɪd 'steɪt ◂ §-əd- ‖ ˌsaːl əd-
sol|idus 'sɒl |ɪd əs -əd- ‖ 'saːl |əd əs **~idi** ɪ daɪ
　-ə-, -diː
Solignum *tdmk* səʊ 'lɪg nəm ‖ soʊ-
Solihull ˌsəʊl i 'hʌl ˌsɒl- ‖ ˌsoʊl-
soliloquis|e, soliloquiz|e sə 'lɪl ə kwaɪz
　səʊ-, sɒ- **~ed** d **~es** ɪz əz **~ing** ɪŋ
soliloq|uy sə 'lɪl ək |wi səʊ-, sɒ- **~uies** wiz
solipsism 'sɒl ɪp ˌsɪz əm 'səʊl-, -əp- ‖ 'saːl əp-
solipsist 'sɒl ɪp sɪst 'səʊl-, -əp-, §-səst
　‖ 'saːl əp səst **~s** s
solipsistic ˌsɒl ɪp 'sɪst ɪk ◂ ˌsəʊl-, -əp-
　‖ ˌsaːl əp- **~ally** ªl‿i
solitaire ˌsɒl ɪ 'teə -ə-, '··· ‖ 'saːl ə ter -tær **~s**
　z
solitarily 'sɒl ɪ ˌt ər əl i '·ɪ-, -ɪ li; ˌ··'teər ə-
　‖ ˌsaːl ə 'ter əl i

solitar|y 'sɒl ə‚tər |i '‚ɪ‚ ‖ 'saːl ə ter |i **~ies** iz
~**iness** i nəs i nɪs
‚solitary con'finement
solitude 'sɒl ə tjuːd -ɪ-, →-tʃuːd ‖ 'saːl ə tuːd
-tjuːd **~s** z
solleret ‚sɒl ə 'ret ‖ ‚saːl- **~s** s
solo 'səʊl əʊ ‖ 'soʊl oʊ **~s** z
soloist 'səʊl əʊ ɪst §-əst ‖ 'soʊl oʊ- **~s** s
Solomon 'sɒl əm ən ‖ 'saːl-
Solomons 'sɒl əm ənz ‖ 'saːl-
Solon 'səʊl ɒn -ən ‖ 'soʊl ən -aːn
solstic|e 'sɒlst ɪs -əs ‖ 'saːlst əs 'soʊlst- **~es** ɪz
əz
Solti 'ʃɒlt i ‖ 'ʃoʊlt i —Hung ['ʃol ti]
solubility ‚sɒl ju 'bɪl ət i ‚jə- -ɪt i
‖ ‚saːl jə 'bɪl ət i
solub|le 'sɒl jʊb |ᵊl -jəb- ‖ 'saːl jəb |ᵊl **~leness**
ᵊl nəs -nɪs **~ly** li
solus 'səʊl əs ‖ 'soʊl əs
solute 'sɒl juːt sɒ 'luːt, -ljuːt ‖ 'saːl- **~s** s
solution sə 'luːʃ ᵊn -'ljuːʃ- **~s** z
Solutrean sə 'luːtr i ‚ən
solvability ‚sɒlv ə 'bɪl ət i -ɪt i
‖ ‚saːlv ə 'bɪl ət i
solvable 'sɒlv əb ᵊl ‖ 'saːlv-
solv|ate v sɒl 'v|eɪt 'sɒlv |eɪt ‖ 'saːlv |eɪt
~**ated** eɪt ɪd -əd ‖ eɪt̬ əd **~ates** eɪts **~ating**
eɪt ɪŋ ‖ eɪt̬ ɪŋ
solvate n 'sɒlv eɪt ‖ 'saːlv- **~s** s
solvation sɒl 'veɪʃ ᵊn ‖ saːl-
Solvay 'sɒlv eɪ ‖ 'saːlv- —Fr [sɔl vɛ]
'Solvay ‚process
solve sɒlv §səʊlv ‖ saːlv **solved** sɒlvd §səʊlvd
‖ saːlvd **solves** sɒlvz §səʊlvz ‖ saːlvz **solving**
'sɒlv ɪŋ §'səʊlv- ‖ 'saːlv ɪŋ
solvency 'sɒlv ᵊn‚s i §'səʊlv- ‖ 'saːlv-
solvent 'sɒlv ᵊnt §'səʊlv- ‖ 'saːlv- **~s** s
'solvent a‚buse
solver 'sɒlv ə §'səʊlv- ‖ 'saːlv ᵊr **~s** z
Solway 'sɒl weɪ ‖ 'saːl-
‚Solway 'Firth
Solzhenitsyn ‚sɒl ʒə 'nɪts ɪn -ʒɪ-, -'niːts-, §-ən
‖ ‚soʊl- —Russ [səl ʒɪ 'nʲi tsɪn]
soma 'səʊm ə ‖ 'soʊm ə
Somali, s~ sə 'maːl i səʊ- ‖ soʊ- **~s** z
Somali|a sə 'maːl i‚ə səʊ- ‖ soʊ- **~an/s** ən/z
~**land** lænd
somatic səʊ 'mæt ɪk ‖ soʊ 'mæt̬ ɪk sə-
somato- comb. form
with stress-neutral suffix |səʊm ət ə
|səʊm ə təʊ; səʊ |mæt ə ‖ |soʊm ət̬ ə
sə 'mæt̬ ə — **somatoplasm**
'səʊm ət əʊ ‚plæz əm səʊ 'mæt ə-
‖ sə 'mæt̬ ə- 'soʊm ət̬ ə-
with stress-imposing suffix ‚səʊm ə 'tɒ +
‖ ‚soʊm ə 'taː + — **somatology**
‚səʊm ə 'tɒl ədʒ i ‖ ‚soʊm ə 'taːl-
somatotype 'səʊm ət əʊ taɪp səʊ 'mæt-
‖ sə 'mæt̬ ə- 'soʊm ət̬ ə- **~s** s
somber, sombre 'sɒm bə ‖ 'saːm bᵊr **~ly** li
~**ness** nəs nɪs
sombrero sɒm 'breər əʊ ‖ saːm 'brer oʊ səm-
~s z

some strong form sʌm, weak form səm —In
stranded (exposed) position only the strong
form is used: I've found some. aɪv 'faʊnd sʌm.
Otherwise the weak form is usual if the word
is unstressed: I've found some coins
aɪv ‚faʊnd səm 'kɔɪnz
-some səm — **burdensome** 'bɜːd ᵊn səm
‖ 'bɜːd- — **eightsome** 'eɪt səm —With this
pronunciation, -some forms adjectives or
collective numerals: compare the following.
-some in biology, 'body' səʊm ‖ soʊm zoʊm —
chromosome 'krəʊm ə səʊm
‖ 'kroʊm ə soʊm -zoʊm —This -some is used
with combining forms and means 'body':
compare the preceding.
somebody 'sʌm bəd i -‚bɒd- ‖ -‚baːd- —There
is also a casual form 'sʌm di
someday 'sʌm deɪ
somehow 'sʌm haʊ —There is also a casual
form 'sʌm aʊ
someone 'sʌm wʌn §-wɒn
‚someone 'clever; ‚someone 'else
someplace 'sʌm pleɪs —Compare the phrase
‚some 'place
Somerfield 'sʌm ə fiːᵊld ‖ -ᵊr-
Somerleyton 'sʌm ə ‚leɪt ᵊn ‖ -ᵊr-
Somers 'sʌm əz ‖ -ᵊrz
somersault 'sʌm ə sɔːlt -sɒlt ‖ -ᵊr- -saːlt **~ed**
ɪd əd **~ing** ɪŋ **~s** s
Somerset 'sʌm ə set -sɪt ‖ -ᵊr-
Somerton 'sʌm ət ən ‖ -ᵊrt ᵊn
Somerville 'sʌm ə vɪl ‖ -ᵊr-
something 'sʌm θɪŋ ∆-θɪŋk; 'sʌmᵖθ ɪŋ,
→'sʌntᵊ-, ∆-ɪŋk ‖ →'sʌmp m —There are
casual forms 'sʌm hɪŋ, 'sʌm ɪŋ
‚something 'else
sometime 'sʌm taɪm (NB not ·'·)—Compare
the phrase some 'time səm 'taɪm, as in I ‚need
some ‚time to 'think
sometimes 'sʌm taɪmz (NB not ·'·)
someway 'sʌm weɪ
somewhat 'sʌm wɒt -hwɒt, §-ət ‖ wʌt -hwʌt,
-waːt, -hwaːt, -wət, -hwət
somewhere 'sʌm weə -hweə ‖ -wer -hwer,
-wær, -hwær **~s** z
‚somewhere 'else
somite 'səʊm aɪt ‖ 'soʊm- **~s** s
Somme sɒm ‖ saːm sʌm —Fr [sɔm]
sommelier sɒ 'mel i‚ə sʌ-, -eɪ; ‚sʌm ᵊl 'jeɪ,
‚sɒm-, '···‖ ‚sʌm ᵊl 'jeɪ —Fr [sɔ mə lje] **~s** z
somnambulant sɒm 'næm bjʊl ənt -bjəl ənt
‖ saːm 'næm bjəl ənt **~s** s
somnambu|late sɒm 'næm bju |leɪt -bjə leɪt
‖ saːm 'naːm bjə- **~lated** leɪt ɪd -əd ‖ leɪt̬ əd
~**lates** leɪts ~**lating** leɪt ɪŋ ‖ leɪt̬ ɪŋ
somnambulation sɒm ‚næm bju 'leɪʃ ᵊn
‚···'··, -bjə'·- ‖ saːm ‚næm bjə-
somnambulism sɒm 'næm bju ‚lɪz əm -'·bjə-
‖ saːm 'næm bjə-
somnambulist sɒm 'næm bjʊl ɪst -'·bjəl-, §-əst
‖ saːm 'næm bjəl əst **~s** s
somniferous sɒm 'nɪf ər əs ‖ saːm-
somnolence 'sɒm nəl ən‚s ‖ 'saːm-

S

somnolent ˈsɒm nəl ənt ‖ ˈsɑːm- **~ly** li
Somoza sə ˈməʊz ə ‖ -ˈmoʊz- -ˈmoʊs- — *AmSp*
[so ˈmo sa]
Sompting ˈsɒmpt ɪŋ ˈsʌmpt- ‖ ˈsɑːmpt-
son *'male child'*, **Son** sʌn (= *sun*) **sons** sʌnz
son *French word, 'sound'*, sɒn ‖ sɔːn soʊn —*Fr*
[sɔ̃] —*see also phrases with this word*
sonagram ˈsəʊn ə græm ˈsɒn- ‖ ˈsoʊn- ˈsɑːn-
~s z
sonagraph, S~ *tdmk* ˈsəʊn ə grɑːf ˈsɒn-, -græf
‖ ˈsoʊn ə græf ˈsɑːn- **~s** s
sonant ˈsəʊn ənt ˈsɒn- ‖ ˈsoʊn- **~s** s
sonar ˈsəʊn ɑː ‖ ˈsoʊn ɑːr **~s** z
sonata sə ˈnɑːt ə ‖ -ˈnɑːt̬- **~s** z
sonatina ˌsɒn ə ˈtiːn ə ‖ ˌsɑːn- **~s** z
sonde sɒnd ‖ sɑːnd **sondes** sɒndz ‖ sɑːndz
Sondheim ˈsɒnd haɪm ‖ ˈsɑːnd-
sone səʊn ‖ soʊn **sones** səʊnz ‖ soʊnz
son et lumiere, son et lumière
ˌsɒn eɪ ˈluːm i eə ˌ·ˌ·ˌ·ˈ· ‖ ˌsɑːn eɪ luːm ˈjeʳr
ˌsoʊn- —*Fr* [sɔ̃ ɛ ly mjeːʁ]
song sɒŋ ‖ sɔːŋ sɑːŋ **songs** sɒŋz ‖ sɔːŋz sɑːŋz
ˌsong and ˈdance; ˈsong thrush
songbird ˈsɒŋ bɜːd ‖ ˈsɔːŋ bɜːd ˈsɑːŋ- **~s** z
songbook ˈsɒŋ bʊk §-buːk ‖ ˈsɔːŋ- ˈsɑːŋ- **~s** s
Songhai ⁽ˌ⁾sɒŋ ˈgaɪ ‖ ⁽ˌ⁾sɔːŋ- ⁽ˌ⁾sɑːŋ- **~s** z
songster ˈsɒŋ stə ˈsɒŋᵏst ə ‖ ˈsɔːŋᵏst ᵊr
ˈsɑːŋᵏst- **~s** z
songstress ˈsɒŋ strəs -strɪs, -stres ‖ ˈsɔːŋᵏs trəs
ˈsɑːŋᵏs- **~es** ɪz əz
songwriter ˈsɒŋ ˌraɪt ə ‖ ˈsɔːŋ ˌraɪt̬ ᵊr ˈsɑːŋ- **~s**
z
Sonia ˈsɒn i ə ˈsəʊn- ‖ ˈsoʊn jə
sonic, Sonic ˈsɒn ɪk ‖ ˈsɑːn ɪk **~s** s
ˌsonic ˈboom
son-in-law ˈsʌn ɪn ˌlɔː §-ən- ‖ -ˌlɑː **sons-in-law**
ˈsʌnz ɪn ˌlɔː §-ən- ‖ -ˌlɑː
Sonja ˈsɒn jə ˈsəʊn- ‖ ˈsoʊn-
sonnet ˈsɒn ɪt -ət ‖ ˈsɑːn ət **~s** s
sonneteer ˌsɒn ɪ ˈtɪə -ə- ‖ ˌsɑːn ə ˈtɪʳr **~s** z
Sonning ˈsɒn ɪŋ ˈsʌn- ‖ ˈsɑːn-
sonn|y, Sonn|y ˈsʌn |i (= *sunny*) **~ies, ~y's** iz
son-of-a-bitch ˌsʌn əv ə ˈbɪtʃ **~es** ɪz əz
sons-of-bitches ˌsʌnz əv ˈbɪtʃ ɪz -əz
son-of-a-gun ˌsʌn əv ə ˈgʌn **sons-of-guns**
ˌsʌnz əv ˈgʌnz
sonogram ˈsəʊn ə græm ˈsɒn- ‖ ˈsoʊn- ˈsɑːn-
~s z
sonograph ˈsəʊn ə grɑːf ˈsɒn-, -græf
‖ ˈsoʊn ə græf ˈsɑːn- **~s** s
Sonoma sə ˈnəʊm ə ‖ -ˈnoʊm-
sonometer səʊ ˈnɒm ɪt ə sɒ-, -ət ə
‖ soʊ ˈnɑːm ət̬ ʳr sə- **~s** z
Sonor|a sə ˈnɔːr |ə ‖ -ˈnoʊr- **~an** ən
sonorant ˈsɒn ər ənt ˈsəʊn- ‖ ˈsoʊn- ˈsɑːn-;
sə ˈnɔːr-, soʊ-, -ˈnoʊr- **~s** s
sonority sə ˈnɒr ət i səʊ-, -ɪt i ‖ sə ˈnɔːr ət̬ i
sə ˈnɑːr-
sonorous ˈsɒn ər əs sə ˈnɔːr- ‖ sə ˈnɔːr əs
-ˈnoʊr-; ˈsɑːn ər- **~ly** li
sons-... —*see* **son-...**
sonsy, sonsie ˈsɒnˢs i ‖ ˈsɑːnˢs i
Sontag ˈsɒn tæg ‖ ˈsɑːn-

Sony *tdmk* ˈsəʊn i ˈsɒn- ‖ ˈsoʊn i —*Jp* [ˈso ɲii]
Sonya ˈsɒn jə ‖ ˈsoʊn-
soon suːn §sʊn **sooner** ˈsuːn ə §ˈsʊn- ‖ -ᵊr
soonest ˈsuːn ɪst §ˈsʊn-, -əst

SOOT

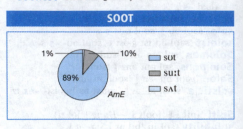

1% 10%

89%

AmE

□ sʊt
□ suːt
□ sʌt

soot sʊt ‖ suːt, sʌt — *Preference poll, AmE:* sʊt
89%, suːt *10%,* sʌt *1%.*
sooth suːθ
soothe suːð **soothed** suːðd **soothes** suːðz
soothing ˈsuːð ɪŋ
soother ˈsuːð ə ‖ -ᵊr **~s** z
soothing ˈsuːð ɪŋ **~ly** li **~ness** nəs nɪs
soothsay|er ˈsuːθ ˌseɪ ə ‖ -ᵊr **~ers** əz ‖ ᵊrz
~ing ɪŋ
soot|y, Sooty ˈsʊt |i ‖ ˈsʊt̬ |i ˈsuːt̬-, ˈsʌt̬- **~ier**
i ə ‖ i ᵊr **~iest** i ɪst i əst **~iness** i nəs i nɪs
sop sɒp ‖ sɑːp **sopped** sɒpt ‖ sɑːpt **sopping**
ˈsɒp ɪŋ ‖ ˈsɑːp ɪŋ **sops** sɒps ‖ sɑːps
Soper ˈsəʊp ə ‖ ˈsoʊp ᵊr
Sophia səʊ ˈfaɪ ə -ˈfiː ə ‖ soʊ ˈfiː ə sə-
Sophie ˈsəʊf i ‖ ˈsoʊf i
sophism ˈsɒf ˌɪz əm ‖ ˈsɑːf-
sophist ˈsɒf ɪst §-əst ‖ ˈsɑːf əst **~s** s
sophister ˈsɒf ɪst ə §-əst- ‖ ˈsɑːf əst ᵊr **~s** z
sophistic sə ˈfɪst ɪk sɒ- ‖ sɑː- **~al** ᵊl **~ally** ᵊl i
sophisti|cate *v* sə ˈfɪst ɪ ˌkeɪt §-ə keɪt **~cated**
keɪt ɪd -əd ‖ keɪt̬ əd **~cates** keɪts **~cating**
keɪt ɪŋ ‖ keɪt̬ ɪŋ
sophisticate *n* sə ˈfɪst ɪ keɪt §-ə-; -ɪk ət, §-ək-,
-ɪt **~s** s
sophistication sə ˌfɪst ɪ ˈkeɪʃ ᵊn §-ə-
sophis|try ˈsɒf ɪs |tri -əs- ‖ ˈsɑːf- **~tries** triz
Sophoclean ˌsɒf ə ˈkliː ən ‖ ˌsɑːf-
Sophocles ˈsɒf ə kliːz ‖ ˈsɑːf-
sophomore ˈsɒf ə mɔː ‖ ˈsɑːf ə mɔːr -moʊr;
ˈsɑːf mɔːr, -moʊr **~s** z
sophomoric ˌsɒf ə ˈmɔːr ɪk ◄ ‖ ˌsɑːf-
Sophronia səʊ ˈfrəʊn i ə ‖ sə ˈfroʊn-
-sophy *stress-imposing* səf i — **philosophy**
fɪ ˈlɒs əf i ‖ -ˈlɑːs-
Sophy ˈsəʊf i ‖ ˈsoʊf i
soporific ˌsɒp ə ˈrɪf ɪk ◄ ˌsəʊp- ‖ ˌsɑːp- ˌsoʊp-
~s s
sopping ˈsɒp ɪŋ ‖ ˈsɑːp ɪŋ
ˌsopping ˈwet◄
sopp|y ˈsɒp |i ‖ ˈsɑːp |i **~ier** i ə ‖ i ᵊr **~iest**
i ɪst i əst **~ily** ɪ li əl i **~iness** i nəs i nɪs
sopranino ˌsɒp rə ˈniːn əʊ ‖ ˌsoʊp rə ˈniːn oʊ
~s z
sopran|o sə ˈprɑːn |əʊ ‖ -ˈpræn |oʊ -ˈprɑːn- **~i**
-iː **~os** əʊz ‖ oʊz
Sopwith ˈsɒp wɪθ ‖ ˈsɑːp-
Soraya sə ˈraɪ ə

sorb, Sorb sɔːb ‖ sɔːrb **sorbs, Sorbs** sɔːbz ‖ sɔːrbz

sorbet 'sɔːb eɪ -ət, -ɪt ‖ 'sɔːrb ət sɔːr 'beɪ **sorbets** 'sɔːb eɪz -əts, -ɪts ‖ 'sɔːrb əts sɔːr 'beɪz

Sorbian 'sɔːb i ən ‖ 'sɔːrb- **~s** z

sorbic 'sɔːb ɪk ‖ 'sɔːrb-

sorbitol 'sɔːb ɪ tɒl -ə- ‖ 'sɔːrb ə tɔːl -taːl, -toʊl

sorbo, Sorbo *tdmk* 'sɔːb əʊ ‖ 'sɔːrb oʊ

Sorbonne ₍ᵢ₎sɔː 'bɒn ‖ sɔːr 'bʌn -'baːn —*Fr* [sɔʁ bɔn]

sorbose 'sɔːb əʊz -əʊs ‖ 'sɔːrb oʊs

sorcerer 'sɔːs ər ə ‖ 'sɔːrs ᵊr ər **~s** z

sorceress 'sɔːs ə res -ər əs, ɪs, ˌsɔːs ə 'res ‖ 'sɔːrs ᵊr əs **~es** ɪz əz

sorcer|y 'sɔːs ər |i ‖ 'sɔːrs- **~ies** iz

sordid 'sɔːd ɪd §-əd ‖ 'sɔːrd əd **~ly** li **~ness** nəs nɪs

sordin|o sɔː 'diːn| əʊ ‖ sɔːr 'diːn|oʊ **~i** iː

sore sɔː ‖ sɔːr soʊr (= *soar*) **sorer** 'sɔːr ə ‖ 'sɔːr ᵊr 'soʊr- **sores** sɔːz ‖ sɔːrz soʊrz **sorest** 'sɔːr ɪst -əst ‖ 'soʊr- ˌsore 'throat

sorehead 'sɔː hed ‖ 'sɔːr- 'soʊr- **~s** z

sore|ly 'sɔː |li ‖ 'sɔːr- 'soʊr- **~ness** nəs nɪs

Sorensen 'sɒr ən sən ‖ 'sɔːr- 'saːr-

sorghum 'sɔːg əm ‖ 'sɔːrg əm

sorites sɒ 'raɪt iːz sə- ‖ soʊ-

Soroptimist, s~ sə 'rɒpt ɪm ɪst -əm-, §-əst ‖ -'raːpt- **~s** s

sororit|y sə 'rɒr ət |i sɒ-, -ɪt i ‖ -'rɔːr ət |i -'raːr- **~ies** iz

Soros 'sɔːr ɒs 'sɒr-, 'ʃɒr-, -ɒʃ, -əs, -əʃ ‖ **-aːs** -oʊs

soros|is sə 'rəʊs| ɪs §-əs ‖ -'roʊs|- **~es** iːz

sorrel 'sɒr əl ‖ 'sɔːr əl 'saːr- **~s** z

Sorrel, Sorrell (i) 'sɒr əl ‖ 'sɔːr əl 'saːr-, (ii) sə 'rel

Sorrento sə 'rent əʊ ‖ -oʊ —*It* [sor 'rɛn to]

sorri|ly 'sɒr |əl i -ɪ li ‖ 'sɔːr- 'saːr- **~iness** i nəs i nɪs

sorrow 'sɒr əʊ ‖ 'sɔːr oʊ 'saːr- **~ed** d **~ing/ly** ɪŋ /li **~s** z

sorrowful 'sɒr əʊ fᵊl -fʊl ‖ 'sɔːr ə- 'saːr-, -oʊ- **~ly** ᵢ **~ness** nəs nɪs

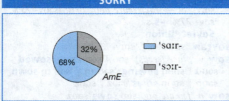

SORRY

32% | 68% | □ 'saːr- □ 'sɔːr- | *AmE*

sorr|y 'sɒr |i ‖ 'saːr |i 'sɔːr- — *Preference poll, AmE:* 'saːr- 68%, 'sɔːr- 32%. **~ier** i ə ‖ i ᵊr **~iest** i ɪst i əst

sort sɔːt ‖ sɔːrt **sorted** 'sɔːt ɪd -əd ‖ 'sɔːrt̬ əd **sorting** 'sɔːt ɪŋ ‖ 'sɔːrt̬ ɪŋ **sorts** sɔːts ‖ sɔːrts

sorta 'sɔːt ə ‖ 'sɔːrt̬ ə

sortal 'sɔːt ᵊl ‖ 'sɔːrt̬ ᵊl **~s** z

sorter 'sɔːt ə ‖ 'sɔːrt̬ ᵊr **~s** z

sortie 'sɔːt i -iː ‖ 'sɔːrt̬ i sɔːr 'tiː **~s** z

sortilege 'sɔːt ɪl ɪdʒ -əl- ‖ 'sɔːrt̬ ᵊl-

sort-out 'sɔːt aʊt ‖ 'sɔːrt̬- **~s** s

sorus 'sɔːr əs ‖ 'soʊr-

SOS ˌes əʊ 'es ‖ -oʊ- **~s, ~'s** ɪz əz

Soskice 'sɒsk ɪs §-əs ‖ 'saːsk-

so-so 'səʊ səʊ ‖ 'soʊ soʊ

sostenut|o ˌsɒst ə 'nuːt |əʊ -ɪ-, -'njuːt- ‖ ˌsaːst ə 'nuːt |oʊ ˌsoʊst- **-i** iː **~os** əʊz ‖ oʊz

sot sɒt ‖ saːt **sots** sɒts ‖ saːts

soteriology səʊ ˌtɪər i 'ɒl ədʒ i sɒ- ‖ soʊ ˌtɪr i 'aːl-

Sotheby 'sʌð ə bi **~'s** z

Sothic 'səʊθ ɪk 'sɒθ- ‖ 'soʊθ ɪk 'saːθ-

Sotho 'suːt uː 'səʊt əʊ ‖ 'soʊt oʊ **~s** z

sottish 'sɒt ɪʃ ‖ 'saːt̬ ɪʃ **~ly** li **~ness** nəs nɪs

sotto voce ˌsɒt əʊ 'vəʊtʃ i ‖ ˌsaːt̬ oʊ 'voʊtʃ i —*It* [ˌsot to 'vo: tʃe]

sou suː **sous** suːz

soubise su 'biːz

soubrette su 'bret **~s** s

soubriquet 'suːb rɪ keɪ -rə-, ˌ·ˈ·

souchong ˌsuː 'tʃɒŋ ◂ -'ʃɒŋ ‖ -'tʃaːŋ ˌsoʊ-, -'ʃaːŋ, '··

souffle '*egg dish*', **soufflé** 'suːf leɪ ‖ su 'fleɪ **~s** z

souffle '*blowing sound*' 'suːf ᵊl **~s** z

Soufriere, Soufrière su 'frɪə 'suːf ri eə ‖ -'frɪᵊr

sough '*sigh, murmur*' saʊ sʌf **soughed** saʊd sʌft **soughing** 'saʊ ɪŋ 'sʌf- **soughs** saʊz sʌfs

sought sɔːt ‖ saːt

sought-after 'sɔːt ˌɑːft ə §-ˌæft- ‖ 'sɔːt̬ ˌæft ᵊr 'saːt̬-

souk suːk **souks** suːks

soul, Soul səʊl →sɒʊl ‖ soʊl (= *sole*) **souls** səʊlz →sɒʊlz ‖ soʊlz 'soul ˌbrother; 'soul mate; 'soul ˌmusic; 'soul ˌsister

Soulbury 'səʊl bər i →'sɒʊl- ‖ 'soʊl ˌber i

Soulby 'səʊl bi →'sɒʊl- ‖ 'soʊl bi

soul-destroying 'səʊl dɪ ˌstrɔɪ ɪŋ də-, §-diː- ‖ 'soʊl-

soulful 'səʊl fᵊl →'sɒʊl-, -fʊl ‖ 'soʊl- **~ly** ᵢ **~ness** nəs nɪs

soulless 'səʊl ləs →'sɒʊl-, -lɪs ‖ 'soʊl- **~ly** li **~ness** nəs nɪs

soul-searching 'səʊl ˌsɜːtʃ ɪŋ →'sɒʊl- ‖ 'soʊl ˌsɜːtʃ ɪŋ

sound saʊnd **sounded** 'saʊnd ɪd -əd **sounding/s** 'saʊnd ɪŋ/z **sounds** saʊndz 'sound ˌbarrier; 'sound bite; 'sounding board; 'sound ˌsystem; 'sound wave

soundboard 'saʊnd bɔːd →'saʊm- ‖ -bɔːrd -boʊrd **~s** z

soundless 'saʊnd ləs -lɪs **~ly** li

soundly 'saʊnd li

soundness 'saʊnd nəs -nɪs

soundproof 'saʊnd pruːf →'saʊm-, §-prʊf **~ed** t **~ing** ɪŋ **~s** s

soundsmith 'saʊnd smɪθ **~s** s

soundstage 'saʊnd steɪdʒ **~s** ɪz əz

soundtrack 'saʊnd træk **~s** s

Souness 'suːn əs -ɪs

S

soup suːp soups suːps
 'soup ˌkitchen; 'soup spoon
soupcon, soupçon 'suːps ɒn -ɒ̃ ‖ -ɑːn
 suːp 'soʊn —Fr [sup sɔ̃] ~s z
souped-up ˌsuːpt 'ʌp ◂
soupy 'suːp i soupier 'suːp i ə ‖ ər soupiest
 'suːp i ɪst əst
sour 'saʊ ə ‖ 'saʊ ʳr soured 'saʊ əd ‖ 'saʊ ʳrd
 sourer 'saʊ ər ə ‖ 'saʊ ʳr ʳr sourest
 'saʊ ər ɪst -əst ‖ 'saʊ ʳr əst souring
 'saʊ ər ɪŋ ‖ 'saʊ ʳr ɪŋ sours 'saʊ əz ‖ 'saʊ ʳrz
 ˌsour 'cream; ˌsour 'grapes
source sɔːs ‖ sɔːrs soʊrs sourced sɔːst ‖ sɔːrst
 soʊrst sources 'sɔːs ɪz -əz ‖ 'sɔːrs əz 'soʊrs-
 sourcing 'sɔːs ɪŋ ‖ 'sɔːrs ɪŋ 'soʊrs-
sourceless 'sɔːs ləs -lɪs ‖ 'sɔːrs- 'soʊrs-
sourdine ˌsʊə 'diːn ‖ sʊr- ~s z
sourdough 'saʊ ə dəʊ ‖ 'saʊ ʳr doʊ ~s z
sour-faced ˌsaʊ ə 'feɪst ◂ '·· ‖ ˌsaʊ ʳr-
sour|ly 'saʊ ə |li ‖ 'saʊ ʳr |li ~ness nəs nɪs
sourpuss 'saʊ ə pʊs ‖ 'saʊ ʳr pʊs ~es ɪz əz
soursop 'saʊ ə sɒp ‖ 'saʊ ʳr sɑːp ~s s
Sousa 'suːz ə
sousaphone 'suːz ə fəʊn ‖ -foʊn ~s z
sous-chef 'suː ʃef ~s s
souse saʊs soused saʊst souses 'saʊs ɪz -əz
 sousing 'saʊs ɪŋ
Sousse suːs
soutach|e su 'tæʃ ~es ɪz əz
soutane su 'tɑːn -'tæn ~s z
Soutar, Souter 'suːt ə ‖ 'suːt̬ ʳr
south, South saʊθ
 ˌSouth 'Africa; ˌSouth A'merica; ˌSouth
 Au'stralia; ˌSouth ˌCaro'lina; ˌSouth
 Da'kota; ˌSouth Gla'morgan; ˌSouth
 'Pole; ˌSouth Sea 'Bubble; ˌSouth
 'Yorkshire
Southall family name 'sʌð ɔːl -ᵊl ‖ -ɑːl
Southall place in London 'saʊθ ɔːl 'saʊð- ‖ -ɑːl
Southam 'saʊð əm
Southampton ˌsaʊθ 'hæmpt ən saʊ 'θæmpt-,
 sə-; sə 'ðæmpt-
Southborough 'saʊθ bər ə ‖ -ˌbɜː oʊ
southbound 'saʊθ baʊnd
Southcott 'saʊθ kɒt -kət ‖ -kɑːt
Southdown 'saʊθ daʊn
southeast, S~ ˌsaʊθ 'iːst ◂
 ˌSoutheast 'Asia
southeaster ˌsaʊθ 'iːst ə ‖ -ʳr ~s z
southeaster|ly ˌsaʊθ 'iːst ə |li -ᵊl i ‖ -ʳr |li
 ~lies liz
southeastern ˌsaʊθ 'iːst ən ‖ -ʳrn
southeastward ˌsaʊθ 'iːst wəd ‖ -wʳrd ~s z
Southend ˌsaʊθ 'end
 ˌSouthend-on-'Sea
souther|ly 'sʌð ə |li ‖ -ʳr- (!) ~lies liz
southern, S~ 'sʌð ən ‖ -ʳrn (!)
 ˌSouthern 'Cross; ˌsouthern 'lights
Southerndown 'sʌð ᵊn daʊn ‖ -ʳrn-
southerner, S~ 'sʌð ᵊn ə ‖ -ʳrn ər -ᵊn ~s z
southernmost 'sʌð ᵊn məʊst →-ᵊm- ‖ -ʳrn moʊst
southernwood 'sʌð ᵊn wʊd ‖ -ʳrn-

Southey (i) 'saʊð i, (ii) 'sʌð i
Southgate 'saʊθ geɪt -gɪt
southing 'saʊð ɪŋ 'saʊθ- ~s z
southland 'saʊθ lænd
southpaw 'saʊθ pɔː ‖ -pɑː ~s z
Southport 'saʊθ pɔːt ‖ -pɔːrt -poʊrt
Southron, s~ 'sʌð rən ~s z
Southsea 'saʊθ siː
southward 'saʊθ wəd ‖ -wʳrd —also naut
 'sʌð əd ‖ -ʳrd ~s z
Southwark 'sʌð ək ‖ -ʳrk (!)
Southwell (i) 'sʌð ᵊl, (ii) 'saʊθ wəl
southwest, S~ ˌsaʊθ 'west ◂ —also naut
 ˌ(ˌ)saʊ-
southwester ˌ(ˌ)saʊθ 'west ə ‖ -ʳr —also naut
 ˌ(ˌ)saʊ- ~s z
southwester|ly ˌ(ˌ)saʊθ 'west ə |li -ᵊl i
 ‖ -ʳr |li —also naut ˌ(ˌ)saʊ- ~lies liz
southwestern, S~ ˌ(ˌ)saʊθ 'west ən ‖ -ʳrn
 —also naut ˌ(ˌ)saʊ-
southwestward ˌ(ˌ)saʊθ 'west wəd ‖ -wʳrd
 —also naut ˌ(ˌ)saʊ- ~s z
Southwick 'saʊθ wɪk —But the places in
 Northants and Hants are sometimes 'sʌð ɪk
Southwold 'saʊθ wəʊld →-wɒʊld ‖ -woʊld
Souttar, Soutter 'suːt ə ‖ 'suːt̬ ʳr
souvenir ˌsuːv ə 'nɪə ◂ '··· ‖ -'nɪʳr ~s z
souvlaki su 'vlɑːk i —ModGk [su 'vla ci] ~a
 ə ~s z
sou'wester saʊ 'west ə ‖ -ʳr ~s z
sovereign 'sɒv rɪn -rən ‖ 'sɑːv rən 'sɑːv ʳr ən
 ~s z
sovereign|ty 'sɒv rən |ti -rɪn- ‖ 'sɑːv-
 'sɑːv ʳr ən |ti ~ties tiz

SOVIET

soviet, S~ 'səʊv i ət 'sɒv-, -et ‖ 'soʊv i et
 'sɑːv-, ət — Preference poll, BrE: 'səʊv- 73%,
 'sɒv- 27%. ~s s
 ˌSoviet 'Union
sovran 'sɒv rən ‖ 'sɑːv-
sow v 'place (seeds)' səʊ ‖ soʊ (= so) sowed
 səʊd ‖ soʊd sowing 'səʊ ɪŋ ‖ 'soʊ ɪŋ sown
 səʊn ‖ soʊn sows səʊz ‖ soʊz
sow n 'female pig' saʊ sows saʊz
sowbread 'saʊ bred
sower 'səʊ ə ‖ 'soʊ ʳr ~s z
Sowerbutts 'saʊ ə bʌts ‖ 'saʊ ʳr bʌts
Sowerby (i) 'saʊ ə bi ‖ 'saʊ ʳr-, (ii) 'səʊ ə bi
 ‖ 'soʊ ʳr-
Soweto sə 'wet əʊ -'weɪt- ‖ -oʊ —Xhosa/Zulu
 [sɔ 'weː tɔ]
sown səʊn ‖ soʊn
sox sɒks ‖ sɑːks (= socks)

soy sɔɪ
  ˌsoy 'sauce, ˈ· ·
soya 'sɔɪ ə
  'soya bean
soybean 'sɔɪ biːn ~s z
Soyinka sɔɪ 'ɪŋk ə
Soyuz sɔɪ 'uːz —*Russ* [sʌ 'jus]
sozzled 'sɒz ᵊld ‖ 'saːz-
spa, Spa spɑː **spas** spɑːz
space speɪs **spaced** speɪst **spaces** 'speɪs ɪz -əz
  spacing 'speɪs ɪŋ
  'space ˌcapsule; ˌspaced 'out◂; 'space
  flight; 'space ˌheater; 'space probe;
  'space ˌshuttle; 'space ˌstation
space-age 'speɪs eɪdʒ
space-bar 'speɪs bɑː ‖ -bɑːr ~s z
spacecraft 'speɪs krɑːft §-kræft ‖ -kræft ~s s
Spacek 'speɪs ek
spacelab 'speɪs læb ~s z
space|man 'speɪs |mæn -mən ~**men** men -mən
spacer 'speɪs ə ‖ -ᵊr ~s z
spaceship 'speɪs ʃɪp →'speɪʃ- ~s s
spacesuit 'speɪs suːt -sjuːt ~s s
space-time ˌspeɪs 'taɪm
spacewalk 'speɪs wɔːk ‖ -wɑːk
space|woman 'speɪs |ˌwʊm ən ~**women**
  ˌwɪm ɪn -ən
spac|ey 'speɪs i ~**ier** i‿ə ‖ i‿ᵊr ~**iest** i‿ɪst ˌəst
spacing 'speɪs ɪŋ ~s z
spacious 'speɪʃ əs ~**ly** li ~**ness** nəs nɪs
spackle 'spæk ᵊl
spade speɪd **spades** speɪdz
spadeful 'speɪd fʊl ~s z
spadework 'speɪd wɜːk ‖ -wɜːk
spadix 'speɪd ɪks **spadices** 'speɪd ɪ siːz -ə-
spag bol ˌspæg 'bɒl ‖ -'bɑːl
spaghetti spə 'get i ‖ -'geṯ-
spahi 'spɑː hiː ~s z
Spain speɪn
spake speɪk
Spalding 'spɔːld ɪŋ ‖ 'spɑːld-
spall spɔːl ‖ spɑːl **spalled** spɔːld ‖ spɑːld
  spalling 'spɔːl ɪŋ ‖ 'spɑːl- **spalls** spɔːlz
  ‖ spɑːlz
spallation spɔː 'leɪʃ ᵊn ‖ spɑː- ~s z
spalpeen 'spæl piːn 'spælp iːn ~s z
spam, Spam *tdmk* spæm **spammed** spæmd
  spamming 'spæm ɪŋ **spams** spæmz
spamblocking 'spæm ˌblɒk ɪŋ ‖ -blɑːk-
spamdexing 'spæm deks ɪŋ
spammer 'spæm ə ‖ -ᵊr ~s z
span spæn **spanned** spænd **spanning**
  'spæn ɪŋ **spans** spænz
Spandau 'spænd aʊ —*Ger* ['ʃpan daʊ]
spandex 'spænd eks
spandrel 'spændr əl ~s z
spangl|e 'spæŋ gᵊl ~**ed** d ~**es** z ~**ing** ɪŋ
Spanglish 'spæŋ glɪʃ
Spaniard 'spæn jəd ‖ -jᵊrd ~s z
spaniel 'spæn jəl ~s z
Spanier 'spæn jeɪ -jə ‖ -jᵊr
Spanish 'spæn ɪʃ
  ˌSpanish 'Main; ˌSpanish 'onion

Spanish-American ˌspæn ɪʃ ə 'mer ɪk ən ◂ ~s
  z
spank spæŋk **spanked** spæŋkt **spanking/s**
  'spæŋk ɪŋ/z **spanks** spæŋks
spanker 'spæŋk ə ‖ -ᵊr ~s z
spanner 'spæn ə ‖ -ᵊr ~s z
spar spɑː ‖ spɑːr **sparred** spɑːd ‖ spɑːrd
  sparring 'spɑːr ɪŋ **spars** spɑːz ‖ spɑːrz
  'sparring ˌpartner
sparaxis spə 'ræks ɪs §-əs
spare speə ‖ speᵊr spæᵊr **spared** speəd
  ‖ speᵊrd spæᵊrd **spares** speəz ‖ speᵊrz spæᵊrz
  sparing 'speər ɪŋ ‖ 'sper ɪŋ 'spær-
  ˌspare 'part; ˌspare-part 'surgery; ˌspare
  'tyre
sparerib 'speə rɪb ˌ·'· ‖ 'sper- 'spær-, -əb ~s z
sparing|ly 'speər ɪŋ |li ‖ 'sper- 'spær- ~**ness**
  nəs nɪs
spark spɑːk ‖ spɑːrk **sparked** spɑːkt ‖ spɑːrkt
  sparking 'spɑːk ɪŋ ‖ 'spɑːrk ɪŋ **sparks**
  spɑːks ‖ spɑːrks
  'sparking plug, 'spark plug
Spark, Sparke spɑːk ‖ spɑːrk **Sparkes** spɑːks
  ‖ spɑːrks
sparkl|e 'spɑːk ᵊl ‖ 'spɑːrk ᵊl ~**ed** d ~**es** z ~**ing**
  ɪŋ
sparkler 'spɑːk lə ‖ 'spɑːrk lᵊr ~s z
Sparklet *tdmk* 'spɑːk lət -lɪt ‖ 'spɑːrk- ~s s
sparkling *adj* 'spɑːk lɪŋ ‖ 'spɑːrk- ~**ly** li
spark|y 'spɑːk| i ‖ 'spɑːrk| i ~**ier** i‿ə ‖ i‿ᵊr
  ~**iest** i‿ɪst i‿əst ~**iness** i nəs i nɪs
sparr... —*see* **spar**
sparrow, S~ 'spær əʊ ‖ -oʊ 'sper- ~s z
sparrowhawk 'spær əʊ hɔːk ‖ -oʊ- 'sper-,
  -hɑːk ~s s
sparse spɑːs ‖ spɑːrs **sparser** 'spɑːs ə
  ‖ 'spɑːrs ᵊr **sparsest** 'spɑːs ɪst -əst ‖ 'spɑːrs-
sparse|ly 'spɑːs |li ‖ 'spɑːrs |li ~**ness** nəs nɪs
sparsity 'spɑːs ət i -ɪt- ‖ 'spɑːrs əṯ i
Spart spɑːt ‖ spɑːrt
Sparta 'spɑːt ə ‖ 'spɑːrṯ ə
Spartacist 'spɑːt əs ɪst §-əst ‖ 'spɑːrṯ- ~s s
Spartacus 'spɑːt ək əs ‖ 'spɑːrṯ-
spartan, S~ 'spɑːt ᵊn ‖ 'spɑːrt ᵊn ~s z
Spartist 'spɑːt ɪst §-əst ‖ 'spɑːrṯ- ~s s
spasm 'spæz əm ~s z
spasmodic spæz 'mɒd ɪk ‖ -'mɑːd- ~**ally** ᵊl_i
spastic 'spæst ɪk ~**ally** ᵊl_i ~s s
spasticity spæ 'stɪs ət i -ɪt i ‖ -əṯ i
spat spæt **spats** spæts
spatchcock 'spætʃ kɒk ‖ -kɑːk ~**ed** t ~**ing** ɪŋ
  ~s s
spate speɪt **spates** speɪts
spathe speɪð **spathes** speɪðz
spathic 'spæθ ɪk
spatial 'speɪʃ ᵊl 'speɪʃ i‿əl ~**ly** i
spatiotemporal ˌspeɪʃ i‿əʊ 'temp ᵊr əl ◂
  ‖ -i‿oʊ- ~**ly** i
Spätlese 'ʃpeɪt ˌleɪz ə —*Ger* ['ʃpɛːt leːz ə,
  ˈʃpeːt-]
spatter 'spæt ə ‖ 'spæṯ ᵊr ~**ed** d **spattering**
  'spæt ᵊr ɪŋ ‖ 'spæṯ ᵊr ɪŋ ~s z
spatterdash 'spæt ə dæʃ ‖ 'spæṯ ᵊr- ~**es** ɪz əz

S

spatterdock 'spæt ə dɒk ‖ 'spæṭ ᵊr dɑːk ~s s
spatula 'spæt jʊl ə §'spætʃ əl ə ‖ 'spætʃ əl̩ ə **~s** z
spavin 'spæv ɪn -ᵊn- **~ed** d
spawn spɔːn ‖ spɑːn **spawned** spɔːnd ‖ spɑːnd **spawning** 'spɔːn ɪŋ ‖ 'spɑːn- **spawns** spɔːnz ‖ spɑːnz
spay speɪ **spayed** speɪd (= spade) **spaying** 'speɪ ɪŋ **spays** speɪz
SPE ˌes piː 'iː
Speaight speɪt
speak spiːk **speaking** 'spiːk ɪŋ **speaks** spiːks **spoke** spəʊk ‖ spoʊk **spoken** 'spəʊk ən ‖ 'spoʊk ən
   ˌspeaking 'clock; 'speaking tube
-speak spiːk — **doublespeak** 'dʌb ᵊl spiːk
speakeas|y 'spiːk ˌiːz ‖i **~ies** iz
speaker, S~ 'spiːk ə ‖ -ᵊr **~s** z
   ˌSpeaker's 'Corner
speakerphone 'spiːk ə fəʊn ‖ -ᵊr foʊn **~s** z
speakership 'spiːk ə ʃɪp ‖ -ᵊr-
-speaking ˌspiːk ɪŋ — **English-speaking** ˈɪŋ glɪʃ ˌspiːk ɪŋ
Spean 'spiːˌən
spear spɪə ‖ spɪᵊr **speared** spɪəd ‖ spɪᵊrd **spearing** 'spɪər ɪŋ ‖ 'spɪr ɪŋ **spears** spɪəz ‖ spɪᵊrz
spearhead 'spɪə hed ‖ 'spɪr- **~ed** ɪd əd **~ing** ɪŋ **~s** z
spear|man, S~ 'spɪə |mən ‖ 'spɪr- **~men** mən men
spearmint 'spɪə mɪnt ‖ 'spɪr-
Spears spɪəz ‖ spɪᵊrz
spearwort 'spɪə wɜːt §-wɔːt ‖ 'spɪr wɜːt -wɔːrt **~s** s
spec spek (= speck) **specs** speks
special 'speʃ ᵊl **~s** z
   'Special Branch; ˌspecial deˈlivery; ˌspecial 'drawing rights; ˌspecial 'licence; ˌspecial 'pleading; 'special school
specialis... —see **specializ...**
specialism 'speʃ ᵊl ˌɪz əm -ə ˌlɪz- **~s** z
specialist 'speʃ ᵊl ɪst §-əst **~s** s
specialit|y ˌspeʃ i 'æl ət ‖i -ɪt i ‖ -əṭ ‖i **~ies** iz
specialization ˌspeʃ əl ˌaɪ 'zeɪʃ ᵊn -ᵊl ɪ- ‖ -əl ə- **~s** z
specializ|e 'speʃ ə laɪz -ᵊl aɪz **~ed** d **~es** ɪz əz **~ing** ɪŋ
specially 'speʃ ᵊl̩ i
special|ty 'speʃ ᵊl |ti **~ties** tiz
speciation ˌspiːs i 'eɪʃ ᵊn ˌspiːʃ-
specie 'spiːʃ i -iː
species 'spiːʃ iːz 'spiːs-, -ɪz —Some speakers pronounce the sing. with -ɪz, the pl with -iːz
speciesism 'spiːʃ iːz ˌɪz əm 'spiːs-, '-ɪz-
specifiable 'spes ə faɪ ˌəb ᵊl '·ɪ-, ˌ·ᵊ'···
specific spə 'sɪf ɪk spɪ- **~ally** ᵊl̩ i **~s** s
   speˌcific 'gravity
specification ˌspes əf ɪ 'keɪʃ ᵊn ˌ·ɪf-, §-ə'·- **~s** z
specificity ˌspes ə 'fɪs ət i ˌ·ɪ-, -ɪt i ‖ -əṭ i
speci|fy 'spes ə |faɪ -ɪ- **~fied** faɪd **~fier/s** faɪ ˌə/z ‖ faɪ ˌᵊr/z **~fies** faɪz **~fying** faɪ ɪŋ
specimen 'spes ə mɪn -ɪ-, -mən **~s** z

specious 'spiːʃ əs **~ly** li **~ness** nəs nɪs
speck spek **specked** spekt **specks** speks
speckl|e 'spek ᵊl **~ed** d **~es** z **~ing** ˌɪŋ
speckless 'spek ləs -lɪs **~ly** li **~ness** nəs nɪs
specs speks
spectacle 'spekt ək ᵊl -ɪk- **~d** d **~s** z
spectacular spek 'tæk jʊl ə -jəl ə ‖ -jəl ᵊr **~ly** li **~s** z
spect|ate spek 't|eɪt 'spekt |eɪt ‖ 'spekt |eɪt **~ated** eɪt ɪd -əd ‖ eɪṭ əd **~ates** eɪts **~ating** eɪt ɪŋ ‖ eɪṭ ɪŋ

spectator, S~ spek 'teɪt ə 'spekt eɪt ə ‖ 'spekt eɪt ᵊr — Preference poll, BrE: ·'·· 91%, '··· 9%. **~s** z
specter 'spekt ə ‖ -ᵊr **~s** z
Spector 'spekt ə ‖ -ᵊr
spectra 'spek trə
spectral 'spek trəl **~ly** i
spectre 'spekt ə ‖ -ᵊr **~s** z
spectro- comb. form
   with stress-neutral suffix ˌspek trəʊ ‖ ˌspek troʊ — **spectrophotometer** ˌspek trəʊ fəʊ 'tɒm ɪt ə -ət ə ‖ -troʊ fə 'tɑːm əṭ ᵊr
   with stress-imposing suffix spek 'trɒ+ ‖ spek 'trɑː+ — **spectrometer** spek 'trɒm ɪt ə -ət ə ‖ -'trɑːm əṭ ᵊr
spectrogram 'spek trəʊ græm ‖ -trə- **~s** z
spectrograph 'spek trəʊ grɑːf -græf ‖ -trə græf **~s** s
spectrographic ˌspek trəʊ 'græf ɪk ◀ ‖ -trə- **~ally** ᵊl̩ i
spectrography spek 'trɒg rəf i ‖ -'trɑːg-
spectroscape 'spek trəʊ skeɪp ‖ -trə- **~s** s
spectroscope 'spek trə skəʊp ‖ -trə skoʊp **~s** s
spectroscopic ˌspek trə 'skɒp ɪk ◀ ‖ -'skɑːp- **~ally** ᵊl̩ i
spectroscopy spek 'trɒsk əp i ‖ -'trɑːsk-
spec|trum 'spek |trəm **~tra** trə
specu|late 'spek ju |leɪt -jə- ‖ -jə- **~lated** leɪt ɪd -əd ‖ leɪṭ əd **~lates** leɪts **~lating** leɪt ɪŋ ‖ leɪṭ ɪŋ
speculation ˌspek ju 'leɪʃ ᵊn -jə- ‖ -jə- **~s** z
speculative 'spek jʊl ət ɪv '·jəl-, -ju leɪt-, -jə leɪt- ‖ -jə leɪṭ- -jə ləṭ- **~ly** li **~ness** nəs nɪs
speculator 'spek ju leɪt ə '·jə- ‖ -jə leɪṭ ᵊr **~s** z
specul|um 'spek jʊl |əm -jəl- ‖ -jəl- **~a** ə **~ums** əmz
sped sped
speech spiːtʃ **speeches** 'spiːtʃ ɪz -əz
   'speech comˌmunity; 'speech day; 'speech deˌfect, '· ˌ·'·; ˌspeech paˈthology;

S

Spelling pronunciation

1 A **spelling pronunciation** of a word is a pronunciation that, unlike the traditional pronunciation, corresponds closely to the spelling.

2 Examples of spelling pronunciations often heard from native speakers of English include **ate** eɪt (rathen than et), **envelope** 'en və ləʊp ‖ -loʊp (rather than 'ɒn- ‖ 'ɑːn-), and **synod** 'sɪn ɒd ‖ -ɑːd (rather than -əd – compare **method**). People whose first encounter with the word **awry** is as a written form sometimes fail to recognize its analysis as prefix **a-** plus stem **wry**, and infer a spelling pronunciation 'ɔːr i rather than the proper ə 'raɪ.

3 Learners of EFL should avoid using spelling pronunciations that native speakers do not use. Do not, for example, use a strong vowel ɔː in the second syllable of **effort** 'ef ət ‖ -ᵊrt, **information** ˌɪnf ə 'meɪʃ ᵊn ‖ -ᵊr-, **Oxford** 'ɒks fəd ‖ 'ɑːks fᵊrd. Do not use ɑː in the first and last syllables of **particular** pə 'tɪk jʊl ə ‖ pᵊr 'tɪk jəl ᵊr. Do not pronounce a b in **climb** klaɪm or **debt** det.

4 British place-names are especially difficult. Spelling pronunciations of **Gloucester**, **Southwark** and **Harwich** sound absurd and would possibly not be understood.

ˌspeech 'synthesis, ˌ· ˌ·· ·; ˌspeech
'synthesizer, ˌ· ˌ· · · ·; ˌspeech ˌtherapist,
ˌ·ˈ· ··; ˌspeech 'therapy, ˌ· ˌ· ··
speechification ˌspiːtʃ ɪf ɪ 'keɪʃ ᵊn §ˌ-əf-, §-ə'--
speechi|fy 'spiːtʃ ɪ |faɪ §-ə- ~fied faɪd ~fier/s
  faɪ ə/z ‖ faɪ ᵊr/z ~fies faɪz ~fying faɪ ɪŋ
speechless 'spiːtʃ ləs -lɪs ~ly li ~ness nəs nɪs
speechwriter 'spiːtʃ ˌraɪt ə ‖ -ˌraɪt ᵊr ~s z
speed spiːd sped sped speeded 'spiːd ɪd -əd
  speeding 'spiːd ɪŋ speeds spiːdz
  'speed ˌlimit; 'speed ˌmerchant; 'speed
  trap
speedball 'spiːd bɔːl ‖ -bɑːl ~s z
speedboat 'spiːd bəʊt →'spiːb- ‖ -boʊt ~s s
speedo 'spiːd əʊ ‖ -oʊ ~s z
speedometer spɪ 'dɒm ɪt ə ₍ᵢ₎spiːd 'ɒm-, -ət ə
  ‖ -'dɑːm ət ᵊr ~s z
speedster 'spiːd stə ‖ -stᵊr ~s z
speed-up 'spiːd ʌp ~s s
speedway 'spiːd weɪ ~s z
speedwell 'spiːd wel ~s z
Speedwriting tdmk 'spiːd ˌraɪt ɪŋ ‖ -ˌraɪt̬-
speed|y 'spiːd |i ~ier i ə ‖ i ᵊr ~iest i ɪst i əst
  ~ily ɪ li əl i ~iness i nəs i nɪs
Speenhamland 'spiːn əm lænd
Speight speɪt
Speir spɪə ‖ spɪᵊr
speiss spaɪs (= spice)
Speke spiːk
spelae... —see spele...
speleological ˌspiːl i ə 'lɒdʒ ɪk ᵊl ◂ ˌspel-
  ‖ -'lɑːdʒ- ~ly ˌi

speleologist ˌspiːl i 'ɒl ədʒ ɪst ˌspel-, §-əst
  ‖ -'ɑːl- ~s s
speleology ˌspiːl i 'ɒl ədʒ i ˌspel- ‖ -'ɑːl-
spell spel spelled speld spelling/s 'spel ɪŋ/z
  spells spelz spelt spelt
  'spelling bee; 'spelling pronunciˌation,
  ˌ· · ˌ··'··
spellbind 'spel baɪnd ~er/s ə/z ‖ ᵊr/z ~ing ɪŋ
  ~s z spellbound 'spel baʊnd
spellcheck 'spel tʃek ~ed t ~er/s ə/z ‖ -ᵊr/z
  ~ing ɪŋ ~s s
speller, S~ 'spel ə ‖ -ᵊr ~s z
Spellman 'spel mən
spelt spelt
spelter 'spelt ə ‖ -ᵊr
spelunk spɪ 'lʌŋk spə-, spiː- ~ed t ~er/s ə/z
  ‖ ᵊr/z ~ing ɪŋ ~s s
Spen spen
Spenborough 'spen bər ə →'spem- ‖ -ˌbɜː oʊ
Spence spenᵗs
Spencer, s~ 'spenᵗs ə ‖ -ᵊr ~s z
Spencerian spen 'sɪər i ən ‖ -'sɪr- ~s z
spend spend spending 'spend ɪŋ spends
  spendz spent spent
spendaholic ˌspend ə 'hɒl ɪk ◂ ‖ -'hɔːl- -'hɑːl-
  ~s s
spender, S~ 'spend ə ‖ -ᵊr ~s z
spending money
  'spending ˌmoney
spendthrift 'spend θrɪft ~s s
Spengler 'speŋ lə -glə ‖ -glᵊr —Ger ['ʃpɛŋ lɐ]

S

Spennymoor 'spen i mɔː -muə ‖ -mɔːr -muʊr,
-mʊr
Spens spenz
Spenser 'spenˢs ə ‖ -ᵊr
Spenserian spen 'sɪər i‿ən ‖ -'sɪr- -'ser-
spent spent
-sperm spɜːm ‖ spɜ˞ːm — **gymnosperm**
    'dʒɪm nəʊ spɜːm ‖ -nə spɜ˞ːm
sperm spɜːm ‖ spɜ˞ːm **sperms** spɜːmz ‖ spɜ˞ːmz
    'sperm bank; 'sperm count; 'sperm oil;
    'sperm whale
spermaceti ˌspɜːm ə 'set i -'siːt i
    ‖ ˌspɜ˞ːm ə 'seṱ i -'siːṱ i
spermatic spɜː 'mæt ɪk ‖ spɜ˞ː 'mæṱ ɪk
spermato- comb. form
    with stress-neutral suffix |spɜːm ət əʊ
    spɜː |mæt- ‖ spɜ˞ː |mæṱ ə — **spermatocyte**
    'spɜːm ət əʊ saɪt spɜː 'mæt- ‖ spɜ˞ː 'mæṱ ə-
    with stress-imposing suffix ˌspɜːm ə 'tɒ +
    ‖ ˌspɜ˞ːm ə 'tɑː + — **spermatolysis**
    ˌspɜːm ə 'tɒl əs ɪs -ɪs -əs, §-əs ‖ ˌspɜ˞ːm ə 'tɑːl-
spermatozo|on ˌspɜːm ət ə 'zəʊ |ɒn -ən
    ‖ ˌspɜ˞ːm əṱ ə 'zoʊ |ən spɜː ˌmæṱ-, -ɑːn ~**a** ə
    ~**al** əl ~**an** ən ~**ic** ɪk
spermicidal ˌspɜːm ɪ 'saɪd ᵊl ◂ -ˌə- ‖ ˌspɜ˞ːm-
spermicide 'spɜːm ɪ saɪd -ə saɪd ‖ 'spɜ˞ːm- ~**s** z
Sperry 'sper i
spew spjuː **spewed** spjuːd **spewing** 'spjuː ɪŋ
    spews spjuːz
Spey speɪ
sphagnum 'sfæg nəm
sphalerite 'sfæl ə raɪt 'sfeɪl-
sphene sfiːn
sphenoid 'sfiːn ɔɪd ~**s** z
sphere sfɪə ‖ sfɪᵊr **spheres** sfɪəz ‖ sfɪᵊrz
-sphere sfɪə ‖ sfɪr — **biosphere** 'baɪ əʊ sfɪə
    ‖ -ə sfɪr
-spheric 'sfer ɪk 'sfɪər ɪk ‖ 'sfɪr ɪk —
    biospheric ˌbaɪ əʊ 'sfer ɪk ◂ -'sfɪər ɪk ‖ -ə-
    -'sfɪr ɪk
spherical 'sfer ɪk ᵊl ‖ 'sfɪr- ~**ly** ‿i ~**ness** nəs nɪs
spheroid 'sfɪər ɔɪd ‖ 'sfɪr- 'sfer- ~**s** z
spheroidal sfɪə 'rɔɪd ᵊl ‖ sfɪ- sfe- ~**ly** i
sphincter 'sfɪŋkt ə ‖ -ᵊr ~**s** z
sphinx, S~ sfɪŋks **sphinxes, Sphinx's**
    'sfɪŋks ɪz -əz
sphragistic sfrə 'dʒɪst ɪk ~**s** s
sphygmo- comb. form
    with stress-neutral suffix |sfɪg məʊ ‖ -mə —
    sphygmogram 'sfɪg məʊ græm ‖ -mə-
    with stress-imposing suffix sfɪg 'mɒ +
    ‖ -'mɑː + — **sphygmography** sfɪg 'mɒg rəf i
    ‖ -'mɑːg-
sphygmomanometer ˌsfɪg məʊ mə 'nɒm ɪt ə
    -ət ə; △ˌsfɪg mə 'nɒm-
    ‖ -moʊ mə 'nɑːm əṱ ᵊr ~**s** z
spic spɪk **spics** spɪks
spica, Spica 'spaɪk ə 'spiːk-
spic-and-span ˌspɪk ən 'spæn ◂ →-ŋ-
spiccato spɪ 'kɑːt əʊ ‖ -'kɑːṱ oʊ —It
    [spik 'ka: to]
spice spaɪs **spiced** spaɪst **spices** 'spaɪs ɪz -əz
    spicing 'spaɪs ɪŋ

spicebush 'spaɪs bʊʃ ~**es** ɪz əz
spick-and-span ˌspɪk ən 'spæn ◂ →-ŋ-
spicule 'spɪk juːl 'spaɪk- ~**s** z
spic|y 'spaɪs |i ~**ier** i‿ə ‖ i‿ᵊr ~**iest** i‿ɪst i‿əst
    ~**ily** ɪ li əl i ~**iness** i nəs i nɪs
spider 'spaɪd ə ‖ -ᵊr ~**s** z
    'spider plant
spider|man, S~ 'spaɪd ə |mæn ‖ -ᵊr- ~**men**
    men
spiderweb 'spaɪd ə web ‖ -ᵊr-
    ~**s** z
spiderwort 'spaɪd ə wɜːt -wɔːt ‖ -ᵊr wɜ˞ːt ~**s** s
spidery 'spaɪd ər i
spie... —see **spy**
spiegeleisen 'spiːg ᵊl aɪz ᵊn
Spiegl 'spiːg ᵊl
spiel ʃpiːᵊl spiːᵊl **spiels** ʃpiːᵊlz spiːᵊlz
Spielberg 'spiːl bɜːg ‖ -bɜ˞ːg
Spier (i) spɪə ‖ spɪᵊr, (ii) 'spaɪ ə ‖ 'spaɪ ᵊr
spiff spɪf **spiffed** spɪft **spiffing** 'spɪf ɪŋ **spiffs**
    spɪfs
spiffli|cate 'spɪf lɪ |keɪt -lə- ~**cated** keɪt ɪd -əd
    ‖ keɪṱ əd ~**cates** keɪts ~**cating** keɪt ɪŋ
    ‖ keɪṱ ɪŋ
spiff|y 'spɪf |i ~**ier** i‿ə ‖ i‿ᵊr ~**iest** i‿ɪst i‿əst
    ~**ily** ɪ li əl i ~**iness** i nəs i nɪs
spignel 'spɪg nᵊl
spigot 'spɪg ət ~**s** s
spik spɪk **spiks** spɪks
spike spaɪk **spiked** spaɪkt **spikes** spaɪks
    spiking 'spaɪk ɪŋ
spikelet 'spaɪk lət -lɪt ~**s** s
spikenard 'spaɪk nɑːd 'spaɪk ə nɑːd ‖ -nɑːrd
spik|y 'spaɪk |i ~**ier** i‿ə ‖ i‿ᵊr ~**iest** i‿ɪst i‿əst
    ~**ily** ɪ li əl i ~**iness** i nəs i nɪs
spile spaɪᵊl **spiled** spaɪᵊld **spiles** spaɪᵊlz
    spiling 'spaɪᵊl ɪŋ
spill spɪl **spilled** spɪld **spilling** 'spɪl ɪŋ **spills**
    spɪlz **spilt** spɪlt
spillag|e 'spɪl ɪdʒ ~**es** ɪz əz
Spillane spɪ 'leɪn §spə-
Spiller 'spɪl ə ‖ -ᵊr
spillikin 'spɪl ɪk ɪn §-ək-, §-ən ~**s** z
spillover 'spɪl ˌəʊv ə ‖ -ˌoʊv ᵊr ~**s** z
spillway 'spɪl weɪ ~**s** z
Spilsbury 'spɪlz bər i ‖ -ˌber i
spilt spɪlt
spin spɪn **span** spæn **spinning** 'spɪn ɪŋ **spins**
    spɪnz **spun** spʌn
    ˌspin 'bowler; 'spin ˌdoctor
spina bifida ˌspaɪn ə 'bɪf ɪd ə -ə 'baɪf-, -əd ə
spinach 'spɪn ɪdʒ -ɪtʃ ‖ -ɪtʃ
spinal 'spaɪn ᵊl ~**ly** i
    ˌspinal 'cord ‖ '· ·
spindle 'spɪnd ᵊl ~**s** z
spindleberry 'spɪnd ᵊl ˌber i
spindleshanks 'spɪnd ᵊl ʃæŋks
spindling 'spɪnd lɪŋ
spind|ly 'spɪnd |li ~**lier** li‿ə ‖ li‿ᵊr ~**liest** li‿ɪst
    li‿əst
spindrift 'spɪn drɪft
spin-|dry ˌspɪn '|draɪ '· · ~**dried** draɪd ~**dries**
    draɪz ~**drying** draɪ ɪŋ

spin-dryer ˌspɪn ˈdraɪ‿ə ˈ··· ‖ -ˈdraɪ‿ʳr ~s z
spine spaɪn spined spaɪnd spines spaɪnz
spine-chiller ˈspaɪn ˌtʃɪl ə ‖ -ʳr ~s z
spine-chilling ˈspaɪn ˌtʃɪl ɪŋ
spinel spɪ ˈnel §spə-
spineless ˈspaɪn ləs -lɪs ~ly li ~ness nəs nɪs
spinet spɪ ˈnet §spə-; ˈspɪn et, -ɪt, §-ət ‖ ˈspɪn ət
~s s
spine-tingling ˈspaɪn ˌtɪŋ gᵊl‿ɪŋ
spinifex ˈspɪn ɪ feks -ə-
Spink spɪŋk
spinnaker ˈspɪn ək ə -ɪk- ‖ -ʳr ~s z
spinner ˈspɪn ə ‖ -ʳr ~s z
spinneret ˈspɪn ə ret ˌ··ˈ· ~s s
spinney ˈspɪn i ~s z
spinning ˈspɪn ɪŋ
  ˌspinning ˈjenny, ˈ·· ˌ··; ˈspinning wheel
spin-off ˈspɪn ɒf -ɔːf ‖ -ɔːf -ɑːf ~s s
spinose ˈspaɪn əʊs spaɪ ˈnəʊs ‖ -oʊs
spinous ˈspaɪn əs
Spinoza spɪ ˈnəʊz ə §spə- ‖ -ˈnoʊz- —Dutch
  [spi ˈnoː zaː]
spinster ˈspɪn⁀st ə ‖ -ʳr ~hood hʊd ~s z
spinsterish ˈspɪn⁀st ər ɪʃ ~ness nəs nɪs
spinthariscope spɪn ˈθær ɪ skəʊp -ə- ‖ -skoʊp
  -ˈθer- ~s s
spinule ˈspaɪn juːl ˈspɪn- ~s z
spin|y ˈspaɪn |i ~ier |i ə ‖ i ʳr ~iest i ɪst i əst
  ~iness i nəs i nɪs
Spion Kop ˌspaɪ ən ˈkɒp → ˌəŋ- ‖ -ˈkɑːp
spiracle ˈspaɪ‿ʳr ək ᵊl ˈspɪr-, -ɪk- ~s s
spiraea spaɪ‿ˈrɪə -ˈriː ə
spiral ˈspaɪ‿ʳr əl ~ed, ~led d ~ing, ~ling ɪŋ ~s
  z
spiral-bound ˈspaɪ‿ʳr əl baʊnd
spirant ˈspaɪ‿ʳr ənt ~s s
spirantisation, spirantization
  ˌspaɪ‿ʳr ənt aɪ ˈzeɪʃ ᵊn -ɪˈ·- ‖ -əˈ·- ~s z
spire ˈspaɪ‿ə ‖ ˈspaɪ‿ʳr spires ˈspaɪ‿əz
  ‖ ˈspaɪ‿ʳrz
spirea spaɪ‿ˈrɪə -ˈriː ə
Spirella tdmk spaɪ‿ˈrel ə
spiril|um spaɪ‿ˈrɪl| əm ~a ə
spir|it, S~ ˈspɪr |ɪt -ət ‖ -|ət ~ited ɪt ɪd -ət-, -əd
  ‖ ət əd ~iting ɪt ɪŋ ət- ‖ ət ɪŋ ~its ɪts əts ‖ əts
  ˈspirit ˌlevel
-spirited ˈspɪr ɪt ɪd -ət-, -əd ‖ -ət̬ əd —
  public-spirited ˌpʌb lɪk ˈspɪr ɪt ɪd ◀ -ət-, -əd
  ‖ -ət̬ əd
spirited|ly ˈspɪr ɪt ɪd |li ˈ·ət-, -əd · ‖ -ət̬ əd |li
  ~ness nəs nɪs
spiritism ˈspɪr ɪt ˌɪz əm -ət- ‖ -ət̬-
spiritist ˈspɪr ɪt ɪst -ət-, §-əst ‖ -ət̬- ~s s
spiritless ˈspɪr ɪt ləs -ət-, -lɪs ~ly li ~ness nəs
  nɪs
spiritous ˈspɪr ɪt əs -ət- ‖ -ət̬-
spiritual ˈspɪr ɪtʃ u‿əl ˈ·ətʃ-; -ɪt ju‿, -ət ju‿
  ‖ ˈspɪr ɪtʃ əl ~s z
spiritualis... —see spiritualiz...
spiritualism ˈspɪr ɪtʃ u ˌlɪz əm ˈ·ətʃ-, ˈ··ə-;
  ˈ···ə‿, ··, ˈ·ɪt ju‿, ˈ·ət-
spiritualist ˈspɪr ɪtʃ ʊl ɪst ˈ·ətʃ-, -əl ·, §-əst;
  ˈ··ʊ‿əl ·, ˈ·ɪt ju‿, ˈ·ət- ~s s

spiritualistic ˌspɪr ɪtʃ u ˈlɪst ɪk ◀ ˌ·ətʃ-, ˌ··ə-;
  ˌ···ə‿·, ·, ˌ·ɪt ju‿, ˌ·ət-
spiritualit|y ˌspɪr ɪtʃ u ˈæl ət |i -ətʃ u-, -ɪt ju‿,
  -ət ju‿, -ɪt i ‖ -ət̬ |i ~ies iz
spiritualization ˌspɪr ɪtʃ ʊl aɪ ˈzeɪʃ ᵊn ˈ·ətʃ-,
  -ɪˈ··; ··u‿əl ·ˈ··, ·ˈ·ɪt ju‿, ·ˈ·ət- ‖ -əˈ·--
spiritualiz|e ˈspɪr ɪtʃ u laɪz -ətʃ u-; ˈ·ɪtʃ u‿ə‿,
  ˈ·ɪt ju‿, ˈ·ət- ~ed d ~es ɪz əz ~ing ɪŋ
spiritually ˈspɪr ɪtʃ ʊl i ˈ·ətʃ-; ˈ··u‿əl i;
  ˈ·ɪt ju‿əl i, -ət ju‿
spirituous ˈspɪr ɪtʃ u‿əs -ətʃ u‿, -ɪt ju‿, -ət ju‿
  ~ness nəs nɪs
spiritus ˈspɪr ɪt əs -ət- ‖ -ət̬-
spirochaete ˈspaɪ‿ʳr əʊ kiːt ‖ -ə- ~s s
spirograph ˈspaɪ‿ʳr əʊ grɑːf -græf ‖ -ə græf ~s
  s
spirogyra ˌspaɪ‿ʳr əʊ ˈdʒaɪ‿ʳr ə ‖ -ə-
spirt spɜːt ‖ spɜːt spirted ˈspɜːt ɪd -əd
  ‖ ˈspɜːt̬ əd spirting ˈspɜːt ɪŋ ‖ ˈspɜːt̬ ɪŋ
  spirts spɜːts ‖ spɜːts
spirula ˈspaɪ‿ʳr ʊl ə -əl ə ‖ -jəl ə
spit spɪt spat spæt spits spɪts spitted ˈspɪt ɪd
  -əd ‖ ˈspɪt̬ əd spitting ˈspɪt ɪŋ ‖ ˈspɪt̬ ɪŋ
  ˌspit and ˈpolish; ˌspitting ˈimage
Spital ˈspɪt ᵊl ‖ ˈspɪt̬ ᵊl
Spitalfields ˈspɪt ᵊl fiːᵊldz ‖ ˈspɪt̬-
spitball ˈspɪt bɔːl ‖ -bɑːl ~s z
spite spaɪt spited ˈspaɪt ɪd -əd ‖ ˈspaɪt̬ əd
  spites spaɪts spiting ˈspaɪt ɪŋ ‖ ˈspaɪt̬ ɪŋ
spiteful ˈspaɪt fᵊl -ful ~ly i ~ness nəs nɪs
spitfire, S~ ˈspɪt ˌfaɪ‿ə ‖ -ˌfaɪ‿ʳr ~s z
Spithead ˌspɪt ˈhed ◀
Spitsbergen ˈspɪts ˌbɜːg ən ˌ·ˈ·· ‖ -ˌbɜːg-
spitt... —see spit
Spittal ˈspɪt ᵊl ‖ ˈspɪt̬ ᵊl
spittle ˈspɪt ᵊl ‖ ˈspɪt̬ ᵊl
spittoon spɪ ˈtuːn §spə- ~s z
spitz, Spitz spɪts —Ger [ʃpɪts] spitzes
  ˈspɪts ɪz -əz
spiv spɪv spivs spɪvz
spivvy ˈspɪv i
splanchnic ˈsplæŋk nɪk
splash splæʃ splashed splæʃt splashes
  ˈsplæʃ ɪz -əz splashing ˈsplæʃ ɪŋ
  ˈsplash guard
splashback ˈsplæʃ bæk ~s s
splashdown ˈsplæʃ daʊn ~s z
splash|y ˈsplæʃ |i ~ier i ə ‖ i ʳr ~iest i ɪst i əst
  ~ily ɪ li əl i ~iness i nəs i nɪs
splat splæt splats splæts
splatter ˈsplæt ə ‖ ˈsplæt̬ ʳr ~ed d splattering
  ˈsplæt ʳr ɪŋ ‖ ˈsplæt̬ ər ɪŋ
splay spleɪ splayed spleɪd splaying ˈspleɪ ɪŋ
  splays spleɪz
splay|foot ˈspleɪ |fʊt ~feet fiːt
splayfooted ˌspleɪ ˈfʊt ɪd ◀ -əd ‖ -ˈfʊt̬- ~ly li
  ~ness nəs nɪs
spleen spliːn
spleenwort ˈspliːn wɜːt §-wɔːt ‖ -wɜːt -wɔːrt
Splenda tdmk ˈsplend ə
splendid ˈsplend ɪd -əd ~ly li ~ness nəs nɪs
splendiferous ₍ᵢ₎splen ˈdɪf ər əs ~ly li ~ness
  nəs nɪs

splendor, splendour 'splend ə ‖ -ᵊr ~s z
splendrous 'splendr əs ~ly li
splenetic splə 'net ɪk spli- ‖ -'neţ ɪk ~ally ᵊl_i
splenic 'splen ɪk 'spliːn-
spleno- *comb. form*
  with stress-neutral suffix |spliːn əʊ ‖ -oʊ
  — **splenomegaly** ˌspliːn əʊ 'meg əl i ‖ ˌ-oʊ-
  with stress-imposing suffix spliː 'nɒ+
  ‖ -'nɑː+ — **splenography** spliː 'nɒg rəf i
  ‖ -'nɑːg-
splice splaɪs **spliced** splaɪst **splices** 'splaɪs ɪz
  -əz **splicing** 'splaɪs ɪŋ
splicer 'splaɪs ə ‖ -ᵊr ~s z
spliff splɪf **spliffs** splɪfs
spline splaɪn **splined** splaɪnd **splines** splaɪnz
  splining 'splaɪn ɪŋ
splint splɪnt **splinted** 'splɪnt ɪd -əd
  ‖ 'splɪnţ əd **splinting** 'splɪnt ɪŋ ‖ 'splɪnţ ɪŋ
  splints splɪnts
splinter 'splɪnt ə ‖ 'splɪnţ ᵊr ~ed d
  splintering 'splɪnt_ər ɪŋ ‖ 'splɪnţ ər ɪŋ ~s z
  'splinter group
splintery 'splɪnt ər i
split, Split splɪt **splits** splɪts **splitting**
  'splɪt ɪŋ ‖ 'splɪţ ɪŋ
  ˌsplit 'end; ˌsplit in'finitive; ˌsplit 'pea;
  ˌsplit ˌperso'nality; ˌsplit 'ring; ˌsplit
  'second
split-level ˌsplɪt 'lev ᵊl ◂
split-second ˌsplɪt 'sek ənd ◂ △-ənt
split-up 'splɪt ʌp ‖ 'splɪţ ʌp ~s s
splodge splɒdʒ ‖ splɑːdʒ **splodges** 'splɒdʒ ɪz
  -əz ‖ 'splɑːdʒ əz
splodg|y 'splɒdʒ |i i ‖ 'splɑːdʒ |i ~ier i_ə ‖ i_ᵊr
  ~iest i_ɪst i_əst ~iness i nəs i nɪs
splosh splɒʃ ‖ splɑːʃ **sploshed** splɒʃt ‖ splɑːʃt
  sploshes 'splɒʃ ɪz -əz ‖ 'splɑːʃ əz **sploshing**
  'splɒʃ ɪŋ ‖ 'splɑːʃ ɪŋ
splotch splɒtʃ ‖ splɑːtʃ **splotched** splɒtʃt
  ‖ splɑːtʃt **splotches** 'splɒtʃ ɪz -əz ‖ 'splɑːtʃ əz
splotch|y 'splɒtʃ |i i ‖ 'splɑːtʃ |i ~ier i_ə ‖ i_ᵊr
  ~iest i_ɪst i_əst ~iness i nəs i nɪs
Splott splɒt ‖ splɑːt
splurge splɜːdʒ ‖ splɝːdʒ **splurged** splɜːdʒd
  ‖ splɝːdʒd **splurges** 'splɜːdʒ ɪz -əz
  ‖ 'splɝːdʒ əz **splurging** 'splɜːdʒ ɪŋ
  ‖ 'splɝːdʒ ɪŋ
splutter 'splʌt ə ‖ 'splʌţ ᵊr ~ed d **spluttering**
  'splʌt_ər ɪŋ ‖ 'splʌţ ər ɪŋ ~s z
Spock spɒk ‖ spɑːk
Spode, spode spəʊd ‖ spoʊd
spodumene 'spɒd ju miːn §'spɒdʒ ə-
  ‖ 'spɑːdʒ ə-
Spofforth 'spɒf əθ -ɔːθ ‖ 'spɑːf ᵊrθ
Spohr spɔː ‖ spɔːr spour —*Ger* [ʃpoːɐ]
spoil spɔɪᵊl **spoiled** spɔɪᵊld **spoiling** 'spɔɪᵊl ɪŋ
  spoils spɔɪᵊlz **spoilt** spɔɪᵊlt
spoilage 'spɔɪᵊl ɪdʒ
spoiler 'spɔɪᵊl ə ‖ -ᵊr ~s z
spoilsport 'spɔɪᵊl spɔːt ‖ -spɔːrt -spourt ~s s
spoilt spɔɪᵊlt
Spokane spəʊ 'kæn ‖ spoʊ- (!)
spoke spəʊk ‖ spoʊk **spokes** spəʊks ‖ spoʊks

-**spoken** 'spəʊk ən ‖ -'spoʊk ən —
  nicely-spoken ˌnaɪs li 'spəʊk ən ◂ ‖ -'spoʊk-
spoken 'spəʊk ən ‖ 'spoʊk ən
spoken-word ˌspəʊk ən 'wɜːd ◂ ‖ -'wɝːd ◂
spokeshave 'spəʊk ʃeɪv ‖ 'spoʊk- ~s z
spokes|man 'spəʊks |mən ‖ 'spoʊks- ~men
  mən men ~people ˌpiːp ᵊl ~person/s
  ˌpɜːs ᵊn/z ‖ ˌpɝːs ᵊn/z ~woman ˌwʊm ən
  ~women ˌwɪm ɪn -ən
spoliation ˌspəʊl i 'eɪʃ ᵊn ‖ ˌspoʊl-
spondaic spɒn 'deɪ ɪk ‖ spɑːn-
spondee 'spɒnd iː ‖ 'spɑːnd iː ~s z
Spondon 'spɒnd ən ‖ 'spɑːnd ən
spondulicks, spondulix spɒn 'duːl ɪks
  -'djuːl-, →-'dʒuːl- ‖ spɑːn 'duːl-
spondylitis ˌspɒnd ɪ 'laɪt ɪs -ə-, §-əs
  ‖ ˌspɑːnd ə 'laɪţ əs
Spong spɒŋ ‖ spɑːŋ
sponge spʌndʒ **sponged** spʌndʒd **sponges**
  'spʌndʒ ɪz -əz **sponging** 'spʌndʒ ɪŋ
  'sponge bag; 'sponge cake; ˌsponge
  'pudding; ˌsponge 'rubber
sponger 'spʌndʒ ə ‖ -ᵊr ~s z
spongiform 'spʌndʒ ɪ fɔːm ‖ -fɔːrm
spong|y 'spʌndʒ |i ~ier i_ə ‖ i_ᵊr ~iest i_ɪst
  i_əst ~iness i nəs i nɪs
sponsion 'spɒnᵗʃ ᵊn ‖ 'spɑːnᵗʃ ᵊn
sponson 'spɒnᵗs ᵊn ‖ 'spɑːnᵗs ᵊn ~s z
sponsor 'spɒnᵗs ə ‖ 'spɑːnᵗs ᵊr ~ed d
  sponsoring 'spɒnᵗs ᵊr ɪŋ ‖ 'spɑːnᵗs ər ɪŋ ~s
  z ~ship ʃɪp
spontaneity ˌspɒnt ə 'neɪ ət i -'niː-, -ɪt i
  ‖ ˌspɑːnt ᵊn 'iː əţ i -'eɪ-
spontaneous ₍₎spɒn 'teɪn i_əs spən- ‖ spɑːn-
  ~ly li ~ness nəs nɪs
Spontex *tdmk* 'spɒnt eks ‖ 'spɑːnt-
spoof spuːf **spoofed** spuːft **spoofing** 'spuːf ɪŋ
  spoofs spuːfs
spook spuːk **spooked** spuːkt **spooking**
  'spuːk ɪŋ **spooks** spuːks
spook|y 'spuːk |i ~ier i_ə ‖ i_ᵊr ~iest i_ɪst i_əst
  ~ily ɪ li əl i ~iness i nəs i nɪs
spool spuːl **spooled** spuːld **spooling** 'spuːl ɪŋ
  spools spuːlz
spoon spuːn **spooned** spuːnd **spooning**
  'spuːn ɪŋ **spoons** spuːnz
spoonbill 'spuːn bɪl →'spuːm- ~s z
Spooner 'spuːn ə ‖ -ᵊr
spoonerism 'spuːn ə ˌrɪz əm ~s z
spoon|feed 'spuːn |fiːd ~fed fed ~feeding
  fiːd ɪŋ ~feeds fiːdz
spoonful 'spuːn fʊl ~s z **spoonsful**
  'spuːnz fʊl
spoor spʊə spɔː ‖ spʊᵊr spɔːr, spour **spoors**
  spʊəz spɔːz ‖ spʊᵊrz spɔːrz, spourz
Sporades 'spɒr ə diːz spə 'rɑːd iːz ‖ 'spɔːr-
sporadic spə 'ræd ɪk spɒ- ~ally ᵊl_i
sporangi|um spə 'rændʒ i_|əm ~a ə
spore spɔː ‖ spɔːr spour **spores** spɔːz ‖ spɔːrz
  spourz
spork spɔːk ‖ spɔːrk **sporks** spɔːks ‖ spɔːrks

S

sporo- *comb. form*
　with stress-neutral suffix |spɔːr əʊ |spɒr-
　‖ |spɔːr ə |spoʊr- — **sporocyst** 'spɔːr əʊ sɪst
　'spɒr- ‖ -ə- 'spoʊr-

sporogeny spɔː 'rɒdʒ ən i spə- ‖ spə 'rɑːdʒ-

sporogony spɔː 'rɒg ən i spə-, -'rɒdʒ-
　‖ spə 'rɑːg-

sporran 'spɒr ən ‖ 'spɔːr ən 'spɑːr- **~s** z

sport spɔːt ‖ spɔːrt spoʊrt **sported** 'spɔːt ɪd -əd
　‖ 'spɔːrt̬ əd 'spoʊrt- **sporting/ly** 'spɔːt ɪŋ /li
　‖ 'spɔːrt̬ ɪŋ /li 'spoʊrt- **sports** spɔːts ‖ spɔːrts
　spoʊrts
　'sports car; **'sports day**; **'sports ,jacket**

sport-fishing 'spɔːt ,fɪʃɪŋ ‖ 'spɔːrt-

sporti... —*see* **sporty**

sportive 'spɔːt ɪv ‖ 'spɔːrt̬ ɪv 'spoʊrt- **~ly** li
　~ness nəs nɪs

sportscast 'spɔːts kɑːst §-kæst ‖ 'spɔːrts kæst
　'spoʊrts- **~er/s** ə/z ‖ -ᵊr/z **~ing** ɪŋ

sports|man 'spɔːts |mən ‖ 'spɔːrts- 'spoʊrts-
　~manlike mən laɪk **~manship** mən ʃɪp
　~men mən **~person** ,pɜːs ᵊn ‖ ,pɜːs ᵊn
　~people ,piːp ᵊl

sportswear 'spɔːts weə ‖ 'spɔːrts wer
　'spoʊrts-, -wær

sports|woman 'spɔːts |,wʊm ən ‖ 'spɔːrts-
　'spoʊrts- **~women** ,wɪm ɪn -ən

sport-utility ,spɔːt ju 'tɪl ət i -ɪt i
　‖ ,spɔːrt ju 'tɪl ət̬ i ,spoʊrt-

sport|y 'spɔːt |i ‖ 'spɔːrt̬ |i 'spoʊrt- **~ier** i ə
　‖ i ᵊr **~iest** i ɪst i əst **~ily** ɪ li əl i **~iness** i nəs
　i nɪs

sporule 'spɒr uːl -juːl ‖ 'spɔːr juːl 'spoʊr- **~s** z

s'pose *nonstandard version of* **suppose** spəʊz
　‖ spoʊz **s'posing** 'spəʊz ɪŋ ‖ 'spoʊz ɪŋ

spot spɒt ‖ spɑːt **spots** spɒts ‖ spɑːts **spotted**
　'spɒt ɪd -əd ‖ 'spɑːt̬ əd **spotting** 'spɒt ɪŋ
　‖ 'spɑːt̬ ɪŋ
　,spot 'check; ‖ '· ·; **,spotted 'dick**

spot-check ,spɒt 'tʃek '· · ‖ 'spɑːt tʃek **~ed** t
　~ing ɪŋ **~s** s

spotless 'spɒt ləs -lɪs ‖ 'spɑːt- **~ly** li **~ness** nəs
　nɪs

spot|light 'spɒt |laɪt ‖ 'spɑːt- **~lighted** laɪt ɪd
　-əd ‖ laɪt̬ əd **~lighting** laɪt ɪŋ ‖ laɪt̬ ɪŋ
　~lights laɪts **~lit** lɪt

spot-on ,spɒt 'ɒn ◂ ‖ ,spɑːt̬ 'ɑːn -'ɔːn

Spotsylvania ,spɒt sɪl 'veɪn i ə ,·sᵊl- ‖ ,spɑːt-

spott... —*see* **spot**

spotter 'spɒt ə ‖ 'spɑːt̬ ᵊr **~s** z
　'spotter plane

Spottiswoode (i) 'spɒts wʊd ‖ 'spɑːts-;
　(ii) 'spɒt ɪs wʊd -ɪz-, -əs- ‖ 'spɑːt-

spott|y 'spɒt |i ‖ 'spɑːt̬ |i **~ier** i ə ‖ i ᵊr **~iest**
　i ɪst i əst **~ily** ɪ li əl i **~iness** i nəs i nɪs

spot-weld 'spɒt weld ‖ 'spɑːt- **~ed** ɪd əd **~ing**
　ɪŋ **~s** z

spousal 'spaʊz ᵊl 'spaʊs ᵊl

spouse spaʊs spaʊz **spouses** 'spaʊs ɪz 'spaʊz-,
　-əz

spout spaʊt **spouted** 'spaʊt ɪd -əd ‖ 'spaʊt̬ əd
　spouting 'spaʊt ɪŋ ‖ 'spaʊt̬ ɪŋ **spouts**
　spaʊts

sprachgefuhl, sprachgefühl, S~
　'ʃprɑːx gə ˌfjuːl 'ʃprɑːk-, -fuːl ‖ 'sprɑːk- —*Ger*
　['ʃpʁɑːx gə ˌfyːl]

sprag spræg **spragged** sprægd **spragging**
　'spræg ɪŋ **sprags** sprægz

Spragge spræg

Sprague spreɪg

sprain spreɪn **sprained** spreɪnd **spraining**
　'spreɪn ɪŋ **sprains** spreɪnz

spraint spreɪnt **spraints** spreɪnts

sprang spræŋ

sprat spræt **sprats** spræts

Sprat|ly 'spræt| li **~lies**, **~lys** liz

Spratt spræt

sprawl sprɔːl ‖ sprɑːl **sprawled** sprɔːld
　‖ sprɑːld **sprawling/ly** 'sprɔːl ɪŋ /li ‖ 'sprɑːl-
　sprawls sprɔːlz ‖ sprɑːlz

spray spreɪ **sprayed** spreɪd **spraying** 'spreɪ ɪŋ
　sprays spreɪz
　'spray gun

spraycan 'spreɪ kæn **~s** z

sprayer 'spreɪ ə ‖ -ᵊr **~s** z

spray-on 'spreɪ ɒn ‖ -ɑːn ◂ -ɔːn
　,spray-on de'odorant

spread spred **spreading** 'spred ɪŋ **spreads**
　spredz

spreadable 'spred əb ᵊl

spread-eagl|e ₍ˌ₎spred 'iːg ᵊl ‖ 'spred ˌiːg ᵊl
　(*) **~ed** d **~es** z **~ing** ɪŋ

spreader 'spred ə ‖ -ᵊr **~s** z

spreadsheet 'spred ʃiːt **~s** s

sprechgesang, S~ 'ʃprex gə ˌzæŋ 'ʃprek-,
　-,zʌŋ ‖ 'sprek- —*Ger* ['ʃpʁɛç gə ˌzaŋ]

sprechstimme, S~ 'ʃprex ˌʃtɪm ə 'ʃprek-
　‖ 'sprek ˌʃtɪm ə —*Ger* ['ʃpʁɛç ˌʃtɪm ə]

spree spriː **sprees** spriːz

sprig sprɪg **sprigged** sprɪgd **sprigging**
　'sprɪg ɪŋ **sprigs** sprɪgz

Sprigg sprɪg

spright|ly 'spraɪt |li **~lier** li ə ‖ li ᵊr **~liest**
　li ɪst li əst **~liness** li nəs -nɪs

spring, S~ sprɪŋ **sprang** spræŋ **springing**
　'sprɪŋ ɪŋ **springs** sprɪŋz **sprung** sprʌŋ
　,spring 'balance; **,spring 'chicken**; **,spring**
　'fever; **,spring 'onion**; **,spring 'roll**;
　,spring 'tide

springboard 'sprɪŋ bɔːd ‖ -bɔːrd -boʊrd **~s** z

springbok, S~ 'sprɪŋ bɒk ‖ -bɑːk **~s** s

Springburn 'sprɪŋ bɜːn ‖ -bɜːrn

spring-clean *v* ,sprɪŋ 'kliːn ◂ **~ed** d **~ing** ɪŋ
　~s z

spring-clean *n* 'sprɪŋ kliːn ,·' **~s** z

springe sprɪndʒ **springes** 'sprɪndʒ ɪz -əz

springer, S~ 'sprɪŋ ə ‖ -ᵊr **~s** z

Springfield 'sprɪŋ fiːᵊld

springlike 'sprɪŋ laɪk

spring-loaded ,sprɪŋ 'ləʊd ɪd ◂ -əd ‖ -'loʊd-

Springs sprɪŋz

Springsteen 'sprɪŋ stiːn

springtail 'sprɪŋ teɪᵊl **~s** z

springtime 'sprɪŋ taɪm

spring|y 'sprɪŋ |i **~ier** i ə ‖ i ᵊr **~iest** i ɪst i əst
　~ily ɪ li əl i **~iness** i nəs i nɪs

S

sprinkl|e 'sprɪŋk ᵊl **~ed** d **~es** z **~ing** ɪŋ
sprinkler 'sprɪŋk lə 'sprɪŋk ᵊl ə || -l ᵊr **~s** z
sprinkling n 'sprɪŋk lɪŋ **~s** z
sprint sprɪnt **sprinted** 'sprɪnt ɪd -əd
|| 'sprɪnt̬ əd **sprinting** 'sprɪnt ɪŋ || 'sprɪnt̬ ɪŋ
   sprints sprɪnts
sprinter 'sprɪnt ə || 'sprɪnt̬ ᵊr **~s** z
sprit sprɪt **sprits** sprɪts
sprite spraɪt **sprites** spraɪts
spritsail 'sprɪt sᵊl -seɪᵊl **~s** z
spritz sprɪts ʃprɪts **spritzed** sprɪtst ʃprɪtst
   spritzes 'sprɪts ɪz 'ʃprɪts-, -əz **spritzing**
   'sprɪts ɪŋ 'ʃprɪts-
spritzer 'sprɪts ə 'ʃprɪts- || -ᵊr **~s** z
Sproat sprəʊt || sproʊt
sprocket 'sprɒk ɪt §-ət || 'sprɑːk ət **~s** s
sprog sprɒg || sprɑːg **sprogs** sprɒgz || sprɑːgz
Sprot, Sprott sprɒt || sprɑːt
Sproughton 'sprɔːt ᵊn || 'sprɑːt-
Sproule (i) sprəʊl || sproʊl, (ii) spruːl
sprout sprəʊt **sprouted** 'sprəʊt ɪd -əd
|| 'sprəʊt̬ əd **sprouting** 'sprəʊt ɪŋ
|| 'sprəʊt̬ ɪŋ **sprouts** sprəʊts
spruce spruːs **spruced** spruːst **sprucer**
   'spruːs ə || 'spruːs ᵊr **spruces** 'spruːs ɪz -əz
   sprucest 'spruːs ɪst -əst **sprucing** 'spruːs ɪŋ
spruce|ly 'spruːs |li **~ness** nəs nɪs
sprue spruː **sprues** spruːz
spruik spruːk **spruiked** spruːkt **spruiker/s**
   'spruːk ə/z || -ᵊr/z **spruiking** 'spruːk ɪŋ
   spruiks spruːks
sprung sprʌŋ
spry, Spry spraɪ **spryer** 'spraɪ_ə || 'spraɪ_ᵊr
   spryest 'spraɪ ɪst -əst **spryly** 'spraɪ li
   spryness 'spraɪ nəs -nɪs
spud spʌd **spuds** spʌdz
spumante spu 'mænt i || -'mɑːnt eɪ —It
   [spu 'man te]
spume spjuːm **spumed** spjuːmd **spumes**
   spjuːmz **spuming** 'spjuːm ɪŋ
spun spʌn
spunk spʌŋk
spunk|y 'spʌŋk |i **~ier** i_ə || i_ᵊr **~iest** i_ɪst i_əst
   ~ily ɪ li əl ɪ **~iness** i nəs i nɪs
spur spɜː || spɝː **spurred** spɜːd || spɝːd
   spurring 'spɜːr ɪŋ || 'spɝː ɪŋ **spurs** spɜːz
   || spɝːz
spurge spɜːdʒ || spɝːdʒ **spurges** 'spɜːdʒ ɪz -əz
   || 'spɝːdʒ əz
Spurgeon 'spɜːdʒ ən || 'spɝːdʒ ən
spurious 'spjʊər i_əs 'spjɔːr- || 'spjʊr- **~ly** li
   ~ness nəs nɪs
Spurling 'spɜːl ɪŋ || 'spɝːl ɪŋ
spurn, Spurn spɜːn || spɝːn **spurned** spɜːnd
   || spɝːnd **spurning** 'spɜːn ɪŋ || 'spɝːn ɪŋ
   spurns spɜːnz || spɝːnz
   ˌSpurn 'Head
spur-of-the-moment
   ˌspɜːr əv ðə 'məʊm ənt ◄ -ə ðə-
   || ˌspɝː əv ðə 'moʊm-
Spurrell 'spʌr əl || 'spɝː_əl
spurrey 'spʌr i || 'spɝː i **~s** z
Spurrier, s~ 'spʌr i_ə || 'spɝː i_ᵊr **~s** z

spurr|y 'spʌr |i || 'spɝː |i **~ies** iz
spurt spɜːt || spɝːt **spurted** 'spɜːt ɪd -əd
|| 'spɜːt̬ əd **spurting** 'spɜːt ɪŋ || 'spɝːt̬ ɪŋ
   spurts spɜːts || spɝːts
sputnik 'spʊt nɪk 'spʌt- || 'spuːt- **~s** s
sputter 'spʌt ə || 'spʌt̬ ᵊr **~ed** d **sputtering**
   'spʌt_ər ɪŋ || 'spʌt̬ ər ɪŋ **~s** z
sputum 'spjuːt əm || 'spjuːt̬ əm
Spuyten Duyvil ˌspaɪt ᵊn 'daɪv ᵊl ◄
   ˌSpuyten ˌDuyvil 'Creek
spy spaɪ **spied** spaɪd **spies** spaɪz **spying**
   'spaɪ ɪŋ
spycatcher 'spaɪ ˌkætʃ ə || -ᵊr **~s** z
spyglass 'spaɪ glɑːs §-glæs || -glæs **~es** ɪz əz
spyhole 'spaɪ həʊl →-hɒʊl || -hoʊl **~s** z
spymaster 'spaɪ ˌmɑːst ə §-ˌmæst- || -ˌmæst ᵊr
   ~s z
spyware 'spaɪ weə || -wer -wær
sq —see **square**
Sqezy tdmk 'skwiːz i
squab skwɒb || skwɑːb **squabs** skwɒbz
   || skwɑːbz
squabbl|e 'skwɒb ᵊl || 'skwɑːb ᵊl **~ed** d **~er/s**
   _ə/z || _ᵊr/z **~es** z **~ing** ɪŋ
squacco 'skwæk əʊ || 'skwɑːk oʊ **~s** z
squad skwɒd || skwɑːd **squads** skwɒdz
   || skwɑːdz
   'squad car
squadd|ie, squadd|y 'skwɒd |i || 'skwɑːd |i
   ~ies iz
squadron 'skwɒdr ən || 'skwɑːdr ən **~s** z
   ˌsquadron 'leader◄, '···
squalid 'skwɒl ɪd §-əd || 'skwɑːl əd 'skwɔːl- **~ly**
   li **~ness** nəs nɪs
squalidity skwɒ 'lɪd ət i -ɪt- || skwɑː 'lɪd ət̬ i
   skwɔː-
squall skwɔːl || skwɑːl **squalled** skwɔːld
   || skwɑːld **squalling** 'skwɔːl ɪŋ || 'skwɑːl-
   squalls skwɔːlz || skwɑːlz
squally 'skwɔːl i || 'skwɑːl-
squalor 'skwɒl ə || 'skwɑːl ᵊr 'skwɔːl-
squam|a 'skweɪm |ə 'skwɑːm- **~ae** iː
Squamish 'skwɑːm ɪʃ || 'skwɔːm- **~es** ɪz əz
squamous 'skweɪm əs **~ly** li **~ness** nəs nɪs
squander 'skwɒnd ə || 'skwɑːnd ᵊr **~ed** d
   squandering 'skwɒnd_ər ɪŋ || 'skwɑːnd ər ɪŋ
   ~s z
squanderer 'skwɒnd_ər ə || 'skwɑːnd ᵊr ər **~s**
   z
Squanto 'skwɒnt əʊ || 'skwɑːnt oʊ
square skweə || skwe ᵊr skwæ ᵊr **squared**
   skweəd || skwe ᵊrd skwæ ᵊrd **squares** skweəz
   || skwe ᵊrz skwæ ᵊrz **squaring** 'skweər ɪŋ
   || 'skwer ɪŋ 'skwær-
   ˌsquare 'bracket; 'square dance; 'square
   knot; ˌsquare 'leg, ˌsquare leg 'umpire;
   ˌsquare 'meal; ˌsquare 'one; ˌsquare 'root
square-bashing 'skweə ˌbæʃ ɪŋ || 'skwer-
   'skwær-
square-danc|e 'skweə dɑːnᵗs §-dænᵗs
   || 'skwer dænᵗs 'skwær- **~er/s** ə/z || ᵊr/z **~ing**
   ɪŋ
squarely 'skweə li || 'skwer li 'skwær-

squareness 'skweə nəs -nɪs ‖ 'skwer- 'skwær-
square-rigged ˌskweə 'rɪgd ◀ ‖ ˌskwer-
ˌskwær-
squarish 'skweər ɪʃ ‖ 'skwer ɪʃ 'skwær-
squash skwɒʃ ‖ skwɑːʃ skwɔːʃ **squashed**
skwɒʃt ‖ skwɑːʃt skwɔːʃt **squashes** 'skwɒʃ ɪz
-əz ‖ 'skwɑːʃ əz 'skwɔːʃ- **squashing**
'skwɒʃ ɪŋ ‖ 'skwɑːʃ ɪŋ 'skwɔːʃ-
squash|y 'skwɒʃ |i ‖ 'skwɑːʃ |i 'skwɔːʃ- **~ier**
i ə ‖ i ³r **~iest** i ɪst i ˌəst **~ily** ɪ li əl i **~iness**
i nəs i nɪs
squat skwɒt ‖ skwɑːt **squats** skwɒts ‖ skwɑːts
squatted 'skwɒt ɪd -əd ‖ 'skwɑːt̬ əd
squatting 'skwɒt ɪŋ ‖ 'skwɑːt̬ ɪŋ
squatter 'skwɒt ə ‖ 'skwɑːt̬ ³r **~s** z
squaw skwɔː ‖ skwɑː **squaws** skwɔːz ‖ skwɑːz
squawk skwɔːk skɔːk ‖ skwɑːk **squawked**
skwɔːkt skɔːkt ‖ skwɑːkt **squawking**
'skwɔːk ɪŋ 'skɔːk- ‖ 'skwɑːk- **squawks**
skwɔːks skɔːks ‖ skwɑːks
squeak skwiːk **squeaked** skwiːkt **squeaking**
'skwiːk ɪŋ **squeaks** skwiːks
squeaker 'skwiːk ə ‖ -³r **~s** z
squeak|y 'skwiːk |i **~ier** i ə ‖ i ³r **~iest** i ɪst
i ˌəst **~ily** ɪ li əl i **~iness** i nəs i nɪs
squeaky-clean ˌskwiːk i 'kliːn ◀
squeal skwiːᵊl **squealed** skwiːᵊld **squealing**
'skwiːᵊl ɪŋ **squeals** skwiːᵊlz
squealer 'skwiːᵊl ə ‖ -³r **~s** z
squeamish 'skwiːm ɪʃ **~ly** li **~ness** nəs nɪs
squeegee 'skwiː dʒiː ˌ·'· **~d** d **~ing** ɪŋ **~s** z
Squeers skwɪəz ‖ skwɪ³rz
squeeze skwiːz **squeezed** skwiːzd **squeezes**
'skwiːz ɪz -əz **squeezing** 'skwiːz ɪŋ
squeezebox 'skwiːz bɒks ‖ -bɑːks **~es** ɪz əz
squeezer 'skwiːz ə ‖ -³r **~s** z
squelch skweltʃ **squelched** skweltʃt
squelches 'skweltʃ ɪz -əz **squelching/ly**
'skweltʃ ɪŋ /li
squelchy 'skweltʃ i
squib skwɪb **squibs** skwɪbz
squid skwɪd **squids** skwɪdz
squidg|y 'skwɪdʒ |i **~ier** i ə ‖ i ³r **~iest** i ɪst
ˌəst **~ily** ɪ li əl i **~iness** i nəs i nɪs
squiff|y 'skwɪf| i **~ier** i ə ‖ i ³r **~iest** i ɪst ˌəst
~ily ɪ li əl i **~iness** i nəs i nɪs
squiggl|e 'skwɪg ³l **~ed** d **~es** z **~ing** ɪŋ
squiggly 'skwɪg ³l i
squill skwɪl **squills** skwɪlz
squillion 'skwɪl jən **~s** z
squinch skwɪntʃ **squinched** skwɪntʃt
squinches 'skwɪntʃ ɪz -əz **squinching**
'skwɪntʃ ɪŋ
squint skwɪnt **squinted** 'skwɪnt ɪd -əd
‖ 'skwɪnt̬ əd **squinting** 'skwɪnt ɪŋ
‖ 'skwɪnt̬ ɪŋ **squints** skwɪnts
squinty 'skwɪnt i ‖ 'skwɪnt̬ i
squirarch|y, squirearch|y 'skwaɪ³r ər ɑːk |i
‖ 'skwaɪ³r ɑːrk |i **~ies** iz
squire, Squire 'skwaɪ³r ə ‖ 'skwaɪ³r **squired**
'skwaɪ³r əd ‖ 'skwaɪ³rd **squires** 'skwaɪ³r əz
‖ 'skwaɪ³rz **squiring** 'skwaɪ³r ɪŋ
‖ 'skwaɪ³r ɪŋ

Squires 'skwaɪ³r əz ‖ 'skwaɪ³rz
squirm skwɜːm ‖ skwɜ·ːm **squirmed** skwɜːmd
‖ skwɜ·ːmd **squirming** 'skwɜːm ɪŋ
‖ 'skwɜ·ːm ɪŋ **squirms** skwɜːmz ‖ skwɜ·ːmz
squirm|y 'skwɜːm| i ‖ 'skwɜ·ːm| i **~ier** i ə
‖ i ³r **~iest** i ɪst ˌəst **~ily** ɪ li əl i **~iness** i nəs
i nɪs
squirrel 'skwɪr əl ‖ 'skwɜ·ː əl (*) **~ed, ~led** d
~ing, ~ling ɪŋ **~s** z
squirrelly, squirrely 'skwɪr əl i ‖ 'skwɜ·ː əl i
squirt skwɜːt ‖ skwɜ·ːt **squirted** 'skwɜːt ɪd -əd
‖ 'skwɜ·ːt̬ əd **squirting** 'skwɜːt ɪŋ
‖ 'skwɜ·ːt̬ ɪŋ **squirts** skwɜːts ‖ skwɜ·ːts
squish skwɪʃ **squished** skwɪʃt **squishes**
'skwɪʃ ɪz -əz **squishing** 'skwɪʃ ɪŋ
squish|y 'skwɪʃ |i **~ier** i ə ‖ i ³r **~iest** i ɪst i ˌəst
~ily ɪ li əl i **~iness** i nəs i nɪs
squit skwɪt **squits** skwɪts
squitters 'skwɪt əz ‖ 'skwɪt̬ ³rz
Sr —*see* **Senior; Señor**
Sranan 'srɑːn ən
Srebrenica ˌsreb rə 'niːts ə
Sri, sri sriː ʃriː —*see also phrases with this word*
Sri Lank|a srɪ 'læŋk |ə ʃrɪ-, ˌsriː-, ˌʃriː-
‖ -'lɑːŋk |ə **~an/s** ən/z
Srinagar srɪ 'nʌg ə 'srɪn ə gɑː ‖ -³r 'srɪn ə gɑːr
—*Hindi* [sɪ riː nə gər]
SS ˌes 'es ◀
ˌSS 'Kittiwake
ssh ʃ
-st *archaic and liturgical second person sing.*
ending **st** — **didst** 'dɪdst —*see* **-est**
St, St. *'Street'* striːt —*In names of*
thoroughfares, unstressed: 'Oxford St
St, St. *'Saint'* sənt sən ‖ seɪnt —*In RP the*
strong form seɪnt *is not customary when* St *is*
prefixed to a name; and of the two weak forms
listed sən *tends to be restricted to cases where*
the following name begins with a consonant.
In GenAm there is no weak form. In French
names St *may be pronounced* sæn, sæ —*Fr*
[sæ̃]. —*Proper names beginning* St *are listed*
in this dictionary alphabetically as St-, *not as*
Saint-.
St 'Anthony; St 'Lawrence, St ˌLawrence
'Seaway
Staaten *Australian river* 'stæt ³n
stab stæb **stabbed** stæbd **stabbing** 'stæb ɪŋ
stabs stæbz
Stabat Mater ˌstɑːb æt 'mɑːt ə ˌstæb-, -ət-
‖ -ɑːt 'mɑːt̬ ³r
stabb... —*see* **stab**
stabber 'stæb ə ‖ -³r **~s** z
St Abb's sənt 'æbz §sən- ‖ seɪnt 'æbz
stabilis... —*see* **stabiliz...**
stability stə 'bɪl ət i -ɪt i ‖ -ət̬ i
stabilization ˌsteɪb əl aɪ 'zeɪʃ ³n ˌ·ɪl-, -ɪ'·-
‖ -ə'·- **~s** z
stabiliz|e 'steɪb ə laɪz -ɪ-; -³l aɪz **~ed** d **~es** ɪz
əz **~ing** ɪŋ
stabilizer 'steɪb ə laɪz ə '·ɪ-; -³l aɪz- ‖ -³r **~s** z

S

stabl|e 'sterb ³l **~ed** d **~er** ₀ə ‖ ər **~es** z **~est**
  ıst əst **~ing** ıŋ
  '**stable boy**; ˌ**stable 'door**
stable|man 'sterb ³l |mæn **~men** men
stablemate 'sterb ³l mert **~s** s
stablish 'stæb lıʃ **~ed** t **~es** ız əz **~ing** ıŋ
staccato stə 'kɑːt əʊ stæ- ‖ -oʊ **~s** z
Stacey, Stacie 'sters i
stack stæk **stacked** stækt **stacking** 'stæk ıŋ
  stacks stæks
Stackhouse 'stæk haʊs
Stacpoole 'stæk puːl
stacte 'stækt i -iː
Stacy 'sters i
stade sterd **stades** sterdz
stadia 'sterd i ə
stadiometer ˌsterd i 'ɒm ıt ə -ət ə
  ‖ -'ɑːm ət ³r **~s** z
stadi|um 'sterd i ˌ|əm **~a** ə **~ums** əmz
staff stɑːf §stæf ‖ stæf **staffed** stɑːft §stæft
  ‖ stæft **staffing** 'stɑːf ıŋ §stæf- ‖ 'stæf ıŋ
  staffs stɑːfs §stæfs ‖ stæfs
  '**staff college**; '**staff nurse**; '**staff ˌofficer**;
  '**staff ˌsergeant**
Staffa 'stæf ə
staffer 'stɑːf ə ‖ 'stæf ³r **~s** z
Stafford 'stæf əd ‖ -³rd **~shire** ʃə ʃɪə ‖ ʃ³r ʃɪr
Staffs, Staffs. stæfs
stag stæg **stagged** stægd **stagging** 'stæg ıŋ
  stags stægz
  '**stag ˌbeetle**; '**stag ˌparty**
stage sterdʒ **staged** sterdʒd **stages** 'sterdʒ ız
  -əz **staging** 'sterdʒ ıŋ
  '**stage diˌrection**; ˌ**stage 'door◄**; ˌ**stage
  door 'Johnny**; '**stage efˌfect**; '**stage
  fright**; ˌ**stage 'manager** ‖ '·ˌ···; '**stage
  name**; ˌ**stage 'whisper** ‖ '·ˌ·; '**staging
  post**
stagecoach 'sterdʒ kəʊtʃ ‖ -koʊtʃ **~es** ız əz
stagecraft 'sterdʒ krɑːft §-kræft ‖ -kræft
stagehand 'sterdʒ hænd **~s** z
stage-manag|e ˌsterdʒ 'mæn ıdʒ '·ˌ··
  ‖ 'sterdʒ ˌmæn ıdʒ **~ed** d **~es** ız əz **~ing** ıŋ
stager 'sterdʒ ə ‖ -³r **~s** z
stagestruck 'sterdʒ strʌk
stag|ey 'sterdʒ |i **~ier** i ə ‖ i ³r **~iest** i ıst i əst
  ~ily ı li əl i **~iness** i nəs i nıs
stagflation ˌstæg 'fleıʃ ³n
Stagg stæg
stagger 'stæg ə ‖ -³r **~ed** d **staggering/ly**
  'stæg ³r ıŋ /li **~s** z
staghorn 'stæg hɔːn ‖ -hɔːrn
staghound 'stæg haʊnd **~s** z
staging 'sterdʒ ıŋ **~s** z
Stagira stə 'dʒaır³r ə 'stædʒ ır ə, -ər ə
Stagirite 'stædʒ ı raıt -ə- **~s** s
stagnancy 'stæg nən°s i
stagnant 'stæg nənt **~ly** li
stag|nate ₍ₒ₎stæg '|neıt '·· ‖ 'stæg |neıt
  ~nated neıt ıd -əd ‖ neıt̬ əd **~nates** neıts
  ~nating neıt ıŋ ‖ neıt̬ ıŋ
stagnation ₍ₒ₎stæg 'neıʃ ³n
St Agnes sənt 'æg nıs §sən-, -nəs ‖ seıṇt-

stag|y 'sterdʒ |i **~ier** i ə ‖ i ³r **~iest** i ıst i əst
  ~ily ı li əl i **~iness** i nəs i nıs
staid sterd (= *stayed*) **staidly** 'sterd li
  staidness 'sterd nəs nıs
stain steın **stained** steınd **staining** 'steın ıŋ
  stains steınz
  ˌ**stained 'glass◄**, ˌ**stained glass 'window**
Stainby 'steın bi →'steım-
stainer, S~ 'steın ə ‖ -³r
Staines steınz
Stainforth 'steın fɔːθ -fəθ ‖ -fɔːrθ -foʊrθ
stainless 'steın ləs -lıs **~ly** li **~ness** nəs nıs
  ˌ**stainless 'steel◄**, ˌ**stainless steel 'cutlery**
Stainton 'steınt ən ‖ -³n
stair steə ‖ ste³r stæ³r **stairs** steəz ‖ ste³rz
  stæ³rz
  '**stair rod**
staircas|e 'steə keıs ‖ 'ster- stær- **~es** ız əz
stairway 'steə weı ‖ 'ster- 'stær- **~s** z
stairwell 'steə wel ‖ 'ster- 'stær- **~s** z
staithe steıð **staithes, S~** steıðz
stake steık **staked** steıkt **stakes** steıks
  staking 'steık ıŋ
stakeholder 'steık ˌhəʊld ə →-ˌhɒʊld-
  ‖ -ˌhoʊld ³r **~s** z
stakeout 'steık aʊt **~s** s
stakhanovism stə 'kæn ə ˌvız əm stæ-, -'kɑːn-
  ‖ -'kɑːn-
stakhanovite stə 'kæn ə vaıt stæ-, -'kɑːn-
  ‖ -'kɑːn- **~s** s
stalactite 'stæl ək taıt ‖ stə 'lækt aıt (*) **~s** s
Stalag 'stæl æg -əg ‖ 'stɑːl ɑːg 'stæl əg —*Ger*
  ['ʃta lak]
stalagmite 'stæl əg maıt ‖ stə 'læg- (*) **~s** s
St Albans sənt 'ɔːlb ənz §sən-, -'ɒlb- ‖ seıṇt-
  -'ɑːlb-
St Aldate's sənt 'ɔːld əts -'ɒld-, -ıts, -eıts
  ‖ seıṇt- -'ɑːld-
stale ster³l **staler** 'ster³l ə ‖ -³r **stalest**
  'ster³l ıst -əst **stalely** 'ster³l li
stale|mate 'ster³l |meıt **~mated** meıt ıd -əd
  ‖ meıt̬ əd **~mates** meıts **~mating** meıt ıŋ
  ‖ meıt̬ ıŋ
staleness 'ster³l nəs -nıs
Stalin 'stɑːl ın 'stæl-, §-ən ‖ -iːn —*Russ*
  ['sta lʲın]
Stalingrad 'stɑːl ın græd 'stæl-, →-ıŋ-, §-ən-
  —*Russ* [stə lʲın 'grat]
Stalinism 'stɑːl ı ˌnız əm 'stæl-, -ə-
Stalinist 'stɑːl ın ıst 'stæl-, -ən-, §-əst **~s** s
stalk stɔːk ‖ stɑːk **stalked** stɔːkt ‖ stɑːkt
  stalking 'stɔːk ıŋ ‖ 'stɑːk- **stalks** stɔːks
  ‖ stɑːks
stalker, S~ 'stɔːk ə ‖ -³r 'stɑːk- **~s** z
stalking-hors|e 'stɔːk ıŋ hɔːs ‖ -hɔːrs 'stɑːk-
  ~es ız əz
Stalky, s~ 'stɔːk i ‖ 'stɑːk-
stall stɔːl ‖ stɑːl **stalled** stɔːld ‖ stɑːld **stalling**
  'stɔːl ıŋ ‖ 'stɑːl- **stalls** stɔːlz ‖ stɑːlz
stallage 'stɔːl ıdʒ
stallholder 'stɔːl ˌhəʊld ə →-ˌhɒʊld-
  ‖ -ˌhoʊld ³r 'stɑːl- **~s** z
stallion 'stæl jən **~s** z

Stallone stə ˈləʊn stæ- ‖ -ˈloʊn
Stallybrass ˈstæl i brɑːs §-bræs ‖ -bræs
stalwart ˈstɔːl wət ˈstɒl- ‖ -wᵊrt ˈstɑːl- **~ly** li
   ~ness nəs nɪs **~s** s
Stalybridge ˈsteɪl i brɪdʒ ˌ·ˈ·ˌ
Stamboul, Stambul ₍ᵢ₎stæm ˈbuːl
stamen ˈsteɪm en -ən **~s** z
Stamford ˈstæmᵖf əd ‖ -ᵊrd
stamina ˈstæm ɪn ə -ən-
stammer ˈstæm ə ‖ -ᵊr **~ed** d **stammering/ly**
   ˈstæm ər ɪŋ /li **~s** z
stamp, Stamp stæmp **stamped** stæmpt
   stamping ˈstæmp ɪŋ **stamps** stæmps
   ˈstamp colˌlection; ˈstamp ˌduty;
   ˈstamping ground
stamped|e ₍ᵢ₎stæm ˈpiːd **~ed** ɪd əd **~es** z **~ing**
   ɪŋ
stamper ˈstæmp ə ‖ -ᵊr **~s** z
Stan stæn
Stanbury ˈstæn bər i →ˈstæm- ‖ -ˌber i
stance stæn⁀ts stɑːn⁀ts **stances** ˈstæn⁀ts ɪz
   ˈstɑːn⁀ts-, -əz
stanch stɑːn⁀tʃ §stæn⁀tʃ ‖ stɔːn⁀tʃ **stanched**
   stɑːn⁀tʃt §stæn⁀tʃt ‖ stɔːn⁀tʃt **stanching**
   ˈstɑːn⁀tʃ ɪŋ §ˈstæn⁀tʃ- ‖ ˈstɔːn⁀tʃ- **stanches**
   ˈstɑːn⁀tʃ ɪz §ˈstæn⁀tʃ-, -əz ‖ ˈstɔːn⁀tʃ-
stanchion ˈstɑːn⁀tʃ ən ˈstæn⁀tʃ- ‖ ˈstæn⁀tʃ ən **~s** z
Stancliffe ˈstæn klɪf →ˈstæŋ-
stand stænd **standing** ˈstænd ɪŋ **stands**
   stændz **stood** stʊd
   ˌstanding ˈorder; ˌstanding oˈvation;
   ˈstanding room
stand-alone ˈstænd ə ˌləʊn ˌ·ˈ· ‖ -ˌloʊn
standard ˈstænd əd ‖ -ᵊrd **~s** z
   ˌstandard ˌdeviˈation; ˈstandard lamp;
   ˌstandard of ˈliving; ˌstandard ˈtime
standard-bearer ˈstænd əd ˌbeər ə →-əb-
   ‖ -ᵊrd ˌber ᵊr -ˌbær- **~s** z
standardis... —*see* **standardiz...**
standard-issue ˌstænd əd ˈɪʃ uː ◂ -ˈɪs juː,
   -ˈɪʃ juː ‖ -ᵊrd ˈɪʃ uː ◂
standardization ˌstænd əd aɪ ˈzeɪʃ ᵊn -ɪˈ--
   ‖ -ᵊrd ə- **~s** z
standardiz|e ˈstænd ə daɪz ‖ -ᵊr- **~ed** d **~es** ɪz
   əz **~ing** ɪŋ
standby ˈstænd baɪ →ˈstæmb- **~s** z
Standedge ˈstæn edʒ ˈstænd-
standee stæn ˈdiː **~s** z
Standen ˈstænd ən
stand-in ˈstænd ɪn **~s** z
Standish ˈstænd ɪʃ
standoff ˈstænd ɒf -ɔːf ‖ -ɔːf -ɑːf **~s** s
   ˌstandoff ˈhalf, ˈ·· ·
standoffish ˌstænd ˈɒf ɪʃ -ˈɔːf- ‖ -ˈɔːf- -ˈɑːf- **~ly**
   li **~ness** nəs nɪs
standout ˈstænd aʊt **~s** s
standpipe ˈstænd paɪp →ˈstæmb- **~s** s
standpoint ˈstænd pɔɪnt →ˈstæmb- **~s** s
St Andrews sənt ˈændr uːz §sən- ‖ seɪnt̬-
   —*locally* sɪn ˈtændr-
standstill ˈstænd stɪl **~s** z
stand-up ˈstænd ʌp
Stanfield ˈstæn fiːᵊld

Stanford ˈstæn fəd ‖ -fᵊrd
Stanford-Binet ˌstæn fəd ˈbiːn eɪ ˌ· ·bɪ ˈneɪ
   ‖ ˌ·fᵊrd bɪ ˈneɪ
   ˌStanford-Biˈnet test
Stanford-le-Hope ˌstæn fəd li ˈhəʊp
   ‖ -fᵊrd lə ˈhoʊp
stang stæŋ
Stanhope, s~ ˈstæn əp -həʊp ‖ -hoʊp **~s, ~'s** s
Stanislas ˈstæn ɪs ləs -əs-; -ɪ slæs, -ə-, -slɑːs
Stanislaus ˈstæn ɪ slaʊs -ə-, -slɔːs ‖ -slɔːs -slɑːs
Stanislavski, Stanislavsky ˌstæn ɪ ˈslæv ski
   -ə- ‖ -ˈslɑːv ski —*Russ* [stə nʲɪ ˈsłaf skʲɪj]
stank stæŋk
Stanley ˈstæn li
   ˌStanley ˈFalls; ˈStanley knife
Stanmore ˈstæn mɔː →ˈstæm- ‖ -mɔːr -moʊr
Stannard ˈstæn əd ‖ -ᵊrd
stannar|y ˈstæn ər |i **~ies** iz
St Anne's sənt ˈænz §sən- ‖ seɪnt̬-
stannic ˈstæn ɪk
stannous ˈstæn əs
Stansfield ˈstænz fiːᵊld ˈstæn's-
Stansgate ˈstænz geɪt
Stansted ˈstæn sted ˈstæn'st ɪd, -əd
St Anthony sənt ˈænt ən i §sən-
   ‖ seɪnt̬ ˈænt ᵊn i -ˈænt̬θ ən i
Stanton ˈstænt ən ‖ -ᵊn
Stanway ˈstæn weɪ
Stanwell ˈstæn wel -wəl
Stanwick, Stanwyck *(i)* ˈstæn ɪk, *(ii)* -wɪk
stanza ˈstænz ə **~s** z
stanzaic stæn ˈzeɪ ɪk
stapelia stə ˈpiːl i ə ‖ -ˈpiːl jə
stapes ˈsteɪp iːz
staph stæf
staphylo- *comb. form*
   with stress-neutral suffix ˌstæf ɪl əʊ -ᵊl- ‖ -ə
   -oʊ — **staphyloplasty** ˈstæf ɪl əʊ ˌplæst i
   ˈ·ᵊl- ‖ -ə,-, -oʊ,--
   with stress-imposing suffix ˌstæf ɪ ˈlɒ+ -ə-
   ‖ -ˈlɑː+ — **staphylorrhaphy** ˌstæf ɪ ˈlɒr əf i
   ˌ·ə- ‖ -ˈlɑːr- -ˈlɔːr-
staphylo|coccus ˌstæf ɪl əʊ ˈkɒk əs ˌ·ᵊl-
   ‖ -ə ˈkɑːk əs -oʊ- **~coccal** ˈkɒk ᵊl ◂
   ‖ -ˈkɑːk ᵊl ◂ **~cocci** ˈkɒks aɪ ˈkɒk-, ˈkɒs-, -iː
   ‖ ˈkɑːks aɪ ˈkɑːk-, -iː
stapl|e ˈsteɪp ᵊl **~ed** d **~es** z **~ing** ɪŋ
Stapleford ˈsteɪp ᵊl fəd ‖ -fᵊrd —*but the place*
   in Leics is ˈstæp-
Staplehurst ˈsteɪp ᵊl hɜːst ‖ -hɝːst
stapler ˈsteɪp lə ‖ -lᵊr **~s** z
Stapleton ˈsteɪp ᵊl tən
star stɑː ‖ stɑːr **starred** stɑːd ‖ stɑːrd **starring**
   ˈstɑːr ɪŋ **stars** stɑːz ‖ stɑːrz
   ˌstar ˈchamber ‖ ˈ· ·,·; ˌStars and ˈStripes;
   ˈstar sign; ˈstar wars
star-apple ˌstɑːr ˈæp ᵊl ˈ·,·· ‖ ˈstɑːr ˌæp ᵊl **~s** z
starboard ˈstɑː bəd -bɔːd ‖ ˈstɑːr bᵊrd
Starbuck ˈstɑː bʌk ‖ ˈstɑːr- **~s, ~'s** s
starburst ˈstɑː bɜːst ‖ ˈstɑːr bɝːst **~s** s
starch stɑːtʃ ‖ stɑːrtʃ **starched** stɑːtʃt ‖ stɑːrtʃt
   starches ˈstɑːtʃ ɪz -əz ‖ ˈstɑːrtʃ əz **starching**
   ˈstɑːtʃ ɪŋ ‖ ˈstɑːrtʃ ɪŋ

S

starch-reduced ˌstɑːtʃ ri ˈdjuːst ◂ -rə-,
→-ˈdʒuːst, '· ·ˌ· ‖ ˌstɑːrtʃ ri ˈduːst ◂ -ˈdjuːst
ˌstarch-reˌduced ˈcrispbread
starch|y ˈstɑːtʃ |i ‖ ˈstɑːrtʃ |i **~ier** i ə ‖ i ˑʳr
~iest i ɪst i əst **~ily** ɪ li əl i **~iness** i nəs i nɪs
star-crossed ˈstɑː krɒst -krɔːst, ˌ·ˈ·
‖ ˈstɑːr krɒst -krɑːst
  stardom ˈstɑː dəm ‖ ˈstɑːr-
stardom ˈstɑː dəm ‖ ˈstɑːr-
stardust ˈstɑː dʌst ‖ ˈstɑːr-
stare steə ‖ steˑʳr stæˑʳr **stared** steəd ‖ steˑʳrd
  stæˑʳrd **stares** steəz ‖ steˑʳrz stæˑʳrz **staring**
  ˈsteər ɪŋ ‖ ˈster ɪŋ ˈstær-
starfish ˈstɑː fɪʃ ‖ ˈstɑːr- **~es** ɪz əz
starfruit ˈstɑː fruːt ‖ ˈstɑːr-
stargazer ˈstɑː ˌgeɪz ə ‖ ˈstɑːr ˌgeɪz ˑʳr **~s** z
stargazing ˈstɑː ˌgeɪz ɪŋ ‖ ˈstɑːr-
staring ˈsteər ɪŋ ‖ ˈster ɪŋ ˈstær- **~ly** li
stark, Stark stɑːk ‖ stɑːrk **starker** ˈstɑːk ə
  ‖ ˈstɑːrk ˑʳr **starkest** ˈstɑːk ɪst -əst
  ‖ ˈstɑːrk əst
starkers ˈstɑːk əz ‖ ˈstɑːrk ˑʳrz
Starkey, Starkie ˈstɑːk i ‖ ˈstɑːrk i
starkly ˈstɑːk li ‖ ˈstɑːrk li
stark-naked ˌstɑːk ˈneɪk ɪd ◂ -əd ‖ ˌstɑːrk-
starkness ˈstɑːk nəs -nɪs ‖ ˈstɑːrk-
starless ˈstɑː ləs -lɪs ‖ ˈstɑːr-
starlet ˈstɑː lət -lɪt ‖ ˈstɑːr- **~s** s
starlight ˈstɑː laɪt ‖ ˈstɑːr-
starling, S~ ˈstɑː lɪ ɪŋ ‖ ˈstɑːrl- **~s** z
starlit ˈstɑː lɪt ‖ ˈstɑːr-
Starr stɑː ‖ stɑːr
starr... —*see* **star**
starr|y ˈstɑːr |i **~ier** i ə ‖ i ˑʳr **~iest** i ɪst i əst
  ~iness i nəs i nɪs
starry-eyed ˌstɑːr i ˈaɪd ◂
starship ˈstɑː ʃɪp ‖ ˈstɑːr- **~s** s
Starsky ˈstɑː ski ˈstɑːsk i ‖ ˈstɑːr ski
star-spangled ˈstɑː ˌspæŋ gˀld ˌ·ˈ··
  ‖ ˌstɑːr ˈspæŋ gˀld ◂
  ˌStar-ˌSpangled ˈBanner
starstruck ˈstɑː strʌk ‖ ˈstɑːr-
star-studded ˈstɑː ˌstʌd ɪd -əd, ˌ·ˈ·· ‖ ˈstɑːr-
star-studded ˈstɑː ˌstʌd ɪd -əd ‖ ˈstɑːr-
start, Start stɑːt ‖ stɑːrt **started** ˈstɑːt ɪd -əd
  ‖ ˈstɑːrt əd **starting** ˈstɑːt ɪŋ ‖ ˈstɑːrt ɪŋ
  starts stɑːts ‖ stɑːrts
  ˈstarting ˌblock; ˈstarting ˌgate; ˈstarting
  ˌpistol; ˈstarting ˌprice
starter ˈstɑːt ə ‖ ˈstɑːrt ˑʳr **~s** z
Startin ˈstɑːt ɪn §-ˀn ‖ ˈstɑːrt ˀn
startl|e ˈstɑːt ˀl ‖ ˈstɑːrt ˀl **~ed** d **~es** z **~ing/ly**
  ɪŋ /li
Start-rite *tdmk* ˈstɑːt raɪt ‖ ˈstɑːrt-
start-up ˈstɑːt ʌp ‖ ˈstɑːrt ʌp **~s** s
starvation ₍ᵢ₎stɑː ˈveɪʃ ˀn ‖ ₍ᵢ₎stɑːr-
  starˈvation ˌwages, ·ˌ··ˈ··
starve stɑːv ‖ stɑːrv **starved** stɑːvd ‖ stɑːrvd
  starves stɑːvz ‖ stɑːrvz **starving** ˈstɑːv ɪŋ
  ‖ ˈstɑːrv ɪŋ
starveling ˈstɑːv lɪ ɪŋ ‖ ˈstɑːrv- **~s** z
starwort ˈstɑː wɜːt §-wɔːt ‖ ˈstɑːr wɜːt -wɔːrt
  ~s s

St Asaph sənt ˈæs əf §sən- ‖ seɪnt̬-
stash stæʃ **stashed** stæʃt **stashes** ˈstæʃ ɪz -əz
  stashing ˈstæʃ ɪŋ
Stasi ˈstɑːz i —*Ger* [ˈʃtɑː zi]
stas|is ˈsteɪs |ɪs ˈstæs-, §-əs **~es** iːz
Stassen ˈstæs ˀn
-stat stæt — **thermostat** ˈθɜːm əʊ stæt
  ‖ ˈθɜːm ə-
state, State steɪt **stated** ˈsteɪt ɪd -əd
  ‖ ˈsteɪt̬ əd **states, States** steɪts **stating**
  ˈsteɪt ɪŋ ‖ ˈsteɪt̬ ɪŋ
  ˈState Deˌpartment; ˌstate's ˈevidence
statecraft ˈsteɪt krɑːft §-kræft ‖ -kræft
statehood ˈsteɪt hʊd
state|house, S~ ˈsteɪt |haʊs **~houses** haʊz ɪz
  -əz
stateless ˈsteɪt ləs -lɪs **~ness** nəs nɪs
state|ly ˈsteɪt |li **~lier** li ə ‖ li ˑʳr **~iest** li ɪst əst
  ~iness li nəs -nɪs
  ˌstately ˈhome
statement ˈsteɪt mənt **~ed** ɪd əd **~ing** ɪŋ **~s** s
Staten ˈstæt ˀn
  ˌStaten ˈIsland
state-of-the-art ˌsteɪt əv ði ˈɑːt ◂ ˌ·ə-
  ‖ ˌsteɪt̬ əv ði ˈɑːrt ◂
stater ˈsteɪt ə ‖ ˈsteɪt̬ ˑʳr **~s** z
stateroom ˈsteɪt ruːm -rʊm **~s** z
stateside ˈsteɪt saɪd
states|man ˈsteɪts |mən **~men** mən
statesman|like ˈsteɪts mən |laɪk **~ship** ʃɪp
states|woman ˈsteɪts ˌwʊm ən **~women**
  ˌwɪm ɪn §-ən
statewide ˌsteɪt ˈwaɪd ◂
Statham (*i*) ˈsteɪθ əm, (*ii*) ˈsteɪð əm
St Athan sənt ˈæθ ˀn §sən- ‖ seɪnt̬-
static ˈstæt ɪk ‖ ˈstæt̬ ɪk **~ally** ˀl i **~s** s
statice ˈstæt ɪs i -əs i; ˈstæt ɪs, §-əs ‖ ˈstæt̬ əs i
  ˈstæt̬ əs
statin ˈstæt ɪn §-ˀn ‖ -ˀn **~s** z
station ˈsteɪʃ ˀn **~ed** d **~ing** ˌɪŋ **~s** z
  ˈstation break; ˈstation house; ˌstations
  of the ˈCross; ˈstation ˌwagon
stationary ˈsteɪʃ ˀn ər i -ˀn̩ər i ‖ -ə ner i
stationer ˈsteɪʃ ˀn̩ə ‖ ˀr **~s** z
stationery ˈsteɪʃ ˀn ər i -ˀn̩ər i ‖ -ə ner i
  (= *stationary*)
stationmaster ˈsteɪʃ ˀn ˌmɑːst ə §-ˌmæst-
  ‖ -ˌmæst ˑʳr **~s** z
statism ˈsteɪt ˌɪz əm ‖ ˈsteɪt̬-
statist '*advocate of state power*' ˈsteɪt ɪst §-əst
  ‖ ˈsteɪt̬ əst **~s** s
statist '*statistician*' ˈstæt ɪst -əst ‖ ˈstæt̬ əst **~s**
  s
statistic stə ˈtɪst ɪk **~s** s
statistical stə ˈtɪst ɪk ˀl **~ly** i
statistician ˌstæt ɪ ˈstɪʃ ˀn -ə- ‖ ˌstæt̬- **~s** z
Statius ˈsteɪʃ i əs ˈsteɪt-
stative ˈsteɪt ɪv ‖ ˈsteɪt̬- **~s** z
stato- *comb. form*
  with stress-neutral suffix |stæt əʊ ‖ |stæt̬ ə
  — **statolith** ˈstæt əʊ lɪθ ‖ ˈstæt̬ ə- -ˀl ɪθ

with stress-imposing suffix stæ ˈtɒ+ ‖ -ˈtɑː+
— **statometer** stæ ˈtɒm ɪt ə -ət ə
‖ -ˈtɑːm ət̬ ər

Staton ˈsteɪt ᵊn

stator ˈsteɪt ə ‖ ˈsteɪt̬ ᵊr ~s z

stats *'statistics'* stæts

statuar|y ˈstætʃ u̯ ər |i ˈstæt ju ‖ -er |i ~ies iz

statue ˈstætʃ u: ˈstæt ju: ~s z

statuesque ˌstætʃ u ˈesk ◂ ˌstæt ju- ~**ly** li

statuette ˌstætʃ u ˈet ˌstæt ju- ~s s

stature ˈstætʃ ə ‖ -ᵊr ~s z

status ˈsteɪt əs ˈstæt- ‖ ˈsteɪt̬ əs ˈstæt̬- ~**es** ɪz əz
  ˌstatus ˈquo

statute ˈstætʃ u:t ˈstæt ju:t ~s s
  ˈstatute ˌbook; ˈstatute ˌlaw

statutor|y ˈstætʃ ʊt ər |i ˈ·u:t ˌ; ˈstæt jʊt ˌ,
ˈ·ju:t ˌ; §stə ˈtju:t ər |i ‖ ˈstætʃ ə tɔːr |i ˈ·u-,
-tour i ~**ily** əl i -ɪ li

St Aubyn sənt ˈɔːb ɪn §sən-, §-æɪ ‖ seɪnt̬- -ˈɑːb-

Staughton ˈstɔːt ᵊn ‖ ˈstɑːt-

St Augustine sənt ɔː ˈɡʌst ɪn §sən-, ˌseɪnt-,
§-ən ‖ ˌseɪnt̬ ɔː- ˌ·ɑː-

staunch *adj* stɔːntʃ ‖ stɑːntʃ —*in RP formerly
also* stɑːntʃ **stauncher** ˈstɔːntʃ ə ‖ -ᵊr ˈstɑːntʃ-
staunchest ˈstɔːntʃ ɪst -əst ‖ ˈstɑːntʃ-

staunch *v* stɔːntʃ stɑːntʃ, §stæntʃ **staunched**
stɔːntʃt stɑːntʃt, §stæntʃt **staunches**
ˈstɔːntʃ ɪz ˈstɑːntʃ-, §ˈstæntʃ-, -əz **staunching**
ˈstɔːntʃ ɪŋ ˈstɑːntʃ-, §ˈstæntʃ-

staunch|ly ˈstɔːntʃ |li ‖ ˈstɑːntʃ- ~**ness** nəs nɪs

Staunton *(i)* ˈstɔːnt ən ‖ ˈstɑːnt-, *(ii)* ˈstænt ən
‖ -ᵊn —*The English family name is (i), as is
the place in IL; the place in VA is (ii)*

staurolite ˈstɔːr ə laɪt ~s s

stauroscope ˈstɔːr ə skəʊp ‖ -skoʊp ~s s

stauroscopic ˌstɔːr ə ˈskɒp ɪk ◂ ‖ -ˈskɑːp-
~**ally** ᵊl_i

St Austell sənt ˈɔːst ᵊl §sən-, -ˈɒst-, -ˈɔːs-
‖ seɪnt̬- -ˈɑːst-

Stavanger stə ˈvæŋ ə ‖ stɑː ˈvɑːŋ ᵊr —*Norw*
[sta ˈvaŋ ər]

stave steɪv **staved** steɪvd **staves** steɪvz
  staving ˈsteɪv ɪŋ **stove** stəʊv ‖ stoʊv

Staveley ˈsteɪv li

Staverton ˈstæv ət ən ‖ -ᵊrt ᵊn

staves *pl of* **staff** steɪvz

stavesacre ˈsteɪvz ˌeɪk ə ‖ -ᵊr ~s z

Stawell stɔːl ‖ stɑːl

stay steɪ **stayed** steɪd *(= staid)* **staying**
ˈsteɪ ɪŋ **stays** steɪz
  ˈstaying ˌpower

stay-at-home ˈsteɪ ət ˌhəʊm ‖ -ˌhoʊm ~s z

stayer ˈsteɪ ə ‖ -ᵊr ~s z
  Stayman ˈsteɪ mən

staysail ˈsteɪ sᵊl -seɪ°l ~s z

St Barts sənt ˈbɑːts ‖ seɪnt ˈbɑːrts

St Bernard sənt ˈbɜːn əd →səm-
‖ ˌseɪnt bᵊr ˈnɑːrd —*Fr* [sæ bɛʁ naːʁ] ~s z
  St ˌBernard ˈPass ‖ ˌSt Ber ˌnard ˈPass

St Briavels sənt ˈbrev ᵊlz →sᵊm- ‖ seɪnt-

St Christopher sənt ˈkrɪst əf ə →sən-
‖ seɪnt ˈkrɪst əf ᵊr

St Clair sənt ˈkleə →sᵊŋ- ‖ seɪnt ˈkleᵊr -ˈklæᵊr
—*but as a family name also* ˈsɪŋ kleə,
ˈsɪn- ‖ -kler, -klær

St Cloud sæŋ ˈkluː —*Fr* [sæ klu] —*but the
place in MN is* seɪnt ˈklaʊd

St Croix sənt ˈkrɔɪ ‖ seɪnt-

STD ˌes tiː ˈdiː

St David's sənt ˈdeɪv ɪdz §-ədz ‖ seɪnt-
  St ˈDavid's ˌday

St Denis sənt ˈden ɪs §-əs ‖ seɪnt- —*but for the
places in Paris and Réunion* ˌsæn də ˈniː,
—*Fr* [sæd ni]

St Dogmaels sənt ˈdɒɡ mᵊlz ‖ seɪnt ˈdɔːɡ-
-ˈdɑːɡ-

St Donat's sənt ˈdɒn əts ‖ seɪnt ˈdɑːn-

stead sted

Stead *(i)* sted, *(ii)* stiːd

steadfast ˈsted fɑːst -fəst, §-fæst ‖ -fæst ~**ly** li
~**ness** nəs nɪs

steading ˈsted ɪŋ ~s z

Steadman ˈsted mən →ˈsteb-

stead|y ˈsted |i ~**ier** i̯ə ‖ i̯ᵊr ~**iest** i̯ɪst i̯əst
~**ily** ɪ li əl i ~**iness** i nəs i nɪs
  ˌsteady ˈstate, ˌsteady ˈstate ˌtheory

steak steɪk *(= stake)* **steaks** steɪks
  ˌsteak tarˈtare

steak|house ˈsteɪk |haʊs ~**houses** haʊz ɪz -əz

steal stiːᵊl *(= steel)* **stealing** ˈstiːᵊl ɪŋ **steals**
stiːᵊlz **stole** stəʊl →stɒʊl ‖ stoʊl **stolen**
ˈstəʊl ən →ˈstɒʊl- ‖ ˈstoʊl ən

stealer ˈstiːᵊl ə ‖ -ᵊr ~s z

stealth stelθ

stealth|y ˈstelθ |i ~**ier** i̯ə ‖ i̯ᵊr ~**iest** i̯ɪst i̯əst
~**ily** ɪ li əl i ~**iness** i nəs i nɪs

steam stiːm **steamed** stiːmd **steaming**
ˈstiːm ɪŋ **steams** stiːmz
  ˈsteam ˌiron; ˈsteam ˌshovel

steamboat ˈstiːm bəʊt ‖ -boʊt ~s s

steamed-up ˌstiːmd ˈʌp ◂

steam-engine ˈstiːm ˌendʒ ɪn §-ˌɪndʒ-, -ən ~s
z

steamer ˈstiːm ə ‖ -ᵊr ~s z

steamroll ˈstiːm ˌrəʊl →-ˌrɒʊl ‖ -ˌroʊl ~**ed** d
~**ing** ɪŋ ~s z

steamroll|er ˈstiːm ˌrəʊl |ə →-ˌrɒʊl-
‖ -ˌroʊl |ᵊr ~**ered** əd ‖ ᵊrd ~**ering** ər ɪŋ ~**ers**
əz ‖ ᵊrz

steamship ˈstiːm ʃɪp ~s s

steam|y ˈstiːm |i ~**ier** i̯ə ‖ i̯ᵊr ~**iest** i̯ɪst i̯əst
~**ily** ɪ li əl i ~**iness** i nəs i nɪs

stearate ˈstɪər eɪt ‖ ˈstiː ə reɪt ˈstɪr eɪt ~s s

stearic sti ˈær ɪk ‖ -ˈer-; ˈstɪr ɪk

stearin ˈstɪər ɪn §-ən ‖ ˈstiː ər ən ˈstɪr ən

Stearn, Stearne stɜːn ‖ stɜːn

stearoptene ˌstɪə ˈrɒpt iːn ‖ ˌstiː ə ˈrɑːpt-

steatite ˈstiː ə taɪt

steatolysis ˌstiː ə ˈtɒl əs ɪs -ɪs ɪs, §-əs ‖ -ˈtɑːl-

steatopygia ˌstiː ət əʊ ˈpaɪdʒ i̯ə -ˈpɪdʒ-
‖ sti ˌæt̬ ə- ˌstiː ət̬ ə-

steatopygous ˌstiː ət əʊ ˈpaɪɡ əs ◂
ˌstiː ə ˈtɒp ɪɡ əs, §-əɡ əs ‖ sti ˌæt̬ ə- ˌstiː ət̬ ə-;
ˌstiː ə ˈtɑːp əɡ əs

steatorrhea, steatorrhoea ˌstiːˌət ə 'riːˌə
‖ sti ˌæt ə-, ˌstiː əʧ ə-
Stebbing 'steb ɪŋ
Stechford 'steʧ fəd ‖ -fərd
stedfast 'sted fɑːst -fəst, §-fæst ‖ -fæst **~ly** li
~ness nəs nɪs
Stedman 'sted mən →'steb-
St Edmunds sənt 'ed məndz §sən-, →-'eb-
‖ seɪnʧ-
steed, Steed stiːd **steeds, Steed's** stiːdz
steel stiːəl **steeled** stiːəld **steeling** 'stiːəl ɪŋ
steels stiːəlz
'steel band; ˌsteel 'wool
Steel, Steele stiːəl
steel-grey, steel-gray ˌstiːəl 'greɪ ◄
steeli... —*see* **steely**
steelmak|er 'stiːəl ˌmeɪk ə ‖ -ər **~ers** əz ‖ ərz
~ing ɪŋ
steelworker 'stiːəl ˌwɜːk ə ‖ -ˌwɜːk ər **~s** z
steelworks 'stiːəl wɜːks ‖ -wɜːks
steel|y 'stiːəl |i **~ier** i‿ə ‖ i‿ər **~iest** i‿ɪst i‿əst
~iness i nəs i nɪs
steelyard 'stiːəl jɑːd 'stɪl-, -jəd ‖ 'stiːəl jɑːrd
'stɪl jərd **~s** z
steely-eyed ˌstiːəl i 'aɪd ◄
Steen stiːn —*but as a Dutch name,* steɪn *Dutch*
[steːn]
steenbok 'stiːn bɒk →'stiːm-, 'steɪn-, 'stɪən-,
-bʌk ‖ -bɑːk **~s** s
steep stiːp **steeper** 'stiːp ə ‖ -ər **steepest**
'stiːp ɪst -əst
steepen 'stiːp ən **~ed** d **~ing** ɪŋ **~s** z
steeple 'stiːp əl **~s** z
steeplechas|e 'stiːp əl ʧeɪs **~er/s** ə/z ‖ -ər/z
~es ɪz əz **~ing** ɪŋ
steeplejack 'stiːp əl dʒæk **~s** s
steep|ly 'stiːp |li **~ness** nəs nɪs
steer stɪə ‖ stɪər **steered** stɪəd ‖ stɪərd
steering 'stɪər ɪŋ ‖ 'stɪr ɪŋ **steers** stɪəz
‖ stɪərz
'steering comˌmittee; 'steering wheel
steerage 'stɪər ɪdʒ ‖ 'stɪr- **~way** weɪ
steers|man 'stɪəz |mən ‖ 'stɪrz- **~men** mən
men
Stefan 'stef ən -æn
Stefanie 'stef ən i
Steffens 'stef ənz
stegodon 'steg ə dɒn ‖ -dɑːn **~s** z
stegosaur 'steg ə sɔː ‖ -sɔːr **~s** z
stegosaurus ˌsteg ə 'sɔːr əs **~es** ɪz əz
Steiff ʃtaɪf
Steiger 'staɪg ə ‖ -ər
stein staɪn —*Ger* [ʃtaɪn] **steins** staɪnz
Stein (i) staɪn, (ii) stiːn —*but as a German
name,* ʃtam —*Ger* [ʃtaɪn]
Steinbeck 'staɪn bek →'staɪm-
Steinberg 'staɪn bɜːg →'staɪm- ‖ -bɜːg
steinbock, steinbok 'staɪn bɒk →'staɪm-,
-bʌk ‖ -bɑːk **~s** s
Steine *place in Brighton, Sx* stiːn
Steinem 'staɪn əm
Steiner 'staɪn ə ‖ -ər —*Ger* ['ʃtaɪ nɐ]
Steinway *tdmk* 'staɪn weɪ **~s** z

stel|a 'stiːl |ə **~ae** iː
Stelazine *tdmk* 'stel ə ziːn
stele (i) 'stiːl i -iː; (ii) stiːəl —*in archaeology
usually* (i), *in botany usually* (ii) **steles**
(i) 'stiːl iz -iːz (ii) stiːəlz
Stella 'stel ə
stellar 'stel ə ‖ -ər
stellate *adj* 'stel eɪt -ət, -ɪt
Stellenbosch 'stel ən bɒs →-əm-, -bɒʃ ‖ -bɑːs
-bɑːʃ
Steller 'stel ə ‖ -ər **~'s** z
ˌSteller's 'jay
St Elmo sənt 'elm əʊ §sən- ‖ seɪnʧ 'elm oʊ **~'s**
z
St ˌElmo's 'fire
stem stem **stemmed** stemd **stemming**
'stem ɪŋ **stems** stemz
stemm|a 'stem |ə **~ata** ət ə ‖ əʧ ə
-stemmed 'stemd — **long-stemmed**
ˌlɒŋ 'stemd ◄ ‖ ˌlɔːŋ- ˌlɑːŋ-
stemware 'stem weə ‖ -wer -wær
Sten sten
'Sten gun
stench stenʧ **stenches** 'stenʧ ɪz -əz
stencil 'stents əl -ɪl **~ed, ~led** d **~ing, ~ling**
ɪŋ **~s** z
Stendhal 'stɒnd ɑːl ‖ sten 'dɑːl —*Fr*
[stɑ̃ dal], *though popularly believed in Britain
to be* [stɔ̃-]
Stenhousemuir ˌsten haʊs 'mjʊə -əs-, -'mjɔː:
‖ -'mjʊər
steno 'sten əʊ ‖ -oʊ **~s** z
steno- *comb. form*
with stress-neutral suffix |sten əʊ ‖ -ə —
stenothermal ˌsten əʊ 'θɜːm əl ◄ ‖ -ə 'θɜːm-
with stress-imposing suffix ste 'nɒ+ stə-
‖ -nɑː+ — **stenophagous** ste 'nɒf əg əs stə-
‖ -nɑːf-
stenograph 'sten ə grɑːf -græf ‖ -græf **~ed** t
~ing ɪŋ **~s** s
stenographer stə 'nɒg rəf ə ste-
‖ -'nɑːg rəf ər **~s** z
stenographic ˌsten ə 'græf ɪk ◄ **~ally** əl i
stenography stə 'nɒg rəf i ste- ‖ -'nɑːg-
stenos|is ste 'nəʊs |ɪs stɪ-, stə-, §-əs ‖ -'noʊs-
~es iːz
stenotype, S~ *tdmk* 'sten əʊ taɪp ‖ -ə- **~s** s
stenotypist 'sten əʊ taɪp ɪst §-əst ‖ '-ə- **~s** s
stenotypy 'sten əʊ taɪp i ‖ '-ə-
stent stent **stented** 'stent ɪd -əd ‖ 'stenʧ əd
stenting 'stent ɪŋ ‖ 'stenʧ ɪŋ **stents** stents
Stentor, s~ 'stent ɔː -ə ‖ 'stent ɔːr 'stenʧ ər **~s**
z
stentorian sten 'tɔːr i‿ən ‖ -'toʊr-
step step **stepped** stept **stepping** 'step ɪŋ
steps steps
step- |step —*Compounds of step- not listed
below mostly have late stress, thus*
ˌstep'grandson
stepbrother 'step ˌbrʌð ə ‖ -ər **~s** z
step-by-step ˌstep baɪ 'step ◄
step|child 'step |ʧaɪld **~children** ˌʧɪldr ən

stepdaughter 'step ˌdɔːt ə ‖ -ˌdɔːʈ ᵊr -ˌdɑːʈ- ~s
z
step-down 'step daʊn ~s z
stepfather 'step ˌfɑːð ə ‖ -ᵊr ~s z
Stepford 'step fəd ‖ -fᵊrd
Stephanie 'stef ən i
stephanotis ˌstef ə 'nəʊt ɪs §-əs ‖ -'noʊʈ əs
Stephen 'stiːv ᵊn
Stephens 'stiːv ᵊnz
Stephenson 'stiːv ᵊn sən
step-in 'step ɪn ~s z
Stepinac 'step ɪ næts -ə- —*Croatian*
[stɛ 'piː nats]
stepladder 'step ˌlæd ə ‖ -ᵊr ~s z
stepmother 'step ˌmʌð ə ‖ -ᵊr ~s z
Stepney 'step ni
   ˌStepney 'Green
stepparent 'step ˌpeᵊr ənt ‖ -ˌper- -ˌpær- ~s s
steppe step (= *step*) **steppes** steps
stepped-up ˌstept 'ʌp ◄
stepper 'step ə ‖ -ᵊr ~s z
stepping-stone 'step ɪŋ stəʊn ‖ -stoʊn ~s z
stepsister 'step ˌsɪst ə ‖ -ᵊr ~s z
stepson 'step sʌn ~s z
Steptoe 'step təʊ ‖ -toʊ
step-up 'step ʌp ~s s
stepwise 'step waɪz
-ster *stress-neutral* stə ‖ stᵊr — **songster**
   'sɒŋᵏst ə 'sɒŋ stə ‖ 'sɔːŋᵏst ᵊr 'sɑːŋᵏst-;
   'sɔːŋ stᵊr, 'sɑːŋ-
Steradent *tdmk* 'ster ə dent
steradian stə 'reɪd i ən ~s z
stercoraceous ˌstɜːk ə 'reɪʃ əs ◄ ‖ ˌstɜːk-

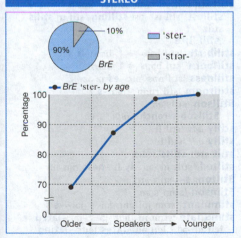

STEREO

10%

90%

BrE

■ 'ster-
■ 'stɪər-

● *BrE* 'ster- *by age*

Percentage

100

90

80

70

0

Older ◄— Speakers —► Younger

---

stereo 'ster i əʊ 'stɪər- ‖ 'ster i oʊ 'stɪr-
   — *Preference poll, BrE:* 'ster- *90%,* 'stɪər-
   10%. ~s z
stereo- *comb. form*
   with stress-neutral suffix ˌster i əʊ ˌstɪər-
   ‖ ˌster i oʊ ˌstɪr- — **stereoisomer**
   ˌster i əʊ 'aɪs əʊm ə ˌstɪər-
   ‖ ˌster i oʊ 'aɪs əm ᵊr ˌstɪr-
   with stress-imposing suffix ˌster i 'ɒ+ ˌstɪər-

‖ ˌster i 'ɑː+ ˌstɪr- — **stereography**
   ˌster i 'ɒg rəf i ˌstɪər- ‖ ˌster i 'ɑːg- ˌstɪr-
stereobate 'ster i əʊ beɪt 'stɪər- ‖ 'ster i oʊ-
   ~s s
stereophonic ˌster i ə 'fɒn ɪk ◄ ˌstɪər-, -i əʊ-
   ‖ ˌster i ə 'fɑːn ɪk ◄ ˌstɪr- ~**ally** ᵊl i **S-s** s
stereoscope 'ster i ə skəʊp 'stɪər-, -i əʊ-
   ‖ 'ster i ə skoʊp 'stɪr- ~s s
stereoscopic ˌster i ə 'skɒp ɪk ◄ ˌstɪər-, -i əʊ-
   ‖ ˌster i ə 'skɑːp ɪk ◄ ˌstɪr- ~**ally** ᵊl i
stereotyp|e 'ster i ə taɪp 'stɪər- ‖ 'stɪr- ~**ed** t
   ~**er/s** ə/z ‖ ᵊr/z ~**es** s ~**ing** ɪŋ
stereotypical ˌster i ə 'tɪp ɪk ᵊl ◄ ˌstɪər-, -i əʊ-
   ‖ ˌstɪr- ~**ly** i
stereotypy 'ster i ə taɪp i ˌstɪər- ‖ 'stɪr-
Stergene *tdmk* 'stɜːdʒ iːn ‖ 'stɜːrdʒ-
steric 'ster ɪk 'stɪər- ‖ 'stɪr-
sterilant 'ster əl ənt -ɪl- ~s s
sterile 'ster aɪᵊl ‖ 'ster əl (*) ~**ly** li ~**ness** nəs
   nɪs
sterilis... —*see* **steriliz...**
sterility stə 'rɪl ət i ste-, -ɪt i ‖ -əʈ i
sterilization ˌster əl aɪ 'zeɪʃ ᵊn ˌ-ɪl-, -ɪ'-- ‖ -ə'--
   ~s z
steriliz|e 'ster ə laɪz -ɪ- ~**ed** d ~**er/s** ə/z ‖ ᵊr/z
   ~**es** ɪz əz ~**ing** ɪŋ
sterling, S~ 'stɜːl ɪŋ ‖ 'stɜːrl ɪŋ
stern stɜːn ‖ stɜːrn **sterner** 'stɜːn ə ‖ 'stɜːrn ᵊr
   sternest 'stɜːn ɪst -əst ‖ 'stɜːrn əst
Stern stɜːn ‖ stɜːrn —*but as a German name,*
   ʃteən ‖ ʃtern —*Ger* [ʃtɛʁn]
sterna 'stɜːn ə ‖ 'stɜːrn ə
Sterne stɜːn ‖ stɜːrn
sternly 'stɜːn li ‖ 'stɜːrn li
sternmost 'stɜːn məʊst →'stɜːm-
   ‖ 'stɜːrn moʊst
sternness 'stɜːn nəs -nɪs ‖ 'stɜːrn-
sternpost 'stɜːn pəʊst →'stɜːm- ‖ 'stɜːrn poʊst
   ~s s
stern|um 'stɜːn |əm ‖ 'stɜːrn |əm ~**a** ə
sternutation ˌstɜːn ju 'teɪʃ ᵊn ‖ ˌstɜːrn jə- ~s z
sternutator|y ˌstɜːn ju 'teɪt ᵊr |i
   stɜː 'njuːt ət ᵊr |i ‖ stᵊr 'nuːʈ ə tɔːr |i -'njuːʈ-,
   -toʊr i ~**ies** iz
steroid 'stɪər ɔɪd 'ster- ‖ 'stɪr- ~s z
sterol 'stɪər ɒl 'ster- ‖ 'stɪr ɔːl -ɑːl, -oʊl ~s z
stertor 'stɜːt ə ‖ 'stɜːrʈ ᵊr
stertorous 'stɜːt ᵊr əs ‖ 'stɜːrʈ- ~**ly** li ~**ness**
   nəs nɪs
stet stet **stets** stets **stetted** 'stet ɪd -əd
   ‖ 'steʈ əd **stetting** 'stet ɪŋ ‖ 'steʈ ɪŋ
stethoscope 'steθ ə skəʊp ‖ -skoʊp ~s s
stethoscopic ˌsteθ ə 'skɒp ɪk ◄ ‖ -'skɑːp-
   ~**ally** ᵊl i
stethoscopy ste 'θɒsk əp i ‖ -'θɑːsk-
stetson, S~ 'stets ən ~s z
Steuart 'stjuː ət →'stʃuː ‖ 'stuː ᵊrt 'stjuː
Steuben 'stjuːb ən →'stʃuːb- ‖ 'stuːb ən
   'stjuːb-; stu 'ben, stju-
Stevas 'stiːv əs -æs
Steve stiːv
stevedore 'stiːv ə dɔː -ɪ- ‖ -dɔːr -doʊr ~**d** d ~**s**
   z **stevedoring** 'stiːv ə dɔːr ɪŋ ˌ·ɪ- ‖ -doʊr ɪŋ

S

Steven 'stiːv ᵊn
Stevenage 'stiːv ən ˌɪdʒ
Stevens 'stiːv ᵊnz
Stevenson 'stiːv ᵊn sən
Steventon 'stiːv ᵊn tən
Stevie 'stiːv i
stew stjuː →stʃuː ‖ stuː stjuː **stewed** stjuːd
→stʃuːd ‖ stuːd stjuːd **stewing** 'stjuː ɪŋ
→'stʃuː ‖ 'stuː ɪŋ 'stjuː- **stews** stjuːz →stʃuːz
‖ stuːz stjuːz
steward, S~ 'stjuː əd →'stʃuː ‖ 'stuː ᵊrd 'stjuː
~**ed** ɪd əd ~**ing** ɪŋ ~**s** z
stewardess ˌstjuː ə 'des →ˌstʃuː ‖ ˈ··· , ə dɪs,
§ˌə dəs ‖ 'stuː ᵊrd əs ~**es** ɪz əz
stewardship 'stjuː əd ʃɪp →'stʃuː
‖ 'stuː ᵊrd ʃɪp 'stjuː ~**s** s
Stewart 'stjuː ət →'stʃuː ‖ 'stuː ᵊrt 'stjuː
stewpan 'stjuː pæn →'stʃuː- ‖ 'stuː 'stjuː- ~**s** z
Steyn family name staɪn
Steyne place name stiːn
Steyning 'sten ɪŋ
St Fagan's sənt 'fæg ənz ‖ seɪnt-
St George sənt 'dʒɔːrdʒ ‖ seɪnt 'dʒɔːrdʒ ~**'s** ɪz
əz
    St ˌGeorge's 'Channel
St Gotthard sənt 'gɒt əd -ɑːd ‖ seɪnt 'gɑːt̬ ᵊrd
    —Ger [zaŋkt 'gɔt haʁt]
St Helena name of saint sənt 'hel ən ə §sən-,
-ɪn ə; -hɪ 'liːn ə, -hə'-- ‖ seɪnt-
St Helena island ˌsent hɪ 'liːn ə sᵊnt-, -hə-,
-'leɪn ə
St. Helena place in CA ˌseɪnt hɪ 'liːn ə sᵊnt-,
-hə- ‖ ˌseɪnt̬ ɪ- ˌseɪnt hɪ-
St Helens sənt 'hel ənz -ɪnz ‖ seɪnt-
St Helier sənt 'hel i ə ‖ seɪnt 'hel jᵊr
sthenic 'sθen ɪk
stibine 'stɪb aɪn ‖ -iːn
stibnite 'stɪb naɪt
Stich ʃtiːk —Ger [ʃtɪç]
stichometry stɪ 'kɒm ətr i §stə-, -ɪtr i
‖ -'kɑːm-
stichomythia ˌstɪk əʊ 'mɪθ i ə ‖ ˌ·ə-
stick stɪk **sticking** 'stɪk ɪŋ **sticks** stɪks **stuck**
stʌk
    'sticking ˌplaster; **'sticking ˌpoint**; **'stick
    ˌinsect**; **'stick ˌshift**
stickball 'stɪk bɔːl ‖ -bɑːl
sticker 'stɪk ə ‖ -ᵊr ~**s** z
stick-in-the-mud 'stɪk ɪn ðə ˌmʌd §'·ən-
‖ 'stɪk ən- ~**s** z
stickleback 'stɪk ᵊl bæk ~**s** s
Sticklepath 'stɪk ᵊl pɑːθ §-pæθ ‖ -pæθ
stickler 'stɪk lə ‖ -lᵊr ~**s** z
stick-on 'stɪk ɒn ‖ -ɑːn -ɔːn
stickpin 'stɪk pɪn ~**s** z
stick-to-it-iveness ˌstɪk 'tuː ɪt ɪv nəs -nɪs
‖ -'tuː ət̬-
stickum 'stɪk əm ~**s** z
stick-up 'stɪk ʌp ~**s** s
stick|y 'stɪk |i ~**ier** i ə ‖ i ᵊr ~**iest** i ɪst i əst
~**ily** ɪ li əl i ~**iness** i nəs i nɪs
    ˌsticky 'end; ˌsticky 'wicket
stie... —see **sty**

stiff stɪf **stiffer** 'stɪf ə ‖ -ᵊr **stiffest** 'stɪf ɪst -əst
    ˌstiff ˌupper 'lip
stiff-arm 'stɪf ɑːm ‖ -ɑːrm ~**ed** d ~**ing** ɪŋ ~**s** z
stiffen 'stɪf ᵊn ~**ed** d ~**ing** ɪŋ ~**s** z
stiffener 'stɪf ᵊn ə ‖ ᵊr ~**s** z
stiffie 'stɪf i ~**s** z
Stiffkey 'stɪf ki: —formerly also 'stjuː k i,
'stuːk i
stiffly 'stɪf li
stiff-necked ˌstɪf 'nekt ◂
stiffness 'stɪf nəs -nɪs ~**es** ɪz əz
stiff|y 'stɪf |i ~**ies** iz
stifl|e 'staɪf ᵊl ~**ed** d ~**es** z ~**ing/ly** ɪŋ /li
stigma 'stɪg mə ~**s** z **stigmata** 'stɪg mət ə
stɪg 'mɑːt ə ‖ stɪg 'mɑːt̬ ə 'stɪg mət̬ ə
stigmatic stɪg 'mæt ɪk ‖ -'mæt̬- ~**s** s
stigmatis... —see **stigmatiz...**
stigmatization ˌstɪg mət aɪ 'zeɪʃ ᵊn -ɪ'--
‖ -mət̬ ə- ~**s** z
stigmatiz|e 'stɪg mə taɪz ~**ed** d ~**es** ɪz əz ~**ing**
ɪŋ
stilb stɪlb
stilbene 'stɪlb iːn
stilbestrol stɪl 'biːs trɒl -'bes-, -trəl
‖ -'bes trɔːl -trɑːl, -troʊl
stilbite 'stɪlb aɪt
stilboestrol stɪl 'biːs trɒl -'bes-, -trəl
‖ -'bes trɔːl -trɑːl, -troʊl
stile staɪᵊl (= style) **stiles** staɪᵊlz
Stiles staɪᵊlz
stiletto stɪ 'let əʊ stə- ‖ -'let̬ oʊ ~**s** z
    stiˌletto 'heel
Stilgoe 'stɪlg əʊ ‖ -oʊ
Stilicho 'stɪl ɪ kəʊ ‖ -koʊ
still stɪl **stilled** stɪld **stiller** 'stɪl ə ‖ 'stɪl ᵊr
stillest 'stɪl ɪst -əst **stilling** 'stɪl ɪŋ **stills**
stɪlz
    ˌstill 'life
stillbirth 'stɪl bɜːθ ˌ·'· ‖ -bɜːθ ~**s** s
stillborn 'stɪl bɔːn ˌ·'· ‖ -bɔːrn
stillness 'stɪl nəs -nɪs ~**es** ɪz əz
stillroom 'stɪl ruːm -rʊm ~**s** z
Stillson 'stɪls ən
    'Stillson ˌwrench tdmk
stilly adv 'stɪl li
stilly adj 'stɪl i
stilt stɪlt **stilts** stɪlts
stilted 'stɪlt ɪd -əd ~**ly** li ~**ness** nəs nɪs
Stilton, s~ 'stɪlt ən
Stimson 'stɪmᵖs ən
stimulant 'stɪm jʊl ənt -jəl- ‖ -jəl- ~**s** s
stimu|late 'stɪm ju |leɪt -jə- ‖ -jə- ~**lated**
leɪt ɪd -əd ‖ leɪt̬ əd ~**lates** leɪts ~**lating**
leɪt ɪŋ ‖ leɪt̬ ɪŋ
stimulation ˌstɪm ju 'leɪʃ ᵊn -jə- ‖ -jə- ~**s** z
stimulative 'stɪm jʊl ət ɪv -ju leɪt ɪv
‖ -jə leɪt̬ ɪv
stimulator 'stɪm ju leɪt ə '·jə- ‖ -jə leɪt̬ ᵊr ~**s** z
stim|ulus 'stɪm |jʊl əs -jəl əs ‖ -|jəl əs ~**uli**
ju laɪ jə-, -liː ‖ jə-
stimy 'staɪm i **stimied** 'staɪm id **stimies**
'staɪm iz **stimying** 'staɪm i ɪŋ

S

sting stɪŋ **stinging** 'stɪŋ ɪŋ **stings** stɪŋz **stung** stʌŋ
  'stinging ˌnettle
stinger 'stɪŋ ə ‖ -ᵊr ~s z
stingi... —*see* **stingy**
stingo 'stɪŋ gəʊ ‖ -goʊ
stingray 'stɪŋ reɪ ~s z
sting|y *'ungenerous'* 'stɪndʒ |i ~ier i ə ‖ iˌᵊr
  ~iest i ɪst i əst ~ily ɪ li əl i ~iness i nəs i nɪs
stingy *'having a sting'* 'stɪŋ i
stink stɪŋk **stank** stæŋk **stinking/ly**
  'stɪŋk ɪŋ /li **stinks** stɪŋks **stunk** stʌŋk
stink-bomb 'stɪŋk bɒm ‖ -bɑːm ~s z
stinker 'stɪŋk ə ‖ -ᵊr ~s z
stinkhorn 'stɪŋk hɔːn ‖ -hɔːrn ~s z
stinkpot 'stɪŋk pɒt ‖ -pɑːt ~s s
stint stɪnt **stinted** 'stɪnt ɪd -əd ‖ 'stɪnt̮ əd
  stinting 'stɪnt ɪŋ ‖ 'stɪnt̮ ɪŋ **stints** stɪnts
stipe staɪp **stipes** staɪps
stipend 'staɪp end -ənd ~s z
stipendiar|y staɪ 'pend i ər i ‖ i stɪ-,
  △-'pendˌər |i ‖ -i er |i ~ies iz
  stiˌpendiary 'magistrate
stipes *sing.* 'staɪp iːz
stippl|e 'stɪp ᵊl ~ed d ~es z ~ing ˌɪŋ
stipu|late *v* 'stɪp ju |leɪt -jə- ‖ -jə- ~lated
  leɪt ɪd -əd ‖ leɪt̮ əd ~lates leɪts ~lating
  leɪt ɪŋ ‖ leɪt̮ ɪŋ
stipulation ˌstɪp ju 'leɪʃ ᵊn -jə- ‖ -jə- ~s z
stipulatory 'stɪp jʊl ət̮ ər i ˌstɪp ju 'leɪt ər i
  ‖ 'stɪp jəl ə tɔːr i -tour i
stipule 'stɪp juːl ~s z
stir stɜː ‖ stɜː: **stirred** stɜːd ‖ stɜː:d **stirring/ly**
  'stɜːr ɪŋ /li ‖ 'stɜː:- **stirs** stɜːz ‖ stɜːz
stir-crazy ˌstɜː 'kreɪz i ‖ ˌstɜː-
stir-|fry ˌstɜː |'fraɪ ‖ ˌstɜː:- ~fried 'fraɪd ◄
  ~fries 'fraɪz ~frying 'fraɪ ɪŋ
Stirling 'stɜːl ɪŋ ‖ 'stɜː:l ɪŋ
stirps stɜːps ‖ stɜːps **stirpes** 'stɜːp iːz
  ‖ 'stɜːp iːz
stirr... —*see* **stir**
stirrer 'stɜːr ə ‖ 'stɜː: ᵊr ~s z
stirrup 'stɪr əp ‖ 'stɜː: əp 'stɪr- (*) ~s s
  'stirrup cup; **'stirrup pump**
stitch stɪtʃ **stitched** stɪtʃt **stitches** 'stɪtʃ ɪz -əz
  stitching 'stɪtʃ ɪŋ
stitchery 'stɪtʃ ər i
stitchwort 'stɪtʃ wɜːt §-wɔːt ‖ -wɜː:t -wɔːrt ~s s
St Ivel *tdmk* sənt 'aɪv ᵊl §sən- ‖ seɪnt̮-
St Ives sənt 'aɪvz §sən- ‖ seɪnt̮-
Stivichall 'staɪtʃ ᵊl -ɔːl (!)
St James sənt 'dʒeɪmz ‖ seɪnt- **St James's**
  sənt 'dʒeɪmz ɪz -əz; sənt 'dʒeɪmz ‖ seɪnt-
St John sənt 'dʒɒn ‖ seɪnt 'dʒɑːn —*but as a*
  surname also 'sɪndʒ ən
St John's sənt 'dʒɒnz ‖ seɪnt 'dʒɑːnz
  St 'John's wort ˌ·ˈ·
St Kilda sənt 'kɪld ə →sᵊŋ- ‖ seɪnt-
St Kitts sənt 'kɪts →sᵊŋ- ‖ seɪnt-
St Kitts-Nevis sənt ˌkɪts 'niːv ɪs →sᵊŋ-, §-əs
  ‖ seɪnt-
St Laurent ˌsæn lɒ 'rɒ̃ -lɔː-, -lə-, -'rɑːnt
  ‖ -loʊ 'rɑːn -lɔː-, -lɑː- —*Fr* [sæ̃ lɔ ʁɑ̃]

St Leger sənt 'ledʒ ə ‖ seɪnt 'ledʒ ᵊr —*but as*
  a surname also 'sel ɪndʒ ə, -əndʒ- ‖ -ᵊr
St Louis sənt 'luːɪs i, §ˌəs ‖ seɪnt-
St Lucia sənt 'luːʃ ə -'luːʃ iˌə, -'luːs- ‖ seɪnt-
St Malo sæ̃ 'maːl əʊ sæn-, sᵊnt-
  ‖ ˌsæn mɑː 'loʊ —*Fr* [sæ̃ ma lo]
St Mary Axe sənt ˌmeər i 'æks ‖ seɪnt ˌmer i-
  -ˌmær- —*formerly* ˌsɪm ər i 'æks
St Moritz ˌsæn mə 'rɪts →sæm-; sənt 'mɒr ɪts
  ‖ -moʊ- —*Ger* Sankt Moritz [zaŋkt 'moː ʁɪts,
  -mo 'ʁɪts]
St Neots sənt 'niːˌəts -'niːts ‖ seɪnt-
stoa 'stəʊ ə ‖ 'stoʊ ə ~s z
stoat stəʊt ‖ stoʊt **stoats** stəʊts ‖ stoʊts
Stobart 'stəʊb ɑːt ‖ 'stoʊb ɑːrt
Stobie 'stəʊb i ‖ 'stoʊb i
stochastic stə 'kæst ɪk stɒ- ‖ stoʊ- ~ally ᵊlˌi
stock, Stock stɒk ‖ stɑːk **stocked** stɒkt
  ‖ stɑːkt **stocking** 'stɒk ɪŋ ‖ 'stɑːk ɪŋ **stocks**
  stɒks ‖ stɑːks
  'stock cerˌtificate; **'stock cube**; **'stock**
  exˌchange; **'stock ˌmarket**
stockad|e stɒ 'keɪd ‖ stɑː- ~ed ɪd əd ~es z
  ~ing ɪŋ
stockbreed|er 'stɒk ˌbriːd ə ‖ 'stɑːk ˌbriːd ᵊr
  ~ers əz ‖ ᵊrz ~ing ɪŋ
Stockbridge 'stɒk brɪdʒ ‖ 'stɑːk-
stockbroker 'stɒk ˌbrəʊk ə ‖ 'stɑːk ˌbroʊk ᵊr
  ~s z
  'stockbroker belt
stockbrokerage 'stɒk ˌbrəʊk ər ɪdʒ
  ‖ 'stɑːk ˌbroʊk ər ˌɪdʒ
stockbroking 'stɒk ˌbrəʊk ɪŋ
  ‖ 'stɑːk ˌbroʊk ɪŋ
stockcar 'stɒk kɑː ‖ 'stɑːk kɑːr ~s z
Stockdale 'stɒk deɪᵊl ‖ 'stɑːk-
stockfish 'stɒk fɪʃ ‖ 'stɑːk-
Stockhausen 'ʃtɒk ˌhaʊz ᵊn 'stɒk- ‖ 'ʃtɑːk-
  —*Ger* ['ʃtɔk hau zᵊn]
stockhold|er 'stɒk ˌhəʊld ə →-ˌhɒʊld-
  ‖ 'stɑːk ˌhoʊld ᵊr ~ers əz ‖ ᵊrz ~ing ɪŋ
Stockholm 'stɒk həʊm §-həʊlm ‖ 'stɑːk hoʊm
  -hoʊlm —*Swed* ['stɔk hɔlm]
stockinet, stockinette ˌstɒk ɪ 'net -ə-
  ‖ ˌstɑːk-
stocking 'stɒk ɪŋ ‖ 'stɑːk ɪŋ ~ed d ~s z
stocking-filler 'stɒk ɪŋ ˌfɪl ə ‖ 'stɑːk ɪŋ ˌfɪl ᵊr
  ~s z
stock-in-trade ˌstɒk ɪn 'treɪd §-ən- ‖ ˌstɑːk ən-
  ˌ·ˈ·
stockist 'stɒk ɪst §-əst ‖ 'stɑːk əst ~s s
stockjobber 'stɒk ˌdʒɒb ə ‖ 'stɑːk ˌdʒɑːb ᵊr
  ~s z
Stockley 'stɒk li ‖ 'stɑːk li
stock|man 'stɒk |mən -mæn ‖ 'stɑːk- ~men
  mən men
stockpil|e 'stɒk paɪᵊl ‖ 'stɑːk- ~ed d ~es z
  ~ing ɪŋ
Stockport 'stɒk pɔːt ‖ 'stɑːk pɔːrt -poʊrt
stockpot 'stɒk pɒt ‖ 'stɑːk pɑːt ~s s
stockroom 'stɒk ruːm -rʊm ‖ 'stɑːk- ~s z
Stocks stɒks ‖ stɑːks
Stocksbridge 'stɒks brɪdʒ ‖ 'stɑːks-

S

stock-still ˌstɒk ˈstɪl ◂ ‖ ˌstaːk-
stocktaking ˈstɒk ˌteɪk ɪŋ ‖ ˈstaːk-
Stockton ˈstɒkt ən ‖ ˈstaːkt ən
Stockton-on-Tees ˌstɒkt ən ɒn ˈtiːz
  ‖ ˌstaːkt ən aːn- -ɔːn-·
Stockwell ˈstɒk wel -wəl ‖ ˈstaːk-
Stockwood ˈstɒk wʊd ‖ ˈstaːk-
stock|y ˈstɒk |i ‖ ˈstaːk |i **~ier** i ə ‖ i ʳr **~iest**
  i ̩ɪst i ̩əst **~ily** ɪ li əl i **~iness** i nəs i nɪs
stockyard ˈstɒk jaːd ‖ ˈstaːk jaːrd **~s** z
Stoddard ˈstɒd əd ‖ ˈstaːd ʳrd
Stoddart ˈstɒd ət ‖ ˈstaːd ʳrt
stodge stɒdʒ ‖ staːdʒ **stodged** stɒdʒd
  ‖ staːdʒd **stodges** ˈstɒdʒ ɪz -əz ‖ ˈstaːdʒ əz
  stodging ˈstɒdʒ ɪŋ ‖ ˈstaːdʒ ɪŋ
stodg|y ˈstɒdʒ |i ‖ ˈstaːdʒ |i **~ier** i ə ‖ i ʳr
  ~iest i ̩ɪst i ̩əst **~ily** ɪ li əl i **~iness** i nəs i nɪs
stoep stuːp stʊp **stoeps** stuːps stʊps
stog|ey, stog|ie, stogly ˈstəʊg |i ‖ ˈstoʊg |i
  ~ies iz
Stogumber stə ˈɡʌm bə stəʊ-; ˈstɒɡ əm- ‖ -bʳr
Stogursey stə ˈɡɜːz i stəʊ- ‖ -ˈɡɜːz i
stoic, Stoic ˈstəʊ ɪk ‖ ˈstoʊ ɪk **~s** s
stoical ˈstəʊ ɪk ʷl ‖ ˈstoʊ- **~ly** ̩i
stoichiometric ˌstɔɪk i ̩ə ˈmetr ɪk ◂ -əʊˈ-
  ‖ -oʊˈ- **~ally** ʷl i
stoichiometry ˌstɔɪk i ˈɒm ətr i ‖ -ˈaːm-
stoicism ˈstəʊ ɪ ˌsɪz əm -ə- ‖ ˈstoʊ ə-
stoke, Stoke stəʊk ‖ stoʊk **stoked** stəʊkt
  ‖ stoʊkt **stokes** stəʊks ‖ stoʊks **stoking**
  ˈstəʊk ɪŋ ‖ ˈstoʊk ɪŋ
  ˌStoke ˈd'Abernon ˈdæb ən ən ˈdaːb- ‖ -ʳrn-;
  ˌStoke ˈMandeville; ˌStoke ˈPoges
  ˈpəʊdʒ ɪz -əz ‖ ˈpoʊdʒ əz
stokehold ˈstəʊk həʊld →-hɒʊld
  ‖ ˈstoʊk hoʊld **~s** z
stokehole ˈstəʊk həʊl →-hɒʊl ‖ ˈstoʊk hoʊl **~s**
  z
Stoke-on-Trent ˌstəʊk ɒn ˈtrent ◂
  ‖ ˌstoʊk aːn- -ɔːn-
stoker ˈstəʊk ə ‖ ˈstoʊk ʳr **~s** z
Stokes stəʊks ‖ stoʊks **Stokes'** stəʊks
  ˈstəʊks ɪz, -əz ‖ stoʊks ˈstoʊks əz
Stokowski stə ˈkɒf ski -ˈkɒv- ‖ -ˈkɔːf- -ˈkaːf-;
  -ˈkaʊsk i
STOL, stol stɒl ˈest ɒl ‖ staːl stɔːl; ˈest ɔːl, -aːl
St Olaves sənt ˈɒl əvz §sən-, -ɪvz ‖ seɪnt ˈaːl-
stole stəʊl →stɒʊl ‖ stoʊl **stoles** stəʊlz
  →stɒʊlz ‖ stoʊlz
stolen ˈstəʊl ən →ˈstɒʊl- ‖ ˈstoʊl ən
stolid ˈstɒl ɪd §-əd ‖ ˈstaːl əd **~ly** li **~ness** nəs
  nɪs
stolidity stə ˈlɪd ət i stɒ-, -ɪt i ‖ -ət i staː-
Stoll (i) stɒl ‖ staːl stɔːl, (ii) stəʊl →stɒʊl
  ‖ stoʊl
stollen ˈstɒl ən ‖ ˈstoʊl ən ˈstɔːl-, ˈstaːl-, ˈstʌl-
  —Ger [ˈʃtɔl ən] **~s** z
stolon ˈstəʊl ɒn -ən ‖ ˈstoʊl ən -aːn **~s** z
Stolport, STOLport ˈstɒl pɔːt ‖ ˈstɔːl pɔːrt
  ˈstaːl-, -poʊrt **~s** s
stoma ˈstəʊm ə ‖ ˈstoʊm ə **~s** z **stomata**
  ˈstəʊm ət ə ˈstɒm-; stəʊ ˈmaːt ə ‖ ˈstoʊm ət̬ ə
  ˈstaːm-; stoʊ ˈmaːt̬ ə

stomach ˈstʌm ək §-ɪk **~ed** t **~s** s **~ing** ɪŋ
  ˈstomach pump
stomachache ˈstʌm ək eɪk §-ɪk- **~s** s
stomach-churning ˈstʌm ək ˌtʃɜːn ɪŋ §-ɪk-
  ‖ -ˌtʃɜːn-
stomacher ˈstʌm ək ə §-ɪk- ‖ -ʳr —formerly
  -ətʃ-, -ədʒ- **~s** z
stomachful ˈstʌm ək fʊl §-ɪk- **~s** z
stomachic stə ˈmæk ɪk stəʊ-; ˈstʌm ək-
stomata ˈstəʊm ət ə ˈstɒm-; stəʊ ˈmaːt ə
  ‖ ˈstoʊm ət̬ ə ˈstaːm-; stoʊ ˈmaːt̬ ə
stomatitis ˌstəʊm ə ˈtaɪt ɪs ˌstɒm-, §-əs
  ‖ ˌstoʊm ə ˈtaɪt̬ əs ˌstaːm-
stomato- comb. form
  with stress-neutral suffix |stəʊm ət ə |stɒm-
  ‖ |stoʊm ət̬ ə stoʊ |mæt̬ ə — **stomatoplasty**
  ˈstəʊm ət ə ˌplæst i ˈstɒm- ‖ ˈstoʊm ət̬-
  stoʊ ˈmæt̬-
  with stress-imposing suffix ˌstəʊm ə ˈtɒ+
  ˌstɒm- ‖ ˌstoʊm ə ˈtaː+ ˌstaːm-
  — **stomatology** ˌstəʊm ə ˈtɒl ədʒ i ˌstɒm-
  ‖ ˌstoʊm ə ˈtaːl- ˌstaːm-
-stome stəʊm ‖ stoʊm — **cyclostome**
  ˈsaɪk ləʊ stəʊm ‖ -lə stoʊm
-stomous stress-imposing stəm əs
  — **monostomous** mɒ ˈnɒst əm əs mə-
  ‖ maː ˈnaːst-
stomp stɒmp ‖ staːmp **stomped** stɒmpt
  ‖ staːmpt **stomping** ˈstɒmp ɪŋ ‖ ˈstaːmp ɪŋ
  stomps stɒmps ‖ staːmps
-stomy stress-imposing stəm i — **colostomy**
  kə ˈlɒst əm i ‖ -ˈlaːst-
stone, Stone stəʊn ‖ stoʊn **stoned** stəʊnd
  ‖ stoʊnd **stones** stəʊnz ‖ stoʊnz **stoning**
  ˈstəʊn ɪŋ ‖ ˈstoʊn ɪŋ
  ˈStone ˌAge; ˈstone ˌfruit; ˈstone ˌmarten;
  ˈstone's throw
stone-blind ˌstəʊn ˈblaɪnd ◂ →ˌstəʊm-
  ‖ ˌstoʊn-
stonebreaker ˈstəʊn ˌbreɪk ə →ˈstəʊm-
  ‖ ˈstoʊn ˌbreɪk ʳr **~s** z
Stonebridge ˈstəʊn brɪdʒ →ˈstəʊm- ‖ ˈstoʊn-
stonechat ˈstəʊn tʃæt ‖ ˈstoʊn- **~s** s
stone-cold ˌstəʊn ˈkəʊld ◂ →ˈstəʊŋ-, →-kɒʊld
  ‖ ˌstoʊn ˈkoʊld ◂
stonecrop ˈstəʊn krɒp →ˈstəʊŋ- ‖ ˈstoʊn kraːp
  ~s s
stonecutter ˈstəʊn ˌkʌt ə →ˈstəʊŋ-
  ‖ ˈstoʊn ˌkʌt̬ ʳr **~s** z
stone-dead ˌstəʊn ˈded ◂ ‖ ˌstoʊn-
stone-deaf ˌstəʊn ˈdef ◂ ‖ ˌstoʊn-
stone-faced ˌstəʊn ˈfeɪst ◂ · · ‖ ˈstoʊn feɪst
stonefish ˈstəʊn fɪʃ ‖ ˈstoʊn- **~es** ɪz əz
stone-ground ˌstəʊn graʊnd →ˈstəʊŋ-, ˌ·ˈ·
  ‖ ˈstoʊn-
Stonehaven ˌstəʊn ˈheɪv ʷn ‖ ˌstoʊn- —There
  is also a local pronunciation ˌsteɪn ˈhaɪ.
Stonehenge ˌstəʊn ˈhendʒ ◂ ‖ ˈstoʊn hendʒ
Stonehouse ˈstəʊn haʊs ‖ ˈstoʊn-
Stoneleigh ˈstəʊn ˈliː ‖ ˌstoʊn-
stoneless ˈstəʊn ləs -lɪs ‖ ˈstoʊn-
stonemason ˈstəʊn ˌmeɪs ʷn →ˈstəʊm-
  ‖ ˈstoʊn- **~s** z

stonewall, S~ ˌstəʊn ˈwɔːl ◂ ˈ· · ‖ ˈstoʊn wɔːl
-waːl **~ed** d **~er/s** ə/z ‖ -ᵊr/z **~ing** ɪŋ **~s** z
stoneware ˈstəʊn weə ‖ ˈstoʊn wer -wær
stonewashed ˈstəʊn wɒʃt ˌ·ˈ· ˈstoʊn wɔːʃt
-waːʃt
stonework ˈstəʊn wɜːk ‖ ˈstoʊn wɜːk
stonk stɒŋk ‖ staːŋk **stonked** stɒŋkt ‖ staːŋkt
    stonking ˈstɒŋk ɪŋ ‖ ˈstaːŋk ɪŋ **stonks**
    stɒŋks ‖ staːŋks
stonker ˈstɒŋk ə ‖ ˈstaːŋk ᵊr **~ed** d **~s** z
stonking ˈstɒŋk ɪŋ ‖ ˈstaːŋk ɪŋ **~ly** li
Stonor (i) ˈstəʊn ə ‖ ˈstoʊn ᵊr, (ii) ˈstɒn ə
    ‖ ˈstaːn ᵊr
ston|y ˈstəʊn |i ‖ ˈstoʊn |i **~ier** i ə ‖ i ᵊr **~iest**
    i ɪst i ᵊst **~ily** ɪ li əl i **~iness** i nəs i nɪs
    ˌstəʊni ˈbroke; ˈStony Brook NY; ˌStony
    ˈPoint
stood stʊd
Stoodley ˈstuːd li
stooge stuːdʒ **stooged** stuːdʒd **stooges**
    ˈstuːdʒ ɪz -əz **stooging** ˈstuːdʒ ɪŋ
stook stuːk stʊk **stooks** stuːks stʊks
stool stuːl **stools** stuːlz
stoolie ˈstuːl i **~s** z
stoolpigeon ˈstuːl ˌpɪdʒ ən -ɪn **~s** z
stoop stuːp **stooped** stuːpt **stooping** ˈstuːp ɪŋ
    stoops stuːps
stop stɒp ‖ staːp **stopped** stɒpt ‖ staːpt
    stopping ˈstɒp ɪŋ ‖ ˈstaːp ɪŋ **stops** stɒps
    ‖ staːps
    ˌstop ˈpress◂
stop-and-go ˌstɒp ən ˈgəʊ →-ᵊŋ-
    ‖ ˌstaːp ən ˈgoʊ
stopcock ˈstɒp kɒk ‖ ˈstaːp kaːk **~s** s
stope stəʊp ‖ stoʊp **stoped** stəʊpt ‖ stoʊpt
    stopes stəʊps ‖ stoʊps **stoping** ˈstəʊp ɪŋ
    ‖ ˈstoʊp ɪŋ
Stopes stəʊps ‖ stoʊps
Stopford ˈstɒp fəd ‖ ˈstaːp fᵊrd
stopgap ˈstɒp gæp ‖ ˈstaːp- **~s** s
stop-go ˌstɒp ˈgəʊ ◂ ‖ ˌstaːp ˈgoʊ ◂
stoplight ˈstɒp laɪt ‖ ˈstaːp- **~s** s
stoploss, stop-loss ˈstɒp lɒs -lɔːs ‖ ˈstaːp lɔːs
    -laːs
stopoff ˈstɒp ɒf -ɔːf ‖ ˈstaːp ɔːf -aːf **~s** s
stopover ˈstɒp ˌəʊv ə ‖ ˈstaːp ˌoʊv ᵊr **~s** z
stoppable ˈstɒp əb ᵊl ‖ ˈstaːp-
stoppag|e ˈstɒp ɪdʒ ‖ ˈstaːp- **~es** ɪz əz
Stoppard ˈstɒp aːd -əd ‖ ˈstaːp aːrd -ᵊrd
stopper ˈstɒp ə ‖ ˈstaːp ᵊr **~ed** d **stoppering**
    ˈstɒp ər ɪŋ ‖ ˈstaːp ər ɪŋ **~s** z
stopwatch ˈstɒp wɒtʃ ‖ ˈstaːp waːtʃ **~es** ɪz əz
storage ˈstɔːr ɪdʒ ‖ ˈstoʊr-
    ˈstorage deˌvice; ˈstorage ˌheater
storax ˈstɔːr æks ‖ ˈstoʊr-
store stɔː ‖ stɔːr stoʊr **stored** stɔːd ‖ stɔːrd
    stoʊrd **stores** stɔːz ‖ stɔːrz stoʊrz **storing**
    ˈstɔːr ɪŋ ‖ ˈstoʊr-
    ˈstore deˌtective
storefront ˈstɔː frʌnt ‖ ˈstɔːr- ˈstoʊr- **~s** s
store|house ˈstɔː |haʊs ‖ ˈstɔːr- ˈstoʊr-
    ~houses haʊz ɪz -əz

storekeeper ˈstɔː ˌkiːp ə ‖ ˈstɔːr ˌkiːp ᵊr ˈstoʊr-
    ~s z
storeroom ˈstɔː ruːm -rʊm ‖ ˈstɔːr- ˈstoʊr- **~s** z
storey, S~ ˈstɔːr i ‖ ˈstoʊr i (= story) **~s** z
-storeyed, -storied ˈstɔːr id ‖ ˈstoʊr id
    — **three-storeyed, three-storied**
    ˌθriː ˈstɔːr id ◂ ‖ -ˈstoʊr-
stori... —see **story**
stori|ate ˈstɔːr i |eɪt ‖ ˈstoʊr- **~ated** eɪt ɪd -əd
    ‖ -eɪţ əd **~ates** eɪts **~ating** eɪt ɪŋ ‖ eɪţ ɪŋ
storiation ˌstɔːr i ˈeɪʃ ᵊn ˌstoʊr-
stork, Stork stɔːk ‖ stɔːrk **storks** stɔːks
    ‖ stɔːrks
storksbill ˈstɔːks bɪl ‖ ˈstɔːrks- **~s** z
storm, Storm stɔːm ‖ stɔːrm **stormed** stɔːmd
    ‖ stɔːrmd **storming** ˈstɔːm ɪŋ ‖ ˈstɔːrm ɪŋ
    storms stɔːmz ‖ stɔːrmz
    ˈstorm cloud; ˈstorm cone; ˈstorm ˌpetrel;
    ˈstorm ˌtrooper
stormbound ˈstɔːm baʊnd ‖ ˈstɔːrm-
Stormont ˈstɔː mənt -mɒnt ‖ ˈstɔːr- -maːnt
stormproof ˈstɔːm pruːf §-prʊf ‖ ˈstɔːrm- **~ed**
    t **~ing** ɪŋ **~s** s
storm|y ˈstɔːm |i ‖ ˈstɔːrm |i **~ier** i ə ‖ i ᵊr
    ~iest i ɪst i ᵊst **~ily** ɪ li əl i **~iness** i nəs i nɪs
    ˌstormy ˈpetrel
Stornoway ˈstɔːn ə weɪ ‖ ˈstɔːrn-
Storr stɔː ‖ stɔːr
Storrington ˈstɒr ɪŋ tən ‖ ˈstɔːr- ˈstaːr-
Storrs stɔːz ‖ stɔːrz
Stortford ˈstɔːt fəd ˈstɔː- ‖ ˈstɔːrt fᵊrd
Storthing, Storting ˈstɔː tɪŋ ‖ ˈstɔːr-
story ˈstɔːr i ‖ ˈstoʊr- **storied** ˈstɔːr id ‖ ˈstoʊr-
    stories ˈstɔːr iz ‖ ˈstoʊr-
    ˈstory line
storyboard ˈstɔːr i bɔːd ‖ -bɔːrd ˈstoʊr i boʊrd
    ~s z
storybook ˈstɔːr i bʊk §-buːk ‖ ˈstoʊr- **~s** s
storytell|er ˈstɔːr i ˌtel ə ‖ -ᵊr ˈstoʊr- **~ers** əz
    ‖ ᵊrz **~ing** ɪŋ
Storyville ˈstɔːr i vɪl ‖ ˈstoʊr-
stoss stɒs ʃtɒs ‖ stoʊs staːs, stɔːs —Ger [ʃtoːs]
St Osyth sənt ˈəʊz ɪθ §-ən-, -ˈəʊs-
    ‖ seɪnt ˈoʊz əθ
stot stɒt ‖ staːt **stots** stɒts ‖ staːts **stotted**
    ˈstɒt ɪd -əd ‖ ˈstaːţ əd **stotting** ˈstɒt ɪŋ
    ‖ ˈstaːţ ɪŋ
stotious ˈstəʊʃ əs ‖ ˈstoʊʃ əs
Stott stɒt ‖ staːt
Stouffer ˈstəʊf ə ‖ ˈstoʊf ᵊr (!)
Stoughton (i) ˈstəʊt ᵊn ‖ ˈstoʊt ᵊn,
    (ii) ˈstaʊt ᵊn, (iii) ˈstɔːt ᵊn ‖ ˈstaːt- —For the
    publishers Hodder & ~, (i) is appropriate,
    although (ii) is probably more often heard.
stoup stuːp (= stoop) **stoups** stuːps
Stour (i) stʊə ‖ ˈstʊᵊr, (ii) ˈstaʊ ə ‖ ˈstaʊ ᵊr,
    (iii) ˈstəʊ ə ‖ ˈstoʊ ᵊr —The river in Suffolk
    and Essex is (i), as, usually, is that in Kent.
    That in Warwickshire is (ii) or (iii). Others
    are mostly (ii).
Stourbridge ˈstaʊ ə brɪdʒ ˈstəʊ ə- ‖ ˈstaʊ ᵊr-
Stourhead (i) ˈstɔː ˈhed ‖ ˈstɔːr- ˌstoʊr-,
    (ii) ˌstaʊ ə ˈhed ‖ ˈstaʊ ᵊr-

S

Stourmouth 'staʊ‿ə maʊθ 'stʊə maʊθ
‖ 'staʊ‿ºr-
Stourport 'staʊ‿ə pɔːt 'stʊə pɔːt ‖ 'staʊ‿ºr pɔːrt
-poʊrt
Stourton (i) 'stɜːt ºn ‖ 'stɜːt ºn, (ii) 'stɔːt ºn
‖ 'stɜːrt ºn 'stoʊrt-
stoush staʊʃ **stoushed** staʊʃt **stoushes**
'staʊʃ ɪz -əz **stoushing** 'staʊʃ ɪŋ
stout, Stout staʊt **stouter** 'staʊt ə ‖ 'staʊt̬ ºr
stoutest 'staʊt ɪst -əst ‖ 'staʊt̬ əst
stouthearted ˌstaʊt 'hɑːt ɪd ◄ -əd ‖ -'hɑːrt̬-
~ly li **~ness** nəs nɪs
stoutish 'staʊt ɪʃ ‖ 'staʊt̬ ɪʃ
stout|ly 'staʊt |li **~ness** nəs nɪs
stove stəʊv ‖ stoʊv **stoves** stəʊvz ‖ stoʊvz
stovepipe 'stəʊv paɪp ‖ 'stoʊv- **~s** s
ˌstovepipe 'hat
stover 'stəʊv ə ‖ 'stoʊv ºr
stow, Stow stəʊ ‖ stoʊ **stowed** stəʊd ‖ stoʊd
stowing 'stəʊ ɪŋ ‖ 'stoʊ ɪŋ **stows** stəʊz
‖ stoʊz
stowage 'stəʊ ɪdʒ ‖ 'stoʊ-
stowaway 'stəʊ ə ˌweɪ ‖ 'stoʊ- **~s** z
Stowe stəʊ ‖ stoʊ
Stowell 'stəʊ əl ‖ 'stoʊ əl
Stowey 'stəʊ i ‖ 'stoʊ i
Stowmarket 'stəʊ ˌmɑːk ɪt §-ət
‖ 'stoʊ ˌmɑːrk ət
Stow-on-the-Wold ˌstəʊ ɒn ðə 'wəʊld
→-'wɒʊld ‖ ˌstoʊ ɑːn ðə 'woʊld -ɔːn-
St Pancras sənt 'pæŋk rəs →səm- ‖ seɪnt-
St Paul sənt 'pɔːl ‖ seɪnt- -'pɑːl **~'s** z
St Peter sənt 'piːt ə ‖ seɪnt 'piːt̬ ºr **~'s** z
St ˌPeter 'Port
St Petersburg sənt 'piːt əz bɜːg
‖ seɪnt 'piːt̬ ºrz bɜːg —Russ Sankt Peterburg
[ˌsankt pʲɪ tʲɪr 'burk]
Strabane strə 'bæn
strabismus strə 'bɪz məs stræ-
Strabo 'streɪb əʊ ‖ -oʊ
Strabolgi strə 'bəʊg i ‖ -'boʊg i
Strachan (i) 'strɔːn ‖ strɑːn, (ii) 'stræk ən
'stræx-
Strachey 'streɪtʃ i 'stræx-
Strad stræd **Strads** strædz
Strada tdmk 'strɑːd ə **~s** z
Stradbroke 'stræd brʊk →'stræb-, -brəʊk
‖ -broʊk
straddl|e 'stræd ºl **~ed** d **~es** z **~ing** ɪŋ
Stradey 'stræd i
Stradivari ˌstræd ɪ 'vɑːr i -ə- ‖ ˌstrɑːd-
Stradivari|us ˌstræd ɪ 'veər i ˌəs ˌ-ə-, -'vɑːr-
‖ -'ver- -'vær- **~i** aɪ
Stradling 'stræd lɪŋ
strafe strɑːf streɪf ‖ streɪf **strafed** strɑːft streɪft
‖ streɪft **strafes** strɑːfs streɪfs ‖ streɪfs
strafing/s 'strɑːf ɪŋ/z 'streɪf- ‖ 'streɪf ɪŋ/z
Strafford 'stræf əd ‖ -ºrd
straggl|e 'stræg ºl **~ed** d **~er/s** ˌə/z ‖ ˌºr/z
~es z **~ing** ɪŋ
straggl|y 'stræg ºl‿|i **~ier** i ə ‖ i ºr **~iest** i ɪst
i əst

straight streɪt (= strait) **straighter** 'streɪt ə
‖ 'streɪt̬ ºr **straightest** 'streɪt ɪst -əst
‖ 'streɪt̬ əst **straights** streɪts
ˌstraight and 'narrow; ˌstraight 'fight;
'straight man
straight-arm 'streɪt ɑːm ‖ 'streɪt̬ ɑːrm **~ed** d
~ing ɪŋ **~s** z
straightaway ˌstreɪt ə 'weɪ ‖ ˌstreɪt̬-
straightedg|e 'streɪt edʒ ‖ 'streɪt̬- **~ed** d **~es**
ɪz əz
straighten 'streɪt ºn **~ed** d **~er/s** ˌə/z ‖ ˌºr/z
~ing ɪŋ **~s** z
straight-faced ˌstreɪt 'feɪst ◄
straightforward ˌstreɪt 'fɔː wəd ◄
‖ -'fɔːr wºrd ◄ **~ly** li **~ness** nəs nɪs
straightjacket 'streɪt ˌdʒæk ɪt §-ət **~s** s
straight-laced ˌstreɪt 'leɪst ◄
straight-out ˌstreɪt 'aʊt ◄ ‖ ˌstreɪt̬-
ˌstraight-out 'answer
straight-to-video ˌstreɪt tə 'vɪd i əʊ ◄ ‖ -oʊ
straightway 'streɪt weɪ ˌ·'·
strain streɪn **strained** streɪnd **straining**
'streɪn ɪŋ **strains** streɪnz
'strain gauge
strainer 'streɪn ə ‖ -ºr **~s** z
strait streɪt **straits** streɪts
straitened 'streɪt ºnd
straitjacket 'streɪt ˌdʒæk ɪt §-ət **~s** s
straitlaced ˌstreɪt 'leɪst ◄
strake streɪk **strakes** streɪks
Straker 'streɪk ə ‖ -ºr
stramonium strə 'məʊn i ˌəm ‖ -'moʊn-
strand, Strand strænd **stranded** 'strænd ɪd
-əd **stranding** 'strænd ɪŋ **strands** strændz
Strang stræŋ
strange, Strange streɪndʒ **stranger**
'streɪndʒ ə ‖ -ºr **strangest** 'streɪndʒ ɪst -əst
strange|ly 'streɪndʒ |li **~ness** nəs nɪs
stranger 'streɪndʒ ə ‖ -ºr **~s** z
Strangeways 'streɪndʒ weɪz
Strangford 'stræŋ fəd ‖ -fºrd
strangl|e 'stræŋ gºl **~ed** d **~es** z **~ing** ɪŋ
stranglehold 'stræŋ gºl həʊld →-hɒʊld
‖ -hoʊld **~s** z
strangler 'stræŋ glə ‖ -glºr **~s** z
strangu|late 'stræŋ gju |leɪt -gjə- ‖ -gjə-
~lated leɪt ɪd -əd ‖ leɪt̬ əd **~lates** leɪts
~lating leɪt ɪŋ ‖ leɪt̬ ɪŋ
strangulation ˌstræŋ gju 'leɪʃ ºn -gjə- ‖ -gjə-
~s z
strangury 'stræŋ gjər i -gjuºr-
Stranraer ⑴stræn 'rɑː strən- ‖ -'rɑːr
strap stræp **strapped** stræpt **strapping**
'stræp ɪŋ **straps** stræps
straphanger 'stræp ˌhæŋ ə ‖ -ºr **~s** z
straphanging 'stræp ˌhæŋ ɪŋ
strapless 'stræp ləs -lɪs
strapline 'stræp laɪn **~s** z
strapper 'stræp ə ‖ -ºr **~s** z
strappy 'stræp i
Strasberg 'stræs bɜːg ‖ -bɜːg

Strasbourg, Strassburg 'stræz bɜːg 'stræs-,
-buəg, -bɔːg ‖ 'straːs bɜːg 'straːz-, -burg —*Fr*
[stʁaz buːʁ], *Ger* Straßburg ['stʁaːs buʁk]
strass stræs
strata 'straːt ə 'streɪt- ‖ 'streɪţ ə 'stræţ- **~s** z
stratagem 'stræt ədʒ əm -ɪdʒ-; -ə dʒem, -ɪ-
‖ 'stræţ- **~s** z
stratal 'straːt ᵊl 'streɪt- ‖ 'straːţ ᵊl
strategic strə 'tiːdʒ ɪk **~al** ᵊl **~ally** ᵊl i
strategist 'stræt ədʒ ɪst -ɪdʒ-, §-əst ‖ 'stræţ- **~s**
s
strateg|y 'stræt ədʒ |i -ɪdʒ- ‖ 'stræţ- **~ies** iz
Stratford 'stræt fəd ‖ -fᵊrd
Stratford-atte-Bowe ˌstræt fəd ˌæt i 'bəʊ -ə'·
‖ -fᵊrd ˌæţ i 'boʊ
Stratford-on-Avon ˌstræt fəd ɒn 'eɪv ᵊn
‖ -fᵊrd ɑːn 'eɪv ɑːn -ɔːn'·-
Stratford-upon-Avon
ˌstræt fəd ə ˌpɒn 'eɪv ᵊn
‖ -fᵊrd ə ˌpɑːn 'eɪv ɑːn -ˌpɔːn-
strath, Strath stræθ straːθ **straths** stræθs
Strath- stræθ straːθ —*For many speakers,* stræθ
functions as the strong form of this prefix,
used in unfamiliar names or careful style, and
stræθ *as the weak form, appropriate for*
familiar names and casual style. This applies
in the entries that follow.
Strathaven *place in Strathclyde* 'streɪv ᵊn (!)
Strathclyde ₍ₜ₎stræθ 'klaɪd straːθ-
Strathcona stræθ 'kəʊn ə straːθ- ‖ -'koʊn ə
Strathearn stræθ 'ɜːn straːθ- ‖ -'ɜːn
Stratheden stræθ 'iːd ᵊn straːθ-
Strathleven stræθ 'liːv ᵊn straːθ-
Strathmore stræθ 'mɔː straːθ- ‖ -'mɔːr -'moʊr
Strathpeffer stræθ 'pef ə straːθ- ‖ -ᵊr
strathspey, S~ stræθ 'speɪ straːθ- ‖ '·· **~s** z
Strathtay stræθ 'teɪ straːθ-
stratification ˌstræt ɪf ɪ 'keɪʃ ᵊn ˌəf-, §-ə'·-
‖ ˌstræţ- **~al** ᵊl **~ally** əl i **~s** z
stratiform 'stræt ɪ fɔːm -ə- ‖ 'stræţ ə fɔːrm
strati|fy 'stræt ɪ |faɪ -ə- ‖ 'stræţ- **-fied** faɪd
~fies faɪz **~fying** faɪ ɪŋ
stratigraphic ˌstræt ɪ 'græf ɪk ◂ §-ə- ‖ ˌstræţ-
~ally ᵊl i
stratigraphy strə 'tɪg rəf i
stratocum|ulus ˌstreɪt əʊ 'kjuːm |jʊl əs
ˌstræt-, -jəl əs ‖ ˌstreɪţ oʊ 'kjuːm |jəl əs
ˌstræţ- **~uli** ju laɪ jə laɪ ‖ jə laɪ
stratopause 'stræt əʊ pɔːz ‖ 'stræţ ə- -paːz
stratosphere 'stræt ə sfɪə -əʊ- ‖ 'stræţ ə sfɪr
stratospheric ˌstræt ə 'sfer ɪk -əʊ- ‖ ˌstræţ-
-'sfɪr-
Stratton 'stræt ᵊn
strat|um 'straːt |əm 'streɪt- ‖ 'streɪţ |əm
'stræţ- **~a** ə
stratus 'streɪt əs ‖ 'streɪţ əs 'stræţ-
Strauli 'strɔːl i ‖ 'straːl-
Strauss straʊs —*Ger* [ʃtʁaʊs]
Stravinsky strə 'vɪnt ski —*Russ*
[stra 'vʲin skʲɪj]
straw strɔː ‖ straː **straws** strɔːz ‖ straːz
ˌstraw 'man; ˌstraw 'poll ‖ '· ·; ˌstraw
'vote ‖ '· ·

strawberr|y, S~ 'strɔː bər ˌ|i ‖ 'strɔː ˌber |i
-bər ˌ|i **~ies** iz
ˌstrawberry 'blonde; 'strawberry mark
strawboard 'strɔː bɔːd ‖ -bɔːrd 'straː-, -boʊrd
straw-colored, straw-coloured
'strɔː ˌkʌl əd ‖ -ᵊrd 'straː-
Strawson 'strɔːs ᵊn ‖ 'straːs-
strawweight 'strɔː weɪt ‖ 'straː-
strawy 'strɔːʳ i ‖ 'strɔː i 'straː i
stray streɪ **strayed** streɪd **straying** 'streɪ ɪŋ
strays streɪz
streak striːk **streaked** striːkt **streaking**
'striːk ɪŋ **streaks** striːks
streaker 'striːk ə ‖ -ᵊr **~s** z
streak|y 'striːk |i **~ier** i ə ‖ i ᵊr **~iest** i ɪst i əst
~ily ɪ li əl i **~iness** i nəs i nɪs
stream striːm **streamed** striːmd **streaming**
'striːm ɪŋ **streams** striːmz
streamer 'striːm ə ‖ -ᵊr **~s** z
streamlet 'striːm lət -lɪt **~s** s
streamlin|e 'striːm laɪn **~ed** d **~es** z **~ing** ɪŋ
Streatfeild, Streatfield 'stret fiːᵊld
Streatham 'stret əm ‖ 'streţ əm
Streatley *place in Berks* 'striːt li
Streep striːp
street, Street striːt **streets** striːts —*Unlike*
all other words referring to thoroughfares,
street *is usually not accented in names:*
'Oxford Street, 'Regent Street (compare
ˌOxford 'Road, ˌRegent 'Crescent)
ˌstreet ˌcredi'bility; 'street light; 'street
smarts; 'street ˌvalue
streetcar 'striːt kaː ‖ -kaːr **~s** z
street-cred ˌstriːt 'kred
Streeter 'striːt ə ‖ 'striːţ ᵊr
street-smart 'striːt smaːt ‖ -smaːrt
streetwalker 'striːt ˌwɔːk ə ‖ -ᵊr -ˌwaːk- **~s** z
streetwise 'striːt waɪz
Streisand 'straɪ sænd -zænd, -sənd
strelitzia stre 'lɪts i ə strə- **~s** z

STRENGTH

Pie chart: 81% / 19%
■ with plosive before θ
■ without
AmE

---

strength streŋᵏθ §strenᵗθ — *Preference poll,*
AmE: with plosive before θ *81%, without 19%.*
strengths streŋᵏθs §strenᵗθs
strengthen 'streŋᵏθ ᵊn §'strenᵗθ- **~ed** d **~er/s**
ə/z ‖ ᵊr/z **~ing** ɪŋ **~s** z
strenuous 'stren ju əs **~ly** li **~ness** nəs nɪs
strep strep
strepto|coccal ˌstrept ə |'kɒk ᵊl ◂
‖ -|'kaːk ᵊl ◂ **~cocci** 'kɒks aɪ 'kɒk-, 'kɒs-, -iː
‖ 'kaːks aɪ 'kaːk-, -iː **~coccus** 'kɒk əs
‖ 'kaːk əs
streptomycin ˌstrept ə 'maɪs ɪn §-ᵊn

streptothricin, streptothrysin
  ˌstrept ə ˈθraɪs ɪn -əʊ-, -ˈθrɪs-, §-ᵊn
-stress strəs strɪs, stres — songstress
  ˈsɒŋᵏs trəs -trɪs, -tres; ˈsɒŋ strəs, -strɪs, -stres
  ‖ ˈsɔːŋᵏs trəs ˈsɑːŋᵏs-; ˈsɔːŋ strəs, ˈsɑːŋ-
stress stres stressed strest stresses ˈstres ɪz
  -əz stressing ˈstres ɪŋ
  ˈstress mark
stressful ˈstres fᵊl -fʊl ~ly _i ~ness nəs nɪs
stress-related ˈstres rɪ leɪt ɪd -rə- ·, -əd ‖ -leɪt̬·
stretch stretʃ stretched stretʃt stretches
  ˈstretʃ ɪz -əz stretching ˈstretʃ ɪŋ
stretchable ˈstretʃ əb ᵊl
stretch|er ˈstretʃ| ə ‖ -ᵊr ~ered əd ‖ ᵊrd
  ~ering ər ɪŋ ~ers əz ‖ ᵊrz
  ˈstretcher ˌparty
stretcher-bearer ˈstretʃ ə ˌbeər ə ‖ -ᵊr ˌber ᵊr
  -ˌbær- ~s z
stretchmark ˈstretʃ mɑːk ‖ -mɑːrk ~s s
stretchy ˈstretʃ i
Stretford ˈstret fəd ‖ -fᵊrd
stretto ˈstret əʊ ‖ ˈstret̬ oʊ —It [ˈstret to] ~s
  z
Stretton ˈstret ᵊn
Strevens ˈstrev ᵊnz
strew struː strewed struːd strewing ˈstruː ɪŋ
  strewn struːn §ˈstruː ən strews struːz
strewth struːθ
stria ˈstraɪ ə striae ˈstraɪ iː
striated straɪ ˈeɪt ɪd -əd ‖ ˈstraɪ eɪt̬ əd (*)
striation straɪ ˈeɪʃ ᵊn ~s z
Strick, strick strɪk
stricken ˈstrɪk ən
Strickland ˈstrɪk lənd
strickl|e ˈstrɪk ᵊl ~ed d ~es z ~ing ɪŋ
strict strɪkt stricter ˈstrɪkt ə ‖ -ᵊr strictest
  ˈstrɪkt ɪst -əst
strict|ly ˈstrɪkt |li ~ness nəs nɪs
stricture ˈstrɪk tʃə ‖ -tʃᵊr ~s z
stride, Stride straɪd stridden ˈstrɪd ᵊn
  strides straɪdz striding ˈstraɪd ɪŋ strode
  strəʊd ‖ stroʊd
stridency ˈstraɪd ᵊnts i
strident ˈstraɪd ᵊnt ~ly li
stridor ˈstraɪd ɔː -ə ‖ ᵊr -ɔːr
stridu|late ˈstrɪd ju |leɪt -jə- ‖ ˈstrɪdʒ ə |leɪt
  ~lated leɪt ɪd -əd ‖ leɪt̬ əd ~lates leɪts
  ~lating leɪt ɪŋ ‖ leɪt̬ ɪŋ
stridulation ˌstrɪd ju ˈleɪʃ ᵊn -jə- ‖ ˌstrɪdʒ ə-
  ~s z
strife straɪf
strigil ˈstrɪdʒ ɪl -əl ~s z
strike straɪk strikes straɪks striking ˈstraɪk ɪŋ
  struck strʌk
  ˈstrike pay
strikebound ˈstraɪk baʊnd
strikebreaker ˈstraɪk ˌbreɪk ə ‖ -ᵊr ~s z
strikebreaking ˈstraɪk ˌbreɪk ɪŋ
strikeout ˈstraɪk aʊt ~s s
striker ˈstraɪk ə ‖ -ᵊr ~s z
striking ˈstraɪk ɪŋ ~ly li ~ness nəs nɪs
  ˈstriking ˌdistance

strim strɪm strimmed strɪmd strimming
  ˈstrɪm ɪŋ strims strɪmz
strimmer, S~ tdmk ˈstrɪm ə ‖ -ᵊr ~s z
Strindberg ˈstrɪnd bɜːg →ˈstrɪmb- ‖ -bɜːg
  —Swed [ˈstrɪnd bærj]
Strine straɪn
string strɪŋ stringing ˈstrɪŋ ɪŋ strings strɪŋz
  strung strʌŋ
  ˌstring ˈbean, ˈ· ·; ˌstringed ˈinstrument
stringency ˈstrɪndʒ ᵊnts i
stringent ˈstrɪndʒ ᵊnt ~ly li
stringer, S~ ˈstrɪŋ ə ‖ -ᵊr ~s z
Stringfellow ˈstrɪŋ ˌfel əʊ ‖ -oʊ
string|y ˈstrɪŋ |i ~ier i ə ‖ i ᵊr ~iest i ɪst i əst
  ~ily ɪ li əl i ~iness i nəs i nɪs
strip strɪp stripped strɪpt stripping ˈstrɪp ɪŋ
  strips strɪps
  ˌstrip carˈtoon; ˈstrip club; ˈstrip
  ˌlighting; ˈstrip ˌmining; ˌstrip ˈpoker
stripe straɪp striped straɪpt stripes straɪps
  striping ˈstraɪp ɪŋ
stripling ˈstrɪp lɪŋ ~s z
stripp... —see strip
strippagram ˈstrɪp ə græm ~s z
stripped-down ˌstrɪpt ˈdaʊn ◂
stripper ˈstrɪp ə ‖ -ᵊr ~s z
stripperama ˌstrɪp ə ˈrɑːm ə ~s z
strippogram ˈstrɪp ə græm ~s z
strip-search ˌstrɪp ˈsɜːtʃ ˈ· · ‖ ˈstrɪp sɜːtʃ ~ed t
  ~es ɪz əz ~ing ɪŋ
striptease ˈstrɪp tiːz ˌ·ˈ·
strip|y ˈstraɪp |i ~ier i ə ‖ i ᵊr ~iest i ɪst i əst
  ~iness i nəs i nɪs
strive straɪv striven ˈstrɪv ᵊn (!) strives
  straɪvz striving/s ˈstraɪv ɪŋ/z strove strəʊv
  ‖ stroʊv
striver ˈstraɪv ə ‖ -ᵊr ~s z
strobe strəʊb ‖ stroʊb strobes strəʊbz
  ‖ stroʊbz
  ˈstrobe light
stroboscope ˈstrəʊb ə skəʊp
  ‖ ˈstroʊb ə skoʊp ~s s
stroboscopic ˌstrəʊb ə ˈskɒp ɪk ◂ ˌstrɒb-
  ‖ ˌstroʊb ə ˈskɑːp ɪk ◂ ~ally ᵊl i
strode, Strode strəʊd ‖ stroʊd
stroganoff ˈstrɒg ə nɒf ‖ ˈstroʊg ə nɔːf
  ˈstrɔːg-, ˈstrɑːg-, -nɑːf
stroke strəʊk ‖ stroʊk stroked strəʊkt
  ‖ stroʊkt strokes strəʊks ‖ stroʊks stroking
  ˈstrəʊk ɪŋ ‖ ˈstroʊk ɪŋ
stroll strəʊl →strɒʊl ‖ stroʊl strolled strəʊld
  →strɒʊld ‖ stroʊld strolling ˈstrəʊl ɪŋ
  →ˈstrɒʊl- ‖ ˈstroʊl ɪŋ strolls strəʊlz →strɒʊlz
  ‖ stroʊlz
stroller ˈstrəʊl ə →ˈstrɒʊl- ‖ ˈstroʊl ᵊr ~s z
strom|a ˈstrəʊm |ə ‖ ˈstroʊm |ə ~ata ət ə
  ‖ ət̬ ə
stromatolite strəʊ ˈmæt ə laɪt -ᵊl aɪt
  ‖ stroʊ ˈmæt̬ ᵊl aɪt ~s s
Stromboli ˈstrɒm bəl i ‖ ˈstrɑːm- —It
  [ˈstrɔm bo li]
Stromness ˈstrɒm nes ˈstrʌm- ‖ ˈstrɑːm-

Stress

1 A **stressed** syllable is one that carries a **rhythmic beat**. It is marked by greater loudness than unstressed syllables, and often by pitch-prominence, or greater duration, or more clearly defined vowel qualities.

2 An **accent** is the placement of intonational pitch-prominence (= higher or lower pitch than the surroundings) on a word. Speakers choose to accent certain words (or to de-accent others) because of the particular meaning they wish to convey in a particular situation. Accents can be located only on stressed syllables. Thus to accent the word **collapse** kə ˈlæps the pitch-prominence goes on the syllable læps, but in **tumble** ˈtʌm bᵊl on the syllable tʌm.

3 The stresses marked in the *Longman Pronunciation Dictionary* (LPD) are **lexical** (= potential) stresses. Whether they are realized as accents depends on intonation.

4 LPD recognizes two levels of stress:

primary stress (ˈ)   When a word is said in isolation, this is where the nuclear tone (= sentence accent) goes. A word or phrase has only one primary stress.

secondary stress (ˌ)   In a word or phrase that potentially has more than one stress, this symbol marks the place of a stress other than the primary one. If this syllable is **before** the primary stress, it may also bear an accent. See STRESS SHIFT.

5 We regard as unstressed the STRONG-vowelled syllables at the end of words such as **hesitate** ˈhez ɪ teɪt, **acorn** ˈeɪk ɔːn.

6 If the primary stress is located on the third or later syllable of a word, then there must also be a secondary stress on one or other of the first two syllables. Thus ˌorganiˈzation has the same stress pattern as ˌExeter ˈstation; asˌsociˈation has the same stress pattern as aˌnother ˈnation.

S

strong, Strong strɒŋ ‖ strɔːŋ strɑːŋ **stronger**
ˈstrɒŋ gə ‖ ˈstrɔːŋ gᵊr ˈstrɑːŋ- **strongest**
ˈstrɒŋ gɪst -gəst ‖ ˈstrɔːŋ gəst ˈ strɑːŋ-
ˌstrong ˈlanguage
strongarm ˈstrɒŋ ɑːm ‖ ˈstrɔːŋ ɑːrm ˈstrɑːŋ-
strongbox ˈstrɒŋ bɒks ‖ ˈstrɔːŋ bɑːks ˈstrɑːŋ-
~**es** ɪz əz
stronghold ˈstrɒŋ həʊld ‖ ˈstrɔːŋ hoʊld
ˈstrɑːŋ- ~**s** z
strongly ˈstrɒŋ li ‖ ˈstrɔːŋ li ˈstrɑːŋ-
strong|man ˈstrɒŋ |mæn ‖ ˈstrɔːŋ- ˈstrɑːŋ-
~**men** men
strong-minded ˌstrɒŋ ˈmaɪnd ɪd ◂ -əd
‖ ˌstrɔːŋ- ˌstrɑːŋ- ~**ly** li ~**ness** nəs nɪs
strongpoint, strong point ˈstrɒŋ pɔɪnt
‖ ˈstrɔːŋ- ˈstrɑːŋ- ~**s** s

strongroom ˈstrɒŋ ruːm -rʊm ‖ ˈstrɔːŋ- ˈstrɑːŋ-
~**s** z
strong-willed ˌstrɒŋ ˈwɪld ◂ ‖ ˌstrɔːŋ- ˌstrɑːŋ-
Stronsay ˈstrɒnz eɪ ‖ ˈstrɑːnz eɪ
strontia ˈstrɒnt i ə ˈstrɒntʃ- ‖ ˈstrɑːntʃ i ə
ˈstrɑːnt̬-
Strontian *place in Highland* ˌ(ˌ)strɒn ˈtiː ən
‖ ˌ(ˌ)strɑːn-
strontium ˈstrɒnt i əm ˈstrɒntʃ-
‖ ˈstrɑːntʃ i əm ˈstrɑːnt̬-
ˌstrontium ˈ90
Strood struːd
strop strɒp ‖ strɑːp **stropped** strɒpt ‖ strɑːpt
stropping ˈstrɒp ɪŋ ‖ ˈstrɑːp ɪŋ **strops**
strɒps ‖ strɑːps

Stress shift

1 Some words seem to change their stress pattern in connected speech. Although in isolation we say **fundamental** with the primary stress on ment and **Japanese** with the primary stress on niːz, in connected speech these words often have a different pattern. For example, there might be greater stress on fʌnd than on ment, or greater stress on dʒæp than on niːz. This phenomenon is known as **stress shift**.

2 A phrase usually receives late stress (see COMPOUNDS AND PHRASES). The placing of primary stress on the last element of the phrase means that the basic stress of the first element is weakened: combining ˈweekly and ˈlessons gives the phrase ˌweekly ˈlessons. So you might expect that ˌfundaˈmental plus miˈstake would give fundaˌmental miˈstake, and that ˌJapaˈnese plus ˈlanguage would give Japaˌnese ˈlanguage.

But these stress patterns are unbalanced. To balance them, native speakers of English usually switch round the stress levels in the first element, and say ˌfundamental miˈstake, ˌJapanese ˈlanguage.

The same thing happens in a phrase such as ˌvery ˈlazy plus ˈpeople. Stress shift produces ˌvery lazy ˈpeople.

3 In principle, stress shift can apply to any word that has a secondary stress before its primary stress. In practice, though, it is most likely to apply to those which are regularly followed in a phrase by a more strongly stressed word: most adjectives, but only certain nouns. As a helpful reminder, in this dictionary the symbol ◄ is attached to the words in which stress shift is most likely.

4 Conversely, the decision whether or not to mark a secondary stress sometimes depends on whether or not stress shift can occur. In some cases usage is divided, and then this dictionary writes the secondary stress mark in parentheses: **antique** is written ₍ˌ₎æn ˈtiːk because in a phrase such as **an antique chair** some speakers stress-shift, saying **an ˌantique ˈchair**, but others do not, saying **an anˌtique ˈchair**.

S

strophanth|in strəʊ ˈfænᵗθ |ɪn strɒ-, §-ᵊn
‖ stroʊ- **~us** əs
strophe ˈstrəʊf i ˈstrɒf-, -iː ‖ ˈstroʊf i **~s** z
strophic ˈstrɒf ɪk ˈstrəʊf- ‖ ˈstroʊf ɪk ˈstrɑːf-
stropp|y ˈstrɒp |i ‖ ˈstrɑːp |i **~ier** i ə ‖ i ᵊr
~iest i ɪst i əst **~ily** ɪ li əl i **~iness** i nəs i nɪs
Stroud, stroud straʊd
Stroudley ˈstraʊd li
strove strəʊv ‖ stroʊv
Strowger ˈstraʊdʒ ə ‖ -ᵊr
struck strʌk
structural ˈstrʌk tʃᵊr_əl -ʃᵊr_ **~ly** i
structuralism ˈstrʌk tʃᵊr_ə ˌlɪz əm ˈ-ʃᵊr_ əl ˌɪz-
structuralist ˈstrʌk tʃᵊr_əl ɪst ˈ-ʃᵊr_, §-əst **~s** s
structure ˈstrʌk tʃə -ʃə ‖ -tʃᵊr **~d** d **~s** z
   structuring ˈstrʌk tʃᵊr_ɪŋ -ʃᵊr_
strudel ˈstruːd ᵊl —*Ger* [ˈʃtʁuː dᵊl] **~s** z

struggl|e ˈstrʌg ᵊl **~ed** d **~er/s** ə/z ‖ ᵊr/z **~es**
z **~ing/ly** _ɪŋ /li
strum strʌm **strummed** strʌmd **strumming**
ˈstrʌm ɪŋ **strums** strʌmz
struma, S~ ˈstruːm ə **~s** z
Strumble ˈstrʌm bᵊl
strumpet ˈstrʌmp ɪt §-ət **~s** s
strung strʌŋ
strung-out ˌstrʌŋ ˈaʊt ◄
strung-up ˌstrʌŋ ˈʌp ◄
strut strʌt **struts** strʌts **strutted** ˈstrʌt ɪd -əd
‖ ˈstrʌt̬ əd **strutting/ly** ˈstrʌt ɪŋ /li
‖ ˈstrʌt̬ ɪŋ /li
struth struːθ
Struthers ˈstrʌð əz ‖ -ᵊrz
Strutt strʌt

Struwwelpeter ˌstruːəl ˈpiːt ə ˈ·ˌ·ˌ·; ˌstruːlˈ·ˌ·ˌ, ˈ·ˌ·ˌ· -ˈpiːt̮ ər —Ger [ˈʃtʀʊv ˀl ˌpeː te]
strychnine ˈstrɪk niːn -nɪn, -naɪn, §-nən ‖ -naɪn -nən, -niːn
Strymon ˈstraɪm ən
Strzelecki Australian name strez ˈlek i —Polish [st-ʃe ˈlets ki]
St Thomas sənt ˈtɒm əs ‖ seɪnt ˈtɑːm əs
St Tropez ˌsæn trəʊ ˈpeɪ ‖ -troʊ- —Fr Saint-Tropez [sæ̃ tʀɔ pe]
Stu stjuː →stʃuː ‖ stuː stjuː
Stuart ˈstjuː ət →ˈstʃuː ‖ ˈstuːrt ˈstjuː
stub stʌb **stubbed** stʌbd **stubbing** ˈstʌb ɪŋ
stubs stʌbz
stubble ˈstʌb əl
stubbly ˈstʌb əl i
stubborn ˈstʌb ən ‖ -ərn **~ly** li **~ness** nəs nɪs
Stubbs stʌbz
stubby ˈstʌb |i **~ier** i ə ‖ i ər **~ies** iz **~iest** i ɪst i əst **~ily** ɪ li əl i **~iness** i nəs i nɪs
stucco ˈstʌk əʊ ‖ -oʊ **~ed** d **~es, ~s** z **~ing** ɪŋ
stuck stʌk
stuck-up ˌstʌk ˈʌp ◄
stud stʌd **studded** ˈstʌd ɪd -əd **studding** ˈstʌd ɪŋ **studs** stʌdz
ˌstud ˈpoker
studbook ˈstʌd bʊk →ˈstʌb-, §-buːk **~s** s
studdingsail ˈstʌd ɪŋ seɪəl —also naut ˈstʌnˈs əl **~s** z
Studebaker ˈstuːd ə beɪk ə ˈstjuːd-, ˈ·ɪ- ‖ -ər **~s** z

STUDENT

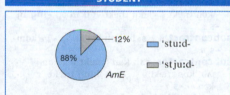

ˈstuːd-

ˈstjuːd-

AmE

88% 12%

student ˈstjuːd ənt →ˈstʃuːd-, §ˈstuːd- ‖ ˈstuːd ənt ˈstjuːd- — Preference poll, AmE: ˈstuːd- 88%, ˈstjuːd- 12%. **~s** s **~ship/s** ʃɪp/s
ˌstudents' ˈunion
studied ˈstʌd id **~ly** li **~ness** nəs nɪs
studio ˈstjuːd i əʊ →ˈstʃuːd-, §ˈstuːd- ‖ ˈstuːd i oʊ ˈstjuːd- **~s** z
ˈstudio couch
studious ˈstjuːd i əs →ˈstʃuːd-, ˈstuːd- ‖ ˈstuːd- ˈstjuːd- **~ly** li **~ness** nəs nɪs
Studland ˈstʌd lənd
Studley ˈstʌd li
study ˈstʌd i **studied** ˈstʌd id **studies** ˈstʌd iz **studying** ˈstʌd i ɪŋ
stuff stʌf **stuffed** stʌft **stuffing/s** ˈstʌf ɪŋ/z **stuffs** stʌfs
ˌstuffed ˈshirt, ˈ· ·
stuffed-up ˌstʌft ˈʌp ◄
stuffy ˈstʌf |i **~ier** i ə ‖ i ər **~iest** i ɪst i əst **~ily** ɪ li əl i **~iness** i nəs i nɪs
Stuka ˈstuːk ə **~s** z —Ger [ˈʃtuː ka, ˈʃtʊ-]
stultification ˌstʌlt ɪf ɪ ˈkeɪʃ ən ˌ·əf-, §-ə·--

stulti|fy ˈstʌlt ɪ |faɪ -ə- **~fied** faɪd **~fies** faɪz **~fying/ly** faɪ ɪŋ /li
stum, stumm 'silent' ʃtʊm
stum 'grape juice' stʌm
stumbl|e ˈstʌm bəl **~ed** d **~es** z **stumbling/ly** ˈstʌm blɪŋ /li
ˈstumbling block
stumblebum ˈstʌm bəl bʌm **~s** z
stumbler ˈstʌm blə ‖ -blər **~s** z
stumer ˈstjuːm ə →ˈstʃuːm- ‖ ˈstuːm ər ˈstjuːm- **~s** z
stumm ʃtʊm
stump stʌmp **stumped** stʌmpt **stumping** ˈstʌmp ɪŋ **stumps** stʌmps
stumpage ˈstʌmp ɪdʒ
stumpy ˈstʌmp |i **~ier** i ə ‖ i ər **~iest** i ɪst i əst **~iness** i nəs i nɪs
stun stʌn **stunned** stʌnd **stunning/ly** ˈstʌn ɪŋ /li **stuns** stʌnz
ˈstun gun
stung stʌŋ
stunk stʌŋk
stunn... —see **stun**
stunner ˈstʌn ə ‖ -ər **~s** z
stunsail, stuns'l ˈstʌn səl **~s** z
stunt stʌnt **stunted** ˈstʌnt ɪd -əd ‖ ˈstʌnt̮ əd **stunting** ˈstʌnt ɪŋ ‖ ˈstʌnt̮ ɪŋ **stunts** stʌnts
ˈstunt man, ˈstunt ˌwoman
stupa ˈstuːp ə **~s** z
stupe stjuːp ‖ stuːp stjuːp **stupes** stjuːps ‖ stuːps stjuːps
stupefaction ˌstjuːp ɪ ˈfæk ʃən ˌstjʊp-, §ˌstuːp-, →ˌstʃuːp-, -ə- ‖ ˌstuːp- ˌstjuːp-
stupe|fy ˈstjuːp ɪ |faɪ ˈstjʊp-, §ˈstuːp-, →ˈstʃuːp-, -ə- ‖ ˈstuːp- ˈstjuːp- **~fied** faɪd **~fier/s** faɪ ə/z faɪ ər/z **~fies** faɪz **~fying** faɪ ɪŋ
stupendous stju ˈpend əs →stʃu-, §stu- ‖ stu- stju- **~ly** li **~ness** nəs nɪs
stupid ˈstjuːp ɪd ˈstjʊp-, §ˈstuːp-, →ˈstʃuːp-, §-əd ‖ ˈstuːp əd ˈstjuːp- **~er** ə ‖ ər **~est** ɪst əst
stupidity stju ˈpɪd ət |i →stʃu-, §stu-, -ɪt i ‖ stu ˈpɪd ət̮ |i stju- **~ies** iz
stupidly ˈstjuːp ɪd |li ˈstjʊp-, §ˈstuːp-, →ˈstʃuːp-, §-əd- ‖ ˈstuːp əd |li ˈstjuːp- **~ness** nəs nɪs
stupor ˈstjuːp ə →ˈstʃuːp-, §ˈstuːp- ‖ ˈstuːp ər ˈstjuːp- **~s** z
sturdy ˈstɜːd |i ‖ ˈstɝːd |i **~ier** i ə ‖ i ər **~iest** i ɪst i əst **~ily** ɪ li əl i **~iness** i nəs i nɪs
Sturge stɜːdʒ ‖ stɝːdʒ
sturgeon, S~ ˈstɜːdʒ ən ‖ ˈstɝːdʒ ən **~s** z
Sturmer ˈstɜːm ə ‖ ˈstɝːm ər
Sturminster ˈstɜː ˌmɪnˈst ə ‖ ˈstɝː ˌmɪnˈst ər
Sturm und Drang ˌʃtʊəm ʊnt ˈdræŋ ‖ ˌʃtʊrm ʊnt ˈdrɑːŋ —Ger [ˌʃtʊʀm ʊnt ˈdʀaŋ]
Sturridge ˈstʌr ɪdʒ ‖ ˈstɝː ɪdʒ
Sturrock ˈstʌr ək ‖ ˈstɝː ək
Sturt stɜːt ‖ stɝːt
Sturtevant, Sturtivant ˈstɜːt ɪv ənt -əv- ‖ ˈstɝːt̮-
Sturton ˈstɜːt ən ‖ ˈstɝːt ən
Stuttaford ˈstʌt ə fəd ‖ ˈstʌt̮ ə fərd

S

Stuttard ˈstʌt əd ‖ ˈstʌt̮ ²rd
stutter ˈstʌt ə ‖ ˈstʌt̮ ²r **~ed** d **stuttering**
  ˈstʌt̮ ər ɪŋ ‖ ˈstʌt̮ ər ɪŋ **~s** z
stutterer ˈstʌt̮ ər ə ‖ ˈstʌt̮ ²r ər →ˈstʌtr ²r **~s** z
Stuttgart ˈʃtʊt gɑːt ‖ -gɑːrt ˈʃtuːt- —*Ger*
  [ˈʃtʊt gaʁt]
Stuyvesant ˈstaɪv əs ənt -ɪs-
St Vincent sənt ˈvɪnˑs ənt ‖ seɪnt-
St Vitus sənt ˈvaɪt əs ‖ seɪnt ˈvaɪt̮ əs **St Vitus',**
  St Vitus's sənt ˈvaɪt əs ɪz -əz; -ˈ·əs
  ‖ seɪnt ˈvaɪt̮ əs əz -ˈ·əs
  St ˌVitus' ˈdance
St Weonards sənt ˈwen ədz ‖ seɪnt ˈwen ²rdz
sty staɪ **sties** staɪz
Styal ˈstaɪ əl staɪ²l
stye staɪ (= *sty*) **styes** staɪz
Stygian, S~ ˈstɪdʒ i ən
style staɪ²l **styled** staɪ²ld **styles** staɪ²lz **styling**
  ˈstaɪ²l ɪŋ
-style staɪ²l — **peristyle** ˈper ɪ staɪ²l -ə-, -i-
Styles staɪ²lz
stylet ˈstaɪl ət ˈstaɪ²l-, -ɪt **~s** s
stylis... —*see* **styliz...**
stylish ˈstaɪl ɪʃ ˈstaɪ²l- **-ly** li **~ness** nəs nɪs
stylist ˈstaɪl ɪst ˈstaɪ²l-, -əst **~s** s
stylistic staɪ ˈlɪst ɪk **~ally** ²l i **~s** s
stylite ˈstaɪl aɪt ˈstaɪ²l- **~s** s
Stylites staɪ ˈlaɪt iːz
stylization ˌstaɪl aɪ ˈzeɪʃ ²n ˌstaɪ²l-, -ɪ- ‖ -ə- **~s**
  z
styliz|e ˈstaɪl aɪz ˈstaɪ²l- **~ed** d **~es** ɪz əz **~ing**
  ɪŋ
stylo ˈstaɪl əʊ ‖ -oʊ **~s** z
stylo- *comb. form*
  with stress-neutral suffix ˌstaɪl əʊ ‖ -oʊ —
    stylohyoid ˌstaɪl əʊ ˈhaɪ ɔɪd ◂ ‖ -oʊ-
  with stress-imposing suffix staɪ ˈlɒ + ‖ -ˈlɑː +
  — **stylography** staɪ ˈlɒg rəf i ‖ -ˈlɑːg-
stylobate ˈstaɪl ə beɪt -əʊ- ‖ -oʊ- **~s** s
stylograph ˈstaɪl əʊ grɑːf -græf ‖ -ə græf **~s** s
styloid ˈstaɪl ɔɪd
stylus ˈstaɪl əs **~es** ɪz əz
stymie, stymy ˈstaɪm i **stymied** ˈstaɪm id
  stymies ˈstaɪm iz **stymieing, stymying**
  ˈstaɪm i ɪŋ
styptic ˈstɪpt ɪk **~s** s
styrax ˈstaɪ²r æks
styrene ˈstaɪ²r iːn
Styri|a ˈstɪr i ǀə **~an/s** ən/z
styrofoam, S~ *tdmk* ˈstaɪ²r ə fəʊm ‖ -foʊm
Styx stɪks
Su suː
suasion ˈsweɪʒ ²n
suave swɑːv —*Formerly also* sweɪv
suave|ly ˈswɑːv ǀli ˈsweɪv- **~ness** nəs nɪs
suavity ˈswɑːv ət i ˈsweɪv-, -ɪt i ‖ -ət̮ i
sub sʌb —*but as a Latin word also* sʊb **subbed**
  sʌbd **subbing** ˈsʌb ɪŋ **subs** sʌbz —*see also*
  phrases with this word
sub- səb, ǀsʌb —*As a productive prefix,* ǀsʌb
  (ˈsubcomˌmittee, ˌ·ˈ·ˌ·); *as a fossilized prefix,*
  usually səb, §sʌb *if the following syllable is*
  stressed (subˈstantial), ǀsʌb *if not* (ˈsubstance) .

subacute ˌsʌb ə ˈkjuːt ◂ **~ly** li
subalpine ˌsʌb ˈælp aɪn ◂
subaltern ˈsʌb ²lt ən ‖ sə ˈbɔːlt ²rn -ˈbɑːlt- (*)
  ~s z
subaqua, sub-aqua ˌsʌb ˈæk wə ‖ -ˈɑːk-
subarachnoid ˌsʌb ə ˈræk nɔɪd ◂
subarctic ˌsʌb ˈɑːkt ɪk ◂ ‖ -ˈɑːrkt- -ˈɑːrt̮-
subarea ˈsʌb ˌeər i ə ‖ -ˌer- -ˌær-
Subaru *tdmk* ˈsuːb ə ruː; ˌ·ˈ· —*Jp* [ˈsɯ ba ɾɯ]
  ~s z
subassem|bly ˈsʌb ə ˌsem ǀbli ˌ·ˈ·· **~blies**
  bliz
subatomic ˌsʌb ə ˈtɒm ɪk ◂ ‖ -ˈtɑːm-
  ˌsubaˌtomic ˈparticles
subb... —*see* **sub**
subbuteo, S~ *tdmk* sə ˈbuːt i əʊ sʌ-, -ˈbjuːt-
  ‖ -ˈbuːt̮ i oʊ
subcategory ˈsʌb ˌkæt ɪg ər i -əg··
  ‖ -ˌkæt̮ ə gɔːr i -goʊr i
subclass ˈsʌb klɑːs §-klæs ‖ -klæs **~ed** t **~es** ɪz
  əz **~ing** ɪŋ
subclinical ˌsʌb ˈklɪn ɪk ²l ◂
subcommittee ˈsʌb kə ˌmɪt i ˌ·ˈ·· ‖ -ˌmɪt̮- **~s**
  z
subcompact ˌsʌb kəm ˈpækt ◂ §-kɒm-;
  -ˈkɒm pækt ‖ ˌsʌb ˈkɑːm pækt **~s** s
subconscious ˌ(ˌ)sʌb ˈkɒnʃ əs ‖ -ˈkɑːnʃ- **~ly** li
  ~ness nəs nɪs
subcontinent ˌsʌb ˈkɒnt ɪn ənt -ən-, ˈ·ˌ···
  ‖ -ˈkɑːnt ²n ənt **~s** s
subcontinental ˌsʌb ˌkɒnt ɪ ˈnent ²l -ə-
  ‖ -ˌkɑːnt ²n ˈent̮ ²l
subcontract *v* ˌsʌb kən ˈtrækt §-kɒn-,
  -ˈkɒn trækt ‖ -ˈkɑːn trækt **~ed** ɪd əd **~ing** ɪŋ
  ~s s
subcontract *n* ˌ(ˌ)sʌb ˈkɒn trækt ˈ·ˌ·· ‖ -ˈkɑːn-
  ~s s
subcontractor ˌsʌb kən ˈtrækt ə §-kɒn-, ˈ·ˌ··ˌ·;
  ˌsʌb ˈkɒn trækt ə ‖ ˌ(ˌ)sʌb ˈkɑːn trækt ²r ˈ·ˌ··ˌ·,
  ˌkən'···· **~s** z
subculture ˈsʌb ˌkʌltʃ ə ‖ -²r **~s** z
subcutaneous ˌsʌb kju ˈteɪn i əs ◂ **~ly** li
subdirector|y ˌsʌb daɪ²rˌrekt ər ǀi ǀˈ·də-, ˈ·dɪ-
  ‖ ˈ·də- **~ies** iz
subdivid|e ˌsʌb dɪ ˈvaɪd -də-, §-diː-; ˈ···· **~ed** ɪd
  əd **~es** z **~ing** ɪŋ
subdivision ˈsʌb dɪ ˌvɪʒ ²n -də-, ˌ·ˈ··· —*The*
  stressing ˌ·ˈ··· *is mostly restricted to the sense*
  'act of subdividing'; a portion resulting from
  this act is a ˈ·ˌ··ˌ·. **~s** z
subdominant ˌsʌb ˈdɒm ɪn ənt -ən ‖ -ˈdɑːm-
  ~s s
subduct səb ˈdʌkt ˌ(ˌ)sʌb- **~ed** ɪd əd **~ing** ɪŋ **~s**
  s
subduction səb ˈdʌk ʃ²n ˌ(ˌ)sʌb- **~s** z
  subˈduction zone
subdu|e səb ˈdjuː §sʌb-, →ˈdʒuː ‖ -ˈduː- -ˈdjuː
  ~ed d **~es** z **~ing** ɪŋ
subdural ˌ(ˌ)sʌb ˈdjʊər əl →-ˈdʒʊər-, -ˈdjɔːr-
  ‖ -ˈdʊr- -ˈdjʊr-
subed|it ˌsʌb ˈed ǀɪt §-ət, ˈ·ˌ·· ‖ -ǀət **~ited** ɪt ɪd
  §ət-, -əd ‖ ²t əd əd **~iting** ɪt ɪŋ §ət- ‖ ²t ɪŋ **~its**
  ɪts §əts ‖ əts

S

subeditor ˌsʌb ˈed ɪt ə §-ət ə, ˈˌˈˌ··· ‖ -əţ ʳr ~s
z
subfamil|y ˈsʌb ˌfæm əl‿|i -ɪl |i ~**ies** iz
subfreezing ˌsʌb ˈfriːz ɪŋ ◂
subfusc ˈsʌb fʌsk ˌˈˌ·
subglottal ˌsʌb ˈglɒt ᵊl ◂ ‖ -ˈglɑːţ-
subgroup ˈsʌb gruːp ~s s
subharmonic ˌsʌb hɑː ˈmɒn ɪk ‖ -hɑːr ˈmɑːn-
~s s
subhead ˈsʌb hed ˌˈˌ· ~**ing/s** ɪŋ/z ~s z
subhuman ˌsʌb ˈhjuːm ən §-ˈjuːm-
Subic ˈsuːb ɪk
subjacency ₍ˌ₎sʌb ˈdʒeɪs ᵊnˈs i
subjacent ₍ˌ₎sʌb ˈdʒeɪs ᵊnt ~**ly** li
subject v səb ˈdʒekt sʌb-; ˈsʌb dʒekt, -dʒɪkt
~**ed** ɪd əd ~**ing** ɪŋ ~s s
subject n, adj ˈsʌb dʒekt -dʒɪkt ~s s
ˈsubject ˌmatter
subjection səb ˈdʒek ʃᵊn sʌb-
subjectival ˌsʌb dʒɪk ˈtaɪv ᵊl ◂ -dʒek-
subjectiv|e səb ˈdʒekt ɪv ₍ˌ₎sʌb- ~**ely** li
~**eness** nəs nɪs ~**ism** ˌɪz əm ~**ist/s** ɪst/s §əst/s
subjectivity ˌsʌb dʒek ˈtɪv ət i -ɪt i ‖ -əţ i
subject-raising ˈsʌb dʒekt ˌreɪz ɪŋ -dʒɪkt-
subjoin ˌsʌb ˈdʒɔɪn ~**ed** d ~**ing** ɪŋ ~s z
sub judice ˌsʌb ˈdʒuːd əs i ˌsʌb-, -ˈjuːd-, -ɪs i;
-ə seɪ, -ɪ-, -keɪ
subju|gate ˈsʌb dʒu |geɪt -dʒə- ‖ -dʒə- ~**gated**
geɪt ɪd -əd ‖ geɪţ əd ~**gates** geɪts ~**gating**
geɪt ɪŋ ‖ geɪţ ɪŋ
subjugation ˌsʌb dʒu ˈgeɪʃ ᵊn -dʒə- ‖ -dʒə-
subjugator ˈsʌb dʒu geɪt ə ˈ-dʒə-
‖ -dʒə geɪţ ᵊr ~s z
subjunct ˈsʌb dʒʌŋkt ~s s
subjunctive səb ˈdʒʌŋkt ɪv §sʌb- ~**ly** li ~s z
subleas|e v ˌsʌb ˈliːs ˈ··· ~**ed** t ~**es** ɪz əz ~**ing**
ɪŋ
subleas|e n ˈsʌb liːs ˌˈˌ· ~**es** ɪz əz
sub|let ˌsʌb ‖ˈlet ~**lets** ˈlets ~**letting** ˈlet ɪŋ
‖ ˈleţ ɪŋ
sublieutenant ˌsʌb lef ˈten ənt -ləf- ‖ -luː- ~s s
subli|mate v ˈsʌb lɪ |meɪt -lə- ~**mated** meɪt ɪd
-əd ‖ meɪţ əd ~**mates** meɪts ~**mating** meɪt ɪŋ
‖ meɪţ ɪŋ
sublimate n ˈsʌb lɪm ət -ləm-, -ɪt; -lɪ meɪt, -lə-
~s s
sublimation ˌsʌb lɪ ˈmeɪʃ ᵊn -lə-
sublim|e sə ˈblaɪm ~**ed** d ~**ely** li ~**eness** nəs
nɪs ~**es** z ~**ing** ɪŋ
subliminal ˌsʌb ˈlɪm ɪn ᵊl sə ˈblɪm-, -ən- ~**ly** i
sublimity sə ˈblɪm ət i -ɪt i ‖ -əţ i
sublingual ˌsʌb ˈlɪŋ gwəl ◂
sublunary ₍ˌ₎sʌb ˈluːn ər i ‖ ˈsʌb luː ner i
submachine gun ˌsʌb mə ˈʃiːn gʌn →-ˈʃiːŋ- ~s
z
submarin|e n, adj ˈsʌb mə riːn ˌˈˌ· —
Preference polls, BrE: ˈ··· 42%, ˌˈˌ· 58%;
AmE: ˈ··· 61%, ˌˈˌ· 39%. ~**ing** ɪŋ ~**es** z
submariner ₍ˌ₎sʌb ˈmær ɪn ə -ən-
‖ ˈsʌb mə riːn ᵊr, ˌˈˌ·· (*) ~s z
submediant ₍ˌ₎sʌb ˈmiːd i‿ənt ~s s
submerg|e səb ˈmɜːdʒ sʌb- ‖ -ˈmɜːdʒ ~**ed** d
~**es** ɪz əz ~**ing** ɪŋ

SUBMARINE

ˈ···   ˌˈˌ·

AmE 42% / 58%
BrE 61% / 39%

submergence səb ˈmɜːdʒ ənˈs sʌb- ‖ -ˈmɜːdʒ-
submerse səb ˈmɜːs sʌb- ‖ -ˈmɜːs ~d t
submersible səb ˈmɜːs əb ᵊl sʌb-, -ɪb- ‖ -ˈmɜːs-
~s z
submersion səb ˈmɜːʃ ᵊn sʌb-, -ˈmɜːʒ- ‖ -ˈmɜːʒ-
-ˈmɜːʃ- ~s z
submission səb ˈmɪʃ ᵊn §sʌb- ~s z
submissive səb ˈmɪs ɪv §sʌb- ~**ly** li ~**ness** nəs
nɪs
sub|mit səb ‖ˈmɪt §sʌb- ~**mits** ˈmɪts ~**mitted**
ˈmɪt ɪd -əd ‖ ˈmɪţ əd ~**mitting** ˈmɪt ɪŋ
‖ ˈmɪţ ɪŋ
subnormal ˌsʌb ˈnɔːm ᵊl ◂ ‖ -ˈnɔːrm- ~**ly** i ~s
z
subnormality ˌsʌb nɔː ˈmæl ət i -ɪt i
‖ -nɔːr ˈmæl əţ i
suborbital ₍ˌ₎sʌb ˈɔːb ɪt ᵊl §-ət- ‖ -ˈɔːrb əţ ᵊl
subordi|nate v sə ˈbɔːd ɪ |neɪt -ə-; -ᵊ|n eɪt
‖ -ˈbɔːrd ᵊ|n eɪt ~**nated** neɪt ɪd -əd ‖ neɪţ əd
~**nates** neɪts ~**nating** neɪt ɪŋ ‖ neɪţ ɪŋ
subordinate adj, n sə ˈbɔːd ɪn ət -ᵊn ət, -ɪt
‖ -ˈbɔːrd- ~**ly** li ~s s
suˌbordinate ˈclause
subordination sə ˌbɔːd ɪ ˈneɪʃ ᵊn -ə-; -ᵊn ˈeɪʃ-
‖ -ˌbɔːrd ᵊn ˈeɪʃ ᵊn
subordinative sə ˈbɔːd ɪn ət ɪv -ˈˌᵊn-
‖ -ˈbɔːrd ᵊn eɪţ ɪv
suborn sə ˈbɔːn sʌ- ‖ -ˈbɔːrn ~**ed** d ~**ing** ɪŋ ~s
z
subornation ˌsʌb ɔː ˈneɪʃ ᵊn ‖ -ɔːr- -ᵊr-
Subotica ˈsuːb ɒ tiːts ə ‖ ˈˌ·ou- —Serbian
[ˈˈsu bɔ ti tsa]
subpar ˌsʌb ˈpɑː ◂ ‖ -ˈpɑːr ◂
subpen|a sə ˈpiːn |ə səb-, ˌsʌb- ~**aed** əd ~**aing**
əˈr ɪŋ ‖ ə ɪŋ ~**as** əz
subplot ˈsʌb plɒt ‖ -plɑːt ~s s
subpoen|a sə ˈpiːn |ə səb-, ˌsʌb- ~**aed** əd
~**aing** əˈr ɪŋ ‖ ə ɪŋ ~**as** əz
sub-post offic|e ˌsʌb ˈpəʊst ˌɒf ɪs §-əs
‖ -ˈpoʊst ˌɔːf əs -ˌɑːf- ~**es** ɪz əz
sub rosa ˌsʌb ˈrəʊz ə ‖ -ˈroʊz ə
subroutine ˈsʌb ruː ˌtiːn ~s z
subscrib|e səb ˈskraɪb §sʌb- ~**ed** d ~**er/s** ə/z
‖ ᵊr/z ~**es** z ~**ing** ɪŋ
subscript ˈsʌb skrɪpt ~**ed** ɪd əd ~s s
subscription səb ˈskrɪp ʃᵊn §sʌb- ~s z
subsection ˈsʌb ˌsek ʃᵊn ~s z
subsequenc|e ˈsequence that is subordinate'
ˈsʌb ˌsiːk wənˈs ~**es** ɪz əz
subsequence ˈbeing subsequent' ˈsʌb sɪk wənˈs
-sək-
subsequent ˈsʌb sɪk wənt -sək- ~**ly** li

subservienc|e səb ˈsɜːv i‿ənˈts sʌb- ‖ -ˈsɜːv- ~y i

subservient səb ˈsɜːv i‿ənt sʌb- ‖ -ˈsɜːv- ~ly li

subset ˈsʌb set ~s s

subsid|e səb ˈsaɪd §sʌb- ~ed ɪd əd ~es z ~ing ɪŋ

SUBSIDENCE

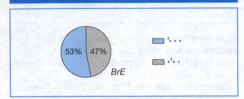

53% 47%

■ ˈ···
■ ·ˈ··

BrE

subsidenc|e səb ˈsaɪd ənts §sʌb-; ˌsʌb sɪd ənts, -səd- — Preference poll, BrE: ·ˈ·· 47%, ˈ··· 53%. ~es ɪz əz

subsidiarity səb ˌsɪd i ˈær ət i ˌsʌb sɪd-, -ɪt i ‖ -ət i -ˈer-

subsidiar|y səb ˈsɪd i‿ər |i §sʌb-; △-ˈsɪd ər‿|i ‖ səb ˈsɪd i er |i ~ies iz ~ily əl i ɪ li

subsidis... —see subsidiz...

subsidization ˌsʌb sɪd aɪ ˈzeɪʃ ən ˌ·səd-, -ɪˈ·-‖ -əˈ·- ~s z

subsidiz|e ˈsʌb sɪ daɪz -sə- ~ed d ~es ɪz əz ~ing ɪŋ

subsid|y ˈsʌb səd |i -sɪd- ~ies iz

subsist səb ˈsɪst §sʌb- ~ed ɪd əd ~ing ɪŋ ~s s

subsistence səb ˈsɪst ənts §sʌb-

　sub'sistence crop; sub'sistence ˌfarmer

subsoil ˈsʌb sɔɪəl ~s z

subsonic ˌsʌb ˈsɒn ɪk ‖ -ˈsɑːn- ~ally əl‿i

subspecies ˈsʌb ˌspiːʃ iːz -ˌspiːs-, -ɪz —see note at species

substanc|e ˈsʌb stənts ~es ɪz əz

substandard ˌsʌb ˈstænd əd ◄ ‖ -ərd ◄

SUBSTANTIAL

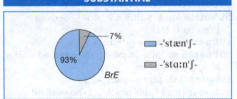

93%　7%

■ -ˈstænˈʃ-
■ -ˈstɑːnˈʃ-

BrE

substantial səb ˈstænʧ əl §sʌb-, -ˈstɑːnˈʃ-
— Preference poll, BrE: -ˈstænˈʃ- 93% (English southerners 90%), -ˈstɑːnˈʃ- 7%. In AmE always -ˈstænˈʃ-. ~ly i

substanti|ate səb ˈstænˈʃ i |eɪt §sʌb-, -ˈstɑːnˈʃ-, -ˈstænˈs- ~ated eɪt ɪd -əd ‖ eɪʈ əd ~ates eɪts ~ating eɪt ɪŋ ‖ eɪʈ ɪŋ

substantiation səb ˌstænˈʃ i ˈeɪʃ ən §sʌb-, -ˌstɑːnˈʃ-, -ˌstænˈs-

substantival ˌsʌb stən ˈtaɪv əl ◄

substantive adj səb ˈstænt ɪv §sʌb-; ˈsʌb stənt- ‖ ˈsʌb stənt ɪv ~ly li ~ness nəs nɪs

substantive n ˈsʌb stənt ɪv səb ˈstænt ɪv, §sʌb- ~s z

substation ˈsʌb ˌsteɪʃ ən ~s z

substitutability ˌsʌb stɪ tjuːt ə ˈbɪl ət i ˌ·stə-, →ˌ·ˌtʃuːt-, -ɪt i ‖ -tuːʈ ə ˈbɪl əʈ i -tjuːʈ-ˈ·-

substitutable ˈsʌb stɪ tjuːt əb əl ˈ·stə-, →-ˈtʃuːt ·ˈ·, ˌ·ˈ·· ‖ -tuːʈ əb əl -tjuːʈ· ·

substi|tute v, n ˈsʌb stɪ |tjuːt -stə-, →-ˈtʃuːt ‖ -|tuːt -tjuːt ~tuted tjuːt ɪd →ˈtʃuːt-, -əd ‖ tuːʈ əd tjuːʈ- ~tutes tjuːts →ˈtʃuːts ‖ tuːts tjuːts ~tuting tjuːt ɪŋ →ˈtʃuːt- ‖ tuːʈ ɪŋ tjuːʈ-

substitution ˌsʌb stɪ ˈtjuːʃ ən -stə-, →-ˈtʃuːʃ-‖ -ˈtuːʃ- -ˈtjuːʃ- ~s z

substitutive ˈsʌb stɪ tjuːt ɪv ˈ·stə-, →tʃuːt ·‖ -tuːʈ ɪv -tjuːʈ-

substrate ˈsʌb streɪt ~s s

substrat|um ˈsʌb ˌstrɑːt |əm -ˌstreɪt-, ˌ·ˈ·· ‖ -ˌstreɪʈ |əm -ˌstræʈ- ~a ə

substructure ˈsʌb ˌstrʌk tʃə -ʃə ‖ -tʃər ~s z

subsum|e səb ˈsjuːm §sʌb-, -ˈsuːm ‖ -ˈsuːm ~ed d ~es z ~ing ɪŋ

subsystem ˈsʌb ˌsɪst əm -ɪm

subteen ˌsʌb ˈtiːn ◄

subtenanc|y ˌsʌb ˈten ənts |i ˈ·ˌ·· ~ies iz

subtenant ˌsʌb ˈten ənt ˈ·ˌ·· ~s s

subtend səb ˈtend §sʌb- ~ed ɪd əd ~ing ɪŋ ~s z

subterfug|e ˈsʌb tə fjuːdʒ -fjuːʒ ‖ -ʈər- ~es ɪz əz

subterranean ˌsʌb tə ˈreɪn i‿ən ◄ ~ly li

subtext ˈsʌb tekst ~s s

subtitl|e ˈsʌb ˌtaɪt əl ‖ -ˌtaɪʈ əl ~ed d ~es z ~ing ɪŋ

subtle ˈsʌt əl ‖ ˈsʌʈ əl (!) ~ness nəs nɪs ~er ə ‖ ər ~est ɪst əst

subtle|ty ˈsʌt əl |ti ‖ ˈsʌʈ- ~ties tiz

subtly ˈsʌt əl‿i ‖ ˈsʌʈ əl i →ˈsʌt li

subtonic ˌsʌb ˈtɒn ɪk ◄ ‖ -ˈtɑːn- ~s s

subtopi|a sʌb ˈtəup i‿|ə ‖ -ˈtoup- ~an ən

subtotal ˈsʌb ˌtəut əl ˌ·ˈ·· ‖ -ˌtouʈ əl ~ed, ~led d ~ing, ~ling ɪŋ ~s z

subtract səb ˈtrækt §sʌb- ~ed ɪd əd ~ing ɪŋ ~s s

subtraction səb ˈtræk ʃən §sʌb- ~s z

subtractive səb ˈtrækt ɪv §sʌb- ~ly li

subtrahend ˈsʌb trə hend ~s z

subtropic ˌsʌb ˈtrɒp ɪk ‖ -ˈtrɑːp- ~al əl ◄ ~s s

subtype ˈsʌb taɪp ~s s

suburb ˈsʌb ɜːb §-əb ‖ -ɝːb ~s z

suburban sə ˈbɜːb ən ‖ -ˈbɝːb-

suburbanite sə ˈbɜːb ə naɪt ‖ -ˈbɝːb- ~s s

suburbia sə ˈbɜːb i‿ə ‖ -ˈbɝːb-

subvariet|y ˈsʌb və ˌraɪ‿ət |i ˌ·ˌ· ˌ· |i ‖ -ˌraɪ əʈ |i ~ies iz

subvention səb ˈvenʧ ən sʌb- ~s z

subversion səb ˈvɜːʃ ən sʌb-, §-ˈvɜːʒ-‖ -ˈvɝːʒ ən -ˈvɝːʃ-

subversive səb ˈvɜːs ɪv sʌb-, §-ˈvɜːz- ‖ -ˈvɝːs- ~ly li ~ness nəs nɪs ~s z

sub|vert səb |ˈvɜːt sʌb- ‖ -|ˈvɝːt ~verted ˈvɜːt ɪd -əd ‖ ˈvɜːʈ əd ~verting ˈvɜːt ɪŋ ‖ ˈvɝːʈ ɪŋ ~verts ˈvɜːts ‖ ˈvɝːts

subway ˈsʌb weɪ ~s z

Suby ˈsuːb i

subzero ˌsʌb ˈzɪər əʊ ◄ ‖ -ˈzɪr ou ◄ ˌsubˌzero ˈtemperatures

succeed sək 'si:d §sʌk- **~ed** ɪd əd **~ing** ɪŋ **~s** z
succes, succès ˌsʊk 'seɪ ◂ sək- —*Fr* [syk sɛ]
　ˌsuccès de scanˈdale, sucˌcès-
　də skɒn 'daːl ‖ -skaːn'- —*Fr* [də skã dal];
　ˌsuccès dˈeˈstime, sucˌcès - de 'stiːm —*Fr*
　[dɛs tim]; ˌsuccès ˈfou, sucˌcès- fuː —*Fr*
　[fu]
success sək 'ses §sʌk- **~es** ɪz əz
　sucˈcess ˌstory
successful sək 'ses fᵊl §sʌk-, -fʊl **~ly** ˌi
succession sək 'seʃ ᵊn §sʌk- **~al** ᵊl **~ally** ᵊl i
　~s z
successive sək 'ses ɪv §sʌk- **~ly** li **~ness** nəs
　nɪs
successor sək 'ses ə §sʌk- ‖ -ᵊr **~s** z
succinate 'sʌks ɪ neɪt -ə-
succinct sək 'sɪŋkt sʌk-, sə- **~ly** li **~ness** nəs
　nɪs
succinic sʌk 'sɪn ɪk sək-
succ|or 'sʌk| ə ‖ -ᵊr (= *sucker*) **~ored** əd ‖ ᵊrd
　~oring ər ɪŋ **~ors** əz ‖ -ᵊrz
succory 'sʌk ər i
succotash 'sʌk ə tæʃ
Succoth 'sʊk əs 'sʌk-; su 'kɒt ‖ su 'koʊs
succ|our 'sʌk| ə ‖ -ᵊr (= *sucker*) **~oured** əd
　‖ ᵊrd **~ouring** ər ɪŋ **~ours** əz ‖ -ᵊrz
succ|uba 'sʌk |jʊb ə -jəb- ‖ -|jəb ə **~ubae**
　ju biː jə-, -baɪ ‖ jə- **~ubi** ju baɪ jə-, -biː ‖ jə-
　~ubus jʊb əs jəb- ‖ jəb-
succulence 'sʌk jʊl ən's -jəl- ‖ -jəl-
succulent 'sʌk jʊl ənt -jəl- ‖ -jəl- **~ly** li
succumb sə 'kʌm **~ed** d **~ing** ɪŋ **~s** z
such *strong form* sʌtʃ, *occasional weak form*
　sətʃ
　ˈsuch and ˌsuch
Suchard *tdmk* 'suːʃ aːd -aː ‖ su 'ʃaːrd —*Fr*
　[sy ʃaːʁ]
Suchet 'suːʃ eɪ
suchlike 'sʌtʃ laɪk
suck sʌk **sucked** sʌkt **sucking** 'sʌk ɪŋ **sucks**
　sʌks
　ˈsucking pig
sucker 'sʌk ə ‖ -ᵊr **~s** z
suckl|e 'sʌk ᵊl **~ed** d **~es** z **~ing** ˌɪŋ
suckling *n*, **S~** 'sʌk lɪŋ **~s** z
sucky 'sʌk i
sucre, Sucre 'suːk reɪ —*Sp* ['suk ɾe] **~s** z
sucrose 'suːk rəʊs 'sjuːk-, -rəʊz ‖ -roʊs
suction 'sʌk ʃᵊn **~ed** d **~ing** ɪŋ **~s** z
　ˈsuction pump
Sudan su 'daːn -'dæn ‖ -'dæn
Sudanese ˌsuːd ə 'niːz ◂ ˌsʊd-, -ᵊn 'iːz ◂
　‖ ˌsuːd ᵊn 'iːz ◂ -'iːs ◂
Sudanic su 'dæn ɪk
sudari|um su 'deər i ˌ|əm sju- ‖ -'der- -'dær- **~a**
　ə
sudatori|um ˌsuːd ə 'tɔːr i ˌ|əm ˌsjuːd- ‖ -'toʊr-
　~a ə
sudator|y 'suːd ət ər |i 'sjuːd- ‖ 'suːd ə tɔːr |i
　-toʊr i **~ies** iz
Sudbury 'sʌd bər ˌi →'sʌb- ‖ -ˌber i
Suddaby 'sʌd əb i

sudden 'sʌd ᵊn **~ly** li **~ness** nəs nɪs
　ˌsudden ˈdeath
Sudeten su 'deɪt ᵊn **~land** lænd
sudoku, su doku su 'dəʊk uː -'dɒk-;
　'suːd ə ku ‖ -'doʊk- —*Jp* [sɯ̥ ɯ do kɯ]
sudorific ˌsuːd ə 'rɪf ɪk ◂ ˌsjuːd-, -ɒ-, -ɔː- **~s** s
suds sʌdz
sudsy 'sʌdz i
sue sjuː suː ‖ suː **sued** sjuːd suːd ‖ suːd **sues**
　sjuːz suːz ‖ suːz **suing** 'sjuː ɪŋ 'suː- ‖ 'suː ɪŋ
Sue suː
suede, suède sweɪd (= *swayed*)
　ˌsuede ˈshoes
suet 'suː ɪt 'sjuː-, §-ət
　ˌsuet ˈpudding
Suetonius ˌsuː ɪ 'təʊn i ˌəs ˌsjuː-, ə'--, swiː'--
　‖ -'toʊn-
Suez 'suː ɪz 'sjuː-, ˌsuː 'ez suː ez (*)
　ˌSuez Caˈnal
suffer 'sʌf ə ‖ -ᵊr **~ed** d **suffering** 'sʌf ər ɪŋ **~s**
　z
sufferab|le 'sʌf ər əb |ᵊl **~ly** li
sufferance 'sʌf ᵊr ən's
sufferer 'sʌf ᵊr ə ‖ -ər **~s** z
suffic|e sə 'faɪs **~ed** t **~es** ɪz əz **~ing** ɪŋ
sufficiency sə 'fɪʃ ᵊn's i
sufficient sə 'fɪʃ ᵊnt **~ly** li
suffix *n* 'sʌf ɪks **~es** ɪz əz
suffix *v* 'sʌf ɪks sə 'fɪks, sʌ- **~ed** t **~es** ɪz əz
　~ing ɪŋ
suffixal 'sʌf ɪks ᵊl sə 'fɪks ᵊl, sʌ-
suffixation ˌsʌf ɪk 'seɪʃ ᵊn
suffo|cate 'sʌf ə |keɪt **~cated** keɪt ɪd -əd
　‖ keɪt̬ əd **~cates** keɪts **~cating/ly** keɪt ɪŋ /li
　‖ keɪt̬ ɪŋ /li
suffocation ˌsʌf ə 'keɪʃ ᵊn
Suffolk 'sʌf ək
suffragan 'sʌf rəg ən ⚠-rædʒ- **~s** z
suffrag|e 'sʌf rɪdʒ **~es** ɪz əz
suffragette ˌsʌf rə 'dʒet -rɪ- **~s** s
suffragist 'sʌf rədʒ ɪst -rɪdʒ-, §-əst **~s** s
suffus|e sə 'fjuːz sʌ- **~ed** d **~es** ɪz əz **~ing** ɪŋ
suffusion sə 'fjuːʒ ᵊn sʌ- **~s** z
Sufi 'suːf i **~s** z
Sufism 'suːf ˌɪz əm
Sugababes 'ʃʊg ə beɪbz
sugar 'ʃʊg ə ‖ -ᵊr (!) **~ed** d **sugaring**
　'ʃʊg ər ɪŋ **~s** z
　ˌsugar ˈbeet, '·· ·; 'sugar bowl; 'sugar
　ˌdaddy
sugarcane 'ʃʊg ə keɪn ‖ -ᵊr-
sugarcoated ˌʃʊg ə 'kəʊt ɪd ◂ -əd
　‖ -ᵊr 'koʊt̬ əd ◂
sugar-free ˌʃʊg ə 'friː ◂ ‖ -ᵊr-
sugariness 'ʃʊg ər i nəs -nɪs
sugarless 'ʃʊg ə ləs -lɪs ‖ -ᵊr-
sugarloaf 'ʃʊg ə ləʊf ‖ -ᵊr loʊf
sugarplum 'ʃʊg ə plʌm ‖ -ᵊr- **~s** z
sugary 'ʃʊg ər i
Sugden 'sʌg dən

S

SUGGEST

with g
without g

AmE
23%
77%

suggest sə ˈdʒest ‖ səg ˈdʒest sə- — *Preference poll, AmE: with* g 77%, *without* g 23%. **~ed** ɪd əd **~ing** ɪŋ **~s** s
suggestibility sə ˌdʒest ə ˈbɪl ət i -ˌɪ-, -ɪt i ‖ səg ˌdʒest ə ˈbɪl əṭ i
suggestible sə ˈdʒest əb əl -ɪb- ‖ səg-
suggestion sə ˈdʒes tʃən →-ˈdʒeʃ- ‖ səg- **~s** z
suggestive sə ˈdʒest ɪv ‖ səg- **~ly** li **~ness** nəs nɪs
Sugrew, Sugrue ˈsuː gruː
Suharto su ˈhɑːt əʊ ‖ -ˈhɑːṛ̥ oʊ
sui ˈsuː aɪ ˈsjuː-, -iː
ˌsui ˈgeneris ˈdʒen ər ɪs ˈgen-; ˌsui ˈjuris ˈdʒʊər ɪs ˈjʊər-
Sui *dynasty* sweɪ ˈsuː i —*Chi* Suí [²sweɪ]
suicidal ˌsuː ɪ ˈsaɪd əl ◂ ˌsjuː̣, ə- **~ly** i
suicide ˈsuː ɪ saɪd ˈsjuː̣, ə- **~s** z
suint swɪnt ˈsuː ɪnt, ˈsjuː̣

SUIT

suːt
sjuːt

BrE
28%
72%

BrE without -j- by age

Percentage
100
80
60
40
0

Older ◄ Speakers ► Younger

suit suːt sjuːt — *Preference poll, BrE:* suːt 72%, sjuːt 28%. *In AmE always* suːt. **suited** ˈsuːt ɪd ˈsjuːt-, -əd ‖ ˈsuːṭ əd **suiting/s** ˈsuːt ɪŋ/z ˈsjuːt- ‖ ˈsuːṭ ɪŋ/z **suits** suːts sjuːts ‖ suːts
suitability ˌsuːt ə ˈbɪl ət i ˌsjuːt-, -ɪt i ‖ ˌsuːṭ ə ˈbɪl əṭ i
suitable ˈsuːt əb əl ˈsjuːt- ‖ ˈsuːṭ- **~leness** əl nəs -nɪs **~ly** li
suitcase ˈsuːt keɪs ˈsjuːt- **~es** ɪz əz
suite swiːt (= *sweet*) —*but in AmE sometimes* suːt *in the sense 'suite of furniture'* **suites** swiːts
suitor ˈsuːt ə ˈsjuːt- ‖ ˈsuːṭ ʰr **~s** z
Sukey, Sukie ˈsuːk i

sukiyaki ˌsuːk i ˈjɑːk i ˌsʊk- —*Jp* [sɯ̥ ˌki ja ki]
Sukkot, Sukkoth su ˈkəʊt ˈsʊk əs, ˈsʌk-, -ət ‖ ˈsʊk oʊt -oʊs, -əs
Sulawesi ˌsuːl ə ˈweɪs i
sulcal ˈsʌlk əl **~ly** i
sulcalis... —*see* **sulcaliz...**
sulcalization ˌsʌlk ə laɪ ˈzeɪʃ ən -lɪˈ· · ‖ ˌ·əl ə
sulcaliz|e ˈsʌlk ə laɪz **~ed** d **~es** ɪz əz **~ing** ɪŋ
sulcate *adj* ˈsʌlk eɪt
sulcus ˈsʌlk əs **sulci** ˈsʌls aɪ ˈsʌlk-, -iː
Suleiman ˌsʊl i ˈmɑːn ˌsuːl-, -eɪ-, ˈ· · ·
sulfa ˈsʌlf ə
ˈsulfa drug
sulfadiazine ˌsʌlf ə ˈdaɪ̣ ə ziːn
sulfaguanidine ˌsʌlf ə ˈgwɑːn ɪ diːn -ˈ·ə-
sulfamic sʌl ˈfæm ɪk
sulfanilamide ˌsʌlf ə ˈnɪl ə maɪd
sulfate ˈsʌlf eɪt **~s** s
sulfathiazole ˌsʌlf ə ˈθaɪ̣ ə zəʊl →-zɒʊl ‖ -zoʊl
sulfide ˈsʌlf aɪd **~s** z
sulfite ˈsʌlf aɪt **~s** s
sulfonamide sʌl ˈfɒn ə maɪd ‖ -ˈfɑːn- -ˈfoʊn-
sulfo|nate ˈsʌlf ə |neɪt **~nated** neɪt ɪd -əd ‖ neɪṭ əd **~nates** neɪts **~nating** neɪt ɪŋ ‖ neɪṭ ɪŋ
sulfone ˈsʌlf əʊn ‖ -oʊn **~s** z
sulfonic sʌl ˈfɒn ɪk ‖ -ˈfɑːn- -ˈfoʊn-
sulfur ˈsʌlf ə ‖ -ʰr
sulfureous sʌl ˈfjʊər i̠ əs -ˈfjɔːr- ‖ -ˈfjʊr-
sulfu|ret ˈsʌlf juʰ |ret -jə-, -ə-; ˌ· ·ˈ· ‖ -ə- **~reted, ~retted** ret ɪd -əd ‖ reṭ əd **~reting, ~retting** ret ɪŋ ‖ reṭ ɪŋ **~rets** rets
sulfuric sʌl ˈfjʊər ɪk -ˈfjɔːr- ‖ -ˈfjʊr- sulˌfuric ˈacid
sulfurous ˈsʌlf ər əs -jʊr- **~ly** li **~ness** nəs nɪs
Sulgrave ˈsʌl greɪv
sulk sʌlk **sulked** sʌlkt **sulking** ˈsʌlk ɪŋ **sulks** sʌlks
sulk|y ˈsʌlk |i **~ier** i̠ ə ‖ i̠ ʰr **~iest** i̠ ɪst i̠ əst **~ily** ɪ li əl i **~iness** i nəs i nɪs
Sulla ˈsʌl ə ˈsʊl-
sullage ˈsʌl ɪdʒ
sullen ˈsʌl ən **~ly** li **~ness** nəs nɪs
sulli... —*see* **sully**
Sullivan ˈsʌl ɪv ən -əv-
Sullom Voe ˌsuːl əm ˈvəʊ ˌsʌl- ‖ -ˈvoʊ
sully, Sully ˈsʌl i **sullied** ˈsʌl id **sullies** ˈsʌl iz **sullying** ˈsʌl i ɪŋ
sulpha ˈsʌlf ə
ˈsulpha drug
sulphadiazine ˌsʌlf ə ˈdaɪ̣ ə ziːn
sulphaguanidine ˌsʌlf ə ˈgwɑːn ɪ diːn -ˈ·ə-
sulphamic sʌl ˈfæm ɪk
sulphanilamide ˌsʌlf ə ˈnɪl ə maɪd
sulphate ˈsʌlf eɪt **~s** s
sulphathiazole ˌsʌlf ə ˈθaɪ̣ ə zəʊl →-zɒʊl ‖ -zoʊl
sulphide ˈsʌlf aɪd **~s** z
sulphite ˈsʌlf aɪt **~s** s
sulphonamide sʌl ˈfɒn ə maɪd ‖ -ˈfɑːn- -ˈfoʊn-

S

sulpho|nate 'sʌlf ə |neɪt ~**nated** neɪt ɪd -əd
‖ neɪ̯t əd ~**nates** neɪts ~**nating** neɪt ɪŋ
‖ neɪ̯t ɪŋ
sulphone 'sʌlf əʊn ‖ -oʊn ~**s** z
sulphonic sʌl 'fɒn ɪk ‖ -'fɑːn- -'foʊn-
sulphur 'sʌlf ə ‖ -ər
sulphureous sʌl 'fjʊər i əs -'fjɔːr- ‖ -'fjʊr-
sulphu|ret 'sʌlf juə |ret -jə-, -ə-; ˌ·ˈ· ‖ -ə-
~**reted, ~retted** ret ɪd -əd ‖ reṭ əd ~**reting,**
~**retting** ret ɪŋ ‖ reṭ ɪŋ ~**rets** rets
sulphuric sʌl 'fjʊər ɪk -'fjɔːr- ‖ -'fjʊr-
sul‚phuric 'acid
sulphurous 'sʌlf ər əs -jʊr- ~**ly** li ~**ness** nəs
nɪs
sultan 'sʌlt ən ‖ -ᵊn ~**s** z
sultana sʌl 'tɑːn ə səl- ‖ -'tæn- ~**s** z
sultanate 'sʌlt ən ət -ɪt; -ə neɪt, -ᵊn eɪt
‖ -ᵊn eɪt ~**s** s
sultr|y 'sʌltr |i -ier i ə ‖ i ᵊr ~iest i ɪst i ̩əst
~ily əl i i li ~iness i nəs i nɪs
Sulu 'suːl uː
Sulwen 'siːᵊl wen -wən —Welsh ['sil wen,
'sil-]
Sulwyn 'siːᵊl wɪn —Welsh ['sil win, 'sil-]
sum sʌm **summed** sʌmd **summing** 'sʌm ɪŋ
sums sʌmz
‚sum 'total
sumac, sumach 'ʃuːm æk 'suːm-, 'sjuːm- ~**s** s
Sumatr|a su 'mɑːtr |ə sju-, sə- ~**an/s** ən/z
Sumburgh 'sʌm bər ə
Sumer 'suːm ə ‖ -ər
Sumerian su 'mɪər i ən sju-, sə-, -'meər-
‖ -'mer- -'mɪr- ~**s** z
Sumitomo ˌsuːm i 'təʊm əʊ ‖ -'toʊm oʊ —Jp
[sɯ ˌmi to mo]
summa 'sʌm ə 'sʊm-, -ɑː
‚summa cum 'laude
summarily 'sʌm ᵊr ‚əl i i ̩l-; sə 'mer-
‖ sə 'mer əl i
summaris|e, summariz|e 'sʌm ə raɪz ~**ed** d
~**es** ɪz əz ~**ing** ɪŋ
summar|y 'sʌm ər ̩|i ~**ies** iz
summat 'sʌm ət —Since this is mainly a North
of England dialect word, in practice it is more
usually 'sʊm-
summation sʌ 'meɪʃ ᵊn sə- ~**s** z
summer 'sʌm ə ‖ -ər ~**s** z
'summer school
Summer 'sʌm ə ‖ -ər ~**s** z
Summerfield 'sʌm ə fiːᵊld ‖ -ər-
Summerhayes 'sʌm ə heɪz ‖ -ər-
Summerhill 'sʌm ə hɪl ‖ -ər-
summer|house 'sʌm ə |haʊs ‖ -ər- ~**houses**
haʊz ɪz -əz
summeriness 'sʌm ər i nəs -nɪs
Summers 'sʌm əz ‖ -ərz
Summerscale 'sʌm ə skerᵊl ‖ -ər-
Summerskill 'sʌm ə skɪl ‖ -ər-
summertime 'sʌm ə taɪm ‖ -ər-
summery 'sʌm ər i
summing-up ˌsʌm ɪŋ 'ʌp **summings-up**
ˌsʌm ɪŋz 'ʌp

summit 'sʌm ɪt §-ət ~**s** s
'summit ‚conference
summiteer ˌsʌm ɪ 'tɪə -ə- ‖ -'tɪᵊr ~**s** z
summitry 'sʌm ɪtr i §-ətr-
summon 'sʌm ən ~**ed** d ~**ing** ɪŋ ~**s** z
summons 'sʌm ənz ~**ed** d ~**es** ɪz əz ~**ing** ɪŋ
summum bonum ˌsʌm əm 'bəʊn əm ˌsʊm-,
-ʊm-, -'bɒn-, -ʊm ‖ -'boʊn-
Sumner 'sʌm nə ‖ -nᵊr
sumo 'suːm əʊ ‖ -oʊ —Jp [sɯ ˌmoo]
sump sʌmp **sumps** sʌmps
sumptuary 'sʌmp tʃu ər i -tju ˌər- ‖ -er i
sumptuous 'sʌmp tʃu əs -tju ̩ ~**ly** li ~**ness** nəs
nɪs
Sumter 'sʌmᵖt ə ‖ -ər
sun sʌn **sunned** sʌnd **sunning** 'sʌn ɪŋ **suns**
sʌnz
'sun god; 'sun ‚lounge; 'sun ‚parlor; 'sun
‚porch; 'sun ‚visor
sunbaked 'sʌn beɪkt →'sʌm-
sunbath|e 'sʌn beɪð →'sʌm- ~**ed** d ~**er/s** ə/z
‖ ᵊr/z ~**es** z ~**ing** ɪŋ
sunbeam, S~ 'sʌn biːm →'sʌm- ~**s** z
sunbed 'sʌn bed →'sʌm- ~**s** z
sunbelt, S~ 'sʌn belt →'sʌm-
sunbird 'sʌn bɜːd →'sʌm- ‖ -bɝːd ~**s** z
sunblind 'sʌn blaɪnd →'sʌm- ~**s** z
sunblock 'sʌn blɒk →'sʌm- -blɑːk ~**s** s
sunbonnet 'sʌn ˌbɒn ɪt →'sʌm-, §-ət
‖ -ˌbɑːn ət ~**s** s
sunburn 'sʌn bɜːn →'sʌm- ‖ -bɝːn ~**ed** d
sunburnt 'sʌn bɜːnt →'sʌm- ‖ -bɝːnt
sunburst 'sʌn bɜːst →'sʌm- ‖ -bɝːst ~**s** s
Sunbury 'sʌn bər i →'sʌm- ‖ -ˌber i
Sunda 'sʌnd ə 'sʊnd-, 'suːnd-
sundae 'sʌnd eɪ -i 'sʊnd-, 'suːnd-
Sundanese ˌsʌnd eɪ 'niːz ◂ ˌsʊnd-, ˌsuːnd-
‖ -'niːs ◂
Sunday 'sʌn deɪ 'sʌnd i —see note at -day ~**s** z
‚Sunday 'best; 'Sunday school
sundeck 'sʌn dek ~**s** s
sunder 'sʌnd ə ‖ -ᵊr ~**ed** d **sundering**
'sʌnd ər ɪŋ ~**s** z
Sunderland 'sʌnd ə lənd →-ᵊl ənd ‖ -ᵊr-
sundew 'sʌn djuː →-dʒuː ‖ -duː -djuː ~**s** z
sundial 'sʌn ˌdaɪ ᵊl ~**s** z
sundown 'sʌn daʊn ~**s** z
sundowner 'sʌn daʊn ə ‖ -ᵊr ~**s** z
sundrenched 'sʌn drentʃt
sundress 'sʌn dres ~**es** ɪz əz
Sundridge 'sʌndr ɪdʒ
sun-dried 'sʌn draɪd ˌ·ˈ· ◂
sundr|y 'sʌndr| i ~**ies** iz
sunfish 'sʌn fɪʃ ~**es** ɪz əz
sunflower 'sʌn ˌflaʊ ə ‖ -ˌflaʊ ᵊr ~**s** z
sung sʌŋ
sunglasses 'sʌn ˌglɑːs ɪz →'sʌŋ-, §-ˌglæs-, -əz
‖ -ˌglæs əz
sunhat 'sʌn hæt ~**s** s
sunk sʌŋk
sunken 'sʌŋk ən
sunkissed, Sunkist tdmk 'sʌn kɪst →'sʌŋ-
sunlamp 'sʌn læmp ~**s** s

sunless 'sʌn ləs -lɪs **~ly** li **~ness** nəs nɪs
sunlight, S~ 'sʌn laɪt
sunlit 'sʌn lɪt
sunlounger 'sʌn ˌlaʊndʒ ə ‖ -ᵊr **~s** z
Sunna 'sʊn ə 'sʌn-
Sunni 'sʊn i 'sʌn- **~s** z
Sunningdale 'sʌn ɪŋ deɪᵊl
Sunnite 'sʊn aɪt 'sʌn- **~s** s
sunn|y, Sunn|y 'sʌn |i **~ier** i‿ə ‖ i‿ᵊr **~iest**
i‿ɪst i‿əst **~ily** ɪ li əl i **~iness** i nəs i nɪs
Sunnyside 'sʌn i saɪd
sunny-side up ˌsʌn i saɪd 'ʌp
sunray 'sʌn reɪ **~s** z
sunris|e 'sʌn raɪz **~es** ɪz əz
   'sunrise ˌindustry
sunroof 'sʌn ruːf -rʊf **~s** s
sunroom 'sʌn ruːm -rʊm **~s** z
sunscreen 'sʌn skriːn **~s** z
sunseeker 'sʌn ˌsiːk ə ‖ -ᵊr **~s** z
sunset 'sʌn set **~s** s
sunshade 'sʌn ʃeɪd **~s** z
sunshine 'sʌn ʃaɪn
sunspot 'sʌn spɒt ‖ -spaːt **~s** s
sunstroke 'sʌn strəʊk ‖ -stroʊk
suntan 'sʌn tæn **~ned** d **~ning** ɪŋ **~s** z
Suntory tdmk 'sʌn tɔːr i ·'·· —Jp ['san to rii]
suntrap 'sʌn træp **~s** s
sun-up 'sʌn ʌp **~s** s
Sun Yatsen ˌsʌn jæt 'sen ‖ -jaːt- —Chi Sūn
Zhōngshān ['swən 'tʂʊŋ 'ʂan]
sup sʌp **supped** sʌpt **supping** 'sʌp ɪŋ **sups**
sʌps
supe suːp **supes** suːps
super 'suːp ə 'sjuːp- ‖ -ᵊr **~s** z
super- ˌsuːp ə ˌsjuːp ə ‖ -ᵊr — **superpower**
'suːp ə ˌpaʊ‿ə 'sjuːp- ‖ 'suːp ᵊr ˌpaʊ‿ᵊr
superabundance ˌsuːp ər‿ə 'bʌnd ən's ˌsjuːp-,
-ə‿ə-
superabundant ˌsuːp ər‿ə 'bʌnd ənt ◄ ˌsjuːp-,
-ə‿ə- **~ly** li
superannu|ate ˌsuːp ər 'æn ju |eɪt ˌsjuːp-
‖ ˌ·ᵊr- **~ated** eɪt ɪd -əd ‖ eɪt̬ əd **~ates** eɪts
~ating eɪt ɪŋ ‖ eɪt̬ ɪŋ
superannuation ˌsuːp ər ˌæn ju 'eɪʃ ᵊn ˌsjuːp-,
‖ ˌ·ᵊr- **~s** z
superb su 'pɜːb sju-, sə- ‖ -'pɝːb **~ly** li **~ness**
nəs nɪs
Superbowl 'suːp ə bəʊl 'sjuːp-, →-bɒʊl
‖ -ᵊr boʊl
superbug 'suːp ə bʌg 'sjuːp ‖ -rᵊ- **~s** z
supercargo ˌsuːp ə 'kaːg əʊ ˌsjuːp-, '···
‖ -ᵊr 'kaːrg oʊ **~s** z
supercharg|e 'suːp ə tʃaːdʒ 'sjuːp-, ˌ·'·
‖ -ᵊr tʃaːrdʒ **~ed** d **~es** ɪz əz **~ing** ɪŋ
supercharger 'suːp ə ˌtʃaːdʒ ə 'sjuːp-, ˌ·'··
‖ -ᵊr ˌtʃaːrdʒ ᵊr **~s** z
supercilious ˌsuːp ə 'sɪl i‿əs ◄ ˌsjuːp- ‖ ˌ·ᵊr- **~ly**
li **~ness** nəs nɪs
supercomputer 'suːp ə kəm ˌpjuːt ə 'sjuːp-,
§-ə kɒm- ‖ 'suːp ᵊr kəm ˌpjuːt̬ ᵊr **~s** z
superconduction ˌsuːp ə kən 'dʌk ʃᵊn ˌsjuːp-,
§-kɒn·- ‖ ˌ·ᵊr-

superconductive ˌsuːp ə kən 'dʌkt ɪv ◄
ˌsjuːp-, §-ə kɒn- ‖ ˌsuːp ᵊr-
superconductivity ˌsuːp ə ˌkɒn dʌk 'tɪv ət i
ˌsjuːp-, -ɪt i ‖ -ᵊr ˌkaːn dʌk 'tɪv ət̬ i
superconductor ˌsuːp ə kən 'dʌkt ə ˌsjuːp-,
§-kɒn·- ‖ -ᵊr kən 'dʌkt ᵊr **~s** z
supercool ˌsuːp ə 'kuːl ◄ ˌsjuːp-, '··· ‖ -ᵊr- **~ed**
d **~ing** ɪŋ **~s** z
Superdrug tdmk 'suːp ə drʌg 'sjuːp- ‖ -rᵊ-
superduper ˌsuːp ə 'duːp ə ◄ ˌsjuːp-
‖ -ᵊr 'duːp ᵊr
superego ˌsuːp ər 'iːg əʊ ˌsjuːp-, -ə-, -'eg-
‖ -'iːg oʊ **~s** z
superelevation ˌsuːp ər ˌel ɪ 'veɪʃ ᵊn ˌ·ə-, -ə'--
supererogation ˌsuːp ər er ə 'geɪʃ ᵊn ˌsjuːp-,
ˌ·ə-
supererogatory ˌsuːp ər er ə 'geɪt ər i ˌsjuːp-,
ˌ·‿ɪ -'rɒg ət· ‖ -'raːg ə tɔːr i -toʊr i
superficial ˌsuːp ə 'fɪʃ ᵊl ◄ ˌsjuːp- ‖ -ᵊr- **~ly** i
~ness nəs nɪs
superficiality ˌsuːp ə ˌfɪʃ i 'æl ət i ˌsjuːp-, -ɪt i
‖ -ᵊr ˌfɪʃ i 'æl ət̬ i
superficies ˌsuːp ə 'fɪʃ iːz ˌsjuːp-, -'fɪʃ i iːz ‖ -ᵊr-
superfine ˌsuːp ə faɪn 'sjuːp-, ˌ·‿·' ‖ -ᵊr- **~ness**
nəs nɪs
superfix 'suːp ə fɪks 'sjuːp- ‖ -ᵊr- **~es** ɪz əz
superfluid 'suːp ə ˌfluːˌɪd 'sjuːp-, §ˌəd ‖ -ᵊr- **~s**
z
superfluidity ˌsuːp ə flu 'ɪd ət i ˌsjuːp-, -ɪt i
‖ -ᵊr flu 'ɪd ət̬ i
superfluit|y ˌsuːp ə 'fluːˌət |i ˌsjuːp-, ɪt i
‖ -ᵊr 'fluː ət̬ |i **~ies** iz
superfluous su 'pɜːf lu‿əs sju- ‖ -'pɝːf- (!) **~ly**
li **~ness** nəs nɪs
Superfund 'suːp ə fʌnd 'sjuːp- ‖ -ᵊr-
super-G 'suːp ə dʒiː 'sjuːp- ‖ -ᵊr-
supergiant 'suːp ə ˌdʒaɪ‿ənt 'sjuːp- ‖ -ᵊr- **~s** s
superglue, Super Glue tdmk 'suːp ə gluː
'sjuːp- ‖ -ᵊr-
supergrass 'suːp ə graːs 'sjuːp-, §-græs
‖ -ᵊr græs **~es** ɪz əz
superhero 'suːp ə ˌhɪər əʊ 'sjuːp-, ˌ·'·‿·
‖ -ᵊr ˌhɪr oʊ -ˌhiː roʊ **~es** z
superhet 'suːp ə het 'sjuːp- ‖ -ᵊr- **~s** s
superhighway ˌsuːp ə 'haɪ weɪ ˌsjuːp-, '·‿·ˌ·
‖ -ᵊr- **~s** z
superhuman ˌsuːp ə 'hjuːm ən ◄ ˌsjuːp-,
§-'juːm- ‖ -ᵊr-
   ˌsuper ˌhuman 'efforts
superimpos|e ˌsuːp ər ɪm 'pəʊz ˌsjuːp-, ˌ·ə-
‖ -'poʊz **~ed** d **~es** ɪz əz **~ing** ɪŋ
superimposition ˌsuːp ər ˌɪmp ə 'zɪʃ ᵊn
ˌsjuːp-, ˌ·ə-
superintend ˌsuːp ər ɪn 'tend ˌsjuːp-, ˌ·ə-,
§ˌ·ᵊn ‖ **~ed** ɪd əd **~ency** ən's i **~ing** ɪŋ **~s** z
superintendent ˌsuːp ər ɪn 'tend ənt ˌsjuːp-,
ˌ·ə-, §ˌ·ən·- **~s** s
superior, S~ su 'pɪər i‿ə sju- ‖ su 'pɪr i‿ᵊr sə-
~ly li **~s** z
superiority su ˌpɪər i 'ɒr ət i sju-, -ɪt i
‖ su ˌpɪr i 'ɔːr ət̬ i sə-, -'aːr-
   suˌperi'ority ˌcomplex

superlative su ˈpɜːl ət ɪv sju- ‖ su ˈpɜːl əţ ɪv
~ly li ~ness nəs nɪs ~s z
supermall ˈsuːp ə mɔːl ˈsjuːp-, -mæl ‖ -ᵊr- -mɑːl
~s z
super|man, S~ ˈsuːp ə |mæn ˈsjuːp- ‖ -ᵊr-
~men men
supermarket ˈsuːp ə ˌmɑːk ɪt ˈsjuːp-, §-ət
‖ -ᵊr ˌmɑːrk ət ~s s
supermen ˈsuːp ə men ˈsjuːp- ‖ -ᵊr-
supermodel ˈsuːp ə ˌmɒd ᵊl ˈsjuːp-
‖ -ᵊr ˌmɑːd ᵊl ~s z
supermom ˈsuːp ə mɒm ˈsjuːp- ‖ -r mɑːm
supernal su ˈpɜːn ᵊl sju- ‖ -ˈpɜːn- ~ly i
supernatural ˌsuːp ə ˈnætʃ ᵊr_əl ◄ ˌsjuːp- ‖ ˌ-ᵊr-
~ly i ~ness nəs nɪs
supernormal ˌsuːp ə ˈnɔːm ᵊl ◄ ˌsjuːp-
‖ -ᵊr ˈnɔːrm- ~ly i
supernov|a ˌsuːp ə ˈnəʊv |ə ˌsjuːp- ‖ -ᵊr ˈnoʊv-
~ae iː ~as əz
supernumerar|y ˌsuːp ə ˈnjuːm ᵊr_ər |i ◄
ˌsjuːp-, △-ˈ·ər |i ‖ ˌsuːp ᵊr ˈnuːm ə rer |i ◄
-ˈnjuːm-, △-ˈ·ər |i ~ies iz
superordinate adj, n ˌsuːp ər ˈɔːd ᵊn_ət ◄
ˌsjuːp-, ɪt, -ɪn ət, -ɪn ɪt; -ə neɪt, -ᵊn eɪt, -ɪ neɪt
‖ -ᵊr ˈɔːrd- ~s s
superphosphate ˌsuːp ə ˈfɒs feɪt ˌsjuːp-
‖ -ᵊr ˈfɑːs- ~s s
superpower ˈsuːp ə ˌpaʊ_ə ˈsjuːp-, ˌ·ˈ··
‖ -ᵊr ˌpaʊˌᵊr ~s z
supersatu|rate ˌsuːp ə ˈsætʃ ə |reɪt ˌsjuːp-,
-ˈsætʃ u-, -ˈsæt juː- ‖ ˌ-ᵊr- ~rated reɪt ɪd -əd
‖ reɪţ əd ~rates reɪts ~rating reɪt ɪŋ ‖ reɪţ ɪŋ
superscript ˈsuːp ə skrɪpt ˈsjuːp- ‖ -ᵊr- ~s s
superscription ˌsuːp ə ˈskrɪp ʃᵊn ˌsjuːp- ‖ -ᵊr-
~s z
supersed|e ˌsuːp ə ˈsiːd ˌsjuːp- ‖ -ᵊr- ~ed ɪd əd
~es z ~ing ɪŋ
supersession ˌsuːp ə ˈseʃ ᵊn ˌsjuːp- ‖ -ᵊr- ~s z
superset ˈsuːp ə set ˈsjuːp- ‖ -ᵊr- ~s s
supersiz|e ˈsuːp ə saɪz ˈsjuːp- ‖ -ᵊr- ~ed d ~es
ɪz əz ~ing ɪŋ
supersonic ˌsuːp ə ˈsɒn ɪk ◄ ˌsjuːp- ‖ -ᵊr ˈsaːn-
~ally ᵊl_i ~s s
superstar ˈsuːp ə stɑː ˈsjuːp- ‖ -ᵊr stɑːr ~dom
dəm ~s z
superstate ˈsuːp ə steɪt ˈsjuːp- ‖ -ᵊr- ~s s
superstition ˌsuːp ə ˈstɪʃ ᵊn ˌsjuːp- ‖ -ᵊr- ~s z
superstitious ˌsuːp ə ˈstɪʃ əs ◄ ˌsjuːp- ‖ -ᵊr- ~ly
li ~ness nəs nɪs
superstore ˈsuːp ə stɔː ˈsjuːp- ‖ -ᵊr stɔːr -stoʊr
~s z
superstrate ˈsuːp ə streɪt ˈsjuːp- ‖ -ᵊr- ~s s
superstring ˈsuːp ə strɪŋ ˈsjuːp- ‖ -ᵊr- ~s z
superstructure ˈsuːp ə ˌstrʌk tʃə ˈsjuːp-, -ʃə
‖ -ᵊr ˌstrʌk tʃᵊr ~s z
supertanker ˈsuːp ə ˌtæŋk ə ˈsjuːp-
‖ -ᵊr ˌtæŋk ᵊr ~s z
supertax ˈsuːp ə tæks ˈsjuːp- ‖ -ᵊr-
supertonic ˌsuːp ə ˈtɒn ɪk ◄ ˌsjuːp-, ˈ·ˌ··
‖ -ᵊr ˈtaːn- ~s s
superven|e ˌsuːp ə ˈviːn ˌsjuːp- ‖ -ᵊr- ~ed d
~es z ~ing ɪŋ

supervis|e ˈsuːp ə vaɪz ˈsjuːp- ‖ -ᵊr- ~ed d ~es
ɪz əz ~ing ɪŋ
supervisee ˌsuːp ə vaɪ ˈziː ˌsjuːp- ‖ ˌ-ᵊr- ~s z
supervision ˌsuːp ə ˈvɪʒ ᵊn ˌsjuːp- ‖ -ᵊr- ~s z
supervisor ˈsuːp ə vaɪz ə ˈsjuːp- ‖ -ᵊr vaɪz ᵊr ~s
z
supervisory ˌsuːp ə ˈvaɪz ər i ◄ ˌsjuːp-, -ˈvɪz-;
ˈ····‖ ˌ-ᵊr-
super|woman ˈsuːp ə |ˌwʊm ən ˈsjuːp- ‖ -ᵊr-
~women ˌwɪm ɪn §-ən
supi|nate ˈsuːp ɪ |neɪt ˈsjuːp-, -ə- ~nated
neɪt ɪd -əd ‖ neɪţ əd ~nates neɪts ~nating
neɪt ɪŋ ‖ neɪţ ɪŋ
supination ˌsuːp ɪ ˈneɪʃ ᵊn ˌsjuːp-, -ə-
supinator ˈsuːp ɪ neɪt ə ˈsjuːp-, ˈ·ə- ‖ -neɪţ ᵊr ~s
z
supine grammatical term ˈsuːp aɪn ˈsjuːp- ~s z
supine 'lying on the back'; 'lazy' ˈsuːp aɪn
ˈsjuːp-; ˌsuː ˈpaɪn, ˌsjuː- ~ly li ~ness nəs nɪs
Suppé ˈsuːp eɪ ‖ su ˈpeɪ —Ger [zʊ ˈpeː]
supper ˈsʌp ə ‖ -ᵊr ~s z
suppertime ˈsʌp ə taɪm ‖ -ᵊr- ~s z
sup|plant sə |ˈplɑːnt §-ˈplænt ‖ -|ˈplænt
~planted ˈplɑːnt ɪd §ˈplænt-, -əd ‖ ˈplænţ əd
~planting ˈplɑːnt ɪŋ §ˈplænt- ‖ ˈplænţ ɪŋ
~plants ˈplɑːnts §ˈplænts ‖ ˈplænts
supple, S~ ˈsʌp ᵊl ~ly li ~ness nəs nɪs
supplejack ˈsʌp ᵊl dʒæk
supplement n ˈsʌp lɪ mənt -lə- ~s s
supple|ment v ˈsʌp lɪ |ment -lə-, ˌ·ˈ·· —see
note at -ment ~mented ment ɪd -əd
‖ menţ əd ~menting ment ɪŋ ‖ menţ ɪŋ
~ments ments
supplemental ˌsʌp lɪ ˈment ᵊl ◄ -lə-
‖ -ˈment ᵊl ~ly i
supplementar|y ˌsʌp lɪ ˈment ᵊr |i ◄ ˌ·lə-
‖ -ˈment ᵊr |i -mentr |i ~ies iz
ˌsupple,mentary 'benefit
supplementation ˌsʌp lɪ men ˈteɪʃ ᵊn ˌ·lə-,
-mən'-
suppletion sə ˈpliːʃ ᵊn
suppletive sə ˈpliːt ɪv ˈsʌp lət ɪv, -lɪt-
‖ sə ˈpliːţ ɪv ˈsʌp ləţ ɪv ~s z
suppliant ˈsʌp li_ənt ~ly li ~s s
supplicant ˈsʌp lɪk ənt -lək- ~s s
suppli|cate ˈsʌp lɪ |keɪt -lə- ~cated keɪt ɪd -əd
‖ keɪţ əd ~cates keɪts ~cating keɪt ɪŋ
‖ keɪţ ɪŋ
supplication ˌsʌp lɪ ˈkeɪʃ ᵊn -lə- ~s z
supplicatory ˈsʌp lɪ ˈkeɪt ər i ◄ ˈ··-;
ˈsʌp lɪk ət ᵊr i ‖ ˈsʌp lɪk ə tɔːr i -toʊr i (*)
supplier sə ˈplaɪ_ə ‖ -ˈplaɪ_ᵊr ~s z
sup|ply v, n sə |ˈplaɪ ~plied ˈplaɪd ~plies
ˈplaɪz ~plying ˈplaɪ ɪŋ
ˌsup,ply and de'mand; sup'ply ,teacher
supply adv of supple ˈsʌp ᵊl li -ᵊl i
supply-sid|e sə ˈplaɪ saɪd ~er/s ə/z ‖ -ᵊr/z
sup|port v, n sə |ˈpɔːt ‖ -|ˈpɔːrt -ˈpoʊrt
~ported ˈpɔːt ɪd -əd ‖ ˈpɔːrţ əd ˈpoʊrt-
~porting ˈpɔːt ɪŋ ‖ ˈpɔːrţ ɪŋ ˈpoʊrt- ~ports
ˈpɔːts ‖ ˈpɔːrts ˈpoʊrts
sup,porting 'part; sup,porting
'programme; sup,porting 'role

supportab|le sə ˈpɔːt əb |ᵊl ‖ -ˈpɔːrt̬- -ˈpoʊrt̬-
  ~ly li
supporter sə ˈpɔːt ə ‖ -ˈpɔːrt̬ ᵊr -ˈpoʊrt̬- **~s** z
  supˈporters' club
supportive sə ˈpɔːt ɪv ‖ -ˈpɔːrt̬- -ˈpoʊrt̬- **~ly** li
  ~ness nəs nɪs
suppos|e sə ˈpəʊz ‖ -ˈpoʊz —*but the phrase* I
  suppose *is often* aɪ ˈspəʊz ‖ -ˈspoʊz **~es** ɪz əz
  ~ing ɪŋ
supposed *in* (be) supposed to '*ought to*'
  sə ˈpəʊst →ˈspəʊst; səˈpəʊzd ‖ -ˈpoʊzd
supposed *past and pp of* **suppose** sə ˈpəʊzd
  ‖ -ˈpoʊzd
supposed *adj* sə ˈpəʊzd -ˈpəʊz ɪd, -əd
  ‖ -ˈpoʊzd -ˈpoʊz əd
supposedly sə ˈpəʊz ɪd li -əd- ‖ -ˈpoʊz-
supposition ˌsʌp ə ˈzɪʃ ᵊn **~s** z
suppositional ˌsʌp ə ˈzɪʃ ᵊn əl **~ly** i
suppositious ˌsʌp ə ˈzɪʃ əs ◂
supposititious sə ˌpɒz ɪ ˈtɪʃ əs ◂ -ə- ‖ -ˌpɑːz-
  ~ly li **~ness** nəs nɪs
suppositive sə ˈpɒz ət ɪv -ɪt- ‖ -ˈpɑːz ət̬- **~ly** li
  ~s z
suppositor|y sə ˈpɒz ɪt ər |i -ˈət ̣
  ‖ sə ˈpɑːz ə tɔːr |i -tour i **~ies** iz
suppress sə ˈpres **~ed** t **~es** ɪz əz **~ing** ɪŋ
suppressant sə ˈpres ᵊnt **~s** s
suppression sə ˈpreʃ ᵊn **~s** z
suppressive sə ˈpres ɪv **~ly** li
suppressor sə ˈpres ə ‖ -ᵊr **~s** z
suppu|rate ˈsʌp juᵊ |reɪt -jə- ‖ -jə- **~rated**
  reɪt ɪd -əd ‖ reɪt̬ əd **~rates** reɪts **~rating**
  reɪt ɪŋ ‖ reɪt̬ ɪŋ
suppuration ˌsʌp juᵊ ˈreɪʃ ᵊn -jə- ‖ -jə-
suppurative ˈsʌp jur ət ɪv -ˈjər-; -ju reɪt ɪv,
  -jə ·· ‖ ˈsʌp jər ət̬ ɪv -jə reɪt̬-; ˈsʌp rət̬ ɪv **~s** z
supra ˈsuːp rə ˈsjuːp-, -rɑː
supra- ˌsuːp rə ˌsjuːp- — **suprarenal**
  ˌsuːp rə ˈriːn ᵊl ◂ ˌsjuːp-
supraglottal ˌsuːp rə ˈglɒt ᵊl ◂ ˌsjuːp- ‖ -ˈglɑːt̬-
  ˌsupra ˌglottal ˈtract
supralapsarian ˌsuːp rə læp ˈseər i ‿ən ◂
  ˌsjuːp- ‖ -ˈser- -ˈsær- **~ism** ˌɪz əm
supranational ˌsuːp rə ˈnæʃ ᵊn əl ◂ ˌsjuːp-
suprasegmental ˌsuːp rə seg ˈment ᵊl ◂
  ˌsjuːp- ‖ -ˈment̬- **~s** z
supremacist su ˈprem əs ɪst sju-, §-əst **~s** s
supremac|y su ˈprem əs |i sju- **~ies** iz
supreme *French word, cooking term,* **suprême**
  su ˈpriːm su-, -ˈprem, -ˈpreɪm —*Fr* [sy pʀɛm]
supreme '*highest*', '*greatest*', '*ultimate*'
  su ˈpriːm sju-, ˌsuː-, ˌsju- **~ly** li **~ness** nəs nɪs
  S~s z
  Suˌpreme ˈBeing; **Suˌpreme ˈCourt**
supremo su ˈpriːm əʊ sju- ‖ -oʊ **~s** z
sur- ˌsɜː ‖ ˌsɜː: *but in certain words* sə ‖ sᵊr
  — **surrejoinder** ˌsɜː rɪ ˈdʒɔɪnd ə -rə-, §-riː-
  ‖ ˌsɜː rɪ ˈdʒɔːɪnd ᵊr
sura ˈsʊər ə ‖ ˈsʊr ə **~s** z
Surabaya ˌsʊər ə ˈbaɪ ə ‖ ˌsʊr ə ˈbɑː jə
surah ˈsʊər ə ‖ ˈsʊr ə **~s** z
sural ˈsjʊər əl ˈsʊər- ‖ ˈsʊr əl
Surbiton ˈsɜːb ɪt ən §-ət- ‖ ˈsɜːb ət ᵊn

S

surceas|e ₍ₗ₎sɜː ˈsiːs ˈ· · ‖ ₍ₗ₎sɜː:- **~ed** t **~es** ɪz əz
  ~ing ɪŋ
surcharg|e *n, v* ˈsɜː tʃɑːdʒ ₍ₗ₎sɜː ˈtʃɑːdʒ
  ‖ ˈsɜː tʃɑːrdʒ **~ed** d **~es** ɪz əz **~ing** ɪŋ
surcingle ˈsɜː ˌsɪŋ gᵊl ‖ ˈsɜː:- **~s** z
surcoat ˈsɜː kəʊt ‖ ˈsɜː koʊt **~s** s
surd sɜːd ‖ sɜːd **surds** sɜːdz ‖ sɜːdz

SURE

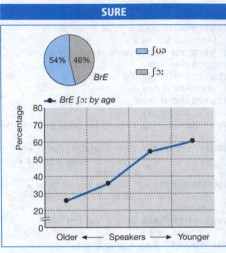

54% 46% BrE

◼ ʃʊə
◼ ʃɔː

● BrE ʃɔː by age

Percentage / Older ◀— Speakers —▶ Younger

sure ʃɔː ʃʊə ‖ ʃʊᵊr ʃɜː: — *Preference poll, BrE:*
  ʃɔː *46% (born since 1973: 60%),* ʃʊə *54%.*
surer ˈʃɔːr ə ˈʃʊər ə ‖ ˈʃʊr ᵊr ˈʃɜː: **surest**
  ˈʃɔːr ɪst ˈʃʊər-, -əst ‖ ˈʃʊr əst ˈʃɜː:-
  ˌsure ˈthing
surefire ˈʃɔː ˌfaɪ ə ˈʃʊə- ‖ ˈʃʊr ˌfaɪ ᵊr ˈʃɜː:-
surefooted ˌʃɔː ˈfʊt ɪd ◂ ˌʃʊə-, -əd
  ‖ ˌʃʊr ˈfʊt̬ əd ◂ ˌʃɜː:-, ˈ·ˌ· · **~ness** nəs nɪs
sure|ly ˈʃɔː |li ˈʃʊə- ‖ ˈʃʊr |li ˈʃɜː:- **~ness** nəs nɪs
suret|y ˈʃɔːr ət |i ˈʃʊər-, -ɪt- ‖ ˈʃʊr ət̬ |i ˈʃɜː:-;
  ˈʃʊrt̬ |i, ˈʃɜː:t̬ i —*in RP formerly also* ˈʃʊət |i
  ~ies iz **~yship/s** i ʃɪp/s
surf sɜːf ‖ sɜːf **surfed** sɜːft ‖ sɜːft **surfing**
  ˈsɜːf ɪŋ ‖ ˈsɜː:f ɪŋ **surfs** sɜːfs ‖ sɜːfs
surfac|e *n, v, adj* ˈsɜːf ɪs -əs ‖ ˈsɜː:f əs **~ed** t
  ~es ɪz əz **~ing** ɪŋ
  ˈsurface ˈmail; ˈsurface ˈnoise; ˈsurface
  ˌstructure; ˌsurface ˈtension
surface-to-air ˌsɜːf ɪs tu ˈeə ◂ ˌəs-
  ‖ ˌsɜː:f əs tə ˈeᵊr ◂ -ˈæᵊr
surface-to-surface ˌsɜːf ɪs tə ˈsɜːf ɪs ◂ -əs tə-,
  -əs ‖ ˌsɜː:f əs tə ˈsɜː:f əs ◂
surfactant sɜː ˈfækt ənt sə-; ˈsɜː fækt ənt ‖ sɜː:-
  ~s s
surfboard ˈsɜːf bɔːd ‖ ˈsɜː:f bɔːrd -bourd **~er/s**
  ə/z ‖ ᵊr/z **~ing** ɪŋ **~s** z
surfboat ˈsɜːf bəʊt ‖ ˈsɜː:f boʊt **~s** s
surf|eit *n, v* ˈsɜːf |ɪt -ət-, -iːt ‖ ˈsɜː:f |ət **~eited**
  ɪt ɪd ət-, iːt-, -əd ‖ ət̬ əd **~eiting** ɪt ɪŋ ət-, iːt-
  ‖ ət̬ ɪŋ **~eits** ɪts əts, iːts ‖ əts
surfer ˈsɜːf ə ‖ ˈsɜː:f ᵊr **~s** z
surfie ˈsɜːf i ‖ ˈsɜː:f i **~s** z
surfing ˈsɜːf ɪŋ ‖ ˈsɜː:f ɪŋ
surfrid|ing ˈsɜːf ˌraɪd |ɪŋ ‖ ˈsɜː:f- **~er/s** ə/z
  ‖ ᵊr/z

surge sɜːdʒ ‖ sɜːdʒ **surged** sɜːdʒd ‖ sɜːdʒd
  surges 'sɜːdʒ ɪz -əz ‖ 'sɜːdʒ əz **surging**
  'sɜːdʒ ɪŋ ‖ 'sɜːdʒ ɪŋ
surgeon 'sɜːdʒ ən ‖ 'sɜːdʒ ən ~**s** z
surger|y 'sɜːdʒ ər‚i ‖ 'sɜːdʒ- ~**ies** iz
surgical 'sɜːdʒ ɪk əl ‖ 'sɜːdʒ- ~**ly** ‚i
  ‚surgical 'spirit
suricate 'sʊər ɪ keɪt 'sjʊər-, -ə- ‖ 'sʊr- ~**s** s
surimi su 'riːm i —Jp [sɯ ‚ri 'mi]
Surinam, Suriname ‚sʊər ɪ 'næm ‚sjʊər-, -ə-;
  '··· ‖ 'sʊr ə nɑːm -næm —Dutch
  [sy ri 'na: mə]
Surinamese ‚sʊər ɪ næ 'miːz ◄ ‚sjʊər-, ‚-ə-,
  -nə'· ‖ ‚sʊr ə nə 'miːz ◄ -'miːs
surly 'sɜːl i ‖ 'sɜːl i **surlier** 'sɜːl i‚ə ‖ 'sɜːl i‚ər
  surliest 'sɜːl i‚ɪst əst ‖ 'sɜːl- **surlily** 'sɜːl ɪl i
  -əl- ‖ 'sɜːl- **surliness** 'sɜːl i nəs -nɪs ‖ 'sɜːl-
surmis|e v, n sə 'maɪz sɜː-; 'sɜː maɪz ‖ sər- ~**ed**
  d ~**es** ɪz əz ~**ing** ɪŋ
sur|mount sə ‖ 'maʊnt sɜː- ‖ sər- ~**mounted**
  'maʊnt ɪd -əd ‖ 'maʊnt əd ~**mounting**
  'maʊnt ɪŋ ‖ 'maʊnt ɪŋ ~**mounts** 'maʊnts
surname 'sɜː neɪm ‖ 'sɜː- ~**d** d ~**s** z
surpass sə 'pɑːs sɜː-, §-'pæs ‖ sər 'pæs ~**ed** t
  ~**es** ɪz əz ~**ing/ly** ɪŋ /li
surplic|e 'sɜːp ləs -lɪs ‖ 'sɜːp- ~**ed** t ~**es** ɪz əz
surplus 'sɜːp ləs ‖ 'sɜː plʌs 'sɜːp ləs ~**es** ɪz əz
surpris|e sə 'praɪz ‖ sər- sə-. ~**ed** d ~**es** ɪz əz
  ~**ing/ly** ɪŋ /li
  sur'prise ‚party
surreal sə 'rɪəl -'riːəl ‖ -'riːəl ~**ly** i
surrealism sə 'rɪəl ‚ɪz əm -'riːəl-
  ‖ sə 'riː ə ‚lɪz əm
surrealist sə 'rɪəl ɪst -'riːəl-, §-əst
  ‖ sə 'riː əl əst ~**s** s
surrealistic sə ‚rɪə 'lɪst ɪk ◄ sjʊ-, -‚riː ə '-
  ‖ sə ‚riː ə 'lɪst ɪk ◄ ~**ally** əl i
surrebutter ‚sʌr i 'bʌt ə -ə- ‖ ‚sɜː ri 'bʌt̬ ər -ɪ-
  ~**s** z
surrejoinder ‚sʌr i 'dʒɔɪnd ə -ə-
  ‖ ‚sɜː ri 'dʒɔɪnd ər -ɪ- ~**s** z
surrender sə 'rend ə ‖ -ər ~**ed** d **surrendering**
  sə 'rend ər ɪŋ ~**s** z
  sur'render ‚value
surreptitious ‚sʌr əp 'tɪʃ əs ◄ -ɪp-, -ep- ‖ ‚sɜː-
  ~**ly** li ~**ness** nəs nɪs
Surrey, s~ 'sʌr i ‖ 'sɜː i ~**s** z
Surridge 'sʌr ɪdʒ ‖ 'sɜː-
surrogacy 'sʌr əg əs i ‖ 'sɜː-
surrogate n, adj 'sʌr əg ət -ɪt, -ə geɪt ‖ 'sɜː- ~**s**
  s ~**ship** ʃɪp
surround sə 'raʊnd ~**ed** ɪd əd ~**ing/s** ɪŋ/z ~**s** z
surround-sound sə 'raʊnd saʊnd
sursum corda ‚sɜːs əm 'kɔːd ə -ʊm-
  ‖ ‚sʊrs əm 'kɔːrd ə -'koʊrd-, -ɑ:
surtax 'sɜː tæks ‖ 'sɜː- ~**ed** t ~**es** ɪz əz ~**ing** ɪŋ
Surtees 'sɜː tiːz ‖ 'sɜː-
surtitle 'sɜː ‚taɪt əl ‖ 'sɜː ‚taɪt̬ əl ~**ed** d ~**ing**
  ɪŋ ~**s** z
Surtsey 'sɜːts i -eɪ ‖ 'sɜːts i —Icelandic
  ['sʏɣ̊ts eɪ]
surveil sə 'verəl ~**led** d ~**ling** ɪŋ ~**s** z

surveillance sə 'veɪl ənts sɜː- ‖ sər- -jənts;
  -'veɪ-
survey n 'sɜːv eɪ ‚·'·, sə 'veɪ ‖ 'sɜːv eɪ sər 'veɪ
  ~**s** z
survey v sə 'veɪ sɜː-; 'sɜːv eɪ ‖ sər- ~**ed** d ~**ing**
  ɪŋ ~**s** z
surveyor sə 'veɪ ə ‖ sər 'veɪ ər ~**s** z
survivability sə ‚vaɪv ə 'bɪl ət i -ɪt i
  ‖ sər ‚vaɪv ə 'bɪl ət̬ i
survivable sə 'vaɪv əb əl ‖ sər-
survival sə 'vaɪv əl ‖ sər- ~**s** z
  sur'vival kit; sur‚vival of the 'fittest;
  sur'vival ‚value
survivalist sə 'vaɪv əl ɪst §-əst ‖ sər- ~**s** s
surviv|e sə 'vaɪv ‖ sər- ~**ed** d ~**es** z ~**ing** ɪŋ
survivor sə 'vaɪv ə ‖ sər 'vaɪv ər ~**s** z ~**ship**
  ʃɪp
sus sʌs **sussed** sʌst **susses** 'sʌs ɪz -əz **sussing**
  'sʌs ɪŋ
Susa 'suːz ə 'suːs-
Susan 'suːz ən
Susann su 'zæn
Susanna, Susannah su 'zæn ə
susceptance sə 'sept ənts
susceptibilit|y sə ‚sept ə 'bɪl ət i‚i -‚ɪ-, -ɪt i
  ‖ -ət̬ ‚i ~**ies** iz
susceptib|le sə 'sept əb |əl -ɪb- ~**leness** əl nəs
  -nɪs ~**ly** li
susceptive sə 'sept ɪv ~**ness** nəs nɪs
susceptivity ‚sʌs ep 'tɪv ət i -ɪt i ‖ -ət̬ i
sushi 'suːʃ i 'sʊʃ-, -iː —Jp [sɯ 'ɕi]
Susie 'suːz i
suslik 'sʊs lɪk 'sʌs-, 'suːs- ~**s** s
suspect v sə 'spekt ~**ed** ɪd əd ~**ing** ɪŋ ~**s** s
suspect n, adj 'sʌsp ekt ~**s** s
suspend sə 'spend ~**ed** ɪd əd ~**ing** ɪŋ ~**s** z
  su‚spended 'sentence
suspender sə 'spend ə ‖ -ər ~**s** z
  su'spender belt
suspense sə 'spents ~**ful** fəl fʊl
suspension sə 'spentʃ ən ~**s** z
  su'spension bridge
suspensive sə 'spents ɪv ~**ly** li ~**ness** nəs nɪs
suspensor|y sə 'spents ər‚i ~**ies** iz
suspicion sə 'spɪʃ ən ~**s** z
suspicious sə 'spɪʃ əs ~**ly** li ~**ness** nəs nɪs
Susquehann|a ‚sʌsk wɪ 'hæn |ə -wə- ~**ock** ək
suss sʌs **sussed** sʌst **susses** 'sʌs ɪz -əz **sussing**
  'sʌs ɪŋ
Sussex 'sʌs ɪks §-əks
Susskind 'sʊs kɪnd 'sʌs-
sustain sə 'steɪn ~**ed** d ~**ing** ɪŋ ~**s** z
sustainability sə ‚steɪn ə 'bɪl ət i -ɪt i ‖ -ət̬ i
sustainable sə 'steɪn əb əl
sustainer sə 'steɪn ə ‖ -ər ~**s** z
sustainment sə 'steɪn mənt →-'steɪm-
sustenance 'sʌst ən ənts -ɪn-
sustentation ‚sʌst en 'teɪʃ ən -ən-
sustention sə 'stenʃ ən
Sustrans 'sʌs trænz -trɑːnz, -trænts, -trɑːnts
  ‖ -trænts -trænz
Sutch sʌtʃ
Sutcliff, Sutcliffe 'sʌt klɪf

Sutherland 'sʌð ə lənd ‖ -ᵊr-
Sutlej 'sʌt lɪdʒ -ledʒ
sutler 'sʌt lə ‖ -lᵊr ~s z
sutra, Sutra 'suːtr ə ~s z
Sutro 'suːtr əʊ ‖ -oʊ
suttee 'sʌt iː sʌ 'tiː —Hindi [sə ʈiː] ~s z
Sutter 'sʌt ə ‖ 'sʌt ᵊr —but the 19th-century
  German-born owner of ˌSutter's 'Mill, CA,
  (Ger Suter ['zuː tɐ]) is sometimes referred to as
  'suːt ə ‖ 'suːt ᵊr
Sutton 'sʌt ᵊn
  ˌSutton 'Coldfield 'kəʊld fiːᵊld →'kɒʊld-;
  ˌSutton 'Hoo
Suttor 'sʌt ə ‖ 'sʌt ᵊr
suture 'suːtʃ ə ‖ 'suːtʃ ᵊr —There are also very
  careful or precious variants 'sjuːt jʊə, 'suːt-,
  -jə ‖ -jʊr, -jᵊr ~d d ~s z suturing 'suːtʃ ər ɪŋ
SUV ˌes juː 'viː ~s z
Suva 'suːv ə
Suwannee sə 'wɒn i su- ‖ -'waːn- -'wɔːn-
Suzanna, Suzannah su 'zæn ə
Suzanne su 'zæn
suzerain 'suːz ə reɪn 'sjuːz-, -ᵊr ən ~s z
suzerain|ty 'suːz ə reɪn |ti 'sjuːz-, -ᵊr ən |ti
  ~ties tiz
Suzette su 'zet
Suzhou ˌsu: 'dʒəʊ ‖ -'dʒoʊ —Chi Sūzhōu
  [¹su ¹ʈsou]
Suzie 'suːz i
Suzman (i) 'sʊz mən, (ii) 'suːz mən
Suzuki tdmk sə 'zuːk i su- —Jp [sɯ ˌdzɯ ki] ~s
  z
Suzy 'suːz i
Svalbard 'svæl baːd 'svaːl-, -baː ‖ 'svaːl baːrd
  -baːr —Norw ['svaːl baɾ]
svarabhakti ˌsfʌr ə 'bʌkt i ˌsfɑːr-;
  ˌsfær ə 'bækt i —Hindi [svər bək ʈi]
svelte sfelt svelt svelter 'sfelt ə 'svelt- ‖ -ᵊr
  sveltest 'sfelt ɪst 'svelt-, -əst
Svengali, s~ sfen 'gɑːl i sven-, →sfeŋ-
Sverdlovsk ˌsfeəd 'lɒfsk -'lɒvsk; '· ·
  ‖ ˌsferd 'lɔːfsk -lɑːfsk —Russ [svʲɪr 'dłɔfsk]
swab swɒb ‖ swɑːb swabbed swɒbd ‖ swɑːbd
  swabbing 'swɒb ɪŋ ‖ 'swɑːb ɪŋ swabs
  swɒbz ‖ swɑːbz
swabber 'swɒb ə ‖ 'swɑːb ᵊr ~s z
Swabi|a 'sweɪb i |ə ~an/s ən/z
Swaby 'sweɪb i
swaddie 'swɒd i ‖ 'swɑːd i ~s z
swaddl|e 'swɒd ᵊl ‖ 'swɑːd ᵊl ~ed d ~es z
  ~ing ˌɪŋ
  'swaddling clothes
swadd|y 'swɒd |i ‖ 'swɑːd |i ~ies iz
Swadlincote 'swɒd lɪn kəʊt →-lɪŋ-, §-lən-
  ‖ 'swɑːd lən koʊt
Swaffer 'swɒf ə ‖ 'swɑːf ᵊr
Swaffham 'swɒf əm ‖ 'swɑːf-
Swaffield 'swɒf iːᵊld ‖ 'swɑːf-
swag swæg
swage sweɪdʒ swaged sweɪdʒd swages
  'sweɪdʒ ɪz -əz swaging 'sweɪdʒ ɪŋ
Swaggart 'swæg ət ‖ -ᵊrt

swagger 'swæg ə ‖ -ᵊr ~ed d swaggering/ly
  'swæg ər ˌɪŋ /li ~s z
  'swagger stick
swaggerer 'swæg ər ə ‖ -ᵊr ᵊr ~s z
swag|man 'swæg |mæn -mən ~men men mən
  —in Australia, -mən
Swahili swə 'hiːl i swɑː- ~s z
swain, Swain sweɪn swains, Swain's sweɪnz
Swainson 'sweɪn sən
Swalcliffe 'sweɪ klɪf
Swale, swale swerᵊl swales swerᵊlz
Swaledale 'swerᵊl derᵊl
Swales swerᵊlz
swallow, S~ 'swɒl əʊ ‖ 'swɑːl oʊ ~ed d ~er/s
  ə/z ‖ ᵊr/z ~ing ɪŋ ~s z
  'swallow dive
swallowtail 'swɒl əʊ terᵊl ‖ 'swɑːl oʊ- -ə- ~ed
  d ~s z
swam swæm
swami, Swami 'swɑːm i —Hindi [svɑː mi] ~s
  z
swamp swɒmp ‖ swɑːmp swɔːmp swamped
  swɒmpt ‖ swɑːmpt swɔːmpt swamping
  'swɒmp ɪŋ ‖ 'swɑːmp ɪŋ 'swɔːmp- swamps
  'swɒmps ‖ swɑːmps swɔːmps
swamper 'swɒmp ə ‖ 'swɑːmp ᵊr 'swɔːmp- ~s
  z
swampland 'swɒmp lænd ‖ 'swɑːmp-
  'swɔːmp- ~s z
swamp|y, S~ 'swɒmp |i ‖ 'swɑːmp |i
  'swɔːmp |i ~ier i ə ‖ i ᵊr ~iest i ɪst i əst
  ~iness i nəs i nɪs
swan, Swan swɒn ‖ swɑːn swanned swɒnd
  ‖ swɑːnd swanning 'swɒn ɪŋ ‖ 'swɑːn ɪŋ
  swans swɒnz ‖ swɑːnz
  'swan dive
Swanage 'swɒn ɪdʒ ‖ 'swɑːn-
Swanee 'swɒn i ‖ 'swɑːn i 'swɔːn i
swank swæŋk swanked swæŋkt swanking
  'swæŋk ɪŋ swanks swæŋks
swank|y 'swæŋk |i ~ier i ə ‖ i ᵊr ~iest i ɪst
  i əst ~ily ɪ li əl i ~iness i nəs i nɪs
Swanley 'swɒn li ‖ 'swɑːn-
Swann swɒn ‖ swɑːn
swanner|y 'swɒn ər |i ‖ 'swɑːn- ~ies iz
Swanscombe 'swɒnz kəm ‖ 'swɑːnz-
swansdown, swan's-down 'swɒnz daʊn
  ‖ 'swɑːnz-
Swansea place in Wales 'swɒnz i ‖ 'swɑːn siː
  'swɑːnz i
Swanson 'swɒnˢs ən ‖ 'swɑːnˢs ən
swansong 'swɒn sɒŋ ‖ 'swɑːn sɔːŋ -sɑːŋ ~s z
Swanton 'swɒnt ən ‖ 'swɑːnt ᵊn
swan-upp|ing ˌswɒn 'ʌp |ɪŋ '·,·· ‖ ˌswɑːn-
  ~er/s ə/z ‖ ᵊr/z
Swanwick 'swɒn ɪk ‖ 'swɑːn-
swap swɒp ‖ swɑːp swapped swɒpt ‖ swɑːpt
  swapping 'swɒp ɪŋ ‖ 'swɑːp ɪŋ swaps
  swɒps ‖ swɑːps
  'swap meet
SWAPO 'swɑːp əʊ 'swɒp- ‖ -oʊ
Swarbrick 'swɔː brɪk ‖ 'swɔːr-

S

sward swɔːd ‖ swɔːrd **swards** swɔːdz
‖ swɔːrdz
sware sweə ‖ sweᵊr swæᵊr
swarf swɔːf swɑːf ‖ swɔːrf
Swarfega tdmk swɔː ˈfiːg ə swɑː- ‖ -ˈrɔːr-
Swarkeston, Swarkestone ˈswɔːkst ən
‖ ˈswɔːrkst-
swarm swɔːm ‖ swɔːrm **swarmed** swɔːmd
‖ swɔːrmd **swarming** ˈswɔːm ɪŋ ‖ ˈswɔːrm ɪŋ
swarms swɔːmz ‖ swɔːrmz
Swarofski tdmk swə ˈrɒf ski ‖ -ˈrɑːf- -ˈrɔːf-
swart, Swart swɔːt ‖ swɔːrt
swarth|y ˈswɔːð |i ‖ ˈswɔːrð |i **~ier** i‿ə ‖ i‿ᵊr
~iest i‿ɪst i‿əst **~ily** ɪ li əl i **~iness** i nəs i nɪs
swash swɒʃ ‖ swɑːʃ swɔːʃ **swashed** swɒʃt
‖ swɑːʃt swɔːʃt **swashes** ˈswɒʃ ɪz -əz
‖ ˈswɑːʃ əz ˈswɔːʃ- **swashing** ˈswɒʃ ɪŋ
‖ ˈswɑːʃ ɪŋ ˈswɔːʃ-
swashbuckl|er ˈswɒʃ ˌbʌk ᵊl̩ |ə
‖ ˈswɑːʃ ˌbʌk ᵊl̩ |ər ˈswɔːʃ- **~ers** əz ‖ ᵊrz **~ing**
ɪŋ
swastika ˈswɒst ɪk ə ‖ ˈswɑːst- **~s** z
swat, Swat, SWAT swɒt ‖ swɑːt (= swot)
swats swɒts ‖ swɑːts **swatted** ˈswɒt ɪd -əd
‖ ˈswɑːt̬ əd **swatting** ˈswɒt ɪŋ ‖ ˈswɑːt̬ ɪŋ
swatch, Swatch tdmk swɒtʃ ‖ swɑːtʃ
swatches ˈswɒtʃ ɪz -əz ‖ ˈswɑːtʃ əz
swath swɒθ swɔːθ ‖ swɑːθ swɔːθ **swaths**
swɒθs swɔːθs, swɔːðz ‖ swɑːθs swɔːθs
swathe sweɪð **swathed** sweɪðd **swathes**
sweɪðz **swathing** ˈsweɪð ɪŋ
Swatow ˌswɑː ˈtaʊ —Chi Shàntóu [⁴ʂan ²tʰou]
swatter ˈswɒt ə ‖ ˈswɑːt̬ ᵊr **~s** z
Swavesey ˈsweɪvz i ˈsweɪv əz i
sway, Sway sweɪ **swayed** sweɪd **swaying/ly**
ˈsweɪ ɪŋ /li **sways** sweɪz
swayback ˈsweɪ bæk **~ed** t
Swayze ˈsweɪz i
Swazi ˈswɑːz i **~s** z
Swaziland ˈswɑːz i lænd
swear sweə ‖ sweᵊr **swearing** ˈsweər ɪŋ
‖ ˈswer ɪŋ **swears** sweəz ‖ sweᵊrz **swore**
swɔː ‖ swɔːr **swour**
swearer ˈsweər ə ‖ ˈswer ᵊr **~s** z
swearing-in ˌsweər ɪŋ ˈɪn ‖ ˌswer-
swearword ˈsweə wɜːd ‖ ˈswer wɜːd **~s** z
sweat swet **sweated** ˈswet ɪd -əd ‖ ˈswet̬ əd
sweating ˈswet ɪŋ ‖ ˈswet̬ ɪŋ **sweats** swets
ˈsweat gland
sweatband ˈswet bænd **~s** z
sweater ˈswet ə ‖ ˈswet̬ ᵊr **~s** z
sweatpants ˈswet pænts
sweatshirt ˈswet ʃɜːt ‖ -ʃɜːt **~s** s
sweatshop ˈswet ʃɒp ‖ -ʃɑːp **~s** s
sweatsuit ˈswet suːt -sjuːt **~s** s
sweat|y ˈswet |i ‖ ˈswet̬ |i **~ier** i‿ə ‖ i‿ᵊr **~iest**
i‿ɪst i‿əst **~ily** ɪ li əl i **~iness** i nəs i nɪs
Swede, swede swiːd **Swedes, swedes** swiːdz
Sweden ˈswiːd ᵊn
Swedenborg ˈswiːd ᵊn bɔːg ‖ -bɔːrg
—Swedish [ˈsveː dən bɔrj]
Swedenborgian ˌswiːd ᵊn ˈbɔːdʒ i ən ◄ -ˈbɔːg-
‖ -ˈbɔːrdʒ- -ˈbɔːrg- **~s** z

Swedish ˈswiːd ɪʃ
Sweeney ˈswiːn i
ˌSweeney ˈTodd
sweeny ˈswiːn i
sweep swiːp **sweeping** ˈswiːp ɪŋ **sweeps**
swiːps **swept** swept
sweeper ˈswiːp ə ‖ -ᵊr **~s** z
sweeping ˈswiːp ɪŋ **~ly** li **~s** z
sweepstake ˈswiːp steɪk **~s** s
sweet, Sweet swiːt **sweeter** ˈswiːt ə
‖ ˈswiːt̬ ᵊr **sweetest** ˈswiːt ɪst -əst ‖ ˈswiːt̬ əst
ˌsweet ˈgum; ˌsweet ˈnothings; ˌsweet
ˈpea ‖ ˈ· ·; ˌsweet ˈpea; ˌsweet poˈtato
‖ ˈ· ·, ·; ˈsweet talk; ˌsweet ˈtooth ‖ ˈ· ·;
ˌsweet ˈwilliam
sweet-and-sour ˌswiːt ᵊn ˈsaʊ ə ◄ -ᵊnd-
‖ -ˈsaʊ ᵊr
sweetbread ˈswiːt bred **~s** z
sweetbriar, sweetbrier ˈswiːt ˌbraɪ ə
‖ -ˌbraɪ ᵊr **~s** z
sweetcorn ˈswiːt kɔːn ‖ -kɔːrn
sweeten ˈswiːt ᵊn **~ed** d **~er/s** ə/z ‖ ᵊr/z **~ing**
ɪŋ **~s** z
Sweetex tdmk ˈswiːt eks
sweetheart ˈswiːt hɑːt ‖ -hɑːrt **~s** s
sweetie ˈswiːt i ‖ ˈswiːt̬ i **~s** z
sweeting, S~ ˈswiːt ɪŋ ‖ ˈswiːt̬ ɪŋ
sweetish ˈswiːt ɪʃ ‖ ˈswiːt̬ ɪʃ
sweetlip ˈswiːt lɪp **~s** s
sweetly ˈswiːt li
sweetmeal ˈswiːt miːᵊl
sweetmeat ˈswiːt miːt **~s** s
sweetness ˈswiːt nəs -nɪs
sweetshop ˈswiːt ʃɒp ‖ -ʃɑːp **~s** s
sweetsop ˈswiːt sɒp ‖ -sɑːp **~s** s
sweet-talk ˈswiːt tɔːk ˌ·ˈ· ‖ -tɑːk **~ed** t **~ing** ɪŋ
~s s
sweet-tempered ˌswiːt ˈtemp əd ◄ ‖ -ᵊrd ◄
swell swel **swelled** sweld **swelling/s**
ˈswel ɪŋ/z **swells** swelz **swollen** ˈswəʊl ən
‖ ˈswoʊl ən
swelter ˈswelt ə ‖ -ᵊr **~ed** d **sweltering/ly**
ˈswelt ᵊr ɪŋ /li **~s** z
swept swept
swept-back ˌswept ˈbæk ◄ ˈ· ·
swept-wing ˌswept ˈwɪŋ ◄
swerve swɜːv ‖ swɜːrv **swerved** swɜːvd
‖ swɜːrvd **swerves** swɜːvz ‖ swɜːrvz **swerving**
ˈswɜːv ɪŋ ‖ ˈswɜːrv ɪŋ
Swetenham, Swettenham ˈswet ᵊn əm
swift, Swift swɪft **swifter** ˈswɪft ə ‖ -ᵊr
swiftest ˈswɪft ɪst -əst **swifts** swɪfts
swiftlet ˈswɪft lət -lɪt **~s** s
swift|ly ˈswɪft |li **~ness** nəs nɪs
swig swɪg **swigged** swɪgd **swigging** ˈswɪg ɪŋ
swigs swɪgz
swill swɪl **swilled** swɪld **swilling** ˈswɪl ɪŋ
swills swɪlz
swim swɪm **swam** swæm **swimming** ˈswɪm ɪŋ
swims swɪmz **swum** swʌm
ˈswimming bath; ˈswimming ˌcostume;
ˈswimming pool; ˈswimming trunks
swimathon ˈswɪm ə θɒn ‖ -θɑːn **~s** z

S

swimmer 'swɪm ə ‖ -ᵊr ~s z
swimmeret 'swɪm ə ret ˌ·'· ~s s
swimmingly 'swɪm ɪŋ li
swimsuit 'swɪm su:t -sju:t ~s s
swimwear 'swɪm weə ‖ -wer -wær
Swinbourne 'swɪn bɔ:n →'swɪm- ‖ -bɔ:rn
-bourn
Swinburn, Swinburne 'swɪn bɜ:n →'swɪm-
‖ -bɜ:n
Swindells (i) 'swɪnd ᵊlz, (ii) ˌ(ˌ)swɪn 'delz
swindl|e 'swɪnd ᵊl ~ed d ~er/s ˌ·ə/z ‖ ᵊr/z ~es
z ~ing ɪŋ
Swindon 'swɪnd ən
swine swaɪn
'swine ˌfever
swineherd 'swaɪn hɜ:d ‖ -hɜ:d ~s z
Swiney (i) 'swaɪn i, (ii) 'swɪn i
swing swɪŋ **swinging** 'swɪŋ ɪŋ **swings** swɪŋz
swung swʌŋ
ˌswing 'door
swingeing 'swɪndʒ ɪŋ ~ly li
swinger 'swɪŋ ə ‖ -ᵊr ~s z
swingl|e 'swɪŋ gᵊl ~ed d ~es z ~ing ɪŋ
Swingler 'swɪŋ glə ‖ -glᵊr
swingletree 'swɪŋ gᵊl tri: ~s z
swingometer ˌ(ˌ)swɪŋ 'ɒm ɪt ə -ət ə
‖ -'ɑ:m ət̬ ᵊr ~s z
swing-wing ˌswɪŋ 'wɪŋ ◂
swinish 'swaɪn ɪʃ ~ly li ~ness nəs nɪs
Swinley 'swɪn li
Swinnerton 'swɪn ət ən ‖ -ᵊrt ᵊn
Swinton 'swɪnt ən ‖ -ᵊn
swipe swaɪp **swiped** swaɪpt **swipes** swaɪps
swiping 'swaɪp ɪŋ
Swire 'swaɪ ə ‖ 'swaɪ ᵊr
swirl swɜ:l ‖ swɜ:l **swirled** swɜ:ld ‖ swɜ:ld
swirling 'swɜ:l ɪŋ ‖ 'swɜ:l ɪŋ **swirls** swɜ:lz
‖ swɜ:lz
swish swɪʃ **swished** swɪʃt **swishes** 'swɪʃ ɪz -əz
swishing 'swɪʃ ɪŋ
swish|y 'swɪʃ |i ~ier i ˌə ‖ i ˌᵊr ~iest i ˌɪst i ˌəst
~ily ɪ li əl i ~iness i nəs i nɪs
Swiss swɪs
ˌSwiss 'chard; ˌSwiss 'cheese; ˌswiss 'roll,
ˈ· ˌ·
Swissair *tdmk* 'swɪs eə ˌ·'· ‖ -er -ær
switch swɪtʃ **switched** swɪtʃt **switches**
'swɪtʃ ɪz -əz **switching** 'swɪtʃ ɪŋ
switchable 'swɪtʃ əb ᵊl
switchback 'swɪtʃ bæk ~s s
switchblade 'swɪtʃ bleɪd ~s z
switchboard 'swɪtʃ bɔ:d ‖ -bɔ:rd -bourd ~s z
switched-on ˌswɪtʃt 'ɒn ◂ ‖ -'ɑ:n ◂ -'ɔ:n-
switchgear 'swɪtʃ gɪə ‖ -gɪr
switch-|hit ˌswɪtʃ |'hɪt ~hits 'hɪts ~hitter/s
'hɪt ə/z ‖ 'hɪt̬ ᵊr/z ~hitting 'hɪt ɪŋ ‖ 'hɪt̬ ɪŋ
switch|man 'swɪtʃ |mən ~men mən men
switchover 'swɪtʃ ˌəʊv ə ‖ -ˌoʊv ᵊr ~s z
Swithin, Swithun 'swɪð ᵊn 'swɪθ-, -ɪn ~'s z
Switzerland 'swɪts ə lənd -ᵊl ˌənd ‖ -ᵊr-
swive swaɪv **swived** swaɪvd **swives** swaɪvz
swiving 'swaɪv ɪŋ

swivel 'swɪv ᵊl ~ed, ~led d ~ing, ~ling ˌɪŋ ~s
z
swiz, swizz swɪz
swizzle 'swɪz ᵊl
'swizzle stick
swob —*see* **swab**
swollen 'swəʊl ən →'swɒʊl- ‖ 'swoʊl-
ˌswollen 'head
swollen-headed ˌswəʊl ən 'hed ɪd ◂
→ˌswɒʊl-, -əd ‖ ˌswoʊl- ~ly li ~ness nəs nɪs
swoon swu:n **swooned** swu:nd **swooning**
'swu:n ɪŋ **swoons** swu:nz
swoop swu:p **swooped** swu:pt **swooping**
'swu:p ɪŋ **swoops** swu:ps
swoosh swu:ʃ swʊʃ **swooshed** swu:ʃt swʊʃt
swooshes 'swu:ʃ ɪz 'swʊʃ-, -əz **swooshing**
'swu:ʃ ɪŋ 'swʊʃ-
a 'swooshing noise
swop swɒp ‖ swɑ:p **swopped** swɒpt ‖ swɑ:pt
swopping 'swɒp ɪŋ ‖ 'swɑ:p ɪŋ **swops**
swɒps ‖ swɑ:ps
sword sɔ:d ‖ sɔ:rd sourd (!) **swords** sɔ:dz
‖ sɔ:rdz sourdz
'sword ˌdance, 'sword ˌdancer; ˌsword of
'Damocles
swordbearer 'sɔ:d ˌbeər ə →'sɔ:b-
‖ 'sɔ:rd ˌber ᵊr 'sourd- ~s z
swordfish 'sɔ:d fɪʃ ‖ 'sɔ:rd- 'sourd- ~es ɪz əz
swordplay 'sɔ:d pleɪ →'sɔ:b- ‖ 'sɔ:rd- 'sourd-
~er/s ə/z ‖ ᵊr/z
swords|man 'sɔ:dz |mən ‖ 'sɔ:rdz- 'sourdz-
~manship mən ʃɪp ~men mən
swordstick 'sɔ:d stɪk ‖ 'sɔ:rd- 'sourd- ~s s
sword-swallower 'sɔ:d ˌswɒl əʊ ə
‖ 'sɔ:rd ˌswɑ:l oʊ ᵊr 'sourd- ~s z
swore swɔ: ‖ swɔ:r swour
sworn swɔ:n ‖ swɔ:rn swourn
swot swɒt ‖ swɑ:t **swots** swɒts ‖ swɑ:ts
swotted 'swɒt ɪd -əd ‖ 'swɑ:t̬ əd **swotting**
'swɒt ɪŋ ‖ 'swɑ:t̬ ɪŋ
swum swʌm
swung swʌŋ
ˌswung 'dash
Swyer, Swyre 'swaɪ ə ‖ 'swaɪ ᵊr
Syal 'saɪ əl
Sybaris 'sɪb ər ɪs §-əs; sɪ 'bɑ:r-
sybarite 'sɪb ə raɪt ~s s
sybaritic ˌsɪb ə 'rɪt ɪk ◂ ‖ -'rɪt̬- ~ally ᵊl i
Sybil 'sɪb ᵊl -ɪl
sycamore 'sɪk ə mɔ: ‖ -mɔ:r -mour ~s z
syce saɪs **syces** 'saɪs ɪz -əz
sycophanc|y 'sɪk əf ᵊn⁀ts |i 'saɪk-, -ə fæn⁀ts |i
‖ 'sɪk ə fæn⁀ts |i ~ies iz
sycophant 'sɪk əf ᵊnt 'saɪk-, -ə fænt ‖ -ə fænt
əf ᵊnt ~s s
sycophantic ˌsɪk əʊ 'fænt ɪk ◂ ˌsaɪk-
‖ -ə 'fænt̬- ~ally ᵊl i
Sydenham 'sɪd ᵊn ˌəm
Sydney 'sɪd ni
Sydneysider 'sɪd ni saɪd ə ‖ -ᵊr ~s z
syenite 'saɪ ə naɪt
Sykes saɪks
Sylheti sɪl 'het i sɪ 'let i ~s z

Syllabic consonants

1 Most syllables contain an obvious vowel sound. Sometimes, though, a syllable consists phonetically only of a consonant or consonants. If so, this consonant (or one of them) is a nasal (usually n) or a liquid (l or, especially in AmE, r). For example, in the usual pronunciation of **suddenly** ˈsʌd n̩ li, the second syllable consists of n alone. Such a consonant is a **syllabic consonant**.

2 Instead of a syllabic consonant it is always possible to pronounce a vowel ə plus an ordinary (non-syllabic) consonant. Thus it is possible, though not usual, to say ˈsʌd ən li rather than ˈsʌd n̩ li.

3 Likely syllabic consonants are shown in the *Longman Pronunciation Dictionary* (LPD) with the symbol ᵊ, thus **suddenly** ˈsʌd ᵊn li. LPD's regular principle is that a raised symbol indicates a sound whose inclusion LPD does not recommend (see OPTIONAL SOUNDS). Hence this notation implies that LPD prefers bare n in the second syllable. Since there is then no proper vowel in this syllable, the n must be syllabic.

4 Similarly, in **middle** ˈmɪd ᵊl LPD recommends a pronunciation with syllabic l, thus ˈmɪd l̩. In **father** ˈfɑːð ə ‖ ˈfɑːð ᵊr LPD recommends for AmE a pronunciation with syllabic r, thus ˈfɑːð r̩.

5 The IPA provides a special diacritic ˌ to show syllabicity. If syllabification is not shown in a transcription, then syllabic consonants need to be shown explicitly, thus n̩. For the syllabic r of AmE, the special symbol ɚ is sometimes used. Because LPD uses spaces to show syllabification, it does not need these conventions. Any nasal or liquid in a syllable in which there is other vowel must automatically be syllabic.

6 Syllabic consonants are also sometimes used where LPD shows italic ə plus a nasal or liquid, thus **distant** ˈdɪst ənt. Although there is a possible pronunciation ˈdɪst nt, LPD recommends ˈdɪst ənt. (In some varieties of English or styles of speech, a syllabic consonant may in fact arise from almost any sequence of ə and a nasal or liquid.)

7 When followed by a weak vowel, a syllabic consonant may lose its syllabic quality, becoming a plain non-syllabic consonant: see COMPRESSION. For example, **threatening** ˈθret ᵊn ɪŋ may be pronounced with three syllables, including syllabic n, thus ˈθret.n̩.ɪŋ; or compressed into two syllables, with plain n, thus ˈθret.nɪŋ.

S

syllabar|y ˈsɪl əb ər‿ˌi ‖ -ə ber ‖i **~ies** iz
syllabi ˈsɪl ə baɪ -biː
syllabic sɪ ˈlæb ɪk sə- **~ally** ᵊl‿i **~s** s
　syl‿labic 'consonant
syllabi|cate sɪ ˈlæb ɪ ‖keɪt sə-, §-ə- **~cated**
　keɪt ɪd -əd ‖ keɪt̬ əd **~cates** keɪts **~cating**
　keɪt ɪŋ ‖ keɪt̬ ɪŋ
syllabication sɪ ˌlæb ɪ ˈkeɪʃ ᵊn sə-, -ə- **~s** z
syllabicity ˌsɪl ə ˈbɪs ət i -ɪt i ‖ -ət̬ i

syllabification sɪ ˌlæb ɪf ɪ ˈkeɪʃ ᵊn sə-, -ˌəf-,
　§-ə'-- **~s** z
syllabi|fy sɪ ˈlæb ɪ ‖faɪ sə-, -ə- **~fied** faɪd **~fies**
　faɪz **~fying** faɪ ɪŋ
syllable ˈsɪl əb ᵊl **~s** z
　'syllable ˌboundary; **'syllable ˌstructure**
syllabub ˈsɪl ə bʌb **~s** z
syll|abus ˈsɪl ‖əb əs **~abi** ə baɪ -biː: **~abuses**
　əb əs ɪz -əz

sylleps|is sɪ 'leps |ɪs sə-, -'liːps-, §-əs **~es** iːz
syllogism 'sɪl ə ˌdʒɪz əm **~s** z
syllogistic ˌsɪl ə 'dʒɪst ɪk ◄ **~ally** ᵊl i
sylph sɪlf **sylphs** sɪlfs
Sylphides sɪl 'fiːd —*Fr* [sil fid]
sylphlike 'sɪlf laɪk
sylvan 'sɪlv ən **~s** z
sylvatic sɪl 'væt ɪk sᵊl- ‖ -'væt̬-
Sylvester sɪl 'vest ə sᵊl- ‖ -ᵊr
Sylvia 'sɪlv i ə
sym- sɪm, ˌsɪm — **sympatric** sɪm 'pætr ɪk
Sym sɪm
symbiont 'sɪm baɪ ɒnt -bi- ‖ -aːnt **~s** s
symbiosis ˌsɪm baɪ 'əʊs ɪs -bi-, §-əs ‖ -'oʊs-
symbiotic ˌsɪm baɪ 'ɒt ɪk ◄ -bi- ‖ -'aːt̬- **~ally**
   ᵊl i
symbol 'sɪm bᵊl **~s** z
symbolic sɪm 'bɒl ɪk ‖ -'baːl- **~al** ᵊl **~ally** ᵊl i
   ~alness ᵊl nəs -nɪs
symbolis... —*see* **symboliz...**
symbolism 'sɪm bə ˌlɪz əm -bʊ- **~s** z
symbolist 'sɪm bəl ɪst -bʊl-, §-əst **~s** s
symbolization ˌsɪm bəl aɪ 'zeɪʃ ᵊn ˌ-bʊl-, -ɪ'--
   ‖ -ə'-- **~s** z
symboliz|e 'sɪm bə laɪz -bʊ- **~ed** d **~es** ɪz əz
   ~ing ɪŋ
symbology sɪm 'bɒl ədʒ i ‖ -'baːl-
Syme saɪm
Symington *(i)* 'saɪm ɪŋ tən, *(ii)* 'sɪm-
symmetric sɪ 'metr ɪk sə-
symmetrical sɪ 'metr ɪk ᵊl sə- **~ly** i
symmetr|y 'sɪm ətr |i -ɪtr- **~ies** iz
Symon 'saɪm ən
Symonds *(i)* 'sɪm əndz, *(ii)* 'saɪm əndz
   ˌSymonds 'Yat ˌsɪm əndz 'jæt
Symons *(i)* 'sɪm ənz, *(ii)* 'saɪm ənz
sympathectom|y ˌsɪmp ə 'θekt əm |i **~ies** iz
sympathetic ˌsɪmp ə 'θet ɪk ◄ ‖ -'θet̬- **~ally**
   ᵊl i
   ˌsympaˌthetic 'magic
sympathis|e, sympathiz|e 'sɪmp ə θaɪz **~ed**
   d **~er/s** ə/z ‖ ᵊr/z **~es** ɪz əz **~ing** ɪŋ
sympath|y 'sɪmp əθ |i **~ies** iz
symphonic sɪm 'fɒn ɪk ‖ -'faːn-
symphonist 'sɪmᵖf ən ɪst §-əst **~s** s
symphon|y 'sɪmᵖf ən |i **~ies** iz
   'symphony ˌorchestra
symph|ysis 'sɪmᵖf |ɪs ɪs -əs-, §-əs **~yses** ɪ siːz
   -ə-
symposia sɪm 'pəʊz i ə ‖ -'poʊz-
symposiac sɪm 'pəʊz i æk ‖ -'poʊz-
symposiarch sɪm 'pəʊz i aːk ‖ -'poʊz i aːrk **~s**
   s
symposiast sɪm 'pəʊz i æst ‖ -'poʊz- **~s** s
symposi|um sɪm 'pəʊz i |əm ‖ -'poʊz- **~a** ə
symptom 'sɪmpt əm **~s** z
symptomatic ˌsɪmpt ə 'mæt ɪk ◄ ‖ -'mæt̬-
   ~ally ᵊl i
syn- sɪn, ˌsɪn — **synonym** 'sɪn ə nɪm
synaer|esis sɪ 'nɪər |əs ɪs sə-, -ɪs-, §-əs ‖ -'nɪr-
   ~eses ə siːz -ɪ-
synaesthesia ˌsɪn iːs 'θiːz i ə ˌ-ɪs-, §ˌ-əs-,
   -ˈθiːʒ ə ‖ ˌsɪn əs 'θiːʒ ə -ˈi̯ə

synagogue 'sɪn ə gɒg ‖ -gaːg **~s** z
synalepha, synaloepha ˌsɪn ə 'liːf ə -'lef- **~s**
   z
synaps|e 'saɪn æps 'sɪn-; sɪ 'næps ‖ 'sɪn æps
   sə 'næps **~es** ɪz əz
synaps|is sɪ 'næps |ɪs **~es** iːz
synaptic sɪ 'næpt ɪk **~ally** ᵊl i
synarthros|is ˌsɪn ɑː 'θrəʊs |ɪs §-əs
   ‖ -ɑːr 'θroʊs- **~es** iːz
synax|is sɪ 'næks |ɪs sə-, §-əs **~es** iːz
sync, synch sɪŋk *(= sink)*
synchro 'sɪŋk rəʊ ‖ -roʊ **~s** z
synchroflash 'sɪŋk rəʊ flæʃ ‖ -roʊ- **~es** ɪz əz
synchromesh 'sɪŋk rəʊ meʃ ‖ -roʊ- **~es** ɪz əz
synchronic sɪn 'krɒn ɪk →sɪŋ- ‖ -'kraːn- **~ally**
   ᵊl i
synchronicity ˌsɪŋ krə 'nɪs ət i ˌsɪn-, ˌ-krɒ-,
   -ɪt i ‖ -ət̬ i ˌkrɑː-
synchronis... —*see* **synchroniz...**
synchronism 'sɪŋk rə ˌnɪz əm
synchronistic ˌsɪŋk rə 'nɪst ɪk ◄ **~ally** ᵊl i
synchronization ˌsɪŋk rən aɪ 'zeɪʃ ᵊn -ɪ'-- **~s** z
synchroniz|e 'sɪŋk rə naɪz **~ed** d **~es** ɪz əz
   ~ing ɪŋ
synchronous 'sɪŋk rən əs **~ly** li **~ness** nəs nɪs
synchron|y 'sɪŋk rən |i **~ies** iz
synchrotron 'sɪŋk rəʊ trɒn ‖ -rə traːn **~s** z
synclinal ˌ(ˌ)sɪŋ 'klaɪn ᵊl ˌ(ˌ)sɪn- **~ly** i
syncline 'sɪŋ klaɪn ‖ 'sɪn- **~s** z
synco|pate 'sɪŋk ə |peɪt **~pated** peɪt ɪd -əd
   ‖ peɪt̬ əd **~pates** peɪts **~pating** peɪt ɪŋ
   ‖ peɪt̬ ɪŋ
syncopation ˌsɪŋk ə 'peɪʃ ᵊn **~s** z
syncope 'sɪŋk əp i **~s** z
syncretic ˌ(ˌ)sɪŋ 'kret ɪk ˌ(ˌ)sɪn- ‖ -'kret̬-
syncretism 'sɪŋk rə ˌtɪz əm -rɪ- **~s** z
syncretistic ˌsɪŋk rə 'tɪst ɪk ◄ -rɪ-
syncretiz|e 'sɪŋk rə taɪz -rɪ- **~ed** d **~es** ɪz əz
   ~ing ɪŋ
syndactyl sɪn 'dækt ɪl -ᵊl, -aɪᵊl **~y** i
syndesis 'sɪnd ɪs ɪs -əs-, §-əs; sɪn 'diːs-
syndesmosis ˌsɪn dez 'məʊs ɪs -des-, §-əs
   ‖ -'moʊs əs
syndetic sɪn 'det ɪk ‖ -'det̬-
syndic 'sɪnd ɪk **~s** s
syndicalism 'sɪnd ɪk ə ˌlɪz əm -ᵊl ˌɪz-
syndicalist 'sɪnd ɪk əl ɪst §-əst **~s** s
syndi|cate *v* 'sɪnd ɪ |keɪt -ə- **~cated** keɪt ɪd
   -əd ‖ keɪt̬ əd **~cates** keɪts **~cating** keɪt ɪŋ
   ‖ keɪt̬ ɪŋ
syndicate *n* 'sɪnd ɪk ət -ək-, -ɪt; -ɪ keɪt, -ə- **~s** s
syndication ˌsɪnd ɪ 'keɪʃ ᵊn -ə- **~s** z
syndiotactic ˌsɪn daɪ ə 'tækt ɪk ◄ -di ə-
Syndonia sɪn 'dəʊn i ə ‖ -'doʊn-
syndrome 'sɪn drəʊm -drəm ‖ -droʊm
   —*Formerly also* -drəʊm i -ə
syndyotactic ˌsɪn daɪ ə 'tækt ɪk ◄ -di ə-
syne saɪn zaɪn
synecdoche sɪ 'nek dək i **~s** z
synecious sɪ 'niːʃ əs
syner|esis sɪ 'nɪər |əs ɪs sə-, -ɪs-, §-əs ‖ -'ner-
   -'nɪr- **~eses** ə siːz -ɪ-
synergic sɪ 'nɜːdʒ ɪk sə- ‖ -'nɜːdʒ-

Syllables

1 In phonetics, a **syllable** is a group of sounds that are pronounced together. Every English word consists of one or more complete syllables.

glad consists of one syllable: glæd

coming consists of two syllables: ˈkʌm and ɪŋ

So does **valley**: ˈvæl and i

tobacco consists of three syllables: tə, ˈbæk, and əʊ or oʊ.

Each syllable contains exactly one vowel. This vowel may be preceded or followed by one or more consonants. The vowel itself may be a short vowel, a long vowel, or a diphthong; or, if it is the weak vowel ə, it may be combined with a nasal or liquid to give a SYLLABIC CONSONANT.

2 **Phonetic** (spoken) syllables must not be confused with **orthographic** (written) syllables. An orthographic syllable is a group of letters in spelling. When a word is split across two lines of writing, it should be broken at an orthographic syllable boundary. (Word processors do this automatically with a **hyphenation** program.) In some cases an orthographic boundary may not correspond exactly to a phonetic syllable boundary. For example, in the word **happen** the spelling includes two **p**s, and the orthographic syllabification is **hap.pen**. But the pronunciation has only a single p, and the syllables are ˈhæp and ᵊn.

3 This Dictionary shows the syllabification of words by putting spaces between successive syllables. See SYLLABIFICATION.

---

synergism ˈsɪn ə ˌdʒɪz əm -ɜː-; sɪ ˈnɜːdʒ ˌɪz əm, sə- ‖ -ᵊr- **~s** z

synergist ˈsɪn ədʒ ɪst -ɜːdʒ-, §-əst; sɪ ˈnɜːdʒ-, sə- ‖ -ᵊrdʒ- **~s** s

synergistic ˌsɪn ə ˈdʒɪst ɪk ◀ -ɜː- ‖ -ᵊr- **~ally** ᵊl i

synerg|y ˈsɪn ədʒ |i ˈsaɪn-, -ɜːdʒ- ‖ -ᵊrdʒ- **~ies** iz

synesis ˈsɪn ɪs ɪs -əs-, §-əs

synesthesia ˌsɪn iːs ˈθiːz i ə ˌ·ɪs-, §,·əs-, -ˈθiːʒ ə ‖ ˌsɪn əs ˈθiːʒ ə -ˈ·i ə

Synge sɪŋ

synizes|is ˌsɪn ɪ ˈziːs |ɪs -ə-, §-əs **~es** iːz

synod ˈsɪn əd -ɒd ‖ -ɑːd **~s** z

synodal ˈsɪn əd ᵊl -ɒd- ‖ -ɑːd-

synodic sɪ ˈnɒd ɪk sə- ‖ -ˈnɑːd- **~al** ᵊl

synoecious sɪ ˈniːʃ əs

synonym ˈsɪn ə nɪm **~s** z

synonymous sɪ ˈnɒn əm əs sə-, -ɪm- ‖ -ˈnɑːn- **~ly** li

synonym|y sɪ ˈnɒn əm |i sə-, -ɪm- ‖ -ˈnɑːn- **~ies** iz

synops|is sɪ ˈnɒps |ɪs sə-, §-əs ‖ -ˈnɑːps- **~es** iːz

synoptic sɪ ˈnɒpt ɪk sə- ‖ -ˈnɑːpt- **~ally** ᵊl i sy,noptic ˈgospels

synovi|a saɪ ˈnəʊv i ‖ə sɪ-, sə- ‖ -ˈnoʊv- **~al** əl

synovitis ˌsaɪn əʊ ˈvaɪt ɪs ˌsɪn-, §-əs ‖ -ə ˈvaɪt̬ əs

syntactic sɪn ˈtækt ɪk **~al** ᵊl **~ally** ᵊl i **~s** s

syntagm ˈsɪn tæm **~s** z

syntag|ma sɪn ˈtæg |mə **~mata** mət ə ‖ mət̬ ə

syntagmatic ˌsɪnt æg ˈmæt ɪk ◀ ‖ -ˈmæt̬- **~ally** ᵊl i

syntax ˈsɪnt æks **~es** ɪz əz

synth sɪnᵗθ **synths** sɪnᵗθs

synth|esis ˈsɪnᵗθ |əs ɪs -ɪs-, §-əs **~eses** ə siːz ɪ- ,synthesis-by-ˈrule

synthesis|e, synthesiz|e ˈsɪnᵗθ ə saɪz -ɪ- **~ed** d **~er/s** ə/z ‖ ᵊr/z **~es** ɪz əz **~ing** ɪŋ

synthespian sɪn ˈθesp i ən **~s** z

synthetic sɪn ˈθet ɪk ‖ -ˈθet̬- **~al** ᵊl **~ally** ᵊl i **~s** s

Syon ˈsaɪ ən

syphilis ˈsɪf əl ɪs -ɪl-, §-əs

syphilitic ˌsɪf ə ˈlɪt ɪk ◀ -ɪ- ‖ -ˈlɪt̬- **~s** s

syphon ˈsaɪf ᵊn **~ed** d **~ing** ɪŋ **~s** z

Syracusan ˌsaɪᵊr ə ˈkjuːz ᵊn ◀ ˌsɪr- **~s** z

Syracuse *place in NY* ˈsɪr ə kjuːs -kjuːz

Syracuse *place in Sicily* 'saɪᵊr ə kjuːz 'sɪr-
Syrah 'sɪər ə ‖ sɪ 'rɑː
Syria 'sɪr i‿ə
Syriac 'sɪr i æk
Syrian 'sɪr i‿ən ~s z
syringa sɪ 'rɪŋ gə sə- ~s z
syring|e *n, v* sɪ 'rɪndʒ sə-; 'sɪr ɪndʒ ~**ed** d ~**es**
ɪz əz ~**ing** ɪŋ
syrinx, S~ 'sɪr ɪŋks ~**es** ɪz əz
syrphid 'sɜːf ɪd §-əd ‖ 'sɜːf- 'sɪrf- ~**s** z
Syrtis 'sɜːt ɪs §-əs ‖ 'sɜːɾ əs

SYRUP

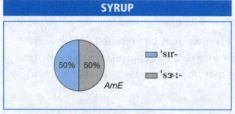

50% | 50%
'sɪr-
'sɜːː-
AmE

syrup 'sɪr əp ‖ 'sɜːː- — *Preference poll, AmE:*
'sɪr- *50%,* 'sɜːː- *50%.* ~**s** s
syrupy 'sɪr əp i ‖ 'sɜːː-
sysadmin 'sɪs ˌæd mɪn 'sɪs əd ˌmɪn ~**s** z
sysop 'sɪs ɒp ‖ -ɑːp ~**s** s

systaltic sɪ 'stælt ɪk sə-
system 'sɪst əm -ɪm ~**s** z
'systems ˌanalyst, ˌ‧‧'‧‧‧
systematic ˌsɪst ə 'mæt ɪk ◂ -ɪ- ‖ -'mæt̬- ~**al** ᵊl
~**ally** ᵊl‿i ~**s** s
systematis... —*see* **systematiz...**
systematist 'sɪst əm ət ɪst sɪ 'stem-, sə-, §-əst
‖ -ət̬ əst ~**s** s
systematization ˌsɪst əm ət aɪ 'zeɪʃ ᵊn ˌ-ɪm-,
-ɪ'‧-; sɪ ˌstem-, sə- ‖ -əm ət̬ ə- ~**s** z
systematiz|e 'sɪst əm ə taɪz sɪ 'stem-, sə-,
-'stiːm- ~**ed** d ~**es** ɪz əz ~**ing** ɪŋ
systemic sɪ 'stiːm ɪk -'stem- ‖ -'stem- ~**ally** ᵊl‿i
~**s** s
systole 'sɪst əl i 'sɪst əʊl
systolic sɪ 'stɒl ɪk ‖ -'stɑːl-
Syston 'saɪst ən
syzyg|y 'sɪz ədʒ |i -ɪdʒ- ~**ies** iz
Szczecin 'ʃtʃetʃ iːn —*Polish* ['ʃtʃe tɕin],
German Stettin [ʃtɛ 'tiːn]
Szechuan, Szechwan ˌsetʃ 'wɑːn ˌseɪtʃ- —*Chi*
Sìchuān [⁴sɯ ¹tʂʰwan]
Szeged 'seg ed —*Hung* ['sɛ gɛd]
Szerelmy sə 'rɛlm i
Szold zəʊld →zɒʊld ‖ zoʊld

Tt

t Spelling-to-sound

1 Where the spelling is **t**, the pronunciation is regularly

t as in **tent** tent.

Less frequently, it is regularly

tʃ as in **nature** ˈneɪtʃ ə ‖ ˈneɪtʃ ᵊr or

ʃ as in **nation** ˈneɪʃ ᵊn.

t may also be part of the digraph **th**.

2 In AmE, t has the variant ţ in certain positions (see T-VOICING). This is shown explicitly in this dictionary's transcriptions, for example **atom** ˈæt əm ‖ ˈæţ əm.

3 Where the spelling is double **tt**, the pronunciation is again t as in **button** ˈbʌt ᵊn, **better** ˈbet ə ‖ ˈbeţ ᵊr.

4 The pronunciation is tʃ in most words ending **-ture**, for example **departure** dɪ ˈpɑːtʃ ə ‖ dɪ ˈpɑːrtʃ ᵊr, **picture** ˈpɪk tʃə ‖ ˈpɪk tʃᵊr. Historically, this pronunciation came about through yod coalescence (see ASSIMILATION). More generally, the pronunciation is usually tʃ wherever the spelling is **t** followed by weak **u** as in **actual** ˈæk tʃu_əl, **situated** ˈsɪtʃ u eɪt ɪd ‖ -eɪţ əd. In some words of this type, however, there is an older or more careful pronunciation with tj, and this is regularly the case where the **u** is strong as in **attitude** ˈæt ɪ tjuːd ‖ ˈæţ ə tuːd. In this latter type, AmE prefers plain t.

In BrE, the pronunciation is also tʃ wherever conservative RP would have tj as in **Tuesday** ˈtjuːz- or ˈtʃuːz-, **tune** tjuːn or tʃuːn.

5 Where **t** at the end of a stressed syllable is followed by **i** plus a vowel within a word, the pronunciation is regularly ʃ as in **partial** ˈpɑːʃ ᵊl ‖ ˈpɑːrʃ ᵊl, **action** ˈæk ʃᵊn, **superstitious** ˌsuːp ə ˈstɪʃ əs ‖ -ᵊr-. When the following vowel is weak as in the examples just given, the **t** is silent; but when it is strong, the pronunciation is i as in **initiate** ɪ ˈnɪʃ i eɪt. Sometimes there is an alternative possibility with s, particularly if the word already contains a ʃ as in **negotiation** -ɡəʊʃ- ‖ -ɡoʊʃ- or -ɡəʊs- ‖ -ɡoʊs-.

6 t is usually silent in two groups of words:

* in **-sten**, **-stle** as in **listen** ˈlɪs ᵊn, **thistle** ˈθɪs ᵊl; also in **Christmas** ˈkrɪs məs, **soften** ˈsɒf ᵊn ‖ ˈsɔːf ᵊn and sometimes in **often** ˈɒf ᵊn or ˈɒft ᵊn ‖ ˈɔːf ᵊn or ˈɔːft ən

* at the end of words recently borrowed from French as in **chalet** ˈʃæl eɪ ‖ ʃæ ˈleɪ.

The sound t is often elided (see ELISION), giving further silent ts in words such as **postman**.

th Spelling-to-sound

1   Where the spelling is the digraph **th**, the pronunciation is regularly
θ as in **thick** θɪk or
ð as in **mother** ˈmʌð ə ‖ ˈmʌð ər.
Exceptionally, it is also
t as in **Thomas** ˈtɒm əs ‖ ˈtɑːm əs.

2   At the beginning of a word, the pronunciation is θ or ð depending on the grammatical class to which the word belongs. In the definite article and other determiners, and in pronouns, conjunctions and pronominal adverbs, it is ð as in **this** ðɪs, **they** ðeɪ, **though** ðəʊ ‖ ðoʊ, **thus** ðʌs. Otherwise it is θ as in **three** θriː, **thing** θɪŋ, **thread** θred.

3   In the middle of a word (provided that **th** is not at the end of a stem), the pronunciation is generally
θ in words of Greek or Latin origin as in **method** ˈmeθ əd, **author** ˈɔːθ-, **ether** ˈiːθ-
ð in words of Germanic origin as in **father** ˈfɑːð-, **together** -ˈgeð-, **heathen** -ˈhiːð-.

4   At the end of a word or stem the pronunciation is usually
θ as in **breath** breθ, **truth** truːθ but
ð in **smooth** smuːð and one or two other words.
In **with**, RP prefers ð, GenAm θ.
Before silent **e**, and in inflected forms of the stems concerned, the pronunciation is regularly
ð as in **breathe** briːð, **soothing** ˈsuːð ɪŋ (from **soothe**).

5   Several stems switch from θ to ð on adding the plural ending (**mouth** maʊθ, **mouths** maʊðz), on adding **-ern** or **-erly** (**northern** ˈnɔːð- , **southerly** ˈsʌð-), or on converting from noun to verb (to **mouth** maʊð).

6   The pronunciation is t in **thyme** taɪm and certain proper names, including **Chatham** ˈtʃæt əm, **Streatham** ˈstret əm ‖ ˈstreţ əm, **Thames** temz, **Thomas** ˈtɒm əs ‖ ˈtɑːm əs. In some cases, however, t has been or is being displaced by θ because of the influence of the spelling.

7   **th** is sometimes silent in **asthma, clothes, isthmus**. It is not a digraph in **hothouse, apartheid**.

T, t tiː (= *tea, tee*) **t's, Ts, T's** tiːz
—*Communications code name:* Tango
'T cell
't t —*see* 'tain't, 'tis, 'twas, 'twere, 'twill, 'twould

ta *'thank you'* tɑː
Taaffe tæf
Taal *'Afrikaans'* tɑːl
Taal *volcano in Philippines* tɑː ˈɑːl

T-voicing

1 For most Americans and Canadians the phoneme t is sometimes pronounced as a voiced sound. Where this is the usual AmE pronunciation it is shown in this dictionary by the symbol ţ.

2 Phonetically, ţ is a voiced alveolar tap (flap). It sounds like a quick English d , and also like the r of some languages. For many Americans, it is actually identical with their d in the same environment, so that AmE **shutter** 'ʃʌţ ᵊr may sound just the same as **shudder** 'ʃʌd ᵊr.

3 Learners of English as a foreign language who take AmE as their model are encouraged to use ţ where appropriate.

4 After n, AmE ţ can optionally be ELIDED. Accordingly, it is shown in this dictionary in italics, as *ţ*. Thus AmE **winter** 'wɪnţ ᵊr can sound exactly the same as **winner** 'wɪn ᵊr. Some Americans, though, consider this pronunciation incorrect.

5 In connected speech, t at the *end of a word* may change to ţ if *both* the following conditions apply:
- the sound before the t is a vowel sound or r
- the next word begins with a vowel sound and follows without a pause.

Thus in AmE **right** raɪt may be pronounced raɪţ in the phrases **right away** ˌraɪţ ə 'weɪ, **right out** ˌraɪţ 'aʊt. But in **right now** ˌraɪt 'naʊ no ţ is possible; nor in **left over** ˌleft 'oʊv ᵊr.

6 Under the same conditions, if the sound before a t at the end of a word is n, the t may change to *ţ* (and therefore possibly disappear): **paint** peɪnt, but **paint it** 'peɪnţ ɪt. Again, some people consider this incorrect.

---

tab tæb **tabbed** tæbd **tabbing** 'tæb ɪŋ **tabs** tæbz

tabard 'tæb ɑːd -əd ‖ -ᵊrd **~s** z

tabasco, T~ *tdmk* tə 'bæsk əʊ ‖ -oʊ
ta ˌbasco 'sauce

Tabatha 'tæb əθ ə

tabbouleh tə 'buːl ə -i, -eɪ

tabb|y 'tæb |i **~ies** iz

tabernacle 'tæb ə næk ᵊl ‖ '-ᵊr- **~s** z

Taberner *(i)* 'tæb ən ə ‖ -ᵊrn ᵊr; *(ii)* tə 'bɜːn ə ‖ -'bɜːn ᵊr

tabes 'teɪb iːz
ˌtabes dor'salis dɔː 'seɪl ɪs -'saːl-, §-əs ‖ -'seɪl- -'sæl-

Tabitha 'tæb ɪθ ə -əθ-

tabla 'tæb lə ‖ 'taːb- —*Hindi* [ʈəb laː] **~s** z

tablature 'tæb lətʃ ə -lɪtʃ-; -lə tjʊə, -lɪ- ‖ -lə tʃʊr -lətʃ ᵊr **~s** z

table 'teɪb ᵊl —*see also phrases with this word*
tabled 'teɪb ᵊld **tables** 'teɪb ᵊlz **tabling** 'teɪb ᵊl ɪŋ

'table ˌlinen; 'table ˌmanners; 'table talk; 'table ˌtennis; 'table wine

tableau 'tæb ləʊ tæ 'bləʊ ‖ tæ 'bloʊ 'tæb loʊ **~s**, **~x** z —*or as sing.*

table|cloth 'teɪb ᵊl |klɒθ -klɔːθ ‖ -|klɔːθ -klaːθ **~cloths** klɒθs klɒðz, klɔːðz, klɔːθs ‖ klɔːðz klɔːθs, klaːðz, klaːθs

table d'hote, table d'hôte ˌtaːb ᵊl 'dəʊt ‖ -'doʊt ˌtæb- —*Fr* [ta blə dot]

tableland 'teɪb ᵊl lænd **~s** z

tablemat 'teɪb ᵊl mæt **~s** s

tablespoon 'teɪb ᵊl spuːn **~s** z

tablespoonful 'teɪb ᵊl spuːn fʊl **~s** z
tablespoonsful 'teɪb ᵊl spuːnz fʊl

tablet 'tæb lət -lɪt **~s** s

tabletop 'teɪb ᵊl tɒp ‖ -taːp **~s** s

tableware 'teɪb ᵊl weə ‖ -wer -wær

tabloid 'tæb lɔɪd **~s** z

taboo tə 'buː ₍ₗ₎tæ- **~ed** d **~ing** ɪŋ **~s** z

tabor 'teɪb ə -ɔː ‖ -ᵊr **~s** z

T

Tabor 'teɪb ɔː -ə ‖ -ᵊr
tabouleh, tabouli tə 'buːl i -ə, -eɪ
tabular 'tæb jʊl ə -jəl- ‖ -jəl ᵊr ~**ly** li
tabula rasa ˌtæb jʊl ə 'rɑːz ə ˌjəl-, -'rɑːs ə ‖ -jəl ə-
tabu|late 'tæb ju |leɪt -jə- ‖ -jə- ~**lated** leɪt ɪd -əd ‖ leɪt əd ~**lates** leɪts ~**lating** leɪt ɪŋ ‖ leɪt ɪŋ
tabulation ˌtæb ju 'leɪʃ ᵊn -jə- ‖ -jə- ~**s** z
tabulator 'tæb ju leɪt ə '·jə- ‖ -jə leɪt ᵊr ~**s** z
tacamahac 'tæk əm ə hæk ~**s** s
tache 'moustache' tæʃ tɑːʃ **taches** 'tæʃ ɪz 'tɑːʃ-, -əz
tachism 'tæʃ ˌɪz əm —Fr tachisme [ta ʃism]
tachistoscope tə 'kɪst ə skəʊp ‖ -skoʊp ~**s** s
tachistoscopic tə ˌkɪst ə 'skɒp ɪk ◂ ‖ -'skɑːp- ~**ally** ᵊl i
tachograph 'tæk ə grɑːf -græf ‖ -græf ~**s** s
tachometer tæ 'kɒm ɪt ə -ət ə ‖ -'kɑːm ət ᵊr ~**s** z
tachycardia ˌtæk i 'kɑːd i ə ‖ -'kɑːrd-
tachymeter tæ 'kɪm ɪt ə -ət ə ‖ -ət ᵊr ~**s** z
tacit 'tæs ɪt §-ət ~**ly** li ~**ness** nəs nɪs
taciturn 'tæs ɪ tɜːn -ə- ‖ -tɝːn ~**ly** li
taciturnity ˌtæs ɪ 'tɜːn ət i ˌ·ə-, -ɪt i ‖ -'tɝːn ət i
Tacitus 'tæs ɪt əs -ət- ‖ -ət əs
tack tæk **tacked** tækt (= tact) **tacking** 'tæk ɪŋ **tacks** tæks (= tax)
tacki... —see **tacky**
tackl|e 'tæk ᵊl —but as a nautical term, often 'teɪk ᵊl ~**ed** d ~**es** z ~**ing** ˌɪŋ
tack|y 'tæk |i ~**ier** i ə ‖ i ᵊr ~**iest** i ɪst i əst ~**ily** ɪ li əl i ~**iness** i nəs i nɪs
taco 'tæk əʊ 'tɑːk- ‖ 'tɑːk oʊ ~**s** z
Tacolneston 'tæk ᵊl stən (!)
Tacoma tə 'kəʊm ə ‖ -'koʊm-
Taconic tə 'kɒn ɪk ‖ -kɑːn-
taconite 'tæk ə naɪt
tact tækt
tactful 'tækt fᵊl -fʊl ~**ly** i ~**ness** nəs nɪs
tactic 'tækt ɪk ~**s** s
-tactic 'tækt ɪk — **morphotactic** ˌmɔːf əʊ 'tækt ɪk ◂ ‖ ˌmɔːrf ə-
tactical 'tækt ɪk ᵊl ~**ly** ˌi
tactician tæk 'tɪʃ ᵊn ~**s** z
tactile 'tækt aɪᵊl ‖ 'tækt ᵊl -aɪᵊl
tactless 'tækt ləs -lɪs ~**ly** li ~**ness** nəs nɪs
tactual 'tæk tʃu əl 'tækt ju əl ~**ly** i
tad, Tad tæd **tads, Tad's** tædz
ta-da, ta-dah tə 'dɑː
Tadcaster 'tæd ˌkæst ə -kəst-, -ˌkɑːst- ‖ -ˌkæst ᵊr
Tadema 'tæd ɪm ə -əm-
Tadhg taɪg teɪg
Tadley 'tæd li
tadpol|e 'tæd pəʊl →'tæb-, →-pɒʊl ‖ -poʊl ~**es** z ~**ing** ɪŋ
Tadzhik tɑː 'dʒiːk 'tɑːdʒ ɪk ~**s** s
Tadzhikistan tɑː ˌdʒiːk ɪ 'stɑːn -ˌdʒɪk-, -ə-, -'stæn ‖ -'·····
Tae Bo ˌtaɪ 'bəʊ ‖ -'boʊ
Taegu ˌteɪ 'guː —Korean ['ɖɛ gu]

tae kwon do, taekwondo ˌtaɪ kwɒn 'dəʊ ˌteɪ-, -'kwɒn dəʊ ‖ ˌtaɪ kwɑːn 'doʊ —Korean [tʰɛ gwɒn do]
tael teɪᵊl (= tail, tale) **taels** teɪᵊlz
ta'en teɪn
taeni|a 'tiːn i |ə ~**ae** iː
Taff tæf
taffeta 'tæf ɪt ə -ət- ‖ -ət ə ~**s** z
taffia, T~ 'tæf i ə
taffrail 'tæf reɪᵊl -rəl, -rɪl ~**s** z
taff|y, Taff|y 'tæf |i ~**ies** iz
tafia 'tæf i ə
Taft tæft tɑːft
tag tæg **tagged** tægd **tagging** 'tæg ɪŋ **tags** tægz
'tag ˌwrestling
Tagalog tə 'gɑːl ɒg -'gæl-, -əg ‖ -əg -ɔːg, -ɑːg ~**s** z
tagalong ˌtæg ə 'lɒŋ ◂ ‖ -'lɔːŋ ◂ -'lɑːŋ ◂ ~**s** z
Tagamet tdmk 'tæg ə met ~**s** s
tagetes tæ 'dʒiːt iːz
tagg... —see **tag**
Taggart 'tæg ət ‖ -ᵊrt
tagliatelle ˌtæl jə 'tel i ˌtæg li ə 'tel i ‖ ˌtɑːl-
tagmeme 'tæg miːm ~**s** z
tagmemic tæg 'miːm ɪk ~**s** s
Tagore tə 'gɔː ‖ -'gɔːr —Bengali [tʰa kur]
tagua 'tɑːg wə
Tagus 'teɪg əs
tahini tə 'hiːn i tɑː-
Tahiti tə 'hiːt i tɑː- ‖ -'hiːt̬i
Tahitian tə 'hiːʃ ᵊn tɑː-, -'hiːt i ən ‖ ~**s** z
Tahoe 'tɑː həʊ ‖ -hoʊ
tahr tɑː ‖ tɑːr (= tar) **tahrs** tɑːz ‖ tɑːrz
Tai taɪ
tai chi, t'ai chi ˌtaɪ 'tʃiː ◂ -'dʒiː —Chi tàijí [⁴tʰai ²tɕi]
ˌt'ai chi 'ch'uan tʃu 'æn ‖ -'ɑːn —Chi quán [²tɕʰɥen]
Taichung, T'ai-chung ˌtaɪ 'tʃʊŋ —Chi Táizhōng [²tʰai ¹tʂʊŋ]
taig, Taig teɪg **taigs, Taigs** teɪgz
taiga 'taɪg ə -ɑː —Russ [tʌj 'ga]
taikonaut 'taɪk əʊ nɔːt ‖ -nɑːt ~**s** s
tail teɪᵊl **tailed** teɪᵊld **tailing/s** 'teɪᵊl ɪŋ/z **tails** teɪᵊlz
ˌtail 'end; 'tail pipe
tailback 'teɪᵊl bæk ~**s** s
tailboard 'teɪᵊl bɔːd ‖ -bɔːrd -boʊrd ~**s** z
tailbone 'teɪᵊl bəʊn ‖ -boʊn ~**s** z
tailcoat ˌteɪᵊl 'kəʊt '·· ‖ -'koʊt ~**s** s
-tailed 'teɪᵊld — **long-tailed** ˌlɒŋ 'teɪᵊld ◂ ‖ ˌlɔːŋ- ˌlɑːŋ-
tail-end ˌteɪᵊl 'end ~**er/s** ə/z ‖ -ᵊr/z ~**s** z
tail|gate 'teɪᵊl |geɪt ~**gated** geɪt ɪd -əd ‖ geɪt̬ əd ~**gater/s** geɪt ə/z ‖ geɪt̬ ᵊr/z ~**gates** geɪts ~**gating** geɪt ɪŋ ‖ geɪt̬ ɪŋ
tailless 'teɪᵊl ləs -lɪs ~**ness** nəs nɪs
taillight 'teɪᵊl laɪt ~**s** s
tailor 'teɪl ə ‖ -ᵊr ~**ed** d **tailoring** 'teɪl ər ɪŋ ~**s** z
tailor-made ˌteɪl ə 'meɪd ◂ ‖ -ᵊr-
tailpiec|e 'teɪᵊl piːs ~**es** ɪz əz

tailpipe 'teɪ⁰l paɪp ~s s
tailplane 'teɪ ⁰l pleɪn ~s z
tailrac|e 'teɪ⁰l reɪs **-es** ɪz əz
tailskid 'teɪ⁰l skɪd ~s z
tailspin 'teɪ⁰l spɪn ~s z
tailwind 'teɪ⁰l wɪnd ~s z
Tain, tain teɪn
Taine teɪn —*Fr* [tɛn]
Taino 'taɪn əʊ taɪ 'iːn-, taː 'iːn- ‖ -oʊ ~s z
taint teɪnt **tainted** 'teɪnt ɪd -əd ‖ 'teɪn̪t̬ əd
　tainting 'teɪnt ɪŋ ‖ 'teɪn̪t̬ ɪŋ **taints** teɪnts
'taint, 'tain't teɪnt
taipan 'taɪp æn ~s z
Taipei, T'aipei ˌtaɪ 'peɪ —*Chi* Táiběi
　[²tʰaɪ ³peɪ]
Taiping ˌtaɪ 'pɪŋ —*Chi* Tàipíng [⁴tʰaɪ ²pʰɪŋ]
Taishan ˌtaɪ 'ʃæn ‖ -'ʃɑːn —*Chi* Tàishān
　[⁴tʰaɪ ¹ʂan]
Tait teɪt
Taittinger ˌteɪt æn 'ʒeɪ '···, -ɪŋ ə —*Fr*
　[tɛ tæ̃ ʒe]
Taiwan, T'aiwan ˌtaɪ 'wɑːn -'wɒn, -'wæn
　—*Chi* Táiwān [²tʰaɪ ¹wan]
Taiwanese ˌtaɪ wə 'niːz ◄ -wɑː- ‖ -'niːs
Taizé 'teɪz eɪ 'tez- ‖ teɪ 'zeɪ te- —*Fr* [tɛ ze]
Tajik tɑː 'dʒiːk 'tɑːdʒ ɪk ~s s
Tajikistan tɑː ˌdʒiːk ɪ 'stɑːn -ˌdʒɪk-, -ə-, -'stæn
　‖ ·'···
tajine tə 'ʒiːn tɑː-, -'dʒiːn ~s z
Taj Mahal ˌtaɪdʒ mə 'hɑːl ˌtɑː-ʒ- —*Hindi*
　[ˌtaːdʒ mə həl]
takahe 'tɑːk ə hiː -ɑː- ~s z
take teɪk △tek **taken** 'teɪk ən △'tek- **takes**
　teɪks △teks **taking** 'teɪk ɪŋ △'tek- **took** tʊk
　§tuːk
takeaway 'teɪk ə ˌweɪ ~s z
takedown 'teɪk daʊn ~s z
take-home pay ˌteɪk həʊm peɪ ˌ·· ', ˌ·· ·
　‖ -hoʊm-
take-it-or-leave-it ˌteɪk ɪt ɔː 'liːv ɪt -ə'--, §ˌ·ət-,
　-ət ‖ ˌteɪk ət ⁳r 'liːv ət
taken 'teɪk ən
takeoff 'teɪk ɒf -ɔːf ‖ -ɔːf -ɑːf ~s s
takeout 'teɪk aʊt ~s s
takeover 'teɪk ˌəʊv ə ‖ -ˌoʊv ⁳r ~s z
taker 'teɪk ə ‖ -⁳r ~s z
take-up, takeup 'teɪk ʌp
takin 'tɑːk iːn ~s z
taking 'teɪk ɪŋ ~ly li ~ness nəs nɪs ~s z
Talacre *place in Clwyd* tæ 'læk reɪ —*Welsh*
　[ta 'lak re]
talapoin 'tæl ə pɔɪn ~s z
Talbot, t~ *(i)* 'tɔːlb ət 'tɒlb- ‖ 'tɑːlb-, *(ii)*
　'tælb ət —*In BrE usually (i), in AmE usually
　(ii).* ~s, ~'s z
talc tælk **talced, talcked** tælkt **talcing,
　talcking** 'tælk ɪŋ **talcs** tælks
Talcott 'tɔːlk ət 'tɒlk-, 'tælk-, -ɒt ‖ 'tɔːl kɑːt
　'tɑːl-, 'tæl-
talcum 'tælk əm
　'talcum ˌpowder
tale teɪ⁰l *(= tail)* **tales** teɪ⁰lz

talebear|er 'teɪ⁰l ˌbeər ə ‖ -ˌber |⁳r -ˌbær-
　~ers əz ‖ -⁳rz **~ing** ɪŋ
talent 'tæl ənt **talented** 'tæl ənt ɪd əd
　‖ -ən̪t̬ əd ~s s
　'talent scout; 'talent ˌspotter
talentless 'tæl ənt ləs -lɪs
tales *'group summoned for jury service'* 'teɪl iːz
　~men mən mæn **~men** mən men
tales *pl of* **tale** teɪ⁰lz
taleteller 'teɪ⁰l ˌtel ə ‖ -⁳r ~s z
Talfan 'tælv ən —*Welsh* ['tal van]
Talgarth 'tæl gɑːθ ‖ -gɑːrθ
tali —*see* **talus**
Taliban 'tæl ɪ bæn 'tɑːl-, -ə-, -bɑːn, ˌ·ˌ·ˈ·
　‖ 'tɑːl ə bɑːn 'tæl-
Taliesin ˌtæl i 'es ɪn ˌtæl 'jes ɪn, §-⁳n —*Welsh*
　[tal 'jes in]
talipes 'tæl ɪ piːz -ə-
talipot 'tæl ɪ pɒt -ə- ‖ -pɑːt ~s s
talisman 'tæl ɪz mən -əz-, -ɪs-, -əs- ‖ -əs- -əz- ~s
　z
talismanic ˌtæl ɪz 'mæn ɪk ◄ -əz-, -ɪs-, -əs-
　‖ -əs- -əz-
Talitha 'tæl ɪθ ə -əθ-
talk tɔːk ‖ tɑːk **talked** tɔːkt ‖ tɑːkt **talking**
　'tɔːk ɪŋ ‖ 'tɑːk- **talks** tɔːks ‖ tɑːks
　**ˌtalking 'head; 'talking point; 'talking
　shop; 'talk show**
talkathon 'tɔːk ə θɒn ‖ -θɑːn 'tɑːk- ~s z
talkative 'tɔːk ət ɪv ‖ -ət̬ ɪv 'tɑːk- ~ly li ~ness
　nəs nɪs
talkback 'tɔːk bæk ‖ 'tɑːk- ~s s
talker 'tɔːk ə ‖ -⁳r 'tɑːk- ~s z
talkie 'tɔːk i ‖ 'tɑːk- ~s z
talking-to 'tɔːk ɪŋ tuː -tu ‖ 'tɑːk- ~s z
talktime 'tɔːk taɪm ‖ 'tɑːk-
talky 'tɔːk i ‖ 'tɑːk i
tall tɔːl ‖ tɑːl **taller** 'tɔːl ə ‖ -⁳r 'tɑːl- **tallest**
　'tɔːl ɪst -əst ‖ 'tɑːl-
　ˌtall 'story
tallage 'tæl ɪdʒ
Tallaght 'tæl ə
Tallahassee ˌtæl ə 'hæs i
tallboy 'tɔːl bɔɪ ‖ 'tɑːl- ~s z
Talleyrand 'tæl i rænd —*Fr* [ta lɛ ʁɑ̃]
Tallin, Tallinn 'tæl ɪn tæ 'lɪn, -'liːn ‖ 'tɑːl ɪn
　—*Estonian* ['tal lin]
Tallis 'tæl ɪs §-əs
tallish 'tɔːl ɪʃ ‖ 'tɑːl-
tallith 'tæl ɪθ 'tɑːl-, -ɪs —*Hebrew* [ta 'liːt]
tallness 'tɔːl nəs -nɪs ‖ 'tɑːl-
tallow 'tæl əʊ ‖ -oʊ
tallowy 'tæl əʊ i ‖ -oʊ-
Tallulah tə 'luːl ə
tally 'tæl i **tallied** 'tæl id **tallies** 'tæl iz
　tallying 'tæl i ɪŋ
tallyho ˌtæl i 'həʊ ‖ -'hoʊ
tally|man 'tæl i |mən **~men** mən men
Talmud 'tæl mʊd -məd, -mʌd ‖ 'tɑːl-
talmudic tæl 'mʊd ɪk -'mjuːd-, -'mʌd- ‖ 'tɑːl-
　~al ⁰l
talon 'tæl ən **~ed** d **~s** z
talus *'anklebone'* 'teɪl əs **tali** 'teɪl aɪ

talus *'slope'* 'teɪl əs 'tæl- **~es** ɪz əz
Talybont, Tal-y-bont ˌtæl i 'bɒnt -ə- ‖ -'bɑːnt
— *Welsh* [tal ə 'bɔnt] —*see note at* -y-
Tal-y-llyn ˌtæl i 'lɪn -ə-, -'θlɪn — *Welsh*
[tal ə 'ɬin, -'ɬɪn] —*see note at* -y-
Tam, tam tæm —*see also phrases with this
word* **tams, Tam's** tæmz
tamable 'teɪm əb əl
tamagotchi ˌtæm ə 'gɒtʃ i ˌtɑːm ə 'goʊtʃ i
-'gɑːtʃ i — *Jp* [ta 'ma got tɕi]
tamale tə 'mɑːl i -eɪ **~s** z
tamandua ˌtæm ən 'duː ə ‖ tə 'mænd u ə
ˌ·ˌ·'ɑː **~s** z
Tamar 'teɪm ɑː -ə ‖ -ər —*the river in Devon and
Cornwall is locally* -ə, §-ər
Tamara *(i)* tə 'mɑːr ə -'mær-, *(ii)* 'tæm ər ə
tamarack 'tæm ə ræk **~s** s
tamarillo ˌtæm ə 'rɪl əʊ ‖ -oʊ **~s** z
tamarin 'tæm ər ɪn §-ən; -ə ræn **~s** z
tamarind 'tæm ər ɪnd §-ənd **~s** z
tamarisk 'tæm ər ɪsk §-əsk **~s** s
tamber 'tæm bə ‖ -bər **~s** z
tambour 'tæm bʊə -bɔː ‖ -bʊr ·ˈ· **~s** z
tamboura tæm 'bʊər ə -'bɔːr- ‖ -'bʊr- **~s** z
tambourin 'tæm bər ɪn **~s** z
tambourine ˌtæm bə 'riːn **~s** z
Tamburlaine 'tæm bə leɪn ‖ -bər-
tame, Tame teɪm **tamed** teɪmd **tamer** 'teɪm ə
‖ -ər **tames** teɪmz **tamest** 'teɪm ɪst -əst
taming 'teɪm ɪŋ
tameable 'teɪm əb əl
tame|ly 'teɪm |li **~ness** nəs nɪs
tamer 'teɪm ə ‖ -ər **~s** z
Tamerlane 'tæm ə leɪn ‖ -ər-
Tameside 'teɪm saɪd
Tamiflu *tdmk* 'tæm ɪ fluː -ə-
Tamika 'tæm ɪk ə
Tamil 'tæm əl -ɪl ‖ 'tɑːm- **~s** z
ˌTamil 'Nadu 'nɑːd uː
Tamla Motown ˌtæm lə 'məʊ taʊn ‖ -'moʊ-
Tammany 'tæm ən i
Tammie, Tammy, t~ 'tæm i
Tam O'Shanter, tam-o'-shanter
ˌtæm ə 'ʃænt ə ‖ -'ʃænt̬ ər **~s, ~'s** z
tamoxifen tə 'mɒks ɪ fen tæ-, -ə-
‖ -'mɑːks əf ən
tamp tæmp **tamped** tæmpt **tamping**
'tæmp ɪŋ **tamps** tæmps
Tampa 'tæmp ə
Tampax *tdmk* 'tæmp æks
tamper 'tæmp ə ‖ -ər **~ed** d **tampering**
'tæmp ər ɪŋ **~s** z
Tampere 'tæmp ə reɪ ‖ 'tɑːmp- —*Finnish*
['tɑm pe ɾe]
tamper-evident ˌtæmp ər 'ev ɪd ənt ◂ -əd·,
§-ɪ dent, §-ə dent ‖ -ˌər-
tamper-proof 'tæmp ə pruːf §-prʊf ‖ -ər-
tamper-resistant ˌtæmp ə rɪ 'zɪst ənt ◂ -ə rə-
‖ ˌtæmp ər-
Tampico tæm 'piːk əʊ ‖ -oʊ tɑːm- —*Sp*
[tam 'pi ko]
tampion 'tæmp i ən **~s** z
tampon 'tæmp ɒn -ən ‖ -ɑːn **~s** z

tamponade ˌtæmp ə 'neɪd **~s** z
Tamsin, Tamsyn *(i)* 'tæm sɪn, *(ii)* -zɪn
Tamworth, t~ 'tæm wɜːθ -wəθ, §-əθ ‖ -wɜːθ
~s, ~'s s
tan tæn **tanned** tænd **tanning** 'tæn ɪŋ **tans**
tænz
tana, Tana 'tɑːn ə
tanager 'tæn ədʒ ə -ɪdʒ- ‖ -ər **~s** z
Tanagra 'tæn əg rə
Tánaiste 'tɔːn əʃ ə tʃə 'tɑːn-, -ɪʃ- —*Irish*
['t̪ʰɑː nʲəç tʲə]
Tanami 'tæn ə maɪ
Tancock 'tæn kɒk →'tæŋ- ‖ -kɑːk
Tancred 'tæŋk rɪd -red, §-rəd
tandem 'tænd əm **~s** z
tandoor 'tænd ʊə -ɔː; tæn 'dʊə, -'dɔː
‖ tɑːn 'dʊər **~s** z
tandoori, tanduri tæn 'dʊər i tʌn-, -'dɔːr-
‖ tɑːn 'dʊr- -'dɜː-
Tandy 'tænd i
Taney 'tɔːn i ‖ 'tɑːn- *(!)*
tang tæŋ **tangs** tæŋz
Tang, T'ang *dynasty* tæŋ tʌŋ ‖ tɑːŋ —*Chi*
Táng [²tʰɑŋ]
tanga, Tanga 'tæŋ gə **~s** z
Tanganyika ˌtæŋ gən 'jiːk ə ˌgæn-
tangelo 'tændʒ ə ləʊ ‖ -loʊ **~s** z
tangent 'tændʒ ənt **~s** s
tangential tæn 'dʒen⸱t ʃəl **~ly** i
tangerine, T~ ˌtændʒ ə 'riːn ◂ · · · **~s** z
tangibility ˌtændʒ ə 'bɪl ət i ˌ·ɪ-, -ɪt i ‖ -ət̬ i
tangib|le 'tændʒ əb əl -ɪb- **~ly** li
Tangier ₍ᵢ₎tæn 'dʒɪə ‖ -'dʒɪ°r
Tangiers ₍ᵢ₎tæn 'dʒɪəz ‖ -'dʒɪ°rz
tangl|e 'tæŋ gəl **~ed** d **~es** z **~ing** ɪŋ
Tanglewood 'tæŋ gəl wʊd
tangly 'tæŋ gli
Tangmere 'tæŋ mɪə ‖ -mɪr
tango 'tæŋ gəʊ ‖ -goʊ **~ed** d **~ing** ɪŋ **~s** z
tangram 'tæn græm →'tæŋ- **~s** z
Tangshan ˌtæŋ 'ʃæn ‖ ˌtɑːŋ 'ʃɑːn —*Chi*
Tángshān [²tʰɑŋ ¹ʂan]
Tanguy 'tæŋ gi ‖ tɑːn 'giː —*Fr* [tɑ̃ gi]
tangy 'tæŋ i
Tangye 'tæŋ gi
tanh θæn tæntʃ, ˌtæn 'eɪtʃ
Tania 'tɑːn i ə ‖ 'tɑːn jə
tank tæŋk **tanked** tæŋkt **tanking** 'tæŋk ɪŋ
tanks tæŋks
ˌtanked 'up; 'tank ˌengine; 'tank top
tanka 'tæŋk ə 'tɑːŋk- ‖ 'tɑːŋk ə —*Jp* ['taŋ ka]
~s z
tankage 'tæŋk ɪdʒ
tankard 'tæŋk əd ‖ -ərd **~s** z
tanker 'tæŋk ə ‖ -ər **~s** z
tankful 'tæŋk fʊl **~s** z
tann... —*see* **tan**
tannate 'tæn eɪt
tanner, T~ 'tæn ə ‖ -ər **~s** z
tanner|y 'tæn ər |i **~ies** iz
Tannhauser, Tannhäuser 'tæn ˌhɔɪz ə -ˌhaʊz-
‖ 'tɑːn ˌhɔɪz ər —*Ger* ['tan hɔy zɐ]
tannic 'tæn ɪk

tannin 'tæn ɪn §-ən ~s z
tannoy, T~ *tdmk* 'tæn ɔɪ ~s z
Tanoan tə 'nəʊ ən 'tɑːn əʊ- ‖ tə 'noʊ ən
    'tɑːn oʊ-
Tanqueray 'tæŋk ər i -ə reɪ
Tansey 'tænz i
tans|y, Tansy 'tænz |i ~ies iz
tantalic tæn 'tæl ɪk
tantalis|e, tantaliz|e 'tænt ə laɪz -ᵊl aɪz
    ‖ 'tænt ᵊl aɪz ~ed d ~es ɪz əz ~ing ɪŋ
tantalous 'tænt əl əs ‖ 'tænt̬-
tantalum 'tænt əl əm ‖ 'tænt̬-
tantalus, T~ 'tænt əl əs ‖ 'tænt̬-
tantamount 'tænt ə maʊnt ‖ 'tænt̬-
tantara tæn 'ra: 'tænt ər ə, tæn 'tɑːr ə
    ‖ tæn 'tær ə
tantiv|y tæn 'tɪv |i ~ies iz
Tantr|a, t~ 'tæntr| ə 'tʌntr| ə ‖ 'tʌntr| ə
    'tɑːntr| ə, 'tæntr| ə ~ic ɪk ~ism ɪz əm
tantrum 'tæntr əm ~s z
Tanya 'tɑːn jə 'tæn-, -i ə
Tanzani|a ˌtæn zə 'niː |ə tæn 'zeɪn i ̩|ə ~an/s
    ən/z
Tao taʊ daʊ —*Chi* Dào [⁴teu]
    ˌTao Te 'Ching teɪ 'tʃɪŋ də 'dʒɪŋ —*Chi* Dào
    dé jīng [⁴teu ²tɤ ¹tɕɪŋ]
Tao Chi ˌtaʊ 'tʃiː
Taoiseach 'tiːʃ ɒk -ək, -əx —*Ir* ['t̪iː ʃax, -ʃɑ,
    -ʃəx]
Taoism 'taʊ ˌɪz əm 'daʊ-; 'teɪ əʊ ̩·, 'tɑː-
Taoist 'taʊ ɪst 'daʊ-, §-əst; 'teɪ əʊ-, 'tɑː- ~s s
Taos taʊs
tap tæp tapped tæpt tapping 'tæp ɪŋ taps
    tæps
    'tap dance; 'tap ˌdancer; tap ˌdancing
tapa 'tɑːp ə
tapas 'tæp æs -əs ‖ 'tɑːp- —*Sp* ['ta pas]
tape teɪp taped teɪpt tapes teɪps taping
    'teɪp ɪŋ
    'tape deck; 'tape ˌmeasure; 'tape
    re̩corder
tapenade, tapénade ˌtæp ə 'nɑːd ‖ ˌtɑːp- ~s
    z —*Fr* [ta pe nad]
taper 'teɪp ə ‖ -ᵊr ~ed d tapering/ly
    'teɪp ər ɪŋ /li ~s z
tape-record 'teɪp ri ̩kɔːd -rə- ‖ -kɔːrd ~ed ɪd
    əd ~er/s ə/z ‖ -ᵊr/z ~ing ɪŋ ~s z
tapes|try 'tæp ɪs |tri -əs- ~tries triz
tapeworm 'teɪp wɜːm ‖ -wɜːm ~s z
tapioca ˌtæp i 'əʊk ə ‖ -'oʊk ə
tapir 'teɪp ə -ɪə ‖ -ᵊr ~s z
tapis 'tæp i -iː ‖ tæ 'piː —*Fr* [ta pi]
Taplin 'tæp lɪn §-lən
Taplow 'tæp ləʊ ‖ -loʊ
Tapp tæp
tapp... —*see* tap
tapper 'tæp ə ‖ -ᵊr ~s z
tappet 'tæp ɪt §-ət ~s s
taproom 'tæp ruːm -rʊm ~s z
taproot 'tæp ruːt ~s s
Tapscott 'tæps kɒt ‖ -kɑːt
Tapsell 'tæps ᵊl
tapster 'tæpst ə ‖ -ᵊr ~s z

taqueria ˌtæk ə 'riː ə ~s z
tar tɑː ‖ tɑːr tarred tɑːd ‖ tɑːrd tarring
    'tɑːr ɪŋ tars tɑːz ‖ tɑːrz
Tara 'tɑːr ə 'tær ə ‖ 'tær ə 'ter ə, 'tɑːr ə
ta-ra tə 'rɑː
taradiddle 'tær ə dɪd ᵊl ‖ 'ter-, ̩·'·· ~s z
Tarahumara ˌtær ə hu 'mɑːr ə ◂
taramasalata, taramosalata
    ˌtær əm ə sə 'lɑːt ə tə ̩rɑːm-, tə 'ræm-
    ‖ 'tɑːr əm ə sə ̩lɑːt̬ ə ̩·····—*ModGk*
    [ta ra mɔ sa 'la ta]
Taranaki ˌtær ə 'næk i
tarantella ˌtær ən 'tel ə ~s z
Tarantino ˌtær ən 'tiːn əʊ ‖ -oʊ ̩ter-
Taranto tə 'rænt əʊ ‖ -oʊ -'rɑːnt-; 'tɑːr ənt-
    —*It* ['ta: ran to]
tarantula tə 'rænt jʊl ə -jəl ə; -'ræntʃ əl-
    ‖ -'ræntʃ əl̩ə -'ræntʃ ᵊl ə ~s z
Tarawa 'tær ə wə
taraxacum, T~ tə 'ræks ək əm
Tarbert 'tɑːb ət ‖ 'tɑːrb ᵊrt
Tarbet 'tɑːb ɪt -ət ‖ 'tɑːrb ət
tarboosh ˌtɑː 'buːʃ ‖ tɑːr- '·· ~es ɪz əz
Tarbuck 'tɑː bʌk ‖ 'tɑːr-
tardigrade 'tɑːd ɪ greɪd §-ə- ‖ 'tɑːrd- ~s z
Tardis 'tɑːd ɪs §-əs ‖ 'tɑːrd-
tard|y 'tɑːd |i ‖ 'tɑːrd |i ~ier i̩ə ‖ i̩ᵊr ~iest
    i ̩ɪst i ̩əst ~ily ɪ li əl i ~iness i nəs i nɪs
tare teə ‖ teᵊr tæᵊr tares teəz ‖ teᵊrz tæᵊrz
Tarentum tə 'rent əm
targ|et 'tɑːg |ɪt §-ət ‖ 'tɑːrg |ət ~eted ɪt ɪd
    §ət-, -əd ‖ ət̬ əd ~eting ɪt ɪŋ §ət- ‖ ət̬ ɪŋ ~ets
    ɪts §əts ‖ əts
    'target ˌlanguage
tariff 'tær ɪf §-əf ‖ 'ter- ~s s
Tariq 'tær ɪk 'tɑːr-
Tarka 'tɑːk ə ‖ 'tɑːrk ə
Tarkington 'tɑːk ɪŋ tən ‖ 'tɑːrk-
Tarleton 'tɑːl tən ‖ 'tɑːrl-
tarmac, T~ *tdmk* 'tɑː mæk ‖ 'tɑːr- ~ked t
    ~king ɪŋ ~s s
tarmacadam ˌtɑː mə 'kæd əm ‖ ˌtɑːr-
tarn, Tarn tɑːn ‖ tɑːrn tarns tɑːnz ‖ tɑːrnz
tarnation tɑː 'neɪʃ ᵊn ‖ tɑːr-
tarnish 'tɑːn ɪʃ ‖ 'tɑːrn ɪʃ ~ed t ~es ɪz əz ~ing
    ɪŋ
taro 'tɑːr əʊ ‖ -oʊ 'tær-, 'ter- ~s z
taroc, tarok 'tær ək -ɒk ‖ -ɑːk 'ter- ~s s
tarot 'tær əʊ ‖ -oʊ 'ter- ~s z
tarp tɑːp ‖ tɑːrp tarps tɑːps ‖ tɑːrps
tarpaper 'tɑː ˌpeɪp ə ‖ 'tɑːr ˌpeɪp ᵊr
tarpaulin ₍ᵢ₎tɑː 'pɔːl ɪn §-ən ‖ tɑːr- -'pɑːl-;
    'tɑːrp əl- ~s z
Tarpeian tɑː 'piː ən ‖ tɑːr-
tarpon 'tɑːp ɒn -ən ‖ 'tɑːrp ɑːn -ən ~s z
Tarporley 'tɑːp əl i ‖ 'tɑːrp ᵊr li
Tarquin 'tɑːk wɪn §-wən ‖ 'tɑːrk-
Tarquinius tɑː 'kwɪn i ̩əs ‖ tɑːr-
Tarr tɑː ‖ tɑːr
tarr... —*see* tar
tarradiddle 'tær ə dɪd ᵊl ‖ 'ter-, ̩·'·· ~s z
tarragon 'tær əg ən ‖ 'ter-

Tarragona ˌtær ə 'gəʊn ə ‖ -'goʊn- ˌter-, ˌtɑːr-
—*Sp* [ta rra 'ɣo na]
Tarrant 'tær ənt ‖ 'ter-
Tarring *place in West Sussex; family name*
'tær ɪŋ ‖ 'ter-
tarr|y *v 'delay'* 'tær |i ‖ 'ter- **~ied** id **~ies** iz
~ying i ɪŋ
tarry *adj 'tar-covered, tar-like'* 'tɑːr i
Tarrytown 'tær i taʊn ‖ 'ter-
tarsal 'tɑːs ᵊl ‖ 'tɑːrs ᵊl **~s** z
Tarshish 'tɑːʃ ɪʃ ‖ 'tɑːrʃ ɪʃ
tarsier 'tɑːs i‿ə ‖ 'tɑːrs i‿ᵊr -ei **~s** z
tars|us, T~ 'tɑːs |əs ‖ 'tɑːrs- **~i** aɪ
tart tɑːt ‖ tɑːrt **tarted** 'tɑːt ɪd -əd ‖ 'tɑːrt̬ əd
tarting 'tɑːt ɪŋ ‖ 'tɑːrt̬ ɪŋ **tarts** tɑːts ‖ tɑːrts
tartan 'tɑːt ᵊn ‖ 'tɑːrt ᵊn **~s** z
tartar, T~ 'tɑːt ə -ɑː ‖ 'tɑːrt̬ ᵊr **~s** z
ˌtartar 'sauce, '···
tartare tɑː 'tɑː ⚠-'teə ‖ tɑːr 'tɑːr
Tartarean tɑː 'teər i‿ən ‖ tɑːr ter- -'ter-
tartaric tɑː 'tær ɪk ‖ tɑːr- -'ter-
tarˌtaric 'acid
Tartarus 'tɑːt ər əs ‖ 'tɑːrt̬-
Tartary 'tɑːt ər i ‖ 'tɑːrt̬-
tartlet 'tɑːt lət -lɪt ‖ 'tɑːrt- **~s** s
tart|ly 'tɑːt |li ‖ 'tɑːrt |li **~ness** nəs nɪs
tartrate 'tɑːtr eɪt ‖ 'tɑːrtr- **~s** s
tartrazine 'tɑːtr ə ziːn ‖ 'tɑːrtr-
Tartuffe ˌtɑː 'tuːf -'ʊf ‖ ˌtɑːr- —*Fr* [taʁ tyf]
tart|y 'tɑːt| i ‖ 'tɑːrt̬| i **~ier** i‿ə ‖ i‿ᵊr **~iest** i‿ɪst
i‿əst **~ily** ɪ li əl i **~iness** i nəs i nɪs
Tarvin 'tɑːv ɪn §-ᵊn ‖ 'tɑːrv ᵊn
Tarzan 'tɑːz ᵊn -æn ‖ 'tɑːrz-
taser 'teɪz ə ‖ -ᵊr **~s** z
Tasha 'tæʃ ə ‖ 'tɑːʃ ə
Tashkent ˌtæʃ 'kent ‖ ˌtɑːʃ- —*Russ* [taʃ 'kʲent]
task tɑːsk §tæsk ‖ tæsk **tasked** tɑːskt §tæskt
‖ tæskt **tasking** 'tɑːsk ɪŋ §'tæsk- ‖ 'tæsk ɪŋ
tasks tɑːsks §tæsks ‖ tæsks
'task force
taskbar 'tɑːsk bɑː ‖ 'tæsk bɑːr **~s** z
Tasker 'tæsk ə ‖ -ᵊr
taskmaster 'tɑːsk ˌmɑːst ə §'tæsk ˌmæst ə
‖ 'tæsk ˌmæst ᵊr **~s** z
taskmistress 'tɑːsk ˌmɪs trəs §'tæsk-, -trɪs
‖ 'tæsk- **~es** ɪz əz
Tasman 'tæz mən
Tasmani|a tæz 'meɪn i‿|ə **~an/s** ən/z
Tass tæs ‖ tɑːs
tassel 'tæs ᵊl **~ed, ~led** d **~s** z
tassie *'cup'* 'tæs i **~s** z
Tassie *'Tasmanian'* 'tæz i **~s** z
Tasso 'tæs əʊ ‖ 'tɑːs oʊ 'tæs- —*It* ['tas so]
taste teɪst **tasted** 'teɪst ɪd -əd **tastes** teɪsts
tasting 'teɪst ɪŋ
'taste bud
tasteful 'teɪst fᵊl -fʊl **~ly** ‿i **~ness** nəs nɪs
tasteless 'teɪst ləs -lɪs **~ly** li **~ness** nəs nɪs
taster 'teɪst ə ‖ -ᵊr **~s** z
tast|y 'teɪst |i **~ier** i‿ə ‖ i‿ᵊr **~iest** i‿ɪst i‿əst
~ily ɪ li əl i **~iness** i nəs i nɪs
tat tæt **tats** tæts **tatted** 'tæt ɪd -əd ‖ 'tæt̬ əd
tatting 'tæt ɪŋ ‖ 'tæt̬ ɪŋ

tata, ta-ta ₍ˌ₎tæ 'tɑː tə-
tatami tə 'tɑːm i tɑː-, tæ- —*Jp* [ta ˌta mi] **~s** z
Tatar 'tɑːt ə ‖ 'tɑːt̬ ᵊr **~s** z
Tatchell 'tætʃ əl
Tate teɪt
tater 'teɪt ə ‖ 'teɪt̬ ᵊr **~s** z
Tatham *(i)* 'tæt əm ‖ 'tæt̬ əm, *(ii)* 'teɪθ əm,
(iii) 'teɪð əm
Tati tæ 'tiː tɑː- ‖ tɑː- —*Fr* [ta ti]
Tatiana ˌtæt i 'ɑːn ə ‖ tɑːt 'jɑːn ə
tatie 'teɪt i ‖ 'teɪt̬ i **~s** z
Tatler *tdmk* 'tæt lə ‖ -lᵊr
Tatra 'tɑːtr ə 'tætr ə
tatter 'tæt ə ‖ 'tæt̬ ᵊr **~ed** d **~s** z
tatterdemalion ˌtæt ə dɪ 'meɪl i‿ən -də'--,
-'mæl- ‖ ˌtæt̬ ᵊr-
Tattersall, t~ 'tæt ə sɔːl -sᵊl ‖ 'tæt̬ ᵊr- -sɑːl **~s,
~'s** z
tattie 'tæt i ‖ 'tæt̬ i **~s** z
tattl|e 'tæt ᵊl ‖ 'tæt̬ ᵊl **~ed** d **~es** z **~ing/ly**
ɪŋ /li
tattler 'tæt ᵊl ə ‖ 'tæt̬ ᵊl ᵊr **~s** z
tattletale 'tæt ᵊl teɪᵊl **~s** z
Tatton 'tæt ᵊn
tattoo tæ 'tuː tə- **~ed** d **~ing** ɪŋ **~s** z
tattooist tæ 'tuː ɪst tə-, §-əst **~s** s
tatt|y 'tæt |i ‖ 'tæt̬ |i **~ier** i‿ə ‖ i‿ᵊr **~iest** i‿ɪst
i‿əst **~ily** ɪ li əl i **~iness** i nəs i nɪs
Tatum 'teɪt əm ‖ 'teɪt̬ əm
Tatung *tdmk* 'tɑː tʊŋ
tau tɔː taʊ ‖ taʊ tɔː, tɑː
taught tɔːt ‖ tɑːt *(= taut)*
taunt tɔːnt ‖ tɑːnt **taunted** 'tɔːnt ɪd -əd
‖ 'tɔːnt̬ əd 'tɑːnt̬- **taunting/ly** 'tɔːnt ɪŋ /li
‖ 'tɔːnt̬- 'tɑːnt̬- **taunts** tɔːnts ‖ tɑːnts
Taunton 'tɔːnt ən ‖ 'tɔːnt ᵊn 'tɑːnt- —*in
Somerset, locally also* 'tɑːnt-
Taunus 'tɔːn əs 'taʊn- ‖ 'taʊn- —*Ger* ['taʊ nʊs]
taupe təʊp ‖ toʊp *(= tope)*
Taurean, t~ 'tɔːr i‿ən tɔː 'riː‿ən **~s** z
taurine *n* '$C_2H_7NO_3S$' 'tɔːr iːn -ɪn
taurine *adj 'bovine'* 'tɔːr aɪn
Taurus 'tɔːr əs
taut tɔːt ‖ tɑːt **tauter** 'tɔːt ə ‖ 'tɔːt̬ ᵊr 'tɑːt̬-
tautest 'tɔːt ɪst -əst ‖ 'tɔːt̬ əst 'tɑːt̬-
tauten 'tɔːt ᵊn ‖ 'tɑːt- **~ed** d **~ing** ɪŋ **~s** z
taut|ly 'tɔːt |li ‖ 'tɑːt- **~ness** nəs nɪs
tauto- *comb. form*
with plain suffix ˌtɔːt əʊ ‖ ˌtɔːt̬- ˌtɑːt̬- —
tautomeric ˌtɔːt ə 'mer ɪk ◄ ‖ ˌtɔːt̬- ˌtɑːt̬-
with stress-imposing suffix tɔː 'tɒ +
‖ tɔː 'tɑː + tɑː- — **tautomerism**
tɔː 'tɒm ər ˌɪz əm ‖ -'tɑːm- tɑː-
tautological ˌtɔːt ə 'lɒdʒ ɪk ᵊl ◄
‖ ˌtɔːt̬ ə 'lɑːdʒ- ˌtɑːt̬- **~ly** ‿i
tautologous tɔː 'tɒl əg əs ⚠-ədʒ əs ‖ -'tɑːl-
tɑː-
tautolog|y tɔː 'tɒl ədʒ |i ‖ -'tɑːl- tɑː- **~ies** iz
tautomer 'tɔːt əm ə ‖ 'tɔːt̬ əm ᵊr 'tɑːt̬- **~s** z
tautonym 'tɔːt ə nɪm -ᵊn ɪm ‖ 'tɔːt̬ ᵊn ɪm 'tɑːt̬-
~s z
tautosyllabic ˌtɔːt əʊ sɪ 'læb ɪk ◄ -sə'--
‖ ˌtɔːt̬ oʊ- ˌtɑːt̬-

Tavare, Tavaré 'tæv ə reɪ
Tavener 'tæv ᵊn ə ‖ -ᵊr
tavern 'tæv ᵊn ‖ -ᵊrn ~s z
taverna tə 'vɜːn ə tæ- ‖ -'vɜːn- —ModGk
[ta 'vɛr na] ~s z
Taverne tə 'vɜːn ‖ -'vɜːn
Taverner 'tæv ᵊn ə ‖ -ᵊrn ər
Tavistock 'tæv ɪ stɒk -ə- ‖ -staːk
Tavy 'teɪv i
taw tɔː ‖ taː tawed tɔːd ‖ taːd tawing 'tɔːⁱ ɪŋ
‖ 'tɔː ɪŋ 'taː- taws tɔːz ‖ taːz
tawdr|y 'tɔːdr |i ‖ 'taːdr- ~ier i ə ‖ i ᵊr ~iest
i ɪst i ᵊst ~ily əl i i li ~iness i nəs i nɪs
Tawe river 'taʊ i -eɪ —Welsh ['ta we]
Tawney 'tɔːn i ‖ 'taːn-
tawn|y 'tɔːn |i ‖ 'taːn- ~ier i ə ‖ i ᵊr ~iest i ɪst
i ᵊst ~iness i nəs i nɪs
tawse tɔːz ‖ taːz
tax tæks taxed tækst taxes 'tæks ɪz -əz
taxing/ly 'tæks ɪŋ /li
'tax e,vasion; 'tax ,exile; 'tax ,haven;
'tax re,turn; 'tax ,shelter; 'tax year
taxa 'tæks ə
taxability ,tæks ə 'bɪl ət i -ɪt i ‖ -əṭ i
taxable 'tæks əb ᵊl ~ness nəs nɪs
taxation tæk 'seɪʃ ᵊn ~s z
tax-deductible ,tæks di 'dʌkt əb ᵊl ◂ -də-,
-ɪb ᵊl; '· ·, · · ·
tax-deferred ,tæks di 'fɜːd ◂ -də- ‖ -'fɜːd ◂
taxeme 'tæks iːm ~s z
taxemic tæk 'siːm ɪk ~s s
tax-exempt ,tæks ɪg 'zempt ◂ -eg-, -əg-, -ɪk-,
-ek-, -ək-
tax-free ,tæks 'friː ◂
taxi 'tæks i ~ed d ~ing ɪŋ ~es, ~s z
'taxi ,driver; 'taxi rank; 'taxi stand
taxicab 'tæks i kæb ~s z
taxiderm|al ,tæks ɪ 'dɜːm| ᵊl ◂ -ə- ‖ -'dɜːm-
~ic ɪk
taxidermist 'tæks ɪ dɜːm ɪst '·ə-, §-əst, ,· ·'· ·;
tæk 'sɪd əm- ‖ 'tæks ə dɜːm əst ~s s
taxidermy 'tæks ɪ dɜːm i '·ə- ‖ -dɜːm i
taximeter 'tæks i ,miːt ə ‖ -,miːṭ ᵊr ~s z
taxis sing. n, Taxis 'tæks ɪs §-əs
taxis pl of taxi 'tæks iz
-taxis 'tæks ɪs §-əs — thermotaxis
,θɜːm əʊ 'tæks ɪs §-əs ‖ ,θɜːm ə-
taxiway 'tæks i weɪ ~s z
tax|man 'tæks |mæn |mæn-men men
taxon 'tæks ɒn ‖ -aːn ~s z taxa 'tæks ə
taxonomic ,tæks ə 'nɒm ɪk ◂ ‖ -'naːm- ~al ᵊl
~ally ᵊl i
,taxo,nomic pho'nemics
taxonomist tæk 'sɒn əm ɪst §-əst ‖ -'saːn- ~s s
taxonom|y tæk 'sɒn əm |i ‖ -'saːn- ~ies iz
taxpayer 'tæks ,peɪ ə ‖ -ᵊr ~s z
taxying 'tæks i ɪŋ
Tay teɪ
tayberr|y 'teɪ bər |i -,ber |i -,ber |i ~ies iz
Tayler, Taylor 'teɪl ə ‖ -ᵊr
Taylorian teɪ 'lɔːr i ən
Taylour 'teɪl ə ‖ -ᵊr
Tayport 'teɪ pɔːt ‖ -pɔːrt -poʊrt

tayra 'taɪᵊr ə ~s z
Tay-Sachs ,teɪ 'sæks
,Tay 'Sachs di,sease
Tayside 'teɪ saɪd
Taz tæz
TB ,tiː 'biː
T-ball 'tiː bɔːl ‖ -baːl
T-bar 'tiː baː ‖ -baːr ~s z
Tbilisi tə 'blɪːs i tə bɪ 'lɪːs i, -bə-
T-bill 'tiː bɪl ~s z
T-bond 'tiː bɒnd ‖ -baːnd ~s z
T-bone 'tiː bəʊn ‖ -boʊn ~s z
T-cell 'tiː sel ~s z
Tchaikovsky tʃaɪ 'kɒf ski ‖ -'kɔːf- -'kaːf-
—Russ [tʃɪj 'kɔf skʲɪj]
TCP tdmk ,tiː siː 'piː
te tiː —see also phrases with this word
tea tiː (= tee) teas tiːz (= tease)
'tea break; 'tea ,caddy; 'tea chest; 'tea
cloth; 'tea ,cosy; 'tea ,party; 'tea
,service; 'tea ,towel; 'tea ,trolley; 'tea
,wagon
teabag 'tiː bæg ~s z
teabread 'tiː bred
teacake 'tiː keɪk ~s s
teach, Teach tiːtʃ taught tɔːt ‖ taːt teaches
'tiːtʃ ɪz -əz teaching/s 'tiːtʃ ɪŋ/z
'teaching ,practice; 'teaching ,hospital
teachability ,tiːtʃ ə 'bɪl ət i -ɪt i ‖ -əṭ i
teachable 'tiːtʃ əb ᵊl
teacher, T~ 'tiːtʃ ə ‖ -ᵊr ~s z
,teacher 'training ,college
teach-in 'tiːtʃ ɪn ~s z
teacup 'tiː kʌp 'tiː kʌp ~s s
teacupful 'tiː kʌp fʊl 'tiː kʌp- ~s z teacupsful
'tiː kʌps fʊl 'tiː kʌps-
teagarden, T~ 'tiː ,gaːd ᵊn ‖ -,gaːrd- ~s z
Teague tiːg
tea|house 'tiː |haʊs ~houses haʊz ɪz -əz
teak tiːk
teakettle 'tiː ,ket ᵊl ‖ -,keṭ- ~s z
teal, Teal tiːᵊl teals tiːᵊlz
tea|leaf 'tiː |liːf ~leaves liːvz
team tiːm (= teem) teamed tiːmd teaming
'tiːm ɪŋ teams tiːmz
,team 'spirit
tea-maker 'tiː ,meɪk ə ‖ -ᵊr ~s z
team-mate 'tiːm meɪt ~s s
teamster 'tiːmᵖst ə ‖ -ᵊr ~s z
teamwork 'tiːm wɜːk ‖ -wɜːk
Tean tiːn
teapot 'tiːp ɒt 'tiː pɒt ‖ 'tiː paːt ~s s
teapoy 'tiːp ɔɪ ~s z
tear 'rip', 'rush' teə ‖ teᵊr tæᵊr (= tare) tearing
'teər ɪŋ ‖ 'ter ɪŋ 'tær- tears teəz ‖ teᵊrz tæᵊrz
tore tɔː ‖ tɔːr toʊr torn tɔːn ‖ tɔːrn toʊrn
tear 'liquid from the eye' tɪə ‖ tɪᵊr tears tɪəz
‖ tɪᵊrz
'tear duct; 'tear gas
tearaway 'teər ə ,weɪ ‖ 'ter- 'tær- ~s z
teardrop 'tɪə drɒp ‖ 'tɪr draːp ~s s
tearful 'tɪəf ᵊl ‖ 'tɪrf ᵊl ~ly ʲi ~ness nəs nɪs

teargas 'tɪə gæs ‖ 'tɪr- **~sed** t **~ses** ɪz əz **~sing** ɪŋ

tearing 'teər ɪŋ ‖ 'ter ɪŋ 'tær-

tearjerker 'tɪə ˌdʒɜːk ə ‖ 'tɪr ˌdʒɜːk ʰr **~s** z

Tearlach 'tʃɑːl əx -ək ‖ 'tʃɑːrl ək —*ScG* ['tʲaːr ləx]

tearless *'unweeping'* 'tɪə ləs -lɪs ‖ 'tɪr- **~ly** li **~ness** nəs nɪs

tearoff 'teər ɒf -ɔːf ‖ 'ter ɔːf 'tær-, -ɑːf

tearoom 'tiː ruːm -rʊm **~s** z

tearstained 'tɪə steɪnd ‖ 'tɪr-

teary 'tɪər i ‖ 'tɪr i

Teasdale 'tiːz derʰl

tease tiːz **teased** tiːzd **teases** 'tiːz ɪz -əz **teasing/ly** 'tiːz ɪŋ /li

teasel 'tiːz ʰl **~ed, ~led** d **~ing, ~ling** ɪŋ **~s** z

teaser 'tiːz ə ‖ -ʰr **~s** z

teashop 'tiː ʃɒp ‖ -ʃɑːp **~s** s

Teasmade *tdmk* 'tiːz meɪd

teaspoon 'tiːsp uːn 'tiː spuːn **~s** z

teaspoonful 'tiːsp uːn fʊl 'tiː spuːn- **~s** z **teaspoonsful** 'tiːsp uːnz fʊl 'tiː spuːnz-

teat tiːt **teats** tiːts

teatime 'tiːt aɪm 'tiː taɪm

tea-tree 'tiː triː **~s** z

tea-urn 'tiː ɜːn ‖ -ɜːn **~s** z

teazel, teazle 'tiːz ʰl **teazeled, teazelled, teazled** 'tiːz ʰld **teazeling, teazelling, teazling** 'tiːz ʰl ɪŋ **teazels, teazles** 'tiːz ʰlz

Tebay *place in Cumbria* 'tiːb eɪ —*but locally* -i

Tebbit, Tebbitt 'teb ɪt §-ət

tec tek **tecs** teks

tech tek

techie 'tek i **~s** z

technetium tek 'niːʃ i əm -'niːs-; -'niːʃ əm

technical 'tek nɪk ʰl 'technical ˌcollege; ˌtechnical 'knockout

technicalit|y ˌtek nɪ 'kæl ət |i ˌ-nə-, -ɪt i ‖ -ət |i **~ies** iz

technically 'tek nɪk ʰl i

technician tek 'nɪʃ ʰn **~s** z

Technicolor *tdmk*, **t~**, **technicolour** 'tek nɪ ˌkʌl ə -nə- ‖ -ʰr

technics, T~ 'tek nɪks

technique ₍ₜ₎tek 'niːk **~s** s

techno 'tek nəʊ ‖ -noʊ

techno- *comb. form* *with stress-neutral suffix* ˌtek nəʊ ‖ -noʊ — **technophobia** ˌtek nəʊ 'fəʊb i ə ‖ -noʊ 'foʊb- *with stress-imposing suffix* tek 'nɒ+ ‖ -'nɑː+ — **technography** tek 'nɒg rəf i ‖ -'nɑːg-

technocrac|y tek 'nɒk rəs |i ‖ -'nɑːk- **~ies** iz

technocrat 'tek nə kræt **~s** s

technocratic ˌtek nə 'kræt ɪk ◄ ‖ -'kræt̬- **~ally** ʰl i

techno-geek 'tek nəʊ giːk ‖ -noʊ- **~s** s

technological ˌtek nə 'lɒdʒ ɪk ʰl ◄ ‖ -'lɑːdʒ- **~ly** i

technologist tek 'nɒl ədʒ ɪst §-əst ‖ -'nɑːl- **~s** s

technolog|y tek 'nɒl ədʒ |i ‖ -'nɑːl- **~ies** iz

technophobe 'tek nəʊ fəʊb ‖ -noʊ foʊb **~s** z

tech|y *'technical enthusiast'* 'tek| i **~ies** iz

Teck tek

tectonic tek 'tɒn ɪk ‖ -'tɑːn- **~s** s

Tecumseh tɪ 'kʌmᵖs ə tə-, -i

Tecwyn 'tek wɪn

ted, Ted ted **tedded** 'ted ɪd -əd **tedding** 'ted ɪŋ **teds** tedz

Tedder, t~ 'ted ə ‖ -ʰr **~s** z

Teddie 'ted i

Teddington 'ted ɪŋ tən

tedd|y, Tedd|y 'ted |i **~ies, ~y's** iz 'teddy ˌbear; 'teddy ˌboy

Te Deum ˌtiː 'diː əm ˌteɪ 'deɪ-, -ʊm **~s** z

tedious 'tiːd i əs §'tiːdʒ əs **~ly** li **~ness** nəs nɪs

tedium 'tiːd i əm

tee tiː **teed** tiːd **teeing** 'tiː ɪŋ **tees** tiːz 'tee ˌshirt

tee-ball 'tiː bɔːl ‖ -bɑːl

teehee ˌtiː 'hiː

teem tiːm **teemed** tiːmd **teeming** 'tiːm ɪŋ **teems** tiːmz

teen tiːn **teens** tiːnz

Teena 'tiːn ə

teenage 'tiːn eɪdʒ **~d** d

teenager 'tiːn eɪdʒ ə ‖ -ʰr **~s** z

teens|y 'tiːnz |i **-ier** i ə ‖ i ʰr **~iest** i ɪst i əst ˌteensy 'weensy◄

teen|y 'tiːn |i **-ier** i ə ‖ i ʰr **~iest** i ɪst i əst ˌteeny 'weeny◄

teenybopper 'tiːn i ˌbɒp ə ‖ -ˌbɑːp ʰr **~s** z

teepee 'tiːp iː **~s** z

Tees tiːz

Teesdale 'tiːz derʰl

Teesside 'tiː saɪd 'tiːz-

teeter 'tiːt ə ‖ 'tiːt̬ ʰr **~ed** d **teetering** 'tiːt ər ɪŋ ‖ 'tiːt̬ ər ɪŋ **~s** z

teeterboard 'tiːt ə bɔːd ‖ 'tiːt̬ ʰr bɔːrd -boʊrd **~s** z

teeter-totter 'tiːt ə ˌtɒt ə ‖ 'tiːt̬ ʰr ˌtɑːt̬ ʰr **~s** z

teeth tiːθ

teethe tiːð **teethed** tiːðd **teethes** tiːðz **teething** 'tiːð ɪŋ 'teething ˌring; 'teething ˌtroubles

teetotal ˌtiː 'təʊt ʰl ◄ ‖ -'toʊt̬ ʰl ◄ ˈˌˌ··

teetotaler, teetotaller ₍ₜ₎tiː 'təʊt ʰl ə ‖ -'toʊt̬ ʰl ʰr **~s** z

tef, t'ef, teff tef

TEFL 'tef ʰl

Teflon *tdmk*, **t~** 'tef lɒn ‖ -lɑːn

teg teg **tegs** tegz

Tegucigalpa te ˌguːs ɪ 'gælp ə -ə- ‖ -'gɑːlp-, -ɑː —*AmSp* [te ɣu si 'ɣal pa]

tegument 'teg ju mənt ‖ -jə- **~s** s

Tehachapi tə 'hætʃ əp i tɪ-

Teheran, Tehran ˌteə 'rɑːn -'ræn; ˌte hə '· ‖ te 'rɑːn -'ræn; ˌteɪ ə '·

Teifi 'taɪv i —*Welsh* ['təi vi]

Teign tiːn tɪn

Teignmouth 'tɪn məθ 'tiːn-, →'tɪm-

Teilhard de Chardin ˌteɪ ɑː də 'ʃɑːd æn ·, ··, ·ˌjɑː-, -ˌʃɑː- 'dæ ‖ teɪ ˌjɑːr də ʃɑːr 'dæn —*Fr* [tɛ jaʁ də ʃaʁ dæ̃]

Te Kanawa ti 'kɑːn ə wə tə-

tektite 'tekt aɪt ~s s
telamon, T~ 'tel əm ən -ə mɒn ‖ -ə mɑːn ~s z
Tel Aviv ˌtel ə 'viːv -'vɪv
telco 'tel kəʊ ‖ -koʊ ~s z
tele 'tel i
tele- *comb form*
　with stress-neutral suffix ˌtel ɪ -ə —*but when*
　an independent prefix ˌtel i ‖ ˌtel ə —
　telephone 'tel ɪ fəʊn -ə- ‖ -ə foʊn
　with stress-imposing suffix tə 'le + tɪ-, te-
　— **telescopy** tə 'lesk əp i tɪ-, te-
telecast *v, n* 'tel i kɑːst -ə-, §-kæst ‖ -ə kæst
　~**ed** ɪd əd ~**ing** ɪŋ ~**s** s
telecom, T~ 'tel i kɒm -ə- ‖ -ə kɑːm ~s z
telecommunication ˌtel i kə ˌmjuːn ɪ 'keɪʃ ᵊn
　ˌ-ə-, -ˌ-ə- ‖ ˌtel ə- ~s z
telecom|mute ˌtel i kə |'mjuːt ‖ ˌtel ə-ˌ-ˌ-
　~**muted** 'mjuːt ɪd -əd ‖ -ˌmjuːt̬ əd ~**muter/s**
　'mjuːt ə/z ‖ ˌmjuːt̬ ᵊr/z ~**mutes** 'mjuːts
　‖ ˌmjuːts ~**muting** 'mjuːt ɪŋ ‖ ˌmjuːt̬ ɪŋ
teleconferenc|e 'tel i ˌkɒn fᵊr ənᵗs ˌ·ˈ···
　‖ -ə ˌkɑːn- ~**es** ɪz əz ~**ing** ɪŋ
teledu *'stinking badger'* 'tel ɪ duː -ə- —*but the*
　Welsh word for 'television', also spelt like this,
　is [te 'le di, -di] ~**s** z
telegenic ˌtel i 'dʒen ɪk ◂ ‖ ˌtel ə-
Telegonus tɪ 'leg ən əs tə-
telegony tɪ 'leg ən i tə-
telegram 'tel ɪ græm -ə- ~**s** z
telegraph *n, v* 'tel ɪ grɑːf -ə-, -græf ‖ -ə græf
　~**ed** t ~**ing** ɪŋ ~**s** s
　'**telegraph pole**; '**telegraph post**
telegrapher tə 'leg rəf ə tɪ-, te- ‖ -ᵊr ~s z
telegraphese ˌtel ɪ grɑːf 'iːz ˌ-ə-, -græf'-, -grəf'-
　‖ -ə græf 'iːz -'iːs
telegraphic ˌtel ɪ 'græf ɪk ◂ -ə- ~**ally** ᵊl i
telegraphist tə 'leg rəf ɪst tɪ-, te-, §-əst ~**s** s
telegraphy tə 'leg rəf i tɪ-, te-
telekinesis ˌtel ɪ kaɪ 'niːs ɪs ˌ-ə-, -kɪ'-, §-kə'-,
　§-əs
Telemachus tə 'lem ək əs tɪ-, te-
Telemann 'teɪl ə mæn 'tel- ‖ -mɑːn —*Ger*
　['teː lə man]
telemark, T~ 'tel i mɑːk -ə- ‖ -ə mɑːrk ~**s** s
telemarketing 'tel i ˌmɑːk ɪt ɪŋ '-ə-, §-ət ɪŋ,
　ˌ·ˈ··· ‖ -ə ˌmɑːrk ət̬ ɪŋ
Telemessag|e *tdmk, t~* 'tel i ˌmes ɪdʒ ‖ -ə-
　~**es** ɪz əz
telemeter tə 'lem ɪt ə tɪ-, te-, §-ət ə;
　'tel ɪ ˌmiːt ə, -ə- ‖ tə 'lem ət̬ ᵊr 'tel ə ˌmiːt̬ ᵊr
　~**ed** d ~**s** z
telemetry tə 'lem ətr i tɪ-, te-, -ɪtr i
teleological ˌtiːl i ə 'lɒdʒ ɪk ᵊl ◂ ˌtel- ‖ -'lɑːdʒ-
　~**ly** i
teleologist ˌtiːl i 'ɒl ədʒ ɪst ˌtel-, §-əst ‖ -'ɑːl-
　~**s** s
teleolog|y ˌtiːl i 'ɒl ədʒ |i ˌtel- ‖ -'ɑːl- ~**ies** iz
teleost 'tiːl i ɒst 'tel- ‖ -ɑːst ~**s** s
telepathic ˌtel ɪ 'pæθ ɪk ◂ -ə- ~**ally** ᵊl i
telepathist tə 'lep əθ ɪst tɪ-, te-, §-əst ~**s** s
telepathy tə 'lep əθ i tɪ-, te-
telepherique, téléphérique ˌtel ɪ fə 'riːk
　ˌ-ə-, ˌ-eɪ-, -fe'- —*Fr* [te le fe ʁik] ~**s** s

telephon|e *n, v* 'tel ɪ fəʊn -ə- ‖ -ə foʊn ~**ed** d
　~**es** z ~**ing** ɪŋ
　'**telephone book**; '**telephone booth**;
　'**telephone box**; '**telephone di,rectory**;
　'**telephone ex,change**; '**telephone ,kiosk**;
　'**telephone ,number**
telephonic ˌtel ɪ 'fɒn ɪk ◂ -ə- ‖ -ə 'fɑːn- ~**ally**
　ᵊl i
telephonist tə 'lef ən ɪst tɪ-, te-, §-əst
　‖ 'tel ə foʊn- ~**s** s
telephony tə 'lef ən i tɪ-, te-
telephoto, Telephoto *tdmk* ˌtel i 'fəʊt əʊ ◂
　-ə- ‖ -ə 'foʊt̬ oʊ ◂ ~**s** z
　ˌtele,photo 'lens
telephotograph ˌtel i 'fəʊt ə grɑːf ˌ-ə-, -græf
　‖ ˌtel ə 'foʊt̬ ə græf ~**s** s
telephotographic ˌtel i ˌfəʊt ə 'græf ɪk ˌ-ə-
　‖ -ə ˌfoʊt̬ ə- ~**ally** ᵊl i
telephotography ˌtel i fə 'tɒg rəf i ˌ-ə-
　‖ -ə fə 'tɑːg-
teleplay 'tel i pleɪ -ə- ~**s** z
telepoint 'tel ɪ pɔɪnt ‖ -ə- ~**s** s
tele|port 'tel ɪ |pɔːt -ə- ‖ -ə |pɔːrt -poʊrt
　~**ported** pɔːt ɪd -əd ‖ pɔːrt̬ əd poʊrt əd
　~**porting** pɔːt ɪŋ ‖ pɔːrt̬ ɪŋ poʊrt ɪŋ ~**ports**
　pɔːts ‖ pɔːrts poʊrts
teleprinter 'tel ɪ ˌprɪnt ə -ə- ‖ -ə ˌprɪnt̬ ᵊr ~**s** z
teleprompter, TelePrompTer *tdmk*
　'tel ɪ ˌprɒmpt ə -ə- ‖ -ə ˌprɑːmpt ᵊr ~**s** z
Teleri tə 'ler i tɪ- —*Welsh* [te 'le ri]
telesales 'tel i seɪᵊlz ‖ -ə-
telescop|e *n, v* 'tel ɪ skəʊp -ə- ‖ -ə skoʊp ~**ed**
　t ~**es** s ~**ing** ɪŋ
telescopic ˌtel ɪ 'skɒp ɪk ◂ -ə- ‖ -ə 'skɑːp-
　~**ally** ᵊl i
telescopist tɪ 'lesk əp ɪst tə-, te-, §-əst ~**s** s
telescopy tɪ 'lesk əp i tə-, te-
teleselling 'tel i ˌsel ɪŋ -ə-, ˌ·ˈ·· ‖ -ə-
teleshopping 'tel i ˌʃɒp ɪŋ ‖ -ə ˌʃɑːp-
teletex, T~ *tdmk* 'tel i teks -ə-
teletext 'tel i tekst -ə-
telethon 'tel ə θɒn -ɪ- ‖ -θɑːn ~**s** z
Teletubb|y 'tel i ˌtʌb| i -ə- ~**ies** iz
teletyp|e, T~ *tdmk* 'tel i taɪp -ə- ‖ -ə- ~**ed** t
　~**es** s ~**ing** ɪŋ
teletypewriter ˌtel i 'taɪp ˌraɪt ᵊr ˌtel ə-
televangelism ˌtel i 'vændʒ ə ˌlɪz əm ˌtel ə-,
　-'vændʒ i- ‖ ˌtel ə-
televangelist ˌtel i 'vændʒ əl ɪst ˌtel ə-, -ɪl-,
　§-əst ‖ ˌtelə- ~**s** s
teleview|er 'tel i vjuːˌə ‖ -ə ˌvjuːˌᵊr ~**ers** əz
　‖ ᵊrz ~**ing** ɪŋ
televis|e 'tel ɪ vaɪz -ə- ‖ -ə- ~**ed** d ~**es** ɪz əz
　~**ing** ɪŋ
television 'tel ɪ ˌvɪʒ ᵊn -ə-, ˌ·ˈ·· ‖ -ə- ~**s** z
　'**television set**, ˌ·ˈ··
televisual ˌtel ɪ 'vɪʒ u əl ◂ ˌ-ə-, -'vɪz ju əl
　‖ -ə 'vɪʒ ᵊl ~**ly** i
telework|er 'tel i ˌwɜːk| ə ‖ -ə ˌwɜːk ᵊr ~**ers**
　əz ‖ ᵊrz ~**ing** ɪŋ
telex *n, v* 'tel eks ~**ed** t ~**es** ɪz əz ~**ing** ɪŋ
telfer, T~ 'telf ə ‖ -ᵊr ~s z
Telford 'telf əd ‖ -ᵊrd

telic 'tel ɪk 'tiːl-

tell, Tell tel telling/ly 'tel ɪŋ /li tells telz
  told təʊld →tɒʊld ‖ toʊld

teller, T~ 'tel ə ‖ -ᵊr ~s z

telling-off ˌtel ɪŋ 'ɒf -'ɔːf ‖ -'ɔːf -'ɑːf
  tellings-off ˌtel ɪŋz 'ɒf -'ɔːf ‖ -'ɔːf -'ɑːf

telltale 'tel teɪᵊl ~s z

tellurian te 'lʊər i ən tɪ-, tə-, -'ljʊer- ‖ -'lʊr- ~s
  z

telluric te 'lʊər ɪk tɪ-, tə-, -'ljʊer- ‖ -'lʊr-

telluride, T~ 'tel juᵊ raɪd ‖ -jə-

tellurium te 'lʊər i əm tɪ-, tə-, -'ljʊer- ‖ -'lʊr-

telly 'tel i tellies 'tel iz

tel|net 'tel| net ~nets nets ~netted net ɪd -əd
  ‖ neţ əd ~netting net ɪŋ ‖ neţ ɪŋ

telomerase 'tiːl ə mɪər eɪz 'tel-
  ‖ 'tel əm ə reɪz

telomere 'tiːl əʊ mɪə 'tel- ‖ 'tel ə mɪr ~s z

telophase 'tiːl ə feɪz

telpher 'telf ə ‖ -ᵊr ~s z

telpherage 'telf ər ɪdʒ

Telscombe 'tels kəm

telson 'tels ᵊn ~s z

Telstar tdmk 'tel stɑː ‖ -stɑːr

Telstra 'tel strə

Telugu 'tel ə guː -u- ~s z

temazepam tɪ 'mæz ɪ pæm te-, tə-, -'meɪz-, -ə-

temblor ˌtem 'blɔː ˈ· ·, '·blə ‖ -'blɔːr -'blour,
  ˈ· ·, '·blᵊr ~s z

temerarious ˌtem ə 'reər i əs ◂ ‖ -'rer- -'rær-

temerity tə 'mer ət i tɪ-, te-, -ɪt i ‖ -əţ i

Temne 'tem ni

temp temp temped tempt temping 'temp ɪŋ
  temps temps

tempe, tempeh 'temp eɪ

Tempe 'temp i

temper 'temp ə ‖ -ᵊr ~ed d tempering
  'temp ər ɪŋ ~s z

tempera 'temp ər ə

temperament 'temp ᵊr ə mənt ~s s

temperamental ˌtemp ᵊr ə 'ment ᵊl ◂
  ‖ -'menţ ᵊl ◂ ~ly i

temperance 'temp ᵊr ənts

temperate 'temp ər ət ɪt ~ly li ~ness nəs nɪs

temperature 'temp ᵊr ətʃ ə ˈtʃ ə ‖ ˌəţ ᵊr
  ə tʃʊr ~s z

-tempered 'temp əd ‖ -ᵊrd — even-tempered
  ˌiːv ᵊn 'temp əd ◂ ‖ -ᵊrd ◂

Temperley 'temp ə li ‖ -ᵊr-

Temperton 'temp ət ən ‖ -ᵊrt ᵊn

tempest 'temp ɪst -əst ~s s

tempestuous tem 'pes tʃu əs təm-, →-'peʃ-;
  -'pest ju əs ~ly li ~ness nəs nɪs

tempi 'temp iː

Templar 'temp lə ‖ -lᵊr ~s z

template 'tem pleɪt 'temp lət, -lɪt ~s s

temple, T~ 'temp ᵊl ~s z

templet 'temp lət -lɪt ~s s

Templeton 'temp ᵊl tən

temp|o 'temp |əʊ ‖ -|oʊ ~i iː ~os əʊz ‖ oʊz

temporal 'temp ᵊr_ᵊl ~ly i

temporalit|y ˌtemp ə 'ræl ət |i -ɪt i ‖ -əţ |i
  ~ies iz

temporarily 'temp ᵊr_ər əl i -ɪ li;
  ˌtemp ə 'rer-, -'reər-; △'temp rəl i
  ‖ ˌtemp ə 'rer-

temporar|y 'temp ᵊr_ər |i §-ə reər i ‖ -ə rer |i
  —in casual speech also 'temp r|i ~ies iz
  ~iness i nəs i nɪs

temporis|e, temporiz|e 'temp ə raɪz ~ed d
  ~es ɪz əz ~ing ɪŋ

tempt tempt tempted 'tempt ɪd -əd
  tempting/ly 'tempt ɪŋ /li tempts tempts

temptation temp 'teɪʃ ᵊn ~s z

tempter 'tempt ə ‖ -ᵊr ~s z

temptress 'temp trəs -trɪs ~es ɪz əz

tempura tem 'pʊər ə 'temp ər ə ‖ tem 'pʊr ə
  -'pɜː- —Jp [te̥m pɯ ra]

tempus fugit ˌtemp əs 'fjuːdʒ ɪt -'fjuːg-,
  -'fuːg-, §-ət

ten ten tens tenz

tenability ˌten ə 'bɪl ət i ˌtiːn-, -ɪt i ‖ -əţ i

tenab|le 'ten əb |ᵊl 'tiːn- ~leness ᵊl nəs -nɪs
  ~ly li

tenac|e 'ten eɪs -əs, -ɪs; te 'neɪs ~es ɪz əz

tenacious tɪ 'neɪʃ əs tə-, te- ~ly li ~ness nəs
  nɪs

tenacity tɪ 'næs ət i tə-, te-, -ɪt i ‖ -əţ i

Tenafly 'ten ə flaɪ

tenanc|y 'ten ənᵗs |i ~ies iz

tenant 'ten ənt ~s s
  ˌtenant 'farmer

tenantr|y 'ten əntr |i ~ies iz

Tenbury 'ten bər_i →'tem-

Tenby 'ten bi →'tem-

tench, Tench tentʃ tenches 'tentʃ ɪz -əz

tend tend tended 'tend ɪd -əd tending
  'tend ɪŋ tends tendz

tendenc|y 'tend ənᵗs |i ~ies iz

tendentious ten 'denᵗʃ əs ~ly li ~ness nəs nɪs

tender 'tend ə ‖ -ᵊr tendered 'tend əd ‖ -ᵊrd
  tenderer/s 'tend ər_ə/z ‖ -ᵊr_ər/z tenderest
  'tend ər_ɪst əst tendering 'tend_ər ɪŋ
  tenders 'tend əz ‖ -ᵊrz

tender|foot 'tend ə |fʊt ‖ -ᵊr- ~feet fiːt

tenderhearted ˌtend ə 'hɑːt ɪd ◂ -əd
  ‖ 'tend ᵊr ˌhɑːrţ əd ~ly li ~ness nəs nɪs

tenderis|e, tenderiz|e 'tend ə raɪz ~ed d
  ~er/s ə/z ‖ -ᵊr/z ~es ɪz əz ~ing ɪŋ

tenderloin 'tend ə lɔɪn ‖ -ᵊr-

tenderly 'tend ə li -ᵊl i ‖ -ᵊr li

tenderness 'tend ə nəs -nɪs ‖ -ᵊr- ~es ɪz əz

tendinitis ˌtend ɪ 'naɪt ɪs -ə-, §-əs ‖ -ə 'naɪţ əs

tendon 'tend ən ~s z

tendonitis ˌtend ə 'naɪt ɪs §-əs ‖ -'naɪţ əs

tendril 'tendr əl -ɪl ~s z

tenebrae, T~ 'ten ə breɪ -ɪ-, -briː, -braɪ

tenebrous 'ten əb rəs -ɪ-

Tenedos 'ten ɪ dɒs -ə- ‖ -dɑːs -doʊs

tenement 'ten ə mənt -ɪ- ~s s

Tenerife, Teneriffe ˌten ə 'riːf —Sp
  [te ne 'ri fe]

tenesmus tɪ 'nez məs tə-

tenet 'ten ɪt 'tiːn-, -et, §-ət ~s s

tenfold 'ten fəʊld →-fɒʊld ‖ -foʊld

ten-gallon hat ˌten ˌgæl ən 'hæt →ˌteŋ- ~s s

tenia 'tiːn i‿ə

Teniers 'ten ɪəz ‖ -jᵊrz —*Dutch* [tə 'niːrs]

Tenison 'ten ɪs ən -əs-

Tenko 'teŋk əʊ ‖ -oʊ

Tennant 'ten ənt

tenner 'ten ə ‖ -ᵊr ~s z

Tennessean, Tennesseean ˌten ə 'siː ən ◂ -ɪ- ~s z

Tennessee ˌten ə 'siː ◂ -ɪ- —*locally also* '·əs i, -ɪs i

Tenniel 'ten i‿əl

tennies 'ten iz

tennis 'ten ɪs §-əs
   'tennis ˌball; ˌtennis 'elbow; 'tennis ˌmatch; 'tennis ˌplayer; 'tennis ˌracquet

Tennison, Tennyson 'ten ɪs ən -əs-

Tennysonian ˌten ɪ 'səʊn i‿ən ˌ·ə- ‖ -'soʊn jən ~s z

tenon 'ten ən ~s z
   'tenon ˌsaw

tenor 'ten ə ‖ -ᵊr (= *tenner*) ~s z

tenpin 'ten pɪn →'tem- ~s z
   ˌtenpin 'bowling

tenrec 'ten rek ~s s

tense tenᵗs **tensed** tenᵗst **tensely** 'tenᵗs li
   tenseness 'tenᵗs nəs -nɪs **tenser** 'tenᵗs ə ‖ -ᵊr
   tenses 'tenᵗs ɪz -əz **tensest** 'tenᵗs ɪst -əst
   tensing 'tenᵗs ɪŋ
   ˌtensed 'up

tensile 'tenᵗs aɪᵊl ‖ -ᵊl (*)

tensility ten 'sɪl ət i -ɪt i ‖ -ət i

tension 'tenʃ ᵊn ~ed d ~ing ɪŋ ~s z

tensity 'tenᵗs ət i -ɪt i ‖ -ət i

tensor 'tenᵗs ə -ɔː ‖ -ᵊr -ɔːr ~s z

ten-speed 'ten spiːd ~s z

tent tent **tented** 'tent ɪd -əd ‖ 'tenţ əd
   tenting 'tent ɪŋ ‖ 'tenţ ɪŋ **tents** tents

tentacle 'tent ək ᵊl -ɪk- ‖ 'tenţ- ~d d ~s z

tentacular ten 'tæk jʊl ə -jəl- ‖ -jəl ᵊr

tentative 'tent ət ɪv ‖ 'tenţ əţ ɪv ~ly li ~ness nəs nɪs

Tenterden 'tent ə dən ‖ 'tenţ ᵊr-

tenterhook 'tent ə hʊk △'tend-, §-huːk ‖ 'tenţ ᵊr- ~s s

tenth tenᵗθ **tenthly** 'tenᵗθ li **tenths** tenᵗθs →tenᵗs

tenu|is 'ten ju‿|ɪs §‿əs ~es iːz eɪz

tenuity te 'njuː ət i tə-, tɪ-, ɪt i ‖ -'nuː əţ i -'njuː-

tenuous 'ten ju‿əs ~ly li ~ness nəs nɪs

tenure 'ten jə -jʊə ‖ -jᵊr ~d d ~s z

tenure-track 'ten jə træk -jʊə- ‖ -jᵊr-

Tenzing 'tenz ɪŋ

teosinte ˌteɪ əʊ 'sɪnt i ‖ -oʊ 'sɪnţ i

tepal 'tep ᵊl 'tiːp- ~s z

tepee 'tiːp iː ~s z

tephra 'tef rə

tephrite 'tef raɪt

tepid 'tep ɪd §-əd ~ly li ~ness nəs nɪs

tepidity te 'pɪd ət i -ɪt i ‖ -əţ i

teppanyaki ˌtep ən 'jæk i →-m- ‖ -'jɑːk i —*Jp* [tep ˌpan ja ki]

tequila tɪ 'kiːl ə tə-, te- ‖ teɪ-

tera- ¦ter ə — **terahertz** 'ter ə hɜːts ‖ -hɜːⁱts

terabyte 'ter ə baɪt ~s s

teraflop 'ter ə flɒp ‖ -flɑːp ~s s

teraph 'ter əf **teraphim** 'ter ə fɪm

teratogenic ˌter ət əʊ 'dʒen ɪk ◂ ‖ -əţ ə-

teratology ˌter ə 'tɒl ədʒ i ‖ -'tɑːl-

teratoma ˌter ə 'təʊm ə ‖ -'toʊm ə ~s z

terbium 'tɜːb i‿əm ‖ 'tɜːb-

terce tɜːs ‖ tɜːs (= *terse*)

tercel 'tɜːs ᵊl ‖ 'tɜːs ᵊl ~s z

Tercel 'tɜːs el ‖ tᵊr 'sel ~s z

tercentenar|y ˌtɜː sen 'tiːn ər |i ˌ·sᵊn-, -'ten- ‖ ˌtɜː sen 'ten ər |i ˌ·'sent ᵊn er i ~ies iz

tercentennial ˌtɜː sen 'ten i‿əl ◂ -ˌsᵊn- ‖ ˌtɜː- ~s z

tercet 'tɜːs ɪt -ət, §-ət; (ˌ)tɜː 'set ‖ 'tɜːs ət ~s s

terebene 'ter ə biːn -ɪ-

terebinth 'ter ə bɪntᵊθ -ɪ- ~s s

teredo tə 'riːd əʊ tɪ-, te-, -'reɪd- ‖ -oʊ ~s z

Terence 'ter ᵊnᵗs

Teresa *(i)* tə 'riːz ə tɪ-, te-, *(ii)* -'reɪz-, *(iii)* -'riːs-, *(iv)* -'reɪs- —*(iii) and (iv) are AmE, but not usually BrE*

Terese *(i)* tə 'riːz tɪ-, te-, *(ii)* -'riːs, *(ii)* -'reɪz

Terfel 'tɜːv ᵊl 'teəv- ‖ 'tɜːv- —*Welsh* ['ter vel]

tergivers|ate 'tɜːdʒ ɪ vɜːs |eɪt -və s|eɪt ‖ tɜː 'dʒɪv ᵊr s|eɪt -'gɪv-; ˌtɜːdʒ ə 'vɜːs |eɪt (*) ~ated eɪt ɪd -əd ‖ eɪţ əd ~ates eɪts ~ating eɪt ɪŋ ‖ eɪţ ɪŋ

tergiversation ˌtɜːdʒ ɪ vɜː 'seɪʃ ᵊn §ˌ·ə-, -və'-- ‖ tɜː ˌdʒɪv ᵊr- -ˌgɪv-; ˌtɜːdʒ ə vɜː- ~s z

teriyaki ˌter i 'æk i ‖ -'jɑːk i —*Jp* [te ˌri ja ki]

Terkel 'tɜːk ᵊl ‖ 'tɜːk ᵊl

term tɜːm ‖ tɜːm **termed** tɜːmd ‖ tɜːmd **terming** 'tɜːm ɪŋ ‖ 'tɜːm ɪŋ **terms** tɜːmz ‖ tɜːmz
   ˌterms of 'reference

termagant 'tɜːm əg ənt ‖ 'tɜːm- ~s s

terminable 'tɜːm ɪn əb ᵊl -ən‿əb- ‖ 'tɜːm- ~ness nəs nɪs

terminal 'tɜːm ɪn ᵊl -ən- ‖ 'tɜːm ᵊn‿əl ~ly i ~s z
   ˌTerminal 'Four

termi|nate 'tɜːm ɪ |neɪt -ə- ‖ 'tɜːm- ~nated neɪt ɪd -əd ‖ neɪţ əd ~nates neɪts ~nating neɪt ɪŋ ‖ neɪţ ɪŋ

termination ˌtɜːm ɪ 'neɪʃ ᵊn -ə- ‖ ˌtɜːm- ~s z

terminative 'tɜːm ɪn ət ɪv -ən-; -ɪ neɪt ɪv, -ə- · ‖ 'tɜːm ə neɪt ɪv ~ly li

terminator 'tɜːm ɪ neɪt ə '·ə- ‖ 'tɜːm ə neɪţ ᵊr ~s z

termini 'tɜːm ɪ naɪ -ə- ‖ 'tɜːm-

terminological ˌtɜːm ɪn ə 'lɒdʒ ɪk ᵊl ◂ ˌ·ən-, -ᵊl 'ɒdʒ- ‖ ˌtɜːm ən ᵊl 'ɑːdʒ- ~ly i

terminolog|y ˌtɜːm ɪ 'nɒl ədʒ |i ˌ·ə- ‖ ˌtɜːm ə 'nɑːl- ~ies iz

term|inus 'tɜːm |ɪn əs -ən- ‖ 'tɜːm- ~ini ɪ naɪ ə-
   ˌterminus ad 'quem æd 'kwem ‖ ɑːd-;
   ˌterminus a 'quo ɑː 'kwəʊ ‖ ɑː 'kwoʊ

termite 'tɜːm aɪt ‖ 'tɜːm- ~s s

termly 'tɜːm li ‖ 'tɜːm-

termtime 'tɜːm taɪm ‖ 'tɜːm-

T

tern tɜːn ‖ tɜːn (= *turn*) terns tɜːnz ‖ tɜːnz
ternar|y 'tɜːn ər |i ‖ 'tɜːn- ~ies iz
terpene 'tɜːp iːn ‖ 'tɜːp- ~s z
terpisichorean, T~ ˌtɜːps ɪk ə 'riː ən ◂ -ɒ'--;
ˌ·ɪ 'kɔːr i ˌən ‖ ˌtɜːps-
Terpsichore tɜːp 'sɪk ər i ‖ tɜːp-
terra, Terra 'ter ə
    ˌterra 'cotta 'kɒt ə ‖ 'kɑːt̬ ə; ˌterra 'firma
'fɜːm ə ‖ 'fɜːm ə; ˌterra in'cognita
ɪn 'kɒg nɪt ə →ɪŋ-; ˌɪŋ kɒg 'niːt ə
‖ ˌɪn kɑːg 'niːt̬ ə ɪn 'kɑːg nət̬ ə; ˌterra
'nullius 'nʊl i ˌəs
terrac|e 'ter əs -ɪs ~ed t ~es ɪz əz ~ing ɪŋ
terracotta ˌter ə 'kɒt ə ◂ ‖ -'kɑːt̬ ə
terrain tə 'reɪn te-, tɪ-; 'ter eɪn
terramycin, T~ *tdmk* ˌter ə 'maɪs ɪn §-ᵊn
terrapin 'ter ə pɪn §-əp ən
terrari|um tə 'reər i ˌ|əm te-, tɪ- ‖ -'rer- -'rær-
    ~a ə ~ums əmz
terrazzo te 'ræts əʊ tə-, tɪ- ‖ -'ræz oʊ -'rɑːts-
Terre Haute ˌter ə 'həʊt ‖ -'hoʊt -'hʌt
Terrence 'ter ənᵗs
terrene 'ter iːn te 'riːn
terrestrial tə 'res tri ˌəl tɪ-, te- ~ly i ~s z
terret 'ter ɪt -ət ~s s
Terri 'ter i
terrible 'ter əb ᵊl -ɪb- ~ness nəs nɪs
terribly 'ter əb li -ɪb-
terrier 'ter i ə ‖ ᵊr ~s z
terrific tə 'rɪf ɪk —*casually also* 'trɪf ɪk ~ally
ᵊl i
terri|fy 'ter ə |faɪ -ɪ- ~fied faɪd ~fies faɪz
    ~fying/ly faɪ ɪŋ /li
terrine te 'riːn tə-; 'ter iːn ~s z
territorial ˌter ə 'tɔːr i ˌəl ◂ ˌ·ɪ- ‖ -'toʊr- ~ly i
    ~s z
    ˌTerri torial 'Army; ˌterri torial 'waters
territoriality ˌter ə ˌtɔːr i ˌæl ət i ˌ·ɪ-, -ɪt i
‖ -ət̬ i -ˌtoʊr-
territor|y 'ter ə ˌtər |i '·ɪ- ‖ -tɔːr |i -toʊr i (*)
    ~ies iz
terror 'ter ə ‖ -ᵊr ~s z
terroris... —*see* terroriz...
terrorism 'ter ər ˌɪz əm
terrorist 'ter ər ɪst §-əst ~s s
terroriz|e 'ter ə raɪz ~ed d ~es ɪz əz ~ing ɪŋ
terror-stricken 'ter ə ˌstrɪk ən ‖ -ᵊr-
terror-struck 'ter ə strʌk ‖ -ᵊr-
terry, Terry 'ter i
terrycloth 'ter i klɒθ -klɔːθ ‖ -klɔːθ -klɑːθ
terse tɜːs ‖ tɜːs tersely 'tɜːs li ‖ 'tɜːs li
    terseness 'tɜːs nəs -nɪs ‖ 'tɜːs nəs terser
'tɜːs ə ‖ 'tɜːs ᵊr tersest 'tɜːs ɪst -əst
‖ 'tɜːs əst
tertian 'tɜːʃ ᵊn 'tɜːʃ i ən ‖ 'tɜːʃ ᵊn
tertiar|y, T~ 'tɜːʃ ər |i -i ər- ‖ 'tɜːʃ i er |i '·ər |i
    ~ies iz
    ˌtertiary ˌedu'cation; ˌtertiary 'stress
tertium quid ˌtɜːʃ i əm 'kwɪd ˌtɜːt- ‖ ˌtɜːʃ-
ˌtɜːt̬-
Tertius 'tɜːʃ i əs ‖ 'tɜːʃ-
Tertullian tɜː 'tʌl i ən tə- ‖ tᵊr-
terylene, T~ *tdmk* 'ter ə liːn -ɪ-

terza rima ˌteəts ə 'riːm ə ˌtɜːts- ‖ ˌterts- —*It*
[ˌter tsa 'riː ma]
Tesco *tdmk* 'tesk əʊ ‖ -oʊ
TESL 'tes ᵊl
Tesla, tesla 'tes lə ~s z
TESOL 'tiːs ɒl ‖ -ɑːl 'tes ᵊl
Tess tes
Tessa, TESSA 'tes ə
tessel|late 'tes ə |leɪt -ɪ- ~lated leɪt ɪd -əd-
‖ leɪt̬ əd ~lates leɪts ~lating leɪt ɪŋ ‖ leɪt̬ ɪŋ
tessellation ˌtes ə 'leɪʃ ᵊn -ɪ- ~s z
tesser|a 'tes ər| ə ~ae iː
tesseract 'tes ə rækt ~s s
Tessie 'tes i
tessitura ˌtes ɪ 'tʊər ə -ə-, -'tjʊər ə ‖ -'tʊr ə
—*It* [tes si 'tuː ra]
test, Test test tested 'test ɪd -əd testing
'test ɪŋ tests tests
    'test ban; 'test card; 'test case; 'testing
    ground; 'test match; 'test ˌpaper; 'test
    ˌpilot; 'test tube
testability ˌtest ə 'bɪl ət i -ɪt i ‖ -ət̬ i
testable 'test əb ᵊl
testament 'test ə mənt ~s s
testamentary ˌtest ə 'ment ˌər i ◂
‖ -'ment̬ ər i →-'mentr i
testamur te 'steɪm ə ‖ -ᵊr ~s z
testate 'test eɪt -ət, -ɪt
testator te 'steɪt ə ‖ 'test eɪt̬ ᵊr te 'steɪt̬ ᵊr ~s z
testatr|ix te 'steɪtr |ɪks ‖ 'test eɪtr- ~ices ɪ siːz
-ə-
test-bed 'test bed
test-|drive 'test |draɪv ~driven drɪv ᵊn
    ~drives draɪvz ~driving draɪv ɪŋ ~drove
drəʊv ‖ droʊv
tester, T~ 'test ə ‖ -ᵊr ~s z
testes 'test iːz
test-|fly 'test|flaɪ ~flew fluː ~flies flaɪz
    ~flown fləʊn §ˌfləʊ ən ‖ floʊn
testicle 'test ɪk ᵊl ~s z
testicular te 'stɪk jʊl ə -jəl- ‖ -jəl ᵊr
testi|fy 'test ɪ |faɪ -ə- ~fied faɪd ~fier/s faɪ ə/z
‖ faɪ ᵊr/z ~fies faɪz ~fying faɪ ɪŋ
testimonial ˌtest ɪ 'məʊn i ˌəl ◂ ˌ·ə- ‖ -'moʊn-
    ~s z
testimon|y 'test ɪ mən |i '·ə- ‖ -ə moʊn |i (*)
    ~ies iz
test|is 'test |ɪs §-əs ~es iːz
testosterone te 'stɒst ə rəʊn ‖ -'stɑːst ə roʊn
test-tube 'test tjuːb →-tʃuːb ‖ -tuːb -tjuːb ~s z
    ˌtest-tube 'baby
testud|o te 'stjuːd |əʊ →-'stʃuːd- ‖ -'stuːd |oʊ
-'stjuːd- ~ines ɪ niːz ə-, -neɪz ~os əʊz ‖ oʊz
test|y 'test |i ~ier i ə ‖ i ᵊr ~iest i ɪst i əst ~ily
ɪ li əl i ~iness i nəs i nɪs
Tet tet
tetanic te 'tæn ɪk tɪ-, tə-
tetanus 'tet ᵊn əs
tetany 'tet ᵊn i
Tetbury 'tet bər ̬i -ˌber i
tetch|y 'tetʃ |i ~ier i ə ‖ i ᵊr ~iest i ɪst i əst
    ~ily ɪ li əl i ~iness i nəs i nɪs

tete-a-tete, tête-à-tête ˌteɪt ə 'teɪt ˌtet-, -ɑː-,
-'tet ‖ ˌteɪt ə 'teɪt ˌtet ə 'tet; '···—*Fr*
[tɛ ta tɛt] **~s** s

tete-beche, tête-bêche ˌteɪt 'beʃ ˌtet-, -'beɪʃ
—*Fr* [tɛd bɛʃ]

tether 'teð ə ‖ -ᵊr **~ed** d **tethering** 'teð ᵊr ɪŋ
~s z

tetherball 'teð ə bɔːl ‖ -ᵊr- -bɑːl

Tethys 'tiːθ ɪs 'teθ-, §-əs

Tetley 'tet li

Teton 'tiːt ᵊn -ɒn ‖ -ɑːn -ᵊn **~s** z

tetra 'tetr ə **~s** z

tetra- *comb form*
with stress-neutral suffix ╷tetr ə —
tetrachloride ˌtetr ə 'klɔːr aɪd ‖ -'klour-
with stress-imposing suffix te 'træ+ —
tetramerous te 'træm ər əs

tetrabrik 'tetr ə brɪk **~s** s

tetrachord 'tetr ə kɔːd ‖ -kɔːrd **~s** z

tetracycline ˌtetr ə 'saɪk liːn -lɪn, -laɪn

tetrad 'tetr æd **~s** z

tetraethyl ˌtetr ə 'iːθ arᵊl -'eθ ɪl, -ᵊl ‖ -ᵊl

tetragrammaton, T~ ˌtetr ə 'græm ət ən
-ə tɒn ‖ -ə tɑːn

tetrahedr|on ˌtetr ə 'hiːdr |ən -'hedr- **~a** ə **~al**
əl **~ons** ənz

tetralog|y te 'træl ədʒ |i ‖ -'trɑːl- **~ies** iz

tetrameter te 'træm ɪt ə -ət ə ‖ -əṯ ᵊr **~s** z

tetrapod 'tetr ə pɒd ‖ -pɑːd **~s** z

tetrarch 'tetr ɑːk ‖ -ɑːrk **~s** s

tetravalent ˌtetr ə 'veɪl ənt

tetrode 'tetr əʊd ‖ -oʊd **~s** z

Tettenhall 'tet ᵊn hɔːl ‖ -hɑːl

tetter 'tet ə ‖ 'teṯ ᵊr

Teucer 'tjuːs ə →'tʃuːs- ‖ 'tuːs ᵊr 'tjuːs-

Teucrian 'tjuːk ri ̩ən →'tʃuːk- ‖ 'tuːk- 'tjuːk- **~s**
z

Teuton 'tjuːt ᵊn →'tʃuːt- ‖ 'tuːt ᵊn 'tjuːt- **~s** z

Teutonic tju 'tɒn ɪk →tʃu- ‖ tu 'tɑːn ɪk tju-

Teversham 'tev əʃ əm ‖ -ᵊrʃ-

Teviot 'tiːv i ̩ət 'tev-

Tew tjuː →tʃuː ‖ tuː tjuː

Tewa 'teɪ wə 'tiː- **~s** z

Tewkesbury 'tjuːks bər i →'tʃuːks-
‖ 'tuːks ˌber i 'tjuːks- —*but locally* -bər i *in*
MA, *just as in Gloucs.*

Tex teks

TeX *software* tek — *although its author Knuth
insists on* tex

Texaco *tdmk* 'teks ə kəʊ ‖ -koʊ -ɪ-

Texan 'teks ᵊn **~s** z

Texas 'teks əs ‖ -əz
   ˌTexas 'Ranger

Texel 'teks ᵊl

Tex-Mex ˌteks 'meks ◂

text tekst **texted** 'tekst ɪd -əd; tekst **texting**
'tekst ɪŋ 'teks- **texts** teksts

text-based 'tekst beɪst ˌ·'◂

textbook 'tekst bʊk §-buːk **~s** s

textile 'tekst arᵊl ‖ -ᵊl **~s** z

textual 'teks tʃu̩əl 'tekst ju̩ **~ly** i

textuality ˌteks tju 'æl ət i -tʃu'--, -ɪt i
‖ ˌteks tʃu 'æl əṯ i

textural 'teks tʃᵊr ̩əl

texture 'teks tʃə ‖ -tʃᵊr **~d** d **texturing**
'teks tʃər ɪŋ **~s** z
   ˌtextured ˌvegetable 'protein

-textured 'teks tʃəd ‖ -tʃᵊrd — **even-textured**
ˌiːv ᵊn 'teks tʃəd ◂ ‖ -tʃᵊrd

Tey teɪ

-th θ — **fourth** fɔːθ ‖ fɔːrθ fourθ

Thabo 'tɑːb əʊ ‖ -oʊ —*Xhosa* ['tʰɑː ɓo]

Thackeray 'θæk ər i -ə reɪ

Thad θæd

Thaddeus 'θæd i̩əs θæ 'diː̩əs

Thai taɪ **Thais** taɪz

Thailand 'taɪ lænd -lənd

Thais, Thaïs *personal name* 'θeɪ ɪs §-əs

Thais *pl of* **Thai** taɪz

thal|amus 'θæl |əm əs **~ami** ə maɪ -miː

thalassaemia, thalassemia ˌθæl ə 'siːm i̩ə

thalassic θə 'læs ɪk

thalassotherapy θə ˌlæs əʊ 'θer əp i θæ-
‖ -·ˌə-

thaler 'tɑːl ə ‖ -ᵊr **~s** z

Thales 'θeɪl iːz

Thalia θə 'laɪ̩ə 'θeɪl i̩ə, 'θæl-

thalidomide θə 'lɪd ə maɪd

thallium 'θæl i̩əm

thall|us 'θæl |əs **~i** aɪ **~uses** əs ɪz -əz

Thame teɪm (*!*)

Thames (i) temz (*!*), (ii) θeɪmz —*The rivers in
England, Canada and NZ are* (i), *the one in
CT usually* (ii).

than *strong form* ðæn, *weak form* ðən

Thanatos 'θæn ə tɒs ‖ -tɑːs

thane θeɪn **thanes** θeɪnz

thaneship 'θeɪn ʃɪp **~s** s

Thanet 'θæn ɪt -ət

thang θæŋ

thank θæŋk **thanked** θæŋkt **thanking**
'θæŋk ɪŋ **thanks** θæŋks
   thank you 'θæŋk ju —*There are also casual
forms such as* 'hæŋk ju, 'ŋk ju

thankful 'θæŋk fᵊl -fʊl **~ly** i **~ness** nəs nɪs

thankless 'θæŋk ləs -lɪs **~ly** li **~ness** nəs nɪs

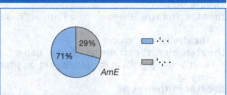

THANKSGIVING

AmE

thanksgiving, T~ 'θæŋks ˌgɪv ɪŋ ˌ·'··
‖ θæŋks 'gɪv ɪŋ '·ˌ·· — *Preference poll, AmE:*
ˌ·'·· 71%, '·ˌ·· 29%. **~s** z
   Thanks'giving Day

thankyou *n, adj* 'θæŋk ju **~s** z

Thapsus 'θæps əs

Tharp θɑːp ‖ θɑːrp

that *determiner (demonstrative adj),
demonstrative pronoun, and adverb* ðæt

—*There is no weak form for* that *in this sense:* that (**ðæt**) man, stop that, not that bad.

that *complementizer (conjunction and relative pronoun): strong form* **ðæt**, *weak form* **ðət** —*Normally, the weak form is used:* say that (**ðət**) she's right, the one that I chose .

thataway ˈðæt ə weɪ ‖ ˈðæt̬-

thatch θætʃ **thatched** θætʃt **thatches** ˈθætʃ ɪz -əz **thatching** ˈθætʃ ɪŋ

Thatcham ˈθætʃ əm

thatcher, T~ ˈθætʃ ə ‖ -ər **~s** z

Thatcherism ˈθætʃ ər ˌɪz əm

Thatcherite ˈθætʃ ə raɪt **~s** s

that'll *strong form* ˈðæt əl ‖ ˈðæt̬ əl, *weak form* ðət əl ‖ ðət̬ əl —*see entries at* that: I think that'll (**ðæt əl**) please you, a thing that'll (**ðət əl**) please you

that's *strong form* ðæts, *weak form* ðəts —*see entries at* that: I think that's (**ðæts**) right, a thing that's (**ðəts**) wrong

thaumatology ˌθɔːm ə ˈtɒl ədʒ i ‖ -ˈtɑːl- ˌθɑːm-

thaumaturg|e ˈθɔːm ə tɜːdʒ ‖ -tɝːdʒ ˈθɑːm- **~es** ɪz əz

thaumaturgic ˌθɔːm ə ˈtɜːdʒ ɪk ◀ ‖ -ˈtɝːdʒ- ˌθɑːm- **~al** əl

thaumaturgy ˈθɔːm ə tɜːdʒ i ‖ -tɝːdʒ i ˈθɑːm-

thaw, Thaw θɔː ‖ θɑː **thawed** θɔːd ‖ θɑːd **thawing** ˈθɔːʳ ɪŋ ‖ ˈθɔː ɪŋ ˈθɑː- **thaws** θɔːz ‖ θɑːz

Thawpit *tdmk* ˈθɔːp ɪt §-ət ‖ ˈθɑːp-

Thayer ˈθeɪ ə θeə ‖ ˈθeɪ ʳr θeʳr, θæʳr

the *strong form* ðiː, *weak forms* ði, ðə —*The EFL learner is advised to use* ðə *before a consonant sound* (the boy, the house), ði *before a vowel sound* (the egg, the hour). *Native speakers, however, sometimes ignore this distribution, in particular by using* ðə *before a vowel (which in turn is usually reinforced by a preceding* ʔ*), or by using* ðiː *in any environment, though especially before a hesitation pause. Furthermore, some speakers use stressed* ðə *as a strong form, rather than the usual* ðiː.

Thea ˈθiːˌə

Theale θiːʳl

theater, theatre ˈθɪət ə θi ˈet ə ‖ ˈθiː ət̬ ʳr **~s** z

ˌtheatre in the ˈround

theatergo|er, theatrego|er ˈθɪət ə ˌgəʊ ə θi ˈet ə ˌgəʊ ə ‖ ˈθiː ət̬ ʳr ˌgoʊ ʳr **~ers** əz ‖ ʳrz **~ing** ɪŋ

theater-in-the-round, theatre-in-the-round ˈθɪət ʳr ɪn ðə ˈraʊnd θi ˌet ər- ‖ ˌθiː ət̬ ʳr-

theaterland, theatreland ˈθɪət ə lænd θi ˈet ə lænd ‖ ˈθiː ət̬ ʳr lænd

theatrical θi ˈætr ɪk ᵊl §-ˈetr- **~ly** i **~ness** nəs nɪs **~s** z

theatricality θi ˌætr ɪ ˈkæl ət i §-ˌetr-, -ˌ-ə-, -ɪt i ‖ -ət̬ i

theatrics θi ˈætr ɪks §-ˈetr-

Thebaid ˈθiːb eɪ ɪd -i-, §-əd

Theban ˈθiːb ən **~s** z

Thebes θiːbz

theca ˈθiːk ə **thecae** ˈθiːs iː ˈθiːk-

thecodont ˈθiːk əʊ dɒnt ‖ -ə dɑːnt **~s** s

thee *strong form* ðiː, *weak form* ði

theft θeft **thefts** θefts

thegn θeɪn *(= thane)* **thegns** θeɪnz

their ðeə §ˈðeɪ ə ‖ ðeʳr ðæʳr —*In GenAm there is also a weak form* ðʳr. *In RP there is either no weak form, or just an occasional weak form* ðr *used only before a following vowel.*

theirs ðeəz §ˈðeɪ əz ‖ ðeʳrz ðæʳrz

theism ˈθiː ˌɪz əm

theist ˈθiː ɪst §-əst **~s** s

theistic θi ˈɪst ɪk **~al** ᵊl **~ally** ᵊl i

Thelma ˈθelm ə

Thelwall ˈθel wɔːl ‖ -wɑːl

Thelwell ˈθel wəl -wel

them *strong form* ðem, *weak form* ðəm

thematic θɪ ˈmæt ɪk θiː- ‖ -ˈmæt̬ ɪk **~ally** ᵊl i

theme θiːm **themes** θiːmz

  ˈtheme park; ˈtheme song; ˈtheme tune

Themis ˈθem ɪs ˈθiːm-, §-əs

Themistocles θə ˈmɪst ə kliːz θɪ-, θe-

themself ðəm ˈself

themselves ðəm ˈselvz —*occasionally also, with contrastive stress,* ˈðem selvz

then ðen

thenar ˈθiːn ə -ɑː ‖ -ʳr -ɑːr **~s** z

thence ðen̩s ‖ θen̩s

thenceforth ˌðen̩s ˈfɔːθ ‖ -ˈfɔːrθ ˌθen̩s-, -ˈfoʊrθ

thenceforward ˌðen̩s ˈfɔː wəd ‖ -ˈfɔːr wʳrd ˌθen̩s-, -ˈfoʊr- **~s** z

theo- *comb. form*

  with stress-neutral suffix ˌθiː əʊ ‖ -ə — **theocentric** ˌθiː əʊ ˈsentr ɪk ◀ ‖ -ə-

  with stress-imposing suffix θiː ˈɒ+ ‖ -ˈɑː+ — **theophagy** θiː ˈɒf ədʒ i ‖ -ˈɑːf-

Theo ˈθiːˌəʊ ‖ -oʊ

Theobald ˈθiːˌə bɔːld ‖ -bɑːld —*Formerly also* ˈtɪb ᵊld **~s** z

theobromine ˌθiː əʊ ˈbrəʊm iːn -ɪn ‖ -ə ˈbroʊm-

theocrac|y θi ˈɒk rəs |i ‖ -ˈɑːk- **~ies** iz

theocrat ˈθiːˌə kræt **~s** s

theocratic ˌθiːˌə ˈkræt ɪk ◀ ‖ -ə ˈkræt̬- **~ally** ᵊl i

Theocritus θi ˈɒk rɪt əs -rət- ‖ -ˈɑːk-

theodic|y θi ˈɒd əs |i -ɪs- ‖ -ˈɑːd- **~ies** iz

theodolite θi ˈɒd ə laɪt -ᵊl aɪt ‖ -ˈɑːd ᵊl aɪt **~s** s

Theodora ˌθiːˌə ˈdɔːr ə ‖ -ˈdoʊr-

Theodorakis ˌθiːˌə dɔː ˈrɑːk ɪs -də'--, §-əs —*ModGk* [θe ɔ ðɔ ˈra cis]

Theodore ˈθiːˌə dɔː ‖ -dɔːr -doʊr

Theodoric θi ˈɒd ər ɪk ‖ -ˈɑːd-

Theodosi|us ˌθiːˌə ˈdəʊs i |əs ‖ -ˈdoʊʃ- **~an** ən

theogon|y θi ˈɒg ən |i ‖ -ˈɑːg- **~ies** iz

theologian ˌθiːˌə ˈləʊdʒ i ˌən -'ʌn ‖ -ˈloʊdʒ- **~s** z

theological ˌθiːˌə ˈlɒdʒ ɪk ᵊl ◀ ‖ -ˈlɑːdʒ- **~ly** i

theolog|y θi ˈɒl ədʒ |i ‖ -ˈɑːl- **~ies** iz

theomachy θi ˈɒm ək i ‖ -ˈɑːm-
theomancy ˈθiː əʊ ˌmænˈs i ‖ -oʊ-
theophan|y θi ˈɒf ən |i ‖ -ˈɑːf- **~ies** iz
Theophilus θi ˈɒf ɪl əs -əl- ‖ -ˈɑːf-
Theophrastus ˌθiː ə ˈfræst əs
theophylline ˌθiː ə ˈfɪl iːn -ɪn, -aɪn; θi ˈɒf ɪ liːn,
    -ə-, -lɪn, -laɪn
theorbo θi ˈɔːb əʊ ‖ -ˈɔːrb oʊ **~s** z
theorem ˈθɪər əm §ˈθi: ər əm ‖ ˈθi: ər əm
    ˈθɪr əm **~s** z
theoretic ˌθɪə ˈret ɪk ◄ §ˌθi: əˈ--
    ‖ ˌθi: ə ˈreṭ ɪk ◄ θɪˈ-- **~al** ⁰l **~ally** ⁰l̩ i **~s** s
theoretician ˌθɪər ə ˈtɪʃ ⁿn -e-, -ɪ-
    ‖ ˌθi: ər ə ˈtɪʃ ⁿn ˌθɪr əˈ· · · **~s** z
theorie... —*see* **theory**
theoris... —*see* **theoriz...**
theorist ˈθɪər ɪst §ˈθi: ər-, §-əst ‖ ˈθi: ər əst
    ˈθɪr əst **~s** s
theoriz|e ˈθɪər aɪz §ˈθi: ə raɪz ‖ ˈθi: ə raɪz **~ed**
    d **~es** ɪz əz **~ing** ɪŋ
theor|y ˈθɪər |i ˈθi: ər |i ‖ ˈθi: ər |i ˈθɪr |i **~ies**
    iz
theosophical ˌθi: ə ˈsɒf ɪk ◄ ‖ -ˈsɑːf- **~ly** i
theosophist θi ˈɒs əf ɪst §-əst ‖ -ˈɑːs- **~s** s
theosoph|y θi ˈɒs əf |i ‖ -ˈɑːs- **~ies** iz
Thera ˈθɪər ə ‖ ˈθɪr ə —*ModGk* [ˈθi ɾa]
therapeutic ˌθer ə ˈpjuːt ɪk ◄ ‖ -ˈpjuːṭ ɪk ◄
    ~ally ⁰l̩ i **~s** s
therapie... —*see* **therapy**
therapist ˈθer əp ɪst §-əst **~s** s
therapsid θə ˈræps ɪd θɪ-, θe-, §-əd **~s** z
therap|y ˈθer əp |i **~ies** iz
Theravada ˌθer ə ˈvɑːd ə
there *existential pronoun (adv): strong form* ðeə
    ‖ ðer ðær, *weak form* ðə ‖ ð⁰r —*Some*
    speakers hardly use the weak form, even
    though the word is never stressed; others
    hardly use the strong form
there *adv of place; interj* ðeə ‖ ðe⁰r ðæ⁰r
thereabout ˌðeər ə ˈbaʊt ˈ· ·, ‖ ˌðer- ˌðær-
thereabouts ˌðeər ə ˈbaʊts ˈ· ·, ‖ ˌðer- ˌðær-
thereafter ₍ₗ₎ðeər ˈɑːft ə §-ˈæft- ‖ ₍ₗ₎ðer ˈæft ⁰r
    ₍ₗ₎ðær-
thereat ˌðeər ˈæt ‖ ˌðer-
thereby ˌðeə ˈbaɪ ˈ· · ‖ ˌðer- ˌðær-
there'd *strong form* ðeəd ‖ ðerd ðærd, *weak*
    form ðəd ‖ ð⁰rd —*See note at* **there**
therefor ˌðeə ˈfɔː ‖ ˌðer ˈfɔːr ˌðær-
therefore ˈðeə fɔː §-fə ‖ ˈðer fɔːr ˈðær-, -four
therefrom ˌðeə ˈfrɒm ‖ ˌðer ˈfrʌm -ˈfrɑːm
therein ˌðeər ˈɪn ‖ ˌðer- ˌðær-
thereinafter ˌðeər ɪn ˈɑːft ə §-ˈæft-
    ‖ ˌðer ɪn ˈæft ⁰r ˌðær-
there'll *strong form* ðeəl ðeər əl ‖ ðerl ðærl,
    ðer əl, ðær əl, *weak form* ðəl ðər əl ‖ ð⁰rl
    ð⁰r əl —*See note at* **there**
theremin, thérémin, T~ ˈθer əm ɪn §-ən **~s** z
thereof ˌðeər ˈɒv ‖ ˌðer ˈʌv ˌðær-, -ˈɑːv
thereon ˌðeər ˈɒn ‖ ˌðer ˈɑːn ˌðær-, -ˈɔːn
there's *strong form* ðeəz ‖ ðerz ðærz, *weak*
    form ðəz ‖ ð⁰rz —*See note at* **there**
Theresa tə ˈriːz ə tɪ-, -ˈreɪz- ‖ -ˈriːs- (*!*)
Therese, Thérèse tə ˈreɪz —*Fr* [te ʁɛːz]

thereto ˌðeə ˈtuː ‖ ˌðer- ˌðær-
theretofore ˌðeə tu ˈfɔː ‖ ˈðerṭ ə fɔːr -four
thereunder ˌðeər ˈʌnd ə ‖ ˌðer ˈʌnd ⁰r ˌðær-
thereupon ˌðeər ə ˈpɒn ˈ· · ‚ ‖ ˌðer ə ˈpɑːn
    ˌðær-, -ˈpɔːn
there've *strong form* ðeəv ‖ ðerv ðærv, *weak*
    form ðəv ðər əv ‖ ð⁰rv ðər əv —*See note at*
    there
therewith ˌðeə ˈwɪð -ˈwɪθ ‖ ˌðer- ˌðær-
therewithal ˈðeə wɪð ɔːl -wɪθ-, ‚ · ˈ· ‖ ˈðer-
    ˈðær-, -ɑːl
therm θɜːm ‖ θɜːm **therms** θɜːmz ‖ θɜːmz
thermal ˈθɜːm ⁰l ‖ ˈθɜːm ⁰l **~ly** i **~s** z
thermic ˈθɜːm ɪk ‖ ˈθɜːm ɪk
Thermidor ˈθɜːm ɪ dɔː §-ə- ‖ ˈθɜːm ə dɔːr —*Fr*
    [tɛʁ mi dɔːʁ]
thermion ˈθɜːm i ən ‖ ˈθɜːm- -aːn **~s** z
thermionic ˌθɜːm i ˈɒn ɪk ◄ ‖ ˌθɜːm i ˈɑːn ɪk ◄
    ~s s
    ˌthermiˌonic ˈvalve
thermistor θɜː ˈmɪst ə ˈθɜːm ɪst ə ‖ θɜː ˈmɪst ⁰r
    ˈθɜːm ɪst- **~s** z
thermite ˈθɜːm aɪt ‖ ˈθɜːm-
thermo- *comb. form*
    with stress-neutral suffix ¦θɜːm əʊ ‖ ¦θɜːm ə
    — **thermographic** ˌθɜːm əʊ ˈgræf ɪk ◄
    ‖ ˌθɜːm ə-
    with stress-imposing suffix θɜː ˈmɒ +
    ‖ θɜː ˈmɑː + — **thermography**
    θɜː ˈmɒg rəf i ‖ θɜː ˈmɑːg-
thermocouple ˈθɜːm əʊ ˌkʌp ⁰l ‖ ˈθɜːm ə- **~s**
    z
thermodynamic ˌθɜːm əʊ daɪ ˈnæm ɪk ◄
    ‖ ˌθɜːm oʊ- **~ally** ⁰l̩ i **~s** s
thermoelectric ˌθɜːm əʊ ɪ ˈlek trɪk ◄ -əˈ--
    ‖ ˌθɜːm oʊ- **~ally** ⁰l̩ i
thermometer θə ˈmɒm ɪt ə -ət-
    ‖ θ⁰r ˈmɑːm əṭ ⁰r **~s** z
thermonuclear ˌθɜːm əʊ ˈnjuːk li ə ◄ §-ˈnuːk-
    ‖ ˌθɜːm oʊ ˈnuːk li ⁰r -ˈnjuːk-, △-jəl ⁰r
thermoplastic ˌθɜːm əʊ ˈplæst ɪk ◄ -ˈplɑːst-
    ‖ ˌθɜːm ə- **~s** s
Thermopylae θə ˈmɒp əl i θɜː-, -ɪl-, -iː
    ‖ θ⁰r ˈmɑːp-
thermos, T~ *tdmk* ˈθɜːm əs -ɒs ‖ ˈθɜːm əs **~es**
    ɪz əz
    ˈthermos flask
thermosetting ˈθɜːm əʊ ˌset ɪŋ ‚ · ˈ· ·
    ‖ ˈθɜːm oʊ ˌseṭ ɪŋ
thermostat ˈθɜːm əʊ stæt ‖ ˈθɜːm ə- **~s** s
thermostatic ˌθɜːm əʊ ˈstæt ɪk ◄
    ‖ ˌθɜːm ə ˈstæṭ ɪk ◄ **~ally** ⁰l̩ i
-thermy ˌθɜːm i ‖ ˌθɜːm i — **diathermy**
    ˈdaɪ ə ˌθɜːm i ‖ -ˌθɜːm i
theropod ˈθer ə pɒd ‖ -pɑːd **~s** z
Theroux θə ˈruː
Thersites θɜː ˈsaɪt iːz ‖ θ⁰r-
thesaur|us θɪ ˈsɔːr |əs θə- **~i** aɪ **~uses** əs ɪz -əz
these ðiːz
theses ˈθiːs iːz
Theseus ˈθiːs juːs ˈθiːs i ˌəs ‖ ˈθiːs i əs ˈθiːs uːs
Thesiger ˈθes ɪdʒ ə ‖ -⁰r

thesis 'θiːs ɪs §-əs —*but as a metrical term,*
sometimes 'θes- **theses** 'θiːs iːz

THESPIAN

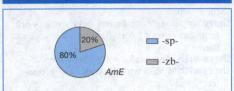

80% 20%

■ -sp-
■ -zb-

AmE

thespian, T~ 'θesp i ən ‖ 'θez bi ən —
Preference poll, AmE: -sp- 80%, -zb- 20%. **~s** z
Thespis 'θesp ɪs §-əs
Thessalian θe 'seɪl i ən θɪ-, θə- **~s** z
Thessalonian ˌθes ə 'ləʊn i ən ◄ ‖ -'loʊn- **~s** z
Thessalonica ˌθes ə 'lɒn ɪk ə ˌθ-ək ə ‖ -'lɑːn-
—*ModGk* Thessaloniki [θε sa lɔ 'ni ci]
Thessaly 'θes əl i
theta 'θiːt ə ‖ 'θeɪt̬ ə 'θiːt̬- **~s** z
Thetford 'θet fəd ‖ -f³rd
thetic 'θet ɪk ‖ 'θet̬ ɪk
Thetis (i) 'θet ɪs §-əs ‖ 'θet̬-, (ii) 'θiːt ɪs -əs
‖ 'θiːt̬- —*The Greek sea goddess is usually* (i),
the personal name (ii)
thew θjuː ‖ θuː θjuː **thews** θjuːz ‖ θuːz θjuːz
they ðeɪ
they'd ðeɪd
Theydon Bois ˌθeɪd ³n 'bɔɪz
they'd've ðeɪd əv
they'll ðeɪ³l ðeəl
they're ðeə §'ðeɪ ə ‖ ðer (= *there*) —*In GenAm*
there is also a weak form ð³r. *There is no RP*
weak form.
they've ðeɪv
thiamin, thiamine 'θaɪ ə miːn -mɪn; §-ə mən
thiazine 'θaɪ ə ziːn -zaɪn
thiazole 'θaɪ ə zəʊl →-zɒʊl ‖ -zoʊl
thick θɪk **thicker** 'θɪk ə ‖ -³r **thickest** 'θɪk ɪst
-əst
thicken 'θɪk ən **~ed** d **~ing** ɪŋ **~s** z
thickener 'θɪk ən ə ‖ -³n ³r **~s** z
thicket 'θɪk ɪt §-ət **~s** s
thickhead 'θɪk hed **~s** z
thickheaded ˌθɪk 'hed ɪd ◄ -əd ‖ ˈ·ˌ·· **~ly** li
~ness nəs nɪs
thickie 'θɪk i **~s** z
thickish 'θɪk ɪʃ
thickly 'θɪk li
thickness 'θɪk nəs -nɪs **~es** ɪz əz
thickset ˌθɪk 'set ◄ ‖ ˈ··
thick-skinned ˌθɪk 'skɪnd ◄ ‖ ˈ··
thick-witted ˌθɪk 'wɪt ɪd ◄ -əd ‖ -'wɪt̬ əd ◄ ˈ·ˌ··
~ly li **~ness** nəs nɪs
thief θiːf **thief's** θiːfs **thieves** θiːvz
Thierry ti 'er i ‖ ˌtiː ə 'riː —*Fr* [tjɛ ʁi]
thieve θiːv **thieved** θiːvd **thieves** θiːvz
thieving 'θiːv ɪŋ
thievery 'θiːv ³r i
thievish 'θiːv ɪʃ **~ly** li **~ness** nəs nɪs
thigh θaɪ **thighs** θaɪz
thighbone 'θaɪ bəʊn ‖ -boʊn **~s** z

thigmo- *comb. form*
with stress-neutral suffix ˌθɪg məʊ ‖ -mə
— **thigmotaxis** ˌθɪg məʊ 'tæks ɪs §-əs
‖ -mə-
with stress-imposing suffix θɪg 'mɒ+
‖ -'mɑː+ — **thigmotropism**
θɪg 'mɒtr ə ˌpɪz əm ‖ -'mɑːtr-, *also*
ˌθɪg məʊ'trəʊp ˌɪz ³m ‖ -mə 'troʊp-
thill θɪl **thills** θɪlz
thimble 'θɪm b³l **~s** z
thimbleful 'θɪm b³l fʊl **~s** z
thimblerig 'θɪm b³l rɪg **~ged** d **~ging** ɪŋ **~s** z
thimerosal θaɪ 'mer ə sæl
Thimphu, Thimbu 'tɪmp uː
thin θɪn **thinned** θɪnd **thinner** 'θɪn ə ‖ -³r
thinnest 'θɪn ɪst -əst **thinning** 'θɪn ɪŋ **thins**
θɪnz
ˌthin 'air
thine ðaɪn
thing θɪŋ **things** θɪŋz
thingama... —*see* **thingummy...**
thingie 'θɪŋ i **~s** z
thinguma... —*see* **thingummy...**
thingumm|y 'θɪŋ əm |i **~ies** iz
thingummybob 'θɪŋ əm i bɒb -ə bɒb
‖ -ə bɑːb **~s** z
thingummyjig 'θɪŋ əm i dʒɪg -ə dʒɪg **~s** z
thing|y 'θɪŋ |i **~ies** iz
think θɪŋk **thinking** 'θɪŋk ɪŋ **thinks** θɪŋks
thought θɔːt ‖ θɑːt
'think piece; 'think tank
thinkable 'θɪŋk əb ³l
thinker 'θɪŋk ə ‖ -³r **~s** z
thinly 'θɪn li
thinn... —*see* **thin**
thinner 'θɪn ə ‖ -³r **~s** z
thinness 'θɪn nəs -nɪs
thin-skinned ˌθɪn 'skɪnd ◄ ‖ ˈ··
thio 'θaɪ əʊ ‖ -oʊ
thio- *comb. form*
with stress-neutral suffix ˌθaɪ əʊ ‖ -ə
— **thiosulfate, thiosulphate**
ˌθaɪ əʊ 'sʌlf eɪt ‖ -ə-
thiokol, T~ *tdmk* 'θaɪ ə kɒl ‖ -kɑːl -kɔːl, -koʊl
thiol 'θaɪ ɒl ‖ -ɑːl -ɔːl, -oʊl **~s** z
thionate 'θaɪ ə neɪt
thiouracil ˌθaɪ əʊ 'jʊər ə sɪl ‖ -oʊ 'jʊr-
third θɜːd ‖ θɝːd **thirds** θɜːdz ‖ θɝːdz
ˌthird de'gree; ˌthird 'party; ˌthird
'person; ˌthird 'reading; ˌThird 'World◄
third-class ˌθɜːd 'klɑːs ◄ →ˌθɜːg-, §-'klæs
‖ ˌθɝːd 'klæs ◄
third-degree ˌθɜːd dɪ 'griː ◄ -də-, §-diː-
‖ ˌθɝːd-
ˌthird-deˌgree 'burns
thirdhand ˌθɜːd 'hænd ◄ ‖ ˌθɝːd-
thirdly 'θɜːd li ‖ 'θɝːd li
third-rate ˌθɜːd 'reɪt ◄ ‖ ˌθɝːd-
Thirkell 'θɜːk ³l ‖ 'θɝːk ³l
Thirlmere 'θɜːl mɪə ‖ 'θɝːl mɪr
Thirsk θɜːsk ‖ θɝːsk

thirst θɜːst ‖ θɝːst **thirsted** 'θɜːst ɪd -əd
‖ 'θɜːst əd **thirsting** 'θɜːst ɪŋ ‖ 'θɜːst ɪŋ
thirsts θɜːsts ‖ θɝːsts
thirst-quenching 'θɜːst‿kwenʃ ɪŋ ‖ 'θɝːst-
thirst|y 'θɜːst |i ‖ 'θɝːst |i **~ier** i ə ‖ i ʲr **~iest**
i ɪst i əst **~ily** ɪ li əl i **~iness** i nəs i nɪs
thirteen ˌθɜː 'tiːn ◂ §ˌθɜːt- ‖ ˌθɝː-ˌθɜːt- **~s** z
thirteenth ˌθɜː 'tiːn'θ ◂ §ˌθɜːt- ‖ ˌθɝː-ˌθɜːt- **~s**
s
thirtieth 'θɜːt i əθ §-ti-, -ɪθ ‖ 'θɝːt i əθ **~s** s
thirt|y 'θɜːt |i §'θɜːt t|i ‖ 'θɝːt |i **~ies** iz
ˌThirty ₍₁₎Years' 'War
thirtyfold 'θɜːt i fəʊld →-fɒʊld ‖ 'θɝːt i foʊld
thirty-nine ˌθɜːt i 'naɪn ◂ §-ti- ‖ ˌθɝːt- **~s** z
ˌThirty-nine 'Articles
thirty-something 'θɜːt i ˌsʌm θɪŋ §-ti-; ˌ·'·· ·
‖ 'θɝːˌt̬i-

this ðɪs —*In BrE some speakers use a weak
form* ðəs *in the expressions ~ afternoon, ~
evening, ~ morning. In AmE, this weak form
is used more widely.* **these** ðiːz

Thisbe 'θɪz bi
thistle 'θɪs ᵊl **~s** z
thistledown 'θɪs ᵊl daʊn
Thistlethwaite 'θɪs ᵊl θweɪt
thistly 'θɪs ᵊl ̩i
thither 'ðɪð ə §'θɪð- ‖ 'θɪð ʲr 'ðɪð- **~ward/s**
wəd/z ‖ wʲrd/z
thixotropic ˌθɪks ə 'trɒp ɪk ◂ ‖ -'trɑːp-
thixotropy θɪk 'sɒtr əp i ‖ -'sɑːtr-
tho, tho' ðəʊ §θəʊ ‖ ðoʊ
Thoday 'θəʊd eɪ ‖ 'θoʊd eɪ
Thody 'θəʊd i ‖ 'θoʊd i
thole θəʊl →θɒʊl ‖ θoʊl **tholes** θəʊlz →θɒʊlz
‖ θoʊlz
tholepin 'θəʊl pɪn →'θɒʊl- ‖ 'θoʊl- **~s** z
Thom tɒm ‖ tɑːm
Thomas 'tɒm əs ‖ 'tɑːm əs (!)
Thomasena, Thomasina ˌtɒm ə 'siːn ə
‖ ˌtɑːm-
Thomism 'təʊm ˌɪz əm ‖ 'toʊm-
Thompson 'tɒmps ən ‖ 'tɑːmps ən
Thomson 'tɒmᵖs ən ‖ 'tɑːmᵖs ən
thon ðɒn ‖ ðɑːn
-thon θɒn ‖ θɑːn — **singathon** 'sɪŋ ə θɒn
‖ -θɑːn —*See note at -on.*
thong θɒŋ ‖ θɔːŋ θɑːŋ **thongs** θɒŋz ‖ θɔːŋz
θɑːŋz
Thor θɔː ‖ θɔːr
Thora 'θɔːr ə
thoraces 'θɔːr ə siːz θɔː 'reɪs iːz ‖ 'θoʊr-
thoracic θɔː 'ræs ɪk θɒ-, θə- ‖ θə-
thoraco- *comb. form*
with stress-neutral suffix |θɔːr ə kəʊ
θɔː |ræk əʊ ‖ -koʊ |θoʊr- — **thoracoplasty**
'θɔːr ə kəʊ ˌplæst i θɔː 'ræk- ‖ -koʊˌ- 'θoʊr-
with stress-imposing suffix ˌθɔːr ə 'kɒ +
‖ -'kɑː + ˌθoʊr- — **thoracotomy**
ˌθɔːr ə 'kɒt əm i ‖ -'kɑːt̬- ˌθoʊr-
thorax 'θɔːr æks ‖ 'θoʊr- **thoraces** 'θɔːr ə siːz
θɔː 'reɪs iːz ‖ 'θoʊr- **~es** ɪz əz
Thorazine *tdmk* 'θɔːr ə ziːn ‖ 'θoʊr-
Thorburn 'θɔː bɜːn ‖ 'θɔːr bɝːn

Thoreau 'θɔːr əʊ θɔː 'rəʊ, θə- ‖ θə 'roʊ θɔː-;
'θɔːr oʊ
thorite 'θɔːr aɪt ‖ 'θoʊr-
thorium 'θɔːr i əm ‖ 'θoʊr-
Thorley 'θɔːl i ‖ 'θɔːrl i
thorn, Thorn θɔːn ‖ θɔːrn **thorns** θɔːnz
‖ θɔːrnz
'thorn ˌapple
Thornaby 'θɔːn əb i ‖ 'θɔːrn-
thornbill 'θɔːn bɪl →'θɔːm- ‖ 'θɔːrn- **~s** z
Thorndike 'θɔːn daɪk ‖ 'θɔːrn-
Thorne θɔːn ‖ θɔːrn
Thorner 'θɔːn ə ‖ 'θɔːrn ʲr
Thorneycroft 'θɔːn i krɒft ‖ 'θɔːrn i krɔːft
-krɑːft
Thornham 'θɔːn əm ‖ 'θɔːrn-
Thornhill 'θɔːn hɪl ‖ 'θɔːrn-
thornless 'θɔːn ləs -lɪs ‖ 'θɔːrn-
Thornley 'θɔːn li ‖ 'θɔːrn-
Thornton 'θɔːn tən ‖ 'θɔːrn tᵊn
thorn|y 'θɔːn |i ‖ 'θɔːrn |i **~ier** i ə ‖ i ʲr **~iest**
i ɪst i əst **~iness** i nəs i nɪs
Thorogood 'θʌr ə gʊd ‖ 'θɝː-
Thorold 'θɒr ᵊld 'θʌr-, -əʊld ‖ 'θɔːr ᵊld 'θɑːr-
thoron 'θɔːr ɒn ‖ -ɑːn 'θoʊr-
thorough 'θʌr ə ‖ 'θɝː oʊ (*)
thoroughbred 'θʌr ə bred ‖ 'θɝː oʊ- -ə- **~s** z
thoroughfare 'θʌr ə feə ‖ 'θɝː oʊ fer -ə-, -fær
~s z
thoroughgoing ˌθʌr ə 'gəʊ ɪŋ ◂
‖ ˌθɝː oʊ 'goʊ ɪŋ ◂ -ə-
thorough|ly 'θʌr ə |li ‖ 'θɝː oʊ |li **~ness** nəs
nɪs
Thorp, Thorpe θɔːp ‖ θɔːrp
Thorpeness ˌθɔːp 'nes ‖ ˌθɔːrp-
those ðəʊz ‖ ðoʊz
Thoth θəʊθ təʊt, θɒθ ‖ θoʊθ toʊt
thou *pronoun* ðaʊ —*In dialectal speech there
may also be a weak form such as* ðə.
thou '*thousand*'; '*thousandth*' θaʊ **thous** θaʊz
though ðəʊ §θəʊ ‖ ðoʊ
thought θɔːt ‖ θɑːt **thoughts** θɔːts ‖ θɑːts
thoughtful 'θɔːt fᵊl -ful ‖ 'θɑːt- **~ly** ̩i **~ness**
nəs nɪs
thoughtless 'θɔːt ləs -lɪs ‖ 'θɑːt- **~ly** li **~ness**
nəs nɪs
thought-out ˌθɔːt 'aʊt ◂ ‖ ˌθɔːt̬- ˌθɑːt̬-
thought-provoking 'θɔːt prə ˌvəʊk ɪŋ
‖ -ˌvoʊk-
thought-reader 'θɔːt ˌriːd ə ‖ -ʲr 'θɑːt̬- **~s** z
Thouless 'θaʊ les
thousand 'θaʊz ᵊnd **~s** z
ˌThousand 'Islands; ˌThousand ˌIsland
'dressing
thousandfold 'θaʊz ᵊnd fəʊld →-fɒʊld
‖ -foʊld
thousandth 'θaʊz ᵊn'θ -ᵊndθ **~s** s
Thrace θreɪs
Thracian 'θreɪʃ ᵊn 'θreɪʃ i ᵊn **~s** z
Thraco-Phrygian ˌθreɪk əʊ 'frɪdʒ i ᵊn ◂ ‖ ˌoʊ-
thraldom 'θrɔːl dəm ‖ 'θrɑːl-
Thrale θreɪᵊl
thrall θrɔːl ‖ θrɑːl

thralldom 'θrɔːl dəm ‖ 'θrɑːl-
thrang θræŋ
thrash θræʃ **thrashed** θræʃt **thrashes** 'θræʃ ɪz
-əz **thrashing** 'θræʃ ɪŋ
thrasher 'θræʃ ə ‖ -ᵊr ~s z
thread θred **threaded** 'θred ɪd -əd **threading**
'θred ɪŋ **threads** θredz
threadbare 'θred beə →'θreb- ‖ -ber -bær
~**ness** nəs nɪs
threadlike 'θred laɪk
Threadneedle ˌθred 'niːd ᵊl '···
threadworm 'θred wɜːm ‖ -wɜːm ~s z
threat θret **threats** θrets
threaten 'θret ᵊn ~**ed** d ~**ing/ly** ɪŋ /li ~**s** z
three θriː **threes** θriːz
ˌthree 'R's
three-cornered ˌθriː 'kɔːn əd ◂ ‖ -'kɔːrn ᵊrd ◂
three-D, 3-D ˌθriː 'diː ◂
three-day ˌθriː 'deɪ ◂
ˌthree-day 'week
three-decker ˌθriː 'dek ə ◂ ‖ -ᵊr ~s z
three-dimensional ˌθriː daɪ 'menᵗʃ ᵊn əl ◂
ˌ-dɪ-, ˌ-də-
threefold 'θriː fəʊld →-fɒʊld, ˌ·'· ‖ -foʊld
three-halfpence ˌθriː 'heɪp ᵊnᵗs →-mᵖs
threeish 'θriː ɪʃ
three-legged ˌθriː 'leg ɪd ◂ -əd; ˌ·'legd
ˌthree-'legged race
three-line ˌθriː 'laɪn ◂
ˌthree-line 'whip
three-peat 'θriː piːt
threepence n '3d' 'θrep ᵊnᵗs 'θrʌp-, 'θrɪp-,
'θrʊp-, →-mᵖs —but meaning '3p', in modern
currency, usually three pence ˌθriː 'penᵗs
threepenny adj '3d' 'θrep ᵊn i 'θrʌp-, 'θrɪp-,
'θrʊp- —but meaning '3p', in modern
currency, usually three-penny ˌθriː 'pen i ◂
ˌthreepenny 'bit
three-piece ˌθriː 'piːs ◂
ˌthree-piece 'suite
three-ply 'θriː plaɪ ˌ·'·
three-point ˌθriː 'pɔɪnt ◂
ˌthree-point 'turn
three-pointer ˌθriː 'pɔɪnt ə ‖ -'pɔɪnt̬ ᵊr ~s z
three-quarter ˌθriː 'kwɔːt ə ◂ -'kɔːt-
‖ -'kwɔːrt̬ ᵊr ◂ ~s z
three-ring ˌθriː 'rɪŋ ◂
ˌthree-ring 'circus
threescore ˌθriː 'skɔː ◂ ‖ -'skɔːr ◂ -'skoʊr
threesome ˌθriː səm ~s z
three-star ˌθriː 'stɑː ◂ ‖ -'stɑːr ◂
ˌthree-star ho'tel
three-way ˌθriː 'weɪ ◂
three-wheeler ˌθriː 'wiːᵊl ə -'hwiːᵊl-
‖ -'hwiːᵊl ᵊr ~s z
Threlfall 'θrel fɔːl ‖ -fɑːl
Threlkeld 'θrel keld
threnody 'θren əd i ‖ 'θriːn- ~**ies** iz
thresh θreʃ **threshed** θreʃt **threshes** 'θreʃ ɪz
-əz **threshing** 'θreʃ ɪŋ
thresher, T~ 'θreʃ ə ‖ -ᵊr ~s z
threshold 'θreʃ həʊld -əʊld, →-hɒʊld ‖ -oʊld
-hoʊld ~s z

threw θruː (= through)
Thribb θrɪb
thrice θraɪs
thrift θrɪft **thrifts** θrɪfts
thriftless 'θrɪft ləs -lɪs ~**ly** li ~**ness** nəs nɪs
thrift|y 'θrɪft |i ~**ier** i ə ‖ i ᵊr ~**iest** i ɪst i əst
~**ily** ɪ li əl i ~**iness** i nəs i nɪs
thrill θrɪl **thrilled** θrɪld **thrilling/ly** θrɪl ɪŋ /li
thrills θrɪlz
thriller 'θrɪl ə ‖ -ᵊr ~s z
thrill-seeker 'θrɪl ˌsiːk ə ‖ -ᵊr ~s z
Thring θrɪŋ
thrips θrɪps
thrive θraɪv **thrived** θraɪvd **thriven** 'θrɪv ᵊn
(!) **thrives** θraɪvz **thriving/ly** 'θraɪv ɪŋ /li
throve θrəʊv ‖ θroʊv
thro, thro' θruː
throat θrəʊt ‖ θroʊt **throats** θrəʊts ‖ θroʊts
throat|y 'θrəʊt |i ‖ 'θroʊt̬ |i ~**ier** i ə ‖ i ᵊr
~**iest** i ɪst i əst ~**ily** ɪ li əl i ~**iness** i nəs i nɪs
throb θrɒb ‖ θrɑːb **throbbed** θrɒbd ‖ θrɑːbd
throbbing/ly 'θrɒb ɪŋ /li ‖ 'θrɑːb ɪŋ /li
throbs θrɒbz ‖ θrɑːbz
throes θrəʊz ‖ θroʊz (= throws)
Throgmorton ₍ᵢ₎θrɒg 'mɔːt ᵊn '···
‖ θrɑːg 'mɔːrt ᵊn
thrombi 'θrɒm baɪ ‖ 'θrɑːm-
thrombin 'θrɒm bɪn §-bən ‖ 'θrɑːm-
thrombo- comb. form
with stress-neutral suffix ¦θrɒm bəʊ
‖ ¦θrɑːm boʊ — **thromboplastic**
ˌθrɒm bəʊ 'plæst ɪk ◂ ‖ ˌθrɑːm boʊ-
with stress-imposing suffix θrɒm 'bɒ+
‖ θrɑːm 'bɑː+ — **thrombolysis**
θrɒm 'bɒl əs ɪs -ɪs-, §-əs ‖ θrɑːm 'bɑːl-
thrombolysis ˌθrɒm bəʊ 'laɪs ɪs
θrɒm 'bɒl əs ɪs, §-əs ‖ ˌθrɑːm boʊ 'laɪs əs
θrɑːm 'bɑːl əs əs
thrombos|e 'θrɒm bəʊz -bəʊs, ·'· ‖ -boʊz -boʊs
~**ed** d ~**es** ɪz əz ~**ing** ɪŋ
thrombos|is θrɒm 'bəʊs |ɪs §-əs
‖ θrɑːm 'boʊs |əs ~**es** iːz
thrombotic θrɒm 'bɒt ɪk ‖ θrɑːm 'bɑːt̬ ɪk
throm|bus 'θrɒm |bəs ‖ 'θrɑːm |bəs ~**bi** baɪ
throne θrəʊn ‖ θroʊn **throned** θrəʊnd
‖ θroʊnd **thrones** θrəʊnz ‖ θroʊnz **throning**
'θrəʊn ɪŋ ‖ 'θroʊn ɪŋ
throng θrɒŋ ‖ θrɔːŋ θrɑːŋ **thronged** θrɒŋd
‖ θrɔːŋd θrɑːŋd **thronging** 'θrɒŋ ɪŋ
‖ 'θrɔːŋ ɪŋ 'θrɑːŋ- **throngs** θrɒŋz ‖ θrɔːŋz
θrɑːŋz
throstle 'θrɒs ᵊl ‖ 'θrɑːs ᵊl ~s z
throttl|e 'θrɒt ᵊl ‖ 'θrɑːt̬ ᵊl ~**ed** d ~**es** z ~**ing**
ɪŋ
through θruː
throughout θru 'aʊt
throughput 'θruː pʊt
throughway 'θruː weɪ ~s z
throve θrəʊv ‖ θroʊv
throw θrəʊ ‖ θroʊ **threw** θruː **throwing**
'θrəʊ ɪŋ ‖ 'θroʊ ɪŋ **thrown** θrəʊn §'θrəʊ ən
‖ θroʊn **throws** θrəʊz ‖ θroʊz
throwaway 'θrəʊ ə ˌweɪ ‖ 'θroʊ- ~s z

throwback 'θrəʊ bæk ‖ 'θroʊ- ~s s
throwdown 'θrəʊ daʊn ‖ 'θroʊ- ~s z
thrower, T~ 'θrəʊ ə ‖ 'θroʊ ʰr ~s z
throw-in 'θrəʊ ɪn ‖ 'θroʊ- ~s z
thrown θrəʊn §'θrəʊ ən ‖ 'θroʊn *(usually = throne)*
thru θruː
thrum θrʌm **thrummed** θrʌmd **thrumming** 'θrʌm ɪŋ **thrums** θrʌmz
thrush θrʌʃ **thrushes** 'θrʌʃ ɪz -əz
thrust θrʌst **thrusting/ly** 'θrʌst ɪŋ /li **thrusts** θrʌsts
thruster 'θrʌst ə ‖ -ʰr ~s z
thruway 'θruː weɪ ~s z
Thucydidean θjuː ˌsɪd ə 'diː ən ◂ -ɪ- ‖ θuː-
Thucydides θjuː 'sɪd ə diːz -ɪ- ‖ θuː-
thud θʌd **thudded** 'θʌd ɪd -əd **thudding** 'θʌd ɪŋ **thuds** θʌdz
thug θʌg **thugs** θʌgz
thuggery 'θʌg ər i
thuggish 'θʌg ɪʃ **~ly** li **~ness** nəs nɪs
thuja 'θjuːdʒ ə 'θuːdʒ-; 'θjuː jə, 'θuː- ‖ 'θuːdʒ ə ~s z
Thule θjuː1l 'θjuːl i, 'θuːl-, -iː ‖ 'θuːl i —*but the base in Greenland is* 'tuːl i
thulium 'θjuːl i əm 'θuːl- ‖ 'θuːl-
thumb θʌm **thumbed** θʌmd **thumbing** 'θʌm ɪŋ **thumbs** θʌmz
    ˌthumbs 'down; ˌthumbs 'up
thumbnail 'θʌm neɪʰl ~s z
thumbprint 'θʌm prɪnt ~s s
thumbscrew 'θʌm skruː ~s z
thumbtack 'θʌm tæk **~ed** t **~ing** ɪŋ **~s** s
thummim 'θʌm ɪm 'θʊm-, 'tʊm-
thump θʌmp **thumped** θʌmpt **thumping/ly** 'θʌmp ɪŋ /li **thumps** θʌmps
thumper 'θʌmp ə ‖ -ʰr ~s z
thunbergia θʌn 'bɜːdʒ i ə θʊn-, ·'·ə ‖ -'bɜːdʒ- ~s z
thunder 'θʌnd ə ‖ -ʰr **~ed** d **thundering/ly** 'θʌnd ʰr ɪŋ /li ~s z
    ˌThunder 'Bay
thunderbird, T~ 'θʌnd ə bɜːd ‖ -ʰr bɜːd ~s z
thunderbolt 'θʌnd ə bəʊlt →-bɒʊlt ‖ -ʰr boʊlt ~s s
thunderclap 'θʌnd ə klæp ‖ -ʰr- ~s s
thundercloud 'θʌnd ə klaʊd ‖ -ʰr- ~s z
thunderer 'θʌnd ʰr ə ‖ ʰr ər
thunder|fly 'θʌnd ə| flaɪ ‖ -ʰr| **~flies** flaɪz
thunderhead 'θʌnd ə hed ‖ -ʰr- ~z z
thunderous 'θʌnd ʰr əs **~ly** li
thundershower 'θʌnd ə ˌʃaʊ‿ə ‖ 'θʌnd ʰr ˌʃaʊ‿ʰr ~s z
thunderstorm 'θʌnd ə stɔːm ‖ -ʰr stɔːrm ~s z
thunderstruck 'θʌnd ə strʌk ‖ -ʰr-
thundery 'θʌn dər i
thunk θʌŋk
Thurber 'θɜːb ə ‖ 'θɜːb ʰr
Thurgarton 'θɜːg ət ən ‖ 'θɜːg ʰrt ʰn
Thurgood 'θɜː gʊd ‖ 'θɜː-
thurible 'θjʊər ɪb ʰl -əb- ‖ 'θʊr- 'θɜː- ~s z
thurifer 'θjʊər ɪf ə -əf- ‖ 'θʊr əf ʰr 'θɜː- ~s z

Thuringi|a θjuʰ 'rɪndʒ i ˌə tuʰ-, -'rɪŋ giː; ·'·ə ‖ θu- **~an/s** ən/z
Thurleigh *place in Bedfordshire* ˌθɜː 'laɪ ‖ ˌθɜː-
Thurlestone 'θɜːl stən ‖ 'θɜːl-
Thurloe, Thurlow 'θɜːl əʊ ‖ 'θɜːl oʊ
Thurman 'θɜːm ən ‖ 'θɜːm-
Thurmond 'θɜːm ənd ‖ 'θɜːm-
Thurrock 'θʌr ək ‖ 'θɜː ək
Thursday 'θɜːz deɪ -di ‖ 'θɜːz- —*See note at* -day ~s z
Thurso 'θɜːs əʊ ‖ 'θɜːs oʊ
Thurston 'θɜːst ən ‖ 'θɜːst ən
thus ðʌs **thusly** 'ðʌs li
thwack θwæk **thwacked** θwækt **thwacking** 'θwæk ɪŋ **thwacks** θwæks
Thwaite θweɪt **Thwaites** θweɪts
thwart θwɔːt ‖ θwɔːrt **thwarted** 'θwɔːt ɪd -əd ‖ 'θwɔːrt̬ əd **thwarting** 'θwɔːt ɪŋ ‖ 'θwɔːrt̬ ɪŋ **thwarts** θwɔːts ‖ θwɔːrts
thy ðaɪ
Thyestean θaɪ 'est i ən
Thyestes θaɪ 'est iːz
thylacine 'θaɪl ə siːn -saɪn ~s z
thyme taɪm *(! = time)*
-thymia 'θaɪm i ˌə — **cyclothymia** ˌsaɪk ləʊ 'θaɪm i ə ‖ ·ˌlə-
thymidine 'θaɪm ɪ diːn -ə-
thymine 'θaɪm iːn
thymol 'θaɪm ɒl ‖ -oʊl -ɔːl, -ɑːl
thymus 'θaɪm əs **~es** ɪz əz
Thynne θɪn
thyratron 'θaɪʰr ə trɒn ‖ -trɑːn ~s z
thyristor θaɪʰ 'rɪst ə ‖ -ʰr ~s z
thyro- *comb. form*
    with stress-neutral suffix ¦θaɪʰr əʊ ‖ -oʊ —
    thyrohyoid ˌθaɪʰr əʊ 'haɪ ɔɪd ◂ ‖ -oʊ-
    with stress-imposing suffix θaɪʰ 'rɒ+ ‖ -'rɑː+
    — **thyropathy** ˌθaɪʰ 'rɒp əθ i ‖ -'rɑːp-
thyroid 'θaɪʰr ɔɪd ~s z
thyroxine θaɪʰ 'rɒks iːn -ɪn, §-ʰn ‖ -'rɑːks-
thyrs|us 'θɜːs |əs ‖ 'θɜːs |əs **~i** aɪ
thyself ðaɪ 'self
Thyssen 'tiːs ʰn —*Ger* ['tʏs ʰn]
ti *'musical note'; 'Cordyline tree'* tiː **tis** tiːz
TI ˌtiː 'aɪ
Tia Maria *tdmk* ˌtiː‿ə mə 'riː‿ə ~s z
Tiananmen ti ˌæn ən 'men ◂ ˌtiː‿ən·, -'mɪn ‖ -ˌɑːn- ·ˌæn-; 'tjen əm ən ən —*Chi* Tiān'ānmén [¹tʰjæn ¹an ²mən]
    Tiˌananmen 'Square
Tianjin ti ˌæn 'dʒɪn -ˌen- ‖ -ˌɑːn- —*Chi* Tiānjīn [¹tʰjæn ¹tɕɪn]
tiara ti 'ɑːr ə ‖ -'ær ə -'er-, -'ɑːr- ~s z
Tibbenham 'tɪb ən‿əm
Tibbett 'tɪb ɪt §-ət
Tibbitts 'tɪb ɪts §-əts
Tibbles 'tɪb ʰlz
Tibbs tɪbz
Tibenham 'tɪb ən‿əm
Tiber 'taɪb ə ‖ -ʰr
Tiberias taɪ 'bɪər i æs -əs ‖ -'bɪr-
Tiberius taɪ 'bɪər i ˌəs ‖ -'bɪr-
Tibet tɪ 'bet §tə- —*Chi* Xīzàng [¹ɕi ⁴tsɑŋ]

T

Tibetan tɪ 'bet ⁿn §tə- ~s z

Tibeto-Burman tɪ ˌbet əʊ 'bɜːm ən ◂ §tə-
‖ tə ˌbeţ oʊ 'bɜːm ən ◂

tibi|a 'tɪb i ˌ|ə ~ae iː ~as əz

Tibullus tɪ 'bʌl əs §tə-, -'bʊl-

tic tɪk (= tick) **tics** tɪks
  ˌtic ˌdoulou'reux ˌduːl ə 'rɜː ‖ -'ruː —Fr
  [tik du lu ʁø]

tice taɪs **tices** 'taɪs ɪz -əz

Ticehurst 'taɪs hɜːst ‖ -hɝːst

Tichborne 'tɪtʃ bɔːn ‖ -bɔːrn -boʊrn

Ticino tɪ 'tʃiːn əʊ ‖ -oʊ —It [ti 'tʃiː no]

tick tɪk **ticked** tɪkt **ticking** 'tɪk ɪŋ **ticks** tɪks
  ˌticking 'off n

ticker 'tɪk ə ‖ -ᵊr ~s z

ticker-tape 'tɪk ə teɪp ‖ -ᵊr-

tick|et 'tɪk |ɪt §-ət ‖ -|ət ~eted ɪt ɪd §ət-, -əd
  ‖ əţ əd ~eting ɪt ɪŋ §ət- ‖ əţ ɪŋ ~ets ɪts §əts
  ‖ əts
  ˌticket ˌagency; ˌticket col,lector; ˌticket
  ˌoffice; ˌticket tout

tickety-boo ˌtɪk ət i 'buː ˌ·ɪt- ‖ -əţ i-

ticking 'tɪk ɪŋ

tickl|e 'tɪk ᵊl ~ed d ~es z ~ing ɪŋ

tickler 'tɪk ᵊlˌə ‖ ər ~s z

ticklish 'tɪk ᵊlˌɪʃ ~ly li ~ness nəs nɪs

tick-over 'tɪk ˌəʊv ə ‖ -ˌoʊv ᵊr

ticktack 'tɪk tæk

tick-tack-toe, tic-tac-toe ˌtɪk tæk 'təʊ ‖ -'toʊ

ticktock 'tɪk tɒk ˌ·'· ‖ -taːk ~ed t ~ing ɪŋ ~s s

ticky-tacky 'tɪk i ˌtæk i

Ticonderoga ˌtaɪ kɒnd ə 'rəʊg ə ·ˌ· ·'· ·
  ‖ ˌtaɪ kaːnd ə 'roʊg ə

tidal 'taɪd ᵊl
  ˌtidal 'wave, '· ·

tidbit 'tɪd bɪt →'tɪb- ~s s

tiddledywink 'tɪd ᵊld i wɪŋk ~s s

tiddler 'tɪd ᵊlˌə ‖ ər ~s z

Tiddles 'tɪd ᵊlz

tiddley, tiddly 'tɪd ᵊlˌi

tiddleywink, tiddlywink 'tɪd ᵊlˌi wɪŋk ~s s

tide taɪd **tided** 'taɪd ɪd -əd **tides** taɪdz **tiding**
  'taɪd ɪŋ
  ˌtide ˌtable

tideland 'taɪd lænd ~s z

tidemark 'taɪd maːk →'taɪb- ‖ -maːrk ~s s

Tidenham 'tɪd ⁿn,əm

Tideswell 'taɪdz wel —Locally also 'tɪdz ᵊl

tidewater 'taɪd ˌwɔːt ə ‖ -ˌwɔːţ ᵊr -ˌwaːţ-

tideway 'taɪd weɪ

tidi... —see **tidy**

tidily 'taɪd ɪ li -əl i

tidiness 'taɪd i nəs -nɪs

tidings 'taɪd ɪŋz

Tidmarsh 'tɪd maːʃ →'tɪb- ‖ -maːrʃ

tidy, Tidy 'taɪd i **tidied** 'taɪd id **tidier**
  'taɪd iˌə ‖ ᵊr **tidies** 'taɪd iz **tidiest** 'taɪd iˌɪst
  əst **tidying** 'taɪd iˌɪŋ

tie taɪ **tied** taɪd **ties** taɪz **tying** 'taɪ ɪŋ
  ˌtie clip; ˌtied 'cottage; ˌtied 'house

tiebreak 'taɪ breɪk ~s s

tiebreaker 'taɪ ˌbreɪk ə ‖ -ᵊr ~s z

tie-dye 'taɪ daɪ ~d d ~s z ~ing ɪŋ

tie-in 'taɪ ɪn ~s z

tie-on 'taɪ ɒn ‖ -aːn -ɔːn ~s z

tiepin 'taɪ pɪn ~s z

Tiepolo ti 'ep ə ləʊ ‖ -loʊ —It ['tjɛː po lo]

tier 'one that ties' 'taɪ ə ‖ 'taɪ ᵊr **tiers** 'taɪ əz
  ‖ 'taɪ ᵊrz

tier 'rank, row' tɪə ‖ tɪᵊr (= tear 'eye-water')
  tiered tɪəd ‖ tɪᵊrd **tiering** 'tɪər ɪŋ ‖ 'tɪr ɪŋ
  tiers tɪəz ‖ tɪᵊrz

tierce tɪəs ‖ tɪᵊrs —but in cards also tɜːs ‖ tɜːs

tiercel 'tɪəs ᵊl 'tɜːs- ‖ 'tɪrs ᵊl ~s z

Tierney 'tɪən i ‖ 'tɪrn i

tierra ti 'eər ə -'er-; 'tɪər ə ‖ ti 'er ə —Sp
  ['tje ɾɾa]
  ti,erra ˌcali'ente ˌkæl i 'ent eɪ ‖ ˌkaːl-;
  Ti,erra del 'Fuego del 'fweɪg əʊ ‖ -oʊ —Sp
  [ðel 'fwe ɣo]; ti,erra 'fria 'friːə —Sp
  ['fri a]; ti,erra he'lada he 'laːd ə —Sp
  [e 'la ða]; ti,erra tem'plada tem 'plaːd ə
  —Sp [tem 'pla ða]

tie-up 'taɪ ʌp ~s s

tiff tɪf **tiffs** tɪfs

Tiffan|y, t~ 'tɪf ən |i ~ies, y's iz

tiffin, T~ 'tɪf ɪn §-ᵊn ~s z

Tiflis 'tɪf lɪs §-ləs

tig tɪg

Tigellinus ˌtɪdʒ ə 'laɪn əs

tiger 'taɪg ə ‖ -ᵊr ~s z
  'tiger cat; ˌtiger ˌlily; 'tiger moth; 'tiger
  shark

tigerish 'taɪg ər ɪʃ ~ly li

Tigger 'tɪg ə ‖ -ᵊr

Tiggy-Winkle 'tɪg i ˌwɪŋk ᵊl ˌ·'· ·

Tighe taɪ

tight taɪt **tighter** 'taɪt ə ‖ 'taɪţ ᵊr **tightest**
  'taɪt ɪst -əst ‖ 'taɪţ əst **tights** taɪts

tighten 'taɪt ⁿn ~ed d ~ing ɪŋ ~s z

tightfisted ˌtaɪt 'fɪst ɪd ◂ -əd

tight-fitting ˌtaɪt 'fɪt ɪŋ ◂ ‖ -'fɪţ ɪŋ ◂

tightie whities ˌtaɪt i 'waɪt iz -'hwaɪt-
  ‖ ˌtaɪţ i 'hwaɪţ iz

tightknit ˌtaɪt 'nɪt ◂ ‖ '· ·

tight-lipped ˌtaɪt 'lɪpt ◂ ‖ '· ·

tight|ly 'taɪt |li ~ness nəs nɪs

tightrope 'taɪt rəʊp ‖ -roʊp ~s s
  'tightrope ˌwalker

tightwad 'taɪt wɒd ‖ -waːd ~s z

Tiglath-pileser ˌtɪg læθ paɪ 'liːz ə -pɪ'·-, -pə'·-
  ‖ -ᵊr

tiglic 'tɪg lɪk

Tignes tiːn —Fr [tiɲ]

tigon 'taɪg ən ~s z

Tigray, Tigre, Tigré 'tɪg reɪ ‖ tiː 'greɪ

tigress 'taɪg rəs -rɪs, -res ~es ɪz əz

Tigrinya tɪ 'grɪn jə -'griːn-

Tigris 'taɪg rɪs -rəs

Tijuana ti 'waːn ə ˌtiːˌə 'waːn-, -'hwaːn-
  ‖ ˌtiːˌə 'waːn ə —Sp [ti 'xwa na]

tike taɪk **tikes** taɪks

tiki 'tiːk i ~s z

tikka 'tiːk ə 'tɪk-
  ˌtikka ma'sala mə 'saːl ə

Tikrit tɪ 'kriːt —Arabic [tɪ 'kriːt]

til *'sesame'* tɪl

'til tɪl *see also* till

tilak 'tɪl æk **~s** s

tilapia tɪ 'læp i̯ ə tə-, -'leɪp- ‖ -'lɑːp- **~s** z

Tilbury, t~ 'tɪl bər̩ i ‖ -ˌber i

tilde 'tɪld ə -i, -eɪ; tɪld **~s** z

Tilden 'tɪld ən

tile taɪᵊl **tiled** taɪᵊld **tiles** taɪᵊlz **tiling** 'taɪl ɪŋ

Tilehurst 'taɪᵊl hɜːst ‖ -hɜːrst

till tɪl *Note: for the prep and conj (not for the noun and verb) there is also an occasional weak form* tᵊl **tilled** tɪld **tilling** 'tɪl ɪŋ **tills** tɪlz

tillage 'tɪl ɪdʒ

Tillamook 'tɪl ə mʊk

tiller, T~ 'tɪl ə ‖ -ᵊr **~s** z

Tilley 'tɪl i

    'Tilley lamp

Tillicoultry ˌtɪl ɪ 'kuːtr i -ə-

Tillie, Tilly 'tɪl i

Tilsit, t~ 'tɪls ɪt 'tɪlz-, §-ət —*Ger* ['tɪl zɪt]

tilt tɪlt **tilted** 'tɪlt ɪd -əd **tilting** 'tɪlt ɪŋ **tilts** tɪlts

tilth tɪlθ

Tilton 'tɪlt ən

Tim tɪm

timbale 'tɪm bᵊl tæm 'baːl, tɪm- —*Fr* [tæ̃ bal] **~s** z

timber 'tɪm bə ‖ -bᵊr **~ed** d **timbering** 'tɪm bər ɪŋ **~s** z

Timberlake 'tɪm bə leɪk ‖ -bᵊr-

timberland, T~ 'tɪm bə lænd ‖ -bᵊr-

timberline 'tɪm bə laɪn ‖ -bᵊr-

timberyard 'tɪm bə jɑːd ‖ -bᵊr jɑːrd **~s** z

timbre 'tæm bə 'tɪm- ‖ -bᵊr —*Fr* [tæ̃ːbʁ] **~s** z

timbrel 'tɪm brᵊl **~s** z

Timbuctoo, Timbuktu ˌtɪm bʌk 'tuː -bək-

time taɪm **timed** taɪmd **times** taɪmz **timing** 'taɪm ɪŋ

    ˌtime and a 'half; ˌtime-and-'motion ˌstudy; 'time bomb; 'time ˌcapsule; 'time clock; 'time exˌposure; 'time fuse; ˌtime immeˈmorial; 'time lag; 'time ˌlimit; 'time lock; 'time maˌchine; ˌtime 'off; 'time sheet; 'time ˌsignal; 'time ˌsignature; 'time span; 'time switch; 'time ˌtrial; 'time warp; 'time zone

time-consuming 'taɪm kən ˌsjuːm ɪŋ §-kɒn-, -ˌsuːm- ‖ -ˌsuːm-

time-honored, time-honoured 'taɪm ˌɒn əd ‖ -ˌɑːn ᵊrd

timekeep|er 'taɪm ˌkiːp ə ‖ -ᵊr **~ers** əz ‖ ᵊrz **~ing** ɪŋ

time-lapse 'taɪm læps

timeless 'taɪm ləs -lɪs **~ly** li **~ness** nəs nɪs

timeline 'taɪm laɪn **~s** z

time|ly 'taɪm |li **~lier** li̯ ə ‖ li̯ᵊr **~liest** li̯ ɪst li̯əst **~liness** li nəs -nɪs

timeous 'taɪm əs **~ly** li

timeout, time-out, time out ˌtaɪm 'aʊt

timepiec|e 'taɪm piːs **~es** ɪz əz

time-poor ˌtaɪm 'pɔː ◂ -'pʊə ‖ -'pʊᵊr ◂ -'pɔːr ◂, -'pʊər ◂

timer 'taɪm ə ‖ -ᵊr **~s** z

Times taɪmz

    ˌTimes 'Roman

timesav|ing 'taɪm ˌseɪv |ɪŋ **~er/s** ə/z ‖ ᵊr/z

timescale 'taɪm skeɪᵊl **~s** z

timeserver 'taɪm ˌsɜːv ə ‖ -ˌsɜːv ᵊr **~s** z

timeserving 'taɪm ˌsɜːv ɪŋ ‖ -ˌsɜːv-

timeshare 'taɪm ʃeə ‖ -ʃer -ʃær **~s** z

time-sharing 'taɪm ˌʃeər ɪŋ ‖ -ˌʃer ɪŋ -ˌʃær-

time-shift 'taɪm ʃɪft **~ed** ɪd əd **~ing** ɪŋ **~s** s

timetabl|e 'taɪm ˌteɪb ᵊl **~ed** d **~es** z **~ing** ɪŋ

timework 'taɪm wɜːk ‖ -wɜːk **~er/s** ə/z ‖ ᵊr/z

timeworn 'taɪm wɔːn ‖ -wɔːrn -woʊrn

Timex *tdmk* 'taɪm eks

timid 'tɪm ɪd §-əd **~ly** li **~ness** nəs nɪs

timidity tɪ 'mɪd ət i -ɪt i ‖ -əṭ i

timing 'taɪm ɪŋ **~s** z

    'timing chain

Timisoara ˌtɪm i 'ʃwɑːr ə ˌtiːm- —*Romanian* Timişoara [ti mi 'ʃoa̯ ra]

Timmie, Timmy 'tɪm i

Timon 'taɪm ən -ɒn

Timor 'tiːm ɔː 'taɪm- ‖ -ɔːr

Timorese ˌtɪm ə 'riːz ◂ -'riːs ◂

timorous 'tɪm ᵊr̩ əs **~ly** li **~ness** nəs nɪs

Timotei *tdmk* 'tɪm ə teɪ

Timothy, t~ 'tɪm əθ i

timpani 'tɪmp ən i -ə niː

timpanist 'tɪm pən ɪst §-əst **~s** s

Timpson 'tɪmps ᵊn

tin tɪn **tinned** tɪnd **tinning** 'tɪn ɪŋ **tins** tɪnz

    ˌtin 'can; ˌtin 'god; ˌtin 'hat; ˌtin 'opener; ˌtin pan 'alley; ˌtin 'whistle

Tina 'tiːn ə

Tinbergen 'tɪn ˌbɜːg ən →'tɪm- ‖ -ˌbɜːg- —*Dutch* ['tɪn bɛr xə]

tinctorial tɪŋk 'tɔːr i̯ əl ‖ -'toʊr-

tincture 'tɪŋk tʃə -ʃə ‖ -tʃᵊr **~d** d **tincturing** 'tɪŋk tʃər ɪŋ -ʃər ɪŋ **~s** z

Tindal 'tɪnd ᵊl

Tindale 'tɪnd ᵊl -erᵊl

Tindall 'tɪnd ᵊl -ɔːl

Tindell 'tɪnd ᵊl 'tɪn del

tinder 'tɪnd ə ‖ -ᵊr

tinderbox 'tɪnd ə bɒks ‖ -ᵊr bɑːks **~es** ɪz əz

tinder-dry ˌtɪnd ə 'draɪ ◂ ‖ -ᵊr-

tine taɪn **tines** taɪnz

tinea 'tɪn i̯ ə

tinfoil 'tɪn fɔɪᵊl

ting, Ting *tdmk* tɪŋ **tinged** tɪŋd **tinging** 'tɪŋ ɪŋ **tings** tɪŋz

tingaling ˌtɪŋ ə 'lɪŋ **~s** z

tinge tɪndʒ **tinged** tɪndʒd **tinges** 'tɪndʒ ɪz -əz **tingeing, tinging** 'tɪndʒ ɪŋ

tinged *past & pp of* **ting**

tinged *past & pp of* **tinge** tɪndʒd

Tingewick 'tɪndʒ wɪk

tingl|e, T~ 'tɪŋ gᵊl **~ed** d **~es** z **~ing** ɪŋ **~y** i

tingly 'tɪŋ gli 'tɪŋ gᵊl i **tinglier** 'tɪŋ gli̯ ə ‖ ᵊr **tingliest** 'tɪŋ gli ɪst ᵊst

Tingwall 'tɪŋ wᵊl

tinhorn 'tɪn hɔːn ‖ -hɔːrn **~s** z

tini... —*see* **tiny**

T

tinker, T~ 'tɪŋk ə ‖ -ᵊr **~ed** d **tinkering**
'tɪŋk ər‿ɪŋ **~s** z
Tinkerbell 'tɪŋk ə bel ‖ -ᵊr-
Tinkertoy *tdmk* 'tɪŋk ə tɔɪ ‖ -ᵊr-
tinkl|e 'tɪŋk ᵊl **~ed** d **~es** z **~ing** ɪŋ
Tinky-Winky ˌtɪŋk i 'wɪŋk i
tinn... —*see* **tin**
Tinney 'tɪn i

TINNITUS

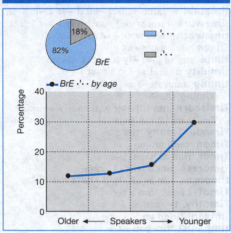

18%
82%
BrE

'...
.'...

● BrE .'·· *by age*

[Line graph: Percentage (y-axis, 0 to 40) against Speakers from Older to Younger (x-axis). Line rises from about 12 at Older, through about 13 and 16 in the middle, to 30 at Younger.]

tinnitus 'tɪn ɪt əs -ət-; tɪ 'naɪt əs, tə- ‖ -ət̬-
— *Preference poll, BrE:* 'tɪn- *82%,* -'naɪt- *18%*
(born since 1981, 30%).
tinny 'tɪn i **tinnier** 'tɪn i ə ‖ ᵊr **tinnies** 'tɪn iz
tinniest 'tɪn i ɪst əst **tinnily** 'tɪn ɪ li -əl i
tinniness 'tɪn i nəs -nɪs
tinplate 'tɪn pleɪt →'tɪm-
tinpot, tin-pot 'tɪn pɒt →'tɪm- ‖ -pɑːt
tinsel 'tɪnˢs ᵊl **~ed, ~led** d **~ing, ~ling** ɪŋ **~s** z
tinselly 'tɪnˢs ᵊl i
Tinseltown 'tɪnˢs ᵊl taʊn
Tinsley 'tɪnz li
tinsmith 'tɪn smɪθ **~s** s
tint tɪnt **tinted** 'tɪnt ɪd -əd ‖ 'tɪnt̬ əd **tinting**
'tɪnt ɪŋ ‖ 'tɪnt̬ ɪŋ **tints** tɪnts
tintack 'tɪn tæk **~s** s
Tintagel tɪn 'tædʒ əl
tinter 'tɪnt ə ‖ 'tɪnt̬ ᵊr **~s** z
Tintern 'tɪnt ən ‖ -ᵊrn
T-intersection 'tiː ˌɪnt ə sek ʃᵊn ‖ -ˌɪnt̬ ᵊr- **~s** z
Tintin 'tɪn tɪn
tintinnabulation ˌtɪn tɪ ˌnæb jʊ ˈleɪʃ ᵊn ˌtə-
‖ -ˌjə- **~s** z
Tintoretto ˌtɪnt ə 'ret əʊ ‖ ˌtɪn tə 'ret̬ oʊ —*It*
[tin to 'ret to] **~s** z
tiny 'taɪn i **tinier** 'taɪn i ə ‖ ᵊr **tiniest**
'taɪn i ɪst əst
-tion *stress-imposing* ʃᵊn — **solution** sə 'luːʃ ᵊn
-'ljuːʃ-
Tio Pepe *tdmk* ˌtiː əʊ 'pep eɪ -i ‖ -oʊ-
-tious *stress-imposing* ʃəs — **fictitious**
fɪk 'tɪʃ əs
tip tɪp **tipped** tɪpt **tipping** 'tɪp ɪŋ **tips** tɪps
tip-and-run ˌtɪp ən 'rʌn →-m-

tipcat 'tɪp kæt
tipi 'tiːp i **~s** z
tip-off 'tɪp ɒf -ɔːf ‖ -ɔːf -ɑːf **~s** s
Tippecanoe ˌtɪp i kə 'nuː ˌ-ə-
tipper 'tɪp ə ‖ -ᵊr **~s** z
'**tipper truck**
Tipperary ˌtɪp ə 'reər i ‖ -'rer i -'rær i
tippet, T~, Tippett 'tɪp ɪt §-ət **~s** s
Tippex, Tipp-Ex *tdmk* 'tɪp eks **~ed** t **~es** ɪz əz
~ing ɪŋ
tippl|e 'tɪp ᵊl **~ed** d **~es** z **~ing** ˌɪŋ
tippler 'tɪp ᵊl ə ‖ ᵊr **~s** z
tippytoes 'tɪp i təʊz ‖ -toʊz
tipstaff 'tɪp stɑːf §-stæf ‖ -stæf **~s** s **tipstaves**
'tɪp steɪvz
tipster 'tɪp stə ‖ -stᵊr **~s** z
tips|y 'tɪps |i **~ier** i ə ‖ i ᵊr **~iest** i ɪst i əst **~ily**
ɪ li əl i **~iness** i nəs i nɪs
tiptoe 'tɪp təʊ ‖ -toʊ **~d** d **~ing** ɪŋ **~s** z
Tipton 'tɪpt ən
tip-top ˌtɪp 'tɒp ◂ ‖ -'tɑːp ◂
Tiptree 'tɪp triː
tip-up 'tɪp ʌp
tirade ₍ˌ₎taɪᵊ 'reɪd tə-, tɪ- ‖ 'taɪᵊr eɪd **~s** z
tiramisu ˌtɪr əm i 'suː ‖ -ə 'mi: suː —*It*
tiramisù [ti ɾa mi 'su]
Tirana tɪ 'rɑːn ə —*Albanian* Tiranë [ti 'ɾa nə]
tire 'taɪᵊ ə ‖ 'taɪ ᵊr **tired** 'taɪ əd ‖ 'taɪ ᵊrd **tires**
'taɪ əz ‖ 'taɪ ᵊrz **tiring** 'taɪᵊr ɪŋ ‖ 'taɪ ᵊr ɪŋ
tired 'taɪ əd ‖ 'taɪ ᵊrd **~ly** li **~ness** nəs nɪs
Tiree ₍ˌ₎taɪᵊ 'riː
tireless 'taɪᵊr ə ləs -lɪs ‖ 'taɪ ᵊr ləs **~ly** li **~ness**
nəs nɪs
Tiresias taɪᵊ 'riːs i æs -'res-, -əs
tiresome 'taɪᵊr ə səm ‖ 'taɪ ᵊr səm **~ly** li **~ness**
nəs nɪs
tiro 'taɪᵊr əʊ ‖ -oʊ **~s** z
Tirol tɪ 'rəʊl tə-, →-'rɒʊl; 'tɪr əl, -əʊl ‖ -'roʊl
—*Ger* [ti 'ʁoːl]
Tirolean ˌtɪr əʊ 'liː ən ◂ tɪ 'rəʊl i ən, tə- ‖ -ə- **~s**
z
Tirolese ˌtɪr əʊ 'liːz ◂ ‖ -ə- -'liːs ◂
Tirpitz 'tɜːp ɪts §-əts ‖ 'tɜːp- —*Ger* ['tɪʁ pɪts]
'**tis** tɪz
tisane tɪ 'zæn tiː- ‖ -'zɑːn **~s** z
Tiscali *tdmk* 'tɪsk əl i
Tishbite 'tɪʃ baɪt **~s** s
Tisiphone taɪ 'sɪf ən i tɪ-
Tissot 'tiːs əʊ ‖ tiː 'soʊ —*Fr* [ti so] **~s** z
tissue 'tɪʃ uː 'tɪs juː, 'tɪʃ juː **~s** z
'**tissue ˌculture**; '**tissue ˌpaper**
tit tɪt **tits** tɪts
ˌtit for 'tat
titan, Titan 'taɪt ᵊn **~s** z
titanate 'taɪt ə neɪt -ᵊn eɪt ‖ -ᵊn eɪt
Titania, t~ tɪ 'tɑːn i ə taɪ-, -'teɪn- ‖ -'teɪn-
titanic, T~ taɪ 'tæn ɪk **~ally** ᵊl i
titanium taɪ 'teɪn i əm tɪ-
titbit 'tɪt bɪt **~s** s
titch tɪtʃ **titches** 'tɪtʃ ɪz -əz
Titchmarsh 'tɪtʃ mɑːʃ ‖ -mɑːrʃ
titch|y 'tɪtʃ |i **~ier** i ə ‖ i ᵊr **~iest** i ɪst i əst
~iness i nəs i nɪs

titer 'ti:t ə 'taɪt- ‖ 'taɪʈ ʳr 'ti:ʈ ʳr ~**s** z
titfer 'tɪt fə ‖ -fʳr ~**s** z
tithe taɪð **tithed** taɪðd **tithes** taɪðz **tithing/s**
  'taɪð ɪŋ/z
Tithonus tɪ 'θəʊn əs taɪ- ‖ -'θoʊn-
titi *monkey* tɪ 'ti: ti: ti: ~**s** z
titi *tree* 'ti: ti: 'taɪ taɪ ~**s** z
Titian, t~ 'tɪʃ ʳn 'tɪʃ i̯ əɪ ~**s** z
Titicaca ˌtɪt ɪ 'kɑːk ə -ˈkɑː kɑː ‖ ˌtɪʈ- —*Sp*
  [ti ti 'ka ka]
titill|ate 'tɪt ɪ l|eɪt -ə-, -ʳl |eɪt ‖ 'tɪʈ ʳl |eɪt
  ~**ated** eɪt ɪd -əd ‖ eɪʈ əd ~**ates** eɪts ~**ating**
  eɪt ɪŋ ‖ eɪʈ ɪŋ
titillation ˌtɪt ɪ 'leɪʃ ʳn -ə-, ˌtɪt ʳl 'eɪʃ-
  ‖ ˌtɪʈ ʳl 'eɪʃ ʳn ~**s** z
titi|vate 'tɪt ɪ |veɪt -ə- ‖ 'tɪʈ- ~**vated** veɪt ɪd
  -əd ‖ veɪʈ əd ~**vates** veɪts ~**vating** veɪt ɪŋ
  ‖ veɪʈ ɪŋ
titivation ˌtɪt ɪ 'veɪʃ ʳn -ə- ‖ ˌtɪʈ- ~**s** z
titlark 'tɪt lɑːk ‖ -lɑːrk ~**s** s
titl|e 'taɪt ʳl ‖ 'taɪʈ ʳl ~**ed** d ~**es** z ~**ing** ɪŋ
  'title deed, ˌ· · '·; 'title page; 'title role,
  ˌ· '·.
titleholder 'taɪt ʳl ˌhəʊld ə →-ˌhɒʊld-
  ‖ 'taɪʈ ʳl ˌhoʊld ʳr ~**s** z
titlist, Titleist *tdmk* 'taɪt ʳl ɪst §-əst ‖ 'taɪʈ- ~**s**
  s
Titmarsh 'tɪt mɑːʃ ‖ -mɑːrʃ
tit|mouse 'tɪt |maʊs ~**mice** maɪs
Titmus 'tɪt məs
Tito 'ti:t əʊ ‖ 'ti:ʈ oʊ ~**ism** ˌɪz əm
titrant 'taɪtr ənt ~**s** s
titr|ate taɪ 'tr|eɪt tɪ-; 'taɪtr |eɪt ‖ 'taɪtr |eɪt
  ~**ated** eɪt ɪd -əd ‖ eɪʈ əd ~**ates** eɪts ~**ating**
  eɪt ɪŋ ‖ eɪʈ ɪŋ
titration taɪ 'treɪʃ ʳn tɪ- ~**s** z
titre 'ti:t ə -taɪt- ‖ 'taɪʈ ʳr 'ti:ʈ ʳr ~**s** z
Tittensor 'tɪt ʳn sə -sɔː ‖ -sʳr -sɔːr
titter 'tɪt ə ‖ 'tɪʈ ʳr ~**ed** d **tittering** 'tɪt ər ɪŋ
  ‖ 'tɪʈ ər ɪŋ ~**s** z
tittiv... —*see* **titiv...**
tittle 'tɪt ʳl ‖ 'tɪʈ ʳl ~**s** z
tittle-tattl|e *n, v* 'tɪt ʳl ˌtæt ʳl ˌ· '··
  ‖ 'tɪʈ ʳl ˌtæʈ ʳl ~**ed** d ~**es** z ~**ing** ɪŋ
tittup 'tɪt əp ‖ 'tɪʈ əp ~**ed, ~ped** t ~**ing, ~ping**
  ɪŋ ~**s** s
titt|y 'tɪt |i ‖ 'tɪʈ |i ~**ies** iz
titubation ˌtɪt ju 'beɪʃ ʳn §ˌtɪʈ ə- ‖ ˌtɪʈ ə-
titular 'tɪtʃ ʊl ə §-əl-; 'tɪt jʊl ə, -jəl- ‖ 'tɪtʃ ʳl ər
  ~**ly** li ~**s** z
titular|y 'tɪtʃ ʊl ər i §-ʳl-; 'tɪt jʊl-, -ˌjəl-
  ‖ 'tɪtʃ ə ler |i ~**ies** iz
Titus 'taɪt əs ‖ 'taɪʈ əs
Tiv tɪv
Tiverton 'tɪv ət ən ‖ -ʳrt ʳn
TiVo *tdmk* 'ti: vəʊ ‖ -voʊ
Tivoli 'tɪv əl i —*It* ['ti: vo li]
Tivy 'taɪv i
Tiwa 'ti: wə ~**s** z
tiz, tizz tɪz
Tizard (i) 'tɪz ɑːd ‖ -ɑːrd, (ii) -əd ‖ -ʳrd
Tizer *tdmk* 'taɪz ə ‖ -ʳr
tizzwazz, tizzwoz 'tɪz wɒz ‖ -wɑːz

tizz|y 'tɪz |i ~**ies** iz
T-junction 'ti: ˌdʒʌŋk ʃʳn ~**s** z
TLC ˌti: el 'si:
Tlingit 'tlɪŋ gɪt -kɪt, §-gət ~**s** s
T-lymphocyte 'ti: ˌlɪmᵖf ə saɪt ~**s** s
tmesis 'tmi:s ɪs 'mi:s-, §-əs; tə 'mi:s-
TNT ˌti: en 'ti:
to *strong form* tu:, *weak forms* tu, tə —*The*
  BrE-oriented EFL learner is advised to use tə
  before a consonant sound, tu *before a vowel*
  sound. Native speakers, however, sometimes
  ignore this distribution, in particular by using
  tə *before a vowel (usually reinforced by a*
  preceding ʔ — *see* HARD ATTACK*) or, in*
  very formal speech, by using tu *even before a*
  consonant. In AmE the weak form tə *is used*
  before both consonants and vowels. In got to,
  ought to, used to, want to, *one* t *may be elided.*
toad təʊd ‖ toʊd **toads** təʊdz ‖ toʊdz
toadflax 'təʊd flæks ‖ 'toʊd- ~**es** ɪz əz
toad-in-the-hole ˌtəʊd ɪn ðə 'həʊl ˌ-ʳn-,
  →-'hɒʊl ‖ ˌtoʊd ʳn ðə 'hoʊl
toadstool 'təʊd stu:l ‖ 'toʊd- ~**s** z
toad|y 'təʊd |i ‖ 'toʊd |i ~**ied** id ~**ies** iz ~**ying**
  i ɪŋ
to-and-fro ˌtu: ən 'frəʊ ‖ -'froʊ
toast təʊst ‖ toʊst **toasted** 'təʊst ɪd -əd
  ‖ 'toʊst əd **toasting** 'təʊst ɪŋ ‖ 'toʊst ɪŋ
  toasts təʊsts ‖ toʊsts
  'toasting fork; 'toast rack
toaster 'təʊst ə ‖ 'toʊst ʳr ~**s** z
toastie 'təʊst i ‖ 'toʊst i ~**s** z
toastmaster 'təʊst ˌmɑːst ə §-ˌmæst-
  ‖ 'toʊst ˌmæst ʳr ~**s** z
toastmistress 'təʊst ˌmɪs trəs -trɪs ‖ 'toʊst-
  ~**es** ɪz əz
toast|y 'təʊst |i ‖ 'toʊst |i ~**ier** i ə ‖ i ʳr ~**iest**
  i ɪst i̯ əst
tobacco tə 'bæk əʊ ‖ -oʊ ~**es, ~s** z
tobacconist tə 'bæk ən ɪst §-əst ~**s** s
Tobago tə 'beɪg əʊ ‖ -oʊ
Tobagonian ˌtəʊb ə 'gəʊn i̯ ən
  ‖ ˌtoʊb ə 'goʊn- ~**s** z
-to-be tə 'bi: tu- — **mother-to-be**
  ˌmʌð ə tə 'bi: -tu'·. ‖ ˌ·ʳr-
Tobermory ˌtəʊb ə 'mɔːr i ‖ ˌtoʊb ʳr-
Tobey 'təʊb i ‖ 'toʊb i
ToBI 'təʊb i ‖ 'toʊb i
Tobias tə 'baɪ əs
Tobin 'təʊb ɪn §-ən ‖ 'toʊb-
Tobit 'təʊb ɪt §-ət ‖ 'toʊb-
Toblerone *tdmk* ˌtəʊb lə 'rəʊn '···
  ‖ ˌtoʊb lə 'roʊn
toboggan tə 'bɒg ən ‖ -'bɑːg- ~**ed** d ~**er/s** ə/z
  ‖ ʳr/z ~**ing** ɪŋ ~**ist/s** ɪst/s §əst/s ‖ əst/s ~**s** z
Tobruk tə 'brʊk
Tob|y, tob|y 'təʊb |i ‖ 'toʊb |i ~**ies, ~y's** iz
  'toby jug
toccata tə 'kɑːt ə tɒ- ‖ -'kɑːʈ ə —*It*
  [tok 'ka: ta] ~**s** z
Toc H ˌtɒk 'eɪtʃ §-'heɪtʃ ‖ ˌtɑːk-
Tocharian tɒ 'kɑːr i̯ ən tə-, -'keər-
  ‖ toʊ 'ker i̯ ən -'kær- ~**s** z

tocopherol tɒ 'kɒf ə rɒl tə- ‖ toʊ 'kɑːf ə rɔːl
  -rɑːl, -roʊl
Tocqueville 'tɒk vɪl 'təʊk- ‖ 'toʊk- —Fr
  [tɔk vil]
tocsin 'tɒks ɪn §-ən ‖ 'tɑːks ən (= toxin) ~s z
tod, Tod tɒd ‖ tɑːd
today tə 'deɪ tu- ~'s z
Todd tɒd ‖ tɑːd
toddl|e 'tɒd əl ‖ 'tɑːd əl ~ed d ~es z ~ing ɪŋ
toddler 'tɒd əl_ə ‖ 'tɑːd əl_ər ~s z
todd|y 'tɒd |i ‖ 'tɑːd |i ~ies iz
todger 'tɒdʒ ə ‖ 'tɑːdʒ ər ~s z
Todhunter 'tɒd ˌhʌnt ə ‖ 'tɑːd ˌhʌnt ər
to-die-for tə 'daɪ fɔː ‖ -fɔːr -fɜr
Todman 'tɒd mən →'tɒb- ‖ 'tɑːd-
Todmorden 'tɒd məd ən -mɔːd-
  ‖ 'tɑːd mɔːrd ən
to-do tə 'duː tu- ~s z
tody 'təʊd |i 'toʊd |i ~ies iz
toe təʊ ‖ toʊ toed təʊd ‖ toʊd toeing 'təʊ ɪŋ
  ‖ 'toʊ ɪŋ toes təʊz ‖ toʊz
  'toe cap
toe-curling 'təʊ ˌkɜːl ɪŋ ‖ 'toʊ ˌkɜːl ɪŋ
TOEFL tdmk 'təʊf əl ‖ 'toʊf əl
toehold 'təʊ həʊld →-hɒʊld ‖ 'toʊ hoʊld ~s z
TOEIC tdmk 'təʊ ɪk ‖ 'toʊ ɪk
toe-in 'təʊ ɪn ‖ 'toʊ- ~s z
toenail 'təʊ neɪəl ‖ 'toʊ- ~s z
toerag 'təʊ ræg ‖ 'toʊ- ~s z
toe-to-toe ˌtəʊ tə 'təʊ ‖ ˌtoʊ tə 'toʊ
toff tɒf ‖ tɑːf toffs tɒfs ‖ tɑːfs
toffee 'tɒf i ‖ 'tɑːf i 'tɔːf- ~s z
  'toffee ˌapple, ˌ· '··
toffee-nosed 'tɒf i nəʊzd ˌ· '··
  ‖ ˌtɑːf i 'noʊzd ◂ ˌtɔːf-
toff|y 'tɒf |i ‖ 'tɑːf |i 'tɔːf- ~ies iz
Toft, toft tɒft ‖ tɑːft tɔːft
Tofts tɒfts ‖ tɑːfts tɔːfts
tofu 'təʊf uː ‖ 'toʊf uː —Jp [to,o 'ɸɯ]
tog tɒg ‖ tɑːg tɔːg togs tɒgz ‖ tɑːgz tɔːgz
toga 'təʊg ə ‖ 'toʊg ə ~ed d ~s z
together tə 'geð ə tu- ‖ -ər ~ness nəs nɪs
togethering tə 'geð ər_ɪŋ
toggl|e 'tɒg əl ‖ 'tɑːg əl ~ed d ~es z ~ing ɪŋ
Togo 'təʊg əʊ ‖ 'toʊg oʊ ~land lænd
Togolese ˌtəʊg əʊ 'liːz ◂ ‖ ˌtoʊg ə- -oʊ-, -'liːs
Tóibín təʊ 'biːn ‖ toʊ- —Irish [ˌtoː bʲiːnʲ]
toil tɔɪəl toiled tɔɪəld toiling 'tɔɪəl ɪŋ toils
  tɔɪəlz
toile twɑːl
toiler 'tɔɪəl ə ‖ -ər ~s z
toil|et 'tɔɪl |ət -ɪt ‖ -|ət ~eted ɪt ɪd §ət-, -əd
  ‖ ət əd ~eting ɪt ɪŋ §ət- ‖ ət ɪŋ ~ets ɪts §əts
  ‖ əts
  'toilet ˌpaper; 'toilet roll; 'toilet
  ˌtraining; 'toilet ˌwater
toiletr|y 'tɔɪl ətr |i ‖ -ɪtr- ~ies iz
toilette twɑː 'let —Fr [twa lɛt]
toilet-trained 'tɔɪl ət treɪnd -ɪt-
toilsome 'tɔɪəl səm ~ly li ~ness nəs nɪs
toilworn 'tɔɪəl wɔːn ‖ -wɔːrn -woʊrn

to-ing and fro-ing ˌtuː ɪŋ ən 'frəʊ ɪŋ
  ‖ -'froʊ ɪŋ to-ings and fro-ings
  ˌtuː ɪŋz ən 'frəʊ ɪŋz ‖ -'froʊ ɪŋz
tokamak 'təʊk ə mæk 'tɒk- ‖ 'toʊk- 'tɑːk- ~s s
Tokay, tokay təʊ 'keɪ tɒ-, -'kaɪ, '· · ‖ toʊ-
  —Hung ['tɒ kɒj] ~s z
toke təʊk ‖ toʊk tokes təʊks ‖ toʊks
Tokelau 'təʊk ə laʊ 'tɒk- ‖ 'toʊk-
token 'təʊk ən ‖ 'toʊk ən ~ed d ~ing ɪŋ ~ism
  ˌɪz əm ~s z
Tokharian tɒ 'kɑːr i_ən tə-, -'keər-
  ‖ toʊ 'ker i_ən -'kær- ~s z
Toklas 'təʊk ləs 'təʊk- ‖ 'toʊk-
Tok Pisin ˌtɒk 'pɪz ɪn §-ən ‖ ˌtɑːk- ˌtɔːk-
Tokyo 'təʊk i_əʊ ‖ 'toʊk i_oʊ —Jp [to,o kjoo]
tola 'təʊl ə ‖ 'toʊl ə ~s z
tolbutamide tɒl 'bjuːt ə maɪd ‖ tɑːl 'bjuːt̬-
told təʊld →tɒʊld ‖ toʊld
tole təʊl →tɒʊl ‖ toʊl —Fr tôle [toːl]
Toledo (i) tə 'liːd əʊ ‖ -oʊ, (ii) tɒ 'leɪd əʊ tə-
  ‖ toʊ 'leɪd oʊ —The place in OH is (i), as is
  the trade name for a car. The place in Spain is
  usually (ii) in BrE. —Sp [to 'le ðo]
tolerab|le 'tɒl ər_əb əl ‖ 'tɑːl- ~leness əl nəs
  -nɪs ~ly li
toleranc|e 'tɒl ər ən's -'r_ən's ‖ 'tɑːl- ~es ɪz əz
tolerant 'tɒl ər ənt -'r_ənt ‖ 'tɑːl- ~ly li
tole|rate 'tɒl ə |reɪt ‖ 'tɑːl- ~rated reɪt ɪd -əd
  ‖ reɪt̬ əd ~rates reɪts ~rating reɪt ɪŋ ‖ reɪt̬ ɪŋ
toleration ˌtɒl ə 'reɪʃ ən ‖ ˌtɑːl-
Tolkien 'tɒl kiːn ‖ 'toʊl- 'tɑːl-
toll təʊl →tɒʊl, §tɒl ‖ toʊl tolled təʊld
  →tɒʊld, §tɒld ‖ toʊld (usually = told) tolling
  'təʊl ɪŋ →'tɒʊl-, §'tɒl- ‖ 'toʊl ɪŋ tolls təʊlz
  →tɒʊlz, §tɒlz ‖ toʊlz
  'toll bridge
toll|booth 'təʊl |buːð →'tɒʊl-, 'tɒl-, -buːθ
  ‖ 'toʊl |buːθ ~booths buːðz buːθs ‖ buːθs
Tollemache 'tɒl mæʃ -mɑːʃ ‖ 'tɑːl-
Tolleshunt 'təʊlz hʌnt →'tɒʊlz- ‖ 'toʊlz-
  Tolleshunt 'd'Arcy 'dɑːs i ‖ 'dɑːrs i
toll-free ˌtəʊl 'friː ◂ →ˌtɒʊl- ‖ ˌtoʊl-
tollgate 'təʊl geɪt →'tɒʊl-, §'tɒl- ‖ 'toʊl- ~s s
toll|house 'təʊl |haʊs →'tɒʊl-, §'tɒl- ‖ 'toʊl-
  ~houses haʊz ɪz -əz
tollway 'təʊl weɪ →'tɒʊl- ‖ 'toʊl- ~s z
Tolman 'təʊl mən →'tɒʊl- ‖ 'toʊl-
Tolpuddle 'tɒl ˌpʌd əl ‖ 'tɑːl- —locally also
  -ˌpɪd-
Tolstoy 'tɒl stɔɪ ‖ 'toʊl- 'tɑːl-, ˌ·'· —Russ
  [tʌɫ 'stɔj]
Toltec 'tɒl tek ‖ 'toʊl- 'tɑːl-
tolu tɒ 'luː təʊ-, -'ljuː ‖ tɑː 'luː tɔː-, tə-
toluene 'tɒl ju iːn ‖ 'tɑːl-
toluic tɒ 'ljuː ɪk təʊ-, -'luː- ‖ tə 'luː ɪk
Tolworth 'tɒl wəθ 'təʊl-, -wɜːθ ‖ 'tɑːl wɜːθ
Tom, tom tɒm ‖ tɑːm toms, Tom's tɒmz
  ‖ tɑːmz
  ˌTom 'Collins; ˌTom, ˌDick, and 'Harry;
  ˌTom 'Thumb
tomahawk 'tɒm ə hɔːk ‖ 'tɑːm- -hɑːk ~s s
Tomalin 'tɒm əl ɪn §-ən ‖ 'tɑːm-
tomato tə 'mɑːt əʊ ‖ tə 'meɪt̬ oʊ (*) ~es z

tomb tuːm *(!)* **tombs** tuːmz

tombac ˈtɒm bæk ‖ ˈtɑːm-

tombola tɒm ˈbəʊl ə ˈtɒm bəl ə ‖ tɑːm ˈboʊl ə

tomboy ˈtɒm bɔɪ ‖ ˈtɑːm- ~**s** z

Tombs tuːmz

tombstone, T~ ˈtuːm stəʊn ‖ -stoʊn ~**s** z

tomcat ˈtɒm kæt ‖ ˈtɑːm- ~**s** s

tome təʊm ‖ toʊm **tomes** təʊmz ‖ toʊmz

-tome təʊm ‖ toʊm — **microtome**
ˈmaɪk rəʊ təʊm ‖ -rə toʊm

tomentose tə ˈment əʊs -əʊz; ˈtəʊm ən təʊs
‖ toʊ ˈment oʊs ˈtoʊm ən toʊs

tomfool ˌtɒm ˈfuːl ◄ ‖ ˌtɑːm-

tomfooler|y ⁽₁⁾ˌtɒm ˈfuːl ər |i ‖ ˌtɑːm- ~**ies** iz

-tomical ˈtɒm ɪk ᵊl ‖ ˈtɑːm- — **anatomical**
ˌæn ə ˈtɒm ɪk ᵊl ◄ ‖ -ˈtɑːm-

Tomintoul ˌtɒm ɪn ˈtaʊl -ən- ‖ ˌtɑːm-

Tomkins ˈtɒmᵖ kɪnz ‖ ˈtɑːmᵖ-

Tomlin ˈtɒm lɪn §-lən ‖ ˈtɑːm-

Tomlinson ˈtɒm lɪn sən §-lən- ‖ ˈtɑːm-

Tommie, Tommy, tommie, tommy ˈtɒm i
‖ ˈtɑːm i **tommies, Tommy's** ˈtɒm iz
‖ ˈtɑːm iz
ˈtommy gun

tommyrot ˈtɒm i rɒt ‖ ˈtɑːm i rɑːt

tomogram ˈtəʊm ə græm ˈtɒm- ‖ ˈtoʊm- ~**s** z

tomography tə ˈmɒg rəf i ‖ toʊ ˈmɑːg-

TOMORROW

-ˈmɑːr-

-ˈmɔːr-

65%   35%

AmE

tomorrow tə ˈmɒr əʊ tu- ‖ tə ˈmɑːr oʊ -ˈmɔːr-
—*In* ~ morning, ~ night *also* -ə, -u; *in* ~
afternoon, ~ evening *also* -**u** — *Preference
poll, AmE:* -ˈmɑːr- *65%,* -ˈmɔːr- *35%.* ~**s,** ~**'s** z
to,morrow ,after'noon; to,morrow
'evening; to,morrow 'morning;
to,morrow 'night

Tompion ˈtɒmp i ̱ən ‖ ˈtɑːmp-

Tomp|kin ˈtɒmp| kɪn ‖ ˈtɑːmp|- ~**kins** kɪnz
~**kinson** kɪn sən

Toms tɒmz ‖ tɑːmz

Tomsk tɒmᵖsk ‖ tɔːmᵖsk tɑːmᵖsk —*Russ*
[tɔmsk]

tomtit ˈtɒm tɪt ˌ·ˈ· ‖ ˈtɑːm- ~**s** s

tom-tom ˈtɒm tɒm ‖ ˈtɑːm tɑːm ~**s** z

-tomy *stress-imposing* təm i — **anatomy**
ə ˈnæt əm i ‖ -ˈnæt̬-

ton *French word 'style'* tɔ̃ ‖ tɔːn toʊn —*Fr* [tɔ̃]

ton *'unit of weight, displacement, or speed'* tʌn
(= *tun*) **tons** tʌnz

tonal ˈtəʊn ᵊl ‖ ˈtoʊn ᵊl ~**ly** i

tonalit|y təʊ ˈnæl ət |i -ɪt i ‖ toʊ ˈnæl ət̬ |i
~**ies** iz

Tonbridge ˈtʌn brɪdʒ →ˈtʌm-

Ton-du *place in MidGlam* ˌtɒn ˈdiː ‖ ˌtɔːn-

tone, Tone təʊn ‖ toʊn **toned** təʊnd ‖ toʊnd
tones təʊnz ‖ toʊnz **toning** ˈtəʊn ɪŋ
‖ ˈtoʊn ɪŋ
'tone ˌlanguage; 'tone ˌpoem

tone-deaf ˌtəʊn ˈdef ◄ ‖ ˈtoʊn def ~**ness** nəs
nɪs

toneless ˈtəʊn ləs -lɪs ‖ ˈtoʊn- ~**ly** li ~**ness**
nəs nɪs

tonematic ˌtəʊn ɪ ˈmæt ɪk ◄ -iː-, -ə-
‖ ˌtoʊn ə ˈmæt̬ ɪk ◄

toneme ˈtəʊn iːm ‖ ˈtoʊn- ~**s** z

tonemic təʊ ˈniːm ɪk ‖ toʊ- ~**ally** ᵊl_i ~**s** s

toner ˈtəʊn ə ‖ ˈtoʊn ᵊr ~**s** z

tonetic təʊ ˈnet ɪk ‖ toʊ ˈnet̬ ɪk ~**ally** ᵊl_i ~**s** s

ton|ey ˈtəʊn| i ‖ ˈtoʊn| i ~**ier** i ə ‖ i ᵊr ~**iest**
i ˌɪst i ˌəst

Tonfanau tɒn ˈvæn aɪ ‖ tɑːn- —*Welsh*
[ton ˈva nai, -nai, -ne, -na]

tong, Tong tɒŋ ‖ tɑːŋ tɔːŋ **tongs** tɒŋz ‖ tɑːŋz
tɔːŋz

tonga ˈtɒŋ gə ‖ ˈtɑːŋ- ~**s** z

Tonga *African people and language* ˈtɒŋ gə
‖ ˈtɑːŋ-

Tonga *place in Polynesia* ˈtɒŋ ə -gə ‖ ˈtɑːŋ-

Tongan ˈtɒŋ ən -gən ‖ ˈtɑːŋ- ~**s** z

Tonge *surname(i)* tɒŋ ‖ tɑːŋ, *(ii)* tɒndʒ
‖ tɑːndʒ, *(iii)* tʌŋ

Tonge *placename* tɒŋ ‖ tɑːŋ

tongs tɒŋz ‖ tɑːŋz tɔːŋz

tongue, T~ tʌŋ §tɒŋ **tongued** tʌŋd **tongues**
tʌŋz **tonguing** ˈtʌŋ ɪŋ
'tongue ˌtwister

tongue-in-cheek ˌtʌŋ ɪn ˈtʃiːk ◄ §ˌtɒŋ-

tongue-lashing ˈtʌŋ ˌlæʃ ɪŋ §ˈtɒŋ-

tongue-tied ˈtʌŋ taɪd §ˈtɒŋ-

Toni ˈtəʊn i ‖ ˈtoʊn i

Tonia ˈtəʊn i ə ‖ ˈtoʊn jə

Tonibell *tdmk* ˈtəʊn i bel ‖ ˈtoʊn-

tonic ˈtɒn ɪk ‖ ˈtɑːn ɪk ~**s** s
ˌtonic ˌsol-'fa; 'tonic ˌwater

tonicit|y təʊ ˈnɪs ət |i tɒ-, -ɪt i ‖ toʊ ˈnɪs ət̬ |i
~**ies** iz

tonight tə ˈnaɪt tu- ~**'s** s

tonite *'tonight'* tə ˈnaɪt

tonite *n 'explosive'* ˈtəʊn aɪt ‖ ˈtoʊn-

tonka, Tonka ˈtɒŋk ə ‖ ˈtɑːŋk ə
'tonka bean

Tonkin *part of Vietnam* ˌtɒn ˈkɪn →ˌtɒŋ-
‖ ˌtɑːn- →ˌtɑːŋ-

Tonkin *family name* ˈtɒŋk ɪn §-ən ‖ ˈtɑːŋk-

Tonks tɒŋks ‖ tɑːŋks

tonnag|e ˈtʌn ɪdʒ ~**es** ɪz əz

tonne tʌn tɒn **tonnes** tʌnz tɒnz

tonneau ˈtɒn əʊ ‖ tə ˈnoʊ ˈtɑːn oʊ ~**s,** ~**x** z

tonogenesis ˌtəʊn əʊ ˈdʒen əs ɪs -ɪs ɪs, §-əs
‖ ˌtoʊn oʊ-

tonology təʊ ˈnɒl ədʒ i ‖ toʊ ˈnɑːl-

tonsil ˈtɒn⌀s ᵊl -ɪl ‖ ˈtɑːn⌀s ᵊl ~**s** z

tonsillectom|y ˌtɒn⌀s ə ˈlekt əm |i ˌ·ɪ-
‖ ˌtɑːn⌀s- ~**ies** iz

tonsillitis ˌtɒn⌀s ə ˈlaɪt ɪs -ɪ-, §-əs
‖ ˌtɑːn⌀s ə ˈlaɪt̬ əs

tonsorial tɒn ˈsɔːr i_əl ‖ tɑːn- -ˈsoʊr-

tonsure 'tɒnʃ ə 'tɒnˈs jʊə ‖ 'tɑːnˈʃ ᵊr **~d** d
 tonsuring 'tɒnʃ ər ɪŋ 'tɒnˈs jʊər ɪŋ
 ‖ 'tɑːnˈʃ ər ɪŋ **~s** z
tontine 'tɒnt aɪn -iːn; ˌtɒn 'tiːn ‖ 'tɑːnt iːn
 tɑːn 'tiːn **~s** z
Tonto 'tɒnt əʊ ‖ 'tɑːnt̬ oʊ
ton-up ˌtʌn 'ʌp ◂
tonus 'təʊn əs ‖ 'toʊn-
ton|y 'təʊn| i ‖ 'toʊn| i **~ier** i ə ‖ i ᵊr **~iest**
 i ɪst i əst
Tony 'təʊn i ‖ 'toʊn i **Tonies, Tony's** 'təʊn iz
 ‖ 'toʊn iz
Tonypandy ˌtɒn ə 'pænd i ˌtəʊn-, -i- ‖ ˌtɑːn-
 —*Welsh* [tɒn ə 'pan di]
Tonyrefail ˌtɒn i 'rev aɪᵊl ‖ ˌtɑːn- —*Welsh*
 [tɒn ər 'e vaɪl]
too tuː —*NB this word has no weak form*
toodle-oo ˌtuːd ᵊl 'uː
toodle-pip ˌtuːd ᵊl 'pɪp
Toogood 'tuː gʊd
took tʊk §tuːk
Took, Tooke tʊk §tuːk
tool tuːl **tooled** tuːld **tooling** 'tuːl ɪŋ **tools**
 tuːlz
toolbar 'tuːl bɑː ‖ -bɑːr **~s** z
toolbox 'tuːl bɒks ‖ -bɑːks **~es** ɪz əz
Tooley 'tuːl i
tool-maker 'tuːl ˌmeɪk ə ‖ -ᵊr **~s** z
toolshed 'tuːl ʃed **~s** z
toon tuːn **toons** tuːnz
toonie 'tuːn i **~s** z
toot *'toilet'; 'paper bag'* tʊt **toots** tʊts
toot *'sound (horn)'; 'spree'* tuːt **tooted** 'tuːt ɪd
 -əd ‖ 'tuːt̬ əd **tooting** 'tuːt ɪŋ ‖ 'tuːt̬ ɪŋ **toots**
 tuːts
Tootal *tdmk* 'tuːt ᵊl ‖ 'tuːt̬ ᵊl
tooth, Tooth tuːθ §tʊθ **teeth** tiːθ **toothed**
 tuːθt tuːðd, §tʊθt **toothing** 'tuːθ ɪŋ §'tʊθ-
 tooths tuːθs §tʊθs
 'tooth ˌpowder
toothache 'tuːθ eɪk §'tʊθ- **~s** s
toothbrush 'tuːθ brʌʃ §'tʊθ- **~es** ɪz əz
toothcomb 'tuːθ kəʊm §'tʊθ- ‖ -koʊm **~s** z
toothed *adj* tuːθt tuːðd, §tʊθt ‖ 'tuːθ əd
Toothill 'tuːt hɪl
toothless 'tuːθ ləs §'tʊθ-, -lɪs **~ly** li **~ness** nəs
 nɪs
toothmug 'tuːθ mʌg §'tʊθ- **~s** z
toothpaste 'tuːθ peɪst §'tʊθ- **~s** s
toothpick 'tuːθ pɪk §'tʊθ- **~s** s
toothsome 'tuːθ səm §'tʊθ- **~ly** li **~ness** nəs
 nɪs
toothwort 'tuːθ wɜːt §'tʊθ-, §-wɔːt ‖ -wɜːt
 -wɔːrt **~s** s
tooth|y 'tuːθ |i §'tʊθ- **~ier** i ə ‖ i ᵊr **~iest** i ɪst
 i əst **~ily** i li əl i **~iness** i nəs i nɪs
Tooting 'tuːt ɪŋ ‖ 'tuːt̬ ɪŋ
tootl|e 'tuːt ᵊl ‖ 'tuːt̬ ᵊl **~ed** d **~es** z **~ing** ˌɪŋ
toots tuːts tʊts
toots|ie, toots|y 'tʊts |i 'tuːts- **~ies** iz
Toowoomba tə 'wʊm bə tu-

top tɒp ‖ tɑːp **topped** tɒpt ‖ tɑːpt **topping**
 'tɒp ɪŋ ‖ 'tɑːp ɪŋ **tops** tɒps ‖ tɑːps
 ˌtop 'brass; ˌtop 'dog; ˌtop 'drawer; ˌtop
 'hat
Topa Inca 'təʊp ᵊ ˌɪŋk ə ‖ 'toʊp-
topaz 'təʊp æz ‖ 'toʊp- **~es** ɪz əz
top-class ˌtɒp 'klɑːs ◂ §-'klæs ◂ ‖ ˌtɑːp 'klæs ◂
Topcliff, Topcliffe 'tɒp klɪf ‖ 'tɑːp-
topcoat 'tɒp kəʊt ‖ 'tɑːp koʊt **~s** s
top-down ˌtɒp 'daʊn ◂ ‖ ˌtɑːp-
top-dress ˌtɒp 'dres '· · ‖ 'tɑːp dres **~ed** t **~es**
 ɪz əz **~ing/s** ɪŋ/z
tope, Tope təʊp ‖ toʊp **toped** təʊpt ‖ toʊpt
 topes təʊps ‖ toʊps **toping** 'təʊp ɪŋ
 ‖ 'toʊp ɪŋ
topee 'təʊp iː -i ‖ 'toʊp iː toʊ 'piː **~s** z
Topeka təʊ 'piːk ə ‖ tə-
top-end 'tɒp end ‖ 'tɑːp-
top-flight 'tɒp 'flaɪt ◂ ‖ ˌtɑːp-
topgallant tɒp 'gæl ənt tə- ‖ ˌtɑːp- —*naut* tə-
top-grossing 'tɒp ˌgrəʊs ɪŋ ‖ 'tɑːp ˌgroʊs ɪŋ
Topham 'tɒp əm ‖ 'tɑːp-
top-heav|y ˌtɒp 'hev |i ◂ ‖ 'tɑːp ˌhev |i
 ~iness i nəs i nɪs
Tophet 'təʊf et ‖ 'toʊf-
toph|us 'təʊf |əs ‖ 'toʊf- **~i** aɪ
topi 'təʊp iː -i ‖ 'toʊp iː toʊ 'piː **~s** z
topiar|y 'təʊp i ər |i ‖ 'toʊp i er |i **~ies** iz
topic 'tɒp ɪk ‖ 'tɑːp ɪk **~s** s
topical 'tɒp ɪk ᵊl ‖ 'tɑːp- **~ly** ˌi
topicalis... —*see* **topicaliz...**
topicality ˌtɒp ɪ 'kæl ət i §ˌ·ə-, -ɪt i
 ‖ ˌtɑːp ə 'kæl ət̬ i
topicalization ˌtɒp ɪk ᵊl aɪ 'zeɪʃ ᵊn -ɪ'··
 ‖ ˌtɑːp ɪk ᵊl ə-
topicaliz|e 'tɒp ɪk ə laɪz -ᵊl aɪz ‖ 'tɑːp- **~ed** d
 ~es ɪz əz **~ing** ɪŋ
topknot 'tɒp nɒt ‖ 'tɑːp nɑːt **~s** s
Toplady 'tɒp ˌleɪd i ‖ 'tɑːp-
topless 'tɒp ləs -lɪs ‖ 'tɑːp-
top-level ˌtɒp 'lev ᵊl ◂ ‖ ˌtɑːp-
topmast 'tɒp mɑːst -məst, §-mæst ‖ 'tɑːp mæst
topmost 'tɒp məʊst ‖ 'tɑːp moʊst
topnotch ˌtɒp 'nɒtʃ ◂ ‖ ˌtɑːp 'nɑːtʃ ◂
topo 'tɒp əʊ ‖ 'tɑːp oʊ **~s** z
topo- *comb. form*
 with stress-neutral suffix |tɒp ə ‖ |tɑːp ə
 — **toponymic** ˌtɒp ə 'nɪm ɪk ◂ ‖ ˌtɑːp-
 with stress-imposing suffix tə 'pɒ+ tɒ-
 ‖ tə 'pɑː+ — **toponymy** tə 'pɒn əm i tɒ-,
 -ɪm i ‖ -'pɑːn-
top-of-the-line ˌtɒp əv ðə 'laɪn ◂ ‖ ˌtɑːp-
top-of-the-range ˌtɒp əv ðə 'reɪndʒ ◂ ‖ ˌtɑːp-
topographer tə 'pɒg rəf ə tɒ- ‖ tə 'pɑːg rəf ᵊr
 ~s z
topographical ˌtɒp ə 'græf ɪk ᵊl ◂ ‖ ˌtɑːp- **~ly**
 ˌi
topograph|y tə 'pɒg rəf |i tɒ- ‖ -'pɑːg- **~ies** iz
topological ˌtɒp ə 'lɒdʒ ɪk ᵊl ◂
 ‖ ˌtɑːp ə 'lɑːdʒ- **~ly** ˌi
topologist tə 'pɒl ədʒ ɪst tɒ-, §-əst ‖ -'pɑːl- **~s**
 s
topolog|y tə 'pɒl ədʒ |i tɒ- ‖ -'pɑːl- **~ies** iz

Topolsky tə ˈpɒl ski ‖ -ˈpɑːl-

toponym ˈtɒp ə nɪm ‖ ˈtɑːp- ~s z

toponymy tə ˈpɒn əm i tɒ-, -ɪm i ‖ -ˈpɑːn-

top|os ˈtɒp |ɒs ‖ ˈtoʊp |ɑːs ~oi ɔɪ

topper, T~ ˈtɒp ə ‖ ˈtɑːp ³r ~s z

topping, T~ ˈtɒp ɪŋ ‖ ˈtɑːp ɪŋ ~s z

topping-out ˌtɒp ɪŋ ˈaʊt ‖ ˌtɑːp-

toppl|e ˈtɒp ³l ‖ ˈtɑːp ³l ~ed d ~es z ~ing ɪŋ

top-quality ˌtɒp ˈkwɒl ət i ◂ -ɪt i ◂
‖ ˌtɑːp ˈkwɑːl ət̬ i ◂

top-|ranked ˌtɒp |ˈræŋkt ◂ ‖ ˌtɑːp- ~ranking
ˈræŋk ɪŋ ◂

top-rated ˌtɒp ˈreɪt ɪd ◂ -əd ◂ ‖ ˌtɑːp ˈreɪt̬ əd ◂

topsail ˈtɒp seɪ³l -s³l ‖ ˈtɑːp- —naut -s³l ~s z

top-secret ˌtɒp ˈsiːk rət ◂ -rɪt ‖ ˌtɑːp-

Topsham ˈtɒps əm ˈtɒpʃ- ‖ ˈtɑːps-

Topshop ˈtɒp ʃɒp ‖ ˈtɑːp ʃɑːp

topside ˈtɒp saɪd ‖ ˈtɑːp-

Topsider tdmk ˈtɒp saɪd ə ‖ ˈtɑːp saɪd ³r ~s z

topsoil ˈtɒp sɔɪ³l ‖ ˈtɑːp- ~s z

topspin ˈtɒp spɪn ‖ ˈtɑːp-

topspinner ˈtɒp spɪn ə ‖ -³r ~s z

Topsy ˈtɒps i ‖ ˈtɑːps i

topsy-turv|y ˌtɒps i ˈtɜːv |i ◂
‖ ˌtɑːps i ˈtɜːv |i ◂ ~idom i dəm ~iness i nəs
i nɪs

top-up n ˈtɒp ʌp ‖ ˈtɑːp- ~s s

toque təʊk ‖ toʊk (= toke) **toques** təʊks
‖ toʊks

tor tɔː ‖ tɔːr **tors** tɔːz ‖ tɔːrz

Torah ˈtɔːr ə ˈtəʊ rə; tɔː ˈrɑː ‖ ˈtoʊr- —Hebrew
[tɔ ˈra]

Torbay ˌtɔː ˈbeɪ ◂ ‖ ˌtɔːr-

torch tɔːtʃ ‖ tɔːrtʃ **torched** tɔːtʃt ‖ tɔːrtʃt
torches ˈtɔːtʃ ɪz -əz ‖ ˈtɔːrtʃ əz **torching**
ˈtɔːtʃ ɪŋ ‖ ˈtɔːrtʃ ɪŋ

torch-bearer ˈtɔːtʃ ˌbeər ə ‖ ˈtɔːrtʃ ˌber ³r
-ˌbær- ~s z

torchlight ˈtɔːtʃ laɪt ‖ ˈtɔːrtʃ-

Torcross ˌtɔː ˈkrɒs -ˈkrɔːs ‖ ˌtɔːr ˈkrɔːs -ˈkrɑːs

Tordoff ˈtɔːd ɒf ‖ ˈtɔːrd ɑːf

tore tɔː ‖ tɔːr toʊr

toreador ˈtɒr i ə dɔː ‖ ˈtɔːr i ə dɔːr ~s z

torero tɒ ˈreər əʊ tə- ‖ tə ˈrer oʊ ~s z

Torfaen ˌtɔː ˈvaɪn ‖ ˌtɔːr- —Welsh [tɔr ˈvain,
-ˈvaɪn]

tori ˈtɔːr aɪ ‖ ˈtoʊr-

toric ˈtɒr ɪk ˈtɔːr- ‖ ˈtɔːr ɪk ˈtɑːr-, ˈtoʊr-

Torie... —see **Tory**

torii ˈtɔːr i iː ‖ ˈtoʊr- —Jp [to ˌrii]

Torino tə ˈriːn əʊ ‖ -oʊ —It [to ˈri no]

torment n ˈtɔː ment ‖ ˈtɔːr- ~s s

tor|ment v ₍ₜ₎tɔː |ˈment ‖ ₍ₜ₎tɔːr |ˈment ··
~**mented/ly** ˈment ɪd /li -əd ‖ ˈment̬-
~**menting/ly** ˈment ɪŋ /li ‖ ˈment̬- ~**ments**
ˈments

tormentil ˈtɔːm ən tɪl ‖ ˈtɔːrm- ~s z

tormentor ₍ₜ₎tɔː ˈment ə ‖ ₍ₜ₎tɔːr ˈment̬ ³r ···
~s z

torn tɔːn ‖ tɔːrn toʊrn

tornado tɔː ˈneɪd əʊ ‖ tɔːr ˈneɪd oʊ ~es, ~s z

toroid ˈtɔːr ɔɪd ‖ ˈtoʊr- ~s z

toroidal tɔː ˈrɔɪd ³l ‖ toʊ-

Toronto tə ˈrɒnt əʊ ‖ -ˈrɑːnt̬ oʊ

torpedo tɔː ˈpiːd əʊ ‖ tɔːr ˈpiːd oʊ ~es z
tor'pedo boat

Torpenhow ˈtɔːp ən haʊ ‖ ˈtɔːrp- —locally also
trɪ ˈpen ə, trə-

torpid ˈtɔːp ɪd §-əd ‖ ˈtɔːrp əd ~ly li ~ness nəs
nɪs ~s z

torpidity tɔː ˈpɪd ət i -ɪt i ‖ tɔːr ˈpɪd ət̬ i

Torpoint ˌtɔː ˈpɔɪnt ‖ ˌtɔːr-

torpor ˈtɔːp ə ‖ ˈtɔːrp ³r

Torquay ˌtɔː ˈkiː ◂ ‖ ˌtɔːr-

torque tɔːk ‖ tɔːrk **torques** tɔːks ‖ tɔːrks

Torquemada ˌtɔːk wɪ ˈmɑːd ə -ɪ-, -wə-
‖ ˌtɔːrk ə- —Sp [tor ke ˈma ða]

Torquil ˈtɔːk wɪl -wəl ‖ ˈtɔːrk-

torr tɔː ‖ tɔːr **torrs** tɔːz ‖ tɔːrz

Torrance ˈtɒr ən¹s ‖ ˈtɔːr- ˈtɑːr-

torrefaction ˌtɒr ɪ ˈfæk ʃ³n -ə- ‖ ˌtɔːr- ˌtɑːr-

torre|fy ˈtɒr ɪ |faɪ -ə- ‖ ˈtɔːr- ˈtɑːr- ~**fied** faɪd
~**fies** faɪz ~**fying** faɪ ɪŋ

Torremolinos ˌtɒr ɪm ə ˈliːn ɒs ˌəm-
‖ ˌtɔːr əm ə ˈliːn oʊs —Sp [to r̝e mo ˈli nos]

Torrens ˈtɒr ənz ‖ ˈtɔːr ənz ˈtɑːr-

torrent ˈtɒr ənt ‖ ˈtɔːr ənt ˈtɑːr- ~s s

torrential tə ˈrenʧ ³l tɒ- ‖ tɔː tə- ~ly i

Torres ˈtɒr ɪs ˈtɔːr-, -ɪz, §-əs ‖ ˈtɔːr əs

Torrey ˈtɒr i ‖ ˈtɔːr i ˈtɑːr-

torrid ˈtɒr ɪd §-əd ‖ ˈtɔːr əd ˈtɑːr- ~ly li ~ness
nəs nɪs

Torrington ˈtɒr ɪŋ tən ‖ ˈtɔːr- ˈtɑːr-

Tórshavn ˈtɔːs haʊn ‖ ˈtɔːrs- —Faroese
[ˈtɔuʂ haun]

torsion ˈtɔːʃ ³n ‖ ˈtɔːrʃ ³n ~al əl

torso ˈtɔːs əʊ ‖ ˈtɔːrs oʊ ~s z

tort tɔːt ‖ tɔːrt **torts** tɔːts ‖ tɔːrts

torte tɔːt ‖ tɔːrt —Ger T~ [ˈtɔʁ tə]

Tortelier tɔː ˈtel i eɪ ‖ ˌtɔːrt el ˈjeɪ —Fr
[tɔʁ tə lje]

tortellini ˌtɔːt ə ˈliːn i -³l ˈiːn- ‖ ˌtɔːrt ³l ˈiːn i
—It [tor tel ˈli ni]

tort-feasor ˌtɔːt ˈfiːz ə ‖ ˌtɔːrt ˈfiːz ³r ~s z

torticollis ˌtɔːt ɪ ˈkɒl ɪs §-ə-, §-əs
‖ ˌtɔːrt̬ ə ˈkɑːl əs

tortilla tɔː ˈtiː ə -jə; -ˈtɪl ə ‖ tɔːr- —Sp
[tor ˈti ʎa, -ja] ~s z

tortious ˈtɔːʃ əs ‖ ˈtɔːrʃ əs ~ly li

tortois|e ˈtɔːt əs §tɔː ˈtɔɪs, §-tɔɪz ‖ ˈtɔːrt̬ əs ~es
ɪz əz

tortoiseshell ˈtɔːt əs ʃel →-əʃ-, -ə- ‖ ˈtɔːrt̬-

Tortola tɔː ˈtəʊl ə ‖ tɔːr ˈtoʊl ə

Tortuga tɔː ˈtuːg ə ‖ tɔːr-

tortuosit|y ˌtɔːt ʃu ˈɒs ət |i ˌtɔːt ju-, -ɪt i
‖ ˌtɔːrtʃ u ˈɑːs ət̬ |i ~**ies** iz

tortuous ˈtɔːt ʃu‿əs ˈtɔːt ju‿əs ‖ ˈtɔːrtʃ u‿əs ~ly
li ~ness nəs nɪs

torture v, n ˈtɔːtʃ ə ‖ ˈtɔːrtʃ ³r ~d d **torturing**
ˈtɔːtʃ ³r ɪŋ ‖ ˈtɔːrtʃ ³r ɪŋ ~s z

torturer ˈtɔːtʃ ³r ə ‖ ˈtɔːrtʃ ³r ³r ~s z

torturous ˈtɔːtʃ ³r əs ‖ ˈtɔːrtʃ- ~ly li

Torun ˈtɔːr uːn ˈtɒr- —Polish Toruń [ˈtɔ ruɲ]

tor|us ˈtɔːr |əs ‖ ˈtoʊr- ~i aɪ

Torvalds ˈtɔːv ælts -ældz ‖ ˈtɔːrv- —Swed
[ˈtuːr valds]

T

Torvill 'tɔː vɪl ‖ 'tɔːr-
Tor|y 'tɔːr |i ‖ 'toʊr- **~ies** iz **~yism** i ˌɪz əm
Tosa, tosa 'təʊz ə 'təʊs ə ‖ 'toʊs ə **~s** z —*Jp*
['to sa]
Toscanini ˌtɒsk ə 'niːn i ‖ ˌtɑːsk- —*It*
[to ska 'niː ni]
tosh, Tosh tɒʃ ‖ tɑːʃ
Toshack 'tɒʃ æk ‖ 'tɑːʃ-
Toshiba *tdmk* tɒ 'ʃiːb ə tə- ‖ tə- toʊ- —*Jp*
[toˌo çi ba]
toss tɒs tɔːs ‖ tɔːs tɑːs **tossed** tɒst tɔːst ‖ tɔːst
tɑːst **tosses** 'tɒs ɪz 'tɔːs-, -əz ‖ 'tɔːs əz 'tɑːs-
tossing 'tɒs ɪŋ 'tɔːs ɪŋ ‖ 'tɔːs ɪŋ 'tɑːs-
tosser 'tɒs ə ‖ 'tɔːs ᵊr 'tɑːs- **~s** z
tosspot 'tɒs pɒt ‖ 'tɔːs pɑːt 'tɑːs- **~s** s
toss-up 'tɒs ʌp 'tɔːs- ‖ 'tɔːs- 'tɑːs- **~s** s
tostada tɒ 'stɑːd ə ‖ toʊ- —*AmSp* [toh 'ta ða]
~s z
tot tɒt ‖ tɑːt **tots** tɒts ‖ tɑːts **totted** 'tɒt ɪd -əd
‖ 'tɑːt̬ əd **totting** 'tɒt ɪŋ ‖ 'tɑːt̬ ɪŋ
total 'təʊt ᵊl ‖ 'toʊt̬ ᵊl **~ed, ~led** d **~ing, ~ling**
ɪŋ **~s** z
totalis... —*see* **totaliz...**
totalitarian təʊ ˌtæl ɪ 'teər i‿ən ◂ ˌtəʊ tæl-,
-ə'- ‖ toʊ ˌtæl ə 'ter- ˌtoʊ tæl- **~ism** ˌɪz əm
totalit|y təʊ 'tæl ət |i -ɪt i ‖ toʊ 'tæl ət̬ |i **~ies**
iz
totalizator 'təʊt əl aɪ zeɪt ə -ɪ· ·
‖ 'toʊt̬ ᵊl ə zeɪt̬ ᵊr **~s** z
totaliz|e 'təʊt ə laɪz -ᵊl aɪz ‖ 'toʊt̬ ᵊl aɪz **~ed** d
~er/s ə/z ‖ ᵊr/z **~es** ɪz əz **~ing** ɪŋ
totally 'təʊt əl i ‖ 'toʊt̬ ᵊl i
totaquine 'təʊt ə kwiːn ‖ 'toʊt̬-
tote təʊt ‖ toʊt **toted** 'təʊt ɪd -əd ‖ 'toʊt̬ əd
totes təʊts ‖ toʊts **toting** 'təʊt ɪŋ ‖ 'toʊt̬ ɪŋ
'tote bag
totem 'təʊt əm ‖ 'toʊt̬- **~ism** ˌɪz əm **~s** z
'totem pole
totemic təʊ 'tem ɪk ‖ toʊ-
tother, t'other 'tʌð ə ‖ -ᵊr
Tothill 'tɒt hɪl -ɪl ‖ 'tɑːt-
Totley 'tɒt li ‖ 'tɑːt-
Totnes 'tɒt nɪs -nəs ‖ 'tɑːt-
toto 'təʊt əʊ ‖ 'toʊt oʊ
Totpak *tdmk* 'tɒt pæk ‖ 'tɑːt- **~s** s
tott... —*see* **tot**
Tottenham 'tɒt ᵊn_əm ‖ 'tɑːt-
ˌTottenham ˌCourt 'Road; ˌTottenham
'Hotspur
totter 'tɒt ə ‖ 'tɑːt̬ ᵊr **~ed** d **tottering/ly**
'tɒt ər ɪŋ /li ‖ 'tɑːt̬ ər ɪŋ /li **~s** z
Totteridge 'tɒt ər ɪdʒ ‖ 'tɑːt̬-
tottery 'tɒt ər i ‖ 'tɑːt̬-
tott|ie, tott|y 'tɒt |i ‖ 'tɑːt̬ |i **~ies** iz
Totton 'tɒt ᵊn ‖ 'tɑːt ᵊn
toucan 'tuːk ən -æn, -ɑːn ‖ -æn -ɑːn; tuː 'kɑːn
~s z
touch tʌtʃ (*!*) **touched** tʌtʃt **touches** 'tʌtʃ ɪz
-əz **touching/ly** 'tʌtʃ ɪŋ /li
'touch judge
Touch *family name* taʊtʃ
Touch *place in Fife* tuːx
touch-and-go ˌtʌtʃ ən 'gəʊ ◂ →-əŋ- ‖ -'goʊ

touchdown 'tʌtʃ daʊn **~s** z
touche, touché 'tuːʃ eɪ ‖ tuː 'ʃeɪ
Touche tuːʃ
touchi... —*see* **touchy**
touchline 'tʌtʃ laɪn **~s** z
touch-me-not 'tʌtʃ mi nɒt ‖ -nɑːt **~s** s
touchpad 'tʌtʃ pæd **~s** z
touchpaper 'tʌtʃ ˌpeɪp ə ‖ -ᵊr
touchstone 'tʌtʃ stəʊn ‖ -stoʊn **~s** z
touch-tone, Touch-Tone *tdmk* 'tʌtʃ təʊn
‖ -toʊn
touch-typ|e 'tʌtʃ taɪp **~ed** t **~es** s **~ing** ɪŋ
ist/s ɪst/s §əst/s
touch-up *n* 'tʌtʃ ʌp **~s** s
touchwood 'tʌtʃ wʊd
touch|y 'tʌtʃ |i **~ier** i ə ‖ i‿ᵊr **~iest** i ɪst i əst
~ily ɪ li əl i **~iness** i nəs i nɪs
touchy-feel|ie, ~y ˌtʌtʃ i 'fiːᵊl i ◂ **~ies** iz
tough tʌf (*!*) (= *tuff*) **tougher** 'tʌf ə ‖ -ᵊr
toughest 'tʌf ɪst -əst
ˌtough 'luck
Tough *place in Grampian* tuːx ‖ tuːk
Tough *family name* (i) tʌf, (ii) tuːx ‖ tuːk
toughen 'tʌf ᵊn **~ed** d **~ing** ɪŋ **~s** z
toughie 'tʌf i **~s** z
toughly 'tʌf li
tough-minded ˌtʌf 'maɪnd ɪd ◂ -əd **~ly** li
~ness nəs nɪs
toughness 'tʌf nəs -nɪs
Toulon (ˌ)tuː 'lɒ̃ ‖ -'lɔːn -'lɑːn —*Fr* [tu lɔ̃]
Toulouse (ˌ)tuː 'luːz tə- —*Fr* [tu luːz]
Toulouse-Lautrec ˌtuː luːz ləʊ 'trek ·ˌ· ·ˈ·, tə-
‖ tuː ˌluːz lə 'trek —*Fr* [tu luz lo tʁɛk]
toupee, toupée 'tuːp eɪ ˌtuː 'peɪ ‖ tuː 'peɪ
—*Fr* toupet [tu pe] **~s** z
tour tʊə tɔː ‖ tʊᵊr **toured** tʊəd tɔːd ‖ tʊᵊrd
touring 'tʊər ɪŋ 'tɔːr- ‖ 'tʊr ɪŋ **tours** tʊəz
tɔːz ‖ tʊᵊrz
ˌtour de 'force —*Fr* [tuʁ də fɔʁs]; ˌTour de
'France —*Fr* [tuʁ də fʁɑ̃ːs]; 'tour ˌoperator
tourer 'tʊər ə 'tɔːr- ‖ 'tʊr ᵊr **~s** z
Tourette tʊ ̍ 'ret **~'s** s
tourism 'tʊər ˌɪz əm 'tɔːr- ‖ 'tʊr-
tourist 'tʊər ɪst 'tɔːr-, §-əst ‖ 'tʊr əst **~s** s
'tourist class
touristic (ˌ)tʊə 'rɪst ɪk (ˌ)tɔː- ‖ tʊ- **~ally** ᵊl i
touristy 'tʊər ɪst i 'tɔːr-, -əst- ‖ 'tʊr-
tourmaline 'tʊəm ə liːn 'tɜːm-, -lɪn ‖ 'tʊrm-
tournament 'tʊən ə mənt 'tɔːn-, 'tɜːn- ‖ 'tʊrn-
'tɔːrn-, 'tɜːn- **~s** s
tournedos *sing.* 'tʊən ə dəʊ 'tɔːn-, 'tɜːn-
‖ ˌtʊrn ə 'doʊ ~ *pl* z
tourney 'tʊən i 'tɔːn-, 'tɜːn- ‖ 'tʊrn i 'tɔːrn-,
'tɜːn- **~ed** d **~ing** ɪŋ **~s** z
tourniquet 'tɔːn ɪ keɪ 'tʊən-, 'tɜːn-, -ə-
‖ 'tɜːn ək ət 'tʊrn-, -ɪk- (***) **~s** z ‖ s
Tours *place in France* tʊə tʊəz, tɔːz ‖ tʊᵊr —*Fr*
[tuʁ]
Tours *English family name* tʊəz tɔːz ‖ tʊᵊrz
tourtière ˌtɔːt i 'eə ‖ ˌtʊrt i 'eᵊr **~s** z
tousl|e 'taʊz ᵊl **~ed** d **~es** z **~ing** ɪŋ
tout *adj, adv, in French expressions* tuːt —*but
before consonants* tuː:

,tout 'court ,tuː 'kʊə -'kɔː ‖ -'kʊər —*Fr*
[tu kuːʁ]; ,tout en'semble ,tuːt ɒn 'sɒm bᵊl
‖ -aːn 'saːm- —*Fr* [tu tɑ̃ sɑ̃ːbl]

tout *v, n* taʊt **touted** 'taʊt ɪd -əd ‖ 'taʊt̬ əd
touting 'taʊt ɪŋ ‖ 'taʊt̬ ɪŋ **touts** taʊts

Tovell 'təʊv ᵊl ‖ 'toʊv-

Tovey *(i)* 'təʊv i ‖ 'toʊv i, *(ii)* 'tʌv i

tow təʊ §taʊ ‖ toʊ *(usually = toe)* **towed** təʊd
§taʊd ‖ toʊd *(usually = toad)* **towing** 'təʊ ɪŋ
§'taʊ- ‖ 'toʊ ɪŋ **tows** təʊz §taʊz ‖ toʊz
'**tow truck**

towage 'təʊ ɪdʒ ‖ 'toʊ-

toward *prep* tə 'wɔːd tu-; tɔːd ‖ tɔːrd toʊrd;
tə 'wɔːrd, twɔːrd, twoʊrd

toward *adj* 'təʊ əd tɔːd ‖ tɔːrd toʊrd **~liness**
li nəs -nɪs **~ly** li **~ness** nəs nɪs

towards tə 'wɔːdz tu-; tɔːdz ‖ tɔːrdz toʊrdz;
tə 'wɔːrdz, twɔːrdz, twoʊrdz

towaway 'təʊ ə ˌweɪ ‖ 'toʊ-

towbar 'təʊ bɑː ‖ 'toʊ bɑːr **~s** z

towboat 'təʊ bəʊt ‖ 'toʊ boʊt **~s** s

Towcester 'təʊst ə ‖ 'toʊst ᵊr

towel 'taʊ əl taʊl ‖ 'taʊ əl **toweled, towelled**
'taʊ əld taʊld ‖ 'taʊ əld **toweling, towelling**
'taʊ əl ɪŋ 'taʊl ɪŋ ‖ 'taʊ əl ɪŋ **towels** 'taʊəlz
taʊlz ‖ 'taʊ əlz

towelette ˌtaʊ ə 'let ˌtaʊ 'let **~s** s

tower, Tower 'taʊ ə ‖ 'taʊ ᵊr **~ed** d **towering**
'taʊ ər ɪŋ ‖ 'taʊ ᵊr ɪŋ **~s** z
'**tower block**; ,Tower 'Bridge◂, ,Tower
,Bridge 'Road; ,Tower 'Hamlets; ,tower of
'strength

Towers 'taʊ əz ‖ 'taʊ ᵊrz

tow-haired ˌtəʊ 'heəd ◂ ‖ ˌtoʊ 'heᵊrd ◂
-'hæᵊrd

towhead 'təʊ hed ‖ 'toʊ- **~ed** ɪd əd **~s** z

Tow Law ˌtaʊ 'lɔː ‖ -'lɑː

towline 'təʊ laɪn §'taʊ- ‖ 'toʊ- **~s** z

town taʊn **towns** taʊnz
,town 'clerk; ,town 'crier; ,town 'hall;
'town house; ,town 'planning

Towne taʊn

Townes taʊnz

townie 'taʊn i **~s** z

Townley 'taʊn li

townscape 'taʊn skeɪp **~s** s

Townsend 'taʊnz end

townsfolk 'taʊnz fəʊk ‖ -foʊk

Townshend 'taʊnz end

township 'taʊn ʃɪp **~s** s

towns|man 'taʊnz |mən **~men** mən men
~people ˌpiːp ᵊl

Townsville 'taʊnz vɪl -vᵊl

towns|woman 'taʊnz ˌwʊm ən **~women**
ˌwɪm ɪn §-ən

tow|path 'təʊ |pɑːθ §'taʊ-, §-pæθ ‖ 'toʊ |pæθ
~paths pɑːðz §pæðz, §pɑːθs, §pæθs ‖ pæðz
pæθs

towrope 'təʊ rəʊp §'taʊ- ‖ 'toʊ roʊp **~s** s

Towy 'taʊ i —*Welsh* ['tə wi, 'to-]

Towyn 'taʊ ɪn 'təʊ- —*Welsh* ['tə wɪn, 'to-,
-wɪn]

toxaemia, toxemia tɒk 'siːm i ə ‖ tɑːk-

toxic 'tɒks ɪk ‖ 'tɑːks ɪk **~ally** ᵊl_i
,toxic 'shock ,syndrome

toxicit|y tɒk 'sɪs ət |i -ɪt i ‖ tɑːk 'sɪs ət̬ |i **~ies**
iz

toxicological ˌtɒks ɪk əʊ 'lɒdʒ ɪk ᵊl ◂
‖ ˌtɑːks ɪk ə 'lɑːdʒ- **~ly** ˌi

toxicologist ˌtɒks ɪ 'kɒl ədʒ ɪst ˌ-ə-, §-əst
‖ ˌtɑːks ɪ 'kɑːl- **~s** s

toxicology ˌtɒks ɪ 'kɒl ədʒ i ˌ-ə-
‖ ˌtɑːks ɪ 'kɑːl-

toxin 'tɒks ɪn §-ən ‖ 'tɑːks ən **~s** z

toxocariasis ˌtɒks əʊ kə 'raɪ_əs ɪs §-əs
‖ ˌtɑːks ə-

toxoid 'tɒks ɔɪd ‖ 'tɑːks- **~s** z

toxophilite tɒk 'sɒf ə laɪt -ɪ- ‖ tɑːk 'sɑːf- **~s** s

toxoplasmosis ˌtɒks əʊ plæz 'məʊs ɪs -əs
‖ ˌtɑːks ə plæz 'moʊs əs ˌ-oʊ-

Toxteth 'tɒkst əθ -ɪθ, -eθ ‖ 'tɑːkst-

toy tɔɪ **toyed** tɔɪd **toying** 'tɔɪ ɪŋ **toys** tɔɪz
'toy ,factory *where toys are made*, ,toy
'factory *for a child to play with*; ,toy 'gun;
,toy 'poodle; ,toy 'soldier

Toya, Toyah 'tɔɪ ə

toyboy 'tɔɪ bɔɪ **~s** z

Toye tɔɪ

toymaker 'tɔɪ ˌmeɪk ə ‖ -ᵊr **~s** z

Toynbee 'tɔɪn bi →'tɔɪm-, -biː

Toyota *tdmk* tɔɪ 'əʊt ə ‖ -'oʊt̬ ə **~s** z —*Jp*
['to jo ta]

toyshop 'tɔɪ ʃɒp ‖ -ʃɑːp **~s** s

Toys "R" Us *tdmk* ˌtɔɪz ᵊr 'ʌs

Tozer 'təʊz ə ‖ 'toʊz ᵊr

T'Pau tə 'paʊ

Trabant *tdmk* 'træb ænt -ənt —*Ger* [tʁa 'bant]

trace treɪs **traced** treɪst **traces** 'treɪs ɪz -əz
tracing 'treɪs ɪŋ
'trace ,element

traceable 'treɪs əb ᵊl

tracer 'treɪs ə ‖ -ᵊr **~s** z

tracer|y 'treɪs ər |i **~ies** iz

Tracey 'treɪs i

trache|a trə 'kiː ˌ|ə 'treɪk i ˌ|ə ‖ 'treɪk i ˌ|ə **~ae** iː
~al əl **~as** əz

tracheitis ˌtreɪk i 'aɪt ɪs ˌtræk-, §-əs ‖ -'aɪt̬ əs

tracheo- *comb. form*
with stress-neutral suffix ˌtreɪk i əʊ ˌtræk-
‖ -oʊ — **tracheocele** 'treɪk i əʊ siːᵊl 'træk-
‖ -i oʊ-
with stress-imposing suffix ˌtreɪk i 'ɒ+ ˌtræk-
‖ -'ɑː+ — **tracheostomy** ˌtreɪk i 'ɒst əm i
ˌtræk- ‖ -'ɑːst-

tracheotom|y ˌtræk i 'ɒt əm |i ˌtreɪk-
‖ ˌtreɪk i 'ɑːt̬- **~ies** iz

trachoma trə 'kəʊm ə ‖ -'koʊm-

tracing 'treɪs ɪŋ **~s** z
'tracing ,paper

track træk **tracked** trækt *(= tract)* **tracking**
'træk ɪŋ **tracks** træks
'track e,vent; 'tracking ,station; 'track
,record; 'track rod

trackage 'træk ɪdʒ

trackball 'træk bɔːl ‖ -bɑːl **~s** z

tracker 'træk ə ‖ -ᵊr **~s** z

T

tracklay|er 'træk ˌleɪ |ə ‖ -|ᵊr **~ers** əz ‖ ᵊrz
~ing ɪŋ
trackless 'træk ləs -lɪs
track|suit 'træk |suːt -sjuːt **~suited** suːt ɪd
sjuːt-, -əd ‖ suːʈ əd **~suits** suːts sjuːts
tract trækt **tracts** trækts
tractability ˌtrækt ə 'bɪl ət i -ɪt i ‖ -əʈ i
tractab|le 'trækt əb |ᵊl **~leness** ᵊl nəs -nɪs **~ly**
li
Tractarian træk 'teər i ‿ən ‖ -'ter- **~s** z
tractate 'trækt eɪt **~s** s
tractile 'trækt aɪᵊl ‖ -ᵊl -aɪᵊl
traction 'træk ʃᵊn
'**traction ˌengine**
tractive 'trækt ɪv
tractor 'trækt ə ‖ -ᵊr **~s** z
tractorfeed 'trækt ə fiːd ‖ -ᵊr-
tractor-trailer 'trækt ə ˌtreɪl ə ‖ -ᵊr ˌtreɪl ᵊr **~s**
z
Tracy 'treɪs i
trad træd
trade treɪd **traded** 'treɪd ɪd -əd **trades** treɪdz
trading 'treɪd ɪŋ
'**trade gap**; '**trade name**; '**trade price**;
'**trade route**; ˌtrade 'secret; ˌTrades
ˌUnion 'Congress; ₍ₗ₎trade 'union; 'trade
wind; 'trading eˌstate; 'trading post;
'trading stamp; ˌtrade(s) 'union ‖ '· ˌ· ·
trade-in 'treɪd ɪn **~s** z
trademark 'treɪd mɑːk →'treɪb- ‖ -mɑːrk **~ed** t
~ing ɪŋ **~s** s
trade-off 'treɪd ɒf -ɔːf ‖ -ɔːf -ɑːf **~s** s
trader 'treɪd ə ‖ -ᵊr **~s** z
Tradescant trə 'desk ənt
tradescantia ˌtræd ɪ 'skænt i‿ə ˌtreɪd-, ˌ-e-,
ˌ-ə-, -'skænʃ- ‖ -'skænʈ- **~s** z
trades|man 'treɪdz |mən **~men** mən men
~people ˌpiːp ᵊl
tradition trə 'dɪʃ ᵊn **~s** z
traditional trə 'dɪʃ ᵊn ᵊl **~ism** ˌɪz əm **~ist/s**
ɪst/s §əst/s ‖ əst/s **~ly** i
traduc|e trə 'djuːs →-'dʒuːs ‖ -'duːs -'djuːs **~ed**
t **~es** ɪz əz **~ing** ɪŋ
Trafalgar trə 'fælg ə ‖ -ᵊr -'fɑːlg- —*But the*
pronunciation ˌtræf ᵊl 'gɑː ◀ ‖ -'gɑːr ◀ *was*
formerly used for the viscountcy and is still
sometimes used for T~ House —near
Salisbury. —Sp [tra fal 'ɣar]
traffic 'træf ɪk **~ked** t **~king** ɪŋ **~s** s
'traffic ˌcircle; 'traffic ˌisland; 'traffic
jam; 'traffic light; 'traffic ˌsignal; 'traffic
ˌwarden
trafficator 'træf ɪ keɪt ə §'·ə- ‖ -keɪʈ ᵊr **~s** z
trafficker 'træf ɪk ə ‖ -ᵊr **~s** z
Trafford 'træf əd ‖ -ᵊrd
tragacanth 'træg ə kænᵗθ 'treɪdʒ-
tragedian trə 'dʒiːd i‿ən **~s** z
tragedienne trə ˌdʒiːd i 'en **~s** z
traged|y 'trædʒ əd |i -ɪd i **~ies** iz
Trager 'treɪg ə ‖ -ᵊr
tragic 'trædʒ ɪk **~ally** ᵊl‿i
tragicomed|y ˌtrædʒ i 'kɒm əd |i ‖ -'kɑːm-
~ies iz

tragicomic ˌtrædʒ i 'kɒm ɪk ◀ ‖ -'kɑːm- **~ally**
ᵊl‿i
tragopan 'træg ə pæn **~s** z
tragus 'treɪg əs **tragi** 'treɪdʒ aɪ 'treɪg-
Traherne trə 'hɜːn ‖ -'hɜːn
trail treɪᵊl **trailed** treɪᵊld **trailing** 'treɪᵊl ɪŋ
trails treɪᵊlz
'trail bike; ˌtrailing 'edge, '· · ·
trailblaz|er 'treɪᵊl ˌbleɪz |ə ‖ -|ᵊr **~ers** əz ‖ ᵊrz
~ing ɪŋ
trailer 'treɪl ə ‖ -ᵊr **~s** z
'trailer camp; 'trailer park
trailhead 'treɪᵊl hed **~s** z
Traill treɪᵊl
train, Train treɪn **trained** treɪnd **training**
'treɪn ɪŋ **trains** treɪnz
'training ˌcollege; 'training course; 'train
set
trainbearer 'treɪn ˌbeər ə →'treɪm- ‖ -ˌber ᵊr
-ˌbær- **~s** z
trainee ˌtreɪ 'niː **~s** z **~ship/s** ʃɪp/s
trainer 'treɪn ə ‖ -ᵊr **~s** z
trainload 'treɪn ləʊd ‖ -loʊd **~s** z
train|man 'treɪn |mən →'treɪm- **~men** mən
men
train-spott|er 'treɪn spɒt| ə ‖ -spɑːʈ| ᵊr **~ers**
əz ‖ ᵊrz **~ing** ɪŋ
traipse treɪps **traipsed** treɪpst **traipses**
'treɪps ɪz -əz **traipsing** 'treɪps ɪŋ
trait treɪ treɪt ‖ treɪt **traits** treɪz treɪts ‖ treɪts
traitor 'treɪt ə ‖ 'treɪʈ ᵊr **~s** z
traitorous 'treɪt ər‿əs ‖ 'treɪʈ ər əs →'treɪtr əs
~ly li **~ness** nəs nɪs
Trajan 'treɪdʒ ən
trajector|y trə 'dʒek tər |i 'trædʒ ɪk-, '-ək-
~ies iz
tra-la trɑː 'lɑː trə-
tra-la-la ˌtrɑːl ɑː 'lɑː -ə-
Tralee trə 'liː
tram træm **trams** træmz
tramcar 'træm kɑː ‖ -kɑːr **~s** z
tramline 'træm laɪn **~s** z
trammel 'træm ᵊl **~ed, ~led** d **~ing, ~ling** ɪŋ
~s z
tramontane trə 'mɒnt eɪn ‖ -'mɑːnt- **~s** z
tramp træmp **tramped** træmᵖt **tramping**
'træmp ɪŋ **tramps** træmᵖs
trampl|e 'træmp ᵊl **~ed** d **~es** z **~ing** ˌɪŋ
trampolin|e 'træmp ə liːn -lɪn, ˌ· ·'· **~ed** d **~es**
z **~ing** ɪŋ
tramway 'træm weɪ **~s** z
trance trɑːnᵗs §trænᵗs ‖ trænᵗs **trances**
'trɑːnᵗs ɪz §'trænᵗs-, -əz ‖ 'trænᵗs əz
tranche trɑːnᵗʃ trɔːnᵗʃ, trænᵗʃ **tranches**
'trɑːnᵗʃ ɪz 'trɔːnᵗʃ-, 'trænᵗʃ-, -əz
trank træŋk **tranks** træŋks
Tranmere 'træn mɪə →'træm- ‖ -mɪr
trann|ie, ~y 'træn |i **~ies** iz
tranquil 'træŋk wɪl -wəl **~ly** li
tranquility, tranquillity træŋ 'kwɪl ət i -ɪt i
‖ træn 'kwɪl əʈ i →træn-

T

tranquiliz|e, tranquillis|e, tranquilliz|e
'træŋk wə laɪz -wɪ- **~ed** d **~er/s** ə/z ‖ -ᵊr/z
~es ɪz əz **~ing** ɪŋ
trans- træn⁵ trænz, trɑːn⁵, trɑːnz —*For EFL
learners, the form* **træns** *is acceptable in all
contexts in all kinds of English. Actual usage
preferences are fairly complex. —In the choice
between* **s** *and* **z** *forms we can distinguish
various phonetic contexts according to the
sound with which the stem begins, as follows.
(1) Before a voiceless sound* (trans'form), **s** *is
usual. (2) Before* l (trans'late) *and before an
unstressed vowel sound* ('transit), **s** *is usual
though a minority use* **z**. *(3) Before other
consonants* (trans'gress, trans'mit), *and before
a stressed vowel sound* (trans'act), *the tendency
is for BrE to prefer* **z**, *but AmE to prefer* **s**.
*This also applies in any word where the prefix
is felt as separate* (ˌtrans.conti'nental). —*For
the vowel, RP prefers* æ, *although a
substantial minority use* ɑː, *and some words
have variants with* ə; *AmE always has* æ.
—*Before a stem beginning with* **s** *the final
consonant sound is often lost* (trans + scribe
giving transcribe **træn ˈskraɪb**).
transact træn 'zækt trɑːn-, trən-, -'sækt;
ˌtræn⁵ 'ækt ‖ -'sækt -'zækt **~ed** ɪd əd **~ing** ɪŋ
~s s
transactinide ˌtræn⁵ 'ækt ɪ naɪd ˌtrɑːn⁵-,
ˌtrænz-, §-ə- **~s** z
transaction træn 'zæk ʃᵊn trɑːn-, trən-, -'sæk-;
ˌtræn⁵ 'æk- ‖ -'sæk- -'zæk- **~al** ᵊl **~s** z
transalpine ₍ᵢ₎trænz 'ælp aɪn ₍ᵢ₎trɑːnz-,
₍ᵢ₎træn⁵- ‖ ₍ᵢ₎træn⁵- ₍ᵢ₎trænz-, -ən **~s** z
transatlantic ˌtrænz ət 'lænt ɪk ◂ ˌtrɑːnz-,
§ˌtræn⁵-, -æt- ‖ ˌtræn⁵ ət 'lænt̬ ɪk ◂ ˌtrænz-
Transcarpathian ˌtrænz kɑː 'peɪθ i ən ◂
ˌtrɑːnz-, ˌtræn⁵- ‖ ˌtræn⁵ kɑːr-
Transcaucasia ˌtrænz kɔː 'keɪz i ə ˌtrɑːnz-,
ˌtræn⁵-, -'keɪʒ ə ‖ ˌtræn⁵ kɔː 'keɪʒ ə -kɑː-,
-'keɪʃ ə
transceiver træn 'siːv ə trɑːn- ‖ -ᵊr **~s** z
transcend træn 'send trɑːn- **~ed** ɪd əd **~ing** ɪŋ
~s z
transcendenc|e træn 'send ən⁵ trɑːn- **~y** i
transcendent træn 'send ənt trɑːn- **~ly** li
transcendental ˌtræn⁵ en 'dent ᵊl ◂ ˌtrɑːn⁵-,
-ᵊn- ‖ -'dent̬ ᵊl ◂ **~ism** ˌɪz əm **~ly** i
ˌtranscen,dental ,medi'tation
transcontinental ˌtrænz ˌkɒnt ɪ 'nent ᵊl
ˌtrɑːnz-, ˌtræn⁵-, -ə-
‖ ˌtræn⁵ ˌkɑːnt ᵊn 'ent̬ ᵊl
transcrib|e ₍ᵢ₎træn 'skraɪb ₍ᵢ₎trɑːn-;
₍ᵢ₎træn⁵ 'skraɪb **~ed** d **~er/s** ə/z ‖ ᵊr/z **~es** z
~ing ɪŋ
transcript 'træn⁵ krɪpt 'trɑːn⁵- **~s** s
transcriptase ₍ᵢ₎træn 'skrɪpt eɪz ₍ᵢ₎trɑːn-, -eɪs;
₍ᵢ₎træn⁵ 'skrɪpt-
transcription ₍ᵢ₎træn 'skrɪp ʃᵊn ₍ᵢ₎trɑːn-;
₍ᵢ₎træn⁵ 'skrɪp- **~al** ᵊl **~ally** ᵊl i **~s** z
transducer ₍ᵢ₎trænz 'djuːs ə ₍ᵢ₎trɑːnz-,
₍ᵢ₎træn⁵-, ₍ᵢ₎trɑːn⁵-, →-'dʒuːs-
‖ ₍ᵢ₎træn⁵ 'duːs ᵊr -'djuːs- **~s** z

transept 'træn⁵ ept 'trɑːn⁵- **~s** s
transeunt 'træn⁵ i ənt 'trɑːn⁵-
transexual træn 'sek ʃu əl trɑːn-, trænz-,
trɑːnz-, ˌtræn⁵-, ˌtrɑːn⁵-, -'seks ju əl, -'sek ʃᵊl
‖ træn⁵- **~ism** ˌɪz əm **~s** z
trans|fer v træn⁵ |'fɜː trɑːn⁵-, trən⁵-, ˈ··
‖ træn⁵ |'fɜː ˈ··· **~ferred** 'fɜːd ‖ 'fɜːd
~ferring 'fɜːr ɪŋ ‖ 'fɜː ɪŋ **~fers** 'fɜːz ‖ 'fɜːz
transfer n 'træn⁵ fɜː 'trɑːn⁵- ‖ -fɜː **~s** z
'transfer fee
transferability ˌtræn⁵ ˌfɜːr ə 'bɪl ət i trɑːn⁵-,
ˌ· ··, ˌfər ə-, -ɪt i ‖ -ˌfɜː ə 'bɪl ət̬ i

TRANSFERABLE

Preference poll, BrE: -'fɜːr- 82%, '···· 18%.

transferable træn⁵ 'fɜːr əb ᵊl trɑːn⁵-, ˌ·-,
trən⁵-; 'træn⁵ fər əb ᵊl, 'trɑːn⁵- ‖ -'fɜː- —
Preference poll, BrE: -'fɜːr- 82%, '···· 18%.
transferal, transferral træn⁵ 'fɜːr əl trɑːn⁵-,
trən⁵- ‖ træn⁵ 'fɜː əl **~s** z
transferas|e 'træn⁵ fə reɪz 'trɑːn⁵-, -reɪs **~es**
ɪz əz
transferee ˌtræn⁵ fɜː 'iː -fər- ‖ -fɜː- **~s** z
transferenc|e 'træn⁵ fᵊr ən⁵ 'trɑːn⁵-;
₍ᵢ₎træn⁵ 'fɜːr ən⁵ ₍ᵢ₎trɑːn⁵-, trən⁵-
‖ træn⁵ 'fɜː ən⁵ '·fᵊr ··· **~es** ɪz əz
transferor, transferrer træn⁵ 'fɜːr ə 'trɑːn⁵-
‖ -'fɜː ᵊr **~s** z
transfiguration, T~ ˌtræn⁵ ˌfɪg ə 'reɪʃ ᵊn
ˌtrɑːn⁵-, ˌ·ˌ·'·, -jə-, -juᵊ- ‖ -jə- **~s** z
transfigure træn⁵ 'fɪg ə trɑːn⁵- ‖ -jᵊr (*) **~d** d
~s z **transfiguring** træn⁵ 'fɪg ᵊr ɪŋ trɑːn⁵-
‖ -jᵊr ɪŋ
transfinite træn⁵ 'faɪn aɪt trɑːn⁵-
transfix træn⁵ 'fɪks trɑːn⁵- **~ed** t **~es** ɪz əz
~ing ɪŋ
transform n 'træn⁵ fɔːm 'trɑːn⁵- ‖ -fɔːrm **~s** z
transform v træn⁵ 'fɔːm trɑːn⁵-, trən⁵-;
'træn⁵ fɔːm, 'trɑːn⁵- ‖ -'fɔːrm **~ed** d **~ing** ɪŋ
~s z
transformable træn⁵ 'fɔːm əb ᵊl trɑːn⁵-,
trən⁵- ‖ -'fɔːrm-
transformation ˌtræn⁵ fə 'meɪʃ ᵊn ˌtrɑːn⁵-,
-fɔː- ‖ -fᵊr- -fɔːr- **~al** ᵊl ◂ **~ally** ᵊl i **~s** z
ˌtransfor,mational 'grammar
transformer træn⁵ 'fɔːm ə trɑːn⁵-, trən⁵-
‖ -'fɔːrm ᵊr '··· **~s** z
transfus|e træn⁵ 'fjuːz trɑːn⁵-, trən⁵- **~ed** d
~es ɪz əz **~ing** ɪŋ
transfusion træn⁵ 'fjuːʒ ᵊn trɑːn⁵-, §trən⁵-
~s z
transgender ˌtrænz 'dʒend ə ˌtrɑːnz-,
ˌtræn⁵-, ˌtrɑːn⁵- ‖ ˌtræn⁵ 'dʒendᵊr ˌtrænz-
transgenic ˌtrænz 'dʒen ɪk ◂ ˌtrɑːnz-, ˌtræn⁵-,
ˌtrɑːn⁵- ‖ ˌtræn⁵- ˌtrænz-

T

transgress trænz ˈgres trɑːnz-, trænˈs-, trɑːnˈs-, trənz- ‖ trænˈs- trænz- ~ed t ~es ɪz əz ~ing ɪŋ

transgression trænz ˈgreʃ ən trɑːnz-, trænˈs-, trɑːnˈs-, §trənz- ‖ trænˈs- trænz- ~s z

transgressor trænz ˈgres ə trɑːnz-, trænˈs-, trɑːnˈs-, §trənz- ‖ trænˈs ˈgres ər trænz- ~s z

tranship trænˈs ˈʃɪp trɑːnˈs-, →trænˈtʃ-, træn-, trɑːn-, trænz-, trɑːnz-, §trənˈs-, →§trənˈtʃ-, §trən-, §trɑːnz- ‖ trænˈs- →trænˈtʃ- ~ped t ~ping ɪŋ ~s s

transhumance trænˈs ˈhjuːm ənˈs trɑːnˈs-, §-ˈjuːm-

transienc|e ˈtrænz i ənˈs ˈtrɑːnz-, ˈtrænˈs-, ˈtrɑːnˈs- ‖ ˈtrænˈtʃ ənˈs, ˈtrænʒ- ~y i

transient ˈtrænz i ənt ˈtrɑːnz-, ˈtrænˈs-, ˈtrɑːnˈs- ‖ ˈtrænˈtʃ ənt, ˈtrænʒ- ~ly li ~ness nəs nɪs

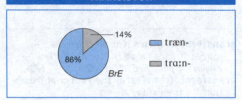

BrE

transistor trænˈzɪst ə trɑːn-, §trən-, -ˈsɪst- ‖ -ᵊr
— *Preference poll, BrE:* træn- 86% *(English southerners 84%),* trɑːn- 14% *(English southerners 16%);* -ˈzɪst- 63%, -ˈsɪst- 37%. ~s z

tranˌsistor ˈradio

transistoris|e, transistoriz|e træn ˈzɪst ə raɪz trɑːn-, §trən-, -ˈsɪst- ~ed d ~es ɪz əz ~ing ɪŋ

trans|it ˈtrænˈs |ɪt ˈtrɑːnˈs-, ˈtrænz-, ˈtrɑːnz-, §-ət ‖ ˈtrænˈs |ət ˈtrænz- ~ited ɪt ɪd §ət-, -əd ‖ əʈ əd ~iting ɪt ɪŋ §ət- ‖ əʈ ɪŋ ~its ɪts §ətsəts

ˈtransit lounge; ˈtransit ˌpassengers; ˈtransit ˌvisa

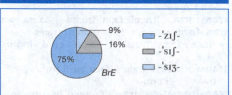

BrE

transition træn ˈzɪʃ ən trɑːn-, trən-, -ˈsɪʃ-, -ˈsɪʒ-
— *Preference poll, BrE:* -ˈzɪʃ- 75%, -ˈsɪʃ- 16%, -ˈsɪʒ- 9%. ~al əl ~ally əl i ~s z

transitive ˈtrænˈs ət ɪv ˈtrɑːnˈs-, ˈtrænz-, ˈtrɑːnz-, -ɪt ɪv ‖ ˈtrænˈs əʈ ɪv ˈtrænz- ~ly li ~ness nəs nɪs ~s z

transitivity ˌtrænˈs ə ˈtɪv ət i ˌtrɑːnˈs-, ˌtrænz-, ˌtrɑːnz-, -ɪ-, -ɪt i ‖ -əʈ i

transitor|y ˈtrænˈs ət_ᵊr |i ˈtrɑːnˈs-, ˈtrænz-, ˈtrɑːnz-, -ˈɪʈ_ ‖ ˈtrænˈs ə tɔːr |i ˈtrænz-, -tour i (*) ~ily əl i ɪ li ~iness i nəs i nɪs

Transkei ˌtrænˈs ˈkaɪ ˌtrɑːnˈs-, ˌtrænz-, ˌtrɑːnz-

translatable trænˈs ˈleɪt əbᵊl trɑːnˈs-, trænz-, trɑːnz-, trənˈs-, trənz- ‖ ˈtræns leɪt əb ᵊl ˈtrænz-, ˌˈ·--

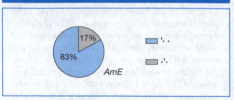

AmE

trans|late trænˈs |ˈleɪt trɑːnˈs-, trænz-, trɑːnz-, trənˈs-, trənz- ‖ ˈtrænˈs |leɪt ˈtrænz-, ˌˈ·
— *Preference poll, AmE:* ˌˈ·· 83%, ˌˈ·· 17%.
~lated ˈleɪt ɪd -əd ‖ leɪʈ əd ~lates ˈleɪts ‖ leɪts ~lating ˈleɪt ɪŋ ‖ leɪʈ ɪŋ

translation trænˈs ˈleɪʃ ən trɑːnˈs-, trænz-, trɑːnz-, trənˈs-, trənz- ‖ trænz- ~al əl ~s z

translator trænˈs ˈleɪt ə trɑːnˈs-, trænz-, trɑːnz-, trənˈs-, trənz- ‖ trænˈs ˈleɪʈ ᵊr trænz-, ˈ···s z

translite|rate trænˈs ˈlɪt ə |reɪt trɑːnˈs-, trænz-, trɑːnz-, ˌ-, trənˈs-, trənz- ‖ trænˈs ˈlɪʈ trænz- ~rated reɪt ɪd -əd ‖ reɪʈ əd ~rates reɪts ~rating reɪt ɪŋ ‖ reɪʈ ɪŋ

transliteration trænˈs ˌlɪt ə ˈreɪʃ ən trɑːnˈs-, trænz-, trɑːnz-, ˌ·ˌ·-, trənz- ‖ trænˈs ˌlɪʈ trænz-, ˌ·ˌ·- ~s z

translo|cate ˈtrænˈs ləʊ| keɪt ˈtrɑːnˈs-, ˈtrænz-, ˈtrɑːnz-, ˌ·ˈ·· ‖ ˈtrænz loʊ|- ˈtrænˈs-, ˌ·ˈ··· ~cated keɪt ɪd -əd ‖ keɪʈ əd ~cates keɪts ~cating keɪt ɪŋ ‖ keɪʈ ɪŋ

translocation ˌtrænˈs ləʊ ˈkeɪʃ ən ˌtrɑːnˈs-, ˌtrænz-, ˌtrɑːnz- ‖ ˌtrænz loʊ- ˌtrænˈs-

translucenc|e trænˈs ˈluːs ənˈs trɑːnˈs-, trænz-, trɑːnz-, -ˈljuːs- ~y i

translucent trænˈs ˈluːs ənt trɑːnˈs-, trænz-, trɑːnz-, -ˈljuːs- ~ly li

transmig|rate ˌtrænz maɪ ˈg|reɪt ˌtrɑːnz-, ˌtrænˈs-, ˌtrɑːnˈs- ‖ ˌtrænˈs ˈmaɪg |reɪt ˌtrænz-, ˈˌ··· (*) ~rated reɪt ɪd -əd ‖ reɪʈ əd ~rates reɪts ~rating reɪt ɪŋ ‖ reɪʈ ɪŋ

transmigration ˌtrænz maɪ ˈgreɪʃ ən ˌtrɑːnz-, ˌtrænˈs-, ˌtrɑːnˈs- ‖ ˌtrænˈs- ˌtrænz- ~s z

transmissibility trænz ˌmɪs ə ˈbɪl ət i trɑːnz-, trænˈs-, trɑːnˈs-, ˌ·ˌ·-, -ɪˈ··-, -ɪt i ‖ trænˈs ˌmɪs ə ˈbɪl əʈ i trænz-, ˌ·ˌ·-

transmissible trænz ˈmɪs əb ᵊl trɑːnz-, trænˈs-, trɑːnˈs-, -ɪb ᵊl ‖ trænˈs- trænz-

transmission trænz ˈmɪʃ ən trɑːnz-, trænˈs-, trɑːnˈs- ‖ trænˈs- trænz- ~s z

transmissive trænz ˈmɪs ɪv trɑːnz-, trænˈs-, trɑːnˈs- ‖ trænˈs- trænz-

transmissivity ˌtrænz mɪ ˈsɪv ət i ˌtrɑːnz-, ˌtrænˈs-, ˌtrɑːnˈs-, -ɪt i ‖ ˌtrænˈs mɪ ˈsɪv əʈ i ˌtrænz-

trans|mit trænz |ˈmɪt trɑːnz-, trænˈs-, trɑːnˈs- ‖ trænˈs- trænz- ~mits ˈmɪts ~mitted ˈmɪt ɪd -əd ‖ ˈmɪʈ əd ~mitting ˈmɪt ɪŋ ‖ ˈmɪʈ ɪŋ

transmittal trænz ˈmɪt ᵊl trɑːnz-, trænˈs-, trɑːnˈs- ‖ trænˈs ˈmɪʈ ᵊl trænz- ~s z

transmittanc|e trænz ˈmɪt ᵊnᵗs trɑːnz-, trænˈs-, trɑːnˈs- ‖ trænˈs- trænz- **~y** i
transmitter trænz ˈmɪt ə trɑːnz-, trænˈs-, trɑːnˈs- ‖ trænˈs ˈmɪt̬ ᵊr trænz-, ˈ‥‥**~s** z
transmogrification trænz ˌmɒg rɪf ɪ ˈkeɪʃ ᵊn trɑːnz-, trænˈs-, trɑːnˈs-, ˌ‥ˌ‥, -rəf ·ˈ‥, §-ə'‥ ‖ trænˈs ˌmɑːg rəf ə- trænz-, ˌ‥ˌ‥ **~s** z
transmogri|fy trænz ˈmɒg rɪ |faɪ trɑːnz-, trænˈs-, trɑːnˈs-, ˌ‥, -rə faɪ ‖ trænˈs ˈmɑːg rə- trænz-, ˌ‥ **~fied** faɪd **~fies** faɪz **~fying** faɪ ɪŋ
transmutation ˌtrænz mju ˈteɪʃ ᵊn ˌtrɑːnz-, ˌtrænˈs-, ˌtrɑːnˈs- ‖ ˌtrænˈs- ˌtrænz- **~s** z
trans|mute trænz |ˈmjuːt trɑːnz-, trænˈs-, trɑːnˈs- ‖ trænˈs- trænz- **~muted** ˈmjuːt ɪd -əd ‖ ˈmjuːt̬ əd **~mutes** ˈmjuːts **~muting** ˈmjuːt ɪŋ ‖ ˈmjuːt̬ ɪŋ
transnational ˌtrænz ˈnæʃ ᵊn ᵊl ◂ ˌtrɑːnz-, ˌtrænˈs-, ˌtrɑːnˈs- ‖ ˌtrænˈs- ˌtrænz- **~s** z
transoceanic ˌtrænz ˌəʊʃ i ˈæn ɪk ˌtrɑːnz-, ˌtrænˈs-, ˌtrɑːnˈs-, -ˌəʊs- ‖ ˌtrænˈs ˌoʊʃ- ˌtrænz-
transom ˈtrænˈs əm **~ed** d **~s** z
transparenc|y trænˈs ˈpær ənˈs |i trɑːnˈs-, trænz-, trɑːnz-, ˌ‥, -ˌ‥, trɑnˈs-, trɑnz-, -ˈpeər- ‖ -ˈper- **~ies** iz
transparent trænˈs ˈpær ənt trɑːnˈs-, trænz-, trɑːnz-, ˌ‥, trɑnˈs-, trɑnz-, -ˈpeər- ‖ -ˈper- **~ly** li **~ness** nəs nɪs
transpiration ˌtrænˈs pə ˈreɪʃ ᵊn ˌtrɑːnˈs-, -pɪ-
tran|spire træn |ˈspaɪ ə trɑːn-, træn-, trɑːn-, §trən- ‖ -|ˈspaɪ ᵊr **~spired** ˈspaɪ əd ‖ ˈspaɪ ᵊrd **~spires** ˈspaɪ əz ‖ ˈspaɪ ᵊrz **~spiring** ˈspaɪ ər ɪŋ ‖ ˈspaɪ ər ɪŋ
trans|plant v ˌtrænˈs |ˈplɑːnt ˌtrɑːnˈs-, §-ˈplænt ‖ ˌtrænˈs |ˈplænt **~planted** ˈplɑːnt ɪd §ˈplænt-, -əd ‖ ˈplænt̬ əd **~planting** ˈplɑːnt ɪŋ §ˈplænt- ‖ ˈplænt̬ ɪŋ **~plants** ˈplɑːnts §ˈplænts ‖ ˈplænts
transplant n ˈtrænˈs plɑːnt ˈtrɑːnˈs-, §-ˈplænt ‖ ˈtrænˈs plænt **~s** s
transplantation ˌtrænˈs plɑːn ˈteɪʃ ᵊn ˌtrɑːnˈs-, -plæn- ‖ ˌtrænˈs plæn- **~s** z
transpolar ˌtrænz ˈpəʊl ə ◂ ˌtrɑːnz-, ˌtrænˈs-, ˌtrɑːnˈs- ‖ ˌtrænˈs ˈpoʊl ᵊr ◂
transponder træn ˈspɒnd ə trɑːn- ‖ træn ˈspɑːnd ᵊr trænˈs ˈpɑːnd- **~s** z
transpontine ˌtrænz ˈpɒnt aɪn ◂ ˌtrɑːnz-, ˌtrænˈs-, ˌtrɑːnˈs- ‖ ˌtrænˈs ˈpɑːnt-
trans|port v trænˈs |ˈpɔːt trɑːnˈs- ‖ trænˈs |ˈpɔːrt -ˈpoʊrt, ·ˈ‥ **~ported** ˈpɔːt ɪd -əd ‖ ˈpɔːrt̬ əd ˈpoʊrt- **~porting** ˈpɔːt ɪŋ ‖ ˈpɔːrt̬ ɪŋ ˈpoʊrt- **~ports** ˈpɔːts ‖ ˈpɔːrts ˈpoʊrts
transport n ˈtrænˈs pɔːt ˈtrɑːnˈs- ‖ ˈtrænˈs pɔːrt -poʊrt **~s** z
ˈtransport ˌcafe
transportable trænˈs ˈpɔːt əb ᵊl trɑːnˈs- ‖ trænˈs ˈpɔːrt̬- -ˈpoʊrt̬-
transportation ˌtrænˈs pɔː ˈteɪʃ ᵊn ˌtrɑːnˈs-, -pə- ‖ ˌtrænˈs pᵊr-
transporter trænˈs ˈpɔːt ə trɑːnˈs- ‖ trænˈs ˈpɔːrt̬ ᵊr -ˈpoʊrt-, ·ˈ‥‥**~s** z
transˈporter ˌbridge

transpos|e trænˈs ˈpəʊz trɑːnˈs- ‖ trænˈs ˈpoʊz **~al** ᵊl **~ed** d **~es** ɪz əz **~ing** ɪŋ
transposition ˌtrænˈs pə ˈzɪʃ ᵊn ˌtrɑːnˈs- **~s** z
transposon trænˈs ˈpəʊz ɒn trɑːnˈs- ‖ trænˈs ˈpoʊz ɑːn **~s** z
transputer trænˈs ˈpjuːt ə trɑːnˈs-, trænz-, trɑːnz- ‖ trænˈs ˈpjuːt̬ ᵊr **~s** z
transsexual træn ˈsek ʃu ᵊl trɑːn-, trænz-, trɑːnz-, ˌtrænˈs-, trɑːnˈs-, -ˈseks ju ᵊl, -ˈsek ʃᵊl ‖ trænˈs- **~ism** ˌɪz əm **~s** z
transship trænˈs ˈʃɪp trɑːnˈs-, →trænˈʃ-, →trɑːnˈʃ-, træn-, trɑːn-, trænz-, trɑːnz-, §trənˈs-, →§trənˈʃ-, §trən-, §trɑnz- ‖ trænˈs- →trænˈʃ- **~ment/s** mənt/s **~ped** t **~ping** ɪŋ **~s** s
Trans-Siberian ˌtrænz saɪ ˈbɪər i ᵊn ◂ ˌtrɑːnz-, ˌtrænˈs saɪ ˈbɪr-
transubstanti|ate ˌtrænˈs əb ˈstænˈtʃ i |eɪt ˌtrɑːnˈs-, §,ˌʌb-, -ˈstɑːnˈtʃ-, -ˈstænˈs- **~ated** eɪt ɪd -əd ‖ eɪt̬ əd **~ates** eɪts **~ating** eɪt ɪŋ ‖ eɪt̬ ɪŋ
transubstantiation ˌtrænˈs əb ˌstænˈtʃ i ˈeɪʃ ᵊn ˌtrɑːnˈs-, §,ˌʌb-, -ˌstɑːnˈtʃ-, -ˌstænˈs-
transudate ˈtrænˈs ju deɪt ˈtrɑːnˈs-, ˈtrænz-, ˈtrɑːnz-, -u- ‖ ˈtrænˈtʃ ə- **~s** s
transudation ˌtrænˈs ju ˈdeɪʃ ᵊn ˌtrɑːnˈs-, trænz-, ˌtrɑːnz-, -u- ‖ ˌtrænˈtʃ ə- **~s** z
transud|e træn ˈsjuːd trɑːn-, -ˈsuːd, -ˈzjuːd, -ˈzuːd ‖ -ˈsuːd **~ed** ɪd əd **~es** z **~ing** ɪŋ
transuranic ˌtrænz juᵊ ˈræn ɪk ◂ ˌtrɑːnz-, ˌtrænˈs-, ˌtrænz- ‖ ˌtrænˈs- ˌtrænz-, →ˌtrænˈtʃ-, →ˌtrænz-, -ə-
Transvaal ˌtrænz vɑːl ˌtrɑːnz-, ˈtrænˈs-, ˈtrɑːnˈs-, ·ˈ‥ ‖ ˌtrænˈs ˈvɑːl ˌtrænz- —*locally also* ˌ-ˈfɑːl **~er/s** ə/z ‖ -ᵊr/z
transvers|e ⁽ˌ⁾trænz ˈvɜːs ⁽ˌ⁾trɑːnz-, ⁽ˌ⁾trænˈs-, ⁽ˌ⁾trɑːnˈs- ‖ ⁽ˌ⁾trænˈs ˈvɜːs ⁽ˌ⁾trænz-, ·ˈ‥ **~al** ᵊl **~ally** ᵊl̬i **~ely** li
transvestism trænz ˈvest ˌɪz əm trɑːnz-, trænˈs-, trɑːnˈs- ‖ trænˈs- trænz-
transvestite trænz ˈvest aɪt trɑːnz-, trænˈs-, trɑːnˈs- ‖ trænˈs- trænz- **~s** s
Transworld *tdmk* ˌtrænz ˈwɜːld ◂ ˌtrɑːnz-, ˌtrænˈs-, ˌtrɑːnˈs- ‖ ˌtrænˈs ˈwɜːld ◂ ˌtrænz-
Transylvani|a ˌtrænˈs ɪl ˈveɪn i ˌjə ˌtrɑːnˈs-, ˌ·ᵊl- **~an/s** ən/z
Trant trænt
Tranter ˈtrænt ə ‖ ˈtrænt̬ ᵊr
trap træp **trapped** træpt **trapping** ˈtræp ɪŋ **traps** træps
trapdoor ˌtræp ˈdɔː ·ˈ‥ ‖ -ˈdɔːr -ˈdoʊr **~s** z
trapes treɪps **trapesed** treɪpst **trapeses** ˈtreɪps ɪz -əz **trapesing** ˈtreɪps ɪŋ
trapez|e trə ˈpiːz ‖ træ- **~es** ɪz əz **traˈpeze ˌartist**
trapezi|um trə ˈpiːz i ˌjəm **~a** ə **~i** aɪ **~ums** əmz **~us/es** əs /ɪz -əz
trapezoid ˈtræp ɪ zɔɪd -ə- **~s** z
Trapp træp
trapp... —*see* **trap**
trapper ˈtræp ə ‖ -ᵊr **~s** z
trappings ˈtræp ɪŋz

T

Trappist 'træp ɪst §-əst **~s** s

trapshooting 'træp ˌʃuːt ɪŋ ‖ -ˌʃuːt̬-

trash træʃ **trashed** træʃt **trashes** 'træʃ ɪz -əz **trashing** 'træʃ ɪŋ

trashcan 'træʃ kæn **~s** z

trash|man 'træʃ |mæn -mən **~men** men mən

trash|y 'træʃ |i **~ier** i ə ‖ i ə̣r **~iest** i ɪst i əst **~ily** ɪ li əl i **~iness** i nəs i nɪs

Trasimene 'træz ɪ miːn -ə-

trass træs

trattoria ˌtræt ə 'riː ə ‖ ˌtrɑːt̬- —*It* trattoría [trat to 'riː a] **~s** z

traum|a 'trɔːm |ə 'traʊm- ‖ 'traʊm |ə 'trɔːm-, 'trɑːm- **~as** əz **~ata** ət ə ‖ ət̬ ə

traumatic trɔː 'mæt ɪk traʊ- ‖ trə 'mæt̬ ɪk traʊ-, trɔː-, trɑː- **~ally** ə̣l i

traumatism 'trɔːm ə ˌtɪz əm 'traʊm- 'traʊm- 'trɔːm-, 'trɑːm- **~s** z

traumatization ˌtrɔːm ət aɪ 'zeɪʃ ə̣n ˌtraʊm-, -ɪ'-- ‖ ˌtraʊm ət̬ ə- ˌtrɔːm-, ˌtrɑːm-

traumatiz|e 'trɔːm ə taɪz 'traʊm- ‖ 'traʊm- 'trɔːm-, 'trɑːm- **~ed** d **~es** ɪz əz **~ing** ɪŋ

travail 'træv eɪə̣l trə 'veɪə̣l **~ed** d **~ing** ɪŋ **~s** z

Travancore ˌtræv ə̣n 'kɔː →-ə̣ŋ- ‖ 'træv ə̣n kɔːr -koʊr

travel 'træv ə̣l **~ed, ~led** d **~ing, ~ling** ɪŋ **~s** z 'travel ˌagency; 'travel ˌagent; 'travel((l)ing) ex,penses; ˌtravel(l)ing 'salesman

travelator 'træv ə leɪt ə -ə̣l eɪt- ‖ -ə̣l eɪt̬ ə̣r **~s** z

Travelcard 'træv ə̣l kɑːd ‖ -kɑːrd **~s** z

traveler, traveller 'træv ə̣l ə ‖ ə̣r **~s** z ˌtraveller's 'cheque ‖ 'traveler's check

Travelodge *tdmk* 'træv ə lɒdʒ ‖ -lɑːdʒ

travelog, travelogue 'træv ə lɒg ‖ -lɔːg -lɑːg **~s** z

travelsick 'træv ə̣l sɪk **~ness** nəs nɪs

Travers 'træv əz ‖ -ə̣rz

travers|e *n* 'træv ɜːs -əs; trə 'vɜːs, træ- ‖ 'træv ɜːs trə 'vɜːs, træ- **~es** ɪz əz

travers|e *v* trə 'vɜːs træ-, 'træv ɜːs, -əs ‖ trə 'vɜːs træ-, 'træv ə̣rs **~ed** t **~es** ɪz əz **~ing** ɪŋ

travertine 'træv ət ɪn §-ən; -ə tiːn ‖ -ə̣r tiːn

travest|y 'træv əst |i -ɪst i **~ies** iz

Traviata ˌtræv i 'ɑːt ə ‖ ˌtrɑːv- —*It* [tra vi 'a: ta, tra 'vja: ta]

Travis 'træv ɪs §-əs

travois *sing.* trə 'vɔɪ 'træv ɔɪ **~** *pl* z

travolator 'træv ə leɪt ə -ə̣l eɪt- ‖ -ə̣l eɪt̬ ə̣r **~s** z

Travolta trə 'vɒlt ə -'vəʊlt- ‖ -'voʊlt ə

trawl trɔːl ‖ trɑːl **trawled** trɔːld ‖ trɑːld **trawling** 'trɔːl ɪŋ ‖ 'trɑːl- **trawls** trɔːlz ‖ trɑːlz 'trawl line

trawler 'trɔːl ə ‖ -ə̣r 'trɑːl- **~man** mən **~men** mən men **~s** z

Trawsfynydd ˌtraʊs 'vʌn ɪð ˌtrɔːz-, -'fɪn-, -ɪd —*Welsh* [traus 'və nið, -nɪð]

tray treɪ **trays** treɪz

Treacher 'triːtʃ ə ‖ -ə̣r

treacherous 'tretʃ ə̣r əs **~ly** li **~ness** nəs nɪs

treacher|y 'tretʃ ə̣r |i **~ies** iz

treacle 'triːk ə̣l **~s** z

treacly 'triːk ə̣l i

tread tred **treading** 'tred ɪŋ **treads** tredz **trod** trɒd ‖ trɑːd **trodden** 'trɒd ə̣n ‖ 'trɑːd ə̣n

treadle 'tred ə̣l **~s** z

treadmill 'tred mɪl →'treb- **~s** z

treason 'triːz ə̣n **~s** z

treasonab|le 'triːz ə̣n əb |ə̣l **~leness** ə̣l nəs -nɪs **~ly** li

treasonous 'triːz ə̣n əs **~ly** li

treas|ure 'treʒ |ə ‖ -|ə̣r 'treɪʒ- **~ured** əd ‖ ə̣rd **~ures** əz ‖ ə̣rz **~uring** ə̣r ɪŋ 'treasure hunt; 'treasure trove

treasure-house 'treʒ ə haʊs ‖ -ə̣r-

treasurer 'treʒ ə̣r ə ‖ ə̣ ̣r 'treɪʒ- **~ship/s** ʃɪp/s **~s** z

treasur|y, T~ 'treʒ ə̣r |i ‖ 'treɪʒ- **~ies** iz 'treasury bill; 'treasury note

treat triːt **treated** 'triːt ɪd -əd ‖ 'triːt̬ əd **treating** 'triːt ɪŋ ‖ 'triːt̬ ɪŋ **treats** triːts

treatable 'triːt əb ə̣l ‖ 'triːt̬-

treatis|e 'triːt ɪz -ɪs, §-əz, §-əs ‖ 'triːt̬ əs **~es** ɪz əz

treatment 'triːt mənt **~s** s

treat|y 'triːt |i ‖ 'triːt̬ |i **~ies** iz 'treaty port

Trebizond 'treb ɪ zɒnd -ə- ‖ -ə zɑːnd

treble 'treb ə̣l **~d** d **~s** z **trebling** 'treb ə̣l̩ ɪŋ ˌtreble 'chance; ˌtreble 'clef

Treblinka tre 'blɪŋk ə trə-

Trebor *tdmk* 'triː bɔː ‖ -bɔːr

trebuchet 'treb ju ʃet -ə-, -ʃeɪ, ˌ·'·

Tredegar trɪ 'diːg ə trə- ‖ -ə̣r

tree, Tree triː **treed** triːd **treeing** 'triː ɪŋ **trees** triːz 'tree ˌdiagram; 'tree fern; 'tree frog; 'tree ˌsurgeon

treecreeper 'triː ˌkriːp ə ‖ -ə̣r **~s** z

tree|house 'triː |haʊs **~houses** haʊz ɪz -əz

tree-hugg|er 'triː ˌhʌg |ə ‖ -|ə̣r **~ers** əz ‖ ə̣rz **~ing** ɪŋ

treeless 'triː ləs -lɪs

treeline 'triː laɪn **~d** d

treen triːn

treetop 'triː tɒp -ˌtɑːp **~s** s

treetrunk 'triː trʌŋk **~s** s

Trefdraeth 'trev draɪθ

Trefeglwys trɪv 'eg lu ɪs

Trefgarne 'tref gɑːn ‖ -gɑːrn

trefoil 'tref ɔɪə̣l 'triː fɔɪə̣l **~ed** d **~s** z

Trefor 'trev ə ‖ -ə̣r —*Welsh* ['tre vor]

Trefusis trɪ 'fjuːs ɪs trə-, §-əs

Tregaron trɪ 'gær ə̣n trə- ‖ -'ger-

Treharris trɪ 'hær ɪs trə-, §-əs ‖ -'her-

Trehearne, Treherne trɪ 'hɜːn trə- ‖ -'hɜːrn

trek trek **trekked** trekt **trekking** 'trek ɪŋ **treks** treks

trekker 'trek ə ‖ -ə̣r **~s** z

trekkie, T~ 'trek i **~s** z

Trelawney trə 'lɔːn i trɪ- ‖ -'lɑːn-

trellis 'trel ɪs §-əs **~ed** t **~es** ɪz əz **~ing** ɪŋ **~work** wɜːk ‖ wɜːrk

Tremain trɪ ˈmeɪn trə-
trematode ˈtrem ə təʊd ˈtriːm- ‖ -toʊd ~s z
tremble ˈtrem b³l ~d d ~s z **trembling/ly**
ˈtrem blɪŋ /li
trembler ˈtrem blə ‖ -bl³r ~s z
trem|bly ˈtrem| bli ~blier bli̯ ə ‖ bli̯ʳr ~bliest
bli̯ ɪst ̩əst
tremendous trə ˈmend əs trɪ-, △-ˈmendʒ- ~ly
li ~ness nəs nɪs
Tremlett ˈtrem lət -lɪt
tremolo ˈtrem ə ləʊ ‖ -loʊ ~s z
tremor ˈtrem ə ‖ -³r —as a medical term, also
ˈtriːm- ~s z
tremulant ˈtrem jʊl ənt -jəl- ‖ -jəl-
tremulous ˈtrem jʊl əs -jəl- ‖ -jəl- ~ly li ~ness
nəs nɪs
trench, T~ trentʃ **trenched** trentʃt **trenches**
ˈtrentʃ ɪz -əz **trenching** ˈtrentʃ ɪŋ
ˈtrench coat
trenchancy ˈtrentʃ ən¹s i
trenchant ˈtrentʃ ənt ~ly li
Trenchard ˈtrentʃ ɑːd -əd ‖ -ɑːrd -³rd
trencher ˈtrentʃ ə ‖ -³r ~s z
trencher|man ˈtrentʃ ə |mən ‖ -³r- ~men mən
men
trend trend **trended** ˈtrend ɪd -əd **trending**
ˈtrend ɪŋ **trends** trendz
trendsett|ing ˈtrend ˌset |ɪŋ ‖ -ˌseţ |ɪŋ ~er/s
ə/z ‖ ³r/z
trend-spott|er ˈtrend ˌspɒt |ə ‖ -ˌspaːţ |³r
~ers əz ‖ ³rz ~ing ɪŋ
trend|y ˈtrend |i ~ier i̯ ə ‖ i̯³r ~iest i̯ ɪst i̯ əst
~ily ɪ li əl i ~iness i nəs i nɪs
Trengganu treŋ ˈgaːn uː
Trent trent
Trentham ˈtrent əm
Trenton ˈtrent ən ‖ -³n
Treorchy tri ˈɔːk i ‖ -ˈɔːrk i
trepan trɪ ˈpæn trə- ~ned d ~ning ɪŋ ~s z
trepang trɪ ˈpæŋ trə-; ˈtriː pæŋ ~s z
trephination ˌtref ɪ ˈneɪʃ ³n §-ə- ~s z
trephin|e trɪ ˈfiːn trə-, tre-, -ˈfaɪn ~ed d ~es z
~ing ɪŋ
trepidation ˌtrep ɪ ˈdeɪʃ ³n §-ə-
treponem|a ˌtrep ə ˈniːm |ə ~ata ət ə ‖ əţ ə
Tresco ˈtresk əʊ ‖ -oʊ
Trescothick trɪ ˈskɒθ ɪk trə- ‖ -ˈskɑːθ-
Tresillian trɪ ˈsɪl i̯ ən trə-
trespass ˈtresp əs §ˈtres paːs, §-pæs ‖ ˈtres pæs
~ed t ~er/s ə/z ‖ ³r/z ~es ɪz əz ~ing ɪŋ
tress tres **tresses** ˈtres ɪz -əz
trestle ˈtres ³l ~s z
Tretchikoff ˈtretʃ ɪ kɒf ‖ -kɔːf -kɑːf
Trethowan trɪ ˈθaʊ ən trə-, -ˈθəʊ-
trevall|y trɪ ˈvæl| i trə- ~ies iz
Trevelyan (i) trɪ ˈvɪl jən trə-, (ii) -ˈvel- —In
Cornwall, (i).
Trevethick trɪ ˈveθ ɪk trə-
Trevino trə ˈviːn əʊ trɪ- ‖ -oʊ
Trevithick ˈtrev ɪθ ɪk -əθ-; trə ˈvɪθ ɪk
Trevor ˈtrev ə ‖ -³r
trews truːz
trey treɪ (= tray) **treys** treɪz

tri- as a productive prefix ˈtraɪ — but in certain
established words ˈtrɪ (see entries)
— **trichromatic** ˌtraɪ krəʊ ˈmæt ɪk ◂
‖ -kroʊ ˈmæţ-
triable ˈtraɪ̯ əb ³l
triad, Triad ˈtraɪ æd ˈtraɪ̯ əd ~s z
triage ˈtriː ɑːʒ ˈtraɪ-, -ɪdʒ ‖ tri ˈɑːʒ
trial ˈtraɪ̯ əl ‖ ˈtraɪ̯ əl ~ed, ~led d ~ing, ~ling
ɪŋ ~s z
ˈtrial court; ˌtrial ˈrun
triangle ˈtraɪ æŋ g³l ~s z
triangular traɪ ˈæŋ gjʊl ə -gjəl- ‖ -gjəl ³r ~ly
li
triangularity traɪ ˌæŋ gju ˈlær ət i ˌˌˌ-,-gjə-,
-ɪt i ‖ -gjə ˈlær əţ i -ˈler-
triangu|late traɪ ˈæŋ gju |leɪt -gjə- ‖ -gjə-
~lated leɪt ɪd -əd ‖ leɪţ əd ~lates leɪts
~lating leɪt ɪŋ ‖ leɪţ ɪŋ
triangulation traɪ ˌæŋ gju ˈleɪʃ ³n ˌˌˌ-, -gjə-
‖ -gjə- ~s z
triassic, T~ traɪ ˈæs ɪk
triathlete ₍₎traɪ ˈæθ liːt ~s s
triathlon ₍₎traɪ ˈæθ lən -lɒn ‖ -lɑːn
tribade ˈtrɪb əd ~s z
tribadism ˈtrɪb əd ˌɪz əm
tribal ˈtraɪb ³l ~ly i ~s z
tribalism ˈtraɪb ə ˌlɪz əm -³l ˌɪz-
tribalistic ˌtraɪb ə ˈlɪst ɪk ◂
tribe traɪb **tribes** traɪbz
Tribeca traɪ ˈbek ə
tribes|man ˈtraɪbz |mən ~men mən men
~people ˌpiːp ³l ~woman ˌwʊm ən ~women
ˌwɪm ɪn §-ən
tribo- comb. form
with stress-neutral suffix ˈtraɪb əʊ ˈtrɪb- ‖ -oʊ
— **triboluminescent**
ˌtraɪb əʊ ˌluːm ɪ ˈnes ³nt ˌtrɪb-, -, ljuːm-, -ə¹--
‖ ˌˌ-oʊ-
with stress-imposing suffix traɪ ˈbɒ+ trɪ-
‖ -ˈbaː+ — **tribology** traɪ ˈbɒl ədʒ i trɪ-
‖ -ˈbaːl-
tribrach ˈtrɪb ræk ˈtraɪ bræk ~s s
tribulation ˌtrɪb ju ˈleɪʃ ³n -jə- ‖ -jə- ~s z
tribunal traɪ ˈbjuːn ³l trɪ- ~s z
tribune ˈtrɪb juːn ‖ trɪ ˈbjuːn ~s z
tributar|y ˈtrɪb jʊt ər |i ‖ -jə ter |i ~ies iz
tribute ˈtrɪb juːt -jət ~s s
trice traɪs
Tricel tdmk ˈtraɪ sel
triceps ˈtraɪs eps
triceratops ₍₎traɪ ˈser ə tɒps ‖ -tɑːps
trichin|a trɪ ˈkaɪn |ə trə- ~ae iː ~as əz
trichinosis ˌtrɪk ɪ ˈnəʊs ɪs -ə-, §-əs ‖ -ˈnoʊs-
trichloroethylene ˌtraɪ ˌklɔːr əʊ ˈeθ ə liːn
-ˌklɒr-, -ɪ liːn, -³l iːn ‖ -oʊ- -ˌklour-
trichological ˌtrɪk ə ˈlɒdʒ ɪk ³l ◂ ‖ -ˈlaːdʒ- ~ly
i
trichologist trɪ ˈkɒl ədʒ ɪst §-əst ‖ -ˈkaːl- ~s s
trichology trɪ ˈkɒl ədʒ i ‖ -ˈkaːl-
trichomoniasis ˌtrɪk əʊ məʊ ˈnaɪ̯ əs ɪs -mə¹--,
§-əs ‖ ˌtrɪk əm ə-
trichotom|y ˌtraɪ ˈkɒt əm |i ‖ -ˈkaːţ- ~ies iz
Tricia ˈtrɪʃ ə ‖ ˈtriːʃ-

tri-city ˌtraɪ 'sɪt i ◂ '·ˌ· ‖ -'sɪt̬-
Tricity *tdmk* 'trɪs ət i -ɪt i ‖ -ət̬ i
trick trɪk **tricked** trɪkt **tricking** 'trɪk ɪŋ **tricks**
 trɪks
  ˌtrick or 'treat
tricker|y 'trɪk ər |i ~**ies** iz
trickl|e 'trɪk ᵊl ~**ed** d ~**es** z ~**ing** ɪŋ
trickle-down 'trɪk ᵊl daʊn
trick-or-treating ˌtrɪk ɔː 'triːt ɪŋ
 ‖ ˌtrɪk ᵊr 'triːt̬ ɪŋ
trickster 'trɪk stə ‖ -stᵊr ~**s** z
tricksy 'trɪks i
trick|y 'trɪk |i ~**ier** i ə ‖ i ᵊr ~**iest** i ɪst i əst
 ~**ily** ɪ li əl i ~**iness** i nəs i nɪs
triclini|um traɪ 'klɪn i |əm trə-, -'klaɪn- ~**a** ə
tricolor, tricolour 'trɪk əl ə ˌtraɪ ˌkʌl ə
 ‖ 'traɪ ˌkʌl ᵊr ~**s** z
tricorn 'traɪ kɔːn ‖ -kɔːrn ~**s** z
tricot 'trɪk əʊ 'triːk- ‖ 'triːk oʊ ~**s** z
tricuspid ₍ₗ₎traɪ 'kʌsp ɪd §-əd ~**s** z
tricycl|e 'traɪs ɪk ᵊl -ək- ~**ed** d ~**es** z ~**ing** ɪŋ
trident, T~ 'traɪd ᵊnt ~**s** s
Tridentine traɪ 'dent aɪn trɪ-, trə-, -iːn, -ɪn
tried traɪd
triennial traɪ 'en i əl ~**ly** i
trienni|um traɪ 'en i |əm ~**a** ə ~**ums** əmz
trier 'traɪ̯ə ‖ 'traɪ̯ᵊr ~**s** z
Trier *place in Germany* trɪə ‖ trɪᵊr —*Ger* [tʁiːɐ]
trierarch 'traɪ̯ə rɑːk ‖ -rɑːrk ~**s** s
tries traɪz
Trieste tri 'est —*It* [tri 'ɛs te]
triffid 'trɪf ɪd §-əd ~**s** z
trifid 'traɪf ɪd §-əd
trifl|e 'traɪf ᵊl ~**ed** d ~**es** z ~**ing** ɪŋ
trifler 'traɪf lə ‖ -lᵊr ~**s** z
trifling *adj* 'traɪf lɪŋ ~**ly** li ~**ness** nəs nɪs
trifocal ˌtraɪ 'fəʊk ᵊl ‖ ˌtraɪ 'foʊk ᵊl ~**s** z
trifori|um traɪ 'fɔːr i |əm ‖ -'foʊr- ~**a** ə
trig, Trig trɪg
trigeminal ₍ₗ₎traɪ 'dʒem ɪn ᵊl -ən ᵊl
trigger, T~ 'trɪg ə ‖ -ᵊr ~**ed** d **triggering**
 'trɪg ər ɪŋ ~**s** z
trigger-happy 'trɪg ə ˌhæp i ‖ -ᵊr-
triglyceride traɪ 'glɪs ə raɪd ~**s** z
triglyph 'trɪg lɪf 'traɪ glɪf ~**s** s
trigonal 'trɪg ən ᵊl ~**ly** i
trigonometric ˌtrɪg ən ə 'metr ɪk ◂ ~**al** ᵊl
 ~**ally** ᵊl̬ i
  ˌtrigonoˌmetric 'function
trigonometry ˌtrɪg ə 'nɒm ətr i -ɪtr i
 ‖ -'nɑːm-
trigraph 'traɪ grɑːf -græf ‖ -græf ~**s** s
trijet 'traɪ dʒet ~**s** s
trike traɪk **trikes** traɪks
trilateral ˌtraɪ 'læt ər əl ◂ ‖ -'læt̬ ər əl
 →-'lætr əl ~**ly** i
trilb|y, T~ 'trɪlb |i ~**ies** iz
  ˌtrilby 'hat
trilingual ˌtraɪ 'lɪŋ gwəl ◂ -gju̯əl ~**ly** i ~**s** z
triliteral ˌtraɪ 'lɪt̬ ər əl ◂ ‖ -'lɪt̬ ər əl →-'lɪtr əl
 ~**s** z
trill trɪl **trilled** trɪld **trilling** 'trɪl ɪŋ **trills** trɪlz
Trilling 'trɪl ɪŋ

trillion 'trɪl jən '·i ən ~**s** z
trillionth 'trɪl jənᵗθ '·i ənᵗθ ~**s** s
trillium 'trɪl i əm
trilobite 'traɪl əʊ baɪt ‖ -ə- ~**s** s
trilog|y 'trɪl ədʒ |i ~**ies** iz
trim, Trim trɪm **trimmed** trɪmd **trimming/s**
 'trɪm ɪŋ/z **trims** trɪmz
trimaran 'traɪm ə ræn ˌ·ˈ· ~**s** z
Trimble 'trɪm bᵊl
trimester traɪ 'mest ə trɪ- ‖ -ᵊr '··· ~**s** z
trimeter 'trɪm ɪt ə -ət- ‖ -ət̬ ᵊr ~**s** z
trimly 'trɪm li
trimm... —*see* **trim**
trimmer 'trɪm ə ‖ -ᵊr ~**s** z
trimness 'trɪm nəs -nɪs
Trina 'triːn ə
Trincomalee ˌtrɪŋk əʊ mə 'liː ‖ -ə mə-
Trinculo 'trɪŋk ju ləʊ -jə- ‖ -jə loʊ
Trinder 'trɪnd ə ‖ -ᵊr
trine traɪn **trines** traɪnz
Tring trɪŋ
Trinidad 'trɪn ɪ dæd -ə-, ˌ·ˈ·
Trinidadian ˌtrɪn ɪ 'dæd i ən ◂ ˌ·ə-, -'deɪd- ~**s** z
trinitarian, T~ ˌtrɪn ə 'teər i ən ◂ ˌ·ɪ- ‖ -'ter-
 ~**ism** ˌɪz əm ~**s** z
trinitrotoluene ˌtraɪ ˌnaɪtr əʊ 'tɒl ju iːn ·ˌ··
 ‖ -oʊ 'tɑːl-
trinity, T~ 'trɪn ət i -ɪt i ‖ -ət̬ i
  ˌTrinity 'College, ˌTrinity ˌCollege
  'Cambridge; ˌTrinity 'House; ˌTrinity
  'Sunday
trinket 'trɪŋk ɪt §-ət ~**s** s
Trinn|ie, Trinn|y 'trɪn i ~**ies** iz
trinomial traɪ 'nəʊm i əl ‖ -'noʊm- ~**s** z
trio 'triː əʊ ‖ -oʊ ~**s** z
triode 'traɪ əʊd ‖ -oʊd ~**s** z
triolet 'triː ə let 'traɪ̯-, -əʊ-, -lət, -lɪt ~**s** s
trioxide ₍ₗ₎traɪ 'ɒks aɪd ‖ -'ɑːks- ~**s** z
trip trɪp **tripped** trɪpt **tripping/ly** 'trɪp ɪŋ /li
 trips trɪps
tripartite ₍ₗ₎traɪ 'pɑːt aɪt ‖ -'pɑːrt-
tripe traɪp **tripes** traɪps
triphammer 'trɪp ˌhæm ə ‖ -ᵊr ~**s** z
triphthong 'trɪf θɒŋ 'trɪp- ‖ -θɑːŋ -θɔːŋ ~**s** z
triphthongal ˌtrɪf 'θɒŋ gᵊl ◂ ˌtrɪp- ‖ -'θɔːŋ-
 -'θɑːŋ- ~**ly** i
tripl|e 'trɪp ᵊl ~**ed** d ~**es** z ~**ing** ɪŋ
  ˌTriple Al'liance; 'triple jump, ·ˌ·ˈ·
triplet 'trɪp lət -lɪt ~**s** s
triplex, T~ *tdmk* 'trɪp leks
triplicate *adj, n* 'trɪp lɪk ət -lək-, -ɪt
tripli|cate *v* 'trɪp lɪ |keɪt -lə- ~**cated** keɪt ɪd
 -əd ‖ keɪt̬ əd ~**cates** keɪts ~**cating** keɪt ɪŋ
 ‖ keɪt̬ ɪŋ
triploid 'trɪp lɔɪd ~**s** z
tripod 'traɪ pɒd ‖ -pɑːd ~**s** z
Tripoli, t~ 'trɪp əl i
Tripolis 'trɪp əl ɪs §-əs
Tripolitania ˌtrɪp əl i 'teɪn i ə -ə'··
tripos 'traɪp ɒs ‖ -ɑːs ~**es** ɪz əz
Tripp trɪp
tripp... —*see* **trip**
tripper 'trɪp ə ‖ -ᵊr ~**s** z

triptan 'trɪpt æn
triptane 'trɪpt eɪn
Triptolemus trɪp 'tɒl ɪm əs -əm- ‖ -'tɑːl-
triptych 'trɪpt ɪk ~s s
triptyque trɪp 'tiːk ~s s
Tripura 'trɪp ʊr ə -ər-
tripwire 'trɪp ˌwaɪ ə ‖ -ˌwaɪ ər ~s z
trireme 'traɪ° riːm ~s z
trisect ˌ(ˌ)traɪ 'sekt ~ed ɪd əd ~ing ɪŋ ~s s
Trish trɪʃ
Trisha 'trɪʃ ə
trishaw 'traɪ ʃɔː ‖ -ʃɑː ~s z
triskaidekaphobia ˌtrɪs kaɪ ˌdek ə 'fəʊb i ə
      ·, ·- ‖ -'foʊb-
triskeli|on trɪ 'skel i |ɒn ˌ(ˌ)traɪ-, ən ‖ -|ɑːn ~a
      ə
trismus 'trɪz məs
trisomy 'trɪs əm i 'traɪ səʊm i ‖ 'traɪ soʊm i
Tristan 'trɪst ən
      ˌTristan da 'Cunha də 'kuːn ə -jə
Tri-Star *tdmk* 'traɪ stɑː ‖ -stɑːr ~s z
tristate 'traɪ steɪt
Tristram 'trɪs trəm
trisyllabic ˌtraɪ sɪ 'læb ɪk ◄ -sə- ~ally ᵊl i
trisyllable ˌtraɪ 'sɪl əb ᵊl '·, ·- ~s z
trite traɪt **triter** 'traɪt ə ‖ 'traɪt̬ ər **tritest**
      'traɪt ɪst -əst ‖ 'traɪt̬ əst
trite|ly 'traɪt |li ~ness nəs nɪs
triticale ˌtrɪt ɪ 'keɪl i -ə- ‖ ˌtrɪt̬ ə-
tritium 'trɪt i_əm ‖ 'trɪt̬- 'trɪʃ-
triton *'nucleus of a tritium atom'* 'traɪt ɒn -ᵊn
      ‖ -ɑːn
Triton *'sea god', 'mollusc', 'satellite of*
      Neptune', t~ 'traɪt ᵊn -ɒn ‖ -ɑːn
tritone 'traɪ təʊn ‖ -toʊn ~s z
triumph *n, v, T~* 'traɪ ʌmᵖf 'traɪˌəmᵖf ~ed t
      ~ing ɪŋ ~s s
triumphal traɪ 'ʌmᵖf ᵊl ~ism ˌɪz əm
triumphant traɪ 'ʌmᵖf ənt ~ly li
triumvir traɪ 'ʌm və tri-, 'traɪˌəm-, -vɜː ‖ -vᵊr
      ~s z
triumvirate traɪ 'ʌm vər ət tri-, -vɪr-, -ɪt ~s s
triune 'traɪ juːn
trivalent ˌ(ˌ)traɪ 'veɪl ənt 'trɪv əl-
Trivandrum trɪ 'vændr əm
trivet 'trɪv ɪt §-ət ~s s
trivia 'trɪv i_ə
trivial 'trɪv i_əl ~ly i
trivialis... *—see* **trivializ...**
trivialit|y ˌtrɪv i 'æl ət |i -ɪt i ‖ -əʈ |i ~ies iz
trivialization ˌtrɪv i_əl aɪ 'zeɪʃ ᵊn -ɪ'·- ‖ -ə'·-
trivializ|e 'trɪv i_ə laɪz ~ed d ~es ɪz əz ~ing
      ɪŋ
trivium 'trɪv i_əm
triweek|ly ˌ(ˌ)traɪ 'wiːk |li ~ies iz
Trixie 'trɪks i
Troad 'trəʊ æd ‖ 'troʊ-
Troas 'trəʊ æs ‖ 'troʊ-
Trobriand 'trəʊb ri_ənd -ænd ‖ 'troʊb-
Trocadero ˌtrɒk ə 'dɪər əʊ ‖ ˌtrɑːk ə 'der oʊ
trocar 'trəʊk ɑː ‖ 'troʊk ɑːr ~s z
trochaic trəʊ 'keɪ ɪk ‖ troʊ- ~s s
trochanter trəʊ 'kænt ə ‖ troʊ 'kænt̬ ər ~s z

troche trəʊʃ 'trəʊk iː ‖ 'troʊk iː **troches**
      'trɒʃ ɪz -əz; 'trəʊk iːz ‖ 'troʊk iːz
trochee ˈtrəʊk iː; -i ‖ 'troʊk- ~s z
trochle|a 'trɒk li ¦ə ‖ 'trɑːk- ~ae iː
trochlear 'trɒk li ə ‖ 'trɑːk li ᵊr
trochoid 'trəʊk ɔɪd 'trɒk- ‖ 'troʊk- 'trɑːk- ~s
trod trɒd ‖ trɑːd
trodden 'trɒd ᵊn ‖ 'trɑːd ᵊn
trog trɒg ‖ trɑːg trɔːg
troglodyte 'trɒg lə daɪt ‖ 'trɑːg- ~s s
troglodytes *sing. 'wren'* ˌtrɒg lə 'daɪt iːz
      trɒ 'glɒd ə tiːz, -ɪ- ‖ ˌtrɑːg-
troglodytic ˌtrɒg lə 'dɪt ɪk ◄
      ‖ ˌtrɑːg lə 'dɪt̬ ɪk ◄
trogon, T~ 'trəʊg ɒn ‖ 'troʊg ɑːn ~s z
troika 'trɔɪk ə 'trəʊ ɪk ə ~s z
troilism 'trɔɪ ˌlɪz əm
Troilus 'trɔɪl əs 'trəʊ ɪl əs, §-əl- ‖ 'troʊ əl-
Trojan 'trəʊdʒ ən ‖ 'troʊdʒ ən ~s z
      ˌTrojan 'horse; ˌTrojan 'War
troll trɒl trəʊl ‖ troʊl —*In BrE both*
      pronunciations shown appear to be in use for
      all the various meanings (both n and v) of the
      word. **trolled** trɒld trəʊld ‖ troʊld **trolling**
      'trɒl ɪŋ 'trəʊl- ‖ 'troʊl ɪŋ **trolls** trɒlz trəʊlz
      ‖ troʊlz
trolley 'trɒl i ‖ 'trɑːl i ~s z
trolleybus 'trɒl i bʌs ‖ 'trɑːl- ~es ɪz əz
trollop 'trɒl əp ‖ 'trɑːl əp ~s s
Trollope 'trɒl əp ‖ 'trɑːl əp
trombone trɒm 'bəʊn ‖ trɑːm 'boʊn '·· ~s z
trombonist trɒm 'bəʊn ɪst §-əst
      ‖ trɑːm 'boʊn- '··· ~s s
tromp trɒmp ‖ trɑːmp **tromped** trɒmpt
      ‖ trɑːmpt **tromping** 'trɒmp ɪŋ ‖ 'trɑːmp ɪŋ
      tromps trɒmps ‖ trɑːmps
trompe l'oeil ˌtrɒmp 'lɔɪ -'ləʊ ɪ, -'lɔː jə
      ‖ ˌtrɔːmp- ˌtrɑːmp-, -'leɪ —*Fr* [tʁɔ̃ plœj]
Tromsø 'trɒm səʊ ‖ 'trɑːm soʊ —*Norw*
      ['trʊm søː]
Trondheim 'trɒnd haɪm 'trɒn- ‖ 'trɑːn heɪm
      —*Norw* ['trɔn heɪm]
Troon truːn
troop truːp **trooped** truːpt **trooping** 'truːp ɪŋ
      troops truːps
      'troop ˌcarrier
trooper 'truːp ə ‖ -ᵊr ~s z
troopship 'truːp ʃɪp ~s s
trope trəʊp ‖ troʊp **tropes** trəʊps ‖ troʊps
-trope trəʊp ‖ troʊp — **heliotrope**
      'hiːl i ə trəʊp ‖ -troʊp
trophic 'trɒf ɪk ‖ 'troʊf ɪk 'trɑːf- ~ally ᵊl i
-trophic 'trɒf ɪk ‖ 'troʊf ɪk 'trɑːf-
      — **hypertrophic** ˌhaɪp ə 'trɒf ɪk ◄
      ‖ -ᵊr 'troʊf- -'trɑːf-
tropho- *comb. form*
      with stress-neutral suffix ¦trɒf əʊ ‖ ¦troʊf ə
      ¦trɑːf ə — **trophoplasm** 'trɒf əʊ ˌplæz əm
      ‖ 'troʊf ə- 'trɑːf-
      with stress-imposing suffix trəʊ 'fɒ+ trɒ-
      ‖ troʊ 'fɑː+ — **trophology** trəʊ 'fɒl ədʒ i
      trɒ- ‖ troʊ 'fɑːl-
troph|y 'trəʊf |i ‖ 'troʊf |i ~ies iz

-trophy *stress-imposing* trəf i — **hypertrophy**
  haɪ 'pɜːtr əf i ‖ -'pɜːtr-
tropic 'trɒp ɪk ‖ 'traːp ɪk **~s** s
-tropic 'trɒp ɪk ‖ 'troʊp ɪk — **heliotropic**
  ˌhiːl i ə 'trɒp ɪk ◄ ‖ ə 'troʊp-
tropical 'trɒp ɪk ᵊl ‖ 'traːp- **~ly** _i
  ˌtropical 'storm
tropicalis|e, tropicaliz|e 'trɒp ɪk ə laɪz
  -ᵊl aɪz ‖ 'traːp- **~ed** d **~es** ɪz əz **~ing** ɪŋ
tropism 'trəʊp ˌɪz əm ‖ 'troʊp- **~s** z
-tropism trə ˌpɪz əm 'trəʊp ˌɪz əm, ˌ···
  —*Usage varies as to whether this suffix is
  stress-imposing or stress-neutral.* —
  heliotropism ˌhiːl i 'ɒtr ə ˌpɪz əm
  əʊ 'trəʊp ˌɪz əm, '···,ˌ··· ‖ -'aːtr ə ˌpɪz əm
  ə 'troʊp ˌɪz əm
tropo- *comb. form*
  with stress-neutral suffix ⎮trɒp əʊ ‖ ⎮troʊp ə
  'traːp- — **tropophyte** 'trɒp əʊ faɪt
  ‖ 'troʊp ə- 'traːp-
  with stress-imposing suffix trɒ 'pɒ + trə-
  ‖ troʊ 'paː + — **tropophilous** trɒ 'pɒf ɪl əs
  trə-, -əl əs ‖ troʊ 'paːf-
tropopause 'trɒp ə pɔːz ‖ 'troʊp- 'traːp-, -paːz
troposphere 'trɒp ə sfɪə ‖ 'troʊp ə sfɪr 'traːp-
-tropous *stress-imposing* trəp əs —
  heterotropous ˌhet ə 'rɒtr əp əs ◄
  ‖ ˌheṭ ə 'raːtr-
troppo 'trɒp əʊ ‖ 'traːp oʊ —*It* ['trɔp po]
Trossachs 'trɒs əks -æks, -əxs ‖ 'traːs-
trot, Trot trɒt ‖ traːt **trots** trɒts ‖ traːts
  trotted 'trɒt ɪd -əd ‖ 'traːṭ əd **trotting**
  'trɒt ɪŋ ‖ 'traːṭ ɪŋ
troth trəʊθ trɒθ ‖ trɔːθ traːθ, troʊθ
Trotsky 'trɒt ski ‖ 'traːt- **~ism** ˌɪz əm
Trotskyist 'trɒt ski ɪst §-əst ‖ 'traːt- **~s** s
Trotskyite 'trɒt ski aɪt ‖ 'traːt- **~s** s
Trott trɒt ‖ traːt
trott... —*see* **trot**
trotter, T~ 'trɒt ə ‖ 'traːṭ ᵊr **~s** z
Trottiscliffe 'trɒz li ‖ 'traːz- (!)
troubadour 'truːb ə dʊə -dɔː ‖ -dɔːr -dʊər
  ~s z
troubl|e 'trʌb ᵊl (!) **~ed** d **~es** z **~ing** ɪŋ
  'trouble spot
trouble-free ˌtrʌb ᵊl 'friː ◄
troublemak|er 'trʌb ᵊl ˌmeɪk| ə ‖ -ᵊr **~ers** əz
  ‖ ᵊrz **~ing** ɪŋ
troubleshoot 'trʌb ᵊl ʃuːt **~s** s
troubleshoot|er 'trʌb ᵊl ˌʃuːt| ə ‖ -ˌʃuːṭ| -ᵊr
  ~ers əz ‖ ᵊrz **~ing** ɪŋ
troublesome 'trʌb ᵊl səm **~ly** li **~ness** nəs nɪs
troublous 'trʌb ləs
Troubridge 'truː brɪdʒ
trough trɒf trɔːf ‖ trɔːf traːf **troughs** trɒfs trɔːfs
  ‖ trɔːfs traːfs
Troughton 'traʊt ᵊn
trounce traʊnⷦs **trounced** traʊnⷦst **trounces**
  'traʊnⷦs ɪz -əz **trouncing** 'traʊnⷦs ɪŋ
troupe truːp (= *troop*) **troupes** truːps
trouper 'truːp ə ‖ -ᵊr **~s** z
troupial 'truːp i əl **~s** z

trouser 'traʊz ə ‖ -ᵊr **~ed** d
  'trouser press; 'trouser suit
trousers 'traʊz əz ⚠ -ɪz- ‖ -ᵊrz
trousseau 'truːs əʊ truː 'səʊ ‖ truː 'soʊ
  'truːs oʊ **~s, ~x** z
trout traʊt **trouts** traʊts
Troutbeck 'traʊt bek
trove trəʊv ‖ troʊv
trow trəʊ traʊ ‖ troʊ
Trowbridge 'trəʊ brɪdʒ ‖ 'troʊ-
trowel 'traʊ əl traʊl ‖ 'traʊ əl **troweled,**
  trowelled 'traʊ əld traʊld ‖ 'traʊ əld
  troweling, trowelling 'traʊ əl ɪŋ 'traʊl ɪŋ
  ‖ 'traʊ əl ɪŋ **trowels** 'traʊ əlz traʊlz
  ‖ 'traʊ əlz
Trowell (i) 'traʊ əl traʊl ‖ 'traʊ əl, (ii) 'trəʊ əl
  ‖ 'troʊ əl
Troy, troy trɔɪ
  'troy weight
truanc|y 'truː ənⷦs |i **~ies** iz
tru|ant 'truː |ənt **~anted** ənt ɪd -əd ‖ əṇṭ əd
  ~anting ənt ɪŋ ‖ əṇṭ ɪŋ **~ants** ənts
Trubenised, Trubenized *tdmk* 'truːb ə naɪzd
Trubetzkoy ˌtruːb ets 'kɔɪ -ɪts-, -əts- —*Russ*
  [tru bʲits 'kɔj]
Trubner, Trübner 'truːb nə ‖ -nᵊr —*Ger*
  ['tʁyːb nɐ]
Trubshaw 'trʌb ʃɔː ‖ -ʃaː
truce truːs **truces** 'truːs ɪz -əz
trucial, T~ 'truːʃ ᵊl 'truːs i_əl
truck trʌk **trucked** trʌkt **trucking** 'trʌk ɪŋ
  trucks trʌks
  'truck farm; 'truck stop
truckage 'trʌk ɪdʒ
Truckee 'trʌk i
trucker 'trʌk ə ‖ -ᵊr **~s** z
truckl|e 'trʌk ᵊl **~ed** d **~es** z **~ing** ˌɪŋ
truckload 'trʌk ləʊd ‖ -loʊd **~s** z
truculence 'trʌk jʊl ənⷦs -jəl- ‖ -jəl-
truculent 'trʌk jʊl ənt -jəl- ‖ -jəl- **~ly** li
Trudeau 'truːd əʊ ‖ truː 'doʊ —*Fr* [tʁy do]
trudge trʌdʒ **trudged** trʌdʒd **trudges**
  'trʌdʒ ɪz -əz **trudging** 'trʌdʒ ɪŋ
Trudgen, t~ 'trʌdʒ ən
Trudgill 'trʌd ɡɪl →'trʌɡ-, §-gᵊl
Trudi, Trudy 'truːd i
true truː **trued** truːd **trueing, truing** 'truː ɪŋ
  truer 'truː ə ‖ ᵊr **trues** truːz **truest** 'truː ɪst
  əst
  ˌtrue 'north
true-blue ˌtruː 'bluː ◄ **~s** z
trueborn ˌtruː 'bɔːn ◄ ‖ -'bɔːrn ◄
true-breeding ˌtruː ˌbriːd ɪŋ
true-false ˌtruː 'fɔːls ◄ -'fɒls ◄ ‖ -'faːls ◄
truehearted ˌtruː 'haːt ɪd ◄ -əd ‖ -'haːrṭ əd ◄
  '···
true-life ˌtruː 'laɪf ◄
truelove, T~ 'truː lʌv **~s** z
Trueman 'truːm ən
trueness 'truː nəs -nɪs
true-to-life ˌtruː tə 'laɪf ◄ ‖ -ṭə-
TrueType *tdmk* 'truː taɪp
Truffaut 'trʊf əʊ 'truːf- ‖ truː 'foʊ —*Fr* [tʁy fo]

truffle ˈtrʌf ᵊl ~s z
trug trʌg **trugs** trʌgz
truism ˈtruː ˌɪz əm ~s z
Trujillo tru ˈhiː jəʊ -ˈhiːl- ‖ -joʊ —Sp
[tru ˈxi ʎo, -jo]
Truk trʌk trʊk
truly ˈtruː li
Truman ˈtruːm ən
Trumbull ˈtrʌm bᵊl
trump, Trump trʌmp **trumped** trʌmpt
trumping ˈtrʌmp ɪŋ **trumps** trʌmps
ˈtrump card
trumped-up ˌtrʌmpt ˈʌp ◂
ˌtrumped-up ˈcharges
trumper|y ˈtrʌmp ər |i ~ies iz
trump|et ˈtrʌmp |ɪt §-ət ‖ -|ət ~eted ɪt ɪd §ət-,
-əd ‖ ət əd ~eting ɪt ɪŋ §ət- ‖ ət ɪŋ ~ets ɪts
§əts ‖ əts
trumpeter ˈtrʌmp ɪt ə §-ət- ‖ -ət ᵊr ~s z
trun|cate trʌn ˈ|keɪt ˈtrʌn|k eɪt ‖ ˈtrʌn|k eɪt
ˈtrʌn |keɪt ~cated keɪt ɪd -əd ‖ keɪt̮ əd ~cates
keɪts ~cating keɪt ɪŋ ‖ keɪt̮ ɪŋ
truncation trʌŋ ˈkeɪʃ ᵊn ~s z
truncheon ˈtrʌntʃ ən ˈtrʌndʒ- ~ed d ~ing ɪŋ
~s z
trundl|e ˈtrʌnd ᵊl ~ed d ~es z ~ing ̩ɪŋ
trunk trʌŋk **trunks** trʌŋks
ˈtrunk call; ˈtrunk road; ˈtrunk route
trunnel ˈtrʌn ᵊl ~s z
trunnion ˈtrʌn i ̩ən ‖ ˈtrʌn jən ~ed d ~s z
Truro ˈtrʊər əʊ ‖ ˈtrʊr oʊ
Truscott ˈtrʌsk ət -ɒt ‖ -ɑːt
truss trʌs **trussed** trʌst (= trust) **trusses**
ˈtrʌs ɪz -əz **trussing** ˈtrʌs ɪŋ
ˈtrust fund; ˈtrust ˌterritory
trustee ˌtrʌ ˈstiː ◂ ~s z
trusteeship ˌtrʌ ˈstiː ʃɪp ~s s
trustful ˈtrʌst fᵊl -fʊl ~ly i
Trusthouse ˈtrʌst haʊs
trusting ˈtrʌst ɪŋ ~ly li
trustworth|y ˈtrʌst ˌwɜːð |i ‖ -ˌwɜːð |i ~ily
ɪ li əl i ~iness i nəs i nɪs
trust|y ˈtrʌst |i ~ier i ̩ə ‖ i ̩ᵊr ~ies iz ~iest i ̩ɪst
i ̩əst ~ily ɪ li əl i ~iness i nəs i nɪs
truth truːθ **truths** truːðz truːθs
ˈtruth drug; ˈtruth ˌtable
truthful ˈtruːθ fᵊl -fʊl ~ly ̩i ~ness nəs nɪs
try traɪ **tried** traɪd **tries** traɪz **trying** ˈtraɪ ɪŋ
—see note at trying
Tryfan ˈtrɪv ᵊn ˈtrɪf-, ˈtrʌv- —Welsh [ˈtrə van]
trying ˈtraɪ ɪŋ ~ly i ~ness nəs nɪs —As a
close-knit expression, trying to has casual weak
forms ˈtraɪ ənt ə ˈtraɪ ̩ən ə ‖ ˈtraɪ ənt̮ ə (or
with final u for ə before a following vowel
sound).
try-on ˈtraɪ ɒn ‖ -ɑːn -ɔːn ~s z
Tryon ˈtraɪ ̩ən
try-out ˈtraɪ aʊt ~s s
trypanosome ˈtrɪp ən ə səʊm trɪ ˈpæn-
‖ -soʊm ~s z

trypanosomiasis ˌtrɪp ən əʊ səʊ ˈmaɪ ̩əs ɪs
trɪ ˌpæn-, §-əs ‖ -ə sə⁻-
trypsin ˈtrɪps ɪn §-ᵊn
tryptophan ˈtrɪpt əʊ fæn ‖ -ə-
tryst trɪst traɪst **trysted** ˈtrɪst ɪd ˈtraɪst-, -əd
trysting ˈtrɪst ɪŋ ˈtraɪst- **trysts** trɪsts traɪsts
tsar zɑː tsɑː ‖ zɑːr tsɑːr **tsars** zɑːz tsɑːz ‖ zɑːrz
tsɑːrz
tsarevich, tsarevitch ˈzɑːr ə vɪtʃ ˈtsɑːr- ~es ɪz
əz
tsarina zɑː ˈriːn ə tsɑː- ~s z
tsar|ism ˈzɑːr ˌɪz əm ˈtsɑːr- ~ist/s ɪst/s §əst/s
TSB tdmk ˌtiː es ˈbiː
tsetse ˈtets i ˈtsets i, ˈsets i
ˈtsetse fly
Tshiluba tʃiː ˈluːb ə
T-shirt, t-shirt ˈtiː ʃɜːt ‖ -ʃɜːt ~s s
Tshwane ˈtʃwɑːn eɪ
Tsimshian ˈsɪm ʃi æn ˈtʃɪm-, -ʃi ̩ən ~s z
Tsing Tao ˌtʃɪŋ ˈdaʊ —Chi Qīngdǎo
[¹tɕʰiŋ ³tɑʊ]
tsk | —This is a conventional spelling for the
alveolar CLICK.
tsotsi ˈtsɒts i ˈtsɑːts i ~s z
T-square ˈtiː skweə ‖ -skwer -skwær ~s z
tsunami tsu ˈnɑːm i su-, -ˈnæm- —Jp
[tsɯ ˌna mi] ~s z
tsutsugamushi ˌtsuːts əg ə ˈmuːʃ i ˌtsʊts-,
ˌsuːts-, ˌuːg-, ˌʊg-, -ˈmʊʃ i —Jp
[tsɯ̥ ˌtsɯ ˈŋa mɯ ɕi, -ˈga-]
ˌtsutsugaˈmushi diˌsease
Tswana ˈtswɑːn ə ˈswɑːn- ~s z
Tuamotu ˌtuː ̩ə ˈməʊt uː ‖ -ˈmoʊt-
Tuareg ˈtwɑːr eg ~s z
tuatara ˌtuː ̩ə ˈtɑːr ə ~s z
tub tʌb **tubbed** tʌbd **tubbing** ˈtʌb ɪŋ **tubs**
tʌbz
tuba ˈtjuːb ə →ˈtʃuːb- ‖ ˈtuːb ə ˈtjuːb- ~s z
tubal ˈtjuːb ᵊl →ˈtʃuːb- ‖ ˈtuːb ᵊl ˈtjuːb-
tubb|y ˈtʌb |i ~ier i ̩ə ‖ i ̩ᵊr ~iest i ̩ɪst i ̩əst
~iness i nəs i nɪs

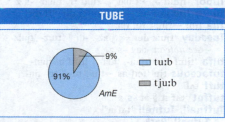

TUBE

AmE

- 91% tuːb
- 9% tjuːb

tube tjuːb →tʃuːb ‖ tuːb tjuːb — Preference poll,
AmE: tuːb 91%, tjuːb 9%. **tubed** tjuːbd
→tʃuːbd ‖ tuːbd tjuːbd **tubes** tjuːbz →tʃuːbz
‖ tuːbz tjuːbz **tubing** ˈtjuːb ɪŋ →ˈtʃuːb-
‖ ˈtuːb ɪŋ ˈtjuːb-
tubeless ˈtjuːb ləs →ˈtʃuːb-, -lɪs ‖ ˈtuːb- ˈtjuːb-
tuber ˈtjuːb ə →ˈtʃuːb- ‖ ˈtuːb ᵊr ˈtjuːb- ~s z
tubercle ˈtjuːb ək ᵊl →ˈtʃuːb- ‖ ˈtuːb ᵊrk ᵊl
ˈtjuːb- ~s z
tubercular tju ˈbɜːk jʊl ə tə-, tu-, →tʃu-, -jəl-
‖ tu ˈbɜːk jəl ᵊr tju-, tə-

T

tuberculin tju ˈbɜːk jʊl ɪn tə-, tu-, →tʃu-, -jəl-,
§-ən ‖ tu ˈbɜːk jəl ən tju-, tə-
tuberculosis tju ˌbɜːk ju ˈləʊs ɪs tə-, tu-,
→tʃu-, -jə-, §-əs ‖ tu ˌbɜːk jə ˈloʊs əs tju-, tə-
tuberculous tju ˈbɜːk jʊl əs tə-, tu-, →tʃu-, -jəl-
‖ tu ˈbɜːk jəl əs tju-, tə-
tuberos|e n ˈtjuːb ə rəʊz →ˈtʃuːb-, ˌ·ˈ·
‖ ˈtuːb ə roʊz tjuːb- —Also, by folk
etymology, ⚠ ˈtjuːb rəʊz →ˈtʃuːb-
‖ ⚠ ˈtuːb roʊz, ˈtjuːb- **~es** ɪz əz
tuberose adj ˈtjuːb ə rəʊs →ˈtʃuːb-
‖ ˈtuːb ə roʊs, ˈtjuːb-
tuberosit|y ˌtjuːb ə ˈrɒs ət |i →ˌtʃuːb-, -ɪt i
‖ ˌtuːb ə ˈrɑːs ət̬ |i ˌtjuːb- **~ies** iz
tuberous ˈtjuːb ər əs →ˈtʃuːb- ‖ ˈtuːb- ˈtjuːb-
tubful ˈtʌb fʊl **~s** z
tubifex ˈtjuːb ɪ feks →ˈtʃuːb-, §-ə- ‖ ˈtuːb-
ˈtjuːb- **~es** ɪz əz
tubiform ˈtjuːb ɪ fɔːm →ˈtʃuːb-, §-ə-
‖ ˈtuːb ə fɔːrm ˈtjuːb-
tubing ˈtjuːb ɪŋ →ˈtʃuːb- ‖ ˈtuːb ɪŋ ˈtjuːb-
Tubingen ˈtjuːb ɪŋ ən tu ˈbɜːk-, →ˈtʃuːb- ‖ ˈtuːb-
—Ger Tübingen [ˈtyː bɪŋ ən]
Tubman ˈtʌb mən
tub-thump|ing ˈtʌb ˌθʌmp |ɪŋ **~er/s** ə/z
‖ ᵊr/z
tubular ˈtjuːb jʊl ə →ˈtʃuːb-, -jəl- ‖ ˈtuːb jəl ᵊr
ˈtjuːb-
tubule ˈtjuːb juːl →ˈtʃuːb- ‖ ˈtuːb- ˈtjuːb- **~s** z
TUC ˌtiː juː ˈsiː
tuck, Tuck tʌk **tucked** tʌkt **tucking** ˈtʌk ɪŋ
tucks tʌks
ˈtuck box; ˈtuck shop
tuckahoe ˈtʌk ə həʊ ‖ -hoʊ **~s** z
tucker, T~ ˈtʌk ə ‖ -ᵊr **~ed** d **~s** z
tuckerbag ˈtʌk ə bæg ‖ -ᵊr- **~s** z
tuckeroo ˌtʌk ə ˈruː **~s** z
tuck-in ˈtʌk ɪn
Tucson ˈtuː sɒn ˌ·ˈ· ‖ -sɑːn (!)
-tude tjuːd →tʃuːd ‖ tuːd tjuːd — **amplitude**
ˈæmp lɪ tjuːd -lə-, →-tʃuːd ‖ -tuːd -tjuːd
Tudor ˈtjuːd ə →ˈtʃuːd- ‖ ˈtuːd ᵊr ˈtjuːd- **~s** z
Tudur ˈtɪd ɪə ‖ -ɪr —Welsh [ˈti dɪr, ˈti dɪr]
Tue tjuː- →tʃuː- ‖ tuː- tjuː-
Tuesday ˈtjuːz deɪ →ˈtʃuːz-, -di ‖ ˈtuːz- ˈtjuːz-
—see note at **-day ~s** z
tufa ˈtjuːf ə →ˈtʃuːf-, ˈtuːf- ‖ ˈtuːf ə ˈtjuːf-
tufaceous tju ˈfeɪʃ əs →tʃuː-, tu- ‖ tu- tju-
tuff tʌf
tuffet ˈtʌf ɪt §-ət **~s** s
Tuffnell, Tufnell ˈtʌf nᵊl
ˌTufnell ˈPark
tuft tʌft **tufted** ˈtʌft ɪd -əd **tufting** ˈtʌft ɪŋ
tufts tʌfts
Tufts tʌfts
tuft|y ˈtʌft |i **~ier** i_ə ‖ i_ᵊr **~iest** i_ɪst i_əst
~iness i nəs i nɪs
tug tʌg **tugged** tʌgd **tugging** ˈtʌg ɪŋ **tugs**
tʌgz
tugboat ˈtʌg bəʊt ‖ -boʊt **~s** s
Tugendhat ˈtuːg ən hɑːt
tugg... —see **tug**
tug-of-love ˌtʌg əv ˈlʌv ◄

tug-of-war ˌtʌg əv ˈwɔː -ə- ‖ -ˈwɔːr
tugrik ˈtuːg rɪk **~s** s
Tuileries ˈtwiːl ər i -iz —Fr [tɥil ʁi]
Tuite (i) tjuːt →tʃuːt ‖ tuːt tjuːt, (ii) ˈtjuː ɪt
→ˈtʃuː, §-ət ‖ ˈtuː ət ˈtjuː-
tuition tju ˈɪʃ ᵊn →tʃu- ‖ tu- tju-
Tuitt ˈtjuː ɪt →ˈtʃuː, §-ət ‖ ˈtuː ət ˈtjuː-
Tuke tjuːk →tʃuːk ‖ tuːk tjuːk
tuk-tuk ˈtʊk tʊk **~s** s
tularaemia, tularemia ˌtuːl ə ˈriːm i_ə ˌtjuːl-
Tulare tu ˈleər i -ˈleə ‖ tu ˈler i -ˈlær-; -ˈleᵊr,
-ˈlæᵊr
Tule, tule ˈtuːl i **~s** z
tulip ˈtjuːl ɪp →ˈtʃuːl-, §-əp ‖ ˈtuːl əp ˈtjuːl- **~s** s
ˈtulip tree
Tull tʌl
Tullamarine ˌtʌl ə mə ˈriːn
tulle tjuːl →tʃuːl ‖ tuːl —Fr [tyl] **tulles** tjuːlz
→tʃuːlz ‖ tuːlz
Tulloch ˈtʌl ək -əx
Tully ˈtʌl i
Tulsa ˈtʌls ə
Tulse tʌls
ˌTulse ˈHill
tum tʌm **tums** tʌmz
tumbl|e ˈtʌm bᵊl **~ed** d **~es** z **~ing** ɪŋ
tumbledown ˈtʌm bᵊl daʊn
tumble-drier, tumble-dryer ˌtʌm bᵊl ˈdraɪ_ə
ˈ·ˌ·· ‖ -ˈdraɪ_ᵊr **~s** z
tumble-|dry ˌtʌm bᵊl |ˈdraɪ ˈ··· **~dried** ˈdraɪd
~dries ˈdraɪz **~drying** ˈdraɪ ɪŋ
tumbler ˈtʌm blə ‖ -blᵊr **~ful/s** fʊl/z **~s** s
tumbleweed ˈtʌm bᵊl wiːd **~s** z
tumbrel, tumbril ˈtʌm brᵊl -brɪl **~s** s
tumefacient ˌtjuːm ɪ ˈfeɪʃ i_ənt ◄ →ˌtʃuːm-,
§ˌ·ə-, -ˈfeɪs-, -ˈfeɪʃ ᵊnt ‖ ˌtuːm- ˌtjuːm-
tumefaction ˌtjuːm ɪ ˈfæk ʃᵊn →ˌtʃuːm-, §-ə-
‖ ˌtuːm- ˌtjuːm-
tume|fy ˈtjuːm ɪ |faɪ →ˈtʃuːm-, -ə- ‖ ˈtuːm-
ˈtjuːm- **~fied** faɪd **~fies** faɪz **~fying** faɪ ɪŋ
tumescence tju ˈmes ᵊn̩s →tʃu- ‖ tu- tju-
tumescent tju ˈmes ᵊnt →tʃu- ‖ tu- tju-
tumid ˈtjuːm ɪd →ˈtʃuːm-, §-əd ‖ ˈtuːm əd
ˈtjuːm- **~ly** li **~ness** nəs nɪs
tumidity tju ˈmɪd ət i →tʃu-, -ɪt- ‖ tu ˈmɪd ət̬ i
tju-
Tummel ˈtʌm ᵊl
tumm|y ˈtʌm |i **~ies** iz
tumor, tumour ˈtjuːm ə →ˈtʃuːm- ‖ ˈtuːm ᵊr
ˈtjuːm- **~s** z
tump tʌmp **tumps** tʌmps
tumuli ˈtjuːm ju laɪ →ˈtʃuːm-, -jə- ‖ ˈtuːm jə laɪ
ˈtjuːm-
tumult ˈtjuːm ʌlt →ˈtʃuːm-, -ᵊlt ‖ ˈtuːm- ˈtjuːm-
~s s
tumultuous tju ˈmʌltʃ u_əs →tʃu-, -ˈmʌlt ju_
‖ tu- tju- **~ly** li **~ness** nəs nɪs
tum|ulus ˈtjuːm |jʊl əs →ˈtʃuːm-, -jəl-
‖ ˈtuːm |jəl əs ˈtjuːm- **~uli** ju laɪ jə- ‖ jə laɪ
tun tʌn **tuns** tʌnz
tuna ˈtjuːn ə ˈtuːn-, →ˈtʃuːn- ‖ ˈtuːn ə ˈtjuːn- **~s**
z
ˈtuna fish; ˌtuna ˈsalad

Tunbridge 'tʌn brɪdʒ →'tʌm-
　　,Tunbridge 'Wells
tundish 'tʌn dɪʃ ~es ɪz əz
tundra 'tʌndr ə

TUNE

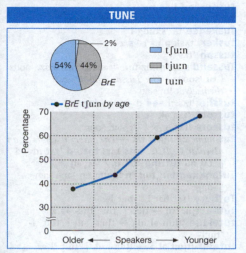

2%

54% 44%

■ tʃuːn
■ tjuːn
■ tuːn

BrE

━●━ *BrE* tʃuːn *by age*

Percentage 70 / 60 / 50 / 40 / 30 / 0

Older ◄━━ Speakers ━━► Younger

tune tjuːn →tʃuːn ‖ tuːn tjuːn — *Preference poll,
BrE:* tʃuːn *54% (born since 1981, 68%),* tjuːn
44%, tuːn *2%.* **tuned** tjuːnd →tʃuːnd ‖ tuːnd
tjuːnd **tunes** tjuːnz →tʃuːnz ‖ tuːnz tjuːnz
tuning 'tjuːn ɪŋ →'tʃuːn- ‖ 'tuːn ɪŋ 'tjuːn-
　'tuning fork; 'tuning peg
tuneful 'tjuːn fᵊl →'tʃuːn-, -fʊl ‖ 'tuːn- 'tjuːn-
~ly i ~ness nəs nɪs
tuneless 'tjuːn ləs →'tʃuːn-, -lɪs ‖ 'tuːn- 'tjuːn-
~ly li ~ness nəs nɪs
tuner 'tjuːn ə →'tʃuːn- ‖ 'tuːn ᵊr 'tjuːn- ~s z
tunesmith 'tjuːn smɪθ →'tʃuːn- ‖ 'tuːn 'tjuːn-
~s s
tune-up 'tjuːn ʌp →'tʃuːn- ‖ 'tuːn- 'tjuːn- ~s s
tung tʌŋ
Tung Chee Hwa ,tʊŋ ,tʃiː 'hwaː —*Chi* Dŏng
Jiànhuá [³tʊŋ ⁴tɕian ²xua], *Cantonese*
[²toŋ ³kiːn ⁴waː]
tungsten 'tʌŋkst ən
Tungus 'tʊŋ ɡʊs tʊŋ 'ɡuːz ~es ɪz əz
Tungusic tʊŋ 'ɡʊs ɪk -'ɡuːz-
tunic 'tjuːn ɪk →'tʃuːn- ‖ 'tuːn ɪk 'tjuːn- ~s s
tunicate 'tjuːn ɪk ət →'tʃuːn-, §-ək-, -ɪt; -ɪ keɪt,
-ə- ‖ 'tuːn- 'tjuːn- ~s s
tunicle 'tjuːn ɪk ᵊl →'tʃuːn-, §-ək- ‖ 'tuːn-
'tjuːn- ~s z
Tunis 'tjuːn ɪs →'tʃuːn-, §-əs ‖ 'tuːn əs 'tjuːn-
Tunisi|a tju 'nɪz i̯|ə →tʃu-, -'nɪs- ‖ tu 'niːʒ |ə
tju-, -'niːʃ-, -'nɪʒ-, -'nɪʃ- (*) ~an/s ən/z ‖ ᵊn/z
tunnel 'tʌn ᵊl ~ed, ~led d ~ing, ~ling ɪŋ ~s z
　,tunnel 'vision, '· ,··
tunneler, tunneller 'tʌn ᵊl ə ‖ -ᵊr ~s z
Tunney 'tʌn i
Tunnicliff, Tunnicliffe 'tʌn i klɪf
tunn|y 'tʌn |i ~ies iz
Tunstall 'tʌnᵗst ᵊl 'tʌn stɔːl
Tuohey, Tuohy 'tuː i -hi
Tuolumne tu 'ɒl əm i -ni ‖ -'ɑːl-

tup tʌp **tupped** tʌpt **tupping** 'tʌp ɪŋ **tups**
tʌps
Tupamaro ,tuːp ə 'mɑːr əʊ ‖ -oʊ ~s z —*Sp*
[tu pa 'ma ro, -s]
tupelo, T~ 'tjuːp ə ləʊ →'tʃuːp- ‖ 'tuːp ə loʊ
'tjuːp- ~s z
Tupi tu 'piː 'tuːp i ~s z
-tuple tjuːp ᵊl tjʊp ᵊl, tʌp ᵊl, →tʃuːp-, →tʃʊp-;
'·· ‖ tuːp ᵊl tjuːp ᵊl, tʌp ᵊl —*usually
unstressed*
tuppenc|e 'tʌp ənᵗs →-mᵖs ~es ɪz əz
tuppenny 'tʌp ən i
　,tuppenny 'ha'penny◄
Tupper 'tʌp ə ‖ -ᵊr
Tupperware *tdmk* 'tʌp ə weə ‖ -ᵊr wer -wær
tuque tuːk **tuques** tuːks
tu quoque ,tuː 'kwɒk wi -'kwəʊk-, -weɪ
‖ -'kwoʊk-
Turandot 'tjʊər ən dɒt 'tʊər-, →'tʃʊər-, -dəʊ
‖ 'tʊr ən dɑːt -doʊ —*It* [tu ran 'dɔt]
Turanian tju͡ə 'reɪn i̯ ən →tʃu͡ə- ‖ tu- tju- ~s z
turban 'tɜːb ən ‖ 'tɜːrb ən ~ed d ~s z
turbar|y 'tɜːb ər |i ‖ 'tɜːrb- ~ies iz
turbid 'tɜːb ɪd §-əd ‖ 'tɜːrb- ~ly li ~ness nəs nɪs
turbidity tɜː 'bɪd ət i -ɪt- ‖ tɜːr 'bɪd ət̬ i
turbinate 'tɜːb ɪn ət -ən-, -ɪt; -ɪ neɪt, -ə-
‖ 'tɜːrb-
turbine 'tɜːb aɪn -ɪn, §-ən ‖ 'tɜːrb- ~s z
turbo 'tɜːb əʊ ‖ 'tɜːrb oʊ ~s z
turbo- ¦tɜːb əʊ ‖ ¦tɜːrb oʊ — **turboelectric**
,tɜːb əʊ ɪ 'lek trɪk ◄ -ə'·- ‖ ,tɜːrb oʊ-
turbocharg|e 'tɜːb əʊ tʃɑːdʒ ‖ 'tɜːrb oʊ tʃɑːrdʒ
~ed d ~er/s ə/z ‖ ᵊr/z ~es ɪz əz ~ing ɪŋ
turbofan 'tɜːb əʊ fæn ,· ·' · ‖ 'tɜːrb oʊ- ~s z
turbojet 'tɜːb əʊ dʒet ‖ 'tɜːrb oʊ- ~s s
turboprop 'tɜːb əʊ prɒp ‖ 'tɜːrb oʊ prɑːp ~s s
turbot 'tɜːb ət ‖ 'tɜːrb ət ~s s
turbulenc|e 'tɜːb jʊl ənᵗs -jəl- ‖ 'tɜːrb jəl- ~y i
turbulent 'tɜːb jʊl ənt -jəl- ‖ 'tɜːrb jəl- ~ly li
Turco- ¦tɜːk əʊ ‖ ¦tɜːrk oʊ — **Turco-Greek**
,tɜːk əʊ 'ɡriːk ◄ ‖ ,tɜːrk oʊ-
turd tɜːd ‖ tɜːrd **turds** tɜːdz ‖ tɜːrdz
tureen tju͡ə 'riːn ,tjʊə-, tu͡ə-, →tʃu͡ə, §→,tʃʊə-,
tjə-, tə- ‖ tə- tju-, tu- ~s z
turf tɜːf ‖ tɜːrf **turfed** tɜːft ‖ tɜːrft **turfing**
'tɜːf ɪŋ ‖ 'tɜːrf ɪŋ **turfs** tɜːfs ‖ tɜːrfs **turves**
tɜːvz ‖ tɜːrvz
　'turf ac,countant
Turgenev tu͡ə 'ɡeɪn jev tɜː-, -'ɡen- ‖ tʊr- tɜː-
—*Russ* [tur 'ɡʲe nʲɪf]
turgid 'tɜːdʒ ɪd §-əd ‖ 'tɜːrdʒ- ~ly li ~ness nəs
nɪs
turgidity tɜː 'dʒɪd ət i -ɪt- ‖ tɜːr 'dʒɪd ət̬ i
turgor 'tɜːg ə ‖ 'tɜːrg ᵊr
Turin ,tjʊə 'rɪn tju͡ə-; 'tʊər ɪn ‖ tu 'rɪn 'tʊr ən,
'tjʊr-, 'tɜː-
　the ,Turin 'shroud
Turing 'tjʊər ɪŋ →'tʃʊər- ‖ 'tʊr ɪŋ 'tjʊr-, 'tɜː-
　'Turing ma,chine
Turk tɜːk ‖ tɜːrk **Turks** tɜːks ‖ tɜːrks
　,Turks and 'Caicos 'keɪk ɒs ‖ -oʊs
Turkestan ,tɜːk ɪ 'stɑːn -ə-, -'stæn ‖ ,tɜːrk-
Turkey, t~ 'tɜːk i ‖ 'tɜːrk i ~s z

turkeycock 'tɜːk i kɒk ‖ 'tɜ·ːk i kɑːk ~s s
Turkic 'tɜːk ɪk ‖ 'tɜ·ːk-
Turkish 'tɜːk ɪʃ ‖ 'tɜ·ːk-
  ˌTurkish 'bath; ˌTurkish deˈlight
Turkmen 'tɜːk men -mən ‖ 'tɜ·ːk-
Turkmeni|a tɜːk ˈmiːn i|ə ‖ tɜ·ːk- ~an/s ˌən/z
Turkmenistan ˌtɜːk men ɪ ˈstɑːn ·ˌ-·, -ə-, -ˈstæn ‖ ˌtɜ·ːk-
Turkoman 'tɜːk əm ən -ə mæn, -ə mɑːn ‖ 'tɜ·ːk- ~s z
Turku 'tʊək uː ‖ 'tʊrk uː —*Finnish* ['tur ku]
Turl, Turle tɜːl ‖ tɜ·ːl
turmeric 'tɜːm ər ɪk ‖ 'tɜ·ːm-
turmoil 'tɜːm ɔɪˀl ‖ 'tɜ·ːm-
turn tɜːn ‖ tɜ·ːn **turned** tɜːnd ‖ tɜ·ːnd **turning** 'tɜːn ɪŋ ‖ 'tɜ·ːn ɪŋ **turns** tɜːnz ‖ tɜ·ːnz
  'turning ˌcircle; 'turning point
turnabout 'tɜːn ə ˌbaʊt ‖ 'tɜ·ːn- ~s s
turnaround 'tɜːn ə ˌraʊnd ‖ 'tɜ·ːn- ~s z
Turnberry 'tɜːn bər i →'tɜːm- ‖ 'tɜ·ːn ˌber i
turnbuckle 'tɜːn ˌbʌk ˀl →'tɜːm- ‖ 'tɜ·ːn- ~s z
Turnbull 'tɜːn bʊl →'tɜːm- ‖ 'tɜ·ːn-
turncoat 'tɜːn kəʊt →'tɜːŋ- ‖ 'tɜ·ːn koʊt ~s s
turncock 'tɜːn kɒk →'tɜːŋ- ‖ 'tɜ·ːn kɑːk ~s s
turndown 'tɜːn daʊn ‖ 'tɜ·ːn-
turner, T~ 'tɜːn ə ‖ 'tɜ·ːn ˀr ~s z
turner|y 'tɜːn ər |i ‖ 'tɜ·ːn- ~ies iz
Turnham 'tɜːn əm ‖ 'tɜ·ːn-
Turnhouse 'tɜːn haʊs ‖ 'tɜ·ːn-
turning 'tɜːn ɪŋ ‖ 'tɜ·ːn ɪŋ ~s z
  'turning point
turnip 'tɜːn ɪp §-əp ‖ 'tɜ·ːn əp ~s s
turnkey 'tɜːn kiː →'tɜːŋ- ‖ 'tɜ·ːn- ~s z
turn-off 'tɜːn ɒf -ɔːf ‖ 'tɜ·ːn ɔːf -ɑːf ~s s
turn-of-the-century ˌtɜːn əv ðə ˈsentʃ ər i ◀ ‖ ˌtɜ·ːn-
turn-on 'tɜːn ɒn ‖ 'tɜ·ːn ɑːn -ɔːn ~s z
turnout 'tɜːn aʊt ‖ 'tɜ·ːn- ~s s
turnover 'tɜːn ˌəʊv ə ‖ 'tɜ·ːn ˌoʊv ˀr ~s z
turnpike 'tɜːn paɪk →'tɜːm- ‖ 'tɜ·ːn- ~s s
turnround 'tɜːn raʊnd ‖ 'tɜ·ːn- ~s z
turnstile 'tɜːn staɪˀl ‖ 'tɜ·ːn- ~s z
turnstone 'tɜːn stəʊn ‖ 'tɜ·ːn stoʊn ~s z
turntable 'tɜːn ˌteɪb ˀl ‖ 'tɜ·ːn- ~s z
turntablist 'tɜːn ˌteɪb ˀl ɪst §ˌ·əst ‖ 'tɜ·ːn- ~s s
turn-up 'tɜːn ʌp ‖ 'tɜ·ːn- ~s s
turpentine 'tɜːp ən taɪn →-m-, -ɪn- ‖ 'tɜ·ːp-
Turpin 'tɜːp ɪn §-ən ‖ 'tɜ·ːp ən
turpitude 'tɜːp ɪ tjuːd -ə-, →-tʃuːd ‖ 'tɜ·ːp ə tuːd -tjuːd
turps tɜːps ‖ tɜ·ːps
turquoise 'tɜːk wɔɪz -wɑːz ‖ 'tɜ·ːk- -ɔɪz
turr|et 'tʌr |ɪt -ət ‖ 'tɜ·ː |ət ~eted ɪt ɪd §ət-, -əd ‖ ət əd ~ets ɪts §əts ‖ əts
Turriff 'tʌr ɪf -əf ‖ 'tɜ·ː əf
turtle 'tɜːt ˀl ‖ 'tɜ·ːt̬ ˀl ~s z
turtledove 'tɜːt ˀl dʌv ‖ 'tɜ·ːt̬- ~s z
turtleneck 'tɜːt ˀl nek ‖ 'tɜ·ːt̬- ~s s
Turton 'tɜːt ˀn ‖ 'tɜ·ːt ˀn
turves tɜːvz ‖ tɜ·ːvz
Turvey 'tɜːv i ‖ 'tɜ·ːv i
Tuscan 'tʌsk ən ~s z
Tuscany 'tʌsk ən i

Tuscarora ˌtʌsk ə ˈrɔːr ə ‖ -ˈroʊr-
tush *interj; n 'tusk'* tʌʃ
tush *n 'buttocks'* tʊʃ **tushes** 'tʊʃ ɪz -əz
tushery 'tʌʃ ər i
tushie 'tʊʃ i ~s z
tusk tʌsk **tusked** tʌskt **tusks** tʌsks
Tuskegee tʌ ˈskiːdʒ i
tusker 'tʌsk ə ‖ -ˀr ~s z
tussah 'tʌs ə
Tussaud's tə ˈsɔːdz tu-, -ˈsəʊdz; 'tuːs ɔːdz, -əʊdz ‖ tu ˈsoʊz —*The Tussaud family call themselves* 'tuːs əʊ
tussl|e 'tʌs ˀl ~ed d ~es z ~ing ɪŋ
tussock 'tʌs ək ~s s
tussore 'tʌs ə -ɔː ‖ -ˀr -ɔːr, -oʊr
tut *name of interj* tʌt —*The interj itself is* ‖, *an alveolar CLICK.* **tuts** tʌts **tutted** 'tʌt ɪd -əd ‖ 'tʌt̬ əd **tutting** 'tʌt ɪŋ ‖ 'tʌt̬ ɪŋ
Tutankhamen ˌtuːt ˀn ˈkɑːm en -əŋ-, -æŋ- ‖ -ɑːŋ-
Tutbury 'tʌt bər i ‖ -ber i
tutee ˌtjuː 'tiː →ˌtʃuː- ‖ ˌtuː- ˌtjuː- ~s z
tutelage 'tjuːt əl ɪdʒ →'tʃuːt-, -ɪl- ‖ 'tuːt̬ ˀl- 'tjuːt̬-
tutelar 'tjuːt əl ə →'tʃuːt-, -ɪl- ‖ 'tuːt̬ ˀl ər 'tjuːt̬-, -ɑːr
tutelary 'tjuːt əl ər i →'tʃuːt-, -ˀl- ‖ 'tuːt̬ ˀl er i 'tjuːt̬-
Tutin 'tjuːt ɪn →'tʃuːt-, §-ˀn ‖ 'tuːt ˀn 'tjuːt-
tutor 'tjuːt ə →'tʃuːt- ‖ 'tuːt̬ ˀr 'tjuːt- ~ed d **tutoring** 'tjuːt ər ɪŋ →'tʃuːt- ‖ 'tuːt̬- 'tjuːt̬- ~s z
tutorage 'tjuːt ər ɪdʒ →'tʃuːt- ‖ 'tuːt̬- 'tjuːt̬-
tutorial tju ˈtɔːr i ˌəl →tʃu- ‖ tu- -ˈtoʊr- ~s z
tutorship 'tjuːt ə ʃɪp →'tʃuːt- ‖ 'tuːt̬ ˀr- 'tjuːt̬- ~s s
tutsan 'tʌts ˀn
Tutsi 'tʊts i 'tuːts-
tutti 'tʊt i 'tuːt-, -iː —*It* ['tut ti] ~s z
tutti-frutti ˌtʊt i 'fruːt i ‖ ˌtuːt̬ i 'fruːt̬ i ~s z
Tuttle 'tʌt ˀl ‖ 'tʌt̬ ˀl
tut-|tut *name of interj; v* ˌtʌt |'tʌt —*The interj itself is* ‖ ‖, *a repeated alveolar CLICK.* **~tuts** 'tʌts **~tutted** 'tʌt ɪd -əd ‖ 'tʌt̬ əd **~tutting** 'tʌt ɪŋ ‖ 'tʌt̬ ɪŋ
tutty 'tʌt i ‖ 'tʌt̬ i
tutu, Tutu 'tuːt uː ~s z
Tuva 'tuːv ə —*Russ* [tu 'va]
Tuvalu tu 'vaːl uː ˌtuːv ə 'luː ~an/s ən/z
tu-whit tu-whoo tə ˌwɪt tə 'wuː tu ˌwɪt tu-, -ˌhwɪt-, -ˈhwuː
tux tʌks **tuxes** 'tʌks ɪz -əz
tuxedo, T~ tʌk 'siːd əʊ ‖ -oʊ ~s z
Tuxford 'tʌks fəd ‖ -fˀrd
Tuzla 'tʊz lə 'tuːz- ‖ 'tuːz- —*S-Cr* ['tuz la]
TV ˌtiː 'viː ◀ **TVs, TV's** ˌtiː 'viːz
  ˌTV 'dinner; ˌT'V ˌprogram(me)
Twaddell *(i)* 'twɒd ˀl ‖ 'twɑːd ˀl, *(ii)* twɒ 'del ‖ twɑː-
twaddle 'twɒd ˀl ‖ 'twɑːd ˀl
twain, Twain tweɪn
twang twæŋ **twanged** twæŋd **twanging** 'twæŋ ɪŋ **twangs** twæŋz

Twankey, Twanky ˈtwæŋk i
ˈtwas *strong form* twɒz ‖ twʌz twɑːz, *weak form* twəz
twat twɒt twæt ‖ twɑːt **twats** twɒts twæts ‖ twɑːts
twayblade ˈtweɪ bleɪd **~s** z
tweak twiːk **tweaked** twiːkt **tweaking** ˈtwiːk ɪŋ **tweaks** twiːks
twee twiː **tweer** ˈtwiː ə ‖ -ər **tweest** ˈtwiː ɪst -əst
tweed, Tweed twiːd **tweeds** twiːdz
Tweeddale ˈtwiːd deɪəl
Tweedie ˈtwiːd i
Tweedledee ˌtwiːd əl ˈdiː
Tweedledum ˌtwiːd əl ˈdʌm
Tweedsmuir ˈtwiːdz mjʊə -mjɔː ‖ -mjʊr
tweed|y ˈtwiːd |i **~ier** i ə ‖ i ər **~iest** i ɪst i əst **~iness** i nəs i nɪs
ˈtween, tween twiːn **tweening** ˈtwiːn ɪŋ
tween|y ˈtwiːn |i **~ies** iz
tweet twiːt **tweeted** ˈtwiːt ɪd -əd ‖ ˈtwiːt̬ əd **tweeting** ˈtwiːt ɪŋ ‖ ˈtwiːt̬ ɪŋ **tweets** twiːts
tweeter ˈtwiːt ə ‖ ˈtwiːt̬ ər **~s** z
tweeze twiːz **tweezed** twiːzd **tweezes** ˈtwiːz ɪz -əz **tweezing** ˈtwiːz ɪŋ
tweezer ˈtwiːz ə ‖ -ər **~s** z
twelfth twelfθ twelθ **twelfthly** ˈtwelfθ li ˈtwelθ- **twelfths** twelfθs twelθs
ˌTwelfth ˈNight ‖ ˈ · ·
twelve twelv **twelves** twelvz
twelvemonth ˈtwelv mʌnθ **~s** s
twelve-tone ˌtwelv ˈtəʊn ◂ ˈ · · ‖ -ˈtoʊn ◂
twelvish ˈtwelv ɪʃ
twentieth ˈtwent i əθ ˈtwen-, θ ‖ ˈtwent̬- **~s** s
twent|y ˈtwent |i ˈtwen i ‖ ˈtwent̬ |i **~ies** iz
twenty-first ˌtwent i ˈfɜːst ◂ ˌtwen- ‖ ˌtwent̬ i ˈfɜːst ◂ **~s** s
twentyfold ˈtwent i fəʊld ˈtwen-, →-fɒʊld ‖ ˈtwent̬ i foʊld
twenty-four ˌtwent i ˈfɔː ◂ ˌtwen- ‖ ˌtwent̬ i ˈfɔːr ◂ -ˈfour
  ˌtwenty-four ˈseven
twenty-one ˌtwent i ˈwʌn ◂ ˌtwen- ‖ ˌtwent̬- **~s** z
twentysomething ˈtwent i ˌsʌm θɪŋ ˈtwen i- ‖ ˈtwent̬ i- **~s** z
twenty-twenty ˌtwent i ˈtwent i ◂ ˌtwen i ˈtwen i ◂ ‖ ˌtwent̬ i ˈtwent̬ i ◂
  ˌtwenty-ˌtwenty ˈvision
twenty-two ˌtwent i ˈtuː ◂ ˌtwen i- ‖ ˌtwent̬i-
ˈtwere *strong form* twɜː tweə ‖ twɜːr, *weak form* twə ‖ twər
twerp twɜːp ‖ twɜːp **twerps** twɜːps ‖ twɜːps
Twi twiː — *Twi* [tɕɥi]
twice twaɪs
twice-told ˌtwaɪs ˈtəʊld ◂ →-ˈtɒʊld ‖ -ˈtoʊld ◂
Twickenham ˈtwɪk ən əm
Twickers ˈtwɪk əz ‖ -ərz
twiddl|e ˈtwɪd əl **~ed** d **~er/s** ə/z ‖ ər/z **~es** z **~ier** i ə ‖ i ər **~iest** i ɪst -əst **~ing** ɪŋ **~y** i
twig twɪg **twigged** twɪgd **twigging** ˈtwɪg ɪŋ **twigs** twɪgz

Twigg twɪg
twigg|y, T~ ˈtwɪg |i **~ier** i ə ‖ i ər **~iest** i ɪst i əst
twilight ˈtwaɪ laɪt
twilit ˈtwaɪ lɪt
ˈtwill twɪl —*sometimes with a weak form* twəl
twill twɪl **twilled** twɪld **twilling** ˈtwɪl ɪŋ **twills** twɪlz
twin twɪn **twinned** twɪnd **twinning** ˈtwɪn ɪŋ **twins** twɪnz
  ˌtwin ˈbed; ˈtwin set
twin-bedded ˌtwɪn ˈbed ɪd ◂ -əd
twine twaɪn **twined** twaɪnd **twines** twaɪnz **twining** ˈtwaɪn ɪŋ
twin-engine ˌtwɪn ˈendʒ ɪn ◂ §-ɪndʒ-, -ən **~d** d
twinge twɪndʒ **twinged** twɪndʒd **twinges** ˈtwɪndʒ ɪz -əz **twingeing, twinging** ˈtwɪndʒ ɪŋ
Twining ˈtwaɪn ɪŋ
twink twɪŋk **twinks** twɪŋks
Twinkie *tdmk* ˈtwɪŋk i **~s** z
twinkl|e ˈtwɪŋk əl **~ed** d **~es** z **~ing** ɪŋ
twinkling *n* ˈtwɪŋk lɪŋ ˈtwɪŋk əl ɪŋ **~s** z
Twinn twɪn
twinset ˈtwɪn set **~s** s
twin-size ˈtwɪn saɪz **~d** d
twin-tub ˌtwɪn ˈtʌb ◂ ‖ ·ˈ·
twirl twɜːl ‖ twɜːl **twirled** twɜːld ‖ twɜːld **twirling** ˈtwɜːl ɪŋ ‖ ˈtwɜːl ɪŋ **twirls** twɜːlz ‖ twɜːlz
twirp twɜːp ‖ twɜːp **twirps** twɜːps ‖ twɜːps
Twisleton ˈtwɪs əl tən
twist twɪst **twisted** ˈtwɪst ɪd -əd **twisting** ˈtwɪst ɪŋ **twists** twɪsts
  ˈtwist grip
twister ˈtwɪst ə ‖ -ər **~s** z
twist|y ˈtwɪst| i **~ier** i ə ‖ i ər **~iest** i ɪst əst
twit twɪt **twits** twɪts **twitted** ˈtwɪt ɪd -əd ‖ ˈtwɪt̬ əd **twitting** ˈtwɪt ɪŋ ‖ ˈtwɪt̬ ɪŋ
twitch twɪtʃ **twitched** twɪtʃt **twitches** ˈtwɪtʃ ɪz -əz **twitching/s** ˈtwɪtʃ ɪŋ/z
twitcher ˈtwɪtʃ ə ‖ -ər **~s** z
Twitchett ˈtwɪtʃ ɪt §-ət
twitch|y ˈtwɪtʃ |i **~ier** i ə ‖ i ər **~iest** i ɪst i əst **~iness** i nəs i nɪs
twite twaɪt **twites** twaɪts
twitter ˈtwɪt ə ‖ ˈtwɪt̬ ər **~ed** d **twittering/ly** ˈtwɪt ər ɪŋ /li ‖ ˈtwɪt̬ ər ɪŋ /li **~s** z
twittery ˈtwɪt ər i ‖ ˈtwɪt̬-
twixt, ˈtwixt twɪkst
twizzler, T~ ˈtwɪz əl ə ‖ -əl ər **~s** z
two tuː (= *too*) **twos** tuːz
  ˌtwo ˈbits
two-bit ˈtuː bɪt
two-by-four ˌtuː bə ˈfɔː -bi-, -baɪ- ‖ -ˈfɔːr -ˈfour
twoc twɒk ‖ twɑːk **twocking** ˈtwɒk ɪŋ ‖ ˈtwɑːk-
two-dimensional ˌtuː daɪ ˈmenʃ ən əl ◂ ·dɪ-, ·də- **~ly** i
two-edged ˌtuː ˈedʒd ◂

two|faced ˌtuː |ˈfeɪst ◂ **~facedly** ˈfeɪs ɪd li -əd-; ˈfeɪst li **~facedness** ˈfeɪs ɪd nəs -əd-, -nɪs; ˈfeɪst nəs, -nɪs
twofer ˈtuːf ə ‖ -ᵊr **~s** z
two-fisted ˌtuː ˈfɪst ɪd ◂ -əd
twofold ˈtuː fəʊld →-fɒʊld ‖ -foʊld
two-four ˌtuː ˈfɔː ‖ -ˈfɔːr -ˈfoʊr **~s** z
two-handed ˌtuː ˈhænd ɪd ◂ -əd **~ly** li **~ness** nəs nɪs
Twohy ˈtuː‿i
two-ish ˈtuː ɪʃ
two-legged ˌtuː ˈleg ɪd ◂ -əd; -ˈlegd ◂
two-man ˌtuː ˈmæn ◂
Twomey ˈtuːm i
two-minute ˌtuː ˈmɪn ɪt ◂ §-ət
 ˌtwo-minute ˈsilence
two-one ˌtuː ˈwʌn §-wɒn **~s** z
twoonie ˈtuːn i **~s** z
two-party ˌtuː ˈpɑːt i ◂ ‖ -ˈpɑːrt̬ i ◂
 ˌtwo-party aˈgreement
twopenc|e *n '2d'* ˈtʌp ənᵗs →-mᵖs *—but meaning '2p', in modern currency, usually* two pence ˌtuː ˈpenᵗs **~es** ɪz əz
twopenn|y *adj '2d', and in figurative senses* ˈtʌp ən‿|i *—but meaning '2p', in modern currency, usually* two-penny ˌtuː ˈpen |i ◂ **~ies** iz
twopenny-halfpenny ˌtʌp ən‿i ˈheɪp ən‿i ◂
two-person ˌtuː ˈpɜːs ᵊn ◂ ‖ -ˈpɜ˞ːs-
 ˌtwo-person ˈhousehold
two-piece ˈtuː piːs
two-ply ˈtuː plaɪ
two-seater ˌtuː ˈsiːt ə ‖ -ˈsiːt̬ ᵊr **~s** z
two-sided ˌtuː ˈsaɪd ɪd ◂ -əd **~ness** nəs nɪs
twosome ˈtuː səm **~s** z
two-star ˈtuː stɑː ˌ·ˈ· ‖ -stɑːr
two-step ˈtuː step **~s** s
two-stroke ˈtuː strəʊk ‖ -stroʊk **~s** s
two-tim|e ˈtuː taɪm **~ed** d **~es** z **~ing** ɪŋ
two-tone ˈtuː təʊn ‖ -toʊn
two-two, 2:2 ˌtuː ˈtuː ◂ **~s** z
'twould twʊd
two-way ˌtuː ˈweɪ ◂
 ˌtwo-way ˈradio
Twyford ˈtwaɪ fəd ‖ -fᵊrd
Ty taɪ *—but in Welsh place names,* tiː *—Welsh* Tŷ [tiː, tiː]
 ˌTy ˈCoch ˌtiː ˈkəʊk -ˈkəʊx ‖ -ˈkoʊk *—Welsh* [ˌtiː ˈkoːχ, ˌtiː-]
-ty ti — **sixty** ˈsɪkst i *—The pronunciation* taɪ *is occasionally used in order to avoid the danger of confusion resulting from the near-homophony of* -ty *and* -teen, *thus* ˈsɪks taɪ
Tybalt ˈtɪb ᵊlt
Tyburn ˈtaɪ bən -bɜːn ‖ -bᵊrn
Tyche ˈtaɪk i
Tycho ˈtaɪk əʊ ‖ -oʊ *—Danish* [ˈty go]
tycoon ₍ˌ₎taɪ ˈkuːn **~s** z
Tye taɪ
tying ˈtaɪ ɪŋ
tyke taɪk **tykes** taɪks
Tyldesley ˈtɪl*dz* li
Tylenol *tdmk* ˈtaɪl ə nɒl ‖ -nɔːl -nɑːl, -noʊl
Tyler ˈtaɪl ə ‖ -ᵊr
tympan ˈtɪmp ən **~s** z
tympana ˈtɪmp ən ə
tympani ˈtɪmp ən i
tympanic tɪm ˈpæn ɪk
tympanist ˈtɪmp ən ɪst §-əst **~s** s
tympan|um ˈtɪmp ən |əm **~a** ə **~ums** əmz **~y** i
Tynan ˈtaɪn ən
Tyndale ˈtɪnd ᵊl ˈtɪn deɪᵊl
Tyndall ˈtɪnd ᵊl
Tyndrum ₍ˌ₎taɪn ˈdrʌm
Tyne taɪn
 ˌTyne and ˈWear ˈwɪə ‖ ˈwɪᵊr
Tynemouth ˈtaɪn maʊθ →ˈtaɪm-, ˈtɪn-, -məθ
Tynesid|e ˈtaɪn saɪd **~er/s** ə/z ‖ ᵊr/z
Tynwald ˈtɪn wəld ˈtaɪn-
-type taɪp — **prototype** ˈprəʊt əʊ taɪp ‖ ˈproʊt̬ ə-
type taɪp **typed** taɪpt **types** taɪps **typing** ˈtaɪp ɪŋ
typebar ˈtaɪp bɑː ‖ -bɑːr **~s** z
typecast ˈtaɪp kɑːst §-kæst ‖ -kæst **~ing** ɪŋ **~s** s
typefac|e ˈtaɪp feɪs **~es** ɪz əz
typescript ˈtaɪp skrɪpt **~s** s
type|set ˈtaɪp |set **~sets** sets **~setting** set ɪŋ ‖ set̬ ɪŋ
typesetter ˈtaɪp ˌset ə ‖ -ˌset̬ ᵊr **~s** z
typewriter ˈtaɪp ˌraɪt ə ‖ -ˌraɪt̬ ᵊr **~s** z
typewriting ˈtaɪp ˌraɪt ɪŋ ‖ -ˌraɪt̬-
typewritten ˈtaɪp ˌrɪt ᵊn
Typhoeus taɪ ˈfiː‿əs -ˈfəʊ juːs
typhoid ˈtaɪf ɔɪd
 ˌtyphoid ˈfever
Typhon ˈtaɪf ᵊn -əʊn, -ɒn ‖ -ɑːn
typhonic taɪ ˈfɒn ɪk ‖ -ˈfɑːn-
Typhoo *tdmk* ₍ˌ₎taɪ ˈfuː
typhoon ₍ˌ₎taɪ ˈfuːn **~s** z
typhus ˈtaɪf əs
-typic ˈtɪp ɪk — **autotypic** ˌɔːt əʊ ˈtɪp ɪk ◂ ‖ ˌɔːt̬ ə- ˌɑːt̬-
typical ˈtɪp ɪk ᵊl **~ness** nəs nɪs
typicality ˌtɪp ɪ ˈkæl ət i ˌ·ə-, -ɪt i ‖ -ət̬ i
typically ˈtɪp ɪk ᵊl‿i
typi|fy ˈtɪp ɪ |faɪ -ə- **~fied** faɪd **~fier/s** faɪ‿ə/z ‖ faɪ‿ᵊr/z **~fies** faɪz **~fying** faɪ ɪŋ
typing ˈtaɪp ɪŋ
 ˈtyping pool
typist ˈtaɪp ɪst §-əst **~s** s
typo ˈtaɪp əʊ ‖ -oʊ **~s** z
typographer taɪ ˈpɒg rəf ə ‖ -ˈpɑːgr əf ᵊr **~s** z
typographic ˌtaɪp ə ˈgræf ɪk ◂ **~al** ᵊl **~ally** ᵊl‿i
typograph|y taɪ ˈpɒg rəf |i ‖ -ˈpɑːg- **~ies** iz
typological ˌtaɪp ə ˈlɒdʒ ɪk ᵊl ◂ ‖ -ˈlɑːdʒ- **~ly** ‿i
typolog|y taɪ ˈpɒl ədʒ |i ‖ -ˈpɑːl- **~ies** iz
-typy ˌtaɪp i *—sometimes treated as stress-imposing,* tɪp i, təp i — **autotypy** ˈɔːt əʊ ˌtaɪp i ɔː ˈtɒt ɪp i, -əp i ‖ ˈɔːt̬ oʊ ˌtaɪp i ˈɑːt̬-; ɔː ˈtɑːt̬ əp i, ɑː-
Tyr tɪə tjʊə ‖ tɪᵊr
tyramine ˈtaɪᵊr ə miːn ˈtɪr-

tyrannical tɪ ˈræn ɪk ᵊl tə-, taɪᵊ- **~ly** ˌi **~ness** nəs nɪs

tyrannicide tɪ ˈræn ɪ saɪd tə-, taɪᵊ-, -ə- **~s** z

tyrannis|e, tyranniz|e ˈtɪr ə naɪz **~ed** d **~es** ɪz əz **~ing** ɪŋ

tyrannosaur tɪ ˈræn ə sɔː tə-, taɪᵊ- ‖ -sɔːr **~s** z

tyrannosaurus tɪ ˌræn ə ˈsɔːr əs ◂ tə-, taɪᵊ- **~es** ɪz əz

   Ty ˌranno ˌsaurus ˈrex

tyrannous ˈtɪr ən əs **~ly** li

tyrann|y ˈtɪr ən |i **~ies** iz

tyrant ˈtaɪᵊr ənt **~s** s

tyre, Tyre ˈtaɪ ə ‖ ˈtaɪ ᵊr (= tire) **tyres** ˈtaɪ əz ‖ ˈtaɪ ᵊrz

Tyrian ˈtɪr i ˌən

Tyrie ˈtɪr i

tyro ˈtaɪᵊr əʊ ‖ -oʊ **~s** z

Tyrol tɪ ˈrəʊl tə-, →-ˈrɒʊl; ˈtɪr əl, -əʊl ‖ -ˈroʊl —Ger Tirol [ti ˈʁoːl]

Tyrolean ˌtɪr əʊ ˈliː ən ◂ tɪ ˈrəʊl i ˌən, tə- ‖ -ə- **~s** z

Tyrolese ˌtɪr əʊ ˈliːz ◂ ‖ -ə- -ˈliːs ◂

Tyrolienne tɪ ˌrəʊl i ˈen tə-, ˌtɪr əʊl- ‖ -ˌrəʊl- **~s** z

Tyrone county in N.Ireland tɪ ˈrəʊn tə- ‖ -ˈroʊn

Tyrone personal name ˈtaɪᵊr əʊn ˌtaɪᵊ ˈrəʊn, tɪ-, tə- ‖ -oʊn

tyrosine ˈtaɪᵊr əʊ siːn ˈtɪr-, -sɪn ‖ -ə-

tyrothricin ˌtaɪᵊr əʊ ˈθraɪs ɪn §-ᵊn ‖ -ə-

Tyrozets tdmk ˈtaɪᵊr ə zets ˈtɪr-

Tyrrell ˈtɪr əl

Tyrrhenian tɪ ˈriːn i ˌən tə-

Tyson ˈtaɪs ᵊn

Tyte taɪt

Tywyn ˈtaʊ ɪn —Welsh [ˈtə win, -win]

Tyzack (i) ˈtaɪz æk -ək, (ii) ˈtɪz-

tzar zɑː tsɑː ‖ zɑːr tsɑːr **tzars** zɑːz tsɑːz ‖ zɑːrz tsɑːrz

tzarina zɑː ˈriːn ə tsɑː- **~s** z

tzar|ism ˈzɑːr ˌɪz əm ˈtsɑːr- **~ist/s** ɪst/s §əst/s

tzatziki tæt ˈsiːk i tsæt- ‖ tɑːt- —ModGk [dza ˈdzi ci]

tzetze ˈtets i ˈtsets i, ˈsets i

Uu

u Spelling-to-sound

1. Where the spelling is **u**, the pronunciation differs according to whether the vowel is short or long, followed or not by **r**, and strong or weak.

2. The 'strong' pronunciation is regularly
   ʌ as in **cup** kʌp ('short U') or
   juː as in **music** ˈmjuːz ɪk ('long U').

3. Less frequently, it is
   ʊ as in **push** pʊʃ (especially before **sh, l**).

4. Where the spelling is **ur**, the 'strong' pronunciation is
   ɜː ‖ ɝː as in **turn** tɜːn ‖ tɝːn or
   jʊə ‖ jʊ as in **pure** pjʊə ‖ pjʊr (in BrE ʊə is often replaced by ɔː, thus pjɔː)
   or, indeed, there may be the regular 'short' pronunciation
   ʌ ‖ ɜː as in **hurry** ˈhʌr i ‖ ˈhɝː i (in most AmE, the ʌ and r coalesce into ɝː).

5. In the case of expected juː, jʊə, jʊ, the j drops out as follows:
   * after the consonant sounds tʃ, dʒ, ʃ, r, j, as in **jury** ˈdʒʊər i ‖ ˈdʒʊr i **rude** ruːd
   * sometimes in BrE, and always in AmE, after l, θ, s, z, as in **assume** ə ˈs(j)uːm ‖ ə ˈsuːm
   * usually in AmE, but not in BrE, after t, d, n as in **tune** tjuːn ‖ tuːn (see also ASSIMILATION for the BrE possibility of tʃuːn).

6. Note the exceptional words **busy** ˈbɪz i, **business** ˈbɪz nəs, **bury** ˈber i.

7. The 'weak' pronunciation is
   jʊ ‖ jə as in **stimulus** ˈstɪm jʊl əs ‖ ˈstɪm jəl əs (but in BrE at the end of a syllable the vowel may be tenser, and in this dictionary is written as ju, thus **stimulate** ˈstɪm ju leɪt ‖ ˈstɪm jə leɪt)
   ə as in **album** ˈælb əm, **Arthur** ˈɑːθ ə ‖ ˈɑːrθ ᵊr or
   jə as in **failure** ˈfeɪl jə ‖ ˈfeɪl jᵊr.
   In the ending **-ure** the vowel is usually weak. Note also **minute** (noun) ˈmɪn ɪt ‖ ˈmɪn ət, **lettuce** ˈlet ɪs ‖ ˈleţ əs, where the BrE vowel sound is ɪ rather than ə.

8. **u** also forms part of the digraphs **au, eu, ou, ue, ui, uy**.

ue Spelling-to-sound

1　Where the spelling is the digraph **ue**, the pronunciation is regularly

ju: as in **cue** kju: or

u: as in **blue** blu:.

(For the dropping of j, see **u** 5 above.)

2　**ue** is not a digraph in **duet**, **cruel**, **pursuer**.

ui Spelling-to-sound

1　Where the spelling is the digraph **ui**, the pronunciation is regularly

ju: as in **nuisance** 'nju:s ⁿn's (AmE usually 'nu:s-) or

u: as in **fruit** fru:t.

(For the dropping of j, see **u** 5 above.)

2　Less frequently, the pronunciation is

ɪ as in **build** bɪld or

aɪ as in **guide** gaɪd, also

ɪ ‖ ə as in **biscuit** 'bɪsk ɪt ‖ 'bɪsk ət (when weak).

3　Note the exceptional case **suite** swi:t.

4　**ui** is not a digraph in **fluid**, **tuition**, nor in **quick**, **quite** (where the digraph **qu** is followed by **i**).

uy Spelling-to-sound

In the rare cases where the spelling is the digraph **uy**, the pronunciation is regularly

aɪ as in **buy** baɪ.

U, u ju: (= you) **U's, u's, Us** ju:z
— *Communications code name:* Uniform
UAE ˌju: eɪ 'i:
UART 'ju: ɑːt ‖ -ɑːrt
UB40 ˌju: ˌbi: 'fɔːt i ‖ -'fɔːrt̬ i
U-bend 'ju: bend ~s z
ubermensch, übermensch 'u:b ə menʃ 'ju:b-
‖ -ᵊr- — *Ger* Ü~ ['y: bɐ mɛnʃ]
ubiquitous ju 'bɪk wɪt əs -wət- ‖ -wət̬ əs **~ly** li
~ness nəs nɪs
ubiquity ju 'bɪk wət i -wɪt- ‖ -wət̬ i
U-boat 'ju: bəʊt ‖ -boʊt ~s s
Ubu Roi ˌu:b u: 'rwɑː
UC ˌju: 'si:

UCAS 'ju:k æs
'UCAS form
Uccello u: 'tʃel əʊ ‖ -oʊ — *It* [ut 'tʃɛl lo]
Uckfield 'ʌk fiːᵊld
UCL ˌju: si: 'el
UCLA ˌju: si: el 'eɪ
UDA ˌju: di: 'eɪ
Udall (i) 'ju:d ᵊl -ɔːl, -æl ‖ 'ju:d ɔːl -ɑːl,
(ii) ju 'dæl -'dɔːl ‖ -'dɔːl, -'dɑːl
udder 'ʌd ə ‖ -ᵊr **~s** z
UDI ˌju: di: 'aɪ
Udimore 'ju:d ɪ mɔː 'ʌd-, -ə- ‖ -mɔːr -moʊr
Udmurt 'ʊd mʊət ·'· ‖ -mʊrt **~s** s
UDR ˌju: di: 'ɑː ‖ -'ɑːr
UEFA ju 'eɪf ə -'iːf-; 'ju:f ə

UFC ˌjuː ef ˈsiː
Uffizi ju ˈfɪts i uː-, -ˈfiːts- —*It* [uf ˈfit tsi]
UFO ˌjuː ef ˈəʊ ˈjuːf əʊ ‖ ˌjuː ef ˈoʊ ˈjuːf oʊ **~s** z
ufolog|y ˌjuː ˈfɒl ədʒ i ‖ -ˈfɑːl- **~ist/s** ɪst/s
Ugand|a ju ˈɡænd |ə ‖ u ˈɡɑːnd |ə **~an/s** ən/z
Ugaritic ˌuːɡ ə ˈrɪt ɪk ◂ ˌjuːɡ- ‖ -ˈrɪt̬-
UGC ˌjuː dʒiː ˈsiː
ugh ʊx ʌɡ, jʌx, ʊə, uː —*and various other
non-speech exclamations typically involving a
vowel in the range* [ɯ, u, ʌ, ɜ] *and sometimes
a consonant such as* [x, ɸ, h]
ugli ˈʌɡ li **~s** z
uglification ˌʌɡ lɪf ɪ ˈkeɪʃ ən ˌ-ləf-, §-ə'--
ugli|fy ˈʌɡ lɪ |faɪ -lə- **~fied** faɪd **~fies** faɪz
~fying faɪ ɪŋ
ugly ˈʌɡ li **uglier** ˈʌɡ li ə ‖ ˀr **ugliest** ˈʌɡ li ɪst
əst **ugliness** ˈʌɡ li nəs -nɪs
ˌugly ˈduckling
Ugrian ˈjuːɡ ri ən ˈuːɡ- **~s** z
Ugric ˈjuːɡ rɪk ˈuːɡ-
U-Haul *tdmk* ˈjuː hɔːl ‖ -hɑːl
UHF ˌjuː eɪtʃ ˈef §-heɪtʃ-
uh huh, uh-huh *'yes'* ˈʌ̃ hʌ̃ ˈʔ̃ hə̃, ˈm m̩m,
ˈn n̩n; ·ˈ· ‖ · ˈ· —*usually with a low-rise tone*
uhlan ˈuːl ɑːn ˈjuːl-, -ən; u ˈlɑːn, ju- **~s** z
uh oh *said when you have made a mistake or
something bad has happened* ˈʔʌʔ əʊ -ɜː
‖ ˈʔʌʔ oʊ ·ˈ· —*usually with the first syllable on
a high level tone, the second on a mid or
low-rising tone*
UHT ˌjuː eɪtʃ ˈtiː ◂ §-heɪtʃ-
Uhu *tdmk* ˈjuː huː ˈuː-
uh uh, uh-uh *'no'* ˈʔʌ̃ʔ ʌ̃ ˈʔɜ̃ʔ ə̃, ˈʔmʔ m
—*always with a falling tone*
Ui ˈuːˌi
U-ie *'U-turn'* ˈjuː i **~s** z
Uig ˈuː ɪɡ ˈjuː-
Uighur, Uigur ˈwiːɡ ə ˌuː i ˈɡʊə ◂ ‖ -r -ʊr;
ˌuː i ˈɡʊˀr ◂ —*Uighur* [ʔʊi ˈʁʊː] **~s** z
Uinta ju ˈɪnt ə ‖ -ˈɪnt̬ ə
Uist ˈjuː ɪst
Uitenhage ˈjuːt ən heɪɡ
UK ˌjuː ˈkeɪ ◂
ukas|e ju ˈkeɪz -ˈkeɪs **~es** ɪz əz
ukelele ˌjuːk ə ˈleɪl i **~s** z
Ukiah *place in CA* ju ˈkaɪ ə
UKIP, Ukip ˈjuːk ɪp
Ukraine ju ˈkreɪn
Ukrainian ju ˈkreɪn iˌən **~s** z
Ukridge ˈjuːk rɪdʒ
ukulele ˌjuːk ə ˈleɪl i **~s** z
Ulaanbaatar, Ulan Bator ˌuːl ɑːn ˈbɑːt ɔː
u ˌlɑːn ·ˈ· ‖ -ɔːr
-ular *stress-imposing* jʊl ə |jəl ə ‖ jəl ˀr —
mandibular mæn ˈdɪb jʊl ə -jəl- ‖ -jəl ˀr
ulcer ˈʌls ə ‖ -ˀr **~s** z
ulce|rate ˈʌls ə |reɪt **~rated** reɪt ɪd -əd
‖ reɪt̬ əd **~rates** reɪts **~rating** reɪt ɪŋ ‖ reɪt̬ ɪŋ
ulceration ˌʌls ə ˈreɪʃ ən **~s** z
ulcerative ˈʌls ər ət ɪv -ə reɪt- ‖ -ə reɪt̬- -ər ət̬-
ulcerous ˈʌls ər əs **~ly** li
Uldall ˈʊl dɔːl
-ule juːl — **globule** ˈɡlɒb juːl ‖ ˈɡlɑːb-

ulema ˈuːl ɪm ə -əm-; -ɪ mɑː, -ə-, ˌ· ˈ· **~s** z
-ulence *stress-imposing* jʊl ənˈs jəl- ‖ jəl- —
opulence ˈɒp jʊl ənˈs -jəl- ‖ ˈɑːp jəl ənˈs
-ulent *stress-imposing* jʊl ənt jəl- ‖ jəl- —
corpulent ˈkɔːp jʊl ənt -jəl- ‖ ˈkɔːrp jəl ənt
Ulfilas ˈʊlf ɪ læs -ə-; -ɪl əs, -əl-
Ulick ˈjuːl ɪk
ullage ˈʌl ɪdʒ
Ullapool ˈʌl ə puːl
Ullman, Ullmann ˈʊl mən
Ullswater ˈʌlz ˌwɔːt ə ‖ -ˌwɔːt̬ ˀr -ˌwɑːt̬-
Ulm ʊlm
ulna ˈʌln ə **ulnae** ˈʌln iː **ulnas** ˈʌln əz
ulnar ˈʌln ə ‖ -ˀr -ɑːr
ulpan ˈʊlp æn -ɑːn
Ulpian ˈʌlp i ən
Ulrich ˈʊl rɪk -rɪx —*Ger* [ˈʔʊl ʁɪç]
Ulrika ʊl ˈriːk ə
Ulster, u~ ˈʌlst ə ‖ -ˀr **~s, ~'s** z
Ulster|man ˈʌlst ə |mən ‖ -ˀr- **~men** mən men
~woman ˌwʊm ən **~women** ˌwɪm ɪn §-ən
ult, ult. ʌlt
ulterior ʌl ˈtɪər iˌə ‖ -ˈtɪr iˌˀr **~ly** li
ultima ˈʌlt ɪm ə -əm-
ultimate ˈʌlt ɪm ət -əm-, -ɪt **~ly** li **~ness** nəs
nɪs
ultimat|um ˌʌlt ɪ ˈmeɪt |əm -ə- ‖ -ˈmeɪt̬ |əm
-ˈmɑːt̬- **~a** ə **~ums** əmz
ultimo ˈʌlt ɪ məʊ -ə- ‖ -moʊ
ultra ˈʌltr ə ˈʊltr-, -ɑː **~s** z
ˌultra ˈvires ˈvaɪˀr iːz ˈvɪər-, -eɪz
ultra- ˌʌltr ə — **ultramodern**
ˌʌltr ə ˈmɒd ˀn ◂ ‖ -ˈmɑːd ˀrn ◂
ultrahigh ˌʌltr ə ˈhaɪ ◂
ˌultrahigh ˈfrequency
ultralight ˌʌltr ə ˈlaɪt ◂
ultramarine ˌʌltr ə mə ˈriːn ◂
ultra-modern ˌʌltr ə ˈmɒd ˀn ◂ ‖ -ˈmɑːd ˀrn ◂
ultramontane ˌʌltr ə ˈmɒnt eɪn ◂ -mɒn ˈteɪn
‖ -ˈmɑːnt eɪn ◂ -mɑːn ˈteɪn
ultranationalist ˌʌltr ə ˈnæʃ ˀn əl ɪst ◂ §-əst
~s s
ultrasonic ˌʌltr ə ˈsɒn ɪk ◂ ‖ -ˈsɑːn- **~ally** ˀlˌi
~s s
ultrasound ˈʌltr ə saʊnd ˌ· ˈ·
ultraviolet ˌʌltr ə ˈvaɪˌəl ət ◂ -ɪt
ULU ˈjuːl uː
ulu|late ˈjuːl ju |leɪt ˈʌl-, -jə- ‖ -jə- **~lated**
leɪt ɪd -əd ‖ leɪt̬ əd **~lates** leɪts **~lating**
leɪt ɪŋ ‖ leɪt̬ ɪŋ
ululation ˌjuːl ju ˈleɪʃ ən ˌʌl-, -jə- ‖ -jə- **~s** z
Uluru ˌuːl ə ˈruː ◂
ˌUluru ˌNational ˈPark
Ulverston, Ulverstone ˈʌlv əst ən ‖ -ˀrst-
Ulysses ju ˈlɪs iːz ˈjuːl ɪ siːz, -ə-
um *hesitation noise* ʌm əm, ɜːm, ə̃ —*usually
with a level tone*
umami u ˈmɑːm i —*Jp* [ɯ ˌma mi]
Umatilla ˌjuːm ə ˈtɪl ə
umbel ˈʌm bˀl **~s** z
umbellifer ʌm ˈbel ɪf ə -əf- ‖ -ˀr **~s** z
umbelliferae ˌʌm bə ˈlɪf ə riː ˌ·be-
umbelliferous ˌʌm bə ˈlɪf ər əs ◂ ˌ·be-

umber ˈʌm bə ‖ -ˈbʳr ~s z
Umberto ʊm ˈbeət əʊ -ˈbɜːt- ‖ -ˈbert oʊ —*It*
[um ˈbɛr to]
umbilical ʌm ˈbɪl ɪk ᵊl -ək-; ˌʌm, bɪ ˈlaɪk ᵊl ◄,
-bə-
umbilicus ʌm ˈbɪl ɪk əs -ək-; ˌʌm bɪ ˈlaɪk əs,
-bə- **umbilici** ʌm ˈbɪl ə saɪ -ɪ-; ˌʌm bɪ ˈlaɪs aɪ,
-bə-
umble ˈʌm bᵊl ~s z
umbo ˈʌm bəʊ ‖ -boʊ **umbones** ʌm ˈbəʊn iːz
‖ -ˈboʊn- **umbos** ˈʌm bəʊz ‖ -boʊz
um|bra ˈʌm |brə ~**brae** briː ~**bras** brəz
umbrage ˈʌm brɪdʒ

UMBRELLA

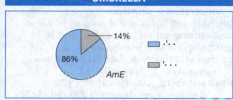

14%
86%
AmE

umbrella ʌm ˈbrel ə ‖ ˈ·ˈ· —*Preference poll,*
AmE: ·ˈ· 86%, ˈ·· 14%. ~**s** z
Umbria ˈʌm bri ə
Umbrian ˈʌm bri ən ~**s** z
Umbriel ˈʌm bri əl
Umbro *tdmk* ˈʌm brəʊ ‖ -broʊ
umiak ˈuːm i æk ~**s** s
UMIST ˈjuːm ɪst
um|laut ˈʊm |laʊt ~**lauted** laʊt ɪd -əd
‖ laʊt̬ əd ~**lauting** laʊt ɪŋ ‖ laʊt̬ ɪŋ ~**lauts**
laʊts
umma, ummah ˈʊm ə —*Arabic* [ˈʔum mah]
ump ʌmp **umps** ʌmps
umpire ˈʌmp aɪ ə ‖ -aɪ ʳr ~**d** d ~**s** z **umpiring**
ˈʌmp aɪ ər ɪŋ ‖ ˈʌmp aɪ ər ɪŋ
umpteen ˌʌmp ˈtiːn ◄
umpteenth ˌʌmp ˈtiːnᵗθ ◄
'un *nonstandard weak form of* **one** ən, ᵊn — **a**
big 'un ə ˈbɪg ən
un- ʌn, ˌʌn —*This prefix may lexically be*
stressed or unstressed. It is unstressed
particularly where it is not a true prefix
(un'wieldy); *it is stressed particularly (a) where*
the initial syllable of the stem does not bear
the primary stress (ˌunaˈshamed), *and (b) in*
verbs (ˌun'coil). *In some words usage is divided*
or uncertain (ˌ(ˌ)un'bearable).
UN ˌjuː ˈen ◄
ˌUN ˈtroops
Una ˈjuːn ə
unabashed ˌʌn ə ˈbæʃt ◄
unabated ˌʌn ə ˈbeɪt ɪd ◄ -əd ‖ -ˈbeɪt̬ əd ◄
unable ʌn ˈeɪb ᵊl ˌ·-
unabridged ˌʌn ə ˈbrɪdʒd ◄
unaccented ˌʌn ək ˈsent ɪd ◄ -æk-, -əd
‖ ˌʌn æk ˈsent̬ əd ◄
unacceptability ˌʌn ək ˌsept ə ˈbɪl ət i ˌ·æk-,
ˌ·ɪk-, -ɪt i ‖ -ət̬ i
unacceptab|le ˌʌn ək ˈsept əb |ᵊl ◄, ˌ·ɪk- ~**ly** li

unaccompanied ˌʌn ə ˈkʌmp ən id ◄
ˌunac,companied ˈchildren
unaccountab|le ˌʌn ə ˈkaʊnt əb |ᵊl ◄
‖ -ˈkaʊnt̬- ~**ly** li
unaccounted-for ˌʌn ə ˈkaʊnt ɪd fɔː ◄ -əd·
‖ -ˈkaʊnt̬ əd fɔːr ◄
unaccusative ˌʌn ə ˈkjuːz ət ɪv ◄ ‖ -ət̬ ɪv ~**s** z
unaccusativity ˌʌn ə ˌkjuːz ə ˈtɪv ət i -ɪt i
‖ -ət̬ i
unaccustomed ˌʌn ə ˈkʌst əmd ◄
ˌunac,customed ˈduty
unacknowledged ˌʌn ək ˈnɒl ɪdʒd ◄ -æk-, -ɪk-
‖ -ˈnɑːl-
unadopted ˌʌn ə ˈdɒpt ɪd ◄ -əd ‖ -ˈdɑːpt-
unadorned ˌʌn ə ˈdɔːnd ◄ ‖ -ˈdɔːrnd ◄
unadulterated ˌʌn ə ˈdʌlt ə reɪt ɪd ◄ -əd
‖ -reɪt̬ əd
unadvised ˌʌn əd ˈvaɪzd ◄ §-æd-
unaffected ˌʌn ə ˈfekt ɪd ◄ -əd
unafraid ˌʌn ə ˈfreɪd ◄
unaided ˌ(ˌ)ʌn ˈeɪd ɪd ◄ -əd
unalienable ˌ(ˌ)ʌn ˈeɪl i ən əb ᵊl ◄
unaligned ˌʌn ə ˈlaɪnd ◄
unalloyed ˌʌn ə ˈlɔɪd ◄
unalterab|le ʌn ˈɔːlt ər əb| ᵊl ◄, ˌʌn-, -ˈɒlt
‖ -ˈɑːlt̬ ~**ly** li
unambiguous ˌʌn æm ˈbɪg ju əs ◄
un-American ˌʌn ə ˈmer ɪk ən ◄ -ək ən
unanalysable, unanalyzable
ˌʌn ˈæn ə laɪz əb ᵊl →-ˈæn ᵊl aɪz-; ˌ·ˌ·ˈ·ˈ·
unanimity ˌjuːn ə ˈnɪm ət i ˌ·æ-, -ɪt i ‖ -ət̬ i
unanimous ju ˈnæn ɪm əs -əm əs ~**ly** li ~**ness**
nəs nɪs
unannounced ˌʌn ə ˈnaʊnst ◄
unanswerable ˌ(ˌ)ʌn ˈɑːns ər əb| ᵊl §-ˈænts-
‖ -ˈænts-
unanswered ˌʌn ˈɑːnts əd ◄ §-ˈænts-
‖ -ˈænts ʳrd ◄
ˌunanswered ˈquestions
unapologetic ˌʌn ə ˌpɒl ə ˈdʒet ɪk ◄
‖ -ˌpɑːl ə ˈdʒet̬ ɪk ◄
unappealing ˌʌn ə ˈpiːᵊl ɪŋ
unappetizing, unappetising
ˌ(ˌ)ʌn ˈæp ɪ taɪz ɪŋ -ə taɪz-
unapproachable ˌʌn ə ˈprəʊtʃ əb ᵊl ◄
‖ -ˈproʊtʃ-
unappropriated ˌʌn ə ˈprəʊp ri eɪt ɪd ◄ -əd
‖ -ˈproʊp ri eɪt̬ əd ◄
unarguab|le ʌn ˈɑːg ju əb| ᵊl ‖ -ˈɑːrg- ~**ly** li
unarmed ˌʌn ˈɑːmd ◄ ‖ -ˈɑːrmd ◄
ˌunarmed ˈcombat
unary ˈjuːn ər i
unashamed ˌʌn ə ˈʃeɪmd ◄
unashamed|ly ˌʌn ə ˈʃeɪm ɪd |li -ˈəd-;
-ˈʃeɪmd |li ~**ness** nəs nɪs
unasked ˌʌn ˈɑːskt ◄ §-ˈæskt ‖ -ˈæskt ◄
unaspirated ˌ(ˌ) ʌn ˈæsp ə reɪt ɪd ◄ -ˈ·ɪ-, -əd
‖ -reɪt̬ əd
unassailable ˌʌn ə ˈseɪl əb ᵊl ◄
unassisted ˌʌn ə ˈsɪst ɪd ◄ -əd
unassuming ˌʌn ə ˈsjuːm ɪŋ ◄ -ˈsuːm-, §-ˈʃuːm-
‖ -ˈsuːm- ~**ly** li ~**ness** nəs nɪs
unattached ˌʌn ə ˈtætʃt ◄

unattainable ˌʌn ə 'teɪn əb ᵊl
unattended ˌʌn ə 'tend ɪd ◂ -əd-
unattractive ˌʌn ə 'trækt ɪv ◂ **-ly** li
unauthorized, unauthorised ʌn 'ɔːθ ə raɪzd
‖ -'ɑːθ-
unavailable ˌʌn ə 'veɪl əb ᵊl ◂
unavailing ˌʌn ə 'veɪl ɪŋ ◂
unavoidab|le ˌʌn ə 'vɔɪd əb |ᵊl ◂ **~leness**
ᵊl nəs -nɪs **~ly** li
unaware ˌʌn ə 'weə ‖ -'weᵊr -'wæᵊr **~s** z
unbalanc|e ˌʌn 'bæl ənˀs →ˌʌm- **~ed** t **~es** ɪz
əz **~ing** ɪŋ
unbar ˌʌn 'bɑː ◂ →ˌʌm- ‖ -'bɑːr ◂ **~red** d
unbarring ˌʌn 'bɑːr ɪŋ →ˌʌm- **~s** z
unbearab|le ₍ˌ₎ʌn 'beər əb |ᵊl →₍ˌ₎ʌm- ‖ -'ber-
-'bær- **~leness** ᵊl nəs -nɪs **~ly** li
unbeatab|le ₍ˌ₎ʌn 'biːt əb |ᵊl →₍ˌ₎ʌm- ‖ -'biːt̬-
~ly li
unbeaten ₍ˌ₎ʌn 'biːt ᵊn
unbecoming ˌʌn bɪ 'kʌm ɪŋ ◂ →ˌʌm-, -bə- **~ly**
li **~ness** nəs nɪs
unbeknown ˌʌn bɪ 'nəʊn ◂ →ˌʌm-, -bə-
‖ -'noʊn ◂
unbeknownst ˌʌn bɪ 'nəʊnˀst →ˌʌm-, -bə-
‖ -'noʊnˀst
unbelief ˌʌn bɪ 'liːf →ˌʌm-, -bə-
unbelievab|le ˌʌn bɪ 'liːv əb |ᵊl ◂ →ˌʌm-, -ˌbə-
~leness ᵊl nəs -nɪs **~ly** li
unbeliever ˌʌn bɪ 'liːv ə →ˌʌm-, -bə- **-ᵊr ~s** z
unbelieving ˌʌn bɪ 'liːv ɪŋ ◂ →ˌʌm-, -bə- **~ly** li
unbend ˌʌn 'bend →ˌʌm- **~ing** ɪŋ **~s** z unbent
ˌʌn 'bent ◂ →ˌʌm-
unbending *adj 'inflexible'* ʌn 'bend ɪŋ →ʌm-
~ly li **~ness** nəs nɪs
unbent ˌʌn 'bent ◂ →ˌʌm-
unbiased, unbiassed ₍ˌ₎ʌn 'baɪ̯ əst →₍ˌ₎ʌm-
~ly li **~ness** nəs nɪs
unbidden ˌʌn 'bɪd ᵊn →ˌʌm-
unbind ˌʌn 'baɪnd →ˌʌm- **~ing** ɪŋ unbound
ˌʌn 'baʊnd ◂
unblemished ʌn 'blem ɪʃt →ʌm, ˌ-
unblinking ˌʌn 'blɪŋk ɪŋ →ˌʌm- **~ly** li
unblock ˌʌn 'blɒk ◂ →ˌʌm- ‖ -'blɑːk ◂ **~ed** t
~ing ɪŋ **~s** s
unblushing ˌʌn 'blʌʃ ɪŋ ◂ →ˌʌm- **~ly** li
unbolt ˌʌn 'bəʊlt ◂ →ˌʌm-, →-'bɒʊlt
‖ -'boʊlt ◂ **~ed** ɪd əd **~ing** ɪŋ **~s** s
unborn ˌʌn 'bɔːn ◂ →ˌʌm- ‖ -'bɔːrn ◂
unbosom ˌʌn 'bʊz əm →ˌʌm-, §-'buːz- **~ed** d
~ing ɪŋ **~s** z
unbound ˌʌn 'baʊnd ◂ →ˌʌm-
unbounded ₍ˌ₎ʌn 'baʊnd ɪd -əd **~ly** li **~ness**
nəs nɪs
unbowed ˌʌn 'baʊd ◂ →ˌʌm-
unbreakable ʌn 'breɪk əb ᵊl →ʌm-
unbridgeable ʌn 'brɪdʒ əb ᵊl →ʌm-
unbridled ₍ˌ₎ʌn 'braɪd ᵊld →₍ˌ₎ʌm-
unbroken ₍ˌ₎ʌn 'brəʊk ən →₍ˌ₎ʌm- ‖ -'broʊk-
~ly li **~ness** nəs nɪs
unbuckl|e ˌʌn 'bʌk ᵊl →ˌʌm- **~ed** d **~es** z **~ing**
ɪŋ
unburden ˌʌn 'bɜːd ᵊn →ˌʌm- ‖ -'bɜːd- **~ed** d
~ing ɪŋ **~s** z

unbutton ˌʌn 'bʌt ᵊn ◂ →ˌʌm- **~ed** d **~ing** ɪŋ
~s z
uncalled-for ₍ˌ₎ʌn 'kɔːld fɔː →₍ˌ₎ʌŋ- ‖ -fɔːr
-'kɑːld-
uncann|y ʌn 'kæn |i →ʌŋ- **~ily** ɪ li əl i **~iness**
i nəs i nɪs
uncap ˌʌn 'kæp →ˌʌŋ- **~ped** t ◂ **~ping** ɪŋ **~s** s
uncared-for ₍ˌ₎ʌn 'keəd fɔː →₍ˌ₎ʌŋ-
‖ -'kerd fɔːr -'kærd-
unceasing ʌn 'siːs ɪŋ ˌ- **~ly** li **~ness** nəs nɪs
unceremonious ˌʌn ˌser ɪ 'məʊn i əs -ˌə-
‖ -'moʊn- **~ly** li **~ness** nəs nɪs
uncertain ʌn 'sɜːt ᵊn ˌ-, -ɪn ‖ -'sɜːt ᵊn **-ly** li
uncertain|ty ʌn 'sɜːt ᵊn |ti -ɪn- ‖ -'sɜːt̬- **~ties**
tiz
un'certainty ˌprinciple
unchain ˌʌn 'tʃeɪn **~ed** d **~ing** ɪŋ **~s** z
unchalleng|ed ʌn 'tʃæl ɪndʒd **~ing** ɪŋ
unchang|ed ʌn 'tʃeɪndʒd ◂ **~ing** ɪŋ
uncharacteristic ʌn ˌkær ɪkt ə 'rɪst ɪk ◂
→ʌŋ-, -əkt ə- ‖ -ˌker- **-ally** ᵊl i
uncharitab|le ₍ˌ₎ʌn 'tʃær ɪt əb |ᵊl ◂ -'-ət-
‖ -'tʃær ət̬- -'tʃer- **~leness** ᵊl nəs -nɪs **~ly** li
uncharted ˌʌn 'tʃɑːt ɪd ◂ -əd ‖ -'tʃɑːrt̬ əd ◂
unchecked ˌʌn 'tʃekt ◂
unchristian ₍ˌ₎ʌn 'krɪs tʃən →₍ˌ₎ʌŋ-, -'krɪst i ən
~ly li
unci 'ʌnˀs aɪ
uncial 'ʌnˀs i əl 'ʌnˀʃ-; 'ʌnˀʃ ᵊl ‖ 'ʌnˀʃ ᵊl -i əl **~s**
z
unciform 'ʌnˀs ɪ fɔːm -ə- ‖ -fɔːrm
uncinate 'ʌnˀs ɪn ət -ən-, -ɪt; -ɪ neɪt, -ə-
uncircumcised ˌʌn 'sɜːk əm saɪzd ◂ ‖ -'sɜːk-
uncircumcision ˌʌn ˌsɜːk əm 'sɪʒ ᵊn ‖ -ˌsɜːk-
uncivilised, uncivilized ₍ˌ₎ʌn 'sɪv ə laɪzd -ɪ-,
-ᵊl aɪzd
unclad ˌʌn 'klæd ◂ →ˌʌŋ-
unclaimed ˌʌn 'kleɪmd ◂ →ˌʌŋ-
ˌunclaimed 'baggage
unclasp ˌʌn 'klɑːsp →ˌʌŋ-, §-'klæsp ‖ -'klæsp
~ed t **~ing** ɪŋ **~s** s
unclassified ˌʌn 'klæs ɪ faɪd ◂ →ˌʌŋ-, -ə-
uncle 'ʌŋk ᵊl **~s** z
ˌUncle 'Sam; ˌUncle 'Tom
unclean ˌʌn 'kliːn ◂ →ˌʌŋ- **~er** ə ‖ ᵊr **~est** ɪst
əst **~ly** li **~ness** nəs nɪs
unclean|ly *adj* ˌʌn 'klen |li →ˌʌŋ- **~liness**
li nəs -nɪs
unclear ˌʌn 'klɪə ◂ →ˌʌŋ- ‖ -'klɪᵊr ◂ **~ly** li
unclench ˌʌn 'klentʃ ◂ →ˌʌŋ- **~ed** t **~es** ɪz əz
~ing ɪŋ
unclog ˌʌn 'klɒg ◂ →ˌʌŋ- ‖ -'klɑːg ◂ **~ged** d
~ging ɪŋ **~s** z
unclothed ʌn 'kləʊðd →ʌŋ- ‖ -'kloʊðd
unclouded ₍ˌ₎ʌn 'klaʊd ɪd ◂ →₍ˌ₎ʌŋ-, -əd
uncluttered ˌʌn 'klʌt əd ◂ →ˌʌŋ- ‖ -'klʌt̬ ᵊrd ◂
unco 'ʌŋk ə -əʊ ‖ -oʊ
uncoil ˌʌn 'kɔɪᵊl ◂ →ˌʌŋ- **~ed** d **~ing** ɪŋ **~s** z
uncolored, uncoloured ˌʌn 'kʌl əd ◂ →ˌʌŋ-
‖ -ᵊrd ◂
uncomfortab|le ʌn 'kʌmᵖft əb |ᵊl →ʌŋ-,
-'kʌmᵖf ət əb |ᵊl ‖ -ᵊrb |ᵊl; -'kʌmᵖf ət̬ əb |ᵊl,
-'-ᵊrt̬- **~leness** ᵊl nəs -nɪs **~ly** li

uncommitted ˌʌn kə ˈmɪt ɪd ◄ →ˌʌŋ-, -əd
‖ -mɪt̬ əd ◄
uncommon ʌn ˈkɒm ən →ʌŋ-, ˌˌ-- ‖ -ˈkɑːm- **~ly**
li **~ness** nəs nɪs
uncommunicative ˌʌn kə ˈmjuːn ɪk ət ɪv ◄
→ˌʌŋ-, §-ˈ-ək-, -eɪt ɪv ‖ -ə keɪt̬ ɪv -ək ət̬- **~ly** li
~ness nəs nɪs
uncompetitive ˌʌn kəm ˈpet ət ɪv ◄ →ˌʌŋ-,
§-ˌkɒm-, -ˈ-ɪt- ‖ -ˈpet̬ ət̬- **~ness** nəs nɪs
uncomplaining ˌʌn kəm ˈpleɪn ɪŋ ◄ →ˌʌŋ-,
§-kɒm- **~ly** li
uncomplicated ˌˌʌn ˈkɒmp lɪ keɪt ɪd
→ˌˌʌŋ-, -lə-ˌ, -əd ‖ ʌn ˈkɑːmp lə keɪt̬ əd
uncomprehending ˌʌn ˌkɒmp ri ˈhend ɪŋ ◄
→ˌʌŋ-, -rə-
uncompromising ʌn ˈkɒmp rə maɪz ɪŋ →ʌŋ-
‖ -ˈkɑːmp- **~ly** li **~ness** nəs nɪs
unconcern ˌʌn kən ˈsɜːn →ˌʌŋ-, §-kɒn- ‖ -ˈsɜːn
~ed d
unconcerned|ly ˌʌn kən ˈsɜːn ɪd |li |-ˈ-əd-;
-ˈsɜːnd |li ‖ -ˈsɜːn- **~ness** nəs nɪs
unconditional ˌʌn kən ˈdɪʃ ᵊn əl ◄ →ˌʌŋ-,
§-ˌkɒn- **~ly** i
unconfirmed ˌʌn kən ˈfɜːmd ◄ →ˌʌŋ-, §-kɒn-
‖ -ˈfɜːmd ◄
ˌunconfirmed reˈports
unconnected ˌʌn kə ˈnekt ɪd →ˌʌŋ-, -əd **~ly** li
~ness nəs nɪs
unconquerab|le ʌn ˈkɒŋk ər əb| ᵊl →ʌŋ-
‖ -ˈkɑːŋk- **~ly** li
unconscionab|le ʌn ˈkɒnᵗ ʃ ᵊn əb | ᵊl →ʌŋ-
‖ -ˈkɑːnᵗʃ- **~leness** ᵊl nəs -nɪs **~ly** li
unconscious ʌn ˈkɒnᵗʃ əs →ʌŋ-, ˌˌ-- ‖ -ˈkɑːnᵗʃ-
~ly li **~ness** nəs nɪs
unconsidered ˌʌn kən ˈsɪd əd ◄ →ˌʌŋ-, §-kɒn-
‖ -ᵊrd ◄
ˌuncon ˌsidered ˈtrifles
unconstitutional ˌʌn ˌkɒnᵗst ɪ ˈtjuːʃ ᵊn əl
→ˌʌŋ-, -ˌˌ-ə-, →-ˈtʃuːʃ- ‖ -ˌkɑːnᵗst ə ˈtuːʃ- -ˈtjuːʃ-
~ly i
uncontested ˌʌn kən ˈtest ɪd ◄ →ˌʌŋ-, §-kɒn-,
-əd
uncontrollab|le ˌʌn kən ˈtrəʊl əb| ᵊl ◄ →ˌʌŋ-,
§-ˌkɒn-, →-ˈtrɒʊl- ‖ -ˈtroʊl- **~ly** li
uncontrolled ˌʌn kən ˈtrəʊld ◄ →ˌʌŋ-, §-kɒn-,
ˈtrɒʊld ◄ ‖ -ˈtroʊld ◄
ˌuncontrolled inˈflation
unconventional ˌʌn kən ˈvenᵗʃ ᵊn əl ◄ →ˌʌŋ-,
§-ˌkɒn- **~ly** i
unconvinced ˌʌn kən ˈvɪnᵗst →ˌʌŋ-
unconvincing ˌʌn kən ˈvɪnᵗs ɪŋ →ˌʌŋ- **~ly** li
uncooked ˌʌn ˈkʊkt ◄ →ˌʌŋ-, §-ˈkuːkt
ˌuncooked ˈfood
uncool ˌʌn ˈkuːl ◄ →ˌʌŋ-
uncooperative ˌʌn kəʊ ˈɒp ər ət ɪv ◄ →ˌʌŋ-,
-ˈɒp ə reɪt ɪv ◄ ‖ ˌʌn koʊ ˈɑːp ᵊr ət̬ ɪv ◄
-ə reɪt̬ ɪv ◄
uncoordinated ˌʌn kəʊ ˈɔːd ɪ neɪt ɪd ◄ →ˌʌŋ-,
-ᵊn eɪt-, -əd ‖ ˌʌn koʊ ˈɔːrd ᵊn eɪt̬ əd ◄
uncork ˌʌn ˈkɔːk ◄ →ˌʌŋ- ‖ -ˈkɔːrk ◄ **~ed** t
~ing ɪŋ **~s** s
uncorroborated ˌʌn kə ˈrɒb ə reɪt ɪd ◄ →ˌʌŋ-,
-əd ◄ ‖ -ˈrɑːb ə reɪt̬ əd ◄

uncount ˈʌn kaʊnt →ˈʌŋ-
uncountable ˌʌn ˈkaʊnt əb ᵊl ◄ →ˌʌŋ-
‖ -ˈkaʊnt̬-
uncounted ˌˌʌn ˈkaʊnt ɪd →ˌˌʌŋ-, -əd
‖ -ˈkaʊnt̬ əd
uncoupl|e ˌʌn ˈkʌp ᵊl →ˌʌŋ- **~ed** d **~es** z **~ing**
ɪŋ
uncouth ʌn ˈkuːθ →ʌŋ-, ˌˌ-- **~ly** li **~ness** nəs
nɪs
uncover ʌn ˈkʌv ə →ʌŋ-, ˌˌ-- ‖ -ᵊr **~ed** d
uncovering ʌn ˈkʌv ər ɪŋ →ʌŋ-, ˌˌ-- **~s** z
uncritical ˌˌʌn ˈkrɪt ɪk ᵊl ◄ →ˌˌʌŋ- ‖ -ˈkrɪt̬- **~ly**
i
uncrowned ˌʌn ˈkraʊnd ◄ →ˌʌŋ-
ˌuncrowned ˈking
uncrushable ˌˌʌn ˈkrʌʃ əb ᵊl
unction ˈʌŋk ʃᵊn
unctuous ˈʌŋk tʃu əs -tju əs **~ly** li **~ness** nəs
nɪs
uncurl ˌʌn ˈkɜːl ◄ →ˌʌŋ- ‖ -ˈkɜːl ◄ **~ed** d **~ing**
ɪŋ **~s** z
uncus ˈʌŋk əs **unci** ˈʌnᵗs aɪ
uncut ˌʌn ˈkʌt ◄ →ˌʌŋ-
undamaged ˌˌʌn ˈdæm ɪdʒd
undamped ˌʌn ˈdæmpt ◄
undated ˌʌn ˈdeɪt ɪd ◄ -əd ‖ -ˈdeɪt̬-
undaunted ˌˌʌn ˈdɔːnt ɪd -əd ‖ -ˈdɔːnt̬ əd
-ˈdɑːnt̬- **~ly** li **~ness** nəs nɪs
undecagon ʌn ˈdek əg ən -ə gɒn ‖ -ə gɑːn **~s**
z
undeceiv|e ˌʌn di ˈsiːv -də- **~ed** d **~es** z **~ing**
ɪŋ
undecided ˌʌn di ˈsaɪd ɪd ◄ -də-, -əd **~ly** li
~ness nəs nɪs
undeclared ˌʌn di ˈkleəd ◄ -də- ‖ -ˈkleᵊrd ◄
-ˈklæᵊrd
undefined ˌʌn di ˈfaɪnd ◄ -də-
undemocratic ˌʌn ˌdem ə ˈkræt ɪk ◄ ‖ -ˈkræt̬-
~ally ᵊl i
undemonstrative ˌʌn di ˈmɒnᵗs trət ɪv ◄ ˌ-də-
‖ -ˈmɑːnᵗs trət̬- **~ly** li **~ness** nəs nɪs
undeniab|le ˌʌn dɪ ˈnaɪ əb | ᵊl ◄ ˌ-də- **~ly** li
undenominational ˌʌn di ˌnɒm ɪ ˈneɪʃ ᵊn əl
ˌ-də-, -ˌˌ-ə- ‖ -ˌnɑːm- **~ly** i
under ˈʌnd ə ‖ -ᵊr
under- ˌʌnd ə ‖ -ᵊr —*but before a vowel sound*
ˌʌnd ər ‖ -ᵊr
underachiev|e ˌʌnd ər ə ˈtʃiːv ‖ ˌ-ᵊr- **~ed** d
~er/s ə/z ‖ ᵊr/z **~es** z **~ing** ɪŋ
underact ˌʌnd ər ˈækt ‖ -ᵊr- **~ed** ɪd əd **~ing** ɪŋ
~s s
underage ˌʌnd ər ˈeɪdʒ ‖ -ᵊr-
ˌunderage ˈdrinking
underarm ˈʌnd ər ɑːm ‖ -ᵊr ɑːrm
underbell|y ˈʌnd ə ˌbel |i ‖ -ᵊr- **~ies** iz
underbid ˌʌnd ə ˈbɪd ‖ -ᵊr- **~ding** ɪŋ **~s** z
underbrush ˈʌnd ə brʌʃ ‖ -ᵊr-
undercapitalis|e, undercapitaliz|e
ˌʌnd ə ˈkæp ɪt ə laɪz §-ˈ-ət-, -ᵊl aɪz
‖ -ᵊr ˈkæp ət̬- **~ed** d **~es** ɪz əz **~ing** ɪŋ
undercarriag|e ˈʌnd ə ˌkær ɪdʒ ‖ -ᵊr- -ˌker-
~es ɪz əz
undercart ˈʌnd ə kɑːt ‖ -ᵊr kɑːrt **~s** s

undercharg|e n ˈʌnd ə tʃɑːdʒ ˌˈ·ˈ· ‖ -ᵊr tʃɑːrdʒ
~es ɪz əz

undercharg|e v ˌʌnd ə ˈtʃɑːdʒ ‖ -ᵊr ˈtʃɑːrdʒ
~ed d **~es** ɪz əz **~ing** ɪŋ

underclass ˈʌnd ə klɑːs §-klæs ‖ -ᵊr klæs **~es**
ɪz əz

underclass|man ˌʌnd ə ˈklɑːs mən §-ˈklæs-
‖ -ᵊr ˈklæs- **~men** mən

underclothes ˈʌnd ə kləʊðz -kləʊz ‖ -ᵊr kloʊz
-kloʊðz

underclothing ˈʌnd ə ˌkləʊð ɪŋ ‖ -ᵊr ˌkloʊð-

undercoat ˈʌnd ə kəʊt ‖ -ᵊr koʊt **~s** s

undercook ˌʌnd ə ˈkʊk §-ˈkuːk ‖ -ᵊr- **~ed** t ◂
~ing ɪŋ **~s** s

under|count v ˌʌnd ə |ˈkaʊnt ‖ -ᵊr- **~counted**
ˈkaʊnt ɪd -əd ‖ ˈkaʊnt̬ əd **~counting**
ˈkaʊnt ɪŋ ‖ ˈkaʊnt̬ ɪŋ **~counts** ˈkaʊnts

undercount n ˈʌnd ə kaʊnt ‖ -ᵊr- **~s** s

undercover ˌʌnd ə ˈkʌv ə ◂ ˈ·ˌ·ˌ·
‖ -ᵊr ˈkʌv ᵊr ◂

undercroft ˈʌnd ə krɒft ‖ -ᵊr krɔːft -krɑːft **~s** s

undercurrent ˈʌnd ə ˌkʌr ənt ‖ -ᵊr ˌkɜː- **~s** s

under|cut v ˌʌnd ə |ˈkʌt ‖ -ᵊr- **~cuts** ˈkʌts
~cutting ˈkʌt ɪŋ ‖ ˈkʌt̬ ɪŋ

undercut n ˈʌnd ə kʌt ‖ -ᵊr- **~s** s

underdevelop ˌʌnd ə dɪ ˈvel əp -də'--, §-diː'--
‖ ˌ·ᵊr- **~ed** t **~ing** ɪŋ **~ment** mənt **~s** s
ˌunderde ˌveloped ˈcountries

underdog ˈʌnd ə dɒg ‖ -ᵊr dɔːg -dɑːg **~s** z

underdone ˌʌnd ə ˈdʌn ◂ ‖ -ᵊr-
ˌunderdone ˈmeat

underdressed ˌʌnd ə ˈdrest ‖ -ᵊr-

underemployed ˌʌnd ᵊr ɪm ˈplɔɪd ◂ -əm'·
‖ ˌ·ᵊr-

underemployment ˌʌnd ᵊr ɪm ˈplɔɪ mənt
-əm'-- ‖ ˌ·ᵊr-

underestimate n ˌʌnd ᵊr ˈest ɪm ət -əm ət, -ɪt;
-ɪ meɪt, -ə meɪt ‖ ˌ·ᵊr- **~s** s

underesti|mate v ˌʌnd ᵊr ˈest ɪ |meɪt -ə·
‖ ˌ·ᵊr- **~mated** meɪt ɪd -əd ‖ meɪt̬ əd **~mates**
meɪts **~mating** meɪt ɪŋ ‖ meɪt̬ ɪŋ

underexpos|e ˌʌnd ᵊr ɪk ˈspəʊz -ək'·, -ek'·
‖ -ᵊr ɪk ˈspoʊz **~ed** d **~es** ɪz əz **~ing** ɪŋ

underexposure ˌʌnd ᵊr ɪk ˈspəʊʒ ə -ək'--,
-ek'-- ‖ -ᵊr ɪk ˈspoʊʒ ᵊr **~s** z

under|feed ˌʌnd ə |ˈfiːd ‖ -ᵊr- **~fed** ˈfed ◂
~feeding ˈfiːd ɪŋ **~feeds** ˈfiːdz

underfelt ˈʌnd ə felt ‖ -ᵊr- **~s** s

underfloor ˌʌnd ə ˈflɔː ◂ ‖ -ᵊr ˈflɔːr ◂ -ˈflʊͬr
ˌunderfloor ˈheating

underfoot ˌʌnd ə ˈfʊt ‖ -ᵊr-

underfund ˌʌnd ə ˈfʌnd ‖ -ᵊr- **~ed** ɪd əd **~ing**
ɪŋ **~s** z

undergarment ˈʌnd ə ˌgɑːm ənt ‖ -ᵊr ˌgɑːrm-
~s s

under|go ˌʌnd ə |ˈgəʊ ‖ -ᵊr |ˈgoʊ **~goes** ˈgəʊz
‖ ˈgoʊz **~gone** ˈgɒn §ˈgɑːn ‖ ˈgɔːn ˈgɑːn
~went ˈwent

undergrad ˈʌnd ə græd ˌˈ·ˈ· ‖ -ᵊr- **~s** z

undergraduate ˌʌnd ə ˈgrædʒ u̯ ət ◂
-ˈgræd ju̯ ət, ɪt, -eɪt ‖ -ᵊr- **~s** s

underground n, **U~** ˈʌnd ə graʊnd ‖ -ᵊr- **~s** z

underground adj, adv ˌʌnd ə ˈgraʊnd ◂ ˈ·ˈ·ˈ·
‖ -ᵊr-
ˌunderground ˈpassages

undergrowth ˈʌnd ə grəʊθ ‖ -ᵊr groʊθ

underhand ˌʌnd ə ˈhænd ◂ ˈ·ˈ·ˈ· ‖ -ᵊr-

underhanded ˌʌnd ə ˈhænd ɪd ◂ -əd ‖ -ᵊr- **~ly**
li **~ness** nəs nɪs

Underhill ˈʌnd ə hɪl ‖ -ᵊr-

underhung ˌʌnd ə ˈhʌŋ ◂ ‖ -ᵊr-

underinsure ˌʌnd ᵊrɪn ˈʃʊə -ˈʃɔːr ‖ -ᵊr ɪn ˈʃʊͬr
-ˈʃɜː **~d** d

underlaid ˌʌnd ə ˈleɪd ‖ -ᵊr-

underlain ˌʌnd ə ˈleɪn ‖ -ᵊr-

underlay n ˈʌnd ə leɪ ‖ -ᵊr- **~s** z

under|lie ˌʌnd ə |ˈlaɪ ‖ -ᵊr- **~lay** ˈleɪ **~lies** ˈlaɪz
~lying/ly ˈlaɪ ɪŋ /li
ˌunderˌlying ˈform

underline n ˈʌnd ə laɪn ˌˈ·ˈ· ‖ -ᵊr- **~s** z

underlin|e v ˌʌnd ə ˈlaɪn ˈ·ˈ· ‖ -ᵊr- **~ed** d **~es**
z **~ing** ɪŋ

underling ˈʌnd ə lɪŋ ‖ -ᵊr- **~s** z

underlying ˌʌnd ə ˈlaɪ ɪŋ ◂ ‖ ˌ·ᵊr- **~ly** li

undermanned ˌʌnd ə ˈmænd ◂ ‖ -ᵊr-

undermentioned ˌʌnd ə ˈmenʃ ᵊnd ◂ ‖ -ᵊr-

undermin|e ˌʌnd ə ˈmaɪn ‖ -ᵊr- **~ed** d **~es** z
~ing ɪŋ

underneath ˌʌnd ə ˈniːθ ◂ ‖ -ᵊr-

undernourish ˌʌnd ə ˈnʌr ɪʃ ‖ -ᵊr ˈnɜː- **~ed** t
~es ɪz əz **~ing** ɪŋ

underpaid ˌʌnd ə ˈpeɪd ◂ ‖ -ᵊr-

underpants ˈʌnd ə pænts ‖ -ᵊr-

underpass ˈʌnd ə pɑːs §-pæs ‖ -ᵊr pæs **~es** ɪz
əz

under|pay ˌʌnd ə |ˈpeɪ ‖ -ᵊr- **~paid** ˈpeɪd
~paying ˈpeɪ ɪŋ **~payment/s** ˈpeɪ mənt/s
~pays ˈpeɪz

underperform ˌʌnd ə pə ˈfɔːm ◂
‖ -ᵊr pᵊr ˈfɔːrm ◂ **~ed** d **~ing** ɪŋ **~s** z

underpin ˌʌnd ə ˈpɪn ‖ -ᵊr- **~ned** d **~ning** ɪŋ
~s z

underpinning n ˌʌnd ə ˈpɪn ɪŋ ˈ·ˌ·ˌ· ‖ -ᵊr- **~s** z

underplay v ˌʌnd ə ˈpleɪ ‖ -ᵊr- **~ed** d **~ing** ɪŋ
~s z

underpowered ˌʌnd ə ˈpaʊ̯ əd ◂
‖ -ᵊr ˈpaʊ̯ ᵊrd ◂

underpric|e v ˌʌnd ə ˈpraɪs ‖ -ᵊr- **~ed** t **~es** ɪz
əz **~ing** ɪŋ

underprivileged ˌʌnd ə ˈprɪv əl ɪdʒd ◂
-ɪl ɪdʒd ‖ -ᵊr-

underproof ˌʌnd ə ˈpruːf ‖ -ᵊr-

under|quote ˌʌnd ə |ˈkwəʊt ‖ -ᵊr |ˈkwoʊt
~quoted ˈkwəʊt ɪd -əd ‖ ˈkwoʊt̬ əd **~quotes**
ˈkwəʊts ‖ ˈkwoʊts **~quoting** ˈkwəʊt ɪŋ
‖ ˈkwoʊt̬ ɪŋ

under|rate ˌʌnd ə |ˈreɪt ‖ -ᵊr- **~rated** ˈreɪt ɪd
-əd ‖ ˈreɪt̬ əd **~rates** ˈreɪts **~rating** ˈreɪt ɪŋ
‖ ˈreɪt̬ ɪŋ

underrepresented ˌʌnd ə ˌrep ri ˈzent ɪd ◂
-rə ˈzent-, -əd ‖ ˌʌnd ᵊr rep rə ˈzent̬ əd ◂

underresourced ˌʌnd ə ri ˈzɔːst ◂ -ə rə-
‖ ˌʌnd ᵊr rə ˈzɔːrst ◂

under|run ˌʌnd ə |ˈrʌn ‖ -ᵊr- **~ran** ˈræn
~running ˈrʌn ɪŋ **~runs** ˈrʌnz

underscore v ˌʌnd ə ˈskɔː ˈ· · · ‖ ˈʌnd ʳr skɔːr
-skoʊr **~d** d **~s** z **underscoring**
ˌʌnd ə ˈskɔːr ɪŋ ˈ· · · · ‖ ˈʌnd ʳr skɔːr ɪŋ
-skoʊr ɪŋ

underscore n ˌʌnd ə skɔː ‖ -ʳr skɔːr -skoʊr **~s**
z

undersea ˌʌnd ə ˈsiː ◂ ˈ· · · ‖ -ʳr-

underseal n, v ˌʌnd ə siːʳl ‖ -ʳr- **~ed** d **~ing** ɪŋ
~s z

undersecretar|y ˌʌnd ə ˈsek rət ʳr |i -ˈrɪt ͵,
⚠-ˈjʊt ͵, ⚠-ˈʳt ͵; -ˈsek rə ter |i, -ˈrɪ-, ⚠-ˈju-,
⚠-ˈʳə- ‖ ˌʌnd ʳr ˈsek rə ter |i **~ies** iz

under|sell ˌʌnd ə |ˈsel ‖ -ʳr- **~selling** ˈsel ɪŋ
~sells selz **~sold** ˈsəʊld →ˈsɒʊld ‖ ˈsoʊld

underserved ˌʌnd ə ˈsɜːvd ◂ ‖ ˌʌnd ʳr ˈsɜːvd ◂

undersexed ˌʌnd ə ˈsekst ◂ ‖ -ʳr-

Undershaft ˈʌnd ə ʃɑːft §-ʃæft ‖ -ʳr ʃæft

undershirt ˈʌnd ə ʃɜːt ‖ -ʳr ʃɜːt **~s** s

under|shoot v ˌʌnd ə |ˈʃuːt ˈ· · · ‖ -ʳr-
~shooting ʃuːt ɪŋ ‖ ʃuːt̬ ɪŋ **~shoots** ʃuːts
~shot ʃɒt ‖ ʃɑːt

undershorts ˈʌnd ə ʃɔːts ‖ -ʳr ʃɔːrts

underside ˈʌnd ə saɪd ‖ -ʳr-

undersigned ˌʌnd ə ˈsaɪnd ◂ ˈ· · · ‖ -ʳr-

undersize ˌʌnd ə ˈsaɪz ◂ ‖ -ʳr- **~d** d

underslung ˌʌnd ə ˈslʌŋ ◂ ‖ -ʳr-

undersold ˌʌnd ə ˈsəʊld →-ˈsɒʊld ‖ -ʳr ˈsoʊld

under|spend ˌʌnd ə |ˈspend ‖ -ʳr- **~spending**
ˈspend ɪŋ **~spends** ˈspendz **~spent** ˈspent

understaffed ˌʌnd ə ˈstɑːft §-ˈstæft ‖ -ʳr ˈstæft

understand ˌʌnd ə ˈstænd ‖ -ʳr- **~ing** ɪŋ **~s** z
understood ˌʌnd ə ˈstʊd ‖ -ʳr-

understandab|le ˌʌnd ə ˈstænd əb |ʳl ‖ -ʳr-
~ly li

understanding ˌʌnd ə ˈstænd ɪŋ ‖ -ʳr- **~ly** li
~s z

under|state ˌʌnd ə |ˈsteɪt ‖ -ʳr- **~stated**
ˈsteɪt ɪd -əd ‖ ˈsteɪt̬ əd **~states** ˈsteɪts
~stating ˈsteɪt ɪŋ ‖ ˈsteɪt̬ ɪŋ

understatement ˌʌnd ə ˈsteɪt mənt ˈ· ·,· · ‖ -ʳr-

understeer v ˌʌnd ə ˈstɪə ˈ· · · ‖ -ʳr ˈstɪʳr **~ed** d
understeering ˌʌnd ə ˈstɪər ɪŋ ‖ -ʳr ˈstɪr ɪŋ
~s z

understeer n ˈʌnd ə stɪə ‖ -ʳr stɪr

understood ˌʌnd ə ˈstʊd ‖ -ʳr-

understorey, understory ˈʌnd ə ˌstɔːr i ‖ -ʳr-
-ˌstɔʊr i

understrapper ˈʌnd ə ˌstræp ə ‖ -ʳr ˌstræp ʳr
~s z

understud|y v, n ˈʌnd ə ˌstʌd |i ‖ -ʳr- **~ied** id
~ies iz **~ying** i ɪŋ

undersubscribed ˌʌnd ə səb ˈskraɪbd ◂
§-ə sʌb- ‖ -ʳr-

under|take ˌʌnd ə |ˈteɪk ‖ -ʳr- **~taken** ˈteɪk ən
~takes ˈteɪks **~taking** ˈteɪk ɪŋ **~took** ˈtʊk
§ˈtuːk

undertaker *'funeral director'* ˈʌnd ə teɪk ə
‖ -ʳr teɪk ʳr **~s** z

undertaking n *'task'; 'promise'* ˌʌnd ə ˈteɪk ɪŋ
ˈ· · ·,· ‖ -ʳr- **~s** z

undertaking n *'funeral direction'*
ˈʌnd ə teɪk ɪŋ ‖ -ʳr-

under-the-counter ˌʌnd ə ðə ˈkaʊnt ə ◂
‖ -ʳr ðə ˈkaʊnt̬ ʳr ◂

undertone ˈʌnd ə təʊn ‖ -ʳr toʊn **~s** z

undertook ˌʌnd ə ˈtʊk §-ˈtuːk ‖ -ʳr-

undertow ˈʌnd ə təʊ ‖ -ʳr toʊ **~s** z

underused ˌʌnd ə ˈjuːzd ◂ ‖ -ʳr-

underutilization, underutilisation
ˌʌnd ə ˌjuːt ɪl aɪ ˈzeɪʃ ʳn -ˌʳl-, -ɪˈ· ·
‖ ˌʌnd ʳr ˌjuːt ʳl ə-

underutilized, underutilised
ˌʌnd ə ˈjuːt ɪ laɪzd ◂ -ʳl aɪzd ◂
‖ ˌʌnd ʳr ˈjuːt ʳl aɪzd ◂

undervalu|e ˌʌnd ə ˈvæl juː ‖ -ʳr- **~ed** d **~es** z
~ing ɪŋ

underwater ˌʌnd ə ˈwɔːt ə ◂ ‖ -ʳr ˈwɔːt̬ ʳr ◂
-ˈwɑːt̬-

underway ˌʌnd ə ˈweɪ ‖ -ʳr-

underwear ˈʌnd ə weə ‖ -ʳr wer -wær

underweight ˌʌnd ə ˈweɪt ◂ ‖ -ʳr-

underwent ˌʌnd ə ˈwent ‖ -ʳr-

underwhelm ˌʌnd ə ˈwelm -ˈhwelm ‖ -ʳr- **~ed**
d **~ing** ɪŋ **~s** z

underwing ˈʌnd ə wɪŋ ‖ -ʳr- **~s** z

underwire ˈʌnd ə ˌwaɪ ə ‖ -ʳr ˌwaɪ ʳr

Underwood, u~ ˈʌnd ə wʊd ‖ -ʳr-

underworld, U~ ˈʌnd ə wɜːld ‖ -ʳr wɜːld **~s** z

under|write ˈʌnd ə |ˈraɪt ˈ· · · ‖ -ʳr- **~writes**
ˈraɪts **~written** ˈrɪt ʳn **~wrote** ˈrəʊt ‖ ˈroʊt

underwriter ˈʌnd ə raɪt ə ‖ -ʳr raɪt̬ ʳr **~s** z

undeserv|ed ˌʌn di ˈzɜːv|d ◂ -də- ‖ -ˈzɜːv|d ◂
~edly ɪd li əd li **~ing** ɪŋ

undesirability ˌʌn di ˌzaɪʳr ə ˈbɪl ət i ˌ·də-,
-ɪt i ‖ -ˌzaɪʳr ə ˈbɪl ət̬ i

undesirable ˌʌn di ˈzaɪʳr əb ʳl ◂ ˌ·də-
‖ -ˈzaɪʳr- **~s** z

undetect|able ˌʌn di ˈtekt |əb ʳl ◂ **~ed** ɪd əd

undetermined ˌʌn di ˈtɜːm ɪnd ◂ -də-, -ənd
‖ -ˈtɜːm-

undeterred ˌʌn di ˈtɜːd ◂ -də- ‖ -ˈtɜːd ◂

undeveloped ˌʌn di ˈvel əpt ◂ ˌ·də-

undeviating ͵₍ᵢ₎ʌn ˈdiːv i eɪt ɪŋ ‖ -eɪt̬ ɪŋ **~ly** li

undid ₍ᵢ₎ʌn ˈdɪd

undies ˈʌnd iz

undifferentiated ˌʌn ˌdɪf ə ˈrenˈʃ i eɪt ɪd ◂
-əd ‖ -eɪt̬-

undignified ʌn ˈdɪg nɪ faɪd -nə-

undiluted ˌʌn daɪ ˈluːt ɪd ◂ -dɪ-, §-də-, -ˈljuːt-,
-əd ‖ -ˈluːt̬ əd ◂

undiminished ˌʌn dɪ ˈmɪn ɪʃt ◂ -də-

Undine, u~ ˈʌnd iːn ʌn ˈdiːn, ʊn- **~s** z

undischarged ˌʌn dɪs ˈtʃɑːdʒd ◂ ‖ -ˈtʃɑːrdʒd ◂
ˌundischarged ˈbankrupt

undisciplined ʌn ˈdɪs əp lɪnd -ɪp-, -lənd

undisclosed ˌʌn dɪs ˈkləʊzd ◂ -dəs-
‖ -ˈkloʊzd ◂
an ˌundisclosed ˈsum

undiscriminating ˌʌn dɪ ˈskrɪm ɪ neɪt ɪŋ ˌ·də-,
-ə · · ‖ -neɪt̬ ɪŋ

undisguised ˌʌn dɪs ˈgaɪzd ◂ -dɪz-, -dəs-

undismayed ˌʌn dɪs ˈmeɪd ◂ -dɪz-

undisputed ˌʌn dɪ ˈspjuːt ɪd ◂ -də-, -əd
‖ -ˈspjuːt̬-

undistinguished ˌʌn dɪ ˈstɪŋ gwɪʃt ◂ ˌdə-, -wɪʃt

undisturbed ˌʌn dɪ ˈstɜːbd ◂ -də- ‖ -ˈstɜːbd ◂

undivided ˌʌn dɪ ˈvaɪd ɪd ˌdə-, -əd

un|do (ˌ)ʌn ˈdu: ~**did** ˈdɪd ~**does** ˈdʌz ~**doing** ˈdu:ˌɪŋ ~**done** ˈdʌn

undocumented ʌn ˈdɒk ju ment ɪd -ˈjə-, -əd ‖ ʌn ˈdɑːk jə ment əd

undomesticated ˌʌn də ˈmest ɪ keɪt ɪd ◂ -ˈ-ə-, -əd ‖ -keɪt əd ◂

undone (ˌ)ʌn ˈdʌn

undoubted ʌn ˈdaʊt ɪd -əd ‖ -ˈdaʊt̬ əd ~**ly** li

undreamed-of ʌn ˈdriːmd ɒv ˌʌn-, -ˈdremᵖt-, -əv ‖ -ʌv -ɑːv

undreamt-of ʌn ˈdremᵖt ɒv ˌʌn-, -əv ‖ -ʌv -ɑːv

undress v, n ʌn ˈdres ˌʌn- ~**ed** t ~**es** ɪz əz ~**ing** ɪŋ

undue ˌʌn ˈdju: ◂ →-ˈdʒu: ‖ -ˈdu: ◂ -ˈdju:

undulant ˈʌnd jʊl ənt ˈʌndʒ ʊl- ‖ ˈʌndʒ əl- ˈʌnd jəl-, -əl-

undu|late ˈʌnd ju ˌleɪt ˈʌndʒ u- ‖ ˈʌndʒ ə- ˈʌnd jə-, -ə- ~**lated** leɪt ɪd -əd ‖ leɪt̬ əd ~**lates** leɪts ~**lating** leɪt ɪŋ ‖ leɪt̬ ɪŋ

undulation ˌʌnd ju ˈleɪʃ ᵊn ˌʌndʒ u- ‖ ˌʌndʒ ə- ˌʌnd jə-, -ə- ~**s** z

undulatory ˈʌnd jʊl ət ər i ˈʌndʒ ʊl-; ˌʌnd ju ˈleɪt ər i, ˌʌndʒ u- ‖ ˈʌndʒ əl ə tɔːr i ˈʌnd jəl-, -əl-, -toʊr i

unduly (ˌ)ʌn ˈdju: li →-ˈdʒu:- ‖ -ˈdu:- -ˈdju:

undying (ˌ)ʌn ˈdaɪ ɪŋ ~**ly** li

unearned ˌʌn ˈɜːnd ◂ ‖ -ˈɜːnd ◂
,**unearned** ˈincome

unearth (ˌ)ʌn ˈɜːθ ‖ -ˈɜːθ ~**ed** t ~**ing** ɪŋ ~**s** s

unearth|ly (ˌ)ʌn ˈɜːθ |li ‖ -ˈɜːθ- ~**lier** li ə ‖ li ̣ᵊr ~**liest** li ̣ɪst əst ~**liness** li nəs nɪs

unease ʌn ˈiːz ˌʌn-

uneas|y ʌn ˈiːz |i ̣i ˌʌn- ~**ier** i ̣ə ‖ i ̣ᵊr ~**iest** i ̣ɪst i ̣əst ~**ily** ɪ li əl i ~**iness** i nəs i nɪs

uneatable ʌn ˈiːt əb ᵊl ‖ -ˈiːt̬-

uneaten ʌn ˈiːt ᵊn

uneconomic ˌʌn ˌiːk ə ˈnɒm ɪk ◂ -ˌek- ‖ -ˈnɑːm- ~**al** ᵊl ~**ally** ᵊl i

unedifying ʌn ˈed ɪ faɪ ɪŋ -ˈ-ə- ~**ly** li

uneducated (ˌ)ʌn ˈed ju keɪt ɪd -ˈedʒ u-, -əd ‖ -ˈedʒ ə keɪt̬ əd

unelected ˌʌn ɪ ˈlekt ɪd ◂ -ə-, -əd

unemotional ˌʌn ɪ ˈməʊʃ ᵊn ᵊl ˌə-, ˌə- ‖ -ˈmoʊʃ- ~**ly** i

unemployable ˌʌn ɪm ˈplɔɪ əb ᵊl ◂ ˌem-, ˌəm- ~**s** z

unemployed ˌʌn ɪm ˈplɔɪd ◂ -em-, -əm-

unemployment ˌʌn ɪm ˈplɔɪ mənt -em-, -əm-
,**unem'ployment ,benefit**

unencumbered ˌʌn ɪn ˈkʌm bəd ◂ →-ŋ-, -ən- ‖ -bᵊrd ◂

unending ʌn ˈend ɪŋ ˌ- ~**ly** li

unendurable ˌʌn ɪn ˈdjʊər əb ᵊl ◂ -en-, ˌən-, →-ˈdʒʊər-, -ˈdjɔː-, →-ˈdʒɔː- ‖ -ˈdʊr- -ˈdjʊr-

unenlightened ˌʌn ɪn ˈlaɪt ᵊnd ◂ -en-, -ən-

unenthusiastic ˌʌn ɪn ˌθjuːz i ˈæst ɪk ◂ ˌen-, -ˈθuːz- ‖ -ˈθuːz-

unenviab|le (ˌ)ʌn ˈen vi əb |ᵊl ~**ly** li

unequal (ˌ)ʌn ˈiːk wəl ~**ed**, ~**led** d ~**ly** i ~**s** z

unequivocal ˌʌn ɪ ˈkwɪv ək ᵊl ◂ ˌ-ə- ~**ly** i

unerring (ˌ)ʌn ˈɜːr ɪŋ §-ˈer- ‖ -ˈer- -ˈɜ:- ~**ly** li

Unesco, UNESCO ju ˈnesk əʊ ‖ -oʊ

unethical ʌn ˈeθ ɪk ᵊl ~**ly** i

uneven (ˌ)ʌn ˈiːv ᵊn ~**ly** li ~**ness** nəs nɪs

uneventful ˌʌn ɪ ˈvent fᵊl ◂ -ə-, -fʊl ~**ly** i ~**ness** nəs nɪs

unexampled ˌʌn ɪg ˈzɑːmp ᵊld ◂ -eg-, -əg-, -ɪk-, -ek-, -ək-, §-ˈzæmp- ‖ -ˈzæmp-

unexceptionab|le ˌʌn ɪk ˈsep ʃᵊn ‿əb |ᵊl ◂ ˌek-, ˌək- ~**leness** ᵊl nəs -nɪs ~**ly** li

unexceptional ˌʌn ɪk ˈsep ʃᵊn əl ˌek-, ˌək- ~**ly** i

unexciting ˌʌn ɪk ˈsaɪt ɪŋ ◂ -ek-, -ək- ‖ -ˈsaɪt̬-

unexcused ˌʌn ɪk ˈskjuːzd ◂ -ek-, -ək-

unexpected ˌʌn ɪk ˈspekt ɪd ◂ -ek-, -ək-, -əd ~**ly** li ~**ness** nəs nɪs

unexplained ˌʌn ɪk ˈspleɪnd ◂ -ek-, -ək-

unexploded ˌʌn ɪk ˈspləʊd ɪd ◂ -ek-, -ək-, -əd ‖ -ˈsploʊd-
an ˌunexploded ˈbomb

unexplored ˌʌn ɪk ˈsplɔːd ◂ -ek-, -ək- ‖ -ˈsplɔːrd ◂ -ˈsploʊrd ◂

unexpurgated (ˌ)ʌn ˈeks pə geɪt ɪd -ˈpɜː-, -əd ‖ -pᵊr geɪt̬ əd

unfailing ʌn ˈfeɪl ɪŋ ~**ly** li

unfair ˌʌn ˈfeə ◂ ‖ -ˈfeᵊr ◂ -ˈfæᵊr ~**ly** li ~**ness** nəs nɪs

unfaithful (ˌ)ʌn ˈfeɪθ fᵊl -fʊl ~**ly** i ~**ness** nəs nɪs

unfaltering (ˌ)ʌn ˈfɔːlt ər ɪŋ -ˈfɒlt- ‖ -ˈfɑːlt̬ ~**ly** li

unfamiliar ˌʌn fə ˈmɪl i ̣ə ‖ ˌ-‿ˈmɪl jᵊr ~**ly** li

unfamiliarity ˌʌn fə ˌmɪl i ˈær ət i -ɪt i ‖ -ˌˈjær ət i -ˈjer-; -ˌi ær-, -ˌi ˈer-

unfashionable ʌn ˈfæʃ ᵊn əb ᵊl

unfasten (ˌ)ʌn ˈfɑːs ᵊn §-ˈfæs- ‖ -ˈfæs- ~**ed** d ~**ing** ˌɪŋ ~**s** z

unfathomab|le ʌn ˈfæð əm ‿əb |ᵊl ~**leness** ᵊl nəs -nɪs ~**ly** li

unfathomed (ˌ)ʌn ˈfæð əmd

unfavorab|le, unfavourab|le (ˌ)ʌn ˈfeɪv ər ‿əb |ᵊl ~**leness** ᵊl nəs -nɪs ~**ly** li

unfazed ˌʌn ˈfeɪzd

unfeasib|le ʌn ˈfiːz əb |ᵊl ~**ly** li

unfeeling ʌn ˈfiːl ɪŋ ~**ly** li ~**ness** nəs nɪs

unfettered ˌʌn ˈfet əd ◂ ‖ -ˈfet̬ ᵊrd ◂

unfilled ˌʌn ˈfɪld ◂

unfinished ˌʌn ˈfɪn ɪʃt ◂

un|fit v, adj (ˌ)ʌn ˈfɪt ~**fitly** ˈfɪt li ~**fitness** ˈfɪt nəs -nɪs ~**fits** ˈfɪts ~**fitted** ˈfɪt ɪd -əd ‖ ˈfɪt̬ əd ~**fitting/ly** ˈfɪt ɪŋ /li ‖ ˈfɪt̬ ɪŋ /li

unflagging (ˌ)ʌn ˈflæg ɪŋ ~**ly** li

unflappab|le (ˌ)ʌn ˈflæp əb |ᵊl ~**ly** li

unflattering ʌn ˈflæt ər ɪŋ ‖ -ˈflæt̬ ᵊr-

unflinching (ˌ)ʌn ˈflɪntʃ ɪŋ ~**ly** li

unfocused, unfocussed ˌʌn ˈfəʊk əst ◂ ‖ -ˈfoʊk-

unfold ʌn ˈfəʊld ˌʌn-, →-ˈfɒʊld ‖ -ˈfoʊld ~**ed** ɪd əd ~**ing** ɪŋ ~**s** z

unforced ˌʌn ˈfɔːst ◂ -ˈfɔːrst ◂ ‖ -ˈfoʊrst ◂

unforeseeable ˌʌn fɔ ˈsiː əb ᵊl ◂ ‖ ˌ-fɔːr- ˌ-foʊr-

unforeseen ˌʌn fɔː 'siːn ◀ -fə- ‖ -fɔːr- -four-,
-fᵊr-

   ˌunforeseen 'circumstances

unforgettab|le ˌʌn fə 'get əb |ᵊl ◀ ‖ -fᵊr 'get̮-
~ly li

unforgiv|able ˌʌn fə 'gɪv| əb ᵊl ◀ ˌʌn fɔː-
‖ ˌʌn fᵊr- **~ably** əb li **~ing** ɪŋ

unformed ˌʌn 'fɔːmd ◀ ‖ -'fɔːrmd ◀

unforthcoming ˌʌn fɔːθ 'kʌm ɪŋ ◀ ‖ -fɔːrθ-

unfortunate ʌn 'fɔːtʃ ən ət -ɪt ‖ -'fɔːrtʃ- **~ly** li
~s s

unfounded ˌʌn 'faʊnd ɪd -əd

unfrequented ˌʌn frɪ 'kwent ɪd ◀ -frə-, -əd
‖ -'kwen̮t̮ əd ◀

   ˌunfreˌquented 'byways

unfriend|ly ˌʌn 'frend |li **~liness** li nəs -nɪs

unfrock ˌʌn 'frɒk ‖ -'frɑːk **~ed** t **~ing** ɪŋ **~s** s

unfulfilled ˌʌn fʊl 'fɪld ◀

unfunded ˌʌn 'fʌnd ɪd ◀ -əd

unfunny ˌʌn 'fʌn i ◀

unfurl ʌn 'fɜːl ‖ -'fɜːl **~ed** d **~ing** ɪŋ **~s** z

unfurnished ˌʌn 'fɜːn ɪʃt ◀ ‖ -'fɜːn-

ungain|ly ˌʌn 'geɪn |li →ˌʌŋ- **~liness** li nəs
-nɪs

Ungava ʌŋ 'gɑːv ə -'geɪv-

ungenerous ˌʌn 'dʒen ər‿əs **~ly** li

ungetatable ˌʌn get 'æt əb ᵊl ◀ →ˌʌŋ-
‖ -get̮ 'æt̮-

unglued ʌn 'gluːd →ʌŋ-

ungod|ly ʌn 'gɒd |li →ʌŋ-, ˌʌn- ‖ -'gɑːd-
~liness li nəs -nɪs

Ungoed (i) 'ɪŋ gɔɪd, (ii) 'ʌŋ gɔɪd

ungovernab|le ˌʌn 'gʌv ən əb |ᵊl →ˌʌŋ-
‖ -ᵊrn əb- **~leness** ᵊl nəs -nɪs **~ly** li

ungracious ˌʌn 'greɪʃ əs →ˌʌŋ- **~ly** li **~ness**
nəs nɪs

ungrammatical ˌʌn grə 'mæt ɪk ᵊl ◀ →ˌʌŋ-
‖ -'mæt̮- **~ly** i

ungrammaticality ˌʌn grə ˌmæt ɪ 'kæl ət i
→ˌʌŋ-, §-ˌ-ə-, -ɪt i ‖ -ˌmæt̮ ə 'kæl ət̮ i

ungrateful ʌn 'greɪt fᵊl →ʌŋ-, ˌʌn-, -fʊl **~ly** i
~ness nəs nɪs

ungrudging ˌʌn 'grʌdʒ ɪŋ →ˌʌŋ- **~ly** li

unguarded ˌʌn 'gɑːd ɪd →ˌʌŋ-, -əd
‖ -'gɑːrd- **~ly** li **~ness** nəs nɪs

unguent 'ʌŋ gwənt 'ʌŋ gju‿ənt, △'ʌnd ʒ ənt
~s s

un|gula 'ʌŋ |gjʊl ə -gjəl- ‖ -|gjᵊl ə **~gulae**
gju liː gjə- ‖ gjə liː

ungulate 'ʌŋ gju leɪt -gjʊl ət, -gjəl-, -ɪt ‖ -gjə-
~s s

unhallowed ˌʌn 'hæl əʊd ‖ -oʊd

unhand ˌʌn 'hænd **~ed** ɪd əd **~ing** ɪŋ **~s** z

unhapp|y ʌn 'hæp |i ˌʌn- **~ily** ɪ li əl i **~iness**
i nəs i nɪs

unharmed ʌn 'hɑːmd ‖ -'hɑːrmd

unhealth|y ʌn 'helθ |i ˌʌn- **~ily** ɪ li əl i **~iness**
i nəs i nɪs

unheard ˌʌn 'hɜːd ‖ -'hɜːd

unheard-of ˌʌn 'hɜːd ɒv -əv ‖ -'hɜːd ʌv -ɑːv

unhelpful ʌn 'help fᵊl -fʊl **~ly** i **~ness** nəs nɪs

unheralded ʌn 'her ᵊld ɪd -əd

unhesitating ʌn 'hez ɪ teɪt ɪŋ -'-ə- ‖ -teɪt̮ ɪŋ
~ly li

unhing|e ˌʌn 'hɪndʒ **~ed** d **~es** ɪz əz **~ing** ɪŋ

unhip ˌʌn 'hɪp

unhitch ˌʌn 'hɪtʃ **~ed** t **~es** ɪz əz **~ing** ɪŋ

unhol|y ˌʌn 'həʊl |i ‖ -'hoʊl |i **~iness** i nəs
i nɪs

   unˌholy al'liance

unhook ˌʌn 'hʊk §-'huːk **~ed** t **~ing** ɪŋ **~s** s

unhoped-for ˌʌn 'həʊpt fɔː ‖ -'hoʊpt fɔːr

unhors|e ˌʌn 'hɔːs ‖ -'hɔːrs **~ed** t **~es** ɪz əz
~ing ɪŋ

unhurried ˌʌn 'hʌr id ◀ ‖ -'hɜː-

unhurt ʌn 'hɜːt ‖ -'hɜːt

unhygienic ˌʌn haɪ 'dʒiːn ɪk ◀

uni 'juːn i **unis** 'juːn iz

uni- |juːn i —but in certain established words
|juːn ɪ, -ə — **unilingual** ˌjuːn i 'lɪŋ gwəl ◀

Uniat 'juːn i æt

Uniate 'juːn i ət ˌɪt, -eɪt

unicameral ˌjuːn i 'kæm ᵊr ᵊl ◀

UNICEF 'juːn i sef -ə-

unicellular ˌjuːn i 'sel jʊl ə ◀ -jəl ə ‖ -jəl ᵊr

Unichem *tdmk* 'juːn i kem

Unicode 'juːn i kəʊd ‖ -koʊd

unicorn 'juːn ɪ kɔːn -ə- ‖ -kɔːrn **~s** z

unicycle 'juːn i ˌsaɪk ᵊl **~s** z

unidentified ˌʌn aɪ 'dent ɪ faɪd ◀ -'-ə-
‖ -'dent̮-

unification ˌjuːn ɪf ɪ 'keɪʃ ᵊn ˌəf-, §-ə'- **~s** z

unifie... —*see* **unify**

uniform 'juːn ɪ fɔːm -ə- ‖ -fɔːrm —*The adj is
occasionally stressed* ˌ·ˈ· **~ed** d **~ly** li **~ness**
nəs nɪs **~s** z

uniformity ˌjuːn ɪ 'fɔːm ət i ˌ-ə-, -ɪt i
‖ -'fɔːrm ət̮ i

uni|fy 'juːn ɪ |faɪ -ə- **~fied** faɪd **~fier/s** faɪ‿ə/z
‖ faɪ‿ᵊr/z **~fies** faɪz **~fying** faɪ ɪŋ

Unigate *tdmk* 'juːn i geɪt

unilateral ˌjuːn i 'læt̮ ᵊr ᵊl ◀ -ˌ-ə- ‖ -'læt̮ ᵊr ᵊl
-'lætr ᵊl **~ism** ˌɪz əm **~ist/s** ɪst/s §əst/s
‖ əst/s **~ly** i

Unilever *tdmk* 'juːn i ˌliːv ə ◀ -ə ‖ -ᵊr

unimagin|able ˌʌn ɪ 'mædʒ ɪn |əb ᵊl ◀
-'mædʒ ən **~ably** əb li **~ative** ət ɪv ◀
‖ ət̮ ɪv ◀

unimagined ˌʌn ɪ 'mædʒ ɪnd ◀ -ənd ◀

unimpaired ˌʌn ɪm 'peəd ◀ ‖ -'peᵊrd ◀
-'pæᵊrd ◀

unimpeachab|le ˌʌn ɪm 'piːtʃ əb |ᵊl ◀ **~ly** li

unimpeded ˌʌn ɪm 'piːd ɪd ◀ -əd

unimportant ˌʌn ɪm 'pɔːt ᵊnt ◀ ‖ -'pɔːrt-

unimpressed ˌʌn ɪm 'prest ◀

unimpressive ˌʌn ɪm 'pres ɪv ◀

unimproved ˌʌn ɪm 'pruːvd ◀

unincorporated ˌʌn ɪn 'kɔːp ə reɪt ɪd ◀
→ˌʌŋ ɪŋ- ‖ -'kɔːrp ə reɪt̮ əd ◀

uninformed ˌʌn ɪn 'fɔːmd ◀ ‖ -'fɔːrmd ◀

uninhabit|able ˌʌn ɪn 'hæb ɪt |əb ᵊl §-'-ət-
‖ -'-ət̮- **~ed** ɪd əd

uninhibited ˌʌn ɪn 'hæb ɪt ɪd ◀ §-ət ɪd, -əd
‖ -ət̮ əd ◀ **~ly** li **~ness** nəs nɪs

uninitiated ˌʌn ɪ 'nɪʃ i eɪt ɪd -əd ‖ -eɪt̮ əd

U

uninspired ˌʌn ɪn ˈspaɪˌəd ◂ ‖ -ˈspaɪˌ°rd ◂
uninspiring ˌʌn ɪn ˈspaɪˌər ɪŋ ‖ -ˈspaɪˌ°r- **~ly**
li
uninstall ˌʌn ɪn ˈstɔːl ◂ ‖ -ˈstɑːl ◂ **~ed** d **~ing**
ɪŋ **~s** z
uninsured ˌʌn ɪn ˈʃʊəd ◂ -ˈʃɔːd ◂ ‖ -ˈʃʊ°rd ◂
-ˈʃɜːd ◂
unintelligib|le ˌʌn ɪn ˈtel ɪdʒ əb |°l ◂ **~ly** li
unintended ˌʌn ɪn ˈtend ɪd ◂ -əd-
unintentional ˌʌn ɪn ˈten°ʃ °n‿əl ◂ **~ly** i
uninterested ˌ(ˌ)ʌn ˈɪntr əst ɪd -ɪst-, -əd;
-ˈɪnt ə rest- ‖ -ˈɪnt̬ ə rest-, -ər əst- **~ly** li **~ness**
nəs nɪs
uninterrupted ˌʌn ˌɪnt ə ˈrʌpt ɪd -əd ‖ -ˌɪnt̬ ə-
~ly li **~ness** nəs nɪs
uninvit|ed ˌʌn ɪn ˈvaɪt |ɪd ◂ -əd ‖ -ˈvaɪt̬- **~ing**
ɪŋ
union ˈjuːn i‿ən ‖ ˈjuːn jən **~s** z
ˈunion card; ˈUnion flag, ˌ···ˈ·; ˌUnion
ˈJack ‖ ˈ···
unionis... —see **unioniz...**
Unionism ˈjuːn i‿ə ˌnɪz əm ən ˌɪz-
‖ ˈjuːn jə ˌnɪz əm
unionist, U~ ˈjuːn i‿ən ɪst §-əst ‖ ˈjuːn jən əst
~s s
unionization ˌjuːn i‿ən aɪ ˈzeɪʃ °n -ɪ-ˈ-
‖ ˌjuːn jə ə ˈzeɪʃ °n
unioniz|e ˈjuːn i‿ə naɪz ‖ ˈjuːn jə naɪz **~ed** d
~es ɪz əz **~ing** ɪŋ
Unipart tdmk ˈjuːn i pɑːt ‖ -pɑːrt
unique ju ˈniːk juː- **~ly** li **~ness** nəs nɪs
Uniroyal tdmk ˈjuːn i ˌrɔɪ əl
unisex ˈjuːn i seks -ə-
unisexual ˌjuːn i ˈsek ʃu‿əl ◂ -ˈseks ju‿əl,
-ˈsek ʃ°l **~ly** i
unison ˈjuːn ɪs ən -ɪz-, -əs-, -əz-
unit ˈjuːn ɪt §-ət **~s** s
ˌunit ˈtrust
UNITA ju ˈniːt ə ‖ -ˈniːt̬ ə
unitard ˈjuːn ɪ tɑːd -ə- ‖ -tɑːrd **~s** z
Unitarian, u~ ˌjuːn ɪ ˈteər i‿ən ◂ ˌˌə- ‖ -ˈter-
-ˈtær- **~s** z
unitary ˈjuːn ɪtˌər i ˈˌət̬ˌ ‖ -ə ter i
Unitas tdmk ˈjuːn ɪ tæs -ə-
u|nite ju |ˈnaɪt ˌjuː- **~nited** ˈnaɪt ɪd -əd
‖ ˈnaɪt̬ əd **~nites** ˈnaɪts **~niting** ˈnaɪt ɪŋ
‖ ˈnaɪt̬ ɪŋ
Uˌnited ˌArab ˈEmirates; Uˌnited
ˈKingdom; Uˌnited ˈNations, Uˌnited
ˈNations Associˌation; Uˌnited Reˈformed
Church; Uˌnited ˈStates◂, Uˌnited ˌStates
of Aˈmerica
unit-linked ˈjuːn ɪt ˈlɪŋkt ◂ §-ət-
unit|y, Unity ˈjuːn ət |i -ɪt- ‖ -ət̬ |i **~ies** iz
Univac tdmk ˈjuːn ɪ væk -ə-
univalve ˈjuːn i vælv **~s** z
univariate ˌjuːn i ˈveər i‿ət ◂ ˌɪt ‖ -ˈver- -ˈvær-
universal ˌjuːn ɪ ˈvɜːs °l ◂ ˌˌə- ‖ -ˈvɜːs- **~s** z
ˌuniˌversal ˈjoint; ˌuniˌversal ˈlanguage
universalism, U~ ˌjuːn ɪ ˈvɜːs ə ˌlɪz əm ˌˌə-,
-°l ˌɪz- ‖ -ˈvɜːs-
universalist, U~ ˌjuːn ɪ ˈvɜːs əl ɪst ˌˌə-, §-əst
‖ -ˈvɜːs- **~s** s

universality ˌjuːn ɪ vɜː ˈsæl ət i ˌˌə-, -ɪt i
‖ -vɜːˈ sæl ət̬ i
universal|ly ˌjuːn ɪ ˈvɜːs °l |i ˌˌə- ‖ -ˈvɜːs-
~ness nəs nɪs
univers|e ˈjuːn ɪ vɜːs -ə- ‖ -vɜːs- **~es** ɪz əz
universit|y ˌjuːn ɪ ˈvɜːs ət |i ˌˌə-, -ɪt i
‖ -ˈvɜːs ət̬ |i **~ies** iz
Unix, UNIX tdmk ˈjuːn ɪks
unjust ˌʌn ˈdʒʌst ◂ **~ly** li **~ness** nəs nɪs
unjustifiab|le ˌʌn ˌdʒʌst ɪ ˈfaɪ əb |°l -ə-ˈ-,
ˌ(ˌ)ˈ····· **~ly** li
unjustified ʌn ˈdʒʌst ɪ faɪd ˌʌn-, -ə- **~ly** li
unkempt ˌʌn ˈkempt ◂ →ˌʌŋ- **~ly** li **~ness** nəs
nɪs
unkind ˌʌn ˈkaɪnd ◂ →ˌʌŋ-, ʌn- **~er** ə ‖ °r **~est**
ɪst əst **~ly** li **~ness** nəs nɪs
unkind|ly ˌ(ˌ)ʌn ˈkaɪnd |li →ˌ(ˌ)ʌŋ- **~lier** li‿ə
‖ li‿°r **~liest** li‿ɪst li‿əst **~liness** li nəs -nɪs
un|knit ˌʌn |ˈnɪt **~knits** ˈnɪts **~knitted** ˈnɪt ɪd
-əd ‖ ˈnɪt̬ əd **~knitting** ˈnɪt ɪŋ ‖ ˈnɪt̬ ɪŋ
un|knot ˌʌn |ˈnɒt ‖ -|ˈnɑːt **~knots** ˈnɒts
‖ ˈnɑːts **~knotted** ˈnɒt ɪd -əd ‖ ˈnɑːt̬ əd
~knotting ˈnɒt ɪŋ ‖ ˈnɑːt̬ ɪŋ
unknowab|le ˌ(ˌ)ʌn ˈnəʊ əb |°l ‖ -ˈnoʊ-
~leness °l nəs -nɪs **~les** °lz **~ly** li
unknowing ˌ(ˌ)ʌn ˈnəʊ ɪŋ ‖ -ˈnoʊ- **~ly** li
unknown ˌʌn ˈnəʊn ◂ ‖ -ˈnoʊn ◂ **~ness** nəs nɪs
~s z
ˌunknown ˈquantity; ˌUnknown ˈSoldier
unlac|e ˌʌn ˈleɪs **~ed** t **~es** ɪz əz **~ing** ɪŋ
unlawful ˌ(ˌ)ʌn ˈlɔː f°l -fʊl ‖ -ˈlɑː- **~ly** i **~ness**
nəs nɪs
unleaded ˌ(ˌ)ʌn ˈled ɪd ◂ -əd
unlearn ˌʌn ˈlɜːn ‖ -ˈlɜːn **~ed** d **~ing** ɪŋ **~s** z
unleash ˌʌn ˈliːʃ **~ed** t **~es** ɪz əz **~ing** ɪŋ
unleavened ˌ(ˌ)ʌn ˈlev °nd ◂
unless ən ˈles ʌn- —occasionally also, for
emphasis, ˌʌn-
unlettered ˌʌn ˈlet əd ◂ ‖ -ˈlet̬ °rd ◂
unlicensed ˌ(ˌ)ʌn ˈlaɪs °n\tst
unlike ˌʌn ˈlaɪk ◂ **~ness** nəs nɪs
unlike|ly ʌn ˈlaɪk |li ˌʌn- **~liness** li nəs -nɪs
unlimited ʌn ˈlɪm ɪt ɪd ˌ·-, §-ət ɪd, -əd ‖ -ət̬ əd
~ly li **~ness** nəs nɪs
unlisted ʌn ˈlɪst ɪd ˌ·-, -əd
unlit ˌʌn ˈlɪt ◂
unload ˌ(ˌ)ʌn ˈləʊd ‖ -ˈloʊd **~ed** ɪd əd **~ing** ɪŋ
~s z
unlock ˌ(ˌ)ʌn ˈlɒk ‖ -ˈlɑːk **~ed** t **~ing** ɪŋ **~s** s
unlooked-for ˌ(ˌ)ʌn ˈlʊkt fɔː ‖ -fɔːr
unloos|e ˌ(ˌ)ʌn ˈluːs **~ed** t **~es** ɪz əz **~ing** ɪŋ
unloosen ˌ(ˌ)ʌn ˈluːs °n **~ed** d **~ing** ɪŋ **~s** z
unlovab|le ʌn ˈlʌv əb |°l **~ly** li
unloved ˌʌn ˈlʌvd ◂
unloving ˌʌn ˈlʌv ɪŋ ◂
unluck|y ˌ(ˌ)ʌn ˈlʌk |i **~ier** i‿ə ‖ i‿°r **~iest** i‿ɪst
i‿əst **~ily** ɪ li əl i **~iness** i nəs i nɪs
unmade ˌʌn ˈmeɪd ◂ →ˌʌm-
unman ˌʌn ˈmæn →ˌʌm- **~ned** d **~ing** ɪŋ **~s** z
unmanageab|le ʌn ˈmæn ɪdʒ əb |°l →ˌʌm- **~ly**
li
unman|ly ˌʌn ˈmæn |li →ˌʌm- **~lier** li‿ə ‖ li‿°r
~liest li‿ɪst əst **~liness** li nəs -nɪs

unmanner|ly ʌn ˈmæn ə |li →ʌm- ‖ -ʲr-
~liness li nəs -nɪs

unmarked ˌʌn ˈmɑːkt ◂ →ˌʌm- ‖ -ˈmɑːrkt ◂
ˌunmarked ˈcar

unmarried ˌʌn ˈmær id ◂ →ˌʌm- ‖ -ˈmer- **~s** z

unmask ˌʌn ˈmɑːsk →ˌʌm-, §-ˈmæsk ‖ -ˈmæsk
~ed t **~ing** ɪŋ **~s** s

unmatched ˌʌn ˈmætʃt ◂ →ˌʌm-

unmeasured ˌʌn ˈmeʒ əd →ˌʌm- ‖ -ʲrd
-ˈmeʒ-

unmediated ˌʌn ˈmiːd i eɪt ɪd →ˌʌm-, -əd
‖ -eɪʈ-

unmentionab|le ʌn ˈmen.tʃ ən əb |ᵊl →ʌm-
~leness ᵊl nəs -nɪs **~les** ᵊlz **~ly** li

unmerciful ʌn ˈmɜːs ɪ fᵊl ˌ-ʲ-, -ə-, -fʊl ‖ -ˈmɜːs-
~ly i **~ness** nəs nɪs

unmet ˌʌn ˈmet ◂ →ˌʌm-

unmindful ˌʌn ˈmaɪnd fᵊl →ˌʌm-, -fʊl **~ly** i
~ness nəs nɪs

unmissable ʌn ˈmɪs əb ᵊl →ʌm-

unmistakab|le, unmistakeab|le
ˌʌn mɪ ˈsteɪk əb |ᵊl ◂ →ˌʌm-, ˌ-mə- **~leness**
ᵊl nəs -nɪs **~ly** li

unmitigated ʌn ˈmɪt ɪ geɪt ɪd →ʌm-, §-ˈ-ə-, -əd
‖ -ˈmɪʈ ə geɪʈ əd **~ly** li

unmixed ˌʌn ˈmɪkst ◂ →ˌʌm-

unmolested ˌʌn mə ˈlest ɪd ◂ →ˌʌm-, -məʊ-,
-əd

unmoved ˌʌn ˈmuːvd →ˌʌm-

unnamed ˌʌn ˈneɪmd ◂

unnatural ˌʌn ˈnætʃ ᵊr_əl **~ly** i **~ness** nəs nɪs

unnecessarily ʌn ˈnes əs ᵊr_əl i ˌʌn-, -ˈɪs-, ɪ li;
ˌʌn ˌnes ə ˈser əl i, ʌn,--, -ˈɪ-, -ɪ li
‖ ˌʌn ˌnes ə ˈser əl i

unnecessar|y ʌn ˈnes əs ər.|i ˌʌn-, -ˈɪs-;
-ə ser i, -ˈɪ- ‖ -ə ser |i **~iness** i nəs i nɪs

unneeded ʌn ˈniːd ɪd -əd

unnerv|e ˌʌn ˈnɜːv ‖ -ˈnɜːv **~ed** d **~es** z **~ing**
ɪŋ

unnoticed ʌn ˈnəʊt ɪst §-əst ‖ -ˈnoʊʈ-

unnumbered ˌʌn ˈnʌm bəd ◂ ‖ -bʲrd

UNO ˈjuːn əʊ ‖ -oʊ

Uno tdmk, car model ˈuːn əʊ ˈjuːn- ‖ -oʊ

unobserved ˌʌn əb ˈzɜːvd ‖ -ˈzɜːvd

unobstructed ˌʌn əb ˈstrʌkt ɪd ◂ §-ɒb-, -əd

unobtainable ˌʌn əb ˈteɪn əb ᵊl §-ɒb-

unobtrusive ˌʌn əb ˈtruːs ɪv ◂ -ɒb-, §-ˈtruːz-
~ly li **~ness** nəs nɪs

unoccupied ˌʌn ˈɒk ju paɪd ‖ -ˈɑːk jə-

unofficial ˌʌn ə ˈfɪʃ ᵊl ◂ §-əʊ- **~ly** i

unopened ʌn ˈəʊp ənd ‖ -ˈoʊp-

unopposed ˌʌn ə ˈpəʊzd ◂ ‖ -ˈpoʊzd ◂

unorganized, unorganised ʌn ˈɔːg ə naɪzd
‖ -ˈɔːrg-

unorthodox ʌn ˈɔːθ ə dɒks ˌʌn-
‖ -ˈɔːrθ ə dɑːks **~ly** li

unorthodox|y ʌn ˈɔːθ ə dɒks |i ˌʌn-
‖ -ˈɔːrθ ə dɑːks |i **~ies** iz

unpack ˌʌn ˈpæk →ˌʌm- **~ed** t **~ing** ɪŋ **~s** s

unpaid ˌʌn ˈpeɪd ◂ →ˌʌm-
ˌunpaid ˈbills

unpalatable ʌn ˈpæl ət əb ᵊl →ʌm-, ˌ-- ‖ -ˈʈ-

unparalleled ˌʌn ˈpær ə leld -əl əld ‖ -ˈper-

unpardonab|le ʌn ˈpɑːd ᵊn_əb |ᵊl →ʌm-
‖ -ˈpɑːrd- **~ly** li

unparliamentary ˌʌn ˌpɑːl ə ˈment ᵊr i
→ˌʌm-, -ˌ-ɪ-, -ˌ-ɪ̯ə'-- ‖ -ˌpɑːrl ə ˈmenʈ-

unpatriotic ˌʌn ˌpætr i ˈɒt ɪk ◂ →ˌʌm-, -ˌpeɪtr-
‖ -ˌpeɪtr i ˈɑːʈ ɪk ◂

unpaved ˌʌn ˈpeɪvd ◂ →ˌʌm-

unpeeled ˌʌn ˈpiːᵊld ◂ →ˌʌm-

unpeg ˌʌn ˈpeg →ˌʌm- **~ged** d **~ging** ɪŋ **~s** z

unperson ˌʌn ˈpɜːs ᵊn →ˌʌm-, ˈ·ˌ·· ‖ -ˈpɜːs- **~s**
z

unperturbed ˌʌn pə ˈtɜːbd ◂ →ˌʌm-
‖ -pʲr ˈtɜːbd ◂

unpick ˌʌn ˈpɪk →ˌʌm- **~ed** t **~ing** ɪŋ **~s** s

unplaced ˌʌn ˈpleɪst →ˌʌm-

unplanned ˌʌn ˈplænd ◂ →ˌʌm-

unplayable ˌʌn ˈpleɪ əb ᵊl →ˌʌm-

unpleasant ʌn ˈplez ᵊnt →ʌm- **~ly** li

unpleasantness ʌn ˈplez ᵊnt nəs →ʌm-, -nɪs
~es ɪz əz

unplug ˌʌn ˈplʌg →ˌʌm- **~ged** d **~ging** ɪŋ **~s** z

unplumbed ˌʌn ˈplʌmd ◂ →ˌʌm-
ˌunplumbed ˈdepths

unpolished ʌn ˈpɒl ɪʃt ‖ -ˈpɑːl-

unpopular ˌʌn ˈpɒp jʊl ə →ˌʌm-, -jəl ə
‖ -ˈpɑːp jəl ʲr **~ly** li

unpopularity ˌʌn ˌpɒp ju ˈlær ət i →ˌʌm-,
-ˌ-jə-, -ɪt i ‖ -ˌpɑːp jə ˈlær əʈ i -ˈler-

unpracticed, unpractised ˌʌn ˈprækt ɪst
→ˌʌm-, §-əst

unprecedented ʌn ˈpres ɪ dent ɪd →ʌm-, ˌ-ˌ-,
-ˈpriːs-, -ˈ-ə-, -ɪd ənt-, -əd ənt-, -əd; ·ˌ·, ·ˈdent·,
ˌ·ˌ·-- ‖ -ˈpres ə denʈ əd **~ly** li

unpredictability ˌʌn pri ˌdɪkt ə ˈbɪl ət i
→ˌʌm-, -ˌprə-, -ɪt i ‖ -əʈ i

unpredictab|le ˌʌn pri ˈdɪkt əb |ᵊl ◂ →ˌʌm-,
-ˌprə- **~leness** ᵊl nəs -nɪs **~ly** li

unprejudiced ˌʌn ˈpredʒ ʊd ɪst →ˌʌm-,
-ˈ-əd-, §-əst, §-aɪst ‖ -əd əst

unpremeditated ˌʌn priː ˈmed ɪ teɪt ɪd ◂
→ˌʌm-, ˌ-prɪ-, -əd ‖ -teɪʈ əd ◂

unprepared ˌʌn pri ˈpeəd ◂ →ˌʌm-, -prə-
‖ -ˈpeʲrd ◂ -ˈpæʲrd ◂

unprepared|ly ˌʌn pri ˈpeər ɪd |li →ˌʌm-,
ˌ-prə-, -əd · ‖ -ˈper əd |li -ˈpær- **~ness** nəs nɪs

unprepossessing ˌʌn ˌpriː pə ˈzes ɪŋ →ˌʌm-;
·ˌ·--; ˌ·ˌ··ˈ····· **~ly** li

unpretentious ˌʌn pri ˈtenʃ əs ◂ →ˌʌm-, -prə-
~ly i **~ness** nəs nɪs

unprincipled ˌʌn ˈprɪn.s əp ᵊld →ˌʌm-, -ɪp-

unprintable ˌʌn ˈprɪnt əb ᵊl →ˌʌm-
‖ -ˈprɪnʈ-

unproductive ˌʌn prə ˈdʌkt ɪv ◂ →ˌʌm- **~ly** li

unprofessional ˌʌn prə ˈfeʃ ᵊn_əl ◂ →ˌʌm- **~ly**
i

Unprofor ˈʌn prə fɔː →ˈʌm- ‖ -fɔːr

unprompted ˌʌn ˈprɒmpt ɪd →ˌʌm-, -əd
‖ -ˈprɑːmpt əd

unpronounceable ˌʌn prə ˈnaʊn.s əb ᵊl
→ˌʌm-

unproven ˌʌn ˈpruːv ᵊn ◂ →ˌʌm-, -ˈprəʊv-

unprovoked ˌʌn prə ˈvəʊkt ◂ →ˌʌm-
‖ -ˈvoʊkt ◂

unpublished ˌʌn 'pʌb lɪʃt ◂ →ˌʌm-

unpunctual ˌʌn 'pʌŋk tʃu əl →ˌʌm-, -tju‿əl **~ly** i

unpunctuality ˌʌn ˌpʌŋk tʃu 'æl ət i -ˌtju-, -ɪt i ‖ -əţ i

unpunished (ˌ)ʌn 'pʌn ɪʃt (ˌ)ʌm-

unputdownable ˌʌn pʊt 'daʊn əb ᵊl →ˌʌm-

unqualified *'lacking qualifications'* ˌʌn 'kwɒl ɪ faɪd ◂ →ˌʌŋ-, -ə- ‖ -'kwɑːl-

unqualified *'downright, not limited'* ʌn 'kwɒl ɪ faɪd →ˌʌŋ-, -ə- ‖ -'kwɑːl-

unquenchable ʌn 'kwentʃ əb ᵊl

unquestionab|le (ˌ)ʌn 'kwes tʃən əb |ᵊl →(ˌ)ʌŋ-, →-'kweʃ-, -'tjən- **~leness** ᵊl nəs -nɪs **~ly** li

unquestioned (ˌ)ʌn 'kwes tʃənd →(ˌ)ʌŋ-, →-'kweʃ-, -tjənd

unquestioning (ˌ)ʌn 'kwes tʃən ɪŋ →(ˌ)ʌŋ-, →-'kweʃ-, -tjən- **~ly** li

unquiet ˌʌn 'kwaɪ ət ◂ →ˌʌŋ- **~ly** li **~ness** nəs nɪs

unquote ˌʌn 'kwəʊt →ˌʌŋ-, -'kəʊt ‖ 'ʌn kwoʊt

unrated ˌʌn 'reɪt ɪd -əd ‖ -'reɪţ-

unravel (ˌ)ʌn 'ræv ᵊl **~ed, ~led** d **~ing, ~ling** ɪŋ **~s** z

unread ˌʌn 'red ◂

unreadab|le (ˌ)ʌn 'riːd əb |ᵊl **~leness** ᵊl nəs -nɪs **~ly** li

unread|y ˌʌn 'red |i **~ily** ɪ li əl i **~iness** i nəs i nɪs

unreal (ˌ)ʌn 'rɪəl -'riːᵊl ‖ -'riː əl

unrealistic ˌʌn rɪə 'lɪst ɪk ‖ ˌʌn ˌriː ə 'lɪst ɪk **~ally** ᵊl i

unreality ˌʌn ri 'æl ət i -ɪt i ‖ -əţ i

unrealized, unrealised ˌʌn 'rɪəl aɪzd ◂ ‖ ˌʌn 'riː ə laɪzd ◂

unreasonab|le (ˌ)ʌn 'riːz ᵊn əb |ᵊl **~leness** ᵊl nəs -nɪs **~ly** li

unreasoning (ˌ)ʌn 'riːz ᵊn ɪŋ **~ly** li

unrecognizab|le, unrecognisab|le ˌʌn 'rek əg naɪz əb |ᵊl -'-ə-; ˌˌ-ˌ-'-- **~ly** li

unrecognized, unrecognised ˌʌn 'rek əg naɪzd ◂ -ə-

unreconstructed ˌʌn ˌriː kən 'strʌkt ɪd ◂ §-kɒn-, -əd

unrecorded ˌʌn ri 'kɔːd ɪd ◂, ˌʌn rə-, -əd ‖ -'kɔːrd-

unrecoverable ˌʌn ri 'kʌv ər əb ᵊl ˌʌn rə-

unreel ˌʌn 'riːᵊl ◂ **~ed** d **~ing** ɪŋ **~s** z

unrefined ˌʌn ri 'faɪnd ◂ -rə-

unregenerate ˌʌn ri 'dʒen ər ət ˌrə-, ɪt, -ə reɪt **~ly** li

unregistered ˌʌn 'redʒ ɪst əd ◂ §-əst ‖ -ᵊrd ◂

unregulated ˌʌn 'reg ju leɪt ɪd -əd ‖ -jə leɪţ əd

unrelated ˌʌn ri 'leɪt ɪd -rə-, -əd ‖ -'leɪţ-

unrelenting ˌʌn ri 'lent ɪŋ ◂ -rə- ‖ -'lenţ ɪŋ ◂ **~ly** li **~ness** nəs nɪs

unreliability ˌʌn ri ˌlaɪ ə 'bɪl ət i ˌrə-, -ɪt i ‖ -əţ i

unreliab|le ˌʌn ri 'laɪ əb |ᵊl ◂, ˌrə- **~leness** ᵊl nəs -nɪs **~ly** li

unrelieved ˌʌn ri 'liːvd ◂ -rə-

ˌunrelieved 'boredom

unremarkable ˌʌn ri 'mɑːk əb ᵊl ◂, ˌʌn rə- ‖ -'mɑːrk-

unremitting ˌʌn ri 'mɪt ɪŋ ◂ -rə- ‖ -'mɪţ ɪŋ ◂ **~ly** li **~ness** nəs nɪs

ˌunremitting 'efforts

unrepeatable ˌʌn ri 'piːt əb ᵊl ◂, ˌʌn rə- ‖ -'piːţ-

unrepentant ˌʌn ri 'pent ənt -rə- ‖ -'penţ-

unreported ˌʌn ri 'pɔːt ɪd ◂ -rə-, -əd ‖ -'pɔːrţ-

unrepresentative ˌʌn ˌrep ri 'zent ət ɪv ◂ -ˌrep rə- ‖ -'zenţ əţ ɪv ◂

unrequited ˌʌn ri 'kwaɪt ɪd ◂ -rə-, -əd ‖ -'kwaɪţ əd ◂

ˌunrequited 'love

unre|served ˌʌn ri |'zɜːvd ◂ -rə- ‖ -|'zɜːvd **~servedly** 'zɜːv ɪd li -əd- ‖ 'zɜːv-

unresisting ˌʌn ri 'zɪst ɪŋ -rə- **~ly** li

unresolved ˌʌn ri 'zɒlvd ◂ -rə-, §-'zəʊlvd, §→-'zɒʊlvd ‖ -'zɑːlvd

unresponsive ˌʌn ri 'spɒn's ɪv ◂ -rə- ‖ -'spɑːn's-

unrest (ˌ)ʌn 'rest

unrestrained ˌʌn ri 'streɪnd ◂ -rə-

unrestrainedly ˌʌn ri 'streɪn ɪd li -'rə-, -əd li

unrestricted ˌʌn ri 'strɪkt ɪd ◂ -rə-, -əd

ˌunrestricted 'access

unrewarded ˌʌn ri 'wɔːd ɪd ◂ -rə-, -əd ‖ -'wɔːrd-

unrip (ˌ)ʌn 'rɪp **~ped** t **~ping** ɪŋ **~s** s

unripe ˌʌn 'raɪp ◂ **~ness** nəs nɪs

unrivaled, unrivalled ʌn 'raɪv ᵊld ˌʌn-

unroll (ˌ)ʌn 'rəʊl →-'rɒl ‖ -'roʊl **~ed** d **~ing** ɪŋ **~s** z

unround ˌʌn 'raʊnd ◂ **~ed** ɪd əd **~ing** ɪŋ **~s** z

unruffled (ˌ)ʌn 'rʌf ᵊld

unrul|y ʌn 'ruːl |i **~iness** i nəs i nɪs

UNRWA ˌʌn rə

unsaddl|e (ˌ)ʌn 'sæd ᵊl **~ed** d **~es** z **~ing** ɪŋ

unsafe (ˌ)ʌn 'seɪf **~ly** li **~ness** nəs nɪs

unsaid (ˌ)ʌn 'sed

unsanitary ˌʌn 'sæn ɪt ər i -ət‿ ‖ -ə ter i

unsatisfactory ˌʌn ˌsæt ɪs 'fækt ər i ◂ -ə- ‖ -ˌsæţ-

unsatisfied ˌʌn 'sæt ɪs faɪd -əs- ‖ -'sæţ-

unsaturated (ˌ)ʌn 'sætʃ ə reɪt ɪd -'‿ʊ, -əd; -'sæt ju- ‖ -reɪţ əd

unsavor|y, unsavour|y (ˌ)ʌn 'seɪv ər |i **~iness** i nəs i nɪs

un|say ˌʌn |'seɪ —*but as contrasted with* say, '‿ ~**said** 'sed **~saying** 'seɪ ɪŋ **~says** 'sez 'seɪz

unscathed (ˌ)ʌn 'skeɪðd

unscheduled ˌʌn 'ʃed juːld ◂ -'sked- ‖ -'skedʒ uːld ◂ -əld

unschooled ˌʌn 'skuːld

unscientific ˌʌn ˌsaɪ ən 'tɪf ɪk **~ally** ᵊl i

Unscom, UNSCOM 'ʌn skɒm ‖ -skɑːm

unscrambl|e (ˌ)ʌn 'skræm bᵊl **~ed** d **~es** z **~ing** ɪŋ

unscrew ˌʌn 'skruː **~ed** d **~ing** ɪŋ **~s** z

unscripted ˌʌn 'skrɪpt ɪd ◂ ʌn-, -əd

unscrupulous ʌn ˈskruːp jʊl əs ˌʌn-, -jəl-
‖ -jəl əs **~ly** li **~ness** nəs nɪs
unseal ˌʌn ˈsiːᵊl **~ed** d **~ing** ɪŋ **~s** z
unseasonab|le ʌn ˈsiːz ᵊn‿əb |ᵊl ˌʌn- **~leness**
ᵊl nəs -nɪs **~ly** li
un|seat ˌʌn |ˈsiːt **~seated** ˈsiːt ɪd -əd ‖ ˈsiːt əd
~seating ˈsiːt ɪŋ ‖ ˈsiːtʃ ɪŋ **~seats** ˈsiːts
unsecured ˌʌn sɪ ˈkjʊəd ◀ -sə-, §-siː-, -ˈkjɔːd
‖ -ˈkjʊᵊrd
‚unsecured ˈloan
unseeded ˌʌn ˈsiːd ɪd -əd
unseeing ˌʌn ˈsiː ɪŋ ◀
unseem|ly ʌn ˈsiːm |li **~liness** li nəs -nɪs
unseen ˌʌn ˈsiːn ◀ **~s** z
unselfish ˌ₍ᵢ₎ʌn ˈself ɪʃ **~ly** li **~ness** nəs nɪs
Unser ˈʌnz ə ‖ -ᵊr
unserviceab|le ˌ₍ᵢ₎ʌn ˈsɜːv ɪs əb |ᵊl §-ˈ-əs-
‖ -ˈsɜːv əs- **~leness** ᵊl nəs -nɪs **~ly** li
unsettl|e ˌ₍ᵢ₎ʌn ˈset ᵊl ‖ -ˈseṭ ᵊl **~ed** d **~es** z
~ing ɪŋ
unsettled adj ˌʌn ˈset ᵊld ◀ ‖ -ˈseṭ ᵊld ◀ **~ness**
nəs nɪs
unsex ˌ₍ᵢ₎ʌn ˈseks **~ed** t **~es** ɪz əz **~ing** ɪŋ
unshakab|le, unshakeab|le ʌn ˈʃeɪk əb |ᵊl
~leness ᵊl nəs -nɪs **~ly** li
unshaken ʌn ˈʃeɪk ən
unshaven ˌʌn ˈʃeɪv ᵊn ◀
unsheath|e ˌ₍ᵢ₎ʌn ˈʃiːð **~ed** d **~es** z **~ing** ɪŋ
unshockable ˌʌn ˈʃɒk əb ᵊl ◀ ‖ -ˈʃɑːk-
unshod ˌʌn ˈʃɒd ◀ ‖ -ˈʃɑːd ◀
unsight|ly ʌn ˈsaɪt |li **~liness** li nəs -nɪs
unsigned ˌʌn ˈsaɪnd ◀
unsinkable ʌn ˈsɪŋk əb ᵊl
unskilled ˌʌn ˈskɪld ◀
unsmiling ˌʌn ˈsmaɪᵊl ɪŋ ◀
unsociab|le ˌ₍ᵢ₎ʌn ˈsəʊʃ əb |ᵊl ‖ -ˈsoʊʃ- **~leness**
ᵊl nəs -nɪs **~ly** li
unsocial ˌʌn ˈsəʊʃ ᵊl ◀ ‖ -ˈsoʊʃ- **~ly** i
‚un‚social ˈhours
unsold ˌʌn ˈsəʊld ◀ →-ˈsɒʊld ‖ -ˈsoʊld ◀
unsolicited ˌʌn sə ˈlɪs ɪt ɪd ◀ §-ət-, -əd
‖ -əṭ əd ◀
unsolved ˌʌn ˈsɒlvd ◀ §-ˈsəʊlvd ◀, §→ˈsɒʊlvd ◀
‖ -ˈsɑːlvd ◀
unsophisticated ˌʌn sə ˈfɪst ɪ keɪt ɪd ◀ §-ˈ-ə-,
-əd ‖ -ə keɪṭ əd ◀
unsound ˌʌn ˈsaʊnd
unsparing ʌn ˈspeər ɪŋ ‖ -ˈsper ɪŋ -ˈspær- **~ly**
li **~ness** nəs nɪs
unspeakab|le ʌn ˈspiːk əb |ᵊl **~leness** ᵊl nəs
-nɪs **~ly** li
unspecified ʌn ˈspes ɪ faɪd -ə-
unspoiled ˌʌn ˈspɔɪᵊld ◀ -ˈspɔɪᵊlt
unspoilt ˌʌn ˈspɔɪᵊlt ◀
unspoken ˌ₍ᵢ₎ʌn ˈspəʊk ən ‖ -ˈspoʊk ən
unsporting ˌʌn ˈspɔːt ɪŋ ‖ -ˈspɔːrṭ- -ˈspoʊrṭ-
unsportsmanlike ʌn ˈspɔːts mən laɪk
‖ -ˈspɔːrts- -ˈspoʊrts-
unspotted ˌʌn ˈspɒt ɪd ◀ -əd ‖ -ˈspɑːṭ əd ◀
~ness nəs nɪs
Unst ʌnˈst
unstab|le ˌ₍ᵢ₎ʌn ˈsteɪb |ᵊl **~leness** ᵊl nəs -nɪs
~ly li

unstated ˌʌn ˈsteɪt ɪd ◀ -əd ‖ -ˈsteɪṭ-
unstead|y ˌ₍ᵢ₎ʌn ˈsted |i **~ied** id **~ier** i‿ə ‖ i‿ᵊr
~ies iz **~iest** i‿ɪst i‿əst **~ily** ɪ li ᵊl i **~iness**
i nəs i nɪs **~ying** i ɪŋ
unstick ˌʌn ˈstɪk **~ing** ɪŋ **~s** s unstuck
ˌʌn ˈstʌk
unstinted ʌn ˈstɪnt ɪd -əd ‖ -ˈstɪnṭ əd
unstinting ʌn ˈstɪnt ɪŋ ‖ -ˈstɪnṭ ɪŋ **~ly** li
unstop ˌʌn ˈstɒp ‖ -ˈstɑːp **~ped** t **~ping** ɪŋ **~s**
s
unstoppab|le ʌn ˈstɒp əb |ᵊl ˌʌn- ‖ -ˈstɑːp-
~leness ᵊl nəs -nɪs **~ly** li
unstreamed ˌʌn ˈstriːmd ◀
unstressed ˌʌn ˈstrest ◀
‚unstressed ˈsyllables
unstructured ˌ₍ᵢ₎ʌn ˈstrʌk tʃəd -ʃəd ‖ -tʃᵊrd **~ly**
li **~ness** nəs nɪs
unstrung ˌʌn ˈstrʌŋ
unstuck ˌʌn ˈstʌk ◀
unstudied ˌʌn ˈstʌd id ◀
unsubscrib|e ˌʌn səb ˈskraɪb §-sʌb- **~ed** d **~es**
z **~ing** ɪŋ
unsubstantiated ˌʌn səb ˈstænᵗʃ i eɪt ɪd ◀
§,-sʌb-, -əd ‖ -eɪṭ-
unsubtle ˌʌn ˈsʌt ᵊl ‖ -ˈsʌṭ ᵊl
unsuccessful ˌʌn sək ˈses fᵊl ◀ §-sʌk-, -fʊl **~ly**
i **~ness** nəs nɪs
unsuitab|le ˌ₍ᵢ₎ʌn ˈsuːt əb |ᵊl -ˈsjuːt- ‖ -ˈsuːṭ-
~leness ᵊl nəs -nɪs **~ly** li
unsuited ʌn ˈsuːt ɪd -ˈsjuːt-, -əd ‖ -ˈsuːṭ-
unsullied ˌʌn ˈsʌl id
unsung ˌʌn ˈsʌŋ ◀
‚unsung ˈhero
unsupervised ˌʌn ˈsuːp ə vaɪzd -ˈsjuːp-
‖ -ᵊr vaɪzd
unsupported ˌʌn sə ˈpɔːt ɪd ◀ -əd
‖ -ˈpɔːrṭ əd ◀ -ˈpoʊrṭ-
unsure ˌʌn ˈʃʊə ◀ -ˈʃɔː ‖ -ˈʃʊᵊr ◀ -ˈʃɔː **~ly** li
~ness nəs nɪs
unsurpassed ˌʌn sə ˈpɑːst ◀ -§ˈpæst
‖ -sᵊr ˈpæst ◀
unsurprising ˌʌn sə ˈpraɪz ɪŋ ◀ ‖ -sᵊr- -sə- **~ly**
li
unsuspected ˌʌn sə ˈspekt ɪd ◀ -əd **~ly** li
unsuspecting ˌʌn sə ˈspekt ɪŋ ◀ **~ly** li
unsustainable ˌʌn sə ˈsteɪn əb ᵊl ◀
unswayed ˌʌn ˈsweɪd ◀
unsweetened ˌʌn ˈswiːt ᵊnd ◀
unswerving ʌn ˈswɜːv ɪŋ ˌʌn- ‖ -ˈswɜːᵊv ɪŋ **~ly**
li
Unsworth ˈʌnz wɜːθ -wəθ ‖ -wɜːθ
unsympathetic ˌʌn ˌsɪmp ə ˈθet ɪk ◀ ‖ -ˈθeṭ-
~ally ᵊl i
unsystematic ˌʌn ˌsɪst ə ˈmæt ɪk ◀ -ɪ- ‖ -ˈmæṭ ɪk
~ally ᵊl i
untainted ˌʌn ˈteɪnt ɪd ◀ -əd ‖ -ˈteɪnṭ-
untalented ˌ₍ᵢ₎ʌn ˈtæl ənt ɪd -əd ‖ -ənṭ əd
untamable, untameable ˌʌn ˈteɪm əb ᵊl ◀
untamed ˌʌn ˈteɪmd ◀
untangl|e ˌ₍ᵢ₎ʌn ˈtæŋ gᵊl **~ed** d **~es** z **~ing** ɪŋ
untapped ˌʌn ˈtæpt ◀
untarnished ˌ₍ᵢ₎ʌn ˈtɑːn ɪʃt ‖ -ˈtɑːrn ɪʃt
untaught ˌʌn ˈtɔːt ◀ ‖ -ˈtɑːt

U

untenable ʌn 'ten əb ᵊl ˌʌn-, -'tiːn-
untested ˌʌn 'test ɪd ◂ -əd
Unthank 'ʌn θæŋk
unthinkab|le ʌn 'θɪŋk əb |ᵊl **~leness** ᵊl nəs
  -nɪs **~ly** li
unthinking ˌʌn 'θɪŋk ɪŋ **~ly** li **~ness** nəs nɪs
unthought-of ʌn 'θɔːt ɒv -əv ‖ -'θɔːt̬ ʌv
  -'θɑːt̬-, -əv
unthought-out ˌʌn θɔːt 'aʊt ◂ -θɔːt̬- -θɑːt̬-
untid|y ˌʌn 'taɪd |i **~ied** id **~ier** i ə ‖ i ᵊr **~ies**
  iz **~iest** i ɪst i əst **~ily** ɪ li əl i **~iness** i nəs
  i nɪs **~ying** i ɪŋ
untie ˌʌn 'taɪ **~d** d **~s** z **untying** ʌn 'taɪ ɪŋ
until ən 'tɪl ˌʌn- —*also occasionally, in*
  STRESS SHIFT environments (ˌuntil 'now),
  'ʌn tᵊl
untime|ly ˌʌn 'taɪm |li **~liness** li nəs -nɪs
untinged ˌʌn 'tɪndʒd
untiring ʌn 'taɪ‿ər ɪŋ ‖ -'taɪ‿ᵊr ɪŋ **~ly** li
untitled ʌn 'taɪt ᵊld ‖ -'taɪt̬-
unto 'ʌn tu —*also, esp before a consonant,* -tə
untold ˌʌn 'təʊld ◂ ʌn-, →-'tɒʊld ‖ -'toʊld ◂
  ˌuntold 'suffering
untouchability ˌʌn ˌtʌtʃ ə 'bɪl ət i -ɪt i ‖ -ət̬ i
untouchable ˌʌn 'tʌtʃ əb ᵊl **~s** z
untouched ˌʌn 'tʌtʃt
untoward ˌʌn tə 'wɔːd ◂ -tu-; ʌn 'təʊ əd
  ‖ ʌn 'tɔːrd -'toʊrd (*) **~ly** li **~ness** nəs nɪs
untrained ˌʌn 'treɪnd ◂
untrammeled, untrammelled
  ˌʌn 'træm ᵊld
untreated ˌʌn 'triːt ɪd ◂ -əd ‖ -'triːt̬-
untried ˌʌn 'traɪd ◂
untrue ˌʌn 'truː
untrustworthy ˌʌn 'trʌst ˌwɜːð i ‖ -ˌwɜːð i
un|truth ˌʌn |'truːθ ' · · **~truths** 'truːðz 'truːθs
untruthful ˌʌn 'truːθ fᵊl -fʊl **~ly** ‿i **~ness** nəs
  nɪs
untuck ˌʌn 'tʌk **~ed** t **~ing** ɪŋ **~s** s
unturned ʌn 'tɜːnd ‖ -'tɜːnd
untutored ˌʌn 'tjuːt əd ◂ →-'tʃuːt-
  ‖ -'tuːt̬ ᵊrd ◂ -'tjuːt̬-
untypical ʌn 'tɪp ɪk ᵊl **~ly** ‿i
unusable ˌʌn 'juːz əb ᵊl
unused '*not made use of* ' ˌʌn 'juːzd ◂
unused '*unaccustomed* ' ˌʌn 'juːst
unusual ʌn 'juːʒ u‿əl ˌʌn-, -ju əl; -'juːʒ ᵊl
unusually ʌn 'juːʒ u‿əl i ˌʌn-, -'ju-; -'juːʒ ᵊl i
unutterab|le ʌn 'ʌt ər əb |ᵊl ‖ -'ʌt̬ ər- **~leness**
  ᵊl nəs -nɪs **~ly** li
unvarnished ˌʌn 'vɑːn ɪʃt ◂ ʌn- ‖ -'vɑːrn ɪʃt ◂
unveil ˌʌn 'veɪᵊl **~ed** d **~ing** ɪŋ **~s** z
unversed ˌʌn 'vɜːst ‖ -'vɜːst
unvoic|e ˌʌn 'vɔɪs ◂ **~ed** t **~es** ɪz əz **~ing** ɪŋ
unwaged ˌʌn 'weɪdʒd ◂
unwanted ˌʌn 'wɒnt ɪd ◂ §-'wʌnt-, -əd
  ‖ -'wɑːnt- -'wɔːnt̬-, 'wʌnt̬-
unwarrantab|le ʌn 'wɒr ənt əb |ᵊl
  ‖ -'wɔːr ənt̬- -'wɑːr- **~ly** li
unwarranted ʌn 'wɒr ənt ɪd -əd
  ‖ -'wɔːr ənt̬ əd -'wɑːr-
unwar|y ˌʌn 'weər |i ‖ -'wer |i -'wær- **~ily**
  əl i ɪ li **~iness** i nəs i nɪs

unwashed ˌʌn 'wɒʃt ◂ -'wɔːʃt -'wɑːʃt
unwavering ʌn 'weɪv ər‿ɪŋ **~ly** li
unwed ˌʌn 'wed ◂
unwelcom|e ʌn 'welk əm ˌʌn- **~ing** ɪŋ
unwell ˌʌn 'wel
unwholesome ˌʌn 'həʊl səm →-'hɒʊl-
  ‖ -'hoʊl- **~ly** li **~ness** nəs nɪs
unwield|y ˌʌn 'wiːld |i **~ily** ɪ li əl i **~iness**
  i nəs i nɪs
unwilling ˌʌn 'wɪl ɪŋ **~ness** nəs nɪs
unwillingly ʌn 'wɪl ɪŋ li
Unwin 'ʌn wɪn
unwind ˌʌn 'waɪnd **~ing** ɪŋ **~s** z **unwound**
  ˌʌn 'waʊnd
unwise ˌʌn 'waɪz ◂ **~ly** li
unwished-for ˌʌn 'wɪʃt fɔː ‖ -fɔːr
unwitting ˌʌn 'wɪt ɪŋ ‖ -'wɪt̬ ɪŋ **~ly** li
unwonted ʌn 'wəʊnt ɪd -əd ‖ -'wɔːnt̬ əd
  -'wɑːnt̬-, -'woʊnt̬-, -'wʌnt̬- (*) **~ly** li **~ness**
  nəs nɪs
unworkable ˌʌn 'wɜːk əb ᵊl ‖ -'wɜːk-
unworld|ly ˌʌn 'wɜːld |li ‖ -'wɜːld- **~liness**
  li nəs -nɪs
unworried ʌn 'wʌr id ˌ·- ‖ -'wɜː id
unworth|y ˌʌn 'wɜːð |i ‖ -'wɜːð |i **~ily** ɪ li
  əl i **~iness** i nəs i nɪs
unwound ˌʌn 'waʊnd
unwrap ˌʌn 'ræp ◂ **~ped** t **~ping** ɪŋ **~s** s
unwritten ˌʌn 'rɪt ᵊn ◂
  ˌunˌwritten 'law
unyielding ˌʌn 'jiːᵊld ɪŋ
unyok|e ˌʌn 'jəʊk ʌn- ‖ -'joʊk **~ed** t **~es** s
  ~ing ɪŋ
Unzen 'ʊn zen —*Jp* ['ʊn dzen]
unzip ˌʌn 'zɪp **~ped** t **~ping** ɪŋ **~s** s
up ʌp **upped** ʌpt **upping** 'ʌp ɪŋ **ups** ʌps
  ˌups and 'downs
up- ˌʌp — **upgrowth** 'ʌp grəʊθ ‖ -groʊθ
up-and-com|ing ˌʌp ən 'kʌm |ɪŋ ◂ -ənd-,
  →-m-, →-əŋ- **~er/s** ə/z ‖ ᵊr/z
up-and-down ˌʌp ən 'daʊn -ənd-, →-m-
up-and-up ˌʌp ən 'ʌp -ənd-
Upanishad u 'pʌn ɪʃ əd ju-, -'pæn-, -əʃ; -ɪ ʃæd
  ‖ u 'pɑːn ɪ ʃɑːd **~s** z
upas 'juːp əs **~es** ɪz əz
upbeat 'ʌp biːt **~s** s
upbraid ʌp 'breɪd **~ed** ɪd əd **~ing** ɪŋ **~s** z
upbringing 'ʌp ˌbrɪŋ ɪŋ
upcast 'ʌp kɑːst §-kæst ‖ -kæst **~s** s
upchuck 'ʌp tʃʌk **~ed** t **~ing** ɪŋ **~s** s
upcoming 'ʌp ˌkʌm ɪŋ ˌ·'··
up-country ˌʌp 'kʌntr i ◂
up|date *v* ˌʌp |'deɪt **~dated** 'deɪt ɪd -əd
  ‖ 'deɪt̬ əd **~dates** 'deɪts **~dating** 'deɪt ɪŋ
  ‖ 'deɪt̬ ɪŋ
update *n* 'ʌp deɪt ˌ·'· **~s** s
Updike 'ʌp daɪk
updraft, updraught 'ʌp drɑːft §-dræft
  ‖ -dræft **~s** s
upend ʌp 'end **~ed** ɪd əd **~ing** ɪŋ **~s** z
upfront ˌʌp 'frʌnt **~ness** nəs nɪs
upgrad|e *v* ˌʌp 'greɪd '·· **~ed** ɪd əd **~ing** ɪŋ
  ~es z

upgrade n 'ʌp greɪd ˌ'· ~s z
upheaval ʌp 'hiːv ᵊl ~s z
upheld ʌp 'held
uphill ˌʌp 'hɪl ◄
  ˌuphill 'struggle
uphold ʌp 'həʊld →-'hɒʊld ‖ -'hoʊld **upheld**
  ʌp 'held ~er/s ə/z ‖ ᵊr/z ~ing ɪŋ ~s z
upholst|er ʌp 'həʊlst |ə əp-, →-'hɒʊlst-
  ‖ ʌp 'hoʊlst |ᵊr ə 'poʊlst- ~ered əd ‖ ᵊrd
  ~ering ər ɪŋ ~ers əz ‖ ᵊrz
upholsterer ʌp 'həʊlst ər ə əp-, →-'hɒʊlst-
  ‖ ʌp 'hoʊlst ᵊr ər ə 'poʊlst- ~s z
upholster|y ʌp 'həʊlst ər |i əp-, →-'hɒʊlst-
  ‖ ʌp 'hoʊlst- ə 'poʊlst- ~ies iz
UPI ˌjuː piː 'aɪ
Upjohn 'ʌp dʒɒn ‖ -dʒɑːn
upkeep 'ʌp kiːp
upland 'ʌp lənd -lænd ~s z
uplift v (ˌ)ʌp 'lɪft '·· ~ed ɪd əd ~ing ɪŋ ~s s
uplift n 'ʌp lɪft ~s s
uplighter 'ʌp ˌlaɪt ə ‖ -ˌlaɪt ᵊr ~s z
upload ˌʌp 'ləʊd ◄ ‖ -'loʊd ◄ ~ed ɪd əd ~ing
  ɪŋ ~s z
up-market ˌʌp 'mɑːk ɪt ◄ §-ət ‖ -'mɑːrk ət ◄
Upminster 'ʌp ˌmɪn'st ə ‖ -ᵊr
upmost 'ʌp məʊst ‖ -moʊst
upon ə 'pɒn ‖ ə 'pɑːn -'pɔːn —*There is also an*
  occasional weak form əp ən
upper 'ʌp ə ‖ -ᵊr ~s z
  ˌupper 'case◄; ˌUpper 'Chamber; ˌupper
  'class◄; ˌupper 'crust◄; ˌupper 'hand;
  ˌUpper 'House
upper-class ˌʌp ə 'klɑːs ◄ §-'klæs ‖ -ᵊr 'klæs ◄
  ~man mən ~men mən ~woman ˌwʊm ən
  ~women ˌwɪm ɪn §-mən
  an ˌupper-class 'accent
uppercut 'ʌp ə kʌt ‖ -ᵊr- ~s s
uppermost 'ʌp ə məʊst ‖ -ᵊr moʊst
Uppingham 'ʌp ɪŋ əm
uppish 'ʌp ɪʃ ~ly li ~ness nəs nɪs
uppity 'ʌp ət i -ɪt- ‖ -əʈ i
Uppsala ʊp 'sɑːl ə ʌp-, '··· —*Swedish*
  ['ʊp sɑː la]
upraised ˌʌp 'reɪzd ◄
up|rate v (ˌ)ʌp |'reɪt ~rated 'reɪt ɪd -əd
  ‖ 'reɪʈ əd ~rates 'reɪts ~rating 'reɪt ɪŋ
  ‖ 'reɪʈ ɪŋ
Uprichard ʌp 'rɪtʃ əd juː-, -ɑːd ‖ -ᵊrd
upright 'ʌp raɪt ˌ'· ~ly li ~ness nəs nɪs ~s s
uprising 'ʌp ˌraɪz ɪŋ ˌ'·· ~s z
upriver ˌʌp 'rɪv ə ◄ ‖ -ᵊr ◄
uproar 'ʌp rɔː ‖ -rɔːr -roʊr ~s z
uproarious ʌp 'rɔːr i əs ‖ -'roʊr- ~ly li ~ness
  nəs nɪs
up|root (ˌ)ʌp |'ruːt '·· ‖ -'rʊt ~rooted 'ruːt ɪd
  -əd ‖ 'ruːʈ əd 'rʊt- ~rooting 'ruːt ɪŋ ‖ 'ruːʈ ɪŋ
  'rʊt- ~roots 'ruːts ‖ 'rʊts
uprush 'ʌp rʌʃ ~es ɪz əz
UPS ˌjuː piː 'es
upsadaisy ˌʌps ə 'deɪz i
upscale ˌʌp 'skeɪᵊl ◄
upset n 'ʌp set ·'· ~s s

upset adj ˌʌp 'set ◄
  ˌupset 'stomach
up|set v ʌp |'set ~sets 'sets ~setting 'set ɪŋ
  ‖ 'seʈ ɪŋ
Upshire 'ʌp ˌʃaɪ‿ə ʌp ʃə ‖ -ˌʃaɪ‿ᵊr 'ʌp ʃᵊr
upshot 'ʌp ʃɒt ‖ -ʃɑːt
upside 'ʌp saɪd ~s z
upside down, upside-down ˌʌp saɪd 'daʊn
  -saɪ-
upsilon juːp 'saɪl ən uːp-, ʊp-, -ɒn; 'juːps ɪl ən,
  'ʌps-, -ɒn ‖ 'uːps ə lɑːn 'juːps-, 'ʌps-, -əl ən
  (*) ~s z
upsiz|e ˌʌp 'saɪz ~ed d ~es ɪz əz ~ing ɪŋ
upskilling 'ʌp ˌskɪl ɪŋ
upstag|e ˌʌp 'steɪdʒ ~ed d ~es ɪz əz ~ing ɪŋ
upstairs ˌʌp 'steəz ◄ ‖ -'steᵊrz -'stæᵊrz
upstanding ˌʌp 'stænd ɪŋ ◄ ʌp- ~ness nəs nɪs
upstart 'ʌp stɑːt ‖ -stɑːrt ~s s
upstate ˌʌp 'steɪt ◄
upstream ˌʌp 'striːm ◄
upstretched ˌʌp 'stretʃt ◄
upstroke 'ʌp strəʊk ‖ -stroʊk ~s s
upsurg|e n 'ʌp sɜːdʒ ‖ -sɜːrdʒ ~es ɪz əz
upswept ˌʌp 'swept ◄ '··
upswing n 'ʌp swɪŋ ~s z
upsy-daisy ˌʌps i 'deɪz i
uptake n 'ʌp teɪk ~s s
up-tempo ˌʌp 'temp əʊ ◄ ‖ -oʊ
upthrust 'ʌp θrʌst ~s s
uptick 'ʌp tɪk ~s s
uptight 'ʌp taɪt ˌ'· ~ness nəs nɪs
uptime 'ʌp taɪm
up-to-date ˌʌp tə 'deɪt ◄ ~ness nəs nɪs
Upton 'ʌpt ən
up-to-the-minute ˌʌp tə ðə 'mɪn ɪt ◄ §-ət
uptown ˌʌp 'taʊn ◄
  an ˌuptown 'bus
uptrend 'ʌp trend ~s z
upturn n 'ʌp tɜːn ‖ -tɜːrn ~s z
upturned ˌʌp 'tɜːnd ◄ ‖ -'tɜːrnd ◄
  ˌupturned 'cars
upward, U~ 'ʌp wəd ‖ -wᵊrd ~ly li
upwardly-mobile ˌʌp wəd li 'məʊb aɪᵊl ◄
  ‖ -wᵊrd li 'moʊb ᵊl ◄ -iːᵊl, -aɪᵊl
upwards 'ʌp wədz ‖ -wᵊrdz
upwind ˌʌp 'wɪnd ◄
Ur *ancient city* ɜː ʊə ‖ ɜːʳ ʊʳr
ur- '*primeval*' ¦ʊə ¦ɜː ‖ ¦ʊr —*Ger* [ʔuːɐ]
  — **Ursprache** 'ʊə ˌʃprɑːx ə 'ɜː-
  ‖ 'ʊr ˌʃprɑːk ə 'ɜː- —*Ger* ['ʔuːɐ ˌʃpʀaː xə]
uracil 'jʊər ə sɪl
uraemia jʊ‿'riːm i ə
Ural 'jʊər əl 'jɔːr- ‖ 'jʊr əl —*Russ* [u 'raɫ] ~s z
Ural-Altaic ˌjʊər əl æl 'teɪ ɪk ◄ ˌjɔːr- ‖ ˌjʊr-
Uralian jʊ‿'reɪl i ən
Uralic jʊ‿'ræl ɪk
Urani|a jʊ‿'reɪn i |ə ~an/s ən/z
uranic jʊ‿'ræn ɪk
uranium jʊ‿'reɪn i‿əm
  u‿ranium 023'5
uranographic ˌjʊər ən əʊ 'græf ɪk ◄ ˌjɔːr-
  ‖ ˌjʊr ən ə-

uranography ˌjʊər ə 'nɒg rəf i ˌjɔːr-
‖ jʊr ə 'nɑːg-

uranous 'jʊər ən əs 'jɔːr- ‖ 'jʊr-

Uranus 'jʊər ən əs 'jɔːr-; jʊ 'reɪn- ‖ 'jʊr-

urban, Urban 'ɜːb ən ‖ 'ɜːb ən

Urbana ɜː 'bæn ə -'bɑːn- ‖ ɜː-

urbane ɜː 'beɪn ‖ ɜː- **~ly** li **~ness** nəs nɪs

urbanis... —*see* **urbaniz...**

urbanite 'ɜːb ə naɪt ‖ 'ɜːb- **~s** s

urbanit|y ɜː 'bæn ət |i -ɪt- ‖ ɜː 'bæn əţ |i **~ies**
iz

urbanization ˌɜːb ən aɪ 'zeɪʃ ᵊn -ɪ'--
‖ ˌɜːb ən ə-

urbaniz|e 'ɜːb ə naɪz ‖ 'ɜːb- **~ed** d **~es** ɪz əz
~ing ɪŋ

urbi et orbi ˌɜːb i et 'ɔːb i ˌʊəb-
‖ ˌɜːb i et 'ɔːrb i

urchin 'ɜːtʃ ɪn §-ən ‖ 'ɜːtʃ ən **~s** z

Urdd Gobaith Cymru ˌɪəð ˌgʊb aɪθ 'kʌm ri
-ˌgəʊb- ‖ ˌɪrð ˌgoʊb- —*Welsh*
[ˌɪrð ˌgo baɪθ 'kəm ri, ˌɪrð-, -ri]

Urdu 'ʊəd uː 'ɜːd- ‖ 'ʊrd uː —*Hindi-Urdu*
[ʊr d̪uː]

Ure jʊə ‖ jʊᵊr

-ure jə jʊə ‖ jᵊr jʊr —*The* j *normally coalesces
with a preceding* t, d, s, z, *to give* tʃ, dʒ, ʃ, ʒ
repectively — **closure** 'kləʊʒ ə ‖ 'kloʊʒ ᵊr

urea jʊᵊ 'riː ə ˌjʊər i ə, 'jɔːr-

ureide 'jʊər i aɪd 'jɔːr- ‖ 'jʊr- **~s** z

uremia jʊᵊ 'riːm i ə

Uren jʊᵊ 'ren

ureter jʊᵊ 'riːt ə ˌjʊər ɪt ə, -ət- ‖ 'jʊr əţ ᵊr
ju 'riːţ ᵊr **~s** z

urethane 'jʊər ə θeɪn 'jɔːr-, -ɪ-, △-θiːn ‖ 'jʊr-

ureth|ra jʊᵊ 'riːθ |rə **~rae** riː **~ras** rəz

urethritis ˌjʊər ə 'θraɪt ɪs ˌjɔːr-, -ɪ-, §-əs
‖ ˌjʊr ə 'θraɪţ əs

Urey 'jʊər i ‖ 'jʊr i

urge ɜːdʒ ‖ ɜːdʒ **urged** ɜːdʒd ‖ ɜːdʒd **urges**
'ɜːdʒ ɪz -əz ‖ 'ɜːdʒ əz **urging/s** 'ɜːdʒ ɪŋ/z
‖ 'ɜːdʒ ɪŋ/z

urgency 'ɜːdʒ ən⁀s i ‖ 'ɜːdʒ-

urgent 'ɜːdʒ ənt ‖ 'ɜːdʒ- **~ly** li

urgh ɜːg ɜːx ‖ jʌk —*or various non-speech
sounds, including* ɯ

-urgy ɜːdʒ i ‖ ɜːdʒ i — **thaumaturgy**
'θɔːm ə tɜːdʒ i ‖ -tɜːdʒ i 'θɑːm- —*but see also*
metallurgy

-uria 'jʊər i ə 'jɔːr- ‖ 'jʊr i ə — **polyuria**
ˌpɒl i 'jʊər i ə -'jɔːr- ‖ ˌpɑːl i 'jʊr i ə

Uriah jʊᵊ 'raɪ ə

uric 'jʊər ɪk 'jɔːr- ‖ 'jʊr ɪk

uridine 'jʊər i diːn -ə-, -daɪn ‖ 'jʊr-

uridylic ˌjʊər ɪ 'dɪl ɪk ◂ ˌjɔːr-, -ə- ‖ ˌjʊr-

Uriel 'jʊər i əl 'jɔːr- ‖ 'jʊr-

urim, Urim 'jʊər ɪm 'jɔːr-, §-əm ‖ 'jʊr əm

urinal jʊᵊ 'raɪn ᵊl 'jʊər ɪn ᵊl, 'jɔːr-, -ən-
‖ 'jʊr ən ᵊl **~s** z

urinalysis ˌjʊər ɪ 'næl əs ɪs 'jɔːr-, ˌ·ə-, -ɪs -, §-əs
‖ ˌjʊr-

urinary 'jʊər ɪn ər i ˌjɔːr-, '·ən- ‖ 'jʊr ə ner i

uri|nate 'jʊər ɪ |neɪt 'jɔːr-, -ə- ‖ 'jʊr ə- **~nated**
neɪt ɪd -əd ‖ neɪţ əd **~nates** neɪts **~nating**
neɪt ɪŋ ‖ neɪţ ɪŋ

urination ˌjʊər ɪ 'neɪʃ ᵊn ˌjɔːr-, -ə- ‖ ˌjʊr ə- **~s**
z

urine 'jʊər ɪn 'jɔːr-, §-ən, §-aɪn ‖ 'jʊr ən

URL juː ɑːr 'el ‖ -ɑːr-

Urmston 'ɜːmᵖst ən ‖ 'ɜːmᵖst-

urn ɜːn ‖ ɜːn (= *earn*) **urns** ɜːnz ‖ ɜːnz

uro- *comb. form*
with stress-neutral suffix ˌjʊər əʊ ˌjɔːr-
‖ ˌjʊr oʊ — **urogenital** ˌjʊər əʊ 'dʒen ɪt ᵊl ◂
ˌjɔːr-, -ət ᵊl ‖ ˌjʊr oʊ 'dʒen əţ ᵊl ◂
with stress-imposing suffix jʊᵊ 'rɒ+ ‖ -'rɑː+
— **uroscopy** jʊᵊ 'rɒsk əp i ‖ -'rɑːsk-

urologist jʊᵊ 'rɒl ədʒ ɪst §-əst ‖ jə 'rɑːl- **~s** s

urology jʊᵊ 'rɒl ədʒ i ‖ -'rɑːl-

Urquhart 'ɜːk ət ‖ 'ɜːk ᵊrt

Ursa 'ɜːs ə ‖ 'ɜːs ə

ˌUrsa 'Major

ursine 'ɜːs aɪn ‖ 'ɜːs-

Ursula 'ɜːs jʊl ə -jəl- ‖ 'ɜːs əl ə

Ursuline 'ɜːs ju laɪn 'ɜːʃ-, -jə-, -lɪn ‖ 'ɜːs əl ən
-ə laɪn, -ə liːn **~s** z

urticaria ˌɜːt ɪ 'keər i ə §ˌ·ə- ‖ ˌɜːţ ə 'ker i ə
-'kær-

Uruguay 'jʊər ə gwaɪ 'ʊər-, 'ʊr-, 'jɔːr-, -ʊ-, ˌ·'·
‖ 'jʊr- 'ʊr-, -gweɪ —*Sp* [u ɾu 'ɣwai]

Uruguayan ˌjʊər ə 'gwaɪ ən ◂ ˌʊər-, ˌʊr-, ˌjɔːr-,
-ʊ-, ‖ ˌjʊr- -'gweɪ- **~s** z

Urumqi, Ürümqi ˌʊr ʊm 'tʃiː ˌjʊr- —*Chi*
Wūlǔmùqí [¹wu ³lu ⁴mu ²tɕʰi]

urus 'jʊər əs 'jɔːr- ‖ 'jʊr əs **~es** ɪz əz

Urwin 'ɜː wɪn ‖ 'ɜː-

us *strong form* ʌs §ʌz, *weak form* əs §əz —*see
also* 's

US juː 'es ◂

ˌUS 'Navy

USA ˌjuː es 'eɪ

usab|le 'juːz əb |ᵊl **~leness** ᵊl nəs -nɪs **~ly** li

USAF ˌjuː es eɪ 'ef

usag|e 'juːs ɪdʒ 'juːz- —*Preference poll, BrE:*
'juːs- 72%, 'juːz- 28%. **~es** ɪz əz

usanc|e 'juːz ᵊn⁀s **~es** ɪz əz

USB ˌjuː es 'biː

Usborne 'ʌz bɔːn ‖ -bɔːrn -bʊərn

USCIS 'ʌsk ɪs

USDAW 'ʌs dɔː 'ʌz- ‖ -dɑː

use *v* juːz (= *yews*) **used** juːzd **uses** 'juːz ɪz -əz
using 'juːz ɪŋ —*See also* **used to**

use *n* juːs **uses** 'juːs ɪz -əz

use-by 'juːz baɪ

ˌpast its 'use-by date

used '*was / were accustomed*' (*expressing a
former fact or state*) **:** **used to** *final or before a
vowel* 'juːst tu, *before a cons* 'juːst tə

used *adj* '*accustomed*' juːst

used '*made use of*' juːzd

usedn't 'juːs ᵊnt 'juːst-

useful 'juːs fᵊl -fʊl **~ly** i **~ness** nəs nɪs

useless 'juːs ləs -lɪs **~ly** li **~ness** nəs nɪs

Usenet 'juːz net

usen't 'juːs ᵊnt

USAGE

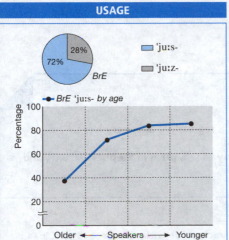

72% 28%

■ 'juːs-
■ 'juːz-

BrE

●— *BrE* 'juːs- *by age*

Percentage (0–100) plotted: Older ◀— Speakers —▶ Younger

---

user 'juːz ə ‖ -ᵊr **~s** z
user-defined ˌjuːz ə dɪ 'faɪnd ◀ -də'- ‖ ˌ-ᵊr-
user-friend|ly ˌjuːz ə 'frend |li ◀ ‖ -ᵊr- **~liness**
   li nəs -nɪs
userid 'juːz ər aɪ ˌdiː **~s** z
username 'juːz ə neɪm ‖ -ᵊr- **~s** z
Ushant 'ʌʃ ᵊnt
usher, Usher 'ʌʃ ə ‖ -ᵊr **~ed** d **ushering**
   'ʌʃ ər ɪŋ **~s** z
usherette ˌʌʃ ə 'ret **~s** s
Usk ʌsk
USN ˌjuːes 'en
USP ˌjuː es 'piː
usquebaugh 'ʌsk wɪ bɔː -wə- ‖ -bɑː
Ussher 'ʌʃ ə ‖ -ᵊr
USSR ˌjuː es es 'ɑː ‖ -'ɑːr
Ustinov 'juːst ɪ nɒf 'uːst-, -ə-, -nɒv ‖ -nɔːf -nɑːf
   —*Russ* [u ˢtⁱi nəf]
usual 'juːʒ u̯əl -juː; 'juːʒ ᵊl **~ness** nəs nɪs
usually 'juːʒ u̯əl i '·juː; 'juːʒ ᵊl i
usufruct 'juːs ju frʌkt 'juːz- ‖ -ə-
usurer 'juːʒ ər ə ‖ -ᵊr ər **~s** z
usurious ju 'zjʊər i̯əs -'ʒʊər-, -'zjɔːr- ‖ -'ʒʊr-
   -'zʊr- **~ly** li **~ness** nəs nɪs
usurp ju 'zɜːp -'sɜːp ‖ ju 'sɜːp -'zɜːp **~ed** t **~ing**
   ɪŋ **~s** s
usurpation ˌjuːz ɜː 'peɪʃ ᵊn ˌjuːs- ‖ ˌjuːs ᵊr-
   ˌjuːz- **~s** z
usur|y 'juːʒ ər |i -ʊər-, -jʊər-, -ʊr- **~ies** iz
ut ʊt ʌt, uːt
Utah 'juːt ɑː -ɔː ‖ -ɑː
Utahan, Utahn 'juːt ɑːn -ɔːn ‖ -ɔːn -ɑːn **~s** z
Ute juːt 'juːt i **Utes** juːts 'juːt iz
utensil ju 'tenˢl ᵊl -ɪl **~s** z
uterine 'juːt ə raɪn -rɪn, -rən ‖ 'juːt̬-
ut|erus 'juːt|ˌər əs ‖ 'juːt̬|- **-eri** ə raɪ
Uther 'juːθ ə ‖ -ᵊr
   Uther Pen'dragon
Utica 'juːt ɪk ə ‖ 'juːt̬-

---

utilis... —*see* **utiliz...**
utilitarian ju ˌtɪl ɪ 'teər i̯ən ◀ ˌjuːt ɪl-, -ə'--
   ‖ -'ter- **~ism** ˌɪz əm **~s** z
utilit|y ju 'tɪl ət |i -ɪt- ‖ -ət̬ |i **~ies** iz
   u'tility room
utilizable 'juːt ɪ laɪz əb ᵊl '·ə-, '·ᵊl aɪz-, ˌ· ·'--
   ‖ 'juːt̬ ᵊl aɪz-
utilization ˌjuːt ɪl aɪ 'zeɪʃ ᵊn ˌ·ᵊl-, -ɪ'--
   ‖ ˌjuːt̬ ᵊl ə- **~s** z
utiliz|e 'juːt ɪ laɪz -ə-, -ᵊl aɪz ‖ 'juːt̬ ᵊl aɪz **~ed**
   d **~es** ɪz əz **~ing** ɪŋ
utmost 'ʌt məʊst -məst ‖ -moʊst
Uto-Aztecan ˌjuːt əʊ 'æz tek ən ◀ -'··
   ‖ ˌjuːt̬ oʊ- **~s** z
utopi|a, U~ ju 'təʊp i̯|ə ‖ -'toʊp- **~an/s** ən/z
   ~anism ən ˌɪz əm **~as** əz
Utrecht 'juːtr ekt -ext; ˌjuː 'trekt, -'trext
   —*Dutch* ['y: trɛxt]
utricle 'juːtr ɪk ᵊl **~s** z
Utrillo ju 'trɪl əʊ ‖ -oʊ —*Fr* [y tʁi jo] **~s** z
Utsira uːt 'sɪər ə ‖ -'sɪr ə —*Norw* [''ʉːt siː ɾa]
Uttar Pradesh ˌʊt ə prə 'deʃ -'deɪʃ ‖ ˌʊt̬ ᵊr-
   —*Hindi* [ʊt̪ t̪ər prə d̪eʃ]
utter 'ʌt ə ‖ 'ʌt̬ ᵊr **uttered** 'ʌt əd ‖ 'ʌt̬ ᵊrd
   uttering 'ʌt ər ɪŋ ‖ 'ʌt̬ ər ɪŋ **utters** 'ʌt əz
   ‖ 'ʌt̬ ᵊrz
utteranc|e 'ʌt ᵊr ənˢts ‖ 'ʌt̬ ər ənˢts **~es** ɪz əz
utterly 'ʌt ə li -ᵊl i ‖ 'ʌt̬ ᵊr li
uttermost 'ʌt ə məʊst ‖ 'ʌt̬ ᵊr moʊst
Uttoxeter ju 'tɒks ɪt ə ʌ-, -ət-; 'ʌks ɪt ə, -ət-
   ‖ ju 'tɑːks ət̬ ᵊr
U-turn 'juː tɜːn ˌ·'· ‖ -tɜːn **~s** z
uuencod|e ˌjuː juː ɪn 'kəʊd ◀ -en'·, -ən'·
   ‖ -'koʊd ◀ **~ed** ɪd əd **~es** z **~ing** ɪŋ
UV ˌjuː 'viː
UVA ˌjuː viː 'eɪ
UVB ˌjuː viː 'biː
uvea 'juːv i̯ə
UVF ˌjuː viː 'ef
uv|ula 'juːv |jʊl ə -jəl- ‖ -jəl ə **~ulae** ju liː jə-
   ‖ jə liː **~ulas** jʊl əz jəl- ‖ jəl əz
uvular 'juːv jʊl ə -jəl- ‖ -jəl ᵊr **~s** z
uvularis... —*see* **uvulariz...**
uvularity ˌjuːv ju 'lær ət i ˌjə-, -ɪt i
   ‖ -jə 'lær ət̬ i -'ler-
uvularization ˌjuːv jʊl ər aɪ 'zeɪʃ ᵊn ˌjəl-, -ɪ'--
   ‖ ˌjəl ər ə-
uvulariz|e 'juːv jʊl ə raɪz '·jəl- ‖ '·jəl- **~ed** d
   ~es ɪz əz **~ing** ɪŋ
UWIST 'juː wɪst
Uxbridge 'ʌks brɪdʒ
uxorial ʌk 'sɔːr i̯əl ‖ -'soʊr-; ʌg 'zɔːr-, -'zoʊr-
uxoricide ʌk 'sɔːr ɪ saɪd §-ə- ‖ -'soʊr-; ʌg 'zɔːr-,
   -'zoʊr- **~s** z
uxorious ʌk 'sɔːr i̯əs ‖ -'soʊr-; ʌg 'zɔːr-, -'zoʊr-
   ~ly li **~ness** nəs nɪs
Uzbek 'ʊz bek -'ʌz- **~s** s
Uzbekistan ˌʊz bek ɪ 'stɑːn -ˌʌz-, -ə'-, -'stæn
   ‖ ʊz 'bek ə stæn -ɪ stæn
Uzi *tdmk* 'uːz i

Vv

V, v viː **V's, v's, Vs** viːz —*Communications code name:* Victor
ˌV and ˈA; ˌVˈO ˌlanguage; ˌVˈU ˌmeter
v *'versus'* ˈvɜːs əs viː ‖ ˈvɜːs-
V-1 ˌviː ˈwʌn §-ˈwɒn **~s** z
V-2 ˌviː ˈtuː **~s** z
Vaal vɑːl
vac væk **vacs** væks
vacanc|y ˈveɪk ən¹s |i →-ŋ¹s- **~ies** iz
vacant ˈveɪk ənt →-ŋt **~ly** li **~ness** nəs nɪs
vacate və ˈkeɪt veɪ- ‖ ˈveɪk eɪt *(*)* **vacated**
və ˈkeɪt ɪd veɪ-, -əd ‖ ˈveɪk eɪt əd **vacates**
və ˈkeɪts veɪ- ‖ ˈveɪk eɪts **vacating** və ˈkeɪt ɪŋ
veɪ- ‖ ˈveɪk eɪt̬ ɪŋ

VACATION

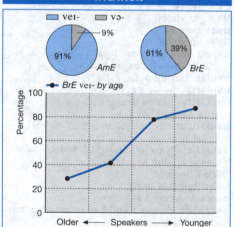

▪ veɪ- ▪ və-

AmE: 91%, 9%
BrE: 61%, 39%

● BrE veɪ- by age

Percentage (y-axis: 0, 20, 40, 60, 80, 100)

Older ◀— Speakers —▶ Younger

vacation veɪ ˈkeɪʃ ᵊn və- — *Preference polls,
AmE:* veɪ- 91%, və- 9%; *BrE:* veɪ- 61%, və-
39%. **~er/s** ə/z ‖ ᵊr/z **~ist/s** ɪst/s §ˌəst/s
‖ ˌəst/s **~s** z
vacci|nate ˈvæks ɪ |neɪt -ə- **~nated** neɪt ɪd -əd
‖ neɪt̬ əd **~nates** neɪts **~nating** neɪt ɪŋ
‖ neɪt̬ ɪŋ
vaccination ˌvæks ɪ ˈneɪʃ ᵊn -ə- **~s** z

vaccinator ˈvæks ɪ neɪt ə -ə- ‖ -neɪt̬ ᵊr **~s** z
vaccine ˈvæks iːn -ɪn ‖ væk ˈsiːn *(*)* **~s** z
vaccinia væk ˈsɪn i ə
Vachel, Vachell *(i)* ˈveɪtʃ ᵊl, *(ii)* ˈvætʃ ᵊl
Vacher ˈvæʃ ə ‖ -ᵊr
vacherin ˈvæʃ ə ræ̃ -ɪn **~s** z —*Fr* [vaʃ ræ̃]
vacil|late ˈvæs ɪ |leɪt -ə- **~lated** leɪt ɪd -əd
‖ leɪt̬ əd **~lates** leɪts **~lating** leɪt ɪŋ ‖ leɪt̬ ɪŋ
vacillation ˌvæs ɪ ˈleɪʃ ᵊn -ə- **~s** z
Vaclav, Václav ˈvɑːt slɑːv ˈvæt-, -slæv, -slɑːf,
-slæf —*also, by those unfamiliar with the
name,* ˈvɑːk-, ˈvæk- —*Czech* [ˈvɑːts laf]
vactor, VActor *tdmk* ˈvækt ə ‖ -ᵊr **~s** z
vacua ˈvæk ju ə
vacuit|y væ ˈkjuː ət |i və-, ɪt i ‖ -ət̬ |i **~ies** iz
vacuole ˈvæk ju əʊl →-ʊʊl ‖ -oʊl **~s** z
vacuous ˈvæk ju əs **~ly** li **~ness** nəs nɪs
vacuum ˈvæk ju əm ˈvæk jʊm, -juːm **~s** z
ˈvacuum ˌcleaner; ˈvacuum flask; ˈvacuum
pump
vacuum-packed ˌvæk ju əm ˈpækt ◂ ˌjʊm▸,
ˌjuːm▸, ˈ···
ˌvacuum-packed ˈcheese
vade mecum ˌvɑːd i ˈmeɪ kəm ˌwɑːd-, ˌeɪ-,
-kʊm; ˌveɪd i ˈmiː-, -kʌm **~s** z
Vaduz vɑː ˈduːts —*Ger* [fa ˈdʊts, va ˈduːts]
vagabond ˈvæg ə bɒnd ‖ -bɑːnd **~s** z
vagabondage ˈvæg ə bɒnd ɪdʒ ‖ -bɑːnd ɪdʒ
vagal ˈveɪg ᵊl
vagar|y ˈveɪg ər |i ‖ və ˈger |i, -ˈgær- —*in BrE
formerly also* və ˈgeər |i **~ies** iz
vagin|a və ˈdʒaɪn |ə **~ae** iː **~as** əz
vaginal və ˈdʒaɪn ᵊl ˈvædʒ ɪn ᵊl, -ən-
‖ ˈvædʒ ən ᵊl **~ly** i
vaginismus ˌvædʒ ɪ ˈnɪz məs -ə-, -ˈnɪs-
vagotom|y veɪ ˈgɒt əm |i və-, væ- ‖ -ˈgɑːt̬-
~ies iz
vagrancy ˈveɪg rən¹s i
vagrant ˈveɪg rənt **~s** s
vague veɪg **vaguely** ˈveɪg li **vagueness**
ˈveɪg nəs -nɪs **vaguer** ˈveɪg ə ‖ -ᵊr **vaguest**
ˈveɪg ɪst -əst
vagus ˈveɪg əs **vagi** ˈveɪdʒ aɪ ˈveɪg-

Vail, vail veɪ^əl *(= veil)* **vailed** veɪ^əld **vailing**
'veɪ^əl ɪŋ **vails** veɪ^əlz

vain veɪn **vainer** 'veɪn ə ‖ -^ər **vainest** 'veɪn ɪst
-əst

vainglorious ₍₎veɪn 'glɔːr i_əs ‖ -'glʊʊr- **~ly** li
~ness nəs nɪs

vainglor|y ₍₎veɪn 'glɔːr |i ‖ -'glʊʊr-; '·,·· **~ies**
iz

vain|ly 'veɪn |li **~ness** nəs nɪs

Vaizey 'veɪz i

Val væl

valanc|e 'væl ən^ts **~ed** t **~es** ɪz əz

Valda 'væld ə

Valdemar 'væld ə maː -ɪ- ‖ 'vaːld ə maːr
'væld-

Valderma *tdmk* væl 'dɜːm ə ‖ -'dɝːm-

Valderrama ,væl də 'raːm ə ‖ ,vaːl- —*Sp*
[bal de 'rra ma]

Valdez *place in AK* væl 'diːz

Val d'Isère ,væl di 'zeə ‖ -'ze^ər —*Fr*
[val di zɛːʁ]

vale *Latin interj, n 'farewell'* 'vaːl eɪ 'væl-,
'veɪl-, -i

vale *n 'valley'* veɪ^əl **vales** veɪ^əlz

valediction ,væl ɪ 'dɪk ʃ^ən -ə- **~s** z

valedictorian ,væl ɪ dɪk 'tɔːr i_ən ,·ə- ‖ -'tʊʊr-
~s z

valedictor|y ,væl ɪ 'dɪk tər |i ◂ ,·ə- **~ies** iz

valenc|e 'veɪl ən^ts **~es** ɪz əz

Valencia *place in Spain* və 'len^tʃ i_ə -'len^ts-,
-'len^tʃ ə —*Sp* [ba 'len θja]

Valenciennes ,væl ən^ts i 'en ,·ɒ̃s-; və ,len^ts-
‖ -'enz —*Fr* [va lɑ̃ sjɛn]

valenc|y 'veɪl ən^ts |i **~ies** iz

Valency *river; family name* və 'len^ts i

Valentia *island in Ireland* və 'len^tʃ i_ə -'len^tʃ ə

valentine, V~ 'væl ən taɪn -tɪn **~s** z

Valentinian ,væl ən 'tɪn i_ən

Valentino ,væl ən 'tiːn əʊ ‖ -oʊ

Valera və 'lɪər ə -'leər- ‖ 'ler- -'lɪr-

valerian, V~ və 'lɪər i_ən -'leər- ‖ -'lɪr- **~s** z

valeric və 'lɪər ɪk -'leər-, -'ler- ‖ -'lɪr- -'ler-

Valerie 'væl ər_i

Valéry ,væl ə 'ri: -eə-, '··· ‖ ,vaːl-, -e- —*Fr*
[va le ʁi]

valet 'væl ɪt -ət, -eɪ ‖ væ 'leɪ —*The traditional
form with t is rivalled by an imitated French
form in* -eɪ. **valeted** 'væl ɪt ɪd -ət-, -əd;
'væl eɪd ‖ 'væl əṭ əd væ 'leɪd **valeting**
'væl ɪt ɪŋ -ət-, -eɪ- ‖ 'væl əṭ ɪŋ væ 'leɪ ɪŋ
valets 'væl ɪts -əts, -eɪz ‖ væ 'leɪz

valetudinarian ,væl ɪ ,tjuːd ɪ 'neər i_ən ,·ə-,
→-,tʃuːd-, -ə'··-, -^ən 'eər- ‖ -,tuːd ^ən 'er-
-,tjuːd- **~s** z

valetudinary ,væl ɪ 'tjuːd ɪn ər_i ◂ ,·ə-,
→-'tʃuːd-, -'·ən- ‖ -'tuːd ^ən er i -'tjuːd-

valgus 'vælg əs **~es** ɪz əz

Valhalla væl 'hæl ə ‖ vaːl 'haːl ə

valiant 'væl i_ənt ‖ 'væl jənt **~ly** li **~ness** nəs
nɪs

valid 'væl ɪd §-əd **~ly** li **~ness** nəs nɪs

vali|date 'væl ɪ |deɪt -ə- **~dated** deɪt ɪd -əd
‖ deɪṭ əd **~dates** deɪts **~dating** deɪt ɪŋ
‖ deɪṭ ɪŋ

validation ,væl ɪ 'deɪʃ ^ən -ə- **~s** z

validit|y və 'lɪd ət i i væ-, -ɪt i ‖ -əṭ |i **~ies** iz

valis|e və 'liːz væ-, -'liːs ‖ -'liːs **~es** ɪz əz

valium, V~ *tdmk* 'væl i_əm **~s** z

Valkyrie 'vælk ər i -ɪr-, -ɪər-; væl 'kɪr i, -'kɪər-,
-'kaɪ^ər- ‖ væl 'kɪr i 'vælk ər i **~s** z

Valladolid ,væl ə dəʊ 'lɪd ‖ -doʊ '· —*Sp*
[ba ʎa ðo 'lið, -ja-]

Vallance, Vallans 'væl ən^ts

Valle Crucis ,væl i 'kruːs ɪs

Vallee 'væl i

Vallejo *place in CA* və 'leɪ əʊ væ-, -həʊ ‖ -oʊ
-hoʊ

Valletta və 'let ə

valley, V~ 'væl i **~s** z

Vallins 'væl ɪnz §-ənz

vallum 'væl əm

Valois 'væl waː ‖ væl 'waː —*Fr* [va lwa] —*but
the place in NY is* və 'lɔɪs

valor, Valor *tdmk* 'væl ə ‖ -^ər

valoris... —*see* **valoriz...**

valorization ,væl ər aɪ 'zeɪʃ ^ən -ɪ'- ‖ -ə'--

valoriz|e 'væl ə raɪz **~ed** d **~es** ɪz əz **~ing** ɪŋ

valorous 'væl ər əs **~ly** li **~ness** nəs nɪs

valour 'væl ə ‖ -^ər

Valparaiso *place in IN* ,væl pə 'reɪz əʊ ‖ -oʊ

Valparaiso *place in Chile* ,væl pə 'raɪz əʊ
-'reɪz- ‖ -oʊ —*Sp* Valparaíso [bal pa ɾa 'i so]

Valpeda *tdmk* væl 'piːd ə

Valpolicella, v~ ,væl pɒl i 'tʃel ə ‖ ,vaːl poʊl-
—*It* [val po li 'tʃel la]

valse vaːls væls, vɔːls **valses** 'vaːls ɪz 'væls-,
'vɔːls-, -əz

valuable 'væl jʊb ^əl -ju,əb ^əl ‖ -jəb- **~ness** nəs
nɪs **~s** z

valuation ,væl ju 'eɪʃ ^ən **~s** z

value 'væl ju: -ju **~d** d **~s** z **valuing** 'væl juː ɪŋ
 'value ˌjudgment

value-added ,væl ju: 'æd ɪd ◂ -əd
 ,value-'added tax, ·,·,·· '·

valueless 'væl ju ləs -lɪs

valuer 'væl ju_ə ‖ ^ər **~s** z

Valujet *tdmk* 'væl ju dʒet

valvate 'vælv eɪt

valve vælv **valved** vælvd **valves** vælvz

Valvoline *tdmk* 'vælv ə liːn

valvular 'vælv jʊl ə -jəl- ‖ -jəl ^ər

vamoos|e və 'muːs væ- **~ed** t **~es** ɪz əz **~ing**
ɪŋ

vamp væmp **vamped** væmpt **vamping**
'væmp ɪŋ **vamps** væmps

vampire 'væmp aɪ_ə ‖ -aɪ_^ər **~s** z
 'vampire ˌbat

vampirism 'væmp aɪ_ər ,ɪz əm ‖ -aɪ_^ər-

vampish 'væmp ɪʃ **~ness** nəs nɪs

van, Van væn **vans** vænz

vanadate 'væn ə deɪt **~s** s

vanadic və 'næd ɪk -'neɪd-

vanadinite və 'næd ɪ naɪt -'neɪd-, -ə-, -^ən aɪt

vanadium və 'neɪd i_əm

vanadous 'væn əd əs və 'neɪd-
Van Allen væn 'æl ən
Vananchal və 'nɑːntʃ əl
Vanbrugh 'væn brə →'væm- ‖ væn 'bruː
Van Buren væn 'bjʊər ən ‖ -'bjʊr- -'bjɜː-
Vance vænˡs vɑːnˡs
Van Cleef væn 'kliːf
vancomycin ˌvæŋk əʊ 'maɪs ɪn -ᵊn
‖ -ə maɪs ᵊn
Vancouver væn 'kuːv ə →væŋ- ‖ -ᵊr
vandal, V~ 'vænd ᵊl ~s z
Vandalia væn 'deɪl i ə ‖ -'deɪl jə
vandalis... —see vandaliz...
vandalism 'vænd ə ˌlɪz əm -ᵊl ˌɪz-
vandaliz|e 'vænd ə laɪz -ᵊl aɪz ~ed d ~es ɪz əz
~ing ɪŋ
Van de Graaff ˌvæn də 'grɑːf ◂ -'græf ‖ -'græf
ˌVan de ˌGraaff 'generator
Vandenberg, Van den Bergh 'vænd ən bɜːg
→-əm- ‖ -bɜːɡ
Vanden Plas ˌvænd ən 'plæs →-əm-, -'plɑːs
Vanderbilt 'vænd ə bɪlt ‖ -ᵊr-
Vanderbyl 'vænd ə baɪᵊl ‖ -ᵊr-
van der Post ˌvæn də 'pɒst ‖ -dᵊr 'pɑːst
Van der Waals ˌvæn də 'wɑːlz ◂ ‖ -dᵊr- -'wɔːlz
—Dutch [vɑn dər 'wɑːls]
ˌVan der ˌWaals 'forces
Van Diemen ₍ᵢ₎væn 'diːm ən
Van Dyck, Vandyke, v~ ₍ᵢ₎væn 'daɪk
vane, Vane veɪn (= vain) vanes veɪnz
Vanessa və 'nes ə
Van Eyck væn 'aɪk
vang væŋ vangs væŋz
Van Gogh væn 'gɒf →væŋ-, -'gɒx ‖ -'goʊ
—Dutch [vɑn 'xɔx]
vanguard 'væn gɑːd →'væŋ- ‖ -gɑːrd ~s z
vanilla və 'nɪl ə ‖ -'nel- ~s z
vanillin və 'nɪl ɪn §-ən; 'væn əl-, -ɪl-
vanish 'væn ɪʃ ~ed t ~es ɪz əz ~ing/ly ɪŋ /li
'vanishing point
vanitory, V~ tdmk 'væn ət ᵊr i 'ɪt ˌ ‖ -ə tɔːr i
-toʊr i
vanit|y 'væn ət |i -ɪt- ‖ -əṭ |i ~ies iz
Van Nuys væ 'naɪz væn-
vanquish 'væŋk wɪʃ ‖ 'væn kwɪʃ ~ed t ~es ɪz
əz ~ing ɪŋ
Vansittart væn 'sɪt ət ‖ -'sɪṭ ᵊrt
van Straubenzee ˌvæn strɔː 'benz i ‖ -strɑː-
vantage 'vɑːnt ɪdʒ §'vænt- ‖ 'vænṭ ɪdʒ
vantagepoint 'vɑːnt ɪdʒ pɔɪnt §'vænt-
‖ 'vænṭ- ~s s
Vanuatu ˌvæn u 'ɑːt uː -'æt-; ˌvæn ə 'wɑːt uː;
'· · · · ‖ ˌvɑːn-
Van Winkle væn 'wɪŋk ᵊl
Van Wyck væn 'waɪk ‖ -'wɪk
Van ˌWyck Ex'pressway
Vanya 'vɑːn jə væn-
Vanzetti væn 'zet i ‖ -'zeṭ i
vapid 'væp ɪd §-əd ~ly li ~ness nəs nɪs
vapidity væ 'pɪd ət i və-, -ɪt- ‖ -əṭ i
vapor... —see vapour...
vaporett|o ˌvæp ə 'ret |əʊ ‖ -'reṭ |oʊ ~i iː ~os
əʊz ‖ oʊz —It [va po 'ret to, -ti]

vaporis... —see vaporiz...
vaporization ˌveɪp ər aɪ 'zeɪʃ ᵊn -ɪ'·- ‖ -ə'·-
vaporiz|e 'veɪp ə raɪz ~ed d ~er/s ə/z ‖ ᵊr/z
~es ɪz əz ~ing ɪŋ
vaporous 'veɪp ər əs ~ly li ~ness nəs nɪs
vapour 'veɪp ə ‖ -ᵊr ~ed d vapouring/s
'veɪp ər ɪŋ/z ~s z
'vapour trail
vapourer 'veɪp ər ə ‖ -ᵊr ər ~s z
vapourware 'veɪp ə weə ‖ -ᵊr weᵊr -ᵊr wæᵊr
vapoury 'veɪp ər i
Varah 'vɑːr ə
Varangian və 'rændʒ i ən ~s z
Varden 'vɑːd ᵊn ‖ 'vɑːrd ᵊn
varec 'vær ek -ɪk
Varèse və 'rez
varia 'veər i ə ‖ 'ver- 'vær-
variability ˌveər i ə 'bɪl ət i -ɪt i
‖ ˌver i ə 'bɪl əṭ i ˌvær-
variab|le 'veər i əb |ᵊl ‖ 'ver- 'vær- ~les ᵊlz
~ly li
varianc|e 'veər i ənˡs ‖ 'ver- 'vær- ~es ɪz əz
variant 'veər i ənt ‖ 'ver- 'vær- ~s s
variate 'veər i ət ɪt, -eɪt ‖ 'ver- 'vær- ~s s
variation ˌveər i 'eɪʃ ᵊn ‖ ˌver- ˌvær- ~s z
variational ˌveər i 'eɪʃ ᵊn ᵊl ◂ ‖ ˌver- ˌvær- ~ly
i
variationist ˌveər i 'eɪʃ ᵊn ɪst §ˌəst ‖ ˌver-
ˌvær- ~s s
varicella ˌvær i 'sel ə ‖ ˌver-
varices 'vær ɪ siːz 'veər-, -ə- ‖ 'ver-
varicocele 'vær ɪ kəʊ siːᵊl '·ə- ‖ -ə koʊ siːᵊl
'ver- ~s z
varicolored, varicoloured 'veər i ˌkʌl əd
‖ 'ver i ˌkʌl ᵊrd 'vær-
varicose 'vær ɪ kəʊs -ə-, -kəʊz, -kəs ‖ -ə koʊs
'ver-
ˌvaricose 'veins
varicosit|y ˌvær ɪ 'kɒs ət |i ˌ·ə-, -ɪt i
‖ -ə 'kɑːs əṭ |i ˌver- ~ies iz
varicotom|y ˌvær ɪ 'kɒt əm |i ˌ·ə- ‖ -ə 'kɑːṭ-
ˌver- ~ies iz
varied 'veər id ‖ 'ver id 'vær- ~ly li
variegated 'veər i ə geɪt ɪd '·ɪ ·· , -əd;
'·ɪ geɪt ·, '·ə- ‖ 'ver ɪ geɪṭ əd 'vær-, '·i ə ··
variegation ˌveər i ə 'geɪʃ ᵊn ˌ·ɪ ·· ·; ˌ·ɪ' ··, ˌ·ə' ··
‖ ˌver i 'geɪʃ ᵊn ˌvær-, ˌ·iˌə' ··
varietal və 'raɪ ət ᵊl ɪt- ‖ -əṭ ᵊl ~ly i
variet|y və 'raɪ ət |i ɪt- ‖ -'raɪ əṭ |i ~ies iz
va'riety show; va'riety store
varifocal 'veər i fəʊk ᵊl ˌ·'·· ‖ 'ver i foʊk ᵊl
ˌ·'·· ~s z
variform 'veər ɪ fɔːm -ə- ‖ 'ver i fɔːrm 'vær-
Varig tdmk 'vær ɪg ‖ 'ver-
variola və 'raɪ əl ə ‖ ˌver i 'oʊl ə
variolate 'veər i ə leɪt ‖ 'ver- 'vær-
variolite 'veər i ə laɪt ‖ 'ver- 'vær-
variometer ˌveər i 'ɒm ɪt ə -ət ə
‖ ˌver i 'ɑːm əṭ ᵊr ˌvær- ~s z
variorum ˌveər i 'ɔːr əm ˌvær- ‖ ˌver- ˌvær-,
-'oʊr-
various 'veər i əs ‖ 'ver i əs 'vær- ~ly li ~ness
nəs nɪs

V

variphone 'veər i fəʊn ‖ 'ver i foʊn 'vær- ~s z
Varityper _tdmk_ 'veər i taɪp ə ‖ 'ver i taɪp ᵊr 'vær- ~s z
varix 'veər ɪks ‖ 'ver- 'vær- **varices** 'vær ɪ siːz 'veər-, -ə- ‖ 'ver-
varlet 'vɑːl ət -ɪt ‖ 'vɑːrl ət ~s s
Varley 'vɑːl i ‖ 'vɑːrl i
varmint 'vɑːm ɪnt -ənt ‖ 'vɑːrm- ~s s
Varney 'vɑːn i ‖ 'vɑːrn i
varnish 'vɑːn ɪʃ ‖ 'vɑːrn ɪʃ ~ed t ~es ɪz əz ~ing ɪŋ
Varro 'vær əʊ ‖ -oʊ 'ver-
varroa və 'rəʊ ə 'vær əʊ ə ‖ -'roʊ-
varsit|y 'vɑːs ət |i -ɪt- ‖ 'vɑːrs ə̯t |i ~ies iz
Varteg 'vɑːt eg ‖ 'vɑːrt-
varus 'veər əs ‖ 'ver əs 'vær- ~es ɪz əz
varve vɑːv ‖ vɑːrv **varves** vɑːvz ‖ vɑːrvz
var|y 'veər |i ‖ 'ver |i 'vær- ~ied id ~ies iz ~ying i ɪŋ
vas væs vɑːs **vasa** 'veɪz ə 'vɑːz-, 'veɪs-, 'vɑːs-
 ˌvas 'deferens 'def ə renz
Vasco da Gama ˌvæsk əʊ də 'gɑːm ə ‖ ˌvɑːsk oʊ- -'gæm- —_Port_ [ˌvaʃ ku ðɐ 'ɣɐ mɐ]
vascul|um 'væsk jʊl |əm -jəl- ‖ -jəl |əm ~a ə ~ar ə ‖ ᵊr
vase vɑːz ‖ veɪs veɪz (*)—_in BrE formerly also_ vɔːz **vases** 'vɑːz ɪz -əz ‖ 'veɪs əz 'veɪz-
vasectom|y və 'sekt əm |i væ- ~ies iz
vaseline, V~ _tdmk_ 'væs ə liːn 'væz-, -ɪ-, -ᵊl iːn, ˌ·ᵊ'·.
Vashti 'væʃt aɪ
vasoconstriction ˌveɪz əʊ kən 'strɪk ʃᵊn §-kɒn'·- ‖ ˌ·oʊ-
vasoconstrictor ˌveɪz əʊ kən 'strɪkt ə §-kɒn'·- ‖ -oʊ kən 'strɪkt ᵊr ~s z
vasodilator ˌveɪz əʊ daɪ 'leɪt ə ‖ -oʊ daɪ 'leɪt ᵊr -də'·-; -'daɪl eɪt ᵊr ~s z
vasomotor ˌveɪz əʊ 'məʊt ə ◂ ‖ -oʊ 'moʊt̯ ᵊr ˌvæs-, -ə-
vasopressin ˌveɪz əʊ 'pres ɪn §-ᵊn ‖ -oʊ- ˌvæs-
vassal, V~ 'væs ᵊl ~s z
vassalage 'væs ᵊl ɪdʒ
Vassar 'væs ə ‖ -ᵊr
vast vɑːst §væst ‖ væst **vaster** 'vɑːst ə §'væst- ‖ 'væst ᵊr **vastest** 'vɑːst ɪst §'væst-, -əst ‖ 'væst əst
vast|ly 'vɑːst |li §'væst- ‖ 'væst |li ~ness/es nəs ɪz nɪs-, -əz
vat væt **vats** væts
VAT ˌviː eɪ 'tiː væt —_But as an informal verb, always_ væt **VAT'd** 'væt ɪd -əd ‖ 'væt̯ əd **VAT'ing** 'væt ɪŋ ‖ 'væt̯ ɪŋ **VAT's** væts
VATable 'væt əb ᵊl ‖ 'væt̯-
Vatersay 'væt ə seɪ ‖ 'væt̯ ᵊr-
Vathek 'vɑːθ ek ‖ 'væθ-
vatic 'væt ɪk ‖ 'væt̯ ɪk
Vatican 'væt ɪk ən ‖ 'væt̯- ˌVatican 'City
vatici|nate væ 'tɪs ɪ |neɪt -ə-, -ᵊ|n eɪt ‖ -ᵊ|n eɪt ~nated neɪt ɪd -əd ‖ neɪt̯ əd ~nates neɪts ~nating neɪt ɪŋ ‖ neɪt̯ ɪŋ
vaticination ˌvæt ɪs ɪ 'neɪʃ ᵊn ˌ·əs-; væ ˌtɪs-, və- ‖ və ˌtɪs- ˌvæt̯ əs- ~s z
VAT|man 'væt mæn ~men men
Vaucluse vəʊ 'kluːz ‖ voʊ- —_Fr_ [vo kly:z]
vaudeville 'vɔːd ə vɪl 'vəʊd-; '·vɪl, -vᵊl ‖ 'vɑːd-
Vaughan, Vaughn vɔːn ‖ vɑːn ˌVaughan 'Williams
vault vɔːlt ‖ vɑːlt **vaulted** 'vɔːlt ɪd vɒlt-, -əd ‖ 'vɑːlt- **vaulting** 'vɔːlt ɪŋ vɒlt- ‖ 'vɑːlt- **vaults** vɔːlts vɒlts ‖ vɑːlts 'vaulting horse
vaunt vɔːnt ‖ vɑːnt **vaunted** 'vɔːnt ɪd -əd ‖ 'vɔːnt̯ əd 'vɑːnt̯- **vaunting/ly** 'vɔːnt ɪŋ /li ‖ 'vɔːnt̯ ɪŋ /li 'vɑːnt̯- **vaunts** vɔːnts ‖ vɑːnts
Vaux (i) vɔːks ‖ vɑːks, (ii) vəʊ ‖ voʊ, (iii) vɒks ‖ vɑːks
Vauxhall 'vɒks ɔːl -hɔːl; vɒk 'sɔːl, ˌvɒks 'hɔːl ‖ 'vɑːks- 'vɔːks-, -ɑːl, -hɔːl, -hɑːl
vavasor, vavasour, V~ 'væv ə sɔː -sʊə, -əs ə ‖ -sɔːr -soʊr ~s z
Vavasseur ˌvæv ə 'sɜː ‖ -'sɜːr
va-va-voom ˌvæv ə 'vuːm ˌvɑː vɑː-
VAX _tdmk_ væks
Vaz væz
VC ˌviː 'siː ~s, ~'s z
V-chip 'viː tʃɪp ~s s
vCJD ˌviː siː dʒeɪ 'diː
VCR ˌviː siː 'ɑː ‖ -'ɑːr ~s, ~'s z
VD ˌviː 'diː
VDT ˌviː diː 'tiː ~s z
VDU, vdu ˌviː diː 'juː ~s z
've əv —_but after a pronoun ending in a vowel sound,_ v — _some've done it_ ˌsʌm əv 'dʌn ɪt, _they've tried_ ˌðeɪv 'traɪd
veal, Veal viːᵊl
Veblen 'veb lən
Vectis 'vekt ɪs §-əs
vector 'vekt ə ‖ -ᵊr ~ed d **vectoring** 'vekt ər ɪŋ ~s z
vectorial vek 'tɔːr i ᵊl ‖ -'toʊr-
Vectra _tdmk_ 'vek trə
Veda 'veɪd ə 'viːd- ~s z
Vedanta vɪ 'dɑːnt ə ve-, veɪ-, və-, -'dænt- —_Hindi_ [veː ɖaːn̪t]
Vedda 'ved ə ~s z
vedette vɪ 'det və- ~s s
Vedic 'veɪd ɪk ‖ 'viːd-
veejay 'viː dʒeɪ ~s z
veep viːp **veeps** viːps
veer vɪə ‖ vɪᵊr **veered** vɪəd ‖ vɪᵊrd **veering** 'vɪər ɪŋ ‖ 'vɪr ɪŋ **veers** vɪəz ‖ vɪᵊrz
veg vedʒ
Vega _name of star_ 'viːg ə 'veɪg-
Vega _Spanish name_ 'veɪg ə —_Sp_ ['be ɣa]
vegan 'viːg ən ~ism ˌɪz əm ~s z
Veganin _tdmk_ 'vedʒ ən ɪn §-ən
Vegas 'veɪg əs
vegeburger 'vedʒ i ˌbɜːg ə ‖ -bɜːg ᵊr ~s z
vegemite, V~ _tdmk_ 'vedʒ ə maɪt -ɪ-
vegetable 'vedʒ təb ᵊl 'vedʒ ət əb ᵊl, '·ɪt- ‖ -ət̯ əb ᵊl ~s z
 'vegetable knife; ˌvegetable 'marrow
vegetal 'vedʒ ɪt ᵊl -ət- ‖ -ət̯ ᵊl

vegetarian ˌvedʒ ə 'teər i ˌən ◂ ˌ·ɪ- ‖ -'ter-
-'tær- **~ism** ˌɪz əm **~s** s

vege|tate 'vedʒ ə |teɪt -ɪ- **~tated** teɪt ɪd -əd
‖ teɪt̬ əd **~tates** teɪts **~tating** teɪt ɪŋ ‖ teɪt̬ ɪŋ

vegetation ˌvedʒ ə 'teɪʃ ᵊn -ɪ-

vegetative 'vedʒ ət ət ɪv -'·ɪt-; -ə teɪt-, -ɪ teɪt-
-ə teɪt̬ ɪv **~ly** li **~ness** nəs nɪs

veggie, veggy, vegie 'vedʒ i **~s** z

veggieburger 'vedʒ i ˌbɜːg ə ‖ -bɝːg ᵊr **~s** z

vehemence 'viː əm ən⌐s 'veɪ-, ˌɪm-, -həm-,
-hɪm-

vehement 'viː əm ənt 'veɪ-, ˌɪm-, -həm-, -hɪm-
~ly li

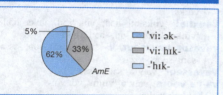

VEHICLE

5% ↓ 62% 33% ▭ 'viː ək-
▭ 'viː hɪk-
▭ -'hɪk-

AmE

vehicle 'viː ˌɪk ᵊl ˌək-, §-hɪk- ‖ 'viː ək ᵊl -hɪk-,
·'hɪk· — *Preference poll, AmE:* 'viː ək- *62%,*
'viː hɪk- *33%;* -'hɪk- *5%.* **~s** z

vehicular vɪ 'hɪk jʊl ə və-, viː-, -jəl-
‖ vɪ 'hɪk jəl ᵊr

veil verᵊl (= *vale*) **veiled** verᵊld **veiling**
'verᵊl ɪŋ **veils** veɪlz

vein veɪn (= *vain*) **veined** veɪnd **veining**
'veɪn ɪŋ **veins** veɪnz

vela, Vela 'viːl ə

velar 'viːl ə ‖ -ᵊr **~s** z

velaric viː 'lær ɪk vɪ- ‖ -'ler-

velaris... —*see* **velariz...**

velarity viː 'lær ət i vɪ-, -ɪt- ‖ -ət̬ i -'ler-

velarization ˌviːl ər aɪ 'zeɪʃ ᵊn -ɪ'·- ‖ -ə'·-

velariz|e 'viːl ə raɪz **~ed** d **~es** ɪz əz **~ing** ɪŋ
ɪz

Velasquez, Velázquez vɪ 'læsk wɪz və-, ve-,
-ɪz, -wez, -wɪθ ‖ və 'lɑːsk eɪs -'læsk-, -əs —*Sp*
[be 'las keθ, -'laθ-]

Velcro *tdmk,* **v~** 'vel krəʊ ‖ -kroʊ **~ed** d

veld, veldt velt felt

veleta və 'liːt ə vɪ- ‖ -'liːt̬ ə **~s** z

Velia 'viːl i ə

velic 'viːl ɪk

Velindre ve 'lɪn dreɪ -'lɪndr ə

velleit|y ve 'liː ət i və-, -ɪt- ‖ -ət̬ i **~ies** iz

vellum 'vel əm

Velma 'velm ə

velocipede və 'lɒs ə piːd vɪ-, -ɪ- ‖ -'lɑːs- **~s** z

velociraptor və ˌlɒs ɪ 'ræpt ə vɪ-, -ə-; ·'····
‖ -ˌlɑːs ə 'ræpt ᵊr ·'····**~s** z

velocit|y və 'lɒs ət i vɪ-, -ɪt- ‖ -'lɑːs ət̬ i **~ies**
iz

velodrome 'vel ə drəʊm 'viːl- ‖ -droʊm **~s** z

velour, velours və 'lʊə ve- ‖ -'lʊᵊr

veloute, velouté və 'luːt eɪ ve- ‖ və ˌluː 'teɪ

velum 'viːl əm **vela** 'viːl ə

Velux *tdmk* 'viː lʌks

Velveeta *tdmk* vel 'viːt ə ‖ -'viːt̬ ə

velvet 'velv ɪt §-ət **~s** s

velveteen ˌvelv ə 'tiːn -ɪ-, '····**~s** z

velvety 'velv ət i -ɪt- ‖ -ət̬ i

vena 'viːn ə **venae** 'viːn iː
ˌvena 'cava 'keɪv ə

Venable 'ven əb ᵊl

Venables 'ven əb ᵊlz

venal 'viːn ᵊl **~ly** i

venality viː 'næl ət i vɪ-, -ɪt- ‖ -ət̬ i

vend vend **vended** 'vend ɪd -əd **vending**
'vend ɪŋ **vends** vendz
'vending maˌchine

Venda 'vend ə

vendace 'vend ɪs -əs, -eɪs

vendee ˌven 'diː **~s** z

vender 'vend ə ‖ -ᵊr **~s** z

vendetta ven 'det ə ‖ -'det̬ ə **~s** z

vendor 'vend ə ‖ -ᵊr —*for contrast also*
-ɔː ‖ -ɔːr, *or* ˌven 'dɔː ‖ -'dɔːr **~s** z

veneer və 'nɪə vɪ- ‖ -'nɪᵊr **~ed** d **veneering**
və 'nɪər ɪŋ vɪ- ‖ -'nɪr ɪŋ **~s** z

venerab|le 'ven ᵊr_əb ᵊl **~leness** ᵊl nəs -nɪs
~ly li

vene|rate 'ven ə |reɪt **~rated** reɪt ɪd -əd
‖ reɪt̬ əd **~rates** reɪts **~rating** reɪt ɪŋ ‖ reɪt̬ ɪŋ

veneration ˌven ə 'reɪʃ ᵊn

venerator 'ven ə reɪt ə ‖ -reɪt̬ ᵊr **~s** z

venereal və 'nɪər i_əl vɪ- ‖ -'nɪr-
veˌnereal di'sease, ·'···· ·ˌ·

venereologist və ˌnɪər i 'ɒl ədʒ ɪst vɪ-, §-əst
‖ -ˌnɪr i 'ɑːl- **~s** s

venereology və ˌnɪər i 'ɒl ədʒ i vɪ-
‖ -ˌnɪr i 'ɑːl-

venery 'ven ᵊr i 'viːn-

Veness və 'nes vɪ-

Venetia və 'niːʃ ə vɪ-, -'niːʃ i_ə

Venetian, v~ və 'niːʃ ᵊn vɪ-, -'niːʃ i_ən **~s** z
veˌnetian 'blind

Venetic və 'net ɪk vɪ-, ve- ‖ -'net̬ ɪk

Venezuel|a ˌven ə 'zweɪl |ə -ɪ-, -e- —*AmSp*
[be ne 'swe la] **~an/s** ən/z

vengeance 'vendʒ ən⌐s

vengeful 'vendʒ fᵊl -fʊl **~ly** i **~ness** nəs nɪs

veni, vidi, vici ˌveɪn iː ˌviːd iː 'viːk iː -'viːtʃ i;
ˌweɪn i ˌwiːd i 'wiːk i

venial 'viːn i_əl **~ly** i **~ness** nəs nɪs

veniality ˌviːn i 'æl ət i -ɪt i ‖ -ət̬ i

Venice 'ven ɪs §-əs

venison 'ven ɪs ᵊn -əs-, -ɪz-, -əz-; 'venz ᵊn

Venite və 'naɪt i vɪ-, ve-, -'niːt eɪ ‖ -'naɪt̬ i
-'niːt eɪ

Venn ven

Venner 'ven ə ‖ -ᵊr

venom 'ven əm

venomous 'ven əm əs **~ly** li **~ness** nəs nɪs

Veno's *tdmk* 'viːn əʊz ‖ -oʊz

venous 'viːn əs **~ly** li

vent vent **vented** 'vent ɪd -əd ‖ 'vent̬ əd
venting 'vent ɪŋ ‖ 'vent̬ ɪŋ **vents** ven ts

Vent-Axia *tdmk* ˌvent 'æks i_ə

Venter 'vent ə ‖ 'vent̬ ᵊr

venti|late 'vent ɪ |leɪt -ə-, -ᵊl ‖ eɪt
‖ 'vent̬ ᵊl ‖ eɪt **~lated** leɪt ɪd -əd ‖ leɪt̬ əd
~lates leɪts **~lating** leɪt ɪŋ ‖ leɪt̬ ɪŋ

ventilation ˌvent ɪ ˈleɪʃ ᵊn -ə-, -ᵊl ˈeɪʃ-
‖ ˌvenṯ ᵊl ˈeɪʃ ᵊn
ventilator ˈvent ɪ leɪt ə -ə-, -ᵊl eɪt-
‖ ˈvenṯ ᵊl eɪṯ ᵊr ~s z
Ventnor ˈvent nə ‖ -nᵊr
Ventolin tdmk ˈvent əʊ lɪn -ᵊl ɪn, §-ən
‖ ˈvenṯ ᵊl ən
ventral ˈventr əl ~ly i
ventricle ˈventr ɪk ᵊl ~s z
ventricular ven ˈtrɪk jʊl ə vən-, -jəl- ‖ -jəl ᵊr
ventriloquial ˌventr ɪ ˈləʊk wi̯ əl ◂ ˌ-ə-
‖ -ˈloʊk-
ventriloquism ven ˈtrɪl ə ˌkwɪz əm
ventriloquist ven ˈtrɪl ək wɪst §-wəst ~s s
ventriloquy ven ˈtrɪl ək wi
Ventris ˈventr ɪs §-əs
Ventura ven ˈtjʊər ə →-ˈtʃʊər ə ‖ -ˈtʊr ə
-ˈtjʊr ə
venture, V~ ˈventʃ ə ‖ -ᵊr ~d d ~s z
   venturing ˈventʃ ər ɪŋ
   ˈventure ˌcapital
venturer ˈventʃ ər ə ‖ -ᵊr ᵊr ~s z
venturesome ˈventʃ ə səm ‖ -ᵊr- ~ly li ~ness
   nəs nɪs
Venturi, v~ ven ˈtjʊər i →-ˈtʃʊər i ‖ -ˈtʊr i ~s
   z
   venˈturi tube
venturous ˈventʃ ər_əs ~ly li ~ness nəs nɪs
venue ˈven juː ~s z
venule ˈven juːl ˈviːn- ~s z
Venus ˈviːn əs ~es, ~'s ɪz əz
   ˌVenus('s) ˈflytrap
Venusian və ˈnjuːz i̯ ən vɪ-, -ˈnjuːs- ‖ -ˈnuːʒ ᵊn
   -ˈnuːʃ-, -ˈnjuːʒ-, -ˈnjuːʃ-, -ˈ·i̯ ən ~s z
Vera ˈvɪər ə ‖ ˈvɪr ə
veracious və ˈreɪʃ əs vɪ-, ve- ~ly li ~ness nəs
   nɪs
veracit|y və ˈræs ət |i vɪ-, ve-, -ɪt- ‖ -əṯ |i ~ies
   iz
Veracruz, Vera Cruz ˌvɪər ə ˈkruːz ˌver-,
   ˌveər- ‖ ˌver- —AmSp [ˌbe ɾa ˈkɾus]
veranda, verandah və ˈrænd ə ~ed d ~s z
verb vɜːb ‖ vɝːb **verbs** vɜːbz ‖ vɝːbz
verbal ˈvɜːb ᵊl ‖ ˈvɝːb ᵊl ~ed, ~led d ~ing,
   ~ling ɪŋ ~ly i ~s z
   ˌverbal ˈnoun
verbalis... —see **verbaliz...**
verbalism ˈvɜːb ə ˌlɪz əm -ᵊl ˌɪz- ‖ ˈvɝːb-
verbalization ˌvɜːb əl aɪ ˈzeɪʃ ᵊn -ɪ'-
   ‖ ˌvɝːb əl ə- ~s z
verbaliz|e ˈvɜːb ə laɪz -ᵊl aɪz ‖ ˈvɝːb- ~ed d
   ~es ɪz əz ~ing ɪŋ
verbatim vɜː ˈbeɪt ɪm -ˈbɑːt-, §-əm
   ‖ vɝː ˈbeɪṯ əm -ɪm
verbena vɜː ˈbiːn ə və- ‖ vɝː-
verbiage ˈvɜːb i ɪdʒ ‖ ˈvɝːb-
verbose və ˈbəʊs ‖ vɝː ˈboʊs ~ly li ~ness nəs
   nɪs
verbosity vɜː ˈbɒs ət i -ɪt- ‖ vɝː ˈbɑːs əṯ i
verboten fə ˈbəʊt ᵊn və- ‖ fᵊr ˈboʊt ᵊn vᵊr-
   —Ger [fɛɐ ˈbo: t̩n]
Vercingetorix ˌvɜːs ɪn ˈdʒet ə rɪks ˌ-ᵊn-, -ˈget-
   ‖ ˌvɝːs ᵊn ˈdʒet- -ˈget-

verd vɜːd ‖ vɝːd
verdancy ˈvɜːd ᵊn̩ts i ‖ ˈvɝːd-
verdant ˈvɜːd ᵊnt ‖ ˈvɝːd- ~ly li
Verde (i) vɜːd veəd ‖ vɝːd, (ii) ˈvɜːd i ˈveəd i
   ‖ ˈvɝːd i ˈverd i — Cape Verde and its islands
   are (i), or an imitation of the Portuguese
   form; the river in AZ is (ii). —Port [ˈver də]
Verdean ˈvɜːd i̯ ən ˈveəd- ‖ ˈvɝːd- ~s z
verderer ˈvɜːd ər ə ‖ ˈvɝːd ᵊr ᵊr ~s z
Verdi ˈveəd i ‖ ˈverd i —It [ˈver di]
verdict ˈvɜːd ɪkt ‖ ˈvɝːd- ~s s
verdigris ˈvɜːd ɪ griː -ə-, -griːs, -grɪs
   ‖ ˈvɝːd ə grɪs -griːs
Verdun vɜː ˈdʌn ‖ vɝː- —Fr [vɛʁ dœ̃, -dæ̃]
verdure ˈvɜːdʒ ə ˈvɜːd jə, -jʊə ‖ ˈvɝːdʒ ᵊr
   (usually = verger)
Vere vɪə ‖ vɪᵊr
verge vɜːdʒ ‖ vɝːdʒ **verged** vɜːdʒd ‖ vɝːdʒd
   verges ˈvɜːdʒ ɪz -əz ‖ ˈvɝːdʒ əz **verging**
   ˈvɜːdʒ ɪŋ ‖ ˈvɝːdʒ ɪŋ
verger ˈvɜːdʒ ə ‖ ˈvɝːdʒ ᵊr ~s z
Vergil ˈvɜːdʒ ɪl -əl ‖ ˈvɝːdʒ əl
Vergilian vɜː ˈdʒɪl i̯ ən və- ‖ vɝː-
veridical və ˈrɪd ɪk ᵊl ve-, vɪ- ~ly ˌi
veridicality və ˌrɪd ɪ ˈkæl ət i ve-, vɪ-, §-ˌ-ə-,
   -ɪt i ‖ -əṯ i
veriest ˈver i̯ ɪst əst
verifiab|le ˈver ɪ faɪ əb |ᵊl ˈ·ə-, ˌ·ˈ·· ~ly li
verification ˌver ɪf ɪ ˈkeɪʃ ᵊn ˌ·əf-, §-əˈ-- ~s z
veri|fy ˈver ɪ |faɪ -ə- ~fied faɪd ~fier/s faɪ ə/z
   ‖ faɪ ᵊr/z ~fies faɪz ~fying faɪ ɪŋ
verily ˈver əl i -ɪ li
verisimilitude ˌver ɪ sɪ ˈmɪl ɪ tjuːd ˌ·ə-, ˌ·i-,
   -sə'--, -ˌ·ə-, →-tʃuːd ‖ -tuːd -tjuːd
verismo ve ˈrɪz məʊ və-, -ˈriːz- ‖ -moʊ —It
   [ve ˈriz mo]
veritab|le ˈver ɪt əb |ᵊl ˈ·ət- ‖ ˈ·əṯ- ~leness
   ᵊl nəs -nɪs ~ly li
verit|y, V~ ˈver ət |i -ɪt- ‖ -əṯ |i ~ies iz
Verizon tdmk və ˈraɪz ᵊn
verjuice ˈvɜː dʒuːs ‖ ˈvɝː-
verkrampte fə ˈkræmpt ə ‖ fᵊr- —Afrikaans
   [fər ˈkram tə] ~s z
Verlaine və ˈleɪn veə- ‖ vᵊr- ver- —Fr [vɛʁ lɛn]
verligte fə ˈlɪxt ə ‖ fᵊr ˈlɪkt ə —Afrikaans
   [fər ˈləx tə] ~s z
Vermeer və ˈmɪə vɜː-, -ˈmeə ‖ vᵊr ˈmɪᵊr
   —Dutch [vər ˈmeːr] ~s z
vermeil ˈvɜːm eɪ₋ᵊl -ɪl, §-ᵊl ‖ ˈvɝːm-
vermicelli ˌvɜːm ɪ ˈtʃel i -ə-, -ˈsel- ‖ ˌvɝːm-
vermicide ˈvɜːm ɪ saɪd -ə- ‖ ˈvɝːm- ~s z
vermiculate vɜː ˈmɪk ju leɪt və-, -jə-
   ‖ vɝː ˈmɪk jə-
vermiculite vɜː ˈmɪk ju laɪt və-, -jə-
   ‖ vɝː ˈmɪk jə-
vermiform ˈvɜːm ɪ fɔːm §-ə- ‖ ˈvɝːm ə fɔːrm
   ˌvermiform apˈpendix
vermifug|e ˈvɜːm ɪ fjuːdʒ §-ə- ‖ ˈvɝːm- ~es ɪz
   əz
vermilion və ˈmɪl i̯ ən vɜː- ‖ vᵊr ˈmɪl jən ~ed
   d ~s z
vermin ˈvɜːm ɪn §-ən ‖ ˈvɝːm ən

verminous 'vɜːm ɪn əs §-ən- ‖ 'vɜːm ən əs **~ly**
li **~ness** nəs nɪs
Vermont və 'mɒnt vɜː- ‖ vᵊr 'mɑːnt
Vermonter və 'mɒnt ə vɜː- ‖ vᵊr 'mɑːnt̬ ᵊr **~s** z
vermouth 'vɜːm əθ -uːθ; və 'muːθ, vɜː-
‖ vᵊr 'muːθ **~s** s
Verna 'vɜːn ə ‖ 'vɜːn ə
vernacular və 'næk jʊl ə -jəl- ‖ vᵊr 'næk jəl ᵊr
və- **~ly** li **~s** z
vernal 'vɜːn ᵊl ‖ 'vɜːn ᵊl **~ly** i
,**vernal 'equinox**
vernalis... —*see* **vernaliz...**
vernalization ,vɜːn əl aɪ 'zeɪʃ ᵊn -ɪ'-
‖ ,vɜːn ᵊl ə-
vernaliz|e 'vɜːn ə laɪz -ᵊl aɪz ‖ 'vɜːn ᵊl aɪz **~ed**
d **~es** ɪz əz **~ing** ɪŋ
Verne vɜːn veən ‖ vɜːn —*Fr* [vɛʀn]
Verner 'vɜːn ə 'veən- ‖ 'vɜːn ᵊr —*Danish*
['vɛʁʔ nɒ] **~'s** z
'**Verner's law**
Verney 'vɜːn i ‖ 'vɜːn i
vernier 'vɜːn iə ‖ 'vɜːn iᵊr **~s** z
vernissag|e ,vɜːn ɪ 'sɑːʒ ‖ ,vɜːn- **-es** ɪz əz
Vernon 'vɜːn ən ‖ 'vɜːn ən
Verona və 'rəʊn ə ve-, vɪ- ‖ -'roʊn- —*It*
[ve 'ro: na]
veronal, V~ *tdmk* 'ver ən ᵊl **~s** z
Veronese ,ver əʊ 'neɪz i ‖ -ə- -'neɪs- —*It*
[ve ro 'ne: se]
veronica, V~ və 'rɒn ɪk ə ve-, vɪ- ‖ -'rɑːn- **~s,**
~'s z
Verrazano ,ver ə 'zɑːn əʊ ‖ -oʊ —*It*
[ver rat 'tsa: no]
,**Verra,zano 'Narrows**
ver|ruca və 'ruːk ə ve-, vɪ- **~rucae** 'ruːs iː
'ruːk-, -aɪ **~rucas** 'ruːk əz
versa 'vɜːs ə ‖ 'vɜːs ə
Versace və 'sɑːtʃ i vɜː- ‖ vᵊr-
Versailles veə 'saɪ vɜː- ‖ ver- —*Fr* [vɛʀ saj]
versant 'vɜːs ᵊnt ‖ 'vɜːs- **~s** s
versatile 'vɜːs ə taɪᵊl ‖ 'vɜːs ət̬ ᵊl (*) **~ly** li
~ness nəs nɪs
versatility ,vɜːs ə 'tɪl ət i -ɪt- ‖ ,vɜːs ə 'tɪl ət̬ i
verse vɜːs ‖ vɜːs **versed** vɜːst ‖ vɜːst **verses**
'vɜːs ɪz -əz ‖ 'vɜːs əz
versicle 'vɜːs ɪk ᵊl ‖ 'vɜːs- **~s** z
versification ,vɜːs ɪf ɪ 'keɪʃ ᵊn ,-əf-, §-ə'-
‖ ,vɜːs- **~s** z
versi|fy 'vɜːs ɪ |faɪ -ə- ‖ 'vɜːs- **~fied** faɪd
~fier/s faɪ ə/z ‖ faɪ ᵊr/z **~fies** faɪz **~fying**
faɪ ɪŋ
version 'vɜːʃ ᵊn 'vɜːʒ- ‖ 'vɜːʒ ᵊn 'vɜːʃ- **~s** z
verso 'vɜːs əʊ ‖ 'vɜːs oʊ **~s** z
versus 'vɜːs əs ‖ 'vɜːs əs
vert vɜːt ‖ vɜːt
vert|ebra 'vɜːt |ɪb rə -əb- ‖ 'vɜːt̬- **~ebrae**
ɪ breɪ ə-, -briː **~ebras** ɪb rəz əb-
vertebral 'vɜːt ɪb rᵊl -əb- ‖ 'vɜːt̬- vɜː 'tiːb-
Vertebrata, v~ ,vɜːt ɪ 'brɑːt ə -ə-, -'breɪt-
‖ ,vɜːt̬ ə 'brɑːt̬ ə -'breɪt̬-
vertebrate 'vɜːt ɪb rət -əb-, -rɪt; -ɪ breɪt, -ə-
‖ 'vɜːt̬- **~s** s

vertex 'vɜːt eks ‖ 'vɜːt̬- **vertices** 'vɜːt ɪ siːz -ə-
‖ 'vɜːt̬-
vertical 'vɜːt ɪk ᵊl ‖ 'vɜːt̬- **~ly** i **~s** z
verticality ,vɜːt ɪ 'kæl ət i ,-ə-, -ɪt i
‖ ,vɜːt̬ ə 'kæl ət̬ i
vertices 'vɜːt ɪ siːz -ə- ‖ 'vɜːt̬-
vertiginous vɜː 'tɪdʒ ɪn əs -ən- əs ‖ vɜː- **~ly** li
~ness nəs nɪs
vertigo 'vɜːt ɪ gəʊ -ə- ‖ 'vɜːt̬ ɪ goʊ **~s** z
Verulam 'ver ʊl əm -jʊl- ‖ -jəl-
Verulamium ,ver u 'leɪm i əm ,ju- ‖ ,jə-
vervain 'vɜːv eɪn ‖ 'vɜːv-
verve vɜːv ‖ vɜːv
vervet 'vɜːv ɪt §-ət ‖ 'vɜːv ət **~s** s
Verwoerd fə 'vʊət feə- ‖ fᵊr 'vʊᵊrt —*Afrikaans*
[fər 'vuːrt]
very 'ver i —*Some speakers use a casual weak
form* vər i **veriest** 'ver i_ɪst əst
,**very ,high 'frequency**
Very 'vɪər i 'ver- ‖ 'ver i 'vɪr-
'**Very light**
Veryan 'ver i_ən
Vesalius və 'seɪl i_əs vɪ-
Vesey 'viːz i
vesic|a 'ves ɪk |ə vɪ 'saɪk |ə, və- **~al** ᵊl **~ant/s**
ənt/s **~as** əz
vesicle 'ves ɪk ᵊl 'viːs- **~s** z
vesicular və 'sɪk jʊl ə ve-, vɪ-, -jəl ə ‖ -jəl ᵊr
~ly li
Vespa *tdmk* 'vesp ə **~s** z
Vespasian ve 'speɪʒ ᵊn -'·i_ən; -'speɪz i_ən
vesper, V~ 'vesp ə ‖ -ᵊr **~s** z
vespertine 'vesp ə taɪn -tiːn ‖ -ᵊr- —*Björk's
album V~ is usually* -tiːn
vespine 'vesp aɪn
Vespucci ve 'spuːtʃ i —*It* [ve 'sput tʃi]
vessel 'ves ᵊl **~s** z
vest vest **vested** 'vest ɪd -əd **vesting** 'vest ɪŋ
vests vests
,**vested 'interest**
Vesta, vesta 'vest ə **~s,** **~'s** z
vestal 'vest ᵊl **~s** z
,**vestal 'virgin**
vestibular ve 'stɪb jʊl ə -jəl- ‖ -jəl ᵊr
vestibule 'vest ɪ bjuːl -ə- **~s** z
vestig|e 'vest ɪdʒ **~es** ɪz əz
vestigial ves 'tɪdʒ i əl -'tɪdʒ əl **~ly** i
vestment 'vest mənt **~s** s
vest-pocket ,vest 'pɒk ɪt ◂ §-ət ‖ -'pɑːk-
ves|try 'ves |tri **~tries** triz
vestry|man 'ves tri |mən **~men** mən men
vesture 'ves tʃə ‖ -tʃᵊr **~d** d **~s** z
Vesuvianite və 'suːv i_ə naɪt vɪ-, -'sjuːv-
Vesuvius və 'suːv i_əs vɪ-, -'sjuːv-
vet vet **vets** vets **vetted** 'vet ɪd -əd ‖ 'vet̬ əd
vetting 'vet ɪŋ ‖ 'vet̬ ɪŋ
vetch vetʃ **vetches** 'vetʃ ɪz -əz
vetchling 'vetʃ lɪŋ **~s** z
veteran 'vet ᵊr ən ‖ 'vet̬ ᵊr ən →'vetr ən **~s** z
'**Veterans Day**
veterinarian ,vet ᵊr ɪ 'neər i_ən -ə'-;
,vet ə 'neər i_ən ‖ ,vet̬ ᵊr ə 'ner i_ən
→,vetr ə 'ner- **~s** z

veterinar|y ˈvet ˌ°r ən ər ˌli -ɪn ər ˌi;
ˈvet ɪn ər ˌli, ˈvet °n ər ˌli ‖ ˈveţ ər ə ner ˌli
→ˈvetr ə ner ˌli, ˈvet °n er ˌli ~**ies** iz
ˌveterinary ˈsurgeon

vetiver ˈvet ɪv ə ‖ -°r

veto ˈviːt əʊ ‖ ˈviːţ oʊ ˈviːt- ~**ed** d ~**es** z ~**ing**
ɪŋ

Vettriano ˌvetr i ˈɑːn əɪ ‖ -oʊ

Veuve vɜːv ‖ vʌv —Fr [vœːv]
ˌ~ **Clicquot** tdmk ˈkliːk əʊ ‖ kli: ˈkoʊ —Fr
[kli ko]

vex veks **vexed** vekst **vexes** ˈveks ɪz -əz
vexing ˈveks ɪŋ

vexation vek ˈseɪʃ °n ~**s** z

vexatious vek ˈseɪʃ əs ~**ly** li ~**ness** nəs nɪs

vexillology ˌveks ɪ ˈlɒl ədʒ i ˌ-ə- ‖ -ˈlɑːl-

V-formation ˈviː fɔː ˌmeɪʃ °n ‖ -fɔːr-

VH1 ˌviː eɪtʃ ˈwʌn

VHF ˌviː eɪtʃ ˈef §-heɪtʃ-

VHS tdmk ˌviː eɪtʃ ˈes §-heɪtʃ-

Vi vaɪ

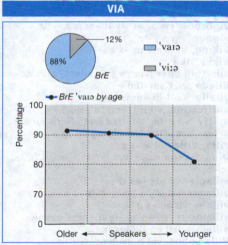

Older ← Speakers → Younger

via ˈvaɪ ə ˈviː ə — *Preference poll, BrE:* ˈvaɪə
88% *(born before 1942, 92%),* ˈviːə 12%. —*see
also phrases with this word*

viability ˌvaɪ ə ˈbɪl ət i -ɪt i ‖ -əţ i

viab|le ˈvaɪ əb |°l ~**ly** li

Viacom tdmk ˈvaɪ ə kɒm ‖ -kɑːm

Via Dolorosa, via d~ ˌviː ə ˌdɒl ə ˈrəʊs ə
‖ -ˌdɑːl ə ˈroʊs- -ˌdoʊl-

viaduct ˈvaɪ ə dʌkt ~**s** s

Viagra tdmk vaɪ ˈæg rə vi- ‖ -ˈɑːg-

vial ˈvaɪ əl ‖ ˈvaɪ °l ~**s** z

via media ˌvaɪ ə ˈmiːd i ə ˌviː ə ˈmeɪd-

viand ˈvaɪ ənd ˈviːˌ ~**s** z

viatic|al vaɪ ˈæt ɪk ‖ °l vi- ‖ -ˈæţ- ~**a** ə ~**um/s**
əm/z

vibe vaɪb **vibes** vaɪbz

vibist ˈvaɪb ɪst §-əst ~**s** s

vibraharp ˈvaɪb rə hɑːp ‖ -hɑːrp ~**s** s

Vibram tdmk ˈvaɪb rəm

vibrancy ˈvaɪb rən̩ts i

vibrant ˈvaɪb rənt ~**ly** li ~**s** s

vibraphone ˈvaɪb rə fəʊn ‖ -foʊn ~**s** z

vib|rate vaɪ ˈb|reɪt ‖ ˈvaɪb |reɪt *(*)* ~**rated**
reɪt ɪd -əd ‖ reɪţ əd ~**rates** reɪts ~**rating**
reɪt ɪŋ ‖ reɪţ ɪŋ

vibratile ˈvaɪb rə taɪ°l ‖ -rəţ °l

vibration vaɪ ˈbreɪʃ °n ~**s** z

vibrational vaɪ ˈbreɪʃ °n ̩əl

vibrationless vaɪ ˈbreɪʃ °n ləs -lɪs

vibrative vaɪ ˈbreɪt ɪv ˈvaɪb rət- ‖ ˈvaɪb rəţ ɪv

vibrato vɪ ˈbrɑːt əʊ §və-, vaɪ-, viː- ‖ -oʊ ~**s** z

vibrator vaɪ ˈbreɪt ə ‖ ˈvaɪb reɪţ °r *(*)* ~**s** z

vibratory vaɪ ˈbreɪt ər i ˈvaɪb rət ər i
‖ ˈvaɪb rə tɔːr i -toʊr i *(*)*

vibrio ˈvɪb ri əʊ ‖ -oʊ ~**s** z

vibriss|a vaɪ ˈbrɪs |ə ~**ae** iː

vibro- |vaɪb rəʊ ‖ -roʊ — **vibromassage**
ˈvaɪb rəʊ ˌmæs ɑːʒ ˌ·ˈ·· ‖ -roʊ mə ˌsɑːʒ ˌ·ˈ··

viburnum vaɪ ˈbɜːn əm ‖ -ˈbɜːn- ~**s** z

Vic vɪk

vicar ˈvɪk ə ‖ -°r ~**s** z

vicarag|e ˈvɪk ər ˌɪdʒ ~**es** ɪz əz

vicarial vɪ ˈkeər i əl və-, vaɪ- ‖ -ˈker- -ˈkær-

vicarious vɪ ˈkeər i əs və-, vaɪ- ‖ -ˈker- -ˈkær-
~**ly** li ~**ness** nəs nɪs

vice n vaɪs **vices** ˈvaɪs ɪz -əz
ˈvice squad

vice prep, Latin ˈvaɪs i -ə; vaɪs, ˈviːs eɪ
ˌvice ˈversa ˈvɜːs ə ‖ ˈvɜːs ə

vice- |vaɪs — **vice-presidency**
ˌvaɪs ˈprez ɪd ən̩ts i -ˈ·əd- ‖ -ə den̩ts i

vice-chair ˌvaɪs ˈtʃeə ‖ -ˈtʃeər -ˈtʃæər ~**man**
mən ~**men** mən ~**person/s** ˌpɜːs °n/z
‖ ˌpɜːs °n/z ~**woman** ˌwʊm ən ~**women**
ˌwɪm ɪn §-ən

vice-chancellor ˌvaɪs ˈtʃɑːn̩ts əl ə §-ˈtʃæn̩ts-
‖ -ˈtʃæn̩ts °l ̩ər ~**ship** ʃɪp ~**s** z

vicegerant ˌvaɪs ˈdʒer ənt -ˈdʒɪər- ‖ -ˈdʒɪr- ~**s**
s

vicelike ˈvaɪs laɪk

viceregal ˌvaɪs ˈriːg °l ◂ ~**ly** i

vicereine ˌvaɪs ˈreɪn ˈ·· ~**s** z

viceroy ˈvaɪs rɔɪ ~**s** z

Vichy ˈviːʃ i ˈvɪʃ- —Fr [vi ʃi]
ˈVichy ˌwater

Vichyite ˈviːʃ i aɪt ˈvɪʃ- ~**s** s

vichyssoise ˌviːʃ i ˈswɑːz ˌvɪʃ- —Fr
[vi ʃi swɑːz]

vicinal ˈvɪs ɪn °l -ən̩°l

vicinit|y və ˈsɪn ət i ˌli vɪ-, -ɪt- ‖ -əţ ˌli ~**ies** iz

vicious ˈvɪʃ əs ~**ly** li ~**ness** nəs nɪs
ˌvicious ˈcircle

vicissitude vaɪ ˈsɪs ɪ tjuːd və-, vɪ-, →-tʃuːd
‖ və ˈsɪs ə tuːd vaɪ-, -tjuːd ~**s** z

Vick vɪk

Vickers ˈvɪk əz ‖ -°rz

Vickery ˈvɪk ər i

Vicki, Vickie ˈvɪk i

Vicksburg ˈvɪks bɜːg ‖ -bɜːg

Vicky ˈvɪk i

victim ˈvɪkt ɪm §-əm ~**hood** hʊd ~**s** z

victimis... —*see* **victimiz...**

victimization ˌvɪkt ɪm aɪ ˈzeɪʃ °n ˌ·əm-, -ɪˈ·-
‖ -əˈ·- ~**s** z

victimiz|e 'vɪkt ɪ maɪz -ə- ‖ -ə- **~ed** d **~es** ɪz əz
  ~ing ɪŋ
victimless 'vɪkt ɪm ləs §-əm-, -lɪs
victor, V~ 'vɪkt ə ‖ -ᵊr **~s** z
  ˌvictor luˈdorum lu 'dɔːr əm
Victoria, v~ vɪk 'tɔːr i‿ə ‖ -'toʊr- —*but the*
  London railway terminus is sometimes
  double-stressed, ˌ·'·◄ **~s, ~'s** z
  Vicˌtoria 'Cross; Vicˌtoria 'Falls; vicˌtoria
  'plum; Vicˌtoria 'Station, ˌ·ˌ-
Victorian vɪk 'tɔːr i‿ən ‖ -'toʊr- **~ism** ˌɪz əm **~s**
  z
Victoriana vɪk ˌtɔːr i ɑː n ə ·‿·'·· ‖ -ˌtoʊr-,
  -'æn-
victorious vɪk 'tɔːr i‿əs ‖ -'toʊr- **~ly** li **~ness**
  nəs nɪs
victor|y 'vɪkt ər |i →ˈvɪk tr|i **~ies** iz
Victory-V *tdmk* ˌvɪk tri 'viː
Victrola *tdmk* vɪk 'trəʊl ə ‖ -'troʊl ə
victual 'vɪt ᵊl (!) **~s** z
victualer, victualler 'vɪt ᵊl‿ə ‖ ᵊr —*Also*
  sometimes a spelling pronunciation
  'vɪk tʃu‿əl ə ‖ -ᵊr **~s** z
vicuna, vicuña vɪ 'kjuːn ə və-, vaɪ-, -'kuːn-, -jə
  —*Sp* [bi 'ku ɲa] **~s** z
Vidal *(i)* vɪ 'dɑːl və-, ˌviː-, -'dæl, *(ii)* 'vaɪd ᵊl
  —*The writer* Gore Vidal *is (i).*
vide 'vaɪd i 'vɪd-, 'viːd-, -eɪ
videlicet vɪ 'diːl ɪ set və-, vaɪ-, -'deɪl-, -'del-,
  -ə-, -ket
video 'vɪd i əʊ ‖ -oʊ **~ed** d **~ing** ɪŋ **~s** z
  'video ˌcamera; 'video game; 'video link;
  'video reˌcorder
videocard 'vɪd i əʊ kɑːd ‖ -oʊ kɑːrd **~s** z
videocassette ˌvɪd i əʊ kə 'set ·'···ˌ ‖ ˌ·i oʊ-
  ˌvideo casˈsette reˌcorder
videoconferenc|e 'vɪd i əʊ ˌkɒn fər‿ən's
  ‖ '··oʊ ˌkɑːn- **~ing** ɪŋ
videodisc 'vɪd i əʊ dɪsk ‖ -oʊ dɪsk **~s** s
videofit 'vɪd i əʊ fɪt ‖ -oʊ· **~s** s
videographer ˌvɪd i 'ɒg rəf ə ‖ -'ɑːg rəf ᵊr **~s**
  z
videophone, V~ *tdmk* 'vɪd i əʊ fəʊn
  ‖ -oʊ foʊn **~s** z
videotap|e 'vɪd i əʊ teɪp ‖ -oʊ teɪp **~ed** t **~es**
  s **~ing** ɪŋ
  'videotape reˌcorder
videotex 'vɪd i əʊ teks ‖ -oʊ teks
videotext 'vɪd i əʊ tekst ‖ -oʊ tekst
vidicon 'vɪd i kɒn ‖ -kɑːn **~s** z
Vidler 'vɪd lə ‖ -lᵊr
vie vaɪ **vied** vaɪd **vies** vaɪz **vying** 'vaɪ ɪŋ
Vienna vi 'en ə
Viennese ˌviː‿ə 'niːz ◄ ‖ -'niːs ◄
Vientiane vi ˌent i 'ɑːn —*Fr* [vjɛn tjan]
Vietcong, Viet Cong ˌvi: et 'kɒŋ ◄ -ɪt-, vi‿ˌet-
  ‖ -'kɑːŋ -'kɔːŋ
Vietminh, Viet Minh ˌvi: et 'mɪn ◄ -ɪt-, vi‿ˌet-
Vietnam, Viet Nam ˌvi: et 'næm ◄ -ɪt-, vi‿ˌet-,
  -'nɑːm ‖ -'nɑːm
Vietnamese vi ˌet nə 'miːz ◄ ˌvi: et-, vi: ɪt-
  ‖ -'miːs ◄

view vju: **viewed** vju:d **viewing** 'vju: ɪŋ
  views vju:z
viewdata, V~ 'vju: ˌdeɪt ə -ˌdɑ:t- ‖ -ˌdeɪt̬ ə
  -ˌdæt̬-, -ˌdɑ:t̬-
viewer 'vju:ˌə ‖ ᵊr **~ship** ʃɪp **~s** z
viewfinder 'vju: ˌfaɪnd ə ‖ -ᵊr **~s** z
Viewgraph *tdmk* 'vju: grɑːf -græf ‖ -græf **~s** s
viewpoint 'vju: pɔɪnt **~s** s
Vigar 'vaɪg ə -ɑ: ‖ -ᵊr -ɑːr
vigesimal vaɪ 'dʒes ɪm ᵊl -əm-
vigil 'vɪdʒ ɪl -əl **~s** z
vigilance 'vɪdʒ əl ən's -ɪl-
  'vigilance comˌmittee
vigilant 'vɪdʒ əl ənt -ɪl- **~ly** li
vigilante ˌvɪdʒ ɪ 'lænt i -ə- ‖ -'lænt̬ i -'lɑ:nt̬- **~s**
  z
vigilantism ˌvɪdʒ ɪ 'lænt ˌɪz əm ‖ -'lænt̬- -ə-
vignette vɪn 'jet vi:n- —*Fr* [vi njɛt] **~s** s
Vigo *(i)* 'viːg əʊ ‖ -oʊ, *(ii)* 'vaɪg- —*Sp* ['bi ɣo]
  —*For the place in Spain, usually (i); as a*
  personal, place or street name in
  English-speaking countries, often (ii).
vigor 'vɪg ə ‖ -ᵊr
vigorous 'vɪg ər‿əs **~ly** li **~ness** nəs nɪs
vigour 'vɪg ə ‖ -ᵊr
Viking, v~ 'vaɪk ɪŋ **~s** z
Vikki 'vɪk i
vile vaɪᵊl **viler** 'vaɪᵊl ə ‖ -ᵊr **vilest** 'vaɪᵊl ɪst -əst
Vileda *tdmk* vaɪ 'liːd ə
vile|ly 'vaɪᵊl |li **~ness** nəs nɪs
vilification ˌvɪl ɪf ɪ 'keɪʃ ᵊn ˌ·əf-, §-ə-'-
vili|fy 'vɪl ɪ |faɪ -ə- **~fied** faɪd **~fier/s** faɪ‿ə/z
  ‖ faɪˌᵊr/z **~fies** faɪz **~fying** faɪ ɪŋ
villa, Villa 'vɪl ə **~s** z
Villa *Spanish name* 'vi:l jə 'vi: ə —*Sp* ['bi ʎa,
  -ja]
villag|e 'vɪl ɪdʒ **~es** ɪz əz
villager 'vɪl ɪdʒ ə §-ədʒ- ‖ -ᵊr **~s** z
villain 'vɪl ən **~s** z
villainous 'vɪl ən əs **~ly** li **~ness** nəs nɪs
villain|y 'vɪl ən |i **~ies** iz
Villa-Lobos ˌvi:l ə 'ləʊb ɒs ˌvi:-, -jə-
  ‖ -'loʊb oʊs -əs, -oʊʃ —*BrPort* [ˌvi la 'lo bus]
villanella ˌvɪl ə 'nel ə **~s** z
villanelle ˌvɪl ə 'nel **~s** z
Villanovan ˌvɪl ə 'nəʊv ᵊn ◄ ‖ -'noʊv-
-ville vɪl — **dullsville** 'dʌlz vɪl
villein 'vɪl eɪn -ɪn, -ən **~s** z
villeinage, villenage 'vɪl ən ɪdʒ -eɪn-, -ɪn-
Villeneuve 'vi:ᵊl nɜ:v ‖ ˌvi:ᵊl 'nu:v —*Fr*
  [vil nœ:v]
villi 'vɪl aɪ
Villiers *(i)* 'vɪl əz ‖ -ᵊrz, *(ii)* 'vɪl i‿əz ‖ ᵊrz
Villon 'vi: ɒ̃ 'vɪl ən ‖ -ɑːn -oʊn —*Fr* [vi jɔ̃, -lɔ̃]
villosit|y vɪ 'lɒs ət |i -ɪt- ‖ vɪ 'lɑːs ət̬ |i **~ies** iz
villous 'vɪl əs **~ly** li
vill|us 'vɪl| əs **~i** aɪ ɪ-
Vilnius, Vilnyus 'vɪl ni‿əs -ʊs
vim, Vim *tdmk* vɪm
Vimto *tdmk* 'vɪm təʊ ‖ -toʊ
vin væ væn —*Fr* [vɛ̃]
  ˌvin 'blanc blɒ̃ blɒŋ ‖ blɑːn —*Fr* [blɑ̃]
vinaceous vaɪ 'neɪʃ əs vɪ-, §və-

Viña del Mar ˌviːn jə del ˈmɑː ‖ -ˈmɑːr
—*AmSp* [ˌbi ɲa ðel ˈmar]
vinaigrette ˌvɪn eɪ ˈgret -ɪ-, -ə- **~s** s
vinca ˈvɪŋk ə **~s** z
Vince vɪnˈs
Vincennes *(i)* væn ˈsen væ̃- —*Fr* [vɛ̃ sɛn]; *(ii)*
vɪn ˈsenz —*In France, (i); in Indiana, (ii).*
Vincent ˈvɪnˈs ənt
Vincentian vɪn ˈsenʃ ᵊn **~s** z
Vinci ˈvɪntʃ i —*It* [ˈvɪn tʃi]
vinculum ˈvɪŋk jʊl əm -jəl- ‖ -jəl-
vindaloo ˌvɪnd ə ˈluː **~s** z
vindi|cate ˈvɪnd ɪ |keɪt §-ə- **~cated** keɪt ɪd -əd
‖ keɪt̬ əd **~cates** keɪts **~cating** keɪt ɪŋ
‖ keɪt̬ ɪŋ
vindication ˌvɪnd ɪ ˈkeɪʃ ᵊn §-ə-
vindictive vɪn ˈdɪkt ɪv **~ly** li **~ness** nəs nɪs
Vindolanda ˌvɪnd əʊ ˈlænd ə ‖ -oʊ- -ˈlɑːnd ə
vin du pays ˌvæn du peɪ ˈiː ˌvæ̃-, ˌdju- —*Fr*
[væ̃ dy pe i]
vine, Vine vaɪn **vines** vaɪnz
vinegar ˈvɪn ɪg ə §-əg- ‖ -ᵊr **~s** z
vinegary ˈvɪn ɪg ər i §ˈ·əg-
Vineland ˈvaɪn lənd
Viner ˈvaɪn ə ‖ -ᵊr
viner|y ˈvaɪn ər |i **~ies** iz
vineyard ˈvɪn jəd -jɑːd ‖ -jᵊrd **~s** z
vingt-et-un ˌvænt eɪ ˈɜ̃ ˌvæ̃t-, -ˈɜːn ‖ -ˈʊn -ˈʌn
—*Fr* [væ̃ te œ̃, -æ̃]
vinho verde ˌviːn əʊ ˈvɜːd i ‖ -oʊ ˈvɛːd i
—*Port* [ˌvi ɲu ˈveʁ di]
vinic ˈvaɪn ɪk ˈvɪn-
viniculture ˈvɪn i ˌkʌltʃ ə ˈvaɪn-, §ˈ·ə- ‖ -ᵊr
Vinland ˈvɪn lənd -lænd
Vinnie ˈvɪn i
vino ˈviːn əʊ ‖ -oʊ
vin ordinaire ˌvæn ˌɔːd ɪ ˈneə -ə-
‖ -ˌɔːrd ᵊn ˈeᵊr —*Fr* [væ̃ nɔʁ di nɛːʁ]
vinosity vaɪ ˈnɒs ət i vɪ-, §və-, -ɪt- ‖ -ˈnɑːs ət̬ i
vinous ˈvaɪn əs
vin rouge ˌvæn ˈruːʒ ˌvæ̃- —*Fr* [væ̃ ʁuʒ]
Vinson ˈvɪnˈs ᵊn
vintag|e ˈvɪnt ɪdʒ ‖ ˈvɪnt̬ ɪdʒ **~es** ɪz əz
ˌvintage ˈcar; ˌvintage ˈyear
vintner ˈvɪnt nə ‖ -nᵊr **~s** z
vinyl ˈvaɪn ᵊl -ɪl **~s** z
ˌvinyl ˈchloride
vinylidene vaɪ ˈnɪl ɪ diːn -ə-
viol ˈvaɪ ᵊl ‖ ˈvaɪ ˌᵊl -oʊl **~s** z
viola *'kind of flower'*, **Viola** *personal name*
ˈvaɪ ᵊl ə ˈviː ˌ, -əʊl ə; vi ˈəʊl ə, vaɪ-
‖ vaɪ ˈoʊl ə vi-; ˈvaɪ əl ə **~s, ~'s** z
viola *'musical instrument'* vi ˈəʊl ə vaɪ-;
ˈviː əl ə ‖ vi ˈoʊl ə **~s** z
vi,ola da ˈgamba də ˈgæm bə ‖ -ˈgɑːm-;
vi,ola d'aˈmore dæ ˈmɔːr i -eɪ ‖ dɑː ˈmɔːr eɪ
vio|late ˈvaɪ ə |leɪt **~lated** leɪt ɪd -əd ‖ leɪt̬ əd
~lates leɪts **~lating** leɪt ɪŋ ‖ leɪt̬ ɪŋ
violation ˌvaɪ ə ˈleɪʃ ᵊn **~s** z
violator ˈvaɪ ə leɪt ə ‖ -leɪt̬ ᵊr **~s** z
violence ˈvaɪ əl ən̍s §ˈvaɪ ən̍s
violent ˈvaɪ əl ənt §ˈvaɪl ənt **~ly** li
violet, V~ ˈvaɪ əl ət -ɪt; §ˈvaɪl ət, -ɪt **~s** s

violin ˌvaɪ ə ˈlɪn ˈ· · · **~s** z
violinist ˌvaɪ ə ˈlɪn ɪst §-əst, ˈ· · · · **~s** s
violist *'viola player'* vi ˈəʊl ɪst §-əst ‖ -ˈoʊl- **~s**
s
violist *'viol player'* ˈvaɪ əl ɪst §-əst **~s** s
violoncellist ˌvaɪ əl ən ˈtʃel ɪst §-əst **~s** s
violoncello ˌvaɪ əl ən ˈtʃel əʊ ‖ -oʊ **~s** z
violone ˈvaɪ ə ləʊn ˈviː ˌ, ˌviː ə ˈləʊn eɪ
‖ ˌviː ə ˈloʊn eɪ -ə **~s** z
Vioxx *tdmk* ˈvaɪ ɒks ‖ -ɑːks
VIP ˌviː aɪ ˈpiː **~s, ~'s** z
viper ˈvaɪp ə ‖ -ᵊr **~s** z
viperine ˈvaɪp ə raɪn
viperish ˈvaɪp ᵊr ɪʃ
viperous ˈvaɪp ᵊr əs
virago və ˈrɑːg əʊ vɪ- ‖ -oʊ **~es, ~s** z
viral ˈvaɪᵊr əl
vire ˈvaɪ ə vɪə ‖ ˈvaɪ ᵊr vɪᵊr **vired** ˈvaɪ əd vɪəd
‖ ˈvaɪ ᵊrd vɪᵊrd **vires** ˈvaɪ əz vɪəz ‖ ˈvaɪ ᵊrz
vɪᵊrz **viring** ˈvaɪ ər ɪŋ ˈvɪər ɪŋ ‖ ˈvaɪ ᵊr ɪŋ
ˈvɪr ɪŋ
virement ˈvaɪ ə mənt ˈvɪə mɒ̃ ‖ ˈvaɪ ᵊr mənt
vɪr ˈmɑːn —*Fr* [viʁ mɑ̃]
vireo ˈvɪr i əʊ ‖ -oʊ **~s** z
vires *Latin, 'powers'* ˈvaɪᵊr iːz
vires *3 sing of vire* ˈvaɪ əz vɪəz ‖ ˈvaɪ ᵊrz vɪᵊrz
Virgil ˈvɜːdʒ ɪl -əl ‖ ˈvɜːdʒ əl
Virgilian vɜː ˈdʒɪl i ən və- ‖ vɜː-
virgin, V~ ˈvɜːdʒ ɪn §-ən ‖ ˈvɜːdʒ ən **~s** z
ˌvirgin ˈbirth; ˈVirgin ˈIslands ‖ , · · ˈ· ·;
ˌVirgin ˈMary; ˌVirgin ˈQueen
virginal ˈvɜːdʒ ɪn ᵊl -ən- ‖ ˈvɜːdʒ- **~s** z
Virginia, v~ və ˈdʒɪn i ə ‖ vᵊr ˈdʒɪn jə
Virˌginia ˈBeach; virˌginia ˈcreeper;
Virˌginia ˈreel
Virginian və ˈdʒɪn i ən ‖ vᵊr ˈdʒɪn jən **~s** z
virginity və ˈdʒɪn ət i vɜː-, -ɪt- ‖ vᵊr ˈdʒɪn ət̬ i
Virgo ˈvɜːg əʊ ‖ ˈvɜːg oʊ **~s** z
ˌvirgo inˈtacta ɪn ˈtækt ə
Virgoan vɜː ˈgəʊ ən ‖ vɜː ˈgoʊ ən **~s** z
virgule ˈvɜːg juːl ‖ ˈvɜːg- **~s** z
viridescence ˌvɪr ɪ ˈdes ᵊnˈs , ·ə-
viridescent ˌvɪr ɪ ˈdes ᵊnt ◂ , ·ə-
viridian və ˈrɪd i ən vɪ-
virile ˈvɪr aɪᵊl ‖ -ᵊl *(*)*
virility və ˈrɪl ət i vɪ-, -ɪt- ‖ -ət̬ i
virion ˈvaɪᵊr i ən ˈvɪr-, -ɒn ‖ -i ɑːn **~s** z
viroid ˈvaɪᵊr ɔɪd ˈvɪr-
Virol *tdmk* ˈvaɪᵊr ɒl ‖ -ɑːl -ɔːl, -oʊl
virologist vaɪᵊ ˈrɒl ədʒ ɪst §-əst ‖ -ˈrɑːl- **~s** s
virology vaɪᵊ ˈrɒl ədʒ i ‖ -ˈrɑːl-
virtu vɜː ˈtuː ‖ vɜː-
virtual ˈvɜːtʃ u əl ˈvɜːt ju ˌ ‖ ˈvɜːtʃ u əl -əl **~ly** i
virtue ˈvɜːtʃ uː ˈvɜːt juː ‖ ˈvɜːtʃ uː **~s** z
virtuosic ˌvɜːtʃ u ˈɒs ɪk ◂ ˌvɜːt ju-, -ˈəʊs-
‖ ˌvɜːtʃ u ˈɑːs ɪk ◂
virtuosity ˌvɜːtʃ u ˈɒs ət i ˌvɜːt ju-, -ɪt i
‖ ˌvɜːtʃ u ˈɑːs ət̬ i
virtuoso ˌvɜːtʃ u ˈəʊs əʊ ◂ ˌvɜːt ju-, -ˈəʊz-
‖ ˌvɜːtʃ u ˈoʊs oʊ ◂ -ˈoʊz- **~s** z
virtuous ˈvɜːtʃ u̯əs ˈvɜːt ju̯ ‖ ˈvɜːtʃ- **~ly** li
~ness nəs nɪs

virulenc|e 'vɪr ʊl ən‹s -jʊl-, -jəl-, -əl- ‖ -əl- -jəl-
~**y** i
virulent 'vɪr ʊl ənt -jʊl-, -jəl-, -əl- ‖ -əl- -jəl-
~**ly** li
virus 'vaɪᵊr əs ~**es** ɪz əz
vis vɪs

VISA

55% 45%
AmE

□ 'viːz-
▨ 'viːs-

visa, Visa tdmk 'viːz ə ‖ 'viːs- — *Preference
poll, AmE:* 'viːz- *55%,* 'viːs- *45%.* ~**ed** d
visaing 'viːz əʳ ɪŋ ‖ 'viːz ə ɪŋ 'viːs- ~**s** z
visag|e 'vɪz ɪdʒ ~**es** ɪz əz
-visaged 'vɪz ɪdʒd — **grim-visaged**
ˌgrɪm 'vɪz ɪdʒd ◄
visagist 'vɪz ədʒ ɪst §-əst ~**s** s
visagiste ˌviːz ɑː 'ʒiːst ~**s** s
Visalia vaɪ 'seɪl i ə vɪ-
vis-a-vis, vis-à-vis ˌviːz ə 'viː ◄ ˌvɪz-, -ɑː-, -æ-
viscacha vɪ 'skɑːtʃ ə -'skætʃ ə ~**s** z
viscera 'vɪs ər ə
visceral 'vɪs ər əl
viscid 'vɪs ɪd §-əd ~**ly** li ~**ness** nəs nɪs
Visconti vɪ 'skɒnt i ‖ -'skɔːnt i -'skɑːnt- —*It*
[vis 'kon ti]
viscose 'vɪsk əʊs -əʊz ‖ -oʊs -oʊz
viscosit|y vɪ 'skɒs ət |i -ɪt- ‖ -'skɑːs əţ |i ~**ies**
iz
viscount 'vaɪ kaʊnt ~**s** s
viscount|cy 'vaɪ kaʊnt |si ~**sies** siz
viscountess ˌvaɪ kaʊn 'tes ◄ 'vaɪ kaʊnt ɪs, -əs
‖ 'vaɪ kaʊnţ əs ~**es** ɪz əz
viscous 'vɪsk əs ~**ly** li ~**ness** nəs nɪs
vise vaɪs (= *vice*) **vises** 'vaɪs ɪz -əz
Vise-Grips tdmk 'vaɪs grɪps
vise-like 'vaɪs laɪk
Vishnu 'vɪʃ nuː
visibilit|y ˌvɪz ə 'bɪl ət |i ˌ-ɪ-, -ɪt i ‖ -əţ |i ~**ies**
iz
visib|le 'vɪz əb |ᵊl -ɪb- ~**les** ᵊlz ~**ly** li
ˌvisible 'speech
VisiCalc tdmk 'vɪz i kælk
Visigoth 'vɪz i ɡɒθ 'vɪs- ‖ -ɡɑːθ ~**s** s
Visine tdmk vaɪ 'ziːn
vision 'vɪʒ ᵊn ~**s** z
visionar|y 'vɪʒ ᵊn ər |i ‖ -ə ner |i ~**ies** iz
vis|it 'vɪz |ɪt §-ət ‖ -|ət ~**ited** ɪt ɪd §ət-, -əd
‖ əţ əd ~**iting** ɪt ɪŋ §ət- ‖ əţ ɪŋ ~**its** ɪts §əts
‖ əts
ˈvisiting card; ˈvisiting ˈfireman; ˌvisiting
proˈfessor
visitant 'vɪz ɪt ənt §-ət- ~**s** s
visitation ˌvɪz ɪ 'teɪʃ ᵊn §-ə- ~**s** z
visitor 'vɪz ɪt ə §-ət- ‖ -əţ ᵊr ~**s** z
ˈvisitors' book
visna 'vɪz nə 'vɪs-

visor 'vaɪz ə ‖ -ᵊr ~**s** z
vista 'vɪst ə ~**s** s
Vistula 'vɪst jʊl ə 'vɪs tʃəl ə ‖ 'vɪs tʃʊl ə
—*Polish* Wisła ['vis wa]
visual 'vɪʒ u əl 'vɪz ju‿, 'vɪʒ ju‿ ~**ly** i ~**s** z
ˌvisual 'aid; ˌvisual diˈsplay ˌunit
visualis... —*see* **visualiz...**
visualization ˌvɪʒ u əl aɪ 'zeɪʃ ᵊn ˌvɪz ju‿,
ˌvɪʒ ju‿, -ɪ'·- ‖ -ə 'zeɪʃ ᵊn ˌvɪʒ əl ə'·‿·‿·‿ ~**s** z
visualiz|e 'vɪʒ u ə laɪz 'vɪz ju‿, 'vɪʒ ju‿
‖ 'vɪʒ ə laɪz ~**ed** d ~**es** ɪz əz ~**ing** ɪŋ
vita 'viːt ə 'vaɪt- ‖ 'viːţ ə 'vaɪţ- ~**s** z
Vitaglass tdmk 'vaɪt ə glɑːs ‖ 'vaɪţ ə glæs
vital 'vaɪt ᵊl ‖ 'vaɪţ ᵊl ~**ly** i ~**s** z
ˌvital caˈpacity; ˌvital ˈsigns; ˌvital
staˈtistics
vitalis... —*see* **vitaliz...**
vitality vaɪ 'tæl ət i -ɪt- ‖ -əţ i
vitaliz|e 'vaɪt ə laɪz -ᵊl aɪz ‖ 'vaɪţ- ~**ed** d ~**es**
ɪz əz ~**ing** ɪŋ
vitally 'vaɪt ᵊl i ‖ 'vaɪţ ᵊl i
vitamin 'vɪt əm ɪn 'vaɪt-, §-ən ‖ 'vaɪţ- ~**s** z
ˌvitamin 'C
VitBe tdmk 'vɪt bi
vitelline vɪ 'tel aɪn -ɪn, §-ən
viti|ate 'vɪʃ i |eɪt ~**ated** eɪt ɪd -əd ‖ eɪţ əd
~**ates** eɪts ~**ating** eɪt ɪŋ ‖ eɪţ ɪŋ
vitiation ˌvɪʃ i 'eɪʃ ᵊn
viticulture 'vɪt i ˌkʌltʃ ə 'vaɪt-, §'·ə-
‖ 'vɪţ ə ˌkʌltʃ ᵊr
Viti Levu ˌviːt i 'lev uː
vitiligo ˌvɪt ɪ 'laɪɡ əʊ -ə-, -ᵊl 'aɪɡ-
‖ ˌvɪţ ᵊl 'aɪɡ oʊ
vitreous 'vɪtr i əs ~**ness** nəs nɪs
vitrifaction ˌvɪtr ɪ 'fæk ʃᵊn -ə-
vitrification ˌvɪtr ɪf ɪ 'keɪʃ ᵊn ˌ·əf-, §-ə'·-
vitri|fy 'vɪtr ɪ |faɪ -ə- ~**fied** faɪd ~**fies** faɪz
~**fying** faɪ ɪŋ
vitriol 'vɪtr i əl -ɒl
vitriolic ˌvɪtr i 'ɒl ɪk ◄ ‖ -'ɑːl- ~**ally** ᵊl‿i
vitro 'viːtr əʊ ‖ -oʊ
Vitruvius vɪ 'truːv i əs və-
Vittel tdmk vɪ 'tel
vittles 'vɪt ᵊlz ‖ 'vɪţ ᵊlz
vitupe|rate vaɪ 'tjuːp ə |reɪt vɪ-, §və-,
→‖-'tʃuːp- ‖ -'tuːp- -'tjuːp-
vituperation vaɪ ˌtjuːp ə 'reɪʃ ᵊn vɪ-, §və-,
→‖-, tʃuːp- ‖ -, tuːp- -, tjuːp-
vituperative vaɪ 'tjuːp ᵊr ət ɪv vɪ-, §və-,
→‖-'tʃuːp-, -ə reɪt- ‖ -'tuːp ᵊr əţ ɪv -'tjuːp-,
-ə reɪţ-
Vitus 'vaɪt əs ‖ 'vaɪţ əs
viva 'long live', **Viva** tdmk 'viːv ə ~**s** z
viva 'oral examination' 'vaɪv ə ~**ed** d **vivaing**
'vaɪv əʳ ɪŋ ‖ 'vaɪv ə ɪŋ ~**s** z
vivace vɪ 'vɑːtʃ i §və-, -eɪ
vivacious vɪ 'veɪʃ əs §və-, vaɪ- ~**ly** li ~**ness** nəs
nɪs
vivacity vɪ 'væs ət i §və-, -ɪt- ‖ -əţ i
Vivaldi vɪ 'væld i ‖ -'vɑːld- —*It* [vi 'val di]
vivari|um vaɪ 'veər i |əm vɪ-, §və- ‖ -'ver-
-'vær- ~**a** ə ~**ums** əmz
vivat 'vaɪv æt 'viːv- ‖ -ɑːt ~**s** s

viva voce ˌvaɪv ə ˈvəʊtʃ i ˌviːv-, -ˈvəʊs-
‖ -ˈvoʊtʃ- -ˈvoʊs-
vivax ˈvaɪv æks
Vivian ˈvɪv i‿ən
vivid ˈvɪv ɪd §-əd **~ly** li **~ness** nəs nɪs
Vivien ˈvɪv i‿ən
Vivienne (i) ˈvɪv i‿ən, (ii) ˌvɪv i ˈen
vivification ˌvɪv ɪf ɪ ˈkeɪʃ ᵊn §ˌ-əf-, §-ə'--
vivi|fy ˈvɪv ɪ |faɪ §-ə- **~fied** faɪd **~fier/s** faɪ‿ə/z
‖ faɪ‿ᵊr/z **~fies** faɪz **~fying** faɪ ɪŋ
viviparous vɪ ˈvɪp ər əs vaɪ-, §və- **~ly** li
vivisect ˈvɪv ɪ sekt -ə-, ˌ·ˈ· **~ed** ɪd əd **~ing** ɪŋ
~s s
vivisection ˌvɪv ɪ ˈsek ʃᵊn §-ə-
vivisectionist ˌvɪv ɪ ˈsek ʃᵊn ɪst §ˌ-ə-, §ˌ_ əst **~s**
s
vixen ˈvɪks ən **~s** z
vixenish ˈvɪks ən ɪʃ
Viyella tdmk vaɪ ˈel ə
viz, viz. vɪz —Usually read aloud as namely
ˈneɪm li
Viz —name of publication vɪz
vizier vɪ ˈzɪə §və-; ˈvɪz ɪə ‖ və ˈzɪᵊr **~s** z
vizsla ˈvɪʒ lə —Hung [ˈviʒ lɒ] **~s** z
VJ ˌviː ˈdʒeɪ **~s** z
Vlach vlɑːk **Vlachs** vlɑːks
Vlad vlæd —Romanian [vlad]
Vladimir ˈvlæd ɪ mɪə -ə- ‖ -ə mɪr —Russ
[vlʌ ˈdʲi mʲɪr], Czech Vladimír [ˈvla dʲi miːr]
Vladivostok ˌvlæd ɪ ˈvɒst ɒk §-ə- ‖ -ˈvɑːst ɑːk
—Russ [vlə dʲi vʌ ˈstɔk]
VLSI ˌviː el es ˈaɪ
Vltava ˈvʊlt əv ə —Czech [ˈvl̩ ta va]
V-neck ˈviː nek ˌ·ˈ· **~ed** t **~s** s
vocab ˈvəʊk æb ‖ ˈvoʊk-
vocabular|y vəʊ ˈkæb jʊl ər |i -ˈ·jəl-; §-ju ler i,
§-ˈ·jə-, §-ˈ·ə- ‖ voʊ ˈkæb jə ler |i və **~ies** iz
vocal ˈvəʊk ᵊl ‖ ˈvoʊk ᵊl **~ly** i **~s** z
ˌvocal ˈcords, ˈ·· ·‖ ˈ·· ·; ˌvocal ˈfolds
‖ ˈ·· ·
vocalic vəʊ ˈkæl ɪk ‖ voʊ- və-
vocalis... —see **vocaliz...**
vocalism ˈvəʊk ə ˌlɪz əm -ᵊl ˌɪz- ‖ ˈvoʊk-
vocalist ˈvəʊk əl ɪst §-əst ‖ ˈvoʊk- **~s** s
vocalization ˌvəʊk əl aɪ ˈzeɪʃ ᵊn -ɪ'--
‖ ˌvoʊk əl ə- **~s** z
vocaliz|e ˈvəʊk ə laɪz -ᵊl aɪz ‖ ˈvoʊk- **~ed** d
~es ɪz əz **~ing** ɪŋ
vocally ˈvəʊk ᵊl i i ‖ ˈvoʊk-
vocation vəʊ ˈkeɪʃ ᵊn ‖ voʊ- **~s** z
vocational vəʊ ˈkeɪʃ ᵊn̩ əl ‖ voʊ- **~ly** i
vocative ˈvɒk ət ɪv ‖ ˈvɑːk əţ ɪv **~s** z
Voce vəʊs ‖ voʊs
vocife|rate vəʊ ˈsɪf ə |reɪt ‖ voʊ- **~rated**
reɪt ɪd -əd ‖ reɪţ əd **~rates** reɪts **~rating**
reɪt ɪŋ ‖ reɪţ ɪŋ
vociferation vəʊ ˌsɪf ə ˈreɪʃ ᵊn ‖ voʊ- **~s** z
vociferous vəʊ ˈsɪf ər‿əs ‖ voʊ- **~ly** li **~ness**
nəs nɪs
vocoder ˌvəʊ ˈkəʊd ə ‖ ˌvoʊ ˈkoʊd ᵊr **~s** z
vocoid ˈvəʊk ɔɪd ‖ ˈvoʊk- **~s** z
vocoidal vəʊ ˈkɔɪd ᵊl ‖ voʊ-

Vodafone tdmk ˈvəʊd ə fəʊn ‖ ˈvoʊd ə foʊn
~s z
vodka ˈvɒd kə ‖ ˈvɑːd kə **~s** z
voe, Voe vəʊ ‖ voʊ **voes** vəʊz ‖ voʊz
Vogt (i) vəʊkt ‖ voʊkt, (ii) vəʊt ‖ voʊt, (iii)
vɒt ‖ vɑːt
vogue vəʊg ‖ voʊg **vogues** vəʊgz ‖ voʊgz
voguish ˈvəʊg ɪʃ ‖ ˈvoʊg- **~ness** nəs nɪs
Vogul ˈvəʊg ʊl -ᵊl ‖ ˈvoʊg- **~s** z
voice vɔɪs **voiced** vɔɪst **voices** ˈvɔɪs ɪz -əz
ˈvoicing ˈvɔɪs ɪŋ
ˈvoice box; ˈvoice mail
-voiced ˈvɔɪst — gruff-voiced ˌgrʌf ˈvɔɪst ◄
voiceless ˈvɔɪs ləs -lɪs **~ly** li **~ness** nəs nɪs
voice-over ˈvɔɪs ˌəʊv ə ˌ·ˈ·· ‖ -ˌoʊv ᵊr **~s** z
voiceprint ˈvɔɪs prɪnt **~s** s
void vɔɪd **voided** ˈvɔɪd ɪd -əd **voiding** ˈvɔɪd ɪŋ
voids vɔɪdz
voidable ˈvɔɪd əb ᵊl **~ness** nəs nɪs
voidance ˈvɔɪd ᵊn̩s
Voight, Voigt vɔɪt
voila, voilà vwæ ˈlɑː vwʌ-, vwɑː- ‖ vwɑː- —Fr
[vwa la]
voile vɔɪᵊl vwɑːl —Fr [vwal]
VoIP vɔɪp
voix vwɑː —Fr [vwa]
ˌvoix ceˈleste, ˌvoix céˈleste sɪ ˈlest sə-
— Fr [se lɛst]
Vojvodina ˌvɔɪv ə ˈdiːn ə —Serbian
[ˈˈvɔj vɔ di na]
vol, vol. vɒl ‖ vɑːl —or as volume
volant ˈvəʊl ənt ‖ ˈvoʊl-
Volapuk, Volapük ˈvɒl ə puːk ˈvəʊl-, -pʊk,
ˌ·ˈ· ‖ ˈvoʊl- ˈvɑːl- —Volapük [vo la ˈpyk]
volatile ˈvɒl ə taɪᵊl ‖ ˈvɑːl əţ ᵊl (*) **~s** z —but
see also **sal volatile**
volatilis... —see **volatiliz...**
volatility ˌvɒl ə ˈtɪl ət i -ɪt i ‖ ˌvɑːl ə ˈtɪl əţ i
volatilization və ˌlæt ɪl aɪ ˈzeɪʃ ᵊn vɒ-, vəʊ-,
-ˌ·əl-, -ɪ'--; ˌvɒl ət- ‖ ˌvɑːl əţ ᵊl ə ˈzeɪʃ ᵊn
volatiliz|e və ˈlæt ɪ laɪz vɒ-, vəʊ-, ˈvɒl ət-,
-ə laɪz, -ᵊl aɪz ‖ ˈvɑːl əţ ᵊl aɪz **~ed** d **~es** ɪz əz
~ing ɪŋ
vol-au-vent ˈvɒl ə vɒ̃ ˈvəʊl-, -əʊ-, -vɒn, -vɒŋ,
ˌ·ˈ· ‖ ˌvɔːl oʊ ˈvɑːn ˌvɑːl- —Fr [vɔ lo vɑ̃] **~s**
z
volcanic vɒl ˈkæn ɪk ‖ vɑːl- **~ally** ᵊl_i
volcanism ˈvɒlk ə ˌnɪz əm ‖ ˈvɑːlk-
volcano vɒl ˈkeɪn əʊ ‖ vɑːl ˈkeɪn oʊ **~s** z
volcanological ˌvɒlk ən ə ˈlɒdʒ ɪk ᵊl ◄
‖ ˌvɑːlk ən ə ˈlɑːdʒ- **~ly** i
volcanologist ˌvɒlk ə ˈnɒl ədʒ ɪst §-əst
‖ ˌvɑːlk ə ˈnɑːl- **~s** s
volcanology ˌvɒlk ə ˈnɒl ədʒ i
‖ ˌvɑːlk ə ˈnɑːl-
Voldemort ˈvɒl də mɔːt ˈvəʊl-, -mɔː
‖ ˈvoʊl də mɔːrt -mɔːr —J.K. Rowling
pronounces this name French-style, with no
final t; the Harry Potter films, however, use
one.
vole vəʊl →vɒʊl ‖ voʊl **voles** vəʊlz →vɒʊlz
‖ voʊlz

volenti non fit injuria
vəʊ ˌlent i ˌnəʊn fɪt ɪn 'dʒʊər i ə vɒ-, -ˌnɒn-,
-'jʊər- ‖ voʊ ˌlent i ˌnɑːn fɪt ɪn 'dʒʊr i ə
Volga 'vɒlg ə ‖ 'vɑːlg ə —*Russ* ['vɒɬ gə]
Volgograd 'vɒlg əʊ græd ‖ 'vɑːlg ə- —*Russ*
[vəɬ gʌ 'grat]
volitant 'vɒl ɪt ənt -ət- ‖ 'vɑːl ət ᵊnt
volition vəʊ 'lɪʃ ᵊn ‖ vʊʊ- və-
volitional vəʊ 'lɪʃ ᵊn əl ‖ vʊʊ- və- ~**ly** i
volitive 'vɒl ət ɪv -ɪt- ‖ 'vɑːl əʈ ɪv
Volk *family name(i)* vɒlk ‖ vɑːlk, *(ii)* vəʊlk
→vɒʊlk ‖ vovlk
Volk *German, 'people'* fɒlk vɒlk ‖ fɔːlk fɑːlk
—*Ger* [fɔlk]
Volkswagen *tdmk* 'vɒlks ˌwæg ən 'vəʊks-,
'fɒlks-, -, wɑːg-, -, vɑːg- ‖ 'voʊks- -, wɑːg- —*Ger*
['fɔlks ˌvaːg ən] ~**s** z
volley 'vɒl i ‖ 'vɑːl i ~**ed** d ~**ing** ɪŋ ~**s** z
volleyball 'vɒl i bɔːl ‖ 'vɑːl- -bɑːl
volplan|e 'vɒl pleɪn ‖ 'vɑːl- ~**ed** d ~**es** z ~**ing**
ɪŋ
Volpone vɒl 'pəʊn i ‖ vɑːl 'poʊn i vɔːl-
Volsci 'vɒls ki -aɪ, -iː ‖ 'vɑːls-
Volscian 'vɒls ki ən ‖ 'vɑːls- ~**s** z
Volstead 'vɒl sted ‖ 'vɑːl-
volt vəʊlt →vɒʊlt, vɒlt ‖ voʊlt **volts** vəʊlts
→vɒʊlts, vɒlts ‖ voʊlts
volta *dance, piece of music, 'time, turn'* 'vɒlt ə
‖ 'voʊlt ə 'vɑːlt- —*It* ['vɔl ta] ~**s** z
Volta *lake and river* 'vɒlt ə ‖ 'voʊlt ə
Volta *physicist* 'vəʊlt ə 'vɒlt- ‖ 'voʊlt ə —*It*
['vɔl ta]
voltag|e 'vəʊlt ɪdʒ →'vɒʊlt-, 'vɒlt- ‖ 'voʊlt-
~**es** ɪz əz
voltaic, V~ vɒl 'teɪ ɪk vəʊl- ‖ vɑːl- voʊl-
Voltaire vɒl 'teə vəʊl-, '·· ‖ voʊl 'teᵊr —*Fr*
[vɔl tɛːʁ]
volte-fac|e ˌvɒlt 'fæs -'fæs ‖ ˌvɔːlt 'fɑːs ˌvɑːlt-,
ˌvoʊlt- —*Fr* [vɔl tə fas] ~**es** ɪz əz —*or as*
sing.
voltmeter 'vəʊlt ˌmiːt ə 'vɒlt- ‖ 'voʊlt ˌmiːʈ ᵊr
~**s** z
volubility ˌvɒl ju 'bɪl ət i ˌjə-, -ɪt i
‖ ˌvɑːl jə 'bɪl əʈ i
volub|le 'vɒl jʊb |ᵊl §-jəb- ‖ 'vɑːl jəb |ᵊl
~**leness** ᵊl nəs -nɪs ~**ly** li
volume 'vɒl juːm -jʊm ‖ 'vɑːl jəm -jʊm, -juːm
~**s** z
volumetric ˌvɒl ju 'metr ɪk ◂ §-jə- ‖ ˌvɑːl jə-
~**ally** ᵊl‿i
voluminous və 'luːm ɪn əs vɒ-, -'ljuːm-, -ən-
~**ly** li ~**ness** nəs nɪs
voluntarily ˌvɒl ən 'ter əl i -'teər-, -'tær-, ɪ li;
'vɒl ənt‿ər əl i, -ɪ li ‖ ˌvɑːl ən 'ter əl i -'tær-;
'· · · · · — *Preference poll, BrE:* -'ter- *41%,* 'vɒl-
32%, -'teər- *15%,* -'tær- *12%.*
voluntarism 'vɒl ənt ə ˌrɪz əm ‖ 'vɑːl-
voluntar|y 'vɒl ənt‿ər |i -ən ter-
‖ 'vɑːl ən ter |i ~**ies** iz ~**iness** i nəs i nɪs
volunteer ˌvɒl ən 'tɪə ‖ ˌvɑːl ən 'tɪᵊr ~**ed** d
volunteering ˌvɒl ən 'tɪər ɪŋ
‖ ˌvɑːl ən 'tɪr ɪŋ ~**s** z

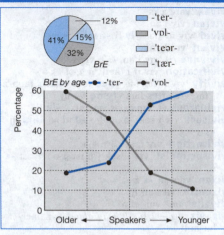

VOLUNTARILY

- -'ter-
- 'vɒl-
- -'teər-
- -'tær-

BrE

BrE by age -●- -'ter- -●- 'vɒl-

volunteerism ˌvɒl ən 'tɪər ˌɪz əm
‖ ˌvɑːl ən 'tɪr-
voluptuar|y və 'lʌp tʃu‿ər |i -'lʌp tju‿,
-'lʌp tʃər |i -tʃu er |i ~**ies** iz
voluptuous və 'lʌp tʃu‿əs -tju‿əs ~**ly** li ~**ness**
nəs nɪs
volute və 'luːt vɒ-, vəʊ-, -'ljuːt ~**s** s
voluted və 'luːt ɪd vɒ-, vəʊ-, -'ljuːt-, -əd
‖ -'luːʈ əd
volution və 'luːʃ ᵊn vɒ-, vəʊ-, -'ljuːʃ-
volv|a 'vɒlv |ə ‖ 'vɑːlv |ə ~**ae** iː
Volvic *tdmk* 'vɒlv ɪk ‖ 'vɑːlv- 'voʊlv-
Volvo *tdmk* 'vɒlv əʊ ‖ 'vɑːlv oʊ 'voʊlv- ~**s** z
volvox 'vɒlv ɒks ‖ 'vɑːlv ɑːks
vomer 'vəʊm ə ‖ 'voʊm ᵊr ~**s** z
vom|it 'vɒm |ɪt §-ət ‖ 'vɑːm |ət ~**ited** ɪt ɪd
§ət-, -əd ‖ əʈ əd ~**iting** ɪt ɪŋ §ət- ‖ əʈ ɪŋ ~**its**
ɪts §əts ‖ əts
vomitori|um ˌvɒm ɪ 'tɔːr i‿|əm ˌ·ə- ‖ ˌvɑːm ə-
-'tʊʊr- ~**a** ə ~**ums** əmz
vomitor|y 'vɒm ɪ tər |i '·ə‿ ‖ 'vɑːm ə tɔːr |i
-tʊʊr i ~**ies** iz
von, Von *in family names* vɒn fɒn ‖ vɑːn
—*Ger* [fɔn]
Vonage 'vɒn ɪdʒ ‖ 'vɑːn ɪdʒ
Von Braun vɒn 'braʊn fɒn- ‖ vɔːn- vɑːn-
—*Ger* [fɔn 'bʁaʊn]
Vonnegut 'vɒn ɪ gʌt -ə- ‖ 'vɑːn- 'vɔːn-
Vono *tdmk* 'vəʊn əʊ ‖ 'voʊn oʊ
voodoo 'vuːd uː ~**ism** ˌɪz əm
Voortrekker 'fʊə ˌtrek ə 'vʊə-, 'fɔː-, 'vɔː-
‖ 'fɔːr ˌtrek ᵊr 'foʊr- —*Afrikaans*
['foːr ˌtrɛk ər] ~**s** z
voracious və 'reɪʃ əs vɒ- ~**ly** li ~**ness** nəs nɪs
voracity və 'ræs ət i vɒ-, -ɪt- ‖ -əʈ i
Vorderman 'vɔːd ə mən ‖ 'vɔːrd ᵊr-
-vorous *stress-imposing* vər əs — **omnivorous**
ɒm 'nɪv ər əs ‖ ɑːm-
Vorsprung durch Technik
ˌvɔː sprʌŋ ˌdɜːx 'tex nɪk -tek 'niːk
‖ ˌvɔːr sprʌŋ dɜːk 'tek nɪk —*Ger*
[ˌfoːɐ ʃpʁʊŋ dʊʁç 'tɛç nɪk]

V

Voiced and voiceless

1 **Voiced** sounds are produced with the vocal folds vibrating – opening and closing rapidly, producing **voice**. **Voiceless** sounds are made with the vocal folds apart, allowing the air to pass freely between them.

2 The sounds p, t, k, tʃ, f, θ, s, ʃ, h are normally voiceless, while the remaining English sounds are classified as voiced.

3 There is a difficulty with this classification, since it refers to PHONEMES – yet in reality a given English phoneme may have both voiced and voiceless ALLOPHONEs. For example, in AmE the 'voiceless' phoneme t includes the voiced allophone ṭ, which is so noticeable that this dictionary gives it a separate symbol (see T-VOICING).

4 Another difficulty arises with b, d, ɡ, dʒ, v, ð, z, ʒ. It is only when they are between other voiced sounds that these consonants are reliably voiced. In other positions there is often little or no actual vibration of the vocal folds during their production. Hence they are sometimes classified as **lenis** rather than as voiced. The corresponding term for p, t, k, tʃ, f, θ, s, ʃ is **fortis**, rather than voiceless.

5 A **devoiced** lenis does not sound quite like a fortis. Quite apart from differences such as those described in the notes at ASPIRATION and CLIPPING, b, d, ɡ etc. have less articulatory force than p, t, k etc. This may be due to the vocal folds, which in the case of a devoiced lenis sound probably remain in the narrowed 'whisper' configuration, distinct from their wide open configuration for a true voiceless (fortis) sound.

---

vortex 'vɔːt eks ‖ 'vɔːrt- **~es** ɪz əz **vortices**
 'vɔːt ɪ siːz -ə- ‖ 'vɔːrt̬-
vorticism 'vɔːt ɪ ˌsɪz əm -ə- ‖ 'vɔːrt̬-
Vortigern 'vɔːt ɪ ɡɜːn -ɪɡ ən ‖ 'vɔːrt̬ ɪ ɡɜːn
Vosburgh 'vɒs bə ˌrə ‖ 'vɑːs-
Vosene *tdmk* 'vəuz iːn ‖ 'vouz-
Vosges vəuʒ ‖ vouʒ —*Fr* [voːʒ]
Voss vɒs ‖ vɑːs vɔːs
Vostok 'vɒst ɒk ‖ 'vɑːst ɑːk —*Russ* [vʌ 'stɔk]
votaress 'vəut ə res -ər əs, -ər ɪs ‖ 'vout̬ ər əs
 ~es ɪz əz
votar|y 'vəut ər |i ‖ 'vout̬- **~ies** iz
vote vəut ‖ vout **voted** 'vəut ɪd -əd ‖ 'vout̬ əd
 votes vəuts ‖ vouts **voting** 'vəut ɪŋ
 ‖ 'vout̬ ɪŋ
 ˌvote of 'thanks; 'voting booth; 'voting
 maˌchine
vote-getter 'vəut ˌɡet ə ‖ 'vout̬ ˌɡet̬ ər **~s** z
voteless 'vəut ləs -lɪs ‖ 'vout̬-
voter 'vəut ə ‖ 'vout̬ ər **~s** z
votive 'vəut ɪv ‖ 'vout̬ ɪv
Votyak 'vɒt jæk 'vəut-, -'i æk ‖ 'vout̬ jɑːk -jæk
vouch vautʃ **vouched** vautʃt **vouches**
 'vautʃ ɪz -əz **vouching** 'vautʃ ɪŋ
voucher 'vautʃ ə ‖ -ər **~s** z

vouchsaf|e ₍ᵢ₎vautʃ 'seɪf '· · **~ed** t **~es** s **~ing**
 ɪŋ
Vouvray 'vuːv reɪ ‖ vuː 'vreɪ —*Fr* [vu vʁɛ]
vow vau **vowed** vaud **vowing** 'vau ɪŋ **vows**
 vauz
vowel 'vau əl vaul ‖ 'vau̯ əl **voweled,**
 vowelled 'vau əld vauld ‖ 'vau̯ əld
 voweling, vowelling 'vau əl ɪŋ 'vaul ɪŋ
 ‖ 'vau̯ əl ɪŋ **vowels** 'vauəlz vaulz ‖ 'vau̯ əlz
vowelless 'vau əl ləs 'vaul ləs; -lɪs ‖ 'vau̯ əl-
vowel-like 'vau əl laɪk 'vaul laɪk ‖ 'vau̯ əl-
Vowles *(i)* vəulz →vɒulz ‖ voulz, *(ii)* vau̯lz
vox vɒks ‖ vɑːks
 ˌvox hu'mana hju 'mɑːn ə; ˌvox 'pop; ˌvox
 'populi 'pɒp ju laɪ -jə-, -liː ‖ 'pɑːp jə-
voyag|e 'vɔɪ ɪdʒ **~ed** d **~es** ɪz əz **~ing** ɪŋ
voyager, V~ 'vɔɪ ɪdʒ ə -ədʒ- ‖ -ᵊr **~s** z
voyeur ₍ᵢ₎vwaɪ 'ɜː ₍ᵢ₎vɔɪ-; ₍ᵢ₎vwɑː 'jɜː; 'vɔɪ ə,
 'vwɔɪ- ‖ vwɑː 'jɜː —*Fr* [vwa jœːʁ] **~s** z
voyeurism ₍ᵢ₎vwaɪ 'ɜː r ˌɪz əm ₍ᵢ₎vɔɪ-;
 ₍ᵢ₎vwɑː 'jɜːr-; 'vɔɪ ər-, 'vwɔɪ- ‖ vwɑː 'jɜː-
voyeuristic ˌvwaɪ ɜː 'rɪst ɪk ◂ ˌvɔɪ-, ˌvwɔɪ-, -ə-;
 ˌvwɑː jɜː- ‖ ˌvwɑː jə- **~ally** ᵊl i
VP ˌviː 'piː **~s** z
VRML 'vɜːm ᵊl ‖ 'vɝːm ᵊl

vroom vruːm vrʊm
vs, vs. 'vɜːs əs ‖ 'vɝːs əs
V-shaped 'viː ʃeɪpt
V-sign 'viː saɪn ~s z
VSO ˌviː es 'əʊ ‖ -'oʊ
  ˌVS'O ˌlanguage
VTOL 'viː tɒl ˌviː tiː əʊ 'el ‖ 'viː tɔːl -tɑːl
VTR ˌviː tiː 'ɑː ‖ -'ɑːr ~s, ~'s z
vug, vugg, vugh vʌg **vuggs, vughs, vugs**
  vʌgz
Vuitton tdmk 'vjuː ɪ tɒn -ɪt ᵊn, §-ət-; 'vwiːt ɒ̃
  ‖ 'vjuː ə tɑːn 'vwiː tɑːn —Fr [vɥi tɔ̃]
Vukovar 'vuːk ə vɑː ‖ -vɑːr —Croatian
  [vu ''kɔ vaːr]
Vulcan 'vʌlk ən
vulcanis... —see **vulcaniz...**
vulcanism 'vʌlk ə ˌnɪz əm
vulcanite 'vʌlk ə naɪt
vulcanization ˌvʌlk ən aɪ 'zeɪʃ ᵊn -ɪ'·- ‖ -ə'·-
vulcaniz|e 'vʌlk ə naɪz ~ed d ~es ɪz əz ~ing
  ɪŋ
vulcanological ˌvʌlk ən ə 'lɒdʒ ɪk ᵊl ◄
  ‖ -'lɑːdʒ- ~ly ˌi
vulcanologist ˌvʌlk ə 'nɒl ədʒ ɪst §-əst
  ‖ -'nɑːl- ~s s
vulcanology ˌvʌlk ə 'nɒl ədʒ i ‖ -'nɑːl-
vulgar 'vʌlg ə ‖ -ᵊr ~ly li ~ness nəs nɪs
  ˌvulgar 'fraction; ˌVulgar 'Latin

vulgarian vʌl 'geər i ən ‖ -'ger- -'gær- ~s z
vulgaris... —see **vulgariz...**
vulgarism 'vʌlg ə ˌrɪz əm ~s z
vulgarit|y vʌl 'gær ət |i -ɪt- ‖ -ət̬ |i -'ger- ~ies
  iz
vulgarization ˌvʌlg ər aɪ 'zeɪʃ ᵊn -ɪ'·- ‖ -ə'·-
vulgariz|e 'vʌlg ə raɪz ~ed d ~es ɪz əz ~ing
  ɪŋ
Vulgate 'vʌlg eɪt -ət, -ɪt
Vulliamy 'vʌl jəm i
vulnerability ˌvʌln ər̩ə 'bɪl ət i ˌvʌn-, -ɪt i
  ‖ -ət̬ i
vulnerab|le 'vʌln ər̩əb |ᵊl 'vʌn- ~leness
  ᵊl nəs -nɪs ~ly li
vulnerary 'vʌln ər ər i ‖ -ə rer i
Vulpecula vʌl 'pek jʊl ə -jəl- ‖ -jəl ə
vulpine 'vʌlp aɪn
vulture 'vʌltʃ ə ‖ -ᵊr ~s z
vulv|a 'vʌlv |ə ~ae iː ~as əz
vulvitis vʌl 'vaɪt ɪs §-əs ‖ -'vaɪt̬ əs
vulvovaginitis ˌvʌlv əʊ ˌvædʒ ɪ 'naɪt ɪs -ə'·-,
  §-əs ‖ -oʊ ˌvædʒ ə 'naɪt̬ əs
VW tdmk ˌviː 'dʌb ᵊl juː -ju ‖ -jə
vying 'vaɪ ɪŋ
Vyrnwy 'vɜːn wi 'vɜːn u i i ‖ 'vɝːn-
Vyvyan 'vɪv i ən

w Spelling-to-sound

1 Where the spelling is **w**,
- either the pronunciation is w as in **swim** swɪm, **away** ə ˈweɪ or else
- the w forms part of one of the digraphs **aw, ew, ow** (see under **a, e, o** respectively) as in **few** fjuː.

2 w is always silent in **wr** at the beginning of a word or stem as in **wreck** rek, **rewrite** (noun) ˈriː raɪt, also in the exceptionally spelled words **two** tuː, **answer** ˈɑːn's ə ‖ ˈæn's ᵊr.

3 w is also regularly written **u** as in **persuade** pə ˈsweɪd ‖ pᵊr- and as part of the digraph **qu** as in **quite** kwaɪt.

wh Spelling-to-sound

1 Where the spelling is the digraph **wh**, the pronunciation in most cases is w, as in **white** waɪt. An alternative pronunciation, depending on regional, social and stylistic factors, is hw, thus hwaɪt. This h pronunciation is usual in Scottish and Irish English, and decreasingly so in AmE, but not otherwise. (Among those who pronounce simple w, the pronunciation with hw tends to be considered 'better', and so is used by some people in formal styles only.) Learners of EFL are recommended to use plain w.

2 Occasionally, the pronunciation is h as in **whole** həʊl ‖ hoʊl, **who** huː.

W, w ˈdʌb ᵊl juː -ju ‖ -jə —*in AmE sometimes reduced to* ˈdʌb jə **W's, w's, Ws** ˈdʌb ᵊl juːz —*Communications code name:* Whisky
ˌWˈC; ˌwˈh ˌquestion; ˌWˌHˈO; ˌWˌPˈC
WAAC wæk
WAAF, Waaf wæf **Waafs** wæfs
Wabash ˈwɔː bæʃ ‖ ˈwɑː-
WAC, Wac wæk **Wacs** wæks
Wace weɪs
wack wæk
wacko ˈwæk əʊ ‖ -oʊ
wack|y ˈwæk |i **-ier** i ə ‖ iᵊr **-iest** i ɪst i ‿əst
~ily ɪ li əl i **~iness** i nəs i nɪs
Waco ˈweɪk əʊ ‖ -oʊ
wad wɒd ‖ wɑːd **wadded** ˈwɒd ɪd -əd
‖ ˈwɑːd əd **wadding** ˈwɒd ɪŋ ‖ ˈwɑːd ɪŋ
wads wɒdz ‖ wɑːdz

Waddell *(i)* ˈwɒd ᵊl ‖ ˈwɑːd ᵊl, *(ii)* wɒ ˈdel wə- ‖ wɑː-
Waddesdon ˈwɒdz dən ‖ ˈwɑːdz-
wadding ˈwɒd ɪŋ ‖ ˈwɑːd ɪŋ
Waddington ˈwɒd ɪŋ tən ‖ ˈwɑːd-
waddl|e ˈwɒd ᵊl ‖ ˈwɑːd ᵊl **~ed** d **~es** z **~ing** ɪŋ
Waddon ˈwɒd ᵊn ‖ ˈwɑːd ᵊn
wadd|y ˈwɒd| i ‖ ˈwɑːd| i **~ies** iz
wade, Wade weɪd **waded** ˈweɪd ɪd -əd **wades** weɪdz **wading** ˈweɪd ɪŋ
ˈwading bird; ˈwading pool
Wadebridge ˈweɪd brɪdʒ →ˈweɪb-
Wade-Giles ˌweɪd ˈdʒaɪᵊlz
ˌWade-ˈGiles ˌsystem
wader ˈweɪd ə ‖ -ᵊr **~s** z

wadge, Wadge wɒdʒ ‖ wɑːdʒ **wadges** 'wɒdʒ ɪz -əz ‖ 'wɑːdʒ əz
Wadham 'wɒd əm ‖ 'wɑːd-
Wadhurst 'wɒd hɜːst ‖ 'wɑːd hɜːst
wadi 'wɒd i 'wɑːd i ‖ 'wɑːd i ~s z
wading —*see* **wade**
Wadsworth 'wɒdz wəθ -wɜːθ ‖ 'wɑːdz wərθ
wad|y 'wɒd |i 'wɑːd- ‖ 'wɑːd |i ~**ies** iz
wafer 'weɪf ə ‖ -ər ~**s** z
wafer-thin ˌweɪf ə 'θɪn ◂ ‖ -ər-
waffl|e 'wɒf əl ‖ 'wɑːf əl ~**ed** d ~**er/s** ə/z ‖ ər/z ~**es** z ~**ing** ɪŋ
  'waffle ˌiron
waffler 'wɒf əl ə ‖ 'wɑːf əl ər ~**s** z
waffly 'wɒf əl i ‖ 'wɑːf əl i
waft wɑːft wɒft, wɔːft, §wæft ‖ wæft **wafted** 'wɑːft ɪd 'wɒft-, 'wɔːft-, -əd ‖ 'wæft-
  wafting 'wɑːft ɪŋ 'wɒft-, 'wɔːft-, §'wæft- ‖ 'wæft- **wafts** wɑːfts wɒfts, wɔːfts, §wæfts ‖ wæfts
wag wæg **wagged** wægd **wagging** 'wæg ɪŋ **wags** wægz
wage weɪdʒ **waged** weɪdʒd **wages** 'weɪdʒ ɪz -əz **waging** 'weɪdʒ ɪŋ
  'wage ˌearner; 'wage ˌpacket; 'wage rate; 'wage rise; 'wage slave
wager 'weɪdʒ ə ‖ -ər ~**ed** d **wagering** 'weɪdʒ ər ɪŋ ~**s** z
Wagg wæg
wagga, Wagga 'wɒg ə ‖ 'wɑːg ə Wagga Wagga '·· ˌ·· ˌ·· '··
waggery 'wæg ər i
waggish 'wæg ɪʃ ~**ly** li ~**ness** nəs nɪs
waggl|e 'wæg əl ~**ed** d ~**es** z ~**ing** ɪŋ
waggly 'wæg əl i
waggon 'wæg ən ~**s** z
waggoner 'wæg ən ə ‖ -ən ər ~**s** z
waggonette ˌwæg ə 'net ~**s** s
waggonload 'wæg ən ləʊd ‖ -loʊd ~**s** z
Waghorn 'wæg hɔːn ‖ -hɔːrn
Wagnall 'wæg nəl
Wagner *German name, composer* 'vɑːg nə ‖ -nər —*Ger* ['vɑːg nɐ]
Wagner *English or American family name* 'wæg nə ‖ -nər
Wagnerian vɑːg 'nɪər i ən ‖ -'nɪr- -'ner- ~**s** z
wagon 'wæg ən ~**s** z
  'wagon train
wagoner 'wæg ən ə ‖ -ən ər ~**s** z
wagonette ˌwæg ə 'net ~**s** s
wagon-lit ˌvæg ɒn 'liː -ō- ‖ ˌvɑːg ən- -ɔːn-, -oʊn- —*Fr* [va gɔ̃ li] ~**s** *same as sing., less commonly* z
wagonload 'wæg ən ləʊd ‖ -loʊd ~**s** z
Wagstaff 'wæg stɑːf §-stæf ‖ -stæf
wagtail 'wæg teɪl ~**s** z
Wahabi, Wahhabi wə 'hɑːb i wɑː-
wahoo wɑː 'huː '·· ~**s** z
wah-wah 'wɑː wɑː ~**s** z
waif weɪf **waifs** weɪfs
waif-like 'weɪf laɪk
Waikato waɪ 'kæt əʊ -'kɑːt- ‖ -'kɑːʈ oʊ
Waikiki 'waɪk ɪ kiː ˌ··'·

wail weɪəl **wailed** weɪəld **wailing** 'weɪəl ɪŋ **wails** weɪəlz
wain weɪn **wains** weɪnz
Wain, Waine weɪn
Wainfleet 'weɪn fliːt
wainscot 'weɪn skət -skɒt ‖ -skɑːt, -skoʊt
  wainscoted, wainscotted 'weɪn skət ɪd -skɒt-, -əd ‖ -skəʈ əd -skɑːʈ-, -skoʊʈ-
  wainscoting, wainscotting 'weɪn skət ɪŋ -skɒt- ‖ -skəʈ ɪŋ -skɑːʈ-, -skoʊʈ- ~**s** s
Wainwright, w~ 'weɪn raɪt ~**s** s
waist weɪst (= *waste*) **waisted** 'weɪst ɪd -əd **waists** weɪsts
waistband 'weɪst bænd ~**s** z
waistcoat 'weɪs kəʊt 'weɪst-; 'wesk ət, -ɪt ‖ 'wesk ət 'weɪst koʊt ~**s** s
waist-deep ˌweɪst 'diːp ◂
waist-high ˌweɪst 'haɪ ◂
waistline 'weɪst laɪn ~**s** z
wait weɪt **waited** 'weɪt ɪd -əd ‖ 'weɪʈ əd
  waiting 'weɪt ɪŋ ‖ 'weɪʈ ɪŋ **waits** weɪts
  'waiting game; 'waiting list; 'waiting room
wait-and-see ˌweɪt ən 'siː -ənd-
Waitangi ˌwaɪ 'tæŋ i
Waite weɪt
waiter 'weɪt ə ‖ 'weɪʈ ər ~**s** z
Waites weɪts
waitlist 'weɪt lɪst ~**ed** ɪd əd ~**ing** ɪŋ ~**s** s
wait|person 'weɪt ˌpɜːs ən ‖ -ˌpɜːs ən ~**people** ˌpiːp əl
waitress 'weɪtr əs -ɪs ~**es** ɪz əz ~**ing** ɪŋ
waitron 'weɪtr ən ~**s** z
Waitrose *tdmk* 'weɪt rəʊz ‖ -roʊz
waitstaff 'weɪt stɑːf §-stæf ‖ -stæf
waive weɪv (= *wave*) **waived** weɪvd **waives** weɪvz **waiving** 'weɪv ɪŋ
waiver 'weɪv ə ‖ -ər (= *waver*) ~**s** z
Wajda 'vaɪd ə —*Polish* ['vai da]
wake, Wake weɪk **waked** weɪkt **wakes** weɪks
  waking 'weɪk ɪŋ **woke** wəʊk ‖ woʊk **woken** 'wəʊk ən ‖ 'woʊk ən
wakeboard 'weɪk bɔːd ‖ -bɔːrd -boʊrd ~**er/s** ə/z ‖ ər/z ~**ing** ɪŋ ~**s** z
Wakefield 'weɪk fiːəld
wakeful 'weɪk fəl -fʊl ~**ly** i ~**ness** nəs nɪs
Wakeham 'weɪk əm
Wakehurst 'weɪk hɜːst ‖ -hɜːst
Wakelin 'weɪk lɪn §-lən
waken 'weɪk ən ~**ed** d ~**ing** ɪŋ ~**s** z
Wakering 'weɪk ər ɪŋ
wake-robin 'weɪk ˌrɒb ɪn §-ən ‖ -ˌrɑːb-
wake-up 'weɪk ʌp
wakey 'weɪk i
  ˌwakey 'wakey!
waking —*see* **wake**
Wakley (i) 'wæk li, (ii) 'weɪk li
Walachi|a wɒ 'leɪk i ə wə- ‖ wɑː- ~**an/s** ən/z
Walberswick 'wɔːlb əz wɪk 'wɒlb- ‖ -ərz- 'wɑːlb-
Walbrook 'wɔːl brʊk 'wɒl- ‖ 'wɑːl-
Walcot, Walcott 'wɔːl kət 'wɒl-, -kɒt ‖ 'wɑːl-, -kɑːt

Waldegrave *(i)* 'wɔːld greɪv 'wɒld- ‖ 'wɑːld-, *(ii)* 'wɔːld ɪ greɪv 'wɒld-, -ə- ‖ 'wɑːld-
Waldemar 'væld ə mɑː 'wɔːld-, -ɪ- ‖ 'vɑːld ə mɑːr —*Ger* ['val də maʁ], *Swed* [-mar]
Walden 'wɔːld ən 'wɒld- ‖ 'wɑːld-
Walden|es wɔːl 'den's |iːz wɒl- ‖ wɑːl- **~ian/s** i ən/z
Waldheim 'vɑːld haɪm ‖ 'wɑːld- —*Ger* ['valt haɪm]
Waldo 'wɔːld əʊ 'wɒld- ‖ -oʊ 'wɑːld-
Waldorf 'wɔːld ɔːf 'wɒld- ‖ -ɔːrf 'wɑːld-
    ˌWaldorf 'salad
Waldron 'wɔːldr ən 'wɒldr- ‖ 'wɑːldr-
Waldstein *(i)* 'væld staɪn 'vɑːld-, 'vɒld- ‖ *(ii)* 'wɔːld staɪn 'wɒld- ‖ 'wɑːld- —*For the Beethoven sonata, and as a German name, (i) —Ger* ['valt ʃtaɪn]; *as an American family name, (ii).*
wale weɪəl **wales** weɪəlz
Wales weɪəlz
Walesa, Wałęsa vɑː 'wen's ə və-, wə-, -'wenz-, -'len's- ‖ wɑː 'len's ə —*Polish* [va 'weu̯ sa]
Waley 'weɪl i
Walford 'wɔːl fəd 'wɒl- ‖ -fərd 'wɑːl-
Walgreens *tdmk* 'wɔːl griːnz 'wɒl- ‖ 'wɑːl-
Walham 'wɒl əm ‖ 'wɑːl-
Walian 'weɪl i ən
walk wɔːk ‖ wɑːk **walked** wɔːkt ‖ wɑːkt
    walking 'wɔːk ɪŋ ‖ 'wɑːk- **walks** wɔːks ‖ wɑːks
    'walking ˌpapers; 'walking shoes; 'walking stick; 'walking tour; ˌwalk of 'life
walkabout 'wɔːk ə ˌbaʊt
walkathon 'wɔːk ə θɒn ‖ 'wɑːk- **~s** z
walkaway 'wɔːk ə ˌweɪ ‖ 'wɑːk- **~s** z
Walkden 'wɔːk dən ‖ 'wɑːk-
walker, W~ 'wɔːk ə ‖ -ər 'wɑːk- **~s** z
walkies 'wɔːk iz ‖ 'wɑːk-
walkie-talkie ˌwɔːk i 'tɔːk i ‖ ˌwɑːk i 'tɑːk i **~s** z
walk-in 'wɔːk ɪn ‖ 'wɑːk- **~s** z
Walkman *tdmk, w~* 'wɔːk mən ‖ 'wɑːk- **~s** z
walk-on 'wɔːk ɒn ‖ -ɑːn 'wɑːk-, -ɔːn **~s** z
walkout 'wɔːk aʊt ‖ 'wɑːk- **~s** s
walkover 'wɔːk ˌəʊv ə ‖ -ˌoʊv ər 'wɑːk- **~s** z
walk-through 'wɔːk θruː ‖ 'wɑːk- **~s** z
walk-up 'wɔːk ʌp ‖ 'wɑːk- **~s** s
walkway 'wɔːk weɪ ‖ 'wɑːk- **~s** z
walky-talk|y ˌwɔːk i 'tɔːk| i ‖ ˌwɑːk i 'tɑːk| i **~ies** iz
wall, Wall wɔːl ‖ wɑːl **walled** wɔːld ‖ wɑːld
    walling 'wɔːl ɪŋ ‖ 'wɑːl- **walls** wɔːlz ‖ wɑːlz
    'wall ˌpainting; 'Wall Street, ˌWall Street 'Journal
walla, Walla 'wɒl ə ‖ 'wɑːl ə
wallab|y 'wɒl əb |i ‖ 'wɑːl- **~ies** iz
Wallace 'wɒl ɪs -əs ‖ 'wɑːl əs 'wɔːl-
Wallachi|a wɒ 'leɪk i ˌ|ə wə- ‖ wɑː- **~an/s** ən/z
wallah 'wɒl ə ‖ 'wɑːl ə **~s** z
wallaroo, W~ ˌwɒl ə 'ruː ‖ ˌwɑːl- **~s** z

Wallasey 'wɒl əs i ‖ 'wɑːl-
wallboard 'wɔːl bɔːd ‖ -bɔːrd 'wɑːl-, -boʊrd **~s** z
wallchart 'wɔːl tʃɑːt ‖ -tʃɑːrt 'wɑːl- **~s** s
Waller *(i)* 'wɒl ə ‖ 'wɑːl ər, *(ii)* 'wɔːl ə ‖ -ər 'wɑːl-
Wallerawang wə 'leər ə wæŋ ‖ -'ler-
wallet 'wɒl ɪt -ət ‖ 'wɑːl ət **~s** s
walleye 'wɔːl aɪ ‖ 'wɑːl- **~s** z
wall-eyed 'wɔːl aɪd ˌ·'· ‖ 'wɑːl-
wallflower 'wɔːl ˌflaʊ ə ‖ ˌ·ʳ 'wɑːl- **~s** z
wallie... —*see* **wally**
Walliker 'wɒl ɪk ə -ək- ‖ 'wɑːl ək ər
Wallingford 'wɒl ɪŋ fəd ‖ 'wɑːl ɪŋ fərd
Wallington 'wɒl ɪŋ tən ‖ 'wɑːl-
Wallis 'wɒl ɪs §-əs ‖ 'wɑːl əs 'wɔːl-
wall-mounted 'wɔːl ˌmaʊnt ɪd -əd ‖ -ˌmaʊnt̬- 'wɑːl-
Wallonia wɒ 'ləʊn i ə wə- ‖ wɑː 'loʊn-
Walloon wɒ 'luːn wə- ‖ wɑː- **~s** z
wallop, W~ 'wɒl əp ‖ 'wɑːl əp **~ed** t **~ing/s** ɪŋ/z **~s** s
wallow 'wɒl əʊ ‖ 'wɑːl oʊ **~ed** d **~er/s** ə/z ‖ ʳr/z **~ing** ɪŋ **~s** z
wallpaper 'wɔːl ˌpeɪp ə ‖ -ʳr 'wɑːl- **~ed** d
    wallpapering 'wɔːl ˌpeɪp ər ɪŋ ‖ 'wɑːl- **~s** z
Walls wɔːlz ‖ wɑːlz
Wallsend 'wɔːlz end ‖ 'wɑːlz-
wall-to-wall ˌwɔːl tə 'wɔːl ◂ -tu- ‖ ˌwɑːl tə 'wɑːl
    ˌwall-to-wall 'carpeting
wallum 'wɒl əm ‖ 'wɑːl-
Wallwork 'wɔːl wɜːk 'wɒl- ‖ -wɜːk 'wɑːl-
wall|y *n*, **Wally** 'wɒl |i ‖ 'wɑːl |i **~ies** iz
Wal-Mart *tdmk* 'wɒl mɑːt 'wɔːl- ‖ 'wɔːl mɑːrt 'wɑːl-, 'wɔː-, 'wɑː-
Walmer 'wɔːlm ə 'wɒlm- ‖ -ʳr 'wɑːlm-
Walmesley, Walmisley, Walmsley 'wɔːmz li ‖ 'wɑːmz-
Walmley 'wɔːm li ‖ 'wɑːm-
Walney 'wɔːln i 'wɒln- ‖ 'wɑːln-
walnut 'wɔːl nʌt ‖ 'wɑːl- **~s** s
Walpamur *tdmk* 'wɔːl pə mjʊə 'wɒl-, -mɜː- ‖ -mjʊr 'wɑːl-
Walpole 'wɔːl pəʊl 'wɒl-, →-pɒʊl ‖ -poʊl 'wɑːl-
Walpurgis væl 'pʊəg ɪs vɑːl-, -'pɜːg-, §-əs ‖ vɑːl 'pʊrg əs
walrus 'wɔːl rəs 'wɒl-, -rʌs ‖ 'wɑːl- **~es** ɪz əz
    ˌwalrus mou'stache ‖ -'··
Walsall 'wɔːl sɔːl 'wɒl-, -sʳl ‖ 'wɑːl sɑːl —*locally also* 'wɔːs ʳl
Walsh wɔːlʃ wɒlʃ ‖ wɑːlʃ
Walsham 'wɔːlʃ əm 'wɒlʃ- ‖ 'wɑːlʃ- —*locally also* 'wɒls əm
Walsingham *(i)* 'wɔːls ɪŋ əm 'wɒls- ‖ 'wɑːls-, *(ii)* 'wɔːlz- 'wɒlz- ‖ 'wɑːlz- —*the personal name is (i), but the place in Nfk is (ii)*
Walt wɔːlt wɒlt ‖ wɑːlt
Walter 'wɔːlt ə 'wɒlt- ‖ -ʳr 'wɑːlt- —*but as a German name,* 'vɑːlt ə ‖ -ʳr —*Ger* ['val tɐ]
    ˌWalter 'Mitty 'mɪt i ‖ 'mɪt̬ i
Walters 'wɔːlt əz 'wɒlt- ‖ -ʳrz 'wɑːlt-

Waltham 'wɔːlθ əm 'wɒlθ- ‖ 'wɑːlθ- —*but
Great W~ and Little W~ in Essex are
traditionally* 'wɔːlt-; *W~ in MA is locally*
'wɔːl θæm
,Waltham 'Forest
Walthamstow 'wɔːlθ əm stəʊ 'wɒlθ- ‖ -stoʊ
'wɑːlθ- —*previously* 'wɔːlt-, 'wɒlt-
Walton 'wɔːlt ən 'wɒlt- ‖ 'wɑːlt-
Walton-le-Dale ,wɔːlt ən li 'deɪəl ,wɒlt-
‖ ,wɑːlt-
Walton-on-the-Naze ,wɔːlt ən ˌɒn ðə 'neɪz
,wɒlt- ‖ -ˌɑːn- ˌwɑːlt-, -ˌɔːn-
waltz wɔːls wɒls, wɔːlts, wɒlts ‖ 'wɔːlts wɑːlts,
wɔːls, wɑːls **waltzed** wɔːlst wɒlst, wɔːltst,
wɒltst ‖ wɔːltst wɑːltst, wɔːlst, wɑːlst **waltzes**
'wɔːls ɪz 'wɒls-, 'wɔːlts-, 'wɒlts-, -əz
‖ 'wɔːlts əz 'wɑːlts-, 'wɔːls-, 'wɑːls- **waltzing**
'wɔːls ɪŋ 'wɒls-, 'wɔːlts-, 'wɒlts- ‖ 'wɔːlts ɪŋ
'wɑːlts-, 'wɔːls-, 'wɑːls-
waltzer 'wɔːls ə 'wɒls-, 'wɔːlts-, 'wɒlts-
‖ 'wɔːlts ər 'wɑːlts-, 'wɔːls-, 'wɑːls- **~s** z
Walvis Bay ,wɔːlv ɪs 'beɪ §-əs- ‖ ,wɑːlv-
Walworth 'wɔːl wəθ 'wɒl-, -wɜːθ ‖ -wərθ 'wɑːl-
Wampanoag ,wɒmp ə 'nəʊ æg
‖ ,wɑːmp ə 'noʊ ɑːg
wampum 'wɒmp əm ‖ 'wɑːmp-
wan '*pale*' wɒn ‖ wɑːn **wanner** 'wɒn ə
‖ 'wɑːn ər **wannest** 'wɒn ɪst -əst ‖ 'wɑːn əst
WAN, wan '*wide area network*' wæn
Wanadoo *tdmk* 'wɒn ə duː ‖ 'wɑːn-
Wanamaker 'wɒn ə meɪk ə ‖ 'wɑːn ə meɪk ər
Wanchai ,wɒn 'tʃaɪ ‖ ,wɑːn- —*Cantonese*
[¹waːn ²tsɐj]
wand wɒnd ‖ wɑːnd **wands** wɒndz ‖ wɑːndz
Wanda 'wɒnd ə ‖ 'wɑːnd ə
wander 'wɒnd ə ‖ 'wɑːnd ər **~ed** d
wandering/s 'wɒnd ər ɪŋ/z ‖ 'wɑːnd ər ɪŋ/z
~s z
,Wandering 'Jew
wanderer 'wɒnd ər ə ‖ 'wɑːnd ər ər **~s** z
wanderlust 'wɒnd ə lʌst ‖ 'wɑːnd ər- —*Ger*
W~ ['van də lʊst]
Wandle 'wɒnd əl ‖ 'wɑːnd əl
Wandsworth 'wɒndz wəθ -wɜːθ
‖ 'wɑːndz wərθ -wɜːθ
wane weɪn **waned** weɪnd **wanes** weɪnz
waning 'weɪn ɪŋ
Wang *tdmk* wæŋ ‖ wɑːŋ
Wanganui ,wɒŋ ə 'nuː i -gə- ‖ ,wɑːŋ-
Wangaratta ,wæŋ gə 'ræt ə ‖ -'ræt̬-
wangl|e 'wæŋ gəl **~ed** d **~es** z **~ing** ɪŋ
wanigan 'wɒn ɪg ən ‖ 'wɑːn- **~s** z
wank wæŋk **wanked** wæŋkt **wanking**
'wæŋk ɪŋ **wanks** wæŋks
Wankel, w~ 'wæŋk əl ‖ 'wɑːŋk əl —*Ger*
['vaŋ kəl]
wanker 'wæŋk ə ‖ -ər **~s** z
wanly 'wɒn li ‖ 'wɑːn li
wanna *casual form of* want to, want a 'wɒn ə
‖ 'wɑːn ə 'wɔːn ə, 'wʌn ə —*not standard in
BrE; the RP equivalent is* 'wɒnt ə. *Before a
vowel sound, also* -u *rather than* -ə

wannabe, wannabee 'wɒn əb i -ə biː
‖ 'wɑːn- 'wɔːn- **~s** z
wanne... —*see* **wan**
wanness 'wɒn nəs -nɪs ‖ 'wɑːn nəs
Wansbeck 'wɒnz bek ‖ 'wɑːnz-
Wanstead 'wɒn stɪd -sted, §-stəd ‖ 'wɑːn-
want wɒnt ‖ wɑːnt wɔːnt, wʌnt **wanted**
'wɒnt ɪd -əd ‖ 'wɑːnt̬əd 'wɔːnt̬-, 'wʌnt̬-
wanting 'wɒnt ɪŋ ‖ 'wɑːnt̬ ɪŋ 'wɔːnt̬-, 'wʌnt̬-
wants wɒnts ‖ wɑːnts wɔːnts, wʌnts —*In the
close-knit phrase* want to *before a verb, the
consonants are often simplified to* 'wɒnt ə,
§'wɒn ə ‖ 'wɑːn ə, 'wɔːn ə, 'wʌn ə —. See also
wanna.
'want ad
Wantage, w~ 'wɒnt ɪdʒ ‖ 'wɑːnt̬ ɪdʒ 'wɔːnt̬-
Wantagh 'wɒnt ɔː ‖ 'wɑːnt- -ɑː
wanton 'wɒnt ən ‖ 'wɑːnt ən 'wɔːnt-, -n **~ly**
li **~ness** nəs nɪs **~s** z
WAP wæp
wapentake 'wɒp ən teɪk 'wæp- ‖ 'wɑːp- **~s** s
wapiti 'wɒp ət i -ɪt- ‖ 'wɑːp ət̬ i **~s** z
Waple 'weɪp əl
Wapner 'wɒp nə ‖ 'wɑːp nər
Wapping 'wɒp ɪŋ ‖ 'wɑːp ɪŋ
Wappingers Falls ,wɒp ɪndʒ əz 'fɔːlz
‖ ,wɑːp əndʒ ərz- -'fɑːlz
war wɔː ‖ wɔːr **warred** wɔːd ‖ wɔːrd **warring**
'wɔːr ɪŋ **wars** wɔːz ‖ wɔːrz
'war bride; 'war clouds; 'war
corre,spondent; 'war crime; 'war cry;
'war dance; 'war game; ,war of 'nerves;
'war paint
waratah 'wɒr ə tɑː; ˌ· '·ˌ ‖ 'wɔːr- **~s** z
Warbeck 'wɔː bek ‖ 'wɔːr-
warbl|e 'wɔːb əl ‖ 'wɔːrb əl **~ed** d **~es** z **~ing**
ɪŋ
'warble fly
warbler 'wɔːb lə ‖ 'wɔːrb lər **~s** z
Warboys 'wɔː bɔɪz ‖ 'wɔːr-
Warburg 'wɔː bɜːg ‖ 'wɔːr bɜːg
Warburton 'wɔːb ət ən 'wɔː ,bɜːt ən
‖ 'wɔːr ,bɜːt ən
warchalking 'wɔː ,tʃɔːk ɪŋ ‖ 'wɔːr- -,tʃɑːk-
ward, Ward wɔːd ‖ wɔːrd **warded** 'wɔːd ɪd
-əd ‖ 'wɔːrd əd **warding** 'wɔːd ɪŋ ‖ 'wɔːrd ɪŋ
wards wɔːdz ‖ wɔːrdz
-ward wəd ‖ wərd — **heavenward**
'hev ən wəd ‖ -wərd
Wardell wɔː 'del ‖ wɔːr-
warden, W~ 'wɔːd ən ‖ 'wɔːrd ən **~s** z **~ship**
ʃɪp
warder 'wɔːd ə ‖ 'wɔːrd ər **~s** z
Wardian 'wɔːd i ən ‖ 'wɔːrd-
Wardle 'wɔːd əl ‖ 'wɔːrd əl
Wardour 'wɔːd ə ‖ 'wɔːrd ər
wardress 'wɔːdr əs -ɪs, -es ‖ 'wɔːrdr- **~es** ɪz əz
wardrobe 'wɔːdr əʊb ‖ 'wɔːrdr oʊb **~s** z
wardroom 'wɔːd ruːm -rʊm ‖ 'wɔːrd- **~s** z
-wards wədz ‖ wərdz — **seawards** 'siː wədz
‖ -wərdz
wardship 'wɔːd ʃɪp ‖ 'wɔːrd- **~s** s

ware, Ware weə ‖ weˑʳr wæˑʳr **wares** weəz
‖ weˑʳrz wæˑʳrz
-ware weə ‖ wer wær — **silverware**
ˈsɪlv ə weə ‖ -ˑʳr wer -wær
Wareham ˈweər əm ‖ ˈwer əm ˈwær-
ware|house ν ˈweə |haʊz -haʊs ‖ ˈwer- ˈwær-
~**housed** haʊzd haʊst ~**houses** haʊz ɪz haʊs-,
-əz ~**housing** haʊz ɪŋ haʊs-
ware|house n ˈweə |haʊs ‖ ˈwer- ˈwær-
~**houses** haʊz ɪz -əz
warehouse|man ˈweə haʊs |mən ‖ ˈwer-
ˈwær- ~**men** mən men
Wareing ˈweər ɪŋ ‖ ˈwer ɪŋ ˈwær-
warfare ˈwɔː feə ‖ ˈwɔːr fer -fær
warfarin ˈwɔːf ər ɪn §-ən ‖ ˈwɔːrf-
Wargrave ˈwɔː greɪv ‖ ˈwɔːr-
warhead ˈwɔː hed ‖ ˈwɔːr- ~**s** z
Warhol ˈwɔː həʊl →-hɒʊl ‖ ˈwɔːr hoʊl
warhors|e ˈwɔː hɔːs ‖ ˈwɔːr hɔːrs ~**es** ɪz əz
wari... —*see* **wary**
Waring ˈweər ɪŋ ‖ ˈwer ɪŋ ˈwær-
Warks —*see* **Warwickshire**
Warkworth ˈwɔːk wəθ -wɜːθ ‖ ˈwɔːrk wɜːθ
ˈwɑːrk-
Warley ˈwɔːl i ‖ ˈwɔːrl i
warlike ˈwɔː laɪk ‖ ˈwɔːr-
Warlingham ˈwɔːl ɪŋ əm ‖ ˈwɔːrl-
warlock, W~ ˈwɔː lɒk ‖ ˈwɔːr lɑːk ~**s** s
warlord ˈwɔː lɔːd ‖ ˈwɔːr lɔːrd ~**ism** ˌɪz əm ~**s**
z
warm wɔːm ‖ wɔːrm **warmed** wɔːmd
‖ wɔːrmd **warmer** ˈwɔːm ə ‖ ˈwɔːrm ˑʳr
warmest ˈwɔːm ɪst -əst ‖ ˈwɔːrm əst
warming ˈwɔːm ɪŋ ‖ ˈwɔːrm ɪŋ **warms**
wɔːmz ‖ wɔːrmz
ˈwarming pan
warm-blooded ˌwɔːm ˈblʌd ɪd ◂ -əd ‖ ˌwɔːrm-
~**ness** nəs nɪs
warm-down ˈwɔːm daʊn ‖ ˈwɔːrm- ~**s** z
warmed-over ˌwɔːmd ˈəʊv ə ◂
‖ ˌwɔːrmd ˈoʊv ˑʳr ◂
warmed-up ˌwɔːmd ˈʌp ◂ ‖ ˌwɔːrmd-
warmer ˈwɔːm ə ‖ ˈwɔːrm ˑʳr ~**s** z
warm-hearted ˌwɔːm ˈhɑːt ɪd ◂ -əd
‖ ˌwɔːrm ˈhɑːrt əd ◂ ~**ly** li ~**ness** nəs nɪs
Warmington ˈwɔːm ɪŋ tən ‖ ˈwɔːrm-
Warminster ˈwɔː mɪnˑst ə ‖ ˈwɔːr mɪnˑst ˑʳr
warmly ˈwɔːm li ‖ ˈwɔːrm li
warmness ˈwɔːm nəs -nɪs ‖ ˈwɔːrm-
warmonger ˈwɔː ˌmʌŋ gə ‖ ˈwɔːr ˌmʌŋ gˑʳr
-ˌmɑːŋ- ~**s** z
warmongering ˈwɔː ˌmʌŋ gər ɪŋ ‖ ˈwɔːr-
-ˌmɑːŋ-
warmth wɔːmᵖθ ‖ wɔːrmᵖθ
warm-up ˈwɔːm ʌp ‖ ˈwɔːrm- ~**s** s
warn wɔːn ‖ wɔːrn **warned** wɔːnd ‖ wɔːrnd
warning/ly ˈwɔːn ɪŋ /li ‖ ˈwɔːrn- **warns**
wɔːnz ‖ wɔːrnz
Warne wɔːn ‖ wɔːrn
Warner ˈwɔːn ə ‖ ˈwɔːrn ˑʳr
Warnham ˈwɔːn əm ‖ ˈwɔːrn-
warning ˈwɔːn ɪŋ ‖ ˈwɔːrn ɪŋ ~**s** z
Warninglid ˈwɔːn ɪŋ lɪd ‖ ˈwɔːrn-

Warnock ˈwɔːn ɒk ‖ ˈwɔːrn ɑːk
warp wɔːp ‖ wɔːrp **warped** wɔːpt ‖ wɔːrpt
warping ˈwɔːp ɪŋ ‖ ˈwɔːrp ɪŋ **warps** wɔːps
‖ wɔːrps
warpath ˈwɔː pɑːθ §-pæθ ‖ ˈwɔːr pæθ
warplane ˈwɔː pleɪn ‖ ˈwɔːr- ~**s** z
Warr wɔː ‖ wɔːr
Warragamba ˌwɒr ə ˈgæm bə ‖ ˌwɔːr-
warr|ant ˈwɒr |ənt ‖ ˈwɔːr |ənt ˈwɑːr- ~**anted**
ənt ɪd -əd ‖ əṭ əd ~**anting** ənt ɪŋ ‖ əṭ ɪŋ
~**ants** ənts
ˈwarrant ˌofficer
warrantab|le ˈwɒr ənt əb| ˑl ‖ ˈwɔːr- ˈwɑːr-
~**ly** li
warrantee ˌwɒr ən ˈtiː ‖ ˌwɔːr- ˌwɑːr- ~**s** z
warrantor ˈwɒr ən tɔː ˌ·ˑ·ˈ· ‖ ˈwɔːr ən tɔːr
ˈwɑːr-, ˌ·ˑ·ˈ· ~**s** z
warrant|y ˈwɒr ənt |i ‖ ˈwɔːr əṭ |i ˈwɑːr- ~**ies**
iz
Warre wɔː ‖ wɔːr
warren, W~ ˈwɒr ən ‖ ˈwɔːr ən ˈwɑːr-
—*formerly also* -ɪn ~**s** z
Warrender ˈwɒr ənd ə ə -ɪnd- ‖ ˈwɔːr ənd ˑʳr
ˈwɑːr-
warrigal ˈwɒr ɪg ˑl -əg- ‖ ˈwɔːr- ˈwɑːr- ~**s** z
warring ˈwɔːr ɪŋ
Warrington ˈwɒr ɪŋ tən ‖ ˈwɔːr- ˈwɑːr-
warrior ˈwɒr i ə ‖ ˈwɔːr i ˑʳr ˈwɑːr- ~**s** z
Warriss ˈwɒr ɪs §-əs ‖ ˈwɔːr əs ˈwɑːr-
Warrumbungle ˌwɒr əm ˈbʌŋ gˑl ‖ ˌwɔːr-
Warsaw ˈwɔː sɔː ‖ ˈwɔːr- -sɑː
ˌWarsaw ˈPact
warship ˈwɔː ʃɪp ‖ ˈwɔːr- ~**s** s
Warsop ˈwɔː sɒp ‖ ˈwɔːr sɑːp
Warspite ˈwɔː spaɪt ‖ ˈwɔːr-
wart wɔːt ‖ wɔːrt **warts** wɔːts ‖ wɔːrts
Wartburg *tdmk* ˈwɔːt bɜːg ˈvɑːt- ‖ ˈwɔːrt bɜːg
—*Ger* [ˈvaʀt buʀk]
warthog ˈwɔːt hɒg ‖ ˈwɔːrt hɔːg -hɑːg ~**s** z
wartime ˈwɔː taɪm ‖ ˈwɔːr-
Warton ˈwɔːt ˑn ‖ ˈwɔːrt ˑn
war-torn ˈwɔː tɔːn ‖ ˈwɔːr tɔːrn -toʊrn
wart|y ˈwɔːt |i ‖ ˈwɔːrṭ |i ~**ier** i ə ‖ i ˑʳr ~**iest**
i ɪst i əst ~**iness** i nəs i nɪs
war-wear|y ˈwɔː ˌwɪər| i ˌ·ˑ·ˈ· ‖ ˈwɔːr ˌwɪr| i
~**iness** i nəs i nɪs
Warwick *(i)* ˈwɒr ɪk ‖ ˈwɔːr ɪk ˈwɑːr-, *(ii)*
ˈwɔː wɪk ‖ ˈwɔːr- —*The English name and the
places in Warks and Queensland are (i); the
place in RI and the American name are
usually (ii).*
Warwickshire ˈwɒr ɪk ʃə -ʃɪə ‖ ˈwɔːr ɪk ʃˑʳr
ˈwɑːr-, -ʃɪr
war|y ˈweər |i ‖ ˈwer |i ˈwær- ~**ier** i ə ‖ i ˑʳr
~**iest** i ɪst i əst ~**ily** əl i ɪ li ~**iness** i nəs i nɪs
was *strong form* wɒz ‖ wʌz wɑːz, *weak form*
wəz
wasabi ˈwɑːs ə biː -ɑː-; wə ˈsɑːb i —*Jp*
[ˈɰa sa bi]
Wasatch ˈwɔː sætʃ ‖ ˈwɑː-
Wasdale ˈwɒs dˑl -deɪˑl ‖ ˈwɑːs-
wash, Wash wɒʃ ‖ wɑːʃ wɔːʃ —*There are also
non-standard AmE forms* wɔːrʃ, wɑːrʃ **washed**

wɒʃt ‖ wɑːʃt wɔːʃt **washes** 'wɒʃ ɪz -əz
‖ 'wɑːʃ əz 'wɔːʃ- **washing** 'wɒʃ ɪŋ ‖ 'wɑːʃ ɪŋ
'wɔːʃ-
  'wash ˌdrawing; 'washing day; 'washing
  maˌchine; 'washing ˌpowder
washable 'wɒʃ əb əl ‖ 'wɑːʃ- 'wɔːʃ-
wash-and-wear ˌwɒʃ ən 'weə ‖ ˌwɑːʃ ən 'weər
  ˌwɔːʃ-
washbasin 'wɒʃ ˌbeɪs ən ‖ 'wɑːʃ- 'wɔːʃ- ~s z
washboard 'wɒʃ bɔːd ‖ 'wɑːʃ bɔːrd 'wɔːʃ-,
  -bourd ~s z
Washbourn, Washbourne 'wɒʃ bɔːn
  ‖ 'wɑːʃ bɔːrn 'wɔːʃ-, -bourn
washbowl 'wɒʃ bəʊl →-bɒʊl ‖ 'wɑːʃ boʊl
  'wɔːʃ- ~s z
Washbrook 'wɒʃ brʊk ‖ 'wɑːʃ- 'wɔːʃ-
Washburn 'wɒʃ bɜːn ‖ 'wɑːʃ bɜːn 'wɔːʃ-
wash|cloth 'wɒʃ |klɒθ -klɔːθ ‖ 'wɑːʃ |klɔːθ
  'wɔːʃ-, -klɑːθ ~**cloths** klɒθs klɔːθs, klɒðz,
  klɔːðz ‖ klɔːðz klɑːðz, klɔːθs, klɑːθs
washday 'wɒʃ deɪ ‖ 'wɑːʃ- 'wɔːʃ- ~s z
washed-out ˌwɒʃt 'aʊt ◂ ‖ ˌwɑːʃt- ˌwɔːʃt-
washed-up ˌwɒʃt 'ʌp ◂ ‖ ˌwɑːʃt- ˌwɔːʃt-
washer 'wɒʃ ə ‖ 'wɑːʃ ər 'wɔːʃ- ~s z
washer-dryer ˌwɒʃ ə 'draɪ ə ‖ ˌwɑːʃ ər 'draɪ ər
  ˌwɔːʃ- ~s z
washer-up ˌwɒʃ ər 'ʌp ‖ ˌwɑːʃ ər 'ʌp ˌwɔːʃ-
  washers-up ˌwɒʃ əz 'ʌp ‖ ˌwɑːʃ ərz 'ʌp
  ˌwɔːʃ-
washer|woman 'wɒʃ ə |ˌwʊm ən ‖ 'wɑːʃ ər-
  'wɔːʃ- ~**women** ˌwɪm ɪn -ən
washer|y 'wɒʃ ər |i ‖ 'wɑːʃ- 'wɔːʃ- ~**ies** iz
wash|house 'wɒʃ |haʊs ‖ 'wɑːʃ- 'wɔːʃ-
  ~**houses** haʊz ɪz -əz
Washington 'wɒʃ ɪŋ tən ‖ 'wɑːʃ- 'wɔːʃ-
Washingtonian ˌwɒʃ ɪŋ 'təʊn i ən ◂
  ‖ ˌwɑːʃ ɪŋ 'toʊn- ˌwɔːʃ- ~s z
washing-up ˌwɒʃ ɪŋ 'ʌp ‖ ˌwɑːʃ- ˌwɔːʃ-
washleather 'wɒʃ ˌleð ə ‖ 'wɑːʃ ˌleð ər 'wɔːʃ-
  ~s z
washload 'wɒʃ ləʊd ‖ 'wɑːʃ loʊd 'wɔːʃ- ~s z
Washoe 'wɒʃ əʊ ‖ 'wɑːʃ oʊ
washout 'wɒʃ aʊt ‖ 'wɑːʃ- 'wɔːʃ- ~s s
washpot 'wɒʃ pɒt ‖ 'wɑːʃ pɑːt 'wɔːʃ- ~s s
washrag 'wɒʃ ræg ‖ 'wɑːʃ- 'wɔːʃ- ~s z
washroom 'wɒʃ ruːm -rʊm ‖ 'wɑːʃ- 'wɔːʃ- ~s z
washstand 'wɒʃ stænd ‖ 'wɑːʃ- 'wɔːʃ- ~s z
washtub 'wɒʃ tʌb ‖ 'wɑːʃ- 'wɔːʃ- ~s z
wash-up 'wɒʃ ʌp ‖ 'wɑːʃ- 'wɔːʃ- ~s s
wash-wipe ˌwɒʃ 'waɪp ‖ ˌwɑːʃ- ˌwɔːʃ-
wash|woman 'wɒʃ |ˌwʊm ən ‖ 'wɑːʃ- 'wɔːʃ-
  ~**women** ˌwɪm ɪn -ən
wash|y 'wɒʃ |i ‖ 'wɑːʃ |i 'wɔːʃ- ~**ier** i ə ‖ i ər
  ~**iest** i ɪst i əst ~**iness** i nəs i nɪs
wasn't 'wɒz ənt ‖ 'wʌz ənt 'wɑːz-
wasp, WASP, Wasp wɒsp ‖ wɑːsp **wasps,**
  WASPs, Wasps wɒsps ‖ wɑːsps
waspish 'wɒsp ɪʃ ‖ 'wɑːsp ɪʃ ~**ly** li ~**ness** nəs
  nɪs
wasp-waisted ˌwɒsp 'weɪst ɪd ◂ -əd, '·,··
  ‖ 'wɑːsp ˌweɪst əd

wasp|y, Wasp|y, WASPly 'wɒsp |i ‖ 'wɑːsp |i
  ~**ier** i ə ‖ i ər ~**iest** i ɪst i əst ~**ily** ɪ li əl i
  ~**iness** i nəs i nɪs
wassail 'wɒs eɪəl -əl ‖ 'wɑːs- ~**ed** d ~**ing** ɪŋ ~**s**
  z
Wassermann 'wæs ə mən 'væs-, 'vɑːs-
  ‖ 'wɑːs ər- —*Ger* ['vas ɐ man]
  'Wassermann test
Wasson 'wɒs ən ‖ 'wɑːs ən
wassup wɒ 'sʌp wə- wɑː-
wast *strong form* wɒst ‖ wɑːst, *weak form* wəst
wastag|e 'weɪst ɪdʒ ~**es** ɪz əz
Wastdale 'wɒs dəl 'weɪst-, 'wɒst-, -deɪəl ‖ 'wɑːst-
waste weɪst (= *waist*) **wasted** 'weɪst ɪd -əd
  wastes weɪsts **wasting** 'weɪst ɪŋ
  ˌwaste 'paper, '·,··; ˌwaste 'paper ˌbasket,
  '·,··,·· ‖ '· ··,·,·; 'waste pipe; 'waste
  ˌproduct
wastebasket 'weɪst ˌbɑːsk ɪt §-,bæsk-, §-ət
  ‖ -,bæsk ət ~s s
wasteful 'weɪst fəl -fʊl ~**ly** i ~**ness** nəs nɪs
wasteland 'weɪst lænd -lənd ~s z
wastepaper ˌweɪst 'peɪp ə '·,··
  ‖ 'weɪst ˌpeɪp ər
wastepipe 'weɪst paɪp ~s s
waster 'weɪst ə ‖ -ər ~s z
wastewater 'weɪst ˌwɔːt ə ‖ -,wɔːt ər -,wɑːt ər
wastrel 'weɪs trəl ~s z
Wastwater 'wɒst ˌwɔːt ə ‖ 'wɑːst ˌwɔːt ər
  -,wɑːt-
Wat, wat wɒt ‖ wɑːt
watch wɒtʃ ‖ wɑːtʃ wɔːtʃ **watched** wɒtʃt
  ‖ wɑːtʃt wɔːtʃt **watches** 'wɒtʃ ɪz -əz
  ‖ 'wɑːtʃ əz 'wɔːtʃ- **watching** 'wɒtʃ ɪŋ
  ‖ 'wɑːtʃ ɪŋ 'wɔːtʃ-
  ˌwatching 'brief; 'watch night
watchable 'wɒtʃ əb əl ‖ 'wɑːtʃ- 'wɔːtʃ-
watchband 'wɒtʃ bænd ‖ 'wɑːtʃ- 'wɔːtʃ- ~s z
watchcas|e 'wɒtʃ keɪs ‖ 'wɑːtʃ- 'wɔːtʃ- ~**es** ɪz
  əz
watchdog 'wɒtʃ dɒg ‖ 'wɑːtʃ dɔːg 'wɔːtʃ-,
  -dɑːg ~s z
watcher 'wɒtʃ ə ‖ 'wɑːtʃ ər 'wɔːtʃ- ~s z
Watchet 'wɒtʃ ɪt §-ət ‖ 'wɑːtʃ ət
watchful 'wɒtʃ fəl -fʊl ‖ 'wɑːtʃ- 'wɔːtʃ- ~**ly** i
  ~**ness** nəs nɪs
watchkeeper 'wɒtʃ ˌkiːp ə ‖ 'wɑːtʃ ˌkiːp ər
  'wɔːtʃ-
watchmaker 'wɒtʃ ˌmeɪk ə ‖ 'wɑːtʃ ˌmeɪk ər
  'wɔːtʃ- ~s z
watch|man 'wɒtʃ |mən ‖ 'wɑːtʃ- 'wɔːtʃ- ~**men**
  mən men
watchnight 'wɒtʃ naɪt ‖ 'wɑːtʃ- 'wɔːtʃ-
watchstrap 'wɒtʃ stræp ‖ 'wɑːtʃ- 'wɔːtʃ- ~s s
watchtower 'wɒtʃ ˌtaʊ ə ‖ 'wɑːtʃ ˌtaʊ ər
  'wɔːtʃ- ~s z
watchword 'wɒtʃ wɜːd ‖ 'wɑːtʃ wɜːd 'wɔːtʃ-
  ~s z
Watendlath wɒ 'tend ləθ ‖ wɑː-
water 'wɔːt ə ‖ 'wɔːt ər 'wɑːt- ~**ed** d **watering**
  'wɔːt ər ɪŋ ‖ 'wɔːt ər ɪŋ 'wɑːt- ~**s** z
  'water bird; 'water ˌbiscuit; 'water
  ˌbuffalo; 'water butt; 'water ˌcannon;

ˌwater 'chestnut ‖ '··ˌ··; 'water ˌcloset;
'water ˌcooler; ˌwatered 'silk; 'water ice;
'watering can; 'watering hole; 'watering
place; 'water jump; 'water ˌlevel; 'water
ˌlily; 'water main; 'water ˌmeadow;
'water pipe; 'water ˌpolo; 'water rat;
'water rate; 'water ˌsoftener; 'water
supˌply; 'water ˌtable; 'water ˌtower;
'water ˌvapour; 'water vole
waterbed 'wɔːt ə bed ‖ 'wɔːt̬ ʳr- 'wɑːt̬ ʳr ~s z
waterborne 'wɔːt ə bɔːn ‖ 'wɔːt̬ ʳr bɔːrn
  'wɑːt̬-, -bourn
waterbuck 'wɔːt ə bʌk ‖ 'wɔːt̬ ʳr- 'wɑːt̬-
Waterbury 'wɔːt ə bər i ‖ 'wɔːt̬ ʳr ˌber i
  'wɑːt̬-, -bər i
watercolor, watercolour 'wɔːt ə ˌkʌl ə
  ‖ 'wɔːt̬ ʳr ˌkʌl ʳr 'wɑːt̬- ~s z
watercolorist, watercolourist
  'wɔːt ə ˌkʌl ər ɪst §-əst ‖ 'wɔːt̬ ʳr ˌkʌl ʳr ɪst
  'wɑːt̬- ~s s
water-cool 'wɔːt ə kuːl ‖ 'wɔːt̬ ʳr- 'wɑːt̬- ~ed d
  ~ing ɪŋ ~s z
watercours|e 'wɔːt ə kɔːs ‖ 'wɔːt̬ ʳr kɔːrs
  'wɑːt̬-, -kours ~es ɪz əz
watercraft 'wɔːt ə krɑːft §-kræft
  ‖ 'wɔːt̬ ʳr kræft 'wɑːt̬- ~s s
watercress 'wɔːt ə kres ‖ 'wɔːt̬ ʳr- 'wɑːt̬-
watered-down ˌwɔːt əd 'daʊn ◂ ‖ ˌwɔːt̬ ʳrd-
  ˌwɑːt̬-
waterfall 'wɔːt ə fɔːl ‖ 'wɔːt̬ ʳr- 'wɑːt̬-, -fɑːl ~s
  z
Waterford 'wɔːt ə fəd ‖ 'wɔːt̬ ʳr fʳrd 'wɑːt̬-
waterfowl 'wɔːt ə faʊl ‖ 'wɔːt̬ ʳr- 'wɑːt̬- ~s z
waterfront 'wɔːt ə frʌnt ‖ 'wɔːt̬ ʳr- 'wɑːt̬- ~s s
Watergate 'wɔːt ə geɪt ‖ 'wɔːt̬ ʳr- 'wɑːt̬-
waterhole 'wɔːt ə həʊl →-hɒʊl ‖ 'wɔːt̬ ʳr hoʊl
  'wɑːt̬- ~s z
Waterhouse 'wɔːt ə haʊs ‖ 'wɔːt̬ ʳr- 'wɑːt̬-
wateriness 'wɔːt ˌər i nəs -nɪs ‖ 'wɔːt̬- 'wɑːt̬-
waterless 'wɔːt ə ləs -lɪs; -ʰl əs, -ɪs
  ‖ 'wɔːt̬ ʳr ləs 'wɑːt̬-
waterline 'wɔːt ə laɪn -ʰl aɪn ‖ 'wɔːt̬ ʳr laɪn
  'wɑːt̬- ~s z
waterlog 'wɔːt ə lɒg -ʰl ɒg ‖ 'wɔːt̬ ʳr lɔːg
  'wɑːt̬-, -lɑːg ~ged d ~ging ɪŋ ~s z
Waterloo ˌwɔːt ə 'luː ◂ -ʰl 'uː ‖ ˌwɔːt̬ ʳr 'luː
  ˌwɑːt̬-, '···
  ˌWaterloo 'Road; ˌWaterloo 'Station
Waterlooville ˌwɔːt ə ˌluː 'vɪl ‖ ˌwɔːt̬ ʳr-
  ˌwɑːt̬-
water|man, W~ 'wɔːt ə |mən ‖ 'wɔːt̬ ʳr- 'wɑːt̬-
  ~men mən men
watermark 'wɔːt ə mɑːk ‖ 'wɔːt̬ ʳr mɑːrk
  'wɑːt̬- ~ed t ~ing ɪŋ ~s s
watermelon 'wɔːt ə ˌmel ən ‖ 'wɔːt̬ ʳr- 'wɑːt̬-
  ~s z
watermill 'wɔːt ə mɪl ‖ 'wɔːt̬ ʳr- 'wɑːt̬- ~s z
waterpower 'wɔːt ə ˌpaʊ ə ‖ 'wɔːt̬ ʳr ˌpaʊ ʳr
  'wɑːt̬-
waterproof 'wɔːt ə pruːf §-prʊf ‖ 'wɔːt̬ ʳr-
  'wɑːt̬- ~ed t ~ing ɪŋ ~s s
water-repellent ˌwɔːt ə rɪ 'pel ənt ◂ -rə'--,
  §-riː'--, '···ˌ·· ‖ ˌwɔːt̬ ʳr rɪ ˌpel ənt 'wɑːt̬-

water-resistant ˌwɔːt ə rɪ 'zɪst ənt ◂ -rə'--,
  §-riː'--, '···ˌ·· ‖ ˌwɔːt̬ ʳr rɪ ˌzɪst ənt 'wɑːt̬-
Waters 'wɔːt əz ‖ 'wɔːt̬ ʳrz 'wɑːt̬-
watershed 'wɔːt ə ʃed ‖ 'wɔːt̬ ʳr- 'wɑːt̬- ~s z
Watership 'wɔːt ə ʃɪp ‖ 'wɔːt̬ ʳr- 'wɑːt̬-
  ˌWatership 'Down
waterside 'wɔːt ə saɪd ‖ 'wɔːt̬ ʳr- 'wɑːt̬-
water-ski 'wɔːt ə skiː ‖ 'wɔːt̬ ʳr- 'wɑːt̬- ~ed d
  ~er/s ə/z ‖ ʳr/z ~ing ɪŋ ~s z
water-soluble 'wɔːt ə ˌsɒl jub ʰl -jəb ʰl
  ‖ 'wɔːt̬ ʳr ˌsɑːl jəb ʰl 'wɑːt̬-
Waterson 'wɔːt əs ən ‖ 'wɔːt̬ ʳrs ən 'wɑːt̬-
waterspout 'wɔːt ə spaʊt ‖ 'wɔːt̬ ʳr- 'wɑːt̬- ~s
  s
Waterstone 'wɔːt ə stəʊn ‖ 'wɔːt̬ ʳr stoʊn
  'wɑːt̬-
watertight 'wɔːt ə taɪt ‖ 'wɔːt̬ ʳr- 'wɑːt̬-
Waterton 'wɔːt ət ən ‖ 'wɔːt̬ ʳrt ʰn 'wɑːt̬-
Watertown 'wɔːt ə taʊn ‖ 'wɔːt̬ ʳr- 'wɑːt̬-
waterway 'wɔːt ə weɪ ‖ 'wɔːt̬ ʳr- 'wɑːt̬- ~s z
waterweed 'wɔːt ə wiːd ‖ 'wɔːt̬ ʳr- 'wɑːt̬- ~s z
waterwheel 'wɔːt ə wiːʰl -hwiːʰl ‖ 'wɔːt̬ ʳr-
  'wɑːt̬- ~s z
waterwings 'wɔːt ə wɪŋz ‖ 'wɔːt̬ ʳr- 'wɑːt̬-
waterworks 'wɔːt ə wɜːks ‖ 'wɔːt̬ ʳr wɜːks
  'wɑːt̬-
Waterworth 'wɔːt ə wɜːθ -wəθ ‖ 'wɔːt̬ ʳr wɜːθ
  'wɑːt̬-
watery 'wɔːt ər i ‖ 'wɔːt̬ ər i 'wɑːt̬-
Wates weɪts
Watford 'wɒt fəd ‖ 'wɑːt fʳrd
Wath wɒθ ‖ wɑːθ
Watkin 'wɒt kɪn ‖ 'wɑːt-
Watkins 'wɒt kɪnz ‖ 'wɑːt-
Watkinson 'wɒt kɪn sən ‖ 'wɑːt-
Watling 'wɒt lɪŋ ‖ 'wɑːt-
  'Watling Street
Watney 'wɒt ni ‖ 'wɑːt ni
WATS wɒts ‖ wɑːts
Watson 'wɒts ʰn ‖ 'wɑːts ʰn
watt, Watt wɒt ‖ wɑːt **watts** wɒts ‖ wɑːts
wattag|e 'wɒt ɪdʒ ‖ 'wɑːt̬ ɪdʒ ~es ɪz əz
Watteau 'wɒt əʊ ‖ wɑː 'toʊ —Fr [va to]
watt-hour ˌwɒt 'aʊ ə ‖ ˌwɑːt̬ 'aʊ ʳr ~s z
wattle 'wɒt ʰl ‖ 'wɑːt̬ ʰl ~d d ~s z
  ˌwattle and 'daub
wattlebird 'wɒt ʰl bɜːd ‖ 'wɑːt̬ ʰl bɜːd ~s z
wattmeter 'wɒt ˌmiːt ə ‖ 'wɑːt ˌmiːt̬ ʳr ~s z
Watts wɒts ‖ wɑːts
Watusi wə 'tuːs i wɑː-, -'tuːz-
Wauchope (i) 'wɒːk əp 'wɒx- ‖ 'wɑːk-, (ii)
  'wɔː hoʊp ‖-hoʊp 'wɑː-
Waugh (i) wɔː ‖ wɑː, (ii) wɒf wɑːf, wɒx ‖ wɑːf
  —The writers Evelyn Waugh and Auberon
  Waugh were (i).
Waunfawr 'waɪn vaʊ ə ‖ -vaʊ ʳr —Welsh
  ['waɪn vaur, 'waɪn-]
WAV, wav wæv
  'wav files
wave weɪv **waved** weɪvd **waves** weɪvz
  waving 'weɪv ɪŋ
  'wave band; 'wave meˌchanics
waveform 'weɪv fɔːm ‖ -fɔːrm ~s z

waveguide 'weɪv gaɪd ~s z
wavelength 'weɪv leŋᵏθ §-lenᵗθ ~s s
wavelet 'weɪv lət -lɪt ~s s
Wavell 'weɪv ᵊl
Waveney 'weɪv ən i
waver 'weɪv ə ‖ -ᵊr ~ed d **wavering/ly**
'weɪv ər ɪŋ /li ~s z
waverer 'weɪv ər ə ‖ -ᵊr ər ~s z
Waverley 'weɪv ə li ‖ -ᵊr-
Wavertree 'weɪv ə tri: ‖ -ᵊr-
waving 'weɪv ɪŋ
wav|y 'weɪv |i ~ier i ə ‖ i ᵊr ~iest i ɪst i əst
~ily ɪ li əl i ~iness i nəs i nɪs
Wawona wɔː 'wəʊn ə ‖ -'woʊn- wɑː-
wax, Wax wæks **waxed** wækst **waxes**
'wæks ɪz -əz **waxing** 'wæks ɪŋ
'waxed ˌpaper; 'wax ˌpaper
waxbill 'wæks bɪl ~s z
waxen 'wæks ᵊn
waxplant 'wæks plɑːnt §-plænt ‖ -plænt ~s s
waxwing 'wæks wɪŋ ~s z
waxwork 'wæks wɜːk ‖ -wɜːk ~s s
wax|y 'wæks |i ~ier i ə ‖ i ᵊr ~iest i ɪst i əst
~iness i nəs i nɪs
way, Way weɪ **ways** weɪz
ˌway 'in; ˌway 'out
waybill 'weɪ bɪl ~s z
wayfarer 'weɪ ˌfeər ə ‖ -ˌfer ᵊr -ˌfær- ~s z
wayfaring 'waɪ ˌfeər ɪŋ ‖ -ˌfer ɪŋ -ˌfær-
'wayfaring tree
waylaid ₍ˌ₎weɪ 'leɪd
Wayland 'weɪ lənd
waylay ₍ˌ₎weɪ 'leɪ **waylaid** ₍ˌ₎weɪ 'leɪd ~ing ɪŋ
~s z
wayleave 'weɪ liːv ~s z
waymark 'weɪ mɑːk ‖ -mɑːrk ~ed t ~ing ɪŋ ~s
s
Wayne weɪn
Waynflete 'weɪn fliːt
way-out adj ˌweɪ 'aʊt ◄
ˌway-out 'fashions
-ways weɪz → **sideways** 'saɪd weɪz
wayside 'weɪ saɪd ~s z
wayward 'weɪ wəd ‖ -wᵊrd ~ly li ~ness nəs
nɪs
Waziristan wə ˌzɪər ɪ 'stɑːn -ə- ‖ -ˌzɪr-
wazoo wə 'zuː wɑː-
we strong form wiː, weak form wi
weak wiːk (= week) **weaker** 'wiːk ə ‖ -ᵊr
weakest 'wiːk ɪst -əst
ˌweaker 'sex, ˌ‧ ‧'‧
weaken 'wiːk ən ~ed d ~ing ɪŋ ~s z
weak-kneed ˌwiːk 'niːd ◄
weakling 'wiːk lɪŋ ~s z
weakly 'wiːk li
weak-minded ˌwiːk 'maɪnd ɪd ◄ -əd ~ly li
~ness nəs nɪs
weakness 'wiːk nəs -nɪs ~es ɪz əz
weak-willed ˌwiːk 'wɪld ◄
weal wiːᵊl **weals** wiːᵊlz
Weald, weald wiːᵊld
wealden, W~ 'wiːᵊld ən
Wealdstone 'wiːᵊld stəʊn ‖ -stoʊn

wealth welθ
wealth|y 'welθ |i ~ier i ə ‖ i ᵊr ~iest i ɪst i əst
~ily ɪ li əl i ~iness i nəs i nɪs
wean wiːn **weaned** wiːnd **weaning** 'wiːn ɪŋ
weans wiːnz
weaner 'wiːn ə ‖ -ᵊr ~s z
weapon 'wep ən ~s z
weaponry 'wep ən ri
wear weə ‖ weᵊr wæᵊr **wearing** 'weər ɪŋ
‖ 'wer ɪŋ 'wær- **wears** weəz ‖ weᵊrz wæᵊrz
wore wɔː ‖ wɔːr woʊr **worn** wɔːn ‖ wɔːrn
woʊrn
ˌwear and 'tear
Wear river wɪə ‖ wɪᵊr
wearability ˌweər ə 'bɪl ət i -ɪt i
‖ ˌwer ə 'bɪl əţ i ˌwær-
wearable 'weər əb ᵊl ‖ 'wer- 'wær-
Weardale 'wɪə deⁱᵊl ‖ 'wɪr-
wearer 'weər ə ‖ 'wer ᵊr 'wær- ~s z
weari... —see **weary**
wearisome 'wɪər i səm ‖ 'wɪr- ~ly li ~ness
nəs nɪs
Wearmouth 'wɪə maʊθ -məθ ‖ 'wɪr-
wear|y 'wɪər |i ‖ 'wɪr |i ~ied id ~ier i ə ‖ i ᵊr
~ies iz ~iest i ɪst i əst ~ily əl i ɪ li ~iness
i nəs i nɪs ~ying i ɪŋ
weasel 'wiːz ᵊl ~ed d ~ing ˌɪŋ ~s z
weaselly 'wiːz ᵊl i
weather 'weð ə ‖ -ᵊr ~ed d **weathering**
'weð ər ɪŋ ~s z
'weather balˌloon; 'weather ˌforecast;
'weather map; 'weather ship; 'weather
ˌstation; 'weather vane
Weatherall 'weð ər ɔːl ‖ -ɑːl
weather-beaten 'weð ə ˌbiːt ᵊn ‖ -ᵊr-
weatherboard 'weð ə bɔːd ‖ -ᵊr bɔːrd -boʊrd
~ing ɪŋ ~s z
weather-bound 'weð ə baʊnd ‖ -ᵊr-
weathercock 'weð ə kɒk ‖ -ᵊr kɑːk ~s s
weatherglass 'weð ə glɑːs §-glæs ‖ -ᵊr glæs
~es ɪz əz
Weatherhead 'weð ə hed ‖ -ᵊr-
weatherization ˌweð ər aɪ 'zeɪʃ ᵊn -ər ɪ-
‖ -ər ə-
weateriz|e 'weð ə raɪz ~ed d ~es ɪz əz ~ing
ɪŋ
weather|man, W~ 'weð ə |mæn ‖ -ᵊr- ~men
men
weatherproof 'weð ə pruːf §-prʊf ‖ -ᵊr- ~ed t
~ing ɪŋ ~s s
weathertight 'weð ə taɪt ‖ -ᵊr-
weave wiːv **weaved** wiːvd **weaves** wiːvz
weaving 'wiːv ɪŋ **wove** wəʊv ‖ woʊv
woven 'wəʊv ᵊn ‖ 'woʊv ᵊn
weaver, W~ 'wiːv ə ‖ -ᵊr ~s z
weaverbird 'wiːv ə bɜːd ‖ -ᵊr bɜːd ~s z
web web **webbed** webd **webbing** 'web ɪŋ
webs webz
ˌweb 'offset; 'web page
Webb web
Webber 'web ə ‖ -ᵊr
webbing 'web ɪŋ
webcam 'web kæm ~s z

Weak forms

1 Many English function words (= articles, pronouns, prepositions, auxiliaries, modals, etc.) have more than one pronunciation. In particular, they have a **strong form**, containing a **strong** vowel, and a **weak form**, containing a **weak** vowel. An example is **at**, with the strong form æt and the weak form ət.

2 The weak form is generally used if the word is unstressed (as is usually the case with function words). The strong form is used only when the word is stressed, usually because it is accented (see STRESS).

Jim's ət **lunch. He'll be back** ət **one.**

We say 'ˈæt **home', not 'in home'.**

I'll invite ðəm **round.**

Tell me how they ˈwɜː ‖ ˈwɜːr.

They wə ‖ wᵊr **delighted.**

3 Nevertheless, the strong form is used for unaccented function words in certain positions:

- usually, for a preposition when it is between a weak syllable and a pronoun, to help the rhythm:

   I'm ˈlooking æt ju. (Compare: **Don't** ˈlook ət mi.)

- always, when a function word is **stranded** (= left exposed by a syntactic operation involving the movement or deletion of the word on which it depends):

   Where does she ˈkʌm frɒm‖frʌm? (...**from X**)

   ˈaɪ kən **speak English better than** ˈjuː kæn. (= **than you can speak**)

   It was ˈeɪmd æt **but not achieved.** (= **they aimed at it**)

4 It is important for learners of English to use weak forms appropriately. Otherwise, listeners may think they are emphasizing a word where this is not really so. Equally, native speakers should not be misled into supposing that careful or declamatory speech demands strong forms throughout. One exception is the pronunciation style used for **singing**, where strong forms are often used. Even here, though, articles are usually weak.

---

webcast ˈweb kɑːst §-kæst ‖ -kæst ~**ing** ɪŋ ~**s** s

webding, W~ ˈweb dɪŋ ~**s** z

weber *unit of magnetic flux* ˈveɪb ə ˈweb- ‖ -ᵊr ~**s** z

Weber *English family name* (i) ˈweb ə ‖ -ᵊr, (ii) ˈwiːb ə ‖ -ᵊr, (iii) ˈweɪb ə ‖ -ᵊr

Weber *German family name; composer, sociologist* ˈveɪb ə ‖ -ᵊr —*Ger* [ˈveː bɐ]

Webern ˈveɪb ɜːn -ən ‖ -ɜːn —*Ger* [ˈveː bɛn]

web|foot ˈweb |fʊt ~**feet** fiːt

web-footed ˌweb ˈfʊt ɪd ◂ -əd, ˈ·ˌ·· ‖ -ˈfʊt əd ◂

webhead ˈweb hed ~**s** z

Webley ˈweb li

webliograph|y ˌweb li ˈɒg rəf |i ‖ -ˈɑːg- ~**ies** iz

weblog ˈweb lɒg ‖ -lɔːg -lɑːg ~**s** z

webmaster ˈweb ˌmɑːst ə §-ˌmæst- ‖ -ˌmæst ᵊr ~**s** z

webology we ˈbɒl ədʒ i ‖ -ˈbɑːl-

Weak vowels

1 Among unstressed syllables it is useful to distinguish between those that nevertheless contain a strong vowel and those that have a weak vowel. This distinction has implications for syllabification, as shown in the *Longman Pronunciation Dictionary* (LPD), and for rhythm.

2 A stressed syllable (shown in words of more than one syllable by one of the marks ' and ˌ) must always contain a **strong** vowel (= any vowel or diphthong except ə, i, u). All the syllables in the following words, whether stressed or unstressed, are strong-vowelled: **red** red, **hope** həʊp ‖ hoʊp, **bedtime** 'bed taɪm, **undone** ˌʌn 'dʌn, **acorn** 'eɪk ɔːn ‖ 'eɪk ɔːrn, **butane** 'bjuːt eɪn.

3 The vowels ə, i, u are always weak. The vowel ɪ, too, is weak in many cases, and also sometimes ʊ in BrE and oʊ in AmE. The unstressed syllables in the following words are all **weak**-vowelled: **allow** ə 'laʊ, **happy** 'hæp i, **situation** ˌsɪtʃ u 'eɪʃ ən, **carelessness** 'keə ləs nəs -lɪs -nɪs ‖ 'ker-, **remember** rɪ 'mem bə rə- ‖ rɪ 'mem bᵊr, **uselessness** 'juːs ləs nəs, **annoying** ə 'nɔɪ ɪŋ, **seductive** sɪ 'dʌkt ɪv, **standard** 'stænd əd ‖ 'stænd ᵊrd, **stimulus** 'stɪm jʊl əs ‖ 'stɪm jəl əs. The weak vowel ə may be realized in the form of a SYLLABIC CONSONANT, as in **suddenly** 'sʌd ᵊn li. If a diphthong is created through the COMPRESSION of weak syllables, it remains weak, as in **annual** 'æn ju ˌəl.

4 The distinction between weak ɪ and ə has the power of distinguishing words in RP. For example, **V. I. Lenin** is 'len ɪn, but **John Lennon** is 'len ən. The words **rabbit** 'ræb ɪt and **abbot** 'æb ət do not rhyme. In certain other kinds of English, however, this distinction may be NEUTRALIZED, with ə used instead of weak ɪ in virtually all positions, or with the choice between ə and ɪ dependent upon the phonetic context. Accordingly, at **rabbit** LPD shows a secondary pronunciation 'ræb ət.

5 Even in RP and in other kinds of English that maintain the distinction between weak ɪ and ə, many words may be heard with either pronunciation, and this is shown in LPD. For example, **carelessness, civil, private** are nowadays more usually pronounced 'keə ləs nəs, 'sɪv ᵊl, 'praɪv ət. A conservative minority say 'keə lɪs nɪs, 'sɪv ɪl, 'praɪv ɪt, and these are given in LPD as secondary pronunciations.

website 'web saɪt ~s s
Webster 'web stə ‖ -stᵊr ~'s z
web-toed ˌweb 'təʊd ◂ ‖ -'toʊd ◂
Wechsler 'weks lə ‖ -lᵊr
wed wed **wedded** 'wed ɪd -əd **wedding** 'wed ɪŋ **weds** wedz
we'd *strong form* wiːd, *weak form* wɪd
Wed —*see* **Wednesday**
wedded 'wed ɪd -əd
Weddell (i) 'wed ᵊl, (ii) wɪ 'del wə- —*For the W~ Sea,* (i)
Wedderburn 'wed ə bɜːn ‖ -ᵊr bɜːn

wedding 'wed ɪŋ ~s z
'wedding ˌbreakfast; 'wedding cake; 'wedding day; 'wedding march; 'wedding ring
wedel 'veɪd ᵊl ~ed, ~led d ~ing, ~ling ɪŋ ~s z
wedeln 'veɪd ᵊln ~ing ɪŋ
wedge wedʒ **wedged** wedʒd **wedges** 'wedʒ ɪz -əz **wedging** 'wedʒ ɪŋ
Wedgewood, Wedgwood 'wedʒ wʊd
wedlock 'wed lɒk ‖ -lɑːk
Wedmore 'wed mɔː →'web- ‖ -mɔːr

Wednesbury 'wenz bər_i ‖ -ˌber i —*There is also a spelling pronunciation* 'wed nız bər_i, 'wed nəz-; *locally also* 'wedʒ bər_i
Wednesday 'wenz deı -di; 'wed ᵊnz deı, -di —*see note at* -day **~s** z
Wednesfield 'wenᵗs fiːᵊld —*There is also a spelling pronunciation* 'wed nıs fiːᵊld, -nəs-; *locally also* 'wedʒ fiːᵊld
Weds —*see* **Wednesday** —*sometimes spoken as* wedz
wee wiː **weed** wiːd **weeing** 'wiː ıŋ **wees** wiːz
Weech wiːtʃ
weed wiːd **weeded** 'wiːd ıd -əd **weeding** 'wiːd ıŋ **weeds** wiːdz
weeder 'wiːd ə ‖ -ᵊr **~s** z
weedi... —*see* **weedy**
weedkiller 'wiːd ˌkıl ə →'wiːg- ‖ -ᵊr **~s** z
Weedon 'wiːd ᵊn
weed|y 'wiːd |i **~ier** i_ə ‖ i_ᵊr **~iest** i_ıst i_əst **~ily** ı li əl i **~iness** i nəs i nıs
Weehawken wiː 'hɔːk ən ‖ -'hɑːk-
Weejuns *tdmk* 'wiːdʒ ənz
week wiːk **weeks** wiːks
weekday 'wiːk deı **~s** z
weekend ˌwiːk 'end ◂ '·· ‖ '·· **~ed** ıd əd **~ing** ıŋ **~s** z
weekender ˌwiːk 'end ə ‖ 'wiːk end ᵊr **~s** z
Weekes wiːks
Weekley 'wiːk li
weeklong 'wiːk lɒŋ ‖ -lɔːŋ -lɑːŋ
week|ly 'wiːk |li **~lies** liz
weeknight 'wiːk naıt **~s** s
Weeks wiːks
ween wiːn
weenie 'wiːn i **~s** z
weensy 'wiːnz i
ween|y 'wiːn |i **~ier** i_ə ‖ i_ᵊr **~ies** iz **~iest** i_ıst i_əst
weenybopper 'wiːn i ˌbɒp ə ‖ -ˌbɑːp ᵊr **~s** z
weep wiːp **weeping** 'wiːp ıŋ **weeps** wiːps **wept** wept ˌweeping 'willow
weeper 'wiːp ə ‖ -ᵊr **~s** z
weep|ie, weep|y 'wiːp |i **~ier** i_ə ‖ i_ᵊr **~ies** iz **~iest** i_ıst i_əst **~iness** i nəs i nıs
Weetabix *tdmk* 'wiːt ə bıks ‖ 'wiːt̬- **~es** ız əz
weever 'wiːv ə ‖ -ᵊr **~s** z
weevil 'wiːv ᵊl -ıl **~s** z
wee-wee 'wiː wiː **~d** d **~ing** ıŋ **~s** z
weft weft
Wehrmacht 'veə mɑːxt -mɑːkt, -mæxt, -mækt ‖ 'ver mɑːkt —*Ger* ['veːʁ maxt]
Weidenfeld 'vaıd ᵊn felt 'waıd-
Weidman 'waıd mən →'waıb-
weigela waı 'dʒiːl ə wı-, wə-, -'dʒel-, -'giːl-; △·'·i_ə; 'waıg ıl ə, -əl- **~s** z
weigh weı (= *way*) **weighed** weıd (= *wade*) **weighing** 'weı ıŋ **weighs** weız
weighbridg|e 'weı brıdʒ **~es** ız əz
Weighell *(i)* 'wiːᵊl, *(ii)* 'weı_əl
weigh-in 'weı ın

weight, W~ weıt (= *wait*) **weighted** 'weıt ıd -əd ‖ 'weıt̬ əd **weighting/s** 'weıt ıŋ/z ‖ 'weıt̬ ıŋ/z **weights** weıts
weightless 'weıt ləs -lıs **~ly** li **~ness** nəs nıs
weightlift|ing 'weıt ˌlıft |ıŋ **~er/s** ə/z ‖ ᵊr/z
Weighton 'wiːt ᵊn
weightwatch|er 'weıt ˌwɒtʃ| ə ‖ -ˌwɑːtʃ| ᵊr **~ers, Weightwatchers** *tdmk* əz ‖ ᵊrz **~ing** ıŋ
weight|y 'weıt |i ‖ 'weıt̬ |i **~ier** i_ə ‖ i_ᵊr **~iest** i_ıst i_əst **~ily** ı li əl i **~iness** i nəs i nıs
Weil, Weill *(i)* vaıᵊl, *(ii)* wiːᵊl —*Ger, Fr* [vaıl]
Weimar 'vaım ɑː ‖ -ɑːr —*Ger* ['vaı maʁ]
Weimaraner, w~ 'vaım ə rɑːn ə 'waım-, ˌ·'··· ‖ -ᵊr **~s** z
Weinberger 'waın bɜːg ə →'waım- ‖ -bɜːg ᵊr
Weinstock 'waın stɒk ‖ -stɑːk
weir, Weir wıə ‖ wıᵊr **weirs** wıəz ‖ wıᵊrz
weird wıəd ‖ wıᵊrd **weirder** 'wıəd ə ‖ 'wırd ᵊr **weirdest** 'wıəd ıst -əst ‖ 'wırd əst
weirdie 'wıəd i ‖ 'wırd i **~s** z
weird|ly 'wıəd |li ‖ 'wırd |li **~ness** nəs nıs
weirdo 'wıəd əʊ ‖ 'wırd oʊ **~es** z
Weismann 'vaıs mən ‖ -mɑːn —*Ger* ['vaıs man]
Weiss *(i)* vaıs, *(ii)* weıs —*Ger* [vaıs]
Weissmuller 'waıs mʌl ə 'vaıs-, -mʊl- ‖ -ᵊr
Weizmann 'vaıts mən ‖ -mɑːn —*Ger* ['vaıts man]
Welbeck 'wel bek
Welbourne 'wel bɔːn ‖ -bɔːrn -boʊrn
Welby 'wel bi
welch weltʃ welʃ **welched** weltʃt welʃt **welches** 'weltʃ ız 'welʃ-, -əs **welching** 'weltʃ ıŋ 'welʃ-
Welch *(i)* weltʃ, *(ii)* welʃ
welcom|e 'welk əm **~ed** d **~es** z **~ing** ıŋ **~eness** nəs nıs **~er/s** ə/z ‖ ᵊr/z
weld, Weld weld **welded** 'weld ıd -əd **welding** 'weld ıŋ **welds** weldz
welder 'weld ə ‖ -ᵊr **~s** z
Weldon 'weld ən
welfare, W~ 'wel feə ‖ -fer -fær ˌwelfare 'state ‖ '···
welfarism 'wel feər ˌız əm ‖ -fer- -fær-
Welford 'wel fəd ‖ -fᵊrd
welkin 'welk ın §-ən
well wel **welled** weld **welling** 'wel ıŋ **wells** welz —*When used as an interjection (but not otherwise) this word has an occasional weak form* wəl
we'll *strong form* wiːᵊl, *weak form* wıl
well-acquainted ˌwel ə 'kweınt ıd -əd ‖ -'kweınt̬-
well-adjusted ˌwel ə 'dʒʌst ıd ◂ -əd
well-advised ˌwel əd 'vaızd ◂ §-æd-
Welland 'wel ənd
well-appointed ˌwel ə 'pɔınt ıd ◂ -əd ‖ -'pɔınt̬ əd ◂
well-attended ˌwel ə 'tend ıd ◂ -əd
well-baby ˌwel 'beıb i
well-balanced ˌwel 'bæl ənᵗst ◂
well-behaved ˌwel bı 'heıvd ◂ -bə-
wellbeing ˌwel 'biː ıŋ '·ˌ··

Wellbeloved 'wel bi lʌvd -bə-
wellborn ˌwel 'bɔːn ◀ ‖ -'bɔːrn ◀
well-bred ˌwel 'bred ◀
well-brought-up ˌwel ˌbrɔːt 'ʌp ◀ ‖ -ˌbrɔːt̬-
-ˌbrɑːt̬-
well-built ˌwel 'bɪlt ◀
well-chosen ˌwel 'tʃəʊz ᵊn ◀ ‖ -'tʃoʊz-
Wellcome 'welk əm
well-connected ˌwel kə 'nekt ɪd ◀ -əd
well-cooked ˌwel 'kʊkt ◀ §-'kuːkt
well-defined ˌwel dɪ 'faɪnd ◀ -də-
well-deserved ˌwel dɪ 'zɜːvd ◀ -də- ‖ -'zɜːvd ◀
well-developed ˌwel dɪ 'vel əpt -də-
well-disposed ˌwel dɪ 'spəʊzd ◀ -də-
‖ -'spoʊzd ◀
well-documented ˌwel 'dɒk ju ment ɪd ◀
-jə ·, -əd ‖ -'dɑːk jə ment̬ əd ◀
well-done ˌwel 'dʌn ◀
well-dressed ˌwel 'drest ◀
well-earned ˌwel 'ɜːnd ◀ ‖ -'ɜːnd ◀
well-educated ˌwel 'ed ju keɪt ɪd ◀ -'edʒ u-,
-'edʒ ə-, -əd ‖ -'edʒ ə keɪt̬ əd ◀
well-endowed ˌwel ɪn 'daʊd ◀ -en-, -ən-
Weller 'wel ə ‖ -ᵊr
Welles welz
Wellesbourne 'welz bɔːn ‖ -bɔːrn -boʊrn
Wellesley 'welz li
well-established ˌwel ɪ 'stæb lɪʃt ◀ -ə-
well-favoured ˌwel 'feɪv əd ◀ ‖ -ᵊrd ◀
well-fed ˌwel 'fed ◀
well-formed ˌwel 'fɔːmd ◀ ‖ -'fɔːrmd ◀
well-formedness ˌwel 'fɔːm ɪd nəs -əd-, -nɪs
‖ -'fɔːrm-
well-found ˌwel 'faʊnd ◀
well-founded ˌwel 'faʊnd ɪd ◀ -əd
well-groomed ˌwel 'gruːmd ◀ -'grʊmd
well-grounded ˌwel 'graʊnd ɪd ◀ -əd
wellhead 'wel hed ~s z
well-heeled ˌwel 'hiːᵊld ◀
well-hung ˌwel 'hʌŋ ◀
wellie 'wel i ~s z
well-informed ˌwel ɪn 'fɔːmd ◀ ‖ -'fɔːrmd ◀
Welling 'wel ɪŋ
Wellingborough 'wel ɪŋ bər ə ‖ -ˌbɝː oʊ
Wellington, w~ 'wel ɪŋ tən —but in New
Zealand, locally usually 'wæl- ~s, ~'s z
ˌwellington 'boot
wellingtonia ˌwel ɪŋ 'təʊn i ə ‖ -'toʊn- ~s z
well-intentioned ˌwel ɪn 'tenʃ ᵊnd ◀
well-kept ˌwel 'kept ◀
well-knit ˌwel 'nɪt ◀
well-known ˌwel 'nəʊn ◀ ‖ -'noʊn ◀
well-liked ˌwel 'laɪkt ◀
well-lined ˌwel 'laɪnd ◀
well-made ˌwel 'meɪd ◀
well-mannered ˌwel 'mæn əd ◀ ‖ -ᵊrd ◀
well-meaning ˌwel 'miːn ɪŋ ◀
well-meant ˌwel 'ment ◀
wellness 'wel nəs -nɪs
well-nigh ˌwel 'naɪ ◀
well-off ˌwel 'ɒf ◀ -'ɔːf ‖ -'ɑːf
well-oiled ˌwel 'ɔɪᵊld ◀
well-ordered ˌwel 'ɔːd əd ◀ ‖ -'ɔːrd ᵊrd ◀

well-paid ˌwel 'peɪd ◀
well-planned ˌwel 'plænd ◀
well-preserved ˌwel prɪ 'zɜːvd ◀ -prə-, §-priː-
‖ -'zɜːvd ◀
well-proportioned ˌwel prə 'pɔːʃ ᵊnd ◀
‖ -'pɔːrʃ- -'poʊrʃ-
well-qualified ˌwel 'kwɒl ɪ faɪd ◀ -ə-
‖ -'kwɑːl-
well-read ˌwel 'red ◀
well-rounded ˌwel 'raʊnd ɪd ◀ -əd
well-run ˌwel 'rʌn ◀
Wells welz
well-set ˌwel 'set ◀
well-spoken ˌwel 'spəʊk ən ◀ ‖ -'spoʊk-
wellspring 'wel sprɪŋ ~s z
well-stocked ˌwel 'stɒkt ◀ ‖ -'stɑːkt ◀
well-suited ˌwel 'suːt ɪd ◀ -'sjuːt-, -əd ‖ -'suːt̬-
well-tempered ˌwel 'temp əd ◀ ‖ -ᵊrd ◀
well-thought-of ˌwel 'θɔːt ɒv ◀ -əv ‖ -'θɔːt̬ ʌv
-'θɑːt̬-, -ɑːv
well-thought-out ˌwel θɔːt 'aʊt ◀ ‖ -θɔːt̬-
-θɑːt̬-
well-thumbed ˌwel 'θʌmd ◀
well-timed ˌwel 'taɪmd ◀
well-to-do ˌwel tə 'duː ◀ -tu-
well-travelled, well-traveled
ˌwel 'træv ᵊld ◀
well-tried ˌwel 'traɪd ◀
well-turned ˌwel 'tɜːnd ◀ ‖ -'tɝːnd ◀
well-turned-out ˌwel ˌtɜːnd 'aʊt ◀ ‖ -ˌtɝːnd-
well-versed ˌwel 'vɜːst ◀ ‖ -'vɝːst ◀
well-wisher 'wel ˌwɪʃ ə ˌ·'·· ‖ -ᵊr ~s z
well-woman ˌwel 'wʊm ən
well-worn ˌwel 'wɔːn ◀ ‖ -'wɔːrn ◀ -'woʊrn
well|y 'wel |i ~ies iz
Welsh, welsh welʃ **welshed** welʃt **welshes**
'welʃ ɪz -əz **welshing** 'welʃ ɪŋ
ˌWelsh 'rabbit, ˌWelsh 'rarebit
welsher 'welʃ ə ‖ -ᵊr ~s z
Welsh|man 'welʃ |mən ~men mən men ~ness
nəs nɪs
Welshpool 'welʃ puːl ˌ·'·
Welsh|woman 'welʃ |ˌwʊm ən ~women
ˌwɪm ɪn §-ən
welt welt **welted** 'welt ɪd -əd **welting**
'welt ɪŋ **welts** welts
weltanschauung 'velt æn ˌʃaʊ ʊŋ -ən-, ˌ·'··
‖ -ɑːn- —Ger W~ ['vɛlt ˌan ʃaʊ ʊŋ]
welter 'welt ə ‖ -ᵊr ~ed d **weltering**
'welt ᵊr ɪŋ ~s z
welterweight 'welt ə weɪt ‖ -ᵊr- ~s s
Welthorpe 'wel θɔːp ‖ -θɔːrp
weltschmerz 'velt ʃmeəts ‖ -ʃmerts —Ger W~
['vɛlt ʃmɛʁts]
Welty 'welt i
welwitschia wel 'wɪtʃ i ə ~s z
Welwyn 'wel ɪn §-ən
Wem wem
Wembley 'wem bli
Wemmick 'wem ɪk
Wemyss wiːmz
wen wen **wens** wenz

W

Wenceslas, Wenceslaus 'wen⸱s əs ləs -ıs-,
⚠-ləs-, -læs ‖ -lɔːs, -lɑːs
wench wentʃ **wenched** wentʃt **wenches**
'wentʃ ız -əz **wenching** 'wentʃ ıŋ
wend, Wend wend **wended** 'wend ıd -əd
  wending 'wend ıŋ **wends, Wends** wendz
Wendell 'wend ᵊl
Wenden 'wend ən
Wendish 'wend ıʃ
Wendon 'wend ən
Wendover 'wend əʊv ə ‖ -oʊv ᵊr
Wendy 'wend i
  'Wendy house
Wenger 'veŋ ə ‖ -ᵊr —*Fr* [vɛ̃ ɡɛːʁ]
Wenham 'wen əm
Wenlock 'wen lɒk ‖ -lɑːk
  Wenlock 'Edge
Wensley 'wenz li 'wen⸱s-
Wensleydale, w~ 'wenz li deıᵊl 'wen⸱s-
Wensum 'wen⸱s əm
went went
wentletrap 'went ᵊl træp **~s** s
Wentworth 'went wəθ -wɜːθ ‖ -wɜːθ
Wenvoe 'wen vəʊ ‖ -voʊ
Weobley 'web li
wept wept

WERE

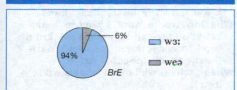

BrE

94%   6%   ☐ wɜː
                    ☐ weə

were *strong forms* wɜː weə ‖ wɜːᵊ, *weak form*
wə ‖ wᵊr — *Preference poll (strong form),*
BrE: wɜː 94%, weə 6%.
we're wıə ‖ wıᵊr (= *weir*)
weren't wɜːnt weənt ‖ wɜːnt
were|wolf 'weə |wʊlf 'wıə-, 'wɜː- ‖ 'wer-
  'wır-, 'wɜː- **~wolves** wʊlvz
Werner 'wɜːn ə ‖ 'wɜːn ᵊr —*Ger* ['vɛʁ nɐ]
Wernicke 'veən ık ə ‖ 'vern- -i —*Ger*
  ['vɛʁ nık ə]
  'Wernicke's ˌarea
wert *strong form* wɜːt ‖ wɜːt, *weak form* wət
  ‖ wᵊrt
Weser 'veız ə ‖ -ᵊr —*Ger* ['veː zɐ]
Wesker 'wesk ə ‖ -ᵊr
Wesley (i) 'wes li, (ii) 'wez li —*The founder of*
  Methodism was actually (i), though often
  pronounced as (ii). **~s, ~'s** z
Wesleyan 'wez li⸱ən 'wes- **~s** z
Wessex 'wes ıks §-əks
Wesson 'wes ᵊn
west, West west
  ˌWest 'Bank; ˌWest 'Coast◂; 'West
  ˌCountry, ⸱ '⸱ ◂; ˌWest 'End◂; ˌWest
  Gla'morgan; (ˌ)West 'Indian, (ˌ)West
  'Indies; ˌWest 'Midlands; ˌWest Vir'ginia;
  ˌWest 'Yorkshire

westbound 'west baʊnd
Westbourne 'west bɔːn -bən ‖ -bɔːrn -boʊrn
Westbrook 'west brʊk
Westbury 'west bər_i ‖ -ˌber i
Westbury-on-Trym ˌwest bər_i ɒn 'trım
  ‖ -ɑːn⸱ -ɔːn⸱
Westclox *tdmk* 'west klɒks ‖ -klɑːks
Westcott 'west kət
wester, W~ 'west ə ‖ -ᵊr **~ed** d **westering**
  'west ər ıŋ **~s** z
Westerham 'west ər əm →'wes trəm
wester|ly 'west ə |li -ᵊ|l i i -ᵊr |li **~lies** liz
western, W~ 'west ən ‖ -ᵊrn **~s** z
  ˌWestern Au'stralia; ˌWestern 'Isles
westerner, W~ 'west ən ə ‖ -ᵊrn ᵊr -ᵊn ər **~s** z
westernis... —*see* **westerniz...**
westernization ˌwest ən aı 'zeıʃ ᵊn -ı⸱-
  ‖ -ᵊrn ə-
westerniz|e 'west ə naız ‖ -ᵊr- **~ed** d **~es** ız əz
  ~ing ıŋ
westernmost 'west ən məʊst →-əm-
  ‖ -ᵊrn moʊst
Westfield 'west fiːᵊld
Westgate 'west geıt -gıt, -gət
Westhoughton ˌwest 'hɔːt ᵊn ‖ -'hɑːt-
Westin 'west ın §-ən
Westinghouse 'west ıŋ haʊs
Westlake 'west leık
Westland *tdmk* 'west lənd **~'s** z
Westmeath ˌwest 'miːð
Westminster 'west mın⸱st ə ˌ⸱'⸱ ⸱;
  ⚠ˌ⸱'mın ıst ə, ⚠-əst ə ‖ -ᵊr
  ˌWestminster 'Abbey
Westmoreland, Westmorland
  'west mə lənd ‖ -mɔːr- -moʊr-
west-northwest ˌwest nɔːθ 'west ‖ -nɔːrθ-
  —*also naut* -nɔː- ‖ -nɔːr-
Westoby (i) 'west əb i, (ii) we 'stəʊb i
  ‖ -'stoʊb-
Weston 'west ən
Westoning 'west ən ıŋ
Weston-super-Mare ˌwest ən ˌsuːp ə 'meə
  -ˌsjuːp-; ⸱ ⸱'⸱ ⸱ ⸱ ‖ -ᵊr 'meᵊr -'mæᵊr
Westphali|a west 'feıl i_|ə **~an/s** ən/z
Westray 'wes treı -tri
west-southwest ˌwest saʊθ 'west —*also naut*
  -saʊ-
westward 'west wəd ‖ -wᵊrd **~s** z
  ˌWestward 'Ho!
Westwood 'west wʊd
wet wet **wets** wets **wetted** 'wet ıd -əd
  ‖ 'weţ əd **wetter** 'wet ə ‖ 'weţ ᵊr **wettest**
  'wet ıst -əst ‖ 'weţ əst **wetting** 'wet ıŋ
  ‖ 'weţ ıŋ
  ˌwet 'blanket ‖ ⸱ '⸱ ⸱; ˌwet 'dream; 'wet
  nurse; 'wet suit; 'wetting ˌagent
wetback 'wet bæk **~s** s
wether 'weð ə ‖ -ᵊr (= *weather*) **~s** z
Wetherall 'weð ər ɔːl -ᵊr ˌəl ‖ -ɑːl
Wetherby 'weð ə bi ‖ -ᵊr-
wetland 'wet lænd -lənd **~s** z
wet-look 'wet lʊk §-luːk
Wetmore 'wet mɔː ‖ -mɔːr

wetness 'wet nəs -nɪs
wett... —*see* **wet**
Wetton 'wet ᵊn
Wetzel 'wets ᵊl
we've *strong form* wiːv, *weak form* wɪv
Wexford 'weks fəd ‖ -fᵊrd
Wexler 'weks lə ‖ -lᵊr
Wey weɪ
Weybridge 'weɪ brɪdʒ
Weyman (i) 'waɪ mən, (ii) 'weɪ mən
Weymouth 'weɪ məθ
whack wæk hwæk **whacked** wækt hwækt
  whacking/s 'wæk ɪŋ/z 'hwæk- **whacks**
  wæks hwæks
  ˌwhacked 'out
whacko ˌwæk 'əʊ ˌhwæk- ‖ '·oʊ
whacky 'wæk i
whale werᵊl hwerᵊl **whales** werᵊlz hwerᵊlz
  'whale of a ˌtime
whaleboat 'werᵊl bəʊt 'hwerᵊl- ‖ -boʊt ~s s
whalebone 'werᵊl bəʊn 'hwerᵊl- ‖ -boʊn
whaler 'werᵊl ə 'hwerᵊl- ‖ -ᵊr ~s z
Whaley 'weɪl i 'hweɪl-
whaling 'werᵊl ɪŋ 'hwerᵊl-
Whalley (i) 'wɒl i 'hwɒl- ‖ 'waːl i 'hwaːl i, (ii)
  'wɔːl i 'hwɔːl i ‖ 'wɔːl i 'waːl i, 'hwaːl i,
  'hwaːl i, (iii) 'weɪl i 'hweɪl- —*The place near
  Blackburn, Lancs., is* (ii), *but W~ Range in
  Manchester is* (i).
wham, Wham wæm hwæm **whammed** wæmd
  hwæmd **whamming** 'wæm ɪŋ 'hwæm-
  whams wæmz hwæmz
whammo 'wæm əʊ 'hwæm- ‖ -oʊ
whamm|y 'wæm |i 'hwæm- ~ies iz
Whampoa ˌwæm 'pəʊ ˌhwæm- ‖ ˌwaːm 'poʊ
  ˌhwaːm- —*Chi* Huángpǔ [²xuaŋ ³pʰu]
whang wæŋ hwæŋ **whanged** wæŋd hwæŋd
  whanging 'wæŋ ɪŋ 'hwæŋ- **whangs** wæŋz
  hwæŋz
whangee ˌwæŋ 'i: ˌhwæŋ-, -'gi: ‖ ˌhwæŋ- ~s z
whare 'wɒr i 'hwɒr i ‖ 'waːr i 'hwaːr i ~s z
wharf wɔːf hwɔːf ‖ wɔːrf hwɔːrf **wharfs** wɔːfs
  hwɔːfs ‖ wɔːrfs hwɔːrfs **wharves** wɔːvz hwɔːvz
  ‖ wɔːrvz hwɔːrvz
wharfage 'wɔːf ɪdʒ 'hwɔːf- ‖ 'wɔːrf- 'hwɔːrf-
Wharfe wɔːf hwɔːf ‖ wɔːrf hwɔːrf
Wharfedale 'wɔːf deɪᵊl 'hwɔːf- ‖ 'wɔːrf-
  'hwɔːrf-
wharfinger 'wɔːf ɪndʒ ə 'hwɔːf-, §-əndʒ-
  ‖ 'wɔːrf əndʒ ᵊr 'hwɔːrf- ~s z
Wharton 'wɔːt ᵊn 'hwɔːt- ‖ 'wɔːrt ᵊn 'hwɔːrt-
wharve wɔːv hwɔːv ‖ wɔːrv hwɔːrv **wharves**
  wɔːvz hwɔːvz ‖ wɔːrvz hwɔːrvz
whassup wɒ 'sʌp wə- waː-
what wɒt hwɒt ‖ wʌt waːt, hwʌt, hwaːt —*Also,
  when followed by weak* do/does/did,
  sometimes wɒ ‖ wʌ, waː, hwʌ, hwaː — *as*
  What do you do? ˌwɒd ə ju 'duː ‖ ˌwʌd-
  ˌwhat 'for
whatchamacallit 'wɒtʃ əm ə ˌkɔːl ɪt §-ət-
  ‖ 'wʌtʃ- 'waːtʃ-, 'hwʌtʃ-, 'hwaːtʃ-, -ˌkaːl-

what-d'you-call-it 'wɒdʒ u ˌkɔːl ɪt 'wɒdʒ ə-,
  'wɒt dʒu-, 'wɒt dʒə-, §-ət ‖ 'wʌdʒ- 'waːdʒ-,
  'hwʌdʒ-, 'hwaːdʒ-, -ˌkaːl-
whate'er wɒt 'eə hwɒt- ‖ wʌt̬ 'eᵊr hwʌt̬-,
  waːt̬-, hwaːt̬-
whatever wɒt 'ev ə hwɒt- ‖ wʌt̬ 'ev ᵊr hwʌt̬-,
  waːt̬-, hwaːt̬-
what-if 'wɒt ɪf 'hwɒt- ‖ 'wʌt̬- 'hwʌt̬-, 'waːt̬-,
  'hwaːt̬- ~s s
Whatmore 'wɒt mɔː 'hwɒt- ‖ 'waːt mɔːr
  'hwaːt-
Whatmough 'wɒt məʊ 'hwɒt-, -mʌf
  ‖ 'waːt moʊ 'hwaːt-
whatnot 'wɒt nɒt 'hwɒt- ‖ 'wʌt naːt 'hwʌt-,
  'waːt-, 'hwaːt- ~s s
what's wɒts hwɒts ‖ wʌts hwʌts, waːts, hwaːts
what's-her-name 'wɒts ə neɪm ‖ 'wʌts ᵊr-
  'hwʌts-, 'waːts-, 'hwaːts-
what's-his-name 'wɒts ɪz neɪm -əz- ‖ 'wʌts-
  'hwʌts-, 'waːts-, 'hwaːts-
whatsit, what's it 'wɒts ɪt 'hwɒts-, §-ət
  ‖ 'wʌts ət 'hwʌts-, 'waːts-, 'hwaːts- ~s s
whatsitsname, what's its name
  'wɒts ɪts neɪm 'hwɒts-, §-əts- ‖ 'wʌts-
  'hwʌts-, 'waːts-, 'hwaːts-
whatsoe'er ˌwɒt səʊ 'eə ˌhwɒt-
  ‖ ˌwʌt soʊ 'eᵊr ˌhwʌt-, ˌwaːt-, ˌhwaːt-
whatsoever ˌwɒt səʊ 'ev ə ˌhwɒt-
  ‖ ˌwʌt soʊ 'ev ᵊr ˌhwʌt-, ˌwaːt-, ˌhwaːt-
Whatton 'wɒt ᵊn 'hwɒt- ‖ 'waːt ᵊn 'hwaːt-
what-you-may-call-it 'wɒdʒ ə mə ˌkɔːl ɪt
  'wɒtʃ-, 'hwɒdʒ-, 'hwɒtʃ-, -'i-, §-ət ‖ 'wʌtʃ-
  'hwʌtʃ-, 'waːtʃ-, 'hwaːtʃ-, -ˌkaːl-
Wheal, wheal wiːᵊl hwiːᵊl **wheals** wiːᵊlz
  hwiːᵊlz
wheat wiːt hwiːt
  'wheat germ
Wheatcroft 'wiːt krɒft 'hwiːt- ‖ -krɔːft -kraːft
wheatear 'wiːt ɪə 'hwiːt- ‖ 'wiːt̬ ɪr 'hwiːt̬- ~s z
wheaten 'wiːt ᵊn 'hwiːt-
Wheathampstead 'wiːt əmp sted 'hwiːt-,
  'wet-, 'hwet- ‖ 'wiːt̬-
Wheaties *tdmk* 'wiːt iz 'hwiːt iz ‖ 'wiːt̬ iz
  'hwiːt̬ iz
Wheatley 'wiːt li 'hwiːt-
wheatmeal 'wiːt miːᵊl 'hwiːt-
Wheatstone 'wiːt stən 'hwiːt-, -stəʊn
  ‖ 'wiːt stoʊn 'hwiːt-
whee wiː hwiː —*usually uttered on a prolonged
  high-fall tone*
wheedl|e 'wiːd ᵊl 'hwiːd- ~ed d ~es z ~ing/ly
  ɪŋ/li
wheel wiːᵊl hwiːᵊl **wheeled** wiːᵊld hwiːᵊld
  wheeling 'wiːᵊl ɪŋ 'hwiːᵊl- **wheels** wiːᵊlz
  hwiːᵊlz
wheelbarrow 'wiːᵊl ˌbær əʊ 'hwiːᵊl-
  -ˌbær oʊ -ˌber oʊ ~s z
wheelbas|e 'wiːᵊl beɪs 'hwiːᵊl- ~es ɪz əz
wheelchair 'wiːᵊl tʃeə 'hwiːᵊl-; ˌ·'· ‖ -tʃer -tʃær
  ~s z
-wheeler 'wiːᵊl ə 'hwiːᵊl- ‖ -ᵊr —
  three-wheeler ˌθriː 'wiːᵊl ə -'hwiːᵊl ə ‖ -ᵊr
Wheeler, w~ 'wiːl ə 'hwiːl- ‖ -ᵊr ~s z

wheeler-dealer ˌwiːl ə 'diːl ə ˌhwiːl-
‖ ˌwiːᵊl ᵊr 'diːlᵊr ˌhwiːl- **~s** z

wheel|house 'wiːᵊl |haʊs 'hwiːᵊl- **~houses**
haʊz ɪz -əz

wheelie 'wiːᵊl i 'hwiːᵊl- **~s** z

wheelwright 'wiːᵊl raɪt 'hwiːᵊl- **~s** s

Wheen wiːn hwiːn

wheeze wiːz hwiːz **wheezed** wiːzd hwiːzd
  wheezes 'wiːz ɪz 'hwiːz-, -əz **wheezing/ly**
  'wiːz ɪŋ /li 'hwiːz-

wheez|y 'wiːz |i 'hwiːz- **~ier** i ə ‖ i ᵊr **~iest**
  i ɪst i əst **~ily** ɪ li əl i **~iness** i nəs i nɪs

Whelan 'wiːl ən 'hwiːl-

whelk welk hwelk —*An initial* hw *in the sense*
  'shellfish' is not supported by the etymology.
  whelks welks hwelks

whelp welp hwelp **whelped** welpt hwelpt
  whelping 'welp ɪŋ 'hwelp- **whelps** welps
  hwelps

when wen hwen —*There is also an occasional*
  weak form wən

whence wen‖s hwen‖s

whene'er wen 'eə hwen-, wən- ‖ -'eᵊr

whenever wen 'ev ə hwen-, wən- ‖ - ᵊr

where weə hweər ‖ weᵊr hweᵊr, wæᵊr, hwæᵊr

whereabouts *n* 'weər ə baʊts 'hweər- ‖ 'wer-
  'hwer-, 'wær-, 'hwær-

whereabouts *interrogative adv*
  ˌweər ə 'baʊts ◂ ˌhweər- ‖ 'wer ə baʊts
  'hwer-, 'wær-, 'hwær-

whereas weər 'æz hweər-, ˌ·'·, wer- ‖ wer-
  hwer-, wær-, hwær-

whereat weər 'æt hweər-, ˌ·'·, wer- ‖ wer-
  hwer-, wær-, hwær-

whereby weə 'baɪ hweə-, ˌ·'· ‖ wer- hwer-,
  wær-, hwær-

where'er weər 'eə hweər-, ˌ·'·, wer- ‖ wer 'eᵊr
  hwer-, wær-, hwær-

wherefore 'weə fɔː 'hweə- ‖ 'wer fɔːr 'hwer-,
  'wær-, 'hwær-, -four **~s** z

wherein weər 'ɪn hweər-, ˌ·'·, wer- ‖ wer-
  hwer-, wær-, hwær-

whereof weər 'ɒv hweər-, ˌ·'·, wer- ‖ wer 'ʌv
  hwer-, wær-, hwær-, -'ɑːv

whereon weər 'ɒn hweər-, ˌ·'·, wer- ‖ wer 'ɑːn
  hwer-, wær-, hwær-, -'ɔːn

where's weəz hweəz ‖ weᵊrz hweᵊrz, wæᵊrz,
  hwæᵊrz

wheresoever ˌweə səʊ 'ev ə ˌhweə-
  ‖ ˌwer soʊ 'ev ᵊr ˌhwer-, ˌwær-, ˌhwær-

whereto weə 'tuː hweə- ‖ wer- hwer-, wær-,
  hwær-

whereunto weər 'ʌn tu hweər-, ˌ·'·; ˌ·'tuː
  ‖ wer-

whereupon ˌweər ə 'pɒn ˌhweər-, '···
  ‖ ˌwer ə 'pɑːn ˌhweər-, ˌwær-, ˌhwær-, -'pɔːn

wherever weər 'ev ə hweər-, ˌ·'·· ‖ wer 'ev ᵊr
  hwer-, wær-, hwær-

wherewithal *n* 'weə wɪð ɔːl 'hweə-, §-wɪθ-,
  ˌ·'·· ‖ 'wer- 'hwer-, 'wær-, 'hwær-, -wɪθ-, -ɑːl

Whernside 'wɜːn saɪd 'hwɜːn- ‖ wɜːn- 'hwɜːn-

wherr|y 'wer |i 'hwer- **~ies** iz

whet wet hwet **whets** wets hwets **whetted**
  'wet ɪd 'hwet-, -əd ‖ 'weṭ əd 'hweṭ- **whetting**
  'wet ɪŋ 'hwet- ‖ 'weṭ ɪŋ 'hweṭ-

whether 'weð ə 'hweð- ‖ -ᵊr

whetstone, W~ 'wet stəʊn 'hwet- ‖ -stoʊn **~s**
  z

whew fjuː hwjuː —*and non-speech sounds such*
  as ʍ, ʍu, ɸ, pɸ:, yụ

Wheway 'wi: weɪ 'hwi:-

Whewell 'hjuːˌəl hjuːl

whey weɪ hweɪ

wheyfaced 'weɪ feɪst 'hweɪ-

which wɪtʃ hwɪtʃ

Whicher 'wɪtʃ ə 'hwɪtʃ- ‖ -ᵊr

whichever wɪtʃ 'ev ə hwɪtʃ-, ˌ·'·· ‖ - ᵊr

whicker, W~ 'wɪk ə 'hwɪk- ‖ -ᵊr **~ed** d
  whickering 'wɪk ər ɪŋ 'hwɪk- **~s** z

whiff wɪf hwɪf **whiffed** wɪft hwɪft **whiffing**
  'wɪf ɪŋ 'hwɪf- **whiffs** wɪfs hwɪfs

Whiffen 'wɪf ɪn 'hwɪf-, §-ᵊn ‖ -ᵊn

whiffl|e 'wɪf ᵊl 'hwɪf- **~ed** d **~es** z **~ing** ɪŋ

whiffleball 'wɪf ᵊl bɔːl ‖ -bɑːl

whiff|y 'wɪf |i 'hwɪf- **~ier** i ə ‖ i ᵊr **~iest** i ɪst
  i əst **~iness** i nəs i nɪs

Whig wɪg hwɪg **Whigs** wɪgz hwɪgz

Whigg|ery 'wɪg| ər i **~ish** ɪʃ **~ism** ɪz əm

while waɪᵊl hwaɪᵊl **whiled** waɪᵊld hwaɪᵊld
  whiles waɪᵊlz hwaɪᵊlz **whiling** 'waɪᵊl ɪŋ
  'hwaɪᵊl-

whilst waɪᵊlst hwaɪᵊlst

whim wɪm hwɪm **whims** wɪmz hwɪmz

whimbrel 'wɪm brəl 'hwɪm- **~s** z

whimper 'wɪmp ə 'hwɪmp- ‖ -ᵊr **~ed** d
  whimpering/ly 'wɪmp ər ɪŋ /li 'hwɪmp- **~s** z

whimsey 'wɪmz i 'hwɪmz- **~s** z

whimsical 'wɪmz ɪk ᵊl 'hwɪmz- **~ly** i

whimsicalit|y ˌwɪmz ɪ 'kæl ət |i ˌhwɪmz-,
  §,-ə-, -ɪt i ‖ -əṭ |i **~ies** iz

whims|y 'wɪmz |i 'hwɪmz- **~ies** iz

whin wɪn hwɪn

whinchat 'wɪn tʃæt 'hwɪn- **~s** s

whine waɪn hwaɪn **whined** waɪnd hwaɪnd
  whines waɪnz hwaɪnz **whining/ly**
  'waɪn ɪŋ /li 'hwaɪn-

whiner 'waɪn ə 'hwaɪn- ‖ -ᵊr **~s** z

whinge wɪndʒ hwɪndʒ **whinged** wɪndʒd
  hwɪndʒd **whinges** 'wɪndʒ ɪz 'hwɪndʒ-, -əz
  whingeing, whinging 'wɪndʒ ɪŋ 'hwɪndʒ-

whinger 'wɪndʒ ə 'hwɪndʒ- ‖ -ᵊr **~s** z

whinn|y 'wɪn |i 'hwɪn- **~ied** id **~ies** iz **~ying**
  i ɪŋ

whinstone 'wɪn stəʊn 'hwɪn- ‖ -stoʊn

whin|y 'waɪn |i 'hwaɪn- **~ier** i ə ‖ i ᵊr **~iest**
  i ɪst -əst **~iness** i nəs -nɪs

whip wɪp hwɪp **whipped** wɪpt hwɪpt
  whipping/s 'wɪp ɪŋ/z 'hwɪp- **whips** wɪps
  hwɪps
  'whip hand, ˌ· '·; **'whipping boy;**
  'whipping cream

whipcord 'wɪp kɔːd 'hwɪp- ‖ -kɔːrd

whiplash 'wɪp læʃ 'hwɪp- **~es** ɪz əz

whipp... —*see* **whip**

whipp|er-in ˌwɪp |ər 'ɪn ˌhwɪp- **~ers-in** əz 'ɪn
‖ ᵊrz-

whippersnapper 'wɪp ə ˌsnæp ə 'hwɪp-
‖ 'wɪp ᵊr ˌsnæp ᵊr 'hwɪp- **~s** z

whippet 'wɪp ɪt 'hwɪp-, §-ət **~s** s

whippoorwill 'wɪp ə wɪl 'hwɪp-, -ʊə-, -pʊə-,
ˌ·'· ‖ -ᵊr- **~s** z

whipp|y 'wɪp |i 'hwɪp- **~ier** i ə ‖ i ᵊr **~iest** i ɪst
i əst

whip-round 'wɪp raʊnd 'hwɪp- **~s** z

whipsaw 'wɪp sɔː 'hwɪp- ‖ -sɑː **~s** z

Whipsnade 'wɪp sneɪd 'hwɪp-

whir wɜː hwɜː ‖ wɜː hwɜː **whirred** wɜːd hwɜːd
‖ wɜːd hwɜːd **whirring** 'wɜːr ɪŋ 'hwɜːr-
‖ 'wɜːˑ ɪŋ 'hwɜːˑ- **whirs** wɜːz hwɜːz ‖ wɜːz
hwɜːz

whirl wɜːl hwɜːl ‖ wɜːl hwɜːl **whirled** wɜːld
hwɜːld ‖ wɜːld hwɜːld **whirling** 'wɜːl ɪŋ
'hwɜːl- ‖ wɜːl ɪŋ hwɜːl- **whirls** wɜːlz hwɜːlz
‖ wɜːlz hwɜːlz

whirligig 'wɜːl i gɪg 'hwɜːl- ‖ 'wɜːl- 'hwɜːl- **~s**
z

whirlpool 'wɜːl puːl 'hwɜːl- ‖ 'wɜːl- 'hwɜːl- **~s**
z

whirlwind 'wɜːl wɪnd 'hwɜːl- ‖ 'wɜːl- 'hwɜːl-
~s z

whirlybird 'wɜːl i bɜːd 'hwɜːl- ‖ 'wɜːl i bɜːd
'hwɜːl- **~s** z

whirr wɜː hwɜː ‖ wɜː hwɜː **whirred** wɜːd hwɜːd
‖ wɜːd hwɜːd **whirring** 'wɜːr ɪŋ 'hwɜːr-
‖ wɜːˑ ɪŋ 'hwɜːˑ- **whirrs** wɜːz hwɜːz ‖ wɜːz
hwɜːz

whisk wɪsk hwɪsk **whisked** wɪskt hwɪskt
whisking 'wɪsk ɪŋ 'hwɪsk- **whisks** wɪsks
hwɪsks

Whiskas *tdmk* 'wɪsk əz 'hwɪsk-

whisker 'wɪsk ə 'hwɪsk- ‖ - ᵊr **~ed** d **~s** z

whiskey 'wɪsk i 'hwɪsk- **~s** z

whisk|y 'wɪsk |i 'hwɪsk- **~ies** iz

whisper 'wɪsp ə 'hwɪsp- ‖ -ᵊr **~ed** d
whispering/s 'wɪsp ər ɪŋ/z 'hwɪsp- **~s** z
'whispering camˌpaign

whisperer 'wɪsp ər ə 'hwɪsp- ‖ -ᵊr ər **~s** z

whist wɪst hwɪst
'whist drive

whistl|e 'wɪs ᵊl 'hwɪs- **~ed** d **~es** z **~ing** ɪŋ
'whistle stop

whistle-blower 'wɪs ᵊl ˌbləʊ ə 'hwɪs-
‖ -ˌbləʊ ᵊr **~s** z

whistler, W~ 'wɪs lə 'hwɪs- ‖ -ᵊr **~s**, **~'s** z

whistle-stop 'wɪs ᵊl stɒp 'hwɪs- ‖ -stɑːp **~ped**
t **~ping** ɪŋ **~s** s
ˌwhistle-stop 'tour

whit, Whit wɪt hwɪt
ˌWhit 'Monday; ˌWhit 'Sunday

Whitaker 'wɪt ək ə 'hwɪt, -ɪk- ‖ 'wɪt̬ ək ᵊr
'hwɪt̬-

Whitbread 'wɪt bred 'hwɪt-

Whitby 'wɪt bi 'hwɪt-

Whitchurch 'wɪt tʃɜːtʃ 'hwɪt- ‖ -tʃɜːtʃ —*in
Wales usually* 'wɪtʃ ɜːtʃ, -ətʃ

Whitcut, Whitcutt 'wɪt kʌt 'hwɪt-

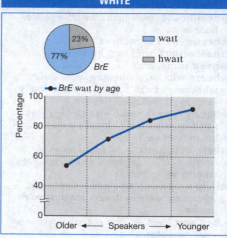

WHITE

Preference poll, BrE: waɪt 77%, hwaɪt 23%.

BrE waɪt by age

---

white, White waɪt hwaɪt — *Preference poll,
BrE:* waɪt 77%, hwaɪt 23%. **whited** 'waɪt ɪd
'hwaɪt-, -əd ‖ 'waɪt̬ əd 'hwaɪt̬- **whiter** 'waɪt ə
'hwaɪt- ‖ 'waɪt̬ ᵊr 'hwaɪt̬- **whites** waɪts hwaɪts
whitest 'waɪt ɪst -əst ‖ 'waɪt̬ əst 'hwaɪt̬-
whiting 'waɪt ɪŋ 'hwaɪt- ‖ 'waɪt̬ ɪŋ 'hwaɪt̬-
ˌwhite 'ant; ˌwhite 'blood cell; ˌwhite
'corpuscle, - cor'puscle; ˌwhited
'sepulchre; ˌwhite 'dwarf; ˌwhite
'elephant; ˌwhite 'flag; ˌwhite goods;
ˌwhite 'heat; 'White House —*This is the
AmE stress pattern for the President's official
residence. In BrE it is sometimes stressed* ˌ· '·;
ˌwhite 'knight; ˌwhite 'lead led; ˌwhite
'lie; ˌwhite 'magic; ˌwhite man; ˌwhite
'meat; ˌwhite 'metal; a ˌwhite 'paper;
ˌwhite 'pepper; ˌwhite 'people; ˌwhite
'sauce ‖ '· ·; ˌwhite 'slavery; ˌwhite
'spirit; ˌwhite 'tie; ˌwhite 'trash; ˌwhite
'water; ˌwhite 'wedding

whitebait 'waɪt beɪt 'hwaɪt-

whitebeam 'waɪt biːm 'hwaɪt- **~s** z

whiteboard 'waɪt bɔːd 'hwaɪt- ‖ -bɔːrd -boʊrd

whitecap 'waɪt kæp 'hwaɪt- **~s** s

Whitechapel 'waɪt ˌtʃæp ᵊl 'hwaɪt-

white-collar ˌwaɪt 'kɒl ə ◄ 'hwaɪt- ‖ -'kɑːl ᵊr ◄

Whitefield (i) 'wɪt fiːᵊld 'hwɪt-, (ii) 'waɪt-
'hwaɪt- —*The family name may be (i) or (ii);
the Methodist evangelist was (i). The place in
Manchester is (ii).*

whitefish 'waɪt fɪʃ 'hwaɪt-

white|fly 'waɪt |flaɪ 'hwaɪt- **~flies** flaɪz

Whitefriars 'waɪt ˌfraɪ əz 'hwaɪt-, ˌ·'· ·
‖ -ˌfraɪ ᵊrz

Whitehall 'waɪt hɔːl 'hwaɪt-, ˌ·'· ‖ -hɑːl

Whitehaven 'waɪt ˌheɪv ᵊn 'hwaɪt-

Whitehead 'waɪt hed 'hwaɪt-

Whitehorn 'waɪt hɔːn 'hwaɪt- ‖ -hɔːrn

Whitehorse 'waɪt hɔːs 'hwaɪt- ‖ -hɔːrs

white-hot ˌwaɪt 'hɒt ◄ ˌhwaɪt- ‖ -'hɑːt ◄

Whitehouse 'waɪt haʊs 'hwaɪt-

white-knuckle ˌwaɪt 'nʌk ᵊl ˌhwaɪt- **~d** d

Whitelaw 'waɪt lɔː 'hwaɪt- ‖ -lɑː
Whiteley 'waɪt li 'hwaɪt-
white-livered ˌwaɪt 'lɪv əd ◂ ˌhwaɪt- ‖ -ˀrd ◂
whiten 'waɪt ˀn 'hwaɪt- **~ed** d **~er/s** ə/z
‖ ˀr/z **~ing** ɪŋ **~s** z
whiteness 'waɪt nəs 'hwaɪt-, -nɪs **~es** ɪz əz
whiteout 'waɪt aʊt 'hwaɪt- ‖ 'waɪt̬ aʊt 'hwaɪt̬-
~s s
white-tailed ˌwaɪt 'teɪld ◂ ˌhwaɪt-
ˌwhite-tailed 'deer
whitethorn 'waɪt θɔːn 'hwaɪt- ‖ -θɔːrn **~s** z
whitethroat 'waɪt θrəʊt 'hwaɪt- ‖ -θroʊt **~s** s
white-tie ˌwaɪt 'taɪ ◂ ˌhwaɪt-
whitewall 'waɪt wɔːl 'hwaɪt- ‖ -wɑːl
whitewash 'waɪt wɒʃ 'hwaɪt- ‖ -wɑːʃ -wɔːʃ **~ed**
t **~es** ɪz əz **~ing** ɪŋ
whitewater, W~ 'waɪt ˌwɔːt ə 'hwaɪt-
‖ -ˌwɔːt̬ ˀr -ˌwɑːt̬-
whitewood 'waɪt wʊd 'hwaɪt-
whitey 'waɪt i 'hwaɪt- ‖ 'waɪt̬ i 'hwaɪt̬ i **~s** z
Whitfield 'wɪt fiːˀld 'hwɪt-
Whitgift 'wɪt ɡɪft 'hwɪt-
whither 'wɪð ə 'hwɪð- ‖ -ˀr
whithersoever ˌwɪð ə səʊ 'ev ə ˌhwɪð-
‖ -ˀr soʊ 'ev ˀr
Whithorn 'wɪt hɔːn 'hwɪt-
whiting, W~ 'waɪt ɪŋ 'hwaɪt- ‖ 'waɪt̬ ɪŋ 'hwaɪt̬-
~s z
whitish 'waɪt ɪʃ 'hwaɪt- ‖ 'waɪt̬ ɪʃ 'hwaɪt̬- **~ness**
nəs nɪs
Whitlam 'wɪt ləm 'hwɪt-
Whitley 'wɪt li 'hwɪt-
Whitlock 'wɪt lɒk 'hwɪt- ‖ -lɑːk
whitlow 'wɪt ləʊ 'hwɪt- ‖ -loʊ **~s** z
Whitman 'wɪt mən 'hwɪt-
Whitmore 'wɪt mɔː 'hwɪt- ‖ -mɔːr
Whitney 'wɪt ni 'hwɪt-
Whitstable 'wɪt stəb ˀl 'hwɪt-
Whitsun 'wɪt sˀn 'hwɪt- **~s** z
Whitsuntide 'wɪt sˀn taɪd 'hwɪt- **~s** z
Whittaker 'wɪt ək ə 'hwɪt-, -ɪk- ‖ 'wɪt̬ ək ˀr
'hwɪt̬-
Whittall 'wɪt ˀl 'hwɪt-, -ɔːl ‖ 'wɪt̬ ˀl 'hwɪt̬-
Whittier 'wɪt i ə 'hwɪt- ‖ 'wɪt̬ i ˀr 'hwɪt̬-
Whittington 'wɪt ɪŋ tən 'hwɪt- ‖ 'wɪt̬- 'hwɪt̬-
whittl|e, W~ 'wɪt ˀl 'hwɪt- ‖ 'wɪt̬ ˀl 'hwɪt̬- **~ed**
d **~es** z **~ing** ɪŋ
Whittle-le-Woods ˌwɪt ˀl lə 'wʊdz ˌhwɪt-, -liˈ-
‖ ˌwɪt̬- ˌhwɪt̬-
Whittlesford 'wɪt ˀlz fəd 'hwɪt- ‖ 'wɪt̬ ˀlz fˀrd
'hwɪt̬-
Whitton 'wɪt ˀn 'hwɪt-
Whitty 'wɪt i 'hwɪt i ‖ 'wɪt̬ i 'hwɪt̬ i
Whitworth 'wɪt wɜːθ 'hwɪt-, -wəθ ‖ -wɜːθ
whit|y 'waɪt |i 'hwaɪt- ‖ waɪt̬ |i 'hwaɪt̬ |i **~ies**
iz
whiz, whizz wɪz hwɪz **whizzed** wɪzd hwɪzd
whizzes 'wɪz ɪz 'hwɪz-, -əz **whizzing** 'wɪz ɪŋ
'hwɪz-
ˌwhiz 'kid, 'whizz kid
whizbang, whizzbang 'wɪz bæŋ 'hwɪz- **~s** z

who strong form **huː**, occasional weak forms **hu**,
u —The weak forms are used, if at all, only
for the relative (not the interrogative).
Who name of pop group **huː**
whoa wəʊ hwəʊ, həʊ ‖ woʊ hwoʊ, hoʊ
Whoberley 'wəʊb ə li 'woʊb ˀr-
who'd strong form **huːd**, occasional weak forms
hud, ud —The weak forms are used, if at all,
only for the relative (not the interrogative).
whodunit, whodunnit ˌhuː 'dʌn ɪt §-ət **~s** s
whoe'er hu 'eə ‖ -'eˀr
whoever hu 'ev ə ‖ -ˀr —also u- when not
clause-initial **~'s** z
whole həʊl →hɒʊl, §huːl ‖ hoʊl (= hole)
wholes həʊlz →hɒʊlz, §huːlz ‖ hoʊlz
ˌwhole 'note; ˌwhole 'number ‖ '· ˌ··
wholefood 'həʊl fuːd →'hɒʊl-, §'huːl- ‖ 'hoʊl-
~s z
wholegrain 'həʊl ɡreɪn →'hɒʊl-, §'huːl-
‖ 'hoʊl-
whole-hearted ˌhəʊl 'hɑːt ɪd ◂ →ˌhɒʊl-,
§ˌhuːl-, -əd ‖ ˌhoʊl 'hɑːrt̬ əd ◂ **~ly** li **~ness**
nəs nɪs
wholemeal 'həʊl miːˀl →'hɒʊl-, §'huːl-
‖ 'hoʊl-
wholeness 'həʊl nəs →'hɒʊl, §'huːl-, -nɪs
‖ 'hoʊl-
wholesale 'həʊl seɪˀl →'hɒʊl-, §'huːl- ‖ 'hoʊl-
wholesaler 'həʊl seɪˀl ə →'hɒʊl-, §'huːl-
‖ 'hoʊl seɪˀl ˀr **~s** z
wholesome 'həʊl səm →'hɒʊl-, §'huːl- ‖ 'hoʊl-
~ly li **~ness** nəs nɪs
wholewheat 'həʊl wiːt →'hɒʊl-, §'huːl-, -hwiːt
‖ 'hoʊl hwiːt
wholistic həʊ 'lɪst ɪk ‖ hoʊ- **~ally** ˀl̬i
who'll strong form **huːl**, occasional weak forms
hul, ul —The weak forms are used, if at all,
only for the relative (not the interrogative).
wholly 'həʊl li →'hɒʊl-; 'həʊl i, §'huːl-
‖ 'hoʊl li -i
whom strong form **huːm**, occasional weak forms
hum, um —The weak forms are used, if at
all, only for the relative (not the interrogative).
whomever huːm 'ev ə ‖ -ˀr
whomp wɒmp hwɒmp ‖ wɑːmp hwɑːmp,
wɔːmp, hwɔːmp **whomped** wɒmpt hwɒmpt
‖ wɑːmpt hwɑːmpt, hwɔːmpt wɔːmpt
whomping 'wɒmp ɪŋ 'hwɒmp- ‖ 'wɑːmp-
'hwɑːmp-, 'wɔːmp-, 'hwɔːmp- **whomps**
wɒmps hwɒmps ‖ wɑːmps hwɑːmps, wɔːmps,
hwɔːmps
whomsoever ˌhuːm səʊ 'ev ə ‖ -soʊ 'ev ˀr
whoop wuːp huːp, wʊp ‖ huːp hʊp, wʊp, wuːp,
hwʊp, hwuːp **whooped** wuːpt huːpt, wʊpt
‖ huːpt hʊpt, wʊpt, wuːpt, hwʊpt, hwuːpt
whooping 'wuːp ɪŋ 'huːp-, 'wʊp- ‖ 'huːp ɪŋ
'hʊp-, 'wʊp-, 'wuːp-, 'hwʊp-, 'hwuːp- **whoops**
wuːps huːps, wʊps ‖ huːps hʊps, wʊps, wuːps,
hwʊps, hwuːps
whoop-de-do ˌwuːp di 'duː ˌhwuːp- ‖ ˌwuːp-
ˌhwuːp- **~s** z
whoopee interj wʊ 'piː hʊ-, ˌwuː- ‖ 'wʊp i
'hwʊp i; wʊ 'piː, hwʊ-, wuː-, hwuː-

whoopee n, **Whoopi** 'wʊp iː 'wu:p-, -i
‖ 'wʊp i 'hwʊp-, 'wu:p-, 'hwu:p-
whooping cough 'hu:p ɪŋ kɒf §'wu:p-, -kɔ:f
‖ 'hu:p ɪŋ kɔ:f 'hʊp-, -kɑ:f
whoops wʊps wu:ps, hwʊps, hwu:ps
whoops-a-daisy ˌwʊps ə 'deɪz i ˌhwʊps-; '·ˌ··
‖ ˌhwʊps-, ˌwu:ps-, ˌhwu:ps-
whoosh wʊʃ wu:ʃ, hwʊʃ, hwu:ʃ ‖ wu:ʃ hwu:ʃ,
wʊʃ, hwʊʃ
whop wɒp hwɒp ‖ wɑ:p hwɑ:p **whopped**
wɒpt hwɒpt ‖ wɑ:pt hwɑ:pt **whopping**
'wɒp ɪŋ 'hwɒp- ‖ 'wɑ:p- 'hwɑ:p- **whops**
wɒps hwɒps ‖ wɑ:ps hwɑ:ps
whopper 'wɒp ə 'hwɒp- ‖ 'wɑ:p ʳr 'hwɑ:p- **~s**
z
whopping 'wɒp ɪŋ 'hwɒp- ‖ 'hwɑ:p ɪŋ
whore hɔ: ‖ hɔ:r hour, hʊʳr (= hoar) **whored**
hɔ:d ‖ hɔ:rd hourd, hʊʳrd (= hoard) **whores**
hɔ:z ‖ hɔ:rz hourz, hʊʳrz **whoring** 'hɔ:r ɪŋ
‖ 'hour-, 'hʊr-
who're 'hu:ˌə ‖ ʳr
whoredom 'hɔ: dəm ‖ 'hɔ:r- 'hour-, 'hʊr-
whore|house 'hɔ: |haʊs ‖ 'hɔ:r- 'hour-, 'hʊr-
~houses haʊz ɪz -əz
whoremaster 'hɔ: ˌmɑ:st ə §-ˌmæst-
‖ 'hɔ:r ˌmæst ʳr 'hour-, 'hʊr- **~s** z
whoremonger 'hɔ: ˌmʌŋ gə §-ˌmɒŋ-
‖ 'hɔ:r ˌmʌŋ gʳr 'hour-, 'hʊr-, -ˌmɑ:ŋ- **~s** z
whoreson 'hɔ: sⁿn ‖ 'hɔ:r- 'hour-, 'hʊr- **~s** z
Whorf wɔ:f hwɔ:f ‖ wɔ:rf hwɔ:rf
whorish 'hɔ:r ɪʃ ‖ 'hour-, 'hʊr- **~ly** li **~ness**
nəs nɪs
whorl wɜ:l hwɜ:l, wɔ:l, hwɔ:l ‖ wɜ:l hwɜ:l,
wɔ:rl, hwɔ:l **whorled** wɜ:ld hwɜ:ld, wɔ:ld,
hwɔ:ld ‖ wɜ:ld hwɜ:ld, wɔ:rld, hwɔ:rld **whorls**
wɜ:lz hwɜ:lz, §wɔ:lz, §hwɔ:lz ‖ wɜ:lz hwɜ:lz,
wɔ:rlz, hwɔ:rlz
whortleberr|y 'wɜ:t ʳl ˌber |i 'hwɜ:t-, -bər i
‖ 'wɜ:t ʳl ˌber |i 'hwɜ:ṭ- **~ies** iz
who's strong form **hu:z**, occasional weak forms
huz, uz —The weak forms are used, if at all,
only for the relative (not the interrogative).
whose strong form **hu:z**, occasional weak forms
huz, uz —The weak forms are used, if at all,
only for the relative (not the interrogative).
whoso 'hu: səʊ ‖ -soʊ
whosoever ˌhu: səʊ 'ev ə ◂ ‖ -soʊ 'ev ʳr ◂
who've strong form **hu:v**, occasional weak
forms **huv, uv** —The weak forms are used, if
at all, only for the relative (not the
interrogative).
whump wʌmp hwʌmp **whumped** wʌmpt
hwʌmpt **whumping** 'wʌmp ɪŋ 'hwʌmp-
whumps wʌmps hwʌmps
whup wʌp hwʌp **whupped** wʌpt hwʌpt
whupping 'wʌp ɪŋ 'hwʌp- **whups** wʌps
hwʌps
why waɪ hwaɪ **whys** waɪz hwaɪz
Whyalla waɪ 'æl ə hwaɪ-
Whyatt 'waɪˌət 'hwaɪˌ
why'd waɪd waɪd
whydah, W~ 'wɪd ə 'hwɪd ə **~s** z
why'll 'waɪˌəl 'hwaɪˌ

why're 'waɪˌə 'hwaɪˌə ‖ 'waɪˌʳr 'hwaɪˌʳr
why's waɪz hwaɪz
Whyte waɪt hwaɪt
Whyteleaf 'waɪt li:f 'hwaɪt-
Whythorne 'waɪt hɔ:n 'hwaɪt- ‖ -hɔ:rn
why've waɪv hwaɪv
Wibberley 'wɪb ə li ‖ -ʳr-
wibbly 'wɪb ʳl i
Wibsey 'wɪb si -zi —The place in WYks is
locally also →'wɪp si
Wicca, wicca 'wɪk ə
Wichita 'wɪtʃ ɪ tɔ: -ə- ‖ -tɑ:
Wichnor 'wɪtʃ nɔ: -nə ‖ -nɔ:r
wick, Wick wɪk **wicks** wɪks
wicked 'wɪk ɪd §-əd **~er** ə ‖ ʳr **~est** ɪst əst **~ly**
li **~ness** nəs nɪs
Wicken 'wɪk ən -ɪn **~s** z
wicker, W~ 'wɪk ə ‖ -ʳr
wickerwork 'wɪk ə wɜ:k ‖ -ʳr wɜ:k
wicket 'wɪk ɪt §-ət **~s** s
    'wicket gate; 'wicket ˌkeeper
Wickham 'wɪk əm
Wickins 'wɪk ɪnz §-ənz
wickiup 'wɪk i ʌp **~s** s
Wicklow 'wɪk ləʊ ‖ -loʊ
Wicks wɪks
Widdecombe, Widdicombe 'wɪd ɪ kəm -ə-
widdershins 'wɪd ə ʃɪnz ‖ -ʳr-
widdl|e 'wɪd ʳl **~ed** d **~es** z **~ing** ɪŋ
Widdowes, Widdows 'wɪd əʊz ‖ -oʊz
Widdowson 'wɪd əʊ sⁿn ‖ -oʊ-
wide waɪd **wider** 'waɪd ə ‖ -ʳr **wides** waɪdz
    widest 'waɪd ɪst -əst
    'wide boy
wide-angle ˌwaɪd 'æŋ gʳl ◂
wide-awake adj ˌwaɪd ə 'weɪk ◂
wide-awake n 'waɪd ə ˌweɪk **~s** s
wide-bod|y 'waɪd ˌbɒd |i 'waɪb- ‖ -ˌbɑ:d- **~ied**
id **~ies** iz
Widecombe 'wɪd ɪ kəm -ə-
wide-eyed ˌwaɪd 'aɪd ◂
Wideford 'waɪd fəd ‖ -fʳrd
widely 'waɪd li
Widemouth 'wɪd məθ →'wɪb-
widen 'waɪd ⁿn **~ed** d **~ing** ɪŋ **~s** z
wideness 'waɪd nəs -nɪs
wide-open ˌwaɪd 'əʊp ən ◂ ‖ -'oʊp-
Wideopen 'waɪd ˌəʊp ən ‖ -ˌoʊp-
wide-ranging ˌwaɪd 'reɪndʒ ɪŋ ◂
wide-scale ˌwaɪd 'skeɪʳl ◂
wide-screen ˌwaɪd 'skri:n ◂ '··
widespread 'waɪd spred ˌ·'·
widgeon 'wɪdʒ ən -ɪn **~s** z
Widgery 'wɪdʒ ər i
widget 'wɪdʒ ɪt §-ət **~s** s
widish 'waɪd ɪʃ
Widlake 'wɪd leɪk
Widmark 'wɪd mɑ:k →'wɪb- ‖ -mɑ:rk
Widmerpool 'wɪd mə pu:l ‖ -mʳr-
Widnes 'wɪd nɪs -nəs
widow 'wɪd əʊ ‖ -oʊ **~ed** d **~ing** ɪŋ **~s** z
widower 'wɪd əʊ ə ‖ -oʊ ʳr **~s** z
widowhood 'wɪd əʊ hʊd ‖ -oʊ-

width wɪdθ wɪtθ **widths** wɪdθs wɪtθs

width|ways ˈwɪdθ |weɪz ˈwɪtθ- **~wise** waɪz

wield wiːˀld **wielded** ˈwiːˀld ɪd -əd **wielding** ˈwiːˀld ɪŋ **wields** wiːˀldz

wielder ˈwiːˀld ə ‖ -ˀr **~s** z

wiener, W~ ˈwiːn ə ‖ -ˀr -i —*but as a German name,* ˈviːn- —*Ger* W~ [ˈviː nɐ] **~s** z

Wiener schnitzel ˌviːn ə ˈʃnɪts ˀl △ -ˈsnɪtʃ- ‖ ˈviːn ˀr ˌ· · ˈwiːn-, -ˌsnɪts- **~s** z

wienie ˈwiːn i **~s** z

Wiesbaden ˈviːs ˌbɑːd ˀn ˈviːz- —*Ger* [ˈviːs baː dˀn]

Wiesenthal ˈwiːz ˀn tɑːl ˈviːz-, -θɔːl —*Ger* [ˈviː zn̩ taːl]

wife waɪf **wife's** waɪfs **wives** waɪvz ˈwife ˌswapping

wife|hood ˈwaɪf hʊd **~less** ləs -lɪs **~like** laɪk **~ly** li

Wiffle *tdmk* ˈwɪf ˀl ˈWiffle ball

Wi-Fi *tdmk* ˈwaɪ faɪ

wig wɪg **wigged** wɪgd **wigging/s** ˈwɪg ɪŋ/z **wigs** wɪgz

Wigan ˈwɪg ən §-ɪn

wigeon ˈwɪdʒ ən -ɪn **~s** z

Wigg wɪg

wigg... —*see* **wig**

Wiggin ˈwɪg ɪn §-ən

Wiggins ˈwɪg ɪnz §-ənz

wiggl|e ˈwɪg ˀl **~ed** d **~es** z **~ing** ɪŋ

Wigglesworth ˈwɪg ˀlz wɜːθ -wəθ ‖ -wɜːθ

wiggly ˈwɪg ˀl i

Wight, wight waɪt

Wightman ˈwaɪt mən

Wightwick ˈwɪt ɪk ‖ ˈwɪt-

Wigley ˈwɪg li

Wigmore ˈwɪg mɔː ‖ -mɔːr

Wigoder ˈwɪg əd ə ‖ -ˀr

Wigram ˈwɪg rəm

Wigston ˈwɪg stən

Wigton ˈwɪg tən

Wigtown ˈwɪg taʊn -tən

wigwag ˈwɪg wæg **~ged** d **~ging** ɪŋ **~s** z

wigwam ˈwɪg wæm ‖ -wɑːm **~s** z

Wii *tdmk* wiː

Wii *tdmk* wiː

Wike waɪk

wiki ˈwɪk i **~s** z

Wikipedia ˌwɪk i ˈpiːd i ə

Wilberforce ˈwɪlb ə fɔːs ‖ -ˀr fɔːrs -foʊrs

Wilbert ˈwɪlb ət ‖ -ˀrt

Wilbraham ˈwɪlb rə həm -hæm; ˈwɪlb rəm

Wilbur ˈwɪlb ə ‖ -ˀr

Wilby, Wilbye ˈwɪl bi

wilco ˈwɪl kəʊ ˌ·ˈ· ‖ -koʊ

Wilcock ˈwɪl kɒk ‖ -kɑːk

Wilcocks, Wilcox ˈwɪl kɒks ‖ -kɑːks

Wilcoxon wɪl ˈkɒks ˀn ‖ -ˈkɑːks-

wild, Wild waɪˀld **wilder** ˈwaɪˀld ə ‖ -ˀr **wildest** ˈwaɪˀld ɪst -əst **wilds** waɪˀldz ˌwild ˈboar; ˈwild ˌflower; ˌwild ˈoats; ˌwild ˈrice; ˌWild ˈWest

Wildblood ˈwaɪˀld blʌd

wild|cat ˈwaɪˀld |kæt **~cats** kæts **~catted** kæt ɪd -əd ‖ kæt̬ əd **~catting** kæt ɪŋ ‖ kæt̬ ɪŋ ˌwildcat ˈstrike

wildcatter ˈwaɪˀld kæt ə ‖ -kæt̬ ˀr **~s** z

Wilde waɪˀld

Wildean ˈwaɪˀld i ən

wildebeest ˈvɪld ə biːst ˈwɪld-, -ɪ-, -bɪəst **~s** s

Wildenstein ˈwɪld ən staɪn —*Ger* [ˈvɪl dˀn ʃtaɪn]

Wilder ˈwaɪˀld ə ‖ -ˀr

wilderness, W~ ˈwɪld ə nəs -nɪs ‖ -ˀr- **~es** ɪz əz

wild-eyed ˌwaɪˀld ˈaɪd ◀ ˈ· ·

Wildfell ˈwaɪld fel

wildfire ˈwaɪˀld ˌfaɪ ə ‖ -ˌfaɪ ˀr

wildfowl ˈwaɪˀld faʊl **~ed** d **~er/s** ə/z ‖ ˀr/z **~ing** ɪŋ **~s** z

wild-goose chase ˌwaɪˀld ˈguːs tʃeɪs

Wilding, w~ ˈwaɪˀld ɪŋ **~s** z

wildland ˈwaɪˀld lænd **~s** z

wildlife ˈwaɪˀld laɪf

wild|ly ˈwaɪˀld |li **~ness** nəs nɪs

wildwood ˈwaɪˀld wʊd **~s** z

wile waɪˀl **wiled** waɪˀld (= *wild*) **wiles** waɪˀlz **wiling** ˈwaɪˀl ɪŋ

Wiley ˈwaɪl i

Wilf wɪlf

Wilford ˈwɪl fəd ‖ -fˀrd

Wilfred, Wilfrid ˈwɪlf rɪd §-rəd

wilful ˈwɪl fˀl -fʊl **~ly** i **~ness** nəs nɪs

Wilhelmina ˌwɪl hel ˈmiːn ə -ə-

wili... —*see* **wily**

wiliness ˈwaɪl i nəs -nɪs

Wilkes wɪlks

Wilkes-Barre *place in PA* ˈwɪlks ˌbær i -ˌber-, -ə

Wilkie ˈwɪlk i

Wilkins ˈwɪlk ɪnz §-ənz

Wilkinson ˈwɪlk ɪnˀs ən §-ən-

Wilks wɪlks

will *modal v: strong form* wɪl, *occasional weak forms* wˀl, ˀl —*see also* **'ll**

will *v* ˈwish, intend', ˈbequeath'; *n* wɪl **willed** wɪld **willing** ˈwɪl ɪŋ **wills** wɪlz

Will wɪl

Willa ˈwɪl ə

Willamette wɪ ˈlæm ɪt wə-, §-ət

Willandra wɪ ˈlændr ə

Willard ˈwɪl ɑːd ‖ -ˀrd

Willcock ˈwɪl kɒk ‖ -kɑːk

Willcocks, Willcox ˈwɪl kɒks ‖ -kɑːks

-willed ˈwɪld — **strong-willed** ˌstrɒŋ ˈwɪld ◀ ‖ ˌstrɔːŋ- ˌstrɑːŋ-

Willenhall ˈwɪl ən hɔːl ‖ -hɑːl

Willesden ˈwɪlz dən

willet ˈwɪl ɪt -ət **~s** s

Willey ˈwɪl i

willful ˈwɪl fˀl -fʊl **~ly** i **~ness** nəs nɪs

William ˈwɪl jəm

Williams ˈwɪl jəmz

Williamsburg ˈwɪl jəmz bɜːg ‖ -bɜːg

Williamson ˈwɪl jəm sən

Williamsport ˈwɪl jəmz pɔːt ‖ -pɔːrt -poʊrt

Willie, w~ 'wɪl i ~s z
willing 'wɪl ɪŋ ~ly li ~ness nəs nɪs
Willis 'wɪl ɪs §-əs
williwaw 'wɪl i wɔː ‖ -wɑː ~s z
Willmott 'wɪl mət -mɒt
Willock 'wɪl ək
will-o'-the-wisp ˌwɪl ə ðə 'wɪsp ~s s
Willoughby 'wɪl ə bi
willow 'wɪl əʊ ‖ -oʊ ~s z
　'willow ˌpattern
willowherb 'wɪl əʊ hɜːb ‖ -oʊ ɝːb ~s z
willowy 'wɪl əʊ i ‖ -oʊ-
willpower 'wɪl ˌpaʊ‿ə ‖ -ˌpaʊ‿ər
Wills wɪlz
Willy, will‖y 'wɪl ‖i ~ies iz
willy-nilly ˌwɪl i 'nɪl i
Wilma 'wɪlm ə
Wilmcote 'wɪlm kəʊt ‖ -koʊt
Wilmer 'wɪlm ə ‖ -ər
Wilmette wɪl 'met
Wilmington 'wɪlm ɪŋ tən
Wilmot, Wilmott 'wɪl mət -mɒt
Wilmslow 'wɪlmz ləʊ ‖ -loʊ
Wilsher 'wɪl ʃə ‖ -ʃər
Wilson 'wɪls ən
Wilsonian wɪl 'səʊn i ən ‖ -'soʊn-
wilt 'wither, droop' wɪlt **wilted** 'wɪlt ɪd -əd
　wilting 'wɪlt ɪŋ **wilts** wɪlts
wilt archaic and liturgical second person sing.
　form of will: strong form **wɪlt**, weak form
　wəlt
Wilton 'wɪlt ən ~s z
Wilts wɪlts
Wiltshire 'wɪlt ʃə -ʃɪə ‖ -ʃ³r -ʃɪr
wil‖y 'waɪl ‖i ~ier i‿ə ‖ i‿³r ~iest i‿ɪst i‿əst
wimble 'wɪm b³l ~s z
Wimbledon 'wɪm b³l dən
Wimborne, Wimbourne 'wɪm bɔːn ‖ -bɔːrn
　-boʊrn
Wimbush 'wɪm bʊʃ
wimin, wimmin 'wɪm ɪn §-ən
Wimmera 'wɪm ³r ə
Wimoweh 'wɪm ə weɪ
wimp wɪmp **wimps** wɪmps
Wimpey 'wɪmp i
wimpish 'wɪmp ɪʃ ~ly li ~ness nəs nɪs
wimple, W~ 'wɪmp ³l ~s z
Wimpole 'wɪm pəʊl →-pɒʊl ‖ -poʊl
wimpy, Wimpy tdmk 'wɪmp i
　'Wimpy bar
Wimsey 'wɪmz i
Wimshurst 'wɪmz hɜːst ‖ -hɝːst
win wɪn **winning** 'wɪn ɪŋ **wins** wɪnz **won**
　wʌn
Winalot tdmk 'wɪn ə lɒt ‖ -lɑːt
Wincanton wɪn 'kænt ən →wɪŋ- ‖ -³n
Wincarnis tdmk wɪn 'kɑːn ɪs →wɪŋ-, §-əs
　‖ -'kɑːrn-
wince wɪnᵗs **winced** wɪnᵗst **winces** 'wɪnᵗs ɪz
　-əz **wincing/ly** 'wɪnᵗs ɪŋ /li
wincey 'wɪnᵗs i ~s z
winceyette ˌwɪnᵗs i 'et

winch, Winch wɪntʃ **winched** wɪntʃt **winches**
　'wɪntʃ ɪz -əz **winching** 'wɪntʃ ɪŋ
Winchelsea 'wɪntʃ ³l si:
Winchester, w~ 'wɪntʃ ɪst ə -əst-,
　§'wɪn ˌtʃest ə ‖ 'wɪn ˌtʃest ³r ~s z
Winchmore 'wɪntʃ mɔː ‖ -mɔːr
wind n 'breeze, moving air' wɪnd **winds** wɪndz
　'wind ˌinstrument; **'wind gauge**; **'wind**
　ˌtunnel; **'wind ˌturbine**
wind n 'bend' waɪnd **winds** waɪndz
wind v 'make breathless', 'give respite to',
　'smell' wɪnd **winded** 'wɪnd ɪd -əd **winding**
　'wɪnd ɪŋ **winds** wɪndz
wind v 'turn'; 'blow on horn' waɪnd **winded**
　'waɪnd ɪd -əd **winding/s** 'waɪnd ɪŋ/z **winds**
　waɪndz **wound** waʊnd
windag‖e 'wɪnd ɪdʒ ~es ɪz əz
windbag 'wɪnd bæg →'wɪmb- ~s z
windblown 'wɪnd bləʊn →'wɪmb- ‖ -bloʊn
wind-borne 'wɪnd bɔːn →'wɪmb- ‖ -bɔːrn
　-boʊrn
windbreak 'wɪnd breɪk →'wɪmb- ~s s
windbreaker, W~ tdmk 'wɪnd ˌbreɪk ə
　→'wɪmb- ‖ -³r ~s z
windburn 'wɪnd bɜːn →'wɪmb- ‖ -bɝːn
windcheater 'wɪnd ˌtʃiːt ə ‖ -ˌtʃiːt̬ ³r ~s z
wind-chill 'wɪnd tʃɪl
winder 'waɪnd ə ‖ -³r ~s z
Windermere 'wɪnd ə mɪə ‖ -³r mɪr
Windeyer 'wɪnd i ə ‖ ³r
windfall 'wɪnd fɔːl ‖ -fɑːl ~s z
windflower 'wɪnd ˌflaʊ ə ‖ -ˌflaʊ ³r ~s z
Windhoek 'wɪnd hʊk 'vɪnd-, 'wɪnt-, 'vɪnt-
windhover 'wɪnd ˌhɒv ə -ˌhʌv- ‖ -ˌhʌv ³r
　-ˌhɑːv- ~s z
windi... —see **windy**
Windies 'wɪnd iz
winding adj, n 'waɪnd ɪŋ ~ly li ~s z
　'winding sheet
winding-up ˌwaɪnd ɪŋ 'ʌp
windjammer 'wɪnd ˌdʒæm ə ‖ -³r ~s z
windlass 'wɪnd ləs ~es ɪz əz
Windlesham 'wɪnd ³l ʃəm
windless 'wɪnd ləs -lɪs
windmill 'wɪnd mɪl →'wɪmb- ~ed d ~ing ɪŋ
　~s z
Windolene tdmk 'wɪnd əʊ liːn ‖ -oʊ-
window 'wɪnd əʊ ‖ -oʊ ~ed d ~ing ɪŋ ~s z
　'window box; **'window ˌdressing**;
　'window seat; **'window shade**
windowless 'wɪnd əʊ ləs -lɪs ‖ -oʊ-
windowpane 'wɪnd əʊ peɪn ‖ -oʊ- -ə- ~s z
Windows tdmk 'wɪnd əʊz ‖ -oʊz
　ˌWindows ˌ9'7
window-shop 'wɪnd əʊ ʃɒp ‖ -oʊ ʃɑːp -ə-
　~ped t ~ping ɪŋ ~s s
windowsill 'wɪnd əʊ sɪl ‖ -oʊ- -ə- ~s z
windpipe 'wɪnd paɪp →'wɪmb- ~s s
windproof 'wɪnd pruːf §-prʊf
windrow 'wɪnd rəʊ ‖ -roʊ ~s z
Windrush 'wɪnd rʌʃ
Windscale 'wɪnd skeɪ³l

windscreen 'wɪnd skriːn ~s z
　'windscreen ˌwiper
windshear 'wɪnd ʃɪə ‖ -ʃɪr
windshield 'wɪnd ʃiːᵊld ~s z
　'windshield ˌwiper
windsock 'wɪnd sɒk ‖ -saːk ~s s
Windsor 'wɪnz ə 'wɪndz- ‖ -ᵊr
　ˌWindsor 'Castle
windstorm 'wɪnd stɔːm ‖ -ˌstɔːrm ~s z
windsurf 'wɪnd sɜːf ‖ -sɜːf ~ed t ~er/s ə/z
　‖ ᵊr/z ~ing ɪŋ ~s s
windswept 'wɪnd swept
wind-up 'waɪnd ʌp ~s s
Windus 'wɪnd əs
windward, W~ 'wɪnd wəd §'wɪn- ‖ -wᵊrd ~s z
wind-whipped 'wɪnd wɪpt -hwɪpt ‖ -hwɪpt
wind|y 'wɪnd |i ~ier i‿ə ‖ i‿ᵊr ~iest i‿ɪst i‿əst
　~ily ɪ li əl i ~iness i nəs i nɪs
wine waɪn wined waɪnd wines waɪnz wining
　'waɪn ɪŋ
　'wine bar; 'wine ˌbottle
winebibber 'waɪn ˌbɪb ə →'waɪm- ‖ -ᵊr ~s z
winebibbing 'waɪn ˌbɪb ɪŋ →'waɪm- ~s z
wineglass 'waɪn glɑːs →'waɪn-, §-glæs ‖ -glæs
　~es ɪz əz
winegrow|er 'waɪn ˌgrəʊ| ə →'waɪn-
　‖ -ˌgroʊ| ᵊr ~ers əz ‖ ᵊrz ~ing ɪŋ
Winehouse 'waɪn haʊs
winemak|er 'waɪn ˌmeɪk| ə →'waɪm- ‖ -ᵊr
　~ers əz ‖ ᵊrz ~ing ɪŋ
winepress 'waɪn pres →'waɪm- ~es ɪz əz
winer|y 'waɪn ər |i ~ies iz
wineskin 'waɪn skɪn ~s z
Winfield 'wɪn fiːᵊld
Winford 'wɪn fəd ‖ -fᵊrd
Winfred 'wɪn frɪd §-frəd
Winfrey 'wɪn fri
Winfrith 'wɪn frɪθ §-frəθ
wing, Wing wɪŋ winged wɪŋd winging
　'wɪŋ ɪŋ wings wɪŋz
　'wing comˌmander; 'wing nut
Wingate 'wɪn geɪt →'wɪŋ-, -gɪt, -gət
wingding 'wɪŋ dɪŋ ~s z
winge 'complain' —see whinge
winged adj 'having wings'; pp of wing wɪŋd
　—but formerly, and sometimes in verse still,
　also 'wɪŋ ɪd, -əd
winger 'wɪŋ ə ‖ -ᵊr ~s z
-winger 'wɪŋ ə ‖ -ᵊr — left-winger
　ˌleft 'wɪŋ ə ‖ -ᵊr
Wingfield 'wɪŋ fiːᵊld
wingless 'wɪŋ ləs -lɪs ~ness nəs nɪs
winglet 'wɪŋ lət -lɪt ~s s
wingspan 'wɪŋ spæn ~s z
wingspread 'wɪŋ spred ~s z
wingtip 'wɪŋ tɪp ~s s
Winifred 'wɪn ɪf rɪd -əf-, §-rəd
wink wɪŋk winked wɪŋkt winking 'wɪŋk ɪŋ
　winks wɪŋks
winker 'wɪŋk ə ‖ -ᵊr ~s z
winkl|e 'wɪŋk ᵊl ~ed d ~es z ~ing ˌɪŋ
winkle-picker 'wɪŋk ᵊl ˌpɪk ə ‖ -ᵊr ~s z
winless 'wɪn ləs -lɪs

Winn wɪn
Winnebago ˌwɪn ɪ 'beɪg əʊ -ə- ‖ -oʊ ~s z
winner, W~ 'wɪn ə ‖ -ᵊr ~s z
Winnie 'wɪn i
Winnie-the-Pooh ˌwɪn i ðə 'puː
winning 'wɪn ɪŋ ~est ɪst əst ~ly li ~ness nəs
　nɪs ~s z
　'winning post
Winnipeg 'wɪn ɪ peg §-ə-
Winnipegosis ˌwɪn ɪ pɪ 'gəʊs ɪs -§,-ə-, -pə'--,
　§-əs ‖ -'goʊs əs
Winnipesaukee ˌwɪn ɪp ə 'sɔːk i ˌ-əp- ‖ -'saːk-
winnow 'wɪn əʊ ‖ -oʊ ~ed d ~er/s ə/z ‖ ᵊr/z
　~ing ɪŋ ~s z
wino 'waɪn əʊ ‖ -oʊ ~s z
Winona wɪ 'nəʊn ə wə- ‖ -'noʊn ə
Winsford 'wɪnz fəd 'wɪnˢ- ‖ -fᵊrd
Winslade 'wɪn sleɪd
Winslet 'wɪnz lɪt -lət
Winslow 'wɪnz ləʊ ‖ -loʊ
winsome, W~ 'wɪnˢ əm ~ly li ~ness nəs nɪs
Winstanley (i) 'wɪnˢt ən li, (ii) wɪn 'stæn li
　—The place in Greater Manchester is (i); the
　family name is usually (ii)
Winston 'wɪnˢt ən
Winston-Salem ˌwɪnˢt ən 'seɪl əm
winter, W~ 'wɪnt ə ‖ 'wɪnt̬ ᵊr ~ed d
　wintering 'wɪnt ər ɪŋ ‖ 'wɪnt̬ ərɪŋ
　→'wɪntr ɪŋ ~s z
　ˌwinter 'sports
Winterbotham, Winterbottom
　'wɪnt ə ˌbɒt əm ‖ 'wɪnt̬ ᵊr ˌbaːt̬ əm
Winterbourn, Winterbourne, w~
　'wɪnt ə bɔːn ‖ 'wɪnt̬ ᵊr bɔːrn -boʊrn ~s z
wintergreen 'wɪnt ə griːn ‖ 'wɪnt̬ ᵊr- ~s z
winterization ˌwɪnt ər aɪ 'zeɪʃ ᵊn -ɪ'--
　‖ ˌwɪnt̬ ᵊr ə-
winteriz|e 'wɪnt ər aɪz ‖ 'wɪnt̬ ᵊr- ~ed d ~es
　ɪz əz ~ing ɪŋ
Winters 'wɪnt əz ‖ 'wɪnt̬ ᵊrz
Winterthur 'wɪnt ə θɜː ‖ 'wɪnt̬ ᵊr θɜːr —Ger
　['vɪn tɐ tuːɐ]
wintertime 'wɪnt ə taɪm ‖ 'wɪnt̬ ᵊr-
Winterton 'wɪnt ət ən ‖ 'wɪnt̬ ᵊrt ᵊn
wintery 'wɪnt ər‿i ‖ 'wɪnt̬ ər i —see also
　wintry
Winthrop 'wɪn θrɒp 'wɪnˢθ rəp ‖ 'wɪnˢθ rəp
Winton 'wɪnt ən ‖ -ᵊn
Wintour 'wɪnt ə ‖ 'wɪnt̬ ᵊr
wintr|y 'wɪntr |i ~ier i‿ə ‖ i‿ᵊr ~iest i‿ɪst i‿əst
　~ily əl i ɪ li ~iness i nəs i nɪs
Winwick 'wɪn ɪk
win-win ˌwɪn 'wɪn
wipe waɪp wiped waɪpt wipes waɪps wiping
　'waɪp ɪŋ
　ˌwiped 'out
wipeout 'waɪp aʊt ~s s
wiper 'waɪp ə ‖ -ᵊr ~s z
wire 'waɪ‿ə ‖ 'waɪ‿ᵊr ~d d ~s z wiring
　'waɪ‿ər ɪŋ ‖ 'waɪ‿ᵊr ɪŋ
　ˌwire 'netting; ˌwire 'wool
wirecutters 'waɪ‿ə ˌkʌt əz ‖ 'waɪ‿ᵊr ˌkʌt̬ ᵊrz

wire|draw 'waɪə |drɔː ‖ 'waɪ ˌ°r- -drɑː
  ~drawing drɔːˑʳ ɪŋ ‖ drɔː ɪŋ drɑː- **~drawn**
  drɔːn ‖ -drɑːn **~draws** drɔːz ‖ drɑːz **~drew**
  druː
wire-haired ˌwaɪə 'heəd ◄ ‖ 'waɪ ˌ°r herd
  -hærd
wireless 'waɪə ləs -lɪs ‖ 'waɪ ˌ°r- **~ed** d **~es** ɪz
  əz **~ing** ɪŋ
wirepuller 'waɪə ˌpʊl ə ‖ 'waɪ ˌ°r ˌpʊl °r **~s** z
wire-rimmed ˌwaɪə 'rɪmd ◄ ‖ ˌwaɪ ˌ°r-
wiretap 'waɪə tæp ‖ 'waɪ ˌ°r- **~s** s
wire-tapping 'waɪə ˌtæp ɪŋ ‖ 'waɪ ˌ°r-
wireworm 'waɪə wɜːm ‖ 'waɪ ˌ°r wɜ·m **~s** z
wiri... —*see* **wiry**
wiring 'waɪər ɪŋ ‖ 'waɪ ˌər ɪŋ **~s** z
Wirksworth 'wɜːks wəθ -wɜːθ ‖ 'wɜ·ks wɜ·θ
Wirral 'wɪr əl ‖ 'wɜ·-
wir|y 'waɪ ˌər |i ‖ 'waɪ ˌər |i **~ier** i ˌə ‖ i ˌ°r **~iest**
  i ˌɪst i ˌəst **~ily** əl i ɪ li **~iness** i nəs i nɪs
Wisbech 'wɪz biːtʃ
Wisconsin wɪ 'skɒnᵗs ɪn §-ən ‖ -'skɑːnᵗs-
Wisconsinite wɪ 'skɒnᵗs ɪ naɪt §-ə- ‖ -'skɑːnᵗs-
  ~s s
Wisden 'wɪz dən
wisdom, W~ 'wɪz dəm
  'wisdom tooth
-wise waɪz — **timewise** 'taɪm waɪz
wise, Wise waɪz **wised** waɪzd **wiser** 'waɪz ə
  ‖ °r **wises** 'waɪz ɪz -əz **wisest** 'waɪz ɪst -əst
  wising 'waɪz ɪŋ
  'wise guy
wiseacre 'waɪz ˌeɪk ə ‖ -°r **~s** z
wisecrack 'waɪz kræk **~ed** t **~ing** ɪŋ **~s** s
wisely 'waɪz li
Wiseman 'waɪz mən
wisent 'viːz ent 'wiːz-, -°nt **~s** s
wish wɪʃ **wished** wɪʃt **wishes** 'wɪʃ ɪz -əz
  wishing 'wɪʃ ɪŋ
Wishart 'wɪʃ ət ‖ -°rt
Wishaw 'wɪʃ ɔː ‖ -ɑː
wishbone 'wɪʃ bəʊn ‖ -boʊn **~s** z
wishful 'wɪʃ fᵊl -fʊl **~ly** i **~ness** nəs nɪs
  ˌwishful 'thinking
wishing-well 'wɪʃ ɪŋ wel **~s** z
wishy-wash|y 'wɪʃ i ˌwɒʃ |i ˌ·'·· ‖ -ˌwɑːʃ |i
  -ˌwɔːʃ- **~iness** i nəs i nɪs
Wisley 'wɪz li
wisp wɪsp **wisps** wɪsps
Wispa *tdmk* 'wɪsp ə
wispy 'wɪsp i
wist wɪst
wistaria, wisteria wɪ 'stɪər i ˌə -'steər- ‖ -'stɪr-
  ~s z
wistful 'wɪst fᵊl -fʊl **~ly** i **~ness** nəs nɪs
Wiston 'wɪst ən
Wistow 'wɪst əʊ ‖ -oʊ
Wistrich 'wɪs trɪtʃ
Wisty 'wɪst i
wit wɪt **wits** wɪts
witch wɪtʃ **witched** wɪtʃt **witches** 'wɪtʃ ɪz -əz
  witching/ly 'wɪtʃ ɪŋ /li
  'witching ˌhour
witchcraft 'wɪtʃ krɑːft §-kræft ‖ -kræft

witchdoctor 'wɪtʃ ˌdɒkt ə ‖ -ˌdɑːkt °r **~s** z
witcher|y 'wɪtʃ ər |i **~ies** iz
witchetty 'wɪtʃ ət i -ɪt- ‖ -əṯ i
witch-hazel 'wɪtʃ ˌheɪz °l **~s** z
witch-hunt 'wɪtʃ hʌnt **~s** s
witenagemot 'wɪt °n ə gɪ ˌməʊt -gə,·, ˌ·ˑ·ˑ·ˑ
  ‖ -gə ˌmoʊt
Wite-out *tdmk* 'waɪt aʊt ‖ 'waɪṯ-

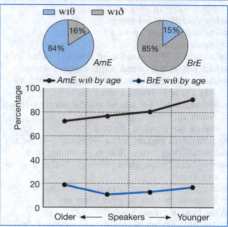

with wɪð §wɪθ ‖ wɪθ wɪð — *Preference polls,*
  AmE: wɪθ *84%,* wɪð *16%; BrE:* wɪð *85%,* wɪθ
  15%. —In Britain, wɪθ *is nevertheless frequent*
  in Scotland (preferred by 82% of Scottish
  respondents). —In some varieties, including
  GenAm but not RP, there may also be a weak
  form wəð, wəθ
withal wɪð 'ɔːl §wɪθ- ‖ -'ɑːl
Witham *river* 'wɪð əm
Witham *family name; place in Essex* 'wɪt əm
  ‖ 'wɪṯ-
with|draw wɪð 'drɔː wɪθ|- ‖ -'drɑː **~drawing**
  'drɔːʳ ɪŋ ‖ 'drɔː ɪŋ -'drɑː ɪŋ **~drawn** 'drɔːn
  ‖ -'drɑːn **~draws** 'drɔːz ‖ 'drɑːz **~drew** 'druː
withdrawal wɪð 'drɔːʳəl wɪθ-, -'drɔːl ‖ -'drɔː ˌəl
  -'drɑː ˌəl **~s** z
  with'drawal ˌsymptoms
withdrawn wɪð 'drɔːn wɪθ- ‖ -'drɑːn
withdrew wɪð 'druː wɪθ-
withe wɪð waɪð, wɪð **withes** wɪðs waɪðz, wɪðz
wither 'wɪð ə ‖ -°r **~ed** d **withering/ly**
  'wɪð ər ɪŋ /li **~s** z
Withernsea 'wɪð °n si ‖ -°rn-
Withers, w~ 'wɪð əz ‖ -°rz
Witherspoon 'wɪð ə spuːn ‖ -°r-
with|hold wɪð |'həʊld wɪθ-, →-'hɒʊld
  ‖ -|'hoʊld **~held** 'held **~holding** 'həʊld ɪŋ
  -→'hɒʊld- ‖ 'hoʊld ɪŋ **~holds** 'həʊldz
  →'hɒʊldz ‖ 'hoʊldz
  with'holding tax
within wɪð 'ɪn §wɪθ-
Withington 'wɪð ɪŋ tən
with-it 'wɪð ɪt 'wɪθ-, §-ət ‖ 'wɪθ- 'wɪð-
without wɪð 'aʊt §wɪθ-

withstand wɪð 'stænd wɪθ- **~ing** ɪŋ **~s** z
  withstood wɪð 'stʊd wɪθ-
with|y, Withy 'wɪð |i §'wɪθ- **~ies** iz
Withycombe 'wɪð i kəm
witless 'wɪt ləs -lɪs **~ly** li **~ness** nəs nɪs
Witley 'wɪt li
witness 'wɪt nəs -nɪs **~ed** t **~es** ɪz əz **~ing** ɪŋ
  'witness box; 'witness stand
Witney 'wɪt ni
-witted 'wɪt ɪd -əd ‖ 'wɪt̬ əd — **slow-witted**
  ˌsləʊ 'wɪt ɪd ◂ -əd ‖ ˌsloʊ 'wɪt̬ əd ◂
Wittenberg 'wɪt ˀn bɜːg ‖ -bɜːg —*Ger*
  ['vɪt ˀn bɛʁk]
witter 'wɪt ə ‖ 'wɪt̬ ˀr **~ed** d **wittering**
  'wɪt ər ɪŋ ‖ 'wɪt̬ ər ɪŋ **~s** z
Wittgenstein 'wɪt gən ʃtaɪn -staɪn
witti... —*see* **witty**
witticism 'wɪt ɪ ˌsɪz əm -ə- ‖ 'wɪt̬ ə- **~s** z
witting 'wɪt ɪŋ ‖ 'wɪt̬ ɪŋ **~ly** li
Witton 'wɪt ˀn
witt|y, Witty 'wɪt |i ‖ 'wɪt̬ |i **~ier** i ə ‖ i ˀr
  ~iest i ɪst i ˌəst **~ily** ɪ li əl i **~iness** i nəs i nɪs
Witwatersrand wɪt 'wɔːt əz rænd ˌ-ˑ-, -'wɑːt-,
  -rɑːnd, -rɒnt, -rɑːnt, ˌ·ˌ·ˑ·, ˌ·ˑ·· ‖ 'wɪt wɔːt̬ ˀrz-
  -'wɑːt̬- —*Afrikaans* [ˌvɪt ˌvɑt ərs 'rɑnt]
Wiveliscombe 'wɪv ə lɪs kəm —*locally also*
  'wɪls kəm
Wivelsfield 'wɪv ˀlz fiːˀld
Wivenhoe 'wɪv ˀn həʊ ‖ -hoʊ
wives waɪvz
Wix wɪks
wiz wɪz
wizard 'wɪz əd ‖ -ˀrd **~s** z
wizardry 'wɪz əd ri ‖ -ˀrd-
wizened 'wɪz ˀnd
woad wəʊd ‖ woʊd
wobbl|e 'wɒb ˀl ‖ 'wɑːb ˀl **~ed** d **~es** z **~ing**
  ɪŋ
wobb|ly, W~ 'wɒb |li ‖ 'wɑːb- **~lier** li ə ‖ li ˀr
  ~lies liz **~liest** li ɪst əst
Wobegon 'wəʊ bɪ gɒn -bə- ‖ 'woʊ bɪ gɔːn
  -gɑːn
Woburn 'wəʊ bɜːn 'wuː-, -bən ‖ 'woʊ bɜːn
Wodehouse 'wʊd haʊs §-əs
Woden 'wəʊd ˀn ‖ 'woʊd ˀn
wodge wɒdʒ ‖ wɑːdʒ **wodges** 'wɒdʒ ɪz -əz
  ‖ 'wɑːdʒ əz
woe wəʊ ‖ woʊ **woes** wəʊz ‖ woʊz
woebegone, Wobegon 'wəʊ bi gɒn -bə-
  ‖ 'woʊ bi gɔːn -gɑːn
woeful 'wəʊ fˀl -fʊl ‖ 'woʊ- **~ly** ˌi **~ness** nəs
  nɪs
wog wɒg ‖ wɑːg wɔːg **wogs** wɒgz ‖ wɑːgz
  wɔːgz
Wogan 'wəʊg ən ‖ 'woʊg ən
woggle 'wɒg ˀl ‖ 'wɑːg ˀl **~s** z
Wojtyla vɔɪ 'tɪl ə —*Polish* Wojtyła [vɔj 'ti wa]
wok wɒk ‖ wɑːk —*Cantonese* [⁶wɔːk] **woks**
  wɒks ‖ wɑːks
woke wəʊk ‖ woʊk
woken 'wəʊk ən ‖ 'woʊk ən
Woking 'wəʊk ɪŋ ‖ 'woʊk ɪŋ
Wokingham 'wəʊk ɪŋ əm ‖ 'woʊk-

wold wəʊld →wɒʊld ‖ woʊld **wolds, Wolds**
  wəʊldz →wɒʊldz ‖ woʊldz
Woldingham 'wəʊld ɪŋ əm →'wɒʊld-
  ‖ 'woʊld-
Woledge 'wʊl ɪdʒ
wolf wʊlf **wolfed** wʊlft **wolfing** 'wʊlf ɪŋ
  wolfs wʊlfs **wolves** wʊlvz
  'wolf cub; 'wolf ˌwhistle
Wolf wʊlf —*but as a German name, also* vɒlf
  ‖ vɔːlf, vɑːlf —*Ger* [vɔlf]
Wolfe wʊlf
Wolfenden 'wʊlf ˀn dən
Wolff wʊlf —*Ger, Fr* [vɔlf]
Wolfgang 'wʊlf gæŋ —*Ger* ['vɔlf gaŋ]
wolfhound 'wʊlf haʊnd **~s** z
wolfish 'wʊlf ɪʃ **~ly** li **~ness** nəs nɪs
Wolfit 'wʊlf ɪt §-ət
wolflike 'wʊlf laɪk
Wolford 'wʊl fəd ‖ -fˀrd
Wolfowitz 'wʊlf ə wɪts
wolfram 'wʊlf rəm
wolframite 'wʊlf rə maɪt
wolfsbane 'wʊlfs beɪn
Wollaston 'wʊl əst ən
wollastonite 'wʊl əst ə naɪt
Wollongong 'wʊl ən gɒŋ →-ˀŋ- ‖ -gɔːŋ -gɑːŋ
Wollstonecraft 'wʊlst ən krɑːft §-kræft
  ‖ -kræft
Wolmer 'wʊlm ə ‖ -ˀr
Wolof 'wɒl ɒf ‖ 'woʊl ɑːf
Wolseley 'wʊlz li
Wolsey 'wʊlz i
Wolsingham 'wʊlz ɪŋ əm 'wɒls- ‖ 'wɑːls-
Wolstenholme 'wʊlst ən həʊm ‖ -hoʊm
Wolverhampton ˌwʊlv ə 'hæmpt ən ˌ·ˑ·ˌ·
  ‖ -ˀr-
wolverine 'wʊlv ə riːn **~s** z
Wolverton 'wʊlv ət ən ‖ -ˀrt ˀn
wolves wʊlvz
woman 'wʊm ən **woman's** 'wʊm ənz **women**
  'wɪm ɪn §-ən **women's** 'wɪm ɪnz §-ənz
  ˌWomen's 'Instutute; ˌwomen's 'lib;
  ˌwomen's ˌlibe'ration; 'women's
  ˌmovement; 'women's ˌstudies
womanhood 'wʊm ən hʊd
womanis... —*see* **womaniz...**
womanish 'wʊm ən ɪʃ **~ly** li **~ness** nəs nɪs
womaniz|e 'wʊm ə naɪz **~ed** d **~er/s** ə/z
  ‖ ˀr/z **~es** ɪz əz **~ing** ɪŋ
womankind 'wʊm ən kaɪnd →-ŋ-, ˌ·ˑ·
woman|ly 'wʊm ən |li **~liness** li nəs -nɪs
woman-to-woman ˌwʊm ən tə 'wʊm ən ◂
womb wuːm (!) **wombs** wuːmz
wombat 'wɒm bæt -bət ‖ 'wɑːm- **~s** s
wombl|e, W~ 'wɒm bˀl ‖ 'wɑːm- **~ed** d **~es** z
  ~ing ɪŋ
Wombourne 'wɒm bɔːn ‖ 'wɑːm bɔːrn -boʊrn
Wombwell 'wʊm wel 'wuːm-, 'wɒm-, -wəl
women 'wɪm ɪn §-ən
womenfolk 'wɪm ɪn fəʊk -ən-, §-fəʊlk ‖ -foʊk
womyn 'wɪm ɪn §-ən
won *Korean currency* wɒn ‖ wɑːn
won *past & pp of* **win** wʌn

wonder, W~ 'wʌnd ə ‖ -ᵊr **~ed** d
  wondering/ly 'wʌnd ‿ər ɪŋ /li **~s** z
Wonderbra *tdmk* 'wʌnd ə brɑː ‖ -ᵊr-
Wonderbread, Wonder Bread *tdmk*
  'wʌnd ə bred ‖ -ᵊr-
wonderful 'wʌnd ə fᵊl -fʊl ‖ -ᵊr- —*In casual*
  AmE also 'wʌn ᵊr- **~ly** ‿i **~ness** nəs nɪs
wonderland 'wʌnd ə lænd ‖ -ᵊr- **~s** z
wonderment 'wʌnd ə mənt ‖ -ᵊr-
wondrous 'wʌndr əs **~ly** li **~ness** nəs nɪs
Wonersh 'wɒn ɜːʃ ‖ 'wɑːn ɜːʃ
Wong wɒŋ ‖ wɑːŋ wɔːŋ —*Cantonese* [⁴wɔːŋ]
wonga 'wɒŋ gə ‖ 'wɑːŋ gə
wonga-wonga 'wɒŋ gə ˌwɒŋ gə ˌ· ·'· ·
  ‖ 'wɑːŋ gə ˌwɑːŋ gə
wonk wɒŋk ‖ wɑːŋk wɔːŋk **wonks** wɒŋks
  ‖ wɑːŋks wɔːŋks
wonk|y 'wɒŋk |i ‖ 'wɑːŋk |i **~ier** i‿ə ‖ i‿ᵊr
  ~iest i‿ɪst i‿əst
wont wəʊnt wɒnt ‖ wɔːnt wɑːnt, woʊnt
won't wəʊnt ‖ woʊnt wʊnt —*Also, esp. before*
  a consonant, wəʊn ‖ woʊn. *This word has no*
  weak form.
wonted 'wəʊnt ɪd -əd ‖ 'wɔːn̬t̬ əd 'wɑːn̬t̬-,
  'woʊn̬t̬-
wonton ˌwɒn 'tɒn ◂ '·· ‖ ˌwɑːn tɑːn
  ˌwonton 'soup
woo wuː **wooed** wuːd **wooing** 'wuː‿ɪŋ **woos**
  wuːz
Woo wuː —*Chi* Wú [²wu], *Cantonese* [⁴wuː]
wood, Wood wʊd **wooded** 'wʊd ɪd -əd
  wooding 'wʊd ɪŋ **woods** wʊdz
  ˌwood 'alcohol; 'wood pulp
Woodall 'wʊd ɔːl ‖ -ɑːl
woodbine 'wʊd baɪn →'wʊb- **~s** z
woodblock 'wʊd blɒk →'wʊb- ‖ -blɑːk **~s** s
Woodbridge 'wʊd brɪdʒ →'wʊb-
Woodburn 'wʊd bɜːn →'wʊb- ‖ -bɜːn
Woodbury 'wʊd bər‿i →'wʊb- ‖ -ˌber i
woodcarv|er 'wʊd ˌkɑːv| ə →'wʊg-
  ‖ -ˌkɑːrv| ᵊr **~ers** əz ‖ ᵊrz **~ing/s** ɪŋ/z
woodchip 'wʊd tʃɪp
woodchuck 'wʊd tʃʌk **~s** s
woodcock, W~ 'wʊd kɒk →'wʊg- ‖ -kɑːk **~s** s
woodcraft 'wʊd krɑːft →'wʊg-, §-kræft
  ‖ -kræft **~s** s
woodcut 'wʊd kʌt →'wʊg- **~s** s
woodcutter 'wʊd ˌkʌt ə →'wʊg- ‖ -ˌkʌt̬ ᵊr **~s**
  z
wooded 'wʊd ɪd -əd
wooden 'wʊd ᵊn **~ly** li **~ness** nəs nɪs
  ˌwooden 'spoon
woodenheaded ˌwʊd ᵊn 'hed ɪd ◂ -əd
Woodford 'wʊd fəd ‖ -fᵊrd
Woodhall 'wʊd hɔːl ‖ -hɑːl
Woodhead 'wʊd hed
Woodhouse 'wʊd haʊs
woodland, W~ 'wʊd lənd -lænd **~s** z
woodlark 'wʊd lɑːk ‖ -lɑːrk **~s** s
Woodlesford 'wʊd ᵊlz fəd ‖ -fᵊrd
Woodley 'wʊd li
Woodliff 'wʊd lɪf
wood|louse 'wʊd |laʊs **~lice** laɪs

wood|man, W~ 'wʊd |mən →'wʊb- **~men**
  mən
woodnote 'wʊd nəʊt ‖ -noʊt **~s** s
Woodnutt 'wʊd nʌt
woodpecker 'wʊd ˌpek ə →'wʊb- ‖ -ᵊr **~s** z
woodpile 'wʊd paɪᵊl →'wʊb- **~s** z
Woodrow 'wʊd rəʊ ‖ -roʊ
woodruff, W~ 'wʊd rʌf **~s** s
Woods wʊdz
woodscrew 'wʊd skruː **~s** z
woodshed 'wʊd ʃed **~s** z
woodsia 'wʊdz i‿ə **~s** z
Woodside ˌwʊd 'saɪd '··
woods|man 'wʊdz |mən **~men** mən
Woodstock 'wʊd stɒk ‖ -stɑːk
woods|y 'wʊdz |i **~ier** i‿ə ‖ i‿ᵊr **~iest** i‿ɪst i‿əst
Woodward 'wʊd wəd ‖ -wᵊrd
woodwind 'wʊd wɪnd
woodwork 'wʊd wɜːk ‖ -wɜːk **~ing** ɪŋ
woodworm 'wʊd wɜːm ‖ -wɜːm
wood|y, Woody 'wʊd |i **~ier** i‿ə ‖ i‿ᵊr **~iest**
  i‿ɪst i‿əst **~iness** i nəs i nɪs
wooer 'wuː‿ə ‖ ᵊr **~s** z
woof *'dog's bark'* wʊf **woofs** wʊfs
woof *'threads'* wuːf ‖ wʊf wuːf **woofs** wuːfs
  ‖ wʊfs wuːfs
woofer 'wʊf ə 'wuːf- ‖ -ᵊr **~s** z
Woofferton 'wʊf ət ən ‖ -ᵊrt ᵊn
woofter 'wʊft ə ‖ -ᵊr **~s** z
Wookey 'wʊk i
wool, Wool wʊl **wools** wʊlz
Woolacombe 'wʊl ə kəm
Woolard 'wʊl ɑːd ‖ -ɑːrd
woolen 'wʊl ən **~s** z
Wooler 'wʊl ə ‖ -ᵊr
Woolf wʊlf
Woolford 'wʊl fəd ‖ -fᵊrd
woolgather|ing 'wʊl ˌgæð ər |ɪŋ ‖ -ᵊr |ɪŋ
  ~er/s ‿ə/z ‖ ‿ᵊr/z
Woolite *tdmk* 'wʊl aɪt
Woollard 'wʊl ɑːd ‖ -ɑːrd
Woollcott 'wʊl kət -kɒt ‖ -kɑːt
woollen 'wʊl ən **~s** z
Woolley 'wʊl i
Woolloomooloo ˌwʊl əm ə 'luː
wooll|y 'wʊl |i **~ier** i‿ə ‖ i‿ᵊr **~ies** iz **~iest** i‿ɪst
  i‿əst **~iness** i nəs i nɪs
woolly-headed ˌwʊl i 'hed ɪd ◂ -əd
Woolmer 'wʊlm ə ‖ -ᵊr
woolpack 'wʊl pæk **~s** s
woolsack 'wʊl sæk **~s** s
Woolton 'wʊlt ən
Woolwich 'wʊl ɪdʒ -ɪtʃ
Woolworth 'wʊl wəθ -wɜːθ ‖ -wɜːθ **~'s** s
Woomera, w~ 'wʊm ər ə 'wuːm- **~s** z
Woon wuːn
Woonsocket wuːn 'sɒk ɪt §-ət ‖ -'sɑːk-
Woore wɔː ‖ wɔːr woʊr
Woosnam 'wuːz nəm
Wooster 'wʊst ə 'wuːst- ‖ -ᵊr
Wootten, Wootton 'wʊt ᵊn
wooz|y 'wuːz |i 'wʊz- **~ier** i‿ə ‖ i‿ᵊr **~iest** i‿ɪst
  i‿əst **~ily** ɪ li əl i **~iness** i nəs i nɪs

W

wop wɒp ‖ wɑːp **wops** wɒps ‖ wɑːps
Worcester 'wʊst ə ‖ -ᵊr **~shire** ʃə ʃɪə ‖ ʃᵊr ʃɪr
 ˌWorcester(shire) 'sauce ‖ '··(·) ·
Worcestershire 'wʊst ə ʃə -ʃɪə ‖ -ᵊr ʃᵊr -ʃɪr
Worcs —*see* **Worcestershire**
word, Word wɜːd ‖ wɜːd **worded** 'wɜːd ɪd -əd
 ‖ 'wɜːd əd **wording/s** 'wɜːd ɪŋ/z
 ‖ 'wɜːd ɪŋ/z **words** wɜːdz ‖ wɜːdz
 'word ˌblindness; 'word class; 'word
 count; 'word ˌorder; 'word ˌprocessing;
 'word ˌprocessor; 'word square
wordag|e 'wɜːd ɪdʒ ‖ 'wɜːd- **~es** ɪz əz
wordbreak 'wɜːd breɪk →'wɜːb- ‖ 'wɜːd- **~s** s
wordless 'wɜːd ləs -lɪs ‖ 'wɜːd ləs **~ly** li **~ness**
 nəs nɪs
word-perfect, WordPerfect *tdmk*
 ˌwɜːd 'pɜːf ɪkt ◂ →ˌwɜːb-, -ekt, §-əkt
 ‖ ˌwɜːd 'pɜːf ɪkt ◂ **~ly** li
wordplay 'wɜːd pleɪ →'wɜːb- ‖ 'wɜːd-
wordsmith 'wɜːd smɪθ ‖ 'wɜːd- **~s** s
Wordstar, WordStar *tdmk* 'wɜːd stɑː
 ‖ 'wɜːd stɑːr
Wordsworth 'wɜːdz wəθ -wɜːθ ‖ 'wɜːdz wɜːθ
 ~'s s
Wordsworthian ˌwɜːdz 'wɜːð i ən -'wɜːθ-
 ‖ ˌwɜːdz 'wɜːθ- -'wɜːð- **~s** z
wordwrap 'wɜːd ræp ‖ 'wɜːd-
word|y 'wɜːd |i ‖ 'wɜːd |i **~ier** i ə ‖ i ᵊr **~iest**
 i ɪst i əst **~ily** ɪ li əl i **~iness** i nəs i nɪs
wore wɔː ‖ wɔːr wʊər
work wɜːk ‖ wɜːk **worked** wɜːkt ‖ wɜːkt
 working/s 'wɜːk ɪŋ/z ‖ 'wɜːk ɪŋ/z **works**
 wɜːks ‖ wɜːks
 ˌworked 'up◂; ˌworking 'class ‖ '·· ·;
 ˌworking 'day ‖ '·· ·; ˌworking
 'knowledge◂; ˌworking 'order ‖ '·· ·;
 'working ˌparty; ˌworking 'week ‖ '···
-work wɜːk ‖ wɜːk — **spadework** 'speɪd wɜːk
 ‖ -wɜːk
workab|le 'wɜːk əb |ᵊl ‖ 'wɜːk- **~leness** ᵊl nəs
 -nɪs **~ly** li
workaday 'wɜːk ə deɪ ‖ 'wɜːk-
workaholic ˌwɜːk ə 'hɒl ɪk ◂
 ‖ ˌwɜːk ə 'hɑːl ɪk ◂ -'hɔːl- **~s** s
workaround 'wɜːk ə ˌraʊnd ‖ 'wɜːk- **~s** z
workbag 'wɜːk bæg ‖ 'wɜːk- **~s** z
workbasket 'wɜːk ˌbɑːsk ɪt §-ˌbæsk-, §-ət
 ‖ 'wɜːk ˌbæsk ət **~s** s
workbench 'wɜːk bentʃ ‖ 'wɜːk- **~es** ɪz əz
workbook 'wɜːk bʊk ‖ 'wɜːk- **~s** s
workbox 'wɜːk bɒks ‖ 'wɜːk bɑːks **~es** ɪz əz
workday 'wɜːk deɪ ‖ 'wɜːk-
worker 'wɜːk ə ‖ 'wɜːk ᵊr **~s** z
worker-priest ˌwɜːk ə 'priːst ‖ ˌwɜːk ᵊr- **~s** s
workfare 'wɜːk feə ‖ 'wɜːk fer -fær
workflow 'wɜːk fləʊ ‖ 'wɜːk floʊ
workforce 'wɜːk fɔːs ‖ 'wɜːk fɔːrs -foʊrs
workhors|e 'wɜːk hɔːs ‖ 'wɜːk hɔːrs **~es** ɪz əz
work|house 'wɜːk |haʊs ‖ 'wɜːk- **~houses**
 haʊz ɪz -əz
work-in 'wɜːk ɪn ‖ 'wɜːk- **~s** z
working-class ˌwɜːk ɪŋ 'klɑːs ◂ §-'klæs
 ‖ 'wɜːk ɪŋ klæs

working-out ˌwɜːk ɪŋ 'aʊt ‖ ˌwɜːk-
Workington 'wɜːk ɪŋ tən ‖ 'wɜːk-
workload 'wɜːk ləʊd ‖ 'wɜːk loʊd **~s** z
work|man, W~ 'wɜːk |mən ‖ 'wɜːk- **~manlike**
 mən laɪk **~manship** mən ʃɪp **~men** mən
workmate, W~ *tdmk* 'wɜːk meɪt ‖ 'wɜːk- **~s** s
workmen 'wɜːk mən ‖ 'wɜːk-
workout 'wɜːk aʊt ‖ 'wɜːk- **~s** s
workpeople 'wɜːk ˌpiːp ᵊl ‖ 'wɜːk-
workplac|e 'wɜːk pleɪs ‖ 'wɜːk- **~es** ɪz əz
workroom 'wɜːk ruːm -rʊm ‖ 'wɜːk- **~s** z
work-sharing 'wɜːk ˌʃeər ɪŋ ‖ 'wɜːk ˌʃer ɪŋ
 -ˌʃær-
worksheet 'wɜːk ʃiːt ‖ 'wɜːk- **~s** s
workshop 'wɜːk ʃɒp ‖ 'wɜːk ʃɑːp **~s** s
workshy 'wɜːk ʃaɪ ‖ 'wɜːk-
Worksop 'wɜːk sɒp ‖ 'wɜːk sɑːp
workspace 'wɜːk speɪs ‖ 'wɜːk-
workstation 'wɜːk ˌsteɪʃ ᵊn ‖ 'wɜːk- **~s** z
work-study 'wɜːk ˌstʌd i ‖ 'wɜːk-
worktable 'wɜːk ˌteɪb ᵊl ‖ 'wɜːk- **~s** z
worktop 'wɜːk tɒp ‖ 'wɜːk tɑːp **~s** s
work-to-rule ˌwɜːk tə 'ruːl -tu- ‖ ˌwɜːk-
workup 'wɜːk ʌp ‖ 'wɜːk- **~s** s
workweek 'wɜːk wiːk ‖ 'wɜːk- **~s** s
world wɜːld ‖ wɜːld **worlds** wɜːldz ‖ wɜːldz
 ˌWorld 'Bank; ˌWorld 'Cup; ˌWorld 'Health
 Organiˌzation; ˌworld 'power; ˌWorld
 'Series; ˌworld 'war; ˌWorld ˌWar 'Two;
 ˌWorld Wide 'Web
world-beater 'wɜːld ˌbiːt ə ‖ 'wɜːld ˌbiːt̬ ᵊr **~s**
 z
world-class ˌwɜːld 'klɑːs ◂ §-'klæs
 ‖ ˌwɜːld 'klæs ◂
world-famous ˌwɜːld 'feɪm əs ◂ ‖ ˌwɜːld- '·ˌ··
worldling 'wɜːld lɪŋ ‖ 'wɜːld- **~s** z
world|ly 'wɜːld |li ‖ 'wɜːld |li **~lier** li ə ‖ li ᵊr
 ~liest li ɪst əst **~liness** li nəs -nɪs
worldly-wise ˌwɜːld li 'waɪz ◂ ‖ ˌwɜːld- '·· ·
worldshaking 'wɜːld ˌʃeɪk ɪŋ ‖ 'wɜːld-
worldview ˌwɜːld 'vjuː ‖ ˌwɜːld- **~s** z
world-wear|y ˌwɜːld 'wɪər |i ◂ '·ˌ··
 ‖ 'wɜːld ˌwɪr |i **~ier** i ə ‖ i ᵊr **~iest** i ɪst i əst
 ~ily əl i ɪ li **~iness** i nəs i nɪs
worldwide ˌwɜːld 'waɪd ◂ ‖ ˌwɜːld-
Worley 'wɜːl i ‖ 'wɜːl i
Worlingham 'wɜːl ɪŋ əm ‖ 'wɜːl-
worm wɜːm ‖ wɜːm **wormed** wɜːmd ‖ wɜːmd
 worming 'wɜːm ɪŋ ‖ 'wɜːm ɪŋ **worms**
 wɜːmz ‖ wɜːmz
 'worm cast; 'worm gear
Wormald 'wɜːm ᵊld ‖ 'wɜːm-
wormcast 'wɜːm kɑːst §-kæst ‖ 'wɜːm kæst **~s**
 s
worm-eaten 'wɜːm ˌiːt ᵊn ‖ 'wɜːm-
wormhole 'wɜːm həʊl →-hɒʊl ‖ 'wɜːm hoʊl
 ~s z
Wormold 'wɜːm əʊld →-ɒʊld, -ᵊld
 ‖ 'wɜːm oʊld
Worms *place in Germany* vɔːmz wɜːmz ‖ wɜːmz
 —*Ger* [vɔʁms]
wormwood, W~ 'wɜːm wʊd ‖ 'wɜːm-
 ˌWormwood 'Scrubs

worm|y 'wɜːm |i ‖ 'wɜːm |i **~ier** i ə ‖ i ̩ᵊr
~iest i ̩ɪst i ̩əst **~iness** i nəs i nɪs
worn wɔːn ‖ wɔːrn woʊrn
worn-out ˌwɔːn 'aʊt ◂ ‖ ˌwɔːrn- ˌwoʊrn-
Worple 'wɔːp ᵊl ‖ 'wɔːrp ᵊl
Worplesdon 'wɔːp ᵊlz dən ‖ 'wɔːrp-
Worrall 'wɒr əl ‖ 'wɔːr- 'wɑːr-
worrie... —see **worry**
worriment 'wʌr i mənt ‖ 'wɜː- ~s s
worrisome 'wʌr i səm ‖ 'wɜː- **~ly** li
worr|it 'wʌr |ɪt §-ət ‖ 'wɜː |ət **~ited** ɪt ɪd §-ət-,
-əd ‖ əţ əd **~iting** ɪt ɪŋ §ət- ‖ əţ ɪŋ **~its** ɪts
§əts ‖ əts
worr|y 'wʌr |i ‖ 'wɜː |i **~ied/ly** id /li **~ier/s**
i ə/z ‖ i ̩ᵊr/z **~ies** iz **~ying/ly** i ̩ɪŋ /li
'**worry beads**
worrywart 'wʌr i wɔːt ‖ 'wɜː i wɔːrt **~s** s
worse wɜːs ‖ wɜːs
worsen 'wɜːs ᵊn ‖ 'wɜːs ᵊn **~ed** d **~ing** ɪŋ **~s**
z
worship, W~ 'wɜːʃ ɪp §-əp ‖ 'wɜːʃ əp **~ed,**
~ped t **~ing, ~ping** ɪŋ **~s** s
worshiper, worshipper 'wɜːʃ ɪp ə §-əp-
‖ 'wɜːʃ əp ᵊr **~s** z
worshipful 'wɜːʃ ɪp fᵊl §-əp-, -fʊl ‖ 'wɜːʃ əp-
~ly i **~ness** nəs nɪs
Worsley 'wɜːs li 'wɜːz- ‖ 'wɜːs-
Worsnip 'wɜːs nɪp §-nəp ‖ 'wɜːs-
worst wɜːst ‖ wɜːst **worsted** 'wɜːst ɪd -əd
‖ 'wɜːst əd **worsting** 'wɜːst ɪŋ ‖ 'wɜːst ɪŋ
worsts wɜːsts ‖ wɜːsts
worst-case ˌwɜːst'keɪs ◂ ‖ ˌwɜːst-
ˌworst-case sce'nario
worsted 'cloth' 'wʊst ɪd -əd ‖ 'wɜːst əd
Worsthorne 'wɜːs θɔːn ‖ 'wɜːs θɔːrn
wort wɜːt §wɔːt ‖ wɜːt wɔːrt
worth wɜːθ ‖ wɜːθ
-worth wəθ wɜːθ ‖ wɜːθ — **poundsworth**
'paʊndz wəθ -wɜːθ ‖ -wɜːθ
Worth wɜːθ ‖ wɜːθ —but as a French name
vɔːt ‖ vɔːrt —Fr [vɔʁt]
worthi... —see **worthy**
Worthing 'wɜːð ɪŋ ‖ 'wɜːð ɪŋ
Worthington 'wɜːð ɪŋ tən ‖ 'wɜːð-
worthless 'wɜːθ ləs -lɪs ‖ 'wɜːθ- **~ly** li **~ness**
nəs nɪs
worthwhile ˌwɜːθ 'waɪᵊl ◂ -'hwaɪᵊl
‖ ˌwɜːθ 'hwaɪᵊl ◂
worth|y, W~ 'wɜːð |i ‖ 'wɜːð |i **~ier** i ə ‖ i ̩ᵊr
~ies iz **~iest** i ̩ɪst i ̩əst **~ily** ɪ li ə l i **~iness**
i nəs i nɪs
-worthy ˌwɜːð i ‖ ˌwɜːð i — **blameworthy**
'bleɪm ˌwɜːð i ‖ -ˌwɜːð-
Wortley 'wɜːt li ‖ 'wɜːt-
Worzel 'wɜːz ᵊl ‖ 'wɜːz ᵊl
wot wɒt ‖ wɑːt
Wotan 'vəʊt ɑːn -æn ‖ 'voʊt- —Ger ['vo: tan]
wotcha, wotcher 'wɒtʃ ə ‖ 'wɑːtʃ ə -ᵊr
Wotton 'wʊt ᵊn 'wɒt- ‖ 'wɑːt-
Wotton-under-Edge ˌwʊt ᵊn ˌʌnd ər 'edʒ
‖ -ᵊr· —locally also ˌ· ·ʌndr ɪdʒ
would strong form wʊd (= wood), occasional
weak forms wəd, əd —see also **'d**

would-be 'wʊd biː →'wʊb-, -bi
wouldn't 'wʊd ᵊnt §'wʊt ᵊnt
wouldst wʊdst wʊtst
would've 'wʊd əv
Woulfe wʊlf
wound past & pp of **wind** waʊnd
wound 'injure, injury' wuːnd **wounded/ly**
'wuːnd ɪd /li -əd /li **wounding/ly**
'wuːnd ɪŋ /li **wounds** wuːndz
wound-up ˌwaʊnd 'ʌp ◂
woundwort 'wuːnd wɜːt §-wɔːt ‖ -wɜːt -wɔːrt
~s s
wove wəʊv ‖ woʊv
woven 'wəʊv ᵊn ‖ 'woʊv ᵊn
wow waʊ **wowed** waʊd **wowing** 'waʊ ɪŋ
wows waʊz
wowser 'waʊz ə ‖ -ᵊr **~s** z
Wozniak 'wɒz ni æk ‖ 'wɑːz- Polish Woźniak
['vɔz ɲak]
Wozzeck 'vɒts ek 'vɔːts- ‖ 'vɔːts- 'vɑːts-
WRAC ræk
wrack ræk (= rack) **wracked** rækt **wracking**
'ræk ɪŋ **wracks** ræks
Wragg, Wragge ræg
wraith, W~ reɪθ **wraiths** reɪθs
wraithlike 'reɪθ laɪk
Wrangel, Wrangell 'ræŋ gᵊl
wrangl|e 'ræŋ gᵊl **~ed** d **~es** z **~ing** ɪŋ
wrangler, W~ tdmk 'ræŋ glə ‖ -glᵊr **~s** z
wrap ræp (= rap) **wrapped** ræpt **wrapping/s**
'ræp ɪŋ/z **wraps** ræps
wraparound 'ræp ə ˌraʊnd **~s** z
wrapper 'ræp ə ‖ -ᵊr (= rapper) **~s** z
wrapround 'ræp raʊnd **~s** z
wrap-up 'ræp ʌp **~s** s
wrasse ræs **wrasses** 'ræs ɪz -əz
wrath, Wrath rɒθ rɔːθ, §rɑːθ, §ræθ ‖ ræθ (*)
Wrathall 'rɒθ ᵊl ‖ 'ræθ ɔːl -ɑːl
wrathful 'rɒθ fᵊl 'rɔːθ-, §'rɑːθ-, §'ræθ-, -fʊl
‖ 'ræθ- **~ly** i **~ness** nəs nɪs
Wray reɪ
Wraysbury 'reɪz bər i ‖ -ber i
wreak riːk §rek (= reek) **wreaked** riːkt
wreaking 'riːk ɪŋ **wreaks** riːks
wreath riːθ **wreaths** riːðz riːθs
wreathe riːð **wreathed** riːðd **wreathes** riːðz
wreathing 'riːð ɪŋ
wreck rek (= reck) **wrecked** rekt **wrecking**
'rek ɪŋ **wrecks** reks (= rex)
wreckage 'rek ɪdʒ
wrecker 'rek ə ‖ -ᵊr **~s** z
Wrekin 'riːk ɪn §-ən
wren, Wren ren **wrens, Wrens, Wren's** renz
wrench, W~ rentʃ **wrenched** rentʃt **wrenches**
'rentʃ ɪz -əz **wrenching** 'rentʃ ɪŋ
Wrenn ren
wrest rest (= rest) **wrested** 'rest ɪd -əd
wresting 'rest ɪŋ **wrests** rests
wrestl|e 'res ᵊl ‖ 'ræs- **~ed** d **~es** z **~ing** ɪŋ
wrestler 'res lə ‖·'·lᵊ ə ‖ 'res lᵊr 'ræs- **~s** z
wretch retʃ **wretches** 'retʃ ɪz -əz
wretched 'retʃ ɪd -əd (!) **~ly** li **~ness** nəs nɪs
Wrexham 'reks əm

wrick rɪk *(= rick)* **wricked** rɪkt **wricking**
'rɪk ɪŋ **wricks** rɪks
wrie... —*see* **ry**
wriggl|e 'rɪg ᵊl **~ed** d **~er/s** ˌə/z ‖ ˌʲr/z **~es** z
~ing ˌɪŋ **~y** ˌi
wright, Wright raɪt *(= right)* **wrights,**
Wright's raɪts
Wrightington 'raɪt ɪŋ tən ‖ 'raɪt̬-
Wrighton 'raɪt ᵊn
Wrigley 'rɪg li **~'s** z
wring rɪŋ *(= ring)* **wringing** 'rɪŋ ɪŋ **wrings**
rɪŋz **wrung** rʌŋ
ˌwringing 'wet◄
wringer 'rɪŋ ə ‖ -ʲr *(= ringer)* **~s** z
wrinkl|e 'rɪŋk ᵊl **~ed** d **~es** z **~ing** ˌɪŋ
wrink|ly 'rɪŋk |li **~lies** liz
Wriothesley 'raɪ ̩əθs li
wrist rɪst **wrists** rɪsts
wristband 'rɪst bænd **~s** z
wristlet 'rɪst lət -lɪt **~s** s
wristwatch 'rɪst wɒtʃ ‖ -wɑːtʃ **~es** ɪz əz
wristy 'rɪst i
writ rɪt **writs** rɪts
writable, writeable 'raɪt əb ᵊl ‖ 'raɪt̬-
write raɪt *(= right)* **writes** raɪts **writing**
'raɪt ɪŋ ‖ 'raɪt̬ ɪŋ **written** 'rɪt ᵊn **wrote** rəʊt
‖ roʊt
write-in 'raɪt ɪn ‖ 'raɪt̬ ɪn **~s** z
write-off 'raɪt ɒf -ɔːf ‖ 'raɪt̬ ɔːf -ɑːf **~s** s
write-protected ˌraɪt prə 'tekt ɪd ◄ -prəʊ-, -əd bi-
‖ -proʊ-
writer 'raɪt ə ‖ 'raɪt̬ ʲr **~s** z
ˌwriter's 'cramp ‖ '·· ·
write-up 'raɪt ʌp ‖ 'raɪt̬ ʌp **~s** s
writhe raɪð **writhed** raɪðd **writhes** raɪðz
writhing 'raɪð ɪŋ
writing 'raɪt ɪŋ ‖ 'raɪt̬ ɪŋ **~s** z
'writing desk; 'writing ˌpaper
written 'rɪt ᵊn
Wroclaw, Wrocław 'vrɒts lɑːv -læv
‖ 'vrɔːts lɑːf 'vrɑːts- —*Polish* ['vrɔts waf]
wrong rɒŋ ‖ rɔːŋ rɑːŋ **wronged** rɒŋd ‖ rɔːŋd
rɑːŋd **wronger** 'rɒŋ ə ‖ 'rɔːŋ ʲr 'rɑːŋ-
wrongest 'rɒŋ ɪst -əst ‖ 'rɔːŋ- 'rɑːŋ-
wronging 'rɒŋ ɪŋ ‖ 'rɔːŋ ɪŋ 'rɑːŋ- **wrongs**
rɒŋz ‖ rɔːŋz rɑːŋz
wrongdoer 'rɒŋ ˌduː ə ˌ·'·· ‖ 'rɔːŋ ˌduː ʲr
'rɑːŋ-; ˌ·'·· **~s** z
wrongdoing 'rɒŋ ˌduː ɪŋ ˌ·'·· ‖ 'rɔːŋ- 'rɑːŋ- **~s**
z
wrong-|foot ˌrɒŋ |'fʊt ‖ ˌrɔːŋ- ˌrɑːŋ- **~footed**
'fʊt ɪd -əd ‖ 'fʊt̬ əd **~footing** 'fʊt ɪŋ ‖ 'fʊt̬ ɪŋ
~foots fʊts
wrongful 'rɒŋ fᵊl -fʊl ‖ 'rɔːŋ- 'rɑːŋ- **~ly** i
~ness nəs nɪs
wrongheaded ˌrɒŋ 'hed ɪd ◄ -əd ‖ ˌrɔːŋ- ˌrɑːŋ-
~ly li **~ness** nəs nɪs
wrong|ly 'rɒŋ |li ‖ 'rɔːŋ |li 'rɑːŋ- **~ness** nəs
nɪs
wrote rəʊt ‖ roʊt *(= rote)*
wroth rəʊθ rɒθ ‖ rɔːθ rɑːθ *(*)*
Wrotham *place in Kent* 'ruːt əm ‖ 'ruːt̬-
Wrottesley 'rɒts li ‖ 'rɑːts-

wrought rɔːt ‖ rɑːt
ˌwrought 'iron◄
wrought-up ˌrɔːt 'ʌp ◄ ‖ ˌrɔːt̬- ˌrɑːt̬-
Wroxeter 'rɒks ɪt ə ‖ 'rɑːks ət̬ ʲr
Wroxham 'rɒks əm ‖ 'rɑːks-
wrung rʌŋ *(= rung)*
wrung-out ˌrʌŋ 'aʊt ◄
wry raɪ *(= rye)* **wrier, wryer** 'raɪ ə ‖ 'raɪ ʲr
wriest, wryest 'raɪ ɪst -əst
wryly 'raɪ li
wryneck 'raɪ nek **~s** s
wryness 'raɪ nəs -nɪs
Wrythe raɪð
Wu wuː —*Chi* Wú [²wu], *Cantonese* [⁴wuː]
Wuhan ˌwuː 'hæn ‖ -'hɑːn —*Chi* Wǔhàn
[³wu ⁴xan]
wulfenite 'wʊlf ə naɪt -ɪ-
Wulfrun 'wʊlf rən
Wulstan 'wʊlst ən
wunderkind 'wʌnd ə kɪnd 'vʊnd- ‖ -ʲr- —*Ger*
['vʊn də kɪnt] **~s** z
Wundt vʊnt
Wuppertal 'vʊp ə tɑːl 'wʊp- ‖ -ʲr- —*Ger*
['vʊp ɐ tɑːl]
Wurlitzer 'wɜːl ɪts ə -əts- ‖ 'wɜːl əts ʲr **~s** z
wurst wɜːst wʊəst, vʊəst ‖ wɜːst wʊrst, wʊst
—*Ger* [vʊʁst]
Wurttemberg, Württemberg 'vɜːt əm bɜːg
'wɜːt- ‖ 'wɜːt̬ əm bɜːg —*Ger* ['vʏʁ təm bɛʁk]
Wurzburg, Würzburg 'vɜːts bɜːg 'wɜːts-
‖ 'wɜːts bɜːg —*Ger* ['vʏʁts bʊʁk]
wuss wʊs **wusses** 'wʊs ɪz -əz
wussy 'wʊs i **wussies** 'wʊs iz
wuthering, W~ 'wʌð ər ɪŋ
ˌWuthering 'Heights
Wuxi ˌwuː 'ʃiː —*Chi* Wúxī [²wu ¹ɕi]
Wyandot, wyandotte 'waɪ ̩ən dɒt ‖ -dɑːt **~s**
s
Wyatt 'waɪ ət
wych-elm 'wɪtʃ elm **~s** z
Wycherley 'wɪtʃ ə li ‖ -ʲr-
wych-hazel 'wɪtʃ ˌheɪz ᵊl **~s** z
Wychwood 'wɪtʃ wʊd
Wyclif, Wycliffe 'wɪk lɪf
Wycliffite 'wɪk lɪ faɪt -lə- **~s** s
Wycombe 'wɪk əm
Wye, wye waɪ *(= Y)* **wyes, Wye's** waɪz
(= wise)
Wyeth 'waɪ ̩əθ
Wyke waɪk
Wykeham 'wɪk əm
Wykehamist 'wɪk əm ɪst §-əst **~s** s
Wyld, Wylde waɪᵊld
Wylfa 'wɪlv ə —*Welsh* ['uɪl va, 'wɪl-]
Wylie, Wyllie, Wylye 'waɪl i
Wyman 'waɪ mən
Wymondham *(i)* 'waɪm ənd əm, *(ii)*
'wɪnd əm, *(iii)* 'wɪm ənd əm —*The place in
Leics is (i), that in Nfk (ii) or (iii).*
Wyn wɪn
wynd waɪnd **wynds** waɪndz
Wyndham 'wɪnd əm
Wynette wɪ 'net wə-

Wynford ˈwɪn fəd ‖ -fərd
Wynn, Wynne wɪn
Wyoming waɪ ˈəʊm ɪŋ ‖ -ˈoʊm-
Wyomingite waɪ ˈəʊm ɪŋ aɪt ‖ -ˈoʊm- ~s s
Wyre *district and river in England* ˈwaɪ ə
‖ ˈwaɪ ər
Wyre *Welsh personal name* ˈwɪr ə

Wyrley ˈwɜːl i ‖ ˈwɜːl i
WYSIWYG, wysiwyg ˈwɪz i wɪg
Wystan ˈwɪst ən
Wytch wɪtʃ
Wythenshawe ˈwɪð ən ʃɔː ‖ -ʃɑː
wyvern ˈwaɪv ən -ɜːn ‖ -ərn ~s z

Xx

x Spelling-to-sound

1 Where the spelling is **x**, the pronunciation is regularly ks as in **six** sɪks. Less commonly, it is gz, and occasionally z or kʃ.

2 The pronunciation gz is found mainly in words beginning **ex-** before a stressed vowel, for example **exist** ɪg ˈzɪst. There is a variant pronunciation with kz. However, in words beginning **exce-**, **exci-**, the pronunciation is ks, with the **c** silent as in **exceed** ɪk ˈsiːd.

3 The pronunciation is regularly z at the beginning of a word as in **xerox** ˈzɪər ɒks ‖ ˈzɪr ɑːks. Note also **anxiety** æŋ ˈzaɪ ət i ‖ -əṭ i.

4 The pronunciation is kʃ in words ending **xious**, **xion**, **xure**, for example **crucifixion**, **anxious** ˈæŋk ʃəs. In **luxury** and its derivatives some speakers use kʃ, some gʒ.

5 ks is also regularly written

    cks as in **kicks** kɪks

    ks as in **thanks** θæŋks and

    cc as in **accident** ˈæks ɪd ənt.

6 **x** is silent in certain names and other words borrowed from French as in **prix** priː.

X, x eks **X's, x's, Xs** ˈeks ɪz -əz
—*Communications code name:* ˈX-ray
ˈX ˌchromosome
X-acto *tdmk* eks ˈækt əʊ ‖ -oʊ
Xan zæn
Xanadu ˈzæn ə duː ˈgzæn-, ˌ·ˈ··· —*Chi*
(Yuán)shàngdū [(²ɕɛn) ⁴ʂɑŋ ¹tu]
xanth- *comb. form before vowel*
  with unstressed suffix ˈzænᵗθ ˈgzænᵗθ —
  xanthene ˈzænᵗθ iːn ˈgzænᵗθ-
  with stressed suffix zæn θ+ gzæn θ+ —
  xanthoma zæn ˈθəʊm ə gzæn- ‖ -ˈθoʊm ə
Xanthe ˈzænᵗθ i ˈgzænᵗθ-
xanthelasma ˌzænᵗθ ɪ ˈlæz mə -ə-
xanthic ˈzænᵗθ ɪk
Xanthippe zæn ˈθɪp i gzæn-, -ˈtɪp-
xantho- *comb. form*
  with stress-neutral suffix ˌzænᵗθ əʊ
  ˌgzænᵗθ əʊ ‖ -ə — **xanthochroic**
  ˌzænᵗθ əʊ ˈkrəʊ ɪk ◂ ˌgzænᵗθ- ‖ -ə ˈkroʊ-
  with stress-imposing suffix zæn ˈθɒ+
  gzæn ˈθɒ+ ‖ -ˈθɑː+ — **xanthochroism**
  zæn ˈθɒk rəʊ ˌɪz əm gzæn- ‖ -ˈθɑːk roʊ-

Xantia *tdmk* ˈzænt i ə
Xantippe zæn ˈtɪp i gzæn-
Xavier ˈzæv i ə ˈzeɪv- ‖ ᵊr —*Sp* [xa ˈβjer]
Xavierian zæ ˈvɪər i ən zeɪ- ‖ -ˈvɪr- **~s** z
x-axis ˈeks ˌæks ɪs §-əs
X-bar ˈeks bɑː ‖ -bɑːr
Xbox *tdmk* ˈeks bɒks ‖ -bɑːks **~es** ɪz əz
X-certificate ˈeks sə ˌtɪf ɪk ət -ɪt ‖ ˈeks sᵊr-
x-coordinate ˈeks kəʊ ˌɔːd ɪn ət -ᵊn ˌət, -ɪt
  ‖ -koʊ ˌɔːrd ᵊn ˌət -eɪt **~s** s
xebek ˈziːb ek ˈzeɪb- **~s** s
Xenia, xenia ˈziːn i ə ˈzen-
Xenical *tdmk* ˈzen ɪ kæl -ə-
Xenix *tdmk* ˈziːn ɪks
xeno- *comb. form*
  with stress-neutral suffix ˌzen əʊ ˈziːn əʊ ‖ -ə
  — **xenophile** ˈzen əʊ faɪᵊl ˈ ˌziːn- ‖ -ə-
  with stress-imposing suffix ze ˈnɒ+ ziː-, zɪ-
  ‖ -ˈnɑː+ — **xenogamy** ze ˈnɒg əm i ziː-, zɪ-
  ‖ -ˈnɑːg-
xenon ˈziːn ɒn ˈzen-, ˈzen- ‖ ˈziːn ɑːn ˈzen-
Xenophanes ze ˈnɒf ə niːz zɪ-, zə- ‖ -ˈnɑːf-

xenophobe 'zen ə fəʊb 'ziːn- ‖ -foʊb **~s** z
xenophobia ˌzen ə 'fəʊb i‿ə ˌziːn- ‖ -'foʊb-
xenophobic ˌzen ə 'fəʊb ɪk ◂ ˌziːn- ‖ -'foʊb-
Xenophon 'zen əf ən -ə fɒn ‖ -ə fɑːn
xenotransplant 'zen əʊ ˌtrænʦ plɑːnt 'ziːn-,
 -ˌtrɑːnʦ-, §-plænt ‖ -oʊ ˌtrænʦ plænt **~s** s
xer- comb. form before vowel
 with unstressed suffix 'zɪər ‖ 'zɪr — **xerarch**
 'zɪər ɑːk ‖ 'zɪr ɑːrk
 with stressed suffix zɪə r+ zɪ r+, zə r+
 ‖ zə r+ zɪ r+ — **xerosis** zɪə 'rəʊs ɪs zɪ-, zə-
 ‖ zə 'roʊs əs zɪ-
xeric 'zɪər ɪk ‖ 'zɪr ɪk
xero- comb. form
 with stress-neutral suffix ¦zɪər əʊ ¦gzɪər əʊ
 ‖ ¦zɪr ə — **xeroderma** ˌzɪər əʊ 'dɜːm ə ˌgzɪər-
 ‖ ˌzɪr ə 'dɝːm ə
 with stress-imposing suffix zɪə 'rɒ+ ze-, zɪ-,
 gzɪə-, gze-, §zi:- ‖ zə 'rɑː+ zɪ- — **xerophilous**
 zɪə 'rɒf ɪl əs ze-, zɪ-, gzɪə-, gze-, §zi:-, §-əl-
 ‖ zə 'rɑːf əl əs zɪ-
xerographic ˌzɪər ə 'græf ɪk ◂ ‖ ˌzɪr- **~ally** ᵊl‿i
xerography zɪə 'rɒg rəf i ze-, zɪ-, §zi:-
 ‖ zə 'rɑːg- zɪ-
xerophthalmia ˌzɪər ɒf 'θælm i‿ə ˌ·ɒp-
 ‖ ˌzɪr ɑːf- ˌ·ɑːp-
xerophyte 'zɪər əʊ faɪt 'gzɪər- ‖ 'zɪr ə- **~s** s
xerox, Xerox tdmk 'zɪər ɒks ‖ 'zɪr ɑːks **~ed** t
 ~es ɪz əz **~ing** ɪŋ
Xerxes 'zɜːks iːz ‖ 'zɝːks-
Xhosa 'kɔːs ə 'kəʊs-, 'kɔːz-, 'kəʊz- ‖ 'koʊs ə
 'hoʊs- —Xhosa ['|ᵏʰɔː sa] **~s** z
xi name of Greek letter saɪ ksaɪ, zaɪ, gzaɪ ‖ zaɪ
 xis, xi's saɪz ksaɪz, zaɪz, gzaɪz ‖ zaɪz
Xia dynasty ʃi 'ɑː —Chi Xià [⁴ɕja]
Xiamen ˌʃɑː 'mʌn ʃi ˌɑː- —Chi Xiàmén
 [⁴ɕja ²mən]
Xian, Xi'an ˌʃiː 'æn ‖ -'ɑːn —Chi Xī'ān
 [¹ɕi ¹an]
Ximenes 'zɪm ə niːz -ɪ- ‖ hɪ 'men ez —Sp
 [xi 'me nes]

 ‖ 'krɔːs ɪŋ 'krɑːs-
Xingu, Xingú ʃɪŋ 'gu: ʃiː ŋ-, '·· —Port [ʃiŋ 'gu]
Xinhua News Agency ˌʃɪn 'hwɑː —Chi Xīnhuá
 [¹ɕin ²xwa]
Xinjiang ˌʃɪn dʒi 'æŋ ‖ -'ɑːŋ —Chi Xīnjiāng
 [¹ɕin ¹tɕjaŋ]
xiphoid 'zɪf ɔɪd
Xmas 'krɪs məs 'eks-
XML ˌeks em 'el ◂
XP Christian symbol, chi-ro ˌkaɪ 'rəʊ ‖ -'roʊ
XP computer operating system ˌeks 'piː
X-rat|ed 'eks ˌreɪt ɪd -əd ‖ -ˌreɪt̬- **~ing** ɪŋ
x-ray, X-ray 'eks reɪ ˌ·'·◂ **~ed** d **~ing** ɪŋ **~s** z
Xsara tdmk 'zɑːr ə
xth eksθ
xyl- comb. form before vowel
 with unstressed suffix zaɪl gzaɪl — **xylyl**
 'zaɪl ɪl 'gzaɪl-, §-əl
 with stressed suffix zaɪ 'l+ gzaɪ 'l+
 — **xylamidine** zaɪ 'læm ɪ diːn gzaɪ-, §-ə-
xylem 'zaɪl əm -em
xylene 'zaɪl iːn 'gzaɪl-
xylidine 'zaɪl ɪ diːn -ə-
xylo- comb. form
 with stress-neutral suffix ¦zaɪl əʊ ¦gzaɪl- ‖ -ə
 — **xylocarpous** ˌzaɪl əʊ 'kɑːp əs ◂ ˌgzaɪl-
 ‖ -ə 'kɑːrp-
 with stress-imposing suffix zaɪ 'lɒ+ gzaɪ-
 ‖ -'lɑː+ — **xylography** zaɪ 'lɒg rəf i gzaɪ-
 ‖ -'lɑːg-
xylol 'zaɪl ɒl 'gzaɪl- ‖ -ɔːl -ɑːl, -oʊl
xylonite, X~ tdmk 'zaɪl ə naɪt 'gzaɪl-
xylophone 'zaɪl ə fəʊn 'zɪl-, 'gzaɪl- ‖ -foʊn **~s**
 z
xylophonist zaɪ 'lɒf ən ɪst 'zaɪl ə fəʊn-, §-əst
 ‖ 'zaɪl ə foʊn əst **~s** s
xylose 'zaɪl əʊz 'gzaɪl-, -əʊs ‖ -oʊs
xyster 'zɪst ə 'gzɪst- ‖ -ᵊr **~s** z

Y y

Y, y *name of letter* waɪ **Y's, y's, Ys** waɪz
—*Communications code name:* Yoke
ˈY ˌchromosome
Y, y *in Welsh expressions* ə
-y i — **panicky** ˈpæn ɪk i
-y- *in Welsh place names* i ə —*Welsh* [ə]
yabber ˈjæb ə ‖ -ᵊr **~ed** d **yabbering**
ˈjæb ər ɪŋ **~s** z
yabb|ie, yabb|y ˈjæb |i **~ies** iz
yacht jɒt ‖ jɑːt **yachted** ˈjɒt ɪd -əd ‖ ˈjɑːt̬ əd
yachting ˈjɒt ɪŋ ‖ ˈjɑːt̬ ɪŋ **yachts** jɒts ‖ jɑːts
yachts|man ˈjɒts |mən ‖ ˈjɑːts- **~manship**
mən ʃɪp **~men** mən **~woman** ˌwʊm ən
~women ˌwɪm ɪn §-ən
yack jæk **yacked** jækt **yacking** ˈjæk ɪŋ **yacks**
jæks
yackety-yak ˌjæk ət i ˈjæk ˌɪt- ‖ ˌjæk ət̬- **~ked**
t **~king** ɪŋ **~s** s
yada yada, yadda yadda ˌjæd ə ˈjæd ə
‖ ˌjɑːd ə ˈjɑːd ə **yada ~, yadda ~** ˌjæd ə
‖ ˌjɑːd ə
yaffle ˈjæf ᵊl **~s** z
Yagi, yagi ˈjɑːg i ˈjæg- —*Jp* [ˈja ŋi, -gi, ·ˌ·] **~s**
z
yah jɑː
yah-boo ˌjɑː ˈbuː ◂
ˌyah-boo ˈsucks
yahoo, Yahoo ₍ˌ₎jɑː ˈhuː jə-, ·ˌ jɑː huː **~s** z
Yahveh ˈjɑː veɪ

Yahweh ˈjɑː weɪ
yak jæk **yaks** jæks
Yakima ˈjæk ɪ mɑː -ə- ‖ -mɔː -mɑː **~s** z
yakitori ˌjæk i ˈtɔːr i ‖ ˌjɑːk- jæk- —*Jp*
[ja ˌki̯ to ɾi]
yakka ˈjæk ə
Yakult *tdmk* ˈjæk ᵊlt
Yakut jə ˈkʊt jæ-, jɑː- ‖ -ˈkuːt **~s** s
Yakutsk jə ˈkʊtsk jæ-, jɑː- ‖ -ˈkuːtsk —*Russ*
[jɪ ˈkutsk]
yakuza jə ˈkuːz ə ˈjæk u zɑː —*Jp* [ˈja kɯ dza]
Yalden ˈjɔːld ən ˈjɒld- ‖ ˈjɑːld-
Yale jeᵊl
y'all jɔːl ‖ jɑːl
Yalta ˈjælt ə ˈjɔːlt-, ˈjɒlt- ‖ ˈjɔːlt ə ˈjɑːlt- —*Russ*
[ˈjaɫ tə]
yam jæm **yams** jæmz
Yamaha *tdmk* ˈjæm ə hɑː -hə ‖ ˈjɑːm- **~s** z
—*Jp* [ja ˌma ha]
Yamani jə ˈmɑːn i
yammer ˈjæm ə ‖ -ᵊr **~ed** d **yammering**
ˈjæm ər ɪŋ **~s** z
Yamoussoukro ˌjæm u ˈsuːk rəʊ
‖ ˌjɑːm u ˈsuːk roʊ —*Fr* [ja mu su kʁo]
yang, Yang jæŋ ‖ jɑːŋ jæŋ
Yangon, Yangôn jæŋ ˈgɒn ‖ jɑːn ˈgoʊn

Yangtse, Yangtze 'jæŋ^kt si ‖ 'jɑːŋ^kt si —*Chi*
Yángzǐ [²jaŋ ³tsɯ]
,**Yangtse Ki'ang, -'Kiang** ki 'æŋ kjæŋ ‖ -'ɑːŋ
—*Chi* Jiāng [¹tɕjaŋ]
Yangzhou jæŋ 'dʒəʊ ‖ jɑːŋ 'dʒoʊ —*Chi*
Yángzhōu [²jaŋ ¹tʂou]
yank, Yank jæŋk **yanked** jæŋkt **yanking**
'jæŋk ɪŋ **yanks, Yanks** jæŋks
Yankee 'jæŋk i **~dom** dəm **~ism/s** ˌɪz əm/z **~s**
z
,**Yankee 'Doodle**
Yaounde, Yaoundé jɑː 'ʊnd eɪ ‖ jɑː ʊn 'deɪ
—*Fr* [ja un de]
yap jæp **yapped** jæpt **yapping/ly** 'jæp ɪŋ /li
yaps jæps
Yap *island* jæp jɑːp ‖ jɑːp
yapok jə 'pɒk ‖ -'pɑːk **~s** s
yapp, Yapp jæp
yapper 'jæp ə ‖ -ᵊr **~s** z
yappy 'jæp i
Yaqui 'jɑːk i ~s z
Yarborough, y~ 'jɑː bər ə ‖ 'jɑːr ˌbɝː oʊ **~s** z
yard jɑːd ‖ jɑːrd **yards** jɑːdz ‖ jɑːrdz
yardag|e 'jɑːd ɪdʒ ‖ 'jɑːrd- **~es** ɪz əz
yardarm 'jɑːd ɑːm ‖ 'jɑːrd ɑːrm **~s** z
yardbird 'jɑːd bɜːd →'jɑːb- ‖ 'jɑːrd bɝːd **~s** z
yardie, Y~ 'jɑːd i ‖ 'jɑːrd i ~s z
Yardley 'jɑːd li ‖ 'jɑːrd-
yardstick 'jɑːd stɪk ‖ 'jɑːrd- **~s** s
yardwork 'jɑːd wɜːk ‖ 'jɑːrd wɝːk
Yare, yare jeə ‖ jeᵊr jæᵊr, jɑːr
Yaren 'jɑːr en 'jær-, -ən
Yarm jɑːm ‖ jɑːrm
Yarmouth 'jɑː məθ ‖ 'jɑːr-
yarmulka, yarmulke 'jɑːm ʊlk ə 'jʌm-, -ᵊlk-
‖ 'jɑːrm- 'jɑːm-, -ək- **~s** z
yarn jɑːn ‖ jɑːrn **yarned** jɑːnd ‖ jɑːrnd
yarning 'jɑːn ɪŋ ‖ 'jɑːrn ɪŋ **yarns** jɑːnz
‖ jɑːrnz
Yarra 'jær ə
Yarralumla ˌjær ə 'lʌm lə
yarrow, Y~ 'jær əʊ ‖ -oʊ 'jer- **~s** z
Yarwood 'jɑː wʊd ‖ 'jɑːr-
yashmak 'jæʃ mæk ‖ 'jɑːʃ mɑːk **~s** s
Yasmin, Yasmine 'jæs mɪn 'jæz-, 'jɑːs-
Yasser, Yassir 'jæs ə ‖ 'jɑːs ᵊr —*Arabic*
['jɑː sir]
yataghan 'jæt əg ən ‖ 'jæt ə gæn -əg ən **~s** z
Yates jeɪts
yatter 'jæt ə ‖ 'jæt ᵊr **~ed** d **yattering**
'jæt ᵊr ɪŋ ‖ 'jæt ᵊr ɪŋ **~s** z
Yaunde jɑː 'ʊnd eɪ ‖ jɑː ʊn 'deɪ —*Fr* Yaoundé
[ja un de]
Yavapai 'jæv ə paɪ ‖ 'jɑːv- -ɑː-
yaw jɔː ‖ jɑː **yawed** jɔːd ‖ jɑːd **yawing/s**
'jɔːʳ ɪŋ/z ‖ 'jɔː ɪŋz 'jɑː- **yaws** jɔːz ‖ jɑːz
yawl jɔːl ‖ jɑːl **yawls** jɔːlz ‖ jɑːlz
yawn jɔːn ‖ jɑːn **yawned** jɔːnd ‖ jɑːnd
yawning/ly 'jɔːn ɪŋ /li ‖ 'jɑːn- **yawns** jɔːnz
‖ jɑːnz
yawp jɔːp ‖ jɑːp **yawped** jɔːpt ‖ jɑːpt **yawping**
'jɔːp ɪŋ ‖ 'jɑːp- **yawps** jɔːps ‖ jɑːps
yaws jɔːz ‖ jɑːz

y-axis 'waɪ ˌæks ɪs §-əs
yclept ɪ 'klept iː-
y-coordinate 'waɪ kəʊ ˌɔːd ɪn ət -ᵊn_ət, -ɪt
‖ -koʊ ˌɔːrd ᵊn_ət -eɪt **~s** s
ye *pronoun strong form* jiː, *weak form* ji
ye *'the'* jiː —*or see* **the**
yea jeɪ **yeas** jeɪz
Yeading 'jed ɪŋ
Yeadon (i) 'jiːd ᵊn, (ii) 'jeɪd ᵊn, (iii) 'jed ᵊn
—*The place in WYks is* (i), *that in PA* (ii).
The family name may be any of the three.
yeah jeə ‖ 'je ə

YEAR

year jɪə jɜː ‖ jɪᵊr — *Preference poll, BrE:* jɪə
80%, jɜː *20%.* **years** jɪəz jɜːz ‖ jɪᵊrz
,**year 'dot**
yearbook 'jɪə bʊk 'jɜː- ‖ 'jɪr- **~s** s
year-end ˌjɪərˈend ◂ ‖ ˌjɪr-
yearling 'jɪə lɪŋ 'jɜː- ‖ 'jɪr- **~s** z
yearlong ˌjɪə 'lɒŋ ◂ jɜː- ‖ ˌjɪr 'lɔːŋ ◂ -'lɑːŋ
yearly 'jɪə li 'jɜː- ‖ 'jɪr li
yearn jɜːn ‖ jɝːn **yearned** jɜːnd ‖ jɝːnd
yearning 'jɜːn ɪŋ ‖ 'jɝːn ɪŋ **yearns** jɜːnz
‖ jɝːnz
yearning 'jɜːn ɪŋ ‖ 'jɝːn ɪŋ **~ly** li **~s** z
year-round ˌjɪə 'raʊnd ◂ jɜː- ‖ ˌjɪr-
yeast jiːst **yeasts** jiːsts
yeast|y 'jiːst |i **~ier** i ə ‖ i ᵊr **~iest** i ɪst i əst
~ily ɪ li əl i **~iness** i nəs i nɪs
Yeates, Yeats jeɪts (*!*)
yecch, yech jex jek, jʌx, jʌk
Yehudi jɪ 'huːd i jə-, je-
yell, Yell jel **yelled** jeld **yelling** 'jel ɪŋ **yells**
jelz
Yelland 'jel ənd
yellow 'jel əʊ ‖ -oʊ **~ed** d **~ing** ɪŋ **~s** z
,**yellow 'fever**; ,**Yellow 'Pages** ‖ '·· ,·· ;
,**yellow ˌrattle**; ,**Yellow 'Sea**
yellowhammer 'jel əʊ ˌhæm ə ‖ -oʊ ˌhæm ᵊr
-ə- **~s** z
yellowish 'jel əʊ ɪʃ ‖ -oʊ-
Yellowknife 'jel əʊ naɪf ‖ -oʊ- -ə-
yellow|ly 'jel əʊ |li ‖ -oʊ- **~ness** nəs nɪs
Yellowstone 'jel əʊ stəʊn ‖ -oʊ stoʊn -ə-
yellowwood 'jel əʊ wʊd ‖ -oʊ- -ə- **~s** z
yellowy 'jel əʊ i ‖ -oʊ-
yelp jelp **yelped** jelpt **yelping** 'jelp ɪŋ **yelps**
jelps
Yeltsin 'jelts ɪn -ᵊn —*Russ* ['jelʲ tsɨn]
Yelverton 'jelv ət ən ‖ -ᵊrt ᵊn
Yemen 'jem ən 'jeɪm-
Yemeni 'jem ən i 'jeɪm- **~s** z
yen *'Japanese currency'* jen —*Jp* ['eɴ]

yen *'long(ing)'* jen **yenned** jend **yenning**
'jen ɪŋ **yens** jenz

Yenisei, Yenisey ˌjen ɪ 'seɪ -ə- —*Russ*
[jɪ nʲɪ 'sʲej]

Yeo jəʊ ‖ joʊ *(!)*

yeo|man 'jəʊ |mən ‖ 'joʊ- **~manly** mən li
~manry mən ri **~men** mən
ˌyeoman 'service ‖ '· · ˌ· ·

Yeovil 'jəʊ vɪl -vəl ‖ 'joʊ-

yep jep —*usually said with no audible release
of the* p

yer *'weak vowel in Slavonic languages'* jɜː ‖ jɜː
yers jɜːz ‖ jɜːz

yer *informal spelling of the weak form of 'your'
or 'you're'* jə ‖ jʲr

yer *informal spelling of the weak form of 'you'
(BrE only)* jə ‖ —

yer *informal 'yes' (BrE only)* jeə jɜː ‖ —

Yerba Buena ˌjeəb ə 'bweɪn ə ˌjɜːb- ‖ ˌjerb-
ˌjɜːb-

Yerevan ˌjer ə 'væn -vɑːn, -ɪ-, '· · · ‖ -'vɑːn
—*Russ* [jɪ rʲɪ 'van]

Yerkes 'jɜːk iːz ‖ 'jɜːk-

yes jes —*Casual variants include* yah, yeah,
yep, yup *(see).* **yeses** 'jes ɪz -əz

yeshiva, yeshivah jə 'ʃiːv ə **~s** z

yes-|man 'jes |mæn **~men** men

yes/no question ˌjes 'nəʊ ˌkwes tʃən -ˌkweʃ-
‖ -'noʊ- **~s** z

yessir 'jes ɜː ‖ -ɜː

yesterday 'jest əd i -ə deɪ; §ˌ· ·'deɪ ‖ -ʲrd i
-ʲr deɪ **~s, ~'s** z

yesteryear 'jest ə jɪə -jɜː, ˌ· ·'· ‖ -ʲr jɪr

yet jet

Yetholm 'jet əm ‖ 'jet̮-

yeti 'jet i ‖ 'jet̮ i **~s** z

Yevtushenko ˌjev tu 'ʃeŋk əʊ -tə- ‖ -oʊ
—*Russ* [jɪf tu 'ʃeŋ kə]

yew juː *(= you, ewe, U)* **yews** juːz *(= use v.)*

Y-front *tdmk* 'waɪ frʌnt **~s** s

Ygdrasil, Yggdrasil 'ɪg drə sɪl

YHA ˌwaɪ eɪtʃ 'eɪ §-heɪtʃ-

yid jɪd **yids** jɪdz

Yiddish 'jɪd ɪʃ

yiddisher, Y~ 'jɪd ɪʃ ə ‖ -ʲr **~s** z

yield jiːəld **yielded** 'jiːəld ɪd -əd **yielding/ly**
'jiːəld ɪŋ /li **yields** jiːəldz

yikes jaɪks

yin, Yin jɪn

yip jɪp **yipped** jɪpt **yipping** 'jɪp ɪŋ **yips** jɪps

yippee ˌ·ˌjɪ 'piː ‖ 'jɪp i

-yl əl ɪl, aɪəl ‖ -iːəl —*in BrE there is an
inconsistent preference for* aɪəl *in* butyl *but* əl *in*
methyl

ylang-ylang ˌiːl æŋ 'iːl æŋ ˌiːl æŋ i 'læŋ;
△jə ˌlæŋ jə 'læŋ ‖ ˌiːl ɑːŋ 'iːl ɑːŋ

YMCA ˌwaɪ em si: 'eɪ

-yne aɪn — **alkyne** 'ælk aɪn

yngling 'ɪŋ lɪŋ **~s** z

Ynys ʌn ɪs △'ɪn- —*Welsh* ['ə nɪs, -nɪs]
ˌYnys 'Mon, ˌYnys 'Môn mɔːn —*Welsh*
[moːn]

Ynys-ddu ˌʌn ɪs 'diː -'ðiː —*Welsh* [ˌə nɪs 'ðiː]

Ynysybwl ˌʌn ɪs ə 'bʊl —*Welsh* [ˌə nɪs ə 'bʊl]

yo jəʊ ‖ joʊ

yob jɒb ‖ jɑːb **yobs** jɒbz ‖ jɑːbz

yobbish 'jɒb ɪʃ ‖ 'jɑːb- **~ly** li **~ness** nəs nɪs

yobbism 'jɒb ˌɪz əm ‖ 'jɑːb-

yobbo 'jɒb əʊ ‖ 'jɑːb oʊ **~s** z

yod jɒd ‖ jɑːd jɔːd, jʊd **yods** jɒdz ‖ jɑːdz jɔːdz,
jʊdz

yodel 'jəʊd əl ‖ 'joʊd əl **~ed, ~led** d **~ing,
~ling** ɪŋ **~s** z

yoga 'jəʊg ə ‖ 'joʊg ə

yogh jɒg jəʊg ‖ joʊg joʊk, joʊx **yoghs** jɒgz
jəʊgz ‖ joʊgz joʊks, joʊxs

yoghourt, yoghurt 'jɒg ət -ʊət ‖ 'joʊg ʲrt *(*)*
~s s

yogi 'jəʊg i ‖ 'joʊg i **~s** z

yogic 'jəʊg ɪk ‖ 'joʊg-

yogurt 'jɒg ət -ʊət ‖ 'joʊg ʲrt *(*)* **~s** s

yo-heave-ho ˌjəʊ ˌhiːv 'həʊ ‖ ˌjoʊ ˌhiːv 'hoʊ

yohimbine jəʊ 'hɪm biːn ‖ joʊ-

yo-ho ˌ·jəʊ 'həʊ ‖ ˌ·joʊ 'hoʊ

yo-ho-ho ˌjəʊ ˌhəʊ 'həʊ ‖ ˌjoʊ ˌhoʊ 'hoʊ

yoicks jɔɪks

yoke jəʊk ‖ joʊk **yoked** jəʊkt ‖ joʊkt **yokes**
jəʊks ‖ joʊks **yoking** 'jəʊk ɪŋ ‖ 'joʊk ɪŋ

yokel 'jəʊk əl ‖ 'joʊk əl **~s** z

Yoknapatawpha ˌjɒk nə pə 'tɔːf ə ‖ ˌjɑːk-
-'tɑːf-

Yoko 'jəʊk əʊ ‖ 'joʊk oʊ —*Jp* ['joo ko]

Yokohama ˌjəʊk əʊ 'hɑːm ə ‖ ˌjoʊk ə- —*Jp*
[jo ˌko ha ma]

Yolanda jəʊ 'lænd ə ‖ joʊ- -'lɑːnd-

yolk jəʊk ‖ joʊk joʊlk, jelk *(= yoke)* **yolks**
jəʊks ‖ joʊks joʊlks, jelks

Yom Kippur ˌjɒm kɪ 'pʊə ·'kɪp ə
‖ ˌjoʊm 'kɪp ʲr ˌjɔːm-, ˌjɑːm-, -kɪ 'pʊʲr

yomp jɒmp ‖ jɑːmp **yomped** jɒmpt ‖ jɑːmpt
yomping 'jɒmp ɪŋ ‖ 'jɑːmp ɪŋ **yomps** jɒmps
‖ jɑːmps

yon jɒn ‖ jɑːn

yond jɒnd ‖ jɑːnd

yonder 'jɒnd ə ‖ 'jɑːnd ʲr

Yonge jʌŋ

yoni 'jəʊn i ‖ 'joʊn i **~s** z

Yonkers 'jɒŋk əz ‖ 'jɑːŋk ʲrz

yonks jɒŋks ‖ jɑːŋks

yoof *non-standard variant of* youth juːf

yoo-hoo juː 'huː '· · ‖ 'juː huː

YOP jɒp ‖ jɑːp

Yorba Linda jɔːb ə 'lɪnd ə ‖ jɔːrb- —*Sp*
[ˌjor βa 'lin da]

yore, Yore jɔː ‖ jɔːr joʊr

Yorick 'jɒr ɪk ‖ 'jɔːr ɪk 'jɑːr-

York, york, Yorke jɔːk ‖ jɔːrk **yorked** jɔːkt
‖ jɔːrkt **yorking** 'jɔːk ɪŋ ‖ 'jɔːrk ɪŋ **yorks,
York's** jɔːks ‖ jɔːrks

yorker 'jɔːk ə ‖ 'jɔːrk ʲr **~s** z

yorkie, Y~ *tdmk* 'jɔːk i ‖ 'jɔːrk i **~s** z

Yorkist 'jɔːk ɪst §-əst ‖ 'jɔːrk- **~s** s

Yorks. jɔːks ‖ jɔːrks

Yorkshire 'jɔːk ʃə -ʃɪə ‖ 'jɔːrk ʃᵊr -ʃɪr **~man** mən **~men** mən men **~s** z **~woman** ˌwʊm ən **~women** ˌwɪm ɪn §-ən
ˌYorkshire 'pudding; **ˌYorkshire 'terrier**

Yorktown 'jɔːk taʊn ‖ 'jɔːrk-

Yoruba 'jɒr ʊb ə ‖ 'jɔːr əb ə **~s** z

Yosemite jəʊ 'sem ət i -ɪt- ‖ joʊ 'sem əţ i

Yossarian jɒ 'seər i‿ən -'sɑːr- ‖ joʊ 'ser- -'sɑːr-

Yost jəʊst ‖ joʊst

you *strong form* juː, *weak forms* ju jə, *before a vowel also* §j *—(1) Learners of BrE are advised not to use weak forms other than* ju; jə *is unusual in RP, while* j *is clearly non-RP. In GenAm, on the other hand, the weak form* jə *is acceptable. —(2) The initial* j *of this word readily coalesces with the final* t *or* d *of a preceding word to give* tʃ *or* dʒ *respectively:* don't you 'dəʊntʃ u ‖ 'doʊntʃ ə, did you 'dɪdʒ u ‖ -ə

you-all ju 'ɔːl jɔːl ‖ jɔːl, ju 'ɑːl, jɑːl

you'd *strong form* juːd, *weak forms* jud jəd *—See note (1) at* you

Youel, Youell 'juː‿əl juːl

Youens 'juː‿ɪnz ənz

Youghal jɔːl ‖ jɑːl

you-know-what ˌjuː nəʊ 'wɒt -'hwɒt ‖ -noʊ 'wʌt -'wɑːt, -'hwʌt, -'hwɑːt

you-know-who ˌjuː nəʊ 'huː ‖ -noʊ-

you'll *strong forms* juːl juː‿əl, *weak forms* jul jəl *—See note (1) at* you

young, Young jʌŋ **younger** 'jʌŋ gə ‖ -gᵊr **youngest** 'jʌŋ gɪst -gəst
ˌyoung 'man; **ˌyoung 'woman**

Younger 'jʌŋ gə ‖ -gᵊr

Younghusband 'jʌŋ ˌhʌz bənd

youngish 'jʌŋ ɪʃ -gɪʃ

youngling 'jʌŋ lɪŋ **~s** z

youngster 'jʌŋᵏst ə ‖ -ᵊr **~s** z

Youngstown 'jʌŋz taʊn

your *strong forms* jɔː jʊə ‖ jʊᵊr jɔːr, joʊr, *weak form* jə ‖ jᵊr *—Learners of BrE are advised not to use the weak form* jə, *which is fairly unusual in RP.*

you're *strong forms* jɔː jʊə ‖ jʊᵊr, *weak form* jə ‖ jᵊr *—Learners of BrE are advised not to use the weak form* jə, *which is fairly unusual in RP. (= your)*

YOURS

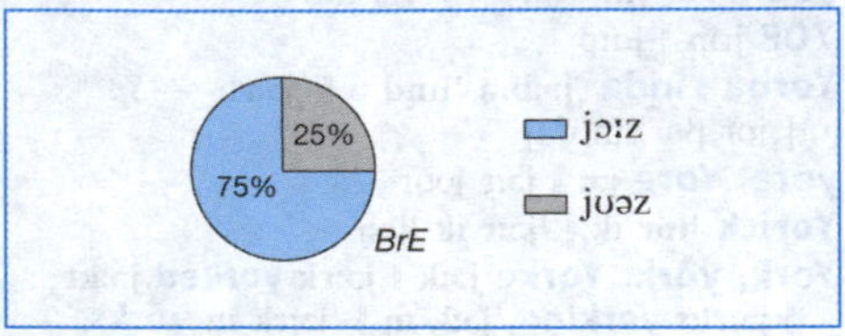

yours jɔːz jʊəz ‖ jʊᵊrz jɔːrz, joʊrz *— Preference poll, BrE:* jɔːz *75%,* jʊəz *25%.*
ˌyours 'truly

your|self jɔː |'self jʊə-, jə- ‖ jʊr- jɔːr-, jᵊr-, joʊr- **~selves** 'selvz

yous, youse *strong form* juːz, *weak forms* jəz, jɪz *—This second person pl pronoun, being non-standard, has no standard pronunciation.*

YOUTHS

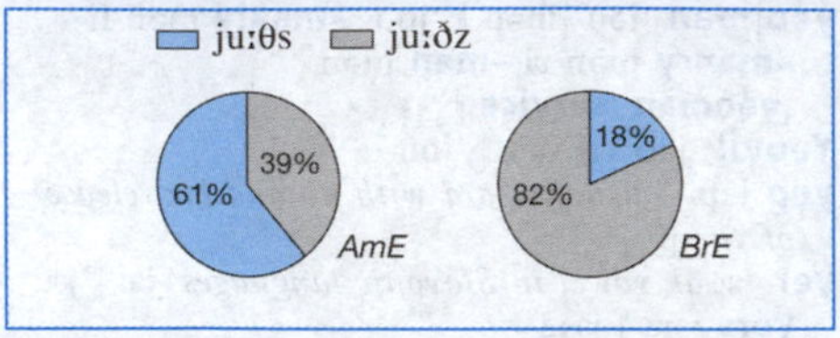

youth juːθ **youths** juːðz juːθs ‖ juːθs juːðz *— Preference polls, AmE:* juːθs *61%,* juːðz *39%; BrE:* juːðz *82%,* juːθs *18%.* **youth's** juːθs
'youth club; **'youth ˌhostel**

youthful 'juːθ fᵊl -fʊl **~ly** i **~ness** nəs nɪs

YouTube 'juː tjuːb →-tʃuːb ‖ -tuːb -tjuːb

you've *strong form* juːv, *weak forms* juv jəv *—See note (1) at* you

yow jaʊ

yowl jaʊl **yowled** jaʊld **yowling** 'jaʊl ɪŋ **yowls** jaʊlz

yoyo, yo-yo, Yo-Yo *tdmk* 'jəʊ jəʊ ‖ 'joʊ joʊ **~s** z

Ypres 'iːp rə -rəz, -əz; iːp; 'waɪp əz *—Fr* [ipχ]

Yr, yr *in Welsh expressions* ər

Ystalyfera ˌʌst əl ə 'ver ə *—Welsh* [ˌəs dal ə 've ra]

Ystrad 'ʌs trəd *—Welsh* ['əs drad]

Ystradgynlais ˌʌs trəd 'gʌn laɪs -træd- *—Welsh* [ˌəs drad 'gən lais]

Ystwyth 'ʌst wɪθ *—Welsh* ['əs duiθ, -duiθ]

Ythan 'aɪθ ᵊn

YTS ˌwaɪ tiː 'es

ytterbium ɪ 'tɜːb i‿əm ‖ -'tɝːb-

yttrium 'ɪtr i‿əm

Yu juː *—Cantonese* [^{4}jyː]

yuan, Yuan ju 'æn -'ɑːn ‖ -'ɑːn *—Chi* yuán [^{2}ɥæn]

Yucatan, Yucatán ˌjʊk ə 'tɑːn ˌjuːk-, -'tæn ‖ ˌjuːk ə 'tæn -'tɑːn *—Sp* [ju ka 'tan]

yucca 'jʌk ə 'juːk- **~s** z

yuck jʌk

yuck|y 'jʌk |i **~ier** i‿ə ‖ i‿ᵊr **~iest** i‿ɪst i‿əst

Yudkin 'juːd kɪn

Yue *(i)* ju 'eɪ *—Chi* Yuè [^{4}ɥɛ]; *(ii)* juː, *Cantonese* [^{4}jyː]

Yugoslav 'juːg əʊ slɑːv ˌ· ·'· ‖ ˌjuːg oʊ 'slɑːv ◂ -'slæv **~s** z

Yugoslavi|a ˌjuːg əʊ 'slɑːv i‿|ə ‖ ˌ·oʊ- **~an/s** ən/z

yuk jʌk **yukked** jʌkt **yukking** 'jʌk ɪŋ **yuks** jʌks

yukk|y 'jʌk |i **~ier** i‿ə ‖ i‿ᵊr **~iest** i‿ɪst i‿əst

Yukon 'juːk ɒn ‖ -ɑːn

yuks jʌks

Yul juːl

yule, Yule juːl
'yule log

yuletide, Y~ 'juːl taɪd

yum jʌm

Yuma 'ju:m ə ~s z
Yuman 'ju:m ən
yumm|y 'jʌm |i ~ier i‿ə ‖ i‿ᵊr ~iest i‿ɪst i‿əst
yum-yum, Yum-Yum ˌjʌm 'jʌm
Yunnan ˌju: 'næn ˌjʊn- ‖ -'nɑ:n —*Chi* Yúnnán [²jyn ²nan]
yup jʌp —*usually said with no audible release of the* p
Yupik 'ju:p ɪk ~s s
yuppie, Y~ 'jʌp i ~s z
yuppification ˌjʌp ɪf ɪ 'keɪʃ ᵊn ˌ·əf-, §-əˈ--

yuppi|fy 'jʌp ɪ |faɪ §-ə- ~**fied** faɪd ~**fies** faɪz ~**fying** faɪ ɪŋ
yupp|y, Yupp|y 'jʌp| i ~**ies** iz
Yuri 'jʊər i ‖ 'jʊr i 'jɜ:- —*Russ* ['ju rʲi]
Yurok 'jʊər ɒk ‖ 'jʊr ɑ:k
yurt jʊət jɜ:t ‖ jʊᵊrt **yurts** jʊəts jɜ:ts ‖ jʊᵊrts
Yussuf 'jʊs ʊf -əf
Yves i:v —*Fr* [i:v]
Yvette ɪ 'vet ₍ᵢ₎i:-
Yvonne ɪ 'vɒn ₍ᵢ₎i:- ‖ -'vɑ:n

Y

Zz

Z, z zed ‖ ziː *(*)* **Z's, z's, Zs** zedz ‖ ziːz
—*Communications code name:* Zulu
-z *alternative, non-standard, spelling of the plural ending -s.* **Bratz** *tdmk* bræts **boyz** bɔɪz
See **-s**
zabaglione ˌzæb ᵊl ˈjəʊn i -æl-, -eɪ
‖ ˌzɑːb ᵊl ˈjoʊn i —*It* zabaione
[dza ba ˈjo: ne] **~s** z
Zachariah ˌzæk ə ˈraɪ ə
Zachary ˈzæk ər i
Zadok ˈzeɪd ɒk ‖ -ɑːk
zaftig ˈzɑːft ɪg ˈzæft- —*Ger* saftig [ˈzaf tɪç]
Zagreb ˈzɑːg reb ˈzæg-, ˌzɑː ˈgreb —*Croatian*
[ˈza greb]
Zaire, Zaïre, zaire ₍ₒ₎zaɪ ˈɪə zɑː- ‖ zɑː ˈɪᵊr
ˈzɑː ɪr
Zairean, Zaïrean zaɪ ˈɪər i‿ən zɑː- ‖ zɑː ˈɪr- **~s**
z
Zak zæk
Zambezi ₍ₒ₎zæm ˈbiːz i
Zambia ˈzæm bi‿ə
Zambian ˈzæm bi‿ən **~s** z
zambuck, Z~, Zam-Buk *tdmk* ˈzæm bʌk **~s** s
Zamenhof ˈzæm ən hɒf -en- ‖ ˈzɑːm ən hoʊf
Zander, z~ ˈzænd ə ‖ -ᵊr **~s** z
Zandra ˈzɑːndr ə ˈzændr-
Zane zeɪn
Zangwill ˈzæŋ wɪl -wəl, -gwɪl, -gwəl
Zantac *tdmk* ˈzænt æk
Zante ˈzænt i
ZANU ˈzɑːn uː ‖ ˈzæn-
Zanuck ˈzæn ək
zan|y ˈzeɪn |i **~ier** i‿ə ‖ i‿ᵊr **~ies** iz **~iest** i‿ɪst
i‿əst **~ily** ɪ li əl i **~iness** i nəs i nɪs

Zanzibar ˈzænz ɪ bɑː -ə-, ˌ‿‿ˈ‿ ‖ -bɑːr
Zanzibari ˌzænz ɪ ˈbɑːr i ◀ -ə- **~s** z
zap zæp **zapped** zæpt **zapping** ˈzæp ɪŋ **zaps**
zæps
Zapata zə ˈpɑːt ə zæ- ‖ -ˈpɑːt̬- —*AmSp*
[sa ˈpa ta]
Zapotec ˈzæp ə tek ˈzɑːp-, ˌ‿‿ˈ‿
zapp... —*see* **zap**
Zappa ˈzæp ə
zapper ˈzæp ə ‖ -ᵊr **~s** z
Zara ˈzɑːr ə
Zaragoza ˌsær ə ˈgɒs ə ‖ ˌzær ə ˈgoʊz ə —*Sp*
[θa ɾa ˈɣo θa]
Zarathustra ˌzær ə ˈθuːs trə ‖ ˌzer-
Zaria ˈzɑːr i‿ə
Zarqawi zɑː ˈkɑː wi ‖ zɑːr- —*Arabic*
[zar ˈqa wiː]
Zatopek ˈzæt ə pek ‖ ˈzæt̬- —*Czech* Zátopek
[ˈza: to pek]
zax zæks **zaxes** ˈzæks ɪz -əz
z-axis ˈzed ˌæks ɪs §-əs ‖ ˈziː-
zeal, Zeal ziːᵊl
Zealand ˈziː lənd
zealot ˈzel ət **~s** s
zealotry ˈzel ət ri
zealous ˈzel əs **~ly** li **~ness** nəs nɪs
Zebedee ˈzeb ə diː -ɪ-
zebra ˈzeb rə ˈziːb- ‖ ˈziːb- — *Preference poll,*
BrE: ˈzeb- *83%,* ˈziːb- *17%.* **~s** z
   ˌzebra ˈcrossing
zebu ˈziːb uː -juː **~s** z
Zebulon, Zebulun ˈzeb jʊl ən ze ˈbjuːl-, zə-
Zechariah ˌzek ə ˈraɪ ə
zed zed **zeds** zedz

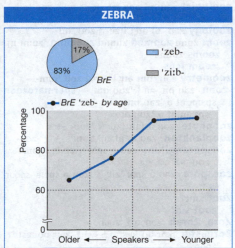

ZEBRA

83% BrE 17%

■ 'zeb-
■ 'ziːb-

BrE 'zeb- by age

Percentage (y-axis: 0, 60, 80, 100)

Older ◀— Speakers —▶ Younger

Zedekiah ˌzed ɪ 'kaɪ ə -ə-
zedoary 'zed əʊ ər i zə 'dəʊ- ‖ -oʊ er i
zee ziː **zees** ziːz
Zeebrugge ˌzeɪ 'brʊg ə ˌziː-, '·ˌ· ·, zɪ'· ·;
'zeɪ bruːʒ —Dutch ['zeː ˌbrʏx ə]
Zeeland 'ziː lənd —Dutch ['zeː lɑnt]
Zeeman 'ziː mən —Dutch ['zeː mɑn]
Zeffirelli ˌzef ə 'rel i -ɪ- —It [dzef fi 'rel li]
Zeiss zaɪs —Ger [tsaɪs]
zeitgeist 'zaɪt gaɪst —Ger Z~ ['tsait gaist]
zek, Zek zek **zeks** zeks
Zelda 'zeld ə
Zeldin 'zeld ɪn §-ən
zelkova 'zelk əv ə zel 'kəʊv ə ‖ zel 'koʊv ə ~s
z
Zellweger 'zel weg ə ‖ -ᵊr
Zelotes zɪ 'ləʊt iːz zə-, ze- ‖ -'loʊt-
Zen zen —Jp ['dzeɴ, dze,ɴ]
ˌZen 'Buddhism
Zena 'ziːn ə
zenana ze 'nɑːn ə zɪ-, zə- ~s z
Zend zend
Zenda 'zend ə
Zeneca tdmk 'zen ɪk ə -ək-
Zener 'ziːn ə 'zen- ‖ -ᵊr
ˌZener 'diode
zenith 'zen ɪθ 'ziːn-, §-əθ ‖ 'ziːn əθ ~s s
zenithal 'zen ɪθ ᵊl 'ziːn-, §-əθ- ‖ 'ziːn əθ ᵊl
Zennor 'zen ə ‖ -ᵊr
Zeno 'ziːn əʊ ‖ -oʊ
Zenobia zɪ 'nəʊb i ə zə-, ze- ‖ -'noʊb-
zeolite 'ziː ə laɪt ~s s
Zephaniah ˌzef ə 'naɪ ə
zephyr 'zef ə ‖ -ᵊr ~s z
Zephyrus 'zef ər əs -ɪr-
zeppelin, Z~ 'zep əl ɪn §-ən —Ger
['tsep ə liːn] ~s z
Zermatt 'zɜː mæt ‖ tser 'mɑːt —Ger
[tsɛʁ 'mat]
zero 'zɪər əʊ 'zɪr- ‖ 'zɪr oʊ 'ziː roʊ ~ed d ~es,
~s z ~ing ɪŋ
ˌzero 'gravity; 'zero ˌhour

zero-coupon ˌzɪər əʊ 'kuːp ɒn ◀
‖ ˌzɪr oʊ 'kuːp ɑːn -'kjuːp-
zero-rated ˌzɪər əʊ 'reɪt ɪd ◀ ˌzɪr-, -əd, '·ˌ··
‖ ˌzɪr oʊ 'reɪt̬ əd ◀ ˌziː roʊ-
zero-sum ˌzɪər əʊ 'sʌm ◀ ‖ ˌzɪr oʊ- '· · ·
zeroth ordinal numeral 'zɪər əʊθ 'zɪr-
‖ 'zɪr oʊθ 'ziː roʊθ
zest zest
zestful 'zest fᵊl -fʊl ~ly i
zest|y 'zest |i ~ier i ə ‖ i ᵊr ~iest i ɪst i əst
zeta, Zeta 'ziːt ə ‖ 'zeɪt̬ ə 'ziːt̬- ~s z
Zetec tdmk 'ziː tek
Zetland 'zet lənd
Zetters 'zet əz ‖ 'zet̬ ᵊrz
zeugma 'zjuːg mə 'zuːg- ‖ 'zuːg- ~s z
Zeus zjuːs zuːs; 'ziːˌəs ‖ zuːs
Zeuxis 'zjuːks ɪs 'zuːks-, §-əs ‖ 'zuːks-
Zewe 'ziː wi
Zhang dʒæŋ ‖ dʒɑːŋ —Chi Zhāng [¹tʂaŋ]
Zhejiang ˌdʒɜ: dʒi 'æŋ ‖ ˌdʒʌdʒ i 'ɑːŋ —Chi
Zhèjiāng [⁴tʂɤ ¹tɕjaŋ]
Zhirinovsky ˌʒɪr ɪ 'nɒf ski -ə- ‖ -'nɑːf- —Russ
[ʒi rʲɪ 'nɔf skʲi]
Zhivago ʒɪ 'vɑːg əʊ ʒə- ‖ -oʊ
Zhou dynasty dʒəʊ tʃəʊ ‖ dʒoʊ tʃoʊ —Chi
Zhōu [¹tʂou]
ˌZhou En'lai ˌtʃəʊ en 'laɪ -ən- ‖ ˌtʃoʊ- —Chi
Zhōu Ēnlái [¹tʂou ¹ən ²lai]
Zhuhai ˌdʒuː 'haɪ —Chi Zhūhǎi [¹tʂu ³xai]
Zhukov 'ʒuːk ɒv -ɒf; -ɔːf -ɑːf —Russ ['ʒu kəf]
zibeline, zibelline 'zɪb ə laɪn -ᵊl aɪn, -ɪn, §-ən
‖ -ə liːn
Zidane zɪ 'dæn -'dɑːn —Fr [zi dan]
Ziegfeld 'zɪg feld 'ziː·g-, -fiːᵊld
Ziegler 'ziːg lə ‖ -lᵊr —Ger ['tsiː glɐ]
ziggurat 'zɪg u ræt -ə- ‖ -ə- ~s s
Ziggy 'zɪg i
zigzag n, v, adv 'zɪg zæg ~ged d ~ging ɪŋ ~s
z
zilch zɪltʃ
zillion 'zɪl jən '·i ən ~s z
Zimbabwe zɪm 'bɑːb wi -'bæb-, -weɪ
Zimbabwean zɪm 'bɑːb wi ən -'bæb-, -weɪ- ~s
z
zimmer, Z~ tdmk 'zɪm ə ‖ -ᵊr ~s z
Zimmerman 'zɪm ə mæn -mən ‖ -ᵊr-
zinc zɪŋk **zinced, zincked** zɪŋkt **zincing,**
zincking 'zɪŋk ɪŋ **zincs** zɪŋks
ˌzinc 'oxide
zincite 'zɪŋk aɪt
zine ziːn **zines** ziːnz
zineb 'zɪn eb 'zaɪn-
Zinédine ˌzɪn eɪ 'diːn ˌziːn-, -i- —Fr
[zi ne din]
zinfandel, Z~ 'zɪn fən del ˌ· ·'· ~s z
zing zɪŋ **zinged** zɪŋd **zinging** 'zɪŋ ɪŋ **zings**
zɪŋz
zinger 'zɪŋ ə ‖ -ᵊr ~s z
zinjanthropus zɪn 'dʒænᵊθ rəp əs
ˌzɪndʒ æn 'θrəʊp- ‖ ˌzɪndʒ æn 'θroʊp-
zinkenite 'zɪŋk ə naɪt
zinnia 'zɪn i ə ~s z

Z

Zinoviev zɪ 'nəʊv i ev zə- ‖ -'noʊv- —*Russ*
[zʲɪ 'no vʲɪf]
Zion 'zaɪ ən
Zionism 'zaɪ ə ˌnɪz əm
Zionist 'zaɪ ən ɪst §-əst **~s** s
zip zɪp **zipped** zɪpt **zipping** 'zɪp ɪŋ **zips** zɪps
'zip code; ˌzip 'fastener
zip-lock, Ziploc *tdmk* 'zɪp lɒk ‖ -lɑːk
zip-on 'zɪp ɒn ‖ -ɑːn -ɔːn
zipper 'zɪp ə ‖ -ᵊr **~ed** d **~s** z
Zippo *tdmk* 'zɪp əʊ ‖ -oʊ
Zipporah 'zɪp ər ə
zipp|y 'zɪp |i **-ier** i ə ‖ i ᵊr **~iest** i ɪst i əst
zip-up 'zɪp ʌp
zircon 'zɜːk ɒn -ən ‖ 'zɜːk ɑːn **~s** z
zirconia zɜː 'kəʊn i ə ‖ zɜː 'koʊn-
zirconium zɜː 'kəʊn i əm ‖ zɜː 'koʊn-
zit zɪt **zits** zɪts
zither 'zɪð ə ‖ -ᵊr 'zɪθ- **~s** z
zizz zɪz
zloty 'zlɒt i ‖ 'zlɔːt̬ i 'zlɑːt̬- —*Polish* ['zwɔ ti]
~s z
-zoa 'zəʊ ə ‖ 'zoʊ ə — **spermatozoa**
ˌspɜːm ət ə 'zəʊ ə ‖ ˌspɜːm ət̬ ə 'zoʊ ə
Zocor *tdmk* 'zəʊ kɔː ‖ -kɔːr
zodiac 'zəʊd i æk ‖ 'zoʊd-
zodiacal zəʊ 'daɪ ək ᵊl ‖ zoʊ-
Zoe, Zoë 'zəʊ i ‖ 'zoʊ i zoʊ
zoetrope 'zəʊ i trəʊp ‖ 'zoʊ i troʊp **~s** s
Zoff *tdmk* zɒf ‖ zɔːf zɑːf
Zoffany 'zɒf ən i ‖ 'zɑːf-
Zog zɒg ‖ zɔːg zɑːg —*Albanian* Zogu ['zo gu]
-zoic 'zəʊ ɪk ‖ 'zoʊ ɪk — **paleozoic**
ˌpæl i əʊ 'zəʊ ɪk ◂ ˌpeɪl- ‖ ˌpeɪl i ə 'zoʊ ɪk ◂
zoisite 'zɔɪs aɪt
Zola 'zəʊl ə ‖ 'zoʊl ə —*Fr* [zɔ la]
Zollner, Zöllner 'zɒl nə ‖ 'zɑːl nᵊr **~'s** z —*Ger*
['tsœl nɐ]
ˌZollner's 'lines
Zomba 'zɒm bə ‖ 'zɑːm-
zombi, zombie 'zɒm bi ‖ 'zɑːm- **~s** z
zonal 'zəʊn ᵊl ‖ 'zoʊn ᵊl **~ly** i
zonation zəʊ 'neɪʃ ᵊn ‖ zoʊ- **~s** z
zone zəʊn ‖ zoʊn **zoned** zəʊnd ‖ zoʊnd **zones**
zəʊnz ‖ zoʊnz **zoning** 'zəʊn ɪŋ ‖ 'zoʊn ɪŋ
zonk zɒŋk ‖ 'zɑːŋk zɔːŋk **zonked** zɒŋkt
‖ 'zɑːŋkt zɔːŋkt **zonking** 'zɒŋk ɪŋ ‖ 'zɑːŋk ɪŋ
'zɔːŋk- **zonks** zɒŋks ‖ zɑːŋks zɔːŋks
Zonta 'zɒnt ə ‖ 'zɑːnt̬ ə
Zontian 'zɒnt i ən ‖ 'zɑːnt̬ i ən **~s** z
zonule 'zɒn juːl 'zəʊn- ‖ 'zoʊn- **~s** z
zoo zuː **zoos** zuːz
zoo- *comb. form*
with stress-neutral suffix ¦zəʊ ə 'zuː ə ‖ ¦zoʊ ə
— **zoophile** 'zəʊ ə faɪᵊl ‖ 'zoʊ-
with stress-imposing suffix zəʊ 'ɒ+ zu 'ɒ+
‖ zoʊ 'ɑː+ — **zoophilous** zəʊ 'ɒf ɪl əs zu-,
-əl- ‖ zoʊ 'ɑːf-
zooid 'zəʊ ɔɪd ‖ 'zoʊ- **~s** z
zoo-keeper 'zuː ˌkiːp ə ‖ -ᵊr **~s** z
zoological ˌzəʊ ə 'lɒdʒ ɪk ᵊl ◂ ˌzuː ə-,
zu 'lɒdʒ- ‖ ˌzoʊ ə 'lɑːdʒ- **~ly** i
ˌzoo‚logical 'gardens

zoologist zəʊ 'ɒl ədʒ ɪst zu-, §-əst ‖ zoʊ 'ɑːl-
~s s
zoology zəʊ 'ɒl ədʒ i zu- ‖ zoʊ 'ɑːl-
zoom zuːm **zoomed** zuːmd **zooming** 'zuːm ɪŋ
zooms zuːmz
'zoom lens
zoometry zəʊ 'ɒm ətr i -ɪtr- ‖ zoʊ 'ɑːm-
-zoon 'zəʊ ɒn -ən ‖ 'zoʊ ɑːn — **spermatozoon**
ˌspɜːm ət ə 'zəʊ ɒn -ən
‖ ˌspɜːm ət̬ ə 'zoʊ ɑːn
zoophyte 'zəʊ ə faɪt 'zuːˌ ‖ 'zoʊ- **~s** s
zooplankton ˌzəʊ ə 'plæŋkt ən '·ˌ··ˌ ‖ ˌzoʊ-
zoosporangi|um ˌzəʊ ə spɔː 'rændʒ i |əm
‖ ˌzoʊ- **~a** ə
zoospore 'zəʊ ə spɔː 'zuːˌ ‖ 'zoʊ ə spɔːr -spoʊr
~s z
zoot zuːt
'zoot suit
Zora, Zorah 'zɔːr ə ‖ 'zoʊr-
Zoroaster ˌzɒr əʊ 'æst ə '····ˌ ‖ 'zɔːr oʊ æst ᵊr
'zoʊr-
Zoroastrian ˌzɒr əʊ 'æs tri ən ◂ ‖ ˌzɔːr oʊ-
ˌzoʊr- **~ism** ˌɪz əm **~s** z
Zorro 'zɒr əʊ ‖ 'zɔːr oʊ —*Sp* ['θo rro, 'so-]
zoster 'zɒst ə ‖ 'zɑːst ᵊr
zouave, Z~ zu 'ɑːv zuː ɑːv, zwɑːv **zouaves, Z~**
zu 'ɑːvz zuː ɑːvz, zwɑːvz
zounds zaʊndz zuːndz
Zovirax *tdmk* zəʊ 'vaɪᵊr æks ‖ zoʊ-
Zsa Zsa 'ʒɑː ʒɑː
Zubes *tdmk* zuːbz zjuːbz
zucchetto zu 'ket əʊ ‖ -'ket̬ oʊ **~s** z
zucchini zu 'kiːn i
Zuckerberg 'zʌk ə bɜːg ‖ -ᵊr bɜːg
Zuckerman 'zʊk ə mən ‖ -ᵊr- 'zʌk-
Zugspitze 'zʊg ˌʃpɪts ə —*Ger* ['tsuːk ˌʃpɪts ə]
zugzwang 'zuːg zwæŋ —*Ger* ['tsuːk tsvaŋ]
Zuider Zee ˌzaɪd ə 'ziː ‖ -ᵊr- —*Dutch*
[ˌzœy dər 'zeː]
Zuleika zu 'leɪk ə -'laɪk-
Zulu 'zuːl uː **~s** z
Zululand 'zuːl uː lænd
Zuni, Zuñi 'zuːn i -ji —*AmSp* ['su ɲi] **~s** s
Zurich, Zürich 'zʊər ɪk 'zjʊər- ‖ 'zʊr ɪk —*Ger*
['tsy: ʁɪç]
Zutphen 'zʌt fən —*Dutch* ['zʏt fən]
Zuyder Zee ˌzaɪd ə 'ziː ‖ -ᵊr- —*Dutch*
[ˌzœy dər 'zeː]
Zwemmer 'zwem ə ‖ -ᵊr
zwieback 'zwiː bæk -bɑːk ‖ 'zwaɪ- 'swiː-,
'swaɪ-, 'zwiː- **~s** s
Zwingli 'zwɪŋ gli -li —*Ger* ['tsvɪŋ li]
Zwinglian 'zwɪŋ gli ən -li ‖ **~s** z
zwitterion 'zwɪt ər ˌaɪ ən 'tsvɪt-, -ɒn
‖ 'zwɪt̬ ə ˌraɪ ən -ɑːn **~s** z
zydeco 'zaɪd ə kəʊ -ɪ- ‖ -koʊ
zyg- *comb. form before vowel*
with unstressed suffix ¦zaɪg — **zygote**
'zaɪg əʊt ‖ -oʊt
with stressed suffix zaɪ g+ zɪ g+ — **zygosis**
zaɪ 'gəʊs ɪs zɪ-, §-əs ‖ -'goʊs-
zygo- *comb. form*
with stress-neutral suffix ¦zaɪg əʊ ¦zɪg əʊ ‖ -ə

Z

— **zygospore** 'zaɪg əʊ spɔː ' ːcɔs
-spoʊr ‖ zɪg- ‖ -ə spɔːr
with stress-imposing suffix zaɪ 'gɒ + zɪ-
‖ -'gɑː + — **zygopteran** zaɪ 'gɒpt ər ən zɪ-
‖ -'gɑːpt-

zygoma zaɪ 'gəʊm ə zɪ- ‖ -'goʊm ə **~s** z

zygomatic ˌzaɪg əʊ 'mæt ɪk ◄ ˌzɪg- ‖ -ə 'mæt̬-

zygote 'zaɪg əʊt 'zɪg- ‖ -oʊt **~s** s

zygotic zaɪ 'gɒt ɪk zɪ- ‖ -'gɑːt̬- **~ally** ᵊl‿i

zym- *comb. form before vowel*
with unstressed suffix ˌzaɪm — **zymurgy**
'zaɪm ɜːdʒ i ‖ -ɜːdʒ-

with stressed suffix zaɪ m + — **zymoma**
zaɪ 'məʊm ə ‖ -'moʊm-

zymase 'zaɪm eɪs -eɪz

zymo- *comb. form*
with stress-neutral suffix ˌzaɪm əʊ ‖ -ə
— **zymolytic** ˌzaɪm əʊ 'lɪt ɪk ◄ ‖ -ə 'lɪt̬-
with stress-imposing suffix zaɪ 'mɒ +
‖ -'mɑː + — **zymolysis** zaɪ 'mɒl əs ɪs -ɪs-,
§-əs ‖ -'mɑːl-

zymosis zaɪ 'məʊs ɪs §-əs ‖ -'moʊs-

zymotic zaɪ 'mɒt ɪk ‖ -'mɑːt̬ ɪk **~ally** ᵊl‿i

Zyrian, Zyryan 'zɪr i‿ən **~s** z

zzz —*sometimes said aloud as* zː

Z

Typographical conventions, stress marks, other symbols

RP Gen
*   Am*

		raised	letters: sounds sometimes optionally inserted
•	•	ᵊl	mid**d**le, to**t**al
•	•	ᵊn	sud**d**enly, serva**n**t
•		ᵊr	fa**th**er, standa**r**d
•	•	mᵖf	emp**h**asis
•	•	nᵗs	fe**nc**e
•	•	ŋᵏs	ga**ng**ster

		italic	letters: sounds sometimes optionally omitted
•	•	ə	dist*a*nt
•		nt∫	lu*n*ch
•	•	ndӡ	hi*n*ge
•		aɪ	f*i*re
•		nt̬	wi*n*ter

ˈ	primary word stress (reˈMEMber)
ˌ	secondary stress (ˌACaˈDEMic; ˈBUTter ˌFINgers)
⁞	(in prefixes) stressed, but level undefined: primary (ˈ) or secondary (ˌ) as appropriate
◄	stress shift possible

‖	GenAm pronunciation follows
§	BrE non-RP
⚠	considered incorrect

+	(in affixes) attracts consonant from next syllable
→	variant derived by automatic rule

‿	possible compression (two syllables become one) of adjacent syllables (ˈliːn i‿ənt) = *lenient* syllable divisions are shown by spaces